K·G·Saur Verlag

THOMSON

International Directory of Arts

28th edition 2004

3 vols., XXIV, 2486 pages, hardbound
€ 278.00 / ISBN 3-598-23095-8

More than 130,000 up-to-date addresses with telephone and fax numbers, e-mail addresses and homepages of museums and organizations dealing with art and antique dealers from all over the world, can be found in this standard reference work. The user can also find useful tips on each specialist field, plus names of curators and senior academic staff of museums, as well as information on the temporary closing of museums.

Up-to-date, reliable and comprehensive!

The entire address contents were revised and updated for this edition following a worldwide questionnaire campaign and by taking into account numerous national and international reference works. Above all the number of e-mail and internet addresses has been considerably increased. Intensive research worldwide uncovered a further ca. 10,000 previously unlisted museums, companies and organizations which have now been included. New in this edition is a chapter providing details of over 400 national and international art and antiques fairs and their organizers.

Clearly set out and logically structured

The clear structure means that users quickly find the address they want. The **International Directory of Arts** is arranged in the following chapters:
Museums and Public Galleries ● Universities, Academies, Schools ● Associations ● Art and Antiques Trade, Numismatics ● Art and Antiques Fairs ● Galleries ● Auctioneers ● Restorers ● Art Publishers ● Art Journals ● Antiquarians and Art Booksellers

Curators, librarians, academics, lecturers at art schools, students, journalists, art and antique dealers, auctioneers, book dealers; in short: all those who are involved in art either professionally or as a hobby will find this work, in which you can find the right address in seconds, indispensable.

www.saur.de

K·G·Saur Verlag
A Part of The Thomson Corporation

Postfach 70 16 20 · 81316 München · Germany
Tel. +49 (0)89 7 69 02-300 · Fax +49 (0)89 7 69 02-150/ 250
e-mail: saur.info@thomson.com   http://www.saur.de

RUE DE LA RÉGENCE 3, 1000 BRUSSELS 
MUSEUM OF ANCIENT ART

PLACE ROYALE 1-2, 1000 BRUSSELS 
MUSEUM OF MODERN ART

RUE DE L'ABBAYE 59, 1050 BRUSSELS 
CONSTANTIN MEUNIER MUSEUM

RUE VAUTIER 62, 1050 BRUSSELS 
ANTOINE WIERTZ MUSEUM

Royal Museums of Fine Arts of Belgium, Brussels

Royal Museums of Fine Arts of Belgium

info: 00 32 2 508 32 11
www.fine-arts-museum.be

Koninklijke Musea voor Schone Kunsten van België
Musées royaux des Beaux-Arts de Belgique

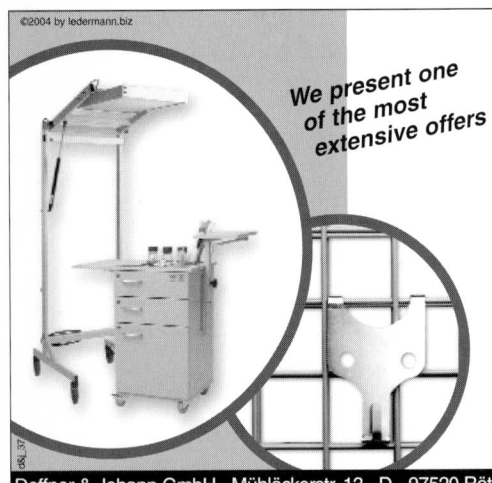
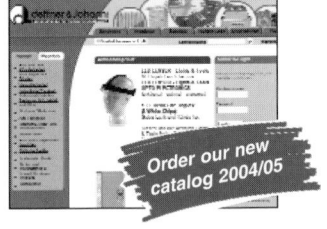

Handbook of International Documentation and Information

Volume 16

Vol. I
Afghanistan
—
United Arab Emirates

Vol. II
United Kingdom
—
Zimbabwe

Indices

Neues Stadtmuseum
Landsberg am Lech

Von-Helfensteingasse 426 · 86899 Landsberg · Tel. 0 81 91/ 94 23 26 · Fax: 0 81 91/ 94 23 27
BAB München-Lindau, Ausfahrt 26
e-mail : neues_stadtmuseum@landsberg.de
Geöffnet täglich, außer montags von 14 bis 17 Uhr, Februar und März geschlossen.

Museums of the World

11th revised and
enlarged edition

Volume II

United Kingdom
—
Zimbabwe

K·G·Saur München 2004

Editor/Redaktion:
Marco Schulze
Boris Eggers

Editorial Office/Redaktionsbüro:
Luppenstr. 1b
D-04177 Leipzig (Germany)
Tel: +49 341 4869911
Fax: +49 341 4869913
Email: marco.schulze@thomson.com

Bibliographic information published by Die Deutsche Bibliothek
Die Deutsche Bibliothek lists this publication in the Deutsche Nationalbibliografie;
detailed bibliographic data is available in the internet at http://dnb.ddb.de.

⊗

Printed on acid-free paper

Data preparation and automatic data processing by
bsix information exchange, Braunschweig
Printed and bound by Strauss GmbH, Mörlenbach

Cover Art by William Pownall

ISSN 0939-1959 (Handbook)
ISBN 3-598-20616-X (2 volumes)

MAN_Museo d'**A**rte Provincia di **N**uoro

via Satta, 15. 08100 Nuoro (Italy)

tel. (+39) 0784 252110_email: man.nuoro@virgilio.it

K · G · Saur Verlag

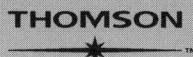

World Guide to Libraries

Book- and CD-ROM-Edition

18th ed. 2003

Book-Edition
(Handbook of International Documentation and
Information, Vol. 8)
2 Volumes, XXX, 1302 pages, hardbound
€428.00 ISBN 3-598-20742-5

What do the "Sächsische Textilforschungsinstitut e.V." in Chemnitz and the "Ministry of Women's Affairs" in Wellington, New Zealand, have in common?

Despite being clearly in possession of both imagination and the powers of deduction, anyone thinking of women's fashion is not in possession of the latest information to be found here: Both institutions maintain their own libraries, detailed entries on which are included in the World Guide to Libraries. A total of 42,954 entries on libraries in 203 countries can be found in the new 17th edition.

From "Summer Institute of Linguistics" in Ukarumpa, Papua New Guinea to the Austrian National Library in Vienna: Libraries all over the World at a glance!
The claim of this comprehensive, 2 volume reference work is to document the library scene right across the globe covering every imaginable type of library, from smaller ones with collections amounting to only a few thousand volumes / media right up to the big libraries with several million volumes.

Clearly structured

The contents are arranged alphabetically by country. Within each country the arrangement is hierarchal according to library types, cities and the names of the institutions. Covered are national libraries, academic libraries, university libraries including subject and institute libraries, school and college libraries, the libraries of authorities, churches and companies, special libraries of other patronage and public libraries.

Fast access using the alphabetical index

All libraries are listed with their place of location, alphabetically sorted by the name of the institution. The index refers to the main part of the work via the consecutively numbered entries.

What is included in each entry in both book and CD-ROM editions?

Name and Address • Telephone, Telefax • E-mail address • URL • Year of Foundation • Library director • Special collections / Special collection areas • Book, Periodical and manuscript holdings • Official publications • Music, maps, films and music media • Microfiche editions • CD-ROMs • Online database services • Inter-library lending • Inter-library lending • Membership of national/international library associations

World Guide to Libraries Plus

8th CD-ROM-Edition 2003
€448.00
(Special price for update purchasers:€420.00)
Also available for network (LAN) use.
ISBN 3-598-40752-1 (1 edition annually)

The most comprehensive reference work for anyone searching for current information about diverse libraries around the world.
The eighth, completely reworked and up-to-date CD-ROM edition World Guide to Libraries PLUS 2003 / 2004 lists approximately 54,000 libraries in 200 countries. Included are national libraries, public libraries, general research libraries, university and college libraries with their sectional and departmental libraries, professional school and school libraries, government libraries, ecclesiastical libraries, corporate or business libraries, and special libraries maintained by other institutions.

View library homepages or send libraries E-mails with a mouse click.

Clicking an URL or an e-mail address allows you to link directly to the internet and to view library homepages or send messages directly to the libraries without having to leave the program.

www.saur.de

K · G · Saur Verlag
A Part of The Thomson Corporation

Postfach 70 16 20 · 81316 München · Germany
Tel. +49 (0)89 7 69 02-300 · Fax +49 (0)89 7 69 02-150/ 250
e-mail: saur.info@thomson.com   http://www.saur.de

Contents

Volume I

Afghanistan	3	Ethiopia	159
Albania	3	Faroe Islands	159
Algeria	3	Fiji	159
American Samoa	4	Finland	159
Andorra	4	France	173
Angola	4	French Guiana	247
Argentina	4	French Polynesia	247
Armenia	13		
Australia	14	Gabon	247
Austria	31	Gambia	248
Azerbaijan	55	Georgia	248
		Germany	248
Bahamas	55	Ghana	347
Bahrain	56	Gibraltar	347
Bangladesh	56	Greece	347
Barbados	56	Greenland	354
Belarus	56	Grenada	355
Belgium	56	Guadeloupe	355
Belize	69	Guam	355
Benin	69	Guatemala	355
Bermuda	69	Guinea	355
Bhutan	70	Guinea-Bissau	355
Bolivia	70	Guyana	355
Bosnia and Herzegovina	70		
Botswana	70	Haiti	355
Brazil	71	Honduras	355
Brunei	81	Hungary	356
Bulgaria	81		
Burkina Faso	87	Iceland	361
Burundi	87	India	362
		Indonesia	369
Cambodia	87	Iran	371
Cameroon	87	Iraq	373
Canada	87	Ireland	373
Cape Verde	119	Israel	377
Central African Republic	119	Italy	380
Chad	119		
Chile	119	Jamaica	427
China, People's Republic	120	Japan	428
China, Republic	125	Jordan	444
Colombia	126		
Comoros	130	Kazakhstan	444
Congo, Democratic Republic	130	Kenya	445
Congo, Republic	130	Korea, Democratic People's Republic	445
Costa Rica	130	Korea, Republic	445
Côte d'Ivoire	130	Kuwait	448
Croatia	131	Kyrgyzstan	448
Cuba	134		
Cyprus	138	Laos	448
Cyprus, Turkish Republic	138	Latvia	448
Czech Republic	139	Lebanon	450
		Lesotho	451
Denmark	148	Liberia	451
Dominican Republic	155	Libya	451
		Liechtenstein	451
East Timor	155	Lithuania	451
Ecuador	156	Luxembourg	452
Egypt	157		
El Salvador	158	Macedonia	452
Equatorial Guinea	158	Madagascar	453
Eritrea	158	Malawi	453
Estonia	158	Malaysia	453
		Maldives	454

Mali	454
Malta	454
Martinique	455
Mauritania	455
Mauritius	455
Mexico	455
Moldova	467
Monaco	467
Mongolia	468
Morocco	468
Mozambique	468
Myanmar	468
Namibia	469
Nepal	469
Netherlands	470
Netherlands Antilles	490
New Caledonia	490
New Zealand	491
Nicaragua	495
Niger	495
Nigeria	495
Niue	496
Norfolk Island	496
Northern Mariana Islands	496
Norway	496
Oman	507
Pakistan	507
Palestine	508
Panama	508
Papua New Guinea	508
Paraguay	509
Peru	511
Philippines	514
Poland	528
Portugal	531
Puerto Rico	531
Qatar	531
Réunion	532
Romania	532

Russia	536
Rwanda	559
St. Lucia	559
St. Pierre and Miquelon	559
Samoa	559
San Marino	559
Sao Tome and Principe	560
Saudi Arabia	560
Senegal	560
Serbia-Montenegro	560
Seychelles	562
Sierra Leone	562
Singapore	563
Slovakia	563
Slovenia	565
Solomon Islands	567
Somalia	567
South Africa	567
Spain	572
Sri Lanka	592
Sudan	593
Suriname	593
Swaziland	593
Sweden	593
Switzerland	604
Syria	622
Tajikistan	622
Tanzania	622
Thailand	623
Togo	623
Tonga	624
Trinidad and Tobago	624
Tunisia	624
Turkey	624
Turkmenistan	628
Uganda	628
Ukraine	628
United Arab Emirates	630

Volume II

United Kingdom	631
Uruguay	687
U.S.A.	688
Uzbekistan	830
Vanuatu	830
Vatican City	830
Venezuela	831
Vietnam	832
Yemen	832
Zambia	833
Zimbabwe	833

Museum Associations	837
Alphabetical Index to Museums	847
Index of Persons	1007
Personality Index	1095
Subject Index	1109
List of Advertisers	1277

United Kingdom

Abercrave

Dan-yr-Ogof Showcaves Museum, Glyntawe, Upper Swansea Valley, Abercrave - T: (01639) 730284, Fax: 730293. Dir.: Ian Gwilim
Natural History Museum - 1964 37927

Aberdare

Cynon Valley Museum, Depot Rd, Gadys, Aberdare CF44 8DL - T: (01685) 886729, Fax: 886730, E-mail: cvm@rhondda-cynon-raff.gov.uk. Cur.: Chris Wilson
Local Museum
Over 200 yrs history of Cynon valley 37928

Aberdeen

Aberdeen Art Gallery, Schoolhill, Aberdeen AB10 1FQ - T: (01224) 523700, Fax: 632133, E-mail: info@aagm.co.uk, Internet: www.aberdeencity.gov.uk. Dir.: Ciaran Monaghan
Fine Arts Museum - 1885
Fine and applied arts (18th-20th c), decorative art since 6th c - library 37929

Aberdeen Arts Centre, 33 King St, Aberdeen AB24 5AA - T: (01224) 635208, Fax: 626390, E-mail: enquiries@aberdeenartscentre.org.uk, Internet: www.aberdeenartscentre.org.uk. Dir.: Arthur Deans
Public Gallery 37930

Aberdeen Maritime Museum, Shiprow, Aberdeen AB11 5BY - T: (01224) 337700, Fax: 213066, E-mail: info@aagm.co.uk, Internet: www.aagm.co.uk. Dir.: John Edwards
Historical Museum - 1984/97
North Sea oil and gas industry, shipping and fishing exhibitions, multi-media and hands-on exhibits 37931

Aberdeen University Natural History Museum, c/o Department of Zoology, Tillydrone Av, Aberdeen AB9 2TN - T: (01224) 272850, Fax: 272396, E-mail: m.gorman@abdn.ac.uk, Internet: www.abdn.ac.uk/zoology. Hon. Cur.: Dr. Martyn Gorman
University Museum / Natural History Museum
Ornithology, entomology, invertebrates/vertebrates coll 37932

Aberdeen University Natural Philosophy Museum, c/o Dept. of Physics, Fraser Noble Bldg, Aberdeen AB24 3UE - T: (01224) 272507, Fax: 272497, E-mail: j.s.reid@abdn.ac.uk, Internet: www.abdn.ac.uk/~nph126. Dir.: Dr. John S. Reid
Science&Tech Museum / University Museum - 1971
Coll of apparatus used during the past 200 years for teaching and demonstrating the traditional branches of physics 37933

Anatomy Museum, c/o Marischal College, University of Aberdeen, Broad St, Aberdeen AB10 1YS - T: (01224) 274320, Fax: 274329, E-mail: i.stewart@abdn.ac.uk. Dir.: Dr. I. Stewart
University Museum / Natural History Museum
Human anatomical specimens and models 37934

The Blairs Museum, South Deeside Rd, Blairs, Aberdeen AB12 5YQ - T: (01224) 863767, Fax: 869424, E-mail: manager@blairsmuseum.com, Internet: www.blairsmuseum.com. Dir.: David Taylor
Fine Arts Museum / Religious Arts Museum
Pictures of Mary Queen of Scots, Stuart portraits and memorabiia, 16th c Church robes, altarware, embroidergd vestments 37935

Geology Department Museum, c/o University of Aberdeen, Meston Bldg, Aberdeen AB24 3UE - T: (01224) 273448, Fax: 272785
Natural History Museum 37936

Gordon Highlanders Museum, Saint Luke's, Viewfield Rd, Aberdeen AB15 7XH - T: (01224) 311200, Fax: 319323, E-mail: museum@gordonhighlanders.com, Internet: www.gordonhighlanders.com. Dir.: Sir Peter Graham, Cur.: Melanie Brooker
Military Museum - 1937
History of Gordon Highlanders regiment, uniforms, medals, pictures, trophies 37937

Grampian Police Museum (closed) 37938

Grays School of Art Gallery and Museum, c/o Faculty of Design, The Robert Gordon University, Garthdee Rd, Aberdeen AB9 2QD - T: (01224) 263506/600
Public Gallery / University Museum 37939

Marischal Museum, Marischal College, University of Aberdeen, Broad St, Aberdeen AB10 1YS - T: (01224) 274301, Fax: 274302, E-mail: museum@abdn.ac.uk, Internet: www.abdn.ac.uk/marischal_museum. Sen. Cur.: Neil Curtis, Margot Wright
University Museum / Local Museum
Local archaeology, art, antiquities, non-western ethnography 37940

Peacock, 21 Castle St, Aberdeen AB11 5BQ - T: (01224) 639539, Fax: 627094, E-mail: peacockprint.co.uk@virgin.net. Dir.: Lindsay Gordon
Public Gallery
Printmaking, photography, digital imaging, video 37941

Provost Skene's House, off Broad St, Guestrow, Aberdeen AB10 1AS - T: (01224) 641086, Fax: 632133, Internet: www.aberdeencity.gov.uk. Dir.: Christine Rew
Decorative Arts Museum - 1953
Scottish furniture, costume, archaeology, painted chapel ceiling (17th c), local history 37942

Robert Gordon University Museum, Heritage Unit, Clarke Bldg, Schoolhill, Aberdeen AB9 2FE - T: (01224) 262599
University Museum 37943

Satrosphere, 179 Constitution St, Aberdeen AB24 5TU - T: (01224) 640340, Fax: 622211, E-mail: satrosphere@satrosphere.net, Internet: www.satrosphere.net. Dir.: Dr. Alistair M. Flett
Science&Tech Museum
Scientific instruments, computers 37944

Aberdovey

Outward Bound Museum (closed) 37945

Aberfeldy

Castle Menzies, Weem, Aberfeldy PH15 2JD - T: (01887) 820982, E-mail: menziesclan@tesco.net, Internet: www.menzies.org. Pres.: G.M. Menzies
Historical Museum
Small Clan-Museum in a 16th c building 37946

Aberford

Lotherton Hall, Leeds Museums and Galleries, Aberford LS25 3EB - T: (0113) 2813259, Fax: 2812100, Internet: www.leeds.gov.uk. Dir.: Nick Winterbotham, Cur.: Adam White
Decorative Arts Museum / Fine Arts Museum - 1969
English and Continental paintings (17th-20th c), furniture, silver, British and oriental ceramics, costume, sculpture 37947

Abergavenny

Abergavenny Museum, Castle, Castle St, Abergavenny NP7 5EE - T: (01873) 854282, Fax: 736004, E-mail: abergavennymuseum@monmouthshire.gov.uk. Dir.: Rachael Rogers
Local Museum - 1959
History and industries of the town and district, kitchen, rural craft, tools, Roman relics from Gobannium site, grocers shop 37948

Aberlady

Myreton Motor Museum, In the Countryside, Aberlady EH32 0PZ - T: (01875) 870288, Fax: (01368) 860199. Dir.: A.P. Dale, Cur.: S. Schwab
Science&Tech Museum - 1966
Cars, motorcycles, bicycles, commercials, period advertising, posters, enamal signs 37949

Abernethy

Abernethy Museum, Cherrybank, Abernethy PH2 9LW - T: (0131) 3177300
Local Museum 37950

Abertillery

Abertillery Museum, Metropole Theater, Market St, Abertillery NP3 1TE - T: (01495) 213806, Internet: www.abertillery-net.co.uk/museum.html. Cur.: Don Bearcroft
Local Museum 37951

Aberystwyth

Aberystwyth Arts Centre, c/o University College of Wales, Penglais, Aberystwyth SY23 3DE - T: (01970) 622882, 622460, Fax: 622883, 622461, E-mail: etr@aber.ac.uk, Internet: www.aber.ac.uk/~arcwww. Dir.: Alan Hewson
University Museum / Fine Arts Museum
ceramics gallery 37952

Aberystwyth Yesterday, Prospect and Vulcan Sts, Aberystwyth - T: (01970) 633088
Special Museum
Replica of 1920's shop 37953

The Ceramic Collection, c/o Arts Centre, University of Wales, Penglais, Aberystwyth SY23 1NE - T: (01970) 622460, Fax: 622461, E-mail: neh@aber.ac.uk, Internet: www.aber.ac.uk. Dir.: Moira Vincentelli
Decorative Arts Museum - 1876
Studio Ceramics 37954

Ceredigion Museum, Coliseum, Terrace Rd, Aberystwyth SY23 2AQ - T: (01970) 633088, Fax: 633084, E-mail: museum@ceredigion.gov.uk, Internet: www.ceredigion.gov.uk/coliseum. Dir.: Michael Freeman
Local Museum - 1972
Alfred Worthington paintings, work of Hutchings, taxidermist 37955

School of Art Gallery and Museum, University of Wales, Buarth Mawr, Aberystwyth SY23 1NG - T: (01970) 622460, Fax: 622461, E-mail: neh@aber.ac.uk, Internet: www.aber.ac.uk/museum. Dir.: Robert Meyrick
Fine Arts Museum / Decorative Arts Museum / University Museum - 1876
Graphic art since 15th c, art in Wales since 1945, 20th c Italian and British photography, pottery (early 20th /contemporary British), slipware, Swansea and Nantgarw porcelain, Oriental ceramics 37956

Abingdon

Abingdon Museum, Old County Hall, Market Pl, Abingdon OX14 3HG - T: (01235) 523703, Fax: 536814, E-mail: enquiries@abingdonmuseum.free-online.co.uk. Dir.: Jill Draper
Local Museum - 1925
Local hist, archaeology, contemporary crafts, 17th c building 37957

Abinger Common

Mesolithic Museum, Abinger Manor, Abinger Common RH5 6JD - T: (01306) 730760. Dir.: Robert Clarke
Historical Museum - 1953
Hut build, flint coll 37958

Accrington

Haworth Art Gallery, Haworth Park, Manchester Rd, Accrington BB5 2JS - T: (01254) 233782, Fax: 301954, E-mail: haworth@hyndburnbc.gov.uk. Cur.: Jennifer A. Rennie
Public Gallery - 1921
19th-20th c paintings, watercolours, largest Tiffany glass coll in Europe 37959

Alcester

Coughton Court, Alcester B49 5JA - T: (01789) 400777, Fax: 765544, E-mail: carol@throckmortons.co.uk, Internet: www.coughton-court.co.uk. Cur.: C. Throckmorton
Decorative Arts Museum / Local Museum
Family portraits, furniture 37960

Ragley Hall, Alcester B49 5NJ - T: (01789) 762090, Fax: 764791, E-mail: info@ragleyhall.com, Internet: www.ragleyhall.com. Owner: Marquess of Hertford
Fine Arts Museum / Decorative Arts Museum
Art 18th c, porcelain, furniture, baroque plasterwork 37961

Aldeburgh

Aldeburgh Museum, The Moot Hall, Aldeburgh IP15 5DS - T: (01728) 452158, E-mail: aldeburgh@museum.freeserve.co.uk
Local Museum - 1911
1862 Anglo-Saxon Ship Burial finds, local history 37962

Moot Hall Museum → Aldeburgh Museum

Alderney

Alderney Railway - Braye Road Station, POB 75, Alderney - T: (01481) 822978
Science&Tech Museum
Two industrial diesel locomotives, 4 petrol Wickham railcars, 2 1938 London transport driving trailer stock 37963

Alderney Society Museum, The Old School, High St, Alderney GY9 3TG - T: (01481) 823222, Fax: 824979, E-mail: alderneymuseum@alderney.net, Internet: www.alderneysociety.org. Pres.: Louis Jean
Local Museum - 1966
Local hist, arts and crafts, hist of the German occupation 1940-1945, Iron Age pottery finds, Elizabethan wreck 37964

Aldershot

Airborne Forces Museum, Browning Barracks, Aldershot GU11 2BU - T: (01252) 349619, Fax: 349203, E-mail: airborneforcesmuseum@army.uk.net. Cur.: Tina Pittock
Military Museum - 1969
World War II operational briefing models, aircraft models, equipment, vehicles, guns 37965

Aldershot Military Museum and Rushmoor Local History Gallery, Queens Av, Aldershot GU11 2LG - T: (01252) 314598, Fax: 342942, E-mail: musmim@hants.gov.uk, Internet: www.hants.gov.uk/museum/aldershot. Cur.: Ian Maine, Asst. Cur.: Sally Day
Military Museum / Local Museum - 1984
Borough of Rushmoor local history coll, vehicle coll 37966

Army Medical Services Museum, Keogh Barracks, Ash Vale, Aldershot GU12 5RQ - T: (01252) 868612, Fax: 868832, E-mail: museum@keogh72.freeserve.co.uk. Cur.: P.H. Starling
Military Museum - 1953
History of Army Medical Service since pre-Tudor times, Crimean relics, memorabilia on Napoleon I (1769-1821) and Wellington (1769-1852), Falklands and Gulfwar military uniforms 37967

Army Physical Training Corps Museum, Queens Av, Aldershot GU11 2LB - T: (01252) 347168, Fax: 340785, E-mail: regtsec@aptc.org.uk, Internet: www.aptc.org.uk. Dir.: A.A. Forbes
Military Museum
History of the Corps since 1860, achievements and personalities - library 37968

Royal Army Dental Corps Historical Museum, Evelyn Woods Rd, Aldershot GU11 2LS - T: (01252) 347976, Fax: 347726. Dir.: C.D. Parkinson
Military Museum / Science&Tech Museum - 1969
Hist of the Corps, developments in dental techniques, connection between dentistry and the Army from the origins of the British Army, following the restoration of the monarchy in 1660 to the present 37969

Royal Army Veterinary Corps Museum, Gallwey Rd, Aldershot GU11 2DQ - T: (01252) 24431 ext 2261
Military Museum 37970

Alexandria

Tobias Smollett Museum, Castle Cameron, Alexandria G83 8QZ - T: (01389) 56226
Special Museum 37971

Alford, Aberdeenshire

Alford Heritage Centre, Mart Rd, Alford, Aberdeenshire AB33 8BZ - T: (019755) 62906
Local Museum 37972

Grampian Transport Museum, Alford, Aberdeenshire AB33 8AE - T: (01975) 562292, Fax: 562180, E-mail: info@g-t-m.freeserve.co.uk, Internet: www.gtm.org.uk. Cur.: Mike Ward
Science&Tech Museum 37973

Alford, Lincolnshire

Alford Manor House Museum, West St, Alford, Lincolnshire LN13 9DJ - T: (01507) 462143, 463073. Dir.: B. Read
Local Museum
Hist of Alford Manor House, Victorian Drawing Room, Shops from the past (Pharmaca, Veterinary Surgery, Bootmaker) Prison Cell, Victorian Schoolroom, coll of Roman finds, displays from the Salt Works and Sweetmakers, costumes and photographs from past local life, Alford's connection with America 37974

Alfriston

Clergy House, The Tye, Alfriston BN26 5TL - T: (01323) 870001, Fax: 871318, E-mail: alfriston@nationaltrust.org.uk, Internet: www.nationaltrust.org.uk. Dir.: Tina Maher
Historic Site 37975

Allerford

West Somerset Rural Life Museum, Old School, Allerford TA24 8HN - T: (01643) 862529. Head: Duncan Osborne
Local Museum
Victorian kitchen, laundry, dairy, school desks, books, toys 37976

Allesley

Jaguar Daimler Heritage Trust, Jaguar Cars, Browns Ln, Allesley CV5 9DR - T: (024) 76402121, Fax: 76202777, E-mail: tokeeffe@jaguar.com, Internet: www.jaguar.com. Dir.: John Maries, Cur.: Tony O'Keeffe
Science&Tech Museum
Vehicles covering Jaguar, Daimler and Lanchester Cars 37977

Alloa

Aberdona Gallery, Aberdona Mains, Alloa FK10 3QP - T: (01259) 752721, Fax: 750276
Public Gallery 37978

Clackmannshire Council Museum, Speirs Centre, 29 Primrose St, Alloa FK10 1JJ - T: (01259) 216913, Fax: 721313, E-mail: smills@clacks.gov.uk, Internet: www.clacksweb.org.uk. Head: Susan Mills, Sc. Staff: Alec Shuttleworth
Local Museum
Alloa pottery, textiles and woolen industry, social and indistrial history 37979

Alloway

Burns Cottage Museum, Alloway KA7 4PY - T: (01292) 441215, Fax: 441750, E-mail: info@burnsheritagepark.com, Internet: www.burnsheritagepark.com. Dir.: Nat Edwards
Special Museum - 1880
Cottage where poet Robert Burns (1759-1796) was born, memorabilia, manuscripts 37980

Tam O'Shanter Experience, Murdoch's Lone, Alloway - T: (01292) 443700, Fax: 441750, E-mail: info@burnsheritagepark.com, Internet: www.burnsheritagepark.com. Dir.: N. Edwards
Local Museum 37981

Alness

Clan Grant Museum, Grants of Dalvey, Alness IV17 0XT - T: (01349) 884111, Fax: 884100
Historical Museum 37982

Alnwick

Bondgate Gallery, 22 Narrowgate, Alnwick NE66 1JG - T: (01665) 576450
Public Gallery
Crafts, visual arts 37983

Fusiliers Museum of Northumberland, Abbots Tower, Alnwick Castle, Alnwick NE66 1NG - T: (01665) 602152, Fax: 605257, E-mail: fusnorthld@aol.com, Internet: www.northumberlandfusiliers.org.uk. Chm.: Tony Adamson
Military Museum - 1929
Artefacts, uniforms, medals, weapons 37984

Museum of Antiquities, Alnwick Castle, Alnwick NE66 1NQ - T: (01665) 510777, Fax: 510876, E-mail: enquiries@alnwickcastle.com, Internet: www.alnwickcastle.com. Cur.: Clare Baxter
Historic Site / Archaeological Museum 37985

Museum of the Percy Tenantry Volunteers 1798-1814, Estate Office, Alnwick Castle, Alnwick NE66 1NQ - T: (01665) 510777, Fax: 510876, E-mail: enquines@alnwickcastle.com, Internet: www.alnwickcastle.com. Cur.: Clare Baxter
Historic Site / Military Museum
Arms and accoutrements of Percy Tenanhy Volunteers formed mainly from people on northern estates of the Duke of Northumberland 37986

Alresford

Mid Hampshire Railway Museum, Railway Station, Alresford SO24 9JG - T: (01962) 733810, Fax: 735448, Internet: www.watercressline.co.uk
Science&Tech Museum
Steam railway 37987

Alston

South Tynedale Railway Preservation Society, Railway Station, Alston CA9 3JB - T: (01434) 381696, Internet: www.strps.org.uk. Dir.: J.M. Sutton
Science&Tech Museum
Steam and diesel narrow-gauge locomotives 37988

Althorp

Althorp Museum, The Stables, Althorp NN7 4HQ - T: (01604) 770107, Fax: 770042, E-mail: mail@althorp.com, Internet: www.althorp.com
Special Museum
Costume, memorabilia of Diana, Princess of Wales 37989

Alton

Allen Gallery, 10-12 Church St, Alton GU34 2BW - T: (01420) 82802, Fax: 84227, E-mail: musmtc@hants.gov.uk, Internet: www.hants.gov.uk/museums. Dir.: Tony Cross
Decorative Arts Museum
Works by W.H. Allen, ceramics from 1550 to the present day, silver - gallery, herb garden 37990

Curtis Museum, 3 High St, Alton GU34 1BA - T: (01420) 82802, Fax: 84227, E-mail: musmtc@hants.gov.uk, Internet: www.hants.gov.uk/museum/curtis. Dir.: Tony Cross
Local Museum - 1855
Local history, archaeology, geology, toys, hop growing, brewing - library 37991

Altrincham

Dunham Massey Hall, Altrincham WA14 4SJ - T: (0161) 9411025, Fax: 9297508, E-mail: mdmsec@smtp.ntrust.org.uk. Dir.: Stephen Adams
Fine Arts Museum / Decorative Arts Museum
Fine coll of paintings, furniture and Huguenot silver - library 37992

Alva

Mill Trail Visitor Centre, West Stirling St, Alva FK12 5EN - T: (01259) 769696, Fax: 763100. Manager: Sharon Harris
Science&Tech Museum
History of weaving industry, spinning wheels and looms 37993

Alyth

Alyth Museum, Perth Museum and Art Gallery, Commercial St, Alyth PH11 8AF - T: (01738) 632488, Fax: 443505, E-mail: museum@pkc.gov.uk
Local Museum
Local histry 37994

Amberley

Amberley Working Museum, Houghton Bridge, Amberley BN18 9LT - T: (01798) 831370, Fax: 831831, E-mail: office@amberleymuseum.co.uk, Internet: www.amberleymuseum.co.uk. Dir.: Howard Stenning
Science&Tech Museum - 1979
Milne electrical coll, Southdown omnibus coll, narrow gauge railways, printing, radio, TV and telephones, concrete technology, roads and roadmaking, industrial buildings - archives 37995

Ambleside

Museum of Ambleside, Rydal Rd, Ambleside LA22 9BL - T: (015394) 31212, Fax: 31313, E-mail: info@armitt.com, Internet: www.armitt.com. Cur.: Michelle Kelly
Local Museum - 1958
Social and economic history, archaeology, geology, natural history, photography, fine art - Library 37996

Rydal Mount, Ambleside LA22 9LU - T: (015394) 33002, Fax: 31738, E-mail: Rydalmount@aol.com. Dir.: Peter Elkington, Marian Elkington
Local Museum - 1970
Portraits, furniture, personal possessions 37997

Amersham

Amersham Museum, 49 High St, Amersham HP7 0DP - T: (01494) 725754, Fax: 725754. Cur.: Monica Mullins
Local Museum
Local hist, fossil and archeaological finds, wall paintings,lace making, strawplait work, brewing, postal services, agriculture 37998

Ancrum

Harestanes Countryside Visitor Centre, Harestanes, Ancrum TD8 6UQ - T: (01835) 830306, Fax: 830734, E-mail: mascott@scotborders.gov.uk
Natural History Museum
Environmental education, natural science, craft 37999

Andover

Andover Museum, 6 Church Close, Andover SP10 1DP - T: (01264) 366283, Fax: 339152, E-mail: musmda@hants.gov.uk, Internet: www.hants.gov.uk/museum/andover. Dir.: David Allen
Local Museum
Local hist, archaeology, natural science 38000

Museum of the Iron Age, 6 Church Close, Andover SP10 1DP - T: (01264) 366283, Fax: 339152, E-mail: musmda@hants.gov.uk, Internet: www.hants.gov.uk/museum/ironagem. Dir.: David Allen
Archaeological Museum
Finds from the excavations, hist of southern Britain in the Iron Age 38001

Annaghmore

Ardress House and Farmyard Museum, Annaghmore BT62 1SQ - T: (028) 38851236. Dir.: Daniel Tennyson
Decorative Arts Museum / Agriculture Museum - 1977
Fine furniture and pictures 38002

Annan

Historic Resources Centre, c/o Annan Museum, Bank St, Annan DG12 6AA - T: (01461) 201384, Fax: 205876, E-mail: info@dumfriesmuseum.demon.co.uk, Internet: www.dumfriesmuseum.demon.co.uk
Local Museum
Ethnography, local history, relics, contemporary art, biographical essays 38003

Anstruther

Scottish Fisheries Museum, Saint Ayles, Habourhead, Anstruther KY10 3AB - T: (01333) 310628, Fax: 310628, E-mail: andrew@scottish-fisheries-museum.org, Internet: www.scottish-fisheries-museum.org. Dir.: Andrew Fox
Special Museum - 1969
History of Scotland's fishing industry and related trades, fishing gear, ship models and gear, fishermen's ethnography, whaling, aquarium, paintings and photographs with marine themes 38004

Antrim

Clotworthy Arts Centre, Castle Gardens, Randalstown Rd, Antrim BT41 4LH - T: (028) 94428000, Fax: 94460360, E-mail: clotworthy@antrim.gov.uk, Internet: www.antrim.gov.uk. Dir.: Kate Wimpress
Fine Arts Museum / Decorative Arts Museum
Art exhibits, scale model of Antrim castle, 17th c Anglo Dutch water garden 38005

Appin

Appin Wildlife Museum (closed) 38006

Appledore, Devon

North Devon Maritime Museum, Odun House, Odun Rd, Appledore, Devon EX39 1PT - T: (01237) 422064, Internet: www.php-net.com/ndmt. Dir.: A.E. Grant
Science&Tech Museum
Scale models of ships using North Devon ports from the 17th c onwards, paintings of ships and maritime scenes, and old photogr of the district and its people 38007

Arbigland

John Paul Jones Birthplace Museum, John Paul Jones Cottage, Arbigland DG2 8BQ - T: (01387) 880613, Fax: 260029, E-mail: postmaster@dumfriesmuseum.demon.co.uk, Internet: www.jpj.demon.co.uk. Chm.: Donald R. Usquhart
Special Museum
Navy history 38008

Arborfield

REME Museum of Technology, Isaac Newton Rd, Arborfield RG2 9NJ - T: (0118) 9763375, Fax: 9763375, E-mail: reme-museum@gtnet.gov.uk, Internet: www.rememuseum.org.uk. Dir.: I.W.J. Cleasby
Science&Tech Museum / Military Museum - 1958
History of the Corps of Royal Electrical and Mechanical Engineers, the British Army's equipment repair corps, documents, photos, equipment and memorabilia, weapons, small arms, electronics, aeronautics engineering, uniforms, medals 38009

Royal Electrical and Mechanical Engineers Museum → REME Museum of Technology

Arbroath

Abbot's House, Arbroath Abbey, Arbroath DD11 1EG - T: (01241) 2443101, Internet: home.clara.net/rabpert/a_house.htm
Archaeological Museum 38010

Arbroath Art Gallery, Library, Hill Terrace, Arbroath DD11 1PU - T: (01241) 875598, Fax: (01307) 462590, E-mail: the.meffan@angus.gov.uk, Internet: www.angus.gov.uk/history.htm. Cur.: N.K. Atkinson
Fine Arts Museum - 1898
Local artists' works, 2 paintings by Breughel 38011

Arbroath Museum, Signal Tower, Ladyloan, Arbroath DD11 1PU - T: (01241) 875598, Fax: 439263, E-mail: signal.tower@angus.gov.uk, Internet: www.angus.gov.uk/history.htm. Cur.: Fiona Guest
Local Museum - 1843
Bell Rock lighthouse artifacts, fishing 38012

Saint Vigeans Museum, Saint Vigeans, Arbroath - T: (01241) 878756, 2443101
Religious Arts Museum - 1960
Picts, stone carvings of particular symbols 38013

Arlington

Arlington Court, Arlington EX31 4LP - T: (01271) 850296, Fax: 851108, E-mail: arlingtoncourt@nationaltrust.org.uk. Dir.: Ana Chylak, Cur.: Patricia Stout (Carriages)
Special Museum
Coll of horse drawn carriages 38014

Armadale

Armadale Community Museum, West Main St, Armadale EH48 2JD - T: (01501) 678400, E-mail: armadale.library@westlothian.org.uk, Internet: www.wlonline.org. Man.: Elizabeth Hunter
Local Museum 38015

Museum of the Isles, Clan Donald Visitor Centre, Armadale Castle, Armadale IV45 8RS - T: (01471) 844227, Fax: 844275
Historical Museum
Story of 1300 years of Clan Donald's hist and of the Lordship of the Isles 38016

Armagh

Armagh County Museum, The Mall East, Armagh BT61 9BE - T: (028) 37523070, Fax: 37522631, E-mail: acm.um@nics.gov.uk, Internet: www.magni.irg.uk. Dir.: Catherine McCullough
Local Museum - 1935
Irish art, hist and natural hist of Armagh County since prehistoric times, local folklore, applied art incl some works and manuscripts by George Russell - library 38017

Hayloft Gallery, Palace Stable Heritage Centre, Palace Demesne, Armagh BT60 4EL - T: (028) 37529629, Fax: 37529630, E-mail: stables@armagh.gov.uk, Internet: www.armagh.gov.uk
Public Gallery 38018

Navan Centre, 81 Killylea Rd, Armagh BT60 4LD - T: (01861) 525550, Fax: 522323, E-mail: info@armagh.gov.uk, Internet: www.armagh.gov.uk
Local Museum
History, archaeology and mythology of Navan Fort (Emain Macha) 38019

Royal Irish Fusiliers Museum, Sovereign's House, The Mall East, Armagh BT61 9DL - T: (028) 37522911, Fax: 37522911. Dir.: Amanda Moreno
Military Museum
Hist of the regiment, uniforms, photographs 38020

Saint Patrick's Trian, 40 English St, Armagh BT61 7BA - T: (028) 37521801, Fax: 37510180, E-mail: education@saintpatrickstrian.com, Internet: www.armaghvisit.com. Dir.: Debbie McCamphill
Local Museum
Local history from prehistory, Celts, Vikings, Brian Boru, Georgian times 38021

Arnol

Arnol Blackhouse Museum, Arnol PA86 9DB - T: (0131) 5568400
Archaeological Museum 38022

Arreton

Arreton Manor, Arreton PO30 3AA - T: (01983) 528134. Dir.: N.H. Schroeder
Decorative Arts Museum - 1961
Manor from period of Henry VIII to Charles I, Jacobean and Elizabethan furniture, dolls, toys, relics, National Wireless museum 38023

Arundel

Arundel Museum and Heritage Centre, 61 High St, Arundel BN18 9AJ - T: (01903) 882456. Cur.: Alan Chapman
Local Museum - 1963 38024

Arundel Toy Museum Dolls House, 23 High St, Arundel BN18 9AD - T: (01903) 883101. Dir.: Diana Henderson
Special Museum - 1978
Britains model toy soldiers and animals/farms, small militaria, dolls houses and contents, games, tintoys, puppets, curiosities 38025

Ashburton

Ashburton Museum, 1 West St, Ashburton TQ13 7DT - T: (01364) 653278
Local Museum - 1954
Local history, American Indian antiques, costumes, arrows, tools 38026

Ashby-de-la-Zouch

Ashby-de-la-Zouch Museum, North St, Ashby-de-la-Zouch LE65 2HU - T: (01530) 560090. Dir.: Kenneth Hillier
Local Museum - 1982 38027

Ashford

Ashford Museum, Church Yard, Ashford - T: (01233) 631511, Fax: 502599, E-mail: a.d.terry@excite.co.uk. Pres.: Countess Mountbatten of Burma
Historical Museum
History of Ashford and the surrounding area, with exhibits reflecting the social and domestic life of the past 150 years, and the occupations carried on in the district 38028

Swanton Mill, Lower Mersham, Ashford TN25 7HS - T: (01233) 720223. Owner: John Bickel
Science&Tech Museum 38029

Ashington

Woodhorn Colliery Museum, Queen Elizabeth II Park, Ashington NE63 9YF - T: (01670) 856968, Fax: 810958, Internet: www.wansbeck.gov.uk. Dir.: Barry Mead
Science&Tech Museum
Coal-mining and socila history of SE Northumberland 38030

Ashton, Oundle

National Dragonfly Biomuseum, Ashton Wold, Ashton, Oundle PE8 5LZ - T: (01832) 272427, E-mail: ndmashton@aol.com, Internet: www.natdragonflymuseum.org.uk
Natural History Museum / Science&Tech Museum
Larva-feeding sessions, dragonflies in art, live larvae in tanks, Victorian hydropower station, vintage farm machinery coll, blacksmith's forge, local crafts, fish coll 38031

Ashton-under-Lyne

Central Art Gallery, Old St, Ashton-under-Lyne OL6 7SG - T: (0161) 3422650, Fax: 3422650, Internet: www.tameside.gov.uk. Dir.: Meg Lewis-Crosby
Public Gallery 38032

Museum of the Manchesters, Town Hall, Market Pl, Ashton-under-Lyne OL6 6DL - T: (0161) 3423078, Fax: 3431732. Dir.: Dr. Alan Wilson
Historical Museum - 1987
Social and regimental hist 38033

Portland Basin Museum, 1 Portland Pl, Ashton-under-Lyne OL7 0QA - T: (0161) 3432878, Fax: 3432869, E-mail: portland.basin@mail.gov.uk, Internet: www.tameside.gov.uk. Dir.: Dr. Alan Wilson
Local Museum 38034

Ashurst

National Dairy Museum, Longdown Dairy Farm, Deerleap Ln, Ashurst SO40 4UH - T: (023) 80293326, Fax: 80293376, E-mail: annette@longdown.uk.com. Dir.: Hannah Field
Agriculture Museum / Special Museum
Coll of horse-drawn and hand-pushed milk prams, history of dairy industry 38035

Ashwell

Ashwell Village Museum, Swan St, Ashwell SG7 5NY - T: (01462) 742956. Cur.: Peter Greener
Local Museum - 1930
Rural village life from the Stone Age to the present,

a Tudor building, snuff and tinder boxes, straw-plaiting tools, lace-making tools, objects formerly used in farming and everyday life, leather eyeglasses 38036

Aston Munslow

White House Museum of Buildings and Country Life, NE Craven Arms, Aston Munslow SY7 9ER
Local Museum 38037

Auchinleck

Boswell Museum and Mausoleum, Church Hill, Auchinleck KA18 2AE - T: (01290) 421185, 420931
Historical Museum
Coll of Boswelliana 38038

Auckengill

Northland Viking Centre (open june-september), Old School House, Auckengill KW1 4XP - T: (01955) 607771, Fax: 604524
Local Museum
Local history 38039

Augrès

Sir Francis Cook Gallery, Rte de la Trinité, Augrès JE3 5JN - T: (01534) 863333, Fax: 864437, E-mail: museum@jerseyheritagetrust.org, Internet: www.jerseyheritagetrust.org
Public Gallery 38040

Avebury

Alexander Keiller Museum, High St, Avebury SN8 1RF - T: (01672) 539250, Fax: 538038, E-mail: Avebury@nationaltrust.org.uk. Cur.: Rosamund Cleal
Archaeological Museum - 1938
Prehistoric artifacts from the world heritage site of Avebury, pottery, flint implements, animal bone, bone implements 38041

Great Barn Museum of Wiltshire Rural Life, Avebury SN8 1RF - T: (01672) 539555. Dir.: Susan Arnold
Local Museum - 1979
Rural and domestic life 38042

Aviemore

Strathspey Railway, Aviemore Station, Dalfaber Rd, Aviemore PH22 1PY - T: (01479) 810725, Fax: 811022, E-mail: information@strathspeyrailway.co.uk, Internet: www.strathspeyrailway.co.uk. Dir.: Laurence Grant
Science&Tech Museum 38043

Axbridge

Axbridge Museum, King John's Hunting Lodge, The Square, Axbridge BS26 2AP - T: (01934) 732012, Fax: (01278) 444076, E-mail: museums@sedgemoor.gov.uk. Dir.: Sarah Harbige
Local Museum
Archaeology 38044

Axminster

Axminster Museum, Old Court House, Church St, Axminster EX13 5LL - T: (01297) 34137, Fax: 32929, E-mail: axminster-museum@ukf.net
Local Museum 38045

Aylesbury

Buckinghamshire County Museum, Church St, Aylesbury HP20 2QP - T: (01296) 331441, Fax: 334884, E-mail: museum@bucksсc.gov.uk, Internet: www.buckscc.gov.uk/museum. Cur.: Sarah Gray, Keeper: Mike Palmer (Natural History), Catherine Weston (Social History), Alexandra MacCulloch (Art, Clothing, Textiles), Brett Thorn (Archaeology), David Erskine (Education, Exhibitions)
Local Museum - 1847
Buckinghamshire artefacts, prints, watercolours, drawings and paintings, studio pottery 38046

Florence Nightingale Museum, Claydon House, Middle Claydon, Aylesbury MK18 2EY - T: (01296) 73349 ext 693
Historical Museum
Objects associated with Florence Nightingale and with the Crimean War during which she became a celebrated public figure 38047

Ayot-Saint-Lawrence

Shaw's Corner, Ayot-Saint-Lawrence AL6 9BX - T: (01438) 820307, Fax: 820307, E-mail: shawscorner@nationaltrust.org.uk, Internet: www.nationaltrust.org/uk/shawscorner
Special Museum
Former home of George Bernard Shaw (1856-1950) from 1906 until his death, memorabilia including Nobel Prize related literature of 1925 and objects concerning the Oscar-winning work 'Pygmalion' 38048

Ayr

Ayrshire Yeomanry Museum, Rozelle House, Monument Rd, Ayr KA7 4NQ - T: (01292) 264091, Internet: www.saw.arts.ed.ac.uk/army/regiments/ayrshire.html
Military Museum 38049

Kyle and Carrick District Library and Museum, 12 Main St, Ayr KA8 8ED - T: (01292) 269141 ext 5227, Fax: 611593. Dir.: David T. Roy
Library with Exhibitions / Local Museum - 1934
Local history, rotating art coll 38050

Maclaurin Art Gallery, Rozelle Park, Monument Rd, Ayr KA7 4NQ - T: (01292) 443708, Fax: 442065. Man.: Elizabeth I. Kwasnik, Cur.: Michael Bailey
Fine Arts Museum - 1976
Maclaurin coll of contemporary art, fine and applied art, sculpture 38051

Rozelle House Galleries, Rozelle Park, Monument Rd, Ayr KA7 4NQ - T: (01292) 445447, 443708, Fax: 442065. Man.: Elizabeth I. Kwasnik
Local Museum / Fine Arts Museum - 1982
Local history, military exhibition, fine and applied art, Tom O'Shanter paintings 38052

Bacup

Natural History Society and Folk Museum, 24 Yorkshire St, Bacup OL13 9AE - T: (01706) 873961. Man.: Ben Ashworth, Cur.: Ken Simpson
Natural History Museum / Local Museum - 1878
Geology, Neolothic objects, local nature, household objects 38053

Baginton

Lunt Roman Fort, Coventry Rd, Baginton CV8 3AJ - T: (024) 76303567, Fax: 76832410, E-mail: luntromanfort@coventry.gov.uk, Internet: www.coventrymuseums.org.uk. Dir.: Roger Vaughan
Historical Museum
Roman cavalry fort 38054

Midland Air Museum, Coventry Airport, Baginton CV8 3AA - T: (024) 76301033, Fax: 76301033
Science&Tech Museum
Sir Frank Whittle Jet Heritage Centre, Wings over Coventry 38055

Bagshot

Archaeology Centre, 4-10 London Rd, Bagshot GU19 5HN - T: (01276) 451181, E-mail: geoffreycole@shaat.netscapeonline.co.uk. Dir.: Geoffrey Cole
Archaeological Museum
Prehistoric, Roman, Saxon, medieval and post-medieval archaeological artefacts 38056

Baildon

Bracken Hall Countryside Centre, Glen Rd, Baildon BD17 5EA - T: (01274) 584140. Dir.: John Dallas
Natural History Museum - 1981
Wildlife, enviroment 38057

Bakewell

Chatsworth House, Bakewell DE45 1PP - T: (01246) 582204, Fax: 583536, E-mail: visit@chatsworth-house.co.uk, Internet: www.chatsworth-house.co.uk
Decorative Arts Museum 38058

Old House Museum, Cunningham Pl, Bakewell DE45 1DD - T: (01629) 813165, 815294, E-mail: bakerwellmuseum@tiscali.co.uk, Internet: www.oldhousemuseum.org.uk
Local Museum - 1959
Costume, craftmen's tools, farming equipment, lacework, toys, cameras 38059

Bala

Bala Like Railway Museum, Station Llanuwchllyn, Bala LL23 7DD - T: (01678) 540666, Fax: 540535, Internet: www.bala-lake-railway.co.uk
Science&Tech Museum 38060

Canolfan Y Plase, Plassey St, Bala LL23 7SW - T: (01678) 520320. Chm.: I.B. Williams
Local Museum
Artwork and local heritage 38061

Ballallan

Museum Cheann A'Loch, School House, Ballallan PA87
Local Museum 38062

Ballasalla

Rushen Abbey, Manx National Heritage, Ballasalla IM9 3DB - T: (01624) 648000, Fax: 648001, E-mail: enquiries@nmh.gov.im, Internet: www.gov.im/mnh
Religious Arts Museum
Cistercian community life, archaeology 38063

Ballindalloch

Glenfarclas Distillery Museum, Ballindalloch AB37 9BD - T: (01807) 500245, Fax: 500234, E-mail: j&ggrant@glenfarclas.demon.co.uk. Dir.: J. Grant
Science&Tech Museum - 1973 38064

Ballycastle

Ballycastle Museum, 59 Castle St, Ballycastle, Co. Antrim - T: (012657) 62942, 62024
Local Museum
Folk and social history 38065

Larrybane and Carrick-A-Rede, Ballintoy, Ballycastle, Co. Antrim - T: (012657) 62178, 31159
Local Museum 38066

Ballygrant

Finlaggan Centre, The Cottage, Ballygrant PA45 7QL - T: (01496) 810629, Fax: 810856, E-mail: LynMags@aol.com, Internet: www.islay.com
Local Museum 38067

Ballymena

Arthur Cottage, c/o Borough Council, 1b, Church St, Ballymena BT43 6DF - T: (028) 25880781, 25638494, Fax: 25660400. Cur.: May Kirkpatrick, Sam Fleming
Historical Museum 38068

Ballymena Museum, 3 Wellington Court, Ballymena BT43 5EJ - T: (028) 256421166, Fax: 25638582. Dir.: William Blair
Local Museum / Folklore Museum
Mixed local history, folklife coll, farm machinery 38069

Royal Irish Regiment Museum, RIR Headquarter, Saint Patrick's Barracks, Ballymena BT43 7NX - T: (028) 25661383/86, Fax: 25661378, E-mail: hqririsht@royalirishregiment.co.uk, Internet: www.royalirishregiment.co.uk. Dir.: M. Hegan
Military Museum
Military history since 1689 38070

Ballymoney

Ballymoney Museum, 33 Charlotte St, Ballymoney BT53 6AY - T: (028) 27662280, Fax: 27667659, E-mail: keith.beattie@ballymoney.gov.uk, Internet: www.1798ballymoney.org.uk
Local Museum
Local history since the earliest settlement in Ireland, motorcycle races, military history, popular culture, art, crafts 38071

Leslie Hill Open Farm, Macfin Rd, Ballymoney BT53 6QL - T: (028) 65663109, 65666803, Fax: 65666803. Dir.: James Leslie
Agriculture Museum
Horse-drawn farm machines 38072

Bamburgh

Bamburgh Castle, Bamburgh NE69 7DF - T: (01668) 214515, Fax: 214060, E-mail: bamburghcastle@aol.com, Internet: www.bamburghcastle.com. Dir.: Francis Watson-Armstrong
Historical Museum 38073

Grace Darling Museum, Radcliffe Rd, Bamburgh NE69 7AE - T: (01668) 214465, Fax: 214465. Cur.: Christine Bell
Historical Museum - 1938 38074

Banbury

Banbury Museum, Spiceball Park Rd, Banbury OX16 2PQ - T: (01295) 259855, Fax: 672652, E-mail: banburymuseum@cherwell-dc.gov.uk, Internet: www.cherwell-dc.gov.uk/banburymuseum. Dir.: Simon Townsend, Sc. Staff: Natalie Chankers (Education), Dale Johnson (Events, Education)
Local Museum - 1958
Local history since 1600, costume, canals and boat building - archives, library 38075

Upton House, Banbury OX15 6HT - T: (01295) 670266, Fax: 670266, E-mail: vuplan@smtp.ntrust.org.uk, Internet: www.ntrustsevern.org.uk. Dir.: Oliver Lane
Fine Arts Museum / Decorative Arts Museum / Historic Site - 1948
Brussels tapestries, porcelain from Sèvres, Chelsea figurines, furniture, coll of internationally important paintings 38076

Banchory

Banchory Museum, Bridge St, Banchory AB31 5SX - T: (01771) 622906, Fax: 622884, E-mail: heritage@aberdeenshire.gov.uk. Dir.: Dr. David M. Bertie
Local Museum - 1977
History of the Banchory area, social and domestic life, life and work of the local musician Scott Skinner, natural history, royal commemorative porcelain 38077

Crathes Castle, Crathes, Banchory AB31 5QJ - T: (01330) 844525, Fax: 844797, E-mail: crathes@nts.org.uk, Internet: www.nts.org.uk. Man.: Alexander Gordon
Decorative Arts Museum - 1951
Furnishings and decoration, painted ceiling from the end of the 16th c - garden 38078

Banff

Banff Museum, High St, Banff AB45 1AE - T: (01771) 622906, Fax: 622884, E-mail: heritage@aberdeenshire.gov.uk. Cur.: William K. Mine, Andrew F. Hill
Local Museum - 1828
Banff silver, arms and armour 38079

Bangor, County Down

North Down Heritage Centre, Town Hall, Bangor Castle, Bangor, County Down BT20 4BT - T: (028) 91270371, 91271200, Fax: 91271370, E-mail: heritage@northdown.gov.uk, Internet: www.northdown.gov.uk/heritage. Dir.: I.A. Wilson
Local Museum - 1984
Local hist 38080

Bangor, Gwynedd

Bangor Museum and Art Gallery, Ffordd Gwynedd, Bangor, Gwynedd LL57 1DT - T: (01248) 353368, Fax: 370426, E-mail: patwest@gwynedd.gov.uk, Internet: www.gwynedd.gov.uk/museums. Dir.: Pat West, Cur.: J.P. Bennyworth
Local Museum - 1884
Archaeology, furniture, costume, textiles, prints 38081

Natural History Museum, c/o School of Biological Sciences, University of Wales, Brambell Bldg, Bangor, Gwynedd LL57 2UW - T: (01248) 351151 ext 2296, Fax: 371644, E-mail: c.bishop@bangor.ac.uk. Cur.: Dr. C. Bishop
Natural History Museum - 1900
Zoology, flowering of North Wales 38082

Penrhyn Castle, Bangor, Gwynedd LL57 4HN - T: (01248) 353084, Fax: 371281, E-mail: ppemsn@smtp.ntrust.org.uk. Dir.: Joan Bayliss
Fine Arts Museum / Decorative Arts Museum - 1952
19th c furnished castle, neo-Norman architecture, industrial railway, dolls, Dutch and Italian masters 38083

Barmouth

Barmouth Sailors' Institute Collection, The Quay, Barmouth LL42 1ET - T: (01341) 241333, Internet: www.cmw.org.uk
Historical Museum
Maritime heritage 38084

Lifeboat Museum (closed) 38085

Ty Gwyn and Ty Crwn, The Quay, Barmouth LL42 1ET - T: (01341) 241333, Internet: www.cmw.org.uk
Local Museum
History of Barmouth as a port 38086

Barnard Castle

The Bowes Museum, Newgate, Barnard Castle DL12 8NP - T: (01833) 690606, Fax: 637163, E-mail: info@bowesmuseum.org.uk, Internet: www.bowesmuseum.org.uk. Dir.: Adrian Jenkins, Sc. Staff: Howard Coutts (Ceramics), Joanna Hashagen (Textiles), Claire Jones (Furniture), Amy Barker (Fine Art), Cons.: Richard Hobson, Anne-Marie Hughes (Textil)
Decorative Arts Museum / Fine Arts Museum / Local Museum - 1892
European painting, works by El Greco, Goya, Tiepolo, Boudin, Fragonard, pottery and porcelain, especially French, textiles, sculpture, furniture, other decorative, European Antiquities arts 38087

Barnet

Museum of Domestic Design and Architecture MODA, Middlesex University, Cat Hill, Barnet EN4 8HT - T: (020) 84115244, Fax: 84115271, E-mail: moda@mdx.ac.uk, Internet: www.moda.mdx.ac.uk. Dir.: Ken Mannering
University Museum / Decorative Arts Museum
Silver studio coll, Sir Richards library, Peggy Anguz archive; Charles Hassler coll, British and American domestic design archive, crown wallpaper archive 38088

Barnoldswick

Bancroft Mill Engine Trust, Gillians Ln, Barnoldswick BB8 5QR - T: (01282) 865626, Internet: www.pendletourism.com. Dir.: T. D. Gill
Science&Tech Museum
Corliss textile mill engine, weaving 38089

Barnsley, South Yorkshire

Cannon Hall Museum, Cawthorne, Barnsley, South Yorkshire S75 4AT - T: (01226) 790270, Fax: www.barnsley.gov.uk, E-mail: cannonhall@barnsley.gov.uk
Fine Arts Museum 38090

Cooper Gallery, Church St, Barnsley, South Yorkshire S70 2AH - T: (01226) 242905, Fax: 297283, E-mail: coopergallery@barnsley.gov.uk, Internet: www.barnsley.gov.uk
Public Gallery - 1980
17th, 18th and 19th c European paintings and English drawings and watercolours 38091

Worsbrough Mill Museum, Worsbrough Bridge, Barnsley, South Yorkshire S70 5LJ - T: (01226) 774527, Fax: 774527. Cur.: Debra L. Bushby
Open Air Museum / Science&Tech Museum - 1976
Working 17th c water powered corn mill, working 19th c oil engine powered corn mill 38092

Barnstaple

Museum of Barnstaple and North Devon, The Square, Barnstaple EX32 8LN - T: (01271) 346747, Fax: 346407, E-mail: alison_mills@northdevon.gov.uk, Internet: www.devonmuseums.net/barnstaple.

Dir.: Alison Miller
Local Museum - 1888
Natural and human history of Northern Devon, industry, decorative arts, archaeology, geology, social history, militaria - inc. the Royal Devon Yeomanry Museum 38093

Saint Anne's Chapel and Old Grammar School Museum (closed) 38094

Barrow-in-Furness

Dock Museum, North Rd, Barrow-in-Furness LA14 2PW - T: (01229) 894444, Fax: 811361, E-mail: dockmuseum@barrowbc.gov.uk, Internet: www.dockmuseum.org.uk. Dir.: Sue Jenkins
Local Museum - 1994
V.S.E.L. glass photographic negative archive, maritime, social hist, archaeology, geology, fine art 38095

Furness Abbey, Barrow-in-Furness LA13 0TJ - T: (01229) 823420, Internet: www.english-heritage.org.uk
Fine Arts Museum
Architectural stonework, sculpture 38096

Barrowford

Pendle Heritage Centre, Park Hill, Barrowford BB9 6JQ - T: (01282) 661704, Fax: 611718. Dir.: E.M.J. Miller
Local Museum 38097

Barton-upon-Humber

Baysgarth House Museum, Baysgarth Leisure Park, Caistor Rd, Barton-upon-Humber DN18 6AH - T: (01652) 632318, Fax: 636659
Local Museum
18th cent mansion house, porcelain, local hist, archeology and geology 38098

Basildon

The Motorboat Museum, Wat Tyler Country Park, Pitsea Hall Ln, Basildon SS16 4UH - T: (01268) 550077, Fax: 581093, 584207, E-mail: julie.graham@basildon.gov.uk, Internet: www.themotorboatmuseum.org. Dir.: Steven Prewer
Science&Tech Museum - 1986
Carstairs coll, Bert Savidge coll, motorboating (sports, leisure), in- and outboard motors, over 35 crafts - library 38099

Potland Museum, Langdon Visitor Centre, Third Av, Lower Dunton Rd, Basildon SS16 6EB - T: (01268) 419103, Fax: 546137, E-mail: melaniel@essexwt.org.uk, Internet: www.essexwt.org.uk
Local Museum - 1933 38100

Basing

Basing House, Redbridge Rd, Basing RG24 7HB - T: (01256) 467294, E-mail: musmat@hants.gov.uk, Internet: www.hants.gov.uk/museum/basingho,. Dir.: Alan Turton
Archaeological Museum
Archaeological material from Basing House 38101

Basingstoke

Milestones: Hampshire's Living History Museum, Basingstoke Leisure Park, Churchill Way W, Basingstoke RG21 6YR - T: (01256) 477766, Fax: 477784, E-mail: milestones@hants.gov.uk, Internet: www.milestones.museum.com. Cur.: Gary Wragg
Historical Museum
Thornycroft and Tasker coll, Hampshire social and domestic hist coll, AA vehicle and memorabilia coll 38102

Stratfield Saye House and Wellington Exhibition, Stratfield Saye House, Stratfield Saye, Basingstoke RG27 0AS - T: (01256) 882882, Fax: 882882, E-mail: info@stratfield-saye.co.uk, Internet: www.stratfield-saye.co.uk
Local Museum
Home of Dukes of Wellington, paintings, captured from Joseph Bonaparte, and the Great Duke's personal belongings - Library 38103

The Vyne, Sherborne Saint John, Basingstoke RG24 9HL - T: (01256) 881337, Fax: 881720, E-mail: thevyne@ntrust.org.uk, Internet: www.nationaltrust.org.uk/southern. Dir.: J. Ingram
Decorative Arts Museum - 1958
Tudor house with renovations (1650-1760), Flemish glass, majolica tiles, panelling, furniture of Charles II, Queen Anne and Chippendale periods, rococo decoration 38104

Willis Museum, Old Town Hall, Market Pl, Basingstoke RG21 7QD - T: (01256) 465902, E-mail: sue.tapliss@hants.gov.uk, Internet: www.hants.gov.uk/museum/willis. Dir.: Sue Tapliss
Local Museum - 1930
Local hist, archaeology, natural sciences 38105

Bath

American Museum in Britain, Claverton Manor, Bath BA2 7BD - T: (01225) 460503, Fax: 469160, E-mail: amibbath@aol.com, Internet: www.americanmuseum.org. Dir.: William McNaught
Decorative Arts Museum - 1961
17th-19th c American decorative art and social hist, furnished period rooms, maritime hist, replica of Captain's cabin, Indian section, 18th c tavern, folk art gallery, New Gallery housing the Dallas Pratt Coll of maps - library 38106

Bath Abbey Heritage Vaults, 13 Kingston Bldgs, Bath BA1 1LT - T: (01225) 422462, Fax: 429990, E-mail: laj@heritagevaults.fsnet.co.uk
Religious Arts Museum 38107

Bath Industrial Heritage Centre → Museum of Bath at Work

Bath Police Museum, Manvers St, Bath BA1 1JN - T: (01225) 444343, 842482, Fax: 842523. Cur.: Bob Allard
Special Museum - 1966
Police helmets and headgear 38108

Bath Postal Museum, 8 Broad St, Bath BA1 5LJ - T: (01225) 460333, Fax: 460333, E-mail: info@bathpostalmuseum.org, Internet: www.bathpostalmuseum.org. Dir.: Patrick Cassels, Cur.: Steve Bailey
Special Museum - 1979
4,000 years of communication, fron Sumarian tablets 2,000 BC to email 38109

Bath Royal Literary and Scientific Institution, 16-18 Queen Sq, Bath BA1 2HN - T: (01225) 312084, Fax: 442460, E-mail: admin@brlsi.org, Internet: www.brlsi.org. Chm.: Nancy Catchpole
Association with Coll - 1824
Moore coll of fossils incl Type Specimens, Jenyns coll of natural hist, material-herbaria, Darwin letters and others from eminent naturalists, geology, ethnology, art, archaeology, mineralogy, early photography - library, archves 38110

Beckford's Tower and Museum, Lansdown Rd, Bath BA1 9BH - T: (01225) 422212, 460705, Fax: 481850, E-mail: beckford@bptrust.demon.co.uk, Internet: www.bath-preservation-trust.org.uk. Dir.: Arnold Wilson
Local Museum - 1977/2000 38111

Book Museum (closed) 38112

Building of Bath Museum, The Countess of Huntingdon's Chapel, The Vineyards, Bath BA1 5NA - T: (01225) 333895, Fax: 445473, E-mail: cathryn@bathmuseum.co.uk, Internet: www.bath-preservation-trust.org.uk. Dir.: Cathryn Spen
Special Museum 38113

Georgian Museum → Number 1 Royal Crescent Museum

Guildhall, High St, Bath BA1 5AW - T: (01225) 477724, Fax: 477442, E-mail: ian_burns@bathnes.gov.uk, Internet: www.bathnes.gov.uk. Dir.: S. Bird
Decorative Arts Museum / Historic Site
18th c Banqueting Room, chandeliers, coll of Royal portraits 38114

Holburne Museum of Art, Great Pulteney St, Bath BA2 4DB - T: (01225) 466669, Fax: 333121, E-mail: holburne@bath.ac.uk, Internet: www.bath.ac.uk/holburne. Dir.: Christopher Woodward, Cur.: Amina Wright
Decorative Arts Museum / Fine Arts Museum - 1893
Decorative and fine art, furniture, silver, miniatures, porcelain, majolica, bronzes, netsukes, paintings by Stubbs, Gainsborough, Guardi and 18th c Old Masters together with 20th c work by leading British artist-craftspeople embracing textiles, ceramics, furniture, calligraphy, sculpture - library 38115

Impossible Microworld Museum, 4 Monmouth St, Bath BA1 2AJ - T: (01225) 333003, Fax: 333633, E-mail: info@theimpossiblemicroworld.com, Internet: www.theimpossiblemicroworld.com
Special Museum
Microscopic sculptures af animals, celebrities, buildings, works of art 38116

Museum of Bath at Work, Camden Works, Julian Rd, Bath BA1 2RH - T: (01225) 318348, Fax: 318348, E-mail: mobaw@hotmail.co.uk, Internet: www.bath-at-work.org.uk. Dir.: Stuart Burroughs
Science&Tech Museum - 1978
Coll of working machinery, hand-tools, brasswork, patterns, bottles and documents of all kinds, displayed as realistically as possible to convey an impression of the working life, local engineering, power generation - archive 38117

Museum of Costume, Bennett St, Bath BA1 2QH - T: (01225) 477789, Fax: 444793, E-mail: costume_enquiries@bathnes.gov.uk, Internet: www.museumofcostume.co.uk. Dir.: R. Harden
Special Museum - 1963
Some pre-18th c costumes, mainly 18th c to present day dress for men, women and children, incl haute couture pcs - study centre 38118

Museum of East Asian Art, 12 Bennett St, Bath BA1 2QJ - T: (01225) 464640, Fax: 461718, E-mail: museum@east-asian-art.freeserve.co.uk, Internet: www.east-asian-art.co.uk. Cur.: Ailisa Laxton
Decorative Arts Museum
Over 1600 art treasures in pottery, stoneware, porcelain, bronze, jade, lacquer 38119

Number 1 Royal Crescent Museum, 1 Royal Crescent, Bath BA1 2LR - T: (01225) 428126, Fax: 481850, E-mail: admin@bptrust.demon.co.uk, Internet: www.bath-preservation-trust.org.uk/museums/no1. Dir.: Michael Briggs, Cur.: Elizabeth Grant
Historical Museum - 1970
Georgian Town House, example of Palladian architecture redecorated and furnished, Beckfords Tower 38120

Roman Baths Museum, Pump Room, Stall St, Bath BA1 1LZ - T: (01225) 477774, Fax: 477243, E-mail: stephen_clews@bathnes.gov.uk, Internet: www.romanbaths.co.uk. Cur.: Stephen Clews
Archaeological Museum - 1895
Archaeological history of Bath in prehistoric, Roman, Saxon, medieval and later times 38121

The Royal Photographic Society Octagon Galleries (closed for re-location), The Octagon, Milsom St, Bath BA1 1DN - T: (01225) 462841, Fax: 469880, E-mail: collection@collection.rps.org, Internet: www.rps.org. Dir.: John Page
Special Museum - 1893/1980
Photography in all its aspects with special emphasis on British 19th and early 20th c photography, equipment and books, periodicals - library, archives 38122

Sally Lunn's Refreshment House and Kitchen Museum, 4 North Parade Passage, Bath BA1 1NX - T: (01225) 811311, 461634, Fax: 811800, E-mail: corsham@ad.com, Internet: www.sallylunns.co.uk. Dir.: Jonathan Overton, Julian Abraham
Historical Museum - 1680
Bakery and kitchen equipment 38123

Victoria Art Gallery, Bridge St, Bath BA2 4AT - T: (01225) 477233, Fax: 477231, E-mail: Jon_Benington@bathnes.gov.uk, Internet: www.victoriagal.org.uk. Cur.: Jon Benington
Fine Arts Museum / Decorative Arts Museum / Public Gallery - 1900
British paintings, sculptures, drawings and prints 18-20th c, ceramics and glass, European and British watches, British miniatures and silhouettes, craft, photography 38124

The William Herschel Museum, 19 New King St, Bath BA1 2BL - T: (01225) 311342, Fax: 446865, Internet: www.bath-preservation-trust.org.uk. Dir.: Prof. Francis Ring, Cur.: Debbie James
Science&Tech Museum - 1978
Astronomy, 18th c music, thermology 38125

Bathgate

Bennie Museum, 9-11 Mansefield St, Bathgate EH48 4HU - T: (01506) 634944, E-mail: thornton@benniemuseum.freeserve.co.uk, Internet: www.benniemuseum.homestead.com. Cur.: William I. Millan
Local Museum
Local hist, early photographs, glass from Bathgate glassworks and Victoriana 38126

Batley

Bagshaw Museum, Wilton Park, Batley WF17 0AS - T: (01924) 326155, 472514, Fax: 326164, 420017, E-mail: bagshaw.museum@kirkleesmc.gov.uk, Internet: www.kirklees.gov.uk/community/museums/museums/shtml. Dir.: Kathryn White, Cur.: Brian Haigh
Local Museum - 1911
Antiquities of Britain and other areas, relics, ethnography, local hist, industries, natural hist, geology, textile industry, Oriental ceramics and finds, egyptology, tropical rainforest 38127

Batley Art Gallery, Market Pl, Batley WF17 5DA - T: (01924) 326090, Fax: 326308, E-mail: robert.hall@kirkleesmc.gov.uk. Dir.: Jenny Hall
Fine Arts Museum - 1948
Local arts and crafts, children's art, 19th-20th c art, works by Francis Bacon and Max Ernst - library 38128

Battle

Battle Abbey, Battle TN33 0AD - T: (014246) 773792, Fax: 775059
Historic Site 38129

Battle Museum of Local History, The Almonry, High St, Battle TN33 0EA - T: (01424) 775955, Fax: 772827, E-mail: ann@battlehill.freeserve.co.uk. Dir.: Anne Ainsley
Local Museum - 1956
Local history, Romano-British ironwork, gunpowder industry, battle artifacts, diorama of the Battle of Hastings and reproductions of the Bayeux Tapestry 38130

Buckleys Museum of Shops → Buckleys Yesterday's World

Buckleys Yesterday's World, 89-90 High St, Battle TN33 0AQ - T: (01424) 775378, 774269, Fax: 775174, E-mail: info@yesterdaysworld.co.uk, Internet: www.yesterdaysworld.co.uk. Dir.: Annette Buckley
Special Museum
Advertising material and the contents of old shops, Victorian and Edwardian social history 38131

Battlesbridge

Battlesbridge Motorcycle Museum, Maltings Rd, Battlesbridge SS11 7RF - T: (01268) 575000, Fax: 575001, E-mail: jimgallie@virgin.net
Science&Tech Museum 38132

Beaconsfield

Royal Army Educational Corps Museum, Wilton Park, Beaconsfield HP9 2RP - T: (01494) 683232
Military Museum
Hist of the RAEC, consists mainly of uniforms, pictorial material and small artefacts, with some weapons 38133

Beaminster

Beaminster Museum, Whitcombe Rd, Beaminster DT8 3NB - T: (01308) 863623, 862880. Dir.: Dr. Murray Rose
Local Museum 38134

Parnham House, Beaminster DT8 3NA - T: (01308) 862204, Fax: 863494
Local Museum 38135

Beamish

Beamish, the North of England Open Air Museum, Beamish DH9 0RG - T: (0191) 3704000, Fax: 3704001, E-mail: museum@beamish.org.uk, Internet: www.beamish.org.uk. Dir.: Miriam Harte
Open Air Museum / Local Museum - 1971
Period areas (1820s and 1913), early railways (1825), Town street, colliery village and farm (1913), manor house (1825) - photographic archive, reference library, trade catalogues 38136

Beaumaris

Beaumaris Castle, Beaumaris LL58 8AB - T: (01248) 810361
Archaeological Museum 38137

Beaumaris Gaol and Courthouse, Steeple Ln, Beaumaris LL58 8ED - T: (01248) 810921, 724444, Fax: 750282, Internet: www.anglesey.gov.uk. Head: Alun Gruffydd
Special Museum 38138

Museum of Childhood Memories, 1 Castle St, Beaumaris LL58 8AP - T: (01248) 712498, Fax: 716869, Internet: www.aboutbritain.com/museumofchildhoodmemories.htm. Dir.: Robert Brown
Special Museum - 1973
Audio and visual entertainment, pottery and glass, trains, cars, clockwork toys, ships and aeroplanes, art, educational toys, dolls, games, money boxes 38139

Beccles

Beccles and District Museum, Leman House, Ballygate, Beccles NR34 9ND - T: (01502) 715722, Internet: www.becclesmuseum.org.uk. Cur.: James Woodrow
Local Museum
Natural history, geology, archaeology 38140

Beckenham

Bethlem Royal Hospital Archives and Museum, Monks Orchard Rd, Beckenham BR3 3BX - T: (020) 87764307, 87764227, Fax: 87764045, E-mail: museum@bethlem.freeserve.co.uk, Internet: www.bethlemheritage.org.uk. Cur.: Patricia Allderidge
Special Museum - 1970
Paintings and drawings by artists who have suffered from mental disorder, incl Richard Dadd, Louis Wain, Vaslav Nijinsky, William Kurelek, historical exhibits relating to Bethlem Hospital (the original 'Bedlam'), and to the history of psychiatry, mental health 38141

Bedale

Bedale Museum, Bedale Hall, Bedale DL8 1AA - T: (01677) 423272, Fax: 423272. Cur.: Denis Stockwell
Local Museum
Local history, clothing, toys, craft tools, hand-drawn fire engine from 1748 38142

Beddgelert

Sygun Copper Mine, Beddgelert LL55 4NE - T: (01766) 510100, Fax: 510102, E-mail: SnowdoniaMine@compuserve.com, Internet: ourworld.compuserve.com/homepages/SnowdoniaMine. Cur.: Sandra Amies
Science&Tech Museum 38143

Beddington

Carew Manor and Dovecote, Church Rd, Beddington SM6 7NH - T: (020) 87704781, Fax: 87704777, E-mail: sutton.museum@ukonline.co.uk, Internet: www.sutton.gov.uk. Man.: Valary Murphy
Historic Site 38144

Bedford

Bedford Central Library Gallery, Harpur St, Bedford MK40 1PG - T: (01234) 350931
Public Gallery 38145

Bedford Museum, Castle Ln, Bedford MK40 3XD - T: (01234) 353323, Fax: 273401, E-mail: bmuseum@bedford.gov.uk, Internet: www.bedfordmuseum.org. Dir.: R.A. Brind

Local Museum - 1959
Local archaeological finds, history, natural history, medieval tile pavement, iron age bronze mirror, lace bobbins 38146

Cecil Higgins Art Gallery, Castle Close, Castle Ln, Bedford MK40 3RP - T: (01234) 211222, Fax: 327149, E-mail: chag@bedford.gov.uk, Internet: www.cecilhigginsartgallery.org. Cur.: Caroline Bacon
Fine Arts Museum / Decorative Arts Museum - 1949
Fine and decorative arts, English watercolours, international prints, English and continental porcelain, glass, furniture, silver, sculptures, lace, costume, Handley-Read coll of Victorian and Edwardian decorative arts, William Burges room 38147

Elstow Moot Hall, Church End, Elstow, Bedford MK42 9XT - T: (01234) 266889, Fax: 228531, E-mail: wilemans@deed.bedfordshire.gov.uk. Dir.: M. Kenworthy
Historical Museum - 1951
17th c cultural history, local history, architecture 38148

John Bunyan Museum, Mill St, Bedford MK40 3EU - T: (01234) 213722, Fax: 213722, E-mail: bmeeting@dialstart.net. Dir.: Doreen Watson
Special Museum - 1947
"The Pilgrim's Progress" in over 170 languages and dialects, artefacts relating to John Bunyan's life and times - library 38149

Beetham

Heron Corn Mill and Museum of Papermaking, Waterhouse Mills, Beetham LA7 7AR - T: (015395) 65027, Fax: 65033, E-mail: nt.stobbs@virgin.net. Dir.: Neil T. Stobbs
Science&Tech Museum - 1975/1988
18th c working water driven corn mill, machinery, displays tell the story of 900 yrs of milling, displays of papermaking separate from Corn Mill in restored carter's barn - Corn mill, Museum of Papermaking 38150

Belfast

Crown Liquor Saloon, Great Victoria St, Belfast, Co. Antrim - T: (01232) 249476
Decorative Arts Museum
Victorian ornamentation, woodwork, glass and tiles 38151

Fernhill House, Glencairn Park, Belfast, Co. Antrim - T: (01232) 715599
Historical Museum
Social, economic and military history 38152

Lagan Lookout Centre, 1 Donegall Quay, Belfast BT1 3EA - T: (028) 90315444, Fax: 90311955, E-mail: lookout@laganside.com, Internet: www.laganside.com
Science&Tech Museum
Hist of Belfast 38153

Natural History Museum, c/o School of Biology and Biochemistry, Queen's University, Medical and Biological Centre, 97 Lisburn Rd, Belfast BT9 7BL - T: (028) 90335786, Fax: 90236505, E-mail: sobb.office@qub.ac.uk, Internet: www.qub.ac.uk/bb/. Dir.: Prof. W.I. Montgomery
Natural History Museum / University Museum
Educational zoology and geology collections 38154

Old Museum Arts Centre, 7 College Sq N, Belfast BT1 6AR - T: (028) 90235053, Fax: 90322912, E-mail: info@oldmuseumartscentre.freeserve.co.uk, Internet: www.oldmuseumartscentre.org. Dir.: Anne McReynolds
Public Gallery 38155

Ormeau Baths Gallery, 18a Ormeau Av, Belfast BT2 8HQ - T: (028) 90321402, Fax: 90312232, E-mail: ormeaubathsgallery@btinternet.com. Dir.: Hugh Mulholland
Fine Arts Museum
Contemporary Irish and international art 38156

The People's Museum, Fernhill House, Glencairn Park, Belfast BT13 3PT - T: (028) 90715599, Fax: 90715582. Dir.: Thomas G. Kirkham
Local Museum
Social and military coll 38157

The Police Museum, Brooklyn, Knock Rd, Belfast BT5 6LE - T: (028) 90650222 ext 22499, Fax: 90700124, E-mail: museum@psni.police.uk, Internet: www.psni.police.uk. Man.: Hugh Forrester
Military Museum
Includes uniforms and equipment, firearms, medals and other items relating to policing in Ireland from the early 19th c to date, database of RIC service records 1822-1922 38158

The Royal Ulster Constabulary Museum → The Police Museum

Royal Ulster Rifles Regimental Museum, The Royal Irish Rangers, 5 Waring St, Belfast BT1 2EW - T: (028) 90232086, Fax: 90232086, E-mail: rurmuseum@yahoo.co.uk. Cur.: J. Knox
Military Museum - 1935
Uniforms, medals, history of the regiment 38159

Ulster Museum, Museums and Galleries of Northern Ireland, Botanic Gardens, Belfast BT9 5AB - T: (028) 90383000, Fax: 90383003, E-mail: john.wilson.um@nics.gov.uk, Internet: www.ulstermuseum.org.uk. Dir.: John Wilson, Sc. Staff: S.B. Kennedy (Fine and Applied Art), R. Warner (Human History), P.S. Doughty (The Sciences)
Local Museum - 1892
International art, Irish painting, contemporary Irish art, silver ceramics, Williamite glass, Irish and European antiquities, treasure from Spanish Armada galleass Girona, Irish botany, zoology, geology, wildlife art, industrial technology and history, numismatics 38160

Whowhatwherewhenwhy W5, Odyssey, 2 Queen's Quay, Belfast BT3 9QQ - T: (028) 90467700, E-mail: [name]@w5online.co.uk, Internet: www.w5online.co.uk. Dir.: Dr. Sally Montgomery
Science&Tech Museum
Siences 38161

Bembridge

Bembridge Maritime Museum and Shipwreck Centre, Providence House, Sherbourne St, Bembridge PO35 5SB - T: (01983) 872223, Fax: 873125, E-mail: museum@isle-of-wight.uk.com, Internet: www.isle-of-wight.uk.com/shipwrecks. Dir.: Martin Woodward
Historical Museum - 1978
Shipwrecks, maritime history, diving equipment, pirate gold and silver, steamship artefacts, salvage, lifeboats, navigational instruments, local history 38162

Benbecula

Museum Nan Eilean, Sgoil Lionacleit, Lionacleit, Benbecula HS7 5PJ - T: (01870) 602864, Fax: 602817, E-mail: danamacphee@cne-siar.gov.uk, Internet: www.cne-siar.gov.uk. Dir.: Richard Langhorne
Local Museum
History and culture of the Islands 38163

Benburb

Blackwater Valley Museum, 89 Milltown Rd, Tullymore Etra, Benburb BT71 7LZ - T: (028) 90311156, Fax: 90311264, E-mail: thelma@ulsterprovidenlofsenet.co.uk. Dir.: Erskine J. Holmes
Local Museum
Set of machinery, spinning, winding, warping, beaming, weaving, forge 38164

Benenden

Mervyn Quinlan Museum, Benenden Hospital, Goddards Green Rd, Benenden TN17 4AX - T: (01580) 240333, Fax: 241877, E-mail: wrichley@benenden.star.co.uk. Cur.: M. Quinlan
Historical Museum
History of the hospital 38165

Benson

Benson Veteran Cycle Museum, 61 Brook St, Benson OX10 6LH - T: (01491) 838414
Science&Tech Museum
600 veteran and vintage cycles (1818-1930) 38166

Berkeley

Berkeley Castle, Berkeley GL13 9BQ - T: (01453) 810332, Fax: 512995, E-mail: info@berkeley-castle.com, Internet: www.berkeley-castle.com. Man.: E.J. Halls
Historical Museum
Paintings, furniture, tapestries, porcelain and silver 38167

Jenner Museum, The Chantry, Church Ln, Berkeley GL13 9BH - T: (01453) 810631, Fax: 811690, E-mail: manager@jennermuseum.com, Internet: www.jennermuseum.com. Dir.: D. Mullin
Special Museum - 1985
Illustration of the life and career of Edward Jenner, coll of memorabilia and personal possessions, computerized exhibition on immunology, medical science as founded by E. Jenner 38168

Berkhamsted

Dacorum Heritage, Museum Store, Clarence Rd, Berkhamsted HP4 3YL - T: (01442) 879525, Fax: 879525, E-mail: dacht@mattwheeler.freeserve.co.uk, Internet: www.hertsmuseums.org.uk/dacorum. Cur.: Matthew Wheeler
Local Museum
History of the borough of Dacorum 38169

Berkswell

Berkswell Village Museum, Lavender Hall Ln, Berkswell CV7 7BJ - T: (01676) 534981, Internet: www.baisley.co.uk. Dir.: D. Tracey
Local Museum
Local artefacts (19th-20th c), Saxon Parish of Berkswell 38170

Bernera

Urras Eachdraibh Sgire Bhearnaraidh, 1 Croir, Bernera PA86 9LZ - T: (01851) 612285
Local Museum 38171

Berwick-upon-Tweed

Berwick Barracks, The Parade, Ravensdowne, Berwick-upon-Tweed TD15 1DE - T: (01289) 304493, Fax: 601999. Cur.: Andrew Morrison
Military Museum
Exhibition on the history of the British infantry, 1660-1880, barrack-room of the 1780s, an Army schoolroom of the 1860s with period figures, and other tableaux 38172

Berwick Borough Museum and Art Gallery, Clock Block, Berwick Barracks, Ravensdowne, Berwick-upon-Tweed TD15 1DQ - T: (01289) 301869, Fax: 330540, E-mail: museum@berwick-upon-tweed.gov.uk. Dir.: Chris Green
Local Museum / Fine Arts Museum - 1867
Local hist, decorative objects in ceramics, bronze and brass, paintings, natural history, archaeology - library 38173

King's Own Scottish Borderers Regimental Museum, The Barracks, Ravensdowne, Berwick-upon-Tweed TD15 1DG - T: (01289) 307426, Fax: 331928. Dir.: C.G.O. Hogg
Military Museum - 1951
Uniforms, medals, trophies, hist of the regiment 38174

Lady Waterford Gallery, Ford Village, Berwick-upon-Tweed TD15 2QA - T: (01890) 820524, Fax: 820384, E-mail: tourism@ford-and-etal.co.uk. Cur.: Fiona Frosdick
Local Museum 38175

Lindisfarne Wine and Spirit Museum, Palace Green, Berwick-upon-Tweed TD15 1HR - T: (01289) 305153, Fax: 302501. Dir.: Ronald Tait
Special Museum 38176

Paxton House, Berwick-upon-Tweed TD15 1SZ - T: (01289) 386291, Fax: 386660, E-mail: info@paxtonhouse.com, Internet: www.paxtonhouse.com. Dir.: Jacky Miller
Special Museum 38177

Bessbrook

Derrymore House, Bessbrook, Co. Down - T: (01693) 830353
Historical Museum
Local history 38178

Betws-y-coed

Betws-y-coed Motor Museum, Betws-y-coed LL24 0AH - T: (01690) 710760
Science&Tech Museum
Vintage and classic vehicles 38179

Conwy Valley Railway Museum, Old Goods Yard, Betws-y-coed LL24 0AL - T: (01690) 710568, Fax: 710132. Cur.: Colin M. Cartwright
Science&Tech Museum / Local Museum - 1973
Historic maps of Conwy Valley, memorabilia from narrow, gauge railways, hist of L.N.W.R. Railway, signalling working models all gauges 38180

Beverley

Beverley Art Gallery, Champney Rd, Beverley HU17 9BQ - T: (01482) 883903, 884956, Fax: 883921. Dir.: Christine Brady
Public Gallery - 1906/1928
Regional art, contemporary art and craft, old paintings, prints, drawings and photographs 38181

Guildhall, Register Sq, Beverley HU17 9XX - T: (01482) 392776, Fax: 884747
Local Museum 38182

Museum of Army Transport, Flemingate, Beverley HU17 0NG - T: (01482) 860445, Fax: 872767. Cur.: Walter Dugan
Military Museum
Coll of Army road, rail, sea and air transport, exhibits of the Second World War, tank transporter train 38183

Bewdley

Bewdley Museum, The Shambles, Load St, Bewdley DY12 2AE - T: (01299) 403573, Fax: 404740, E-mail: bewdley.museum@wyreforestdc.gov.uk. Dir.: Monica Rees, St. Staff: Liz Cowley
Historical Museum / Local Museum - 1972
Crafts and industries of the Wyre Forest, pewter brass 38184

Severn Valley Railway, Railway Station, Bewdley DY12 1BG - T: (01299) 403816, Fax: 400839, Internet: www.svr.co.uk
Science&Tech Museum
Steam locomotives and pre-nationalisation coaches 38185

Bexhill-on-Sea

Bexhill Museum, Egerton Rd, Bexhill-on-Sea TN39 3HL - T: (01424) 787950, Fax: 787950, E-mail: museum@rother.gov.uk, Internet: www.bexhillmuseum.co.uk. Cur.: Julian Porter
Local Museum - 1914
Regional, natural and social history, geology, antiquities, ethnography 38186

Bexhill Museum of Costume and Social History, Manor Gardens, Upper Sea Rd, Bexhill-on-Sea TN40 1RL - T: (01424) 210045
Special Museum 38187

Bibury

Arlington Mill Museum, Arlington, Bibury GL7 5NL - T: (01285) 740368, 740199, Fax: 740368
Folklore Museum / Science&Tech Museum
Mill machinery, Victorian way of life 38188

Bickenhill

National Motorcycle Museum, Coventry Rd, Bickenhill B92 0EJ - T: (01675) 443311, Fax: 443310, E-mail: sales@nationalmotorcyclemuseum.co.uk. Dir.: W.R. Richards
Science&Tech Museum - 1984
Coll of 700 British motorcycles dating from 1898 to the present day 38189

Bickleigh

Bickleigh Castle, Bickleigh EX16 8RP - T: (01884) 855363. Owner: Michael Boxall
Historical Museum
Agricultural objects and toys, model ships, civil war arms and armour 38190

Bideford

The Burton Art Gallery and Museum, Kingsley Rd, Bideford EX39 2QQ - T: (01237) 471455, Fax: 473813, E-mail: burtonartgallery@torridge.gov.uk, Internet: www.burtongallery.co.uk. Cur.: John Butler
Public Gallery - 1951/1994
Watercolour paintings Hubert Coop and Ackland, Edwards, oils by Hunt, Opie, Fisher et al, ceramics, pewter, porcelain, Napoleonic ship models, local artefacts, touring exhibits 38191

Hartland Quay Museum, Hartland Quay, Bideford EX39 6DU - T: (01288) 331353
Local Museum
History of the quay, coastal trades and industries, shipwreck, life-saving, Hartland Point Lighthouse, smuggling, geology and natural history 38192

Biggar

Biggar Gasworks Museum, c/o Biggar Museums Trust, Moat Park, Biggar ML12 6 DT - T: (01899) 221050, Fax: 221050
Science&Tech Museum
Original 1914 equipment of gasworks, early history of the gas industry 38193

Brownsbank Cottage, Moat Park, Biggar ML12 6DT - T: (01899) 221050, Fax: 221050
Special Museum - 1992
Home of Hugh MacDiarmid, 1951-1978 38194

Crawfordjohn Heritage Venture, Crawfordjohn Church, Main St, Biggar ML12 6SS - T: (01864) 504206, Fax: 504206, E-mail: crawfordjohn-heritage@culturalprojects.co.uk. Cur.: Robert A. Clark
Local Museum
Traditional way of life, hill farms and community activity 38195

Gladstone Court Museum, North Back Rd, Biggar ML12 6DT - T: (01899) 221050, Fax: 221050, E-mail: margaret@bmtrust.freeserve.co.uk, Internet: www.biggar-net.co.uk. Dir.: Margaret Brown
Local Museum - 1968
Reconstructed street with various shops and trades 38196

Greenhill Covenanter's House, Burn Braes, Biggar ML12 6DT - T: (01899) 221050, Fax: 221050, E-mail: margaret@bmtrust.freeserve.co.uk, Internet: www.biggar-net.co.uk. Dir.: Margaret Brown
Historical Museum - 1981
17th c furniture and artefacts 38197

Moat Park Heritage Centre, Kirkstyle, Biggar ML12 6DT - T: (01899) 221050, Fax: 221050, E-mail: margaret@bmtrust.freeserve.co.uk, Internet: www.biggar-net.co.uk/museums. Dir.: Margaret Brown
Local Museum - 1988
Embroidery, archaeology - local archives 38198

Billericay

Barleylands Farm Museum, Barleylands Rd, Billericay CM11 2UD - T: (01268) 532253, Fax: 290222, E-mail: museum@barleylands.co.uk, Internet: www.barleylands.co.uk. Dir.: Chris Philpot
Agriculture Museum - 1984 38199

Cater Museum, 74 High St, Billericay CM12 9BS - T: (01277) 622023. Cur.: Christine Brewster
Local Museum - 1960
Local and regional history, Victorian room settings, WWII exhibition, Zeppelin airship L32 which was destroyed near Billericay in 1916 38200

Billingham

Billingham Art Gallery, Queensway, Billingham TS23 2LN - T: (01642) 397590, Fax: 397594, E-mail: billinghamartgallery@stocuton.gov.uk. Dir.: Graham Bowen, Sc. Staff: Mark Rowland Jones, Kirstie Garbutt
Public Gallery 38201

Birchington

Patterson Heritage Museum and Family History Centre, 4 Station Approach, Birchington CT7 9RD - T: (01843) 841649. Head: J.J. Patterson-O'Regan
Historical Museum
Social History 38202

Powell-Cotton Museum, Quex House and Gardens, Quex Park, Birchington CT7 0BH - T: (01843) 842168, Fax: 846661, E-mail: powell-cotton.museum@virgin.net, Internet: www.powell-cottonmuseum.co.uk. Dir.: C. Powell-Cotton, Cur.: John Harrison
Ethnology Museum / Natural History Museum / Decorative Arts Museum - 1896
African and Asian natural hist and ethnography, primates, bovidae, dioramas of African and Asian animals, archaeology, firearms, oriental fine arts, European & English ceramics, Chinese imperial porcelain - library 38203

Birkenhead

Birkenhead Priory and Saint Mary's Tower, Priory St, Birkenhead CH41 5JH - T: (0151) 6661249, Fax: 6663965
Religious Arts Museum
History of the building and its development 38204

Birkenhead Tramways and Taylor Street Large Object Collections, 1 Taylor St, Birkenhead CH41 1BG - T: (0151) 6472128. Dir.: Kevin Johnson
Science&Tech Museum
Transport related objects incl. trams, buses, motorcycles and cars 38205

Shore Road Pumping Station, Hamilton St, Birkenhead CH41 6DN - T: (0151) 6501182, Fax: 6663965
Science&Tech Museum
Giant restored steam engine 38206

Williamson Art Gallery and Museum, Slatey Rd, Birkenhead CH43 4UE - T: (0151) 6524177, Fax: 6700253, E-mail: wag@museum-service.freeserve.co.uk. Dir.: Colin M. Simpson
Fine Arts Museum / Decorative Arts Museum - 1928
Paintings, sculpture, etchings, pottery, porcelain, glass, silver, furniture, local history, geology, numismatics, porcelain, shipping history, motor vehicle history - archive 38207

Wirral Museum, Town Hall, Hamilton St, Birkenhead CH41 5BR - T: (0151) 6664010, Fax: 6663965. Dir.: David Hillhouse
Local Museum - 2001
Social, industrial and commercial history 38208

Birmingham

Aston Hall, Birmingham Museums, Trinity Rd, Aston, Birmingham B6 6JD - T: (0121) 3270062, Fax: 3277162, Internet: www.bmag.org.uk. Dir.: Christopher Rice
Decorative Arts Museum - 1864
Jacobean house dating from 1616-1635, period furniture and rooms 38209

Aston Manor Transport Museum, Old Tram Depot, 208-216 Witton Ln, Birmingham B6 6QE - T: (0121) 3223398, Fax: 3080544
Science&Tech Museum
Over 100 vehicles, two unrestored tramcars, scale model tram, trolleybus layout 38210

Barber Institute of Fine Arts, c/o University of Birmingham, Edgbaston Park Rd, Birmingham B15 2TS - T: (0121) 4147333, Fax: 4143370, E-mail: info@barber.org.uk, Internet: www.barber.org.uk. Dir.: Prof. Richard Verdi, Sen. Cur.: Dr. P. Spencer-Longhurst
Fine Arts Museum - 1932
European art up to the 20th c, works by Bellini, Veronese, Rubens, Rembrandt, Frans Hals, Gainsborough, Reynolds, Degas, Gauguin 38211

Biological Sciences Collection, c/o School of Biological Sciences, University of Birmingham, Birmingham B15 2TT - T: (0121) 4145465, Fax: 4145925. Cur.: James Hamilton
Natural History Museum
herbarium 38212

Birmingham Institute of Art and Design, c/o University of Central England, Gosta Green, Birmingham B4 7DX - T: (0121) 3315800/01, Fax: 3317876, E-mail: helen.staples@uce.ac.uk, Internet: www.biad.uce.ac.uk. Dean: Prof. Mick Durman
Fine Arts Museum 38213

Birmingham Museum and Art Gallery, Chamberlain Sq, Birmingham B3 3DH - T: (0121) 3032834, Fax: 3031394, E-mail: bmag-enquiries@birmingham.gov.uk, Internet: www.bmag.org.uk. Dir.: Graham Allen, Cur.: Jane Farrington (Art), Philip Watson (Human History)
Fine Arts Museum / Decorative Arts Museum / Local Museum / Ethnology Museum / Archaeological Museum - 1885
British and European painting and sculpture, Pre.Raphaelite paintings and drawings, contemporary art, drawings and watercolours, ceramics, metalwork, costume and textiles, jewellery and stained glass, coll from India, China, Japan and the Far East, archaeology and ethnography - picture library 38214

Birmingham Nature Centre, Pershore Rd, Edgbaston, Birmingham B5 7RL - T: (0121) 4727775, Fax: 4723040. Dir.: John Needle
Natural History Museum
Birdwatching, apiary culture, fishing, house pets, bird dioramas, African bush reconstruction 38215

Birmingham Railway Museum, 670 Warwick Rd, Tyseley, Birmingham B11 2HL - T: (0121) 7074696, Fax: 7644645. Dir.: C.M. Whitehouse
Science&Tech Museum / Open Air Museum - 1969
Steam locomotives, passenger trains driving exp. 38216

Blakesley Hall, Blakesley Rd, Yardley, Birmingham B25 8RN - T: (0121) 4648193, Fax: 4640400, E-mail: bmag.enquiries@bcc.gov.uk, Internet: www.bmag.org.uk. Dir.: Irene de Boo
Historical Museum - 1935
Historic and archaeological objects, period rooms in Tudor house 38217

Bournville Centre for Visual Arts, Linden Rd, Birmingham B30 1JX - T: (0121) 3315777, Fax: 3315779, E-mail: tom.jones@uce.ac.uk, Internet: www.uce.ac.uk. Dir.: Prof. Tom Jones
University Museum / Public Gallery 38218

Chamberlain Museum of Pathology, c/o Medical School, University of Birmingham, Edgbaston, Birmingham B15 2TT - T: (0121) 4144014, Fax: 4144019, E-mail: e.l.jones@bham.ac.uk. Dir.: Prof. E.L. Jones
Special Museum
History of medical education, human organs, anatomical coll 38219

Danford Collection of West African Art and Artefacts, c/o Centre of West African Studies, University of Birmingham, Edgbaston, Birmingham B15 2TT - T: (0121) 4145128, Fax: 4143228, E-mail: cwas@bham.ac.uk, Internet: www.cwas.bham.ac.uk. Cur.: Dr. S. Brown, Dr. James Hamilton
Ethnology Museum / University Museum
Carvings, metalwork, textiles, paintings, domestic objects 38220

English Heritage West Midlands Region, 112 Colmore Row, Birmingham B3 3AG - T: (0121) 6256820, Fax: 6256821, Internet: www.english-heritage.org.uk
Association with Coll 38221

Ikon Gallery, 1 Oozells Sq, Brindleyplace, Birmingham B1 2HS - T: (0121) 2480708, Fax: 2480709, E-mail: art@ikon-gallery.co.uk, Internet: www.ikon-gallery.co.uk. Dir.: Jonathan Watkins, Dep. Dir.: Graham Halstead, Cur.: Michael Stanley, Deborah Kermode, Nigel Prince, Saira Holmes
Public Gallery 38222

Lapworth Museum of Geology, c/o Earth Sciences, University of Birmingham, Edgbaston Park Rd, Birmingham B15 2TT - T: (0121) 4147294, Fax: 4144942, E-mail: lapmus@bham.ac.uk, Internet: www.earthsciences.bham.ac.uk/museum. Dir.: Dr. M.P. Smith, Cur.: J.C. Clatworthy
University Museum / Natural History Museum - 1880
Palaeozoic fossils of the West Midlands and Welsh Borders, UK, fossil fish, minerals, stone implements - archive 38223

Midlands Art Centre, Cannon Hill Park, Egbaston, Birmingham B12 9QH - T: (0121) 4403838, Fax: 4464372, E-mail: enquiries@mac-birmingham.org.uk, Internet: www.mac-birmingham.org.uk. Dir.: Dorothy Wilson
Public Gallery 38224

Museum of the Jewellery Quarter, 77-79 Vyse St, Hockley, Birmingham B18 6HA - T: (0121) 5543598, Fax: 5549700, Internet: www.bmag.org.uk. Cur.: Victoria Emmanuel
Special Museum
Old family run jewellery making factory, history of Birmingham jewellery industry 38225

Patrick Collection Motor Museum, 180 Lifford Ln, Birmingham B30 3NK - T: (0121) 4863399, Fax: 4863388. Dir.: J.A. Patrick
Science&Tech Museum - 1985
Motor vehicles since 1904 - reference library 38226

Sarehole Mill, Colebank Rd, Hall Green, Birmingham B13 0BD - T: (0121) 7776612, Fax: 3032891, Internet: www.bmag.co.uk. Dir.: Kristina Sayle
Science&Tech Museum - 1969
Restored water mill (1760), hist of rural life, corn production, connections with Matthew Bovlton and J.R.R. Tolkien 38227

Selly Manor Museum, Cnr Maple and Sycamore Rds, Birmingham B30 2AE - T: (0121) 4720199, Fax: 4714101, E-mail: gillianellis@bvt.org.uk, Internet: www.sallymanor.mus. Cur.: Gillian Ellis
Decorative Arts Museum
Laurence Cadbury coll of Vernacular furniture (1500-1730) 38228

Soho House, Soho Av, off Soho Rd, Birmingham B18 5LB - T: (0121) 5549122, Fax: 5545929, Internet: www.bmag.co.uk
Science&Tech Museum
Industrial pioneer Matthew Boulton (1766-1809), Lunar Society, scientists, engineers and thinkers 38229

Thinktank, The Museum of Science and Discovery, Millennium Point, Curzon St, Birmingham B4 7XG - T: (0121) 2022222, Fax: 2022280, E-mail: findout@thinktank.ac, Internet: www.thinktank.ac. Dir.: Stewart Dobson
Science&Tech Museum - 2001
Science, history 38230

University Archaeology Museum, c/o Dept. Ancient History and Archaeology, University of Birmingham, Birmingham B15 2TT - T: (0121) 4145497, Fax: 4143595, E-mail: j.h.hamilton@bham.ac.uk. Cur.: James Hamilton
Archaeological Museum
Study coll, about 1,700 Greek, Mycenean, Roman and Egyptian artefacts 38231

Weoley Castle, Selly Oak, Birmingham B29 5RX, mail addr: c/o Birmingham Museum and Art Gallery, Chamberlain Sq, Birmingham B3 3DH - T: (0121) 3031675, 3034698, E-mail: bmag_enquiries@birmingham.gov.uk, Internet: www.bmag.org.uk/woeley_castle
Historical Museum 38232

West Midlands Police Museum, 641 Stratford Rd, Sparkhill, Birmingham B11 6EA - T: (0121) 6267181, Fax: 6267066, E-mail: museumwmidpol@btinternet.com
Historical Museum
Police memorabilia 38233

Birsay

Orkney Farm and Folk Museum, Kirbister Hill, Birsay KW17 2LR - T: (01856) 771268, Fax: 771268, Internet: www.orkneyislands.com/guide/museums/farm.html. Cur.: Katrina Mainland
Agriculture Museum / Folklore Museum 38234

Birstall

Oakwell Hall Country Park, Nutter Ln, Birstall WF17 9LG - T: (01924) 326240, Fax: 326249, E-mail: oakwell.hall@kirkleesmc.gov.uk. Dir.: Eric Brown
Historic Site - 1928
Elizabethan Manor House displayed as a family home of the 1690s, 17th c furniture, decorations - gardens 38235

Bishop Auckland

Binchester Roman Fort, Bishop Auckland DL13 - T: (01388) 663089, Fax: (0191) 3841336, E-mail: niall.hammond@durham.gov.uk, Internet: www.durham.gov.uk. Keeper: Niall Hammond (Archaeology)
Archaeological Museum
Roman fort of Vinovia 38236

Bishopbriggs

Thomas Muir Museum, Huntershill Recreation Centre, Crowhill Rd, Bishopbriggs G66 1RW - T: (0141) 7751185
Historical Museum
Displays illustrating the life of the 18th c Scottish radical and reformer, Thomas Muir 38237

Bishop's Castle

House on Crutches Museum, Tan House, Church St, Bishop's Castle SY9 5AA - T: (01588) 630007, E-mail: hocmuseum@tan-house.demon.co.uk
Local Museum
Agricultural tools, household objects, clothing, shop goods 38238

Bishop's Stortford

Bishop's Stortford Local History Museum, Cemetery Lodge, Apton Rd, Bishop's Stortford CM23 3SU
Local Museum
Local trades, archaeology, architecture, local and family history 38239

Rhodes Memorial Museum and Commonwealth Centre, South Rd, Bishop's Stortford CM23 3JG - T: (01279) 651746, Fax: 467171, E-mail: rhodesmuseum@freeuk.com, Internet: www.hertsmuseums.org.uk. Cur.: Hannah Kay
Special Museum - 1938
Life and work of statesman Cecil John Rhodes, his birthplace, memorabilia, photos, documents, African ethnography and artwork 38240

Bishop's Waltham

Bishops Waltham Museum, Brook St, Bishop's Waltham S032 1EB - T: (01489) 894970. Cur.: John Bosworth
Local Museum
Local history, Victorian pottery, brick making, brewing, local trades, shops 38241

Blackburn, Lancashire

Blackburn Museum and Art Gallery, Museum St, Blackburn, Lancashire BB1 7AJ - T: (01254) 667130, Fax: 685541, E-mail: paul.flintoff@blackburn.gov.uk, Internet: www.blackburnworld.com. Dir.: S. Rigby, Sc. Staff: Paul Flintoff, Nick Harling
Fine Arts Museum / Historical Museum - 1874
Natural hist, geology, ethnography, applied and fine arts, Hart coll of coins, philatelics, medieval illuminated manuscripts, books, local hist, Lewis coll of Japanese prints, ornithology 38242

East Lancashire Regiment Museum (closed) 38243

Lewis Textile Museum, 3 Exchange St, Blackburn, Lancashire BB1 7AJ - T: (01254) 667130, Fax: 685541, E-mail: paul.flintoff@blackburn.gov.uk, Internet: www.blackburn.gov.uk/museum. Dir.: S. Rigby, Sc. Staff: Paul Flintoff, Nick Harling
Decorative Arts Museum / Science&Tech Museum - 1938
18th and 19th c cotton machinery, art gallery, hist of textile production 38244

Blackgang

Blackgang Sawmill and Saint Catherine's Quay, Blackgang PO38 2HN - T: (01983) 730330, Fax: 731267, E-mail: vectisventuresltd@btinternet.com, Internet: www.blackgangchine.com. Dir.: Simon Dabell
Historical Museum 38245

Blackpool

Grundy Art Gallery, Queen St, Blackpool FY1 1PX - T: (01253) 478170, Fax: 478172, E-mail: grundyartgallery@blackpool.gov.uk, Internet: www.blackpool.gov.uk. Dir.: Paul Flintoff
Fine Arts Museum - 1911
Contemporary paintings, watercolors, ivory, porcelain, Victorian and Edwardian oils, modern British painting 38246

Blackridge

Blackridge Community Museum, Library, Craig Inn Centre, Blackridge EH48 3RJ - T: (01506) 776347, Fax: 776190, E-mail: museums@westlothian.org.uk, Internet: www.wlonline.org
Local Museum 38247

Blaenau Ffestiniog

Gloddfa Ganol Slate Mine, Blaenau Ffestiniog LL41 3NB - T: (01766) 830664
Science&Tech Museum 38248

Llechwedd Slate Caverns, Blaenau Ffestiniog LL41 3NB - T: (01766) 830306, Fax: 831260, E-mail: llechwedd@aol.com. Dir.: R.H. Davies
Science&Tech Museum - 1972
The earliest slate extraction, sawing and dressing equipment, coll of narrow gauge railway stock 38249

Blaenavon

Big Pit National Mining Museum of Wales, Blaenavon NP4 9XP - T: (01495) 790311, Fax: 792618, E-mail: bigpit@nmgw.ac.uk, Internet: www.nmgw.ac.uk/bigpit. Man.: Peter Walker, Cur.: C. Thomson
Science&Tech Museum - 1983
Preserved colliery shaft, winding engine and underground areas giving public guess & a former working colliery 38250

Pontypool and Blaenavon Railway, Council Office, High St, Blaenavon NP4 9XP - T: (01495) 792263, Internet: www.pontypool-and-blaenavon.co.uk
Science&Tech Museum
Locomotives, coaches 38251

Blair Atholl

Atholl Country Life Museum, Old School, Blair Atholl PH18 5SP - T: (01796) 481232, Fax: 473639, E-mail: janet.cam@virgin.net, Internet: www.blairatholl.org.uk. Cur.: John Cameron
Local Museum - 1982 38252

Blair Castle, Blair Atholl PH18 5TL - T: (01796) 481207, Fax: 481487, E-mail: office@blair-castle.co.uk, Internet: www.blair-castle.co.uk
Historical Museum
Furniture, paintings, arms and armour, china, lace and embroidery, masonic regalia and other treasures 38253

Blairgowrie

Errol Station Railway Heritage Centre, c/o Errol Station Trust, 48 Moyness Park Dr, Blairgowrie PH10 6LX - T: (015754) 222
Science&Tech Museum
Station from 1847 on the main Aberdeen-Glasgow line 38254

Blandford Forum

Blandford Forum Museum, Bere's Yard, Market Pl, Blandford Forum DT11 7HQ - T: (01258) 450388, E-mail: andrewsnhm@aol.com, Internet: www.blandford-town.co.uk. Cur.: Dr. Peter Andrews, Dep. Cur.: Michael le Bas
Historical Museum
Illustration of the life and occupations of people in Blandford and its neighbourhood from prehistoric times to the present day, good coll of domestic equipment, local militaria and Victorian and Edwardian costumes 38255

Cavalcade of Costume, Lime Tree House, The Plocks, Blandford Forum DT11 7AA - T: (01258) 453006
Special Museum
Costumes and accessories from 18th c to 1960s 38256

Royal Signals Museum, Blandford Camp, Blandford Forum DT11 8RH - T: (01258) 482248, Fax: 482084, E-mail: info@royalsignalsmuseum.com, Internet: www.royalsignalsmuseum.com. Dir.: Cliff Walters, Cur.: Stella McIntyre

Military Museum - 1935
Communication equipment, uniforms, prints and photos relating to the Royal Signals and Army communications 38257

Blantyre

David Livingstone Centre, 165 Station Rd, Blantyre G72 9BT - T: (01698) 823140, Fax: 821424, E-mail: kcarruthers@nts.org.uk. Dir.: Karen Carruthers
Special Museum - 1929
Memorabilia on explorer David Livingstone in the house of his birth 38258

Bletchley

Bletchley Park Exhibition, Wilton Av, Bletchley MK3 6EF - T: (01908) 640404, Fax: 274381, E-mail: info@bletchleypark.org.uk, Internet: www.bletchleypark.org.uk. Dir.: Christine Large
Science&Tech Museum / Historical Museum
Cryptography, WW 2 codebreaking computer, radar and electronics, WW 2 memorabilia 38259

Blindley Heath

National Museum of Baking → Past Times

Past Times, Bannisters Bakery, Eastbourne Rd, Blindley Heath RH7 6LQ - T: (01342) 832086, E-mail: enquiries@bannistersbakery.co.uk, Internet: www.bannistersbakery.co.uk. Owner: R. Bannister
Special Museum
Household and rural bakery 38260

Bloxham

Bloxham Village Museum, Courthouse, Church St, Bloxham OX15 4ET - T: (01295) 721256, 720801, E-mail: peter.barwell@tesco.net. Chm.: John Phillips
Local Museum
Past life in this village 38261

Bodelwyddan

Bodelwyddan Castle Museum, Castle, Bodelwyddan LL18 5YA - T: (01745) 584060, Fax: 584563, E-mail: k.mason@btconnect.com. Dir.: Dr. Kevin Mason, Dep. Dir.: Charles Jenkins, Cur.: Deborah Davies
Fine Arts Museum
Portraits, sculptures, furniture 38262

Bodmin

Bodmin and Wenford Railway, General Station, Bodmin PL31 1AQ - T: (01208) 73666, Fax: 77963, E-mail: manager@bodminandwenfordrailway.co.uk, Internet: www.bodminandwenfordrailway.co.uk. Dir.: Roger J. Webster
Science&Tech Museum
Various locomotives, carriages, wagons and steam crane 38263

Bodmin Town Museum, Mount Folly Sq, Bodmin PL31 2HQ - T: (01208) 77067, Fax: 79268, E-mail: bodmin.museum@ukonline.co.uk. Cur.: M. Tooze
Historical Museum / Natural History Museum
Artefacts, documents, photographs and text illustrating Bodmin's Local und social hist 38264

Duke of Cornwall's Light Infantry Museum, The Keep, Bodmin PL31 1EG - T: (01208) 72810, Fax: 72810, E-mail: dcli@talk21.com, Internet: www.digiserve.com/msyoung/dcli.htm. Dir.: Richard Vyvyan-Robinson
Military Museum - 1923
Armaments, uniforms, military hist of the regiment, small arms, medals, badges, pictures 38265

Lanhydrock, Bodmin PL30 5AD - T: (01208) 265950, Fax: 265959, E-mail: lanhydrock@nationaltrust.org.uk, Internet: www.nationaltrust.org.uk. Dir.: Andrea Marchington
Historical Museum
18th c and Brussels and Mortlake tapestries, family portraits painted by Kneller and Romney, books, furniture, kitchens, nurseries, interiors 38266

Pencarrow House, Washaway, Bodmin PL30 3AG - T: (01208) 841369, Fax: 841722, E-mail: pencarrow@aol.com, Internet: www.pencarrow.co.uk. Dir.: Lady Iona Molesworth-Saint Aubyn
Fine Arts Museum / Decorative Arts Museum
Family portraits, including works by Reynolds, Northcote, Raceburn, Hudson and Devis, paintings by Samuel Scott and Richard Wilson, furnitures of the 18th and early 19th c 38267

Bognor Regis

Bognor Regis Museum, 69 High St, Bognor Regis PO21 1RY - T: (01243) 865636, Fax: (01903) 725254, E-mail: stephen_hill@arun.gov.uk. Dir.: Eve May
Local Museum
Social and local history (19th-20th c) 38268

Bolton

Bolton Museum and Art Gallery, Le Mans Crescent, Bolton BL1 1SE - T: (01204) 332211, Fax: 332241, E-mail: museums@bolton.gov.uk, Internet: www.boltonmuseums.org.uk. Dir.: Steve Garland, Cur.: J. Shaw (Art), Angela Thomas (Human History)
Natural History Museum / Fine Arts Museum / Local Museum / Ethnology Museum / Archaeological Museum / Decorative Arts Museum / Historical Museum - 1893
Natural hist, geology, fossils, archaeology, Egyptian coll, early English watercolors, British sculpture with works by Epstein, Moore, Hepworth, costumes, papers of inventor Samuel Crompton, local and social hist 38269

Bolton Steam Museum, off Chorley Old Rd, Bolton BL1 4EU, mail addr: John Phillp, 84 Watkin Rd, Clayton-le-Woods PR6 7PX - T: (01257) 265003, E-mail: john.phillp@btinternet.com, Internet: www.nmes.org. Head: John Phillp
Science&Tech Museum - 1992
Stationary steam engines from textile industry, cotton mill 38270

Hall-I'Th'-Wood Museum, Green Way, off Crompton Way, Bolton BL1 8UA - T: (01204) 332370, E-mail: museum@bolton.gov.uk, Internet: www.boltonmuseums.co.uk. Head: Harold Farrell
Historical Museum - 1902
Manor dating from 1483-1648, furnishings, memorabilia of inventor Samuel Crompton 38271

Smithills Hall Museum, Smithills Dean Rd, Bolton BL1 7NP - T: (01204) 332377, E-mail: museum@bolton.gov.uk, Internet: www.boltonmuseums.co.uk. Head: Harold Farrell
Historical Museum - 1962
16th-19th c timbered manor, furnishings 38272

Bolventor

Potter's Museum of Curiosity and Smugglers's Museum, Old School, Jamaica Inn, Bolventor PL15 7TS - T: (01566) 86838, Fax: 86838, E-mail: jamaicainn@eclipse.co.uk, Internet: www.jamaicainn.co.uk. Cur.: Rose Mullins
Special Museum - 1861
Museum founded by Walter Potter, Victorian naturalist and taxidermist, Daphne Du Maurie' novel 'Jamaica Inn', smuggling history 38273

Bo'ness

Bo'ness and Kinneil Railway, Bo'ness Station, off Union St, Bo'ness EH51 9AQ - T: (01506) 822298, Fax: 828766, E-mail: railway@srps.org.uk, Internet: www.srps.org.uk. Cur.: John Crompton
Science&Tech Museum
Scottish railways history 38274

Bo'ness Heritage Area, 17-19 North St, Bo'ness EH51 9AQ - T: (01506) 825855, Fax: 828766
Local Museum 38275

Kinneil Museum and Roman Fortlet, Duchess Anne Cottages, Kinneil Estate, Bo'ness EH51 0PR - T: (01506) 778530. Dir.: Maria Gillespie, Sheila Smith
Historical Museum / Archaeological Museum - 1976
Estate history, medieval village and church, excavations 38276

Museum of Communication, POB 12556, Bo'ness EH51 9YX - T: (01506) 823424. Pres.: Prof. C.W. Davidson
Science&Tech Museum
Coll of telephones, radio, telegraphy, computing, televion covering 20th c 38277

Boosbeck

Margrove - South Cleveland Heritage Centre, Margrove Park, Boosbeck TS12 3BZ - T: (01287) 610368, Fax: 610368
Local Museum / Natural History Museum
Moors, valley and coast of South Cleveland, historic maps 38278

Bootle

Art Gallery and Museum, Central Library, Stanley Rd, Bootle L20 6AG
Fine Arts Museum / Decorative Arts Museum
Pottery, ceramics, rotating exhibits, English porcelain 38279

Boroughbridge

Aldborough Roman Town Museum, Main St, Aldborough, Boroughbridge YO2 3PH - T: (01423) 322768, Internet: www.english-heritage.org.uk
Archaeological Museum / Historic Site 38280

Boscombe

Museum of Childhood, 39 Ashley Rd, Boscombe BH5 - T: (01202) 33173
Special Museum
Dolls, comics, Meccano sets, Hornby trains, model ships and boats, jigsaws, games, toys and books 38281

Boston

Boston Guildhall Museum, South St, Boston PE21 6HT - T: (01205) 365954, E-mail: heritage@originalboston.freeserve.co.uk. Cur.: Andrew Crabtree
Local Museum - 1926
15th c building with medieval kitchen, cells used by Pilgrim Fathers pending trial in 1607, Council Chamber, Courtroom & Banqueting Hall Displays on archaeology, costume & textiles, ceramics, militaria, coins & tokens & Boston's maritime heritage 38282

Botley, Hampshire

Hampshire Farm Museum, Country Park, Brook Ln, Botley, Hampshire SO3 2ER - T: (01489) 787055. Dir.: Barbara Newbury
Agriculture Museum - 1984
Tools, implements machinery, domestic buildings 38283

Bourn

Wysing Arts, Fox Rd, Bourn CB3 7TX - T: (01954) 718881, Fax: 718500, E-mail: info@wysing.demon.co.uk, Internet: www.wysing.demon.co.uk. Dir.: Trystan Hawkins
Fine Arts Museum 38284

Bournemouth

Bournemouth Natural Science Society Museum, 39 Christchurch Rd, Bournemouth BH1 3NS - T: (01202) 553525, E-mail: administrator@bnss.org.uk, Internet: www.bnss.org.uk. Chm.: V.E. Copp, Cur.: H. Wilson
Natural History Museum - 1903
Local natural hist, archaeology, zoology, herbarium (Dorset plants) entomology, geology, egyptology - botanical garden, library 38285

Russell-Cotes Art Gallery and Museum, East Cliff, Bournemouth BH1 3AA - T: (01202) 451800, Fax: 451851, E-mail: diane.edge@bournemouth.gov.uk, Internet: www.russell-cotes.bournemouth.gov.uk. Dir.: Victoria Pirie
Fine Arts Museum / Ethnology Museum - 1922
Victorian painting, Japanese coll, ethnography from Oceania, New Zealand and Africa 38286

Bourton-on-the-Water

Cotswold Motoring Museum and Toy Collection, Old Mill, Bourton-on-the-Water GL5 2BY - T: (01451) 821255, E-mail: motormuseum@csma-netlink.co.uk. Dir.: Michael Tambini
Science&Tech Museum - 1978
Vintage enamel advertising signs, toys, cars 38287

Bovey Tracey

Devon Guild of Craftsmen Gallery, Riverside Mill, Bovey Tracey TQ13 9AF - T: (01626) 832223, Fax: 834220, E-mail: devonguild@crafts.org.uk, Internet: www.crafts.org.uk. Dir.: Alexander Murdin
Historical Museum
Craftwork, changing exhibits invited contributors work in the gallery, guilds 38288

Bovington

Tank Museum, Bovington BH20 6JG - T: (01929) 405096, Fax: 405360, E-mail: info@tankmuseum.co.uk, Internet: www.tankmuseum.co.uk. Dir.: John Woodward
Military Museum - 1923
Hist of tank units, small arms and ammunition 38289

Bowness-on-Windermere

Blackwell - The Arts and Crafts House, Bowness-on-Windermere LA23 3JR - T: (015394) 46139, Fax: 88486, E-mail: info@blackwell.org.uk, Internet: www.blackwell.org.uk. Dir.: Edward King
Decorative Arts Museum - 2001
Rare surviving house from the arts and crafts movement, original interior, furniture, applied arts, crafts 38290

Steamboat Museum, Rayrigg Rd, Bowness-on-Windermere LA23 1BN - T: (015394) 45565, E-mail: info@steamboat.co.uk, Internet: www.steamboat.co.uk. Dir.: Tony Jackson
Science&Tech Museum 38291

Bracknell

Look Out Discovery Centre, Nine Mile Ride, Bracknell RG12 7QW - T: (01344) 354400, Fax: 354422, E-mail: thelookout@bracknell-forest.gov.uk, Internet: www.bracknell-forest.gov.uk/lookout
Science&Tech Museum 38292

South Hill Park Arts Centre, Bracknell RG12 7PA - T: (01344) 427272, Fax: 411427, E-mail: visual.art@southhillpark.org.uk
Public Gallery 38293

Bradford

Bolling Hall Museum, Bowling Hall Rd, Bradford BD4 7LP - T: (01274) 723057, Fax: 726220, Internet: www.bradford.gov.uk. Dir.: Mark Suggitt
Local Museum - 1915
House with historic furniture, 17th and 18th c plaster ceilings, 17th-18th c furniture, local history 38294

Bradford Industrial Museum and Horses at work, Moorside Rd, Eccleshill, Bradford BD2 3HP - T: (01274) 631756, Fax: 636362, E-mail: industrial.museum@bradford.gov.uk. Head: Paul W.G. Lawson
Science&Tech Museum / Historical Museum
History of local industry, industrial archaeology, wool, textiles, transport, horses, victorian mill 38295

Cartwright Hall Art Gallery, Lister Park, Bradford BD9 4NS - T: (01274) 431212, Fax: 481045, E-mail: cartwright.hall@bradford.gov.uk, Internet: www.bradford.gov.uk/tourism/museums. Head: Mark Suggitt
Fine Arts Museum - 1904
Old and modern British painting, drawings, watercolors, modern prints 38296

Colour Museum, 1 Providence St, Bradford BD1 2PW - T: (01274) 390955, Fax: 392888, E-mail: museum@sdc.org.uk, Internet: www.sdc.org.uk. Dir.: Sarah Burge
Special Museum - 1978
Textile industry 38297

Gallery II, c/o University of Bradford, Chesham Bldg, off Great Horton Rd, Bradford BD7 1DP - T: (01274) 383365, Fax: 305340
Fine Arts Museum / University Museum 38298

National Museum of Photography, Film and Television, Manchester Rd and Hallings, Bradford BD1 1NQ - T: (01274) 202030, Fax: 723155, E-mail: talk.nmpft@nmsi.ac.uk, Internet: www.nmpft.org.uk. Head: Armanda Nevill
Science&Tech Museum - 1983
Art, history and science of photography, film, television and digital imaging 38299

Peace Museum, 10 Piece Hall Yard, Bradford BD1 - T: (01274) 434009, Fax: 422618, E-mail: peacemuseum@bradford.gov.uk, Internet: www.peacemuseum.org.uk. Cur.: Peter Nias
Historical Museum
Peace, non-violence and conflict resolution 38300

Bradford-on-Avon

Bradford-on-Avon Museum, Bridge St, Bradford-on-Avon BA15 1BY - T: (01225) 863280. Cur.: Roger Clark
Local Museum
Local history 38301

Bradford-on-Tone

Sheppy's Farm and Cider Museum, c/o R.J. Sheppy & Son, Three Bridges, Bradford-on-Tone TA4 1ER - T: (01823) 461233, Fax: 461712, E-mail: info@sheppyscider.com, Internet: www.sheppyscider.com. Dir.: Richard Sheppy
Agriculture Museum
Old cidermaking equipment, agricultural implements, coopers' and other craftsmen's tools, video of cidermaker's year 38302

Brading

Aylmer Military Collection, Nunwell House, Brading PO36 0JQ - T: (01983) 407240. Cur.: John Alymer
Military Museum 38303

Isle of Wight Wax Works, 46 High St, Brading PO36 0DQ - T: (01983) 407286, Fax: 402112, E-mail: info@iwwaxworks.co.uk, Internet: www.iwwaxworks.co.uk
Special Museum - 1965
Wax tableaux of Island, national and international from Roman times to present day, includes the oldest house on the Island part dating 1066 AD instruments of torture from the Royal castle of Nuremberg, world of nature 38304

Lilliput Antique Doll and Toy Museum, High St, Brading PO36 0DJ - T: (01983) 407231, E-mail: lilliput.museum@btconnect.com, Internet: www.lilliputmuseum.com. Dir.: Graham K. Munday
Special Museum - 1974 38305

Roman Villa, Morton Old Rd, Brading PO36 0EN - T: (01983) 406223, Fax: 406223, Internet: www.brading.co.uk/romanvilla.html. Dir.: N.J. Carr
Archaeological Museum 38306

Braemar

Braemar Castle, Invercauld Rd, Braemar AB35 5XR - T: (013397) 41219, Fax: 41219, E-mail: invercauld@freenet.co.uk, Internet: www.braemarcastle.co.uk. Cur.: Bruce McCudden
Historical Museum / Historic Site
Historic seat of the Farquharsons of Invercauld 38307

Braintree

Braintree District Museum, Manor St, Braintree CM7 3HW - T: (01376) 325266, Fax: 344345, Internet: www.braintree.gov.uk/museum. Head: Jean Grice
Local Museum
Textile and engineering industries, archaeology, social history, textiles, large photographic coll - Textile archive 38308

Bramhall

Bramall Hall, Bramhall Park, Bramhall SK7 3NX - T: (0161) 4853708, Fax: 4866959, E-mail: bramall.hall@stockport.gov.uk, Internet: www.stockport.gov.uk/heritageattractions. Man.: Caroline Egan
Historic Site
14th to 16th c half-timbered Hall 38309

Brandon

Brandon Heritage Museum, George St, Brandon IP27 0BX - T: (01225) 863280, Fax: (01204) 391352
Local Museum - 1991
Flint, fur and forestry industries, local history 38310

Braunton

Braunton and District Museum, Bakehouse Centre, Caen St, Braunton EX33 1AA - T: (01271) 816688, E-mail: braunton@devonmuseums.net, Internet: www.devonmuseums.net/braunton. Cur.: Kathy Lehan
Local Museum
Maritime, agriculture and village life 38311

Breamore

Breamore Countryside Museum, Breamore SP6 2DF - T: (01725) 512468, Fax: 512858, E-mail: breamore@ukonline.co.uk, Internet: www.breamorehouse.com. Dir.: Sir Edward Hulse, Cur.: Philip Crowter
Agriculture Museum / Open Air Museum - 1972
Hand tools, tractors, steam engines, blacksmith's and wheel-wright's shops, brewery, dairy, farmworkerscottage, harnessmakers, boot makers, village general store, village school, laundry, coopers', baker's and clockmaker's shop, village garage 38312

Breamore House Museum, near Fordingbridge, Breamore SP6 2DF - T: (01725) 512233, Fax: 512858, E-mail: breamore@ukonline.co.uk, Internet: www.breamorehouse.com. Dir.: E. Hulse
Fine Arts Museum / Decorative Arts Museum / Folklore Museum - 1953
17th and 18th c furniture and paintings (mainly Dutch), tapestries, porcelain, 14 paintings of the intermingling of Indian races (c 1725), development of agricultural machinery, farm implements, aspects of a self-sufficient village 38313

Brechin

Brechin Museum, Town House, High St, Brechin DD9 7AA - T: (01307) 464123, Fax: 462590, E-mail: montrose.museum@angus.gov.uk, Internet: www.angus.gov.uk/history.htm
Local Museum
Local history, antiquities 38314

Glenesk Folk Museum, The Retreat, Glenesk, Brechin DD9 7YT - T: (01356) 670254. Cur.: A. Robertson
Folklore Museum - 1955
Local rural life, period rooms, Victoriana 38315

Brecon

Brecknock Museum and Art Gallery, Captain's Walk, Brecon LD3 7DW - T: (01874) 624121, E-mail: brecknock.museum@powys.gov.uk, Internet: www.powymuseums.powy.gov.uk. Dir.: David Moore
Local Museum - 1928
Natural and local hist, archaeology, ceramics, costumes, early Christian monuments, art - art gallery 38316

Howell Harris Museum, Trefeca, Brecon LD3 0PP - T: (01874) 711423, Fax: 712212, E-mail: post@trefeca.org.uk, Internet: www.trefeca.org.uk. Dir.: T. Lewis
Local Museum - 1957
Local and religious hist, Howell Harris (1714-1773) 38317

South Wales Borderers and Monmouthshire Regimental Museum of the Royal Regiment of Wales, The Barracks, Brecon LD3 7EB - T: (01874) 613310, Fax: 613275, E-mail: swb@rrw.org.uk, Internet: www.rrw.org.uk. Dir.: Martin Everett
Military Museum - 1934
Regimental hist, medals, armaments, Anglo-Zulu War 1879 - archive 38318

Brentwood

Brentwood Museum, Cementery Lodge, Lorne Rd, Brentwood CM14 5HH - T: (01277) 224012. Cur.: Pam Guiver, Audrey Puddy, Mary Humphreys
Local Museum
Social and domestic items, memorabilia from world wars, toys, games, furniture and costumes 38319

Bridgend

South Wales Police Museum, Cowbridge Rd, Bridgend CF31 3SU - T: (01656) 655555. Cur.: Julia Mason
Special Museum - 1950
Policing in Glamorgan from the Celts to the present day, Edwardian police station, wartime tableau 38320

Bridgnorth

Bridgnorth Northgate Museum, Burgess Hall, High St, Bridgnorth WV16 4ER - T: (01746) 761859. Cur.: Alan Webb
Local Museum
Local history, firemarks, tokens, coins, agriculture 38321

Childhood and Costume Museum, Newmarket Bldg, Postern Gate, Bridgnorth WV16 4AA - T: (01746) 764636. Cur.: Jayne Griffiths
Folklore Museum - 1951
Clothes and accessories (1860-1960), toys, games, Victorian nursery, textiles, mineral coll 38322

Midland Motor Museum, Stanmore House, Stourbridge Rd, Bridgnorth WV15 6DT - T: (01746) 761761
Science&Tech Museum 38323

Bridgwater

Blake Museum, Blake St, Bridgwater TA6 3NB - T: (01278) 456127, Fax: 446412, E-mail: museums@sedgemoor.gov.uk, Internet: www.sedgemoor.gov.uk. Officer: Jessica Vale, Asst.: Carolyn Cudbill
Historical Museum - 1926
Local hist (18th c), archaeology, work of Admiral Blake (1598-1657) in the supposed place of his birth, relics on the Battle of Sedgemoor, photos 38324

Somerset Brick and Tile Museum, East Quay, Bridgwater TA6 3NB - T: (01278) 426088, Fax: 320229, E-mail: county-museum@somerset.gov.uk, Internet: www.somerset.gov.uk/museums. Dir.: David Dawson
Historical Museum
Brick and tile industry 38325

Westonzoyland Pumping Station Museum, Hoopers Ln, Westonzoyland, Bridgwater, mail addr: c/o A. Derrick, 4 Hillside Cottages, Barrow Gurney BS48 3RX - T: (01275) 472385, E-mail: webmaster@wzlet.org, Internet: www.wzlet.org
Science&Tech Museum - 1977
Land drainage, steam pumps and engines 38326

Bridlington

Bayle Museum, Bayle Gate, Bridlington YO16 5TW - T: (01262) 674308, E-mail: charity@themail.co.uk. Dir.: B.R. Langton
Local Museum - 1920
Victorian kitchen, Green Howard's Regemental room, courtroom of 1388, the monastic gatehouse of the Augustinian Priory 38327

Bridlington Harbour Museum, Harbour Rd, Bridlington YO15 2NR - T: (01262) 670148, Fax: 602041
Historical Museum 38328

Sewerby Hall Art Gallery and Museum, Museum of East Yorkshire, Church Ln, Sewerby, Bridlington YO15 1EA - T: (01262) 677874, Fax: 674265, E-mail: sewerbyhall@yahoo.com, Internet: www.bridlington.net/sewerby. Dir.: J. Ginnever (Education, Leisure and Libraries), Sc. Staff: N.C. Adams, W.M. Foley, G.J. Harvey, Dr. D.J. Marchant, Jane Bielby, J. Tierney, S. Ramsden
Local Museum / Fine Arts Museum - 1936
19th c marine paintings by Henry Redmore of Hull, early 19th c local watercolours, local archaeology, farm implements, vintage motorcycles, horse-drawn vehicles, military uniforms with local associations, fossils from the nearby chalk cliffs, the various seabirds and waders found in the area, memorabilia on air-woman Amy Johnson 38329

Bridport

Bredy Farm Old Farming Collection, Bredy Farm, Burton Bradstock, Bridport DT6 4ND - T: (01308) 897229. Cur.: Justin Mallinson
Agriculture Museum
A coll of yeaster-year farm 38330

Bridport Museum, South St, Bridport DT6 3NR - T: (01308) 422116, Fax: 420659. Cur.: J.E. Burrell
Local Museum
Local hist, archaeology, natural hist, geology, trades, costumes, Victorian relics, net weaving 38331

Harbour Life Exhibition, Salt House, West Bay, Bridport DT6 4SA - T: (01308) 422807, Fax: 421509
Local Museum
Industry, history of Bridport Harbour 38332

Brierfield

Neville Blakey Museum of Locks, Keys and Safes, Burnley Rd, Brierfield BB9 5AD - T: (01282) 613593, Fax: 617550, E-mail: sales@blakeys.fsworld.co.uk. Dir.: W.H. Neville Blakey
Special Museum 38333

Brierley Hill

Brierley Hill Glass Museum, Moor St, Brierley Hill
Decorative Arts Museum - 1923
Local and foreign glass work, cameo glass by George Woodall 38334

Brighouse

Smith Art Gallery, Halifax Rd, Brighouse HD6 2AA - T: (01484) 719222, Fax: 719222. Cur.: Barry Sheridan
Public Gallery - 1907
Paintings, English watercolors, 19th c woodcarvings 38335

Brightlingsea

Brightlingsea Museum, 1 Duke St, Brightlingsea CO7 0EA - T: (01206) 303286. Cur.: Margaret Stone
Local Museum
Maritime and oyster industry, local history 38336

Brighton

Barlow Collection of Chinese Ceramics, Bronzes and Jades, c/o University of Sussex, Falmer, Brighton BN1 9QU - T: (01273) 606755 ext 3506, E-mail: k.mcloughlin@sussex.ac.uk, Internet: www.sussex.ac.uk/library/gen-info/barlow.html. Cur.: Kevin McLoughlin
Decorative Arts Museum
Chinese jades, bronzes, porcelain and ceramics 38337

Booth Museum of Natural History, 194 Dyke Rd, Brighton BN1 5AA - T: (01273) 292777, Fax: 292778, E-mail: boothmus@pavilion.co.uk. Dir.: Dr. G. Legg (Biology and Firearms), Sc. Staff: J.M. Adams (Natural Sciences)
Natural History Museum - 1874
British birds, dioramas, butterflies, nymphalid butterflies, fossils, vertebrate skeletons - library 38338

Brighton Fishing Museum, 201 Kings Rd Arches, Brighton BN1 1NB - T: (01273) 723064, E-mail: brightonfishingmuseum@btinternet.com. Dir.: Andy Durr
Special Museum - 1994
Boats, artifacts, pictures - film and historical archive 38339

Brighton Museum and Art Gallery, Royal Pavilion Gardens, Brighton BN1 1EE - T: (01273) 290900, Fax: 292841, E-mail: museums@brighton-hove.gov.uk, Internet: www.brighton.virtualmuseum.info. Dir.: Jessica Rutherford
Fine Arts Museum / Decorative Arts Museum / Local Museum - 1873
Fine coll of local and practical importance, Art Nouveau and Art Deco, fine art and non-Western art, costumes, Willett coll of pottery and porcelain - My Brighton - interactive local hist project 38340

Fabrica, 40 Duke St, Brighton BN1 1AG - T: (01273) 778646, Fax: 778646, E-mail: info@fabrica.org.uk, Internet: www.fabrica.org.uk
Association with Coll
Artist-led space promoting the understanding of contemporary art in a regency church, site specific commissions with four exhibitions a year: craft, material based, lens based and digital 38341

Preston Manor, Preston Park, Brighton BN1 6SD - T: (01273) 292770, Fax: 292771, E-mail: david.beevers@brighton-hove.gov.uk, Internet: www.museums.brighton-hove.gov.uk. Dir.: David Beevers
Decorative Arts Museum - 1933
Macquoid bequest English and Continental period furniture, silver, pictures, panels of stained glass, 16th-19th c original 17th leather wall-hangings - archives 38342

Rottingdean Grange Art Gallery and National Toy Museum, The Rottingdean Green, Brighton BN2 7HA - T: (01273) 301004
Fine Arts Museum / Special Museum 38343

Royal Pavilion, 4-5 Pavilion Bldgs, Brighton BN1 1EE - T: (01273) 290900, Fax: 292871, E-mail: visitor.services@brighton-hove.gov.uk, Internet: www.royalpavilion.org.uk. Dir.: Jessica Rutherford
Fine Arts Museum / Decorative Arts Museum - 1851
Seaside palace of George IV - designed by John Nash, exterior - Indian design - interiors in Chinese taste, items on loan from H.M. The Queen, 18th c gardens 38344

Stanmer Rural Museum, Stanmer Park, Brighton BN1 7HN - T: (01273) 509563. Head: R.A. Stopps
Folklore Museum - 1975
Rare horse trave, rural tools, local archaeological finds, agricultural implements 38345

University of Brighton Gallery, Grand Parade, Brighton - T: (01273) 643012, Fax: 643038, E-mail: c.l.matthews@bton.ac.uk, Internet: www.bton.ac.uk/gallery-theatre/. Dir.: Sir David Watson
Public Gallery 38346

Bristol

Arnolfini, 16 Narrow Quai, Bristol BS1 4QA - T: (0117) 9299191, Fax: 9253876, E-mail: arnolfini@arnolfini.demon.co.uk, Internet: www.arnolfini.demon.co.uk. Dir.: Caroline Collier, Dep. Dir.: Helen Parson, Cur.: Catsou Roberts
Fine Arts Museum / Public Gallery
Contemporary and 20th c art 38347

Ashton Court Visitor Centre, Stable Block, Ashton Court Estate, Long Ashton, Bristol BS41 9JN - T: (0117) 9639174, Fax: 9532143. Dir.: Cellan Rhys-Michael
Local Museum
History of this landscape, temporary exhibits 38348

At-Bristol, Anchor Rd, Harbourside, Bristol BS1 5DB - T: (0845) 3451235, Fax: (0117) 9157200, E-mail: information@at-bristol.org.uk, Internet: www.at-bristol.org.uk
Natural History Museum / Science&Tech Museum
Nature and sciene 38349

Blaise Castle House Museum, Henbury Rd, Henbury, Bristol BS10 7QS - T: (0117) 9039818, Fax: 9039820, E-mail: general_museum@bristol-city.gov.uk, Internet: www.bristol-city.gov.uk/museums. Dir.: David J. Eveleigh
Local Museum - 1947
Regional social history, agricultural history, domestic life, costumes, toys, dairy 38350

Bristol City Museum and Art Gallery, Queens Rd, Bristol BS8 1RL - T: (0117) 9223571, Fax: 9222047, E-mail: general_museum@bristol-city.gov.uk, Internet: www.bristol-city.gov.uk/museums. Dir.: Stephen Price, Cur.: Roger Clark (Geology), Samantha Trebilczok (Biology), David J. Eveleigh (Social History), Andy King (Industrial and Maritime History), Sheena Stoddard (Fine Art), Karin Walton (Applied Art), Sue Giles (Ethnography), Gail Boyle, Les Good (Archaeology), Kate Newnham (Eastern Art)
Local Museum / Fine Arts Museum - 1905
Archaeology, geology, natural hist, transportation and technology of the area, ethnography, Classical and Egyptian finds, numismatics, local hist, fine art, ceramics, Eastern art, marine history 38351

Bristol Industrial Museum, Princes Wharf, Wapping Rd, Bristol BS1 4RN - T: (0117) 9251470, Fax: 9297318, E-mail: andy_king@bristol-city.gov.uk, Internet: www.bristol-city.gov.uk/museums. Cur.: Andy King, Cons.: Chris West
Science&Tech Museum - 1978
Models of early ships, flight deck of Concorde, buses, cars and motorcycles, ships, cranes and railway stock, slave trade 38352

British Empire and Commonwealth Museum, Clock Tower Yard, Temple Meads, Bristol BS1 6QH - T: (0117) 9254980, 9292688, Fax: 9254983, E-mail: staff@empiremuseum.co.uk, Internet: www.empiremuseum.co.uk. Dir.: Dr. G. Griffiths
Historical Museum
Social history, photographies - library, oral history archive 38353

English Heritage South West Region, 29 Queen Sq, Bristol BS1 4ND - T: (0117) 9750700, Fax: 9750701, Internet: www.english-heritage.org.uk
Association with Coll
Archaeological artefacts and furnishings 38354

Georgian House, 7 Great George St, Bristol BS1 5RR - T: (0117) 9211362, Fax: 9222047, E-mail: general_museum@bristol-city.gov.uk, Internet: www.bristol-city.gov.uk/museums. Cur.: Karin Walton
Decorative Arts Museum - 1937
Period furnishings 38355

Guild Gallery, 68 Park St, Bristol BS1 5JY - T: (0117) 9265548, Fax: 9255659, E-mail: bristolguild@70parkst.freeserve.co.uk. Dir.: Mark Bunce
Public Gallery
Paintings, prints, crafts, sculptures a.o. visual arts 38356

Harvey's Wine Museum, 12 Denmark St, Bristol BS1 5DQ - T: (0117) 9275036, Fax: 9275001, E-mail: alun.cox@adswed.com, Internet: www.j-harvey.co.uk. Dir.: Juliet Hawkes
Special Museum - 1965
18th c English drinking glass, antique delanters, bottles, corkscrews, bottle tickets and other wine-related artefacts and furniture 38357

Kings Weston Roman Villa, c/o City Museum and Art Gallery, Queens Rd, Bristol BS8 1RL - T: (0117) 9223571, Fax: 9222047, E-mail: general_museum@bristol-city.gov.uk, Internet: www.bristol-city.gov.uk/museums
Archaeological Museum
Farmhouse with bathhouse 38358

Maritime Heritage Centre → SS Great Britain Museum

Red Lodge, Park Row, Bristol BS1 5LJ - T: (0117) 9211360, Fax: 9222047, E-mail: general_museum@bristol-city.gov.uk, Internet: www.bristol-city.gov.uk/museums. Cur.: Karin Walton
Decorative Arts Museum
Elizabethan house, modified 18th c, furnishings 38359

SS Great Britain Museum, Wapping Wharf, Gasferry Rd, Bristol BS1 6TY - T: (0117) 9260680, Fax: 9255788, E-mail: enquiries@ss-great-britain.com, Internet: www.ss-great-britain.com. Dir.: Matthew Tanner
Science&Tech Museum
Iron steam-ship 'Great Britain' and its designer I.K. Brunel, iron ship-building, paddle ships 'Great Western'- 'Great Eastern', passenger emigration to Australia 38360

University of Bristol Theatre Collection, c/o Department of Drama, Cantocks Close, Bristol BS8 1UP - T: (0117) 9287836, Fax: 9287832, E-mail: theatre-collection@bristol.ac.uk, Internet: www.bris.ac.uk/theatrecollection. Keeper: Jo Elsworth
Performing Arts Museum / University Museum
Written and graphic material, theatre history - archives, library 38361

Brixham

Brixham Museum, Bolton Cross, Brixham TQ5 8LZ - T: (01803) 856267, E-mail: mail@brixhamheritage.org.uk, Internet: www.brixhamheritage.org.uk. Cur.: Dr. Philip L. Armitage, Cust.: Brian Ogle
Local Museum - 1958
Fishing, shipping, maritime and local history, archaeology 38362

Golden Hind Museum, The Quay, Habour, Brixham TQ5 8AW - T: (01803) 856223, E-mail: postmaster@goldenhind.co.uk, Internet: www.goldenhind.co.uk
Special Museum
Full sized replica of Sir Francis Drake's ship (16th c) 38363

Broadclyst

Paulise de Bush Costume Collection, Killerton House, Broadclyst EX5 3LE - T: (01392) 881345, Fax: 883112, E-mail: sherley.tobin@nationaltrust.org.uk, Internet: www.nationaltrust.org.uk. Cur.: Shelley Tobin
Decorative Arts Museum - 1978
Coll of costumes, which is displayed in a series of rooms furnished in different periods, from the 18th c to the present day 38364

Broadstairs

Bleak House, Fort Rd, Broadstairs CT10 1HD - T: (01843) 862224. Dir.: L.A. Longhi
Special Museum - 1958
Memorabilia on writer Charles Dickens (1811-1870) in the house where he wrote 'David Copperfield' and 'Bleak House' 38365

Crampton Tower Museum, Broadway, Broadstairs CT10 2AB - T: (01843) 864446. Cur.: Robert Tolhurst
Science&Tech Museum - 1978
Thomas Russell Crampton memorabilia, designer of locomotives, submarine telegraphic cable, gas and water works 38366

Dickens House Museum Broadstairs, 2 Victoria Parade, Broadstairs CT10 1QS - T: (01843) 863453, 861232, Fax: 863453, E-mail: aleeeault@aol.com. Dir.: Lee Ault
Special Museum - 1973
Dickens memorabila, costume and Victoriana 38367

Broadway

Broadway Magic Experience, 76 High St, Broadway WR12 7AJ - T: (01386) 858323, E-mail: janicelonghi@hotmail.com. Dir.: Janice Longhi
Special Museum
Automated childhood scenes, Teddy bears 38368

Snowshill Manor, Snowshill, Broadway WR12 7JU - T: (01386) 852410, Fax: 842822, E-mail: snowshill@smtp.ntrust.org.uk, Internet: www.nationaltrust.org.uk
Decorative Arts Museum - 1951
Wade Coll, Chinese and Japanese objects, nautical instruments, Japanese Samurai armour, musical instruments, costumes, toys, spinning and weaving tools, bicycles, farm wagon models 38369

Brockenhurst

Beaulieu Abbey Exhibition of Monastic Life, Beaulieu, Brockenhurst SO42 7ZN - T: (01590) 612345, Fax: 612624, E-mail: susan.tomkins@beaulieu.co.uk, Internet: www.beaulieu.co.uk. Chm.: Lord Montagu of Beaulieu
Religious Arts Museum - 1952
Story of daily life for the Cistercian Monks, who founded the Abbey in 1204 38370

National Motor Museum, John Montagu Bldg, Beaulieu, Brockenhurst SO42 7ZN - T: (01590) 612345, Fax: 612655, E-mail: info@beaulieu.co.uk, Internet: www.beaulieu.co.uk. Chm.: Lord Montagu of Beaulieu
Science&Tech Museum - 1952
Cars, motorcycles, commercial vehicles, racing cars, photographs, books, film - archives 38371

Brodick

Arran Heritage Museum, Rosaburn, Brodick KA27 8DP - T: (01770) 302636, E-mail: arranmuseum@btinternet.com. Dir.: A. Sillaks
Local Museum
Agricultural machinery, geology, archaeology, smiddy, naval photos 38372

Brodick Castle, Brodick KA27 8HY - T: (01770) 302202, Fax: 302312, E-mail: brodickcastle@nts.org.uk, Internet: www.thenationaltrustforscotland.org.uk. Dir.: Ken Thorburn
Fine Arts Museum / Decorative Arts Museum
Beckford silver, porcelain, paintings, Duke of Hamilton and Earl of Rochford sport photos and trophies - garden 38373

Brokerswood

Phillips Countryside Museum, Woodland Park, Brokerswood BA13 4EH - T: (01373) 823880, Fax: 858474. Dir.: Barry Capon
Natural History Museum - 1971
Natural history and forestry, botany, ornithology 38374

Bromham

Bromham Mill and Art Gallery, Bridge End, Bromham MK43 8LP - T: (01234) 824330, Fax: 228531, E-mail: wilemans@deed.bedfordshire.gov.uk, Internet: www.bedfordshire.gov.uk. Dir.: M. Kenworthy
Public Gallery
Art, industrial heritage, natural environment 38375

Bromsgrove

Avoncroft Museum of Historic Buildings, Redditch Rd, Stoke Heath, Bromsgrove B60 4JR - T: (01527) 831886, Fax: 876934, E-mail: avoncroft1@compuserve.com, Internet: www.avoncroft.org.uk. Dir.: Simon Penn
Open Air Museum - 1969
16th c inn, 19th c post mill, granary and barn, 15th c merchant's house, hand-made nail and chain workshops, medieval guesten hall roof, 17th c cockpit, 18th c ice-house, perry mill, National Telephone Kiosk coll, 20th c pre-fab 38376

Bromsgrove Museum, 26 Birmingham Rd, Bromsgrove B61 0DD - T: (01527) 831809, Fax: 831809, Internet: www.bromsgrove.gov.uk
Historical Museum - 1972
Social and industrial hist of the area, with exhibits covering glass, button, nail and salt-making, social hist of the 19th and early 20th c 38377

Bronwydd

Gwili Steam Railway, Bronwydd Arms Station, Bronwydd SA33 6HT - T: (01267) 230666, Internet: www.gwili-railway.co.uk
Science&Tech Museum
Steam and diesel locomotives, carriages and wagons 38378

Broseley

Clay Tobacco Pipe Museum, The Flat, Duke St, Broseley TF8 7AW - T: (01952) 433522, Fax: 432204, E-mail: info@ironbridge.org.uk, Internet: www.ironbridge.org.uk. Cur.: Michael Vanns
Special Museum
Clay tobacco pipe factory 38379

Buckfastleigh

Buckfast Abbey, Buckfastleigh TQ11 0EE - T: (01364) 642519, Fax: 643891
Local Museum 38380

South Devon Railway, The Station, Buckfastleigh TQ11 0DZ - T: (01364) 642338, 643536, Fax: 642170, Internet: www.southdevonrailway.org. Cur.: Harold Eldridge
Science&Tech Museum
17 steam locomotives, 3 heritage diesels, 27 carriages, 35 freight wagons 38381

The Valiant Soldier, 79 Fore St, Buckfastleigh TQ11 0BS - T: (01364) 644522, E-mail: enquiries@valiantsoldier.org.uk. Head: Stuart Barker
Local Museum
Pub fittings, furniture, bar ephemera, promotional and domestic items, history coll 38382

Buckhaven

Buckhaven Museum, Library, College St, Buckhaven KY1 1LD - T: (01592) 412860, Fax: 412870
Historical Museum
History and techniques of the local fishing industry, life of families who earned a living from it, recreations of interiors of home of past generations of Buckhaven people 38383

Buckie

Buckie Drifter Maritime Museum, Freuchny Rd, Buckie AB56 1TT - T: (01542) 834646, Fax: 835995, E-mail: buckie.drifter@moray.gov.uk, Internet: www.moray.org/area/bdrifter/mbdrifter.html
Historical Museum
History of the town of Buckie, fishing industry, boats and techniques employed, navigation, achievements of the local lifeboat 38384

Peter Anson Gallery, Townhouse West, Cluny Pl, Buckie AB56 1HB - T: (01542) 832121, Fax: (01309) 675863, E-mail: alasdair.joyce@techleis.moray.gov.uk, Internet: www.moray.org/museums/ansongal
Fine Arts Museum
Watercolours by marine artist Peter Anson 38385

Buckingham

Buckingham Movie Museum, Printers Mews, Market Hill, Buckingham MK18 1JX - T: (01280) 816758
Special Museum
Coll of 200 projectors and 100 cine-cameras and accessories 38386

Old Gaol Museum, Market Hill, Buckingham MK18 1JX - T: (01280) 823020, Fax: 823020. Man.: John Roberts
Local Museum
Story of Buckingham, military history 38387

Buckler's Hard

Buckler's Hard Village Maritime Museum, Beaulieu, Buckler's Hard SO42 7XB - T: (01590) 616203, Fax: 616283. Dir.: Mike Lucas
Science&Tech Museum - 1963
Shipping, 18th c naval vessels, model of Hard in 1803, memorabilia on Nelson, Sir Francis Chichester, display cottages 18th c, recreation of vinage life, with models 38388

Bude

Bude-Stratton Museum, The Wharf, Bude EX23 8LG - T: (01288) 353576, Fax: 353576, E-mail: theclerk@bstc.freeserve.co.uk. Cur.: Harvey Kendall
Historical Museum - 1976
Hist and working of the canal, by means of early photographs, models, drawings, plans and maps, development of Bude, shipwrecks and hist of the local lifeboat, railway, military and social hist 38389

Budleigh Salterton

Fairlynch Museum, 27 Fore St, Budleigh Salterton EX9 6NP - T: (01395) 442666, E-mail: fairlynch@eclipse.co.uk, Internet: www.devonmuseums.net/fairlynch. Pres.: Priscilla Hull
Local Museum
Prehistory, art, local history, ecology of Lower Otter Valley, geology 38390

Otterton Mill Centre and Working Museum, Fore Otterton St, Budleigh Salterton EX9 7HG - T: (01395) 568521, Fax: 568521, E-mail: ottertonmill@ukonline.co.uk, Internet: www.ottertonmill.co.uk. Dir.: Dr. Desna Greenhow
Science&Tech Museum - 1977
Use of water to drive mill machinery, production processes of flour, displays of crafts, fine arts and historical items - gallery, lace exhibition 38391

Bulwell

South Nottinghamshire Hussars Museum, TA Centre, Hucknall Ln, Bulwell NG6 8AQ - T: (0115) 9272251, Fax: 975420. Cur.: G.E. Aldridge
Military Museum
Regimental uniforms, models of vehicles and guns from WW II, paintings and trophies 38392

Bunbury

Bunbury Watermill, Mill Ln, off Bowes Gate Rd, Bunbury CW6 9PP - T: (01829) 261422, Fax: 261422, Internet: www.bunbury-mill.org. Dir.: Dennis Buchanan
Science&Tech Museum 38393

Bungay

Bungay Museum, Council Office, Bungay NR35 1EE - T: (01986) 893155, 894463, Fax: 892176, E-mail: chris.reeve@waveney.gov.uk. Cur.: Christopher R.M. Theol
Local Museum
Local history, fossils, flint implements, coins, J.B. Scott memorabilia 38394

Burford

Tolsey Museum, 126 High St, Burford OX18 4QU - T: (01993) 823196. Dir.: Christopher Walker
Local Museum - 1960
Local governmental history, local crafts, social history 38395

Burghead

Burghead Museum, 16-18 Grant St, Burghead IV36 1PH - T: (01309) 673701, E-mail: alasdair.joyce@techleis.moray.gov.uk, Internet: www.moray.gov.uk/museums/homepage.htm
Local Museum 38396

Burnham-on-Crouch

Burnham Museum, Coronation Rd, Burnham-on-Crouch CM0 8AA - T: (01621) 782670, E-mail: pfhammond@btinternet.com, Internet: www.burnham.gov.uk
Local Museum - 1981
archives 38397

Mangapps Farm Railway Museum, Mangapps Farm, Burnham-on-Crouch CM0 8QQ - T: (01621) 784898, Fax: 783833, Internet: www.mangapps.co.uk
Science&Tech Museum
Good wagons, carriages, steam and diesel locomotives, railway artefacts 38398

Burnley

Museum of Local Crafts and Industries, Towneley Holmes Rd, Burnley BB11 3RQ - T: (01282) 424213, Fax: 436138, E-mail: towneleyhall@burnley.gov.uk, Internet: www.towneleyhall.gov.uk
Historical Museum
Social and industrial history, textiles, street scene, home life, a pub 38399

Queen Street Mill Textile Museum, Queen St, Harle Syke, Burnley BB10 2HX - T: (01282) 412555, Fax: 430220, E-mail: queenstreet.mill@mus.lancscc.gov.uk, Internet: www.lancashire.com/lcc/museums. Dir.: Edmund Southworth
Science&Tech Museum
Steam powered textile mill 38400

Towneley Hall Art Gallery and Museums, Towneley Holmes Rd, Burnley BB11 3RQ - T: (01282) 424213, Fax: 436138, E-mail: towneleyhall@burnley.gov.uk, Internet: www.towneleyhall.org. Cur.: Susan Bourne
Fine Arts Museum / Local Museum - 1902
Paintings, water colours, furnishings, period house, archaeology, local hist, natural hist, decorative arts, military 38401

Weavers' Triangle Visitor Centre, 85 Manchester Rd, Burnley BB11 1JZ - T: (01282) 452403. Dir.: Brian Hall
Historical Museum - 1980
Burnley's cotton industry and its workers, Victorian industrial area 38402

Burntisland

Burntisland Museum, 102 High St, Burntisland KY3 9AS - T: (01592) 412860, Fax: 412870, E-mail: kirkcaldy.museum@fife.gov.uk. Dir.: Dallas Mechan
Local Museum 38403

Bursledon

Bursledon Windmill, Windmill Ln, Bursledon SO31 8BG - T: (023) 80404999, E-mail: musmgb@hants.gov.uk, Internet: hants.gov.uk/museums/windmill. Cur.: Dr. Gavin Bowie
Science&Tech Museum 38404

Manor Farm, Pylands Ln, Bursledon SO31 1BH - T: (01489) 787055, Internet: www.hants.gov.uk/countryside/manorfarm. Man.: Barbara Newbury
Agriculture Museum
Farm with machinery, woodworking, blacksmithing, farmhouse, living history displays 38405

Burston, Diss

Burston Strike School, The Firs, Burston, Diss IP22 5TP - T: (01379) 741565, Internet: www.burstonstrikeschool.org
Historical Museum
Events in 1914 which lead to the longest strike in history 38406

Burton Agnes

Burton Agnes Hall, Burton Agnes YO25 4NB - T: (01262) 490324, Fax: 490513, E-mail: burton.agnes@fannline.com, Internet: www.burton-agnes.com. Dir.: E.S. Cunliffe-Lister
Fine Arts Museum / Decorative Arts Museum - 1946
Elizabethan house with ceilings, overmantels, paintings by Reynolds, Gainsborough, Cotes, Marlow, Reinagle, also modern French paintings 38407

Burton-upon-Trent

Bass Museum of Brewing, Horninglow St, Burton-upon-Trent DE14 1YQ - T: (0845) 6000598, (01283) 511000, Fax: (01283) 513509, E-mail: enquiries@bass-museum.com, Internet: www.bass-museum.com. Dir.: Mike Maryon, Cur.: Diana Lay
Science&Tech Museum - 1977
Company records of Bass and Co. (Brewers) 38408

Burwash

Bateman's Kipling's House, Batemaris Ln, Burwash TN19 7DS - T: (01435) 882302, Fax: 882811, E-mail: batemans@nationaltrust.org.uk. Man.: Elaine Francis
Special Museum - 1939
Work and living rooms of writer Rudyard Kipling (1865-1936) in his former home, built 1634, manuscripts, Kiplings Rolls Royce, working water mill - Library 38409

Burwell

Burwell Museum, Mill Close, Burwell CB5 0HJ - T: (01638) 605544, 741713
Local Museum
Local history 38410

Bury, Lancashire

Bury Art Gallery and Museum (closed until 2005), Moss St, Bury, Lancashire BL9 0DR - T: (0161) 2535878, Fax: 2535915, E-mail: artgallery@bury.gov.uk, Internet: www.bury.gov.uk. Cur.: Richard Burns
Fine Arts Museum / Decorative Arts Museum / Local Museum
British paintings and drawings, local hist, natural hist, ornithology, archaeology, Wedgwood and local pottery, Bronze Age finds 38411

Bury Transport Museum, Castlecrof Rd, off Bolton St, Bury, Lancashire BL9 0LN - T: (01225) 333895, Fax: (01424) 775174
Science&Tech Museum
Road and rail transport, buses, lorries, traction engines 38412

Fusiliers' Museum Lancashire, Wellington Barracks, Bolton Rd, Bury, Lancashire BL8 2PL - T: (0161) 7642208, Fax: 7642208, E-mail: rrflhq@aol.com, Internet: www.thefusiliers.org. Cur.: John O'Grady
Military Museum - 1934
History of the regiment since 1688, uniforms, medals, militaria, Napoleonic relics 38413

Bury Saint Edmunds

Abbey Visitor Centre (closed) 38414

Bury Saint Edmunds Art Gallery, Market Cross, Bury Saint Edmunds IP28 7EF - T: (01284) 762081, Fax: 750774, E-mail: e.enquiries@burysted-artgall.org, Internet: www.burystedmundsartgallery.org. Dir.: Barbara Taylor
Public Gallery 38415

John Gershom-Parkington Collection of Timekeeping Instruments, Manor House, Honey Hill, Bury Saint Edmunds IP33 1HF - T: (01284) 757076, Fax: 757079, E-mail: manor.house@burybo.stedsbc.gov.uk, Internet: www.stedmundsbury.gov.uk. Dir.: Viscount Midleton
Science&Tech Museum / Fine Arts Museum - 1953
Technological hist of timekeeping instruments, costume, fine art 38416

Moyse's Hall Museum, Cornhill, Bury Saint Edmunds IP33 1DX - T: (01284) 706183, Fax: 765373, E-mail: maggie.goodger@stedsbc.gov.uk, Internet: www.stedmundsbury.gov.uk. Dir.: Margaret Goodger
Local Museum - 1899
Prehistoric-medieval finds, regional natural history, local history, 12th c Norman building, Suffolk Regiment 38417

Suffolk Regiment Museum, nr Galz St, Bury Saint Edmunds IP33 3RN - T: (01284) 752394, Fax: 752026. Dir.: A.G.B. Cobbold
Military Museum - 1935
Regimental history 38418

West Stow Anglo-Saxon Centre, The Visitor Centre, Icklingham Rd, West, Bury Saint Edmunds IP28 6HG - T: (01284) 728718, Fax: 728277, E-mail: weststow@stedsbc.gov.uk, Internet: www.stedmundsbury.gov.uk/weststow. Man.: Alan Baxter
Archaeological Museum
Early Anglo-Saxon archaeology from the West Stow settlement (c 450-650 AD) and cemetary, along with other local material from the same period, also mesolithic, Bronze Age, Iron Age and Roman material, reconstructed Anglo-Saxon village on original site 38419

Buscot

Buscot House, Buscot SN7 8BU - T: (01367) 20786
Fine Arts Museum
Coll of paintings 38420

Bushey

Bushey Museum and Art Gallery, Rudolph Rd, Bushey WD23 3HW - T: (020) 84204057, 89503233, Fax: 84204923, E-mail: busmt@bushey.org.uk, Internet: www.busheymuseum.org. Cur.: Bryen Wood
Local Museum / Fine Arts Museum
Local history, Monro circle of artists Herkomer and Kemp-Welch art schools - local study centre 38421

Bushmead

John Dony Field Centre, Hancock Dr, Bushmead LU2 7SF - T: (01582) 486983, Fax: 422805, E-mail: tweent@luton.gov.uk, Internet: www.luton.gov.uk
Natural History Museum
Natural history, enviroment 38422

Bushmills

Causeway School Museum, 52 Causeway Rd, Bushmills BT57 8SU - T: (028) 20731777, Fax: 20732142. Head: Vivienne Quinn
Historical Museum 38423

Giant's Causeway and Bushmills Railway, Runkerry Rd, Bushmills BT57 8SZ - T: (028) 20732844, Fax: 20732844. Dir.: D.W. Laing
Science&Tech Museum 38424

Giants Causeway Visitor Centre, 44a Causeway Rd, Bushmills, Co. Antrim - T: (012657) 31582
Natural History Museum
World Heritage Centre and National Nature Reserve 38425

Bute Town

Drenewydd Museum, 26-27 Lower Row, Bute Town NP2 5QH - T: (01443) 864224, Fax: 864228, E-mail: morgacl@caerphilly.gov.uk, Internet: www.caerphilly.gov.uk. Dir.: Chris Morgan
Local Museum
Ironworker's cottages, domestic and household objects 38426

Buxton

Buxton Museum and Art Gallery, Peak Bldgs, Terrace Rd, Buxton SK17 6DA - T: (01298) 24658, Fax: 79394, E-mail: buxton.museum@derbyshire.gov.uk, Internet: www.derbyshire.gov.uk/libraries&heritage. Man.: Ros. Westwood
Fine Arts Museum / Natural History Museum / Local Museum - 1891
Prehistoric cave finds, geology, mineralogy, archaeology, art, craft, local hist 38427

Cadbury

Fursdon House, Cadbury EX5 5JS - T: (01392) 860860, Fax: 860126, E-mail: enquiries@fursdon.co.uk, Internet: www.fursdon.co.uk. Dir.: E.D. Fursdon
Special Museum
Coll of family possessions, furniture, portraits, everyday items, family costumes, coll of Iron Age and Roman material, old estate maps 38428

Cadeby

Cadeby Experience, Boston Collection and Brass Rubbing Centre, Old Rectory, Cadeby CV13 0AS - T: (01455) 290462. Dir.: J. Audrey Boston
Local Museum 38429

Cadeby Light Railway, Old Rectory, Cadeby CV13 0AS - T: (01455) 290462. Dir.: A. Boston
Science&Tech Museum - 1962
Railway relics, trains, locomotives, steam traction engine, steam rollers - library 38430

Caerleon

Roman Legionary Museum, High St, Caerleon NP18 1AE - T: (01633) 423134, Fax: 422869, E-mail: post@nmgw.ac.uk, Internet: www.nmgw.ac.uk/rlm. Dir.: P. Guest
Archaeological Museum - 1850
Finds from excavations at the fortress of the Second Augustan Legion 38431

Caernarfon

Caernarfon Maritime Museum, Victoria Dock, Caernarfon LL55 1SR - T: (01248) 752083. Pres.: F. Whitehead
Local Museum / Science&Tech Museum
History of Caernarfon as a harbour and port since Roman times, maritime education, trade and industry of the port, steam engine Seiont II, HMS Conway exhibits 38432

Gwynedd Education and Culture, Archives, Museums and Galleries, County Offices, Caernarfon LL55 1SH - T: (01286) 679088, 678098, Fax: 679637, E-mail: archives@gwynedd.gov.uk, Internet: www.gwynedd.gov.uk. Ass. Dir.: Gareth H. Williams
Historical Museum
Social hist 38433

Royal Welch Fusiliers Regimental Museum, Queen's Tower, The Castle, Caernarfon LL55 2AY - T: (01286) 673362, Fax: 677042, E-mail: rwfusiliers@callnetuk.com. Dir.: P.A. Crocker
Military Museum - 1960
Hist of the regiment since 1689, documents, portraits, medals, weapons, uniforms, badges and pictures 38434

Segontium Roman Museum, Beddgelert Rd, Caernarfon LL55 1AT - T: (01286) 675625, Fax: 678416
Archaeological Museum - 1937
Finds from excavations at the former Roman fort Segontium, inscriptions, medals, urns, tools, armaments, pottery, household objects 38435

Caerphilly

Caerphilly Castle, Caerphilly CF2 1UF - T: (029) 20883143, Internet: www.castleswales.com/caerphil.html
Historical Museum
Full scale replica, working medieval siege engines 38436

Calbourne

Calbourne Water Mill and Rural Museum, Calbourne PO30 4JN - T: (01983) 531277, Fax: 531227, Internet: www.calbournewatermill.co.uk
Local Museum / Science&Tech Museum
War and country life 38437

Caldicot

Caldicot Castle, Church Rd, Caldicot NP26 4HU - T: (01291) 420241, Fax: 435094, E-mail: caldicotcastle@monmouthshire.gov.uk, Internet: www.caldicotcastle.co.uk. Man.: Sarah Finch
Historic Site 38438

Callander

Rob Roy and Trossachs Victor Centre, Acaster Sq, Callander FK17 8ED - T: (01877) 330342, Fax: 330784. Man.: Janet Michael
Historical Museum
Story of the highland folk hero Rob Roy MacGregor 38439

Calne

Atwell-Wilson Motor Museum, Stockley Ln, Calne SN11 0NF - T: (01249) 813119, Fax: 813119, E-mail: stoned@stonehenge.co.uk, Internet: www.atwell-museum.freeuk.com
Science&Tech Museum
Coll of post vintage and classic vehicles, motorcycles 38440

Bowood House and Gardens, Derry Hill, Calne SN11 0LZ - T: (01249) 812102, Fax: 821757, E-mail: houseandgardens@bowood.org, Internet: www.bowood.org. Cur.: Dr. Kate Fielden
Decorative Arts Museum / Fine Arts Museum / Historical Museum
Fine and decorative arts, paintings, watercolours, furniture, sculptures, architecture - library, archive 38441

Calverton

Calverton Folk Museum, Main St, Calverton NG14 6FQ - T: (0115) 9654843, Fax: (0870) 1370332, E-mail: cps@bay47.clara.net, Internet: www.welcome.to/calverton
Folklore Museum
Hosiery industry, framework knitting machine - Library 38442

Camberley

National Army Museum, Sandhurst Outstation, Royal Military Academy Sandhurst, Camberley GU15 4PQ - T: (01276) 63344 ext 2457, Fax: 686316, E-mail: info@national-army-museum.ac.uk, Internet: www.national-army-museum.ac.uk
Military Museum
Indian army memorial room, study coll of uniforms and equipment 38443

Royal Military Academy Sandhurst Collection, Royal Military Academy, Camberley GU15 4PQ - T: (01276) 412489, Fax: 412595, E-mail: drthwaites@rmas.nod.uk. Cur.: Dr. Peter Thwaites
Military Museum
History of the academy 38444

Staff College Museum, Camberley GU15 4NP - T: (01276) 412602, 412643, Fax: 412718. Dir.: Stephen Connelly
Historical Museum - 1958
History of college 1799-1990, staff uniforms 38445

Surrey Heath Museum, Surrey Heath House, Knoll Rd, Camberley GU15 3HD - T: (01276) 707284, Fax: 671158, E-mail: museum@sureyheath.gov.uk, Internet: www.sureyheath.gov.uk/leisure. Dir.: Sharon Cross
Local Museum - 1935
Local 19th and 20th c social hist, costume, natural hist, local photographs 38446

Cambo

Wallington Hall, Cambo NE61 4AR - T: (01670) 774283, Fax: 774420, E-mail: nwapir@smtp.ntrust.org.uk, Internet: www.nationaltrust.org.uk. Dir.: Bill Pashley
Decorative Arts Museum / Fine Arts Museum - 1688
House built in 1688 with 18th c furnishings, rococo plaster decorations, porcelain, needlework, 19th c hall decorated by W. Scott, Ruskin and others, Scott's pre-Raphaelite paintings 38447

Camborne

Camborne Museum, Cross St, Camborne TR14 8HA - T: (01209) 713544. Dir.: Janet Spargo
Local Museum / Archaeological Museum
Stone Age finds, Iron and Bronze Age pottery, Roman Villa excavation finds, Mexican and Egyptian antiquities, old china and silver, numismatics, geology, mineralogy, local history, mining 38448

Trevithick Cottage, Penponds, Camborne TR14 0QG - T: (01209) 612154, Fax: 612142, E-mail: info@trevithicktrust.com, Internet: www.trevithicktrust.com. Cust.: L. Humphrey
Historical Museum / Fine Arts Museum
Oil paintings of himself, wife and family 38449

Cambridge

Cambridge and County Folk Museum, 2-3 Castle St, Cambridge CB3 0AQ - T: (01223) 355159, Fax: 576301, E-mail: info@folkmuseum.org.uk, Internet: www.folkmuseum.org.uk. Cur.: Cameron Hawke-Smith, Ass. Cur.: Rebecca Proctor
Local Museum - 1936
Hist of Cambridge and Cambridgeshire county since the 17th c, looking at the everyday life of people in the area, wide-ranging colls, strengths, domestic items, toys, tools 38450

Cambridge Museum of Technology, Old Pumping Station, Cheddars Ln, Cambridge CB5 8LD - T: (01223) 368650, Internet: www.museumoftechnology.com. Dir.: Alan Denney
Science&Tech Museum
Local industry 38451

Cambridge University Collection of Air Photographs, Mond Bldg, Free School Ln, Cambridge CB2 3RF - T: (01223) 334578, Fax: 763300, E-mail: aerial-photography@lists.cam.ac.uk, Internet: www.aerial.cam.ac.uk. Dir.: Dr. B.J. Devereux
Special Museum
Air-photographs of the British Isles record both the natural environment and the effects of human activity from prehistoric times to the present day, substantial Irish coll and smaller collections of photographs taken over northern France, Denmark and the Netherlands 38452

Cavendish Laboratory, c/o University of Cambridge, Dept. of Physics, Madingley Rd, Cambridge CB3 0HE - T: (01223) 337420, 337200, Fax: 766360, E-mail: clh29@phy.cam.ac.uk, Internet: www.phy.cam.ac.uk
Science&Tech Museum
Scientific instruments 38453

Fitzwilliam Museum, c/o University of Cambridge, Trumpington St, Cambridge CB2 1RB - T: (01223) 332900, Fax: 332923, E-mail: fitzmuseum-enquiries@lists.cam.ac.uk, Internet: www.fitzmuseum.cam.ac.uk. Dir.: Duncan Robinson, Sc. Staff: Dr. L. Burn (Antiquities), J. Dawson (Antiquities, Conservation), Dr. S. Ashton (Antiquities), J.E. Poole (Applied Arts), M.A.S. Blackburn (Coins and Medals), Dr. A. Popescu (Coins and Medals), Dr. S. Panayotova (Manuscripts and Printed Books), D.E. Scrase (Paintings and Drawings), J.A. Munro (Paintings and Drawings), C. Hartley (Prints), Cons.: R. Proctor, B. Clarke, C. Withycombe
University Museum - 1816
Egyptian, Greek and Roman antiquities, numismatics, paintings, drawings, bronze objects, pottery, porcelain, ceramics, armaments, furniture - Hamilton Kerr Institute for the Conservation of Paintings 38454

Herbarium, Department of Plant Sciences, Downing St, Cambridge CB2 3EA - T: (01223) 333900 ext 30211, Fax: 333953, E-mail: jgm23@cus.cam.ac.uk, Internet: www.plantsci.ac.uk/plantsci. Cur.: Prof. John S. Parker
Natural History Museum
Coll of 1.2 m pressed, mounted plant specimens, Charles Darwin's plant specimens from the voyage of the Beagle, the John Lindley coll of plant from expeditions 38455

Imperial War Museum Duxford, Cambridge CB2 4QR - T: (01223) 835000, Fax: 837267, E-mail: duxford@iwm.org.uk, Internet: www.iwm.org.uk. Dir.: Edward Inman
Military Museum - 1976
Largest coll of civil and military aircraft in EU also tanks, guns, naval exhibits, aircraft ranging from WWI biplanes, spitfires to concorde 38456

Kettle's Yard, c/o University of Cambridge, Castle St, Cambridge CB3 0AQ - T: (01223) 352124, Fax: 324377, E-mail: mail@kettlesyard.cam.ac.uk, Internet: www.kettlesyard.co.uk. Dir.: Michael Harrison
Fine Arts Museum / University Museum - 1957
20th c art incl Ben Nicholson, Alfred Wallis, David Jones, Christopher Wood, Henri Gaudier-Brzeska 38457

Lewis Collection, Corpus Christi College, Cambridge CB2 1RH - T: (01223) 338000, Fax: 338061, E-mail: http://www.corpus.cam.nc.uk. Dir.: Dr. Christopher Kelly (Greek and Roman Art, Archaeology, Numismatics)
Archaeological Museum / Decorative Arts Museum / University Museum
Classical and neo-classical gems, Greek and Roman coins, Greek and Roman figurines and pottery 38458

Museum of Classical Archaeology, c/o University of Cambridge, Sidgwick Av, Cambridge CB3 9DA - T: (01223) 335153, Fax: 335409, E-mail: jd125@cam.ac.uk, Internet: www.classics.cam.ac.uk/ark.html. Cur.: Prof. Martin Millett, Asst. Cur.: John Donaldson
Archaeological Museum - 1884 38459

New Hall Women's Art Collection, Huntingdon Rd, Cambridge CB3 0DF - T: (01223) 762297, Fax: 763110, E-mail: art@newhall.cam.ac.uk, Internet: www.newhall.cam.ac.uk. Cur.: Dr. Aya Soika
Fine Arts Museum 38460

Scott Polar Research Institute Museum, c/o University of Cambridge, Lensfield Rd, Cambridge CB2 1ER - T: (01223) 336540, 336555, Fax: 336549, E-mail: rkh10@cam.ac.uk, Internet: www.spri.cam.ac.uk. Cur.: R.K. Headland
Natural History Museum - 1920
Polar exploration and research, material from Antarctic expeditions of Captain Scott and from other historical British polar expeditions, exploration of the NW-Passage, relics, manuscripts, paintings, photographs, Eskimo art, ethnological coll - library, archives 38461

Sedgwick Museum of Geology, c/o University of Cambridge, Dept. of Earth Sciences, Downing St, Cambridge CB2 3EQ - T: (01223) 333456, Fax: 333450, E-mail: sedgmus@esc.cam.ac.uk, Internet: www.sedgwickmuseum.org. Dir.: Dr. D.B. Norman, Cur.: Dr. R.B. Rickards, Dr. M.A. Carpenter, M. Dorling
Natural History Museum / University Museum - 1728/1904
Local, British, foreign rocks, fossils, minerals, memorabilia of scientist Adam Sedgwick, John Woodward coll (oldest intact geological coll), Darwin's Rocks - conservation laboratory, Sedgwick library 38462

University Museum of Archaeology and Anthropology, c/o University of Cambridge, Downing St, Cambridge CB2 3DZ - T: (01223) 333516, Fax: 333517, E-mail: cumaa@hermes.cam.ac.uk, Internet: museum.archanth.cam.ac.uk. Dir.: Prof. David W. Phillipson
Archaeological Museum / University Museum / Ethnology Museum - 1884
Prehistoric archaeology of all parts of the world, the archaeology of the Cambridge region from the paleolithic period to recent times, ethnographic material from all regions of the world with a particular emphasis on Oceania 38463

University Museum of Zoology, c/o University of Cambridge, Downing St, Cambridge CB2 3EJ - T: (01223) 336650, Fax: 336676, E-mail: umzc@zoo.cam.ac.uk, Internet: www.zoo.cam.ac.uk/museum. Dir.: Prof. Michael Akam
Natural History Museum - 1814
Zoology: birds, fossil tetrapods, invertebrates, mammals, fish, reptiles and amphibians 38464

Whipple Museum of the History of Science, Free School Ln, Cambridge CB2 3RH - T: (01223) 330906, Fax: 334554, E-mail: hps-whipple-museum@lists.cam.ac.uk, Internet: www.hps.cam.ac.uk/whipple.html. Dir.: Liba Taub (Early Scientific Instruments and Cosmology)
Historical Museum / University Museum - 1944
Old scientific instruments, 16th-20th c books 38465

Camelford

British Cycling Museum, The Old Station, Camelford PL32 9TZ - T: (01840) 212811, Fax: 212811, Internet: www.chycor.co.uk. Owner: J.W. Middleton, S.I. Middleton
Science&Tech Museum
Cycling history, 400 cycles, over 1,000 cycling medals, enamel signs and posters 38466

North Cornwall Museum and Gallery, The Clease, Camelford PL32 9PL - T: (01840) 212954, Fax: 212954, E-mail: camelfordtic@eurobell.co.uk. Dir.: Sally Holden
Local Museum / Folklore Museum 38467

Campbeltown

Campbeltown Museum, Public Library, Hall St, Campbeltown PA28 6BS - T: (01586) 552366 ext 2237, Fax: 552938, 705797, E-mail: mvhelmond@abc-museums.demon.co.uk, Internet: www.abc-museums.demon.co.uk. Dir.: Mary van Helmond
Local Museum - 1898 38468

Canterbury

Buffs Museum, National Army Museum, 18 High St, Canterbury CT1 2RA - T: (01227) 452747, Fax: 455047, E-mail: museums@canterbury.gov.uk, Internet: www.canterbury-museum.co.uk
Military Museum / Fine Arts Museum
Royal East Kent Regiment story, uniforms, weapons, medals, sporting and leisure pursuits 38469

Canterbury Cathedral Archives and Library, The Precincts, Canterbury CT1 2EH - T: (01227) 865330, 865287, Fax: 865222, E-mail: library@canterbury-cathedral.org, Internet: www.canterbury-cathedral.org. Head: Keith M.C. O'Sullivan
Library with Exhibitions 38470

Canterbury Heritage Museum, Poor Priests' Hospital, Stour St, Canterbury CT1 2RA - T: (01227) 452747, Fax: 455047, Internet: www.canterbury-museum.co.uk. Dir.: K.G.H. Reedie
Local Museum
History of Canterbury's 2000 years 38471

Canterbury Roman Museum, Longmarket, Butchery Ln, Canterbury CT1 2RA - T: (01227) 785575, Fax: 455047, Internet: www.canterbury-museum.co.uk. Dir.: K.G.H. Reedie
Archaeological Museum / Historical Museum / Historic Site
Round a Roman site, excavated finds, mosaic floors, hands-on area 38472

Ethnic Doll and Toy Museum, Cogan House, 53 Saint Peter St, Canterbury CT1 2BE - T: (01227) 472986
Special Museum 38473

Royal Museum and Art Gallery, 18 High St, Canterbury CT1 2RA - T: (01227) 452747, Fax: 455047, E-mail: museums@canterbury.gov.uk, Internet: www.canterbury-artgallery.co.uk
Fine Arts Museum / Decorative Arts Museum / Public Gallery - 1899
Decorative arts, picture coll, cattle paintings 38474

Saint Augustine's Abbey, Longport, Canterbury CT1 1TF - T: (01227) 767345, Fax: 767345, E-mail: dan.dennis@english-heritage.org.uk, Internet: www.english-heritage.org.uk. Cur.: Jan Summerfield
Religious Arts Museum
Religious art 38475

West Gate Towers, Saint Peters St, Canterbury - T: (01227) 452747, Fax: 455047, E-mail: museums@canterbury.gov.uk, Internet: www.canterbury-museum.co.uk
Historical Museum - 1906
British and foreign armaments, relics in 14th c medieval gate 38476

Canvey Island

Castle Point Transport Museum, 105 Point Rd, Canvey Island SS8 7TP - T: (01268) 684272
Science&Tech Museum
Busses, coaches, commercial, military & emergency vehicles (1944-1972) 38477

Cardiff

Cardiff Castle, Castle St, Cardiff CF10 3RB - T: (029) 20878100, Fax: 20231417, E-mail: cardiffcastle@cardiff.gov.uk, Internet: www.cardiff-info.com/castle
Fine Arts Museum / Historical Museum
Architectural drawings, ceramics, painting, furniture, Burges coll, De Morgan coll 38478

Howard Gardens Gallery, University of Wales Institute, Howard Gardens, Cardiff CF24 0SP - T: (029) 20416678, Fax: 20416678, E-mail: wwarrilow@uwic.ac.uk. Dir.: Walt Warrilow
Public Gallery 38479

IBRA Collection, International Bee Research Association, 18 North Rd, Cardiff CF10 3DT - T: (029) 20372409, Fax: 20665522, E-mail: museum@ibra.org.uk, Internet: www.ibra.org.uk. Dir.: Richard Jones
Special Museum / Agriculture Museum
Bees and bee keeping - library 38480

National Museum and Gallery, Cathays Park, Cardiff CF10 3NP - T: (029) 20397951, Fax: 20373219, E-mail: post@nmgw.ac.uk, Internet: www.nmgw.ac.uk/nmgc. Dir.: Michael Tooby, Sc. Staff: R. Brewer (Archaeology), Dr. M.G. Bassett (Geology), Dr. Graham Oliver (Biodiversity and systematic Biology), Oliver Fairclough (Art)
Archaeological Museum / Natural History Museum / Fine Arts Museum - 1907
Geology, mineralogy, fossils, botany, plant ecology, Welsh zoology, mollusks, entomology, Welsh archaeology up to the 16th c, numismatics, industrial history, European painting, sculpture, applied art, decorative objects, French art 38481

Regimental Museum of 1st The Queen's Dragoon Guards, Cardiff Castle, Cardiff CF10 2RB - T: (029) 20781271, Fax: 20781384, E-mail: curator@qdg.org.uk, Internet: www.qdg.org.uk. Cur.: Clive Morris
Military Museum 38482

Saint David's Hall, The Hayes, Cardiff CF1 2SH - T: (029) 20878500, Fax: 20878599
Public Gallery 38483

Techniquest, Stuart St, Cardiff CF10 5BW - T: (029) 20475475, Fax: 20482517, E-mail: info@techniquest.org, Internet: www.techniquest.org. Dir.: Colin Johnson
Science&Tech Museum
Science discovery centre - Planetarium 38484

The Welch Regiment Museum (41st/ 69th Foot) of the Rpyal Regiment of Wales, Black and Barbican Towers, Cardiff Castle, Cardiff CF10 2RB - T: (029) 20229367, Internet: www.rrw.org.uk. Cur.: John Dart
Military Museum 38485

Cardigan

Cardigan Heritage Centre, Teifi Wharf, Castle St, Cardigan SA43 3AA - T: (01239) 614404, Fax: 614404
Local Museum
Town history 38486

Carlisle

Border Regiment and King's Own Royal Border Regiment Museum, Queen Mary's Tower, Castle, Carlisle CA3 8UR - T: (01228) 532774, Fax: 521275, E-mail: RHQ@kingsownborder.demon.co.uk, Internet: www.army.mod.uk/army/press/museums/details/m.36bord.htm. Cur.: S.A. Eastwood
Military Museum - 1932
Uniforms, badges, medals, pictures, silver, arms, dioramas, documents, trophies, militaria, photogr - archives 38487

Cathedral Treasury Museum, Carlisle Cathedral, 7 The Abbey, Carlisle CA3 8TZ - T: (01228) 548151, Fax: 547049, E-mail: office@carlislecathedral.org.uk, Internet: www.carlislecathedral.org.uk. Dir.: D.W.V. Weston
Religious Arts Museum / Archaeological Museum
Articles connected with the site from Roman times to the present day, 15th to 20th c Church plate 38488

Guildhall Museum, Greenmarket, Carlisle CA2 4PW - T: (01228) 534781, 819925, Fax: 810249, E-mail: enquiries@tullie-house.co.uk, Internet: www.tulliehouse.co.uk. Dir.: Hilary Wade
Local Museum
History of the medieval Guilds and on the building itself, medieval iron-bound muniment chest and town bell, two 1599 silver bells, medieval measures and pottery, civic regalia, the pillory and stocks, wearing, local history 38489

Tullie House - City Museum and Art Gallery, Castle St, Carlisle CA3 8TP - T: (01228) 534781, Fax: 810249, E-mail: enquirires@tullie-house.co.uk, Internet: www.tulliehouse.co.uk. Dir.: Hilary Wade
Local Museum - 1892
Regional antiquities, natural history, Lake District specimens, pre-Raphaelite, 19th c painting, modern paintings, English porcelain, Roman finds, ornithology, historic railways, local history 38490

Carlton Colville

East Anglia Transport Museum, Chapel Rd, Carlton Colville NR33 8BL - T: (01502) 518459, Fax: 584658, E-mail: enquiries@eatm.org.uk, Internet: www.eatm.org.uk
Science&Tech Museum
Trams, trolleybuses and a narrow gauge railway 38491

Carmarthen

Carmarthen Heritage Centre, The Quay, Carmarthen SA31 3AN - T: (01267) 223788, Fax: 223830, E-mail: cdelaney@carmarthenshire.gov.uk, Internet: www.carmarthenshire.gov.uk
Local Museum
History of the River Tywi and the port of Carmarthen 38492

Carmarthen Museum → Carmarthenshire County Museum

Carmarthenshire County Museum, Abergwili, Carmarthen SA31 2JG - T: (01267) 231691, Fax: 223830, E-mail: chrisdelaney@carmarthenshire.gov.uk. Dir.: Chris Delaney, Sc. Staff: C.J. Delaney, A.G. Dorsett (Arts), G.H. Evans (Archaeology)
Archaeological Museum / Folklore Museum - 1905
Folklore, archaeology - library 38493

Carnforth

Leighton Hall, Carnforth LA5 9ST - T: (01524) 734474, Fax: 720357, E-mail: leightonhall@yahoo.co.uk, Internet: www.leightonhall.co.uk. Owner: R.G. Reynolds
Local Museum
Manor house dating from the 13th c with old and modern painting, antique furniture, Gillow family portraits 38494

Steamtown Railway Museum, Warton Rd, Carnforth LA5 9HX - T: (01524) 732100, Fax: 735518. Dir.: W.D. Smith
Science&Tech Museum 38495

Carrbridge

Landmark Forest Heritage Park, Main St, Carrbridge PH23 3AJ - T: (01479) 841613, Fax: 841384, E-mail: landmarkcentre@compuserve.com, Internet: www.landmark-centre.co.uk. Dir.: David Hayes
Natural History Museum - 1970
Hist, natural environment and wildlife of the Highlands, nature trails, microscopy, steampowered sawmill, working horse and woodcraft centre 38496

Carrickfergus

Flame!, The Gasworks Museum of Ireland, 44 Irish Quarter West, Carrickfergus BT38 8AT - T: (028) 93369575, E-mail: info@flamegasworks.fsnet.co.uk, Internet: www.gasworksflame.com. Dir.: Sam Gault
Science&Tech Museum 38497

Carshalton

Carshalton Water Tower, West St, Carshalton SM5 2NR - T: (020) 86470984. Chm.: Jean Knight
Science&Tech Museum
An early 18th-c water tower with a small suite of rooms incl bathroom, pump chamber, orangery and saloon, also a few related prints 38498

Castle Cary

Castle Cary and District Museum, Market House, High St, Castle Cary BA7 7AL - T: (01663) 350680, Internet: www.southsomerset.gov.uk
Local Museum 38499

Castle Combe

Castle Combe Museum, Combe Cottage, Castle Combe SN14 7HU - T: (01249) 782250, Fax: 782250, E-mail: abishop@northwilts.gov.uk. Cur.: Adrian Bishop
Local Museum
Artefacts and historical displays 38500

Castle Donington

Donington Grand Prix Collection, Donington Park, Castle Donington DE74 2RP - T: (01332) 811027, Fax: 812829, E-mail: enquiries@doningtoncollection.co.uk, Internet: www.doningtoncollection.com. Dir.: F.B. Wheatcroft
Special Museum - 1973
Coll of Grand Prix Racing cars, McLarren, BRM, Lotus, Ferrari, Vanwalls, Williams, amazing coll of helmets, Formula 1 racing 38501

Castle Douglas

Castle Douglas Art Gallery, King St, Castle Douglas DG7 1AE - T: (01556) 30291, Fax: 331643, E-mail: davidd@dumgal.gov.uk, Internet: www.dumfriesmuseum.demon.co.uk. Dir.: David Devereux
Public Gallery
Paintings by Ethel S.G. Bristowe, local artists 38502

Castleford

Castleford Museum Room, Library, Carlton St, Castleford WF10 2BB - T: (01924) 305351, Fax: 305353. Dir.: Colinn MacDonald
Historical Museum - 1935
Archaelogy in Castlefort 38503

Castlerock

Downhill Castle, Mussenden Rd, Castlerock, Co. Antrim - T: (012658) 848728
Historical Museum 38504

Castleton

Castleton Village Museum, Methodist Schoolroom, Buxton Rd, Castleton S33 8WX - T: (01433) 620950. Cur.: Christine Thorpe
Local Museum
Local crafts, lead mining, rope-making, agriculture, Garland Ceremony and Blue John Caverns 38505

Castletown

Castle Rushen, Manx National Heritage, The Quay, Castletown IM9 1AB - T: (01624) 648000, Fax: 648001, E-mail: enquiries@mnh.gov.im, Internet: www.gov.im/mnh. Man.: Iain A. McKinlay
Historical Museum
Story of the Kings and Lords of Man, castle keep, draw bridge and dungeons 38506

Dunnet Pavilion, Dunnet Bay Caravan Site, Castletown KW14 8XD - T: (01847) 821531, Fax: 821531, E-mail: mary.legg@highland.gov.uk
Natural History Museum 38507

Nautical Museum, Manx National Heritage, Castletown IM9 1AB - T: (01624) 648000, Fax: 648001, E-mail: enquiries@mnh.gov.im, Internet: www.gov.im/mnh. Man.: Iain McKinley
Historical Museum
Maritime life and trade in the days of sail, armed yacht "Peggy" (1791), sailmakers loft, ship model, photos 38508

Old Grammar School, Manx National Heritage, Quay Ln, Castletown IM9 1LE - T: (01624) 648000, Fax: 648001, E-mail: enquiries@mnh.gov.im, Internet: www.gov.im/mnh. Man.: Iain McKinley
Historical Museum
Hist of Manx education, Victorian school life 38509

Old House of Keys, Manx National Heritage, Parliament Sq, Castletown IM9 1LA - T: (01624) 648000, Fax: 648001, E-mail: enquiries@mnh.gov.im, Internet: www.gov.im/mnh
Historical Museum
Assambly and debating chamber for Manx parliament, Manx politics 38510

Câtel

Folk Museum, Saumarez Park, Câtel GY5 7UJ - T: (01481) 255384, Fax: 255384, E-mail: folkmuseumntgsy@cwgsy.net, Internet: www.nationaltrust-gsy.org.gg. Dir.: Tamara Scharf
Folklore Museum - 1968
Agriculture tools of the island, horse drawn machinery, farmhouse interior, domestic ang Guernsey fishermans' life (19th-20th c), trades, tools 38511

Caterham

East Surrey Museum, 1 Stafford Rd, Caterham CR3 6JG - T: (01883) 340275, E-mail: es@emuseums.freeserve.co.uk, Internet: www.tandridgedc.gov. Cur.: Anthea Hopkins
Local Museum
Local History 38512

Cavendish

Sue Ryder Museum, Cavendish CO10 8AY - T: (01787) 282591, Fax: 282991
Local Museum - 1979
Life and work of Lady Ryder of Warsaw 38513

Cawdor

Cawdor Castle, Cawdor IV12 5RD - T: (01667) 404401, Fax: 404674, E-mail: info@cawdorcastle.com, Internet: www.cawdorcastle.com
Decorative Arts Museum 38514

Cawthorne

Regimental Museum of the 13th/18th Royal Hussars and Kent Dragoons, Cannon Hall Museum, Cawthorne S75 4AT - T: (01226) 790270, Fax: 792117, E-mail: cannonhall@barnsley.gov.uk. Dir.: Dr. J. Whittaker
Military Museum
library 38515

Victoria Jubilee Museum, Taylor Hill, Cawthorne S75 4HQ - T: (01226) 790545. Pres.: G.B. Jackson
Local Museum - 1884
Local history, example of Cruck formation timbered building, Victoriana, domestic bygones 38516

Cenarth

National Coracle Centre, Cenarth Falls, Cenarth SA38 9JL - T: (01239) 710980, E-mail: martinfowler@btconnect.com, Internet: www.coraclecentre.co.uk. Cur.: Martin Fowler
Science&Tech Museum
Boat coll of coracles from Wales and other parts of the world 38517

Ceres

Fife Folk Museum, Weigh House, High St, Ceres KY15 5NF - T: (01334) 828180, E-mail: fifefolkmuseum@btopenworld.com. Dir.: Dr. Paula Martin
Folklore Museum / Historical Museum - 1968
Tools, scales, agricultural equipment, domestic items 38518

Chalfont Saint Giles

Chiltern Open Air Museum, Newland Park, Gorelands Ln, Chalfont Saint Giles HP8 4AD - T: (01494) 871117, 872163, Fax: 872774, E-mail: coamuseum@netscape.net, Internet: www.

coam.org.uk. Dir.: Joanna Ruddock
Open Air Museum - 1976
Historic buildings, iron age house, Victorian farm 38519

Milton's Cottage, Deanway, Chalfont Saint Giles HP8 4JH - T: (01494) 872313, Fax: 873936, E-mail: info@miltonscottage.org, Internet: www.miltonscottage.org. Dir.: E.A. Dawson
Special Museum - 1887
Life and times of writer John Milton (1608-1674), editions of Milton's work, portraits and engravings of Milton, memorabilia 38520

Chapel Brampton

Northampton and Lamport Railway, Pitsford and Brampton Station, Pitsford Rd, Chapel Brampton NN6 8BA - T: (01604) 820327, E-mail: info@nlr.org.uk, Internet: www.nlr.org.uk
Science&Tech Museum
Steam trains 38521

Chard

Chard and District Museum, Godworthy House, 15 High St, Chard TA20 1QL - T: (01460) 65091, Internet: www.southsomerset.gov.uk. Dir.: P. Wood
Local Museum - 1970
John Stringfellow Pioneer of powered flight, James Gillingham maker of artificial limbs 38522

Forde Abbey, Chard TA20 4LU - T: (01460) 220231, Fax: 220296, E-mail: forde.abbay@virgin.net, Internet: www.fordeabbay.co.uk. Dir.: Mark Roper
Religious Arts Museum 38523

Hornsbury Mill, Hornsbury Hill, Chard TA20 3AQ - T: (01460) 63317, Fax: 63317, E-mail: hornsburymill@btclick.com, Internet: www.hornsburymill.co.uk. Dir.: S.J. Lewin
Science&Tech Museum - 1970
Milling machinery and equipment, agricultural implements, craftsmen's tools, domestic equipment and clothing 38524

Charlbury

Charlbury Museum, Corner House Community Centre, Market St, Charlbury OX7 3PN - T: (01608) 810060. Cur.: R. Prew
Local Museum
Traditional crafts and industry 38525

Charney Basset

Charney Bassett Mill, 7 Clement Close, Charney Basset OX12 7ED - T: (01235) 868677, 223354, E-mail: bruce.hedge@virgin.net
Science&Tech Museum
19th c watermill 38526

Chartwell

Chartwell House, Mapleton Rd, Chartwell TN16 1PS - T: (01732) 866368, Fax: 868193, E-mail: kchxxx@smtp.ntrust.org.uk, Internet: www.bigginhill.co.uk/chartwell.htm. Man.: Carole Kenwright
Historical Museum
Sir Winston Churchill's family house 38527

Chatham

Fort Amherst Heritage Museum, Dock Rd, Chatham ME4 4UB - T: (01634) 847747, Fax: 847747
Historical Museum
Napoleonic fortress, WWII, military artefacts 38528

Historic Dockyard Chatham, Dock Rd, Chatham ME4 4TZ - T: (01634) 823800/07, Fax: 823801, E-mail: info@chdt.org.uk, Internet: www.chdt.org.uk
Historical Museum
Georgian dockyard, warships incl HMS Cavalier, submarine Ocelot, HMS Gannet, ropery, lifeboats coll 38529

Kent Police Museum, Dock Rd, Chatham ME4 4TZ - T: (01634) 403260, Fax: 403260, E-mail: kentpolmus@aol.com, Internet: www.kent-police-museum.co.uk. Cur.: John Endicott
Historical Museum 38530

Medway Heritage Centre, Dock Rd, Chatham ME4 4SH - T: (01634) 408437. Cur.: R. Ingle
Local Museum
Artefacts and photographs to River Medway 38531

Royal Engineers Museum, Brompton Barracks, Chatham ME4 4UG - T: (01634) 822839, Fax: 822006, E-mail: mail@re-museum.co.uk, Internet: www.royalengineers.org.uk. Dir.: Richard Dunn, Cur.: Rebecca Cheney
Science&Tech Museum / Military Museum - 1873
Hist of engineers' work, military engineering science, memorabilia on General 'Chinese' Gordon and Field Marshal Lord Kitchener of Khartoum 38532

Chawton

Jane Austen's House, Winchester Rd, Chawton GU34 1SD - T: (01420) 83262, Fax: 83262, Internet: www.janeaustenmuseum.org.uk. Head: T.F. Carpenter, Asst.: Ann Channon
Special Museum - 1949
Memorabilia of writer Jane Austen (1775-1817) 38533

Cheam

Whitehall, 1 Malden Rd, Cheam SM3 8QD - T: (020) 86431236, Fax: 87704777, E-mail: curators@whitehallcheam.fsnet.co.uk, Internet: www.sutton.gov.uk. Cur.: Laurel Joseph, Helen Henkens-Lewis
Historical Museum - 1978
Arts, crafts and local history centre, displays of material from the excavations at Nonsuch Palace, Cheam Pottery and Cheam School, works by or featuring William Gilpin (caricatured by Rowlandson as Dr. Syntax) inside a timber-framed house build c 15th 38534

Cheddar

Cheddar Man and the Cannibals, Cheddar Caves and Gorge, Cheddar BS27 3QF - T: (01934) 742343, Fax: 744637, E-mail: caves@cheddarcaves.co.uk, Internet: www.cheddarcaves.co.uk
Archaeological Museum / Natural History Museum - 1934
Archaeology and zoology of Cheddar Gorge area, paleolithic pleistocene finds, artefacts from local caves 38535

Cheddleton

Cheddleton Flint Mill, Leek Rd, Cheddleton ST13 7HL - T: (01782) 502907. Head: Ted Royle
Science&Tech Museum - 1967
Prime movers for the grinding of raw materials for the pottery industry, steam engines, transportation, grinding equipment 38536

Chelmsford

Chelmsford Museum, Oaklands Park, Moulsham St, Chelmsford CM2 9AQ - T: (01245) 615100, Fax: 268545, E-mail: oaklands@chelmsfordbc.gov.uk, Internet: www.chelmsfordmuseums.co.uk. Man.: N.P. Wickenden, Sc. Staff: A. Lutyens-Humfrey (Art), T. Walentowicz (Natural Sciences), G. Bowles (Science and Industry), M.D. Bedenham (Social History), I.D. Hook (Essex Regiment Museum), C. Hammer (Education)
Local Museum / Military Museum - 1835
Natural hist, geology, archaeology, local hist, coins,decorative arts, paintings, glass, costume, military hist, developing science and technology museum 38537

Engine House Project, Chelmsford Museums, Sandford Mill, Chelmsford CM2 6NY - T: (01245) 475498, Fax: 475498, E-mail: engine.house@chelmsfordbc.gov.uk. Dir.: G. Bowles (Science and Industry)
Science&Tech Museum
Industrial coll 38538

Essex Police Museum, Headquarters Springfield, Chelmsford CM2 6DA - T: (01245) 491491 ext 50771, Fax: 452456, Internet: www.essex.police.uk. Cur.: Elizabeth Farnhill
Special Museum
Police history since 1836 38539

Essex Regiment Museum, Oaklands Park, Moulsham St, Chelmsford CM2 9AQ - T: (01245) 615100, Fax: 262428, E-mail: pompadour@chelmsfordbc.gov.uk, Internet: www.chelmsfordbc.gov.uk/museums/index.shtml. Head: I.D. Hook
Military Museum
Regimental hist 38540

Cheltenham

Axiom Centre for Arts, 57-59 Winchcombe St, Cheltenham GL52 2NE - T: (01242) 253183, Fax: 253183
Public Gallery 38541

Bugatti Trust, Prescott Hill, Gotherington, Cheltenham GL52 9RD - T: (01242) 677201, Fax: 674191, E-mail: trust@bugatti.co.uk, Internet: www.bugatti.co.uk/trust. Cur.: Richard Day
Science&Tech Museum
Bugatti artefacts, technical drawings - photographic archive 38542

Chedworth Roman Villa Museum, Yanworthn Villa, Cheltenham GL54 3LJ - T: (01242) 890256
Archaeological Museum - 1865
Ruins of Roman villa, finds 38543

Cheltenham Art Gallery and Museum, Clarence St, Cheltenham GL50 3JT - T: (01242) 237431, Fax: 262334, E-mail: artgallery@cheltenham.gov.uk, Internet: www.cheltenham.artgallery.museum. Sc. Staff: Steven Blake (Collections), Helen Brown, Mary Greensted (Visitor Service), Paul McKee (Arts), Sophia Wilson (Exhibitions), Julien Parsons (Documentation), Susan Welsh (Environment and Conservation), Virginia Adsett, Faye Little (Education and Outreach)
Fine Arts Museum / Decorative Arts Museum - 1907
Dutch, Flemish and English paintings, watercolours, local prints, English pottery and porcelain, geology, Cotswold area history, Chinese porcelain, memorabilia on Edward Wilson, internationally important coll of the Arts and Crafts Movement, furniture, metalwork, textiles 38544

Holst Birthplace Museum, 4 Clarence Rd, Pittville, Cheltenham GL52 2AY - T: (01242) 524846, Fax: 580182, E-mail: holstmuseum@btconnect.com, Internet: www.holstmuseum.org.uk. Cur.: Dr. Joanna Archibald
Music Museum
Musical instruments, Victorian history 38545

Chepstow

Chepstow Museum, Gwy House, Bridge St, Chepstow NP16 5EZ - T: (01291) 625981, Fax: 635005, E-mail: chepstowmuseum@monmouthshire.gov.uk. Dir.: Anne Rainsbury
Local Museum - 1949
Local and social history - education resource centre, paper and object conservation (social history, archaeology & ethnography) 38546

Tintern Abbey, Tintern Abbey Information Centre, Chepstow NP6 6SE - T: (01291) 689251
Religious Arts Museum
Ruins 38547

Chertsey

Chertsey Museum, The Cedars, 33 Windsor St, Chertsey KT16 8AT - T: (01932) 565764, Fax: 571118, E-mail: enquiries@chertseymuseum.org.uk, Internet: www.chertseymuseum.org.uk. Cur.: Stephen Nicholls
Local Museum / Decorative Arts Museum - 1965
Olive Matthews coll of English dress and accessories, local history, archaeology, ancient Greek pottery, horology 38548

Chesham

Chesham Town Museum, Library, Elgiva Ln, Chesham HP5 2JB - T: (01494) 783183. Dir.: Adrian Kerwood
Local Museum
Historical items 38549

Chester

Cheshire Military Museum, The Castle, Chester CH1 2DN - T: (01244) 327617, Fax: 401700, E-mail: r.corners@chester.ac.uk, Internet: www.chester.ac.uk/militarymuseum. Cur.: N.A. Hine
Military Museum - 1924
Memorabilia on the 22nd Cheshire Regiment, Cheshire Yeomanry, Battle of Meeanee 1843, memorabilia of Sir Charles Napier, Eaton Hall Officer Cadet School - archives 38550

Dewa Roman Experience, Pierpoint Ln, Off Bridge St, Chester CH1 1NL - T: (01244) 343407, Fax: 347737. Man.: Lesley Wilson
Archaeological Museum
Streets of Roman Chester 38551

Grosvenor Museum, 27 Grosvenor St, Chester CH1 2DD - T: (01244) 402008, Fax: 347587, E-mail: s.woolfall@chestercc.gov.uk, Internet: www.chestercc.gov.uk/heritage/museum. Dir.: Steve Woolfall, Keeper: Peter Boughton (Art, Architecture), Sophie Fowler (Local and Social History), Dan Robinson (Archaeology)
Local Museum
Roman archaeology. local history, natural history, art, clocks, coins, silver, costume 38552

Chester-le-Street

Anker's House Museum, Church Chare, Chester-le-Street DH3 3QB - T: (0191) 3883295, Internet: www.ris.niaa.org.uk/museums/anker.htm. Dir.: Mike Rutter
Archaeological Museum
Roman and Anglo-Saxon artefacts 38553

Chesterfield

Chesterfield Museum and Art Gallery, Saint Mary's Gate, Chesterfield S41 7TD - T: (01246) 345727, Fax: 345720, E-mail: museum@chesterfieldbc.gov.uk, Internet: www.chesterfieldbc.co.uk. Dir.: A.M. Knowles
Historical Museum - 1994
Locally produced salt glazed pottery (19th-20th c) 38554

Hardwick Hall, Doe Lea, Chesterfield S44 5QJ - T: (01246) 850430, Fax: 854200, E-mail: hardwickhall@nationaltrust.org.uk, Internet: www.nationaltrust.org.uk. Man.: Denise Edwards
Decorative Arts Museum - 1597
Furniture, tapestry, needlework, and portraits of the Cavendish family, late 16th c house, greatest of all Elizabethan houses and garden, corn mill and parkland 38555

Peacock Heritage Centre, Low Pavement, Chesterfield S40 1PB - T: (01246) 345777/78, Fax: 345770, E-mail: publicity@chesterfieldbc.gov.uk
Local Museum 38556

Revolution House, Hight St, Old Whittington, Chesterfield - T: (01246) 345727, Fax: 345720. Dir.: A.M. Knowles
Historical Museum - 1938
Restored 17th c building with 17th c furnishings, hist of the Revolution of 1688 38557

Chichester

Cathedral Treasury, Royal Chantry, Cathedral Cloisters, Chichester PO19 1PX - T: (01243) 782595, Fax: 812499, E-mail: visitors@chichestercathedral.org.uk, Internet: www.chichestercathedral.org.uk. Head: M.J. Moriarty
Religious Arts Museum
Historical ecclesiastical plate from diocese and cathedral 38558

Chichester District Museum, 29 Little London, Chichester PO19 1PB - T: (01243) 784683, Fax: 776766, E-mail: districtmuseum@chichester.gov.uk, Internet: www.chichester.gov.uk/museum. Dir.: Dr. I. Friel, Sc. Staff: Rosemary Gilmour, Simon Kitchin, Jane Seddon
Historical Museum - 1964
Local archaeology and social hist 38559

Fishbourne Roman Palace and Museum, The Sussex Archaeological Society, Salthill Rd, Fishbourne, Chichester PO19 3QR - T: (01243) 785859, Fax: 539266, E-mail: adminfish@sussexpast.co.uk, Internet: www.sussexpast.co.uk. Dir.: David J. Rudkin
Archaeological Museum - 1968
Roman ruins and finds, Britains largest coll of 'in-situ' Roman mosaic floors and other architectural and artefactural remains, formal Roman garden planted to its original plan 38560

Goodwood House, Goodwood, Chichester PO18 0PX - T: (01243) 755000, Fax: 755005, E-mail: housevisiting@goodwood.co.uk, Internet: www.goodwood.co.uk. Dir.: Earl of March and Kinrara
Fine Arts Museum / Decorative Arts Museum - 1616
Family portraits, Sèvres porcelain, French furniture, Gobelin tapestries, paintings by Van Dyck, Canaletto 38561

Guildhall Museum, Priory Park, Chichester PO19 1PB, mail addr: 29 Little London, Chichester PO19 1PB - T: (01243) 784683, Fax: 776766, E-mail: districtmuseum@chichester.gov.uk, Internet: www.chichester.gov.uk/museum. Dir.: Dr. I. Friel, Sc. Staff: Simon Kitchin, Rosemary Gilmour, Asst. Cur.: Jane Seddon
Historical Museum - 1930
Hist of the site/building, large stones from Roman Chichester 38562

Mechanical Music and Doll Collection, Church Rd, Portfield, Chichester PO19 4HN - T: (01243) 372646, Fax: 370299. Dir.: Lester Jones, Clive Jones
Music Museum / Special Museum - 1983
Disc musical boxes, mechanical musical instruments 38563

Pallant House Gallery, 9 North Pallant, Chichester PO19 1TJ - T: (01243) 774557, Fax: 536038, E-mail: info@pallant.org.uk, Internet: www.pallant.org.uk. Dir.: Stefan Van Raay, Cur.: Frances Guy
Fine Arts Museum - 1982
20th c British art 38564

Royal Military Police Museum, Roussillon Barracks, Broyle Rd, Chichester PO19 4BN - T: (01243) 534225, Fax: 534288, E-mail: museum@rhqrmp.freeserve.co.uk, Internet: www.rhqrmp.freeserve.co.uk. Dir.: P.H.M. Squier
Military Museum - 1946
Military police, uniforms, medals, history, books, pictures, arms - archives 38565

Chicksands

Museum of Military Intelligence, Intelligence Corps Museum and Medmenham Collection, Defence Intelligence and Security Centre, Chicksands SG17 5PR - T: (01462) 752297, 752340, Fax: 752297, E-mail: dinticacorpssec-e1@disc.mod.uk. Cur.: J.D. Woolmore
Military Museum
Hist of Intelligence Corps, hist of air photography, Y service 1940-45 38566

Chiddingstone

Chiddingstone Castle, Chiddingstone TN8 7AD - T: (01892) 870347. Sc. Staff: Ruth Eldridge
Historical Museum / Fine Arts Museum - 1956
Stuart royal letters and memorabilia, Jacobite coll, portraits, manuscripts, medals, Japanese boxes, swords, lacquer, armaments and metal objects, Buddhistic art, Egyptian objects 4000 BC-Roman times 38567

Chippenham

Chippenham Museum and Heritage Centre, 10 Market Pl, Chippenham SN15 3HF - T: (01249) 705020, Fax: 705025, E-mail: heritage@chippenham.gov.uk. Cur.: Mike Stone
Local Museum - 2000 38568

Yelde Hall Museum → Chippenham Museum and Heritage Centre

Chipping Campden

Woolstaplers Hall Museum (closed) 38569

Chipping Norton

Chipping Norton Museum of Local History, Westgate Centre, High St, Chipping Norton OX7 5AD - T: (01608) 643779, E-mail: museum@cn2001.fsnet.co.uk. Cur.: D. Morris
Local Museum
Agricultural tools and horse harnesses, local industries, tweed, brewing and agricultural engineering, baseball 38570

Chirk

Castell y Waun (Chirk Castle), Chirk LL14 5AF - T: (01691) 777701, Fax: 774706, E-mail: pcwmsn@smtp.ntrust.org.uk. Dir.: M.V Wynne
Decorative Arts Museum / Fine Arts Museum
Paintings, decorative art, history, 16th, 17th, 18th and early 19th c decorations 38571

Chittlehampton

Cobbaton Combat Collection, Chittlehampton EX37 9RZ - T: (01769) 540740, 540414, Fax: 540141, E-mail: info@cobbatoncombat.co.uk, Internet: www.cobbatoncombat.co.uk. Dir.: Preston Isaac
Military Museum - 1980
60 Second World War British and Canadian tanks, trucks, guns and armoured cars, which have been restored to running order 38572

Chollerford

Clayton Collection Museum, Chesters Roman Fort, Chollerford NE46 4EP - T: (01434) 681379, Internet: www.english-heritage.org.uk. Dir.: Georgina Plowright
Archaeological Museum - 1903
Roman coll from sites along central sector of hadrian's wall 38573

Chorley

Astley Hall Museum and Art Gallery, Astley Park, Chorley PR7 1NP - T: (01257) 515555, Fax: 515556, E-mail: astleyhall@lineone.net, Internet: www.astleyhall.co.uk. Dir.: Nigel Wright
Fine Arts Museum / Decorative Arts Museum - 1924
Jacobean furniture, paintings and etchings, Flemish tapestries, Leeds pottery, 18th c English glass, magnificent plaster ceilings 38574

Christchurch

Bournemouth Transport Museum, Aviation Park West, Bournemouth International Airport, Christchurch BH23 6NW
Science&Tech Museum
Coll of busses 38575

Christchurch Tricycle Museum, Quay Rd, Christchurch BH23 1BY - T: (01202) 479849
Science&Tech Museum 38576

Museum of Electricity, Old Power Station, Bargates, Christchurch BH23 1QE - T: (01202) 480467, Fax: 480468. Cur.: Eric Jones
Science&Tech Museum
Working models of orginal experiments by Faraday, Richie and Barlow 38577

Red House Museum and Art Gallery, Quay Rd, Christchurch BH23 1BU - T: (01202) 482860, Fax: 481924, E-mail: musmjh@hants.gov.uk, Internet: www.hants.gov.uk/museums. Cur.: Jim Hunter
Local Museum - 1951
Paleolithic to medieval local archaeology, local hist, geology and natural hist, costumes, toys, dolls, domestic equipment, agricultural equipment, fashion plates, Victoriana, paintings, drawings, prints and photographs of local interest - library, herb garden 38578

Saint Michael's Loft Museum, Priory, Quay Rd, Christchurch BH23 1BU - T: (01202) 485804, E-mail: uk.edlunds@ntlworld.com, Internet: www.christchurchpriory.org.uk. Cur.: D. Edlund
Religious Arts Museum
Stonework and carving from Saxon to Tudor times, church memorabilia, map and models, tomb of Knight Tempian Stephen de Strapplebrugge, watercolours 38579

Chudleigh

Ugbrooke House, Chudleigh TQ13 0AD - T: (01626) 852179, Fax: 853322. Dir.: L.A. Martin
Military Museum / Decorative Arts Museum
Private military coll, portraits 38580

Church Stretton

Acton Scott Historic Working Farm, Wenlock Lodge, Acton Scott, Church Stretton SY6 6QN - T: (01694) 781306, Fax: 781569, E-mail: acton.scott.museum@shropshire-cc.gov.uk, Internet: www.shropshire-cc.gov.uk/museum.nsf. Dir.: Mike Barr, Cur.: Nigel Nixon
Open Air Museum / Agriculture Museum - 1975
Stock, crops and machinery (1870-1920), agriculture, rural crafts (wheelwright, farrier, blacksmith), dairy, period cottage - library, technical workshops, education 38581

Cirencester

Bingham Library Trust Art Collection, 3 Dyer St, Cirencester GL7 2PP - T: (01285) 655646, Fax: 643843, E-mail: clerk@cirencester.gov.uk, Internet: binghamlibrarytrust.org.uk/artcollection. Cur.: David Viner
Fine Arts Museum
Oil paintings, watercolours, prints and drawings 38582

Cirencester Lock-Up, Trinity Rd, Cirencester GL7 1BR - T: (01285) 655611, Fax: 643286, E-mail: john.paddock@costwold.gov.uk, Internet: www.cotswold.gov.uk
Local Museum 38583

Corinium Museum, Park St, Cirencester GL7 2BX - T: (01285) 655611, Fax: 643286, E-mail: john.paddock@cotswold.gov.uk, Internet: www.cotswold.gov.uk. Dir.: Dr. J.M Paddock
Archaeological Museum / Local Museum - 1856
Romano-British antiquities from the site of Corinium Dobunnorum, archaeology, local history, military 38584

Clare

Clare Ancient House Museum, High St, Clare CO10 8NY - T: (01787) 277662, Fax: 277662, E-mail: clareah@btinternet.com, Internet: www.clare-ancient-house-museum.co.uk. Dir.: David J. Ridley
Local Museum
Clare people and industries, exhibits from prehistoric to Victorian times 38585

Clatteringshaws

Clatteringshaws Forest Wildlife Centre, c/o Galloway Deer Museum, New Galloway, Castle Douglas, Clatteringshaws DG7 3SQ - T: (01671) 402420, Fax: 403708. Man.: Ann Smith
Natural History Museum
Red deer, roe deer, wild goats, local wildlife, geology of the district 38586

Claydon

Bygones Museum, Butlin Farm, Claydon OX17 1EP - T: (01295) 690258, E-mail: bygonesmuseum@yahoo.com, Internet: www.bygonesmuseum.moonfruit.com. Dir.: Catherine Fox
Agriculture Museum
Domestic equipment, agricultural implements, tools once used by rural craftsmen 38587

Cleethorpes

Humber Estuary Discovery Centre, The Lakeside, Kings Rd, Cleethorpes DN35 0AG - T: (01472) 323232, Fax: 323233, E-mail: discovery.centre@nelincs.gov.uk, Internet: www.time-discoverycentre.co.uk. Man.: Lisa Edinborough
Historical Museum 38588

Clevedon

Clevedon Court, Tickenham Rd, Clevedon BS21 6QU - T: (01275) 872257
Decorative Arts Museum
Eltonware ceramics, Nailsea glass, prints of bridges 38589

Clitheroe

Castle Museum, Castle, Clitheroe BB7 1BA - T: (01200) 424635, Fax: 424568, E-mail: museum@ribblevalley.gov.uk, Internet: www.ribblevalley.gov.uk. Cust.: D. Mary Hornby
Local Museum
20 000 Geology specimens: International coll of rocks, minerals and fossils, local hist - earth science educational project 38590

North West Sound Archive, Old Steward's Office, Castle Crounds, Clitheroe BB7 1AZ - T: (01200) 427897, Fax: 427897, E-mail: nwsa@ed.lancscc.gov.uk, Internet: www.lancashire.gov.uk/education/lifelong/recordindex.shtm
Music Museum
100,000 recordings on all aspects of north west life, specialist coll incl folk music, radio astronomy, the survey of English dialects 38591

Clun

Clun Local History Museum, Town Hall, The Square, Clun SY7 8JA - T: (01588) 640681, Fax: 640681, E-mail: ktomey@fish.co.uk. Dir.: J.K. Tomey
Archaeological Museum / Local Museum - 1934
Over 1000 flint artefacts Palaeolithic to Bronze Age 38592

Clydebank

Clydebank Museum, Old Town Hall, Dumbarton Rd, Clydebank G81 1UE - T: (01389) 738702, Fax: 738689, E-mail: curator@clydebankmuseum.sol.co.uk, Internet: www.west-dumbarton.gov.uk. Cur.: Mary Land
Local Museum
Local industry and social history, with special coll of ship models and sewing machines, shipbuilders history 38593

Coalbrookdale

Darby Houses, Rosehill and Dale House, Darby Rd, Coalbrookdale TF8 7EL - T: (01952) 432551, Fax: 432551, E-mail: info@ironbridge.org.uk, Internet: www.ironbridge.org.uk. Cur.: John Challen
Historical Museum
Quaker ironmasters, Abraham Darby III, builder of the Iron Bridge 38594

Long Warehouse, Coalbrookdale TF8 7EL - T: (01952) 432141, Fax: 432751, E-mail: coalbrookdale@ironbridge.org.uk, Internet: www.ironbridge.org.uk. Cur.: John Challen
Fine Arts Museum / Historical Museum
Elton coll of industrial art - library, archive 38595

Museum of Iron and Darby Furnace, Coalbrookdale TF8 7NR - T: (01952) 433418, Fax: 432237, E-mail: coalbrookdale@ironbridge.org.uk, Internet: www.ironbridge.org.uk. Cur.: John Challen
Science&Tech Museum 38596

Coalport

Coalport China Museum, High St, Coalport TF8 7AW - T: (01952) 580650, Fax: 432204, E-mail: info@ironbridge.org.uk, Internet: www.ironbridge.org.uk. Cur.: Ruth Denison
Decorative Arts Museum
History of China manufacturesince 1776, coll of Coalport and Caughley china 38597

Tar Tunnel, High St, Coalport TF8 7HS - T: (01952) 580627, Fax: 432204, E-mail: info@ironbridge.org.uk, Internet: www.ironbridge.org.uk. Dir.: Glen Lawes
Science&Tech Museum
18th c mining tunnel, natural bitumen 38598

Coalville

Snibston Discovery Park, Ashby Rd, Coalville LE67 3LN - T: (01530) 278444, Fax: 813301, E-mail: snibston@leics.gov.uk, Internet: www.leics.gov.uk/museum. Cur.: Steph N. Mastoris
Science&Tech Museum
Transport, engineering, fashion, science, colliery, toys 38599

Coatbridge

Summerlee Heritage Park, Heritage Way, Coatbridge ML5 1QD - T: (01236) 431261, Fax: 440429, Internet: www.summerlee.co.uk. Man.: Carol Haddow
Local Museum / Historic Site - 1988
Social and industrial hist of Scotland's iron and steel and heavy engineering industries, coll of machinery and equipment, a steam winding engine, railway locomotives, two steam cranes, underground coalmine, recreated miner's cottages, Scotland's only electric tramway, art gallery 38600

Coate

Agricultural Museum (closed) 38601

Cobham

Cobham Bus Museum, Redhill Rd, Cobham KT11 1EF - T: (01932) 868665, Fax: (01743) 358411, Internet: www.geocities.com/MotorCity/Downs/9026
Science&Tech Museum
London buses from 1925 to 1973 38602

Cockermouth

Cumberland Toy and Model Museum, Bank's Court, Market Pl, Cockermouth CA13 9NG - T: (01900) 827606, E-mail: rodmoore42@hotmail.com, Internet: www.toyandmodelmuseum.grb.cc. Dir.: Rod Moore
Special Museum - 1989
British toys from 1900 to present 38603

Printing House Museum, 102 Main St, Cockermouth CA13 9LX - T: (01900) 824984, Fax: 823124, E-mail: printinghouse@uk2.net, Internet: www.printinghouse.co.uk. Dir.: David R. Winkworth
Science&Tech Museum - 1979
Hist of printing 15th c to 1970 (letterpress era), iron presses, platen presses, automatic presses, type founding machinery, stone and etching press 38604

Wordsworth House, Main St, Cockermouth CA13 9RX - T: (01900) 824805, Fax: 824805, E-mail: wordsworthhouse@nationaltrust.org.uk, Internet: www.wordsworthhouse@org.uk
Special Museum - 1937
Fine Georgian townhouse, birthplace and childhood home of William Wordsworth 38605

Cockley Cley

Iceni Village and Museums, Estate Office, Cockley Cley PE37 8AG - T: (01760) 721339, 24588, Fax: 721339. Dir.: Sir Samuel Roberts
Local Museum / Agriculture Museum - 1971
Carriage and farm implements, engines 38606

Coggeshall

Coggeshall Heritage Centre and Museum, Saint Peter's Hall, Stoneham St, Coggeshall CO6 1QG - T: (01376) 563003, E-mail: spratcliffe@btinternet.com, Internet: www.btinternet.com/~coggeshall/. Cur.: Shirley Ratcliffe
Local Museum
Local hist 38607

Colchester

Castle Museum, c/o Museum Resource Centre, 14 Ryegate Rd, Colchester CO1 1YG - T: (01206) 282931/2, 282939, Fax: 282925, Internet: www.colchestermuseum.org.uk. Dir.: Peter Berridge, Sc. Staff: J. Bowdery (Natural History), Tom Hodgson (Social History), Philip Wise (Archaeology)
Archaeological Museum - 1860
Material from Iron Age and Roman Colchester, Roman military tombstones, Roman pottery, bronze figure of Mercury, civil war - library 38608

East Anglian Railway Museum, Chappel and Wakes Colne Station, Colchester CO6 2DS - T: (01206) 242524, Fax: 242524, E-mail: info@earm.co.uk, Internet: www.earm.co.uk
Science&Tech Museum 38609

Firstsite at the Minories Art Gallery, 74 High St, Colchester CO1 1UE - T: (01206) 577067, Fax: 577161, E-mail: info@firstsite.uk.net, Internet: www.firstsite.uk.net. Dir.: Katherine Wood
Public Gallery - 1956/ 1992
Contemporary visual arts 38610

Hollytrees Museum, High St, Colchester CO1 1UG - T: (01206) 282931/2, 282940, Fax: 282925. Dir.: Tom Hodgson
Historical Museum - 1928
Georgian town house built in 1718 housing domestic displays of toys, costumes and decorative arts from the 18th, 19th and early 20th c - library 38611

Mansfield Costume Study Centre, 38 Churchfields, West Mersea, Colchester CO5 8QJ - T: (01206) 382513, E-mail: sarah@shehadeh1.freeserve.co.uk
Special Museum
Private costume coll, archive of books, slides, patterns - conservation workshop 38612

Natural History Museum, All Saints Church, High St, Colchester CO1 1YG - T: (01206) 282931/2, 282941, Fax: 282925. Dir.: Jeremy Bowdrey
Natural History Museum - 1958
Natural history of Essex 38613

Tymperleys Clock Museum, Trinity St, Colchester CO1 1JN - T: (01206) 282931/2, 282943, Fax: 282925
Science&Tech Museum - 1987
216 clocks and 12 watches 38614

University of Essex Exhibition Gallery, Wivenhoe Park, Colchester CO4 3SQ - T: (01206) 872074, 873333, Fax: 873598, E-mail: kennj@essex.ac.uk, Internet: www.essex.ac.uk. Dir.: Jessica Kenny
Fine Arts Museum / University Museum
150 works with regional focus, sited sculpture, contemporary Latin American art 38615

Coldstream

Coldstream Museum, 12 Market Sq, Coldstream TD12 4BD - T: (01890) 882630, Fax: 882631, E-mail: jthompson@scotborders.gov.uk. Dir.: Ian Brown
Local Museum - 1971
Social and domestic hist of the Coldstream area, hist of the Coldstream guards regiment, raised in the town, 1659 38616

Hirsel Homestead Museum, The Hirsel, Coldstream TD12 4LP - T: (01890) 882834, Fax: 882834, E-mail: rogerdodd@btinternet.com. Dir.: Roger Dodd
Historical Museum
Archaeology, farming, forestry, the estate workshops, the laundry, the gardens, the dovecote, and natural history 38617

Coleraine

Hezlett House, 107 Sea Rd, Castlerock, Coleraine, Co. Derry - T: (01265) 848567
Historical Museum / Agriculture Museum
Victorian style, farm implements 38618

Colne

British in India Museum, Newtown St, Colne BB8 0JJ - T: (01282) 870215, 613129, Fax: 870215. Dir.: Henry Nelson
Historical Museum / Military Museum - 1972
Model soldiers, photographs, documents, paintings, postage stamps, letters, military uniforms - library 38619

Combe Martin

Combe Martin Museum, The Parade, Seaside, Combe Martin EX34 0AP - T: (01271) 882441. Chm.: Jean Griffiths
Local Museum
Local industries, silver/lead mining, lime quarrying and burning, maritime, social history, photographs, documents - archives 38620

Compton, Surrey

Watts Gallery, Down Ln, Compton, Surrey GU3 1DQ - T: (01483) 810235. Cur.: Richard Jefferies
Fine Arts Museum - 1903
Paintings and sculptures by artist G.F. Watts 38621

Compton Verney

Compton Verney Collections, Compton Verney CV35 9HZ - T: (01926) 645500, Fax: 642224, E-mail: cvht@comptonverney.org.uk, Internet: www.comptonverney.org.uk. Dir.: Richard Gray
Fine Arts Museum
Old master paintings and British folk art 38622

Congleton

Little Moreton Hall, Congleton CW12 4SD - T: (01260) 272018, Fax: 292802, E-mail: mlmsca@smtp.ntrust.org.uk. Dir.: Dean V. Thomas
Decorative Arts Museum - 1937
Elizabethan house with woodwork, plaster decorations, oak furniture, pewter objects 38623

Coniston

Brantwood, Coniston LA21 8AD - T: (015394) 41396, Fax: 41263, E-mail: enquiries@brantwood.org.uk, Internet: www.brantwood.org.uk. Dir.: Howard Hull
Fine Arts Museum / Decorative Arts Museum
Former Ruskin's home, filled with Ruskin's watercolours and drawings, works by some of his friends, incl T.M. Rooke, Sir Edward Burne-Jones and William Holman Hunt, furniture, his personal possessions, books - library 38624

Ruskin Museum, Coniston Institute, Yewdale Rd, Coniston LA21 8DU - T: (015394) 41164, Fax: 41132, E-mail: vjm@ruskinmuseum.com, Internet: www.ruskinmuseum.com. Dir.: V.A.J. Slowe, Cur.: J. Dawson
Fine Arts Museum / Natural History Museum / Local Museum - 1900
Memorabilia of John Ruskin (1819-1900), incl watercolours, drawings, sketchbooks geology, slate and coppermines, Malcolm & Donald Campbell personalia and Bluebird memorabilia, water speed record 38625

Conwy

Aberconwy House, 2 Castle St, Conwy LL32 8AY - T: (01492) 592246, Fax: 860233. Dir.: Linda Thorpe
Local Museum
Medieval house that dates from the 14th c, now houses the Conwy Exhibition, depicting the life of the borough from Roman times to the present day 38626

Plas Mawr, High St, Conwy LL32 8DE - T: (01492) 593413. Dir.: L.H.S. Mercer
Historic Site
Plas Mawr is an Elizabethan mansion, built 1577-80, in virtually its original condition 38627

Royal Cambrian Academy of Art, Crown Ln, Conwy LL32 8AN - T: (01492) 593413, Fax: 593413, E-mail: rca@rcaconwy.org, Internet: www.rcaconwy.org. Dir.: Gwyneth Jones
Fine Arts Museum - 1881
Paintings, sculpture 38628

Cookham

Stanley Spencer Gallery, King's Hall, High St, Cookham SL6 9SJ - T: (01628) 523484, 471885, Internet: www.stanleyspencer.org.uk. Dir.: Richard Hurley
Fine Arts Museum - 1962
Paintings and drawings by Stanley Spencer, reference works 38629

Cookstown

Wellbrook Beetling Mill, 20 Wellbrook Rd, Corkhill, Cookstown BT80 9RY - T: (028) 86748210, 86751735, E-mail: uspest@smtp.ntrust.org.uk
Science&Tech Museum
Last working mill 38630

Corbridge

Corbridge Roman Site Museum, Roman Site, Corbridge NE45 5NT - T: (01434) 632349, Fax: 633168, E-mail: georgiana.plowright@english-heritage.org.uk, Internet: www.english-heritage.org.uk. Cur.: Georgina Plowright, Sarah Lawrance
Archaeological Museum - 1929
Roman inscriptions and other finds from the Roman town of Corstopitum 38631

Corfe Castle

Corfe Castle Museum, West St, Corfe Castle BH20 5HB - T: (01929) 480181. Cur.: W.J. Carter
Historical Museum
Early agricultural and clay working implements, clay and stone industries 38632

Cornhill-on-Tweed

Heatherslaw Mill, Ford and Etal Estates, Cornhill-on-Tweed TD12 4TJ - T: (01890) 820338, Fax: 820384, E-mail: tourism@ford-and-etal.co.uk. Head: Julia Nolan
Science&Tech Museum
Traditional milling of wheat 38633

Cornwall

Museum of Witchcraft, Boscastle, Cornwall PL35 0HD - T: (01840) 250111, E-mail: museum-witchcraft@aol.com, Internet: www.museumofwitchcraft.com. Dir.: Graham King
Special Museum
Displays on cursing, charms and spells, stone circles and ancient sacred sites, modern witchcraft, the persecution of witches 38634

Corpach

Treasures of the Earth, Rd fo the Isles A830, Corpach PH33 7JL - T: (01397) 772283, Fax: 772133
Natural History Museum
Coll of crystals, gemstones and fossils, simulation of cave, cavern and mining scene 38635

Corsham

Corsham Court, Corsham SN13 0BZ - T: (01249) 701610, Fax: 701610. Dir.: Pat Wallace
Fine Arts Museum / Decorative Arts Museum
Paintings by various old masters incl Filippo Lippi, Rubens, van Dyck, Reynolds, Guido Reni, furniture by Chippendale, Adam, Cobb, Johnson 38636

Hartham Park - Underground Quarry Museum, Park Ln, Corsham SN13 0QR - T: (01380) 828645. Dir.: David Pollard
Science&Tech Museum - 1989
Quarring, working and transport 38637

Cottesmore

Rutland Railway Museum, Ashwell Rd, Cottesmore LE15 7BX - T: (01572) 813203
Science&Tech Museum
Industrial railways, locomotives and wagons associated with local iron ore quarries 38638

Cotton

Mechanical Music Museum and Bygones, Blacksmith Rd, Cotton IP14 4QN - T: (01449) 613876, E-mail: clarkeqff@aol.com, Internet: www.visitbritain.com. Dir.: Phyllis Keeble
Music Museum - 1982
Music boxes, polyphons, organettes, street pianos, barrel organs, pipe organs, fair organs, gigantic cafe organ, the Wurlitzer theatre pipe organ and many unusual items 38639

Cousland

Cousland Smiddy, 21 Hadfast Rd, Cousland EH22 2NZ - T: (0131) 6631058, Fax: 6632730, E-mail: smiddy@cousland99.freeserve.co.uk, Internet: www.propeller.net/cousland
Local Museum
Blacksmithing tools, farm machinery and tools 38640

Coventry

Coventry Toy Museum, Whitefriars Gate, Much Park St, Coventry CV1 2LT - T: (024) 76227560. Dir.: Ron Morgan
Special Museum
Coll of dolls, toys, games dating from 1750 to 1960, a display of amusement machines 38641

Coventry Watch Museum, POB 1714, Coventry CV3 6ZS - T: (024) 76402331, 76502916, E-mail: 100624.1127@compuserve.com, Internet: www.coventry.watches.org.uk
Science&Tech Museum
Coventry made clocks and watches, tools, watch industry, factories, and people at work 38642

Herbert Art Gallery and Museum, Jordan Well, Coventry CV1 5QP - T: (024) 76832381, 76832565, Fax: 76832410, E-mail: artsandheritage@coventry.gov.uk, Internet: www.coventrymuseum.org.uk. Dir.: Roger Vaughan (Arts, Heritage), Sc. Staff: Robin Johnson (Lifelong Learning), David Shaw (Outreach), Rosie Addenbrooke (Exhibitions), Ron Clarke (Visual Arts), Martin Roberts (Social History), Huw Jones (Industry), Paul Thompson (Archaeology), Steve Lane (Natural History), Cons.: Judi Browes (Works on Paper), Gillian Irving (Easel Paintings), Martin Grahn
Fine Arts Museum / Local Museum / Archaeological Museum / Natural History Museum - 1960
Sutherland sketches used in making Coventry Cathedral tapestry, local art, topography, local natural hist, silk ribbons, archaeology, social and industrial hist - Lunt Roman Fort 38643

Mead Gallery, c/o Warwick Arts Centre, University of Warwick, Gibbet Hill Rd, Coventry CV4 7AL - T: (024) 76522589, Fax: 76572664, E-mail: meadgallery@warwick.ac.uk, Internet: www.warwickartscentre.co.uk. Cur.: Sarah Shalgosky
Fine Arts Museum
British post-war paintings, photographs, prints, sculpture 38644

Museum of British Road Transport, Saint Agnes Lane, Hales St, Coventry CV1 1PN - T: (024) 76832425, Fax: 76832465, E-mail: museum@mbrt.co.uk, Internet: www.mbrt.co.uk. Dir.: Barry Littlewood
Science&Tech Museum - 1980
230 bicycles, 75 motorcycles, more than 220 motor vehicles, a wide range of equipment and accessories - archives 38645

Whitefriars (closed) 38646

Coverack

Poldowrian Museum of Prehistory, Poldowrian, Coverack TR12 6SL - T: (01326) 280468, E-mail: vjhadley@talk21.com. Dir.: V.J. Hadley
Archaeological Museum 38647

Cowbridge

Cowbridge and District Museum, Town Hall Cells, Cowbridge CF71 7AD - T: (01446) 775139. Cur.: D. Keith Jones
Local Museum
Local history, archaeology of Cowbridge 38648

Cowes

Cowes Maritime Museum, Beckford Rd, Cowes PO31 7SG - T: (01983) 293341/394, Fax: 293341, E-mail: tony.butler@iow.gov.uk. Cur.: Tony Butler
Science&Tech Museum - 1975
Items and archives from J. Samuel White & Co Ltd. shipbuilders, 5 small boats designed by Uffa Fox, yachting photos by Kirk of Cowes - library 38649

Sir Max Aitken Museum, 83 High St, Cowes PO31 7AJ - T: (01983) 295144, 293800, Fax: 200253
Special Museum
Paintings of maritime subjects, half models and full models of ships, including a number of Sir Max Aitken's own yachts, and souvenirs of former royal yachts 38650

Coxwold

Byland Abbey, Coxwold YO6 4BD - T: (01347) 868614, Internet: www.english-heritage.org.uk. Cur.: Andrew Morrison
Religious Arts Museum 38651

Shandy Hall, Coxwold YO61 4AD - T: (01347) 868465, Fax: 868465, E-mail: mazu73@dial.pipex.com, Internet: www.shandy-hall.org.uk. Chm.: Dr. Nicolas Barker, Cur.: Patrick Wildgust
Special Museum
Place where Laurence Sterne wrote his 2 novels, relevant prints, paintings, books 38652

Cradley Heath

Haden Hall, Halesowen Rd, Cradley Heath B64 5LP - T: (01384) 569444, Fax: 412623
Historical Museum
Paintings, books etc 38653

Haden Hill House, Off Barrs Rd, Cradley Heath B64 7EX - T: (01384) 569444, Fax: 412623, Internet: www.sandwellmbc.broadnet.co.uk
Historical Museum 38654

Craigavon

Craigavon Museum, Pinebank House, 2 Tullygally Rd, Craigavon, Co. Armagh - T: (01762) 341635
Agriculture Museum
Hist farming and a Georgian farmhouse 38655

Crail

Crail Museum, 62-64 Marketgate, Crail KY10 3TL - T: (01333) 450869, Fax: 450869. Cur.: Susan Bradman
Historical Museum - 1979
H.M.S. Jackdaw (world war II fleer air arm station) 38656

Crakehall

Crakehall Water Mill, Little Crakehall, Crakehall DL8 1HU - T: (01677) 423240, Internet: www.crakehall.org.uk
Science&Tech Museum 38657

Cranbrook

Cranbrook Museum, Carriers Rd, Cranbrook TN17 3JX - Internet: www.localmuseum.freeserve.com. Dir.: Brian Brent
Local Museum
Local trades, social, domestic and community exhibits, Boyd Alexander Bird Coll - archives 38658

Crawley

Crawley Museum Centre, Goffs Park House, Old Horsham Rd, Southgate, Crawley RH11 8PE - T: (01293) 539088. Admin.: Nadine Hygate
Local Museum
Local history 38659

Ifield Watermill, Hydr Dr, Ifield, Crawley RH11 8PE - T: (01293) 539088. Dir.: Nick Sexton
Science&Tech Museum
Milling machinery, rural crafts and local history 38660

Creetown

Creetown Exhibition Centre, 91 Saint John's St, Creetown DG8 7JE - T: (01671) 820471. Chm.: Andrew Ward
Local Museum 38661

Creetown Gem Rock Museum, Chain Rd, Creetown DG8 7HJ - T: (01671) 820357, Fax: 820554, E-mail: gem.rock@btinternet.com, Internet: www.gemrock.net. Dir.: Tim Stephenson
Natural History Museum - 1971
Scottish agate coll, British minerals, dinosaur egg fossil, cut gemstones, meteorite 38662

Cregneash

Cregneash Folk Village, Cregneash IM9 5PX - T: (01624) 648000, Fax: 648001, E-mail: enquiries@mnh.gov.im, Internet: www.gov.im/mnh. Man.: Chris Page
Folklore Museum 38663

Cremyll

Mount Edgcumbe House, Cremyll PL10 1HZ - T: (01752) 822236, Fax: 822199, E-mail: mt.edgcumbe@plymouth.gov.uk, Internet: www.cornwalltouristboard.co.uk
Special Museum
Paintings, furniture, Plymouth porcelain 38664

Crewe

Museum of Primitive Methodism, Englesea Brook, Englesea Brook Methodist Chapel, Crewe CW2 5QW - T: (01270) 820836, E-mail: engleseabrook-methodist-museum@supanet.com, Internet: www.engleseabrook-museum.org.uk. Dir.: Stephen Hatcher
Religious Arts Museum
Early pipe organ, printing press and chest of drawers pulpit, pottery, banners 38665

Railway Age, Vernon Wy, Crewe CW1 2DB - T: (01270) 212130
Science&Tech Museum
railway archives 38666

Crewkerne

Crewkerne and District Museum, Heritage Centre, Market Sq, Crewkerne TA18 7JU - T: (01460) 77079
Local Museum
Social and industrial history 38667

Criccieth

Criccieth Castle, off A497, Criccieth LL52 0AA - T: (01766) 522227
Archaeological Museum 38668

Cricklade

Cricklade Museum, 16 Calcutt St, Cricklade SN6 6BB - T: (01793) 750756. Cur.: T. Ramsden-Binks
Local Museum
Social history, Roman, Saxons, finds, photographs - archives 38669

Cromarty

Cromarty Courthouse Museum, Church St, Cromarty IV11 8XA - T: (01381) 600418, Fax: 600408, E-mail: courthouse@mail.cali.co.uk, Internet: www.cali.co.uk/users/freeway/courthouse. Cur.: David Alston
Local Museum
Cromarty's rule in the history of Scotland 38670

Hugh Miller's Cottage, Church St, Cromarty IV11 8XA - T: (01381) 600245, Fax: 600391, E-mail: fgostwick@nts.org.uk. Dir.: Martin Gostwick
Special Museum - 1890
Birthplace of Scottish geologist Hugh Miller (1802-1852), memorabilia, equipment, letters, fossil coll 38671

Cromer

Cromer Museum, East Cottages, Tucker St, Cromer NR27 9HB - T: (01263) 513543, Fax: 511651, E-mail: cromer.museum@norfolk.gov.uk, Internet: www.norfolk.gov.uk/tourism/default.htm. Head: Vanessa Trevelyan
Local Museum - 1978 38672

Henry Blogg Lifeboat Museum, The Gangway, Cromer NR27 9HE - T: (01263) 511294, Fax: 511294, E-mail: rfmuirhead@csma.netlink.co.uk. Cur.: Frank H. Muirhead
Historical Museum
Houses the lifeboat, H F Bailey 777, History of the lifeboat station from 1804, models 38673

Cromford

The Arkwright Society, Sir Richard Arkwright's Cromfort Mill, Mill Ln, Cromford DE4 3RQ - T: (01629) 823256, Fax: 823256, E-mail: info@cromfordmill.co.uk, Internet: www.arkwrightsociety.org.uk. Dir.: Dr. Christopher Charlton
Historic Site 38674

Cromford Mill, Mill Ln, Cromford DE4 3RQ - T: (01629) 824297, Fax: 823256, E-mail: info@arkwrightsociety.org.uk, Internet: www.arkwrightsociety.org.uk. Dir.: Dr. Christopher Charlton, Pres.: Sir George Kenyon
Science&Tech Museum - 1979
Water powered cotton spinning mill 38675

Crosby-on-Eden

Solway Aviation Museum, Aviation House, Carlisle Airport, Crosby-on-Eden CA6 4NW - T: (01228) 573823, Fax: 573823, E-mail: info@solway-aviation-museum.org.uk, Internet: www.solway-aviation-museum.org.uk. Dir.: David Kirkpatrick
Science&Tech Museum
Local aviation heritage and the Blue Streak Project at Spadeadam 38676

Croydon

Croydon Museum, Croydon Clocktower, Katherine St, Croydon CR9 1ET - T: (020) 82531022, Fax: 82531003, E-mail: museum@croydon.gov.uk, Internet: www.croydon.gov.uk/museum. Head: Rachel Hasted
Local Museum / Decorative Arts Museum
Local people's lives, Riesco coll of Chinese porcelain 38677

Croydon Natural History and Scientific Society Museum, 96a Brighton Rd, Croydon CR2 6AD - T: (020) 86691501. Dir.: John Greig
Local Museum
Archaeology, geology, social history, ethnography 38678

Cuckfield

Cuckfield Museum, Queen's Hall, High St, Cuckfield RH17 5EL - T: (01444) 454276. Cur.: Marilyn McInnes
Local Museum
Local history 38679

Cullyhanna

Cardinal Ó Fiaich Heritage Centre, Áras an Chairdiméil Ó Fiaich, Slatequarry Rd, Cullyhanna BT35 0JH - T: (01693) 868757, E-mail: info@ofiaichcentre-cullyhanna.com, Internet: www.ofiaichcentre-cullyhanna.com
Religious Arts Museum 38680

Culross

Culross Palace, Sandhaven, Royal Burgh of Culross, Culross KY12 8JH - T: (01383) 880359, Fax: 882675, E-mail: cwilson@nts.org.uk, Internet: www.nts.org.uk. Head: Robin Pellen, Cur.: Christine Wilson
Decorative Arts Museum - 1932
17th c wood panelling, painted ceilings and furniture 38681

Dunimarle Castle, Culross KY12 8JN - T: (01383) 229
Decorative Arts Museum
Palace (1597-1611) with wood-panelling, tempera ceiling 38682

Town House, Sandhaven, Royal Burgh of Culross, Culross KY12 8HT - T: (01383) 880359, Fax: 882675, E-mail: cwilson@nts.org.uk, Internet: www.nts.org.uk. Head: Robin Pellen, Cur.: Christine Wilson
Local Museum 38683

Cumbernauld

Cumbernauld Museum, 8 Allander Walk, Cumbernauld G67 1EE - T: (01236) 725664, Fax: 458350
Local Museum 38684

Lenziemill Archive Store, 10 Kelvin Rd, Cumbernauld G67 2BA - T: (01236) 737114, Fax: 781762. Man.: Richard Devaney
Music Museum
Archives and public records relating to area defined as North Lanarkshire 38685

Cumnock

Baird Institute Museum, 3 Lugar St, Cumnock KA18 1AD - T: (01290) 421701, Fax: 421701, E-mail: baird@east-ayrshire.gov.uk, Internet: www.east-ayrshire.gov.uk. Dir.: Charles J. Woodward
Decorative Arts Museum / Local Museum - 1891
Cumnock pottery, Mauchline boxware, Ayrshire embroidery and the "Lochnorris Collection" of artefacts mining equipment, photos, local and social history 38686

Cupar

Five Council Museums East Headquarters, County Bldgs, Saint Catherine St, Cupar KY15 4TA - T: (01334) 412933, 412934, Fax: 413214, E-mail: fifecouncil@museumseast.fsnet.co.uk. Cur.: Marion Wood
Local Museum
Local hist, militaria, ethnography (Oceania and Southern Africa), fife archaeology and geology, social history 38687

Hill of Tarvit Mansion House, Cupar KY15 5PB - T: (01334) 653127, Fax: 653127, E-mail: hilloftarvit@nts.org.uk, Internet: www.nts.org.uk. Dir.: K. Caldwell
Decorative Arts Museum / Fine Arts Museum / Historic Site
French, Chippendale and vernacular furniture, Dutch paintings and pictures by Scottish artists Raeburn and Ramsay, Flemish tapestries, Chinese porcelain and bronzes 38688

Cwmbran

Llanyrafon Farm, Llanfrecfa Way, Cwmbran NP44 6HT - T: (01633) 861810
Agriculture Museum
Story of farming in East Gwent 38689

Dagenham

Valence House Museum and Art Gallery, Becontree Av, Dagenham RM8 3HT - T: (020) 82275293, Fax: 82275293, E-mail: valencehousemuseum@hotmail.com, Internet: www.bardaglea.org.uk/4-valence. Dir.: Sue Curtis, Cur.: Mark Watson
Local Museum / Fine Arts Museum - 1938
Local hist, art gallery, herb garden - archives 38690

Dalbeattie

Dalbeattie Museum, Southwick Rd, Dalbeattie DG5 4HA - T: (01556) 610437. Cur.: D.T. Henderson
Local Museum
Local granite quarrying industy, shipping, the railway, mills history 38691

Dalkeith

Dalkeith Arts Centre, White Hart St, Dalkeith EH22 1OAE - T: (0131) 6636986, 2713970, Fax: 4404635, E-mail: alan.reid@midlothian.gov.uk. Man.: Alan Reid
Public Gallery 38692

Dalmellington

Cathcartston Visitor Centre, Dalmellington KA6 7QY - T: (01292) 550633, Fax: 550937, E-mail: stanley.sarsfield@east-ayrshire.gov.uk. Officer: Stanley Sarsfield
Local Museum
Hand-loom weaving, local coal, Iron and brockwork industries 38693

Scottish Industrial Railway Centre, Minnivey Colliery, Burnton, Dalmellington KA6 7PU - T: (01292) 531144. Dir.: Charles Robinson
Science&Tech Museum - 1980
Steam and diesel locomotives, rolling stock and cranes 38694

Darlington

Darlington Art Centre, Vane Terrace, Darlington DL3 7AX - T: (01325) 483271, Fax: 365794
Fine Arts Museum
Chiefly 19th c topographical and 20th c works 38695

Darlington Art Gallery (closed) 38696

Darlington Railway Centre and Museum, North Road Station, Darlington DL3 6ST - T: (01325) 460532, Fax: 287746, E-mail: museum@darlington.gov.uk, Internet: www.drcm.org.uk. Cur.: John Wilks
Science&Tech Museum - 1975
Material relating to the Stockton and Darlington Railway, Ken Hoole coll, North Eastern Railway Association Library - Ken Hoole Study Centre 38697

Raby Castle, Staindrop, Darlington - T: (01833) 660202, Fax: 660169, E-mail: admin@rabycastle.com, Internet: www.rabycastle.com
Fine Arts Museum
Dutch and Flemish paintings 38698

Dartford

Brooking Collection, c/o School of Land and Construction Management, University of Greenwich, Oakfield Ln, Dartford DA1 2SZ - T: (020) 83319897, Fax: 83319305. Cur.: Charles Brooking
Science&Tech Museum
Architectural detail and fittings, including doors, windows, staircase sections, timber mouldings, small ironmongery and fire grates 38699

Dartford Borough Museum, Market St, Dartford DA1 1EU - T: (01322) 343555, Fax: 343209. Asst. Cur.: Chris Baker (Archaeology)
Local Museum - 1908
Natural hist, geology, prehistoric finds, Roman, Saxon and medieval finds, Saxon finds from Horton Kirby site 38700

Dartmouth

Dartmouth Castle, Dartmouth TQ6 0JN - T: (01803) 833588, Internet: www.english-heritage.org.uk. Cur.: Tony Musty
Military Museum
Historic artillery and military items 38701

Dartmouth Museum, 6 The Butterwalk, Dartmouth TQ6 9PZ - T: (01803) 832923, E-mail: darmouth@devonmuseums.net, Internet: www.devonmuseums.net/darmouth. Cur.: C. Ruddlesden
Local Museum
Local and maritime hist, ship models, 17th c panelling 38702

Newcomen Engine House, Mayors Av, adj to The Butterwalk, Dartmouth TQ6 9YY - T: (01803) 834224, Fax: 835631, E-mail: enquire@dartmouth-tic.demon.co.uk, Internet: www.dartmouth-information.co.uk
Science&Tech Museum
Pressure/steam engine of 1725 38703

Darwen

Sunnyhurst Wood Visitor Centre, off Earnsdale Rd, Darwen BB3 - T: (01254) 701545, Fax: 701545, E-mail: countryside@blackburn.gov.uk
Public Gallery 38704

Daventry

Daventry Museum, Moot Hall, Market Sq, Daventry NN11 4BH - T: (01327) 302463, 71100, Fax: 706035, E-mail: vgabbitas@daventrydc.gov.uk. Cur.: Victoria Gabbitas
Local Museum - 1986 38705

Dawlish

Dawlish Museum, The Knowle, Barton Terrace, Dawlish EX7 9QH - T: (01626) 888557, Internet: www.devonmuseumnet/dawlish. Dir.: Brenda French
Local Museum - 1969
Local history, railway, industry, military, toys, clothes 38706

Deal

Deal Archaeological Collection, Library, Broad St, Deal - T: (01304) 374726
Archaeological Museum
Archaeological finds of the Deal area - library 38707

Deal Castle, Victoria Rd, Deal CT14 7BA - T: (01304) 372762, E-mail: sue.pearson@english-heritage.org.uk, Internet: www.english-heritage.org.uk. Cur.: Nick Moore
Historical Museum 38708

Deal Maritime and Local History Museum, 22 Saint George's Rd, Deal CT14 6BA - T: (01304) 381344, Fax: 373684, E-mail: dealmuseum@lineone.net, Internet: home.freeuk.com/deal-museum
Historical Museum / Local Museum
Local history, people, boats, life jackets, Deals maritime history, pilots, social history, fishing, trade, ship-to-shore communications 38709

Timeball Tower, Victoria Parade, Beach St, Deal CT14 7BP - T: (01304) 360897, 201200
Science&Tech Museum
Telegraphy and semaphores 38710

Dedham

Sir Alfred Munnings Art Museum, Castle House, Dedham CO7 6AZ - T: (01206) 322127, Fax: 322127. Dir.: Claire Woodage
Fine Arts Museum - 1970
Coll of paintings, sketches, studies of racehorses and of racing, equestrian portraits and hunting scenes, house, studios and grounds where Sir Alfred Munnings lived and painted for 40 yrs, large coll of his works 38711

Deepcut

Royal Logistic Corps Museum, Princess Royal Barracks, Deepcut GU16 6RW - T: (01252) 833371, Fax: 833484, E-mail: query@rlcmuseum.freeserve.co.uk, Internet: www.army-rlc.co.uk/museum. Cur.: S. Lines
Military Museum
Military artefacts 38712

Denbigh

Denbigh Castle Museum, Denbigh - T: (01745) 713979
Historical Museum
History of Denbigh, methods of castle warfare, the campaigns and castles of Edward I in North Wales, Richard Dudley, Earl of Leicester 38713

Denbigh Museum and Gallery, Hall Sq, Denbigh LL16 3NU - T: (01745) 816313, Fax: 816427, E-mail: manon.edwards@denbighshire.gov.uk. Dir.: Kevin Matthias
Local Museum / Fine Arts Museum
Social, industrial and economical growth, cultural heritage 38714

Derby

Derby Industrial Museum, Silk Mill Ln, off Full St, Derby DE1 3AR - T: (01332) 255308, Fax: 716670, E-mail: David.Fraser@derby.gov.uk, Internet: www.derby.gov.uk/museums. Dir.: Roger Shelley
Science&Tech Museum - 1974
Rolls-Royce aero engine coll, items relating to the Midland Railway and especially to Railway Research carried out in Derby 38715

Derby Museum and Art Gallery, The Strand, Derby DE1 1BS - T: (01332) 716659, Fax: 716670, E-mail: David.Fraser@derby.gov.uk, Internet: www.derby.gov.uk/museums. Dir.: David Fraser, Cur.: Anneke Bambery, Elizabeth Spencer, Janine Derbyshire (Decorative Arts), Sarah Allard (Fine Art), Bill Grange, Nick Moyes (Natural History), Roger Shelly (Social History), Chris Kennedy, Louise Dunning, Maggie Cullen (Exhibitions), Jonathan Wallis (Collections)
Fine Arts Museum / Local Museum - 1879
Paintings of Joseph Wright, history, natural history, porcelain, paintings, drawings, engravings, numismatics 38716

The Eastern Museum, Kedleston Hall, Derby DE22 5JH - T: (01332) 842191, Fax: 841972, E-mail: ehdxxx@sntp.ntrust.org.uk
Ethnology Museum - 1927
Eastern silver, textiles, ceramics, metalworks, ivory, furniture 38717

Pickford's House Museum, 41 Friar Gate, Derby DE1 1DA - T: (01332) 255363, Fax: 255277, E-mail: David.Fraser@derby.gov.uk, Internet: www.derby.gov.uk/museums. Dir.: Janine Derbyshire, Elizabeth Spencer
Decorative Arts Museum - 1988
Georgian town house, historic costumes, toy theatres, decorative art, domestic life 38718

Regimental Museum of the 9th/12th Royal Lancers, The Strand, Derby DE1 1BS - T: (01332) 716656, Fax: 716670, E-mail: David.Fraser@derby.gov.uk, Internet: www.derby.gov.uk/museums. Cur.: A. Tarnowski
Military Museum 38719

Royal Crown Derby Museum, 194 Osmaston Rd, Derby DE23 8JZ - T: (01332) 712800, Fax: 712899, E-mail: enquiries@royal-crown-derby.co.uk, Internet: www.royal-crown-derby.co.uk. Cur.: Jaqueline Banks
Decorative Arts Museum - 1969
Hist of ceramics production in Derby since 1748 38720

Dereham

Hobbies Museum of Fretwork, 34-36 Swaffham Rd, Dereham NR19 2QZ - T: (01362) 692985, Fax: 699145, E-mail: enquire@hobbies-dereham.co.uk, Internet: www.hobbies-dereham.co.uk
Special Museum
Machines and tools, fretwork articles 38721

Derry

The Calgach Centre, Butcher St, Derry, Co. Derry - T: (01504) 373177
Local Museum
Local history 38722

Upperlands Eco-Museum, 55 Kilrea Rd, Upperlands, Derry, Co. Derry - T: (01648) 43265
Historical Museum / Open Air Museum
History 38723

Dervaig

The Old Byre Heritage Centre, Dervaig PA75 6QR - T: (01688) 400229, E-mail: theoldbyre@lineone.net. Dir.: J.M. Bradley
Natural History Museum / Local Museum
Natural history and history of Mull, geology, wildlife 38724

Devizes

Devizes Museum → Wiltshire Heritage Museum and Gallery

Kennet and Avon Canal Trust Museum, Devizes Wharf, Couch Ln, Devizes SN10 1EB - T: (01380) 721279, 729489, Fax: 727870, E-mail: administrator@katrust.org, Internet: www.katrust.org. Dir.: Clive Hackford, Cur.: Warren Berry
Science&Tech Museum
History of the Kennet and Avon Canal from 1788 38725

Wiltshire Heritage Museum and Gallery, 41 Long St, Devizes SN10 1NS - T: (01380) 727369, Fax: 722150, E-mail: wanhs@wiltshireheritage.org.uk, Internet: www.wiltshireheritage.org.uk. Dir.: Dr. Paul Robinson, Sc. Staff: Andrew Tucker (Natural Sciences), Dr. Lorna Haycock (Library)
Archaeological Museum / Historical Museum / Fine Arts Museum / Local Museum / Natural History Museum - 1853
Archaeology, Stourhead Bronze age coll, geological fossils, paintings by John Buckler, etchings by Robin Tanner - library 38726

Wiltshire Regiment Museum, Le Marchant Barracks, Devizes
Military Museum - 1933
Militaria on 62nd and 99th Regiment of Foot, Wiltshire Regiment and Militaria 38727

Dewsbury

Dewsbury Museum, Crow Nest Park, Heckmondwike Rd, Dewsbury WF13 0AS - T: (01924) 325100, E-mail: cultural-hq@geo2.poptel.org.uk, Internet: www.kirkleesmc.gov.uk. Dir.: Brian Haigh
Local Museum
Local history and childhood 38728

Dickleburgh

100th Bomb Group Memorial Museum, Common Rd, Dickleburgh IP21 4PH - T: (01379) 740708. Dir.: S.P. Hurry
Military Museum 38729

Didcot

Didcot Railway Centre, Didcot OX11 7NJ - T: (01235) 817200, Fax: 510621, E-mail: didrlyc@globalnet.co.uk, Internet: www.didcotrailwaycentre.org.uk. Dir.: M. Dean
Science&Tech Museum - 1967
Great Western Railway locomotives and carriages 38730

Dingwall

Dingwall Museum, Town House, High St, Dingwall IV15 9RY - T: (01349) 865366. Dir.: Kate MacPherson
Local Museum - 1975
Local hist, military exhibits 38731

Disley

Lyme Hall, Lyme Park, Disley SK12 2NX - T: (01663) 762023, Fax: 765035, E-mail: mlyrec@smtp.ntrust.org.uk, Internet: www.nationaltrust.org.uk. Dir.: Kevin Reid
Decorative Arts Museum - 1946
16th c house, remodelled in 18th c in Palladian style interiors of many architectural fashions, Mortlake tapestries, limewood carvings, Heraldic glass, English clocks 38732

Diss

Bressingham Steam Museum, Thetford Rd, Bressingham, Diss IP22 2AB - T: (01379) 687386/82, Fax: 688085, E-mail: info@bressingham.co.uk, Internet: www.bressingham.co.uk. Dir.: Alan Bloom, David D. Ward, Mervyn Thompson
Science&Tech Museum - 1964/1973
Coll of steam engines, road and industrial engines, a steam-operated Victorian roundabout, steamhauled narrow gauge railways, locomotives, mechanical organ, fire fighting equipment dating from 1800's 38733

Diss Museum, The Shambles, Market Pl, Diss IP22 3AB - T: (01379) 650618, Fax: 643848. Man.: Denise Beale
Local Museum
History and prehistory of the market town 38734

Ditchling

Ditchling Museum, Church Ln, Ditchling BN6 8TB - T: (01273) 844744, Fax: 844744, E-mail: ditchling.museum@mistral.co.uk, Internet: www.ditchling-museum.com. Dir.: Ann Phillips
Local Museum / Fine Arts Museum - 1985
Calligraphy, engraving, typography 38735

Dobwalls

The John Southern Gallery, Dobwalls Family Adventure Park, Dobwalls PL14 6HB - T: (01579) 320325, 321129, Fax: dobwallsadventurepark@hotmail.com. Cur.: John Southern
Fine Arts Museum
Steven Townsend (born 1955), Britain's dog painter, his limited prints, Carl Brenders (born 1937) nature paintings and his limited prints 38736

Thorburn Gallery → The John Southern Gallery

Doddington

Doddington Hall, Doddington LN6 4RU - T: (01522) 694308, Fax: 685259, E-mail: fionawatson@doddingtonhall.free-online.co.uk, Internet: www.doddingtonhall.free-online.co.uk. Dir.: Antony Jarvis
Association with Coll
China, glass, furniture, textiles, pictures 38737

Dollar

Dollar Museum, Castle Campbell Hall, 1 High St, Dollar FK14 7AY - T: (01259) 742895, 743239, Fax: 742895, E-mail: janet.carolan@btinternet.com. Cur.: Janet Carolan
Local Museum
Local hist, Dollar academy, Devon Valley railway, castle hist 38738

Dolwyddelan

Ty Mawr Wybrnant, Dolwyddelan LL25 0HJ
Special Museum
Birthplace of Bishop William Morgan who translated the Bible into Welsh which was the foundation of modern Welsh literature 38739

Doncaster

Brodsworth Hall & Gardens, Brodsworth, Doncaster DN5 7XJ - T: (01302) 722598, Fax: 337165, E-mail: michael.constantine@english-heritage.org.uk, Internet: www.english-heritage.org.uk. Dir.: Peter Gordon-Smith, Cur.: Caroline Carr-Whitworth, Dr. Crosby Stevens
Historical Museum
Paintings, Italian sculpture, furnishings, kitchen equipment - gardens 38740

Doncaster Museum and Art Gallery, Chequer Rd, Doncaster DN1 2AE - T: (01302) 734293, Fax: 735409, E-mail: museum@doncaster.gov.uk, Internet: www.doncaster.gov.uk/museums. Dir.: Geoff Preece, Sc. Staff: Carolyn Dalton, Cons.: Libby Finney
Local Museum / Fine Arts Museum - 1899
Regional hist, archaeology, natural hist, fine and decorative art, temporary exhibitions 38741

King's Own Yorkshire Light Infantry Regimental Museum, Chequer Rd, Doncaster DN1 2AE - T: (01302) 734293, Fax: 735409, E-mail: museum@doncaster.gov.uk, Internet: www.doncaster.gov.uk/museums. Dir.: C.M.J. Deedes
Military Museum - 1950
History of King's Own Yorkshire Light Infantry, medals, armaments, uniforms 38742

Museum of South Yorkshire Life, Cusworth Hall, Cusworth Ln, Doncaster DN5 7TU - T: (01302) 782342, Fax: 782342, E-mail: museum@duncaster.gov.uk, Internet: www.doncaster.gov.uk. Dir.: Frank Carpenter
Historical Museum - 1967
Social history of South Yorkshire, coll illustrate life over last 200 years (domestic life, costume, childhood, transport) 38743

Sandtoft Transport Centre, Belton Rd, Sandtoft, Doncaster DN8 5SX - T: (01724) 711391, Internet: freespace.virgin.net/neil.worthington/sandtoft98.htm
Science&Tech Museum
Trolleybuses, motorbus, miniature railway, coll of small exhibits relating to trolleybus 38744

Donington-le-Heath

Manor House, Manor Rd, Donington-le-Heath LE67 2FW - T: (01530) 831259, Fax: 831259, E-mail: museums@leics.gov.uk, Internet: www.leics.gov.uk/lcc/tourism/attractions_museums.html. Dir.: Peter Liddle
Decorative Arts Museum 38745

Dorchester

Athelhampton House, Athelhampton, Dorchester - T: (01305) 848363, Fax: 848135, E-mail: enquiry@athelhampton.co.uk, Internet: www.athelhampton.co.uk. Dir.: Patrick Cooke
Historic Site - 1957
House with 15th-16th c furniture - architectural garden, library 38746

Dinosaur Museum, Icen Way, Dorchester DT1 1EW - T: (01305) 269880, 269741, Fax: 268885, E-mail: info@thedinosaurmuseum.com, Internet: www.thedinosaurmuseum.com. Dir.: Jackie D. Ridley, Cur.: Tim Batty
Natural History Museum - 1984 38747

Dorset County Museum, High West St, Dorchester DT1 1XA - T: (01305) 262735, Fax: 257180, E-mail: dorsetcountymuseum@dor-mus.demon.co.uk, Internet: www.dorsetcountymuseum.org. Dir.: Judy Lindsay, Cur.: Peter Woodward
Local Museum - 1846
County archaeology, geology, biology, local and regional history, memorabilia, literature incl Thomas Hardy coll - library 38748

Dorset Teddy Bear Museum, Teddy Bear House, Antelope Walk, Dorchester DT1 1BE - T: (01305) 263200, 26974, Fax: 268885, E-mail: info@teddybearhouse.co.uk, Internet: www.teddybearhouse.co.uk. Dir.: Jackie D. Ridley
Special Museum 38749

Military Museum of Devon and Dorset, The Keep, Bridport Rd, Dorchester DT1 1RN - T: (01305) 264066, Fax: 250373, E-mail: keep.museum@talk21.com, Internet: www.keepmilitarymuseum.org. Cur.: R.A. Leonard, Cust.: J. Murphy
Military Museum - 1927
Uniforms, weapons, militaria, exhibits of Devon Regiment, Dorset Regiment, local militia and volunteers, Queens Own Dorset Yeomanry and Devonshire and Dorset Regiment - library, archives 38750

Old Crown Court and Shire Hall, 58-60 High West St, Dorchester DT1 1UZ - T: (01305) 252241, Fax: 257039, E-mail: tourism@westdorset-dc.gov.uk, Internet: www.westdorset.com
Historical Museum
Law and order (Rough Justice), Tolpuddle Martyrs 38751

Terracotta Warriors Museum, High East St, Dorchester DT1 1JU - T: (01305) 266040, Fax: 268885, E-mail: info@terracottawarriors.co.uk, Internet: www.terracottawarriors.co.uk. Dir.: Jacqeline Ridley
Archaeological Museum - 2002 38752

Tutankhamun Exhibition, High West St, Dorchester DT1 1UW - T: (01305) 269571, 269741, Fax: 268885, E-mail: info@tutankhamun-exhibition.co.uk, Internet: www.tutankhamun-exhibition.co.uk. Dir.: Dr. Michael Ridley
Archaeological Museum - 1987 38753

Dorchester-on-Thames

Dorchester Abbey Museum, Abbey Guest House, Dorchester-on-Thames OX10 7HH - T: (01865) 340751, E-mail: richard.riddell@freenet.co.uk, Internet: www.dorchester-abbey.org.uk. Dir.: Dr. Richard Riddell
Local Museum
Local history since prehistoric time 38754

Dorking

Dorking and District Museum, 62a West St, Dorking RH4 1BS - T: (01306) 876591
Local Museum
Toys, domestic and agricultural displays, fossil coll, minerals, photographes 38755

Polesden Lacey, Dorking RH5 6BD - T: (01372) 453401, 452048, Fax: 452023, E-mail: polesdenlacey@nationaltrust.org.uk, Internet: www.nationaltrust.org.uk/polesdenlacey. Dir.: Sue Saville
Decorative Arts Museum
Pictures, furniture, tapestries, art objects 38756

Dornie

Eilean Donan Castle Museum, Dornie IV40 8DX - T: (01599) 555202, Fax: 555262
Local Museum 38757

Dornoch

Dornoch Heritage Museum, Struie Rd, Ardoch, Dornoch - T: (01862) 810754
Local Museum 38758

Dorset

Museum of Net Manufacture, Bridgeacre, Uploders, Bridport, Dorset DT6 4PF - T: (01308) 485349, Fax: 485621. Cur.: Jacquie Summers
Historical Museum
Documents, ledgers, traditional tools, samples of natural fibres, historic trade 38759

Douglas, Isle of Man

Manx Museum, Manx National Heritage, Kingswood Grove, Douglas, Isle of Man IM1 3LY - T: (01624) 648000, Fax: 648001, E-mail: enquiries@mnh.gov.im, Internet: www.gov.im/mnh. Dir.: Stephen Harrison
Local Museum / Historical Museum / Fine Arts Museum
Manx history and story of Mann, natural history, archaeology, social development of the island, famous Manx artists - archive, library 38760

Douglas, Lanarkshire

Douglas Heritage Museum, Saint Sophia's Chapel, Bells Wynd, Douglas, Lanarkshire ML11 0QH - T: (01555) 851243
Local Museum
Village history, Douglas family 38761

Doune

Doune Motor Museum, Carse of Cambus, Doune FK16 6DF - T: (01786) 841203, Fax: 842070
Science&Tech Museum 38762

Dover

Agricultural Museum Brook, Old Post Office, Slip Ln, Alkham, Dover CT15 7DE - T: (01304) 824969, E-mail: brianwimsett@hotmail.com, Internet: www.agriculturalmuseumbrook.org.uk. Cur.: Brian Wimsett
Agriculture Museum
Old farm equipment, medieval barn and oast house 38763

Crabble Corn Mill, Lower Rd, River, Dover CT17 0UY - T: (01304) 823292, 362569, Fax: 826040, E-mail: mill@invmed.demon.co.uk, Internet: www.invmed.demon.co.uk. Chairman: Alan Davies
Science&Tech Museum 38764

Dover Castle, Dover CT16 1HN - T: (01304) 201628, 211067, Fax: 214739, E-mail: tracey.wahdan@english-heritage.org.uk, Internet: www.english-heritage.org.uk. Man.: Tracey Wahdan
Historical Museum
Medieval fortress 38765

Dover Museum, Market Sq, Dover CT16 1PB - T: (01304) 201066, Fax: 241186, E-mail: museum@dover.gov.uk, Internet: www.dover.gov.uk/museum. Cur.: Jon Iveson
Local Museum / Archaeological Museum / Public Gallery - 1836
Local history, ceramics, geology, transportation, embroidery, cameras, natural history, bronze age archaeology 38766

Dover Old Town Goal, Town Hall, Biggin St, Dover CT16 1DQ - T: (01304) 202723, 242766, Fax: 201200
Historical Museum
Courtroom, cells, Victorian prison 38767

Grand Shaft, South Military Rd, Dover CT17 9BZ - T: (01304) 201200, 201066, Fax: 201200, Internet: www.dover.gov.uk/museum/g_shaft/home.htm. Dir.: Trevor Jones
Military Museum
Vast military fortification 38768

Princess of Wales's Royal Regiment and Queen's Regiment Museum, 5 Keep Yard, Dover Castle, Dover CT16 1HU - T: (01304) 240121, Fax: 240121, E-mail: pwrrqueensmuseum@tinyworld.co.uk. Cur.: J.-C. Rogerson
Military Museum 38769

Queen's Regiment Museum → Princess of Wales's Royal Regiment and Queen's Regiment Museum

Roman Painted House, New St, Dover CT17 9AJ - T: (01304) 203279. Dir.: B.J. Philp
Archaeological Museum 38770

Wye College Museum of Agriculture → Agricultural Museum Brook

Downe

Darwin Museum → Down House

Down House, Home of Chales Darwin, Luxted Rd, Downe BR6 7JT - T: (01689) 859119, Fax: 862755, Internet: www.english-heritage.org.uk. Dir.: Margaret Speller
Special Museum / Natural History Museum - 1929/1998
Memorabilia of biologist Charles Darwin, his study, portraits 38771

Downpatrick

Castle Ward, Strangford, Downpatrick, Co. Down - T: (01396) 881204
Historical Museum
18th c house, fortified tower, cornmill 38772

Down County Museum, The Mall, Downpatrick BT30 6AH - T: (028) 44615218, Fax: 44615590, E-mail: museum@downdc.gov.uk, Internet: www.downdc.gov.uk. Cur.: Michael D. King
Local Museum - 1981 38773

Downpatrick Railway Museum, Railway Station, Market St, Downpatrick BT30 6LZ - T: (01396) 615779, E-mail: drm@downrail.freeserve.co.uk, Internet: www.uel.ac.uk/pers/1278/rly-pres/drm. Dir./ Cur.: G. Cochrane
Science&Tech Museum
Steam and diesel locomotives, historic carriages and wagons, signal box, water tower, goods shed, travelling Post Office 38774

Draperstown

Plantation of Ulster Visitor Centre, 50 High St, Draperstown BT45 7AD - T: (028) 79627800, Fax: 79627732, E-mail: info@theflightoftheearlsexperience.com, Internet: www.theflightoftheearlsexperience.com. Man.: Frank Larey
Agriculture Museum
Story of plantation of Ulster, Irish history from 1595 38775

Droitwich

Droitwich Spa Heritage Centre, Saint Richard's House, Victoria Sq, Droitwich WR9 8DS - T: (01905) 774312, Fax: 794226. Dir.: R.G. Pharo
Local Museum
Local artefacts from Roman times to the 17th c 38776

Hanbury Hall, School Rd, Droitwich WR9 7EA - T: (01527) 821214, Fax: 821251, E-mail: hanbury@smtp.ntrust.org.uk, Internet: www.ntrustsevern.org.uk
Fine Arts Museum 38777

Drumnadrochit

Loch Ness 2000 Exhibition, Official Loch Ness Centre, Drumnadrochit IV63 6TU - T: (01456) 450573, Fax: 450770, E-mail: info@loch-ness-scotland.com, Internet: www.loch-ness-scotland.com. Dir.: R.W. Bremner, Cur.: Gary Richardson
Special Museum 38778

Urquhart Castle, Drumnadrochit IV3 6TX - T: (01456) 450551. Cust.: Cameron McKenzie
Historical Museum
Ruins 38779

Drumoak

Drum Castle, Drumoak AB3 5EY - T: (01330) 811204, Fax: 811962, E-mail: agordon@nts.org.uk, Internet: www.drum-castle.org.uk. Dir.: Alec Gordon
Historical Museum 38780

Dudley

Black Country Living Museum, Tipton Rd, Dudley DY1 4SQ - T: (0121) 5579643, Fax: 5574242, E-mail: info@bclm.co.uk, Internet: www.bclm.co.uk. Dir.: Ian N. Walden
Historical Museum - 1975
Social and industrial history of Black Country 38781

Dudley Museum and Art Gallery, Saint James's Rd, Dudley DY1 1HU - T: (01384) 815575, Fax: 815576, E-mail: museum.pls@dudley.gov.uk, Internet: www.dudley.gov.uk. Dir.: Charles R. Hajdamach, Keeper: Roger C. Dodsworth (Glass and Fine Art), Graham Worton (Geology)
Natural History Museum / Fine Arts Museum 38782

Royal Brierley Crystal Museum, Tipton Rd, Dudley DY1 4SH - T: (0121) 5305600, Fax: 5305590, E-mail: sales@royalbrierley.com, Internet: www.royalbrierley.com. Dir.: T.G. Westbrook
Decorative Arts Museum 38783

Dufftown

Glenfiddich Distillery Museum, Glenfiddich Distillery, Dufftown AB5 4DH - T: (01340) 20373
Science&Tech Museum
19th-c furniture, many of the distillery ledgers, coopers' tools, and distillery equipment used in the past 38784

Dumbarton

Denny Ship Model Experiment Tank, Scottish Maritime Museum, Castle St, Dumbarton G82 1QS - T: (01389) 763444, Fax: 743093. Dir.: J.M. Tildesley
Science&Tech Museum
First ship model testing tank by William Froude (1883), drawing office, clay model moulding beds and shaping machinery 38785

Dumfries

Crichton Museum (temporary closed because of moving), Easterbrook Hall, Bankend Rd, Dumfries DG1 4TG - T: (01387) 244228, Fax: 269696, E-mail: Morag.Williams@btinternet.com, Internet: www.john.l.l.williams.btinternet.com. Cur.: Morag Williams
Historical Museum / Special Museum - 1989
Hist of Health Care, esp Mental Health Care in SW Scotland, Dumfries and Galloway, Art therapy creative work by patients 1839-1860 38786

Dumfries and Galloway Aviation Museum, Former Control Tower, Heathhall Industrial Estate, Dumfries DG2 3PH - T: (01387) 256680. Chm.: David Reid
Science&Tech Museum
Engines and aeronautica 38787

Dumfries Museum, Observatory, Corberry Hill, Dumfries DG2 7SW - T: (01387) 253374, Fax: 265081, E-mail: elainek@dumgal.gov.uk, Internet: www.dumgal.gov.uk/museums. Dir.: David Lockwood, Cur.: Elaine Kennedy
Local Museum - 1835
Geology, paleontology, mineralogy, botany, zoology, ethnography, costumes, photos, archaeology, social history 38788

Gracefield Arts Centre, 28 Edinburgh Rd, Dumfries DG1 1NW - T: (01387) 262084, Fax: 255173, Internet: www.artandcraftsouthwest.scotland.com. Dir.: D. Henderby (Arts)
Fine Arts Museum
Coll of Scottish paintings (19th-20th c), programme of contemporary art and craft exhibitions 38789

Old Bridge House Museum, Mill Rd, Dumfries DG2 7BE - T: (01387) 256904, Fax: 265081, E-mail: dumfriesmuseum@dumgal.gov.uk, Internet: www.dumgal.gov.uk/museums. Dir.: David Lockwood, Cur.: Ian Rennie
Decorative Arts Museum - 1959/1960
Period furnishings, interiors, various rooms, ceramics, costumes, toys, books 38790

Robert Burns Centre, Mill Rd, Dumfries DG2 7BE - T: (01387) 264808, Fax: 264808, E-mail: dumfriesmuseum@dumgal.gov.uk, Internet: www.dumgal.gov.uk/museums. Dir.: David Lockwood, Cur.: Jennifer Taylor
Special Museum - 1986
Exhibitions, including an audio-visual presentation on Robert Burns and his life in Dumfries, and on the growth of interest in his life and poetry 38791

Robert Burns House, Burns St, Dumfries DG1 2PS - T: (01387) 255297, Fax: 265081, E-mail: dumfriesmuseum@dumgal.gov.uk, Internet: www.dumgal.gov.uk/museums. Man.: David Lockwood, Attendant: Paul Cowley
Special Museum
House in which Robert Burns lived for three years prior to his death 38792

Dunbar

Dunbar Town House Museum, High St, Dunbar EH42 1ER - T: (01368) 863734, Fax: 828201, E-mail: elms@elothian-museums.demon.co.uk, Internet: www.dunbarmuseum.org
Local Museum
16th c house, archeology, photographs of old Dunbar 38793

John Muir's Birthplace, 126 High St, Dunbar EH42 1JJ - T: (01386) 865899, E-mail: jmoulin@jmbt.org.uk, Internet: www.jmbt.org.uk
Special Museum
Father of the conservation movement John Muir 38794

Dunbeath

Laidhay Croft Museum, Laidhay, Dunbeath KW6 6EH - T: (01593) 731244, Fax: 721548. Dir.: Elizabeth Cameron
Agriculture Museum - 1974
Examples of early agricultural machinery, household artefacts 38795

Dunblane

Dunblane Museum, 1 The Cross, Dunblane FK15 0AQ - T: (01786) 823440, 825691. Cur.: M.P. Davies
Local Museum - 1943
Paintings, prints, medieval carvings, letters of Bishop Robert Leighton, Communion Tokens - library 38796

Dundee

Broughty Castle Museum, Broughty Ferry, Dundee DD5 2TF - T: (01382) 436916, Fax: 436951, E-mail: broughty@dundeecity.gov.uk, Internet: www.dundeecity.gov.uk/broughtycastle. Cur.: Ruth Neave
Historical Museum / Local Museum - 1969
Local history, fishing, Dundee's former whaling industry tourism, the wildlife of the Tay estuary, weapons and armour, military history 38797

Duncan of Jordanstone College of Art and Design Exhibition → University of Dundee Exhibitions Department

Dundee City Council Arts and Heritage, Dundee Contemporary Arts, 152 Nethergate, Dundee DD1 4DY - T: (01383) 432322, Fax: 432252, E-mail: john.stewart-young@dundeecity.gov.uk, Internet: www.dundeecity.gov.uk
Association with Coll
Operates three registered museums, see individual venue entries 38798

Frigate Unicorn, Victoria Dock, Dundee DD1 3JA - T: (01382) 200900, Fax: 200923, E-mail: frigateunicorn@hotmail.com, Internet: www.frigateunicorn.org.uk. Chm.: Earl of Dalhousie
Military Museum
Oldest British-built warship still afloat 'HMS Unicorn', Royal Navy coll 38799

McManus Galleries, Albert Sq, Dundee DD1 1DA - T: (01382) 432084, Fax: 432052, E-mail: arts.heritage@dundeecity.gov.uk, Internet: www.dundeecity.gov.uk. Man.: J. Stewart-Young, Sc. Staff: R. Brinklow (Facilities), C. Young (Art), A. Zealand (Archaeology, Ethnography)
Fine Arts Museum / Local Museum - 1873
19th c Scottish fine art, Dundee & Edinburgh silver, contemporary Scottish art & photography & crafts, local hist, civil, church & history material, archaeology, whaling material, etc. natural hist of the region incl taywhale skeleton, botany, geology, entomology, zoology 38800

Mills Observatory Museum, Balgay Park, Glamis Rd, Dundee DD2 2UB - T: (01382) 435846, Fax: 435962, E-mail: mills.observatory@dundeecity.gov.uk, Internet: www.dundeecity.gov.uk/mills. Dir.: Dr. Bill Samson
Science&Tech Museum
Astronomy, space flight - planetarium 38801

North Carr Lightship, Victoria Dock, Dundee DD1 3HW - T: (01382) 350353, Fax: 350353, E-mail: brian.callison@steamship.co.uk. Head: Brian Callison
Science&Tech Museum
Last manned light vessel North Carr (1933-1974) with contemporary furniture, fittings and machinery 38802

Old Steeple, Nethergate, Dundee DD1 4DG - T: (01382) 206790, Fax: 206790, E-mail: info@dundeeheritage.sol.co.uk, Internet: www.oldsteeple.co.uk
Public Gallery 38803

Royal Research Ship Discovery, Discovery Point, Discovery Quay, Dundee DD1 4XA - T: (01382) 201245, Fax: 225891, E-mail: info@dundeeheritage.co.uk, Internet: www.rrsdiscovery.com. Dir.: Gill Poulter
Special Museum
Ship used by Robert Falcon Scott on the Antarctic Expedition of 1901-1904 38804

University Museum, University of Dundee, Dundee DD1 4HN - T: (01382) 344310, Fax: 344310, E-mail: museum@dundee.ac.uk, Internet: www.dundee.ac.uk/museum/. Cur.: Matthew Jarron
Fine Arts Museum / University Museum / Natural History Museum / Science&Tech Museum
Scientific and medical instr, natural hist, historic and contemporary fine arts and design 38805

University of Dundee Exhibitions Department, Perth Rd, Dundee DD1 4HT - T: (01382) 345330, Fax: 345192, E-mail: exhibitions@dundee.ac.uk, Internet: www.dundee.ac.uk/exhibitions
Public Gallery 38806

Verdant Works, 27 West Henderson's Wynd, Dundee DD1 5BT - T: (01382) 225282, Fax: 221612, E-mail: info@dundeeheritage.co.uk, Internet: www.verdantworks.com. Dir.: Gill Poulter
Science&Tech Museum - 1996
Museum of Dundee's textile industries, 19th c flax and jute mill, historic textile machinery 38807

Dunfermline

Andrew Carnegie Birthplace Museum, Moodie St, Dunfermline KY12 7PL - T: (01383) 724302, Fax: 721862, E-mail: carnegiebirthplace@hotmail.com, Internet: www.carnegiemuseum.com. Dir.: Lorna Owers
Special Museum - 1928
Birthplace of industrialist-philanthropist Andrew Carnegie with memorabilia, costumes, decorative arts 38808

Dunfermline Museum, Viewfield Terrace, Dunfermline KY12 7HY - T: (01383) 313838, Fax: 313837, E-mail: lesley.botten@fife.gov.uk
Local Museum - 1961
Local industrial, social and natural history, significant local linen coll 38809

Pittencrieff House Museum, Pittencrieff Park, Dunfermline KY12 8QH - T: (01383) 722935, 313838
Local Museum
Costume 19th-20th c, local history, major arts, photographics 38810

Dungannon

The Argory, 144 Derrycaw Rd, Moy, Dungannon BT70 - T: (028) 87784753
Historical Museum 38811

Heritage World Centre, 26 Market Sq, Dungannon BT70 1AB - T: (028) 87724187, Fax: 87752141, E-mail: irishworld@iol.ie, Internet: www.heritagewld.com
Historical Museum
Genealogy, religious register for research 38812

United States Grant Ancestral Homestead, Dergenagh Rd, Dungannon BT70 1TW - T: (028) 87767259, Fax: 87767911, E-mail: killymaddy@nitic.net, Internet: www.dungannon.gov.uk. Man.: Libby McLean
Historical Museum
19th c agricultural implements, Ulysses Simpson Grant, 18th President of the USA 38813

Dunkeld

Dunkeld Cathedral Chapter House Museum, Cathedral St, Dunkeld PH8 0AW - T: (01350) 728732, Fax: 728732. Dir.: Eileen Cox
Local Museum
Ecclesiastical artefacts, an cross slab from the 9th-c, the Pictish Apostles Stone from the 9th c, temporary displays reflecting different aspect of social history - Archives 38814

Little Houses, High St, Dunkeld PH8 0AN - T: (013502) 727460. Dir.: Gillian Kelly
Local Museum 38815

Dunoon

Dunoon and Cowal Museum, Castle House, Dunoon PA23 7HH - T: (01369) 701422
Local Museum 38816

Dunrossnes

Shetland Croft House Museum, Voe, Boddam, Dunrossnes ZE2 9JG - T: (01595) 695057, Fax: 696729, E-mail: museum@sic.shetland.gov.uk, Internet: www.shetland-museum.org.uk. Dir.: T. Watt
Agriculture Museum - 1972 38817

Duns

Biscuit Tin Museum, Manderston, Duns TD11 3PP - T: (01361) 883450, Fax: 882010, E-mail: palmer@manderston.co.uk, Internet: www.manderston.co.uk. Dir.: Lord Palmer
Decorative Arts Museum 38818

Duns Area Museum, 49 Newtown St, Duns TD11 3AU - T: (01361) 884114, Fax: 884104, E-mail: jthompson@scotborders.gov.uk. Cur.: Ian Brown
Local Museum 38819

Jim Clark Room, 44 Newtown St, Duns TD11 3AU - T: (01361) 883960, 884114, Fax: 884104, E-mail: jthompson@scotborders.gov.uk. Dir.: Ian Brown
Historical Museum - 1969
Trophies and other memorabilia, world champion of motor racing 38820

Dunster

Dunster Castle, Dunster TA24 6SL - T: (01643) 821314, Fax: 823000, E-mail: dunstercastle@ntrust.org.uk. Dir.: William Wake
Historical Museum 38821

Dunvegan

Dunvegan Castle, Dunvegan IV55 8WF - T: (01470) 521206, Fax: 521205, E-mail: info@dunvegancastle.com, Internet: www.dunvegancastle.com. Dir.: John Lambert
Historical Museum 38822

Dunwich

Dunwich Museum, Saint James' St, Dunwich IP17 3EA - T: (01728) 648796. Dir.: M. Caines
Historical Museum - 1972
Local history, natural history of the seashore, marshes, heathland and woodland 38823

Durham

Durham Cathedral Treasures of Saint Cuthbert, Cloisters, off the Cathedral, Durham DH1 3EH - T: (0191) 3864266, Fax: 3864267, E-mail: enquiries@durhamcathedral.co.uk, Internet: www.durhamcathedral.co.uk. Dir.: Dr. M. Kitchen
Religious Arts Museum - 1978
17th and 18th c altar plate, opus anglicanum embroidery, manuscripts, medieval bronze work, Saint Cuthbert relics 38824

Durham Heritage Centre and Museum, Saint Mary-le-Bow, North Bailey, Durham DH1 3ET - T: (0191) 3868719, 3845589. Dir.: J.M. Jones
Historical Museum - 1975 38825

Durham Light Infantry Museum and Durham Art Gallery, Aykley Heads, Durham DH1 5TU - T: (0191) 3842214, Fax: 3861770, E-mail: dli@durham.gov.uk, Internet: www.durham.gov.uk/dli_website. Man.: Steve Shannon, Officer: Dennis Hardingham (Exhibitions, Collections)
Military Museum / Fine Arts Museum - 1969/2000
Medals, uniforms, weapons, documents, arts 38826

Monks' Dormitory Museum, The Chapter Library, The College, Durham DH1 3EH - T: (0191) 3862489, 3864266, Fax: 3864267, Internet: www.durhamcattedral.co.uk
Religious Arts Museum 38827

Museum of Archaeology, c/o University of Durham, Old Fulling Mill, The Banks, Durham DH1 3EB - T: (0191) 3341823, Fax: 3747911, E-mail: fulling.mill@durham.ac.uk, Internet: www.dur.ac.uk/fulling.mill. Cur.: Linda Brewster
Archaeological Museum - 1833
Oswald Plicque coll of Samian pottery, Roman stone inscriptions from Hadrian's Wall 38828

Oriental Museum, c/o University of Durham, Elvet Hill, Durham DH1 3TH - T: (0191) 3345694, Fax: 3345694, E-mail: oriental.museum@durham.ac.uk, Internet: www.dur.ac.uk/oriental.museum. Cur.: Linda Brewster
Fine Arts Museum / Decorative Arts Museum - 1960
Chinese ceramics, ancient Egyptian antiquities, Indian paintings and sculptures, Tibetan paintings and decorative art, hist of writing 38829

Duxford

Royal Anglian Regiment Museum, Imperial War Museum, Airfield, Duxford CB2 4QR - T: (01223) 835000, Fax: 837267. Head: George Boss
Military Museum
Military coll of the East Anglian Regiments and the Royal Anglian Regiment, customs, uniforms, operations, weapons 38830

Dymchurch

New Hall, New Hall Close, Dymchurch TN29 0LF - T: (01303) 873897, Fax: 874788
Local Museum
Local artefacts, pottery, muskets, cannon balls, rifles and general miscellany 38831

Dysart

John McDouall Stuart Museum, Rectory Ln, Dysart KY1 2TP - T: (01592) 412860, Fax: 412870, E-mail: kirkcaldy.museum@fite.gov.uk. Cur.: Dallas Machan
Historical Museum
Australian exploration by John McDouall, history of Dysart 38832

Earby

Museum of Yorkshire Dales Lead Mining, Old Grammar School, School Ln, Earby BB8 - T: (01282) 841422, Fax: 841422, E-mail: earby.leadmines@bun.com, Internet: www.ex.ac.uk/~rburt/minhistnet/emrg.html. Dir.: Peter R. Hart
Science&Tech Museum
Mining, miners' tools and equipment, photos 38833

Eardisland

Burton Court, Eardisland HR6 9DN - T: (01544) 388231, E-mail: helenjsimpson@hotmail.com. Dir.: Helen J. Simpson
Local Museum - 1967
Oriental and European costumes dating from the 16th c, natural history, ship and railway models, local history 38834

Earls Barton

Earls Barton Museum of Local Life, 26 The Square, Earls Barton NN6 0HT. Chairman: I.D. Flanagan
Local Museum
Local cottage industries, lace, boot and shoe making 38835

Easdale Island

Easdale Island Folk Museum, Easdale Island PA34 4TB - T: (01852) 300370, Fax: 300370, E-mail: pwithall@aaol.co.uk, Internet: www.slate.co.uk. Dir.: Jean Adams
Folklore Museum - 1980
Industrial and domestic life of the Slate Islands during the 19th c 38836

East Budleigh

Countryside Museum, Bicton Park Botanical Gardens, East Budleigh EX9 7BJ - T: (01395) 568465, Fax: 568374, E-mail: museum@bictongardens.co.uk, Internet: www.bictongardens.co.uk. Dir.: Simon Listen
Local Museum - 1967
Agricultural and estate memorabilia 38837

East Carlton

East Carlton Steel Heritage Centre, Park, East Carlton LE16 8YF - T: (01536) 770977, Fax: 770661. Dir.: Chris Smith
Science&Tech Museum
Living room of 1930's steel worker, model of Corby Steel Works 38838

East Cowes

Osborne House, East Cowes PO32 6JY - T: (01983) 200022, Fax: 297281, 281380. Dir.: Alan Lock
Fine Arts Museum / Decorative Arts Museum - 1954
Queen Victoria's seaside home, build in 1845, mementoes of royal travel abroad, Indian plaster decoration, furniture, 400 works of art, pictures 38839

East Dereham

Bishop Bonner's Cottage Museum, Saint Withburga Ln, East Dereham NR19 1AA - T: (01362) 692736
Local Museum / Folklore Museum
Victorian clothing, pictures, toys, farm implements and local trades 38840

East Grinstead

Town Museum, East Court, College Ln, East Grinstead RH19 3LT - T: (01342) 712087. Cur.: D.A. Hatswell
Historical Museum
Coll of local handicrafts, 19th and 20th-c pottery 38841

East Hendred

Champs Chapel Museum, Chapel Sq, East Hendred OX12 8JN - T: (01235) 833312, Fax: 833312, E-mail: jstevehendred@cs.com, Internet: www.hendred.org
Local Museum
Material of local interest 38842

East Kilbride

Calderglen County Park, Strathaven Rd, East Kilbride G75 0QZ - T: (01355) 236644, Fax: 247618
Historical Museum
Calderglen is made of two former estates of Torrance and Calderwood and opened in 1982 as a country park, Torrance house, which dates back to the 17th c and its courtyard (18th c) are now used as a combined private residence and visitor centre 38843

Hunter House, Maxwellton Rd, Calderwood, East Kilbride G74 3LU - T: (01355) 261261. Dir.: Kirsty Lingstadt
Special Museum
Exhibition portraying the lives of John and William Hunter, 18th c scientists 38844

Museum of Scottish Country Life, National Museums of Scotland, Philipshill Rd, Wester Kittochside, East Kilbride G76 9HR - T: (01355) 224181, Fax: 571290, E-mail: kittochside@nms.ac.uk, Internet: www.nms.ac.uk/countrylife. Man.: Duncan Dornan
Agriculture Museum - 2001
History of farming and rural life throughout Scotland 38845

East Linton

Preston Mill and Phantassie Doocot, East Linton - T: (01620) 860426
Science&Tech Museum 38846

East Molesey

Embroiderers' Guild Museum Collection, Apt 41, Hampton Court Palace, East Molesey KT8 9AU - T: (020) 89431229, Fax: 89779882, E-mail: administrator@embroiderersguild.com, Internet: www.embroiderersguild.com. Dir.: Michael Spender, Cur.: Lynn Szygenda
Special Museum 38847

Hampton Court Palace, East Molesey KT8 9AU - T: (020) 87819500, Fax: 87819509, Internet: www.hrp.org.uk
Fine Arts Museum - 1514
Royal palace, original furnishings, Italian, Flemish, German, Dutch, Spanish paintings 38848

Mounted Branch Museum, Imber Court, East Molesey KT8 0BY - T: (020) 82475480
Special Museum
Uniforms and equipment, saddles, harness, paintings and photographs 38849

East Tilbury

Thameside Aviation Museum, Coalhouse Fort, East Tilbury, Essex - T: (01277) 655170, Fax: (0113) 2470219
Science&Tech Museum
Aviation archaeology 38850

East Winterslow

New Art Centre, Roche Court, Sculpture Park and Gallery, East Winterslow SP5 1BG - T: (01980) 862244, Fax: 862447, E-mail: nac@globalnet.co.uk, Internet: www.sculpture.uk.com. Dir.: Madeleine Bessborough
Fine Arts Museum 38851

Eastbourne

Eastbourne Heritage Centre, 2 Carlisle Rd, Eastbourne BN21 4JJ - T: (01323) 411189, 721825. Chm.: Owen Boydell
Local Museum 38852

Museum of Shops, 20 Cornfield Tce, Eastbourne BN21 4NS - T: (01323) 737143. Owner: Graham Upton, Owner: Jan Upton
Special Museum
Victorian-style shops 38853

Museum of the Royal National Lifeboat Institution, King Edward Parade, Eastbourne BN21 4BY - T: (01323) 730717. Dir.: I.M. Shearer
Special Museum - 1937
Hist of Eastbourne lifeboats from 1853 to present, lifeboat models, many photogr 38854

Queen's Royal Irish Hussars Museum, c/o Sussex Combined Services Museum, Redoubt Fortress, Royal Parade, Eastbourne BN22 7AQ - T: (01323) 410300, Fax: 732240, E-mail: eastbourne_museums@breathmail.net. Cur.: Richard Callaghan
Military Museum
Medals, uniforms, prints and memorabilia 38855

Royal Sussex Regiment Museum, Redoubt Fortress, Royal Parade, Eastbourne BN21 4BP - T: (01323) 410300, Fax: 732240, E-mail: eastbourne_museums@breathemail.net. Cur.: Richard Callaghan
Military Museum
Uniforms, medals, weapons, equipment and campaign medals illustrate the history of the former Royal Sussex Regiment from 1701 to 1966, photographs, books and documentary material 38856

Sussex Combined Services Museum, Redoubt Fortress, Royal Parade, Eastbourne BN22 7AQ - T: (01323) 410300, Fax: 732240, E-mail: eastbourne_museums@breathemail.net. Cur.: Richard Callaghan
Military Museum
Uniforms, medals and other military artefacts 38857

Towner Art Gallery and Local Museum, High St, Old Town, Eastbourne BN20 8BB - T: (01323) 417961, 411688, Fax: 648182, E-mail: townergallery@eastbourne.gov.uk, Internet: www.eastbourne.gov.uk. Cur.: Matthew Rowe
Fine Arts Museum / Historical Museum - 1923
History of Eastbourne from prehistory onwords to the original station clock and an original Victorian kitchen British art of mainly 19th and 20th cc, coll of contemporary art 38858

Wishtower Puppet Museum, King Edward's Parade, Eastbourne BN21 4BY - T: (01323) 410400, Fax: 411620. Dir.: Mel Myland, Conny Myland
Special Museum - 1996
Victorian puppets of England, old TV and film puppets, shadow puppets of Asia, Judy & Punch 38859

Eastleigh

Eastleigh Museum, The Citadel, 25 High St, Eastleigh SO50 5LF - T: (023) 80643026, Fax: 80653582, E-mail: musmst@hants.gov.uk, Internet: www.hants.gov.uk/museum/eastlmus/. Cur.: Alan Johnston
Local Museum
Local hist, railway, art gallery 38860

Royal Observer Corps Museum, 8 Roselands Close, Fair Oak, Eastleigh SO50 8GN - T: (02380) 693823, E-mail: xrocmunc@hants.gov.uk. Cur.: N.A. Cullingford
Military Museum 38861

Easton

Easton Farm Park, Easton IP13 0EQ - T: (01728) 746475, Fax: 747861, E-mail: easton@eastonfarmpark.co.uk, Internet: www.eastonfarmpark.co.uk. Dir.: John Kerr
Agriculture Museum
Farm buildings, dairy, farm machinery 38862

Easton-on-the-Hill

Priest's House, 40 West St, Easton-on-the-Hill PE9 3LS. Chm.: Paul Way
Local Museum
Local artefacts 38863

Eastwood

D.H. Lawrence Birthplace Museum, 8a Victoria St, Eastwood NG16 3AN - T: (01773) 717353, Fax: 713509, E-mail: durban@broxbcl.demon.co.uk, Internet: www.broxtowe.gov.uk. Dir.: Sally Rose
Special Museum - 1975
Three original watercolours by D.H. Lawrence, original items of furniture owners by the Lawrence family, birthplace of D.H. Lawrence 38864

D.H. Lawrence Heritage Centre, Durban House, Mansfield Rd, Eastwood NG16 3DZ - T: (01773) 717353, Fax: 713509, E-mail: durban@broxbcl.demon.co.uk, Internet: www.broxtowe.gov.uk. Dir.: Sally Rose
Historical Museum
Local coal owners, D.H. Lawrence 38865

Ecclefechan

Thomas Carlyle's Birthplace, The Arches House, High St, Ecclefechan DG11 3DG - T: (01576) 300666. Head: Fiona Auchterlonie
Special Museum
Birthplace of writer Thomas Carlyle, coll of his belongings and copy manuscript letters, local artisan dwelling, 38866

Edenbridge

Eden Valley Museum, Church House, High St, Edenbridge TN8 5AR - T: (01732) 868102, E-mail: curator@evmt.org.uk, Internet: www.evmt.org.uk. Cur.: Jane Higgs
Local Museum
Changing fashions, social structures, economic history of the Eden Valley, coll photographs, paintings and engravings 38867

Hever Castle and Gardens, Hever, Edenbridge TN8 7NG - T: (01732) 865224, Fax: 866796, E-mail: mail@hevercastle.co.uk, Internet: www.hevercastle.co.uk. Dir.: Robert Pullin
Decorative Arts Museum
Furniture, paintings, tapestries, 16th c portraits 38868

Kent and Sharpshooters Yeomanry Museum, Hever Castle, Edenbridge TN8 7DB - T: (01732) 865224, E-mail: ksymuseum@aol.com, Internet: www.ksymuseum.org.uk. Cur.: B. Mollo
Military Museum 38869

Edinburgh

Braidwood and Rushbrook Museum, Fire Stn, McDonald Rd, Edinburgh EH7 4NN - T: (0131) 2282401, Fax: 2298359, E-mail: csg@lothian.fire-uk.org, Internet: www.lothian.fire-uk.org. Dir.: I. McMurtie
Historical Museum
Engines, manual, horse drawn, steam and motorised pumps from 1806, fire related items since 1426 38870

Brass Rubbing Centre, Trinity Apse, Chalmers Close, High St, Edinburgh - T: (0131) 5564664, Fax: 5583103, Internet: www.cac.org.uk
Special Museum 38871

Camera Obscura, Outlook Tower, Castlehill, Edinburgh EH1 2LZ - T: (0131) 2263709, Fax: 2254239. Dir.: Andrew Johnson
Special Museum 38872

City Art Centre, 2 Market St, Edinburgh EH1 1DE - T: (0131) 5293993, Fax: 5293977, E-mail: enquiries@city-art-centre.demon.co.uk, Internet: www.cac.org.uk. Sc. Staff: Ian O'Riordan
Public Gallery - 1980
19th and 20th c artists, mostly Scottish 38873

Cockburn Museum, c/o Dept of Geology & Geophysics, University of Edinburgh, King's Bldg, West Mains Rd, Edinburgh EH9 3JF - T: (0131) 6508527, Fax: 6683184, E-mail: peder.aspen@glg.ac.uk. Cur.: Pedeŕ Aspen
Natural History Museum / University Museum
Rocks, fossils and minerals 38874

The Danish Cultural Institute, 3 Doune Terrace, Edinburgh EH3 6DY - T: (0131) 2257189, Fax: 2206162, E-mail: dci@dancult.demon.co.uk, Internet: www.dancult.demon.co.uk. Dir.: Kim Caspersen
Public Gallery
Danish paintings, prints, photography and craft 38875

Dean Gallery, 73 Belford Rd, Edinburgh EH4 3DS - T: (0131) 6246200, Fax: 3433250, E-mail: enquiries@nationalgalleries.org, Internet: www.nationalgalleries.org. Cur.: Richard Calvocoressi
Fine Arts Museum 38876

Edinburgh Printmakers Workshop and Gallery, Wash-House, 23 Union St, Edinburgh EH1 3LR - T: (0131) 5572479, Fax: 5588418, E-mail: printmakers@ednet.co.uk, Internet: www.edinburgh-printmakers.co.uk. Dir.: David Watt
Public Gallery
Lithography, screenprinting, relief, etching fine art prints 38877

Edinburgh Scout Museum, 7 Valleyfield St, Edinburgh EH3 9LP - T: (0131) 2293756, Fax: 2219905
Special Museum
History of scout mouvement, memorabilia of movement in Edinburgh and worldwide 38878

Edinburgh University Anatomy Museum, c/o Department of Anatomy, University Medical School, Teviot Pl, Edinburgh EH8 9AG
Natural History Museum 38879

Edinburgh University Collection of Historic Musical Instruments, Reid Concert Hall, Bristo Sq, Edinburgh EH8 9AG - T: (0131) 6502422, Fax: 6502425, E-mail: euchmi@ed.ac.uk, Internet: www.music.ed.ac.uk/euchmi. Dir./Cur.: Dr. Arnold Myers, Ass. Cur.: Dr. Raymond Parks
Music Museum / University Museum
Display of over 1,000 musical instruments showing 400 years of hist of folk and domestic music, bands and orchestras - Sound Laboratory 38880

Edinburgh University Natural History Collections, c/o ICAPB, Ashworth Laboratories, King' Bldgs, West Mains Rd, Edinburgh EH9 3JT - T: (0131) 6501000, Fax: 6506564, E-mail: pat.preston@ed.ac.uk, Internet: www.nhc.ed.ac.uk. Cur.: Dr. B.E. Matthews, Dr. P.M. Preston
Natural History Museum 38881

Fruitmarket Gallery, 45 Market St, Edinburgh EH1 1DF - T: (0131) 2252383, Fax: 2203130, E-mail: info@fruitmarket.co.uk, Internet: www.fruitmarket.co.uk. Dir.: Fiona Bradley
Public Gallery
Contemporary art 38882

Gallery of the Royal Scottish Academy, The Mound, Princes St, Edinburgh EH2 2EL - T: (0131) 2256671, Fax: 2252349. Dir.: An McKenzie Smith
Fine Arts Museum - 1826
Scottish painting & sculpture of the 19th & 20th c 38883

The Georgian House, 7 Charlotte Sq, Edinburgh EH2 4DR - T: (0131) 2252160, 2263318, Fax: 2263318, E-mail: thegeorgianhouse@nts.org.uk, Internet: www.nts.org.uk. Man.: Dr. Shéonagh Martin
Decorative Arts Museum - 1975
Georgian house, furniture, life in Edinburgh (late 18th/ early 19th c) 38884

The Grand Lodge of Scotland Museum, 96 George St, Edinburgh EH2 3DH - T: (0131) 2255304, Fax: 2253953, E-mail: grandsecretary@sol.co.uk, Internet: www.grandlodgescotland.com. Cur.: Robert L.D. Cooper
Special Museum
Ceramics, glassware, artefacts relating to Freemasonry, manuscripts - library 38885

Granton Centre, National Museums of Scotland, 242 W Granton Rd, Edinburgh EH5 1JA - T: (0131) 2474470, Fax: 5514106, E-mail: info@nms.ac.uk, Internet: www.nms.ac.uk. Dir.: Dr. Gordon Rintoul
Local Museum 38886

Heriot-Watt University Museum and Archive, Mary Burton Centre, Riccarton, Edinburgh EH14 4AS - T: (0131) 4513218, Fax: 4513164, Internet: www.hw.ac.uk/archive. Dir.: Ann Jones
University Museum / Historical Museum / Fine Arts Museum
History of the University, scientific and tachnical education in Scotland, art and artefacts, artists of the Edinburgh School 38887

Historic Scotland, Hist. Scotland Conservation Centre, 3 Stenhouse Mill Ln, Edinburgh EH11 3LR - T: (0131) 4435635, Fax: 4558260, E-mail: robert.wilmot@scotland.gsi.gov.uk, Internet: www.historic-scotland.gov.uk. Man.: Robert Wilmot, Cons.: Michael Pearce
Historical Museum 38888

Huntly House Museum, 142 Canongate, Edinburgh EH8 8DD - T: (0131) 5294143, Fax: 5573346, Internet: www.cac.org.uk
Local Museum / Decorative Arts Museum - 1932
Local history, Scottish pottery, local glass and silver, paintings, prints 38889

John Knox's House, 45 High St, Edinburgh EH1 1SR - T: (0131) 5569579, Fax: 5575224. Dir.: Dr. Donald Smith
Special Museum - 1849
Memorabilia on John Knox, memorabilia on James Mossman, goldsmith to Mary, Queen of Scots, memorabilia on Mary, information on 16th c Edinburgh 38890

Lauriston Castle, 2a Cramond Rd South, Edinburgh EH4 5QD - T: (0131) 3362060, Fax: 3127165, Internet: www.cac.org.uk. Dir.: David Scarratt
Decorative Arts Museum - 1926
"Blue John" Derbyshire Spar, wool mosaics, castle with period furnishings, tapestries, decorative arts 38891

Museum of Childhood, 42 High St, Royal Mile, Edinburgh EH1 1TG - T: (0131) 5294142, Fax: 5583103, E-mail: admin@musenmotchildhood.fsnet.co.uk, Internet: www.cac.org.uk. Dir.: John Heyes
Special Museum - 1955
Social hist of childhood, hobbies, education, toys, dolls, games 38892

Museum of Fire, c/o Lothian and Borders Fire Brigade Headquarters, Lauriston Pl, Edinburgh EH3 9DE - T: (0131) 2282401, Fax: 2298359, E-mail: csg@lothian.fire-uk.org, Internet: www.lothian.fire-uk.org. Dir.: I. McMurtrie
Science&Tech Museum - 1966
Fire engines and fire-fighting equipment dating from the early 19th c to the present day, coll of badges, medals, photographs and records relating to fire-fighting 38893

Museum of Lighting, 59 Saint Stephen St, Edinburgh EH3 5AG - T: (0131) 5564503. Cur.: W.M. Purves
Science&Tech Museum - 1972
All types of lighting equipment, hand-operated machines from the 19th-c lampmakers, Bocock - archive 38894

Museum of Scotland, National Museums of Scotland, Chambers St, Edinburgh EH1 1JF - T: (0131) 2474219, 2474422, Fax: 2204819, E-mail: info@nms.ac.uk, Internet: www.nms.ac.uk. Dir.: Dr. Gordon Rintoul
Historical Museum 38895

Museum of the Royal College of Surgeons of Edinburgh, 18 Nicholson St, Edinburgh EH8 9DW - T: (0131) 5271649, Fax: 5576406, E-mail: museum@rcsed.ac.uk, Internet: www.rcsed.ac.uk. Pres.: Prof. J. Temple
Special Museum - 1699
Surgery, pathology and medicine, dentistry 38896

Museum on the Mound, HBOS, The Mound, Edinburgh EH1 1YZ - T: (0131) 5291288, Fax: 5291307, E-mail: archives@hbosplc.com, Internet: www.hbosplc.com. Head: Helen Redmond-Cooper
Special Museum 38897

National Gallery of Scotland, The Mound, Edinburgh EH2 2EL - T: (0131) 6246200, Fax: 2200917, E-mail: enquiries@nationalgalleries.org, Internet: www.nationalgalleries.org. Gen. Dir.: Timothy Clifford, Sc. Staff: Michael Clarke, Christopher Baker, Helen Smailes, Aidan Weston-Lewis, Emilie Gordenker, Valerie Hunter, Libr.: Penelope Carter
Fine Arts Museum - 1850

Paintings, drawings and prints by the greatest artists from the Renaissance to Post-Impressionism, incl Velazquez, El Greco, Rembrandt, Vermeer, Turner, Constable, Monet and Van Gogh, Botticelli, Titian, Rubens, Van Dyck, Goya, Pousssin, Raphael 38898

National Museums of Scotland, Chambers St, Edinburgh EH1 1JF - T: (0131) 2257534, Fax: 2204819, E-mail: info@nms.ac.uk, Internet: www.nms.ac.uk. Dir.: Dr. Gordon Rintoul 1781 38899

National War Museum of Scotland, National Museums of Scotland, The Castle, Edinburgh EH1 2NG - T: (0131) 2257534, Fax: 2253848, Internet: www.nms.ac.uk. Cur.: A.L. Carswell
Military Museum - 1930
Military history of Scotland and the experiance of war and military service, uniforms, weapons, paintings, sculpture, ptints 38900

Nelson Monument, Calton Hill, Edinburgh EH7 5AA, mail addr: CAC, 2 Market St, Edinburgh EH1 1DE - T: (0131) 5562716, Fax: 2205057, Internet: www.cac.org.uk. Cust.: Karen Bootman
Historical Museum
Artefacts relating to Admiral Lord Nelson 38901

Newhaven Heritage Museum, 24 Pier Pl, Edinburgh EH6 4LP - T: (0131) 5514165, Fax: 5573346, Internet: www.cac.org.uk. Man.: Denise Brace
Historical Museum - 1994 38902

Palace of Holyroodhouse, Royal Collection, The Royal Mile, Edinburgh EH8 8DX, mail addr: Stable Yard House, Saint James's Palace, London SW1A 1JR - T: (0131) 5565100, Fax: 5575256, E-mail: holyroodhouse@royalcollection.org.uk, Internet: www.royal.gov.uk
Fine Arts Museum
Royal residence 38903

People's Story Museum, 163 Canongate, Royal Mile, Edinburgh EH8 8BN - T: (0131) 5294057, Fax: 5563439, E-mail: helen.peoplestory@virgin.net, Internet: www.cac.org.uk. Dir.: Helen Clark
Historical Museum - 1989
Social history material representing the life and work of Edinburgh's people over the past 200 years, coll of Trade Union banners, oral tape recordings, photos 38904

Pharmaceutical Society Late Victorian Pharmacy, 36 York Pl, Edinburgh EH1 3HU - T: (0131) 5564386, Fax: 5588850, E-mail: info@rpsis.com
Historical Museum 38905

Portfolio Gallery (closed) 38906

The Queen's Gallery, Royal Collection, Palace of Holyroodhouse, The Royal Mile, Edinburgh EH8 8DX, mail addr: Stable Yard House, Saint James's Palace, London SW1A 1JR - T: (0131) 5565100, Fax: 5575256, E-mail: holyroodhouse@royalcollection.org.uk, Internet: www.royal.gov.uk
Fine Arts Museum 38907

Regimental Museum of the Royal Scots Dragoon Guards, The Castle, Edinburgh EH1 2YT - T: (0131) 2204387, Internet: www.scotsdg.com
Military Museum 38908

Royal Incorporation of Architects in Scotland Gallery, 15 Rutland Sq, Edinburgh EH1 2BE - T: (0131) 2297545, Fax: 2282188, E-mail: acarolan@rias.org.uk, Internet: www.rias.org.uk. Dir.: Sebastian Tombs
Public Gallery
Architecture, design, visual arts 38909

Royal Museum, National Museums of Scotland, Chambers St, Edinburgh EH1 1JF - T: (0131) 2474219, Fax: 2204819, E-mail: info@nms.ac.uk, Internet: www.nms.ac.uk. Dir.: Dr. Gordon Rintoul
Archaeological Museum / Natural History Museum / Ethnology Museum / Science&Tech Museum - 1855
Archaeology, natural history, geology, technology, Oriental arts, ethnography of Plains Indians, Eastern Island and Maori cultures, Baule figures, minerals , fossils, mining and metallurgy, power industries, shipping, aeronautics, radiation, primitive arts, British birds - library 38910

Royal Scots Regimental Museum, Castle, Edinburgh EH1 2YT - T: (0131) 3105014, Fax: 3105019, E-mail: rhqroyalscots@edinburghcastle.fsnet.co.uk, Internet: www.theroyalscots.co.uk. Dir.: R.P. Mason, Sc. Staff: D. Murphy
Military Museum - 1951
History, uniforms, medals, weapons, trophies of the regiment, militaria 38911

Royal Scottish Academy Collections, Dean Gallery, 73 Belford Rd, Edinburgh EH4 3DS - T: (0131) 6246277, Fax: 2206016, E-mail: info@royalscottishacademy.org, Internet: www.royalscottishacademy.org. Cur.: Joanna Soden
Fine Arts Museum
Visual arts, fine art - library and archives 38912

Russell Collection of Early Keyboard Instruments, University of Edinburgh, Saint Cecilia's Hall, Niddry St, Cowgate, Edinburgh EH1 1LJ - T: (0131) 6502805, Fax: 6502812, E-mail: russell.collection@music.ed.ac.uk, Internet: www.music.ed.ac.uk/russell. Dir.: Dr. G.G. O'Brien
Music Museum - 1968
Harpsichords, virginals, spinets, clavichords, chamber organs and early pianos 38913

Scotch Whisky Heritage Centre, 354 Castlehill, The Royal Mile, Edinburgh EH1 2NE - T: (0131) 2200441, Fax: 2206288, E-mail: enquiries@whisky-heritage.co.uk, Internet: www.whisky-heritage.co.uk
Special Museum 38914

Scott Monument, Princes St, Edinburgh EH2 2EJ - T: (0131) 5294068, Fax: 2205057, Internet: www.cac.org.uk. Man.: Paul McAuley
Fine Arts Museum
National monument to Sir Walter Scott 38915

Scottish National Gallery of Modern Art Gallery, Belford Rd, Edinburgh EH4 3DR - T: (0131) 6246200, Fax: 3432802, 3433250, E-mail: enquiries@nationalgalleries.org, Internet: www.nationalgalleries.org. Gen. Dir.: Timothy Clifford, Dir.: Richard Calvocoressi, Cur.: Philip Long, Fiona Pearson (Paolozzi Collection), Alice Dewey, Patrick Elliott, Keith Hartley, Nicole Giles, Ann Simpson
Public Gallery / Fine Arts Museum - 1960
20th c paintings, sculpture and graphic art incl works by Vuillard, Matisse, Kirchner, Picasso, Magritte, Miró, Dali and Ernst, coll of 20th c Scottish art - sculpture garden, conservation 38916

Scottish National Portrait Gallery, 1 Queen St, Edinburgh EH2 1JD - T: (0131) 6246200, Fax: 5583691, E-mail: pginfo@nationalgalleries.org, Internet: www.nationalgalleries.org. Dir.: James Holloway, Asst. Keeper: Nicola Kalinsky, Sara Stevensen, Stephen Lloyd, Julie Lawson, Duncan Forbes
Fine Arts Museum - 1882
Portraits in various media illustrating the hist of Scotland from the 16th c up to the present day, portraits of Scots but not all by Scots but by van Dyck, Gainsborough, Copley, Thorvaldsen, Rodin and Kokoschka 38917

Scottish Rugby Union Museum, Murrayfield Stadium, Edinburgh EH12 5PJ - T: (0131) 3465000, Fax: 3465001, E-mail: library@sru.org.uk, Internet: www.sru.org.uk. Dir.: William S. Watson
Special Museum
History and development of the game and the Scottish Rugby Union, jerseys, caps, balls, trophies, photos 38918

Stills Gallery, 23 Cockburn St, Edinburgh - T: (0131) 6226200, Fax: 6226201, E-mail: info@stills.org, Internet: www.stills.org. Dir.: Kate Tregaskis
Public Gallery 38919

Talbot Rice Gallery, c/o University of Edinburgh, Old College, South Bridge, Edinburgh EH8 9YL - T: (0131) 6502211, Fax: 6502213, E-mail: info.talbotrice@ed.ac.uk, Internet: www.trg.ed.ac.uk. Dir.: Prof. Duncan Macmillan
Fine Arts Museum / University Museum / Public Gallery
Coll of bronzes and paintings, esp Dutch and Italian contemporary Scottish art 38920

The Writers' Museum, Lady Stair's House, Lady Stair's Close, Lawnmarket, Edinburgh EH1 2PA - T: (0131) 5294901, Fax: 2205057, E-mail: enquiries@writersmuseum.demon.co.uk, Internet: www.cac.org.uk. Dir.: Herbert Coutts
Special Museum - 1907
Memorabilia of writers Robert Burns, Sir Walter Scott, Robert Louis Stevenson 38921

Egham

Egham Museum, Literary Institute, High St, Egham TW20 9EW - T: (01344) 843047. Cur.: John Mills
Historical Museum / Archaeological Museum
Archaeology and history of Egham, Thorpe and Virginia Water, displays relating to Magna Carta, which was sealed nearby at Runnymede 38922

Royal Holloway College Picture Gallery, Egham Hill, Egham - T: (01784) 34455, Fax: 473285, E-mail: m.cowling@rhul.ac.uk, Internet: www.rhul.ac.uk. Cur.: Dr. Mary Cowling
Fine Arts Museum / University Museum - 1887
Paintings by Frith, Fildes, Maclise, Landseer, Millais and others 38923

Egremont

Florence Mine Heritage Centre, Egremont CA22 2NR - T: (01946) 820683, Fax: 820683, E-mail: info@florencmine.com, Internet: www.florencmine.com. Cur.: J. Askew
Science&Tech Museum
Mining artefacts and geological displays 38924

Elgin

Elgin Museum, 1 High St, Moray, Elgin IV30 1EQ - T: (01343) 543675, Fax: 543675, E-mail: curator@elginmuseum.org.uk, Internet: www.elginmuseum.org.uk. Pres.: Richard Mabon, Cur.: Susan Bennett
Archaeological Museum - 1843
Local antiquities, Triassic and Permian reptile fossils, Devonian fish fossils, archaeology - scientific archive 38925

Ellesmere Port

Boat Museum, South Pier Rd, Ellesmere Port CH65 4FW - T: (0151) 3555017, Fax: 3554079, E-mail: bookings@boatmuseum.freeserve.co.uk. Dir.: Tracey McNaboe
Science&Tech Museum
60 canal and river craft, icebreakers, traditional boat-building techniques in progress, story of canal building, life of dock workers, working engines, canal hist 38926

Hooton Park Exhibition Centre, Hangars, West Rd, Hooton Park Airfield, Ellesmere Port CH65 1BQ - T: (0151) 3502598, Fax: 3502598. Dir.: D. Beckett, R. Frost, A. Terry, J. Graham
Science&Tech Museum
Classic vehicles (military and civil), aeronautical items, aircraft 38927

Ellisland

Ellisland Farm, Hollywood Rd, Ellisland DG2 0RP - T: (0138774) 426
Special Museum
Exhibits connected with the poet Robert Burns and his family, farming life 38928

Ellon

Museum of Farming Life, Pitmedden Garden, Ellon AB41 7PD - T: (01651) 842352, Fax: 843188, E-mail: sburgess@nts.org.uk, Internet: nts.org.uk/garden. Dir.: Susan M. Burgess
Agriculture Museum - 1982
Coll of farm tools and domestic equipment, a furnished farmhouse and bothy, restored outbuildings, hist of Scottish farming 38929

Elsham

Clocktower Museum, Elsham Hall, Elsham DN20 0QZ - T: (01652) 688698, Fax: 688240, Internet: www.brigg.com/elsham.htm
Fine Arts Museum / Decorative Arts Museum
Resident artists and working craft 38930

Elvaston

Elvaston Castle Working Estate Museum (closed) 38931

Elvington

Yorkshire Air Museum, Halifax Way, Elvington YO41 4AU - T: (01904) 608595, Fax: 608246, E-mail: museum@yorksairmuseum.co.uk, Internet: www.yorkshireairmuseum.co.uk. Dir.: Ian Reed
Science&Tech Museum / Military Museum
Coll of WWII memorabilia, historical airframes and replica's (early days of aviation to modern military jets) - library 38932

Ely

Ely Museum, The Old Gaol, Market St, Ely CB7 4LS - T: (01353) 666655. Cur.: Zara Matthews
Local Museum
Social and natural history of the Isle of Ely, local archeology 38933

Oliver Cromwell's House, 29 Saint Mary's St, Ely CB7 4HF - T: (01353) 662062, Fax: 668518, E-mail: tic@eastcambs.co.uk, Internet: www.elyeastcambs.co.uk
Special Museum
Rooms incl kitchen, palour, Civil War exhibition, Cromwell's study and a haunted room, fen drainage 38934

Stained Glass Museum, South Triforium, Ely Cathedral, Ely CB7 4DN - T: (01353) 660347, Fax: 665025, E-mail: curator@stainedglassmuseum.com, Internet: www.stainedglassmuseum.com. Dir.: Viscount Churchill, Cur.: Susan Mathews
Decorative Arts Museum / Special Museum - 1972
100 windows from medieval to modern times, a photographic display of the styles and techniques of medieval glass, and models of a modern stained glass workshop, 19th-c glass, with examples of work from all the leading studios and designers 38935

Emsworth

Emsworth Museum, 10b North St, Emsworth PO10 7DD - T: (01243) 378091
Local Museum
Local history, sea-faring families, oyster fishermen and coastal trade in grain and coal, P.G. Woodhouse, Sir Peter Blake memorabilia 38936

Enfield

Forty Hall Museum, Forty Hill, Enfield EN2 9HA - T: (020) 83638196, Fax: 83639098. Man.: Nick Lane
Decorative Arts Museum - 1955
Ceramics, history childhood, Middlesex maps, furniture, paintings, teaching 38937

Enniskillen

Castle Coole, Enniskillen, Co. Fermanagh - T: (01365) 322690
Historical Museum
Furniture and textiles 38938

Fermanagh County Museum at Enniskillen Castle, Castle Barracks, Enniskillen BT74 7HL - T: (028) 66325000, Fax: 66327342, E-mail: castle@fermanagh.gov.uk, Internet: www.enniskillencastle.co.uk. Dir.: Helen Lanigan Wood
Local Museum
Regional history, archaeology, fine and applied art 38939

Florence Court House, Florence Court, Enniskillen BT92 1DB - T: (028) 66348249, 66348788, Fax: 66348873, E-mail: florencecourt@ntrust.org.uk, Internet: www.ntni.org.uk
Local Museum 38940

Royal Inniskilling Fusiliers Regimental Museum, The Castle, Enniskillen BT74 7HL - T: (028) 66323142, Fax: 66320359, E-mail: museum@inniskilling.com, Internet: www.inniskilling.com. Dir.: J.M. Dunlop
Military Museum - 1931
Hist of the Royal Inniskilling Fusiliers (1689-1968) and associated Fermanagh, Tyrone and Donegal militia regiments, displays on 6th Inniskilling Dragoons (cavalry regiment) - library 38941

Shellin Antiques and Irish Lace Museum, Bellanaleck, Enniskillen, Co. Fermanagh - T: (01365) 348052, E-mail: info@irishlacemuseum.com, Internet: www.irishlacemuseum.com. Dir.: Rosemary Cathcart
Special Museum
Coll of Irish Lace 38942

Epping

North Weald Airfield Museum and Memorial, Astra House, Hurricane Way, North Weald, Epping CM16 6AA - T: (01922) 714162, Fax: 713193, E-mail: 106051.3271@compuserve.com, Internet: www.fly.to/northweald
Science&Tech Museum - 1989
Historic and vintage flying aircraft in a 1940 period setting 38943

Epsom

College Museum, Epsom College, Epsom KT17 4QJ - T: (01372) 728862. Sc. Staff: Dr. D.J. Young (owls)
University Museum / Natural History Museum 38944

Epworth

Epworth Old Rectory, 1 Rectory St, Epworth DN9 1HX - T: (01427) 872268, E-mail: epworth@oldrectory63.freeserve.co.uk, Internet: www.epworthrectory.freeserve.co.uk. Cur.: Andrew Milson
Historical Museum
Portraits, Prints, Furniture, Wesley family items - library 38945

Erith

Erith Museum, Library, Walnut Tree Rd, Erith DA8 1RS - T: (01322) 336582
Local Museum - 1934
History of the town of Erith, archaeology and social history of Erith, with a reproduction of an Edwardian kitchen and a special section on local industries 38946

Errol

Megginch Castle, Errol PH1 - T: (01821) 2222
Historical Museum 38947

Etchingham

Bateman's, Kipling's House, Burwash, Etchingham TN19 7DS - T: (01435) 882302, Fax: 882811, E-mail: kbaxxx@smtp.ntrust.org.uk. Man.: Jan Wallwork-Wright
Local Museum
Home of the Rudyard Kipling from 1902-36: Kipling's rooms and study are left as they were during his lifetime, the coll incl his Rolls-Royce 38948

Haremere Hall, Etchingham TN19 7QJ - T: (01580) 81145, Internet: members.tripod.com/~harmer1/reunion78c.html
Decorative Arts Museum - 1978 38949

Eton

Eton College Natural History Museum, Eton College, Eton SL4 6EW - T: (01753) 671288, Fax: 671159, E-mail: d.smith@etoncollege.org.uk, Internet: www.etoncollege.com. Cur.: Dr. David A.S. Smith, Sc. Staff: Derek Sainsbury
Natural History Museum / University Museum - 1875
Fossils, insects, molluscs, birds, mammals, fishes, plants - Herbarium 38950

Museum of Eton Life, c/o Eton College, Eton SL4 6DB - T: (01753) 671177, Fax: 671265. Cur.: P. Hatfield
Historical Museum - 1985
Daily life and duties, food and living conditions, punishments, uniforms, and school books and equipment, history of rowing at the College and the Officer Training Corps 38951

Myers Museum, Brewhouse Gallery, Eton College, Eton SL4 6DW - T: (01753) 801538, Fax: 801538, E-mail: n.reeves@etoncollege.org.uk. Cur.: Dr. Nicholas Reeves (Egyptian and Classical Art)
Archaeological Museum
Coll of Egyptian archaeology by Major W.J. Myers (1883-1899), objects dating from Predynastic times to the Coptic period, faience, wooden models from tombs and a preserved panel portrait from a mummy of the 2nd c A.D. 38952

Evesham

Almonry Heritage Centre, Abbey Gate, Evesham WR11 4BG - T: (01386) 446944, Fax: 442348, E-mail: tic@almonry.ndo.co.uk, Internet: www.evesham.uk.com
Local Museum / Archaeological Museum
History of the Vale of Evesham from prehistoric times to the present day, Romano-British, Anglo-Saxon and medieval items, together with material illustrating the history of the monastery, coll of agricultural implements 38953

Ewell

Bourne Hall Museum, Spring St, Ewell KT17 1UF - T: (020) 83941734, Fax: 87867265, E-mail: j.harte@bournehall.free-online.co.uk, Internet: www.epsom.townpage.co.uk. Dir.: Jeremy Harte
Decorative Arts Museum / Special Museum - 1969
Coll of some of the earliest wallpapers ever made (c 1690) and the Ann Hull Grundy coll of costume jewellery, prehistoric material found in the vicinity, Victorian and more modern costumes and accessories, and early cameras and radio sets, Roman archaeology, tools - library 38954

Exeter

Devon and Cornwall Constabulary Museum, Devon & Cornwall Constabulary Headquarters, Exeter EX2 7HQ - T: (01392) 203025, Fax: 426496
Special Museum
The coll comprises of documents and artefacts relating to the hist of policing throughout Devon & Cornwall, incl photographs, uniforms, equipment and memorabilia 38955

Guildhall, High St, Exeter - T: (01392) 277888, 665500, Fax: 201329, E-mail: guildhall@exeter.gov.uk, Internet: www.exeter.gov.uk
Local Museum 38956

Royal Albert Memorial Museum and Art Gallery, Queen St, Exeter EX4 3RX - T: (01392) 665858, Fax: 421252, E-mail: ramm@exeter.gov.uk, Internet: www.exeter.gov.uk/residents/arts/museums. Dir.: Camilla Hampshire, Sc. Staff: John Madin (Art), John Allan (Antiquities), David Bolton (Natural History), Len Pole (Ethnography)
Fine Arts Museum / Natural History Museum / Ethnology Museum / Historical Museum / Archaeological Museum - 1865
Natural hist, butterflies, birds, local geology, fine art, local artists, applied arts, Exeter silver, Devon pottery, Devon lace, ethnography, Polynesian, N. American Indian material, Yoruba sculptures, 18th and early 19th c Eskimo and N.W. Coast material, Benin head and Staff mount, 18th c Tahitian morning dress, flute glass 'Exeter flute' c 1660, harpsichord by Vincentius Sodi 38957

Saint Nicholas Priory, The Mint, off Fore St, Exeter EX4 3RX - T: (01392) 665858, Fax: 421252
Religious Arts Museum 38958

Underground Passages, High St, Exeter EX1 1JJ - T: (01392) 265887, Fax: 265695, E-mail: upassages@exeter.gov.uk, Internet: www.exeter.gov.uk/tourism
Science&Tech Museum
Introductory exhibition and video, scheduled ancient monument, vaulted medieval passages build in the 14th c unterground tour shows how water was brought into the city 38959

Exmouth

Exmouth Museum, Sheppards Row, Exeter Rd, Exmouth EX8 1PW. Cur.: Tom Haynes
Local Museum 38960

World of Country Life, Sandy Bay, Exmouth EX8 5BU - T: (01395) 274533, Fax: 273457, E-mail: worldofcountrylife@hotmail.com, Internet: www.worldofcountrylife.co.uk
Folklore Museum / Science&Tech Museum
Vintage cars, classic motorbikes and steam traction engines, Fire engines, moving farm machinery, gypsy caravan 38961

Eyam

Eyam Museum, Hawkhill Rd, Eyam S32 5QP - T: (01433) 631371, Fax: 631371, Internet: www.eyam.org.uk. Chm.: P. Horsnall
Local Museum - 1994
Village heroism when in 1665 they had Bubonic Plague and quarantined themselves - C. Daniel Collection 38962

Eyemouth

Eyemouth Museum, Auld Kirk, Manse Rd, Eyemouth TD14 5JE - T: (01890) 750678. Hon. Cur.: Jean Bowle
Local Museum
History of the Eyemouth area and its people, with a special emphasis on the fishing industry, farming and the traditional trades and handicrafts 38963

Eynsford

Lullingstone Roman Villa, Eynsford DA4 0JA - T: (01322) 863467, E-mail: karen.hawkins@english-heritage.org.uk, Internet: www.english-heritage.org.uk. Cur.: Nick Moore
Archaeological Museum
Artefacts from the excavations of the 1960s 38964

Fair Isle

Auld Sköll, Utra, Fair Isle ZE2 9JU - T: (01595) 760209
Historical Museum 38965

Fakenham

Fakenham Museum of Gas and Local History, Hempton Rd, Fakenham NR21 9EP - T: (01328) 863507, E-mail: em@bridges3.fslife.co.uk, Internet: www.fakenham.org.uk. Chm.: Dr. E.M. Bridges
Science&Tech Museum / Local Museum
Local history, coal gas industry and trade, industrial archaeology 38966

Thursford Collection, Thursford Green, Fakenham NR21 0AS - T: (01328) 878477, Fax: 878415, E-mail: admin@thursfordcollection.co.uk. Dir.: J.R. Cusming
Science&Tech Museum / Music Museum - 1947
Steam and locomotives including showman's traction and ploughing engines, steam wagons, mechanical musical organs, Wurlitzer theater organ, concert organ, German organ Karl Frei 38967

Falkirk

Callendar House, Callendar Estate, Falkirk FK1 1YR - T: (01324) 503770, Fax: 503771, E-mail: callendar.house@falkirk.gov.uk. Dir.: Sve Selwyn
Historical Museum - 1991
Mansion, working kitchen of 1825, social coll, archaeology - Falkirk Council Archives 38968

Park Gallery, Callendar Park, Falkirk FK1 1YR - T: (01324) 503789, Fax: 503771
Fine Arts Museum
Coll of contemporary visual art and craft incl work by national, international and local artists 38969

Falkland

Falkland Palace and Garden, High St, Falkland KY7 7BY - T: (01337) 857397, Fax: 857980. Man.: Judith A. Fisken
Historical Museum - 1952
Chapel Royal, Royal Tennis Court (1539), Flemish tapestries 38970

Falmer

Gardner Arts Centre, University of Sussex, Falmer BN1 9RA - T: (01273) 685447, Fax: 678551, E-mail: marketing@gardnerarts.co.uk, Internet: www.gardnerarts.co.uk
Public Gallery 38971

Falmouth

Falmouth Art Gallery, Municipal Buildings, The Moor, Falmouth TR11 2RT - T: (01326) 313863, Fax: 312662, E-mail: falag@uknetworks.co.uk, Internet: www.falmouthartgallery.com. Dir.: Brian Stewart
Fine Arts Museum / Public Gallery - 1978
Late 19th and early 20th c paintings (mainly British) donated by Alfred de Pass 38972

National Maritime Museum Cornwell, Discovery Quay, Falmouth TR11 3QY - T: (01326) 313388, Fax: 317878, E-mail: enquiries@nmmc.co.uk, Internet: www.nmmc.co.uk. Dir.: Jonathan Griffin
Historical Museum / Science&Tech Museum - 2002
Maritime history of Cornwall and the Falmouth Packet Service, models, photographs, navigational instruments, ship-building tools, boat coll of 120 historic vessels - Database of Cornish built vessels 1786-1914, Bartlett library 38973

Pendennis Castle, Falmouth TR11 4LP - T: (01326) 316594, Fax: 319911, Internet: www.english-heritage.org.uk. Cur.: Tony Musty
Historical Museum
Arms and uniforms, artillery, furnished interiors and discovery centre 38974

Fareham

Royal Armouries at Fort Nelson, Fort Nelson, Portsdown Hill, Down End Rd, Fareham PO17 6AN - T: (01329) 233734, Fax: 822092, E-mail: nelson@rmplc.co.uk, Internet: www.resort-guide/portsmouth/fort-nelson. Sen. Cur.: Christopher Henry
Historical Museum / Military Museum - 1988
19th c fortress home of the Royal armouries coll of artillery (worldwide 15th-20th c), regular exhibitions and firing days - Conservation education centre 38975

Westbury Manor Museum, 84 West St, Fareham PO16 0JJ - T: (01329) 824895, Fax: 825917, E-mail: musmop@hants.gov.uk, Internet: hants.gov.uk/museum/westbury. Cur.: Oonagh Palmer
Local Museum 38976

Faringdon

Buscot Park House, Faringdon SN7 8BU - T: (01367) 240786, Fax: 241794, E-mail: estbuscot@aol.com, Internet: www.buscot-park.com. Dir.: Lord Faringdon
Fine Arts Museum
Georgian house in park, containing Faringdon Coll of the English and Continental schools (Rembrandt, Murillo and Reynolds), 18th c furniture, porcelain, objets d'art 38977

Farleigh Hungerford

Farleigh Hungerford Castle, Farleigh Hungerford BA3 6RS - T: (01225) 754026, Internet: www.english-heritage.org.uk. Cur.: Tony Musty
Archaeological Museum
Ruins of a fortified manor house containing a furnished chapel and a small collection of architectural fragments 38978

Farndon

Stretton Water Mill, Stretton, Farndon CH3 6LN - E-mail: cheshiremuseums@cheshire.gov.uk. Cur.: William Miller
Science&Tech Museum 38979

Farnham

Farnhem Maltings Gallery, Farnham Maltings, Bridge Sq, Farnham GU9 7QR - T: (01252) 726234, Fax: 718177, E-mail: FarnMAlt@aol.com, Internet: www.farnhammaltings.com. Dir.: Tozzy Bridger
Public Gallery 38980

Foyer Gallery/James Hockey Gallery, Falkner Rd, Farnham GU9 7DS - T: (01252) 892668/46, Fax: 892667, E-mail: ckapteijn@surrart.ac.uk, Internet: www.surrart.ac.uk
Public Gallery 38981

Museum of Farnham, Willmer House, 38 West St, Farnham GU9 7DX - T: (01252) 715094, Fax: 715094, E-mail: fmuseum@waverley.gov.uk. Cur.: Anne Jones
Decorative Arts Museum - 1960
House (1718) with English decorative arts, local history, archaeology, 18th c furniture, costumes, William Cobbett memorabilia - Reference library 38982

Rural Life Centre, Reeds Rd, Tilford, Farnham GU10 2DL - T: (01252) 795571, Fax: 795571, E-mail: rural.life@argonet.co.uk, Internet: www.surreyweb.uk/rural-life. Dir.: Henry Jackson
Agriculture Museum - 1972
Waggons, farm implements, hand tools, dairy, kitchen, trades and crafts, rural life 1800-1950, arboretum, wheel whight 38983

Faversham

Fleur de Lis Heritage Centre, 10-13 Preston St, Faversham ME13 8NS - T: (01795) 534542, Fax: 533261, E-mail: faversham@btinternet.com, Internet: www.faversham.org/society/museum.html. Dir.: Arthur Percival
Local Museum - 1977
Telephones, explosives hist 38984

Maison Dieu, Water Lane, Ospringe, Faversham ME13 8TW - T: (01795) 533751, Fax: 533261, Internet: www.english-heritage.co.uk
Historical Museum - 1925
Medieval bldg, once part of complex which served as Royal lodge, pilgrims' hostel, hospital and almshouse for retired Royal retainers, now housing Roman finds and new displays illustrating Ospringe's eventful hist 38985

Ferniegair

Chatelherault, Ferniegair ML3 7UE - T: (01698) 426213, Fax: 421532
Historical Museum
Historic park, ruined Cadzow Castle, remains of coal mines 38986

Museums of South Lanarkshire, Chatelherault, Ferniegair ML3 7UE - T: (01698) 426213, Fax: 421532. Man.: Alison Reid
Local Museum 38987

Fetlar

Fetlar Interpretive Centre, Beach of Houbie, Fetlar ZE2 9DJ - T: (01957) 733206, Fax: 733219
Local Museum 38988

Filching

Motor Museum, Filching Manor, Filching BN26 5QA - T: (01323) 487838, Fax: 486331
Science&Tech Museum
Wealden Hall house, car coll, 1893-1997 karting circuit 38989

Filey

Filey Museum, 8-10 Queen St, Filey YO14 9HB - T: (01723) 515013. Cur.: Margaret Wilkins
Local Museum
Fishing, lifeboats, the seashore, rural and domestic objects 38990

Filkins

Swinford Museum, Filkins GL7 3JQ - T: (01367) 860209, 860334. Cur.: Mervyn Swinford
Agriculture Museum / Folklore Museum - 1931
Household and farm tools, stone craft 38991

Firle

Charleston Trust, Charleston, Firle BN8 6LL - T: (01323) 811626, 811265, Fax: 811628, E-mail: info@charleston.org.uk, Internet: www.charleston.org.uk. Dir.: Alastair Upton, Cur.: Dr. Wendy Hitchmough
Decorative Arts Museum - 1981
Domestic decorative art of Vanessa Bell and Duncan Grant 38992

Firle Place, Firle BN8 6LP - T: (01273) 858335, Fax: 858188, E-mail: gage@firleplace.co.uk
Decorative Arts Museum
Home of Viscount Gage, old masters, Sevres and English porcelain, fine French and English furniture 38993

Fishguard

West Wales Arts Centre, 16 West St, Fishguard SA65 9AE - T: (01348) 873867, E-mail: westwalesarts@btconnect.com, Internet: home.btconnect.com/west-wales-arts
Public Gallery
Paintings, sculpture, ceramics, jewllery and glass 38994

Fleetwood

Fleetwood Museum, Queen's Terrace, Fleetwood FY7 6BT - T: (01253) 876621, Fax: 878088, E-mail: fleedwoodmuseum@museumoflancs.org.uk, Internet: www.lancashire.com/lcc/museums. Cur.: Simon Hayhow
Natural History Museum - 1974
County Museum Service biology collections 38995

Flintham

Flintham Museum, Inholms Rd, Flintham NG23 5LF - T: (01636) 525111, E-mail: flintham.museum@lineone.net, Internet: www.flintham-museum.org.uk
Local Museum
Rural life, toys, postcards, pharmeceuticals, tobacco products, bike accessories, haberdashery and hardware - archive 38996

Flixton

Norfolk and Suffolk Aviation Museum, East Anglia's Aviation Heritage Centre, Buckeroo Way, The Street, Flixton NR35 1NZ - T: (01986) 896644, E-mail: nsam.flixton@virgin.net, Internet: www.aviationmuseum.net. Pres.: W.-C.K.H. Wallis
Science&Tech Museum - 1972
Coll of over 36 aircraft and items from Pre-WW I to present day, civil and military 38997

Fochabers

Fochabers Folk Museum, Pringle Church, High St, Fochabers IV32 7DU - T: (01343) 821204, Fax: 821291. Dir.: Gordon A. Christie
Folklore Museum - 1984
Hist of the village of Fochabers since the late 18th c, coll of horse gigs and carts 38998

Folkestone

Elham Valley Railway Museum, Peene Yard, Peene, Newington, Folkestone CT18 8BA - T: (01303) 273690, Fax: 873939, E-mail: evlt.museum@btopenworld.com, Internet: www.elhamvalleylinetrust.org. Chm.: George Wright
Science&Tech Museum
Winston Churchill brought the Bochbuster railway gun during the war 38999

Folkestone Museum and Art Gallery, 2 Grace Hill, Folkestone CT20 1HD - T: (01303) 256710, Fax: 256710, E-mail: janet.adamson@kent.gov.uk, Internet: www.kent-museums.org.uk/folkston.html. Cur.: J. Adamson
Historical Museum - 1868
Natural hist, geology, local archaeology 39000

Metropole Gallery, The Leas, Folkestone CT20 2LS - T: (01303) 244706, Fax: 851353, E-mail: info@metropole.org.uk, Internet: www.metropole.org.uk. Dir.: Sue Jones
Public Gallery 39001

Fordingbridge

Rockbourne Roman Villa, Rockbourne, Fordingbridge SP6 3PG - T: (01725) 518541, E-mail: musuijh@hants.gov.uk, Internet: www.hants.gov.uk/museum/rockbourne. Cur.: Jim Hunter
Archaeological Museum
Mosaics and hypocaust exposed 39002

Fordyce

Fordyce Joiner's Visitor Centre, Fordyce AB45 2SL - E-mail: heritage@aberdeenshire.gov.uk, Internet: www.aberdeenshire.gov.uk/heritage
Special Museum
Rural joiner's workshop, woodworking tools 39003

Forest

German Occupation Museum, Les Houards, Forest GY8 0BG - T: (01481) 238205. Dir.: R.L. Heaume
Military Museum / Historical Museum
The museum tells the story of the German occupation with audio-visual tableaux including an occupation street, kitchen and bunker rooms etc, also restored German fortifications can be visited 39004

Forfar

Museum and Art Gallery, Meffan Institute, 20 West High St, Forfar DD8 1BB - T: (01307) 464123, 467017, Fax: 468451, E-mail: the.meffan@angus.gov.uk, Internet: www.angus.gov.uk/history. Dir.: Margaret H. King
Local Museum / Fine Arts Museum - 1898
Local hist, archaelogy, art esp. pictish stones 39005

Forncett Saint Mary

Forncett Industrial Steam Museum, Low Rd, Forncett Saint Mary NR16 1JJ - T: (01508) 488277, Internet: www.oldenginehouse.demon.co.uk/forncett.htm. Dir.: Dr. R. Francis
Science&Tech Museum
147 hp Cross Compound engine which was used to open Tower Bridge, 85t triple expansion water pump 39006

Forres

Brodie Castle, Brodie, Forres IV36 2TE - T: (01309) 641371, Fax: 641600, E-mail: brodiecastle@nts.org.uk. Dir.: Fiona Dingwall
Decorative Arts Museum / Fine Arts Museum - 1979
French furniture, English, Continental and Chinese porcelain and an important coll of 17th-c Dutch and 18th-c English paintings 39007

Falconer Museum, Tolbooth St, Forres IV36 1PH - T: (01309) 673701, Fax: 673701, E-mail: museums@moray.gov.uk, Internet: www.moray.org/museums
Local Museum - 1871
Specialized herbaria, local history, natural history, Peter Anson, Hugh Fallconer archive - library, archive 39008

Nelson Tower, Grant Park, Forres IV36 1PH - T: (01309) 673701, Fax: 675863, E-mail: alasdair.joyce@techleis.moray.gov.uk, Internet: www.moray.gov.uk/museums
Fine Arts Museum 39009

Fort William

Glenfinnan Station Museum, Glenfinnan Railway Station, Fort William PH37 4LT - T: (01397) 722295, Fax: 722291
Science&Tech Museum 39010

West Highland Museum, Cameron Sq, Fort William PH33 6AJ - T: (01397) 702169, Fax: 701927, E-mail: info@westhighlandmuseum.org.uk, Internet: www.westhighlandmuseum.org.uk. Dir.: Fiona C. Marwick
Local Museum - 1922
Many aspects of the district and its hist, including geology, wildlife, tartans, maps and a coll of items connected with the 1745 Jacobite rising 39011

Foxton

Foxton Canal Museum, Middle Lock, Foxton LE16 7RA - T: (01858) 466185, E-mail: mike@foxcm.freeserve.co.uk, Internet: www.foxcanal.fsnet.co.uk. Cur.: Mike Beech
Historical Museum
Canal items, 1793-1950, boat life and locks 39012

Framlingham

390th Bomb Group Memorial Air Museum and British Resistance Organisation Museum, Parham Airfield, Framlingham IP13 9AF - T: (01473) 711275. Dir.: Peter Kindred
Military Museum
Engines and other components of crashed U.S. and Allied aircraft, and many photographs and mementoes of the wartime life of both airmen and civilians, reconstructions of a radio hut and of a wartime office 39013

Lanman Museum, Castle, Framlingham IP13 9BP - T: (01728) 724189, Fax: 724324. Dir.: T.J. Gilder
Local Museum
Objects of historical, educational or artistic interest connected with the town of Framlingham and the surrounding villages 39014

Fraserburgh

Fraserburgh Museum, 37 Gralton Pl, Fraserburgh AB51 7LD
Local Museum 39015

Museum of Scottish Lighthouses, Kinnaird Head, Fraserburgh AB43 9DU - T: (01346) 511022, Fax: 511033, E-mail: enquiries@lighthousemuseum.demon.co.uk. Dir.: David Bett
Special Museum
Extensive collection of items relating to lighthouses in Scotland and the work of the Northern Lighthouse Board 39016

Freshwater

Dimbola Lodge, Terrace Ln, Freshwater PO40 9QE - T: (01983) 756814, Fax: 755578, E-mail: administrator@dimbola.co.uk, Internet: www.dimbola.co.uk. Cur.: Dr. Brian Hinton
Decorative Arts Museum / Fine Arts Museum
Original Cameron images, Isle ogf Wight Pop festival, photography, applied and visual arts, Julia Margaret Cameron coll - library 39017

Frodsham

Castle Park Arts Centre, Fountain Ln, Frodsham WA6 6SE - T: (01928) 735832, Internet: www.castle-park-arts.co.uk
Fine Arts Museum 39018

Frome

Frome Museum, 1 North Parade, Frome BA11 1AT
Local Museum
History of local industries, including cloth-making, metal-casting, printing and quarrying, local geological section - library 39019

Fyvie

Fyvie Castle, Fyvie AB53 8JS - T: (01651) 891266, Fax: 891107. Man.: Robert Lovie
Local Museum
Coll of portraits including works by Batoni, Raeburn, Gainsborough, arms and armour, 16th c tapestries 39020

Gainsborough

Gainsborough Old Hall, Parnell St, Gainsborough DN21 2NB - T: (01427) 612669, Fax: 612779, E-mail: gainsborougholdhall@lincolnshire.gov.uk, Internet: www.lincolnshire.gov.uk
Local Museum - 1974
In building dating from 1460, medieval room settings & kitchens, 17th c furniture 39021

Gairloch

Gairloch Heritage Museum, Achtercairn, Gairloch IV21 2BP - T: (01445) 712287, E-mail: info@GairlochHeritageMuseum.org.uk, Internet: www.GairlochHeritageMuseum.org.uk. Chairman: Roy Macintyre
Local Museum - 1977
Archaeology, wildlife, agriculture, dairying, wood processing and the domestic arts, family hist section - archive, library 39022

Galashiels

Galashiels Museum, Woollen Mill, Huddersfield St, Galashiels TD1 3BA - T: (01896) 2091
Local Museum
History of Galashiels, emphasising its close involvement with the woollen trade, all aspects of production, from spinning to the finished article 39023

Old Gala House, Scott Crescent, Galashiels TD1 3JS - T: (01750) 720096, Fax: 723282, E-mail: ssinclair@scotborckrs.gov.uk. Sen. Cur.: Ian Brown
Historical Museum
Home of Lairds of Gala, painted ceiling (1635) and wall (1988) 39024

Garlogie

Garlogie Mill Power House Museum, Garlogie AB32 6RX - T: (01771) 622906, Fax: 622884, E-mail: heritage@aberdeenshire.gov.uk, Internet: www.aberdeenshire.gov.uk/heritage. Dir.: Dr. David M. Bertie
Science&Tech Museum
19th c beam engine, 20th c turbine 39025

Gateshead

Bowes Railway Heritage Museum, Springwell Village, Gateshead NE9 7QJ - T: (0191) 4161847, 4193349, E-mail: alison_gibson77@hotmail.com, Internet: www.bowesrailway.co.uk. Chm.: Phillip Dawe
Science&Tech Museum - 1976
Coll of historic colliery rolling stock, rope haulage equipment, coll of historic colliery buildings dating from 19th c 39026

The Gallery, Prince Consort Rd, Gateshead Central Library, Gateshead NE8 4LN - T: (0191) 4773478, Fax: 4771495
Public Gallery - 1917 39027

Shipley Art Gallery, Prince Consort Rd, Gateshead NE8 4JB - T: (0191) 4771495, Fax: 4787917, E-mail: shipley@tyne-wear-museums.org.uk, Internet: www.twmuseums.org.uk. Cur.: Ann Fletcher-Williams
Fine Arts Museum / Decorative Arts Museum / Local Museum - 1917
17th-20th c British painting, also French, Flemish, German, Dutch and Italian painting, Schufelein Altar, contemporary craft, local glass, local industrial hist 39028

Gaydon

Heritage Motor Centre, Banbury Rd, Gaydon CV35 0BJ - T: (01926) 641188, Fax: 641555, E-mail: enquiries@heritage-motor-centre.co.uk, Internet: www.heritage-motor-centre.co.uk. Dir.: Julie Tew
Science&Tech Museum - 1993
Coll of over 200 historic cars, incl prototypes, concept vehicles, record breakers - archive, photographic library 39029

Gerston

Castletown Museum, Mingulay, Gerston KW12 6XQ
Local Museum 39030

Gillingham, Dorset

Gillingham Museum, Chantry Fields, Gillingham, Dorset SP8 4UA - T: (01747) 823176, E-mail: davidlloyd@btinternet.com, Internet: www.brwebsites.com/gillingham.museum/. Cur.: Lyn Light
Local Museum - 1958
Articles manufactured, used or found in Gillingham and documents from the 13th century to the present 39031

Gillingham, Kent

Gillingham Library Gallery, High St, Gillingham, Kent ME7 1BG - T: (01634) 281066, Fax: 855814
Public Gallery 39032

Royal Engineers Museum, Prince Arthur Rd, Gillingham, Kent ME4 4UG - T: (01634) 406397, Fax: 822371, E-mail: remuseum.rhqre@gtnet.gov.uk, Internet: www.royalengineers.org.uk. Dir.: John Nowers, Cur.: John Rhodes
Ethnology Museum
Lives and works, worldwide, of Britain's soldier-engineers from 1066, scientific and engineering equipment, medals, weapons and uniforms, ethnography, decorative arts, esp. Chinese and Sudanese material 39033

Girvan

McKechnie Institute, Dalrymple St, Girvan KA26 9AE - T: (01465) 713643, Fax: 713643
Local Museum / Fine Arts Museum
Local history, community arts centre in a octagonal tower 39034

Penkill Castle, Girvan KA26 9TQ - T: (01465) 871219, Fax: 871215, E-mail: psbfd2@aol.com. Dir.: P.S.B.F. Dromgoole
Historic Site - 1978
Pre Raphaelite 39035

Glamis

Angus Folk Museum, Kirkwynd Cottages, Glamis DD8 1RT - T: (01307) 840288, Fax: 840233. Dir.: Kathleen Ager
Folklore Museum - 1957
Local 17th c stone-roofed cottages, agricultural implements, domestic artefacts 39036

Glamis Castle, Glamis DD8 1RJ - T: (01307) 840393, Fax: 840733, E-mail: enquiries@glamis-castle.co.uk, Internet: www.glamis-castle.co.uk. Admin.: David Adams
Historical Museum
Remodelled castle (17th c), historic pictures, furniture, porcelain and tapestries 39037

Glandford

Glandford Shell Museum, Glandford NR25 7JR - T: (01263) 740081, Fax: 740081, E-mail: sushell@dircon.co.uk. Dir.: S. Hullah
Special Museum - 1915
Sir Alfred Jodrell shell collection, jewelry, pottery, tapestry 39038

Glasgow

Burrell Collection, Pollok Country Park, 2060 Pollokshaws Rd, Glasgow G43 1AT - T: (0141) 2872550, Fax: 2872597, Internet: www.lasgow.gov.uk/cls. Dir.: Bridget McConnell, Mark O'Neill
Fine Arts Museum / Decorative Arts Museum / Museum of Classical Antiquities - 1983
Paintings, watercolors by Glasgow artists, ceramics, pottery, tapestries, antiquities, Islamic art, stained glass, sculpture, arms and armour, Oriental art, furniture, textiles 39039

CCA-Centre for Contemporary Arts, 350 Sauchiehall St, Glasgow G2 3JD - T: (0141) 3327521, Fax: 3323226, E-mail: gen@cca-glasgow.com, Internet: www.cca-glasgow.com. Dir.: Graham McKenzie, Head: Vivienne Gaskin (Artistic Program, Education)
Public Gallery 39040

Clydebuilt, Scottish Maritime Museum, Kins Inch Rd, Glasgow G51 4BN - T: (0141) 8861013, Fax: 8861015, E-mail: clydebuilt@tinyworld.co.uk. Dir.: J.M. Tildesley
Science&Tech Museum
Story of the river Clyde, ships 39041

Collins Gallery, c/o University of Strathclyde, 22 Richmond St, Glasgow G1 1XQ - T: (0141) 5482558, Fax: 5524053, E-mail: collinsgallery@strath.ac.uk. Cur.: Laura Hamilton
Science&Tech Museum / Public Gallery / University Museum - 1973
Anderson coll of scientific instruments, contemporary Scottish art, prints 39042

Eastwood House, Eastwood Park, Giffnoclk, Glasgow G46 6UG - T: (0141) 6381101
Public Gallery 39043

Fossil Grove, Victoria Park, Glasgow G14 1BN - T: (0141) 9501448, Internet: www.glasgow.gov.uk/cls
Local Museum
330 million year old fossilised tree stumps 39044

Gallery of Modern Art, Royal Exchange 50, Glasgow G1 3AH - T: (0141) 2291996, Fax: 2045316, Internet: www.glasgowmuseums.com
Fine Arts Museum - 1996
Paintings, sculptures and installations from around the world, artists represented include John Bellamy, Alan Davie, Peter Howson and Alison Watt 39045

Glasgow Art Gallery and Museum (closed until 2006), Kelvingrove, Glasgow G3 8AG - T: (0141) 2872699, Fax: 2872690, Internet: www.glasgowmuseums.com. Dir.: Mark O'Neill
Fine Arts Museum / Local Museum - 1902
British and European paintings including pictures by Rembrandt and Giorgione, 19th c French Impressionists, Scottish painting, sculpture, costume, silver, pottery and porcelain, arms and armour, wildlife and story of man in Scotland 39046

Glasgow Print Studio, 22-25 King St, Glasgow G1 5QP - T: (0141) 5520704, Fax: 5522919, E-mail: gallery@gpsart.co.uk, Internet: www.gpsart.co.uk. Dir.: John Mackechnie
Public Gallery
Work of Paolozzi, Bellany, Blackadder, Howson, Wiszniewski - printmaking workshop, Three Gallery 39047

Glasgow School of Art - Mackintosh Collection, 167 Renfrew St, Glasgow G3 6RQ - T: (0141) 3534500, Fax: 3534746, E-mail: info@gsa.ac.uk, Internet: www.gsa.ac.uk. Dir.: Prof. Seona Reid, Cur.: Peter Trowles
University Museum
Coll of furniture, watercolours and architectural designs and drawings by Charles Rennie Mackintosh and other GSA-artists 39048

Heatherbank Museum of Social Work, c/o Glasgow Caledonian University, City Campus, Cowcaddens Rd, Glasgow G4 0BA - T: (0141) 33138637, Fax: 3313005, E-mail: a.ramage@gcal.ac.uk, Internet: www.lib.gcal.ac.uk/heatherbank. Dir.: Alastair Ramage
Historical Museum - 1975
Photographic coll of historic pictures, some archive material and ephemera - library, picture library, social work archives 39049

Hunterian Art Gallery, c/o University of Glasgow, 82 Hillhead St, Glasgow G12 8QQ - T: (0141) 3305431, Fax: 3303618, E-mail: hunter@museum.gla.ac.uk, Internet: www.hunterian.gla.ac.uk. Dep. Dir.: Mungo Campbell, Cur.: Pamela B. Robertson (Charles Rennie Mackintosh and Scottish Art), Asst. Cur.: Jo Anthony
Fine Arts Museum / University Museum - 1980
Paintings, drawings, prints, furniture, sculpture, works by Charles Rennie Mackintosh, James McNeill Whistler 39050

Hunterian Museum, c/o University of Glasgow, University Av, Glasgow G12 8QQ - T: (0141) 3304221, Fax: 3303617, E-mail: hunter@museum.gla.ac.uk., Internet: www.hunterian.gla.ac.uk
Ethnology Museum / Natural History Museum / Archaeological Museum / University Museum - 1807
Coll of the celebrated physician and anatomist Dr. William Hunter, geology, rocks, minerals and fossils, incl 'Bearsden shark', archaeology - early civilizations in Scotland, ethnography, Greek, Roman and Scottish coins, scientific instruments 39051

Hunterian Museum, Zoology Section, c/o University of Glasgow, Graham Kerr Bldg, Glasgow G12 8QQ - T: (0141) 3304772, Fax: 3305971, E-mail: mreilly@museum.gla.ac.uk, Internet: www.hunterian.gla.ac.uk. Cur.: Margaret T. Reilly
Natural History Museum
Animal kingdom from microscopic creatures to elephants and whales 39052

Kelly Gallery, 118 Douglas St, Glasgow G2 4ET - T: (0141) 2486386, Fax: 2210417
Public Gallery 39053

McLellan Galleries, 270 Sauchiehall St, Glasgow G2 3EH - T: (0141) 3311854, Fax: 3329957. Dir.: Bridget McConnell
Public Gallery 39054

Museum of Anatomy, c/o IBLS, University of Glasgow, Laboratory of Human Anatomy, Glasgow G12 8QQ - T: (0141) 3305869, Fax: 3304299, E-mail: a.payne@bio.gla.ac.uk
Natural History Museum 39055

Museum of Piping, 30-34 McPhater St, Cowcadden, Glasgow G3 - T: (0141) 3530220, Fax: 3531570, E-mail: ysamson@thepipingcentre.co.uk, Internet: www.thepipingcentre.co.uk. Dir.: Roddy McLeod
Music Museum
Bagpipes, piping artefacts 39056

Museum of Transport, Kelvin Hall, 1 Bunhouse Rd, Glasgow G3 8DP - T: (0141) 2872720, Fax: 2872692
Science&Tech Museum - 1964
Railroad locomotives, bicycles, motorcycles, streetcars, automobiles, models, fire engines, baby carriages, steam road vehicles, horse-drawn carriages 39057

Pearce Institute, 840 Govan Rd, Glasgow G51 3UT - T: (0141) 4451941
Public Gallery 39058

People's Palace Museum, Glasgow Green, Glasgow G40 1AT - T: (0141) 5540223, Fax: 5500892, Internet: www.glasgow.gov.uk/cls. Cur.: Fiona Hayes
Historical Museum - 1898
Glaswegian social, economic and political hist since 1175, exhibits on popular culture, public art 39059

Pollok House, 2060 Pollokshaws Rd, Glasgow G43 1AT - T: (0141) 6166410, Fax: 6166521. Dir.: Robert S. Ferguson
Fine Arts Museum / Decorative Arts Museum - 1968
Stirling Maxwell coll incl Spanish school of painting El Greco, Goya, Murillo, British school, principally William Blake, decorative arts, furniture, pottery, porcelain, silver, bronzes 39060

Provan Hall House, Auchinlea Park, Auchinlea Rd, Glasgow G34 - T: (0141) 7711538
Decorative Arts Museum - 1983/2000 39061

Provand's Lordship, 3 Castle St, Glasgow G4 0RB - T: (0141) 5528819, Fax: 5524744, Internet: www.glasgowmuseums.com. Dir.: Bridget McConnell
Historical Museum
Medieval building of 1471 39062

Royal Glasgow Institute of the Fine Arts, 5 Oswald St, Glasgow G1 4QR - T: (0141) 2487411, Fax: 2210417
Public Gallery 39063

Royal Highland Fusiliers Regimental Museum, 518 Sauchiehall St, Glasgow G2 3LW - T: (0141) 3320961, Fax: 3531493, E-mail: assregseg@rhr.org.uk, Internet: www.rhr.org.uk. Dir.: W. Shaw
Military Museum - 1969
History of the regiment since 1678, medals, uniforms, regimental silver, militaria 39064

Saint Mungo Museum of Religious Life and Art, 2 Castle St, Glasgow G4 0RH - T: (0141) 5532557, Fax: 5524744, Internet: www.glasgowmuseums.com. Dir.: Bridget McConnell
Religious Arts Museum - 1993
Objects associated with different religious faiths - Japanese Zen garden 39065

Scotland Street School Museum, 225 Scotland St, Glasgow G5 8QB - T: (0141) 2870500, Fax: 2870515, Internet: www.glasgow.gov.uk/cls. Dir.: Bridget McConnell
Historical Museum - 1990
Hist of education in Scotland from 1872, several historical classrooms, Edwardian cookery room, school hist, architectural hist (designed by Charles Rennie Mackintosh) 39066

Scottish Football Museum, c/o Museum of Transport, Kelvin Hall, 1 Bunhouse Rd, Glasgow G3 9DP - T: (0141) 2872697, Fax: 2872692, Internet: www.scottishfa.co.uk
Special Museum
Football memorabilia coll from SFA since 1873 39067

Scottish Jewish Museum, Garnethill Synagogue, 127 Hill St, Glasgow G3 6UB - T: (0141) 9562973
Historical Museum
archives 39068

Tenement House, 145 Buccleuch St, Glasgow G3 6QN - T: (0141) 3330183, Fax: 3329368, Internet: www.nts.org.uk. Dir.: Lorna Hepburn
Local Museum
Typical lower middle class Glasgow tenement flat of the turn of the century with original furnishings and fittings. 39069

Glastonbury

Glastonbury Abbey Museum, Abbey Gatehouse, Magdalene St, Glastonbury BA6 9EL - T: (01458) 832267, Fax: 832267, E-mail: info@glastonburyabbey.com, Internet: www.glastonburyabbey.com
Religious Arts Museum - 1908
Coll of tiles, carved stonework and miscellaneous artefacts from the site of the ruined Abbey, together with a model showing how the Abbey may have looked in 1539, before the Dissolution 39070

Glastonbury Lake Village Museum, The Tribunal, 9 High St, Glastonbury BA6 9DP - T: (01458) 832954, Fax: 832949, E-mail: glastonbury.tic@ukonline.co.uk, Internet: www.glastonburytic.co.uk
Local Museum
Local history 39071

Somerset Rural Life Museum, Abbey Farm, Chilkwell St, Glastonbury BA6 8DB - T: (01458) 831197, Fax: 834684, E-mail: mcgryspeerdt@somerset.gov.uk, Internet: somerset.gov.uk/museums. Dir.: David A. Walker
Local Museum - 1976
Agricultural machinery, tools, waggons and carts, baskets and basket making tools, cider making equipment, chedder cheese making presses and equipment, kitchen and general domestic colls, Somerset furniture, contrymen's smocks 39072

Glenavy

Ballance House, 118a Lisburn Rd, Glenavy BT29 4NY - T: (028) 92648492, Fax: 92648098, E-mail: ballancenz@aol.com, Internet: www.geocities.com/heartland/prairie/8890. Cur.: Keri Wilson
Historical Museum / Ethnology Museum
John Ballance (New Zealand premier 1891-93), ethnographical material, fine art, journals, books, furniture 39073

Glencoe

Glencoe and North Lorn Folk Museum, Glencoe PH49 4HP - T: (01855) 811664. Pres.: Rachel Grant, Vice Pres.: A. Smith
Local Museum
MacDonald and Jacobite relicts, domestic bygones, weapons, embroidery, costumes, agricultural items, Ballachulish slate industry, ethnology, military 39074

Glenesk

Glenesk Folk Museum, The Retreat, Glenesk DD9 7YT - T: (01356) 670254, Fax: 670321, E-mail: retreat@angusglens.co.uk, Internet: www.angusglens.co.uk. Cur.: Muriel McIntosh
Local Museum
Local history, costume coll 39075

Glenluce

Glenluce Motor Museum, Glenluce DG8 0NY - T: (01581) 300534, Fax: 300258
Science&Tech Museum
Vintage and classic cars, motor cycles memorabilia and old type garage 39076

Glenrothes

Corridor Gallery, Viewfield Rd, Glenrothes KY6 2RB - T: (01592) 415700
Public Gallery 39077

Glossop

Glossop Heritage Centre, Bank House, Henry St, Glossop SK13 8BW - T: (01457) 869176. Man.: Peggy Davies
Local Museum
Local newspapers, local history 39078

Gloucester

Archaeology Unit and Transport Museum, Old Fire Station, Barbican Rd, Gloucester GL1 2JF - T: (01452) 526342, Fax: 503050. Dir.: Amanda Wadsley
Archaeological Museum / Science&Tech Museum
Horse-drawn manual fire-engine of c 1895,a horse-drawn tram of 1880, a Gloucestershire type of farm wagon, three Dursley-build Pedersen cycles, Morris Commercial of 1926, Cotton motorcycle of ca. 1923, various cycles from 18th and 19th c, J.E.S. motorcycle of 1912, Leyland Metz Fire Engine of ca. 1938, responsibility for the archaeology service and county-wide collections of Gloucester City Council 39079

City Museum and Art Gallery, Brunswick Rd, Gloucester GL1 1HP - T: (01452) 396131, Fax: 410898, E-mail: city.museum@gloucester.gov.uk, Internet: www.mylife.gloucester.gov.uk. Dir.: Linda Coode, Cur.: Louise Allen, Sue Byrne, David Rice
Archaeological Museum / Fine Arts Museum / Decorative Arts Museum / Natural History Museum - 1860
Archaeology, geology, botany, natural hist, English pottery, glass and silver objects, numismatics, art 39080

Gloucester Folk Museum, 99-103 Westgate St, Gloucester GL1 2PG - T: (01452) 396467, Fax: 330495, E-mail: folk.museum@gloucester.gov.uk, Internet: www.mylife.gloucester.gov.uk. Head: C.I. Morris, Cur.: N.R. Cox (Social history)
Local Museum - 1935
Local hist since 1500, crafts, trades, farming tools, fishing, shops and workshops, toys and games, laundry and household equipment, steam engines, model aircraft, pewter, glass, pottery 39081

Gloucester Prison Museum, Barrack Sq, Gloucester GL1 2DN - T: (01452) 529551, Fax: 309320, E-mail: museum@breathmail.net, Internet: www.hmprisonservice.gov.uk. Head: Rita Goode
Historical Museum
History and development of Her Majesty Prison Gloucester 39082

National Waterways Museum, Llanthony Warehouse, Gloucester Docks, Gloucester GL1 2EH - T: (01452) 318200, Fax: 318202, E-mail: bookingsnwm@thewaterwaystrust.org, Internet: www.nwm.org.uk. Dir.: Mike Brooksbank
Science&Tech Museum / Historical Museum - 1988
Inland waterways and its transport - archive 39083

Nature in Art, Wallsworth Hall, Tewkesbury Rd, Gloucester GL2 9PA - T: (01452) 731422, Fax: 730937, E-mail: ninart@globalnet.co.uk, Internet: www.nature-in-art.org.uk. Dir.: Simon H. Trapnell
Fine Arts Museum
Fine, decorative and applied art inspired by nature, any period, and country in all media 39084

Soldiers of Gloucestershire Museum, Custom House, Gloucester Docks, Gloucester GL1 2HE - T: (01452) 522682, Fax: 311116. Cur.: George C. Streatfield
Military Museum - 1989
Uniforms, medals, badges, paintings, arts and crafts - archives 39085

Glyn Ceiriog

Ceiriog Memorial Institute, High St, Glyn Ceiriog LL20 7EH - T: (01691) 718910, 718383
Special Museum 39086

Godalming

Charterhouse School Museum, Charterhouse, Godalming GU7 2DX - T: (01483) 421006, 291515, Fax: 291594, E-mail: dsh@charterhouse.org.uk
Local Museum
Local hist, ethnography, archaeology, natural hist 39087

Godalming Museum, 109a High St, Godalming GU7 1AQ - T: (01483) 426510, Fax: 523495, E-mail: museum@godalming.ndo.co.uk, Internet: www.godalming-museum.org.uk. Cur.: Alison Pattison
Local Museum - 1920
Local hist and industries, Gertrude Jekyll and Edwin Lutyens coll - local studies library 39088

Golcar

Colne Valley Museum, Cliffe Ash, Golcar HD7 4PY - T: (01484) 659762
Local Museum
Restored 19th century weavers' cottages. Demonstration of hand-loom weaving, working spinning jenny, spinning on saxony wheel and clog-making in gas-lit clogger's workshop 39089

Goldhanger

Maldon and District Agricultural and Domestic Museum, 47 Church St, Goldhanger CM9 8AR - T: (01621) 788647, Fax: 788647
Agriculture Museum / Folklore Museum
Coll of vintage farm machinery and tools, domestic bygones, printing machinery, photographs 39090

Golspie

Dunrobin Castle Museum, Dunrobin Castle, Golspie KW10 6SF - T: (01408) 633177, Fax: 634081, E-mail: dunrobin.est@btinternet.com, Internet: www.great-houses-scotland/dunrobin. Dir.: Keith Jones
Decorative Arts Museum
Victorian castle, formerly a summerhouse, collections of game trophies and Pictish stones, local history, ornithology, geology, ethnography 39091

Gomersal

Red House Museum, Oxford Rd, Gomersal BD19 4JP - T: (01274) 335100, Fax: 335105, Internet: www.kirkleesmc.gov.uk/community/museums. Dir.: Helga Hughes
Historical Museum
Regency house with Brontë connections 39092

Gomshall

Gomshall Gallery, Station Rd, Gomshall GU5 9LB - T: (01483) 203795, Fax: 203282
Public Gallery 39093

Goole

Goole Museum and Art Gallery, Carlisle St, Goole DN14 5BG, mail addr: Eryc Offices, Church St, Goole DN14 5BG - T: (01482) 392777, Fax: 392782, E-mail: janet.tierney@eastriding.gov.uk. J. Tierney
Local Museum / Fine Arts Museum - 1968
Local history, shipping, paintings 39094

Waterways Museum, Sobriety Project, Dutch River Side, Goole DN14 5TB - T: (01405) 768730, Fax: 769868, E-mail: waterwaysmuseum@btinternet.com, Internet: www.waterwaysmuseumandadventurecentre.co.uk. Dir.: Bob Watson
Historical Museum
Photographs, documents, industrial and waterways heritage, Aire and Calder navigation, Goole port, Yorkshire waterways 39095

Gordon

Mellerstain House, Mellerstain, Gordon TD3 6LG - T: (01573) 410225, Fax: 410636, E-mail: mellerstain.house@virgin.net, Internet: www.muses.calligrafix.co.uk/mellerstain. Dir.: Earl of Haddington
Local Museum - 1952
Robert Adam architecture, old master paintings, antique dolls - Library 39096

Gorey

Mont Orgueil Castle, Rte de la Côte, Gorey JE3 6DN - T: (01534) 853292, Fax: 854303, E-mail: museum@jerseyheritagetrust.org, Internet: www.jerseyheritagetrust.org. Dir.: Michael Day
Historic Site / Archaeological Museum - 1907
Medieval castle, local archaeological finds 39097

Gosport

Fort Brockhurst, Gunner's Wy, Elson, Gosport PO12 4DS - T: (023) 92581059, Internet: www.english-heritage.org.uk. Cur.: Nick Moore
Military Museum
Artillery coll 39098

Gosport Museum, Walpole Rd, Gosport PO12 1NS - T: (023) 92588035, Fax: 92501951, E-mail: musmop@hants.gov.uk, Internet: www.hants.gov.uk/museums/gosport. Head: Oonagh Palmer
Local Museum - 1974
Local hist, geology 39099

Hovercraft Museum, Argus Gate, Chark Ln, Gosport PO13 9NY - T: (023) 92552090, Fax: 92552090, E-mail: brian@hovercraft-museum.org, Internet: www.hovercraft-museum.org. Man.: Brian J. Russell
Historical Museum / Science&Tech Museum
44 hovercraft and history 39100

The Museum of Naval Firepower, Priddy's Hard, Gosport PO12 4LE - T: (023) 92505600, Fax: 92505605, E-mail: info@explosion.org.uk, Internet: www.explosion.org.uk. Cur.: Chris Henry
Science&Tech Museum / Special Museum
Small arms, cannon and large guns, shells and munitions, mines, torpedoes and modern missiles 39101

Royal Navy Submarine Museum, Haslar Jetty Rd, Gosport PO12 2AS - T: (02392) 510354, Fax: 511349, E-mail: rnsubs@rnsubmus.co.uk, Internet: www.rnsubmus.co.uk. Dir.: J.J. Tall
Military Museum - 1963
Models of all British submarines from 1879 to the present day, H.M. Submarine Alliance, Holland I - library, photographic archive, diving museum 39102

SEARCH-Centre, 50 Clarence Rd, Gosport PO12 1BU - T: (023) 92501957, Fax: 92501921, E-mail: musmjw@hants.gov.uk, Internet: www.hants.gov.uk/museum/search. Man.: Janet Wildman
Historical Museum / Natural History Museum
History and natural history 39103

Gott

Tingwall Agricultural Museum, 2 Veensgarth, Gott ZE2 9SB - T: (01595) 840344
Agriculture Museum
18th c farming 39104

Goudhurst

Finchcocks, Living Museum of Music, Goudhurst TN17 1HH - T: (01580) 211702, Fax: 211007, E-mail: katrina@finchcocks.co.uk, Internet: www.finchcocks.co.uk. Dir.: Richard Burnett
Music Museum - 1971
Coll of historical keyboard instruments, chamber organs, and a wide range of early pianos, musical furniture 39105

Gower

Gower Heritage Centre, Y Felin Ddwr, Parkmill, Gower SA3 2EM - T: (01792) 371206, Fax: 371471, E-mail: info@gowerheritagecentre.sagehost.co.uk, Internet: www.gowerheritagecentre.sagehost.co.uk
Local Museum / Agriculture Museum
Milling and wheelwrights equipment, agriculture and farming 39106

Grange-over-Sands

Lakeland Motor Museum, Holker Hall, Cark-in-Cartmel, Grange-over-Sands LA11 7PL - T: (015395) 58509, Fax: 58509, E-mail: info@lakelandmotormuseum.co.uk, Internet: www.lakelandmotormuseum.co.uk. Dir.: D.J. Sidebottom
Science&Tech Museum - 1978
Classic and vintage cars, motor-cycles, cycles, tractors, engines and automobilia, 1920's garage re-creation, Campbell Bluebird exhibition, 39107

Grangemouth

Grangemouth Museum, Bo'ness Rd, Grangemouth FK1 1YR - T: (01324) 504699
Local Museum
Scotlands earliest planned industrial town, petroleum and chemical industries 39108

Workshop and Stores, 7-11 Abbotsinch Rd, Abbotsinch Industrial Estate, Grangemouth FK3 9UX - T: (01324) 504689, Fax: 504689, E-mail: carol.whittaker@falkirk.gov.uk
Local Museum
Extensive industrial collection, machines, hand tools, transport items 39109

Grantham

Belton House, Grantham NG32 2LS - T: (01476) 566116, Fax: 579071, E-mail: belton@smtp.ntrust.org.uk. Man.: Duncan Bowen
Fine Arts Museum / Decorative Arts Museum
Plasterwork ceilings by Edward Goudge, wood carvings of the Grinling Gibbons School, portraits, furniture, tapestries, oriental porcelain 39110

Grantham Museum, Saint Peter's Hill, Grantham NG31 6PY - T: (01476) 568783, Fax: 592457, E-mail: grantham.museum@lincolnshire.gov.uk, Internet: www.lincolnshire.gov.uk/granthammuseum. Keeper: A. Brearley
Local Museum - 1926
Local history from prehistoric to modern times, two special exhibitions are devoted to the town's famous personalities - Isaac Newton and Margaret Thatcher 39111

The Queen's Royal Lancers Regimental Museum, Belvoir Castle, Grantham NG32 1PD - T: (0115) 9573295, Fax: 9573195, E-mail: hhqandmuseumqrl@ukonline.co.uk, Internet: www.qrl.uk.com. Cur.: J.M. Holtby, Asst. Cur.: T. Brighton
Military Museum - 1963
Arms, uniforms, paintings, silver, medals - archives 39112

Grantown-on-Spey

Grantown Museum, Burnfield House, Burnfield Av, Grantown-on-Spey PH26 3HH - T: (01479) 872478, Fax: 872478, E-mail: molly.duckett@btinternet.com, Internet: grantownmuseum.com. Dir.: Angus Miller
Local Museum 39113

Grasmere

Dove Cottage and the Wordsworth Museum, Centre for British Romanticism, Town End, Grasmere LA22 9SH - T: (015394) 35544, Fax: 35748, E-mail: enquiries@wordsworth.org.uk, Internet: www.wordsworth.org.uk. Dir.: Dr. Robert Woof
Special Museum - 1890/1935
Former home of William Wordsworth (1770-1850) with memorabilia of the poet, books and manuscripts of major Romantic figures, lake district fine art and topography 39114

Grassington

Upper Wharfdale Folk Museum, 6 The Square, Grassington BD23 5AQ - T: (01756) 752801
Folklore Museum
History of the Dales, with a special emphasis on farming, lead mining and domestic life 39115

Gravesend, Kent

Gravesham Museum, High St, Gravesend, Kent DA12 0BQ - T: (01474) 365600. Head: Georgina Hammond
Local Museum
Local archaeology and history, paintings 39116

Grays

Thurrock Museum, Thameside Complex, Orsett Rd, Grays RM17 5DX - T: (01375) 382555, Fax: 392666, E-mail: jcatton@thurrock.gov.uk, Internet: www.thurrock.gov.uk/museum. Dir.: Jonathan Catton, Cur.: Terry J. Carney
Local Museum - 1956
Local history and archaeology, maritime - Borough archives 39117

Great Ayton

Captain Cook Schoolroom Museum, 101 High St, Great Ayton TS9 6NB - T: (01642) 724296, Internet: www.captaincookschoolroommuseum.co.uk
Historical Museum - 1928 39118

Great Bardfield

Great Bardfield Cage, Bridge St, Great Bardfield CM7 4UA - T: (01371) 810516, E-mail: stellaherbert@hotmail.com. Dir.: Peter Cott
Local Museum 39119

Great Bardfield Cottage Museum, Dunmow Rd, Great Bardfield CM7 4UA - T: (01371) 810516. Chairman: Charles Holden
Local Museum
19th and 20th c domestic and agricultural artefacts, rural crafts 39120

Great Bookham

Polesden Lacey, Great Bookham RH5 6BD - T: (01372) 458203, 452048, Fax: 452023, E-mail: spljxd@smtp.ntrust.org.uk, Internet: www.nationaltrust.org.uk/regions/southern. Man.: J.A.C. McElwee
Decorative Arts Museum
Fine paintings, furniture, porcelain and silver 39121

Great Malvern

Malvern Museum, Abbey Gateway, Abbey Rd, Great Malvern WR14 3ES - T: (01684) 567811, E-mail: cora@malvernspa.com. Cur.: M.J. Hebden
Local Museum - 1979
Geology, water-cure, radar 39122

Great Yarmouth

Elizabethan House Museum, 4 South Quay, Great Yarmouth NR30 2QH - T: (01493) 855746, Fax: 745459, E-mail: rachelkirk@mus.norfolk.gov.uk. Dir.: Dr. Sheila Watson
Historical Museum - 1975
Tudor merchant's house of 1596 with displays of social hist and domestic life, Victorian kitchen and scullery 39123

Great Yarmouth Museums, Tolhouse St, Great Yarmouth NR30 2SH - T: (01493) 745526, Fax: 745459. Dir.: Dr. Sheila Watson
Public Gallery - 1961 39124

Maritime Museum for East Anglia, 25 Marine Parade, Great Yarmouth NR30 2EN - T: (01493) 842267, Fax: 745459. Dir.: Dr. Sheila Watson
Historical Museum - 1967
Maritime hist of the district, fishing, historic racing lateener (1829), life saving 39125

Old Merchant's House and Row 111 Houses, South Quay, Great Yarmouth NR30 2RQ - T: (01493) 857900, Internet: www.english-heritage.org.uk. Cur.: Sara Lunt
Local Museum
Two 17th c town houses, original fixtures and displays of local architectural fittings salvaged from bombing in 1942/43 39126

Tolhouse Museum and Brass Rubbing Centre, Tolhouse St, Great Yarmouth NR30 2SH - T: (01493) 858900, Fax: 745459. Dir.: Dr. Sheila Watson
Historical Museum - 1976
Victorian prison cells 39127

Greenfield

Greenfield Valley Museum, Basingwerk House, Heritage Park, Greenfield CH8 7QB - T: (01352) 714172, Fax: 714791, Internet: www.greenfieldvalley.com. Dir.: John Richards
Science&Tech Museum / Agriculture Museum
Farm machinery and industrial heritage 39128

Greenford

London Motorcycle Museum, Ravenor Farm, 29 Oldfield Ln S, Greenford UB6 9LB - T: (020) 85756644, E-mail: thelmm@hotmail.com, Internet: www.london-motorcycle-museum.org. Dir.: Bill Crosby
Science&Tech Museum - 1999
80 motorcycles (incl. many prototypes and Crosby Coll of Triumphs) 39129

Greenhead

Roman Army Museum, Carvoran, Greenhead CA6 7JB - T: (016977) 47485, Fax: 47487, E-mail: vinolandatrust@btinternet.com, Internet: www.yell.co.uk/sites/vinolanda
Military Museum 39130

Greenock

McLean Museum and Art Gallery, 15 Kelly St, Greenock PA16 8JX - T: (01475) 715624, Fax: 715626, E-mail: val.boa@inverclyde.gov.uk, Internet: www.inverclyde.gov.uk. Cur.: Valerie N.S. Boa
Local Museum - 1876
Caird and McKellar coll of pictures, shipping, objects of J. Watt 39131

Gressenhall

Norfolk Rural Life Museum and Union Farm → Roots of Norfolk at Gressenhall

Roots of Norfolk at Gressenhall, Gressenhall NR20 4DR - T: (01362) 860563, Fax: 860385, E-mail: gressenhall.museum@norfolk.gov.uk, Internet: www.museums.norfolk.gov.uk. Man.: Stuart Gillis
Open Air Museum / Agriculture Museum - 1976
Rural and Norfolk life, working traditional farm 39132

Grimsby

National Fishing Heritage Centre, Alexandra Dock, Grimsby DN31 1UZ - T: (01472) 323345, Fax: 323555
Special Museum 39133

Welholme Galleries, Welholme Rd, Grimsby DN32 9LP - T: (01472) 323575, Fax: 323577. Dir.: Richard Doughty
Local Museum / Fine Arts Museum 39134

Guildford

English Heritage South East Region, Eastgate Ct, 195-205 High St, Guildford GU1 3EH - T: (01483) 252000, Fax: 252001, Internet: www.english-heritage.org.uk
Association with Coll
Archaeological artefacts and furnishings 39135

Guildford Cathedral Treasury, Stag Hill, Guildford GU2 5UP - T: (01483) 565287, Fax: 303350. Cur.: Ann Wickham
Religious Arts Museum
Cathedral plate and other artefacts 39136

Guildford House Gallery, 155 High St, Guildford GU1 3AJ - T: (01483) 444742, Fax: 444742, E-mail: guildfordhouse@guildford.gov.uk, Internet: www.guildfordhouse.co.uk
Public Gallery - 1959
Topographical paintings, drawings and prints from the 18th to 20th centuries including pastel and oil portraits by local artist John Russell, 20th century craft collection, textiles, glass, ceramics - library 39137

Guildford Museum, Castle Arch, Guildford GU1 3SX - T: (01483) 444751, Fax: 532391, E-mail: museum@guildford.gov.uk, Internet: www.guildfordmuseum.co.uk. Dir.: Sue Roggero
Local Museum - 1898
County archaeology, history, needlework, ethnography, Saxon cemetery finds from Guildtown 39138

Lewis Elton Gallery, c/o University of Surrey, Guildford GU2 7XH - T: (01483) 300800, 879167, Fax: 300803, E-mail: gallery@surrey.ac.uk, Internet: www.surrey.ac.uk. Cur.: Patricia Grayburn
Public Gallery / University Museum 39139

Loseley House, Estate Office, Loseley Park, Guildford GU3 1HS - T: (01483) 304440, Fax: 302036, E-mail: enquiries@loseley-park.com, Internet: www.loseley-park.com. Owner: Michael More-Molyneux
Decorative Arts Museum
House (1562) with Elizabethan architecture, works of art, furniture, paintings, ceilings 39140

Queen's Royal Surrey Regiment Museum, Clandon Park, Guildford GU4 7RQ - T: (01483) 223419, Fax: 224636, Internet: www.surrey-online.co.uk/queenssurreys
Military Museum
Militaria, medals, photographs and reference material relating to the Infantry Regiments of Surrey 39141

Haddington

Jane Welsh Carlyle's House, Lodge St, Haddington EH41 3DX - T: (01620) 823738, Fax: 825147. Dir.: Garth Morrison
Local Museum
House from the middle of the 18th century 39142

Lennoxlove House, Lennoxlove Estate, Haddington EH41 4NZ - T: (01620) 823720, Fax: 825112, E-mail: enquiries@lennoxlove.com, Internet: www.lennoxlove.com. Cur.: Duke of Hamilton
Fine Arts Museum 39143

Hagley

Hagley Hall, Hagley DY9 9LG - T: (01562) 882408, Fax: 882632, E-mail: enquiries@hagleyhall.info, Internet: www.hagleyhall.com
Fine Arts Museum
Pictures - library 39144

Hailes

Cistercian Museum, Hailes Abbey, Hailes GL54 5PB - T: (01242) 602398, Internet: www.englishheritage.org.uk. Cur.: Tony Musty
Religious Arts Museum
Medieval sculpture, coll of 13th c roof bosses, medieval tiles, manuscripts, pottery and iron work 39145

Hailsham

Hailsham Heritage Centre, Blackman's Yard, Market St, Hailsham BN27 2AE - T: (01323) 840947. Dir.: M. Alder
Local Museum - 1962 39146

Michelham Priory, Upper Dicker, Hailsham BN27 3QS - T: (01323) 844224, Fax: 844030, E-mail: smomich@sussexpast.co.uk, Internet: www.sussexpast.co.uk. Dir.: Henry Warner, Officer: Helen Poole
Decorative Arts Museum / Agriculture Museum / Historical Museum - 1960
Medieval and Tudor-Jacobean furniture, 17th c tapestries, 16th-17th c ironwork, glass, 18th c paintings, agricultural and wheelwright tools and equipment, buildings date from 1229 and include 16th c Great Barn and working watermill 39147

Halesworth

Halesworth and District Museum, Railway Station, Station Rd, Halesworth IP19 8BZ - T: (01986) 873030. Cur.: Michael Fordham
Local Museum
Local geology and archaeology 39148

Halifax

Bankfield Museum, Akroyd Park, Boothtown Rd, Halifax HX3 6HG - T: (01422) 354823, 352334, Fax: 349020, E-mail: bankfield-museum@calderdale.gov.uk, Internet: www.caldendale.gov.uk. Ass. Dir.: Rosemary Crook, Sc. Staff: June Hill
Local Museum / Military Museum / Decorative Arts Museum - 1887
Textiles, crafts, militaria, toys, ethnography 39149

Calderdale Industrial Museum (closed) 39150

The Dean Clough Galleries, Dean Clough, Halifax HX3 5AX - T: (01422) 250250, Fax: 341148, E-mail: linda@design-dimension.co.uk, Internet: www.DeanClough.com. Dir.: Roger Standen, Cur.: Doug Binder, Coord.: Chris Taylor (Arts)
Public Gallery 39151

Eureka! The Museum for Children, Discovery Rd, Halifax HX1 2NE - T: (01422) 330069, Fax: 330275, E-mail: info@eureka.org.uk, Internet: www.eureka.org.uk. Dir.: Leigh-Anne Stradeski
Special Museum - 1992 39152

Museum of The Duke of Wellington's Regiment, Boothtown Rd, Halifax HX3 6HG - T: (01422) 352334, Fax: 349020, E-mail: bankfield-museum@calderdale.gov.uk. Dir.: Philippa Mackenzie
Military Museum - 1959
History of the regiment, memorabilia on the first Duke of Wellington (1769-1852) 39153

Piece Hall Art Gallery, Piece Hall, Halifax HX1 1RE - T: (01422) 358300, Fax: 349310, E-mail: piece.hall@calderdale.gov.uk, Internet: www.calderdale.gov.uk. Dir.: Rosie Crook
Public Gallery
Temporary exhibition program, regular artists in residence, complementary workshops, educational programs 39154

Pre-Industrial Museum (closed) 39155

Shibden Hall Museum, West Yorkshire Folk Museum, Shibden Hall, Lister's Rd, Halifax HX3 6XG - T: (01422) 352246, Fax: 348440. Asst. Dir.: Barry Sheridan
Folklore Museum - 1937
15th c house with 17th-19th c furnishings, other old buildings, workshops, farm tools, vehicles, musical instruments, local pottery 39156

Hallaton

Hallaton Museum, Hog Ln, Hallaton LE16 8UE - T: (01858) 555416. Chm.: J. Morison
Local Museum
Local history, village life, agricultural artefacts 39157

Halstead

Brewery Chapel Museum, Adams Court, off Trinity St, Halstead CO9 1LF - T: (01787) 478463
Local Museum 39158

Halton

County Museum Technical Centre, Tring Rd, Halton HP22 5PJ - T: (01296) 696012, Fax: 694519, E-mail: museum@buckscc.gov.uk, Internet: www.buckscc.gov.uk/museum
Local Museum
Hist 39159

Hamilton

District Museum and Cameronians Regimental Museum → Hamilton Low Parks Museum

Hamilton Low Parks Museum, 129 Muir St, Hamilton ML3 6BJ - T: (01698) 328232, Fax: 328412. Dir.: Kirsty Lingstadt
Military Museum / Local Museum - 1996
History of the Cameronians regiment, costumes, weaving, industrial and local history, musician gallery 39160

Harewood

Harewood House, c/o Harewood House Trust, Moor House, Harewood LS17 9LQ - T: (0113) 2181010, Fax: 2181002, E-mail: business@harewood.org, Internet: www.harewood.org. Dir.: Terence Suthers
Decorative Arts Museum 39161

Terrace Gallery → Harewood House

Harlech

Harlech Castle, Harlech LL46 2YH - T: (01766) 780552, Fax: 780552
Historic Site 39162

Harlow

Harlow Museum, Third Av, Harlow CM18 6YL - T: (01279) 446422, 454959, Fax: 626094, E-mail: richard.bartlett@harlow.gov.uk. Dir.: R.W. Bartlett, Sc. Staff: C.L. Hooper (Education, Local History)
Local Museum - 1973
Roman, post-medieval pottery - library 39163

Mark Hall Cycle Museum, Muskham Rd, Harlow CM20 2LF - T: (01279) 439680. Dir.: Ken Kilvington
Science&Tech Museum - 1982
Over 75 cycles and accessories illustrating the history of the bicycle from 1818 to the present day 39164

Museum of Harlow, Muskham Rd, Off First Av, Harlow CM20 2LF - T: (01279) 454959, Fax: 442789. Man.: Chris Lydamore
Archaeological Museum
Archaeological, social hist and archival coll 39165

Harray

Orkney Farm and Folk Museum, Corrigall, Harray KW15 1DH - T: (01856) 771411, Fax: 771411, Internet: www.orkneyislands.com/guide/. Cust.: Harry Flett
Local Museum
Series of restored Orkney farm buildings, visitors can see the traditional use of local resources - stone, straw, heather and horn, poultry, native sheep 39166

Harrington

Carpetbagger Aviation Museum, Sunnyvale Farm, off Lamport Rd, Harrington NN6 9PF - T: (01604) 686608, E-mail: cbaggermuseum@aol.com, Internet: www.harringtonmuseum.org.uk. Dir.: J. Bernard Tebbutt
Science&Tech Museum / Military Museum
Memorabilia of 801st-492nd, BG. USAAF Royal Observer Corps, Thor Rocket site 39167

Harrogate

Harlow Carr Museum of Gardening, Royal Horticultural Society, Crag Ln, Harrogate HG3 1QB - T: (01423) 565418, Fax: 530666, E-mail: education-harlowcarr@rhs.org.uk, Internet: www.rhs.org.uk. Chm.: Fred Dunning
Agriculture Museum - 1989
Old gardening equipment, gardening ephemera, large coll available to students 39168

Mercer Art Gallery, Swan Rd, Harrogate HG1 2SA - T: (01423) 566188, Fax: 566130, E-mail: lg12@harrogate.gov.uk, Internet: www.harrogate.gov.uk. Dir.: Mary J. Icershaw
Fine Arts Museum - 1991
Paintings, watercolors, lithographs, drawings, prints, reproductions 39169

Nidderdale Museum, Council Offices, King St, Pateley Bridge, Harrogate HG3 5LE - T: (01423) 711225
Local Museum - 1975
Domestic, farming and industrial material, costumes, a cobbler's shop, solicitor's office, general store, a Victorian parlour 39170

Royal Pump Room Museum, Crown Pl, Harrogate HG1 2RY - T: (01423) 566130, Fax: 840026, E-mail: LG12@harrogate.gov.uk, Internet: www.harrogate.gov.uk/museums. Dir.: Mary J. Kershaw
Science&Tech Museum - 1953
History of sulphur and mineral wells, costumes, pottery, archaeology, local social life 39171

War Room and Motor House Collection, 30 Park Parade, Harrogate HG1 5AG - T: (01423) 500704. Keeper: Brian Jewell
Historical Museum / Science&Tech Museum
Exhibits from two WW's transport and architectural models 39172

Harrow

Harrow Museum, Headstone Manor, Pinner View, Harrow HA2 6PX - T: (020) 88612626, Fax: 88636407, E-mail: davidw@hacserve.tcom.co.uk, Internet: www.harrowarts.org.uk. Cur.: David Whorlow
Local Museum
History of Harrow 39173

Hartland

Hartland Quay Museum, Hartland Quay, Hartland EX39 6DU - T: (01288) 331353. Dir.: M.R. Myers, M. Nix
Local Museum - 1980
Geological and natural hist, a marine aquarium, maritime hist, shipwrecks, local hist, coastal industry - aquarium 39174

Hartlepool

Hartlepool Art Gallery, Church Sq, Hartlepool TS24 8EQ - T: (01429) 869706, Fax: 523408, E-mail: arts-museums@hartlepool.gov.uk, Internet: www.thisishartlepool.com
Fine Arts Museum
19th and 20th century paintings, oriental antiquities, displays of local history and the history of Christ Church - Japanese gallery 39175

HMS Trincomalee, Jackson Dock, Hartlepool TS24 0SQ - T: (01429) 223193, Fax: 864385, E-mail: office@hms-trincomalee.co.uk, Internet: www.hms-trincomalee.co.uk. Gen. Man.: Bryn Huges
Science&Tech Museum - 1817
Historic warship 39176

Museum of Hartlepool, Jackson Dock, Hartlepool TS24 0SQ - T: (01429) 860077, Fax: 867332, E-mail: arts-museum@hartlepool.gov.uk, Internet: www.thisishartlepool.com
Local Museum - 1995
Local history stone age to present, natural history, fishing, shipbuilding, archaeology, local sailing craft 39177

Tees Archaeology, Sir William Gry House, Clarence Rd, Hartlepool TS24 8BT - T: (01429) 523455, Fax: 523477, E-mail: tees-archaeology@hartlepool.gov.uk. Dir.: R. Daniels
Archaeological Museum 39178

Harwich

Harwich Maritime Museum and Harwich Lifeboat Museum, Harwich Green, Harwich CO12 3NC - T: (01255) 503429, Fax: 503429, E-mail: theharwichsociety@quista.net, Internet: www.harwich-society.com. Dir.: T. Beirne (Maritime), C. Farnell (Lifeboat)
Science&Tech Museum 39179

Harwich Redoubt Fort, Main Rd, Harwich CO12 3LT - T: (01255) 503429, Fax: 503429, E-mail: theharwichsociety@quista.net, Internet: www.harwich-society.com. Dir.: A. Rutter
Historical Museum
180ft diameter circular fort built 1808 against Napoleonic invasion, 11 guns/battlements 39180

National Vintage Wireless and Television Museum, The High Lighthouse, Harwich - T: (07796) 280980. Cur.: Anthony O'Neill
Special Museum
Large coll of vintage wirelesses, televisions and broadcasting items, tracing the history of broadcasting from Baird and Marconi to the present day 39181

Haslemere

Haslemere Educational Museum, 78 High St, Haslemere GU27 2LA - T: (01428) 642112, Fax: 645234, E-mail: haslemeremuseum@aol.com, Internet: www.haslemeremuseum.co.uk. Cur.: Julia Tanner
Local Museum - 1888
Natural history, geology, ornithology, botany, prehistory, local history, peasant art 39182

Hastings

Fishermen's Museum, Rock-a-Nore Rd, Hastings TN34 3DW - T: (01424) 461446, Fax: 461446. Keeper: Philip Ornsby
Historical Museum
Hastings fishing industry, maritime hist 39183

Hastings Museum and Art Gallery, Bohemia Rd, Hastings TN34 1ET - T: (01424) 781155, Fax: 781165, E-mail: museum@hastings.gov.uk, Internet: www.hastings.gov.uk/museum. Cur.: Victoria Williams
Fine Arts Museum / Ethnology Museum - 1890
Paintings, Oriental art, Pacific and American Indian ethnography, geology, zoology, archaeology, history, folklore, topography, Durbar Hall, Hawaiian feather cloak, majolica dish of 1594, Sussex pottery - library, archives, two North American Indian galleries 39184

Museum of Local History, Old Town Hall, High St, Hastings TN34 1EW - T: (01424) 781166, Fax: 781165, E-mail: museum@hastings.gov.uk, Internet: www.hastings.gov.uk/museum. Dir.: Victoria Williams
Historical Museum - 1949
Local archaeology and history, topography 39185

Shipwreck Heritage Centre, Rock-a-Nore Rd, Hastings TN34 3DW - T: (01424) 437452, Fax: 437452. Dir.: Peter Marsden
Archaeological Museum - 1986
Objects from historic and ancient shipwrecks around southern England, prehistoric, Roman, medieval and later 39186

Hatfield

Art and Design Gallery, c/o Faculty of Art & Design, University of Hertfordshire, College Ln, Hatfield AL10 9AB - T: (01707) 285376, Fax: 285310, E-mail: m.b.shaul@herts.ac.uk, Internet: www.herts.ac.uk/artdes. Dir.: Chris McIntyre
Public Gallery
Fine and applied arts, design and craft 39187

Mill Green Museum and Mill, Mill Green, Hatfield AL9 5PD - T: (01707) 271362, Fax: 272511, E-mail: museum@welhar.gov.uk, Internet: www.hersmuseums.org.uk. Dir.: Carol Rigby
Local Museum / Science&Tech Museum - 1973
18th c brick-built, three-storey watermill, with early 19th c wood and iron machinery, 18th-c miller's house, the social hist of the Welwyn-Hatfield area, archaeology, domestic life, the railways, industry, farming and wartime, Belgic and Roman pottery from Welwyn, pottery from Hatfield - library 39188

Havant

Havant Museum, East St, Havant PO9 1BS - T: (023) 92451155, Fax: 92498707, E-mail: musmcp@hants.gov.uk, Internet: www.hants.gov.uk/museum/havant. Dir.: Dr. C.J. Palmer
Local Museum - 1977
Vokes Coll of sporting firearms, Havant local industries and local hist 39189

Havenstreet

Isle of Wight Steam Railway and Isle of Wight Railway Heritage Museum, Railway Station, Havenstreet PO33 4DS - T: (01983) 882204, Fax: 884515, Internet: www.iwsteamrailway.co.uk. Dir.: Hugh Boynton
Science&Tech Museum - 1971
Locomotives and rolling stock from early Isle of Wight-railways, oldest vehicle built in 1864, oldest locomotive built in 1876 - Documentary and photographic archive 39190

Haverfordwest

Scolton Manor Museum, Spittal, Haverfordwest SA62 5QL - T: (01437) 731328, Fax: 731457. Dir.: Mark Thomas
Local Museum - 1967
Social hist, costume, photographs, military hist, fine art, decorative art, natural hist, coins & numismatics, geology, archaeology 39191

Haverhill

Haverhill and District Local History Centre, Town Hall Arts Centre, High St, Haverhill CB9 8AR - T: (01440) 714962, E-mail: haverhillhistuk@aol.com
Local Museum
Photographs of local area, newspaper on microfilm 39192

Hawes

Dales Countryside Museum, Station Yard, Hawes DL8 3NT - T: (01969) 667494, Fax: 667165, E-mail: dcm@yorkshiredales.co.uk. Cur.: Fiona Rosher
Local Museum - 1979
History, agriculture, industry, local crafts transport, communications , telling the story of the people and landscape of the Dales 39193

Hawick

Drumlanrig's Tower, 1 Tower Knowe, Hawick TD9 9EN - T: (01450) 377615, Fax: 378506. Cur.: Fiona Colton
Local Museum / Fine Arts Museum
Borders history, local traditions, Tom Scott Gallery of late Victorian watercolours 39194

Hawick Museum, Wilton Lodge Park, Hawick TD9 7JL - T: (01450) 373457, Fax: 378506. Cur.: Fiona Colton
Local Museum / Fine Arts Museum - 1856/1975
Scottish history, natural history, militaria, coins, knitwear industry, 19th-20th c paintings 39195

The Scott Gallery, Hawick Museum, Wilton Lodge Park, Hawick TD9 7JL - T: (01450) 373457, Fax: 378506, E-mail: fionacolton@hotmail.com. Cur.: Fiona Colton
Public Gallery 39196

Hawkinge

Kent Battle of Britain Museum, Aerodrome Rd, Hawkinge CT18 7AG - T: (01303) 893140, E-mail: kentbattleofbritainmuseum@btinternet.com, Internet: www.kbobm.org. Cur.: Mike Llewellyn
Military Museum
Battle of Britain artefacts, aircraft, vehicles, weapons, flying equipment, prints and relics from over 600 crashed aircraft 39197

Hawkshead

Beatrix Potter Gallery, The National Trust, Main St, Hawkshead LA22 0NS - T: (015394) 36355, Fax: 36187, E-mail: rhabpg@smtp.ntrust.org.uk, Internet: www.nationaltrust.org.uk. Dir.: Liz Hunter
Fine Arts Museum
Beatrix Potter's original drawings and illustrations of her children's storybooks 39198

Haworth

Brontë Parsonage Museum, Church St, Haworth BD22 8DR - T: (01535) 642323, Fax: 674131, E-mail: bronte@bronte.org.uk, Internet: www.bronte.info. Dir.: Alan Bentley
Special Museum - 1895
Books, manuscripts, letters, paintings, drawings, furniture and personal treasures of the Brontë family 39199

Keighley and Worth Valley Railway Museum, Station, Haworth BD22 8NJ - T: (01535) 645214, 647777, Fax: 647317, Internet: www.kwvr.co.uk
Science&Tech Museum
Engines and rolling stock, Pullman train, vintage carriages and steam locomotives, station signs 39200

Haywards Heath

Lindfield Parvise Museum (closed) 39201

Headcorn

Lashenden Air Warfare Museum, Aerodrome, Headcorn TN27 9HX - T: (01622) 890226, 206783, Fax: 206783, E-mail: lashairwar@aol.com. Man.: D. Campbell
Science&Tech Museum
Aviation relics, uniforms, civilians at war, prisoners of war 39202

Heathfield

Sussex Farm Museum, Horam Manor, Heathfield TN21 0JB - T: (01435) 812597, Fax: 813716. Dir.: M.R.R. Goulden
Agriculture Museum
Farming and farm life since 1900 39203

Hebden Bridge

Automobilia, Billy Ln, Old Town, Wadsworth, Hebden Bridge HX7 8RY - T: (01422) 844775, Fax: 842884
Science&Tech Museum
Coll of cars, motorcycles, bicycles hr 39204

Heckington

Heckington Windmill, Hale Rd, Heckington NG34 9JW - T: (01529) 461919, Internet: www.visitlincolnshire.com
Science&Tech Museum
Ancillary machinery 39205

Hednesford

Museum of Cannock Chase, Valley Rd, Hednesford WS12 1TD - T: (01543) 877666, Fax: 428272, E-mail: museum@cannockchase.gov.uk, Internet: www.museumofcannockchase.co.uk. Dir.: Adrienne Whitehouse
Local Museum
Social history, industry, coal mining 39206

Hedon

Hedon Museum, Town Hall Complex, Saint Augustine's Gate, Hedon HU12 8EX - T: (01482) 890908, E-mail: hedon.museum@widerhorizon.net
Local Museum 39207

Helensburgh

Hill House, Upper Colquhoun St, Helensburgh G84 9AJ - T: (01436) 673900, Fax: 674685, E-mail: crostek@nts.org.uk, Internet: www.nts.org.uk. Cur.: Charlotte Rostek
Decorative Arts Museum
Domestic architecture of Charles Rennie Mackintosh, furniture, interior design, new domestic design (annual exhibition) 39208

Portico Gallery, 78 W Clyde St, Helensburgh G84 0AB - T: (01436) 671821, Fax: 677553
Fine Arts Museum 39209

Helmsdale

Timespan Museum and Art Gallery, Dunrobin St, Helmsdale KW8 6JX - T: (01431) 821327, Internet: www.timespan.org.uk
Local Museum / Public Gallery
Highland's people, natural hist, rare and medicinical plants - garden 39210

Helmshore

Helmshore Textile Museums, Holcombe Rd, Helmshore BB4 4NP - T: (01706) 226459, Fax: 218554, E-mail: helmshoremuseum@museumoflancs.org.uk, Internet: www.lancashire.com/lcc/museums. Dir.: Edmund Southworth
Science&Tech Museum - 1967
Platt coll of early textile machinery, Lancs textile industry 39211

Helston

Cornwall Aero Park, Clodgey Ln, Helston TR13 0QA - T: (01326) 573404, Fax: 573344, E-mail: flambards@connexions.co.uk, Internet: www.flambards.co.uk. Dir.: J.K. Hale
Science&Tech Museum - 1976
Flying machines, several aircraft, motorcycles motorcars and vehicles, historic streets, shops, houses, coaches, dresses, Victorian village, Britain in the Blitz historical aviation pioneers 39212

Flambards Victorian Village and Gardens, Culdrose Manor, Helston TR13 0QA - T: (01326) 573404, Fax: 573344, E-mail: info@flambards.co.uk, Internet: www.flambards.co.uk. Dir.: James Kingsford Hale
Science&Tech Museum
Flambards Victorian Village and Britain in The Blitz, life-sized recreations, aeropark coll, aviation in peace and war 39213

Helston Folk Museum, The Old Butter Market, Market Pl, Helston TR13 8TH - T: (01326) 564027, Fax: 569714, E-mail: enquiries@helstonmuseum.org.uk, Internet: www.helstonmuseum.org.uk. Cur.: Martin Matthews
Local Museum - 1949
Local history 39214

National Museum of Gardening, Trevarno Estate and Gardens, Helston TR13 0RU - T: (01326) 574274, Fax: 574282, E-mail: enquiries@trevarnoestateandgardens.co.uk, Internet: www.trevarnoestateandgardens.co.uk. Cur.: Marye Porter
Special Museum
Garden tools, implements, requisites, memorabilia and ephemera 39215

Poldark Mine and Heritage Complex, Wendron, Helston TR13 0ER - T: (01326) 573173, 563166, Fax: 563166, E-mail: info@poldark-mine.co.uk, Internet: www.poldark-mine.co.uk. Dir.: Richard Williams
Science&Tech Museum - 1971
18th c tin mine heritage, Cornish beam engine, machinery 39216

Hemel Hempstead

Old Town Hall, High St, Hemel Hempstead HP1 3AE - T: (01442) 228095, Fax: 234072
Local Museum 39217

Henfield

Henfield Museum, Village Hall, Coopers Yard, Henfield BN5 9DB - T: (01273) 492546, Fax: 494898, E-mail: office@henfield.gov.uk, Internet: www.henfield.gov.uk. Dir.: Marjorie W. Carreck
Local Museum - 1948
Local hist, costume, agricultural and domestic bygones, local paintings and photographs, uniforms 39218

Henley-on-Thames

Fawley Court Historic House and Museum, Fawley Court, Henley-on-Thames RG9 3AE - T: (01491) 574917, Fax: 411587. Hon. Cur.: Henry Lipinski
Historical Museum / Military Museum
Books from 15th to 19th century in a few European languages, religious and secular paintings, early manuscripts, Polish documents, rare collections of European, Far and Middle Eastern militaria and arms 39219

River and Rowing Museum, Mill Meadows, Henley-on-Thames RG9 1BF - T: (01491) 415600, Fax: 415601, E-mail: museum@rrm.co.uk, Internet: www.rrm.co.uk. Dir.: Paul E. Mainds
Historical Museum
History, ecology and archaeology of the River Thames, development of the international sport of rowing and the town of Henley-on-Thames 39220

Stonor Park, Henley-on-Thames RG9 6HF - T: (01491) 638587, Fax: 638587, E-mail: jweaver@stonor.com, Internet: www.stonor.com. Dir.: Lord Camoys
Fine Arts Museum 39221

Heptonstall

Heptonstall Museum, Old Grammar School, Heptonstall HX7 7PL - T: (01422) 843738
Local Museum 39222

Hereford

Churchill House Museum and Hatton Gallery, Venns Ln, Aylestone Hill, Hereford HR1 1DE - T: (01432) 260693, Fax: 342492. Dir.: Judy Stevenson, Sc. Staff: Althea Mackenzie
Fine Arts Museum / Decorative Arts Museum - 1966
Costumes 1700-1980, furniture, early English watercolors, local art, glass, toys 39223

Cider Museum, Pomona Pl, Whitecross Rd, Hereford HR4 0LW, mail addr: 21 Ryelands St, Hereford HR4 0LW - T: (01432) 354207, Fax: 371641, E-mail: info@cidermuseum.co.uk, Internet: www.cidermuseum.co.uk. Dir.: Margaret Thompson
Agriculture Museum - 1981
Farm cider making, the evolution of the modern cider factory 39224

Hereford City Museum and Art Gallery, Broad St, Hereford HR4 9AU - T: (01432) 364691, 260692, Fax: 342492, Internet: www.herfordshire.gov.uk. Man.: Jenny Williams
Local Museum / Fine Arts Museum - 1874
Roman remains, agricultural implements, natural hist, paintings and prints, glass and china, militaria, coins 39225

Herefordshire Light Infantry Regimental Museum, TA Centre, Harold St, Hereford - T: (01432) 272914
Military Museum
History and achievements of the Regiment, uniforms, weapons, medals, Colours and documents 39226

Mappa Mundi and Chained Library, 5 College Cloisters, Cathedral Close, Hereford HR1 2NG - T: (01432) 374202, Fax: 374220, E-mail: visits@herefordcathedral.co.uk, Internet: www.herefordcathedra.co.uk. Man.: Christine Quinto
Library with Exhibitions - 1996
Medieval world map, chained medieval books, Anglo-Saxon gospels, Hereford breviary and the Wycliffe Cider Bible 39227

Old House, High Town, Hereford HR1 2AA - T: (01432) 260694, Fax: 342492. Dir.: David Llewellyn
Historical Museum - 1928
17th c furniture, model of the city (1640), civil war displays, Jacobean domestic architecture 39228

Piano Museum Collection, c/o Royal National College for the Blind, College Rd, Hereford HR1 1EB - T: (01432) 265725, Fax: 376628, E-mail: info@rncb.ac.uk, Internet: www.rncb.ac.uk. Dir.: Roisin Burge
Music Museum
Early keyboard instruments 39229

Saint John and Coningsby Medieval Museum, Coningsby Hospital, Widemarsh St, Hereford HR4 9HN - T: (01432) 358134
Historical Museum
History of the Order of St John and the wars during the 300 years of the Crusades, armour and emblazons, also models, in period dress and bandages, of the Coningsby pensioners who used the hospital 39230

Waterworks Museum - Hereford, Broomy Hill, Hereford, mail addr: Llancraugh Cottage, Marstow, Ross-on-Wye HR9 6EH - T: (01432) 344062, Fax: (01600) 890009, E-mail: info@waterworksmuseum.org.uk, Internet: www.waterworksmuseum.org.uk. Dir.: Dr. Noel Meeke
Science&Tech Museum
Hist of drinking water supplies, wide range of working pumping engines (steam, diesel, gas) incl a triple-expansion condensing steam engine by Worth, McKenzie & Co (1895) 39231

Herne Bay

Herne Bay Museum and Gallery, 12 William St, Herne Bay CT6 5EJ - T: (01227) 367368, Fax: 742560, E-mail: museums@canterbury.gov.uk, Internet: www.hernebay-museum.co.uk
Local Museum / Fine Arts Museum
Displays about the town, about Reculver Roman Fort, archaeology and fossils 39232

Public Library and Museum, High St, Herne Bay CT6 5JY - T: (01227) 374896
Local Museum
Local history, natural history, Roman finds from Reculver 39233

Hertford

Hertford Museum, 18 Bull Plain, Hertford SG14 1DT - T: (01992) 582686, Fax: 534797, Internet: www.hertford.net/museum. Cur.: Helen Gurney
Local Museum - 1902
Geology, natural history, archaeology, history of East Hertfordshire, militaria, Saxon coins, ethnography 39234

Hethersett

Fire Service Museum, Fire Service Headquarters, Norwich Rd, Hethersett HR9 3DM - T: (01603) 810351
Science&Tech Museum - 1985 39235

Hexham

Border History Museum, The Old Gaol, Hallgate, Hexham NE46 3NH - T: (01434) 652351, Fax: 652425, E-mail: lted@tynedale.gov.uk. Dir.: Janet Goodridge
Historical Museum - 1980
Weapons and armour 39236

Chesterholm Museum Roman Vindolanda, Bardon Mill, Hexham NE47 7JN - T: (01434) 344277, Fax: 344060, E-mail: info@vindolanda.com, Internet: www.vindolanda.com. Dir.: Robin Birley
Historical Museum / Archaeological Museum
Roman leather, textilles and wooden objects 39237

Housesteads Roman Fort and Museum, Haydon Bridge, Hexham NE47 6NN - T: (01434) 344363, Internet: www.english-heritage.org.uk. Dir.: Georgina Plowright
Archaeological Museum - 1936
Inscriptions, sculptures, small finds, arm from Housesteads Roman Fort Arms 39238

Heywood

The Corgi Heritage Centre, 53 York St, Heywood OL10 4NR - T: (01706) 365812, Fax: 627811, E-mail: corgi@zen.co.uk, Internet: www.zen.co.uk/home/page/corgi
Special Museum
Model vehicle, history of Corgi toys 39239

High Wycombe

Hughenden Manor, High Wycombe HP14 4LA - T: (01494) 755573, 755565, Fax: 474284. Man.: Roslyn Lee
Special Museum - 1948
Home of Prime Minister Benjamin Disraeli (1848-1881), containing much of his furniture, pictures, books 39240

Wycombe Museum, Castle Hill House, Priory Av, High Wycombe HP13 6PX - T: (01494) 421895, Fax: 421897, E-mail: enquiries@wycombemuseum.demon.co.uk, Internet: www.wycombe.gov.uk/museum. Dir.: Vicki Wood
Local Museum / Historical Museum - 1932
Windsor chair making industry, lace, local hist, domestic furniture - library 39241

Higher Bockhampton

Hardy's Cottage, Higher Bockhampton DT2 8OJ
Special Museum
Memorabilia of writer Thomas Hardy (1840-1928) 39242

Hillsborough

The Art Gallery, 34 Lisburn St, Hillsborough BT26 6AB - T: (028) 92689896, Fax: 92688433, E-mail: theartgallery@whiteimage.com, Internet: www.whiteimage.com
Fine Arts Museum
Irish art, contemporary pieces, watercolours, oils, etchings, drawings 39243

Hillside

Sunnyside Museum, Sunnyside Royal Hospital, Hillside DD10 9JP - T: (01674) 830361, Fax: 830251. Cur.: Dr. P. Thompson
Special Museum
Administrative records from 1797, clinical records from 1815, photographs taken in Victorian and Edwardian times, medical instruments, a straitjacket, firefighting uniforms, replicas of nursing uniforms, examples of patients' craftwork 39244

Himley

Himley Hall, Himley Park, Himley DY3 4DF - T: (01902) 326665, Fax: 894163, E-mail: himley.pls@mbc-dudley.gov.uk, Internet: www.dudley.gov.uk. Dir.: Charles Hajdamach
Decorative Arts Museum - 1995
Temporary exhibitions programme 39245

Hinckley

Hinckley and District Museum, Framework Knitters' Cottage, Lower Bond St, Hinckley LE10 1QX - T: (01455) 251218. Chm.: H.A. Beavin
Local Museum
Hosiery and boot and shoe industries of Hinckley and district, machines, social history, WW I and II, pickering coll, local archaeological finds 39246

Hindley

Hindley Museum, Market St, Hindley WN2 3AU - T: (01942) 55287
Local Museum 39247

Hitchin

Hitchin Museum and Art Gallery, Paynes Park, Hitchin SG5 1EQ - T: (01462) 434476, Fax: 431316, E-mail: nhdc@hitchin.gov.uk, Internet: www.north.herts.gov.uk. Dir.: Gillian Riding, Cur.: Caroline Frith
Local Museum - 1939
Local history, militaria, costumes, paintings by Samuel Lucas, Victorian chemist shop and physic garden 39248

Museum Education for Letchworth Museum and Hitchin Museum, Museum Resources Centre, Bury Mead Rd, Hitchin SG5 1RT - T: (01462) 422946, Fax: 434883, E-mail: fran.brown@nhdc.gov.uk, Internet: www.nhdc.gov.uk
Association with Coll
Teaching coll 39249

Natural History Department, Museums Resources Centre, Bury Mead Rd, Hitchin SG5 1RT - T: (01462) 435197, Fax: 434883, Internet: www.ndhc.gov.uk
Natural History Museum
Natural sciences coll relating to northern Hertfordshire, Herdfordshire county herbarium - Library 39250

Hoddesdon

Lowewood Museum, High St, Hoddesdon EN11 8BH - T: (01992) 445596, E-mail: lowewood@tesco.net, Internet: www.homepages.tesco.net/~hdp. Cur.: Neil Robbins
Local Museum - 1948
Archaeology, geology and social history 39251

Hollingbourne

Eyhorne Manor Laundry Museum, Hollingbourne ME17 1UU - T: (01627) 80514
Historical Museum - 1971
Laundry 39252

Holm

Norwood Museum, Graemshall, Holm KW17 2RX - T: (01856) 78217
Local Museum
Coll of Norris Wood 39253

Holmfirth

Postcard Museum, Huddersfield Rd, Holmfirth HD7 1JH - T: (01484) 682231
Special Museum - 1987
Slides, postcards, and films 39254

Holsworthy

Holsworthy Museum, Manor Office, Holsworthy EX22 6JG - T: (01409) 259337, E-mail: holsworthy@devonmuseum.net, Internet: www.devonmuseums.net/holsworthy. Cur.: Emma Bond
Local Museum
Local history, social, domestic and agricultural items 39255

Holy Island

Lindisfarne Priory, Holy Island TD15 2RX - T: (01289) 389200, Internet: www.english-heritage.org.uk. Cur.: Andrew Morrison
Archaeological Museum
Anglo-Saxon sculpture and archaeological finds from the Priory 39256

Holyhead

Holyhead Maritime Museum, 8 Llainfain Estate, Llaingoch, Holyhead LL65 1NF - T: (01407) 769745, Fax: 769745, E-mail: jonncave4@aol.com, Internet: www.geocities.com/dickburnell. Dir.: William B. Carroll
Historical Museum
Photographs, plans, ship-models, marine tools 39257

Holywood

Ulster Folk and Transport Museum, Cultra, Holywood BT18 0EU - T: (028) 90428428, Fax: 90428728, E-mail: uftm@nidex.com, Internet: www.nidex.com/uftm. Dir.: Marshall McKee
Folklore Museum / Science&Tech Museum - 1958
History and social life of Northern Ireland, aviation, maritime, road and rail transport, reconstructed buildings, homes and shops, paintings, rural life, agriculture, fishing, crafts, music, textiles - archive, library 39258

Honiton

Allhallows Museum of Lace and Antiquities, High St, Honiton EX14 1PG - T: (01404) 44966, Fax: 46591, E-mail: info@honitonmuseum.co.uk, Internet: www.honitonmuseum.co.uk
Local Museum - 1945
Honiton Pottery, antiquities, fossils, local history, industry, Doll's House, Honiton lace 39259

Horndean

Goss and Crested China Centre, 62 Murray Rd, Horndean PO8 9JL - T: (023) 92597440, Fax: 92591975, E-mail: info@gosschinaclub.demon.co.uk, Internet: www.gosscrestedchina.co.uk. Dir.: Lynda Pine
Decorative Arts Museum
Souvenir china from Victorian and Edwardian times to WWI 39260

Hornsea

Hornsea Museum of Village Life, 11-13 Newbegin, Hornsea HU18 1AB - T: (01964) 533443, Internet: www.hornseamuseum.com. Dir.: Catherine Walker
Local Museum
Representations of the dairy, kitchen, parlour and bedroom of a c ago, tools of local craftsmen, photographs and postcards of local scenes, local industry, Hornsea Brick and Tile Works (c 1868-96), Hull and Hornsea Railway (1864-1964) 39261

Horringer

Ickworth House, The Rotunda, Horringer IP29 5QE - T: (01284) 735270, Fax: 735175. Man.: Kate Carver
Decorative Arts Museum - 1957
House dating from 1795-1830 with 18th c French furniture, silver, paintings 39262

Horsham

Christ's Hospital Museum, Counting House, Christ's Hospital, Horsham RH13 7YP - T: (01403) 247444. Cur.: Nicholas Plumley
Historical Museum
Boys boarding school, manuscripts, models, statues, ephemera 39263

Horsham Arts Centre, North St, Horsham RH12 1RL - T: (01403) 259708, 268689, Fax: 211502
Public Gallery 39264

Horsham Museum, Causeway House, 9 Causeway, Horsham RH12 1HE - T: (01403) 254959, Fax: 217581, E-mail: museum@horsham.gov.uk. Cur.: Jeremy Knight
Local Museum - 1893
Costumes, toys, old bicycles, local crafts and industries, reconstructed shops, in 16th c house, Shelley, geology, saddlery, farming - archives 39265

Horsham Saint Faith

City of Norwich Aviation Museum, Old Norwich Rd, Horsham Saint Faith NR10 3JF - T: (01603) 893080, Internet: www.cnam.co.uk
Science&Tech Museum / Military Museum
Aviation history of Norfolk, Vulcan bomber and some military and civil aircraft 39266

Houghton

Houghton Hall Soldier Museum, Houghton Hall, Houghton PE31 6UE - T: (01485) 528569, Fax: 528167, E-mail: administrator@houghtenhall.comm, Internet: www.houghtenhall.com
Military Museum - 1978 39267

Hove

British Engineerium, Nevill Rd, Hove BN3 7QA - T: (01273) 559583, Fax: 566403, E-mail: info@britishengineerium.com, Internet: www.britishengineerium.com. Dir.: Dr. Jonathan E. Minns
Science&Tech Museum
Restored Victorian pumping station 39268

Hove Museum and Art Gallery, 19 New Church Rd, Hove BN3 4AB - T: (01273) 290200, Fax: 292827, E-mail: visitor.services@brighton-hove.gov.uk. Dir.: Abigail Thomas
Fine Arts Museum / Local Museum - 1927
Early film material, toys, contemporary and decorative arts (all media), 20th c English art 39269

West Blatchington Windmill, Holmes Av, Hove BN3 7LE - T: (01273) 776017. Dir.: Peter Hill
Science&Tech Museum - 1979
Artefacts of milling and agricultural hist 39270

Hoy

Scapa Flow Museum, Hoy KW16 3NT - T: (01856) 791300, E-mail: museum@orkney.gov.uk, Internet: www.orkneyheritage.com. Cur.: Lewis Munro
Military Museum
Large military vehicles, boats, cranes, field artillery and railway rolling stock 39271

Huddersfield

Huddersfield Art Gallery, Princess Alexandra Walk, Huddersfield HD1 2SU - T: (01484) 221964, 221962, Fax: 221952, E-mail: robert.hall@kirkleesmc.gov.uk. Head: Robert Hall
Fine Arts Museum - 1898
British paintings, drawings, prints and sculpture since 1850 (Bacon, Hockney), changing exhibitions of contemporary art by regional and national artists in all media 39272

Kirklees Collection of Photographs, Huddersfield Library, Princess Alexandra Walk, Huddersfield HD1 2SU - T: (01484) 223800, Fax: 223805
Special Museum
Photographs, glass plate negatives 39273

Tolson Memorial Museum, Ravensknowle Park, Wakefield Rd, Huddersfield HD5 8DJ - T: (01484) 223830, Internet: www.kirkleesmc.gov.uk/community/museums/museums/shtml. Dir.: Jenny Salton, J.H. Rumsby, Cur.: S. Cooper
Local Museum / Folklore Museum - 1920
Local history, natural history, mineralogy, geology, botany, zoology, local life in Stone Age, Bronze Age, Iron Age, Roman and medieval periods, dolls, English glass, woolens, old vehicles, money scales, Ronnie The Raven's puzzlepath 39274

Victoria Tower, Castle Hill, Lumb Ln, Almondbury, Huddersfield HD5 8DJ - T: (01484) 223830, Internet: www.kirkleesmc.gov.uk/community/museums/museums.shtml
Historical Museum
Prehistoric hill-fort and medieval earthworks 39275

Humshaugh

Clayton Collection Museum, Roman Fort Chollerford, Humshaugh NE49 4EP - T: (01434) 681379. Cur.: Georgina Plowright
Archaeological Museum
Roman inscriptions, sculpture, weapons, tools and ornaments from several forts 39276

Huntingdon

Cromwell Museum, Grammar School Walk, Huntingdon PE29 3LF - T: (01480) 375830, Fax: 459563, E-mail: john.goldsmith@cambridgeshire.gov.uk, Internet: edweb.camcnty.gov.uk/cromwell. Dir.: John Goldsmith
Historical Museum / Special Museum - 1962
Documents on Cromwell's time, portraits, memorabilia on Oliver Cromwell (1599-1658) 39277

Hinchingbrooke House, Brampton Rd, Huntingdon PE18 6BN - T: (01480) 451121. Cur.: J.J. Cronin
Historical Museum
Cromwell family and the Earls of Sandwich 39278

Huntly

Brander Museum, The Square, Huntly AB54 8AE - T: (01771) 622906, Fax: 622884, E-mail: heritage@aberdeenshire.gov.uk. Dir.: W.K. Milne
Local Museum
Communion tokens, author George MacDonald memorabilia 39279

Leith Hall, Kennethmont, Huntly AB54 4NQ - T: (01464) 831216, Fax: 831594, E-mail: lpadgett@nts.org.uk, Internet: www.nts.org.uk/leith.html. Dir.: Robin Pellow
Historic Site / Military Museum
Exhibit 'For Crown and Country', Leith Hay family's military memorabilia 39280

Hutton-le-Hole

Ryedale Folk Museum, Hutton-le-Hole Y062 6UA - T: (01751) 417367. Cur.: Martin Watts
Open Air Museum / Folklore Museum - 1966
Tools, spinning, weaving, reconstructions of a 15th c Cruck house, 16th c manor house, 18th c cottage, 16th c glass furnace, agricultural coll of folk life 39281

Hynish

Skerryvore Museum, Upper Sq, Hynish PA77 6UQ - T: (01879) 2691, 220606, Fax: (01865) 311593. Cur.: C.D. Plant
Local Museum
Lighthouse story, pictures 39282

Hythe, Kent

Hythe Local History Room, Stade St, Oaklands, Hythe, Kent CT21 6BG - T: (01303) 266152/53, Fax: 262912, E-mail: admin@hythe-kent.com, Internet: www.hythe-kent.com. Cur.: J. Adamson
Local Museum - 1933
Local history, archaeology, paintings, mititary history 39283

Ilchester

Ilchester Museum, Town Hall and Community Centre, High St, Ilchester BA22 8NQ - T: (01935) 841247. Cur.: Graham Mottram
Local Museum
Prehistory, Roman, Saxon, Medieval, Post Medieval history 39284

Ilfracombe

Ilfracombe Museum, Wilder Rd, Ilfracombe EX34 8AF - T: (01271) 863541, E-mail: ilfracombe@devonmuseums.net, Internet: www.devonmuseums.net. Dir.: Sue Pullen
Local Museum - 1932
Local history, archaeology, ethnography, natural history, fauna, Victorian relics, shipping, armaments, militaria 39285

Ilkeston

Erewash Museum, High St, Ilkeston DE7 5JA - T: (0115) 9071141, Fax: 9071121, E-mail: museum@erewash.gov.uk, Internet: www.erewash.gov.uk. Cur.: Julie Biddlecombe
Local Museum - 1981/82
Listed Georgian and Victorian town house with kitchen and scullery display and other rooms containing civic, local and social hist collections, Long Eaton Town Hall 39286

Ilkley

Manor House Museum and Art Gallery, Castle Yard, Ilkley LS29 9DT - T: (01943) 600066, Fax: 817079. Dir.: Paul Lawson
Local Museum - 1961
Local hist, Roman finds from Olicana Roman Fort, temporary art exhibitions in Elizabethan Manor House 39287

Ilminster

Perry's Cider Mills, Dowlish Wake, Ilminster TA19 0NY - T: (01460) 52681, Internet: www.perryscider.co.uk
Folklore Museum
Old farm tools, wagons, cider-making equipment, stone jars and related country living items 39288

Immingham

Immingham Museum, Margaret St, Immingham DN40 1LE - T: (01469) 577066, E-mail: immingham@bmummery.freeserve.co.uk, Internet: www.ukwebwizard.co.uk. Dir.: Brian Mummery
Historical Museum
Coll of the Great Central Railway Society, creation of a port - archive 39289

Ingatestone

Ingatestone Hall, Ingatestone CM4 9NR
Historical Museum / Decorative Arts Museum - 1953
Essex history, furniture, china 39290

Innerleithen

Traquair House, Innerleithen EH44 6PW - T: (01896) 830323, Fax: 830639, E-mail: enquiries@traquair.co.uk, Internet: www.traquair.co.uk. Dir.: Catherine Maxwell Stuart
Decorative Arts Museum / Historical Museum - 1963
16th-17th c embroidery, Jacobite glass, silver, manuscripts, books, household objects, furniture, musical instruments, memorabilia of Mary, Queen of Scotland, 18th c Brew House 39291

Inveraray

Auchindrain Museum of Country Life, Auchindrain, Inveraray PA32 8XN - T: (01499) 500235. Cur.: John McDonald
Open Air Museum
West Highland farming township buildings, agricultural, domestic and social history 39292

Inveraray Bell Tower, All Saints' Episcopal Church, Inveraray PA32 8XJ - T: (01499) 302259
Religious Arts Museum 39293

Inveraray Castle, Cherry Park, Inveraray PA32 8XE - T: (01499) 302203, Fax: 302421, E-mail: enquiries@inveraray-castle.com, Internet: www.inveraray-castle.com. Dir.: A. Montgomery
Decorative Arts Museum 39294

Inveraray Jail, Church Sq, Inveraray PA32 8TX - T: (01499) 302381, Fax: 302195, E-mail: inverarayjail@btclick.com, Internet: www.inverarayjail.co.uk. Dir.: Jim Linley
Special Museum
19th c Scottish prison 39295

Inveraray Maritime Museum, The Pier, Inveraray PA32 8UY - T: (01499) 302213
Historical Museum
Clyde maritime memorabilia, three masted schooner 39296

Inverkeithing

Inverkeithing Museum, The Friary, Queen St, Inverkeithing KY11 1LS - T: (01383) 313594, E-mail: lesley.botton@fife.gov.uk
Local Museum
Social and local history 39297

Inverness

Culloden Visitor Centre, Culloden Moor, Inverness IV2 5EU - T: (01463) 790607, Fax: 794294, E-mail: culloden@nts.org.uk, Internet: www.nts.org.uk. Man.: Deirdre Smyth
Historical Museum - 1970
Historical display of the Battle of Culloden (1745/46), Jacobite exhibition - Old Leanach Cottage 39298

Eden Court Art Gallery, Eden Court Theatre, Bishops Rd, Inverness IV3 5SA - T: (01463) 234234, E-mail: ecmail@cali.co.uk
Public Gallery 39299

Inverness Museum and Art Gallery, Castle Wynd, Inverness IV2 3EB - T: (01463) 237114, Fax: 225293, E-mail: inverness.museum@highland.gov.uk, Internet: www.highland.gov.uk/cl/publicservices/museumdetails/inverness.htm. Cur.: Catharine Niven
Local Museum - 1825
Local hist, archaeology, paleontology, geology, bagpipes, local prints and paintings, old kitchen, silver, uniforms, costumes, weapons 39300

Regimental Museum The Highlanders, The Queen's Own Highlanders Collection, Fort George, Inverness IV2 7TD - T: (01463) 224380, E-mail: rhqthe-highlanders@btopenworld.com, Internet: www.saw.arts.ed.ac.uk/army/regiments/queensownhighlanders.html
Military Museum
Chronological display of uniforms, pictures, equipment, medals, pipe banners 39301

Inverurie

Carnegie Museum, The Square, Inverurie AB51 3SN - T: (01771) 622906, (01779) 477778, Fax: (01771) 622884, E-mail: heritage@aberdeenshire.gov.uk, Internet: www.aberdeenshire.gov.uk/heritage. Dir.: Dr. David M. Bertie
Local Museum - 1884
Local archaeology, geology, paleontology of Northern Scotland and England, coins, shells, natural history, North American Eskimo anthropological coll 39302

Ipswich

Christchurch Mansion, Soane St, Ipswich IP4 2BE - T: (01473) 433554, Fax: 433564, E-mail: christchurch.mansion@ipswich.gov.uk, Internet: www.ipswich.gov.uk. Dir.: Tim Heyburn (Culture)
Fine Arts Museum / Decorative Arts Museum / Public Gallery - 1896
English pottery, porcelain, glass, paintings (Gainsborough, Constable, Wilson Steer), prints, sculptures, furniture, in 16th c house 39303

HMS Ganges Association Museum, Old Sail Loft, Shotley Marina, Shotley Gate, Ipswich IP9 1QJ - T: (01473) 684749, E-mail: georgeathroll@appliedonline.co.uk, Internet: www.hmsgangesassoc.org. Cur.: Ron Catchpole
Fine Arts Museum / Military Museum
Photographs, artefacts, memorabilia of The Royal Navy and HMS Ganges - the premier boy entrants training ship 1905-1976 39304

Ipswich Museum, High St, Ipswich IP1 3QH - T: (01473) 433550/53, Fax: 433558, E-mail: museums@ipswich.gov.uk, Internet: www.ipswich.gov.uk/tourism/guide/museum.htm. Dir.: Tim Heyburn, Sc. Staff: D.L. Jones (Human History), D. Lampard (Botany), S. Dummer (Collections, Registration), R. Entwistle (Cons.), T. Butler (Public Services), M.R. Hayward (Design), E. Dodds (Design), R. Weaver (Exhibitions), Catherine Richardson (Art Education), M. Swift (Christchurch Mansion), E. Richardson (Ipswich Museum)
Local Museum / Natural History Museum - 1881
Archaeology, geology, natural history, ethnology, wildlife 39305

Ipswich Transport Museum, Old Trolleybus Depot, Cobham Rd, Ipswich IP3 9JD - T: (01473) 715666, Fax: 832260, Internet: www.ipswichtransportmuseum.co.uk. Chm.: Brian Dyes
Science&Tech Museum
Road transport, built or used in the Ipswich area, on air, water and rail transport - archive, library 39306

Suffolk City Council Libraries and Heritage, Ipswich Library, Northgate St, Ipswich IP1 3DE - T: (01473) 584564, Fax: 584549, E-mail: Lyn.gash@libher.suffolkcc.gov.uk, Internet: www.suffolkmuseums.org.uk. Off.: Alexander Hayward
Local Museum
Library 39307

Ironbridge

Ironbridge Gorge Museum, The Wharfage, Ironbridge TF8 7AW - T: (01952) 433522, 432405, Fax: 432204, E-mail: info@ironbridge.org.uk, Internet: www.ironridge.org.uk. Dir.: Glen Lawes, Cur.: John Challen
Decorative Arts Museum / Open Air Museum - 1967/1997
Elton coll of industrial art (items representing the hist and growth of industry through paintings, engravings and books), decorative tiles, porcelain, iron - archives, library 39308

Ironbridge Tollhouse, Ironbridge TF8 7AW - T: (01952) 433522, Fax: 432204, E-mail: info@ironbridge.org.uk, Internet: www.ironbridge.org.uk. Cur.: David de Haan
Science&Tech Museum
First iron bridge, erected in 1779 39309

Teddy Bear Shop and Museum, Dale End, Ironbridge TF8 7AQ - T: (01952) 433029, E-mail: info@ironbridge.org.uk, Internet: www.merrythought.co.uk. Man.: Barbara Stewart
Special Museum
Famous teddy bear factory, modern Merrythought products, historical coll of soft toys 39310

Irvine

Irvine Burns Club Museum, Fairburn, 5 Burns St, Irvine KA12 8RW - T: (01294) 274511
Special Museum
Flax dresser works, letters from Honorary Members Dickens, Garibaldi, Tennyson 39311

Scottish Maritime Museum, Laird Forge Bldgs, Gottries Rd, Irvine KA12 8QE - T: (01294) 278283, Fax: 313211, E-mail: smm@tildesley.fsbusiness.co.uk, Internet: www.scottishmaritimemuseum.org. Dir.: J.M. Tildesley, David Thomson
Science&Tech Museum
Traditional maritime skills, shipbuilding, equipment, tools, boats, a Puffer 'Spartan', a tug 'Garnock', steam yacht 'Carola' - archives 39312

Vennel Gallery, 4-10 Glasgow Vennel, Irvine KA12 0BD - T: (01294) 275059, Fax: 275059, E-mail: vennel@globalnet.co.uk, Internet: www.northayrshiremuseums.org.ukl
Special Museum / Fine Arts Museum
Robert Burns' heckling shop and lodging house where he worked and lived, international art 39313

Isle-of-Barra

Dualchas-Museum Bharraigh Agus Bhatarsaidh, Castlebay, Isle-of-Barra HS9 5XD - T: (01871) 810413, Fax: 810413. Chm.: Malcolm MacNeil
Local Museum 39314

Isle-of-Iona

Infirmary Museum, Saint Ronan's Church Museum and Columba Centre, Iona Abbey, Isle-of-Iona PA76 6SN - T: (01828) 640411, Fax: 640217, E-mail: iona_abbay@compuserve.com, Internet: ourworld.compuserve.com/homepages/iona_abbay
Religious Arts Museum
Celtic gravestones and crosses, Celtic artefacts 39315

Iona Abbey Museum → Infirmary Museum, Saint Ronan's Church Museum and Columba Centre

Iona Heritage Centre, Isle-of-Iona PA76 6SJ - T: (01681) 700576, Fax: 700580, E-mail: heritage@ionagallery.com, Internet: www.isle-of-iona.com. Cur.: Mary Hay
Historical Museum
Social history 39316

Isle-of-Lewis

Dell Mill, North Dell, Ness, Isle-of-Lewis PA86 0SN
Science&Tech Museum
Equipment, machinery, local grain production 39317

Isle-of-Skye

Staffin Museum, 6 Ellishadder, Staffin, Isle-of-Skye IV51 9JE - T: (01470) 562321. Dir.: Dugald Alexander Ross
Archaeological Museum
Fossils from Skye (Jurassic age), incl the only dinosaur bones from Scotland (these represent five species incl the world's oldest recorded Stegosaur), 18th c implements and furniture, old glass and eartheware bottles, geological and mineralogical specimens, horse-drawn implements of the 19th c, archaeological exhibits incl neolithic flint arrowheads and pottery 39318

Isle-of-Tiree

An Iodnlann, Am Bagh, Isle-of-Tiree PA77 6UN - T: (01879) 220323, Fax: 220893, E-mail: doc.holliday@dial.pipex.com. Dir.: Dr. John Holliday
Local Museum 39319

Isleworth

Osterley Park House, Jersey Rd, Isleworth TW7 4RB - T: (020) 85687714, Fax: 85687714, E-mail: tosgen@smtp.ntrust.org.uk
Decorative Arts Museum - 1949
18th c villa, neo-classical interior decoration and furnishings designed by Robert Adam, landscaped park 39320

Ivinghoe

Ford End Watermill, Ivinghoe LU6 3QB - T: (01582) 600391, Internet: www.thechilterns.co.uk. Man.: David Lindsey
Science&Tech Museum
Milling machines and artefacts 39321

Jackfield

Jackfield Tile Museum, Jackfield TF8 7JX - T: (01952) 882030, Fax: 432204, E-mail: info@ironbridge.org.uk, Internet: www.ironbridge.org.uk. Cur.: Michael Vanns
Decorative Arts Museum
Decorative wall and floor tiles 39322

Jarrow

Bede's World, Church Bank, Jarrow NE32 3DY - T: (0191) 4892106, Fax: 4282361, E-mail: visitor.info@bedesworld.co.uk, Internet: www.bedesworld.co.uk. Dir.: Keith Merrin, Cur.: Laura M. Sole
Archaeological Museum - 1974
Finds from the Anglo-Saxon and medieval monastic site of St. Paul's, Anglo-Saxon demonstration farm - library 39323

Jedburgh

Jedburgh Castle Jail Museum, Castlegate, Jedburgh TD8 6QD - T: (01835) 864750, Fax: 864750. Dir.: Rosi Capper
Historical Museum - 1965
19th c prison life, local history coll 39324

Mary Queen of Scots' House, Queen St, Jedburgh TD8 6EN - T: (01835) 863331, Fax: 863331. Cur.: Fiona Colton
Special Museum
Facility for the 400th anniversary of the death of Mary Stuart 39325

Kegworth

Kegworth Museum, 52 High St, Kegworth DE74 2DA - T: (01509) 672886, 214460
Local Museum
Village life and trades 39326

Keighley

Cliffe Castle Museum, Spring Gardens Ln, Keighley BD20 6LH - T: (01535) 618231, Fax: 610536, E-mail: alison.armstrong@bradford.gov.uk, Internet: www.bradford.gov.uk/tourism/museums. Dir.: Jane Glaister, Keeper: Alison C. Armstrong (Geology and Education)
Local Museum / Natural History Museum - 1899
Paintings, sculpture, applied arts, household and farm tools, natural history, geology, archaeology, reconstructed craft shops, militaria, sports, toys, costumes 39327

East Riddlesden Hall, Bradford Rd, Keighley BD20 5EL - T: (01535) 607075, Fax: 691462, E-mail: eastriddlesdenhall@ntrust.org.uk. Dir.: Lloyd Taylor
Decorative Arts Museum
Coll of furniture, textiles, embroidery, pweter 39328

Ingrow Loco Museum, South St, Keighley BD21 5AV, mail addr: 296 Didsbury Rd, Stockport SK4 3JH - T: (01535) 690739
Science&Tech Museum - 1968
Locomotive Museum, Coaltank Locomotiv No 1054 39329

Keighley and Worth Valley Light Railway Museum → Ingrow Loco Museum

Museum of Rail Travel, Ingrow, Keighley BD22 8NJ - T: (01535) 680425, Fax: 610796, E-mail: admin@vintagecarriagestrust.org, Internet: www.vintagecarriagestrust.org. Dir.: Michael W. Cope
Science&Tech Museum
Coll of historic railway coaches 39330

Kelevedon

Feering and Kelvedon Local History Museum, Aylett's School, Maldon Rd, Kelevedon CO5 9AH - T: (01376) 571206, Fax: 573163, E-mail: alipes@dial.pipex.com. Dir.: G.H. Wheldon
Local Museum
Local history, Roman remains, manorial history, agricultural and domestic, schools, transport, post 39331

Kelmscott

Kelmscott Manor, Kelmscott GL7 3HJ - T: (01367) 252486, Fax: 253754, E-mail: admin@kelmscottmanor.co.uk, Internet: www.kelmscottmanor.co.uk. Cust.: Sue Ashworth
Decorative Arts Museum
Home of William Morris, coll of textiles, furniture and drawings 39332

Kelso

Floors Castle, Roxburghe Estate's Office, Kelso TD5 7SF - T: (01573) 223333, Fax: 226056, E-mail: marketing@floorscastle.com, Internet: www.floorscastle.com. Dir.: Duke of Roxburghe
Fine Arts Museum 39333

Kelso Museum and Turret Gallery, Turret House, Abbey Court, Kelso TD5 7JA - T: (01573) 223464, Fax: 373993. Dir.: Ian Brown
Local Museum - 1983
Growth of Kelso and its importance as a market town, hist of the local skinning industry 39334

Kelvedon Hatch

Kelvedon Hatch Secret Nuclear Bunker, Kelvedon Hall Ln, Kelvedon Hatch CM14 5TL - T: (01277) 364883, Fax: 372562, E-mail: bunker@japar.demon.co.uk, Internet: www.japar.demon.co.uk. Cur.: M. Parrish
Historical Museum
Cold war artefacts 39335

Kendal

Abbot Hall Art Gallery, Kendal LA9 5AL - T: (01539) 722464, Fax: 722494, E-mail: info@abbothall.org.uk, Internet: www.abbothall.org.uk. Dir.: Edward King
Fine Arts Museum - 1962
18th c furnished rooms, paintings, sculpture, pottery, portraits by Kendal painters, Romney, works by Schwitters, Ruskin, Riley, Turner and Nicholson, watercolours of the English Lake District 39336

Kendal Museum, Station Rd, Kendal LA9 6BT - T: (01539) 721374, Fax: 737976, E-mail: info@kendalmuseum.org.uk, Internet: www.kendalmuseum.org.uk
Local Museum - 1796
Local history, archaeology, geology, natural history, British birds and mounted mammals 39337

Museum of Lakeland Life, Abbot Hall, Kendal LA9 5AL - T: (01539) 722464, Fax: 722494, E-mail: info@lakelandmuseum.org.uk, Internet: www.lakelandmuseum.org.uk. Dir.: Edward King
Local Museum - 1970
Local cultural hist of Lake District area, industry, period rooms, costumes, trades, farming, printing presses, weaving equipment, photogr coll, Simpson furniture, Arthur Ransome Society 39338

Sizergh Castle, Sizergh, Kendal LA8 8AE - T: (015395) 60070, Fax: 60951, E-mail: sizergh@nationaltrust.org.uk, Internet: www.nationaltrust.org.uk
Local Museum 39339

Kenton

Powderham Castle, Kenton EX6 8JQ - T: (01626) 890243, Fax: 890729, E-mail: castle@powderham.co.uk, Internet: www.powderham.co.uk. Dir.: Tim Faulkner
Fine Arts Museum 39340

Kerriemuir

Kirriemuir Gateway to the Glens Museum, The Townhouse, 32 High St, Kerriemuir DD8 4BB - T: (01575) 575479, Fax: 462590, E-mail: kirriegateway@angus.gov.uk, Internet: www.angus.gov.uk/history.htm. Cur.: Fiona Guest
Local Museum
Archaeology and social hist town and western angus glens, wildlife and multimedia programme 39341

Keswick

Cars of the Stars Motor Museum, Standish St, Keswick CA12 5LS - T: (017687) 73757, Fax: 72090, E-mail: cotsmm@aol.com, Internet: www.carsofthestars.com. Cur.: John Nelson, Philip Nelson
Science&Tech Museum
Celebrity TV and film vehicles 39342

Cumberland Pencil Museum, Southey Works, Greta Bridge, Keswick CA12 5NG - T: (017687) 73626, Fax: 74679, E-mail: museum@acco-uk.co.uk, Internet: www.pencils.co.uk. Dir.: D.J. Sharrock
Special Museum - 1981
Process of pencil manufacture, history of pencils using 39343

Keswick Museum and Art Gallery, Fitz Park, Station Rd, Keswick CA12 4NF - T: (017687) 73263, Fax: 80390, E-mail: hazel.davison@allerdale.gov.uk. Cur.: Hazel Davison
Local Museum / Fine Arts Museum - 1873
Keswick's social hist, natural hist, archeology, lit coll, geology 39344

Mirehouse, Underskiddaw, Keswick CA12 4QE - T: (017687) 72287, Fax: 72287, E-mail: info@mireho.freeserve.co.uk. Dir.: J.H.F. Spedding
Fine Arts Museum
Pictures, furniture, works by Constable, Turner, De Wint, Hearne, Girtin, Romney, Morland, coll of papers and books of Francis Bacon 39345

Kettering

Alfred East Art Gallery, Sheep St, Kettering NN16 0AN - T: (01536) 534274, Fax: 534370, E-mail: museum@kettering.gov.uk, Internet: www.kettering.gov.uk. Dir.: Su Davies
Public Gallery - 1913
English paintings, watercolors, drawings and prints since 1800, Sir Alfred East, Thomas Cooper-Gotch 39346

Boughton House, Kettering NN14 1BJ - T: (01536) 515731, Fax: 417255, E-mail: llt@boughtonhouse.org.uk, Internet: www.boughtonhouse.org.uk. Dir.: Gareth Fitzpatrick
Fine Arts Museum
Paintings of Van Dyck, English and Flemish tapestries, Armoury 39347

Manor House Museum, Sheep St, Kettering NN16 0AN - T: (01536) 534219, Fax: 534370, E-mail: museum@kettering.gov.uk, Internet: www.kettering.gov.uk. Dir.: Su Davies
Local Museum
History of Kettering Borough, geology, archaeology, social and industrial history 39348

Kew

Kew Bridge Steam Museum, Green Dragon Ln, Brentford, Kew TW8 0EN - T: (020) 85684757, Fax: 85699978, E-mail: info@kbsm.org, Internet: www.kbsm.org. Dir.: Lesley Bossine
Science&Tech Museum - 1975
Cornish beam engines dating from 1820 plus other stationary steam engines, all housed in a Victorian waterworks, 'Water for Life' exhibition on London's water supply 39349

Kew Palace Museum of the Royal Botanic Gardens (temporary closed), Royal Botanic Gardens, Kew TW9 3AB - T: (020) 87819500, Fax: 89481197, Internet: www.hrp.org.uk. Dir.: Prof. Peter Crane
Natural History Museum - 1759
Tropical Plant Species, economic botany coll 39350

Museum - Treasures from the National Archives, Ruskin Av, Kew TW9 4DU - T: (020) 83925279, Fax: 83925345, E-mail: events@pro.gov.uk, Internet: www.pro.gov.uk. Man.: Claire Bertrand
Special Museum - 1902
Millenium treasure 39351

Kidderminster

Kidderminster Railway Museum, Station Approach, Comberton Hill, Kidderminster DY10 1QX - T: (01562) 825316, Fax: 861039
Science&Tech Museum
Railways of the British Isles, signalling equipment 39352

Worcestershire County Museum, Hartlebury Castle, Kidderminster DY11 7XZ - T: (01299) 250416, Fax: 251890, E-mail: Museum@worcestershire.gov.uk, Internet: www.worcestershire.gov.uk/museum. Dir.: Robin Hill
Local Museum - 1966
Horse-drawn vehicles including gypsy caravans, glass, crafts, toys, costumes, folk life, archaeology, coll from the Victorian period, including costume, transport, domestic life, agriculture and crafts and trades - library 39353

Kidwelly

Kidwelly Industrial Museum, Broadford, Kidwelly SA17 4LW - T: (01554) 891078
Science&Tech Museum
Local history, tinplate industry, local coal industry, gear and steam winding engine from Morlais colliery, geology, 39354

Kilbarchan

Weaver's Cottage, The Cross, Kilbarchan PA10 2JG - T: (01505) 705588, E-mail: gmurray@nts.org.uk. Man.: Grace Murrey
Historical Museum - 1954
18th c cottage, handloom weaver, looms, weaving equipment, domestic utensils, local history 39355

Kildonan

Kildonan Museum, South Uist, Kildonan HS8 5RY - T: (01878) 710343
Local Museum / Ethnology Museum
Artefacts, photographs, genealogical information, local archaeology 39356

Museum Chill Donnan, Old School, Kildonan PA81 5R2
Local Museum 39357

Killiecrankie

Pass of Killiecrankie Visitor Centre, Killiecrankie PH16 5LG - T: (01796) 473233, Fax: 473233
Historical Museum / Natural History Museum
Historic battle of 1689, natural history 39358

Killin

Breadalbane Folklore Centre, Falls of Dochart, Killin FK21 8XE - T: (01567) 820254, Fax: 820764. Man.: Lynne Liddell
Folklore Museum
Folklore, legends and myths of Breadalbane, contains the healing stones of St Fillan, exhibition on clan heritage, area wildlife and audio visual presentations 39359

Killingworth

John Sinclair Railway Collection, Dial Cottage, Great Lime Rd, West Moor, Killingworth NE12 5BA - T: (01670) 355899, E-mail: peterdonnelly@iname.com. Dir.: Peter Donnelly
Science&Tech Museum
Signalling, booking office, lamps, signs, the permanent way, posters 39360

Kilmarnock

Dean Castle, Dean Rd, off Glasgow Rd, Kilmarnock KA3 1XB - T: (01563) 554702, Fax: 554720, E-mail: donna.chisholm@east-ayrshire.gov.uk. Dir.: Donna Chrisholm
Historical Museum - 1976
Medieval arms and armour, musical instruments, tapestries 39361

Dick Institute Museum and Art Gallery, 14 Elmbank Av, Kilmarnock KA1 3BU - T: (01563) 554343, Fax: 554344, E-mail: jason.sutcliffe@east-ayrshire.gov.uk, Internet: www.east-ayrshire.gov.uk. Dir.: Adam Geary
Natural History Museum / Fine Arts Museum - 1901
Geology, ethnography, archaeology, conchology, armaments, numismatics, church and trade relics, paintings, etchings, sculptures, old bibles, incunabula, fine art, local and social history 39362

Kilmartin

Museum of Ancient Culture, Kilmartin House, Kilmartin PA31 8RQ - T: (01546) 510278, Fax: 510330, E-mail: museum@kilmartin.org, Internet: www.kilmartin.org. Dir.: Colin Schafer
Historical Museum / Archaeological Museum
Archaeology, landscape interpretation, prehistory, early Schotish history, neolithic, bronze age, Dalriada, rock art, ancient monuments 39363

Kilmaurs

Kilmaurs Historical Society Museum, 13 Irvine Rd, Kilmaurs KA3 2RJ
Historical Museum 39364

Kilsyth

Colzium Museum, Colzium House, Colzium-Lennox Estate, Kilsyth G65 0PY - T: (01236) 735077, Fax: 781407
Local Museum
Local hist, battle of Kilsyth - garden, woodland walk, chilren's zoo 39365

Kilsyth's Heritage, Library, Burngreen, Kilsyth G65 0HT - T: (01236) 735077, Fax: 781407
Local Museum
History of Kilsyth from the 18th c 39366

Kilwinning

Dalgarven Mill, Museum of Ayrshire Country Life and Costume, Dalry Rd, Kilwinning KA13 6PL - T: (01294) 552448, Fax: 552448, E-mail: admin@dalgarvenmill.org.uk, Internet: www.dalgarvenmill.org.uk. Dir.: Moira Ferguson
Science&Tech Museum / Folklore Museum
Water-driven flour mill, agricultural and domestic implements, costume 39367

Kilwinning Abbey Tower, Main St, Kilwinning KA13 6AN, mail addr: c/o North Ayrshire Museum, Manse St, Saltcoats KA21 5AA - T: (01294) 464174, Fax: 464174, E-mail: namuseum@north-ayrshire.gov.uk
Local Museum
Local and social history 39368

King's Lynn

King's Lynn Arts Centre, 29 King St, King's Lynn - T: (01553) 779095, Fax: 766834, E-mail: ifalconbridge@west-norfolk.gov.uk, Internet: www.kingslynnarts.org.uk. Man.: Liz Falconbridge
Public Gallery 39369

King's Lynn Museum, Market St, King's Lynn PE30 1NL - T: (01553) 775001, Fax: 775001, E-mail: lynn.museum@norfolk.gov.uk, Internet: www.norfolk.gov.tourism/museums. Dir.: Robin Hanley, Cur.: Timothy Thorpe
Local Museum - 1904
Natural hist, archaeology, local hist, geology, temporary exhibition gallery 39370

Tales of the Old Gaol House, Saturday Market Pl, King's Lynn PE30 5DQ - T: (01553) 774297, Fax: 772361, E-mail: gaolhouse@west-norfolk.gov.uk, Internet: www.west-norfolk.gov.uk
Historical Museum
History of crime and punishment in Lynn, King John Cup (1340), King John Sword 39371

Town House Museum of Lynn Life, 46 Queen St, King's Lynn PE30 5DQ - T: (01553) 773450, Fax: 775001, E-mail: townhouse.museum@norfolk.gov.uk, Internet: www.norfolk.gov.uk/tourism/museums. Dir.: Robin Hanley
Folklore Museum - 1992
Ceramic and glass, furniture, Victoriana 39372

True's Yard Fishing Heritage Centre, North St, King's Lynn PE30 1QW - T: (01553) 770479, Fax: 765100, E-mail: trues.yard@virgin.net, Internet: welcome.to/truesyard. Cur.: Dr. Andrew Lane
Historical Museum 39373

Kingsbridge

Cookworthy Museum of Rural Life in South Devon, 108 Fore St, Kingsbridge TQ7 1AW - T: (01548) 853235, E-mail: wcookworthy@talk21.com. Chair.: Margaret Lorenz
Local Museum - 1971
Cookworthy's porcelain and work as a chemist, costumes, craft tools, photos, agricultural machinery, Edwardian pharmacy, Victorian kitchen - library, archives 39374

Kingston-upon-Hull

Arctic Corsair, 25 High St, Kingston-upon-Hull HU1 3DX, mail addr: c/o Ferens Art Gallery, Queen Victoria Sq, Kingston-upon-Hull HU1 3RA - T: (01482) 613902, Fax: 613710, E-mail: museums@hullcc.gov.uk. Dir.: Arthur G. Credland
Science&Tech Museum
Deep sea trawler (1960) 39375

Burton Constable Hall, Skirlaugh, Kingston-upon-Hull HU11 4LN - T: (01964) 562400, Fax: 563229, E-mail: enquires@burtonconstable.com, Internet: www.burtonconstable.com. Dir.: Dr. D.P. Connell
Decorative Arts Museum
Paintings, furniture 39376

Ferens Art Gallery, Hull City Museum & Art Gallery, Queen Victoria Sq, Kingston-upon-Hull HU1 3RA - T: (01482) 613902, Fax: 613710, E-mail: museums@hullcc.gov.uk, Internet: www.hullcc.gov.uk/museums. Keeper: Kirsten Simister (Art), Brian Hayton (Culture), Asst. Keeper: Laura Turner (Collections), Christine Brady (Exhibitions)
Fine Arts Museum - 1927
Coll of old masters (British, Dutch, Flemish, French, Italian), portraits (16th c to present), marine painting, 19th & 20th c British art, contemporary British painting, sculpture and photography 39377

Hands on History, South Church Side, Kingston-upon-Hull HU1 1RR, mail addr: c/o Ferens Art Gallery, Queen Victoria Sq, Kingston-upon-Hull HU1 3RA - T: (01482) 613902, Fax: 613710, E-mail: museums@hullcc.gov.uk, Internet: www.hullcc.gov.uk/museums. Dir.: Jayne Tyler (Social History)
Historical Museum - 1988
Hull and its people, Victorian Britain, ancient Egypt 39378

Hull and East Riding Museum, 36 High St, Kingston-upon-Hull HU1 1PS, mail addr: c/o Ferens Art Gallery, Queen Victoria Sq, Kingston-upon-Hull HU1 3RA - T: (01482) 613902, Fax: 613710, E-mail: museum@hullcc.demon.co.uk, Internet: www.hullcc.gov.uk/museums. Keeper: Craig Barclay (Archaeology), Asst. Keeper: Martin Foreman (Arcaeology), Matt Stephens (Natural History)
Archaeological Museum - 1925
Prehistoric and early hist of Humberside, mosaics found at the Roman villa at Horkstow, material from Iron Age chariot burials on the Worlds 39379

Hull Maritime Museum, Queen Victoria Sq, Kingston-upon-Hull HU1 3DX - T: (01482) 613902, Fax: 613710, E-mail: arthur.credland@hullcc.gov.uk, Internet: www.hullcc.gov.uk/museums. Dir.: Arthur G. Credland
Special Museum - 1975
Whaling, shipbuilding, weapons, gear, maritime history, marine paintings, shipmodels, scrimshaw work - library 39380

Hull University Art Collection, Middleton Hall, University Cottingham Rd, Kingston-upon-Hull HU6 7RX - T: (01482) 465035, Fax: 465192, E-mail: j.g.bernasconi@hull.ac.uk, Internet: www.hull.ac.uk/artcoll. Dir.: John G. Bernasconi
Public Gallery / Decorative Arts Museum - 1963
Art in Britain 1890-1940, the Thompson Collections of Chinese porcelain 39381

Old Grammar School Museum → Hands on History

Spurn Lightship, Castle St, Hull Marina, Kingston-upon-Hull HU1 3JT, mail addr: c/o Ferens Art Gallery, Queen Victoria Sq, Kingston-upon-Hull HU1 3RA - T: (01482) 613902, Fax: 613710, E-mail: museum@hullcc.gov.uk, Internet: www.hullcc.gov.uk/museums. Dir.: Arthur G. Credland
Science&Tech Museum 39382

Streetlife Museum, Hull Museum of Transport, 26 High St, Kingston-upon-Hull HU1 1PS, mail addr: c/o Ferens Art Gallery, Queen Victoria Sq, Kingston-upon-Hull HU1 3RA - T: (01482) 613902, Fax: 613710, E-mail: museum@hullcc.gov.uk, Internet: www.hullcc.gov.uk/museums. Dir.: Clare Parsons, Matt Stephens
Science&Tech Museum 39383

Wilberforce House, 25 High St, Kingston-upon-Hull HU1 1NQ, mail addr: c/o Ferens Art Gallery, Queen Victoria Sq, Kingston-upon-Hull HU1 3RA - T: (01482) 613902, Fax: 613710, E-mail: museums@hullcc.gov.uk, Internet: www.hullcc.gov.uk/museums. Dir.: Jayne Tayler (Social History)
Historical Museum - 1906
Silver, costume, dolls, slavery, slave trade and abolition, items relating to William Wilberforce, born here in 1759 - library 39384

Kingston-upon-Thames

Kingston Museum, Wheatfield Way, Kingston-upon-Thames KT1 2PS - T: (020) 85465386, Fax: 85476747, E-mail: king.mus@rbk.kingston.gov.uk, Internet: www.kingston.gov.uk/museum. Dir.: Tracey Mardles
Local Museum - 1904
Archaeology, oral hist, social hist, borougn archives, Eadweard Muybridge colls, Martin Brothers (art pottery) 39385

The Stanley Picker Gallery, Middle Mill Island, Knights Park, Kingston-upon-Thames KT1 2QJ - T: (020) 85478074, Fax: 85478068, E-mail: picker@kingston.ac.uk, Internet: www.kingston.ac.uk/picker. Dir.: Prof. Bruce Russell
Public Gallery 39386

Kingswinford

Broadfield House Glass Museum, Compton Dr, Kingswinford DY6 9NS - T: (01384) 812745, Fax: 812746, E-mail: glass.pls@mbc@dudley.gov.uk, Internet: www.dudley.gov.uk. Dir.: Emma Warren
Decorative Arts Museum
Coll of British glass from the 17th c to the present 39387

Kingussie

Highland Folk Museum, Am Fasgadh, Duke St, Kingussie PH21 1JG - T: (01540) 661307, Fax: 661631, E-mail: highland.folk@highland.gov.uk, Internet: www.highlandfolk.com. Cur.: Bob Powell
Open Air Museum - 1934
Agriculture, costume, furniture, tartans, folklore, social history, vehicles of Scotland 39388

Kinnesswood

Michael Bruce Cottage Museum, The Cobbles, Kinnesswood KY13 9HL - T: (01592) 840203. Dir.: Dr. David M. Munro
Special Museum - 1906
Manuscripts by poet Michale Bruce, local articles 39389

Kinross

Kinross Museum, temporary closed, 108-110 High St, Kinross KY13 7DA, mail addr: N. Walker, 2 Muirpark Rd, Kinross KY13 7AS - T: (01738) 632488, Fax: 443505, E-mail: kinross-museum@tulbol.demon.co.uk, Internet: www.tulbol.demon.co.uk
Local Museum 39390

Kirkcaldy

Kirkcaldy Museum and Art Gallery, War Memorial Gardens, Kirkcaldy KY1 1YG - T: (01592) 412860, Fax: 412870, E-mail: kirkcaldy.museum@fite.gov.uk. Dir.: Dallas Wemyss
Local Museum - 1926
Local ceramics (ware), paintings by W.M. McTaggart and S.J. Peploe, Adam Smith items, archaeology, history, natural sciences 39391

Kirkcudbright

Broughton House and Garden, 12 High St, Kirkcudbright DG6 4JX - T: (01557) 330437, Fax: 330437, E-mail: fscott@nts.org.uk, Internet: www.nts.org.uk. Dir.: F.E. Scott
Special Museum - 1950
18th c town house, photographs, paintings by Hornel, Dumfries and Galloway history and literature - library 39392

The Stewartry Museum, 6 Saint Mary St, Kirkcudbright DG6 4AQ - T: (01557) 331643, Fax: 331643, E-mail: DavidD@dumgal.gov.uk, Internet: www.dumgal.gov.uk/museums. Dir.: David Devereux
Local Museum - 1881
Items concerning the Stewartry of Kirkcudbright, natural history, geology, archaeology, fine art 39393

Tolbooth Art Centre, High St, Kirkcudbright DG6 4JL - T: (01557) 331556, Fax: 331643, E-mail: davidd@dumgal.gov.uk, Internet: www.dumgal.gov.uk/museums. Dir.: David Devereux
Public Gallery
Paintings from the art colony, contemporary art 39394

Kirkintilloch

Auld Kirk Museum, Auld Kirk and Barony Chambers, Cowgate, The Cross, Kirkintilloch G66 1AB - T: (0141) 7751185, 5780144, Fax: 7777649, 5780140. Dir.: Susan Jeffrey, Cur.: Cecilia McDaid
Local Museum
Local history, art and craft living conditions of working-class families (early 20th c), weaving, mining, boatbuilding and ironfounding industries, displays of tools, equipment and photographs 39395

Kirkoswald

Souter Johnnie's House, Main St, Kirkoswald KA19 8HY - T: (01655) 760603
Special Museum
Home of John Daidson, village cobbler and original Souter 39396

Kirkwall

Orkney Museum, Tankerness House, Broad St, Kirkwall KW15 1DH - T: (01856) 873191, Fax: 871560, E-mail: museum@orkney.gov.uk, Internet: www.orkneyislands.com/guide/museums/tanker.html. Dir.: Janette A. Park
Archaeological Museum / Historical Museum - 1968
Extensive archaeological coll, social history 39397

Orkney Wireless Museum, Kiln Corner, Junction Rd, Kirkwall KW15 1LB - T: (01856) 871400, 874272, Internet: www.owm.org.uk. Dir.: Peter MacDonald
Science&Tech Museum - 1983
Coll of wartime radio and defences used at Scapa Flow, also hist of domestic wireless in Orkney 39398

Kirriemuir

Barrie's Birthplace, 9 Brechin Rd, Kirriemuir DD8 4BX - T: (01575) 572646, Fax: 575461. Dir.: K. Gilmour, S. Philp
Special Museum - 1963
Life and work of writer Sir James M. Barrie (1860-1937), memorabilia, manuscripts 39399

Knaresborough

Knaresborough Castle and Old Courthouse Museum, Castle Grounds, Knaresborough HG5 8AS - T: (01423) 556188, Fax: 556130, E-mail: lg12@harrogate.gov.uk, Internet: www.harrogate.gov.uk
Local Museum / Fine Arts Museum
Medieval castle with King's Tower, underground sallyport, tudor courthouse, civil war gallery, local history, site archaeology, art 39400

Saint Robert's Cave, Abbay Rd, Knaresborough HG5 8AS - T: (01423) 556188, Fax: 556130, E-mail: lg12@harrogate.gov.uk
Religious Arts Museum 39401

Knebworth

Knebworth House, Park, Knebworth SG3 6PY - T: (01438) 812661, Fax: 811908, E-mail: info@knebworthhouse.com, Internet: www.knebworthhouse.com. Dir.: Martha Lytton Cobbold
Decorative Arts Museum
Tudor to Victorian, Gothic and 20th c interior, wallpapers, rustic wall paintings, literary coll 39402

Knutsford

First Penny Farthing Museum, 92 King St, Knutsford WA16 6ED - T: (01565) 653974
Science&Tech Museum
Largest coll of penny farthing bicycle in the UK 39403

Knutsford Heritage Centre, 90a King St, Knutsford WA16 6ED - T: (01565) 650506. Man.: Pat Heath
Local Museum 39404

Tabley House Collection, Tabley House, Knutsford WA16 0HB - T: (01565) 750151, Fax: 653230, E-mail: inquiries@tableyhouse.co.uk, Internet: www.tableyhouse.co.uk. Cur.: Peter Cannon-Brookes
Fine Arts Museum / Historic Site
Coll of British paintings (1790's to 1826) formed by Sir John-Flemming Leicester Bart 39405

Tatton Park, Knutsford WA16 6QN - T: (01625) 534400, Fax: 534403, E-mail: tatton@cheshire.gov.co.uk, Internet: www.tattonpark.org.uk. Man.: Brendan Flanagan
Decorative Arts Museum
Coll Gillow furniture, pictures by Canaletto, Carracci, De Heem, Poussin, Nazzari, Van Dyck, silver by Paul Storr, porcelain, European, English and Chinese, carpet 39406

Kyle

Raasay Heritage Museum, 6 Osgaig Park, Raasay, Kyle W40 8PB - T: (01478) 660207, Fax: (0870) 1227170, E-mail: osgaig@lineone.net, Internet: www.angelfire.com/ilz/raasayheritagetrust/index.htm. Chm.: F. Maclennan
Local Museum 39407

Lacock

Fox Talbot Museum, Lacock SN15 2LG - T: (01249) 730459, Fax: 730501, E-mail: m.w.gray@bath.ac.uk, Internet: www.nationaltrust.org.uk/lacock. Dir.: Michael Gray
Science&Tech Museum - 1975
Coll of manuscripts, documents, correspondence and photographs relating to the invention and discovery of the positive/negative photographic process by William Henry Fox Talbot (1800-1877), photographic technology - research and documentation facilities 39408

Lackham Museum of Agriculture and Rural Life, Wiltshire College Lackham, Lacock SN15 2NY - T: (01249) 466847, Fax: 444474, E-mail: daviaj@wiltscoll.ac.uk, Internet: www.lackham.co.uk. Dir.: Andrew Davies
Agriculture Museum - 1946
Agricultural tools, machinery, rural life displays, historic farm buildings 39409

Lanark

Lanark Museum, 8 Westport, Lanark ML11 9HD - T: (01555) 666681, Internet: www.biggar-net.co.uk/lanarkmuseum
Local Museum
Lanark history, 19th c costume, photographs, maps and plans 39410

Lancaster

Cottage Museum, 15 Castle Hill, Lancaster LA1 1YS - T: (01524) 64637, Fax: 841692, E-mail: lancaster.citymuseum@mus.lancscc.gov.uk, Internet: www.lancaster.gov.uk/council/museums. Dir.: Edmund Southworth
Decorative Arts Museum - 1978
Artisan cottage, furnished in the style of the 1820s 39411

Judges' Lodgings, Church St, Lancaster LA1 1YS - T: (01524) 32808, 846315, Fax: 846315, E-mail: judgeslodgings.lcc@btinternet.com, Internet: www.lancashire.com/lcc/museums. Dir.: Edmund Southworth, Keeper: John Rayment
Decorative Arts Museum / Special Museum
Local hist, toys, dolls, games, costumes, coll of Gillow furniture (18th-20th c) 39412

King's Own Royal Regiment Museum, Market Sq, Lancaster LA1 1HT - T: (01524) 64637, Fax: 841692, E-mail: kingsownmuseum@iname.com, Internet: www.lancaster.gov.uk/council/museums. Dir.: Edmund Southworth, Cur.: Peter Donnelly
Military Museum - 1929
Archives, medals, photographs, uniforms, memorabilia 39413

Lancaster City Museum, Old Town Hall, Market Sq, Lancaster LA1 1HT - T: (01524) 64637, Fax: 841692, E-mail: lancaster.citymuseum@mus.lancscc.gov.uk, Internet: www.lancaster.gov.uk/council/museums. Dir.: Edmund Southworth, Sc. Staff: S. Ashworth (Collections), P. Thompson (Visitor Service), P. Donelly (Military History)
Local Museum / Decorative Arts Museum / Military Museum / Archaeological Museum - 1923
Local hist, decorative arts, Roman finds, weights and measures, Gillow furniture, drawings, local paintings 39414

Lancaster Maritime Museum, Custom House, Saint George's Quay, Lancaster LA1 1RB - T: (01524) 382264, Fax: 841692, E-mail: lancaster.citymuseum@mus.lancscc.gov.uk, Internet: www.lancaster.gov.uk/council/museums. Dir.: Edmund Southworth
Science&Tech Museum - 1985
Ship models, ship fittings, navigational aids, customs equipment, charts 39415

Peter Scott Gallery, c/o University of Lancaster, Lancaster LA1 4YW - T: (01524) 593057, Fax: 592603, E-mail: m.p.gavagan@lancaster.ac.uk, Internet: www.peterscottgalllery.com. Dir.: Mary Gavagan
Fine Arts Museum / Decorative Arts Museum / University Museum
Art, pottery, ceramics, sculptures 39416

Roman Bath House, Vicarage Field, Lancaster LA1 1HN - T: (01524) 64637, Fax: 841692, E-mail: lancaster.citymuseum@mus.lancscc.gov.uk, Internet: www.lancaster.gov.uk/council/museums. Dir.: Edmund Southworth
Archaeological Museum 39417

Ruskin Library, c/o Lancaster University, Lancaster LA1 4YH - T: (01524) 593587, Fax: 593580, E-mail: ruskin.library@lancaster.ac.uk, Internet: www.lancs.ac.uk/users/ruskinlib. Dir.: S.G. Wildman
Library with Exhibitions / Fine Arts Museum / University Museum - 1997
Memorabilia of the writer John Ruskin, paintings, drawings by artists associated with him, photographs, letters - library 39418

Lancing

College Museum (closed) 39419

Langbank

The Dolly Mixture, Finlaystone Country Estate, Langbank PA14 6TJ - T: (01475) 540505, Fax: 540285, E-mail: info@finlaystone.co.uk, Internet: www.finlaystone.co.uk. Dir.: C.J. MacMillan
Special Museum - 1996
Finlaystone Doll Collection - The Dolly Mixture - All sorts of dolls from around the world 39420

Langholm

Clan Armstrong Museum, Lodge Walk, Castleholm, Langholm DG13 0NY - T: (013873) 81610, Fax: 81243, E-mail: info@armstrongclan.org, Internet: www.armstrongclan.org
Historical Museum
Armstrong artefacts, maps, documents, portraits, weapons, armour, ancient Reiver clan of the Scottish border - library 39421

Langton Matravers

Coach House Museum → Langton Matravers Museum

Langton Matravers Museum, Saint George's Close, Langton Matravers BH19 3HZ - T: (01929) 423168, Fax: 427534, E-mail: langtonia@cwcom.net, Internet: www.langton.mcmail.com. Dir.: R.J. Saville
Science&Tech Museum - 1974
History of the local stone industry from Roman times to the present day, quarrying equipment, stone-masons' tools, model of a section of underground working, test pieces, photographs, social history exhibits 39422

Lanreath

Farm and Folk Museum (closed) 39423

Lapworth

Packwood House, Lapworth B94 6AT - T: (01564) 782024, Fax: 782912
Decorative Arts Museum - 1941
17th c country house with tapestries, needlework, English antique furniture, topiary 39424

Largs

Largs Museum, Kirkgate House, Manse Court, Largs KA30 8AW - T: (01475) 687081, E-mail: mike.mackenzie2@virgin.net, Internet: freespace.virgin.net/mike.mackenzie2/LDHSoc.htm
Local Museum - 1973
Local hist 39425

Larne

Larne Museum, Carnegie Bldg, 2 Victoria Rd, Larne BT40 1RN - T: (028) 28279482, Fax: 28260660. Head: Joan Morris
Local Museum
Local history colls incl country kitchen, smithy, agricultural implements, old photographs, old newspapers, maps 39426

Latheron

Clan Gunn Museum, Old Parish Church, Latheron KW1 4DD - T: (01593) 721325, Fax: 721325
Local Museum
Hist of Orkney and the North 39427

Lauder

Thirlestane Castle, Lauder TD2 6RU - T: (01578) 722430, Fax: 722761, E-mail: admin@thirlestanecastle.co.uk, Internet: www.thirlestanecastle.co.uk. Dir.: P.D. Jarvis
Local Museum 39428

Laugharne

Dylan Thomas Boathouse, Dylan's Walk, Laugharne SA33 4SD - T: (01994) 427420, Fax: 427420
Special Museum
Dylan Thomas' writing hut, memorabilia 39429

Launceston

Launceston Steam Railway, Saint Thomas Rd, Launceston PL15 8DA - T: (01566) 775665
Science&Tech Museum
Locomotives, vintage cars and motorcycles, stationary steam engines, machine tools 39430

Lawrence House Museum, 9 Castle St, Launceston PL15 8BA - T: (01566) 773277. Cur.: Jean Brown
Local Museum
Local history, WWII and home front, coins, feudal dues, rural and domestic Victorian life, costume 39431

Laxey

Great Laxey Wheel and Mines Trail, Manx National Heritage, Laxey IM4 7AH - T: (01624) 648000, Fax: 648001, E-mail: enquiries@mnh.gov.im, Internet: www.gov.im/mnh. Man.: Phil Hollis
Science&Tech Museum
Largest working water wheel in the world, pump water from the lead and zinc mines, Victorial engineering 39432

Murray's Motorcycle Museum, The Bungalow, Snaefell, Laxey IM4 - T: (01624) 861719
Science&Tech Museum
Over 120 motorcycles (1902-1961), motoring memorabilia 39433

Vintage Motor Cycle Museum → Murray's Motorcycle Museum

Laxfield

Laxfield and District Museum, The Guildhall, Laxfield IP13 8DU - T: (01986) 798026
Local Museum
Rural domestic and working life, local archaeology, costumes and natural history 39434

Leadhills

Leadhills Miners' Library Museum, 13 Main St, Leadhills ML12 8SU - Fax: 504206, E-mail: leadhills-library@culturalprojects.co.uk. Chm.: Harry Shaw
Library with Exhibitions
Original book stock, library holds objects, photos 39435

Leamington Spa

Leamington Spa Art Gallery and Museum, Royal Pump Rooms, The Parade, Leamington Spa CV32 4AA - T: (01926) 742700, Fax: 742705, E-mail: prooms@warwickdc.gov.uk, Internet: www.royal-pump-rooms.co.uk. Dir.: Jeffrey Watkin
Fine Arts Museum / Local Museum / Historical Museum - 1928
British, Dutch, Flemish paintings (16th-20th c), ceramics from Delft, Wedgwood-Whieldon, Worchester, 18th c drinking glasses, costumes, photography, ethnography, social hist 39436

Leatherhead

Leatherhead Museum of Local History, 64 Church St, Leatherhead KT22 8DP - T: (01372) 386348, E-mail: museum@localhistory.free-online.co.uk, Internet: www.freespace.virgin.net/frank.haslam/sites/ladlhistsoc. Chm.: Peter Tarplee
Local Museum
Local history, coll of Art Deco Ashtead pottery 39437

Ledaig

Lorn Museum, An Sailean, Ledaig PA37 1QS - T: (01631) 720282. Dir.: Catherine MacDonald
Local Museum 39438

Ledbury

Eastnor Castle, Ledbury HR8 1RN - T: (01531) 633160, Fax: 631776, E-mail: EastnorCastle@btinternet.com. Dir.: James & Sarah Hervey Bathurst
Decorative Arts Museum / Fine Arts Museum - 1850
Armour, Italian furniture, pictures, tapestries - library 39439

Leeds

Abbey House Museum, Leeds Museums and Galleries, Kirkstall Rd, Leeds LS5 3EH - T: (0113) 2305492, Fax: 2305499, E-mail: abbeyhouse.museum@virgin.net. Dir.: N. Winterbotham, Cur.: Samantha Flavin
Decorative Arts Museum / Local Museum - 1926
Reconstructions of 3 street scenes (19th c) cottages, Victorian city, childhood, Kirkstall abbey 39440

Art Library, Municipal Bldgs, Leeds LS1 3AB - T: (0113) 2478247
Library with Exhibitions 39441

City Art Gallery, Leeds Museums and Galleries, The Headrow, Leeds LS1 3AA - T: (0113) 2478248, Fax: 2449689, E-mail: city.art.gallery@leeds.gov.uk, Internet: www.leeds.gov.uk/artgallery. Dir.: Nick Winterbotham, Cur.: Corinne Miller, Alexander Robertson (Fine Art), Nigel Walsh (Exhibitions), Matthew Whitey (Sculpture), Amanda Phillips (Education)
Fine Arts Museum - 1888
Victorian paintings, early English watercolours, British 20th c paintings and sculpture 39442

City Museum, Leeds Museums and Galleries, The Headrow, Calverley St, Leeds LS1 3AA - T: (0113) 2478275, Fax: 2342300, E-mail: evelyn.silber@leeds.gov.uk. Dir.: Dr. Evelyn Silber, Cur.: Adrian Norris
Local Museum - 1820
Natural science, archaeology, anthropology, local history 39443

Department of Semitic Studies Collection, c/o University of Leeds, Leeds LS2 9JT
Archaeological Museum - 1960
Biblical history, Palestina archaeology, Near Eastern ethnology, manuscripts 39444

Henry Moore Institute, 74 The Headrow, Leeds LS1 3AH - T: (0113) 2343158, 2467467, Fax: 2461481, E-mail: hmi@henry-moore.ac.uk, Internet: www.henry-moore-fdn.co.uk. Head: Penelope Curtis
Fine Arts Museum
Sculpture production and reception, drawings, letters - research facilities 39445

Horsforth Village Museum, 3-5 The Green, Horsforth, Leeds LS18 5JB - T: (0113) 2819877, E-mail: horsforthmuseum@hotmail.com, Internet: www.yourhorseforth.co.uk/history.htm
Local Museum
Local history 39446

Leeds Industrial Museum, Leeds Museums and Galleries, Armley Mills, Canal Rd, Leeds LS12 2QF - T: (0113) 2637861, 2244362, Fax: 2244365, E-mail: armleymills.indmuseum@virgin.net, Internet: www.leeds.gov.uk/tourinfo/attract/museum/armley. Dir.: Nick Winterbotham, Cur.: Daru Rooke, Neil Dowlan (Engineering), Gwendolen Powell (Social and Industrial History)
Science&Tech Museum / Local Museum
Large woollen mill, textiles, printing 39447

Leeds Metropolitan University Gallery, Woodhouse Ln, Leeds LS1 3HE - T: (0113) 2833130, Fax: 2835999, E-mail: m.innes@lmu.ac.uk, Internet: www.lmu.ac.uk/arts. Cur.: Moira Innes
Public Gallery 39448

Museum of the History of Education, c/o University of Leeds, Parkinson Court, Leeds LS2 9JT - T: (0113) 2431751 ext 4665, Fax: 2431751 ext 4541, E-mail: e.j.foster@education.ac.uk, Internet: education.leeds.ac.uk/~edu/inted/museum.htm. Dir.: Dr. E.J. Foster
Historical Museum / Special Museum - 1951
Hist of education in England, old school books, samplers, equipment, portraits, foundation charters, local school hist, text books, photographs 39449

Royal Armouries Museum, Armouries Dr, Leeds LS10 1LT - T: (0113) 2201940, Fax: 2201934, E-mail: enquiries@armouries.org.uk, Internet: www.armouries.org.uk. Chief Ex.: Paul Evan (Master of the Armouries), Keeper: G.J. Rimer (Weapons), R.T. Richardson (Armour and Oriental Collection), Cons.: R.D. Smith, Libr.: P. Abbott
Military Museum - 1996
Arms and armour coll, five galleries describe the evolution of arms and armour in war, tournament, oriental, self-defence and hunting, computer programmes and films on this topic - Conservation, library, education centre 39450

Second World War Experience Centre, 5 Feast Field, Horsforth, Leeds LS18 4TJ - T: (0113) 2584993, Fax: 2582557, E-mail: enquiries@war-experience.org, Internet: www.war-experience.org. Dir.: Dr. Peter Liddle
Historical Museum
Soldiers, sailors and airmen, daily civilian and military experience, women and children in every community during wartime 39451

Temple Newsam House, Leeds Museums and Galleries, Temple Newsham Rd, off Selby Rd, Leeds LS15 0AE - T: (0113) 2647321, Fax: 2602285, E-mail: nick.winterbotham@leeds.gov, Internet: www.leeds.gov.uk. Dir.: Nick Winterbotham, Sc. Staff: Anthony Wells-Cole (Historic Interiors, Crafts), James Lomax (Silver), Adam White (Ceramics), Helen Bower (Textiles)
Fine Arts Museum / Decorative Arts Museum - 1922
English and Continental paintings (16th-20th c), furniture, silver, ceramics, country house from 1490 39452

Tetley's Brewery Wharf, The Waterfront, Leeds LS1 1QG - T: (0113) 2420666, Fax: 2594125. Man.: Ian Glenholme
Science&Tech Museum
History of Joshua Tetley & Son Brewery, brewing and allied trades 39453

Thackray Museum, Beckett St, Leeds LS9 7LN - T: (0113) 2444343, Fax: 2470219, E-mail: info@thackraymuseum.org, Internet: www.thackraymuseum.org. Dir.: Fiona Elliott, Cur.: Joanne Stewardson, Libr.: Alan Humphries
Historical Museum
History of surgery, medicine, health care and medical supply trades 39454

Thwaite Mills Watermill, Thwaite Ln, Stourton, Leeds LS10 1RP - T: (0113) 2496453, Fax: 2776737. Dir.: Nick Winrerborham
Science&Tech Museum
Working water-powered mill 39455

University Gallery Leeds, Parkinson Bldg, Woodhouse Ln, Leeds LS2 9JT - T: (0113) 3432777, Fax: 3435561, E-mail: gallery@leeds.ac.uk, Internet: www.leeds.ac.uk/gallery. Dir.: Hilary Diaper, Dr. Hilary Diaper
Public Gallery / University Museum
British paintings, drawings and prints (16th-20th c), Bloomsbury group 39456

Leek

Leek Art Gallery, Nicholson Institute, Stockwell St, Leek ST13 6DW - T: (01538) 483732, Fax: 483733, E-mail: alison.strauss@staffsmoorlands.gov.uk, Internet: www.staffmoorlands.gov.uk
Public Gallery - 1884 39457

Leicester

Abbey Pumping Station Museum, Corporation Rd, off Abbey Ln, Leicester LE4 5PX - T: (0116) 2995111, Fax: 2995125, Internet: www.leicestermuseums.ac.uk. Dir.: Stuart Warburton
Science&Tech Museum
Horse drawn vehicles, bicycles, motorcycles, motor vehicles, 1891 Beam pumping engines 39458

Belgrave Hall and Gardens, Church Rd, off Thurcaston Rd, Leicester LE4 5PE - T: (0116) 2666590, Fax: 2613063, E-mail: haro001@leicester.gov.uk, Internet: www.leicestermuseums.ac.uk. Dir.: Sarah Leritt, Cur.: Stuart Warburton
Decorative Arts Museum
Queen Anne House with 18th-19th c furniture, botanical/ historical gardens 39459

City Gallery, 90 Granby St, Leicester LE1 1DJ - T: (0116) 2540595, Fax: 2540593
Public Gallery 39460

Guildhall, Guildhall Ln, Leicester LE1 5FQ - T: (0116) 2532569, Fax: 2539626, Internet: www.leicestermuseums.ac.uk. Dir.: Nick Ladlow
Historical Museum
Medieval timber construction 39461

Jewry Wall Museum, Saint Nicholas Circle, Leicester LE1 4LB - T: (0116) 2254971, Fax: 2254966, E-mail: lucaj001@leicester.gov.uk, Internet: www.leicestermuseums.ac.uk. Dir.: S. Levitt
Archaeological Museum - 1966
Roman wall dating from the 2nd c, local archaeology, Roman milestone, mosaics and painted wallplaster 39462

Leicestershire CCC Museum, County Ground, Grace Rd, Leicester LE2 8AD - T: (0116) 2832128, Fax: 2440363, E-mail: leicestershireccc@ukonline.co.uk, Internet: www.leicestershireccc.co.uk. Man.: Angus Mackay
Special Museum
Coll of cricket memorabilia to the Leicestershire County Cricket Club 39463

Museum and Art Gallery Leicester, 53 New Walk, Leicester LE1 7EA - T: (0116) 2554100, Fax: 2473057, E-mail: hidemool@leicester.gov.uk, Internet: www.leicestermuseums.ac.uk. Dir.: J.G. Martin, Cur.: Adrienne Avery-Gray (Fine Art), Nick Gordon (Natural Science)
Fine Arts Museum / Decorative Arts Museum / Natural History Museum - 1849
Geology, natural hist, mammalogy, ornithology, ichthyology, biology, English painting, German expressionists, French painting (19th-20th c), old masters, English ceramics, silver, egyptology - library 39464

Museum of the Royal Leicestershire Regiment, Magazine Gateway, Oxford St, Leicester LE2 7BY - T: (0116) 2473222, Fax: 2470403. Dir.: S. Levitt, Cur.: J.A. Legget
Military Museum - 1969
Hist of the Royal Leicestershire Regiment, in building from 1400, medieval gateway - closed till 1998 for refurbishment 39465

The National Gas Museum, c/o British Gas, Aylestone Rd, Leicester LE2 7QH - T: (0116) 2503190, Fax: 2503190, E-mail: information@gasmuseum.co.uk, Internet: www.gasmuseum.co.uk. Cur.: M. Martin
Science&Tech Museum - 1977
Gas production (tools and equipment), gas lighting, meters, gas appliances (heating, cooking etc.) 39466

National Space Centre, Exploration Drive, Leicester LE4 5NS - T: (0116) 2582111, Fax: 2582100, E-mail: info@spacecentre.co.uk, Internet: www.spacecentre.co.uk. Dir.: George Barnett
Science&Tech Museum 39467

Newarke Houses Museum, The Newarke, Leicester LE2 7BY - T: (0116) 2473222, Fax: 2470403, Internet: www.leicestermuseums.ac.uk. Dir.: Nick Ladlow, Cur.: Jane May (Decorative Art), Cons.: Libby Finney, Fiona Graham
Music Museum / Science&Tech Museum - 1940
Clock making, mechanical musical instruments, reconstructed 19th c street, reconstructed workshop of 18th c clockmaker Samuel Deacon, sewing accessories, fans, tokens, toys, Gimson furniture 39468

Record Office for Leicestershire, Leicester and Rutland, Long St, Leicester LE18 2AH - T: (0116) 2571080, Fax: 2571120, E-mail: recordoffice@leics.gov.uk, Internet: www.leics.gov.uk
Fine Arts Museum
Official, public and private archives and local studies library, from medieval times to date, serves Leicestershire, the City of Leicester and Rutland, jointly supported by Leicestershire County Council, Leicester City Council and Rutland County Council 39469

William Carey Museum, Central Baptist Church, Charles St, Leicester LE1 1LA - T: (0116) 2766862, Internet: www.central-baptist.org.uk
Religious Arts Museum
Life of William Carey (1762-1834), modern Overseas missions 39470

Leigh, Lancashire

Turnpike Gallery, Civic Sq, Leigh, Lancashire WN7 1EB - T: (01942) 404469, Fax: 404447, E-mail: turnpikegallery@wlct.org, Internet: www.wlct.org. Officer: Martyn Lucas
Public Gallery
20th c prints, contemporary art 39471

Leigh-on-Sea

Leigh Heritage Centre, 13A High St, Old Town, Leigh-on-Sea SS9 2EN - T: (01702) 470834. Chr.: Richard Owen
Fine Arts Museum
Leigh photographs and artefacts 39472

Leighton Buzzard

Ascott House, Ascott Estate, Office Wing, Leighton Buzzard LU7 0PS - T: (01296) 688242, Fax: 681904, E-mail: info@ascottestate.co.uk, Internet: www.ascottestate.co.uk
Decorative Arts Museum
French and Chippendale furniture, original needlework, paintings by Rubens, Hogarth, Gainsborough, Hobbema, Oriental porcelain, former possession of Anthony de Rothschild 39473

Leighton Buzzard Railway, Page's Park Station, Billington Rd, Leighton Buzzard LU7 4TN - T: (01525) 373888, Fax: 377814, E-mail: info@buzzrail.co.uk, Internet: www.buzzrail.co.uk. Chm.: Mervyn Leah
Science&Tech Museum
Over 50 unique and historic locomotives 39474

Leiston

Long Shop Museum, Main St, Leiston IP16 4ES - T: (01728) 832189, Fax: 832189, E-mail: longshop@care4free.net, Internet: www.longshop.care4free.net. Dir.: Stephen Mael
Science&Tech Museum - 1980
History of Richard Garrett eng works for over 200 years 1778-1980, display of Leiston air base occupied by 357th fighter group USAAF World War II 39475

Leominster

Croft Castle, Leominster HR6 9PW - T: (01568) 780246
Fine Arts Museum 39476

Leominster Folk Museum, Etnam St, Leominster HR6 8AL - T: (01568) 615186. Cur.: Lynne Moult
Folklore Museum / Local Museum
Local trades and industry, cider house, dairy, costume, social history 39477

Lerwick

Böd of Gremista Museum, Gremista, Lerwick ZE1 0PX - T: (01595) 694386, Fax: 696729, E-mail: museum@sic.shetland.gov.uk, Internet: www.shetland-museum.org.uk. Dir.: T. Watt
Historical Museum
Birthplace of Arthur Anderson 39478

Shetland Museum, Lower Hillhead, Lerwick ZE1 0EL - T: (01595) 695057, Fax: 696729, E-mail: museum@sic.shetland.gov.uk, Internet: www.shetland-museum.org.uk. Dir.: T. Watt
Local Museum - 1970 39479

Letchworth

First Garden City Heritage Museum, 296 Norton Way S, Letchworth SG6 1SU - T: (01462) 482710, Fax: 486056, E-mail: fgchm@letchworth.com, Internet: www.letchworthge.com. Cur.: Robert Lancaster
Historical Museum - 1977 39480

Museum and Art Gallery, Broadway, Letchworth SG6 3PF - T: (01462) 685647, Fax: 481879, E-mail: letchworth.museum@north-herts.gov.uk, Internet: www.north-herts.gov.uk. Dir.: Rosamond Allwood
Local Museum / Fine Arts Museum - 1914
Archaeology, natural hist, local hist, fine and decorative art, costume 39481

North Hertfordshire Museums, North Herts District Council, Gernon Rd, Letchworth SG6 3JF - T: (01462) 474274, Fax: 474500
Association with Coll 39482

Lewes

Anne of Cleves House Museum, 52 Southover High St, Lewes BN7 1JA - T: (01273) 474610, Fax: 486990, E-mail: anne@sussexpast.co.uk, Internet: www.sussexpast.co.uk. Cur.: Steve Watts
Decorative Arts Museum / Folklore Museum
Furniture, domestic equipment and a wide range of material illustrating the everyday life of local people during the 19th and early 20th c 39483

Lewes Castle and Barbican House Museum, 169 Hihg St, Lewes BN7 1YE - T: (01273) 486290, Fax: 486990, E-mail: castle@sussexpast.co.uk, Internet: www.sussexpast.co.uk. Man.: Jill Allen
Local Museum
The castle was built on the orders of William the Conqueror soon after the conquest of 1066, the museum, next door, incl exhibits and a computer touch-screen history of the area 39484

Military Heritage Museum, 7-9 West St, Lewes BN7 2NJ - T: (01273) 480208, Fax: 476562, E-mail: WallisandWallis@inatos.co.uk. Cur.: S.R. Butler
Military Museum - 1977
Roy Butler Coll - Hist of the British army 1650-1914 39485

Museum of Sussex Archaeology, Barbican House, 169 High St, Lewes BN7 1YE - T: (01273) 486290, Fax: 486990, E-mail: castle@sussexpast.co.uk, Internet: www.sussexpast.co.uk. Dir.: Hannah Crowdy
Archaeological Museum
Prehistoric, Roman and Saxon archaeology, watercolors 39486

Leyland

British Commercial Vehicle Museum, King St, Leyland PR5 1LE - T: (01772) 451011, Fax: 623404. Dir.: Andrew Buchan
Science&Tech Museum - 1983
Historic commercial vehicles and buses, truck and bus building 39487

South Ribble Museum and Exhibition Centre, Old Grammar School, Church Rd, Leyland PR5 1EJ - T: (01772) 422041, Fax: 625363. Dir.: Dr. D.A. Hunt
Local Museum
Archaeological material from excavations at the Roman site at Walton-le-Dale, and a wide range of smaller items relating to the history of the town and the area 39488

Lichfield

Friary Art Gallery, The Friary, Lichfield WS13 6QG - T: (01543) 510700, Fax: 510716, E-mail: lichfield.library@staffordshire.gov.uk. Dir.: Elizabeth Rees-Jones, Fiona Bailey
Library with Exhibitions - 1859
Crafts, textiles 39489

Hanch Hall, Lichfield WS13 8HH - T: (01543) 490308. Dir.: Colin Lee, Linda Lee
Local Museum 39490

Lichfield Heritage Centre, Market Sq, Lichfield WS13 6LG - T: (01543) 256611, Fax: 414749, E-mail: heritage@lichfield.gov.uk, Internet: www.lichfield.gov.uk/heritage. Pres.: J.E. Rackham
Local Museum 39491

Samuel Johnson Birthplace Museum, Breadmarket St, Lichfield WS13 6LG - T: (01543) 264972, Fax: 414779, E-mail: sjmuseum@lichfield.gov.uk, Internet: www.lichfield.gov.uk
Special Museum - 1901
Memorabilia of Dr. Samuel Johnson (1709-1784), paintings, association books, documents, letters of Johnson, Boswell, Anna Seward - library 39492

Staffordshire Regiment Museum, Whittington Barracks, Lichfield WS14 9PY - T: (0121) 3113240, Fax: 3113205, E-mail: museum@rhqstaffords.fsnet.co.uk, Internet: www.armymuseums.org.uk. Dir.: E. Green, Cur.: Sarah Elsom
Military Museum - 1963
Hist of the regiment, medals, armaments, uniforms, exterior WWI trench, Anderson shelters 39493

Wall Roman Site and Museum - Letocetum, Watling St, Lichfield WS14 0AW - T: (01543) 480768, Internet: www.english-heritage.org.uk. Cur.: Sara Lunt, Cust.: Kevin Lynch
Archaeological Museum - 1912
Roman finds, pottery, coins, tools, glass 39494

Lifton

Dingles Steam Village, Lifton PL16 0AT - T: (01566) 783425, Fax: 783584, E-mail: richard@dinglesteam.co.uk, Internet: www.dinglesteam.co.uk
Science&Tech Museum
Steam and other early road rollers, lorries, fairground engines and industrial engines, old road signs, fairground art, belt driven machinery 39495

Lincoln

City and County Museum, 12 Friars Ln, Lincoln LN2 5AL - T: (01522) 530401, Fax: 530724, E-mail: librarian@lincolncathedral.com. Dir.: Dr. Nicholas Bennett
Historical Museum
Perhistoric, Roman and medievial Lincolnshire, armoury 39496

Lawn, Union Rd, Lincoln LN1 3BL - T: (01522) 560330
Science&Tech Museum
Sir Joseph Banks Conservatory and aquarium 39497

Lincoln Cathedral Treasury, Cathedral, Lincoln - T: (01522) 552222 ext 2805, 811308. Dir.: O.T. Griffin
Religious Arts Museum 39498

Lincolnshire Road Transport Museum, Whisby Rd, off Doddington Rd, Lincoln LN6 3QT - T: (01522) 689497
Science&Tech Museum - 1959/93
Vehicles dating from 1920s to 1960s, mostly restored and with local connections 39499

Museum of Lincolnshire Life, Old Barracks, Burton Rd, Lincoln LN1 3LY - T: (01522) 528448, Fax: 521264, E-mail: finchj@lincolnshire.gov.uk. Dir.: Jon Finch
Local Museum - 1969
Agricultural and industrial machinery, horse-drawn vehicles, displays devoted to domestic, community and commercial life within the county, crafts and trades, Royal Lincolnshire Regiment - windmill archive 39500

Old Toy Show, 26 Westgate, Lincoln LN1 3BD - T: (01522) 520534
Special Museum
Toys from the 1790's to the 1970's 39501

Royal Lincolnshire Regiment Museum, Burton Rd, Lincoln LN1 3LY - T: (01522) 528448, Fax: 521264, E-mail: finchj@lincolnshire.gov.uk. Dir.: Jon Finch
Military Museum - 1986
Hist of the regiment, uniforms, medals, war trophies, armaments, social history coll relating to Lincolnshire 39502

Usher Gallery, Lindum Rd, Lincoln LN2 1NN - T: (01522) 527980, Fax: 560165, E-mail: usher.gallery@lincolnshire.gov.uk, Internet: www.lincolnshire.gov.uk/ushergallery
Fine Arts Museum / Decorative Arts Museum - 1927
Paintings, watercolours, watches, miniatures, silver, porcelain, manuscripts and memorabilia of Alfred Lord Tennyson (1809-1892) 39503

Linford

Walton Hall Museum, Walton Hall Rd, Linford SS17 0RH - T: (01375) 671874, Fax: 641268
Science&Tech Museum
Historic farm machinery, gypsy caravan, motor rollers 39504

Linlithgow

Canal Museum, Canal Basin, Manse Rd, Linlithgow EH49 6AJ - T: (01506) 671215, E-mail: info@lucs.org.uk, Internet: www.lucs.org.uk
Science&Tech Museum / Historic Site 39505

House of the Binns, Linlithgow EH49 7NA - T: (01506) 834255. Dir.: Kathleen Dalyell
Historical Museum / Decorative Arts Museum - 1944
Historic home of the Dalyells, 17th c moulded plaster ceilings, paintings, porcelain, furniture 39506

Linlithgow Palace, Edinburgh Rd, Linlithgow EH49 6QS - T: (01506) 842896
Decorative Arts Museum 39507

Linlithgow Story, Annet House, 143 High St, Linlithgow EH49 7JH - T: (01506) 670677
Local Museum 39508

Liphook

Hollycombe Steam Collection, Iron Hill, Liphook GU30 7UP - T: (01428) 724900, Fax: 723682, E-mail: info@hollycombe.co.uk, Internet: www.hollycombe.co.uk. Dir.: Brian Gooding
Science&Tech Museum 39509

Lisburn

Irish Linen Centre and Lisburn Museum, Market Sq, Lisburn BT28 1AG - T: (028) 92663377, Fax: 92672624, E-mail: irishlinencentre@lisburn.gov.uk, Internet: www.lisburn.gov.uk/irishlinencentre. Cur.: Brian Mackey
Special Museum
Linen, archaeology, social history, art and industry of the Lagan valley - specialist library 39510

Lisnaskea

Folklife Display, Library, Lisnaskea BT92 0AD - T: (028) 67721222
Local Museum 39511

Litcham

Litcham Village Museum, Fourways, Mileham Rd, Litcham PE32 2NZ - T: (01328) 701383. Chm.: R.W. Shaw
Local Museum
Local artefacts 39512

Little Walsingham

Shirehall Museum, Common Pl, Little Walsingham NR22 6BP - T: (01328) 820510, Fax: 820098, E-mail: walsingham.museum@farmline.com, Internet: www.walsingham.uk.com
Historical Museum
Local and village history, pilgrimages to Walsingham, court 39513

Littlehampton

Littlehampton Museum, Manor House, Church St, Littlehampton BN17 5EW - T: (01903) 738100, Fax: 731690, E-mail: Littlehamptonmuseum@arun.gov.uk
Local Museum - 1928
Nautical and maritime exhibits, photography 39514

Liverpool

Anfield Museum, c/o LFC, Anfield Rd, Liverpool L4 0TH - T: (0151) 2606677, 2632361, Fax: 2608813, Internet: www.liverpoolfc.tv/lfc_story/tour_museum
Special Museum
Football history in Liverpool 39515

Conservation Centre Presentation, Whitechapel, Liverpool L3 - T: (0151) 4784999, Internet: www.conservationcentre.org.uk
Special Museum
Works of museum conservators 39516

Croxteth Hall, Croxteth Hall Ln, Liverpool L12 0HB - T: (0151) 2285311, Fax: 2282817, E-mail: croxteth-countrypark@liverpool.gov.uk, Internet: www.croxteth.co.uk. Dir.: Irene Vickers, Cur.: Julia Carder
Decorative Arts Museum
Edwardian furnishings 39517

Her Majesty Customs and Excise National Museum, c/o Merseyside Maritime Museum, Albert Dock, Liverpool L3 4AQ - T: (0151) 4784499, Fax: 4784590, Internet: www.customsandexcisemuseum.org.uk. Cur.: Karen Bradbury
Special Museum
Battle between smugglers and duty men since the 1700's 39518

Lark Lane Motor Museum, 1 Hesketh St, Liverpool
Science&Tech Museum
Cars, motorcycles and a wide range of mechanical devices 39519

Liverpool Museum, William Brown St, Liverpool L3 8EN - T: (0151) 4784399, Fax: 4784390, Internet: www.liverpoolmuseum.org.uk. Dir.: R.A. Foster, Keeper: E.F. Greenwood, Secr.: M. Harrison, Sc. Staff: Edmund Southworth (Antiquities), R. Cowell (Archaeology), L. Stumpe (Ethnology), I. Wallace (Zoology), J. Edmondson (Botany), Martin Suggett (Earth and Physical Sciences)
Local Museum - 1851
Archaeology, astronomy, botany, ethnology, geology, ceramics, decorative arts, zoology, musical instruments, vivarium and aquarium, natural history 39520

Liverpool Scottish Regimental Museum, Forbes House, Score Ln, Childwall, Liverpool L16 2NG - T: (0151) 7727711. Cur.: Dennis Reeves
Military Museum
Uniforms, weapons, equipment, photographs and documents, history of the Regiment from 1900 to the present day 39521

Merseyside Maritime Museum, Albert Dock, Liverpool L3 4AQ - T: (0151) 4784499, Fax: 4784590, Internet: www.merseysidemaritimemuseum.org.uk. Dir.: Michael Stammers
Science&Tech Museum - 1980
Coll of full-size craft, incl the pilot boat, Edmund Gardner (1953), coll of models, paintings, marine equipment, the history of cargo-handling in the Port of Liverpool, the develop and operation of the encl dock system 39522

Museum of Archaeology, Classics and Oriental Studies, c/o University of Liverpool, 14 Abercromby Sq, Liverpool L69 7WZ - T: (0151) 7942467, Fax: 7942226, E-mail: winkerpa@liverpool.ac.uk, Internet: www.liv.ac.uk/archaeology_classics. Head: Elizabeth A. Slater
Archaeological Museum
Objects from the excavations in Egypt and the Near East, classical Aegean and prehistoric antiquities, coins 39523

Museum of Dentistry, c/o School of Dental Surgery, University of Liverpool, Pembroke Pl, Liverpool L69 3BX - T: (0151) 7065279, 7062000, Fax: 7065809. Cur.: John Cooper
Special Museum - 1880
History of dentistry, dentistal education, equipment 39524

Museum of Liverpool Life, Pier Head, Liverpool L3 1PZ - T: (0151) 4784060, Fax: 4784090, Internet: www.museumofliverpoollife.org.uk. Dir.: Graham Boxer, Keeper: Mike Stammers
Historical Museum - 1993
Displays on Making a Living, Demanding a Voice and Mersey Culture, forthcoming developments: Phase 2 - Homes and Communities, Phase 3 - The King's Regiment 39525

Open Eye Photography Gallery, 28-32 Wood St, Liverpool L1 4AQ - T: (0151) 7099460, Fax: 7093059, E-mail: info@openeye.org.uk, Internet: www.openeye.co.uk. Dir.: David Williams
Public Gallery 39526

Speke Hall, The Walk, Liverpool L24 1XD - T: (0151) 4277231, Fax: 4279860. Dir.: S. Osborne
Decorative Arts Museum - 1970
Decorative art, social history, interior design (16th-19th c), furniture (17th-19th c), Victorian furnishings (19th c) 39527

Sudley House, Mossley Hill Rd, Liverpool L18 8BX - T: (0151) 7243245, Fax: 7290531, Internet: www.sudleyhouse.org.uk. Dir.: Julian Treuherz
Fine Arts Museum - 1986
British paintings 39528

Tate Liverpool, Albert Dock, Liverpool L3 4BB - T: (0151) 7027400, Fax: 7027401, E-mail: liverpoolinfo@tate.org.uk, Internet: www.tate.org.uk/liverpool. Dir.: Christoph Grunenberg, Head of Exhibitions: Simon Groom
Public Gallery - 1988
National coll of 20th c art 39529

University of Liverpool Art Gallery, 3 Abercromby Sq, Liverpool L69 7WY - T: (0151) 7942348, Fax: 7942343, E-mail: artgall@liverpool.ac.uk, Internet: www.liv.ac.uk/artgall
Fine Arts Museum / University Museum - 1977
Watercolours by Turner, Girtin, Cozens, Cotman, early English porcelain, oil paintings by Turner, Audubon, Joseph Wright of Derby, Augustus John, sculpture by Epstein 39530

The Walker, William Brown St, Liverpool L3 8EL - T: (0151) 4784199, Fax: 4784190, E-mail: walker@nmgm.org, Internet: www.thewalker.org.uk. Keeper: Julian Treuherz
Fine Arts Museum - 1877
European painting, sculpture, drawings, watercolors and prints since 1300, Italian, Dutch and Flemish paintings (13th-17th c), British paintings (17th-19th c), 19th c Liverpool art, contemporary painting 39531

Walker Art Gallery → The Walker

Western Approaches, 1 Rumford St, Liverpool L2 8SZ - T: (0151) 2272008, Fax: 2366913
Historical Museum
Visit the labyrinth in the 50,000 sq ft headquarters beneath the streets of Liverpool, incl main operations room, Anderson Shelter, teleprinters, educational centre, admiral's office etc 39532

Livingston

Almond Valley Heritage Centre, Millfield, Kirkton North, Livingston EH54 7AR - T: (01506) 414957, Fax: 497771, E-mail: rac@almondvalley.co.uk, Internet: www.almondvalley.co.uk. Cur.: Dr. Robin Chesters
Local Museum - 1990
Agriculture, Scottish shale oil industry, local & social history 39533

Llanberis

Electric Mountain - Museum of North Wales, Amgueddfa'r Gogledd, Llanberis LL55 4UR - T: (01286) 870636, Fax: 873001. Dir.: Eluned Davies, Keeper: Dr. Dafydd Roberts
Local Museum
Art, temporary exhibitions, underground trips to Dinorwig pumped storage power station 39534

Llanberis Lake Railway, Gilfach Ddu, Llanberis LL55 4TY - T: (01286) 870549, Fax: 870549, E-mail: info@lake-railway.co.uk, Internet: www.lake-railway.co.uk
Science&Tech Museum 39535

Welsh Slate Museum, Pardarn Country Park, Llanberis LL55 4TY - T: (01286) 870630, Fax: 871906, E-mail: slate@nmgw.ac.uk, Internet: www.nmgw.ac.uk/wsm. Dir.: Dr. Dafydd Roberts
Natural History Museum - 1971
Geology, industry, slate, engineering, victorian technology, social history, mining, quarrying 39536

Llandrindod Wells

Museum of Local History and Industry, Temple St, Llandrindod Wells LD1 5DL - T: (01686) 412605. Cur.: Chris Wilson
Local Museum / Archaeological Museum
Castell Collen Roman Fort, archaeology, local history and industry, dolls, life in Llanidloes 19th-20th c 39537

National Cycle Collection, Automobile Palace, Temple St, Llandrindod Wells - T: (01597) 825531, Fax: 825531, E-mail: cycle.museum@care4free.net, Internet: www.cyclemuseum.org.uk. Cur.: David Higman
Science&Tech Museum
Bicycle since 1818, photographs, early lighting art, racing stars 39538

Radnorshire Museum, Temple St, Llandrindod Wells LD1 5DL - T: (01597) 824513, Fax: 825781, E-mail: radnorshire.museum@powys.gov.uk. Cur.: Rachel Sholl
Local Museum 39539

Llandudno

Great Orme Tramway, Victoria Station, Church Walks, Llandudno LL30 1AZ - T: (01492) 575350, Fax: 879346, E-mail: eng@greatormetramway.com, Internet: www.greatormetramway.com
Science&Tech Museum
Cable-hauled street tramway (only one in the world outside San Francisco), 4 tramcars working in 2 pairs, trams built by Hurst Nelson in 1902/3 39540

Llandudno Museum and Art Gallery, Chardon House, 17-19 Gloddaeth St, Llandudno LL30 2DD - T: (01492) 876517, Fax: 876517, E-mail: llandudno.museum@lineone.net. Cust.: Richard Ll. Hughes
Local Museum / Fine Arts Museum
Archaeology, history and early industry of the area, with a special section on early 20th-c tourism and entertainment 39541

Oriel Mostyn Gallery, 12 Vaughan St, Llandudno LL30 1AB - T: (01492) 879201, 870875, Fax: 878869, E-mail: post@mostyn.org, Internet: www.mostyn.org. Dir.: Martin Barlow
Public Gallery 39542

Llandysul

Museum of the Welsh Woollen Industry, Dre-fach Felindre, Llandysul SA44 5UP - T: (01559) 370929, Fax: 371592, E-mail: post@nmgw.ac.uk, Internet: www.nmgw.ac.uk/mwwi
Science&Tech Museum
Manufacture of woollen cloth from fleece to fabric, development of Wales' most important rural industry from its domestic beginnings to the 19th and early 20th-c factory units, coll of textile machinery and tools, a working waterwheel 39543

Teifi Valley Railway, Henllan Station Yard, Henllan, Llandysul SA44 5TD - T: (01559) 371077, Fax: 371077, E-mail: teifivr@f9.co.uk, Internet: www.teifivr@f9.uk
Science&Tech Museum
Steam locomotive, Motorail diesel units 39544

Llanelli

Bwlch Farm Stable Museum, Bwlch Farm, Bynea, Llanelli SA14 9ST - T: (01554) 772036
Agriculture Museum
Roman archaeological material found in the area, farm implements and tools, and relics of the Second World War 39545

Parc Howard Museum and Art Gallery, Parc Howard, Felinfoel Rd, Llanelli SA15 3AS - T: (01554) 772029, Fax: (01267) 223830, E-mail: chrisdelaney@carmarthenshire.gov.uk,

Internet: www.carmarthenshire.gov.uk. Cur.: A.G. Dorsett
Decorative Arts Museum / Fine Arts Museum / Local Museum - 1912
Pottery, art 39546

Public Library Gallery, Vaughan St, Llanelli SA15 3AS - T: (01554) 773538, Fax: 750125. Dir.: D.F. Griffiths
Public Gallery 39547

Llanfair Caereinion

Welshpool and Llanfair Light Railway, The Station, Llanfair Caereinion SY21 0SF - T: (01938) 810441, Fax: 810861, E-mail: info@wllr.org.uk, Internet: www.wllr.org.uk
Science&Tech Museum
Narrow gauge steam railway 39548

Llanfairpwll

Plas Newydd, Llanfairpwll LL61 6DQ - T: (01248) 714795, Fax: 713673, E-mail: ppnmsn@smtp.ntrust.org.uk. Dir.: Paul Carr-Griffin
Historical Museum
Wall paintings, relics of the 1st Marquess of Anglesey and the Battle of Waterloo, and the Ryan coll of military uniforms and headdresses 39549

Llangefni

Oriel Ynys Môn (Anglesey Heritage Gallery), Rhosmeirch, Llangefni LL77 7TQ - T: (01248) 724444, Fax: 750282, E-mail: agxlh@anglesey.gov.uk. Head: Alun Gruffydd
Local Museum
Tunnicliffe wildlife art coll, Welsh art, archaeology, geology, social history 39550

Llangernyw

Sir Henry Jones Museum, Y Cwm, Llangernyw LL22 8PR - T: (01492) 575371, Fax: 513664. Chm.: John Hughes
Local Museum
Furniture and domestic items, craft tools, books, photographs and costume relating to Sir Henry Jones and village life 39551

Llangollen

Canal Museum, The Wharf, Llangollen LL20 8TA - T: (01978) 860702, Fax: 860799, E-mail: sue@horsedrawnboats.co.uk, Internet: www.horsedrawnboats.co.uk. Dir.: D.R. Knapp, S. Knapp
Historical Museum - 1974
Canals and canals boats 39552

Llangollen Motor Museum, Pentrefelin, Llangollen LL20 8EE - T: (01978) 860324, E-mail: llangollen-motormuseum@hotmail.com, Internet: www.llangollenmotormuseum@hotmail.co.uk. Owner: Ann Owen, Gwilym Owen
Science&Tech Museum
Cars, motorcycles, memorabilia from 1910-1970's, history of Britain's canals 39553

Llangollen Railway, The Station, Abbey Rd, Llangollen LL20 8SN - T: (01978) 860979, Fax: 869247, Internet: www.llangollen-railway.co.uk. Dir.: Gordon Heddon
Science&Tech Museum
Locomotive, passenger stock and goods vehicles in its possession and care 39554

Plas Newydd, Hill St, Llangollen LL20 8AW - T: (01978) 861314, Fax: 708258, E-mail: rose.mcmahon@denbighshire.gov.uk. Dir.: Rose MacMahon
Special Museum
Home of the Ladies of Llangollen 39555

Llanidloes

Llanidloes Museum, Town Hall, Great Oak St, Llanidloes SY18 6BU, mail addr: c/o Powysland Museum, Canal Wharf, Welshpool SY21 7AQ - T: (01938) 554656, Fax: 554656, E-mail: powysland@powys.gov.uk, Internet: po-wysmuseums.powys.gov.uk. Dir.: Eva B. Bredsdorff
Local Museum - 1933 39556

Llantrisant

Model House Gallery, Bull Ring, Llantrisant CF72 8EB - T: (01443) 237758, Fax: 224718
Public Gallery 39557

Llanycefn

Penrhos Cottage, Llanycefn SA66 7XT - T: (01437) 731328
Local Museum
Traditional Welsh thatched cottage with original furniture 39558

Llanystumdwy

Lloyd George Museum and Highgate, Llanystumdwy LL52 0SH - T: (01766) 522071, Fax: 522071, E-mail: amgveddfalloydgeotge@gwynedd.gov.uk, Internet: www.gwynedd.gov.uk/museums. Dir.: Dafydd Whittall
Historical Museum - 1948
Caskets, original punch cartoons, original archives concerning Versailles Peace Treaty 39559

Llwynypia

Rhondda Museum, Glyncornel Environmental Study Centre, Llwynypia CF40 2HT - T: (01443) 431727
Local Museum 39560

Lochwinnoch

Lochwinnoch Community Museum, High St, Lochwinnoch PA12 4AB - T: (01505) 842615, Fax: 8899240. Dir.: Martine Morletta
Local Museum - 1984
Local agriculture, industry and village life 39561

Lockerbie

Rammerscales, Lockerbie DG11 1LD - T: (01387) 811988
Fine Arts Museum
20th c paintings, tapestries, sculpture 39562

London

198 Gallery, 194-198 Railton Rd, Herne Hill, London SE24 0LU - T: (020) 79788309, Fax: 77379315, E-mail: gallery@198gallery.co.uk, Internet: www.198gallery.co.uk. Dir.: Lucy Davies
Public Gallery
Contemporary art by artists from diverse cultural backgrounds - education centre 39563

Alexander Fleming Laboratory Museum, Saint Mary's Hospital, Praed St, London W2 1NY - T: (020) 78866528, Fax: 78866739, E-mail: kevin.brown@st-marys.nhs.uk, Internet: www.st-marys.org.uk/about/fleming-museum.htm. Dir.: Kevin Brown
Science&Tech Museum - 1993
Reconstruction of the laboratory in which Fleming discovered Penicillin in 1928 39564

All Hallows Undercroft Museum, Byward St, London EC3R 5BJ - T: (020) 74812928, Fax: 74883333
Religious Arts Museum
Roman pavement in situ, classical tombstones, a model of the Roman city, ancient registers, a Crusader Altar 39565

Anaesthetic Museum, c/o Dept. of Anaesthesia, Saint Bartholomew's Hospital, London EC1A 7BE - T: (020) 76017518. Owner: D.J. Wilkinson
Historical Museum
Encompasses apparatus general, local anaesthetics since 1800's 39566

Apsley House, Hyde Park Cnr, London W1J 7NT - T: (020) 74995676, Fax: 74936576, Internet: www.apsleyhouse.org.uk. Dir.: Alicia Robinson
Decorative Arts Museum / Fine Arts Museum - 1952
Art coll, decorative objects, paintings, silver, sculpture, porcelain 39567

Architecture Foundation, 30 Bastwick St, London EC1V 3TN - T: (020) 72533334, Fax: 72533335, E-mail: mail@architecturefoundation.org.uk, Internet: www.architecturefoundation.org.uk
Public Gallery 39568

Arsenal Museum, Highbury, London N5 1BU - T: (020) 77044000, Fax: 77044001
Special Museum 39569

Baden-Powell House, 65-67 Queen's Gate, London SW7 5JS - T: (020) 75847031, Fax: 75906902, E-mail: bph.hostel@scout.org.uk, Internet: www.scoutbase.org.uk
Special Museum - 1961
Life and work of Lord Robert Baden-Powell (1857-1941), founder of the Boy Scouts 39570

Bank of England Museum, Threadneedle St, London EC2R 8AH - T: (020) 76015545, Fax: 76015808, E-mail: museum@bankofengland.co.uk, Internet: www.bankofengland.co.uk/museum. Dir.: John Keyworth
Special Museum - 1988
Banknotes, coins and medals, photographs, pictures, prints and drawings, statuary, artefacts, Roman and medieval 39571

Bankside Gallery, 48 Hopton St, London SE1 9JH - T: (020) 79287521, Fax: 79282820, E-mail: info@banksidegallery.com, Internet: www.banksidegallery.com. Dir.: Judy Dixey
Public Gallery 39572

Banqueting House, Whitehall, London SW1A 2ER - T: (0870) 7515178, Fax: (020) 79308268, Internet: www.banqueting-house.org.uk. Cust: Irma Hay, Dep. Cust.: SimonWhite Lumley
Fine Arts Museum
Historic building, completed in 1622 to a design by Inigo Jones, ceiling paintings by Rubens installed in 1635 39573

Barbican Art, Barbican Centre, Silk St, London EC2Y 8DS - T: (020) 73827105, Fax: 76282308, E-mail: artinfo@barbican.org.uk, Internet: www.barbican.org.uk. Dir.: Carol Brown (Head of Art Galleries)
Public Gallery 39574

Barnet Museum, 31 Wood St, Barnet, London EN5 4BE - T: (020) 84408066. Dir.: Dr. Gilian Gear
Local Museum - 1935
Barnet district history, costume photogr - library 39575

BBC Experience (closed) 39576

Ben Uri Gallery, London Jewish Museum of Art, 108a Boundary Rd, Saint Johns Wood, London NW8 0RH - T: (020) 76043991, Fax: 76043992, E-mail: info@benuri.org.uk, Internet: www.benuri.com. Dir.:

Richard Aronowitz-Mercer
Public Gallery / Fine Arts Museum
Contemporary art by Jewish artists, paintings, drawings, sculptures 39577

Benjamin Franklin House, 36 Craven St, London WC2N 5NF - T: (020) 79309121, Fax: 79309124, E-mail: BenjaminFranklinHouse@msn.com, Internet: www.rsa.org.uk/franklin
Historical Museum 39578

Bexley Museum, Hall Pl, Bourne Rd, Bexley, London DA5 1PQ - T: (01322) 526574, Fax: 522921, E-mail: janice@bexleymuseum.freeserv.co.uk, Internet: www.hallplaceandgardens.com. Dir.: Martin Purslow
Historical Museum - 1934
Local geology, archaeology, fauna and flora, minerals, Roman finds, local history and industries 39579

Black Cultural Archives, 378 Coldharbour Ln, London SW9 8LF - T: (020) 77384591, Fax: 77387168, E-mail: info@aambh.org.uk. Dir.: Sam Walker
Local Museum
Biographies, music manuscripts, slave documents, photographs, British parliamentary records, volumes of "Crisis" and "Messenger" 39580

BOC Museum, The Charles King Collection, 9 Bedford Sq, London WC1B 3RE - T: (020) 76318806, Fax: 76314352, E-mail: trishwillis@aagbi.org, Internet: www.aagbi.org. Dir.: Patricia Willis
Historical Museum
Historic anaesthetic equipment 39581

Bramah Tea and Coffee Museum, 40 Southwark St, London SE1 1UN - T: (020) 74035650, Fax: 74035650, E-mail: e.bramah@virgin.net, Internet: www.bramahmuseum.co.uk. Dir.: Edward Bramah
Special Museum - 1992
Large coll of teapots and coffee making machinery 39582

British Dental Association Museum, 64 Wimpole St, London W1M 8AL - T: (020) 75634549, Fax: 79356492, E-mail: r.fea@bda-dentistry.org.uk, Internet: www.bda.dentistry.org.uk
Historical Museum
History, art and science of dental surgery 39583

British Film Institute Collections, 21 Stephen St, London W1T 1LN - T: (020) 72551444, Fax: 75807503, E-mail: gail.nolan@bfi.org.uk, Internet: www.bfi.org.uk. Dir.: Jon Teckman, Cur.: Gail Nolan (Museum of the Moving Image), Anne Fleming (National Film and Television Archive), Registrar: Shirley Collier, Keeper: David Meeker (Feature Film), James Patterson (Documentary Film), Steve Bryant (Television), Head: Caroline Ellis (Collections), Heather Stewart (Access), Rod Molinare (Sales), Erich Sargeant (Video Publishing), Karen Alexander (Marketing)
Special Museum 39584

British Library, 96 Euston Rd, London NW1 2DB - T: (020) 74127332, Fax: 74127340, E-mail: visitor-services@bl.uk, Internet: www.bl.uk. Chief Ex.: Lynne Brindley
Library with Exhibitions
Permanent display: Magna Carta, first folio of Shakespeare's works, Gutenberg Bible 39585

The British Museum, Great Russell St, London WC1B 3DG - T: (020) 73238000, Fax: 73238616, E-mail: information@thebritishmuseum.ac.uk, Internet: www.thebritishmuseum.ac.uk. Dir.: Neil MacGregor, Sc. Staff: Dr. W.V. Davies (Ancient Egypt and Sudan), Dr. A. Burnett (Coins and Medals), Dr. D. Williams (Greek and Roman), A. Griffiths (Prints and Drawings), R. Knox (Asia), Dr. J. Curtis (Ancient Near East), Dr. S. Bowman (Conservation, Documentation, Science), J. Mack (Ethnography)
Museum of Classical Antiquities - 1753
Coins and medals, ancient Egypt and Sudan ethnography, Greek and Roman antiquities, Japanese antiquities, prehistory and Europe prints & drawings, Ancient Near East 39586

British Optical Association Museum, College of Optometrists, 42 Craven St, London WC2N 5NG - T: (020) 77664353, Fax: 78396800, E-mail: museum@college-optometrists.org, Internet: www.college-optometrists.org/college/museum/index.htm. Cur.: Neil Handley
Historical Museum / Science&Tech Museum
Optical and ophthalmic items, incl. spectacles, pince- nez, lorgnettes, spyglasses, lenses and artificial eyes, diagnostic instruments, fine art, ceramics, oil paintings - library 39587

British Red Cross Museum and Archives, 9 Grosvenor Crescent, London SW1X 7EJ - T: (020) 72015153, Fax: 72356456, E-mail: enquiry@redcross.org.uk, Internet: www.redcross.org.uk/museum&archives. Dir.: Sir Nicholas Young
Special Museum
Uniforms, medals, badges, textiles, medical equipment and humanitarian aid - archives 39588

Bruce Castle Museum, Lordship Ln, Tottenham, London N17 8NU - T: (020) 88088772, Fax: 88084118, E-mail: museum.services@haringey.gov.uk, Internet: www.haringey.gov.uk. Dir.: Sian Harrington
Local Museum - 1906
Haringey Libraries, archives 39589

Brunei Gallery, c/o SOAS, Thornhaugh St, Russell Sq, London WC1H 0XG - T: (020) 78984915, 78984046, Fax: 78984259, E-mail: gallery@soas.ac.uk, Internet: www.soas.ac.uk/gallery. Dir.: John Hollingworth
Public Gallery / University Museum
Historical and contemporary works of and from Asia and Africa 39590

Brunel Engine House, Railway Av, Rotherhithe, London SE16 4LF - T: (020) 72313840, E-mail: robert.hulse@brunelenginehouse.org.uk, Internet: www.brunelenginehouse.org.uk. Dir.: Robert Hulse
Historic Site - 1974
Unique compound horizontal V steam engine, model and watercolours of Sir Marc Brunel's tunnel (1st underwater thoroughfare) 39591

BT Museum (closed) 39592

Buckingham Palace, Royal Collections, London SW1A 1AA, mail addr: Stable Yard House, Saint James's Palace, London SW1A 1JR - T: (020) 73212233, Fax: 79309625, E-mail: buckinghampalace@royalcollection.org.uk, Internet: www.royal.gov.uk
Fine Arts Museum / Decorative Arts Museum
State appartments, royal coll 39593

Cabaret Mechanical Theatre (temporary closed), c/o Sarah Alexander, 95 Wilton Rd, London SW1V 1BZ - T: (020) 85163134, Fax: 86937664, E-mail: barecat@cabaret.co.uk, Internet: www.cabaret.co.uk. Dir.: Susan Jackson
Science&Tech Museum - 1984
Coll of contemporary automata and mechanical sculpture, Paul Spooner, Keith Newstead, Ron Fuller, Peter Markey, Tim Hunkin 39594

Cabinet War Rooms, Clive Steps, King Charles St, London SW1A 2AQ - T: (020) 79306961, Fax: 78395897, E-mail: cwr@imw.org.uk, Internet: www.iwm.org.uk. Dir.: Philip Reed
Historical Museum - 1984
Churchill's underground Headquarter, 21 rooms for Churchill and his staff, including the Cabinet Room, the Map Room, Churchill's bedroom and the Transatlantic Telephone Room 39595

Camden Arts Centre, Arkwright Rd, London NW3 6DG - T: (020) 74352643, 74355224, Fax: 77943371, E-mail: info@camdenartscentre.org, Internet: www.camdenartscentre.org. Dir.: Jenni Lomax
Public Gallery
Contemporary art, painting and pottery 39596

Canada House Gallery, Trafalgar Sq, London SW1Y 5BJ - T: (020) 72586537, Fax: 72586434, Internet: www.dfait-maeci.gc.ca. Dir.: Michael Regan
Public Gallery 39597

Carlyle's House, 24 Cheyne Row, London SW3 5HL - T: (020) 73527087, Fax: 73525108, Internet: www.nationaltrust.org.uk. Cust.: Lin Skippings
Special Museum - 1895
Home of Thomas and Jane Carlyle with furniture, books, letters, personal effects and portraits - library 39598

Carshalton Water Tower, West St, Carshalton, London SM5 3PN - T: (020) 786470984. Dir.: Jean Knight
Science&Tech Museum
18th c water tower, bathroom, pump chamber, saloon, prints 39599

A Celebration of Immigration, 19 Princelet St, London E1 6QH - T: (020) 72475352, Fax: 73751490, E-mail: information@19princeletstreet.org.uk, Internet: www.19princeletstreet.org.uk
Historical Museum
Various waves of immigration through the East End of London, religious textiles of the Jewish life - archive 39600

Centre for the Magic Arts, 12 Stephenson Wy, Euston, London NW1 2ND - T: (020) 73875114, E-mail: henry.lewis@classictm.net, Internet: www.themagiccircle.co.uk
Fine Arts Museum
Original posters ephemera, apparatus of conjurours and illusionists 39601

Chapter House, East Cloister, Westminster Abbey, London SW1P 3PE - T: (020) 72225897, Fax: 72220960, Internet: www.english-heritage.org.uk
Fine Arts Museum
Medieval sculture, wall paintings 39602

Chartered Insurance Institute's Museum, The Hall, 20 Aldermanbury, London EC2V 7HY - T: (020) 74174412, Fax: 77260131, E-mail: customer.service@cii.co.uk, Internet: www.cii.co.uk. Dir.: K. Clayden
Special Museum - 1934
History of insurance, insurance company fire brigades, fire marks, early firefighting equipment - library 39603

Chelsea Physic Garden, 66 Royal Hospital Rd, London SW3 4HS - T: (020) 73525646, Fax: 73763910, E-mail: sue@cpgarden.demon.co.uk, Internet: www.cpgarden.demon.co.uk. Cur.: Sue Minter
Special Museum
Second oldest botanic garten in the country, particularly strong on collections of medicinal plants 39604

Chisenhale Gallery, 64 Chisenhale Rd, London E3 5QZ - T: (020) 89814518, Fax: 89807169, E-mail: mail@chisenhale.org.uk, Internet: www.chisenhale.org.uk. Dir.: John Gill
Public Gallery 39605

Chiswick House, Burlington Ln, Chiswick, London W4 2RP - T: (020) 89950508, 87421978, Fax: 87423104, Internet: www.english-heritage.org.uk. Cur.: Cathy Power
Decorative Arts Museum
18th century furniture and interiors, paintings collection from 17th-19th century 39606

Church Farmhouse Museum, Greyhound Hill, Hendon, London NW4 4JR - T: (020) 82030130, Fax: 8896804, E-mail: gerrard.roots@barnet.gov.uk, Internet: www.barnet.gov.uk/cultural_services. Dir.: Gerrard Roots, WM: Hugh Petrie (Archivist)
Local Museum - 1955
Period furniture, local hist 39607

Cinema Museum, 2 Dugard Way, Kennington, London SE11 4TH - T: (020) 78402200, Fax: 78402299, E-mail: martin@cinemamuseum.org.uk. Dir.: Martin Humphries
Performing Arts Museum
History of cinemas since 1896 39608

City of London Police Museum, 37 Wood St, London EC2P 2NQ - T: (020) 76012747. Cur.: Roger Appleby
Historical Museum
Police and the policing of the city, insignia truncheons, tipstaves, uniforms and photographs 39609

Clink Prison Museum, 1 Clink St, London SE1 9DG - T: (020) 73781558, Fax: 74035813, E-mail: museum@clink.co.uk, Internet: www.clink.co.uk. Owner: Ray Rankin
Local Museum 39610

Clipper Ship Cutty Sark, King William Walk, London SE10 9HT - T: (020) 88583445, Fax: 88533589, E-mail: info@cuttysark.org.uk, Internet: www.cuttysark.org.uk. Man.: Julia Parker
Historical Museum - 1957
Restored ship, launched 1869, with figureheads, ship hist 39611

Collection of the Worshipful Company of Clockmakers, Clock Room, Guildhall Library, Aldermanbury, London EC2P 2EJ - T: (020) 7606303 ext 1865/66. Keeper: Sir George White
Science&Tech Museum
Clocks, watches and marine timekeepers, the majority dating between late 16th c and the mid of 19th c - library 39612

College Art Collections, University College London, Gower St, London WC1 6BT - T: (020) 76792540, Fax: 78132803, E-mail: college.art@ucl.ac.uk, Internet: collections.ucl.ac.uk
Association with Coll
Formerly known as the Strang print room, the collection incl plaster models and drawings by Flaxman, George Grote's family coll of 16th-18th c German drawings, old master prints with an emphasis on the German school, early English watercolours and prints from the 17th-19th c, bequethed by Henry Vaughan, Japanese Ukiyo-e prints of the 19th and early 20th c; the Slade coll, illustrating the history of the Slade School 39613

Commonwealth Institute, Kensington High St, London W8 6NQ - T: (020) 76034535, Fax: 76027374, E-mail: information@commonwealth.org.uk, Internet: www.commonwealth.org.uk. Dir.: David French, Sc. Staff: Karen Peters (Information and Resources)
Public Gallery - 1962
Exhibitions of commonwealth countries, commonwealth artists, culture, literature, books, artefacts from commonwealth countries - library, educational programmes 39614

Courtauld Institute Gallery, Somerset House, Strand, London WC2R 0RN - T: (020) 78482526, Fax: 78482589, E-mail: galleryinfo@courtauld.ac.uk, Internet: www.courtauld.ac.uk. Dir.: Prof. James Cuno, Cur.: Helen Braham, Ernst Vegelin Van Claerbergen
Fine Arts Museum - 1932
French Impressionists, Post-Impressionists and European Old Masters (14th-18th c) 39615

Crafts Council Collection, 44a Pentonville Rd, Islington, London N1 9BY - T: (020) 72787700, Fax: 78736891, E-mail: reference@craftscouncil.org.uk, Internet: www.craftscouncil.org.uk. Dir.: Dr. Louise Taylor
Decorative Arts Museum - 1971
Crafts - gallery, education workshop, picture and reference libraries 39616

The Crossness Engines, Old Works Thames Water, Belvedere Rd, Abbey Wood, London SE2 9AQ - T: (020) 83113711, Fax: 83036723, E-mail: mail@crossness.org.uk, Internet: www.crossness.org.uk
Science&Tech Museum
Four 1865 James Watt rotative beam engines, sanitation ware 39617

Crystal Palace Museum, Anerley Hill, London SE19 2BA - T: (020) 86760700, Fax: 86760700, E-mail: museum@thecrystalpalace.fsnet.co.uk. Dir.: K. Kiss
Historical Museum
Oil paintings, ceramics, medals, papers, 3-dimensional objects, history of the Crystal Palace 39618

Cuming Museum, 155-157 Walworth Rd, London SE17 1RS - T: (020) 77011342, Fax: 77037415, E-mail: cumming.museum@southwark.gov.uk, Internet: southwark.gov.uk. Dir.: Sophie Perkins
Archaeological Museum / Decorative Arts Museum - 1902
Roman and medieval remains from archaeological excavations, coll of London superstitions, worldwide coll of the Cuming family 39619

De Morgan Centre, 38 West Hill, Wandsworth, London SW18 1RZ - T: (020) 88711144, E-mail: info@demorgancentre.org.uk, Internet: www.demorgan.org.uk. Pres.: Jon Catleugh
Fine Arts Museum
Paintings and drawings by Evelyn De Morgan, ceramics by William De Morgan 39620

Delfina, 50 Bermondsey St, London SE1 3UD - T: (020) 73576600, Fax: 73570250
Public Gallery
Modern and contemporary art 39621

Department of Geological Sciences Collection, c/o University College London, Gower St, London WC1E 6BT - T: (020) 76797900, Fax: 73871612, E-mail: w.kirk@ucl.ac.uk. Cur.: Wendy Kirk
Natural History Museum
Geological specimens, rocks, minerals and fossils 39622

Design Museum, Shad Thames, London SE1 2YD - T: (0870) 8339955, Fax: 9091909, E-mail: info@designmuseum.org, Internet: www.designmuseum.org. Dir.: Alice Rawsthorn
Fine Arts Museum - 1989 39623

The Dickens House Museum, 48 Doughty St, London WC1N 2LX - T: (020) 74052127, Fax: 78315175, E-mail: dhmuseum@rmplc.co.uk, Internet: www.dickensmuseum.com. Dir.: Andrew Xavier
Special Museum / Library with Exhibitions / Historic Site - 1925
Former home of the writer Charles Dickens (1812-1870), memorabilia, manuscripts, letters, first editions, furniture - library 39624

Dr. Johnson's House, 17 Gough Sq, London EC4A 3DE - T: (020) 73533745, Fax: 73533745, E-mail: curator@drjohnsonshouse.org, Internet: www.drjohnsonshouse.org. Chairman: Lord Harmsworth, Cur.: Natasha McEnroe
Special Museum - 1912
Memorabilia on Samuel Johnson (1709-1784) 39625

Drawings Collection, Royal Institute of British Architects, 21 Portman Sq, London W1H 6LP - T: (020) 73073698, Fax: 74863797, E-mail: drawings@inst.riba.org, Internet: www.architecture.com. Dir.: Charles Hind
Fine Arts Museum 39626

Dulwich Picture Gallery, Gallery Rd, Dulwich Village, London SE21 7AD - T: (020) 86935254, Fax: 82998700, E-mail: info@dulwichpicturegallery.org.uk, Internet: www.dulwichpicturegallery.org.uk. Dir.: Desmond Shawe-Taylor
Fine Arts Museum - 1811
Paintings by Poussin, Gainsborough, Canaletto Rembrandt, Rubens, building by Sir John Soane 39627

Dunhill Museum, 48 Jermyn St, Saint James, London SW1Y 6LX - T: (020) 78388233, Fax: 78388304, E-mail: peter.tilley@dunhill.com, Internet: www.dunhill.com. Cur.: Peter Tilley
Decorative Arts Museum / Special Museum
Dunhill antique products, incl. motoring accessories, pens, compendiums, lighters, watches - archive 39628

Ealing College Gallery, 83 The Avenue, London W3 8UX - T: (020) 82316303, Internet: www.etc.ac.uk
University Museum 39629

East Ham Nature Reserve, Norman Rd, London E6 4HN - T: (020) 84704525. Man.: Barry Graham
Local Museum
Local and natural hist 39630

Eltham Palace, Court Yard, Eltham, London SE9 5QE - T: (020) 82942548, 82482577, Fax: 82942621, E-mail: eltham.palace@english-heritage.org.uk, Internet: www.english-heritage.org.uk
Decorative Arts Museum / Historical Museum - 1999
Rare 1930's Art Deco house, build for Edvard IV and medieval Great Hall build for Edvard IV and Henry VIII - gardens 39631

Estorick Collection of Modern Italian Art, 39a Canonbury Sq, Islington, London N1 2AN - T: (020) 77049522, Fax: 77049531, E-mail: curator@estorickcollection.com, Internet: www.estorickcollection.com. Dir.: Alexandra Noble
Fine Arts Museum 39632

Fan Museum, 12 Crooms Hill, Greenwich, London SE10 8ER - T: (020) 88587879, 83051441, Fax: 82931889, E-mail: fan.museum@virgin.net, Internet: www.fan-museum.org. Dir.: H.E. Alexander
Decorative Arts Museum - 1985
European 17th and 18th c fans, fan leaves, important oriental export fans 39633

Fenton House, Hampstead Grove, Hampstead, London NW3 6RT - T: (020) 74353471, Fax: 74353471, E-mail: fenton@nationaltrust.org.uk
Music Museum / Decorative Arts Museum - 1953
Benton-Fletcher coll of early musical instruments, Binning coll of porcelain, Georgian furniture, needlework 39634

Fire Power, the Royal Artillery Museum, Number One St, Royal Arsenal, Woolwich, London SE18 6ST - T: (020) 88557755, Fax: 88557100, E-mail: info@firepower.org.uk, Internet: www.firepower.org.uk
Military Museum - 2001
Fuses, ammunition, artillery instruments, rockets, edge weapons, display of artillery from the 14th c to present day 39635

Florence Nightingale Museum, Saint Thomas's Hospital, 2 Lambeth Palace Rd, London SE1 7EW - T: (020) 76200374, Fax: 79281760, E-mail: juwa@florence-nightingale.co.uk, Internet: www.florence-nightingale.co.uk. Dir.: Alex Attewell
Historical Museum - 1989
Nightingale memorabilia 39636

Foundation for Women's Art, 11 Northburgh St, London EC1V 0AH - T: (020) 72514881, Fax: 72514882, E-mail: admin@fwa-uk.org, Internet: www.fwa-uk.org. Dir.: Monica Petzal
Fine Arts Museum
archives 39637

Foundling Museum, 40 Brunswick Sq, London WC1N 1AZ - T: (020) 78413600, Fax: 78378084, E-mail: rhian@foundlingmuseum.org.uk. Dir.: Rhian Harris
Fine Arts Museum
London's first art gallery, works by Hogarth, Gainsborough and Reynolds, social history 39638

Freud Museum, 20 Maresfield Gardens, Hampstead, London NW3 5SX - T: (020) 74352002, Fax: 74315452, E-mail: freud@gn.apc.org, Internet: www.freud.org.uk. Dir.: Erica Davies
Special Museum - 1986
Sigmund Freud's complete working environment, including the famous couch, his library and coll of 2000 Greek, Roman and Egyptian antiquities 39639

Fusiliers London Volunteers' Museum, 213 Balham High Rd, London SW17 7BQ - T: (020) 86721168. Cur.: A.H. Mayle
Military Museum 39640

Geffrye Museum, Kingsland Rd, Shoreditch, London E2 8EA - T: (020) 77399893, Fax: 77295647, E-mail: info@geffrye-museum.org.uk, Internet: www.geffrye-museum.org.uk. Dir.: David Dewing
Decorative Arts Museum - 1914
English domestic interiors from 1600-2000, walled herb garden and period garden rooms fom 17th to 20th c - library 39641

Gilbert Collection, Somerset House, Strand, London WC2R 1LN - T: (020) 74209400, Fax: 74209400, E-mail: info@gilbert-collection.org.uk, Internet: www.gilbert-collection.org.uk. Dir.: Tom L. Freudenheim
Fine Arts Museum / Decorative Arts Museum - 2000
Decorative art, European silver, gold snuff boxes, Italian mosaics 39642

Golden Hinde Educational Museum, Saint Mary Overie Dock, Cathedral St, London SE1 9DE - T: (020) 74030123, Fax: 74075908, Internet: www.goldenhinde.co.uk. Dir.: Roddy Coleman
Historical Museum
16th-c warship in which Sir Francis Drake circumnavigated the world between 1577 and 1580 39643

Goldsmiths' Hall, Foster Lane, London EC2V 6BN - T: (020) 76067010, Fax: 76061511, E-mail: the.clerk@thegoldsmiths.co.uk, Internet: www.thegoldsmiths.co.uk. Dir.: R. Buchanan-Dunlop, Cur.: Rosemary Ransome Wallis
Decorative Arts Museum
English silver, modern jewelry since 1960 - library 39644

Gordon Museum, Saint Thomas St, London SE1 9RT - T: (020) 79554358, E-mail: william.edwards@kcl.ac.uk. Keeper: William Edwards
Special Museum
Specimens of human disease, wax models of anatomical dissection and skin diseases 39645

Government Art Collection, c/o Department for Culture, Media and Sport, 2-4 Cockspur St, London SW1Y 5DH - T: (020) 72116200, Fax: 72116032, E-mail: enquiries@culture.gov.uk, Internet: www.gac.culture.gov.uk. Dir.: Penny Johnson
Fine Arts Museum - 1898
British art from the 16th c to the present day 39646

Grange Museum of Community History, Neasden Ln, Neasden, London NW10 1QB - T: (020) 84528311, Fax: 82084233, E-mail: grangemuseum@brent.gov.uk, Internet: www.brent.gov.uk. Cur.: Victoria Barlow
Historical Museum - 1977
Archive of the British Empire exhibition held at Wembley 1924, historical displays relating to Brent people 39647

Grant Museum of Zoology and Comparative Anatomy, c/o Biology Department, University College London, Darwin Bldg, Gower St, London WC1E 6BT - T: (020) 76792647, Fax: 76797096, E-mail: zoology.museum@ucl.ac.uk, Internet: www.collections.ucl.ac.uk/zoology. Dir.: Dr. H.J. Chatterjee
Natural History Museum / University Museum - 1828
Robert Edmund Grant, T.H. Huxley, E. Ray Lankester, DMS Watson, J. Cloudsly Thompson colls, Quagga skeleton and many rare, endangered and extinct animals, extensive skeletal and fossil coll 39648

Greenwich Borough Museum → Greenwich Heritage Centre

Greenwich Heritage Centre, The Royal Arsenal, Woolwich, London SE18 4DX - T: (020) 88542452, Fax: 88542490, E-mail: beverley.burford@greenwich.gov.uk, Internet: www.greenwich.gov.uk. Cur.: Beverley Burford
Local Museum - 1919
Local history, natural history 39649

Greenwich Local History Centre, 90 Mycenae Rd, Blackheath, London SE3 7SE - T: (020) 88584631, Fax: 82934721, E-mail: local.history@greenwich.gov.uk, Internet: www.greenwich.gov.uk/council/publicsevices/lhistory.html. Man.: Julian Watson
Local Museum - 1972
A.R. Martin coll of documents relating to Greenwich, Blackheath and Charlton 39650

Greenwich Theatre Art Gallery, Crooms Hill, London SE10 8ES - T: (020) 88584447, Fax: 88588042
Performing Arts Museum 39651

The Guards Museum, Wellington Barracks, Birdcage Walk, London SW1E 6HQ - T: (020) 74143271, Fax: 74143429. Cur.: David Horn
Military Museum
Uniforms, weapons, memorabilia illustratings 39652

Guide Heritage Centre, 17-19 Buckingham Palace Rd, London SW1W 0PT - T: (020) 75921818, Fax: 78288317, E-mail: heritage@guides.org.uk, Internet: www.guides.org.uk
Historical Museum
archive 39653

Guildhall Art Gallery, 2 Guildhall Yard, London EC2P 2EJ - T: (020) 73323700, Fax: 73323342, E-mail: guildhall.artgallery@corpoflondon.gov.uk, Internet: www.guildhall-art-gallery.org.uk. Dir.: David Bradbury, Cur.: V.M. Knight
Fine Arts Museum - 1886
London paintings, 19th c works of art, portraits, sculpture, Sir Matthew Smith Studio coll 39654

Guinness Archives (closed) 39655

Gunnersbury Park Museum, Gunnersbury Park, Popes Ln, London W3 8LQ - T: (020) 89921612, Fax: 87520686, E-mail: gp-museum@cip.org.uk. Cur.: Seán Sherman
Local Museum / Archaeological Museum / Historic Site - 1929
Local archaeology, Sadler coll of flints, Middlesex maps and topography, costumes, toys and dolls, transportation, local crafts and industries - library 39656

Hackney Museum, 1 Reading Ln, Hackney, London E8 1GQ - T: (020) 83563500, Fax: 89857600, E-mail: hmuseum@hackney.gov.uk, Internet: www.hackney.gov.uk/hackneymuseum. Cur.: Fiona Davison, Man.: Laura Williams
Local Museum
History of Hackney, Chalmers Bequest coll of artworks 39657

Hamilton's Gallery, 13 Carlos Pl, London W1Y 5AG - T: (020) 74999493/94, Fax: 76299919, Internet: www.art-on-line.com/hamiltons
Fine Arts Museum 39658

Hampstead Museum, Burgh House, New End Sq, London NW3 1LT - T: (020) 74310144, Fax: 74358817, E-mail: hamsteadmuseum@talk21.com. Cur.: Marilyn Greene
Local Museum - 1979
Local history, Helen Allingham coll, Isokon furniture 39659

Handel House Museum, 25 Brook St, London W1K 4HB - T: (020) 74951685, Fax: 74951759, E-mail: mail@handelhouse.org, Internet: www.handelhouse.org. Dir.: Jacqueline Riding
Music Museum
Decorative arts, musical instruments, furniture and 18th-c editions of Handel's music 39660

Haringey Museum → Bruce Castle Museum

Hayward Gallery, Belvedere Rd, London SE1 8XZ - T: (020) 79604242, E-mail: visual_arts@hayward.org.uk, Internet: www.hayward.org.uk. Dir.: Susan Ferleger Brades
Fine Arts Museum - 1968
Arts Council coll, National Touring exhibitions 39661

Her Majesty Tower of London, Tower Hill, London EC3N 4AB - T: (0870) 7566060, Internet: www.tower-of-london.org.uk. Chief.: Michael Day
Historical Museum / Decorative Arts Museum / Historic Site
Royal palace and fortress, White Tower, towers and ramparts, royal lodgings, Chapel Royal of Saint Peter at Vincula, crown jewels, Royal amouries 39662

Heritage Royal Mail Collection, Freeling House, Phoenix Pl, London WC1X 0DL - T: (020) 72392570, Fax: 72392576, E-mail: heritage@royalmail.com, Internet: www.royalmail.com/heritage. Dir.: Martin Rush
Special Museum - 1965
Philatelics, British stamps since 1840, world coll since 1878, special display on the creation of the One Penny Black 1840, Postal services and artefacts 39663

Hermitage Rooms, South Bldg, Somerset House, Strand, London WC2R 1LA - T: (020) 78454630, 78454631, Fax: 78454637, E-mail: joy@somerset-house.org.uk, Internet: www.hermitagerooms.com. Dir.: Timothy Stevens
Special Museum
Rotating coll from the State Hermitage Museum in St Petersburg 39664

HMS Belfast, Morgans Ln, off Tooley St, London SE1 2JH - T: (020) 79406300, Fax: 74030719, E-mail: hmsbelfast@iwm.org.uk, Internet: www.iwm.org.uk. Dir.: Brad King
Military Museum - 1971
Armoured warship of WWII, Royal Navy 39665

Hogarth's House, Hogarth Ln, Great West Rd, Chiswick, London W4 2QN - T: (020) 89946757, Fax: 85834595. Cust.: L.J. Channer
Fine Arts Museum - 1904
Prints, engravings 39666

Honeywood Heritage Centre, Honeywood Walk, Carshalton, London SM5 3NX - T: (020) 87704297, Fax: 87704777, E-mail: ibshoneywood@netscapeonline.co.uk, Internet: www.sutton.gov.uk/lfl/heritage
Local Museum
Hist of London borough Sutton 39667

Horniman Museum, 100 London Rd, Forest Hill, London SE23 3PQ - T: (020) 86991872, Fax: 82915506, E-mail: enquiry@horniman.ac.uk, Internet: www.horniman.ac.uk. Dir.: Janet Vitmayer
Local Museum / Ethnology Museum / Music Museum - 1890
Anthropology, natural history, musical instruments - library, gardens, Living Waters aquarium, conservation 39668

House Mill, Three Mill Ln, Bromley-by-Bow, London E3 3DU - T: (020) 89804626, Fax: 82150051, E-mail: lowerlea@netscape.online.co.uk, Internet: www.riverlee.org.uk
Science&Tech Museum
Original machinery incl millstones and waterwheels 39669

Hunterian Museum (closed until end of 2004), 35-43 Lincoln's Inn Fields, London WC2A 3PN - T: (020) 78696560, Fax: 78696564, E-mail: museum@rcseng.ac.uk, Internet: www.rcseng.ac.uk/museums
Special Museum - 1813
Anatomy, physiology and pathology from the coll of John Hunter (1728-1793) historical surgical instruments 39670

Imperial War Museum, Lambeth Rd, London SE1 6HZ - T: (020) 74165000, Fax: 74165374, E-mail: mail@iwm.org.uk, Internet: www.iwm.org.uk. Gen. Dir.: R.W.K. Crawford, Dir.: J. Carmichael (Collections), Keeper: A. Weight (Art), R.W.A. Suddaby (Documents), Cur.: Philip Reed (Cabinet War Rooms)
Historical Museum - 1917
Wars since 1914, armaments, documents, books involving Britain and the Commonwealth, films, records, photographs, drawings, paintings, sculpture - library, reference dept, archives 39671

Inns of Court and City Yeomanry Museum, 10 Stone Bldgs, Lincoln's Inn, London WC2A 3TG - T: (020) 74058112, Fax: 74143496. Dir.: M.J. O'Beirne
Military Museum
Hist of 2 regiments, the Inns of Court Regiment and City of London Yeomanry from 1780 to date 39672

Institute of Contemporary Arts, The Mall, London SW1Y 5AH - T: (020) 79303647, Fax: 78730051, E-mail: info@ica.org.uk, Internet: www.ica.org.uk. Dir.: Philip Dodd
Public Gallery 39673

Islington Education Artefacts Library, Barnsbury Complex, Barnsbury Park, London N1 1QG - T: (020) 75275524, Fax: 75275564, E-mail: artefacts@iels.demon.co.uk, Internet: www.objectlessions.org
Historical Museum
History, science, natural history, religion and multiculture, costume coll 39674

Islington Museum, Foyer Gallery, Islington Town Hall, Upper St, London N1 2UD - T: (020) 73549442, Fax: 75273049, E-mail: valerie.munday@islington.gov.uk, Internet: www.islington.gov.uk/localinfo/leisure/museum. Dir.: Alison Lister
Local Museum
Local and social history of Islington borough, popular culture 39675

Jewel Tower, Abingdon Rd, Westminster, London SW1P 3JY - T: (020) 72222219, Fax: 72222219, Internet: www.english-heritage.org.uk
Local Museum 39676

Jewish Museum, Raymond Burton House, 129-131 Albert St, London NW1 7NB - T: (020) 72841997, Fax: 72679008, E-mail: admin@jmus.org.uk, Internet: www.jewishmuseum.org.uk. Dir.: Rickie Burman
Religious Arts Museum / Historical Museum - 1932
Jewish ceremonial art and hist 39677

Jewish Museum Finchley, 80 East End Rd, London N3 2SY - T: (020) 83491143, Fax: 83432162, E-mail: jml.finchley@lineone.net, Internet: www.jewmusm.ort.net. Dir.: Rickie Burman
Religious Arts Museum / Historical Museum
History of Jewish immigration and settlement in London 39678

Keats House, Keats Grove, Wentworth Pl, London NW3 2RR - T: (020) 74352062, Fax: 74319293, E-mail: keatshouse@corpoflondon.org.uk, Internet: www.keatshouse.org.uk. Dir.: Christina M. Gee
Special Museum - 1925
Life and work of the poet John Keats (1795-1821), manuscripts, relics, furniture - library 39679

Kenwood, The Iveagh Bequest, Hampstead Ln, London NW3 7JR - T: (020) 83481286, Fax: 87933891, Internet: www.english-heritage.org.uk. VSM: Susan Coventry, Cur.: Laura Houliston
Fine Arts Museum - 1927
Paintings by Rembrandt, Vermeer, Gainsborough, Reynolds and others, 18th c furniture and sculpture 39680

Kingsgate Gallery, 114 Kingsgate Rd, London NW6 2JG - T: (020) 73287878, Fax: 73287878, E-mail: mail@kingsgateworkshops.org.uk, Internet: www.kingsgateworkshops.org.uk. Dir.: Stephen Williams
Public Gallery
Contemporary art 39681

Kirkaldy Testing Museum, 99 Southwark St, Southwark, London SE1 0JF - T: (020) 76201580
Science&Tech Museum
David Kirkaldy's original all-purpose testing machine 39682

Kufa Gallery, 26 Westbourne Grove, London W2 5RH - T: (020) 72291928, Fax: 72438513, E-mail: kufa@dircon.co.uk, Internet: www.kufa.dircon.co.uk. Man.: Walid Atiyeh
Public Gallery
Islamic and Middle Eastern Art and architecture 39683

Lauderdale House, Waterlow Park, Highgate Hill, London N6 5HG - T: (020) 83488716, Fax: 84429099, E-mail: admin@lauderdale.org.uk, Internet: www.lauderdale.org.uk. Dir.: Carolyn Naish
Local Museum
Fine art, photography, local hist 39684

Leighton House Museum, 12 Holland Park Rd, Kensington, London W14 8LZ - T: (020) 76023316, Fax: 73712467, E-mail: leightonhousemuseum@rbkc.gov.uk, Internet: www.rbkc.gov.uk/leightonhousemuseum. Cur.: Daniel Robbins
Special Museum - 1898
Leighton drawings coll, Leighton letters and archive 39685

Lewisham Local Studies Centre, c/o Lewisham Library, 199-201 Lewisham High St, London SE13 6LG - T: (020) 82970682, Fax: 82971169, E-mail: local.studies@lewisham.gov.uk, Internet: www.lewisham.gov.uk/localStudies
Library with Exhibitions
Coll of archives, printed materials (incl newspapers), maps, pictorial materials and objects 39686

Library and Collection of the Worshipful Company of Clockmakers, Clock Room, Guildhall Library, Aldermanbury, London EC2P 2EJ - T: (020) 73321865, E-mail: keeper@clockmakers.org, Internet: www.clockmakers.org. Keeper: Sir George White
Special Museum - 1813
Old clocks, marine chronometers, watch keys 39687

Library Drawings Collection, c/o Royal Institute of British Architects, 21 Portman Sq, London W1H 6LP - T: (020) 73073698, Fax: 74863797, E-mail: dwgs@inst.riba.org, Internet: www.architecture.com. Cur.: Charles Hind
Fine Arts Museum
500,000 architectural drawings c1480 to the present together with engravings, models, portraits etc 39688

Linley Sambourne House, 18 Stafford Terrace, Kensington, London W8 7BH - T: (020) 76023316, Fax: 73712467, Internet: www.rbkc.gov.uk/linleysambournehouse
Decorative Arts Museum
Edward Linley Sambourne, political cartoonist at punch magazine, funishings 39689

Little Holland House, 40 Beeches Av, Carshalton, London SM5 3LW - T: (020) 87704781, Fax: 87704777, E-mail: valary.murphy@sutton.gov.uk, Internet: www.sutton.gov.uk. Dir.: Valary Murphy
Decorative Arts Museum - 1974
Furniture, paintings and craft by Frank R. Dickinson 39690

Livesey Museum for Children, 682 Old Kent Rd, London SE15 1JF - T: (020) 76395604, Fax: 72775384, E-mail: livesey.museum@southwark.gov.uk, Internet: www.liveseymuseum.org.uk. Dir.: Theresa Dhaliwal
Special Museum - 1974
Interactive childrens museum 39691

Lloyd's Nelson Collection, c/o Lloyd's, Lime St, London EC3M 7HA - T: (020) 76237100, Fax: 73276400
Special Museum
Silver, documents, letters, objects of art associated with Admiral Lord Nelson and his contemporaries 39692

London Brass Rubbing Centre, The Crypt, Saint Martin-in-the-Fields Church, Trafalgar Sq, London WC2N 4JJ - T: (020) 79309306, Fax: 79309306, Internet: www.visitlondon.co.uk. Dir.: A. Dodwell, P. Dodwell
Decorative Arts Museum
Coll of facsimile monumental church brasses from the medieval and Tudor periods portraying kings, knights, merchants and families, designs from Celtic sources 39693

London Canal Museum, 12-13 New Wharf Rd, King's Cross, London N1 9RT - T: (020) 77130836, Fax: 76896679, E-mail: enq@canalmuseum.org.uk, Internet: www.canalmuseum.org.uk. Chm.: Margaret Gralter
Historical Museum
Inland waterways of the London region 39694

London Fire Brigade Museum, 94a Southwark Bridge Rd, Southwark, London SE1 0EG - T: (020) 75872894, Fax: 75872878, E-mail: museum@lfcda.org.uk. Cur.: Esther Mann
Historical Museum
Fire appliances, equipment, clothing, medals and miscellanea (17th-20th c), fire-related art 39695

London Institute Gallery, 65 Davies St, London W1K 5DA - T: (020) 75148083, Fax: 75146131, E-mail: gallery@linst.ac.uk, Internet: www.linst.ac.uk/events/eventdef.htm. Man.: Lynne Trembath
Public Gallery
Art and design 39696

London Irish Rifles Regimental Museum, Duke of York Headquarters, Kings Rd, Chelsea, London SW3 4RX
Military Museum 39697

London Scottish Regimental Museum, 95 Horseferry Rd, London SW1P 2DX - T: (020) 76301639, Fax: 72337909
Military Museum
History of the regiment 39698

London Sewing Machine Museum, 292-312 Balham High Rd, Tooting Bec, London SW17 7AA - T: (020) 86827916, Fax: 87674726, E-mail: wimbledonsewingmachinecoltd@btinternet.com, Internet: www.sewantique.com. Cur.: Ray Rushton
Science&Tech Museum
Industrial and domestic sewing machines from 1850-1950 39699

London Toy and Model Museum, 21-23 Craven Hill, London W2 3EN - T: (020) 77068000, Fax: 77068823, E-mail: gba67@dial.pipex.com, Internet: www.londontoy.com. Manager: Glen Sharman
Special Museum - 1982
Including dolls, bears, tinplate toys, model, tains, antique coalmine model, garden railway 39700

London's Transport Museum, Covent Garden Piazza, London WC2E 7BB - T: (020) 73796344, Fax: 75657254, E-mail: contact@ltmuseum.co.uk, Internet: www.ltmuseum.co.uk. Dir.: Sam Mullins
Science&Tech Museum - 1980
London transport history, coll of historic vehicles and artefacts - photographic library, reference library 39701

Madame Tussaud's, Marylebone Rd, London NW1 5LR - T: (0870) 4003000, Fax: (020) 74650862, E-mail: firstname.lastname@madame-tussauds.com, Internet: www.madame-tussauds.com. Man.: Peter Philipson, Diane Moon (Press and Publicity)
Special Museum - 1770
Wax figures, planetarium - Planetarium 39702

Mall Galleries, The Mall, 17 Carlton House Terrace, London SW1Y 5BD - T: (020) 79306844, Fax: 78397830, E-mail: info@mallgalleries.com, Internet: www.mallgalleries.org.uk. Dir.: Bob Boas
Public Gallery - 1971 39703

Mander and Mitchenson Theatre Collection, c/o Jerwood Library, Trinity College of Music, Old Royal Naval College, King Charles Court, London SE10 9JF - T: (020) 83054426, Fax: 83053993, E-mail: rmangan@tcm.ac.uk, Internet: www.tcm.ac.uk. Dir.: Richard Mangan
Performing Arts Museum
Theatre, music hall, pantomime, circus, opera, ballet, incl. posters, playbills, programmes, engravings, photo- graphs, paintings, manuscripts, china and unique ephemera 39704

Markfield Beam Engine and Museum, Markfield Rd, South Tottenham, London N15 4RB - T: (020) 88020680, Fax: 88020680. Dir.: A.J. Spackman
Science&Tech Museum
Beam pumping engine, public health engineering 39705

MCC Museum, Lord's Cricket Ground, Saint John's Wood, London NW8 8QN - T: (020) 72891611, Fax: 74321062, E-mail: glenys.williams@mcc.org.uk, Internet: www.uk.cricket.org.uk/link_to_database/national/eng/clubs/mcc/mccmuseum.html. Dir.: Adam Chadwick
Historical Museum - 1953
History of cricket, pictures, relics, trophies, art objects - library 39706

Metropolitan Police Historical Museum, 4th Fl. Victoria Embankment, London SW1A 2JL - T: (020) 83052824, Fax: 82936692. Cur.: Ray Seal
Historical Museum
Beat duty equipment, uniforms, books, documents, photos, medals, paintings, police station furnishings 39707

Michael Faraday's Laboratory and Museum, The Royal Institution of Great Britain, 21 Albemarle St, London W1S 4BS - T: (020) 74092992, Fax: 76293569, E-mail: ri@ri.ac.uk, Internet: www.rigb.org. Dir.: Prof. Susan Greenfield
Science&Tech Museum - 1972
Unique coll of Faraday's original apparatus, diaries 39708

Millwall FC Museum, Millwall Football Club, Zampa Rd, London SE16 3LN - T: (020) 86980793, Fax: 86980793. Cur.: Chris Bethell
Special Museum
Football and social history from 1885 to date 39709

MoCHA, 61 Malmesbury Terrace, London E3 2EB - T: (020) 89830820, Fax: 89830820, E-mail: develoopment@mocha.co.uk, Internet: www.mocha.co.uk
Special Museum
Embryonic coll of culinary history and recipe books, ephemera and journals, Susan Campbell coll 39710

Morley Gallery, Art Centre, Morley College, 61 Westminster Bridge Rd, London SE1 7HT - T: (020) 74509226, Fax: 79284074, E-mail: janet.browne@morleycollege.ac.uk. Sc. Staff: Jane Hartwell (Exhibitions Organisation)
Public Gallery / University Museum 39711

Museum of Childhood at Bethnal Green, Cambridge Heath Rd, London E2 9PA - T: (020) 89802415, Fax: 89835225, E-mail: k.bines@vam.ac.uk, Internet: www.museumofchildhood.org.uk. Dir.: Diane Lees
Special Museum - 1872
Toys, dolls, games, puppets, children's books, doll's houses, teddy bears, toy soldiers, trains, nursery coll incl children's costume and furniture, baby equipment 39712

Museum of Freemasonry, Freemasons Hall, Great Queen St, London WC2B 5AZ - T: (020) 73959257, Fax: 74047418, E-mail: libmus@ugle.org.uk, Internet: www.freemasonry.london.museum. Dir.: D.E. Clements
Special Museum - 1837
Coll of class, porcelain, silver, furniture, paintings - Library 39713

Museum of Fulham Palace, Bishop's Av, London SW6 6EA - T: (020) 77363233, Fax: 77363233
Historical Museum
Archaeology, paintings, stained glass, history of the Palace 39714

Museum of Garden History, Saint Mary at Lambeth, Lambeth Palace Rd, London SE1 7LB - T: (020) 74018865, Fax: 74018869, E-mail: info@museumgardenhistory.org, Internet: www.museumgardenhistory.org. Dir.: Rosemary Nicholson
Historical Museum - 1977
Historic garden tools 39715

Museum of Installation, 171 Deptford High St, London SE8 3NU - T: (020) 84694140, E-mail: moi@dircon.co.uk, Internet: www.moi.org.uk. Dir.: Nicolas de Oliveira, Nicola Oxley, Michael Petry, Jeremy Wood
Fine Arts Museum
Installations - archive 39716

Museum of Instruments, Royal College of Music, Prince Consort Rd, South Kensington, London SW7 2BS - T: (020) 75914346, Fax: 75897740, E-mail: museum@rcm.ac.uk, Internet: www.rcm.ac.uk. Cur.: Elizabeth Wells
Music Museum - 1883
Old stringed, wind and keyboard instruments 39717

Museum of London, London Wall, London EC2Y 5HN - T: (020) 76003699, Fax: 76001058, E-mail: info@museumoflondon.org.uk, Internet: www.museumoflondon.org.uk. Dir.: Dr. Simon Thurley, Asst. Dir.: Michael Launchbury (Early London Dept.), Sc. Staff: Hedley Swain (Early London Dept.), Dr. Cathy Ross (Later London Dept.), Kate Starling (Cur. Division), Taryn Nixon (Museum of London Archaeology Service (MOLAS))
Historical Museum - 1912
Prehistoric, Roman and medieval antiquities, costumes, decorative art objects, topography, history and social life of London, royal relics, Parliament and legal history, Cromwellian period relics, objects relating to the Great Fire of London, toys, fire engines, glass, suffragettes 39718

Museum of Mankind (closed) 39719

Museum of Methodism, 49 City Rd, London EC1Y 1AU - T: (0207) 2532262, Fax: 6083825, E-mail: museum@wesleyschapel.org.uk, Internet: www.wesleyschapel.org.uk. Cur.: Heather Carson
Religious Arts Museum - 1984
Wesleyana, paintings, manuscript letters, social history 39720

Museum of the Moving Images, South Bank, Waterloo, London SE1 8XT - T: (020) 74012636, 79283535, Fax: 79287938, E-mail: Caroline.Ellis@bfi.org.uk, Internet: www.bfi.org.uk/museum. Dir.: Caroline Ellis
Historical Museum - 1988
Early optical toys, costumes from modern science fiction films, Charlie Chaplin's hat and cane, Fred Astaire's tail coat, the IBA coll of period television sets, the world's first fourscreen unit 39721

Museum of the Order of Saint John, Saint John's Gate, Saint John's Ln, Clerkenwell, London EC1M 4DA - T: (020) 72536644, Fax: 73360587, E-mail: museum@nhq.sja.org.uk, Internet: www.sja.org.uk/history. Dir.: Pamela Willis
Religious Arts Museum / Historical Museum - 1915
Silver, coins, armaments, medals, furniture, documents on the order of Saint John, manuscripts, uniforms, glass, ceramics, paintings, prints, cartography, textiles, Saint John Ambulance, hist of religious military order - library 39722

Museum of the Royal College of Physicians, 11 Saint Andrews Pl, Regent's Park, London NW1 4LE - T: (020) 79351174 ext 510, Fax: 74863729, E-mail: info@rcplondon.ac.uk, Internet: www.rcplondon.ac.uk. Dir.: Prof. C.M. Black
Fine Arts Museum
History of the college and the physician's profession, portraits of fellows a.o., Symon's coll of medical instr, William Harvey's demonstration rod, anatomical tables 39723

Museum of the Royal College of Surgeons → Hunterian Museum

Museum of the Royal Pharmaceutical Society of Great Britain, 1 Lambeth High St, London SE1 7JN - T: (0207) 7359141 ext 354, Fax: 7930232, E-mail: museum@rpsgb.org.uk, Internet: www.rpsgb.org.uk. Dir.: Caroline M. Reed
Special Museum - 1841
History of pharmacy, 17th-18th c drugs, English Delft drug jars, mortars, retail and dispensing equipment 39724

Museums and Study Collection, Central Saint Martins College of Art and Design, Southampton Row, London WC1B 4AP - T: (020) 75147146, Fax: 75147024, E-mail: s.backemeyer@csm.linst.ac.uk, Internet: www.csm.linst.ac.uk
Fine Arts Museum / Decorative Arts Museum 39725

Musical Museum, 368 High St, Brentford, London TW8 0BD - T: (020) 85608108, Internet: www.musicalmuseum.co.uk. Dir.: Michael J. Ryder, Cur.: Richard Cole
Music Museum - 1963
Automatic musical instruments in working order, pianos, music rolls, Welte Philharmonic Reprocuding Pipe Organ Model, Wurlitzer Theater Organ, Double Mills Violano Virtuoso, Hupfeld Phonoliszt Violina, Hupfeld Animatic Clavitist Sinfonie-Jazz and orchestra, Edison Phonograph, Hupfeld Piano, Street Barrel Pianos and Organs, Broadwood Grand Piano 39726

Narwhal Inuit Art Gallery, 55 Linden Gardens, Chiswick, London W4 2EH - T: (020) 87421268, Fax: 87421268, E-mail: narwhalman@blueyonder.co.uk, Internet: www.niaef.com. Dir.: Ken Mantel
Ethnology Museum
Canadian, Russian and Greenlandic Inuit art 39727

National Army Museum, Royal Hospital Rd, London SW3 4HT - T: (020) 77300717, Fax: 78236573, E-mail: info@national-army-museum.ac.uk, Internet: www.national-army-museum.ac.uk. Dir.: I. Robertson, Asst. Dir.: Dr. P. Boyden, D. Smurthwaite, Dr. A. Guy
Military Museum - 1960
Hist of the British Army 1415-2000, Indian Army until 1947, colonial forces, uniforms, weapons, medals, British military painting, early photographs - library 39728

National Gallery, Trafalgar Sq, London WC2N 5DN - T: (020) 77472885, Fax: 77472423, E-mail: information@ng-london.org.uk, Internet: www.nationalgallery.org.uk. Dir.: Neil MacGregor, Cur.: Dr. Nicholas Penny, Dr. Dillian Gordon, Dr. Susan Foister, Christopher Riopelle, Dr. Gabriele Finaldi, Dr. Humphrey Wine, Axel Rüger, Lorne Campbell, Sarah Herring, Carol Plazotta, Xavier Bray, Sc. Staff: Dr. Ashok Roy, Raymond Wise, Jo Kirby, Marika Spring, Dr. David Saunders, John Cupitt, Jo Atkinson, Ruven Pillay, Chief Rest.: Martin Wyldster, Exhibition and Display: Michael Wilson, Libraries and Archive: Elspeth Hattrick, Cons.: Anthony Reeve, David Bomford, Jill Dunkerton, Larry Keith, Paul Ackroyd, David Thomas, Rachel Billinge, David Godkin
Fine Arts Museum - 1824
Western European paintings from 1250-1900 incl works by Leonardo, Rembrandt, and others, British painters from Hogarth to Turner, 19th c French painting such as Cézanne, Van Gogh 39729

National Hearing Aid Museum, Royal Throat, Nose and Ear Hospital, Grays Inn Rd, London WC1X 1DA - T: (020) 79151390, Fax: 79151646, E-mail: p.turner@ucl.ac.uk. Cur.: Peggy Chalmers
Science&Tech Museum
Hearing aids and test equipment, the first cochlea implant device to be fitted in the United Kingdom 39730

National Maritime Museum, Park Row, Greenwich, London SE10 9NF - T: (020) 88584422, Fax: 83126632, Internet: www.nmm.ac.uk. Dir.: Roy Clare
Historical Museum - 1934
Maritime hist of Britain, Navy, Merchant Service, yachting, ship models and plans 1700-1990, oil paintings, Nelson memorabilia, astronomical instruments (17th-20th c), globes since 1530, rare books from 1474, manuscripts, charts, atlases - library 39731

National Portrait Gallery, 2 Saint Martin's Pl, London WC2H 0HE - T: (020) 73060055, Fax: 73060056, Internet: www.npg.org.uk. Dir.: Sandy Naivne
Fine Arts Museum - 1856
National coll of portraits (15th-21st c), incl paintings, sculptures, miniatures, engravings and photographs - archive, library; Montacute House, Beningbrough Hall, Bodelwyddan Castle 39732

Natural History Museum, Cromwell Rd, London SW7 5BD - T: (020) 79425000, Fax: 79389290, E-mail: information@nhm.ac.uk, Internet: www.nhm.ac.uk. Dir.: Sir Neil Chalmers, Sc. Staff: Prof. P. Rainbow (Zoology), R. Vane-Wright (Entomology), Dr. R. Cocks (Palaeontology), Dr. A. Fleet (Mineralogy), Dr. Richard Bateman (Botany), Head: Sharon Ament (Development/ Communication), Dierdre Candlin (Visitor/Operational Services)
Natural History Museum - 1881
Botany, entomology, mineralogy, palaeontology, zoology, ornithology 39733

Newham Heritage Centre, Old Dispensary, 30 Romford Rd, London E15 4BZ - T: (020) 84306393, Fax: 84306392, E-mail: tom.mcallister@newham.gov.uk, Internet: www.newham.gov.uk/leisure/museums/mmp.htm. Man.: Sean Sherman
Local Museum - 2002
Archaeology, local history, Bow porcelain, work of Madge Gill (local outsider artist) - museum education 39734

North Woolwich Old Station Museum, Pier Rd, North Woolwich, London E16 2JJ - T: (020) 74747244, Fax: 74736065, E-mail: kathy.taylor@newham.gov.uk, Internet: www.newham.gov.uk/leisure/museums/. Man.: Kathy Taylor
Science&Tech Museum 39735

Odontological Museum, c/o Royal College of Surgeons of England, 35-43 Lincoln's Inn Fields, London WC2A 3PE - T: (020) 778696562, Fax: 78696564, E-mail: museums@rcseng.ac.uk
Special Museum
Coll of 6,000 animal skulls, of which 2,000 are pathological, 3,500 human casts, skulls and jaws, 200 dentures, 300 dental instruments 39736

Old Operating Theatre, Museum and Herb Garret, London's Museums of Health and Medicine, 9a Saint Thomas St, London SE1 9RY - T: (020) 79554791, Fax: 73788383, E-mail: curator@thegarret.org.uk, Internet: www.thegarret.org.uk. Dir.: Kevin Flude, Cur.: Karen Howell
Special Museum - 1957
Medicine, surgery, hospitals, Florence Nightingale, herbal medicine 39737

Old Speech Room Gallery, Harrow School, High St, Harrow, London HA1 3HP - T: (020) 88128205, 88728000, Fax: 84233112, E-mail: bmiller@harrowschool.org.uk, Internet: www.harrowschool.wwood.co.uk. Cur.: Carolyn R. Leder
Fine Arts Museum / Museum of Classical Antiquities
School's coll (Egyptian and Greek antiquities, watercolours, printed books) 39738

Painters's Hall, Little Trinity Ln, London EC4V 2AD - T: (020) 72366258, Fax: 72360500, E-mail: beadle@painters-hall.co.uk, Internet: www.painters-hall.co.uk. Keeper: E. Drocklehurst
Decorative Arts Museum / Fine Arts Museum
Miscellaneous portraits, coll of silver 39739

Palace of Westminster, Houses of Parliament, London SW1A 0AA - T: (020) 72196218, 72195503, Fax: 72194250, E-mail: curator@parliament.uk. Cur.: Malcolm Hay
Decorative Arts Museum
Coll of Victorian wall paintings depicting scenes from British history, coll of political portraits, and works of art, coll of Gothic Revival furniture 39740

Pathological Museum, Saint Bartholomew's, Royal London School of medicine Smithfield, London EC1A 7BE - T: (020) 76018537, Fax: 76018530, E-mail: d.g.lowe@mds.qmw.ac.uk, Internet: www.mds.qmw.ac.uk/. Cur.: Dr. D. Lowe
Special Museum 39741

Percival David Foundation of Chinese Art, School of Oriental and African Studies, University of London, 53 Gordon Sq, London WC1H 0PD - T: (020) 73873909, Fax: 73835163, E-mail: sp17@soas.ac.uk, Internet: www.pdfmuseum.org.uk. Cur.: Stacey Pierson
Decorative Arts Museum - 1950
Finest coll of Chinese ceramics outside China, dating mainly to the period 10th-18th c - subscription reference library 39742

Petrie Museum of Egyptian Archaeology, University College London, Malet Pl, London WC1E 6BT - T: (020) 76792884, Fax: 76792886, E-mail: petrie.museum@ucl.ac.uk, Internet: www.petrie.ucl.ac.uk. Dir.: S. MacDonald, Ass. Cur.: S. Quirke (Papyri, Ostraca, Hieroglyphic Texts)
Archaeological Museum / University Museum - 1913
Archaeology, hieroglyphic texts, Sir William M. Flinders Petrie (1853-1942) 39743

Photographers' Gallery, 5-8 Great Newport St, London WC2H 7HY - T: (020) 78311772, Fax: 78369704, E-mail: info@photonet.org.uk, Internet: www.photonet.org.uk. Dir.: Paul Wombell
Public Gallery 39744

Pitzhanger Manor-House and Gallery, Walpole Park, Mattlock Ln, Ealing, London W5 5EQ - T: (020) 85671227, Fax: 85670595, E-mail: pmgallery&house@ealing.gov.uk, Internet: www.ealing.gov.uk/pmgallery&house. Dir.: Sir John Soane
Decorative Arts Museum / Local Museum
Contemporary art exhibitions, Martinware pottery 39745

Polish Cultural Institution Gallery, 34 Portland Pl, London W1N 4HQ - T: (020) 76366032, Fax: 76372190. Dir.: Aleksandra Czapiewska
Public Gallery
Polish paintings, graphics, photography, posters, tapestry, folk art 39746

Pollock's Toy Museum, 1 Scala St, London W1T HTL - T: (020) 76363452, E-mail: info@pollocksmuseum.co.uk, Internet: www.pollocksmuseum.co.uk. Cur.: Veronica Sheppard
Special Museum / Historical Museum - 1956
Old toys and games, toytheatres 39747

POSK Gallery, 238-246 King St, London W6 0RF - T: (020) 87411940, Fax: 87463798, E-mail: admin@posk.org, Internet: www.posk.org. Dir.: Janina Baranowska
Association with Coll - 1980
Posk coll of 80 paintings by Polish Artists working in Great Britain, Motz coll: engravings, maps, tin plate, armour, Polish paintings (19th-20th c) 39748

Pump House Gallery, Battersea Park, London SW11 4NJ - T: (020) 88717572, Fax: 82289062
Public Gallery
Contemporary art 39749

Pumphouse Educational Museum, Lavender Pond and Nature Park, Lavender Rd, Rotherhithe, London SE16 5DZ - T: (020) 72312976, Fax: 72312976. Dir.: Caroline Marais
Local Museum
Dockers tools, life in Rotherhithe, replica 6ft Queen Elizabeth II wedding cake 39750

Queen Elizabeth's Hunting Lodge, Rangers Rd, Chingford, London E4 7QH - T: (020) 85296681, Fax: 85298209. Cur.: Jeffrey Seddon
Historical Museum - 1895
Local history, archaeology, forestry, zoology, botany 39751

The Queen's Gallery, Royal Collection, Buckingham Palace, London SW1A 1AA, mail addr: Stable Yard House, Saint James's Palace, London SW1A 1JR - T: (020) 73212233, Fax: 79309625, E-mail: buckinghampalace@royalcollection.org.uk, Internet: www.royal.gov.uk. Dir.: Sir Hugh Roberts
Fine Arts Museum - 1962
Paintings, drawings, artworks from Royal coll, furniture, clocks, porcelain, silver, scientific instruments, books, miniatures, gems 39752

Ragged School Museum, 46-50 Copperfield Rd, London E3 4RR - T: (020) 89806405, Fax: 89833481, E-mail: enquiries@raggedschoolmuseum.org.uk, Internet: www.raggedschoolmuseum.org.uk. Dir.: Dr. Claire Seymour
Special Museum - 1990
Victorian school room, social history 39753

Royal Academy of Arts Gallery, Burlington House, Piccadilly, London W1J 0BD - T: (020) 73008000, Fax: 73008001, Internet: www.royalacademy.org.uk. Pres.: Prof. Phillip King, Sc. Staff: Prof. Leonard MacComb
Public Gallery - 1768
Temporary exhibitions of painting, sculpture, architecture and engraving 39754

Royal Air Force Museum, Grahame Park Way, London NW9 5LL - T: (020) 82052266, Fax: 83584981, E-mail: info@rafmuseum.com, Internet: www.rafmuseum.com. Dir. Gen.: Dr. Michael A. Fopp
Military Museum - 1972
Sister Museum at Cosford, reserve coll at Cosford, one of the best WWII fighter coll in the world, 70 aircraft on permanent display 39755

Royal Armouries, Tower of London, London EC3N 4AB - T: (020) 74806358, Fax: 74812922, E-mail: enquiries@armouries.org.uk, Internet: www.armouries.org.uk. Dir.: Paul Evans (Master of the Armouries), Keeper: Dr. G. Parnell (Tower History), Libr.: B. Clifford
Historical Museum / Military Museum / Decorative Arts Museum
Eight galleries tell the story of the evolution of the Tower and the Armouries itself over the centuries, incl weapons of the historic Tower arsenal, Royal Tudor and Stuart armours, coll 16th-19th c - Education centre, archives 39756

Royal Bank of Scotland Art Collection, Drapers Garden, 12 Throgmorton St, London EC2N 2DL - T: (020) 79205493, Fax: 74546613. Cur.: Rosemary Harris, Asst. Cur.: James Pidcock
Fine Arts Museum / Public Gallery
Works from the 17th c to the present day with focus on the 20th c post-war British art 39757

Royal British Society of Sculptors, 108 Old Brompton Rd, London SW7 3RA - T: (020) 73738615, Fax: 73703721, E-mail: info@rbs.org.uk, Internet: www.rbs.org.uk. Pres.: Derek Morris
Public Gallery 39758

Royal Ceremonial Dress Collection, Kensington Palace, London W8 4PX - T: (020) 79379561, Fax: 73760198, Internet: www.hrp.org.uk. Dir.: Nigel Arch
Special Museum
Royal and ceremonial dress 39759

Royal College of Art, Kensington Gore, London SW7 2EU - T: (020) 75904444, Fax: 75904124, E-mail: info@rca.ac.uk, Internet: www.rca.ac.uk. Dir.: Prof. Christopher Frayling
Public Gallery 39760

Royal College of Obstetricians and Gynaecologists Collection, 27 Sussex Pl, Regent's Park, London NW1 4RG - T: (020) 77726309, Fax: 72628331, E-mail: library@rcog.org.uk, Internet: www.rcog.org.uk. Cur.: Ian L.C. Fergusson

Historical Museum / Science&Tech Museum / Association with Coll / Special Museum
Obstetrical and gynaecological instruments, incl. original Chamberlen instruments 39761

Royal Fusiliers Regimental Museum, Tower of London, London EC3N 4AB - T: (020) 74885612, Fax: 74811093. Dir.: C.P. Bowes-Crick
Military Museum - 1949
History of regiment 1685-1968, silver, documents, armaments, uniforms 39762

Royal Hospital Chelsea Museum, Royal Hospital Rd, Chelsea, London SW3 4SR - T: (020) 78815203, Fax: 78815463, E-mail: info@chelsea.pensioners.org.uk
Historical Museum
Royal hospital artefacts, medals and uniforms, veteran soldiers 39763

Royal London Hospital Archives and Museum, Newark St, Whitechapel, London E1 2AA - T: (020) 73777608, Fax: 73777413, E-mail: jonathan.evans@bartsandthelondon.nhs.uk, Internet: www.brlcf.org.uk. Head: Jonathan Evans
Historical Museum - 1989
Medical science history 39764

The Royal Mews, Royal Collection, Buckingham Palace, London SW1A 1AA, mail addr: Stable Yard House, Saint James's Palace, London SW1A 1JR - T: (020) 73212233, Fax: 79309625, E-mail: buckinghampalace@royalcollection.org.uk, Internet: www.royal.gov.uk. Dir.: Hugh Roberts
Historical Museum - 1825
The Monarch's magnificent gilded State carriages and coaches, incl the unique Gold State Coach are housed here together with their horses and State liveries 39765

Royal Mint Sovereign Gallery, 7 Grosvenor Gardens, London SW1W 0BH - T: (020) 75928601, E-mail: charmaine.boga@salves.royalmint.gov.uk, Internet: www.royalmint.com
Special Museum 39766

Royal Observatory Greenwich, National Maritime Museum, Greenwich, London SE10 9NF - T: (020) 88584422, Fax: 83126632, Internet: www.nmm.ac.uk. Dir.: Roy Clare
Science&Tech Museum 39767

RSA Library (closed) 39768

Saatchi Gallery, County Hall, Belvedere Rd, Southbank, London SE1 7PB - T: (020) 78232363, 72894440, Fax: 72860313, Internet: www.saatchi-gallery.co.uk. Cur., William Miller
Public Gallery 39769

Saint Bartholomew's Hospital Museum, West Smithfield, London EC1A 7BE - T: (020) 76018152, E-mail: barts.archives@bartsandthelondon.nhs.uk, Internet: www.brlcf.org.uk
Historical Museum
Archives 39770

Saint Bride's Crypt Museum, Saint Bride's Church, Fleet St, London EC4Y 8AU - T: (020) 74270133, Fax: 75834867, E-mail: info@stbrides.com. Dir.: James Irving
Religious Arts Museum - 1957
History of Fleet Street, Roman ruins, former church ruins 39771

Salvation Army International Heritage Centre (temporary closed), House 14, William Booth College, Denmark Hill, London SE5 8BQ - T: (020) 77373327, Fax: 77374127, E-mail: heritage@salvationarmy.org, Internet: www.salvationarmy.org/history.htm. Dir.: Christine Clement
Historical Museum
library, archives 39772

Science Museum, The National Museum of Science & Industry, Exhibition Rd, South Kensington, London SW7 2DD - T: (020) 79424777, 79424445, Fax: 79424302, E-mail: sciencemuseum@nmsi.ac.uk, Internet: www.sciencemuseum.org.uk. Dir.: Dr. Lindsay Sharpe
Science&Tech Museum / Historical Museum - 1857
Hist of science and industry, agriculture, astronomy, air, sea and land transport, civil, electrical, marine and mechanical engineering, jet engines, geophysics, telcommunications, domestic appliances, spacetechnology, chemistry, medicine, interactive galleries 39773

Serpentine Gallery, Kensington Gardens, London W2 3XA - T: (020) 72981515, Fax: 74024103, E-mail: information@serpentinegallery.org, Internet: www.serpentinegallery.org. Dir.: Julia Peyton-Jones
Public Gallery - 1970 39774

Shakespeare's Globe Exhibition and Tour, 21 New Globe Walk, Bankside, London SE1 9DT - T: (020) 79021500, Fax: 79021515, E-mail: exhibit@shakespearesglobe.com, Internet: www.shakespeares-globe.org. Gen. Dir.: Peter Kyle, Dir.: Mark Rylance
Fine Arts Museum
The largest exhibition in the world dedicated to Shakespeare in his workplace, incl a tour of today's working theatre 39775

Sherlock Holmes Museum, 221b Baker St, London NW1 6XE - T: (020) 79358866, Fax: 77381269, E-mail: sherlock@easynet.co.uk, Internet: www.sherlock-holmes.co.uk. Dir.: Grace Riley
Special Museum - 1990
Victorian memorabilia 39776

Sir John Soane's Museum, 13 Lincoln's Inn Fields, London WC2A 3BP - T: (020) 74052107, Fax: 78313957, E-mail: will.palin.soane3@ukgateway.net, Internet: www.soane.org. Dir.: Margaret Richardson
Fine Arts Museum / Decorative Arts Museum - 1833
Sir John Soane's private art and antiquities coll, paintings (Hogarth, Turner), architectural and other drawings - library 39777

The Sladmore Gallery of Sculpture, 32 Bruton Pl, Berkeley Sq, London W1X 7AA - T: (020) 74990365, Fax: 74091381, E-mail: sculpture@sladmore.com, Internet: www.sladmore.com
Fine Arts Museum
19th and 20th c bronze sculptures 39778

Small Mansions Arts Centre, Gunnersbury Park, Popes Ln, London W3 8IQ - T: (020) 89938312
Fine Arts Museum 39779

South London Gallery, 65 Peckham Rd, London SE5 8UH - T: (020) 77036120, Fax: 72524730, E-mail: mail@southlondonart.com, Internet: www.southlondongallery.org. Dir.: Margot Heller
Fine Arts Museum - 1891
Victorian paintings and drawings, small coll of contemporary British art, coll of 20th c original prints, topographical paintings and drawings 39780

Southside House, Wimbledon Common, London SW19 4RJ - T: (020) 89467643, Fax: 89467643, E-mail: info@southsidehouse.com. Dir.: Adam Munthe
Decorative Arts Museum 39781

Spencer House, 27 Saint James's Pl, London SW1A 1NR - T: (020) 74998620, 75141964, Fax: 74092952, Internet: www.spencerhouse.co.uk. Dir.: Jane Rick
Fine Arts Museum / Decorative Arts Museum
Built in 1756-66, London's finest surviving private palace, 18th c furniture and paintings 39782

Stephens Collection, Av House, East End Rd, Finchley, London N3 3QE - T: (020) 83467812. Chairman: Norman Burgess
Historical Museum
History of the Stephens Ink Company 39783

Strang Print Room, University College London, Gower St, London WC1E 6BT - T: (020) 738737050 ext 2540, Fax: 78132803, E-mail: college.art@ucl, Internet: www.collections.ucl.ac.uk
Fine Arts Museum
Coll of fine german drawings,old master prints, plaster models, drawings by Flaxman, early english watercolours and english prints, japanese ukiyo-e prints, history of the slade school 39784

Studio Glass Gallery, 63 Connaught St, London W2 2AE - T: (020) 77063013/69
Public Gallery 39785

Syon House, Syon Park, Brentford, London TW8 8JF - T: (020) 85600882, Fax: 85680936, E-mail: info@@syonpark.co.uk, Internet: www.syonpark.co.uk
Historic Site - 1415
Robert Adam furniture and decoration, famous picture coll, home of the Dukes of Northumberland 39786

Tate Britain, Millbank, London SW1P 4RG - T: (020) 78878000, Fax: 78878007, E-mail: information@tate.org.uk, Internet: www.tate.org.uk. Dir.: Sir Nicholas Serota (Tate), Stephen Deuchar (Tate Britain), Head: Celia Clear (Publications), Sheena Wagstaff (Exhibitions and Displays), Richard Humphreys (Education and Interpretation), Peter Wilson (Building and Gallery Services)
Fine Arts Museum - 1897
National art coll of British Art from 15th c to the present, Turner bequest, Pre-Raphaelites - library and archive of 20th c art 39787

Tate Gallery of British Art → Tate Britain

Tate Modern, Bankside, London SE1 9TG - T: (020) 78878000, Fax: 74015052, E-mail: information@tate.org.uk, Internet: www.tate.org.uk/modern. Dir.: Sir Nicholas Serota, Head: Celia Clear (Publications), Sheena Wagstaff (Exhibitions and Displays), Toby Jackson (Education and Interpretation), Peter Wilson (Building and Gallery Services)
Fine Arts Museum - 2000
International 20th c art incl major works by some of the most influential artists of this century such as Picasso, Matisse, Dalí, Duchamp, Moore, Bacon, Gabo, Giacometti and Warhol 39788

Thames Police Museum, Wapping Police Station, 98 Wapping High St, London E1 9NE - T: (020) 72754421, Fax: 72754490, E-mail: thames.metpol@gtnet.gov.uk
Special Museum
Uniforms and items 39789

Theatre Museum, Victoria and Albert Museum, Russell St, London WC2E 7PR - T: (020) 79434700, Fax: 79434777, E-mail: tmenquiries@vam.ac.uk, Internet: theatermuseum.org. Dir.: Geoff Marsh
Performing Arts Museum - 1974
Stage models, costumes, prints, drawings, puppets, props and memorabilia 39790

Tower Bridge Exhibition, Tower Bridge, London SE1 2UP - T: (020) 74033761, Fax: 73577935, E-mail: enquiries@towerbridge.org.uk, Internet: www.towerbridge.org.uk. Dir.: David White
Science&Tech Museum - 1982
Original Victorian steam machinery, glass walkways above the Thames 39791

TWO 10 Gallery, 183 Euston Rd, London NW1 2BE - T: (020) 76118888, Fax: 76118545, E-mail: k.arnold@wellcome.ac.uk, Internet: www.wellcome.ac.uk. Dir.: Dr. Ken Arnold
Natural History Museum / Fine Arts Museum
Exhibitions on the interaction between medical scienes and art 39792

United Grand Lodge of England Library and Museum → Museum of Freemasonry

Vestry House Museum, Vestry Rd, Walthamstow, London E17 9NH - T: (020) 85091917, E-mail: vestry.house@lbwf.gov.uk, Internet: www.lbwf.gov.uk/intro/vestry_intro.stm
Local Museum - 1931
Bremer car, built between 1892-94 - local studies library and archives 39793

Veterinary Museum, c/o Library, Royal Veterinary College, Royal College St, London NW1 0TU - T: (020) 74685162, Fax: 74685162, Internet: www.rvc.ac.uk
Historical Museum - 1992
Development of veterinary education and science, veterinary instruments, print and manuscript items, pictures, history of veterinary medicine in the UK 39794

Victoria and Albert Museum, Cromwell Rd, South Kensington, London SW7 2RL - T: (020) 79422000, Fax: 79422496, E-mail: vanda@vam.ac.uk, Internet: www.vam.ac.uk. Dir.: Mark Jones, Dep. Dir.: David Anderson (Learning, Visitor Services), Ian Blatchford (Finance), John McCaffrey (Development), Gwyn Miles (Projects), Debby Swallow (Collections), Nick Umney (Collections Services), Damien Whitmore (Public Affairs), Michael Cass (V & A Enterprises), Gillian Henchley (Personnel), Keeper: Susan Lambert (PDP/ NAL), Paul Williamson (Sculpture, Metalwork, Ceramics and Glass)
Decorative Arts Museum - 1852
European and early medieval art, Gothic art and tapestries, Italian Renaissance art, Raphael cartoons, continental art from 1500-1800, British art (1500-1900) and watercolors, Far Eastern and Islamic art, Indian art, applied arts, jewellery, costumes, musical instruments, textiles, embroidery, metalwork, armour, stained glass, pottery and porcelain, Limoges enamels, earthenware, alabasters, casts, furniture, bookart, miniatures - library 39795

Vintage Museum of Photography, Kirkdale Corner, London SE26 4NL - T: (020) 87785416, Fax: 87785841, E-mail: sales@vintagecameras.co.uk, Internet: www.vintagecameras.co.uk/lkd
Special Museum 39796

Vintage Wireless Museum (by appointment only), 23 Rosendale Rd, West Dulwich, London SE21 8DS - T: (020) 86703667. Cur.: Gerald Wells
Science&Tech Museum / Historical Museum
Broadcast receiving history, TV and radio 39797

The Wallace Collection, Hertford House, Manchester Sq, London W1U 3BN - T: (020) 75639500, Fax: 72242155, E-mail: information@wallacecollection.rg, Internet: www.wallacecollection.org. Dir.: Rosalind J. Savill, Cur.: Paul Tear
Fine Arts Museum - 1900
Paintings of all European schools, 17th c Dutch painting, incl works by Titian, Rubens, Van Dyck, Rembrandt, 18th c French art, sculpture, goldsmith art, porcelain, majolica, European and Oriental armaments, French furniture 39798

Wandsworth Museum, Courthouse, 11 Garratt Ln, London SW18 4AQ - T: (020) 88717074, Fax: 88714602, E-mail: wandsworthmuseum@wandsworth.gov.uk. Dir.: Patricia Astley Cooper
Local Museum - 1986 39799

Wellcome Library for the History and Understanding of Medicine, 183 Euston Rd, London NW1 2BE - T: (020) 76118582, Fax: 76118369, E-mail: library@wellcome.ac.uk, Internet: library.wellcome.ac.uk
Library with Exhibitions
Oriental coll, archives and manuscripts coll, iconographic coll, early printed book coll 39800

Wellcome Museum of Anatomy and Pathology, c/o Royal College of Surgeons of England, 35-43 Lincoln's Inn Fields, London WC2A 3PE - T: (020) 778696562, Fax: 78696564, E-mail: museums@rcseng.ac.uk
Special Museum / University Museum
Human anatomy and systemic pathology, histological and histopathological microscope slides 39801

Wellcome Museum of Medical Science → Wellcome Library for the History and Understanding of Medicine

Wellington Arch, Hyde Park Cnr, London W1J 7JZ - T: (020) 79302726, Fax: 79251019, Internet: www.english-heritage.org.uk
Historical Museum
Arch and Buckingham palace history 39802

Wellington Museum → Apsley House

Wernher Collection at Ranger's House, Chesterfield Walk, Blackheath, London SE10 8QX - T: (020) 88530035, Fax: 88530090, Internet: www.english-heritage.org.uk. Dir.: John Jacob
Decorative Arts Museum - 1688
Sevres porcelain, renaissance jewellery, limoges, enamels 39803

Wesley's House and Museum, 47 City Rd, London EC1Y 1AU - T: (0207) 2532262, Fax: 6083825, E-mail: museum@wesleyschapel.org.uk, Internet: www.wesleyschapel.org.uk. Dir.: Heather Carson
Special Museum - 1898
John Wesley's library, personal memorabilia, largest coll of Wesleyana in the world 39804

Westminster Abbey Museum, Westminster Abbey, London SW1P 3PA - T: (020) 72225152, Fax: 72332072
Religious Arts Museum - 1987 39805

Westminster Dragoons Museum, Cavalry House, Duke of York's Headquarter, Chelsea, London SW3 4SC - T: (020) 88567995. Cur.: John Annett
Military Museum
Uniforms and artefacts of the Westminster Dragoons 39806

Whitechapel Art Gallery, 80-82 Whitechapel High St, London E1 7QX - T: (020) 75227878, Fax: 73771685, E-mail: info@whitechapel.org, Internet: www.whitechapel.org. Dir.: Iwona Blazwick
Public Gallery - 1901 39807

William Morris Gallery and Brangwyn Gift, Lloyd Park, Forest Rd, London E17 4PP - T: (020) 85273782, Fax: 85277070, Internet: www.lbwf.gov.uk/wmg. Dir.: Norah Gillow
Decorative Arts Museum - 1950
19th/early 20th c English arts & crafts, decorative arts, life & work of socialist poet William Morris 1834-1896, incl work by Morris & Co. and the Pre-Raphaelites - library, archive 39808

The William Morris Society, Kelmscott House, 26 Upper Mall, London W6 9TA - T: (020) 87413735, Fax: 87485207, E-mail: william.morris@care4free.net, Internet: www.morrissociety.org. Dir.: Linda Parry
Association with Coll 39809

Wimbledon Lawn Tennis Museum, All England Lawn Tennis Club, Church Rd, Wimbledon, London SW19 5AE - T: (020) 89466131, Fax: 89446497, E-mail: museum@aeltc.com, Internet: www.wimbledon.org/museum. Dir.: Honor Godfrey
Special Museum - 1977
Prints, photos, pictures on Wimbledon, objects, pictures etc. relating to the history of tennis - Kenneth Ritchie Wimbledon Library 39810

Wimbledon Society Museum of Local History, 22 Ridgway, Wimbledon, London SW19 4QN - T: (020) 82969914, Fax: 89446497, E-mail: cyril.maidment@clara.net, Internet: www.wimbledonmuseum.org.uk. Dir.: Charles Toase
Historical Museum - 1916
Flints, artefacts, prints, watercolours, maps, photographs, manuscripts, natural hist, ephemera 39811

Wimbledon Windmill Museum, Windmill Rd, Wimbledon Common, London SW19 5NR - T: (020) 89472825. Dir.: N. Plastow
Science&Tech Museum - 1976 39812

Woodlands Art Gallery, 90 Mycenae Rd, Blackheath, London SE3 7SE - T: (020) 88585847, Fax: 88585847, E-mail: a.walton@cwcom.net, Internet: www.wag.co.uk. Dir.: Colin Boothman
Public Gallery 39813

Young's Brewery Museum, The Ram Brewery, Wandsworth High St, London SW18 4JD - T: (020) 88757000, Fax: 88757100
Science&Tech Museum
Brewing equipment of 19th and 20th c, drinking vessels 16th-20th c 39814

Londonderry

Foyle Valley Railway Museum, Foyle Rd, Londonderry BT48 6SQ - T: (028) 71265234, Fax: 71370080. Dir.: Harriet Purkis
Science&Tech Museum
Local railway memorabilia and rolling stock 39815

Harbour Museum, Harbour Sq, Londonderry BT48 6AF - T: (028) 71377331, Fax: 71377633, E-mail: museum@derrycity.gov.uk, Internet: www.derrycity.gov.uk. Dir.: Harriet Purkis
Local Museum
History of the city, maritimes 39816

Orchard Gallery, 21 Orchard St, Londonderry BT48 6EG, mail addr: 98 Strand Rd, Londonderry BT48 7NN - T: (028) 71269675, Fax: 71267273, Internet: www.derrycity.gov.uk. Dir.: Brendan McMenamin
Fine Arts Museum 39817

Tower Museum, Union Hall Pl, Londonderry BT48 6LU - T: (028) 71372411, Fax: 71377633, E-mail: tower.museum@derrycity.gov.uk. Dir.: Harriet Purkis
Local Museum - 1992
Local history 39818

Workhouse Museum, Glendermott Rd, Waterside, Londonderry BT47 6BG - T: (028) 71318328, Fax: 71377633. Dir.: Dermot Francis
Historical Museum
Protection of North Atlantic convoys during WW II, Workhouse Guardians, comparisons between Irish and African famines 39819

Long Eaton

Long Eaton Town Hall, Derby Rd, Long Eaton NG10 1HU - T: (0115) 9071141,
E-mail: erewashmuseum@free4all.co.uk,
Internet: www.erewash.gov.uk
Local Museum / Fine Arts Museum
Paintings, mostly 18th and 19th c oils, local history 39820

Long Hanborough

Combe Mill Beam Engine and Working Museum, Long Hanborough OX8 8ET - T: (01608) 643377. Dir.: Bob Staunton
Science&Tech Museum
19th c sawmill, working forge, 19th c artifacts 39821

Oxford Bus Museum Trust, Old Station Yard, Main Rd, Long Hanborough OX29 8LA - T: (01993) 883617, 881662, E-mail: colin@print-rite.u-net. com, Internet: www.oxfordbusmuseum.org.uk
Science&Tech Museum
Public transport from Oxford and Oxfordshire, local buses, horse trams, vehicles 39822

Long Melford

Melford Hall, Long Melford CO10 9AA - T: (01787) 880286
Decorative Arts Museum
Coll of furniture and porcelain 39823

Long Wittenham

Pendon Museum, Long Wittenham OX14 4QD - T: (01865) 407365, 408143, Internet: www. pendonmuseum.com. Chm.: Chris Webber
Historical Museum - 1954
The Vale Scene, based on the Vale of White Horse, with model buildings illustrating a cross-section of local building styles and materials over the years 39824

Looe

Old Guildhall Museum, Higher Market St, Looe PL13 1BP - T: (01503) 263709, Fax: 265674
Local Museum
Looe history, fishing, smuggling, stocks, courthouse, ceramics, model boats 39825

Lossiemouth

Lossiemouth Fisheries and Community Museum, Pitgaveny St, Lossiemouth IV31 6AA - T: (01343) 543221
Local Museum 39826

Lostwithiel

Lostwithiel Museum, 16 Fore St, Lostwithiel PL22 0BW - T: (01208) 872079. Chm.: Jeanne Jones
Local Museum
Former town jail, houses local domestic and agricultural exhibits 39827

Loughborough

Bellfoundry Museum, Freehold St, Loughborough LE11 1AR - T: (01509) 233414, 212241, Fax: 263305, E-mail: museum@taylorbells.co.uk, Internet: www.taylorbells.co.uk. Cur.: Robert Bracegirdle
Special Museum
Bells and bellfounding 39828

Charnwood Museum, Granby St, Loughborough LE11 3DU - T: (01509) 233754, 233737, Fax: 268140, E-mail: museum@leics.gov.uk, Internet: www. charnwoodbc.gov.uk/tourism.museum.htm. Cur.: Susan Cooke
Local Museum
Natural history of Charnwood borough, social and cultural history 39829

Great Central Railway Museum, Great Central Station, Loughborough LE11 1RW - T: (01509) 230726, Fax: 239791, E-mail: booking-office@ gcrailway.co.uk, Internet: www.gcrailway.co.uk. Dir.: Graham Oliver
Special Museum
Station signs, loco's name and number plates, cast iron notices, silverware, signalling equipment, maps and diagrams, models, photos 39830

Old Rectory Museum, Rectory Pl, Loughborough LE11 1UW - T: (01509) 634704, Fax: 262370
Archaeological Museum
Local archaeological finds 39831

War Memorial Carillon Tower and Military Museum, Queen's Park, Loughborough LE11 2TT - T: (01509) 263370, 634704, Fax: 262370
Military Museum 39832

Loughgall

Dan Winters House - Ancestral Home, 9 The Diamond, Derryloughan Rd, Loughgall BT61 8PH - T: (028) 38851344, E-mail: winter@orangenet.org, Internet: www.orangenet.org/winter. Owner: Hilda Winter
Historical Museum
17th c family chair, Rushlamp, thatching needle, 1903 pram, guns and lead shot, sword from The Battle of the Diamond 1795, churn, milk separator 39833

Louth

Louth Museum, 4 Broadbank, Louth LN11 0EQ - T: (01507) 601211, Internet: www.louth.org.uk. Pres.: D.N. Robinson, Cur.: J. Howard
Local Museum - 1910
Impressions of seals collected by G.W. Gordon, architect James Fowler (1828-92), woodcarver Thomas Wilkinson Wallis (1821-1903) 39834

Lower Broadheath

The Elgar Birthplace Museum, Crown East Ln, Lower Broadheath WR2 6RH - T: (01905) 333224, Fax: 333426, Internet: www.elgar.org. Dir.: Catherine Sloan
Music Museum - 1938
Memorabilia of composer Edward Elgar (1857-1934), manuscripts, clippings, photos 39835

Lower Methil

Lower Methil Heritage Centre, 272 High St, Lower Methil KY8 3EQ - T: (01333) 422100, Fax: 422101, Internet: www.virtual-pc.com/museum/methil
Local Museum 39836

Lower Stondon

Stondon Museum, Station Rd, Lower Stondon SG16 6JN - T: (01462) 850339, Fax: 850824, E-mail: enquiries@transportmuseum.co.uk, Internet: www.transportmuseum.co.uk. Dir.: Maureen Hird
Science&Tech Museum
Coll of transport, replica of Captain Cooks ship HM Bark Endeavour, over 100 years of motoring from 1896-1996 39837

Lowestoft

Lowestoft and East Suffolk Maritime Museum, Fisherman's Cottage, Sparrows Nest Park, Whapload Rd, Lowestoft NR32 1XG - T: (01502) 561963. Dir.: P. Parker
Historical Museum - 1968
Hist of local fishing (1900-1995), evolution of R.N. lifeboats, marine art gallery, ship and boat models 39838

Lowestoft Museum, Broad House, Nicholas Everitt Park, Oulton Broad, Lowestoft NR33 9JR - T: (01502) 511457, 5133795. Dir.: J. Reed
Local Museum - 1972
Lowestoft porcelain, archaeology, history 39839

Royal Naval Patrol Service Association Museum, Europa Room, Sparrows Nest, Lowestoft NR32 1XG - T: (01502) 586250
Historical Museum / Military Museum
Naval uniforms, memorabilia, records, log books, photos, working models 39840

Ludham

Toad Hole Cottage Museum, How Hill, Ludham NR29 5PG - T: (01692) 678763, Fax: 678763
Local Museum
Home and working life on the Broads marshes 39841

Ludlow

Ludlow Museum, Shropshire County Museum, Castle St, Ludlow SY8 1AS - T: (01584) 875384, 873857, Fax: 872019, E-mail: ludlow.museum@shropshire-cc.gov.uk, Internet: www.shropshire-cc.gov.uk/museum.nsf. Dir.: Daniel Lockett
Local Museum 39842

Luton

Bedfordshire and Hertfordshire Regiment Association Museum Collection, Wardown Park, Luton LU2 7HA - T: (01582) 746723, Fax: 746763, E-mail: worrellk@luton.gov.uk
Military Museum
Medals, memorabilia, uniforms, equipment - library 39843

The Gallery, c/o Luton Cental Library, Saint George's Sq, Luton LU1 2NG - T: (01582) 419584, Fax: 459401
Public Gallery 39844

Luton Museum and Art Gallery, Wardown Park, Old Bedford Rd, Luton LU2 7HA - T: (01582) 746722, Fax: 746763, E-mail: hampson@luton.gov.uk, Internet: www.museums.co.uk/luton. Dir.: Leslie Hampson, Sc. Staff: Marian Nicols (Collections), Siobhan Kirrane (Public Service), Dr. Elizabeth Adey (Local History), Dr. P. Hyman (Natural History), Eleanor Markland (Education), Dr. Trevor Taylor (Field Centre), Alison Taylor (Costume)
Local Museum / Fine Arts Museum - 1928
Regional social hist, archaeology, industrial hist, local art, lace, textiles, costumes, toys, rural trades, crafts, porcelain, glass, furniture, household objects 39845

Stockwood Craft Museum and Mossman Gallery, Stockwood Park, Farley Hill, Luton LU1 4BH - T: (01582) 738714, Fax: 746763, E-mail: worrellk@ luton.gov.uk, Internet: www.luton.gov.uk. Dir.: Marian Nicols
Local Museum
Horse-drawn vehicles, rural life, crafts and trades 39846

Lutterworth

Percy Pilcher Museum, Stanford Hall, Lutterworth LE17 6DH - T: (01788) 860250, Fax: 860870, E-mail: enquiries@stanfordhall.co.uk, Internet: www.stanfordhall.co.uk. Dir.: Robert G. Thomas
Science&Tech Museum
First man in England to fly using unpowered flight, replica 1898 fliying machine, rare photos 39847

Sherrier Resources Centre, Church St, Lutterworth LE17 4AG - T: (0116) 2656783, Fax: (01455) 552845, E-mail: museums@leics.gov.uk. Dir.: Eleanor Thomas
Local Museum
Natural, life, working, archaeology, domestic life, artworks 39848

Stanford Hall Motorcycle Museum, Stanford Hall, Lutterworth LE17 6DH - T: (01788) 860250, Fax: 860870, E-mail: enquiries@stanfordhall.co.uk, Internet: www.stanfordhall.co.uk. Dir.: Robert G. Thomas
Science&Tech Museum - 1962
Old motorcycles, bicycles, engines, photos 39849

Lydd

Lydd Town Museum, Old Fire Station, Queens Rd, Lydd TN29 9DF - T: (01797) 366566, E-mail: boxallas@onetel.net
Local Museum
Old fire engine, horse bus and unique beach cart, the army, agriculture, fishing and the fire service 39850

Lydney

Norchard Railway Centre, Dean Forest Railway Museum, Forest Rd, New Mill, Lydney GL15 4ET - T: (01594) 843423, 845840, Fax: 845840, Internet: www.deanforestrailway.co.uk. Cur.: Fergus Scoon
Science&Tech Museum
Last remaining part of original Severn and Wye railway, railway artefacts since 1809 39851

Lyme Regis

Dinosaurland, Coombe St, Lyme Regis DT7 3PY - T: (01297) 443541. Dir.: Steve Davies, Jenny Davies
Natural History Museum - 1995
Fossils, models and live animals, coll of Jurassic fossils 39852

Lyme Regis Philpot Museum, Bridge St, Lyme Regis DT7 3QA - T: (01297) 443370, E-mail: info@ lymeregismuseum.co.uk, Internet: www. lymeregismuseum.co.uk. Hon. Cur.: Max Habditch, Cur.: Jo Draper
Local Museum
Geology, local history, literary 39853

Lymington

Saint Barbe Museum and Art Gallery, New St, Lymington SO41 9BH - T: (01590) 676969, Fax: 679997, E-mail: office@stbarbe-museum.org. uk, Internet: www.stbarbe-museum.org.uk. Cur.: Steven Marshall
Local Museum / Fine Arts Museum
Local history, boat building, fishing, engineering, social history and archaeology 39854

Lyndhurst

New Forest Museum and Visitor Centre, High St, Lyndhurst SO43 7NY - T: (023) 80283914, Fax: 80284236, E-mail: nfmuseum@lineone.net, Internet: www.hants.gov.uk/leisure/museums/new. Dir.: Louise Bessant
Natural History Museum
History, traditions, character and wildlife of New Forest 39855

Lynton

Lyn and Exmoor Museum, Saint Vincent's Cottage, Market St, Lynton EX35 6AF - T: (01598) 752219, Internet: www.devonmuseum.net/lynton. Chm.: John Pedder
Local Museum
Arts, crafts, implements depicting history and life, railway, lifeboat, flood features, Victorian doll's house 39856

Lyth

Lyth Arts Centre, Wick, Caithness, Lyth KW1 4UD - T: (01955) 641270, Internet: www.caithness.org/. Dir.: William Wilson
Fine Arts Museum
Coll of visual art 39857

Lytham Saint Anne's

Lytham Hall, Ballam Rd, Lytham Saint Anne's FY8 4LE - T: (01253) 736652, Fax: 737656. Dir.: E.M.J. Miller
Decorative Arts Museum
Portraits of the Clifton family, landscape pictures, Gillow furniture 39858

Lytham Heritage Centre, 2 Henry St, Lytham Saint Anne's FY8 5LE - T: (01253) 730787, Fax: 730767. Chm.: Alan Ashton
Local Museum
Lytham history, local artists and art societies 39859

Lytham Lifeboat Museum, East Beach, Lytham Saint Anne's FY8 5EQ - T: (01253) 730155, Internet: www.legendol.freeserve.co.uk/lythrnli. html. Cur.: Frank Kilroy
Historical Museum 39860

Lytham Windmill Museum, East Beach, Lytham Saint Anne's FY8 5EQ - T: (01253) 794879
Science&Tech Museum
History of mills and milling 39861

Toy and Teddy Bear Museum (closed) 39862

Macclesfield

Gawsworth Hall, Church Ln, Macclesfield SK11 9RN - T: (01260) 223456, Fax: 223469, E-mail: gawsworth@lineone.net, Internet: www. gawsworth.com
Decorative Arts Museum 39863

Jodrell Bank Science Centre and Arboretum, Lower Withington, Macclesfield SK11 9DL - T: (01477) 571339, Fax: 571695, E-mail: visitorcentre@jb. man.ac.uk, Internet: www.jb.man.ac.uk/scicen. Dir.: Sylvia Chaplin
Science&Tech Museum - 1880
Lovell radio telescope, displays on astronomy, space, energy and satellites, planetarium, arboretum 39864

Macclesfield Silk Museum, Heritage Centre, Roe St, Macclesfield SK11 6XD - T: (01625) 613210, Fax: 617880, E-mail: silkmuseum@tiscali.co.uk, Internet: www.silk-macclesfield.org. Dir.: Richard de Peyer
Historical Museum / Local Museum - 1987
Hist of the building and of the Macclesfield Sunday School, religious, educational and social life of the town, silk industry, social and industrial change 39865

Paradise Mill Silk Industry Museum, Paradise Mill, Old Park Ln, Macclesfield SK11 6TJ - T: (01625) 612045, Fax: 612048, E-mail: silkmuseum@tiscali. co.uk, Internet: www.silk-maaclesfield.org. Dir.: Ricard de Peyer
Science&Tech Museum - 1984/2002
Silk industry, machinery, photos, textiles, silk mill, jacquard handlooms 39866

West Park Museum and Art Gallery, Prestbury Rd, Macclesfield SK10 3BJ - T: (01625) 619831, Fax: 617880, E-mail: silkmuseum@tiscali.co.uk, Internet: www.silk-macclesfield.org. Dir.: Louanne Collins
Local Museum / Decorative Arts Museum / Fine Arts Museum - 1898
Art, Egyptian antiquities, local coll 39867

Machynlleth

Corris Railway Museum, Station Yard, Corris, Machynlleth SY20 9SH - T: (01654) 761624, E-mail: alfo@corris.co.uk, Internet: www.corris.co. uk
Science&Tech Museum - 1970
Locomotives, brake van, coaches, a number of wagons, hist and photogr of the railway 39868

The Museum of Modern Art, Y Tabernacl, Heol Penrallt, Machynlleth SY20 8AJ - T: (01654) 703355, Fax: 702160, E-mail: info@momawales. org.uk, Internet: www.momawales.org.uk. Head: Ruth Lambert
Fine Arts Museum
British/Welsh paintings 20th c 39869

Madeley

Blists Hill Victorian Town Open Air Museum, Legges Way, Madeley TF8 7AW - T: (01952) 586063, 583003, Fax: 588016, E-mail: info@ ironbridge.org.uk, Internet: www.ironbridge.org.uk. Dir.: Michael Ward
Open Air Museum
Working Victorian town: foundry, candle factory, saw mill, printing shop 39870

Magherafelt

Bellaghy Bawn, Castle St, Bellaghy, Magherafelt BT45 8LA - T: (028) 79386812, Fax: 79386556, E-mail: bellaghy.bawn@doeni.gov.uk
Local Museum
Plantation coll, local artefacts, literature 39871

Springhill House, 20 Springhill Rd, Moneymore, Magherafelt, Co. Derry - T: (016487) 48210
Decorative Arts Museum
Furniture, paintings and an important costume coll 39872

Maidenhead

Courage Shire Horse Centre (closed) 39873

Royal Borough Collection, Town Hall, Saint Ives Rd, Maidenhead SL6 1QS - T: (01628) 798888
Fine Arts Museum 39874

Maidstone

Dog Collar Museum, Leeds Castle, Maidstone ME17 1PL - T: (01622) 765400, Fax: 767838, E-mail: enquiries@leeds-castle.co.uk, Internet: www.leeds-castle.co.uk
Special Museum
Coll of dog collars, of iron, brass, silver and leather from 16th c 39875

Maidstone Library Gallery, Saint Faith's St, Maidstone ME14 1LH - T: (01622) 752344, Fax: 754980
Public Gallery 39876

Maidstone Museum and Bentlif Art Gallery, Saint Faith's St, Maidstone ME14 1LH - T: (01622) 754497, 756405, Fax: 685022, Internet: www.museum.maidstone.gov.uk. Sc. Staff: V. Tonge (Fine and Applied Art), Prof. Dr. E. Jarzembowski (Natural History), Giles Guthrie (Human History)
Local Museum / Archaeological Museum / Fine Arts Museum / Natural History Museum / Ethnology Museum - 1858
17 c & 18 c furniture in Elizabethan setting, costume, musical instruments, military coll, 17th c Dutch and Italian paintings, watercolors, archaeology, ethnography (SW Pacific), esp. china and glass, natural history, local history & industry, numismatics, carriages 39877

Queen's Own Royal West Kent Regimental Museum, Saint Faith's St, Maidstone ME14 1LH - T: (01622) 602842, Fax: 685022, E-mail: qorwkmuseum@maidstone.gov.uk. Dir.: H.B.H. Waring
Military Museum - 1961
Regiment's artifacts 39878

Tyrwhitt-Drake Museum of Carriages, Archbishop's Stables, Mill St, Maidstone ME15 6YE - T: (01622) 602835, Fax: 685022, E-mail: museuminfo@maidstone.qov.uk. Dir.: Simon Lace
Science&Tech Museum - 1946
Horse-drawn coaches and carriages (17th to 19th c) 39879

Maldon

Maldon District Museum, 47 Mill Rd, Maldon CM9 5HX - T: (01621) 842688, E-mail: bygones@maldonmuseum.fsnet.co.uk, Internet: www.maldonmuseum.fsnet.co.uk. Dir.: M. Derek Maldon Fitch
Local Museum
Social history 39880

Mallaig

Mallaig Heritage Centre, Station Rd, Mallaig PH41 4PY - T: (01687) 462085, Fax: 462085, E-mail: info@mallaigheritage.org.uk, Internet: www.mallaigheritage.org.uk. Dir.: Trish Macintyre
Local Museum
Local history, social history of West Lochaber, railway, steamers, fishing, agriculture 39881

Malmesbury

Athelstan Museum, Town Hall, Cross Hayes, Malmesbury SN16 9BZ - T: (01666) 829258, Fax: 829258, E-mail: athelstanmuseum@northwilts.gov.uk. Cur.: J.R. Prince
Local Museum - 1979
Malmesbury lacemaking industry, Malmesbury branch railway, costume, local engineering company, bicycles, coins and the new educational/hands-on activity facility for children and their families, prints, drawings 39882

Malton

Eden Camp, Modern History Theme Museum, Eden Camp, Malton YO17 6RT - T: (01653) 697777, Fax: 698243, E-mail: admin@edencamp.co.uk, Internet: www.edencamp.co.uk. Dir.: S.A. Jaques
Historical Museum - 1987
History of the British wartime, series of reconstructed scenes, story of civilian life during World War II 39883

Malton Museum, Old Town Hall, Market Pl, Malton YO17 7LP - T: (01653) 695136, 692610
Archaeological Museum
Roman finds, coins, Samian ceramics, iron, bronze and stone objects 39884

Manchester

Chethams's Hospital and Library, Long Millgate, Manchester M3 1SB - T: (0161) 8347961, Fax: 8395797, E-mail: librarian@chethams.org.uk, Internet: www.chethams.org.uk. Head: Michael Powell
Historical Museum
Printed books, manuscripts, ephemera, newspapers, photographs, prints, maps, drawings, paintings, furniture 39885

Gallery of Costume, Manchester City Art Gallery, Platt Hall, Rusholme, Manchester M14 5LL - T: (0161) 2245217, Fax: 2563278, Internet: www.cityartgalleries.org.uk. Dir.: Anthea Jarvis
Special Museum - 1947
History of costumes since 1700, housed in a 1760s building - library 39886

Greater Manchester Police Museum, Newton St, Manchester M1 1ES - T: (0161) 8563287, Fax: 8563286. Cur.: Duncan Broady, Asst. Cur.: David Tetlow
Historical Museum - 1981 39887

Heaton Hall, Manchester City Art Gallery, Heaton Park, Prestwich, Manchester M25 5SW - T: (0161) 7731231, Fax: 2367369, E-mail: r.shrigley@notes.manchester.gov.uk, Internet: www.cityartgalleries.org.uk. Dir.: Virginia Tandy, Cur.: Ruth Shrigley
Fine Arts Museum / Decorative Arts Museum - 1906
Neo-classical interiors, furniture, ceramics, paintings, plasterwork, musical instruments 39888

Holden Gallery, c/o Faculty of Art and Design, Manchester Metropolitan University, Cavendish St, Manchester M15 6BR - T: (0161) 2476225, Fax: 2476870
Fine Arts Museum 39889

Imperial War Museum North, The Quays, Trafford Wharf Rd, Trafford Park, Manchester M17 1TZ - T: (0161) 8364000, Fax: 8364012, E-mail: info@iwmnorth.org.uk, Internet: www.iwm.org.uk. Gen. Dir.: Robert Crawford, Dir.: Jim Forrester
Historical Museum - 2002
Material showing people's experience of war and the impact of war on society from 1914 to the present day 39890

John Rylands Library, 150 Densgate, Manchester M3 3EH - T: (0161) 8345343, Fax: 8345574, E-mail: spcoll72@fs1.li.man.ac.uk, Internet: www.rylibweb.man.ac.uk. Dir.: Christopher J. Hunt
Library with Exhibitions
Coll of rare books and manuscripts - Library 39891

Manchester Art Gallery, Mosley St, Manchester M2 3JL - T: (0161) 2358888, Fax: 2358899, E-mail: k.gowland@notes.manchester.gov.uk, Internet: www.manchestergalleries.org. Dir.: Virginia Tandy, Asst. Dir.: Moira Stevenson, Cur.: Howard Smith (Head), Anthea Jarvis (Costume), Sandra Martin (Fine Art), Ruth Shrigley (Decorative Arts), Tim Wilcox (Exhibitions), Cons.: Amanda Wallace
Fine Arts Museum / Decorative Arts Museum - 1882
British art, painting, drawing, sculptures, decorative arts 39892

Manchester Jewish Museum, 190 Cheetham Hill Rd, Manchester M8 8LW - T: (0161) 8349879, Fax: 8349801, E-mail: info@manchesterjewishmuseum.com, Internet: www.manchesterjewishmuseum.com
Historical Museum / Religious Arts Museum
Hist of Manchester's Jewish community over the past 250 years 39893

Manchester Museum, c/o University of Manchester, Oxford Rd, Manchester M13 9PL - T: (0161) 2752634, Fax: 2752676, E-mail: murecep@man.ac.uk, Internet: www.museum.man.ac.uk. Dir.: Tristram Besterman (Earth Sciences), Sc. Staff: Dr. A.J.N.W. Prag (Archaeology), Dr. S.R. Edwards (Botany), Dr. A.R. David (Egyptology), C. Johnson (Entomology), Dr. G. Bankes (Ethnology), Dr. J.R. Nudds (Geology), Dr. D. Green (Mineralogy), K. Sugden (Numismatics), Wendy Hodkinson (Archery)
Archaeological Museum / Natural History Museum / University Museum / Ethnology Museum
Egyptian coll, geology, zoology, entomology, botany, ethnology, numismatics, archaeology 39894

Manchester Museum of Transport, Boyle St, Cheetham, Manchester M8 8UW - T: (0161) 2052122, Fax: 2052122, E-mail: gmtsenquire@btinternet.com, Internet: www.gmts.co.uk. Dir.: Dennis Talbot
Science&Tech Museum - 1979
Transports, buses, trams 39895

Manchester United Museum and Tour Centre, Sir Matt Busby Way, Old Trafford, Manchester M16 0RA - T: (0810) 4421994, Fax: 8688861, E-mail: tours@manutd.co.uk. Dir.: Mike Maxfield
Special Museum - 1986
British Football - education dept 39896

Manchester University Medical School Museum, Medical Admin., Stopford Bldg, Oxford Rd, Manchester M13 9PT - T: (0161) 2755027, Fax: 2755584, E-mail: peter.mohr@srht.nhs.uk. Cur.: Peter Mohr, Julie Mohr
Historical Museum / University Museum
Medical, surgical and pharmaceutical equipment, instruments, trade catalogues, photographs 39897

Museum of Science and Industry in Manchester, Liverpool Rd, Castlefield, Manchester M3 4FP - T: (0161) 8322244, Fax: 6060104, E-mail: marketing@msim.org.uk, Internet: www.msim.org.uk. Acting Dir.: Bob Scott
Science&Tech Museum - 1983
World's oldest passenger railway station, steam engines, electricity, gas, air and space, textiles - library, restoration workshop, coll centre 39898

National Museum of Labour History, 103 Princess St, Manchester M1 6DD - T: (0161) 2287212, Fax: 2375965, E-mail: admin@peoplehistorymuseum.org.uk, Internet: www.peoplehistorymuseum.org.uk. Dir.: Nicholas Mansfield
Historical Museum
Working class life and institutions, labour and women's movements, banners, photographs, badges, tools, regalia, paintings 39899

North West Film Archive, c/o Manchester Metropolitan University, Minshull House, 47-49 Chorlton St, Manchester M1 3EU - T: (0161) 2473097, Fax: 2473098, E-mail: n.w.filmarchiv@mmu.ac.uk, Internet: www.nwfa.mmu.ac.uk. Dir.: Maryann Gomes
Performing Arts Museum
Film coll 39900

Pankhurst Centre, 60-62 Nelson St, Chorlton-on-Medlock, Manchester M13 9WP - T: (0161) 2735673, Fax: 2743525, E-mail: pankhurst@zetnet.co.uk, Internet: www.thepankhurstcentre.org.uk. Dir.: Yvonne Edge
Historical Museum
Women's suffrage movement 39901

People's History Museum, Pump House, Left Bank, Bridge St, Manchester M3 3ER - T: (0161) 8396061, Fax: 8396027, E-mail: info@peopleshistorymuseum.org.uk, Internet: www.peopleshistorymuseum.org.uk. Dir.: Nicholas Mansfield
Historical Museum - 1994
Banners 39902

Portico Library and Gallery, 57 Mosley St, Manchester M2 3HY - T: (0161) 2366785, Fax: 2366803, E-mail: librarian@theportico.org.uk, Internet: www.theportico.org.uk
Public Gallery 39903

The Whitworth Art Gallery, c/o University of Manchester, Oxford Rd, Manchester M15 6ER - T: (0161) 2757450, Fax: 2757451, E-mail: whitworth@man.ac.uk, Internet: www.whitworth.man.ac.uk. Dir.: Alistair Smith, Cur.: Jennifer Harris (Textiles), David Morris (Prints), Mary Griffiths (Modern Art), Frances Pritchard (Textiles), Christine Woods (Wallpapers), Charles Nugent (Watercolours), Admin.: Julian Tomlin, Cons.: Nicola Walker (Works on Paper), Ann French (Textiles), Carly Wong, Angela Conley (Marketing), Esmé Ward (Education)
Fine Arts Museum / University Museum - 1889
British water colors and drawings, Old Master prints and drawings, Japanese prints, textiles, contemporary British art, wallpapers - library 39904

Wythenshawe Hall, Manchester City Art Gallery, Wythenshawe Park, Northenden, Manchester M23 0AB - T: (0161) 2341456, Fax: 2367369, E-mail: r.shrigley@notes.manchester.gov.uk, Internet: www.cityartgalleries.org.uk. Dir.: Virginia Tandy
Decorative Arts Museum / Fine Arts Museum - 1930
17th-19th c furniture and pictures housed in country manor 39905

Mansfield

Mansfield Museum and Art Gallery, Leeming St, Mansfield NG18 1NG - T: (01623) 463088, Fax: 412922, E-mail: mansfield_museum@hotmail.com, Internet: www.mansfield-dc.gov.uk. Cur.: E. Weston
Local Museum / Fine Arts Museum - 1904
Natural hist, local hist, art works, ceramics, archaeology, Buxton watercolors, Wedgwood and Pinxton China 39906

Marazion

Giant's Castle, Saint Michael's Mount, Marazion TR17 0HT - T: (01736) 710507, Fax: 719930, E-mail: godolphin@manor-office.co.uk
Special Museum 39907

March

March and District Museum, High St, March PE15 9JJ - T: (01354) 655300, Fax: 653714
Local Museum
Coll of domestic and agricultural artefacts 39908

Margam

Abbey and Stones Museum, Port Talbot, Margam - T: (01639) 891548, Fax: 891548
Religious Arts Museum 39909

Margate

Lifeboat House, The Rendezvous, Margate Harbour, Margate CT9 1AA - T: (01843) 221613
Special Museum 39910

Margate Caves, 1 Northdown Rd, Margate CT9 2RN - T: (01843) 220139, Fax: 834428. Cur.: Iris Harvey
Historical Museum 39911

Old Town Hall Museum, Market Pl, Margate CT9 1ER - T: (01843) 231213, E-mail: margatemuseum@bonkers16.freeserve.co.uk. Cur.: Bob Bradley
Local Museum 39912

Tudor House, Hosking Memorial Museum (temporary closed), King St, Margate CT9 1DA - T: (01843) 225511 ext 2520
Local Museum 39913

Market Bosworth

Bosworth Battlefield Visitor Centre and Country Park, Sutton Cheney, Market Bosworth CV13 0AD - T: (01455) 290429, Fax: 292841, E-mail: bosworth@leics.gov.uk, Internet: www.leics.gov.uk
Historical Museum 39914

Market Harborough

Harborough Museum, Council Offices, Adam and Eve St, Market Harborough LE16 7AG - T: (01858) 821085, Fax: 821086, E-mail: harboroughmuseum@uklink.net. Dir.: H.E. Broughton, Cur.: L. Souster
Local Museum 39915

Rockingham Castle, Market Harborough LE16 8TH - T: (01858) 770240, Fax: (01536) 771692, E-mail: estateoffice@rockinghamcastle.com, Internet: www.rockinghamcastle.com
Fine Arts Museum
Fine pictures, furniture 39916

Market Lavington

Market Lavington Village Museum, Church St, Market Lavington SN10 4DP - T: (01380) 818736, Fax: 816222. Cur.: Peggy Gye
Local Museum
Life in the village 39917

Maryport

Maryport Maritime Museum, 1 Senhouse St, Maryport CA15 6AB - T: (01900) 813738, Fax: 819496, E-mail: maryport.museum@allerdale.gov.uk, Internet: www.allerdale.gov.uk/heritage&arts
Historical Museum / Science&Tech Museum - 1976
Maryport local hist, maritime hist 39918

Senhouse Roman Museum, Sea Brows, Maryport CA15 6JD - T: (01900) 816168, Fax: 816168, E-mail: romans@senhouse.freeserve.co.uk, Internet: www.senhousemuseum.co.uk. Man.: Jane Laskey
Archaeological Museum 39919

Matlock

Caudwell's Mill & Craft Centre, Rowsley, Matlock DE4 2EB - T: (01629) 734374, Fax: 734374, E-mail: raymarjoran@compuserve.com, Internet: caudwellsmill.museum.com. Man.: Lesley Wyld
Science&Tech Museum - 1982
Flour mill machinery 39920

Model Railway Museum (closed) 39921

National Tramway Museum, Crich Tramway Village, Matlock DE4 5DP - T: (01773) 852565, Fax: 852326, E-mail: info@tramway.co.uk, Internet: www.tramway.co.uk. Dir.: David Senior
Science&Tech Museum - 1959
Coll of tramcars, built between 1873 and 1969, from Britain and abroad - library, restoration workshop 39922

Peak District Mining Museum, The Pavilion, Matlock DE4 3NR - T: (01629) 583834, E-mail: mail@peakmines.co.uk, Internet: www.peakmines.co.uk. Dir.: Robin Hall
Science&Tech Museum - 1978
Artifacts relating to the history of lead mining from the Roman period to present day, mining tools, water pressure engine built in 1819 39923

Peak Rail Museum, Station, Matlock DE4 3NA - T: (01629) 580381, Fax: 760645, E-mail: peakrail@peakrail.co.uk, Internet: www.peakrail.co.uk. Dir.: J.T. Starham
Science&Tech Museum
Standard gauge, railway 39924

Mauchline

Burns House Museum, Castle St, Mauchline KA5 5BS - T: (01290) 550045. Dir.: D.I. Lyell, Sc. Staff: J. Kelso
Special Museum - 1969
Memorabilia on Poet Robert Burns, Mauchline Boxware, curling stones 39925

Maud

Maud Railway Museum, Station, Maud AB42 5LY - T: (01224) 664228, E-mail: heritage@aberdeenshire.gov.uk, Internet: www.aberdeenshire.gov.uk/heritage/
Science&Tech Museum 39926

Maybole

Culzean Castle and Country Park, Culzean Castle, Maybole KA19 8LE - T: (01655) 884455, Fax: 884503, E-mail: culzean@nts.org.uk, Internet: www.nts.org.uk. Dir.: Michael L. Tebbutt
Decorative Arts Museum - 1945
Interiors, fittings designed by Robert Adam, staircase, plaster ceilings, 18th c castle built by Robert Adam 39927

Measham

Measham Museum, High St, Measham DE12 7HZ - T: (01530) 273956, Fax: 273986. Chm.: Denise Mulka
Local Museum
Local history, Measham ware pottery, mining artefacts, Hart coll, pictures 39928

Meigle

Meigle Museum of Sculptured Stones, Dundee Rd, Meigle PH12 8SB - T: (01828) 640612, Fax: 640612, E-mail: hs.explorer@scotland.gsi.gov.uk, Internet: www.historic-scotland.gov.uk
Archaeological Museum - ca 1890
Pictish and early Christian stone objects 39929

Melbourne

Melbourne Hall, Church Sq, Melbourne DE73 1EN - T: (01332) 862502, Fax: 862263, E-mail: gillweston@melbhall.globalnet.co.uk. Cur.: Gill Weston
Fine Arts Museum 39930

Melrose

Abbotsford House, Melrose TD6 9BQ - T: (01896) 752043, Fax: 752916, E-mail: abbotsford@melrose.border.et.co.uk
Special Museum / Historical Museum
Relics of Sir Walter Scott - library 39931

Melrose Abbey Museum, Melrose - T: (01896) 822562
Religious Arts Museum
Abbey pottery, floor, tiles, stone sculpture 39932

Melton Mowbray

Melton Carnegie Museum, Thorpe End, Melton Mowbray LE13 1RB - T: (01664) 569946, Fax: 564060, E-mail: museums@leics.gov.uk, Internet: www.leics.gov.uk/museum. Dir.: Jenny Dancey
Local Museum - 1977
Local history, hunting pictures 39933

Meopham

Meopham Windmill, Wrotham Rd, Meopham DA13 0QA - T: (01474) 813779, Fax: 813779, E-mail: p.tennyson@btinternet.com, Internet: www.meopham.org
Science&Tech Museum 39934

Mere

Mere Museum, Barton Ln, Mere BA12 6JA - T: (01747) 861444, E-mail: curator@meremuseum.fsnet.co.uk. Cur.: Dr. D. Longbourne
Local Museum 39935

Merthyr Tydfil

Brecon Mountain Railway, Pant Station, Dowlais, Merthyr Tydfil CF4 2UP - T: (01685) 722988, Fax: 384854
Science&Tech Museum
Locomotives from three continents built between 1894 and 1930 39936

Cyfarthfa Castle Museum and Art Gallery, Brecon Rd, Merthyr Tydfil CF47 8RE - T: (01685) 723112, Fax: 723112, E-mail: museum@cyfarthfapark.freeserve.co.uk. Cur.: Scott Reid
Decorative Arts Museum / Fine Arts Museum - 1910
Paintings, ceramics, silver, natural history, geology, ethnology, local history, industrial history 39937

Joseph Parry's Cottage, 4 Chapel Row, Merthyr Tydfil CF48 1BN - T: (01685) 721858, 723112, Fax: 723112. Cur.: Scott Reid
Music Museum - 1979
Story of the Welsh composer Joseph Parry 39938

Merton

Barometer World Museum, Quicksilver Barn, Merton EX20 3DS - T: (01805) 603443, Fax: 603344, E-mail: barometerworld@barometerworld.co.uk, Internet: www.barometerworld.co.uk. Cur.: Philip Collins
Special Museum
Barometers 39939

Methil

Methil Heritage Centre, 272 High St, Methil KY8 3EQ - T: (01333) 422100, Fax: 422101. Dir.: Kevan Brown
Local Museum
Local history 39940

Methlick

Haddo House, Methlick AB41 7EQ - T: (01651) 851440, Fax: 851888, E-mail: haddo@nts.gov.uk, Internet: www.nts.org.uk. Dir.: Lorraine Hesketh-Campbell
Decorative Arts Museum
Earls of Aberdeen mansion 39941

Mevagissey

Folk Museum, Frazier House, East Quay, Mevagissey PL26 6PP - T: (01726) 843568. Cur.: Ron Forder
Folklore Museum 39942

Mickley

Thomas Bewick's Birthplace, Station Bank, nr Stocksfield, Mickley NE43 7DD - T: (01661) 843276. Cur.: Hugh Dixon
Special Museum / Fine Arts Museum - 1990
Engravings and prints from Bewick's wood blocks 39943

Middle Claydon

Claydon House, Middle Claydon MK18 2EY - T: (01296) 730349, Fax: 738511, E-mail: todgen@smtp.ntrust.org.uk, Internet: www.nationaltrust.org.uk
Decorative Arts Museum
Rococo State rooms with carving and decoration by Luke Lightfoot and plasterwork by Joseph Rose the younger 39944

Middle Wallop

Museum of Army Flying, Middle Wallop SO20 8DY - T: (01980) 674421, Fax: (01264) 781694, E-mail: enquiries@flying-museum.org.uk, Internet: www.flying-museum.org.uk. Dir.: Dr. Edward Tait
Military Museum
British Army's flying history, balloons in Bechuanaland, helicopters in the Falklands campaign of 1982, Army helicopters and fixed-wing aircraft, a captured Huey helicopter, British WWII assault gliders 39945

Middlesbrough

Captain Cook Birthplace Museum, Stewart Park, Marton, Middlesbrough TS7 8AT - T: (01642) 311211, Fax: 317419, E-mail: captcookmuseum@middlesbrough.gov.uk, Internet: www.middlesbrough.gov.uk. Dir.: Phil Philo
Special Museum - 1978
The life of Cook, a reconstruction of the below-deck accomodation in his famous ship, the Endeavour, galleries illustrating countries he visited until his death in Hawaii in 1779, ethnographical material 39946

Cleveland Crafts Centre, 57 Gilkes St, Middlesbrough TS1 5EL - T: (01642) 262376, Fax: 226351. Head: Tracey Taylor
Decorative Arts Museum
Decorative arts (16th-20th c), contemporary drawings, glass, ceramics, textiles, works of wood, pottery, non-precious contemporary jewellery 39947

Dorman Memorial Museum, Linthorpe Rd, Middlesbrough TS5 6LA - T: (01642) 813781, Fax: 358100, E-mail: dormanmuseum@middlesborough.gov.uk, Internet: www.dormanmuseum.co.uk. Dir.: Godfrey Worsdale, Sc. Staff: Ken Sedman
Local Museum - 1904
Natural hist, industrial and social hist, pottery, conchology, archaeology, world cultures 39948

Middlesbrough Art Gallery, 320 Linthorpe Rd, Middlesbrough TS1 4AW - T: (01642) 358139, Fax: 358138. Dir.: Julia Bell, Cur.: Lisa Movan
Public Gallery - 1958
20th c British works, contemporary international art 39949

Newham Grange Leisure Farm Museum, Coulby Newham, Middlesbrough TS1 - T: (01642) 300261, Fax: 300276
Agriculture Museum
History of farming in Cleveland, reconstructions of a farmhouse kitchen, a veterinary surgeon's room, a saddler's shop, coll of farm tools, implements and equipment 39950

Middleton-by-Wirksworth

Middleton Top Engine House, Middleton-by-Wirksworth DE4 4LS - T: (01629) 823204, Fax: 825336
Science&Tech Museum - 1974
Restored Beam Winding Engine of 1830 39951

Mildenhall, Suffolk

Mildenhall and District Museum, 6 King St, Mildenhall, Suffolk IP28 7EX - T: (01638) 716970, E-mail: chris.mycock@stedsbc.gov.uk
Local Museum
Local history, history of RAF Mildenhall, archaeology 39952

Milford Haven

Milford Haven Museum, Old Customs House, Sybil Way, The Docks, Milford Haven SA73 3AF - T: (01646) 694496
Local Museum
History of the town and waterway, fishing port 39953

Milford, Staffordshire

Shugborough Estate Museum, Milford, Staffordshire ST17 0XB - T: (01889) 881388, Fax: 881323, Internet: www.staffordshire.gov.uk/shugboro/shugpark.htm. Dir.: Geoff Elkin
Local Museum - 1966
The social and agricultural history of rural Staffordshire, stables, laundry, ironing room, brewhouse, coachhouse, coll of horse-drawn vehicles ranges from family coaches and carriages to farm carts 39954

Millom

Folk Museum, The Station Building, Station Rd, Millom LA18 4DD - T: (01229) 772555, Fax: 772555, Internet: www.visitcumbria.com/wc/milmmus.htm
Folklore Museum 39955

Millport

Museum of the Cumbraes, Garrison House, Garrison Grounds, Millport KA28 0DG - T: (01475) 531191, Fax: 531191, E-mail: museum@north-ayrshire.gov.uk, Internet: www.northayrshire.gov.uk/museums. Dir.: John Travers, Man.: Morag McNicol, Asst. Man.: Margaret Weir, Manager: Debra L. Keasal, Asst.: Kathryn Valentine
Local Museum
Local history in a reconstructed wash house 39956

Robertson Museum and Aquarium, c/o University Marine Biological Station, Millport KA28 0EG - T: (01475) 530581, Fax: 530601, E-mail: donna.murphy@millport.gla.ac.uk, Internet: www.gla.ac.uk/acad/marine. Dir.: Dr. Rupert Ormond
Natural History Museum / University Museum - 1900
Local marine life 39957

Milngavie

Lillie Art Gallery, Station Rd, Milngavie G62 8BZ - T: (0141) 5788847, Fax: 5700244, E-mail: museums@eastdunbarton.gov.uk. Dir./ Cur.: Hildegarde Berwick
Fine Arts Museum - 1962
Paintings 20th c, paintings water colors and etchings by Robert Lillie, drawings by Joan Eardley 39958

Milnrow

Ellenroad Engine House, Elizabethan Way, Milnrow OL16 4LG - T: (01706) 881952, Fax: (0161) 6880634, E-mail: ellenroad@aol.com
Science&Tech Museum 39959

Milton Abbas

Park Farm Museum, Park Farm, Blanford, Milton Abbas DT11 0AX - T: (01258) 880216
Agriculture Museum 39960

Milton Keynes

Milton Keynes Gallery, 900 Midsummer Blvd, Milton Keynes MK9 3QA - T: (01908) 676900, Fax: 676900, E-mail: info@mk-g.org, Internet: www.mk-g.org. Dir.: Stephen Snoddy
Public Gallery 39961

Milton Keynes Museum, McConnell Dr, Wolverton, Milton Keynes MK12 5EL - T: (01908) 316222, Fax: 319148, E-mail: enquiries@mkmuseum.org.uk, Internet: www.mkmuseum.org.uk. Dir.: Bill Griffiths
Local Museum
Industry, agriculture, social history, retailing, railways 39962

Warner Archive, Bradbourne Dr, Tilbrook, Milton Keynes MK7 8BE - T: (01908) 658021, Fax: 658020, E-mail: sue_kerry@walkergreenbank.com
Historical Museum / Decorative Arts Museum
Textiles, designs, Warner Fabrics, Wilson, Keith, Norris, Walters, Scott Richmond and Helios 39963

Minehead

West Somerset Railway, Station, Minehead TA24 5BG - T: (01643) 704996, 707650, Fax: 706349, E-mail: info@west-somerset-railway.co.uk, Internet: www.west-somerset-railway.co.uk. Dir.: Mark Smith
Science&Tech Museum
Colls of Great Western Railway artefacts, Somerset and Dorset Railway artefacts 39964

Minera

Minera Lead Mines, Wern Rd, Minera LL11 3DU - T: (01978) 753400, E-mail: museum@wrexham.gov.uk. Man.: Hilary Williams
Science&Tech Museum
19th c lead mine, beam engine house, geology 39965

Minster

Minster Abbey, Church St, Minster CT12 4HF - T: (01843) 821254
Religious Arts Museum 39966

Mintlaw

Aberdeenshire Farming Museum, Aden Country Park, Mintlaw AB42 5FQ - T: (01771) 622906, Fax: 622884, E-mail: heritage@aberdeenshire.gov.uk. Cur.: William K. Milne, Sc. Staff: Dr. David M. Bertie
Open Air Museum / Agriculture Museum
Agricultural colls, history of farming in NE Scotland 39967

Mistley

Essex Secret Bunker Museum (closed) 39968

Mitcham

Wandle Industrial Museum, Vestry Hall Annexe, London Rd, Mitcham CR4 3UD - T: (020) 86480127, Fax: 86850249, E-mail: curator@wandle.org, Internet: www.wandle.org
Science&Tech Museum
Life and industries of the River Wandle 39969

Moffat

Moffat Museum, The Neuk, Church Gate, Moffat DG10 9EG - T: (01683) 220868
Local Museum 39970

Moira

Moira Furnace, Furnace Ln, Moira DE12 6AT - T: (01283) 224667, Fax: 224667. Dir.: Brian Waring
Science&Tech Museum
Cast iron goods produced at the furnace foundary, foundryman's tools, social history 39971

Mold

Daniel Owen Museum, Earl Rd, Mold CH7 1AP - T: (01352) 754791, Fax: 754655. Man.: Nia Jones (Library)
Library with Exhibitions / Public Gallery 39972

Oriel Gallery, Clwyd Theatr Cymru, Mold CH7 1YA - T: (01352) 756331, Fax: 701558, E-mail: oriel@clwyd-theatr-cymru.co.uk. Dir.: Jonathan Le Vay
Public Gallery 39973

Moneymore

Springhill Costume Museum, Magherafelt, Springhill, Moneymore BT45 7NQ - T: (028) 86747927, Fax: 86747927, E-mail: UPSET@smpt.ntrust.org.uk
Special Museum 39974

Moniaive

James Paterson Museum, Meadowcroft, North St, Moniaive DG3 4HR - T: (01848) 200583, Internet: www.lepad.demon.co.uk/pater-j.html. Cur.: Anne Paterson
Special Museum 39975

Maxwelton House Museum, Maxwelton, Moniaive DG3 4DX - T: (01848) 200385. Cur.: Roderick Stenhouse
Local Museum - 1973 39976

Monmouth

Castle and Regimental Museum, The Castle, Monmouth NP25 3BS - T: (01600) 772175, Fax: 711428, E-mail: curator@monmouthcastlemuseum.org.uk, Internet: www.monmouthcastlemuseum.org.uk. Dir.: P. Lynesmith
Military Museum 39977

Nelson Museum and Local History Centre, Priory St, Monmouth NP25 3XA - T: (01600) 713519, Fax: 775001, E-mail: monmouthmuseum@monmouthshite.gov.uk. Dir.: Andrew Helme
Historical Museum - 1924
Documents and material concerning Nelson, local coll including the Hon. Charles Stuart Rolls (of Rolls Royce Fame) - commercial conservation service 39978

Montacute

National Portrait Gallery, Montacute House, Montacute TA15 6XP - T: (01935) 823289, Fax: 826921, E-mail: wmogen@smtp.ntrust.org.uk
Decorative Arts Museum
Furniture, tapestries, wood panelling, amorial glass, portraits of Tudor and Jacobean courts 39979

Montgomery

Old Bell Museum, Arthur St, Montgomery SY15 6RA - T: (01686) 668313
Local Museum
Local history, railway, industry 39980

Montrose

House of Dun, Montrose DD10 9LQ - T: (01674) 810264, Fax: 810722
Historic Site
Georgian house built in 1730, exhibition on the architecture of house and garden 39981

Montrose Air Station Museum, Waldron Rd, Broomfield, Montrose DD10 9BB - T: (01674) 673107, 674210, Fax: 674210, E-mail: pd.mams@btopenworld.com, Internet: www.rafmontrose.org.uk. Chm.: David Butler
Military Museum
Aircrafts, wartime artefacts 39982

Montrose Museum and Art Gallery, Panmure Pl, Montrose DO10 8HE - T: (01674) 673232, Fax: (01307) 462590, E-mail: montrose.museum@angus.gov.uk, Internet: www.angus.gov.uk. Cur.: Rachel Benvie
Local Museum / Fine Arts Museum - 1837
Social history, ethnography, natural science, fossils, watercolours, sculpture and etchings, geology, molluscs 39983

William Lamb Memorial Studio, 24 Market St, Montrose DD10 8NB - T: (01674) 673232, Fax: (01307) 462590, E-mail: montrose.museum@angus.gov.uk, Internet: www.angus.gov.uk. Cur.: R. Benvie
Fine Arts Museum
Sculptures, wood carvings, etchings, drawings, watercolours 39984

Moreton-in-Marsh

Wellington Aviation Museum, British School House, Broadway Rd, Moreton-in-Marsh GL56 0BG - T: (01608) 650323, Fax: 650323. Dir.: Gerry V. Tyack
Local Museum / Military Museum
Royal Air Force treasures, local history 39985

Moreton Morrell

Warwickshire Museum of Rural Life, Warwickshire College of Agriculture, Moreton Morrell - T: (01926) 493431 ext 2021
Agriculture Museum
Implements, equipment, important farming activities such as ploughing, sowing, harvesting and dairying, locally made ploughs 39986

Morpeth

Chantry Bagpipe Museum, Bridge St, Morpeth NE61 1PJ - T: (01670) 500717, Fax: 500710, E-mail: anne.moore@castlemorphet.gov.uk. Dir.: Anne Moore
Music Museum - 1987
W.A. Cocks Coll of bagpipes and manuscripts 39987

Motherwell

Motherwell Heritage Centre, High St, Motherwell ML1 3HU - T: (01698) 251000, Fax: 268867, E-mail: heritage@mhc158.freeserve.co.uk, Internet: www.motherwell.museum.com. Man.: Carol Haddow
Local Museum - 1996
Heritage from the Roman period, the rise and fall of heavy industry, present days - study room, exhibition gallery 39988

Mottistone

Bembridge Windmill Museum, Strawberry Ln, Mottistone PO30 4EA - T: (01983) 873945
Science&Tech Museum 39989

Mouldsworth

Mouldsworth Motor Museum, Smithy Ln, Mouldsworth CH3 8AR - T: (01928) 731781
Science&Tech Museum
Automobilia, motoring, art, enamel signs 39990

Much Hadham

Forge Museum, The Forge, High St, Much Hadham SG10 6BS - T: (01279) 843301, Fax: 843301, E-mail: christinaharrison@hotmail.com, Internet: www.hertsmuseum.org.uk. Cur.: Christina Harrison
Science&Tech Museum
Tools, blacksmith's shop and works, beekeeping equipment 39991

Much Marcle

Hellen's House, off A449, Much Marcle HR8 2LY - T: (01531) 660504, Fax: 660416, E-mail: info@hellensmanor.com, Internet: www.hellensmanor.com. Dir.: Adam Munthe
Decorative Arts Museum 39992

Much Wenlock

Much Wenlock Museum, The Square, High St, Much Wenlock TF13 6HR - T: (01952) 727773. Dir.: Nigel Nixon, Cur.: K.J. Andrew (Natural Sciences)
Local Museum
Modern Olympics 39993

Mullach Ban

Mullach Ban Folk Museum, Tullymacrieve, Mullach Ban BT35 9XA - T: (028) 30888278, Fax: 30888100, E-mail: micealsdsa@dial.pipex.com
Folklore Museum / Agriculture Museum
Past agricultural way of life 39994

Mytchett

Basingstoke Canal Exhibition, Mytchett Place Rd, Mytchett GU16 6DD - T: (01252) 370073, Fax: 371758, E-mail: info@bastingstoke-canal.co.uk, Internet: www.basingstokecanal1.freeserve.co.uk. Dir.: Leigh Thornton
Historical Museum
200 year history of the Basingstoke Canal 39995

Nairn

Nairn Fishertown Museum, Viewfield House, Viewfield Dr, Nairn IV12 4EE - T: (01667) 456798, Fax: 455399, E-mail: manager@nairnmuseum.freeserve.co.uk, Internet: www.nairnmuseum.co.uk. Chairman: David M. Ellen
Local Museum
Domestic life of the fishertown, fishing industry around Moray Firth 39996

Nairn Museum, Viewfield House, Viewfield Dr, Nairn IV12 4EE - T: (01667) 456798, Fax: 455399, E-mail: manager@nairnmuseum.freeserve.co.uk, Internet: www.nairnmuseum.co.uk
Local Museum - 1985
Literary Institute's coll, folk life, Rocks minerals, fossiles, natural history 39997

Nantgarw

Nantgarw China Works Museum, Tyla Gwyn, Nantgarw CF15 7TB - T: (01443) 841703, Fax: 841826. Dir.: Gerry Towell
Decorative Arts Museum
William Billingsley, 19th-c porcelain maker and decorator 39998

Nantwich

Nantwich Museum, Pillory St, Nantwich CW5 5BQ - T: (01270) 627104
Local Museum 39999

Narberth

Blackpool Mill, Canaston Bridge, Narberth SA67 8BL - T: (01437) 541233
Science&Tech Museum 40000

Wilson Museum of Narberth, 13 Market Sq, Narberth SA67 7AU - T: (01834) 861719. Cur.: Pauline Griffiths
Local Museum
Local history, brewery items, local shops and businesses, costume, toys, postcards and domestic items 40001

Naseby

Battle and Farm Museum, Purlieu Farm, Naseby NN6 7DD - T: (01604) 740241, Fax: 740800, Internet: www.hillyer.demon.co.uk/museum.htm
Military Museum / Agriculture Museum - 1975
Battle of 1645, agriculture 40002

Near Ripon

Norton Conyers, Near Ripon HG4 5EQ - T: (01765) 640333, Fax: 640333, E-mail: norton.conyers@ripon.org. Dir.: Sir James Graham, Lady Graham
Local Museum / Fine Arts Museum / Decorative Arts Museum 40003

Neath

Cefn Coed Colliery Museum, Neath Rd, Crynant, Neath SA10 8SN - T: (01639) 750556, Fax: 750556. Dir.: Robert Merrill
Historical Museum - 1980
Mining of coal, story of men and machines 40004

Neath Museum, Gwyn Hall, Orchard St, Neath SA11 1DT - T: (01639) 645741, 645726, Fax: 645726
Local Museum
Local history, archaeology, natural history, art gallery 40005

Nefyn

Lleyn Historical and Maritime Museum, Old Saint Mary's Church, Church St, Nefyn LL53 6HE - T: (01758) 720270
Military Museum
Model ships, lifeboats, maritime paintings, local hist and items on the fishing industry 40006

Nelson

Llancaiach Fawr Living History Museum, Llancaiach Fawr Manor, Nelson CF46 6ER - T: (01443) 412248, Fax: 412688, E-mail: allens@caerphilly.gov.uk, Internet: www.caerphilly.gov.uk/visiting. Man.: Suzanne Allen
Local Museum
Social history, decorative arts, archaeology 40007

Nenthead

Nenthead Mines Heritage Centre, Nenthead CA9 3PD - T: (01434) 382037, Fax: 382294, E-mail: administration.office@virgin.net, Internet: www.npht.com
Science&Tech Museum
History and geology of this lead mining area 40008

Ness

Ionad Dualchais Nis, Lionel Old School, Ness PA86
Historical Museum
Crofting, past domestic life - archives 40009

Nether Stowey

Coleridge Cottage, 35 Lime St, Nether Stowey TA5 1NQ - T: (01278) 732662, E-mail: stc1798@aol.com. Cust.: Derrick Woolf
Special Museum - 1909
Memorablia of poet Samuel Taylor Coleridge (1772-1834) 40010

New Abbey

Museum of Costume, National Museums of Scotland, Shambellie House, New Abbey DG2 8HQ - T: (01387) 850375, Fax: 850461, Internet: www.nms.ac.uk/costume. Dir.: Dale Idiens, Cur.: Mark Jones
Special Museum - 1977
Costumes from 1850 to 1950, European fashionable dress 40011

New Lanark

New Lanark World Heritage Village, New Lanark Mills, New Lanark ML11 9DB - T: (01555) 661345, Fax: 665738, E-mail: visit@newlanark.org, Internet: www.newlanark.org. Dir.: J. Arnold
Historical Museum - 1785
New Millennium experience, 19th c textile machinery, period housing and shop 40012

New Mills

New Mills Heritage and Information Centre, Rock Mill Ln, New Mills SK22 3BN - T: (01663) 746904, Fax: 746904, Internet: www.newmills.org.uk
Association with Coll
3-D items in display cases and wall displays of New Mills material describing the Torrs, the pre-industrial history incl Domesday and the royal forest of Peak, the story of the "New Mill" and the growth of communications, goal mining and the textile industry, reconstruction of a coal mine tunnel, and engraver's workshop, and a model of the town in 1884 40013

New Milton

Sammy Miller Motorcycle Museum, Bashley Cross Road, New Milton BH25 5SZ - T: (01425) 620777, Fax: 619696, E-mail: info@sammymiller.co.uk, Internet: www.sammymiller.co.uk. Dir.: Sammy Miller
Science&Tech Museum
Motorcycles of the world, rare and exotic phototypes 40014

New Pitsligo

Northfield Farm Museum, New Pitsligo AB43 6PX - T: (01771) 653504
Agriculture Museum
Coll of historic farm machinery and household impl 40015

New Romney

Romney Toy and Model Museum, Romney Hythe and Dymchurch Railway, New Romney Station, New Romney TN28 8PL - T: (01797) 362353, Fax: 363591, E-mail: danny.martin2@btinternet.com, Internet: www.rhdr.demon.co.uk. Dir.: Danny Martin
Special Museum
World's smallest public railway, traditional toys 40016

New Tredegar

Elliot Colliery Winding House, White Rose Way, New Tredegar NP24 6DF - T: (01443) 864224, 822666, Fax: 838609, E-mail: museum@caerphilly.gov.uk, Internet: www.caerphilly.gov.uk. Dir.: Chris Morgan
Science&Tech Museum
Thornewill and Warham steam engine, history of mining in Caerphilly county borough 40017

Newark-on-Trent

Castle Story, Gilstrap Heritage Centre, Castlegate, Newark-on-Trent NG24 1BG - T: (01636) 611908, Fax: 612274, E-mail: gilstrap@newark-sherwooddc.gov.uk, Internet: www.newark-sherwooddc.gov.uk
Local Museum 40018

Gilstrap Heritage Centre, Castlegate, Newark-on-Trent NG24 1BG - T: (01636) 611908, Fax: 612274, E-mail: gilstrap@newark-sherwooddc.gov.uk, Internet: www.newark-sherwooddc.gov.uk
Historical Museum 40019

Millgate Museum, 48 Millgate, Newark-on-Trent NG24 4TS - T: (01636) 655730, Fax: 655735, E-mail: museums@newark-sherwooddc.gov.uk, Internet: www.newark-sherwooddc.gov.uk. Dir.: Melissa Hall
Folklore Museum - 1978
Items mid-19th c-1950's relating to everyday life 40020

Newark Air Museum, Airfield Winthorpe, Newark-on-Trent NG24 2NY - T: (01636) 707170, Fax: 707170, E-mail: newarkair@lineone.net, Internet: www.newarkairmuseum.co.uk. Dir.: H.F. Heey
Science&Tech Museum
Aircraft, instruments, avionics, memorabilia, uniforms 40021

Newark Museum, Appleton Gate, Newark-on-Trent NG24 1JY - T: (01636) 655740, Fax: 655745, E-mail: museums@newark-sherwooddc.gov.uk, Internet: www.newark-sherwooddc.gov.uk. Dir.: M.J. Hall
Local Museum - 1912
Archaeology, social hist, art, natural science, photogr, coins, documents 40022

Newark Town Treasures and Art Gallery, Market Pl, Newark-on-Trent NG24 1DU - T: (01636) 680333, Fax: 680350, E-mail: post@newark.gov.uk, Internet: www.newarktowntreasures.co.uk. Cur.: Patty Temple
Historical Museum / Fine Arts Museum
Civic plate, insignia, regalia, gifts and fine art 40023

Saint Mary Magdalene Treasury, Parish Church, Newark-on-Trent - T: (01636) 706473
Religious Arts Museum 40024

The Time Museum, Upton Hall, Upton, Newark-on-Trent NG23 5TE - T: (01636) 813795/96, Fax: 812258, E-mail: clocks@bhi.co.uk, Internet: www.bhi.co.uk. Man.: M. Taylor
Special Museum - 1858 40025

Vina Cooke Museum of Dolls and Bygone Childhood, Old Rectory, Cromwell, Newark-on-Trent NG23 6JE - T: (01636) 821364. Dir.: Vina Cooke
Special Museum - 1984
Dolls, costume, general items associated with childhood 40026

Newburgh

Laing Museum, High St, Newburgh KY14 6DX - T: (01337) 883017, Fax: (01334) 413214, E-mail: museums.east@fife.gov.uk. Cur.: Lin Collins
Local Museum 40027

Newburn

Newburn Hall Motor Museum, 35 Townfield Gardens, Newburn NE15 8PY - T: (0191) 2642977. Dir.: D.M. Porrelli
Science&Tech Museum
Cars and motorcycles, model cars 40028

Newbury

British Balloon Museum, c/o West Berkshire Museum, The Wharf, Newbury RG14 5AS - T: (01635) 30511, E-mail: tjthafb@aol.com, Internet: www.britishballoonmuseum.or.uk. Cur.: John Baker
Special Museum / Science&Tech Museum
Cloud-hopper balloon, two baskets, model of hot air burner built 1904, balloon envelopes, baskets and related items - library 40029

West Berkshire Museum, The Wharf, Newbury RG14 5AS - T: (01635) 30511, Fax: 38535, E-mail: heritage@westberks.gov.uk, Internet: www.westberks.gov.uk. Cur.: A. Loaring, P. Cannon
Local Museum - 1904
Archaeology, medieval hist, natural hist, Bronze Age objects, local pottery, costume, pewter, local and social hist 40030

Newcastle-under-Lyme

Borough Museum and Art Gallery, Brampton Park, Newcastle-under-Lyme ST5 0QP - T: (01782) 619705, Fax: 626857, E-mail: nulmuseum@newcastle-staffs.gov.uk, Internet: www.newcastle-staffs.gov.uk. Dir.: Delyth Enticott
Local Museum / Decorative Arts Museum / Fine Arts Museum / Public Gallery - 1943
Staffordshire pottery, weapons, clocks, toys, local and civic hist, English paintings from 18th c to present 40031

Newcastle-upon-Tyne

A Soldier's Life, Regimental Museum of the 15th/19th The King's Royal Hussars and Northumberland Hussars and Light Dragoons, Blandford Sq, Newcastle-upon-Tyne NE1 4JA - T: (0191) 2326789, 2772262, Fax: 2302614, E-mail: ralph.thompson@twmuseums.org.uk. Cur.: A. Wilson
Military Museum 40032

Bessie Surtees House, 41-44 Sandhill, Newcastle-upon-Tyne NE1 3JF - T: (0191) 2691200, Fax: 2611130, Internet: www.english-heritage.org.uk
Archaeological Museum
Archaeological artefacts and furnishings 40033

Castle Keep Museum, Castle Garth, Newcastle-upon-Tyne NE1 1RQ - T: (0191) 2327938
Local Museum 40034

Discovery Museum, Blandford House, Blandford Sq, Newcastle-upon-Tyne NE1 4JA - T: (0191) 2326789, Fax: 2302614, E-mail: discovery@twmuseums.org.uk, Internet: www.twmuseums.org.uk. Dir.: Alec Coles
Special Museum / Local Museum
Local history, science and technology, fashion and textiles, maritime history 40035

Hancock Museum, Barras Bridge, Newcastle-upon-Tyne NE2 4PT - T: (0191) 2226765, Fax: 2226753, E-mail: hancock.museum@ncl.ac.uk, Internet: www.twmuseums.org.uk/hancock. Dir.: Iain Watson, Cur.: Steve McLean (Geology), Keeper: L. Jessop (Biology), Asst. Keeper: E. Morton (Biology), Sylvia Humphrey (Geology), Sc. Staff: G. Mason (Education)
Natural History Museum / University Museum - 1829
Natural hist, mounted birds, Hutton fossilised plants, Hancock and Atthey fossilised vertebrates, N.J. Winch herbarium 40036

Hatton Gallery, c/o University of Newcastle, The Quadrangle, Newcastle-upon-Tyne NE1 7RU - T: (0191) 2226057, Fax: 2226057, E-mail: hatton-gallery@ncl.ac.uk, Internet: www.ncl.ac.uk/hatton. Cur.: Lucy Whetstone
Fine Arts Museum / University Museum - 1926
14th-18th c European paintings, 16th-18th c Italian art, contemporary English drawings, Uhlman coll of African sculpture, Kurt Schwitters' Elterwater 'Merzbau' 40037

Laing Art Gallery, New Bridge St, Newcastle-upon-Tyne NE1 8AG - T: (0191) 2327734, Fax: 2220952, E-mail: julie.milne@tyne-wear-museums.org.uk. Dir.: Alec Coles, Cur.: Julie Milne, Sc. Staff: Sarah Richardson, Asst.: Natalie Frost (Exhibition), Ruth Trotter (Fine and Decorative Art), Julie Watson (Education)
Fine Arts Museum / Decorative Arts Museum - 1904
British paintings and water colours, pottery, porcelain, silver, glass and pewter 40038

Military Vehicle Museum, Exhibition Park Pavilion, Newcastle-upon-Tyne NE2 4PZ - T: (0191) 2817222, Fax: (01962) 73544, E-mail: miltmuseum@aol.com, Internet: www.military-museum.org.uk
Military Museum
Military vehicles and artefakt since 1900, soldiers life 40039

Museum of Antiquities, c/o University of Newcastle-upon-Tyne, The Quadrangle, Newcastle-upon-Tyne NE1 7RU - T: (0191) 2227846/9, Fax: 2228561, E-mail: m.o.antiquities@ncl.ac.uk, Internet: www.ncl.ac.uk/antiquities. Dir.: L. Allason-Jones
Archaeological Museum / University Museum - 1813
Roman inscriptions, sculptures, small finds, prehistoric and Anglo Saxon, antiquities from north Britain (from Paleolithic period to Tudors and Stuarts) - library 40040

Shefton Museum of Greek Art and Archaeology, c/o University of Newcastle, Dept. of Classics, Armstrong Bldg, Newcastle-upon-Tyne NE1 7RU - T: (0191) 2228996, Fax: 2228561, E-mail: m.o.antiquities@ncl.ac.uk, Internet: www.ncl.ac.uk/shefton-museum. Dir.: L. Allason-Jones
Fine Arts Museum / Archaeological Museum / University Museum - 1956
Classical art and archaeology, Corinthian bronze helmet, Apulian helmet, 6th c Laconian handles, Greek bronze hand mirrors, 7th c B.C. Etruscan bucchero, Pelike by Pan Painter, Italic late archaic carved amber, Tarantine and Sicilian terra cotta 40041

Trinity House, 29 Broad Chare, Quayside, Newcastle-upon-Tyne NE1 3DQ - T: (0191) 2328226, Fax: 2328448, E-mail: ncl_trinityhouse@hotmail.com
Science&Tech Museum 40042

The University Gallery, c/o University of Northumbria, Sandyford Rd, Newcastle-upon-Tyne NE1 8ST - T: (0191) 2274424, Fax: 2274718, E-mail: mara-helen.wood@unn.ac.uk, Internet: www.northumbria.ac.uk/universitygallery. Dir.: Mara-Helen Wood
Public Gallery
1977 40043

Newent

Shambles Museum, 16-24 Church St, Newent GL18 1PP - T: (01531) 822144, Fax: 821120. Dir.: H. Chapman
Historical Museum
Complete Victorian town layout with shops, houses, gardens 40044

Newhaven

Local and Maritime Museum, Paradise Leisure Park, Avis Rd, Newhaven BN9 9EE - T: (01273) 612530. Pres.: Lord Greenway, Hon. Cur.: Robert Bailey
Local Museum / Science&Tech Museum 40045

Newhaven Fort, Fort Rd, Newhaven BN9 9DL - T: (01273) 517622, Fax: 512059, E-mail: info@newhavenfort.org.uk, Internet: www.newhavenfort.org.uk
Military Museum 40046

Planet Earth Museum, Paradise Park, Avis Rd, Newhaven BN9 0DH - T: (01273) 512123, Fax: 616005, E-mail: enquiries@paradisepark.co.uk, Internet: www.paradisepark.co.uk
Natural History Museum
Fossils, minerals and crystals from around the world 40047

Newlyn

Pilchard Works, Tolcarne, Newlyn TR18 5QH - T: (01736) 332112, Fax: 332442, E-mail: nick@pilchardworks.co.uk, Internet: www.pilchardworks.co.uk. Dir.: N. Howell
Science&Tech Museum 40048

Newmarket

BSAT Gallery, British Sporting Art Trust, 99 High St, Newmarket CB8 8JL - T: (01264) 710344, Fax: 710114, E-mail: BSATrust@aol.comom, Internet: www.bsat.co.uk
Fine Arts Museum 40049

National Horseracing Museum, 99 High St, Newmarket CB8 8JL - T: (01638) 667333, Fax: 665600, Internet: www.nhrm.co.uk. Dir.: H. Bracegirdle
Special Museum - 1983
Archive, Hands on gallery 40050

Newport, Gwent

Museum and Art Gallery, John Frost Sq, Newport, Gwent NP20 1PA - T: (01633) 840064, Fax: 222615, E-mail: museum@newport.gov.uk. Sc. Staff: Robert Trett (Collections and Archaeology), Bruce Campbell (Collections and Natural Science)
Local Museum / Decorative Arts Museum / Fine Arts Museum - 1888
Local archaeology, Roman caerwent, natural sciences, geology, zoology, local history, social & industrial, art, 18th & 19th British watercolours, 20th c British oil paintings, ceramics including teapots 40051

Tredegar House and Park, Coedkernew, Newport, Gwent NP10 8YW - T: (01633) 815880, Fax: 815895, E-mail: tredegar.house@newport.gov.uk
Archaeological Museum 40052

Newport, Isle of Wight

Carisbrooke Castle Museum, Carisbrooke Castle, Newport, Isle of Wight PO30 1XY - T: (01983) 523112, E-mail: carismus@lineone.net, Internet: www.carisbrookecastlemuseum.org.uk. Dir.: Rosemary Cooper
Historical Museum - 1898
Isle of Wight hist, material associated with Charles I and the Civil War, objects owned by Alfred Lord Tennyson 40053

Cothey Bottom Heritage Centre, Guildhall, High St, Newport, Isle of Wight PO30 1TY - T: (01983) 823822, Fax: 823841, E-mail: mike.bishop@iow.gov.uk. Dir.: Dr. Michael Bishop
Local Museum 40054

Museum of Island History, The Guildhall, High St, Newport, Isle of Wight PO30 1TY - T: (01983) 823366, Fax: 823841, E-mail: tony.butler@iow.gov.uk. Dir.: Michael Bishop, Cur.: Tony Butler
Local Museum
Archaeology, geology, palaeontology, social history and fine art 40055

Newport Roman Villa, Cypress Rd, Newport, Isle of Wight PO30 1HE - T: (01983) 529720, Fax: 823841, E-mail: rachel.silverson@iow.gov.uk. Dir.: Dr. Mike Bishop
Archaeological Museum / Historic Site - 1963
Roman finds, villa ruins, mosaics 40056

Newport Pagnell

Beatty Museum (open only at certain times of the year), Chicheley Hall, Newport Pagnell MK16 9JJ - T: (01234) 391252, Fax: 391388, E-mail: enquiries@chicheleyhall.co.uk, Internet: www.chicheleyhall.co.uk
Military Museum
Memorabilia and photographs of Admiral Beatty 40057

Newport Pagnell Historical Society Museum, Chandos Hall, Silver St, Newport Pagnell MK16 8ET - T: (01908) 610852/53
Local Museum
Archaeological, domestic and trade artefacts 40058

Newquay

Lappa Valley Steam Railway, Saint Newlyn East, Newquay TR8 5HZ - T: (01872) 510317, E-mail: steam@lappa.freeserve.co.uk, Internet: www.lappa-railway.co.uk. Owner: Amanda Booth
Science&Tech Museum 40059

Trerice, Kestle Mill, Newquay TR8 4PG - T: (01637) 875404
Local Museum 40060

Newry

Newry and Mourne Arts Centre and Museum, 1a Bank Parade, Newry BT35 6HP - T: (028) 30266232, Fax: 30266839, E-mail: noreen.cunningham@newryandmourne.gov.uk, Internet: www.newryandmourne.gov.uk. Dir.: Mark Hughes, Cur.: Noreen Cunningham
Public Gallery / Local Museum 40061

Newry Museum, 1a Bank Parade, Newry BT35 6HP - T: (01693) 66232, Fax: 66839. Cur.: Noreen Cunningham
Local Museum 40062

Newton Abbot

Newton Abbot Town and Great Western Railway Museum, 2a Saint Paul's Rd, Newton Abbot TQ12 2HP - T: (01626) 201121, Fax: 201119, E-mail: museum@newtonabbot-tc.gov.uk, Internet: www.newtonabbot-tc.gov.uk. Cur.: Felicity Cole
Local Museum / Science&Tech Museum
Local social history, Aller Vale Art pottery coll, Mapleton Butterfly Coll, signal box, railway memorabilia 40063

Newton Aycliffe

Aycliffe and District Bus Preservation Society, 110 Fewston Close, Newton Aycliffe DL5 7HF. Chm.: John Gibson
Science&Tech Museum
Vintage united automobile services vehicles, Darlington Corporation busses 40064

Newton Stewart

The Museum, York Rd, Newton Stewart DG8 6HH - T: (01671) 402472, E-mail: jmclay@argonet.co.uk. Dir.: D. Ferries
Local Museum - 1978 40065

Newtongrange

Scottish Mining Museum, Lady Victoria Colliery, Newtongrange EH22 4QN - T: (0131) 6637519, Fax: 6541618, E-mail: enquiries@scottishminingmuseum.org, Internet: www.scottishminingmuseum.com. Dir.: F. Waters
Science&Tech Museum
Machinery and artefacts relating to 900 yrs of Scottish coal mining, historic 'A-listed' Victorian colliery - Library 40066

Newtonmore

Clan Macpherson House and Museum, Main St, Newtonmore PH20 1DE - T: (01540) 673332, Fax: 673332, E-mail: macphersonmuseum@btopenworld.com, Internet: www.clan-macpherson.org. Cur.: O. Ormiston
Special Museum
Family hist, relicts associated with Prince Charles Edward Stuart (Bonnie Prince Charlie) 40067

Highland Folk Museum, Aultlarie Croft, Newtonmore PH20 1AY - T: (01540) 661307, Fax: 661631, E-mail: highland.folk@highland.gov.uk, Internet: www.highlandfolk.com. Cur.: R. Ross Noble
Open Air Museum - 1934
Working farm, historic buildings 40068

Newtown, Powys

Newtown Textile Museum, 5-7 Commercial St, Newtown, Powys SY16 2BL, mail addr: c/o Powysland Museum, Canal Wharf, Welshpool SY21 7AQ - T: (01938) 554656, Fax: 554656, E-mail: powysland@powys.gov.uk, Internet: powysmuseums.powys.gov.uk. Dir.: Eva B. Bredsdorff
Special Museum - 1964
Crafts, Newtown woollen industry 1790-1910 40069

Oriel Davies Gallery, The Park, Newtown, Powys SY16 2NZ - T: (01686) 625041, Fax: 623633, E-mail: enquiries@orieldavies.org, Internet: www.orieldavies.org. Dir.: Amanda Farr
Public Gallery - 1985 40070

Robert Owen Memorial Museum, Broad St, Newtown, Powys SY16 2BB - T: (01686) 626345, E-mail: johnd@robert-owen.midwales.com, Internet: www.robert-owen.midwales.com. Dir.: John H. Davidson
Special Museum - 1929
Life of socialist Robert Owen (1771-1858) 40071

W.H. Smith Museum, c/o W.H. Smith & Son Ltd., 24 High St, Newtown, Powys SY16 2NP - T: (01686) 626280. Dir.: H. Hyde
Historical Museum
Original oak shop front, tiling and mirrors, plaster relief decoration, models, photographs and a variety of historical momentoes, history of W.H. Smith from its beginning in 1792 until the present day 40072

Newtownards

Ards Art Centre, Town Hall, Conway Sq, Newtownards BT23 4DB - T: (028) 91810803, Fax: 91823131, E-mail: arts@ards-council.gov.uk. Dir.: Eilis O'Baoill
Public Gallery 40073

Mount Stewart House, Greyabbey, Newtownards, Co. Down - T: (012477) 88387
Historical Museum
Home of Lord Castlereagh, statues, plants, furniture - Temple of the Winds, garden 40074

Somme Heritage Centre, 233 Bangor Rd, Newtownards BT23 7PH - T: (028) 91823202, Fax: 91823214, E-mail: sommeassociation@dnet.co.uk, Internet: www.irishsoldier.org. Manager: Carol Walker
Military Museum
WW I through 10th and 16th (Irish) Divisions and 36th (Ulster) Division, Battle of the Somme, uniforms and artefacts 40075

Newtownbutler

Crom Estate, Newtownbutler, Co. Fermanagh - T: (0139657) 38118
Historical Museum / Archaeological Museum
History, archaeology 40076

North Berwick

Museum of Flight, National Museums of Scotland, East Fortune Airfield, North Berwick EH39 5LF - T: (01620) 880308, Fax: 880355, E-mail: museum_of_flight@sol.co.uk, Internet: www.nms.ac.uk/flight
Science&Tech Museum - 1971
Aircrafts on a WW II airfield 40077

North Berwick Museum, School Rd, North Berwick EH39 4JU - T: (01620) 895457, Fax: 828201, E-mail: elms@northberwickmuseum.org, Internet: www.northberwickmuseum.org. Head: Peter Gray
Local Museum - 1957
Local and domestic hist, natural hist, archaeology, hist of the Royal Burgh of North Berwick 40078

North Leverton

North Leverton Windmill, West View, Sturton Rd, North Leverton DN22 0AB - T: (01427) 880662, 880573. Man.: Keith Barlow
Science&Tech Museum
Coll of stationary barn engines 40079

North Shields

Stephenson Railway Museum, Middle Engine Lane, West Chirton, North Shields NE29 8DX - T: (0191) 2007145, Fax: 2007144, E-mail: sharon.grenville@tyne-wear-museums.org.uk, Internet: www.twmuseums.org.uk. Cur.: Sharon Granville
Science&Tech Museum 40080

Northampton

Abington Museum, Abington Park, Northampton NN1 5LW - T: (01604) 631454, Fax: 238720, E-mail: museums@northampton.gov.uk, Internet: www.northampton.gov.uk/museums. Dir.: Peter Field
Local Museum
Local history 40081

Museum of the Northamptonshire Regiment, Abington Park, Northampton NN1 5LW - T: (01604) 631454, Fax: 238720, E-mail: museums@northamton.gov.uk, Internet: www.northampton.gov.uk/museums. Dir.: Peter Field
Military Museum
Military coll 40082

National Fairground Museum, Riverside Park, Northampton
Local Museum
Photographs, works drawings and social history 40083

Northampton Museum and Art Gallery, Guildhall Rd, Northampton NN1 1DP - T: (01604) 838111, Fax: 838720, E-mail: museums@northampton.gov.uk, Internet: www.northampton.gov.uk/museums. Dir.: Peter Field, Sc. Dir.: W. Brown (Information, Resources), S. Constable (Shoe Heritage), A. Cowling (Art, Exhibitions), J. Minchinton (Records, Resoures), S. Pevereit (Senior Community Heritage, Education), K. Grünzweil (Community History)
Local Museum / Fine Arts Museum - 1865
Northampton archaeology, geology, natural history, ethnography, Italian and modern English paintings, decorative arts, boots and shoes, leathercraft 40084

Northleach

Cotswold Heritage Centre, Fosseway, Northleach GL54 3JH - T: (01451) 860715, Fax: 860091, E-mail: john.poddock@cotswold.gov.uk, Internet: www.cotswold.co.uk. Dir.: Dr. John Paddock
Agriculture Museum - 1981
Agricultural hist, horse-drawn, implements and tools, Lloyd Baker coll of farm waggons 40085

Keith Harding's World of Mechanical Music, Oak House, High St, Northleach GL54 3ET - T: (01451) 860181, Fax: 861133, E-mail: keith@mechanicalmusic.co.uk, Internet: www.mechanicalmusic.co.uk. Dir.: Keith Harding
Music Museum - 1977
Self-playing musical instruments, clocks - restoration workshops 40086

Northwich

Lion Salt Works, Ollershaw Ln, Marston, Northwich CW9 6ES - T: (01606) 41823, Fax: 41823, E-mail: afielding@lionsalt.demon.co.uk, Internet: www.lionsaltworkstrust.co.uk. Dir.: Andrew Fielding
Science&Tech Museum 40087

Salt Museum, 162 London Rd, Northwich CW9 8AB - T: (01606) 41331, Fax: 350420, E-mail: cheshiremuseums@cheshire.gov.uk, Internet: www.cheshire.gov.uk/saltmuseum. Cur.: Stephen Penney
Special Museum
Salt making in Cheshire 40088

Norwich

Blickling Hall, Buckling, Norwich NR11 6NF - T: (01263) 738030, Fax: 731660, E-mail: abgusr@smtp.ntrust.org.uk, Internet: www.nationaltrust.org.uk. Man.: Peter Griffiths
Local Museum
Jacobian architecture, plaster ceilings, tapestries, furniture, pictures 40089

Bridewell Museum, Bridewell Alley, Norwich NR2 1AQ - T: (01603) 629127, E-mail: museums@norfolk.gov.uk, Internet: www.museums.norfolk.gov.uk. Cur.: John Renton
Historical Museum - 1925
Textiles, shoes, timepieces, printing, brewing and iron founding, pharmacy, manufacturing industries 40090

Castle Museum, Castle, Norwich NR1 3JU - T: (01603) 493625, Fax: 765651, Internet: www.ecn.co.uk/norfolkcc/tourism/museums/museums.htm. Dir.: Vanessa Travelyan
Decorative Arts Museum / Fine Arts Museum - 1894
Fine and applied arts, archaeology, geology, natural hist, social hist, Norwich paintings, porcelain, silver, coins 40091

East Anglian Film Archive, University of East Anglia, Centre of East Anglian Studies, Norwich NR4 7TJ - T: (01603) 592664, Fax: 458553, E-mail: EAFA@uea.ac.uk, Internet: www.uea.ac.uk/eafa. Dir.: David Cleveland
Performing Arts Museum
Film and videotape of East Anglian life (official regional film archive for the counties of Bedfordshire, Cambridgeshire, Essex, Hertfordshire, Norfolk and Suffolk) plus museum of film-making and projection equipment 40092

Felbrigg Hall, Roughton, Norwich NR11 8PR - T: (01263) 837444, Fax: 837032, E-mail: afgusr@smtp.ntrust.org.uk
Decorative Arts Museum
Historic country house with complete furnishings and fittings 40093

Inspire - Hands-on Science Centre, Saint Michael's Church, Coslany St, Norwich NR3 3DT - T: (01603) 612612, Fax: 616721, E-mail: inspire@science-project.org, Internet: www.science-project.org. Dir.: Ian Simmons
Science&Tech Museum 40094

John Jarrold Printing Museum, Whitefriars, Norwich NR3 1SH - T: (01603) 660211, Fax: 630162
Science&Tech Museum - 1982 40095

Mustard Shop Museum, 15 Royal Arcade, Norwich NR2 1NQ - T: (01603) 627889, Fax: 762142, Internet: www.mustardshop.com. Dir.: Avril Houseago
Special Museum - 1973
Colman's mustard manufaturing history 40096

Norwich Gallery, c/o Norwich School of Art and Design, Saint George St, Norwich NR3 1BB - T: (01603) 610561, Fax: 615728, E-mail: info@norwichgallery.co.uk, Internet: www.norwichgallery.co.uk. Cur.: Lynda Morris
University Museum / Public Gallery 40097

Royal Air Force Air Defence Radar Museum, RAF Neatishead, Norwich NR12 8YB - T: (01692) 633309, Fax: 633214, Internet: www.neatishead.raf.mod.uk. Man.: Doug Robb
Science&Tech Museum / Military Museum
History of radar and air defence since 1935, radar engineering, military communications systems, Cold War operations room, Royal Observer Corps rooms, ballistic missile and space defence, Bloodhound missile systems, radar vehicles 40098

Royal Norfolk Regimental Museum, Shirehall, Market Av, Norwich NR1 3JQ - T: (01603) 493649, Fax: 765651. Cur.: Kate Thaxton
Military Museum - 1933
Hist of regiment, medals, uniforms, hist of British Army 40099

Sainsbury Centre for Visual Arts, c/o University of East Anglia, Norwich NR4 7TJ - T: (01603) 593199, Fax: 259401, E-mail: scva@uea.ac.uk, Internet: www.uea.ac.uk/scva. Dir.: Nichola Johnson
Fine Arts Museum / Association with Coll / University Museum - 1978
Robert and Lisa Sainsbury coll, Anderson coll of Art Nouveau, coll of abstract/constructivist art and Design 40100

Saint Peter Hungate Church Museum, Princes St, Norwich NR3 1AE - T: (01603) 667231, Fax: 493623
Religious Arts Museum - 1936
In 15th c church, hist of parish life, illuminated manuscripts, church musical instruments 40101

Strangers Hall Museum of Domestic Life, Charing Cross, Norwich NR2 4AL - T: (01603) 667229, Fax: 765651, E-mail: museum@norfolk.gov.uk, Internet: www.norfolk.gov.uk/tourism/museums. Dir.: Vanessa Trevelyan, Cur.: H.E. Rowles
Decorative Arts Museum - 1922
House with parts dating from 14th c, period rooms, toys, transportation, tapestries 40102

Nottingham

Angel Row Gallery, Central Library Bldg, 3 Angel Row, Nottingham NG1 6HP - T: (0115) 9152869, Fax: 9152860, E-mail: angelrow.info@nottighamcity.gov.uk, Internet: www.angelowgallery.com. Man.: Deborah Dean
Public Gallery
Temporary exhibitions 40103

Brewhouse Yard Museum, Castle Blvd, Nottingham NG7 1FB - T: (0115) 9153600, 9153640, Fax: 9153601, E-mail: bhyoffice@notmusghy.demon.co.uk, Internet: www.nottinghamcity.gov.uk. Dir.: Michael Williams, Asst. Dir.: Brian Ashley, Cur.: Suella Postles
Local Museum - 1977
Daily life material in Nottingham, local working, domestic, community, personal life from 1750 to present 40104

Djanogly Art Gallery, c/o Arts Centre, University of Nottingham, University Park, Nottingham NG7 2RD - T: (0115) 9513192, Fax: 9513194, E-mail: neil.bennison@nottingham.ac.uk, Internet: www.nottingham.ac.uk/artscentre. Dir.: Joanne Wright, Sc. Staff: Neil Walker (Exhibitions)
Fine Arts Museum / University Museum - 1956
Duke of Newcastle coll: a bequest of family portraits from the 17th to 19th c, Glen Bott Bequest: a coll of watercolours and drawings of the British School (19th-20th c) 40105

Galleries of Justice, Shire Hall, High Pavement, Lace Market, Nottingham NG1 1HN - T: (0115) 9520555, Fax: 9939828, E-mail: info@galleriesofjustice.org.uk, Internet: www.galleriesofjustice.org.uk. Cur.: Louise Connell
Historical Museum
Gaol, court rooms and 1905 police station, crime and punishment, prisons 40106

Green's Mill and Science Centre, Windmill Ln, Sneinton, Nottingham NG2 4QB - T: (0115) 9156878, Fax: 9156875, E-mail: enquiries@greenmill.org.uk, Internet: www.greensmill.org.uk. Man.: Jo Kemp
Science&Tech Museum - 1985
Mathematics, physics, mills and milling, science 40107

Industrial Museum, Courtyard Bldgs, Wollaton Park, Nottingham NG8 2AE - T: (0115) 9153910, Fax: 9153941, Internet: www.nottinghamcity.gov.uk/museums. Dir.: Michael Williams
Science&Tech Museum - 1971
Lace machinery, bicycles, telecommunications, steam engines 40108

Museum of Costume and Textiles, 51 Castle Gate, Nottingham NG1 6AF - T: (0115) 9153500, Fax: 9153599
Special Museum
Dresses, laces, textiles 40109

Museum of Nottingham Lace, 3-5 High Pavement, Nottingham NG1 1HF - T: (0115) 9897365, Fax: 9897301, E-mail: info@nottinghamlace.org, Internet: www.nottinghamlace.org. Dir.: V. Hatcher
Special Museum - 1980
Complete history of Nottingham lace 40110

Natural History Museum, Wollaton Hall, Nottingham NG8 2AE - T: (0115) 9153900, Fax: 9153932, E-mail: wollaton@ncmg.demon.co.uk. Sc. Staff: G.P. Walley (Team Leader Natural Sciences), Keeper: Dr. S. Wright (Biology), C.D. Paul (Biology), N.S. Turner (Geology)
Natural History Museum - 1867
Mounted British and foreign birds, birds eggs, herbaria, European Diptera, lepidoptera, British aculeates, British beetles, mounted African big game heads, paleontology, fossils, Nottinghamshire plant and animal coll - library, Nottinghamshire Enironmental Archive, City Wildlife Database 40111

Nottingham Castle, off Friar Ln, Nottingham NG1 6EL - T: (0115) 9153700, Fax: 9153653, E-mail: castle@ncmg.demon.co.uk. Dir.: Michael Williams, Asst. Dir.: Brian Ashley
Decorative Arts Museum / Fine Arts Museum - 1878
Fine and applied arts, archaeology, militaria, medieval alabaster, English glass and silver, ceramics 40112

Nottingham University Museum, University Park, Nottingham NG7 2RD - T: (0115) 9514820, 9514813, Fax: 9514812, E-mail: roger.wilson@nottingham.ac.uk. Dir.: Prof. R.J.A. Wilson
University Museum / Archaeological Museum
Prehistoric, Roman and medieval artefacts from Eastern England, Bronze Age and Greek Mediterranean ceramics 40113

Regimental Museum of the Sherwood Foresters, Castle, Nottingham NG1 6EL - T: (0115) 9465415, Fax: 9469853, E-mail: rhqwfr-nottm@lineone.net, Internet: www.wfrmuseum.org.uk. Cur.: I. O. M. Hackett
Military Museum - 1964
History of Worcestershire and Sherwood Foresters Regiment since 1741, armaments, medals, uniforms 40114

William Booth Birthplace Museum, 14 Notintone Pl, Sneiton, Nottingham NG2 4QG - T: (0115) 9503927, Fax: 9598604, E-mail: djepson@salvationarmy.ndo.co.uk. Dir.: D. Jepson
Special Museum 40115

Yard Gallery, Wollaton Park, Nottingham NG8 2AE - T: (0115) 9153920, Fax: 9153932
Public Gallery 40116

Nuneaton

George Eliot Hospital Museum, College St, Nuneaton CV10 7JD - T: (024) 763511351, E-mail: ann.cahill@geh.tr-wmids.nhs.uk. Cur.: Ann Cahill
Special Museum
Coll of medical equipment, photographs and archival documents 40117

Museum and Art Gallery, Riversley Park, Nuneaton CV11 5TU - T: (024) 76350720, Fax: 76343559, E-mail: museum@nuneaton-bedworthbc.gov.uk, Internet: www.nuneatonandbedworth.gov.uk
Local Museum - 1917
Roman to late-medieval archaeology, ethnography, George Eliot Coll, Baffin Land Inuit material, miniatures, oil painting and watercolours 40118

Nunnington

Carlisle Collection of Miniature Rooms, Nunnington Hall, Attic Rm, Nunnington YO62 5UY - T: (01439) 748283, Fax: 748284, E-mail: nunningtonhall@ntrust.org.uk
Special Museum - 1981 40119

Oakham

Normanton Church Museum, Rutland Water, Oakham LE15 8PX - T: (01572) 653026/27, Fax: 653027
Local Museum - 1985
Fossils, Anglo Saxon artefacts 40120

Oakham Castle, Rutland County Museum, Market Pl, Oakham LE15 6HW - T: (01572) 758440, Fax: 758445, E-mail: museum@rutland.gov.uk, Internet: www.rutnet.co.uk/rcc/rutlandmuseums. Dir.: Simon Davies
Historical Museum
12th c Great Hall of Norman Castle, coll of horseshoes 40121

Rutland County Museum, Catmose St, Oakham LE15 6HW - T: (01572) 758440, Fax: 758445, E-mail: museum@rutland.gov.uk, Internet: www.rutnet.co.uk/rcc/rutlandmuseums. Dir.: Simon Davies
Local Museum - 1967
Local history and archaeology, Anglo-Saxon and other finds, farm tools, rural trades 40122

Oban

McCaig Museum (closed) 40123

War and Peace Exhibition, North Pier, Oban PA34 - T: (01631) 563977, 563452. Dir.: Ronald MacIntyre
Historical Museum / Military Museum 40124

Okehampton

Finch Foundry Working Museum, Sticklepath, Okehampton EX20 2NW - T: (01837) 840046, Fax: 840046. Dir.: Matthew Applegate
Science&Tech Museum - 1966
Working water powered tilt hammers 40125

Museum of Dartmoor Life, 3 West St, Okehampton EX20 1HQ - T: (01837) 52295, Fax: 52295, E-mail: dartmoormuseum@eclipse.co.uk, Internet: www.museumofdartmoorlife.eclipse.co.uk. Cur.: Maurie Webber
Folklore Museum 40126

Museum of Waterpower → Finch Foundry Working Museum

Old Warden

Shuttleworth Collection, Aerodrome, Old Warden SG18 9EP - T: (01767) 627288, Fax: 627053, E-mail: enquiries@shuttleworth.org, Internet: www.shuttleworth.org
Science&Tech Museum
Classic grass aerodrome, historic aeroplanes, aviation from a 1909 Bleriot XI to a 1942 Spitfire, veteran and vintage cars, motorcycles and horse-drawn carriages 40127

Oldham

Gallery Oldham, Greaves St, Oldham OL1 1AL - T: (0161) 9114657, Fax: 9114669, E-mail: ecs.galleryoldham@oldham.gov.uk, Internet: www.oldham.gov.uk. Dir.: Sheena MacFarlane
Fine Arts Museum / Local Museum - 1883/2002
Social, industrial and natural history of the region, 19th-20th c British paintings and sculpture, English watercolors, glass, Oriental art objects 40128

Oldland

Artemis Archery Collection, 29 Batley Court, Oldland BS30 8YZ - T: (0117) 9323276, Fax: 9323276. Dir.: H.D. Hewitt
Special Museum
British longbows and arrows (since 18th c), related artifacts and ephemera - research library 40129

Olney

Cowper and Newton Museum, Orchardside, Market Pl, Olney MK46 4AJ - T: (01234) 711516, Fax: (0870) 1640662, E-mail: museum@onley.co.uk, Internet: www.cowperandnewtonmuseum.org. Cust.: Joan McKillop
Special Museum - 1900
Memorabilia of writer William Cowper (1731-1800), memorabilia of the hymn writer, antislave campaigner and ev. preacher Reverend John Newton (1725-1807), lace industry 40130

Omagh

Ulster-American Folk Park, Museums and Galleries of Northern Irland, 2 Mellon Rd, Castle Town, Omagh BT78 5QY - T: (028) 82243292, Fax: 82242241, E-mail: uafp@iol.ie, Internet: www.folkpark.com. Dir.: J.A. Gilmour, Cur.: Dr. P. Mowat, P. O'Donnell, L. Corry, Sc. Staff: J. Bradley, E. Cardwell (Education), A.C. O'Rawe (Education)
Open Air Museum / Folklore Museum / Historical Museum - 1976
Series of buildings representing life in Ulster and North America in the 18th and 19th c, exhibitions on emigration and the Atlantic crossing, ship and dockside gallery, a reconstruction of an early 19th c sailing brig - library 40131

Ulster History Park, Cullion, Omagh BT79 7SU - T: (028) 81648188, Fax: 81648011, E-mail: uhp@omagh.gov.uk, Internet: www.historypark.org. Man.: Anthony Candon
Historical Museum
Models of homes and monuments (17th c) 40132

Onchan

Groudle Glen Railway, Groudle Glen, Onchan, mail addr: 29 Hawarden Av, Douglas IM1 4BP - T: (01624) 670453, E-mail: tbear@manx.net
Science&Tech Museum
Narrow gauge steam railway, steam loco Sea Lion, built in 1896 40133

Orpington

Crofton Roman Villa, Crofton Rd, Orpington BR6 8AD - T: (020) 84624737, E-mail: bromley.museum@bromley.gov.uk, Internet: www.bromley.gov.uk. Man.: Brian Philp
Archaeological Museum 40134

London Borough of Bromley Museum, The Priory, Church Hill, Orpington BR6 0HH - T: (01689) 873826, E-mail: bromley.museum@bromley.gov.uk, Internet: www.bromley.gov.uk/museums. Cur.: Dr. Alan Tyler
Local Museum - 1965
Avebury coll 40135

Ospringe

Maison Dieu, Water Ln, Ospringe ME13 9DW - T: (01795) 533751, Internet: www.english-heritage.org.uk. Cur.: Nick Moore
Historical Museum
Roman pottery and other finds from the local cemetry, finds from the medieval hospital 40136

Oswestry

Oswestry Transport Museum, Oswald Rd, Oswestry SY11 1RE - T: (01691) 671749, E-mail: hignetts@enterprise.net, Internet: www.cambrianline.co.uk
Science&Tech Museum
Railway, coll of 105 bicycles 40137

Otley

Otley Museum, Civic Centre, Cross Green, Otley LS21 1HP - T: (01943) 461052
Local Museum - 1962
Archives relating to the printing machine industry in Otley, large coll of flints from the region 40138

Oundle

Oundle Museum, The Courthouse, Mill Rd, Oundle PE8 4BW - T: (01832) 272741, 273871, Fax: 273871, E-mail: jim.irving@virgin.net
Local Museum 40139

Owermoigne

Mill House Cider Museum and Dorset Collection of Clocks, Owermoigne DT2 8HZ - T: (01305) 852220, Fax: 854760. Dir.: D.J. Whatmoor
Special Museum
Horology, cider mills and presses, long case and Turret clocks 40140

Oxford

Ashmolean Museum of Art and Archaeology, Oxford University, Beaumont St, Oxford OX1 2PH - T: (01865) 278000, Fax: 278018, Internet: www.ashmol.ox.ac.uk. Dir.: Dr. Christopher Brown, Chief Cons.: Mark Normann
Archaeological Museum / Fine Arts Museum / University Museum / Decorative Arts Museum / Historical Museum / Religious Arts Museum - 1683
Archaeology of Britain, Europe, the Mediterranean, Egypt, the Near East, Italian, French, Dutch, Flemish and English paintings, Old Master drawings, modern drawings, watercolours, prints, miniatures, European ceramics, sculpture, bronze and silver, engraved portraits, numismatics, Oriental art, Indian and Islamic arts and crafts 40141

Bate Collection of Historical Instruments, Faculty of Music, Saint Aldatés, Oxford OX1 1DB - T: (01865) 276139, Fax: 76128, E-mail: bate.collection@music.ox.ac.uk, Internet: www.ashmol.ox.ac.uk/bcmipage.html. Cur.: Dr. Hélèna LaRue
Music Museum / University Museum 40142

British Telecom Museum, 35 Speedwell St, Oxford OX1 1RH - T: (01865) 246601, Fax: 790428
Science&Tech Museum
Telephone and telegraph equipment illustrating the history and evolution of telecommunications, 150 telephones from Alexander Graham Bell's 'Gallows' telephone of 1875 to modern instruments 40143

Christ Church Cathedral Treasury, Christ Church, Oxford OX1 1DP - T: (01865) 201971, Fax: 276277, E-mail: edward.evans@christ-church.ox.ac.uk. Cur.: Edward Evans
Religious Arts Museum
Church plate 40144

Christ Church Picture Gallery, Christ Church, Canterbury Quadrangle, Oxford OX1 1DP - T: (01865) 202429, Fax: 202429, E-mail: picturegallery@chch.ox.ac.uk, Internet: www.chch.ox.ac.uk. Dir.: Jacqueline Thalmann (Pictures), Cur.: Dr. Ian Watson
Public Gallery - 1968
Old Master paintings and drawings 1300-1750 40145

The Crypt - Town Hall Plate Room, Town Hall, Saint Aldate's, Oxford OX1 1BX - T: (01865) 249811, Fax: 252388, E-mail: dclark@oxford.gov.uk, Internet: www.oxford.gov.uk

Decorative Arts Museum
Historic civic plate, large silver gilt mace, two Sear-geant's maces, gold porringer, cups and covers 40146

Modern Art Oxford, 30 Pembroke St, Oxford OX1 1BP - T: (01865) 722733, 813830, Fax: 722573, E-mail: info@modernartoxford.org.uk, Internet: www.modernartoxford.org.uk. Dir.: Andrew Nairne, Cur.: Suzanne Cotter, Press, PR: Rachel Tomkins, Admin. Head: Caroline Winnicott, Development: Kirsty Brackenridge
Fine Arts Museum - 1965
Temporary exhibitions 40147

Museum of Modern Art → Modern Art Oxford

Museum of Oxford, Saint Aldates, Oxford OX1 1DZ - T: (01865) 252761, 815539, Fax: 202447, E-mail: museum@oxford.gov.uk, Internet: www.oxford.gov.uk. Dir.: V. Collett, Cur.: Dr. John Lange
Local Museum - 1975
Objects relating to the hist of the city and University of Oxford 40148

Museum of the History of Science, c/o University of Oxford, Broad St, Oxford OX1 3AZ - T: (01865) 277280, Fax: 277288, E-mail: museum@mhs.ox. ac.uk, Internet: www.mhs.ox.ac.uk. Dir.: James A. Bennett, Asst. Cur.: Stephen Johnston, Photographer: Giles Hudson
Science&Tech Museum / University Museum - 1924
Historic scientific instruments (astrolabes, armillary spheres, sundials, clocks and watches, microscopes and telescopes, various apparatus) - library 40149

The Oxford Story, Broad St, Oxford OX1 3AJ - T: (01865) 728822, Fax: 791716, E-mail: oxfordstory@uk2.net, Internet: www. oxfordstory.co.uk
Historical Museum
Review of Oxford's past 40150

Oxford University Museum of Natural History, Park Rd, Oxford OX1 3PW - T: (01865) 272950, 272966, Fax: 272970, E-mail: info@oum.ac.uk, Internet: www.oum.ox.ac.uk. Dir.: Prof. K.S. Thomson, Cur.: Prof. W.J. Kennedy (Geology and Mineralogy), Dr. T.S. Kemp (Zoology), Prof. S.J. Simpson (Entomology)
University Museum / Natural History Museum - 1860
Entomology, geology, mineralogy, zoology 40151

Oxford University Press Museum, Walton St, Oxford OX2 6DP - T: (01865) 267527, Fax: 267908, E-mail: mawma@oup.co.uk. Cur.: Dr. Martin Maw
Special Museum
OUP's history from the middle ages to the age of techno- logy, historical printing and typographical artefacts - archives 40152

Pitt Rivers Museum, c/o University of Oxford, South Parks Rd, Oxford OX1 3PP - T: (01865) 270927, Fax: 270943, E-mail: prm@pitt-rivers-museum. oxford.ac.uk, Internet: www.prm.ox.ac.uk. Dir.: Dr. Michael O'Hanlon, Cur.: Dr. Hélène LaRue (Ethnomusicology), Dr. Laura Peers (Social Anthropology, Central and South America), Dr. Chris Gosden (European and Pacific Archaeology and Archaeological Method/Theory, Central Asia and ironage sites in Oxfordshire), Dr. Peter Mitchell (African Archaeology), Dr. C. Harris (Art, Anthropology, Asia esp. Tibet)
Ethnology Museum / University Museum - 1884
Prehistoric archaeology, musical instruments, Captain Cook's material collected 1773-1774, African art, North American, Arctic, Pacific material, masks, textiles, arms and armour, amulets, charms, costumes, pottery, lamps and jewellery - archives, Balfour Library 40153

Regimental Museum of the Oxfordshire and Buckinghamshire Light Infantry, T.A. Centre, Slade Park, Headington, Oxford OX3 7JJ - T: (01865) 780128
Military Museum 40154

Paddock Wood

Hop Farm, Beltring, Paddock Wood TN12 6PY - T: (01622) 872068, Fax: 872630. Cur.: Brent Pollard
Agriculture Museum
Exhibits of rural crafts, hop-growing and processing, agricultural tools and implements, and horse harness and equipment 40155

Padiham

Rachel Kay Shuttleworth Textile Collections, Gawthorpe Hall, Padiham BB12 8UA - T: (01282) 773963. Sc. Staff: G. Newbery (Trustee), L. Rogerson (Librarian, Archivist)
Decorative Arts Museum
Embroideries from 17th c including goldwork, whitework, canvas work, quilts, lacework, costumes from 1750 - library 40156

Padstow

Padstow Museum, The Institute, Market Pl, Padstow PL28 8AD - T: (01841) 532470. Chm.: John Buckingham
Local Museum 40157

Paignton

Compton Castle, Marldon, Paignton TQ3 1TA - T: (01803) 875740, Fax: 875740, Internet: www. nationaltrust.org.uk
Historic Site
Historic house and garden 40158

Kirkham House, Kirkham St, Paignton TQ3 3AX - T: (0117) 9750700, Fax: 9750701, Internet: www. english-heritage.org.uk. Cur.: Tony Musty
Decorative Arts Museum
Coll of reproduction furniture 40159

Paignton and Dartmouth Steam Railway, Queen's Park Station, Torbay Rd, Paignton TQ4 6AF - T: (01803) 555872, Fax: 664313, E-mail: pdsr@ talk21.com
Science&Tech Museum 40160

Paisley

Paisley Museum and Art Gallery, High St, Paisley PA1 2BA - T: (0141) 8893151, Fax: 8899240, Internet: www.cqm.co.uk/www/rdc/leisurestart. Dir.: Andrea J. Kerr, Sc. Staff: Jane Kidd (Art), Shona Allan (Natural History), Valerie A. Reilly (Textiles), Chris Lee (Social History)
Local Museum / Fine Arts Museum - 1870
Art, local history, natural history, local weaving art, Paisley Shawl Coll - observatory 40161

Palacerigg

Palacerigg House (closed) 40162

Patna

Dunaskin Open Air Museum, Waterside, Dalmellington Rd, Patna KA6 7JF - T: (01292) 531144, Fax: 532314, E-mail: dunaskin@ btconnect.com, Internet: www.yell.co.uk/sites/ dunaskin
Open Air Museum / Science&Tech Museum
Ironworks, coal mining, brickworks, social and industrial history 40163

Paulerspury

Sir Henry Royce Memorial Foundation, The Hunt House, Paulerspury NN12 7NA - T: (01327) 811048, Fax: 811797, E-mail: shrmf@rrec.co.uk, Internet: www.henry-royce.org. Cur.: Philip Hall
Science&Tech Museum
Life and work of Henry Royce, Rolls-Royce cars 40164

Peebles

Cornice Museum of Ornamental Plasterwork, Innerleithen Rd, Peebles EH45 8BA - T: (01721) 720212, Fax: 720212
Special Museum 40165

Tweeddale Museum, c/o Chambers Institute, High St, Peebles EH45 8AQ - T: (01721) 724820, Fax: 724424, E-mail: rhannay@scotborders.gov.uk. Dir.: Rosemary Hannay
Natural History Museum / Archaeological Museum / Local Museum - 1859
Geology coll and local prehistoric material 40166

Peel

House of Manannan, Manx National Heritage, Peel IM5 1TA - T: (01624) 648000, Fax: 648001, E-mail: enquiries@mnh.gov.im, Internet: www.gov. im/mnh. Man.: Nick Corkill
Historical Museum
Celtic, Viking and maritime traditions, art' technology 40167

Peel Castle, Manx National Heritage, Peel IM5 1TB - T: (01624) 648000, Fax: 648001, E-mail: enquiries@mnh.gov.im, Internet: www.gov. im/mnh. Man.: Nick Corkill
Religious Arts Museum / Historic Site
History, mystory and suspence of Peel castle, Viking heritage 40168

Pembroke

Castle Hill Museum → The Museum of the Home

The Museum of the Home, 7 Westgate Hill, Pembroke SA71 4LB - T: (01646) 681200. Dir.: Judy Stimson
Historical Museum - 1986
Domestic equipment, games and toys 40169

Penarth

Turner House Gallery, Plymouth Rd, Penarth CF64 3DM - T: (029) 20708870, E-mail: post@nmgw.ac. uk, Internet: www.nmgw.ac.uk/thg. Dir.: A. Southall
Fine Arts Museum / Decorative Arts Museum / Public Gallery
Fine and applied arts 40170

Pendeen

Geevor Tin Mining Museum, Geevor Tin Mine, Pendeen TR19 7EW - T: (01736) 788662, Fax: 786059, E-mail: pch@geevor.com, Internet: www.geevor.com. Dir.: W.G. Lakin
Science&Tech Museum
History of tin mining in Cornwall, geology, Cornish minerals, mining artefacts 40171

Pendeen Lighthouse, Pendeen TR19 7ED - T: (01736) 788418, Fax: 786059, E-mail: info@ trevithicktrust.com, Internet: www.trevithicktrust. com
Science&Tech Museum
Engine room with sounder 40172

Pendine

Museum of Speed, Pendine SA33 4NY - T: (01994) 453488
Science&Tech Museum
Hist of Pendine sands 40173

Penicuik

Scottish Infantry Divisional Museum, The Scottish Division Depot, Glencorse Barracks, Milton Bridge, Penicuik EH26 0NP - T: (01968) 72651 ext 239
Military Museum
History of infantry weapons 40174

Penrith

Dalemain Historic House, Penrith CA11 0HB - T: (017684) 86450, E-mail: admin@dalemain.com, Internet: www.dalemain.com
Historical Museum 40175

Penrith Museum, Robinson's School, Middlegate, Penrith CA11 7PT - T: (01768) 212228, Fax: 891754, E-mail: museum@eden.gov.uk, Internet: www.eden.gov.uk. Cur.: Judith Clarke, Dr. S.T. Chapman
Local Museum - 1990 40176

Steam Museum (closed) 40177

Penshurst

Penshurst Place and Toy Museum, Penshurst TN11 8DG - T: (01892) 870307, Fax: 870866, E-mail: enquiries@penshurstplace.com, Internet: www.penshurstplace.com. Dir.: Viscount de L'Isle
Special Museum 40178

Penzance

Cornwall Geological Museum, Saint John's Hall, Alverton St, Penzance TR18 2QR - T: (01736) 332400, Fax: 332400, E-mail: honsec@geological. org.uk, Internet: www.geological.nildram.co.uk. Pres.: David Freegman
Natural History Museum - 1914
Mineralogy, petrography, paleontology, Cornwall geology 40179

Natural History and Antiquarian Museum → Penlee House Gallery and Museum

Newlyn Art Gallery, New Rd, Newlyn, Penzance TR18 5PZ - T: (01736) 363715, Fax: 331578, E-mail: mail@newlynartgallery.co.uk, Internet: www.newlynartgallery.co.uk. Dir.: Elizabeth Knowles
Public Gallery - 1895 40180

Penlee House Gallery and Museum, Morrab Rd, Penzance TR18 4HE - T: (01736) 363625, Fax: 361312, E-mail: info@penlee-house.demon. co.uk, Internet: www.penleehouse.org.uk. Dir.: Alison LLoyd
Fine Arts Museum / Local Museum / Archaeological Museum
Archaeology, local history, natural history, Bronze Age pottery, Newlyn school paintings 40181

Penzance and District Museum → Penlee House Gallery and Museum

Trinity House National Lighthouse Centre, Wharf Rd, Penzance TR18 4BN - T: (01736) 360077, Fax: 364292. Man.: Alan Renton
Science&Tech Museum - 1990
Coll of lighthouse equipment 40182

Perranporth

Perranzabuloe Folk Museum, Oddfellows Hall, Ponsmere Rd, Perranporth TR6 0BW
Local Museum
History of mining, fishing, farming 40183

Perth

Fergusson Gallery, Marshall Pl, Perth PH2 8NU - T: (01738) 441944, Fax: 621152, E-mail: museum@pkc.gov.uk, Internet: www.pkc. gov.uk/ah/fergussongallery.htm. Head: Michael Taylor, Sc. Staff: J. Kinnear (Arts)
Fine Arts Museum 40184

Perth Museum and Art Gallery, 78 George St, Perth PH1 5LB - T: (01738) 632488, Fax: 443505, E-mail: museum@pkc.gov.uk, Internet: www.pkc. gov.uk/ah. Dir.: M.A. Taylor, Sc. Staff: Robin Rodger (Fine and Applied Art), Fiona Slattery (Applied Art), Susan Payne (Human History), Robert Jarvie (Design), Barbara Hamilton (Education), Mark Hall (Archaeology), Mark Simmons (Natural Sciences)
Local Museum / Fine Arts Museum / Natural History Museum / Public Gallery - 1935
Scottish and other paintings, applied art (Perth silver and glass), regional natural history, ethnography, archaeology, geology, antiquities 40185

Regimental Museum of the Black Watch, Balhousie Castle, Hay St, Perth PH1 5HR - T: (0131) 3108530, Fax: (01738) 643245, E-mail: museum@ theblackwatch.co.uk. Dir.: S.J. Lindsay

Military Museum - 1924
History of Black Watch, related regiments, paintings, royal relics, uniforms, trophies from 1740 to the present 40186

Scone Palace, Perth PH2 6BD - T: (01738) 552300, Fax: 552588, E-mail: visits@scone-palace.co.uk, Internet: www.scone-palace.co.uk. Head: Elspeth Bruce
Decorative Arts Museum
Finest French furniture, china, clocks, ivories, needlework, vases, several historic rooms, halls and galleries 40187

Peterborough

Peterborough Museum and Art Gallery, Priestgate, Peterborough PE1 1LF - T: (01733) 343329, Fax: 341928, E-mail: museum@peterborough.gov. uk, Internet: www.peterboroughheritage.org.uk. Dir.: Mike Dillon, Cur.: Maggie Warren
Local Museum - 1880
Archaeology, history, geology, marine reptils, natural history, ceramics, glass, portraits, paintings, finds from Castor, Napoleonic P.O.W. coll from Norman cross, bone carving, straw marquetry 40188

Railworld, Oundle Rd, Peterborough PE2 9NR - T: (01733) 344240, Fax: 344240, E-mail: mail@ railworld.net, Internet: www.railworld.net. Dir.: Richard Paten
Science&Tech Museum - 1993
Exhibits on worldwide modern trains, transport environmental factors, Maglev trains, the age of steam 40189

Southwick Hall, Peterborough PE8 5BL - T: (01832) 274064. Man.: Greg Bucknill
Fine Arts Museum
Hall dates from the 14th c, from which two stair turrets and adjoining rooms remain, illustrates the development of the English manor house comprising medieval, Elizabethan, Georgian and 19th-c architectural styles, incl coll of Victorian and Edwardian artefacts and exhibitions of local hist 40190

Peterhead

Arbuthnot Museum, Saint Peter St, Peterhead AB42 1QD - T: (01771) 622906, Fax: 622884, E-mail: heritage@aberdeenshire.gov.uk. Dir.: Dr. David M. Bertie
Local Museum - 1850
Local hist, fishing, shipping and whaling, coin and medal coll, 19th c Inuit ethnography 40191

Petersfield

Bear Museum, 38 Dragon St, Petersfield GU31 4JJ - T: (01730) 265108, Fax: 266119, Internet: www. bearmuseum.co.uk. Dir.: Judy Sparrow, John Sparrow
Special Museum - 1984
The world's first museum of teddy bears 40192

Flora Twort Gallery, Church Path, 21 The Square, Petersfield GU32 1HS - T: (01730) 260756, E-mail: musmtc@hants.gov.uk, Internet: www. hants.gov.uk/floratwo
Public Gallery 40193

Petersfield Museum, The Old Courthouse, Saint Peters Rd, Petersfield GU32 3HX - T: (01730) 262601, E-mail: museum@petersfield.org
Local Museum 40194

Uppark Exhibition, South Harting, Petersfield GU31 5QR - T: (01730) 825415, Fax: 825873, E-mail: uppark@nationaltrust.org.uk, Internet: www.nationaltrust.org.uk/uppark. Man.: D.W. Evans
Special Museum
The fire of 1989 and subsequent restoration work 40195

Petworth

Coultershaw Beam Pump, Station Rd, Petworth GU28 0JE - T: (01798) 865774, Fax: 865672, E-mail: rlwconsult@compuserve.com, Internet: www.coultershaw..co.uk. Cur.: Robin Wilson
Science&Tech Museum
Waterwheel-driven pump, other pumps 40196

The Petworth Cottage Museum, 346 High St, Petworth GU28 0AU - T: (01798) 342100, Internet: www.petworthcottagemuseum.co.uk. Cur.: Jacqueline Golden
Historical Museum
Restored as an estate cottage occupied by a seamstress employed by the Le Consfield estate (1910) 40197

Petworth House and Park, Church St, Petworth GU28 0AE - T: (01798) 342207, Fax: 342963, E-mail: petworth@nationaltrust.org.uk, Internet: www.nationaltrust.org.uk/petworth
Fine Arts Museum
Old Masters (Turner, Van Dyck, Laguerre), ancient and neo-classical sculpture 40198

Pevensey

Court House and Museum, High St, Pevensey BN24 5LF - T: (01323) 762309. Cur.: G.J.H. Dent
Local Museum 40199

Pewsey

Pewsey Heritage Centre, Whatleys Old Foundry, Avonside Works, High St, Pewsey SN9 5AF - T: (01672) 56240, 562617, E-mail: mikeasbury@aol.com. Man.: Michael J. Asbury
Local Museum
Farming, commerce, the home, engineering 40200

Pickering

Beck Isle Museum of Rural Life, Bridge St, Pickering YO18 8DU - T: (01751) 473653, Fax: 475996, E-mail: beckislemuseum@aol.com, Internet: www.beckislemuseum.com. Dir.: G. Clitheroe
Local Museum - 1967
Reconstructed rooms and shops, photographic work of the late "Sidney Smith", works of Rex Whistler 40201

North Yorkshire Moors Railway, Station, Pickering YO18 7AJ - T: (01751) 472508, Fax: 476970, E-mail: admin@nymrpickering.fsnet.co.uk, Internet: www.northyorkshiremoorsrailway.com
Science&Tech Museum 40202

Pinxton

John King Workshop Museum, Victoria Rd, Pinxton NG16 6LR - T: (01773) 860137
Science&Tech Museum
Mining, engineering, railway artifacts 40203

Pitlochry

Clan Donnachaidh Museum, Bruar, Pitlochry PH18 5TW - T: (01796) 483264, Fax: 483338. Dir.: Ann McBay
Historical Museum
Items related to the Jacobite rising of 1745 40204

Pitlochry Festival Theatre Art Gallery, Port-na-Craig, Pitlochry PH16 5DR - T: (01796) 484600, Fax: 484616, E-mail: boxoffice@pitlochry.org.uk. Dir.: Roy Wilson
Performing Arts Museum - 1951 40205

Pitstone

Pitstone Green Farm Museum, Vicarage Rd, Pitstone LU7 9EY - T: (01296) 668223
Agriculture Museum 40206

Pittenweem

Kellie Castle, Pittenweem KY10 2RF - T: (01333) 720271. Head: M. Pirnie
Decorative Arts Museum 40207

Plumridge

Sperrin Heritage Centre, 274 Glenelly Rd, Plumridge BT79 8LS - T: (028) 81648142, Fax: 81648143
Local Museum
Treasure, ghosts, gold and poteen 40208

Plymouth

City Museum and Art Gallery, Drake Circus, Plymouth PL4 8AJ - T: (01752) 304774, Fax: 304775, E-mail: plymouth.museum@plymouth.gov.uk, Internet: www.plymouthmuseum.gov.uk. Cur.: Nicola Moyle, Dep. Cur.: M. Tosdevin, Cons.: J. Tamblin
Local Museum / Fine Arts Museum - 1897
Porcelain, cotton coll, paintings, drawings, prints, early printed books, 17th c portraits, ceramics, personalia of Sir Francis Drake, archaeology, ethnography, model ships, Oceanic coll, tokens, photography, minerals, herbarium 40209

Merchant's House Museum, 33 Saint Andrew's St, Plymouth - T: (01752) 304774, Fax: 304775, E-mail: plymouth.museum@plymouth.gov.uk, Internet: www.plymouthmuseum.gov.uk. Dir.: N. Moyle
Historical Museum - 1977
Social, economic and maritime history of Plymouth 40210

Plymouth Arts Centre, 38 Looe St, Plymouth PL4 8AJ - T: (01752) 221450
Public Gallery 40211

Saltram House, Plympton, Plymouth PL7 1UH - T: (01752) 333500, Fax: 336474, E-mail: saltram@nationaltrust.org.uk, Internet: www.nationaltrust.org.uk. Manager: Susan M. Baumbach
Fine Arts Museum / Decorative Arts Museum / Historic Site / Association with Coll 40212

Smeaton's Tower, The Hoe, Plymouth PL1 2NZ - T: (01752) 603300, Fax: 256361, E-mail: plymouth.dome@plymouth.gov.uk
Science&Tech Museum
Historic lighthouse 40213

Pocklington

Stewart Collection, Burnby Hall Gardens, Pocklington YO4 2QF - T: (01759) 302068, E-mail: burnbyhallgardens@hotmail.com, Internet: www.burnbyhallgardens.co.uk
Local Museum 40214

Point Clear Bay

Museum of the 40's, Martello Tower, Point Clear Bay CO16 8NG
Military Museum / Science&Tech Museum
Navy in WW II 40215

Polegate

Windmill and Milling Museum, Park Croft, Polegate BN26 5LB - T: (01323) 734496. Dir.: Lawrence Stevens
Science&Tech Museum 40216

Pontefract

Pontefract Castle Museum, Castle Chain, Pontefract WF8 1QH - T: (01977) 723440. Dir.: Colin MacDonald
Historical Museum 40217

Pontefract Museum, 5 Salter Row, Pontefract WF8 1BA - T: (01977) 722740, Fax: 722742
Local Museum
Archaeology, local history 40218

Ponterwyd

Llywernog Silver-Lead Mine Museum, Ponterwyd SY23 3AB - T: (01970) 890620, Fax: (01545) 570823, E-mail: silverrivermine@cs.com. Dir.: Peter Lloyd Harvey
Science&Tech Museum
Coll of mining artefacts 40219

Pontypool

Junction Cottage, Lower Mill, off Fontain Rd, Pontymoile, Pontypool NP4 0RF - T: (0800) 5422663, Fax: (01495) 755877, E-mail: junctioncottage@messages.co.uk, Internet: www.junctioncottage.co.uk
Special Museum 40220

Pontypool Museums, Park Bldgs, Pontypool NP4 6JH - T: (01495) 752036, Fax: 752043, E-mail: pontypoolmuseum@hotmail.com. Cur.: D. Wildgust
Local Museum - 1978 40221

Torfaen Museum, Park Bldgs, Pontypool NP4 6JH - T: (01495) 752036, Fax: 752043. Dir.: Martin Buckridge
Local Museum
Social and industrial history of Torfaen 40222

Pontypridd

Pontypridd Museum, Bridge St, Pontypridd CF37 4PE - T: (01443) 409748, Fax: 490746, E-mail: bdavies@pontypriddmuseum.org.uk, Internet: www.pontypriddmuseum.org.uk. Cur.: Brian Davies
Local Museum
Social history, industry, agriculture, culture and recreation 40223

Pool

Camborne School of Mines Geological Museum and Art Gallery, c/o University of Exeter, Pool TR15 3SE - T: (01209) 714866, Fax: 716977, E-mail: l.atkinson@csm.ex.ac.uk, Internet: www.ex.ac.uk/csm/museum2.htm. Cur.: Lesley Atkinson
Natural History Museum / Public Gallery
Rocks and minerals, incl. fluorescent, radioactive, gem and ore minerals, art exhibitions 40224

Cornish Mines, Engines and Cornwall Industrial Discovery Centre, Pool TR15 3NP - T: (01209) 315027, Fax: 315027, E-mail: info@trevithicktrust.com, Internet: www.trevithicktrust.com
Science&Tech Museum
Cornish beam-engines used for mine winding and pumping 40225

Poole

Lighthouse Poole Centre for the Arts, Kingland Rd, Poole BH15 1UG - T: (01202) 665334, Fax: 670016, E-mail: oliviah@lighthousepoole.co.uk, Internet: www.lighthousepoole.co.uk. Dir.: Olivia Hamilton
Public Gallery 40226

Old Lifeboat Museum, East Quay, Poole - Internet: www.rnli.org.uk
Historical Museum
1938 lifeboat Thomas Kirk Wright 40227

Royal National Lifeboat Institution Headquarters Museum, West Quay Rd, Poole BH15 1HZ - T: (01202) 663000, Fax: 662243, Internet: www.rnli.org.uk. Dir.: Andrew Freemantle
Historical Museum
Lifeboat, models, paintings, fundraising artifacts 40228

Scaplen's Court Museum, High St, Poole BH15 1BW - T: (01202) 262600, Fax: 262622, E-mail: museums@poole.gov.uk, Internet: www.poole.gov.uk/culturalservices/museums. Dir.: Clive Fisher
Special Museum / Historical Museum - 1932 40229

Waterfront Museum, 4 High St, Poole BH15 1BW - T: (01202) 262600, Fax: 262622, E-mail: museums@poole.gov.uk, Internet: www.poole.gov.uk/culturalservices/museums. Dir.: Clive Fisher
Historical Museum - 1989
Boats and shipping, local hist, archaeology 40230

Port Charlotte

Museum of Islay Life, Port Charlotte PA48 7UN - T: (01496) 850358, Fax: 850358, E-mail: imt@islaymuseum.freeserve.co.uk, Internet: www.islaymuseum.freeserve.co.uk. Cur.: Margot Perrons
Local Museum - 1977
Victorian domestic items, industry, carved stone coll 6th to 16th c - lapidarium, library 40231

Port-of-Ness

Ness Historical Society Museum, Old School, Lionel, Port-of-Ness PA86 0TG - T: (01851) 81576
Local Museum
History and occupations of the Ness area of Lewis, coll of photographic, printed and written material, fishing equipment, domestic utensils, implements used in crofting 40232

Port Saint Mary

Cregneash Village Folk Museum, Manx National Heritage, Cregneash, Port Saint Mary IM9 5PT - T: (01624) 648000, Fax: 648001, E-mail: enquiries@mnh.gov.im, Internet: www.gov.im/mnh
Folklore Museum
Manx crofting and fishing 19th-20th c, traditional cooking and spinning, farming 40233

Sound Visitor Centre, Manx National Heritage, The Sound, Port Saint Mary IM9 5PT - T: (01624) 648000, 838123, Fax: 648001, E-mail: enquiries@mnh.gov.im, Internet: www.gov.im/mnh
Natural History Museum
Natural wonders of the Sound and the Calf of Man 40234

Port Sunlight

Lady Lever Art Gallery, Lower Rd, Port Sunlight CH62 5EQ - T: (0151) 4784136, Fax: 4784140, Internet: www.ladyleverartgallery.uk. Dir.: Dr. David Fleming
Fine Arts Museum - 1922
British and other paintings, watercolors, sculpture, porcelain, furniture 40235

Port Sunlight Heritage Centre, 95 Greendale Rd, Port Sunlight CH62 4XE - T: (0151) 6446466, Fax: 6448973
Historical Museum / Special Museum
Story of William Hesketh Lever, his soap factory, period soap packaging 40236

Port Talbot

Margam County Park, Margam, Port Talbot SA13 2TJ - T: (01639) 881635, Fax: 895897. Ass. Dir.: Raymond Butt
Natural History Museum
Over 800 acres of parkland, orangery, castle, sculpture coll, nursery rhyme village for children under 8, large hedge maze 40237

South Wales Miner's Museum, Afan Argoed Country Park, Cynonville, Port Talbot SA13 3HG - T: (01639) 850564, Fax: 850446. Dir.: Mair Boast
Science&Tech Museum 40238

Portchester

Portchester Castle, Castle St, Portchester PO16 9QW - T: (023) 92378291, Internet: www.english-heritage.org.uk. Cur.: Nick Moore
Local Museum 40239

Porthcawl

Porthcawl Museum, Old Police Station, John St, Porthcawl CF36 3DT - T: (01656) 782111
Local Museum
Local and maritime hist, military hist of 49th Recce Regiment, costume, photographs - archives 40240

Porthcurno

Museum of Submarine Telegraphy → Porthcurno Telegraph Museum

Porthcurno Telegraph Museum, Eastern House, Porthcurno TR19 6JX - T: (01736) 810966, 810478, Fax: 810966, E-mail: mark@tunnels.demon.co.uk, Internet: www.porthcurno.org.uk. Dir.: Mary Godwin
Science&Tech Museum
Working submarine telegraphy equipment, underground WW II tunnels, local hist - archive 40241

Porthmadog

Porthmadog Maritime Museum, The Harbour, Porthmadog LL49 9LU - T: (01766) 513736
Historical Museum 40242

Welsh Highland Railway Museum, Gelert's Farm Works, Porthmadog LL49 9DY - T: (01766) 513402, Fax: 514024, E-mail: dw@allan89.fsnet.co.uk, Internet: www.whr.co.uk/whr/whr.html. Chm.: David Allan
Science&Tech Museum - 1985
History of Festiniog and allied railway systems, steam locomotives and quarry wagons, tramway horse, drawn tramcar 40243

Portland

Portland Castle, Castletown, Portland DT5 1AZ - T: (01305) 820539, Fax: 860853, Internet: www.english-heritage.org.uk. Cur.: Tony Musty
Local Museum 40244

Portland Museum, 217 Wakeham, Portland DT5 1HS - T: (01305) 821804, Fax: 761654, E-mail: tourism@weymouth.gov.uk, Internet: www.weymouth.gov.uk
Natural History Museum - 1930
Cunnington, fossil coll (c 1925) of national importance being the best coll of faunal fossils from the Portlandian rocks 40245

Portree

Skye and Lochalsh Area Museums, Tigh na Sgire, Park Ln, Portree IV51 9GP - T: (01478) 613857, Fax: 613751
Association with Coll
Prints, mapts, archives, archaeology - Library 40246

Portslade-by-Sea

Foredown Tower, Foredown Rd, Portslade-by-Sea BN41 2EW - T: (01273) 292092, Fax: 292092, E-mail: visitor.services@brighton-hove.gov.uk
Natural History Museum
Camera obscura, astronomy, gallery of surrounding countryside 40247

Portsmouth

Charles Dickens Birthplace Museum, 393 Old Commercial Rd, Portsmouth PO1 4QL - T: (023) 92827261, Fax: 92875276, E-mail: david.evans@portsmouthcc.gov.uk, Internet: www.portsmouthmuseums.co.uk. Dir.: Sarah Quail
Special Museum - 1904
Birthplace of writer Charles Dickens (1812-1870), furniture, memorabilia, prints 40248

City Museum and Records Office, Museum Rd, Portsmouth PO1 2LJ - T: (023) 92827261, Fax: 92875276, E-mail: david.evans@portsmouthcc.gov.uk, Internet: www.portsmouthmuseums.co.uk. Dir.: Sarah Quail
Local Museum / Decorative Arts Museum / Fine Arts Museum / Historical Museum - 1972
Local history, ceramics, sculpture, paintings, wood engravings, prints, furniture, glass 40249

D-Day Museum and Overlord Embroidery, Clarence Esplanade, Southsea, Portsmouth PO5 3NT - T: (023) 92827261, Fax: 92875276, E-mail: david.evans@portsmouthcc.gov.uk, Internet: www.ddaymuseum.co.uk. Dir.: Sarah Quail
Military Museum - 1984
"The Overlord embroidery" D-day military hist 40250

Eastney Beam Engine House, Henderson Rd, Eastney, Portsmouth PO4 9JF - T: (023) 92827261, Fax: 92875276, E-mail: david.evans@portsmouthcc.gov.uk, Internet: www.portsmouthmuseums.co.uk. Dir.: Sarah Quail
Science&Tech Museum 40251

Fort Widley, A333, Portsdown Hill, Portsmouth PO6 3LS - T: (023) 92324553
Military Museum
Bunker, tunnels, the Great Ditch 40252

HMS Victory, HM Naval Base, Portsmouth PO1 3PZ - T: (023) 92819604, Internet: www.flagship.org.uk
Military Museum
Flagship of Lord Nelson at the Battle of Trafalgar 40253

HMS Warrior 1860, Victory Gate, HM Naval Base, Portsmouth PO1 3QX - T: (023) 92778600, Fax: 92778601, E-mail: info@hmswarrior.org, Internet: www.hmswarrior.org. Dir.: David Newbery
Military Museum - 1987
Historic warship 40254

Mary Rose Museum, HM Naval Base, College Rd, Portsmouth PO1 3LX - T: (023) 92750521, Fax: 92870588, E-mail: maryrose@cix.co.uk, Internet: www.maryrose.org. Dir.: Charles Payton
Military Museum
Objects recovered from the wreck of Henry VIII's warship, the 'Mary Rose', surviving portion of the ship's hull 40255

Natural History Museum, Cumberland House, Eastern Parade, Southsea, Portsmouth PO4 9RF - T: (023) 92827261, Fax: 92875276, E-mail: david.evans@portsmouthcc.gov.uk, Internet: www.portsmouthmuseums.co.uk. Dir.: Sarah Quail, Sc. Staff: Clare Stringer
Natural History Museum 40256

Royal Marines Museum, Eastney, Southsea, Portsmouth PO4 9PX - T: (023) 92819385, Fax: 92838420, E-mail: info@royalmarinesmuseum.co.uk, Internet: www.royalmarinesmuseum.co.uk. Dir.: C. Newbery
Military Museum - 1958/1975
Documents, paintings, weapons, uniforms, campaign relics since 1664, band and music paraphernalia 40257

Royal Naval Museum Portsmouth, HM Naval Base, PP66, Portsmouth PO1 3NH - T: (023) 92727562, Fax: 92727575, E-mail: information@royalnavalmuseum.org, Internet: www.royalnavalmuseum.org. Dir.: H. Campbell McMurray, Dep. Dir.: C.S. White
Historical Museum - 1911
Figureheads, ship models, ship furniture, memorabilia of Lord Nelson, panorama of the Battle of Trafalgar, history of the Royal Navy from earliest times to present - library, full research facilities 40258

Southsea Castle, Clarence Esplanade, Southsea, Portsmouth PO5 3PA - T: (023) 92827261, Fax: 92875276, E-mail: david.evans@portsmouthcc.gov.uk, Internet: www.portsmouthmuseums.co.uk. Dir.: Sarah Quail
Military Museum - 1967
History of Portsmouth fortress, tudor, civilwar, Victorian military hist 40259

Treadgolds Museum, 1 Bishop St, Portsmouth PO1 3DA - T: (023) 92824745, Fax: 92837310, Internet: www.hants.gov.uk/museums. Man.: Peter Lawton
Special Museum
Machine and hand tools, materials, business archives, Treadgolds, ironmongers and engineers 40260

Potterne

Wiltshire Fire Defence Collection, Fire Brigade Headquarters, Manor House, Potterne SN10 5PP - T: (01380) 723601, Fax: 727000, Internet: www.withshirefirebrigade.com
Science&Tech Museum 40261

Potters Bar

Potters Bar Museum, Wyllotts Pl, Darkes Ln, Potters Bar EN6 4HN - T: (01707) 645005 ext 20. Cur.: Arnold Davey
Local Museum
History and archaeology of Potters Bar, telephones, Potters Bar Zeppelin 40262

Prescot

Museum of Clock and Watch Making, 34 Church St, Prescot L34 3LA - T: (0151) 4307787, Fax: 4307219
Science&Tech Museum 40263

Prescot Museum, 34 Church St, Prescot L34 3LA - T: (0151) 4307787, Fax: 4307219. Dir.: R. John Griffiths
Science&Tech Museum - 1982
Horology, earthenware 40264

Presteigne

The Judge's Lodging, Broad St, Presteigne LD8 2AD - T: (01544) 260650/51, Fax: 260652, E-mail: info@judgeslodging.org.uk, Internet: www.judgeslodging.org.uk. Dir.: Gabrielle Rivers
Local Museum - 1980
Victorian domestic life, law and order, local/regional hist 40265

Preston

Harris Museum and Art Gallery, Market Sq, Preston PR1 2PP - T: (01772) 258248, Fax: 886764, E-mail: harris.museum@preston.gov.uk, Internet: www.visitpreston.com/harris. Dir.: Alexandra Walker, Sc. Staff: James Green (Exhibition), Francis Marshall (Fine Art), Emma Heslewood (Social History), Amanda Draper (Decorative Art), Hilary Ryan (Development), Lisa Watson (Education), Dawn Workington (Education), Paula Simpson (Access)
Fine Arts Museum / Decorative Arts Museum / Local Museum - 1893
Fine art, Devis Coll of 18th c paintings, Newsham Bequest of 19th c British paintings, Haslam Bequest of 19th c watercolors, decorative art, costumes, ceramics, porcelain, social hist, archaeology, skeleton of Mesolithic elk, photogr 40266

Museum of Lancashire, Stanley St, Preston PR1 4YP - T: (01772) 264075, Fax: 264079, E-mail: museum.enquiries@mus.lancscc.co.uk. Dir.: Edmund Southworth
Local Museum / Natural History Museum 40267

National Football Museum, Sir Tom Finney Wy, Deepdale, Preston PR1 6RU - T: (01772) 908442, Fax: 908443, E-mail: enquiries@nationalfootballmuseum.com, Internet: www.nationalfootballmuseum.com. Dir.: Kevin Moore
Special Museum
Hist of football 40268

Queen's Lancashire Regiment Museum, Fulwood Barracks, Watling St Rd, Preston PR2 8AA - T: (01772) 260362, Fax: 260583. Dir.: Mike Glover
Military Museum - 1926
Regimental history, uniforms, silver, trophies, weapons - library, archive 40269

Prestongrange

Prestongrange Museum, Morison's Haven, Prestongrange EH32 9RX - T: (0131) 6532904, Fax: (01620) 828201, E-mail: elms@prestongrangemuseum.org, Internet: www.prestongrangemuseum.org. Head: Peter Gray
Science&Tech Museum
History of Prestongrange colliery and brickworks, colliery locomotives, 800 years mining history 40270

Prickwillow

Prickwillow Drainage Engine Museum, Main St, Prickwillow CB7 4UN - T: (01353) 688360, Fax: 723456. Chm.: Les Walton
Science&Tech Museum
Memorabilia, artefacts, diesel engines 40271

Pudsey

Moravian Museum, 55-57 Fulneck, Pudsey LS28 8NT - T: (0113) 564862, 2564147. Cur.: Eunice Harrison
Special Museum
Moravian lace and emboidery, ethnography 40272

Pulborough

Parham Elizabethan House & Gardens, Parham Park, Pulborough RH20 4HS - T: (01903) 744888, Fax: 746557, E-mail: enquiries@parhaminsussex.co.uk, Internet: www.parhaminsussex.co.uk
Fine Arts Museum - 1577
Historical portraits, needlework, Equestrian portrait of Henry Frederick, Prince of Wales, Kangaroo by Stubbs 40273

Roman Villa Museum at Bignor, Bignor Ln, Pulborough RH20 1PH - T: (01798) 869259, Fax: 869259, E-mail: bignorromanvilla@care4free.net. Dir.: J. Tupper
Archaeological Museum - 1960
Samian pottery, tiles, finds from 1811 excavations, mosaics 40274

Quainton

Buckinghamshire Railway Centre, Quainton Road Station, Quainton HP22 4BY - T: (01296) 655720, Fax: 655720, Internet: www.bucksrailcentre.org.uk. Dir.: D. Bratton
Science&Tech Museum
Steam/Diesel locomotives, carriages, wagons, railway artefacts 40275

Quatt

Dudmaston House, Quatt WV15 6QN - T: (01746) 780866, Fax: 780744, E-mail: mduefe@smtp.ntrust.org.uk
Decorative Arts Museum
Dutch flower paintings, fine furniture 40276

Radstock

Midsomer Norton and District Museum, Market Hall, Wateroo Rd, Radstock BA3 3ER - T: (01761) 437722, Fax: 420470, E-mail: radstockmuseum@ukonline.co.uk, Internet: www.radstockmuseum.co.uk
Local Museum
Local history, industrial archaeology, mining 40277

Rainham

Rainham Hall, The Broadway, Rainham RM13 9YN - T: (01494) 528051, Fax: 463310
Decorative Arts Museum
Plasterworks, carved porch and interor 40278

Ramsey, Cambridgeshire

Ramsey Rural Museum, Wood Lane, Ramsey, Cambridgeshire PE26 2TY - T: (01487) 815715
Local Museum
Victorian kitchen, sitting room, bedroom, schoolroom, farm machinery 40279

Ramsey, Isle of Man

Grove Rural Life Museum, Manx National Heritage, Andreas Rd, Ramsey, Isle of Man IM8 3UA - T: (01624) 648000, Fax: 648001, E-mail: enquiries@mnh.gov.im, Internet: www.gov.im/mnh
Historical Museum
Victorian time capsule, period furnishings, costume, farming, 19th c vehicles 40280

Ramsgate

Maritime Museum, Pier Yard, Royal Harbour, Ramsgate CT11 8LS - T: (01843) 587765, Fax: 582359. Dir.: Michael Cates
Science&Tech Museum - 1984
Artifacts from H.M.S. Stirling Castle wrecked on the Goodwin sands in the great storm of 1703, historic ship coll includes steam tug Cervia and Dunkirk little ship motor yacht Sundowner 40281

Motor Museum, Westcliff Hall, Ramsgate CT11 9JX - T: (01843) 581948. Dir.: D. Sharpe
Science&Tech Museum 40282

Ramsgate Museum, Guildford Lawn, Ramsgate CT11 9AY - T: (01843) 593532, Fax: 852692, Internet: www.kent.gov.uk. Dir.: Beth Thomson, Sc. Staff: Sheena Watson
Local Museum - 1912
library 40283

Spitfire and Hurricane Memorial Museum, The Airfield, Manston Rd, Ramsgate CT12 5DF - T: (01843) 821940, Fax: 821940, E-mail: thetrust@spitfire752.freeserve.co.uk, Internet: www.spitfire-museum.com. Chm.: Sid Farmer
Science&Tech Museum / Military Museum
Spitfire and hurricane fighters, aviation-related artefacts relating to WW II period (battle of Britain) 40284

Ravenglass

Muncaster Castle, Ravenglass CA18 1RQ - T: (01229) 717614, Fax: 717010, E-mail: info@muncaster.co.uk, Internet: www.muncaster.co.uk. Dir.: Peter Frost-Pennington
Fine Arts Museum 40285

Muncaster Watermill, Ravenglass CA18 1ST - T: (01229) 717232, Internet: www.muncaster.co.uk/mill
Science&Tech Museum 40286

Railway Museum, c/o Ravenglass and Eskdale Railway Co. Ltd., Ravenglass CA18 1SW - T: (01229) 717171, Fax: 717011, E-mail: rer@netcomuk.co.uk, Internet: www.ravenglass.railway.co.uk
Science&Tech Museum - 1978
History of the Ravenglass and Eskdale Railway since 1875 and its effect on the area 40287

Ravenshead

Gordon Brown Collection, Longdale Craft Centre, Longdale Ln, Ravenshead NG15 9AH - T: (01623) 794858, 796952, Fax: 794858, E-mail: longdale@longdale.co.uk, Internet: www.longdale.co.uk. Dir.: Gordon Brown
Decorative Arts Museum 40288

Longdale Craft Centre and Museum, Longdale Ln, Ravenshead NG15 9AH - T: (01623) 794858, Fax: 794858, Internet: www.longdale.co.uk. Dir.: Gordon Brown
Science&Tech Museum 40289

Newstead Abbey, Newstead Abbey Park, Ravenshead NG15 8NA - T: (01623) 455900/03, Fax: 455904, Internet: www.newsteadabbey.org.uk
Special Museum - 1170
Roe-Byron Coll: Poet's possessions and furniture, manuscripts, letters and first editions, 18th and 19th c furniture - library 40290

Papplewick Pumping Station, Longdale Ln, Ravenshead NG15 9AJ - T: (0115) 9632938, Fax: 9632938, E-mail: director@papplewickpumpingstation.co.uk, Internet: www.papplewickpumpingstation.co.uk. Dir.: Ian Smith
Science&Tech Museum
Boilers, beam engines, working forge, colliery winding engine, 7.25" gauge passenger carrying steam railway 40291

Rawtenstall

Rossendale Footware Heritage Museum, Greenbridge Works, Fallbarn Rd, Rawtenstall BB4 7NY - T: (01706) 235155, Fax: 229643
Special Museum 40292

Rossendale Museum, Whitaker Park, Haslingden Rd, Rawtenstall BB4 6RE - T: (01706) 217777, 244682, Fax: 250037. Dir.: Sandra Cruise
Local Museum - 1902
Local history, fine and decorative arts, natural history 40293

Reading

Blake's Lock Museum → Riverside Museum at Blake's Lock

Cole Museum of Zoology, c/o School of Animal and Microbial Science, University of Reading, Whiteknights, Reading RG6 6AJ - T: (0118) 3786409, E-mail: s.p.hopkin@reading.ac.uk, Internet: www.ams.rdg.ac.uk/zoology/hopkin. Dir.: Dr. Steve hopkin
Natural History Museum - 1906
Form and function in the animal kingdom 40294

Museum of English Rural Life, Whiteknights, Reading RG6 6AG, mail addr: c/o Rural History Centre, University of Reading, POB 229, Reading RG6 6AG - T: (0118) 9318660, Fax: 9751264, E-mail: rhc@reading.ac.uk, Internet: www.ruralhistory.org. Dir.: Prof. R.W. Hoyle
Agriculture Museum - 1951
Farming development, history of local rural life - library 40295

Museum of Reading, Town Hall, Blagrave St, Reading RG1 1QH - T: (0118) 9399800, Fax: 9399881, E-mail: mail@readingmuseum.org, Internet: www.readingmuseum.org. Dir.: Karen Hull
Decorative Arts Museum / Archaeological Museum / Local Museum - 1993
Britain's only full-size replica of the Bayeux Tapestry, the Silchester coll (Roman artefacts from Callera Atrebatum, now Silchester) 40296

Reading Abbay Gateway, The Forbury, Reading RG1 1QH - T: (0118) 9399809/05, Fax: 9566719
Religious Arts Museum 40297

Riverside Museum at Blake's Lock, Gas Works Rd, off Kenavon Dr, Reading RG1 3DH - T: (0118) 9399800, Fax: 9399881, E-mail: mail@readingmuseum.org.uk, Internet: www.readingmuseum.org.uk. Dir.: Karen Hull
Historical Museum - 1985
Waterways (rivers Thames and Kennet), traders and industries of Reading 40298

Ure Museum of Greek Archaeology, c/o Dept. of Classics, Faculty of Letters, University of Reading, Humanities Bldg, Whiteknights, Reading RG6 6AA - T: (0118) 3786599, Fax: 3786661, E-mail: ure@reading.ac.uk, Internet: www.rdg.ac.uk/ure. Dir.: Dr. Amy C. Smith
Archaeological Museum / Museum of Classical Antiquities / University Museum - 1922
Greek, Egyptian antiquities, Boeotian and South Italian vases 40299

Redcar

Kirkleatham Museum, Kirkleatham, Redcar TS10 5NW - T: (01642) 479500, Fax: 474199, E-mail: museum_services@redcar-cleveland.gov.uk. Dir.: P. Philo
Local Museum - 1981
Local 19th c artists (the staithes group incl Dame Laura Knight), commondale pottery, poster coll (some international from Poland and Germany), photographic coll, maritime hist incl lifeboats of the north east coast, iron stone mining, iron making, fishing 40300

Zetland Lifeboat Museum, 5 King St, Redcar TS10 3PF - T: (01642) 486952
Historical Museum - 1969
Shipping and fishing, industrial development, sea rescue, oldest lifeboat, ship models, marine paintings, scientific instruments 40301

Redditch

Forge Mill Needle Museum and Bordesley Abbey Visitor Centre, Needle Mill Ln, Riverside, Redditch B98 8HY - T: (01527) 62509, Fax: 66721, E-mail: museum@redditchbc.gov.uk, Internet: www.redditchbc.gov.uk. Dir.: Gillian Wilson
Science&Tech Museum / Archaeological Museum - 1983
Needles and fishing tackle from the Redditch needle-making district - Bordesley Abbey archaeological archive 40302

Redruth

Geological Museum and Art Gallery, University of Exeter, Camborne School of Mines, Redruth TR15 3SE - T: (01209) 714866, Fax: 716977, E-mail: scamm@csm.ex.ac.uk, Internet: geo-server.ex.ac.uk. Dir.: Simon Camm
Natural History Museum - 1888
Robert Hunt Coll of minerals, flurorescent minerals, ore specimens, Cornish minerals, fossils, worldwide coll of rocks and minerals, shows by local artists - library 40303

Tolgus Tin Mill and Streamworks, c/o Trevithick Trust, Pool, Redruth TR15 3NP - T: (01209) 210900, Fax: 210900, E-mail: trevithicktrust@aol.com, Internet: www.trevithicktrust.com. Dir.: William Barnes
Science&Tech Museum - 1921
Tin-streaming machinery in operation incl Cornish stamps (water powered), tin-mining - library 40304

Reeth

Swaledale Folk Museum, Village Green, Reeth DL11 6QT - T: (01748) 884373. Dir.: Erica Law
Folklore Museum - 1975
Folk exhibits, social hist and traditions of the Dale, sheep farming, lead mining 40305

Reigate

Fire Brigades Museum, Saint David's, 70 Wray Park Rd, Reigate RH2 0EJ - T: (01737) 242444, Fax: 224095. Man.: Derek Chinery
Science&Tech Museum
A coll of vintage fire engines, photographs and general information related to fire fighting in Surrey from 1754 to modern times 40306

Museum of the Holmesdale Natural History Club, 14 Croydon Rd, Reigate RH2 0PG - Internet: www.hnhc.co.uk
Natural History Museum / Local Museum - 1857
Fossils, local archaeological finds, coll of British birds, herbarium, coll of photographs and postcards, local history, geology 40307

Reigate Priory Museum, Reigate Priory, Bell St, Reigate RH2 7RL - T: (01737) 222550
Historical Museum
The coll incl domestic memorabilia, local hist and costume 40308

Renishaw

Renishaw Hall Museum and Art Gallery, Renishaw Park, Renishaw S21 3WB - T: (01246) 432310, Fax: 430760, E-mail: info@renishaw-hall.co.uk, Internet: www.sitwell.co.uk. Head: Stephen David Fidler
Fine Arts Museum
Art, John Piper music and theatre exhibits, Sitwell memorabilia 40309

Retford

Bassetlaw Museum and Percy Laws Memorial Gallery, Amcott House, 40 Grove St, Retford DN22 6JU - T: (01777) 713749, Fax: 713749. Cur.: Malcolm J. Dolby
Local Museum / Fine Arts Museum - 1986
Local archaeology, civic, social and agricultural history, fine and applied art 40310

Rhayader

Rhayader and District Museum, Bank House, East St, Rhayader LD6 5DL - T: (01597) 810800, Fax: 810194, E-mail: rachel@caradchronicles.fsnet.co.uk, Internet: www.carad.org.uk. Cur.: T.G.B. Lawrence
Local Museum
History and archaeology of the area 40311

Rhuddlan

Rhuddlan Castle, Rhuddlan LL18 5AE - T: (01745) 590777
Archaeological Museum 40312

Rhyl

Rhyl Library, Museum and Arts Centre, Church St, Rhyl LL18 3AA - T: (01745) 353814, Fax: 331438. Cur.: Rose Mahon
Local Museum
Town's role, firstly as a fishing village and later as a seaside resort, maritime and social history 40313

Ribchester

Ribchester Roman Museum, Riverside, Bremetennacum, Ribchester PR3 3XS - T: (01254) 878261, E-mail: ribchestermuseum@btconnect.com, Internet: www.ribchestermuseum.org. Dir.: Patrick Tostevin
Archaeological Museum - 1914
Prehistoric and Roman finds from the Ribble Valley and the fort and civilian settlement at Ribchester 40314

Richmond, North Yorkshire

Georgian Theatre Royal Museum, Victoria Rd, Richmond, North Yorkshire DL10 4DW - T: (01748) 823710, 825252, Fax: (0870) 7064494, E-mail: admin@georgiantheatreroyal.co.uk, Internet: www.georgiantheatreroyal.co.uk. Dir.: Vaughn Curtis
Performing Arts Museum
Coll of original playbills from 1792 to the 1840s, the oldest and largest complete set of painted scenery in Britain, dating from 1836, displays of model theatres, photographs 40315

Green Howards Museum, Trinity Church Sq, Richmond, North Yorkshire DL10 4QN - T: (01748) 826561, Fax: 826561, E-mail: greenhowardsmus@aol.com, Internet: www.greenhowards.org.uk. Dir.: J.R. Chapman
Military Museum - 1973
History of the regiment since 1688, uniforms, medals, equipment, paintings, photographs & memorabilia 40316

Richmondshire Museum, Ryder's Wynd, Richmond, North Yorkshire DL10 4JA - T: (01748) 825611
Local Museum
Development of the Richmond area since 1071, earlier archaeological material, Anglo-Saxon carved stones, farming and craftsmen's tools and equipment, leadmining relics, costumes, needlework, reconstructions of a carpenter's and a blacksmith's shop, model of Richmond railway station, old photographs and prints 40317

Richmond, Surrey

Ham House, Ham St, Petersham, Richmond, Surrey TW10 7RS - T: (020) 89401950, Fax: 83326903, E-mail: shhgen@smtp.ntrust.org.uk, Internet: www.nationaltrust.org.uk/southern
Local Museum
19th-c kitchen, textiles, paintings and tapestries 40318

Museum No 1, Royal Botanic Gardens, Kew, Richmond, Surrey TW9 3AE - T: (020) 83325706, Fax: 83325768, E-mail: h.prendergast@rbgkew.org.uk, Internet: www.rbgkew.org.uk/collections/ecbot.html. Cur.: Dr. D.V. Prendergast
Natural History Museum
Economic botany coll, useful plants and their products worldwide, wood coll 40319

Museum of Richmond, Old Town Hall, Whittaker Av, Richmond, Surrey KT9 1TP - T: (020) 83321141, Fax: 89487570, E-mail: musrich@globalnet.co.uk, Internet: www.museumofrichmond.com. Cur.: Simon Lace
Local Museum
Local history 40320

Queen Charlotte's Cottage, Kew Gardens, Kew Rd, Richmond, Surrey TW9 3AB - T: (0870) 7515179, Internet: www.hrp.org.uk
Historical Museum
Royal picnic house 40321

Rickmansworth

Batchworth Lock Canal Centre, 99 Church St, Rickmansworth WD3 1JD - T: (01923) 778382, Fax: 710903
Science&Tech Museum
Visitor centre, maps, information, books, photographs of old Batchworth, working boats on canal, canal trips on summer sunday afternoons 40322

Three Rivers Museum and Local History, Basing House, Rickmansworth WD3 8QH - T: (01923) 710365
Local Museum
Collection of photographs 40323

Rievaulx

Rievaulx Abbay, Rievaulx YO6 5LB - T: (01439) 798340, Fax: 798480, E-mail: yorknu@smtp.ntrust.org.uk. Cur.: Andrew Morrison
Decorative Arts Museum / Religious Arts Museum
English landscape design in the 18th c, medieval tiles, everyday items 40324

Ripley, Derbyshire

Midland Railway Centre, Butterley Station, Ripley, Derbyshire DE5 3QZ - T: (01773) 747674, Fax: 570721, E-mail: info@midlandrailwaycentre.co.uk. Cur.: Dudley Fowkes
Science&Tech Museum 40325

Ripley, North Yorkshire

Ripley Castle, Ripley, North Yorkshire HG3 3AY - T: (01423) 770152, Fax: 771745, E-mail: enquiries@ripleycastle.co.uk, Internet: www.ripleycastle.co.uk. Dir.: Sir Thomas C.W. Ingilby
Historical Museum - 1307
Civil War armour, Elizabethan panelling 40326

Ripon

Newby Hall, Ripon HG4 5AE - T: (01765) 322583, Fax: (01423) 324452, E-mail: info@newbyhall.com, Internet: www.newbyhall.com. Dir.: Richard Compton
Fine Arts Museum / Decorative Arts Museum
Classical statuary, Chippendale furniture, chamber pots, Gobelin tapestries 40327

Ripon Prison and Police Museum, Saint Marygate, Ripon HG4 1LX - T: (01765) 690799, 603006. Dir.: J.K. Whitehead
Historical Museum
Police mementoes and equipment from the 17th c to the present day, illustration of the 17th to 19th-c methods of confinement and punishment 40328

Ripon Workhouse Museum, Sharow View, Allhallowgate, Ripon HG4 1LX. Cur.: Ralph Lindley
Historical Museum
Victorian poor law artefacts 40329

Robertsbridge

Bodiam Castle, Robertsbridge TN32 5UA - T: (01580) 830436, Fax: 830398, E-mail: bodiamcastle@nationaltrust.org.uk, Internet: www.nationaltrust.org.uk/places/bodiamcastle
Historical Museum - 1926
Relics connected with Bodiam castle 40330

Robin Hood's Bay

Robin Hood's Bay and Fylingdale Museum, Fisherhead, Robin Hood's Bay YO22 4ST - T: (01947) 880097
Local Museum
Local social history, geology 40331

Rochdale

Rochdale Art and Heritage Centre, Esplanade, Rochdale OL16 1AQ - T: (01706) 342154, Fax: 712723, E-mail: artgallery@rochdale.gov.uk. Dir.: Andrew Pearce
Fine Arts Museum / Local Museum - 1903
British paintings and watercolours, contemporary paintings, local social history 40332

Rochdale Pioneers Museum, 31 Toad Ln, Rochdale OL12 0NU - T: (01706) 524920, Fax: (0161) 2462946, E-mail: museum@co-op.ac.uk, Internet: museum.co-op.ac.uk. Cur.: Gillian Lonergan
Historical Museum - 1931
Formation of the Rochdale Equitable Pioneers Society, which marked the beginning of the worldwide co-operative movement, Co-operative Wholesale Society, celebrations (1944 and 1994) celebrations, international social reformer and co-operator Robert Owen 40333

Rochester

Charles Dickens Centre, Eastgate House, High St, Rochester ME1 1EW - T: (01634) 844176, Fax: 844676
Special Museum - 1903
Victorian furniture, memorabilia of Charles Dickens 40334

Guildhall Museum, High St, Rochester ME1 1PY - T: (01634) 848717, Fax: 832919, E-mail: guildhall.museum@medway.gov.uk. Dir.: Peter Boreham, Sc. Staff: Steve Nye (Archaeology, Collections), N. Waghorne (Clerical and Admin. support), A. Freeman (Display and Technic), Jeremy Clarke (Education)
Historical Museum
18th-19th c prison hulks, prisoner-of-war ship models 40335

Medway Towns Gallery, Civic Centre, Strood, Rochester ME20 4AW - T: (01634) 727777
Public Gallery 40336

Strood Library Gallery, 32 Bryant Rd, Strood, Rochester ME2 3EP - T: (01634) 718161, Fax: 718161
Public Gallery 40337

Rolvenden

C.M. Booth Collection of Historic Vehicles, c/o Falstaff Antiques, 63-67 High St, Rolvenden TN17 4LP - T: (01580) 241234. Dir.: C.M. Booth
Science&Tech Museum - 1972
Morgan 3-wheel cars 40338

Romney Marsh

Brenzett Aeronautical Museum, Ivychurch Rd, Brenzett, Romney Marsh TN29 0EE - T: (01797) 344747, Internet: www.kent2do.com/brenzettaeronautical. Chm.: Frank J. Beckley, Adviser: Ron Pain
Military Museum / Historical Museum - 1972
Former Womens Land Army Hostel, coll incl engines and other relicts from British ,American and German wartime aircraft, the 4 1/2 ton dam-buster bomb, designed by Sir Barnes Wallis in 1943, Vampire MKII, Dakota Nose, Canberra 40339

Brenzett Museum → Brenzett Aeronautical Museum

Romsey

Mountbatten Exhibition, Broadlands, Romsey SO51 9ZD - T: (01794) 505010, Fax: 518605, E-mail: admin@broadlands.net, Internet: www.broadlands.net
Historical Museum
Lives and careers of Lord and Lady Mountbatten 40340

Rosemarkie

Groam House Museum, High St, Rosemarkie IV10 8UF - T: (01381) 620961, Fax: 621730, E-mail: groamhouse@ecosse.net. Cur.: Susan Seright
Archaeological Museum - 1989
13 Pictish sculptured stones & Rosemarkie Pictish cross-slab, artistic impressions of Ross and Cromarty Pictish stones, photographs of all the Pictish carved stones in Scotland, celtic art by George Bain 40341

Roslin

Rosslyn Chapel, Roslin EH25 9PU - T: (0131) 4402159, Fax: 4401979, E-mail: rosslych@aol.com, Internet: www.rosslynchapel.org.uk. Dir.: Stuart Beattie
Historic Site 40342

Rothbury

Cragside House, Rothbury NE65 7PX - T: (01669) 620150, Fax: 620066, E-mail: ncrvmx@smtp.ntrust.org.uk
Decorative Arts Museum
Original furniture and fittings, stained glass, earliest wallpaper, Lord Armstrong's first hydro-electric lighting 40343

Rotherham

Clifton Park Museum, Clifton Ln, Rotherham S65 2AA - T: (01709) 823635, Fax: 823631, E-mail: steve.blackbourn@rotherham.gov.uk, Internet: www.rotherham.gov.uk. Dir.: Di Billups
Local Museum - 1893
Rockingham porcelain, Roman archaeology 40344

Rotherham Art Gallery, Walker Pl, Rotherham S65 1JH - T: (01709) 823621, Fax: 823653, E-mail: wendyfoster@rotherham.gov.uk, Internet: www.roterham.gov.uk. Dir.: David Gilbert
Public Gallery - 1893
Fine and decorative art 40345

York and Lancaster Regimental Museum, Arts Centre, Walker Pl, Rotherham S65 1JH - T: (01709) 382121 ext 3633, Fax: 823631, E-mail: steve.blackbourn@rotherham.gov.uk, Internet: www.rotherham.gov.uk. Dir.: Di Billups
Military Museum - 1930
Uniform, orders, medals and effects of field marshal Viscount H.C.O. Plumer of Messines 40346

Rothesay

Bute Museum, Stuart St, Rothesay PA20 0BR - T: (01700) 502248, E-mail: thomas.clegg@btinternet.com. Dir.: Alexandra Montgomery, Cur.: Ivor Gibbs
Local Museum - 1905
Local archaeology, geology, mineralogy, natural history, social history 40347

Royston

Royston and District Museum, Lower King St, Royston SG8 5AL - T: (01763) 242587. Cur.: Carole Kaszak
Local Museum
Local archaeology, social history, local art 40348

Wimpole Hall and Home Farm, Arrington, Royston SG8 0BW - T: (01223) 207257, Fax: 207838, E-mail: aweusr@smtp.ntrust.org.uk, Internet: www.wimpole.org. Cust.: Georges Potirakis
Local Museum / Agriculture Museum 40349

Ruddington

Nottingham Transport Heritage Centre, Mere Way, Ruddington NG11 6NX - T: (0115) 9405705, Fax: 9405909, Internet: www.nthc.org.uk. Dir.: Alan Kemp
Science&Tech Museum
Steam railway and bus, signal boxes and sundry railwayana 40350

Ruddington Framework Knitters' Museum, Chapel St, Ruddington NG11 6HE - T: (0115) 9846914, Fax: 9841174, E-mail: jack@smirfitt.demon.co.uk, Internet: www.rfkm.org. Pres.: Prof. Stanley Chapman
Special Museum - 1971
Textile machinery 40351

Ruddington Village Museum, Saint Peters Rooms, Church St, Ruddington NG11 6HA - T: (0115) 9146645. Cur.: Gavin Walker
Local Museum - 1968
Village history, fish and chips shop, pharmacy 40352

Rufford

Rufford Old Hall, nr Ormskirk, Rufford L40 1SG - T: (01704) 821254, Fax: 821254, E-mail: rrufoh@smtp.ntrust.org.uk, Internet: www.nationaltrust.org.uk. Man.: Nick Ralls
Folklore Museum - 1936
Antique furniture, tapestries, armaments 40353

Rugby

HM Prison Service Museum, Newbold Revel, Rugby CV23 0TH - T: (01788) 834167/68, Fax: 834186, E-mail: museum@breathemail.net, Internet: www.hmprisonservice.gov.uk. Cur.: Elizabeth Cheetham
Special Museum - 1982
Irons, fetters, gyves, a door from cells visited by the Wesley brothers at Oxford Prison, original tools, uniforms, photographs, objects - archives 40354

James Gilbert Rugby Football Museum, 5 Saint Matthews St, Rugby CV21 3BY - T: (01788) 333889, Fax: 540795, E-mail: sales@james-gilbert.com, Internet: www.james-gilbert.com. Dir.: Pat Kidd
Special Museum - 1985
History of the development of Rugby football 40355

Rugby Art Gallery and Museum, Little Gborow St, Rugby CV21 3BZ - T: (01788) 533201, Fax: 533204, E-mail: rugbyartgallery&museum@rugby.gov.uk, Internet: www.rugbygalleryandmuseum.org.uk. Dir.: Wendy Parry
Public Gallery / Local Museum - 2000
Rugby coll, British art (20th c), Tripontium 40356

Rugby School Museum, 10 Little Church St, Rugby CV21 3AW - T: (01788) 556109, E-mail: museum@rugbyschool.net. Man.: Rusty MacLean
Historical Museum / Special Museum
School history and artefacts, early Rugby Football memorabilia, art colls 40357

Rugeley

Brindley Bank Pumping Station and Museum, Wolseley Rd, Rugeley WS15 2EU - T: (01922) 38282
Science&Tech Museum
Flowmeters, pumps, maps, documents and other items illustrating the history of the Waterworks and the public water supply in the area 40358

Runcorn

Norton Priory Museum, Manor Park, Tudor Rd, Runcorn WA7 1SX - T: (01928) 569895, Fax: 589743, E-mail: info@nortonpriory.org, Internet: www.nortonpriory.org. Dir.: Steven Miller
Religious Arts Museum - 1975
Medieval decorated floor tiles, medieval carved stonework, remains of medieval priory, medieval mosaic tile floor (70 sq.m.), statue of St. Christopher, 12th c undercroft, contemporary sculpture - priory remains, gardens 40359

Rustington

Rustington Heritage Exhibition Centre, 34 Woodlands Av, Rustington BN16 3HB - T: (01903) 784792
Local Museum
Social history 40360

Ruthin

Ruthin Craft Centre, Park Rd, Ruthin LL15 1BB - T: (01824) 704774, Fax: 702060. Dir.: Philip Hughes, Jane Gerrard
Decorative Arts Museum 40361

Ruthwell

Savings Banks Museum, Ruthwell DG1 4NN - T: (01387) 870640, E-mail: info@savingsbanksmuseum.co.uk, Internet: www.savingsbanksmuseum.co.uk. Cur.: Linda Williams
Special Museum - 1974
History of savings banks movement, coll of money boxes, bank memorabilia, familiy history, Runic stone - archive 40362

Rye

Rye Art Gallery, Ockman Ln and East St, Rye TN31 7JY - T: (01797) 223218, 222433, Fax: 225376. Dir.: Eric Money
Fine Arts Museum / Decorative Arts Museum
Contemporary fine art and craft 40363

Rye Castle Museum, 3 East St, Rye TN31 7JY - T: (01797) 226728. Dir.: A.V Downend
Local Museum - 1928
Medieval Rye pottery, modern Rye pottery, prints and drawings local scenes, costumes, cinque ports regalia, 18th c fire engine, toys, maritime history of Rye 40364

Rye Heritage Centre Town Model, Strand Quay, Rye TN31 7AY - T: (01797) 226696, Fax: 223460, E-mail: ryetic@rother.gov.uk, Internet: www.visitrye.co.uk. Dir.: J. Arkley
Local Museum 40365

Saffron Walden

Audley End House, Saffron Walden CB11 4JF - T: (01799) 522842, Fax: 521276, Internet: www.english-heritage.org.uk. Cur.: Gareth Hughes
Decorative Arts Museum
House history, Howard, Neville and Cornwallis coll, early neo-classical furniture, British Portraits, natural history, silver coll 40366

Fry Public Art Gallery, Bridge End Gardens, Castle St, Saffron Walden CB10 1BD - T: (01799) 513779, Fax: 520212, E-mail: gcummings@totalise.co.uk, Internet: www.fryartgallery.org. Dir.: Nigel Weaver
Fine Arts Museum - 1985
Works by 20th c artists from the area of North West Essex, incl Ravilious, Bawden, Rothenstein, Aldridge, Rowntree, Cheese, Hoyle a.o. 40367

Saffron Walden Museum, Museum St, Saffron Walden CB10 1JL - T: (01799) 510333, Fax: 510334, E-mail: museum@uttlesford.gov.uk. Cur.: Carolyn Wingfield, Sc. Staff: Sarah Kenyon (Natural History), Cons.: Lynn Morrison
Local Museum - 1832
Local archaeology, hilt of a 6th c ring sword, unique viking pendant necklace from saxon walden cemetery, social and natural hist, geology, ethnography, ceramics, glass, costumes, furniture, dolls 40368

Saint Albans

Clock Tower, Market Pl, Saint Albans AL1 - T: (01727) 751810, 751820, Fax: 859919, E-mail: museum@stalbans.gov.uk, Internet: www.stalbansmuseums.org.uk
Historical Museum
A 15th-c town belfry 40369

De Havilland Aircraft Heritage Centre, Mosquito Aircraft Museum, Salisbury Hall, London Colney, Saint Albans AL2 1EX - T: (01727) 822051, 826400, Fax: 826400, E-mail: wa050@dhamt.freeserve.co.uk, Internet: www.dehavillandmuseum.co.uk. Dir.: Ralph Steiner
Science&Tech Museum - 1959
Displays of de Havilland aircraft, Mosquito prototype - Library, photo archive 40370

Hypocaust, Verulamium Park, Saint Albans AL3 4SW - T: (01727) 751810, Fax: 859919, E-mail: museum@stalbans.gov.uk, Internet: www.stalbansmuseums.org.uk. Dir.: Chris Green
Historic Site
Roman hypocaust system and mosaic floor 40371

Kingsbury Watermill Museum, Saint Michaels Village, Saint Albans AL3 4SJ - T: (01727) 853502, Fax: 832662. Man.: Andrew Spratt
Science&Tech Museum / Agriculture Museum
Old farm implements 40372

Kyngston House Museum, Inkerman Rd, Saint Albans AL1 3BB - T: (01727) 819338, Fax: 836282, E-mail: museum@stalbans.gov.uk, Internet: www.stalbansmuseums.org.uk
Local Museum / Archaeological Museum
Social hist coll, archaeology 40373

Margaret Harvey Gallery, c/o Faculty of Art & Design, University of Herfordshire, 7 Hatfield Rd, Saint Albans AL1 3RS - T: (01707) 285376, Fax: 285310, E-mail: s.moore@herts.ac.uk. Dir.: Chris McIntyre
Public Gallery 40374

Museum of Saint Albans, Hatfield Rd, Saint Albans AL1 3RR - T: (01727) 819340, Fax: 837472, E-mail: museum@stalbans.gov.uk, Internet: www.stalbansmuseums.org.uk. Dir.: Chris Green
Local Museum - 1898
Salaman coll of trade and craft tools, social and local history, natural sciences, temporary exhibitions 40375

Roman Theatre of Verulamium, Gorhambury Dr, off Bluehouse Hill, Saint Albans AL3 6AH - T: (01727) 835035, Fax: 843657
Performing Arts Museum
Theatre discovered on the Gorhambury estate in 1847, fully excavated by Dr Kathleen Kenyon in 1935, first constructed in AD 160, the theatre was altered and modified during 2 centuries and was used for religious processions, ceremonies and plays 40376

Saint Albans Organ Museum, 320 Camp Rd, Saint Albans AL1 5PE - T: (01727) 851557, 869693, Fax: 851557. Dir.: Bill Walker
Music Museum - 1959
Two theatre pipe organs, four Belgian cafe organs, music boxes, mills violino vertuoso, player pianos, player reed organs 40377

Sopwell Nunnery, Cottonmill Ln, Saint Albans AL3 4SW - T: (01727) 751810, 751820, Fax: 859919, E-mail: museum@stalbans.gov.uk, Internet: www.stalbansmuseums.org.uk
Historical Museum
Ruins of house built by Sir Richard Lee in the mid-16th c 40378

Verulamium Museum, Saint Michael's, Saint Albans AL3 4SW - T: (01727) 751810, Fax: 859919, E-mail: museum@stalbans.gov.uk, Internet: www.stalbansmuseums.org.uk. Dir.: Chris Green
Archaeological Museum - 1939
Iron Age & Roman, excavated at Verulamium, c. 100 BC-AD 450, Roman hypocaust 40379

Saint Andrews

Bell Pettigrew Museum, c/o University of Saint Andrews, Bute Medical Bldg, Saint Andrews KY16 9TS - T: (01334) 463498, Fax: 462401, E-mail: asel@st-and.ac.uk, Internet: medialab.st-and.ac.uk/bellpet. Cur.: Prof. P.G. Willmer
Natural History Museum / University Museum 40380

British Golf Museum, Bruce Embankment, Saint Andrews KY16 9AB - T: (01334) 460046, Fax: 460064, E-mail: hilrywebster@randagc.org, Internet: www.britishgolfmuseum.co.uk. Dir.: Kathryn Baker, Cur.: Angela Morrison
Special Museum
Golf history in Britain since the middle ages, clubs, balls, trophies, costume, paintings 40381

Crawford Arts Centre, 93 North St, Saint Andrews KY16 9AD - T: (01334) 474610, Fax: 479880, E-mail: crawfordarts@crawfordarts.free-online.co.uk, Internet: www.crawfordarts.free-online.co.uk. Dir.: Diana A. Sykes
Public Gallery 40382

Saint Andrews Cathedral Museum, Saint Andrews - T: (0131) 2443101
Religious Arts Museum - 1950
Early Christian crosses, medieval cathedral relics, pre-Reformation tomb stones, 9th-10th c sarcophagus 40383

Saint Andrews Museum, Doubledykes Rd, Saint Andrews KY16 9DP - T: (01334) 412690, Fax: 413214, E-mail: museums.east@fife.gov.uk
Local Museum
Social history, archaeology 40384

Saint Andrews Preservation Museum, 12 North St, Saint Andrews - T: (01334) 477629, Internet: www.standrewspreservationtrust.co.uk. Cur.: Susan Keracher
Local Museum 40385

Saint Andrews University Museum Collections, University of Saint Andrews, Saint Andrews KY16 9TR - T: (01334) 462417, Fax: 462401, E-mail: hcr1@st-andrews.ac.uk, Internet: www.st-and.ac.uk/services/muscoll. Keeper: Prof. Ian A. Carradice
Natural History Museum / University Museum
Fine and applied art, silver, furniture, anatomy, pathology, chemistry, ethnography, geology, psychology, zoology, natural history, Amerindians, scientific apparatus and instruments 40386

Scotland's Secret Bunker, Troywood, Saint Andrews KY16 8QH - T: (01333) 310301, Fax: 312040, E-mail: mod@secretbunker.co.uk, Internet: www.secretbunker.co.uk
Historical Museum
Underground secret nuclear command bunker 40387

Saint Asaph

Saint Asaph Cathedral Treasury, The Cathedral, Saint Asaph LL19 0RD - T: (01745) 583429, Internet: www.stasaphcathedral.org.uk
Religious Arts Museum
Relics relating to the Clwyd area 40388

Saint Austell

Charlestown Shipwreck and Heritage Centre, Charlestown Harbour, Saint Austell PL25 3NJ - T: (01726) 69897, Fax: 68025. Dir.: John Brian Kneale
Historical Museum - 1976
Town and port hist, largest coll of shipwreck artefacts in UK, Richard Larn (diver) 40389

Wheal Martyn Cornwall's Museum of the Clay, Carthew, Saint Austell PL26 8XG - T: (01726) 850362, Fax: 850362, E-mail: info@wheal-martyn.com, Internet: www.wheal-martyn.com. Dir.: Peter Jennings, Cur.: Elisabeth Chald
Historical Museum 40390

Saint Brelade

Noirmont Command Bunker, Noirmont Point, Saint Brelade JE3 8JA, mail addr: M.P. Costard, Rte de Vinchelez, Saint Ouen JE3 2DJ - T: (01534) 746795, E-mail: m.costard@spoor.co.uk. Dir.: Matthew P. Costard
Historical Museum / Military Museum
German artillery command bunker 40391

Saint Dominick

Cotehele House, Saint Dominick PL12 6TA - T: (01579) 351346, Fax: 351222, E-mail: cotehele@nationaltrust.org.uk, Internet: www.nationaltrust.org.uk
Special Museum
Armour, tapestries and furniture 40392

Jersey Heritage Trust, Clarence Rd, Saint Dominick JE3 5HQ - T: (01534) 833300, Fax: 833301, E-mail: archives@jerseyheritagetrust.org, Internet: www.jerseheritagetrust.org
Association with Coll - 1993
Royal Court, H E Lieutenant Governor, parishes, churches, societies and individuals relating to the island 40393

Shamrock and Cotehele Quay Museum, National Maritime Museum Outstation, Cotehele Quay, Saint Dominick PL12 6TA - T: (01579) 350830. Dir.: Peter Allington
Science&Tech Museum - 1979
Historic sailing barge Shamrock 40394

Saint Fagans

Museum of Welsh Life, Saint Fagans CF5 6XB - T: (029) 20573500, Fax: 20573490, E-mail: mwl@nmgw.ac.uk, Internet: www.nmgw.ac.uk/mwl. Dir.: John Williams-Davies, Keeper: Dr. Beth Thomas
Open Air Museum / Folklore Museum / Agriculture Museum / Ethnology Museum - 1948
Farmhouses, cottages, Victorian shop complex, tollhouse, tannery, smithy, corn mill, woollen mill, bakehouse, pottery 40395

Saint Helens

Citadel's Artspace, Waterloo St, Saint Helens WA10 1PX - T: (01744) 735436, Internet: www.citadel.org.uk
Public Gallery 40396

Saint Helens Transport Museum (temporary closed), 51 Hall St, Saint Helens WA10 1DU - T: (01744) 451681, E-mail: nwmot@btinternet.com, Internet: www.sthelens-transport-museum.co.uk
Science&Tech Museum 40397

World of Glass, Chalon Way E, Saint Helens WA10 1BX - T: (01744) 22766, Fax: 616966, E-mail: info@worldofglass.com, Internet: www.worldofglass.com. Cur.: John Messner
Decorative Arts Museum / Local Museum
History of glass manufacture and design, local glass industry, local history, oils and waterclours 40398

Saint Helier

Barreau Le Maistre Art Gallery, Jersey Museum, The Weighbridge, Saint Helier JE2 3NF - T: (01534) 633300, Fax: 633301, E-mail: museum@jerseyheritagetrust.org, Internet: www.jerseyheritagetrust.org. Dir.: Michael Day
Fine Arts Museum 40399

Elizabeth Castle, Saint Aubins Bay, Saint Helier JE2 6QN - T: (01534) 723971, Fax: 610338, E-mail: museum@jerseyheritagetrust.org, Internet: www.jerseyheritagetrust.org. Dir.: Michael Day
Fine Arts Museum / Local Museum / Military Museum / Historic Site - 1923
Jersey militia, numismatic coll, silver, German occupation, regional hist, hist. tableaux, paintings by Jersey Artists 40400

Jersey Museum, The Weighbridge, Saint Helier JE2 3NF - T: (01534) 633300, Fax: 633301, E-mail: museum@jerseyheritagetrust.org.uk, Internet: www.jerseyheritagetrust.org. Dir.: Michael Day
Local Museum - 1992
Archaeology, German occupation, prison hist, rural life, finance, art 40401

Jersey Photographic Museum, Hôtel de France, Saint Saviour Rd, Saint Helier JE1 7PX - T: (01543) 614700, Fax: 887342, E-mail: ian.parker@jerseymail.co.uk, Internet: www.style2000.com
Science&Tech Museum
Cameras, images, processing, history of photography since 1840 40402

La Hougue Bie Museum, Grouville, Saint Helier JE2 3NF - T: (01534) 853823, Fax: 856472, E-mail: museum@jerseyheritagetrust.org, Internet: www.jerseyheritagetrust.org
Historical Museum / Archaeological Museum
Main coll of geological and archaeological artefacts 40403

Occupation Tapestry Gallery and Maritime Museum, New North Quay, Saint Helier JE2 3ND - T: (01534) 811043, Fax: 874099, E-mail: museum@jerseyheritagetrust.org, Internet: www.jerseyheritagetrust.org. Dir.: Michael Day
Decorative Arts Museum / Special Museum - 1996
Twelve-panel tapestry depicting the occupation of Jersey during WWII by Germany 40404

Saint Ives, Cambridgeshire

Norris Museum, 41 The Broadway, Saint Ives, Cambridgeshire PE17 5BX - T: (01480) 497314, E-mail: bob@norrismuseum.fsnet.co.uk. Cur.: R.I. Burn-Murdoch
Local Museum - 1931
Archaeology of all periods, French prisoner-of-war material from Norman Cross, ice-skates, 18th c fire engine, local prints, paintings, newspapers, paleolithic finds, lace production - library 40405

Saint Ives, Cornwall

Barbara Hepworth Museum and Sculpture Garden, Barnoon Hill, Saint Ives, Cornwall TR26 1TG - T: (01736) 796226, Fax: 794480, E-mail: ina.cole@tate.org.uk, Internet: www.tate.org.uk. Dir.: Susan Daniel McElroy, Sc. Staff: Bill Pashley (Gallery), Susan Lamb (Education), Ina Cole (Press and Publicity)
Fine Arts Museum - 1976
A selection of sculptures devoted to the work of Barbara Hepworth (1903-75) 40406

Penwith Galleries, Back Rd W, Saint Ives, Cornwall TR26 1NL - T: (01736) 795579. Cur.: Kathleen Watkins
Fine Arts Museum - 1949
Paintings, sculpture, pottery 40407

Saint Ives Museum, Wheal Dream, Saint Ives, Cornwall TR26 1PR - T: (01736) 796005
Local Museum - 1951
Local industries, arts, crafts, fishing, mining, paintings, folklore 40408

Saint Ives Society of Artists Members Gallery (Norway Gallery) and Mariners Gallery, Old Mariners Church, Norway Sq, Saint Ives, Cornwall TR26 1NA - T: (01736) 795582, E-mail: gallery@stisa.co.uk, Internet: www.stisa.co.uk. Dir.: Nicola Tilley, Cur.: Judy Joel
Public Gallery - 1926
Paintings, sculpture, cards, prints 40409

Tate Saint Ives, Porthmeor Beach, Saint Ives, Cornwall TR26 1TG - T: (01736) 796226, Fax: 794480, E-mail: ina.cole@tate.org.uk, Internet: www.tate.org.uk. Dir.: Susan Daniel McElroy, Sc. Staff: Bill Pashley (Gallery), Susan Lamb (Education), Alex Lambley (Development, Marketing), Ina Cole (Press, Information)
Public Gallery - 1993
Changing displays of 20th c art in the context of Cornwall focusing on the modern tradition for which St Ives is famous. Major exhibitions of work by contemporary artist 40410

Saint Lawrence

German Underground Hospital, c/o Paul Simmonds, Les Charrières Malorey, Meadowbank, Saint Lawrence JE3 1FU - T: (01534) 863442, Fax: 865970. Dir.: James McScowan
Military Museum
Wartime occupation, arms 40411

Hamptonne Country Life Museum, Rue de la Patente, Saint Lawrence JE3 1HG - T: (01534) 863955, Fax: 863935, E-mail: museum@jerseyheritagetrust.org, Internet: jerseyheritagetrust.org
Agriculture Museum - 1993
Restored farm complex tracing its hist through centuries of development 40412

Saint Margaret's Bay

Saint Margaret's Museum, Beach Rd, Saint Margaret's Bay CT15 6DZ - T: (01304) 852764, Fax: 853626, Internet: www.pinesgardenandmuseum.co.uk
Local Museum
Marine and local history, ships' badges 40413

Saint Margaret's Hope

W. Hourston Smithy Museum, Cromarty Sq, Saint Margaret's Hope KW17 2RH - T: (01856) 831558
Historical Museum
Blacksmiths equipment, machinery, tools, horse-drawn implements and smith-made articles 40414

Saint Mary's

Isles of Scilly Museum, Church St, Saint Mary's TR21 0JT - T: (01720) 422337, Fax: 422337, E-mail: info@iosmuseum.org, Internet: www.iosmuseum.org. Cur.: Amanda Martin
Local Museum
Scilly archaeology, history, shipwrecks, birds, flowers and lichens 40415

Saint Neots

Saint Neots Museum, 8 New St, Saint Neots PE19 1AE - T: (01480) 388921, Fax: 388791, Internet: www.stneotsmuseum.freeserve.co.uk. Cur.: Anna Mercer
Local Museum
Local history, local archaeology, crafts and trades, home and community life 40416

Saint Osyth

East Essex Aviation Society and Museum of the 40's, Martello Tower, Point Clear, Saint Osyth
Historical Museum
Military hist 40417

Saint Ouen

Channel Islands Military Museum, The Five Mile Rd, Saint Ouen JE2 4SL - T: (01534) 723136, Fax: 485647, E-mail: damienhorn@jerseymail.co.uk. Owner: Damian Horn, Ian Cabot
Historical Museum / Military Museum
Civilian and military items (June 1940-May 1945), WW2 German optical equipment, weapons, enigma decoding machine, Axis military motorcycles 40418

Jersey Battle of Flowers Museum, La Robeline, Mont des Corvees, Saint Ouen JE3 2ES - T: (01534) 482408. Cur.: Florence Bechelet
Special Museum
Animals and birds, made with dried wildflowers 40419

Saint Peter

Jersey Motor Museum (closed) 40420

Saint Peter's Bunker, German Occupation Museum, Saint Peter JE3 7AF - T: (01534) 481048
Military Museum - 1965
Military items of the German Army in WWII, seven rooms in an original underground bunker, German 'Enigma' decoding machine 40421

Saint Peter Port

Castle Cornet Military and Maritime Museums, Castle Emplacement, Saint Peter Port GY1 1AU - T: (01481) 721657, Fax: 714021, E-mail: admin@museum.guernsey.net, Internet: www.museum.gov.gg. Dir.: P.M. Sarl
Military Museum / Historical Museum / Historic Site - 1950
Royal militia coll 40422

Fort Grey and Shipwreck Museum, Rocquaine Bay, Saint Peter Port GY7 9BY - T: (01481) 265036, Fax: 263279, E-mail: admin@museum.guernsey.net, Internet: www.museum.guernsey.net. Dir.: P.M. Sarl
Military Museum / Historical Museum - 1976
Shipwrecks, Martello tower 40423

Guernsey Museum and Art Gallery, Candie Gardens, Saint Peter Port GY1 1UG - T: (01481) 726518, Fax: 715177, E-mail: admin@museum.guernsey.net, Internet: www.museum.guernsey.net. Dir.: P.M. Sarl, Sc. Staff: M. Harvey (Social History), H. Sebire (Archaeology), A.C. Howell (Natural History), P. Le Tissier (Project Development), S. Hamilton (Historic Sites), L. Ashton (Education)
Archaeological Museum / Local Museum / Fine Arts Museum
Natural hist, local watercolours, Frederick Corbin Lukis, Joshua Gosselin 40424

Hauteville House, Maison de Victor Hugo Paris, 38 Hauteville, Saint Peter Port GY1 1DG - T: (01481) 721911, Fax: 715913, E-mail: hugohouse@cwgsy.net. Dir.: Anne Blanchette, Cur.: Danielle Molinari
Special Museum
Exile House of Victor Hugo, in which he lived from 1856 to 1870, decorated in his very own unique style, using tapestries, Delft tiles carvings, chinoiseries, etc - garden 40425

Royal Air Force Museum 201 Squadron, Castle Cornet, Saint Peter Port GY1 1AU - T: (01481) 721657, Fax: 714021, E-mail: admin@museum.guernsey.net, Internet: www.museum.gov.gg. Dir.: P.M. Sarl
Military Museum - 2001
Hist of Guernsey's own Squadron 40426

Story of Castle Cornet, Castle Cornet, Saint Peter Port GY1 1AU - T: (01481) 721657, Fax: 714021, E-mail: admin@museum.guernsey.net, Internet: www.museum.gov.gg. Dir.: P.M. Sarl
Fine Arts Museum - 1997
Objects and paintings depicting the hist of the Castle 40427

Salcombe

Overbeck's Museum → Salcombe Maritime Museum

Salcombe Maritime Museum, Town Hall, Market St, Salcombe TQ8 8DE - T: (01548) 843080
Historical Museum - 1938
Secret childrens room, doll coll, Britain's lead soldier coll, paper conservation/illustration 40428

Salford

Chapman Gallery, University of Salford, Crescent, Salford M5 4WT - T: (0161) 7455000 ext 3219
Public Gallery 40429

The Lowry Gallery, Quays, Pier 8, Salford M50 3AZ - T: (0161) 8762020, Fax: 8762021, E-mail: info@thelowry.com, Internet: www.thelowry.com. Dir.: Lindsay Brooks, Cur.: Ruth Salisbury
Fine Arts Museum
Coll of paintings and drawings by L.S. Lowry 40430

Ordsall Hall Museum, Ordsall Ln, Salford M5 3AN - T: (0161) 8720251, Fax: 8724951, E-mail: admin@ordsallhall.org.uk, Internet: www.ordsallhall.org.uk. Dir.: Cindy Shaw
Folklore Museum - 1972
Folk life, leather figures, sword made in Solingen 40431

Salford Museum and Art Gallery, Crescent Peel Park, Salford M5 4WU - T: (0161) 7362649, Fax: 7459490, E-mail: salford.museum@salford.gov.uk, Internet: www.salford.gov.uk. Cur.: Nicola Power (Heritage Service), Julie Allsop (Heritage Development), Peter Ogilive (Collections), Meg Ashworth (Exhibitions), K. Craven (Research), Jo Clarke (Learning), A. Monaghan (Outreach)
Local Museum / Fine Arts Museum - 1850
Fine and applied arts, social and local history 40432

Salisbury

Edwin Young Collection, c/o Salisbury Library and Galleries, Market Pl, Salisbury SP1 1BL - T: (01722) 410614, Fax: 413214, E-mail: peterriley@wiltshire.gov.uk. Cur.: Peter Riley
Fine Arts Museum
Victorian and Edwardian oils and watercolours, contemporary paintings 40433

John Creasey Museum, c/o Salisbury Library and Galleries, Market Pl, Salisbury SP1 1BL - T: (01722) 324145, Fax: 413214, E-mail: peterriley@wiltshire.gov.uk. Cur.: Peter Riley
Special Museum / Fine Arts Museum
John Creasey's work, a local author - all editions, all languages, all pseudonyms (23 in all), contemporary art 40434

Mompesson House, The Close, Salisbury SP1 2EL - T: (01722) 335659, Fax: 321559, E-mail: mompessonhouse@nationaltrust.org.uk, Internet: www.nationaltrust.org.uk. Man.: Karen Rudd
Fine Arts Museum / Decorative Arts Museum
18th c drinking glasses, furniture, ceramics 40435

Royal Gloucestershire, Berkshire and Wiltshire Regiment Museum, 58 The Close, Salisbury SP1 2EX - T: (01722) 414536, Fax: 421626, E-mail: curator@thewardrobe.org.uk, Internet: www.thewardrobe.org.uk. Dir.: D.G. Chilton
Military Museum - 1982
History of the Regiment over a period of more than 200 years, include uniforms, weapons, equipment, campaign relics, medals and Regimental silver 40436

Salisbury and South Wiltshire Museum, The Kings House, 65 The Close, Salisbury SP1 2EN - T: (01722) 332151, Fax: 325611, E-mail: museum@salisburymuseum.org.uk, Internet: www.salisburymuseum.org.uk. Dir.: P.R. Saunders, Asst. Cur.: J. Standen, M. Wright
Local Museum / Archaeological Museum / Decorative Arts Museum - 1860
Archaeology, ceramics, English china, glass, Pitt Rivers coll, Brixie Jarvis coll of Wedgwood, Lace, Salisbury Giant - library 40437

Saltash

Saltash Heritage Centre, 17 Lower Fore St, Saltash PL12 6JQ - T: (01752) 848466. Cur.: David Coles
Local Museum
Local history 40438

Saltcoats

North Ayrshire Museum, Manse St, Kirkgate, Saltcoats KA21 5AA - T: (01294) 464174, Fax: 464234, E-mail: namuseum@globalnet.co.uk, Internet: www.northayrshiremuseums.org.uk. Cur.: Dr. Martin Bellamy
Local Museum - 1957
Local history, stone carvings, old kitchen 40439

Sandal

Sandal Castle, Manygates Ln, Sandal WF1 5PD - T: (01924) 305352
Historical Museum 40440

Sandford Orcas

Manor House, Sandford Orcas DT9 4SB - T: (01963) 220206. Dir.: Sir Mervyn Medlycott
Fine Arts Museum / Decorative Arts Museum
Queen Anne and Chippendale furniture, 17th c Dutch and 18th c English pictures, coll medieval stained glass 40441

Sandhurst, Berkshire

National Army Museum Sandhurst Departments, Royal Military Academy, Sandhurst, Berkshire GU15 4PQ - T: (01276) 63344 ext 2457. Dir.: I.G. Robertson, Cur.: S.K. Hopkins
Military Museum 40442

Sandling

Museum of Kent Life, Lock Ln, Sandling ME14 3AU - T: (01622) 763936, Fax: 662024, E-mail: enquiries@museum-kentlife.co.uk, Internet: www.museum-kentlife.co.uk. Dir.: Nigel Chew
Open Air Museum / Local Museum - 1983
Agricultural rural coll mainly from Kent: hopping industry darling buds of May exhibit, life in Kent exhibit, hop, herb and kitchen gardens, oast, granary, barn, farmhouse, farmyard, village hall 40443

Sandown

Dinosaur Isle, Culver Parade, Sandown PO36 8QA - T: (01983) 404344, Fax: 407502, E-mail: dinosaur@iow.gov.uk, Internet: www.dinosaurisle.com. Dir.: Martin Munt
Natural History Museum - 1913
Fossils, dinosaurs, local rocks 40444

Museum of Isle of Wight Geology → Dinosaur Isle

Sandringham

Sandringham House Museum, Sandringham PE35 6EN - T: (01553) 772675, Fax: (01485) 541571, Internet: www.sandringhamestate.co.uk. Dir.: G. Pattinson
Local Museum / Science&Tech Museum
Photogr, commemorative china, Royal Daimler cars, fire engine 40445

Sandwich

Guildhall Museum, Cattle Market, Sandwich CT13 9AN - T: (01304) 617197, Fax: 620170, E-mail: sandwichtowncouncil@btopenworld.com, Internet: www.sandwichtowncouncil.co.uk. Cur.: C.A. Wanostrocht
Historical Museum - 1930
Victorian photogr by a Sandwich photographer 1869 to 1897, 50 Nazi propaganda photogr of the German Army in the field, as distributed to their Embassies worldwide in the 1939-45 War 40446

Richborough Castle - Roman Fort, Richborough Rd, Sandwich CT13 9JW - T: (01304) 612013, Fax: 612013, E-mail: susan.harris@english-heritage.org.uk, Internet: www.english-heritage.org.uk. Dir.: Tracey Wahdan, Cur.: Nick Moore
Archaeological Museum - 1930
Roman finds, pottery, tools, coins, ornaments 40447

White Mill Rural Heritage Centre, Ash Rd, Sandwich CT13 9JB - T: (01304) 612076, Internet: www.kent.museums.org.uk/whitemill/home.htm. Head: R.G. Barber
Science&Tech Museum
Agricultural implements, artefacts and craft workers' tools, domestic artefacts, blacksmith forge, models 40448

Sanquhar

Sanquhar Tolbooth Museum, High St, Sanquhar DG4 5BN - T: (01659) 50186, E-mail: info@dumfriesmuseum.demon.co.uk, Internet: www.dumfriesmuseum.demon.co.uk. Dir.: Robert Martin
Local Museum
1735 town house, local history, geology knitting 40449

Sauchen

Castle Fraser, Sauchen AB51 7LD - T: (01330) 833463, Fax: 833819, E-mail: castlefraser@nts.org.uk. Man.: Nicola Hansen
Historical Museum 40450

Sawrey

Hill Top, Sawrey LA22 0LF - T: (015394) 36269, Fax: 36118, E-mail: rpmht@smtp.ntrust.org.uk, Internet: www.nationaltrust.org.uk. Man.: Caroline Binder
Special Museum
Beatrix Potter wrote many "Peter Rabbit" books here, furniture, china and other possessions 40451

Saxtead

Saxtead Green Post Mill, Saxtead Green, Saxtead IP13 9QQ - T: (01728) 685789, Internet: www.english-heritage.org.uk
Science&Tech Museum
Milling equipment, tools 40452

Scalloway

Scalloway Museum, Main St, Scalloway
Local Museum
Coll of objects relating to Scalloway and the nearby islands, dating from Neolithic times to the present day, a large photographic archive, Scalloway's role in the WWII 40453

Scarborough

Crescent Arts, The Crescent, Scarborough YO11 2PW - T: (01723) 371461, Fax: 506674, E-mail: info@crescentarts.co.uk, Internet: www.crescentarts.co.uk. Head: Mary Butter
Public Gallery 40454

Rotunda Museum of Archaeology and Local History, Museum Terrace, Vernon Rd, Scarborough YO11 2NN - T: (01723) 374839, Fax: 376941, E-mail: scab.meg@pop3.poptel.org.uk, Internet: www.scarboroughmuseum.org.uk. Dir.: Karen Snowden
Archaeological Museum / Local Museum - 1829
Regional archaeological coll, esp mesolithic, Bronze Age and medieval, fine surviving example of early purpose-built museums 40455

Scarborough Art Gallery, The Crescent, Scarborough YO11 2PW - T: (01723) 232323, Fax: 376941. Dir.: Helen Watson
Fine Arts Museum - 1947
Paintings (17th-20th c), local paintings (19th c), contemporary prints 40456

Wood End Museum, Londesborough Lodge, The Crescent, Scarborough YO11 2PW - T: (01723) 367326, Fax: 376941. Dir.: Karen Snowden
Natural History Museum - 1951
Regional fauna, flora and geology, entomology, conchology, vertebrates 40457

Scunthorpe

Normanby Hall, Normanby Hall Country Park, Scunthorpe DN15 9HU - T: (01724) 720588, Fax: 720337, E-mail: adam.smith@northlincs.gov.uk, Internet: www.northlincs.gov.uk/museums. Dir.: Susan Hopkinson
Decorative Arts Museum - 1964
Period furniture, decorations, costume galleries - Normanby park farming museum 40458

Normanby Park Farming Museum, Normanby Hall, Country Park, Scunthorpe DN15 9HU - T: (01724) 720588, Fax: 720337, E-mail: adam.smith@northlincs.gov.uk, Internet: www.northlincs.gov.uk/museums. Dir.: Susan Hopkinson
Agriculture Museum - 1989
Rural crafts and industry, transport, agriculture - Normanby Hall 40459

North Lincolnshire Museum, Oswald Rd, Scunthorpe DN15 7BD - T: (01724) 843533, Fax: 270474, E-mail: steve.thompson@northlincs.gov.uk, Internet: www.northlincs.gov.uk/museums. Cur.: K.A. Leahy, Keeper: S. Thompson, Susan Hopkinson
Local Museum - 1909
Geology, history and natural hist, archaeology, agriculture 40460

Seaford

Seaford Museum of Local History, Martello Tower, Esplanade, Seaford BN25 1JH - T: (01323) 898222, E-mail: museumseaford@tinyonline.co.uk, Internet: www.seafordmuseum.org
Local Museum - 1970
Housing register, huge photographic coll, Connie Brewer coll, television and radio 40461

Seaton

Seaton Delaval Hall, Estate Office, Seaton NE26 4QR - T: (0191) 2371493. Owner: Lord Hastings
Decorative Arts Museum
Pictures and documents 40462

Seaview

National Wireless Museum, Puckpool Park, Seaview PO34 5AR - T: (01983) 567665. Cur.: Douglas Byrne
Science&Tech Museum
History of wireless communications 40463

Seething

448th Bomb Group Memorial Museum, Airfield, Seething NR2 4HB - T: (01603) 614041
Military Museum 40464

Selborne

Gilbert White's House and the Oates Museum, The Wakes, Selborne GU34 3JH - T: (01420) 511275, Fax: 511040, E-mail: gilbertwhite@btinternet.com. Dir.: Maria Newbery
Special Museum - 1955
Restored 18th c home of Gilbert White, travels of Frank Oates in Africa, Cpt. L. Oates Antarctic fame - library 40465

Oates Memorial Museum and Gilbert White Museum → Gilbert White's House and the Oates Museum

Romany Folklore Museum and Workshop, Selborne GU34 3JW - T: (01420) 50486
Folklore Museum
Coll of living vans, other vehicles undergoing restoration in the workshop, the early history, language, music, dress and crafts of the gypsies 40466

Selkirk

Bowhill Collection, Selkirk TD7 5ET - T: (01750) 722204, Fax: 722204, E-mail: bht@buccleuch.com, Internet: www.heritageontheweb.co.uk. Cur.: Duke of Buccleuch
Decorative Arts Museum / Fine Arts Museum
Art coll, French furniture, silver, porcelain, relicts of Duke of Monmouth, Queen Victoria ans Sir Walter Scott 40467

Halliwell's House Museum, Halliwell's Close, Market Pl, Selkirk TD7 4BC - T: (01750) 20096, 20054, Fax: 23282, E-mail: museums@scotborders.gov.uk. Dir.: Ian Brown
Local Museum - 1984
Late 19th/early 20thc domestic ironmongery 40468

James Hogg Exhibition, Bowhill, Selkirk TD7 5ET - T: (01750) 722204, Fax: 722204, E-mail: bht@buccleuch.com. Cur.: Duke of Buccleuch
Special Museum
Life and work of the Scottish writer James Hogg 40469

Robson Gallery, Halliwells House Museum, Market Pl, Selkirk TD7 4BC - T: (01750) 20096, Fax: 23282, E-mail: museums@scotborders.gov.uk. Dir.: Ian Brown
Public Gallery 40470

Sir Walter Scott's Courtroom, Town Hall, Market Pl, Selkirk TD7 4BT - T: (01750) 720096, Fax: 723282, E-mail: museums@scotborders.gov.uk. Dir.: Ian Brown
Local Museum - 1994 40471

Selsey

Selsey Lifeboat Museum, Kingsway, Selsey PO20 0DL - T: (01243) 602387, Fax: 607790, E-mail: terry@kaytel.fsnet.co.uk
Historical Museum 40472

Settle

Museum of North Craven Life, The Folly, Settle BD24 9RN
Local Museum
Local history 40473

Sevenoaks

Knole, Sevenoaks TN15 0RP - T: (01732) 462100, 450608, Fax: 465528, E-mail: kknxxx@smtp.ntrust.org.uk. Dir.: Jane Sedge
Decorative Arts Museum
State rooms, paintings, furniture, tapestries, silver 40474

Sevenoaks Museum and Gallery, Library, Buckhurst Ln, Sevenoaks TN13 1LQ - T: (01732) 453118, 452384, Fax: 742682
Local Museum
Local geology, history, archaeology, local fossils, paintings 40475

Shackerstone

Shackerstone Railway Museum, Shackerstone Station, Shackerstone CV13 6NW - T: (01827) 880754, Fax: 881050, Internet: www.battlefield-line-railway.co.uk. Pres.: John C. Jacques Mbe
Science&Tech Museum
Coll of railway items, signalbox equipment, station signs, timetables from 1857 and dining-car crockery, eighteen paraffin lamps, a coll of WWII-railway posters 40476

Shaftesbury

Shaftesbury Abbey and Museum, Park Walk, Shaftesbury SP7 8JR - T: (01747) 852910, Fax: 852910, E-mail: user@shaftesburyabbey.fsnet.co.uk. Dir.: Anna McDowell
Archaeological Museum - 1951
Tiles, stone finds, Saxon relics, reconstruction of old church 40477

Shaftesbury Town Museum, Gold Hill, Shaftesbury SP7 8JW - T: (01747) 852157. Cur.: Pat Gates
Local Museum 40478

Shallowford

Izaak Walton's Cottage, Worston Ln, Shallowford ST15 0PA - T: (01785) 760278, Fax: 760278. Man.: Gillian Bould
Local Museum / Special Museum
Local history, fishing, material on Izaak Walton (1593-1683) author of 'The Compleat Angler' 40479

Sheerness

Minster Abbey Gatehouse Museum, Minster, Union Rd, Sheerness ME12 2HW - T: (01795) 872303, 661119, Internet: www.swaketiyrusn.ci.yi. Chairman: Jonathan Fryer
Local Museum
Local memorabilia, fossils, tools, costume, telephones, radios, photographs, toys 40480

Sheffield

Abbeydale Industrial Hamlet, Abbeydale Rd S, Sheffield S7 2QW - T: (0114) 2367731, Fax: 2353196, E-mail: postmaster@simt.co.uk, Internet: www.simt.co.uk. Dir.: John Hamshere
Science&Tech Museum - 1970
A fully restored 18th c water-powered skythe and steel works, four working water wheels, craftsmen on site, science, production of steel tools, development of steel manufacturing 40481

Bishops' House Museum, Norton Lees Ln, Sheffield S8 9BE - T: (0114) 2782600, Fax: 2782604, E-mail: info@sheffieldgalleries.org.uk, Internet: www.sheffieldgalleries.org.uk. Dir.: Dr. Gordon Rintoul
Special Museum - 1976
16th and 17th c oak furniture 40482

Fire Police Museum, 101-109 West Bar, Sheffield S3 8PT - T: (0114) 2491999, Fax: 2491999, Internet: www.hedgepig.freeserve.co.uk
Historical Museum
Fire fighting, police coll, Charlie Peace exhibition 40483

Graves Art Gallery, Surrey St, Sheffield S1 1XZ - T: (0114) 2782600, Fax: 2782604, E-mail: info@sheffieldgalleries.org.uk, Internet: www.sheffieldgalleries.org.uk. Dir.: Dr. Gordon Rintoul, Sc. Staff: Anne Goodchild (Visual Art)
Fine Arts Museum 40484

Handsworth Saint Mary's Museum, Handsworth Parish Centre, Rectory Grounds, Sheffield S13 9BZ - T: (0114) 2692537
Local Museum
Coll of photographs, artefacts and documents of the local community 40485

Kelham Island Museum, Alma St, off Corporation St, Sheffield S3 8RY - T: (0114) 2722106, Fax: 2757847, E-mail: postmaster@simt.co.uk, Internet: www.simt.co.uk. Dir.: John Hamshere
Historical Museum / Science&Tech Museum - 1982
Story of Sheffield, industry and life, working steam engine, workshops, working cutlers and craftspeople - library; lecture room 40486

Millennium Galleries, Arundel Gate, Sheffield S1 2PP - T: (0114) 2782600, Fax: 2782604, E-mail: info@sheffieldgalleries.org.uk, Internet: www.sheffieldgalleries.org.uk. Dir.: Dr. Gordon Rintoul, Sc. Staff: Caroline Krzesinska (Exhibitions, Collections), Dorian Church (Decorative Art)
Fine Arts Museum / Decorative Arts Museum - 2001
Metalworks, Ruskin coll, craft, design, visal art 40487

Ruskin Gallery → Millennium Galleries

Sheffield Bus Museum, Tinsley Tram Sheds, Sheffield Rd, Tinsley, Sheffield S9 2FY - T: (0114) 2553010, E-mail: webmaster@sheffieldbusmuseum.com, Internet: www.sheffieldbusmuseum.com. Dir.: David Roberts, Eric Wilson, Mike Greenwood, Keith Beeden
Science&Tech Museum
Buses from Sheffield area, tramcars 40488

Sheffield City Museum and Mappin Art Gallery (closed for edvelopment until 2005), Weston Park, Sheffield S10 2TP - T: (0114) 2782600, Fax: 2782604, E-mail: info@sheffieldgalleries.org.uk, Internet: www.sheffieldgalleries.org.uk. Dir.: Nick Dodd, Sc. Staff: Paul Richards (Natural History), Gill Woolrich (Archaeology and Ethnography), Kim Streets (Social History)
Local Museum / Fine Arts Museum - 1875
Archaeology, antiquities, armaments, applied arts, natural hist, relics, ethnography, geology, glass, entomology, numismatics, porcelain, paintings (16th- 19th c) 40489

Shepherd Wheel, Whiteley Woods, off Hangingwater Rd, Sheffield S11 - T: (0114) 2367731, Fax: 2353196, Internet: www.smit.co.uk
Science&Tech Museum - 1973
Old water-driven cutlery-grinding shop 40490

Traditional Heritage Museum, 605 Ecclesall Rd, Sheffield S11 8PR - T: (0114) 2226296, E-mail: j.widdowson@sheffield.ac.uk, Internet: www.shef.ac.uk/english/natcect. Cur.: Prof. J.D.A. Widdowson
University Museum
Life and work in Sheffield area, Muir Smith puppet coll, handicrafted trades - archives 40491

Shepton Mallet

East Somerset Railway, Cranmore Station, Shepton Mallet BA4 4QP - T: (01749) 880417, Fax: 880764, E-mail: info@eastsomersetrailway.org, Internet: www.EastSomersetRailway.org
Science&Tech Museum
Steam and diesel locomotives 40492

Shepton Mallet Museum, Council Offices, Great Ostry, Shepton Mallet
Local Museum / Natural History Museum / Archaeological Museum - 1900
Geology, fossils, Roman kiln and jewelry 40493

Sherborne

Sherborne Castle, New Rd, Sherborne DT9 5NR - T: (01935) 813182, Fax: 816727, E-mail: enquiries@sherbornecastle.com, Internet: www.sherbornecastle.com. Cur.: Ann Smith, Man.: Ian Pollard (Events)
Fine Arts Museum / Decorative Arts Museum - 1594
Oriental and European porcelain, painting 'Procession of Elizabeth I' attributed to Peake the Elder, furniture, pictures, miniatures - library 40494

Sherborne Museum, Abbeygate House, Church Ln, Sherborne DT9 3BP - T: (01935) 812252, E-mail: admin@shermus.fsnet.co.uk. Cur.: N. Darling-Finan
Local Museum - 1966
Local history, prehistoric finds, geology, Roman and medieval relics, silk production, 20th c fiberglass, local architecture and 14th c wall painting 40495

Worldwide Butterflies and Lullingstone Silk Farm, Compton House, Sherborne DT9 4QN - T: (01935) 74608, Fax: 29937
Natural History Museum - 1960 40496

Sheringham

North Norfolk Railway Museum, Station, Sheringham NR26 8RA - T: (01263) 822045, Fax: 823794
Science&Tech Museum
Steam locomotives, rolling stock, station buildings 40497

Sheringham Museum, Station Rd, Sheringham NR26 8RE - T: (01263) 821871, Fax: 825741, E-mail: peterbrooks@amserve.com. Dir.: Mary Blyth
Local Museum
Local history, customs and development, local families, boat building, lifeboats, fishing industry, geology, art gallery 40498

Shifnal

Royal Air Force Museum, Cosford, Shifnal TF11 8UP - T: (01902) 376200, Fax: 376211, E-mail: cosford@rafmuseum.com, Internet: www.cosfordairshow.co.uk. Dir.: John Francis, Cur.: Al McLean
Historical Museum
Military and civil aircraft, including the Victor and Vulcan bombers, the Hastings, the York, the Bristol 188, the last airworthy Britannia and other airliners used by British Airways, Missiles and aero engines also on display 40499

Shildon

Timothy Hackworth Victorian Railway Museum, Soho Cottages, Hackworth Close, Shildon DL4 1PQ - T: (01388) 777999, Fax: 777999, Internet: www.hackworthmuseum.co.uk. Dir.: Alan Pearce
Science&Tech Museum - 1975
Sans Pareil locomotive, family memorabilia, Stockton and Darlington railway, Soho works beam engine, Braddyil Locomotive C 1836 40500

Shipley

Museum of Victorian Reed Organs and Harmoniums, Victoria Hall, Victoria Rd, Saltaire, Shipley BD18 3JS - T: (01274) 585601, E-mail: phil@harmoniumservice.demon.co.uk. Dir.: Phil Fluke, Pam Fluke
Music Museum - 1986
Coll of around 100 instruments, Harmoniums of all types and styles 40501

Shoreham

Shoreham Aircraft Museum, High St, Shoreham TN14 7TB - T: (01959) 524416, Fax: 524416, E-mail: geoff@aviartnutkins.com, Internet: www.shoreham-aircraft-museum.co.uk. Cur.: Geoff Nutkins
Historical Museum / Military Museum
Aviation relics from crashed British and German aircrafts (shot down over Southern England 1940), flying equipment, home front memorabilia 40502

Shoreham-by-Sea

Marlipins Museum, 36 High St, Shoreham-by-Sea BN43 5DA - T: (01273) 462994, Fax: (01323) 844030, E-mail: smomich@sussexpast.co.uk, Internet: www.sussexpast.co.uk. Cur.: Helen E. Poole
Local Museum - 1922/1928
Local history, paintings of ships, ship models, in a 12th-14th c building 40503

Shoreham Airport Historical Exhibition, Terminal Bldg, Shoreham Airport, Shoreham-by-Sea - T: (01273) 441061, Fax: 440146
Science&Tech Museum
Hist of Shoreham Airport 40504

Shotts

Shotts Heritage Centre, Benhar Rd, Shotts ML27 5EN - T: (01501) 821556
Local Museum
Iron and coal industries and social history, local studies 40505

Shrewsbury

Attingham Park, Atcham, Shrewsbury SY4 4TP - T: (01743) 708162, 708123, Fax: 708175, E-mail: matsec@smtp.ntrust.org.uk. Man.: Jane Alexander
Decorative Arts Museum
Italian furniture (c 1810), silver and pictures, printed pottery 40506

Clive House Museum, College Hill, Shrewsbury SY1 1LT - T: (01743) 354811, Fax: 358411, E-mail: museums@shrewsbury-atcham.gov.uk, Internet: www.shrewsburymuseums.com
Local Museum
Archaeology, geology of Shropshire, paintings and prints, prehistory, local and regional social history, natural history 40507

Coleham Pumping Station, Longden Coleham, Shrewsbury SY3 7DB - T: (01743) 361196, Fax: 358411, E-mail: museums@shrewsbury-atcham.gov.uk, Internet: www.shrewsburymuseums.com
Science&Tech Museum 40508

Radbrook Culinary Museum, Centre for Catering and Management Studies, Radbrook Rd, Shrewsbury SY3 9BL - T: (01743) 232686, Fax: 271563, E-mail: mail@s-cat.ac.uk, Internet: www.s-cat.ac.uk. Head: Sue Warton, Library: F. Bates
Special Museum - 1985
Food, nutrition, housecraft, education 40509

Rowley's House Museum → Shrewsbury Museum and Art Gallery

Shrewsbury Castle, Castle St, Shrewsbury SY1 2AT - T: (01743) 358516, Fax: 270023, E-mail: museums@shrewsbury-atcham.gov.uk, Internet: www.shrewsburymuseums.com. Cust.: L. Cliffe
Decorative Arts Museum 40510

Shrewsbury Museum and Art Gallery, Rowley's House, Barker St, Shrewsbury SY1 1QH - T: (01743) 361196, Fax: 358411, E-mail: museums@shrewsbury-atcham.gov.uk, Internet: www.shrewsburymuseums.com. Man.: Peter Boyd (Collections), Mary White (Operations), Sc. Staff: Mike Stokes (Archaeology)
Local Museum / Archaeological Museum / Decorative Arts Museum - 1935
Main repository of excavated material from Viroconium, Shropshire geology and prehist, natural hist incl Shropshire herbarium, costume, decorative arts incl Shropshire manufacturers 40511

Shropshire Regimental Museum, Castle, Shrewsbury SY1 2AT - T: (01743) 262292, 358516, Fax: 270023, E-mail: shropsrm@zoom.co.uk, Internet: www.shropshireregimental.co.uk. Cur.: Peter Duckers
Military Museum 40512

Shropshire

Boscobel House, Brewood, Bishop's Wood, Shropshire ST19 9AR - T: (01902) 850244, Internet: www.english-heritage.org.uk. Head: Peter Trickett
Local Museum
Furniture, textiles, agricultural machinery, forge, dairy and salting room 40513

Sibsey

Trader Windmill, off A16, W of Sibsey, Sibsey PE22 0UT, mail addr: c/o Ian Ansell, Pear Tree Cottage, Pitcher Row Ln, Algarkirk PE20 2LJ - T: (01205) 460647, E-mail: traderwindmill@sibsey.fsnet.co.uk, Internet: www.sibsey.fsnet.co.uk/trader_wind-mill_sibsey.htm
Science&Tech Museum
Flour milling related machinery and bygones 40514

Sidmouth

Sidmouth Museum, Hope Cottage, Church St, Sidmouth EX10 8LY - T: (01395) 516139. Cur.: Dr. Robert F. Symes
Local Museum
Local history 40515

Vintage Toy and Train Museum, Field's Department Store, Market Pl, Sidmouth EX10 8LU - T: (01395) 515124 ext 208. Dir.: R.D.N. Salisbury
Special Museum - 1982
Coll of metal and mechanical toys made between 1925 and 1975, coll of French Hornby trains, made at the Meccano factory in Paris between 1930 and 1950, sets of GWR wooden jigsaw puzzles 40516

Silchester

Calleva Museum, Bramley Rd, Silchester RG7 2LU, mail addr: 11 Romans Gate, Pamber Heath RG26 3EH - T: (0118) 9700825. Dir.: Prof. M.G. Fulford
Archaeological Museum - 1951
Roman period 40517

Silsoe

Wrest Park, Silsoe MK45 4HS - T: (01525) 860152, Internet: www.english-heritage.org.uk. Cur.: Gareth Hughes
Local Museum
18th c sculpture in a landscaped garden 40518

Singleton

Weald and Downland Open Air Museum, Singleton PO18 0EU - T: (01243) 811348, Fax: 811475, E-mail: wealddown@mistral.co.uk, Internet: www.wealddown.co.uk. Dir.: Richard Harris
Open Air Museum / Agriculture Museum - 1967
40 historic buildings, plumbing, carpentry, wheelwrighting, blacksmithing and shepherding equipment, working watermill, medieval farmstead 40519

Sittingbourne

Court Hall Museum, High St, Milton Regis, Sittingbourne ME10 1RW - T: (01795) 478446
Local Museum
Documents, objects and photographs 40520

Dolphin Sailing Barge Museum, Crown Quay Ln, Sittingbourne ME10 3SN - T: (01795) 423215, 470598, Internet: www.kentacces.org.uk/artmuse/dolphin/home.html. Dir.: Peter J. Morgan
Science&Tech Museum - 1969

Sailing barge artefacts, photographs, maps, documents, brickmaking tools, sample bricks, moored in our basin is the Thames Sailingbarge Cambria 40521

Sittingbourne and Kemsley Light Railway, POB 300, Sittingbourne ME10 2DZ - T: (0871) 8714606, E-mail: info@sklr.net, Internet: www.sklr.net
Science&Tech Museum
Narrow gauge locomotives and wagons, photographs, industrial archaeology, papermaking 40522

Sittingbourne Heritage Museum, 67 East St, Sittingbourne ME10 4BQ - T: (01795) 423215
Local Museum
Archaeological finds, local history 40523

Skegness

Church Farm Museum, Church Rd S, Skegness PE25 2ET - T: (01754) 766658, Fax: 898243, E-mail: walkerr@lincolnshire.gov.uk, Internet: www.lincolnshire.gov.uk. Dir.: Heather Cummins
Open Air Museum / Agriculture Museum - 1976 40524

Skidby

Skidby Windmill and Museum of East Riding Rural Life, Beverley Rd, Skidby HU16 5TF - T: (01482) 848405, Fax: 848432, E-mail: janet.tierney@eastriding.gov.uk. Dir.: Janet Tierney, Jane Bielby
Historical Museum / Agriculture Museum - 1974
Alex West (agricultural exhibits) 40525

Skinningrove

Cleveland Ironstone Mining Museum, Deepdale, Skinningrove TS13 4AP - T: (01287) 642877, Fax: 642970, E-mail: visits@ironstonemuseum.co.uk, Internet: www.ironstonemuseum.co.uk. Dir.: Peter Tuffs, Kate Brennan
Science&Tech Museum
Social history, tools, minestone face 40526

Skipton

Craven Museum, Town Hall, High St, Skipton BD23 1AH - T: (01756) 706407, Fax: 706412, E-mail: museum@cravendc.gov.uk, Internet: www.cravendc.gov.uk. Dir.: Andrew Mackay
Local Museum - 1928 40527

Embsay Bolton Abbey Steam Railway, Bolton Abbey Station, Skipton BD23 6AF - T: (01756) 710614, Fax: 710720, E-mail: embsay.steam@btinternet.com, Internet: www.embsayboltonabbeyrailway.org.uk. Dir.: Stephen Walker
Science&Tech Museum - 1968
Coll of industrial steam locomotives in Britain, items of passenger and freight rolling stock, photogr and documents illustrates the hist of the line and of the Trust which operates it 40528

Sledmere

Sledmere House, Sledmere YO25 3XG - T: (01377) 236637, Fax: 236500
Fine Arts Museum 40529

Slough

Slough Museum, 278-286 High St, Slough SL1 1NB - T: (01753) 526422, Fax: 526422, E-mail: info@sloughmuseum.co.uk, Internet: www.sloughmuseum.co.uk. Dir.: Joanna Follett
Local Museum 40530

Smethwick

Avery Historical Museum, c/o Avery Weigh-Tronix, Foundry Ln, Smethwick B66 2LP - T: (0870) 9034343, Fax: (0121) 5652677, E-mail: info@avery-berkel.com, Internet: www.averyweigh-tronix.com. Cur.: J. Doran
Historical Museum - 1928
Coll of scales, weights and records relating to the hist of weighing 40531

Soudley

Dean Heritage Museum, Camp Mill, Soudley GL14 2UB - T: (01594) 822170, Fax: 823711, E-mail: deanmuse@btinternet.com, Internet: www.deanheritagemuseum.com. Dir.: Kate Biggs
Local Museum - 1982
Forest of dean, foresty, royal hunting, clocks, mining, geology, archaeology, social/industrial history - reference library 40532

South Molton

South Molton and District Museum, Guildhall, South Molton EX36 3AB - T: (01769) 572951, Fax: 574008, E-mail: curatorsouthmolton@lineone.net, Internet: www.devonmuseums.net/southmolton. Cur.: Ruth Spires
Local Museum - 1951
Local hist, farming and mining, pewter, fire engines, cider presses, local painting, pottery, original royal charters 40533

South Queensferry

Dalmeny House, South Queensferry EH30 9TQ - T: (0131) 3311888, Fax: 3311788, E-mail: events@dalmeny.co.uk, Internet: www.dalmeny.co.uk
Decorative Arts Museum
French furniture, tapestries, porcelain from Mentmore, Napleonic coll, British portraits 40534

Hopetoun House, South Queensferry EH30 9SL - T: (0131) 3312451, Fax: 3191885. Dir.: P. Normand
Decorative Arts Museum / Fine Arts Museum - 1700
Paintings, mid-18th c furniture, sculpture, manuscripts, costumes, tapestries, architecture 40535

Queensferry Museum, 53 High St, South Queensferry EH30 9HP - T: (0131) 3315545, Fax: 5573346, Internet: www.cac.org.uk. Cur.: Denise Brace
Local Museum - 1951
History of the Royal Burgh 40536

South Shields

Arbeia Roman Fort and Museum, Baring St, South Shields NE33 2BB - T: (0191) 4561369, Fax: 4276862, E-mail: liz.elliott@twmuseums.org.uk. Dir.: Alec Coles, Cur.: Paul Bidwell (Archaeology)
Archaeological Museum - 1953
Roman finds from the fort 40537

South Shields Museum and Art Gallery, Ocean Rd, South Shields NE33 2JA - T: (0191) 4568740, Fax: 4567850, E-mail: alisdair.wilson@tyne-wear-museums.org.uk, Internet: www.twmuseums.org.uk
Local Museum / Fine Arts Museum - 1876
Glass, natural hist, local hist, watercolours - Catherine Cookson Gallery 40538

South Witham

Geeson Brothers Motor Cycle Museum, 4-6 Water Ln, South Witham NG33 5PH - T: (01572) 767280, 768195
Science&Tech Museum
85 British bikes, automobilia 40539

Southall

Collection of Martinware Pottery, Southall Library, Osterley Park Rd, Southall UB2 4BL - T: (020) 85743412, Fax: 85717629. Head: Neena Sohal
Decorative Arts Museum 40540

Saint Bernard's Hospital Museum and Chapel, c/o Hammersmith and Fulham Mental Health Trust, Saint Bernard's Hospital, Uxbridge Rd, Southall UB1 3EU - T: (020) 83548183/8109, Fax: 83548035. Man.: Pauline May
Historical Museum
Hospital records, incl. leather restraints and padded cell 40541

Southampton

Ancient Order of Foresters, College Pl, Southampton SO15 2FE - T: (023) 80229655, Fax: 80229657, E-mail: mail@foresters.ws
Religious Arts Museum / Historical Museum
Regalia, certificates, photographs, badges, banners, memorabilia and court room furniture, mural self-help 40542

Bitterne Local History Centre, 225 Peartree Av, Bitterne, Southampton SO19 7RD - T: (023) 80490948, E-mail: jimbrown@byterne.screaming.net, Internet: www.bitterne2.freeserve.co.uk
Local Museum
Lives of the people, gentry and traders of Bitterne 40543

Hawthorns Urban Wildlife Centre, Hawthorns Centre, Southampton Common, Southampton SO15 7NN - T: (023) 80671921, Fax: 80676859, E-mail: l.hand@southampton.gov.uk, Internet: www.southampton.gov.uk/leisure
Natural History Museum - 1980
Biological records 40544

John Hansard Gallery, University of Southampton, Highfield, Southampton SO17 1BJ - T: (023) 80592158, Fax: 80594192, E-mail: info@hansardgallery.org.uk, Internet: www.hansardgallery.org.uk. Dir.: Stephen Foster
Public Gallery 40545

Southampton City Art Gallery, Civic Centre, Southampton SO14 7LP - T: (023) 80832277, Fax: 80832153, E-mail: art.gallery@southampton.gov.uk, Internet: www.southampton.gov.uk/leisure/arts. Dir.: Tim Craven (Collections), Sc. Staff: Esta Mion-Jones (Exhibitions), Charlotte Baber (Cons.), Rosie Shirley (Education)
Public Gallery - 1939
18th-20th c English paintings, Continental Old Masters 14th-18th c, modern French paintings, incl the Impressionist, also sculpture and ceramics, paintings and drawings, contemporary British art 40546

Southampton Hall of Aviation, Albert Rd S, Southampton SO1 3FR - T: (023) 80635830, Fax: 80223383, E-mail: spitfirehome@compuserve.com. Dir.: Alan Jones
Science&Tech Museum - 1982
History of Solent aviation, story of 26 aircraft companies 40547

Southampton Maritime Museum, Wool House, Town Quay, Bugle St, Southampton SO14 2AR - T: (023) 80635904, 80237584, Fax: 80339601, E-mail: historic.sites@southampton.gov.uk, Internet: www.southampton.gov.uk/leisure/heritage. Cur.: Alastair Arnott
Science&Tech Museum - 1962
Models of the great liners and shipping ephemera, Titanic to Queen Mary, docks model showing the port c 1938 and associated displays, in 14th c warehouse 40548

Tudor House Museum, Bugle St, Southampton SO14 2AD - T: (023) 80635904, 80332513, Fax: 80339601, E-mail: s.hardy@southampton.gov.uk, Internet: www.southampton.gov.uk/leisure/heritage. Dir.: Sian Jones, Cur.: Alastair Arnott (Local Collections)
Local Museum - 1912
Furniture, domestic artefacts, paintings and drawings of Southampton, costumes and decorative arts, in a late medieval town house 40549

Southborough

Salomons Memento Rooms, David Salomons House, Broomhill Rd, Southborough TN3 0TG - T: (01892) 515152, Fax: 539102, E-mail: enquiries@salomons.org.uk, Internet: www.salomonscentre.org.uk. Head: A. Ironside
Religious Arts Museum
Mementoes of three David Salomons 40550

Southend-on-Sea

Beecroft Art Gallery, Station Rd, Westcliff-on-Sea, Southend-on-Sea SS0 7RA - T: (01702) 347418, Fax: 215631, Internet: www.beecroft-art-gallery.co.uk. Dir.: Clare Hunt, Keeper: C.F. Leming (Art)
Fine Arts Museum - 1953
Permanent coll by artists as Constable, Molenaer, Bright, Epstein, Weight, Lear and Seago, Thorpe-Smith coll of local works, Todman coll, drawings of Nubia by Alan Sorrell 40551

Focal Point Gallery, Southend Central Library, Victoria Av, Southend-on-Sea SS2 6EX - T: (01702) 612621 ext 207, Fax: 469241, E-mail: admin@focalpoint.org.uk, Internet: www.focalpoint.org.uk. Dir.: Lesley Farrell
Public Gallery 40552

Prittlewell Priory Museum, Priory Park, Victoria Av, Southend-on-Sea SS1 2TF - T: (01702) 342878, Fax: 349806, E-mail: southendmuseum@hotmail.com, Internet: www.southendmuseums.co.uk. Dir.: J.F. Skinner
Local Museum - 1922
Natural history of South East Essex, medieval life, printing, radios and television 40553

Southchurch Hall Museum, Southchurch Hall Close, Southend-on-Sea - T: (01702) 467671, Fax: 349806, E-mail: soutendmuseum@hotmail.com, Internet: www.southendmusuems.co.uk. Dir.: Richard Pace
Historical Museum - 1974
Medieval manor house with 17th c furnishings, built in 1340 40554

Southend Central Museum, Victoria Av, Southend-on-Sea SS2 6EW - T: (01702) 215131, 434449, Fax: 349806, E-mail: southendmuseum@hotmail.com, Internet: www.southendmuseums.co.uk. Dir.: J.F. Skinner, Keeper: K.L. Crowe (Human History), C. Hunt (Art), Asst. Keeper: R.G. Payne (Natural History), D.I. Mitchell (Human History), Cons.: C. Reed
Local Museum
Natural and human history of south-east Essex, Planetarium 40555

Southend Pier Museum, Southend Pier, Western Esplanade, Southend-on-Sea SS1 2EQ - T: (01702) 611214, 614553. Dir.: Peggy Dowie
Historical Museum
History of the pier, buildings, staff, illuminations, pleasure boats, war years, lifeboats, disasters, pier transport and railway 40556

Southport

Atkinson Art Gallery, Lord St, Southport PR8 1DH - T: (01704) 533133 ext 2110, Fax: (0151) 9342109, E-mail: atkinson.gallery@leisure.sefton.gov.uk. Keeper: Joanna Jones
Public Gallery - 1878
Paintings, drawings, watercolours, prints, sculptures 40557

Botanic Gardens Museum, Churchtown, Southport PR8 7NB - T: (01704) 227547, Fax: 224112. Sc. Staff: Joanna Denton
Natural History Museum - 1938
Toys, Liverpool porcelain, natural hist, Victorian artefacts 40558

British Lawnmower Museum, 106-114 Shakespeare St, Southport PR8 5AJ - T: (01704) 501336, Fax: 500564, E-mail: info@lawnmowerworld.co.uk, Internet: www.lawnmowerworld.co.uk. Cur.: B. Radam
Special Museum
Garden machinery, 200 lawnmowers 40559

Southwick

Manor Cottage Heritage Centre, Southwick St, Southwick BN42 4TE - T: (01273) 465164, E-mail: nigel.divers@unisonfree.net
Historical Museum / Decorative Arts Museum
Coll of modern, specially worked needlework panels depicting the history of Southwick 40560

Southwold

Southwold Museum, 9-11 Victoria St, Southwold IP18 6HZ - T: (01502) 723374, Fax: 723379, E-mail: david@de-kretser.fsnet.co.uk. Dir.: M. Child
Local Museum - 1933
Local hist, Southwold railway relics, natural hist, battle of Sole Bay, tokens, coins, watercolours 40561

Spalding

Ayscoughfee Hall Museum, Churchgate, Spalding PE11 2RA - T: (01775) 725468, Fax: 762715, Internet: www.sholland.gov.uk. Dir.: S. Sladen
Local Museum
Medieval manor house, local and social history, bird coll 40562

Pinchbeck Marsh Engine and Land Drainage Museum, Pinchbeck Marsh of West Marsh Rd, Spalding PE11 3UW - T: (01775) 725861, 725468, Fax: 767689, Internet: www.sholland.gov.uk
Science&Tech Museum
Drain pipes, pumps, gas and oil engines, a dragline excavator, hand tools, digging tools, turf cutters, weed cutters, fishing spears, plank road equipment, lamps, steam engine, punt 40563

Spalding Gentlemen's Society Museum, Broad St, Spalding PE11 1TB - T: (01775) 724658. Pres.: J. W. Belsham
Local Museum - 1710
Local history, ceramics, glass, coins, medals, trade tokens 40564

Sparkford

Haynes Motor Museum, Castle Cary Rd, Sparkford BA22 7LH - T: (01963) 440804, Fax: 441004, E-mail: mike@haynesmotormuseum.co.uk, Internet: www.haynesmotormuseum.co.uk. Dir.: John H. Haynes, Cur.: Michael Penn
Science&Tech Museum - 1985
1905 Daimler detachable top limousine, the 1965 AC Cobra, motoring and motorcycling items of historical and cultural interest, American coll, Red coll of sports cars, William Morris Garages, 1929 model J. Deusenberg, Derham bodied tourster, V16 Cadillac, speedway motorcycles 40565

Spean Bridge

Clan Cameron Museum, Achnacarry, Spean Bridge PH34 4EJ - T: (01397) 712090, E-mail: museum@achnacarry.fsnet.co.uk, Internet: www.clan-cameron.org. Dir.: Sir Donald Cameron of Lochiel
Historical Museum
Hist of Cameron Clan and their involvement in the Bonnie Prince Charlie rising 40566

Spey Bay

Tugnet Ice House, Tugnet, Spey Bay IV32 7PS - T: (01309) 673701, Fax: 675863, E-mail: alasdair.joyce@techleis.moray.gov.uk, Internet: www.moray.gov.uk/museums/homepage.htm
Special Museum
Salmon fishing and boat building on the River Spey 40567

Staffin

Staffin Museum, 6 Ellishadder, Staffin IV51 9JE - T: (01470) 562321. Dir.: Dugald Alexander Ross
Historical Museum - 1977
The only fossilized dinosaur bone from Scotland, it was found in Skye in 1994, neolithic arrowheads and axeheads 40568

Stafford

Ancient High House, Greengate St, Stafford ST16 2JA - T: (01785) 619131, Fax: 619132, E-mail: ahh@staffordbc.gov.uk, Internet: staffordbc.gov.uk. Dir.: Jill Fox
Historic Site
England's largest timber-framed town house built in 1595, period room settings 40569

Royal Air Force Museum Reserve Collection, RAF Stafford, Beaconside, Stafford ST18 0AQ - T: (01785) 258200, Fax: 220080, Internet: www.rafmuseum.com. Keeper: Ken Hunter
Military Museum / Science&Tech Museum 40570

Shire Hall Gallery, Market Sq, Stafford ST16 2LD - T: (01785) 278345, Fax: 278327, E-mail: shirehallgallery@staffordshire.gov.uk, Internet: www.staffordshire.gov.uk/shirehallgallery. Dir.: Kim Tudor
Fine Arts Museum / Decorative Arts Museum - 1927
Works by Staffordshire artists and of subjects in the county, contemporary jewellery coll by British makers 40571

Stafford Castle and Visitor Centre, Newport Rd, Stafford ST16 1DJ - T: (01785) 257698, Fax: 257698, E-mail: castlebc@btconnect.com. Dir.: Nicholas Thomas
Historical Museum / Archaeological Museum
Archaeological display 40572

Staines

Spelthorne Museum, Old Fire Station, Market Sq, Staines TW18 4RH - T: (01784) 461804, E-mail: staff@spelthorne.free-online.co.uk. Cur.: Ralph Parsons

Local Museum
Archaeology, local history and social history, Roman town model, Victorian kitchen, 1738 fire engine 40573

Stalybridge

Astley-Cheetham Art Gallery, Trinity St, Stalybridge SK15 2BN - T: (0161) 3382708, 3383831, Fax: 3431732. Sc. Staff: Dr. A. Wilson
Public Gallery
Art, craft, photograpgy 40574

Stamford

Burghley House, Stamford PE9 3JY - T: (01780) 752451, Fax: 480125, E-mail: burghley@burghley. co.uk, Internet: www.burghley.co.uk. Dir.: D.M. Parratt
Fine Arts Museum / Decorative Arts Museum
Italian paintings 17th c, fine oriental ceramics, European furniture, works of art 40575

Stamford Brewery Museum, All Saints St, Stamford PE9 2PA - T: (01780) 52186
Science&Tech Museum
Victorian steam brewery 40576

Stamford Museum, Broad St, Stamford PE9 1PJ - T: (01780) 766317, Fax: 480363, E-mail: stamford_museum@lincolnshire.gov.uk, Internet: www.lincolnshire.gov.uk/stamfordmuseum. Keeper: Tracey Crawley
Local Museum - 1961
Archaeology, medieval pottery, social history relating to town of Stamford 40577

Stansted Mountfitchet

House on the Hill Museums Adventure, Stansted Mountfitchet CM24 8SP - T: (01279) 813567, Fax: 816391, E-mail: gold@enta.net, Internet: www.gold.enta.net. Dir.: Jeremy Goldsmith
Special Museum - 1991
Action man coll, star wars coll, toys, books, games since late Victorian times 40578

Mountfitchet Castle and Norman Village, Mountfitchet Castle, Stansted Mountfitchet CM24 8SP - T: (01279) 813237, Fax: 816391. Dir.: A. Goldsmith
Historic Site - 1986 40579

Stansted Mountfitchet Windmill, Millside, Stansted Mountfitchet CM24 8BL - T: (01279) 813214
Science&Tech Museum
Tower mill, machinery 40580

Staplehurst

Brattle Farm Museum, Five Oak Ln, Staplehurst TN12 0HE - T: (01580) 891222, Fax: 891222. Owner: Brian Thompson
Agriculture Museum / Historical Museum
Vintage cars, motorcycles, bicycles, tractors, wagons, horse-drawn machinery, hand tools and crafts, war items, laundry and dairy 40581

Stevenage

Boxfield Gallery, Stevenage Arts and Leisure Centre, Stevenage SG1 1LZ - T: (01438) 766644, Fax: 766675
Public Gallery 40582

Stevenage Museum, Saint George's Way, Stevenage SG1 1XX - T: (01438) 218881, Fax: 218882, E-mail: museum@stevenage.gov.uk, Internet: www. stevenage.gov.uk. Dir.: Maggie Appleton
Local Museum - 1954
Local hist, archaeology, natural hist, geology 40583

Stevington

Stevington Windmill, Stevington MK43 7QB - T: (01234) 824330, Fax: 228531
Science&Tech Museum 40584

Stewarton

Stewarton and District Museum, Council Chambers, Avenue Sq, Stewarton KA3 5AB, mail addr: 17 Grange Terrace, Kilmarnock KA1 2JR - T: (01563) 524748, Fax: www.stewarton.org, E-mail: ianhmac@aol.com. Dir.: I.H. Macdonald
Local Museum - 1980
Local industry, bonnet-making 40585

Steyning

Steyning Museum, Church St, Steyning BN44 3YB - T: (01903) 813333. Cur.: Chris Tod
Historical Museum
Hist of Steyning from Saxon times to the present day, photographs, documents and objects 40586

Stibbington

Nene Valley Railway, Wansford Station, Stibbington PE8 6LR - T: (01780) 784444, Fax: 784440, E-mail: nvrorg@aol.com, Internet: www.nvr.org.uk
Science&Tech Museum
Steam and diesel locomotives and rolling stock, railwayana 40587

Sticklepath

Museum of Rural Industry, Oakhampton, Sticklepath EX20 2NW - T: (01837) 840286
Science&Tech Museum
Agriculture 40588

Stirling

Argyll and Sutherland Highlanders Regimental Museum, Castle, Stirling FK8 1EH - T: (01786) 475165, Fax: 446038, E-mail: museum@argylls.co. uk, Internet: www.argylls.co.uk. Cur.: C.A. Campbell
Military Museum - 1961
History of regiment since 1794, medals, pictures, silver armours, uniforms 40589

Art Collection, c/o University of Stirling, Stirling FK9 4LA - T: (01786) 466050, Fax: 466866, E-mail: v.a. m.fairweather@stir.ac.uk, Internet: www.stir.ac.uk/ artcol. Cur.: Valerie A. Fairweather
Fine Arts Museum
Paintings, prints, sculptures, tapestries, J.D. Fergusson 40590

Bannockburn Heritage Centre, Glasgow Rd, Stirling FK7 0LJ - T: (01786) 812664, Fax: 810892, E-mail: bannockburn@nts.org.uk, Internet: www. nts.org.uk
Historical Museum - 1987
Scottish history 40591

MacRobert Gallery, c/o University of Stirling, MacRobert Arts Centre, Stirling FK9 4LA - T: (01786) 467155, Fax: 451369, E-mail: macrobert-arts@stirling.ac.uk, Internet: www.stir.ac.uk/macrobert. Dir.: Liz Moran
Public Gallery 40592

National Wallace Monument, Abbey Craig, Hillfoots Rd, Stirling FK9 5LF - T: (01786) 472140, Fax: 461332. Man.: Eleanor Muir
Historical Museum
Scotlands National hero Sir William Wallace, famous Scots, countryside, history 40593

Stirling Old Town Jail, Saint John St, Stirling FK8 1EA - T: (01786) 450050, Fax: 471301, E-mail: otjua@aillst.ossian.net, Internet: www. visitscottishheartlands.com. Man.: Neil Craig
Historical Museum 40594

Stirling Smith Art Gallery and Museum, 40 Albert Pl, Dumbarton Rd, Stirling FK8 2RQ - T: (01786) 471917, Fax: 449523, E-mail: museum@ smithartgallery.demon.co.uk, Internet: www. smithartgallery.demon.co.uk. Dir.: Elspeth King
Local Museum / Fine Arts Museum - 1874
Local hist, archaeology, ethnology, geology, paintings, watercolors 40595

Stockport

Hat Works, Museum of Hatting, Wellington Mill, Wellington Rd S, Stockport SK3 0EU - T: (0161) 8557770, Fax: 4808735, E-mail: angela.stead@ stockpart.gov.uk, Internet: www.hatworks.org.uk. Dir.: John Baker
Special Museum - 2000
Hatting coll, machinery, historical and contemporary hats 40596

Stockport Art Gallery, Wellington Rd S, Stockport SK3 8AB - T: (0161) 4744453/54, Fax: 4804960, E-mail: stockport.artgallery@stockport.gov.uk, Internet: www.stockport.gov.uk/tourism/artgallery. Dir.: John Sculley
Fine Arts Museum - 1924
Paintings, sculptures, bronze of Yehudi Menuhin by Epstein 40597

Stockport Museum, Vernon Park, Turncroft Ln, Stockport SK1 4AR - T: (0161) 4744460, Fax: 4744449. Dir.: John Baker, Keeper: Frank Galvin (Social and Industrial History), Sc. Staff: Collette Curry (Education)
Local Museum - 1860
Local history, natural history, applied arts, example of a window made from 'Blue John' fluorspar 40598

Stockton-on-Tees

Green Dragon Museum, Theatre Yard, off Silver St, Stockton-on-Tees TS18 1AT - T: (01642) 393938, Fax: 391433. Dir.: Alan Cracket
Local Museum - 1973
Social, industrial and administrative development, ship models, coll of local pottery 40599

Preston Hall Museum, Preston Park, Yarm Rd, Stockton-on-Tees TS18 3RH - T: (01642) 781184, Fax: 393479, Internet: www.train.stockton.gov.uk. Dir.: Mark Rowland Jones
Local Museum - 1953
Arms, working crafts, Victorian life, toys 40600

Stockton-on-Tees Museums and Heritage Service, Municipal Bldgs, Church Rd, Stockton-on-Tees TS18 1XE - T: (01642) 415385, Fax: 393479, E-mail: mark.rowlandjones@stockton-bc.gov.uk, Internet: www.stockton.gov.uk
Local Museum 40601

Stoke Bruerne

Canal Museum, Stoke Bruerne NN12 7SE - T: (01604) 862229, Fax: 864199, E-mail: british. waterways@sosb.globalnet.co.uk
Historical Museum - 1963
Canal history, 200 years of inland waterways 40602

Stoke-on-Trent

Chatterley Whitfield Mining Museum, Tunstall, Stoke-on-Trent ST6 8UN - T: (01782) 813337. Dir.: P. Gifford
Science&Tech Museum
2.000-foot deep Hesketh shaft, different methods of extraction used over the past 150 years 40603

Etruria Industrial Museum, Lower Bedford St, Etruria, Stoke-on-Trent ST4 7AF - T: (01782) 287557, Fax: 260192. Dir.: Hadley Perry
Science&Tech Museum - 1991
Ceramic processing, steam beam engine (1820), grinding machinery (1856), blacksmithing coll 40604

Flaxman Gallery, c/o Staffordshire Polytechnic, College Rd, Stoke-on-Trent ST4 2DE - T: (01782) 744531
Fine Arts Museum / Decorative Arts Museum 40605

Ford Green Hall, Ford Green Rd, Smallthorne, Stoke-on-Trent ST6 1NG - T: (01782) 233195, Fax: 233194, Internet: www.stoke.gov.uk/ fordgreenhall. Dir.: Angela Graham
Decorative Arts Museum - 1952
In 17th c framed house, period furniture, household objects 40606

Gladstone Working Pottery Museum, Uttoxeter Rd, Longton, Stoke-on-Trent ST3 1PQ - T: (01782) 319232, 311378, Fax: 598640, E-mail: gladstone@ stoke.gov.uk, Internet: www.stoke.gov.uk/gladstone. Dir.: H. Wood
Special Museum
Story of the British pottery industry, the history of the industry in Staffordshire, social history, tiles and tilemaking, sanitary ware, colour and decoration 40607

Minton Museum, Visitor Centre, Nile St, Burslem, Stoke-on-Trent ST6 2AJ - T: (01782) 292400, Fax: 292499, E-mail: jmjones@royal-doulton.com. Cur.: Joan Jones
Decorative Arts Museum
Porcelain, ceramics 40608

The Potteries Museum and Art Gallery, Bethesda St, Stoke-on-Trent ST1 3DW - T: (01782) 232323, Fax: 232500, E-mail: museums@stoke.gov.uk, Internet: www.stoke.gov.uk/museums. Head: I. Lawley
Archaeological Museum / Fine Arts Museum / Decorative Arts Museum / Natural History Museum - 1956
Staffordshire pottery and porcelain, Continental and Oriental pottery, sculpture, natural history, local history, 18th c watercolors, English paintings, contemporary art 40609

Sir Henry Doulton Gallery, c/o Royal Doulton Ltd., Visitor Centre, Nile St, Burslem, Stoke-on-Trent ST6 2AJ - T: (01782) 292433/34, Fax: 292499, 292424, E-mail: visitor@royal-doulton.com, Internet: www. royal-doulton.com. Dir.: Joan Jones
Decorative Arts Museum - 1984
Hist and development of Royal Doulton, Royal Doulton figures 40610

Spode Museum, Church St, Stoke-on-Trent ST4 1BX - T: (01782) 744011, Fax: 572526, E-mail: spodemuseum@spode.co.uk, Internet: www.spode.co.uk. Dir.: Pam Woolliscroft
Decorative Arts Museum - 1938
Spode & Copeland ceramics since 1780, bone china and transfer printed wares 40611

Wedgwood Museum, Barlaston, Stoke-on-Trent ST12 9ES - T: (01782) 282818, Fax: 223315, E-mail: info@wedgwoodmuseum.org.uk, Internet: www.wedgwoodmuseum.com. Dir.: Gaye Blake Roberts
Decorative Arts Museum - 1906
Wedgwood family hist, ceramics, paintings and manuscripts, mason's ironstone, historical pottery, comprehensive coll of the works of Wedgwood - library, archives 40612

Stonehaven

Tolbooth Museum, Old Pier, Stonehaven AB39 2JU - T: (01771) 622906, Fax: 622884, E-mail: heritage@ aberdeenshire.gov.uk. Dir.: Dr. David M. Bertie
Local Museum - 1963 40613

Stornoway

An Lanntair, Town Hall, South Beach, Stornoway HSI 2BX - T: (01851) 703307, Fax: 703307, E-mail: lanntair@sol.co.uk, Internet: www.lanntair. com. Dir.: Roddy Murray
Public Gallery 40614

Museum Nan Eilean, Steornabhagh, Francis St, Stornoway HS1 2NF - T: (01851) 703773 ext 266, Fax: 706318, E-mail: rlanghorne@cne-siar.gov.uk, Internet: www.cne-siar.gov.uk. Cur.: Richard Langhorne
Archaeological Museum / Historical Museum
Archeology of Lewis and Harris, history of the islands, maritime, fishing, crofting coll 40615

Stourbridge

Red House Glass Cone Museum, High St, Wordsley, Stourbridge DY8 4AZ - T: (01384) 812750. Off.: Charles Hajdamach
Special Museum
A glassmaking site dating from the late 18th c and

in use until 1936, a 90' high glassmaking cone, built in 1790 and one of only four left in the UK, is surrounded by buildings related to the Victorian glass industry 40616

Stourton

Stourhead House, Stourton BA12 6QH - T: (01747) 842020, E-mail: gary.calland@nationaltrust.org.uk. Man.: Gary Calland
Fine Arts Museum / Decorative Arts Museum - 1720
Furniture, paintings, porcelain, furniture designed by Thomas Chippendale, the Younger 40617

Stowmarket

Museum of East Anglian Life, Abbot's Hall, Stowmarket IP14 1DL - T: (01449) 612229, Fax: 672307, E-mail: meal@meal.fsnet.co.uk, Internet: www.suffolkcc.gov.uk/central/meal. Dir.: Miriam Stead
Historical Museum - 1965
Rural life in East Anglia, household equipment, farm and craft tools, re-erected watermill, wind pump, smithy 40618

Strabane

Gray's Printing Press, 49 Main St, Strabane, Co. Tyrone - T: (01504) 884094
Science&Tech Museum
18th c printing press, 19th c printing machines 40619

Strachur

Strachur Smiddy Museum, The Clachan, Strachur PA27 8DG - T: (01369) 860565. Dir.: Cathie Montgomery
Science&Tech Museum 40620

Stranraer

Castle of Saint John, Castle St, Stranraer DG9 7RT - T: (01776) 705088, Fax: 705835, E-mail: JohnPic@ dumgal.gov.uk, Internet: www.dumfriesmuseums. demon.co.uk. Dir.: John Pickin
Historical Museum
Castle hist, town jail in the 18th and 19th c 40621

Stranraer Museum, 55 George St, Stranraer DG9 7JP - T: (01776) 705088, Fax: 705835, E-mail: JohnPic@dumgal.gov.uk, Internet: www. dumfriesmuseum.demon.co.uk. Dir.: John Pickin
Local Museum - 1939
Social and local history, archaeology, art, numismatics, costume, photos - archive 40622

Stratfield Saye

Stratfield Saye House and Wellington Exhibition, Stratfield Saye RG27 0AS - T: (01256) 882882, Fax: 882882, Internet: www.stratfield-saye.co.uk
Historical Museum
Bonaparte coll, paintings 40623

Stratford-upon-Avon

Anne Hathaway's Cottage, Shakespeare Birthplace Trust, Shottery, Stratford-upon-Avon CV37 9HH - T: (01789) 292100, Fax: 296083, E-mail: info@ shakespeare.org.uk, Internet: www.shakespeare. org.uk. Dir.: Roger Pringle
Special Museum
Thatched farmhouse, home of Anne Hathaway before her marriage to Shakespeare in 1582, period furniture since 16th c with traditional English cottage garden and orchard 40624

Hall's Croft, Shakespeare Birthplace Trust, Old Town, Stratford-upon-Avon CV37 6BG - T: (01789) 292107, Fax: 296083, E-mail: info@shakespeare. org.uk, Internet: www.shakespeare.org.uk. Dir.: Roger Pringle
Special Museum - 1847
Home of Shakespeare's daughter Susanna and her husband Dr. John Hall, Tudor and Jacobean furniture, period medical Exhibition 40625

Harvard House, Shakespeare Birthplace Trust, High St, Stratford-upon-Avon CV37 - T: (01789) 204507, Fax: 296083, E-mail: info@shakespeare.org.uk, Internet: www.shakespeare.org.uk. Dir.: Roger Pringle
Special Museum
Neish Pewter Coll 40626

Mary Arden's House and the Countryside Museum, Shakespeare Birthplace Trust, Wilmcote, Stratford-upon-Avon CV37 9UN - T: (01789) 293455, Fax: 296083, E-mail: info@shakespeare.org.uk, Internet: www.shakespeare.org.uk. Dir.: Roger Pringle
Special Museum
Tudor farmhouse, home of Mary Arden (Shakespeare's mother) before her marriage to John Shakespeare, exhibitions and displays of life and work on the land over the centuries 40627

Nash's House and New Place, Shakespeare Birthplace Trust, Chapel St, Stratford-upon-Avon CV37 6EP - T: (01789) 292325, Fax: 296083, E-mail: info@shakespeare.org.uk, Internet: www. shakespeare.org.uk. Dir.: Roger Pringle
Special Museum
Nash's House, former home of Thomas Nash, husband of Elizabeth Hall (Shakespeare's grand-

daughter), adjacent to stunning Elizabethan-style Knott garden set in foundations of New Place, Shakespeare's home from 1597 until he died in 1616 40628

Royal Shakespeare Company Collection, Royal Shakespeare Theatre, Waterside, Stratford-upon-Avon CV37 6BB - T: (01789) 296655, Fax: 262870, E-mail: david.howells@RSC.org.uk. Cur.: David Howells
Performing Arts Museum - 1881
Relics of famous actors and actresses, portraits of actors, paintings of scenes from Shakespeare's plays, sculptures, scenery and costume designs, costume coll plus props, production photographs, programmes, posters, stage equipment - archive 40629

Shakespeare Birthplace Trust, Shakespeare Centre, Henley St, Stratford-upon-Avon CV37 6QW - T: (01789) 204016, Fax: 296083, E-mail: info@shakespeare.org.uk, Internet: www.shakespeare.org.uk. Dir.: Roger Pringle
Special Museum - 1847
16th c timbered house, Shakespeare's birthplace, memorabilia, ceramics, books, documents, pictures - specialist Shakespeare library, records office, education department 40630

The Teddy Bear Museum, 19 Greenhill St, Stratford-upon-Avon CV37 6LF - T: (01789) 293160, Fax: 87413454, E-mail: info@theteddybearmuseum.com, Internet: www.theteddybearmuseum.com. Dir.: Sylvia Coote
Special Museum - 1988 40631

Strathaven

John Hastie Museum, 8 Threestanes Rd, Strathaven ML10 6DX - T: (01357) 521257
Historical Museum / Decorative Arts Museum
History of Strathaven, with special displays on the weaving industry, Covenanting and the Radical Uprising, coll of porcelain 40632

Strathpeffer

Highland Museum of Childhood, The Old Station, Strathpeffer IV14 9DH - T: (01997) 421031, Fax: 421031, E-mail: info@highlandmuseumofchildhood.org.uk, Internet: www.highlandmuseumofchildhood.org.uk. Cur.: Jennifer Maxwell
Special Museum - 1992
Dolls, toys, children's costume 40633

Strathpeffer Spa Pumping Room Exhibition, Park House Studio, The Square, Strathpeffer IV14 9DL - T: (01997) 420124
Science&Tech Museum 40634

Street

Shoe Museum, c/o C. & J. Clark Ltd., 40 High St, Street BA16 0YA - T: (01458) 842169, Fax: 843110, E-mail: janet.targett@clarks.com. Dir.: John Keery
Special Museum - 1974 40635

Stretham

Stretham Old Engine, Green End Ln, Stretham CB6 3LE - T: (01353) 649210, 648106. Dir.: E. Langford
Science&Tech Museum
Pumping station (1831) 40636

Stromness

Pier Arts Centre, 28-30 Victoria St, Stromness KW16 3AA - T: (01856) 850209, Fax: 851462, E-mail: info@pierartscentre.com. Cur.: Neil Firth
Public Gallery - 1979
20th c art, paintings, Barbara Hepworth, Naum Gabo, Ben Nicholson, Alfred Wallis 40637

Stromness Museum, 52 Alfred St, Stromness KW16 3DF - T: (01856) 850025, Internet: www.orknet.co.uk/stromness-museum. Cur.: B. Wilson
Local Museum - 1837
Orkney maritime and local history, natural history, birds and fossils, Stone Age finds, ship models, Invit carvings, fishing 40638

Stroud

The Museum in the Park, Stratford Park, Stratford Rd, Stroud GL5 4AF - T: (01453) 763394, Fax: 752400, E-mail: museum@stroud.gov.uk, Internet: www.stroud.gov.uk. Cur.: Susan P. Hayward
Local Museum - 1899
Geology, archaeology, fine and decorative arts, social hist 40639

Stroud Museum → The Museum in the Park

Styal

Quarry Bank Mill, Styal SK9 4LA - T: (01625) 527468, Fax: 539267, E-mail: reception.quarrybank@nationaltrust.org.uk, Internet: www.quarrybankmill.org.uk. Head: Andrew Backhouse
Science&Tech Museum - 1976
Working textile museum, hist of cotton, skilled machine demonstrators and costumed interpreters 40640

Sudbury, Derbyshire

Museum of Childhood, Sudbury Hall, Sudbury, Derbyshire DE6 5HT - T: (01283) 585305, Fax: 585139, E-mail: esucah@smtp.ntrust.org.uk. Dir.: Carolyn Aldridge
Special Museum - 1974
Betty Cadbury coll of playthings past - education dept. 40641

Sudbury, Suffolk

Gainsborough's House, 46 Gainsborough St, Sudbury, Suffolk CO10 2EU - T: (01787) 372958, Fax: 376991, E-mail: mail@gainsborough.org, Internet: www.gainsborough.org. Cur.: Hugh Belsey
Fine Arts Museum - 1958
Paintings, drawings and prints by Thomas Gainsborough 40642

Sulgrave

Sulgrave Manor, Manor Rd, Sulgrave OX17 2SD - T: (01295) 760205, Fax: 768056, E-mail: sulgrave-manor@talk21.com, Internet: www.sulgravemanor.org.uk. Dir.: Martin Sirot Smith
Historic Site
Tudor furniture and artefacts, Queen Anne furniture and artefacts, Washington memorabilia 40643

Sunderland

Monkwearmouth Station Museum, North Bridge St, Sunderland SR5 1AP - T: (0191) 5677075, Fax: 5109415, E-mail: juliet.horsley@tyne-wear-museums.org.uk, Internet: www.twmuseums.org.uk. Dir.: Juliet Horsley
Science&Tech Museum - 1973
Land transport in North East England, rail exhibits and other land transport items 40644

National Glass Centre, Liberty Way, Sunderland SR6 0GL - T: (0191) 5155555, Fax: 5155556, E-mail: info@nationalglasscentre.com, Internet: www.nationalglasscentre.com. Dir.: Jules Preston
Decorative Arts Museum 40645

North East Aircraft Museum, Old Washington Rd, Sunderland SR5 3HZ - T: (0191) 5190662, Internet: www.neam.co.uk. Dir.: William Fulton
Science&Tech Museum 40646

Northern Gallery for Contemporary Art, Fawcett St, Sunderland SR1 1RE - T: (0191) 5141235, Fax: 5148444, Internet: www.ngca.co.uk. Cur.: Ele Carpenter
Public Gallery 40647

Ryhope Engines Museum, Pumping Station, Ryhope, Sunderland SR2 0ND - T: (0191) 5210235, E-mail: keith-bell@beeb.net, Internet: www.g3wte.demon.co.uk
Science&Tech Museum - 1973
Mechanical engineering design and construction, beam engines and pumps, history of water supply, pair of beam engines (1868) complete with boilers, chimneys etc. 40648

Saint Peter's Church, Vicarage, Saint Peter's Way, Sunderland SR6 0DY - T: (0191) 5673726, 5160135, Fax: 5160135, E-mail: stuart.hill@durham.anglican.org
Religious Arts Museum / Historic Site 40649

Sunderland Museum, Burdon Rd, Sunderland SR1 1PP - T: (0191) 5532323, Fax: 5537828, E-mail: sheryl.muxworthy@tyne-wear-museums.org.uk, Internet: www.twmuseums.org.uk. Dir.: Alec Coles, Cur.: Juliet Horsley (Fine and Applied Art), M.A. Routledge (Social History), Sc. Staff: Jo Cunningham, H.M. Sinclair (Education)
Decorative Arts Museum / Fine Arts Museum / Natural History Museum - 1846
Pottery and glass, Wearside paintings, prints, etchings and photographs, Wearside maritime history, British silver, zoology, botany, geology, industries, archaeology 40650

Sutton, Norwich

Sutton Windmill and Broads Museum, Mill Rd, Sutton, Norwich NR12 9RZ - T: (01692) 581195. Cur.: Chris Nunn
Local Museum
Social history, tricycles, engines, pharmacy, tobacco 40651

Sutton-on-the-Forest

Sutton Park, Main St, Sutton-on-the-Forest YO61 1DP - T: (01347) 810249, Fax: 811251, E-mail: suttonpark@fsbdial.co.uk, Internet: www.statelyhome.co.uk. Dir.: Sir Reginald Sheffield
Fine Arts Museum / Decorative Arts Museum
Furniture, paintings, porcelain, plasterwork by Cortese 40652

Swaffham

Swaffham Museum, 4 London St, Swaffham PE37 7DQ - T: (01760) 721230, Fax: 720469. Man.: Patricia Finch
Local Museum
Local and social history, hand crafted figures from English literature 40653

Swalcliffe

Swalcliffe Barn, Shipston Rd, Swalcliffe OX15 5ET - T: (01295) 788278
Local Museum
Agricultural and trade vehicles, local history 40654

Swanage

Swanage Railway, Station House, Swanage BH19 1HB - T: (01929) 425800, Fax: 426680, E-mail: general@swanrail.freeserve.co.uk, Internet: www.swanagarailway.co.uk. Man.: Michael Scott
Science&Tech Museum
Coll of goods vehicles, locomotives 40655

Tithe Barn Museum and Art Centre, Church Hill, Swanage BH19 1HU - T: (01929) 427174. Dir.: David Haysom
Local Museum / Fine Arts Museum / Archaeological Museum - 1976
Fossils of the area, examples of the various beds of Purbeck stone, exhibitions of archaeological, architectural and social history material relating to the district, paintings and sculpture 40656

Swansea

Egypt Centre, c/o University of Wales Swansea, Singleton Park, Swansea SA2 8PP - T: (01792) 295960, Fax: 295739, E-mail: c.a.graves-Brown@swansea.ac.uk, Internet: www.swansea.ac.uk/egypt. Cur.: Carolyn Graves-Brown, Dep. Cur.: W. Goodridge
University Museum / Historical Museum / Archaeological Museum - 1998 40657

Glynn Vivian Art Gallery, Alexandra Rd, Swansea SA1 5DZ - T: (01792) 655006, 651738, Fax: 651713, E-mail: glynn.vivian.gallery@swansea.gov.uk, Internet: www.swansea.gov.uk. Dir.: Jenni Spencer-Davies
Fine Arts Museum - 1911
Swansea and Nantgarw pottery and porcelain, glass, 20th c Welsh art 40658

Maritime and Industrial Museum (closed for renovation until spring 2005), Maritime Quarter, Museum Sq, Swansea SA1 1SN - T: (01792) 653763, Fax: 652585, E-mail: swansea.museum@swansea.gov.uk, Internet: www.swansea.gov.uk. Cur.: Rosalyn Gee
Science&Tech Museum 40659

Mission Gallery, Gloucester Pl, Maritime Quarter, Swansea SA1 1TY - T: (01792) 652016, Fax: 652016. Dir.: Keith Bayliss
Public Gallery
Contemporary arts and crafts 40660

Swansea Museum, Victoria Rd, Maritime Quarter, Swansea SA1 1SN - T: (01792) 653763, Fax: 652585, E-mail: swansea.museum@swansea.gov.uk, Internet: www.swansea.gov.uk. Cur.: Rosalyn P. Gee
Local Museum - 1835
Social history, archaeology, ceramics, natural history, Welsh ethnography, numismatic, maps, topography, photography, manuscripts - library 40661

Swindon

Great Western Railway Museum → STEAM Museum of the Great Western Railway

Lydiard House, Lydiard Tregoze, Swindon SN5 3PA - T: (01793) 770401, Fax: 877909. Dir.: Sarah Finch-Crisp
Fine Arts Museum / Decorative Arts Museum - 1955
Palladian mansion, ancestral home of the Viscount of Bolingbroke, furniture, family portrait coll - 17th c parish church 40662

Purton Museum, Library, High St, Purton, Swindon SN5 4AA - T: (01793) 770648, E-mail: curator@purtonmuseum.com, Internet: www.purtonmuseum.com. Cur.: Rick Dixon
Local Museum
Local history, archaeological material, agricultural hand tools 40663

Railway Village Museum, c/o STEAM - Museum of the Great Western Railway, 34 Faringdon Rd, Swindon SN1 5BJ - T: (01793) 466553, Fax: 484073, Internet: www.steam-museum.org.uk. Cur.: Tim Bryan
Science&Tech Museum - 1980
The Railway Village built in the 1840s 40664

Richard Jefferies Museum, Marlborough Rd, Swindon SN3 6AA - T: (01793) 466556, Fax: 484141. Dir.: Robert Dickinson
Special Museum - 1962
Memorabilia on Richard Jefferies, manuscripts, memorabilia on local poet Alfred Williams 40665

Royal Wiltshire Yeomanry Museum, Yeomanry House, Church Pl, Swindon SN1 5EH - T: (01793) 523865, Fax: 529350
Military Museum
Military uniforms, militaria 40666

STEAM Museum of the Great Western Railway, Kemble Dr, Swindon SN2 2TA - T: (01793) 466646, Fax: 466615, E-mail: steampostbox@swindon.gov.uk, Internet: www.steam-museum.org.uk. Cur.: Tim Bryan
Science&Tech Museum - 1962/2000
Hist of railway, hist locomotives, models, illustrations 40667

Swindon Museum and Art Gallery, Bath Rd, Swindon SN1 4BA - T: (01793) 466556, Fax: 484141, Internet: www.swindon.gov.uk. Dir.: Robert Dickinson, Cur.: Isobel Thompson, Rosalyn Thomas (Art Gallery)
Local Museum / Fine Arts Museum - 1920
Numismatics, natural hist, ethnography, 20th-21th c British paintings, local archaeology and social history 40668

Symbister

Hanseatic Booth or The Pier House, Symbister ZE2 9AA - T: (01806) 566240. Dir.: J.L. Simpson
Local Museum 40669

Tain

Tain and District Museum, Castle Brae, Tower St, Tain IV19 1DY - T: (01862) 894089, Fax: 894089, E-mail: info@tainmuseum.demon.co.uk, Internet: www.tainmuseum.demon.co.uk. Dir.: Estelle Quick
Historical Museum - 1966 40670

Tamworth

Tamworth Castle Museum, The Holloway, Tamworth B79 7NA - T: (01827) 709626, Fax: 709630, E-mail: heritage@tamworth.gov.uk, Internet: www.tamworthcastle.co.uk. Head: Frank Caldwell
Local Museum - 1899
Local hist, archaeology, Saxon and Norman coins, costumes, heraldry, arms - archives 40671

Tangmere

Military Aviation Museum, Tangmere Airfield, Tangmere PO20 2ES - T: (01243) 775223, Fax: 789490, E-mail: admin@tangmere-museum.org.uk, Internet: www.tangmere-museum.org.uk. Dir.: Alan Bower
Military Museum
British world speed record aircraft-Meteorand Hunter - Library 40672

Tarbert

An Tairbeart Museum, Campbeltown Rd, Tarbert - T: (01880) 820190
Local Museum 40673

Tarbolton

Bachelor's Club, Sandgate St, Tarbolton KA5 5RB - T: (01292) 541940. Man.: David Rodger
Special Museum - 1938
Memorabilia of Robert Burns and his friends, period furnishings, free masonery 40674

Tarporley

Beeston Castle, Tarporley CW6 9TX - T: (01829) 260464, Internet: www.english-heritage.org.uk. Cur.: Andrew Morrison
Archaeological Museum
Archeological finds 40675

Tattershall

Guardhouse Museum, Tattershall Castle, Tattershall LN4 4LR - T: (01526) 342543, Fax: 342543, E-mail: etcxxx@smtp.ntrust.org.uk
Archaeological Museum
Model of the Castle (17th c), Lord Curzon artefacts, fossils, axe-heads, archaeological material, pottery, glass and metal objects 40676

Taunton

Somerset County Museum, The Castle, Castle Green, Taunton TA1 4AA - T: (01823) 320200, Fax: 320229, E-mail: county-museums@somerset.gov.uk, Internet: www.somerset.gov.uk/museums. Dir.: David Dawson
Local Museum
Archaeology, geology, biology, pottery, costume and textiles and other applied crafts 40677

Somerset Cricket Museum, 7 Priory Av, Taunton TA1 1XX - T: (01823) 275893. Man.: Tony Stedall
Special Museum
Cricket memorabilia - library 40678

Somerset Military Museum, Taunton Castle, Taunton TA1 4AA - T: (01823) 320201, Fax: 320229, E-mail: info@sommilmuseum.org.uk, Internet: www.sommilmuseum.org.uk. Dir.: D. Eliot
Military Museum - 1921
Militaria 40679

Tavistock

Morwellham Quay Historic Port & Copper Mine, Morwellham, Tavistock PL19 8JL - T: (01822) 832766, Fax: 833808, E-mail: enquiries@morwellham-quay.co.uk, Internet: www.mrwellham-quay.co.uk. Dir.: Peter Kenwright
Open Air Museum - 1970
George and Charlotte Copper Mine, industry, archaeology, local hist, River Port 40680

Teignmouth

Teignmouth and Shaldon Museum, 29 French St, Teignmouth TQ14 8ST - T: (016267) 777041, 862265, E-mail: museum@teign24.freeserve.co.uk,

Internet: website.lineone.net/~teignmuseum. Dir.: B.R. King
Local Museum - 1978
Spanish Armada Patache/Zabra, bronze swivel guns, pottery, copper cooking and caulking pots, other items of iron, Church Rocks Wreck, Church Rocks Teignmouth Devon, local/maritime history, lace, lifeboats, Haldon aerodrome, Brunerl athmospheric railway 40681

Templepatrick

Patterson's Spade Mill, 751 Antrim Rd, Templepatrick, Co. Antrim - T: (013967) 51467
Science&Tech Museum
Last surviving water driven spade mill in Ireland 40682

Tenbury Wells

Tenbury and District Museum, Goff's School, Cross St, Tenbury Wells WR15 8EF - T: (01299) 832143. Cur.: John Greenhill
Local Museum
Local history, bath and fountain from spa, farming, Victorian kitchen 40683

Tenby

Tenby Museum and Art Gallery, Castle Hill, Tenby SA70 7BP - T: (01834) 842809, Fax: 842809, E-mail: tenbymuseum@hotmail.com, Internet: www.tenbymuseum.free-online.co.uk. Cur.: Jon Beynon
Fine Arts Museum / Local Museum / Natural History Museum - 1878
Geology, archaeology, natural an social hist of Pembrokeshire, local hist of Tenby 40684

Tenterden

Colonel Stephens Railway Museum, Station, Station Rd, Tenterden TN30 6HE - T: (01580) 765350, Fax: 763468. Cur.: John Miller
Special Museum
Paperwork from the 16 light railways associated with Lt Colonel Holman F. Stephens, railway promoter, engineer and manager, his railway and military career 40685

Ellen Terry Memorial Museum, Smallhythe Pl, Tenterden TN30 7NG - T: (01580) 762334, Fax: 761960, E-mail: smallhytheplace@ntrust.org.uk
Performing Arts Museum - 1929
Memorabilia on actress Dame Ellen Terry, costumes, Edith Craig archive 40686

Kent and East Sussex Railway, Tenterden Town Station, Station Rd, Tenterden TN30 6HE - T: (01580) 765155, Fax: 765654, E-mail: kesroffice@aol.com, Internet: www.kesr.org.uk
Science&Tech Museum
Engines, carriages, goods vehicles 40687

Tenterden and District Museum, Station Rd, Tenterden TN30 6HN - T: (01580) 764310, Fax: 766648, Internet: www.ukpages.net/kent/museums.htm. Cur.: Debbie Greaves
Local Museum - 1976
Hist of Tenterden, weights and measures of the former Borough, scale model of the town as it was in the mid 19th c, domestic and business life of Tenterden in the 18th and 19th c 40688

Tetbury

Tetbury Police Museum, 63 Long St, Tetbury GL8 8AA - T: (01666) 504670, Fax: 504670, E-mail: tetburypolicemuseum@btinternet.com. Cur.: Brian E. Toney
Historical Museum
Cells, artefacts, uniforms, history of the Gloucestershire force 40689

Tewkesbury

John Moore Countryside Museum, 41 Church St, Tewkesbury GL20 5SN - T: (01684) 297174, E-mail: myecrofte@aol.com, Internet: www.gloster.demon.co.uk/jmcm. Cur.: Simon R. Lawton
Special Museum
Row of medieval cottages, furnishings, domestic environment, British woodland and wetland wildlife, writer and naturalist John Moore 40690

Little Museum, 45 Church St, Tewkesbury GL20 5SN - T: (01684) 297174. Dir.: Simon R. Lawton
Local Museum 40691

Tewkesbury Museum, 64 Barton St, Tewkesbury GL20 5PX - T: (01684) 292901, Fax: 292277, E-mail: museum@tewkgl20.fsnet.co.uk, Internet: mysite.freeserve.com/tewkesburymuseum. Dir.: Chris Kirby
Local Museum / Archaeological Museum - 1962
Hist, trades and industries of Tewkesbury, a diorama of the Battle of Tewkesbury in 1471, models of fairground machines, coll of woodworking tools 40692

Thaxted

Guildhall, Town St, Thaxted CM6 24D - T: (01371) 831339, Fax: 830418, Internet: www.thaxted.co.uk. Chairman: P.G. Leeder
Local Museum
Thaxted archives coll and old Thaxted photographs 40693

Thetford

Ancient House Museum, White Hart St, Thetford IP24 1AA - T: (01842) 752599, Fax: 752599, E-mail: oliver.bone.mus@norfolk.gov.uk, Internet: www.norfolk.gov.uk/tourism.museums. Cur.: Oliver Bone
Local Museum - 1924
Early tudor house, local history and industries 40694

Duleep Singh Picture Collection, c/o Ancient House Museum, White Hart St, Thetford IP24 IAA - T: (01842) 752599
Fine Arts Museum - 1924
Timber framed house from 1480, displays of Thetford and Breckland life, Roman treasure hoard, herb garden 40695

Euston Hall, Thetford IP24 2QP - T: (01842) 766366, Internet: www.eustonhall.co.uk. Dir.: Duke of Grafton
Fine Arts Museum 40696

Thirsk

Sion Hill Hall (closed) 40697

Thirsk Museum, 14-16 Kirkgate, Thirsk YO7 1PQ - T: (01845) 527707, 524510, E-mail: thirskmuseum@supanet.com, Internet: thirskmuseum.org. Dir.: J.C. Harding
Local Museum - 1975
Local life, hist and industry, exhibits of cobblers' and blacksmith's tools, veterinary and medical equipment, Victorian clothing, esp underwear, children's games, archaeological finds, medieval pottery, cameras and cricket mementoes, agricultural implements, pharmaceutical products and equipment, photographs 40698

Thornbury, Gloucestershire

Thornbury and District Museum, 4 Chapel St, Thornbury, Gloucestershire BS35 2BJ - T: (01454) 857774, Fax: 281638, E-mail: enquiries@thornburymuseum.org.uk, Internet: www.thornburymuseum.org.uk. Cur.: Vic Hallett
Local Museum
Local social history, landscape history, local crafts and industry, farming - archive 40699

Thorney

Thorney Heritage Centre, The Tankyard, Station Rd, Thorney PE6 0QE - T: (01733) 270908, E-mail: dot.thorney@tesco.net, Internet: www.thorney-museum.org.uk
Local Museum
History of the village 40700

Thornhaugh

Sacrewell Farm and Country Centre, Sacrewell, Thornhaugh PE8 6HJ - T: (01780) 782254, Fax: 782254, E-mail: info@sacrewell.fsnet.co.uk, Internet: www.sacrewell.org.uk. Dir.: Peter Thompson
Agriculture Museum - 1987 40701

Thornhill, Central

Farmlife Centre, Dunaverig, Ruskie, Thornhill, Central FK8 3QW - T: (01786) 850277, Fax: 850404. Dir.: Sarah Stewart
Agriculture Museum
A small mixed farm, the story of the parish of Ruskie from ancient times to the present day, models, photographs, charts, implements 40702

Thornhill, Dumfriesshire

Alex Brown Cycle History Museum, Drumlanrig Castle, Thornhill, Dumfriesshire DG3 4AQ - T: (01848) 31555, E-mail: aleyx@calderbrown.com. Dir.: Alex Brown
Science&Tech Museum 40703

Drumlanrig Castle, Thornhill, Dumfriesshire DG3 4AQ - T: (01848) 330248, Fax: 331682, E-mail: bre@drumlanrigcastle.org.uk, Internet: www.drumlanrigcastle.org.uk. Dir.: Claire Fisher
Decorative Arts Museum 40704

Threlkeld

Threlkeld Quarry and Mining Museum, Quarry, Threlkeld CA12 4TT - T: (017687) 79747. Dir.: Ian Hartland
Science&Tech Museum
Minerals, steam cranes, geological and industrial history 40705

Throwley

Belmont Collection, Belmont Park, Throwley ME13 0HH - T: (01795) 890202, Fax: 890042, E-mail: belmondadmin@cwcom.net. Cur.: Jonathan Betts
Science&Tech Museum
Clocks and watches coll 40706

Thurgoland

Wortley Top Forge, Thurgoland S30 7DN - T: (0114) 2887576. Cur.: Ken Hawley
Science&Tech Museum
Iron works, water wheels, hammers, cranes, stationary steam engine coll 40707

Thurso

Strathnaver Museum, Clachan, Bettyhill, Thurso KW14 7SS - T: (01641) 521418, E-mail: strathnavermus@ukonline.co.uk. Dir.: Thomas Mackay
Local Museum - 1976
Highland clearances of Strathnaver, clan Mackay 40708

Thurso Heritage Museum, Town Hall, High St, Thurso KW14 8AG - T: (01847) 62459. Dir.: E. Angus
Local Museum - 1970
Pictish stones 40709

Tilbury

Tilbury Fort, 2 Office Block, The Fort, Tilbury RM18 7NR - T: (01375) 858489, Internet: www.english-heritage.org.uk. Cur.: Jan Summerfield
Military Museum 40710

Tiptree

Tiptree Museum, Tiptree CO5 0RF - T: (01621) 814524, Fax: 814555, E-mail: tiptree@tiptree.com, Internet: www.tiptree.com
Local Museum
Jam making equipment, story of village life 40711

Tiverton

Tiverton Museum of Mid Devon Life, Beck's Sq, Tiverton EX16 6PJ - T: (01884) 256295, E-mail: tiverton@eclipse.co.uk, Internet: www.tivertonmuseum.org.uk. Dir.: Patrick Brooke, Cur.: John Leach
Science&Tech Museum / Local Museum / Agriculture Museum - 1960
Wagons, agricultural implements, railway, clocks, industries, crafts - library 40712

Tobermory

Mull Museum, Columbia Bldg, Main St, Tobermory PA75 6NY - T: (01688) 302493. Chm.: Dr. W.H. Clegg
Local Museum
Isle of Mull history - library, archives 40713

Toddington

Gloucestershire Warwickshire Railway, Railway Station, Toddington GL54 5DT - T: (01242) 621405, Internet: www.gwsr.plc.uk
Science&Tech Museum
Stand and gauge steam and diesel locomotives, carriages, wagons 40714

Tolpuddle

Tolpuddle Martyrs Museum, TUC Memorial Cottages, Tolpuddle DT2 7EH - T: (01305) 848237, Fax: 848237, E-mail: jpickering@tuc.org.uk, Internet: www.tolpuddlemartyrs.org.uk. Head: Nigel Costely
Historical Museum
Story of the six agricultural workers transported to Australia in 1834 after forming a trade union 40715

Tomintoul

Tomintoul Museum, The Square, Tomintoul AB3 9ET - T: (01807) 580440, Fax: 675863, E-mail: alasdair.joyce@techleis.moray.gov.uk, Internet: www.moray.org/museums/tomintou. Dir.: R. Inglis
Local Museum
Local and natural hist, geology 40716

Topsham

Topsham Museum, Holman House, 25 The Strand, Topsham EX3 0AX - T: (01392) 873244, E-mail: museum@topsham.org, Internet: www.devonmuseums.net/topsham
Local Museum - 1967
Local history, crafts, shipbuilding, lacemaking, fishing 40717

Torquay

Torquay Museum, 529 Babbacombe Rd, Torquay TQ1 1HG - T: (01803) 293975, Fax: 294186. Dir.: Ros Palmer
Local Museum - 1844
Geology, entomology, botany, folk life, social history - local studies, library 40718

Torre Abbey Historic House and Gallery, The King's Dr, Torquay TQ2 5JE - T: (01803) 293593, Fax: 215948, E-mail: torre-abbey@torbay.gov.uk, Internet: www.torre-abbey.org.uk. Dir.: Dr. Michael Rhodes, Cur.: Leslie Retallick
Fine Arts Museum / Historic Site - 1930
Paintings, furniture, glass, archaeology, historic building, the most complete medieval monastery in Devon and Cornwall 40719

Torrington

Dartington Crystal Glass Museum, Torrington EX38 7AN - T: (01805) 626242, Fax: 626263, E-mail: tours@dartington.co.uk, Internet: www.dartington.co.uk. Dir.: Jon Courtiour
Decorative Arts Museum - 1987
Dartington Crystal production from 1967 to present, non Dartington Crystal, historical glass from 1650 to today 40720

Torrington Museum, Town Hall, High St, Torrington EX38 8HN - T: (01805) 624324. Dir.: Emma Bond
Local Museum
Local and social history, trade - archive 40721

Totnes

British Photographic Museum, Bowden House, Totnes TQ9 7PW - T: (01803) 863664. Cur.: Christopher Petersen
Science&Tech Museum - 1974
Moving-picture photographic equipment of the period 1875 to 1960 40722

Totnes Costume Museum, Bogan House, 43 High St, Totnes TQ9 5NP - T: (01803) 862857. Cur.: Peter Clapham, Julie Fox
Special Museum
Coll of period costume since mid 18th c 40723

Totnes Elizabethan Museum, 70 Fore St, Totnes TQ9 5RU - T: (01803) 863821, Fax: 863821, E-mail: totnesmuseum@btconnect.com, Internet: www.devonmuseums.net/totnes. Dir.: Kristin Saunders
Local Museum - 1961
Period furniture, costumes, farm and household objects, archaeology, toys, computers - library, archive 40724

Trehafod

Rhondda Heritage Park, Lewis Merthyr Colliery, Coed Cae Rd, Trehafod CF37 7NP - T: (01443) 682036, Fax: 687420, E-mail: info@rhonddaheritagepark.com, Internet: www.rhonddaheritagepark.com. Dir.: John Harrison
Local Museum
Social, cultural and industrial history of the Rhondda and South Wales Valleys 40725

Tresco

Valhalla Museum, Tropical Garden, Tresco TR24 0QH - T: (01720) 424108, Fax: 422807
Special Museum
Figureheads and ships' carvings from wrecks 40726

Tring

Natural History Museum, Akeman St, Tring HP23 6AP - T: (020) 79426158, Fax: 79426150, E-mail: r.prys-jones@nhm.ac.uk. Man.: Dr. R. Prys-Jones
Natural History Museum
Coll of birds 40727

Walter Rothschild Zoological Museum, Akeman St, Tring HP23 6AP - T: (020) 79426171, Fax: 79426150, E-mail: terw@nhm.ac.uk, Internet: www.nhm.ac.uk. Dir.: Dr. Neil R. Chalmers, Cur.: Iain R. Bishopone
Natural History Museum - 1892
Ornithological coll of the Natural History Museum, London SW (research coll, not open to the public), zoological specimens, most of which were collected by Walter Rothschild (open to the public) 40728

Trowbridge

Trowbridge Museum, The Shires, Court St, Trowbridge BA14 8AT - T: (01225) 751339, Fax: 754608, E-mail: staff@trowbridgemuseum.co.uk, Internet: www.trowbridgemuseum.co.uk. Dir.: Clare Lyall
Science&Tech Museum - 1976
Textile machinery, West of England woollen industry 40729

Truro

Royal Cornwall Museum, River St, Truro TR1 2SJ - T: (01872) 272205, Fax: 240514, E-mail: royal-cornwall-museum@freeserve.co.uk, Internet: www.royalcornwallmuseum.org.uk. Dir.: Caroline Dudley
Local Museum - 1818
Philip Rashleigh coll of minerals, John Opie, artist, Newlyn School paintings, old master drawings - Courtney library and archives 40730

Saint Mawes Castle, Saint Mawes, Truro TR2 3AA - T: (01326) 270526, Internet: www.english-heritage.org.uk. Head Cust: Keith Robson
Local Museum
A well preserved, clover leaf design Tudor coastal fort situated in a strategic position overlooking the entrance to the Carrick Rd anchorage 40731

Tunbridge Wells

Tunbridge Wells Museum and Art Gallery, Civic Centre, Mount Pleasant, Tunbridge Wells TN1 1JN - T: (01892) 554171, Fax: 554131, E-mail: museum@tunbridgewells.gov.uk, Internet: www.tunbridgewells.gov.uk/museum. Man.: Caroline Ellis, Cur.: Dr. Ian Beavis
Local Museum / Public Gallery - 1885
Victorian paintings, local hist, natural hist, prints, drawings, dolls, toys, Tunbridge ware, archaeology, historic costume 40732

Turriff

Delgatie Castle, Turriff AB53 5TD - T: (01888) 563479, Fax: 563479. Dir.: Joan Johnson
Historical Museum / Fine Arts Museum / Decorative Arts Museum
Arts, arms and armour, paintings, furniture, history 40733

Old Post Office Museum, 24 High St, Turriff AB53 4DS - T: (01888) 563451. Dir.: Anna E. Cormack
Local Museum - 1999
Local goverment and history 40734

Session Cottage Museum, Session Close, Castle St, Turriff AB53 4AS - T: (01888) 563369, Fax: 568445. Dir.: Anna E. Cormack
Historical Museum - 1982
Lighting, domestic irons 40735

Turton Bottoms

Turton Tower, Chapeltown Rd, Turton Bottoms BL7 0HG - T: (01204) 852203, Fax: 853759, E-mail: turtontower.lcc@btinternet.com, Internet: www.lancashire.com/lcc/museums. Dir.: Martin Robinson-Dowland
Decorative Arts Museum - 1952
National coll, furniture, 16th, 17th and 19th c, arms and armour, metalwork, paintings 40736

Tweedoale

John Buchan Centre, Broughton, Tweedoale ML12 6HQ - T: (01899) 830223, 221050
Special Museum
Carrier and achievements of John Buchan as a novelist, lawyer, politician, soldier, historian, biographer and Governor-General of Canada, photographs, books, personal possessions of John Buchan and his family 40737

Twickenham

Marble Hill House, Richmond Rd, Twickenham TW1 2NL - T: (020) 88925115, Fax: 86079976, Internet: www.english-heritage.org.uk. Cur.: Julius Bryant
Fine Arts Museum - 1966
Overdoor and overmantel paintings by G.P. Painini 40738

Museum of Rugby, Rugby Football Union, Rugby Rd, Twickenham TW1 1DZ - T: (020) 88928877, Fax: 88922817, E-mail: museum@rfu.com, Internet: www.rfu.com. Cur.: J. Smith
Special Museum
Rugby memorabilia, photographs and books 40739

Museum of the Royal Military School of Music, Kneller Hall, Twickenham TW2 7DU - T: (020) 88985533, Fax: 88987906. Dir.: R.G. Swift
Music Museum - 1935
Old music instruments 40740

Orleans House Gallery, Riverside, Twickenham TW1 3DJ - T: (020) 88920221, Fax: 87440501, E-mail: r.tranter@richmond.gov.uk, Internet: www.richmond.gov.uk/depts/opps/leisure/arts/orleanshouse. Cur.: Rachel Tranter, Asst. Cur.: Mark de Novellis
Local Museum / Fine Arts Museum - 1972
Nearly 800 topographical paintings, prints and photographs of Richmond, Twickenham Hampton court area, Sir Richard Burton coll (paintings, portraits, photos, letters, personal objects, 1821-1890) 40741

Tywyn

Narrow Gauge Railway Museum, Wharf Station, Tywyn LL36 9EY - T: (01654) 710472, E-mail: curator@ngrm.org.uks.co.uk, Internet: www.talyllyn.co.uk/ngrm. Dir.: A.C. White
Science&Tech Museum - 1956
Locomotives and wagons of Narrow Gauge Railways of Britain and Ireland 40742

Uckfield

Bluebell Railway, Sheffield Park Station, Uckfield TN22 3QL - T: (01825) 720800, Fax: 720804, E-mail: info@blueball-railway.co.uk, Internet: www.bluebell-railway.co.uk. Cur.: J.E. Potter
Science&Tech Museum - 1960
Train tickets, badges, timetables 40743

Heaven Farm Museum, Heaven Farm, Danehill, Uckfield TN22 3RG - T: (01825) 790226, Fax: 790881, Internet: www.heavenfarm.co.uk. Cur.: Joan Ward
Agriculture Museum
A large coll of small farm tools and implements displayed in several Victorian farm buildings incl a barn, cowshed and oast house 40744

Uffculme

Coldharbour Mill, Working Wool Museum, Uffculme EX15 3EE - T: (01884) 840960, Fax: 840858, E-mail: info@coldharbourmill.org.uk, Internet: www.coldharbourmill.org.uk. Cur.: Jill E. Taylor
Science&Tech Museum - 1982
Turn-of-the-c worsted spinning machinery, spinning mule and looms, steam engine, new world tapestry 40745

Uffington

Tom Brown School Museum, Broad St, Uffington SN7 7RA - T: (01367) 820259, E-mail: museum@uffington.net, Internet: www.uffington.net/museum. Dir.: Sharon Smith
Historical Museum - 1984
150 editions of Tom Brown's schoolday by Thomas Hughes 40746

Ullapool

Ullapool Museum, 7-8 West Argyle St, Ullapool IV26 2TY - T: (01854) 612987, Fax: 612987, E-mail: ulmuseum@waverider.co.uk. Head: Alex Eaton
Local Museum - 1988/96
Village tapestry and quilt, natural hist, education, genealogy, archaeology, social hist, fishing, religion, emigration - archive 40747

Ulverston

Laurel and Hardy Museum, 4c Upperbrook St, Ulverston LA12 7BH - T: (01229) 582292, Fax: 582292. Cur.: Marion Grave
Special Museum
Memorabilia of Stan Laurel and Lucille Hardy, waxwork models 40748

Stott Park Bobbin Mill, Low Stott Park, Ulverston LA12 8AX - T: (015395) 31087, Fax: (015394) 43742. Dir.: M.J. Nield
Science&Tech Museum - 1983
Bobbin turning with Victorian machinery, working Victorian static steam engine 40749

Upminster

Upminster Mill, Saint Mary's Ln, Upminster RM14 1AU - T: (01708) 226040, E-mail: bobsharp@ukonline.co.uk, Internet: www.upminsterwindmill.co.uk. Head: R.W.D. Sharp
Science&Tech Museum 40750

Upminster Tithe Barn Museum, Agricultural and Folk Museum, Hall Ln, Upminster RM14 1AU, mail addr: 123 Victor Close, Hornchurch RM12 4XH - T: (07855) 633917. Head: M.L. Cullen
Agriculture Museum / Folklore Museum - 1978 40751

Uppermill

Saddleworth Museum and Art Gallery, High St, Uppermill OL3 6HS - T: (01457) 874093, Fax: 870336, E-mail: curator@saddleworthmuseum.net, Internet: www.saddleworthmuseum.net. Dir.: Kirsty Mairs
Science&Tech Museum / Fine Arts Museum - 1962
Textile machinery, transport, art - archive 40752

Usk

Usk Rural Life Museum, Malt Barn, New Market St, Usk NP5 1AU - T: (01291) 673777, E-mail: uskrurallife.museum@virgin.net, Internet: uskmuseum.members.easyspace.com. Dir.: J. Evares
Agriculture Museum - 1966
Agricultural and rural artefacts, vintage machinery 40753

Uttoxeter

Uttoxeter Heritage Centre, 34-36 Carter St, Uttoxeter ST14 8EU - T: (01889) 567176, Fax: 568426
Local Museum
Local history 40754

Ventnor

Museum of Smuggling History, Botanic Garden, Ventnor PO38 1UL - T: (01983) 853677. Cur.: J.R. Dowling
Special Museum - 1972
The only museum in the world depicting methods of smuggling in England over 700 years to the present 40755

Ventnor Heritage Museum, 11 Spring Hill, Ventnor PO38 1PE - T: (01983) 855407. Cur.: Graham Bennett
Local Museum
Local history, old photographs, prints 40756

Waddesdon

Waddesdon Manor, The Rothschild Collection, Waddesdon HP18 0JH - T: (01296) 653203, Fax: 653212, Internet: www.waddesdon.org.uk. Exec. Dir.: Fabia Bromovsky, Head: Pippa Shirley (Collections)
Decorative Arts Museum / Fine Arts Museum - 1959
French decorative arts, English portraits, Dutch and Flemish painting, majolica, design drawings, textiles, glass, Renaissance jewellery, European arms, French, Italian and Flemish illuminated manuscripts, French books and bindings 40757

Wainfleet

Magdalen Museum, Saint John St, Wainfleet PE24 4DL - T: (01754) 881548
Historical Museum 40758

Wakefield

Clarke Hall, Aberford Rd, Wakefield WF1 4AL - T: (01924) 302700, Fax: 302700, E-mail: info@clark-hall.co.uk, Internet: www.clarke-hall.co.uk. Dir.: Susan Morton
Decorative Arts Museum
17th c gentleman farmer's house 40759

National Arts Education Archive, c/o Lawrence Batley Centre & Gallery, Bretton Hall, West Bretton, Wakefield WF4 4LG - T: (01924) 832020, Fax: 832077, E-mail: skielty@bretton.ac.uk, Internet: www.bretton.ac.uk. Dir.: Prof. Ron George
Fine Arts Museum
Paintings, drawings, books, sculpture, ceramics, magazines, papers and letters, games, puzzles, videos, audiotapes, films, photographs and slides 40760

National Coal Mining Museum for England, Caphouse Colliery, New Rd, Overton, Wakefield WF4 4RH - T: (01924) 848806, Fax: 844567, E-mail: info@ncm.org.uk, Internet: www.ncm.org.uk. Dir.: Dr. Margaret Faull
Science&Tech Museum - 1988
Colliery site buildings incl original twin-cylinder steam winding engine, mining in the English coalfields, mining literature, photos, mine safety lamps, mining related coll - research library, photographic coll 40761

Nostell Priory, Doncaster Rd, Wakefield WF4 1QE - T: (01924) 863892, Fax: 865282, Internet: www.ukindex.co.uk/nationaltrust/
Special Museum
Chippendale coll, Robert Adam's finest interiors 40762

Stephen G. Beaumont Museum, Fieldhead Hospital, Ouchthorpe Ln, Wakefield WF1 3SP - T: (01924) 328654, Fax: 327340, E-mail: sarahgarner@wpchtr.northy.nhs.uk, Internet: www.wpch.tr.northy.nhs.uk. Cur.: A. Lawrence Ashworth
Historical Museum
Originally West Riding Pauper Lunatic Asylum, plans, records, documents, scale model of 1818, surgical and medical equipment, tradesmen's tools 40763

Wakefield Art Gallery, Wentworth Terrace, Wakefield WF1 3QW - T: (01924) 305796, 305900, Fax: 305770. Dir.: Antonino Vella
Public Gallery - 1934
20th c British and other paintings, sculpture 40764

Wakefield Museum, Wood St, Wakefield WF1 2EW - T: (01924) 305351, Fax: 305353, Internet: www.wakefield.gov.uk/culture/museums. Dir.: Colinn MacDonald
Local Museum - 1920
Local history, natural history, costumes, photogr - Resource Centre 40765

Walkerburn

Scottish Museum of Woollen Textiles, Tweedvale Mill, Walkerburn EH43 6AH - T: (0189687) 281/83
Special Museum
Weaver's cottage and weaver's shed, appropriate furnishings and equipment, examples of 18th to 20th-c wool and cloth patterns 40766

Wallingford

Wallingford Museum, Flint House, High St, Wallingford OX10 0DB - T: (01491) 835065. Dir.: S. Dewey
Local Museum
History of the town, items date from the 19th and 20th c, Civil War relics, a model of Wallingford Castle 40767

Wallsend

Buddle Arts Centre, 258b Station Rd, Wallsend NE28 8RH - T: (0191) 2007132, Fax: 2007142, E-mail: buddle@ntyneearts.demon.co.uk
Public Gallery
Prints 40768

Segedunum Roman Fort, Baths and Museum, Buddle St, Wallsend NE28 6HR - T: (0191) 2369347, Fax: 2955858, E-mail: segedunum@twmuseums.org.uk, Internet: www.twmuseums.org.uk. Cur.: Geoff Woodward
Archaeological Museum 40769

Wallsend Heritage Centre → Segedunum Roman Fort, Baths and Museum

Walmer

Walmer Castle, Kingsdown Rd, Walmer CT14 7LJ - T: (01304) 364288, Fax: 364826, E-mail: sally.mewton-hynds@english-heritage.org.uk, Internet: www.english-heritage.org.uk. Cur.: Jan Summerfield, Cust.: Sally Mewton-Hynds
Decorative Arts Museum
Wellington memorabilia 40770

Walsall

Birchills Canal Museum, Old Birchills, Walsall WS3 8QD - T: (01922) 645778, Fax: 632824, E-mail: museum@walsall.gov.uk, Internet: www.walsall.gov.uk/museums. Man.: Louise Troman
Historical Museum
Life and work on the canals 40771

Jerome K. Jerome Birthplace Museum, Belsize House, Bradford St, Walsall WS1 1PN - T: (01922) 627686, 629000, Fax: 721065, E-mail: tonygray@jkj.demon.co.uk, Internet: www.jeromekjerome.com. Pres.: Jeremy Nicholas
Special Museum
Story of the life and work of the famous author 40772

The New Art Gallery Walsall, Gallery Sq, Walsall WS2 8LG - T: (01922) 654400, Fax: 654401, E-mail: info@artatwalsall.org.uk, Internet: www.artatwalsall.org.uk. Dir.: Deborah Robinson, Sc. Staff: Jo Digger (Fine Art), Deborah Robinson (Exhibitions), Oliver Buckley (Interpretation)
Public Gallery - 1887/2000
Garman Ryan Coll: works by Matisse, Modigliani, Pissarro, Manet, Constable, Van Gogh, prints and sculpture; non-Western artefacts, social and local hist of Walsall 40773

Walsall Leather Museum, Littleton St W, Walsall WS2 8EQ - T: (01922) 721153, Fax: 725827, E-mail: leathermuseum@walsall.gov.uk, Internet: www.walsall.gov.uk/leathermuseum. Dir.: Michael Glasson
Special Museum - 1988
Designer leatherwork, lethergoods, saddlery, harness trades - library, photo archive 40774

Walsall Local History Centre, Essex St, Walsall WS2 7AS - T: (01922) 721305, Fax: 634954, E-mail: localhistorycentre@walsall.gov.uk, Internet: www.earl.org.uk/partners/walsall
Local Museum
Archives 40775

Walsall Museum, Lichfield St, Walsall WS1 1TR - T: (01922) 653116, Fax: 632824, E-mail: museum@walsall.gov.uk, Internet: www.walsall.gov.uk/museums. Man.: Louise Troman
Local Museum
Locally made goods, social history, costume, contemporary colls 40776

Walsall Museum and Art Gallery → The New Art Gallery Walsall

Waltham Abbey

Epping Forest District Museum, 39-41 Sun St, Waltham Abbey EN9 1EL - T: (01992) 716882, Fax: 700427, E-mail: museum@efdc.fsnet.co.uk, Internet: www.eppingforestdistrictmuseum.org.uk. Dir.: Tony O'Connor
Local Museum
Objects, documents, photographs and pictures relating to the social history of the area, an bi-annual 'Art in Essex' exhibition of work by county artists 40777

Royal Gunpowder Mills, Beaulieu Dr, Waltham Abbey EN9 1JY - T: (01992) 707370, Fax: 707372, E-mail: info@royalgunpowdermills.com, Internet: www.royalgunpowdermills.com. Dir.: Trevor Knapp
Science&Tech Museum
Gunpowder a.o. explosives production since the 1660s, largest heronry in Essex, producers, transport equipment for the internal canal and railway network 40778

Walton-on-the-Naze

Walton Maritime Museum, Old Lifeboat House, East Tce, Walton-on-the-Naze CO14 8AA - T: (01255) 678259
Historical Museum / Local Museum
Geology, fossils, flints, military history, local lifeboats, piers, old mills 40779

Wanlockhead

Museum of Lead Mining, Wanlockhead ML12 6UT - T: (01659) 74387, Fax: 74481, E-mail: ggodfrey@goldpan.co.uk, Internet: www.leadminingmuseum.co.uk. Dir.: Gerard Godfrey
Science&Tech Museum / Natural History Museum - 1974
Rare mineral coll, unique mining engines - library 40780

Wantage

Charney Basset Mill, Charney Basset, Wantage OX12 0EN - T: (01235) 868677, 763752
Science&Tech Museum
Watermill, machinery and millwrighting coll, dressing machine 40781

Vale and Downland Museum, Church St, Wantage OX12 8BL - T: (01235) 771447, Fax: 764316, E-mail: museum@wantage.com, Internet: www.wantage.com/museum. Cur.: Richard Halliwell
Local Museum - 1983 40782

Ware

Ware Museum, The Priory Lodge, Ware SG12 9AL - T: (01920) 487848. Cur.: David Perman
Local Museum
Local and historical objects, archaeology, malting industry, railcar manufacturers   40783

Wareham

Wareham Town Museum, Town Hall, East St, Wareham BH20 4NS - T: (01929) 553448, Fax: 553521. Cur.: Michael O'Hara
Local Museum   40784

Warminster

Dewey Museum, Library, Three Horseshoes Mall, Warminster BA12 9BT - T: (01985) 216022, Fax: 846332, E-mail: deweywar@ukonline.co.uk. Dir.: G.A. Hardy
Local Museum - 1972
History of Warminster and the surrounding area, the geology of the area   40785

Infantry and Small Arms School Corps Weapons Collection, Warminster Training Centre, Warminster BA12 0DJ - T: (01985) 222487, Fax: 222211
Military Museum - 1853
Coll of infantry firearms, dating from the 16th c to the present day, and ranging from small pocket pistols to heavy anti-tank weapons - documentation   40786

Longleat House, Warminster BA12 7NW - T: (01985) 844400, Fax: 844885, E-mail: enquiries@longleat. co.uk, Internet: www.longleat.co.uk. Dir.: Marquess of Bath
Historical Museum / Fine Arts Museum - 1541
6th Marquess of Bath's coll of Churchilliana and Hitleriana and children's books; incunabula, medieval manuscripts, porcelain, Italian/Dutch paintings, English portraits, French/Italian/English furniture - library, archives   40787

Warrington

Walton Hall Heritage Centre, Walton Hall Gardens, Walton Lea Rd, Warrington WA4 6SN - T: (01925) 601617, Fax: 861868, E-mail: waltonhall@ warrington.gov.uk, Internet: www.warrington.gov. uk/waltongardens. Dir.: Keith Webb
Local Museum - 1995   40788

Warrington Museum and Art Gallery, Bold St, Warrington WA1 1JG - T: (01925) 442733, Fax: 443257, E-mail: museum@warrington.gov.uk, Internet: www.warrington.gov.uk/museum
Local Museum / Public Gallery - 1848
Local hist, Romano-British finds from Wilderspool, prehistory, ethnology, natural hist, local industries, early English watercolours, ceramics, local longcase clocks, temporary exhibits   40789

Warwick

Midland Warplane Museum (closed)   40790

Queen's Own Hussars Museum, Lord Leycester Hospital, High St, Warwick CV34 4BH - T: (01926) 492035, Fax: 492035, E-mail: qohmuseum@ netscapeonline.co.uk, Internet: www.army.mod.uk. Dir.: P.J. Timmons
Military Museum - 1966
History of regiments, uniforms, medals, silver goblets - library   40791

Royal Regiment of Fusiliers Museum, Saint John's House, Warwick CV34 4NF - T: (01926) 491653, Fax: (01869) 257633, E-mail: areasecretary@ rrfmuseumwarwick.demon.co.uk. Head: R.G. Mills
Military Museum
County Infantry Regiment   40792

Saint John's House, Saint John's, Warwick CV34 4NF - T: (01926) 412021, E-mail: museum@ warwickshire.gov.uk, Internet: www.warwickshire. gov.uk. Dir.: Dr. Helen Maclagan
Historical Museum - 1961
Social hist, costume, domestic artefacts   40793

Warwick Castle, Castle Hill, Warwick CV34 4QU - T: (0870) 4422000, Fax: (01926) 401692, E-mail: custumer.information@warwick-castle.com, Internet: www.warwick-castle.co.uk. Gen. Man.: S.E. Montgomery
Historic Site
Over 1000 items of armour & weaponry, "A Royal Weekend Party 1898", award-winning wax exhibit by Madame Tussauds depicting a weekend party, "Kingmaker-Preparation for Battle 1471" from Richard Neville   40794

Warwick Doll Museum, Oken's House, Castle St, Warwick CV34 4BP - T: (01926) 495546, 412500, Fax: 419840, E-mail: museum@warwickshire.gov. uk, Internet: www.warwickshire.gov.uk/museum. Dir.: Helen Maclagan
Special Museum - 1955
Old dolls and toys, Teddy Bears   40795

Warwickshire Museum, Market Pl, Warwick CV34 4SA - T: (01926) 412500, Fax: 419840, E-mail: museum@warwickshire.gov.uk, Internet: www.warwickshire.gov.uk/museum. Dir.: Helen Maclagan
Local Museum - 1836
Archaeology, geology, natural history, musical instruments, tapestry map   40796

Warwickshire Yeomanry Museum, Court House, Jury St, Warwick CV34 4EW - T: (01926) 492212, Fax: 411694, E-mail: wtc.admin@btclick.com. Dir.: Michael Burman
Military Museum
History of the Yeomanry from 1794 to 1968, uniforms, swords, firearms, pictures and paintings relating to the Regiment, campaign relics   40797

Washford

Somerset and Dorset Railway Trust Museum, Railway Station, Washford TA23 0PP - T: (01984) 640869, E-mail: info@sdrt.org, Internet: www.sdrt. org. Cur.: Michael Gates
Science&Tech Museum
Locomotives, rolling stock, railway buildings, signs, small artefacts, plans, railway signal box   40798

Washington, Tyne and Wear

Arts Centre, Biddick Ln, Fatfield, Washington, Tyne and Wear NE38 8AB - T: (0191) 2193455, Fax: 2193466
Public Gallery   40799

Washington Old Hall, The Avenue, District 4, Washington, Tyne and Wear NE38 7LE - T: (0191) 4166879, Fax: 4192065, Internet: www. washington.co.uk
Special Museum
Ancestral home of the first President of the United States   40800

Watchet

Watchet Market House Museum, Market St, Watchet TA23 0AN - T: (01984) 631345. Dir.: W.H. Norman
Local Museum - 1979
Maritime history of the port of Watchet, archaeology, Saxon Mint, industry, railways, mining   40801

Waterbeach

Farmland Museum and Denny Abbey, Ely Road, Waterbeach CB5 9PQ - T: (01223) 860988, Fax: 860988, E-mail: f.m.denny@tesco.net, Internet: www.dennyfarmlandmuseum.org.uk. Cur.: Kate Brown, Corinna Bower (Curatorial Officer), Jeremy Ressiter (Education)
Agriculture Museum / Historic Site - 1997
Interactive displays on farming, esp village life in the 1940/50s, Denny Abbey   40802

Watford

Watford Museum, 194 High St, Watford WD1 2HG - T: (01923) 232297, Fax: 244772, E-mail: museum@artsteam-watford.co.uk, Internet: www.watford.gov.uk/leisure. Cur.: Victoria Barlow
Fine Arts Museum / Local Museum - 1981
Fine art coll (17th-18th c), North European genre painting, 19th c English landscape, sculpture by Sir Jacob Epstein, African art coll, local hist, archaeology   40803

Weardale

Killhope, the North of England Lead Mining Museum, Cowshill, Weardale DL13 1AR - T: (01388) 537505, Fax: 537617, E-mail: killhope@ durham.gov.uk, Internet: www.durham.gov.uk/ killhope
Science&Tech Museum
Lead mining, waterwheels, minerals of the North Pennines, spar boxes   40804

Weardale Museum, Ireshopeburn, Weardale DL14 - T: (01388) 537417, E-mail: dtheaherington@ argonet.co.uk. Chm.: Peter Bowes
Local Museum
Typical Weardale cottage room, geology, farming, railways, water resources and early settlement   40805

Wednesbury

Wednesbury Museum and Art Gallery, Holyhead Rd, Wednesbury WS10 7DF - T: (0121) 5560683, Fax: 5051625, Internet: www.sandwell.gov.uk/ heritage. Dir.: Raj Pal, Cur.: Emma Cook
Local Museum / Fine Arts Museum - 1891
William Howson-Taylor-Ruskin pottery, Helen Caddick ethnography coll, George Robbins geological coll, English 19th c oil paintings and watercolours, ethnography, local hist, geology, decorative arts   40806

Welbeck

Creswell Crags Museum and Education Centre, off Crags Rd, Welbeck S80 3LH - T: (01909) 720378, Fax: 724726, E-mail: info@creswell-crags.org.uk, Internet: www.creswell-crags.org.uk. Cur.: Nigel Mills
Archaeological Museum
Ecofacts and artefacts of Pleistocene research   40807

Harley Gallery, Welbeck S80 3LW - T: (01909) 501700, Fax: 488747, E-mail: info@harley-welbeck.co.uk, Internet: www.harleygallery.org.uk. Dir.: Gill Wilson
Fine Arts Museum
Contemporary visual arts   40808

Wellesbourne

Wellesbourne Wartime Museum, Airfield, Control Tower Entrance, Wellesbourne CV35 9EU - T: (01926) 855031. Man.: D. Paddock
Historical Museum
Underground bunker, roll of honour 316 airmen killed while serving at Wellesbourne 1941-45   40809

Wellingborough

Irchester Narrow Gauge Railway Museum, Irchester Country Park, Wellingborough MK43 0EX, mail addr: c/o RUC Office, 71 Bedford Rd, Cranfield MK43 0EX - T: (01234) 750469, E-mail: irchester@ kingstonray.freeserve.co.uk, Internet: www. ikingston.demon.co.uk/ingrt
Science&Tech Museum
8 steam and diesel locomotives   40810

Wellingborough Heritage Centre, Croyland Hall, Burstead Pl, Wellingborough NN8 1AH - T: (01933) 276838
Local Museum   40811

Wells

Wells Museum, 8 Cathedral Green, Wells BA5 2UE - T: (01749) 673477, Fax: 675337, E-mail: wellsmuseum@ukonline.co.uk, Internet: www.yell.co.uk/sites/wellsmuseum. Cur.: Estelle Jakeman
Local Museum / Archaeological Museum - 1893
Archaeology, natural history, geology, speleology, social history, needlework samplers   40812

Wells-next-the-Sea

Bygones at Holkham, Holkham Park, Wells-next-the-Sea NR23 1AB - T: (01328) 713112, Fax: 711707, Internet: www.holkham.co.uk. Cur.: Eric Absolon
Historical Museum
Agricultural Bygones, craft, domestic items, steam and motor vehicles, farming   40813

Wells Walsingham Light Railway, Stiffkey Rd, Wells-next-the-Sea NR23 1QB - T: (01328) 710631. Cur.: Dr. R.W. Francis
Science&Tech Museum
Garratt steam locomotive, carriages   40814

Welshpool

Andrew Logan Museum of Sculpture, Berriew, Welshpool SY21 8PJ - T: (01686) 640689, Fax: 640764, E-mail: info@andrewlogan.com, Internet: www.andrewlogan.com. Dir.: Anne Collins
Decorative Arts Museum
Sculpture, Alternative Miss World memorabilia   40815

Powis Castle, Welshpool SY21 8RF - T: (01938) 551944, Fax: 554336, E-mail: powiscastle@ nationaltrust.org.uk, Internet: www.nationaltrust. org.uk. Dir.: Anna Orton
Decorative Arts Museum / Historic Site / Natural History Museum - 1987
Plasterwork and panelling, paintings, tapestries, sculpture, early Georgian furniture, Clive Museum of Indian artifacts - garden   40816

Powysland Museum and Montgomery Canal Centre, Canal Wharf, Welshpool SY21 7AQ - T: (01938) 554656, Fax: 554656, E-mail: powysland@powys.gov.uk, Internet: po-wysmuseums.powys.gov.uk. Dir.: Eva B. Bredsdorff
Local Museum - 1874
Archiological finds, social history   40817

Welwyn

Welwyn Roman Baths Museum, By Pass, Welwyn AL6 9HT - T: (01707) 271362, Fax: 272511, E-mail: museum@welhat.gov.uk, Internet: www. welhal.gov.uk/leisure. Dir.: Carol Rigby, Cur.: Caroline Rawle
Archaeological Museum - 1975
Remains of a 3rd c AD bath house   40818

Wensleydale

Yorkshire Museum of Carriages and Horse Drawn Vehicles, Yore Bridge, Aysgarth Falls, Wensleydale DL8 3SR - T: (01969) 663399, Fax: 663399. Dir.: David Kiely, Ann Kiely, Cur.: Elizabeth Shaw
Science&Tech Museum
Coll of both everyday and more lavish horse-drawn vehicles in Britain today   40819

West Bretton

Yorkshire Sculpture Park, Bretton Hall, West Bretton WF4 4LG - T: (01924) 830302, Fax: 832600, E-mail: info@ysp.co.uk, Internet: www.ysp.co.uk. Dir.: Peter Murray, Cur.: Clare Lilley
Public Gallery   40820

West Bromwich

Bishop Asbury Cottage, Newton Rd, Great Barr, West Bromwich B43 6HN - T: (0121) 5530759, Fax: 5255167, Internet: www.sandwell.gov.uk/ heritage
Historical Museum
18th c cottage, childhood home of Francis Asbury (early Methodist pioneer in United States), contains period furniture and Methodist ephemera   40821

Oak House Museum, Oak Rd, West Bromwich B70 8HJ - T: (0121) 5530759, Fax: 5255167, E-mail: oakhouse@sandloell.gov.uk, Internet: www. sandwell.gov.uk/heritage. Dir.: Raj Pal, Cur.: Emma Cook
Historical Museum - 1898
Fine coll of oak furniture of 16th c and 17th c, 17th c interiors, Tudor Yoeman farmers house with period furniture   40822

West Clandon

Queen's Royal Surrey Regiment Museum, Clandon Park, West Clandon GU4 7RQ - T: (01483) 223419, Fax: 223419, E-mail: queenssurrey@care4free.net, Internet: www.queensroyalsurreys.org.uk
Military Museum   40823

West Hoathly

Priest House, North Ln, West Hoathly RH19 4PP - T: (01342) 810479, E-mail: priest@sussexpast.co. uk, Internet: www.sussexpast.co.uk. Cur.: Antony Smith
Local Museum - 1908
Vernacular furniture, domestic implements, embroidery   40824

West Kilbride

West Kilbride Museum, Public Hall, Arthur St, West Kilbride KA23 9EN - T: (01294) 882987
Local Museum   40825

West Malling

Outreach Collection, KCC, Gibson Dr, Kings Hill, West Malling ME19 4AL - T: (01622) 671411 ext 5226, 605226, Fax: 605221, E-mail: peter.divall@kent. gov.uk, Internet: www.kent.gov.uk/arts/libserv/ loan1.html
Historical Museum
Models and replicas which illustrate the history, natural history and development of Kent and of the wider world   40826

West Mersea

Mersea Island Museum, High St, West Mersea CO5 8QD - T: (01206) 385191. Dir.: David W. Gallifant
Local Museum   40827

West Walton

Fenland and West Norfolk Aviation Museum, Old Lynn Rd, West Walton PE14 7DA - T: (01945) 584440, Fax: 581984, E-mail: petewinning@ btinternet.com, Internet: www.fawnaps.co.uk. Chm.: Richard Mason
Science&Tech Museum
Aircraft crash sites, Boeing 747 flight deck, general aviation memorabilia   40828

West Wycombe

West Wycombe Motor Museum, Chorley Rd, West Wycombe
Science&Tech Museum   40829

West Wycombe Park House, West Wycombe HP14 3AJ - T: (01494) 52441
Fine Arts Museum
Contemporary frescos, painted ceilings   40830

Westbury

Woodland Heritage Museum, Woodland Park, Brokerswood, Westbury BA13 4EH - T: (01373) 823880, Fax: 858474, E-mail: woodland.park@ virgin.net. Dir.: S.H. Capon
Natural History Museum
Wildlife diorama, a bird wall and exhibits on forestry, bird eggs, natural history   40831

Westerham

Quebec House, National Trust Chartwell, Quebec Sq, Westerham TN16 1TD - T: (01959) 562206. Hon. Cur.: David Boston
Historical Museum
General Wolfe's early years, battle of Quebec 40832

Squerryes Court, Goodley Stock Rd, Westerham TN16 1SJ - T: (01959) 562345, 563118, Fax: 565949, E-mail: squerryes.court@squerryes. co.uk, Internet: www.squerryes.co.uk
Fine Arts Museum
Paintings (Dutch 17th c, English 18th) tapestries, furniture, porcelain, General James Wolfe 40833

Weston-super-Mare

The Helicopter Museum, Heliport, Locking Moor Rd, Weston-super-Mare BS24 8PP - T: (01934) 635227, Fax: 645230, E-mail: office@helimuseum.fsnet.co. uk, Internet: www.helicoptermuseum.freeserve.co. uk. Dir.: Elfan Rees
Science&Tech Museum - 1979
Bristol Belvedere, Cierva C-30A, Fairey Rotodyne, Mil Mi-1, PZL Swidnik SM-2, Westland Lynx 3, Sud Super Frelon, MBB Bo-102, Mil M.24D, Queens Flight Wessex XV 733   40834

North Somerset Museum, Burlington St, Weston-super-Mare BS23 1PR - T: (01934) 621028, Fax: 612526, E-mail: museum.service@n-somerset.gov.uk, Internet: www.n-somerset.gov.uk/museum. Dir.: Nick Goff
Local Museum 40835

Time Machine, Burlington St, Weston-super-Mare BS23 1PR - T: (01934) 621028, Fax: 612526, E-mail: museum.service@n-somerset.gov.uk, Internet: www.n-somerset.gov.uk/museum
Archaeological Museum / Local Museum
Archaeology, hist (esp seaside holidays), wildlife and geology of north Somerset 40836

Weston-under-Lizard

Weston Park, Weston-under-Lizard TF11 8LE - T: (01952) 850207, Fax: 850430, E-mail: enquiries@weston-park.com, Internet: www.weston-park.com. Dir.: Colin Sweeney
Decorative Arts Museum / Fine Arts Museum - 1671
House built 1671 with English, Flemish and Italian paintings, furniture, books, tapestries, art objects 40837

Wetheringsett

Museum of the Mid-Suffolk Light Railway, Brockford Station, Wetheringsett IP14 5PW - T: (01449) 766899
Science&Tech Museum
Artefacts, railway station, photographs of mid-Suffolk railway 40838

Weybourne

Muckleburgh Collection, Weybourne Military Camp, Weybourne NR25 7EG - T: (01263) 588210, Fax: 588425, E-mail: info@muckleburgh.co.uk, Internet: www.muckleburgh.co.uk. Dir.: Christine Swettenham
Military Museum
Military, Suffolk and Norforlk Yeomanry 40839

Weybridge

Brooklands Museum, Brooklands Rd, Weybridge KT13 0QN - T: (01932) 857381, Fax: 855465, E-mail: info@brooklandsmuseum.com, Internet: www.brooklandsmuseum.com. Dir.: Allan Winn
Science&Tech Museum
British motorsport and aviation, Brooklands cars, aircraft, motorcycles, cycles, John Cobb's 24-litre Napier-Railton, Wellington bomber of Loch Ness 40840

Elmbridge Museum, Church St, Weybridge KT13 8DE - T: (01932) 843573, Fax: 846552, E-mail: info@elm-mus.datanet.co.uk, Internet: www.elmbridge.history.museum. Dir.: Michael Rowe
Local Museum - 1909/1996
Local history, archaeology, excavated material from Oatlands palace, costume, natural history 40841

Weymouth

Deep Sea Adventure and Diving Museum, Custom House Quay, Weymouth - T: (01305) 760690, Fax: 760690
Special Museum 40842

Nothe Fort Museum of Coastal Defence, Barrack Rd, Weymouth DT4 8UF - T: (01305) 766626, Fax: 766465, E-mail: fortressweymouth@btconnect.com, Internet: www.weymouth.gov.uk/nothe.htm. Dir.: Alisdair Murray
Military Museum - 1979
Coastal fortress, coll of guns, weapons and equipment, military badges, torpedos, uniforms 40843

Tudor House, Weymouth Civic Soc, 3 Trinity St, Weymouth DT4 8TW - T: (01305) 779711
Historical Museum
17th c life 40844

Water Supply Museum, Sutton Poyntz, Pumping Station, Weymouth DT3 6LT - T: (01305) 832634, Fax: 834287, E-mail: museum@wessexwater.co.uk, Internet: www.wessexwater.co.uk
Science&Tech Museum
Water turbine pump from 1857, pumping plant and artefacts 40845

Weymouth Museum, Timewalk and Brewery Museum, Brewer's Quay, Hope Sq, Weymouth DT4 8TR - T: (01305) 777622, 752323, Fax: 761680. Cur.: Rodney Alcock
Historical Museum
Local and social history, costume, prints, paintings, Bussell coll - archives 40846

Whaley Thorns

Whaley Thorns Heritage Centre and Museum, Cock Shut Ln, Whaley Thorns NG20 9HA - T: (01623) 742525, Fax: (01246) 813200. Cur.: John Hyatt
Agriculture Museum
Old farming, sheep shearing and many more implements 40847

Whaplode

Museum of Entertainment, Rutland Cottage, Millgate, Whaplode PE12 6SF - T: (01406) 540379. Cur.: Iris Tunnicliff
Performing Arts Museum
History of entertainment, mechanical music, the fairground, radio, TV, cinema, theatre 40848

Whitburn

Whitburn Community Museum, Library, Union Rd, Whitburn EH47 0AR - T: (01506) 776347, Fax: 776190, E-mail: museums@westlothian.org.uk, Internet: www.wlonline.org. Man.: Hilda Gibson
Local Museum
Whitburn and its mining past 40849

Whitby

Captain Cook Memorial Museum, Grape Ln, Whitby YO22 4BA - T: (01947) 601900, Fax: 601900, E-mail: captcookmuseumwhitby@ukgateway.net, Internet: www.cookmuseumwhitby.co.uk. Dir.: Dr. Sophie Forgan
Historical Museum
House where Captain Cook lodged as an apprentice 1746-49, paintings,drawings, artifacts from the voyages, documents 40850

Museum of Victorian Whitby, 4 Sandgate, Whitby YO22 4DB - T: (01947) 601221. Man.: T.J. Ruff
Local Museum
Life in Victorian Whitby, whaling, jet mining and jewellery manufacturing 40851

Sutcliffe Gallery, 1 Flowergate, Whitby YO21 3BA - T: (01947) 602239, Fax: 820287, E-mail: photographs@sutcliffe-gallery.fsnet.co.uk, Internet: www.sutcliffe-gallery.co.uk
Fine Arts Museum
Prints, photofraphy, negative coll of works by Frank Meadow (19th c) 40852

Whitby Abbey Museum, Whitby YO22 4JT - T: (01947) 603568, Fax: 825561. Cur.: Andrew Morrison
Archaeological Museum - 2001
Architectural material from the abbey 40853

Whitby Museum, Pannett Park, Whitby YO21 1RE - T: (01947) 602908, Fax: 897638, E-mail: graham@durain.demon.co.uk, Internet: www.durain.demon.co.uk. Dir.: Lady Normanby
Local Museum - 1823
Local history, archaeology, geology, natural history, shipping, fossils, paintings, ceramics, costumes, Scoresby, Captain Cook, toys and dolls, militaria - library, archives 40854

Whitchurch, Hampshire

Whitchurch Silk Mill, 28 Winchester St, Whitchurch, Hampshire RG28 7AL - T: (01256) 892065, Fax: 893882, E-mail: silkmill@btinternet.com, Internet: www.whitchurchsilkmill.org.uk. Man.: Stephen Bryer
Science&Tech Museum
Textile watermill, 19th-c machinery 40855

Whitehaven

The Beacon Whitehaven, West Strand, Whitehaven CA28 7LY - T: (01946) 592302, Fax: 598150, E-mail: thebeacon@copelandbc.gov.uk, Internet: www.thebeacon-whitehaven.co.uk
Local Museum / Fine Arts Museum - 1996
Maritime hist, coal mining, pottery, social hist - library 40856

Haig Colliery Mining Museum, Solway Rd, Kells, Whitehaven CA28 9BG - T: (01946) 599949, Fax: 61896, E-mail: museum@haig1.freeserve.co.uk, Internet: www.haig1.freeserve.co.uk
Science&Tech Museum
Standard gauge Huslet locomotive and coal waggons, mining history 40857

Whitehaven Museum and Art Gallery → The Beacon Whitehaven

Whitehead

Railway Preservation Society of Ireland, Whitehead Excursion Station, Castleview Rd, Whitehead BT39 9NA - T: (028) 28260803, Fax: 28260803, E-mail: rpsitrains@hotmail.com, Internet: www.rpsi-online.org
Association with Coll
9 steam locomotives, 2 diesel locomotives, over 25 coaches, wagons, steam crane 40858

Whitfield

Dover Transport Museum, White Cliffs Business Park, Port Zone, Whitfield CT16 2HJ - T: (01304) 822409, 204612. Dir.: Colin Smith
Science&Tech Museum
Local transport history by land, sea and air 40859

Whithorn

Whithorn - Cradle of Christianity, 45-47 George St, Whithorn DG8 8NS - T: (01988) 500508, Fax: 500508
Religious Arts Museum 40860

Whithorn Priory and Museum, Bruce St, Whithorn DG8 8P4 - T: (0131) 24431010. Dir.: Michael Lyons
Archaeological Museum - 1908
Early Christian medieval stonework, Latins Stone 450 AD to mid 5th c, St Peters Cross, 7th c, 10th c Monrieith Cross, fine coll of other crosses 40861

Whitstable

Whitstable Museum and Gallery, Oxford St, Whitstable CT5 1DB - T: (01227) 276998, Fax: 772379, E-mail: museums@canterbury.gov.uk, Internet: www.whitstable-museum.co.uk
Historical Museum / Fine Arts Museum
Seafaring tradition (oyster industry, divers), fine coll of maritime art 40862

Whitstable Oyser and Fishery Exhibition, Harbour, East Quay, Whitstable CT5 1AB - T: (01227) 280753, Fax: 264829, E-mail: bayes@seasalter.evnet.co.uk. Man.: Norman Goodman
Special Museum
Traditional oyster and fishing industry, oyster farming, science and technology 40863

Whittlesey

Whittlesey Museum, Town Hall, Market St, Whittlesey PE7 1BD - T: (01733) 840968. Cur.: Maureen Watson
Local Museum
Local trades and industry 40864

Whittlesford

Peppin Brown Art Gallery, Old School, High St, Whittlesford CB2 4LT - T: (01223) 836394
Fine Arts Museum 40865

Whitworth

Whitworth Historical Society Museum, North St, Whitworth OL12 8RE - T: (01706) 853655
Local Museum
Coll of quarry tools, photographs, books, local council records 40866

Wick

Caithness District Museum, Bruce Bldg, Sinclaire Terrace, Wick KW1 5AB - T: (01955) 607771, Fax: 604524
Local Museum 40867

Wick Heritage Centre, 20 Bank Row, Wick KW1 5EY - T: (01955) 605393, Fax: 605393
Local Museum / Fine Arts Museum
Coll of photographs of 115 years history, art gallery 40868

Widnes

Catalyst, Science Discovery Centre, Gossage Bldg, Mersey Rd, Widnes WA8 0DF - T: (0151) 4201121, Fax: 4952030, E-mail: info@catalyst.org.uk, Internet: www.catalyst.org.uk. Dir.: C. Allison
Science&Tech Museum - 1989 40869

Wigan

History Shop, Library St, Wigan WN1 1NU - T: (01942) 828128, Fax: 827645, E-mail: heritage@wiganmbc.gov.uk, Internet: www.wiganmbc.gov.uk/pub/leis/info/leisure/heritage. Dir.: A. Gillies
Local Museum - 1992
Local and family hist, archaeology, numismatics, local art, industries 40870

Opie's Museum of Memories, Wigan Pier Experience, Trencherfield Mill, Wigan WN3 4EF - T: (01942) 323666, E-mail: info@robertopie-collection.com, Internet: www.themuseum.co.uk. Cur.: Robert Opie
Special Museum - 1984
Hist of British consume product development 40871

Robert Opie Collection → Opie's Museum of Memories

Wigan Pier, Trencherfield Mill, Wigan WN3 4EU - T: (01942) 323666, Fax: 701927, E-mail: wiganpier@wiganmbc.gov.uk, Internet: www.wigangov.co.uk. Dir.: Carole Tydesley, Paul David (Art)
Local Museum
Social and industrial life in Wigan in 1900 40872

Willenhall

Willenhall Lock Museum, 54-56 New Rd, Willenhall WV13 2DA - T: (01902) 634542, Fax: 634542, Internet: members.tripod.co.uk/lock_museum/. Dir.: John Whistance
Science&Tech Museum - 1987
17th-20th c locks and keys, early 20th c womens childrens's clothing 40873

Willenhall Museum, Above Willenhall Library, Walsall St, Willenhall WV13 2EX - T: (01922) 653116, Fax: 632824, E-mail: museum@walsall.gov.uk, Internet: www.walsall.gov.uk/museums. Man.: Louise Troman
Local Museum
History of this Midland town 40874

Williton

Bakelite Museum, Orchard Mill, Williton TA4 4NS - T: (01984) 632133, 632322, E-mail: info@bakelitemuseum.com, Internet: www.bakelitemuseum.co.uk. Cur.: Patrick Cook
Decorative Arts Museum
Design 40875

Wilmington

Wilmington Priory, Polegate, Wilmington BN26 5SW - T: (01323) 870537
Agriculture Museum - 1925
Old agricultural implements 40876

Wilton, Marlborough

Wilton Windmill, Wilton, Marlborough SN8 3SP - T: (01672) 870266, Fax: 870401, E-mail: jctalbot@waitrose.com, Internet: www.wiltonwindmill.com. Chairman: Dick Marchant Smith
Science&Tech Museum
Working windmill 40877

Wilton, Salisbury

Wilton House, Wilton, Salisbury SP2 0BJ - T: (01722) 746720, Fax: 744447, E-mail: tourism@wiltonhouse.com, Internet: www.wiltonhouse.com
Historic Site
Paintings, interior, art coll, marble bustos 40878

Wimborne Minster

Priest's House Museum, 23-27 High St, Wimborne Minster BH21 1HR - T: (01202) 882533, Fax: 882533, E-mail: priestshouse@hotmail.com. Cur.: Emma Ayling, Ass. Cur.: Caitlin Griffiths, Librarian: Julia Wenham
Local Museum - 1962
Local hist, archaeology, Bronze Age and Romano-British finds, toys 40879

Wincanton

Wincanton Museum, 32 High St, Wincanton BA9 9JF - T: (01963) 34063. Cur.: H.C. Rodd
Local Museum 40880

Winchcombe

Sudeley Castle, Winchcombe GL54 5JD - T: (01242) 602308, Fax: 602959, E-mail: marketing@sudeley.org.uk, Internet: www.sudeleycastle.co.uk. Dir.: Timothy Baylis
Historical Museum
Relics and art, paintings by Turner, Van Dijk, Rubens 40881

Winchcombe Folk and Police Museum, Old Town Hall, High St, Winchcombe GL54 5LJ - T: (01242) 609151, Internet: www.winchcombemuseum.org.uk. Cur.: Barbara Edward
Local Museum / Historical Museum
Local hist, police uniforms and equipment 40882

Winchcombe Railway Museum, 23 Gloucester St, Winchcombe GL54 - T: (01242) 620641. Dir.: Tim Petchey
Science&Tech Museum - 1968
Tickets, labels, horsedrawn railway road vehicles, mechanical signalling, lineside notices 40883

Winchelsea

Winchelsea Museum, Court Hall, Winchelsea TN36 4EN - T: (01797) 226382. Cur.: G. Alexander
Local Museum - 1945
Cinque Ports, town history, maps, seals, coins, pictures, pottery, clay pipes, model of the town in 1292 40884

Winchester

Adjutant General's Corps Museum, Worthy Down, Winchester SO21 2RG - T: (01962) 887435, 887919, Fax: 887690, E-mail: agc.regtsec@virgin.net. Dir.: J. Mills
Military Museum
Uniforms, badges and medals, old office machines, documents related to Royal Army Pay Corps, Educational Corps, Military Provost Corps, Army Legal Corps, Women' Royal Army Corps 40885

Balfour Museum of Hampshire Red Cross History, Red Cross House, Stockbridge Rd, Winchester SO22 5JD - T: (01962) 865174, Fax: 869721
Historical Museum
History of the British Red Cross, Hampshire branch - archives 40886

Guildhall Gallery, Broadway, Winchester SO23 9LJ - T: (01962) 848289, Fax: 848299, E-mail: museums@winchester.gov.uk, Internet: www.winchester.gov.uk/heritage/heritage.htm. Dir.: Geoffrey Denford, Cons.: Christopher Bradbury
Public Gallery - 1969 40887

Gurkha Museum, Peninsula Barracks, Romsey Rd, Winchester SO23 8TS - T: (01962) 842832, 843657, Fax: 877597, E-mail: curator@thegurkhamuseum.co.uk, Internet: www.thegurkhamuseum.co.uk. Cur.: Christopher Bullock
Military Museum / Ethnology Museum
Story of Gurkha since 1815, ethnographic objects from Nepal, India, Tibet and Afghanistan 40888

The King's Royal Hussars Museum, Peninsula Barracks, Romsey Rd, Winchester SO23 8TS - T: (01962) 828539, Fax: 828538, E-mail: beresford@krhmuseum.freeserve.co.uk, Internet: www.hans.gov.uk/leisure/museums/royalhus. Dir.: P. Beresford
Military Museum - 1980
Story of the Regiment from the raising of the 10th and 11th Hussars (originally Light Dragoons) in 1715, armoured vehicles, uniforms, equipment, medals, photographs and campaign relics 40889

Light Infantry Museum, Peninsula Barracks, Romsey Rd, Winchester SO23 8TS - T: (01962) 828550, 828530, Fax: 828534, Internet: www.army.doc.uk/army/press/museums/details/m158light.html. Man.: Patrick Kirkby
Military Museum
Modern military museum, elite regiment, Berlin wall, Gulf war, Bosnia exhibition 40890

Royal Green Jackets Museum, Peninsula Barracks, Romsey Rd, Winchester SO23 8TS - T: (01962) 828549, Fax: 828500, E-mail: museum@royalgreenjackets.co.uk. Dir.: K. Grai
Military Museum - 1926
Regimental history, pictures, silver, medals 40891

Royal Hampshire Regiment Museum, Serle's House, Southgate St, Winchester SO23 9EG - T: (01962) 863658, Fax: 888302. Dir.: H.D.H. Keatinge
Military Museum - 1933
History of the regiment - archive 40892

Textile Conservation Centre, University of Southampton, Winchester Campus, Park Av, Winchester SO23 8DL - T: (023) 80597100, Fax: 80597101, E-mail: tccuk@soton.ac.uk, Internet: www.soton.ac.uk/~wsart/tcc.htm. Dir.: Nell Hoare
Special Museum
Karen Finch Library 40893

Westgate Museum, High St, Winchester - T: (01962) 848269, Fax: 848299, E-mail: museums@winchester.gov.uk, Internet: www.winchester.gov.uk. Dir.: Dr. G.T. Denford
Local Museum - 1898
Medieval building: coll of weights and standards 40894

Winchester Cathedral Triforium Gallery, Cathedral, South Transept, Winchester SO23 9LS - T: (01962) 857223, Fax: 841519, E-mail: john.hardacre@winchester-cathedral.org.uk, Internet: www.winchester-cathedral.org.uk. Dir.: John Hardacre
Religious Arts Museum
Artistic and archeological material from the Cathedral, stone and wooden sculpture 40895

Winchester City Museum, The Square, Winchester SO23 7DW - T: (01962) 848269, Fax: 848299, E-mail: museum@winchester.gov.uk, Internet: www.winchester.gov.uk/heritage/heritage.htm. Dir.: Kenneth Qualmann
Archaeological Museum / Local Museum - 1847
Archeology and history of Winchester 40896

Winchester College Treasury, College St, Winchester SO23 9NA - T: (01962) 866079, Fax: 843005. Dir.: Victoria Hebron
Fine Arts Museum
Historic documents, antique silver, ceramics, Egyptian and Central American objects, antique scientific instruments, modern crafts 40897

Windermere

Windermere Steamboat Museum, Rayrigg Rd, Windermere LA23 1BN - T: (015394) 45565, Fax: 48769, E-mail: info@steamboat.co.uk, Internet: www.steamboat.co.uk. Dir.: Tony Jackson
Science&Tech Museum - 1977
Coll of 35 steam, sail and motorboats undercover in a purpose built wet dock made on Lake Windermere - art gallery, library 40898

Windsor

Dorney Court, Dorney, Windsor SL4 6QP - T: (01628) 604638, Fax: 665772, E-mail: palmer@dorneycourt.co.uk, Internet: www.dorneycourt.co.uk. Dir.: Peregrine Palmer
Historical Museum - 1440 40899

Frogmore House, Royal Collections, Windsor SL4 1NJ, mail addr: Stable Yard House, Saint James's Palace, London SW1A 1JR - T: (01753) 868286, Fax: 832290, E-mail: windsorcastle@royalcollection.org.uk, Internet: www.royal.gov.uk
Fine Arts Museum / Decorative Arts Museum
Royal coll 40900

Household Cavalry Museum, Combermere Barracks, Windsor SL4 3DN - T: (01753) 755112, Fax: 755161, E-mail: homehq@householdcavalry.co.uk. Sc. Staff: S.F. Sibley, K.C. Hughes
Military Museum - 1952
Regimental history, uniforms, armaments, pictures 40901

Royal Berkshire Yeomanry Cavalry Museum, Territorial Army Centre, Bolton Rd, Windsor SL4 3JG - T: (01753) 860600, Fax: 854946. Cur.: A.P. Verey
Military Museum 40902

Royal Borough Museum Collection, Tinkers Ln, Windsor SL4 4LR - T: (01628) 796829, Fax: 796859, E-mail: museum.collections@rbwm.gov.uk, Internet: www.rbwm.gov.uk. Dir.: Olivia Goodend
Local Museum
Royal borough of Windsor and Maidenhead history 40903

Town and Crown Exhibition, Royal Windsor Information Centre, 24 High St, Windsor SL4 1LH - T: (01753) 743918, Fax: 743917, E-mail: museum.collections@rbwm.gov.uk. Cur.: Judith Hunter
Local Museum / Special Museum
History of the town of Windsor 40904

Windsor Castle, Royal Collections, Windsor SL4 1NJ, mail addr: Stable Yard House, Saint James's Palace, London SW1A 1JR - T: (01753) 868286, Fax: 832290, E-mail: windsorcastle@royalcollection.org.uk, Internet: www.royal.gov.uk
Fine Arts Museum / Decorative Arts Museum
Royal coll, state apartments - Royal library 40905

Wisbech

Peckover House, North Brink, Wisbech PE13 1JR - T: (01945) 583463, Fax: 583463, E-mail: aprigx@smtp.ntrust.org.uk
Decorative Arts Museum 40906

Wisbech and Fenland Museum, 5 Museum Sq, Wisbech PE13 1ES - T: (01945) 583817, Fax: 589050. Cur.: Dr. Jane Hubbard
Local Museum / Decorative Arts Museum - 1835
Pottery and porcelain, figures, local photographs, manuscripts by Dickens and Lewis, calotypes by Samuel Smith, early Madagascar photos, parish records, african ethnography, geology, Fenland hist and folklife, coins, applied art, fossils - library, archives 40907

Withernsea

Withernsea Lighthouse Museum, Hull Rd, Withernsea HU19 2DY - T: (01964) 614834, E-mail: with-lighthouse@www.com, Internet: www.yell.co.uk/sites/wsealighthousemuseum. Admin.: Janet Standley
Science&Tech Museum 40908

Witney

Bishop of Winchester's Palace Site, Mount House, The Green, Witney - T: (01993) 772602, Fax: 813239, E-mail: oxonmuseum@oxfordshire.gov.uk, Internet: www.oxfordshire.gov.uk
Historic Site
12th c palace 40909

Cogges Manor Farm Museum, Church Ln, Cogges, Witney OX28 3LA - T: (01993) 772602, Fax: 703056, E-mail: info@cogges.org, Internet: www.cogges.org. Dir.: Clare Pope
Agriculture Museum - 1976
Historic Manor House with Victorian period room displays, 17th c study with original painted panelling, agricultural history, tools, wagon coll 40910

Witney and District Museum and Art Gallery, Gloucester Court Mews, High St, Witney OX8 6LX - T: (01993) 775915
Local Museum
Social history, fine art, military history, photographic coll 40911

Woburn

Woburn Abbey, Woburn MK17 9WA - T: (01525) 290666, Fax: 290271, E-mail: enquiries@woburnabbay.co.uk, Internet: www.woburnabbay.co.uk. Cur.: Lavinia Wellicome
Historical Museum
Coll of English and French furniture (18th c), paintings by Canaletto, Reynolds, Van Dyck 40912

Woking

The Galleries, Chobham Rd, Woking GU21 1JF - T: (01483) 725517, Fax: 725501, E-mail: the.galleries@pipex.com. Dir.: Amana Devonshire
Local Museum
Life in Woking past and present, arts and crafts 40913

Wollaston

Wollaston Heritage Museum, 102-104 High St, Wollaston NN29 7RJ - T: (01933) 664468. Dir.: D. Hall, Cur.: I. Walker
Local Museum
Farming implements, archaeological finds from the area, village life, paintings by local artists, footware manufacture, lace making 40914

Wolverhampton

Bantock House, Bantock Park, Finchfield Rd, Wolverhampton WV3 9LQ - T: (01902) 552195, Fax: 552196, Internet: www.wolverhamptonart.org.uk. Dir.: Nicholas Dodd
Decorative Arts Museum / Local Museum
Enamels, steel jewellery, japanned ware 40915

Bilston Craft Gallery, Mount Pleasant, Bilston, Wolverhampton WV14 7LU - T: (01902) 552507, Fax: 552504, E-mail: bilstoncraftgallery@dial.pipex.com, Internet: www.wolverhamptonart.org.uk. Cur.: Nicki Gardner, Sc. Staff: Emma Daker, Val Plummer, Anne Hardy
Local Museum / Public Gallery - 1937
Local hist, enamels, contemporary crafts, glass, jewellry, sculptures 40916

Wightwick Manor, Wightwick Bank, Wolverhampton WV6 8EE - T: (01902) 761400, Fax: 764663, E-mail: wightwickmanor@nationaltrust.org.uk. Cur.: T.A. Clement
Local Museum 40917

Wolverhampton Art Gallery, Lichfield St, Wolverhampton WV1 1DU - T: (01902) 552055, Fax: 552053, E-mail: info.wag@dial.pipex.com, Internet: www.wolverhamptonart.org.uk. Dir.: Nicholas Dodd
Fine Arts Museum - 1884
British 18th-20th c paintings and sculpture, British and American Pop Art and contemporary paintings, geology, interactive display "ways of seeing" 40918

Woodbridge

Suffolk Punch Heavy Horse Museum, Market Hill, Woodbridge IP12 4LU - T: (01394) 380643, E-mail: sec@suffolkhousesociety.org.uk
Special Museum 40919

Woodbridge Museum, 5a Market Hill, Woodbridge IP12 4LP - T: (01394) 380502. Dir.: P. Hayworth
Local Museum - 1981 40920

Woodchurch

Woodchurch Village Life Museum, Susans Hill, Woodchurch TN26 3RE - T: (01233) 860240, Internet: www.woodchurchmuseum.fsnet.com. Cur.: G. Loynes
Local Museum
Social history of the village, vehicles, agricultural equipment, ceramics, coins, household items, books, papers and photographs 40921

Woodhall Spa

Woodhall Spa Cottage Museum, Bungalow, Iddesleigh Rd, Woodhall Spa LN10 6SH - T: (01526) 353775
Local Museum
History of Woodhall Spa, geology 40922

Woodley

Museum of Berkshire Aviation, Mohawk Wy, Woodley RG5 4UE - T: (0118) 9448089, E-mail: museumofberkshireaviation@fly.to, Internet: fly.tomuseumofberkshireaviation. Dir.: Trevor Hensley
Local Museum
Aircraft, models, archives, photographs 40923

Woodstock

Blenheim Palace, Woodstock OX20 1PX - T: (01993) 811091, Fax: 813527, E-mail: admin@blenheimpalace.com, Internet: www.blenheimpalace.com. Dir.: Julian Blades
Fine Arts Museum / Decorative Arts Museum
Tapestries, paintings, sculpture, porcelain, fine furniture 40924

The Oxfordshire Museum, Fletcher's House, Park St, Woodstock OX20 1SN - T: (01993) 811456, Fax: 813239, E-mail: oxon.museum@oxfordshire.gov.uk, Internet: www.oxfordshire.gov.uk/the_oxfordshire_museum. Cur.: Carol Anderson
Local Museum - 1965
Archaeology, history and natural environment of Oxfordshire, county's innovative industry 40925

Wookey Hole

Wookey Hole Cave Diving and Archaeological Museum, Wookey Hole BA5 1BB - T: (01749) 672243, Fax: 677749, E-mail: witch@wookey.co.uk, Internet: www.wookey.co.uk. Dir.: Peter Haylings
Natural History Museum / Archaeological Museum - 1980
Archaeological finds, cave exploration, geology, cave diving, myth and legends 40926

Woolpit

Woolpit and District Museum, The Institute, Woolpit IP30 9QH - T: (01359) 240822. Dir.: John Wiley
Local Museum - 1983
Coll of items from the village and its immediate surroundings 40927

Worcester

Commandery Museum, Sidbury, Worcester WR1 2HU - T: (01905) 361821, Fax: 361822, E-mail: thecommandery@cityofworcester.gov.uk, Internet: www.cityofworcester.gov.uk. Dir.: Amanda Lunt
Local Museum - 1977
Local hist, english Civil War, 15th c wall paintings 40928

Museum of Local Life (closed) 40929

Museum of the Worcestershire Regiment, Foregate St, Worcester WR1 1DT - T: (01905) 25371, Fax: 722350, E-mail: rhq_wfr@lineone.net. Cur.: D.W. Reevees
Military Museum
History of the regiment, medals, uniforms, equipment 40930

Museum of Worcester Porcelain, Severn St, Worcester WR1 2NE - T: (01905) 746000, Fax: 617807, E-mail: museum@royal-worcester.co.uk, Internet: www.worcesterporcelainmuseum.org. Dir.: Amanda Savidge, Chm.: T.G. Westbrook, Cur.: Wendy Cook
Decorative Arts Museum - 1946
Worcester porcelain since 1751 40931

Worcester City Museum and Art Gallery, Foregate St, Worcester WR1 1DT - T: (01905) 25371, Fax: 616979, E-mail: artgalleryandmuseum@cityofworcester.gov.uk, Internet: www.worcestercitymuseums.org.uk
Local Museum / Fine Arts Museum - 1833
Area hist, geology, natural hist, archaeology, glass, ceramics, local prints, watercolors 40932

Worcestershire Yeomanry Cavalry Museum, Foregate St, Worcester WR1 1DT - T: (01905) 25371, Fax: 616979, E-mail: tbridges@cityofworcester.gov.uk. Head: Tim Bridges
Military Museum - 1929
Hist of regiment, medals, uniforms, decorations, documents and prints 40933

Workington

Helena Thompson Museum, Park End Rd, Workington CA14 4DE - T: (01900) 326255, Fax: 326256, E-mail: helena.thompson@allerdale.gov.uk, Internet: www.allerdale.dov.uk. Dir.: Philip Crouch, Cur.: Janet Baker
Local Museum - 1940
Workington's social and industrial hist, costume, ceramics, other decorative art 40934

Worksop

Mr. Straw's House, 7 Blyth Grove, Worksop S81 0JG - T: (01909) 482380, E-mail: mrstrawshouse@nationaltrust.org.uk, Internet: www.nationaltrust.org.uk. Manager: Philippa Caurie
Historical Museum
Family ephemera, costume, furniture and household objects from 19th and 20th c 40935

Worksop Museum, Memorial Av, Worksop S80 2BP - T: (01777) 713749, Fax: 713749. Cur.: Malcolm J. Dolby
Local Museum
Local history, archaeology, natural history, Stone Age finds 40936

Worthing

Worthing Museum and Art Gallery, Chapel Rd, Worthing BN11 1HP - T: (01903) 239999 ext 1150, Fax: 236277, E-mail: museum@worthing.gov.uk, Internet: www.worthing.gov.uk. Cur.: Dr. Sally White (Antiquities), Asst. Cur.: Ann Wise (Costumes and Textiles), Laura Kidner (Art and Exhibitions)
Local Museum / Decorative Arts Museum / Fine Arts Museum - 1908
Archaeology, geology, local history, costumes, paintings, decorative arts, toys 40937

Wotton-under-Edge

Wotton Heritage Centre, The Chipping, Wotton-under-Edge GL12 7AD - T: (01453) 521541, E-mail: wootonhs@freeuk.com. Cur.: Beryl A. Kingan
Local Museum
Local and family history - library 40938

Wrexham

Bersham Heritage Centre and Ironworks, Bersham, Wrexham LL14 4HT - T: (01978) 261529, Fax: 361703. Dir.: Alan Watkin, Sc. Staff: Hilary Williams
Science&Tech Museum / Local Museum - 1983/1992 40939

Erddig Agricultural Museum, Felin Puleston, Wrexham LL13 0YT - T: (01978) 355314, Fax: 313333, E-mail: erddig@ntrust.org.uk, Internet: www.nationaltrust.org.uk. Dir.: Gavin Hogg
Decorative Arts Museum
Furniture, domestic outbuildings, vehicles 40940

Geological Museum of North Wales, Bwlchgwyn Quarry, Wrexham LL11 5UY - T: (01978) 757573
Natural History Museum 40941

King's Mill Visitor Centre, King's Mill Rd, Wrexham LL13 0NT - T: (01978) 358916
Science&Tech Museum
Restored mill featuring life and work in an 18th c mill, waterwheel, by appointment 40942

Wrexham Arts Centre, Rhosddu Rd, Wrexham LL11 1AU - T: (01978) 292093, Fax: 292611, E-mail: arts.centre@wrexham.gov.uk, Internet: www.wrexham.gov.uk. Dir.: Tracy Simpson
Public Gallery 40943

Wrexham County Borough Museum, County Bldgs, Regent St, Wrexham LL11 1RB - T: (01978) 317970, Fax: 317982, E-mail: museum@wrexham.gov.uk. Dir.: Steve Grenter, Cur.: Joanne Neri
Local Museum
Local hist, iron and coal industry (18th-19th c), bronze age skeleton of Brymbo man, archeology 40944

Wroughton

Science Museum Wroughton, The National Museum of Science & Industry, Wroughton Airfield, Wroughton SN4 9NS - T: (01793) 814466, Fax: 813569, E-mail: f.riccini@nmsi.ac.uk, Internet: www.nmsi.ac.uk/wroughton. Dir.: Lindsay Sharp
Science&Tech Museum 40945

Wroxeter

Viroconium Museum, Wroxeter Roman City, Roman Site, Wroxeter SY5 6PH - T: (01743) 761330. Cur.: Sara Lunt
Archaeological Museum
Archeological finds, pottery, coins, metalwork 40946

Wylam

Wylam Railway Museum, Falcon Centre, Falcon Terrace, Wylam NE41 8EE - T: (01661) 852174. Dir.: Philip R.B. Brooks
Science&Tech Museum - 1981
Railway hist. 40947

Wymondham

Wymondham Heritage Museum, 10 The Bridewell, Norwich Rd, Wymondham NR18 0NS - T: (01953) 600205, Internet: www.wymondham-norfolk.co.uk. Man.: Adrian D. Hoare
Local Museum / Historic Site
Local history 40948

Y Bala

Canolfan Y Plase, Plassey St, Y Bala LL23 7YD - T: (01678) 520320. Chm.: I.B. Williams
Local Museum
Exhibitions of artwork and local heritage topics 40949

Yanworth

Chedworth Roman Villa, Yanworth GL54 3LJ - T: (01242) 890256, Fax: 890544, E-mail: chedworth@smtp.ntrust.org.uk, Internet: www.ntrustseern.org.uk. Dir.: Philip Bethell
Archaeological Museum - 1865
Roman walls, mosaic floors, bath suites, wooden buildings, heating in Roman houses, Roman gardens, religion in Roman times, archaeology, classical history 40950

Yarmouth

Maritime Heritage Exhibition, Fort Victoria Museum, Fort Victoria Country Park, off Westhill Ln, Yarmouth PO41 0RW - T: (01983) 761214, Fax: (023) 80593052, E-mail: hwtma@mail.soc.soton.ac.uk, Internet: www.soc.coton.ac.uk/hwtma. Cur.: Paul Blake
Historical Museum 40951

Yell

Old Haa, Burravoe, Yell ZE2 9AY - T: (019577) 22339. Dir.: A. Nisbet
Local Museum
Arts and crafts, local history, tapes of Shetland music and folklore, Bobby Tulloch collection, genealogy 40952

Yelverton

Buckland Abbey, Yelverton PL20 6EY - T: (01822) 853607, Fax: 855448, E-mail: buckland.abbey@nationaltrust.org.uk, Internet: www.nationaltrust.org.uk. Man.: Michael Coxson
Historic Site - 1952
Drakes drum, standards, portraits and family pictures, furniture and ship navigation equipment 40953

Yelverton Paperweight Centre, 4 Buckland Tce, Leg O'Mutton Cnr, Yelverton PL20 6AD - T: (01822) 854250, Fax: 854250, E-mail: paperweightcentre@btinternet.com, Internet: www.paperweightcentre.co.uk
Fine Arts Museum
Work of glass artists and others 40954

Yeovil

Country Life Museum, Priest House, Brympton d'Evercy, Yeovil BA22 8TD - T: (01935) 862528
Folklore Museum
Coll of old domestic appliances 40955

Museum of South Somerset, Hendford, Yeovil BA20 1UN - T: (01935) 424774, Fax: 475281, E-mail: marion.barnes@southsomerset.gov.uk, Internet: www.zynet.co.uk/somerset/altrac/sout_mus.html. Dir.: Marion Barnes
Local Museum - 1928
Archaeology, industries, household and farm tools, topography, armaments, glass, costumes 40956

Yeovilton

Fleet Air Arm Museum - Concorde, The National Museum of Science & Industry, D6, Royal Naval Air Station, Yeovilton BA22 8HT - T: (01935) 840565, Fax: 842630, E-mail: enquires@fleetairarm.com, Internet: www.fleetairarm.com. Dir.: Graham Mottram
Military Museum - 1964
Paintings, photographs, weapons, medals and uniforms, coll of model aircraft and model ships, the ultimate "carrier" experience a flight deck on land with eleven carrier-borne aircraft 40957

York

Archaeological Resource Centre, Saint Saviourgate, York - T: (01904) 543403, Fax: 627097, E-mail: enquiries@vikingjorvik.com, Internet: www.vikingjorvik.com/arc
Archaeological Museum 40958

Beningbrough Hall, Beningbrough, York YO30 1DD - T: (01904) 470666, Fax: 470002, E-mail: ybblmb@smtp.ntrust.org.uk. Man.: Ray Barker
Fine Arts Museum - 1979
Restored early Georgian country house, National portrait gallery 40959

Castle Museum, Eye of York, nr Clifford's Tower, Coppergate, York YO1 9RY - T: (01904) 653611, Fax: 671078, E-mail: castle.museum@york.gov.uk, Internet: www.york.gov.uk. Dir.: Keith Matthews
Ethnology Museum / Historical Museum - 1938
Yorkshire ethnology, period rooms, household and farm tools, militaria, costumes, crafts 40960

Divisional Kohima Museum, Imphal Barracks, Fulford Rd, York YO1 4AU - T: (01904) 662381, Fax: 662744. Cur.: Robin McDermott
Military Museum 40961

Fairfax House Museum, Castlegate, York YO1 9RN - T: (01904) 655543, Fax: 652262, E-mail: peterbrown@fairfaxhouse.co.uk, Internet: www.fairfaxhouse.co.uk. Dir.: Peter B. Brown
Decorative Arts Museum / Fine Arts Museum - 1984
18th c English furniture, clocks, dining room, silver, paintings and glass, elaborate stucco ceilings 40962

Impressions Gallery of Photography, 29 Castlegate, York YO1 9RN - T: (01904) 654724, Fax: 651509, E-mail: enquiries@impressions-gallery.com, Internet: www.impressions-gallery.com. Dir.: Anne E. McNeill
Public Gallery
Contemporary photography 40963

Jorvik Museum, Coppergate, York YO1 9WT - T: (01904) 543400, Fax: 627097, E-mail: jorvik@yorkarchaeology.co.uk, Internet: www.vikingjorvik.com. Dir.: John Walker
Archaeological Museum / Historical Museum
Viking life and trade 40964

Merchant Adventurers' Hall, Fossgate, York YO1 9XD - T: (01904) 654818, Fax: 654818, E-mail: the.clerk@mahall-york.demon.co.uk, Internet: www.theyorkcompany.sagenet.co.uk. Dir.: James Finlay
Decorative Arts Museum
Early furniture, silver and portraits, pottery and other objects 40965

National Railway Museum, The National Museum of Science and Industry, Leeman Rd, York YO26 4XJ - T: (01904) 621261, Fax: 611112, 631319, E-mail: nrm@nmsi.ac.uk, Internet: www.nrm.org.uk. Head: Andrew Scott, Man.: Chris Allender, Dep. Head: Janice Murray, Sc. Staff: Colin Divall (Research), Su Matthewman (Marketing), Graham Stratfold (Visitor Service), Camilla Harrison (Press, PR), Richard Gibbon (Engineering), Dieter Hopkin (Photographic Archive and Arts Collections)
Science&Tech Museum - 1975
Mallard - the world's fastest steam locomotive, Queen Victoria's Royal Carriage, Working Replica of Stephenson's Rocket, Japanese Bullet train, Chinese 4-8-4 locomotive - library, archives and picture archives 40966

Regimental Museum of the Royal Dragoon Guards and the Prince of Wales's Own Regiment of Yorkshire, 3a Tower St, York YO1 9SB - T: (01904) 642036, Fax: 642036, Internet: www.army.mod.uk. Cur.: W.A. Henshall
Military Museum
Uniforms, paintings, pictures, medals, horse furniture, weapons, soldiers' personal memorabilia, regiments history 40967

Treasurer's House, Minster Yard, York YO1 2JL - T: (01904) 624247, Fax: 647372, E-mail: yorkth@smtp.ntrust.org.uk. Dir.: Norma Sutherland
Decorative Arts Museum - 1930
Furniture 17th-18th c, pictures, glass, ceramics 40968

Viking City of Jorvik → Jorvik Museum

York City Art Gallery, Exhibition Sq, York YO1 7EW - T: (01904) 551861, Fax: 551866, E-mail: art.gallery@york.gov.uk, Internet: www.york.gov.uk/heritage/museums/art. Dir.: Richard Green, Sc. Staff: Lara Goodband (Exhibitions and Publicity), Victoria Osborne (Art)
Fine Arts Museum - 1879
European painting 1350-1930, topographical prints and drawings, Italian paintings, English stoneware pottery - library 40969

York Minster Undercroft Treasury and Crypt, York Minster, Deangate, York YO1 7JF - T: (01904) 557216, Fax: 557218, E-mail: visitors@yorkminster.org, Internet: www.yorkminster.org. Man.: Louise Hampson
Religious Arts Museum
Coll of diocesan church plate (13th-20th c), archaeological artefacts 40970

York Racing Museum, Racecourse, The Knavesmire, York YO23 1EX - T: (01904) 620911, Fax: 611071, E-mail: info@yorkracecourse.co.uk, Internet: www.yorkracecourse.co.uk. Dir.: Scott Brown, Cur.: Dede Marks
Special Museum - 1965
Horce racing 40971

York Story, Saint Mary Castlegate, York YO1 9RN - T: (01904) 628632
Local Museum
Social and architectural history of York 40972

Yorkshire Museum, Museum Gardens, York YO1 7FR - T: (01904) 551800, Fax: 551802, E-mail: yorkshire.museum@york.gov.uk, Internet: www.york.gov.uk. Cur.: Paul Howard
Local Museum - 1822
Archaeology, decorative art, pottery, biology, mammals, entomology, herbarium, geology, fossils, minerals, numismatics, figures - library 40973

Yorkshire Museum of Farming, Murton Park, York YO19 5UF - T: (01904) 489966, Fax: 489159
Agriculture Museum - 1982
Viking village, Roman fort, Celtic houses, 200 years farm machinery and equipment 40974

Zennor

Wayside Folk Museum, Old Mill House, Zennor TR26 3DA - T: (01736) 796945. Cur.: Th. Priddle
Folklore Museum - 1935
Mining, household objects, milling, fishing, archaeology, wheelwrights and carpenters shop, blacksmiths, agriculture, millers cottage kitchen, childhood memories, the sea, village dairy, cobblers shop working water wheels, photographs 40975

Uruguay

Canelones

Museo Fernando García, Calle Camino Carrasco 7075, 90000 Canelones - T: (033) 6019228, 618527
Natural History Museum 40976

La Barra

Museo del Mar, 20001 La Barra - Internet: www.turismo.gub.uy/mumar_s.html
Historical Museum 40977

Madonado

Museo de Artes Plásticas, Casona de Don Antonio Lussich, 20000 Madonado
Fine Arts Museum 40978

Museo del Azulejo Francés, Casona de Don Antonio Lussich, 20000 Madonado
Decorative Arts Museum - 1997 40979

Maldonado

Museo de Arte Americano de Maldonado, Calle Treinta y Tres 823, 20000 Maldonado - T: (042) 22276
Fine Arts Museum 40980

Museo Didáctico Artiguista, Cuartel de Dragones, Calle 18 de Julio 871, 20000 Maldonado - T: (042) 25378
Special Museum 40981

Museo Regional Francisco Mazzoni, Calle Ituzaigó 789, 20000 Maldonado - T: (042) 21107
Local Museum 40982

Mercedes

Museo de Mercedes, 75000 Mercedes
Natural History Museum / Ethnology Museum
Natural history, palaeontology, geology, ethnography of Venezuela 40983

Montevideo

Casa de Lavalleja, Museo Histórico Nacional, Calle Zabala 1469, 11000 Montevideo - T: (02) 951028
Historical Museum 40984

Casa del General José Garibaldi, Museo Histórico Nacional, Calle 25 de Mayo 314, 11000 Montevideo - T: (02) 9154257
Historical Museum 40985

Casa Rivera, Museo Histórico Nacional (National Historical Museum), Calle Rincón 437, 11000 Montevideo - T: (02) 9151051, Fax: 9156863, E-mail: mhistoricnac@mixmail.com. Dir.: Prof. Enrique Mena Segarra
Historical Museum - 1900
Prehistoric and colonial Indian cultural hist, Uruguay political hist, military, armaments, music 40986

Centro de Artistas Plásticos, Calle Charrúa 2009, 11200 Montevideo - T: (02) 4080262, Fax: 4087224, E-mail: agranese@adinet.com.uy
Fine Arts Museum 40987

Centro Municipal de Exposiciones Subste, Av 18 de Julio y Julio Herrera y Obes, 11400 Montevideo - T: (02) 9087643, Fax: 4095701, E-mail: kikebada@adinet.com.uy. Dir.: Enrique Badaró Nadal
Public Gallery 40988

Galería de Cinemateca, Calle Dr. Lorenzo Carnelli 1311, 11200 Montevideo
Special Museum 40989

Galería Pocitos, Calle Alejandro Chucarro 1036, 11300 Montevideo - T: (02) 7082957
Public Gallery 40990

Museo Aeronáutico, Calle Dámaso Antonio Larrañaga 4045, 12000 Montevideo - T: (02) 2152039
Science&Tech Museum 40991

Museo Antártico, Calle 8 de Octubre 2958, Montevideo - T: (02) 4878341
Natural History Museum 40992

Museo Botánico, Calle 19 de Abril 1181, 11000 Montevideo - T: (02) 3364005
Natural History Museum 40993

Museo de Armas, Fortaleza del Cerro de Montevideo, 11000 Montevideo
Military Museum
Military, armaments 40994

Museo de Arte Contemporáneo, Calle 18 de Julio 965, 11000 Montevideo - T: (02) 9006662
Fine Arts Museum 40995

Museo de Arte Industrial, Calle San Salvador 1674, 12000 Montevideo
Decorative Arts Museum
Applied arts, crafts 40996

Museo de Descubrimiento, Calle Zabala y Calle Piedras, 11000 Montevideo
Historical Museum
Evokes the journeys of Cristobal Colón, the meeting of the two worlds, maps, dioramas and photographs 40997

Museo del Automóvil, Calle Colonia y Yi, 11000 Montevideo - T: (02) 9024792
Science&Tech Museum 40998

Museo del Azulejo, Calle Cavia 3080, 11300 Montevideo - T: (02) 7096352, Internet: www.artemercosur.com.uy/azulejo
Special Museum 40999

Museo del Círculo de Estudios Ferroviarios del Uruguay, Calle Paraguay 1763, Montevideo
Science&Tech Museum 41000

Museo del Gaucho y de la Moneda, Calle 18 de Julio 998, 11000 Montevideo - T: (02) 908764, Internet: www.turismo.gub.uy/gaucho_s.html
Ethnology Museum / Special Museum 41001

Museo Egipcio, Parque Battle, Montevideo - T: (02) 6280743
Museum of Classical Antiquities / Archaeological Museum 41002

Museo Ernesto Laroche, Calle General Gregorio Suárez 2716, Punta Carretas, 11000 Montevideo - T: (02) 700637, 704166. Dir.: Walter Ernesto Laroche
Local Museum
Local history 41003

Museo Geológico del Uruguay, Calle Hervidero 2861, 11800 Montevideo - T: (02) 2001951/53, Fax: 2094905, E-mail: secretaria@dinamige.gub.uy, Internet: www.dinamige.gub.uy. Dir.: Felipe Puig
Science&Tech Museum / Natural History Museum - 1934
Geology, mining, rock coll 41004

Museo Histórico Nacional Luis A. de Herrera, Calle Luis Alberto de Herrera 3760, Montevideo - T: (02) 2008832
Historical Museum 41005

Museo Juan Manuel Blanes, Av Millán 4015, 11700 Montevideo - T: (02) 362248. Dir.: María del Carmen Heguerte de Soria, Jorge Satut
Fine Arts Museum
Sculpture, paintings, drawings, graphic arts, woodcarvings 41006

Museo Juan Zorrilla de San Martín, Calle J.L. Zorrilla de San Martín 96, 11300 Montevideo - T: (02) 7101818
Special Museum
Life and work of Juan Zorilla de San Martín 41007

Museo Marítimo-Ecológico Malvín, Calle Amazonas 1525, Montevideo - T: (02) 6193370
Natural History Museum 41008

Museo Martin Perez, Calle Solis esq Cerrito, Parroquia San Francisco, 11000 Montevideo
Local Museum 41009

Museo Municipal Cabildo de Montevideo, Calle Juan Carlos Gómez 1362, 11000 Montevideo - T: (02) 9159685. Dir.: Jorge Rodriguez Delucchi
Local Museum - 1915
Paintings, jewelry, icons, furniture, documents, maps - library, archive 41010

Museo Municipal de Bellas Artes Juan Manuel Blanes, Calle Millán 1415, 11700 Montevideo - T: (02) 3362248, Internet: www.artemercosur.com.uy/museos/uruguay/bla.html. Dir.: Mario C. Tempone
Fine Arts Museum - 1928
Paintings, graphic arts, sculpture, woodcarvings 41011

Museo Municipal de Historia del Arte, Calle Ejido 1326, 11200 Montevideo - T: (02) 9089252 int 457, Internet: www.artemercosur.com.uy/museos/uruguay/his.html
Fine Arts Museum 41012

Museo Municipal de la Construcción, Calle Piedras 528, 11000 Montevideo - T: (02) 954087
Science&Tech Museum 41013

Museo Municipal Precolombino y Colonial, Calle Ejido 1326, 11200 Montevideo - T: (02) 9089252, Internet: www.artemercosur.com.uy/museos/uruguay/pre.html
Fine Arts Museum 41014

Museo Nacional de Antropología, Av de las Instrucciones 948, 12900 Montevideo - T: (02) 393353
Ethnology Museum 41015

Museo Nacional de Artes Visuales, Calle Julio Herrera y Reissig s/n, Parque Rodó, 11300 Montevideo - T: (02) 7116124/27, Fax: 7116054, Internet: www.zfm.com/mnav
Fine Arts Museum
library 41016

Museo Nacional de Bellas Artes, Av Tomás E. Giribaldi 2283, Parque Rodó, 11300 Montevideo - T: (02) 43800. Dir.: Angel Kalenberg
Fine Arts Museum
Paintings, sculptures, graphic arts of Uruguay and America, works by Joaquín Torres García - library 41017

Museo Nacional de Historia Natural y Antropología, Calle Juan Carlos Gómez 1436, 11000 Montevideo, mail addr: Casilla de Correro 399, 11000 Montevideo - T: (02) 9160908, 9167825, Fax: 9170213, E-mail: mnhn@internet.com.uy, Internet: www.mec.gub.uy/natura. Dir.: Prof. Alvaro Mones
Natural History Museum - 1837
Botany, zoology, anthropology, geology, paleontology, history of science - library 41018

Museo Naval, Rambla Charles de Gaulle s/n, esq Luis Alberto de Herrera, Montevideo - T: (02) 6221084
Historical Museum 41019

Museo Parque de Esculturas, Edificio Libertad, Calle Luis Alberto de Herrera 3350, Montevideo
Ethnology Museum / Folklore Museum 41020

Museo Pedagógico José Pedro Varela, Pl de Cagancha 1175, 11100 Montevideo - T: (02) 9004744, 9020915, Fax: 9084131, E-mail: lemamc@adinet.com.uy, Internet: www.crnti.edu.uy/museo. Dir.: María del Carmen Lema Pensado
Special Museum - 1889
Educational hist 41021

Museo Romántico, Calle 25 de Mayo 428, Montevideo - T: (02) 9155361
Fine Arts Museum 41022

Museo Severino Pose, Calle Eduardo Acevedo Díaz 1229, 11200 Montevideo - T: (02) 483563
Local Museum 41023

Museo Torres García, Peatonal Sarandí 683, 11000 Montevideo - T: (02) 9162663, Fax: 9152635, E-mail: torresgarcia@montevideo.com.uy, Internet: www.torresgarcia.org.uy. Dir.: Dr. Jimena Perera Diaz Díaz
Fine Arts Museum 41024

Museo Virtual de Artes el País, Pl de Cagancha 1164, 11000 Montevideo - T: (02) 9006662, Internet: www.diarioelpais.com/muva
Fine Arts Museum 41025

Museo y Biblioteca Blanco Acevedo, Calle Zabala 1469, 11000 Montevideo
Local Museum 41026

Museo y Centro Cultural AGADU, Calle Héctor Gutiérrez Ruiz 1181, Montevideo - T: (02) 9012773
Folklore Museum 41027

Museo y Jardín Botánico Profesor Atilio Lombardo, Av 19 de Abril 1181, 11700 Montevideo - T: (02) 3364005, Fax: 3366488, E-mail: botanico@adinet.com.uy, Internet: www.uruguay.com/jardinbotanico. Dir.: Carlos A. Brussa
Natural History Museum - 1902
Botany 41028

Museo Zoológico Dámaso A. Larrañaga, Rambla República de Chile 4215, 11400 Montevideo - T: (02) 6220258. Dir.: Juan Pablo Cuello
Natural History Museum - 1956
Zoology - library 41029

Museos del Gaucho y de la Moneda, Banco de la República Oriental del Uruguay, Calle 18 de Julio No 998, 11100 Montevideo - T: (02) 908764. Dir.: Frederico Slinger
Special Museum
Banknotes, coins, history of banking 41030

Palacio Taranco, Museo de Artes Decorativas, Calle 25 de Mayo 376, Montevideo - T: (02) 9156060, 9151101, Fax: 9156060, E-mail: taranco@mec.gub.uy, Internet: chana.mec.gub.uy/museum/taranco
Decorative Arts Museum / Archaeological Museum
Archaeology, art 41031

Sala de Arte Carlos F. Sáez, Calle Rincón 575, 11000 Montevideo
Fine Arts Museum 41032

Piriápolis

Museo de Piria, Ruta 37, 20200 Piriápolis - T: (043) 3268
Local Museum 41033

Punta Ballena

Museo Antonio Lussich, 20003 Punta Ballena - T: (042) 28077, Internet: www.artemercosur.com.uy/lussich
Natural History Museum 41034

Punta del Este

Museo Ralli, Calle Los Arrayanes y Jacaranda, Barrio Beverly Hills, 20100 Punta del Este - T: (042) 83476/77, Fax: 87378
Fine Arts Museum 41035

Rivera

Museo Municipal de Artes Plásticas, Calle Artigas 1019, Rivera - T: (062) 31900, E-mail: osantos@netgate.com.uy, Internet: www.turismo.gub.uy/plasti.htm. Dir.: Osmar Santos
Fine Arts Museum - 1970 41036

Museo Municipal de Historia y Arqueología, Calle Artigas 1019, Rivera - T: (062) 31900, E-mail: osantos@netgate.com.uy. Dir.: Osmar Santos
Local Museum / Archaeological Museum - 1946 41037

Salto

Museo Histórico Municipal, Calle Amorín 55, 50000 Salto
Local Museum
Local history 41038

San Carlos

Museo Regional de San Carlos, Calle Carlos Reyles y Leonardo Olivera, 20400 San Carlos - T: (042) 23781/82
Local Museum 41039

San Gregorio de Polanco

Museo San Gregorio de Polanco, 45200 San Gregorio de Polanco
Fine Arts Museum 41040

San José de Mayo

Museo de Bellas Artes Departamental de San José, Calle Dr Julián Beccerro de Bengoa 493, 80000 San José de Mayo - T: 3642. Dir.: César Bernesconi
Fine Arts Museum - 1947
Paintings, sculptures, graphic art, ceramics - library 41041

Tacuarembó

Museo del Indio y del Gaucho, Calle 25 de Mayo 315, 45000 Tacuarembó. Dir.: Washington Escobar
Ethnology Museum
Indian and Gaucho arts and crafts, armaments, implements 41042

Treinta y Tres

Museo de Bellas Artes Agustin Araujo, Pablo Zufriategui 1272, Treinta y Tres - Internet: www.turismo.gub.uy/araujo.htm
Fine Arts Museum 41043

U.S.A.

Abercrombie ND

Fort Abercrombie Historic Site, 816 Broadway St, Abercrombie, ND 58001 - T: (701) 553-8513, E-mail: histsoc@state.nd.us, Internet: www.discovernd.com/hist. Head: June Singer
Historical Museum - 1905 41044

Aberdeen SD

Dacotah Prairie Museum and Lamont Art Gallery, 21 S Main St, Aberdeen, SD 57402-0395 - T: (605) 626-7117, Fax: (605) 626-4026, E-mail: bcmuseum@midco.net, Internet: www.brown.sd.us/museum. Dir.: Sue Gates, Cur.: Lora Schaunaman (Exhibits), Sherri Rawstern (Education)
Local Museum - 1964
Local hist, American Indian art - Ruth Bunker Memorial library 41045

Northern Galleries, Northern State University, 1200 S Jay St, Aberdeen, SD 57401 - T: (605) 626-2596, Fax: (605) 626-2263, E-mail: mulvaner@wolf.northern.edu. Dir.: Rebecca Mulvaney
Fine Arts Museum - 1902
Drawings, paintings, prints, photography, sculpture 41046

Aberdeen Proving Ground MD

United States Army Ordnance Museum, c/o U.S. Army Ordnance Center and School, 2601 Aberdeen Blvd, Aberdeen Proving Ground, MD 21005 - T: (410) 278-3602, 278-2396, Fax: (410) 278-7473, E-mail: museum@ocs.apg.army.mil, Internet: www.ordmusfound.org. Dir./Cur.: William F. Atwater
Military Museum - 1919
Military history 41047

Abilene KS

Dickinson County Heritage Center, 412 S Campbell St, Abilene, KS 67410 - T: (785) 263-2681, Fax: (785) 263-0380, E-mail: heritagecenter@access-one.com, Internet: www.heritagecenterk.com. Dir.: Jeff Sheets
Local Museum - 1928
Local history - telephone hist 41048

Dwight D. Eisenhower Library-Museum, SE 4th St, Abilene, KS 67410 - T: (913) 263-4751, Fax: (913) 263-4218, E-mail: eisenhower.library@nara.gov, Internet: www.eisenhower.utexas.edu/. Dir.: Daniel D. Holt, Cur.: Dennis H.J. Medina
Library with Exhibitions - 1962
Presidential library 41049

Greyhound Hall of Fame, 407 S Buckeye, Abilene, KS 67410 - T: (913) 263-3000, Fax: (785) 263-2604, E-mail: ghf@ikansas.com, Internet: www.greyhoundhalloffame.com. Pres.: Vey O. Weaver, Dir.: Edward Scheele, Exec. Asst.: Kathryn Lounsbury
Special Museum - 1963
Greyhound sports and animal 41050

Museum of Independent Telephony, 412 S Campbell, Abilene, KS 67410 - T: (785) 263-2681, Fax: (785) 263-0380, E-mail: dchs@ikansas.com, Internet: www.geocities.com/museumofindependenttelephony. Dir.: Robin Sherck, Cur.: Janet Groninga
Science&Tech Museum - 1973
Telephonic history 41051

Western Museum, 201 SE 6th, Abilene, KS 67410 - T: (913) 263-4612. Head: B.G. French
Local Museum
Local history, housed in Rock Island Railroad Stn 41052

Abilene TX

Grace Museum, 102 Cypress St, Abilene, TX 79601 - T: (915) 673-4587, Fax: (915) 675-5993, E-mail: info@thegracemuseum.org, Internet: www.thegracemuseum.org. Exec. Dir.: Judith Godfrey
Local Museum / Fine Arts Museum - 1937
American paintings and prints, local history, T&P railway coll 41053

Ryan Fine Arts Center, c/o McMurry University, 514th and Sayles Blvd, Abilene, TX 79697 - T: (915) 793-3823, Fax: (915) 793-4662, Internet: www.mcm.edu
University Museum / Fine Arts Museum - 1970 41054

Abingdon VA

William King Regional Arts Center, 415 Academy Dr, Abingdon, VA 24212 - T: (276) 628-5005, Fax: (276) 628-3922, E-mail: info@wkrac.org, Internet: www.wkrac.org. Dir.: Betsy K. White, Dep. Dir.: Suzanne G. Brewster, Cur.: Heather McBride
Fine Arts Museum - 1979 41055

Abington MA

Dyer Memorial Library, 28 Centre Av, Abington, MA 02351 - T: (781) 878-8480. Cur.: Joice Himawan
Library with Exhibitions - 1932
Civil war monographs 41056

Abiquiu NM

Florence Hawley Ellis Museum of Anthropology, Ghost Ranch Conference Center, Abiquiu, NM 87510-9601 - T: (505) 685-4333 ext 118, Fax: (505) 685-4519, Internet: www.newmexico-ghostranch.org. Dir.: Cheryl Muceus
Ethnology Museum - 1980
Anthropology 41057

Piedra Lumbre Visitors Center, Ghost Ranch Living Museum, US Hwy 84, Abiquiu, NM 87510 - T: (505) 685-4312. Dir.: Ray Martinez
Fine Arts Museum - 1959
Paintings and prints related to natural resources 41058

Ruth Hall Museum of Paleontology, Ghost Ranch Conference Center, Abiquiu, NM 87510-9601 - T: (505) 685-4333 ext 118, Fax: (505) 685-4519, Internet: www.newmexico-ghostranch.org. Dir./Cur.: Cheryl Muceus (Anthropology), Cur.: Alex Downs (Paleontology)
Natural History Museum - 1980
Paleontology, geology 41059

Accokeek MD

The Accokeek Foundation, 3400 Bryan Point Rd, Accokeek, MD 20607 - T: (301) 283-2113, Fax: (301) 283-2049, E-mail: accofound@accokeek.org, Internet: www.accokeek.org. Pres.: Wilton C. Corkern
Agriculture Museum - 1958
Agriculture 41060

Acme MI

The Music House, 7377 U.S. 31 N, Acme, MI 49610 - T: (616) 938-9300, Fax: (616) 938-3650, E-mail: musichouse@coslink.net, Internet: www.musichouse.org. Pres.: Robert L. Jackson, Dir.: David L. Stiffler
Music Museum - 1983
Music, musical instrument 41061

Acton MA

The Discovery Museums, 177 Main St, Acton, MA 01720 - T: (978) 264-4200, Fax: (978) 264-0210, E-mail: discover@ultranet.com, Internet: www.ultranet.com/~discover. Dir.: Deborah J. Gilpin, Geoff Nelson (Exhibits), Denise LeBlanc (Education Science Discovery Museum), Lauren Kotkin (Education Children's Discovery Museum), Ass. Dir.: Maria Conley (Education Science Discovery Museum), Amy Leonard (Education Children's Discovery Museum)
Special Museum / Science&Tech Museum - 1981
Children's museums, Sea of Clouds 41062

Ada MN

Memorial Museum, 2nd St and 2nd Av E, Ada, MN 56510-1604 - T: (218) 784-4989, 784-4141, Fax: (218) 784-3475. Dir.: R. De Floren, Cur.: Ruby Miller
Local Museum - 1957
Village museum 41063

Addison VT

Chimney Point Tavern, 7305 VT Rte 125, Addison, VT 05491 - T: (802) 759-2412, Fax: (802) 759-2547, E-mail: chimneypoint@dca.state.vt.us, Internet: www.historicvermont.org. Head: Elsa Gilbertson
Local Museum - 1968
Historic building 41064

John Strong Mansion, 6656 Rte 17, Addison, VT 05491 - T: (802) 545-2153, E-mail: sbutton@together.net. Cur.: Polly Schwenker
Local Museum - 1934
Historic house 41065

Adrian MI

Klemm Gallery, Siena Heights University, 1247 Siena Heights Dr, Adrian, MI 49221 - T: (517) 264-7860, Fax: (517) 265-3380, E-mail: pbarr@sienahts.edu, Internet: www.sienahts.edu/~arts. Dir.: Dr. Peter J. Barr
Fine Arts Museum - 1919
National artists 41066

Stubnitz Gallery, Adrian College, 110 S Madison, Adrian, MI 49221 - T: (517) 265-5161 ext 454, Fax: (517) 264-3331, E-mail: croyer@adrian.edu, Internet: www.adrian.edu/art
Public Gallery 41067

Aiken SC

Aiken County Historical Museum, 433 Newberry St SW, Aiken, SC 29801 - T: (803) 642-2017, Fax: (803) 642-2016, E-mail: acmuseum@duesouth.net, Internet: www.duesouth.net. Dir.: Carolyn W. Miles, C.E.O.: Owen Clary
Local Museum - 1970
Regional hist 41068

Aiken Thoroughbred Racing Hall of Fame and Museum, Whiskey Rd and Dupree Pl, Aiken, SC 29801 - T: (803) 642-7758, 642-7650, Fax: (803) 642-7639, E-mail: howeeks@aiken.net. Dir./Cur.: Joan B. Tower
Special Museum - 1979
Horse races 41069

Ainsworth NE

Coleman House Museum, 456 Old Highway #7, Ainsworth, NE 69210
Local Museum - 1973
Local hist 41070

Akron CO

Washington County Museum, 34445 Hwy 63, Akron, CO 80720 - T: (970) 345-6446. Cur.: Mildred Starlin
Local Museum - 1958
Local history, Burlington northern school house 41071

Akron OH

Akron Art Museum, 70 E Market St, Akron, OH 44308-2084 - T: (330) 376-9185, Fax: (330) 376-1180, E-mail: mail@akronartmuseum.org, Internet: www.akronartmuseum.org. Dir.: Mitchell Kahan, Chief Cur.: Barbara Tannenbaum, Ass. Cur.: Kathryn Wat
Fine Arts Museum - 1922 41072

National Inventors Hall of Fame, 221 S Broadway, Akron, OH 44308 - T: (800) 968-4332, (330) 762-6565, Fax: (330) 762-6313, Internet: www.invent.org. Pres.: David G. Fink, Dir.: Cornelia Eichorn
Science&Tech Museum - 1973
Science 41073

Stan Hywet Hall and Gardens, 714 N Portage Path, Akron, OH 44303-1399 - T: (330) 836-5533, Fax: (330) 836-2680, Internet: www.stanhywet.org. C.E.O.: Harry P. Lynch
Decorative Arts Museum / Historical Museum - 1957 41074

Summit County Historical Society Museum, 550 Copley Rd, Akron, OH 44320 - T: (330) 535-1120, Fax: (330) 376-6868, E-mail: schs@akronschs.org, Internet: www.akronschs.org. Pres.: Charles Pierson, Dir.: Paula G. Moran
Historical Museum - 1924 41075

University Galleries, 302 Buchtel Mall, Akron, OH 44325 - T: (330) 972-5950, Fax: (330) 972-5960, E-mail: bengston@uakron.edu, Internet: www.uakron.edu. Dir.: Rod Bengston
University Museum / Fine Arts Museum - 1974
Contemporary photography, Southeast Asian ceramics and artifacts 41076

Alamogordo NM

New Mexico Museum of Space History, Top of New Mexico, Hwy 2001, Alamogordo, NM 88310 - T: (505) 437-2840, Fax: (505) 434-2245, E-mail: spacepr@zianet.com, Internet: www.spacefame.org. C.E.O.: Mark Santiago, Cur.: George M. House, Ass. Cur.: Kimberly Merrill
Science&Tech Museum - 1973 41077

The Space Center → New Mexico Museum of Space History

Tularosa Basin Historical Society Museum, 1301 White Sands Blvd, Alamogordo, NM 88310 - T: (505) 434-4438, E-mail: tbhs@zianet.com, Internet: www.alamogordo.com/tbhs. Dir.: Mildred Evascovich
Historical Museum - 1971 41078

Alamosa CO

Adams State College Luther Bean Museum, Richardson Hall, Alamosa, CO 81102 - T: (719) 587-7011, Fax: (719) 587-7522, E-mail: lsrelyea@adams.edu. Dir.: Shelly L. Andrews
Historical Museum - 1968
Anthropology, ethnology, Indian, history 41079

Albany GA

Albany Civil Rights Movement Museum, 326 Whitney Av, Albany, GA 31701 - T: (229) 432-1698, Fax: (229) 432-2150, E-mail: mtzion@surfsouth.com, Internet: albanycivilrights.org. Cur.: Angela M. Whitmal
Historical Museum - 1994 41080

Albany Museum of Art, 311 Meadowlark Dr, Albany, GA 31707 - T: (912) 439-8400, Fax: (912) 439-1332, E-mail: curator@albanymuseum.com, Internet: www.albanymuseum.com. Dir.: Aaron Berger, Cur.: Kristen Miller Zohn (Art), Kristin Caso
Fine Arts Museum - 1964
Archaeology, ethnography, costumes and textiles, decorative arts, paintings, photographs, prints, drawings, graphic arts, sculpture 41081

Thronateeska Heritage Foundation, 100 W Roosevelt Av, Albany, GA 31701 - T: (912) 432-6955, Fax: (912) 435-1572, E-mail: info@heritagecenter.org, Internet: www.heritagecenter.org. Pres.: Jimmy Lindsey, Dir.: Tommy Gregors
Local Museum - 1974
Local history - planetarium 41082

Albany NY

Albany Institute of History and Art, 125 Washington Av, Albany, NY 12210-2296 - T: (518) 463-4478, Fax: (518) 462-1522, E-mail: information@albanyinstitute.org, Internet: www.albanyinstitute.org. Dir.: Christine M. Miles, Chief Cur.: Tammis K. Groft, Cur.: Wesley Balla (History)
Fine Arts Museum / Historical Museum - 1791 41083

Historic Cherry Hill, 523 1/2 S Pearl St, Albany, NY 12202 - T: (518) 434-4791, Fax: (518) 434-4806, E-mail: housemus@kick.net, Internet: www.historiccherryhill.org. Pres.: Michael Breiter, Dir.: Liselle LaFrance
Decorative Arts Museum / Historical Museum - 1964 41084

New York State Museum, 3099 Cultural Education Center, Empire State Plaza, Albany, NY 12230 - T: (518) 474-5877, Fax: (518) 486-3696, E-mail: cryan@mail.nysed.gov, Internet: www.nysm.nysed.gov. Dir.: Clifford A. Siegfried, Sc. Staff: Robert H. Fakundiny (Geology), Jeanine Grinage, John Hard (Collections)
Local Museum - 1870 41085

Schuyler Mansion, 32 Catherine St, Albany, NY 12202 - T: (518) 434-0834, Fax: (518) 434-3821, E-mail: marcy.shaffer@oprhp.state.ny.us, Internet: www.nysparks.com/hist. Dir.: Marcy Shaffer
Historical Museum - 1911 41086

Shaker Heritage Society Museum, 1848 Shaker Meeting House, Albany Shaker Rd, Albany, NY 12211 - T: (518) 456-7890, Fax: (518) 452-7348, E-mail: shakerwv@crisny.org, Internet: crisny.org/notforprofit-shakerwv. Dir.: Henry G. Williams
Local Museum - 1977
Local hist 41087

Ten Broeck Mansion, 9 Ten Broeck Pl, Albany, NY 12210 - T: (518) 436-9826, Fax: (518) 436-1489, E-mail: history@tenbroeck.org, Internet: www.tenbroeck.org. Pres.: John MacAffer
Decorative Arts Museum / Historical Museum - 1947
Local hist, decorative arts 41088

University Art Museum, c/o State University of New York at Albany, 1400 Washington Av, Albany, NY 12222 - T: (518) 442-4035, Fax: (518) 442-5075, Internet: www.albany.edu/museum. Dir.: Marijo Dougherty
Fine Arts Museum / University Museum - 1967 41089

Albany OR

Albany Regional Museum, 136 Lyon St SW, Albany, OR 97321 - T: (541) 967-7122
Local Museum 41090

Albany TX

The Old Jail Art Center, 201 S Second St, Albany, TX 76430 - T: (915) 762-2269, Fax: (915) 762-2260, E-mail: ojac@camalott.com, Internet: www.oldjailartcenter.org. Exec. Dir.: Margaret Blagg
Fine Arts Museum - 1977
Art 41091

Albemarle NC

Morrow Mountain State Park Museum, 49104 Morrow Mountain Rd, Albemarle, NC 28001 - T: (704) 982-4402. Head: Timothy McCree
Natural History Museum - 1962 41092

Stanly County Historic Museum, 245 E Main St, Albemarle, NC 28001 - T: (704) 986-3777, Fax: (704) 986-3778, E-mail: cdwyer@co.stanly.nc.us, Internet: www.co.stanly.nc.us/departments/museum. Dir.: Christine M. Dwyer
Historical Museum - 1972 41093

Albert Lea MN

Freeborn County Historical Museum, 1031 Bridge Av, Albert Lea, MN 56007 - T: (507) 373-8003, Fax: (507) 373-4172, E-mail: fchm@smig.net, Internet: www.smig.net/fchm. Dir.: Bev Jackson
Local Museum / Open Air Museum - 1948
Regional history, pioneer village - library 41094

Albion IN

Old Jail Museum, 215 W Main St, Albion, IN 46701 - T: (219) 636-2428, Internet: www.noblehistoricalsociety.org
Historical Museum - 1968 41095

Albion MI

Bobbitt Visual Arts Center, 805 Cass St, Albion, MI 49224 - T: (517) 629-0246, Fax: (517) 629-0752, E-mail: rkreger@albion.edu, Internet: www.albion.edu. Head: Prof. Lynne Chytilo, Cur.: Pati Scobey
Fine Arts Museum / University Museum - 1835
Contempotary artists 41096

Brueckner Museum, 13725 Starr Commonwealth Rd, Albion, MI 49224-9580 - T: (517) 629-5591, Fax: (517) 629-2317, E-mail: info@starr.org, Internet: www.starr.org. Pres.: Arlin E. Ness
Fine Arts Museum - 1956 41097

Gardner House Museum, 509 S Superior St, Albion, MI 49224 - T: (517) 629-5100, Internet: www.forks.org/history. C.E.O.: Marorie Ulbrich
Local Museum - 1958
Local history 41098

Albuquerque NM

The Albuquerque Museum of Art and History, 2000 Mountain Rd NW, Albuquerque, NM 87104 - T: (505) 243-7255, Fax: (505) 764-6546, E-mail: jmoore@cabq.gov, Internet: www.cabq.gov/museum. Dir.: James C. Moore, Cur.: Ellen Landis (Art), Thomas C. Lark (Collections), Bob Woltman (Exhibits), Deb Slaney (History), Chris Steiner (Education)
Fine Arts Museum / Historical Museum - 1967 41099

Explora Science Center and Children's Museum, 2100 Louisiana Blv, Albuquerque, NM 87110-5410 - T: (505) 842-1537, Fax: (505) 842-5915, E-mail: exploralnfo@esccma.org, Internet: www.explora.mus.nm.us. C.E.O.: Paul Tatter
Science&Tech Museum - 1996
Science 41100

Indian Pueblo Cultural Center, 2401 12th St NW, Albuquerque, NM 87104 - T: (505) 843-7270, Fax: (505) 842-6959, Internet: www.indianpueblo.org. Dir.: Ron Solimon, Cur.: Pat Reck
Ethnology Museum / Historical Museum - 1976
Indian hist 41101

Institute of Meteoritics Meteorite Museum, c/o University of New Mexico, Albuquerque, NM 87131 - T: (505) 277-2747, Fax: (505) 277-3577, Internet: epswww.unm.edu/iom. Dir.: Dr. James J. Papike, Chief Cur.: Rhian Jones
University Museum / Natural History Museum - 1944 41102

Jonson Gallery, University of New Mexico Art Museum, 1909 Las Lomas NE, Albuquerque, NM 87131 - T: (505) 277-4967, Fax: (505) 277-3188, E-mail: jonsong@unm.edu, Internet: www.unm.edu/~jonsong. Cur.: Robert Ware
Fine Arts Museum / University Museum - 1950 41103

Maxwell Museum of Anthropology, c/o University of New Mexico, Albuquerque, NM 87131-1201 - T: (505) 277-4405, Fax: (505) 277-1547, E-mail: gbawden@unm.edu, Internet: www.unm.edu/~maxwell. Dir.: Dr. Garth L. Bawden, Ian Wagoner (Exhibits), Patricia Cyman (Education), Chief Cur.: Mari Lyn Salvador, Cur.: Marian Rodee (South West Ethnology), Debra Komarl (Osteology), Michael Lewis (Archaeology)
University Museum / Ethnology Museum / Archaeological Museum / Science&Tech Museum / Folklore Museum - 1932 41104

Museum of Southwestern Biology, c/o Biology Department, University of New Mexico, Albuquerque, NM 87131 - T: (505) 277-3781, Fax: (505) 277-0304, E-mail: tlowrey@unm.edu, Internet: www.unm.edu/~museum. Dir.: Timothy K. Lowrey (Herbarium), Cur.: Dr. J. David Ligon (Birds), Dr. Howard L. Snell (Reptiles and Amphibians), Dr. Manuel C. Molles (Anthropods), Dr. Thomas F. Turner (Fishes), Dr. Terry L. Yates (Mammals), Dr. Michael A. Bogan (BRD), Ass. Cur.: Dr. Robert W. Dickerman (Birds)
University Museum / Natural History Museum - 1930
Birds, mammals, plants, arthropods, fishes, reptiles, amphibians - frozen tissues coll 41105

National Atomic Museum, 1905 Mountain Rd NW, Albuquerque, NM 87104 - T: (505) 284-3243, Fax: (505) 284-3244, E-mail: info@atomicmuseum.com, Internet: www.atomicmuseum.com. Dir.: Jim Walther, Ass. Dir.: Merri Lewis, Sc. Staff: Sam Bono (History)
Science&Tech Museum - 1969
Energy, science, weapons, history, aircraft, robotics, medicine 41106

New Mexico Museum of Natural History and Science, 1801 Mountain Rd NW, Albuquerque, NM 87104-1375 - T: (505) 841-2823, Fax: (505) 841-2866, E-mail: mtanner@nmmnh.state.nm.us, Internet: www.nmmnh.state.nm.us. Dir.: Adrian P. Hunt, Sc. Staff: David Mandel (Exhibits), Jackie McConachie (Collections), Jayne Aubele (Education)
Natural History Museum / Science&Tech Museum - 1986 41107

Rattlesnake Museum, 202 San Felipe, Albuquerque, NM 87104-1426 - T: (505) 242-6569, Fax: (505) 242-6569, E-mail: zoomuseum@aol.com, Internet: www.rattlesnakes.com. Dir.: Bob Myers
Natural History Museum - 1990
Herpetology 41108

Telephone Pioneer Museum of New Mexico, 110 Fourth St NW, Albuquerque, NM 87103 - T: (505) 842-2937, Internet: www.nmculture.org. Dir.: Neal Roch
Science&Tech Museum - 1961 41109

Turquoise Museum, 2107 Central NW, Albuquerque, NM 87104 - T: (505) 247-8650, Fax: (505) 247-8765
Special Museum
Turquoise coll, hist, mining, geology, cutting, marketing 41110

University Art Museum, University of New Mexico, UNM Center for the Arts, Albuquerque, NM 87131-1416 - T: (505) 277-4001, Fax: (505) 277-7315, E-mail: lbahm@unm.edu, Internet: unmartmuseum.unm.edu. Dir.: Peter Walch, Ass. Dir.: Linda Bahm, Cur.: Lee Savary (Exhibits), Kathleen Howe (Prints and Photos), Michael Certo (Education), Ass. Cur.: Bonnie Verardo (Prints and Photos)
Fine Arts Museum / University Museum - 1963
Johnson Gallery 41111

Very Special Arts Gallery, 4904 Fourth St NW, Albuquerque, NM 87107 - T: (505) 345-2872, Fax: (505) 345-2896, E-mail: info@vfranm.org. Dir.: Beth Rudolph
Fine Arts Museum - 1994
Drawings, paintings, ceramics, crafts, folk art 41112

Alden KS

Atchinson, Topeka and Santa Fe Depot, POB 158, Alden, KS 67512 - T: (316) 534-2425, E-mail: prflrcraft@aol.com. Dir.: Sara Fair Sleeper
Science&Tech Museum - 1970
Transportation 41113

Alden NY

Alden Historical Society Museum, 13213 Broadway, Alden, NY 14004 - T: (716) 937-7606. Dir.: Ronald Savage, Cur.: Laura Airey, Ruth Davis
Historical Museum - 1965 41114

Aledo IL

Essley-Noble Museum, Mercer County Historical Society, 1406 SE 2nd Av, Aledo, IL 61231 - T: (309) 584-4820. Pres.: Alicia Ives, Cur.: Shirley Crawford
Local Museum - 1959
Local history 41115

Aledo TX

Living Word National Bible Museum, 3909 Snow Creek Dr, Aledo, TX 76008 - T: (817) 244-4504, Fax: (817) 244-4504, E-mail: johnhellstern@charter.net, Internet: www.flash.net/~bibleetc/. C.E.O.: Dr. John R. Hellstern
Religious Arts Museum - 1991 41116

Alexandria LA

Alexandria Museum of Art, 933 Main St, Alexandria, LA 71301 - T: (318) 443-3458, Fax: (318) 443-0545, E-mail: dnovotny@themuseum.org, Internet: www.themuseum.org. Dir.: Deborah Novotny, Cur.: Roy de Ville (Art)
Fine Arts Museum - 1977
Art, housed in a old Bank Bldg 41117

University Gallery, c/o Louisiana State University at Alexandria, Student Ctr, Hwy 71 S, Alexandria, LA 71302 - T: (318) 473-6449. Cur.: Roy V. de Ville
Fine Arts Museum / University Museum - 1960 41118

Alexandria MN

Runestone Museum, 206 N Broadway, Alexandria, MN 56308 - T: (320) 763-3160, Fax: (320) 763-9705, E-mail: bigole@rea-alp.com, Internet: www.runestonemuseum.org. Dir.: LuAnn W. Patton
Archaeological Museum - 1958
History, youth 41119

Alexandria VA

Alexandria Archaeology Museum, 105 N Union St, 327, Alexandria, VA 22314 - T: (703) 838-4399, Fax: (703) 838-6491, E-mail: archaeology@ci.alexandria.va.us, Internet: www.alexandriaarchaeology.org. Dir.: Dr. Pamela J. Cressey
Archaeological Museum - 1977
Archaeology 41120

Alexandria Black History Resource Center, 638 N Alfred St, Alexandria, VA 22314 - T: (703) 838-4356, Fax: (703) 706-3999, E-mail: blackhistory@ci.alexandria.va.us, Internet: alexblackhistory.org. Dir.: Louis Hicks, Ass. Dir.: Audrey P. Davis, Sc. Staff: Lillian Patterson
Local Museum - 1983
African American hist 41121

The Athenaeum, 201 Prince St, Alexandria, VA 22314 - T: (703) 548-0035, Fax: (703) 768-7471, Internet: www.alexandria-athenaeum.org. Exec. Dir.: Mary Gaissert Jackson
Fine Arts Museum - 1964
Art 41122

Carlyle House, 121 N Fairfax St, Alexandria, VA 22314 - T: (703) 549-2997, Fax: (703) 549-5738, E-mail: mrcoleman@juno.com, Internet: www.carlylehouse.org. Dir.: Mary Ruth Coleman, Cur.: Pam Hardin
Local Museum - 1976
Historic house 41123

Collingwood Museum on Americanism, 8301 E Boulevard Dr, Alexandria, VA 22308 - T: (703) 765-1652, Fax: (703) 765-8390, E-mail: clmal@arols.com. Cur.: Warren L. Baker, Ass. Cur.: Barbara J. Baker
Historical Museum - 1977
American hist 41124

Fort Ward Museum and Historic Site, 4301 W Braddock Rd, Alexandria, VA 22304 - T: (703) 838-4848, Fax: (703) 671-7350, E-mail: fort.ward@ci.alexandria.va.us, Internet: www.fortward.org. Dir.: Wanda S. Dowell, Cur.: Susan G. Cumbey
Military Museum - 1964
Military hist, Civil War coll and Union Fort 41125

Friendship Firehouse, 107 S Alfred St, Alexandria, VA 22314 - T: (703) 838-3891, Fax: (703) 838-4997, Internet: ci.alexandria.va.us/oha/. Dir.: Jean Federico
Science&Tech Museum - 1993 41126

Gadsby's Tavern Museum, 134 N Royal St, Alexandria, VA 22314 - T: (703) 838-4242, Fax: (703) 838-4270, E-mail: gadsbys.tavern@ci.alexandria.va.us, Internet: www.gadsbystavern.org. Dir.: Gretchen M. Bulova
Local Museum - 1976
Historic buildings 41127

Gallery West, 205 S Union St, Alexandria, VA 22314 - T: (703) 549-7359. Dir.: Craig Snyder
Fine Arts Museum - 1979 41128

George Washington Masonic National Memorial, 101 Callahan Dr, Alexandria, VA 22301 - T: (703) 683-2007, Fax: (703) 519-9270, E-mail: gseghers@gwmemorial.org, Internet: www.gwmemorial.org. Pres.: George D. Seghers
Historical Museum - 1910
History 41129

The John Q. Adams Center for the History of Otolaryngology - Head and Neck Surgery, 1 Prince St, Alexandria, VA 22314 - T: (703) 836-4444, Fax: (703) 683-5100, E-mail: tsullivan@

entnet.org, Internet: www.entnet.org/museum. Dir.: Tracy L. Sullivan
Special Museum - 1990
Medical hist 41130

Lee-Fendall House, 614 Oronoco St, Alexandria, VA 22314 - T: (703) 548-1789, Fax: (703) 548-0931, E-mail: staff@leefendallhouse.org, Internet: www.leefendallhouse.org. Dir.: Kristin Miller
Local Museum - 1974
Historic house 41131

The Lyceum - Alexandria's History Museum, 201 S Washington St, Alexandria, VA 22314 - T: (703) 838-4994, Fax: (703) 838-4997, E-mail: lyceum@ci.alexandria.va.us, Internet: alexandriahistory.org. Dir.: Jim Mackay, Ass. Dir.: Kristin B. Lloyd
Historical Museum - 1974
History 41132

Ramsay House, 221 King St, Alexandria, VA 22314 - T: (703) 838-4200 ext 212, Fax: (703) 838-4683, E-mail: jmitchell@funside.com, Internet: www.funside.com. Dir.: Joanne Mitchell, Dep. Dir.: Laura Overstreet
Local Museum - 1962
Historic house 41133

Stabler-Leadbeater Apothecary Museum, 105-107 S Fairfax St, Alexandria, VA 22314 - T: (703) 836-3713, Fax: (703) 836-3713, E-mail: slamuseum@juno, Internet: www.apothecary.org. Dir.: Sara Becker
Special Museum - 1792
Pharmacy 41134

Torpedo Factory Art Center, 105 N Union St, Alexandria, VA 22314 - T: (703) 838-4199, 838-4565, Fax: (703) 838-0088, E-mail: director@torpedofactory.org, Internet: www.torpedofactory.org. Pres.: Joan Menard
Fine Arts Museum / Folklore Museum - 1974
Art 41135

Woodlawn Plantation, 9000 Richmond Hwy, Alexandria, VA 22309 - T: (703) 780-4000, Fax: (703) 780-8509, E-mail: woodlawn@nthp.org, Internet: www.nthp.org/main/sites/woodlawn.htm. Dir.: Ross Randall, Asst. Dir.: Gail Donahue, Historian: Craig Tuminaro
Local Museum - 1951
Historic house 41136

Alfred NY

The Scein-Joseph International Museum of Ceramic Art, New York State College of Ceramics at Alfred University, Alfred, NY 14802 - T: (607) 871-2421, Fax: (607) 871-2615, E-mail: ceramicsmuseum@alfred.edu, Internet: www.ceramicsmuseum.alfred.edu. Dir./Chief Cur.: Dr. Margaret Carney
Decorative Arts Museum - 1900
Ceramics 41137

Alice TX

South Texas Museum, 66 S Wright St, Alice, TX 78332 - T: (512) 668-8891, Fax: (512) 664-3327, E-mail: stmuseum@sbcglobal.com. Chm.: Mary Dru Burns
Local Museum - 1975
Local hist 41138

Aline OK

Sod House Museum, Rte 1, Aline, OK 73716 - T: (580) 463-2441. C.E.O.: DeAnn McGahen
Historical Museum - 1968 41139

Allaire NJ

Historic Allaire Village, Allaire State Park, Rte 524, Allaire, NJ 07727-3715 - T: (732) 919-3500, 938-2253, Fax: (732) 938-3302, E-mail: allairevillage@bytheshore.com, Internet: www.allairevillage.org. Dir.: John Curtis
Open Air Museum / Local Museum - 1957 41140

Allegan MI

Allegan County Historical and Old Jail Museum, 113 Walnut St, Allegan, MI 49010 - T: (616) 673-8292, 673-4853. Pres.: Robert Hoyt, Dir.: Marguerite Miller
Local Museum - 1952
Regional history, former county jail and sheriff's home 41141

Allentown NJ

Artful Deposit Galleries, 1 Church St, Allentown, NJ 08505 - T: (609) 259-3234, Internet: www.theartfuldeposit.com. Owner: C.J. Mugavero
Fine Arts Museum - 1986
Works by Patrick Antonelle, Joseph Dawley, Hanneke de Neve and Ken McIndoe 41142

Allentown PA

Allentown Art Museum, Fifth and Court Sts, Allentown, PA 18105 - T: (610) 432-4333 ext 10, Fax: (610) 434-7409, E-mail: marketing@allentownartmuseum.org, Internet: www.allentownartmuseum.org. Pres.: Stanford T. Beldon, Dep. Dir.: Lisa Miller (Admin.), Rachel Osborn (Advancement), Lisa Dubé (Education), Cur.: Christine I. Oaklander (Collections, Exhibitions), Ruta Saliklis (Textiles)
Fine Arts Museum - 1934 41143

Allied Air Force Museum, Queen City Airport, 1730 Vultee St, Allentown, PA 18103 - T: (610) 791-5122, Fax: (610) 791-5453. Dir./Cur.: Joseph B. Fillman
Military Museum / Science&Tech Museum - 1984
Aeronautics 41144

Lehigh County Historical Society Museum, Hamilton at Fifth St, Allentown, PA 18101 - T: (610) 435-1074, Fax: (610) 435-9812. Dir.: Bernard P. Fishman, Cur.: Andree Miller (Collections), Sarah E. Nelson (Education)
Historical Museum - 1904
Reninger House (c. 1860), Elverson House (c. 1910), Gruber House (c. 1912), Trout Hall (1770), Haines Mill (1760), David O. Saylor Cement Industry Museum (Coplay, 1892), Lock Ridge Furnace Museum (Alburtis, 1868), One-Room-Schoolhouse (Claussville, 1893) 41145

Martin Art Gallery, c/o Muhlenberg College, 2400 Chew St, Allentown, PA 18104-5586 - T: (484) 664-3467, Fax: (484) 664-3234, E-mail: gallery@muhlenberg.edu, Internet: www.muhlberg.edu. Dir.: Dr. Lori Verderame
Fine Arts Museum - 1976
Master prints, Rembrandt, Durer, Whistler, Goya, 20th c American contemporary art 41146

Museum of Indian Culture, 2825 Fish Hatchery Rd, Allentown, PA 18103-9801 - T: (610) 797-2121, Fax: (610) 797-2801, E-mail: lenape@epixi.net, Internet: www.lenape.org. C.E.O.: Carla Messinger
Ethnology Museum - 1981
Lenni Lenape Indians, early Pennsylvania German artifacts 41147

Alliance NE

Knight Museum of High Plains Heritage, 908 Yellowstone, Alliance, NE 69301 - T: (308) 762-2384, 762-5400 ext 261, Fax: (308) 762-7848, E-mail: museum@panhandle.net, Internet: www.cityofalliance.com. C.E.O.: Richard Cayer
Local Museum - 1965
Local hist 41148

Allison IA

Butler County Historical Museum, Little Yellow Schoolhouse, Fair Grounds, 714 Elm St, Allison, IA 50602 - T: (319) 267-2255, 278-4321. Pres.: Deb Bochmann
Local Museum - 1956
Local history 41149

Allison Park PA

Depreciation Lands Museum, 4743 S Pioneer Rd, Allison Park, PA 15101 - T: (412) 486-0563
Historical Museum - 1974 41150

Alma CO

Alma Firehouse and Mining Museum, 1 W Buckskin Rd, Alma, CO 80420-0336 - T: (719) 836-3413, 836-3117. Dir.: Don Gostisha
Historical Museum - 1976
Fire fighting 41151

Alma KS

Wabaunsee County Historical Museum, Missouri and Third Sts, Alma, KS 66401, mail addr: POB 387, Alma, KS 66401 - T: (913) 765-2200. C.E.O./Pres.: Gertrude Gehrt, Cur.: Rayonna Mock
Local Museum - 1968
Regional history 41152

Almond NY

Hagadorn House Museum, 7 N Main St, Almond, NY 14804 - T: (607) 276-6781, E-mail: dodomo@infoblvd.net, Internet: www.rootsweb.com/~nyahs/almondhs.html. Pres.: Charlotte Baker
Historical Museum - 1965 41153

Alpena MI

Jesse Besser Museum, 491 Johnson St, Alpena, MI 49707-1496 - T: (989) 356-2202, Fax: (989) 356-3133, E-mail: jbmuseum@northland.lib.mi.us, Internet: www.oweb.com/upnorth/museum/. Exec. Dir.: Dr. Janice V. McLean
Local Museum - 1962
Art, history and science of Northeast Michigan, anthropology, natural history 41154

Alpine TX

Museum of the Big Bend, Sul Ross State University, Alpine, TX 79832 - T: (915) 837-8143, Fax: (915) 837-8381, E-mail: francell@sulross.edu, Internet: www.sulross.edu/~museum/. Dir.: Larry Francell, Cur.: Mary Bridges
Local Museum - 1926
Regional hist 41155

Altenburg MO

Perry County Lutheran Historical Society Museum, 866 Hwy C, Altenburg, MO 63732 - T: (573) 824-5542. Pres.: Leonard A. Kuehnert
Historical Museum / Religious Arts Museum - 1910 41156

Alton IL

Alton Museum of History and Art, 2809 College Av, Alton, IL 62002 - T: (618) 462-2763, Fax: (618) 462-6390, E-mail: altonmuseum@618connect.com, Internet: www.altonweb.com/museum/index.html. Pres.: Lois Lobbig
Fine Arts Museum / Historical Museum - 1971
History, art 41157

Altoona PA

Railroader's Memorial Museum, 1300 Ninth Av, Altoona, PA 16602 - T: (814) 946-0834, Fax: (814) 946-9457, E-mail: info@railroadcity.com, Internet: www.railroadcity.com. Dir.: R. Cummins McNitt, Ass. Dir.: Clifford P. Kendall, Cur.: Janice Hartman
Science&Tech Museum - 1980 41158

Alturas CA

Modoc County Historical Museum, 600 S Main St, Alturas, CA 96101 - T: (530) 233-9944. Dir.: Paula Murphy
Local Museum - 1967
Regional history 41159

Altus OK

Museum of the Western Prairie, 1100 Memorial Dr, Altus, OK 73521 - T: (580) 482-1044, Fax: (580) 482-0128, E-mail: muswestpr@ok-history.mus.ok.us, Internet: members.staroffice.com/www/muswestprmasnum18.htm. Dir.: Burna Cole, Cur.: Bart McClenny
Historical Museum - 1970 41160

Alva OK

Cherokee Strip Museum, 901 14 St, Alva, OK 73717 - T: (580) 327-2030, E-mail: dansh@alva.net. Pres.: Daniel A. Shorter
Local Museum - 1961 41161

Northwestern Oklahoma State University Museum, Jesse Dunn Hall, 709 Oklahoma Blvd, Alva, OK 73717 - T: (580) 327-1700 ext 8513, Fax: (580) 327-1881, E-mail: vnpowders@nwosu.edu, Internet: www.nwosu.edu. Dir.: Dr. Vernon Powders
University Museum - 1902 41162

Amana IA

Museum of Amana History, 4310 220th Trail, Amana, IA 52203 - T: (319) 622-3567, Fax: (319) 622-6481, E-mail: amherit@juno.com, Internet: www.amanaheritage.org. Dir.: Lanny Haldy, Cur.: Catherine Engelkemier
Local Museum / Folklore Museum - 1969
Local hist 41163

Amarillo TX

Amarillo Museum of Art, 2200 S Van Buren, Amarillo, TX 79109 - T: (806) 371-5050, Fax: (806) 373-9235, E-mail: amoa@arn.net, Internet: www.amarilloart.org. Dir.: Patrick McCracken, Cur.: Mark Morey (Education)
Fine Arts Museum - 1972
Art 41164

American Quarter Horse Heritage Center and Museum, 2601 I-40, E, Amarillo, TX 79104 - T: (806) 376-5181, Fax: (806) 376-1005, E-mail: museum@aqha.org, Internet: www.aqha.org. C.E.O.: Billy Brewer, Dir.: James May
Special Museum - 1991
Equine, Hall of Fame 41165

Don Harrington Discovery Center, 1200 Streit Dr, Amarillo, TX 79106 - T: (806) 355-9547 ext 20, Fax: (806) 355-5703, E-mail: dhdc.org, Internet: www.dhdc.org. Exec. Dir.: Tom Halliday, Greg Shuman (Exhibits)
Science&Tech Museum - 1968
Science and technology 41166

Texas Pharmacy Museum, c/o Texas Tech School of Pharmacy, 1300 Coulter, Amarillo, TX 79106 - T: (806) 356-4000 ext 268, Fax: (806) 356-4017, Internet: www.texas.pharmacy.museum. Cur.: Paul Katz
Historical Museum - 1968
Pharmacy in Texas, the US and Western Europe, products and delivery systems, pharmacy art, Texas practitioners, laboratory, glassware, medical items 41167

Ambridge PA

Old Economy Village Museum, 14-16 and Church Sts, Ambridge, PA 15003 - T: (724) 266-4500, Fax: (724) 266-7506, E-mail: mlandis@phmc.state.pa.us, Internet: www.oldeconomyvillage.org. Dir.: Mary Ann Landis
Open Air Museum / Historical Museum - 1919
18 buildings of the original town of Economy (now Ambridge), PA, built between 1824 and 1831 41168

American Falls ID

Massacre Rocks State Park Museum, 3592 Park Lane, American Falls, ID 83211-5555 - T: (208) 548-2672, Fax: (208) 548-2671, E-mail: mas@idpr.state.id.us, Internet: www.idahoparks.org
Natural History Museum - 1967 41169

Ames IA

Brunnier Art Museum, Iowa State University, 290 Scheman Bldg, Iowa State University, Ames, IA 50011 - T: (515) 294-3342, Fax: (515) 294-7070, E-mail: museums@adp.iastate.edu, Internet: www.museums.iastate.edu. Dir.: Lynette Pohlman, Cur.: Matthew DeLay (Education)
Decorative Arts Museum / Fine Arts Museum / University Museum - 1975
Decorative and fine arts 41170

Farm House Museum, Iowa State University, Knoll Rd, Iowa State University Campus, Ames, IA 50011 - T: (515) 294-3342, 294-7426, Fax: (515) 294-7070, Internet: www.museums.iastate.edu. Dir.: Lynette Pohlman, Cur.: Mary Atherly, Matthew Delay (Education)
University Museum / Agriculture Museum - 1976 41171

Gallery 181, Iowa State University, 134 College of Design Bldg, Iowa State University, Ames, IA 50011 - T: (515) 294-7428, Fax: (515) 294-9755, E-mail: isutoded@iastate.edu, Internet: www.design.iastate.edu. Dir.: Dean Mark. Engelbrecht
Fine Arts Museum / University Museum - 1978
Art 41172

The Octagon Center for the Arts, 427 Douglas Av, Ames, IA 50010-6281 - T: (515) 232-5331, Fax: (515) 232-5088, E-mail: directorart@isunet.net, Internet: www.octagonarts.org
Fine Arts Museum - 1966
Art, Feinberg Mask collection 41173

Amesbury MA

The Bartlett Museum, 270 Main St, Amesbury, MA 01913 - T: (978) 388-4528, 388-7950. Pres.: John McCone
Local Museum - 1968
History, housed in a Old Victorian School house 41174

John Greenleaf Whittier Home, Whittier Home Association, 86 Friend St, Amesbury, MA 01913 - T: (508) 388-1337. Pres.: Sally Ann Lavery, Cur.: Stephen McDonough
Special Museum - 1898
Home of poet and abolitionist John Greenleaf Whittier 41175

Amherst MA

Amherst History Museum, Strong House, 67 Amity St, Amherst, MA 01002 - T: (413) 256-0678, Fax: (413) 256-0678, E-mail: amhersthistory@go.com, Internet: www.amhersthistory.org. Dir.: Melinda LeLacheur
Local Museum - 1899
Local hist 41176

Dickinson Homestead, 280 Main St, Amherst, MA 01002 - T: (413) 542-8161, E-mail: csdickinson@amherst.edu, Internet: www.dickensonhomestead.org. Dir.: Cindy Dickinson
Special Museum - 1965
Literature, local hist 41177

Mead Art Museum, Amherst College, Amherst, MA 01002-5000 - T: (413) 542-2335, Fax: (413) 542-2117, E-mail: mead@amherst.edu, Internet: www.amherst.edu/~mead. Dir.: Jill Meredith, Cur.: Trinkett Clarck (American Art), Jill Meredith (European Art), Carol Solomon Kiefer (Prints)
Fine Arts Museum / University Museum - 1821
American art 41178

Museum of Zoology, University of Massachusetts, Dept. of Biology, Amherst, MA 01003 - T: (413) 545-2902, Fax: (413) 545-3243, E-mail: mmnh@bio.umass.edu, Internet: snapper.bio.umass.edu/vmmnh. Dir./Cur.: William Bemis (Fish), Cur.: Alan Richmond (Amphibians and Reptiles), Doug Smith (Invertebrates), Jim Meng (Mammals)
University Museum / Natural History Museum - 1863
Zoology, fishes, amphibians and reptiles, invertebrates, mammals, birds 41179

National Yiddish Book Center, Harry and Jeanette Weinberg Bldg, 1021 West St, Amherst, MA 01002-3375 - T: (413) 256-4900 ext 103, Fax: (413) 256-4700, E-mail: yiddish@bikher.org, Internet: www.yiddishbookcenter.org. Pres.: Aaron Lansky
Historical Museum / Religious Arts Museum - 1980
Yiddish culture 41180

The Pratt Museum of Natural History, Amherst College, Amherst, MA 01002 - T: (413) 542-2165, Fax: (413) 542-2713, E-mail: llthomas@amherst.edu, Internet: www.amherst.edu/~pratt/. Cur.: Linda L. Thomas, Dr. Margery C. Coombs, Dr. Walter A. Coombs (Vertebrate Paleontology), Dr. Gerald P. Brophy (Mineralogy), Dr. John T. Cheney (Petrology)
University Museum / Natural History Museum - 1848
Natural history, paleontology, mineralogy, petrology 41181

University Gallery, University of Massachusetts at Amherst, Fine Arts Center, 151 Presidents Dr, Amherst, MA 01003-9331 - T: (413) 545-3670, Fax: (413) 545-2018, E-mail: ugallery@acad.umass.edu, Internet: www.umass.edu/fac/universitygallery. Dir.: Betsy Siersma, Cur.: Regina Coppola
Fine Arts Museum / University Museum - 1975
Art gallery 41182

Amherst NY

Amherst Museum, 3755 Tonawanda Creek Rd, Amherst, NY 14228 - T: (716) 689-1440, Fax: (716) 689-1409, E-mail: amhmuseum@adelphia.net, Internet: www.amherstmuseum.org. Dir.: Lynn S. Beman, Cur.: Jessica A. Norton, Kristine Rhoback (Textiles), Cur.: Jean W. Neff (Education)
Local Museum - 1970
Local history and culture, historic buildings 41183

Amherst VA

Amherst County Museum, 154 S Main St, Amherst, VA 24521 - T: (804) 946-9068, E-mail: achmuseum@aol.com, Internet: members.aol.com/achmuseum/achmhis.htm. Dir.: Meghan Wallace
Local Museum / Folklore Museum - 1973
Local hist 41184

Amityville NY

Lauder Museum, 170 Broadway, Amityville, NY 11701-0764. C.E.O.: William T. Lauder
Local Museum - 1973 41185

Amory MS

Amory Regional Museum, 715 Third St, Amory, MS 38821 - T: (601) 256-2761. Dir.: Gene Pierce, Cur.: Mildred Ritter
Local Museum - 1976 41186

Amsterdam NY

Walter Elwood Museum, 300 Guy Park Av, Amsterdam, NY 12010-2228 - T: (518) 843-5151, Fax: (518) 843-6098, Internet: www.walterelwood.com. Dir.: Mohawk Valley
Local Museum - 1940 41187

Anaconda MT

Copper Village Museum and Arts Center, 401 E Commercial, Anaconda, MT 59711 - T: (406) 563-2422. Dir.: Carol Jette
Fine Arts Museum / Historical Museum - 1971
library 41188

Anacortes WA

Anacortes Museum, 1305 8th, Anacortes, WA 98221 - T: (360) 293-1915, Fax: (360) 293-1929, E-mail: museum@cityofanacortes.org, Internet: www.anacorteshistorymuseum.org. Dir.: Garry Cline, Cur.: Will Sarvis
Local Museum - 1957
Local hist 41189

Anadarko OK

Anadarko Philomathic Museum, 311 E Main St, Anadarko, OK 73005 - T: (405) 247-3240. C.E.O. & Pres.: Linda Taylor, Cur.: Lee Reeves
Local Museum - 1936 41190

Indian City U.S.A., Hwy 8, 2 1/2 miles SE of Anakarko, Anadarko, OK 73005 - T: (405) 247-5661, Fax: (405) 247-2467, E-mail: indiancity@aol.com, Internet: www.indiancityusa.com. Pres.: Linda Poolaw
Historical Museum / Natural History Museum / Ethnology Museum - 1955 41191

National Hall of Fame for Famous American Indians, Hwy 62 E, Anadarko, OK 73005 - T: (405) 247-5555, Fax: (405) 247-5571, E-mail: dailynews@tanet.net. C.E.O.: Joe McBride
Historical Museum - 1952 41192

Southern Plains Indian Museum, 715 E Central Blvd, Anadarko, OK 73005, mail addr: POB 749, Anadarko, OK 73005 - T: (405) 247-6221, Fax: (405) 247-7593. Cur.: Rosemary Ellison
Ethnology Museum / Folklore Museum - 1947 41193

Anaheim CA

Anaheim Museum, 241 S Anaheim Blvd, Anaheim, CA 92805 - T: (714) 778-3301, Fax: (714) 778-6740, E-mail: joycemuse@aol.com, Internet: www.anaheimmuseum.net. Dir./Cur.: Joyce Franklin
Local Museum / Historical Museum - 1982
Local history, art works 41194

Anaktuvuk Pass AK

Simon Paneak Memorial Museum, 341 Mekiana Rd, Anaktuvuk Pass, AK 99721 - T: (907) 661-3413, Fax: (907) 661-3414, E-mail: vweber@co.north-slope.ak.us, Internet: www.nsbsd.k12.ak.us/villages/akp/museum/paneak.htm. Dir.: George N. Ahmaogak, Cur.: Grant Spearman, Vera Weber
Local Museum - 1986
Local history, ethnography 41195

Anchorage AK

Alaska Aviation Heritage Museum, 4721 Aircraft Dr, Anchorage, AK 99502 - T: (907) 248-5325, Fax: (907) 248-6391, E-mail: aahm@gci.net, Internet: home.gci.net/~aahm. Dir.: Kerry Eielson, Cur.: Don Robinson
Science&Tech Museum - 1988 41196

Anchorage Museum of History and Art, 121 W Seventh Av, Anchorage, AK 99501 - T: (907) 343-6172, Fax: (907) 343-6149, E-mail: museum@ci.anchorage.ak.us, Internet: www.anchoragemuseum.org. Dir.: Patricia B. Wolf, Dep. Dir.: Suzi Jones, Cur.: Walter Van Horn (Collections), David Nicholls (Exhibits), Jocelyn Young (Public Art)
Fine Arts Museum / Historical Museum / Ethnology Museum - 1968
History, art 41197

Cook Inlet Historical Society Museum, 121 W Seventh Av, Anchorage, AK 99501-3696 - T: (907) 343-4326, Fax: (907) 343-6149. Pres.: James K. Barnett
Local Museum - 1955
Local history 41198

Heritage Library and Museum, 301 W Northern Lights Blvd, Anchorage, AK 99503 - T: (907) 265-2834, Fax: (907) 265-2860, E-mail: holling@wellsfargo.com. Dir./Cur.: Gail Hollinger
Fine Arts Museum / Ethnology Museum - 1968 41199

The Imaginarium, 737 W Fifth Av, Ste G, Anchorage, AK 99501 - T: (907) 276-3179, Fax: (907) 258-4306, E-mail: info@imaginarium.org, Internet: www.imaginarium.org. Exec. Dir.: Christopher B. Cable
Science&Tech Museum - 1987
Science, technology 41200

Oscar Anderson House Museum, 420 M St, Anchorage, AK 99501 - T: (907) 274-2336, 333-6563, Fax: (907) 274-3610, Internet: www.customcpu.com/np/ahpi. Man.: Mary A. Flaherty
Historical Museum - 1982 41201

Anderson IN

Alford House-Anderson Fine Arts Center, 32 W Tenth St, Anderson, IN 46016-1406 - T: (765) 649-1248, Fax: (765) 649-0199, E-mail: andersnart@netdirect.net, Internet: www.andersonart.org/index.html. Pres.: Dave Harbert, C.E.O.: Deborah McBratney-Stapleton
Fine Arts Museum - 1966 41202

Gustav Jeeninga Museum of Bible and Near Eastern Studies, Theology Bldg, 1123 Anderson University Blvd, Anderson, IN 46012-3495 - T: (765) 649-9071, Fax: (765) 641-3005, E-mail: dneidert@anderson.edu, Internet: www.anderson.edu. Dir.: David Neidert
University Museum / Archaeological Museum / Religious Arts Museum - 1963
Archaeology, religion 41203

Anderson SC

Anderson County Arts Center, 405 N Main St, Anderson, SC 29621 - T: (864) 224-8811, Fax: (864) 224-8864, E-mail: info@andersonartscenter.org, Internet: www.andersonartscenter.org. Exec. Dir.: Kimberly Spears
Public Gallery - 1972 41204

Anderson County Museum, 202 E Greenville St, Anderson, SC 29624 - T: (864) 260-4737, Fax: (864) 260-4044, E-mail: acm@andersoncountysc.org, Internet: www.andersoncountysc.org/museum.htm. Dir.: Paula Reel
Military Museum - 1983
Local hist 41205

Andersonville GA

Andersonville Prison, 496 Cemetery Rd, Andersonville, GA 31711 - T: (912) 924-0343, Fax: (912) 928-9640, Internet: www.nps.ande.gov
Historical Museum - 1971
P.O.W. camps, Civil War and later conflicts, monuments and sculptures 41206

Andover MA

Addison Gallery of American Art, Phillips Academy, Andover, MA 01810 - T: (978) 749-4015, Fax: (978) 749-4025, E-mail: addison@andover.edu, Internet: www.addisongallery.org. Dir.: Adam D. Weinberg, Cur.: Susan Faxon, Ass. Cur.: Allison Kemmerer
Fine Arts Museum - 1931
American art 41207

Andover Historical Society Museum, 97 Main St, Andover, MA 01810 - T: (978) 475-2236, Fax: (978) 470-2741, E-mail: info@andhist.org, Internet: www.andhist.org. Dir.: Diane Hender, Ass. Dir.: Juliet Mofford
Local Museum - 1911
Local history 41208

Robert S. Peabody Museum of Archaeology, 175 Main St, Andover, MA 01810 - T: (978) 749-4490, Fax: (978) 749-4495, E-mail: rpeabody@andover.edu, Internet: www.andover.edu. Dir./Cur.: Malinda S. Blustain
Archaeological Museum - 1901
Archaeology 41209

Angleton TX

Brazoria County Historical Museum, 100 E Cedar, Angleton, TX 77515 - T: (919) 864-1208, Fax: (919) 864-1217, E-mail: bchm@bchm.org, Internet: www.bchm.org. Dir.: Jackie Haynes, Cur.: Alison G. Van Wagner
Historical Museum - 1983
Local hist 41210

Angola IN

General Lewis B. Hershey Museum, Tri-State University, Ford Memorial Library, 1 University Av, Angola, IN 46703 - T: (219) 665-4162, 665-4100, Fax: (219) 665-4283, E-mail: brewerk@tristate.edu, Internet: www.tristate.edu. Pres.: Dr. Earl Brooks
University Museum / Military Museum - 1970
Military 41211

Angwin CA

Rasmussen Art Gallery, Pacific Union College, 1 Angwin Av, Angwin, CA 94508 - T: (707) 965-6311, E-mail: enroll@puc.edu, Internet: www.puc.edu
Public Gallery 41212

Ann Arbor MI

Ann Arbor Art Center, 117 W Liberty, Ann Arbor, MI 48104 - T: (734) 994-8004 ext 110, Fax: (734) 994-3610, E-mail: a2artcen@aol.com, Internet: www.annarborartcenter.org. Dir.: Deborah Campbell
Fine Arts Museum - 1909
Art 41213

Ann Arbor Hands-On Museum, 220 E Ann St, Ann Arbor, MI 48104 - T: (313) 995-5439, Fax: (313) 995-1188, Internet: www.aahom.org. Dir.: James P. Frenza, Ass. Dir.: Carol Knauss
Science&Tech Museum - 1982
Science, technology, central firehouse 41214

Artrain, 1100 N Main St, Ste 106, Ann Arbor, MI 48104 - T: (734) 747-8300, Fax: (734) 742-8530, E-mail: drwartrain@aol.com, Internet: www.artrainusa.org. Dir.: Debra Polich
Fine Arts Museum - 1971
Traveling art, housed in five railroad cars 41215

Exhibit Museum of Natural History, University of Michigan, 1109 Geddes Av, Ann Arbor, MI 48109-1079 - T: (734) 763-4190, 764-0478, Fax: (734) 647-2767, E-mail: dmadaj@umich.edu, Internet: www.exhibits.lsa.umich.edu. Dir.: Amy Harris
University Museum / Natural History Museum - 1881
Natural history - planetarium 41216

Jean Paul Slusser Gallery, University of Michigan, School of Art and Design, Arts/Architecture Bldg, N Campus, 2000 Bonisteel Blvd, Ann Arbor, MI 48109-2069 - T: (734) 936-2082, Fax: (734) 615-6761, E-mail: slussergallery@umich.edu, Internet: www.art-design.umich.edu. Dir.: Todd M. Cashbaugh
University Museum / Fine Arts Museum
Art, design, architecture 41217

Kelsey Museum of Ancient Archaeology, 434 S State St, Ann Arbor, MI 48109 - T: (734) 764-9304, Fax: (734) 763-8976, Internet: www.isa.umich.edu/kelsey/. Dir.: Sharon C. Herbert, Cur.: Elaine K. Gazda (Conservation), Margaret Root (Greece and Near East), Elaine K. Gazda (Hellenistic and Roman Empire), Ass. Cur.: Lauren Talalay, Thelma Thomas (Late Antique and Textiles Post Classical), Janet Richards, Terry Wilfong (Dynastic Egypt), Robin Meador-Woodruff (Slides and Photographs)
University Museum / Archaeological Museum / Museum of Classical Antiquities - 1928
Archaeology, Hellenic, Roman and Egypt antiques, photos 41218

Museum of Anthropology, University of Michigan, 4009 Ruthven Museums Bldg, Ann Arbor, MI 48109 - T: (734) 764- 0485, Fax: (734) 763-7783, E-mail: anthro-museum@umich.edu, Internet: www.umma.lsa.umich.edu. Dir./Cur.: Robert Whallon (Mediterranean Archaeology), Cur.: C. Sinopoli (South and Southeast Archaeology), John D. Speth (North American Archaeology), Jeffrey R. Parsons (Ethnology), Richard I. Ford (Ethnology), C. Loring Brace (Physical Anthropology), Kent V. Flannery (Environmental Archaeology), John O'Shea (Great Lakes Archaeology), Henry T. Wright (Old World Civilization), Joyce Marcus (Mayan and Central American Archaeology), Dr. William R. Farrand (Analytical Collections)
University Museum / Ethnology Museum / Archaeological Museum - 1922
Anthropology, archaeology, old world civilization 41219

Museum of Zoology, University of Michigan, 1109 Geddes, Ann Arbor, MI 48109-1079 - T: (734) 764-0476, Fax: (734) 763-4080. Dir.: Prof. David P. Mindell, Sc. Staff: Prof. R.A. Nussbaum, Prof. Reeve M. Bailey, Prof. Lacey Knowles, Prof. John B. Burch, Prof. Richard D. Alexander, Prof. Thomas E. Moore, Prof. Robert B. Payne, Prof. Robert W. Storer, Prof. Arnold G. Kluge, Prof. William L. Fink, Prof. Philip Myers, Prof. Barry M. Oconnor, Prof. Priscilla K. Tucker, Prof. David P. Mindell, Prof. Diarmaid O'Foighil
University Museum / Natural History Museum - 1838
Zoology 41220

Stearns Collection of Musical Instruments, University of Michigan, School of Music, Ann Arbor, MI 48109-2085 - T: (734) 647-9471, 764-0583, Fax: (734) 647-1897, Internet: www.music.umich.edu/resources/sterns. Dir.: Joseph Lamb
Music Museum - 1899 41221

University of Michigan Museum of Art, 525 S State St, Ann Arbor, MI 48109-1354 - T: (734) 763-8662, 764-0395, Fax: (734) 764-3731, E-mail: umma.info@umich.edu, Internet: www.umich.edu/~umma/. Dir.: James Steward, Ass. Dir.: Carole McNamara, Sen. Cur.: Maribeth Graybill (Asian Art), Cur.: Annette Dixon (Western Art), Sean Ulmer (Modern and Contemporary Art)
Fine Arts Museum / University Museum - 1946
Western paintings and sculptures 12th c to the present, Old Master prints and contemporary prints and drawings, photography, Asian, African, Oceanic art, Islamic ceramics 41222

Annandale MN

Minnesota Pioneer Park Museum, 725 Pioneer Park Trail, Annandale, MN 55302 - T: (320) 274-8489, Fax: (320) 274-9612, E-mail: pioneerp@lkdlink.net, Internet: www.pioneerpark.org. Pres.: Julie Oldenburger
Historical Museum - 1972
Memorabilia from 1850-1910 41223

Annandale-on-Hudson NY

Center for Curatorial Studies, Bard College, Annandale-on-Hudson, NY 12504-5000 - T: (845) 758-7598, Fax: (845) 758-2442, E-mail: ccs@bard.edu, Internet: www.bard.edu/ccs. Dir.: Norton Batkin
Fine Arts Museum - 1990
Contemporary art 41224

Annapolis MD

Cardinal Gallery, 801 Chase St, Annapolis, MD 21401 - T: (410) 263-5544, Fax: (410) 263-5114, E-mail: mdhall@annap.infi.net, Internet: www.mdhallarts.org. Exec. Dir.: Linnell R. Bowen
Fine Arts Museum - 1979
Drawings, photography, sculpture, watercolors, woodcarvings, woodcuts, Afro-American art 41225

Charles Carroll House of Annapolis, 107 Duke of Gloucester St, Annapolis, MD 21401 - T: (410) 269-1737, Fax: (410) 269-1746, E-mail: ccarroll@toad.net. Dir.: Sandria B. Ross
Historic Site - 1987 41226

Elizabeth Myers Mitchell Art Gallery, Saint John's College, 60 College Av, Annapolis, MD 21401 - T: (410) 263-2371, (410) 626-2556, Fax: (410) 626-2886, E-mail: h-schaller@sjea.edu, Internet: www.sjca.edu. Dir.: Hydee Schaller
Fine Arts Museum / University Museum - 1989
Art gallery 41227

Hammond-Harwood House Museum, 19 Maryland Av, Annapolis, MD 21401 - T: (410) 263-4683, Fax: (410) 267-6891, E-mail: hammondharwood@annapolis.net, Internet: www.hammondharwoodhouse.org. Pres.: Pamela McKee, Exec. Dir.: Carter C. Lively
Historical Museum / Folklore Museum - 1938 41228

Historic Annapolis Foundation, 18 Pinkney St, Annapolis, MD 21401 - T: (410) 267-7619, Fax: (410) 267-6189, Internet: www.annapolis.org. Pres./C.E.O.: Brian Alexander, Dir.: William Sherman (Conservation), Sibley Jennings (Preservation)
Local Museum - 1952
Local history, 1715 Shiplap House 41229

United States Naval Academy Museum, 118 Maryland Av, Annapolis, MD 21402-5034 - T: (410) 293-2108, Fax: (410) 293-5220, Internet: www.usna.edu/museum. Cur.: James W. Cheevers, Cur.: Robert F. Sumrall (Ship Models), Sigrid Trumpy (Beverly R. Robinson Collection)
Fine Arts Museum / Historical Museum - 1845
Naval hist 41230

Anniston AL

Anniston Museum of Natural History, 800 Museum Dr, Anniston, AL 36202 - T: (256) 237-6766, Fax: (256) 237-6776, E-mail: info@annistonmuseum.org, Internet: www.annistonmuseum.org. Dir.: Cheryl H. Bragg, Renee Morrison (Education), Cur.: Robert Price (Exhibits), Daniel Spaulding (Collections)
Natural History Museum - 1930 41231

Anoka MN

Anoka County Historical and Genealogical Museum, 2135 Third Av S, Anoka, MN 55303 - T: (612) 421-0600, Fax: (323) 323-0218. Pres.: John Weaver, Dir.: Vickie Wendel
Local Museum - 1934
Regional history 41232

Ansted WV

Hawks Nest State Park, Rte 60, Ansted, WV 25812 - T: (304) 658-5212, 658-5196, Fax: (304) 658-4549, E-mail: hawknest@citynet.net, Internet: www.hawknestsp.com. Head: Thomas L. Shriver
Local Museum - 1935
Local hist 41233

Antigo WI

Langlade County Historical Society Museum, 404 Superior St, Antigo, WI 54409 - T: (715) 627-4464, E-mail: lchs@newnorth.net, Internet: www.newnorth/ichs
Local Museum - 1929
Local hist 41234

Antwerp OH

Ehrhart Museum, 118 N Main St, Antwerp, OH 45813 - T: (419) 258-2665, Fax: (419) 258-2665. Pres.: Randy Shaffer
Natural History Museum - 1963 41235

Apalachicola FL

John Gorrie Museum, 46 6th St and Avenue D, Apalachicola, FL 32329, mail addr: POB 267, Apalachicola, FL 32329-0267 - T: (850) 653-9347, Internet: www.baynavigator.com. Dir.: Fran P. Mainella
Science&Tech Museum - 1955
Inventor of machine tomate ice, fore-runner of refrigerator and air conditioning 41236

Apple Valley CA

Victor Valley Museum and Art Gallery, 11873 Apple Valley Rd, Apple Valley, CA 92308 - T: (760) 240-2111, Fax: (760) 240-5290. Pres.: Calvin Camara, C.E.O.: Carl Mason
Fine Arts Museum / Local Museum - 1976
Natural hist, art, archaeology, geography 41237

Appleton WI

Appleton Art Center, 111 W College Av, Appleton, WI 54911 - T: (920) 733-4089, Fax: (920) 733-4149, E-mail: info@appletonartcenter.org, Internet: www.appletonartcenter.org. Pres.: Elizabeth Nevitt, Dir.: Tracey Jenks
Fine Arts Museum - 1960
Art 41238

Hearthstone Historic House Museum, 625 W Prospect Av, Appleton, WI 54911 - T: (920) 730-8204, Fax: (920) 730-8266, E-mail: hearthstonemuseum@athenet, Internet: www.hearthstonemuseum.org. Dir.: Beverly Harrington
Historical Museum / Science&Tech Museum - 1986
First residence in the world to be lighted from a central hydroelectric powerplant using the Edison system in 1882 41239

Outagamie Museum and Houdini Historical Center, 330 E College Av, Appleton, WI 54911 - T: (920) 733-8445, Fax: (920) 733-8636, E-mail: ochs@foxvalleyhistory.org, Internet: www.foxvalleyhistory.org. Dir.: Terry Bergen, Cur.: Matthew Carpenter
Local Museum - 1872
Hist of technology, regional hist 41240

Wriston Art Center Galleries, Lawrence University, 613 E College Av, Appleton, WI 54912-0599 - T: (414) 832-6621, Fax: (414) 832-7362, E-mail: nadine.wassman@lawrence.edu, Internet: www.lawrence.edu/news/wriston.shtml. Cur.: Frank C. Lewis
University Museum / Fine Arts Museum - 1989 41241

Appomattox VA

Appomattox Court House, POB 218, Appomattox, VA 24522 - T: (804) 352-8987, Fax: (804) 352-8330, Internet: www.nps.gov/apco
Local Museum - 1940
Civil War, historic buildings 41242

Arapahoe NE

Furnas-Gosper Historical Society Museum, 401 Nebraska Av, Arapahoe, NE 68922. C.E.O. & Pres.: Robert Trosper
Local Museum - 1966 41243

Arcade NY

Arcade Historical Museum, 331 W Main St, Arcade, NY 14009 - T: (716) 492-4466
Local Museum - 1956
Crafts, local hist, household items, toys 41244

Arcadia MI

Arcadia Township Historical Museum and Furniture Museum, Lake St, Arcadia, MI 49613 - T: (616) 889-4830, 889-3389, Internet: www.arcadiami.com
Local Museum - 1992
Lumbertown, Sawmill furniture factory, mirror works 41245

Arcata CA

Humboldt State University Natural History Museum, 1315 G St, Arcata, CA 95521 - T: (707) 826-4479, Fax: (707) 826-4477, E-mail: mlz1@axe.humboldt.edu, Internet: www.humboldt.edu/~natmus/. Dir.: Melissa L. Zielinski
University Museum / Natural History Museum - 1989
Natural hist 41246

Reese Bullen Gallery, Humboldt State University, 1 Harpst St, Arcata, CA 95521 - T: (707) 826-5802, Fax: (707) 826-3628, E-mail: mm1@humboldt.edu, Internet: www.humboldt.edu/~rbg. Dir.: Martin Morgan
University Museum / Fine Arts Museum - 1970
20th c American and African art 41247

Archbold OH

Historic Sauder Village, 22611 State Rd 2, Archbold, OH 43502 - T: (419) 446-2541, Fax: (419) 445-5251, E-mail: village@bright.net, Internet: www.saudervillage.com. Exec. Dir.: Carolyn Sauder
Historical Museum - 1971
Farm equip, woodworking tools, household, smith, potter, glassblower, spinning and weaving, broommaking, basket maker, grist mill 41248

Archer City TX

Archer County Museum, Old County Jail, Archer City, TX 76351 - T: (940) 423-6426. Cur.: Jack Loftin
Local Museum - 1974
Lizard fossils, art and western paintings, old clothing, farm machinery, vehicles, Indian artifacts, early pictures 41249

Arco ID

Craters of the Moon, 18 mi SW of Arco on Hwy 26, Arco, ID 83213, mail addr: POB 29, Arco, ID 83213 - T: (208) 527-3257, Fax: (208) 527-3073, E-mail: crmo_resource_management@nps.gov, Internet: www.nps.gov/crmo
Natural History Museum - 1924
Local geology, hist 41250

Ardmore OK

Charles B. Goddard Center for Visual and Performing Arts, 401 First Av and D St SW, Ardmore, OK 73401 - T: (580) 226-0909, Fax: (580) 226-8891, E-mail: godart@brightok.net, Internet: www.godart.org. Dir.: Mort Hamilton
Fine Arts Museum / Performing Arts Museum - 1969 41251

Eliza Cruce Hall Doll Museum, 320 E Northwest, Ardmore, OK 73401 - T: (580) 223-8290. Dir.: Carolyn J. Franks
Special Museum - 1971 41252

Tucker Tower Nature Center Park Museum, 3310 S Lake Murray Dr, Ardmore, OK 73401 - T: (405) 223-2109, Fax: (405) 223-2109, E-mail: Markttnc@aol.com
Natural History Museum - 1952
Fossils, minerals, meteorite, nature exhibits 41253

Argonia KS

Salter Museum, 220 W Garfield, Argonia, KS 67004, mail addr: POB 116, Argonia, KS 67004 - T: (316) 435-6376. Pres.: Laura High, Chief Cur.: Helen Nafziger
Historical Museum - 1961
Home of America's first woman mayor Susanna M. Salter 41254

Arkadelphia AR

Henderson State University Museum, The Stone House, Henderson and 10th, Arkadelphia, AR 71923 - T: (870) 246-7311, Fax: (870) 246-3199. Cur.: Dr. Ann M. Early
University Museum / Local Museum - 1953 41255

Arkansas City KS

Cherokee Strip Land Rush Museum, Hwy 77 S, Box 778, Arkansas City, KS 67005 - T: (316) 442-6750, Fax: (316) 441-4332, E-mail: museum@arkcity.org, Internet: www.arkcity.org/csm.html. Dir.: Tom Junkins
Historical Museum - 1966
Cherokee Strip Run, Indian and military coll, Hardy Jail 41256

Arlington MA

Arlington Historical Society, 7 Jason St, Arlington, MA 02476 - T: (781) 648-4300, Internet: www.arlhs.org. Pres.: Howard Winkler
Historical Museum - 1897
Local history 41257

Old Schwamb Mill, 17 Mill Ln, Arlington, MA 02476-4189 - T: (781) 643-0554, Fax: (781) 648-8809, E-mail: schwambmil@aol.com, Internet: www.oldschwambill.org. C.E.O.: Bruce Wheltle
Science&Tech Museum - 1969
Industrial history, waterpowered mill 41258

Arlington TX

Arlington Museum of Art, 201 W Main St, Arlington, TX 76010 - T: (817) 275-4600, Fax: (817) 860-4800, E-mail: ama@arlingtonmuseum.org, Internet: www.arlingtonmuseum.org. Pres.: Jeff Hansen, Dir./Cur.: Anne Allen
Fine Arts Museum - 1987 41259

The Gallery at UTA, c/o University of Texas at Arlington, 502 S Cooper St, Arlington, TX 76019 - T: (817) 272-5658, 272-3143, Fax: (817) 272-2805, E-mail: bhuerta@uta.edu, Internet: www.uta.edu/art. Dir.: Benito Huerta
Fine Arts Museum / University Museum - 1976
Contemporary art 41260

Legends of the Game Baseball Museum, 1000 Ballpark Way, Arlington, TX 76011 - T: (817) 273-5059, Fax: (817) 273-5093, E-mail: museum@texasrangers.com, Internet: museum.texasrangers.com. Dir.: Amy E. Polley
Special Museum - 1994
National baseball hist, Texas League, Texas Rangers, Negro Leagues 41261

River Legacy Living Science Center, 703 NW Green Oaks Blvd, Arlington, TX 76006 - T: (817) 860-6752, Fax: (817) 860-1595, E-mail: rlegacy@earthlink.net, Internet: www.riverlegacy.org. C.E.O.: Phyllis Snider
Natural History Museum - 1996
Animals, botany, archaeology, geology 41262

Arlington VA

Arlington Arts Center, 3550 Wilson Blvd, Arlington, VA 22201 - T: (703) 524-1494, Fax: (703) 527-4050, E-mail: artcenter@erols.com, Internet: www.onwashington.com/groups-arlingtonartscenter. Dir.: Carole Sullivan, Cur.: Julie Mangis
Fine Arts Museum - 1976
Art 41263

Arlington Historical Museum, 1805 S Arlington Ridge Rd, Arlington, VA 22202 - T: (703) 892-4204, 812-9479, E-mail: arlhistory@aol.com, Internet: www.arlingtonhistoricalsociety.org. Pres.: Gerald Laporte, Dir.: Dr. Harold Handerson
Local Museum - 1956
Local hist 41264

Arlington House - The Robert E. Lee Memorial, Arlington National Cemetery, Arlington, VA 22211 - T: (703) 535-1530, Fax: (703) 535-1546, E-mail: gwmp-arlingtonhouse@nps.gov, Internet: www.nps.gov/arho. Dir.: Terry Carustrom
Local Museum - 1925
Historic house, residence of Gen. Robert E. Lee 41265

The Newseum, c/o The Freedom Forum Newseum, 1101 Wilson Blvd, Arlington, VA 22209 - T: (703) 284-3700, 888-639-7386, Fax: (703) 284-3777, E-mail: newseum@freedomforum.org, Internet: www.newseum.org. Dir.: Joe Urschel, Dep. Dir.: Jim Thompson, Cur.: Cara Sutherland
Historical Museum - 1997
History and present time 41266

US Patent and Trademark Office - Museum, 2121 Crystal Dr, Arlington, VA 22202 - T: (703) 305-8341, Fax: (703) 308-5258, E-mail: mscott@invent.org, Internet: www.uspto.gov. C.E.O.: Richard Maulsby
Science&Tech Museum / Special Museum - 1995
Hist of the patent and trademark systems, models 41267

Arlington Heights IL

Arlington Heights Historical Museum, 110 W Fremont St, Arlington Heights, IL 60004 - T: (847) 255-1225, Fax: (847) 255-1570, E-mail: susan@ahpd.org, Internet: www.ahmuseum.org. Cur.: Mickey Horndasch
Local Museum - 1957
Local history 41268

Armonk NY

North Castle Historical Society Museum, 440 Bedford Rd, Armonk, NY 10504 - T: (914) 273-4510. C.E.O.: Judy Early
Local Museum - 1971
History 41269

Armour SD

Douglas County Museum Complex, Courthouse Grounds, Armour, SD 57313 - T: (605) 724-2129. Dir.: Laverne Vanderwerff, Pres. & Cur.: Sharon A. Wiese, Dep. Dir.: Erna Putnam, Ass. Dir.: Dot Hoveng
Local Museum - 1958
Local hist 41270

Arrow Rock MO

Arrow Rock State Historic Site, Fourth and Van Buren, Arrow Rock, MO 65320 - T: (660) 837-3330, Fax: (660) 837-3300, E-mail: dsparro@mail.dnr.state.mo.us, Internet: www.arrowrock.org. C.E.O.: Michael Dickey
Historical Museum / Open Air Museum - 1923 41271

Artesia NM

Artesia Historical Museum and Art Center, 505 Richardson Av, Artesia, NM 88210 - T: (505) 748-2390, Fax: (505) 746-3886, E-mail: ahmac@pvtnetworks.net. Dir.: Nancy Dunn, Registrar: Merle Rich
Historical Museum - 1970 41272

Arthurdale WV

Arthurdale Heritage Museum, Q and A Rds, Arthurdale, WV 26520 - T: (304) 864-3959, Fax: (304) 864-4602, E-mail: ahi1934@aol.com, Internet: www.arthurdaleheritage.org. Pres.: Randall Weaver, Dir.: Deanna Hornyak
Local Museum - 1987
Local hist 41273

Arvada CO

Arvada Center for the Arts and Humanities, 6901 Wadsworth Blvd, Arvada, CO 80003 - T: (303) 431-3080, Fax: (303) 431-3083, E-mail: kathy-a@arvadacenter.org, Internet: www.arvadacenter.org. Dir.: Deborah L. Ellerman, Kathy Andrews
Fine Arts Museum / Historical Museum - 1976
Art, history 41274

Asheville NC

Asheville Art Museum, 2 S Pack Sq, Asheville, NC 28801 - T: (828) 253-3227, Fax: (828) 257-4503, E-mail: mailbox@ashevilleart.org, Internet: www.ashevilleart.org. Dir.: Pamela L. Myers, Cur.: Frank E. Thomson
Fine Arts Museum - 1948 41275

Biltmore Estate, 1 N Pack Sq, Asheville, NC 28801 - T: (828) 255-1776, Fax: (828) 255-1111, E-mail: rking@biltmore.com, Internet: www.biltmore.com. C.E.O.: William A.V. Cecil
Local Museum - 1930 41276

Black Mountain College Museum and Arts Center, POB 18912, Asheville, NC 28814 - T: (828) 299-9306, Fax: (828) 229-9306, E-mail: bmcmac@bellsouth.net, Internet: www.blackmountaincollege.org. C.E.O.: Connie Bostic
Historical Museum / Fine Arts Museum - 1993
Artwork, photographs, books 41277

Colburn Gem and Mineral Museum, 2 S Pack Sq, Asheville, NC 28801 - T: (828) 254-7162, Fax: (704) 251-5652, (828) 257-4505, E-mail: ddmowrey@yahoo.com, Internet: main.nc/colburn. Pres.: Kempton Roll, Exec. Dir.: Debbie Mowrey, Cur.: Christian Richart
Natural History Museum - 1960 41278

Estes-Winn Antique Automobile Museum, 111 Grovewood Rd, Asheville, NC 28804 - T: (828) 253-7651, Fax: (828) 254-2489, E-mail: automuseum@grovewood.com, Internet: www.grovewood.com. Pres.: S.M. Patton
Science&Tech Museum - 1970 41279

Folk Art Center → Southern Highland Craft Guild at the Folk Art Center

Grovewood Gallery, 111 Grovewood Rd, Asheville, NC 28804 - T: (828) 253-7651, Fax: (828) 254-2489, E-mail: homespun@grovewood.com, Internet: grovewood.com. Pres.: S.M. Patton
Special Museum - 1992 41280

Health Adventure, 2 S Pack Sq, Asheville, NC 28802-0180 - T: (828) 254-6373, Fax: (828) 257-4521, E-mail: info@thehealthadventure.org, Internet: www.thehealthadventure.org. C.E.O.: Todd Boyette, Dir.: Maralee Gollberg
Special Museum - 1968 41281

Smith-McDowell House Museum, 283 Victoria Rd, Asheville, NC 28801 - T: (828) 253-9231, Fax: (828) 253-5518, E-mail: smithmcdowellhouse@msn.com, Internet: www.wnchistory.org. Pres.: Edward Metz, Exec. Dir.: Rebecca B. Lamb, Dir.: Ellen Shaylor
Historic Site - 1981 41282

Southern Highland Craft Guild at the Folk Art Center, Milepost 382, Blue Ridge Pkwy, Asheville, NC 28815 - T: (828) 298-7928, Fax: (828) 298-7962, E-mail: shcg@buncombe.main.nc.us, Internet: www.southernhighlandguild.org. Man.: Madeline Parker, Exec. Dir.: Ruth Summers
Folklore Museum - 1930
Robert W. Gray library and archives 41283

Thomas Wolfe Memorial, 52 N Market St, Asheville, NC 28801 - T: (828) 253-8304, Fax: (828) 252-8171, E-mail: wolfememorial@worldnet.att.net, Internet: www.wolfememorial.home.att.net. Dir.: Steve Hill
Historical Museum - 1949 41284

Ashland KS

Pioneer-Krier Museum, 430 W 4th, Ashland, KS 67831 - T: (620) 635-2227, Fax: (620) 635-2227, E-mail: pioneer@ucom.net, Internet: history.cc.ukans.edu/heritage/kshs/places/. CEO: Charles Walter Couch
Local Museum - 1968
Kitchen equip, dolls and toys, bits and spurs, guns, musical instruments, furniture, military, pioneer pictures, farm machinery, fossils, aerobatic airplanes 41285

Pioneer-Krier Museum, 430 W Fourth St, Ashland, KS 67831-0862 - T: (316) 635-2227, Fax: (316) 635-2227, E-mail: rogers@ucom.net. Cur.: Floretta Rogers
Local Museum / Historical Museum - 1967
Archeology, early settlers, elephant and gun colls 41286

Ashland KY

Highlands Museum and Discovery Center, 1620 Winchester Av, Ashland, KY 41101 - T: (606) 329-8888, Fax: (606) 324-3218, E-mail: highlandsmuseum@yahoo.com, Internet: www.highlandsmuseum.com. CEO: Dr. Kenneth Hauswald
Local Museum - 1984
Clothing, transportation, communication, industry, country music, medical and military since WW 2 41287

Ashland MA

Ashland Historical Museum, 2 Myrtle St, Ashland, MA 01721 - T: (508) 881-8183, 881-3319. Pres.: Clifford Wilson, Cur.: Catherine Powers
Local Museum - 1905
Local history 41288

Ashland ME

Ashland Logging Museum, Box 866, Ashland, ME 04732 - T: (207) 435-6039, Fax: (207) 435-6579. Cur.: Ed Chase
Ethnology Museum - 1964
Reproduction of an early logging camp 41289

Ashland Logging Museum, POB 866, Ashland, ME 04732 - T: (207) 435-6039. Cur.: Ed Chase
Science&Tech Museum - 1964
Lombard steam andgas log haules, log hauler sleds, bateau, tote wagon, pine log 41290

Ashland NE

Strategic Air Command Museum → Strategic Air & Space Museum

Strategic Air & Space Museum, 28210 W Park Hwy, Ashland, NE 68003 - T: (800) 358-5029, Fax: (402) 944-3160, E-mail: staff@strategicairandspace.com, Internet: www.strategicairandspace.com. Dir.: Scott Hazelrigg, Dep. Dir.: Steve Prall, Cur.: Brian York
Military Museum - 1959
Aerospace 41291

Ashland NH

Ashland Railroad Station Museum, 69 Depot St, Ashland, NH 03217
Science&Tech Museum - 1999 41292

Pauline E. Glidden Toy Museum, Pleasant St, Ashland, NH 03217-9401 - T: (603) 968-7289. Dir.: Shirley Splaine
Special Museum - 1990
Toys 41293

Whipple House Museum, 14 Pleasant St, Ashland, NH 03217-0175 - T: (603) 968-7716, Fax: (603) 968-7716. Pres.: David Ruell, Cur.: Wilma Garland
Local Museum / Historical Museum - 1970
Local history, home of George Hoyt Whipple, Nobel Prize for medicine 41294

Ashland OH

The Coburn Gallery, Ashland College Arts & Humanities Gallery, 401 College Ave, Ashland, OH 44805 - T: (419) 289-4142. Dir.: Larry Schiemann
Fine Arts Museum / Public Gallery
Contemporary works 41295

Ashland OR

Schneider Museum of Art, Southern Oregon University, 1250 Siskiyou Blvd, Ashland, OR 97520 - T: (541) 552-6245, Fax: (541) 552-8241, E-mail: schneider_museum@sou.edu, Internet: www.sou.edu/sma. Dir.: Mary N. Gardiner
University Museum / Fine Arts Museum - 1986 41296

Southern Oregon University Museum of Vertebrate Natural History, 1250 Siskiyou Blvd, Ashland, OR 97520 - T: (541) 552-6341, Fax: (541) 552-6415, E-mail: stonek@sou.edu. Cur.: Karen Stone
University Museum / Natural History Museum - 1969 41297

Ashland PA

Museum of Anthracite Mining, Pine and 17 Sts, Ashland, PA 17921 - T: (570) 875-4708, Fax: (570) 875-3732, Internet: www.phmc.state.pa.us. Dir.: Steven Ling, Cur.: Chester Kulesa
Science&Tech Museum / Historical Museum - 1970 41298

Ashland WI

Ashland Historical Society Museum, 509 W Main, Ashland, WI 54806 - T: (715) 682-4743, E-mail: ashlandhistory@centurytel.net
Local Museum - 1954
Costumes, hist, military 41299

Ashley ND

McIntosh County Historical Society Museum, 117 3rd Av, Ashley, ND 58413 - T: (701) 288-3388. Pres.: Ronald J. Meidinger
Local Museum - 1977
Local hist 41300

Ashley Falls MA

Colonel Ashley House, Cooper Hill Rd, Ashley Falls, MA 01222 - T: (413) 229-5024, Fax: (413) 298-5239, E-mail: wgarrison@ttor.org, Internet: www.thetrustees.org. Exec. Dir.: Andrew Kendall
Historical Museum - 1972
Oldest house in Berkshire County 41301

Ashtabula OH

Ashtabula Arts Center, 2928 W 13 St, Ashtabula, OH 44004 - T: (440) 964-3396, Fax: (440) 964-3396, E-mail: aac@suite224.net, Internet: www.ashartscenter.org. Pres.: Judy Robson, Exec. Dir.: Elizabeth Koski
Fine Arts Museum - 1953 41302

Ashville OH

Slate Run Living Historical Farm, Metro Parks, 9130 Marcy Rd, Ashville, OH 43103 - T: (614) 833-1880, Fax: (614) 837-3809, Internet: www.metroparks.co.franklin.ohius/slaterunfarmsched.htm. C.E.O.: John O'Meara
Local Museum / Agriculture Museum - 1976
Local hist 41303

Askov MN

Pine County Historical Society Museum, 3851 Glacier Rd, Askov, MN 55704 - T: (320) 838-3792, E-mail: lizesp@juno.com. Pres.: Elizabeth Espointour
Local Museum - 1948
Agriculture, manuscripts, folklore - archives, library 41304

Aspen CO

Aspen Art Museum, 590 N Mill St, Aspen, CO 81611 - T: (970) 925-8050, Fax: (970) 925-8054, E-mail: info@aspenartmuseum.org, Internet: www.aspenartmuseum.org. Dir.: Dean Sobel, Ass. Dir.: Mary Ann Igna
Fine Arts Museum - 1979 41305

Aspen Historical Society Museum, 620 W Bleeker St, Aspen, CO 81611 - T: (970) 925-3721, Fax: (970) 925-5347, E-mail: ahistory@rof.net, Internet: www.aspenhistory.org. Dir.: Grace Gary, Cur.: Sarah Oates
Local Museum - 1969
Local history, Wheeler-Stallard house 41306

Astoria NY

American Museum of the Moving Image, 35th Av at 36th St, Astoria, NY 11106 - T: (718) 784-4520, Fax: (718) 784-4681, Internet: www.ammi.org. Dir.: Rochelle Slovin, Chief Cur.: David Schwartz (Film and Video), Cur.: Carl Goodman (Digital Media), Dana Sergent Nemeth (Popular Culture)
Special Museum - 1977 41307

Astoria OR

Captain George Flavel House Museum, 441 Eighth St, Astoria, OR 97103 - T: (503) 325-2203, Fax: (503) 325-7727, E-mail: cchs@seasurf.net, Internet: www.clatsophistoricalsociety.org. Dir.: Scott Reuter, Cur.: Lisa Penner (Collections)
Historical Museum 41308

Columbia River Maritime Museum, 1792 Marine Dr, Astoria, OR 97103 - T: (503) 325-2323, Fax: (503) 325-2331, E-mail: information@crmm.org, Internet: www.crmm.org. Dir.: Jerry Ostermiller, Cur.: Dave Pearson
Historical Museum / Science&Tech Museum - 1962 41309

Fort Clatsop National Memorial, Rte 3, Astoria, OR 97103 - T: (503) 861-2471, Fax: (503) 861-2585, E-mail: focl_administration@nps.gov, Internet: www.nps.gov/focl. Head: Don Striker
Open Air Museum / Military Museum - 1958 41310

The Heritage Museum, Clatsop Historical Society, 1618 Exchange St, Astoria, OR 97103 - T: (503) 338-4849, Fax: (503) 338-6265, E-mail: cchs@seasurf.net, Internet: www.clatsophistoricalsociety.org. Dir.: Scott Reuter, Cur.: Liisa Penna (Collections)
Local Museum - 1985
Local history 41311

Uppertown Firefighters Museum, 30th and Marine Dr, Astoria, OR 97103 - T: (503) 325-2203, Fax: (503) 325-7727, E-mail: cchs@seasurf.net, Internet: www.clatsophistoricalsociety.org. Dir.: Scott Reuter, Cur.: Lisa Penner (Collections)
Historical Museum - 1990
Firefighting 41312

Atascadero CA

Atascadero Historical Society Museum, 6500 Palma Av, Atascadero, CA 93422 - T: (805) 466-8341, Fax: (805) 461-0606. Dir.: Mike Lindsay, Cur.: Marjorie R. Mackey, Bill Smith
Local Museum - 1965
Local history 41313

Atchison KS

Amelia Earhart Birthplace Museum, 223 North Tce, Atchison, KS 66002 - T: (816) 554-2567, (913) 367-4217, Fax: (816) 554-3239
Special Museum - 1984
Women pilots 41314

Atchison County Historical Society Museum, 200 S 10th St, Santa Fe Depot, Atchison, KS 66002 - T: (913) 367-6238, E-mail: gowest@atchisonhistory.org, Internet: www.atchisonhistory.org. Exec. Dir.: Chris Taylor
Local Museum - 1966
Local history, westward expansion, Lewis O'Clark, Amelia Barhart 41315

The Muchnic Gallery, 704 N 4th, Atchison, KS 66002 - T: (913) 367-4278, Fax: (913) 367-2939, E-mail: atchart@ponyexpress.net, Internet: www.atchison-art.org. Dir./Cur.: Gloria Conkle Davis
Public Gallery - 1970
Art gallery 41316

Athens GA

Church-Waddel-Brumby House Museum, 280 E Dougherty St, Athens, GA 30601 - T: (706) 353-1820, Fax: (706) 353-1770, E-mail: athenswc@negia.net, Internet: www.visitathensga.com. Dir.: Mary Beth Justus
Historical Museum - 1968 41317

Georgia Museum of Art, University of Georgia, 90 Carlton St, Athens, GA 30602-6719 - T: (706) 542-4662, Fax: (706) 542-1051, E-mail: buramsey@arches.uga.edu, Internet: www.uga.edu/gamuseum/. Dir.: William U. Eiland, Cur.: Romita Ray (Prints and Drawings), Ashley Brown (Decorative Arts)
Fine Arts Museum / University Museum - 1945
Prints, drawings, paintings, photographs, graphics 41318

Georgia Museum of Natural History, University of Georgia, Natural History Bldg, Athens, GA 30602-1882 - T: (706) 542-1663, Fax: (706) 542-3920, E-mail: musinfo@arches.uga.edu, Internet: museum.nhm.uga.edu/. Dir./Cur.: Dr. E. Reitz (Zooarchaeology), Cur.: B.J. Freeman (Fish), Dr. D.J. Hally (Archaeology), Dr. D. Giannasi (Botany), Dr. J. McHugh (Entomology), Dr. D. Crowe (Geology), Dr. R. Hanlin (Mycology), W. Zomlefer (Botany), S. Kowalewski (Archaeology), P. Schroeder (Geology), M. Williams (Archaeology)
University Museum / Natural History Museum - 1977
Zooarchaeology, botany, paleontology, geology, mycology, palynology, entomology 41319

Lyndon House Art Center, 293 Hoyt St, Athens, GA 30601 - T: (706) 613-3623, Fax: (706) 613-3627. Dir.: Claire Benson, Cur.: Nancy Lukasiewicz
Fine Arts Museum / Decorative Arts Museum - 1973 41320

Sed Gallery, University of Georgia, c/o School of Environmental Design, G14 Caldwell Hall, Athens, GA 30602 - T: (706) 542-8292, Fax: (706) 542-4485, E-mail: rds@arches.uga.edu, Internet: www.sed.uga.edu/events. C.E.O.: Rene D. Shoemaker
Fine Arts Museum / University Museum - 1993
Architecture 41321

Taylor-Grady House, 634 Prince Av, Athens, GA 30601 - T: (706) 549-8688, Fax: (706) 613-0860, E-mail: jlathens@aol.com. Pres.: Jill Bateman
Historical Museum - 1968
1844 Henry W. Grady home 41322

United States Navy Supply Corps Museum, 1425 Prince Av, Athens, GA 30606-2205 - T: (706) 354-7349, Fax: (706) 354-7239, E-mail: roth_dan@nscs.com, Internet: www.nscs.com. Dir.: Dan Roth
Military Museum - 1974
Naval Museum housed in 1910 Carnegie Library 41323

Athens OH

Kennedy Museum of Art, Lin Hall, Ohio University, Athens, OH 45701-2979 - T: (740) 593-1304, Fax: (740) 593-1305, E-mail: kenmus@www.cats.ohiou.edu, Internet: www.ohiou.edu/museum. Dir.: James Wyman, Cur.: Sally Delgado (Education), Jennifer McLerran
Fine Arts Museum / University Museum - 1993 41324

Seigfred Gallery, Ohio University, School of Art, Seigfred Hall 528, Athens, OH 45701 - T: (740) 593-4290, Fax: (740) 593-0457. Dir.: Jenita Landrum-Bittle
Fine Arts Museum - 1993 41325

Athens PA

Tioga Point Museum, 724 S Main St, Athens, PA 18810 - T: (717) 888-7225, E-mail: tiogapoint@exotrope.net. Pres.: Dr. Donald W. Hunt, Dir./Cur.: Shannon O'Shea Schmieg
Local Museum - 1895
Native american art, archaeology 41326

Athens TN

McMinn County Living Heritage Museum, 522 W Madison Av, Athens, TN 37303 - T: (423) 745-0329, Fax: (423) 745-0329, E-mail: livher@usit.net, Internet: www.usit.com/livher/. Dir.: Ann Davis
Decorative Arts Museum / Local Museum - 1982
Local hist 41327

Atlanta GA

Apex Museum, 135 Auburn Av NE, Atlanta, GA 30303 - T: (404) 523-2739, Fax: (404) 523-3248, E-mail: apexmuseum@aol.com, Internet: www.apexmuseum.org. Pres.: Dan Moore, Dir.: Dan Moore jr.
Fine Arts Museum / Historical Museum - 1978 41328

Art Gallery, c/o Georgia State University, 10 Peachtree Center Av, Rm 117, Atlanta, GA 30303 - T: (404) 651-2257, Fax: (404) 651-1779. Dir.: Teri Williams
Fine Arts Museum / University Museum 41329

The Atlanta College of Art, 1280 Peachtree St, NE, Atlanta, GA 30309 - T: (404) 733-5001, Fax: (404) 733-5201, Internet: www.aca.edu. Pres.: Ellen L. Meyer
Fine Arts Museum / Library with Exhibitions - 1928
Artist's books 41330

Atlanta Contemporary Art Center and Nexus Press, 535 Means St NW, Atlanta, GA 30318 - T: (404) 688-1970, Fax: (404) 577-5856, E-mail: gallery@thecontemporary.org, Internet: www.thecontemporary.org. Dir.: Sam Gappmayer, Helena Reckitt, Dir.: Teresa Bramlette
Fine Arts Museum - 1973 41331

The Atlanta Cyclorama, 800-C Cherokee Av SE, Atlanta, GA 30315 - T: (404) 658-7625, Fax: (404) 658-7045, E-mail: atlcyclorama@mindspring.com, Internet: www.bcaatlanta.org. Dir.: Pauline M. Smith, Ass. Dir.: Keith G. Lauer
Fine Arts Museum / Historical Museum - 1898
Art, Civil War, c.1886 Cyclorama that depicts the July 22, 1864 Battle of Atlanta 41332

Atlanta History Museum, 130 W Paces Ferry Rd NW, Atlanta, GA 30305-1366 - T: (404) 814-4000, Fax: (404) 814-4186, Internet: www.atlantahistorycenter.com. Dir.: Rick Beard, Sc. Staff: Franklin M. Garrett (History)
Historical Museum / Military Museum / Open Air Museum - 1926
Local history, historic houses, gardens - library 41333

Atlanta International Museum of Art and Design, 285 Peachtree Center Av, Atlanta, GA 30303 - T: (404) 688-2467 ext 307, Fax: (404) 521-9311, E-mail: info@atlantainternationalmuseum.org, Internet: www.atlantainternationalmuseum.org. Dir.: John Johnes
Fine Arts Museum - 1989 41334

Atlanta Museum, 537-39 Peachtree St, NE, Atlanta, GA 30308 - T: (404) 872-8233. Dir.: J.H. Elliott, Cur.: Mary Gene Elliott
Local Museum - 1938
General Museum 41335

Callanwolde Fine Arts Center, 980 Briarcliff Rd NE, Atlanta, GA 30306 - T: (404) 872-5338, Fax: (404) 872-5175, E-mail: callanwolde@mindspring.com, Internet: www.callanwolde.org. Dir.: Laurie Allan (Gallery)
Fine Arts Museum - 1973 41336

Center for Puppetry Arts, 1404 Spring St, Atlanta, GA 30309 - T: (404) 873-3089 ext 110, Fax: (404) 873-9907, E-mail: puppet@mindspring.com, Internet: www.puppet.org. Exec. Dir.: Vincent Anthony
Special Museum - 1978
Puppetry 41337

City Gallery at Chastain, 135 W Wieuca Rd NW, Atlanta, GA 30342 - T: (404) 257-1804, Fax: (404) 851-1270. Dir.: Lynn Ho
Local Museum
Contemporary art by local, regional and national artists and designers 41338

City Gallery East, 675 Ponce de Leon Av NE, Atlanta, GA 30308 - T: (404) 817-6981, Fax: (404) 817-6827, E-mail: citygalleryeast@mindspring.com. Dir.: Karen Comer
Fine Arts Museum
Contemporary fine art 41339

Clark Atlanta University Art Galleries, Trevor Arnett Hall, Atlanta, GA 30314, mail addr: 223 James P Brawley Dr SW, Atlanta, GA 30314 - T: (404) 880-6102, Fax: (404) 880-6968, E-mail: tdunkley@cau.edu, Internet: www.cau.edu/artgalleries. Dir.: Tina Dunkley
Fine Arts Museum - 1942
African-American art 41340

Fernbank Museum of Natural History, 767 Clifton Rd NE, Atlanta, GA 30307-1221 - T: (404) 929-6300, 929-6400, Fax: (404) 378-8140, 370-8087, Internet: www.fernbank.edu/museum. Pres.: Susan E. Neugent
Natural History Museum / Archaeological Museum - 1992
Jewelry, costumes, textiles, Georgia minerals, gemstones, plants, shells, animals, dinosaurs, argentinosaurus, gigantosaurus 41341

Fernbank Science Center, 156 Heaton Park Dr NE, Atlanta, GA 30307-1398 - T: (404) 378-4311, Fax: (404) 370-1336, E-mail: fernbank@fernbank.edu, Internet: fsc.fernbank.edu. Dir.: William M. Sudduth
Natural History Museum - 1967 41342

Folk Art and Photography Galleries, High Museum of Art, 133 Peachtree St NE, Atlanta, GA 30303 - T: (404) 577-6940, 733-4400, Fax: (404) 653-0916, E-mail: dean.walcott@woodruffcenter.org, Internet: www.high.org. Dir.: Dr. Michael E. Shapiro
Fine Arts Museum / Folklore Museum - 1986
Photographic art, folk art 41343

Georgia Capitol Museum, Georgia State Capitol Rm 431, Atlanta, GA 30334 - T: (404) 651-6996, Fax: (404) 657-3801, E-mail: dolson@sos.state.ga.us, Internet: www.sos.ga.us. Dir.: Dorothy Olson
Historical Museum - 1895 41344

Georgia State University Art Gallery, University Plaza, 10 Peachtree Center Av, Atlanta, GA 30303 - T: (404) 651-2257, 651-3424, Fax: (404) 651-1779, E-mail: cathybyrd@gsu.edu, Internet: www.gsu.

edu/~wwwart/pages/const_gallery.html. Dir.: Cathy Byrd, Cur.: Ann England
Public Gallery / Fine Arts Museum / University Museum - 1970 41345

Gilbert House, 2238 Perkerson Rd SW, Atlanta, GA 30315 - T: (404) 766-9049, Fax: (404) 765-2806. Dir.: Erin Bailey
Decorative Arts Museum / Historical Museum - 1984 41346

Global Health Odyssey, 1600 Clifton Rd, NE-MS A14, Atlanta, GA 30333 - T: (404) 639-0830, Fax: (404) 639-0834, E-mail: global@cdc.gov, Internet: www.cdc.gov/global. Dir.: Judy M. Gantt
Historical Museum - 1996
Hist of Public Health Service and Disease Control, protection of health 41347

High Museum of Art, 1280 Peachtree St NE, Atlanta, GA 30309 - T: (404) 733-4000, Fax: (404) 733-4529, Internet: www.high.org. Dir.: Michael Shapiro, Chief Cur.: David Brenneman, Cur.: Carrie Przybilla (Modern and Contemporary Art), Stephen Harrison (Decorative Arts), Sylvia Yount (American Art), Tom Southall (Photography), Linda Dubler (Media Arts), Lynne Spriggs (Folk Arts), Carol Thompson (African Art)
Fine Arts Museum - 1926
Audiovisual and film, decorative arts, paintings, photographs, prints, drawings, graphic arts, sculpture 41348

The Margaret Mitchell House and Museum, 990 Peachtree St, Atlanta, GA 30309-3964 - T: (404) 249-7015, Fax: (404) 249-9388, E-mail: mary_rosetaylor@gwtw.org, Internet: www.gwtw.org. C.E.O.: Mary Rose Taylor
Historical Museum - 1990 41349

Martin Luther King jr. Center for Nonviolent Social Change, 449 Auburn Av NE, Atlanta, GA 30312 - T: (404) 526-8900, Fax: (404) 526-8969, E-mail: information@thekingcenter.org, Internet: www.thekingcenter.org. Pres.: Dexter Scott King
Historical Museum - 1968
History at the Martin Luther King, Jr. National Historic Site - educational center, archives 41350

Martin Luther King jr. National Historic Site and Preservation District, 450 Auburn Av NE, Atlanta, GA 30312 - T: (404) 331-5190, Fax: (404) 730-3112, Internet: www.nps.gov/malu. Dir.: Frank Catroppa, Sc. Staff: Dean Rowley (History)
Historical Museum / Historic Site - 1980
Neighborhood in which Dr. Martin Luther King, Jr. grew up, incl birthplace, boyhood home, church and gravesite 41351

Michael C. Carlos Museum, Emory University, 571 S Kilgo St, Atlanta, GA 30322 - T: (404) 727-4282, Fax: (404) 727-4292, E-mail: aghirsc@emory.edu, Internet: www.emory.edu/carlos. Dir.: Catherine Howett Smith, Cur.: Dr. Peter Lacovara (Ancient Art), Dr. Bonna D. Wescoat (Classical Art), Dr. Gay Robins (Egyptian Art), Dr. Rebecca Stone-Miller (Pre-Columbian Art), Dr. Monique Seefried (Near Eastern Art), Dr. Sidney Kasfir (African Art), Sc. Staff: Therese O'Gorman (Conservation)
Fine Arts Museum / University Museum / Archaeological Museum - 1920
Arts, archaeology 41352

Museum of the Jimmy Carter Library, 441 Freedom Pkwy, Atlanta, GA 30307 - T: (404) 331-3942, Fax: (404) 730-2215, E-mail: library@carter.nara.gov, Internet: www.jimmycarterlibrary.org. Dir.: Jay E. Hakes, Cur.: Sylvia Mansour Naguib
Library with Exhibitions - 1986
Presidential library 41353

Nexus Contemporary Art Center → Atlanta Contemporary Art Center and Nexus Press

Oglethorpe University Museum of Art, 4484 Peachtree Rd NE, Atlanta, GA 30319 - T: (404) 364-8555, Fax: (404) 364-8556, E-mail: museum@oglethorpe.edu, Internet: museum.oglethorpe.edu. Dir.: Lloyd Nick
Fine Arts Museum / University Museum - 1993 41354

Photographic Investments Gallery, 3977 Briarcliff Rd, Atlanta, GA 30345 - T: (404) 320-1012, Fax: (404) 320-3465, E-mail: ecsymmes@aol.com. Dir.: Edwin C. Symmes
Fine Arts Museum - 1979
Photography Art 41355

Robert C. Williams American Museum of Papermaking, 500 10th St NW, Atlanta, GA 30318 - T: (404) 894-7840, Fax: (404) 894-4778, E-mail: cindy.bowden@ipst.edu, Internet: www.ipst.edu/amp. Dir.: Cindy Bowden, Cur.: Teri Williams
Science&Tech Museum - 1936
Paper technology 41356

Salvation Army Southern Historical Museum, 1032 Metropolitan Pkwy SW, Atlanta, GA 30310-3488 - T: (404) 752-7578, Fax: (404) 753-1932, E-mail: salmerritt@aol.com, Internet: www.salvationarmysouth.org/history.htm. Dir.: Jacklyn Campbell
Religious Arts Museum - 1986
Religion 41357

Science and Technology Museum of Atlanta, 395 Piedmont Av NE, Atlanta, GA 30308 - T: (404) 522-5500 ext 202, Fax: (404) 525-6906, E-mail: tsmith@scitrek.org, Internet: www.scitrek.org. Pres./ C.E.O.: Lewis Massey
Natural History Museum / Science&Tech Museum - 1988 41358

Southeast Arts Center, 215 Lakewood Way SE, Atlanta, GA 30315 - T: (404) 658-6036, Fax: (404) 624-0746. Dir.: Alberta Ward
Fine Arts Museum
Photography, ceramics, handbuilt pottery and Raku Firing, jewelry-making, sewing, art for youth 41359

Spelman College Museum of Fine Art, 350 Spelman Ln SW, Atlanta, GA 30314 - T: (404) 681-3643, Fax: (404) 223-7665, E-mail: museum@spelman.edu, Internet: museum.spelman.edu. C.E.O.: Andrea D. Barnwell
Fine Arts Museum - 1996
African American and European art, African sculpture, textiles, crafts 41360

Spruill Gallery, 4681 Ashford Dunwoody Rd, Atlanta, GA 30338 - T: (770) 394-4019, Fax: (770) 394-3987, E-mail: sprgalry@bellsouth.net, Internet: www.spruillarts.org. Exec. Dir.: Sandra Bennett
Public Gallery - 1975 41361

William Breman Jewish Heritage Museum, 1440 Spring St NW, Atlanta, GA 30309 - T: (404) 873-1661, Fax: (404) 881-4009, E-mail: jleavey@atljf.org, Internet: atlantajewishmuseum.org. Dir.: Jane Leavey
Historical Museum - 1996
Georgia Jewish hist since 1845, Holocaust 41362

Wren's Nest House Museum, 1050 R.D. Abernathy Blvd SW, Atlanta, GA 30310-1812 - T: (404) 753-7735 ext 1, Fax: (404) 753-8535, E-mail: wrensnest@mindspring.com, Internet: www.accessatlanta.com/community/groups/wrensnest. Exec. Dir.: Sharon Crutchfield
Special Museum - 1909
Home of Joel Chandler Harris, creator of Uncle Remus and chronicler of stories 41363

Atlantic Beach NC

Fort Macon, E Fort Macon Rd, Atlantic Beach, NC 28512 - T: (919) 726-3775, Fax: (919) 726-2497, E-mail: ftmacon@starfishnet.com, Internet: www.clis.com/friends. Head: Jody A. Merritt
Historical Museum - 1924 41364

Atlantic City NJ

Atlantic City Historical Museum, New Jersey Av and The Boardwalk, Garden Pier, Atlantic City, NJ 08401 - T: (609) 347-5839, 344-1943, Fax: (609) 347-5284, E-mail: princetn@earthlink.net, Internet: www.acmuseum.org. Dir.: Vicki Gold Levi
Local Museum - 1982
Local hist 41365

Historic Gardner's Basin, 800 N New Hampshire Av, Atlantic City, NJ 08401 - T: (609) 348-2880, Fax: (609) 345-4238, Internet: www.oceanlifecenter.com. Exec. Dir.: Jack Keith
Local Museum - 1976 41366

Attleboro MA

Attleboro Area Industrial Museum, 42 Union St, Attleboro, MA 02703-2911 - T: (508) 222-3918, E-mail: info@industrialmuseum.com, Internet: www.industrialmuseum.com
Historical Museum - 1975 41367

Attleboro Museum, 86 Park St, Attleboro, MA 02703 - T: (508) 222-2644, Fax: (508) 226-4401, E-mail: museum@naisp.net, Internet: www.attleboromuseum.org. Pres.: Gerry Hickman, C.E.O.: Dore Van Dyke
Fine Arts Museum / Public Gallery - 1929
Regional American prints, paintings, civil war coll 41368

Atwater CA

Castle Air Museum, 5050 Santa Fe Rd, Atwater, CA 95301 - T: (209) 723-2178, Fax: (209) 723-0323, E-mail: cam@elite.net, Internet: www.elite.net/castle-air. Dir.: Jack Gotcher, Cur.: Dale Griffin
Military Museum / Science&Tech Museum - 1981
Aircraft history, 40 aircrafts esp. SR-71, B-17 41369

Auburn IN

Auburn-Cord-Duesenberg Museum, 1600 S Wayne St, Auburn, IN 46706 - T: (219) 925-1444, Fax: (219) 925-6266, Internet: www.acdmuseum.org. Pres.: Robert Sbarge
Science&Tech Museum - 1973
Transportation 41370

National Automotive and Truck Museum of the United States, 1000 Gordon M. Buehrig Pl, Auburn, IN 46706-0686 - T: (219) 925-9100, Fax: (219) 925-8695, E-mail: natmus@ctlnet.com, Internet: www.natmus.com
Science&Tech Museum - 1989 41371

Auburn ME

Androscoggin Historical Society Museum, County Bldg, 2 Turner St, Auburn, ME 04210-5978 - T: (207) 784-0586, E-mail: ltigapa@aol.com, Internet: www.rootsweb.com/~meandrhs. Pres. & Chm.: A.B. Palmer
Local Museum / Historical Museum - 1923
County history 41372

Auburn NY

Cayuga Museum, 203 Genesee St, Auburn, NY 13021 - T: (315) 253-8051, Fax: (315) 253-9829, E-mail: cayugamuseum@cayuganet.org, Internet: www.cayuganet.org/cayugamuseum. Dir.: Eileen McHugh, Cur.: Gina Stankiritz
Local Museum - 1936
Indian artefacts, history 41373

Schweinfurth Memorial Art Center, 205 Genesee St, Auburn, NY 13021 - T: (315) 255-1553, Fax: (315) 255-0871, E-mail: smac@baldcom.net, Internet: www.cayuganet.org/smac. Dir.: Donna Lamb, Cur.: Stephanie Bielejec
Fine Arts Museum - 1975 41374

Seward House, 33 South St, Auburn, NY 13021 - T: (315) 253-3351, Fax: (315) 253-3351, E-mail: info@sewardhouse.org, Internet: www.sewardhouse.org. Dir.: David Emerson, Cur.: Jeniffer Haines, Ass. Cur.: Paul McDonald
Local Museum - 1951 41375

Ward O'Hara Agricultural Museum of Cayuga County, E Lake Rd, Auburn, NY 13021 - T: (315) 252-7644, Fax: (315) 252-7644, E-mail: mrr423@dreamscape.com, Internet: www.cayuganet.org. C.E.O.: Norman Riley
Agriculture Museum - 1975
Agricultural 41376

Auburn WA

White River Valley Museum, 918 H St SE, Auburn, WA 98002 - T: (253) 939-2590, Fax: (253) 939-4523, Internet: www.wrvmuseum.org. C.E.O.: Patricia Cosgrove
Local Museum - 1959
Life of Native Americans and settlers, railroading, farming 41377

Auburn Hills MI

Walter P. Chrysler Museum, 1 Chrysler Dr, Auburn Hills, MI 48327-2766 - T: (248) 944-0432, Fax: (248) 944-0460, E-mail: BD28@daimlerchrysler.com, Internet: www.chryslerheritage.com. C.E.O.: Barry Dressel
Science&Tech Museum / Historical Museum
Founder of the automotive industry, historical vehicles 41378

Audubon PA

Mill Grove, The Audubon Wildlife Sanctuary, 1201 Audubon and Pawlings Rds, Audubon, PA 19407-7125 - T: (610) 666-5593, Fax: (610) 666-1490, E-mail: millgrove@mail.montcopa.org, Internet: www.montcopa.org/historicsites. C.E.O.: Linda S. Boice
Fine Arts Museum / Natural History Museum / Historical Museum - 1951 41379

Augusta GA

Augusta Museum of History, 560 Reynolds St, Augusta, GA 30901 - T: (706) 722-8454, Fax: (706) 724-5192, E-mail: amh@csra.net, Internet: www.augustamuseum.org. Dir.: Scott W. Loehr
Historical Museum - 1937
The past of Augusta, Georgia and its environs 41380

Augusta Richmond County Museum → Augusta Museum of History

Ezekiel Harris House, 1822 Broad St, Augusta, GA 30904 - T: (706) 724-0436, Fax: (706) 724-3083. C.E.O.: Erick D. Montgomery
Historical Museum - 1965 41381

Fort Discovery, 1 Seventh St, Augusta, GA 30901 - T: (800) 325-5445, Fax: (706) 821-0648, E-mail: info@www.nscdiscovery.org, Internet: www.nationalsciencecenter.org
Science&Tech Museum - 1997 41382

Gertrude Herbert Institute of Art, 506 Telfair St, Augusta, GA 30901 - T: (706) 722-5495, Fax: (706) 722-3670, E-mail: ghia@ghia.org, Internet: www.ghia.org. Pres.: Cheryl W. O'Keeffe, Dir.: Amy E. Meybohm
Fine Arts Museum - 1937
Paintings, sculptures, graphics 41383

Lucy Craft Laney Museum of Black History, 1116 Philips St, Augusta, GA 30901 - T: (706) 724-3576, E-mail: lclmuseum@4tscomputers.com, Internet: lucycraftmuseum.com. Exec. Dir.: Christine Miller-Betts
Ethnology Museum / Folklore Museum - 1991
African Americans from the Augusta and Central Savannah River area education, religion, science sports, entertainment and medicine 41384

Meadow Garden Museum, 1320 Independence Dr, Augusta, GA 30901-1038 - T: (706) 724-4174
Historical Museum
1791-1804 residence of George Walton, signer of the Declaration of Independence 41385

Morris Museum of Art, 1 Tenth St, Augusta, GA 30901-0100 - T: (706) 724-7501, Fax: (706) 724-7612, E-mail: mormuse@themorris.org, Internet: www.themorris.org. Dir.: Louise Keith Claussen
Fine Arts Museum - 1985 41386

Augusta KS

Augusta Historical Museum, 303 State, Augusta, KS 67010 - T: (316) 775-5655, E-mail: augustahm@earthlink.net. Exec. Dir.: Diana Herrman, Pres.: Virginia Belt
Local Museum - 1938
Local history, genealogy 41387

Augusta ME

Blaine House, 192 State St, Augusta, ME 04330 - T: (207) 287-2121. Head: Sue J. Plummer
Local Museum
Blaine House, governer's mansion of Maine 41388

Jewett Hall Gallery, c/o University of Maine at Augusta, 46 University Dr, Augusta, ME 04330 - T: (207) 61-3243, Fax: (207) 621-3293, E-mail: kareng@maine.edu. Dir.: Karen Gilg
Fine Arts Museum - 1970
Drawings, painting, outdoor sculpture 41389

Maine State Museum, 83 State House Station, State House Complex, Augusta, ME 04333-0083 - T: (207) 287-2301, Fax: (207) 287-6633, E-mail: museum@state.me.us, Internet: www.state.me.us/museum/. Dir.: Joseph R. Phillips, Archaeologist: Bruce Bourque, Steven Cox, Robert Lewis, Cur.: Edwin Churchill, Julia Hunter (Fine Arts, Graphic Arts and Archives), Laurie LaBar (Historic Collections), Gary Hoyle (Natural History)
Local Museum - 1837
History, natural history, archaeology, fine arts, graphics 41390

Old Fort Western, 16 Cony St, Augusta, ME 04330 - T: (207) 626-2385, Fax: (207) 626-2304, E-mail: oldfort@oldfortwestern.org, Internet: www.oldfortwestern.org. Dir./Cur.: Jay Adams
Historical Museum - 1922
Historic house 41391

Auriesville NY

Kateri Galleries, National Shrine of the North American Martyrs, off Rte 5S, Auriesville, NY 12016 - T: (518) 853-3033, Fax: (518) 853-3051, E-mail: office@martyshrine.org, Internet: www.martyshrine.org. Dir.: John G. Marzolf, Ass. Dir.: John J. Paret, Cur.: Owen Smith
Religious Arts Museum - 1950 41392

Aurora CO

Aurora History Museum, 15001 E Alameda Dr, Aurora, CO 80012-1547 - T: (303) 739-6660, Fax: (303) 739-6657, E-mail: auroramuseum@ci.aurora.co.us, Internet: www.aurora-museum.org. Dir.: Gordon Davis, Sc. Staff: Gordon Davis, Peter Faris, Michelle Bahe, Mary Ellen Schoonover
Local Museum - 1979
History 41393

Aurora IL

Aurora Historical Museum, Cedar and Oak Sts, Aurora, IL 60506 - T: (630) 897-9029, Fax: (630) 906-0657, E-mail: ahs@pdqlink.com, Internet: www.aurora.il.us/ahs. Dir.: John R. Jaros, Cur.: Dennis Buck
Local Museum - 1906
Local history 41394

Aurora Public Art Commission, 20 E Downer Pl, Aurora, IL 60507 - T: (630) 844-3623, 906-0654, Fax: (630) 892-0741, E-mail: rchurch@ci.aurora.il.us. Dir./Cur.: Rena J. Church
Fine Arts Museum - 1996
Art 41395

Blackberry Farm-Pioneer Village, 100 S Barnes Rd, Aurora, IL 60506 - T: (630) 264-7408, Fax: (630) 892-1661, E-mail: fupd@aol.com, Internet: www.foxvalleyparkdistrict.org. Dir.: Lorraine Beasley, Cur.: Carol Nordbrock
Historical Museum / Agriculture Museum - 1969
Village, agriculture 41396

Grand Army of the Republic Memorial and Veteran's Military Museum, 23 E Downer Pl, Aurora, IL 60505 - T: (630) 897-7221. Pres.: Charles Gates
Military Museum - 1875
Civil, Spanish American, Korean, Vietnam wars, WW 1 and 2 colls 41397

Schingoethe Center for Native American Cultures, Aurora University, Dunham Hall, 347 S Gladstone, Aurora, IL 60506-4892 - T: (630) 844-5402, Fax: (630) 844-8884, E-mail: museum@aurora.edu, Internet: www.aurora.edu/museum. Dir.: Michael P. Sawdey, Cur.: Mary C. Kennedy (Collections), Meg Bero (Education)
University Museum / Ethnology Museum / Folklore Museum - 1989
Native American cultures 41398

Scitech, 18 W Benton, Aurora, IL 60506 - T: (630) 859-3434 ext 210, Fax: (630) 859-8692, E-mail: ronen@scitech.mus.il.us, Internet: scitech.mus.il.us. Exec. Dir.: Dr. Ronen Mir
Science&Tech Museum / Natural History Museum - 1988
Weather, light and color, heat, mathematics, sound and music, magnets and electricity, physics, chemistry, biology, astronomy and nuclear physics 41399

Aurora IN

Hillforest House Museum, 213 Fifth St, Aurora, IN 47001 - T: (812) 926-0087, Fax: (812) 926-1075, E-mail: hillforest@seidata.com, Internet: www.hillforest.org. Pres.: Deannaopher Hacker
Historical Museum - 1956
Victorian Ohio River Valley mansion 41400

Aurora NE

Plainsman Museum, 210 16th St, Aurora, NE 68818 - T: (402) 694-6531, E-mail: smpolak@hamilton.net, Internet: www.plainsmanmuseum.org. Pres.: Wesley C. Huenefeld, Dir./Cur.: Sarah Polak
Local Museum - 1935 41401

Aurora OH

Aurora Historical Society Museum, 115 E Pioneer Trail, Aurora, OH 44202 - T: (330) 562-6502, E-mail: lsc5128446@aol.com. Pres.: Lois H. Schoch
Local Museum - 1968 41402

Austin MN

The Spam Museum, 1937 Spam Blvd, Austin, MN 55912 - T: (507) 437-5100
Special Museum
Cans of SPAM from around the world, photographs 41403

Austin TX

Austin Children's Museum, 201 Colorado St, Austin, TX 78701-3922 - T: (512) 472-2494, 2499, Fax: (512) 472-2495, E-mail: griderg@austinkids.org, Internet: www.austinkids.org. C.E.O.: Gwendolyn Crider
Special Museum - 1983 41404

Austin History Center, 810 Guadalupe St, Austin, TX 78701 - T: (512) 499-7480, Fax: (512) 499-7483, E-mail: ahc@coa1.ci.austin.tx.us, Internet: www.ci.austin.tx.us. Pres.: Amalia Rodriguez-Mendoza
Local Museum - 1955
Local history - library 41405

Austin Museum of Art, 823 Congress Av, Ste 100, Austin, TX 78701 - T: (512) 495-9224, Fax: (512) 495-9029, E-mail: info@amoa.org, Internet: www.amoa.org. Dir.: Dana Friis-Hansen, Cur.: Judith Sims (Film and Video), Eva Buttacavoli (Education)
Fine Arts Museum - 1961
Art 41406

Austin Nature and Science Center, 301 Nature Center Dr, Austin, TX 78746 - T: (512) 327-8180 ext 25, Fax: (512) 327-8745, Internet: www.ci.austin.tx.us/naturescience
Natural History Museum - 1960
Native Texas mammals, fish, birds, reptiles and insects, microscope tables, Eco-Detective 41407

Center for American History, c/o University of Texas, Sid Richardson Hall, Unit 2, Austin, TX 78712 - T: (512) 495-4515, Fax: (512) 495-4542, E-mail: cahref@uts.cc.utexas.edu, Internet: www.cah.utexas.edu. Dir.: Dr. Don Carleton, H.G. Dulaney (Sam Rayburn Library and Museum), Ass. Dir.: Kate Adams, Alison Beck, Cur.: Lynn Bell
Historical Museum
History 41408

Elisabet Ney Museum, 304 E 44th St, Austin, TX 78751 - T: (512) 458-2255, Fax: (512) 453-0638, E-mail: enm@ci.anstin.tx.us, Internet: www.cityofaustin/elisabetney. Dir./Cur.: Mary Collins Blackmon
Fine Arts Museum - 1911
Sculptures 41409

Fine Arts Exhibitions, c/o Saint Edward's University, 3001 S Congress Av, Austin, TX 78704 - T: (512) 488-8400 ext 1338, Fax: (512) 448-8492. Dir.: Stan Irvin
University Museum / Public Gallery - 1961 41410

The French Legation Museum, 802 San Marcos St, Austin, TX 78702 - T: (512) 472-8180, Fax: (512) 472-9457, E-mail: dubois@french-legation.mus.tx.us, Internet: www.french-legation.mus.tx.us. Head: Pete Wehmeyer
Historical Museum - 1956
History 41411

Jack S. Blanton Museum of Art, c/o University of Texas at Austin, 23rd and San Jacinto, Austin, TX 78712-1205 - T: (512) 471-7324, Fax: (512) 471-7023, E-mail: blantonmuseum@utexas.edu, Internet: www.blantonmuseum.org. Dir.: Jessie Otto Hite, Cur.: Jonathan Bober (Prints and Drawings, European Painting), Annette DiMeo Carlozzi (American Art), Anne Manning (Education), Cons.: Sara McElroy
Fine Arts Museum / University Museum - 1963
Art 41412

Jones Center for Contemporary Art, c/o Texas Fine Arts Association, 3809-B W 35th St, Austin, TX 78701 - T: (512) 453-5312, Fax: (512) 459-4830, E-mail: txfineart@aol.com, Internet: www.tfaa.org. Dir.: Sue Graze
University Museum / Fine Arts Museum - 1911 41413

Jourdan-Bachman Pioneer Farm, 11418 Sprinkle Cut Off Rd, Austin, TX 78754 - T: (512) 837-1215, Fax: (512) 837-4503, E-mail: john.hirsch@ci.austin.tx.us, Internet: www.pioneerfarm.org. Dir.: John Hirsch
Agriculture Museum - 1975
Historical agriculture 41414

Julia C. Butridge Gallery, 1110 Barton Springs Rd, Austin, TX 78704 - T: (512) 397-1455, Fax: (512) 397-1460, E-mail: megan.weiler@ci.austin.tx.us, Internet: www.ci.austin.tx.us/dougherty/butridge.htm
Public Gallery 41415

Lyndon Baines Johnson Museum, 2313 Red River St, Austin, TX 78705-5702 - T: (512) 916-5137 ext 0, Fax: (512) 916-5170, E-mail: library.johnson@nara.gov, Internet: www.lbjlib.utexas.edu. Dir.: Betty Sue Flowers, Cur.: Sandor Cohen
Library with Exhibitions - 1971
Presidential library 41416

Mexic-Arte Museum, 419 Congress St, Austin, TX 78701 - T: (512) 480-9373, Fax: (512) 480-8626, E-mail: mexicarte@inetmail.att.net, Internet: www.main.org/mexic-arte. Exec. Dir.: Sylvia Orozco
Fine Arts Museum - 1984
Art, focus on Mexican and Latin American culture 41417

Neill-Cochran Museum House, 2310 San Gabriel St, Austin, TX 78705 - T: (512) 478-2335, E-mail: ncmuseum@flash.net, Internet: www.neill-cochranmuseum.com. Head: Kathleen Peterson-Moussaid
Local Museum - 1956
Historic house 41418

O. Henry Home and Museum, 409 E. 5th St, Austin, TX 78701 - T: (512) 472-1903, Fax: (512) 472-7102, E-mail: valerie.bennett@ci.austin.tx.us, Internet: www.ci.austin.tx.us/parks/ohenry.htm. Dir.: Valerie Bennett
Local Museum - 1934
Historic house 41419

Texas Governor's Mansion, 1010 Colorado, Austin, TX 78701 - T: (512) 463-5518, 463-5516, Internet: www.txfgm.org
Local Museum
Historic house 41420

Texas Memorial Museum of Science and History, 2400 Trinity, Austin, TX 78705 - T: (512) 232-5504, Fax: (512) 232-5504, E-mail: tmmweb@uts.cc.utexas.edu, Internet: www.texasmemorialmusem.org. Dir.: Edward C. Theriot, Timothy Rowe (Vertebrate Paleontology Lab), Cur.: Dean A. Hendrickson (Ichthyology), Chris J. Durden (Entomology), James R. Reddell (Anthropods), David C. Cannatella (Herpetology)
Historical Museum / Ethnology Museum / Natural History Museum - 1936
Natural Science, cultural hist 41421

Texas Military Forces Museum, 2200 W 35th St, Austin, TX 78703 - T: (512) 782-5659, Fax: (512) 782-6750, E-mail: museum@agd.state.tx.us, Internet: www.kwanah.com/txmilmus. Cur.: John C.L. Scribner
Military Museum - 1992
Paintings, military hist of Texas, vehicles, equip, uniforms 41422

Texas Music Museum, 1109 E 11th St, Austin, TX 78761 - T: (512) 472-8891, Fax: (512) 471-9600, E-mail: cshorkey@mail.utexas.edu, Internet: www.texasmusicmuseum.org
Music Museum - 1984
Music instrument-makers, recording and reproduction devices, music art 41423

Umlauf Sculpture Garden and Museum, 605 Robert E. Lee Rd, Austin, TX 78704 - T: (512) 445-5582, Fax: (512) 445-5583, E-mail: info@umlaufsculpture.org, Internet: www.umlaufsculpture.org. Dir.: Nelie Plourde
Fine Arts Museum - 1991
Sculpture 41424

Women and Their Work, 1710 Lavaca St, Austin, TX 78701 - T: (512) 477-1064, Fax: (512) 477-1090, E-mail: wtw@eden.com, Internet: www.womenandtheirwork.org. Dir.: Chris Cowden
Fine Arts Museum - 1978 41425

Avalon CA

Catalina Island Museum, Casino Bldg, Avalon, CA 90704 - T: (310) 510-2414, Fax: (310) 510-2780, E-mail: museum@catalinas.net, Internet: www.catalina.com/museum. Dir.: Stacey A. Otte
Historical Museum / Archaeological Museum - 1953
Regional history 41426

Avella PA

Meadowcroft Museum of Rural Life, Historical Society of Western Pennsylvania, 401 Meadowcroft Rd, Avella, PA 15312 - T: (724) 587-3412, E-mail: mcroft@cobweb.net, Internet: www.meadowcroftmuseum.org
Local Museum
History of Life on the land in Western Pennsylvania, archeological site, 19th c village 41427

Avon CT

Avon Historical Society Museum, 8 E Main St, Avon, CT 06001 - T: (860) 678-7621, E-mail: oakeshoward@aol.com, Internet: www.avonct.com. C.E.O.: Nora Howard
Local Museum
Local hist - archives 41428

Aztec NM

Aztec Museum and Pioneer Village, 125 N Main Av, Aztec, NM 87410-1923 - T: (505) 334-9829, Fax: (505) 334-7648, E-mail: aztecmuseum@cyberport.com, Internet: www.aztecnm.com/museum/museum-index.htm. Dir.: Barry Coopen
Historical Museum - 1963 41429

Aztec Ruins, Ruins Rd, Aztec, NM 87410 - T: (505) 334-6174, Fax: (505) 334-6372, E-mail: azru_curatorial@nps.gov, Internet: www.nps.gov/azru
Archaeological Museum - 1923
Archaeological materials of Chaco and Mesa Verde Anasazi 41430

Bahama NC

Historic Stagville, 5825 Old Oxford Hwy, Bahama, NC 27503 - T: (919) 620-0120, Fax: (919) 620-0422, E-mail: stagvill@sprynet.com, Internet: www.ah.dcr.state.nc.us/sections/do/stagvill/
Agriculture Museum - 1977
Period furnishings, farm implements, plantation house, slave cabins, barn 41431

Bailey NC

The Country Doctor Museum, 6629 Vance St, Bailey, NC 27807 - T: (252) 235-4165. Pres.: Isabel H. Gover, C.E.O.: Carolyn B. Bissette
Historical Museum - 1967
Practice of medicine 18th-19th c 41432

Bainbridge OH

Dr. John Harris Dental Museum, 208 W Main St, Bainbridge, OH 45612 - T: (513) 561-7009, E-mail: jgotts@cinci.rr.com. Pres.: Dr. Jack W. Gottschalk
Special Museum - 1939 41433

Baird TX

Callahan County Pioneer Museum, 100 W 4th, B-1, Baird, TX 79504-5305 - T: (915) 854-1718, Fax: (915) 854-1227, E-mail: callahancl@bitstreet.com. C.E.O.: Joyce McAuley, Cur.: Sonia Walker
Local Museum - 1940
Local hist 41434

Baker MT

O'Fallon Historical Museum, 723 S Main St, Baker, MT 59313 - T: (406) 778-3265, Internet: www.midrivers.com/~bakelo. Pres.: Harold Jensen, Dir.: Lora Heyen
Historical Museum - 1968 41435

Baker NV

Great Basin National Park, 100 Great Basin, Baker, NV 89311-9701 - T: (775) 234-7331, Fax: (775) 234-7269, E-mail: grba_administration@nps.gov, Internet: www.nps.gov/grba
Natural History Museum - 1986
Speleothems, historical found in cave, botany 41436

Baker City OR

National Historic Oregon Trail Interpretive Center, Oregon Hwy 86, Baker City, OR 97814 - T: (541) 523-1845, Fax: (541) 523-1834, E-mail: nhotic@or.blm.gov, Internet: www.or.blm.gov/nhotic. Dir.: Gay Ernst, Cur.: Sarah LeCompte
Local Museum - 1992 41437

Oregon Trail Regional Museum, 2180 Grove St, Baker City, OR 97814 - T: (541) 523-9308, Fax: (541) 523-0244, E-mail: jjmotrm@oregontrail.net, Internet: www.bakercounty.org
Historical Museum - 1982
Original settlers artifacts 41438

Bakersfield CA

Bakersfield Museum of Art, 1930 R St, Bakersfield, CA 93301 - T: (661) 323-7219, Fax: (661) 323-7266, Internet: www.bmao.org. Exec. Dir.: Charles G. Meyer
Fine Arts Museum - 1987
Paintings, sculpture, graphics, Marion Osborn Cunningham coll, serigraphs 41439

Kern County Museum, 3801 Chester Av, Bakersfield, CA 93301 - T: (661) 852-5000, Fax: (661) 322-6415, E-mail: kcmuseum@kern.org, Internet: www.kcmuseum.org. Dir.: Carola Rupert Enriquez, Cur.: Jeff Nickell
Local Museum - 1945
Local history, culture - children's museum 41440

Todd Madigan Gallery, California State University Bakersfield, 9001 Stockdale Hwy, Bakersfield, CA 93311 - T: (661) 664-3093, Fax: (661) 665-6901, Internet: www.csub.edu/Art
Public Gallery 41441

Baldwin NY

Baldwin Historical Society Museum, 1980 Grand Av, Baldwin, NY 11510 - T: (516) 223-6900. Dir.: Jack Bryck, Cur.: Gary R. Hammond
Local Museum - 1971 41442

Baldwin City KS

Old Castle Museum, Baker University, 515 Fifth St, Baldwin City, KS 66006, mail addr: POB 65, Baldwin City, KS 66006-0065 - T: (913) 594-6809, Fax: (913) 594-2522, E-mail: day@harvey.bakeru.edu, Internet: www.bakeru.edu. Dir.: Brenda Day, Asst. Dir.: Jane Richards, Pres.: Dan Lembert
Historical Museum - 1953
Original Santa Fe Trail Post Office, replica of Kibbee cabin 41443

William A. Quayle Bible Collection, Baker University, Collins Library, Spencer Quayle Wing, 8th and Grove Sts, Baldwin City, KS 66006 - T: (913) 594-8414, Fax: (913) 594-6721. Dir.: Dr. John M. Forbes
University Museum / Religious Arts Museum / Library with Exhibitions - 1925
Rare Bibles 41444

Ballston Spa NY

Brookside Saratoga County Historical Society, 6 Charlton St, Ballston Spa, NY 12020 - T: (518) 885-4000, Fax: (518) 885-7085, E-mail: info@brooksidemuseum.org, Internet: www.brooksidemuseum.org. Dir.: Susie Kilpatrick, Cur.: Linda Gorham
Local Museum - 1962 41445

Balsam Lake WI

Polk County Museum, Main St, Balsam Lake, WI 54810 - T: (715) 485-3292, E-mail: darose@centurytel.net, Internet: www.co.polk.wi.us/museum.. C.E.O.: Darrell Kittleson, Cur.: Willis D. Erickson
Local Museum - 1960
Local hist 41446

Baltimore MD

The Albin O. Kuhn Gallery, University of Maryland-Baltimore County, 1000 Hilltop Circle, Baltimore, MD 21250 - T: (410) 455-2270, Fax: (410) 455-1153, Internet: www.umbc.edu/library. Chief Cur.: Tom Beck, Cur.: Cynthia Wayne
University Museum / Fine Arts Museum - 1975
Art 41447

American Visionary Art Museum, 800 Key Hwy, Baltimore, MD 21230 - T: (410) 244-1900, Fax: (410) 244-5858, E-mail: AVAM.org, Internet: www.avam.org. Pres.: Rebecca Hoffberger, Dir.: Mark Ward
Fine Arts Museum - 1995
Art 41448

Archaeological Collection, c/o Johns Hopkins University, 3400 North Charles St, Baltimore, MD 21218 - T: (410) 516-7561. Dir.: Dr. Betsy Bryan (Near Eastern and Egyptian Art), Cur.: Dr. Eunice Maguire
Archaeological Museum / University Museum - 1876
Egyptian, Roman antiquities 41449

The B & O Railroad Museum, Smithsonian Institution, 901 W Pratt St, Baltimore, MD 21223 - T: (410) 752-2490, Fax: (410) 752-2499, E-mail: info@borail.org, Internet: www.borail.org. Dir.: Courtney B. Wilson, Chief Cur.: Ed Williams, Cur.: Shawn Herne
Historical Museum / Science&Tech Museum - 1953
Transport, site of c.1830 B & O Railroad's Mt Clare shops, site of first common carrier rail service in the US, which received SFB Morse's first long distance telegraph message in 1844 41450

Babe Ruth Birthplace & Museum, 216 Emory St, Baltimore, MD 21230 - T: (410) 727-1539, Fax: (410) 727-1652, Internet: www.baberuthmuseum.com. Dir.: Michael L. Gibbons, Cur.: Gregory Schwalenberg
Special Museum / Fine Arts Museum - 1974
Sports 41451

Baltimore Civil War Museum, 601 President St, Baltimore, MD 21202 - T: (410) 385-5188, E-mail: Museum@mdhs.org, Internet: www.mdhs.org. Dir.: Paul O'Neil
Historical Museum / Military Museum - 1995 41452

Baltimore Maritime Museum, Pier 3, Pratt St, Baltimore, MD 21202 - T: (410) 396-3453, Fax: (410) 396-3393, E-mail: admin@baltomaritimemuseum.org, Internet: www.baltomaritimemuseum.org. Dir.: John Kellett
Historical Museum - 1982
Coast Guard cutter, WW II submarine, lightship, lighthouse 41453

The Baltimore Museum of Art, 10 Art Museum Dr, Baltimore, MD 21218-3898 - T: (410) 396-7100, Fax: (410) 396-7153, Internet: www.artbma.org. Dir.: Doreen Bolger, Dep. Dir.: Allison Perkins (Education, Interpretation), Robin Churchill (Finance, Planning), Becca Seitz (Marketing), Judith Gibbs (Development), Alan Dirican (Operations), Jay Fisher (Cultural Affairs, Cur. Prints, Drawings, Photographs), Cur.: James Abbott (Decorative Art), Susan Dackerman (Prints, Drawings, Photographs), Frederick Lamp (Arts of Africa, Asia, the Americas and Oceania), Sona Johnston (Painting, Sculpture before 1900), Katherine Rothkopf (Painting,

Sculpture), Assoc. Cur.: Anita Jones (Textiles), Darsie Alexander (Prints, Drawings, Photographs), Frances Klapthor (Arts of Africa, Asia, the Americas and Oceania)
Fine Arts Museum - 1914
Arts of America, Africa, Asia, Oceania, decorative arts, drawings, prints, photography - sculpture gardens 41454

Baltimore Museum of Industry, 1415 Key Hwy, Inner Harbour S, Baltimore, MD 21230 - T: (410) 727-4808, Fax: (410) 727-4869, E-mail: chboyd@thebmi.org, Internet: www.thebmi.org. Dir.: William H. Cole
Historical Museum / Science&Tech Museum - 1981
History, industry, housed in a water front oyster cannery 41455

Baltimore Public Works Museum, 751 Eastern Av, Baltimore, MD 21202 - T: (410) 396-1509, 396-5565, Fax: (410) 545-6781, E-mail: bpwm@erols.com. Exec. Dir.: Mari B. Ross, Dir.: Vince Pompa
Historical Museum / Science&Tech Museum - 1982
Urban environmental history, sewage pumping stn 41456

Baltimore Streetcar Museum, 1901 Falls Rd, Baltimore, MD 21211 - T: (410) 547-0264, Fax: (410) 547-0264, Internet: www.baltimoremd.com/streetcar. Pres.: John J. O'Neill
Special Museum / Science&Tech Museum - 1966
Transport, RR Terminal 41457

Baltimore's Black American Museum, 1767 Carswell St, Baltimore, MD 21218 - T: (410) 243-9600
Ethnology Museum / Historical Museum 41458

The Benjamin Banneker Museum, 300 Oella Av, Baltimore, MD 21228 - T: (410) 887-1081, Fax: (410) 203-2747, Internet: www.thefriendsofbanneker.org. Dir.: Steven Lee
Fine Arts Museum / Natural History Museum - 1998
Traditional and contemporary art from Africa and the Americas, plants 41459

Community College Art Gallery, 2901 Liberty Heights Av, Baltimore, MD 21215 - T: (410) 462-8000, Fax: (410) 462-7614
Fine Arts Museum - 1965 41460

Contemporary Museum, 100 W Centre St, Baltimore, MD 21201 - T: (410) 783-5720, Fax: (410) 783-5722, E-mail: info@contemporary.org, Internet: www.contemporary.org. Dir.: Gary Sangster, Dep. Dir.: Dana Johns, Ass. Cur.: Adam Lerner
Fine Arts Museum - 1989 41461

Cylburn Nature Museum, 4915 Greenspring Av, Baltimore, MD 21209 - T: (410) 367-2217, Fax: (410) 367-7112, E-mail: caa4915@bcpl.net, Internet: www.cylburnorganization.org. Pres.: Jane Baldwin, Dir.: Patsy Perlman
Natural History Museum - 1954
Natural history, horticulture 41462

Dr. Samuel D. Harris National Museum of Dentistry, 31 S Greene St, Baltimore, MD 21201 - T: (410) 706-8314, Fax: (410) 706-8313, E-mail: rfetter@dentalmuseum.umaryland.edu, Internet: www.dentalmuseum.org. Exec. Dir.: Rosemary Fetter, Cur.: Dr. John M. Hyson
Special Museum - 1840
Dentistry 41463

Edgar Allan Poe House and Museum, 203 N Amity St, Baltimore, MD 21223 - T: (410) 396-7932, Fax: (410) 396-5662, E-mail: eapo@baltimorecity.gov. Cur.: Jeff Jerome
Special Museum - 1923
Home of Edgar Allan Poe 41464

Eubie Blake National Jazz Museum and Cultural Center, 847 N Howard St, Baltimore, MD 21201 - T: (410) 225-3110, Fax: (410) 225-3139, E-mail: eubieblake@erols.com, Internet: www.eubieblake.org. Pres.: James Crokett, Exec. Dir.: Kenny Murphy
Music Museum - 1983 41465

Evergreen House, Johns Hopkins University, 4545 N Charles St, Baltimore, MD 21210 - T: (410) 516-0341, Fax: (410) 516-0864, E-mail: ckelly@jhu.edu, Internet: www.jhu.edu/historichouses. Dir.: Cindy Kelly, Ass. Dir.: Jane Katz
Historical Museum - 1952
Historic House, purchased for the Garrett family in 1878 41466

Fort McHenry, End of E Fort Av, Baltimore, MD 21230-5393 - T: (410) 962-4290, Fax: (410) 962-2500, E-mail: fomc_superintendent@nps.gov., Internet: www.nps.gov/fomc. Dir.: Laura Joss, Sc. Staff: Scott Sheads (History)
Historic Site / Historical Museum / Military Museum - 1933
Site of bombardment which inspired Francis Scott Key to write "The Star-Spangled Banner", 1861-65 site of Union Prison Camp, 1917-25 U.S. Army General Hospital 2 41467

Great Blacks in Wax Museum, 1601-03 E North Av, Baltimore, MD 21213-1409 - T: (410) 563-3404, Fax: (410) 675-5040, E-mail: jmartin@greatblacksinwax.org, Internet: www.greatblacksinwax.org. Dir.: Dr. Joanne M. Martin, Dep. Dir.: Trevis Henson
Historical Museum / Decorative Arts Museum - 1983
History, wax figures 41468

Heritage Museum, Hamlet Court, 4509 Prospect Circle, Baltimore, MD 21216 - T: (410) 664-6711, Fax: (410) 664-6711, E-mail: heritagemuseum@startpower.net. Dir.: Steven Lee
Historical Museum - 1991
Hist and culture 41469

Homewood House Museum, Johns Hopkins University, 3400 N Charles St, Baltimore, MD 21218 - T: (410) 516-5589, Fax: (410) 516-7859, E-mail: homewood@jhu.edu, Internet: www.jhu.edu/historichouses. Dir.: Cindy Kelly, Cur.: Catherine Arthur
University Museum / Historical Museum / Museum of Classical Antiquities - 1987 41470

James E. Lewis Museum of Art, Morgan State University, Carl Murphy Fine Arts Center, Coldspring Ln and Hillen Rd, Baltimore, MD 21251 - T: (410) 319-3030, Fax: (410) 319-4024, E-mail: gtenabe@moac.morgan.edu, Internet: www.morgan.edu. Dir.: Gabriel S. Tenabe
Fine Arts Museum / University Museum - 1955
Arts 41471

Jewish Museum of Maryland, 15 Lloyd St, Baltimore, MD 21202 - T: (410) 732-6400, Fax: (410) 732-6451, E-mail: info@jewishmuseummd.org, Internet: www.jewishmuseummd.org. Dir.: Avi Y. Decter, Simone Ellin (Program), Deborah Cardin (Education), Cur.: Melissa Martens
Historical Museum - 1960
Two restored synagogues - research archives, library 41472

The Johns Hopkins University Archaeological Collection, 129 Gilman Hall, 34th and Charles, Baltimore, MD 21218 - T: (410) 516-8402, Fax: (410) 516-5218. Cur.: Dr. Bryan Betsy (Classical, Near Eastern and Egyptian Antiquities), Cur.: Dr. Eunice Daughterman-Maguire
Museum of Classical Antiquities / University Museum / Archaeological Museum - 1884
Classical art, archaeology 41473

The Lacrosse Museum and National Hall of Fame, 113 W University Pkwy, Baltimore, MD 21210 - T: (410) 235-6882 ext 122, Fax: (410) 366-6735, E-mail: info@lacrosse.org, Internet: www.lacrosse.org. Dir.: Joshua W. Christian (Men's Division)
Folklore Museum / Special Museum - 1959
National Hall of Fame 41474

Lovely Lane Museum, 2200 Saint Paul St, Baltimore, MD 21218 - T: (410) 889-4458, Fax: (410) 889-1501, E-mail: lovinmus@bcpl.net, Internet: www.bwconf/org/archivehistory. Pres.: Dennis Whitmore, C.E.O.: Suni Johnson
Religious Arts Museum - 1855
Religion, methodist history, Strawbridge shrine 41475

Maryland Art Place, 8 Market Pl, Ste 100, Baltimore, MD 21202 - T: (410) 962-8565, Fax: (410) 244-8017, E-mail: map@mdartplace.org, Internet: www.mdartplace.org. Dir.: Julie Ann Cavnor
Public Gallery - 1982 41476

Maryland Historical Society Museum, 201 W Monument St, Baltimore, MD 21201 - T: (410) 685-3750, Fax: (410) 385-2105, E-mail: web.comments@mdhs.org, Internet: www.mdhs.org
Local Museum - 1844
Maryland portraits and landscapes, furniture, silver, China, glass, costumes, clocks, uniforms, textiles, Chesapeake Bay maritime coll, Civil War, prints, architectural drawings 41477

Maryland Institute Museum, College of Art Exhibitions, 1300 Mount Royal Av, Baltimore, MD 21217 - T: (410) 225-2280, Fax: (410) 225-2396, E-mail: whipps@mica.edu, Internet: www.mica.edu. Pres.: Fred Lazarus, Dir.: Will Hipps
Fine Arts Museum / University Museum - 1826
Art 41478

Maryland Science Center, 601 Light St, Baltimore, MD 21230 - T: (410) 685-5225, Fax: (410) 545-5974, E-mail: crowett@mdsci.org, Internet: www.mdsci.org. Exec. Dir.: Gregory Paul Andorfer
Science&Tech Museum - 1797
Science, technology - planetarium 41479

Meredith Gallery, 805 N Charles St, Baltimore, MD 21201 - T: (410) 837-3575, Fax: (410) 837-3577, Internet: www.meredithgallery.com. Dir.: Judith Lippman
Decorative Arts Museum - 1977 41480

Mount Clare Museum House, 1500 Washington Blvd, Baltimore, MD 21230 - T: (410) 837-3262, Fax: (410) 837-0251, E-mail: mtclare@msn.com, Internet: www.erols.com/mountclaremuseumhouse. Dir.: Jim Bartlinski
Historical Museum / Decorative Arts Museum - 1917
Mansion 41481

Mount Vernon Museum of Incandescent Lighting, 717 Washington Pl, Baltimore, MD 21201 - T: (410) 752-8586. Dir.: Hugh Francis Hicks
Science&Tech Museum - 1963
Science, technology, development of the electronic light bulb (1878-now) 41482

Museum for Contemporary Arts → Contemporary Museum

Museum of Maryland History, Maryland Historical Society, 201 W Monument St, Baltimore, MD 21201 - T: (410) 685-3750, Fax: (410) 385-2105, E-mail: mray@mdhs.org, Internet: www.mdhs.org. Dir.: Dennis A. Fiori, Cur.: Nancy Davis
Local Museum - 1844
Regional history - library 41483

National Museum of Ceramic Art and Glass, 2406 Shelleydale Dr, Baltimore, MD 21209 - T: (410) 764-1042, Fax: (410) 764-1042. Pres.: Richard Taylor
Decorative Arts Museum - 1989
Ceramic art, glass 41484

Port Discovery - Children's Museum in Baltimore, 35 Market Pl, Ste 905, Baltimore, MD 21202 - T: (410) 864-2700, Fax: (410) 727-3042, E-mail: info@portdiscovery.org, Internet: www.portdiscovery.org. Pres./C.E.O.: Alan Leberknight, Pres./Chm.: Douglas L. Becker
Ethnology Museum - 1977 41485

Rosenberg Gallery, Goucher College, 1021 Dulaney Valley Rd, Baltimore, MD 21204 - T: (410) 337-6073, Fax: (410) 337-6405, E-mail: lburns@goucher.edu, Internet: www.goucher.edu/rosenberg. Dir.: Laura Burns
University Museum / Fine Arts Museum - 1885 41486

Star-Spangled Banner Flag House and 1812 Museum, 844 E Pratt St, Baltimore, MD 21202 - T: (410) 837-1793, Fax: (410) 837-1812, E-mail: info@flaghouse, Internet: www.flaghouse.org. Dir.: Sally Johnston
Historical Museum - 1927
Home of Mary Pickersgill, maker of the 30'x42' banner which flew over Fort McHenry during the War of 1812 41487

Steamship Collection, University of Baltimore, Library, 1420 Maryland Av, Baltimore, MD 21201-5779 - T: (410) 837-4334, Fax: (410) 837-4330, E-mail: ahouse@ubmail.ubalt.edu, Internet: www.ubalt.edu/archives/ship/ship.htm. Pres.: Tim Dacey
University Museum / Library with Exhibitions - 1940 41488

Walters Art Museum, 600 N Charles St, Baltimore, MD 21201-5185 - T: (410) 547-9000, Fax: (410) 783-7969, 752-4797, E-mail: gvikan@thewalters.org, Internet: www.thewalters.org. Dir.: Dr. Gary Vikan, Terry Drayman-Weisser (Conservation), Jackie Copeland (Education), Nancy Zinn (Exhibitions), Ass. Dir./Cur.: William R. Johnston (18th/ 19th c Art), Hiram Woodward (Asian Art), Cur.: Joaneath Spicer (Renaissance/ Baroque Art), Regine Schulz (Ancient Art), Ass. Cur.: William Noel (Manuscripts, Rare Books), Eik Kahng (18th/ 19th c Art)
Fine Arts Museum / Museum of Classical Antiquities - 1931
Art, rare books 41489

Bancroft NE

John G. Neihardt Center, Nebraska State Historical Society, Elm and Washington, Bancroft, NE 68004 - T: (402) 648-3388, Fax: (402) 648-3388, E-mail: neihardt@gpcom.net, Internet: www.neihardt.com. Dir.: Nancy S. Gillis
Special Museum / Historical Museum - 1976
library 41490

Bandera TX

Frontier Times Museum, 510 31th St, Bandera, TX 78003 - T: (830) 796-3864. Dir.: Bob Perry
Historical Museum - 1933
Texas' early pioneer days, western paintings, antiques, photographs 41491

Bangor ME

Bangor Historical Society Museum, 159 Union St, Bangor, ME 04401 - T: (207) 942-5766, Fax: (207) 941-0266, E-mail: bangorhistorical@hotmail.com, Internet: www.bairnet.org. Exec. Dir.: Margaret Puckett
Local Museum - 1864
Local history 41492

Cole Land Transportation Museum, 405 Perry Rd, Bangor, ME 04401 - T: (207) 990-3600, Fax: (207) 990-2653, E-mail: mail@colemuseum.com, Internet: www.colemuseum.org. Dir.: Garrett Cole, Cur.: Mark R. Burnett
Science&Tech Museum - 1990 41493

Isaac Farrar Mansion, 17 Second St, Bangor, ME 04401 - T: (207) 941-2808, Fax: (207) 941-2812. Dir.: Lynda Clyve, Peggy Wentworth, Cur.: Margaret Jane Moore
Local Museum - 1972
Historic house 41494

Banning CA

Malki Museum, 11-795 Fields Rd, Banning, CA 92220 - T: (909) 849-7289, 849-8304. Pres.: Katherine Saubel
Historical Museum / Ethnology Museum / Folklore Museum - 1964
Indian tribe artifacts e.g. Cahuilla 41495

Bar Harbor ME

Abbe Museum at Downtown, 26 Mount Desert St, Bar Harbor, ME 04609 - T: (207) 288-3519, Fax: (207) 288-8979, E-mail: abbe@midmaine.com, Internet: www.abbemuseum.org. Dir.: Diane Kopec, Cur.: Becky Cole-Will
Ethnology Museum / Archaeological Museum - 2001
Archaeology, anthropology, ethnology 41496

Abbe Museum at Sieur de Monts Spring, Sieur de Monts Spring, Acadia National Park, Bar Harbor, ME 04609 - T: (207) 288-3519, Fax: (207) 288-8979, E-mail: abbe@midmaine.com, Internet: www.abbemuseum.org. Dir.: Diane Kopec, Cur.: Becky Cole-Will
Ethnology Museum / Archaeological Museum - 1928
Archaeology, anthropology, ethnology 41497

Bar Harbor Historical Society Museum, 33 Ledgelawn Av, Bar Harbor, ME 04609 - T: (207) 288-3807, 288-0000. Cur.: Deborah Dyer
Local Museum - 1946
Local history 41498

George B. Dorr Museum of Natural History, College of the Atlantic, 105 Eden St, Bar Harbor, ME 04609 - T: (207) 288-5015, Fax: (207) 288-2917, E-mail: museum@ecology.coa.edu, Internet: www.coamuseum.org. Dir.: Dr. Stephen Ressel, Cur.: Dianne Clendaniel (Program), Gail LaRosa (Operations)
Natural History Museum - 1982
Natural history 41499

Baraboo WI

Circus World Museum, 550 Water St, Baraboo, WI 53913 - T: (608) 356-8341, Fax: (608) 356-1800, E-mail: ringmaster@circusworldmuseum.com, Internet: www.circusworldmuseum.com. Exec. Dir.: Larry Fisher
Performing Arts Museum - 1959 41500

International Crane Foundation Museum, E 11376 Shady Lane Rd, Baraboo, WI 53913-0447 - T: (608) 356-9462, Fax: (608) 356-9465, E-mail: cranes@savingcranes.org, Internet: www.savingcranes.org. Pres.: James T. Harris, Sc. Staff: Jeb Barzen (Ecology), Cur.: Michael Putnam
Natural History Museum - 1973
Ornithology 41501

Sauk County Historical Museum, 531 4th Av, Baraboo, WI 53913 - T: (608) 356-1001, E-mail: schist@shopstop.net, Internet: www.saukcounty.com/schs. Dir.: Peter Shrake, Cur.: Mary Farrell Stieve
Local Museum - 1906
Local hist 41502

Bardstown KY

My Old Kentucky Home, 501 E Stephen Foster Av, Bardstown, KY 40004 - T: (502) 348-3502, 323-7803, Fax: (502) 349-0054, Internet: www.kystateparks.com. Head: Alice Heaton
Special Museum - 1922
Home of Judge John Rowan, where Stephen Foster wrote My Old Kentucky Home 41503

Oscar Getz Museum of Whiskey History, 114 N Fifth St, Bardstown, KY 40004-1402 - T: (502) 348-2999, E-mail: bourbonmuseum@cube3.net. Chm.: Francis X. Smith, Cur.: Mary Ellin Hamilton, Flaget Nally
Local Museum / Special Museum - 1984
Local history, Whiskey history 41504

Barkers Island WI

S.S. Meteor Maritime Museum, 300 Marina Dr, Barkers Island, WI 54880 - T: (715) 392-5742, 394-5712, Fax: (715) 394-3810, Internet: www.superiorpublicmuseums.org. C.E.O.: Susan K. Anderson
Science&Tech Museum - 1973
Whaleback, boat models, ship equip and building hist 41505

Barnesville OH

Gay 90's Mansion Museum, 532 N Chestnut St, Barnesville, OH 43713 - T: (614) 425-2926. Pres.: Marietta Martin, Dir.: Howard Lemasters
Historical Museum - 1966 41506

Barnet VT

Barnet Historical Society Museum, Goodwille House, Barnet, VT 05821 - T: (802) 633-2611. Pres.: Hazel McLaren
Local Museum - 1967
Local hist 41507

Barnstable MA

Donald G. Trayser Memorial Museum, 3353 Main St, Barnstable, MA 02630, mail addr: 230 South St Town Hall, Hyannis, MA 02601 - T: (617) 362-2092, 790-6270. Dir.: Tom Broaderick
Local Museum - 1960
History, Old Customs House 41508

Olde Colonial Courthouse, Main St, Rte 6A, Barnstable, MA 02630 - T: (508) 362-9056, Fax: (508) 362-9056, Internet: www.capehistory.com. Pres.: Carol Clarke Di Vico
Historical Museum - 1949
Sachem Iyanough's gravesite dedicated to early Indians who befriended Pilgrims 41509

Barnwell SC

Barnwell County Museum, Hagood and Marlboro Aves, Barnwell, SC 29812 - T: (803) 259-1916, 259-3277, E-mail: barnwellmuseum@barnwellsc.com. Cur.: Pauline Zidlick
Local Museum - 1978
Local hist 41510

Barre MA

Barre Historical Museum, 18 Common St, Barre, MA 01005 - T: (978) 355-4067. Pres.: Mary Ellen Radziewicz, Cur.: Bertyne Smith
Local Museum - 1955
Local history 41511

Barrington IL

Barrington Area Historical Museum, 212 W Main St, Barrington, IL 60010 - T: (708) 381-1730, Fax: (708) 381-1766. Pres.: Dean Maiben, Exec. Dir.: Michael J. Harkins
Local Museum - 1969
Local history, housed in two Folk Victorian Houses 41512

Bartlesville OK

Bartlesville Area History Museum, 401 S Johnstone, Bartlesville, OK 74005 - T: (918) 337-5336, Fax: (918) 337-5338, E-mail: kkswoods@bartlesville.org, Internet: www.cityofbartlesville.org. Dir.: Karen Smith Woods
Local Museum - 1964
Early settlers and Native Indian tribes 41513

Frank Phillips Home, 1107 S Cherokee, Bartlesville, OK 74003 - T: (918) 336-2491, Fax: (918) 336-3529, E-mail: fphillipshome@ok-history.mus.ok.us. Dir.: J. Blake Wade, Cur.: Susan J. Lacey
Local Museum - 1973 41514

Price Tower Arts Center, 510 S Dewey, Bartlesville, OK 74003 - T: (918) 336-4949, Fax: (918) 336-7117, E-mail: director@pricetower.org, Internet: www.pricetower.org. Exec. Dir.: Richard P. Townsend
Fine Arts Museum / Decorative Arts Museum - 1985
Frank Lloyd Wright and Bruce Goff 41515

Woolaroc Museum, State Hwy 123, Bartlesville, OK 74003 - T: (918) 336-0307 ext 10, Fax: (918) 336-0084, E-mail: woolaroc1@aol.com, Internet: www.woolaroc.org. Dir.: Robert R. Lansdown, Cur.: Linda Stone (Art), Kenneth Meek (Collections)
Fine Arts Museum / Historical Museum - 1929 41516

Barton VT

Crystal Lake Falls Historical Museum, 97 Water St, Barton, VT 05822 - T: (802) 525-3583, 525-6251, Fax: (802) 525-3583, E-mail: jbrown@kingcon.com. Pres.: Avis Harper
Local Museum / Science&Tech Museum - 1984
Local hist and industry 41517

Basking Ridge NJ

Environmental Education Center, 190 Lord Stirling Rd, Basking Ridge, NJ 07920 - T: (908) 766-2489, Fax: (908) 766-2687, Internet: www.park.co.somerset.nj.us. Head: Catherine Schrein
Natural History Museum - 1970 41518

Bastrop LA

Snyder Museum and Creative Arts Center, 1620 E Madison Av, Bastrop, LA 71220 - T: (318) 281-8760. Pres.: Madeline Herring, Dir.: Helen T. Landress
Fine Arts Museum / Local Museum - 1974
Local history, art 41519

Batavia IL

Batavia Depot Museum, 155 Houston, Batavia, IL 60510 - T: (630) 406-5253, Fax: (630) 879-9537, E-mail: carlah@batpkdist.org, Internet: www.bataviahistoricalsociety.org. Dir.: Carla Hill
Local Museum - 1960
Local history, housed in 1854 Batavia Depot, one of the oldest railroad station on the Burlington Line 41520

Batavia NY

Holland Land Office Museum, 131 W Main St, Batavia, NY 14020 - T: (716) 343-4727, Fax: (716) 345-0023, E-mail: info@hollandoffice.com, Internet: www.hollandoffice.com. Pres.: Don Burkel, Cur.: Patrick Weissend
Local Museum - 1894
Local hist 41521

Bath ME

Maine Maritime Museum, 243 Washington St, Bath, ME 04530 - T: (207) 443-1316, Fax: (207) 443-1665, Internet: www.bathmaine.com/. Dir.: Thomas R. Wilcox, Cur.: Anne Witty, Libr.: Nathan Lipfert
Historical Museum - 1964
Maritime, historic shipyard 41522

Bath NC

Historic Bath State Historic Site, 207 Carteret St, Bath, NC 27808 - T: (252) 923-3971, Fax: (252) 923-0174, E-mail: historicbath@tri-countynet.net, Internet: www.ah.dcr.state.nc.us/sections/hs/bath/bath.htm. C.E.O.: Gerald Butler
Historic Site - 1963 41523

Bath OH

Hale Farm and Village, 2686 Oak Hill Rd, Bath, OH 44210 - T: (330) 666-3711, Fax: (330) 666-9497, E-mail: srusher@wrhs.org, Internet: www.wrhs.org. C.E.O.: Dr. Richard Ehrlich
Open Air Museum / Agriculture Museum - 1957 41524

Baton Rouge LA

Baton Rouge Gallery, 1442 City Park Av, Baton Rouge, LA 70808-1037 - T: (225) 383-1470, Fax: (225) 336-0943. Dir.: Kathleen Pheney
Fine Arts Museum - 1966
Contemporary art 41525

Enchanted Mansion Doll Museum, 190 Lee Dr, Baton Rouge, LA 70808 - T: (225) 769-0005, Fax: (225) 766-6822, E-mail: termansion@bellsouth.net, Internet: www.angelfire.com/la2/enchantedmansion. CEO: Rosemary Sedberry
Decorative Arts Museum - 1995 41526

Louisiana Arts and Science Center, 100 S River Rd, Baton Rouge, LA 70802 - T: (225) 344-5272, 344-9478, Fax: (225) 344-9477, Internet: www.lasm.org. Dir.: Carol Sommerfeldt Gikas, Ass. Dir.: Sam Losavio, Cur.: Elizabeth Chubbuck Weinstein
Fine Arts Museum / Science&Tech Museum - 1960
Art, science, former Illinois Central Railroad Station 41527

Louisiana Naval War Memorial U.S.S. Kidd, 305 S River Rd, Baton Rouge, LA 70802 - T: (225) 342-1942, Fax: (225) 342-2039, E-mail: kidd661@aol.com, Internet: www.usskidd.com. Dir./Cur.: H. Maury Drummond, Cur.: Timothy C. Rizzuto
Military Museum - 1981
Maritime, historic ship 41528

Louisiana Old State Capitol, Center for Political and Governmental History, 100 North Blvd, Baton Rouge, LA 70801 - T: (225) 342-0500, (800) 488-2968, Fax: (225) 342-0316, E-mail: osc@sec.state.la.us, Internet: www.sec.state.la.us. Dir.: Mary Louise Prudhomme, Ass. Dir.: Sailor Jackson (Film, Video), Cur.: Dr. Florent Hardy
Historical Museum - 1990
Louisiana State history 41529

Louisiana State University Museum of Art, Memorial Tower, Baton Rouge, LA 70803 - T: (225) 578-4003, Fax: (225) 578-9288, E-mail: indiana@lsu.edu. Exec. Dir.: Steven W. Rosen
Fine Arts Museum / University Museum - 1959
Art 41530

Magnolia Mound Plantation, 2161 Nicholson Dr, Baton Rouge, LA 70802 - T: (504) 343-4955, Fax: (504) 343-6739, E-mail: marketmmp@aol.com, Internet: magnoliamound.org. Pres.: Suzette Tannehill, Dir.: Dorinda Hilbun
Open Air Museum / Local Museum - 1968
Plantation house and outbuildings 41531

Museum of Natural Science, 119 Foster Hall, LSU, Baton Rouge, LA 70803 - T: (225) 578-2855, Fax: (225) 578-3075, E-mail: namark@lsu.edu, Internet: www.museum.lsu.edu. Dir.: Dr. Mark S. Hafner (Mammals), Cur.: Dr. J. Michael Fitzsimons (Fishes), Dr. J.V. Remsen (Birds), Dr. Jim A. McGuire (Reptiles), Dr. Jennifer L. Chidsey (Science Education), Dr. Judith A. Schiebout (Paleontology), Dr. Rebecca A. Saunders (Anthropology), Dr. Frederick H. Sheldon (Genetic Resources)
University Museum / Natural History Museum - 1936
Paleontology, anthropology, mammals, birds, fishes, reptiles 41532

Old Bogan Central Firefighters Museum → Robert A. Bogan Fire Museum

Robert A. Bogan Fire Museum, 427 Laurel St, Baton Rouge, LA 70801 - T: (225) 344-8558, Fax: (225) 344-7777, E-mail: gnadler@acgbr.com, Internet: www.383arts.org. Pres.: Hank Saurage, Dir.: Genny Nadler Thomas
Historical Museum - 1924
Fire fighting 41533

Rural Life Museum and Windrush Gardens, 4600 Essen Ln, Baton Rouge, LA 70809 - T: (225) 765-2437, Fax: (225) 765-2639, E-mail: rulife1@lsu.edu, Internet: www.rurallife.lsu.edu. Dir.: David Floyd
Local Museum - 1970
Local hist 41534

School of Art Gallery, c/o Louisiana State University, 123 Art Bldg, Baton Rouge, LA 70803-0001 - T: (225) 578-5411, Fax: (225) 578-5424, E-mail: mdaughi@isu.edu, Internet: lsuart.org. Dir.: Michael Crespo
Fine Arts Museum / University Museum - 1934
Contemporary graphic works, prints, drawings 41535

Union Art Gallery, c/o Louisiana State University, Nicholson Dr, Baton Rouge, LA 70803 - T: (225) 3885162, 388-5117, Internet: www.lib.lsu.edu. Dir.: Judith R. Stahl
Fine Arts Museum / University Museum - 1964 41536

Battle Creek MI

Art Center of Battle Creek, 265 E Emmett St, Battle Creek, MI 49017 - T: (616) 962-9511, Fax: (616) 969-3838, E-mail: acbc@net-link.net. Dir.: Lorrie Zorbo
Fine Arts Museum - 1948
Art gallery of Michigan artists 41537

Kimball House Museum, 196 Capital Av NE, Battle Creek, MI 49017 - T: (616) 965-2613, Fax: (616) 966-2495, E-mail: bchist@net-link.net. Dir.: Michael Evans, Sc. Staff: Mary Butler (History)
Local Museum - 1966 41538

Kingman Museum of Natural History, W Michigan Av at 20th St, Battle Creek, MI 49017 - T: (616) 965-5117, Fax: (616) 962-5610. Cur.: D. Thomas Johnson (Exhibits), Kathy Ward (Collections)
Natural History Museum - 1869
Natural history 41539

Battle Ground IN

Tippecanoe Battlefield, 200 Battle Ground Av, Battle Ground, IN 47920 - T: (765) 567-2147, Fax: (765) 567-2149, E-mail: info@tcha.mus.in.us, Internet: www.tcha.mus.in.us. Dir.: James Turley
Historic Site - 1972
Keththpecanuk, a lonf forgotten settlement, Tippecanoe and Tyler, Two 41540

Baudette MN

Lake of the Woods County Museum, 8th Av SE, Baudette, MN 56623 - T: (218) 634-1200. Cur.: Marlys Hirst
Local Museum - 1978
County history 41541

Baxter Springs KS

Baxter Springs Heritage Center and Museum, 740 East Av, Baxter Springs, KS 66713 - T: (620) 856-2385, E-mail: heritagectr@4state.com, Internet: home.4state.com/~heritagectr/. Cur.: Phyliss Abbott
Local Museum / Military Museum - 1962
Civil War coll, Oct 1863 Baxter Massacre of General Blunt's men, quilt coll, mining 41542

Bay City MI

Historical Museum of Bay County, 321 Washington Av, Bay City, MI 48708 - T: (989) 893-5733, Fax: (989) 893-5741, Internet: www.bchsmuseum.org. Dir.: Gay McInerney
Historical Museum - 1919
County history 41543

Bay City TX

Matagorda County Museum, 2100 Av F, Bay City, TX 77414-0851 - T: (409) 245-7502, Fax: (409) 245-1233, E-mail: mcma@tgn.net. C.E.O.: Jack Hollister
Local Museum - 1965
Regional history 41544

Bay View MI

Bay View Historical Museum, Bay View Association Encampment, Bay View, MI 49770 - T: (231) 347-6225, 347-8182, Fax: (231) 347-4337, E-mail: bvarod@freeway.net. Pres.: Roy Talley
Local Museum - 1970
Local hist 41545

Bay Village OH

Baycrafters, 28795 Lake Rd, Bay Village, OH 44140 - T: (440) 871-6543, Fax: (440) 871-0452. Dir.: Sally Irwin Price
Fine Arts Museum / Science&Tech Museum - 1948
Coll of paintings, Nickel Plate Railroad Station, Norfolk and Western Caboose 41546

Lake Erie Nature and Science Center, 28728 Wolf Rd, Bay Village, OH 44140 - T: (440) 871-2900, Fax: (440) 871-2901, Internet: www.lensc.org. Dir.: Larry D. Richardson
Natural History Museum - 1945
Astronomy, botany, geology, physical science, zoology, ecology 41547

Rose Hill Museum, 27715 Lake Rd, Bay Village, OH 44140 - T: (440) 871-7338, E-mail: mail@bayhistorical.com, Internet: www.bayhistorical.com. Pres.: Eric Eakin
Historical Museum - 1960 41548

Bayside NY

QCC Art Gallery, 222-05 56th Av, Bayside, NY 11364-1497 - T: (718) 631-6396, Fax: (718) 631-6620, E-mail: qccgallery@aol.com, Internet: qcc.cuny.edu. Dir.: Faustino Quintanilla
University Museum / Fine Arts Museum - 1966 41549

Beachwood OH

Temple Museum of Religious Art, 26000 Shaker Blvd, Beachwood, OH 44122 - T: (216) 831-3233 ext 108, E-mail: makeck@hotmail.com. Dir.: Susan Koletsky
Religious Arts Museum - 1950
Antique Torah hangings, Holyland pottery, Israel stamps, paintings, sculpture, stained glass, Torah ornaments 41550

Beacon NY

Beacon Historical Society Museum, 477 Main St, Beacon, NY 12508, mail addr: POB 89, Beacon, NY 12508 - T: (914) 831-1877. Cur.: Joan Van Voorhis
Local Museum - 1976 41551

Dia:Beacon, Dia Art Foundation, 3 Beekman St, Beacon, NY 12508 - T: (845) 440-0100, Fax: (845) 440-0092, E-mail: info@diaart.org, Internet: www.diabeacon.org. Dir.: Michael Govan, Asst. Dir.: Stephen Dewhurst, Amy S. Weisser, Cur.: Lynne Cooke, Sc. Staff: Patrick Heilman (Digital Media), Laura Fields (Graphics), Steven Evans (Gallery)
Fine Arts Museum - 1974
Contemporary American/European art 41552

Madam Brett Homestead, 50 Van Nydeck Av, Beacon, NY 12508 - T: (914) 831-6533. Dir.: Denise Doring Van Buren, Cur.: Linda Shedd
Local Museum - 1954 41553

Bear Mountain NY

Bear Mountain Trailside Museums Wildlife Center, Bear Mountain State Park, Bear Mountain, NY 10911 - T: (845) 786-2701 ext 263, Fax: (845) 786-7157, Internet: www.trailsidenewyork.com. Head: John Focht
Natural History Museum - 1927 41554

Beatrice NE

Gage County Historical Museum, 101 N Second, Beatrice, NE 68310 - T: (402) 228-1679, E-mail: gagecountymuseum@beatricene.com, Internet: www.beatricene.com/gagecountymuseum. Dir.: Lesa Arterburn, Ass. Dir./Cur.: Rita Clawson
Historical Museum - 1971 41555

Homestead National Monument of America, 8523 W State Hwy, Beatrice, NE 68310 - T: (402) 223-3514, Fax: (402) 228-4231, Internet: www.nps.gov
Agriculture Museum - 1936 41556

Beaufort NC

Beaufort Historic Site, 138 Turner St, Beaufort, NC 28516 - T: (252) 728-5225, Fax: (252) 728-4966, E-mail: bha@bmd.clis.com, Internet: www.historicbeaufort.com. Exec. Dir.: Patricia Suggs
Local Museum - 1960 41557

North Carolina Maritime Museum, 315 Front St, Beaufort, NC 28516 - T: (252) 728-7317, Fax: (252) 728-2108, E-mail: maritime@ncmail.net, Internet: www.ah.dcr.state.nc.us/sections/maritime. Dir.: Dr. George Ward Shannon, Cur.: Jeannie W. Kraus, Scott Kucra (Natural Science), Roger Allen (Boatbuilding Technology), Paul Fontenoy (Watercraft and Maritime Research), Jerry Heiser (Exhibits), JoAnne Powell (Education)
Natural History Museum / Science&Tech Museum - 1975 41558

Beaufort SC

Beaufort Museum, 713 Craven St, Beaufort, SC 29902 - T: (843) 525-7077, 525-7005, Fax: (843) 379-3331, E-mail: bftmuseum@islc.net, Internet: www.cityofbeaufort.crglmuseum.htm. Dir.: Margaret Anne Lane, C.E.O.: Jefferson Mansell
Fine Arts Museum / Local Museum - 1939
Local hist 41559

University of South Carolina Beaufort Art Gallery, 801 Carteret St, Beaufort, SC 29902 - T: (843) 521-4145, E-mail: info@beaufortarts.com, Internet: www.beaufortarts.com. Exec. Dir.: Eric V. Holowacz
University Museum / Fine Arts Museum - 1990 41560

The Verdier House, 801 Bay St, Beaufort, SC 29902 - T: (843) 379-3331, Fax: (843) 379-3371, E-mail: histbft@hargray.com. Exec. Dir.: Jefferson Mansell
Local Museum - 1977
Historic house 41561

Beaumont TX

Art Museum of Southeast Texas, 500 Main St, Beaumont, TX 77701 - T: (409) 832-3432, Fax: (409) 832-8508, E-mail: info@amset.org, Internet: www.amset.org. Exec. Dir.: Lynn P. Castle, Cur.: Janis Zigler Becker (Education)
Fine Arts Museum - 1950
Art 41562

The Art Studio, 720 Franklin St, Beaumont, TX 77701-4424 - T: (409) 838-5393, Fax: (409) 838-4695, E-mail: gregb@artstudio.org, Internet: www.artstudio.org. Dir.: Greg Busceme, Ass. Dir.: Tracy Danna
Fine Arts Museum - 1983
Art 41563

Babe Didrikson Zaharias Museum, I-10 W, MLK Blvd, Exit 854, Beaumont, TX 77701 - T: (409) 880-3749, 833-4622, Fax: (409) 880-3750, E-mail: khughes@ci.beaumont.tx.us, Internet: www.beaumontcvb.com. Cur.: Rosemary Cox
Special Museum - 1976
Sports trophies, golf clubs, Olympic medals 41564

Beaumont Art League, 2675 Gulf St, Fairgrounds, Beaumont, TX 77703 - T: (409) 833-4179, Fax: (409) 832-1563, E-mail: abarr91511@aol.com. Pres.: Frank Gerrietts
Fine Arts Museum - 1943
Art 41565

Dishman Art Gallery, 1030 Lavaca, Beaumont, TX 77705 - T: (409) 880-8959, Fax: (409) 880-1799, E-mail: dishman_art@hal.lamar.edu. Dir.: Dr. Lynne Lokensgard
Fine Arts Museum / Public Gallery - 1983
Art 41566

Edison Plaza Museum, 350 Pine St, Beaumont, TX 77701 - T: (409) 839-3089, Fax: (409) 839-3077. Chm.: Michael Barnhill
Local Museum - 1980
Local hist 41567

Fire Museum of Texas, 400 Walnut at Mulberry, Beaumont, TX 77701 - T: (409) 880-3927, Fax: (409) 880-3914, E-mail: firemuseum@ci.beaumont.tx.us. Cur.: Linda Gaudio
Science&Tech Museum - 1986 41568

John Jay French House, 3025 French Rd, Beaumont, TX 77706 - T: (409) 898-0348, Fax: (409) 898-8487. Dir.: Nell Truman, Ass. Dir.: Gladys E. Manning
Local Museum - 1968
Historic house 41569

McFaddin-Ward House, 1906 McFaddin Av, Beaumont, TX 77701 - T: (409) 832-1906, Fax: (409) 832-3483, E-mail: info@mcfaddin-ward.org, Internet: www.mcfaddin-ward.org. Dir.: Metthew White, Cur.: Sherri Birdsong
Local Museum - 1982
Historic house 41570

Spindletop and Gladys City Boomtown Museum, Hwy 69 at University Dr, Beaumont, TX 77705 - T: (409) 835-0823, Fax: (409) 838-9107. Cur.: Christy Mariono
Local Museum - 1975
Oilfield machinery and tools, furniture, textiles, glass items 41571

Texas Energy Museum, 600 Main St, Beaumont, TX 77701 - T: (409) 833-5100, Fax: (409) 833-4282, E-mail: smithtem@msn.com, Internet: www.texasenergymuseum.orgum/. Dir.: D. Ryan Smith
Science&Tech Museum - 1987
Industry history 41572

Beaver Dam WI

Dodge County Historical Society Museum, 105 Park Av, Beaver Dam, WI 53916 - T: (920) 887-1266, E-mail: dchs@internetwis.com. C.E.O.: Christine Cross
Local Museum - 1938
Local hist 41573

Beaver Island MI

Beaver Island Historical Museum, 26275 Main St, Beaver Island, MI 49782 - T: (906) 448-2254, Fax: (906) 448-2106, E-mail: news@beaverisland.net, Internet: beaverisland.net. Pres.: James Willis, Dir.: William Cashman
Local Museum - 1957
Local history 41574

Beaverdam VA

Scotchtown, 16120 Chiswell Ln, Beaverdam, VA 23015 - T: (804) 227-3500, Fax: (804) 227-3559, E-mail: scotchtownAPVA@aol.com. C.E.O.: Susan Nepomuceno
Decorative Arts Museum - 1958 41575

Becker MN

Sherburne County Historical Museum, 13122 First St, Becker, MN 55308 - T: (612) 261-4433, Fax: (612) 261-4437, E-mail: schs@sherbtel.net, Internet: www.rootsweb.com/mnschs. Pres.: Craig Schwarzkopf, Exec. Dir.: Kurt K. Kragness
Local Museum - 1972
Regional history 41576

Beckley WV

Youth Museum of Southern West Virginia, New River Park, Beckley, WV 25802 - T: (304) 252-3730, Fax: (304) 252-3764, E-mail: ymswv@citynet.net. Exec. Dir.: Sandi Parker
Special Museum - 1977 41577

Bedford IN

Antique Auto and Race Car Museum, 3348 16th St, Bedford, IN 47421 - T: (812) 275-0556, Fax: (812) 279-1916, E-mail: retail@autoracemuseum.com, Internet: www.autoracemuseum.com. Cur.: Eddie L. Evans
Science&Tech Museum - 1994
Antique, race and special interest cars 41578

Lawrence County Historical Museum, Rm 12, Court House, Bedford, IN 47421 - T: (812) 275-4141. Cur.: Helen Burchard
Local Museum - 1928
Local history 41579

Bedford NY

Museum of the Bedford Historical Society, 38 Village Green, Bedford, NY 10586 - T: (914) 234-9751, Fax: (914) 234-5461, E-mail: bedhist@bestweb.net, Internet: www.bedhistoricalsociety.org. Pres.: Linda DeMenocal, Dir.: Lynne Ryan
Local Museum - 1916
Local hist 41580

Bedford OH

Bedford Historical Society Museum, 30 Squire Pl, Bedford Commons, Bedford, OH 44146 - T: (440) 232-0796, Internet: bedfordohio.com/history. C.E.O.: Richard J. Squire
Local Museum - 1955
Americana, archaeology, period furniture, glass, local and Ohio hist, Indian artifacts, railway - library 41581

Bedford PA

Fort Bedford Museum, Fort Bedford Dr, Bedford, PA 15522 - T: (814) 623-8891, Fax: (814) 623-2011, E-mail: fbm@nb.net, Internet: www.nb.net/fbm. Pres.: William H. Clark
Local Museum - 1958 41582

Bedford VA

Bedford City/County Museum, 201 E Main St, Bedford, VA 24523 - T: (540) 586-4520. Dir.: Ellen A. Wandrei, Cur.: Bernice Sizemore
Local Museum - 1932
Local hist 41583

Bedford Corners NY

Westmoreland Sanctuary, 260 Chestnut Ridge Rd, Bedford Corners, NY 10549 - T: (914) 666-8448, Fax: (914) 242-1175, E-mail: mail@westmorelandsanctuary.org, Internet: www.westmorelandsanctuary.org. Dir.: Stephen A. Ricker
Natural History Museum - 1957 41584

Belchertown MA

The Stone House Museum, 20 Maple St, Belchertown, MA 01007 - T: (413) 289-2010, E-mail: stonehousmuseum@yhoo.com, Internet: www.stonehousemuseum.org. Pres.: Jim Phaneuy, Dir./Cur.: Caren Anne Harrington
Historical Museum - 1904
Historic house 41585

Belcourt ND

Turtle Mountain Chippewa Heritage Center, Hwy 5, Belcourt, ND 58316 - T: (701) 477-6140, Fax: (701) 477-0065, E-mail: tmchc@utma.com, Internet: chippewa.etma.com. Dir.: Dorene Bruce
Fine Arts Museum / Historical Museum - 1985
History, art 41586

Belhaven NC

Belhaven Memorial Museum, 211 E Main St, Belhaven, NC 27810 - T: (252) 943-3055, Fax: (252) 943-2357, Internet: www.beaufort-county.com/Belhaven/museum. Pres.: Peg McKnight
Historical Museum - 1965 41587

Bellefontaine OH

Logan County Historical Society Museum, 521 E Columbus Av, Bellefontaine, OH 43311 - T: (937) 593-7557, E-mail: lchsmuse@logan.net, Internet: www.logancountymuseum.org. Dir.: Todd McCormick
Local Museum - 1945
Household appliances, tools, clothing, cameras, music, firearms, uniforms, railroad, military and pioneer costumes, geology, Warren Cushman art 41588

Bellefonte PA

Centre County Library Historical Museum, 203 N Allegheny St, Bellefonte, PA 16823 - T: (814) 355-1516, Fax: (814) 355-2700, E-mail: paroom@centrecountylibrary.org, Internet: www.ccfpl.org. Dir.: Charlene K. Brungard
Local Museum - 1939 41589

Belleville IL

Saint Clair County Historical Museum, 701 E Washington St, Belleville, IL 62220 - T: (618) 234-0600. Pres.: Robert Fietsam
Local Museum - 1905
Regional history 41590

Belleville KS

Republic County Historical Society Museum, 2726 Hwy 36, Belleville, KS 66935 - T: (785) 527-5971, E-mail: repcomuse@nckcn.com, Internet: www.nckcn.com/homepage/republic_co/repmus.htm. Cur.: Patricia Walter
Local Museum - 1985
Pioneer historic tools, rail road caboose 41591

Belleville MI

Belleville Area Museum, 405 Main St, Belleville, MI 48111 - T: (734) 697-1944, Fax: (734) 697-1944. Pres.: Fred Hudson, Dir.: Diane Wilson
Historical Museum - 1989
Local history 41592

Yankee Air Museum, Willow Run Airport, H-2041 A St, Belleville, MI 48111 - T: (734) 483-4030, Fax: (734) 483-5076, E-mail: yankeeairmuseum@provide.net, Internet: www.yankeeairmuseum.org. Pres.: Jon Stevens, Dep. Dir./Cur.: Gayle Roberts-Walker
Military Museum / Science&Tech Museum - 1981
Aeronautics, Ford Willow Run bomber plant airplane hangar - research library, aircraft restoration 41593

Bellevue NE

Sarpy County Historical Museum, 2402 Clay St, Bellevue, NE 68005-3932 - T: (402) 292-1880. Dir.: Gary Iske
Local Museum - 1970 41594

Bellevue OH

Historic Lyme Village, 5001 State Rte 4, Bellevue, OH 44811 - T: (419) 483-4949, 483-6052, Internet: www.lymmevillage.com
Historical Museum - 1972 41595

Bellevue PA

John A. Hermann jr. Memorial Art Museum, 318 Lincoln Av, Bellevue, PA 15202 - T: (412) 761-8008, Internet: www.borough.bellevue.pa.us/hermann/hermann.html. Dir.: Donald F. Gust
Fine Arts Museum - 1940 41596

Bellevue WA

Bellevue Art Museum, 510 Bellevue Wayne, Bellevue, WA 98004 - T: (425) 519-0770, Fax: (425) 637-1799, E-mail: bam@bellevueart.org, Internet: www.bellevueart.org. Dir.: Kathleen Harleman, Cur.: Greg Ginger
Fine Arts Museum - 1975
Art 41597

Iquest Children's Museum, 4055 Factona Mall SE, Bellevue, WA 98006 - T: (425) 829-5148, E-mail: info@iquestmuseum.org, Internet: www.iquestmuseum.org. Exec. Dir.: Putter Bert
Science&Tech Museum / Natural History Museum - 1997 41598

Rosalie Whyel Museum of Doll Art, 1116 108th Av, NE, Bellevue, WA 98004 - T: (425) 455-1116, Fax: (425) 455-4793, E-mail: dollart@dollart.com, Internet: www.dollart.com. Dir.: Rosalie Whyel, Cur.: Jill Gorman
Special Museum - 1989
Dolls, games, books, photographs, costumes 41599

Bellflower IL

Bellflower Genealogical and Historical Society Museum, Latcha St, Bellflower, IL 61724 - T: (309) 722-3757, 722-3467. Pres.: Dorothy Woliung, Phyllis Kumler
Local Museum - 1976
Early 1900 Illinois Central Railroad Depot 41600

Bellingham WA

American Museum of Radio, 1312 Bay St, Bellingham, WA 98225 - T: (360) 738-3886, Fax: (360) 738-3472, E-mail: jwinter@americanradiomuseum.org, Internet: www.antique-radio.org
Science&Tech Museum - 1982
Hist of radio and electricity, radios, televisions, recording devices and players 41601

Viking Union Gallery, Western Washington University, 516 High St, Bellingham, WA 98225 - T: (360) 650-3450, Fax: (360) 650-6507, E-mail: aspart@cc.wwu.edu, Internet: www.edu/asp/gallery. Dir.: Caroline Knebelsberger
Fine Arts Museum / University Museum - 1899
Art 41602

Western Gallery, Western Washington University, Bellingham, WA 98225-9068 - T: (360) 650-3900, Fax: (360) 650-6878, E-mail: sarah.clarklangager@wwu.edu, Internet: www.westerngallery.wwu.edu. Dir.: Sarah Clark-Langager, Sc. Staff: Paul Brower (Preparator)
University Museum / Fine Arts Museum - 1950
Fine and performing art 41603

Whatcom Museum of History and Art, 121 Prospect St, Bellingham, WA 98225 - T: (360) 676-6981, Fax: (360) 738-7409, E-mail: museuminfo@cob.org, Internet: www.city-govt.ci.bellingham.wa.us/museum.htm. Dir.: Thomas A. Livesay, Cur.: Janis Olson
Local Museum - 1940
Art, history 41604

Bellows Falls VT

Adams Old Stone Grist Mill, Mill St, Bellows Falls, VT 05101 - T: (802) 463-3734, E-mail: facades@sover.net. Cur.: Robert Ashcroft
Local Museum / Open Air Museum - 1965
Local hist 41605

Rockingham Free Museum, 65 Westminster St, Bellows Falls, VT 05101 - T: (802) 463-4270, E-mail: rockingham@dol.state.vt.us. C.E.O.: Devik Wyman
Historical Museum - 1909
Local hist 41606

Bellport NY

Bellport-Brookhaven Historical Society Museum, 31 Bellport Ln, Bellport, NY 11713 - T: (516) 286-0888, E-mail: robinastarbuck@aol.com. Pres.: Francis G. Fosmine, Cur.: robin Starbuck
Historical Museum - 1963
Local hist 41607

Belmont CA

The San Mateo County Arts Council, 1219 Ralston Av, Belmont, CA 94002 - T: (650) 593-1816, Fax: (650) 593-4716, E-mail: smcoarts@aol.com, Internet: www.smcoarts.org. Pres.: Peter Weiglin, Exec. Dir.: Matias Varela
Fine Arts Museum - 1972
Contemporary gallery 41608

The Wiegand Gallery, Notre Dame de Namur University, 1500 Ralston Av, Belmont, CA 94002 - T: (650) 508-3595, 593-1601, Fax: (650) 508-3488, E-mail: elainek@ndnu.edu, Internet: www.ndnu.edu. Dir.: Charles Strong, Cur.: Robert Poplack
Public Gallery / University Museum - 1970 41609

Belmont NY

Allegany County Museum, 11 Wells St, Belmont, NY 14813 - T: (716) 268-9293, Fax: (716) 268-9446, E-mail: historian@alleganyco.com. Dir.: Craig R. Braack
Local Museum - 1970 41610

Americana Manse, Whitney-Halsey Home, 39 South Stney Pl, Belmont, NY 14813 - T: (716) 268-5130. C.E.O.: Ruth Czankus
Local Museum - 1964 41611

Belmont VT

Community Historical Museum of Mount Holly, Tarbelville Rd, Belmont, VT 05730 - T: (802) 259-2460. Cur.: Janice Bamforth
Local Museum - 1968
Local hist 41612

Beloit KS

Little Red Schoolhouse-Living Library, Roadside Park, N Walnut and Hwy 24, Beloit, KS 67420 - T: (913) 738-5301. Chairman: Mildred Peterson
Historical Museum - 1976
Education, one-room school 41613

Beloit WI

Beloit Historical Society Museum, 845 Hackett St, Beloit, WI 53511 - T: (608) 365-7835, Fax: (608) 365-5999, E-mail: beloiths@ticon.net, Internet: www.ticon.net/~beloiths. Dir.: Paul K. Kerr
Local Museum - 1910 41614

Logan Museum of Anthropology, 700 College St, Beloit, WI 53511 - T: (608) 363-2677, Fax: (608) 363-2248, Internet: www.beloit.edu/~museum/logan. Dir.: Dr. William Green (North American Archaeology), Sc. Staff: Karla Wheeler, Nicolette Meister
University Museum / Ethnology Museum / Archaeological Museum - 1892
Anthropology 41615

Wright Museum of Art, 700 College St, Beloit, WI 53511 - T: (608) 363-2095, Fax: (608) 363-2248, E-mail: newlandj@beloit.edu, Internet: www.beloit.edu/libmuseum.html. Cur.: Judy Newland
Fine Arts Museum / University Museum - 1892
Art 41616

Belton SC

South Carolina Tennis Hall of Fame, Belton, SC 29627 - T: (864) 338-7751, Fax: (864) 338-4034, E-mail: rexmaynard@statecom.net, Internet: www.beltonsc.com. Head: Rex Maynard
Special Museum - 1984
Tennis 41617

Belton TX

Bell County Museum, 201 N Main St, Belton, TX 76513 - T: (254) 933-5243, Fax: (254) 933-5756, E-mail: museum@vvm.com, Internet: www.vvm.com/~museum. Dir.: Stephanie Turnham
Local Museum - 1975
Local hist 41618

Belvidere IL

Boone County Historical Society Museum, 311 Whitney Blvd, Belvidere, IL 61008 - T: (815) 544-8391, Fax: (815) 544-8391. Pres.: Kenneth Strate
Local Museum - 1968
Local history - library 41619

Bement IL

Bryant Cottage, 146 E Wilson Av, Bement, IL 61813 - T: (217) 678-8184. Head: Marilyn L. Ayers
Historical Museum - 1925
1856 Bryant Cottage where the Lincoln-Douglas Debates were verbally agreed to be part of the 1858 Senate campaigns 41620

Bemidji MN

Beltrami County Historical Museum, 130 Minnesota Av, Bemidji, MN 56619 - T: (218) 444-3376, Fax: (218) 444-3377, E-mail: depot@paulbunyan.net, Internet: www.paulbunyan.net/users/depot/index.html. Dir.: Wanda Hoyum
Local Museum - 1949
Regional history 41621

Bend OR

Deschutes County Historical Society Museum, 129 NW Idaho Av, Bend, OR 97701 - T: (541) 389-1813, Fax: (541) 317-9345, E-mail: dchsmuseum@aol.com
Local Museum - 1975
County hist exhibits 41622

High Desert Museum, 59800 S Hwy 97, Bend, OR 97702-7963 - T: (541) 382-4754, Fax: (541) 382-5256, E-mail: info@highdesert.org, Internet: www.highdesert.org. Cur.: Vivian Adams (Native American Heritage), Robert Boyd (Western Heritage)
Ethnology Museum / Natural History Museum / Historical Museum - 1974 41623

Benicia CA

Benicia Historical Museum, 2024 Camel Rd, Benicia, CA 94510 - T: (707) 745-5435, 745-5869, Fax: (707) 745-2135, E-mail: info@beniciahistoricalmuseum.org, Internet: www.beniciahistoricalmuseum.org. Interim Dir.: Beverly Phelan, Cur.: Harry Wassmann
Historical Museum - 1985
Local history 41624

Benjamin TX

Knox County Museum, Courthouse, Benjamin, TX 79505 - T: (940) 454-2229, Fax: (940) 454-2229, E-mail: kchc@nts-online.net, Internet: www.knoxcountytexas.com. C.E.O.: Mary Jane Young
Local Museum - 1966
Local hist 41625

Benkelman NE

Dundy County Historical Society Museum, 522 Araphahoe, Benkelman, NE 69021 - T: (308) 423-2750. Pres.: Betty Deyle, Dee Fries
Local Museum - 1970 41626

Bennettsville SC

Jennings-Brown House Female Academy, 119 S Marlboro St, Bennettsville, SC 29512 - T: (843) 479-5624, E-mail: marlborough@mecsc.net. Exec. Dir.: Lucille Carabo
Local Museum - 1967
Historic house 41627

Marlboro County Historical Museum, 123 S Marlboro St, Bennettsville, SC 29512 - T: (843) 479-5624, E-mail: marlborough@mecse.net. Pres.: Ron J. Munnerlyn, Dir.: Lucille Carabo
Local Museum - 1970
Local hist 41628

Bennington VT

The Bennington Museum, W Main St, Bennington, VT 05201 - T: (802) 447-1571, Fax: (802) 442-8305, E-mail: executivedirector@benningtonmuseum.com, Internet: www.benningtonmuseum.com. Dir.: Richard Borges, Cur.: Carissa Amash
Fine Arts Museum / Decorative Arts Museum / Local Museum - 1875
Art, decorative arts, local hist 41629

Southern Vermont College Art Gallery, 982 Mansion Dr, Bennington, VT 05201 - T: (802) 442-5427, Fax: (802) 447-4695. Dir.: Greg Winterhalter
Fine Arts Museum / University Museum - 1979
Art 41630

Benson MN

Swift County Historical Museum, 2135 Minnesota Av, Bldg 2, Benson, MN 56215 - T: (320) 843-4467, E-mail: historical.society@co.swift.mn.us. Pres.: George Clemens, Exec. Dir.: Marlys Gallagher
Historical Museum - 1929
Regional history 41631

Benton WI

Swindler's Ridge Museum, 25 W Main St, Benton, WI 53803 - T: (608) 759-5182. Dir.: Peg Roberts
Historical Museum - 1993 41632

Benton Harbor MI

Morton House Museum, 501 Territorial, Benton Harbor, MI 49022 - T: (616) 925-7011, Internet: www.parrett.net/~morton. Pres.: Miriam Pede
Local Museum - 1966
Local hist 41633

Benzonia MI

Benzie Area Historical Museum, 6941 Traverse Av, Benzonia, MI 49616 - T: (231) 882-5539, Fax: (231) 882-5539, E-mail: museum@t-one.net. Dir.: Debbra Eckhout
Local Museum - 1969
Local hist 41634

Berea KY

Berea College Burroughs Geological Museum, Main St, Berea, KY 40404 - T: (859) 985-3893, Fax: (859) 985-3303, E-mail: larry_lipchinsky@berea.edu, Internet: www.berea.edu/. Cur.: Zelek L. Lipchinsky
University Museum / Natural History Museum - 1920
Geology 41635

Berea College Doris Ulmann Galleries, Corner of Chestnut and Elipse St, Berea, KY 40404 - T: (606) 986-9341 ext 5530, Fax: (859) 985-3541, E-mail: robert_boyce@berea.edu, Internet: www.berea.edu/. Dir.: John Zhang
Fine Arts Museum / University Museum - 1975
Art 41636

Berea OH

Fawick Art Gallery, Baldwin-Wallace College, 275 Eastland Rd, Berea, OH 44017 - T: (440) 826-2152, Fax: (440) 826-3380, Internet: www.baldwinwallacecollege.com. Dir.: Prof. Paul Jacklitch
Fine Arts Museum
Drawings and prints from 16th - 20th c, paintings, sculptures by American Midwest artists 41637

Bergen NY

Bergen Museum of Local History, 7547 Lake Rd, Bergen, NY 14416 - T: (716) 494-1121. Pres.: Raymond MacConnell, Sc. Staff: Tracy Miller
Local Museum - 1964
Local hist 41638

Berkeley CA

Badè Institute of Biblical Archaeology and Howell Bible Collection, 1798 Scenic Av, Berkeley, CA 94709 - T: (510) 849-1272, 849-0528, Fax: (510) 845-8948, E-mail: bade@psr.edu, Internet: www.psr.edu/bade. C.E.O.: Ruth Ohm
Religious Arts Museum / Archaeological Museum - 1926
Archaeology, religion, rare bibles 41639

Berkeley Art Center, 1275 Walnut St, Berkeley, CA 94709 - T: (510) 644-6893, Fax: (510) 540-0343, Internet: www.berkeyartcenter.org. Dir.: Robbin L. Henderson, Cur.: Patrice Wagner
Fine Arts Museum - 1967
Contemporary art 41640

Berkeley Art Museum, University of California, Berkeley, CA 94710 - T: (510) 642-0808, Fax: (510) 642-4889. Dir.: Jacquelynn Bass
University Museum / Fine Arts Museum - 1963
Pacific film archive 41641

Essig Museum of Entomology, University of California, Berkeley, 211 and 311 Wellman Hall, Berkeley, CA 94720 - T: (510) 643-0804, Fax: (510) 642-7428, E-mail: cbarr@nature.berkeley.edu, Internet: www.mip.berkeley.edu/essig/. Dir.: Rosemarie G. Gillespie, Cur.: Cheryl B. Barr, Ass. Cur.: F.A.H. Sperling
University Museum / Natural History Museum - 1939
Entomology, esp arachnids and other terreestrial arthropods 41642

Judah L. Magnes Museum → The Magnes Museum

Kala Art Institute, 1060 Heinz Av, Berkeley, CA 94710 - T: (510) 549-2977, Fax: (510) 540-6914, E-mail: kala@kala.org, Internet: www.kala.org. Dir.: Yuzo Nakano, Archana Horsting
Library with Exhibitions - 1974 41643

Lawrence Hall of Science, University of California, 1 Centennial Dr, Hall of Science, Berkeley, CA 94720-5200 - T: (510) 642-5132, Fax: (510) 642-1055, E-mail: lhsinfo@uclink.berkeley.edu, Internet: www.laurencehallofscience.edu. Dir.: Dr. Ian Carmichael, Dep. Dir.: Susan Gregory, Ass. Dir.: Barbara Ando, Craig Strang, Jacquey Barber
Natural History Museum / Science&Tech Museum
Science, technology 41644

The Magnes Museum, 2911 Russell St, Berkeley, CA 94705 - T: (510) 549-6950, Fax: (510) 849-3673, E-mail: info@magnesmuseum.org, Internet: www.magnesmuseum.org. Dir.: Susan Morris, Cur.: Michal Friedlander (Judaica), Ruth Eis (Special Projects), Florence Helzel (Prints and Drawings), William Chayes (Photography and Video), Sheila Braufman (Paintings and Sculpture)
Fine Arts Museum / Religious Arts Museum - 1962
Judaica, historic Berkeley mansion, prints, drawings, paintings, sculptures, Western US Jewish history 41645

Museum of Paleontology, University of California at Berkeley, 1101 Valley Life Sciences Bldg, Berkeley, CA 94720-4780 - T: (510) 642-1821, Fax: (510) 642-1822, E-mail: ucmpwebmaster@uclink.berkeley.edu, Internet: www.ucmp.berkeley.edu. Dir.: David R. Lindberg, Cur.: Jere Lipps, William B. Berry, Carole S. Hickman, Kevin Padian, Walter Alvarez, Roger Byrne, William A. Clemens, Roy Caldwell, David R. Lindberg, James W. Valentine, Tim White, Anthony Barnosky, Joseph Gregory, Lynn Ingram
Natural History Museum - 1921
Vertebrates, plants, invertebrates, microfossils 41646

Museum of Vertebrate Zoology, University of California, 3101 Valley Life Sciences Bldg, Berkeley, CA 94720-3160 - T: (510) 642-3567, Fax: (510) 643-8238, Internet: www.mip.berkeley.edu/mvz/. Dir.: Craig Moritz, Cur.: David B. Wake (Herpetology), Ned K. Johnson (Birds), Ass. Cur.: Eileen A. Lacey (Mammalogy)
University Museum / Natural History Museum - 1908
Zoology, herpetology, mammology 41647

Phoebe Apperson Hearst Museum of Anthropology, University of California, 103 Kroeber Hall, Berkeley, CA 94720-3712 - T: (510) 642-3682, Fax: (510) 642-6271, E-mail: pahma@uclink.berkeley.edu, Internet: hearstmuseum.berkeley.edu. Dir.: Rosemary Joyce, Patrick V. Kirch, Cons.: Madeleine Fang
University Museum / Ethnology Museum / Archaeological Museum - 1901
Anthropology 41648

University of California Berkeley Art Museum, 2626 Bancroft Way, Berkeley, CA 94720-2250 - T: (510) 642-0808, Fax: (510) 642-4889, E-mail: rmacneil@uclink.berkeley.edu, Internet: www.bampfa.berkeley.edu. Dir.: Kevin Consey, Ass. Dir.: Stephen Gong, Cur.: Constance Lewallen (Exhibitions), Lucinda Barnes (Collections), Heidi Jacobson Zuckerman (Matrix)
Fine Arts Museum / University Museum - 1965
Art, film, video - Pacific film archive 41649

Berkeley Springs WV

Museum of the Berkeley Springs, POB 99, Berkeley Springs, WV 25411 - T: (304) 258-3743. Head: Hettie G. Hawvermale
Local Museum - 1984 41650

Berlin MA

Berlin Art and Historical Collections, 4 Woodward Av, Berlin, MA 01503 - T: (978) 838-2502. Dir.: Barry W. Eager
Local Museum / Fine Arts Museum - 1950
Art, history 41651

Berlin WI

Berlin Historical Society Museum of Local History, 111 S Adams Av, Berlin, WI 54923 - T: (920) 361-3636, Fax: (920) 361-5439, E-mail: berlinc@vbe.com, Internet: www.1berlin.com. Pres.: Dan Friemark, Vice Pres.: Jim Petersen
Local Museum - 1962
Local hist 41652

Bermuda LA

Beau Fort Plantation Home, 4078 Hwy 494 and Hwy 119, Bermuda, LA 71456 - T: (318) 352-9580, 352-8352, Fax: (318) 352-7280, E-mail: beaufort@worldnetla.net
Folklore Museum - 1790
1790 Creole one and one-half cottage type building 41653

Berrien Springs MI

Courthouse Museum, 313 N Cass, Berrien Springs, MI 49103 - T: (616) 471-1202, Fax: (616) 471-7412, E-mail: bcha@berrienhistory.org, Internet: www.berrienhistory.org. Dir.: Leo J. Goodsell
Local Museum - 1967
County hist 41654

Siegfried H. Horn Archaeological Museum, Andrews University, Berrien Springs, MI 49104-0990 - T: (616) 471-3273, Fax: (616) 471-3619, E-mail: hornmusm@andrews.edu, Internet: www.andrews.edu/archaeology. Dir.: Randall W. Younker, Cur.: David Merling, Ass. Cur.: Efrain Velazquez
Archaeological Museum - 1970
Archaeology 41655

Berryville AR

Saunders Memorial Museum, 113-15 E Madison St, Berryville, AR 72616 - T: (870) 423-2563. Head: Hazel Prentice Burkett
Museum of Classical Antiquities / Special Museum - 1955
Gun, period furnishings 41656

Berryville VA

Clarke County Historical Museum, 32 E Main St, Berryville, VA 22611 - T: (540) 955-2600, Fax: (540) 955-0285, E-mail: ccha@visuallink.com, Internet: www.visuallink.net/ccha. Pres./Cur.: Sarah P. Trumbower
Local Museum - 1983
Regional history 41657

Bessemer AL

Bessemer Hall of History, 1905 Alabama Av, Bessemer, AL 35020 - T: (205) 426-1633, Fax: (205) 426-1633. Dir.: Dominga N. Toner
Local Museum - 1970 41658

Bethany WV

Historic Bethany, Bethany College, Bethany, WV 26032 - T: (304) 829-7285, Fax: (304) 829-7287, E-mail: historic@mail.bethanywv.edu, Internet: www.bethanywv.edu. C.E.O.: Dr. D. Duane Cummins
University Museum / Historical Museum - 1840 41659

Bethel AK

Yugtarvik Regional Museum, Third Av, Bethel, AK 99559, mail addr: POB 388, Bethel, AK 99559 - T: (907) 543-2098, Fax: (907) 543-2255
Local Museum - 1967
Native culture, lifestyle of the Central Yupik Eskimos of the Yukon-Kuskokwin delta 41660

Bethel ME

Bethel Historical Society's Regional History Center, 10-14 Broad St, Bethel, ME 04217-0012 - T: (207) 824-2908, Fax: (207) 824-0882, E-mail: info@bethelhistorical.org, Internet: bethelhistorical.org. Exec. Dir.: Dr. Stanley Russell Howe
Historical Museum - 1974
Regional history of Northern New England, federal style house - Research library, period house museum, 41661

Bethesda MD

DeWitt Stetten Jr. Museum of Medical Research, National Institutes of Health, Bldg 31, Bethesda, MD 20892-2092 - T: (301) 496-6610, Fax: (301) 402-1434, E-mail: museum@nih.gov, Internet: www.nih.gov/od/museum. Dir.: Victoria A. Harden, Cur.: Michele Lyons
Historical Museum - 1987
Medicine, Warren Grant Magnuson Clinical Center 41662

Bethlehem NH

Crossroads of America, 6 Trudeau Rd, Bethlehem, NH 03574 - T: (603) 869-3919, E-mail: Roger.Hinds@fothBBS. C.E.O.: Roger Hinds
Special Museum - 1981
Model railroad, toy 41663

Bethlehem PA

Burnside Plantation, 1461 Schoenersville Rd, Bethlehem, PA 18018 - T: (610) 868-5044, Fax: (610) 882-5044, E-mail: histbeth2@hotmail.com, Internet: www.historicbethlehem.org. Exec. Dir.: Charlene Donchez Mowers
Decorative Arts Museum - 1986
Farming, domestic crafts and decorative arts 41664

Colonial Industrial Quarter, 459 Old York Rd, Bethlehem, PA 18018 - T: (610) 882-0450, Fax: (610) 882-0460, E-mail: histbeth2@hotmail.com, Internet: www.historicbethlehem.org. Exec. Dir.: Charlene Donchez Mowers
Historical Museum - 1957 41665

Historic Bethlehem → Colonial Industrial Quarter

Kemerer Museum of Decorative Arts, 427 N New St, Bethlehem, PA 18018 - T: (610) 868-6868, Fax: (610) 332-2459, E-mail: histbeth2@hotmail.com, Internet: www.historicbethlehem.org. Exec. Dir.: Charlene Donchez Mowers
Decorative Arts Museum - 1954 41666

Lehigh University Art Galleries/Museum, Zoellner Arts Center, 420 E Packer Av, Bethlehem, PA 18015 - T: (610) 758-3615, Fax: (610) 758-4580, E-mail: rv02@lehigh.edu, Internet: www.lehigh.edu/luag. Dir./Cur.: Ricardo Viera, Asst. Dir.: Denise Stangl, Cur./Prep.: Robert Lopata
Fine Arts Museum / University Museum - 1864 41667

Moravian Museum of Bethlehem, 66 W Church St, Bethlehem, PA 18018 - T: (610) 867-0173, Fax: (610) 694-0960, E-mail: histbeth2@hotmail.com, Internet: www.historicbethlehem.org. Exec. Dir.: Charlene Donchez Mowers
Local Museum / Religious Arts Museum - 1938 41668

Payne Gallery, c/o Moravian College, Main and Church Sts, Bethlehem, PA 18018 - T: (610) 861-1675, 861-1680, Fax: (610) 861-1682, E-mail: medjr01@moravian.edu, Internet: www.moravian.edu. Dir.: Dr. Diane Radycki
Fine Arts Museum - 1982
Drawings, paintings, photography, prints, watercolors, woodcuts 41669

Bettendorf IA

Family Museum of Arts and Science, 2900 Learning Campus Dr, Bettendorf, IA 52722 - T: (563) 344-4106, Fax: (563) 344-4164, Internet: www.familymuseum.org. Dir.: Tracey K. Kuehl
Fine Arts Museum / Natural History Museum - 1974
Children's museum 41670

Beverly MA

Beverly Historical Museum, 117 Cabot St, Beverly, MA 01915 - T: (508) 922-1186, Fax: (508) 922-7387, E-mail: info@beverlyhistory.org, Internet: www.beverlyhistory.org. Exec. Dir.: Paige W. Roberts, Pres.: Doreen Ushakoff
Local Museum - 1891
Local history, John Cabot mansion, John Balch house, Hale farm - genealogical research 41671

Beverly OH

Oliver Tucker Historic Museum, State Rte 60, Beverly, OH 45715 - T: (614) 984-2489. Pres.: Greg Holdren, Cur.: Mary A. Irvin
Local Museum - 1971 41672

Beverly WA

Wanapum Dam Heritage Center, Hwy 243, Beverly, WA 98823 - T: (509) 754-3541, Fax: (509) 754-2522, E-mail: sjohns1@gcpud.org. Dir.: Leon Hoepner
Local Museum / Folklore Museum - 1966
Local hist 41673

Beverly WV

Randolph County Museum, Main St, Beverly, WV 26253 - T: (304) 636-0841. Dir.: Randy Allan, Cur.: Donald Rice
Local Museum - 1924 41674

Beverly Hills CA

The Academy Gallery, c/o Academy of Motion Picture Arts and Sciences, 8949 Wilshire Blvd, Beverly Hills, CA 90211-1972 - T: (310) 247-3000, Fax: (310) 247-3610, E-mail: gallery@oscars.org, Internet: www.oscars.org. Dir.: Robert Smolkin
Public Gallery - 1970 41675

California Museum of Ancient Art, POB 10515, Beverly Hills, CA 90213 - T: (818) 762-5500, E-mail: cmaa@earthlink.net. Pres.: John D. Hofbauer, Dir./Cur.: Jerôme Berman
Archaeological Museum - 1983
Near Eastern art and archaeology (Egypt, Mesopotamia, the Holy Land) 41676

Museum of Television and Radio, 465 N Beverly Dr, Beverly Hills, CA 90210 - T: (310) 786-1000, 786-1025, Fax: (310) 786-1086, E-mail: lramos@mtr.org, Internet: www.mtr.org. Dir.: Steve Bell
Science&Tech Museum - 1996
Communication 41677

Bexley OH

Bexley Historical Society Museum, 2242 E Main St, Bexley, OH 43209-2319 - T: (614) 235-8694, Fax: (614) 235-3420. Dir.: Edward L. Hamblin, Cur.: Debbie McCue
Local Museum - 1974 41678

Big Cypress Seminole Indian Reservation FL

Ah-Tah-Thi-Ki Museum, County Rd 833 and W. Boundary Rd, Big Cypress Seminole Indian Reservation, FL 33440 - T: (863) 902-1115, Fax: (863) 902-1117, E-mail: museum@semtribe.com, Internet: www.seminotribe.com/museum. Dir.: Billy L. Cypress
Historical Museum - 1989 41679

Big Horn WY

Bradford Brinton Memorial, 239 Brinton Rd, Big Horn, WY 82833 - T: (307) 672-3173, Fax: (307) 672-3258, E-mail: kls_bbm@vcn.com, Internet: www.bradfordbrintonmemorial.com. Dir./Kur.: Kenneth L. Schuster, Cur.: Dwight Layton
Fine Arts Museum - 1961
Art 41680

Big Pool MD

Fort Frederick, 11100 Fort Frederick Rd, Big Pool, MD 21711 - T: (301) 842-2155, Fax: (301) 842-0028, Internet: www.dwr.state.md.us
Fine Arts Museum / Military Museum - 1922
Historic building and site 41681

Big Rapids MI

Mecosta County Historical Museum, 129 S Stewart St, Big Rapids, MI 49307 - T: (616) 592-5091, 796-6360
Local Museum - 1957
Agriculture, costumes, folklore, Indian artifacts, numismatic, logging and lumbering, toys 41682

Big Spring TX

Heritage Museum and Potton House, 510 Scurry, Big Spring, TX 79720 - T: (915) 267-8255, Fax: (915) 267-8255, E-mail: heritage@crcom.net, Internet: www.bondwebs.com. Cur.: Angela Way, Ass. Cur.: Nancy Raney
Local Museum - 1971
Local hist 41683

Big Stone Gap VA

Southwest Virginia Museum, 10 W First St N, Big Stone Gap, VA 24219 - T: (276) 523-1322, Fax: (276) 523-6616, Internet: www.dcr.state.va.us/parks/swvamus.htm
Historical Museum - 1948
Early hist and pioneer period of Southwest Virginia, industrial develop, coal bboom 41684

Big Timber MT

Crazy Mountain Museum, Exit 367 Cemetery Rd, Hwy I-90, Big Timber, MT 59011 - T: (406) 932-5126. Dir.: Fran Elgen
Local Museum - 1990
Hist of Sweet Grass County 41685

Bigfork MT

Butter Pat Museum, 265 Eagle Bend Dr, Bigfork, MT 59911-6235. Dir.: Mary Dessoie Stephen Weppner
Decorative Arts Museum / Special Museum
2000 butter pats (miniature plates used to hold an individual portion of butter), 19th c China 41686

Biglerville PA

National Apple Museum, 154 W Hanover St, Biglerville, PA 17307-0656 - T: (717) 677-4556, Internet: www.uasd.k12.pa.us/upperadams/appmus. Pres.: Dick Mountfort
Agriculture Museum - 1990
Agriculture 41687

Billings MT

Moss Mansion Museum, 914 Division St, Billings, MT 59101 - T: (406) 256-5100, Fax: (506) 252-0091, E-mail: mossmansion@mossmansion.com, Internet: www.mossmansion.com. C.E.O.: Ruth Towe
Decorative Arts Museum - 1986 41688

Northcutt Steele Gallery, Montana State University Billings, 1500 N 30th St, Billings, MT 59101-0298 - T: (406) 657-2324, Fax: (406) 657-2187, E-mail: njussila@msu-b.edu. Dir.: Neil Jussila
Fine Arts Museum
Visual art 41689

Peter Yegen Jr. Yellowstone County Museum, 1950 Terminal Circle, Logan Field, Billings, MT 59105 - T: (406) 256-6811, Fax: (406) 256-6031, E-mail: ycm@pyjrycm.org, Internet: www.pyjrycm.org. Dir.: Robin Urban
Local Museum - 1953
Indian artifacts, Western memorabilia, military items, dinosaur bones, Leory Greene paintings 41690

Western Heritage Center, 2822 Montana Av, Billings, MT 59101 - T: (406) 256-6809 ext 21, Fax: (406) 256-6850, E-mail: heritage@ywhc.org, Internet: www.ywhc.org. Dir.: Kevin Kooistra-Manning, Cur.: Dorla Brunner
Historical Museum - 1971 41691

Yellowstone Art Museum, 401 N 27 St, Billings, MT 59101 - T: (406) 256-6804, Fax: (406) 256-6817, E-mail: artinfo@artmuseum.org, Internet: yellowstone.artmuseum.org. Dir.: Robert Knight
Fine Arts Museum - 1964
Contemporary art and prints, abstract expresionists art 41692

Biloxi MS

Beauvoir, Jefferson Davis Home and Presidential Library, 2244 Beach Blvd, Biloxi, MS 39531 - T: (228) 388-9074, Fax: (228) 388-7082, E-mail: majedwards@aol.com, Internet: www.beauvoir.org. Asst. Dir./Cur.: Patrick Hotard
Historical Museum / Military Museum / Historic Site - 1941 41693

George E. Ohr Arts and Cultural Center → The Ohr-O'Keefe Museum of Art

Mardi Gras Museum, 119 Rue Magnolia, Biloxi, MS 39530 - T: (228) 435-6245, Fax: (228) 435-6246, E-mail: museums@biloxi.ms.us. Dir.: Lolly Barnes
Historical Museum
History Museum, housed in the restored antebellum 1847 Magnolia Hotel 41694

Maritime and Seafood Industry Museum, 115 First St, Biloxi, MS 39530 - T: (228) 435-6320, Fax: (228) 435-6309, E-mail: museums@biloxi.ms.us. Pres.: Gavin Schmidt, Dir.: Robin Krohn
Historical Museum / Science&Tech Museum - 1986
Maritime and seafood industry 41695

Museum of Biloxi → Maritime and Seafood Industry Museum

Museum of Biloxi → Mardi Gras Museum

The Ohr-O'Keefe Museum of Art, 136 George E. Ohr St, Biloxi, MS 39530 - T: (228) 374-5547, Fax: (228) 436-3641, E-mail: info@georgeohr.org, Internet: www.georgeohr.com. Dir.: Marjorie E. Gowdy
Fine Arts Museum - 1989
Art, ceramics 41696

Tullis-Toledano Manor, 360 Beach Blvd, Biloxi, MS 39530 - T: (228) 435-6293, 435-6308, Fax: (228) 435-6246, E-mail: museums@biloxi.ms.us, Internet: www.biloxi.ms.us. Dir.: Ed Miles
Decorative Arts Museum 41697

Binghamton NY

Broome County Historical Society Museum, 30 Front St, Binghamton, NY 13905 - T: (607) 772-0660, Fax: (607) 771-8905, E-mail: broomehistory@tier.net, Internet: www.sites.tier.net/broomehistory/. Pres.: David J. Dixon
Local Museum - 1919 41698

Discovery Center of the Southern Tier, 60 Morgan Rd, Binghamton, NY 13903 - T: (607) 773-8750, Fax: (607) 773-8019, E-mail: info@discoverycenter.org, Internet: www.thediscoverycenter.org. Dir.: Elaine Kelly (Exhibits), Dr. Michael Grenis (Education), Ass. Dir.: Martha J. Steed
Special Museum - 1983
Fossils, artifacts, textiles, 41699

Roberson Museum and Science Center, 30 Front St, Binghamton, NY 13905 - T: (607) 772-0660, Fax: (607) 771-8905, Internet: www.roberson.org. Dir.: Leon Horwitz, Cur.: Catherine Schwoeffermann (Folklife)
Fine Arts Museum / Historical Museum / Science&Tech Museum - 1954 41700

University Art Museum, State University of New York at Binghamton, Binghamton, NY 13902-6000 - T: (607) 777-2634, Fax: (607) 777-2613, E-mail: hogan@binghamton.edu. Dir.: Lynn Gamwell, Ass. Dir.: Jacqueline Hogan, Ass. Cur.: Silvia Ivanova
Fine Arts Museum / University Museum - 1967 41701

Birdsboro PA

Daniel Boone Homestead, 400 Daniel Boone Rd, Birdsboro, PA 19508 - T: (610) 582-4900, Fax: (610) 582-1744. Pres.: Gerald Vermeesch
Local Museum / Folklore Museum / Open Air Museum - 1937 41702

Birmingham AL

Agnes Gallery, 1919 15th Av S, Birmingham, AL 35205 - T: (205) 939-3393, Fax: (205) 393-0063, E-mail: agnesgalle@aol.com, Internet: www.agnesgallery.com. Dir.: Jon Coffelt, Shawn Boley
Fine Arts Museum - 1993 41703

Arlington Museum, 331 Cotton Av SW, Birmingham, AL 35211 - T: (205) 780-5656, Fax: (205) 788-0585. Dir.: Daniel F. Brooks
Local Museum - 1953 41704

Birmingham Civil Rights Institute Museum, 520 16th St N, Birmingham, AL 35203 - T: (205) 328-9696, Fax: (205) 323-5219, E-mail: bcri.info@bcri.bham.al.us, Internet: www.bcri.bham.al.us. Exec. Dir.: Dr. Lawrence Pijeaux
Historical Museum - 1991 41705

Birmingham Museum of Art, 2000 8th Av N, Birmingham, AL 35203 - T: (205) 254-2566, Fax: (205) 254-2714, E-mail: jhatchett@artsBMA.org, Internet: www.artsBMA.org. Dir.: Gail Andrews Trechsel, Cur.: Dr. Donald A. Wood (Asian Art), Dr. Anne Forschler (Decorative Arts), Dr. David Moos (Painting and Sculpture Works on Paper), Asst. Dir.: Barbara Kelley (Education), Libr.: Grace Reid
Fine Arts Museum - 1951
American, European and Asian art, decorative art, renaissance art - Hanson library 41706

McWane Center, 200 19th St N, Birmingham, AL 35203 - T: (205) 714-8300, Fax: (205) 714-8400, E-mail: mwright@mcwane.org, Internet: www.mcwane.org
Science&Tech Museum - 1997
Science, technology 41707

Red Mountain Museum → McWane Center

Sloss Furnaces National Historic Landmark, First Av N and 32nd St, Birmingham, AL 35222 - T: (205) 324-1911, Fax: (205) 324-6758, E-mail: ron@slossfurnaces.com, Internet: www.slossfurnaces.com. Dir.: Robert R. Rathburn, Cur.: Karen Utz
Science&Tech Museum - 1983
Industry, ironmaking plant incl blast furnaces, blowing engines, power house, boilers 41708

Southern Museum of Flight, 4343 N 73rd St, Birmingham, AL 35206-3642 - T: (205) 833-8226, Fax: (205) 836-2439, E-mail: southernmuseumofflight@compuserve.com, Internet: www.southernmuseumofflight.org. Dir.: Dr. J. Dudley Pewitt, Ass. Dir.: Dr. Donald B. Dodd
Science&Tech Museum - 1965
Aviation, transportation 41709

Space One Eleven, 2409 Second Av N, Birmingham, AL 35203-3809 - T: (205) 328-0553, Fax: (205) 328-0533, E-mail: soe@artswire.org, Internet: www.spaceoneleven.org. Dir.: Anne Arrasmith, Peter Prinz
Public Gallery - 1988 41710

Visual Arts Gallery, University of Alabama at Birmingham, Birmingham, AL 35294-1260 - T: (205) 934-4941, Fax: (205) 975-2836, Internet: www.uab.edu. Dir.: Antoinette Spanos Nordan
Fine Arts Museum / University Museum - 1972
Art 41711

Birmingham MI

Birmingham Bloomfield Art Center, 1516 S Cranbrook Rd, Birmingham, MI 48009 - T: (248) 644-0866, Fax: (248) 644-7904, Internet: www.bbartcenter.org. Dir.: Janet E. Torno, Ass. Dir.: Cynthia K. Mills
Fine Arts Museum - 1956
Art 41712

Birmingham Historical Museum, 556 W Maple, Birmingham, MI 48009 - T: (248) 642-2817, Fax: (248) 642-5551, E-mail: bmcelhone@ci.birmingham.mi.us, Internet: www.ci.birmingham.mi.us. Dir.: William K. McElhone
Historical Museum
Local history, furnishings, hist buildings 41713

Bisbee AZ

Bisbee Mining and Historical Museum, 5 Copper Queen Plaza, Bisbee, AZ 85603 - T: (520) 432-7071, 432-7848, Fax: (520) 432-7800, E-mail: carrie@bisbeemuseum.org, Internet: www.bisbeemuseum.org. Dir.: Carrie Gustavson, Cur.: Boyd Nicholl (Archival Colls), Margaret Harnett (Colls)
Historical Museum / Science&Tech Museum - 1971
Local hist, mining 41714

Bishop CA

Laws Railroad Museum, Silver Canyon Rd, Bishop, CA 93515 - T: (760) 873-5950, E-mail: lwasmuseum@aol.com, Internet: www.thesierraweb.com/bishop/laws. Pres.: Denton Sonke
Local Museum / Historical Museum / Historic Site - 1966
Laws Railroad Depot and 22 other buildings 41715

Bishop Hill IL

Bishop Hill Colony, POB 104, Bishop Hill, IL 61419 - T: (309) 927-3345, Fax: (309) 927-3345, Internet: www.bishophill.com. Man.: Martha J. Downey
Local Museum - 1946
Colony artifacts-agricultural items, furnitures, household items, textiles and tools, Olof Krans coll of folk art paintings 41716

Bishop Hill Heritage Museum, 103 N Bishop Hill St, Bishop Hill, IL 61419 - T: (309) 927-3899, Fax: (309) 927-3010, E-mail: bhha@winco.net, Internet: www.bishophill.net. Pres.: Morris Nelson, Dir.: Michael G. Wendel
Local Museum - 1962
Local history, Swedish communal settlement founded in 1846 by religious dissenters 41717

Bishopville SC

South Carolina Cotton Museum, 121 W Cedar Ln, Bishopville, SC 29010 - T: (803) 484-4497, Fax: (803) 484-5203, E-mail: scottonmus@ftc-i.net, Internet: www.sccotton.org. Exec. Dir.: Janson L. Cox
Special Museum - 1993
Economic, social and political impact of cotton 41718

Bismarck ND

Camp Hancock, First and Main St, Bismarck, ND 58505 - T: (701) 328-9664, Internet: www.discovernd.com/hist
Local Museum - 1951
Local hist, railroad steam engine 41719

De Mores State Historic Site, North Dakota Heritage Center, Bismarck, ND 58505-0830 - T: (701) 328-2666, Fax: (701) 328-3710, Internet: www.state.nd.us/hist/. Dir.: Merl Paaverud
Local Museum - 1936 41720

Former Governors' Mansion, 320 Av B East, Bismarck, ND 58501 - T: (701) 255-3819, 328-2666, Fax: (701) 328-3710, Internet: www.discovernd.com/hist. Dir.: Merlan E. Paaverud
Local Museum - 1895
Historic house 41721

State Historical Society of North Dakota Museum, c/o North Dakota Heritage Center, 612 E Blvd, Bismarck, ND 58505 - T: (701) 328-2666, Fax: (701) 328-3710, E-mail: histsoc@state.nd.us, Internet: www.discovernd.com/hist. Dir.: Merlan E. Paaverud
Local Museum - 1895 41722

Black Hawk CO

Lace House Museum, 161 Main St, Black Hawk, CO 80422 - T: (303) 582-5221, Fax: (303) 582-0429
Historical Museum - 1976 41723

Black River Falls WI

Jackson County Historical Society Museum, 13 S First and 321 Main St, Black River Falls, WI 54615-0037 - T: (715) 284-4927, Internet: www.blackriverfalls.com
Local Museum - 1916
Costumes, tools, school artifacts, glass plates, furniture, dairy 41724

Blacksburg SC

Kings Mountain National Military Park, 2625 Park Rd, Blacksburg, SC 29702 - T: (864) 936-7921, Fax: (864) 936-9897, Internet: www.nps.gov/kimo.htm. Head: D. Broadbert
Military Museum - 1931
Military hist 41725

Blacksburg VA

Armory Art Gallery, c/o Virgina Polytechnic Institute and State University, 201 Draper Rd, Blacksburg, VA 24061 - T: (540) 231-4859, 231-5547, Fax: (540) 231-7826
Fine Arts Museum / University Museum - 1969 41726

Historic Smithfield, 1000 Smithfield Plantation Rd, Blacksburg, VA 24060 - T: (540) 231-3947, Fax: (540) 231-3006, E-mail: smithfield.plantation@vt.edu, Internet: www.civic.bev.net/smithfield. Dir.: Belva Collins
Local Museum - 1964
Historic house 41727

Museum of the Geological Sciences, Virginia Polytechnic Institute and State University, Derring Hall, Blacksburg, VA 24061 - T: (540) 231-6029, Fax: (540) 231-3386, E-mail: seriksn@vt.edu. Dir./Cur.: Susan C. Eriksson
University Museum / Natural History Museum - 1969
Geology, mineralogy 41728

Perspective Gallery, c/o Virgina Polytechnic Institute and State University, Squires Student Center, Blacksburg, VA 24061 - T: (540) 231-5431, 231-6040, Fax: (540) 231-5430. Dir.: Tom Butterfield
Fine Arts Museum / University Museum - 1969 41729

Blackwell OK

Top of Oklahoma Historical Museum, 303 S Main St, Blackwell, OK 74631 - T: (405) 363-0209, Fax: (580) 363-0209. Pres.: George Glaze
Local Museum - 1972 41730

Blairsville GA

Union County Historical Society Museum, 1 Town Sq, Blairsville, GA 30512 - T: (706) 745-5493, Fax: (706) 745-5493, E-mail: history1@alltel.net. Dir.: Ann Farabee
Local Museum - 1988
Local history 41731

Blakely GA

Kolomoki Mounds State Park Museum, Indian Mounds Rd, off US-Hwy 27 and Kolomoki Rds, Blakely, GA 31723 - T: (229) 724-2150/51, Fax: (229) 724-2152, E-mail: kolomoki@alltel.net, Internet: www.gastateparks.org
Archaeological Museum - 1951
13th-century Indian burial mound and village 41732

Blanding UT

Edge of the Cedars State Park, 660 West, 400 N, Blanding, UT 84511 - T: (435) 678-2238, Fax: (435) 678-3348, E-mail: edgeofthecedars@utah.gov, Internet: www.parks.state.ut.us/parks/www1.edgh.htm. Cur.: Deborah Westfall
Ethnology Museum - 1978
Remains of 700 AD to 1220 AD structures, ancient dwellings of the Anasazi Indian culture 41733

Bloomfield NJ

Historical Society of Bloomfield Museum, 90 Broad St, Bloomfield, NJ 07003 - T: (973) 566-6220, Fax: (973) 566-6220, E-mail: bloomfhist@aol.com. Pres.: Ina Campbell, Cur.: Dorothy E. Johnson
Local Museum - 1966 41734

Bloomfield NM

San Juan County Museum, 6131 US Hwy 64, Bloomfield, NM 87413 - T: (505) 632-2013, Fax: (505) 632-1707, E-mail: salmonruin@outerbounds.net. Exec. Dir.: Larry L. Baker
Local Museum - 1973
History, archaeology, anthropology 41735

Bloomfield NY

A.W.A. Electronic-Communication Museum, 2 South Av, Bloomfield, NY 14469 - T: (585) 392-3088, Fax: (716) 392-3088, E-mail: k2mp@etnet.net, Internet: www.antiquewireless.org. Dir.: Thomas Peterson, Cur.: Edward Gable
Science&Tech Museum - 1953 41736

Bloomfield Academy Museum, 8 South Av, Bloomfield, NY 14443 - T: (716) 657-7244, Fax: (716) 657-7244, E-mail: ebhs1838@hotmail.com. Pres.: Charles Thomas, C.E.O.: Carl J. Elsbree
Historical Museum - 1967 41737

Bloomfield Hills MI

Cranbrook Art Museum, 39221 Woodward Av, Bloomfield Hills, MI 48303-0801 - T: (248) 645-3323, 645-3361, Fax: (248) 645-3324, E-mail: artmuseum@cranbrook.edu, Internet: www.cranbrook.edu/museum. Dir.: Gregory M. Wittkopp, Cur.: Irene Hofmann
Fine Arts Museum - 1927
Contemporary art, architecture and design - library 41738

Cranbrook House and Gardens Auxiliary, 380 Lone Pine Rd, Bloomfield Hills, MI 48303-0801 - T: (248) 645-3149, Fax: (248) 645-3151, E-mail: mkrygier@cranbrook.edu, Internet: www.cranbrook.edu
Local Museum - 1971
Home of George Gough and Ellen Scripps Booth 41739

Cranbrook Institute of Science, 39221 Woodward, Bloomfield Hills, MI 48303-0801 - T: (248) 645-3200, Fax: (248) 645-3050, Internet: www.cranbrook.edu. Dir.: Talbert B. Spence, Cur.: Lawrence Hutchinson
Natural History Museum / Science&Tech Museum - 1932
Science 41740

Bloomington IL

Children's Discovery Museum of Central Illinois, 716 E Empire, Bloomington, IL 61701 - T: (309) 829-6222, Fax: (309) 829-2292, E-mail: staff@cdmci.org. CEO: Shari Spaniol Buckellew
Natural History Museum / Science&Tech Museum - 1994 41741

The David Davis Mansion, 1000 E Monroe Dr, Bloomington, IL 61701 - T: (309) 828-1084, Fax: (309) 828-3493, E-mail: davismansion@yahoo.com, Internet: www.davismansion.org. Dir.: Dr. Marcia Young, Cur.: Jeff Saulsbery
Historical Museum - 1960
David Davis' Second Empire Italianate brick mansion (Abraham Lincoln's campaign manager) 41742

McLean County Arts Center, 601 N East St, Bloomington, IL 61701 - T: (309) 829-0011, Fax: (309) 829-4928, E-mail: mcac@dave-world.net, Internet: www.mcac.org. Exec. Dir.: Catherine Sutloff, Cur.: Alison Hatcher
Fine Arts Museum - 1922 41743

McLean County Museum of History, 200 N Main, Bloomington, IL 61701 - T: (309) 827-0428, Fax: (309) 827-0100, E-mail: gregkoos@mchistory.org, Internet: www.mchistory.org. Exec. Dir.: Greg Koos, Cur.: Susan Hartzold
Local Museum - 1892
Library and Archives 41744

Bloomington IN

Elizabeth Sage Historic Costume Collection, Memorial Hall E 232, Indiana University, Bloomington, IN 47405 - T: (812) 855-4627, 855-5223, Fax: (812) 855-0362, E-mail: rowold@indiana.edu. Dir.: Nelda M. Christ, Cur.: Kathleen L. Rowold
Special Museum - 1935
Textiles, costume 41745

Indiana University Art Museum, 1133 E Seventh St, Bloomington, IN 47405 - T: (812) 855-5445, Fax: (812) 855-1023, E-mail: iuartmus@indiana.edu, Internet: www.indiana.edu/~iuam. Dir.: Adelheid M. Gealt, Ass. Dir.: Brian Kearney (Development), Diane Pelrine (Curatorial Services), Danae Thimme (Conservation)
Fine Arts Museum - 1941 41746

Monroe County Historical Society, 202 E Sixth St, Bloomington, IN 47408 - T: (812) 332-2517, Fax: (812) 355-5593, E-mail: mchm@kiva.net, Internet: www.kiva.net/~mchm/museum.htm. Dir.: Samuel D. Bohl, Cur.: Michelle Hill
Local Museum - 1980
County history 41747

School of Fine Arts Gallery, Indiana University Bloomington, 1201 E Seventh St, 123 Fine Arts Bldg, Bloomington, IN 47405 - T: (812) 855-8490, Fax: (812) 855-7498, E-mail: sofa@indiana.edu, Internet: www.fa.indiana.edu. Dir.: Betsy Stirratt, Georgia Strange
Fine Arts Museum / University Museum - 1987
Paintings, graphics, drawings, sculptures, decorative arts 41748

William Hammond Mathers Museum, 416 N Indiana Av, Bloomington, IN 47405 - T: (812) 855-6873, Fax: (812) 855-0205, E-mail: mathers@indiana.edu, Internet: www.indiana.edu/~mathers/. Dir.: Geoffrey Conrad, Cur.: Thomas Kavanagh (Collections), Ellen Sieber Kirk (Education), Cons.: Judith Sylvester
Folklore Museum / Historical Museum / Ethnology Museum / University Museum - 1963
Anthropology, history, folklore 41749

Wylie House Museum, 307 E 2nd St, Bloomington, IN 47401, mail addr: 317 E 2nd St, Bloomington, IN 47401 - T: (812) 855-6224. Dir.: Jo Burgess
Historical Museum
Indiana University's first president 41750

Bloomington MN

Bloomington Art Center, 10206 Penn Av S, Bloomington, MN 55431 - T: (952) 563-4777, Fax: (952) 563-8744, E-mail: info@bloomingtonartcenter.com, Internet: www.bloomingtonartcenter.com. Dir.: Susan M. Anderson, Dep. Dir.: Rachel Flentje (Exhibitions), Judith Yerhot (Education), Cur.: Elizabeth R. Greenbaum
Fine Arts Museum / Performing Arts Museum - 1976
Multi-Disciplinary art, performing and visual, Rachel Flentje (exhibitions) 41751

Bloomington Historical Museum, 10200 Penn Av, S, Bloomington, MN 55431 - T: (612) 948-8881. Pres.: Vonda Kelly
Local Museum - 1964
Regional history 41752

Bloomsburg PA

Columbia County Museum, 225 Market St, Bloomsburg, PA 17815-0360 - T: (570) 784-1600, Internet: www.colcohist-gensoc.org. Exec. Dir.: Bonnie Farver, Dir.: Julia Driskell
Local Museum - 1914
Local hist 41753

Haas Gallery of Art, c/o Bloomsburg University of Pennsylvania, Arts Dept., Old Science Hall, Bloomsburg, PA 17815 - T: (570) 389-4646, Fax: (570) 389-4459, E-mail: rhuber@bloomu.edu, Internet: www.bloomu.edu. Dir.: Vincent Hron
University Museum / Fine Arts Museum - 1966 41754

Blue Earth MN

Wakefield House Museum, 405 E Sixth St, Blue Earth, MN 56013 - T: (507) 526-5421. Cust.: Agnes Schaal
Local Museum - 1948 41755

Blue Hill ME

Parson Fisher House, Jonathan Fisher Memorial, Mines Rd, Blue Hill, ME 04614 - T: (207) 374-2159, E-mail: parsonfisher@hypernet.com, Internet: www.hypernet.com/fischer/about.htm. Pres.: Eric Linnel
Folklore Museum / Local Museum - 1954 41756

Blue Mounds WI

Little Norway, 3576 Hwy JG N, Blue Mounds, WI 53517 - T: (608) 437-8211, Fax: (608) 437-7827, Internet: www.littlenorway.com
Historical Museum - 1926
Farmstead buildings, Norwegian and pioneer artifacts 41757

Blue Mountain Lake NY

Adirondack Museum, Rts 28N and 30, Blue Mountain Lake, NY 12812-0099 - T: (518) 352-7311 ext 101, Fax: (518) 352-7653, E-mail: acaroll@adkmuseum.org, Internet: www.adirondakmuseu.org. Dir.: John Collins, Chief Cur.: Caroline Welsh, Cur.: Hallie Bond
Local Museum - 1952 41758

Bluefield WV

Science Center of West Virginia, 500 Bland St, Bluefield, WV 24701 - T: (304) 325-8855, Fax: (304) 324-0513. Pres.: Patty Wilkinson, Dir.: Thomas R. Willmitch
Natural History Museum / Science&Tech Museum - 1994 41759

Bluffton IN

Wells County Historical Museum, 420 W Market St, Bluffton, IN 46714 - T: (219) 824-9956, E-mail: jcsturgeon@adamswells.com, Internet: www.parlorcity.com. Pres.: Laura Sawyer
Local Museum - 1935
Local history 41760

Blunt SD

Mentor Graham Museum, 103 N Commercial Av, Blunt, SD 57522
Local Museum - 1950
Local hist 41761

Boalsburg PA

Boal Mansion Museum, Business Rte 322, Boalsburg, PA 16827 - T: (814) 466-6210, E-mail: boalmus@vicon.net, Internet: www.boalmuseum.com. Pres.: Christopher Lee, Mathilde Boal Lee
Fine Arts Museum / Historical Museum - 1952 41762

Pennsylvania Military Museum and 28th Division Shrine, Rtes 322 and 45, Boalsburg, PA 16827 - T: (814) 466-6263, Fax: (814) 466-6618, E-mail: wleech@state.pa.us, Internet: www.psu.edu/dept/aerospace/museum. Pres.: Michael Siggins, Dir./Cur.: William J. Leech
Military Museum - 1969 41763

Boca Raton FL

Boca Raton Historical Society Museum, 71 N Federal Hwy, Boca Raton, FL 33432 - T: (561) 395-6766, Fax: (561) 395-4049, E-mail: info@bocahistory.org, Internet: www.bocahistory.org. Dir.: Mary Csar
Historical Museum - 1972 41764

Boca Raton Museum of Art, 501 Plaza Real, Boca Raton, FL 33432 - T: (561) 392-2500 ext 200, Fax: (561) 391-6410, E-mail: info@bocamuseum.org, Internet: www.bocamuseum.org. Dir.: George S. Bolge, Cur.: Courtney P. Curtiss (Exhibitions), Richard J. Frank (Education)
Fine Arts Museum - 1950 41765

Children's Museum of Boca Raton, 498 Crawford Blvd, Boca Raton, FL 33432 - T: (561) 368-6875, Fax: (561) 395-7764. Exec. Dir.: Poppi Mercier
Special Museum - 1979 41766

International Museum of Cartoon Art, 201 Plaza Real, Boca Raton, FL 33432 - T: (561) 391-2200, Fax: (561) 391-2721, E-mail: correspondance@cartoon.org, Internet: www.cartoon.org. Dir.: Abigail Roeloffs, Cur.: Charla Stephen
Fine Arts Museum - 1974
Art, cartoons, comic strips and books, magazine illustration - Library 41767

Jewish Institute for the Arts, 9557 Islamorade Tce, Boca Raton, FL 33496 - T: (561) 883-5023, Fax: (561) 883-5019, E-mail: jiarts@aol.com, Internet: www.jiarts.org. Cur.: Shalom Goldberg
Fine Arts Museum - 1966
Paintings, sculpture and works on paper 41768

University Gallery, c/o Florida Atlantic University, 777 Glades Rd, Boca Raton, FL 33431-0991 - T: (561) 297-2966, 297-3406, Fax: (561) 297-2166, E-mail: wfaulds@fau.edu, Internet: www.fau.edu/galleries. Dir.: W. Rod Faulds
Fine Arts Museum - 1970
Artinian coll, Albert Binny Backus paintings 41769

Boerne TX

Kuhlmann King Historical House and Museum, 402 E Blanco, Boerne, TX 78006 - T: (830) 249-2030, E-mail: edmond@gsinternet.net, Internet: www.nootsweb.com/~txkendal
Local Museum 41770

Boise ID

Boise Art Museum, 670 S Julia Davis Dr, Boise, ID 83702 - T: (208) 345-8330, Fax: (208) 345-2247, E-mail: comments@boiseartmuseum.org, Internet: www.boiseartmuseum.org. Dir.: Lucinda Barnes, Ass. Dir.: Marilyn Allen, Cur.: Sandy Harthorn (Exhibitions), Andrea Potochick (Education), Ass. Cur.: Cynthia Sewell
Fine Arts Museum - 1931
General Arts 41771

Discovery Center of Idaho, 131 Myrtle St, Boise, ID 83702 - T: (208) 343-9895, Fax: (208) 343-0105, E-mail: discover@scidaho.org, Internet: www.scidaho.org. Exec. Dir.: Rika Clement
Science&Tech Museum - 1986 41772

Idaho Museum of Mining and Geology, 2455 Old Penitentiary Rd, Boise, ID 83712 - T: (208) 343-3315, E-mail: idahomuseum@hotmail.com. Pres.: Edward D. Fields
Natural History Museum / Science&Tech Museum - 1989
Mining, mineralogy 41773

Idaho State Historical Museum, 610 N Julia Davis Dr, Boise, ID 83702 - T: (208) 334-2120, Fax: (208) 334-4059, E-mail: jochoa@shs.state.id.us, Internet: www.state.id.us/ishs/. Dir.: Steve Guerber, Cur.: Joe Toluse
Historical Museum - 1881
History 41774

Bolinas CA

Bolinas Museum, 48 Wharf Rd, Bolinas, CA 94924 - T: (415) 868-0330, Fax: (415) 868-0607, E-mail: info@bolinasmuseum.org, Internet: www.bolinasmuseum.org. Dir.: Dolores Richards
Fine Arts Museum / Local Museum - 1982
Art, local history 41775

Bolivar OH

Fort Laurens State Memorial, 11067 Fort Laurens Rd NW, Bolivar, OH 44612 - T: (330) 874-2059, Fax: (330) 874-2936, E-mail: kmfzoar@compuserve.com, Internet: ohiohistory.org/places/ftlaurens. Dir.: Kathleen M. Fernández
Military Museum - 1972 41776

Bolton MA

Bolton Historical Museum, Sawyer House, 676 Main St, Bolton, MA 01740 - T: (508) 779-6392. Dir.: Tim Feihler, Sc. Staff: Deborah Kellett, Elaine Wetzel
Local Museum - 1962
Local history, farm/barn blacksmith shop 41777

Bolton Landing NY

Marcella Sembrich Opera Museum, 4800 Lake Shore Dr, Bolton Landing, NY 12814-0417 - T: (518) 644-2492, Fax: (518) 644-2191, E-mail: sembrich@webtv.net, Internet: www.

operamuseum.org. Dir.: Anita Behr Richards, Cur.: Richard Wargo
Music Museum - 1937
Golden age of Opera 41778

Bonham TX

Fort Inglish, Hwy 56 and Chinner St, Bonham, TX 75418 - T: (903) 583-3943, 640-2228. Pres.: Emily Porter
Military Museum - 1976
Military hist 41779

The Sam Rayburn Museum, 800 W Sam Rayburn Dr, Bonham, TX 75418 - T: (903) 583-2455, Fax: (903) 583-7394. Dir.: H.G. Dulaney
Local Museum - 1957
Local hist 41780

Bonner Springs KS

The National Agricultural Center and Hall of Fame, 630 Hall of Fame Dr, Bonner Springs, KS 66012 - T: (913) 721-1075, Fax: (913) 721-1202, Internet: www.aghalloffame.com. C.E.O.: Tim Nimz, Pres.: Chris Bernat, Chairman: Robert Carlson
Agriculture Museum / Science&Tech Museum / Historical Museum - 1958
Agriculture 41781

Wyandotte County Museum, 631 N 126th St, Bonner Springs, KS 66012 - T: (913) 721-1078, Fax: (913) 721-1394, E-mail: wycomus@toto.net. Dir.: Trish Schurkamp, Cur.: Rebecca J. Phipps
Local Museum - 1889
Regional history 41782

Boone IA

Boone County Historical Center, 602 Story St, Boone, IA 50036 - T: (515) 432-1907, E-mail: bchs@opencominc.com. Pres.: Jerry Ober, Dir.: Charles W. Irwin
Folklore Museum / Historical Museum / Natural History Museum - 1965 41783

Iowa Railroad Historical Museum, 225 10th St, Boone, IA 50036 - T: (515) 432-4249, Fax: (515) 432-4253, E-mail: B&svrr@tdsi.net.com, Internet: www.scenic-valley.com. Pres.: Sally Courter, C.E.O.: Fenners W. Stevenson
Science&Tech Museum - 1983 41784

Kare Shelley Railroad Museum, 1198 232nd St, Boone, IA 50036 - T: (515) 432-1907, E-mail: bchs@opencominc.com. Pres.: Carmen Jungbluth, Dir.: Charles W. Irwinnson
Science&Tech Museum / Historic Site - 1976 41785

Mamie Doud Eisenhower Birthplace, 709 Carroll St, Boone, IA 50036 - T: (515) 432-1896, Fax: (515) 432-3097, E-mail: mamiedoud@opencominc.com, Internet: www.booneiowa.com/mamie. C.E.O./Cur.: Larry Adams
Historic Site - 1970 41786

Boonesboro MO

Boone's Lick Site, State Rd 187, Arrow Rock, Boonesboro, MO 65233 - T: (660) 837-3330, Fax: (660) 837-3300, E-mail: dsparro@mail.dnr.state.mo.us, Internet: www.mostateparks.com/booneslick.htm
Archaeological Museum - 1960 41787

Boonsboro MD

Boonsborough Museum of History, 113 N Main St, Boonsboro, MD 21713-1007 - T: (301) 432-6969, Fax: (301) 416-2222. Dir.: Douglas G. Bast
Historical Museum - 1975 41788

Boonville IN

Warrick County Museum, 217 S First St, Boonville, IN 47601 - T: (812) 897-3100, Fax: (812) 897-6104. Pres.: Jo Ann Baum, Dir.: Virginia S. Allen
Local Museum - 1976
Local hist 41789

Boothbay ME

Boothbay Railway Village, Rte 27, Boothbay, ME 04537 - T: (207) 633-4727, Fax: (207) 633-4733, E-mail: staff@railwayvillage.org, Internet: www.railwayvillage.org. Dir.: Robert Ryan
Science&Tech Museum / Open Air Museum / Historical Museum - 1962
Transportation 41790

Boothbay Harbor ME

Boothbay Region Art Foundation, 7 Townsend Av, Boothbay Harbor, ME 04538 - T: (207) 633-2703, E-mail: localart@gwi.net, Internet: www.boothbayartists.org. Pres.: Robert McCarthy
Fine Arts Museum - 1964 41791

Boothwyn PA

Real World Computer Museum, c/o US Ikon Naaman Creek Center, 7 Creek Pkwy, Boothwyn, PA 19061 - T: (610) 494-9000, Fax: (610) 494-2090, E-mail: museum@phila.usconnect.com, Internet: uscphl.com/museum. Head: Craig Collins
Science&Tech Museum - 1990
Computer 41792

Bordentown NJ

Bordentown Historical Society Museum, 211 Crosswicks St, Bordentown, NJ 08505 - T: (609) 298-1740. Cur.: L.A. LeJambre
Local Museum - 1930 41793

Borger TX

Hutchinson County Museum, 618 N Main, Borger, TX 79007 - T: (806) 273-0130, Fax: (806) 273-0128, E-mail: museum@nts-online.net. Dir.: Edward Benz
Local Museum - 1977
Local hist 41794

Borrego Springs CA

Anza-Borrego Desert Museum, 200 Palm Cyn Dr, Borrego Springs, CA 92004 - T: (760) 767-4037, Fax: (760) 767-3427, Internet: www.anzaborrego.statepark.org. Head: David Van Cleve
Ethnology Museum / Archaeological Museum - 1979
Archaeology, paleontology 41795

Boston MA

Ancient and Honorable Artillery Company Museum, Armory, Faneuil Hall, Boston, MA 02109 - T: (617) 227-1638, Fax: (617) 227-7221, E-mail: vze28mb@verizon.net. Cur.: John F. McCauley
Military Museum - 1638
Military hist 41796

The Art Institute of Boston Main Gallery, 700 Beacon St, Boston, MA 02215 - T: (617) 262-1223, Fax: (617) 437-1226, E-mail: robinson@aiboston.edu, Internet: www.aiboston.edu. C.E.O.: Bonnell Robinson
Fine Arts Museum / Public Gallery / University Museum
Art gallery 41797

Boston Athenaeum, 10 1/2 Beacon St, Boston, MA 02108 - T: (617) 227-0270, Fax: (617) 227-5266, E-mail: starzyk@bostonathenaeum.org, Internet: www.bostonathenaeum.org. Dir.: Richard Wendorf, Ass. Dir.: John Lannon, Ruth Oliver Joliffe, Cur.: Sally Pierce (Prints and Photographs), Cons.: Stanley Cushing
Fine Arts Museum / Library with Exhibitions - 1807
Library with art coll 41798

Boston Fire Museum, 344 Congress St, Boston, MA 02210 - T: (617) 482-1344, 776-1288, Fax: (617) 666-1431. Chm.: Theodore Gerber, Cur.: John Vahey
Historical Museum - 1977
Fire fighting history, Congress Street Fire Station 41799

Boston National Historical Park, Charlestown Navy Yard, Boston, MA 02129 - T: (617) 242-5648, Fax: (617) 241-8650, E-mail: marty_blatt@nps.gov, Internet: www.nps.gov/bost/. Dir.: Terry Savage, Sc. Staff: Phillip Hunt
Historic Site / Archaeological Museum - 1974 41800

Boston Public Library Art Collections, 700 Boylston St, Boston, MA 02116 - T: (617) 536-5400, Fax: (617) 236-4306, E-mail: fine_arts@bpl.org, Internet: www.bpl.org. Dir.: Bernard Margolis, Head: Janice Chadbourne (Fine Arts Reference), Keeper: Sinclair Hitchings (Prints)
Fine Arts Museum / Library with Exhibitions - 1852
Library with art colls 41801

Boston University Art Gallery, 855 Commonwealth Av, Boston, MA 02215 - T: (617) 353-4672, Fax: (617) 353-4509, E-mail: gallery@bu.edu, Internet: www.bu.edu/art. Dir.: John R. Stomberg, Cur.: Stacey McCarroll
Fine Arts Museum / University Museum - 1960
Art gallery 41802

Bromfield Art Gallery, 560 Harrison Av, Boston, MA 02118-2436 - T: (617) 451-3605, E-mail: bromfieldartgallery@earthlink.net, Internet: www.bromfieldartgallery.com. Pres.: Florence Montgomery
Public Gallery - 1974 41803

The Children's Museum, Museum Wharf, 300 Congress St, Boston, MA 02210-1034 - T: (617) 426-6500, Fax: (617) 426-1944, E-mail: info@bostonkids.org, Internet: www.bostonkids.org. Pres.: Louis B. Casagrande
Ethnology Museum - 1913 41804

Commonwealth Museum, 220 William T. Morrissey Blvd, Boston, MA 02125 - T: (617) 727-2816, Fax: (617) 228-8429, E-mail: stephen.kenney@sec.state.ma.us, Internet: www.state.ma.us/sec/mus. Dir.: Maxine Trost
Historical Museum - 1986
State history 41805

Federal Reserve Bank of Boston Collection, POB 2076, Boston, MA 02106-2076 - T: (617) 973-3454, 973-3368, Fax: (617) 973-4272, Internet: www.bos.frb.org
Fine Arts Museum - 1978
Coll on US art since the mid-1950s 41806

Fleet Boston Financial Gallery, 100 Federal St, Boston, MA 02110 - T: (617) 434-2200, 434-6314, Fax: (617) 434-6280, E-mail: llambrechts@bkb.com. Dir./ Cur.: Lilian Lambrechts
Fine Arts Museum / Historical Museum
Paintings, historical docs, textiles, photography, sculpture 41807

Gibson House Museum, 137 Beacon St, Boston, MA 02116 - T: (617) 267-6338, Fax: (617) 267-5121, E-mail: gibsonmuseum@aol.com, Internet: www.thegibsonhouse.org. Exec. Dir.: Barbara Thibault
Historical Museum - 1957
Historic house, decorative art, paintings, sculptures, Victorian furniture 41808

Harrison Gray Otis House, 141 Cambridge St, Boston, MA 02114 - T: (617) 227-3956, Fax: (617) 227-9204, E-mail: pzea@spnea.org, Internet: www.spnea.org. Pres.: Jane Nylander, (Library and Archives)
Decorative Arts Museum / Historic Site - 1910
New England antiquities 41809

Institute of Contemporary Art, 955 Boylston St, Boston, MA 02115-3194 - T: (617) 266-5152, Fax: (617) 266-4021, E-mail: info@icaboston.org, Internet: www.icaboston.org. Dir.: Jill Medvedow, Cur.: Jessica Morgan
Fine Arts Museum - 1936 41810

Isabella Stewart Gardner Museum, 280 The Fenway, Boston, MA 02115 - T: (617) 566-1401, Fax: (617) 566-7653, E-mail: collection@isgm.org, Internet: www.gardnermuseum.org. Dir.: Anne Hawley, Cur.: Alan Chong, Pieranna Cavalchini (Contemporary Art), Cons.: Valentine Talland, Kathy Francis
Fine Arts Museum - 1903
Art, housed in 15th-century Venetian style bldg 41811

John F. Kennedy Presidential Library-Museum, Columbia Point, Boston, MA 02125 - T: (617) 929-4500, Fax: (617) 929-4538, E-mail: library@kennedy.nara.gov, Internet: www.jfklibrary.org. C.E.O.: John Shattuck, Cur.: Frank Rigg
Special Museum - 1979
History, presidential library, documents, film, photos 41812

Kaji Aso Studio Gallery Nature and Temptation, 40 Saint Stephen St, Boston, MA 02115 - T: (617) 247-1719, Fax: (617) 267-4920, E-mail: kajiasostudio@rcn.com
Fine Arts Museum - 1973
Watercolor, oil and Sumi Painting 41813

Massachusetts Historical Society Museum, 1154 Boylston St, Boston, MA 02215 - Fax: (617) 859-0074, E-mail: library@masshist.org, Internet: www.masshist.org. Pres.: Levin Campbell, C.E.O.: William M. Fowler
Historical Museum - 1791
State history - library 41814

Mobius Gallery, 354 Congress St, Boston, MA 02210 - T: (617) 542-7416, Fax: (617) 451-2910, E-mail: mobius@mobius.org, Internet: www.mobius.org. Dir.: Jed Speare
Fine Arts Museum - 1977 41815

Museum of Afro-American History, 8 Smith Ct and 46 Joy St, Boston, MA 02114 - T: (617) 725-0022, Fax: (617) 720-5225, E-mail: history@afroammuseum.org, Internet: www.afroammuseum.org. Exec. Dir.: Beverly Morgan-Welch
Ethnology Museum / Folklore Museum - 1966
Afro-Americans in New England, papers on civil rights and civic organizations, Black family papers, sculptures, Civil War, artworks 41816

Museum of Fine Arts, 465 Huntington Av, Boston, MA 02115-5519 - T: (617) 267-9300, E-mail: webmaster@mfa.org, Internet: www.mfa.org. Dir.: Malcolm Rogers, Pres.: Susan W. Paine, Dep. Dir./Cur.: Katherine Getchell, Cur.: Rita E. Freed (Ancient Egyptian, Nubian and Near Eastern Art), Elliot Davis (Art Americas), Clifford S. Ackley (Prints, Drawings and Photographs), Wu Tung (Asiatic Art), George T. M. Shackelford (Europe Arts), John Herrmann (Classical Art), Arthur C. Beale (Conservation), Patricia Loiko (Registrar), Cheryl Brutvan (Contemporary Art)
Fine Arts Museum - 1870
Ancient Egyptian, Nubian and Near Eastern art, decorative art, Asiatic art, drawings, photography, European and American paintings, contemporary art 41817

Museum of Science, Science Park, Boston, MA 02114-1099 - T: (617) 589-0100, Fax: (617) 589-0454, E-mail: webteam@www.mos.org, Internet: www.mos.org. Pres./Dir.: David W. Ellis
Natural History Museum / Science&Tech Museum - 1830
Science technology 41818

Museum of the National Center of Afro-American Artists, 300 Walnut Av, Boston, MA 02119 - T: (617) 442-8614, 442-8014, Fax: (617) 445-5525. Dir./ Cur.: Edmund B. Gaither
Fine Arts Museum - 1969
Afro-American art 41819

Nichols House Museum, 55 Mount Vernon St, Boston, MA 02108 - T: (617) 227-6993, Fax: (617) 723-8026, E-mail: nhm@channel1.com, Internet: www.nicholshousemuseum.org. Dir.: Flavia Cigliano
Decorative Arts Museum / Historical Museum - 1961
Decorative arts, former Beacon Hill home of Rose Standish Nichols 41820

Old South Meeting House, 310 Washington St, Boston, MA 02108 - T: (617) 482-6439, Fax: (617) 482-9621, Internet: www.oldsouthmeetinghouse.org. Pres.: Catherine E. C. Henn, Exec. Dir.: Emily Curran
Historical Museum / Historic Site - 1877 41821

Old State House, 206 Washington St, Boston, MA 02109 - T: (617) 720-1713, Fax: (617) 720-3289, E-mail: bostoniansociety@bostonhistory.org, Internet: www.bostonhistory.org. C.E.O.: Robert H. Summersgill, Libr.: Nancy Richard
Historical Museum - 1881
History - library 41822

Paul Revere House, 19 North Sq, Boston, MA 02113 - T: (617) 523-2338, Fax: (617) 523-1775, E-mail: staff@paulreverehouse.org, Internet: www.paulreverehouse.org. Dir.: Nina Zannieri, Ass. Dir.: Andrew Alexander, Cur.: Edith Steblecki
Historical Museum - 1907
History, c.1680 Paul Revere house (Boston's oldest) 41823

Photographic Resource Center, 602 Commonwealth Av, Boston, MA 02215 - T: (617) 353-0700, Fax: (617) 353-1662, E-mail: prc@bu.edu, Internet: www.prc.boston.org. Pres.: Richard Grossman, Dep. Dir.: Terrence Morash
Public Gallery / Fine Arts Museum - 1976 41824

Revolving Museum, 288-300 A St, Boston, MA 02210 - T: (617) 439-8617, Fax: (617) 439-4718, E-mail: info@revolvingmuseum.org, Internet: www.revolvingmuseum.org. Dir.: Jerry Beck
Fine Arts Museum 41825

Shirley-Eustis House, 33 Shirley St, Boston, MA 02119 - T: (617) 442-2275, Fax: (617) 442-2270, Internet: www.shirleyeustushouse.org. Pres.: Brian Pfeiffer, Exec. Dir.: Tamsen E. George
Historical Museum - 1913
1747 Georgian country house, furnished according to Gov. William Eustis inventory 1825, 1806 Gardner Carriage House 41826

Society of Arts and Crafts Exhibition Gallery, 175 Newbury St, Boston, MA 02116 - T: (617) 266-1810, Fax: (617) 266-5654, E-mail: exhibitiongallery@societyofcrafts.org, Internet: www.societyofcrafts.org. Man.: Margaret Pace-DeBruin
Public Gallery - 1897 41827

The Sports Museum of New England, 1175 Soldiers Field Rd, Boston, MA 02134 - T: (617) 624-1105, Fax: (617) 624-1326, Internet: www.sportsmuseum.org. Exec. Dir.: Bill Galatis, Cur.: Richard Johnson
Special Museum - 1977 41828

Tremont Gallery, c/o Chinese Culture Institute, 276 Tremont St, Boston, MA 02116 - T: (617) 542-4599, Fax: (617) 338-4274, E-mail: internationalsociety@yahoo.com, Internet: www.internationalsociety.org. Dir.: Doris Chu
Fine Arts Museum - 1980 41829

Urbanarts, 140 Clarendon St, Boston, MA 02116 - T: (617) 536-2880. Pres.: Pamela Worden
Fine Arts Museum 41830

USS Constitution Museum, Boston National Historical Park, Charlestown Navy Yard, Boston, MA 02129-1797 - T: (617) 426-1812, Fax: (617) 242-0496, E-mail: info@ussconstitutionmuseum.org, Internet: www.ussconstitutionmuseum.org. Dir.: Burt Logan, Cur.: Margherita Desy
Military Museum - 1972
Historic ship, old ironsides, launched 1797, world's oldest commissioned warship afloat 41831

Boubonnais IL

Exploration Station, A Children's Museum, 1095 W Perry St, Boubonnais, IL 60914 - T: (815) 933-9905, Fax: (815) 933-5468. Dir.: Bruce Baum
Special Museum - 1987 41832

Boulder CO

Boulder History Museum, 1206 Euclid Av, Boulder, CO 80302 - T: (303) 449-3464, Fax: (303) 938-8322, E-mail: info@boulderhistory.org, Internet: www.boulderhistorymuseum.org. Dir.: DeAnne Butterfield
Local Museum - 1944
Local history 41833

Colorado University Art Galleries, 318 UCB, Sibell Wolle Fine Arts Bldg, Boulder, CO 80309-0318 - T: (303) 492-8300, Fax: (303) 735-4197, E-mail: gilmore@colorado.edu, Internet: www.colorado.edu/cuartgalleries. Dir.: Susan Krane, Jerry Gilmore
Fine Arts Museum - 1939
Colorado coll 41834

Colorado University Heritage Center, Campus, Old Main St, Boulder, CO 80309 - T: (303) 492-6329, Fax: (303) 492-6799, E-mail: oltmans_k@cufund.colorado.edu. Dir.: Kay Oltmans, Ass. Dir.: Nancy Lee Miller
University Museum / Local Museum - 1985
Local hist 41835

Leanin' Tree Museum of Western Art, 6055 Longbow Dr, Boulder, CO 80301 - T: (303) 530-1442 ext 299, Fax: (303) 581-2152, E-mail: artmuseum@leanintree.com, Internet: www.leanintree.com. Dir.: Edward P. Trumble, Assoc. Dir.: Sara Sheldon
Fine Arts Museum - 1974
Art of the American West 41836

University of Colorado Museum, Broadway, between 15th and 16th St, Boulder, CO 80309 - T: (303) 492-6892, Fax: (303) 492-4195, E-mail: susan.reinke@colorado.edu, Internet: www.colorado.edu/cumuseum. Dir.: Prof. Linda S. Cordell, Ass. Dir.: Barbara Kelly, Lisa J. Spiegel, Cur.: Prof. Frederick W. Lange, Prof. Thomas A. Ranker, Prof. M. Deane Bowers (Entomology), Prof. Peter Robinson

(Geology), John R. Rohner (Museography), Prof. Judith A. Harris (Osteology), Prof. Shi-Kuei Wu (Zoology), Prof. Alan DeQueiroz (Zoology), Steve Lekson (Museum Studies), Ass. Cur.: Tim Hogan, Nan Lederer, Virginia Scott (Entomology), Rosanne Humphrey (Zoology)
University Museum / Natural History Museum / Local Museum - 1902
Natural history, anthropology, botany, zoology, geology, entomology, osteology, textiles, archaeology 41837

Boulder UT

Anasazi State Park, 460 North Hwy 12, Boulder, UT 84716 - T: (435) 335-7308, Fax: (435) 335-7352, E-mail: nrdpr.ansp@tate.ut.us. Dir.: Cortland Nelson, Cur.: Bill Latady
Archaeological Museum - 1970
1050-1200 AD, excavated Anasazi Indian Village 41838

Boulder City NV

Boulder City-Hoover Dam Museum, 1305 Arizona St, Boulder City, NV 89005 - T: (702) 294-1988, Fax: (702) 294-4380, E-mail: bcmha@yahoo.com, Internet: www.lvc.com/bcmha. Pres.: Bruce Anderson
Science&Tech Museum - 1981 41839

Bourbonnais IL

Exploration Station, A Children's Museum, 1095 W Perry St, Bourbonnais, IL 60914 - T: (815) 933-9905, Fax: (815) 933-5468, E-mail: rose@btpd.org, Internet: www.btpd.org
Science&Tech Museum - 1987
Aircraft, NASA replicas 41840

Bourne MA

Aptucxet Trading Post Museum, 24 Aptucxet Rd, Bourne, MA 02532-0795 - T: (508) 759-8167, E-mail: info@bournehistoricalsoc.org, Internet: www.bournehistoricalsoc.org. C.E.O.: Judith McAlister, Cur.: Eleanor A. Hammond
Historical Museum - 1921
Trading post, reconstructed on original 1627 site 41841

Bowie AZ

Fort Bowie, 13 mi S of Bowie, on Apache Pass Rd, Bowie, AZ 85605, mail addr: POB 158, Bowie, AZ 85605 - T: (520) 847-2500, Fax: (520) 847-2221, E-mail: fobo_operations@nps.gov, Internet: www.nps.gov/fobo
Historical Museum / Military Museum - 1964
Ruins of military structures, Apache Pass Overland Mail Station 41842

Bowie MD

Belair Mansion, 12207 Tulip Grove Dr, Bowie, MD 20715 - T: (301) 809-3089, Fax: (301) 809-2308, E-mail: museums@cityofbowie.org, Internet: www.cityofbowie.org/comserv/museum.htm. Cur.: Stephen E. Patrick
Decorative Arts Museum - 1968
Furniture and decorative artcs c 1730-1957 41843

Belair Stable Museum, 2835 Belair Dr, Bowie, MD 20715 - T: (301) 809-3089, Fax: (301) 809-2308, E-mail: museums@cityofbowie.org, Internet: www.cityofbowie.org/comserve/museums.htm. Dir.: Stephen E. Patrick
Science&Tech Museum / Agriculture Museum - 1968
Thoroughbred racing, farming, carriage coll 41844

Bowie Railroad Station and Huntington Museum, 8614, Chestnut Av, Bowie, MD 20715 - T: (301) 809-3089, Fax: (301) 809-2308, E-mail: museums@cityofbowie.org, Internet: www.cityofbowie.org/comserv/museums.htm. Dir.: Stephen E. Patrick
Science&Tech Museum / Local Museum - 1994 41845

City of Bowie Museums, 12207 Tulip Grove Dr, Bowie, MD 20715 - T: (301) 809-3088, Fax: (301) 809-2308, E-mail: museums@cityofbowie.org, Internet: www.cityofbowie.org/comserv/museum.htm. Dir.: Stephen E. Patrick, Ass. Dir.: Pamela Williams
Local Museum - 1968
Local hist 41846

Radio-Television Museum, 2608 Mitchellville Rd, Bowie, MD 20716 - T: (301) 809-3088, Fax: (301) 809-2308, E-mail: museums@cityofbowie.org, Internet: www.radiohistory.org. Dir.: Stephen E. Patrick
Science&Tech Museum - 1999
Broadcast hist 1900-present 41847

Bowling Green FL

Paynes Creek Historic State Park, 888 Lake Branch Rd, Bowling Green, FL 33834 - T: (863) 375-4717, Fax: (863) 375-4510, E-mail: paynes.creek@dep.state.fl.us, Internet: www.dep.state.fl.us
Historical Museum / Folklore Museum - 1981
Fort Chokonikla, Seminole Indian War Fort 41848

Bowling Green KY

The Kentucky Museum, Western Kentucky University, 1 Big Red Way, Bowling Green, KY 42101 - T: (502) 745-6258, Fax: (502) 745-4878, E-mail: Riley.Handy@wku.edu; nancy.baird@wku.edu, Internet: www2.wku/edu/www/library/museum/. Cur.: Donna Parker (Exhibits), Sandra Staebell (Collections), Laura Harper Lee (Education)
University Museum / Local Museum - 1931
Regional history 41849

National Corvette Museum, 350 Corvette Dr, Bowling Green, KY 42101 - T: (270) 781-7973, Fax: (270) 781-5286, E-mail: strode@corvettemuseum.com, Internet: www.corvettemuseum.com. Dir.: Wendell Strode, Cur.: Dick Yanko
Science&Tech Museum - 1989 41850

Riverview at Hobson Grove, 1100 W Main Av, Bowling Green, KY 42102-4859 - T: (270) 843-5565, Fax: (270) 843-5557, E-mail: rivervw@bowlinggreen.net, Internet: www.bgky.org/riverview.htm. Exec. Dir.: Levi Word, Pres.: Jane Coleman
Decorative Arts Museum / Historical Museum / Historic Site - 1972 41851

Western Kentucky University Gallery, Rm 441, Ivan Wilson Center for Fine Arts, Bowling Green, KY 42101 - T: (270) 745-3944, Fax: (270) 745-5932, E-mail: art@wku.edu, Internet: www.wku.edu/dept/academic/ahss/art. Head: Kim Chalmers
Fine Arts Museum / Public Gallery / University Museum - 1973
Art 41852

Bowling Green OH

Bowling Green State University Fine Arts Center Galleries, Fine Arts Center, Bowling Green State University, Bowling Green, OH 43403-0211 - T: (419) 372-8525, Fax: (419) 372-2544, E-mail: jnathan@bgnet.bgsu.edu, Internet: www.bgsu.edu/departments/art/main/2galler.html. Dir.: Jaqueline S Nathan
Fine Arts Museum / University Museum - 1960 41853

Wood County Historical Center, 13660 County Home Rd, Bowling Green, OH 43402 - T: (419) 352-0967, Fax: (419) 352-6220, E-mail: wchisctr@wcnet.org, Internet: www.woodcountyhistory.org. Dir.: Stacey Hann-Ruff
Local Museum - 1955 41854

Boyertown PA

Boyertown Museum of Historic Vehicles, 85 S Walnut St, Boyertown, PA 19512-1415 - T: (610) 367-2090, Fax: (610) 367-9712, E-mail: museum@enter.net, Internet: www.boyertownmuseum.org. Pres.: Dennis E. Leh, Exec. Dir.: Kenneth D. Wells
Science&Tech Museum - 1968
Vehicle building in Southeastern Pennsylvania 41855

Boys Town NE

Boys Town Hall of History & Father Flanagan House, 14057 Flanagan Blvd, Boys Town, NE 68010 - T: (402) 498-1185, Fax: (402) 498-1159, E-mail: lyncht@boystown.org, Internet: www.boystown.org. C.E.O.: Thomas J. Lynch
Historic Site - 1986
History 41856

Bozeman MT

Helen E. Copeland Gallery, Montana State University, MSU School of Art, Haynes Hall, Bozeman, MT 59717 - T: (406) 994-4501, Fax: (406) 994-3680, E-mail: dungan@montana.edu, Internet: www.montana.edu/wwwart. Dir.: Erica Howe Dungan
Fine Arts Museum / University Museum - 1974
Japanese patterns, native American ceramics, prints 41857

Museum of the Rockies, 600 W Kagy, Bozeman, MT 59717 - T: (406) 994-5283, Fax: (406) 994-2682, E-mail: sfischer@montana.edu, Internet: www.museumoftherockies.org. Dir.: Marilyn F. Wessel, Cur.: Dr. Leslie B. Davis (Archaeology and Ethnology), John R. Horner (Paleontology), Steven B. Jackson (Art and Photography), Margaret M. Woods (Textiles and History), Ass. Cur.: Kenneth W. Karsmizki (Historical Archeology and History), Ass. Cur.: Dr. Christopher L. Hill (Prehistory and Geology)
Local Museum - 1956
American Western and Indian art, drawings, anthropology, archaeology, ethnology, decorative arts 41858

School of Art - Gallery, Montana State University, 213 Haynes Hall, Bozeman, MT 59717 - T: (406) 994-4501, Fax: (406) 994-3680, E-mail: schoolofart@montana.edu, Internet: www.montana.edu/wwwart. Dir.: Richard Helzer
Public Gallery 41859

Bradenton FL

Art League of Manatee County, 209 Ninth St W, Bradenton, FL 34205 - T: (941) 746-2862, Fax: (941) 746-2319, E-mail: artleague@almc.org, Internet: www.almc.org. Dir.: Patricia Richmond
Fine Arts Museum - 1937 41860

Desoto National Memorial, 75th St NW, Bradenton, FL 34209, mail addr: POB 15390, Bradenton FL 34280-5390 - T: (941) 792-0458, Fax: (941) 792-5094, E-mail: deso_ranger_activities@nps.gov, Internet: www.nps.gov/deso/
Historical Museum - 1948
6th-c European military artifacts, pre-historic Native American artifacts 41861

Manatee Village Historical Park Museum, 604 15th St E, Bradenton, FL 34208 - T: (941) 749-7165, Fax: (941) 708-5924, Internet: www.manateeclerk.com
Historic Site - 1974
Local history 41862

South Florida Museum, 201 10th St W, Bradenton, FL 34205 - T: (941) 746-4131 ext 14, Fax: (941) 746-2556, E-mail: info@southfloridamuseum.org, Internet: www.southfloridamuseum.org. Pres.: Mike Carter, C.E.O.: Dr. Peter Bennett
Local Museum / Natural History Museum - 1946 41863

Bradford PA

Zippo and Case Visitors Center Company Museum, 1932 Zippo Dr, Bradford, PA 16701, mail addr: 33 Barbour St, Bradford, PA 16701 - T: (814) 368-1932, 368-2711, Fax: (814) 368-2874, E-mail: lmeabon@zippo.com, Internet: www.zippo.com
Historical Museum - 1994
Zippo lighters and other Zippo products, company hist, case knives 41864

Bradford VT

Bradford Historical Society Museum, Town Hall, Main St, Bradford, VT 05033 - T: (802) 222-4727, 222-9026. Cur.: Phyllis Lavelle
Local Museum - 1959
Local hist 41865

Brainerd MN

Crow Wing County Historical Museum, 320 W Laurel St, Brainerd, MN 56401 - T: (218) 829-3268, Fax: (218) 828-4434, E-mail: cwchistsoc@brainerdonline.com. Dir.: Mary Lou Moudry
Local Museum - 1927
Local history 41866

Braintree MA

Braintree Historical Society Museum, 31 Tenney Rd, Braintree, MA 02184-6512 - T: (781) 848-1640, Fax: (781) 380-0731, E-mail: genthyer@aol.com, Internet: www.braintreehistorical.com. Dir.: Brian A. Kolner, Cur.: Dr. Robert H. Downey, Libr.: Marjorie P. Maxham
Local Museum - 1930
History, decorative arts, antique furniture, American and Japanese fans 41867

Branchville SC

Branchville Railroad Shrine and Museum, 7505 Freedom Rd, Branchville, SC 29432 - T: (803) 274-8821, Fax: (803) 274-8760. Pres.: Luther Folk, C.E.O.: Johnny Norris
Science&Tech Museum - 1969
Transportation 41868

Brandon OR

Coquille River Museum, 270 Fillmore and Hwy 101, Brandon, OR 97411 - T: (541) 347-2164, Fax: (541) 347-2164, E-mail: jnrknox@harborside.com. Dir.: Judy Knox
Local Museum - 1977
Native Americans, fires, period clothing, businesses and schools 41869

Branford CT

Harrison House, 124 Main St, Branford, CT 06405 - T: (203) 488-4828. Pres.: William B. Davis
Local Museum - 1960
Local hist, farm tools 41870

Branson MO

The Roy Rogers-Dale Evans Museum, 3950 Green Mountain Dr, Branson, MO 65616 - T: (417) 339-1900, E-mail: administrator@royrogers.com, Internet: www.royrogers.com. C.E.O.: Roy Dusty Rogers jr
Performing Arts Museum / Ethnology Museum - 1967
Costumes, cowboy and western memorabilia, awards, gun coll - Theater 41871

Brattleboro VT

Brattleboro Museum and Art Center, 10 Vernon St, Brattleboro, VT 05301 - T: (802) 257-0124, Fax: (802) 258-9182, E-mail: bmac@sover.net, Internet: www.brattlebowmuseum.org. Dir.: Christine Holderness
Fine Arts Museum / Local Museum - 1972
Visual art, local hist 41872

Brazosport TX

Brazosport Museum of Natural Science, 400 College Dr., Brazosport, TX 77566 - T: (409) 265-7831. Pres.: J.H. McIver
Natural History Museum / Science&Tech Museum - 1962
Natural science 41873

Brea CA

City of Brea Gallery, 1 Civic Center Circle, Brea, CA 92821-5732 - T: (714) 990-7730, 990-7600, Fax: (714) 990-2258, Internet: www.ci.brea.ca.us. Dir.: Dianna Rivera
Fine Arts Museum / Public Gallery - 1980 41874

Breckenridge CO

Fine Arts Gallery, c/o Colorado Mountain College, 103 S Harris St, Breckenridge, CO 80424 - T: (970) 453-6757, Fax: (970) 451-2209
Public Gallery - 1980 41875

Breckenridge MN

Wilkin County Historical Museum, 704 Nebraska Av, Breckenridge, MN 56520 - T: (218) 643-1303. Pres.: Gordon Martinson
Local Museum - 1965
Regional history 41876

Breckenridge TX

Swenson Memorial Museum of Stephens County, 116 W Walker, Breckenridge, TX 76424 - T: (254) 559-8471. Dir.: Freda Mitchell
Local Museum - 1970
Local hist 41877

Bremerton WA

Bremerton Naval Museum, 402 Pacific Av, Bremerton, WA 98337 - T: (360) 479-7447, Fax: (360) 377-4186, E-mail: bremnavmuseum@silverlink.net. C.E.O.: Charleen Zettl
Military Museum - 1954
Naval hist 41878

Kitsap Museum, 280 4th St, Bremerton, WA 98337 - T: (360) 479-6226, Fax: (360) 415-9294, E-mail: kchsm@telebyte.net, Internet: www.waynes.net/kchsm/. Cur.: Gail Campbell-Ferguson
Historical Museum - 1949
Local hist 41879

Brenham TX

Texas Baptist Historical Center Museum, 10405 FM 50, Brenham, TX 77833 - T: (409) 836-5117, Fax: (409) 836-2929. Dir./Cur.: D.H. Strickland
Religious Arts Museum - 1965
Religion 41880

Brevard NC

Spiers Gallery, Brevard College, c/o Sims Art Center, 400 N Broad St, Brevard, NC 28712 - T: (828) 883-8292 ext 2245, Fax: (828) 884-3790, E-mail: lydamike@brevard.edu, Internet: www.brevard.edu. Dir.: Bill Byers
Fine Arts Museum / University Museum 41881

Brewster MA

Cape Cod Museum of Natural History, 869 Rte 6A, Brewster, MA 02631 - T: (508) 896-3867, Fax: (508) 896-8844, E-mail: info@ccmnh.org, Internet: www.ccmnh.org. Dir.: George Stevens, Sc. Staff: Fred Dunford (Archaeology)
Natural History Museum - 1954
Natural history 41882

New England Fire and History Museum, 1439 Main St, Rte 6A, Brewster, MA 02631 - T: (508) 896-5711, 432-2450, Internet: www.cape.cod.us. Pres./Dir.: Joan Frederici
Local Museum - 1972
Fire fighting, local history 41883

Brewster NY

Southeast Museum, 67 Main St, Brewster, NY 10509 - T: (845) 279-7500, Fax: (845) 279-1992, E-mail: sem@bestweb.net, Internet: www.southeastmuseum.org. Exec. Dir.: Samantha M. Ligon
Local Museum / Science&Tech Museum - 1963
McLane Railroad, hist of the Harlem Line, Borden Condensed Milk Factory coll, local hist 41884

Brewton AL

Thomas E. McMillan Museum, c/o Jefferson Davis College, 220 Alco Dr, Brewton, AL 36426 - T: (251) 809-1607, Fax: (251) 867-7399, E-mail: jpowell@acet.net. Dir.: John T. Powell
Decorative Arts Museum / University Museum / Archaeological Museum - 1978
Archaeology, Indian artifacts, trading wares, Civil war 41885

Bridgehampton NY

Bridgehampton Historical Society Museum, 2368 Main St, Bridgehampton, NY 11932-0977 - T: (631) 537-1088, Fax: (631) 537-4225, E-mail: bhhs@hamptons.com, Internet: www.hamptons.com/bhhs. Pres.: Paul Brennan
Historical Museum - 1956 41886

Bridgeport AL

Russell Cave Museum, 3729 County Rd 98, Bridgeport, AL 35740 - T: (256) 495-2672, Fax: (256) 495-9220, E-mail: cave@trailler.com, Internet: nps.gov/ruca. Head: Bill Springer
Archaeological Museum - 1961
Archaeology 41887

Bridgeport CA

Bodie State Historic Park, Hwy 395, Bridgeport, CA 93517, mail addr: POB 515, Bridgeport, CA 93517 - T: (760) 647-6445, Fax: (760) 647-6486, E-mail: bodie@qnet.com, Internet: www.ceres.ca.gov/sierradsp/bodie.html. Cur.: Judith K. Polanich
Historic Site / Open Air Museum - 1962
1859-1942 Gold Rush Mining Boom Town 41888

Bridgeport CT

Barnum Museum, 820 Main St, Bridgeport, CT 06604 - T: (203) 331-1104, Fax: (203) 339-4341, Internet: www.barnum-museum.org. Cur.: Kathleen Maher
Performing Arts Museum - 1893
Circus history 41889

The Discovery Museum, 4450 Park Av, Bridgeport, CT 06604 - T: (203) 372-3521, Fax: (203) 374-1929, E-mail: audley@discoverymuseum.org, Internet: www.discovery.museum.org. Pres.: Paul Audley, Dir.: Lynn Hamilton, Cur.: Wendy Kelly
Fine Arts Museum / Science&Tech Museum - 1958
Art, science - planetarium 41890

Housatonic Museum of Art, 900 Lafayette Blvd, Bridgeport, CT 06604-4704 - T: (203) 332-5000, Fax: (203) 332-5123, E-mail: ho_zella@commnet.edu, Internet: www.hctc.commnet.edu. Dir./Cur.: Robbin Zella
Fine Arts Museum / University Museum - 1967
European and American art 19th-20th c, contemporary Latinamerican and Connecticut art 41891

University Art Gallery, Bernhard Arts and Humanities Center, 84 Iranistan Av, Bridgeport, CT 06601-2449 - T: (203) 576-4402, 576-4419, Fax: (203) 576-4051, E-mail: tjuliusb@cr2.nai.net. Dir.: Thomas Juliusburger
Fine Arts Museum / University Museum - 1972
Art gallery 41892

Bridgeton NJ

New Sweden Farmstead Museum, City Park, Bridgeton, NJ 08302 - T: (609) 653-1271, Internet: www.biderman.net/nj/new.htm. C.E.O.: Michael Tartaglio
Historical Museum / Agriculture Museum - 1983
Reproduction of 17th-century farmstead 41893

Woodruff Museum of Indian Artifacts, 150 E Commerce St, Bridgeton, NJ 08302 - T: (856) 451-2620
Ethnology Museum - 1976 41894

Bridgewater VA

Reuel B. Pritchett Museum, Bridgewater College, E College St, Bridgewater, VA 22812 - T: (540) 828-5462, 828-5414, Fax: (540) 828-5482, E-mail: tbarkley@bridgewater.edu, Internet: www.bridgewater.edu. Cur.: Terry Barkley
Decorative Arts Museum / University Museum / Ethnology Museum - 1954 41895

Bridgton ME

Bridgton Historical Museum, Gibbs Av, Bridgton, ME 04009 - T: (207) 647-3699, E-mail: bhs@megalink.net, Internet: www.megalink.net/~bhs. Pres.: Dan Abbott
Local Museum / Folklore Museum - 1953
Local history 41896

Brigham City UT

Brigham City Museum-Gallery, 24 N 300 W, Brigham City, UT 84302 - T: (435) 723-6769, Fax: (435) 723-6769. Pres.: Colleen Bradford, Dir.: Larry Douglass
Local Museum - 1970
Art, historical coll focussing the Mormon Communitarian Society in Brigham City 1865-1881 41897

Golden Spike National Historic Site, POB 897, Brigham City, UT 84302 - T: (435) 471-2209, Fax: (435) 471-2341, E-mail: gosp_interpretation@nps.gov, Internet: www.nps.gov/gosp. Head: Bruce Powell
Local Museum - 1965
Local hist 41898

Brighton CO

Adams County Museum, 9601 Henderson Rd, Brighton, CO 80601-8100 - T: (303) 659-7103, Fax: (303) 659-7103, E-mail: dnvrdixie@aol.com. Pres.: Virginia Eppinger
Local Museum / Agriculture Museum - 1987
Prehistoric life and geology, native Americans, early Western settlement 41899

Bristol CT

American Clock and Watch Museum, 100 Maple St, Bristol, CT 06010 - T: (860) 583-6070, Fax: (860) 583-1862, Internet: www.clockmuseum.org. Dir.: Donald Muller, Sc. Staff: Chris H. Bailey (Horology)
Special Museum - 1952
Horology 41900

New England Carousel Museum, 95 Riverside Av, Bristol, CT 06010 - T: (860) 585-5411, Fax: (860) 314-0483, E-mail: caramuse@aol.com, Internet: www.thecarouselmuseum.com. Exec. Dir.: Louise L. DeMars
Special Museum - 1989 41901

Bristol IN

Elkhart County Historical Museum, 304 W Vistula St, Bristol, IN 46507 - T: (574) 535-6458, 848-4322, Fax: (584) 848-5703, E-mail: ECHM@Juno.com. Dir.: Tina Mellott
Local Museum - 1896
Agriculture, railroad hist, furnishings, apparel, military, Native Americans 41902

Bristol RI

Asri Environmental Education Center, 1401 Hope St, Bristol, RI 02809 - T: (401) 949-5454, Fax: (401) 949-5788, Internet: www.asri.org. C.E.O.: Lee C. Schisler jr
Special Museum - 1897
Flora, fauna and natural hist of Rhode Island 41903

Bristol Historical and Preservation Society Museum, 48 Court St, Bristol, RI 02809 - T: (401) 253-7223, Fax: (401) 253-7223. Cur.: Reinhard Battcher
Local Museum - 1936
Local hist 41904

Coggeshall Farm Museum, Rte 114, Poppasquash Rd, Bristol, RI 02809 - T: (401) 253-9062, E-mail: coggmuseum@aol.com. Exec. Dir.: Walter Katkevich
Historical Museum - 1968
Rural life on a RI coastal farm 41905

Haffenreffer Museum of Anthropology, Brown University, Mount Hope Grant, 300 Tower St, Bristol, RI 02809-4050 - T: (401) 253-8388, 253-1287, Fax: (401) 253-1198, E-mail: kathleen_luke@Brown.edu, Internet: www.haffenreffermuseum.org. Dir.: Shepard Krech, Dep. Dir. & Chief Cur.: Kevin P. Smith, Cur./Res.: Douglas Anderson, Ass. Cur.: Thierry Gentis, David Gregg
University Museum / Ethnology Museum - 1956
Anthropology 41906

Herreshoff Marine Museum/America's Cup Hall of Fame, 1 Burnside St, Bristol, RI 02809 - T: (401) 253-5000, Fax: (401) 253-6222, E-mail: b.knowles@herreshoff.org, Internet: www.herreshoff.org. C.E.O. & Pres.: Halsey C. Herreshoff, Cur.: John Palmeiri
Historical Museum - 1971
Maritime hist 41907

Brockport NY

Tower Fine Arts Gallery, SUNY Brockport, Tower Fine Arts Bldg, Brockport, NY 14420 - T: (716) 395-2209, Fax: (716) 395-2588, E-mail: llonnen@po.brockport.edu, Internet: cc.brockport.edu/~art/arthome.htm. Dir.: Debra Fisher
University Museum / Fine Arts Museum - 1964 41908

Brockton MA

Fuller Museum of Art, 455 Oak St, Brockton, MA 02301-1395 - T: (508) 588-6000, Fax: (508) 587-6191, Internet: www.fullermuseum.org. Dir.: Jennifer Atkinson, Cur.: Denise Markonish
Fine Arts Museum - 1969
Art 41909

Joseph A. Driscoll Art Gallery, 304 Main St, Brockton, MA 02301 - T: (508) 580-7890. Dir.: Diane Pacheco
Fine Arts Museum
19th-20th c American paintings 41910

Broken Bow NE

Custer County Historical Society Museum, 455 S 9th St, Broken Bow, NE 68822 - T: (308) 872-2203, Fax: (custer.county.history@navix.net, E-mail: www.rootsweb.com/~necuster
Local Museum - 1962 41911

Broken Bow OK

Oklahoma Forest Heritage Center Forestry Museum, US-259A, Broken Bow, OK 74728, mail addr: POB 157, Broken Bow, OK 74728 - T: (580) 494-6497, Fax: (580) 494-6689, E-mail: fhc@beaversbend.com, Internet: www.beaversbend.com
Natural History Museum - 1876
Forestry tools, Caddo Indian papermaking, lumbering 41912

Bronx NY

Bartow-Pell Mansion Museum, 895 Shore Rd, Pelham Bay Park, Bronx, NY 10464 - T: (718) 885-1461, Fax: (718) 885-9164, E-mail: bartowpell@aol.com, Internet: www.bartowpellmansionmuseum.org. Dir.: Robert Engel
Local Museum - 1914 41913

Bronx County Historical Society Museum, 3309 Bainbridge Av, Bronx, NY 10467 - T: (718) 881-8900, Fax: (718) 881-4827, Internet: www.bronxhistoricalsociety.org. Dir.: Dr. Gary D. Hermalyn, Cur.: Kathleen A. McAuley, Sc. Staff: Prof. Lloyd Ultan (History), Dr. Stephen Stertz (Research)
Local Museum - 1897 41914

Bronx Museum of the Arts, 1040 Grand Concourse, Bronx, NY 10456 - T: (718) 681-6000, Fax: (718) 681-6181, E-mail: bxarts@bronxview.com, Internet: www.bronxview.com/museum. Sen. Cur.: Marysol Nieves, Cur.: Lydia Yee
Fine Arts Museum - 1971 41915

Brooklyn Arts Council Gallery, 195 Cadman Plaza W, Bronx, NY 11201 - T: (718) 625-0080. Dir.: Pamela Billig
Association with Coll
Junior Children's Museum of Art 41916

City Island Nautical Museum, 190 Fordham St, Bronx, NY 10464 - T: (718) 885-0008, E-mail: barbaurn@att.net, Internet: www.cityislandmuseum.org. Cur.: Tom Nye
Historical Museum - 1964 41917

Edgar Allan Poe Cottage, Poe Park, Grand Concourse, E Kingsbridge Rd, Bronx, NY 10458 - T: (718) 881-8900, Fax: (718) 881-4827, E-mail: kmcauley@bronxhistoricalsociety.org, Internet: www.bronxhistoricalsociety.org. Dir.: Dr. Gary D. Hermalyn, Cur.: Kathleen A. McAuley
Local Museum - 1955
Historic house 41918

Glyndor Gallery and Wave Hill House Gallery, 675 W 252nd St, Bronx, NY 10471 - T: (718) 549-3200, Fax: (718) 884-8952, E-mail: arts@wavehill.org, Internet: www.wavehill.org/arts
Fine Arts Museum 41919

Hall of Fame for Great Americans, Bronx Community College, University Av and W 181 St, Bronx, NY 10453 - T: (718) 220-5162, Fax: (718) 220-6287, Internet: www.bcc.cuny.edu. Dir.: Ralph Rourke
Historical Museum - 1900
American hist, beaux arts archtitecture and sculpture 41920

Judaica Museum of the Hebrew Home for the Aged at Riverdale, 5961 Palisade Av, Bronx, NY 10471 - T: (718) 581-1787, Fax: (718) 581-1009, E-mail: judaicamuseum@aol.com, Internet: www.hebrewhome.org/museum. Dir.: Karen S. Franklin
Folklore Museum / Religious Arts Museum - 1982 41921

Lehman College Art Gallery, 250 Bedford Park Blvd W, Bronx, NY 10468-1589 - T: (718) 960-8731, Fax: (718) 960-8212, E-mail: susan@alpha.lehman.cuny.edu, Internet: ca80.lehman.cuny.edu/gallery/wet/ag. Dir.: Susan Hoeltzel, Ass. Dir.: Mary Ann Siano
Fine Arts Museum / University Museum - 1985
Art 41922

Museum of Bronx History, Varian Park, 3266 Bainbridge Av at E 208th St, Bronx, NY 10467 - T: (718) 881-8900, Fax: (718) 881-4827, E-mail: DocHermalyn@bronxhistoricalsociety.org, Internet: www.bronxhistoricalsociety.org. Dir.: Dr. Gary D. Hermalyn, Cur.: Kathleen A. McAuley
Local Museum - 1955
Local hist 41923

Museum of Migrating People, Harry S. Truman High School, 750 Baychester Av, Bronx, NY 10475 - T: (718) 904-5400. Cur.: Peter Lerner
Local Museum - 1974 41924

North Wind Undersea Institute, 610 City Island Av, Bronx, NY 10464 - T: (718) 885-0701, Fax: (718) 885-1008, Internet: www.northwind.org. Dir.: Michael Sandlofer, Irene Sullivan, Cur.: Lee Clodfelter
Natural History Museum - 1976
Marine hist 41925

Van Cortlandt House Museum, Van Cortlandt Park, Bronx, NY 10471 - T: (718) 543-3344, Fax: (718) 543-3315, E-mail: vancortlandthouse@juno.com, Internet: www.vancortlandhouse.org. Pres.: Ana Duff, Dir.: Laura Carpenter Correa
Historical Museum - 1896
House built by Frederick Van Cortlandt 41926

Bronxville NY

Eastchester Historical Society Museum, 388 California Rd, Bronxville, NY 10708 - T: (914) 793-1900, E-mail: eastchesterhistoricalsociety@juno.com
Local Museum - 1959
Toys, costumes, photos, furniture, school artifacts 41927

Brookfield CT

Brookfield Craft Center, Rte 25, Brookfield, CT 06804, mail addr: POB 122, Brookfield, CT 06804 - T: (203) 775-4526, Fax: (203) 740-7815, E-mail: brkfldcrft@aol.com, Internet: www.brookfieldcraftcenter.org. Exec. Dir.: John I. Russell
Decorative Arts Museum - 1954
Craft, old grist mill 41928

Brookfield VT

Brookfield Museum, Ridge Rd, Brookfield, VT 05036 - T: (802) 276-3959. Cur.: Jacalin W. Wilder
Local Museum - 1933
Local hist 41929

Marvin Newton House, 1133 Ridge Rd, Brookfield, VT 05036 - T: (802) 276-3277. Cur.: Jacalin W. Wilder
Local Museum - 1935
Historic house 41930

Brookings SD

Brookings Arts Council, 524 Fourth St, Brookings, SD 57006 - T: (605) 692-4177, Fax: (605) 692-8298, E-mail: arts@brookings.net, Internet: www.mjts.com/bac. Dir.: Nancy Hartenhoff
Fine Arts Museum / Folklore Museum - 1977
Cultural arts 41931

South Dakota Art Museum, Harvey Dunn St and Medary Av, Brookings, SD 57007-0999 - T: (605) 688-5423, Fax: (605) 688-4445, E-mail: sdsu_sdam@sdstate.edu, Internet: sdartmuseum.sdstate.edu. Dir.: M. Lynn Verschoor, Cur.: Lisa Scholten (Collections), Nancy Rexwinkel (Education), John Rychtarik (Exhibitions)
Fine Arts Museum - 1969
Art 41932

State Agricultural Heritage Museum, South Dakota State University, 925 11th St, Brookings, SD 57007 - T: (605) 688-6226, Fax: (605) 688-6303, E-mail: sdsu_agmuseum@sdstate.edu, Internet: www.agmuseum.com. Dir.: John C. Awald, Cur.: William D. Lee, Carrie Lavarnway, Michelle Glanzer, Dawn Stephens
Agriculture Museum / University Museum - 1967
Agricultural hist 41933

Brookline MA

Brookline Historical Society Museum, 347 Harvard St, Brookline, MA 02146 - T: (617) 566-5747. Pres.: John Little, Cur.: Walter F. Eayrs
Local Museum - 1901
Local history 41934

Frederick Law Olmsted Historic Site, 99 Warren St, Brookline, MA 02445 - T: (617) 566-1689, Fax: (617) 232-3964, E-mail: olmsted_archives@nps.gov, Internet: www.nps.gov/frla. Head: Myra Harrison
Historic Site - 1979
Home and office of Frederick Law Olmsted, landscape plans and drawings 41935

John Fitzgerald Kennedy House, 83 Beals St, Brookline, MA 02146 - T: (617) 566-7937, Fax: (617) 232-3964, E-mail: frla_kennedy_nhs@nps.gov, Internet: www.nps.gov/jofi. Head: Myra Harrison
Historical Museum - 1969
Birthplace of John F. Kennedy 41936

Larz Anderson Auto Museum, 15 Newton St, Brookline, MA 02445 - T: (617) 522-6547, Fax: (617) 524-0170, Internet: www.mot.org. Dir.: John Sweeney, Cur.: Evan Ide
Science&Tech Museum - 1952
Transport 41937

Museum of Afro-American History, 138 Mountfork St, Brookline, MA 02446 - T: (617) 739-1200, Fax: (617) 739-1285, E-mail: tmckin1751@aol.com, Internet: www.afroammuseum.org. Exec. Dir.: Sylvia Watts McKinney
Historical Museum - 1966
African American hist 41938

Museum of Transportation → Larz Anderson Auto Museum

Brooklyn CT

Museum Necca and New England Center for Contemporary Art, 248 Pomfret Rd, Brooklyn, CT 06234 - T: (860) 774-8899, Fax: (860) 779-9291, E-mail: museum@museum-necca.org, Internet: www.museum-necca.org. Dir.: Henry Riseman, Cur.: John Roth, Xue Jian Xin (Chinese Art)
Fine Arts Museum - 1975
Contemporary art 41939

Brooklyn NY

Brooklyn Children's Museum, 145 Brooklyn Av, Brooklyn, NY 11213 - T: (718) 735-4400, Fax: (718) 604-7442, E-mail: acanty@bchildmus.org, Internet: www.bchildmus.org. Pres.: Peggi Einhorn, Exec. Dir.: Carol Enseki, Dir.: Cheryl Bartholow (Programs), Beth Alberty (Collections), Paul Pearson (Exhibitions)
Special Museum - 1899 41940

Brooklyn Museum of Art, 200 Eastern Pkwy, Brooklyn, NY 11238-6052 - T: (718) 638-5000, Fax: (718) 638-5931, E-mail: information@brooklynmuseum.org, Internet: www.

brooklynmuseum.org. Chairman Board of Trustees: Robert S. Rubin, Chief Cur.: Kevin Stayton, Cur.: Richard Fazzini (Egyptian and Classical Art), Elizabeth Easton (European Paintings and Sculpture), Linda Ferber (American Paintings and Sculpture), Charlotta Kotik (Contemporary Art), Amy Poster (Asian Art), Kevin Stayton (Decorative Arts), William Siegmann (Arts of Africa and Pacific)
Fine Arts Museum - 1823 41941

Harbor Defense Museum of New York City, Bldg 230, Fort Hamilton, Brooklyn, NY 11252-5701 - T: (718) 630-4349, Fax: (718) 630-4888, E-mail: coxr@hamilton-emhl.army.mil, Internet: www.hamilton.army.mil. Cur.: Richard Cox (Technic)
Military Museum - 1966 41942

KBCC Art Gallery, Kingsborough Community College, 2001 Oriental Blvd, Art & Science Bldg, Brooklyn, NY 11235 - T: (718) 368-5449, Fax: (718) 368-4872, E-mail: pmalone@kbcc.cuny.edu, Internet: www.kbcc.cuny.edu/academicdepartments/art/gallery. Dir.: Peter Malone
Fine Arts Museum 41943

The Kurdish Museum, 144 Underhill Av, Brooklyn, NY 11238 - T: (718) 783-7930, Fax: (718) 398-4365, E-mail: kurdishlib@aol.com. Dir.: Dr. Vera Beaudin Saeedpour
Ethnology Museum / Folklore Museum - 1988
Ethnology 41944

Lefferts Homestead, 95 Prospect Park W, Brooklyn, NY 11215 - T: (718) 789-2822, Fax: (718) 789-4724, Internet: www.prospectpark.org. Dir.: Maria Cobo, Ass. Dir.: Erica Catlin
Local Museum - 1918 41945

Lesbian Herstory Educational Foundation, 14th St, Brooklyn, NY 11215, mail addr: POB 1258, New York, NY 10116 - T: (718) 768-3953, Fax: (718) 768-4663, Internet: www.datalounge.net/lha/
Special Museum - 1974
Lesbian hist and culture 41946

Marian and Religious Museum, 545 74th St, Brooklyn, NY 11209 - T: (718) 238-4113, Fax: (718) 238-4113. Dir.: Armand J. Williamson
Folklore Museum / Religious Arts Museum - 1978
Religious art and folk art 41947

New York Transit Museum, Boerum Pl and Schermerhorn St, Brooklyn, NY 11201, mail addr: 130 Livingston St, Brooklyn, NY 11201 - T: (718) 694-5100, Fax: (718) 694-4290, E-mail: casolan@nyct.com, Internet: www.mta.info/museum. Dir.: Gabrielle Shubert, Dep. Dir.: Carlos Gutierrez-Solana, Sen. Cur.: Charles L. Sachs
Science&Tech Museum - 1976
Urban transportation 41948

Pieter Claesen Wyckoff House Museum, 5816 Clarendon Rd, Brooklyn, NY 11203 - T: (718) 629-5400, Fax: (718) 629-3125, E-mail: info@wyckoffassociation.org, Internet: wyckoffassociation.org. C.E.O.: Sean Sawyer
Decorative Arts Museum - 1982
Colonial and early American furniture 41949

Rotunda Gallery, 33 Clinton St, Brooklyn, NY 11201 - T: (718) 875-4047, Fax: (718) 488-0609, E-mail: rotunda@brooklynx.org, Internet: www.brooklynx.org/rotunda. Dir.: Janet Riker
Public Gallery - 1981 41950

Rubelle and Norman Schafler Gallery, 200 Willoughby Av, Brooklyn, NY 11205 - T: (718) 636-3517, Fax: (718) 636-3785, E-mail: exhibits@pratt.edu, Internet: www.pratt.edu/exhibitions. Dir.: Loretta Yarlow
Fine Arts Museum / University Museum - 1967
Art 41951

Waterfront Museum and Showboat Barge, 699 Columbia St, Brooklyn, NY 11231 - T: (718) 624-4719, Fax: (718) 624-4719, Internet: www.waterfrontmuseum.org
Historical Museum - 1998 41952

Brooklyn OH

Brooklyn Historical Society Museum, 4442 Ridge Rd, Brooklyn, OH 44144-3353 - T: (216) 749-2804. Pres.: Barbara Stepic
Local Museum - 1970 41953

Brooklyn Park MN

Art Gallery, North Hennepin Community College, 7411 85th Ave N, Brooklyn Park, MN 55445 - T: (612) 424-0702, Fax: (612) 424-0929, Internet: www.nh.cc.mn.us. Dir.: Susan McDonald
Fine Arts Museum
Student works and local artists 41954

Brookneal VA

Red Hill-Patrick Henry National Memorial, 1250 Red Hill Rd, Brookneal, VA 24528 - T: (804) 376-2044, Fax: (804) 376-2647, E-mail: RedHill@lynchburg.net, Internet: www.redhill.org. Dir.: Dr. Jon Kukla
Historical Museum - 1944
Local hist 41955

Brooks OR

Pacific Northwest Truck Museum, 3995 Brooklake Rd NE, Brooks, OR 97305 - T: (503) 678-5108, 463-8701, Fax: (503) 678-2953, E-mail: delh@integrity.com, Internet: www.pacificnwtruckmuseum.org
Science&Tech Museum - 1989
Truck, manufacturing and transportation industries, photographs, drawings, patents 41956

Brooks Air Force Base TX

Edward H. White II Memorial Museum, 311 ABG/MU, Brooks Air Force Base, TX 78235-5329 - T: (210) 536-2203, Fax: (210) 240-3224, E-mail: museum@brooks.af.mil, Internet: www.brooks.af.mil/abg/mh/general/html. Dir./Cur.: Ulysses S. Rhodes
Science&Tech Museum / Historical Museum - 1966
Aeronautics 41957

Brookville IN

Franklin County Museum, 5th and Mill St, Brookville, IN 47012 - T: (765) 647-5182, E-mail: mick@sur-seal.com, Internet: www.franklinchs.com. Pres.: Mick Wilz
Local Museum - 1969
Local history, housed in a original Franklin County Seminary bldg 41958

Brookville NY

Hillwood Art Museum, Long Island University, C.W. Post Campus, 720 Northern Blvd, Brookville, NY 11548 - T: (516) 299-4073, Fax: (516) 299-2787, E-mail: museum@cwpost.liu.edu, Internet: www.liu.edu/museum. Pres.: Dr. David Steinberg, C.E.O.: Barry Stern
Fine Arts Museum / University Museum - 1973
Precolumbian and African art, contemporary photography, prints 41959

Browning MT

Museum of the Plains Indian, Junction of Hwys 2 and 89 W, Browning, MT 59417 - T: (406) 338-2230, Fax: (406) 338-7404, E-mail: mpi@3rivers.net, Internet: www.iacb.doi.gov. Dir.: Meridith Z. Stanton, Cur.: Loretta Pepion
Folklore Museum - 1941
American Indian artefacts and crafts 41960

Scriver Museum of Montana Wildlife and Hall of Bronze, POB 172, Browning, MT 59417 - T: (406) 338-5425, Fax: (406) 338-5425. Cur.: Dr. Robert M. Scriver, Ass. Cur.: Lorraine Scriver
Natural History Museum - 1953 41961

Brownington VT

The Old Stone House Museum, 28 Old Stone House Rd, Brownington, VT 05860 - T: (802) 754-2022, E-mail: osh@together.net, Internet: oldstonehousemuseum.org. Pres.: Alfred W. Fuller, C.E.O.: Tracy N. Martin
Local Museum - 1916
Local hist 41962

Browns Valley MN

Sam Brown Memorial Park, West Broadway, Browns Valley, MN 56219 - T: (320) 695-2110
Historical Museum - 1932
Log cabin of 1863, one room country school house 41963

Brownsville OR

Linn County Historical Museum and Moyer House, 101 Park Av, Brownsville, OR 97327 - T: (503) 466-3390, 446-3070, Fax: (541) 466-5312, E-mail: jmoyer@peak.org, Internet: lchm-friends.peak.org. C.E.O.: Brian Carrol
Local Museum / Folklore Museum - 1962
Local hist 41964

Brownsville TX

Brownsville Museum of Fine Art, 230 Neale Dr, Brownsville, TX 78520 - T: (956) 542-0941, Fax: (956) 542-7094, E-mail: balart@prodigy.net, Internet: brownsvilleartleague.netfirms.com. Pres.: Tencha Sloss
Fine Arts Museum - 1935
Art 41965

Brownville NE

Brownville Historical Society Museum, Main St, Brownville, NE 68321 - T: (402) 825-6001, Internet: www.cibrownville.ne.us. Cur.: Lola Vice (Bailey House), Jenny Wheeldon (Carson House and Cur. CB&Q Depot), Robert Lutz (Agriculture), Jane Smith (Dental Office)
Local Museum - 1956 41966

Meriwether Lewis Dredge Museum, RR 1, Brownville State Recreation Area, Brownville, NE 68321 - T: (402) 825-3341. Cur.: Clay W. Kennedy
Local Museum - 1977 41967

Brownville NY

General Jacob Brown Historical Museum, 216 Brown Blvd, Brownville, NY 13615 - T: (315) 782-4508, Fax: (315) 786-1178, E-mail: bville@gisco.net. Pres.: Constance G. Hoard
Military Museum - 1978 41968

Brunswick GA

Hofwyl-Broadfield Plantation, 5556 US-Hwy 17 N, Brunswick, GA 31525 - T: (912) 264-7333, E-mail: hofwyl@darientel.net
Agriculture Museum - 1974
Historic plantation 41969

Brunswick MD

Brunswick Railroad Museum, 40 W Potomac St, Brunswick, MD 21716 - T: (301) 834-7100, E-mail: moppy6@juno.com, Internet: www.brrm.org. Pres.: Ed Moss, Cur.: Vicki Dearing, Sue Richwagen
Science&Tech Museum - 1974
Transportation 41970

Brunswick ME

Bowdoin College Museum of Art, Walker Art Bldg, 9400 College Station, Brunswick, ME 04011-8494 - T: (207) 725-3275, Fax: (207) 725-3762, E-mail: artmuseum@bowdoin.edu, Internet: www.bowdoin.edu/artmuseum. Dir.: Katy Kline, Cur.: Alison Ferris
Fine Arts Museum / University Museum - 1811
Art 41971

The Peary-MacMillan Arctic Museum, Bowdoin College, 9500 College Stn, Brunswick, ME 04011-8495 - T: (207) 725-3416, 725-3062, Fax: (207) 725-3499, Internet: www.bowdoin.edu/arcticmuseum. Dir.: Dr. Susan A. Kaplan, Cur.: Dr. Geneviève LeMoine
Ethnology Museum / University Museum - 1967
Ethnology, archaeology, natural history 41972

Pejepscot Historical Society Museum, 159 Park Row, Brunswick, ME 04011 - T: (207) 729-6606, Fax: (207) 729-6012, E-mail: pejepscot@curtislibrary.com, Internet: www.curtislibrary.com/pejepscot.htm. Dir.: Deborah A. Smith, Cur.: Jarrod Roll
Local Museum - 1888
Regional history 41973

Bryan TX

Brazos Valley Museum of Natural History, 3232 Briarcrest Dr, Bryan, TX 77802 - T: (409) 776-2195, Fax: (409) 774-0252, E-mail: bvmnh@myriad.net, Internet: bvmuseum.myriad.net. Dir.: Thomas F. Lynch, Sc. Staff: Nivia Maldonado (Biology), Amy Witte (Collections, Exhibitions)
Natural History Museum - 1961
Natural hist 41974

Bryant Pond ME

Woodstock Historical Society Museum, 70 S Main St, Bryant Pond, ME 04219 - T: (207) 665-2450. Cur.: Larry Billings
Historical Museum - 1979
Local hist 41975

Bryn Athyn PA

Glencairn Museum, 1001 Cathedral Rd, Bryn Athyn, PA 19009-0757 - T: (215) 938-2600, Fax: (215) 914-2986, E-mail: dfcarey@newchurch.edu, Internet: www.glencairnmuseum.org. Dir.: Stephen H. Morley, Cur.: C. Edward Gyllenhaal
Religious Arts Museum - 1878
History. religious art 41976

Bucksport ME

Bucksport Historical Museum, Main St, Bucksport, ME 04416 - T: (207) 567-3623. Pres.: Frances D. Beamis
Local Museum - 1964
Local history, Old Maine Central Railroad Station 41977

Bucyrus OH

Bucyrus Historical Society Museum, 202 S Walnut St, Bucyrus, OH 44820 - T: (419) 562-6386. Dir.: Dr. John K. Kurtz, Cur.: Linda Blicke
Local Museum - 1969 41978

Buena Park CA

Buena Park Historical Society Museum, 6631 Beach Blvd, Buena Park, CA 90621 - T: (714) 562-3570, Internet: www.historicalsociety.org. Cur.: Dee Cavenee, Jane Mueller
Local Museum - 1967 41979

Buffalo MN

Wright County Historical Museum, 2001 Hwy 25 N, Buffalo, MN 55313 - T: (763) 682-7323, Fax: (612) 682-6178. Cur.: Maureen Galvin
Local Museum - 1967
Regional history 41980

Buffalo NY

Albright-Knox Art Gallery, 1285 Elmwood Av, Buffalo, NY 14222-1096 - T: (716) 882-8700, Fax: (716) 882-1958, E-mail: corlick@albrightknox.org, Internet: www.albrightknox.org. Dir.: Douglas G. Schultz, Cur.: Douglas Dreishpoon, Kenneth Wayne, Jennifer Bayles, Claire Schneider, Mariann Smith, Libr.: Susana Tejada
Fine Arts Museum - 1862
Painting, sculpture, photography, works on paper 41981

Benjamin and Dr. Edgar R. Cofeld Judaic Museum of Temple Beth Zion, 805 Delaware Av, Buffalo, NY 14209 - T: (716) 836-6565, Fax: (716) 831-1126, E-mail: tbz@webt.com, Internet: www.tbz.org. Dir.: Mortimer Spiller, Dep. Dir.: Harriet Spiller
Special Museum / Religious Arts Museum - 1981 41982

Buffalo and Erie County Historical Society Museum, 25 Nottingham Ct, Buffalo, NY 14216 - T: (716) 873-9644, Fax: (716) 873-8754, E-mail: bechs@buffnet.net, Internet: www.bechs.org. Pres.: Richard A. Wiesen, Exec. Dir.: William Siener, Dir.: Walter Mayer
Local Museum - 1862 41983

Buffalo and Erie County Naval and Military Park, One Naval Park Cove, Buffalo, NY 14202 - T: (716) 847-1773, Fax: (716) 847-6405, E-mail: navalpark@ch.ci.buffalo.ny.us, Internet: www.buffalonavalpark.org. Dir.: Patrick J. Cunningham
Military Museum - 1979
Military hist 41984

Buffalo Museum of Science, 1020 Humboldt Pkwy, Buffalo, NY 14211 - T: (716) 896-5200, Fax: (716) 897-6723, E-mail: dchesebrough@sciencebuff.org, Internet: www.buffalomuseumofscience.org. Dir.: David Chesebrough, Cur.: Dr. Richard S. Laub (Geology), Ass. Cur.: Kevin Smith (Anthropology)
Natural History Museum - 1861 41985

Burchfield-Penney Art Center, Buffalo State College, 1300 Elmwood Av, Buffalo, NY 14222 - T: (716) 878-6011, Fax: (716) 878-6003, E-mail: burchfld@buffalostate.edu, Internet: www.burchfield-penney.org. Dir.: Ted Pietrzak, Nancy Weekly (Curatorial Sevices)
Fine Arts Museum - 1966
Western New York art and craft, watercolors by Charles E. Burchfield 41986

Center for Exploratory and Perceptual Art, 617 Main St, Buffalo, NY 14203 - T: (716) 856-2717, Fax: (716) 270-0184, E-mail: cepa@aol.com, Internet: cepagallery.com. Dir.: Lawrence F. Brose
Fine Arts Museum - 1974 41987

El Museo Francisco Oller y Diego Rivera, 91 Allen St, Buffalo, NY 14202 - T: (716) 884-9693, Fax: (716) 884-9362, E-mail: elmuseubuffalo@aol.com, Internet: www.buffalo.com/elmuseobuffalo
Fine Arts Museum 41988

Theodore Roosevelt Inaugural National Historic Site, 641 Delaware Av, Buffalo, NY 14202 - T: (716) 884-0095, Fax: (716) 884-0330, Internet: www.nps.gov/thri/. Dir.: Molly Quackenbush, Ass. Dir.: Janice Tomaka, Cur.: Leonora Henson
Historical Museum - 1971
Buffalo Barracks, the site of the inauguration of Pres. Theodore Roosevelt in 1901 41989

University at Buffalo Art Galleries, 201A Center for the Arts, Buffalo, NY 14260-6000 - T: (716) 645-6912, Fax: (716) 645-6912, E-mail: rihauser@acsu.buffalo.edu, Internet: www.artgallery.buffalo.edu. Dir.: Sandra H. Olsen, Cur.: Reine Hauser
Fine Arts Museum / University Museum - 1994
Art 41990

Buffalo WY

Jim Gatchell Museum, 100 Fort St, Buffalo, WY 82834 - T: (308) 684-9331, Fax: (307) 684-0354, E-mail: jmuseum@trib.com, Internet: www.jimgatchell.com
Local Museum - 1957
Military, pioneer, Indian hist, mineralogy, paintings 41991

Buford GA

Lanier Museum of Natural History, 2601 Buford Dam Rd, Buford, GA 30518 - T: (770) 932-4460, Fax: (770) 932-3055, E-mail: patterma@co.gwinnett.ga.us, Internet: co.gwinnett.ga.us. Dir.: Dr. Mark A. Patterson
Natural History Museum - 1978
Botany, zoology, geology, paleontology 41992

Burfordville MO

Bollinger Mill State Historic Site, 113 Bollinger Mill Rd, Burfordville, MO 63739 - T: (573) 243-4591, Fax: (573) 243-5385
Open Air Museum / Local Museum - 1967 41993

Burley ID

Cassia County Museum, East Main and Highland Av, Burley, ID 83318 - T: (208) 678-7172
Local Museum - 1972
Train car, farm machinery, county covered wagon 41994

Burlington IA

The Apple Trees Museum, 1616 Dill St, Burlington, IA 52601 - T: (319) 753-2449, E-mail: dmcohist@interl.net. Pres.: Avis Long
Historical Museum / Agriculture Museum - 1972
Charles E. Perkins mansion 41995

Art Guild of Burlington Gallery, Seventh and Washington, Burlington, IA 52601 - T: (319) 754-8069, Fax: (319) 754-4731, E-mail: arts4living@aol.com. Pres.: Burton Prugh, Dir.: Lois Rigdon
Public Gallery - 1966 41996

Hawkeye Log Cabin, 2915 S Main St, Burlington, IA 52601 - T: (319) 753-2449, E-mail: dmcohist@interl.net. Pres.: Keith Erts
Special Museum - 1971
1909 log cabin, furnishings, pioneer tools 41997

Phelps House, 521 Columbia, Burlington, IA 52601 - T: (319) 753-5880, E-mail: dmcohist@interl.net. Pres.: Ellen Fuller
Decorative Arts Museum - 1974
1851 Victorian mansion 41998

Burlington KY

Dinsmore Homestead History Museum, 5656 Burlington Pike, Burlington, KY 41005 - T: (859) 586-6117, Fax: (859) 334-3690, E-mail: info@dinsmorefarm.org, Internet: www.dinsmorefarm.org. Exec. Dir.: Marty McDonald
Historical Museum - 1986 41999

Burlington MA

Burlington Historical Museum, Town Hall, 29 Center St, Burlington, MA 01803 - T: (781) 272-1049, E-mail: archives@burlmass.org, Internet: www.burlington.org/archives. C.E.O.: Norman Biggart
Local Museum - 1970
Primitive agriculture, costumes, dolls, furniture, WW 1, toys, paintings, town hist 42000

Burlington Historical Museum, 106 Bedford St, Burlington, MA 01803 - T: (781) 270-1600, Fax: (781) 270-1608, E-mail: archives@burlmass.org, Internet: www.burlington.org/archives. Dir.: Joyce Fay
Local Museum / Historic Site - 1970
Historical and todays artifacts 42001

Burlington ME

Stewart M. Lord Memorial Museum, Burlington, ME 04448 - T: (207) 732-4121. Cur.: Fern P. Cummings
Historical Museum / Folklore Museum - 1968
History , restored tavern, housing wagons, surry boat 42002

Burlington NC

Alamance Battleground, 5803 S NC Rte 62, Burlington, NC 27215 - T: (336) 227-4785, Fax: (336) 227-4787, E-mail: alamance@ncsl.dcr.state.nc.us, Internet: www.ah.dcr.state.nc.us/sections/hs/alamance. Head: Bryan Dalton
Open Air Museum / Military Museum - 1955 42003

Burlington NJ

Burlington County Historical Society Museum, 451 High St, Burlington, NJ 08016 - T: (609) 386-4773, Fax: (609) 386-4828, E-mail: bchsnj@earthlink.net. Dir.: Douglas E. Winterick
Historical Museum - 1915
Decorative arts, clocks, quilts, Delaware River Decoys 42004

Colonial Burlington Foundation, 213 Wood St, Burlington, NJ 08016 - T: (609) 239-2266, Fax: (609) 386-3415, E-mail: jacques@colorite-resins.com. Pres.: Gary E. Jacques
Local Museum - 1939 42005

Hoskins House, 202 High St, Burlington, NJ 08016 - T: (609) 386-0200, Fax: (609) 386-0214, Internet: www.tourburlington.org
Local Museum / Folklore Museum - 1975
Local history 42006

Burlington VT

The Children's Discovery Museum of Vermont, 1 College St, Burlington, VT 05401 - T: (802) 864-1848, Fax: (802) 864-6832, E-mail: lcbsc@together.net, Internet: www.uvm.edu/~lcbsc/. Dir.: Betsy Rosenbluth
Special Museum - 1995
Children's museum 42007

Francis Colburn Gallery, c/o University of Vermont, Art Department, Williams Hall, Burlington, VT 05405 - T: (802) 656-2014, Fax: (802) 656-2064
Fine Arts Museum / University Museum - 1975
Art 42008

Robert Hull Fleming Museum, c/o University of Vermont, Colchester Av, Burlington, VT 05405-0064 - T: (802) 656-0750, Fax: (802) 656-8059, E-mail: fleming@zoo.uvm.edu, Internet: www.uvm.edu/~fleming. Dir.: Ann Porter, Ass. Dir./Cur.: Janie Cohen
Fine Arts Museum / University Museum / Ethnology Museum - 1931
Art, anthropology 42009

Burnet TX

Fort Croghan Museum, 703 Buchanan Dr, Burnet, TX 78611 - T: (512) 756-8281, Fax: (512) 756-2548, E-mail: piejoy@tstar.net, Internet: www.fortcroghan.org. Dir.: Neva Clark
Local Museum / Historic Site - 1957
Local hist 42010

Burns OR

Harney County Historical Museum, 18 W D St, Burns, OR 97720 - T: (503) 573-1461, Fax: (541) 573-5618, E-mail: dpurdy@centurytel.net, Internet: www.burnsmuseum.com. C.E.O. & Pres.: Dorothea Purdy, Cur.: Kathy Elsbury
Local Museum - 1960 42011

Burr Oak IA

Laura Ingalls Wilder Museum, 3603 236th Av, Burr Oak, IA 52101 - T: (319) 735-5916, Fax: (319) 735-5916, Internet: bluffcountry.com/liwbo.htm. Pres.: Heidi Hotvedt
Natural History Museum / Special Museum - 1976 42012

Burton OH

Century Village Museum, 14653 E Park St, Burton, OH 44021 - T: (216) 834-4012, Fax: (216) 834-4012, E-mail: gchs@jmzcomputer.com, Internet: www.geavgahistorical.org. Pres.: Kurt Updegraff Mary Bennett
Open Air Museum / Historical Museum - 1938 42013

Burwell NE

Fort Hartsuff, RR 1, Burwell, NE 68823 - T: (308) 346-4715, Fax: (308) 346-4715, E-mail: forthartsuff@nctc.net, Internet: www.ngpc.state.ne.us
Military Museum - 1874
Period furniture, arch. coll, Great Plains military hist - Military Museum 42014

Bushnell FL

Dade Battlefield Historic State Park, 7200 County Rd 603, Bushnell, FL 33513 - T: (352) 793-4781, Fax: (352) 793-4230, E-mail: dbshs@sum.net, Internet: www.floridastateparks.com. Dir.: Barbara Webster
Historic Site / Historical Museum - 1921
Site of a battle between Seminole and US soldiers on Dec. 28, 1835 42015

Butte MT

Butte Silver Bow Arts Chateau, 321 W Broadway, Butte, MT 59701 - T: (406) 723-7600, Fax: (406) 723-5083, E-mail: glenv@in-tch.com, Internet: www.artschateau.org. Dir.: Glenn Bodish
Fine Arts Museum - 1977
Contemporary regional art 42016

Copper King Mansion, 219 W Granite, Butte, MT 59701 - T: (406) 782-7580. Head: John Thompson
Fine Arts Museum / Decorative Arts Museum - 1966 42017

Mineral Museum, University of Montana, Montana Tech., 1300 W Park St, Butte, MT 59701-8997 - T: (406) 496-4414, Fax: (406) 496-4451, E-mail: dberg@mtech.edu, Internet: mbmg.mtech.edu/museum.htm. Cur.: Dr. Richard B. Berg
University Museum / Natural History Museum / Science&Tech Museum - 1900 42018

World Museum of Mining, West End of Park St, Butte, MT 59702 - T: (406) 723-7211, E-mail: director@miningmuseum.org, Internet: www.miningmuseum.org. Dir.: Robin Urban
Science&Tech Museum - 1964 42019

Buzzards Bay MA

Captain Charles H. Hurley Library Museum, 101 Academy Dr, Buzzards Bay, MA 02532 - T: (508) 830-5000, 830-5035, Fax: (508) 830-5074, E-mail: mbosse@bridge.mma.mass.edu, Internet: www.mma.mass.edu/mma.html. Dir.: Maurice Bosse
Historical Museum - 1980
Maritime naval museum - library 42020

Byron NY

Byron Historical Museum, 6407 Town Line Rd, Byron, NY 14422 - T: (585) 548-9008, E-mail: byron-historian@juno.com. Sc. Staff: Beth Wilson (History)
Local Museum - 1967
General coll 42021

Cable WI

Cable Natural History Museum, County Hwy M and Randysek Rd, Cable, WI 54821 - T: (715) 798-3890, Fax: (715) 798-3828, E-mail: mail@cablemuseum.org, Internet: www.cablemuseum.org. Exec. Dir.: Allison D. Slavick
Natural History Museum - 1968
Natural hist 42022

Cabot VT

Cabot Historical Society Museum, 193 McKinistry St, Cabot, VT 05647 - T: (802) 563-2558, 563-2547. Pres.: Leonard H. Spencer, Cur.: Eric Ginette
Local Museum - 1966
Local hist 42023

Cadillac MI

Wexford County Historical Museum, 127 Beech St, Cadillac, MI 49601 - T: (231) 775-1717, Fax: (231) 775-0888. Pres.: Ronald D. Jones
Local Museum - 1978
Local hist 42024

Cahokia IL

Cahokia Courthouse State Historic Site, 107 Elm St, Cahokia, IL 62206 - T: (618) 332-1782, Fax: (618) 332-1737. Head: Molly McKenzie
Historical Museum - 1940
Residence build 1737 42025

Cairo IL

Magnolia Manor Museum, 2700 Washington Av, Cairo, IL 62914 - T: (618) 734-0201, Fax: (618) 734-0201. Cur.: Tim Slapinski
Local Museum - 1952 42026

Caldwell ID

Kiwanis Van Slyke Museum Foundation, Caldwell Municipal Park, Grant and Kimball Sts, Caldwell, ID 83605 - T: (208) 459-2229. Chm.: Mac McCann
Local Museum / Agriculture Museum - 1958 42027

Rosenthal Gallery of Art, Albertson College of Idaho, 2112 Cleveland Blvd, Caldwell, ID 83605 - T: (208) 459-5321, Fax: (208) 454-2077, E-mail: gclassen@albertson.edu, Internet: www.acofi.edu/art/galleries/rosenthal.htm. Dir.: Garth Claassen
Fine Arts Museum / University Museum - 1891
Art 42028

Caldwell NJ

Grover Cleveland Birthplace, 207 Bloomfield Av, Caldwell, NJ 07006 - T: (973) 226-0001, Fax: (973) 226-1810
Local Museum - 1913 42029

Visceglia Art Gallery, Caldwell College, 9 Ryerson Av, Caldwell, NJ 07006 - T: (973) 618-3457, Internet: www.caldwell.edu/news/art_index. Dir.: Kendall Baker
Fine Arts Museum - 1970 42030

Caldwell TX

Burleson County Historical Museum, Burleson County Courthouse, Caldwell, TX 77836 - T: (979) 567-7196, Fax: (979) 567-0366. Chm.: Bill Giesenschlag
Local Museum - 1968
Local hist 42031

Caledonia NY

Big Springs Museum, 3089 Main St, Caledonia, NY 14423 - T: (585) 538-9880. Pres.: Jeanne Guthrie, Cur.: Patty Garret
Local Museum - 1936
History 42032

Calhoun GA

New Echota, 1211 Chatsworth Hwy NE, Calhoun, GA 30701 - T: (706) 624-1321, Fax: (706) 624-1323, E-mail: n_echoda@innerx.net, Internet: www.innerx.net/~newechota
Historic Site / Open Air Museum
1825 capital town of Cherokee Nation 42033

Calistoga CA

Sharpsteen Museum, 1311 Washington St, Calistoga, CA 94515 - T: (707) 942-5911, Fax: (707) 942-6325, E-mail: sdblomq@aol.com, Internet: www.sharpsteen-museum.org. Pres.: Shirley Blomquist
Local Museum - 1978 42034

Calumet MI

Coppertown U.S.A., 109 Red Jacket Rd, Calumet, MI 49913 - T: (906) 337-4354, Internet: www.uppermichigan.com/coppertown. Pres.: Richard Dana
Science&Tech Museum - 1973
Restored Mining Co. Complex, former Calumet and Hecla Mining Co 42035

Calverton NY

Grumman Memorial Park, Rte 25 and 25A, Calverton, NY 11933, mail addr: POB 147, Calverton, NY 11933 - T: (631) 369-9488, Fax: (631) 369-9489, E-mail: grummanpk@aol.com, Internet: www.grummanpark.org
Military Museum
Military aircraft 42036

Cambridge MA

Arthur M. Sackler Museum, 485 Broadway, Cambridge, MA 02138 - T: (617) 495-2397
Fine Arts Museum 42037

Botanical Museum of Harvard University, 26 Oxford St, Cambridge, MA 02138 - T: (617) 495-2326, Fax: (617) 495-5667, Internet: www.hmnh.harvard.edu. Cur.: Andrew H. Knoll (Paleobotany)
University Museum / Natural History Museum - 1858
Botany 42038

Cambridge Historical Museum, 159 Brattle St, Cambridge, MA 02138 - T: (617) 547-4252, Fax: (617) 661-1623, E-mail: camhistory@aol.com, Internet: www.cambridgehistory.org. Pres.: M. Wyllis Bibbins, Exec. Dir.: Sally Purrington-Hild
Local Museum - 1905
Local history 42039

Gallery 57, 51 Inman St, Cambridge, MA 02139 - T: (617) 349-4380, Fax: (617) 349-6357, E-mail: cac@ci.cambridge.ma.us, Internet: www.ci.cambridge.ma.us. Dir.: Donna Marcantonio
Public Gallery - 1973 42040

Harvard Museum of Natural History, 24-26 Oxford St, Cambridge, MA 02138 - T: (617) 496-8204, Fax: (617) 496-8206, E-mail: hmnh@oeb.harvard.edu, Internet: www.hmnh.harvard.edu. Exec. Dir.: Joshua Basseches
University Museum / Natural History Museum - 1995
University's three natural history institutions: Botanical Museum, Museum of Comparative Zoology, Mineralogical Museum 42041

Harvard University Art Museums, Fogg Art Museum, Arthur M. Sackler Museum, Busch-Reisinger Museum, 32 Quincy St, Cambridge, MA 02138 - T: (617) 495-9400, Fax: (617) 496-9762, E-mail: huam@fas.harvard.edu, Internet: www.artmuseums.harvard.edu. Acting Dir.: Marjorie B. Cohn, Cur.: Mary McWilliams (Islamic and Later Indian Art), Theodore Stebbins (American Art), Robert Mowry (Chinese Art), Harry Cooper (Modern Art), Linda Norden (Contemporary Art), David Mitten (Ancient Art), Deborah Kao (Photography), Marjorie B. Cohn (Prints), Ivan Gaskell (Paintings, Sculpture, Decorative Arts), William Robinson (Drawings), Peter Nisbet (Busch-Reisinger)
Fine Arts Museum / University Museum - 1895
Art 42042

Harvard University Semitic Museum, 6 Divinity Av, Cambridge, MA 02138 - T: (617) 495-4631, Fax: (617) 496-8904, E-mail: stager@fas.harvard.edu, Internet: www.fas.harvard.edu/~semitic/. Dir.: Prof. Lawrence Stager, Ass. Dir.: Joseph A. Greene, Cur.: Prof. Piotr Steinkeller, Ass. Cur.: James A. Armstrong
University Museum / Archaeological Museum - 1889
Ancient and medieval Near East archaeology 42043

Longfellow National Historic Site, 105 Brattle St, Cambridge, MA 02138 - T: (617) 876-4491, Fax: (617) 876-6014, E-mail: frla_longfellow@nps.gov, Internet: www.nps.gov/long. Cur.: Janice Hodson
Historical Museum - 1972
Home of Henry Wadsworth Longfellow, headqaurters of George Washington 1775-1776 - library 42044

Margaret Hutchinson Compton Gallery, 77 Massachusetts Av, Bldg 10, Cambridge, MA 02139-4307 - T: (617) 253-4444, Fax: (617) 253-8994, Internet: web.mit.edu/museum. Dir.: Jane Pickering
Fine Arts Museum / Science&Tech Museum - 1978
Technology 42045

Mineralogical Museum of Harvard University, 24 Oxford St, Cambridge, MA 02138 - T: (617) 495-4758, Fax: (617) 495-8839. Dir.: Prof. Michael B. McElroy, Cur.: Dr. Carl A. Francis, Ass. Cur.: William C. Metropolis
Natural History Museum - 1784
Scientific referance coll, rocks 42046

MIT-List Visual Arts Center, 20 Ames St, Wiesner Bldg E15-109, Cambridge, MA 02139 - T: (617) 253-4680, 253-4400, Fax: (617) 258-7265, E-mail: freilach@mit.edu, Internet: web.mit.edu/lvac. Dir.: Jane Farver, Cur.: Bill Arning, Kathleen Goncharov
Fine Arts Museum / University Museum - 1963
Art 42047

The MIT Museum, 265 Massachusetts Av, Cambridge, MA 02139-4307 - T: (617) 253-5927, Fax: (617) 253-8994, E-mail: museum@mit.edu, Internet: web.mit.edu/museum. Dir.: Jane Pickering, Ass. Dir.: Mary Leen, Cur.: Kurt Hasselbalch (Hart Nautical Collections), Gary Van Zante (Architecture)
University Museum / Science&Tech Museum - 1971
Science, technology, architecture 42048

Peabody Museum of Archaeology and Ethnology, 11 Divinity Av, Cambridge, MA 02138 - T: (617) 496-1027, Fax: (617) 495-7535, Internet: www.peabody.harvard.edu. Dir.: Dr. Rubie Watson, Cur.: Diane Loren
University Museum / Ethnology Museum / Archaeological Museum - 1866
Anthropology, archaeology, ethnology 42049

Cambridge MD

Dorchester County Historical Society Museum, 902 LaGrange Av, Cambridge, MD 21613 - T: (410) 228-7953, Fax: (410) 228-2947, E-mail: dchs@fastol.com, Internet: www.bluecrab.org/dchs/index.html. Pres.: Thomas F. Collins
Local Museum - 1953 42050

Cambridge MN

Isanti County Museum, 1400 Hwy 293, McBroom, Cambridge, MN 55008 - T: (763) 689-4229, Fax: (763) 689-4229, E-mail: varrow2@ecenet.com, Internet: www.braham.com. Dir.: Valorie Stavem Arrowsmith
Local Museum - 1865
Pioneer artifacts 1870 to 1930, household and farm equip 42051

Cambridge NE

Cambridge Museum, 612 Penn St, Cambridge, NE 69022 - T: (308) 697-4385. Pres.: Marilyn Kester, Cur.: Marjorie Ridpath
Fine Arts Museum / Local Museum - 1938
Local history 42052

Cambridge OH

Cambridge Glass Museum, 812 Jefferson Av, Cambridge, OH 43725 - T: (614) 432-3045. Dir.: Harold D. Bennett, Dep. Dir.: Dorthy E. Bennett
Decorative Arts Museum - 1973 42053

Degenhart Paperweight and Glass Museum, 65323 Highland Hills Rd, Cambridge, OH 43725 - T: (614) 432-2626, E-mail: degmus@clover.net, Internet: www.degenhartmuseum.com. Cur.: Erna Burris
Decorative Arts Museum / Special Museum - 1978
Ohio Valley midwestern pattern glass, 20th-c paperweights, artglass, decorative items 42054

Guernsey County Museum, 218 N Eighth St, Cambridge, OH 43725 - T: (740) 439-5884. Cur.: Calvin Rice
Local Museum - 1964
Regional hist, county hall of fame, military 42055

Cambridge City IN

Huddleston Farmhouse Inn Museum, 838 National Rd, Mt Auburn, Cambridge City, IN 47327 - T: (765) 478-3172, Fax: (765) 478-3410, E-mail: huddleston@historiclandmarks.org, Internet: www.historiclandmarks.org. Pres.: J. Reid Williamson, Dir.: Brady Kress
Historical Museum / Agriculture Museum - 1977
Federal style brick, 3-story farmhouse 42056

Camden AR

McCollum-Chidester House Museum, 926 Washington St, NW, Camden, AR 71701 - T: (870) 836-9243, 836-4580. Dir.: Clara Freeland, Cur.: Kathrin Boyette
Historical Museum - 1847
Stage Coach House, Union general quartered here during Battle at Poison Springs, furniture and personal effects of family (1863-1963) - Leake-Ingham library 42057

Camden ME

Old Conway Homestead Museum and Mary Meeker Cramer Museum, US Rte 1, Camden-Rockport Ln, Camden, ME 04843, mail addr: POB 747, Rockport, ME 04856 - T: (207) 236-2257, E-mail: crmuseum@midcoast.com. C.E.O.: Marlene Hall
Local Museum - 1962
Paintings, books, photographs, costumes, folklore, local hist, marine, musical instruments, agriculture 42058

Camden NJ

Camden County Historical Society Museum, Park Blvd and Euclid Av, Camden, NJ 08103 - T: (856) 964-3333, Fax: (856) 964-0378, Internet: www.cchsnj.org. Dir.: John R. Seitter, Cur.: Judith Synder, Libr.: Joanne Diogo
Local Museum - 1899 42059

Stedman Art Gallery, Rutgers State University of New Jersey, Camden, NJ 08102 - T: (856) 225-6245, Fax: (609) 225-6330, E-mail: arts@camdenrutgers.edu, Internet: seca.camdenrutgers.edu. Dir.: Virginia Oberlin Steel, Cur.: Nancy Maguire (Exhibits), Noreen Scott Garrity (Education)
Fine Arts Museum - 1975
Modern and Contemporary art 42060

Walt Whitman House, 328 Mickle Blvd, Camden, NJ 08103 - T: (609) 964-5383, Fax: (856) 964-1088, E-mail: whitmanshs@snip.net. Cur.: Leo D. Blake
Historical Museum - 1946 42061

Camden NY

Carriage House Museum, 2 N Park St, Camden, NY 13316 - T: (315) 245-4652, E-mail: historycamden@a-znet.com. Pres.: Elaine Norton
Historical Museum - 1975 42062

Camden SC

Camden Archives and Museum, 1314 Broad St, Camden, SC 29020-3535 - T: (803) 425-6050, Fax: (803) 424-4053, Internet: www.mindspring.com/~camdenarchives/index.html. Dir.: Agnes Corbett
Local Museum - 1973
Local hist 42063

Fine Arts Center of Kershaw County, 810 Lyttleton St, Camden, SC 29020 - T: (803) 425-7676, Fax: (803) 425-7679, E-mail: fackc@infoave.net, Internet: www.fineartscenter.org. Dir.: Dianne Pantoja
Fine Arts Museum - 1976
Art 42064

Historic Camden Revolutionary War Site, 222 Broad St, Camden, SC 29020 - T: (803) 432-9841, Fax: (803) 432-3815. Dir.: Joanna Craig
Local Museum - 1967
Local hist 42065

Kershaw County Historical Society Museum, 811 Fair St, Camden, SC 29020 - T: (803) 425-1123, E-mail: kchistory@mindspring.com, Internet: www.mindspring.com/~kchistory. Dir.: Kathleen P. Stahl
Local Museum - 1954
Local hist 42066

Cameron TX

Milam County Historical Museum, Main and Fannin Sts, Cameron, TX 76520 - T: (254) 697-4770, 697-8963, Fax: (254) 697-7028, E-mail: milamco@tlab.net, Internet: www.cameron-tx.com. Dir.: Charles King
Local Museum - 1977
Local hist 42067

Cameron WI

Barron County Historical Society's Pioneer Village Museum, 1 1/2 mile west of Cameron on Museum Rd, Cameron, WI 54822 - T: (715) 458-2841, Internet: www.chibardun.net/~museum. Pres.: Ken Mosenstine
Local Museum - 1960
State and local hist 42068

Camp Douglas WI

Wisconsin National Guard Memorial Library and Museum, 101 Independence Dr, Camp Douglas, WI 54618 - T: (608) 427-1280, Fax: (608) 427-1399, E-mail: eric.lent@dva.state.wi.us. C.E.O.: Raymond Boland, Cur.: Eric Lent
Military Museum - 1984
Military hist 42069

Campbell CA

Ainsley House, 300 Grant St, Campbell, CA 95008 - T: (408) 866-2118, Fax: (408) 866-2795, Internet: www.ci.campbell.ca.us. Dir.: Robert Pedretti, Cur.: Karen Brey
Historical Museum - 1964 42070

Campbell Historical Museum, 51 N Central Av, Campbell, CA 95008 - T: (408) 866-2119, Fax: (408) 866-2795, Internet: www.ci.campbell.ca.us. Dir.: Robert Pedretti, Cur.: Karen Brey
Historical Museum - 1964 42071

Campbellsport WI

Henry S. Reuss Ice Age Visitor Center, DNR, Kettle Moraine State Forest N 2875 Hwy 67, Campbellsport, WI 53010 - T: (920) 533-8322, (262) 626-2116, Fax: (262) 626-2117, Internet: www.DNR.state.wi.us
Natural History Museum - 1980
Glacial geology 42072

Canaan NY

Canaan Historical Society Museum, Warner's Crossing Rd, Canaan, NY 12029 - T: (518) 781-4228. Cur.: Anna Mary Dunton
Local Museum - 1963 42073

Canajoharie NY

Canajoharie Library and Art Gallery, 2 Erie Blvd, Canajoharie, NY 13317 - T: (518) 673-2314, Fax: (518) 673-5243, E-mail: etrahan@sals.edu, Internet: www.clag.org. Dir.: Eric Trahan, Cur.: James Crawford
Fine Arts Museum / Library with Exhibitions - 1929 42074

Canal Fulton OH

Canal Fulton Heritage Society Museum, 103 Tuscarawas St, Canal Fulton, OH 44614 - Fax: (330) 854-2902. Pres.: Rochelle Rossi
Local Museum - 1968 42075

Canandaigua NY

Granger Homestead Society Museum, 295 N Main St, Canandaigua, NY 14424 - T: (716) 394-1472, Fax: (716) 394-6958, E-mail: ghomestead@aol.com, Internet: www.grangerhomestead.org. Dir.: Saralinda Hooker
Local Museum - 1946 42076

Ontario County Historical Society Museum, 55 N Main St, Canandaigua, NY 14424 - T: (716) 394-4975, Fax: (716) 394-9351, E-mail: director@ochs.org, Internet: www.ochs.org. Dir.: Edward Varno, Cur.: Wilma T. Townsend
Historical Museum - 1902 42077

Canby OR

Canby Depot Museum, 888 NE Fourth Av, Canby, OR 97013, mail addr: POB 160, Canby, OR 97013 - T: (503) 266-6712, Fax: (503) 266-9775, E-mail: depotmuseum@canby.com, Internet: www.canby.com/chamber/depot.htm
Local Museum - 1984
Hist of Canby, caboose, speeder car, railroading, agriculture and daily living 42078

Caney KS

Caney Valley Historical Society Museum, West Fourth St, Caney, KS 67333, mail addr: POB 354, Caney, KS 67333 - T: (316) 879-5198
Local Museum - 1984
Education, medical, post office, military, municipal, religious, industry and domestic items 42079

Cannon Falls MN

Cannon Falls Area Historical Museum, 208 W Mill St, Cannon Falls, MN 55009 - T: (507) 263-4080, E-mail: cfmuseum@rconnect.com. Pres.: John Otto, Dir.: Heidi Holmes Helgren
Local Museum - 1979
Regional history, town fire hall 42080

Canon City CO

Canon City Municipal Museum, 612 Royal Gorge Blvd, Canon City, CO 81212 - T: (719) 276-5279, Fax: (719) 269-9017, E-mail: museum@canoncity.org. Dir.: Ann Swim
Local Museum - 1928
Local history 42081

Canterbury CT

Prudence Crandall Museum, Rts 14 and 169, Canterbury Green, Canterbury, CT 06331-0058 - T: (860) 546-9916, Fax: (860) 546-7803, E-mail: crndll@snet.net. Cur.: Kazimiera Kozlowski
Historical Museum - 1984
New England life in 19th c, abolitionism, education 42082

Canterbury NH

Canterbury Shaker Village, 288 Shaker Rd, Canterbury, NH 03224 - T: (603) 783-9511, Fax: (603) 783-9152, E-mail: info@shakers.org, Internet: www.shakers.org. Pres.: Scott T. Swank, Chief Cur.: Shery N. Hack
Open Air Museum / Historical Museum / Historic Site - 1969 42083

Canton MA

Canton Historical Museum, 1400 Washington St, Canton, MA 02021 - T: (781) 828-8537, Internet: www.canton.org. Pres.: James Roche
Local Museum - 1893
Local history 42084

Canton NY

Pierrepont Museum, 868 State Hwy 68, Canton, NY 13617 - T: (315) 386-8311, Fax: (315) 379-0415. Sc. Staff: Charlotte Ragan (History)
Decorative Arts Museum - 1977 42085

Richard F. Brush Art Gallery and Permanent Collection, Saint Lawrence University, 23 Romoda Dr, Canton, NY 13617 - T: (315) 229-5174, Fax: (315) 229-7445, E-mail: ctedford@stlawu.edu, Internet: www.stlawu.edu/gallery. Dir.: Catherine L. Tedford
Fine Arts Museum / University Museum - 1967 42086

Silas Wright Jr. Historic House, 3 E Main St, Canton, NY 13617 - T: (315) 386-8133, Fax: (315) 386-8134, E-mail: slcha@northnet.org, Internet: www.slcha.org. C.E.O.: Trent Trulock
Local Museum - 1947
archive 42087

Canton OH

Canton Classic Car Museum, Market Av and 6th St SW, Canton, OH 44702 - T: (330) 455-3603, Fax: (330) 455-0363, E-mail: cccm@cantonclassiccar.org, Internet: www.cantonclassiccar.org. Dir.: Robert C. Lichty
Science&Tech Museum - 1978 42088

Canton Museum of Art, 1001 Market Av N, Canton, OH 44702 - T: (330) 453-7666, Fax: (330) 452-4477, E-mail: staff@cantonart.orgom, Internet: www.cantonart.org. Pres.: Jack Hank, C.E.O.: M.J. Albacete
Fine Arts Museum - 1935 42089

McKinley Museum and McKinley National Memorial, 800 McKinley Monument Dr NW, Canton, OH 44708 - T: (330) 455-7043, Fax: (330) 455-1137, E-mail: mmuseum@neo.rr.com, Internet: www.mckinleymuseum.org. Dir.: Joyce Yut, Dep. Dir.: Chris Kenney (Education), Cur.: Kimberley Kenney
Historical Museum / Science&Tech Museum / Natural History Museum - 1946
planetarium 42090

National Football Museum, 2121 George Halas Dr NW, Canton, OH 44708 - T: (330) 456-8207, Fax: (330) 456-8175, E-mail: jaikens@profootballhof.com, Internet: www.profootballhof.com. Exec. Dir.: John Bankert
Special Museum - 1963 42091

Canyon TX

Panhandle-Plains Historical Museum, 2503 Fourth Av, Canyon, TX 79015 - T: (806) 651-2244, Fax: (806) 651-2250, E-mail: museum@wtamu.edu, Internet: www.panhandleplains.org. Dir.: Walter R. Davis, Ass. Dir.: Lisa Shippee Lambert, Cur.: Michael R. Grauer (Art), Dr. William E. Green (History), Dr. Jeff Indeck (Archaeology)
Local Museum - 1921
Local hist 42092

Canyon City OR

Grant County Historical Museum, 101 S Canyon City Blvd, Canyon City, OR 97820 - T: (541) 575-0362, 575-1993
Local Museum - 1953
Pioneer antiques and relics, Indian artifacts 42093

Cape Coral FL

The Children's Science Center, 2915 NE Pine Island Rd, Cape Coral, FL 33909 - T: (239) 997-0012, Fax: (239) 997-7215, E-mail: scicenter@hotmail.com, Internet: www.cyberstreet.com/csc. C.E.O.: Jeff Rodgers
Science&Tech Museum - 1989 42094

Cape Girardeau MO

Glenn House, 325 S Spanish, Cape Girardeau, MO 63701
Decorative Arts Museum 42095

Southeast Missouri State University Museum, 1 University Pl, Cape Girardeau, MO 63701 - T: (573) 651-2260, Fax: (573) 651-5909, E-mail: museum@semovm.semo.edu. Dir.: Stanley I. Grand, Cur.: James Phillips, Andreu Morrill (Education)
University Museum - 1976 42096

Cape May NJ

Mid-Atlantic Center for the Arts, 1048 Washington St, Cape May, NJ 08204-0340 - T: (609) 884-5404, Fax: (609) 884-2006, E-mail: mac4arts@capemaymac.org, Internet: www.capemaymac.org. Dir.: B. Michael Zuckerman, Cur.: Elizabeth Bailey
Fine Arts Museum - 1970 42097

Cape May Court House NJ

Cape May County Historical Museum, 504 Rte 9 N, Cape May Court House, NJ 08210 - T: (609) 465-3535, Fax: (609) 465-4274, E-mail: museum@co.cape-may.nj.us, Internet: www.cmcmuseum.org. Pres.: James Waltz, Cur.: Rachel A. Rodgers
Local Museum - 1927 42098

Leaming's Run Garden and Colonial Farm, 1845 Rte 9 N, Cape May Court House, NJ 08210 - T: (609) 465-5871, Internet: njsouth.com/index-leamingsrun.htm. Dir.: Gregg Aprill
Agriculture Museum - 1978
Agriculture 42099

Cape Vincent NY

Cape Vincent Historical Museum, James St, Cape Vincent, NY 13618 - T: (315) 654-4400. Pres.: J. Thompson, Dir.: Mary Hamilton, Peter Margrey
Local Museum - 1968 42100

Capitola Village CA

Capitola Historical Museum, 410 Capitola Av, Capitola Village, CA 95010 - T: (408) 464-0322, Fax: (408) 479-8879. Head: Carolyn Swift
Historical Museum - 1967 42101

Carbondale IL

University Museum, Southern Illinois University, 2469 Faner Hall N, Carbondale, IL 62901-4508 - T: (618) 453-5388, Fax: (618) 453-7409, E-mail: museum@siu.edu, Internet: www.museum.siu.edu/. Dir.: Dona R. Bachman, Cur.: Dr. Brooks M. Burr (Zoology), Dr. Donald Ugent (Botany), Harvey Henson (Geology)
University Museum / Local Museum - 1869
University history 42102

Caribou ME

Nylander Museum, 657 Main St, Caribou, ME 04736 - T: (207) 493-4209, E-mail: nylander@mfx.net, Internet: www.nylandermuseum.org. Dir.: Jeanie L. McGowan
Natural History Museum - 1938
Natural history 42103

Carlisle PA

Hamilton Library and Two Mile House, 21 N Pitt St, Carlisle, PA 17013 - T: (717) 249-7610, Fax: (717) 258-9332, E-mail: info@historicalsociety.com, Internet: www.historicalsociety.com. Dir.: Linda F. Witmer, Libr.: Christa Bassett
Historical Museum / Library with Exhibitions - 1874   42104

Trout Gallery, High St, Carlisle, PA 17013, mail addr: c/o Dickinson College, POB 1773, Carlisle, PA 17013-2896 - T: (717) 245-1344, Fax: (717) 245-8929, Internet: www.dickinson.edu/departments/trout. C.E.O.: Dr. Phillip Earenfight
Fine Arts Museum - 1983
Prints, Oriental and decorative arts, African art   42105

United States Army Heritage and Education Center, 22 Ashburn Dr, Carlisle, PA 17013-5008 - T: (717) 245-3611, Fax: (717) 245-4370, E-mail: usamhi@ carlisle.army.mil, Internet: carlisle-www.army.mil/ usamhi. Dir.: Russell J. Hall, Cur.: Michael J. Winey, Ass. Cur.: Randy Hackenburg
Military Museum - 1967   42106

United States Army Military History Institute Museum → United States Army Heritage and Education Center

Carlsbad CA

Carlsbad Children's Museum → Children's Discovery Museum of North San Diego

Children's Discovery Museum of North San Diego, 300 Carlsbad Village Dr, Carlsbad, CA 92008 - T: (760) 720-0737, Fax: (760) 720-0336, E-mail: vaavoom@aol.com, Internet: www. museumforchildren.org. C.E.O.: Catherine Boyle
Special Museum - 1992   42107

Carlsbad NM

Carlsbad Caverns National Park, 3225 National Parks Hwy, Carlsbad, NM 88220 - T: (505) 785-2232 ext 437, Fax: (505) 785-2302, E-mail: DavidKayser@nps.gov, Internet: www.nps. gov
Archaeological Museum / Natural History Museum - 1923
Hist of the caverns, botany, entomology, geology, paleontology, archaeology, herpetology   42108

Carlsbad Museum and Art Center, 418 W Fox St, Carlsbad, NM 88220 - T: (505) 887-0276, Fax: (505) 885-8809, E-mail: virginia_dodier@ carlsbadmuseum.org, Internet: www. carlsbadmuseum.org. Dir.: Virginia Dodier
Fine Arts Museum / Archaeological Museum / Historical Museum / Science&Tech Museum - 1931   42109

Carmel CA

Mission San Carlos Borromeo del Rio Carmelo, 3080 Rio Rd, Carmel, CA 93923 - T: (831) 624-3600, Fax: (831) 624-0658, Internet: www. carmelmission.org. Cur.: Richard J. Menn
Historical Museum / Religious Arts Museum - 1770   42110

Carmi IL

White County Historical Museums, Ratcliff Inn, L.Haas Store, Matsel Cabin, Robinson-Stewart House, 203 N Church St, Carmi, IL 62821 - T: (618) 382-8425, E-mail: cbconly@midwest.net, Internet: www.rootsweb.com/~ilwcohs. Pres.: Jim Pumphrey
Local Museum - 1957
Local history   42111

Carpinteria CA

Carpinteria Valley Museum of History, 956 Maple Av, Carpinteria, CA 93013 - T: (805) 684-3112, Fax: (805) 684-4721. Pres.: Bradley R. Miles, Dir./Cur.: David W. Griggs
Historical Museum - 1959   42112

Carrollton MS

Merrill Museum, Rte 1, Carrollton, MS 38917 - T: (662) 237-9254. Pres.: Kay Slocum
Local Museum - 1961
Local history   42113

Carrollton OH

Civil War Museum, McCook House, Public Sq, Carrollton, OH 44615 - T: (330) 627-3345, Fax: (330) 627-5366, E-mail: ohswww@winslo. ohio.gov, Internet: www.ohiohistory.org/places/ mcookhse/. Pres.: Thomas Konst
Historical Museum - 1963   42114

Carson CA

The Printing Museum, 315 Torrence Blvd, Carson, CA 92745 - T: (714) 523-2070. Pres./Dir.: Mark Barbour
Science&Tech Museum - 1988
Typography, printing machinery   42115

University Art Gallery, CSU Dominguez Hills, 1000 E Victoria St, Carson, CA 90747 - T: (310) 243-3334, Fax: (310) 217-6967, E-mail: kzimmerer@csudh. edu, Internet: www.csudh.edu/art. Dir.: Kathy Zimmerer
University Museum / Fine Arts Museum - 1978   42116

Carson City NV

Bowers Mansion, 4005 US 395 N, Carson City, NV 89704 - T: (702) 849-0201, Fax: (775) 849-9568. Cur.: Betty Hood
Historical Museum - 1946   42117

Nevada State Museum, 600 N Carson St, Carson City, NV 89701 - T: (775) 687-4810, Fax: (775) 687-4168, Internet: www.nevadaculture.org. Dir.: Jim Barmore, Cur.: George Baumgardner (Natural History), Gene Hattori (Anthropology), Bob Nylen (History), Jan Loverin (Clothing and Textiles)
Historical Museum / Natural History Museum - 1939   42118

Nevada State Railroad Museum, 2180 S Carson St, Carson City, NV 89701 - T: (702) 687-6953, Fax: (702) 687-8294, E-mail: jballwe@lahontan. clan.lib.nv.us, Internet: www.nsrm-friends.org. Cur.: John Ballweber
Science&Tech Museum - 1980
Virginia and Truckee railway coll, cars and locomotives, railroad equip   42119

Stewart Indian Cultural Center, 1329 Stanford Dr, Carson City, NV 89701 - T: (702) 882-1808
Folklore Museum / Ethnology Museum   42120

Cartersville GA

Bartow History Center, 13 N Wall St, Cartersville, GA 30120 - T: (770) 382-3818, Fax: (770) 382-0288, Internet: www.etowah.org. Dir.: Michele Rodgers
Historical Museum - 1987
Local hist   42121

Etowah Indian Mounds Historical Site, 813 Indian Mounds Rd SE, Cartersville, GA 30120 - T: (770) 387-3747, Fax: (770) 387-3972, E-mail: etowahl@ innerx.net. Head: Elizabeth Bell
Ethnology Museum / Archaeological Museum - 1953
Indian, archaeology   42122

Rose Lawn Museum, 224 W Cherokee Av, Cartersville, GA 30120 - T: (770) 387-5162, E-mail: roselawn@mindspring.com, Internet: www. roselawnmuseum.com. Dir.: Steven Ellis
Religious Arts Museum - 1973
Victorian mansion, former home of evangelist Samuel Porter Jones   42123

Carterville IL

John A. Logan College Museum, 700 Logan College Rd, Carterville, IL 62918 - T: (618) 985-3741, Fax: (618-985-2248, E-mail: museum@jal.cc.il.us, Internet: www.jal.cc.il.us/museum/index.html
Fine Arts Museum / Decorative Arts Museum - 1967
Contemporary regional art and craft, international ethnic crafts, relating to the life of General John A Logan memorabilia   42124

Carthage IL

Hancock County Historical Museum, 306 Walnut, Carthage, IL 62321. Pres.: Barbara Cochran
Local Museum - 1968
1906-8 Stone Courthouse, on historical site in Carthage   42125

Carthage MO

Powers Museum, 1617 Oak St, Carthage, MO 64836 - T: (417) 358-2667, Fax: (417) 359-9627, E-mail: Info@powersmuseum.com, Internet: www. powersmuseum.com. Dir.: Michele Hansford
Local Museum - 1982
Local hist   42126

Casa Grande AZ

Casa Grande History Museum, 110 W Florence Blvd, Casa Grande, AZ 85222-4033 - T: (520) 836-2223, Fax: (520) 836-5065, E-mail: cgvhs@hotmail.com. Dir.: Gloria A. Smith, Cur.: Kay Benedict
Local Museum - 1964
Local history - library   42127

Cashmere WA

Chelan County Historical Museum, 600 Cotlets Way, Cashmere, WA 98815 - T: (509) 782-3230, Fax: (509) 782-8905, E-mail: cchspvm@aol.com. Dir.: Penny Brouillette
Local Museum - 1956
Local hist   42128

Casper WY

Fort Caspar Museum, 4001 Fort Caspar Rd, Casper, WY 82604 - T: (307) 235-8462, Fax: (307) 235-8464, E-mail: ftcaspr@trib.com, Internet: www. fortcasparwyoming.com. C.E.O.: Richard L. Young, Cur.: Dana Schaar
Military Museum - 1936
Military hist   42129

Nicolaysen Art Museum, 400 East Collins Dr, Casper, WY 82601 - T: (307) 235-5247, Fax: (307) 235-0923, E-mail: nic_art@trib.com, Internet: www. thenic.org. Dir.: Joe Ellis, Cur.: Joe Ramirez
Fine Arts Museum - 1967
Art   42130

Tate Geological Museum, c/o Casper College, 125 College Dr, Casper, WY 82601 - T: (307) 268-2447, Fax: (307) 268-2514, E-mail: dbrown@ caspercollege.edu, Internet: www.caspercollege. edu/tate/webpage.htm. Dir.: David Brown
Natural History Museum - 1979   42131

Caspian MI

Iron County Museum, Brady at Museum Rd, Caspian, MI 49915 - T: (906) 265-2617, E-mail: icmuseum@ up.net, Internet: www.ironcountymuseum.com. Dir.: Harold O. Bernhardt
Local Museum - 1962
Lumbering, mining and farm tools   42132

Cassville WI

Stonefield Historic Site, 12195 County Rd V V, Cassville, WI 53806 - T: (608) 725-5210, Fax: (608) 725-5919, E-mail: stonefld@pcll.net. Dir.: Allen Schroeder, Cur.: Judith Meyerdierks
Agriculture Museum / Open Air Museum - 1952
Agriculture   42133

Castalian Springs TN

Historic Cragfont, 200 Cragfront Rd, Castalian Springs, TN 37031 - T: (615) 452-7070, Internet: www.srlab.net/cragfort/
Local Museum - 1958
Historic house, home of General James Winchester   42134

Castile NY

William Pryor Letchworth Museum, 1 Letchworth State Park, Castile, NY 14427 - T: (716) 493-3617, Fax: (716) 493-5272, Internet: www.nysparks.state. us. Dir.: Brian Scriven
Natural History Museum - 1913   42135

Castine ME

Castine Scientific Society Museum, 107 Perkins St, Castine, ME 04421 - T: (207) 326-9247, Fax: (207) 326-8545, E-mail: admin@wilsonmuseum.org. Dir.: Norman Doudiet, Cur.: Patricia Hutchins
Natural History Museum / Historical Museum - 1921
Science   42136

Castleton VT

Castleton Historical Society Museum, The Higley Homestead, Main St, Castleton, VT 05735-0219 - T: (802) 468-5523. Pres.: Mary Williamson
Local Museum - 1973
Local hist   42137

Catasauqua PA

George Taylor House, Lehigh and Poplar Sts, Catasauqua, PA 18032 - T: (610) 435-4664, Fax: (610) 435-9812. Pres.: Robert M. McGovern, Exec. Dir.: Andree Miller
Local Museum - 1904   42138

Catawissa PA

Catawissa Railroad Museum, 119 Pine St, Catawissa, PA 17820 - T: (570) 356-2675, Fax: (570-356-7876, E-mail: caboosenut.com
Science&Tech Museum
Railroad cabooses, track, railroad memorabilia   42139

Cathlamet WA

Wahkiakum County Historical Museum, 65 River St, Cathlamet, WA 98612 - T: (360) 795-3954. Pres.: Ralph Keyser
Local Museum - 1956
Local hist   42140

Catonsville MD

Alumni Museum, Spring Grove Hospital Center, Wade Av, Garrett Bldg, Catonsville, MD 21228 - T: (410) 402-7786, 402-7856, Fax: (410) 402-7050, Internet: www.springgrove.com/history.html
Historical Museum
Tools, furniture, photos   42141

Cattaraugus NY

Cattaraugus Area Historical Center, 23 Main St, Cattaraugus, NY 14719 - T: (716) 257-3312. Dir.: Dawn D. Waite
Local Museum - 1955   42142

Cavalier ND

Pioneer Heritage Center, 13571 Hwy 5, Cavalier, ND 58220 - T: (701) 265-4561, Fax: (701) 265-4443, E-mail: isp@state.nd.us, Internet: www.state.nd.us. ndparks. Pres.: Alice Olson
Local Museum - 1989
Local hist, settlement story (1870-1920)   42143

Cazenovia NY

Cazenovia College Chapman Art Center Gallery, Cazenovia College, Cazenovia, NY 13035 - T: (315) 655-7162, Fax: (315) 655-2190, E-mail: jaistars@ cazcollege.edu, Internet: www.cazcollege.edu. Dir.: John Aistars
Fine Arts Museum / University Museum - 1978   42144

Lorenzo State Historic Site, 17 Rippleton Rd, Cazenovia, NY 13035 - T: (315) 655-3200, Fax: (315) 655-4304, E-mail: lincklaen@juno.com. Head: Pam Ellis, Cur.: Jackie Vizirito
Historic Site - 1968
History   42145

Cedar City UT

Braithwaite Fine Arts Gallery, Southern Utah University, Cedar City, UT 84720 - T: (435) 586-5432, Fax: (435) 865-8012, E-mail: museums@ suu.edu, Internet: www.suu.edu/pva/artgallery. Dir.: Lydia Johnson
Fine Arts Museum / University Museum - 1976
18th-20th c American art   42146

Iron Mission Museum, 635 N Main St, Cedar City, UT 84720 - T: (435) 586-9290, Fax: (435) 8665-6830, E-mail: nrdpr.ironmiss@state.ut.us. Dir.: Todd Prince, Cur.: Ryan Paul
Historical Museum - 1973
Pioneer hist   42147

Cedar Falls IA

Cedar Falls Historical Museum, 303 Franklin St, Cedar Falls, IA 50613 - T: (319) 266-5149, 277-8817, Fax: (319) 268-1812, E-mail: cfhs_schmitz@ cfu.net, Internet: www.cedarfallshistorical.org. Pres.: Robert Hardman, C.E.O.: Doris Schmitz
Local Museum - 1962
Local history   42148

Gallery of Art, University of Northern Iowa, Kamerick Art Bldg, Cedar Falls, IA 50614-0362 - T: (319) 273-2077, Fax: (319) 273-7333, E-mail: galleryofart@ uni.edu, Internet: www.uni.edu/artdept. Dir.: Darrell Taylor
Fine Arts Museum / University Museum - 1978
20th c American and European art   42149

James and Meryl Hearst Center for the Arts, 304 W Seerley Blvd, Cedar Falls, IA 50613 - T: (319) 273-8641, Fax: (319) 273-8659, E-mail: huberm@ci. cedar-falls.ia.us, Internet: www.hearstartscenter. com. Dir.: Mary Huber, Cur.: Everett Cole
Fine Arts Museum / Open Air Museum / Public Gallery - 1989
Arts - sculpture garden   42150

University of Northern Iowa Museum Museums & Collections, 3219 Hudson Rd, Cedar Falls, IA 50614-0199 - T: (319) 273-2188, Fax: (319) 273-6924, E-mail: doris.mitchell@uni.edu, Internet: www.uni.edu/museum. Dir.: Sue Grosboll
University Museum - 1892
Ethnological and zoological coll   42151

Cedar Grove NJ

Cedar Grove Historical Society Museum, 903 Pompton Av, Cedar Grove, NJ 07009 - T: (973) 239-5414
Local Museum - 1968
Farming, sports equip, textiles   42152

Cedar Key FL

Cedar Key Historical Society Museum, 2nd St at State Rd 24, Cedar Key, FL 32625 - T: (352) 543-5549, E-mail: ckhistory@inetw.net. Cur.: Peggy Rix
Local Museum - 1979
Fossils, shells, pencil and lumber industry, railroad hist, maps, Indian hist, commercial fishing industry   42153

Cedar Key State Park Museum, 12231 SW 166 Court, Cedar Key, FL 32625 - T: (352) 543-5350, 543-5567, Fax: (352) 543-6315, E-mail: charles. neese@dep.state.fl.us, Internet: www.dep.state.fl. us/parks. Exec. Dir.: David B. Struhs
Local Museum / Natural History Museum - 1962   42154

Cedar Lake IN

Lake of the Red Cedars Museum, 7808 W 138th St, Constitution Av, Cedar Lake, IN 46303 - T: (219) 374-6157, Fax: (219) 374-6157. Pres. & C.E.O.: Mildred Schreiber, Dir.: Anne Zimmerman
Local Museum - 1977
Local history   42155

Cedar Rapids IA

Brucemore, 2160 Linden Dr SE, Cedar Rapids, IA 52403 - T: (319) 362-7375, Fax: (319) 362-9481, E-mail: mail@brucemore.org, Internet: www. brucemore.org. Dir.: Peggy Whitworth, Ass. Dir.: David Janssen, Sc. Staff: Jennifer Puste (History)
Historical Museum / Historic Site - 1981
Historic Site, culture, housed in 21-room Queen Anne-style mansion   42156

Cedar Rapids Museum of Art, 410 Third Av, SE, Cedar Rapids, IA 52401 - T: (319) 366-7503, Fax: (319) 366-4111, E-mail: crma@earthlink.net, Internet: www.crma.org. Dir.: Terence Pitts
Fine Arts Museum - 1905
Art 42157

Eaton-Buchan Gallery and Marvin Cone Gallery, c/o Coe College, 1220 First Av NE, Cedar Rapids, IA 52402 - T: (319) 399-8217, Fax: (319) 399-8557, E-mail: dchance@coe.edu, Internet: www.coe.edu. Dir.: Delores Chance
Fine Arts Museum - 1942
Art works, paintings, contemporary art 42158

Iowa Masonic Library and Museum, 813 1st Av, SE, Cedar Rapids, IA 52402 - T: (319) 365-1438, Fax: (319) 365-1439, E-mail: gliowa@qwest.net, Internet: www.showcase.nctins.net/web/iowamasons
Local Museum - 1845
Local history - library 42159

Linn County Historical Society Museum, 615 First Av, Cedar Rapids, IA 52401-2022 - T: (319) 362-1501, Fax: (319) 362-6790, E-mail: linda@historycener.org, Internet: www.historycenter.org. Dir.: Linda Langston, Cur.: Christina Kastell
Local Museum - 1969 42160

National Czech and Slovak Museum, 30 16th Av SW, Cedar Rapids, IA 52404 - T: (319) 362-8500, Fax: (319) 363-2209, Internet: www.ncsml.org. Cur.: Carmen Langel, Libr.: David Muhlena
Special Museum - 1974
Ethnic museum, 1880-1900 restored Czech immigrant home 42161

Science Station Museum, 427 First St, SE, Cedar Rapids, IA 52401 - T: (319) 366-0968, Fax: (319) 366-4590, E-mail: gdganpat@mcleodusa.net, Internet: www.sciencestation.org. Pres.: Barb Rhamie, Exec. Dir.: Ganesh Ganpat
Science&Tech Museum - 1986
Science, housed in a fire station bldg 42162

Cedarburg WI

Ozaukee Art Center, W 62 N 718 Riveredge Dr, Cedarburg, WI 53012 - T: (414) 377-8230, E-mail: ozaukeeartcenter@pauljyank.com. Pres.: Lon Horton, Dir.: Paul Yank
Fine Arts Museum - 1971
Art 42163

Cedartown GA

Polk County Historical Museum, 205 N College St, Cedartown, GA 30125 - T: (404) 748-0073
Local Museum - 1974
Regional history 42164

Celina OH

Mercer County Historical Museum, 130 E Market, Celina, OH 45822-0512 - T: (419) 586-6065, E-mail: histalig@bright.net. Exec. Dir.: Joyce L. Alig
Historical Museum - 1959 42165

Centennial WY

Nici Self Museum, Hwy 130, 28 miles west of Laramie, Centennial, WY 82055 - T: (307) 742-7158, Fax: (307) 634-4955, E-mail: houmavrick@aol.com. Pres.: Jim Chase
Local Museum - 1974
Local hist 42166

Center ND

Fort Clark Trading Post, 1074 27th Av SW, Center, ND 58530 - T: (701) 794-8832, 328-2666, Internet: www.state.nd.us/hist
Special Museum - 1965
Mandan Indian villages, fur trading 42167

Center Sandwich NH

Sandwich Historical Society Museum, 4 Maple St, Center Sandwich, NH 03227 - T: (603) 284-6269, Fax: (603) 284-6269, E-mail: shistory@worldpath.net, Internet: sandwichnh.com/history. Pres.: D. Bruce Montgomery, Dir.: Rick Fabian
Local Museum / Fine Arts Museum - 1917
Paintings, furniture 42168

Centerport NY

Suffolk County Vanderbilt Museum, 180 Little Neck Rd, Centerport, NY 11721 - T: (516) 854-5562, Fax: (516) 854-5527 and 5591, E-mail: vanderbilt@webscope.com, Internet: www.webscope.com/vanderbilt. Exec. Dir.: J. Lance Mallamo, Pres.: Steve Gittelman
Natural History Museum - 1950 42169

Centerville MA

Centerville Historical Museum, 513 Main St, Centerville, MA 02632 - T: (508) 775-0331, Fax: (508) 862-9211, E-mail: chsm@capecod.net. Cur.: Britt Steen-Zuniga
Local Museum - 1952
Costumes, quilts, military, marine, tools, toys, Dodge MacKnight watercolors, decorative arts 42170

Centerville OH

Walton House Museum, 89 W Franklin St, Centerville, OH 45459 - T: (937) 433-0123, Fax: (937) 432-9296, E-mail: cwhistorical@aol.com, Internet: www.mvcc.net/centerville/histsoc. Dir.: Jane Beach
Local Museum - 1967 42171

Central City CO

Central City Opera House Museum, 124 Eureka St, Central City, CO 80427 - T: (303) 292-6500, Fax: (303) 292-4958, E-mail: marketing@centralcityopera.org, Internet: www.centralcityopera.org. Gen. Dir.: Pelham G. Pearce
Performing Arts Museum - 1932
Theater museum, housed in Teller House Hotel Museum 42172

Gilpin History Museum, 228 E High St, Central City, CO 80427-0247 - T: (303) 582-5283, Fax: (303) 582-5283, E-mail: gchs@ecentral.com, Internet: www.coloradomuseums.org/gilpin.htm. Pres.: Linda Jones, Dir.: James J. Prochaska
Local Museum - 1971
Regional history 42173

Chadds Ford PA

Brandywine Battlefield, US Rte 1, Chadds Ford, PA 19317 - T: (610) 459-3342, Fax: (610) 459-9586, Internet: www.ushistory.org/brandywine. Head: Elisabeth Rump
Military Museum / Historic Site / Open Air Museum - 1947 42174

Brandywine River Museum, US Rte 1 at PA Rte 100, Chadds Ford, PA 19317 - T: (610) 388-2700, Fax: (610) 388-1197, E-mail: inquiries@brandywine.org, Internet: www.brandywinemuseum.org.. Dir.: James H. Duff, Cur.: Gene E. Harris, Ass. Cur.: Virginia Herrick O'Hara, Christine B. Podmaniczky (N.C. Wyeth Collections)
Fine Arts Museum - 1971 42175

Christian C. Sanderson Museum, Rte 100 N, Chadds Ford, PA 19317 - T: (610) 388-6545, Internet: www.sandersonmuseum.org. Pres. & C.E.O.: Richard A. McLellan
Local Museum - 1967 42176

Chadron NE

Chadron State College Main Gallery, 1000 Main St, Chadron, NE 69337 - T: (308) 432-6326, Fax: (308) 432-3561, E-mail: rbird@csc.edu. Dir.: Richard Bird
Fine Arts Museum - 1967 42177

Dawes County Historical Society Museum, 341 Country Club Rd, Chadron, NE 69337 - T: (308) 432-4999, 432-2309, Internet: www.chadron.com/dchm. C.E.O. & Pres.: Dean Carpenter, Chm./Cur.: Belvadine Lecher
Local Museum - 1964
Local history 42178

Eleanor Barbour Cook Museum of Geology, Chadron State College, Math & Science Bldg, 1000 Main St, Chadron, NE 69337 - T: (308) 432-6293, Fax: (308) 432-6434, E-mail: mleite@csc1.csc.edu, Internet: www.csc.edu. Dir.: Prof. Michael Leite
University Museum / Natural History Museum - 1939 42179

Museum of the Fur Trade, 6321 E Hwy 20, Chadron, NE 69337 - T: (308) 432-3843, Fax: (308) 432-5943, E-mail: museum@furtrade.org, Internet: www.furtrade.org. Pres.: William R. Hanson, C.E.O. & Dir.: Gail DeBuse Potter
Historical Museum - 1955 42180

Chagrin Falls OH

Chagrin Falls Historical Society Museum, 21 Walnut St, Chagrin Falls, OH 44022 - T: (440) 247-4695. Cur.: Pat E. Zalba, Libr.: Dorothy Pauly
Local Museum - 1949 42181

Chamberlain SD

Akta Lakota Museum, Saint Joseph's Indian School, Chamberlain, SD 57325 - T: (605) 734-3452, Fax: (605) 734-3388, E-mail: aktalakota@stjo.org, Internet: www.stjo.org. Dir.: Dixie Thompson
Historical Museum / Folklore Museum - 1991 42182

South Dakota Hall of Fame, 1480 S Main, Chamberlain, SD 57325 - T: (605) 734-4216, Fax: (605) 734-4216, E-mail: sdhof@midstatesd.net, Internet: www.sdhalloffame.com
Historical Museum - 1974
Biographical info, artwork, pioneer and Indian days 42183

Chambersburg PA

Fort Loudoun, 1720 Brooklyn Rd, Chambersburg, PA 17021 - T: (717) 369-3473, Fax: (717) 783-1073
Historical Museum - 1968 42184

Old Brown's Mill School, 1051 S Coldbrook Av, Chambersburg, PA 17201 - T: (717) 705-0559, Fax: (717) 783-1073
Local Museum - 1956 42185

Champaign IL

Champaign County Historical Museum, 102 E University Av, Champaign, IL 61820 - T: (217) 356-1010, E-mail: director@champaignmuseum.org, Internet: www.champaignmuseum.org. Dir.: Paul Idleman
Historical Museum - 1972
Local history 42186

Krannert Art Museum, University of Illinois, 500 E Peabody Dr, Champaign, IL 61820 - T: (217) 333-1861, Fax: (217) 333-0883, E-mail: schumach@uiuc.edu, Internet: www.art.uiuc.edu/kam/. Dir.: Dr. Josef Helfenstein, Ass. Dir.: Karen Hewitt, Cur.: Kerry Morgan
Fine Arts Museum - 1961
Art 42187

Parkland College Art Gallery, 2400 W Bradley, Champaign, IL 61821 - T: (217) 351-2485, 2200, Fax: (217) 373-3899, E-mail: dseif@parkland.cc.il.us, Internet: www.parkland.cc.il.us/gallery. Dir.: Denise Seif, Ass. Dir.: Marsha Daniels
Fine Arts Museum - 1980 42188

Champion NE

Champion Mill, POB 117, Champion, NE 69023 - T: (308) 882-5860, 394-5118, E-mail: anderssra@ngpc.state.ne.us
Science&Tech Museum - 1969
Milling machinery, tools 42189

Chandler AZ

Chandler Museum, 178 E Commonwealth Av, Chandler, AZ 85225 - T: (480) 782-2717. Cur.: Al Wiatr
Local Museum - 1969
Local history 42190

Chandler OK

Lincoln County Historical Society Museum of Pioneer History, 717 Manvel Av, Chandler, OK 74834 - T: (405) 258-2425, Fax: (405) 258-2809, E-mail: lchs@brightok.net. Dir.: Treva Lee Lindsey, Cur.: Jeanette Haley
Local Museum - 1954 42191

Chanute KS

Imperato Collection of West African Artifacts, Safari Museum, 111 N Lincoln Av, Chanute, KS 66720 - T: (620) 431-2730, Fax: (620) 431-3848, E-mail: osajohns@safarimuseum.com, Internet: www.safarimuseum.com. Dir.: Conrad G. Froehlich
Ethnology Museum - 1974
West African sculpture, masks, ancestor figures and ritual objects, household items, musical instruments 42192

Johnson Collection of Photographs, Movies and Memorabilia, Safari Museum, 111 N Lincoln Av, Chanute, KS 66720 - T: (620) 431-3848, Fax: (620) 431-3848, E-mail: osajohns@safarimuseum.com, Internet: www.safarimuseum.com. Dir.: Conrad G. Froehlich
Special Museum 42193

Martin and Osa Johnson Safari Museum, 111 N Lincoln Av, Chanute, KS 66720 - T: (620) 431-2730, Fax: (620) 431-3848, E-mail: osajohns@safarimuseum.com, Internet: www.safarimuseum.com. Dir.: Conrad G. Froehlich, Cur.: Barbara E. Henshall, Jaquelyn L. Borgeson
Special Museum - 1961
Biography, ethnography, film/photo, Santa Fe Train Depot 42194

Selsor Gallery of Art, Safari Museum, 111 N Lincoln Av, Chanute, KS 66720 - T: (620) 431-2730, Fax: (620) 431-3848, E-mail: osajohns@safarimuseum.com, Internet: www.safarimuseum.com. Dir.: Conrad G. Froehlich
Fine Arts Museum - 1981 42195

Chapel Hill NC

Ackland Art Museum, c/o University of North Carolina, 9302 Columbia and Franklin Sts, Chapel Hill, NC 27599 - T: (919) 966-5736, Fax: (919) 966-1400, E-mail: ackland@email.unc.edu, Internet: www.ackland.org. Dir.: Gerald D. Bolas, Cur.: Timothy A. Riggs, Barbara Matilsky (Exhibitions), Carolyn Wood (Education), Cons.: Lyn Koehnline
Fine Arts Museum - 1958 42196

Chappaqua NY

Horace Greeley House, 100 King St, Chappaqua, NY 10514 - T: (914) 238-4666, Fax: (914) 238-1296, E-mail: newcastlehs@aol.com. Pres.: Albert Hutin, Exec. Dir.: Betsy Towl
Local Museum - 1966 42197

Chappell NE

Chappell Art Gallery, 289 Babcock St, Chappell, NE 69129 - T: (308) 874-2626
Fine Arts Museum - 1935
Aaron Pyle coll, art works from many countries - Memorial library 42198

Chappell Hill TX

Chappell Hill Historical Society Museum, 9220 Poplar St, Chappell Hill, TX 77426 - T: (979) 836-6033, Fax: (979) 836-7438, E-mail: chmuseum@alpha1.net, Internet: www.chappellhillmuseum.org. Dir.: Ladonna Vest
Local Museum / Historical Museum - 1964
Local hist 42199

Charles City IA

Floyd County Historical Museum, 500 Gilbert St, Charles City, IA 50616-2738 - T: (641) 228-1099, Fax: (641) 228-1157, E-mail: fchs@fiai.net, Internet: www.floydcountymuseum.org. Pres.: Robert Baron, Dir.: Frank B. McKinney
Local Museum / Historical Museum - 1961
Local history 42200

Charles City VA

Berkeley Plantation, 12602 Harrison Landing Rd, Charles City, VA 23030 - T: (804) 829-6018, Fax: (804) 829-6757, Internet: www.berkeleyplantation.com. Head: Grace Eggleston Jamieson
Local Museum - 1619
Historic house 42201

Sherwood Forest Plantation, 14501 John Tyler Memorial Hwy, Charles City, VA 23030 - T: (804) 829-5377, Fax: (804) 829-2947, E-mail: ktylerl@sherwoodforest.org, Internet: www.sherwoodforest.org. Pres.: Frances P.B. Tyler, Dir.: Kay Montgomery Tyler
Historic Site - 1975
Historic house, home of President John Tyler 42202

Shirley Plantation, 501 Shirley Plantation Rd, Charles City, VA 23030 - T: (804) 829-5121, Fax: (804) 829-6322, E-mail: information@shirleyplantation.com, Internet: www.shirleyplantation.com. Head: Charles Hill Carter
Local Museum - 1613
Historic house 42203

Westover House, 7000 Westover Rd, Charles City, VA 23030 - T: (804) 829-2882, Fax: (804) 829-5528. Man.: F.S. Fisher
Historical Museum 42204

Charleston IL

Tarble Arts Center, Eastern Illinois University, S 9th St at Cleveland Av, Charleston, IL 61920-3099 - T: (217) 581-2787, Fax: (217) 581-7138, E-mail: cfmw@eiu.edu, Internet: www.eiu.edu/~tarble. Dir.: Michael Watts
Fine Arts Museum / University Museum - 1982
Art 42205

Charleston MO

Mississippi County Historical Society Museum, 403 N Main, Charleston, MO 63834 - T: (314) 683-4348. Pres.: Tom Graham
Historical Museum - 1966 42206

Charleston SC

American Military Museum, 44 John St, Charleston, SC 29403 - T: (803) 723-9620, E-mail: ammilmus@aol.com. Dir./Cur.: George E. Meagher
Military Museum - 1987
Military hist 42207

Avery Research Center for African American History and Culture, College of Charleston, 125 Bull St, Charleston, SC 29424 - T: (843) 953-7609, Fax: (843) 953-7607, Internet: www.cofc.edu/~avery.rsc. Dir.: W. Marvin Dulaney, Curtis J. Franks (Education and Exhibits)
Historical Museum - 1985
History 42208

Best Friend of Charleston Museum, 456 King St, Charleston, SC 29403 - T: (843) 973-7269. Cur.: J.M. LeCato
Science&Tech Museum - 1968
Railroad 42209

Charles Towne Landing 1670, 1500 Old Town Rd, Charleston, SC 29407 - T: (843) 852-4200, Fax: (803) 852-4205, E-mail: charles_towne_landing_sp@scprt.com, Internet: www.southcarolinaparks.com. Head: Ron Fischer
Historic Site / Historical Museum - 1970
1670 site of the first permanent English settlement in South Carolina 42210

The Charleston Museum, 360 Meeting St, Charleston, SC 29403-6297 - T: (803) 722-2996, Fax: (843) 722-1784, Internet: www.charlestonmuseum.com. Dir.: Dr. John R. Brumgardt, Ass. Dir.: R. Brien Varnado, Cur.: Dr. Albert E. Sanders (Natural History), Dr. William Post (Ornithology), Martha Zierden (Historical Archaeology), J. Grahame Long (History), Libr.: Sharon Bennett
Local Museum - 1773
Local hist, ceramics, decorative art, furniture, glass - library 42211

The Citadel Archives and Museum, The Military College of South Carolina, 171 Moultrie St, Charleston, SC 29409 - T: (843) 953-6846, Fax: (843) 953-6956, E-mail: yatesj@citadel.edu,

Internet: www.citadel.edu/archivesandmuseum. Dir.: Jane M. Yates
Historical Museum - 1842
History 42212

City Hall Council Chamber Gallery, 80 Broad St, Charleston, SC 29401 - T: (843) 724-3799, 577-6970, Fax: (843) 720-3827. Dir.: Joseph P. Riley, Cur.: Carol Ezell-Gilson
Fine Arts Museum / Historical Museum - 1818
Art, history 42213

Drayton Hall, 3380 Ashley River Rd, Hwy 61, Charleston, SC 29414 - T: (843) 769-2600, Fax: (803) 766-0878, E-mail: dhmail@draytonhall.org, Internet: www.draytonhall.org. Dir.: George W. McDaniel, Ass. Dir.: Wade Lawrence
Historic Site - 1974
Historic house 42214

Elizabeth O'Neill Verner Studio Museum, 38 Tradd St, Charleston, SC 29401 - T: (803) 722-4246, Fax: (803) 722-1763, E-mail: info@vernergallery.com, Internet: www.vernergallery.com. C.E.O. & Pres.: David Hamilton, Cur.: Elizabeth Verner Hamilton
Fine Arts Museum - 1970
Works by E. O'Neill Verner 42215

Gibbes Museum of Art, 135 Meeting St, Charleston, SC 29401 - T: (843) 722-2706, Fax: (843) 720-1682, E-mail: marketing@gibbes.com, Internet: www.gibbes.com. Dir.: Elizabeth A. Fleming, Cur.: Angela Mack
Fine Arts Museum - 1858
Portraits, Japanese woodblock prints, contemporary American art - library 42216

Halsey Gallery, College of Charleston, School of the Arts, 66 George St, Charleston, SC 29424-0001 - T: (843) 953-5680, Fax: (843) 953-7890, E-mail: halseygal@cofc.edu. Dir.: Mark Sloan
Fine Arts Museum / University Museum - 1978 42217

Heyward-Washington House, 87 Church St, Charleston, SC 29401 - T: (843) 722-0354, Fax: (843) 722-1784, Internet: www.charlestonmuseum.com
Historical Museum - 1929 42218

Historic Charleston Foundation, 40 E Bay, Charleston, SC 29401 - T: (843) 723-1623, Fax: (843) 577-2067, E-mail: krobinson@historiccharleston.org, Internet: historiccharleston.org. C.E.O.: Katharine S. Robinson, Dir.: Jonathan Poston, Stephen Hanson
Local Museum - 1947
Local hist 42219

John Rivers Communications Museum, College of Charleston, 58 George St, Charleston, SC 29424 - T: (843) 953-5810, Fax: (843) 953-5815, E-mail: evansc@cofc.edu, Internet: www.cofc.edu/~jrmuseum. Dir./Cur.: Cathy Evans
Science&Tech Museum / University Museum - 1989
Communications 42220

Joseph Manigault House, 350 Meeting St, Charleston, SC 29403 - T: (843) 723-2926, Fax: (843) 722-1784, Internet: www.charlestonmuseum.com
Decorative Arts Museum - 1773
Charleston silver, furniture, textiles, fossils, porcelain 42221

Macaulay Museum of Dental History, Medical University of South Carolina, 175 Ashley Av, Charleston, SC 29425 - T: (843) 792-2288, Fax: (843) 792-8619, Internet: www.waring.library.musc.edu. Cur.: Jane Brown
Special Museum - 1975
Dental hist 42222

Magnolia Plantation, 3550 Ashley River Rd, Charleston, SC 29414 - T: (843) 571-1266, Fax: (843) 571-5346, E-mail: tours@magnoliaplantation.com, Internet: www.magnoliaplantation.com. Dir.: J. Drayton Hastie
Fine Arts Museum / Local Museum / Natural History Museum / Historic Site - 1676
Historic house 42223

Middleton Place Foundation, 4300 Ashley River Rd, Charleston, SC 29414 - T: (843) 556-6020, Fax: (843) 766-4460, E-mail: ttodd@middletonplace.org, Internet: www.middletonplace.org. Pres.: Charles H.P. Duell
Decorative Arts Museum / Historical Museum - 1974
Historic House: restored 1755 structure 42224

Old Exchange and Provost Dungeon, 122 East Bay St, Charleston, SC 29401 - T: (843) 727-2165, Fax: (843) 727-2163, E-mail: oldexchange@infoave.net, Internet: www.oldexchange.com. Exec. Dir.: Frances McCarthy
Historic Site - 1976
Local hist 42225

Powder Magazine, 79 Cumberland St, Charleston, SC 29401 - T: (843) 723-1623, Fax: (843) 577-2067, Internet: www.historiccharleston.org. Pres.: Harold Pratt Thomas, Exec. Dir.: Katharine S. Robinson
Local Museum - 1713
Local hist 42226

South Carolina Historical Society Museum, 100 Meeting St, Charleston, SC 29401 - T: (843) 723-3225, Fax: (843) 723-8584, E-mail: info@schistory.org, Internet: www.schistory.org. Dir.: David O. Percy, Ass. Dir.: Daisy R. Bigda, Libr.: Ashley Yandle
Historical Museum - 1855
Regional history, Robert Mills Bldg 42227

University Medical Museum, Medical University of South Carolina, 175 Ashley Av, Charleston, SC 29425 - T: (843) 792-2288, Fax: (843) 792-8619, Internet: waring.library.musc.edu. Dir.: W. Curtis Washington jr
Historical Museum / University Museum - 1966
Doctors' saddle bags, medicine chests, amputation kits, electro-therapeutic machines, bleeding instruments, obstatrical specula and forceps, pharmaceutical items 42228

Charleston WV

Charles M. Auampato Discovery Museum, Leon Sullivan Way, Charleston, WV 25311 - T: (304) 344-8035, Fax: (304) 344-8038, E-mail: sunrise@citynet.net, Internet: www.sunrisemuseum.org. C.E.O.: Judith Wellington
Fine Arts Museum - 1961
American painting, sculpture, works on paper 42229

Frankenberger Art Gallery, c/o University of Charleston, 2300 MacCorkle Av SE, Charleston, WV 25304 - T: (304) 357-4870, E-mail: swatts@ucwv.edu, Internet: www.ucwv.edu
Public Gallery 42230

Sunrise Museum, 746 Myrtle Rd, Charleston, WV 25314 - T: (304) 344-8035, Fax: (304) 344-8038, E-mail: sunrise@citynet.net, Internet: www.sunrisemuseum.org. Chief Cur.: Richard Ambrose, Cur.: Denise Deegan
Fine Arts Museum - 1961
Art 42231

West Virginia State Museum, 1900 Kanawha Blvd, Charleston, WV 25305 - T: (304) 558-0220, Fax: (304) 558-2779, E-mail: charles.morris@wvculture.org, Internet: www.wvculture.org. C.E.O.: Nancy Herholdt, Fredrick Armstrong (Archives and History), Cur.: James Mitchell, Sc. Staff: Richard Ressmeyer (Art), Stephanie Lilly (Exhibitions), Charles Morris (Collections),
Local Museum - 1905
Local hist 42232

Charlestown MA

Bunker Hill Museum, 43 Monument Sq, Charlestown, MA 02129 - T: (617) 242-5641, Internet: www.mps.gov/bost. Pres.: Arthur L. Hurley
Historical Museum - 1975
Bunker Hill Monument grounds 42233

Charlestown NH

Old Fort Number 4 Associates, Springfield Rd, Rte 11, Charlestown, NH 03603 - T: (603) 826-5700, Fax: (603) 826-3368, E-mail: fortat4@cyberportal.net, Internet: www.fortat.4.com. C.E.O.: Roberto M. Rodriguez
Local Museum - 1948 42234

Charlotte MI

Courthouse Square Museum, 100 W Lawrence Av, Charlotte, MI 48813 - T: (517) 543-6999, Fax: (517) 543-6999, E-mail: preserve@ia4u.net, Internet: www.visitcourthsquare.org. Dir.: Mindie M. Dings
Local Museum - 1993
Military, textiles, government records, political coll, agriculture 42235

Charlotte NC

Afro-American Cultural Center, 401 N Myers St, Charlotte, NC 28202 - T: (704) 374-1565, Fax: (704) 374-9273, Internet: www.aacc.charlotte.org. Exec. Dir.: Cynthia Lewis Schaal
Folklore Museum - 1974
African American culture 42236

Carolinas Aviation Museum, 4108 Airport Dr, Charlotte, NC 28208 - T: (704) 359-8442, Fax: (704) 359-0429, E-mail: chacboss@aol.com, Internet: www.chacweb.com. Pres.: Floyd S. Wilson
Science&Tech Museum - 1991
Aviation 42237

Charlotte Museum of History and Hezekiah Alexander Homesite, 3500 Shamrock Dr, Charlotte, NC 28215 - T: (704) 568-1774, Fax: (704) 566-1817, E-mail: info@charlottemuseum.org, Internet: www.charlottemuseum.org. Pres.: William P. Massey, Ass. Dir.: Kristina Carmichael
Local Museum - 1976 42238

Discovery Place, 301 N Tryon St, Charlotte, NC 28202 - T: (704) 372-6261, Fax: (704) 337-2670, Internet: www.discoveryplace.org. Pres.: John L. Mackay
Natural History Museum / Science&Tech Museum - 1981 42239

Historic Rosedale, 3427 N Tryon St, Charlotte, NC 28206 - T: (704) 335-0325, Fax: (704) 335-0384, E-mail: roseplan@bellsouth.net. C.E.O: Elaine Wood
Decorative Arts Museum - 1989
Decorative arts of the Catawba River Valley, family hist 42240

Levine Museum of the New South, 200 E Seventh St, Charlotte, NC 28202 - T: (704) 333-1887, Fax: (704) 333-1896, E-mail: info@museumofthenewsouth.org, Internet: www.museumofthenewsouth.org. Dir.: Emily F. Zimmern, Cur.: Jean Johnson
Historical Museum - 1991 42241

Light Factory, 809 West Hill St, Charlotte, NC 28208 - T: (704) 333-9755, Fax: (704) 333-5910, E-mail: info@lightfactory.org, Internet: www.lightfactory.org. C.E.O.: Mary Anne Redding
Performing Arts Museum - 1972
Light-generated media incl photography, video and film 42242

Mint Museum of Art, 2730 Randolph Rd, Charlotte, NC 28207 - T: (704) 337-2000, Fax: (704) 337-2101, E-mail: pbusher@mintmuseum.org, Internet: www.mintmuseum.org. Dep. Dir.: Charles Mo (Collections and Exhibitions), Harry Creemers (Development), Carolyn Mints (Community Relations), Cheryl Palmer (Education), Cur.: Michael Whittington (Pre-Columbian and African Art), Libr.: Sara Wolf
Fine Arts Museum - 1933 42243

Mint Museum of Craft and Design, 220 N Tryon St, Charlotte, NC 28202 - T: (704) 337-2000, Fax: (704) 337-2101, E-mail: pbusher@mintmuseum.org, Internet: www.mintmuseum.org. Dir.: Mark Leach
Decorative Arts Museum - 1999 42244

Nature Museum, 1658 Sterling Rd, Charlotte, NC 28209 - T: (704) 372-6261, Fax: (704) 333-8948, Internet: www.discoveryplace.org. C.E.O.: John L. Mackay
Natural History Museum - 1947 42245

Charlottesville VA

Ash Lawn-Highland, College of William and Mary, 1000 James Monroe Pkwy, Charlottesville, VA 22902 - T: (804) 293-9539, Fax: (804) 293-8000, E-mail: ashlawnjm@aol.com, Internet: avenue.org/ashlawn. Dir.: Carolyn C. Holmes, Cur.: James E. Wootton
Decorative Arts Museum / Historic Site - 1930
Historic house 42246

Bayly Art Museum of the University of Virginia → University of Virginia Art Museum

Children's Health Museum, Primary Care Center, Lee St and Park Pl, Charlottesville, VA 22908 - T: (804) 924-1593, Fax: (804) 982-4379, E-mail: epv4p@virginia.edu, Internet: nsc.virginia.edu/medcntr/health-museum. Dir.: Ellen Vaughan
Historical Museum - 1982
Children's health 42247

Historic Michie Tavern, 683 Thomas Jefferson Pkwy, Rte 53, Charlottesville, VA 22902 - T: (804) 977-1234, Fax: (804) 296-7203, E-mail: info@michietavern.com, Internet: www.michietavern.com. Cur.: Cynthia Conte
Local Museum - 1928
Historic house 42248

Monticello, Home of Thomas Jefferson, Rte 53 Thomas Jefferson Pkwy, Charlottesville, VA 22902 - T: (434) 984-9808, Fax: (434) 977-7751, E-mail: djordan@monticello.org, Internet: www.monticello.org. Cur.: Susan R. Stein
Historical Museum - 1923
Art objects, manuscripts, personal items, slavery artifacts, American independence declaration 42249

The Rotunda, University of Virginia, Charlottesville, VA 22903 - T: (804) 924-7969, 924-1019, Fax: (804) 924-1364, Internet: www.virginia.edu/~urelat/Tours/rotunda. Head: Carolyn Laquatra
University Museum / Local Museum - 1819
Historic buildings, site of Thomas Jefferson's original academical village 42250

Second Street Gallery, 201 Second St, Charlottesville, VA 22902 - T: (804) 977-7284, Fax: (804) 979-9793, E-mail: ssg@cstone.net, Internet: www.avenue.org/ssg. Dir.: Leah Stoddard
Fine Arts Museum - 1973
Contemporary art 42251

Thomas Jefferson House Monticello, POB 316, Charlottesville, VA 22902 - T: (804) 984-9801, Fax: (804) 977-7757, E-mail: administration@monticello.org, Internet: www.monticello.org. Pres.: Daniel P. Jordan
Natural History Museum / Historical Museum - 1923 42252

University of Virginia Art Museum, 155 Rugby Rd, Charlottesville, VA 22904-4119 - T: (434) 924-3592, Fax: (434) 924-6321, E-mail: cjh6r@virginia.edu, Internet: www.virginia.edu/artmuseum. Dir.: Jill Hartz, Cur.: Stephen N. Margulies (Prints), Suzanne Foley
Fine Arts Museum / University Museum - 1935
Art 42253

The Virginia Discovery Museum, 524 E Main St, Charlottesville, VA 22902 - T: (804) 977-1025, Fax: (804) 977-9681, E-mail: vdm@cstone.net, Internet: www.vadm.org. C.E.O.: Peppy G. Linden
Special Museum - 1981
Childrens' Museum 42254

Chase City VA

MacCallum More Museum, 603 Hudgins St, Chase City, VA 23924 - T: (804) 372-0502, 372-3120, Fax: (804) 372-3483, E-mail: mmmg@meckcom.net, Internet: www.mmmg.org. Pres.: Gay Butler, C.E.O.: Brenda Arriaga
Ethnology Museum - 1991
Anthropology 42255

Chatham MA

Old Atwood House Museum, 347 Stage Harbor Rd, Chatham, MA 02633 - T: (508) 945-2493, Fax: (508) 945-1205, E-mail: chs2002@msn.com, Internet: www.atwoodhouse.org
Local Museum - 1923
Harold Brett, Harold Dunbar and Frederick Wright paintings, sandwich glass, 17th-18th c furnishings, antique tools, China 42256

Chatsworth GA

Vann House, 82 Hwy 225 N, Chatsworth, GA 30705 - T: (706) 695-2598, Fax: (706) 517-4255, E-mail: vannhouse@alltel.net. Pres.: Marcia Kendrick
Historical Museum - 1952 42257

Chattanooga TN

Chattanooga African-American Museum, 200 E Martin Luther King Blvd, Chattanooga, TN 37403 - T: (423) 267-8658, Fax: (423) 267-1076, E-mail: caami@bellsouth.net, Internet: www.caamhistory.com. Dir.: Vilma S. Fields
Historical Museum - 1983 42258

Chattanooga Regional History Museum, 400 Chestnut St, Chattanooga, TN 37402 - T: (423) 265-3247, Fax: (423) 266-9280, E-mail: office@chattanoogahistory.com, Internet: www.chattanoogahistory.com. Dir.: R. Brit. Brantley, Cur.: Patrice Glass
Local Museum - 1978
Regional hist 42259

Creative Discovery Museum, 321 Chestnut St, Chattanooga, TN 37402 - T: (423) 756-2738, Fax: (423) 267-9344, E-mail: hhs@tennis.org, Internet: www.cdmfun.org. C.E.O.: Henry H. Schulson
Special Museum - 1995 42260

Cress Gallery of Art, c/o University of Tennessee at Chattanooga, Dept. of Art, Fine Arts Center, 615 McCallie Av, Chattanooga, TN 37403 - T: (423) 425-4178, Fax: (423) 425-2101, E-mail: ruth-grover@utc.edu, Internet: www.utc.edu/~artdept. Cur.: Ruth Grover
Fine Arts Museum / University Museum - 1952
Graphics, paintings, student's works 42261

Houston Museum of Decorative Arts, 201 High St, Chattanooga, TN 37403 - T: (423) 267-7176. Dir.: Amy H. Frierson
Decorative Arts Museum - 1949
American decorative arts 1750-1930 42262

Hunter Museum of American Art, 10 Bluff View, Chattanooga, TN 37403-1197 - T: (423) 267-0968, Fax: (423) 267-9844, E-mail: robkret@huntermuseum.org, Internet: www.huntermuseum.org. Dir.: Robert A. Kret, Cur.: Ellen Simak (Collections), Sherry Babic (Education)
Fine Arts Museum - 1952
American paintings, photography, prints, sculpture, glass 42263

Medal of Honor Museum of Military History, 400 Georgia Av, Chattanooga, TN 37403 - T: (423) 267-1737, Fax: (423) 266-7771, Internet: www.smoky.com/medalofhonor
Military Museum - 1987
Uniforms, pre-Civil War to present, weapons, military prints and paintings, medals, badges, Nuremburg coll, Confederate coll, currency coll, helmets 42264

Siskin Museum of Religious and Ceremonial Art, 101 Carter St, Chattanooga, TN 37403 - T: (423) 634-1700, Fax: (423) 634-1717
Religious Arts Museum - 1950
Religious art 42265

Tennessee Valley Railroad Museum, 4119 Cromwell Rd, Chattanooga, TN 37421 - T: (423) 894-8028, Fax: (423) 894-8029, E-mail: info@tvrail.com, Internet: www.tvrail.com. Pres. & C.E.O.: Robert M. Soule
Science&Tech Museum - 1961
Railroad 42266

Chattsworth GA

Fort Mountain, 181 Fort Mountain Park Rd, Chattsworth, GA 30705 - T: (706) 695-2621, Fax: (706) 517-3520, Internet: www.gastateparks.org
Archaeological Museum - 1938
Pre-historic stone wall 42267

Chazy NY

Alice T. Miner Colonial Collection, 9618 Main St, Chazy, NY 12921 - T: (518) 846-7336, Fax: (518) 846-8771, E-mail: minermuseum@westelcom.com, Internet: www.minermuseum.org. Pres.: Joan T. Burke, Dir./Cur.: Frederick G. Smith
Local Museum - 1924 42268

Chehalis WA

Lewis County Historical Museum, 599 NW Front Way, Chehalis, WA 98532 - T: (360) 748-0831, Fax: (360) 740-5646, E-mail: lchm@lewiscountymuseum.org, Internet: www.lewiscountymuseum.org. Dir.: Barbara Laughton
Local Museum - 1979
Local hist 42269

Chelmsford MA

Chelmsford Historical Museum, 40 Byam Rd, Chelmsford, MA 01824 - T: (978) 256-2311. Cur.: Rebecca Warren
Local Museum - 1930
Local history, housed in Barrett-Byam homestead 42270

Chelsea MI

Gerald E. Eddy Discovery Center, 17030 Bush Rd, Chelsea, MI 48118 - T: (734) 475-3170, Fax: (734) 475-6421, E-mail: eddy.geoctr@juno.com, Internet: www.dnr.state.mi.us
Natural History Museum - 1976
Geology 42271

Gerald E. Eddy Geology Center → Gerald E. Eddy Discovery Center

Cheraw SC

Cheraw Lyceum Museum, 200 Market St, Cheraw, SC 29520 - T: (843) 537-8425, Fax: (843) 537-8407, E-mail: townofcherawtour@mindspring.com, Internet: www.cheraw.com. Dir.: J. William Taylor, Cur.: Sarah C. Spruill
Local Museum - 1962
Local hist 42272

Cherokee IA

Joseph A. Tallman Museum, Mental Health Institute, 1205 W Cedar Loop, Cherokee, IA 51012 - T: (712) 225-6922, Fax: (712) 225-6969, E-mail: larmstrl@dhs.state.IA.us. Head: Dr. Tom Deiker
Historical Museum - 1961
Psychiatry 42273

Sanford Museum, 117 E Willow St, Cherokee, IA 51012 - T: (712) 225-3922, Fax: (712) 225-0446, E-mail: sanford@cherokee.k12.ia.us, Internet: www.whs.cherokee.K12.ia.us/mainfolder/sanford/sanhome.htm. Dir.: Linda Burkhart, Ass. Dir.: Michele Deiber-Kumm
Local Museum - 1941
General museum - planetarium 42274

Cherokee NC

Mountain Farm Museum, 1194 Newfound Gap Rd, Cherokee, NC 28719 - T: (828) 497-1900, Fax: (828) 497-1910, Internet: www.nps.gov/grsm
Agriculture Museum - 1945 42275

Museum of the Cherokee Indian, 589 Tsali Blvd, Cherokee, NC 28719 - T: (828) 497-3481, Fax: (828) 497-4985, E-mail: littlejohn@cherokeemuseum.org, Internet: www.cherokeemuseum.org. Dir.: Ken Blankenship
Historical Museum / Ethnology Museum - 1948 42276

Cherokee County TX

Caddoan Mounds, State Hwy 21 W, Cherokee County, TX 75925 - T: (409) 858-3218, Fax: (409) 858-3227
Local Museum - 1983 42277

Cherry Valley CA

Edward Dean Museum, 9401 Oak Glen Rd, Cherry Valley, CA 92223 - T: (909) 845-2626, Fax: (909) 845-2628. Dir.: Belinda J. McLaughlin
Decorative Arts Museum - 1958
Decorative arts, paintings, prints, sculpture, ceramics, glass, textiles, 16th-19th c furniture - gardens 42278

Cherry Valley NY

Cherry Valley Museum, 49 Main St, Cherry Valley, NY 13320 - T: (607) 264-3303, E-mail: museum@celticart.com, Internet: www.cherryvalleymuseum.com. Pres.: James Johnson
Local Museum - 1958 42279

Cherryville NC

C. Grier Beam Truck Museum, 111 N Mountain St, Cherryville, NC 28021 - T: (704) 435-3072, Fax: (704) 445-9010, E-mail: gfisher@bellsouth.net, Internet: www.beamtruckmuseum.com. Pres.: Michael N. Beam
Science&Tech Museum - 1982 42280

Chesapeake Beach MD

Chesapeake Beach Railway Museum, 4155 Mears Av, Chesapeake Beach, MD 20732 - T: (410) 257-3892
Science&Tech Museum / Local Museum - 1979
Early railroad era of 1900-1935, local hist 42281

Chesnee SC

Cowpens National Battlefield, POB 308, Chesnee, SC 29323 - T: (864) 461-2828, Fax: (864) 461-7077, E-mail: cowp-information@nps.gov, Internet: www.nps.gov/cowp/
Historic Site / Military Museum - 1933
Military hist, site of the 1781 Battle of Cowpens 42282

Chester MT

Liberty County Museum, Second St E and Madison, Chester, MT 59522 - T: (406) 759-5256. Pres.: Shirley Lybeck
Local Museum - 1969 42283

Liberty Village Arts Center and Gallery, 410 Main St, Chester, MT 59522 - T: (406) 759-5652, Fax: (406) 759-5652
Folklore Museum - 1976
Paintings, quilts by local artists 42284

Chester PA

Widener University Art Collection and Gallery, 14th and Chestnut Sts, Chester, PA 19013 - T: (610) 499-1189, Fax: (610) 499-4425, E-mail: rebecca.m.warda@widener.edu, Internet: www.widener.edu/campuslife.edu. Head: Rebecca M. Warda
Fine Arts Museum / University Museum - 1970 42285

Chester SC

Chester County Museum, 107 McAliley St, Chester, SC 29706 - T: (803) 385-2330, 581-4354. Dir.: Gary Roberts
Historical Museum - 1959
Local hist 42286

Chester VT

Chester Art Guild, The Green, Main St, Chester, VT 05143 - T: (802) 875-3767. Pres.: Doris Ingram
Fine Arts Museum - 1960
Art 42287

Chesterfield MA

Edwards Memorial Museum, 3 North Rd, Chesterfield, MA 01012 - T: (413) 296-4750. Pres.: Naomi Sturtevant
Folklore Museum - 1950
Woodworking and agricultural tools 42288

Chesterfield MO

River Hills Park Museum, 800 Guy Park Dr, Chesterfield, MO 63005 - T: (314) 458-3813, Fax: (314) 458-9105. Head: George Hosack
Natural History Museum - 1972 42289

Thornhill Historic Site and 19th Century Village, 15185 Olive Blvd, Chesterfield, MO 63017-1805 - T: (636) 532-1030, Fax: (314) 532-0604, Internet: www.st-louiscountyparks.com. Dir.: Jim Foley, Cur.: Jesse Francis
Local Museum - 1968
Local hist 42290

Chesterfield VA

Chesterfield County Museum → Chesterfield Historical Society of Verginia Museum

Chesterfield Historical Society of Verginia Museum, Courthouse Sq, Chesterfield, VA 23832 - T: (804) 777-9663, Fax: (804) 777-9643, E-mail: farmerdp@co.chesterfield.va.us, Internet: www.chesterfieldhistory.com. Dir.: Dennis Farmer, Dep. Dir.: Jim Holloman
Local Museum - 1961
Local hist 42291

Chestertown MD

Historical Society of Kent County Museum, 101 Church Alley, Chestertown, MD 21620 - T: (410) 778-3499, Fax: (410) 788-3747, E-mail: hskcmd@friend.ly.net, Internet: www.kentcounty.com/historicalsociety
Historical Museum
Indian artifacts, furniture, paintings, maps 42292

Chestnut Hill MA

Longyear Museum, 1125 Boylston St, Chestnut Hill, MA 02467 - T: (617) 278-9000, Fax: (617) 278-9003, E-mail: letters@longyear.org, Internet: www.longyear.org. Dir.: John Baehrend (Exec.), Stephen R. Howard (Cur.), Sandra J. Houston (Activities)
Historical Museum / Religious Arts Museum - 1923
History 42293

McMullen Museum of Art, Boston College, Devlin Hall 108, Chestnut Hill, MA 02467 - T: (617) 552-8587, Fax: (617) 552-8577, E-mail: netzer@bc.edu, Internet: www.bc.edu/artmuseum. Dir.: Dr. Nancy Netzer, Cur.: Alston Conley
Fine Arts Museum / Public Gallery / University Museum - 1986
Art 42294

Chetopa KS

Chetopa Historical Museum, 419 Maple St, Chetopa, KS 67336 - T: (316) 236-7121. Cur.: Fannie Bassett
Local Museum - 1881
Local history 42295

Cheyenne OK

Black Kettle Museum, Intersection of US 283 and State Hwy 47, Cheyenne, OK 73628 - T: (405) 497-3929, Fax: (580) 497-3537, E-mail: bkmus@ok-hstory.mus.ok.us
Local Museum - 1958 42296

Cheyenne WY

Cheyenne Frontier Days Old West Museum, 4610 N Carey Av, Cheyenne, WY 82001 - T: (307) 778-7290, Fax: (307) 778-7288, Internet: www.oldwestmuseum.org. Dir.: Wayne Hansen, Cur.: John Gavin
Local Museum - 1978 42297

Historic Governors' Mansion, 300 E 21st St, Cheyenne, WY 82001 - T: (307) 777-7878, Fax: (307) 635-7077, E-mail: sphs@state.wy.us, Internet: www.wyospcr.state.wy.us. Dir.: Bill Gentle, Cur.: Timothy J. White
Local Museum - 1904
Historic building 42298

Wyoming Arts Council Gallery, 2320 Capitol Av, Cheyenne, WY 82002 - T: (307) 777-7742, Fax: (307) 777-5499, E-mail: lfranc@state.wy.us, Internet: www.wyoarts.states.wy.us. Dir.: John G. Coe
Fine Arts Museum - 1976
Art 42299

Wyoming State Museum, Barrett Bldg, 2301 Central Av, Cheyenne, WY 82002 - T: (307) 777-7022, Fax: (307) 777-5375, E-mail: wsm@state.wy.us, Internet: www.wyomuseum.state.wy.us. Dir.: Marie Wilson-McKee, Cur.: Mike Fox, Jim Allison (Exhibits), Cons.: Anna Bechtel
Historical Museum - 1895
State hist 42300

Chicago IL

American Police Center and Museum, 1926 S Canalport Av, Chicago, IL 60616-1071 - T: (312) 455-8770. CEO: Joseph P. Pecoraro
Historical Museum - 1974
Uniforms, weapons, photos, documents 42301

A.R.C. Gallery, 734 N Milwaukee Av, Chicago, IL 60622 - T: (312) 733-2787, Fax: (312) 733-2787, E-mail: arcgallery@yahoo.com, Internet: www.arcgallery.com. Pres.: Carolyn King
Public Gallery - 1973 42302

ARC Gallery, 734 N Milwaukee Av, Chicago, IL 60622 - T: (312) 733-2787, Fax: (312) 733-2787, Internet: www.icsp.net/asc. Pres.: Nancy Bechtol
Public Gallery - 1973
American paintings, sculpture 42303

The Art Institute of Chicago, 111 S Michigan Av, Chicago, IL 60603-6110 - T: (312) 443-3600, Fax: (312) 443-0849, Internet: www.artic.edu. Pres./Dir.: James N. Wood, Asst. Dir.: Dorothy Schroeder (Exhibition), Cur.: Douglas Druick (Prints, Drawings and European Painting), Suzanne McCullagh (Prints and Drawings), Richard F. Townsend (African and American Indian Art), John Zukowsky (Architecture), Christa C. Mayer-Thurman (Textiles), Judith A. Barter (American Arts), David Travis (Photography), Jay Xu (Asian Art), Martha Wolff (European Painting Before 1750), Larry Feinberg, Gloria Groom (European Painting), Ian Wardropper, G. Zelleke (European Decorative Arts), Ass. Cur.: Courtney G. Donnell, James Rondeau, Daniel Schulman (Modern and Contemporary Art), Martha Tedeschi, Mark Pascale, Jay Clarke (Prints and Drawings), Kathleen Bickford-Berzock (African Art), Martha Thorne (Architecture), Colin Westerbeck, Sylvia Wolf (Photography), Bernd Jesse, Elinor L. Pearlstein (Asian Art), James Rondeau, Daniel Schulman Jesse
Fine Arts Museum - 1879
Architecture, paintings, drawings, prints, photos, decorative art, art from America, Asia, Europe - Ryerson and Burnham libraries, art school 42304

Artemisia Gallery, 700 N Carpenter, Chicago, IL 60622 - T: (312) 226-7323, Fax: (312) 226-7756, E-mail: artemisi@enteract.com, Internet: www.artemisia.org. Pres.: Marji Vecchio
Public Gallery - 1973 42305

Australian Exhibition Center, 114 W Kinzie St, Chicago, IL 60610 - T: (312) 645-1948, Fax: (312) 222-4119, E-mail: exhibit@aec-chicago.com.au, Internet: www.aec-chicago.com.au
Public Gallery 42306

Balzekas Museum of Lithuanian Culture, 6500 S Pulaski Rd, Chicago, IL 60629 - T: (773) 582-6500, Fax: (773) 582-5133, E-mail: editor@lithuanian-museum.org, Internet: www.lithuanian-museum.org. Dir.: Stanley Balzekas, Robert Balzekas (Genealogy), Edward Mankus (Audio Visual Department), Val Martis (Periodicals Collection), Karile Vaitkute (Education), Cur.: Edward Pocius (Cartography), Frank Zapolis (Folk Art), R. Balzekas (Genealogy)
Historical Museum / Folklore Museum / Fine Arts Museum - 1966
Ethnology, folklore, numismatics, folk art - library, archive 42307

Beverly Art Center, 2407 W 111th St, Chicago, IL 60655 - T: (773) 445-3838, Internet: www.beverlyartcenter.org
Public Gallery 42308

Boulevard Arts Center, 1525 W 60th St, Chicago, IL 60636 - T: (773) 476-4900, Fax: (773) 476-5951. Dir.: Pat Devine-Reed, Marti Price
Fine Arts Museum - 1986
Visual arts, wood carving, stone carving 42309

Carlson Tower Gallery, c/o North Park University, 3225 W Foster, Chicago, IL 60625 - T: (773) 244-6200, Fax: (773) 244-5230, Internet: www.northpark.edu. Dir.: Tim Lowly
Fine Arts Museum / University Museum
Contemporary Christian, Illinois and Scandinavian art 42310

Center for Intuitive and Outsider Art, 756 N Milwaukee Av, Chicago, IL 60622 - T: (312) 243-9088, Fax: (312) 243-9089, E-mail: intuit@art.org, Internet: www.outsider.art.org. Exec. Dir.: Jeff Cory
Ethnology Museum / Fine Arts Museum - 1991 42311

Charnley-Persky House Museum, 1365 N Astor St, Chicago, IL 60610-2144 - T: (312) 573-1365, Fax: (312) 573-1141, E-mail: psaliga@sah.org, Internet: www.sah.org. Pres.: Diane Favro, C.E.O.: Pauline Saliga
Local Museum - 1998
Local hist 42312

The Chicago Academy of Sciences Peggy Notebaert Nature Museum, 2060 N Clark St, Chicago, IL 60614 - T: (773) 549-0606, Fax: (773) 549-5199, E-mail: cas@chias.org, Internet: www.chias.org. Dir.: Micheal Sarna, Cur.: Dr. Douglas Taron (Biology)
Natural History Museum - 1857
Natural science 42313

Chicago Architecture Foundation, 224 S Michigan Av, Ste 368, Chicago, IL 60604-2507 - T: (312) 922-3432 ext 224, Fax: (312) 922-2607, E-mail: losmond@architecture.org, Internet: www.architecture.org. Pres.: Lynn Osmond
Fine Arts Museum - 1966
Architecture 42314

The Chicago Athenaeum - Museum of Architecture and Design, 307 N Michigan Av, Chicago, IL 60601 - T: (312) 372-1083, Fax: (312) 372-1085, E-mail: info@athenaeum.cncdsl.com, Internet: www.chi-athenaeum.org/. Dir.: Christian K. Warkiewicz Laine
Fine Arts Museum - 1988
Architecture and design 42315

Chicago Children's Museum, 700 E Grand Av, Ste 127, Navy Pier, Chicago, IL 60611 - T: (312) 527-1000, Fax: (312) 527-9082, Internet: www.chichildrensmuseum.org
Special Museum - 1982 42316

Chicago Cultural Center, 78 E Washington St, Chicago, IL 60602 - T: (312) 744-6630, Fax: (312) 744-7482, E-mail: culture@cityofchicago.org, Internet: www.cityofchicago.org/CulturalAffairs/. Dir.: Gregory Knight, Cur.: Lanny Silverman, Asst. Cur.: Sofia Zutautas
Public Gallery - 1897
Paintings, sculptures photographs, ceramics, graphics, design, mixed media, installations 42317

Chicago Historical Society, Clark St at North Av, Chicago, IL 60614-6099 - T: (312) 642-4600, Fax: (312) 266-2077, E-mail: bunch@chicagohistory.org, Internet: www.chicagohistory.org. Pres.: Lonnie G. Bunch
Historical Museum - 1856
History of Chicago 42318

Clarke House Museum, 1821 S Indiana Av, Chicago, IL 60616 - T: (312) 745-0040, Fax: (312) 745-0077, E-mail: clarkehouse@interaccess.com, Internet: www.cityofchicago.org/culturalaffairs. Cur.: Eduard M. Maldonado
Local Museum - 1984
Greek Revival building, oldest home in Chicago 42319

Columbia College Art Gallery, 72 E Eleventh St, Chicago, IL 60605-2312 - T: (312) 663-1600 ext 7104, Fax: (312) 344-8067. Dir.: Denise Miller, Dr. John Mulvany, Ass. Dir.: Nancy Fewkes
Fine Arts Museum / University Museum - 1984 42320

Contemporary Art Workshop, 542 W Grant Pl, Chicago, IL 60614 - T: (773) 472-4004, Fax: (773) 472-4505. Pres.: John Kearney, Dir.: Lynn Kearney
Public Gallery 42321

The David and Alfred Smart Museum of Art, University of Chicago, 5550 S Greenwood Av, Chicago, IL 60637 - T: (773) 702-0200, Fax: (773) 702-3121, E-mail: smart-museum@uchicago.edu, Internet: smartmuseum.uchicago.edu. Dir.: Kimerly Rorschach, Ass. Dir.: David Robertson, Cur.: Richard Born, Elizabeth Rodini, Stephanie Smith
Fine Arts Museum / University Museum - 1974 42322

DePaul University Art Gallery, 2350 N Kenmore, Chicago, IL 60614 - T: (773) 325-7506, Fax: (773) 325-4506, E-mail: llincoln@wppost.depaul.edu, Internet: www.depaul.edu/~gallery. Dir./Cur.: Louise Lincoln
Fine Arts Museum / University Museum - 1987 42323

Dusable Museum of African-American History, 740 E 56th Pl, Chicago, IL 60637 - T: (773) 947-0600, Fax: (773) 947-0677, E-mail: awright@dusablemuseum.org, Internet: www.dusablemuseum.org. Chief Cur.: Selean Holmes
Historical Museum / Ethnology Museum - 1961
Ethnography 42324

Field Museum, 1200 S Lake Shore Dr, Chicago, IL 60605 - T: (312) 665-7932, Fax: (312) 922-0741, Internet: www.fieldmuseum.org. Pres.: John W. McCarte jr.
Natural History Museum - 1893
Anthropology, botanic, geology, zoology 42325

Field Museum of Natural History, 1400 S Lake Shore Dr, Chicago, IL 60605 - T: (312) 922-9410, Fax: (312) 922-0741, E-mail: jmcarter@fmnh.org, Internet: www.fieldmuseum.org. Pres.: John W. McCarter
Natural History Museum - 1893
Natural history, zoology, geology, botany 42326

First National Bank of Chicago Art Collection, 1 Bank One Plaza, Chicago, IL 60670 - T: (312) 732-5935. Dir./ Cur.: Lisa K. Erf
Fine Arts Museum / Archaeological Museum - 1968
Art from Africa, America, Asia, Australia, the Caribbean Basin, Europe, Latin America, Near East and the South Seas since 16th c 42327

Frederick C. Robie House, 5757 S Woodlawn Av, Chicago, IL 60637 - T: (773) 834-1847, Fax: (773) 834-1538, E-mail: mercuri@wrightplus.org, Internet: www.wrightplus.org. Pres.: Joan B. Mercuri
Historical Museum - 1974
Residence of Frederick C. Robie 42328

Gallery 2, c/o School of the Art Institute of Chicago, 847 W Jackson Blvd, Chicago, IL 60607 - T: (312) 563-5162, Fax: (312) 563-0510, E-mail: saicg2@artic.edu, Internet: www.artic.edu/saic/art/galleries/gallery2.html. Dir.: Anthony Wight
Fine Arts Museum / University Museum - 1988 42329

Gallery 400, c/o University of Illinois at Chicago, 400 S Peoria St, Chicago, IL 60607-7034 - T: (312) 996-6114, Fax: (312) 355-3444, E-mail: kareni@uic.edu, Internet: www.uic.edu/aa/artd/g400.html. Dir.: Lorelei Stewart
Fine Arts Museum / University Museum - 1983 42330

Glessner House Museum, 1800 S Prairie Av, Chicago, IL 60616-1333 - T: (312) 326-1480, Fax: (312) 326-1397, Internet: www.glessnerhouse.org. Dir./Cur.: Corina Carusi, Pres.: Susan Baldwin, Man.: Betsy Hutula
Historical Museum - 1994
Home designed by H.H. Richardson 42331

Hellenic Museum and Cultural Center, 168 N Michigan Av, Chicago, IL 60610 - T: (312) 726-1234, Fax: (312) 726-8539, E-mail: hellenicmu@aol.com, Internet: www.hellenicmuseum.org. Pres.: Konstantinos Armiros, Exec. Dir.: Jeanne Costopoulos Weeks
Folklore Museum / Historical Museum / Museum of Classical Antiquities / Archaeological Museum - 1987 42332

Hyde Park Art Center, 5307 S Hyde Park Blvd, Chicago, IL 60615 - T: (312) 324-5520, Fax: (312) 324-6641, E-mail: info@hydeparkart.org, Internet: www.hydeparkart.org. Exec. Dir.: Chuck Thurow
Fine Arts Museum - 1939
Art gallery 42333

Illinois Art Gallery, 100 W Randolph, Ste 2-100, Chicago, IL 60601 - T: (312) 814-5322, Fax: (312) 814-3471, E-mail: ksmith@museum-state.il.us, Internet: www.museum.state.il.us/ismsites/chicago/. Dir.: Kent Smith, Ass. Dir.: Jane Stevens
Fine Arts Museum / Public Gallery - 1985 42334

International Museum of Surgical Science, 1524 N Lake Shore Dr, Chicago, IL 60610 - T: (312) 642-6502, Fax: (312) 642-9516, E-mail: info@imss.org, Internet: www.imss.org. Pres.: Raymond Dieter
Special Museum - 1953
Medicine 42335

Jane Addams' Hull-House Museum, University of Illinois Chicago, 800 S Halsted St, Chicago, IL 60607-7017 - T: (312) 413-5353, Fax: (312) 413-2092, E-mail: jahh@uic.edu, Internet: www.uic.edu/jaddams/hull/hull_house. Dir.: Margaret Strobel
Historical Museum - 1967
Hull Mansion occupied by Jane Addams in 1889, serving as the first settlement building of Hull House complex 42336

John H. Vanderpoel Art Gallery, 9625 S Longwood Dr, Ridge Park, Chicago, IL 60643 - T: (312) 239-8320
Fine Arts Museum
About 500 paintings, prints and works of sculpture 42337

The Lithuanian Museum, 5620 S Claremont Av, Chicago, IL 60636-1039 - T: (773) 434-4545, Fax: (773) 434-9363, E-mail: lithuanianresearch@ameritech.net. Dir.: Skirmante Miglinas, Milda Budrys, (Medical Museum), Cur.: Peter Paul Zansitis
Fine Arts Museum / Historical Museum - 1989
Lithuanian history 42338

The Martin D'Arcy Museum of Art, Loyola University Museum of Medieval, Renaissance and Baroque Art, 6525 N Sheridan Rd, Chicago, IL 60626 - T: (773) 508-2679, Fax: (773) 508-2993, Internet: darcy.luc.edu. Dir.: Dr. Sally Metzler, Ass. Dir.: Rachel Baker
Fine Arts Museum / University Museum - 1969
European art 42339

Marwen Foundation, 833 N Orleans St, Chicago, IL 60610 - T: (312) 944-2418, Fax: (312) 944-6696, Internet: www.marwen.org. Dir.: Antonia Contro, Asst. Dir.: Jesse McClelland
Public Gallery - 1987 42340

Mexican Fine Arts Center Museum, 1852 W 19th St, Chicago, IL 60608 - T: (312) 738-1503, Fax: (312) 738-9740, E-mail: carlost@mfacmchicago.org, Internet: www.mfacmchicago.org. Exec. Dir.: Carlos Tortolero
Fine Arts Museum / Folklore Museum - 1982
Art 42341

Museum of Ancient Artifacts, 2528 N Luna St, Chicago, IL 60639 - T: (773) 385-9840. Cur.: Michael J. Kurban
Natural History Museum - 1990
Rare photographs and gems, tapestries, artwork - botanical garden 42342

The Museum of Broadcast Communications, 78 E Washington St, Chicago, IL 60602-9837 - T: (312) 629-6000, Fax: (312) 629-6009, E-mail: archives@museum.tv, Internet: www.museum.tv. Pres.: Bruce DuMont
Special Museum - 1987
Historic and contemporary radio and TV memorabilia - archives 42343

Museum of Contemporary Art, 220 E Chicago Av, Chicago, IL 60611-2604 - T: (312) 280-2660, Fax: (312) 397-4095, E-mail: pr@machicago.org, Internet: www.mcachicago.org. Dir.: Robert Fitzpatrick, Chief Cur.: Elizabeth Smith
Fine Arts Museum - 1967
Contemporary art 42344

The Museum of Contemporary Photography, Columbia College Chicago, 600 S Michigan Av, Chicago, IL 60605-1901 - T: (312) 663-5554, Fax: (312) 344-8067, E-mail: mocp@aol.com, Internet: www.mocp.org. Dir.: Sara McNear, Ass. Dir.: Nancy Fewkes
University Museum - 1976
Photography 42345

Museum of Cosmetology, c/o National Cosmetology Assn, 401 N Michigan Av, Chicago, IL 60611 - T: (312) 527-6765. Exec. Dir.: Gordon Miller
Special Museum - 1990
History of American hair and cosmetics fashion 42346

Museum of Decorative Art, 4611 N Lincoln Av, Chicago, IL 60625 - T: (773) 989-4310
Decorative Arts Museum 42347

Museum of Holography, 1134 W Washington Blvd, Chicago, IL 60607 - T: (312) 829-2292, Fax: (312) 829-9636, E-mail: hologram@flash.net, Internet: holographiccenter.com. Dir.: Loren Billings, John Hoffmann (Research)
Special Museum - 2001
Holography 42348

Museum of Science and Industry, 57th S Lake Shore Dr, Chicago, IL 60637 - T: (773) 684-9844, Fax: (773) 684-7141, Internet: www.msichicago.org. Pres.: David R. Mosena, Dir.: Dr. Barry Aprison
Natural History Museum / Science&Tech Museum - 1926
Science, technology, housed in classic Greek structure constructed as the Palace of Fine Arts for the World's Fair Columbian Exposition of 1893 in Chicago 42349

NAB Gallery, 1117 W Lake, Chicago, IL 60607 - T: (312) 738-1620. Dir.: Craig Anderson, Robert Horn
Fine Arts Museum - 1974 42350

The National Time Museum, 57th St and Lake Shore Dr, Chicago, IL 60637-2093 - T: (312) 742-1412. Dir.: Michael Lash
Science&Tech Museum - 2001
Horology 42351

National Vietnam Veterans Art Museum, 1801 S Indiana Av, Chicago, IL 60616 - T: (312) 326-0270, Fax: (312) 326-9767, E-mail: nvvamart@cs.com
Fine Arts Museum 42352

The Nature Museum of the Chicago Academy of Sciences → The Chicago Academy of Sciences Peggy Notebaert Nature Museum

Northeastern Illinois University Art Gallery, 5500 N Saint Louis Av, Chicago, IL 60625 - T: (773) 583-4050, Fax: (773) 442-4920, Internet: www.neiu.edu
Fine Arts Museum / University Museum - 1973 42353

Northern Illinois University Art Gallery in Chicago, 215 W Superior St, Chicago, IL 60610 - T: (312) 642-6010, Fax: (312) 642-9635, E-mail: juliec@niu.edu, Internet: www.vpa.niv.edu/museum. Dir.: Julie Charmelo
Fine Arts Museum / University Museum - 1984 42354

Oriental Institute Museum, University of Chicago, 1155 E 58th St, Chicago, IL 60637 - T: (773) 702-9514, Fax: (773) 702-9853, E-mail: oi-museum@uchicago.edu, Internet: www.oi.uchicago.edu/oi/. Dir.: Karen L. Wilson, Cur.: Raymond D. Tindel, Cons.: Laura D'Alessandro
Fine Arts Museum / Archaeological Museum / University Museum - 1894
Archaeology, ancient history, art 42355

The Palette and Chisel, 1012 N Dearborn St, Chicago, IL 60610 - T: (312) 642-4149, Fax: (312) 642-4317, E-mail: finearts@paletteandchisel.org, Internet: www.paletteandchisel.org. Pres.: Linda Boatman, Exec. Dir.: William Ewers
Fine Arts Museum / Public Gallery - 1895
Art Academy, paintings, sculptures 42356

The Peace Museum, 100 N Central Park Av, Chicago, IL 60610-1912 - T: (773) 638-6450, Fax: (312) 440-1267, E-mail: virginia@peacemuseum.org, Internet: www.peacemuseum.org. Dir.: Virginia Albaneso
Fine Arts Museum / Special Museum - 1981 42357

Polish Museum of America, 984 N Milwaukee Av, Chicago, IL 60622-4104 - T: (773) 384-3352 and 3731, Fax: (773) 384-3799, E-mail: pma@prcua.org, Internet: www.prcua.org/pma. Dir.: Jan McLorys, Pres.: Joan Kosinski, Ass. Cur.: Bohdan Gorczynski, Libr.: Malgorzata Kot
Folklore Museum / Ethnology Museum - 1937
Polonica, Paderewski memorabilia, world fair 1939, art 42358

Pullman Museum, Historic Pullman Foundation, 11141 S Cottage Grove Av, Chicago, IL 60628-4614 - T: (773) 785-8901, Fax: (773) 785-8182, E-mail: PullmanHPF@aol.com, foundation@pullmanil.org, Internet: www.pullmanil.org. Pres.: Cynthia McMahon, Exec. Dir.: Deborah Bellamy-Jawor
Historical Museum - 1973
Historic District, first planned model industrial community in 1880 42359

The Renaissance Society at the University of Chicago, 5811 S Ellis Av, Chicago, IL 60637 - T: (773) 702-8670, Fax: (773) 702-9669, Internet: www.renaissancesociety.org. Pres.: Timothy Flood, Dir.: Susanne Ghez
Fine Arts Museum - 1915 42360

Roy Boyd Gallery, 739 N Wells St, Chicago, IL 60610 - T: (312) 642-1606, Fax: (312) 642-2143. Dir.: Roy Bod
Fine Arts Museum
Contemporary American paintings, Russian and Baltic photography, sculpture and works on paper 42361

School of the Art Institute of Chicago Gallery, 847 W. Jackson Blvd, Chicago, IL 60603 - T: (312) 899-5219, Fax: (312) 899-1840, Internet: www.artic.edu/saic. Dir.: Meg Duguid
Public Gallery 42362

Spertus Museum, 618 S Michigan Av, Chicago, IL 60605 - T: (312) 322-1747, Fax: (312) 922-3934, E-mail: musm@spertus.edu, Internet: www.spertus.edu. Dir.: Mark Akgulian, Cur.: Olga Weiss
Archaeological Museum / Religious Arts Museum - 1968
Culture, art, archaeology 42363

Stephen A. Douglas Tomb, 636 E 35th St, Chicago, IL 60616 - T: (312) 225-2620, Fax: (312) 225-7855, E-mail: stephenadouglas@aol.com. Head: Michael Carson
Historic Site - 1865
1866-1881 Stephen A. Douglas Tomb 42364

Swedish American Museum Association of Chicago Museum, 5211 N Clark St, Chicago, IL 60640 - T: (312) 728-8111, Fax: (312) 728-8870, E-mail: museum@samac.org, Internet: www.samac.org. Pres.: Margareta Alexander, Exec. Dir.: Kerstin Lane
Folklore Museum - 1976
Swedish history 42365

TBA Exhibition Space, c/o Thomas Blackman Assoc., 230 W Huron St, Ste 3E, Chicago, IL 60610 - T: (312) 587-3300, Fax: (312) 587-3304. Dir.: Heather Hubbs, Cur.: Pedro Velez
Public Gallery 42366

Terra Museum of American Art, 666 N Michigan Av, Chicago, IL 60611, mail addr: 664 N Michigan Av, Chicago, IL 60611 - T: (312) 664-3939 ext 1233, Fax: (312) 664-2052, E-mail: terra@terramuseum.org, Internet: www.terramuseum.org. Dir.: Elizabeth Glassman, Cur.: Elizabeth Kennedy
Fine Arts Museum - 1979 42367

The Time Museum → The National Time Museum

Ukrainian National Museum, 721 N Oakley Blvd, Chicago, IL 60612 - T: (312) 421-8020, Fax: (773) 772-2883, E-mail: hankewych@msn.com, Internet: www.ukrntlmuseum.org. C.E.O.: Jaroslaw J. Hankewych
Folklore Museum - 1952
Folk art 42368

Chico CA

1078 Gallery, 738 W Fifth St, Chico, CA 95928 - T: (916) 343-1973. Dir.: Lynette Krehe, John Ferrell
Public Gallery 42369

Bidwell Mansion, 525 Esplanade, Chico, CA 95926 - T: (530) 895-6144, Fax: (530) 895-6699. Head: Paul Holman
Historical Museum - 1964 42370

Chico Museum, 141 Salem St, Chico, CA 95928 - T: (530) 891-4336, Fax: (530) 891-4336, E-mail: chicomuseum@chico.com, Internet: www.chicomuseum.org. Pres.: Beulah Robinson, Cur.: Paul Russell
Local Museum - 1980
Local history, Chinese Taoist temple 42371

Janet Turner Print Museum, California State University-Chico, 400 W First St, Chico, CA 95929-0820 - T: (530) 898-4476, Fax: (530) 898-5581, E-mail: csullivan@exchange.csuchico.edu, Internet: www.csuchico.edu/art/galleries/turnergallery.html. Cur.: Catherine Sullivan Sturgeon
University Museum / Fine Arts Museum - 1981
Fine art prints 42372

Museum of Anthropology, California State University-Chico, Chico, CA 95929-0400 - T: (530) 898-5397, Fax: (530) 898-6143, E-mail: anthromuseum@csuchico.edu. Dir.: Dr. Stacy Schaefer, Dr. Georgia Fox, Cur.: Adrienne Scott
University Museum / Ethnology Museum - 1969 42373

University Art Gallery, c/o California State University Chico, Chico, CA 95929-0820 - T: (530) 898-5864, E-mail: jtannen@csuchico.edu. Chm.: Jason Tannen
Fine Arts Museum / University Museum 42374

Childress TX

Childress County Heritage Museum, 210 Third St, Childress, TX 79201 - T: (940) 937-2261, Fax: (940) 937-3188, E-mail: cchm@srcaccess.net. Pres.: John Preston, C.E.O.: Jenny Lou Taylor
Local Museum - 1976
Local hist 42375

Chillicothe MO

George W. Somerville Historical Library, Livingston County Library, 450 Locust, Chillicothe, MO 64601 - T: (660) 646-0547, Fax: (660) 646-5504, E-mail: ugy001@mail.connect.more.net, Internet: www.livcolibrary.org. Pres.: Patricia Henry, Dir.: Karen Hicklin
Library with Exhibitions - 1966 42376

Grand River Historical Society Museum, 1401 Forest Dr, Chillicothe, MO 64601 - T: (816) 646-3430. Pres.: Dr. Frank Stark, Cur.: Dr. John R. Neal
Historical Museum - 1959 42377

Chillicothe OH

Adena State Memorial, Home of Thomas Worthington, Adena Rd, Chillicothe, OH 45601 - T: (740) 772-1500, Fax: (740) 775-2746, E-mail: amansion@bright.com, Internet: www.ohiohistory.org/places/adena/. Man.: Mary Anne Brown
Local Museum - 1946 42378

Hopewell Culture National Historic Park, 16062 State Rte 104, Chillicothe, OH 45601-8694 - T: (740) 774-1125, Fax: (740) 774-1140, E-mail: hocu_superintendent@nps.gov, Internet: www.nps.gov/hocu. Sc. Staff: Jennifer Pederson (Archaeology)
Ethnology Museum - 1923
200 B.C.-500 A.D. Hopewell Indian mound enclosure 42379

Pump House Center for the Arts, POB 1613, Chillicothe, OH 45601-5613 - T: (740) 772-5783, Fax: (740) 772-5783, E-mail: pumpart@bright.net, Internet: www.bright.net/~pumpart. Exec. Dir.: Beverly J. Mullen
Decorative Arts Museum / Fine Arts Museum - 1986
Baskets, fine art, designer crafts, glass, prints, quilts, woodcarving 42380

Ross County Historical Society Museum, 45 W Fifth St, Chillicothe, OH 45601 - T: (740) 772-1936, E-mail: info@rosscountyhistorical.org, Internet: www.rosscountyhistorical.org. Pres.: Eric Picciano, C.E.O.: Thomas G. Kuhn
Local Museum - 1896 42381

Chiloquin OR

Collier Memorial State Park and Logging Museum, 46000 Hwy 97 N, 30 miles north of Klamath Falls, Chiloquin, OR 97624 - T: (541) 783-2471, Fax: (541) 783-2707, Internet: www.pdr.state.or.us. Cur.: Lowell N. Jones
Historical Museum - 1945 42382

Chincoteague VA

The Oyster and Maritime Museum of Chincoteague, 7125 Maddox Blvd, Chincoteague, VA 23336 - T: (804) 336-6117. C.E.O.: Gerald C. West
Natural History Museum / Science&Tech Museum / Historical Museum - 1966
Natural science, maritime hist, Fresnel lens 42383

Chino CA

Yorba-Slaughter Adobe Museum, 17127 Pomona Rincon Rd, Chino, CA 91710 - T: (909) 597-8332, Fax: (909) 307-0539 http://www.co.san-bernardino.ca.us/museum, E-mail: tbothel@sbcm.sbcounty.gov. Dir.: Robert McKernan, Cur.: Dr. Ann Deegan
Historical Museum - 1976
Decoratibve arts, farm equipment, photos 42384

Chinook MT

Blaine County Museum, 501 Indiana, Chinook, MT 59523 - T: (406) 357-2590, Fax: (406) 357-2199, E-mail: blmuseum@mtintouch.net, Internet: www.chinookmontana.com. Dir.: Stuart C. MacKenzie, Cur.: Jude Sheppard
Local Museum - 1977 42385

Chinook WA

Fort Columbia House Museum, Fort Columbia State Park, Hwy 101, Chinook, WA 98614 - T: (360) 777-8221, Fax: (360) 642-4216
Decorative Arts Museum - 1954 42386

Chiriaco Summit CA

General Patton Memorial Museum, 62-510 Chiriaco Rd, Chiriaco Summit, CA 92201 - T: (760) 227-3483, Fax: (760) 227-3483. Dir.: Jan Roberts
Military Museum - 1988
Military, headquarters of WW II Desert Training Areas 42387

Chisholm MN

Ironworld Discovery Center, Hwy 169 W, Chisholm, MN 55719 - T: (218) 254-7959, Fax: (218) 254-7972, E-mail: yourroots@ironworld.com, Internet: www.ironworld.com. Dir.: Marianne Bouska
Local Museum / Science&Tech Museum - 1977
Mining, regional history 42388

Chittenango NY

Chittenango Landing Canal Boat Museum, 7010 Lakeport Rd, Chittenango, NY 13037 - T: (315) 687-3801, Fax: (315) 687-3801, Internet: www.canalboatmuseum.org. Pres.: Joan DiChristina Hager, Cur.: Laura Alvud
Science&Tech Museum - 1986 42389

Choteau MT

Old Trail Museum, 823 Main St, Choteau, MT 59422 - T: (406) 466-5332, E-mail: otm@3rivers.net, Internet: www.oldtrailmuseum.org. Dir.: Corlene Martin, Cur.: Rebecca Hanna
Agriculture Museum - 1985 42390

Christiansburg VA

Montgomery Museum and Lewis Miller Regional Art Center, 300 S Pepper St, Christiansburg, VA 24073 - T: (540) 382-5644, Fax: (540) 382-9127, E-mail: info@montgomerymuseum.org, Internet: www.montgomerymuseum.org. Dir.: Shearon Campbell, Cur.: Tina Ruus
Local Museum / Fine Arts Museum - 1983
Local hist, art 42391

Christmas FL

Fort Christmas, 1300 Fort Christmas Rd, Christmas, FL 32709 - T: (407) 568-4149, Fax: (407) 568-6629, Internet: parks.onetgov.net. Cur.: Vickie Prewett
Military Museum - 1977
Military artifacts 42392

Chula Vista CA

Southwestern College Art Gallery, 900 Otay Lakes Rd, Chula Vista, CA 91910 - T: (935) 421-6700, Fax: (935) 421-6372, E-mail: pturley@swc.cc.ca.us. Dir.: G. Pasha Turley
Public Gallery - 1961 42393

Church Rock NM

Red Rock Museum, Red Rock State Park, Church Rock, NM 87311 - T: (505) 863-1337, Fax: (505) 863-1297, E-mail: rrsp@ci.gallup.nm.us, Internet: www.ci.gallup.nm.us/rrsp. Head: Joe Athens, Sc. Staff: Maxine Armstrong Touchine
Ethnology Museum / Natural History Museum / Public Gallery - 1951 42394

Cimarron NM

Old Mill Museum, 220 W 17th St, Rte 1, Cimarron, NM 87714 - T: (505) 376-2913, Fax: (505) 376-2417. Cur.: F.E. Morse
Local Museum - 1967 42395

The Philmont Museum, Seton Memorial Library and Kit Carson Museum, Philmont Scout Ranch, Cimarron, NM 87714 - T: (505) 376-2281 ext 46, Fax: (505) 376-2602, E-mail: jschubert@philmontscoutranch.org. Dir.: Jason Schubert, Libr.: Seth McFarland
Fine Arts Museum / Local Museum - 1967 42396

Cincinnati OH

American Classical Music Hall of Fame and Museum, 4 W Fourth St, Cincinnati, OH 45202 - T: (513) 621-3263, Fax: (513) 621-1563, E-mail: info@classicalhall.org, Internet: www.classicalhall.org. C.E.O.: Stefan A. Skirtz Althea Warren
Music Museum - 1995
Classical music in US 42397

Betts House Research Center, 416 Clark St, Betts-Longworth Historic District, Cincinnati, OH 45203-1420 - T: (513) 651-0734, Fax: (513) 651-2143, E-mail: BettsHouse@Juno.com, Internet: www.bettshouse.org. Dir.: Susan Vesio-Steinkamp, Cur.: Elisabeth Tuttle Miller
Local Museum - 1995
Local hist 42398

Cary Cottage, 7000 Hamilton Av, Cincinnati, OH 45231 - T: (513) 522-3860, Fax: (513) 728-3946, E-mail: clovernook@clovernook.org, Internet: www.clovernook.org. C.E.O.: Jeff Brasie
Historical Museum - 1903 42399

Cincinnati Art Museum, 953 Eden Park Dr, Cincinnati, OH 45202-1596 - T: (513) 639-2995, Fax: (513) 639-2888, E-mail: information@cincyart.org, Internet: www.cincinnatiartmuseum.org. Dir.: Timothy Rub, Cur.: Anita Ellis (Decorative Arts), Kristin Spangenberg (Prints, Drawings), Betsy Wieseman (European Art), Glenn Markoe (Classical, Near Eastern), Cur.: Julie Aronson (American Art), Ass. Cur.: Dennis Kiel (Photography), Libr./Archive: Mona Chapin
Fine Arts Museum / Decorative Arts Museum - 1881 42400

Cincinnati Fire Museum, 315 W Court St, Cincinnati, OH 45202 - T: (513) 621-5553, Fax: (513) 621-1456, Internet: www.cincyfiremuseum.com. Pres.: Rick Jahnigen, Exec. Dir.: Barbara M. Hammond
Special Museum - 1979 42401

Cincinnati Museum Center, 1301 Western Av, Cincinnati, OH 45203 - T: (513) 287-7000, Fax: (513) 287-7029, Internet: www.cincymuseum.org. Pres.: Douglass W. McDonald, Dir.: Sandra Shipley (Exhibits), Elisabeth Jones (Touring Exhibits)
Ethnology Museum / Local Museum / Natural History Museum / Science&Tech Museum - 1835 42402

Contemporary Arts Center, 115 E Fifth St, Cincinnati, OH 45202-3998 - T: (513) 345-8412, Fax: (513) 721-7418, E-mail: admin@spiral.org, Internet: www.spiral.org. Dir.: Charles Desmarais, Cur.: Thom Collins, Sue Spaid
Fine Arts Museum - 1939 42403

DAAP Galleries, c/o University of Cincinnati, 2624 Clifton Av, Cincinnati, OH 45221-0016 - T: (513) 556-4933, Fax: (513) 556-3288, E-mail: daap.galleries@uc.edu, Internet: www.daap.uc.edu/gallery/gallery.html. Dir.: Anne Timpano
Fine Arts Museum / University Museum - 1993
Art 42404

Fine Arts Department Gallery, Xavier University, 3800 Victory Pkwy, Cincinnati, OH 45207-7311 - T: (513) 745-1098, Internet: www.xu.edu/art-dept
Public Gallery 42405

Hebrew Union College-Jewish Institute of Religion Skirball Museum, 3101 Clifton Av, Cincinnati, OH 45220 - T: (513) 221-1875, Fax: (513) 221-1842, E-mail: jlucas@cnhuc.edu, Internet: www.huc.edu. Cur.: Judith S. Lucas
Religious Arts Museum - 1913 42406

Hillel Jewish Student Center Gallery, 2615 Clifton Av, Cincinnati, OH 45220-2885 - T: (513) 221-6728, Fax: (513) 221-7134, Internet: www.hillelcincinnati.org. Exec. Dir.: Abie Ingber
Fine Arts Museum - 1982
Jewish art, antique Judaica 42407

Indian Hill Historical Society Museum, 8100 Given Rd, Cincinnati, OH 45243 - T: (513) 891-1873, Fax: (513) 891-1873, E-mail: ihhist@one.net, Internet: www.indianhill.org. Pres.: Margaret Gillespie
Local Museum - 1973 42408

Studio San Giuseppe Art Gallery, c/o College of Mount Saint Joseph, 5701 Delhi Rd, Cincinnati, OH 45233-1670 - T: (513) 244-4203, Fax: (513) 244-4942, E-mail: Jerry-Bellas@mail.msj.edu, Internet: www.msj.edu. Dir.: Gerald M. Bellas
Fine Arts Museum / University Museum / Public Gallery - 1962 42409

Taft Museum of Art, 316 Pike St, Cincinnati, OH 45202-4293 - T: (513) 241-0343, Fax: (513) 241-7762, E-mail: taftmuseum@taftmuseum.org, Internet: www.taftmuseum.org. Dir.: Phillip C. Long, Chief Cur.: David T. Johnson
Fine Arts Museum - 1932
Furnishings, coll of Duncan Phyfe furniture, paintings, old masters 42410

Trailside Nature Center and Museum, Brookline Dr, Burnet Woods Park, Cincinnati, OH 45220 - T: (513) 321-6070, Fax: (513) 751-3679, E-mail: vivian.wagner@cinparks.rcc.org, Internet: www.cinci-parks.org. Dir.: Willie F. Carden, Vivian Wagner
Natural History Museum - 1930 42411

William Howard Taft National Historic Site, 2038 Auburn Av, Cincinnati, OH 45219 - T: (513) 684-3262, Fax: (513) 684-3627, E-mail: wiho_superintendent@nps.gov, Internet: www.nps.gov/wiho/index.html. Man.: E. Ray Henderson
Historical Museum - 1969 42412

Xavier University Art Gallery, 3800 Victory Pkwy, Cincinnati, OH 45207-7311 - T: (513) 745-3811, Fax: (513) 745-1098. Dir.: Kitty Uetz
University Museum / Fine Arts Museum - 1831 42413

Circle MT

McCone County Museum, 1507 Av B, Circle, MT 59215 - T: (406) 485-2414. Cur.: Donald Zahn
Local Museum - 1953 42414

City of Industry CA

Workman and Temple Family Homestead Museum, 15415 E Don Julian Rd, City of Industry, CA 91745 - T: (626) 968-8492, Fax: (626) 968-2048, E-mail: info@homesteadmuseum.org, Internet: www.homesteadmuseum.org. Dir.: Karen Graham Wade
Historical Museum - 1981 42415

Clackamas OR

Oregon Military Museum, Camp Withycombe, Clackamas, OR 97015 - T: (503) 557-5359, Fax: (503) 557-5202
Military Museum - 1974
Military uniforms, vehicles, weapons, Oregon National Guard, US Army 42416

Claremont CA

Clark Humanities Museum, Humanities Bldg, Scripps College, 1030 Columbia Av, Claremont, CA 91711 - T: (909) 607-3606, Fax: (909) 607-7143. Head: Dr. Eric T. Haskell
Fine Arts Museum / University Museum - 1970
Paintings, prints,cloisonne, African sculpture, drawings 42417

Montgomery Gallery → Pomona College Museum of Art

Petterson Museum of Intercultural Art, 730 Plymouth Rd, Claremont, CA 91711 - T: (909) 399-5544, 621-9581, Fax: (909) 399-5508
Fine Arts Museum / Decorative Arts Museum - 1968
International folk and fine art 42418

Pomona College Museum of Art, 330 N College Av, Claremont, CA 91711 - T: (909) 621-8283, Fax: (909) 621-8989, E-mail: mharth@pomona.edu, Internet: www.pomona.edu/museum. Dir.: Marjorie L. Harth, Ass. Dir.: Steve Comba, Cur.: Rebecca McGrew
Fine Arts Museum / University Museum - 1958 42419

Raymond M. Alf Museum of Paleontology, 1175 W Base Line Rd, Claremont, CA 91711 - T: (909) 624-2798, Fax: (909) 624-2798, E-mail: dlofgren@webb.org, Internet: www.alfmuseum.org. Dir.: Donald Lofgren
Natural History Museum - 1937 42420

Claremont NH

Claremont Museum, 26 Mulberry St, Claremont, NH 03743 - T: (603) 543-1400. Pres.: Colin J. Sanborn
Local Museum - 1966 42421

Claremore OK

J.M. Davis Arms and Historical Museum, 333 N Lynn Riggs Blvd, Claremore, OK 74017 - T: (918) 341-5707, Fax: (918) 341-5771, E-mail: american@onenet.net, Internet: www.state.ok.us/~jmdavis/. Dir.: Duane Kyler, Cur.: Dennis Duval
Local Museum - 1965 42422

Will Rogers Memorial Museums, 1720 W Will Rogers Blvd, Claremore, OK 74018-0157 - T: (918) 341-0719, Fax: (918) 343-8119, E-mail: wrinfo@willrogers.com, Internet: www.willrogers.com. Dir.: Michelle Lefebvre-Canter, Cur.: Gregory Malak
Historical Museum - 1938 42423

Clarence NY

Town of Clarence Museum, 10465 Main St, Clarence, NY 14031 - T: (716) 759-8575. Pres.: Lorna Helm, Cur.: Alicia L. Braaten
Local Museum - 1954 42424

Clarion IA

4-H Schoolhouse Museum, 302 S Main, Clarion, IA 50525 - T: (515) 532-2256, Fax: (515) 532-2511, E-mail: clchamb@trvnet.net, Internet: www.trvnet.net/~clchamb/clarion. Exec. Dir.: Nancy Nail
Historical Museum - 1955 42425

Clarion PA

Hazel Sandford Gallery → University Galleries

Sutton-Ditz House Museum, 18 Grant St, Clarion, PA 16214 - T: (814) 226-4450, Fax: (814) 226-7106, E-mail: cchs@csonline.net, Internet: www.csonline.net/cchs/. Dir./Cur.: Lindsley A. Dunn
Local Museum - 1955 42426

University Galleries, Clarion University of Pennsylvania, c/o Carlson Library A-4, Clarion, PA 16214 - T: (814) 393-2523, 393-2412, Fax: (814) 393-2168, E-mail: gallery@clarion.edu. Interim Dir.: Joe Thomas
Fine Arts Museum / University Museum - 1982
Art gallery 42427

Clark CO

Hahns Peak Area Historical Museum, Hahns Peak Village, Clark, CO 80428 - T: (970) 879-6781. Cur.: Mallory Pollock
Local Museum - 1972
Regional history, Old Horse Barn, one room school house 42428

Clark NJ

Dr. William Robinson Plantation, 593 Madison Hill Rd, Clark, NJ 07066 - T: (732) 381-3081. Pres.: Eleanor Warren, Dir.: Constance Brewer
Local Museum - 1974 42429

Clark SD

Beauvais Heritage Center, Hwy 212, Clark, SD 57225 - T: (605) 532-3722, 532-5216. C.E.O. & Pres.: Ailene Luckhurst
Local Museum - 1978
Cultural hist, pioneer home, depot, store, military, religion, machine, tool 42430

Clarksdale MS

Delta Blues Museum, 114 Delta Av, Clarksdale, MS 38614 - T: (662) 627-6820, Fax: (662) 627-7263, E-mail: dbmuseum@clarksdale.com, Internet: www.deltabluesmuseum.org. C.E.O.: Tony Czech
Music Museum - 1979 42431

Clarkson NE

Clarkson Historical Museum, 221 Pine St, Clarkson, NE 68629 - T: (402) 892-3854. Dir.: Evelyn D. Podany
Local Museum - 1967 42432

Clarkston MI

Yesteryear House-Central Mine, 7995 Perry Lake Rd, Clarkston, MI 48348 - T: (248) 625-4296, (906) 337-2092
Science&Tech Museum - 1860
Local copper mining hist 42433

Clarkston WA

Valley Art Center, 842 6th St, Clarkston, WA 99403 - T: (509) 758-8331, E-mail: valleyarts@clarkston.com, Internet: www.valleyarts.qpg.com. Exec. Dir.: Pat Rosenberger
Fine Arts Museum - 1968
Art 42434

Clarksville TN

Clarksville-Montgomery County Museum-Customs House Museum, 200 S Second St, Clarksville, TN 37040 - T: (931) 648-5780, Fax: (931) 553-5179, E-mail: cvillemuse@aol.com. Dir.: Ned Crouch, Ass. Dir.: Linda Maki, Cur.: Janelle Strandberg Aieta
Local Museum - 1984
Local hist 42435

Mabel Larson Fine Arts Gallery, Austin Peay State University, POB 4677, Clarksville, TN 37044 - T: (615) 648-7333
Fine Arts Museum - 1994
Drawings 42436

Margaret Fort Trahern Gallery, College and Eighth Sts, Clarksville, TN 37044 - T: (931) 221-7333, Fax: (931) 221-5997, 221-7219, E-mail: holteb@apsu02.apsu.edu. Dir.: Bettye Holte
Fine Arts Museum / University Museum - 1974
Art 42437

Clarksville VA

Prestwould Foundation, U.S. 15, 2 miles N of Clarksville, Clarksville, VA 23927 - T: (804) 374-8672, Fax: (434) 374-3060. Dir.: Dr. Julian D. Hudson
Local Museum - 1963
Local hist 42438

Clawson MI

Clawson Historical Museum, 41 Fisher Ct, Clawson, MI 48017 - T: (248) 588-9169. Chief Cur.: Delorise M. Kumler
Local Museum - 1973
Local history 42439

Clay City KY

Red River Historical Society Museum, 4541 Main St, Clay City, KY 40312 - T: (606) 663-2555, Internet: www.redriverky.com. Dir.: Larry G. Meadows, Cur.: John Faulkner (Archaeology), Steve Abner (Photography), Jim Spencer (History), Doug Morton (Genealogy)
Local Museum - 1966
Local history, archaeology, photography, genealogy 42440

Clayton ID

Custer Museum, Yankee Fork Ranger District Museum, Clayton, ID 83227 - T: (208) 838-2201, Fax: (208) 838-3329. Pres.: Craig Wolford
Historical Museum - 1961
Located on site of 1870 Gold Rush 42441

Clayton MO

Hanley House, 7600 Westmoreland Rd, Clayton, MO 63105 - T: (314) 290-8501, Fax: (314) 290-8517
Decorative Arts Museum 42442

Clayton NY

American Handweaving Museum → Handweaving Museum and Arts Center

Antique Boat Museum, 750 Mary St, Clayton, NY 13624 - T: (315) 686-4104, Fax: (315) 686-2775, E-mail: info@abm.org, Internet: www.abm.org. Dir.: John Summers, Cur.: Rebecca Hopfinger
Historical Museum - 1964 42443

Handweaving Museum and Arts Center, 314 John St, Clayton, NY 13624 - T: (315) 686-4123, Fax: (315) 686-3459, E-mail: hmac@gisco.net, Internet: www.hm-ac.org. Dir.: Beth Conlon, Cur.: Sonja Wahl
Special Museum - 1966 42444

Thousand Islands Museum of Clayton, 312 James St, Clayton, NY 13624 - T: (315) 686-5794, Fax: (315) 686-4867, E-mail: timuseum@gisco.net, Internet: www.thousandislands.com/timuseum. Dir.: Linda Schleher
Historical Museum - 1964 42445

Cle Elum WA

Carpenter Home Museum, 221 E 1st St, Cle Elum, WA 98922 - T: (509) 674-5702. Pres.: Sarah Engdahl
Historical Museum / Special Museum - 1990
Home, with ballroom and a special maid's room 42446

Cle Elum Telephone Museum, 221 E 1st St, Cle Elum, WA 98922 - T: (509) 674-5702. Pres.: Sarah Engdahl
Science&Tech Museum - 1967
Communications 42447

Clear Lake IA

Kinney Pioneer Museum, 9184 G 265th St, Clear Lake, IA 50428 - T: (641) 423-1258. Dir.: Fran Tagesen
Local Museum - 1964
Local hist, Indian artifacts, fossil coll, dolls and toys 42448

Clear Lake WI

Clear Lake Area Historical Museum, 450 Fifth Av, Clear Lake, WI 54005 - T: (715) 263-3050, 263-2042. Pres./Cur.: Charles T. Clark
Local Museum - 1977
Local hist 42449

Clearfield PA

Clearfield County Historical Society Museum, 104 E Pine St, Clearfield, PA 16830 - T: (814) 765-6125. Cur.: Harry Reickart
Local Museum - 1955 42450

Clearmont WY

Big Red Barn Gallery, 30 Big Red Ln, Clearmont, WY 82835 - T: (307) 737-2291, Fax: (307) 737-2322, E-mail: ucross@wyoming.com. Exec. Dir.: Sharon Dynak
Decorative Arts Museum - 1981
Quilts by Linda Behar 42451

Clearwater FL

Napoleonic Society of America, 1115 Ponce de Leon Blvd, Clearwater, FL 33756 - T: (727) 586-1779, Fax: (727) 581-2578, E-mail: napoleonic1@juno.com, Internet: www.napoleonicsociety.org. Pres.: Robert M. Snibbe
Historical Museum / Military Museum - 1983
library 42452

Ruth Eckerd Hall, 1111 McMullen-Booth d, Clearwater, FL 33759 - T: (727) 791-7060, Fax: (727) 791-6020, Internet: www.rutheckerdhall.net. Exec. Dir.: Robert A. Freedman
Public Gallery - 1978 42453

Cleburne TX

Layland Museum, 201 N Caddo, Cleburne, TX 76031 - T: (817) 645-0940, Fax: (817) 641-4161, E-mail: museum@cleburne.net, Internet: www.cleburne.net. Cur.: Julie P. Backer
Historical Museum - 1964
History of domestic life, photographs, archives 42454

Clemson SC

Bob Campbell Geology Museum, Clemson University, 103 Garden Trail, Clemson, SC 29634-0130 - T: (864-4600, Fax: (864) 656-6230, E-mail: dcheech@clemson.edu, Internet: www.clemson.edu/geomuseum. Cur.: David Cicimurri
Natural History Museum - 1989
Minerals, gems, fossils, meteorites, mining artifacts 42455

Fort Hill - The John C. Calhoun House, Clemson University, Fort Hill St, Clemson, SC 29634 - T: (864) 656-2475, 656-4789, Fax: (864) 656-1026, E-mail: hiottw@clemson.edu, Internet: www.clemson.edu/welcome/history/forthill.htm. Dir.: William D. Hiott
Local Museum - 1889
Historic house, home of John C. Calhoun 42456

Hanover House, Clemson University, c/o South Carolina Botanical Garden,, Perimeter Rd, Clemson, SC 29634 - T: (864) 656-2241, 656-2475, Fax: (803) 656-1026, E-mail: hiottw@clemson.edu, Internet: www.clemson.edu/welcome/history/hanover.htm. Dir.: William D. Hiott
Local Museum - 1941
Historic house 42457

Rudolph E. Lee Gallery, College of Architecture, Arts and Humanities Lee Hall, Clemson University, Clemson, SC 29634 - T: (864) 656-3883, Fax: (864) 656-7523. Dir.: David Houston
Fine Arts Museum / University Museum - 1956
Architecture, graphics, paintings 42458

Clermont IA

Montauk, POB 372, Clermont, IA 52135 - T: (319) 423-7173, Fax: (319) 423-7378, E-mail: nwest@max.state.ia.us
Historical Museum - 1968
Home of William Larrabee, Iowa's 12th Governor 42459

Clermont NY

Clermont State Historic Site, 1 Clermont Av, Clermont, NY 12526 - T: (518) 537-4240, Fax: (518) 537-6240, E-mail: fof@valstar.net, Internet: www.friendsofclermont.org. Dir.: Bruce E. Naramore, Cur.: Travis Bowman
Local Museum - 1962 42460

Cleveland GA

White County Historical Society Museum, Cleveland Sq, Cleveland, GA 30528 - T: (706) 865-3225, Internet: www.georgiamagazine.com. Pres.: Janet Cox
Local Museum - 1965
Civil War, local pictures, historic papers 42461

Cleveland MS

Fielding L. Wright Art Center, Delta State University, Cleveland, MS 38733 - T: (662) 846-4720, Fax: (662) 846-4016, E-mail: bherisn@dsu.deltast.edu. Dir.: Patricia Brown
Fine Arts Museum / University Museum - 1924 42462

Cleveland OH

African American Museum, 1765 Crawford Rd, Cleveland, OH 44106 - T: (216) 791-1700, Fax: (216) 791-1774, E-mail: ourstory@aamcleveland.org, Internet: www.ben.net/aamuseum. C.E.O.: Nancy Nolan Jones
Folklore Museum - 1953 42463

The Children's Museum of Cleveland, 10730 Euclid Av, Cleveland, OH 44106-2200 - T: (216) 791-7114, Fax: (216) 791-8838, Internet: www.museum4kids.com. Exec. Dir.: Karen L. Prasser
Special Museum - 1986 42464

Cleveland Center for Contemporary Art, 8501 Carnegie Av, Cleveland, OH 44106 - T: (216) 421-8671, Fax: (216) 421-0737, E-mail: jwilhelm@contemporaryart.org, Internet: www.contemporaryart.org. Dir.: Jill Snyder, Cur.: Kristin Chambers
Fine Arts Museum - 1968 42465

Cleveland Museum of Art, 11150 East Blvd, Cleveland, OH 44106 - T: (216) 421-7350, (888) 242-0033, Fax: (216) 421-0411, E-mail: info@CMA-oh.org, Internet: www.clevelandart.org. Dir.: Katharine Lee Reid, Dep. Dir.: Susan Jaros (Development, External Affairs), Janet Ashe (Admin., Treasurer), Chief Cur.: Henry Hawley, Cur.: George P. Bickford, Stanislaw Czuma (Southeast Asian Art and Indian Art), Ju-Hsi Chou (Chinese Art), Michael R. Cunningham (Japanese and Korean Art), Jane Glaubinger (Prints), Louise Mackie (Textiles and Islamic Art), Henry Adams (American Painting), Tom E. Hinson (Photography), Assoc. Cur.: Michael Bennett (Greek and Roman Art), Carter Foster (Drawings), William H. Robinson (Paintings - modern, 1900-1945)
Fine Arts Museum - 1913 42466

Cleveland Museum of Natural History, 1 Wade Oval Dr, Cleveland, OH 44106-1767 - T: (216) 231-4600 ext 235, Fax: (216) 231-5919, E-mail: info@cmnh.org, Internet: www.cmnh.org. Dir.: Dr. Bruce Latimer, Dep. Dir.: Dr. Brian Redmond (Science), Harvey Webster (Wildlife Resources), Thomas Zak (Exhibits), Cur.: Dr. Joseph Hannibal (Invertebrate Paleontology), Dr. Michael Williams (Vertebrate Paleontology), Dr. Timothy Matson (Vertebrate Zoology), Dr. Shya Chitaley (Paleobotany), James Bissell (Botany), Ass. Cur.: Dr. David (Mineralogy), Sharon Dean (Cultural Anthropology), Dr. Joe Keiper (Invertebrate Zoology)
Natural History Museum - 1920 42467

Cleveland Police Museum, 1300 Ontario St, Cleveland, OH 44113-1600 - T: (216) 623-5055, Fax: (216) 623-5145, E-mail: museum@stratos.net, Internet: www.clevelandpolicemuseum.org. Dir.: David C. Holcombe, Cur.: Anne T. Kmieck
Special Museum - 1983
Police hist 42468

Cleveland State University Art Gallery, 2307 Chester Av, Cleveland, OH 44114-3607 - T: (216) 687-2103, Fax: (216) 687-2275, E-mail: artgallery@csuohio.edu, Internet: www.csuohio.edu/art/gallery. Dir.: Robert Thurmer, Pres.: Michael Schwartz
Fine Arts Museum / University Museum - 1973 42469

Crawford Auto-Aviation Museum, 10825 East Blvd, Cleveland, OH 44106 - T: (216) 721-5722, Fax: (216) 721-0645, Internet: www.wrhs.org. Cur.: Chris Dawson
Science&Tech Museum - 1963
Autos and aircraft transportation documents 42470

Dittrick Museum of Medical History, Case Western Reserve University, 11000 Euclid Av, Cleveland, OH 44106-1714 - T: (216) 368-3648, Fax: (216) 368-6421, E-mail: jme3@po.cwru.edu, Internet: www.cwru.edu/artsci/dittrick/home.htm. Dir./Cur.: Dr. James M. Edmonson
Historical Museum - 1926
Library 42471

Dunham Tavern Museum, 6709 Euclid Av, Cleveland, OH 44103 - T: (216) 431-1060. Pres.: Barbara Peterson, C.E.O.: Raymond L. Cushing
Local Museum - 1939 42472

Great Lakes Science Center, 601 Erieside Av, Cleveland, OH 44114 - T: (216) 694-2000, Fax: (216) 696-2140, E-mail: pamblancom@glsc.org, Internet: www.greatscience.com. Dir.: Richard F. Coyne
Natural History Museum / Science&Tech Museum - 1988 42473

Health Museum of Cleveland, 8911 Euclid Av, Cleveland, OH 44106 - T: (216) 231-5010, Fax: (216) 231-5129, E-mail: marks@healthmuseum.org, Internet: healthmuseum.org. Chm.: Theodore J. Castele
Special Museum - 1936 42474

International Women's Air and Space Museum, 1501 N Marginal Rd, Cleveland, OH 44114 - T: (216) 623-1111, Fax: (216) 623-1113, E-mail: cluhta@iwasm.org, Internet: www.iwasm.org. Pres.: Caroline Luhta
Science&Tech Museum - 1976
History of Women in Air and space 42475

NASA Lewis Research Center's Visitor Center, 21000 Brookpark Rd, MS 8-1, Cleveland, OH 44135 - T: (216) 433-6689, Fax: (216) 433-3061, E-mail: david.lowenfeld@lere.nasa.gov, Internet: www.grc.nasa.gov/internal. Man.: David Lowenfeld
Science&Tech Museum - 1976 42476

Oberlin College Gallery, 1305 Euclid Av, Cleveland, OH 44115 - T: (216) 861-0748, Internet: www.oberlin.edu/herehere
Public Gallery
Contemporary art, sculpture, installations 42477

Reinberger Galleries, Cleveland Institute of Art, 11141 East Blvd, Cleveland, OH 44106 - T: (216) 421-7407, Fax: (216) 421-7438, Internet: www.cia.edu. Dir.: Bruce Checefsky
Public Gallery 42478

The Rock and Roll Hall of Fame and Museum, 1 Key Plaza, Cleveland, OH 44114-1022 - T: (216) 781-7625, Fax: (216) 781-1832, E-mail: director@rockhall.org, Internet: www.rockhall.com. Chief Cur.: James Henke
Music Museum - 1985
Rock and Roll music 42479

Romanian Ethnic Art Museum, 3256 Warren Rd, Cleveland, OH 44111 - T: (216) 941-5550, Fax: (216) 941-3368, E-mail: dobreaart@aol.com, Internet: www.smroc.org. Dir.: George Dobrea
Ethnology Museum - 1960
Folk art, Romanian art, costumes, ceramics, painters, rugs, silver & woodwork 42480

Spaces, 2220 Superior Viaduct, Cleveland, OH 44113 - T: (216) 621-2314, Fax: (216) 621-2314, E-mail: spaces@apk.net, Internet: www.spacesgallery.org. Dir.: Susan R Channing
Public Gallery
Special exhibitions of contemporary artists 42481

Steamship William G. Mather Museum, 1001 E Ninth St Pier, Cleveland, OH 44114 - T: (216) 574-9053, Fax: (216) 574-2536, E-mail: wgmather@aol.com, Internet: little.nhlink.net/wgm. C.E.O.: Holly Holcombe
Science&Tech Museum - 1991
Freighter and flagship, Great Lakes shipping 42482

Temple Museum of Religious Art, 1855 Ansel Rd, Cleveland, OH 44106 - T: (216) 831-3233, Fax: (216) 831-4216, Internet: www.ttti.org. C.E.O.: Jeremy Handler
Religious Arts Museum - 1950 42483

Ukrainian Museum, 1202 Kenilworth Av, Cleveland, OH 44113 - T: (216) 781-4329, Fax: (216) 781-5844, E-mail: staff@umacleveland.org, Internet: www.umacleveland.org. C.E.O.: Andrew Fedynsky
Fine Arts Museum / Folklore Museum / Historical Museum - 1952 42484

Western Reserve Historical Society Museum, 10825 East Blvd, Cleveland, OH 44106-1788 - T: (216) 721-5722, Fax: (216) 721-8934, Internet: www.wrhs.org. Pres.: Patrick H. Reymann, Exec. Dir.: Richard L. Ehrlich
Historical Museum - 1867 42485

Cleveland TN

Red Clay State Historical Park, 1140 Red Clay Park Rd, SW, Cleveland, TN 37311 - T: (423) 478-0339. Head: Lois I. Osborne
Historic Site - 1979
Historic site, seat of the former Cherokee government and site of eleven general councils national affairs 42486

Clewiston FL

Clewiston Museum, 112 S Commercio St, Clewiston, FL 33440-3706 - T: (941) 983-2870. Dir./Cur.: Joel McCrary
Local Museum - 1984 42487

Clifton KS

Clifton Community Historical Society, 108 Clifton St, Clifton, KS 66937-0223
Local Museum - 1976
Military and scout clothing, photos, schools records, China, tools 42488

Clifton NJ

Hamilton House Museum → Hamilton van Wogener Museum

Hamilton van Wogener Museum, 971 Valley Rd, Clifton, NJ 07013 - T: (973) 744-5707. Cur.: Genevieve Generalli
Local Museum - 1974 42489

Clifton Forge VA

Alleghany Highlands Arts and Crafts Center, 439 E Ridgeway St, Clifton Forge, VA 24422 - T: (540) 862-4447. Pres.: Annette Anderson, Exec. Dir.: Nancy Newhard-Farrar
Decorative Arts Museum - 1984
Arts, crafts 42490

Clinton IA

River Arts Center, 229 Fifth Av S, Clinton, IA 52733-0132 - T: (319) 242-3300, 242-8055, E-mail: gwenwes@webtv.net. Dir.: Gwen Chrest
Fine Arts Museum - 1968
Painting, beaded loin cloth, photographs, lithography, engraving, sculptures, etching, prints, pottery, fabric, pencil, wood 42491

Clinton IL

C.H. Moore Homestead, 219 E Woodlawn St, Clinton, IL 61727 - T: (217) 935-6066, Fax: (217) 935-0553, E-mail: chmoure@davesword.net, Internet: www.chmoorehomestead.org. C.E.O.: Shirley Strange
Historic Site - 1967
General museum housed in C.H. Moore home 42492

Clinton MD

Surratt House Museum, 9118 Brandywine Rd, Clinton, MD 20735 - T: (301) 868-1121, Fax: (301) 868-8177, Internet: www.surrat.org. Dir.: Laurie Verge
Historical Museum - 1976
Historic house, Civil Warand Lincoln assassination 42493

Clinton MI

Wings of Love, 12803 E Michigan Av, Clinton, MI 49236 - T: (517) 456-8800, Fax: (517) 456-8800. Dir.: Dr. Khristina Smith-Speelman
Fine Arts Museum 42494

Clinton MO

Henry County Museum and Cultural Arts Center, 203 W Franklin St, Clinton, MO 64735 - T: (660) 885-8414, Fax: (660) 890-2228, E-mail: hcmus@mid-america.net. Dir.: Alta Dulaban
Decorative Arts Museum / Local Museum - 1974
Architecture, drawings, archaeology, ethnology, costumes, decorative art, Eskimo art, dolls, Oriental, Persian and Greek antiquities 42495

Clinton MS

Mississippi Baptist Historical Commission Museum, Mississippi College, Library-College St, Clinton, MS 39058 - T: (601) 925-3434, Fax: (601) 925-3435, E-mail: mbhc@mc.edu, Internet: www.mc.edu. C.E.O.: Edward McMillan
Religious Arts Museum / University Museum - 1887 42496

Clinton NJ

Hunterdon Historical Museum → Red Mill Museum Village

Hunterdon Museum of Art, 7 Lower Center St, Clinton, NJ 08809 - T: (908) 735-8415, Fax: (908) 735-8416, E-mail: info@hunterdonmuseumofart.org, Internet: www.hunterdonmuseumofart.org. Exec. Dir.: Marjorie Frankel Nathanson, Dir.: Donna Gustafson (Exhibitions)
Fine Arts Museum - 1952
Print coll 42497

Red Mill Museum Village, 56 Main St, Clinton, NJ 08809-0005 - T: (908) 735-4101, Fax: (908) 735-0914, E-mail: hhmredmill@yahoo.com. Pres. & C.E.O.: Jo-an' Van Doren, Dir.: Dr. Charles Speierl
Local Museum - 1960 42498

Clinton NY

Emerson Gallery, Hamilton College, 198 College Hill Rd, Clinton, NY 13323 - T: (315) 859-4396, Fax: (315) 859-4687. Dir.: David Nathans, Ass. Cur.: Thomas Mazzullo
Fine Arts Museum / University Museum - 1982 42499

Clinton OK

Oklahoma Route 66 Museum, 2229 Gary Blvd, Clinton, OK 73601 - T: (580) 323-7866, Fax: (580) 323-2870, E-mail: rt66mus@ok-history.mus.ok.us, Internet: www.route66.org. Dir.: Pat A. Smith, Cur.: Andy Watson
Local Museum - 1967 42500

Clintonville WI

Four Wheel Drive Foundation, E 11th St, Clintonville, WI 54929 - T: (715) 823-2141, Fax: (715) 823-5768, E-mail: rich@seagrave.com, Internet: www.fwd/seagrave.com
Science&Tech Museum - 1948
Racing and passenger cars, trucks, fire engines 42501

Cloquet MN

Carlton County Historical Museum and Heritage Center, 406 Cloquet Av, Cloquet, MN 55720-1750 - T: (218) 879-1938, Fax: (218) 879-1938, E-mail: cchs@cpinternet.com, Internet: www.carltoncountyhs.org. Pres.: Milo Rasmusen, Dir.: Marlene Wisuri
Historical Museum - 1949
Regional history 42502

Cloucester Point VA

Virginia Institute of Marine Science, Fish Collection, Rte 1208, Great Rd, Cloucester Point, VA 23062 - T: (804) 684-7000, Fax: (804) 684-7327, E-mail: jmusick@vims.edu, Internet: www.vims.edu. Cur.: Melanie M. Harbin
Agriculture Museum - 1969
Preserved fishes, scientific ichthyology coll 42503

Cloudcroft NM

Sacramento Mountains Historical Museum, 1000 Hwy 82, Cloudcroft, NM 88317 - T: (505) 682-2932. C.E.O. & Pres.: Patrick Rand
Local Museum - 1977 42504

Cloutierville LA

The Kate Chopin House and Bayou Folk Museum, 243 Hwy 495, Cloutierville, LA 71416 - T: (318) 379-2233, Fax: (318) 379-0055. Pres.: Julia Hildebran, Dir.: Amanda Chenault
Special Museum - 1965
Home of Creole writer Kate Chopin from 1880-1884 42505

Clute TX

Brazosport Museum of Natural Science, 400 College Dr, Clute, TX 77531 - T: (979) 265-7831, Fax: (979) 265-6022, E-mail: bmns@bcfas.org, Internet: bcfas.org
Natural History Museum - 1962
Archaeology, botany, geology, malacology, marine, mineralogy, paleontology, zoology 42506

Cockeysville MD

Baltimore County Historical Museum, 9811 Van Buren Ln, Cockeysville, MD 21030 - T: (410) 666-1876 and 1878, Fax: (410) 666-5276, E-mail: bchistory@msn.com, Internet: www.baltocohistsoc.com. C.E.O.: Ann Rutledge, Exec. Dir.: Kristi Alexander
Local Museum - 1959
Regional history 42507

Cocoa FL

Brevard Museum, 2201 Michigan Av, Cocoa, FL 32926-5618 - T: (321) 632-1830, Fax: (321) 631-7551, E-mail: brevardmuseum@palmnet.net, Internet: www.brevardmuseum.com. Dir.: Ann L. Lawton, Cur.: Kay Davis (History), Winnifred Mendenhall (Science)
Local Museum / Natural History Museum - 1969
History, natural history 42508

Coconut Grove FL

Barnacle Historic State Park, 3485 Main Hwy, Coconut Grove, FL 33133 - T: (305) 448-9445, Fax: (305) 448-7484, Internet: www.floridastateparks.org
Historical Museum - 1973
Memorabilia of pioneer Commodore Ralph Middleton Munroe, marine, photographs, cameras, furniture 42509

Cody WY

Buffalo Bill Historical Center, 720 Sheridan Av, Cody, WY 82414 - T: (307) 587-4771 ext 0, Fax: (307) 578-4066, E-mail: janj@bbhc.org, Internet: www.bbhc.org. Dir.: Dr. Robert E. Shimp, Assoc. Dir.: Eugene Reber, Dr. Judi A. Winchester (Buffalo Bill Museum), Simeon Stoddart (Cody Firearms Museum), Dr. Sarah E. Boehme (Whitney Gallery of Western Art), Emma Hansen (Plains Indian Museum), Dr. Charles R. Preston (Draper Museum of Natural History)
Historical Museum / Fine Arts Museum - 1917
American history coll, art 42510

Coeur d'Alene ID

Museum of North Idaho, 115 NW Blvd, Coeur d'Alene, ID 83814 - T: (208) 664-3448, E-mail: museumni@nidlink.com, Internet: www.museumni.org. Dir.: Dorothy Dahlgren
Local Museum - 1968
Region's hist, logging, mining and steamboat, textiles, firearms, Native American artifacts, hist of Fort Sherman 42511

Coffeyville KS

Dalton Defenders Museum, 113 E 8th, Coffeyville, KS 67337 - T: (316) 251-5944, Fax: (316) 251-5448, E-mail: chamber@coffeyville.com, Internet: www.coffeyville.com. Pres.: Lue Barndollar
Historical Museum - 1954
History 42512

Cohasset MA

Caleb Lothrop House, 14 Summer St, Cohasset, MA 02025 - T: (781) 383-1434, E-mail: tla@dreamcom.net. Pres.: Kathleen O'Malley, Cur.: David H. Wadsworth
Historical Museum - 1928
Federal house 42513

David Nichols-Captain John Wilson House, 4 Elm St, Cohasset, MA 02025 - T: (781) 383-1434, E-mail: tlg@dreamcom.net. Pres.: Kathleen O'Malley, Cur.: David H. Wadsworth
Historical Museum - 1936
Furniture, artwork, toys 42514

Maritime Museum, 4 Elm St, Cohasset, MA 02025 - T: (781) 383-1434, E-mail: tlg@dreamcom.net. Pres.: Kathleen O'Malley, Cur.: David H. Wadsworth
Historical Museum / Folklore Museum - 1928
Maritime hist 42515

Cokato MN

Cokato Museum and Akerlund Photography Studio, 175 W 4th St, Cokato, MN 55321 - T: (320) 286-2427, Fax: (320) 286-5876, E-mail: cokatomuseum@cmgate.com, Internet: www.cokato.mn.us/cmhs/. Dir.: Mike Worcester
Local Museum - 1976
Businesses, Finnish culture, agriculture, immigration artifacts 42516

Colby KS

The Prairie Museum of Art and History, 1905 S Franklin, Colby, KS 67701, mail addr: POB 465, Colby, KS 67701 - T: (913) 462-4590, Fax: (785) 462-4592, E-mail: prairiem@colby.ixks.com, Internet: www.prairiemuseum.org. Dir.: Sue Ellen Taylor
Local Museum - 1959
Local hist - archives 42517

Cold Spring NY

Putnam County Historical Society and Foundry School Museum, 63 Chestnut St, Cold Spring, NY 10516 - T: (914) 265-4010, Fax: (914) 265-2884, E-mail: office@pchs-fsm.org, Internet: www.pchs-fsm.org. Dir.: Martha Waters, Sc. Staff: Minette Gunther (History)
Local Museum - 1906 42518

Cold Spring Harbor BY

SPLIA Gallery, 161 Main St, Cold Spring Harbor, BY 11724 - T: (631) 692-4664, Fax: (631) 692-5265, E-mail: splia@aol.com, Internet: splia.org. Dir.: Robert B. MacKay
Local Museum - 1948
Decorative arts, textiles, ceramics, glass, photos, paintings, prints, manuscripts 42519

Cold Spring Harbor NY

Cold Spring Harbor Whaling Museum, Main St, Cold Spring Harbor, NY 11724 - T: (516) 367-3418, Fax: (516) 692-7037, E-mail: cshwm@optonline.net, Internet: www.cshwhalingmuseum.org. Dir.: Paul B. DeOrsay
Special Museum - 1936 42520

Colfax IA

Trainland U.S.A., 3135 Hwy 117 N, Colfax, IA 50054 - T: (515) 674-3813, Fax: (515) 674-3813, Internet: www.trainland.usa.com. Pres.: Leland Atwood
Decorative Arts Museum - 1981
Toys 42521

College Park MD

Art Gallery, c/o University of Maryland, 1202 Art-Sociology Bldg, College Park, MD 20742 - T: (301) 405-2763, Fax: (301) 314-7774, E-mail: cg17@umail.umd.edu. Dir.: Terry Gips
Fine Arts Museum / University Museum - 1966
20th c paintings, prints and drawings 42522

The Art Gallery, University of Meryland, 1202 Art-Sociology Bldg, College Park, MD 20742 - T: (301) 405-2763, Fax: (301) 314-7774, E-mail: artgal@umail.umd.edu, Internet: www.artgallery.umd.edu. Dir.: Scott Habes
Fine Arts Museum / University Museum - 1966
Art 42523

College Park Aviation Museum, 1985 Cpl. Frank Scott Dr, College Park, MD 20740-3836 - T: (301) 864-6029, Fax: (301) 927-6472, Internet: www.pgparks.com. Dir.: Catherine Allen, Cur.: Jane Welsh (Education), Anne Smallman (Collections), Susan Fite (Program)
Science&Tech Museum / Historical Museum - 1982
Aviation, oldest continually operating airport in the world 42524

College Station TX

George Bush Presidential Library and Museum, 1000 George Bush Dr W, College Station, TX 77845-3906 - T: (979) 260-9552, Fax: (979) 260-9557, E-mail: library@bush.nara.gov, Internet: bushlibrary.tamu.edu. C.E.O.: Dr. David E. Alsobrook
Historical Museum - 1992 42525

J. Wayne Stark University Center Galleries, Mem. Student Center, College Station, TX 77844 - T: (979) 845-6081, Fax: (979) 862-3381, E-mail: uart@stark.tamu.edu, Internet: stark.tamu.edu. Cur.: Catherine A. Hastedt
Fine Arts Museum / University Museum - 1973
Art 42526

MSC Forsyth Center Galleries, Texas A & M University, Memorial Student Center, Joe Routt Blvd, College Station, TX 77844-9081 - T: (409) 845-9251, Fax: (409) 845-5117, E-mail: fcg@msc.tamu.edu, Internet: forsyth.tamu.edu. Dir.: Timothy Novak
Fine Arts Museum / Decorative Arts Museum / University Museum - 1989
Art 42527

Collegeville PA

Philip and Muriel Berman Museum of Art, Ursinus College, 601 East Main St, Collegeville, PA 19426-1000 - T: (610) 409-3500, Fax: (610) 409-3664, E-mail: lhanover@ursinus.edu, Internet: www.ursinus.edu. Dir./Cur.: Lisa Tremper Hanover, Ass. Dir.: Laura Steen, Head: Andrea Cooper (Collections)
Fine Arts Museum / University Museum - 1987
Art 42528

Collingswood NJ

Film Forum - Film Archives, 579A Haddon Av, Collingswood, NJ 08108-1445 - T: (856) 854-3221. Dir.: David J. Grossman
Performing Arts Museum / Special Museum - 1989
Color design, social issues on film 42529

Collinsville IL

Cahokia Mounds State Historic Site, 30 Ramey St, Collinsville, IL 62234 - T: (618) 346-5160, Fax: (618) 346-5162, E-mail: cahokiamounds@ezl.com, Internet: www.cahokiamounds.com. C.E.O.: Christina Pallozola
Ethnology Museum / Archaeological Museum - 1930
Archaeology, 800-1500 A.D., site of largest prehistoric Indian city in North America 42530

Collinsville OK

Collinsville Depot Museum, 115 S 10th St, Collinsville, OK 74021 - T: (918) 371-3540. Pres.: William T. Thomas
Historical Museum - 1975 42531

Colonial Beach VA

George Washington Birthplace National Monument, 1732 Popes Creek Rd, Colonial Beach, VA 22443 - T: (804) 224-1732, Fax: (804) 224-2142, E-mail: gewa_park_information@nps.gov, Internet: www.nps.gov/gewa. Head: John J. Donahue
Local Museum - 1932
Birthplace of George Washington 42532

Colorado City TX

Heart of West Texas Museum, 340 E 3rd St, Colorado City, TX 79512 - T: (915) 728-8285, Fax: (915) 728-8944, E-mail: wtmuseum@colorado.net, Internet: www.coloradocity.net/museumheartofwesttexas. Pres.: Jay McCollum, Dir.: Louise Crenshaw
Local Museum - 1960
Local hist 42533

Colorado Springs CO

Carriage House Museum, 16 Lake Circle, Colorado Springs, CO 80906 - T: (719) 634-7711 ext 5353. Cur.: Franeis Pittz, Bill MacEnulty, Ed Singleton
Science&Tech Museum - 1941
Transportation 42534

Colorado Springs Fine Arts Center, Taylor Museum, 30 W Dale St, Colorado Springs, CO 80903 - T: (719) 634-5581, Fax: (719) 634-0570, E-mail: info@csfineartscenter.org, Internet: www.csfineartscenter.org. Dir.: David Turner
Fine Arts Museum - 1936
Historic and contemporary art, Southwestern U.S. culture 42535

Colorado Springs Museum, 215 S Tejon, Colorado Springs, CO 80903 - T: (719) 385-5990, Fax: (719) 385-5645, E-mail: cosmuseum@ci.colospgs.co.us, Internet: www.cspm.org. Dir.: William C. Holmes, Matthew Mayberry, Cur.: Katie Davis Gardner
Local Museum - 1937
Local history 42536

Gallery of Contemporary Art, University of Colorado, 1420 Austin Bluffs Pkwy, Colorado Springs, CO 80918 - T: (719) 262-3567, Fax: (719) 262-3183, E-mail: griggs@uccs.edu, Internet: harpy.uccs.edu/gallery. Dir.: Gerry Riggs
Fine Arts Museum / University Museum - 1981
Contemporary art 42537

McAllister House Museum, 423 N Cascade Av, Colorado Springs, CO 80903 - T: (719) 635-7925, Fax: (719) 528-5869, E-mail: patric@oldcolo.com, Internet: oldcolo.com/~mcallister. Cur.: Patric Fox, Barbara Gately
Historical Museum - 1961
Major Henry McAllister home, Victorian furnishings 42538

May Natural History Museum and Museum of Space Exploration, 710 Rock Creek Canyon Rd, Colorado Springs, CO 80926-9799 - T: (719) 576-0450, Fax: (719) 576-3644, Internet: www.maymuseum-camp-rvpark.com. Pres./ Dir.: John M. May
Science&Tech Museum / Natural History Museum - 1941
Natural history, entomology, space exploration 42539

Museum of the American Numismatic Association, 818 N Cascade Av, Colorado Springs, CO 80903 - T: (719) 632-2646, Fax: (719) 634-4085, E-mail: anamus@money.org, Internet: www.money.org. Dir.: Edward C. Rochette, Cur.: Lawrence Lee
Special Museum - 1967
Numismatics 42540

Pro Rodeo Hall of Fame and Museum of the American Cowboy, 101 Pro Rodeo Dr, Colorado Springs, CO 80919 - T: (719) 528-4761, Fax: (719) 548-4874, E-mail: phildebrand@prorodeo.com, Internet: www.prorodeo.com. C.E.O.: Steven J. Hatchell
Special Museum - 1979
Rodeo and Cowboy history 42541

Western Museum of Mining and Industry, 125 N Gate Rd, Colorado Springs, CO 80921 - T: (719) 488-0880, Fax: (719) 488-9261, E-mail: westernmuseum@aol.com, Internet: www.wmmi.org. Dir.: Linda D. LeMieux, Cur.: Terry Girouard
Science&Tech Museum - 1970
Mining, technology history 42542

World Figure Skating Museum and Hall of Fame, 20 First St, Colorado Springs, CO 80906 - T: (719) 635-5200, Fax: (719) 635-9548, E-mail: museum@usfsa.org, Internet: www.worldskatingmuseum.org. Dir.: John LeFevre, Cur.: Beth Davis
Special Museum - 1964
Sports 42543

Colter Bay Village WY

Colter Bay Indian Arts Museum, Visitor Center, Grand Teton National Park, Colter Bay Village, WY 83012 - T: (307) 739-3399, Fax: (307) 739-3504, E-mail: danna_kinsey@nps.gov, Internet: www.nps.gov/grte/. Cur.: Danna Kinsey
Fine Arts Museum - 1972 42544

Colton CA

Colton Area Museum, 380 N La Cadena Dr, Colton, CA 92324 - T: (909) 824-8814. Dir.: Paula Olson
Local Museum / Historic Site - 1984
Indian artifacts 42545

Colton Point MD

Saint Clements Island-Potomac River Museum, 38370 Pointbreeze Rd, Colton Point, MD 20626 - T: (301) 769-2222, Fax: (301) 769-2225, E-mail: pineypoint@erols. Dir.: Michael E. Humphries, Ass. Dir.: Lydia Wood
Historic Site / Historical Museum / Archaeological Museum - 1975
Archaeology, history, 1634 landing site of Maryland colonists, first Roman Catholic mass in English colonies 42546

Columbia CA

Columbia State Historic Park, 22708 Broadway, Columbia, CA 95310 - T: (209) 532-4301, Fax: (209) 532-5064, E-mail: calavera@goldrush.com, Internet: www.sierra.parks.state.ca.us
Historical Museum / Special Museum - 1945 42547

Columbia MD

African Art Museum of Maryland, 5430 Vantage Point Rd, Columbia, MD 21044-0105 - T: (410) 730-7105, Fax: (410) 715-3047, E-mail: africanartmuseum@erols.com, Internet: www.africanartmuseum.org. Dir.: Doris H. Ligon
Fine Arts Museum / Ethnology Museum - 1980
African art 42548

Howard County Center of African American Culture, 5434 Vantage Point Rd, Columbia, MD 21044 - T: (410) 715-1921, Fax: (410) 715-8755, E-mail: hccaacmd@Juno.com. Dir.: Wylene Sims-Burch
Folklore Museum - 1987 42549

Columbia MO

Davis Art Gallery, Stephens College, Columbia, MO 65215 - T: (573) 876-4267, Fax: (573) 876-7248, Internet: www.stephens.edu. Dir.: Robert Friedman, Cur.: Irene O. Alexander
Fine Arts Museum / University Museum - 1962 42550

Lewis, James and Nellie Stratton Gallery, Stephens College, 1200 E Braodway, Columbia, MO 65215 - T: (573) 876-7267, Fax: (573) 876-7248. Dir.: Robert Friedman, Cur.: Irene O. Alexander
Fine Arts Museum
Modern graphics and paintings, primitive sculpture 42551

Museum of Anthropology, University of Missouri, 104 Swallow Hall, Columbia, MO 65211 - T: (573) 882-3573, Fax: (573) 884-1435, E-mail: FrenchME@missouri.edu, Internet: coas.missouri.edu/anthromuseum. Dir.: Michael J. O'Brien, Cur.: Mary French
University Museum / Ethnology Museum - 1949 42552

Museum of Art and Archaeology, University of Missouri-Columbia, Pickard Hall, University Av and S Ninth St, Columbia, MO 65211 - T: (573) 882-3591, Fax: (573) 884-4039, Internet: www.research.missouri.edu/museum. Dir.: Marlene Perchinske, Assoc. Cur.: Joan Stack (European and American Art), Asst. Cur.: Benton Kidd (Ancient Art)
Fine Arts Museum / University Museum / Archaeological Museum - 1957 42553

State Historical Society of Missouri Museum, 1020 Lowry St, Columbia, MO 65201-7298 - T: (573) 882-7083, Fax: (573) 884-4950, E-mail: shsofmo@umsystem.edu, Internet: www.system.missouri.edu/shs. Dir.: Dr. James W. Goodrich, Cur.: Sidney Larson
Fine Arts Museum - 1898 42554

Columbia PA

National Watch and Clock Museum, 514 Poplar St, Columbia, PA 17512-2130 - T: (717) 684-8261, Fax: (717) 684-0878, E-mail: nconnelly@nawcc.org, Internet: www.nawcc.org. Dir.: Nancy Connelly, Cur.: Scott Sagar, Libr.: Beth Bisbano
Science&Tech Museum - 1971 42555

Wright's Ferry Mansion, 38 S Second St, Columbia, PA 17512 - T: (717) 684-4325. Dir.: Thomas Cook, Cur.: Elizabeth Meg Schaefer
Local Museum - 1974 42556

Columbia SC

Columbia Fire Department Museum, 1800 Laurel St, Columbia, SC 29201 - T: (803) 733-8350, Fax: (803) 733-8311, Internet: www.columbia.net/city/fire.htm. C.E.O.: John D. Jansen jr
Historical Museum - 1996
Metropolitan horse drawn steamer, hist of fire service 42557

Columbia Museum of Art, Main and Hampton Sts, Columbia, SC 29201, mail addr: POB 2068, Columbia, SC 29202 - T: (803) 799-2810, Fax: (803) 343-2150, E-mail: margaret@colmusart.org, Internet: www.columbiamuseum.org. Dir.: Michael Roh, Interim Chief Cur.: Kevin W. Tucker
Fine Arts Museum - 1950
Art 42558

Edventure, 1728 Gervais St, Columbia, SC 29201 - T: (803) 779-3100 ext 10, Fax: (813) 779-3144, E-mail: info@edventure.org, Internet: www.edventure.org
Natural History Museum / Science&Tech Museum - 1994 42559

Governor's Mansion, 800 Richland St, Columbia, SC 29201 - T: (803) 737-1710, Fax: (803) 737-3860, Internet: www.scgovernorsmansion.org/history.htm. Dir.: Ryan Zimmerman, Cur.: Nancy B. Bunch
Historic Site - 1855
Historic house 42560

Hampton-Preston Mansion, 1615 Blanding St, Columbia, SC 29201 - T: (803) 252-1770, Fax: (803) 929-7695. Pres.: Dr. John G. Sproat, Exec. Dir.: Arrington Cox
Historical Museum - 1961
Historic house 42561

Historic Columbia Foundation, 1601 Richland St, Columbia, SC 29201 - T: (803) 252-7742, Fax: (803) 929-7695, Internet: www.historiccolumbia.org. Pres.: Richard C. Stanland, Dir.: John Sherrer
Local Museum - 1961
Local hist 42562

McKissick Museum, University of South Carolina, Pendleton and Bull Sts, Columbia, SC 29208 - T: (803) 777-7251, Fax: (803) 777-2829, E-mail: lynn.robertson@sc.edu, Internet: www.cla.sc.edu/mcks. Dir.: Lynn Robertson, Chief Cur.: Jay Williams (Exhibitions), Saddler Taylor (Folklife and Research), Cur.: Jason Shaiman (Traveling Exhibitions), Karen Swager (Collections), Alice Booknight (Education)
Folklore Museum / University Museum - 1976
Folk art, natural sciences, material culture 42563

Mann-Simons Cottage, 1403 Richland St, Columbia, SC 29201 - T: (803) 252-1770, Fax: (803) 252-5001. Pres.: Dr. John G. Sproat, C.E.O.: Arrington Cox
Historical Museum - 1961
House dedicated to free African American Celia Mann and her family who lived here until 1970 42564

Robert Mills Historic House and Park, Historic Columbia Foundation, 1601 Richland St, Columbia, SC 29201 - T: (803) 252-1770, Fax: (803) 929-7695. Pres.: Roger D. Poston, Exec. Dir.: Cynthia Moses Nesmith
Local Museum - 1961
Local hist 42565

South Carolina Confederate Relic Room and Museum, 301 Gervais St, Columbia, SC 29201 - T: (803) 737-8095, Fax: (803) 737-8099, E-mail: sschoon@crr.state.sc.us, Internet: www.state.sc.us/crr. Dir.: W. Allen Roberson
Historical Museum - 1896
History 42566

South Carolina Law Enforcement Officers Hall of Fame, 5400 Broad River Rd, Columbia, SC 29212 - T: (803) 896-8199, Fax: (803) 896-8067, Internet: www.state.sc.us/dps/cja.htm. Admin.: Marsha T. Ardila
Special Museum / Historical Museum - 1979
Law enforcement artifacts 42567

South Carolina Military Museum, 1 National Guard Rd, Columbia, SC 29201-4766 - T: (803) 806-4440, Fax: (803) 806-2103, E-mail: 1982. Dir.: Ewell G. Sturgis jr
Military Museum
SC military and National Guard, artillery 42568

South Carolina State Museum, 301 Gervais St, Columbia, SC 29201 - T: (803) 898-4921, Fax: (803) 898-4917, E-mail: artcurator@museum.state.sc.us, Internet: www.museum.state.sc.us. Dir.: William Callahan, Cur.: Fritz Hamer (History), Jim Knight (Natural History), Ronald G. Shelton (Science and Technology), Paul Matheny (Art)
Local Museum - 1973
Local hist, culture, art, natural history, science, technology 42569

Columbia TN

James K. Polk Ancestral Home, 301 W 7th St, Columbia, TN 38401 - T: (931) 388-2354, Fax: (931) 388-5971, E-mail: jkpolk@usit.net, Internet: www.jameskpolk.com. Dir.: John C. Holtzapple, Cur.: Thomas E. Price
Historic Site - 1924
Historic house 42570

Columbia City IN

Whitley County Historical Museum, 108 W Jefferson, Columbia City, IN 46725 - T: (219) 244-6372, Fax: (219) 244-6384, E-mail: wcmuseum@whitleynet.org, Internet: www.whitleynet.org/historical/. Dir.: Ruth Kirk, Cur.: Susan Richey
Local Museum - 1963
County history 42571

Columbia Falls ME

Ruggles House, 1/4m off U.S. Rte 1, Columbia Falls, ME 04623 - T: (207) 483-4637, 546-7429, E-mail: ruggles@midmaine.com, Internet: www.midmaine.com/~ruggles/. Pres.: Richard Grant
Historical Museum - 1949 42572

Columbiana OH

Columbiana-Fairfield Township Museum, 10 E Park Av, Columbiana, OH 44408 - T: (330) 482-2983. Pres.: Leonard Pritchard, Cur.: Nora Salmen, Sc. Staff: Ada Wilhelm (Genealogy)
Local Museum - 1953 42573

Columbus GA

The Columbus Museum, 1251 Wynnton Rd, Columbus, GA 31906 - T: (706) 649-0713, Fax: (706) 649-1070, E-mail: colmuseum@mcsd.ga.net, Internet: www.columbusmuseum.com. Dir.: Charles Thomas Butler, Cur.: Frank Schnell (Archeology)
Fine Arts Museum / Historical Museum - 1952
Archaeology, costumes and textiles, decorative arts, paintings, photos, prints, drawings, graphics, sculpture, furnishings, personal artifacts 42574

Historic Columbus Foundation, 700 Broadway, Columbus, GA 31901 - T: (706) 322-0756, Fax: (706) 576-4760, E-mail: hcf.inc@minspring.com, Internet: www.historiccolumbus.com. Pres.: Stephen G. Gunby, Exec. Dir.: Virginia T. Peebles
Historical Museum - 1966
Five house museums incl c.1870 first brick house in original residential part of city 42575

Port Columbus National Civil War Naval Center, 1002 Victory Dr, Columbus, GA 31902 - T: (706) 324-7334, Fax: (706) 324-7225, E-mail: cwnavy@portcolumbus.org, Internet: www.portcolumbus.org. Exec. Dir.: Bruce Smith
Military Museum - 1962
Naval Museum 42576

Columbus IN

Bartholomew County Historical Museum, 524 Third St, Columbus, IN 47201 - T: (812) 372-3541, Fax: (812) 372-3113, E-mail: bchs@hsonline.net, Internet: www.bchs.hsonline.com. Interim Dir.: Virginia Rouse, Cur.: Sandy Greenlee
Local Museum - 1921
Local History 42577

Indianapolis Museum of Art - Columbus Gallery, 390 The Commons, Columbus, IN 47201-6764 - T: (812) 376-2597, Fax: (812) 375-2724, E-mail: jhandley@imacg.org, Internet: www.imacg.org. Pres.: Em Rodway, Dir.: Jerry Handley
Fine Arts Museum - 1974
Art 42578

Columbus KY

Columbus-Belmont Civil War Museum, 350 Park Rd, Columbus, KY 42032 - T: (502) 677-2327, Fax: (502) 677-4013, E-mail: cindy.lynch@state.ky.us, Internet: www.kystateparks.com/angencies/parks/columbus.htm. Head: Cindy Lynch
Historical Museum / Military Museum - 1934
History, civil war, military 42579

Columbus MS

Blewitt-Harrison-Lee Museum, 316 Seventh St N, Columbus, MS 39701 - T: (662) 329-3533. Cur.: Caroline Neault
Local Museum - 1960
Local artifacts, furniture, jewelry, pictures, portraits 42580

Fine Arts Gallery, c/o Mississippi University for Women, Fine Arts Bldg, 1100 College St, Columbus, MS 39701 - T: (662) 329-7341, 241-6976, Fax: (662) 241-7815. Dir.: Lawrence Feeney
Fine Arts Museum / University Museum - 1948
American art, paintings, sculpture, photographs, drawings, ceramics, prints 42581

Florence McLeod Hazard Museum, 316 Seventh St N, Columbus, MS 39701 - T: (662) 327-8888, Internet: www.historic-columbus.org. Pres.: Libba Johnson, Dir.: Heather Roland
Historical Museum - 1959 42582

Mississippi University for Women Museum, Fant Library, Columbus, MS 39701 - T: (662) 329-7332, Fax: (662) 329-7348, E-mail: fdavison@muw.edu, Internet: www.muw.edu. Pres.: Dr. Clyda S. Rent
University Museum - 1978 42583

Columbus NJ

Georgetown Museum, 3121 Rte 206, Columbus, NJ 08022-2043 - T: (609) 298-4174
Local Museum - 1976
Township hist 42584

Columbus OH

ACME Art Gallery, 1129 N High St, Columbus, OH 43201 - T: (614) 299-4003, Internet: www.acmeart.com. Dir.: Margaret Evans
Fine Arts Museum 42585

Columbus Cultural Arts Center, 139 W Main St, Columbus, OH 43215 - T: (614) 645-7047, Fax: (614) 645-5862, E-mail: jljohnson@cmhmetro.net, Internet: www.culturalartscenteronline.com. Pres.: Richard Wissler, Dir.: Jennifer L. Johnson
Fine Arts Museum / Folklore Museum / Historical Museum - 1978 42586

Columbus Museum of Art, 480 E Broad St, Columbus, OH 43215 - T: (614) 221-6801, Fax: (614) 221-0226, E-mail: info@cmaohio.org, Internet: www.columbusart.mus.oh.us. Dir.: Irvin M. Lippman, Sen. Cur.: Nannette V. Maciejunes, Cur.: Annegreth T. Nill (20th-Century and Contemporary Art), Catherine Evans (Photography)
Fine Arts Museum - 1878 42587

COSI Columbus, 333 W Broad St, Columbus, OH 43215-2738 - T: (614) 228-2674, Fax: (614) 228-6363, E-mail: cosi@cosi.org, Internet: www.cosi.org. Pres.: Kathryn D. Sullivan
Science&Tech Museum - 1964 42588

Kelton House Museum, 586 E Town St, Columbus, OH 43215-4888 - T: (614) 464-2022, Fax: (614) 464-3346, E-mail: Keltonhouse@cs.com, Internet: www.keltonhouse.com. Cur.: Joseph Lowe
Special Museum / Folklore Museum - 1976
Historic house 42589

Ohio Historical Center → Ohio Historical Society Museum

Ohio Historical Society Museum, 1982 Velma Av, Columbus, OH 43211-2497 - T: (614) 297-2300, Fax: (614) 297-2318, E-mail: ohsref.ohiohistory.org, Internet: www.ohiohistory.org. C.E.O.: Gary C. Ness, Cur.: Martha Otto (Archaeology), William Gates (History)
Historical Museum - 1885 42590

Orton Geological Museum, Ohio State University, 155 S Oval Mall, Columbus, OH 43210 - T: (614) 292-6896, Fax: (614) 292-1496, E-mail: gnidovec@geology.ohio-state.edu. Dir.: Prof. Stig M. Bergstrom, Cur.: Dale Gnidovec
University Museum / Natural History Museum - 1892 42591

Schumacher Gallery, c/o Capital University, 2199 E Main St, Columbus, OH 43209 - T: (614) 236-6319, Fax: (614) 236-6490, Internet: www.capital.edu/cc/gall/index.shtml. Dir.: Dr. Cassandra Tellier
Fine Arts Museum / University Museum - 1964 42592

Wexner Center for the Arts, c/o Ohio State University, 1871 N High St, Columbus, OH 43210-1393 - T: (614) 292-0330, Fax: (614) 292-3369, E-mail: wexnercenter@osu.edu, Internet: www.wexarts.org. Dir.: Sherri Geldin, Cur.: Jeffrey Kipnis (Exhibitions), Charles Helm (Performing Arts), Patricia Trumps (Education), William Horrigan (Media Arts)
Fine Arts Museum / University Museum / Performing Arts Museum - 1989 42593

Commack NY

Long Island Culture History Museum, Hoyt Farm Park, New Hwy, Commack, NY 11725, mail addr: POB 1542, Stony Brook, NY 11790 - T: (516) 929-8725, Fax: (516) 929-6967, E-mail: gstone@msn.com. Dir.: Gaynell Stone
Historical Museum / Archaeological Museum / Open Air Museum - 1986
History, archaeology 42594

Commerce TX

University Gallery, Texas A & M University, POB 3011, Commerce, TX 75429 - T: (903) 886-5208, Fax: (214) 886-5415, E-mail: BarbaraFrey@tamu-commerce.edu. Dir.: Barbara Frey
Fine Arts Museum - 1979 42595

Comstock TX

Seminole Canyon State Historical Park, U.S. Hwy 90 West, Comstock, TX 78837 - T: (915) 292-4464, Fax: (915) 292-4596, Internet: www.tpwd.state.tx.us
Archaeological Museum - 1980
Archaeology site, containing 4,000-year old pictographs 42596

Concord MA

Concord Art Association Museum, 37 Lexington Rd, Concord, MA 01742 - T: (508) 369-2578, Fax: (508) 371-2496, E-mail: concordart@concentric.net, Internet: www.concordart.org. Dir.: Elizabeth Adams
Fine Arts Museum - 1922
Art gallery 42597

Concord Museum, 200 Lexington Rd, Concord, MA 01742 - T: (978) 369-9763, Fax: (978) 369-9660, E-mail: cm1@concordmuseum.org, Internet: www.concordmuseum.org. Dir.: Desiree Caldwell, Cur.: David Wood
Decorative Arts Museum / Local Museum / Historical Museum - 1886
Local history, decorative arts 42598

Minute Man National Historical Park, 174 Liberty St, Concord, MA 01742 - T: (978) 369-6993, Fax: (978) 371-2483, E-mail: mima_info@nps.gov, Internet: www.nps.gov/mima. Dir.: Nancy Nelson, Cur.: Teresa Wallace
Historical Museum / Archaeological Museum - 1959
Along 1775 battle road, 19th c wayside, Nathaniel Hawthorne, Alcott and Lothrop family home 42599

The Old Manse, 269 Monument St, Concord, MA 01742, mail addr: POB 572, Concord, MA 01742 - T: (978) 369-3909, Fax: (978) 287-6154, E-mail: oldmanse@ttor.org, Internet: www.thetrustees.org
Historical Museum - 1939
Site of the 1st major skirmish of the Revolutionary War 1775, home to Ralph Waldo Emerson and Nathaniel Hawthorne 42600

Orchard House - Home of the Alcotts, 399 Lexington Rd, Concord, MA 01742 - T: (978) 369-5617, Fax: (978) 369-1367, E-mail: louisa@acunet.net, Internet: www.louisamayalcott.org. Dir.: Jan Turnquist
Special Museum - 1911
House where Louisa May Alcott wrote Little Women, Bronson Alcott's School of Philosophy, American history, art 42601

Ralph Waldo Emerson House, 28 Cambridge Turnpike at Lexington Rd, Concord, MA 01742 - T: (978) 369-2236. Pres.: William Bancroft, Dir.: Barbara Mongan
Historical Museum - 1930 42602

Concord MI

Historic Mann House, 205 Hanover St, Concord, MI 49237 - T: (517) 524-8943, 373-1979. Sc. Staff: Patrick Murphy (History)
Historical Museum - 1970 42603

Concord NH

Art Center In Hargate, Saint Paul's School, 325 Pleasant St, Concord, NH 03301 - T: (603) 229-4644, Fax: (603) 229-5696, E-mail: ccallaha@sps.edu, Internet: www.sps.edu/arts/hargate/index.shtml. Dir.: Colin J. Callahan
Fine Arts Museum - 1967
Drawings, graphics, paintings, sculpture, school gifts - Ohrstrom library 42604

Museum of New Hampshire History, 6 Eagle Sq, Concord, NH 03301 - T: (603) 228-6688, Fax: (603) 228-6308, E-mail: jdesmarais@nhhistory.org, Internet: www.nhhistory.org. Dir.: John L. Frisbee, Cur.: Janet Deranian, Libr.: William N. Copeley
Decorative Arts Museum / Historical Museum - 1823 42605

Pierce Manse, 14 Penacook St, Concord, NH 03301 - T: (603) 224-5954, 255-4555. C.E.O.: Florence Holden
Historical Museum - 1966
1842-1848 home of President Franklin Pierce 42606

Concordia KS

Cloud County Historical Museum, 635 Broadway, Concordia, KS 66901 - T: (913) 243-2866. Pres.: Don Kaufmann, Cur.: Linda Palmquist
Local Museum - 1959
Local history 42607

Condon OR

Depot Museum Complex, Hwy 19 at Burns Park, Condon, OR 97823 - T: (541) 384-4233
Local Museum - 1985
County hist, farm machinery 42608

Conneaut OH

Conneaut Railroad Museum, Depot St, Conneaut, OH 44030 - T: (440) 599-7878
Science&Tech Museum - 1962
Engines, hopper car, wood caboose, Red River Line, Ashtabula disaster 1876, models 42609

Connersville IN

Henry H. Blommel Historic Automotive Data Collection, 427 E County Rd, 215 S, Connersville, IN 47331 - T: (317) 825-9259. Cur.: Henry H. Blommel
Science&Tech Museum - 1928
Automotive industry 42610

Constantine MI

John S. Barry Historical Society Museum, 300 N Washington, Constantine, MI 49042 - T: (616) 435-5825, 435-5385. Pres.: Dr. Vercler
Local Museum - 1945
Local history, 1835-1847 Governor Barry House 42611

Conway AR

Faulkner County Museum, Courthouse Sq, 805 Locust St, Conway, AR 72032 - T: (501) 329-5918, E-mail: fcm@conwaycorp.net. Dir.: Lyntia Langley-Ware
Local Museum - 1992
Local history 42612

Conway SC

Horry County Museum, 428 Main St, Conway, SC 29526 - T: (803) 248-1282, Fax: (843) 248-1854, E-mail: hcmuseum@sccoast.net. C.E.O.: Stewart J. Pabst, Dep. Dir.: Terri Hooks
Historical Museum / Ethnology Museum / Archaeological Museum - 1979
Anthropology, history, archaeology 42613

Cookeville TN

Cookeville Art Gallery, 186 S Walnut, Cookeville, TN 38501 - T: (615) 526-2424. Pres.: Linda McGraw
Public Gallery - 1961 42614

Cookeville Depot Museum, 116 W Broad St, Cookeville, TN 38503 - T: (931) 528-8570, Fax: (931) 526-1167, E-mail: depot@ci.cookeville.tn.us. Dir.: Judy Duke
Science&Tech Museum - 1984
Transportation, railroads 42615

Coolidge AZ

Casa Grande Ruins, 1100 Ruins Dr, Coolidge, AZ 85228 - T: (520) 723-3172, Fax: (520) 723-7209, E-mail: peggy_carter@nps.gov, Internet: www.cagr.nps.gov
Historic Site / Archaeological Museum - 1892
Archaeology, located on Hohokam village, approx. A.D. 500-1450 42616

Coolspring PA

Coolspring Power Museum, Main St, Coolspring, PA 15730 - T: (814) 849-6883, Fax: (814) 849-5495, E-mail: coolspring@penn.com, Internet: www.coolspringpowermuseum.org. Dir.: John Wilcox, Weldon Forman, Preston Foster, Edward Kuntz, Vance Packard, John Kline, Dir./Cur.: Paul Harvey
Science&Tech Museum - 1985
Internal combustion engine technology, electric generators, oil field technology 42617

Cooperstown NY

The Farmers' Museum, Lake Rd, Cooperstown, NY 13326 - T: (607) 547-1450, Fax: (607) 547-1499, E-mail: info@nysha.org, Internet: www.farmersmuseum.org. Dir.: Dr. Gilbert T. Vincent, Chief Cur.: Paul D'Ambrosio, Cons.: C.R. Jones
Open Air Museum / Agriculture Museum - 1943
Early 19th-century Village, agricultural tools and implements 42618

Fenimore Art Museum, Lake Rd, Cooperstown, NY 13326 - T: (607) 547-1400, Fax: (607) 547-1404, E-mail: info@nysha.org, Internet: www.nysha.org. Dir.: Dr. Gilbert T. Vincent, Cons.: C.R. Jones, Cur.: Paul D'Ambrosio
Fine Arts Museum - 1899 42619

National Baseball Hall of Fame and Museum, 25 Main St, Cooperstown, NY 13326 - T: (607) 547-7200, Fax: (607) 547-2044, E-mail: info@baseballhalloffame.org., Internet: www.baseballhalloffame.org. Cur.: Peter P. Clark (Collections), Ted Spencer (Exhibits), Libr.: Jim Gates
Special Museum - 1936 42620

Coopersville MI

The Coopersville Area Historical Society Museum, 363 Main St, Coopersville, MI 49404 - T: (616) 837-6978, Internet: www.coopersville.com. C.E.O.: Lillian Budzynski
Local Museum
Railroad, gold records, Del Shannon, an early rock-n-roll star 42621

Coos Bay OR

Coos Art Museum, 235 Anderson, Coos Bay, OR 97420 - T: (541) 267-3901, Fax: (541) 267-4877, Internet: www.coosart.org. Pres.: Lynda Shapiro
Fine Arts Museum - 1950 42622

Copper Center AK

George I. Ashby Memorial Museum, Mile 101, Old Richardson Hwy, Copper Center Loop Rd, Copper Center, AK 99573 - T: (907) 822-5285. Pres.: Fred Williams
Local Museum 42623

Copper Harbor MI

Fort Wilkins Historic Complex, Fort Wilkins, Copper Harbor, MI 49918 - T: (906) 289-4215, Fax: (906) 289-4939, Internet: www.michiganhistory.org. Head: Dan Plesher
Local Museum - 1923
Outdoor museum incl Fort Wilkins, Pittsburgh and Boston Co. Mine, lighthouse 42624

Coral Gables FL

Coral Gables Merrick House, 907 Coral Way, Coral Gables, FL 33134 - T: (305) 460-5361, 460-5095, Fax: (305) 460-5097, E-mail: cmcgeehan@citybeautiful.net, Internet: www.citybeautiful.net
Decorative Arts Museum - 1976
Plantation house belonging to family of founder of Coral Gables 42625

Creatabilitoys! - Museum of Advertising Icons, 1550 Madruga Av, Coral Gables, FL 33146 - T: (305) 663-7374, Fax: (305) 669-0092, E-mail: info@creatability.com, Internet: www.toymuseum.com. Dir.: Ritchie Lucas, Cur.: Carmen Rodriguez
Decorative Arts Museum - 1995
Toys and dolls 42626

The Florida Museum of Hispanic and Latin American Art, 4006 Aurora St, Coral Gables, FL 33126-1414 - T: (305) 444-7060, Fax: (305) 261-6996, E-mail: Hispmuseum@aol.com, Internet: www.latinoweb.com/museo/. Pres.: Raul M. Oyuela
Fine Arts Museum - 1991
Art 42627

Lowe Art Museum, University of Miami, 1301 Stanford Dr, Coral Gables, FL 33124-6310 - T: (305) 284-3603, Fax: (305) 284-2024, E-mail: bdursum@miami.edu, Internet: www.lowemuseum.org. Dir./Chief Cur.: Brian A. Dursum, Cur.: Margaret Jackson (Pre-Columbian Art), Marcilene Wittmer (African Art), Perri L. Roberts (Renaissance)
Fine Arts Museum / University Museum - 1950 42628

Coral Springs FL

Coral Springs Museum of Art, 2855 Coral Springs Dr, Coral Springs, FL 33065 - T: (954) 340-5000, Fax: (954) 346-4424, E-mail: ctbok@coral-springs.com, Internet: www.coralsprings.org/arts/museum/htm. Dir.: Barbara K. O'Keefe
Fine Arts Museum - 1997
Visual arts of Florida residents 42629

Coralville IA

Johnson County Historical Society Museum, 310 Fifth St, Coralville, IA 52241 - T: (319) 351-5738, Fax: (319) 351-5310, E-mail: joctyhistsociety@yahoo.com. Pres.: John Chadima, Exec. Dir.: Laurie Robinson
Local Museum - 1973
Local history 42630

Cordele GA

Georgia Veterans Memorial Museum, 2459-A Hwy 280 W, Cordele, GA 31015 - T: (912) 276-2371, Fax: (912) 276-2372, E-mail: gavets@sowega.net. Head: Charles Luther
Military Museum - 1962
Military hist 42631

Cordova AK

Cordova Historical Museum, 622 First St, Cordova, AK 99574 - T: (907) 424-6665, Fax: (907) 424-6666, E-mail: cdvmsm@ptialaska.net. Dir.: Cathy R. Sherman
Local Museum - 1966
Fishing artifacts, railway, lighthouse, Native Americans 42632

Corinth MS

Jacinto Courthouse, Corinth, MS 38835-1174 - T: (601) 286-8662, Fax: (601) 286-6777
Historical Museum - 1966 42633

Northeast Mississippi Museum, 204 E 4th St, Corinth, MS 38834 - T: (662) 287-3120, Fax: (662) 287-3120, E-mail: nemma@tsixroads.com. Cur.: Kristy White
Local Museum - 1980
Fossils, American Indian, Civil War, railroad, local arts and crafts 42634

Corning NY

Benjamin Patterson Inn Museum Complex, 59 W Pulteney St, Corning, NY 14830-2212 - T: (607) 937-5281, Fax: (607) 937-5281, E-mail: benpatt@juno.com. Pres.: Theone Gestwicki, Dir.: Roger Grigsby
Historical Museum - 1976 42635

Corning Glass Center, 1 Museum Way, Corning, NY 14830 - T: (607) 937-5371, Fax: (607) 974-8470, E-mail: cmg@cmog.org, Internet: www.cmog.org. Dir.: David B. Whitehouse, Cur.: Dr. Jutta Annette
Decorative Arts Museum - 1951 42636

Corning Museum of Glass, 1 Corning Glass Center, Corning, NY 14830-2253 - T: (607) 937-5371, Fax: (607) 974-8470, E-mail: cmg@cmog.org, Internet: www.cmog.org. Dir.: David B. Whitehouse, Dep. Dir.: Jane S. Spillman, Cur.: Dr. Jutta Annette Page, Libr.: Patricia Rogers
Decorative Arts Museum - 1951 42637

Rockwell Museum of Western Art, 111 Cedar St, Corning, NY 14830-2694 - T: (607) 937-5386, Fax: (607) 974-4536, E-mail: info@rockwellmuseum.org, Internet: www.rockwellmuseum.org. Dir.: Kristin Swain, Sc. Staff: Joyce Penn
Fine Arts Museum / Decorative Arts Museum - 1976 42638

Cornish NH

Saint Gaudens National Historic Site, Saint Gaudens Rd, Cornish, NH 03745 - T: (603) 675-2175, Fax: (603) 675-2701, E-mail: saga@nps.gov, Internet: www.nps.gov/saga/index.html. Dir.: John Dryfhout, Cur.: Henry J. Duffy
Fine Arts Museum - 1926 42639

Cornwall CT

Cornwall Historical Museum, 7 Pine St, Cornwall, CT 06753. Pres.: Michael R. Gannett
Local Museum - 1964
Local history 42640

Cornwall PA

Cornwall Iron Furnace, Rexmont Rd at Boyd St, Cornwall, PA 17016 - T: (717) 272-9711, Fax: (717) 272-0450. Head: Stephen G. Somers
Science&Tech Museum - 1931 42641

Cornwall-on-Hudson NY

Museum of the Hudson Highlands, The Boulevard, Cornwall-on-Hudson, NY 12520 - T: (845) 534-5506, Fax: (845) 534-4581, E-mail: rzito@museumhudsonhighlands.org, Internet: www.museumhudsonhighlands.org. Chm.: Ed Hoyd
Fine Arts Museum / Natural History Museum - 1962 42642

Corpus Christi TX

Art Museum of South Texas, 1902 N Shoreline, Corpus Christi, TX 78401 - T: (361) 825-3500, Fax: (361) 825-3520, E-mail: stiaweb@mail.tamucc.edu, Internet: www.stia.org. Dir.: Dr. William G. Otton, Ass. Dir.: Marilyn Smith, Ass. Cur.: Michelle Locke
Fine Arts Museum - 1960
Art 42643

Asian Cultures Museum, 1809 N Champarral St, Corpus Christi, TX 78401 - T: (361) 882-2641, Fax: (361) 882-5718, E-mail: asiancm@yahoo.com, Internet: www.geocities.com/asiancm. C.E.O.: Dongwol Kim Robertson
Decorative Arts Museum - 1973 42644

Corpus Christi Museum of Science and History, 1900 N Chaparral, Corpus Christi, TX 78401 - T: (512) 883-2862, Fax: (512) 884-7392, Internet: www.ci.corpus-christi.tx.us/services/museum. Dir.: Richard R. Stryker, Cur.: Donald P. Zuris, Jane Deisler-Seno (Science)
Local Museum - 1957
Local hist 42645

Joseph A. Cain Memorial Art Gallery, c/o Del Mar College, 101 Baldwin, Corpus Christi, TX 78404-3897 - T: (361) 698-1216, Fax: (361) 698-1511, E-mail: elambert@delmar.edu, Internet: www.delmar.edu. Dir.: William E. Lambert
Fine Arts Museum - 1932
Drawings and small sculpture 42646

USS Lexington Museum on the Bay, 2914 N Shoreline Blvd, Corpus Christi, TX 78402 - T: (800) ladylex, Fax: (361) 883-8361, Internet: www.usslexington.com. Exec. Dir.: Frank Montesano, Dir.: M. Charles Reustle
Military Museum - 1991
Naval military hist 42647

Weil Art Gallery, c/o Texas A&M University, 6300 Ocean Dr, Corpus Christi, TX 78412 - T: (361) 825-2314/17, Fax: (361) 994-6097, E-mail: anderson@falcon.tamucc.edu, Internet: www2.tamurc.edu/~dvpa/artsite/gallery. Dir.: Mark Anderson
Fine Arts Museum / University Museum - 1979
Contemporary Texas and Mexican art 42648

Corry PA

Corry Area Historical Society Museum, 937 Mead Av, Corry, PA 16407 - T: (814) 664-4749, Internet: www.tbscc.com. Pres.: James R. Nelson
Local Museum - 1965
locomotive, generalogy research 42649

Corsicana TX

Navarro County Historical Society Museum, 912 W Park Av, Corsicana, TX 75110 - T: (903) 654-4846. Cur.: Bobbie Young
Local Museum - 1958
8 log buildings contructed in Navarro County during 1838-1865 42650

Cortez CO

Crow Canyon Archaeological Center, 23390 County Rd K, Cortez, CO 81321 - T: (970) 565-8975, Fax: (970) 565-4859, E-mail: cleoncini@crowcanyon.org, Internet: www.crowcanyon.org. C.E.O.: Ricky Lightfoot
Archaeological Museum - 1983
Archaeology 42651

Cortland NY

1890 House-Museum and Center for Victorian Arts, 37 Tompkins St, Cortland, NY 13045-2555 - T: (607) 756-7551. Pres.: Joseph Puzo, C.E.O.: Teresa Roberts
Decorative Arts Museum / Fine Arts Museum - 1975 42652

Bowers Science Museum, Bowers Hall, State University of New York at Cortland, Cortland, NY 13045 - T: (607) 753-2900, Fax: (607) 753-2927, Internet: www.cortland.edu. Dir./Cur.: Dr. Peter K. Ducey
University Museum / Natural History Museum / Science&Tech Museum - 1964 42653

Cortland County Historical Society Museum, 25 Homer Av, Cortland, NY 13045 - T: (607) 753-4216, Fax: (607) 753-5728, E-mail: graffa@cortland.edu, Internet: www.cortland.edu/art/dowd.html. Dir.: Allison Graff
Local Museum - 1925
library 42654

Dowd Fine Arts Gallery, State University of New York, Suny Cortland, Cortland, NY 13045 - T: (607) 753-4216, Fax: (607) 753-5728, E-mail: graffa@cortland.edu, Internet: www.cortland.edu/art/dowd.html. Dir.: Allison Graff
Fine Arts Museum / University Museum - 1967
Art gallery 42655

Corvallis OR

Corvallis Art Center, Oregon State University, 700 SW Madison, Corvallis, OR 97331-4501 - T: (541) 754-1551
Public Gallery 42656

Fairbanks Gallery, c/o Oregon State University, 106 Fairbank Hall, Corvallis, OR 97331-4501 - T: (541) 737-5009, Fax: (541) 737-5372, E-mail: drussell@orst.edu. Dir.: Douglas Russell
Fine Arts Museum / University Museum 42657

Giustina Gallery, c/o Oregon State University, La Sells Stewart Center, 875 SW 26th St, Corvallis, OR 97331-4501 - T: (541) 737-2402, Fax: (541) 737-3187. Dir.: Melanie Fahrenbruch
Fine Arts Museum / University Museum 42658

Greensward Gallery, Oregon State University, 968 NW Circle Blvd, Corvallis, OR 97331-4501 - T: (541) 754-0204
Public Gallery 42659

Memorial Union Art Gallery, c/o Oregon State University, Memorial Union, Corvallis, OR 97331-4501 - T: (541) 737-8511, Fax: (541) 737-1565, E-mail: kent.sumner@mu.orst.edu, Internet: www.osumu.org/mu/events_coucourse1.htm. Dir.: Kent Sumner
Fine Arts Museum / University Museum
Paintings, sculptur, prints 42660

Corydon IA

Prairie Trails Museum of Wayne County, Hwy 2 E, Corydon, IA 50060 - T: (641) 872-2211, Fax: (641) 872-2664. Pres.: Hal Greenlee
Local Museum - 1942
General museum 42661

Coshocton OH

Johnson-Humrickhouse Museum, Roscoe Village, 300 N Whitewoman St, Coshocton, OH 43812 - T: (740) 622-8710, Fax: (740) 622-8710, E-mail: jhmuseum@clover.net, Internet: jhm.lib.oh.us. Dir.: Patti Malenke
Local Museum - 1931
American Indian, Japanese, Chinese, American and European decorative arts, weapon, Ohio history 42662

Roscoe Village Foundation, 381 Hill St, Coshocton, OH 43812 - T: (740) 622-9310, Fax: (614) 623-6555, E-mail: rvmarketing@coshocton.com, Internet: www.roscoevillage.com. Dir.: John Rodriguez (Landscaping), Thomas Mackie (History and Education), Sc. Staff: Wilma Hunt (History)
Historic Site / Open Air Museum - 1968 42663

Cottage Grove OR

Cottage Grove Museum, 147 High St and Birch Av, Cottage Grove, OR 97424 - T: (541) 942-3963. Head: Isabelle S. Woolcott
Local Museum - 1961
Local hist 42664

Cottonwood ID

The Historical Museum at Saint Gertrude, Keuterville Rd, Cottonwood, ID 83522-9408 - T: (208) 962-7123, Fax: (208) 962-8647, E-mail: museum@velocitus.net, Internet: www.historicalmuseumatstgertrude.com. Dir.: Lyle Wirtanen, Cur.: Mary Cay Henry
Local Museum - 1931 42665

Cottonwood Falls KS

Chase County Museum, 301 Broadway, Cottonwood Falls, KS 66845 - T: (620) 273-8500, Internet: skyways.lib.ks.us/genweb/society/cottonwd/
Local Museum - 1934
Old tools, household items 42666

Roniger Memorial Museum, 315 Union, Cottonwood Falls, KS 66845 - T: (316) 273-6310, 273-6412, Fax: (316) 273-6671, E-mail: dcroy@kansas.net. Pres./Cur.: David E. Croy
Historical Museum / Special Museum - 1959
History, old courthouse 42667

Cotuit MA

Cahoon Museum of American Art, 4676 Falmouth Rd, Cotuit, MA 02635 - T: (508) 428-7581, Fax: (508) 420-3709, E-mail: cmaa@cahoonmuseum.org, Internet: www.cahoonmuseum.org. C.E.O.: Cindy Nickerson
Fine Arts Museum - 1984 42668

Historical Society of Santuit and Cotuit, 1148 Main St, Cotuit, MA 02635 - T: (508) 428-0461. Pres.: Jessica Grassetti
Local Museum - 1954
Restored home of village carpenter, local history 42669

Cotulla TX

Brush Country Museum, 201 S Stewart, Cotulla, TX 78014 - T: (830) 879-2429, Internet: www.historicdistrict.com/museum. Cur.: Gwendolyn Cavanaugh
Local Museum - 1982 42670

Coudersport PA

Potter County Historical Society Museum, 308 N Main St, Coudersport, PA 16915 - T: (814) 274-4410, E-mail: pottercohist@adelphia.net, Internet: www.pottercountypa.net/history. Pres.: Leon B. Reed
Local Museum - 1919 42671

Coulee City WA

Dry Falls Interpretive Center, Sun Lakes State Park, 34875 Park Lake Rd NE, Coulee City, WA 99115 - T: (509) 632-5583, Fax: (509) 632-5971. Dir.: Mike Sternback
Local Museum - 1965
Local geological events, archaeology, anthropology, ethnology, Indian artifacts 42672

Council Bluffs IA

Historic General Dodge House, 605 3rd St, Council Bluffs, IA 51503 - T: (712) 322-2406, Fax: (712) 322-3504, E-mail: generaldodgehouse@alltel.net, Internet: www.councilbluffsiowa.com. Exec. Dir.: Kori L. Nielsen
Local Museum / Decorative Arts Museum - 1961
Historic house 42673

Council Grove KS

Kaw Mission, 500 N Mission, Council Grove, KS 66846 - T: (620) 767-5410, Fax: (620) 767-5816, E-mail: kawmission@cgtelco.net, Internet: www.kawmission.org. Cur.: Ron Parks
Ethnology Museum - 1951
19th c America, plains Indians 42674

Coupeville WA

Fort Casey Interpretive Center, 1280 Engle Rd, Coupeville, WA 98239 - T: (360) 679-7391, 678-4519, Fax: (360) 679-7327
Historical Museum / Military Museum
Coast artillery, natural history, sea life 42675

Gallery at the Wharf, Coupeville Arts Center, Coupeville, WA 98239, mail addr: POB 171, Coupeville, WA 98239 - T: (360) 678-3396, Fax: (360) 678-7420, E-mail: cac@whidbey.net. Exec. Dir.: Judy G. Lynn
Fine Arts Museum - 1989
Paintings, photography 42676

Island County Historical Society Museum, 908 NW Alexander St, Coupeville, WA 98239 - T: (360) 678-3310, Fax: (360) 678-1702, E-mail: ichscpul@whidbey.net
Local Museum - 1949 42677

Courtland VA

Rawls Museum Arts, 22376 Linden St, Courtland, VA 23837 - T: (757) 653-0754, Fax: (757) 653-0341, E-mail: rma@beldar.com, Internet: www.rawlsart.cjb.net. Dir.: Barbara Easton-Moore
Fine Arts Museum - 1958
Art, visual arts 42678

Coventry RI

Western Rhode Island Civic Museum, 7 Station St, Coventry, RI 02816 - T: (401) 821-4095. Pres.: Lynda Hawkins
Local Museum - 1945
Local hist 42679

Covington KY

Behringer-Crawford Museum, 1600 Montague Rd, Devou Park, Covington, KY 41012 - T: (859) 491-4003, Fax: (859) 491-4006. Dir.: Laurie Risch
Local Museum - 1950
Local hist 42680

The Railway Exposition, 315 W Southern Av, Covington, KY 41015 - T: (513) 761-3500
Science&Tech Museum - 1975
Railway 42681

Covington LA

Saint Tammany Art Gallery, 129 N New Hampshire St, Covington, LA 70433 - T: (985) 892-8650, Fax: (985) 898-0976, E-mail: staa1@juno.com
Public Gallery 42682

Covington TN

Tipton County Museum, 751 Bert Johnston Av, Covington, TN 38019 - T: (901) 476-0242, Fax: (901) 476-0261. Dir.: Alice Fisher
Local Museum
Military history, environmental education 42683

Coweta OK

Mission Bell Museum, 201 South Av B, Coweta, OK 74429 - T: (918) 486-2513, Fax: (918) 486-2513, E-mail: CowetaCham@aol.com
Local Museum - 1977 42684

Coxsackie NY

Bronck Museum, 90 County Rte 42, Coxsackie, NY 12051 - T: (518) 731-6490, Fax: (518) 731-7672, Internet: www.gchistory.org. C.E.O.: Robert Hallock
Local Museum - 1929
Vedder library 42685

Cozad NE

The 100th Meridian Museum, 206 E Eighth St, Cozad, NE 69130 - T: (308) 784-1100, 784-2704. Pres.: Morrie Andres, Rec.Sec.: Glenda France
Local Museum - 1994 42686

Craig CO

Museum of Northwest Colorado, 590 Yampa Av, Craig, CO 81625 - T: (970) 824-6360, Fax: (970) 824-7175, E-mail: musnwco@quik.com, Internet: www.museumnwco.org. Dir.: Dan Davidson, Ass. Dir.: Jan Gerber
Local Museum - 1964
Regional history 42687

Cranbury NJ

Cranbury Historical and Preservation Society Museum, 4 Park Pl E, Cranbury, NJ 08512 - T: (609) 395-0702, E-mail: historycenter@comcast.net, Internet: www.cranburylions.org/museum.htm. Pres.: Becky Beauregrand, Cur.: Don Jo Swanagan, Jerry Pevahouse
Historical Museum / Local Museum - 1967
History center, library 42688

Crawford NE

Fort Robinson Museum, US Hwy 20, Crawford, NE 69339 - T: (308) 665-2919, Fax: (308) 665-2917, E-mail: fortrob@bbc.net. Cur.: Thomas R. Buecker
Military Museum - 1956 42689

Crawfordsville IN

Ben-Hur Museum, Pike St at Wallace Av, Crawfordsville, IN 47933 - T: (765) 362-5769, 364-5175, Fax: (765) 364-5179, E-mail: study@wico.net, Internet: www.ben-hur.com. Dir.: Cheryl Keim
Historical Museum / Library with Exhibitions - 1896
1896 General Lew Wallace Study, author of 'Ben-Hur' - library 42690

The Lane Place, 212 S Water St, Crawfordsville, IN 47933 - T: (765) 362-3416, E-mail: mchs@wico.net. Pres.: Conrad Harvey, C.E.O.: Michael D. Hall
Historical Museum / Decorative Arts Museum - 1911
Home of Henry S. Lane, governor and senator of Indiana 42691

The Old Jail Museum, c/o Montgomery County Cultural Foundation, 225 N Washington, Crawfordsville, IN 47933 - T: (765) 362-5222, Fax: (765) 362-5222, E-mail: oldjail@tctc.com, Internet: crawfordsville.org/jail.html. Pres.: Sam Smith
Historical Museum - 1975
1882 Old Jail only remaining rotating circular jail still in working condition 42692

Crawfordville GA

Confederate Museum, 456 Alexander St, Crawfordville, GA 30631 - T: (706) 456-2221, 456-2602, Fax: (706) 456-2396, E-mail: ahsst@nu-2.net, Internet: www.g-net.net/~ahssp/
Historical Museum - 1952
History Museum 42693

Crazy Horse SD

Indian Museum of North America, Av of the Chiefs, Crazy Horse, SD 57730-9506 - T: (605) 673-4681, Fax: (605) 673-2185, E-mail: memorial@crazyhorse.org, Internet: www.crazyhorse.org. Dir.: Anne Ziolkowski
Ethnology Museum - 1972
Indian culture 42694

Crescent City CA

Del Norte County Historical Society Museum, 577 H St, Crescent City, CA 95531 - T: (707) 464-3922, E-mail: dnhissoc@northcoast.com. Pres.: Loren Bommerlyn
Local Museum - 1951 42695

Cresson TX

Pate Museum of Transportation, Hwy 377, Cresson, TX 76035, mail addr: 1227 W Magnolia Av, Ste 420, Fort Worth, TX 76104 - T: (817) 922-9504, Fax: (817) 922-9536. Cur.: Sue Baker
Science&Tech Museum - 1969
Antique and classic autos, aircraft, railroad artifacts, space exhibits 42696

Crestline OH

Crestline Shunk Museum, 211 Thoman St, Crestline, OH 44827 - T: (419) 683-3410. Pres.: Nancy Everly
Local Museum - 1947 42697

Creston IA

Union County Historical Complex, McKinley Park, Creston, IA 50801 - T: (515) 782-4247. Pres.: Paul Roeder
Local Museum / Open Air Museum - 1966
General and village museum, 10 pioneer bldgs 42698

Crestview KY

TM Gallery, c/o Thomas More College, 333 Thomas More Pkwy, Crestview, KY 41017 - T: (606) 344-3419/20, Fax: (606) 344-3345. Dir.: Barb Rauf
Fine Arts Museum
Drawings, graphics, photography, sculpture, ceramics 42699

Crestwood MO

Thomas Sappington House Museum, 1015 S Sappington Rd, Crestwood, MO 63126 - T: (314) 822-8171, Fax: (314) 129-4794, E-mail: lblumer@ci.crestwood.mo.us, Internet: www.ci.crestwood.mo.us. Pres.: Betty Oberhaus
Historical Museum - 1965 42700

Creswell NC

Somerset Place, 2572 Lake Shore Rd, Creswell, NC 27928 - T: (919) 797-4560, Fax: (919) 797-4171, E-mail: somerset@coastalnet.com, Internet: www.ah.dcr.state.nc.us/hs/somerset/somerset.htm. Head: Dorothy Spruill Redford
Local Museum - 1969 42701

Cripple Creek CO

Cripple Creek District Museum, 500 E Bennett Av, Cripple Creek, CO 80813 - T: (719) 689-9540, Fax: (719) 689-0512, E-mail: ccdistrictmuseum@aol.com, Internet: www.cripple-creek.co.us. Dir.: Erik Swanson
Fine Arts Museum / Local Museum - 1953
Local history, historic camp where gold was discovered in 1890 42702

Critz VA

Reynolds Homestead, 463 Homestead Ln, Critz, VA 24082 - T: (703) 694-7181, Fax: (703) 694-7183, E-mail: registrar.reynolds.homestead@vt.edu, Internet: www.cis.vt.edu/reynolds_homestead/defualt.html. Dir.: Joanne McNeal, Ass. Dir.: Carolyn Beale
Fine Arts Museum / Local Museum - 1970
Historic house 42703

Crockett TX

Discover Houston County Visitors Center-Museum, 303 S First St, Crockett, TX 75835 - T: (936) 544-9520, Fax: (936) 544-8053. Cur.: Eliza H. Bishop
Local Museum - 1983
Local hist 42704

Croghan NY

American Maple Museum, POB 81, Croghan, NY 13327 - T: (315) 346-1107. Pres.: Vernon Lyndaker, Cur.: Rene Moser
Agriculture Museum - 1977 42705

Crookston MN

Polk County Historical Museum, Hwy 2 E, Crookston, MN 56716 - T: (218) 281-1038, E-mail: polkcomuseum@rru.net, Internet: www.crookston.com. Pres./Cur.: Allen Brolsma
Local Museum - 1930
Regional history 42706

Crosby MN

Cuyuna Range Museum, 101 First St NE, Crosby, MN 56441 - T: (218) 546-5435
Local Museum - 1970 42707

Crosby ND

Divide County Historical Society Museum, Pioneer Village, Crosby, ND 58730 - T: (701) 965-6297. Pres.: Perry E. Rosenquist
Local Museum - 1969
Regional history 42708

Crosbyton TX

Crosby County Pioneer Memorial Museum, 101 W Main intersection U.S. 82 and F.M. 651, Crosbyton, TX 79322 - T: (806) 675-2331, 675-2906, Fax: (806) 675-7012, E-mail: ccpmm@door.net, Internet: www.crosbycountymuseum.com. Pres.: Gary Mitchel, Dir.: Linda Jones
Local Museum - 1958
Local hist 42709

Cross Creek FL

Marjorie Kinnan Rawlings Historic State Park, 187000 S County Rd 325, Cross Creek, FL 32640 - T: (352) 466-9273, Fax: (352) 466-4743, E-mail: mkrshs@bellsouth.net, Internet: www.dep.state.fl.us/parks/district2/marjoriekinnan
Historical Museum / Agriculture Museum - 1970
1930's citrus farm and home of Marjorie Kinnan Rawlings, a rambling Cracker farmhouse 42710

Cross River NY

Trailside Nature Museum, Ward Pound Ridge Reservation, Cross River, NY 10518 - T: (914) 864-7322, Fax: (914) 864-7321. Cur.: Beth Herr
Natural History Museum - 1937 42711

Crow Agency MT

Little Bighorn Battlefield Museum, I-90 and Hwy 212, Crow Agency, MT 59022, mail addr: POB 39, Crow Agency, MT 59022-0039 - T: (406) 638-2621 ext 110, Fax: (406) 638-2623, E-mail: Neil_Mangum@nps.gov, Internet: www.nps.gov. Cur.: Kitty Deernose
Historical Museum / Military Museum - 1940
Indian and military items, Sioux War 1876-90 42712

Crowley LA

Crowley Art Association and Gallery, 220 N Parkerson, Crowley, LA 70527-2003 - T: (337) 783-3747, Fax: (337) 783-3747
Fine Arts Museum / Decorative Arts Museum - 1980
Art gallery, crafts 42713

The Rice Museum, 6428 Airport Rd, Crowley, LA 70527-1176 - T: (337) 783-6417, Fax: (318) 788-0123, E-mail: crpwright@cs.com, Internet: www.crystalrice.com. Pres.: Diane Hoffpauer
Special Museum - 1970 42714

Crown Point NY

Crown Point State Historic Site, Bridge Rd, Crown Point, NY 12928 - T: (518) 597-3666, Fax: (518) 597-4668, E-mail: williamfarrar@oprhe.state.ny.us. Head: Bill Farar
Military Museum - 1910
1734 remains of French fort, 1759 British Fort Crown Point and Outwork fortifications controlling Lake Champlain 42715

Crystal River FL

Coastal Heritage Museum, 532 Citrus Av, Crystal River, FL 34429 - T: (352) 795-1755, 341-6428, Fax: (352) 341-6445. Dir.: Kathy Thompson
Local Museum - 1986
Citrus County hist, Aboriginal and Seminole Indian artifacts, archaeology 42716

Crystal River State Archaeological Site, 3400 N Museum Pt, Crystal River, FL 34428 - T: (352) 795-3817, Fax: (352) 795-6061, E-mail: crsas@flanet.com, Internet: www.floridastateparks.org
Archaeological Museum - 1965 42717

Cuddebackville NY

Neversink Valley Area Museum, D and H Canal Park, Hoag Rd, Cuddebackville, NY 12729 - T: (845) 754-8870, E-mail: nvam@magiccarpet.com, Internet: www.neversinkmuseum.org. C.E.O.: Stephen. Skye
Local Museum / Natural History Museum - 1964 42718

Cuero TX

DeWitt County Historical Museum, 312 E Broadway, Cuero, TX 77954 - T: (361) 275-6322, Internet: www.cuero.org. Chm.: Elizabeth Haun
Local Museum - 1973
Local hist 42719

Culbertson MT

Culbertson Museum, Hwy 2 E, Culbertson, MT 59218, mail addr: POB 95, Culbertson, MT 59218-0095 - T: (406) 787-6320, 787-5337
Local Museum - 1990
Hist in northeastern Montana 42720

Northeastern Montana Threshers and Antique Association Museum, POB 12, Culbertson, MT 59218 - T: (406) 787-5265, E-mail: elk1@nemontel.net. Vice Pres.: David Krogedal
Agriculture Museum - 1964 42721

Cullman AL

Cullman County Museum, 211 Second Av NE, Cullman, AL 35055 - T: (256) 739-1258, Fax: (256) 737-8782, E-mail: efuller@hiwaay.net, Internet: www.cullman.com/museum. Dir.: Elaine L. Fuller
Local Museum - 1975
Local history, housed in replica of 1873 home of Col. John G. Cullman, founder of Cullman 42722

Cullowhee NC

Mountain Heritage Center, Western Carolina University, Cullowhee, NC 28723 - T: (828) 227-7129, Internet: www.wcu.edu/mhc. Dir.: H. Tyler Blethen, Cur.: Suzanne McDowell
Historical Museum / University Museum - 1975 42723

Cumberland MD

Allegany County Historical Museum, 218 Washington St, Cumberland, MD 21502 - T: (301) 777-8678, Fax: (301) 777-8678 ext 51, E-mail: hhouse@allconet.org, Internet: historyhouse.allconet.org. Dir.: Sharon Nealis, Cur.: Wilma Thompson
Local Museum - 1937
Historic house, regional history 42724

Cumberland Theatre Arts Gallery, 101-103 N Johnson St, Cumberland, MD 21502 - T: (301) 759-4990, Fax: (301) 777-7092, E-mail: ctdon@mindspring.com, Internet: www.cumberlandtheatre.com
Performing Arts Museum - 1987 42725

George Washington's Headquarters, Greene St, Cumberland, MD 21502 - T: (301) 759-6636, Fax: (301) 759-3223, E-mail: djohnson@allconet.org, Internet: www.ci.cumberland.md.us. Dir.: Diane Johnson
Historical Museum - 1925
1755 log cabin built during the French and Indian war 42726

Cummington MA

Kingman Tavern Historical Museum, 41 Main St, Cummington, MA 01026 - T: (413) 634-5527, 634-5335. Head: Stephen Howese
Local Museum - 1967
Local history, frame bldg used as a post office, Masonic Lodge meeting hall and tavern 42727

William Cullen Bryant Homestead, 207 Bryant Rd, Cummington, MA 01026 - T: (413) 634-2244, Fax: (413) 296-5239, E-mail: bryanthomestead@ttor.org, Internet: www.therrustees.org. C.E.O.: Andy Kendall
Special Museum - 1928
Boyhood home and stuff summer residence of literary figure William Cullen Bryant 42728

Cupertino CA

Cupertino Historical Museum, 10185 N Stelling Rd, Cupertino, CA 95014 - T: (408) 973-1495, Fax: (408) 973-1495, E-mail: cuphistorysoc@juno.com. Dir.: Ethel Worn
Local Museum - 1990
Local history, farming, blacksmith tools, furniture, clothing - archive 42729

Euphrat Museum of Art, De Anza College, 21250 Stevens Creek Blvd, Cupertino, CA 95014 - T: (408) 864-8836, Fax: (408) 864-8738. Dir.: Jan Rindfleisch
University Museum / Fine Arts Museum - 1971
Contemporary paintings, prints and photographs, sculpture 42730

Currie MN

End-O-Line Railroad Museum, 440 N Mill St, Currie, MN 56123-1004 - T: (507) 763-3708, 763-3113, Fax: (507) 763-3708, E-mail: louise@endoline.com, Internet: www.endoline.com. Dir.: Louise Gervais, Ass. Dir.: David J. Hansen
Science&Tech Museum - 1972
Railroads 42731

Currie NC

Moores Creek National Battlefield, 40 Patriots Hall Dr, Currie, NC 28435 - T: (910) 283-5591, Fax: (910) 283-5351, Internet: www.nps.gov/mocr. Dir.: Ann Childress
Open Air Museum / Military Museum - 1926 42732

Cushing OK

Cimarron Valley Railroad Museum, South Kings Hwy, Cushing, OK 74023 - T: (918) 225-3936, 225-1657. Cur.: Robert F. Read
Science&Tech Museum - 1970 42733

Custer SD

Custer County 1881 Courthouse Museum, 411 Mount Rushmore Rd, Custer, SD 57730 - T: (605) 673-2443, Fax: (605) 673-2443. C.E.O.: Dan McPherson
Local Museum - 1974
Local hist 42734

National Museum of Woodcarving, Hwy 16 W, Custer, SD 57730 - T: (605) 673-4404, Fax: (605) 673-3843, E-mail: woodcarv@gwtc.net, Internet: www.blackhills.com/woodcarving/index. C.E.O.: Dale Schaffer
Fine Arts Museum - 1966
Woodcarvings 42735

Cuyahoga Falls OH

Richard Gallery and Almond Tea Gallery, 2250 Front St, Cuyahoga Falls, OH 44221 - T: (330) 929-1575, E-mail: jrichard@gallery.com. Dir.: Jack Richard
Fine Arts Museum - 1960
Local, regional and national works of art 42736

Cypress CA

Fine Arts Gallery, c/o Cypress College, 9200 Valley View St, Cypress, CA 90630 - T: (714) 484-7133, Fax: (714) 527-8238. Dir.: Betty Disney
Fine Arts Museum - 1969 42737

Dade City FL

Pioneer Florida Museum, 15602 Pioneer Museum Rd, Dade City, FL 33523 - T: (352) 567-0262, Fax: (352) 567-1262, E-mail: pioneer@innet.com, Internet: www.dadecity.com/museum. Pres.: Eileen Herman, Cur.: Donna Swart
Historical Museum / Agriculture Museum - 1961 42738

Dahlonega GA

Dahlonega Courthouse Gold Museum, 1 Public Sq, Dahlonega, GA 30533 - T: (706) 864-2257, Fax: (706) 864-8370, E-mail: dgmgold@alltel.net, Internet: www.ngeorgia.com/parks/dahlonega.html. Head: Sharon Johnson
Historical Museum / Science&Tech Museum - 1966
Tools and equipment, personal artefacts, furnishings 42739

Dakota City IA

Humboldt County Historical Association Museum, 905 First Av N, Dakota City, IA 50529 - T: (515) 332-5280, 332-3449. Dir.: Bette Newton
Local Museum - 1962 42740

Dalhart TX

Dallam-Hartley XIT Museum, 108 E 5th St, Dalhart, TX 79022 - T: (806) 244-4838, Fax: (806) 244-3031, E-mail: xitmusm@xit.net. Dir.: Nicky L. Olson
Local Museum - 1975
Local history and ranching 42741

Dallas NC

Gaston County Museum of Art and History, 131 W Main St, Dallas, NC 28034 - T: (704) 922-7681, Fax: (704) 922-7683, E-mail: museum@co.gaston.nc.us, Internet: www.gastoncountymuseum.org. Dir.: Barbara H. Brose
Fine Arts Museum / Local Museum - 1975 42742

Dallas TX

African American Museum, 3536 Grand Av, Dallas, TX 75210, mail addr: POB 150153, Dallas, TX 75315 - T: (214) 565-9026, Fax: (214) 421-8204
Folklore Museum / Historical Museum - 1974
African American fine art and folk art, Texas Black hist 42743

The Age of Steam Railroad Museum, 1105 Washington St, Fair Park, Dallas, TX 75210 - T: (214) 428-0101, Fax: (214) 426-1937, E-mail: info@dallasrailwaymuseum.com, Internet: www.dallasrailwaymuseum.com. Pres.: Robert Willis, Exec. Dir.: Robert LaPrelle
Science&Tech Museum - 1963
Railroad 42744

American Museum of the Miniature Arts, 2201 N Lamar St, Dallas, TX 75202 - T: (214) 969-5502, 969-5997, Fax: (214) 969-5997, E-mail: minimuseum@aol.com. Exec. Dir.: Janet Wilhite
Decorative Arts Museum - 1988
Dolls, house designs, miniature room boxes, vignettes, antique toys, militaria scenes 42745

Biblical Arts Center, 7500 Park Ln, Dallas, TX 75225 - T: (214) 691-4662, Fax: (214) 691-4752, E-mail: rjmach329@aol.com, Internet: www.biblicalarts.org. Dir.: Ronnie L Roese, Cur.: Susan E Metcalf, Scott Peck
Religious Arts Museum - 1966
Religious art 42746

Cultural Heritage Center, Davy Crockett School, 401 N Carroll, Dallas, TX 75246 - T: (214) 841-5355. Dir.: Dr. Doris Freeling
Decorative Arts Museum - 1976
Decorative arts 42747

The Dallas Center for Contemporary Art, 2801 Swiss Av, Dallas, TX 75204-5925 - T: (214) 821-2522, Fax: (214) 821-9103, E-mail: thecontemporary@mindspring.com, Internet: www.thecontemporary.net. Exec. Dir.: Joan Davidow
Fine Arts Museum / Public Gallery - 1981 42748

Dallas Historical Society Museum, Hall of State, Fair Park, 3939 Grand Av, Dallas, TX 75315 - T: (214) 421-4500, Fax: (214) 421-7500, E-mail: dhs@dallashistory.org, Internet: www.dallashistory.org. Dir.: Lisa Hemby
Local Museum - 1922
Local hist 42749

Dallas Holocaust Memorial Center, 7900 Northaven, Dallas, TX 75230 - T: (214) 750-4654, Fax: (214) 750-4672, E-mail: info@dallasholocaustmemorialcenter.org, Internet: www.dallasholocaustmemorialcenter.org. Pres.: Michael Schiff, Exec. Dir.: Elliott Dlin
Historical Museum - 1984
Holocaust memorial - library 42750

Dallas Museum of Art, 1717 N Harwood St, Dallas, TX 75201 - T: (214) 922-1200, 954-0234, Fax: (214) 922-1350, E-mail: judyc@cdm-art.org, Internet: www.dallasmuseumofart.org. Dir.: Dr. John R. Lane, Cur.: Charles Wylie (Contemporary Art), Dr. Dorothy Kosinski (European Art), Dr. Anne Bromberg (Ancient Art), Carol Robbins (New World and Pacific Cultures), Suzanne Weaver (Contemporary Art), Bonni Pitman (Deputy Director)
Fine Arts Museum - 1903 42751

Dallas Museum of Natural History, Fair Park, 3535 Grand Av, Dallas, TX 75210 - T: (214) 421-3466 ext 200, Fax: (214) 428-4356, E-mail: www.@dmnhnet.org, Internet: www.dallasdino.org. C.E.O.: Nicole G. Small, Cur.: Avelino Segura (Exhibits), Alex Barker (Archaeology), Anthony Fiorillo (Paleontology)
Natural History Museum - 1935
Natural hist 42752

Frontiers of Flight Museum, 8008 Cedar Springs Blvd, Dallas, TX 75235 - T: (214) 350-3600, 350-1651, Fax: (214) 351-0101, E-mail: info@flightmuseum.com, Internet: www.flightmuseum.com. Dir.: Dan Hamilton, Cur.: Knox Bishop
Science&Tech Museum - 1988
Aeronautical history 42753

International Museum of Cultures, 7500 W Camp Wisdom Rd, Dallas, TX 75236 - T: (972) 708-7537, Fax: (972) 708-7341, E-mail: imc_museum@sil.org, Internet: www.sil.org/imc/. Dir.: Marie Fae Kamm, Cur.: Gary Eastty
Ethnology Museum - 1974
Anthropology 42754

Meadows Museum, c/o Southern Methodist University, 5900 Bishop Blvd, Dallas, TX 75205 - T: (214) 768-2516, Fax: (214) 768-1688, E-mail: amyd@mail.smu.edu, Internet: www.meadowsmuseum.smu.edu. Dir.: Greg Warden, Cur.: Dr. Mark Roglán-Kelly
Fine Arts Museum / University Museum - 1965
Spanish art 42755

Old City Park - The Historical Village of Dallas, 1717 Gano St, Dallas, TX 75215 - T: (214) 421-5162, Fax: (214) 428-6351, E-mail: dagns@airmail.net, Internet: www.oldcitypark.org. Dir.: Gary N. Smith, Jennifer Bransom, Cur.: Hal Simon
Local Museum - 1966
Historic village 42756

Sixth Floor Museum at Dealey Plaza, 411 Elm St, Ste 120, Dallas, TX 75202 - T: (214) 747-6660, Fax: (214) 747-6662, E-mail: jfk@jfk.org, Internet: www.jfk.org. C.E.O.: Jeff West
Historical Museum - 1989
John F. Kennedy and the memory of a nation 42757

The Southland Art Collection, 2711 N Haskell, Dallas, TX 75221-0711 - T: (214) 828-7011. Cur.: Richard Allen
Fine Arts Museum
Paintings, sculpture, photography, works on paper 42758

Southwest Museum of Science and Technology, 1318 Second Av in Fair Park, Dallas, TX 75210 - T: (214) 428-5555, Fax: (214) 428-2033, E-mail: dhueter@scienceplace.org, Internet: www.scienceplace.org. C.E.O.: Diana Hueter
Science&Tech Museum - 1946
Science and technology 42759

Trammell and Margaret Crow Collection of Asian Art, 2010 Flora St, Dallas, TX 75201-2335 - T: (214) 979-6432, Fax: (214) 979-6439, E-mail: education@crowollection.com, Internet: crowcollection.org
Fine Arts Museum - 1998
Arts from Japan, China, Cambodia, India, Thailand, Myanmar and Tibet 42760

Women's Museum, 3800 Parry Av, Dallas, TX 75226 - T: (214) 915-0887, Fax: (214) 915-0870, E-mail: bbooker@thewomensmuseum.org, Internet: www.thewomensmuseum.org
Historical Museum - 1998 42761

The Dalles OR

Fort Dalles Museum, 500 W 15th St, The Dalles, OR 97058 - T: (541) 296-4547. Head: Sam Woolsey
Military Museum - 1951 42762

Wasco County Historical Museum, 5000 Discovery Dr, The Dalles, OR 97058 - T: (541) 296-8600, Fax: (541) 298-8660, E-mail: perry@gorgediscovery.org, Internet: www.gorgediscovery.org. Dir.: Michael L. Perry
Local Museum - 1997
Local hist 42763

Wonder Works Children's Museum, 419-East Second, The Dalles, OR 97058 - T: (541) 296-2444, Fax: (541) 298-1408. Pres.: Betsy Hege
Special Museum / Science&Tech Museum - 1977 42764

Dalton GA

Creative Arts Guild, 520 W Waugh St, Dalton, GA 30722-1485 - T: (706) 278-0168, Fax: (706) 278-6996, Internet: www.creativeartsguild.org. Pres.: John Hutchison
Fine Arts Museum - 1963
Paintings, prints, drawings, photos, sculptures 42765

Crown Gardens Museum, 715 Chattanooga Av, Dalton, GA 30720 - T: (706) 278-0217. Pres.: Marvin Sowder, Dir.: Marcelle White
Local Museum - 1977
1848 Blunt House, 1908 Wright Hotel-Chatsworth, 1840 John Hamilton House-Chatsworth Depot - archives 42766

Dalton MA

Crane Museum, Rtes 8 and 9, Dalton, MA 01226 - T: (413) 684-6481, Fax: (413) 684-0817, E-mail: info@crane.com, Internet: www.crane.com. Cur.: Charles Wellspeak, Carol Shea
Historical Museum / Science&Tech Museum - 1930
Industry, 1844 old stone mill 42767

Damariscotta ME

Round Top Center for the Arts - Arts Gallery, POB 1316, Damariscotta, ME 04543 - T: (207) 563-1507, E-mail: rtca@lincoln.midcoast.com, Internet: www.lincoln.midcoast.com/~artca
Fine Arts Museum - 1988 42768

Dana IN

Ernie Pyle House, 107 Maple, Dana, IN 47847-0338 - T: (765) 665-3633, Fax: (765) 665-9312, E-mail: erniepyle@abcs.com. Cur.: Rick Bray
Historical Museum - 1976
Birthplace of Ernie Pyle, noted WW II journalist 42769

Danbury CT

Danbury Museum, 43 Main St, Danbury, CT 06810 - T: (203) 743-5200, Fax: (203) 743-1131, E-mail: dmhs@danburyhistorical.org, Internet: www.danburyhistorical.org. Exec. Dir.: Birgid Durkin
Local Museum - 1942
Local history, Charles Ives birthplace 42770

Military Museum of Southern New England, 125 Park Av, Danbury, CT 06810 - T: (203) 790-9277, Fax: (203) 790-0420, E-mail: mmsne@juno.com, Internet: www.usmilitarymuseum.org. Exec. Dir.: Bernardo Ferreira
Military Museum - 1985
Military hist 42771

Danbury WI

Forts Folle Avoine Historic Park, 8500 County Rd U, Danbury, WI 54830 - T: (715) 866-8890, E-mail: fahp@centuryitel.net, Internet: www.mwd.com/burnett/. Dir.: Kevin Klucas
Local Museum - 1945
Fur trade 42772

Dania Beach FL

Graves Museum of Archaeology and Natural History → South Florida Museum of Natural History

South Florida Museum of Natural History, 481 S Federal Hwy, Dania Beach, FL 33004 - T: (954) 925-7770, Fax: (954) 925-7064, E-mail: digit@sfmuseumnh.org, Internet: www.sfmuseumnh.org. Dir.: Sharon McMorris, Cons.: James J. Sinclair (Marine Archaeology)
Archaeological Museum / Natural History Museum - 1980
Archaeology, paleontology, natural history 42773

Danvers MA

Danvers Historical Society Exhibition, 9 Page St, Danvers, MA 01923 - T: (978) 777-1666, Fax: (978) 777-5028, E-mail: danvershistoricalsociety@yahoo.com, Internet: www.danvershistory.org. Dir.: Glenn Uminowicz
Historical Museum - 1889
Local history 42774

Rebecca Nurse Homestead, 149 Pine St, Danvers, MA 01923 - T: (978) 774-8799, Internet: www.rebeccanurse.org/. Pres.: William Clemens, Cur.: Richard B. Trask
Historical Museum - 1974
1678 home of Rebecca Nurse, hanged as a witch in 1692 42775

Danville CA

Eugene O'Neill National Historic Site, POB 280, Danville, CA 94526 - T: (925) 838-0249, Fax: (925) 838-9471
Historical Museum - 1976
Clothing, jewelry, paintings, letters, photos, furnishings 42776

Danville IL

Vermilion County Museum, 116 N Gilbert St, Danville, IL 61832-8506 - T: (217) 442-2922, 442-2001, Fax: (217) 442-2001, Internet: www.vilmilioncountymuseum.org. Pres.: Donald Richter
Local Museum - 1964
History, housed in 1855 Dr. Fithian Home, doctor's residence, often visited by Abraham Lincoln 42777

Danville KY

Constitution Square, 134 S Second St, Danville, KY 40422 - T: (859) 239-7089, Fax: (859) 239-7894, E-mail: brenda.willoughby@mail.state.ky.us, Internet: www.kystateparks.com/agencies/parks/constsq2.htm. Head: Brenda Willoughby
Historic Site - 1937
Historic site 42778

McDowell House and Apothecary Shop, 125 S Second St, Danville, KY 40422 - T: (859) 236-2804, Fax: (859) 236-2804, E-mail: mcdhse@kih.net, Internet: www.mcdowellhouse.org. Dir.: Carol J. Senn, Cur.: George Grider
Historical Museum / Historic Site - 1939
McDowell House 1800, 1795 Apothecary shop 42779

Danville VA

Danville Museum of Fine Arts and History, 975 Main St, Danville, VA 24541 - T: (804) 793-5644, Fax: (804) 799-6145, E-mail: dmfah@gamewood.net, Internet: www.danvillemuseum.org. Exec. Dir.: Lynne Bjarnesen, Pres.: Robert Sexton
Fine Arts Museum / Historical Museum - 1974
Art, history 42780

Daphne AL

American Sport Art Museum and Archives, 1 Academy Dr, Daphne, AL 36526-7055 - T: (334) 626-3303, Fax: (334) 621-2527, E-mail: asama@ussa-sport.ussa.edu, Internet: www.asama.org. Cur.: Kay Daughdrill
Fine Arts Museum / University Museum / Special Museum - 1985 42781

Darien CT

Bates-Scofield Homestead, 45 Old King's Hwy, N, Darien, CT 06820 - T: (203) 655-9233. Dir.: Judith Geoppa, Cur.: Babs White (Cosumes), Lois Hofmann (Quilts)
Historical Museum - 1954 42782

Darien GA

Fort King George Historic Site, Fort King George Dr, Darien, GA 31305 - T: (912) 437-4770, Fax: (912) 437-5479, E-mail: ftkgeo@darientel.net, Internet: www.darientel.net/~ftkgeo. Head: Ken Akins
Historic Site / Historical Museum / Military Museum - 1961
Archaeology, photos, ethnography 42783

Darlington SC

Joe Weatherly Museum, 1301 Harry Byrd Hwy, Darlington, SC 29532 - T: (803) 395-8821, Fax: (803) 393-3911, E-mail: cmock@darlingtonraceway.com, Internet: www.darlingtonraceway.com
Science&Tech Museum - 1965
Stock cars 42784

Davenport IA

Davenport Museum of Art, 1737 W 12th St, Davenport, IA 52804 - T: (563) 326-7804, Fax: (563) 326-7876, E-mail: asc@ci.davenport.ia.us, Internet: www.art-dma.org. Dir.: Dr. William Steven Bradley, Cur.: Michelle Robinson, Libr.: Sheryl Haut
Fine Arts Museum - 1925
Art 42785

Putnam Museum of History and Natural Science, 1717 W 12th St, Davenport, IA 52804 - T: (563) 324-1933, Fax: (563) 324-6638, E-mail: museum@putnam.org, Internet: www.putnam.org. Dir.: Christopher J. Reich, Chief Cur.: Eunice Schlicting, Christine Chandler (Natural Science)
Historical Museum / Ethnology Museum / Natural History Museum - 1867
History, natural science, anthropology 42786

Davenport WA

Fort Spokane Visitor Center and Museum, HCR 11, POB 51, Davenport, WA 99122 - T: (509) 725-2715, 633-3836, Fax: (509) 633-3834
Military Museum - 1965
Military hist 42787

Lincoln County Historical Museum, 7th and Park, Davenport, WA 99122 - T: (509) 725-6711
Local Museum - 1972
Early agricultural tools, combine harvester, steam engine, cameras, printing tools, costumes, guns, Indian artifacts, railroad 42788

Davidson NC

William H. Van Every jr. and Edward M. Smith Galleries, c/o Davidson College, 315 N Main St, Davidson, NC 28036-1720 - T: (704) 894-2519, Fax: (704) 894-2691, E-mail: brthomas@davidson.edu, Internet: www.davidson.edu. Dir.: Brad Thomas
Fine Arts Museum - 1993
Graphics 42789

Davie FL

Young at Art Children's Museum, 11584 W State Rd 84, Davie, FL 33325 - T: (954) 424-0085 ext 21, Fax: (954) 370-5057, E-mail: postmaster@youngatartmuseum.org, Internet: www.youngatartmuseum.org. Dir.: Mindy Shrago, Ass. Dir.: Esther Shrago
Special Museum - 1985
Hands-On Children's museum 42790

Davis CA

Davis Art Center, 1919 F St, Davis, CA 95616 - T: (530) 756-4100, Fax: (530) 756-3041, E-mail: davisart@dcn.davis.ca.us. Dir.: Jackie Steven
Fine Arts Museum - 1959
Contemporary art 42791

Memorial Union Art Gallery, Memorial Union Bldg, University of California, Davis, CA 95616 - T: (530) 752-2885, Fax: (530) 754-4387, E-mail: hmmikolaj@ucdavis.edu, Internet: campus-recreation.ucdavis.edu. Dir.: Roger Hankins, Ass. Dir.: Martha Brundin
Fine Arts Museum / University Museum - 1965 42792

Pence Gallery, 212 D St, Davis, CA 95616 - T: (530) 758-3370, Fax: (530) 758-4670, E-mail: pencegallery@davis.com, Internet: www.pencegallery.org. Dir.: Nancy M. Servis
Fine Arts Museum / Public Gallery - 1975 42793

Richard L. Nelson Gallery and the Fine Arts Collection, University of California, Department of Art, Davis, CA 95616 - T: (530) 752-0522, Fax: (530) 754-9122, E-mail: nelsongallery@ucdavis.edu, Internet: art.ucdavis.edu/nelson. Cur.: Melissa Chandon
Fine Arts Museum / University Museum - 1976
16th c present paper, prints, drawings and paintings, contemporary art, Southeast Asian, European and American art, ceramics 42794

R.M. Bohart Museum of Entomology, University of California, Dept of Entomology, 1 Shields Av, Davis, CA 95616-8584 - T: (530) 752-0493, Fax: (530) 752-9464, E-mail: bohart@ucdavis.edu, Internet: cbshome.ucdavis.edu/bohart/. Dir.: Dr. Lynn S. Kimsey
University Museum / Natural History Museum - 1946 42795

Daviston AL

Horseshoe Bend National Military Park, 11288 Horseshoe Bend Rd, Daviston, AL 36256 - T: (256) 234-7111, Fax: (256) 329-9905, E-mail: hobeadministration@nps.gov, Internet: www.nps.gov/hobe
Historic Site / Historical Museum - 1959
Horseshoe Bend Battlefield, location of final battle of the Creek Indian War of 1813-1814 42796

Davisville MO

Dillard Mill State Historic Site, 142 Dillard Mill Rd, Davisville, MO 65456 - T: (573) 244-3120, Fax: (573) 244-5672, E-mail: dillmill@misn.com, Internet: www.dnr.state.mo.us/dsp. Head: Jerry Wilson
Historical Museum - 1975 42797

Dawson Springs KY

Dawson Springs Museum and Art Center, 127 S Main St, Dawson Springs, KY 42408 - T: (270) 797-3503, 797-3891. Pres./Cur.: Claude A. Holeman
Fine Arts Museum / Decorative Arts Museum / Historical Museum - 1986
Art, hist 42798

Dayton OH

Boonshoft Museum of Discovery, 2600 DeWeese Pkwy, Dayton, OH 45414 - T: (937) 275-7431, Fax: (937) 275-5811, E-mail: info@boonshoftmuseum.org, Internet: www.boonshoftmuseum.org. Dir.: Mark Meister, Dept. Dir.: Cheryl Adams (Astronomy), Cur.: Elizabeth Toth (Live Animals), Lynn Simonelli (Anthropology), Asst. Cur.: William Kennedy
Archaeological Museum / Natural History Museum / Science&Tech Museum - 1893 42799

Carillon Historical Park, 1000 Carillon Blvd, Dayton, OH 45409 - T: (937) 293-2841 ext 100, Fax: (937) 293-5798, E-mail: chpdayton@aol.com, Internet: www.carillonpark.org. Exec. Dir.: Mary Mathews, Dir.: Jeanne Palermo
Historical Museum - 1950 42800

Dayton Art Institute, 456 Belmonte Park N, Dayton, OH 45405 - T: (937) 223-5277, Fax: (937) 223-3140, E-mail: info@daytonartinstitue.org, Internet: www.daytonartinstitute.org. Dir.: Alexander Lee Nyerges, Chief Cur.: Michael Komanecky, Cur.: Li Jian (Asian Art)
Fine Arts Museum - 1919 42801

Dayton Museum of Discovery → Boonshoft Museum of Discovery

Dayton Visual Arts Center, 40 W Fourth St, Dayton, OH 45387-0416 - T: (937) 224-3822, E-mail: dvac@gemair.com, Internet: www.sinclair.edu/community/dvac. Exec. Dir.: Kay Koeninger
Fine Arts Museum - 1991 42802

Montgomery County Historical Society Center, 224 North St.Clair St, Dayton, OH 45402 - T: (937) 228-6271, Fax: (937) 331-7160, E-mail: mchsdayton@aol.com, Internet: www.daytonhistory.org. Dir.: Brian Hackett, Ass. Dir.: Claudia Watson
Historical Museum - 1896
archive 42803

Patterson Homestead, 1815 Brown St, Dayton, OH 45409 - T: (937) 222-9724, Fax: (937) 222-0345, Internet: www.pattersonhome.com. Dir.: Denise L. Darling, Cur.: Rays Shook
Decorative Arts Museum / Historical Museum - 1953 42804

Paul Laurence Dunbar State Memorial, 219 N Paul Laurence Dunbar St, Dayton, OH 45407 - T: (937) 224-7061, Fax: (937) 224-5625, 224-7051, E-mail: pldunbar@coax.net, Internet: www.ohiohistory.org. Head: LaVerne Sci
Historical Museum / Historic Site - 1936 42805

Sunwatch Indian Village - Archaeological Park, 2301 W River Rd, Dayton, OH 45418 - T: (937) 268-8199, Fax: (937) 268-1760, E-mail: sunwatch@archaeologist.com, Internet: www.sunwatch.org. Exec. Dir.: Mark Meister
Historical Museum / Archaeological Museum - 1988
Prehistory 42806

Wright State University Art Galleries, 3640 Colonel Glenn Hwy, Dayton, OH 45435 - T: (937) 775-2896, Fax: (937) 775-4082, E-mail: cmartin@desire.wright.edu, Internet: www.wright.edu/artgalleries/. Head: Barbara Siwecki
Fine Arts Museum / University Museum - 1974 42807

Dayton VA

Shenandoah Valley Folk Art and Heritage Center, 382 High St, Dayton, VA 22821 - T: (540) 879-2616, Fax: (540) 879-2616, E-mail: heritag1@shentel.net, Internet: www.heritagecenter.com. Pres.: Shelvie Carr
Local Museum / Folklore Museum - 1895
Local hist, folk art, civil war 42808

Dayton WA

Dayton Historical Depot Society Museum, 222 E Commercial St, Dayton, WA 99328 - T: (509) 382-2026, Fax: (509) 382-4726. Pres.: Russell P. Markus
Local Museum - 1974 42809

Daytona Beach FL

Halifax Historical Museum, 252 S Beach St, Daytona Beach, FL 32114 - T: (904) 255-6976, Fax: (904) 255-7605, E-mail: mail@halifaxhistorical.org, Internet: www.halifaxhistorical.org. Dir.: Cheryl Atwell
Local Museum - 1949
Local history 42810

The Museum of Arts and Sciences, 1040 Museum Blvd, Daytona Beach, FL 32114 - T: (904) 255-0285, Fax: (904) 255-5040, E-mail: moas@n-jcenter.com, Internet: www.moas.org. Dir.: Michael M. Brothers, Dep. Dir.: Patricia Thalheimer, Cur.: Richard Lussky
Fine Arts Museum / Local Museum / Natural History Museum - 1971
American, European, African and Cuban fine, folk and decorative art 42811

Southeast Museum of Photography, Daytona Beach Community College, 1200 W International Speedway Blvd, Daytona Beach, FL 32114 - T: (904) 947-3165, Fax: (904) 254-4487, E-mail: millerk@dbcc.edu, Internet: www.smponline.org. Dir.: Alison Devine Nordstrom, Kevin R. Miller, Ass. Dir.: Martha Carden
Fine Arts Museum / Science&Tech Museum - 1979
Photography 42812

De Land FL

De Land Museum of Art, 600 N Woodland Blvd, De Land, FL 32720-3447 - T: (386) 734-4371, Fax: (386) 734-7697, E-mail: info@delandmuseum.com, Internet: www.delandmuseum.com. Dir.: Jennifer Coolidge, Head: Dorthory Dansberger (Operations)
Fine Arts Museum - 1951 42813

The Duncan Gallery of Art, Stetson University, 421 N Woodland Blvd, De Land, FL 32723 - T: (386) 822-7266, Fax: (386) 822-7268, E-mail: cnelson@stetson.edu, Internet: www.stetson.edu/departments/art. Dir.: Dan Gunderson
Fine Arts Museum / University Museum - 1965 42814

Gillespie Museum of Minerals, Stetson University, 234 E Michigan Av, De Land, FL 32720 - T: (386) 822-7330, Fax: (386) 822-7328, E-mail: hvanter@stetson.edu, Internet: www.gillespiemuseum.stetson.edu. Dir.: Dr. Robert S. Chauvin, Ass. Dir.: Holli M. Vanater, Cur.: Dr. Bruce C. Bradford
University Museum / Natural History Museum - 1958
Mineralogy 42815

De Pere WI

Oneida Nation Museum, W892 County Trunk EE, De Pere, WI 54115 - T: (920) 869-2768, Fax: (920) 869-2959, E-mail: LMiller@oneidanation.org, Internet: www.oneidanation.org. Dir.: Katherine Hill
Ethnology Museum - 1979
Oneida Nation and Iroquois Confederacy, Indian artifacts, Civil War 42816

White Pillars Museum, 403 N Broadway, De Pere, WI 54115 - T: (920) 336-3877. Dir.: Pete Safford
Local Museum - 1970
Local hist 42817

De Smet SD

De Smet Depot Museum, 104 Calumet Ave NE, De Smet, SD 57231 - T: (605) 854-3991. C.E.O.: Gary Wolkow
Local Museum - 1965
Local hist 42818

Deadwood SD

Adams House, 22 Van Buren St, Deadwood, SD 57732 - T: (605) 578-1928, Fax: (605) 578-1194, E-mail: director@adamsmuseumandhouse.org, Internet: www.adamsmuseumandhouse.org. Dir.: Mary A. Kopco, Asst Dir.: Deborah Gangloff
Historical Museum 42819

Adams Museum, 54 Sherman St, Deadwood, SD 57732 - T: (605) 578-1714, 578-1928, Fax: (605) 578-1194, E-mail: director@adamsmuseumandhouse.org, Internet: www.adamsmuseumandhouse.org. Dir.: Mary A. Kopco, Cur.: Darrel Nelson (Exhibits), Arlette Hansen
Local Museum - 1930
Local hist 42820

House of Roses, Senator Wilson Home, 15 Forest Av, Deadwood, SD 57732 - T: (605) 722-1879. Pres./ Dir.: Michael Bockwoldt
Historical Museum - 1976
Historic house, antique Victorian furniture, paintings, old prints 42821

Dearborn MI

Automotive Hall of Fame, 21400 Oakwood Blvd, Dearborn, MI 48124 - T: (313) 240-4000, Fax: (313) 240-8641, Internet: www.automotivehalloffame.org. Pres.: Jeffrey K. Leestma
Science&Tech Museum - 1939 42822

Dearborn Historical Museum, 915 Brady St, Dearborn, MI 48124 - T: (313) 565-3000, Fax: (313) 565-4848, E-mail: hmuseum@ci.dearborn.mi.us, Internet: www.cityofdearborn.org. Chief Cur.: Mary V. MacDonald
Historical Museum - 1950
Local history, ex powder magazine 42823

Henry Ford Estate, Universty of Michigan-Dearborn, Evergreen Rd, Dearborn, MI 48128 - T: (313) 593-5590, 593-5128, 593-5593, Fax: (313) 593-5243, Internet: www.henryfordestate.org
Local Museum - 1957
Historic house, former home of Henry Ford 42824

Henry Ford Museum and Greenfield Village, 20900 Oakwood Blvd, Dearborn, MI 48124 - T: (313) 271-1620, Fax: (313) 982-6250, E-mail: barbh@hfmgv.org, Internet: www.hfmgv.org. Pres.: Steven K. Hamp, Dir.: Denise Thal
Historical Museum - 1929
History 42825

Death Valley CA

Death Valley National Park Visitor Center and Museum, on Hwy 190, Death Valley, CA 92328 - T: (760) 786-2331, Fax: (760) 786-3283, E-mail: blair-davenport@nps.gov, Internet: www.nps.gov/deva
Local Museum / Ethnology Museum / Archaeological Museum / Historical Museum - 1933 42826

Decatur AL

The Art Gallery, John C. Calhoun State Community College, Hwy 31 N, Fine Arts Bldg, Decatur, AL 35609-2216 - T: (256) 306-2500, 306-2699, Fax: (256) 306-2889, E-mail: kab@calhoun.cc.al.us, Internet: www.calhoun.cc.al.us. Pres.: Dr. Richard Carpenter
Fine Arts Museum / University Museum - 1965 42827

Department of Fine Arts Gallery, John C. Calhoun State Community College, Hwy 31 N, Decatur, AL 35609-2216 - T: (256) 306-2702, Fax: (256) 306-2925, E-mail: jtc@calhoun.cc.al.us, Internet: www.calhoun.cc.al.us
Public Gallery 42828

Decatur GA

Dalton Gallery, Agnes Scott College, E College Av, Decatur, GA 30030 - T: (404) 471-6000, Fax: (404) 471-5369, E-mail: aparry@agnesscott.edu, Internet: www.agnesscott.edu. Chm.: Dr. Donna Sadler
Fine Arts Museum / University Museum - 1957
Decorative art, paintings, sculptures 42829

DeKalb Historical Society Museum, 101 E Court Sq, Decatur, GA 30030 - T: (404) 373-1088, Fax: (404) 373-8287, E-mail: dhs@dekalbhistory.org, Internet: www.dekalbhistory.us. Exec. Dir.: Sue Ellen Owens
Local Museum - 1947
Local history, Old Courthouse, personal artefacts, costumes, photos 42830

Decatur IL

Birks Museum, c/o Millikin University, 1184 W Main, Decatur, IL 62522 - T: (217) 424-6337, Fax: (217) 424-3993, E-mail: ewalker@mail.millikin.edu, Internet: www.millikin.edu. Dir.: Edwin G. Walker
Decorative Arts Museum / University Museum - 1981
China, glass, paper weights 42831

Kirkland Fine Arts Center-Perkinson Gallery, c/o Millikin University, 1184 W Main St, Decatur, IL 62522 - T: (217) 424-6227, Fax: (217) 424-3993, E-mail: jschietinger@mail.millikin.edu. Dir.: James Schietinger, Ass. Dir.: Lyle Salmi
Fine Arts Museum / University Museum - 1969 42832

Macon County Museum Complex, 5580 N Fork Rd, Decatur, IL 62521 - T: (217) 422-4919, Fax: (217) 422-4773, E-mail: mchs@fgi.net, Internet: www.fgi.net/~mchs. Pres.: Ary Anderson, C.E.O.: Christopher D. Gordy
Local Museum - 1973
Local history 42833

Perkinson Gallery, c/o Millikin University, 1184 W Main St, Decatur, IL 62522 - T: (217) 424-6227, Fax: (217) 424-3993, Internet: www.millikin.edu. Dir.: Jim Schitinger
Fine Arts Museum / University Museum - 1970
Drawings, painting, prints, sculpture, watercolors 42834

Decatur IN

Adams County Historical Museum, 420 W Monroe St, Decatur, IN 46733 - T: (219) 724-2341, E-mail: goble@adamswells.net. Pres.: Rebecca Goble
Local Museum - 1965
Local history, in Charles Dugan Home 42835

Decatur MI

Historic Newton Home, 20689 Marcellus Hwy, Decatur, MI 49045 - T: (616) 445-9016. Head: Abigail Schten
Historical Museum 42836

Decatur TX

Wise County Heritage Museum, 1602 S Trinity, Decatur, TX 76234 - T: (940) 627-5586, E-mail: wisemuseum@ntws.net. Pres.: George Beeson, C.E.O.: Rosalie Gregg
Local Museum - 1967
Local hist 42837

Decorah IA

Fine Arts Collection, 700 College Dr, Luther College Library, Decorah, IA 52101-1042 - T: (563) 387-1195, Fax: (563) 387-1657, E-mail: kempjane@luther.edu, Internet: www.luther.edu/~library/. Head: Jane Kemp, Gallery Coord.: David Kamm
Fine Arts Museum / University Museum
Art 42838

Vesterheim Norwegian-American Museum, 523 W Water St, Decorah, IA 52101-0379 - T: (563) 382-9681, Fax: (319) 382-8828, E-mail: vesterheim@vesterheim.org, Internet: vesterheim.org. Dir.: Janet Blohm Pultz, Chief Cur.: Darrell D. Henning, Cur.: Laurann Gilbertson (Textiles), Tova Brandt, Steven Johnson (Jacobson Farmstead), Libr.: Carol Hasvold
Ethnology Museum / Folklore Museum - 1877
Ethnology, genealogy 42839

Dedham MA

Dedham Historical Museum, 612 High St, Dedham, MA 02027-0215 - T: (781) 326-1385, Fax: (781) 326-5762, E-mail: society@dedhamhistorical.org, Internet: www.dedhamhistorical.org. C.E.O.: Ronald F. Frazier
Fine Arts Museum / Decorative Arts Museum / Local Museum - 1859
Local history, pottery, Katharine Pratt silver, fine arts, furniture 42840

Fairbanks House, 511 East St, Dedham, MA 02026 - T: (781) 326-1170, Fax: (781) 326-2147, E-mail: fairbankshouse@aol.com, Internet: www.fairbankshouse.org. Pres.: Lynn Fairbank, Cur.: Julie Letendre
Historical Museum / Museum of Classical Antiquities - 1903
Oldest surviving timber frame house in North America, built for Fairbanks family, furnishings 42841

Museum of Bad Art, 580 High St, Dedham, MA 02026, mail addr: 73 Parker Rd, Needham, MA 02494 - T: (781) 444-6757, Fax: (781) 433-9991, E-mail: moba@world.std.com, Internet: glyphs.com/moba. C.E.O.: Louise R. Sacco
Fine Arts Museum - 1993
Works of exuberant, although crude, execution by artists barely in control of the brush 42842

Deer Isle ME

Deer Isle-Stonington Historical Society Museum, Rte 15A, Deer Isle, ME 04627 - T: (207) 348-2897. Pres.: Paul Stubing
Historical Museum - 1959
Local history 42843

Haystack Mountain School of Crafts Gallery, 89 Haystack School Dr, Deer Isle, ME 04627-0518 - T: (207) 348-2306, Fax: (207) 348-2307, Internet: www.haystack-mtn.org. Dir.: Stuart J. Kestenbaum
Historical Museum - 1950 42844

Deer Lodge MT

Grant-Kohrs Ranch National Historic Site, 210 Missouri Av, Deer Lodge, MT 59722 - T: (406) 846-2070, Fax: (406) 846-3962, E-mail: darlene_koontz@nps.gov, Internet: www.nps.gov/grko. Dir.: Darlene Koontz, Cur.: Chris Ford
Historic Site - 1972 42845

Montana Auto Museum, 1106 Main St, Deer Lodge, MT 59722 - T: (406) 846-3111, Fax: (406) 846-3156, E-mail: oldprisonmuseums@in-tch.com. Dir.: Andrew C. Towe, Cur.: James R. Haas
Historical Museum - 1980 42846

Old Prison Museum, 1106 Main St, Deer Lodge, MT 59722 - T: (406) 846-3111, Fax: (406) 846-3156, E-mail: oldprisonmuseums@in-tch.com. Dir.: Andrew C. Towe, Cur.: James R. Haas
Historical Museum - 1980 42847

Powell County Museum, 1193 Main St, Deer Lodge, MT 59722 - T: (406) 846-1694, Fax: (406) 846-3156, E-mail: oldprisonmuseums@in-tch.com. Dir.: Andrew C. Towe, Cur.: James R. Haas
Local Museum - 1964 42848

Deerfield MA

Historic Deerfield, The Street, Deerfield, MA 01342 - T: (413) 774-5581, Fax: (413) 773-7415, E-mail: tours@historic-deerfield.org, Internet: www.historic-deerfield.org. Dir.: Donald R. Friary, Cur.: Philip Zea, Edward F. Maeder, Joshua W. Lane
Decorative Arts Museum / Folklore Museum / Local Museum - 1952
Local history 42849

Memorial Hall Museum, 8 Memorial St, Deerfield, MA 01342 - T: (413) 774-7476, Fax: (413) 774-5400, E-mail: pvma@shaysnet.com, Internet: www.old-deerfield.org. Dir.: Timothy C. Neumann, Cur.: Suzanne Flynt, Libr.: David Bosse
Decorative Arts Museum / Local Museum - 1870
Local history, decorative arts, Deerfield Academy Building 42850

Deerfield Beach FL

Deerfield Beach Historical Society Museum, 380 E Hillsboro Blvd, Deerfield Beach, FL 33443 - T: (954) 429-0378, Fax: (954) 429-0378, E-mail: fdallen49@earthlink.net. Exec. Dir.: Dale Allen
Local Museum - 1973
Photographs, oral histories, costumes, period furnishings - archives, library 42851

Defiance MO

Historic Daniel Boone Home and Boonesfield Village, Lindenwood University, 1868 Hwy F, Defiance, MO 63341 - T: (314) 798-2005, Fax: (314) 798-2914, Internet: www.lindenwood.edu. Dir.: Jim Gladwin, Pam Jensen, Greta Maxheimer
Open Air Museum / Local Museum - 1803 42852

Defiance OH

Au Glaize Village, 12296 Krouse Rd, Defiance, OH 43512, mail addr: 15806 Campbell Rd, Defiance, OH 43512 - T: (419) 784-0107, Internet: www.defiance-online.com/auglaize. C.E.O.: Lynn Lanth
Local Museum - 1966
Local hist, farming, household, clothing, military uniforms, natural hist, archaeology, model trains 42853

DeKalb IL

Anthropology Museum, Northern Illinois University, DeKalb, IL 60115 - T: (815) 753-0230, Fax: (815) 753-7027, E-mail: awparsons@niu.edu, Internet: www.niu.edu/anthro_museum. Exec. Dir.: Winifred Creamer, Dir.: Ann Wright-Parsons
University Museum / Ethnology Museum / Archaeological Museum - 1964
Anthropology, archaeology 42854

Ellwood House Museum, 509 N First St, DeKalb, IL 60115 - T: (815) 756-4609, Fax: (815) 756-4645, E-mail: ellwoodhouse@hcnet.com, Internet: www.ellwoodhouse.org. Dir.: Gerald J. Brauer, Cur.: Francine Larson
Historical Museum - 1965 42855

Niu Art Museum, Northern Illinois University, Altgeld Hall, DeKalb, IL 60115 - T: (815) 753-1936, Fax: (815) 753-7897, E-mail: pdoherty@niu.edu, Internet: www.vpa.niu.edu/museum. Dir.: Peggy M. Doherty, Ass. Dir.: Jo Burke
Fine Arts Museum / University Museum - 1970
Art 42856

Northern Illinois University Art Museum, Altgeld Hall, DeKalb, IL 60115 - T: (815) 753-1936. Dir.: Peggy M. Doherty
Fine Arts Museum - 1970
Contemporary and modern paintings, prints, sculptures and photographs, Burmese art, native American art 42857

Del Rio TX

Whitehead Memorial Museum, 1308 S Main St, Del Rio, TX 78840 - T: (830) 774-7568, Fax: (830) 768-0223, E-mail: director@whitehead-museum.com, Internet: www.whitehead.museum.com. Pres.: Charles Chandler, C.E.O.: Lee Lincoln
Local Museum - 1962
Local hist 42858

Delafield WI

Hawks Inn, 426 Wells St, Delafield, WI 53018 - T: (414) 646-4794, Internet: www.hawksinn.org. Pres.: Mary Daniel
Local Museum - 1960
Historic building 42859

Saint John's Northwestern Military Academy Museum, 1101 N Genesee St, Delafield, WI 53018 - T: (414) 646-7191, Fax: (414) 646-7155, E-mail: alumni@sjnma.org, Internet: www.sjnma.org. C.E.O.: Margaret H. Koller
Military Museum - 1984
Military hist 42860

Delano CA

Delano Heritage Park, 330 Lexington at Garces Hwy, Delano, CA 93215 - T: (661) 725-6730, Fax: (559) 757-2344, E-mail: dmuseum@lightspeed.net. Pres.: James Sevier
Local Museum / Natural History Museum - 1961
Local history, agriculture, arboretum 42861

Delaware City DE

Fort Delaware Society Museum, 108 Old Reedy Point Bridge Rd, Delaware City, DE 19706 - T: (302) 834-1630, E-mail: ftdsociety@del.net, Internet: www.del.net/org/fort. Pres.: William G. Robelen
Military Museum - 1950
Military hist 42862

Delray Beach FL

Cornell Museum, 51 N Swinton Av, Delray Beach, FL 33444 - T: (561) 243-7922, Fax: (561) 243-7022, E-mail: museum@oldschool.org, Internet: www.oldschool.org/oldschool. Dir.: Gloria Rejune Adams
Fine Arts Museum - 1990
Fine art, sculpture 42863

The Morikami Museum and Japanese Gardens, 4000 Morikami Park Rd, Delray Beach, FL 33446 - T: (561) 495-0233, Fax: (561) 499-2557, E-mail: morikami@co.palm-beach.fl.us, Internet: www.morikami.org. Dir.: Larry Rosensweig, Cur.: Thomas Gregersen
Ethnology Museum / Folklore Museum - 1977
Ethnology, Japanese culture 42864

Delta CO

Delta County Museum, 251 Meeker St, Delta, CO 81416 - T: (970) 874-8721, E-mail: deltamuseum@aol.com. Dir.: James K. Wetzel, Bernice Musser
Local Museum - 1964
Regional history 42865

Delta UT

Great Basin Museum, 328 W 100 N, Delta, UT 84624 - T: (801) 864-5013, Fax: (801) 864-2446, E-mail: greatbasin@hubwest.com. Dir.: Charlotte K. Morrison, Cur.: Sindy McMichael
Local Museum - 1988 42866

Delton MI

Bernard Historical Museum, 7135 W Delton Rd, Delton, MI 49046 - T: (616) 623-5451. Pres.: Richard Martin
Local Museum - 1962
Local history 42867

Deming NM

Luna Mimbres Museum, 301 S Silver St, Deming, NM 88030 - T: (505) 546-2382, Fax: (505) 544-0121, E-mail: dlm-museum@zianet.com, Internet: www.cityofdeming.org/museum.html. Dir.: Sharon Lein
Local Museum / Decorative Arts Museum - 1955
Local hist, vintage clothing, Mimbres Indian artifacts, American Indian art, anthropology, folk art, decorative art 42868

Demopolis AL

Gaineswood, 805 S Cedar Av, Demopolis, AL 36732 - T: (334) 289-4846, Fax: (334) 289-1027, E-mail: gaineswood@demopolis.com, Internet: www.demopolis.com/gaineswood/. Dir.: Matthew D. Hartzell
Historical Museum / Historic Site - 1975
History 42869

Denison TX

Eisenhower Birthplace, 208 E Day, Denison, TX 75020 - T: (903) 465-8908, Fax: (903) 465-8988, E-mail: eisenhower@texoma.net, Internet: www.eisenhowerbirthplace.org. Pres.: Wayne Jamison
Local Museum - 1946
Historic house where Dwight D. Eisenhower was born 42870

Dennis MA

Cape Museum of Fine Arts, 60 Hope Lane Rt 6A, Dennis, MA 02638 - T: (508) 385-4477, Fax: (508) 385-7933, E-mail: cmfa@capecod.net. Pres.: Joseph A. Signore, Exec. Dir.: Donald E. Knuab
Fine Arts Museum / Public Gallery - 1981
Art 42871

Dennison OH

Dennison Railroad Depot Museum, 400 Center St, Dennison, OH 44621 - T: (740) 922-6776, Fax: (740) 922-0105, E-mail: depot@tusco.net, Internet: www.dennisondepot.org
Science&Tech Museum / Local Museum - 1984
Railroad, WW 2 Canteen site, local hist, model train, Keystone exhibit, rolling stock 42872

Denton MD

Museum of Rural Life, 16 N Second St, Denton, MD 21629, mail addr: POB 514, Denton, MD 21629 - T: (410) 479-2055, Fax: (410) 479-4513
Folklore Museum 42873

Denton TX

Dar Museum First Ladies of Texas Historic Costumes Collection, Texas Woman's University, Denton, TX 76204 - T: (940) 898-3350, Fax: (940) 898-3306, Internet: www.twu.edu. Pres.: Ann Stuart
Special Museum - 1940
Costumes 42874

Denton County Historical Museum, 5800 North I-35, Denton, TX 76201 - T: (940) 380-0877, Fax: (940) 380-1699, E-mail: dchminc@earthlink.net. Dir.: Judy Selph
Local Museum - 1977
Local hist 42875

Texas Woman's University Art Galleries, 1200 Frame St, Denton, TX 76204 - T: (940) 898-2530, Fax: (940) 898-2496, E-mail: visualarts@twu.edu, Internet: www.twu.edu. Dir.: Corky Stuckenbruck
Fine Arts Museum / University Museum - 1901
Art 42876

University of North Texas Art Gallery, School of Visual Arts, Mulberry at Welch, Denton, TX 76203 - T: (940) 565-4005, Fax: (940) 565-4717, E-mail: block@art.unt.edu, Internet: www.art.unt.edu. Dir.: Diana Block
University Museum / Fine Arts Museum - 1972 42877

Denver CO

Black American West Museum and Heritage Center, 3091 California St, Denver, CO 80205 - T: (303) 292-2566, Fax: (303) 382-1981, E-mail: bawmhc@aol.com, Internet: www.coax.net/people/lwf/bawmus.htm. Dir.: Ottawa Harris
Historical Museum - 1971
African American hist 42878

Byers-Evans House Museum, 1310 Bannock St, Denver, CO 80204 - T: (303) 620-4933, Fax: (303) 620-4795, E-mail: byer@rmi.net, Internet: www.coloradohistory.org/byers-evans. Dir.: Kevin Gramer
Historical Museum - 1990 42879

Center for the Visual Arts, c/o Metropolitan State College of Denver, 1734 Wazee St, Denver, CO 80202 - T: (303) 294-5207, Fax: (303) 294-5210, E-mail: banker@mscd.edu, Internet: www.mscd.edu/news/cva. C.E.O.: Sally L. Perisho, Amy Banker
Fine Arts Museum / University Museum - 1991
Art 42880

Children's Museum of Denver, 2121 Children's Museum Dr, Denver, CO 80211 - T: (303) 433-7444, Fax: (303) 433-9520, E-mail: lindaf@cmdenver.org, Internet: www.cmdenver.org. Dir.: Dr. Linda E. Farley
Special Museum - 1973 42881

Colorado Historical Society Museum, 1300 Broadway, Denver, CO 80203 - T: (303) 866-3682, Fax: (303) 866-5739, E-mail: webmaster@chs.state.co.us, Internet: www.coloradohistory.org. Dir.: Georgianna Contiguglia, Cur.: Moya Hansen (Decorative and Fine Arts), Eric Paddock (Photography), Bridget Burke (Books and Manuscripts)
Historical Museum - 1879
State history 42882

Colorado Photographic Arts Center, 1513 Boulder St, Denver, CO 80211 - T: (303) 433-9591, Fax: (303) 278-3693. Pres.: R. Skip
Public Gallery 42883

Core, 2045 Larimer St, Denver, CO 80205 - T: (303) 297-8428, E-mail: rgarriott@electricstores.com, Internet: www.corenwartspace.com. Dir.: Dave Griffin
Public Gallery 42884

Denver Art Museum, 100 W 14th Av Pkwy, Denver, CO 80204 - T: (720) 865-5001, Fax: (720) 865-5028, 913-0001, E-mail: web-mail@denverartmuseum.org, Internet: www.denverartmuseum.org. Dir.: Lewis I. Sharp, Dep. Dir.: Cynthia Ford, Chief Cur.: Timothy Standring (Paintings, Sculpture), Cur.: Ronald Otsuka (Asian Art), Nancy Blomberg (Native Arts), Dianne Vanderlip (Modern and Contemporary Art), Donna Pierce (New World-Spanish Colonial Art), Margaret Young-Sanchez (New World-PreColumbian Art), R. Craig Miller (Architecture, Design and Graphics), Alice Zrebiec (Textile Art), Joan Carpenter Troccoli (Institute of Western American Art)
Fine Arts Museum - 1893
Native art, contemporary and modern art, architecture, paintings, graphics, sculptures 42885

Denver Museum of Miniatures, Dolls and Toys, 1880 Gaylord St, Denver, CO 80206 - T: (303) 322-1053, Fax: (303) 322-3704, E-mail: bazyl57@yahoo.com, Internet: www.dmmdt.homepage.com. Dir.: Bevyn L. Hazelwood
Special Museum - 1981 42886

Denver Museum of Nature and Science, 2001 Colorado Blvd, Denver, CO 80205 - T: (303) 322-7009, Fax: (303) 370-8384, E-mail: jtaylor@dmns.org, Internet: www.dmns.org. Pres.: Raylene Decatur, Chief Cur.: Dr. Rusell W. Graham, Cur.: Dr. Kirk R. Johnson (Earth Sciences, Paleontology), Dr. Ella Maria Ray (Anthropology), Joyce L. Herold (Ethnology), Dr. Cheri A. Jones (Mammalogy), Dr. Jack A. Murphy (Geology), Dr. Kirk R. Johnson, Dr. Stephen Holen (Archaeology), Dr. Laura Danly (Space Sciences), Dr. Paula E. Cushing (Entomology, Arachnology)
Natural History Museum - 1900
Natural history, archaeology, paleontology, mammals, entomology, earth and space sciences 42887

Forney Transportation Museum, 4303 Brighton Blvd, Denver, CO 80216 - T: (303) 297-1113, Fax: (970) 498-9505, E-mail: forney@info2000.net, Internet: www.forneymuseum.com. Pres.: Jack D. Forney
Science&Tech Museum - 1961
Transport 42888

Ginny Williams Family Foundation, 299 Fillmore St, Denver, CO 80206 - T: (303) 321-4077
Fine Arts Museum 42889

Grant-Humphreys Mansion, 770 Pennsylvania St, Denver, CO 80203 - T: (303) 894-2505, Fax: (303) 894-2508, E-mail: gran@rmi.net, Internet: www.coloradohistory.org/grant_humphreys. Dir.: Kevin Gramer
Historical Museum - 1976
Historic Beaux-Arts style home 42890

Mizel Museum of Judaica, 350 S Dahela St, Denver, CO 80246 - T: (303) 316-6400, Fax: (303) 316-6403, E-mail: epremack@jccdenver.org, Internet: www.mizelmuseum.org. Dir.: Ellen Premack, Dep. Dir.: Ellen Rosenthal (Education)
Religious Arts Museum - 1982
Religious art and culture 42891

Molly Brown House Museum, 1340 Pennsylvania St, Denver, CO 80203 - T: (303) 832-4092 ext 16, Fax: (303) 832-2340, E-mail: admin@mollybrown.org, Internet: www.mollybrown.org. Dir.: Kerri Atter, Cur.: Elizabeth Owen Walker
Historical Museum - 1970 42892

Museo de Las Americas, 861 Santa Fe Dr, Denver, CO 80204 - T: (303) 571-4401, Fax: (303) 607-9761, E-mail: jose@museo.org, Internet: www.museo.org. Exec. Dir.: José Aguayo
Fine Arts Museum / Historical Museum - 1991
Art and history 42893

Museum of Anthropology, c/o University of Denver, 2000 Asbury Av, Ste 146, Denver, CO 80208 - T: (303) 871-2406, Fax: (303) 871-2437, E-mail: ckreps@du.edu, Internet: www.du.edu/duma. Dir.: Dr. Christina Kreps
University Museum / Ethnology Museum - 1932
Anthropology, ethnology, textiles 42894

Museum of Contemporary Art Denver, 1275 19th St, Denver, CO 80202 - T: (303) 298-754, Fax: (303) 298-7553, E-mail: moca@mocadenver.com, Internet: www.mocadenver.com. Dir.: Sidney Payton
Fine Arts Museum - 1997 42895

Pirate Contemporary Art Oasis, 1370 Verbana, Denver, CO 80220 - T: (303) 458-6058. Dir.: Phil Bender
Public Gallery 42896

Rocky Mountain College of Art and Design Galleries, 6875 E Evans Av, Denver, CO 80224 - T: (303) 753-6046, Fax: (303) 759-4970, E-mail: lspival@rmcad.edu, Internet: www.rmcad.edu. Dir.: Steven Steele, Cur.: Lisa Spivak
Fine Arts Museum / University Museum - 1963 42897

Rocky Mountain Conservation Center, University of Denver, 2420 S University Blvd, Denver, CO 80208 - T: (303) 733-2508, Fax: (303) 733-2508, E-mail: lmellon@du.edu, Internet: www.du.edu/rmcc. Dir.: Lori A. Mellon
Special Museum
Photography, textiles, archaeologie, ethnology, maps 42898

School of Art and Art History Gallery, c/o University of Denver, 2121 E Asbury Av, Denver, CO 80210 - T: (303) 871-2846, Fax: (303) 871-4112, Internet: www.du.edu/art. Dir.: Shannen Hill
Fine Arts Museum / University Museum - 1940
European and regional masters art 42899

Spark Gallery, 1535 Platte St, Denver, CO 80202 - T: (303) 455-4435
Public Gallery
Drawings, photography, prints, sculptures 42900

Trianon Museum and Art Gallery, 335 14th St, Denver, CO 80202 - T: (303) 623-0739
Fine Arts Museum / Public Gallery 42901

Vance Kirkland Museum, 1311 Pearl St, Denver, CO 80203 - T: (303) 832-8576, Fax: (303) 832-8404, E-mail: info@vancekirkland.org, Internet: www.vancekirkland.org. Dir.: Hugh Grant, Cons.: Dean Sartori
Fine Arts Museum / Decorative Arts Museum - 1932
Paintings by Colorado artists, Vance Kirkland, works by Frank Lloyd Wright, Russel and Mary Wright, Eva Zeisel 42902

Denville NJ

Blackwell Street Center for the Arts, POB 808, Denville, NJ 07834 - T: (201) 337-2143, Fax: (201) 337-2143, E-mail: wblakeart@nac.net, Internet: www.blackwell-st-artists.org. Dir.: Annette Adrian Hanna
Public Gallery - 1983
Professional gallery for NJ/NY artists 42903

Des Arc AR

Prairie County Museum, 2009 W Main St, Des Arc, AR 72040 - T: (870) 256-3711, Fax: (870) 256-9202, E-mail: prairieco@arkansas.com. Dir.: Neva Boatright
Local Museum - 1971
County history 42904

Des Moines IA

Des Moines Art Center, 4700 Grand Av, Des Moines, IA 50312 - T: (515) 277-4405, Fax: (515) 271-0357, E-mail: marketing@desmoinesartcenter.org, Internet: www.desmoinasartcenter.org. Dir.: Susan Lubowsky Talbott, Ass. Dir.: M. Jessica Rowe, Sen. Cur.: Jeff Fleming, Amy N. Worthen (Prints), Assoc. Cur.: Chris Gilbert
Fine Arts Museum - 1933
19th-20th c art 42905

Hoyt Sherman Place, 1501 Woodland Av, Des Moines, IA 50309 - T: (515) 244-0507, Fax: (515) 237-3582, E-mail: barcus@hoytsherman.org, Internet: www.hoytsherman.org. Dir.: Leisha Barcus, Cur.: Reva Cash
Fine Arts Museum - 1907
Art 42906

Polk County Heritage Gallery, 3 Court Av, Des Moines, IA 50309 - T: (515) 286-3215, Fax: (515) 286-3082, Internet: www.co.polk.ia.us. Pres.: Mel Shivvers, C.E.O.: Gene Phillips
Public Gallery - 1980
Art 42907

Polk County Historical Society, 317 SW 42nd St, Des Moines, IA 50312 - T: (515) 255-6657. Pres.: Robert Simon
Local Museum - 1938
Local history, Fort Des Moines II 42908

Salisbury House, 4025 Tonawanda Dr, Des Moines, IA 50312 - T: (515) 274-1777, Fax: (515) 274-0184, E-mail: salhouse@dwx.com, Internet: www.salisburyhouse.org. Dir.: Scott Brunscheen, Ass. Dir.: Ann Pross
Historical Museum / Special Museum - 1993 42909

Science Center of Iowa, 4500 Grand Av, Greenwood-Ashworth Park, Des Moines, IA 50312-2499 - T: (515) 274-4138, Fax: (515) 274-3404, E-mail: info@sciowa.org, Internet: www.sciowa.org. Exec. Dir.: Mary B. Sellers
Science&Tech Museum - 1965
Science, technology 42910

State Historical Society of Iowa Museum, 600 E Locust St, Des Moines, IA 50319 - T: (515) 281-6412, Fax: (515) 282-0502, Internet: www.iowahistory.org. C.E.O.: Anita Walker, Chief Cur.: Michael O. Smith, Cur.: William M. Johnson (Natural History), John C. Lufkin (History), Cons.: Peter Sixbey
Local Museum - 1892
Regional history, natural history 42911

Terrace Hill Historic Site and Governor's Mansion, 2300 Grand Av, Des Moines, IA 50312 - T: (515) 281-7205, Fax: (515) 281-7267, E-mail: david.cordes@igov.state.ia.us, Internet: www.terracehill.org. Pres.: Mike Blouin, C.E.O.: David Cordes
Local Museum - 1971 42912

Des Plaines IL

Des Plaines Historical Museum, 789 Pearson St, Des Plaines, IL 60016-4506 - T: (847) 391-5399, 4741, Fax: (847) 297-1710, E-mail: dphslibrary@juno.com, Internet: nsn.nslsilus.org/dpkhome/dphs. Dir.: Joy A. Matthiessen, Cur.: Lynne Micklim
Local Museum - 1967
Local history 42913

Desert Hot Springs CA

Cabot's Old Indian Pueblo Museum, 67-616 E Desert View Av, Desert Hot Springs, CA 92240 - T: (760) 329-7610, Internet: www.cabotsmuseum.org. Man.: Edna Wells
Fine Arts Museum - 1968 42914

Detroit MI

Black Legends of Professional Basketball Museum, 8900 E Jefferson, Detroit, MI 48202, mail addr: POB 02384, Detroit, MI 48214 - T: (313) 822-8208, Fax: (313) 822-8227, E-mail: blbpf@cs.com, Internet: www.projectbait.com/legends. Pres.: Dr. John Kline
Special Museum - 1997 42915

Casa de Unidad (Unity House), 1920 Scotten, Detroit, MI 48209 - T: (313) 843-9598, Fax: (313) 843-7307, E-mail: casadeu@www-net.com, Internet: www.casadeu.com. Dir.: Marta Lagos, David Conklin
Public Gallery - 1981
Works of Latino artists 42916

Center Galleries, c/o College for Creative Studies, 301 Frederick Douglas Av, Detroit, MI 48202 - T: (313) 664-7800, Fax: (313) 664-7880, Internet: www.ccscad.edu. Dir.: Michelle M. Perron
Fine Arts Museum / University Museum - 1989 42917

Charles H. Wright Museum of African American History, 315 E Warren Av, Detroit, MI 48201 - T: (313) 494-5800, Fax: (313) 494-5855, Internet: www.maah-detroit.org. Pres.: Christy Matthews, Cur.: Patrina Chatman
Folklore Museum / Historical Museum - 1965
History, ethnography, folk art 42918

Children's Museum, 6134 Second Av., Detroit, MI 48202 - T: (313) 873-8100, Fax: (313) 873-3384, Internet: wmwc.detroit.k12.mi.usffindex.htm. Dir.: Dwight R. Levens
Ethnology Museum - 1917 42919

Community Arts Gallery, c/o Dept. of Arts, Wayne State University, 150 Community Arts Bldg, Dept of Art, Detroit, MI 48202 - T: (313) 577-2423, 577-2203, Fax: (313) 577-8935, E-mail: s.dupret@wayne.edu, Internet: www.art.wayne.edu. Cur.: Sandra Dupret
Fine Arts Museum / University Museum - 1958
American and European graphics, paintings, sculpture 42920

Detroit Artists Market, 4719 Woodward Av, Detroit, MI 48201 - T: (313) 832-8540, Fax: (313) 832-8543, E-mail: detroitartists@juno.com, Internet: www.detroitartistsmarket.org. Exec. Dir.: Aaron Timlin
Fine Arts Museum - 1932
Paintings, photographs, prints, drawings, sculpture, ceramics, glass 42921

Detroit Focus Gallery, 33 E Grand River, Detroit, MI 48232-0823 - T: (313) 533-2900. Dir.: Robert Crise jr.
Fine Arts Museum
Michigan visual artists 42922

Detroit Historical Museum, 5401 Woodward Av, Detroit, MI 48202 - T: (313) 833-1805, Fax: (313) 833-5342, Internet: www.detroithistorical.org. Dir.: Dr. Dennis Zembala, Cur.: Cynthia Young (Social History), John Polacsek (Marine History), Amy DeWys-VanHecke (Education), James Conway (Programs), Catherine Klingman, Jill Grannan, Bruce MacMillan, Ass. Cur.: Fred Stubbs, Registrar: Patience Nauta
Historical Museum / Local Museum - 1928
History, social and marine history 42923

The Detroit Institute of Arts, 5200 Woodward Av, Detroit, MI 48202 - T: (313) 833-7900, Fax: (313) 833-2357, Internet: www.dia.org. Dir.: Graham W.J. Beal, Cur.: William H. Peck (Ancient Art), David Penney (Native American Art), MaryAnn Wilkinson (20th-Century Art), Jim Tottis (American Art), Alan P. Darr (European Sculpture and Decorative Arts), George S. Keyes (European Paintings), Ellen Sharp (Graphic Arts), Elsie Peck (Near Eastern Art), Elliot Wilhelm (Film Theatre), Cons.: Barbara Heller
Fine Arts Museum - 1885
Ancient American, African, Near Eastern and Asien art, modern and contemporary art and design, New World culture, graphics, European sculpture, painting and decorative art, photgraphy 42924

Detroit Repertory Theatre Gallery, 13103 Woodrow Wilson, Detroit, MI 48238 - T: (313) 868-1347, Fax: (313) 868-1705. Dir.: Gilda Snowden
Fine Arts Museum / Decorative Arts Museum - 1957 42925

Detroit Science Center, 5020 John R. St, Detroit, MI 48202 - T: (313) 577-8400 ext 440, Fax: (313) 832-1623, E-mail: info@sciencedetroit.org, Internet: www.sciencedetroit.org. Pres & C.E.O.: Sharon M. Kahle
Science&Tech Museum - 1970
Science 42926

Dossin Great Lakes Museum, 100 Strand Dr, Belle Isle, Detroit, MI 48207 - T: (313) 852-4051, Fax: (313) 822-4610, Internet: www.glmi.org. Cur.: John F. Polacsek
Local Museum - 1948
Great Lakes history 42927

Gospel Music Hall of Fame and Museum, 18301 W McNichols St, Detroit, MI 48219 - T: (313) 592-0017, Fax: (313) 592-8762, E-mail: gmhfm@cs.com, Internet: www.gmhf.org. Pres.: David Gough, C.E.O.: Phyllis Siders, Chief Cur.: Sherry Dupree
Music Museum - 1995 42928

The Heritage Museum of Fine Arts for Youth, 110 E Ferry Av, Detroit, MI 48202 - T: (313) 871-1667. Dir.: Josephine Harreld Love
Decorative Arts Museum / Fine Arts Museum - 1969
Fine arts for Youth, toys, games, puppets, children's music - library 42929

International Institute of Metropolitan Detroit, 111 E Kirby St, Detroit, MI 48202 - T: (313) 871-8600, Fax: (313) 871-1651. Pres.: Adrian Ladi, Exec. Dir.: Richard G. Thipodeau
Fine Arts Museum / Folklore Museum - 1919
International and ethnic folk art 42930

Michigan Chapter Gallery, National Conference of Artists, 216 Fisher Bldg, 3011 W Grand Blvd, Detroit, MI 48202 - T: (313) 875-0923, Fax: (313) 875-7537, E-mail: gallery@ncamich.org, Internet: www.ncamich.org. Dir.: Esther Vivian Brewer, Cur.: Shirley Woodson
Fine Arts Museum
African Americam artists 42931

Michigan Sports Hall of Fame, Cobo Center, 1 N Washington Blvd, Detroit, MI 48226, mail addr: 32985 Hamilton Court, Ste 218, Farmington Hill, MI 48334 - T: (248) 374-8455, Fax: (248) 374-8447,

E-mail: misportshof@aol.com. Pres.: William F. McLaughlin
Special Museum - 1955
Sports 42932

Motown Historical Museum, 2648 W Grand Blvd, Detroit, MI 48208-1237 - T: (313) 875-2264, Fax: (313) 875-2267, E-mail: motownmus@aol.com. C.E.O.: Esther Gordy Edwards
Music Museum - 1988
Hist of Motown Records, recording artists 42933

Pewabic Pottery Museum, 10125 E Jefferson St, Detroit, MI 48214 - T: (313) 822-0954 ext.108, Fax: (313) 822-6266, E-mail: pewabic@pewabic.com, Internet: www.pewabic.com. Dir.: Terese Ireland
Decorative Arts Museum - 1903
Arts, crafts, pottery factory 42934

Swords Into Plowshares Peace Center and Gallery, 33 E Adams St, Detroit, MI 48226 - T: (313) 963-7575, Fax: (313) 963-2569, E-mail: swordsinto-plowshares@msn.com, Internet: www.swordsinto-plowshares.org
Special Museum - 1985
Peace art coll 42935

Wayne State University Museum of Anthropology, 4841 Cass Av, Detroit, MI 48202 - T: (313) 577-2598, Fax: (313) 577-9759, E-mail: tamara.bray@wayne.edu, Internet: www.cla.wayne.edu/anthro/museum/homepage.html. Dir.: Tamara Bray
University Museum / Ethnology Museum / Archaeological Museum - 1958
Anthropology, ethnography, archaeology 42936

Wayne State University Museum of Natural History, Biological Sciences Bldg, 5047 Gullen Mall, Detroit, MI 48202 - T: (313) 577-2872, Fax: (313) 577-6891, E-mail: wmoore@biologybiosci.wayne.edu. Dir.: William S. Moore, Cur.: Jesheskel Shoshani (Vertebrates), Stanley K. Gangwere (Insects), D. Carl Freeman (Herbarium)
University Museum / Natural History Museum - 1972
Natural History - herbarium 42937

Your Heritage House → The Heritage Museum of Fine Arts for Youth

Detroit Lakes MN

Becker County Historical Museum, Summit and W Front St, Detroit Lakes, MN 56501 - T: (218) 847-2938, Fax: (218) 847-5048, E-mail: bolerud@tekstar.com. Dir.: Becky Olerud
Local Museum - 1883
Local history 42938

Devils Tower WY

Devils Tower Visitor Center, State Hwy 110, Bldg 170, Devils Tower, WY 82714 - T: (307) 467-5283, Fax: (307) 467-5350, Internet: www.nps.gov/deto. Cur.: Jim Cheatham
Local Museum - 1906
Geology, hist, botany, Indian artifacts 42939

Dewey OK

Dewey Hotel, 801 N Delaware, Dewey, OK 74029 - T: (918) 532-4416
Local Museum - 1967 42940

Tom Mix Museum, 721 N Delaware, Dewey, OK 74029 - T: (918) 534-1555. Pres.: Colleen Burne
Local Museum - 1973 42941

Dexter ME

Dexter Historical Society Museum, 3 Water St, Dexter, ME 04930 - T: (207) 924-3043, 924-5721, E-mail: dexhist@panax.com, Internet: www.dextermaine.org. Dir./Cur.: Richard Whitney
Local Museum - 1966
Local history, Grist mill, Millers house, Carr school 42942

Dexter MI

Dexter Area Museum, 3443 Inverness, Dexter, MI 48130 - T: (734) 426-2519, E-mail: dexmuseum@aol.com, Internet: www.hvcn.org/info/dextermuseum. Dir.: Nina Doletsky-Rackham
Local Museum - 1976
Local hist 42943

Diamond MO

George Washington Carver House, 5646 Carver Rd, Diamond, MO 64840 - T: (417) 325-4151, Fax: (417) 325-4231, E-mail: gwca_superintendent@nps.gov
Science&Tech Museum / Agriculture Museum - 1943
Scientist George Washington Carver 42944

Dickinson ND

Dakota Dinosaur Museum, 200 Museum Dr, Dickinson, ND 58601 - T: (701) 225-3466, Fax: (701) 227-0534, E-mail: info@dakotadino.com, Internet: www.dakotadino.com. C.E.O.: Alice League
Science&Tech Museum - 1991
Paleontology, geology 42945

Gallery of Art, Dickinson State University, Dickinson, ND 58601-4896 - T: (701) 483-2312, Fax: (701) 483-2006, E-mail: sharon_linnehan@dsu.nodak.edu. Dir.: Sharon Linnehan
Fine Arts Museum
Contemporary graphics, Zoe Bailer paintings, American art 42946

Dighton KS

Lane County Historical Museum, 333 N Main St, Dighton, KS 67839 - T: (316) 397-5652. Pres.: Joanie Trebilcock, Cur.: Virginia Johnston
Local Museum - 1976
Regional history 42947

Dillingham AK

Samuel K. Fox Museum, Seward and D Sts, Dillingham, AK 99576 - T: (907) 842-5610, Fax: (907) 842-5691, Internet: www.nushtel.com/~dlgchmbr. Dir.: Tim Troll
Ethnology Museum - 1974
Alaskan Native and Indian museum 42948

Dillon MT

Beaverhead County Museum, 15 S Montana, Dillon, MT 59725-2433 - T: (406) 683-5027, E-mail: bvhdmuseum@bmt.net. Pres.: Stan Smith
Historical Museum - 1947 42949

Western Art Gallery and Museum, The University of Montana, 710 S Atlantic St, Dillon, MT 59725-3598 - T: (406) 683-7232, Fax: (406) 683-7493, E-mail: R_Horst@umwestern.edu, Internet: www.umwestern.edu. Dir.: Randy Horst
Fine Arts Museum / University Museum - 1986
Seidensticker wildlife trophy coll - Lucy Carson Library 42950

Dillon SC

James W. Dillon House Museum, W Main St, Dillon, SC 29536 - T: (843) 774-9051, Fax: (843) 774-5521, E-mail: jru@multi-forms.com. Dir.: Don Barclay
Local Museum
Local hist 42951

Dixon IL

John Deere House, 8393 S Main, Grand Detour, Dixon, IL 61021-9406 - T: (815) 652-4551, Fax: (815) 652-3835, E-mail: timmermanlynna@johndeere.com. Pres./Dir.: James H. Collins
Archaeological Museum / Historic Site - 1953 42952

Ronald Reagan Boyhood Home, 816 S Hennepin Av, Dixon, IL 61021 - T: (815) 288-3830, Fax: (815) 288-6757. Chm.: Norm Wymbs
Historic Site - 1980
Historic house 42953

Dodge City KS

Boot Hill Museum, Front St, Dodge City, KS 67801 - T: (316) 227-8188, Fax: (316) 227-7673, E-mail: frontst@pld.com, Internet: www.boothill.org. C.E.O.: Tammy Moody, Chairman: Gwen Nelson, Chief Cur.: David N. Kloppenborg, Cur.: Susan Dame (Exhibitions)
Historical Museum - 1947
Western history, located on Boot Hill 42954

Home of Stone, Ave A and Vine St, Dodge City, KS 67801 - T: (620) 227-6791, E-mail: glaugh@pld.com, Internet: www.ukans.edu/kansas/ford/index.html
Local Museum - 1965
Kerosene lamps, clocks, picture coll 42955

The Kansas Teachers' Hall of Fame, 603 5th Av, Dodge City, KS 67801 - T: (316) 225-7311. Dir.: Nancy Tramer
Historical Museum - 1977 42956

Dolores CO

Anasazi Heritage Center, 27501 Hwy 184, Dolores, CO 81323 - T: (970) 882-4811, Fax: (970) 882-7035, E-mail: marilynn_eastin@co.blm.gov, Internet: www.co.blm.gov/ahc/hmepge.htm. Dir.: LouAnn Jacobson
Ethnology Museum / Archaeological Museum - 1988
Archaeology 42957

Dora AL

Alabama Mining Museum, 120 East St, Dora, AL 35062 - T: (205) 648-2442. Dir.: Bonnie Sue Groves, Cur.: Florence Wiley
Historical Museum / Science&Tech Museum - 1982
Mining, 1905 steam locomotive, ore car and caboose; c.1900 Oakman, Alabama railroad depot bldg, c.1930 U.S. post office 42958

Dorchester NE

Saline County Historical Society Museum, Hwy 33, S of Main St, Dorchester, NE 68343 - T: (402) 947-2911, Fax: (402) 947-2911. Pres.: Norma Knoche
Local Museum - 1956 42959

Dothan AL

Landmark Park, Hwy 431 N, Dothan, AL 36302, mail addr: POB 6362, Dothan, AL 36302 - T: (334) 794-3452, Fax: (334) 677-7229, Internet: www.landmarkpark.com. Dir.: William M. Holman
Agriculture Museum - 1976
Official Museum of Agriculture for the State of Alabama 42960

Wiregrass Museum of Art, 126 Museum Av, Dothan, AL 36303-1624 - T: (334) 792-1746, Fax: (334) 792-9035, E-mail: wmuseum@snowhill.com, Internet: www.wiregrassmuseumofart.org. Exec. Dir.: Sam W. Kates
Fine Arts Museum - 1988
Art 42961

Douglas AZ

Slaughter Ranch Museum, 6153 Geronimo Trail, Douglas, AZ 85608 - T: (520) 558-2474, Fax: (602) 933-3777, E-mail: sranch@vtc.net, Internet: www.vtc.net/~sranch. Dir.: Harvey Finks, Cur.: John Lavanchy, Sc. Staff: Dr. Reba Grandrud (History)
Local Museum - 1982
Local hist 42962

Douglas MI

Steamship Keewatin, Harbour Village, Union St & Blue Star Hwy, Douglas, MI 49406 - T: (616) 857-2464, 857-2151, Fax: (616) 857-2107, Internet: www.keewatinmaritimemuseum. Pres.: R.J. Peterson
Historical Museum / Science&Tech Museum - 1965
Historic Ship, former 1907 Great Lakes passenger steamship of the Canadian Pacific Railroad 42963

Douglas WY

Fort Fetterman State Museum, 752 Hwy 93, Douglas, WY 82633 - T: (307) 358-2864, 684-7629, Fax: (307) 358-2864, E-mail: rwilso@missc.state.wy.us. Head: Bill Gentle
Military Museum - 1963
Military hist, life of the native Americans (Dakota, Cheyenne, Shoshone) 42964

Wyoming Pioneer Memorial Museum, Wyoming State Fairgrounds, 400 W Center St, Douglas, WY 82633 - T: (307) 358-9288, Fax: (307) 358-9293. Dir./Cur.: Arlene E. Earnst
Local Museum - 1956
Local hist 42965

Douglass KS

Douglass Historical Museum, 318 S Forest, Douglass, KS 67039 - T: (316) 746-2319, 746-2122. Dir./Cur.: Francis Renfro
Historical Museum - 1949
Pioneer museum 42966

Dover DE

Biggs Museum of American Art, 406 Federal St, Dover, DE 19901, mail addr: POB 711, Dover, DE 19903 - T: (302) 674-2111, Fax: (302) 674-5133, E-mail: biggs@delaware.net, Internet: www.biggsmuseum.org. Dir.: Karol A. Schmiegel, Cur.: Roxanne M. Stanulis
Fine Arts Museum - 1989
Art Museum housed in 1858 County Office Building 42967

Delaware Agricultural Museum, 866 N Dupont Hwy, Dover, DE 19901 - T: (302) 734-1618, Fax: (302) 734-0457, E-mail: damv@dol.net, Internet: www.agriculturalmuseum.org. Dir.: Linda Chatfield, Cur.: Jennifer Griffin
Local Museum / Agriculture Museum - 1974
Rural life, agricultural hist and technology 42968

Delaware State Museums, Rose Cottage, 102 S State St, Dover, DE 19901 - T: (302) 739-5316, Fax: (302) 739-6712, E-mail: jistewart.de.us, Internet: www.destatemuseums.org. Cur.: Claudia Melson (Collections Management), Edward R. McWilliams (Exhibits), Madeline Dunn (Education)
Local Museum - 1931
Local hist 42969

Dover MA

Caryl House, 107 Dedham St, Dover, MA 02030 - T: (508) 785-1832, Fax: (508) 785-0789. C.E.O.: Paul H. Tedesco, Cur.: Priscilla Pitt Jones
Local Museum - 1920
Historic house 42970

Sawin Memorial Building, 80 Dedham St, Dover, MA 02030 - T: (508) 785-1832, Fax: (508) 785-0789. C.E.O.: Paul H. Tedesco, Cur.: Shirley McGill, Glenda Mattes
Local Museum - 1907
Regional history 42971

Dover NH

Annie E. Woodman Institute, 182 Central Av, Dover, NH 03821-0146 - T: (603) 742-1038. Cur.: Raoul F. Couture, Ass. Cur.: Llyr E. Couture
Local Museum - 1916 42972

Dover OH

J.E. Reeves Home and Museum, 325 E Iron Av, Dover, OH 44622 - T: (330) 343-7040, (800) 815-2794, Fax: (330) 343-6290, E-mail: reeves@tusco.net, Internet: web.tusco.net/reeves. Pres.: James D. Nixon, Dir.: Chris Nixon
Local Museum - 1958 42973

Warther Museum, 331 Karl Av, Dover, OH 44622 - T: (330) 343-7513, E-mail: info@warthers.com, Internet: www.warthers.com. Pres./Dir.: David R. Warther
Decorative Arts Museum / Agriculture Museum - 1936 42974

Dover TN

Fort Donelson National Battlefield Museum, 120 Fort Donelson Rd, Dover, TN 37058 - T: (931) 232-5706, Fax: (931) 232-6331, E-mail: fodo_ranger_-activities@nps.gov
Military Museum - 1928
Civil War 42975

Dover-Foxcroft ME

Blacksmith Shop Museum, 100 Dawes Rd, Dover-Foxcroft, ME 04426 - T: (207) 564-8618, E-mail: dblockwood@hotmail.com. Cur.: Dave Lockwood
Historical Museum - 1963 42976

Dowagiac MI

Heddon Museum, 414 West St, Dowagiac, MI 49047 - T: (616) 782-5698, E-mail: heddonmuseum@lyonsindustries.com. Dir.: Joan Lyons, Don Lyons
Science&Tech Museum - 1995
History Museum in the original Heddon factory 42977

Southwestern Michigan College Museum, 58900 Cherry Grove Rd, Dowagiac, MI 49047 - T: (616) 782-1374, Fax: (616) 782-1460, E-mail: museum@smc.cc.mi.us, Internet: smc.cc.mi.us. Dir.: Jill P. Dixon, Cur.: Steve Arseneau (History)
University Museum / Historical Museum / Science&Tech Museum - 1982
History Museum and Science Center 42978

Downers Grove IL

The Downers Grove Park District Museum, 831 Maple Av, Downers Grove, IL 60515 - T: (630) 963-1309, Fax: (630) 963-0496, E-mail: mharmon@xnet.com, Internet: www.dgparks.org. Dir.: Mark S. Harmon
Local Museum - 1968
Local history 42979

Downey CA

Downey Museum of Art, 10419 S Rives Av, Downey, CA 90241 - T: (562) 861-0419, Fax: (562) 861-0419. Dir.: Kate Davies, Sachia Long
Fine Arts Museum - 1957
Paintings, sculpture, graphics, photographs 42980

Downieville CA

Downieville Museum, 330 Main St, Downieville, CA 95936 - T: (530) 289-3423, Fax: (530) 289-1501, E-mail: arniekej@sccn.net. Dir.: Kevel Jane Gutman
Local Museum - 1932 42981

Doylestown PA

Fonthill Museum of the Bucks County Historical Society, E Court St, Doylestown, PA 18901 - T: (215) 348-9461, Fax: (215) 348-9462, E-mail: info@fonthillmuseum.org, Internet: www.fonthillmuseum.org. C.E.O.: Douglas C. Dolan, Dir.: Jennifer Sliwinski
Decorative Arts Museum / Historical Museum - 1930
Home of Henry C. Mercer (1856-1930), noted archeologist, arts and crafts 42982

Heritage Conservancy, 85 Old Dublin Pike, Doylestown, PA 18901 - T: (215) 345-7020, Fax: (215) 345-4328, E-mail: cdavid@heritageconservancy.org, Internet: www.heritageconservancy.org
Fine Arts Museum / Decorative Arts Museum - 1958
Artwork of local artists, decorative arts, photographs 42983

James A. Michener Art Museum, 138 S Pine St, Doylestown, PA 18901 - T: (215) 340-9800, Fax: (215) 340-9807, E-mail: jamam1@mitchenerartmuseum.org, Internet: www.michenerartmuseum.org. Dir.: Bruce Katsiff, Ass. Dir.: Judy Hayman, Sen. Cur.: Brian Peterson, Cur.: Adrienne Neszmelyi (Education), Zoriana Siokalo (Public Programs)
Fine Arts Museum - 1987
Pennsylvania impressionism 20th c 42984

Mercer Museum of the Bucks County Historical Society, 84 S Pine St, Doylestown, PA 18901-4999 - T: (215) 345-0210, Fax: (215) 230-0823, E-mail: info@mercermuseum.org, Internet: www.mercermuseum.org. Dir.: Douglas C. Dolan, Ass. Dir.: Molly W. Lowell, Cur.: Cory Amsler, Libr.: Betsy Smith
Folklore Museum / Historical Museum / Science&Tech Museum - 1916 42985

Dragoon AZ

The Amerind Foundation, 2100 N Amerind Rd, Dragoon, AZ 85609, mail addr: POB 400, Dragoon, AZ 85609 - T: (520) 586-3666, Fax: (520) 586-4679, E-mail: amerind@amerind.org, Internet: www.amerind.org. Pres.: William Duncan Fulton, Dir.: Dr. Anne I. Woosley
Local Museum - 1937
Archaeology, ethnology, art 42986

Dresden ME

Pownalborough Court House, Rte 128, Dresden, ME 04342 - T: (207) 882-6817, E-mail: lcha@wiscasset.net, Internet: www.lincolncountyhistory.org. Dir.: Margaret M. Shiels
Decorative Arts Museum - 1954 42987

Drummond Island MI

Drummond Island Historical Museum, Water St, Drummond Island, MI 49726 - T: (906) 493-5746. Dir.: Harry Ropp, John Lowe, Michael McDonald, Rosalie Sasso, Catherine Ashley, Cur.: Audrey Moser
Local Museum - 1961
Local history 42988

Dublin GA

Dublin-Laurens Museum, 311 Academy Av, Dublin, GA 31021 - T: (478) 272-9242, E-mail: history@nlamerica.com. Dir.: Scott Thompson
Special Museum - 1979
Archaeology, geology, paintings, photos, artefacts, housed in 1904 restored Carnegie Library 42989

Dubois WY

Wind River Historical Center Dubois Museum, 909 West Ramshorn, Dubois, WY 82513 - T: (307) 455-2284, Fax: (307) 455-3852, E-mail: wrh@wyoming.com, Internet: www.windriverhistory.org. Dir.: Dr. Sharon Kahin
Local Museum - 1976
Local hist, natural hist - Lucius Burch Center for Western Traditions 42990

Dubuque IA

Dubuque Museum of Art, 701 Locust St, Dubuque, IA 52001 - T: (563) 557-1851, Fax: (319) 557-7826, E-mail: dbqartmuseum@mcleodusa.net, Internet: www.dbqartmuseum.com. Dir.: Nelson Britt, Pres.: Tim Conlon
Fine Arts Museum / Folklore Museum - 1874
Art 42991

Mathias Ham House, 2241 Lincoln Av, Dubuque, IA 52001 - T: (563) 557-9545, Fax: (563) 583-1241, E-mail: rivermuse@mwci.net, Internet: www.mississippirivermuseum.com. Dir.: Jerome A. Enzler
Historical Museum - 1964
Local history 42992

Mississippi River Museum, 350 E 3rd St, Dubuque, IA 52001 - T: (563) 557-9545, Fax: (563) 583-1241, E-mail: rivermuseum@mwci.net, Internet: www.mississippirivermuseum.com. Dir.: Jerome A. Enzler, Cur.: Tacie N. Campbell
Historical Museum - 1950
Maritime and naval history, Mississippi Riverboats - archives 42993

Dugger IN

Dugger Coal Museum, 8178 E Main St, Dugger, IN 47848. Cur.: Martha Marlow
Science&Tech Museum - 1980
Deep coal mines and strip mines, tools, clothing, protective gear, old mining reports 42994

Duluth GA

Gwinettt Fine Arts Center → Jacqueline Casey Hudgens Center for the Arts

Jacqueline Casey Hudgens Center for the Arts, 6400 Sugarloaf Pkwy, Bldg 300, Duluth, GA 30097 - T: (770) 623-6002, Fax: (770) 623-3555, E-mail: elliott@hudgenscenter.org, Internet: www.hudgenscenter.org. Dir.: Nancy Gullickson, Cur.: Lucy Elliott
Fine Arts Museum - 1981 42995

Southeastern Railway Museum, 3595 Peachtree Rd, Duluth, GA 30096 - T: (770) 476-2013, Fax: (770) 622-7269, E-mail: admin@srmduluth.org, Internet: www.srmduluth.org. Dir.: Lesa Campbell
Science&Tech Museum / Historical Museum - 1968
Rail cars and locomotives 1910 - present, rail-related artefacts 42996

Duluth MN

Duluth Art Institute, 506 W Michigan St, Duluth, MN 55802 - T: (218) 733-7560, Fax: (218) 733-7506, Internet: www.duluthartinstitute.org. Dir.: John Steffl
Fine Arts Museum 42997

Duluth Children's Museum, 506 W Michigan St, Duluth, MN 55802 - T: (218) 733-7544, Fax: (218) 733-7547, E-mail: explore@duluthchildrensmuseum.org, Internet: www.duluthchildrensmuseum.org. Dir./Cur.: Bonnie A. Cusick
Local Museum / Special Museum - 1930
Children's, youth, Saint Louis County heritage, arts 42998

Glensheen Historic Estate, 3300 London Rd, Duluth, MN 55804 - T: (218) 726-8910, Fax: (218) 726-8911, E-mail: glen@d.umn.edu, Internet: www.d.umn.edu/glen. Dir.: William K. Miller
Historical Museum - 1979
Historic neo-Jacobean mansion, carriage house, original furnishings 42999

Lake Superior Maritime Visitors Center, 600 Lake Av, Duluth, MN 55802 - T: (218) 727-2497, Fax: (218) 720-5270, E-mail: Thomas.R.Holden@Lre02.usace.army.mil. Dir.: Thomas Holden
Historical Museum / Science&Tech Museum - 1973
Marine hist 43000

Lake Superior Railroad Museum, 506 W Michigan St, Duluth, MN 55802 - T: (218) 733-7590, Fax: (218) 733-7596, E-mail: museum@lsrm.org, Internet: www.lsrm.org. Cur.: Thomas Gannon
Historical Museum - 1974
Railroad, Duluth Union Depot Bldg 43001

Saint Louis County Historical Museum, 506 W Michigan St, Duluth, MN 55802 - T: (218) 733-7580, Fax: (218) 733-7585, E-mail: history@chartemi.net, Internet: www.vets-hall.org. Pres.: Nick Wognum, Dir.: JoAnne Coombe
Local Museum - 1922
Regional history, E. Johnson coll of drawings and paintings, Ojibwe and Sioux beadwork, quillwork, furniture 43002

Tweed Museum of Art, University of Minnesota, 10 University Dr, Duluth, MN 55812 - T: (218) 726-8222, Fax: (218) 726-8503, E-mail: tma@d.umn.edu, Internet: www.d.umn.edu/tma/. Dir.: Martin DeWitt
Fine Arts Museum / University Museum - 1950
Johnathan Sax coll (American prints), George P. Tweed coll (paintings), sculpture 43003

Dumas AR

Desha County Museum, Hwy 165 E, Dumas, AR 71639, mail addr: POB 141, Dumas, AR 71639 - T: (870) 382-4222. Dir.: Mary C. Martin, Cur.: Charlotte Shexnayder
Local Museum - 1979
Local history 43004

Dumas TX

Moore County Historical Museum, 1820 S Dumas Av, Dumas, TX 79029-4329 - T: (806) 935-3113, Fax: (806) 934-3621. C.E.O.: Kurt Stallwitz
Local Museum - 1976
Local hist 43005

Dumfries VA

Weems-Botts Museum, 3914 Cameron St, Dumfries, VA 22026 - T: (703) 221-2218, Fax: (703) 221-2218, E-mail: weemsbotts@msn.com, Internet: www.geocities.com/hdvine. Pres.: Barry K. Ward, Dir.: Kimberley D. Ward
Local Museum - 1974
Local hist 43006

Duncan OK

Chisholm Trail Heritage Center Museum, 1000 N 29th St, Duncan, OK 73534 - T: (580) 252-6692, 252-6563, Fax: (580) 252-6567, E-mail: statue@texhoma.net, Internet: www.onthechistholmtrial.com. Exec. Dir.: Dr. Chris Jefferies
Historical Museum
Cowboy, cavalry, Native American clothing, cattle trails, sculptures 43007

Stephens County Historical Society Museum, Hwy 81 and Beech, Fuqua Park, Duncan, OK 73533 - T: (580) 252-0717, Fax: (580) 251-3195. Dir.: PeeWee Cary, Ass. Dir.: Vickie Zimmerman, Pat Hale, Marge Rigdon, Sharleen Johns, Teresa Fritts
Local Museum - 1971 43008

Dundee IL

Dundee Township Historical Society Museum, 426 Highland Av, Dundee, IL 60118 - T: (847) 428-6996, Internet: www.nothstarnet.org/dukhome/DTHS. Pres.: Kristie Benedik
Local Museum - 1964
Local history 43009

Dunedin FL

Dunedin Fine Arts and Cultural Center, 1143 Michigan Blvd, Dunedin, FL 34698 - T: (727) 298-3322, E-mail: info@dfac.org
Public Gallery 43010

Dunedin Historical Society Museum, 349 Main St, Dunedin, FL 34697-2393 - T: (727) 736-1176, Fax: (727) 738-1871, E-mail: dunhist@compuserve.com, Internet: www.ci.dunedin.fl.us. Dir.: Vincent Luisi
Local Museum - 1969
Local history, 1920 Atlantic Coastline Passenger Station, Old Freight Warehouse 43011

Dunkirk IN

The Glass Museum, 309 S Franklin, Dunkirk, IN 47336 - T: (765) 768-6872, Fax: (765) 768-6872, E-mail: marynewsome@netscape.net, Internet: www.dunkirkpubliclibrary.com. Dir.: Ailesia Franklin, Cur.: Mary Newsome
Decorative Arts Museum - 1979
Glass 43012

DuPont WA

DuPont Historical Museum, 207 Barksdale Av, DuPont, WA 98327 - T: (253) 964-2399, 964-3492, Fax: (253) 964-3554, E-mail: info@dupontmuseum.com, Internet: www.dupontmuseum.com. Pres.: Lorraine Overmyer
Local Museum - 1976
Local hist 43013

Durango CO

Animas Museum, 3065 W 2nd Av, Durango, CO 81301 - T: (970) 259-2402, Fax: (970) 259-4749, E-mail: animasmuseum@frontier.net, Internet: www.frontier.net/~animasmuseum. Dir.: Robert McDaniel, Cur.: Charles A. DiFerdinando
Local Museum - 1978
Local hist 43014

Strater Hotel, 699 Main Av, Durango, CO 81301 - T: (970) 247-4431, 375-7121, Fax: (970) 259-2208, E-mail: info@strater.com, Internet: www.strater.com. C.E.O.: Rod Barker
Historical Museum - 1887
Walnut antiques 43015

Durant OK

Fort Washita, 15 miles east of Madill, Durant, OK 74701 - T: (580) 924-6502, Fax: (580) 924-6502, E-mail: ftwashita@ok-history.mus.ok.us, Internet: www.texoma-ok.com/trooper/1842.htm. C.E.O.: Dr. Bob Blackburn
Historic Site / Open Air Museum / Military Museum - 1967 43016

Durham NC

Bennett Place State Historic Site, 4409 Bennett Memorial Rd, Durham, NC 27705 - T: (919) 383-4345, Fax: (919) 383-4349, E-mail: bennettplace@mindspring.com, Internet: www.ah.dcr.state.nc.us/hs/bennett/bennett.htm. Man.: Davis Waters
Local Museum - 1962 43017

Duke Homestead State Historic Site, 2828 Duke Homestead Rd, Durham, NC 27705 - T: (919) 477-5498, Fax: (919) 479-7092, E-mail: dukehomestead@verizon.net, Internet: duke.ncsl.dcr.state.nc.us. Pres.: Walker S. Stone
Historical Museum - 1974 43018

Duke University Museum of Art, Buchanan Blvd at Trinity, Durham, NC 27708 - T: (919) 684-5135, Fax: (919) 681-8624, E-mail: brevans@duke.edu, Internet: www.duke.edu/duma/. Dir.: Dr. Michael P. Mezzatesta, Ass. Dir.: David L. Roselli, Cur.: Dr. Sarah W. Schroth, Ass. Cur.: Dr. Anne Schroder
Fine Arts Museum / University Museum - 1968 43019

Duke University Union Museum and Brown Art Gallery, Bryan Center, Science Dr, Durham, NC 27708 - T: (919) 684-2911, Fax: (919) 684-8395, Internet: www.duke.edu/web/duu/. Dir.: Regan Bedouin
University Museum / Fine Arts Museum 43020

Durham Art Guild, 120 Morris St, Durham, NC 27701 - T: (919) 560-2713, Fax: (919) 560-2754, E-mail: artguild1@yahoo.com, Internet: www.durhamartguild.org. Dir.: Lisa Morton
Public Gallery 43021

History of Medicine Collections, Duke University Medical Center Library, Durham, NC 27710 - T: (919) 660-1143, Fax: (919) 681-7599, E-mail: porte004@mc.duke.edu, Internet: www.mc.duke.edu/mclibrary. Cur.: Suzanne Porter
Library with Exhibitions - 1956 43022

North Carolina Central University Art Museum, c/o North Carolina Central University, 1801 Fayetteville Stal University, Durham, NC 27707 - T: (919) 560-6211, Fax: (919) 560-5012, E-mail: Krodgers@wpo.nccu.edu, Internet: www.nccu.edu/artmuseum/. Dir.: Kenneth G. Rodgers
Fine Arts Museum / University Museum - 1971 43023

North Carolina Museum of Life and Science, 433 Murray Av, Durham, NC 27704 - T: (919) 220-5429, Fax: (919) 220-5575, E-mail: contactus@ncmls.org, Internet: www.ncmls.org. C.E.O.: Dr. Thomas H. Krakauer
Science&Tech Museum / Natural History Museum - 1946 43024

Durham NH

The Art Gallery, University of New Hampshire, Paul Creative Arts Center, 30 College Rd, Durham, NH 03824-3538 - T: (603) 862-3712, Fax: (603) 862-2191, E-mail: art.gallery@unh.edu, Internet: www.unh.edu/art-gallery. Dir.: Vicki C. Wright, Ass. Dir.: Astrida Schaeffer, Cur.: Amanda Tappan (Education, Publicity)
Fine Arts Museum / University Museum - 1960 43025

Durham Historic Association Museum, Newmarket Rd and Main St, Durham, NH 03824 - T: (603) 868-5436. Pres.: Marion E. James, C.E.O.: Alexander Amell
Local Museum - 1851 43026

Duxbury MA

Alden House Museum, 105 Alden St, Duxbury, MA 02332 - T: (781) 934-9092, Fax: (781) 934-9149, E-mail: curator@alden.org, Internet: www.alden.org. Dir.: Charles R. Coombs
Local Museum - 1906
Pilgrims John Alden and Priscilla Mullins, founders of Duxbury 43027

Art Complex Museum, 189 Alden St, Duxbury, MA 02331 - T: (781) 934-6634, Fax: (781) 934-5117, E-mail: info@artcomplex.org, Internet: www.artcomplex.org. Dir.: Charles A. Weyerhaeuser, Cur.: Catherine Mayes, Laura Doherty (Communication)
Fine Arts Museum - 1971
Art 43028

Duxbury Ma

Duxbury Rural and Historical Society, 479 Washington St, Duxbury, Ma 02331 - T: (781) 934-6106, Fax: (781) 934-5730, E-mail: pbrowne@duxburyhistory.org, Internet: www.duxburyhistory.org. Exec. Dir.: Patrick Browne
Local Museum - 1883
Decorative arts, textiles, relics of 1869 French-American cable 43029

Dyersville IA

National Farm Toy Museum, 1110 16th Av Ct SE, Dyersville, IA 52040 - T: (563) 875-2727, Fax: (563) 875-8467, E-mail: farmtoys@dyersville.com, Internet: www.nftmonline.com. Cur.: Anne Reitzler
Special Museum - 1986
Trucks, life size toy tractor display 43030

Eagle WI

Old World Wisconsin, S103 W37890 Hwy 67, Eagle, WI 53119 - T: (262) 594-6300, Fax: (262) 594-6342, E-mail: oww@whs.wisc.edu, Internet: www.swisconsinhistory.org. Dir.: Peter S. Arnold, Ass. Dir.: John W. Reilly, Cur.: Martin Perkins (Collections), Carol Smith
Agriculture Museum / Historical Museum / Historic Site - 1976
Ethnology 43031

Eagle City AK

Eagle Historical Society and Museums, Third and Chamberlain Rd, Eagle City, AK 99738 - T: (907) 547-2325, Fax: (907) 547-2232, E-mail: ehsmuseums@aptalaska.net, Internet: www.eagleak.org. Pres.: Elva Scott
Local Museum - 1961
Local military and Indians history 43032

Eagle Harbor MI

Keweenaw County Historical Society Museum, Lighthouse Street, M-26, Eagle Harbor, MI 49950 - T: (906) 289-4990, 296-2561, Fax: (906) 296-9767. Pres.: Peter Van Pelt
Historical Museum / Science&Tech Museum - 1981
Marine hist 43033

Eagle River AK

Alaska Museum of Natural History, 11723 Old Glenn Hwy, Eagle River, AK 99577 - T: (907) 694-0819, Fax: (907) 694-0919, E-mail: info@alaskamuseum.org, Internet: www.alaskamuseum.org. Dir.: Kurt Johnson, Ass. Dir.: Elaine M. Hughes, Cur.: Jim Pray (Minerals), Anne Pasch (Exhibits), Cons.: Melissa Engel
Natural History Museum - 1992 43034

East Aurora NY

Elbert Hubbard-Roycroft Museum, 363 Oakwood Av, East Aurora, NY 14052, mail addr: POB 472, East Aurora, NY 14052-0472 - T: (716) 652-4735. Cur.: M. Fisher, Geneviève Steffen, Bruce F. Bland, Maryann Myers
Local Museum / Decorative Arts Museum - 1962
Books, leathercraft, metal work, furniture, artglass, arts and crafts movement 43035

Millard Fillmore House, 24 Shearer Av, East Aurora, NY 14052 - T: (716) 652-8875, Internet: www.millardfilmorehouse.org. Pres.: Diane Meade, Cur.: Marie Schnurr, Lyn Chemera
Local Museum - 1951 43036

East Brunswick NJ

East Brunswick Museum, 16 Maple St, East Brunswick, NJ 08816 - T: (732) 257-2313, 257-1508. Pres.: Mark Nonesteid
Local Museum - 1978
Local and regional hist 43037

East Durham NY

Durham Center Museum, Star Rte 1, East Durham, NY 12423 - T: (518) 239-8461, Fax: (518) 239-4081, E-mail: dougsancie@aol.com. Dir.: Dan Clifton, Cur.: Sanciea Thomsen, Douglas Thomsen
Local Museum - 1960 43038

Irish American Heritage Museum, 2267 Rte 145, East Durham, NY 12423 - T: (518) 432-6598, Fax: (518) 634-7497, E-mail: irishamermuseum@cs.com, Internet: www.irishamericanheritagemuseum.org. C.E.O.: Joseph J. Dolan
Folklore Museum - 1986
Ethnic museum 43039

East Greenwich RI

James Mitchell Varnum House and Museum, 57 Peirce St, East Greenwich, RI 02818 - T: (401) 884-1776, E-mail: k8bcm@home.com, Internet: www.varnumcontinentals.org. Dir.: Bruce C. MacGunnigle
Local Museum - 1938
Historic house 43040

New England Wireless and Steam Museum, 1300 Frenchtown Rd, East Greenwich, RI 02818 - T: (401) 885-0545, Fax: (401) 884-0683, E-mail: newsm@ids.net, Internet: users.ids.net/~newsm. Pres.: Robert W. Merriam
Science&Tech Museum - 1964
Engineering 43041

Varnum Memorial Armory and Military Museum, 6 Main St, East Greenwich, RI 02818 - T: (401) 884-4110, E-mail: k8bcm@cox.net, Internet: www.varnumcontinentals.org. Dir.: Bruce C. MacGunnigle, Cur.: Donald Marcum
Military Museum - 1913
Military hist 43042

East Hampton NY

Clinton Academy Museum, 151 Main St, East Hampton, NY 11937 - T: (516) 324-6850, Fax: (516) 324-9885, E-mail: ehhs@optonline.net, Internet: www.easthamptonhistory.org. Dir.: Dr. Karen Hensel
Historical Museum - 1784 43043

East Hampton Historical Society Museum, 101 Main St, East Hampton, NY 11937 - T: (516) 324-6850, Fax: (516) 324-9885, E-mail: ehhs@optonline.net, Internet: www.easthamptonhistory.org. Exec. Dir.: Dr. Karen Hensel
Local Museum - 1921 43044

East Hampton Town Marine Museum, 101 Main St, East Hampton, NY 11937 - T: (516) 267-6544, Fax: (516) 324-9885, E-mail: ehhs@optonline.net, Internet: www.easthamptonhistory.org. Exec. Dir.: Dr. Karen Hensel
Natural History Museum - 1966 43045

Guild Hall Museum, 158 Main St, East Hampton, NY 11937 - T: (631) 324-0806, Fax: (631) 329-5043, E-mail: pr@guildhall.org, Internet: guildhall.org. Dir.: Ruth Appelhof, Cur.: Simon Taylor, Ass. Cur.: Farrin Cary
Fine Arts Museum - 1931 43046

Home Sweet Home Museum, 14 James Ln, East Hampton, NY 11937 - T: (613) 324-0713, Fax: (613) 324-0713, Internet: www.easthampton.com/homesweethome. Dir.: Hugh R. King
Decorative Arts Museum / Local Museum / Historic Site - 1928 43047

Mulford House and Farm, 10 James Ln, East Hampton, NY 11937 - T: (516) 324-6850, Fax: (516) 324-9885, E-mail: ehhs@optonline.net, Internet: www.easthamptononline.org. Dir.: Dr. Karen Hensel
Agriculture Museum / Open Air Museum - 1948
Farm implements 43048

Osborn-Jackson House, 101 Main St, East Hampton, NY 11937 - T: (516) 324-6850, Fax: (516) 324-9885, E-mail: ehhs@optonline.net, Internet: www.easthamptonhistory.org. Dir.: Dr. Karen Hensel
Decorative Arts Museum / Local Museum - 1979
Decorative and fine arts 43049

East Haven CT

Shore Line Trolley Museum, 17 River St, East Haven, CT 06512-2519 - T: (203) 467-6927, Fax: (203) 467-7635, E-mail: berasltm@aol.com, Internet: www.bera.org. Pres.: Donald J. Engel, Dir.: George Boucher, Theodore Eickmann (Vehicle Collection), Frederick Sherwood (Exhibits)
Science&Tech Museum - 1945
Transport technology, operating railway 43050

East Islip NY

Islip Art Museum, 50 Irish Ln, East Islip, NY 11730 - T: (631) 224-5402, Fax: (631) 224-5417, E-mail: info@islipartmuseum.org, Internet: www.islipartmuseum.org. Dir.: Mary Lou Cohalan, Susan Simmons, Cur.: Karen Shaw
Fine Arts Museum - 1973
Art 43051

East Jordan MI

East Jordan Portside Art and Historical Museum, 1787 S M-66 Hwy, East Jordan, MI 49727 - T: (616) 536-2393, Fax: (616) 536-2051, E-mail: JPardee2@Juno.com. Pres.: Jean Pardee, C.E.O.: Cygred Riley
Fine Arts Museum / Local Museum - 1976
Local hist, art 43052

East Lansing MI

Kresge Art Museum, Michigan State University, East Lansing, MI 48824 - T: (517) 353-9834, Fax: (517) 355-6577, E-mail: kamuseum@msu.edu, Internet: www.msu.edu/unit/kamuseum. Dir.: Dr. Susan J. Bandes, Cur.: April Kingsley
Fine Arts Museum / University Museum - 1959
Drawings, graphics, bronzes, African art, ethnology, ceramics, etchings and engravings, Afro-American art, Eskimo art, decorative arts, baroque art, antiquities 43053

Michigan State University Museum, W Circle Dr, East Lansing, MI 48824-1045 - T: (517) 355-2370, Fax: (517) 432-2846, E-mail: dewhurs1@pilot.msu.edu, Internet: museum.msu.edu. Pres.: Max Hoffman, Dir.: Dr. C. Kurt Dewhurst, Cur.: Dr. Barbara Lundrigan (Mammalogy), Dr. Pamela Rasmussen (Ornithology), Dr. William Lovis (Anthropology), Dr. Michael Gottfried (Vertebrate Paleontology), Dr. Jodie O'Gorman (Great Lakes Archaeology), Val Berryman (History), Dr. Marsha MacDowell (Folk Arts), Dr. Yvonne Lockwood (Folklife), Juan Alvarez (Exhibits), Dr. Kris Morrissey (Education), Ass. Cur.: Terry Shaffer (History), LuAnne Kozma (Folk Arts), Dr. Susan Krouse (Anthropology), Brian Kirschensteiner, Tammy Stone-Gordon (Exhibits)
University Museum / Local Museum - 1857
Science, cultural history, folk art, history, archaeology, ethnology, anthropology, paleontology, mammalogy, ornitology 43054

East Liverpool OH

Lou Holtz and Upper Ohio Valley Hall of Fame, 120 E Fifth St, East Liverpool, OH 43920 - T: (330) 386-5443, Fax: (330) 382-0244, E-mail: gulutz@raex.com, Internet: www.louholtzhalloffame.com
Special Museum / Local Museum - 1998 43055

Museum of Ceramics, 400 E Fifth St, East Liverpool, OH 43920 - T: (330) 386-6001, Fax: (330) 386-0488, E-mail: ceramics@clover.net, Internet: www.ohiohistory.org. Cur.: Mark Twyford
Decorative Arts Museum - 1980 43056

Museum of Ceramics at East Liverpool → Museum of Ceramics

East Meredith NY

Hanford Mills Museum, County Routes 10 and 12, East Meredith, NY 13757 - T: (607) 278-5744, Fax: (607) 278-6299, E-mail: hanford1@hanfordmills.org, Internet: www.hanfordmills.org. Dir.: Elizabeth Callahan
Science&Tech Museum - 1973
Sawmilling, woodworking, gristmilling equip 43057

East Poultney VT

East Poultney Museum, The Green, East Poultney, VT 05741, mail addr: 148 Upper Rd, Poultney, VT 05764 - T: (802) 287-5268
Local Museum - 1954
Early Poultney hist, costumes, farming 43058

East Springfield NY

Boswell Museum of Music, 5748 US Hwy 20, East Springfield, NY 13333 - T: (607) 264-3321, Fax: (607) 264-3321, E-mail: boswell@telenet.net, Internet: www.boswellmuseum.org
Music Museum - 1990
Recorded sound, clothing, furnishings 43059

Hyde Hall, Mill Rd, Near Glimmerglass State Park, East Springfield, NY 13333, mail addr: Friends of Hyde Hall, POB 721, Cooperstown, NY 13326 - T: (607) 547-5098, Fax: (607) 547-8462, E-mail: hydehall@wpe.com, Internet: www.hydehall.org
Historical Museum - 1964 43060

East Tawas MI

Iosco County Historical Museum, 405 W Bay St, East Tawas, MI 48730 - T: (989) 362-8911, E-mail: klenowr@alpena.cc.mi.us. Pres.: Rosemary E. Klenow
Local Museum - 1976
Local history, bldg built by J.D. Hawks, 1st president of the Detroit and Mackinaw Railway 43061

East Troy WI

East Troy Electric Railroad Museum, POB 943, East Troy, WI 53120-0943 - T: (262) 642-3263, Fax: (262) 642-3197, E-mail: JFTrolley@aol.com, Internet: www.easttroyrr.org
Science&Tech Museum - 1975
Trolley cars, electric railway cars 43062

East Windsor CT

Connecticut Trolley Museum, 58 North Rd, East Windsor, CT 06088-0360 - T: (860) 627-6540, Fax: (860) 627-6510, E-mail: information@ceraonline.org, Internet: www.ceraonline.org. Pres.: Alex P. Goff
Science&Tech Museum - 1940
Trolley transport system 43063

Scantic Academy Museum, 169 Wells Rd, East Windsor, CT 06088 - T: (860) 623-5327. Pres.: Michael Hunt
Local Museum - 1965
Industry, agriculture, transpotation, paintings 43064

Eastlake OH

Croatian Heritage Museum, 34900 Lakeshore Blvd, Eastlake, OH 44095 - T: (440) 946-2044, Fax: (216) 991-3051, E-mail: banjelacic@worldnet.att.net. Cur.: Branka Malinar
Ethnology Museum / Folklore Museum - 1983
Croatian textiles, folk costumes, wood carvings, sculpture, metal work, leather work, paintings - library 43065

Easton MD

Academy Art Museum, 106 South St, Easton, MD 21601 - T: (410) 822-2787, Fax: (410) 822-5997, E-mail: Academy@goeaston.net, Internet: www.art-academy.org. Dir.: Christopher J. Brownawell
Fine Arts Museum - 1958
Multi-disciplinary arts 43066

Historical Museum of Talbot County, 25 S Washington St, Easton, MD 21601 - T: (410) 822-0773, Fax: (410) 822-7911, E-mail: director@hstc.org, Internet: www.hstc.org. Pres.: Fred Dallam, Dir.: Joan R. Hoge
Local Museum - 1954
Regional history 43067

Easton PA

Lafayette College Art Gallery, Hamilton and High St, Easton, PA 18042-1768 - T: (610) 330-5361, Fax: (610) 330-5642, E-mail: okayam@lafayette.edu, Internet: www.lafayette.edu. Dir./Cur.: Michiko Okaya
Fine Arts Museum / Public Gallery / University Museum - 1983
Art 43068

National Canal Museum, 30 Centre Sq, Easton, PA 18042-7743 - T: (610) 559-6613, Fax: (610) 559-6686, E-mail: ncm@canals.org, Internet: canals.org. Dir.: J. Steven Humphrey, Sc. Staff: Lance Metz (History), Cur.: Kelly Austin
Science&Tech Museum - 1970 43069

Northampton County Historical and Genealogical Society Museum, 107 S Fourth St, Easton, PA 18042 - T: (610) 253-1222, Fax: (610) 253-1224, E-mail: ruta@northamptonctymuseum.org, Internet: northamptonctymuseum.org. Pres.: Grace Fried, Exec. Dir.: Ruta Saliklis
Local Museum - 1906 43070

Eastsound WA

Orcas Island Historical Museum, 181 North Beach Rd, Eastsound, WA 98245 - T: (360) 376-4849, Fax: (360) 376-2994, E-mail: orcasmuseum@rockisland.com, Internet: www.orcasisland.org. Pres.: Linda Trtheway, Dir.: Jennifer Vollmer
Local Museum - 1950
Local hist 43071

Eatonton GA

Uncle Remus Museum, 360 Oak St, Hwy 441 S, Eatonton, GA 31024 - T: (706) 485-6856. Pres./Cur.: Norma Watterson
Historical Museum - 1963
House c.1820 slave cabin, furnishings 43072

Eatonville WA

Pioneer Farm Museum and Ohop Indian Village, 7716 Ohop Valley Rd E., Eatonville, WA 98328 - T: (360) 832-6300, Fax: (360) 832-4533, E-mail: pioneer@mashell.com, Internet: www.pioneerfarmmuseum.org. Head: Dean Carpenter
Local Museum / Agriculture Museum - 1975
Agriculture, local hist 43073

Eau Claire WI

Chippewa Valley Museum, 1204 Carson Park Dr, Eau Claire, WI 54703 - T: (715) 834-7871, Fax: (715) 834-6624, E-mail: anyone@cvmuseum.com, Internet: www.cvmuseum.com. Dir.: Susan M. McLeod
Local Museum - 1966 43074

Foster Gallery, University of Wisconsin-Eau Claire, 121 Water St, Eau Claire, WI 54702-5008 - T: (715) 836-2328, Fax: (715) 836-4882, E-mail: wagenetk@uwec.edu, Internet: www.uwec.edu. Dir.: Thomas K. Wagner
Fine Arts Museum / University Museum - 1970 43075

Paul Bunyan Logging Camp, 1110 Carson Park Dr, Eau Claire, WI 54703 - T: (715) 835-6200, Fax: (715) 835-6293, E-mail: paulbunyancamp@mail.paulbunyancamp.org, Internet: www.paulbunyancamp.org. Pres.: Gordon Wall
Science&Tech Museum - 1934
Logging and lumbering 43076

Ebensburg PA

Cambria County Historical Society Museum, 615 N Center, Ebensburg, PA 15931 - T: (814) 472-6674, E-mail: info@cambriacountyhistorical.com, Internet: www.cambriacountyhistorical.com. C.E.O. & Pres.: Fremont McKenrick, Cur.: Kathy Jones
Local Museum - 1925 43077

Echo OR

Chinese House Museum, 230 W Bridge and 33208 Marble, Echo, OR 97826 - T: (541) 376-84111, Fax: (541) 376-8218, E-mail: ecpl@centurytel.net, Internet: www.echo-oregon.com. C.E.O.: Diane Berry
Religious Arts Museum - 1987 43078

Echo Historical Museum, 76502 Echo Meadows Rd, Echo, OR 97826 - T: (541) 376-8150. Cur.: Elaine Attum
Local Museum - 1981
Umatilla County hist, guns, musical instruments, Indian artifacts, dolls 43079

Eckley PA

Eckley Miners' Village, Main St, Eckley, PA 18255 - T: (570) 636-2070, Fax: (570) 636-2938, Internet: www.phmc..state.pa.us. Dir.: David Dubick, Cur.: Chester Kulesa
Historical Museum - 1969
54 houses built in the 1850s as coal patch town including Roman Catholic Church, Episcopal Church, doctor's office, coal breaker, visitor's center and mule barn 43080

Edenton NC

Historic Edenton State Historic Site, 108 N Broad St, Edenton, NC 27932 - T: (252) 482-2637, Fax: (252) 482-3499, E-mail: edentonshs@inteliport.com, Internet: www.ah.dcr.state.nc.us/sections/hs/iredell. Man.: Linda Jordan Eure
Historical Museum - 1951 43081

Edgartown MA

Martha's Vineyard Historical Society Exhibition, Thomas Cooke House, Cooke and School Sts, Edgartown, MA 02539 - T: (508) 627-4441, Fax: (508) 627-4436, E-mail: mvhist@vineyard.net, Internet: www.marthasvineyardhistory.org. Dir.: Matthew Stackpole, Chief Cur.: Jill Bouck
Open Air Museum / Local Museum - 1922
Thomas Cooke House, 2nd Captain Francis Pease House - library 43082

Edgerton KS

Lanesfield School, 18745 S Dillie Rd, Edgerton, KS 66021 - T: (913) 893-6645, Fax: (913) 631-6359, Internet: www.digitalhistory.com. Dir.: Mindi Love
Historical Museum - 1967
One-room schoolhouse restored to 1904 appearance 43083

Edgerton WI

Albion Academy Historical Museum, 605 Campus Ln, Edgerton, WI 53534 - T: (608) 884-3940. Pres.: Clifford Townsend
Local Museum - 1959
Local hist 43084

Edgewater MD

Historic London Town, 839 Londontown Rd, Edgewater, MD 21037 - T: (410) 222-1919, Fax: (410) 222-1918, E-mail: londntown@historiclondontown.com, Internet: www.historiclondontown.com. Pres.: Louise Hayman, C.E.O.: Gregory Stiverson
Historical Museum / Archaeological Museum - 1971
Significant archaelogical site 43085

Edina MN

Mhiripiri Gallery, 3519 W 70th St, Edina, MN 55343 - T: (952) 285-9684, Internet: www.shonasculpturemhiripiri.com
Fine Arts Museum - 1986 43086

Edina MO

Knox County Historical Society Museum, Court House, 107 N Fourth St, Edina, MO 63537 - T: (660) 397-2349, Fax: (660) 397-3331. Pres.: Brent Karhoff
Historical Museum - 1967 43087

Edinburg TX

Hidalgo County Historical Museum, 121 E McIntyre St, Edinburg, TX 78539 - T: (210) 383-6911, Fax: (210) 381-6911, E-mail: hchm@hiline.net, Internet: www.riograndeborderlands.org. Dir.: Shan Rankin, Asst. Dir.: Thomas A. Fort
Local Museum - 1967
Local hist 43088

University Galleries, Art Dept., University of Texas Pan American, 1201 W University Dr, Edinburg, TX 78539 - T: (210) 381-2655, Fax: (210) 384-5072, E-mail: galleries@panam.edu, Internet: www.panam.edu/dept/art/pages/artgall.html. Dir.: Dindy Reich
Fine Arts Museum 43089

Edisto Island SC

Edisto Island Historic Preservation Society Museum, 8123 Chisolm Plantation Rd, Edisto Island, SC 29438 - T: (843) 869-1954, Fax: (843) 869-1954. Dir.: Karen Nickles
Archaeological Museum - 1986
Prehistoric low country 43090

Edmond OK

Edmond Historical Society Museum, 431 S Blvd, Edmond, OK 73034 - T: (405) 340-0078, Fax: (405) 340-2771, Internet: www.edmondhistory.org. Pres.: Linda Hopkins, Dir.: Brenda Granger, Iris Muno Jordan
Local Museum - 1983
Local hist 43091

Edmonds WA

Edmonds Arts Festival Museum, 700 Main St, Edmonds, WA 98020, mail addr: POB 699, Edmonds, WA 98020 - T: (425) 771-6412, Fax: (425) 673-7700, E-mail: hardarmc@cmc.net, Internet: www.edmondsartsfestival.com. Cur.: Darlene McLellan
Fine Arts Museum - 1979
Fine arts 43092

Edmonds South Snohomish County Historical Society Museum, 118 Fifth Av N, Edmonds, WA 98020 - T: (425) 774-0900, Fax: (425) 774-6507, Internet: www.historicedmonds.org. Dir.: Joni L. Sein, Cur.: Mike Wilcox
Local Museum - 1973
Local hist 43093

Edna KS

Edna Historical Museum, 100 S Delaware, Edna, KS 67342
Local Museum - 1978 43094

Edna TX

Texana Museum, 403 N Wells, Edna, TX 77957 - T: (361) 782-5431. Pres.: Lois Cunning, Lee Doersch
Local Museum - 1967
Local hist 43095

Edwards Air Force Base CA

Air Force Flight Test Center Museum, 95 ABW/MU, 1100 Kincheloe, Edwards Air Force Base, CA 93524-1850 - T: (805) 277-8050, Fax: (805) 277-8051, E-mail: museum@edwards.af.mil, Internet: afftc.edwards.af.mil/341.html. Dir./Cur.: Doug Nelson
Military Museum / Science&Tech Museum - 1986
Aeronautics 43096

Edwardsville IL

Madison County Historical Museum, 715 N Main St, Edwardsville, IL 62025-1111 - T: (618) 656-7562, Internet: www.plantnet.com/museum. Dir.: Suzanne Dietrich, Libr.: Marion Sperling
Local Museum - 1924
Local history, housed in John H. Weir home - library 43097

The University Museum, Southern Illinois University Edwardsville, Edwardsville, IL 62026 - T: (618) 650-2996, Fax: (618) 650-2995, E-mail: ebarnet@siue.edu, Internet: www.siue.edu/art/museum.html. Dir.: Eric B. Barnett, Cur.: Michael E. Mason
Local Museum / University Museum - 1959 43098

Egg Harbor WI

Chief Oshkosh Native American Arts, 7631 Egg Harbor Rd, Egg Harbor, WI 54209 - T: (920) 868-3240. Dir.: Coleen Bins
Fine Arts Museum - 1975
Native American art 43099

Cupola House, 7836 Egg Harbor Rd, Egg Harbor, WI 54209 - T: (800) 871-1871, Fax: (920) 868-1710, E-mail: cupolahouse@itol.com, Internet: www.cupolahouse.com
Decorative Arts Museum - 1871 43100

Eglin Air Force Base FL

Air Force Armament Museum, 100 Museum Dr, Eglin Air Force Base, FL 32542-1497 - T: (850) 882-4062, 882-4189, Fax: (850) 882-3990, E-mail: sneddon@eglin.af.mil, Internet: www.wg53.eglin.af.mil/armmus. C.E.O.: Russell C. Sneddon
Military Museum - 1985
Military 43101

Egypt PA

Troxell-Steckel House and Farm Museum, 4229 Reliance St, Egypt, PA 18052 - T: (610) 435-1074, Fax: (610) 435-9812. Cur.: Andree Miller
Local Museum / Agriculture Museum - 1904 43102

Ekalaka MT

Carter County Museum, 100 Main St, Ekalaka, MT 59324 - T: (406) 775-6886. Dir.: Warren O. White
Local Museum / Ethnology Museum / Natural History Museum / Folklore Museum - 1936 43103

El Cajon CA

Hyde Art Gallery, Grossmont Community College, 8800 Grossmont College Dr, El Cajon, CA 92020 - T: (619) 644-7299, Fax: (619) 644-7922, E-mail: teresa.markey@gcccd.net, Internet: www.grossmont.net/artgallery. Dir.: Ron Tatro, Cur.: James Wilsterman, Ben Aubert
University Museum / Fine Arts Museum - 1961 43104

El Campo TX

El Campo Museum of Natural History, 2350 N Mechanic St, El Campo, TX 77437 - T: (979) 543-6885, Fax: (979) 543-5788, E-mail: museum@wcnet.net, Internet: www.elcampomuseum.com. Pres.: Phyllis Laughlin, Cur.: Denise Prochazka
Natural History Museum - 1978
Natural hist 43105

El Dorado AR

South Arkansas Arts Center, 110 E Fifth St, El Dorado, AR 71730 - T: (870) 862-5474, Fax: (870) 862-4921, E-mail: saac@arkansas.net, Internet: www.saac-arts.org. Exec. Dir.: Beth James
Fine Arts Museum - 1962
Art gallery 43106

El Dorado KS

Butler County Museum and Kansas Oil Museum, 383 E Central Av, El Dorado, KS 67042 - T: (316) 321-9333, Fax: (316) 321-3619, E-mail: bchs@powwwer.net, Internet: www.skyways.org/museums/kom. Dir.: Rebecca Matticks, Cur.: Debbie Amend (Education), Brad Amend (Collections), Dale Wilson (Projekt Dir.)
Local Museum / Science&Tech Museum - 1956
Kansas oil history, local history 43107

Coutts Memorial Museum of Art, 110 N Main St, El Dorado, KS 67042-0001 - T: (316) 321-1212, Fax: (316) 321-1215, E-mail: coutts@southwind.com, Internet: skyways.lib.ks.us/museums/coutts/. Pres.: Rhoda Hodges, Dir.: Terri Scott
Fine Arts Museum - 1970
Fine art, Frederic Remington sculpture coll 43108

El Monte CA

El Monte Historical Society Museum, 3150 Tyler Av, El Monte, CA 91731 - T: (626) 444-3813, Fax: (626) 444-8142. Cur.: Donna Crippen
Local Museum - 1958 43109

El Paso CO

United States Air Force Academy Museum, 2346 Academy Dr, USAF Academy, El Paso, CO 80840-9400 - T: (719) 333-2569, Fax: (719) 333-4402
University Museum / Military Museum - 1961
Military 43110

El Paso TX

Americana Museum, 5 Civic Center Plaza, El Paso, TX 79901-1153 - T: (915) 542-0394, Fax: (915) 542-4511. Cur.: William Kwiecinski, Ass. Cur.: Victor Gomez
Folklore Museum / Historical Museum 43111

Bridge Center for Contemporary Art, 1 Union Fasion Center, El Paso, TX 79902 - T: (915) 532-6707, Internet: utminers.utep.edu/amit/thebridge/index. Dir.: Richard Baron
Public Gallery - 1986 43112

The Centennial Museum at the University of Texas at El Paso, University Av, Wiggins Rd, El Paso, TX 79968-0533 - T: (915) 747-5565, Fax: (915) 747-5411, E-mail: museum@utep.edu, Internet: www.utep.edu/museum/. Dir.: Florence Schwein, Cur.: Scott Cutler
University Museum / Natural History Museum - 1936
Natural hist 43113

Chamizal National Memorial, 800 S San Marcial, El Paso, TX 79905 - T: (915) 532-7273, Fax: (915) 532-7240, Internet: www.nps.gov/cham
Local Museum - 1967
Local hist 43114

El Paso Holocaust Museum, 401 Wallenberg Dr, El Paso, TX 79912 - T: (915) 833-5656, Fax: (915) 833-9523, E-mail: mholocau@elp.rr.com, Internet: www.txtolerance.org. Exec. Dir.: Sylvia Cohen
Historical Museum - 1992 43115

El Paso Museum of Art, 1 Arts Festival Plaza, El Paso, TX 79901 - T: (915) 532-1707, Fax: (915) 532-1010, E-mail: rodriguezx@elpasoartmuseum.org, Internet: www.elpasoartmuseum.org. Dir.: Becky Duval Reese, Cur.: Teresa H. Ebie
Fine Arts Museum - 1930
Art 43116

El Paso Museum of History, 12901 Gateway West, El Paso, TX 79928 - T: (915) 858-1928, Fax: (915) 858-4591, Internet: www.ci.el-paso.tx.us/mohistory.htm. Dir.: René Harris, Cur.: Barbara J. Angus
Historical Museum - 1974
History 43117

Glass Gallery and Main Gallery, University of Texas at El Paso, Department of Art, 500 W University Av, El Paso, TX 79968 - T: (915) 747-5181, Fax: (915) 797-6749, E-mail: bonansin@utep.edu, Internet: www.utep.edu/arts. Dir.: Kate Bonansinga
Public Gallery - 1940 43118

Insights - El Paso Science Center, 505 N Santa Fe, El Paso, TX 79901 - T: (915) 534-0000, Fax: (915) 532-7416, E-mail: contact@insightsmuseum.org, Internet: www.insightsmuseum.org. Pres.: Blanca Orona, Exec. Dir.: Carol Munoz
Science&Tech Museum - 1979
Science 43119

International Museum of Art, 1211 Montana St, El Paso, TX 79902 - T: (915) 543-6747, Fax: (915) 543-9222. Dir.: Michael Kirkwood
Fine Arts Museum
Western, African and Heritage gallery, William Kolliker Gallery 43120

Magoffin Home, 1120 Magoffin Av, El Paso, TX 79901 - T: (915) 533-5147, Fax: (915) 544-4398, Internet: www.tpwd.state.tx.us/tpwd.htm. Pres.: Prestene Dehrkoop, Exec. Dir.: Andrew Sansom, Dir.: Zane Morgan
Local Museum - 1976
Historic house 43121

National Border Patrol Museum and Memorial Library, 4315 Transmountain Rd, El Paso, TX 79924 - T: (915) 759-6060, Fax: (915) 759-0992, E-mail: nbpm@dzn.com, Internet: www.nationalbpmuseum.org. Cur.: Brenda Tisdale
Historical Museum - 1985 43122

People's Gallery, 2 Civic Center Plaza, El Paso, TX 79901 - T: (915) 541-4481, Fax: (915) 541-4902, E-mail: fierrole@ci.el-paso.tx.us, Internet: www.artsresources.org. Dir.: Alejandrina Drew
Fine Arts Museum - 1979 43123

Wilderness Park Museum, 4301 Transmountain Rd, El Paso, TX 79924 - T: (915) 755-4332, Fax: (915) 759-6824. Dir.: Marc Thompson
Archaeological Museum - 1977 43124

El Reno OK

Canadian County Historical Museum, 300 S Grand, El Reno, OK 73036 - T: (405) 262-5121. Pres.: Vicki Proctor, Cur.: Pat Reuter
Local Museum - 1969 43125

Elberta AL

Baldwin County Heritage Museum, 25521 Hwy 98, Elberta, AL 36530 - T: (251) 986-8375. Head: June Taylor
Local Museum / Agriculture Museum - 1986
Rural hist (farming, forestry and associated crafts) 43126

Elberton GA

Elberton Granite Museum, 1 Granite Plaza, Elberton, GA 30635 - T: (706) 283-2551, Fax: (706) 283-6380, E-mail: granite@egaonline.com, Internet: www.egaonline.com. Dir.: Thomas A. Robinson
Local Museum - 1981
Local hist, granite monuments 43127

Elbow Lake MN

Grant County Historical Museum, Hwy 79 E, Elbow Lake, MN 56531 - T: (218) 685-4864, E-mail: gcmnhist@runestone.net. Dir./Cur.: Patricia Benson
Historical Museum - 1944
Regional history 43128

Elgin IL

Elgin Public Museum, 225 Grand Blvd, Elgin, IL 60120 - T: (847) 741-6655, Fax: (847) 931-6787, E-mail: epm@mc.net, Internet: www.elginpublicmuseum.org. Pres.: Marty Kellams, Exec. Dir.: Nancy J. Epping
Ethnology Museum / Natural History Museum - 1904
Natural hist 43129

Elgin ND

Grant County Museum, 119 Main St, Elgin, ND 58533 - T: (701) 584-2900, E-mail: gcn@westriv.com. Head: Duane Schatz
Local Museum - 1970 43130

Elizabeth WV

Beauchamp Newman Museum, Court St, Elizabeth, WV 26143 - T: (304) 275-6534. Cur.: Jean Daley
Decorative Arts Museum - 1950
Furniture, costumes, domestic artifacts 43131

Elizabeth City NC

Museum of the Albemarle, 1116 US Hwy 17 S, Elizabeth City, NC 27909-9806 - T: (252) 335-1453, Fax: (252) 335-0637, E-mail: ncs1583@mindspring.com, Internet: www.albemarle-nc.com. Pres.: Ed Merrell
Historical Museum - 1963 43132

Elizabethtown KY

Coca-Cola Memorabilia Museum of Elizabethtown, 321 Peterson Dr, Elizabethtown, KY 42701-9375 - T: (270) 769-3320 ext 328, Fax: (270) 769-3323. Cur.: Channing C. Hardy
Science&Tech Museum - 1977
Company museum 43133

Elizabethtown NY

Adirondack Center Museum, Court St, Elizabethtown, NY 12932 - T: (518) 873-6466, E-mail: echs@northnet.org. Pres.: James Rogers, Dir.: Margaret Gibbs
Local Museum - 1954 43134

Elk City OK

National Route 66 Museum and Old Town Museum, 2717 W Hwy 66, Elk City, OK 73644 - T: (405) 225-6266, Fax: (580) 225-3234. Cur.: Lucy Stansberry
Local Museum - 1966 43135

Elk Grove Village IL

Elk Grove Farmhouse Museum, 399 Biesterfield Rd, Elk Grove Village, IL 60007 - T: (847) 437-9494, Fax: (847) 228-3508, Internet: www.elkgrove.org/egpd. Dir.: Tammy Miller, Cur.: Peggy Rogers, Karen David
Local Museum - 1976 43136

Elk Horn IA

Danish Immigrant Museum, 2212 Washington St, Elk Horn, IA 51531 - T: (712) 764-7001, Fax: (712) 764-7002, E-mail: dkmus@metc.net, Internet: dkmuseum.org. CEO: Rick Burns
Ethnology Museum - 1983
Culture and diversity of Danish-American immigrants 43137

Elk River MN

Oliver Kelley Farm, 15788 Kelley Farm Rd, Elk River, MN 55330 - T: (612) 441-6896, Fax: (612) 441-6302, E-mail: Jim.Mattson@MNHS.ORG, Internet: www.mnhs.org/sites/ohkf.html. Head: James Mattson
Local Museum / Agriculture Museum - 1849
Agriculture 43138

Elkhart IN

CTS Turner Museum, 905 N West Blvd, Elkhart, IN 46514 - T: (574) 293-7511 ext 296, Fax: (574) 293-6146, E-mail: turnermuseum@ctscorp.com, Internet: www.cts.com. Dir.: Joseph Carlson, Ass. Dir.: William Lantz
Science&Tech Museum - 1979
Company history, technology 43139

Midwest Museum of American Art, 429 S Main St, Elkhart, IN 46515 - T: (219) 293-6660, Fax: (219) 293-6660, E-mail: mdwstmsam@aol.com, Internet: www.midwestmuseum.org. Dir.: Jane Burns, Ass. Cur.: Brian Byrn
Fine Arts Museum - 1978 43140

National New York Central Railroad Museum, 721 S Main St, Elkhart, IN 46516 - T: (219) 294-3001, Fax: (219) 295-9434, E-mail: artscul@michiana.org, Internet: nycrrmuseum.railfan.net. C.E.O.: David M. Bird
Science&Tech Museum - 1987 43141

Ruthmere House Museum, 302 E Beardsley Av, Elkhart, IN 46514 - T: (219) 264-0330, Fax: (219) 266-0474, E-mail: dwiegand@ruthmere.com, Internet: www.ruthmere.com. Dir.: Dawn Michelle Wiegand
Special Museum - 1969 43142

RV/MH Heritage Foundation, 801 Benham Av, Elkhart, IN 46516-3369 - T: (219) 293-2344, Fax: (219) 293-3466, E-mail: rvmhhall@aol.com, Internet: rv-mh-hall-of-fame.org. Pres.: Carl A. Ehry
Science&Tech Museum - 1972 43143

S. Ray Miller Auto Museum, 2130 Middlebury St, Elkhart, IN 46516 - T: (219) 522-0539, Fax: (219) 522-0358, E-mail: millermuseum@earthlink.net, Internet: www.miller.automuseum.org. CEO: Linda L. Miller
Science&Tech Museum / Folklore Museum - 1987
Automobile, vintage clothing, antiques 43144

Elkhorn WI

Webster House Museum, 9 E Rockwell, Elkhorn, WI 53121 - T: (414) 723-4248, E-mail: walcohistsoc@elknet.net, Internet: www.geocites.com/walcohistory. Pres.: Doris M. Reinke
Decorative Arts Museum / Local Museum - 1955
Local hist 43145

Elko NV

Northeastern Nevada Museum, 1515 Idaho St, Elko, NV 89801 - T: (775) 738-3418, Fax: (775) 778-9318, E-mail: museum@nenv-museum.org, Internet: www.nenv-museum.org. C.E.O.: Dr. Thomas H. Gallagher, Dir.: Claudia Wines, Cur.: Jan Petersen
Fine Arts Museum / Historical Museum / Natural History Museum - 1968
History, natural history, wildlife, art - library, archives 43146

Elkton MD

Historical Museum of Cecil County, 135 E Main St, Elkton, MD 21921 - T: (410) 398-1790, E-mail: history@cchistory.org, Internet: www.cchistory.org. Pres.: Paula H. Newton
Local Museum - 1931
Regional history 43147

Ellensburg WA

Clymer Museum of Art, 416 N Pearl St, Ellensburg, WA 98926 - T: (509) 962-6416, Fax: (509) 962-6424, E-mail: clymermuseum@charter.net, Internet: www.clymermuseum.com. Dir.: Diana Tasker, Cur.: Randall Sharp
Fine Arts Museum - 1991 43148

CWU Anthropology Department Collection, c/o Central Washington University, Farrell Hall, Ellensburg, WA 98926-7544 - T: (509) 963-3201, Fax: (509) 963-3215, E-mail: anthro@cwu.edu, Internet: www.cwu.edu/~anthro/dept
Ethnology Museum / University Museum - 1972
Ethnography from New Guinea, Mexico, Western Plateau, San Blas Islands, Panama, Africa, SW and NW Coast US 43149

Gallery One, 408 1/2 N Pearl St, Ellensburg, WA 98926 - T: (509) 925-2670. Dir.: Eveleth Green
Fine Arts Museum - 1968
Oil paintings, enamel paintings, watercolors, wood sculpture 43150

Olmstead Place State Park, 921 N Ferguson Rd, Ellensburg, WA 98926 - T: (509) 925-1943, Fax: (509) 925-1943
Local Museum / Agriculture Museum - 1968
Local hist 43151

Sarah Spurgeon Gallery, c/o Central Washington University, 400 E Eighth Av, Ellensburg, WA 98926-7564 - T: (509) 963-2665, Fax: (509) 963-1918, E-mail: chinnm@cwu.edu, Internet: www.cwu.edu/~art. Dir.: James Sahlstrand
University Museum / Public Gallery - 1970 43152

Ellenton FL

The Judah P. Benjamin Confederate Memorial at Gamble Plantation, 3708 Patten Av, Ellenton, FL 34222 - T: (941) 723-4536, Fax: (941) 723-4538, E-mail: charles.dickerman@dep.state.fl.us, Internet: www.fcn.state.fl.us
Local Museum / Agriculture Museum - 1926
Home of Robert Gamble, main house of the Gamble sugar plantation 43153

Ellerbe NC

Rankin Museum, 131 Church St, Ellerbe, NC 28338 - T: (910) 652-6378, Internet: www.rankinmuseum.com. Cur.: P.R. Rankin jr
Fine Arts Museum / Historical Museum
Southeastern Indian artifacts, Arts of Amhzonia, Melanesian art 43154

Ellicott City MD

B & O Railroad Station Museum, 2711 Maryland Av, Ellicott City, MD 21043 - T: (410) 461-1945, E-mail: ECBOstation@aol.com, Internet: www.b-orrstationmuseum.org. Pres.: Lisa Mason-Chaney, Dir.: Ed Williams
Science&Tech Museum - 1976
Transport, railroad stn, first terminus in the U.S 43155

Bagpipe Music Museum, 840 Oella Av, Ellicott City, MD 21043 - T: (410) 313-9311. C.E.O.: James Coldren
Music Museum - 1997 43156

Firehouse Museum, 3829 Church Rd, Ellicott City, MD 21043 - T: (410) 465-0232. Dir.: Carolyn Klein
Science&Tech Museum - 1991 43157

Howard County Historical Society Museum, 8328 Court Av, Ellicott City, MD 21041, mail addr: POB 109, Ellicott, MD 21041 - T: (410) 750-0370, Fax: (410) 750-0370, E-mail: hchs@clark.net. Dir.: Phyllis Knill
Local Museum - 1957
County's hist, furniture, weapons 43158

Ellis KS

Walter P. Chrysler Boyhood Home and Museum, 102 W 10th, Ellis, KS 67637 - T: (785) 726-3636, Fax: (785) 726-3636, E-mail: chrysler@eaglecom.net
Special Museum - 1954 43159

Ellis Grove IL

Pierre Menard Home - State Historic Site, 4230 Kaskaskta Rd, Ellis Grove, IL 62241-9702, mail addr: 4372 Park Rd, Ellis Grove, IL 62241-9704 - T: (618) 859-3031, Fax: (618) 859-3741, E-mail: menrdhom@midwest.net. C.E.O.: Robert Coomer
Historical Museum - 1927
Home of Pierre Menard, the first Lt. Governor of Illinois and U.S. Agent of Indian Affairs 43160

Ellison Bay WI

Newport State Park, 475 City Hwy NP, Ellison Bay, WI 54210 - T: (920) 854-2500, Fax: (920) 854-1914, Internet: www.dcty.com/newport
Local Museum
Local hist 43161

Ellsworth KS

Ellsworth County Museum, Hodgen House Museum, 104 W South Main, Ellsworth, KS 67439 - T: (785) 472-3059, E-mail: echs@informatics.net. Pres.: Patricia L. Bender
Local Museum - 1961
Folklore, Indian, agriculture, archaeology, costumes 43162

Rogers House Museum and Gallery, 102 E Main S, Ellsworth, KS 67439 - T: (913) 472-5674. Dir.: Robert Rogers
Fine Arts Museum / Public Gallery - 1968
Paintings, prints, art 43163

Ellsworth ME

Woodlawn Museum, 17 Black House Dr, Ellsworth, ME 04605 - T: (207) 667-8671, Fax: (207) 667-7950, E-mail: info@woodlawnmuseum.com, Internet: www.woolawnmuseum.com. Exec. Dir.: Joshua C. Torrance
Local Museum - 1928 43164

Elmhurst IL

Elmhurst Art Museum, 150 Cottage Hill Av, Elmhurst, IL 60126 - T: (630) 834-0202, Fax: (630) 834-0234, E-mail: nbremer@elmhurstartmusesum.org, Internet: www.elmhurstartmuseum.org. Dir.: D. Neil Bremer, Ass. Dir.: Heather Pastore, Cur.: Teresa Parker
Fine Arts Museum - 1981
Art 43165

Elmhurst Historical Museum, 120 E Park Av, Elmhurst, IL 60126 - T: (630) 833-1457, Fax: (630) 833-1326, E-mail: ehm@elmhurst.org, Internet: www.elmhurst.org. Dir.: Brian F. Bergheger, Cur.: Marcia Lautanen-Raleigh
Local Museum - 1952
Local history 43166

Lizzadro Museum of Lapidary Art, 220 Cottage Hill Av, Elmhurst, IL 60126 - T: (630) 833-1616, Fax: (630) 833-1225, E-mail: lizzardromuseum@earthlink.net, Internet: www.lizzardromuseum.org. Dir.: John S. Lizzadro, Ass. Dir.: Dorothy J. Asher
Special Museum - 1962
Chinese jades, hardstone carvings, gemstones, minerals, earth science 43167

Milano Model and Toy Museum, 116 Park Av, Elmhurst, IL 60126 - T: (630) 279-4422, Internet: www.toys-n-cars.com. CEO: Dean Milano
Special Museum - 2002
Model cars, 1930s-1960s vintage toys 43168

Elmira NY

Arnot Art Museum, 235 Lake St, Elmira, NY 14901 - T: (607) 734-3697, Fax: (607) 734-5687, Internet: www.artotartmuseum.org. Pres.: Laurie Liberatore, Dir./Cur.: John D. O'Hern, Cur.: Karen Kucharski, Sc.Staff: Michael Sampson (Registrar)
Fine Arts Museum - 1913 43169

Chemung Valley History Museum, 415 E Water St, Elmira, NY 14901 - T: (607) 734-4167, Fax: (607) 734-1565, E-mail: history@exotrope.net, Internet: www.chemungvalleymuseum.org. Pres.: George L. Howell, Cur.: Amy Wilson
Local Museum - 1923
Civil war and Indian artifacts 43170

National Soaring Museum, Harris Hill, 51 Soaring Hill Dr, Elmira, NY 14903-9204 - T: (607) 734-3128, Fax: (607) 732-6745, E-mail: nsm@soaringmuseum.org, Internet: www.soaringmuseum.org. Pres.: Robert Gaines, Exec. Dir.: L. Little
Science&Tech Museum - 1969 43171

Elsah IL

School of Nations Museum, Principia College, Elsah, IL 62028 - T: (618) 314-2100, 374-5236, Fax: (618) 275-3519, E-mail: bkh@prin.edu. Dir.: Dan Hanna
University Museum / Folklore Museum - 1930
Local history, arts, crafts 43172

Village of Elsah Museum, 26 LaSalle, Elsah, IL 62028 - T: (618) 374-5238, Fax: (618) 374-2625, E-mail: jhp@prin.edu, Internet: www.elsah.org. C.E.O.: Marjorie A. Doerr
Local Museum - 1978
Local history housed in 1857 school 43173

Elverson PA

Hopewell Furnace National Historic Site, 2 Mark Bird Ln, Elverson, PA 19520 - T: (610) 582-8773, Fax: (610) 582-2768, E-mail: hofu_superintendent@nps.gov, Internet: www.nps.gov/hofu/index.html. Head: William A. Sanders
Science&Tech Museum - 1938 43174

Ely NV

East Ely Railroad Depot Museum, 1100 Avenue A, Ely, NV 89301 - T: (775) 289-1663, Fax: (775) 289-1664, E-mail: esm@the-onramp.net
Science&Tech Museum / Historical Museum - 1992
Mining and transportation, industrial development, right of way maps 43175

White Pine Public Museum, 2000 Aultman St, Ely, NV 89301 - T: (775) 289-4710, Fax: (775) 289-4710, E-mail: wpmuseum@idsely.com, Internet: www.webpanda.com. Head: Tom Puckett
Local Museum / Natural History Museum - 1957
Local hist 43176

Elyria OH

Hickories Museum, 509 Washington Av, Elyria, OH 44035 - T: (216) 322-3341, Fax: (440) 322-2817, E-mail: thehickories@alltel.net. Pres.: George Strom
Historical Museum - 1889 43177

Spirit of '76 Museum, 509 Washington Av, Elyria, OH 44035 - T: (216) 647-4367. Cur.: Diane Stanley
Historical Museum - 1970
Archibald M. Willard memorabilia 43178

Elysian MN

Lesueur County Historical Museum, NE Frank and Second St, Elysian, MN 56028-0240 - T: (507) 267-4620, 362-8350, Fax: (507) 267-4750, E-mail: museum@lchs.mus.mn.us, Internet: www.lchs.mus.mn.us. Pres.: Pat Nusbaum
Local Museum - 1966 43179

Emmaus PA

Shelter House, 601 S Fourth St, Emmaus, PA 18049 - T: (610) 965-9258. Pres.: R. Mitchell Freed
Local Museum - 1951 43180

Empire MI

Empire Area Heritage Group - History Museum, 11544 S La Core, Empire, MI 49630 - T: (231) 326-5568. Pres.: Gerard Boiseneau
Local Museum - 1972
Local hist 43181

Emporia KS

Emporia State University Geology Museum, 1200 Commercial St, Emporia, KS 66801 - T: (316) 341-5330, Fax: (316) 341-6055. Dir.: Dr. Michael Morales
Natural History Museum - 1983
Geology 43182

Lyon County Museum, 118 E 6th Av, Emporia, KS 66801 - T: (316) 342-0933, E-mail: lycomu@birch.net. Pres.: Lisa Goldstein, Dir.: J. Greg Jordon, Chm.: Annette Rice, Sc. Staff: Laura Dodge (Education), Jake Dalton (Registrar), Carolyn Eckstrom (Asst. Registrar)
Local Museum - 1937
County history, Carnegie library and Richard Howe home 43183

Norman R. Eppink Art Gallery, Emporia State University, 1200 Commercial, Emporia, KS 66801 - T: (316) 341-5246, Fax: (316) 341-6246, E-mail: schwarml@emporia.edu, Internet: www.emporia.edu/m/www/art/eppink.htm. C.E.O.: Kay Schallenkamp, Dir.: Larry W. Schwarm
Fine Arts Museum / University Museum - 1939
Art gallery 43184

Richard H. Schmidt Museum of Natural History, Emporia State University, 1200 Commercial St, Emporia, KS 66801 - T: (316) 341-5311, Fax: (316) 341-5607, E-mail: mooredwiQemporia.edu. Dir.: Dr. Dwight Moore
University Museum / Natural History Museum - 1959
Natural history 43185

Encampment WY

Grand Encampment Museum, 817 Barnett Av, Encampment, WY 82325 - T: (307) 327-5558 327-5308, Fax: (307) 327-5427, E-mail: gemuseum@aol.com, Internet: www.encampment.1wyo.net/gemuseum. Pres.: Doug Tiescen, Cur.: Rick Martin
Science&Tech Museum - 1965
Mining 43186

Encinitas CA

San Dieguito Heritage Museum, 561 S Vulcan Av, Encinitas, CA 92024 - T: (760) 632-9711, Fax: (760) 632-9711. Pres.: Alice Jacobson, Exec. Dir.: Carol Ann Jensen
Local Museum / Historical Museum - 1988 43187

Enfield NH

Enfield Historical Society Museum, Rte 4A, Enfield, NH 03749 - T: (603) 632-7740. Pres.: John Goodwin
Local Museum - 1991
Local hist 43188

Enfield Shaker Museum, Rte 4A, Enfield, NH 03748 - T: (603) 632-4346, Fax: (603) 632-4346, E-mail: chosen.vale@valley.net, Internet: www.shakermuseum.org. Exec. Dir.: Robert Rudd
Local Museum / Historical Museum - 1986
Historic village 43189

Lockehaven Schoolhouse Museum, E Hill Rd., Enfield, NH 03748 - T: (603) 632-7740. C.E.O.: John Goodwin
Local Museum - 1947 43190

Englewood CO

The Museum of Outdoor Arts, 1000 Englewood Pkwy, Ste 2-230, Englewood, CO 80110 - T: (303) 806-0444, Fax: (303) 806-0504, Internet: www.moaonline.org. Exec. Dir.: Cynthia Madden Leitner
Fine Arts Museum - 1982
Art 43191

Enid OK

Museum of the Cherokee Strip, Oklahoma Historical Society, 507 S Fourth St, Enid, OK 73701 - T: (580) 237-1907, Fax: (580) 242-2874, E-mail: mcs1@onenet.net, Internet: www.ok-history.mus.ok.us. C.E.O.: Dr. Bob Blackburn, Cur.: Steve Dortch
Historical Museum - 1951 43192

Ephraim WI

Ephraim Foundation Museums, Thomas Goodletson House, Pioneer School House, Anderson Store Museum, Anderson Barn Museum, 3060 Anderson Ln, Ephraim, WI 54211 - T: (920) 854-9688, Fax: (920) 854-7232, E-mail: efoundation@itol.com, Internet: www.ephraim.org. Dir.: Sally Jacobson
Local Museum - 1949 43193

Ephrata PA

Cocalico Valley Museum, 249 W Main St, Ephrata, PA 17522 - T: (717) 733-1616. Pres.: Jill Berkes
Historical Museum - 1957 43194

Ephrata Cloister, 632 W Main St, Ephrata, PA 17522-1717 - T: (717) 733-6600, Fax: (717) 733-4364, E-mail: tocollins@state.pa.us, Internet: www.state.pa.us. Pres.: Scott L. Shonk, Dir.: Toni I. Collins
Open Air Museum / Religious Arts Museum / Historic Site - 1732
Religious Village Museum comprising of 12 mid-18th century buildings of Germanic architectural style, located on original site of a celibate religious community 43195

Ephrata WA

Grant County Historical Museum, 742 Basin St NW, Ephrata, WA 98823 - T: (509) 754-3334
Local Museum - 1951 43196

Epping ND

Buffalo Trails Museum, Main St, Epping, ND 58843 - T: (701) 859-4361, Fax: (701) 859-4361, E-mail: buffalotrails@dia.net. Pres.: Duane Syverson
Local Museum - 1966 43197

Epworth IA

Father Weyland Gallery, c/o Divine Word College, 102 Jacoby Dr SW, Epworth, IA 52045-0380 - T: (319) 876-3353, Fax: (319) 876-3353
Fine Arts Museum - 1985
Art of Africa and Papua New Guinea 43198

Erie KS

Mem-Erie Historical Museum, 225 S Main St, Erie, KS 66733 - T: (316) 244-3218, Fax: (316) 244-3332, E-mail: ruthmc@terraworld.net. Pres.: Ruth McKinney-Tandy
Local Museum - 1994
Local hist 43199

Erie PA

Erie Art Museum, 411 State St, Erie, PA 16501 - T: (814) 459-5477, Fax: (814) 452-1744, E-mail: contact@erieartmuseum.org, Internet: www.erieartmuseum.org. Pres.: Dr. Kirk W. Steehler, Exec. Dir.: John L. Vanco
Fine Arts Museum - 1898 43200

Erie Historical Museum → Watson-Curtze Mansion

Erie History Center, 417-419 State St, Erie, PA 16501 - T: (814) 454-1813, Fax: (814) 452-1744, E-mail: echs@velocity.net, Internet: www.eriecountyhistory.org
Local Museum - 1903 43201

Experience Children's Museum, 420 French St, Erie, PA 16507 - T: (814) 453-3743, Fax: (814) 459-9735, E-mail: junep@erie.net, Internet: www.erie.childrensmuseum.org. Exec. Dir.: June Pintea
Ethnology Museum
Children,Youth 43202

United States Brig Niagara, Homeport Erie Maritime Museum, 150 E Front St, Ste 100, Erie, PA 16507 - T: (814) 452-2744, Fax: (814) 455-6760, E-mail: sail@brigniagara.org, Internet: www.brigniagara.org. Dir.: Walter P. Rybka, John Beebe
Military Museum - 1943 43203

Watson-Curtze Mansion, 356 W Sixth St, Erie, PA 16507 - T: (814) 871-5790, Fax: (814) 879-0988, E-mail: ehmp@erie.net, Internet: www.eriecountyhistory.org
Local Museum - 1899 43204

Escanaba MI

Delta County Historical Society Museum, Sand Point, Ludington Park, Escanaba, MI 49829 - T: (906) 786-3428, Fax: (906) 786-3428. Pres.: Peter Strom, Dir.: Mrs. Robert Ham
Local Museum - 1947 43205

Sandpoint Lighthouse, Delta County Historical Society, Sandpoint, Ludington Park, Escanaba, MI 49829 - T: (906) 786-3763. Pres.: Peter Strom, Dir.: Mrs. Robert Mosenfelder
Historical Museum - 1990 43206

William Bonifas Fine Arts Center, 700 First Av S, Escanaba, MI 49829 - T: (906) 786-3833, Fax: (906) 786-3840, E-mail: bonifas@bonifasarts.org, Internet: www.bonifasarts.org. Dir.: Samantha Gibb Roff, Pasqua Warstler, Cust.: Jesse Farkas
Fine Arts Museum - 1974
Arts 43207

Escondido CA

California Center for the Arts, 340 N Escondido Blvd, Escondido, CA 92025 - T: (760) 839-4120, 839-4138, Fax: (760) 739-0205, E-mail: ftracey@ci.escondido.ca.us, Internet: www.artcenter.org/ccae. Dir.: Ellen Fleurov
Fine Arts Museum - 1994
Contemporary art - library 43208

Escondido Historical Museum → Heritage Walk Museum

Heritage Walk Museum, 321 N Broadway, Escondido, CA 92025 - T: (760) 743-8207, Fax: (760) 743-8267, E-mail: ehs@connectnet.com. Exec. Dir.: Wendy Barker
Historical Museum - 1956
Local history, railroad car with model train layout, furnishing, blacksmith shop 43209

Museum California Center for the Arts Escondido, 340 N Escondido Blvd, Escondido, CA 92025 - T: (760) 839-4170, Fax: (760) 743-6472, Internet: www.artcenter.org. Dir.: Ellen Fleurov, Cur.: Catherine Gleason
Fine Arts Museum - 1992
Art 43210

Essex CT

Connecticut River Museum, 67 Main St, Essex, CT 06426 - T: (860) 767-8269, Fax: (860) 767-7028, E-mail: crm@ctrivermuseum.org, Internet: www.connix.com/~crm. Dir.: Stuart Parnes, Cur.: John Bodinger, Alison Guinness
Historical Museum / Folklore Museum - 1974
Maritime and River Museum: housed in 1878 wooden warehouse 43211

Essex Historical Museum, 22 Prospect St, Essex, CT 06426 - T: (860) 767-0681, Internet: www.essexhistory.org. Pres.: Ned Rogin
Local Museum - 1955
Local history 43212

Essex MA

Essex Shipbuilding Museum, 66 Main St, Essex, MA 01929, mail addr: POB 277, Essex, MA 01929 - T: (978) 768-7541, Fax: (978) 768-2541, E-mail: info@essexshipbuildingmuseum.org, Internet: www.essexshipbuildingmuseum.org. Pres.: Suzanne O'Brien, Cur.: Courtney Ellis-Peckham
Historical Museum / Science&Tech Museum - 1976
Hearse house, maritime history, old Story Yard site where A.D. Story launched 300 fishing schooners 43213

Essington PA

Governor Printz Park, Second and Taylor Aves, Essington, PA 19029 - T: (610) 583-7221, Fax: (610) 459-9586. C.E.O.: Brent D. Glass
Local Museum - 1937 43214

Estero FL

Koreshan Historic Site, US 41 at Corkscrew Rd, Estero, FL 33928 - T: (941) 992-0311, Fax: (941) 992-1607, E-mail: j_parks.kshs@juno.com, Internet: www.dep.state.fl.us/parks. Head: John Robinson
Special Museum - 1961
Historic buildings, 1894-1977 utopian settlement 43215

Estes Park CO

Estes Park Area Historical Museum, 200 Fourth St, Estes Park, CO 80517 - T: (970) 586-6256, Fax: (970) 586-6909, E-mail: bkilsdonk@estes.org, Internet: estes.on-line.com/epmuseum. Dir.: Betty Kilsdonk, Cur.: Lisel Goetze
Local Museum - 1962
General museum, regional history 43216

Rocky Mountain National Park Museum, 1000 Hwy 36, Estes Park, CO 80517 - T: (970) 586-1340, Fax: (970) 586-1310, E-mail: christine_baker@nps.gov
Natural History Museum - 1915
Natural history, archaeology, botany, zoology, history 43217

Estherville IA

H.G. Albee Memorial Museum, 1720 Third Av, S, Estherville, IA 51334 - T: (712) 362-2750. Pres.: David Kaltved
Special Museum - 1964 43218

Eufaula AL

Shorter Mansion Museum, 340 N Eufaula Av, Eufaula, AL 36027 - T: (334) 687-3793, Fax: (334) 687-1836, E-mail: info@eufaulapilgrimage.com, Internet: www.eufaulapilgrimage.com. Pres.: Calvin Wingo, C.E.O.: John Martin
Local Museum - 1965
Local history 43219

Eugene OR

Aperture Photo Gallery and EMU Art Gallery, c/o University of Oregon, EMU, Eugene, OR 97403-1228 - T: (541) 346-4373, Fax: (541) 346-4400, Internet: www.darkwing.uoregon.edu/~cultural
University Museum / Fine Arts Museum - 1981 43220

Lane Community College Art Gallery, 4000 E 30th Av, Eugene, OR 97405 - T: (541) 747-4501, Fax: (541) 744-4185. Dir.: Nancy LaValle
University Museum / Fine Arts Museum - 1970 43221

Lane County Historical Museum, 740 W 13th Av, Eugene, OR 97402 - T: (541) 682-4242, Fax: (541) 682-7361, E-mail: lchm@efn.org, Internet: www.ichmuseum.org. Dir.: Evearad Stelfox
Historical Museum - 1951 43222

Maude I. Kerns Art Center, 1910 E 15th Av, Eugene, OR 97403 - T: (541) 345-1571, Fax: (541) 345-6248, E-mail: mkart@efn.org, Internet: www.mkartcenter.org. Exec. Dir.: Karen Pavelec
Fine Arts Museum / Public Gallery - 1962 43223

Museum of Natural History, University of Oregon, 1680 E 15th Av, Eugene, OR 97403-1224 - T: (541) 346-3024, Fax: (541) 346-5334, E-mail: mnh@oregon.uoregon.edu, Internet: natural-history.uoregon.edu. Dir.: C. Melvin Aikens, Patricia Krier (Program), Thomas Connolly (Research for Archaeology), Sc. Staff: Pamela Endzweig (Archaeology)
Natural History Museum / Ethnology Museum / Archaeological Museum - 1935
Natural history, archaeology 43224

New Zone Virtual Gallery, 2740 Onyx St, Eugene, OR 97403 - T: (541) 343-5651, E-mail: ross@newzone.org, Internet: www.newzone.org. Dir.: Jerry Ross
Fine Arts Museum - 1978
Etchings, abstract figurative, oils, landscape, portraits 43225

Oregon Air and Space Museum, 90377 Boeing Dr, Eugene, OR 97402 - T: (541) 461-1101, Fax: (541) 689-3593, E-mail: Thomasewinn@cs.com, Internet: oasm.org. Pres.: Gary Holcomb
Science&Tech Museum - 1987
Aviation, space 43226

The Science Factory, 2300 Leo Harris Pkwy, Eugene, OR 97401 - T: (541) 682-7882, 682-7882, Fax: (541) 484-9027, E-mail: info@sciencefactory.org, Internet: www.sciencefactory.org. Dir.: Meg Trendler
Science&Tech Museum - 1960 43227

University of Oregon Museum of Art (closed until fall 2004), 1430 Johnson Ln, Eugene, OR 97403 - T: (541) 346-3027, Fax: (541) 346-0976, E-mail: uoma@darkwing.uoregon.edu, Internet: uoma.uoregon.edu. Dir.: Del Hawkins, Ass. Dir.: Lawrence Fong
Fine Arts Museum / University Museum - 1930 43228

Willamette Science and Technology Center, 2300 Leo Harris Pkwy, Eugene, OR 97401 - T: (541) 682-7888, Fax: (541) 484-9027, E-mail: wistec@efn.org, Internet: www.efn.org/~wistec. Exec. Dir.: Meg Trendler
Natural History Museum / Science&Tech Museum - 1960 43229

Eureka CA

Clarke Memorial Museum, 240 E St, Eureka, CA 95501 - T: (707) 443-1947, Fax: (707) 443-0290, Internet: www.tidepool.com/~clarke. Dir./Cur.: Pam Service
Local Museum - 1960 43230

Morris Graves Museum of Art, Cnr 7th and F Sts, Eureka, CA 95501 - T: (707) 442-0278, Fax: (707) 442-2040, E-mail: humboldt@telis.org, Internet: www.humboldtarts.org. Dir.: Sally Arnot
Fine Arts Museum 43231

Eureka KS

Greenwood County Historical Society Museum, 120 W 4th St, Eureka, KS 67045-1445 - T: (316) 583-6682, E-mail: gwhistory@correct-connect.com. Pres.: Robert E. Honeyman
Local Museum - 1973
Local hist 43232

Eureka SD

Eureka Pioneer Museum of McPherson County, 1610 J Av, Eureka, SD 57437 - T: (605) 284-2711. Dir./Cur.: Edmund Opp
Local Museum - 1978
Local hist 43233

Eureka UT

Tintic Mining Museum, POB 218, Eureka, UT 84628 - T: (435) 433-6842. Dir.: J.L. McNulty, Ass. Dir.: E.C. McNulty
Historical Museum - 1974
Mining 43234

Eureka Springs AR

Rosalie House, 282 Spring St, Eureka Springs, AR 72632 - T: (501) 253-7377, E-mail: rosalie@arkansas.net, Internet: www.rosaliehouse.com
Historical Museum / Science&Tech Museum - 1973
Home belonging to J.W. Hill, housed first phone system 43235

Eustis FL

Eustis Historical Museum, 536 N Bay St, Eustis, FL 32726-3439 - T: (352) 483-0046, E-mail: EustisHist@aol.com, Internet: www.eustis.org. Cur.: Alice M. Davis
Historical Museum - 1983
Florida hist and culture 43236

Evanston IL

Charles Gates Dawes House, Evanston Historical Society Museum, 225 Greenwood St, Evanston, IL 60201 - T: (847) 475-3410, Fax: (847) 475-3599, E-mail: evanstonhs@nwu.edu, Internet: www.evanstonhistorical.org. Dir.: Lee A. Cabot
Local Museum - 1898
Restored 1894 national historic landmark, home of former Vice President and Nobel laureate Dawes, original 1920s furnishings 43237

Evanston Art Center, 2603 Sheridan Rd, Evanston, IL 60201 - T: (847) 475-5300, Fax: (847) 475-5330, Internet: www.evanstonartcenter.org. Dir.: Brooke Marler
Fine Arts Museum - 1929
Contemporary art 43238

The Kendall College Mitchell Museum of the American Indian, 2600 Central Park, Evanston, IL 60201 - T: (847) 495-1030, Fax: (847) 495-0911, E-mail: mitchellmuseum@mindsprung.com, Internet: www.mitchellmuseum.org. Dir.: Janice B. Klein
University Museum / Historical Museum / Ethnology Museum - 1977 43239

Levere Memorial Temple, 1856 Sheridan Rd, Evanston, IL 60201-3837 - T: (847) 475-1856, Fax: (847) 475-2250, E-mail: lburrows@sae.net, Internet: www.saefraternity.org, www.sae.net. Pres.: William Woods, C.E.O.: Thomas Goodale
Historical Museum - 1929 43240

Mary and Leigh Block Museum of Art, Northwestern University, 1967 South Campus Dr, Evanston, IL 60208-2410 - T: (847) 491-4000, Fax: (847) 491-2261, E-mail: block-museum@nortwestern.edu, Internet: www.blockmuseum.northwestern.edu. Dir.: David Mickenberg, Ass. Dir.: Mary Stewart
Fine Arts Museum / University Museum - 1851 43241

Mitchell Museum of the American Indian, 2600 Central Park, Evanston, IL 60201 - T: (847) 475-1030, Fax: (847) 475-0911, E-mail: mitchellmuseum@mindspring.com, Internet: www.mitchellmuseum.org. Dir.: Janice B. Klein
Ethnology Museum / Folklore Museum - 1977
Cultures of the Woodlands, Plains, Arctic, Southwest and Northwest coast 43242

The Willard House, WCTU Museum, 1730 Chicago Av, Evanston, IL 60201-4585 - T: (847) 328-7500. C.E.O.: B. A. Church
Special Museum - 1946
Home of Frances E. Willard (1865-1898) 43243

Evansville IN

Angel Mounds Historic Site, 8215 Pollack Av, Evansville, IN 47715 - T: (812) 853-3956, Fax: (812) 858-7686, E-mail: curator@angelmounds.org, Internet: www.angelmounds.org. Cur.: Mike Linderman, Ass. Cur.: William Salvador Spellazza
Archaeological Museum / Folklore Museum - 1972
Archaeology, pre-historic middle Mississippian Indian site 43244

Evansville Museum of Arts and Science, 411 SE Riverside Dr, Evansville, IN 47713 - T: (812) 425-2406, Fax: (812) 421-7506, E-mail: mary@emuseum.org, Internet: www.emuseum.org. Dir.: John W. Streetman, Cur.: Thomas R. Lonnberg (History), Mary S. Schnepper (Collections), Susan F. Donahue (Education)
Local Museum / Fine Arts Museum - 1926
General museum - planetarium 43245

Reitz Home Museum, 224 SE First St, Evansville, IN 47713 - T: (812) 426-1871, Fax: (812) 426-2179, E-mail: reitz@evansville.net, Internet: www.reitzhome.evansville.net. Dir.: Tess C. Grimm, Cur.: Mary Bower
Local Museum - 1974 43246

Evansville WY

Reshaw Exhibit, 235 Curtis, Evansville, WY 82636 - T: (307) 234-6530, Fax: (307) 266-5109
Science&Tech Museum - 1963 43247

Eveleth MN

United States Hockey Hall of Fame, 801 Hat Trick Av, Eveleth, MN 55734 - T: (218) 744-5167, Fax: (218) 744-2590, E-mail: kuitunen@ushockeyhall.com, Internet: www.ushockeyhall.com. Exec. Dir.: Tom Sersha
Special Museum - 1969
Sports 43248

Evergreen CO

Hiwan Homestead Museum, 4208 S Timbervale Dr, Evergreen, CO 80439 - T: (303) 674-6262, Fax: (303) 670-7746, E-mail: jsteinle@co.jefferson.co.us, Internet: www.co.jefferson.co.us/dpt/openspac/hiwan. Cur.: Brian Lang
Ethnology Museum / Historical Museum / Historic Site - 1974
Local history, Camp Neosho, later renamed Hiwan Ranch Inetrnational antique Doll collection, Southwestern native american pottery - Archiv of local hist 43249

Excelsior MN

Excelsior-Lake Minnetonka Historical Museum, 420 3rd Av, Excelsior, MN 55331 - T: (612) 474-8956. Pres.: Phillip Hallen
Local Museum - 1972
Local history 43250

Exeter NH

American Independence Museum, 1 Governors Ln, Exeter, NH 03833-2420 - T: (603) 772-2622, Fax: (603) 772-0861, E-mail: info@independencemuseum.org, Internet: www.independencemuseum.org. Exec. Dir.: Funi Burdick, Cur.: Laura Gowing, Debbie Kane (Development), Elizabeth Pappas (Special Events, Programs Manager), Debbie Kanner (Museumseducator)
Historical Museum - 1991 43251

Gilman Garrison House, 12 Water St, Exeter, NH 03833 - T: (603) 436-3205, Fax: (617) 227-9204, E-mail: ezopes@spnea.org, Internet: www.spnea.org. Dir.: Elaine Zopes
Local Museum - 1965 43252

The Lamont Gallery, Phillips Exeter Academy, Frederic R. Mayer Bldg, 20 Main St, Exeter, NH 03833 - T: (603) 777-3461, Fax: (603) 777-4371, E-mail: gallery@exeter.edu, Internet: www.exeter.edu. Interim Dir.: Steve Lewis
Fine Arts Museum / University Museum - 1953 43253

Exira IA

Courthouse Museum, Washington St, Exira, IA 50076 - T: (712) 563-3984, E-mail: aced@netins.net
Local Museum - 1960
Indian hist, flood memorabilia 43254

Exton PA

Thomas Newcomen Museum, 412 Newcomen Rd, Exton, PA 19341 - T: (610) 363-6600, Fax: (610) 363-0612, E-mail: mewcomen@libertynet.org, Internet: www.libertynet.org/~newcomen/. Pres.: C. Daniel Hayes, C.E.O.: Edward Kottcamp
Science&Tech Museum - 1923 43255

Fabius NY

Pioneer Museum, Highland Forest Rte 80, Fabius, NY 13063 - T: (315) 453-6767, Fax: (315) 453-6762, E-mail: stemarie@nysnet.net, Internet: www.ongov.net/parks. Head: Valerie Bell
Local Museum - 1959 43256

Fairbanks AK

Alaska Centennial Center for the Arts, Fairbanks Arts Association, 2300 Airport Way, Fairbanks, AK 99707, mail addr: POB 72786, Fairbanks, AK 99707 - T: (907) 456-6485, Fax: (907) 456-4112, E-mail: fairbanksarts@mosquitonet.com, Internet: www.fairbanksarts.org
Public Gallery 43257

University of Alaska Museum, 907 Yukon Dr, Fairbanks, AK 99775-6960 - T: (907) 474-7505, 474-6939, Fax: (907) 474-5469, E-mail: ffaj@uaf.edu, Internet: www.uaf.edu/museum. Dir.: Aldona Jonaitis, Cur.: Amy Denton (Herbarium), Roland Gangloff (Earth Sciences), Gordon Haas (Ichthyology), Gordon Jarrell (Mammals), Leonard Kamerling (Alaska Center for Docu Film), James Kruse (Entomology), Molly Lee (Ethnology, History), Daniel Odess (Archaeology), Kevin Winter (Ornithology), Coord.: Barry McWayne (Fine Arts)
Fine Arts Museum / University Museum / Local Museum / Natural History Museum / Ethnology Museum - 1929
Natural history, fine art, photography, ethnograpgy, archaeology, paleontology, geology, ornitology, mammals - herbarium 43258

Fairbury NE

Rock Creek Station State Historic Park, 57425 710 Rd, Fairbury, NE 68352 - T: (402) 729-5777, Internet: www.ngpc.state.ne.us. Head: Wayne Brandt
Local Museum / Open Air Museum - 1980 43259

Fairfax VA

Fairfax Museum and Visitor Center, 10209 Main St, Fairfax, VA 22030 - T: (703) 385-8414, Fax: (703) 385-8692, E-mail: sgray@ci.fairfax.va.us, Internet: www.ci.fairfax.va.us. C.E.O.: Susan Inskeep Gray
Historical Museum / Natural History Museum - 1992 43260

National Firearms Museum, 11250 Waples Mill Rd, Fairfax, VA 22030 - T: (703) 267-1620, Fax: (703) 267-3913, E-mail: nfmstaff@nrahq.org, Internet: www.nrahq.org. Pres.: Charlton Heston, Cur.: Doug Wicklund
Science&Tech Museum - 1871
Firearms 43261

Fairfield CO

The Gallery of Contemporary Art, Sacred Heart University, 5151 Park Av, Fairfield, CO 06825-1000 - T: (203) 365-7650, Fax: (203) 396-8361, E-mail: gevass@sacredheart.edu, Internet: artgallery.sacredheart.edu. Dir.: Sophia Gevas
Public Gallery 43262

Fairfield CT

Connecticut Audubon Birdcraft Museum, 314 Unquowa Rd, Fairfield, CT 06430 - T: (203) 259-0416, Fax: (203) 259-1344, E-mail: birdcraft@snet.net, Internet: www.ctaudubon.org. Dir.: Christopher B. Nevins
Natural History Museum - 1914
Bird life, eggs, insects 43263

Ogden House, 636 Old Post Rd, Fairfield, CT 06430 - T: (203) 259-1598, Fax: (203) 255-2716, E-mail: asaintpierre@fairfieldhs.org, Internet: www.fairfieldhistoricalsociety.org. Dir.: Steve Young, Cur.: Adrienne Saint-Pierre
Local Museum - 1902
Local history - library 43264

Thomas J. Walsh Art Gallery and Regina A. Quick Center for the Arts, Fairfield University, N Benson Rd, Fairfield, CT 06430 - T: (203) 254-4242, Fax: (203) 254-4113, E-mail: dmille@fairfield.edu, Internet: www.fairfield.edu/quick. Dir.: Dr. Diana Dimodica Mille, Thomas V. Zingarelli
Fine Arts Museum / University Museum - 1990 43265

Fairfield IA

Carnegie Historical Museum, 114 S Court, Fairfield, IA 52556 - T: (641) 472-2485
Local Museum - 1870
Indian, Iowa pioneer artifacts, mounted birds, mammals, rocks 43266

Fairfield Art Museum, POB 904, Fairfield, IA 52556 - T: (515) 472-2688, 472-6551. Pres.: Diane Boltesilverman
Fine Arts Museum - 1964
Paintings and sculpture by Iowa and Midwest artists 43267

Fairfield TX

Freestone County Historical Museum, 302 E Main St, Fairfield, TX 75840 - T: (903) 389-3738, E-mail: fcmuseum@airmail.net, Internet: www.fairfield.tx.com. Dir.: Kathleen McKee, Cur.: Molly Fryer
Historical Museum - 1967
Local hist, telephones 43268

Fairfield UT

Camp Floyd, 18035 W 1540 N, Fairfield, UT 84013 - T: (801) 768-8932, Fax: (801) 768-1731, E-mail: marktrotter@utah.gov, Internet: www.parks.state.ut.us. Head: Mark A. Trotter
Local Museum - 1855
Historic site, former Army of Utah camp 43269

Fairfield VT

President Chester A. Arthur Historic Site, Chester Arthur St, Fairfield, VT 05455 - T: (802) 828-3051, Fax: (802) 828-3206, E-mail: jdumville@dca.state.vt.us, Internet: www.historicvermont.org. Head: John P. Dumville
Local Museum - 1953
Local hist 43270

Fairhope AL

Eastern Shore Art Center, 401 Oak St, Fairhope, AL 36532 - T: (334) 928-2228, Fax: (334) 928-5188, E-mail: esac@mindspring.com, Internet: www.easternshoreartcenter.com. Dir.: Robin Fitzhugh
Fine Arts Museum - 1958
Contemporary American paintings 43271

Fairmont MN

Pioneer Museum, 304 E Blue Earth Av, Fairmont, MN 56031 - T: (507) 235-5178. Cur.: Helen Simon
Local Museum - 1929
Regional history 43272

Fairmont WV

Pricketts Fort, Rte 3, Fairmont, WV 26554 - T: (304) 363-3030, Fax: (304) 363-3857, E-mail: pfort@host.dmsc.net, Internet: www.picketsfort.org. C.E.O.: Richard D. Brown
Local Museum - 1976 43273

Fairplay CO

South Park City Museum, 100 Fourth, Fairplay, CO 80440 - T: (719) 836-2387, Internet: www.southparkcity.org. Pres.: Raymond Dellacroce, Dir.: Carol A. Davis
Open Air Museum / Local Museum - 1957
Historic village, Colorado mining town 43274

Fairport NY

Fairport Historical Museum, 18 Perrin St, Fairport, NY 14450-2122 - T: (716) 223-3989, Fax: (716) 425-1962, Internet: www.angelfire.com/ny5/fairporthistmuseum. Dir.: Matson Ewell
Local Museum - 1935
Local lore, Native Americans, industry, farm 43275

Fairport Harbor OH

Fairport Marine Museum, 129 Second St, Fairport Harbor, OH 44077 - T: (440) 354-4825, E-mail: fhhs@ncweb.com, Internet: www.fairportlighthouse.com. Pres.: Valerie Laczko
Special Museum - 1945 43276

Fairview UT

Fairview Museum of History and Art, 85 N 100 E, Fairview, UT 84629 - T: (435) 427-9216, Internet: www.sanpete.com. Dir.: Ron Staker
Local Museum - 1966 43277

Falcon Heights MN

Gibbs Farm Museum, 2097 W Larpenteur Av, Falcon Heights, MN 55113 - T: (651) 646-8629, Fax: (651) 223-8539, E-mail: admin@rchs.com, Internet: www.rchs.com. Pres.: Howard Guthman, C.E.O.: Priscilla Farnham
Agriculture Museum - 1949 43278

Gibbs Museum of Pioneer and Dakotah Life, 2097 W Larpenteur Av, Falcon Heights, MN 55113 - T: (651) 646-8629, 659-0345, Fax: (651) 223-8539, E-mail: admin@rchs.com, Internet: www.rchs.com
Agriculture Museum / Local Museum - 1949
Hist of the Gibbs family 1835-1940, Dakota Native Americans, agriculture 43279

Falfurrias TX

The Heritage Museum at Falfurrias, 415 N Saint Mary's St, Falfurrias, TX 78355 - T: (512) 325-2907. Cur.: E. Cabrera
Local Museum - 1965
Local hist 43280

Fall River MA

Battleship Cove - Maritime Heritage Museums, Battleship Cove, Fall River, MA 02721 - T: (508) 678-1100, Fax: (508) 674-5597, E-mail: battleship@battleshipcove.com, Internet: www.battleshipcove.org. Head: Ernst E. Cummings, Cur.: Christopher J. Nardi
Historical Museum / Military Museum / Historic Site - 1965
Historic ships 43281

Fall River Historical Society Museum, 451 Rock St, Fall River, MA 02720 - T: (508) 679-1071, Fax: (508) 675-5754, Internet: www.lizzieborden.org. Pres.: Elizabeth Denning, Cur.: Michael Martins, Ass. Cur.: Dennis Binette
Local Museum - 1921
Local history 43282

Marine Museum at Fall River, 70 Water St, Fall River, MA 02721 - T: (508) 674-3533, Fax: (508) 674-3534, E-mail: staff@marinemuseum.org, Internet: www.marinemuseum.org. Chm.: James Haskins
Historical Museum - 1968
Marine, restored machine shop 43283

Fall River Mills CA

Fort Crook Historical Museum, Fort Crook Av and Hwy 299, Fall River Mills, CA 96028 - T: (530) 336-5110, E-mail: ftcrook@yahoo.com, Internet: www.geocities.com/ftcrook. Cur.: Susan Knoch, Bill Ingram
Historical Museum - 1934 43284

Fallon NV

Churchill County Museum and Archives, 1050 S Maine St, Fallon, NV 89406 - T: (775) 423-3677, Fax: (775) 423-3662, E-mail: ccmuseum@phonewave.net, Internet: ccmuseum.org. Dir./Cur.: Jane Pieplow
Local Museum - 1967 43285

Fallsington PA

Historic Fallsington, 4 Yardley Av, Fallsington, PA 19054 - T: (215) 295-6567, Fax: (215) 295-6567, E-mail: histfals@pop.erols.com. Pres.: Robert L.B. Harman, Exec. Dir.: Erica Armour
Open Air Museum / Local Museum - 1953 43286

Falmouth MA

Falmouth Historical Museum, 55-65 Palmer Av at Village Green, Falmouth, MA 02541 - T: (508) 548-4857, Fax: (508) 540-0968, E-mail: rfitzpa24@aol.com, Internet: www.falmouthhistoricalsociety.org. Dir.: Ann Sears, Cur.: Judith McAlister
Local Museum - 1900
Local history 43287

Far Hills NJ

Golf Museum, 77 Liberty Corner Rd, Far Hills, NJ 07931 - T: (908) 234-2300, Fax: (908) 234-0319, Internet: www.usga.org. Dir.: David Fay, Cur.: Rand Jerris
Special Museum - 1935
Golf 43288

Fargo GA

Stephen C. Foster State Park, Rte 1, Fargo, GA 31631, mail addr: POB 131, Fargo, GA 31631 - T: (912) 637-5274, Fax: (912) 637-5587, E-mail: scfost@planttel.net
Natural History Museum - 1954
Folk culture, personal artefacts, lumbering, turpentining 43289

Fargo ND

Children's Museum at Yunker Farm, 1201 28th Av N, Fargo, ND 58102 - T: (701) 232-6102, Fax: (701) 232-4605, E-mail: ynasset@hotmail.com, Internet: www.childrensmuseum-yunker.org. Pres.: Lisa Drake, Exec. Dir.: Yvette Nasset
Special Museum - 1989 43290

Fargo Air Museum, 1609 19th Av N, Fargo, ND 58109 - T: (701) 293-8043, Fax: (701) 293-8103, Internet: www.fargoairmuseum.org. Dir.: Gerald Beck
Science&Tech Museum 43291

Memorial Union Gallery, Memorial Union-North Dakota State University, Fargo, ND 58105-5476 - T: (701) 231-8239, Fax: (701) 231-8043, E-mail: peg-furshong@ndsu.nodak.edu, Internet: www.ndsu.nodak.edu/memorial_union/gallery. Dir.: Peg Furshong
University Museum / Fine Arts Museum - 1975 43292

Plains Art Museum, 704 First Av N, Fargo, ND 58102 - T: (701) 232-3821, Fax: (701) 293-1082, E-mail: museum@plainsart.org, Internet: www.plainsart.org. Chm.: Kim Kemmer, C.E.O.: Todd Smith
Fine Arts Museum - 1973
Contemporary American, American Indian and West African art, fine arts, Woodland and Plain Indian art 43293

Faribault MN

Rice County Museum of History, 1814 NW 2nd Av, Faribault, MN 55021 - T: (507) 332-2121, Fax: (507) 332-2121. Dir.: Maynard A. Spitzack
Local Museum / Agriculture Museum - 1926
Local history, agricultural 43294

Farmington CT

Hill-Stead Museum, 35 Mountain Rd, Farmington, CT 06032 - T: (860) 677-4787, Fax: (860) 677-0174, E-mail: hillstead@hillstead.org, Internet: www.hillstead.org. Dir.: Linda Stagleder
Fine Arts Museum - 1946
French impressionist painting, prints, sculpture, porcelain, furniture 43295

Museum of the University of Connecticut Health Center, c/o School of Dental Medicine, 263 Farmington Av, Farmington, CT 06030 - T: (860) 679-3211. Head: Jay Christian
University Museum / Special Museum - 1979
Dental antiques 43296

Stanley-Whitman House, 37 High St, Farmington, CT 06032 - T: (860) 677-9222, Fax: (860) 677-7758, E-mail: lisa@stanleywhitman.org, Internet: www.stanleywhitman.org. Dir.: James Bennett
Local Museum - 1936
Interpretation of 18th-c Farmington 43297

Farmington ME

Nordica Homestead Museum, 116 Nordica Ln, Farmington, ME 04938 - T: (207) 778-2042. Pres.: Tom Sawyer
Local Museum - 1927
Regional history 43298

Farmington NM

Farmington Museum, 3041 E Main St, Farmington, NM 87402 - T: (505) 599-1174, Fax: (505) 326-7572, E-mail: rwelch@fmtn.org, Internet: www.farmingtonmuseum.org. Dir.: Richard Welch, Cur.: Bart Wilsey, Sc. Staff: Catherine Davis
Ethnology Museum / Local Museum - 1980 43299

Farmington PA

Fort Necessity National Battlefield, 1 Washington Pkwy, Farmington, PA 15437 - T: (724) 329-5512, Fax: (724) 329-8682, E-mail: fone_Superintendent@nps.gov, Internet: www.nps.gov/fone/. Dir.: Joanne Hanley, Cur.: Lawren Dunn
Open Air Museum / Military Museum - 1931 43300

Touchstone Center for Crafts, RR 1, Box 60, Farmington, PA 15437-9707 - T: (724) 329-1370, Fax: (724) 329-1371, E-mail: tcc@hhs.net, Internet: www.touchstonecrafts.com
Decorative Arts Museum - 1972
Ceramics, jewelry 43301

Farmington UT

Pioneer Village, 375 N Lagoon Ln, Farmington, UT 84025 - T: (801) 451-8050, Fax: (801) 451-8015. Dir.: Peter Freed, Dep. Dir.: Howard Freed
Local Museum / Open Air Museum - 1954
Historic village 43302

Farmville NC

May Museum and Park, 213 S Main St, Farmville, NC 27828 - T: (252) 753-5814, Fax: (252) 753-3910, E-mail: maymuseum@farmville.ng.com. Dir.: Clifford P. Kendall, Cur.: John S. Rossi
Local Museum - 1991
Local history, decorative art, textiles 43303

Farmville VA

Longwood Center for the Visual Arts, 129 N Main St, Farmville, VA 23901 - T: (434) 395-2206, Fax: (434) 392-6441, E-mail: kjbowles@longwood.lwc.edu, Internet: web.longwood.edu/lcva. Dir.: Kay Johnson Bowles
Fine Arts Museum / University Museum - 1971
Art 43304

Fayette AL

Fayette Art Museum, 530 Temple Av N, Fayette, AL 35555 - T: (205) 932-8727, Fax: (205) 932-8788, E-mail: fam@fayette.net. Dir./Cur.: Jack Black
Fine Arts Museum - 1969 43305

Fayette MO

Ashby-Hodge Gallery of American Art, 411 CMC Sq, Fayette, MO 65248 - T: (660) 248-6324, Fax: (660) 248-2622, E-mail: jgeist@coin.org, Internet: www.cmc.edu. Cur.: Dr. Joseph E. Geist
Fine Arts Museum / University Museum - 1994 43306

Stephens Museum, Central Methodist College, Fayette, MO 65248 - T: (660) 248-6370, 248-6334, Fax: (660) 248-2622, E-mail: delliot@cmc2.cmc.edu, Internet: www.cmc.edu. Dir./Cur.: Dana R. Elliott
Natural History Museum / Religious Arts Museum / University Museum - 1879 43307

Fayetteville AR

The University Museum, University of Arkansas, Museum Bldg, Rm 202, Fayetteville, AR 72701 - T: (501) 575-3466, Fax: (501) 575-8766, Internet: www.uark.edu/~museinfo/. Dir.: Dr. Johnnie L. Gentry, Cur.: Mary Suter (Collections), Ass. Cur.: Dr. Nancy G. McCartney (Zoology)
University Museum / Ethnology Museum / Natural History Museum - 1873
Ethnology, anthropology, zoology - herbarium 43308

Fayetteville NC

Airborne and Special Operations Museum, 100 Bragg Blvd, Fayetteville, NC 28301 - T: (910) 483-3003 ext 221, Fax: (910) 483-8232, E-mail: aarsenj@bragg.army.mil. Dir.: John Aarsen
Military Museum - 2000
Military artifacts, uniforms, weapons, WW 2 airplane, helicopter 43309

Arts Council of Fayetteville, 301 Hay St, Fayetteville, NC 28302 - T: (910) 323-1776, Fax: (910) 323-1727, E-mail: admin@theartscouncil.com, Internet: www.theartscouncil.com. Exec. Dir.: Deborah Martin Mintz
Fine Arts Museum - 1974 43310

Fayetteville Museum of Art, 839 Stamper Rd, Fayetteville, NC 28303 - T: (910) 485-5121, Fax: (910) 485-5233, E-mail: fmastar@infi.net, Internet: www.fayettevillemuseumart.org. Pres.: Rebecca Eatman-Jackson, Dir.: Tom Grubb
Fine Arts Museum / Public Gallery - 1971 43311

Museum of the Cape Fear Historical Complex, Corner of Bradford and Arsenal Aves, Fayetteville, NC 28305 - T: (910) 486-1330, Fax: (910) 486-1585, E-mail: mcfhc@infi.net, Internet: www.ncmuseumofhistory.org. Pres.: Sam T. Snowdon
Historical Museum - 1985
History 43312

Fergus Falls MN

Otter Tail County Historical Museum, 1110 Lincoln Av W, Fergus Falls, MN 56537 - T: (218) 736-6038, Fax: (218) 739-3075. Dir.: Chris Schuelke, Cur.: Kathy M. Lindberg
Local Museum - 1927
Regional history 43313

Fernandina Beach FL

Amelia Island Museum of History, 233 S Third St, Fernandina Beach, FL 32034 - T: (904) 261-7378, Fax: (904) 261-9701, E-mail: aimh@net-magic.net, Internet: www.ameliaislandmuseumofhistory.org. Pres.: Carol Ann Atwood, Dir.: W. David Mallery
Historical Museum - 1986 43314

Fort Clinch, 2601 Atlantic Av, Fernandina Beach, FL 32034 - T: (904) 277-7274, Fax: (904) 277-7249, Internet: www.floridastateparks.org. C.E.O.: Virginia Wetherell
Historical Museum - 1935 43315

Ferrisburgh VT

Rokeby Museum, Rowland Evans Robinson Memorial Association, 4334 Rte 7, Ferrisburgh, VT 05456 - T: (802) 877-3406, E-mail: rokeby@globalnetisp.net, Internet: www.rokeby.org. Dir.: Jane Williamson
Historic Site - 1962
Historic house 43316

Ferrum VA

Blue Ridge Institute and Museum, c/o Ferrum College, Rt 40, Ferrum, VA 24088 - T: (540) 365-4416, Fax: (540) 365-4419, E-mail: bri@ferrum.edu, Internet: www.ferrum.edu. Dir.: J. Roderick Moore, Ass. Dir.: Vaughan Webb
Folklore Museum - 1971
Farming, folklife 43317

Fessenden ND

Wells County Museum, 305 First St S, Fessenden, ND 58450 - T: (701) 984-2688. Pres.: Lorraine Rau, Cur.: Lorraine Rau
Local Museum - 1972 43318

Fifield WI

Old Town Hall Museum, W 7213 Pine St, Fifield, WI 54524 - T: (715) 762-4571. Cur.: Patricia Schroeder
Local Museum / Historical Museum - 1969
Local hist, logging and farming tools, clothing, books, household 43319

Fillmore CA

Fillmore Historical Museum, 350 Main St, Fillmore, CA 93016 - T: (805) 524-0948, Fax: (805) 524-0516, E-mail: museum@csiway.com
Local Museum - 1971 43320

Fillmore UT

Territorial Statehouse State Museum, 50 W Capitol Av, Fillmore, UT 84631 - T: (435) 743-5316, Fax: (435) 743-4723. Head: Gordon Chatland
Historical Museum - 1930
Regional hist 43321

Findlay OH

Dudley and Mary Marks Lea Gallery, c/o University of Findlay, 1000 N Main St, Findlay, OH 45840 - T: (419) 424-4577, Fax: (419) 424-4757. Dir.: Doug Salveson
Fine Arts Museum / University Museum - 1962 43322

Hancock Historical Museum, 422 W Sandusky St, Findlay, OH 45840 - T: (419) 423-4433, Fax: (419) 423-2154. Pres.: Tim Brugeman, C.E.O.: Sue Tucker
Local Museum - 1970 43323

Fishers IN

Conner Prairie Living History Museum, 13400 Allisonville Rd, Fishers, IN 46038 - T: (317) 776-6000, Fax: (317) 776-6014, E-mail: info@connerprairie.org, Internet: www.connerprairie.org. Pres.: John H. Herbst, Dep. Dir.: Dan Freus (Programs)
Historical Museum - 1964
William Conner home; living history, natural history area 43324

Fishkill NY

Van Wyck Homestead Museum, 504 Rte 9, Fishkill, NY 12524 - T: (845) 896-9560, E-mail: vanwyckhomestead@hotmail.com. Dir.: Roy Jorgensen, Chair: Susan Dexter
Historical Museum / Local Museum - 1962
Artefacts of Rev. war, Hudson valley painting 43325

Fitchburg MA

Fitchburg Art Museum, Merriam Pkwy, Fitchburg, MA 01420, mail addr: 185 Elm St, Fitchburg, MA 01420 - T: (978) 345-4207, Fax: (978) 345-2319, E-mail: info@fitchburgartmuseum.org, Internet: www.fitchburgartmuseum.org. Dir.: Peter Timms (Program), Roger Dell (Education), Cur.: Pamela Russell
Fine Arts Museum - 1925
Art 43326

Fitchburg Historical Society Museum, 50 Grove St, Fitchburg, MA 01420 - T: (978) 345-1157, Fax: (978) 345-2229, E-mail: fitchburghistory@aol.com. Pres.: Helen Obermeyer Simmons, Exec. Dir.: Betsy Hannula
Historical Museum - 1892
Local history, civil war coll 43327

Flagstaff AZ

Arizona Historical Society Pioneer Museum, 2340 N Fort Valley Rd, Flagstaff, AZ 86001 - T: (520) 774-6272, Fax: (520) 774-1596, E-mail: ahsnad@infomagic.net, Internet: www.infomagic.net/ahsnad. Dir.: Joseph M. Meehan, Cur.: Susan Wilcox
Historical Museum - 1953 43328

Museum of Northern Arizona, 3101 N Fort Valley Rd, Flagstaff, AZ 86001 - T: (928) 774-5213, Fax: (928) 779-1527, E-mail: info@mna.mus.az.us, Internet: www.musnaz.org. C.E.O.: Eugene M. Hughes, Vice Pres.: Dr. Edwin L. Wade (Programs), Cur.: Dr. David D. Gillette (Paleontology), Dr. L. Barry Albright (Geology), Dr. David R. Wilcox (Anthropology)
Local Museum - 1928
Local history, anthropology, geology, biology, fine art 43329

Northern Arizona University Art Museum and Galleries, Knoles and McMullen Circle, Bldg 10, N NAU Campus, Flagstaff, AZ 86011-6021 - T: (928) 523-3471, Fax: (928) 523-1424, E-mail: linda.stromberg@nau.edu, Internet: www.nau.edu/art_museum. Dir.: John Burton
University Museum / Fine Arts Museum / Public Gallery - 1961
Paintings, graphics, ceramics, sculpture, furniture 43330

Riordan Mansion, 409 Riordan Rd, Flagstaff, AZ 86001 - T: (928) 779-4395, Fax: (928) 556-0253, E-mail: jschreiber@pr.state.az.us, Internet: www.pr.state.az.us
Local Museum - 1983
Local hist, coll of original craftsman furnishings 43331

Walnut Canyon National Monument, 6400 N Hwy 89, Flagstaff, AZ 86004 - T: (928) 526-1157, Fax: (928) 526-4259. Head: Sam R. Henderson
Historic Site / Archaeological Museum - 1915
Site of prehistoric Indian ruins of the Sinagua Indian culture 43332

Wupatki National Monument, 6400 N Hwy. 89, Flagstaff, AZ 86004 - T: (928) 526-1157, Fax: (928) 526-4259. Cur.: Jeri DeYoung
Historic Site / Archaeological Museum - 1924
Over 2,600 archaeological sites dating from approx. 1100 A.D., Hopi ancestral homeland 43333

Flandreau SD

Moody County Museum, 706 East Pipestone Av, Flandreau, SD 57028 - T: (605) 997-3191, Internet: www.rootsweb.com/~sdmoody. Dir.: Roberta Williamson
Local Museum - 1965
Local hist 43334

Flat Rock NC

Carl Sandburg Home, 1928 Little River Rd, Flat Rock, NC 28731 - T: (704) 693-4178, Fax: (704) 693-4179, E-mail: carl_administration@nps.gov, Internet: www.nps.gov/carl. C.E.O./Cur.: Connie Backlund
Local Museum - 1969 43335

Fleming CO

Fleming Historical Museum, Heritage Museum Park, Fleming, CO 80728 - T: (970) 265-3721, 265-2591. C.E.O.: Helen Lambert
Local Museum - 1965
Local history 43336

Flemington NJ

Doric House, 114 Main St, Flemington, NJ 08822 - T: (908) 782-1091. Pres.: Richard H. Stothoff
Local Museum - 1885 43337

Flint MI

Buckham Fine Arts Project Gallery, 134 1/2 W Second St, Flint, MI 48502 - T: (810) 239-6334. Pres.: Suzanne M. Brodie
Fine Arts Museum - 1984
Contemporary arts since 1984 43338

Flint Institute of Arts, 1120 E Kearsley St, Flint, MI 48503 - T: (810) 234-1695, Fax: (810) 234-1692, E-mail: info@flintarts.org, Internet: www.flintarts.org. Dir.: John B. Henry
Fine Arts Museum - 1928
African, American, Asian and European art, decorative arts 43339

Sloan Museum, 1221 E Kearsley St, Flint, MI 48503 - T: (810) 237-3450, Fax: (810) 237-3451, E-mail: sloandir@tir.com; tshickles@flintcultural.org, Internet: www.sloanmuseum.com. Dir.: Tim Shickles, Ass. Dir.: James L. Johnson, Cur.: Jeff Taylor (Collections), Jim Berry (Programs)
Historical Museum / Science&Tech Museum - 1966 43340

Flora MS

Mississippi Petrified Forest Museum, 124 Forest Park Rd, Flora, MS 39071 - T: (601) 879-8189, Fax: (601) 879-8165, E-mail: mspforest@aol.com, Internet: www.mspetrifiedforest.com. Dir.: C. J. McNamara
Natural History Museum - 1963 43341

Floral Park NY

Queens County Farm Museum, 73-50 Little Neck Pkwy, Floral Park, NY 11004 - T: (718) 347-3276, Fax: (718) 347-3243, E-mail: afischetti@queensfarm.org, Internet: www.queensfarm.org. Dir.: Amy Fischetti
Agriculture Museum - 1975 43342

Florence AL

Kennedy-Douglass Center for the Arts, 217 E Tuscaloosa St, Florence, AL 35630 - T: (256) 760-6379, Fax: (256) 760-6382, E-mail: bbroach@floweb.com. Dir.: Barbara K. Broach
Fine Arts Museum - 1976 43343

Pope's Tavern Museum, 203 Hermitage Dr, Florence, AL 35630 - T: (256) 760-6439. Cur.: Jo Parkhurst
Local Museum - 1968
One of oldest structures in Florence, one-time stagecoach stop, tavern and inn, hospital by Confederate and Union forces 43344

W.C. Handy Home Museum, 620 W College St, Florence, AL 35630 - T: (256) 760-6434, Fax: (256) 760-6382, E-mail: bbroach@floweb.com. Dir.: Barbara K. Broach, Cur.: Pearley Woods
Historical Museum - 1968
library 43345

Florence CO

Florence Price Pioneer Museum, Pikes Peak Av and Front St, Florence, CO 81226 - T: (719) 784-3157. C.E.O.: Frank W. Tedesko, Cur.: Leona Blackman
Local Museum - 1964 43346

Florence KS

Harvey House Museum, 221 Marion, Florence, KS 66851 - T: (316) 878-4296, E-mail: timm2@marionco.net. Pres.: Kristal Timm
Special Museum - 1971
Antique furniture, pictures, dishes, tools, 43347

Florence SC

Florence Museum of Art, Science and History, 558 Spruce St, Florence, SC 29501 - T: (843) 662-3351, E-mail: flomuseum@bellsouth.net, Internet: www.florenceweb.com/museum.htm. Dir.: Betsy Olsen
Fine Arts Museum / Natural History Museum / Historical Museum - 1936
Art, science, history 43348

Florissant MO

Florissant Valley Historical Society Museum, 1896 S Florissant Rd, Florissant, MO 63031 - T: (314) 524-1100, E-mail: fredmary2@aol.com. Pres.: Lorelei Cromer
Historical Museum - 1958 43349

Old Saint Ferdinand's Shrine, 1 Rue Saint François, Florissant, MO 63031 - T: (314) 831-4237, Fax: (314) 830-0075, E-mail: Bill052946@aol.com. Pres.: Bill Bray
Religious Arts Museum - 1958 43350

Flovilla GA

Indian Springs State Park Museum, Hwy 42, 5 Miles S of Jackson, Flovilla, GA 30216, mail addr: 678 Lake Clark Rd, Flovilla, GA 30216 - T: (770) 504-2277, Fax: (770) 504-2178. Head: Don Coleman
Natural History Museum - 1825
History, photos 43351

Flushing NY

Bowne House, 37-01 Bowne St, Flushing, NY 11354 - T: (718) 359-0528. Pres.: Douglas F. Bauer
Local Museum - 1945 43352

Frances Godwin and Joseph Ternbach Museum → Godwin and Ternbach Museum

Godwin and Ternbach Museum, Queens College, 65-30 Kissena Blvd, Flushing, NY 11367 - T: (718) 997-5000 ext 4747, Fax: (718) 997-4734, Internet: www.qc.edu/art/gtmus.html. C.E.O.: Amy Winter
Fine Arts Museum / University Museum - 1957
Art 43353

Kingsland Homestead, Queens Historical Society, Weeping Beech Park, 143-35 37th Av, Flushing, NY 11354 - T: (718) 939-0647, Fax: (718) 539-9885, E-mail: qhs@juno.com, Internet: www.preserve.org/queens. Pres.: Stanley Cogan, Exec. Dir.: Mitchell Grubler
Historical Museum - 1968
Photographs, postcards, maps, personal papers, architectural renderings, 43354

New York Hall of Science, 47-01 111th St, Flushing, NY 11368 - T: (718) 699-0005, Fax: (718) 699-1341, E-mail: wbrez@nyscience.org, Internet: www.nyhallsci.org. Dir.: Dr. Alan J. Friedman, Dep. Dir.: Harold Chapnick (Internal Affairs), Marilyn Hoyt (External Affairs), Eric Siegel (Planning, Programs), Martin Weiss (Biology), Preeti Gupta (Education), PR: Wendy Brez
Science&Tech Museum - 1964
library 43355

Queens Historical Museum, 143-35 37th Av, Flushing, NY 11354 - T: (718) 939-0647, Fax: (718) 539-9885, E-mail: qhs@juno.com, Internet: www.preserve.org/queens. Pres.: Stanley Cogan, Exec. Dir.: Joyce A. Cook
Local Museum - 1968
Local history, Kingsland homestead 43356

Queens Museum of Art, New York City Bldg, Flushing Meadows Corona Park, Flushing, NY 11368-3398 - T: (718) 592-9700, Fax: (718) 592-5778, Internet: www.queensmuse.org. Dir.: Laurene Buckley, Cur.: Sharon Vatksy
Fine Arts Museum - 1972
Paintings, sculpture, prints, photography 43357

Folsom CA

Folsom History Museum, 823 Sutter St, Folsom, CA 95630 - T: (916) 985-2707, Fax: (916) 985-7288, E-mail: folsom_history_museum@msn.com, Internet: www.folsomhistorymuseum.org. Dir.: Karen Mehring
Local Museum - 1960 43358

Folsom NM

Folsom Museum, Main St, Folsom, NM 88419 - T: (505) 278-3616, E-mail: bkthompson@bacavalley.com, Internet: www.geocities.com/folsom_museum. Pres.: Vinita Brown
Archaeological Museum - 1967 43359

Fond du Lac WI

Galloway House and Village, 336 Old Pioneer Rd, Fond du Lac, WI 54935 - T: (414) 922-6390. Chief Cur.: Jim Glassel, Cur.: William J. Weinshrott
Local Museum - 1955
Historic village 43360

Fonda NY

Native American Exhibit, National Kateri Shrine, Rte 5, 1/2 mile West of Fonda, Fonda, NY 12068 - T: (518) 853-3646, Fax: (518) 853-3371, E-mail: kkenny@nycap.rr.com, Internet: www.katerishrine.com. Dir.: Kevin Kenny, Ass. Dir.: Florence Guiffre
Historical Museum / Archaeological Museum / Folklore Museum / Religious Arts Museum - 1949
1666-1693 staked out Mohawk Indian castle and 1666-1676 residence of Kateri Tekakwitha 43361

Forest Grove OR

Pacific University Museum, Pacific University, 2043 College Way, Forest Grove, OR 97116 - T: (503) 359-2211, Fax: (503) 359-2252, E-mail: ur@pacificu.edu, Internet: www.pacificu.edu
University Museum / Historical Museum / Folklore Museum - 1949 43362

Forked River NJ

Lacey Historical Society Museum, Rte 9, Old Schoolhouse, Forked River, NJ 08731 - T: (609) 971-0467
Local Museum - 1962 43363

Forsyth MT

Rosebud County Pioneer Museum, 1335 Main St, Forsyth, MT 59327 - T: (406) 356-7547. Pres.: Cal MacConnel
Local Museum - 1966 43364

Fort Atkinson WI

Hoard Historical Museum, 407 Merchant Av, Fort Atkinson, WI 53538 - T: (920) 563-7769, Fax: (920) 568-3203, E-mail: hartwick@hoardmuseum.org, Internet: www.hoardmuseum.org. Dir.: Sue Hartwick, Cur.: Karen O'Connor
Local Museum - 1933
Local hist 43365

Fort Benning GA

National Infantry Museum, c/o US Army Infantry School, Bldg 396, Baltzell Av, Fort Benning, GA 31905-5593 - T: (706) 545-2958, Fax: (706) 545-5158, E-mail: hannerz@benning.army.mil, Internet: www.benningmwr.com. Dir.: Frank Hanner
Military Museum - 1959
Military history 43366

Fort Benton MT

Fort Benton Museum of the Upper Missouri, 1801 Front St, Fort Benton, MT 59442 - T: (406) 622-5316, Fax: (406) 622-3725, E-mail: fbmusuems@hotmail.com. Head: John G. Lepley
Local Museum - 1957 43367

Museum of the Northern Great Plains, 20th and Washington, Fort Benton, MT 59442 - T: (406) 622-5133, Fax: (406) 622-3725, E-mail: fbmuseums@hotmail.com. Dir.: John G. Lepley
Historical Museum - 1989 43368

Fort Bliss TX

Fort Bliss Museum, Pleasonton and Sheridan Rds, Fort Bliss, TX 79916-3802 - T: (915) 568-6940, Fax: (915) 568-6941, E-mail: jroger@bliss.army.mil. Dir.: Peter M. Poessiger, Chief Cur.: James R. Rogers
Military Museum - 1954
Military hist, local installation hist 43369

United States Army Air Defense Artillery Museum, Bldg 5000, Pleasanton Rd, Fort Bliss, TX 79916 - T: (915) 568-5412, Fax: (915) 568-6941, E-mail: rossd@emhio.bliss.army.mil. Cur.: David A. Ross
Military Museum - 1975
Military hist 43370

Fort Bragg NC

82nd Airborne Division War Memorial Museum, Gela and Ardennes Sts, Fort Bragg, NC 28307 - T: (910) 432-5307, Fax: (910) 436-4440. Chief Cur.: Robert Anzuoni
Military Museum - 1945 43371

JFK Special Warfare Museum, Ardennes and Marion Sts, Bldg D-2502, Fort Bragg, NC 28307 - T: (910) 432-1533, Fax: (910) 432-4062, E-mail: merrittr@soc.mil. Cur.: Roxanne M. Merritt
Military Museum - 1963 43372

Fort Bridger WY

Fort Bridger State Museum, 37,000 Business Loop I-80, Fort Bridger, WY 82933 - T: (307) 782-3842, Fax: (307) 782-7181, E-mail: lnewma@missc.state.wy.us, Internet: www.wyospcr.state.wy.us. Dir.: Bill Gentle, Cur.: Cecil Sanderson
Historical Museum / Historic Site - 1843
Local hist 43373

Fort Calhoun NE

Fort Atkinson State Historical Park, 1 mile E of Hwy 75, Fort Calhoun, NE 68023 - T: (402) 468-5611, Fax: (402) 468-5066, E-mail: ftatkin@ngpc.state.ne.us, Internet: ngpc.state.ne.us. Head: John Slader
Military Museum - 1963 43374

Washington County Historical Association Museum, 104 N 14, Fort Calhoun, NE 68023 - T: (402) 468-5740, Fax: (402) 468-5741, E-mail: info@newashcohist.org, Internet: www.newashcohist.org. Cur.: Agnes L. Smith
Local Museum - 1938 43375

Fort Campbell KY

Don F. Pratt Museum, 5702 Tennessee Av, Fort Campbell, KY 42223-5335 - T: (270) 798-4986, Fax: (502) 798-2605, E-mail: boggsr@emh2.army.mil, Internet: www.campbell.army.mil/pratt/. Dir./Cur.: Rex Boggs, Sc. Staff: John O'Brian (History)
Military Museum - 1956
Airborne military, history of 101st ABN Division 43376

Fort Carson CO

Third Cavalry Museum, Bldg 2160, Barkeley Rd, Fort Carson, CO 80913-5000 - T: (719) 526-1404, 526-2028, Fax: (719) 526-6573, E-mail: paul.martin@carson.army.mil. Dir.: Paul Martin
Military Museum - 1959
Military hist 43377

Fort Collins CO

Curfman Gallery and Duhesa Lounge, Colorado State University, Fort Collins, CO 80523 - T: (970) 491-6444, 491-5838, Fax: (970) 491-3746, E-mail: mshelmer@otis.sc.colostate.edu, Internet: www.colostate.edu. Dir.: Miriam B. Harris
Fine Arts Museum / Public Gallery - 1968 43378

Discovery Center Science Museum, 703 E Prospect Rd, Fort Collins, CO 80525 - T: (970) 472-3990, Fax: (970) 472-3997, E-mail: dcsm@psd.k12.co.us, Internet: www.dcsm.org. Exec. Dir.: Diane White
Science&Tech Museum - 1989
Science 43379

Fort Collins Museum, 200 Matthews, Fort Collins, CO 80524 - T: (970) 221-6738, Fax: (970) 416-2236, E-mail: bhiggins@fcgov.com, Internet: www.fcgov.com/museum. Dir.: Jill Gardner-Stilwell
Local Museum - 1940 43380

Gustafson Gallery, Colorado State University, 314 Gifford St, Fort Collins, CO 80523 - T: (970) 491-1983, Fax: (970) 491-4376, E-mail: carlson@cahs.colostate.edu, Internet: www.colostate.edu/depts/dm. Dir.: Dr. Kevin Oltjenbruns, Cur.: Linda Carlson
Special Museum / University Museum - 1986
Historical costume and textile 43381

Hatton Gallery, Colorado State University, Visual Arts Bldg, Fort Collins, CO 80523 - T: (970) 491-6774, Fax: (970) 491-0505, E-mail: linda.frickman@colostate.edu, Internet: www.colostate.edu. Dir.: Linda Frickman
Fine Arts Museum / University Museum - 1970
Art gallery, Japanese prints, contemporary posters, African art 43382

Museum of Contemporary Art, 201 S College Av, Fort Collins, CO 80524 - T: (970) 482-2787, Fax: (970) 482-0804, E-mail: fcmoca@frii.com. Dir.: Jeanne Shoaff, Ass. Dir.: Michele Carle
Fine Arts Museum - 1990 43383

One West Art Center → Museum of Contemporary Art

Fort Davis TX

Fort Davis, Hwy 17-118, Fort Davis, TX 79734 - T: (915) 426-3224 ext 27, Fax: (915) 426-3122, E-mail: foda_superintendent@nps.gov, Internet: www.nps.gov/foda. Cur.: Elaine Harmon
Military Museum / Historical Museum - 1963
Military hist, Indians wars Western frontier history 43384

Neill Museum, 7th and Court St, Fort Davis, TX 79734 - T: (915) 426-3838, 426-3969. Dir.: Teda W. Neill
Local Museum - 1960
Local hist 43385

Fort DeRussy HI

United States Army Museum of Hawaii, Battery Randolph, Kalia Rd, Fort DeRussy, HI 96815 - T: (808) 438-2821, Fax: (808) 438-2819, E-mail: mclaughlinje@shafter.army.mil. Dir./Cur.: Thomas M. Fairfull
Historical Museum / Military Museum - 1976
Military history, Battery Randolph, a Pre-WWI coast artillery defense bastion 43386

Fort Dix NJ

Fort Dix Museum, AFRC-FA-KPS, Fort Dix, NJ 08640 - T: (609) 562-6983, Fax: (609) 562-2164, E-mail: daniel.zimmerman@dix.army.mil. Dir.: Daniel W. Zimmerman, Cur.: Robert McCully
Military Museum - 1984 43387

Fort Dodge IA

Blanden Memorial Art Museum, 920 Third Av, S, Fort Dodge, IA 50501 - T: (515) 573-2316, Fax: (515) 573-2317, E-mail: blanden@dodgenet.com, Internet: www.blanden.org. Pres.: M. Peters, Dir.: Charles P. Helsell
Fine Arts Museum - 1930
Art 43388

Fort Dodge Historical Museum, Museum Rd, Fort Dodge, IA 50501 - T: (515) 573-4231, Fax: (515) 573-4231, E-mail: thefort@frontiernet.net, Internet: www.fortmuseum.com. Pres.: Dr. E. Ryan, Exec. Dir.: David Parker
Military Museum / Local Museum - 1962
Local and military history 43389

Fort Douglas UT

Fort Douglas Military Museum, 32 Potter St, Fort Douglas, UT 84113 - T: (801) 581-1710, Fax: (801) 581-9846, E-mail: fdouglas@webquyinternet.com, Internet: www.fortdouglas.org. Dir.: Robert Voyles, Cur.: Jay Nielson
Military Museum - 1975
Military history, weapons, equipment, uniforms 43390

Fort Duchesne UT

Cultural Rights and Protection/Ute Indian Tribe, Hwy 40, Fort Duchesne, UT 84026 - T: (801) 722-4992, Fax: (801) 722-2083. Dir.: Betsy Chapoose
Ethnology Museum - 1976
Indian hist 43391

Fort Edward NY

Old Fort House Museum, 29 Lower Broadway, Fort Edward, NY 12828 - T: (518) 747-9600, Fax: (518) 747-7790, E-mail: old-fort-house-museum@juno.com, Internet: www.ftedward.com. Pres.: Dr. John A. Matochik, C.E.O.: R. Paul McCarty
Local Museum - 1925 43392

Fort Eustis VA

United States Army Transportation Museum, Besson Hall, Bldg 300, Fort Eustis, VA 23604 - T: (757) 878-1115, Fax: (757) 878-5656, E-mail: bowerba@eustis.army.mil, Internet: www.eustis.army.mil/dptmsec/museum.htm. Dir.: Barbara A. Bower, Cur.: David S. Hanselman
Military Museum / Science&Tech Museum - 1959
Military transportation 43393

Fort Garland CO

Old Fort Garland, S of US-160, on Hwy 159, Fort Garland, CO 81133 - T: (719) 379-3512, Fax: (719) 379-3479, E-mail: rick.manzanares@state.co.us. Dir.: Rick Manzanares
Historical Museum / Military Museum - 1858
Military, pioneer and Indian artifacts 43394

Fort Gibson OK

Fort Gibson Historic Site, 907 N Garrison Av, Fort Gibson, OK 74434 - T: (918) 478-4088, Fax: (918) 478-4089, E-mail: fortgibson@ok-history.mus.ok.us, Internet: www.geocities.com/fortgibson-historicsite. Dir.: Chris Morgan
Military Museum - 1936
Military, acoutrements, weapons 43395

Fort Gordon GA

United States Army Signal Corps and Fort Gordon Museum, Bldg 29807, Fort Gordon, GA 30905-5735 - T: (706) 791-2818, 791-3856, Fax: (706) 791-6069, E-mail: wiset@gordon.army.mil, Internet: www.gordon.army.mil/museums. Dir.: Theodore F. Wise, Cur.: Michael W. Rodgers
Military Museum / Science&Tech Museum - 1965
Military, technology, photos 43396

Fort Hood TX

4th Infantry Division Museum, Bldg 418, 761st Tank Bn Av and 27th St, Fort Hood, TX 76544 - T: (254) 287-8811, Fax: (254) 287-3833, E-mail: strattonc@hood.emh3.army.mil. Dir.: Ceilia M. Stratton
Military Museum / Science&Tech Museum - 1949
Military vehicles, tank destroyers, III corps 43397

First Cavalry Division Museum, 2218 Headquarters Av, Bldg 2218, Fort Hood, TX 76545 - T: (254) 287-3626, Fax: (254) 287-6423, E-mail: steven.draper@hood.army.mil, Internet: www.METROT.com/~harry/1st-Team/FtMuseum. Dir./Cur.: Steven C. Draper
Military Museum - 1971
Military hist 43398

Fort Huachuca AZ

Fort Huachuca Museum, Boyd and Grierson Sts, Fort Huachuca, AZ 85613-6000 - T: (520) 533-3898, 533-3638, Fax: (520) 533-5736, E-mail: smpp.tuttleb@huachuca-emh1.army.mil, Internet: 138.27.35.32/history.html. Dir.: James P. Finley, Cur.: Barbara Tuttle
Historical Museum / Military Museum - 1960
Local history, 1877 fort, national historic landmark 43399

Fort Hunter NY

Schoharie Crossing, 129 Schoharie St, Fort Hunter, NY 12069-0140 - T: (518) 829-7516, Fax: (518) 829-7491
Historical Museum - 1966
Hist of transportation in the Mohawk Valley 43400

Fort Jackson SC

Fort Jackson Museum, 4442 Jackson Blvd, Fort Jackson, SC 29207-5325 - T: (803) 751-7419, Fax: (803) 751-4434. Cur.: Judith M. Matteson
Military Museum - 1974
Military hist 43401

United States Army Chaplain Museum, 10100 Lee Rd, Fort Jackson, SC 29207-7090 - T: (803) 751-8827, Fax: (803) 751-8740, E-mail: mcmanusm@usaches.army.mil. Dir./Cur.: Marcia McManus
Military Museum - 1957 43402

United States Army Finance Corps Museum, ATSG-FSM, Bldg 4392, Fort Jackson, SC 29207 - T: (803) 751-3771, Fax: (803) 751-1749, E-mail: carnesw@jackson.army.mil. Cur.: William H. Carnes
Military Museum / Special Museum - 1954
Military 43403

Fort Johnson NY

Old Fort Johnson, 14 Tessiero Dr, Fort Johnson, NY 12070 - T: (518) 843-0300, E-mail: museum@oldfortjohnson.org, Internet: www.telenet.net/commercial/fortjohnson. Pres.: David Bellinger
Local Museum - 1905 43404

Fort Jones CA

Fort Jones Museum, 11913 Main St, Fort Jones, CA 96032-0428 - T: (530) 468-5568, Fax: (530) 468-2598. Dir.: Cecelia Reuter
Local Museum - 1947 43405

Fort Knox KY

Patton Museum of Cavalry and Armor, 4554 Fayette Av, Fort Knox, KY 40121-0208 - T: (502) 624-3812, Fax: (502) 624-2364, E-mail: museum@knox.army.mil, Internet: www.generalpatton.org. Dir.: Frank Jardim, Cur.: C.R. Lemons, Libr.: Candy Fuller
Military Museum - 1948
Military 43406

Fort Laramie WY

Fort Laramie, HC72, Box 389, Fort Laramie, WY 82212 - T: (307) 837-2221, Fax: (307) 837-2120, Internet: www.nationalparks.org/guide/parks/fort-laramie-1986.htm. Cur.: Louise Samson
Historic Site - 1938
Military hist 43407

Fort Lauderdale FL

Bonnet House, 900 N Birch Rd, Fort Lauderdale, FL 33304-3326 - T: (954) 563-5393, Fax: (954) 561-4174, E-mail: bobk@bonnethouse.com, Internet: www.bonnethouse.com. Dir.: Robert R. Kauth, Cur.: Denyse M. Cunningham
Local Museum / Historic Site - 1987 43408

Broward County Historical Museum, 151 SW Second St, Fort Lauderdale, FL 33301 - T: (954) 765-4670, Fax: (954) 765-4437, Internet: www.cobroward.fl.us/history.htm. Cur.: Denyse M. Cunningham
Local Museum - 1972
Historic Commission 43409

International Swimming Hall of Fame, One Hall of Fame Dr, Fort Lauderdale, FL 33316 - T: (954) 462-6536, Fax: (954) 525-4031, E-mail: ishof@ishof.org, Internet: www.ishof.org. Cur.: Bob Duenkel, Libr.: Preston Levi
Special Museum - 1965
Swimming sports 43410

Museum of Art, 1 E Las Olas Blvd, Fort Lauderdale, FL 33301 - T: (954) 525-5500, Fax: (954) 524-6011, E-mail: museumofart@hotmail.com, Internet: www.museumofart.org. Dir.: R. Andrew Maass, Cur.: Jorge Santis, Fran Mulcahy
Fine Arts Museum - 1958
20th c European and American art 43411

Museum of Discovery and Science, 401 SW Second St, Fort Lauderdale, FL 33312-1707 - T: (954) 467-6637 ext 311, Fax: (954) 467-0046, E-mail: kcavendish@mods.net, Internet: www.gsni.com/discsci. Pres.: Kim L. Cavendish, Dir.: Paul Siboroski, Joe Cytacki, Woody Wilkes
Science&Tech Museum - 1976
Science, technology 43412

Old Fort Lauderdale Museum of History, 219 SW Second Av, Fort Lauderdale, FL 33301 - T: (954) 463-4431, Fax: (954) 523-6228, E-mail: ftlaud_hist_soc@hotmail.com, Internet: www.oldfortlauderdale.org. Dir.: Joan Mikus, Dep. Dir.: Merrilyn Rathbun (Research)
Local Museum - 1962
Local history 43413

Stranahan House, 335 SE Sixth Av, Fort Lauderdale, FL 33301 - T: (954) 524-4736, Fax: (954) 525-2838, E-mail: stranahanl@aol.com, Internet: www.stranahanhouse.com. Dir.: Barbara W. Keith
Local Museum - 1981 43414

Fort Leavenworth KS

Fort Leavenworth Historical Museum and Post Museum, Reynolds and Gibbons Sts, Fort Leavenworth, KS 66027 - T: (913) 651-7440
Special Museum / Local Museum - 1950
Local history, postal hist 43415

Frontier Army Museum, 100 Reynolds Av, Fort Leavenworth, KS 66027-2334 - T: (913) 684-3767, 684-3553, Fax: (913) 684-3192, E-mail: allies@leav-emhi.army.mil, Internet: leav-www.army.mil/museum. Dir.: Stephen J. Allie, Sc. Staff: George Moore (Exhibitions), Richard W. Frank (Collection)
Military Museum - 1938
Military 43416

Fort Lee NJ

Fort Lee Historic Park and Museum, Hudson Terrace, Fort Lee, NJ 07024 - T: (201) 461-1776, Fax: (201) 461-7275, E-mail: flhp@intac. Pres.: Jim Hall, C.E.O.: Carol Ash, Dir.: John Muller
Local Museum - 1976
Local hist 43417

Fort Lee VA

The United States Army Quartermaster Museum, Bldg 5218, A Av, Fort Lee, VA 23801-1601 - T: (804) 734-4203, Fax: (804) 734-4359, Internet: www.qmmuseum.lee.army.mil. Dir.: Tim O'Gorman, Cur.: Luther D. Hanson
Military Museum - 1957
Military hist 43418

United States Army Women's Museum, A Av and 22nd St, Fort Lee, VA 23801 - T: (804) 734-4327, Fax: (804) 734-4337, E-mail: burgessj@lee.army.mil, Internet: www.amw.lee.army.mil. Pres.: Vickie Longenecker, C.E.O.: Jerry G. Burgess
Military Museum - 1955
Women military history 43419

Women's Army Corps Museum → United States Army Women's Museum

Fort Leonard Wood MO

United States Army Engineer Museum, Bldg 1607, Fort Leonard Wood, MO 65473 - T: (573) 596-0131, Fax: (573) 596-0169, E-mail: combsk@wood.army.mil, Internet: www.Wood.Army.Mil/Museum. Dir.: Robert K. Combs, Cur.: Wilfried W. H. Rust, Stephen D. Wells
Military Museum - 1972 43420

US Army Military Police Corps Museum, 495 Dakota Av, Fort Leonard Wood, MO 65473 - T: (573) 596-0604, Fax: (573) 596-0603, E-mail: wilsonj@wood.army.mil, Internet: www.wood.army.mil/museum. Dir.: Scott L. Norton
Military Museum - 1960
Uniforms, weapons, flags, insignia, badges, military artifacts from allied countries 43421

Fort Lewis WA

Fort Lewis Military Museum, Bldg 4320, Fort Lewis, WA 98433-5000 - T: (206) 967-7206, E-mail: museum@foxisland.net, Internet: www.foxisland.net. Dir./Cur.: Alan H. Archambault
Military Museum - 1970
Military hist 43422

Fort McKavett TX

Fort McKavett State Historic Park, POB 68, Fort McKavett, TX 76841 - T: (915) 396-2358, Fax: (915) 396-2818, E-mail: mckavett@airmail.net, Internet: www.tpwd.state.tx.us. Head: Michael A. Garza
Military Museum - 1968
Military hist 43423

Fort McNair DC

United States Army Center of Military History, 103 Third Av, Bldg 35, Fort McNair, DC 20319-5058 - T: (202) 685-2453, Fax: (202) 685-2113, E-mail: judson.bennett@hqda.army.mil, Internet: www.army.mil/cmh-pg. Chief Cur.: Judson E. Bennett
Military Museum / Fine Arts Museum - 1946
Military hist 43424

Fort Madison IA

North Lee County Historic Center and Santa Fe Depot Museum Complex, 10th and Av H, Fort Madison, IA 52627 - T: (319) 372-7661, 372-7363, Fax: (319) 372-7363. Pres.: Tom Barr, Dir.: Sheila Sallen
Local Museum / Fine Arts Museum - 1962
Historic Center, located in Santa Fe Railroad depot, caboose, country school, Brush College, 1993 Flood museum, Louis Koch Gallery of historic paintings, furniture 43425

Fort Meade MD

Fort George G. Meade Museum, 4674 Griffin Av, Fort Meade, MD 20755-5094 - T: (301) 677-6966, 677-7054, Fax: (301) 677-2953, E-mail: johnsonr@emh1.ftmeade.army.mil, Internet: www.ftmeade.army.mil/museum. Cur.: Robert S. Johnson
Military Museum - 1963
Military hist 43426

National Cryptologic Museum, Colony 7 Rd, Fort Meade, MD 20755-6000 - T: (301) 688-5848, 588-5849, Fax: (301) 688-5847, E-mail: www.museum@nsa.gov, Internet: www.nsa.gov:8080/museum/. Cur.: Jack E. Ingram
Military Museum - 1993
Cryptology 43427

Fort Meade SD

Old Fort Meade Museum, POB 164, Fort Meade, SD 57741 - T: (605) 347-9822, E-mail: ftmeade@rapidnet.com, Internet: www.fortmeademuseum.org. Pres.: Michael Jackley, Dir.: Charles Rambow
Military Museum - 1964
Military hist 43428

Fort Mitchell KY

Vent Haven Museum, 33 W Maple, Fort Mitchell, KY 41011 - T: (859) 341-0461, 331-9500, Fax: (859) 341-0461, E-mail: venthaven@home.com, Internet: www.venthaven.org. Cur.: Lisa Sweasy
Performing Arts Museum - 1973
Ventriloquial figures and memorabilia 43429

Fort Monmouth NJ

United States Army Communications-Electronics Museum, Kaplan Hall, Bldg 275, Fort Monmouth, NJ 07703 - T: (732) 532-1682, Fax: (732) 532-2637. Dir.: Mindy Rosewitz
Military Museum / Science&Tech Museum - 1976 43430

Fort Monroe VA

Casemate Museum, 20 Bernard Rd, Fort Monroe, VA 23651-0341 - T: (757) 788-3391, Fax: (757) 788-3886, E-mail: mroczkod@monroe.army.mil, Internet: www.tradoc.monroe.army.mil/museum. Pres.: Richard E. Mackin, Dir.: Dennis P. Mroczkowski
Military Museum - 1951
Military hist 43431

Fort Morgan CO

Fort Morgan Museum, 414 Main City Park, Fort Morgan, CO 80701 - T: (970) 867-6331, Fax: (970) 542-3008, E-mail: ftmormus@ftmorganmus.org, Internet: www.ftmorganmus.org/. Dir.: Marne Jurgemeyer
Local Museum / Music Museum - 1969
General museum, music Glen Miller 43432

Fort Myer VA

The Old Guard Museum, 204 Lee Av, 3rd US Infantry, Fort Myer, VA 22211-1199 - T: (703) 696-6670, 696-4168, Fax: (703) 696-4256, E-mail: bogana@fmmc.army.mil, Internet: www.mdw.army.mil/oldguard/. Dir.: Alan Bogan, Sc. Staff: John Manes, Kirk Heflin
Military Museum - 1962
Military hist 43433

Fort Myers FL

Edison and Ford Winter Estates, 2350 McGregor Blvd, Fort Myers, FL 33901 - T: (239) 334-7419, Fax: (239) 332-6684, E-mail: info@edison-ford-estate.com, Internet: edison-ford-estate.com. Man.: Chris Pendleton, Cur: James Hagler
Historic Site - 1947
1886 wooden vernacular, pre-cut in Maine, brought to Florida by schooner, early light bulbs, early phonographs laboratory with equipment, Edison papers/rubber research 43434

Edison Community College Gallery of Fine Art, 8099 College Pkwy SW, Fort Myers, FL 33919, mail addr: POB 60210, Fort Myers, FL 33906 - T: (941) 489-9313, Fax: (941) 489-9482, E-mail: rbishop@edison.edu, Internet: www.edison.edu/. Cur.: Ron Bishop
Fine Arts Museum / Public Gallery / University Museum - 1979
Art 43435

Fort Myers Historical Museum, 2300 Peck St, Fort Myers, FL 33901 - T: (941) 332-5955, 332-4276, Fax: (941) 332-6637, E-mail: msantiago@cityftmyers.com, Internet: www.tntonline.com/dtown/muse.htm. Dir.: Mildred Santiago, Dr. Jacquelyn S. Kent
Local Museum / Historical Museum - 1982
Local history, in a 1924 ACL Railroad Depot 43436

Imaginarium Hands-On Museum, 2000 Cranford Av, Fort Myers, FL 33916 - T: (941) 337-3332, Fax: (941) 337-2109, E-mail: cpendleton@cityftmyers.com, Internet: www.cityftmyers.com. Dir.: Chris Pendleton
Science&Tech Museum - 1989
Science and technology 43437

Fort Oglethorpe GA

Chickamauga-Chattanooga National Military Park, 3370 LaFayette Rd, US 27 S, Fort Oglethorpe, GA 30742 - T: (706) 866-9241, Fax: (423) 752-5215, Internet: www.nps.gov/chch. Dir.: Patrick H. Reed
Military Museum - 1890
Military, communication 43438

Fort Peck MT

Fort Peck Museum, Fort Peck Power Plant, Fort Peck, MT 59223 - T: (406) 526-3431, Fax: (406) 526-3477, E-mail: John.E.Daggett@usace.army.mil
Natural History Museum 43439

Fort Pierce FL

Harbor Branch Oceanographic Institution, 5600 US 1 N, Fort Pierce, FL 34946 - T: (561) 465-2400 ext 306, Fax: (561) 465-5415, E-mail: tours@hboi.edu, Internet: www.hboi.edu. Dir.: Richard Herman, Cur.: Dr. Dennis Hanisak
Natural History Museum / Science&Tech Museum - 1975
Natural hist 43440

Saint Lucie County Historical Museum, 414 Seaway Dr, Fort Pierce, FL 34949 - T: (561) 462-1795, Fax: (561) 462-1877, Internet: www.st-lucie.lib.fl.us/museum.htm. C.E.O.: Iva Jean Maddox
Local Museum - 1965 43441

UDT-SEAL Museum, 3300 N State Rd A1A, Fort Pierce, FL 34949-8520 - T: (561) 595-5845, Fax: (561) 595-5847, Internet: www.udt-sealmuseum.org. Pres.: James H. Barnes, Exec. Dir.: H.T. Aldhizer
Military Museum - 1985
Military, site where the Navy first trained Frogmen (underwater demolition teams), artifacts, weapons 43442

Fort Plain NY

Fort Plain Museum, 389 Canal St, Fort Plain, NY 13339 - T: (518) 993-2527. Dir.: G. Wetterau
Local Museum - 1963 43443

Fort Polk LA

Fort Polk Military Museum, Bldg 917, S Carolina Av, Fort Polk, LA 71459-0916 - T: (337) 531-7905, 531-4840, Fax: (337) 531-4202, E-mail: binghamd@polk.army.mil, Internet: polk.army.mil. Dir./Cur.: David S. Bingham
Military Museum - 1972
Military 43444

Fort Ransom ND

Bjarne Ness Gallery, Bear Creek Hall, Fort Ransom, ND 58033 - T: (701) 973-4461
Fine Arts Museum
American painting, woodcarvings, paintings of Bjarne Ness 43445

Ransom County Historical Society Museum, 101 Mill Rd SE, Fort Ransom, ND 58033-9740 - T: (701) 678-2045, Fax: (701) 678-2045, E-mail: rbower@northpro.net, Internet: www.members.tripod.com/rchsmuseum. Pres.: Richard Birklid, Cur.: George Anderson
Local Museum - 1972 43446

Fort Recovery OH

Fort Recovery Museum, 1 Fort Site St, Fort Recovery, OH 45846 - T: (800) 283-8920, Fax: (419) 375-4629, E-mail: bmeiring@columbus.rr.com. Dir.: Barbara Meiring
Military Museum / Ethnology Museum - 1982 43447

Fort Riley KS

First Territorial Capitol of Kansas, Bldg 693, Huebner Rd, K-18, Fort Riley, KS 66442 - T: (785) 784-5535, Internet: www.kshs.org. Cur.: Gary R. Dierking
Historical Museum - 1928
Historic House Museum 43448

United States Cavalry Museum, Bldg. 205, Fort Riley, KS 66442 - T: (785) 239-2737, Fax: (785) 239-6243, E-mail: vanmetet@riley.army.mil, Internet: www.kshs.org. Dir.: William McKale, Sc. Staff: Steven Ruhnke (Exhibitions)
Military Museum - 1957
Military, housed in a old hospital 1855-1890 (post headquarters 1890-1948), 1st Infantry and 1st Armored division 43449

Fort Rucker AL

United States Army Aviation Museum, Bldg 6000, Fort Rucker, AL 36362-0610 - T: (334) 255-3036, Fax: (334) 255-3054, E-mail: avnmuseum@alanet.com, Internet: www.aviationmuseum.org. Dir.: R.S. Maxham, Cur.: Harford Edwards jr.
Military Museum / Science&Tech Museum - 1962 43450

Fort Sam Houston TX

Fort Sam Houston Museum, 1210 Stanley Rd, Fort Sam Houston, TX 78234-5002 - T: (210) 221-1886, Fax: (210) 221-1311, E-mail: ftsammuseum@amedd.army.mil, Internet: www.army.mil/dptmsec/muse/htm. Dir.: John M. Manguso, Sc. Staff: Jacqueline B. Davis, Martin L. Callahan
Military Museum / Historical Museum / Historic Site - 1967
Military hist 43451

United States Army Medical Department Museum, Bldg 1046, 2310 Stanley Rd, Fort Sam Houston, TX 78234 - T: (210) 221-6358, Fax: (210) 221-6781, E-mail: ameddmus@aol.com, Internet: www.samhou-usag.army.mil. Dir.: Thomas O. McMasters
Military Museum / Historical Museum - 1955
Military medicine 43452

Fort Scott KS

Fort Scott National Historic Site, Old Fort Blvd, Fort Scott, KS 66701 - T: (620) 223-0310, Fax: (620) 223-0188, E-mail: fosc_superintendent@nps.gov, Internet: www.nps.gov/fosc
Historic Site - 1978
Restored and reconstructed Fort Scott 43453

Historic Preservation Association of Bourbon County, 117 S Main, Fort Scott, KS 66701 - T: (316) 223-1557, E-mail: ldrdevon@ckt.net. Pres.: Don Miller
Local Museum / Military Museum - 1973
History, military 43454

Fort Sill OK

Fort Sill, 437 Quanah Rd, Fort Sill, OK 73503-5100 - T: (580) 442-5123, Fax: (580) 442-8120, E-mail: spiveyt@sill.army.mil, Internet: www.sill.army.mil/museum. Dir./Cur.: Towana Spivey
Military Museum / Historic Site - 1934
archives 43455

Fort Smith AR

Fort Smith, 301 Parker Av, Fort Smith, AR 72901 - T: (501) 783-3961, Fax: (501) 783-5307, E-mail: fosm_interpretation@nps.gov, Internet: www.nps.gov./fosm. Superint.: William N. Black, Cur.: Emily Lovick, Sc. Staff: Julie Galonska (History)
Historical Museum - 1961
1817-24 Fort Smith, became the Federal Courthouse and Jail 1871-1896 43456

Fort Smith Art Center, 423 N Sixth St, Fort Smith, AR 72901 - T: (501) 784-2787, Fax: (501) 784-9071, E-mail: ftsartcenter@aol.com, Internet: www.ftsartcenter.com. Dir.: Kathy Williams, Michael Richardson
Fine Arts Museum - 1948
Arts 43457

Fort Smith Museum of History, 320 Rogers Av, Fort Smith, AR 72901 - T: (501) 783-7841, Fax: (501) 783-3244, Internet: www.fortsmith.com/museum. Dir.: Ellen F. Campbell
Historical Museum - 1910 43458

Patent Model Museum, 400 N 8th St, Fort Smith, AR 72901 - T: (501) 782-9014, Fax: (501) 782-1555. Dir.: Carolyn Pollan, Ass. Dir.: Dorothy Williams
Museum of Classical Antiquities - 1976
Rogers-Tilles House 43459

Fort Stewart GA

Fort Stewart Museum, 2022 Frank Cochran Dr, Fort Stewart, GA 31314 - T: (912) 767-7885, Fax: (912) 767-4480
Military Museum - 1977
Military 43460

Fort Stockton TX

Annie Riggs Memorial Museum, 301 S Main St, Fort Stockton, TX 79735 - T: (915) 336-2167, Fax: (915) 336-2402, E-mail: TXRousse@aol.com. Exec. Dir.: Leanna S. Biles
Local Museum - 1955
Local hist 43461

Historic Fort Stockton, 300 E Third, Fort Stockton, TX 79735 - T: (915) 336-2400, Fax: (915) 336-2402, E-mail: hfs@ci.fort-stockton.tx.us. Dir./Cur.: LeAnna S. Biles
Historic Site / Open Air Museum / Military Museum - 1990 43462

Fort Sumner NM

Fort Sumner, Billy the Kid Rd, Fort Sumner, NM 88119-0356 - T: (505) 355-2573, Fax: (505) 355-2573, E-mail: hweeldi@plateautel.net
Historical Museum - 1968 43463

Fort Totten ND

Fort Totten State Historic Museum, Pioneer Daughters Museum, Fort Totten, ND 58335 - T: (701) 766-4441, Fax: (701) 766-4882, E-mail: histsoc@state.nd.us
Local Museum / Open Air Museum - 1960
Local hist 43464

Fort Towson OK

Fort Towson Military Park, HC 63, Box 1580, Fort Towson, OK 74735-9273 - T: (580) 873-2634, Fax: (580) 873-9385, E-mail: johndavis@ok-history.mus.ok.uk. Dir.: William Vandever, Cur.: John Davis
Military Museum / Archaeological Museum - 1972 43465

Fort Valley GA

A.L. Fetterman Educational Museum, 100 Massee Ln, Fort Valley, GA 31030 - T: (912) 967-2358, 967-2722, Fax: (912) 967-2083, E-mail: acs@alltel.net, Internet: www.camellias-acs.com. Pres.: Arthur Gonos, Dir.: Ann Walton
Decorative Arts Museum - 1989
Porcelain, paintings, prints, books, sculpture 43466

Fort Walton Beach FL

Indian Temple Mound Museum, 139 Miracle Strip Pkwy SE, Fort Walton Beach, FL 32548 - T: (850) 833-9595, Fax: (850) 833-9675, Internet: www.fwb.org. Dir.: Anna M. Peele
Historical Museum / Ethnology Museum - 1962
Anthropology, ethnology of Indian, Indian Temple Mound of Fort Walton Culture, prehistoric Native American cultures of local area 43467

Fort Washakie WY

Shoshone Tribal Cultural Center, 31 First St, Fort Washakie, WY 82514 - T: (307) 332-9106, Fax: (307) 332-3055, E-mail: rteran@mail.washakie.net. C.E.O.: Reba Jo Teran
Folklore Museum
Indian culture 43468

Fort Washington MD

Fort Washington, 13551 Fort Washington Rd, Fort Washington, MD 20744 - T: (301) 763-4600, Fax: (301) 763-1389, Internet: www.nps.gov/fowa
Military Museum - 1940
Military, Commandant's house 43469

Fort Washington PA

Childventure Museum, 430 Virginia Dr, Fort Washington, PA 19034 - T: (215) 643-9906. Dir.: Nina Kardon, Beverly Levine
Special Museum - 1989 43470

Fort Washington Museum, 473 Bethlehem Pike, Fort Washington, PA 19034 - T: (215) 646-6065. Head: Betty Mackinlay
Historical Museum / Historic Site - 1935
1801 Clifton House 43471

Highlands, 7001 Sheaff Ln, Fort Washington, PA 19034 - T: (215) 641-2687, Fax: (215) 641-2556, E-mail: highlandshistorical@earthlink.net. Dir.: Margaret Bleecker Blades, Cur.: Laura Koloski
Local Museum - 1975 43472

Hope Lodge and Mather Mill, 553 S Bethlehem Pike, Fort Washington, PA 19034 - T: (215) 646-1595, Fax: (215) 628-9471, E-mail: hkrueger@state.pa.us, Internet: www.ushistory.org/hope. Pres.: William Lutz, C.E.O.: Hilary Folwell Krueger, Cur.: Jennifer Glass
Local Museum / Historic Site / Open Air Museum - 1957 43473

Fort Wayne IN

Allen County-Fort Wayne Historical Society Museum, 302 E Berry St, Fort Wayne, IN 46802 - T: (219) 426-2882, Fax: (219) 424-4419, E-mail: histsociety@fwi.net, Internet: www.fwhistorycenter.com. Cur.: Walter Font
Local Museum - 1921
Local history 43474

Fort Wayne Firefighters Museum, 226 W Washington Blvd, Fort Wayne, IN 46802 - T: (219) 426-0051
Science&Tech Museum
Hist of the Fort Wayne Fire Department, apparatus, equip, patch coll 43475

Fort Wayne Museum of Art, 311 E Main St, Fort Wayne, IN 46802 - T: (219) 422-6467, Fax: (219) 422-1374, E-mail: mail@fwmoa.org, Internet: www.fwmoa.org. Dir.: Patricia Watkinson, Cur.: Bob Schroeder, Ass. Cur.: Sachi Yanari
Fine Arts Museum - 1922
Art 43476

John E. Weatherhead Gallery, University of Saint Francis, 2701 Spring St, Fort Wayne, IN 46808 - T: (219) 434-3235, Fax: (219) 434-3194, E-mail: rcartwright@sf.edu, Internet: www.sf.edu/art
Public Gallery 43477

The Lincoln Museum, 200 E Berry, Fort Wayne, IN 46801-7838 - T: (219) 455-3864, Fax: (219) 455-6922, E-mail: thelincolnmuseum@lnc.com, Internet: www.thelincolnmuseum.org. C.E.O.: Joan L. Flinspach
Historical Museum - 1928
History, civil war 43478

Fort Worth TX

American Airlines C.R. Smith Museum, 4601 Hwy 360 at FAA Rd, Fort Worth, TX 76155 - T: (817) 967-5905, 967-5904, Fax: (817) 967-5737, E-mail: benkristy@aa.com, Internet: www.crsmithmuseum.org. Cur.: Ben Kristy
Science&Tech Museum / Historical Museum - 1993
American Airlines hist 43479

Amon Carter Museum, 3501 Camp Bowie Blvd, Fort Worth, TX 76107-2695 - T: (817) 738-1933, Fax: (817) 989-5079, E-mail: carol.noel@cartermuseum.org, Internet: www.cartermuseum.org. Dir.: Rick Stewart, Dep. Dir.: Robert Workman, Chief Cur.: Jane Myers, Cur.: Barbara McCandless, Patricia Junker, Ass. Cur.: John Rohrbach, Rebecca Lawton
Fine Arts Museum / Folklore Museum - 1961
Art 43480

Atrium Gallery, c/o University of North Texas Health Science Center, 3500 Camp Bowie Blvd, Fort Worth, TX 76109-2699 - T: (817) 735-2000, E-mail: jsager@hsc.unt.edu, Internet: www.hsc.unt.edu/artcompetition. Head: Judy Sager
Fine Arts Museum - 1986
Watercolors 43481

Bank One Fort Worth Collection, 500 Throckmorton, Fort Worth, TX 76102 - T: (817) 884-4000, Fax: (817) 870-2454
Fine Arts Museum - 1974
Sculpture, drawings, graphics, paintings, prints and tapestries 43482

Cattle Raisers Museum, 1301 W 7th St, Fort Worth, TX 76102-2665 - T: (817) 332-8551, Fax: (817) 332-8749, E-mail: museum@texascattleraisers.org, Internet: www.cattleraisersmuseum.org. Dir.: Dr. Cheri L. Wolfe
Local Museum - 1981
Local hist 43483

Contemporary Art Center of Fort Worth, 500 Commerce St, Fort Worth, TX 76102 - T: (817) 877-5550
Public Gallery 43484

Fort Worth Museum of Science and History, 1501 Montgomery St, Fort Worth, TX 76107 - T: (817) 255-9300 ext 0, Fax: (817) 732-7635, E-mail: webmaster@fwmshz.org, Internet: www.fortworthmuseum.org. Dir.: James P. Diffily, Dennis Gabbard, Chief Cur.: William J. Voss (Science), Ass. Cur.: Wesley Hathaway (Science), Renee Erwin (History)
Historical Museum / Science&Tech Museum - 1941
General Museum 43485

Fort Worth Public Library Arts and Humanities, Fine Arts Section, 500 W Third Rd, Fort Worth, TX 76102 - T: (817) 871-7737, Fax: (817) 871-7734, E-mail: tstone@fortworthlibrary.org, Internet: www.fortworthlibrary.org. Man.: Thelma Stone
Library with Exhibitions - 1902 43486

Kimbell Art Museum, 3333 Camp Bowie Blvd, Fort Worth, TX 76107-2792 - T: (817) 332-8451 ext 224, Fax: (817) 877-1264, E-mail: gottlieb@kimbellmuseum.org, Internet: www.kimbellart.org. Dir.: Timothy Potts, Cur.: Malcolm Warner, Jennifer R. Casler (Asian and Non-Western Art), Nancy E. Edwards (European Art), Patricia C. Loud (Architecture), Libr.: Chia-Chun Shih
Fine Arts Museum - 1972
Art 43487

Log Cabin Village, 2100 Log Cabin Village Lane, Fort Worth, TX 76109 - T: (817) 926-5881, Fax: (817) 922-0246, E-mail: director@logcabinvillage.org, Internet: www.logcabinvillage.org. Dir.: Kelli L. Pickard, Cur.: Dulce Ivette Ray
Local Museum / Open Air Museum - 1965
Historic village 43488

Modern Art Museum of Fort Worth, 3200 Darnell St at University Dr, Fort Worth, TX 76110 - T: (817) 738-9215, Fax: (817) 735-1161, E-mail: carriann@mamfw.org, Internet: www.themodern.org. Dir.: Dr. Marla J. Price, Chief Cur.: Michael Auping, Ass. Cur.: Andrea Karnes
Fine Arts Museum - 1892
Art 43489

Moudy Exhibition Hall, c/o Texas Christian University, Dept. of Art and Art History, Campus Box 298000, Fort Worth, TX 76129 - T: (817) 257-7643, Fax: (817) 257-7399, E-mail: r.watson@tcu.edu. Dir.: Ronald Watson
University Museum / Fine Arts Museum - 1874 43490

National Cowgirl Museum and Hall of Fame, 1720 Gendy, Fort Worth, TX 76107 - T: (817) 336-4475, Fax: (817) 336-2470, E-mail: susan@cowgirl.net, Internet: www.cowgirl.net. Dir.: Pat Riley, Cur.: Jennifer Nielsen
Historical Museum - 1975/2002
Hist of Western American women 43491

Sid Richardson Collection of Western Art, 309 Main St, Fort Worth, TX 76102 - T: (817) 332-6554, Fax: (817) 332-8671, E-mail: info@sidrmuseum.org, Internet: www.sidrmuseum.org. Dir.: Jan Brenneman, Ass. Dir.: Monica Herman
Fine Arts Museum - 1982
Art 43492

Forty Fort PA

Nathan Denison House, 35 Denison St, Forty Fort, PA 18704-4390 - T: (717) 288-5531. Pres.: Louise Robinson
Local Museum - 1970 43493

Fossil OR

Fossil Museum, First and Main Sts, Fossil, OR 97830 - T: (541) 763-2113, Fax: (541) 763-2026
Local Museum - 1966 43494

Fostoria OH

Fostoria Area Historical Museum, 123 W North St, Fostoria, OH 44830. C.E.O.: Leonard Skonecki
Local Museum - 1972 43495

Fountain MN

Fillmore County Historical Museum, 202 County Rd, Ste 8, Fountain, MN 55935 - T: (507) 268-4449. Dir.: Jerry D. Henke
Local Museum - 1934 43496

Fountain City IN

Levi Coffin House, 113 U.S. 27 North, Fountain City, IN 47341 - T: (765) 847-2432, Fax: (765) 847-2498, E-mail: coffinha@infocom.com, Internet: www.waynet.org. Pres.: Janice McGuire
Historical Museum - 1967 43497

Four Oaks NC

Bentonville Battleground State Historic Site, 5466 Harper House Rd, Four Oaks, NC 27524 - T: (910) 594-0789, Fax: (910) 594-0222, E-mail: bentonville@intrstar.net, Internet: www.ah.dcr.state.nc.us/hs/bentonri/bentonri.htm. Man.: Donald B. Taylor
Military Museum / Open Air Museum - 1961 43498

Fox Island WA

Fox Island Historical Society Museum, 1017 Ninth Av, Fox Island, WA 98333 - T: (253) 549-2239, Fax: (253) 549-2461, E-mail: museum@foxisland.net, Internet: www.foxisland.net. Pres.: David McHughs
Local Museum - 1895
Local hist 43499

Fox Lake WI

Fox Lake Historical Museum, 211 Cordelia St and S College Av, Fox Lake, WI 53933 - T: (920) 928-2172. Pres./Cur.: Donald Frank
Local Museum / Science&Tech Museum - 1970
Railroad, local hist 43500

Framingham MA

Danforth Museum of Art, 123 Union Av, Framingham, MA 01702 - T: (508) 620-0050, Fax: (508) 872-5542, E-mail: dmadev@conversent.net, Internet: www.danforthmuseum.org. Dir.: Ronald L. Crusan, Asst. Cur.: Laura McCarty
Fine Arts Museum - 1975
Art 43501

Framingham Historical Society and Museum, 16 Vernon St, Framingham, MA 01701, mail addr: POB 2032, Framingham, MA 01703-2032 - T: (508) 872-3780, Fax: (508) 872-3780, E-mail: framhist@juno.com, Internet: www.framinghamhistory.org. Dir.: Joan Mickelson-Lukach, Cur.: Dana Dautermann Ricciardi
Local Museum - 1888
Local history 43502

Frances E. Warren Air Force Base WY

Warren ICBM and Heritage Museum, 7405 Marne Loop, 90th SW/MU, Frances E. Warren Air Force Base, WY 82005 - T: (307) 773-2980, Fax: (307) 773-2791, E-mail: paula.taylor@warren.af.mil, Internet: www.pawnee.com/fewmuseum. Dir./Cur.: Paula Bauman Taylor
Military Museum - 1967
Military hist 43503

Franconia NH

New England Ski Museum, Franconia Notch State Park, Pkwy Exit 2, Franconia, NH 03580 - T: (603) 823-7177, Fax: (603) 823-9505, E-mail: staff@skimuseum.org, Internet: www.skimuseum.org. Pres.: Glenn Parkinson, Exec. Dir.: Jeffrey R. Leich
Special Museum - 1977 43504

Frankenmuth MI

Frankenmuth Historical Museum, 613 S Main, Frankenmuth, MI 48734 - T: (517) 652-9701, Fax: (517) 652-9701, E-mail: frankenmuthmuseum@yahoo.com, Internet: www.dtimmons.com/frankenmuthmuseum. Pres.: Mary Anne Ackerman, C.E.O.: Sally D. Van Ness
Local Museum / Folklore Museum - 1963
Regional history 43505

Frankfort IN

Clinton County Museum, 301 E Clinton St, Frankfort, IN 46041 - T: (765) 659-2030, 659-4079, Fax: (765) 654-7773, E-mail: elosrebe@aol.com, Internet: www.cchsm.cjb.net. Dir.: Nancy Hart
Local Museum - 1980
Local history, housed in Old Stoney, former Frankfort High School building 43506

Frankfort KY

The Executive Mansion, 704 Capitol Av, Frankfort, KY 40601 - T: (502) 564-8004, Fax: (502) 564-5022, E-mail: rlyons@mail.state.ky.us, Internet: www.state.ky.us/agencies/gov./mansion. Dir.: Rex Lyons
Local Museum - 1914
Historic house, residence of 22 of Kentucky's governors 43507

Jackson Hall Gallery, c/o Kentucky State University, Frankfort, KY 40601 - T: (502) 597-5994/95, E-mail: jalexandra@qwmail.kysu.edu. Head: John Bater
Fine Arts Museum / University Museum - 1886
African art 43508

Kentucky Historical Society Museum, 100 W Broadway, Frankfort, KY 40601 - T: (502) 564-1792, Fax: (502) 564-4701, Internet: www.kyhistory.org. Dir.: J. Kevin Graffagnino, Ass. Dir.: James E. Wallace
Historical Museum - 1836
History, housed in the Kentucky History Center and 1869 Old State Capitol Annex 43509

Kentucky Military History Museum, Old State Arsenal, E Main St, Frankfort, KY 40601 - T: (502) 564-1792, ext. 4498, Fax: (502) 564-4054, E-mail: bill.bright@mail.state.ky.us, Internet: www.kyhistory.org. Cur.: Bill Bright
Military Museum - 1974
Military 43510

Kentucky New State Capitol, 700 Capitol Av, Frankfort, KY 40601 - T: (502) 564-3000 ext 222, Fax: (502) 564-6505, Internet: www.state.ky.us/agencies/finance/attract/capitol2.htm. Cur.: Lou Karibo
Decorative Arts Museum
First Lady, miniature dolls, oil paintings of chief justices 43511

Liberty Hall, 218 Wilkinson St, Frankfort, KY 40601 - T: (502) 227-2560, Fax: (502) 227-3348, E-mail: libhall@dcr.net, Internet: www.libertyhall.org. Dir.: Sara Farley-Harger
Decorative Arts Museum - 1937
Formerly the home of the Kentucky Senator John Brown 43512

The Old Governor's Mansion, 420 High St, Frankfort, KY 40601 - T: (502) 564-5500, Fax: (502) 564-4099, E-mail: Frankie.McNulty@mail.state.ky.us. Dir.: F.M. McNulty, Cur.: John Downs
Local Museum - 1798
Historic house 43513

Orlando Brown House, Liberty Hall Museum, 220 Wilkinson St, Frankfort, KY 40601 - T: (502) 875-4952, Fax: (502) 227-3348, Internet: www.libertyhall.org. Dir.: Sara Harger
Fine Arts Museum / Decorative Arts Museum - 1956
Paul Sawyier paintings, original furnishings 43514

Vest-Lindsey House, 401 Wapping St, Frankfort, KY 40601 - T: (502) 564-3000, 564-6980, Fax: (502) 564-6505, E-mail: helen.evans@mail.state.ky.us. Dir.: Helen H. Evans, Cur.: Lou Karibo
Local Museum - 1978
Historic house 43515

Frankfort SD

Fisher Grove Country School, 17250 Fishers Ln, Frankfort, SD 57440 - T: (605) 472-1212
Local Museum - 1884
Historic building 43516

Franklin IN

Johnson County History Museum, 135 N Main St, Franklin, IN 46131 - T: (317) 736-4655, Fax: (317) 736-5451, E-mail: map@netdirect.net, Internet: www.johnsoncountymuseum.com. Dir.: Mary Ann Plummer, Cur.: Jill Hasprunar
Local Museum - 1931
County history 43517

Franklin ME

Franklin Historical Society Museum, Rte 200, Franklin, ME 04634 - T: (207) 565-2223. Dir.: Lawrence Button, Cur.: Helen Cantor
Local Museum - 1960
Local hist 43518

Franklin NJ

Franklin Mineral Museum, 32 Evans St, Franklin, NJ 07416 - T: (973) 827-3481, Fax: (973) 827-0149, E-mail: funrocks@warwick.net, Internet: www.franklinmineralmuseum.com. Pres.: Steven Phillips, Cur.: John Cianciulli
Natural History Museum / Science&Tech Museum - 1965
Geology, mining 43519

Franklin OH

Harding Museum, 302 Park Av, Franklin, OH 45005 - T: (513) 746-8295. Pres.: Phyllis McDaniel
Local Museum - 1965 43520

Franklin TN

Carnton Plantation, 1345 Carnton Ln, Franklin, TN 37064 - T: (615) 794-0903, Fax: (615) 794-6563, E-mail: carnton@mindspring.com, Internet: www.carnton.org. Exec. Dir.: Angela Calhoun
Local Museum - 1977
Historic house 43521

The Carter House, 1140 Columbia Av, Franklin, TN 37064 - T: (615) 791-1861, Fax: (615) 794-1327, E-mail: museum@carter-house.org, Internet: www.carterhouse.org. Exec. Dir./Cur.: Thomas Cartwright, Cur.: John Wallwork
Local Museum - 1951
Local hist 43522

Franklin Center PA

Franklin Mint Museum, Franklin Mint, Rte 1, Franklin Center, PA 19091 - T: (610) 459-6881 ext 6348, Fax: (610) 459-6463, E-mail: hpowers@franklinmint.com, Internet: www.franklinmint.com. Cur.: Heather Powers
Science&Tech Museum / Special Museum - 1973 43523

Franklinville NY

Ischua Valley Historical Society, 9 Pine St, Franklinville, NY 14737 - T: (716) 676-5651. Pres.: Gertrude H. Schnell
Local Museum - 1966 43524

Frederick MD

Barbara Fritchie House, 154 W Patrick St, Frederick, MD 21701 - T: (301) 698-0630, Fax: (301) 698-8994
Decorative Arts Museum - 1927
Furnishings, distribution and transportation, paintings 43525

The Children's Museum of Rose Hill Manor Park, 1611 N Market St, Frederick, MD 21701-4304 - T: (301) 694-1648, Fax: (301) 694-2595, E-mail: parksrec@co.frederick.md.us, Internet: www.co.frederick.md.us/parks/rosehill. Dir.: A. Colin Clevenger
Historical Museum - 1972 43526

Historical Museum of Frederick County, 24 E Church St, Frederick, MD 21701 - T: (301) 663-1188, Fax: (301) 663-0526, E-mail: director@fwp.net, Internet: www.fwp.net/hsfc. Dir.: Mark S. Hudson, Cur.: Heidi Campbell-Shoaf
Local Museum - 1888
Regional history 43527

Monocacy National Battlefield, 4801 Urbana Pike, Frederick, MD 21704 - T: (301) 662-3515, 432-7677, Fax: (301) 662-3420, E-mail: cathy_beeler@nps.gov, Internet: www.nps.gov/mono/mo_visit.htm. Head: John Howard
Historic Site - 1907
Dedicated to soldiers who fought in the Battle of Monocacy, July 9, 1864 43528

National Museum of Civil War Medicine, 48 E Patrick St, Frederick, MD 21701 - T: (301) 695-1864, Fax: (301) 695-6823, E-mail: museum@civilwarmed.org, Internet: www.CivilWarMed.org. Pres.: Robert E. Gearinger, Exec. Dir.: JaNeen M. Smith
Special Museum - 1990
Medical hist 43529

Schifferstadt Architectural Museum, 1110 Rosemont Av, Frederick, MD 21701 - T: (301) 663-3885, Fax: (301) 663-4807, E-mail: fredcolandmark.aol.com, Internet: www.fredericklandmarks.org. Pres.: Joe Luboznski
Fine Arts Museum - 1974
Architecture 43530

Fredericksburg TX

Admiral Nimitz National Museum of the Pacific War, 340 E Main St, Fredericksburg, TX 78624 - T: (830) 997-4379 ext 225, Fax: (830) 997-8220, E-mail: nimitzm@ktc.com, Internet: www.nimitz-museum.org. Dir.: Joe Cavanaugh
Military Museum - 1967
Local hist 43531

Pioneer Museum and Vereins Kirche, Gillespie County Historical Society, 309 W San Antonio St, Fredericksburg, TX 78624 - T: (830) 997-2835, Fax: (830) 997-3891, E-mail: gchs@ktc.com, Internet: www.pioneermuseum.com. Pres.: Kathy Harrison, Dir.: Paul Camfield
Local Museum - 1936
History 43532

Fredericksburg VA

Belmont, Gari Melchers Estate and Memorial Gallery, 224 Washington St, Fredericksburg, VA 22405 - T: (540) 654-1842, Fax: (540) 654-1785, E-mail: belmont@mwc.edu, Internet: www.mwc.edu/belmont. Dir.: David S. Berreth, Cur.: Joanna D. Catron
Fine Arts Museum - 1975
Art 43533

Fredericksburg and Spotsylvania National Military Park, 120 Chatham Ln, Fredericksburg, VA 22405 - T: (540) 371-0802, Fax: (540) 371-1907, Internet: www.nps.gov/frsp. Sc. Staff: Robert K. Krick, Donald C. Pfanz (History)
Military Museum - 1927
Military hist 43534

Fredericksburg Area Museum and Cultural Center, 907-911 Princess Anne St, Fredericksburg, VA 22401 - T: (540) 371-5668, 371-3037, Fax: (540) 373-6569, E-mail: famcc@fls.infi.net, Internet: www.famcc.org. Dir.: Edwin W. Watson, Cur.: Mary H. Dellinger
Local Museum - 1985
Local hist 43535

Historic Kenmore, 1201 Washington Av, Fredericksburg, VA 22401 - T: (540) 373-3381, Fax: (540) 371-6066, E-mail: mailroom@kenmore.org, Internet: www.kenmore.org. Pres.: W. Vernon Edenfield
Local Museum - 1922
Local hist 43536

James Monroe Museum and Memorial Library, 908 Charles St, Fredericksburg, VA 22401-5810 - T: (540) 654-1043, Fax: (540) 654-1106, E-mail: jmmuseum@mwc.edu, Internet: www.JamesMonroeMuseum.mwc.edu. Dir.: John N. Pearce, Ass. Dir./Cur.: David B. Voelkel
Historical Museum / Library with Exhibitions / Historic Site - 1928
Presidential library, local hist, James Monroe (1785 - 1831, 5th president of the USA) 43537

Kenmore Plantation and George Washington's Ferry Farm → Historic Kenmore

Mary Washington College Galleries, College Av at Seacobeck St, Fredericksburg, VA 22401-5358 - T: (540) 654-1013, Fax: (540) 654-1171, E-mail: gallery@mwc.edu. Dir.: Dr. Thomas P. Somma
Fine Arts Museum - 1956
European, American and Asian art 43538

Mary Washington House, 1200 Charles St, Fredericksburg, VA 22401 - T: (540) 373-1569, Fax: (540) 373-1569, Internet: www.apva.org. Dir.: Gail G. Braxton
Local Museum - 1772
Historic house 43539

Ridderhof Martin Gallery, College Av at Seacobeck St, Fredericksburg, VA 22401-5358 - T: (540) 654-1013, Fax: (540) 654-1171, E-mail: gallery@mwc.edu, Internet: www.mwc.edu. Dir.: Dr. Thomas P. Somma
Fine Arts Museum / University Museum - 1956 43540

Rising Sun Tavern, 1304 Caroline St, Fredericksburg, VA 22401 - T: (540) 371-1494, Internet: www.apva.org. Dir.: Gail G. Braxton
Decorative Arts Museum - 1760 43541

Saint James' House, 1300 Charles St, Fredericksburg, VA 22401 - T: (703) 373-1569, Internet: www.apva.org. Dir.: Gail G. Braxton
Local Museum - 1760
Historic house 43542

Fredonia KS

Stone House Gallery, 320 N 7th St, Fredonia, KS 66736 - T: (316) 378-2052, E-mail: stonehouse@twinmounds.com. Pres.: Joyce Fulghum
Fine Arts Museum - 1967
Art 43543

Wilson County Historical Society Museum, 420 N 7th, Fredonia, KS 66736 - T: (316) 378-3965
Local Museum - 1961
Local history, located in old county jail 43544

Fredonia NY

Historical Museum of the D.R. Barker Library, 20 E Main St, Fredonia, NY 14063 - T: (716) 672-2114, Fax: (716) 679-3547, E-mail: BarkerMu@netsync.net, Internet: www.netsync.net/users/barkermu. Pres.: Peter Clark, C.E.O./Cur.: Kathryn Courtney
Library with Exhibitions - 1884 43545

Michael C. Rockefeller Arts Center Gallery, State University College, Fredonia, NY 14063 - T: (716) 673-4897, Fax: (716) 673-3810, E-mail: gaaschc@fredonia.edu, Internet: www.fredonia.edu. Dir.: Cynnie Gaasch
Fine Arts Museum / University Museum - 1826 43546

Freehold NJ

Monmouth County Historical Museum, 70 Court St, Freehold, NJ 07728 - T: (908) 462-1466, Fax: (908) 462-8346, E-mail: mcha@monmouth.com, Internet: www.monmouthhistory.org. Dir.: Lee Ellen Griffith
Local Museum - 1898
History of the county, decorative arts, folk art, paintings, silver, furniture, glass, ceramics, toys 43547

Freeman SD

Heritage Hall Museum and Archives, 748 S Main St, Freeman, SD 57029 - T: (605) 925-4237. Cur.: Cleon Graber
Local Museum / Ethnology Museum - 1976
Local history, ethnology - archives 43548

Freeport IL

Freeport Arts Center, 121 N Harlem Av, Freeport, IL 61032 - T: (815) 235-9755, Fax: (815) 235-6015, E-mail: artscenter@aeroinc.net. Dir.: Stephen H. Schwartz
Fine Arts Museum - 1975 43549

Silvercreek Museum, 2954 Walnut Rd, Freeport, IL 61032 - T: (815) 232-2350, E-mail: ike.sue@gte.net, Internet: www.journalstandard.com/community. Pres.: Larry Buttel, Dir.: Russel Bawinkel, Duane Johnsen, Betty Bawinkel
Local Museum / Agriculture Museum - 1988
Regional history, in 1906 county poor farm 43550

Stephenson County Historical Society Museum, 1440 S Carroll Av, Freeport, IL 61032 - T: (815) 232-8419, Fax: (815) 297-0313, E-mail: director@stephcohs.org, Internet: www.stephcohs.org. Exec. Dir.: Suzy Beggin
Historical Museum - 1944
Local and regional history, Jane Addams, Abraham Licoln, underground railroad, school, agriculture 43551

Freeport ME

Freeport Historical Society Museum, 45 Main St, Freeport, ME 04032 - T: (207) 865-3170, Fax: (207) 865-9055, E-mail: FRPHistory@aol.com. C.E.O.: Randall Wade Thomas
Library with Exhibitions - 1969
Local hist 43552

Fremont CA

Olive Hyde Art Gallery, 123 Washington Blvd, Fremont, CA 94537 - T: (510) 791-4357, 494-4228, Fax: (510) 494-4753, E-mail: kbach@ci.fremont.ca.us. Dir.: Kim Bach
Fine Arts Museum - 1964 43553

Fremont NC

Charles B. Aycock Birthplace, 264 Governor Aycock Rd, Fremont, NC 27830 - T: (919) 242-5581, Fax: (919) 242-6668, E-mail: cbaycock@esn.net, Internet: www.ah.dcr.state.nc.us/hs/Aycock/Aycock.htm. Head: Charlotte Brow
Local Museum - 1959 43554

Fremont NE

Louis E. May Museum, 1643 N Nye, Fremont, NE 68025 - T: (402) 721-4515, Fax: (402) 721-8354, E-mail: maymuseum@juno.com, Internet: www.connectfremont.org. Pres.: Russel Uehling, Cur.: Patty Manhart
Historical Museum - 1969 43555

Fremont OH

Rutherford B. Hayes Presidential Center, Spiegel Grove, Fremont, OH 43420-2796 - T: (419) 332-2081, Fax: (419) 332-4952, E-mail: admin@rbhayes.org, Internet: www.rbhayes.org. Exec. Dir.: Roger D. Bridges, Chief Cur.: James B. Snider, Cur.: Nan Card (Manuscript), Gil Gonzales (Photography)
Historical Museum / Library with Exhibitions - 1916
Books, manuscripts, photographic prints 43556

Fresno CA

Discovery Center, 1944 N Winery Av, Fresno, CA 93703 - T: (209) 251-5533, Fax: (209) 251-5531, Internet: www.gemworld.com/discoverycenter. Exec. Dir.: Rick Kruytz
Ethnology Museum / Historical Museum / Natural History Museum / Science&Tech Museum - 1956 43557

Fresno Art Museum, 2233 N First St, Fresno, CA 93703-9955 - T: (559) 441-4221, Fax: (559) 441-4227, E-mail: fam@qnis.net, Internet: www.fresnoartmuseum.com. Dir.: Mary LaFollette, Cur.: Jacquelin Pilar, Yumi Kinoshita
Fine Arts Museum - 1949
Pre-Columbian, Mexican, Peruvian and Californian works of art 43558

Fresno Metropolitan Museum, 1555 Van Ness Av, Fresno, CA 93721 - T: (209) 441-1444, Fax: (209) 441-8607, E-mail: marketing@fresnomet.org, Internet: www.fresnomet.org. Dir.: Kim Cline, Ass. Dir.: Sally Fouhse, Cur.: Kristina Hornback
Fine Arts Museum / Local Museum / Natural History Museum - 1984 43559

Kearney Mansion Museum, 7160 W Kearney Blvd, Fresno, CA 93706 - T: (559) 441-0862, Fax: (559) 441-1372, E-mail: frhistsoc@aol.com, Internet: www.valleyhistory.org. Exec. Dir.: Jill Moffat
Local Museum - 1919 43560

Friday Harbor WA

San Juan Historical Society Museum, 405 Price St, Friday Harbor, WA 98250 - T: (360) 378-3949, Fax: (360) 378-3949, E-mail: curator@sjmuseum.org, Internet: www.sjmuseum.org. Dir.: Jennifer Fleming
Local Museum - 1961
Island hist, town jail, log cabin, farmhouse, milk house 43561

San Juan Island National Historical Park, 125 Spring St, Friday Harbor, WA 98250 - T: (360) 378-2240, Fax: (360) 378-2615, E-mail: sajh@nps.gov
Military Museum
Pig War 1859-72, US Army and British Royal Marines 43562

Whale Museum, 62 First St N, Friday Harbor, WA 98250 - T: (360) 378-4710, Fax: (360) 378-5790, E-mail: whale@rockisland.com, Internet: www.whalemuseum.com. Exec. Dir.: Clark McAlpine
Natural History Museum - 1978 43563

Frisco CO

Frisco Historical Society Museum, 120 Main St, Frisco, CO 80443 - T: (970) 668-3428, Fax: (970) 668-3428, E-mail: museum@colorado.net. Dir.: Rita Bartram
Local Museum - 1983 43564

Frisco NC

Frisco Native American Museum and Natural History Center, 53536 Hwy 12, Frisco, NC 27936 - T: (252) 995-4440, Fax: (252) 995-4030, E-mail: bfriend1@mindspring.com, Internet: www.nativeamericanmuseum.org. Exec. Dir.: Carl Bornfriend
Ethnology Museum - 1986 43565

Fritch TX

Lake Meredith Aquatic and Wildlife Museum, 103 N Robey St, Fritch, TX 79036 - T: (806) 857-2458, Fax: (806) 857-3229, E-mail: lmmuseum@infinitytx.net. Chm.: Robin Dickerson
Natural History Museum - 1976
Natural hist 43566

Fromberg MT

The Little Cowboy Bar and Museum, 105 W River, Fromberg, MT 59029 - T: (406) 668-9502, E-mail: diehard@imt.net, Internet: www.littlecowboy.com. Dir.: Shirley Smith
Local Museum - 1990
Local hist and culture 43567

Front Royal VA

Warren Rifles Confederate Museum, 95 Chester St, Front Royal, VA 22630 - T: (540) 636-6982, 635-2219, Fax: (540) 635-2219, E-mail: silwood@rmaonline.net. Dir.: Suzanne Silek
Military Museum - 1959
Military hist 43568

Frostburg MD

Stephanie Ann Roger Gallery, c/o Frostburg State University, 1011 Braddock Rd, Frostburg, MD 21532 - T: (301) 687-4797, Fax: (301) 687-3099, E-mail: ddavis@frostburg.edu. Chm.: Dustin P. Davis
University Museum / Fine Arts Museum / Decorative Arts Museum - 1972
Folk, art, prints 43569

Thrasher Carriage Museum, 19 Depot St, Frostburg, MD 21532 - T: (301) 689-3380, Fax: (301) 689-3882, E-mail: info@thrashercarriagemuseum.com, Internet: www.thrashercarriagemuseum.com
Science&Tech Museum - 1992
Horse-drawn conveyances 43570

Fryeburg ME

The Fryeburg Fair Farm Museum, Rte 5 N, Fryeburg, ME 04037 - T: (207) 935-3268, Fax: (207) 935-3662, E-mail: info@fryeburgfair.com, Internet: www.fryefair.com. Cur.: Edward Jones
Agriculture Museum - 1970
Agriculture 43571

Fullerton CA

Fullerton Museum Center, 301 N Pomona Av, Fullerton, CA 92832 - T: (714) 738-6545, 738-5319, Fax: (714) 738-3124, E-mail: fmc@ci.fullerton.ca.us, Internet: www.ci.fullerton.ca.us/museum. Dir.: Joseph Felz
Local Museum - 1971 43572

Main Art Gallery, Department of Art, California State University, 800 N State College Blvd, Fullerton, CA 92634-6850 - T: (714) 773-3471, 2783262, Fax: (714) 773-3005, E-mail: mmcgee@fullerton.edu, Internet: www.art.fullerton.edu. Dir.: Prof. Mike McGee
Public Gallery / University Museum - 1967
Contemporary prints, sculpture 43573

Muckenthaler Cultural Center Gallery, 1201 W Malvern, Fullerton, CA 92633 - T: (714) 738-6595, Fax: (714) 738-6366, Internet: www.muckenthaler.org
Public Gallery - 1966 43574

Museum of Anthropology, California State University, Fullerton, CA 92834-6846 - T: (714) 278-2844, 278-3564, Fax: (714) 278-7046, Internet: www.anthro.fullerton.edu. Dir.: Susan Parman
Ethnology Museum - 1970
Anthropology 43575

Fulton MO

William Woods University Art Gallery, 1 University Av, Fulton, MO 65251 - T: (573) 592-4245. Dir.: Terry Martin
Fine Arts Museum 43576

Winston Churchill Memorial and Library in the United States, Westminster College, 501 Westminster Av, Fulton, MO 65251 - T: (573) 592-5369, Fax: (573) 592-5222, E-mail: henslej@jaynet.wcmo.edu, Internet: www.churchillmemorial.org. Dir.: Dr. Jerry Morelock
University Museum / Historical Museum - 1962 43577

Gadsden AL

Center for Cultural Arts, 501 Broad St, Gadsden, AL 35901 - T: (256) 543-2787, Fax: (256) 546-7435, E-mail: bobwelsh@culturalarts.org, Internet: www.culturalarts.org. Dir.: Robert M. Welch, Cur.: Dennis Sears
Fine Arts Museum / Folklore Museum - 1987
Art 43578

Gadsden Museum of Fine Arts, 2829 W Meighan Blvd, Gadsden, AL 35904-1717 - T: (256) 546-7365, Fax: (256) 546-7365, E-mail: gadmusa@internetpro.net. Dir.: Jim Loftin
Fine Arts Museum - 1965 43579

Gaffney SC

Winnie Davis Museum of History, Limestone College, 1115 College Dr, Gaffney, SC 29340 - T: (864) 488-8399, Fax: (864) 487-7151, E-mail: chayward@saint.limestone.edu, Internet: www.limestone.edu
Historical Museum / University Museum - 1976
History 43580

Gainesville FL

Florida Museum of Natural History, SW 34th St and Hull Rd, Gainesville, FL 32611-7800, mail addr: POB 117800, Gainesville, FL 32611-7800 - T: (352) 392-1721, 846-2000, Fax: (352) 392-8783, 846-0253, E-mail: cosmith@flmnh.ufl.edu, Internet: flmnh.ufl.edu. Dir.: Dr. Douglas S. Jones, Ass. Dir: Dr. Graig D. Shaak (Operations), Dr. B.J. MacFadden (Exhibits, Public Programs, Vertebrate Paleontology), Dr. D.W. Steadman (Research, Collections, Ornithology), Sc. Staff: Dr. J.S. Albert (Ichthyology), Dr. K.A. Deagan (Spanish Colonial Archaeology), Dr. D.L. Dilcher (Paleobotany), Dr. K.F. Emery (Environmental Archaeology), L.R. Franz jr. (Ecology), Dr. Douglas S. Jones (Invertebrate Paleontology), Dr. W.F. Keegan (Caribbean Archaeology), Dr. F.W. King (Herpetology), Dr. S.R. Manchester (Paleobotany), Dr. W.H. Marquardt, Dr. J.T. Milanich (Florida Archaeology), Dr. S. Milbrath (Ethnography), Dr. L.D. Miller, Dr. J.Y. Miller (Lepidoptera), Dr. M.A. Nickerson (Herpetology), Dr. G. Paulay (Marine Malacology), Dr. C.M. Porter (History of Science), Dr. J.P. Ross (Herpetology), Dr. P.S. Soltis (Molecular Systematics), Dr. F.G. Thompson (Malacology), Dr. K.J. Walker (Florida Archaeology), Dr. S.D. Webb (Vertebrate Paleontology), Dr. N.H. Williams (Herbarium)
University Museum / Natural History Museum - 1917
Paleontology, archaeology, ornitology, botany, mammalogy, herpetlogy, art 43581

Matheson Museum, 513 E University Av, Gainesville, FL 32601 - T: (352) 378-2280, Fax: (352) 378-1246, E-mail: mathesonmuseum@usa.net. Dir.: Lisa B. Auel
Local Museum - 1994
Local culture and hist 43582

Morningside Nature Center, 3540 E University Av, Gainesville, FL 32641 - T: (352) 334-2170, Fax: (352) 334-2248, Internet: www.natureoperations.org. Dir.: Dr. Clifford Crawford
Agriculture Museum / Open Air Museum / Natural History Museum - 1972 43583

Samuel P. Harn Museum of Art, University of Florida, Gainesville, FL 32611-2700 - T: (352) 392-9826, Fax: (352) 392-3892, Internet: www.harn.ufl.edu. Dir.: Rebecca Nagy, Cur.: Larry David Perkins
Fine Arts Museum / University Museum - 1981
Art 43584

Santa Fe Gallery, Santa Fe Community College, 3000 NW 83rd St, Gainesville, FL 32606 - T: (352) 395-5000, Fax: (352) 395-4432, E-mail: treey.klenk@santafe.cc.fl.us, Internet: inst.santafe.cc.fl.us/~cah
Fine Arts Museum - 1978 43585

Thomas Center Galleries, 302 NE 6th Av, Gainesville, FL 32601 - T: (352) 334-5064, Fax: (352) 334-2314, E-mail: cultural@ci.gainesville.fl.us, Internet: www.state.fl.us/gvl/arts_culture. Dir.: Amy Dickerson
Public Gallery 43586

University Gallery, University of Florida, Gainesville, FL 32611, mail addr: POB 115803, Gainesville, FL 32611-5803 - T: (352) 392-0201, Fax: (352) 846-0266, E-mail: wyman@ufl.edu, Internet: www.arts.ufl.edu. Dir.: James Wyman
Fine Arts Museum / University Museum - 1965 43587

Gainesville GA

Brenau University Galleries, 1 Centennial Circle, Gainesville, GA 30501 - T: (770) 534-6299, Fax: (770) 538-4599, E-mail: jwestmacott@lib.brenau.edu, Internet: www.brenau.edu. Dir./Cur.: Jean Westmacott
Fine Arts Museum / University Museum - 1983
Paintings, drawings, prints, sculpture, photos, craft works 43588

Georgia Mountains History Museum, c/o Brenau University, 311 Green St SE, Gainesville, GA 30501 - T: (770) 536-0889, Fax: (770) 534-9488, E-mail: gamthist@bellsouth.net, Internet: www.gamtshistorymuseum.org
Historical Museum / University Museum - 1981
Textile, poultry, medical, African-American, Indian, firefighting, arts and crafts, Ed Dodd, Mark Trail 43589

Gainesville TX

Morton Museum of Cooke County, 210 S Dixon St, Gainesville, TX 76240 - T: (940) 668-8900, Fax: (940) 668-0533, E-mail: mortonmuseum@nortexinfo.net, Internet: www.martonmuseum.org. Cur.: Shana Powell
Local Museum - 1968
Local hist 43590

Gaithersburg MD

The London Brass Rubbing Centre in Washington D.C., 11808 Silent Valley Ln, Gaithersburg, MD 20878 - T: (301) 279-7046, E-mail: me2you@starpower.net. Pres.: Richard A. Etches, C.E.O.: Karen L. Hammond
Decorative Arts Museum - 1977
Arts, crafts 43591

Galax VA

Jeff Matthews Memorial Museum, 606 W Stuart Dr, Galax, VA 24333 - T: (540) 236-7874. Cur.: Rita Edwards
Local Museum - 1974
Local hist 43592

Galena IL

Galena-Jo Daviess County Historical Museum, 211 S Bench St, Galena, IL 61036 - T: (815) 777-9129, Fax: (815) 777-9131, E-mail: ghmuseum@galenalink.net, Internet: www.galenahistorymuseum.org. Exec. Dir.: Daryl Watson
Local Museum - 1938
Local history, civil war, lead mining, clothing, geology, dolls and toys 43593

Old Market House, Market Sq, Galena, IL 61036 - T: (815) 777-3310, Fax: (815) 777-3310, E-mail: granthome@granthome.com, Internet: www.granthome.com. Chm.: Daniel F. Tindell
Historical Museum - 1947
Greek Revival-style Market House 43594

United States Grant's Home, 500 Bouthillier St, Galena, IL 61036 - T: (815) 777-3310, Fax: (815) 777-3310, E-mail: granthome@granthome.com, Internet: www.granthome.com. Man.: Terry J. Miller
Historical Museum - 1932
Italianate bracketed style house presented to Gen. Grant in 1865 43595

Galena KS

Galena Mining and Historical Museum, 319 W Seventh St, Galena, KS 66739 - T: (316) 783-2192
Science&Tech Museum / Historical Museum - 1984
Lead and zinc mine artifacts, tools, lamps, pictures, paintings, mineral, locomotive, caboose, helicopter, tank 43596

Galesburg IL

Carl Sandburg State Historic Site, 331 E 3rd St, Galesburg, IL 61401 - T: (309) 342-2361, Fax: (309) 342-2141, E-mail: carl@sandburg.org, Internet: www.sandburg.org. Man.: Steve Holden
Historical Museum - 1945
Immigrant railroad worker's cottage 43597

Galesburg Civic Art Center, 114 E Main St, Galesburg, IL 61401 - T: (309) 342-7415, E-mail: artcenter@misslink.net, Internet: www.artcenter.com, www.gallatinriver.net. C.E.O.: Heather L. Norman
Public Gallery - 1923 43598

Illinois Citizen Soldier Museum, 1001 Michigan Av, Galesburg, IL 61401 - T: (309) 342-1181. Cur.: Kenneth R. Johnson
Military Museum - 1988 43599

Galesville MD

Carrie Weedon Natural Science Museum, 911 Galesville Rd, Galesville, MD 20765 - T: (410) 222-1625, Fax: (410) 867-0588. Dir.: Dotty Cheney
Natural History Museum / Science&Tech Museum - 1988
Natural history and science 43600

Galeton PA

Pennsylvania Lumber Museum, US Rte 6, Galeton, PA 16922 - T: (814) 435-2652, Fax: (814) 435-6361, Internet: www.lumbermuseum.org. Pres.: Robert Currin
Historical Museum / Natural History Museum - 1970 43601

Galion OH

Brownella Cottage, 132 S Union St, Galion, OH 44833 - T: (419) 468-9338. Pres.: Jerry A. Lantz
Local Museum - 1981 43602

Galion Historical Museum, 132 S Union St, Galion, OH 44833 - T: (419) 468-9338. Dir.: Dr. Bernard M. Mansfield
Local Museum - 1956 43603

Gallipolis OH

French Art Colony, 530 First Av, Gallipolis, OH 45631 - T: (740) 446-3834, Fax: (740) 446-3834, E-mail: facart@zoomnet.net. Dir.: Mary Bea McCalla, Cur.: Janice M. Thaler
Fine Arts Museum - 1971 43604

Our House State Memorial, 434 First Av, Gallipolis, OH 45631 - T: (740) 446-0586. Cur.: Janice Layne
Historical Museum - 1933 43605

Galveston TX

Ashton Villa, 2328 Broadway, Galveston, TX 77550-2014 - T: (409) 762-3933, Fax: (409) 762-1904, E-mail: foundation@galvestonhistory.org, Internet: www.galvestonhistory.org. Cur.: Christy Carl
Local Museum - 1974
Historic house 43606

The Bishop's Palace, 1402 Broadway, Galveston, TX 77550 - T: (409) 762-2475, Fax: (409) 762-1810. Dir.: Tom Hunter, Cur.: Joseph Fiorenza
Local Museum - 1886
Historic building 43607

Galveston Arts Center, 2127 Strand, Galveston, TX 77550 - T: (409) 763-2403, Fax: (409) 763-0531, E-mail: galartsctr@aol.com. Exec. Dir.: Clint Willour
Fine Arts Museum
Art 43608

Galveston County Historical Museum, 2219 Market St, Galveston, TX 77550 - T: (409) 766-2340, Fax: (409) 795-2157, E-mail: christy.carl@galvestonhistory.org, Internet: www.galvestonhistory.org. Dir.: Christine S. Carl, Cur.: Robin Munson
Historical Museum - 1972
Local hist 43609

Harris Art Gallery, James M. Lykes Maritime Gallery and Hutchings Gallery, c/o Rosenberg Library, 2310 Sealy Av, Galveston, TX 77550 - T: (409) 763-8854, Fax: (409) 763-0275, Internet: www.rosenberg-library.org. Exec. Dir.: Nancy Milnor, Cur.: Lise Darst
Fine Arts Museum / Local Museum 43610

John Sydnor's 1847 Powhatan House, 3427 Avenue O, Galveston, TX 77550 - T: (409) 763-0077, Fax: (409) 744-1456, E-mail: ewhorton@utmb.edu. C.E.O.: Dwayne Johnson
Local Museum - 1938
Historic house 43611

Lone Star Flight Museum/Texas Aviation Hall of Fame, 2002 Terminal Dr, Galveston, TX 77552 - T: (409) 740-7722, Fax: (409) 740-7612, E-mail: flight@lsfm.org, Internet: www.lsfm.org. Dir.: Ralph Royce, Cur.: Darla Harmon
Military Museum / Science&Tech Museum - 1986
Aeronautics 43612

Moody Mansion Museum, 2618 Broadway, Galveston, TX 77550 - T: (409) 762-7668, 765-9770, Fax: (409) 762-7055. Pres.: Edward L. Protz, Cur.: Catherine L. Campbell
Historical Museum / Decorative Arts Museum - 1991
History, decorative arts, costume, textiles 43613

Texas Seaport Museum, Pier 21, 8, Galveston, TX 77550 - T: (409) 763-1877, Fax: (409) 763-3037, E-mail: elissa@galvestonhistory.org, Internet: www.tsm-elissa.org. C.E.O.: Gina Spagnola, Dir.: Kurt Voss
Historical Museum - 1982
Maritime hist 43614

Gambier OH

Olin Art Gallery, c/o Kenyon College, Olin Library, Gambier, OH 43022 - T: (740) 427-5000, Fax: (740) 427-5272, Internet: www.cycle.kenyon.edu
Fine Arts Museum 43615

Ganado AZ

Hubbell Trading Post, Hwy 264, Ganado, AZ 86505, mail addr: POB 150, Ganado, AZ 86505 - T: (928) 755-3475, Fax: (928) 755-3405, E-mail: e_chamberlin@nps.gov, Internet: www.nps.gov/hutr/. Head: Nancy E. Stone, Cur.: Edward M. Chamberlin
Historical Museum / Historic Site - 1967
Historic Site 43616

Garden City KS

Finney County Kansas Historical Museum, Finnup Park, 403 S 4th, Garden City, KS 67846-0796 - T: (316) 272-3664, Fax: (316) 272-3664, E-mail: fico.historical@gcnet.com. Dir.: Mary Regan, Cur.: Laurie Oshel
Historical Museum - 1949
Local history - library 43617

Garden City NY

Firehouse Art Gallery, Nassau Community College, 1 Education Dr, Garden City, NY 11530 - T: (516) 572-7165, Fax: (516) 572-7302. Cur.: Lynn R. Casey
University Museum / Fine Arts Museum - 1965 43618

Long Island Children's Museum, 550 Stewart Av, Garden City, NY 11530 - T: (516) 222-0217, Fax: (516) 222-0225, E-mail: licm1@aol.com, Internet: www.licm.org. Pres.: Robert Lemle, Dir.: Bonnie Dixon
Special Museum - 1990 43619

Long Island Museum of Science and Technology, Museum Row, Mitchel Field, Garden City, NY 11530 - T: (516) 227-1994, E-mail: bparris@limsat.org, Internet: www.limsat.org
Science&Tech Museum - 1982 43620

Gardiner NY

Locust Lawn and Terwilliger House, 400 Rte 32 S, Gardiner, NY 12525 - T: (845) 255-1660, Fax: (845) 255-0376, E-mail: hhsoffice@hhs-newpaltz.org, Internet: www.hhs-newpaltz.org. Dir.: John Braunlein
Decorative Arts Museum / Historical Museum - 1894
Queen Anne-early Victorian furnishings, China, fabrics, laces, textiles, toys, paintings, coaches, tools 43621

Mohonk Preserve, 3197 Rte 44/55, Gardiner, NY 12525-0715, mail addr: POB 715, New Paltz, NY 12561 - T: (845) 255-0919, Fax: (845) 255-5646, E-mail: info@mohonkpreserve.org, Internet: mohonkpreserve.org
Historical Museum / Natural History Museum - 1963
Natural hist, Northern Shawanqunk Ridge hist 43622

Gardner MA

Gardner Museum, 28 Pearl St, Gardner, MA 01440 - T: (978) 632-3277. Pres.: Donald Gearan
Fine Arts Museum / Local Museum - 1978
Local history, Richardson Romanesque brick bldg 43623

Mount Wachusett Community College Art Galleries, 444 Green St, Gardner, MA 01440 - T: (978) 632-6600 ext 168, Internet: www.mwcc.mass.edu
Fine Arts Museum - 1971
Color art posters and reproductions, prints, ceramic, student coll 43624

Garfield AR

Pea Ridge National Military Park, 15930 Hwy 62, Garfield, AR 72732 - T: (501) 451-8122, Fax: (501) 451-8635, Internet: www.nps.gov/peri. Head: John Scott
Military Museum - 1960
Reconstructed Elkhorn tavern 43625

Garnavillo IA

Garnavillo Historical Museum, 205 N Washington, Garnavillo, IA 52049 - T: (563) 964-2341, Fax: (563) 964-2485, E-mail: gmaomie@alpine.com.net. Pres.: Kurt Kuenzel
Local Museum - 1965
Local history, housed in a church 43626

Garnett KS

Anderson County Historical Museum, W 6th St, Garnett, KS 66032-0217 - T: (785) 867-2966, 448-5740, E-mail: ancohiso@ecksor.net. Pres.: Dorothy L. Lickteig
Local Museum / Folklore Museum - 1968
Local hist, home and carriage house of Dr. Harris, Longfellow school building 43627

Walker Art Collection of the Garnett Public Library, 125 W 4th Av, Garnett, KS 66032 - T: (913) 448-3388, Fax: (913) 448-3936, E-mail: garnett@kanza.net, Internet: www.kanza.net/garnett. Chm.: Terry J. Solander
Fine Arts Museum - 1965
Art gallery 43628

Garrett IN

Garrett Historical Museum, Heritage Park, 300 N Randolph St, Garrett, IN 46738 - T: (219) 357-5575, E-mail: jmohre@locl.net, Internet: www.garretthistoricalsociety.org. Cur.: Robert Parker
Local Museum / Science&Tech Museum - 1971
Local history, 3 railroad cars, diesel locomotive 43629

Garrison NY

Boscobel Restoration, 1601 Rte 9D, Garrison, NY 10524 - T: (845) 265-3638, Fax: (845) 265-4405, E-mail: info@boscobel.org, Internet: www.boscobel.org. Dir.: Charles T. Lyle
Decorative Arts Museum / Historical Museum - 1955 43630

Garryowen MT

Custer Battlefield Museum, Town Hall, Garryowen, MT 59031-0200 - T: (406) 638-1876, Fax: (406) 638-2019, E-mail: chris@custermuseum.org, Internet: www.custermuseum.org. C.E.O.: Christopher Kortlander
Military Museum - 1994
Paintings, rare books, Battle of the Little Bighorn 43631

Gastonia NC

Schiele Museum of Natural History, 1500 E Garrison Blvd, Gastonia, NC 28054-5199 - T: (704) 866-6908, Fax: (704) 866-6041, E-mail: dbrose@schielemuseum.org, Internet: www.schielemuseum.org. Dir.: David S. Brose, Cur.: J. Alan May (Archaeology), Adj. Cur.: Allein Stanley (Mycology), Kay K. Moss (18th c Lifeways Studies), Toni Superchi (Paleontology)
Natural History Museum / Ethnology Museum - 1960
Natural hist, ethnography, colonial hist 43632

Gate OK

Gateway to the Panhandle, Main St, Gate, OK 73844 - T: (405) 934-2004. Dir.: L. Ernestine Maphet, Dep. Dir.: Karen Bond, Charlene Husted, Louise Hein
Local Museum / Historical Museum - 1975 43633

Gates Mills OH

Gates Mills Historical Society Museum, 7580 Old Mill Rd, Gates Mills, OH 44040 - T: (440) 423-4808, Fax: (440) 423-4808. Pres.: Harriet Leedy
Local Museum - 1946 43634

Gatlinburg TN

Arrowmont School of Arts and Crafts Collection, 556 Pkwy, Gatlinburg, TN 37738 - T: (865) 436-5860, Fax: (865) 430-4101, E-mail: info@arrowment.org, Internet: www.arrowmont.org. Dir.: David Willard, Cur.: Billi R.S. Rothove
Fine Arts Museum / Decorative Arts Museum - 1945
Arts and crafts 43635

Gaylord MI

Call of the Wild Museum, 850 S Wisconsin Av, Gaylord, MI 49735 - T: (517) 732-4336, Fax: (517) 732-3749, Internet: www.gocallofthewild.com. Dir.: William C. Johnson, Judy Fleet, Pres.: Janis Vollmer
Natural History Museum - 1957
Natural history 43636

Geddes SD

Geddes Historic District Village, Box 97, Geddes, SD 57342 - T: (605) 337-2501, Fax: (605) 337-3535, E-mail: dufsdfek@midstate.net, Internet: www.geddes.org. Pres.: John Steckley, C.E.O.: Mike Dufek
Local Museum - 1969
Local hist, old items from 1850-1910 era 43637

Geneseo NY

Bertha V.B. Lederer Fine Arts Gallery, SUNY at Geneseo, Fine Arts Bldg, 1 College Circle, Geneseo, NY 14454 - T: (716) 245-5814, Fax: (716) 245-5815, E-mail: shanahan@uno.cc.geneseo.edu. C.E.O.: Carl Shanahan
Fine Arts Museum / University Museum - 1967 43638

Livingston County Historical Society Museum, 30 Center St, Geneseo, NY 14454 - T: (716) 243-2281, Internet: www.livingstoncountyhistoricalsociety.org. Pres.: Alberta Dunn
Historical Museum - 1876 43639

Geneva IL

Fabyan Villa Museum and Dutch Windmill, Rtes 31 and 25 at Fabyan Pkwy, Geneva, IL 60134, mail addr: 1925 S Batavia Av, Geneva, IL 60134 - T: (630) 232-4811, Fax: (630) 377-6424. Cur.: Diana Malakar
Decorative Arts Museum / Science&Tech Museum - 1941
Oriental porcelains, Fabyan hist, Frank Lloyd Wright furniture 43640

Geneva IN

Limberlost State Historic Site, 200 East 6th St, Geneva, IN 46740 - T: (219) 368-7428, Fax: (219) 368-7007, E-mail: limberlost@adamswells.com, Internet: www.genestrattonporter.net. Cur.: Rebecca Smith, Randall Lehmann, Becky Smith
Special Museum - 1947
Home of Gene Stratton-Porter, author and naturalist 43641

Geneva NY

Prouty-Chew Museum, 543 S Main St, Geneva, NY 14456 - T: (315) 789-5151, Fax: (315) 789-0314, E-mail: info@genevahistoricalsociety.com, Internet: www.genevahistoricalsociety.com. C.E.O.: Charles C. W. Bauder, Cur.: John C. Marks (Collections), Anne F. Dealy (Education)
Historical Museum - 1883 43642

Rose Hill Mansion, Rte 96A, Geneva, NY 14456 - T: (315) 789-5151, Fax: (315) 789-0314, E-mail: info@genevehistoricalsociety.com, Internet: www.genevehistoricalsociety.com. C.E.O./Cur.: H. Merrill Roenke
Historical Museum - 1968
History 43643

Geneva OH

Platt R. Spencer Special Collections and Archival Room, 860 Sherman St, Geneva, OH 44041-9101 - T: (440) 466-4521 ext 107, Fax: (440) 466-0162, E-mail: acgs@ashtabulagen.org, Internet: www.ashtabula.lib.oh.us/geneva.htm. Dir.: William Tokarczyk
Special Museum - 1988
Archive 43644

Shandy Hall, 6333 S Ridge, Geneva, OH 44041 - T: (216) 466-3680, Internet: www.wrhs.org. Cur.: Byron Robertson
Historical Museum - 1937 43645

Geneva-on-the-Lake OH

Ashtabula County Historical Society Museum, 5685 Lake Rd, Geneva-on-the-Lake, OH 44041 - T: (440) 466-7337
Local Museum 43646

Gentryville IN

Colonel William Jones House, 3/4 m W of U.S. Hwy 231, on Boone St, Gentryville, IN 47537 - T: (812) 937-2802, Fax: (812) 937-7038, E-mail: coljones@psci.net, Internet: www.state.in.us/ism/sites/jones. Cur.: Peggy Brooks
Historical Museum - 1976 43647

Georgetown CO

Historic Georgetown, 305 Argentine, Georgetown, CO 80444 - T: (303) 569-2840, Fax: (303) 569-2111, E-mail: preservation@historicgeorgetown.org, Internet: www.historicgeorgetown.org. Dir.: Dana Abrahamson, Cur.: Deirdre Baldwin
Open Air Museum / Local Museum - 1970
William A. Hamill house and office bldg, stable and carriage house, Bowman-White house; Tucker-Rutherford house; Miner's cottage, log cabin 43648

Hotel de Paris Museum, 409 Sixth Av, Georgetown, CO 80444 - T: (303) 569-2311, Fax: (303) 756-8768, E-mail: mrc6118@aol.com, Internet: www.hoteldeparismuseum.org
Historical Museum - 1875
Furniture, dishes and kitchen utensils - library 43649

Georgetown DE

Treasures of the Sea Exhibit, Delaware Technical and Community College, Rte 18, Seashore Hwy, Georgetown, DE 19947-0610 - T: (302) 856-5700, Fax: (302) 858-5462, E-mail: treasures@dtcc.edu, Internet: www.treasuresofthesea.org. Dir.: Barbara S. Ridgely
Natural History Museum - 1988 43650

Georgetown KY

Georgetown College Gallery, Mullberry and College Sts, Georgetown, KY 40324 - T: (502) 863-8106, 863-8399, E-mail: jean_ippolito@georgetowncollege.edu. Dir.: Christine Huskisson
Fine Arts Museum - 1959
Contemporary graphics, painting and sculpture, crafts 43651

Ward Hall, 1782 Frankfort Pike, Georgetown, KY 40324 - T: (859) 233-0525. Cur.: Frances Susong Jenkins
Decorative Arts Museum - 1979 43652

Georgetown SC

Hopsewee Plantation, 494 Hopsewee Rd, Georgetown, SC 29440 - T: (803) 546-7891, Internet: www.hopsewee.com. Dir.: Helen B. Maynard
Local Museum - 1970
Historic house, birthplace of Thomas Lynch Jr., signer of the Declaration of Independence 43653

Kaminski House Museum, 1003 Front St, Georgetown, SC 29440 - T: (843) 546-7706, Fax: (843) 545-4062, E-mail: klawrimore@cityofgeorgetownsc.com. C.E.O.: Katrina P. Lawrimore, Pres.: Alice Williams
Local Museum - 1973
Historic house 43654

The Rice Museum, Lafayette Park, Front and Screven Sts, Georgetown, SC 29440 - T: (843) 546-7423, Fax: (843) 545-9093, Internet: www.distrand.com/rice. Dir.: James A. Fitch, Cur.: Sarah Johnson, Chris Boyle
Historical Museum - 1968
History 43655

Gering NE

North Platte Valley Museum, 11 and J Sts, near Hwys 92 and 71, Gering, NE 69341 - T: (308) 436-5411, Fax: (308) 436-2592, E-mail: npvm@actcom.net, Internet: www.npum.org. Dir.: John Versluis
Local Museum - 1969 43656

Oregon Trail Museum, Scotts Bluff National Monument, Hwy 92 W, Gering, NE 69341 - T: (308) 436-4340, 436-2975, Fax: (308) 436-7611, Internet: www.nps.gov/scbl
Historical Museum - 1919
Geology, prehistory, archaeology, ethnological history, history of Western migration 43657

Scotts Bluff National Monument, 190276 Hwy 92, Gering, NE 69341-0027 - T: (308) 436-4340, Fax: (308) 436-7611
Archaeological Museum - 1919
History 43658

Germantown TN

P.T. Boat Museum, 1384 Cordova Rd, Germantown, TN 38138 - T: (901) 755-8440, Fax: (901) 751-0522, E-mail: ptboats@pop.net, Internet: www.ptboats.org. C.E.O.: Alyce N. Guthrie
Military Museum - 1946
Battleship Cove, WW 2 PT boats 43659

P.T. Boat Museum, POB 38070, Germantown, TN 38138 - T: (901) 755-8440, Fax: (901) 751-0522, Internet: www.ptboats.org. Dir.: Alyce N. Guthrie
Historical Museum / Military Museum - 1946
Maritime, naval history, at Battleship Cove, WW II - archives 43660

Gettysburg PA

Adams County Historical Society Museum, 111 Seminary Ridge, Gettysburg, PA 17325 - T: (717) 334-4723, Fax: (717) 334-4723, E-mail: info@achs-pa.org. Dir.: Arthur Weaner
Local Museum - 1934 43661

Eisenhower National Historic Site, 250 Eisenhower Farm Ln, Gettysburg, PA 17325 - T: (717) 338-9114, Fax: (717) 338-0821, E-mail: eise_site_manager@nps.gov, Internet: www.nps.gov/eise. Dir.: Dr. John A. Latschar, Cur.: Michael R. Florer, Historian: Carol A. Hegeman
Historical Museum - 1967
Presidential and retirement home of Dwight D. Eisenhower 43662

Gettysburg National Military Park, 97 Taneytown Rd, Gettysburg, PA 17325 - T: (717) 334-1124, Fax: (717) 334-1891, E-mail: gett_curator@nps.gov, Internet: www.nps.gov/gett. Dir.: Dr. John A. Latschar, Cur.: Michael L. Vice
Historic Site / Military Museum / Open Air Museum - 1895 43663

Lincoln Train Museum, 425 Steinwehr Av, Gettysburg, PA 17325 - T: (717) 334-5678, Fax: (717) 334-9100, Internet: www.gettysburgbattlefieldtours.com
Special Museum
Model train of Abe Lincoln, railroad dioramas 43664

Soldiers National Museum, 777 Baltimore St, Gettysburg, PA 17325 - T: (717) 334-4890, Internet: www.gettysburgbattlefieldtours.com
Military Museum - 1950
Military, confederate encampment 43665

Ghent NY

Parker-O'Malley Air Museum, 1571 Rte 66, Ghent, NY 12075 - T: (518) 392-7200, Fax: (518) 392-2408, E-mail: jmcmahon@parkeromalley.org. C.E.O.: James E. McMahon
Science&Tech Museum - 1991
Aeronautics 43666

Gig Harbor WA

Gig Harbor Peninsula Historical Society Museum, 4218 Harborview Dr, Gig Harbor, WA 98332 - T: (253) 858-6722, Fax: (253) 853-4211, E-mail: info@gigharbormuseum.org, Internet: www.gigharbormuseum.org. Dir.: Chris Fiala Erlich
Historical Museum - 1962
Local hist 43667

Gillett AR

Arkansas Post Museum, 5530 Hwy 165 S, Gillett, AR 72055 - T: (870) 548-2634, Fax: (870) 548-3003, E-mail: arkpost@futura.net, Internet: www.arkansas.com. Dir.: Thomas E. Jordan
Local Museum - 1960
Local history 43668

Arkansas Post National Memorial, 1741 Old Post Rd, Gillett, AR 72055 - T: (870) 548-2207, Fax: (870) 548-2431, E-mail: arpo_superintendant@nps.gov, Internet: www.gov.nps./arpo. Head: Edward Wood
Historical Museum - 1964
Statehood period, civil war 43669

Gillette WY

Campbell County Rockpile Museum, 900 W 2nd St, Gillette, WY 82716 - T: (307) 682-5723, Fax: (307) 686-8528, E-mail: rockpile@vcn.com, Internet: www.gillettewyoming.com/rockpile/. Dir.: Robert J. Kothe
Local Museum - 1974
Local hist 43670

Gills Rock WI

Door County Maritime Museum, 12724 Wisconsin Bay Rd, Gills Rock, WI 54210 - T: (920) 854-1844, 743-5958, Fax: (920) 743-9483, E-mail: dcmm@itol.com, Internet: www.dcmm.org
Historical Museum - 1969
Sailing, Coast Guard, commercial fishing, shipbuilding industry 43671

Gilmanton NH

Carpenter Museum of Antique Outboard Motors, POB 459, Gilmanton, NH 03237-0459 - T: (603) 524-7611, Fax: (603) 524-7611, E-mail: amc@cyberportal.net
Special Museum / Science&Tech Museum - 1976
Marine technology 43672

Carpenter Museum of Antique Outboard Motors, POB 459, Gilmanton, NH 03237-0459 - T: (603) 524-7611, Fax: (603) 524-7611, E-mail: amc@cyberportal.net
Science&Tech Museum - 1976
Outboard motors, marine 43673

Gilroy CA

Gavilan Community College Art Gallery, 5055 Santa Teresa Blvd, Gilroy, CA 95020 - T: (408) 846-4946, Fax: (408) 846-4927, Internet: www.gavilan.cc.ca.us.
Public Gallery - 1967 43674

Gilroy Historical Museum, 195 Fifth St, Gilroy, CA 95020 - T: (408) 848-0470, 846-0460, Fax: (408) 842-2409, E-mail: lsolorzano@ci.gilroy.ca.us, Internet: www.ci.gilroy.ca.us. Head: Cathy Mirelez
Local Museum - 1958
Local history 43675

Girard PA

Battles Museums of Rural Life, 436 Walnut St, Girard, PA - T: (814) 774-4788, Fax: (814) 452-1744, E-mail: gdomow1962@aol.com, Internet: www.eriecountyhistory.org
Historical Museum - 1989
Battles family 43676

Glasgow MT

Valley County Pioneer Museum, Hwy 2 W, Glasgow, MT 59230 - T: (406) 228-8692, E-mail: vcmuseum@nemontel.net, Internet: www.valleycountymuseum.com. Dir.: Lenore Hinerman, Cur.: Carol Cotton
Historical Museum - 1964 43677

Glastonbury CT

Glastonbury Museum, 1944 Main St, Glastonbury, CT 06033 - T: (860) 633-6890, Fax: (860) 633-6890, E-mail: hsglastonbury@netzero.net. Dir.: James Bennett
Historical Museum - 1936 43678

Glen Allen VA

Meadow Farm Museum, 3400 Mountain Rd, Glen Allen, VA 23060, mail addr: POB 27032, Richmond, VA 23273 - T: (804) 501-5520, Fax: (804) 501-5284, Internet: www.co.henrico.va.us/rec
Decorative Arts Museum / Folklore Museum - 1981
19th-20th c folk art 43679

Glen Echo MD

Clara Barton Home, 5801 Oxford Rd, Glen Echo, MD 20812 - T: (301) 492-6245, Fax: (301) 492-5330, E-mail: gwmp_clara_barton_nhs@nps.gov, Internet: www.nps.gov/clba
Historical Museum - 1975
Home of Clara Barton, founder of the American Red Cross 43680

Glen Ellen CA

Jack London State Historic Park, House of Happy Walls, 2400 London Ranch Rd, Glen Ellen, CA 95442 - T: (707) 938-5216, Fax: (707) 938-4827, E-mail: jacklondonshp@aol.com, Internet: www.parks.sonoma.net
Local Museum - 1959
History, paintings, sculpture 43681

Glen Ellyn IL

Stacy's Tavern Museum and Glen Ellyn Historical Society, 557 Geneva Rd, Glen Ellyn, IL 60137, mail addr: POB 283, Glen Ellyn, IL 60138 - T: (630) 858-8696, Fax: (630) 858-8696, Internet: www.glen-ellyn.com/historical/. Pres.: John Costersian, Dir.: Barbara Bishop
Local Museum - 1976
1846 Moses Stacy House and Inn, local Glen Ellyn history - archive 43682

Glen Rose TX

Barnard's Mill Art Museum, 307 SW Barnard St, Glen Rose, TX 76043 - T: (817) 897-2611. Dir.: Richard H. Moore
Fine Arts Museum - 1989
Art 43683

Dinosaur Valley State Park, FM 205, Glen Rose, TX 76043 - T: (817) 897-4588, Fax: (817) 897-3409, E-mail: dinosaur@hcnews.com, Internet: www.tpwd.state.tx.us. Head: Billy P. Baker
Natural History Museum - 1969
Paleontology 43684

Somervell County Museum, Elm & Vernon Sts, Glen Rose, TX 76043 - T: (254) 897-4529. Dir.: Jeanne P. Mack
Local Museum - 1966
Local hist 43685

Glencoe MO

Wabash Frisco and Pacific Association Museum, 199 Grand Av, Glencoe, MO 63038, mail addr: 1569 Ville Angela Ln, Hazelwood, MO 63042-1630 - T: (636) 587-3538, (314) 351-9385, E-mail: tiel4@msn.com, Internet: www.wfprr.com
Science&Tech Museum - 1939
Miniature steam locomotives, trank, hopper and gondola cars, wooden benched flat cars and gondolas, passenger cars, milling machines 43686

Glendale CA

Brand Library and Art Galleries, 1601 W Mountain St, Glendale, CA 91201-1200 - T: (818) 548-2051, Fax: (818) 548-5079, Internet: library.ci.glendale.ca.us/brand. Dir.: Jill Conner
Library with Exhibitions / Fine Arts Museum - 1956 43687

Casa Adobe de San Rafael, 1330 Dorothy Dr, Glendale, CA 91202 - T: (818) 548-2000, Fax: (818) 548-3789, E-mail: dzabinski@ci.glendale.ca.us. Dir.: Nello Iaconoy
Historical Museum - 1867
California furniture 43688

Forest Lawn Museum, 1712 S Glendale Av, Glendale, CA 91205 - T: (323) 254-3131, Fax: (323) 551-5329. Dir.: Margaret Burton
Historical Museum - 1951 43689

Glenford OH

Flint Ridge State Memorial Museum, 7091 Brownsville Rd SE, Glenford, OH 43739-9609 - T: (800) 283-8707, E-mail: moundbuilders@cgate.net. Man.: James Kingery
Natural History Museum - 1933 43690

Glenn Dale MD

Marietta House Museum, 5626 Bell Station Rd, Glenn Dale, MD 20769 - T: (301) 464-5291, Fax: (301) 456-5654, E-mail: susan.wolfe@pgparks.com, Internet: www.pgparks.com. Pres.: Susan Wolfe
Local Museum - 1978
Federal style brick home 43691

Glens Falls NY

Chapman Historical Museum, 348 Glen St, Glens Falls, NY 12801 - T: (518) 793-2826, Fax: (519) 793-2831, Internet: www.chapmanmuseum.com. Dir.: Timothy Weidner, Cur.: Rebecca Gereau
Historical Museum - 1967 43692

Hyde Collection Art Museum, 161 Warren St, Glens Falls, NY 12801 - T: (518) 792-1761, Fax: (518) 792-9197, E-mail: info@hydeartmuseum.org, Internet: www.hydeartmuseum.org. Dir.: Randall Suffolk

Fine Arts Museum - 1952
European and American art by Raphael, Da Vinci, Rubens, Rembrandt, Cézanne, Renoir, Van Gogh, Picasso, Whistler, Eakins, Homer 43693

Glenside PA

Arcadia University Art Gallery, Church and Easton Rds, Glenside, PA 19038 - T: (215) 572-2131, Fax: (215) 881-8774, E-mail: torchia@beaver.edu, Internet: www.beaver.edu. Dir.: Richard Torchia
University Museum / Fine Arts Museum - 1853 43694

Beaver College Art Gallery → Arcadia University Art Gallery

Glenview IL

Glenview Area Historical Museum, 1121 Waukegan Rd, Glenview, IL 60025 - T: (847) 724-2235, Fax: (847) 724-2235. Cur.: James Milius
Local Museum - 1965
Local history, housed in original 1864 farm house - library 43695

Hartung's Auto and License Plate Museum, 3623 W Lake St, Glenview, IL 60025 - T: (847) 724-4354. C.E.O.: Lee Hartung
Science&Tech Museum - 1971
Automotive, over 150 antique cars, trucks, tractors and motorcycles 43696

Glenville NY

Empire State Aerosciences Museum, 250 Rudy Chase Dr, Glenville, NY 12302 - T: (518) 377-9121, Fax: (518) 377-1959, E-mail: esam@ensam.org, Internet: www.esam.org. Pres.: Rowland Whiteman
Science&Tech Museum - 1984
Aerosciences and airplane 43697

Glenwood IA

Mills County Museum, Glenwood Lake Park, Glenwood, IA 51534, mail addr: POB 255, Glenwood, IA 51534 - T: (712) 527-9221, 712-9533, E-mail: carriemerritt@hotmail.com. Pres.: Carrie Merrit
Local Museum - 1957
Machinery hall, dolls, guns, household furniture, glass and china, Indian artifacts 43698

Glenwood MN

Pope County Historical Museum, 809 S Lakeshore Dr, Glenwood, MN 56334-1115 - T: (320) 634-3293, Fax: (320) 634-3293, E-mail: pcmuseum@runestone.net. Dir.: Merlin Peterson
Fine Arts Museum / Historical Museum / Open Air Museum - 1931
Regional history, native American crafts 43699

Globe AZ

Gila County Historical Museum, 1330 N Broad St, Globe, AZ 85502 - T: (928) 425-7385. C.E.O.: Dr. Bill Haak
Local Museum / Archaeological Museum - 1972 43700

Gloucester MA

Beauport-Sleeper-McCann House, 75 Eastern Point Blvd, Gloucester, MA 01930, mail addr: 141 Cambridge St, Boston, MA 02114 - T: (978) 283-0800, (617) 227-3956, Fax: (617) 277-2904, E-mail: beauporthouse@spnea.org, Internet: www.spnea.org
Historical Museum - 1942
40-room summer cottage 43701

Cape Ann Historical Museum, 27 Pleasant St, Gloucester, MA 01930 - T: (978) 283-0455, Fax: (978) 283-4141, Internet: www.cape-ann.com/historical-museum. Dir.: Judith McCulloch, Pres.: Harold Bell
Historical Museum / Fine Arts Museum - 1873
Maritime history, art 43702

Hammond Castle Museum, 80 Hesperus Av, Gloucester, MA 01930 - T: (508) 283-7673, 283-2080, Fax: (508) 283-1643, Internet: www.hammondcastle.org. Cur.: John W. Pettibone
Historical Museum - 1930
Castle built in 1928 43703

The North Shore Arts Association, 197 E Main St at Pirate's Ln, Gloucester, MA 01930 - T: (978) 283-1857, Fax: (978) 282-9189, E-mail: arts@gis.net, Internet: www.northshoreartsassoc.net. Dir.: Trudy J. Allen, Pres.: Anne Krapish
Association with Coll - 1922
Art gallery 43704

Sargent House Museum, 49 Middle St, Gloucester, MA 01930 - T: (978) 281-2432, Fax: (978) 281-2432, E-mail: sargenthouse@cove.com, Internet: sargenthouse.org. Dir.: Martha Oaks
Fine Arts Museum / Decorative Arts Museum - 1919
Furniture, decorative and fine arts, coll of works by John Singer Sargent 43705

Glover VT

Bread & Puppet Museum, 753 Heights Rd, Rte 122, Glover, VT 05839 - T: (802) 525-3031, 525-6972, Fax: (802) 525-3618. Dir.: Peter Schumann
Decorative Arts Museum - 1975
Puppets 43706

Gnadenhutten OH

Gnadenhutten Historical Park and Museum, 352 S Cherry St, Gnadenhutten, OH 44629 - T: (740) 254-4143, Fax: (740) 254-4992, E-mail: gnadmuse@tusc.net, Internet: www.tusco.net/gnaden. C.E.O.: Jack J. McKeown
Local Museum - 1963 43707

Goehner NE

Seward County Historical Society Museum, I-80 Exit 373, Goehner, NE - T: (402) 643-4935, 523-4055, E-mail: drouss//@connect.ccsn.edu. Pres.: Larry Hansen
Local Museum / Agriculture Museum - 1978
Local history, agriculture 43708

Goessel KS

Mennonite Heritage Museum, 200 N Poplar St, Goessel, KS 67053 - T: (316) 367-8200, E-mail: mhmuseum@futureks.net. Pres.: Dwight Schmidt, Dir./Cur.: Kristine Schmucker
Historical Museum - 1974
History 43709

Gold Beach OR

Curry Historical Society Museum, 29419 Ellensburg Av, Gold Beach, OR 97444 - T: (541) 247-6113, E-mail: hissoc@gb.wave.net, Internet: curryhistory.com
Local Museum - 1974
Local hist, animal life, local beach ecosystem, Rogue River Indian artifacts 43710

Golden CO

Astor House Hotel Museum, 822 12th St, Golden, CO 80401 - T: (303) 278-3557, Fax: (303) 278-8916, E-mail: info@astorhousemuseum.org, Internet: www.astorhousemuseum.org. C.E.O.: Cindy Nasky, Cur.: Angela Rayne, Kristen Mortimer
Historical Museum - 1972 43711

Buffalo Bill Memorial Museum, 987.5 Lookout Mountain Rd, Golden, CO 80401 - T: (303) 526-0747, Fax: (303) 526-0197, Internet: www.buffalobill.org. Dir.: Steve Friesen, Cur.: Steve Friesen, Carey Southwell (Collection)
Historical Museum - 1921
Founded by Johnny Baker, a close friend of Buffalo Bill and an important member of Buffalo Bill's Wild West Show 43712

Colorado Railroad Museum, 17155 W 44th Av, Golden, CO 80403 - T: (303) 279-4591, Fax: (303) 279-4229, E-mail: mail@crrm.org, Internet: www.crrm.org. Dir.: William Gould
Science&Tech Museum - 1958
Rolling stock of Colorado railroads, interior 43713

Colorado School of Mines Geology Museum, 16th and Maple, Golden, CO 80401-1887 - T: (303) 273-3823, 273-3815, Fax: (303) 273-3859, E-mail: pbartos@mines.edu, Internet: magma.mines.edu/academics/geology/museum. Cur.: Paul I. Bartos
University Museum / Natural History Museum - 1874
Geology, mineralogy 43714

Rocky Mountain Quilt Museum, 1111 Washington Av, Golden, CO 80401 - T: (303) 277-0377, Fax: (303) 215-1636, E-mail: rmqm@att.net, Internet: www.rmqm.org. Dir.: Janet Finley
Folklore Museum / Special Museum - 1982
Quilts, fabric and quilt-related items 43715

Goldendale WA

Klickitat County Historical Society Museum, 127 W Broadway, Goldendale, WA 98620 - T: (509) 773-4303. C.E.O.: Bonny Beeks
Local Museum - 1958
Local hist 43716

Maryhill Museum of Art, 35 Maryhill Museum Dr, Goldendale, WA 98620 - T: (509) 773-3733, Fax: (509) 773-6138, E-mail: maryhill@maryhillmuseum.org, Internet: www.maryhillmuseum.org. Dir.: Colleen Schafroth, Cur.: Betty Long, Lee Musgrave
Fine Arts Museum - 1923
Art 43717

Goldsboro NC

Arts Council of Wayne County, 901 E Ash St, Goldsboro, NC 27530 - T: (919) 736-3300, Fax: (919) 736-3335, E-mail: arts@esn.net, Internet: www.esn.net/arts. Dir.: Alice Strickland
Fine Arts Museum - 1964 43718

Community Arts Council Museum → Arts Council of Wayne County

Goleta CA

Air Heritage Museum of Santa Barbara/Goleta, 601 Firestone Rd, Goleta, CA 93117 - T: (805) 683-8936. Pres.: H. Ben Walsh
Military Museum / Science&Tech Museum - 1989
Military hist, aviation 43719

South Coast Railroad Museum at Goleta Depot, 300 N Los Carneros Rd, Goleta, CA 93117 - T: (805) 964-3540, Fax: (805) 964-3549, E-mail: director@goletadepot.org, Internet: www.goletadepot.org. Dir.: Gary B. Coombs, Asst. Dir.: Phyllis J. Olsen
Science&Tech Museum - 1983
Southern Pacific railroad depot 43720

Stow House, Museum of Goleta Valley History, 304 N Los Carneros Rd, Goleta, CA 93117 - T: (805) 964-4407, Fax: (805) 681-7217, E-mail: staff@goletahistory.org, Internet: www.goletahistory.org
Historical Museum / Local Museum - 1967 43721

Goliad TX

Goliad State Historical Park, 108 Park Rd, Goliad, TX 77963 - T: (361) 645-3405, Fax: (361) 645-8538, E-mail: james.hudnall@tpwd.state.tx.us, Internet: www.tpwd.state.tx.us. Dir.: Andrew Sansom, Cur.: Luis Cazarez-Rueda
Local Museum / Folklore Museum - 1931
Local hist 43722

Presidio La Bahia, Refugio Hwy, 1 mile south of Goliad on Hwy 183, Goliad, TX 77963 - T: (512) 645-3752, Fax: (512) 645-1706, Internet: www.nazarethtoday.com/mhs. Dir.: Newton M. Warzecha
Military Museum / Historic Site / Archaeological Museum - 1966
Military hist 43723

Gonzales TX

Gonzales Memorial Museum, E Saint Lawrence St, Gonzales, TX 78629 - T: (210) 672-6350. Cur.: Mary Bea Arnold
Local Museum - 1936
Local hist 43724

Goochland VA

Goochland County Museum, POB 602, Goochland, VA 23063 - T: (804) 556-3966, Fax: (804) 556-4617. Cur.: Kathleen Cabell
Library with Exhibitions - 1968
Land grant parents (1700's) 43725

Goochland County Museum, 2875 River Rd West, Goochland, VA 23063 - T: (804) 556-3966, Fax: (804) 556-4617, E-mail: gchsadmin@earthlink.net, Internet: www.goochlandh.story.org
Local Museum - 1968
Folklore, archaeology, maps, medical instruments 43726

Goodland KS

High Plains Museum, 1717 Cherry, Goodland, KS 67735 - T: (913) 899-4595. Dir.: Linda Holton
Historical Museum - 1959
History 43727

Goodwell OK

No Man's Land Historical Museum, 207 W Sewell St, Goodwell, OK 73939 - T: (580) 349-6697, Fax: (580) 349-2670, E-mail: nmlhs@ptsi.net. Dir.: Dr. Kenneth R. Turner, Pres.: Gerald Dixon
Historical Museum - 1932 43728

Gordonsville VA

Exchange Hotel Civil War Museum, 400 S Main St, Gordonsville, VA 22942 - T: (540) 832-2944, E-mail: sturkhntr@aol.com, Internet: www.hgiexchange.org. Pres.: Andy Daniel
Historical Museum / Military Museum - 1971
Civil war, railroad hotel used as a Confederate receiving hospital 43729

Gorham ME

Baxter House Museum, 71 South St, Gorham, ME 04038 - T: (207) 839-5031, Fax: (207) 839-7749. Pres.: Linda M. Frinsko
Local Museum - 1908 43730

USM Art Gallery, Campus, 37 College Av, Gorham, ME 04038 - T: (207) 780-5008, Fax: (207) 780-5759, E-mail: cexler@usm.maine.edu, Internet: www.usm.maine.edu/~gallery. C.E.O.: Carolyn Eyler
Fine Arts Museum / University Museum - 1965
Art 43731

Goshen CT

Goshen Historical Society Museum, 21 Old Middle Rd, Goshen, CT 06756 - T: (860) 491-9610. Pres.: Margaret K. Wood, Cur.: Henrietta Horray
Historical Museum - 1955 43732

Goshen NY

Harness Racing Museum and Hall of Fame, 240 Main St, Goshen, NY 10924 - T: (845) 294-6330, Fax: (845) 294-3463, E-mail: hrm@frontiernet.net, Internet: www.harnessmuseum.com. Dir.: Gail C. Cunard
Special Museum - 1951 43733

Gothenburg NE

Sod House Museum, I-80 and Hwy 47, Gothenburg, NE 69138 - T: (308) 537-2680, E-mail: sodlady2001@hotmail.com. Dir.: Merle Block
Local Museum - 1988
Local hist 43734

Gouverneur NY

Gouverneur Historical Association Museum, 30 Church St, Gouverneur, NY 13642 - T: (315) 287-0570. Pres./Cur.: Joseph Laurenza, Cur.: Jean Tyler (Acquisitions)
Historical Museum - 1974
History 43735

Grafton MA

Willard House and Clock Museum, 11 Willard St, Grafton, MA 01536 - T: (508) 839-3500, Fax: (508) 839-3599, E-mail: info@willardhouse.org, Internet: www.willardhouse.org. Dir.: Dr. Roger W. Robinson, Cur.: John R. Stephens
Science&Tech Museum - 1971
Horology 43736

Grafton VT

Grafton Museum, 147 Main St, Grafton, VT 05146 - T: (802) 843-2489, 843-1010. Cur.: Elisha Prouty
Local Museum - 1962
Local hist 43737

Grafton Museum of Natural History → Nature Museum at Grafton

Nature Museum at Grafton, 186 Townshend Rd, Grafton, VT 05146 - T: (802) 843-2111, Fax: (802) 843-1164, E-mail: info@nature-museum.org, Internet: www.nature-museum.org. Cur.: Donald Clark
Natural History Museum - 1987
Natural hist 43738

Granby CT

Salmon Brook Historical Society Museum, 208 Salmon Brook St, Granby, CT 06035 - T: (860) 653-9713, Internet: www.salmonbrookhistorical.org. Cur.: Christine Hanauer
Local Museum - 1959 43739

Grand Canyon AZ

Grand Canyon National Park Museum Collection, Albright Maintenance Area, South Rim, Grand Canyon, AZ 86023, mail addr: POB 129, Grand Canyon, AZ 86023 - T: (928) 638-7769, Fax: (928) 638-7797, E-mail: grca_museum_collection@nps.gov, Internet: www.nps.gov/grca/photos/museum.htm. Dir.: Joseph Alston
Natural History Museum - 1919
Deep gorge of the Colorado River, 277 mi long, 1-18 mi wide, 1 mi deep 43740

Grand Forks ND

Grand Forks County Historical Society Museum, 2405 Belmont Rd, Grand Forks, ND 58201 - T: (701) 775-2216, E-mail: gfchs@infi.net, Internet: www.home.infi.net/~gfchs. Pres.: Suellen Bateman, Dir.: Leah Byzewski
Historical Museum - 1970 43741

Hughes Fine Arts Center, c/o Univerisity of North Dakota, Dept of Visual Arts, Rm 127, Grand Forks, ND 58202-7099 - T: (701) 777-2257
University Museum / Fine Arts Museum - 1979
Prints, drawings 43742

North Dakota Museum of Art, Centennial Dr, Grand Forks, ND 58202 - T: (701) 777-4195, Fax: (701) 777-4425, E-mail: ndmuseum@infi.net, Internet: www.ndmoa.com. Dir.: Laurel J. Reuter, Asst. Dir.: Brian Lofthus, Dept. Dir.: Bonnie Sobolik (Development), Greg Vettel (Exhibitions, Collections)
Fine Arts Museum - 1970 43743

University of North Dakota Zoology Museum, Dept of Biology, University of North Dakota, Grand Forks, ND 58202 - T: (701) 777-2621, Fax: (701) 777-2623, Internet: www.und.edu/dept/biology/undergrad/bio_undergrad.html. Cur.: Dr. Richard Crawford (Vertebrates), Rick Sweitzer (Vertebrates), Dr. Jefferson Vaughan (Invertebrates)
University Museum / Natural History Museum - 1883 43744

Grand Haven MI

Tri-Cities Museum, 1 N Harbor, Grand Haven, MI 49417 - T: (616) 842-0700, Fax: (616) 842-3698, E-mail: tcmuseum@grandhaven.com, Internet: www.grandhaven.com/museum. Dir.: Dennis W. Swartout
Local Museum - 1962
Regional history 43745

Grand Island NE

Stuhr Museum of the Prairie Pioneer, 3133 W Hwy 34, Grand Island, NE 68801 - T: (308) 385-5316, Fax: (308) 385-5028, Internet: www.stuhrmuseum.org. C.E.O.: Susan Gallagher, Asst. Dir.: Warren D. Rodgers (Education), John Adamik, Cur.: Joe Black, Deb Arenz
Local Museum - 1961 43746

Grand Junction CO

Doozoo Children's Museum, 421 Colorado Av, Grand Junction, CO 81501 - T: (970) 241-5225, 241-0971, Fax: (970) 241-8510. Dir.: Valerie Johns
Special Museum - 1984 43747

Museum of Western Colorado, 462 Ute Av, Grand Junction, CO 81502-5020 - T: (970) 242-0971, Fax: (970) 242-3960, E-mail: info@wcmuseum.org, Internet: www.wcmuseum.org. Dir.: Richard S. Helm, Cur.: David Bailey
Local Museum - 1966
Cultural and natural history, paleontology, farming 43748

Western Colorado Center for the Arts, 1803 N Seventh, Grand Junction, CO 81501 - T: (970) 243-7337, Fax: (970) 243-2482, E-mail: arts@gjct.net, Internet: www.gjartcenter.org. Dir.: Dan W. Patten
Fine Arts Museum / Decorative Arts Museum - 1953
Arts, crafts 43749

Grand Lake CO

Grand Lake Area Historical Museum, Kauffman House, Lake Av at Pitkin St, Grand Lake, CO 80447-0656 - T: (970) 627-9277, 887-1210, Fax: (970) 887-0163
Local Museum - 1973
Regional history 43750

Grand Marais MN

Cook County Historical Museum, 5 S Broadway, Grand Marais, MN 55604 - T: (218) 387-2883, E-mail: cchristsoc@boreal.org. Dir.: Pat Zankman
Local Museum - 1966
Regional history 43751

Grand Portage, 315 S Broadway, Grand Marais, MN 55604 - T: (218) 387-2788, Fax: (218) 387-2790, E-mail: grpo_admin_clerk@nps.gov, Internet: www.nps.gov/grpo. Head: Tim Cochrane
Historical Museum - 1958
18thc reconstructed NW Co. fur trading depot 43752

Johnson Heritage Post, 115 W Wisconsin St, Grand Marais, MN 55604 - T: (218) 387-2314, E-mail: cchristsoc@boreal.org. Dir.: D. Anderson
Fine Arts Museum - 1966
Art gallery 43753

Grand Rapids MI

Center Art Gallery, c/o Calvin College, 3201 Burton St SE, Grand Rapids, MI 49546 - T: (616) 957-66271, Fax: (616) 957-8551, E-mail: bullock@calvin.edu, Internet: www.calvin.edu/academic/art/gallery. Dir.: Charles Young
Fine Arts Museum / University Museum - 1974
Drawings, prints, sculpture, textiles, ceramics 43754

Gerald R. Ford Library Museum, 303 Pearl St NW, Grand Rapids, MI 49504 - T: (616) 451-9263 ext 21, Fax: (616) 451-9570, E-mail: ford.museum@nara.gov, Internet: www.ford.utexas.edu. Dir.: Dennis Daellenbach, Cur.: James R. Kratsas
Library with Exhibitions / Historical Museum - 1980
Presidential library 43755

Grand Rapids Art Museum, 155 Division N, Grand Rapids, MI 49503 - T: (616) 831-1000, 831-2929, Fax: (616) 559-0422, E-mail: pr@gr-artmuseum.org, Internet: www.gramonline.org. Dir.: Celeste M. Adams, Cur.: Richard Avsom (Prints, Drawings), Asst. Cur.: Jennifer Nienur, Registrar: Katleen Ferres
Fine Arts Museum - 1910
Art 43756

Grand Rapids Children's Museum, 11 Sheldon Av, Grand Rapids, MI 49503 - T: (616) 235-4726, Fax: (616) 235-4728, E-mail: akinsman@grcm.org, Internet: www.grcm.org. Dir.: Teresa L. Thome
Special Museum - 1992 43757

Kendall Gallery, 17 Fountain St NW, Grand Rapids, MI 49503 - T: (800) 676-2787 ext 138, Fax: (616) 451-9867, E-mail: josephs@ferris.edu, Internet: www.kcad.edu. Dir.: Sarah Joseph
Public Gallery 43758

Public Museum of Grand Rapids, 272 Pearl St NW, Grand Rapids, MI 49504-5371 - T: (616) 456-3977, Fax: (616) 456-3873, E-mail: staff@grmuseum.org, Internet: www.grmuseum.org. Dir.: Timothy J. Chester, Asst. Dir.: Kay A. Zuris, Cur.: Mannie Gentile (Education), David L. DeBruyn (Astronomy), Christian G. Carron (Collections), Veronica Kandl (History), Eric Alexander (Natural History, Ethnology), Tom Bantle (Exhibits)
Local Museum - 1854
Local history, ethnology, natural history, astronomy 43759

Urban Institute for Contemporary Arts, 41 Sheldon Blvd SE, Grand Rapids, MI 49503 - T: (616) 454-7000, Fax: (616) 454-9395, E-mail: info@uica.org, Internet: www.uica.org. Dir.: Gail Philbin, Pres.: Tom Clinton, Sc. Staff: Linda Potter (Film), Jennifer Steensma (Visual Arts), Shannon McMaster (Literature), Carolyn Heines (Music), Dawn Mcllhargey-Wigert (Dance), Bob Hubbard (Performace and visual arts)
Fine Arts Museum - 1977 43760

Grand Rapids MN

Forest History Center, 2609 County Rd 76, Grand Rapids, MN 55744 - T: (218) 327-4482, Fax: (218) 327-4483, E-mail: foresthistory@mnhs.org, Internet: www.mnhs.org
Natural History Museum - 1978
Natural hist 43761

Itasca Heritage Center Museum, 10-5th St NW, Grand Rapids, MN 55744-0664 - T: (218) 326-6431, Fax: (218) 326-7083, E-mail: ichs@paulbunyan.net, Internet: www.itascahistorical.org. Pres.: Art Toms
Local Museum - 1948
Local history 43762

Grandview MO

Harry's Truman Farm Home, 12301 Blue Ridge Blvd, Grandview, MO 64030 - T: (816) 254-2720, Fax: (816) 254-4491, E-mail: james_sanders@nps.gov, Internet: www.nps.gov/hstr/
Agriculture Museum / Historical Museum - 1994
Life of Harry S. Truman, local agriculture and rural life 43763

Grandview WA

Ray E. Powell Museum, 313 S Division, Grandview, WA 98930 - T: (509) 882-2070. Chm.: Jack Norting
Local Museum - 1969
Local hist 43764

Granite Falls MN

Yellow Medicine County Historical Museum, Hwy 67 and 23, Granite Falls, MN 56241, mail addr: POB 145, Granite Falls, MN 56241 - T: (320) 564-4479, Fax: (320) 564-4146, E-mail: ymchs@kilowatt.net, Internet: www.kilowatt.net/ymchs/
Local Museum - 1952
Geology, archaeology, pioneer artifacts 43765

Grant NE

Perkins County Historical Society Museum, Central Av, Grant, NE 69140 - T: (308) 352-4019. Pres./Chm.: Delores Swan
Local Museum - 1964 43766

Grants Pass OR

Grants Pass Museum of Art, 229 SW G St, Grants Pass, OR 97526 - T: (541) 479-3290, Fax: (541) 479-0508, E-mail: museum@grantspass.net, Internet: www.gpmuseum.org. Dir.: Don Brown
Fine Arts Museum / Folklore Museum / Public Gallery - 1979 43767

Schmidt House Museum, 508 SW 5th St, Grants Pass, OR 97526 - T: (541) 479-7827, Fax: (541) 472-8928, E-mail: jchs@terragon.com, Internet: www.webtrail.com/jchs. C.E.O.: Rose Scott
Decorative Arts Museum - 1960
Furniture, toys, clothes, photos 43768

Wiseman and Fire House Galleries, Rogue Community College, 3345 Redwood Hwy, Grants Pass, OR 97527 - T: (541) 956-7339, Fax: (541) 471-3588, E-mail: tdrake@rogue.cc.or.us, Internet: www.rogue.cc.or.us/. Dir.: Tommi Drake
Fine Arts Museum / University Museum - 1988
Art 43769

Granville NY

Pember Museum of Natural History, 33 W Main St, Granville, NY 12832 - T: (518) 642-1515, Fax: (518) 642-3097, E-mail: pember@adelphia.net, Internet: www.pembermuseum.com. Dir.: Patricia E. Bailey, Pres.: Dan Wilson
Natural History Museum - 1909 43770

Slate Valley Museum, 17 Water St, Granville, NY 12832 - T: (518) 642-1417, Fax: (518) 642-1417, E-mail: mail@slatevalleymuseum.org, Internet: www.slatevalleymuseum.org. Dir.: Mary Lou Willits
Science&Tech Museum / Local Museum - 1994
Slate quarrying and slate industry, geological specimens, prints, paintings 43771

Granville OH

Denison University Art Gallery, Burke Hall, Granville, OH 43023 - T: (740) 587-6255, Fax: (740) 587-5701, E-mail: vanderheijde@cc.denison.edu, Internet: www.denison.edu/art/artgallery. Dir.: Merijn Van Der Heijden
Fine Arts Museum / University Museum - 1946 43772

Granville Historical Museum, 115 E Broadway, Granville, OH 43023 - T: (740) 587-3951, E-mail: granvillehistorical@juno.com. Pres.: Maggie Brooks, Cur.: Cynthia Cort
Historical Museum - 1885 43773

Robbins Hunter Museum, Avery-Downer House, 221 E Broadway, Granville, OH 43023 - T: (740) 587-0430, Fax: (740) 587-0430. Pres.: David Neel
Historical Museum - 1981 43774

Grass Lake MI

Waterloo Area Farm Museum, 9998 Waterloo-Munith Rd, Grass Lake, MI 49240 - T: (734) 426-9135, E-mail: diannemoulton@webtv.net, Internet: scs.k12_mi.us/~waterloo
Agriculture Museum - 1962 43775

Grass Valley CA

North Star Mining Museum, Allison Ranch Rd, Grass Valley, CA 95959 - T: (916) 273-4255. Dir.: Glenn Jones
Science&Tech Museum
World largest Pelton wheel, models, machinery, tools 43776

Video Museum and Theater, Central Av, Memorial Park, Grass Valley, CA 95959 - T: (916) 274-1126. Dir.: Ron Sturgell
Science&Tech Museum 43777

Great Barrington MA

Doreen Young Art Gallery, c/o Simon's Rock College of Bard, 84 Alford Rd, Great Barrington, MA 01230 - T: (413) 528-7420, Fax: (413) 528-7365, E-mail: wjackson@simons-rock.edu, Internet: www.simons-rock.edu
Fine Arts Museum - 1964
Drawing, paintings, graphics, sculpture and crafts 43778

Great Bend KS

Barton County Historical Society Village and Museum, 85 S Hwy 281, Great Bend, KS 67530 - T: (316) 793-5125, Fax: (316) 793-5125, Internet: www.greatbend.net/gbcc/tourism/bchs. Chm.: Beverly Komarek
Local Museum / Open Air Museum - 1963
Historic Village 43779

Great Falls MT

C.M. Russell Museum, 400 13 St N, Great Falls, MT 59401 - T: (406) 727-8787, Fax: (406) 727-2402, Internet: www.cmrussell.org. Dir.: Barbara Moe, Cur.: Elizabeth Dear
Fine Arts Museum - 1953
Latin American, Mexican and American Indian art, decorative arts, archaeology, ethnology, folk art 43780

High Plains Heritage Center, 422 2nd St S, Great Falls, MT 59405 - T: (406) 452-3462, Fax: (406) 761-3805, E-mail: hphc@highplainsheritage.org, Internet: www.highplainsheritage.org. Dir.: Cindy Kittredge, Cur.: Michelle Reid
Local Museum - 1976
archive 43781

Paris Gibson Square Museum of Art, 1400 First Av N, Great Falls, MT 59401 - T: (406) 727-8255, Fax: (406) 727-8256, E-mail: pgsmoa@mcn.net. Pres.: Bennett Carter, Exec. Dir.: Bonnie Laing-Malcolmson, Cur.: Jessica Hunter (Art), Susan Thomas (Education)
Fine Arts Museum - 1976
American art, folk art, decorative art 43782

Greeley CO

Centennial Village Museum, 1475 A St, Greeley, CO 80631 - T: (970) 350-9224, Fax: (970) 350-9570, E-mail: museums@ci.greeley.co.us, Internet: www.greeleymuseums.com. Dir.: Jil Rosentrater
Open Air Museum / Historical Museum - 1976
28 historic structures illustrating the hist of Colorado 43783

Historic Centennial Village → Centennial Village Museum

John Mariani Art Gallery, c/o University of Northern Colorado, Eighth Av and 18 St, Greeley, CO 80639 - T: (970) 351-2184, Fax: (970) 351-2299. Dir.: Patricia Reublin, Ass. Dir.: Rebecca Telltingsrude
Fine Arts Museum / University Museum - 1972 43784

Meeker Home Museum, 1324 9th Av, Greeley, CO 80631 - T: (970) 350-9220, Fax: (970) 350-9570, E-mail: museums@ci.greeley.co.us, Internet: www.greeleymuseums.com. Dir.: Chris Dill, Head: Nina Johnson, Cur.: Peggy A. Ford (Education), Jim Rakke (Collections)
Historical Museum - 1929
Home of Nathan Cook Meeker, founder of Greeley 43785

Plumb Farm Museum, 955 39th Av, Greeley, CO 80634 - T: (970) 350-9220, Fax: (970) 350-9570, E-mail: museum@ci.greeley.co.us, Internet: www.greeleymuseums.com. Dir.: Chris Dill
Agriculture Museum - 1997
Farming history 43786

Green Bay WI

The Children's Museum of Green Bay, Port Plaza Mall, 320 N Adams St, Green Bay, WI 54301 - T: (920) 432-4397, Fax: (920) 432-4566, E-mail: gbcmuseum@yahoo.com, Internet: www.cmuseumgb.org. C.E.O.: Bobbie Schuette
Special Museum - 1989 43787

Great Expectations → The Children's Museum of Green Bay

Green Bay Packer Hall of Fame, 855 Lombardi Av, Green Bay, WI 54307 - T: (920) 499-4281, Fax: (920) 405-5564, Internet: www.packerhalloffame.com. Pres.: Mike Gage, Dir.: Kelly Schiltz
Special Museum - 1969
Sports 43788

Heritage Hill State Park, 2640 S Webster Av, Green Bay, WI 54301 - T: (920) 448-5150 ext 10, Fax: (920) 448-5127, Internet: www.heritagehillgb.org. Dir.: Doug Browns, Cur.: Randy Klemm (Collections), Jack Moga
Local Museum - 1976
Local hist 43789

Lawton Gallery, University of Wisconsin-Green Bay, 2420 Nicolet Dr, Green Bay, WI 54311-7001 - T: (920) 465-2916, Fax: (920) 465-2890, E-mail: perkinss@uwgb.edu, Internet: www.uwgb.edu. Cur.: Stephen Perkins
Public Gallery 43790

National Railroad Museum, 2285 S Broadway, Green Bay, WI 54304-4832 - T: (920) 437-7623, Fax: (920) 437-1291, E-mail: staff@nationalrrmuseum.org, Internet: www.nationalrrmuseum.org. Dir.: Julie Lopas
Science&Tech Museum - 1957
Railroad 43791

Neville Public Museum of Brown County, 210 Museum Pl, Green Bay, WI 54303 - T: (920) 448-4460 ext 0, Fax: (920) 448-4458, E-mail: bc_museum@co.brown.wi.us, Internet: www.nevillepublicmuseum.org. Dir.: Eugene Umberger, Cur.: John Moga (Art), Michael Talzrow (History), Matt Welter (Education), John Jacobs (Science), Louise Pfotenhauer (Collections)
Local Museum - 1915
Local hist 43792

Green Lane PA

Goschenhoppen Folklife Museum, Rte 29, Red Men's Hall, Green Lane, PA 18054-0476 - T: (610) 367-8286, E-mail: redmens_hall@goschenhoppen.org, Internet: www.goschenhoppen.org. C.E.O.: George Spotts
Ethnology Museum / Folklore Museum / Historical Museum - 1965
Folk art and love, local history 43793

Green River WY

Sweetwater County Historical Museum, 80 W Flaming Gorge Way, Green River, WY 82935 - T: (307) 872-6435, Fax: (307) 872-6469, E-mail: swchm@sweetwater.net, Internet: www.sweetwatermuseum.org. Dir.: Ruth Lauritzen
Local Museum - 1967
Local hist 43794

Green Valley AZ

Titan Missile Museum, Duval Mine Rd, Green Valley, AZ 85614 - T: (520) 625-7736, Fax: (520) 625-9845
Science&Tech Museum - 1986
Intercontinental ballistic missiles, Titan II 43795

Greenbelt MD

Greenbelt Museum, 15 Crescent Rd, Greenbelt, MD 20770 - T: (301) 474-1936, 507-6582, Fax: (301) 441-8248, E-mail: greenbeltmuseum@ci.greenbelt.md.us, Internet: ci.greenbelt.md.us. Cur.: Katie Scott-Childress
Historical Museum - 1987
Local history, culture of the 1930s, planned communities 43796

Greenbush WI

Wade House and Wesley Jung Carriage Museum, W 7747 Plank Rd, Greenbush, WI 53026 - T: (920) 526-3271, Fax: (920) 526-3626, E-mail: wadehous@danet.net, Internet: wadehouse.shsw.wisc.edu. Dir.: Jeffrey Schultz, Cur.: Mark Knipping, Jeffrey Murray
Science&Tech Museum - 1953
Transportation 43797

Greencastle IN

DePauw University Anthropology Museum, Harrison Hall, Rm 206, Greencastle, IN 46135 - T: (765) 658-4800, Fax: (765) 658-4177. Cur.: Danielle Brain
University Museum / Ethnology Museum - 1984 43798

DePauw University Art Center, 10 W Hauna St, Greencastle, IN 46135 - T: (765) 658-4336, Fax: (765) 658-6552. Cur.: Kaytie Johnson
Fine Arts Museum - 1984 43799

Greencastle PA

Allison-Antrim Museum, 365 S Ridge Av, Greencastle, PA 17225-1157 - T: (717) 597-9325, E-mail: aamuseum@greencastlemuseum.org, Internet: www.greencastlemuseum.org
Historical Museum - 1995
20th-c paintings, historic artifacts, Henry P Fletcher US diplomat 43800

Greeneville TN

Andrew Johnson National Historic Site, 101 N College St, Greeneville, TN 37743 - T: (423) 638-3551, 639-3711, Fax: (423) 638-9194, 798-0754, E-mail: jim_small@nps.gov, Internet: www.nps.gov/anjo/. Dir.: Jim Small, Cur.: Elaine R. Clark, Superint.: Mark Corey

Historical Museum - 1942
Memorabilia of Andrew Johnson (US-President), history, civil war, furnishings - Tailor Shop Museum 43801

Doak House Museum, Tusculum College, Greeneville, TN 37743 - T: (423) 636-8554, 636-7348, Fax: (423) 638-7166, E-mail: clucas@tusculum.edu, Internet: www.tusculum.edu/museum/doak.html. Dir.: E. Alvin Gerhardt, Assoc. Dir. & Cur.: Cynthia L. Lucas
University Museum / Historical Museum
History 43802

President Andrew Johnson Museum, Tusculum College, Greeneville, TN 37743 - T: (423) 636-7348, Fax: (423) 638-7166, E-mail: gcollins@tusculum.edu, Internet: www.tusculum.edu/museum/johnson.html. Dir.: George Collins, Assoc. Dir. & Cur.: Cynthia L. Lucas
University Museum / Historical Museum - 1993
History 43803

Greenfield IA

Iowa Aviation Museum, 2251 Airport Rd, Greenfield, IA 50849 - T: (641) 343-7184, E-mail: aviation@mddc.com, Internet: www.flyingmuseum.com. Dir.: Lee Ann Nelson, Pres.: Ron Havens
Science&Tech Museum - 1990
Aviation 43804

Greenfield IN

James Whitcomb Riley Birthplace and Museum, Riley Home, 250 W Main St, Greenfield, IN 46140 - T: (317) 462-8539, Fax: (317) 462-8556, E-mail: parks_rec@greenfieldin.org, Internet: www.hccn.org/parks/rileyhouse.htm. Cur.: Clark Ketchum
Historical Museum - 1937 43805

Old Log Jail and Chapel Museums, Rte 40 and Apple St, Greenfield, IN 46140, mail addr: POB 375, Greenfield, IN 46140 - T: (317) 462-7780, 787-5474. Dir.: Greg Roland
Ethnology Museum - 1966
Indian arrowhead coll, coverlets, pictures, agriculture 43806

Greenfield MA

Greenfield Museum, Corner of Church & Union St, Greenfield, MA 01301 - T: (413) 774-3663. Pres.: Joan Vander, Cur.: Tim Blagg
Local Museum - 1907
Local history - library 43807

Greenfield WI

Greenfield Historical Society Museum, 57th and Layton Av, Greenfield, WI 53220 - T: (262) 679-5016, Internet: www.greenfieldlibrary.org/greenfield_history.htm. Cur.: Carol Pingel
Local Museum - 1965 43808

Greenport NY

East and Seaport Museum, 3rd St at Ferry Dock, Greenport, NY 11944 - T: (631) 477-2100, Fax: (631) 477-3422, E-mail: eseaport@aol.com, Internet: www.eastendseaport.org
Science&Tech Museum - 1990
Shipbuilding in Greenport during WW 2, tools, models, lighthouse 43809

Greensboro AL

Magnolia Grove-Historic House Museum, 1002 Hobson St, Greensboro, AL 36744 - T: (334) 624-8618, Fax: (334) 624-8618, E-mail: maggrove@westal.net. Dir.: Eleanor W. Cunningham
Historical Museum - 1943
Birthplace of Rear Admiral Richmond Pearson Hobson 43810

Greensboro NC

Green Hill Center for North Carolina Art, 200 N Davie St, Greensboro, NC 27401 - T: (336) 333-7460, Fax: (336) 333-2612, E-mail: info@greenhillcenter.org, Internet: www.greenhillcenter.org. Dir.: Jennifer Moore
Fine Arts Museum - 1974 43811

Greensboro Artists' League Gallery, 200 N Davie St, Greensboro, NC 27401 - T: (336) 333-7485, Fax: (336) 373-7553, E-mail: gal@vacgreensboro.org, Internet: www.people-places.com/gal. Dir.: Susan Andrews, Cur.: Corrie Lisk-Hurst
Fine Arts Museum - 1956 43812

Greensboro Historical Museum, 130 Summit Av, Greensboro, NC 27401-3016 - T: (336) 373-2043, Fax: (336) 373-2204, E-mail: linda.evans@ci.greensboro.nc.us, Internet: www.greensborohistory.org. Dir.: William J. Moore, Asst. Dir.: Gayle H. Fripp, Cur.: Donald C. Henderson, Susan Webster
Historical Museum - 1924 43813

Guilford College Art Gallery, 5800 W Friendly Av, Greensboro, NC 27410 - T: (336) 316-2438, Fax: (336) 316-2950, E-mail: thammond@guilford.edu, Internet: www.guilford.edu/artgallery. Dir.: Theresa N. Hammond
Fine Arts Museum - 1990
Art gallery 43814

Guilford Courthouse National Military Park, 2332 New Garden Rd, Greensboro, NC 27410-2355 - T: (336) 288-1776, Fax: (336) 282-2296, E-mail: guco_administration@nps.gov, Internet: www.nps.gov/guco
Military Museum - 1917 43815

Irene Cullis Gallery, c/o Greensboro College, 815 W Market St, Greensboro, NC 27401-1875 - T: (336) 272-7102 ext 301, Fax: (336) 271-6634, E-mail: bkowski@gborocollege.edu. Dir.: Robert Kowski
Fine Arts Museum / University Museum - 1838 43816

Mattye Reed African Heritage Center, N.C.A. & T. State University, Greensboro, NC 27411 - T: (336) 334-3209, Fax: (336) 334-4378, 334-7837, E-mail: ndegec@ncat.edu. Dir.: Conchita F. Ndege, Cur.: Vandorn Hinnant
Decorative Arts Museum / University Museum / Historical Museum / Folklore Museum - 1968 43817

Natural Science Center of Greensboro, 4301 Lawndale Dr, Greensboro, NC 27455 - T: (336) 288-3769, Fax: (336) 288-0545, E-mail: nscg@nr.infi.net, Internet: www.greensboro.com/sciencecenter. C.E.O.: Edward J. von der Lippe, Cur.: Richard G. Bolling, Patricia Day, Peggy V. Ferebee, Kenneth A. Schneidmiller, Roger D. Joyner, Richard A. Betton
Natural History Museum - 1957 43818

Weatherspoon Art Museum, University of North Carolina at Greensboro, Spring Garden and Tate St, Greensboro, NC 27402-6170 - T: (336) 334-5770, Fax: (336) 334-5907, E-mail: weatherspoon@uncg.edu, Internet: www.weatherspoon.uncg.edu. Dir.: Nancy Doll, Cur.: Ronald Platt, Pamela K. Hill
Fine Arts Museum / University Museum - 1942 43819

Greensburg KS

Big Well, 315 S Sycamore, Greensburg, KS 67054
Natural History Museum - 1937
World's largest Pallasite meteorite 43820

Greensburg PA

Westmoreland Museum of American Art, 221 N Main St, Greensburg, PA 15601-1898 - T: (724) 837-1500, Fax: (724) 837-2921, E-mail: info@wmuseumaa.org, Internet: www.wmuseumaa.org. Dir.: Judith H. O'Toole, Cur.: Barbara L. Jones
Fine Arts Museum - 1949 43821

Greentown IN

Greentown Glass Museum, 112 N Meridian, Greentown, IN 46936 - T: (317) 628-6206, Internet: www.easternk12.in.us/gpl/musmhist.htm. Head Cur.: Norma Jean David, Cur.: Annette LaRowe
Decorative Arts Museum - 1969
Glass 43822

Greenville IL

Bond County Museum → Hoiles-Davis Museum

Hoiles-Davis Museum, 318 W Winter St, Greenville, IL 62246 - T: (618) 664-1590, E-mail: duke36prod@hotmail.com
Local Museum - 1955
Local history 43823

Greenville MS

Old Firehouse Museum, 340 Main St, Greenville, MS 38701 - T: (662) 378-1538, Fax: (662) 378-1564, E-mail: ctyofgvl@tecinfo.com. C.E.O.: Paul C. Artman jr
Historical Museum - 1994
Firefighting equip 43824

Greenville NC

Greenville Museum of Art, 802 S Evans St, Greenville, NC 27834 - T: (252) 758-1946, Fax: (252) 758-1946, E-mail: art@greenvillenc.com, Internet: gma.greenvillenc.com. Dir.: C. Barbour Strickland, Asst. Dir.: Amber M. Young, Sc. Staff: Christopher Daniels
Fine Arts Museum - 1956 43825

Wellington B. Gray Gallery, c/o East Carolina University, Jenkins Fine Arts Center, Greenville, NC 27858-4353 - T: (252) 328-6336, Fax: (252) 328-6441, E-mail: adamsk@mail.ecu.edu, Internet: www.ecu.edu/art/home.html. Dir.: Gilbert Leebrick
Fine Arts Museum / University Museum - 1978 43826

Greenville OH

Garst Museum, 205 N Broadway, Greenville, OH 45331-2222 - T: (937) 548-5250, Fax: (937) 548-7645, Internet: www.garstmuseum.org. Dir.: Judy Logan
Historical Museum - 1903 43827

Greenville PA

Weyers-Sampson Art Gallery, c/o Thiel College, 75 College Av, Greenville, PA 16125 - T: (724) 589-2095, Fax: (724) 589-2021
Fine Arts Museum - 1971
Paintings, prints 43828

Greenville SC

Bob Jones University Museum and Gallery, 1700 Wade Hampton Blvd, Greenville, SC 29614 - T: (864) 242-5100 ext 1050, Fax: (864) 770-1306, E-mail: art_gallery@bju.edu, Internet: www.bju.edu/art_gallery. Dir.: Erin Jones, Cur.: John Nolen
Fine Arts Museum / Religious Arts Museum - 1951
Coll of old masters, icons, antiquities, furniture, tapestries 43829

Greenville County Museum of Art, 420 College St, Greenville, SC 29601 - T: (864) 271-7570, Fax: (864) 271-7579, E-mail: info@greenvillemuseum.org, Internet: www.greenvillemuseum.org. Dir.: Thomas W. Styron, Cur.: Martha R. Severens
Fine Arts Museum - 1963
18th & 19th century southern art 43830

Greenville TX

American Cotton Museum, 600 I-30 E, Greenville, TX 75401 - T: (903) 450-4502, 454-1990, Fax: (903) 454-1990, E-mail: staff@cottonmuseum.com, Internet: www.cottonmuseum.com. Dir.: Adrien Witkofsky
Historical Museum - 1987
Cotton tools and machinary, cotton production hist 43831

Greenwich CT

Historical Society Museum of the Town of Greenwich, 39 Strickland Rd, Greenwich, CT 06807 - T: (203) 869-6899, Fax: (203) 861-9720, E-mail: dmecky@hstg.org, Internet: www.hstg.org. C.E.O.: Debra Walker Mecky
Local Museum - 1931
Local history - archives 43832

Putnam Cottage, 243 E Putnam Av, Greenwich, CT 06830 - T: (203) 869-9697. Chm.: Eugene Fox
Historical Museum - 1900 43833

Greenwich NJ

Cumberland County Historical Society Museum, 960 YeGreate St, Greenwich, NJ 08323 - T: (856) 455-4055, Fax: (856) 455-8580, E-mail: lummis2@juno.com, Internet: www.co.cumberland.nj.us. Pres.: Sara C. Watson
Local Museum - 1908 43834

Greenwood MS

Cottonlandia Museum, 1608 Hwy 82 W, Greenwood, MS 38930 - T: (662) 453-0925, Fax: (662) 455-7556. Exec. Dir.: Robin Seage Person, Pres.: Carolyn Manning
Agriculture Museum / Archaeological Museum / Fine Arts Museum / Local Museum / Historical Museum - 1969 43835

Florewood State Park, Fort Loring Rd, Greenwood, MS 38930 - T: (662) 455-3821, Fax: (662) 453-2459, E-mail: florew@tecinfo.com, Internet: www.mdwfp.com. Dir.: Myra Castle
Local Museum - 1976
Furniture, household accessories, food preparations utensils, blacksmith and carpentry tools, farm implements, steam engines, mill, wagons 43836

Greenwood SC

Greenwood Museum → The Museum

The Museum, 106 Main St, Greenwood, SC 29646 - T: (864) 229-7093, Fax: (864) 229-9317, E-mail: themuseum@greenwood.net. Pres.: Ken Hartlage, Dir.: M. Lyda Carroll
Local Museum - 1968
Local hist 43837

Gresham OR

Gresham History Museum, 410 N Main Av, Gresham, OR 97030 - T: (503) 661-0347. Dir.: Pat Stone
Local Museum - 1976
Local history 43838

Greybull WY

Greybull Museum, 325 Greybull Av, Greybull, WY 82426 - T: (307) 765-2444. Dir.: Wanda L. Bond
Local Museum - 1967
Local hist 43839

Grinnell IA

Faulconer Gallery at Grinnell College, 1108 Park St, Grinnell, IA 50112 - T: (641) 269-4660, Fax: (641) 269-4626, E-mail: strongdj@grinnell.edu, Internet: www.grinnell.edu/faulconergallery. Dir.: Lesley Wright, Assoc. Dir.: Dan Strong, Cur.: Kay Wilson Jenkins
Fine Arts Museum / University Museum - 1998
Art 43840

Grinnell College Art Gallery, Grinnell, IA 50112 - T: (641) 269-3371, Fax: (641) 269-4283, E-mail: jenkins@grinnell.edu. Cur.: Kay Wilson
Fine Arts Museum - 1983
Works of art on paper 43841

Grinnell Historical Museum, 1125 Broad St, Grinnell, IA 50112 - T: (641) 236-3252. Chm.: Jeff Garland
Historical Museum - 1954
History 43842

Grosse Ile MI

Grosse Ile Historical Museum, East River and Grosse Ile Pkwy, Grosse Ile, MI 48138 - T: (734) 675-1250. Pres.: Mark McPherson
Local Museum - 1959
Local history 43843

Grosse Pointe Shores MI

Edsel and Eleanor Ford House, 1100 Lake Shore Rd, Grosse Pointe Shores, MI 48236 - T: (313) 884-4222, Fax: (313) 884-5977, E-mail: info@fordhouse.org, Internet: www.fordhouse.org. Pres.: John Miller
Local Museum / Decorative Arts Museum / Historic Site - 1978
Historic house, decorative art, design, automotive, architecture, landscape design 43844

Groton CT

Submarine Force Museum and Historic Ship Nautilus, 1 Crystal Lake Rd, Groton, CT 06349-5571 - T: (860) 449-3558, Fax: (860) 449-4150, Internet: www.ussnautilus.org. Cur.: Stephen Finnigan
Military Museum / Science&Tech Museum - 1954 43845

Groton MA

Groton Historical Museum, 172 Main St, Groton, MA 01450 - T: (978) 448-2046, Fax: (978) 448-5589. Cur.: Isabel C. Beal
Historical Museum - 1894
Governor Boutwell House 43846

Grove OK

Har-Ber Village, 4404 W 20th St, Grove, OK 74344 - T: (918) 786-6446, 786-3488, Fax: (918) 787-6213, E-mail: harbervil@aol.com, Internet: www.har-bervillage.com. Pres.: Gary Smith, Dir.: Jan Norman
Local Museum - 1968
Pottery, China, toys, natural hist, furniture, lamps, dolls, farm machinery, stagecoaches, prairie schooner, steam engines, wagons, guns, musical instruments, clothing 43847

Groveport OH

Motts Military Museum, 5075 S Hamilton Rd, Groveport, OH 43125 - T: (614) 836-1500, Fax: (614) 836-5110, E-mail: info@mottsmilitarymuseum.org, Internet: www.mottsmilitarymuseum.org
Military Museum - 1988
Military items from the Civil War, WW 1 and 2, Korea, Vietnam and Desert Storm 43848

Groversville NY

Fulton County Museum, 237 N Kingsboro Av, Groversville, NY 12078 - T: (518) 725-2203. C.E.O.: Elwood A. Stowell
Historical Museum - 1891
History 43849

Guernsey WY

Lake Guernsey Museum, U.S. 26 to State Hwy 317, Guernsey, WY 82214 - T: (307) 836-2334, 836-2900, Fax: (307) 836-3088. Interim Dir.: John Keck
Local Museum - 1936
Local hist 43850

Guilford CT

Henry Whitfield State Historical Museum, 248 Old Whitfield St, Guilford, CT 06437 - T: (203) 453-2457, Fax: (203) 453-7544, E-mail: whitfieldmuseum@snet.net, Internet: www.chc.state.ct.us. Dir.: Michael A. McBride
Historical Museum - 1899
First state-owned museum in Connecticut (1899) 43851

Gulf Shores AL

Fort Morgan Museum, 51 Hwy 180 W, Gulf Shores, AL 36542 - T: (251) 540-7202, Fax: (251) 540-7665, E-mail: bricfort@gulftel.com. Dir.: Blanton Blankenship, Cur.: Michael Bailey
Military Museum - 1967 43852

Gunnison CO

Gunnison County Pioneer and Historical Museum, S Adams St and Hwy 50, Gunnison, CO 81230 - T: (970) 641-4530. Dir.: C.J. Miller
Local Museum - 1930
Regional history, geology, minerals, costume, railroad, agriculture 43853

Gurdon AR

Hoo-Hoo International Forestry Museum, 207 Main St, Gurdon, AR 71743 - T: (870) 353-4997, Fax: (870) 353-4151, E-mail: hoohoo@dancooks.com, Internet: www.hoo-hoo.org. Head: Beth A. Thomas
Ethnology Museum / Fine Arts Museum - 1981
Logging, lumber 43854

Guthrie OK

Oklahoma Territorial Museum, 402 E Oklahoma Av, Guthrie, OK 73044 - T: (405) 282-1889. Dir.: Michael Bruce, Cur.: Helen Stiefmiller, Ass. Cur.: Nathan Turner
Historical Museum - 1970 43855

State Capital Publishing Museum, 301 W Harrison Av, Guthrie, OK 73044 - T: (405) 282-4123, E-mail: guthriecomplex@ok-history.mus.ok.us. Dir.: Michael Bruce, Cur.: Helen Stiefmiller, Ass. Cur.: Nathan Turner
Special Museum / Science&Tech Museum - 1976 43856

Hackensack NJ

Bergen Museum of Art and Science, 25 E Salem St, Ste 405, Hackensack, NJ 07601 - T: (201) 968-1001, Fax: (201) 265-2536, E-mail: BergenMuse@aol.com, Internet: www.thebergenmuseum.com. Dir.: David J. Messer
Fine Arts Museum / Natural History Museum - 1956 43857

New Jersey Naval Museum, 78 River St, Hackensack, NJ 07601 - T: (201) 342-3268, Fax: (201) 342-3268, E-mail: njnavalmus@aol.com, Internet: www.njnm.com. Dir.: Ronald J. Pellegrino, C.E.O.: Chris Buermeyer, Cur.: Joseph Wallace
Military Museum - 1974
Naval military hist 43858

Hackettstown NJ

Hackettstown Historical Society Museum, 106 Church St, Hackettstown, NJ 07840 - T: (908) 852-8797. Pres.: Raymond Lamasters, Cur.: Helen G. Montfort
Local Museum - 1975
Local history, genealogy - library 43859

Haddonfield NJ

Haddonfield Museum, 343 Kings Hwy E, Haddonfield, NJ 08033 - T: (856) 429-7375, E-mail: hadhistsoc@netcarrier.com, Internet: www.08033.com. Dir.: Robert A. Marshall, Cur.: Dianna H. Snodgrass
Historical Museum - 1914
library 43860

Indian King Tavern Museum, 233 King's Hwy E, Haddonfield, NJ 08033 - T: (856) 429-6792, Internet: www.levins.com/tavern.html. Cur.: William J. Mason
Historic Site - 1903 43861

Hadley MA

Hadley Farm Museum, 147 Russell St, Hadley, MA 01035 - T: (413) 586-1812. Pres.: Thomas West, Cur.: Norman Barstow
Agriculture Museum - 1930 43862

Porter-Phelps-Huntington Foundation, 130 River Dr, Hadley, MA 01035 - T: (413) 584-4699. Dir.: Susan J. Lisk, Pres.: Peter Wells
Historical Museum - 1955
Womens history studies 43863

Hagerstown IN

Wilbur Wright Birthplace and Interpretive Center, 1525 N County Rd 750 E, Hagerstown, IN 47346 - T: (765) 332-2495, Internet: www.wilburwright-birthplace.org
Historical Museum - 1929 43864

Hagerstown MD

Jonathan Hager House and Museum, 110 Key St, Hagerstown, MD 21740 - T: (301) 739-8393. Cur.: John Nelson
Folklore Museum - 1962 43865

Miller House Museum, 135 W Washington St, Hagerstown, MD 21740 - T: (301) 797-8782, Fax: (301) 797-9509, E-mail: histsoc@intrepid.nrt, Internet: www.rootsweb.com/~mdwchs. Exec. Dir.: Melinda Marsden, Cur.: Elizabeth Graff, John Nelson
Local Museum - 1911
Antiques, local history 43866

Washington County Museum of Fine Arts, City Park, 91 Key St, Hagerstown, MD 21741 - T: (301) 739-5727, Fax: (301) 745-3741, E-mail: wcmfa@aol.com, Internet: www.washcomuseum.org. Dir.: Jean Woods, Cur.: Amy Metzger
Fine Arts Museum - 1929
19th and 20th c american art 43867

Hailey ID

Blaine County Historical Museum, 218 N Main St, Hailey, ID 83333 - T: (208) 726-4226 & 8405, E-mail: teddie@micron.net. Chm.: Ivan Swaner
Local Museum - 1964
Regional history 43868

Haines AK

Alaska Indian Arts, Historic Bldg 13, Fort Seward, Haines, AK 99827 - T: (907) 766-2160, Fax: (907) 766-2105, 766-2160, E-mail: aia@wytbear.com, Internet: www.alaskaindianarts.com. Dir.: Lee D. Heinmiller, Asst. Dir.: Charles Jimmie (Culture), John Hagen (Art)
Ethnology Museum - 1957
Indian living village 43869

Sheldon Museum, 11 Main St, Haines, AK 99827 - T: (907) 766-2366, Fax: (907) 766-2368, E-mail: curator@sheldonmuseum.org, Internet: www.sheldonmuseum.org. Dir.: Cynthia L. Jones
Historical Museum / Ethnology Museum - 1924
History, ethnography, Tlingit Indian culture, Eldred Rock Lighthouse Lense 43870

Haines OR

Eastern Oregon Museum on the Old Oregon Trail, Third and Wilcox, Haines, OR 97833 - T: (503) 856-3233, E-mail: mrifer@eoni.com, Internet: www.hainesoregon.com/eomuseum.. Pres.: Viola Perkins
Local Museum / Historical Museum - 1958 43871

Haledon NJ

American Labor Museum, 83 Norwood St, Haledon, NJ 07508 - T: (973) 595-7953, Fax: (973) 595-7291, E-mail: labormuseum@aol.com, Internet: community.nj.com/cc/labormuseum. Dir.: Angelica M. Santomauro
Historical Museum - 1982 43872

Halifax NC

Historic Halifax, Saint David and Dobb Sts, Halifax, NC 27839 - T: (252) 583-7191, Fax: (252) 583-9241, E-mail: histhalifax@coastalnet.com, Internet: www.ah.dcr.state.nc.us/sections/hs
Local Museum - 1955
Archaeology, hist 43873

Hallowell ME

Harlow Gallery, Kennebec Valley Art Association, 160 Water St, Hallowell, ME 04347 - T: (207) 622-3813. Pres.: Amy Bliss Coleman, Val Howard
Fine Arts Museum / Public Gallery - 1963
Art 43874

Halstead KS

Kansas Health Museum, Kansas Learning Center for Health, 505 Main St, Halstead, KS 67056 - T: (316) 835-2662, Fax: (316) 835-2755, E-mail: reservations@learningcenter.org, Internet: www.learningcenter.org. Dir.: Megan E. Evans
Historical Museum - 1965
Health, education 43875

Hamden CT

Eli Whitney Museum, 915 Whitney Av, Hamden, CT 06517 - T: (203) 777-1833, Fax: (203) 777-1229, E-mail: wb@eliwhitney.org, Internet: www.eliwhitney.org. Pres.: Beverly Hodgson, Dir.: William Brown
Science&Tech Museum - 1976 43876

Hamilton MT

Ravalli County Museum, 205 Bedford, Hamilton, MT 59840 - T: (406) 363-3338, Fax: (406) 363-3338, E-mail: rcmuseum@cybernet1.com, Internet: www.cybernet1.com/rcmuseum. Dir.: Helen Ann Bibler
Local Museum - 1955
Early life of Bitterroot Valley, Indian, railroads 43877

Hamilton NJ

Grounds For Sculpture, 18 Fairgrounds Rd, Hamilton, NJ 08619 - T: (609) 586-0616, Fax: (609) 586-0968, E-mail: info@groundsforsculpture.org, Internet: www.groundsforsculpture.org. Dir. & Cur.: Brooke Barrie, Cur.: Christine Finkelstein (Education)
Fine Arts Museum - 1992
Sculptures 43878

International Sculpture Center, 14 Fairground Rd, Ste B, Hamilton, NJ 08619-3447 - T: (609) 689-1051, Fax: (609) 689-1061, E-mail: Kristine@sculpture.org, Internet: www.sculpture.org. Dir.: Kristine Smith
Public Gallery / Association with Coll - 1960 43879

John Abbott II House, 2200 Kuser Rd, Hamilton, NJ 08690 - T: (609) 585-1686, E-mail: Thomglo@aol.com. Pres.: Thomas Glover
Historical Museum - 1976 43880

Kuser Farm Mansion, 390 Newkirk Av, Hamilton, NJ 08610 - T: (609) 890-3630, Fax: (609) 890-3632, E-mail: comments@hamiltonnj.com, Internet: www.hamiltonnj.com. Cur.: Denise Dale Zemlansky
Historical Museum - 1979 43881

Hamilton NY

Picker Art Gallery, Colgate University, 13 Oak Dr, Hamilton, NY 13346 - T: (315) 228-7634, Fax: (315) 228-7932, E-mail: pickerart@mail.colgate.edu, Internet: picker.colgate.edu. Dir.: Dewey F. Mosby
Fine Arts Museum - 1966 43882

Hamilton OH

Butler County Museum, 327 N Second St, Hamilton, OH 45011 - T: (513) 896-9930, Fax: (513) 896-9936, E-mail: bcomuseum@fuse.net, Internet: home.fuse.net/butlercountymuseum/. Dir.: Marjorie Brown
Historical Museum - 1934 43883

Pyramid Hill Sculpture Park and Museum, 1763 Rte 128, Hamilton, OH 45013 - T: (513) 868-8336, Fax: (513) 868-3585, E-mail: pyramid@pyramidhill.org, Internet: www.pyramidhill.org
Fine Arts Museum - 1997
Sculptures, art 43884

Hamlet NC

National Railroad Museum and Hall of Fame, 2 Main St, Hamlet, NC 28345 - T: (910) 582-3317
Science&Tech Museum - 1976
Maps, model railroad, rolling stock, SAL locomotive 43885

Hammond IN

Hammond Historical Museum, 564 State St, Hammond, IN 46320 - T: (219) 931-5100, 852-2255, Fax: (219) 931-3474, E-mail: longs@hammond.lib.in.us, Internet: www.hammond.lib.in.us.com. Dir.: Margaret Evans
Local Museum - 1960
Local history - library 43886

Purdue University Calumet Library Gallery, POB 2590, Hammond, IN 46323-2094 - T: (219) 989-2249, Fax: (219) 989-2070
Decorative Arts Museum - 1976
Chinese scroll coll 43887

Hammondsport NY

Glenn H. Curtiss Museum, 8419 Rte 54, Hammondsport, NY 14840 - T: (607) 569-2160, Fax: (607) 569-2040, E-mail: curtiss@linkny.com, Internet: www.linkny.com/curtissmuseum. Dir.: Douglas Robb, Cur.: Kirk House
Historical Museum / Science&Tech Museum - 1961 43888

Wine Museum of Greyton H. Taylor, 8843 Greyton H. Taylor Memorial Dr, Hammondsport, NY 14840 - T: (607) 868-4814, Fax: (607) 868-3205, E-mail: bullyhil@ptd.net, Internet: www.bullyhill.com. Pres.: Lillian Taylor
Agriculture Museum - 1967
Hist of wine 43889

Hammonton NJ

Batsto Village, 4110 Nesco Rd, Hammonton, NJ 08037 - T: (609) 561-0024, Fax: (609) 567-8116, E-mail: whartonsf@netzero.com, Internet: www.batstovillage.org. Dir.: Patricia A. Martinelli
Historic Site / Decorative Arts Museum - 1954
33 historic buildings built in the 1800s 43890

Hampden-Sydney VA

The Esther Thomas Atkinson Museum, College Rd, Hampden-Sydney, VA 23943 - T: (804) 223-6134, 223-6000, Fax: (804) 223-6344, E-mail: lmastemaker@hsc.edu, Internet: www.hsc.edu/museum/. Cur.: Lorie Mastemaker
University Museum / Historical Museum - 1968 43891

Hampton NH

Tuck Museum, 40 Park Av, Hampton, NH 03842 - T: (603) 926-2543, E-mail: hhs@nh.ultranet.com, Internet: www.nhultranet.com/~hhs/hhshome.htm. Pres.: Bennett Moore
Historical Museum - 1925 43892

Hampton SC

Hampton County Historical Museum, 702 1st West, 601 South, Hampton, SC 29924 - T: (803) 943-5484. C.E.O. & Pres.: James Dreyfuss, Cur.: Mildred B. Rivers
Local Museum / Folklore Museum - 1979
Local hist 43893

Hampton VA

Air Power Park and Museum, 413 W Mercury Blvd, Hampton, VA 23666 - T: (757) 727-1163. Dir.: Jim Wilson
Military Museum / Science&Tech Museum - 1964
Military aircraft 43894

Charles H. Taylor Arts Center, 4205 Victoria Blvd, Hampton, VA 23669 - T: (757) 727-1490, Fax: (757) 727-1167, E-mail: artscom@city.hampton.va.us, Internet: www.hampton.va.us/arts. Dir.: Michael P. Curry
Fine Arts Museum - 1989
Regional and national artists 43895

Hampton University Museum, Hampton University, Hampton, VA 23668 - T: (757) 727-5308, Fax: (757) 727-5170, E-mail: museum@hamptonu.edu, Internet: www.hamptonu.edu. Dir.: Ramona Austin, Dept. Dir.: Dr. Paulette Molin (American Indian Educational Opportunities Program), Cur.: Mary Lou Hultgren, Jeffrey Bruce, Cur.: Vanessa Thaxton-Ward (History)
Fine Arts Museum / University Museum / Historical Museum / Ethnology Museum - 1868
Art, history 43896

Saint John's Church and Parish Museum, 100 W Queensway, Hampton, VA 23669 - T: (757) 722-2567, Fax: (757) 722-0641, Internet: homestead.juno.com/stjohns-hampton. Cur.: Beverly F. Gundry
Local Museum / Historic Site - 1976
Local hist 43897

Virginia Air and Space Center, 600 Settlers Landing Rd, Hampton, VA 23669 - T: (757) 727-0900, Fax: (757) 727-0898, E-mail: tbridgfo@vasc.org, Internet: www.vasc.org. Dir.: Todd C. Bridgford, Pres.: Duncan McIver
Local Museum / Science&Tech Museum - 1991
Aerospace, regional history 43898

Hamtramck MI

Ukrainian-American Archives and Museum, 11756 Charest St, Hamtramck, MI 48212 - T: (313) 366-9764. Dir./Cur.: Danylo Dmytrykiw
Folklore Museum / Local Museum / Historical Museum / Special Museum - 1958
Cultural Center 43899

Hana, Maui HI

Hana Cultural Center, 4974 Uakea Rd, Hana, Maui, HI 96713 - T: (808) 248-8622, Fax: (808) 248-8620, E-mail: hccm@aloha.net, Internet: planet-hawaii.com/hana. Exec. Dir.: Coila Eade
Local Museum - 1971 43900

Hancock NH

Hancock Historical Society Museum, 7 Main St, Hancock, NH 03449-6008 - T: (603) 525-9379, E-mail: hancockhistsoc@monaj.net. Cur.: Eleanor Amidon
Local Museum / Historical Museum - 1903 43901

Hancock's Bridge NJ

Hancock House, 1 Main St, Hancock's Bridge, NJ 08038 - T: (856) 935-4373, Fax: (856) 925-7818, E-mail: fortmott@snip.net, Internet: www.nj.us/dep/forestry/hitsite.htm
Historical Museum 43902

Hanford CA

Fort Roosevelt Natural Science and History Museum, Spruce Court, Hanford, CA 93230 - T: (559) 582-0919, Fax: (559) 582-8970. Dir.: Heidi Arroues
Natural History Museum / Historical Museum - 1969 43903

Hannibal MO

Mark Twain Home and Museum, 208 Hill St, Hannibal, MO 63401 - T: (573) 221-9010, Fax: (573) 221-7975. Dir.: Henry Sweets, Pres.: Herbert S. Parham
Historical Museum - 1936 43904

Hanover KS

Hollenberg Pony Express Station Museum, 2889 23rd Rd, Kansas Hwy 243, Hanover, KS 66945-9634 - T: (913) 337-2635, E-mail: hollenberg@ksk.org, Internet: www.history.cc.ukans.edu/heritage/kshs/places/howlenbg. Cur.: Duane R. Durst
Special Museum
1857 Pony Express stn, comprised of general store, tavern and stage stn 43905

Hanover MI

Conklin Reed Organ and History Museum, 105 Fairview, Hanover, MI 49241 - T: (517) 563-8927, Internet: www.community.mlive.com/cc/hanover. Pres.: Ronald McClain
Local Museum / Museum of Classical Antiquities / Music Museum - 1977 43906

Lee Conklin Antique Organ History Museum → Conklin Reed Organ and History Museum

Hanover NH

Hood Museum of Art, Dartmouth College, Hanover, NH 03755 - T: (603) 646-2808, Fax: (603) 646-1400, E-mail: hood.museum@dartmouth.edu, Internet: www.dartmouth.edu/~hood/menu.html. Dir.: Derrick R. Cartwright, Cur.: T. Barton Thurber (European Art), Lesley Wellman (Education), Barbara Thompson (African, Oceanic and Native American Art), Evelyn Marcus (Exhibitions), Katherine Hart (Academic Programming), Barbara J. MacAdam (American Art), Margaret E. Spicer (Costumes)
Fine Arts Museum / University Museum - 1772
Fine arts, anthropology 43907

Hanover VA

Hanover Historical Society Museum, Hwy 301, Court Green, Hanover, VA 23069 - T: (804) 537-5815. Cur.: W.C. Wickham
Local Museum - 1967
Local hist 43908

Harbor Springs MI

Andrew J. Blackbird Museum, 368 E Main St, Harbor Springs, MI 49740 - T: (231) 526-0612, Fax: (231) 526-6865, E-mail: cityhs@freeway.net. Dir.: Joyce Shagonaby
Historical Museum / Ethnology Museum - 1952
Indians 43909

Hardwick MA

Hardwick Historical Museum, On Hardwick Common, Hardwick, MA 01037 - T: (413) 477-8734. Cur.: Leon Thresher
Local Museum - 1959
Local history 43910

Hardy VA

Booker T. Washington National Monument, 12130 Booker T. Washington Hwy, Hardy, VA 24101 - T: (540) 721-2094, Fax: (540) 721-8311, 721-5128, Internet: www.nps.gov/bowa. C.E.O.: Rebecca Harriett
Special Museum - 1956
Birthplace & early home of Booker T. Washington 43911

Harleysville PA

Mennonite Heritage Center, 565 Yoder Rd, Harleysville, PA 19438 - T: (215) 256-3020, Fax: (215) 256-3023, E-mail: info@mhep.org, Internet: www.mhep.org/. Cur.: Joel D. Alderfer
Local Museum / Religious Arts Museum - 1974
Local hist - library 43912

Harlingen TX

Lon C. Hill Home, Boxwood at Raintree, Harlingen, TX 78550 - T: (956) 430-8500, Fax: (956) 430-8502, E-mail: rgvmuse@hiline.net, Internet: hiline.net/rgvmuse. Dir.: Linn Keller
Local Museum - 1905
Historic house 43913

Rio Grande Valley Museum, Boxwood at Raintree, Harlingen, TX 78550 - T: (956) 430-8500, Fax: (956) 430-8502, E-mail: rgvmuse@hiline.net, Internet: www.hiline.net/rgvmuse. Dir.: Linn Keller
Local Museum - 1967
Local hist 43914

Harlowtown MT

Upper Musselshell Historical Society Museum, 11 S Central, Harlowtown, MT 59036 - T: (406) 632-5519, E-mail: museum@mtintouch.net, Internet: harlowtonmuseum.com
Local Museum - 1985 43915

Harper KS

Harper City Historical Museum, 804 E 12th St, Harper, KS 67058 - T: (316) 896-2824. Pres.: Gail Bellar
Local Museum - 1959
Local history, housed in a German Apostolic Church 43916

Harpers Ferry IA

Effigy Mounds Museum, 151 Hwy 76, Harpers Ferry, IA 52146 - T: (563) 873-3491, Fax: (563) 873-3743, E-mail: efmo_superintendent@nps.gov, Internet: www.nps.gov/efmo. Head: Phyllis Ewing
Archaeological Museum - 1949
Archaeology 43917

Harpers Ferry WV

Harpers Ferry National Historical Park, Fillmore St, Harpers Ferry, WV 25425 - T: (304) 535-6224, Fax: (304) 535-6244, Internet: www.nps.gov/hafe/home.htm. Dir.: Terry Carlstrom, Cur.: Marsha B. Starkey
Local Museum - 1944
56 restored buildings and Civil War fortifications 43918

John Brown Wax Museum, 168 High St, Harpers Ferry, WV 25425 - T: (304) 535-2792. Pres.: D.D. Kilham
Decorative Arts Museum - 1964 43919

Harpursville NY

Colesville and Windsor Museum at Saint Luke's Church, Maple Av, Harpursville, NY 13787 - T: (607) 655-3174. Pres.: Fran Bromley, Cur.: Marjory Hinman
Historical Museum - 1971
American Indian artifacts 43920

Harrisburg NE

Banner County Historical Museum, 200 N Pennsylvania Av, Harrisburg, NE 69156 - T: (308) 783-1660. Pres.: Harold L. Brown, C.E.O.: George Penick, Cur.: Norris Leafdale
Local Museum / Agriculture Museum - 1969
Regional history 43921

Harrisburg PA

Art Association of Harrisburg, 21 N Front St, Harrisburg, PA 17101 - T: (717) 236-1432, Fax: (717) 236-6631, E-mail: carrie@artassocofhbg.com, Internet: www.artassocofhbg.com. Pres.: Carrie Wissler-Thomas
Public Gallery - 1926 43922

Fort Hunter Mansion, 5300 N Front St, Harrisburg, PA 17110 - T: (717) 599-5751, Fax: (717) 599-5838, Internet: www.forthunter.org. Dir.: Carl A. Dickson, Cur.: Julia Hair
Decorative Arts Museum / Local Museum - 1933
Historic house 43923

The John Harris/Simon Cameron Mansion, Dauphin County Museum, 219 S Front St, Harrisburg, PA 17104 - T: (717) 233-3462, Fax: (717) 233-6059, Internet: www.dauphincountyhistoricalsociety.org. Exec.Dir.: Gary D. Smith, Dir.Coll.: Robert D. Hill
Local Museum - 1869 43924

State Museum of Pennsylvania, Third and North Sts, Harrisburg, PA 17120-0024 - T: (717) 787-4980, Fax: (717) 783-4558, E-mail: museum@statemuseumpa.org, Internet: www.statemuseumpa.org. Dir.: Anita D. Blackaby, Cur.: Dr. Robert M. Sullivan (Paleontology, Geology), N. Lee Stevens (Art colls), Albert G. Mehring (Natural Science), John Zwierzyna (Industry and Technology, Military and Political History), Stephen G. Warfel (Archaeology), Curt Miner (Popular Culture), Dr. Walter Mehaska (Zoology, Botany)
Local Museum / Historical Museum - 1905
Archaeology, fine and decorative arts, natural science, paleontology, geology, industry, technology, military history, mammals, native American village, civil war - planetarium, dino lab 43925

Susquehanna Art Museum, 301 Market St, Harrisburg, PA 17101 - T: (717) 233-8668, Fax: (717) 233-8155, Internet: www.squart.org. Pres.: William Lehr, Cur.: Jonathon Van Dyke
Fine Arts Museum - 1989 43926

Whitaker Center for Science and the Arts, 301 Market St, Kunkel Bldg, Harrisburg, PA 17101 - T: (717) 221-8201, Fax: (717) 221-8208, E-mail: info@whitakercenter.org, Internet: www.whitakercenter.org. C.E.O.: Byron Quann
Natural History Museum / Fine Arts Museum - 1993
Physical, natural and life science 43927

Harrison OH

American Watchmakers-Clockmakers Institute, 701 Enterprise Dr, Harrison, OH 45030 - T: (513) 367-9800, Fax: (513) 367-1414, E-mail: jlubic@awi-net.org, Internet: www.awi-net.org. C.E.O.: James E. Lubic
Special Museum - 1977
Watches, clocks, tools 43928

Village Historical Society Museum, 10659 New Biddinger Rd, Harrison, OH 45030 - T: (513) 367-9379. C.E.O.: Betty Cookendorfer
Local Museum - 1962 43929

Harrisonburg VA

D. Ralph Hostetter Museum of Natural History, c/o Eastern Mennonite University, 1200 Park Rd, Harrisonburg, VA 22802-2462 - T: (540) 432-4400, 432-4000, Fax: (540) 432-4488, E-mail: mellinac@emu.edu, Internet: www.emu.edu/. Dir.: Christine C. Hill, Cur.: A. Clair Mellinger
University Museum / Natural History Museum - 1968
Natural hist 43930

Sawhill Gallery, Duke Hall, James Madison University, Main and Grace St, Harrisonburg, VA 22807 - T: (540) 568-6407, Fax: (540) 568-6598. Dir.: Stuart Downs
Fine Arts Museum / University Museum - 1967
Art 43931

Harrodsburg KY

Morgan Row Museum, 220 S Chiles St, Harrodsburg, KY 40330 - T: (859) 734-5985, Fax: (859) 734-5985. Pres.: George Neal
Local Museum - 1907 43932

Old Fort Harrod Museum, US 68, Harrodsburg, KY 40330 - T: (859) 734-3314, Fax: (859) 734-0794, E-mail: joanhuffman@mail.state.ky.us, Internet: www.oldfortharrod.com
Local Museum - 1934
Costumes, decorative arts, glass, hist, Indian artifacts, music 43933

Old Fort Harrod State Park Mansion Museum, POB 156, Harrodsburg, KY 40330 - T: (859) 734-3314, Fax: (859) 734-0794, E-mail: joan.huffman@mail.state.ky.us, Internet: www.state.ky.us/agencies/park/ftharrod2.htm. Dir.: Joan Huffman
Historical Museum - 1925
1830 Greek revival mansion, replica of original fort 43934

Shaker Village of Pleasant Hill, 3501 Lexington Rd, Harrodsburg, KY 40330 - T: (859) 734-5411, Fax: (859) 734-7278, E-mail: lcurry@shakervillageky.org, Internet: www.shakervillageky.org. Dir.: Larrie Spier Curry, Sc. Staff: Ralph E. Ward (Historic Farming)
Local Museum / Open Air Museum - 1961
Village, agriculture 43935

Harrogate TN

Abraham Lincoln Museum, Lincoln Memorial University, Hwy 25 E, Cumberland Gap Pkwy, Harrogate, TN 37752 - T: (423) 869-6235, Fax: (423) 869-6350, E-mail: museum@lmunet.edu, Internet: www.lmunet.edu/museum. Dir.: Dr. Charles M. Hubbard, Cur.: Steven Wilson
Historical Museum - 1897
History - Library 43936

Hartford CT

Antiquarian and Landmarks Society Museum, 66 Forest St, Hartford, CT 06105-3204 - T: (860) 247-8996, Fax: (860) 249-4907, E-mail: als@hartnet.org, Internet: www.hartnet.org/als. Dir.: William Hosley, Assoc. Dir.: Karin E. Peterson
Historical Museum - 1936 43937

Connecticut Historical Society Museum, 1 Elizabeth St, Hartford, CT 06105 - T: (860) 236-5621, Fax: (860) 236-2664, E-mail: ask_us@chs.org, Internet: www.chs.org. Dir.: David M. Kahn, Cur.: Nancy Finlay (Graphics)
Fine Arts Museum / Decorative Arts Museum / Local Museum / Historical Museum - 1825 43938

Harriet Beecher Stowe Center, 77 Forest St, Hartford, CT 06105 - T: (860) 522-9258, Fax: (860) 522-9259, E-mail: stowelib@hartnet.org, Internet: www.harrietbeecherstowe.org. Dir.: Katherine Kane, Cur.: Dawn C. Adiletta
Historical Museum - 1941 43939

Mark Twain House, 351 Farmington Av, Hartford, CT 06105-4498 - T: (860) 247-0998, Fax: (860) 278-8148, E-mail: lynn_gregor@hartnet.org, Internet: www.marktwainhouse.org. Dir.: John Vincent Boyer, Dep. Dir.: Debra Petke, Cur.: Marianne J. Curling
Historical Museum - 1929 43940

Menczer Museum of Medicine and Dentistry, 230 Scarborough St, Hartford, CT 06105 - T: (860) 236-5613, Fax: (860) 236-8401, Internet: library.uchc.edu/hms. Cur.: Bernard Kosta
Special Museum - 1974 43941

Museum of Connecticut History, Connecticut State Library, 231 Capitol Av, Hartford, CT 06106 - T: (860) 757-6535, Fax: (860) 757-6533, Internet: www.cslib.org. Cur.: Howard L. Miller, David J. Corrigan
Historical Museum - 1910 43942

Old State House, 800 Main St, Hartford, CT 06103 - T: (860) 522-6766, Fax: (860) 522-2812, E-mail: info@sharect.org, Internet: www.ctosh.org. Dir.: Wilson H. Faude
Fine Arts Museum / Historical Museum - 1975 43943

Wadsworth Atheneum, 600 Main St, Hartford, CT 06103-2990 - T: (860) 278-2670, Fax: (860) 527-0803, E-mail: info@wadsworthatheneum.org, Internet: www.wadsworthatheneum.org. Dir.: Kate M. Sellers, Cur.: Elizabeth Mankin Kornhauser (American Painting and Sculpture), Eric Zafran (European Painting and Sculpture), Linda H. Roth (European Decorative Arts), Deirdre Bibby (African American Art), Carol Dean Krute (Costume, Textiles), Nicholas Baume (Contemporary Art), Thomas Denenberg (American Decorative Arts), Eugene R. Gaddis (Austin House), Ass. Cur.: Amy Ellis (American Art), Cynthia Roman (European Art), Trina Bowman (American Decorative Arts), Joanna Marsh (Contemporary Art)
Fine Arts Museum - 1842 43944

Widener Gallery, c/o Trinity College, Austin Arts Center, 300 Summit St, Hartford, CT 06106 - T: (860) 297-5232, Fax: (860) 297-5349, E-mail: felice.caivano@mail.trincoll.edu, Internet: www.trincoll.edu. Dir.: Noreen Channels, Cur.: Felice Caivano
Fine Arts Museum / University Museum - 1964 43945

Hartford WI

Hartford Heritage Auto Museum → Wisconsin Automotive Museum

Wisconsin Automotive Museum, 147 N Rural St, Hartford, WI 53027 - T: (414) 673-7999, E-mail: automu@netwurx.net. Dir.: Dale W. Anderson
Science&Tech Museum - 1982
Transportation 43946

Hartsville SC

Cecelia Coker Bell Gallery, Coker College, Art Dept., 300 E College Av, Hartsville, SC 29550 - T: (843) 383-8156, Fax: (843) 383-8048, E-mail: lmerriman@pascal.coker.edu, Internet: www.coker.edu/art/gallery.html. Dir.: Larry Merriman
University Museum / Fine Arts Museum - 1983 43947

Hartsville Museum, 222 N Fifth St, Hartsville, SC 29550 - T: (843) 383-3005, Fax: (843) 383-2477, E-mail: info@hartsvillemuseum.org, Internet: www.hartsvillemuseum.org. Dir.: Patricia J. Wilmot
Local Museum / Fine Arts Museum - 1980
Local hist, art 43948

Jacob Kelley House Museum, 2585 Kellytown Rd, Hartsville, SC 29551 - T: (843) 332-6401, 339-9093, Fax: (843) 332-8017. Dir.: Horace F. Rudisill
Decorative Arts Museum
Handcrafted furniture, decorative arts 43949

Robinson Visitors Center, 3581 West Entrance Rd, Hartsville, SC 29550 - T: (843) 857-5291, Fax: (843) 857-1319, E-mail: mike.mccracken@cpk.com
Science&Tech Museum - 1968
Nuclear and coal generation of electricity 43950

Harvard IL

Greater Harvard Area Historical Society, 308 N Hart Blvd, Harvard, IL 60033 - T: (815) 943-6770, 943-6141. C.E.O.: Brian Schultz, Cur.: Elaine Fideucci
Local Museum - 1977
Local history 43951

Harvard MA

Fruitlands Museums, 102 Prospect Hill Rd, Harvard, MA 01451 - T: (978) 456-3924, Fax: (978) 456-8078, E-mail: fruitlands@fruitlands.org, Internet: www.fruitlands.org. Pres.: Martin Fay, Deputy Dir.: Peggy Kempton, Cur.: Michael Volmar (Archaeology)
Fine Arts Museum / Local Museum / Natural History Museum - 1914
Regional history 43952

Harvard Historical Society Collection, 215 Still River Rd, Harvard, MA 01451 - T: (508) 456-8285. Cur.: Joyce Verrando
Historical Museum - 1897
History 43953

Harwich MA

Brooks Academy Museum, 80 Parallel St, Harwich, MA 02645 - T: (508) 432-8089, E-mail: harwichhistoricalsociety@capecod.com, Internet: www.capecod.com/history. Dir.: James A. Brown
Local Museum - 1954
Local history 43954

Hastings MI

Historic Charlton Park Village and Museum, 2545 S Charlton Park Rd, Hastings, MI 49058 - T: (616) 945-3775, Fax: (616) 945-0390, E-mail: forsbergp@earthlink.net, Internet: ch-arltonpark.org. Dir.: Dr. Peter K. Forsberg, Cur.: Sara Feldbauer
Local Museum / Open Air Museum - 1936
Regional history 43955

Hastings NE

Hastings Museum, 1330 N Burlington, Hastings, NE 68901 - T: (402) 461-2399, Fax: (402) 461-2379, E-mail: hastingsmuseum@alltel.com, Internet: www.hastingsnet.com/museum. Dir.: Terry Hunter, Cur.: Teresa Kreutzer
Local Museum / Natural History Museum - 1926 43956

Hattiesburg MS

Hahs Museum, 723 Main St, Hattiesburg, MS 39401 - T: (601) 582-5460
Local Museum - 1970 43957

Turner House Museum, 500 Bay, Hattiesburg, MS 39401 - T: (601) 582-1771. Dir./Cur.: David Sheley
Fine Arts Museum / Decorative Arts Museum - 1970
18th c furniture, silver, Persian rugs, paintings (old masters), tapestries 43958

Hatton ND

Hatton-Eielson Museum, 405 Eielson St, Hatton, ND 58240 - T: (701) 543-3726, Fax: (701) 543-4013. Pres.: Arden Johnson, Cur.: Eileen Mork
Historical Museum - 1973 43959

Haverford PA

Main Line Art Center, Old Buck Rd and Lancaster Av, Haverford, PA 19041 - T: (610) 525-0272, Fax: (610) 525-5036, E-mail: jherman@mainlineart.org, Internet: www.mainlineart.org. Exec. Dir.: Judy Herman
Public Gallery - 1937 43960

Haverhill MA

Haverhill Historical Museum, 240 Water St, Haverhill, MA 01830 - T: (978) 374-4626, Fax: (978) 521-9176, Internet: www.haverhillhistory.org. Dir.: Joanne Sullivan
Local Museum - 1893
Local history 43961

Haverhill Public Library Special Collections, 99 Main St, Haverhill, MA 01830 - T: (978) 373-1586 ext 642, Fax: (978) 373-8466, E-mail: library@haverhill.com, Internet: www.haverhillpl.org. Cur.: Greg Laing
Public Gallery / Library with Exhibitions
Paintings, manuscripts, prints, photos 43962

Havertown PA

Haverford Township Historical Society Museum, Karakung Dr, Powder Mill Valley Park, Havertown, PA 19083 - T: (610) 789-5169, Internet: www.delcohistory.org/hths. Cur.: Carolyn Joseph
Local Museum - 1939
Costumes, glass photographic plates of railroads, engines 43963

Havre MT

H. Earl Clack Museum, 306 Third Av, Havre, MT 59501 - T: (406) 265-4000, Fax: (406) 265-7258
Archaeological Museum - 1964 43964

Havre de Grace MD

Havre de Grace Decoy Museum, 215 Giles St, Havre de Grace, MD 21078 - T: (410) 939-3739, Fax: (410) 939-3775, E-mail: decoymuseum@aol.com, Internet: www.decoymuseum.com. Pres.: Dr. Patrick Vincenti, Dir.: Debra Pence, Cur.: Diane Rees
Folklore Museum - 1983 43965

Steppingstone Museum, 461 Quaker Bottom Rd, Havre de Grace, MD 21078 - T: (410) 939-2299, (888) 419-1762, Fax: (410) 939-2321, E-mail: steppingstonemuseum@msn.com, Internet: www.steppingstonemuseum.org. Dir.: Linda M. Noll
Decorative Arts Museum / Agriculture Museum - 1968
Arts and crafts 43966

Susquehanna Museum of Havre de Grace, 817 Conesteo St, Havre de Grace, MD 21078 - T: (410) 939-5780, E-mail: susqmuseum@erols.com, Internet: users.erols.com/susqmuseum/Index.html
Local Museum - 1970
Local hist 43967

Hawaii National Park HI

Volcano Art Center, POB 104, Hawaii National Park, HI 96718 - T: (808) 967-8222, Fax: (808) 967-8512, E-mail: vacadm@verizon.net, Internet: www.volcanoartcenter.org. Dir.: Marilyn L. Nicholson
Fine Arts Museum / Folklore Museum - 1974 43968

Hays KS

Fort Hays, 1472 Hwy 183, Alt., Hays, KS 67601-9212 - T: (913) 625-6812, Fax: (785) 625-4785, E-mail: thefort@kshs.org, Internet: www.kshs.org/places/forthays.htm. Dir.: Robert Wilhelm
Military Museum - 1965
Military hist 43969

Moss-Thorns Gallery of Arts, c/o Fort Hays State University, 600 Park St, Hays, KS 67601 - T: (785) 628-4247, Fax: (785) 628-4087, E-mail: ctaylor@fhsu.edu, Internet: www.fhsu.edu. Chm.: Leland Powers
Fine Arts Museum / University Museum - 1953
Contemporary prints, small paintings, prints and drawings, Oriental scroll coll 43970

Sternberg Museum of Natural History, Fort Hays State University, 3000 Sternberg Dr, Hays, KS 67601-2006 - T: (785) 628-5516, Fax: (785) 628-4518, E-mail: jchoate@fhsu.edu, Internet: www.fhsu.edu/sternberg/. Dir.: J.R. Choate (Mammals), Asst. Dir.: G. Liggett, Chief Cur.: R.J. Zakrzewski, Cur.: J.R. Thomasson (Plants), Asst. Cur.: G. Farley (Birds), R. Packauskas (Insects), Travis Taggart (Herptiles), William Stark (Fishes), J.R. Choate (Mammals)
University Museum / Natural History Museum - 1926
Mammals, birds, insects, plants, fossils, amphibians, reptiles, fishes - library 43971

University Gallery, Fort Hays State University, 600 Park St, Hays, KS 67601 - T: (785) 628-4247, Fax: (785) 628-4087, E-mail: ctaylor@fhsu.edu, Internet: www.fhsu.edu/art
Public Gallery 43972

Hayward CA

C.E. Smith Museum of Anthropology, California State University, 25800 Carlos B Blvd, Hayward, CA 94542-3039 - T: (510) 885-3168, 885-3104, Fax: (510) 885-3353, E-mail: gmiller@csuhayward.edu, Internet: www.csuhayward.edu/cesmith. Dir.: Prof. George Miller
Ethnology Museum - 1974 43973

Sulphur Creek Nature Center, 1801 D St, Hayward, CA 94541 - T: (510) 881-6749, Fax: (510) 881-6763, E-mail: slphrcreek@aol.com, Internet: www.hard.dst.ca.us
Natural History Museum - 1961 43974

Sun Gallery, Hayward Area Forum of the Arts, 1015 E St, Hayward, CA 94541 - T: (510) 581-4050, Fax: (510) 581-3384, E-mail: sungallery@value.net, Internet: www.sungallery.org. Dir.: Maria Ochoa
Fine Arts Museum - 1975 43975

Hayward WI

National Fresh Water Fishing Hall of Fame, Hall of Fame Dr, Hayward, WI 54843 - T: (715) 634-4440, Fax: (715) 634-4440, E-mail: fishhall@win.bright.net, Internet: www.freshwater-fishing.org. Pres.: Harold Tiffany
Special Museum - 1960
Fishing 43976

Hazelwood MO

Museum of the Western Jesuit Missions, 700 Howdershell Rd, Hazelwood, MO 63031 - T: (314) 837-3525. Dir.: William B. Faherty, Cust.: Mark Fischer
Religious Arts Museum - 1971 43977

Hazleton PA

Greater Hazleton Historical Society Museum, 55 N Wyoming St, Hazleton, PA 18201 - T: (570) 455-8576. C.E.O. & Pres.: Jean Coll Gormley
Local Museum - 1983
Local hist 43978

Healdton OK

Healdton Oil Museum, 315 E Main St, Healdton, OK 73438 - T: (580) 229-0900, Fax: (580) 229-0900. Cur.: Claude N. Woods
Special Museum / Science&Tech Museum - 1973
Technology Museum 43979

Heavener OK

Peter Conser House, Hodgens off Hwy 59, Heavener, OK 74937 - T: (918) 653-2493, E-mail: hawhope@clnk.com. C.E.O.: Blake Wade
Historical Museum - 1970 43980

Helena AR

Delta Cultural Center, 141 Cherry St, Helena, AR 72342 - T: (870) 338-4350, Fax: (870) 338-4358, E-mail: info@deltaculturalcenter.com, Internet: www.deltaculturalcenter.com. Dir.: Katie Harrington
Folklore Museum - 1990
Folk culture 43981

Phillips County Museum, 623 Pecan St, Helena, AR 72342 - T: (870) 338-7790, Fax: (870) 338-7732, E-mail: helenamuseum@hnb.com. Cur.: Danielle Burch
Local Museum / Military Museum - 1929
County history, military 43982

Helena MT

Holter Museum of Art, 12 E Lawrence St, Helena, MT 59601 - T: (406) 442-6400, Fax: (406) 442-2404, E-mail: holter@mt.net, Internet: www.holtermuseum.org. Dir.: Peter Held, Cur.: Katie Knight
Fine Arts Museum - 1987
Contemporary regional art 43983

Montana Historical Society Museum, 225 N Roberts, Helena, MT 59620, mail addr: POB 201201, Helena, MT 59620-1201 - T: (406) 444-2694, Fax: (406) 444-2696, E-mail: klambert@state.mt.us, Internet: www.montanahistoricalsociety.org. Dir.: Dr. Arnold Olsen, Cur.: Kirby Lambert
Local Museum - 1865
library 43984

Hellertown PA

Gilman Museum, At the Cave, POB M, Hellertown, PA 18055 - T: (610) 838-8767, Fax: (610) 838-2961, E-mail: info@lostcave.com, Internet: www.lostcave.com. Dir.: Robert G. Gilman, Chief Cur.: Beverly L. Rozewicz
Local Museum - 1955
Natural hist, antique weapons 43985

Helvetia WV

Helvetia Museum, POB 42, Helvetia, WV 26224 - T: (304) 924-6435
Local Museum - 1969 43986

Hempstead NY

Hofstra Museum, 112 Hofstra University, Hempstead, NY 11549-1120 - T: (516) 463-5672, Fax: (516) 463-4743, E-mail: elgkta@hofstra.edu. Dir.: David C. Christman, Cur.: Eleanor Rait, Karen T. Albert
Fine Arts Museum / University Museum - 1963 43987

Henderson KY

John James Audubon Museum, Audubon State Park, U.S. Hwy 41 N, Henderson, KY 42419-0576 - T: (270) 827-1893, Fax: (270) 826-2286, E-mail: jaudubon@henderson.net; curator@henderson.net, Internet: www.state.ky.us/agencies/parks/parkhome.htm. Cur.: Don Boarman
Special Museum - 1938
Nr migratory bird route, coll on life and work of John James Audubon 43988

Henderson MN

Sibley County Historical Museum, 700 Main St W, Henderson, MN 56044 - T: (507) 248-3434, 248-3234, E-mail: schs@prairie.lakes.com, Internet: www.history.sibley.mn.us. Pres.: Jerome Petersen
Historical Museum - 1940
Regional history late 1800's to early 1900's, household, agriculture, music, tools 43989

Henderson NV

Clark County Museum, 1830 S Boulder Hwy, Henderson, NV 89015 - T: (702) 455-7955, Fax: (702) 455-7948, E-mail: ryz@co.clark.nv.us, Internet: www.co.clark.nv.us. Admin.: Mark Ryzdynski, Cur.: Dawna Jolliff (Exhibitions), Christie Leavitt (Education), Assist.Cur.: Kitty Heckendorf (Education)
Historical Museum / Science&Tech Museum - 1968 43990

Howard W. Cannon Aviation Museum, 1830 S Boulder Hwy, Henderson, NV 89015 - T: (702) 455-7968, Fax: (702) 455-7948, E-mail: mhp@co.clark.nv.us, Internet: www.co.clark.nv.us/parkrec/aviation.htm. C.E.O. & Dir.: Mark P. Hall-Patton
Science&Tech Museum - 1993 43991

Henderson TX

The Depot Museum Complex, 514 N High St, Henderson, TX 75652 - T: (903) 657-4303, Fax: (903) 657-2679, E-mail: depot514@qte.net, Internet: www.depotmuseum.com. Dir.: Susan Weaver
Historical Museum - 1979
Local hist 43992

Howard-Dickinson House Museum, 501 S Main St, Henderson, TX 75654 - T: (903) 657-6925, Fax: (903) 657-9283, E-mail: lslov@worldnet.att.net. C.E.O.: Louise Slover
Agriculture Museum / Historical Museum - 1964 43993

Hendersonville NC

Mineral and Lapidary Museum of Henderson County, 400 N Main St, Hendersonville, NC 28792 - T: (828) 698-1977, Fax: (828) 698-1977, E-mail: minlap@henderson.main.nc.us, Internet: www.minmuseum.org. Chm.: Larry Hauser
Natural History Museum / Special Museum - 1996
Minerals, fossils 43994

Hendricks MN

Lincoln County Pioneer Museum, 610 W Elm, Hendricks, MN 56136 - T: (507) 275-3537. Pres.: Allen Johnson
Local Museum - 1969
Regional history 43995

Henniker NH

New England College Gallery, 7 Main St, Henniker, NH 03242 - T: (603) 428-2329, Fax: (603) 428-2266, E-mail: jhb@nec1.nec.edu. Dir.: Jan Hodges Baer
Fine Arts Museum / University Museum - 1988 43996

Hereford AZ

Coronado National Memorial, 4101 E Montezuma Canyon Rd, Hereford, AZ 85615 - T: (520) 366-5515, Fax: (520) 366-5705, Internet: www.nps.gov/coro. Head: James Bellamy
Historical Museum - 1952
Tools and Equipment for Science and technology, costumes, paintings 43997

Hereford TX

Deaf Smith County Museum, 400 Sampson, Hereford, TX 79045 - T: (806) 363-7070. Dir.: Paula Edwards
Local Museum - 1966
Local hist 43998

Herington KS

Tri-County Historical Society and Museum, 800 S Broadway, Herington, KS 67449-3060 - T: (913) 258-2842, E-mail: trimusda@ikansas.com. Pres.: Royna L. Brockmeier
Local Museum / Science&Tech Museum - 1975
Local hist, railroad hist 43999

Herkimer NY

Herkimer County Historical Society Museum, 400 N Main St, Herkimer, NY 13350 - T: (315) 866-6413, E-mail: herkimerhistory@yahoo.com, Internet: www.rootsweb.com/~nyhchs. Pres.: Jeffrey Steele
Historical Museum - 1896 44000

Hermann MO

Deutschheim State Historic Site, 109 W Second St, Hermann, MO 65041 - T: (573) 486-2200, Fax: (573) 486-2249, E-mail: dspdeut@mail.dnr.state.mo.us, Internet: www.mostateparks.com/deutschheim.html
Historical Museum - 1979
German Heritage Museum 44001

Historic Hermann Museum, Fourth and Schiller Sts, Hermann, MO 65041 - T: (573) 486-2017, Fax: (573) 486-2017, Internet: www.mo.provider/depteconomicdevelopment. C.E.O.: Mollye C. Mundwiller
Local Museum - 1956 44002

Hermitage TN

The Hermitage - Home of President Andrew Jackson, 4580 Rachel's Ln, Hermitage, TN 37076 - T: (615) 889-2941, Fax: (615) 889-9289, E-mail: info@thehermitage.com, Internet: www.thehermitage.com. Exec. Dir.: Patricia Leach, Dir. & Chief Cur.: Marsha A. Mullin, Cur.: B. Anthony Guzzi
Local Museum - 1889
Historic house 44003

Hershey PA

Hershey Museum, 170 W Hersheypark Dr, Hershey, PA 17033 - T: (717) 520-5722, Fax: (717) 534-8940, E-mail: info@hersheymuseum.org, Internet: www.hersheymuseum.org. Dir.: David L. Parke, Assoc. Dir.: Mary D. Houts, Cur.: Lois Miklas, Tanya Richter, James McMahon
Decorative Arts Museum / Historical Museum / Local Museum - 1933
History 44004

Hibbing MN

Hibbing Historical Museum, 400 23rd St and 5th Av E, Hibbing, MN 55746 - T: (218) 263-8522, Fax: (775) 878-1706, E-mail: hibbhist@uslink.net. Head: Terry Moore
Local Museum - 1958
Local history 44005

Hickory NC

Catawba Science Center, 243 Third Av NE, Hickory, NC 28601 - T: (828) 322-8169, Fax: (828) 322-1585, E-mail: msinclair@catawbascience.org, Internet: www.catawbascience.org. Dir.: Mark E. Sinclair, Asst. Dir.: Tricia Little
Natural History Museum / Science&Tech Museum - 1975 44006

Hickory Museum of Art, 243 Third Av NE, Hickory, NC 28601 - T: (828) 327-8576, Fax: (828) 327-7281, E-mail: hma@w3link.com, Internet: www.hickorymuseumofart.org. Dir.: Arnold Cogswell, Pres.: Bob Williams
Fine Arts Museum - 1944 44007

Propst House and Marple Grove, 542 5th Av NE, Hickory, NC 28601 - T: (828) 322-4731, Fax: (828) 327-9096, E-mail: hls@abts.net, Internet: hickorylandmarks.org
Decorative Arts Museum - 1968
Victorian period furniture 44008

Hickory Corners MI

Gilmore-CCCA Museum, 6865 W Hickory Rd, Hickory Corners, MI 49060 - T: (616) 671-5089, Fax: (616) 671-5843, E-mail: gcccam@gilmorecarmuseum.org, Internet: www.gilmorecarmuseum.org/. Dir.: Thomas A. Kayser
Science&Tech Museum - 1964
Cars 44009

Hicksville NY

Hicksville Gregory Museum, Heitz Pl, Hicksville, NY 11801 - T: (516) 822-7505, Fax: (516) 822-3227, E-mail: gregorymuseum@earthlink.net, Internet: members.aol.com/hgmuseum. Dir.: William P. Bennett, Cur.: Donald Curran, Historian: Richard Evers
Historical Museum / Natural History Museum - 1963 44010

Hidalgo TX

Hidalgo Pumphouse Heritage, 902 S Second St, Hidalgo, TX 78557 - T: (956) 843-8686, Fax: (956) 843-6519, E-mail: chuck_snyder@hotmail.com, Internet: www.hidalgotexas.com
Science&Tech Museum - 1999
Pumps driven by two double action, steam engines, diesel engine and pump 44011

Hiddenite NC

Hiddenite Center, 316 Church St, Hiddenite, NC 28636 - T: (828) 632-6966, Fax: (828) 632-3783, E-mail: hidnight@aol.com, Internet: www.hiddenitecenter.com. Exec. Dir.: Dwaine C. Coley
Fine Arts Museum / Local Museum - 1981
General museum, art 44012

Higginsville MO

Confederate Memorial State Historic Site, 211 W First St, Higginsville, MO 64037 - T: (660) 584-2853, Fax: (660) 584-5134, Internet: www.mostateparks.com
Local Museum - 1925 44013

High Falls NY

Delaware and Hudson Canal Museum, 23 Mohonk Rd, High Falls, NY 12440 - T: (845) 687-9311, Fax: (845) 687-2340, E-mail: info@canalmuseum.org, Internet: www.canalmuseum.org. Dir.: Jennifer Dodd
Historical Museum / Science&Tech Museum - 1966 44014

High Point NC

High Point Museum, 1859 E Lexington Av, High Point, NC 27262 - T: (336) 885-1859, Fax: (336) 883-3284, Internet: www.highpointmuseum.org. Dir.: Barbara E. Taylor, Cur.: Amy E. Lorek, John C. Marks
Historical Museum - 1966 44015

Springfield Museum of Old Domestic Life, 555 E Springfield Rd, High Point, NC 27263 - T: (910) 889-4911. Dir.: Brenda Haworth
Historical Museum - 1935 44016

Highland KS

Native American Heritage Museum at Highland Mission, 1737 Elgin Rd, Highland, KS 66035 - T: (913) 442-3304, E-mail: nahm@kshs.org, Internet: www.kshs.org. Pres.: Suzanne Heck, Cur.: Suzette McCord-Rogers
Historical Museum / Folklore Museum - 1943
House serving as a mission, dormitory and school for the Iowa, Sac and Fox Indians 44017

Highland Heights KY

Museum of Anthropology, Northern Kentucky University, University Dr, Highland Heights, KY 41099-6210 - T: (859) 572-5259, Fax: (859) 572-5566, Internet: www.nku.edu/~anthro/. Dir.: Dr. James F. Hopgood
Ethnology Museum / Archaeological Museum - 1976
Anthropology 44018

Northern Kentucky University Art Galleries, Nunn Dr, Highland Heights, KY 41099 - T: (859) 572-5148, Fax: (859) 572-6501, E-mail: knight@nku.edu, Internet: www.nku.edu/~art. Dir.: David J. Knight
University Museum / Fine Arts Museum - 1968 44019

Highland Park IL

Highland Park Historical Museum, 326 Central Av, Highland Park, IL 60035 - T: (847) 432-7090, Fax: (847) 432-7307, E-mail: hphistoricalsociety@worldnet.att.net, Internet: www.highlandpark.org/histsoc. C.E.O.: Ellsworth Mills, Pres.: Charlotte. Shields
Local Museum - 1966
Local history 44020

Hill Air Force Base UT

Hill Aerospace Museum, 7961 Wardleigh Rd, Hill Air Force Base, UT 84506-5842 - T: (801) 777-6868, Fax: (801) 777-6386, Internet: www.hill.af.mil/museum. Dir.: Carol Nash, Cur.: Carol Nash
Military Museum / Science&Tech Museum - 1985
Aerospace 44021

Hill City SD

Black Hills Museum of Natural History, 217 Main St, Hill City, SD 57745 - T: (605) 574-4505, Fax: (605) 574-2518, E-mail: ammoniteguy@bhigr.com. Dir./Cur.: Neal L. Larson, Pres.: Joe Harris, Cur.: Robert A. Farrar
Natural History Museum - 1990
Natural hist 44022

Hilllsboro WV

Pearl S. Buck Birthplace, POB 126, Hilllsboro, WV 24946 - T: (304) 653-4430, Internet: www.wvnet.edu.80/~omb00996/
Special Museum 44023

Hillsboro KS

Hillsboro Museum, 501 S Ash St, Hillsboro, KS 67063 - T: (316) 947-3775. C.E.O.: Peggy Goertzen, Cur.: Dave Wiebe
Local Museum / Agriculture Museum - 1958
Local history, pioneer adobe house, typical Mennonite dwelling 44024

Hillsboro ND

Traill County Historical Society Museum, 306 Caledonia W Av, Hillsboro, ND 58045 - T: (701) 436-5571. Pres.: John Wright, Cur.: Aagot Nysveen
Historical Museum - 1965 44025

Hillsboro OH

Fort Hill Museum, 13614 Fort Hill Rd, Hillsboro, OH 45133 - T: (937) 588-3221, Internet: www.ohiohistory.org. Head: Keith Bengtson
Historical Museum 44026

Highland House Museum, 151 E Main St, Hillsboro, OH 45133 - T: (937) 393-3392. Pres.: Jeff Hoskins, Dir.: M. Van Frank
Historical Museum - 1965 44027

Hillsboro TX

Texas Heritage Museum, c/o Hill College, 112 Lamar Dr, Hillsboro, TX 76645 - T: (254) 582-2555 ext 258, Fax: (254) 582-5740, E-mail: patterson@hill-college.cc.tx.us, Internet: hillcollege.hill-college.cc.tx.us. Dir.: Dr. T. Lindsay Baker
Military Museum - 1963
Military hist 44028

Hillsboro WI

Hillsboro Area Historical Society Museum, Maple St, Hillsboro, WI 54634 - T: (608) 489-3322. Pres.: Don Schiefelbein
Local Museum - 1958
Local hist 44029

Hillsborough NC

Orange County Historical Museum, 201 N Churton St, Hillsborough, NC 27278 - T: (919) 732-2201, Fax: (919) 732-6322, E-mail: alliance@historichillsborough.org, Internet: www.historichillsborough.org. Cur.: Angela Beeker, Robert Lucas
Local Museum - 1957 44030

Hillsborough NH

Franklin Pierce Homestead, Second N.H. Turnpike, Hillsborough, NH 03244 - T: (603) 478-1081, 478-3165, Fax: (603) 464-5401
Historical Museum - 1804
Childhood home of Franklin Pierce, 14th U.S. President 44031

Hilo HI

Lyman House Memorial Museum, 276 Haili St, Hilo, HI 96720 - T: (808) 935-5021, Fax: (808) 969-7685, E-mail: info@lymanmuseum.org, Internet: www.lymanmuseum.org. Dir.: Dr. Marie D. Strazar
Local Museum / Folklore Museum - 1931 44032

Hilton Head Island SC

Coastal Discovery Museum, 100 William Hilton Pkwy, Hilton Head Island, SC 29926-3497 - T: (843) 689-6767, Fax: (843) 689-6769, E-mail: info@coastaldiscovery.org, Internet: www.coastaldiscovery.org. Pres. & C.E.O.: Michael J. Marks
Historical Museum / Science&Tech Museum - 1985
History and science 44033

Hinckley ME

L.C. Bates Museum, c/o Good Will-Hinckley Home For Boys and Girls, Rte 201, Hinckley, ME 04944 - T: (207) 238-4250, Fax: (207) 238-4007, E-mail: lcbates@gwh.org, Internet: www.gwh.org. Dir./ Cur.: Deborah Staber
Local Museum - 1911
General museum 44034

Hinckley MN

Hinckley Fire Museum, 106 Old Hwy 61, Hinckley, MN 55037 - T: (320) 384-7338, Fax: (320) 384-7338, E-mail: hfire@ecenet.com, Internet: www.ci.hinckleyfire.com. Dir.: Jeanne Coffey
Historical Museum - 1976
Fire fighting, Saint Paul & Duluth Railroad Depot 44035

Hingham MA

Bare Cove Fire Museum, POB 262, Hingham, MA 02043 - T: (781) 749-0028, E-mail: barecov-efiremuseum.org. Cur.: Andrew Addoms
Historical Museum - 1976
Hand and horse motored antique fire engines, equip 44036

Old Ordinary Museum, 21 Lincoln St, Hingham, MA 02043 - T: (781) 749-0013, 749-7721, E-mail: info@hinghamhistorical.org, Internet: www.hinghamhistorical.org. Pres.: Willis Ertman
Historical Museum - 1922 44037

Hinsdale IL

Hinsdale Historical Society Museum, 15 S Clay St, Hinsdale, IL 60521 - T: (630) 789-2600, Internet: www.hinsdalehistory.org. Cur.: Kim Morrison
Local Museum / Historical Museum - 1981 44038

Hinton WV

Bluestone Museum, Rte 87, Hinton, WV 25951 - T: (304) 466-1454
Natural History Museum - 1972 44039

Ho-Ho-Kus NJ

Bergen Museum of Art and Science, Ho-Ho-Kus, NJ 07423, mail addr: 96 Linwood Plaza, Ste 443, Fort Lee, NJ 07024 - T: (201) 968-0470, Fax: (201) 265-2536, E-mail: bergenmuseum@hotmail.com, Internet: www.thebergenmuseum.com. C.E.O.: Peter Knipe
Fine Arts Museum / Natural History Museum / Science&Tech Museum - 1956
Paintings, prints, sculpture, Hackensack and Dwarskill mastodons, minerals, shell, fossils, aviation 44040

The Hermitage, 335 N Franklin Turnpike, Ho-Ho-Kus, NJ 07423 - T: (201) 445-8311, Fax: (201) 445-0437, E-mail: info@thehermitage.org, Internet: www.thehermitage.org. Dir.: T. Robins Brown
Historical Museum - 1972
Clothing ant textiles 44041

Hobart IN

Hobart Historical Society Museum, 706 E Fourth St, Hobart, IN 46342 - T: (219) 942-0970. Dir.: Dorothy Ballantyne
Local Museum - 1968
Life in the Hobart are, wheelwright and woodworking tools, agriculture 44042

Hobbs NM

Lea County Cowboy Hall of Fame and Western Heritage Center, 5317 Lovington Hwy, Hobbs, NM 88240 - T: (505) 392-1275, 657-6260, Fax: (505) 392-5871, E-mail: lburnett@nmjc.cc.nm.us. Dir.: La Jean Burnett
Historical Museum - 1978
History 44043

New Mexico Wing-Commemorative Air Force, U.S. Hwy 62-180, Hobbs, NM 88240 - T: (505) 393-6696, Fax: (505) 392-1441, E-mail: hafnau@aol.com. C.E.O.: Harold Brown, Exec. Officer: Phill Ross
Military Museum - 1968
World War II aircraft 44044

Hobson MT

Utica Museum, HC 81, Hobson, MT 59452 - T: (406) 423-5531. Pres.: Charles Nicholsen
Historical Museum - 1965 44045

Hodgenville KY

Abraham Lincoln Birthplace, 2995 Lincoln Farm Rd, Hodgenville, KY 42748 - T: (270) 358-3137, Fax: (270) 358-3874, Internet: www.nps.gov/abli. Head: Kenneth Apschnikat
Special Museum - 1916
Lincoln family homestead 44046

Hogansburg NY

Akwesasne Museum, 321 State Rte 37, Hogansburg, NY 13655-3114 - T: (518) 358-2240, 358-2461, Fax: (518) 358-2649, E-mail: akwmuse@northnet.org, Internet: www.nc3r.org/akwlibr/
Local Museum - 1972
Local hist, folklife 44047

Hohenwald TN

Meriwether Lewis National Monument, 189 Meriwether Lewis Park, Hohenwald, TN 38462 - T: (931) 796-2675, Fax: (931) 796-5417
Historical Museum - 1936
Death and burial site of Meriwether Lewis 44048

Holbrook NY

Sachem Historical Society Museum, 59 Crescent Circle, Holbrook, NY 11741 - T: (516) 588-3967
Historical Museum - 1963 44049

Holderness NH

Squam Lakes Natural Science Center, Rte 113, Holderness, NH 03245 - T: (603) 968-7194, Fax: (603) 968-2229, E-mail: info@nhnature.org, Internet: www.nhnature.org. Dir.: Will Abbott
Natural History Museum - 1966 44050

Holdrege NE

Nebraska Prairie Museum, Phelps County Historical Society, N Burlington Hwy 183, Holdrege, NE 68949-0164 - T: (308) 995-5015, Fax: (308) 995-3955, E-mail: pchs@nebi.com, Internet: www.nebraskaprairie.org. C.E.O./Pres.: Harry Dahlstrom
Local Museum - 1966
Local history - library 44051

Phelps County Museum → Nebraska Prairie Museum

Holland MI

Cappon House Museum, 228 W 9th St, Holland, MI 49423 - T: (616) 392-6740, Fax: (616) 394-4756, E-mail: museum@hope.edu, Internet: www.hollandmuseum.org. C.E.O.: Ann Kiewel
Historical Museum - 1986
Home of Holland's first mayor 44052

DePree Art Center and Gallery, Hope College, 275 Columbia Av, Holland, MI 49423 - T: (616) 395-7000, Fax: (616) 395-7499, Internet: hope.edu/academic/art/depree. Dir.: Dr. John Hanson
University Museum / Fine Arts Museum - 1982 44053

First Michigan Museum of Military History, U.S. 31 and New Holland St, Holland, MI 49424 - T: (616) 399-1955. Pres.: Craig DeSeyter
Military Museum - 1953
Military history 44054

Holland Area Arts Council, 150 W 8th St, Holland, MI 49423 - T: (616) 396-3278, Fax: (616) 396-6298. Pres.: Robert Frieling, Exec. Dir.: Jason Kalajainen
Fine Arts Museum / Public Gallery - 1967
Arts 44055

Holland Museum, 31 W 10th St, Holland, MI 49423 - T: (616) 394-1362, Fax: (616) 394-4756, E-mail: hollandmuseum@macatawa.com, Internet: www.hollandmuseum.org. Dir.: Ann Kiewel, Cur.: Joel Lefever
Local Museum - 1937
Dutch heritage, local history 44056

Windmill Island Municipal Park Museum, 7th St and Lincoln Av, Holland, MI 49423 - T: (616) 355-1030, Fax: (616) 355-1035, E-mail: ad@windmillisland.org, Internet: www.windmillisland.org. Dir.: Ad Van den Akker
Local Museum - 1965
Dutch windmill 44057

Holland VT

Holland Historical Society Museum, Gore Rd, Holland, VT 05830 - T: (802) 895-2917, Fax: (802) 895-4440. Dir.: Julia Carter, Martha Judd, Howard Nelson, Julia Carter, Cyril Worth
Local Museum - 1972
Local hist 44058

Holly Springs MS

Marshall County Historical Museum, 220 E College Av, Holly Springs, MS 38635 - T: (601) 252-3669. C.E.O. & Cur.: Lois Swanee
Historical Museum - 1970 44059

Hollywood FL

Art and Culture Center of Hollywood, 1650 Harrison St, Hollywood, FL 33020 - T: (954) 921-3274, Fax: (954) 921-3273, E-mail: acch@bellsouth.net. Dir.: Cynthia Berman-Miller, Head of Visual Arts: Kenn Piatrowski, Head: Kathleen Lowell (Marketing)
Fine Arts Museum / Folklore Museum - 1976
Multi-disciplinary Arts Center 44060

Hollywood MD

Sotterley Plantation Museum, Rte 245, Hollywood, MD 20636 - T: (301) 373-2280, (800) 681-0850, Fax: (301) 373-8474, E-mail: sotterleyoffice@mail.ameritel.net, Internet: www.sotterley.com. Dir.: Carolyn J. Laray, Sc. Staff: Judith O'Brien, Carol Wilson, Carole Wible, Elizabeth Harman
Historic Site - 1961
1710 Manor House, outbuildings, illustrating Tidewater Plantation culture 44061

Holmdel NJ

Longstreet Farm, Holmdel Park, Longstreet Rd, Holmdel, NJ 07733 - T: (732) 946-3758, 842-4000, Fax: (732) 946-0750, E-mail: info@monmouthcountyparks.com, Internet: www.monmouthcountyparks.com. Cur.: Kevin Guinn
Agriculture Museum - 1967 44062

Vietnam Era Educational Center, 1 Memorial Ln, Holmdel, NJ 07733 - T: (800) 648-8387, Fax: (732) 335-1107, E-mail: klwatts@njvvmf.org, Internet: www.njvvmf.org. Exec. Dir.: Kelly Watts
Military Museum / Historical Museum - 1998 44063

Holyoke CO

Phillips County Museum, 109 S Campbell Av, Holyoke, CO 80734 - T: (970) 854-2129, Fax: (970) 854-3811, E-mail: statz@henge.com, Internet: www.rootsweb.com/cophilli. Pres.: Carol Haynes
Local Museum - 1967
Regional history, agriculture, doll coll, weapons 44064

Holyoke MA

Children's Museum, 444 Dwight St, Holyoke, MA 01040 - T: (413) 536-7048, Fax: (413) 533-2999, E-mail: landry@javanet.com. Dir.: Kathleen McCreary
Special Museum - 1981
Cultural and natural hist 44065

Wistariahurst Museum, 238 Cabot St, Holyoke, MA 01040 - T: (413) 534-2216, Fax: (413) 534-2344, Internet: www.holyoke.org. Dir.: Olivia Mausel
Local Museum / Historical Museum - 1959
Mansion and carriage house, former home of local silk manufacturer William Skinner 44066

Homer AK

Bunnell Street Gallery, 106 W Bunnel, Ste A, Homer, AK 99603 - T: (907) 235-2662, Fax: (907) 235-1530, E-mail: bunnell@xyz.net, Internet: www.xyz.net/~bunnell
Public Gallery - 1994 44067

Pratt Museum, 3779 Bartlett St, Homer, AK 99603 - T: (907) 235-8635, Fax: (907) 235-2764, E-mail: info@prattmuseum.org, Internet: www.prattmuseum.org. Dir.: Michael C. Hawfield
Local Museum - 1968
Natural history, Alaskan history, ethnography, archaeology, local art 44068

Homer NY

Homerville Museum, 49 Clinton St, Homer, NY 13077-1024 - T: (607) 749-3105. Head: Kenneth M. Eaton
Historical Museum / Military Museum - 1976 44069

Hominy OK

Drummond Home, 305 N Price, Hominy, OK 74035 - T: (918) 885-2374. Dir.: Blake Wade
Historical Museum - 1986
Original furnishing of Drummond family 44070

Honesdale PA

Wayne County Museum, 810 Main St, Honesdale, PA 18431 - T: (570) 253-3240, Fax: (717) 253-5204, E-mail: wchs@ptd.net-director, Internet: www.waynehistorypa.org. Dir.: Sally Talaga
Historical Museum / Historic Site - 1917
History, hist of the Delaware and Hudson Canal - Research library, Farm Museum, room of a county school 44071

Honolulu HI

Bernice Pauahi Bishop Museum, 1525 Bernice St, Honolulu, HI 96817-2704 - T: (808) 847-3511, Fax: (808) 841-8968, E-mail: ktama@bishop.org, Internet: www.bishopmuseum.org. Chm.: Marcus Polifka
Local Museum / Ethnology Museum / Natural History Museum / Special Museum - 1889
Cultury, natural history 44072

The Contemporary Museum, 2411 Makiki Heights Dr, Honolulu, HI 96822 - T: (808) 526-1322, Fax: (808) 536-5973, E-mail: info@tcmhi.org, Internet: www.tcmhi.org. Dir.: Georgiana Lagoria, Assoc. Dir.: James Jensen, Dir. Development: Kathleen Hong, Asst. Cur.: Allison Wong
Fine Arts Museum - 1961
Contemporary fine art, historic house, gardens 44073

The Contemporary Museum at First Hawaiian Center, 999 Bishop St, Honolulu, HI 96813, mail addr: 2411 Makiki Heights Dr, HI 96822 - T: (808) 526-1322, Fax: (808) 536-5973, E-mail: info@tcmhi.org, Internet: www.tcmhi.org. Dir.: Georgiana Lagoria, Assoc. Dir.: James Jensen, Cur.: Allison Wong
Fine Arts Museum - 1989
Contemporary art 44074

East-West Center, 1601 East-West Rd, Honolulu, HI 96848-1601 - T: (808) 944-7111, Fax: (808) 944-7070, E-mail: feltzb@ewc.hawaii.edu, Internet: www.ewc.hawaii.edu. Cur.: Jeanette Bennington
Fine Arts Museum / Historical Museum / Natural History Museum / Folklore Museum - 1961 44075

Hawaii Children's Discovery Center, 111 Ohe St, Honolulu, HI 96813 - T: (808) 592-5437, Fax: (808) 592-5400. Pres.: Loretta Yajima
Special Museum - 1985 44076

Hawaii Maritime Center, Pier 7, Honolulu, HI 96813 - T: (808) 523-6151, Fax: (808) 536-1519, E-mail: bmoore@bishopmuseum.org. C.E.O.: Dr. William Brown
Historical Museum - 1988
Maritime history 44077

Hawaii Pacific University Gallery, 1164 Bishop St, Honolulu, HI 96813 - T: (808) 544-0200, Fax: (808) 544-1136, E-mail: nellis@hpu.edu, Internet: www.hpu.edu. Dir.: Sanit Khewhok
University Museum / Fine Arts Museum - 1983 44078

Honolulu Academy of Arts Museum, 900 S Beretania St, Honolulu, HI 96814 - T: (808) 532-8700, Fax: (808) 532-8787, E-mail: webmaster@honoluluacademy.org, Internet: www.hoholuluacademy.org. Dir.: George R. Ellis, Cur.: Julia White (Asian Art), Jennifer Saville (Western Art), Reiko Brandon (Textiles), Don Brown (Film), Karen Thompson (Education), Carol D. Khewhok (Art Center)
Fine Arts Museum - 1922
Art - library 44079

Iolani Palace, King and Richards Sts, Honolulu, HI 96813 - T: (808) 522-0822, Fax: (808) 532-1051, E-mail: kanaina@iolanipalace.org, Internet: www.iolanipalace.org. Dir.: Deborah F. Dunn
Historical Museum / Historic Site - 1966
Iolani Palace c. 1982 erected as state residence for Hawaii's last king Kalakaua, Iolani Barracks of the Royal Guard, paintings 44080

Japanese Cultural Center of Hawaii, 2454 S Beretania St, Honolulu, HI 96826 - T: (808) 945-7633, Fax: (808) 944-1123, E-mail: jcch@lava.net, Internet: www.jcch.com. Pres.: Susan Kodani
Historical Museum - 1987 44081

King Kamehameha V - Judiciary History Center, 417 S King St, Honolulu, HI 96813 - T: (808) 539-4999, Fax: (808) 539-4996, E-mail: jhc@aloha.net, Internet: jhchawaii.org. Exec. Dir.: Paris K. Chai
Historical Museum - 1989
History, Ali'iolani Hale, Hawaii Supreme Court Bldg 44082

Lassen Museum Waikiki, 2250 Kalakaua Av, Honolulu, HI 96815 - T: (808) 923-3435, Internet: www.lassenwaikiki.com
Fine Arts Museum 44083

Mission Houses Museum, 553 S King St, Honolulu, HI 96813 - T: (808) 531-0481, Fax: (808) 545-2280, E-mail: mhm@lava.net, Internet: www.lava.net/~mhm/main.htm. Cur.: Deborah F. Dunn
Historical Museum - 1920 44084

Moanalua Gardens Foundation, 1352 Pineapple Pl, Honolulu, HI 96819 - T: (808) 839-5334, Fax: (808) 839-3658, E-mail: mgf@pixi.com, Internet: mgf-hawaii.com. Dir.: Marilyn Schoenke
Archaeological Museum - 1970
Archaeology 44085

Queen Emma Gallery, 1301 Punchbowl St, Honolulu, HI 96802-0861 - T: (808) 547-4397, Fax: (808) 547-4646, E-mail: efubuda@queens.org, Internet: www.queens.org. Dir.: Masa Morioka Tira
Decorative Arts Museum - 1977
Nicholas Bleecker sculptures, Hawaiian moon calender, Queen Emma's medallion, linocut prints, batik hangings, glass spheres 44086

Queen Emma Summer Palace, 2913 Pali Hwy, Honolulu, HI 96817 - T: (808) 595-3167, Fax: (808) 595-4395, E-mail: doh@pixi.com, Internet: www.daughtersofhawaii.org
Historical Museum / Decorative Arts Museum - 1915
Former home of Queen Emma and King Kamehameha IV 44087

Ramsay Museum, 1128 Smith St, Honolulu, HI 96817-5194 - T: (808) 537-2787, Fax: (808) 531-6873, E-mail: ramsey@lava.net, Internet: www.ramsaymuseum.org. Dir.: Russ Sowers
Fine Arts Museum
Drawings, painting-American, photography, prints, sculpture 44088

Tennent Art Foundation Gallery, 203 Prospect St, Honolulu, HI 96813 - T: (808) 531-1987. Dir.: Elaine Tennent
Fine Arts Museum - 1954 44089

University of Hawaii Art Gallery, 2535 The Mall, Honolulu, HI 96822 - T: (808) 956-6888, Fax: (808) 956-9659, E-mail: gallery@hawaii.edu, Internet: www.hawaii.edu/artgallery. Dir.: Tom Klobe, Assoc. Dir.: Sharon Tasaka
Fine Arts Museum / Public Gallery / University Museum - 1976 44090

University of Hawaii at Manoa Art Gallery, 2535 The Mall, Honoiulu, HI 96822 - T: (808) 956-6888, Fax: (808) 956-9659, E-mail: gallery@hawaii.edu, Internet: www.hawaii.edu/artgallery. Dir.: Tom Klobe
Fine Arts Museum - 1976
Japanese and Polish posters 44091

USS Arizona Memorial, 1 Arizona Memorial Pl, Honolulu, HI 96818 - T: (808) 422-2771, Fax: (808) 483-8608, Internet: www.nps.gov/usar. Cur.: Marshall Owens, Sc. Staff: Daniel Martinez (History)
Military Museum - 1980
Military, WW II Memorial 44092

USS Bowfin Submarine Museum, 11 Arizona Memorial Dr, Honolulu, HI 96818 - T: (808) 423-1341, Fax: (808) 422-5201, E-mail: info@bowfin.org, Internet: www.bowfin.org. Dir.: Gerald Hofwolt, Cur.: Nancy Richards
Historical Museum / Military Museum - 1978
Military ship 44093

Hood VA

Roaring Twenties Antique Car Museum, Rte 230 W, Hood, VA 22623 - T: (540) 948-6290, Fax: (540) 948-6290, E-mail: info@roaring-twenties.com, Internet: www.roaring_twenties.com. C.E.O.: Clarissa Dudley
Science&Tech Museum - 1967 44094

Hood River OR

Hood River County Historical Museum, 300 E Port Marina Dr, Hood River, OR 97031 - T: (541) 386-6772, Fax: (541) 386-6722, E-mail: hrchm@gorge.net
Local Museum - 1907 44095

Hope ND

Steele County Museum, 301 Steele Av, Hope, ND 58046 - T: (701) 945-2394, Fax: (701) 945-2394, E-mail: culture@ictc.com, Internet: www.museum.com. Pres.: Duane Anderson, Dir.: Tracy D. Anderson
Local Museum - 1966 44096

Hope NJ

Hope Historical Society Museum, High St, Rte 519, Hope, NJ 07840 - T: (908) 637-4120, Fax: (908) 637-4120, E-mail: cleopatra@nac.net. Pres.: Tessa McDonald
Historical Museum - 1950 44097

Hopewell NJ

Hopewell Museum, 28 E Broad St, Hopewell, NJ 08525 - T: (609) 466-0103. Pres.: David M. Mackey, Cur.: Beverly Weidl
Local Museum - 1924
Colonial furniture, Indian handicrafts, antique china, glass, silver and pewter, parlors, early needlework 44098

Hopewell VA

Flowerdew Hundred Foundation, 1617 Flowerdew Hundred Rd, Hopewell, VA 23860 - T: (804) 541-8897, Fax: (804) 458-7738, E-mail: flowerdew@firstsaga.com, Internet: www.flowerdew.org. Cur.: Karen K. Shriver
Archaeological Museum - 1978
Archaeology 44099

Hopkinsville KY

Pennyroyal Area Museum, 217 E Ninth St, Hopkinsville, KY 42240 - T: (270) 887-4270, Fax: (270) 887-4271, E-mail: pennyroyal@aol.com. Exec. Dir.: Donna K. Stone
Local Museum - 1975
Local history 44100

Hopkinton NH

New Hampshire Antiquarian Society Museum, 300 Main St, Hopkinton, NH 03229 - T: (603) 746-3825. Dir.: Elaine P. Loft
Local Museum - 1859 44101

Hoquiam WA

Polson Park and Museum, 1611 Riverside Av, Hoquiam, WA 98550 - T: (360) 533-5862, E-mail: jbl@polsonmuseum.org, Internet: www.polsonmuseum.org. Dir.: John Larson
Local Museum - 1976
Local hist 44102

Horicon WI

Satterlee Clark House, 322 Winter St, Horicon, WI 53032 - T: (414) 485-2011. Pres.: Alferna Dobbratz
Local Museum - 1972
Historic house 44103

Hornby NY

Hornby Museum, County Rte 41, Hornby, NY 14813 - T: (607) 962-4471. Pres.: Susan J. Moore
Local Museum - 1958 44104

Horseheads NY

National Warplane Museum, 17 Aviation Dr, Horseheads, NY 14845 - T: (607) 739-8200 ext 221, Fax: (607) 739-8374, E-mail: nwm@warplane.org, Internet: www.warplane.org. Dir.: Vincent Azzarelli, Asst. Dir.: Ed Kittner (Restoration), Cur.: Julie Munson
Science&Tech Museum / Military Museum - 1983 44105

Regional Science and Discovery Center, 3300 Chambers Rd, Horseheads, NY 14844 - T: (607) 739-5297, Fax: (607) 739-5297, E-mail: scenter@stny.rr.com, Internet: www.sdcsciencecenter.org
Natural History Museum - 1996
Physical and biological sciences 44106

Horsham PA

Graeme Park/Keith Mansion, 859 County Line Rd, Horsham, PA 19044 - T: (215) 343-0965, Fax: (215) 343-2223, E-mail: pmousley@state.pa.us, Internet: www.state.pa.us. Dir.: Patricia K. Mousley
Local Museum - 1958
Local hist 44107

Hot Springs AR

Fine Arts Center of Hot Springs, 405 Park Av, Hot Springs, AR 71901 - T: (501) 624-0489, E-mail: taube@ndak.net. Dir.: Barbara Huckaby
Public Gallery - 1947 44108

Mid-America Science Museum, 500 Mid America Blvd, Hot Springs, AR 71913 - T: (501) 767-3461, Fax: (501) 767-1170, E-mail: masm@direclynx.net, Internet: www.direclynx.net/~masm. Dir.: Glenda Eshenroder
Science&Tech Museum - 1971
Science 44109

Hot Springs SD

Fall River County Historical Museum, Rte 1, Hot Springs, SD 57747 - T: (605) 745-5147. Dir./Cur.: Paul Hickock
Local Museum / Decorative Arts Museum - 1961
Local hist 44110

Mammoth Site of Hot Springs, 1800 Highway 18, Bypass, Hot Springs, SD 57747 - T: (605) 745-6017, Fax: (605) 745-3038, E-mail: mammoth@mammothsite.com, Internet: www.mammothsite.com. C.E.O.: Joe Muller
Natural History Museum - 1975
Paleontology 44111

Hot Sulphur Springs CO

Grand County Museum, 110 E Byers, Hot Sulphur Springs, CO 80451 - T: (970) 725-3939, Fax: (970) 725-0129, E-mail: gcha@rkymtnhi.com, Internet: www.grandcountymuseum.com. Pres.: Barbara Mitchell
Local Museum - 1974
Regional history, settlement 44112

Houghton MI

A.E. Seaman Mineral Museum, Michigan Technological University, 1400 Townsend Dr, Houghton, MI 49931 - T: (906) 487-2572, Fax: (906) 487-3027, E-mail: sjdyl@mtu.edu, Internet: www.geo.mtu.edu/museum/. Dir.: Stanley J. Dyl, Cur.: Dr. George W. Robinson
University Museum / Natural History Museum - 1902
Mineralogy - library 44113

Houma LA

Terrebonne Museum, 1208 Museum Dr, Houma, LA 70360 - T: (985) 851-0154, Fax: (985) 868-1476, E-mail: southdown@mobiltel.com, Internet: www.southdownmuseum.org. Dir.: Karen Hart
Folklore Museum - 1975
Hist and culture of Terrebonne Parish 44114

Houston TX

Art League of Houston, 1953 Montrose Blvd, Houston, TX 77006-1243 - T: (713) 523-9530, Fax: (713) 523-4053, E-mail: artleagh@neosoft.com, Internet: www.artleaguehouston.org. Exec. Dir.: Claudia Solis, Pres.: Margaret Poissant
Fine Arts Museum - 1948
Art 44115

Bayou Bend Collection, 1 Westcott, Houston, TX 7707 - T: (713) 639-7750, Fax: (713) 639-7770, E-mail: dwarren@mfah.org, Internet: www.mfah.org. Dir.: David B. Warren
Fine Arts Museum / Decorative Arts Museum - 1956
American decorative arts, paintings, English ceramics 44116

The Children's Museum of Houston, 1500 Binz, Houston, TX 77004-7112 - T: (713) 522-1138 ext 215/200, Fax: (713) 522-5747, E-mail: staylor@cmhouston.org, Internet: www.cmhouston.org. Dir.: Tammie Kahn, Dept. Dir.: Cheryl McCallum, Cur.: Niobe Ngozi (Arts Education)
Special Museum - 1981
Children's Museum 44117

Contemporary Arts Museum, 5216 Montrose Blvd, Houston, TX 77006-6598 - T: (713) 284-8250, Fax: (713) 284-8275, Internet: www.camh.org. Dir.: Marti Mayo, Asst. Dir.: Michael Reed, Cur.: Lynn M. Herbert, Valerie Cassell, Paola Morsiani
Fine Arts Museum - 1948
Art 44118

Cy Twombly Gallery, 1501 Branard St, Houston, TX 77006 - T: (713) 525-9400, Fax: (713) 525-9444, E-mail: public_affairs@menil.org, Internet: www.menil.org. Dir.: Paul Winkler
Fine Arts Museum - 1995
Art 44119

Diverse Works, 1117 E Freewy, Houston, TX 77002 - T: (713) 223-8346, Fax: (713) 223-4608, E-mail: info@diverseworks.org, Internet: www.diverseworks.org. Exec. Dir.: Sara Kelner
Performing Arts Museum - 1983 44120

The Heritage Society Museum, 1100 Bagby, Houston, TX 77002 - T: (713) 655-1912, Fax: (713) 655-7527, E-mail: efle@heritagesociety.org, Internet: www.heritagesociety.org. C.E.O.: Tina Medlin, Cur.: Wallace Saage, Eve Fleishman
Local Museum - 1954
Local hist 44121

Holocaust Museum Houston, 5401 Caroline St, Houston, TX 77004 - T: (713) 942-8000 ext 100, Fax: (713) 942-7953, E-mail: sjohnson@hmh.org, Internet: www.hmh.org. C.E.O.: Susan Llanes-Myers
Historical Museum - 1996
Diaries, photographs, maps, prison uniforms, bricks from Auschwitz and the Warsaw ghetto 44122

Houston Fire Museum, 2403 Milam St, Houston, TX 77006 - T: (713) 524-2526, Fax: (713) 520-7566, E-mail: hfmi@houstonfiremuseum.org, Internet: www.houstonfiremuseum.org. Dir.: Emily Ponte, Cur.: Timothy B. Kirwin
Historical Museum - 1982
Fire fighting 44123

Houston Museum of Natural Science, 1 Hermann Circle Dr, Houston, TX 77030-1799 - T: (713) 639-4601, 639-4614, 639-4629, Fax: (713) 523-4125, Internet: www.hmns.org. C.E.O.: Rebecca A. McDonald
Natural History Museum / Science&Tech Museum - 1909
Natural science 44124

Houston Police Museum, 17000 Aldine Westfield Rd, Houston, TX 77073 - T: (281) 230-2360, Fax: (281) 230-2334. Dir.: Denny G. Hair
Historical Museum - 1981
Police hist 44125

The Menil Collection, 1515 Sul Ross, Houston, TX 77006 - T: (713) 525-9400, Fax: (713) 525-9444, E-mail: info@menil.org, Internet: www.menil.org. Cur.: Matthew Drutt, Cons.: Elizabeth Lunning, Registrar: Anne Adams
Fine Arts Museum - 1980
Art, antiquities, art books 44126

Midtown Art Center, 3414 La Branch St, Houston, TX 77004-3841 - T: (713) 521-8803, Fax: (713) 521-8803. Dir.: Ida Thompson
Public Gallery - 1982 44127

Museum of American Architecture and Decorative Arts, c/o Houston Baptist University, 7502 Fondren Rd, Houston, TX 77074 - T: (281) 649-3311, -3000, Fax: (281) 649-3489. Dir.: Lois Miller
Decorative Arts Museum - 1964
Architecture, decorative arts 44128

The Museum of Fine Arts, 1001 Bissonnet, Houston, TX 77265 - T: (713) 639-7300, Fax: (713) 639-7395, E-mail: pr@mfah.org, Internet: www.mfah.org. Dir.: Peter C. Marzio, Assoc. Dir.: David B. Warren (Bayou Bend), Joseph Havel (Glassell School of Art), Gwendolyn H. Goffe (Finance, Admin.), Cur.: Barry Walker (Prints, Drawings), Tina Llorente (Textiles, Costumes), James Clifton (Renaissance,

Baroque Painting and Sculpture, Blaffer coll), Edgar Peters Bowron (European Painting and Sculpture), Alison de Lima Greene, Alivia Wardlaw (Modern and Contemporary Art), Anne W. Tucker (Photography, Gus and Lyndall Wortham), Katherine S. Howe (Decorative Arts), Michael K. Brown (Bayou Bend Coll), Marian Lutz (Film and Video), Emily Neff (American Paintings and Sculpture), Frances Marzio (Glassell coll), Mari Carmen Ramirez (Latin American Art), Cons.: Wynne Phelan
Fine Arts Museum - 1900
Multicultural art, European ancient art, American and European decorative art, impressionist and post- impressionist art, African gold, prints, pre-columbian drawings, photos 44129

Museum of Health and Medical Science, 1515 Hermann Dr, John P. McGovern Bldg, Houston, TX 77004-7126 - T: (713) 942-7054, Fax: (713) 526-1434, E-mail: info@mhms.org, Internet: www.mhms.org. Dir.: Randy W. Ray
Science&Tech Museum - 1969 44130

Museum of Printing History, 1324 W Clay, Houston, TX 77019 - T: (713) 522-4652, Fax: (713) 522-5694, Internet: www.printingmuseum.org. Exec. Dir.: Elizabeth P. Griffin
Special Museum / Science&Tech Museum - 1983
Hist of communication, tools and machines 44131

National Museum of Funeral History, 415 Barren Springs Dr, Houston, TX 77090 - T: (281) 876-3063, Fax: (281) 876-4403, E-mail: info@nmfh.org, Internet: www.nmfh.org. Dir.: Georg Favell
Historical Museum - 1992 44132

Rice University Art Gallery, 6100 Main St, Sewall Hall, Houston, TX 77005 - T: (713) 348-6069, Fax: (713) 348-5980, E-mail: ruag@rice.edu, Internet: www.rice.edu/ruag. Dir.: Kimberly Davenport
University Museum / Public Gallery - 1971
Contemporary art, installation 44133

Robert A. Vines Environmental Science Center, 8856 Westview Dr, Houston, TX 77055 - T: (713) 365-4175, Fax: (713) 365-4178, E-mail: harrisp@springbranchisd.com, Internet: www.springbranchisd.com. Dir.: Randell A. Beavers
Natural History Museum
Natural science 44134

Rothko Chapel, 3900 Yupon, 1490 Sul Ross, Houston, TX 77006 - T: (713) 524-9839, E-mail: info@rothkochapel.org, Internet: www.rothkochapel.org. Dir.: Suna Umari
Religious Arts Museum - 1971
Religious art 44135

Sarah Campbell Blaffer Foundation, 5601 Main St, Houston, TX 77006 - T: (713) 639-7741, Fax: (713) 639-7742, E-mail: jclifton@mfah.org, Internet: riceinfo.rice.edu/projects/blaffer/index.html. Dir.: Dr. James Clifton, Pres.: Charles W. Hall
Fine Arts Museum - 1964
Art 44136

Sarah Campbell Blaffer Gallery, Art Museum of the University of Houston, 120 Fine Arts Bldg, Houston, TX 77204-4018 - T: (713) 743-9521, Fax: (713) 743-9525, E-mail: tsultan@uh.edu, Internet: www.blaffergallery.org. Dir.: Terrie Sultan
Fine Arts Museum / University Museum - 1973
Art 44137

Space Center Houston, 1601 NASA Road One, Houston, TX 77058-3696 - T: (281) 244-2105, Fax: (281) 283-7724, Internet: www.spacecenter.org. Pres.: Richard Allen
Science&Tech Museum - 1992
Space technology 44138

Howell NJ

Howell Historical Society & Committee Museum, 427 Lakewood-Farmingdale Rd, Howell, NJ 07731 - T: (732) 938-2212, E-mail: howellhist@aol.com, Internet: www.howellnj.com/historic/. Pres.: Steve Meyer
Historical Museum - 1971 44139

Howes Cave NY

Iroquois Indian Museum, Caverns Rd, Howes Cave, NY 12092 - T: (518) 296-8949, Fax: (518) 296-8955, E-mail: info@iroquoismuseum.org, Internet: www.iroquoismuseum.org. Dir.: Erynne Ansell, Cur.: Neal B. Keating, Mike Tarbell
Ethnology Museum / Folklore Museum - 1980
Contemporary Iroquois art, ethnology, archaeology 44140

Hubbardton VT

Hubbardton Battlefield Museum, Monument Hill Rd, Hubbardton, VT 05749 - T: (802) 759-2412, 828-3051, Fax: (802) 828-3206, E-mail: jdumville@dca.state.vt.us, Internet: www.historicvermont.org. Head: John P. Dumville
Historic Site - 1948
Historic site 44141

Hudson NY

American Museum of Fire Fighting, Firemen's Home, 125 Harry Howard Av, Hudson, NY 12534 - T: (518) 828-7695, Fax: (518) 828-1092, Internet: www.warrenstreet.com. Cur.: R. Dennis Randall
Science&Tech Museum - 1925 44142

Olana State Historic Site, 5720 Rte 9-G, Hudson, NY 12534 - T: (518) 828-0135, Fax: (518) 828-6742, Internet: www.olana.org. Dir.: Linda E. McLean, Cur.: Evelyn Trebilcock, Asst. Cur.: Valerie Balist, Head: Geraldine Weidel (Education), Archivist: Ida Brier
Fine Arts Museum / Historical Museum - 1966 44143

Hudson OH

Historical Society Museum, 22 Aurora St, Hudson, OH 44236-2947 - T: (330) 653-6658, Fax: (330) 650-4693, Internet: www.hudsonlibrary.org. Dir.: E. Leslie Polott
Historical Museum - 1910 44144

Hudson WI

The Octagon House, 1004 Third St, Hudson, WI 54016 - T: (715) 386-2654. Dir.: Catherine Hawhsford
Local Museum - 1948
Local hist 44145

Hugo CO

Headlund Museum, 7th St and 3rd Av, Hugo, CO 80821 - T: (719) 743-2485, Fax: (719) 743-2447, E-mail: twbndee@yahoo.com. Head: Garald Ensign
Local Museum - 1972
Local hist 44146

Lincoln County Museum → Headlund Museum

Hugo OK

Choctaw Museum, 309 N B St, Hugo, OK 74743 - T: (580) 326-6630, Fax: (580) 326-6686, E-mail: npence@sailfish.net. Pres.: Noel Pence
Science&Tech Museum - 1978
Railroad Museum 44147

Hugoton KS

Stevens County Gas and Historical Museum, 905 S Adams, Hugoton, KS 67951 - T: (316) 544-8751, E-mail: svcomus@pld.com. Pres.: Richard Barnes, Cur.: Gladys Renfro
Historical Museum / Science&Tech Museum - 1961
Original A.T.S.F. depot country store, incl barber shop, grocery store, agricultural and automotive displays 44148

Hull MA

Hull Lifesaving Museum, The Museum of Boston Harbor Heritage, 1117 Nantasket Av, Hull, MA 02045, mail addr: POB 221, Hull, MA 02045 - T: (781) 925-5433, Fax: (781) 925-0992, E-mail: hullmuseum@channel1.com, Internet: www.bostonharborheritage.org
Special Museum - 1978
Prints, clothing, lifesaving vessels, logs, fleet of traditional small crafts 44149

Humboldt IA

Humboldt County Historical Association Museum, POB 162, Humboldt, IA 50548 - T: (515) 332-5280, 332-3449. Pres.: Tim Smith, Dir.: Bette Newton
Local Museum - 1962
County history 44150

Humboldt KS

Humboldt Historical Museum, Second and Charles Sts, Humboldt, KS 66748 - T: (620) 473-2250, 365-8267, E-mail: rrthompson504@yahoo.com, Internet: www.usd258.net~humbmuseum
Local Museum - 1966
Farm equip, Civil War cannon, original jail cell, horse-drawn adult and infant hearse 44151

Huntersville NC

Historic Latta Plantation, 5225 Sample Rd, Huntersville, NC 28078 - T: (704) 875-2312, Fax: (704) 875-1794, Internet: www.lattaplanation.org. Dir.: Duane Smith
Historical Museum - 1972 44152

Huntingdon PA

Huntingdon County Museum, 106 4th St, Huntingdon, PA 16652 - T: (814) 643-5449, Fax: (814) 643-2711, E-mail: hchs@vicon.net, Internet: www.huntingdon.net/hchs. Dir.: Nancy S. Shedd, Pres.: Judith A. Heberling
Local Museum - 1937
Local hist 44153

Juniata College Museum of Art, Moore and 17th St, Huntingdon, PA 16652 - T: (814) 641-3505, Fax: (814) 641-3607, E-mail: earenfight@juniata.edu, Internet: www.juniata.edu/museum. Dir.: Philip Earenfight, Cur.: Nancy Siegel
Fine Arts Museum - 1998
American portrait miniatures, contemporary works on paper, paintings, prints 44154

Swigart Museum, Museum Park, Rte 22 E, Huntingdon, PA 16652 - T: (814) 643-0885, Fax: (814) 643-2857, E-mail: tours@swigartmuseum.com, Internet: www.swigartmuseum.com. Pres.: Patricia B. Swigart, Dir.: Marjorie E. Cutright
Science&Tech Museum - 1927
Automobiles 44155

Huntington IN

Dan Quayle Center and Museum, 815 Warren St, Huntington, IN 46750 - T: (219) 356-6356, Fax: (219) 356-1455, E-mail: info@quaylemuseum.org, Internet: www.quaylemuseum.org. CEO: Daniel Johns
Historical Museum - 1993 44156

Huntington County Historical Society Museum, 315 Court St, Huntington, IN 46750 - T: (219) 356-7264, Fax: (219) 356-7264. Dir.: Robert McKinley, Cur.: Helen Shock
Historical Museum - 1932
Local history 44157

Wings of Freedom, 1365 Warren Rd, Huntington, IN 46750 - T: (219) 356-1945, Fax: (219) 356-1315, E-mail: scatvii@aol.com, Internet: www.members.aol.com. Pres.: John Shuttleworth
Military Museum / Science&Tech Museum - 1996
Aeronautics, military hist 44158

Huntington NY

David Conklin Farmhouse, 2 High St, Huntington, NY 11743 - T: (631) 427-7045, Fax: (631) 427-7056, E-mail: judy@huntingtonhistoricalsociety.org, Internet: www.huntingtonhistoricalsociety.org. Dir.: Judith Estes
Decorative Arts Museum - 1903
Furnished in Colonial, Empire and Victorian styles, dols, toys, pottery 44159

Dr Daniel W. Kissam House, 434 Park Av, Huntington, NY 11743 - T: (631) 427-7045, Fax: (631) 427-7056, E-mail: judy@huntingtonhistoricalsociety.org, Internet: www.huntingtonhistoricalsociety.org. Dir.: Judith Estes
Historical Museum - 1903
Early physicians home 44160

Heckscher Museum of Art, 2 Prime Av, Huntington, NY 11743-7702 - T: (516) 351-3250, Fax: (516) 423-2145, E-mail: info@heckscher.org, Internet: www.heckscher.org. C.E.O.: Beth E. Levinthal, Cur.: Anne DePietro
Fine Arts Museum - 1920
Art 44161

Huntington Historical Society Museum, 209 Main St, Huntington, NY 11743 - T: (516) 427-7045, Fax: (516) 427-7056, E-mail: judy@huntingtonhistoricalsocietymuseum.org, Internet: www.huntingtonhistoricalsocietymuseum.org. Pres.: Peter Demidovich, Cur.: Judith Estes
Local Museum - 1903
History 44162

Huntington VT

Birds of Vermont Museum, 900 Sherman Hollow Rd, Huntington, VT 05462 - T: (802) 434-2167, Fax: (802) 434-2167, E-mail: birdsvt@together.net, Internet: www.ejhs.k12.vt.us/homepages/birds. Pres.: Craig Reynolds, C.E.O.: Robert N. Spear
Natural History Museum - 1986 44163

Huntington WV

Geology Museum, Marshall University, 3rd Av & Hal Greer Blvd, Huntington, WV 25755 - T: (304) 696-6720, Fax: (304) 696-2600. Dir.: Dr. Dewey D. Sanderson, Sc. Staff: Dr. Richard B. Bonnett, Dr. Ronald L. Martino
University Museum / Natural History Museum / Science&Tech Museum - 1837
Geology 44164

Huntington Museum of Art, 2033 McCoy Rd, Huntington, WV 25701 - T: (304) 529-2701, Fax: (304) 529-7447, E-mail: jgillisp@hmoa.org, Internet: www.hmoa.org. Dep. Dir.: Katherine Cox (Education), Mike Beck (Horticulture), Chief Cur.: Jenine Culligan
Fine Arts Museum - 1947
Art 44165

Huntington Railroad Museum, 14th St W, River Park, Huntington, WV 25705 - T: (304) 453-1641, Fax: (304) 453-6140, E-mail: railtwo@aol.com, Internet: www.newrivertrain.com
Science&Tech Museum - 1962
Steam locomotive caboose, diesel locomotive cab, working pump handcar on track 44166

Museum of Radio and Technology, 1640 Florence Av, Huntington, WV 25701 - T: (304) 525-8890
Science&Tech Museum - 1992 44167

Huntington Beach CA

Huntington Beach Art Center, 538 Main St, Huntington Beach, CA 92648 - T: (714) 374-1650, Fax: (714) 374-5304, E-mail: deangel@surfcity-hb.org. Dir.: Michael Mudd
Public Gallery - 1995 44168

Huntington Beach International Surfing Museum, 411 Olive Av, Huntington Beach, CA 92648 - T: (714) 960-3483, Fax: (714) 960-1434, E-mail: intsurfing@earthlink.net, Internet: www.surfingmuseum.org. Dir.: Natalie Kotsch
Special Museum - 1987
Surfing, restored Art Deco bldg 44169

Huntington Station NY

Walt Whitman Birthplace State Historic Site, 246 Old Walt Whitman Rd, Huntington Station, NY 11746-4148 - T: (516) 427-5240, Fax: (516) 427-5247, Internet: www.liglobal.com/walt. Dir.: Barbara M. Bart
Historical Museum - 1949 44170

Huntsville AL

Art Galleries at UAH, Dept of Art and Art History, Huntsville, AL 35899 - T: (256) 824-6114, Fax: (256) 890-6411, E-mail: fromk@email.uah.edu, Internet: www.artuniversityalabama.com. Head: Kristy From-Brown
Fine Arts Museum / University Museum - 1975
Print coll 44171

Burritt on the Mountain, A Living Museum, 3101 Burritt Dr, Huntsville, AL 35801 - T: (256) 536-2882, Fax: (256) 532-1784, E-mail: bm-recep@ci.huntsville.al.us, Internet: www.burrittmuseum.com. Dir.: James L. Powers, Asst. Dir.: Pat Robertson, Cur.: Emma Eckenrode-Lewis
Local Museum / Historical Museum / Natural History Museum - 1955 44172

Earlyworks Museum Complex, 404 Madison St, Huntsville, AL 35801 - T: (256) 564-8100, Fax: (256) 564-8151, E-mail: info@earlyworks.com, Internet: www.earlyworks.com. Dir.: Dana Lee Tatum
Historical Museum - 1982 44173

Huntsville Museum of Art, 300 Church St S, Huntsville, AL 35801 - T: (256) 535-4350 ext 200, Fax: (256) 532-1743, E-mail: info@hsvmuseum.org, Internet: www.hsvmuseum.org. Exec. Dir.: Deborah Taylor, Cur.: Peter J. Baldaia
Fine Arts Museum - 1970 44174

United States Space and Rocket Center, 1 Tranquility Base, Huntsville, AL 35805 - T: (256) 837-3400, Fax: (256) 837-6137, 721-7180, E-mail: info@spacecamp.com, Internet: www.spacecamp.com. C.E.O.: Larry Capps
Science&Tech Museum - 1968
Aviation, early space history to space shuttle, missiles, Apollo artefacts 44175

Huntsville TX

Sam Houston Memorial Museum, 1836 Sam Houston Av, Huntsville, TX 77341 - T: (936) 294-1832, Fax: (409) 294-3670, E-mail: SMM_PBN@shsu.edu, Internet: www.samhouston.org. Dir.: Patrick B. Nolan, Cur.: Mac Woodward, Derrick Birdsall, David Wight
Historical Museum - 1927
History, memorabilia of Sam Houston (1793 - 1863) 44176

Hurley NY

Hurley Patentee Manor, 464 Old Rte 209, Hurley, NY 12443 - T: (845) 331-5414, Fax: (845) 331-5414. Dir.: Carolyn M. Waligurski, Stephen S. Waligurski
Historical Museum - 1968 44177

Hurley WI

Old Iron County Courthouse Museum, Wisconsin State Historical Society, 303 Iron St, Hurley, WI 54534 - T: (715) 561-2244. Pres.: Bernice Miles
Local Museum / Historic Site - 1976
Local hist, iron mining, loging, early family living, historical records 44178

Hurleyville NY

Sullivan County Historical Society Museum, 265 Main St, Hurleyville, NY 12747-0247 - T: (845) 434-8044, Fax: (845) 434-8056, E-mail: schs@warwick.net, Internet: www.sullivancountyhistory.org. Pres.: Allan Dampman
Local Museum - 1898 44179

Huron SD

Dakotaland Museum, State Fair Grounds, Huron, SD 57350 - T: (605) 352-4626. Pres.: K.O. Kauth, Dir.: Ruby Johannsen
Local Museum - 1960
Bird and animals (stuffed), Local hist 44180

Hurricane UT

Hurricane Valley Heritage Park Museum, 35 W State, Hurricane, UT 84737 - T: (435) 635-3245, Fax: (435) 635-4696. C.E.O.: Verdell Hinton
Local Museum - 1989
Local pioneer and Indian culture, dools, tools, family histories, town military men 44181

Hurricane WV

Museum in the Community, 3 Valley Park Dr, Hurricane, WV 25526 - T: (304) 562-0484, Fax: (304) 562-4733, E-mail: info@museuminthecommunity.org, Internet: www.museuminthecommunity.org. Dir.: Kelly S. Burns, Pres.: Judy Ross
Fine Arts Museum / Folklore Museum / Ethnology Museum - 1983
Art 44182

Hutchinson KS

Kansas Cosmosphere and Space Center, 1100 N Plum, Hutchinson, KS 67501-1499 - T: (316) 662-2305, Fax: (316) 662-3693, E-mail: info@cosmo.org, Internet: www.cosmo.org. Pres.: Jeff Ollenburger
Science&Tech Museum - 1962
Space museum 44183

Reno County Museum, 100 S Walnut, Hutchinson, KS 67501-0664 - T: (620) 662-1184, Fax: (620) 662-0236, E-mail: rcmuseum@swbell.net, Internet: renocounty.museum.com. Dir.: Jay Smith, Cur.: Barbara Ulrich-Hicks, Pat Garwood
Local Museum - 1961
County history 44184

Hyannis NE

Grant County Museum, Grant County Courthouse, 105 E Harrison, Hyannis, NE 69350-9706 - T: (308) 458-2371, Fax: (308) 458-2485. C.E.O.: Merle Hayward
Local Museum - 1963 44185

Hyde Park NY

Eleanor Roosevelt National Historic Site, Rte 9 G, Hyde Park, NY 12538 - T: (914) 229-9115, Fax: (914) 229-0739, E-mail: rova-superintendent@nps.gov, Internet: www.nps.gov/elro
Local Museum - 1977
Home of Eleanor Roosevelt from 1945-1962 44186

Franklin D. Roosevelt Library-Museum, 4079 Albany Post Rd, Hyde Park, NY 12538 - T: (845) 229-8114, Fax: (845) 229-0872, E-mail: library@roosevelt.nara.gov, Internet: www.fdrlibrary.marist.edu. Dir.: Cynthia M. Koch
Historical Museum / Library with Exhibitions - 1940
Culture coll, manuscripts, books, film, photographs, White House records 44187

Home of Franklin D. Roosevelt, Rte 9, Hyde Park, NY 12538 - T: (914) 229-9115, Fax: (914) 229-0739, E-mail: rova_superintendent@nps.gov., Internet: www.nps.gov/fofr
Local Museum - 1946 44188

Vanderbilt Mansion National Museum, Rte 9, Hyde Park, NY 12538 - T: (914) 229-9115, Fax: (914) 229-0739, Internet: www.nps.gov/vana
Historical Museum - 1940 44189

Idabel OK

Museum of the Red River, 812 E Lincoln Rd, Idabel, OK 74745 - T: (508) 286-3616, Fax: (508) 286-3616, E-mail: motrr@hotmail.com, Internet: www.museumoftheredriver.org. Dir.: Henry Moy, Cur.: Mary Herron, Mario Rivera
Ethnology Museum / Archaeological Museum / Fine Arts Museum / Natural History Museum - 1974 44190

Idaho Springs CO

Argo Gold Mine and Mill Museum, 2350 Riverside Dr, Idaho Springs, CO 80452 - T: (303) 567-2421, Fax: (303) 567-9304, Internet: www.historicargotours.com. Dir.: Robert N. Maxwell
Science&Tech Museum - 1977
Mining history 44191

Heritage Museum, 2060 Colorado Blvd, Idaho Springs, CO 80452 - T: (303) 567-4382, Fax: (303) 567-4605. Cur.: Chee Chee Bell
Local Museum - 1964 44192

Underhill Museum, 1318 Miner Rd, Idaho Springs, CO 80452 - T: (303) 567-4709, Fax: (303) 567-4605. Cur.: Chee Chee Bell
Science&Tech Museum
Mining, U.S. Mineral Surveyor James Underhill 44193

Ignacio CO

Southern Ute Indian Cultural Center, Hwy 172 N, Ignacio, CO 81137, mail addr: POB 737CO 81137, Ignacio - T: (970) 563-9583, Fax: (970) 563-4641, E-mail: sum@frontier.net, Internet: www.southernutemuseum.org. Dir.: Cheryl A. Frost, Cur.: Liz Kent
Historical Museum / Ethnology Museum / Folklore Museum - 1972
Native American history, ethnology, Indian reservation 44194

Ilion NY

Remington Firearms Museum and Country Store, 14 Hoefler Av, Ilion, NY 13357 - T: (315) 895-3301, Fax: (315) 895-3543, E-mail: wittmanc@remington.com, Internet: www.remington.com. Cur.: Dennis Sanita
Science&Tech Museum / Special Museum - 1959 44195

Ilwaco WA

Ilwaco Heritage Museum, 115 SE Lake St, Ilwaco, WA 98624-0153 - T: (360) 642-3446, Fax: (360) 642-4615, E-mail: ihm@willapabay.org. Dir.: Hobe Kytr, Man.: Barbara Minard (Collections)
Fine Arts Museum / Historical Museum - 1983
History, art 44196

Independence CA

Eastern California Museum, 155 Grant St, Independence, CA 93526 - T: (760) 878-0364, Fax: (760) 878-0412, E-mail: ecmuseum@qnet.com. Dir.: William H. Michael
Local Museum / Historical Museum / Ethnology Museum / Natural History Museum - 1928 44197

Independence KS

Independence Historical Museum, 8th and Myrtle, Independence, KS 67301 - T: (316) 331-3515, E-mail: museum@comgen.com
Local Museum - 1882
Fred Hudiburg coll, coll of Christmas plates, glass, hist, Indian artifacts, paintings, black pottery 44198

Independence MO

1859 Jail-Marshal's Home and Museum, 217 N Main St, Independence, MO 64050 - T: (816) 252-1892, Fax: (816) 461-7792, E-mail: jail@jchs.org, Internet: www.jchs.org. Dir.: Susan Church
Local Museum - 1958
Jackson county history, furnishings of mid-19th c 44199

Community of Christ Musuem, The Temple, River and Walnut, Independence, MO 64051 - T: (816) 833-1000, Fax: (816) 521-3089, E-mail: bgunderson@cofchrist.org, Internet: www.cofchrist.org. Dir.: Robert A. Gunderson
Religious Arts Museum - 1956 44200

Harry S. Truman Home, 223 N Main St, Independence, MO 64050 - T: (816) 254-2720, Fax: (816) 254-4491, E-mail: james_sanders@nps.gov, Internet: www.nps.gov/hstr/. Dir.: James Sanders, Cur.: Carol J. Dage
Historical Museum - 1982
Former farm home young Harry S Truman 44201

Harry S. Truman Library Museum, 500 W Hwy 24 and Delaware Rd, Independence, MO 64050 - T: (816) 833-1400, Fax: (816) 833-4368, E-mail: truman.library@nara.gov, Internet: www.trumanlibrary.org. Dir.: Scott Roley, Cur.: Clay R. Bauske
Historical Museum - 1957
library 44202

Harry S. Truman Office and Courtroom, Main and Lexington St, Independence, MO 64050 - T: (816) 795-8200 ext 1260, Fax: (816) 795-7938, E-mail: juligor@gw.co.jackson.mo.us, Internet: www.co.jackson.mo.us
Historical Museum - 1973
Judge Truman 44203

Independence Visitors Center, 937 W Walnut St, Independence, MO 64050 - T: (816) 836-3466, Fax: (816) 252) 6256, E-mail: vcindepend@ldschurch.org, Internet: www.ldschurch.org. Dir.: George G. Romney
Folklore Museum - 1971
Art, Mormon life in Missouri from 1831-1839 44204

John Wornall House Museum, 6115 Wornall Rd, Independence, MO 64113 - T: (816) 444-1858, Fax: (816) 361-8165, E-mail: jwornall@crn.org, Internet: www.wornallhouse.org. Exec. Dir.: Lori Cox-Paul
Historical Museum / Decorative Arts Museum - 1972
Decorative arts, furniture, architecture 44205

Mormon Visitors Center, 937 W Walnut St, Independence, MO 64050-0000 - T: (816) 836-3466, Fax: (816) 252-6256, Internet: www.lds.org. Dir.: George Romney
Religious Arts Museum - 1970
30 ft mural of Christ, painting, reproductions 44206

National Frontier Trails Center, 318 W Pacific, Independence, MO 64050 - T: (816) 325-7575, Fax: (816) 325-7579, Internet: www.frontiertrailscenter.com. Dir.: John Mark Lambertson, Cur.: David Aamodt
Historical Museum - 1990 44207

Vaile Mansion - Dewitt Museum, 1500 N Liberty St, Independence, MO 64050 - T: (816) 325-7111, Fax: (816) 325-7400, Internet: www.ci.independence.mo.us. C.E.O. & Pres.: Ron Potter, Cur.: Cathy Offutt
Local Museum / Historic Site - 1983
Local hist 44208

Indian Rocks Beach FL

Gulf Beach Art Center, 1515 Bay Palm Blvd, Indian Rocks Beach, FL 37785 - T: (727) 596-4331. Dir.: Betsy Choetf
Fine Arts Museum - 1978
Art gallery 44209

Indiana PA

Historical and Genealogical Society of Indiana County, 200 S Sixth St, Indiana, PA 15701-2999 - T: (724) 463-9600, Fax: (724) 463-9899, E-mail: ichs@ptd.net, Internet: www.rootsweb.com/~paicgs/. Pres.: Scott E. Decker, Exec. Dir.: Coleen B. Chambers
Local Museum - 1938
Local hist 44210

The Jimmy Stewart Museum, 845 Philadelphia St, Indiana, PA 15701 - T: (724) 349-6112, Fax: (724) 349-6140, E-mail: curator@jimmy.org, Internet: www.jimmy.org. Dir.: Elizabeth Salome
Special Museum / Performing Arts Museum - 1994
Cinematography 44211

Kipp Gallery, Indiana University of Pennsylvania, 470 Sprowls Hall, 11th St, Indiana, PA 15705 - T: (412) 357-7930, Fax: (412) 357-7778, Internet: www.arts.iup.edu/museum. Dir.: Dr. Richard Field
Fine Arts Museum / University Museum - 1970 44212

The University Museum, Indiana University of Pennsylvania, Sutton Hall, 1011 South Dr, Indiana, PA 15705-1087 - T: (724) 357-7930, Fax: (724) 357-7778, Internet: www.arts.iup.edu/museum. Pres.: Joseph Mack, Dir.: Michael Hood
Fine Arts Museum / University Museum - 1981
Art 44213

Indianapolis IN

Center for Agricultural Science and Heritage, 1201 E 38th St, Indianapolis, IN 46205 - T: (317) 925-2410, Fax: (317) 925-7277, E-mail: thebarn@iquest.net. Exec. Dir.: Betsy Kranz
Agriculture Museum - 1994 44214

The Children's Museum of Indianapolis, 3000 N Meridian St, Indianapolis, IN 46208 - T: (317) 334-4000, Fax: (317) 921-4122, E-mail: tcmi@childrensmuseum.org, Internet: www.childrensmuseum.org. Pres.: Dr. Jeffrey Patchen
Ethnology Museum / Local Museum / Natural History Museum - 1925 44215

Clowes Fund Collection, 1200 W 38th St, Indianapolis, IN 46208 - T: (317) 923-1331, Fax: (317) 931-1978, E-mail: ima@ima-art.org. Dir.: Bret Waller
Fine Arts Museum
Italian painting 44216

Eiteljorg Museum of American Indians and Western Art, 500 W Washington, Indianapolis, IN 46204 - T: (317) 636-9378, Fax: (317) 264-1724, E-mail: museum@eiteljorg.org, Internet: www.eiteljorg.org. Pres.: John Vanausdall, Cur.: James H. Nottage, Bob Tucker, Ray Gonyea (Native American Art and Culture), Jennifer Complo (Contemporary Art)
Fine Arts Museum / Ethnology Museum / Folklore Museum - 1989
Art Museum 44217

Emil A. Blackmore Museum of the American Legion, 700 N Pennsylvania St, Indianapolis, IN 46204 - T: (317) 630-1356, Fax: (317) 630-1241, E-mail: library@legion.org, Internet: www.legion.org/library.htm. Dir.: Joseph J. Hovish
Military Museum
Military hist 44218

Herron Gallery, Indiana University - Purdue University Indianapolis, 1701 N Pennsylvania St, Indianapolis, IN 46202 - T: (317) 920-2416, Fax: (317) 920-2401, E-mail: Herrart@iupui.edu, Internet: www.herron.iupui.edu
Public Gallery 44219

Historic Landmarks Foundation of Indiana, 340 W Michigan St, Indianapolis, IN 46202-3204 - T: (317) 639-4534, Fax: (317) 639-6734, Internet: www.historiclandmarks.org. Pres.: J. Reid Williamson
Historical Museum - 1960
Historic Landmarks Headquarters, Morris-Butler House, Huddleston Farmhouse Inn Museum, Cambridge City, Kemper House Wedding Cake House 44220

Hoosier Salon Gallery, 6434 N College Av C, Indianapolis, IN 46220 - T: (317) 253-5340, Fax: (317) 259-1817, E-mail: hoosiersalon@iquest.net, Internet: www.hoosiersalon.org. Dir.: Ginger Bievenour
Public Gallery - 1926
Art 44221

Indiana Historical Society Museum, 450 W Ohio St, Indianapolis, IN 46202-3269 - T: (317) 232-1882, 234-1830, Fax: (317) 233-3109, Internet: www.indianahistory.org. Dir.: Peter T. Harstad
Historical Museum - 1830
History - library, exhibition programs 44222

Indiana Medical History Museum, 3045 W Vermont St, Indianapolis, IN 46222 - T: (317) 635-7329, Fax: (317) 635-7349, E-mail: edenharter@aol.com, Internet: www.imhm.org. Dir.: Virginia L. Terpening
Historical Museum - 1969
Medicine, housed in c.1896 pathology laboratory 44223

Indiana State Museum, 202 N Alabama St, Indianapolis, IN 46204 - T: (317) 232-1637, Fax: (317) 232-7090, E-mail: inmuseum@ismhs.org, Internet: www.in.gov. Dir.: Douglas R. Noble, Asst. Dir.: Kathleen McLary, Bill Bruggen, Jeff Myers, Cur.: Bill Wepler (Anthropology), James May (Cultural History), Ron Richards (Natural History), Dale Ogden (Popular Culture)
Local Museum / Historical Museum / Natural History Museum - 1869
General museum, former Indianapolis City Hall, anthropology, culture and natural history 44224

Indiana War Memorials Museum, 431 N Meridian St, Indianapolis, IN 46204 - T: (317) 232-7615, Fax: (317) 233-4285, Internet: www.state.in.us/iwm. Dir.: Bill Sweeney, Sc. Staff: Donna Schmink, Ethan Wright, Kenneth Chandler, David Buchanan, Pam Chandler, Steve Hill
Historic Site / Military Museum - 1927
Military, war history, housed in 1927 Indiana War Memorial 44225

Indianapolis Art Center, Churchman-Fehsenfeld-Gallery, 820 E 67th St, Indianapolis, IN 46220 - T: (317) 255-2464, Fax: (317) 254-0486, E-mail: inartctr@netdirect.net, Internet: www.indplsartcenter.org/. Pres. & Dir.: Joyce A. Sommers, Julia Muney Moore
Fine Arts Museum - 1934
Art Teaching Center 44226

Indianapolis Motor Speedway Hall of Fame Museum, 4790 W 16th St, Indianapolis, IN 46222 - T: (317) 481-8500, Fax: (317) 484-6449, E-mail: ebireley@brickyard.com, Internet: www.brickyard.com. Dir.: Ellen K. Bireley
Special Museum / Science&Tech Museum - 1956 44227

Indianapolis Museum of Art, 4000 Michigan Rd, Indianapolis, IN 46208-3326 - T: (317) 923-1331, Fax: (317) 931-1978, E-mail: ima@ima-art.org, Internet: www.ima-art.org. Dir.: Anthony G. Hirschel, Chief Cur.: Ellen W. Lee, Cur.: Theodore Celenko (African, South Pacific and Precolumbian Art), Dr. James J. Robinson (Asian Art), Martin F. Krause (Prints, Drawings and Photographs), Barry L. Shifman (Decorative Arts), Niloo Imami-Paydar (Textiles and Costumes), Ronda J. Kasl (Painting and Sculpture to 1800), Ass. Cur.: John Teramoto (Asian Art)
Fine Arts Museum / Historic Site / Folklore Museum - 1883
Contemporary art, decorative art, paintings, sculptures, drawings, prints, photos, textiles and costumes - library 44228

Iupui Cultural Arts Gallery, 815 W Michigan St, Indianapolis, IN 46202-5164 - T: (317) 274-3931, Fax: (317) 274-7099, Internet: life.iupui.edu/campcomm
Fine Arts Museum
Paintings, sculpture 44229

Lockerbie Street Home of James Whitcomb Riley, 528 Lockerbie St, Indianapolis, IN 46202 - T: (317) 631-5885, Fax: (317) 634-4478, E-mail: rileyhome@rileymem.org, Internet: www.rileymem.org. Dir.: Sandra Crain
Historical Museum - 1922 44230

Morris-Butler House Museum, 1204 N Park Av, Indianapolis, IN 46202 - T: (317) 636-5409, Fax: (317) 636-2630, E-mail: mbhouse@historiclandmarks.org, Internet: www.historiclandmarks.org. Pres.: J. Reid Williamson
Decorative Arts Museum - 1969 44231

National Art Museum of Sport, University Pl, 850 W Michigan St, Indianapolis, IN 46202-5198 - T: (317) 274-3627, Fax: (317) 274-3878, E-mail: arein@iupui.edu, Internet: www.namos.iupui.edu. Pres.: John D. Short
Fine Arts Museum / Special Museum - 1959
Sports art 44232

Phi Kappa Psi Fraternity-Heritage Hall, 510 Lockerbie St, Indianapolis, IN 46202 - T: (317) 632-1852, Fax: (317) 637-1898, E-mail: pkp_hq@phikappapsi.com, Internet: www.phikappapsi.com. Dir.: Tom C. Pennington
Local Museum - 1978 44233

President Benjamin Harrison Home, 1230 N Delaware St, Indianapolis, IN 46202-2598 - T: (317) 631-1888, Fax: (317) 632-5488, E-mail: Harrison@surf-ici.com, Internet: www.surf-ici.com/harrisonhttp://www.presidentbenjaminharrison.org. Dir.: Phyllis Geeslin, Cur.: Jennifer Capps, Cust.: Ruben Meza
Historical Museum - 1937 44234

Indianola IA

Farnham Galleries, Simpson College, 701 N C St, Indianola, IA 50125 - T: (515) 961-6251, 961-1561, Fax: (515) 961-1498, E-mail: heinicke@storm.simpson.edu. Pres.: Dr. Kevin Lagree, Dir.: Dr. Janet Heinicke
Fine Arts Museum / University Museum - 1982 44235

Ingalls KS

Santa Fe Trail Museums of Gray County, 204 S Main St, Ingalls, KS 67853 - T: (620) 335-5220, E-mail: dlmkwend@ucom.net. Dir.: Kyleen Lacy, Cur.: Candice Wendel, Debra Mitne
Local Museum - 1973
Local hist 44236

Ingram TX

Duncan-McAshan Visual Arts Center, Hwy 39, Ingram, TX 78025, mail addr: POB 1169, Ingram, TX 78025 - T: (830) 367-5121, 367-5120, Fax: (830) 367-5725, E-mail: artdept@hcaf.com, Internet: www.pointtheatre.com. Exec. Dir.: George Eychner
Fine Arts Museum / Public Gallery - 1958
Contemporary paintings, prints, photographs and sculpture 44237

Interlaken NY

Interlaken Historical Society Museum, Main St, Interlaken, NY 14847 - T: (607) 532-8505. Pres.: Allan Buddle, Cur.: Louise Akins
Historical Museum - 1960 44238

International Falls MN

Grand Mound History Center, 6749 Hwy 11, International Falls, MN 56649 - T: (218) 285-3332, Fax: (218) 285-3332, Internet: www.mnhs.org
Folklore Museum - 1849
Woodland, Laurel and Blackduck cultures, American Indian lifeways 44239

Koochiching County Historical Society Museum, 214 Sixth Av, International Falls, MN 56649 - T: (218) 283-4316, Fax: (218) 286-5237. Dir.: Edgar S. Oerichbauer
Local Museum - 1958
Regional history, paintings, football memorabilia 44240

Voyageurs National Park Museum, 3131 Hwy 53, International Falls, MN 56649-8904 - T: (218) 283-9821, Fax: (218) 285-7407, E-mail: voyasu-perintendent@nps.gov. Head: Barbara West
Natural History Museum - 1975 44241

Inverness FL

Museum of Citrus County History-Old Courthouse → Old Courthouse Heritage Museum

Old Courthouse Heritage Museum, 532 Citrus Av, Crystel River, Inverness, FL 34450 - T: (352) 341-6428/29, Fax: (352) 341-6445. Dir.: Kathy Turner
Local Museum - 1985
Regional history 44242

Iola KS

Allen County Historical Museum, 207 N Jefferson, Iola, KS 66749 - T: (316) 365-3051. Cur.: Michael Anderson
Local Museum - 1956
Local history 44243

The Major General Frederick Funston Boyhood Home and Museum, 14 S Washington Av, Iola, KS 66749 - T: (316) 365-3051, 365-6728, Internet: www.frederickfunston.org. Dir.: Michael Anderson, Pres.: Bob Hawk
Local Museum - 1995
Local hist 44244

Iowa City IA

Hospitals and Clinics Medical Museum, University of Iowa, 200 Hawkins Dr, 8014 RCP, Iowa City, IA 52242 - T: (319) 356-1616, 356-7106, Fax: (319) 356-3862, E-mail: adrienne-drapkin@uiowa.edu, Internet: www.ulhealthcare.com/medmuseum. Dir.: Adrienne Drapkin
Historical Museum - 1989
Medicine 44245

Plum Grove Historic Home, 1030 Carroll St, Iowa City, IA 52240 - T: (319) 351-5738, Fax: (319) 351-5310, E-mail: johctyhistscty@yahoo.com. Exec. Dir.: Margaret Wieting
Historical Museum - 1944
Home of Robert Lucas, first governor of Territory of Iowa 44246

Project Art-University of Iowa and Clinics, 200 Hawkins Dr, Iowa City, IA 52242-1009 - T: (319) 356-1616, Fax: (319) 356-3862, E-mail: carl-lindquist@uiowa.edu, Internet: www.uihc.uiowa.edu/pubinfo/projart.htm. Dir.: Carl Lindquist
Fine Arts Museum - 1967
American art, historic and modern Native American art 44247

University of Iowa Museum of Art, 150 N Riverside Dr, Iowa City, IA 52242 - T: (319) 335-1727, Fax: (319) 335-3677, E-mail: uima@uiowa.edu, Internet: www.uiowa.edu/uima. Dir.: Howard Collinson, Cur.: Pam Trimpe (Painting, Sculpture), Kathy Edwards (Graphics), Victoria Rovine (Arts of Africa, Oceania and the Americas)
Fine Arts Museum - 1967
International art 44248

University of Iowa Museum of Natural History, 10 Macbride Hall, Iowa City, IA 52242 - T: (319) 335-0481, Fax: (319) 335-0653, E-mail: mus-nat-hist@uiowa.edu, Internet: www.uiowa.edu/~nathist. Cur.: Julia Golden (Collections), Bruce A. Scherting (Exhibitions)
University Museum / Natural History Museum - 1858
Natural history 44249

Iowa Falls IA

Callkins Field Museum, 18335 135th St, Iowa Falls, IA 50126-8511 - T: (641) 648-9878, Fax: (641) 648-9878, E-mail: calkins@hotmail.com, Internet: www.hardincounty.net. Dir.: Duane Rieken
University Museum / Natural History Museum - 1890
Natural science, history 44250

Ipswich MA

Ipswich Historical Society Museum, 54 S Main St, Ipswich, MA 01938 - T: (978) 356-2811, Fax: (978) 356-2817, E-mail: ihs@cove.com, Internet: www.ipswichma.com. Dir.: Stefanie J. Muscat, Cur.: Amanda Nelson
Local Museum - 1890
Local history 44251

Ipswich SD

J.W. Parmely Historical Home Museum, Hwy 12 and Hwy 45, Ipswich, SD 57451 - T: (605) 426-6949. C.E.O. & Pres.: Phyllis M. Herrick
Local Museum - 1931
Local hist 44252

Iraan TX

Iraan Museum, Alley Oop Fantasy Land Park, West City Limits Off Hwy 190, Iraan, TX 79744 - T: (915) 639-8895. Cur.: Morine Collett, Asst. Cur.: Pansy Smart
Historical Museum / Archaeological Museum - 1965
Archaeology, history 44253

Ironton OH

Lawrence County Gray House Museum, 506 S Sixth St, Ironton, OH 45638-0073 - T: (614) 532-1222, E-mail: lchsmus@cloh.net. Pres.: Naomi Deer
Local Museum / Historic Site - 1925/1988 44254

Ironwood MI

Ironwood Area Historical Museum, 150 N Lowell St, Ironwood, MI 49938 - T: (906) 932-0287, Internet: www.ironwood.org. Dir.: Gary Harrington, Cur.: Ray Maurin
Local Museum - 1970
Local hist 44255

Irvine CA

Irvine Fine Arts Center, 14321 Yale Av, Irvine, CA 92604-1901 - T: (949) 724-6880, Fax: (949) 552-2137. Dir.: Toni Pang
Public Gallery - 1980 44256

Irvine Museum, 18881 Von Karman, Ste 100, Irvine, CA 92612 - T: (949) 476-0294, Fax: (949) 476-2437, Internet: www.irvinemuseum.org. Dir.: Jean Stern
Fine Arts Museum - 1992 44257

University Art Gallery, Claire Trevor School of the Arts, Beall Center for Art and Technology, 712 Arts Plaza, Irvine, CA 92967-2775 - T: (714) 824-6206, Fax: (714) 824-4197, E-mail: indi@uci.edu, Internet: www.beallcenter.uci.edu. Dir.: Nohema Fernandez
Fine Arts Museum / University Museum - 1965 44258

Irving TX

Irving Arts Center, 3333 N MacArthur Blvd, Irving, TX 75062 - T: (972) 252-7558, Fax: (972) 570-4962, E-mail: minman@ci.irving.tx.us, Internet: www.ci.irving.tx.us/arts. Exec. Dir.: Richard E. Huff
Fine Arts Museum - 1990
Sculpture garden, works by Jesus Bautista Moroles and Michael Manjarris 44259

Irving Arts Center, 3333 N MacArthur Blvd, Irving, TX 75062 - T: (972) 252-7558, Fax: (972) 570-4962, E-mail: iac@airmail.net, Internet: www.ci.irving.tx.us. Exec. Dir.: Richard E. Huff
Fine Arts Museum - 1990
Paintings, sculpture, pottery, woodcuts 44260

The National Museum of Communications (closed) 44261

National Scouting Museum, 1329 W Walnut Hill Ln, Irving, TX 75015-2079 - T: (800) 303-3047, Fax: (972) 580-2020, E-mail: nsmuseum@netbsa.org, Internet: www.bsamuseum.org. Dir.: Dan Matkin
Special Museum - 1959
History of the Boy Scouts of America, uniforms, Norman Rockwell oils, patches 44262

Ishpeming MI

United States National Ski Hall of Fame and Museum, 610 Palms, Ishpeming, MI 49849 - T: (906) 485-6323, Fax: (906) 486-4570, E-mail: skihall@uplogon.com, Internet: www.skihall.com. Pres.: Richard Goetzman, Cur.: Raymond Leverton
Special Museum - 1954
Sports 44263

Island Falls ME

John E. and Walter D. Webb Museum of Vintage Fashion, Sherman St, Rte 2, Island Falls, ME 04747 - T: (207) 862-3797, 463-2404, Internet: www.coffeenews.net/webbmuseum. C.E.O.: Frances R. Stratton
Special Museum - 1983 44264

Isle La Motte VT

Isle La Motte Historical Society Museum, 283 School St, Isle La Motte, VT 05463 - T: (802) 928-3173, Fax: (802) 928-3342, E-mail: rgmcewen@together.net. Vice Dir.: Bob McEwen, Gloria McEwen, Cur.: Allen Fales
Local Museum - 1925
Local hist 44265

Isleford ME

Isleford Historical Museum, Little Cranberry Island, Isleford, ME 04646 - T: (207) 288-5463, Fax: (207) 288-5507, E-mail: brooke_childrey@nps.gv, Internet: www.nps.gov/acad/home.html. Cur.: Brooke Childrey
Local Museum
Maritime hist and settlement 44266

Islesboro ME

Islesboro Historical Museum, 388 Main Rd, Islesboro, ME 04848 - T: (207) 734-6733
Local Museum - 1964
Local history 44267

Sailor's Memorial Museum, Grindle Point, Islesboro, ME 04848-0076 - T: (207) 734-2253, Fax: (207) 734-8394
Historical Museum - 1936
Maritime, 1850 Lighthouse 44268

Issaquah WA

Gilman Town Hall Museum, 165 SE Andrews, Issaquah, WA 98027 - T: (425) 392-3500, Fax: (425) 392-3500, E-mail: info@issaquahhistory.org, Internet: www.issaquahhistorical.org. Dir.: Erica S. Maniez
Historical Museum - 1972 44269

Ithaca NY

DeWitt Historical Society Museum, 401 E State St, Ithaca, NY 14850 - T: (607) 273-8284, Fax: (607) 273-6107, E-mail: dhs@lakenet.org, Internet: www.lakenet.org/dewitt. Dir.: Matthew Braun
Historical Museum - 1935 44270

Handwerker Gallery of Art, 1170 Gannett Ctr, Ithaca College, Ithaca, NY 14850-7276 - T: (607) 274-3018, Fax: (607) 274-1484, E-mail: jstojanovic@ithaca.edu, Internet: www.ithaca.edu/handwerker. Dir.: Jelena Stojanovic
Fine Arts Museum / University Museum - 1977
Art Gallery 44271

Herbert F. Johnson Museum of Art, Cornell University, Ithaca, NY 14853 - T: (607) 255-6464, Fax: (607) 255-9940, E-mail: museum@cornell.edu, Internet: www.museum.cornell.edu. Dir.: Franklin W. Robinson, Cur.: Nancy Green (Prints, Drawings and Photographs), Ellen Avril (Asian Art), Cathy Klimaszewski (Education), Andrea Inselmann (Modern and Contemporary Art)
Fine Arts Museum / University Museum - 1973 44272

Hinckley Foundation Museum, 410 E Seneca St, Ithaca, NY 14850 - T: (607) 273-7053. Dir.: Nicole M. Carrier, Pres.: Tim Bumgardner
Historical Museum / Folklore Museum / Special Museum - 1972 44273

Sciencenter, 601 First St, Ithaca, NY 14850 - T: (607) 272-0600, Fax: (607) 277-7469, E-mail: info@sciencenter.org, Internet: www.sciencenter.org. Dir.: Charles H. Trautmann, Dept. Dir.: Barbara Thorp (Operations)
Science&Tech Museum - 1983
Science and technology 44274

Jacksboro TX

Fort Richardson, Hwy 281 S, Jacksboro, TX 76458 - T: (940) 567-3506, Fax: (940) 567-5488, E-mail: fortrich@digitalpassage.com. Dir.: Andrew Sansom
Local Museum - 1968
Local history 44275

Jackson MI

Ella Sharp Museum, 3225 Fourth St, Jackson, MI 49203 - T: (517) 787-2320, Fax: (517) 787-2933, E-mail: ellasharp@dmci.net
Fine Arts Museum / Local Museum - 1964 44276

Jackson MS

Chimneyville Crafts Gallery, c/o Mississippi Agriculture and Forestry Museum, 1150 Lakeland Dr, Jackson, MS 39216 - T: (601) 981-2499, Fax: (601) 981-0488, E-mail: mscrafts@mscraftsmensguild.org, Internet: www.mscraftsmensguild.org
Historical Museum - 1989 44277

Manship House Museum, 420 E Fortification St, Jackson, MS 39202-2340 - T: (601) 961-4724, Fax: (601) 354-6043, E-mail: manship@mdah.state.ms.us, Internet: www.mdah.state.ms.us. C.E.O.: Elbert R. Hillard, Dir.: Marilyn Jones
Historical Museum - 1980 44278

Mississippi Governor's Mansion, 300 E Capitol, Jackson, MS 39201 - T: (601) 359-3175, Fax: (601) 359-6473. Dir.: Elbert R. Hilliard, Cur.: Mary Lohrenz
Historical Museum - 1842 44279

Mississippi Museum of Art, 201 E Pascagoula St, Jackson, MS 39201 - T: (601) 960-1515, Fax: (601) 960-1505, E-mail: mmart@netdoor.com, Internet: www.msmuseumart.org. Dir.: Betsy Bradley, Cur.: Rene Paul Barilleaux, J. Marshall Adams, Preparator: Paul L.C. Tucker
Fine Arts Museum - 1911 44280

Mississippi Museum of Natural Science, 2148 Riverside Dr, Jackson, MS 39202 - T: (601) 354-7303, Fax: (601) 354-7227, Internet: www.mdwfp.state.ms.us/museum. Dir.: Libby Hartfield, Sc. Staff: Mark Woodrey (Ornithology), Dr. Eleanor Daly (Paleontology), Georgia Spencer (Project WILD), Dr. Robert Jones (Zoology)
Natural History Museum - 1934
library 44281

Mississippi Agriculture and Forestry/National Agricultural Aviation Museum, 1150 Lakeland Dr, Jackson, MS 39216 - T: (601) 713-3365, Fax: (601) 982-4292, Internet: www.mdac.state.us.ms.org. C.E.O.: Mike Brinkley, Cur.: Jim McDonald
Agriculture Museum - 1973 44282

Museum of the Southern Jewish Experience, 4915 I-55 N, Ste 204B, Jackson, MS 39206 - T: (601) 362-6357, Fax: (601) 366-6293, E-mail: information@msje.org, Internet: www.msje.org. C.E.O.: Macy B. Hart
Religious Arts Museum - 1989 44283

Oaks House Museum, 823 N Jefferson St, Jackson, MS 39202 - T: (601) 353-9339. Dir.: Dr. Kathryn Breese
Historical Museum / Local Museum / Special Museum - 1960 44284

Old Capitol Museum of Mississippi History, 100 S State, Jackson, MS 39201 - T: (601) 359-6920, Fax: (601) 359-6981, E-mail: ocmuseum@mdah.state.ms.us, Internet: www.mdah.state.ms.us. Dir.: Lucy Allen, Dept. Dir.: Clay Williams (Exhibits), Cur.: John Gardner, Michael Wright (Collections), Historian: David Morgan, Carol Rietvelt
Historical Museum - 1961
State history, household objects, textiles (quilts, clothing), folk art, craft, civil war flags, swords 44285

Smith Robertson Museum, 528 Bloom St, Jackson, MS 39202-4005 - T: (601) 960-1457, Fax: (601) 960-2070. Cur.: Turry Flucker
Historical Museum - 1977
Public funds for Blacks in Jackson 44286

Jackson TN

Casey Jones Home and Railroad Museum, Casey Jones Village, 30 Casey Ln, Jackson, TN 38305 - T: (731) 668-1222, Fax: (731) 664-7782, E-mail: casey@caseyjones.com, Internet: www.caseyjonesvillage.com. C.E.O.: J. Lawrence Taylor
Science&Tech Museum - 1956
Railroads 44287

University Art Gallery, Union University, 1050 Union University Dr, Jackson, TN 38305 - T: (731) 668-1818 ext 5075, Fax: (731) 664-7476, Internet: www.uu.edu/dept/art
Public Gallery 44288

Jackson WY

Jackson Hole Historical Museum, 105 Mercill Av, Jackson, WY 83001 - T: (307) 733-2414, Fax: (307) 739-9019, E-mail: jhhsm@rmisp.com, Internet: www.jacksmholehistory.org. Dir.: Lokey Lytjen
Local Museum - 1958
Archaeology, regional prehistory, Plains Indians, fur trade, game heads, regional hist 44289

National Museum of Wildlife Art, 2820 Rungius Rd, Jackson, WY 83001 - T: (307) 733-5771, 733-5328, Fax: (307) 733-5787, E-mail: info@wildlifeart.org, Internet: www.wildlifeart.org. Dir.: Dr. Francine Carraro, Cur.: Jane Lavino (Education), Adam Duncan Harris (Art)
Fine Arts Museum - 1987
Art 44290

Jacksonville AL

Dr. Francis Medical and Apothecary Museum, 207 Gayle Av SW, Jacksonville, AL 36265 - T: (256) 435-4970, Fax: (256) 435-4103. Dir.: Barbara B. Johnson
Historical Museum - 1968 44291

Jacksonville FL

Alexander Brest Museum, 2800 University Blvd N, Jacksonville, FL 32211 - T: (904) 745-7371, Fax: (904) 745-7375, E-mail: dlauder@ju.edu. Dir.: David Lauderdale
Fine Arts Museum / University Museum - 1977
Art 44292

Cummer Museum of Art, 829 Riverside Av, Jacksonville, FL 32204 - T: (904) 356-6857, Fax: (904) 353-4101, E-mail: info@cummer.org, Internet: www.cummer.org. Dir.: Dr. Maarten Van de Guchte, Asst. Dir.: Jean Hall-Dodd, L. Vance Shrum
Fine Arts Museum - 1958
Art - gardens 44293

Fort Caroline Memorial Museum, 13165 Mount Pleasant Rd, Jacksonville, FL 32225 - T: (904) 641-7155, Fax: (904) 641-3798, E-mail: timu-operations@nps.gov, Internet: www.nps.gov/timu. Dir.: Barbara Goodman
Historical Museum / Natural History Museum - 1988
History, natural history 44294

Jacksonville Fire Museum, 146 Gator Bowel Blvd, Jacksonville, FL 32202 - T: (904) 630-0618, Fax: (904) 630-4202, E-mail: jpeavy@coj.net. Cur.: John M. Peavy
Historical Museum - 1974
Antique fire apparatus, fire fighting hist 44295

Jacksonville Museum of Modern Art, 333 N Laura St, Jacksonville, FL 32202 - T: (904) 366-6911, Fax: (904) 366-6901, E-mail: jmomapres@mindspring.com. Dir.: Jane Craven
Fine Arts Museum - 1948
American painting, sculpture, graphics, contemporary and modern art since 1920 44296

Kent Campus Museum and Gallery, c/o Florida Community College, 3939 Roosevelt Blvd, Jacksonville, FL 32205 - T: (904) 381-3400, 381-3674, Fax: (904) 381-3690, E-mail: kwarren@fccj.org, Internet: www.fccj.org
Fine Arts Museum / University Museum - 1971 44297

Kingsley Plantation, 11676 Palmetto Av, Jacksonville, FL 32226 - T: (904) 251-3537, Fax: (904) 251-3577, E-mail: timu_kingsley_-plantation@nps.gov, Internet: www.nps.gov/timu
Historical Museum / Historic Site - 1955
Historic site 44298

Museum of Science and History of Jacksonville, 1025 Museum Circle, Jacksonville, FL 32207-9053 - T: (904) 396-7062, 396-6674, Fax: (904) 396-5799, E-mail: moshfac@jax-inter.net, Internet: www.themosh.org. Dir.: Margo Dundon, Cur.: Wanda Edwards (Humanities Coll), James Ashley (Natural Science Coll)
Historical Museum / Science&Tech Museum - 1941
Planetarium 44299

Museum of Southern History, 4304 Herschel St, Jacksonville, FL 32210 - T: (904) 388-3574, E-mail: gevans12@juno.com. C.E.O.: Michael B. Snyder
Historical Museum - 1975
Black soldiers in Confederate service 44300

Jacksonville IL

David Strawn Art Gallery, Art Association of Jacksonville, 331 W College Av, Jacksonville, IL 62651-1213 - T: (217) 243-9390, Fax: (217) 245-7445, E-mail: strawn@myhtn.net, Internet: www.japl.lib.il.us/community/strawn. Pres.: Dana Ryan, Chm.: Sue Freeman
Fine Arts Museum / Public Gallery - 1873 44301

Jaffrey NH

Jaffrey Civic Center, 40 Main St, Jaffrey, NH 03452 - T: (603) 532-6527. Dir.: Scott Cunningham, Kim Cunningham
Folklore Museum / Local Museum - 1964 44302

Jamaica NY

Chung-Cheng Art Gallery, Saint John's University, 8000 Utopia Pkwy, Sun Yat Sen Hall, Jamaica, NY 11439 - T: (718) 990-6250, 990-7476, Fax: (718) 990-2075, E-mail: artdept@stjohns.edu, Internet: www.stjohns.edu
Public Gallery 44303

Jamaica Center for Arts, 161-04 Jamaica Av, Jamaica, NY 11432 - T: (718) 658-7400, Fax: (718) 658-7922, Internet: www.jcal.org. Dir.: Alexander Campos
Fine Arts Museum / Decorative Arts Museum - 1972
Art 44304

King Manor, 150-03 Jamaica Av, King Park, Jamaica, NY 11432 - T: (718) 206-0545, Fax: (718) 206-0541
Historical Museum - 1900
Rufus King, signer of the US constitution, senator from NY state and ambassador to Great Britain under four presidents 44305

Queens Library Gallery, 89-11 Merrick Blvd, Jamaica, NY 11432 - T: (718) 990-8665, Fax: (718) 291-8936, E-mail: mkrazmien@queenslibrary.org, Internet: www.queenslibrary.org/gallery. Sc. Staff: Mindy Krazmien
Public Gallery - 1995
Art 44306

Jamestown ND

Frontier Village Museum, 17th St SE, Jamestown, ND 58401 - T: (701) 252-7492, 252-8089, Fax: (701) 252-8089. Pres.: Charles Tanata
Local Museum - 1959
Local hist 44307

Stutsman County Memorial Museum, 321 Third Av SE, Jamestown, ND 58401-1002 - T: (701) 252-6741. Head: Leah Mitchell
Local Museum / Historical Museum - 1964 44308

Jamestown NY

Art Gallery, James Prendergast Library, 509 Cherry St, Jamestown, NY 14701 - T: (716) 484-7135, Fax: (716) 487-1148, E-mail: reference@cclslib.org, Internet: www.cclslib.org/prendergast/. Dir.: Murray L. Bob, Asst. Dir.: Catherine A. Way
Fine Arts Museum - 1880 44309

CCC Weeks Gallery, 525 Falconer St, Jamestown, NY 14701-0020 - T: (716) 665-9188, Fax: (716) 665-7023, E-mail: jimcolby@mail.sunyjcc.edu, Internet: www.sunyjcc.edu/gallery. Dir.: James Colby
Public Gallery - 1969 44310

Fenton History Center-Museum and Library, 67 Washington St, Jamestown, NY 14701 - T: (716) 664-6256, Fax: (716) 483-7524, E-mail: information@fentonhistorycenter.org, Internet: www.fentonhistorycenter.org. Dir.: Christin L. Stein, Exec. Dir.: Sara W. Reale, Cur.: Wendy Chadwick-Case (Exhibits), Norman P. Carlson (Collections), Nancy Kerrin (Exhbtion design), Registrar: Sylvia Lobb, Libr.: Karen E. Livsey
Historical Museum - 1964 44311

Forum Gallery, 525 Falconer St, Jamestown, NY 14701 - T: (716) 665-5220 ext 478, Fax: (716) 665-7023, E-mail: colbyjd@jccw22.cc.sunyjcc.edu. Dir.: James Colby
Public Gallery - 1969 44312

Roger Tory Peterson Institute of Natural History Museum, 311 Curtis St, Jamestown, NY 14701 - T: (716) 665-2473, Fax: (716) 665-3794, E-mail: webmaster@rtpi.org, Internet: www.rtpi.org. C.E.O.: James M. Berry
Natural History Museum - 1984 44313

Jamestown RI

Jamestown Museum, 92 Narragansett Av, Jamestown, RI 02835 - T: (401) 423-0784. Pres.: John H. Howard
Local Museum - 1972
Local hist 44314

Watson Farm, 455 North Rd, Jamestown, RI 02835 - T: (401) 423-0005, (617) 227-3956, Fax: (617) 227-9204, E-mail: pzea@spnea.org, Internet: www.spnea.org. Vice Pres.: Philip Zea, Head: Don Minto, Heather Minto
Folklore Museum / Agriculture Museum
Historic farm 44315

Jamestown VA

Jamestown Visitor Center Museum, Colonial National Historical Park, Jamestown, VA 23081 - T: (757) 229-1733, Fax: (757) 229-4273, Internet: www.nps.gov/colo. Dir.: Alec Gould, Historian: Diane G. Stallings
Local Museum - 1930
Local hist, first permanent English settlement at Jamestown 44316

Janesville MN

Farmamerica, Minnesota Agricultural Interpretive Center, 7367 360th Av, Janesville, MN 56048 - T: (507) 835-2052, Fax: (507) 835-2053, E-mail: farmamer@mnic.net, Internet: www.farmamerica.org
Agriculture Museum - 1978 44317

Janesville WI

The Lincoln-Tallman Restorations, 440 N Jackson St, Janesville, WI 53545 - T: (608) 752-4519, 756-4509, Fax: (608) 741-9596, Internet: www.lincolntallman.org. C.E.O.: Jason Josvai, Pres.: Madge Murphy, Cur.: Anamani Golf
Local Museum - 1951
Historic house 44318

Rock County Historical Society Museum, 426 N Jackson St, Janesville, WI 53545 - T: (608) 756-4509, Fax: (608) 741-9596, E-mail: rchs@ticon.net, Internet: www.lincolntallman.org. C.E.O.: Jason Josvai, Cur.: Anamani Golf
Local Museum - 1948
Local hist 44319

Jeannette PA

Bushy Run Battlefield Museum, Rte 993, Jeannette, PA 15644 - T: (724) 527-5584, Fax: (724) 527-5610, E-mail: davmiller@state.pa.us, Internet: www.bushyrunbattlefield.com
Military Museum - 1933
18th-c military 44320

Jefferson GA

Crawford W. Long Museum, 28 College St, Jefferson, GA 30549 - T: (706) 367-5307, Fax: (706) 367-5307, E-mail: tinaharris@crawfordlong.org, Internet: www.crawfordlong.org. Dir.: Tina B. Harris
Historical Museum - 1957
Medical history 44321

Jefferson IA

Jefferson Telephone Museum, 105 W Harrison, Jefferson, IA 50129 - T: (515) 386-2626, 386-4141, Fax: (515) 386-2600. Dir.: James Daubendiek
Science&Tech Museum - 1960 44322

Jefferson OH

Dezign House, 4090 Lenox-New Lyme Rd, Jefferson, OH 44047 - T: (440) 294-2778. Dir.: Ramon Jan Elias
Decorative Arts Museum - 1962
Western decorative art and furniture 44323

Jefferson TX

Excelsior House, 211 W Austin St, Jefferson, TX 75657 - T: (903) 665-2513, Fax: (903) 665-9389, E-mail: excelsior@jeffersontx.com, Internet: texasmonthly.com/mag/1991/jun/excelsior/html
Decorative Arts Museum - 1850 44324

Jefferson Historical Museum, 223 W Austin, Jefferson, TX 75657 - T: (903) 665-2775. Chm.: Bill McCay
Local Museum - 1948
Local hist 44325

Jefferson WI

Aztalan Museum, N 6264 Hwy Q, Jefferson, WI 53549 - T: (414) 648-4362. Pres.: Dr. Cheryl D. Peterson, Cur.: Steve Steigerwald
Local Museum - 1941
Local hist 44326

Jefferson City MO

Cole County Historical Museum, 109 Madison, Jefferson City, MO 65101 - T: (573) 635-1850. Pres.: Charles B. Blackmar, William Tackett
Historical Museum - 1941 44327

Elizabeth Rozier Gallery, State Capitol, Rm B-2, Jefferson City, MO 65101 - T: (573) 751-4210, Fax: (573) 526-2927. Dir.: Molly Strode
Public Gallery - 1981 44328

Missouri State Museum, Missouri State Capitol, Capitol Av, Jefferson City, MO 65101 - T: (573) 751-2854, Fax: (573) 526-2927, Internet: www.mostateparks.com. Dir.: Molly O'Donnell, Cur.: L.T. Shelton, Gina Mills
Historical Museum - 1919 44329

Jeffersonville IN

Howard Steamboat Museum, 1101 E Market St, Jeffersonville, IN 47130-0606 - T: (812) 283-3728, Fax: (812) 283-6049, Internet: www.steamboatmuseum.org. Dir.: Yvonne Knight, Cur.: John T. Smith, Forrest F. Steinlage
Historical Museum / Science&Tech Museum - 1958
Home of Edmonds J. Howard, son of James E. Howard, founder of the Howard Shipyards 1834 44330

Jekyll Island GA

Jekyll Island Museum, Stable Rd, Jekyll Island, GA 31520, mail addr: 381 Riverview Dr, Jekyll Island, GA 31527 - T: (912) 635-2119, 635-2236, Fax: (912) 635-4420, E-mail: jekyllisland@compuserve.com, Internet: www.jekyllisland.com. Dir.: F. Warren Murphey, Cur.: John Hunter
Local Museum - 1954
Local history 44331

Jemez Springs NM

Jemez State Monument, 1 mile N of Jemez Springs, State Hwy 4, Jemez Springs, NM 87025 - T: (505) 829-3530, Fax: (505) 829-3530, E-mail: giusewaq-sulphurcanyon.com. Dir.: Jose Cisneros
Local Museum - 1935
Local hist 44332

Jenkintown PA

Abington Art Center, 515 Meetinghouse Rd, Jenkintown, PA 19046 - T: (215) 887-4882, Fax: (215) 887-1402, Internet: www.abingtonartcenter.org. Dir.: Laura Burnham
Fine Arts Museum - 1939 44333

Jennings LA

The Zigler Museum, 411 Clara St, Jennings, LA 70546 - T: (318) 824-0114, Fax: (318) 824-0120, E-mail: zigler-museum@charter.net, Internet: www.jeffdavis.org. Cur.: Dolores Spears, Pres.: Gregory Marcantel
Fine Arts Museum - 1963
European and American art 44334

Jericho Corners VT

Jericho Historical Society Museum, Rte 15, Jericho Corners, VT 05465 - T: (802) 899-3225, Internet: www.jerichohistoricalsociety.com. Pres.: Ann Squires
Local Museum - 1971
Local hist 44335

Jerome AZ

Jerome State Historic Park, Douglas Rd, Jerome, AZ 86331 - T: (928) 634-5381, Fax: (928) 639-3132, Internet: www.pr.state.az.us. Head: Jon Clow
Historical Museum - 1962
History, mining 44336

Jerome ID

Jerome County Historical Society, 220 N Lincoln, Jerome, ID 83338 - T: (208) 324-5641, Fax: (208) 324-7694, E-mail: info@historicaljeromecounty.com, Internet: www.historicaljeromecounty.com. C.E.O.: Francis Egbert jr
Local Museum / Agriculture Museum - 1981
Antique farm machinery, hist of Jerome County 44337

Jersey City NJ

Afro-American Historical Society Museum, 1841 Kennedy Blvd, Jersey City, NJ 07305 - T: (201) 547-5262, Fax: (201) 547-5392. Dir.: Neal E. Brunson, Cons.: Theodore Brunson
Historical Museum - 1977
History 44338

Courtney and Lemmerman Galleries, New Jersey City University, 2039 Kennedy Blvd, Jersey City, NJ 07305 - T: (201) 200-3214, Fax: (201) 200-3224, E-mail: hbastidas@njcu.edu. Dir.: Hugo Xavier Bastidas
Fine Arts Museum
Prints, drawings 44339

Jersey City Museum, 350 Montgommery St, Jersey City, NJ 07302 - T: (201) 413-0303, Fax: (201) 413-9922, E-mail: info@jerseycitymuseum.org, Internet: www.jerseycitymuseum.org. Exec. Dir.: Marion Grzesiak, Cur.: Rocio Aranda-Alvarado
Fine Arts Museum / Local Museum - 1901
Local artifacts, regional art (19th-20th c) 44340

Saint Peter's College Art Gallery, 2641 Kennedy Blvd, Jersey City, NJ 07306 - T: (201) 915-9000, Fax: (201) 413-1669. Dir.: Oscar Magnan
Fine Arts Museum - 1971
Different art trends 44341

Jewell KS

Palmer Museum, POB 314, Jewell, KS 66949
Local Museum / Historical Museum - 1991
Printing machines, city hist 44342

Jim Thorpe PA

Asa Packer Mansion, Packer Hill, Jim Thorpe, PA 18229-0108 - T: (717) 325-3229, Fax: (717) 325-8154, Internet: www.asapackermansion. Dir.: Ron Sheehan
Local Museum - 1913
Local hist, 1860 Victorian mansion 44343

Johnson City TN

Carroll Reece Museum, East Tennessee State University, Gilbreath Dr, Johnson City, TN 37614 - T: (423) 439-4392, Fax: (423) 439-4283, E-mail: whiteb@etsu.edu, Internet: cass.etsu.edu/museum. Dir./Cur.: Blair H. White
Fine Arts Museum / University Museum / Historical Museum - 1965
History, art 44344

Elizabeth Slocumb Galleries, Carrol Reece Museum, c/o Dept. of Art, East Tennessee State University, POB 70708, Johnson City, TN 37614-0708 - T: (423) 439-5315, Fax: (423) 439-4393, E-mail: ropp@access.etsu-tn.edu, Internet: www.etsu-tenn-st.edu/design/. Dir.: Ann Ropp
Fine Arts Museum / University Museum - 1965
Art 44345

Hands On! Regional Museum, 315 E Main St, Johnson City, TN 37601 - T: (423) 928-6508, 928-6509, Fax: (423) 928-6915, E-mail: handson@handsonmuseum.org, Internet: www.handsonmuseum.org. Pres.: Duffie Jones
Special Museum / Science&Tech Museum - 1986
Children's museum 44346

Museum at Mountain Home, c/o East Tennessee State University, POB 70693, Johnson City, TN 37614-0693 - T: (423) 439-8069, Fax: (423) 431-7025, E-mail: whaleym@etsu.edu. Cur.: Martha Whaley
Historical Museum / Military Museum / University Museum - 1994
Medical and military artifacts 44347

Tipton-Haynes Museum, 2620 S Roan St, Johnson City, TN 37604 - T: (423) 926-3631, E-mail: information@tipton-haynes.org, Internet: www.tipton-haynes.org
Agriculture Museum / Local Museum - 1965
Agriculture, hist, folklore 44348

Johnson City TX

Lyndon B. Johnson National Historical Park, 100 Ladybird Ln, Johnson City, TX 78636 - T: (830) 868-7128, Fax: (830) 868-0810, Internet: www.nps.gov/lyjo. Dir.: Leslie Starr Hart, Cur.: Virginia Kilby
Local Museum - 1969
Local hist 44349

Johnstown NY

Johnson Hall, Hall Av, Johnstown, NY 12095 - T: (518) 762-8712, Fax: (518) 762-2330, E-mail: wanda.burch@oprhp.state.ny.us, Internet: www.nysparks.com. Head: Wanda Burch
Historical Museum - 1763 44350

Johnstown Historical Society Museum, 17 N William St, Johnstown, NY 12095 - T: (518) 762-7076. Pres.: Frederick Linus, Cur.: James F. Morrison
Historical Museum - 1892 44351

Johnstown PA

Flood Museum, 304 Washington St, Johnstown, PA 15907, mail addr: POB 1889, Johnstown, PA 15907 - T: (814) 539-1889, Fax: (814) 535-1931, E-mail: info@jaha.org, Internet: www.jaha.org. Dir.: Richard A. Burkert, Cur.: Daniel Ingram
Local Museum - 1971
Local hist 44352

Heritage Discover Center, Broad St and Seventh Av, Johnstown, PA 15907, mail addr: POB 1889, Johnstown, PA 15907 - T: (814) 539-1889, Fax: (814) 535-1931, E-mail: jaha@ctcnet.net, Internet: www.jaha.org. Dir.: Richard A. Burkert, Cur.: Daniel Ingram
Local Museum - 2001
Local hist 44353

Southern Alleghenies Museum of Art at Johnstown, c/o University of Pittsburgh at Johnstown, Pasquerilla Performing Arts Center, Johnstown, PA 15904 - T: (814) 269-7234, Fax: (814) 269-7240, E-mail: ncward@pitt.edu, Internet: www.sama-sfc.org. Cur.: Nancy Ward
Fine Arts Museum - 1982 44354

Joliet IL

Joliet Area Historical Museum, Cass & Ottawa Sts, Joliet, IL 60431 - T: (815) 280-1500, Fax: (815) 722-7225, E-mail: susan.english@jolietmuseum.org, Internet: www.jolietmuseum.org. Head: Gene Bogdan
Local Museum - 1981/1999
Local history 44355

Laure A. Sprague Art Gallery, c/o Joliet Junior College, J Bldg, 1215 Houbolt Rd, Joliet, IL 60436-8938 - T: (815) 729-9020 ext 2423, Fax: (815) 744-5507, Internet: www.jjc.cc.il.us. Dir.: Joe B. Milosevich
Fine Arts Museum - 1978 44356

Jolon CA

San Antonio Missions Museum, Mission Creek Rd, Jolon, CA 93928 - T: (408) 385-4478, Fax: (408) 386-9332, Internet: www.missionsanantoniopadua.com. Dir.: John Gini
Religious Arts Museum - 1771
Indian relicts, wine press of Spanish colonial period, manuscripts - archive 44357

Jonesboro AR

Arkansas State University Art Gallery, Caraway Rd, Jonesboro, AR 72467 - T: (870) 972-3050, Fax: (870) 972-3932, E-mail: csteele@aztec.astate.edu, Internet: www.astate.edu/docs/acad/art. Chm.: Curtis Steele
Fine Arts Museum / University Museum - 1967
Prints, drawings, paintings, sculpture 44358

Arkansas State University Museum, 110 Cooley Dr, Jonesboro, AR 72401 - T: (870) 972-2074, Fax: (870) 972-2793, E-mail: rhawkins@astate.edu. Dir.: Dr. Ruth Hawkins, Cur.: Brenda Keech
University Museum / Historical Museum / Public Gallery - 1936
University hist 44359

Jonesborough TN

Jonesborough-Washington County History Museum, 117 Boone St, Jonesborough, TN 37659 - T: (423) 753-1015, Fax: (423) 753-6129, E-mail: jbwchm@tricon.net, Internet: jonesborough.tricon.net/museum.html. Dir.: Jill Sauceman
Local Museum - 1982
Local hist 44360

Joplin MO

Dorothea B. Hoover Historical Museum, Schifferdecker Park, Joplin, MO 64802 - T: (417) 623-1180, Fax: (417) 623-6393, E-mail: jopmusm@ipa.net. Dir.: Brad Belk, Cur.: Christopher Wiseman
Local Museum - 1973
Local history 44361

George A. Spiva Center for the Arts, 222 W Third St, Joplin, MO 64801 - T: (417) 623-0183, Fax: (417) 623-3805, E-mail: spiva@spivaarts.com, Internet: www.spivaarts.com. Dir.: Darlene Brown
Fine Arts Museum - 1957 44362

Tri-State Mineral Museum, Schifferdecker Park, Joplin, MO 64801 - T: (417) 623-1180, Fax: (417) 623-6393, E-mail: jopmusm@ipa.net. Dir.: Brad Belk, Cur.: Christopher Wiseman
Natural History Museum - 1931 44363

Julesburg CO

Depot Museum and Fort Sedgwick Museum, 202 W First St, Julesburg, CO 80737 - T: (970) 474-2061, Fax: (970) 474-2061, E-mail: history@kcl.net
Local Museum - 1940
Union Pacific Railroad depot, agriculture, archaeology, folklore, military, local and natural history, Indian artifacts 44364

Juliette GA

Jarrell Plantation Georgia, 711 Jarrell Plantation Rd, Juliette, GA 31046-2515 - T: (912) 986-5172, Fax: (912) 986-5919, E-mail: jarrell_plantation_park@mail.dnr.state.ga.us, Internet: www.dnr.state.ga.us/dnr/parks
Agriculture Museum - 1974
Living farm 44365

Junction TX

Kimble County Historical Museum, 101 N 4th St, Junction, TX 76849 - T: (915) 446-4219, Fax: (915) 446-2871, E-mail: burtwyatt@ctesc.net. Cur.: Frederica Wyatt
Local Museum - 1966
Local hist 44366

Junction City OR

Junction City Historical Society Museum, 655 Holly St, Junction City, OR 97448 - T: (541) 998-2924, Fax: (541) 998-2924, E-mail: cgoodin@aol.com, Internet: www.junctioncity.com/history. Cur.: Kitty Goodin
Historical Museum - 1971 44367

Juneau AK

Alaska State Museum, 395 Whittier St, Juneau, AK 99801-1718 - T: (907) 465-2901, Fax: (907) 465-2976, E-mail: bkato@educ.state.ak.us, Internet: www.museum.state.ak.us. Dir.: Karen R. Crane, Cur.: Bruce Kato, Steve Henrikson, Mark Daughhetee, Kenneth Deroux, Cons.: Scott Carroll
Local Museum / Folklore Museum - 1900
General State museum 44368

House of Wickersham, 213 Seventh St, Juneau, AK 99801 - T: (907) 465-4563, Fax: (907) 465-5330, E-mail: separks@alaska.net, Internet: dnr.state.ak.us/parks. Dir.: William Garry
Historical Museum / Historic Site - 1984 44369

Juneau-Douglas City Museum, 114 4th St, Juneau, AK 99801 - T: (907) 586-3572, Fax: (907) 586-3203, E-mail: mary_pat_wyatt@ci.juneau.ak.us, Internet: www.juneau.lib.ak.us.parksrec/. Dir.: Mary Pat Wyatt, Cur.: Ellen Carrlee
Local Museum - 1976
Local history, culture 44370

Jupiter FL

Florida History Museum, 805 N US Hwy 1, Jupiter, FL 33477 - T: (561) 747-6639, Fax: (561) 575-3292, E-mail: fhcm3@bellsouth.net
Historical Museum - 1971
General History, lighthouse, historic homes 44371

Hibel Museum of Art - Jupiter, 1200 Town Center Dr, Jupiter, FL 33458 - T: (561) 622-1380, Fax: (561) 622-3475, E-mail: hibelmuseumjupiter@excite.com, Internet: www.hibel.org. Dir.: Lynne Zuback
Fine Arts Museum / Decorative Arts Museum - 1977
Paintings, sculptures, drawings, graphics, porcelain art, crystal art and dolls by Edna Hibel, furniture 44372

Kadoka SD

Jackson-Washabaugh Historical Museum, S Main St, Kadoka, SD 57543 - T: (605) 837-2229, E-mail: kadokacity@wcenet.com
Local Museum - 1980
Local hist 44373

Kailua-Kona HI

Hulihee Palace, 75-5718 Alii Dr, Kailua-Kona, HI 96740 - T: (808) 329-1877, Fax: (808) 329-1321, E-mail: hulihee@ilhawaii.net, Internet: www.huliheepalace.org
Decorative Arts Museum / Natural History Museum - 1928
Residence for Hawaiian royalty 44374

Kake AK

Kake Tribal Heritage Foundation, 422 Totem Way, Kake, AK 99830 - T: (907) 785-3258, Fax: (907) 790-3258. Dir.: Henrich Kadake
Open Air Museum / Local Museum - 1986
Local hist 44375

Kalamazoo MI

Alamo Township Museum-John E. Gray Memorial, 8119 N 6th St, Kalamazoo, MI 49009 - T: (616) 344-2107. Pres.: Mary Gobel
Ethnology Museum / Local Museum - 1969 44376

Gallery II, Western Michigan University, College of Fine Arts, 1903 W Michigan Av, Kalamazoo, MI 49008 - T: (616) 387-2455, 387-2436, Fax: (616) 387-2477, E-mail: exhibitions@wmich.edu, Internet: www.wmich.edu/art/exhibitions/. Dir.: Jacquelyn Ruttinger, Cur.: Holly Stephenson
Public Gallery / University Museum - 1975
Prints, sculptures 44377

Kalamazoo Aviation History Museum, 3101 E Milham Rd, Kalamazoo, MI 49002 - T: (616) 382-6555, Fax: (616) 382-1813, E-mail: airzoo@airzoo.org, Internet: www.airzoo.org. Dir.: Robert E. Ellis, Pres.: Suzanne D. Parish, Cur.: Bill Painter, Restoration: Dick Schaus
Military Museum / Historical Museum - 1977
Aviation 44378

Kalamazoo Institute of Arts, 314 S Park St, Kalamazoo, MI 49007-5102 - T: (616) 349-7775, Fax: (616) 349-9313, E-mail: museum@kiarts.org, Internet: www.kiarts.org. Dir.: James A. Bridenstine, Cur.: Don Desmet, Susan Eckhardt
Fine Arts Museum - 1924
Art - school 44379

Kalamazoo Valley Museum, Kalmazzo Valley Community College, 230 N Rose St, Kalamazoo, MI 49007 - T: (616) 373-7990, Fax: (616) 373-7997, E-mail: pnorris@kvcc.edu, Internet: www.kvcc.edu/kvm/. Dir.: Dr. Patrick Norris, Asst. Dir.: Elspeth Inglis, Cur.: Thomas A. Dietz, Jean Stevens (Design)
Local Museum / Science&Tech Museum / Historical Museum - 1927
Participatory, science, technology - planetarium 44380

Kalaupapa HI

Kalaupapa Historical Park, 7 Puahi St, Kalaupapa, HI 96742, mail addr: POB 2222, Kalaupapa, HI 96742 - T: (808) 567-6802, Fax: (808) 567-6729, E-mail: kala-superintendent@nps.gob, Internet: www.nps.gov/kala/gov. Head: Tom Workmann
Historic Site - 1980
Site of the 1886-present Molokai Island leprosy settlement 44381

Kalida OH

Putnam County Historical Society Museum, 201 E Main St, Kalida, OH 45853 - T: (419) 532-3008. Pres.: Joe Balbaugh, Cur.: Carol Wise
Local Museum - 1873 44382

Kalispell MT

Conrad Mansion Museum, Between Third and Fourth Sts and Woodland Av, Kalispell, MT 59901 - T: (406) 755-2166, E-mail: paivaa@altavista.net, Internet: www.conradmansion.com. Chm.: Rita Fitzsimmons
Historical Museum - 1975 44383

Hockaday Museum of Arts, 302 Second Av E at Third St, Kalispell, MT 59901 - T: (406) 755-5268, Fax: (406) 755-2023, E-mail: hockaday@aboutmontana.net, Internet: www.hockadayartmuseum.org. Pres.: William R. Hanson, C.E.O./Dir.: Gail DeBuse Potter
Fine Arts Museum - 1968 44384

Kalkaska MI

Kalkaska County Historical Museum, 335 S Cedar St, Kalkaska, MI 49646, mail addr: POB 1178, Kalkaska, MI 49646 - T: (616) 258-7840. Pres.: Don F. Darke
Local Museum - 1967
Regional history, Grand Rapids and Indiana Railroad depot 44385

Kampsville IL

Center for American Archeology, Hwy 100, Kampsville, IL 62053 - T: (618) 653-4316, Fax: (618) 653-4232, E-mail: csutton@caa-archeology.org, Internet: www.caa-archeology.org. Dir.: Cynthia Sutton
Archaeological Museum - 1954/1970
Archaeology 44386

Kane PA

Thomas L. Kane Memorial Chapel, 30 Chestnut St, Kane, PA 16735 - T: (814) 837-9729, Fax: (814) 837-2213
Religious Arts Museum - 1970
Religious hist, historic chapel 44387

Kankakee IL

Kankakee County Historical Society Museum, 801 South Eighth Av, Kankakee, IL 60901 - T: (815) 932-5279, Fax: (815) 932-5204, E-mail: museum@daily-journal.com, Internet: www.kankakeecountymuseum.com. C.E.O.: Norman S. Stevens
Local Museum - 1906
Local history 44388

Kannapolis NC

Cannon Village Visitor Center, 200 West Av, Kannapolis, NC 28081 - T: (704) 938-3200, Fax: (704) 933-5403
Local Museum - 1974
Textile art, historic artifacts, antique handloom 44389

Kanopolis KS

Fort Harker Museum, 309 W Ohio St, Kanopolis, KS 67454 - T: (785) 472-3059, E-mail: echs@informatics.net. Head: Tyra Denny
Military Museum - 1961
Military 44390

Kansas City KS

The Children's Museum of Kansas City, 4601 State Av, Kansas City, KS 66102 - T: (913) 287-8888, Fax: (913) 287-8332, E-mail: childrens-museumofkc@hotmail.com, Internet: www.kidmuzm.org. Pres.: David Raymond, Dir.: Marty Porter, Sc. Staff: Elizabeth Schwartz (Exhibitions), Janene Brown (Admin.)
Special Museum - 1984 44391

Clendening History of Medicine Library and Museum, University of Kansas Medical Center, 3901 Rainbow Blvd, Kansas City, KS 66160-7311 - T: (913) 588-7244, Fax: (913) 588-7060, E-mail: nhulston@kumc.edu, Internet: www.kumc.edu. Chm.: Robert L. Martensen, Cur.: Nancy Hulston
University Museum / Historical Museum - 1945
Medicine 44392

Grinter Place, 1420 S 78th St, Kansas City, KS 66111 - T: (913) 299-0373, Fax: (913) 788-8046, E-mail: grinter@kshs.org, Internet: www.kshs.org. Cur.: Eric Page
Historical Museum - 1968
Historic house, built by Moses Grinter, culture, domestic life 44393

Kansas City MO

American Jazz Museum, 1616 E 18th St, Kansas City, MO 64108-1610 - T: (816) 474-8463 ext 204, Fax: (816) 474-0074, E-mail: jmoore@kcjazz.org, Internet: www.americanjazzmuseum.com. Exec. Dir.: Juanita Moore
Music Museum - 1994
Jazz masters Louis Armstrong, Duke Ellington, Ella Fitzgerald and Charlie Parker 44394

American Royal Museum, 1701 American Royal Court, Kansas City, MO 64102 - T: (816) 221-9800, Fax: (816) 221-8189, E-mail: amroyal@birch.net, Internet: www.americanroyal.com. Dir.: Nancy Perry
Agriculture Museum - 1992
Agriculture, horses 44395

Commerce Bancshares Fine Art Collection, 1000 Walnut St, Kansas City, MO 64199 - T: (816) 760-7885, Fax: (816) 234-2356, E-mail: robin.trafton@commercebank.com. Dir.: Laura Kemper Fields
Fine Arts Museum - 1964
Contemporary American realist art, paintings and drawings 44396

Creative Arts Center, 4525 Oak St, Kansas City, MO 64111 - T: (816) 751-1236, Fax: (816) 761-7154. Dir.: Marc F. Wilson
Fine Arts Museum 44397

Gallery of Art → John Maxine Belger Center

John Maxine Belger Center, University of Missouri-Kansas City, 203 Fine Arts, 5100 Rockhill Rd, Kansas City, MO 64110-2499 - T: (816) 235-1502, Fax: (816) 235-6528, E-mail: csubler@umkc.edu, Internet: www.umkc.edu/gallery. Dir.: Craig A. Subler
Fine Arts Museum / University Museum - 1975
Contemporary art (20th-21st c) 44398

Kaleidoscope, 2501 McGee, Kansas City, MO 64108 - T: (816) 274-8301, 274-8934, Fax: (816) 274-3148, E-mail: lavery1@hallmark.com, Internet: www.hallmarkkaleidoscope.com. Admin.: Regi Ahrens
Special Museum - 1969
Children's participatory art exhibit 44399

Kansas City Museum/Science City at Union Station, 30 W Pershing Rd, Kansas City, MO 64123-1199 - T: (816) 460-2000, Fax: (816) 460-2260, E-mail: info@sciencecity.com, Internet: www.kcmuseum.com; www.sciencecity.com. Dir.: Turner White, Dep. Dir.: Gaye Clemenson (History)
Ethnology Museum / Historical Museum / Natural History Museum / Science&Tech Museum - 1939 44400

Kemper Museum of Contemporary Art, 4420 Warwick Blvd, Kansas City, MO 64111-1821 - T: (816) 753-5784, Fax: (816) 753-5806, E-mail: info@kemperart.org, Internet: www.kemperart.org. Dir.: Rachael Blackburn, Cur.: Dana Self
Fine Arts Museum - 1994
Contemporary art 44401

Leedy-Voulke's Art Center, 2012 Baltimore Av, Kansas City, MO 64108 - T: (816) 474-1919, Fax: (816) 474-1919. Dir.: Sherry Leedy
Public Gallery
Contemporary arts and crafts 44402

Liberty Memorial Museum of World War One, 100 W 26th St, Kansas City, MO 64108 - T: (816) 784-1918, Fax: (816) 784-1929, E-mail: staff@libertymemorialmuseum.org, Internet: www.libertymemorialmuseum.org. Dir.: Doran L. Cart
Historical Museum - 1919
World War I memorabilia - archives 44403

The Nelson-Atkins Museum of Art, 4525 Oak St, Kansas City, MO 64111-1873 - T: (816) 561-4000, Fax: (816) 561-7154, Internet: www.nelson-atkins.org. Dir.: Marc F. Wilson (Oriental Art), Chief Cur.: Deborah Emont Scott, Cur.: Ian Kennedy (European Art), Cur.: Christina Futter (European and American Decorative Arts), Cur.: Dr. Robert Cohon (Ancient Art), Margaret Conrads (American Art), Gaylord Torrence (American Indian Art), Xiaoneng Yang (Early Chinese Art), Jan Schall (20th c Art), George L. McKenna (Prints and Photographs), Cons.: Elisabeth

Batchelor, Scott Heffley (Paintings), Kathleen Garland (Objects)
Fine Arts Museum - 1933
English pottery, Oriental ceramics, paintings, sculpture, contemporary artworks, Oriental art and furniture 44404

Print Consortium, 6121 NW 77th St, Kansas City, MO 64151 - T: (816) 587-1986, E-mail: eickhorst@griffon.nwic.edu. Exec. Dir.: Dr. William S. Eickhorst
Fine Arts Museum - 1983
Prints by established professional artists 44405

Roger Guffey Gallery, Federal Reserve Bank of Kansas City, 925 Grand Blvd, Kansas City, MO 64198 - T: (816) 881-2554, Fax: (816) 881-2007, Internet: www.kc.frb.org. Pres.: Thomas M. Hoenig
Fine Arts Museum / Public Gallery - 1985 44406

Shoal Creek Living History Museum, 7000 NE Barry Rd, Kansas City, MO 64156 - T: (816) 792-2655, Fax: (816) 792-3469, E-mail: shoalcreeklhm@aol.com, Internet: www.kcmo.org. Cur.: Alisha Moore Cole
Open Air Museum - 1975
Architecture, material culture 19th c 44407

Society for Contemporary Photography, 2016 Baltimore Av, Kansas City, MO 64108, mail addr: POB 32284, Kansas City, MO 64171 - T: (816) 471-2115, Fax: (816) 471-2462, E-mail: spc@sky.net, Internet: www.spconline.org. Dir.: Kathy Aron
Fine Arts Museum - 1984 44408

Steamboat Arabia Museum, 400 Grand Av, Kansas City, MO 64106 - T: (816) 471-1856, Fax: (816) 471-1616, E-mail: info@1856.com, Internet: www.1856.com. Cur.: Greg Hawley
Fine Arts Museum - 1991
Tools, textiles, leather, glassware, China, tin, international goods, equip from the steamboat 44409

Thomas Hart Benton Home and Studio, 3616 Belleview, Kansas City, MO 64111 - T: (816) 931-5722, Fax: (816) 931-5722, E-mail: dspbhome@@mail.dnr.state.mo.us, Internet: www.mostateparks.com/benton.htm
Historical Museum - 1977 44410

Thornhill Gallery, Avila College, 11901 Wornall Rd, Kansas City, MO 64145 - T: (816) 942-8400 ext 2443, Fax: (816) 846-4726, E-mail: chrismanga@mail.avila.edu, Internet: www.avila.edu. Dir.: Dr. Carol Coburn, Cur.: Lisa Ann Sugimoto
Fine Arts Museum / University Museum - 1978
Japanese woodblock prints 44411

Toy and Miniature Museum of Kansas City, 5235 Oak St, Kansas City, MO 64112 - T: (816) 333-9328, Fax: (816) 333-2055, E-mail: toynmin@swbell.net, Internet: www.umkc.edu/tmm. Dir.: Roger Berg, Cur.: Mary Wheeler
Decorative Arts Museum - 1981
Toys 44412

Kapaa HI

Kauai Children's Discovery Museum, 6458 B. Kahuna Rd, Kapaa, HI 96746 - T: (808) 823-8222, Fax: (808) 821-2558, E-mail: robin@kcdm.org, Internet: www.kcdm.org. Dir.: Robin Mazor
Special Museum - 1994 44413

Katonah NY

Caramoor Center for Music and the Arts, Girdle Ridge Rd, Katonah, NY 10536 - T: (914) 232-5035, Fax: (914) 232-5521, E-mail: museum@caramoor.com, Internet: www.caramoor.com. C.E.O.: Erich Vollmer
Fine Arts Museum / Decorative Arts Museum / Performing Arts Museum - 1946
Eastern and Western art and furnishings, jade coll 44414

John Jay Homestead, 400 Rte 22, & Jay St, Katonah, NY 10536 - T: (914) 232-5651, Fax: (914) 232-8085, E-mail: julia.warger@oprhp.state.ny.us. Pres.: Wendy Ross
Historical Museum - 1958
Home and farm of chief justice John Jay, portraits, farming 44415

Katonah Museum of Art, Rte 22 at Jay St, Katonah, NY 10536 - T: (914) 232-9555, Fax: (914) 232-3128, Internet: www.katonah-museum.org. Dir.: Susan H. Edwards, Assoc. Dir.: Nancy Wallach, Nancy Hilzhood (Registrar)
Fine Arts Museum - 1953
Art 44416

Kauai HI

Koke'e Natural History Museum, Kokee State Park, Kauai, HI 96752, mail addr: POB 100, Kekaha, HI 96752 - T: (808) 335-9975, Fax: (808) 335-6131, E-mail: kokee@aloha.net, Internet: www.aloha.net/~kokee/. Exec. Dir.: Marsha Erickson
Natural History Museum - 1952
Kaua'i's ecology, geology, climatology 44417

Kaukauna WI

Charles A. Grignon Mansion, 1313 Augustine St, Kaukauna, WI 54130 - T: (920) 766-3122, Fax: (920) 766-9834, E-mail: ochs@foxvalleyhistory.org, Internet: www.foxvalleyhistory.org. C.E.O.: Terry Bergen
Local Museum / Folklore Museum - 1837
Historic house 44418

Kawaihae HI

Puukohola Heiau National Historic Site, 62-3601 Kawaihae Rd, Kawaihae, HI 96743, mail addr: POB 44340, Kawaihae, HI 96473 - T: (808) 882-7218, Fax: (808) 882-1215, E-mail: ernest_young@nps.gov, Internet: www.nps.gov/puhe. Superint.: Daniel Kawaiaea, Cur.: Ernest Young, Daniel Kawaiaea
Archaeological Museum - 1972
Ruins of Puukohola Heiau, Temple on the hill of the Puukohla Whale, war temple built 1790-1791 44419

Kearney MO

Jesse James Farm and Museum, 21216 Jesse James Farm Rd, Kearney, MO 64060 - T: (816) 628-6065, Fax: (816) 628-6676, E-mail: jessejames@claycogov.com, Internet: home.co.clay.mo.us. Head: Elizabeth Gilliam-Beckett
Local Museum - 1978 44420

Kearney NE

Fort Kearney Museum, 131 S Central Av, Kearney, NE 68847 - T: (308) 234-5200. Dir.: Marlo L. Johnson
Military Museum - 1950 44421

Fort Kearny State Historical Park, 1020 V Rd, Kearney, NE 68847 - T: (308) 865-5305, Fax: (308) 865-5306, E-mail: ftkrny@ngpsun.ngpc.state.ne.us. Dir.: Eugene A. Hunt
Military Museum / Historic Site - 1929 44422

Kearney Area Children's Museum, 2013 Av A, Kearney, NE 68847 - T: (308) 236-5437. C.E.O.: Peggy Abels
Special Museum - 1989 44423

Museum of Nebraska Art, 2401 Central Av, Kearney, NE 68847 - T: (308) 865-8559, Fax: (308) 865-8104, E-mail: monet@unk.edu, Internet: monet.unk.edu/mona. Dir.: Audrey S. Kauders, Cur.: Josephine Martins
Fine Arts Museum - 1986 44424

Keene NH

Cheshire County Museum, 246 Main St, Keene, NH 03431 - T: (603) 352-1895, Fax: (603) 352-9226, E-mail: hscc@cheshire.net. Dir.: Alan F. Rumrill
Local Museum - 1927
Local hist, furniture, glass, pottery, maps, photos, silver, toys, paintings 44425

Horatio Colony House Museum, 199 Main St, Keene, NH 03431 - T: (603) 352-0460, E-mail: colonymuseum@webryders.com
Decorative Arts Museum 44426

Thorne-Sagendorph Art Gallery, Keene State College, Wyman Way, Keene, NH 03435-3501 - T: (603) 358-2720, Fax: (603) 358-2238, Internet: www.keene.edu/tsag. Dir.: Maureen Ahern
Fine Arts Museum - 1965 44427

Kellogg IA

Kellogg Historical Society Museum, 218 High St, Kellogg, IA 50135
Local Museum - 1980
Pitcher coll, farming 44428

Kelly WY

Murie Museum, 1 Ditch Creek Rd, Kelly, WY 83011 - T: (307) 733-4765, Fax: (307) 739-9388, E-mail: info@tetonscience.org, Internet: www.tetonscience.org. Dir.: John C. Shea
Natural History Museum - 1973
Natural hist 44429

Kelso WA

Cowlitz County Historical Museum, 405 Allen St, Kelso, WA 98626 - T: (360) 577-3119, Fax: (360) 423-9987, E-mail: freeced@co.cowlitz.wa.us, Internet: www.co.cowlitz.wa/museum. Pres.: Sarah Koss, Dir.: David W. Freece
Local Museum - 1953
Local hist 44430

Kemmerer WY

Fossil Country Museum, 400 Pine, Kemmerer, WY 83101 - T: (307) 877-6551, Fax: (307) 877-6552, E-mail: museum@hamsfork.net, Internet: www.hamsfork.net/~museum. Dir.: Hilary Barton Billman
Local Museum - 1989
Local hist, coal mine, genuine whiskey stills 44431

Kenilworth IL

Kenilworth Historical Society Museum, 415 Kenilworth Av, Kenilworth, IL 60043-1134 - T: (847) 251-2565, Fax: (847) 251-2565, E-mail: kenilworthhistory@earthlink.net, Internet: www.kenilworthhistory.org. Pres.: Ray Drexler
Local Museum - 1922
Local history 44432

Kenly NC

Tobacco Farm Life Museum, Hwy 301 N, 709 Church St, Kenly, NC 27542 - T: (919) 284-3431, Fax: (919) 284-9788, E-mail: tobmuseum@bbnp.com, Internet: www.tobmuseum.bbnp.com. C.E.O.: Lynn Wagner, Cur.: Harold Jacobson
Local Museum - 1983
Agriculture, heritage, Eastern NC farm family 44433

Kennebunk ME

Brick Store Museum, 117 Main St, Kennebunk, ME 04043 - T: (207) 985-4802, Fax: (207) 985-6887, E-mail: info@brickstoremuseum.org, Internet: www.brickstoremuseum.org. Dir.: Marcene J. Molinaro, Asst. Dir.: Jan Fisk
Historical Museum - 1936
Paintings, works on paper, fueniture, photographs, costumes, maritime related objekts, 44434

Kennebunkport ME

Kennebunkport Historical Museum, 125 North St, Kennebunkport, ME 04046 - T: (207) 967-2751, Fax: (207) 967-1205, E-mail: kporths@gwi.net, Internet: www.kporthistory.org. C.E.O.: William Clark
Local Museum - 1952
Local history 44435

Seashore Trolley Museum, 195 Log Cabin Rd, Kennebunkport, ME 04046-1690 - T: (207) 967-2712, Fax: (207) 967-2800, E-mail: carshop@gwi.net, Internet: www.trolleymuseum.org. Pres.: Peter Folger
Science&Tech Museum - 1939
Electric railway history and technology, steetcars, mass transit 44436

Kennesaw GA

Kennesaw Civil War Museum, 2829 Cherokee St, Kennesaw, GA 30144 - T: (770) 427-2117, Fax: (770) 429-4538, E-mail: kcwm@juno.com, Internet: www.thegeneral.org. Dir.: Dr. Jeffrey A. Drobney, Harper Harris
Historic Site / Historical Museum / Science&Tech Museum - 1972
Civil war, trains, site where the Great Locomotive chase began, the locomotive General 44437

Kennesaw Mountain National Battlefield Park, 900 Kennesaw Mountain Dr, Kennesaw, GA 30152 - T: (770) 427-4686, Fax: (770) 528-8399, E-mail: kmha@mindspring.com, Internet: www.nps.gov. Cur.: Retha Stephens
Historical Museum / Military Museum - 1917
Civil war history 44438

Kennett MO

Dunklin County Museum, 122 College, Kennett, MO 63857 - T: (573) 888-6620, E-mail: cbrown@sheltonbbs.com. Dir.: Charles B. Brown
Historical Museum - 1976 44439

Kenosha WI

Kenosha County Museum, 2202 51 St Pl, Kenosha, WI 53143 - T: (262) 654-5770, Fax: (414) 654-1730, E-mail: kchs@acronet.net, Internet: www.kenoshahistorycenter.org. Pres.: Barbara Riley, Cur.: Cindy J. Nelson
Local Museum - 1878
Local hist 44440

Kenosha Public Museum, 5500 First Av, Kenosha, WI 53140 - T: (262) 653-4140, Fax: (262) 653-4437, E-mail: mpaulat@kenosha.org, Internet: www.kenosha.org. Dir.: Paula Touhey, Cur.: Dan Joyce, Nancy Mathews
Fine Arts Museum / Decorative Arts Museum / Natural History Museum - 1933
Natural hist, art 44441

Kensington CT

New Britain Youth Museum at Hungerford Park, 191 Farmington Av, Kensington, CT 06037 - T: (860) 827-9064, Fax: (860) 827-1266, E-mail: newb@snet.net, Internet: www.newbritainyouthmuseum.org. Dir.: Ann F. Peabody
Special Museum - 1984
Farming, geological and agricultural tools 44442

Kent CT

Kent Art Association, 21 S Main St, Kent, CT 06757 - T: (860) 927-3989, E-mail: kent.art.assoc@snet.net. Pres.: David Fouts
Public Gallery - 1923 44443

Sloane-Stanley Museum and Kent Furnace, Rte 7, Kent, CT 06757, mail addr: POB 917, Kent, CT 06757 - T: (860) 927-3849, Fax: (860) 927-2152, E-mail: sloanestanley.museum@snet.net, Internet: www.chc.state.ct.us. Dir.: Karin Peterson
Science&Tech Museum - 1969
Iron industry, paintings 44444

Kent OH

Kelso House, 1106 Old Forge Rd, Kent, OH 44240 - T: (330) 673-1058, E-mail: pegparwink@aol.com. Dir.: Edgar L. McCormick, Cur.: Michelle Wardle
Historical Museum - 1963 44445

Kent State University Art Galleries, School of Art, Kent State University, Kent, OH 44242-0001 - T: (330) 672-2444, 672-2192, Fax: (330) 672-2192, E-mail: fsmith@kentvm.kent.edu, Internet: www.kent.edu/art/soa-gallery/index.html. Dir.: Fred T. Smith
Fine Arts Museum / University Museum - 1950 44446

Kent State University Museum, Rockwell Hall, Corner of E Main & S Lincoln Sts, Kent, OH 44242-0001 - T: (330) 672-3450, Fax: (330) 672-3218, E-mail: museum@kent.edu, Internet: www.kent.edu/museum/. Dir.: Jean Druesedow, Sc. Staff: Anne Bissonnette
Decorative Arts Museum - 1981
Costumes and decorative arts 44447

Kentfield CA

College of Marin Art Gallery, College Av, Kentfield, CA 94904 - T: (415) 485-9494, Internet: www.marin.edu. Dir.: Francis Arnold
Fine Arts Museum - 1970 44448

Kenton OH

Hardin County Historical Museum, 215 N Main St, Kenton, OH 43326 - T: (419) 673-7147, Fax: (419) 675-3547, E-mail: hchm@dbscorp.net, Internet: www.kenton.com/keller.hchm. Dir.: Shirley Ray
Historical Museum - 1991 44449

Kenyon MN

Gunderson House, 107 Gunderson Blvd, Kenyon, MN 55946 - T: (507) 789-6141, 789-6329. Pres.: Lois Easton
Historical Museum - 1895 44450

Keokuk IA

Keokuk Art Center, 300 Main St, Keokuk, IA 52632 - T: (319) 524-8354. Dir.: Thomas Seabold
Fine Arts Museum - 1954
Paintings, sculptures 44451

Keokuk River Museum, Foot of Johnson St, Victory Park, Keokuk, IA 52632 - T: (319) 524-4765, Fax: (319) 524-2642, Internet: www.geomuerity.org. Dir.: Charles Pietscher
Historical Museum - 1962
Maritime history, housed in Geo. M. Verity Mississippi River Steamboat 44452

Keosauqua IA

Van Buren County Historical Society Museum, First St, Keosauqua, IA 52565 - T: (319) 293-3211. Pres.: Vel Luse
Local Museum - 1960
Local history 44453

Kerby OR

Kerbyville Museum, 24195 Redwood Hwy, Kerby, OR 97531 - T: (541) 592-5252, Fax: (541) 592-5252, E-mail: kerbyvillemuseum@mail.com, Internet: www.kerbyvillemuseum.com. C.E.O. & Pres.: Sandra J.. Hare
Local Museum - 1959 44454

Kerrville TX

Cowboy Artists of America Museum → National Center for American Western Art

Hill Country Museum, 226 Earl Garrett St, Kerrville, TX 78028-5305 - T: (830) 896-8633. Dir.: Griffiths Carnes
Local Museum - 1983
Local hist 44455

L.D. Brinkman Art Foundation, 444 Sidney Baker St S, Kerrville, TX 78028 - T: (830) 257-2000, Fax: (830) 257-2030. Dir.: L.D. Brinkman, Byron C. Smith, Charles C. Thomas
Fine Arts Museum - 1985
Art 44456

National Center for American Western Art, 1550 Bandera Hwy, Kerrville, TX 78028 - T: (830) 896-2553, Fax: (830) 896-2556, E-mail: caam@ktc.com, Internet: www.caamuseum.com. Exec. Dir.: Michael W. Duty
Fine Arts Museum - 1983
Art 44457

Ketchikan AK

City of Ketchikan Museum, 629 Dock St, Ketchikan, AK 99901 - T: (907) 225-5900, Fax: (907) 225-5901, E-mail: museumdir@city.ketchikan.ak.us. Dir.: Michael Naab, Cur.: Victoria A. Lord
Local Museum - 1976 44458

Tongass Historical Museum, 629 Dock St, Ketchikan, AK 99901 - T: (907) 225-5600, Fax: (907) 225-5602, E-mail: museumdir@city.ketchikan.ak.us, Internet: city.ketchikan.ak.us. Dir.: Michael Naab, Cur.: Victoria Lord, Christopher Hanson
Local Museum - 1961
Regional history 44459

Kewaunee WI

Kewaunee County Historical Museum, Court House Sq, 613 Dodge St, Kewaunee, WI 54216 - T: (920) 388-7176, Internet: www.rootsweb.com/~wikewaun. Dir.: Gerald Abitz, Cur.: Tom Schuller
Local Museum - 1970
Local hist   44460

Key West FL

Audubon House, 205 Whitehead St, Key West, FL 33040 - T: (305) 294-2116, Fax: (305) 294-4513, E-mail: audubon@flakeysol.com, Internet: www.audubonhouse.com. Cur.: Tom Greenwood
Historical Museum - 1960
Early 19th-century home of Capt. John H. Geiger which commemorates John James Audubon visit to Key West in 1832 - gardens   44461

Donkey Milk House, 613 Eaton St, Key West, FL 33040 - T: (305) 296-1866, Fax: (305) 296-0922. C.E.O.: Denison Tempal
Decorative Arts Museum - 1992   44462

East Martello Museum, 3501 S Roosevelt Blvd, Key West, FL 33040 - T: (305) 296-3913, Fax: (305) 296-6206, Internet: www.kwahs.org. Dir.: Kevin J. O'Brien, Claudia L. Pennington, Cur.: Collen Martin
Historical Museum - 1951
History, art, housed in 1861 brick fort   44463

Ernest Hemingway House Museum, 907 Whitehead, Key West, FL 33040 - T: (305) 294-1136, 294-1575, Fax: (305) 294-2755, E-mail: hemingwayhome@prodigy.net, Internet: www.hemingwayhome.com. Dir.: Mike Morawski
Special Museum / Historic Site - 1964
1931-1961 Ernest Hemingway Home in Spanish Colonial Style   44464

Fort Zachary Taylor, End of Southard St, Truman Annex, Key West, FL 33040, mail addr: POB 6560, Key West, FL 33041 - T: (305) 292-6713, Fax: (305) 292-6881, 292-6850, E-mail: foft1985@yahoo.com
Military Museum - 1985
Civil War, Spanish-American war, WW 12   44465

Harry S. Truman Little White House Museum, 111 Front St, Key West, FL 33040 - T: (305) 294-9911, Fax: (305) 294-9988, E-mail: bwolz@historictours.com, Internet: www.trumanlittlewhitehouse.com. Exec. Dir.: Robert J. Wolz
Historical Museum - 1991   44466

Key West Lighthouse Museum, 938 Whitehead, Key West, FL 33040 - T: (305) 296-3913, Fax: (305) 296-6206. Dir.: Kevin J. O'Brien
Science&Tech Museum - 1966
Housed in 1887 lighthouse keepers home, 1846 lighthouse   44467

Key West Museum of Art and History, 281 Front St, Key West, FL 33040 - T: (305) 295-6649. Dir.: Claudia L. Pennington
Fine Arts Museum / Historical Museum - 1951   44468

Mel Fisher Maritime Heritage Museum, 200 Greene St, Key West, FL 33040 - T: (305) 294-2633, Fax: (305) 294-5671, E-mail: info@melfisher.org, Internet: www.melfisher.org. Dir.: Madeleine H. Burnside, Cur.: Corey Malcom (Archaeology)
Historical Museum - 1982   44469

The Oldest House Museum, 322 Duval St, Key West, FL 33040 - T: (305) 294-9502. Dir.: David L. Roumm
Historical Museum / Folklore Museum - 1975
Maritime, Conch house, home of local sea captain and wrecker   44470

Ripley's Believe it or not!, 527 Duval St, Key West, FL 33040 - T: (305) 295-9686, Fax: (305) 293-9709, Internet: www.ripleys.com. Cur.: James R. McGarry
Museum of Classical Antiquities / Decorative Arts Museum - 1927
Asian and primitive tribal artifacts, human oddities, arcane art   44471

Keyport NJ

Steamboat Dock Museum, POB 312, Keyport, NJ 07735 - T: (732) 264-7822. Cur.: Angela Jeandron
Local Museum - 1976
Business ledgers, photographs of commercial, industrial and domestic life   44472

Keyport WA

Naval Undersea Museum, Garnett Way, Keyport, WA 98345-7610 - T: (360) 396-4148, Fax: (360) 396-7944, Internet: num.kpt.nuwc.navy.mil. Dir.: Bill Galvani, Cur.: Barbara Moe
Science&Tech Museum / Military Museum - 1979   44473

Keystone SD

Big Thunder Gold Mine, 604 Blair, Keystone, SD 57751 - T: (605) 666-4847, Fax: (605) 666-4566, Internet: www.bigthundergoldmine.com. C.E.O.: Charles McLain
Science&Tech Museum - 1958
1880s gold mine's equipment   44474

Keystone Area Museum, 410 3rd St, Keystone, SD 57751 - T: (605) 666-4494, Fax: (605) 666-4824, E-mail: keygadfly@aol.com, Internet: www.keystonehistory.com. Pres.: Betty Jo Sagdalen
Local Museum - 1983
Local hist   44475

Mount Rushmore National Memorial, Hwy 244, Keystone, SD 57751 - T: (605) 574-2523, Fax: (605) 574-2307, E-mail: jim_popovich@nps.gov, Internet: www.nps.gov/moru/. Cur.: Bruce Weisman
Historical Museum - 1925
Massive granite sculpture, carved into a mountainside, memorializing the likenesses of the Presidents Washington, Jefferson, Theodore Roosevelt & Lincoln   44476

Parade of Presidents Wax Museum, Highway 609 16-A, Keystone, SD 57751 - T: (605) 666-4455, Fax: (605) 666-4455. Dir.: Mary Ann Riordan
Decorative Arts Museum - 1970
Wax figures   44477

Keytesville MO

General Sterling Price Museum, 412 Bridge St, Keytesville, MO 65261 - T: (660) 288-3204. Pres.: Sarah Weaver
Local Museum - 1964   44478

Kilgore TX

East Texas Oil Museum at Kilgore College, Hwy 259 at Ross St, Kilgore, TX 75662 - T: (903) 983-8531, 983-8295, Fax: (903) 983-8600, Internet: www.easttexasoilmuseum.com. Dir.: Joe L. White
Science&Tech Museum / University Museum - 1980
Oil industry   44479

Kill Devil Hills NC

Wright Brothers National Memorial, Virginia Dare Trail-US 158, Kill Devil Hills, NC 27948 - T: (919) 441-7430, Fax: (919) 441-7730, Internet: www.nps.gov/wrbr. Head: Mary H. Doll
Science&Tech Museum - 1927   44480

Kimberly OR

John Day Fossil Beds National Monument, HCR 82, Box 126, Kimberly, OR 97848 - T: (541) 987-2333, Fax: (541) 987-2336, E-mail: joda_interpretation@nps.gov, Internet: www.nps.gov/joda/. Cur.: T. Fremd (Paleontology)
Natural History Museum / Archaeological Museum - 1975
Fossils, geology, cenozoic   44481

Kinderhook NY

Columbia County Historical Society Museum, 5 Albany Av, Kinderhook, NY 12106-0311 - T: (518) 758-9265, Fax: (518) 758-2499. Dir.: Sharon S. Palmer, Cur.: Helen M. McLallen
Historical Museum / Local Museum - 1916   44482

Martin Van Buren Historic Site, Rte 9H, Kinderhook, NY 12106 - T: (518) 758-9689, Fax: (518) 758-6986, E-mail: superintendent@nps.gov/mava, Internet: www.nps.gov/mava. C.E.O.: Steven Beatty, Cur.: Dr. Patricia West
Historical Museum - 1974   44483

King WI

Wisconsin Veterans Museum King, Wisconsin Veterans Home, Hwy QQ, King, WI 54946 - T: (608) 266-1009, Fax: (608) 264-7615. Chm.: Don Heiliger, Cur.: Mary Bade
Military Museum - 1935
Military hist   44484

Kingfield ME

Stanley Museum, 40 School St, Kingfield, ME 04947 - T: (207) 265-2729, Fax: (207) 265-4700, E-mail: maine@stanleymuseum.org, Internet: www.stanleymuseum.org. Pres.: Susan S. Davis
Historical Museum / Science&Tech Museum - 1981
History, transportation, steam car   44485

Kingfisher OK

Chisholm Trail Museum, 605 Zellers Av, Kingfisher, OK 73750 - T: (405) 375-5176, Fax: (405) 375-5176 (call first), E-mail: reneem@ok-history.mus.ok.us, Internet: www.ok-history.mus.ok.us/. Cur.: Renee Mitchell
Local Museum - 1970   44486

Governor Seay Mansion, 605 Zellers Av, Kingfisher, OK 73750 - T: (405) 375-5176, Fax: (405) 375-5176, E-mail: reneem@ok-history.mus.ok.us, Internet: www.ok-history.mus.ok.us/. Cur.: Renee Mitchell
Historical Museum - 1967   44487

Kingman AZ

Mohave Museum of History and Arts, 400 W Beale, Kingman, AZ 86401 - T: (520) 753-3195, Fax: (520) 753-3195, E-mail: mocohist@ctaz.com, Internet: www.ctaz.com/mehovist/museum. Dir.: Chambers Jaynell, Shannon Rossiter
Local Museum / Fine Arts Museum - 1961
History, archaeology, art   44488

Kingman KS

Kingman County Historical Museum, 400 N Main, Kingman, KS 67068 - T: (316) 532-2627. C.E.O.: John Trollope, Cur.: June Walker
Local Museum - 1969
County history, housed in 1888 City Hall   44489

Kings Point NY

American Merchant Marine Museum, United States Merchant Marine Academy, Kings Point, NY 11024-1699 - T: (516) 773-5515, Fax: (516) 482-5340, E-mail: ammmuaeum@aol.com, Internet: www.usmma.edu. C.E.O.: Dennis Sanucci
Historical Museum / Science&Tech Museum - 1978
American Merchant Marine hist   44490

Kingsport TN

Netherland Inn House Museum, 2144 Netherland Inn Rd, Kingsport, TN 37660 - T: (615) 247-4043, E-mail: jgibson@naxs.net
Local Museum - 1966
Costumes, guns, musical instruments, toys, farm equip, tools, flatboat replica, railroading, forts, antique dolls, antique furniture, wagons   44491

Kingston MA

Major John Bradford House, Maple St and Landing Rd, Kingston, MA 02364 - T: (617) 585-5622. Chm.: Lilias Cingolani
Historical Museum - 1921   44492

Kingston NY

Hudson River Maritime Museum, 1 Rondout Landing, Kingston, NY 12401 - T: (914) 338-0071, Fax: (914) 338-0583, E-mail: hrmm@ulster.net, Internet: www.ulster.net/~hrmm. C.E.O.: Gregory Bell, Cur.: Allynne Lange
Historical Museum - 1980   44493

Senate House, 296 Fair St, Kingston, NY 12401 - T: (914) 338-2786, Fax: (914) 334-8173, Internet: www.nysparks.com
Fine Arts Museum / Historic Site / Historical Museum - 1887   44494

Trolley Museum of New York, 89 E Strand, Kingston, NY 12401 - T: (845) 331-3399, E-mail: info@tmny.org, Internet: tmny.org
Science&Tech Museum - 1955
Trolley, subway cars, photos   44495

Volunteer Firemen's Mall and Museum of Kingston, 265 Fair St, Kingston, NY 12401 - T: (845) 331-0866, 338-1247
Historical Museum - 1980
Personal and firemanic artifacts, fire engines, hose carriages   44496

Kingston RI

Pettaquamscutt Museum, 2636 Kingstown Rd, Kingston, RI 02881 - T: (401) 783-1328. Dir.: Christpher P. Bickford
Local Museum - 1958
Local hist   44497

University of Rhode Island Fine Arts Center Galleries, University of Rhode Island, 105 Upper College Rd, Ste 1, Kingston, RI 02881-0820 - T: (401) 874-2775, Fax: (401) 874-2007, E-mail: jtolnick@uri.edu, Internet: www.uri.edu/artsci/art/gallery. Dir.: Judith E. Tolnick
University Museum / Fine Arts Museum - 1968   44498

Kingsville TX

John E. Conner Museum, c/o Texas A&M University, 905 W Santa Gertrudis St, Kingsville, TX 78363 - T: (361) 593-2810, Fax: (361) 593-2112. Dir.: Hal Hau, Cur.: Kate Hogue
Local Museum - 1925
Local hist   44499

Kinsley KS

Edwards County Historical Museum, POB 64, Kinsley, KS 67547 - T: (316) 659-2420. Cur.: Maxine Blank
Local Museum - 1967
County history   44500

Kinzers PA

Rough and Tumble Engineers Museum, Rte 30 1/2 E of Kinzers, Kinzers, PA 17535 - T: (717) 442-4249, Internet: www.roughandtumble.org. C.E.O. & Pres.: Lewis Frantz
Agriculture Museum / Science&Tech Museum - 1948
Agricultural and mechanical technology and hist   44501

Kirksville MO

E.M. Violette Museum, Truman State University, Kirksville, MO 63501-4221 - T: (660) 785-4532, Fax: (660) 785-7415, E-mail: emdoak@truman.edu, Internet: library.truman.edu/Violette-Museum/mainpage.htmviolette-mus.html. Dir.: Richard J. Coughlin, Cur.: Elaine M. Doak
University Museum / Historical Museum - 1913
Pickler library, University archives   44502

Still National Osteopathic Museum, 800 W Jefferson, Kirksville, MO 63501 - T: (660) 626-2359, Fax: (660) 626-2984, E-mail: museum@kcom.edu, Internet: www.kcom.edu/museum. Dir.: Jason Haxton
Special Museum - 1978   44503

Kirtland OH

Kirtland Temple Historic Center, 9020 Chillicothe Rd, Kirtland, OH 44094 - T: (440) 256-3318, E-mail: temple@ncweb.com, Internet: www.kirtlandtemple.org. Dir.: Dr. Lachlin MacKay
Historic Site   44504

Kirtland Hills OH

Lake County Historical Society Museum, 8610 Mentor Rd, Kirtland Hills, OH 44060 - T: (440) 255-8979, Fax: (440) 255-8980, Internet: www.lakehistory.org
Local Museum - 1936
Decorative arts, costumes, photographs, tools   44505

Kit Carson CO

Kit Carson Historical Society Museum, Park St, Kit Carson, CO 80825 - T: (719) 962-3306. Dir.: Polly Johnson
Local Museum - 1968
Local history   44506

Kittery ME

Kittery Historical and Naval Museum, Rogers Rd, Kittery, ME 03904, mail addr: POB 453, Kittery, ME 03904 - T: (207) 439-3080, Fax: (207) 439-3080. Dir.: Wayne Manson
Local Museum / Historical Museum - 1976
Local hist, ship models, decorative arts, crafts, regional archaeology, shipbuilding   44507

Klamath Falls OR

Favell Museum of Western Art and Indian Artifacts, 125 W Main St, Klamath Falls, OR 97601 - T: (541) 882-9996, Fax: (541) 850-0125, E-mail: favmusem@internetcds.com, Internet: www.favellmuseum.com. Dir.: Gene H. Favell, C.E.O.: Bev Cornwall
Fine Arts Museum / Ethnology Museum / Archaeological Museum - 1972   44508

Klamath County Museum, 1451 Main St, Klamath Falls, OR 97601 - T: (541) 883-4208, Fax: (541) 884-5710, E-mail: tourklco@cdsnet.net. Dir.: Kim Bellavia
Historical Museum - 1953
Baldwin Hotel Museum Annex   44509

Knoxville IA

National Sprint Car Hall of Fame and Museum, 1 Sprint Capital Pl, Knoxville, IA 50138 - T: (641) 842-6176, Fax: (641) 842-6177, E-mail: sprintcarhof@sprintcarhof.com, Internet: www.sprintcarhof.com. Dir.: Thomas J. Schmeh
Science&Tech Museum - 1986
Sprint car racing, open wheel racers, big car racing   44510

Knoxville IL

Knox County Museum, c/o City Hall, Public Sq, Knoxville, IL 61448 - T: (309) 289-2814, Fax: (309) 289-8825, E-mail: tbould@wmco.net, Internet: www.webwinco.net/~tbould. C.E.O.: Peg Bivens, Cur.: Sally Hutchcrot
Local Museum - 1954
Local history   44511

Knoxville TN

Beck Cultural Exchange Center, 1927 Dandridge Av, Knoxville, TN 37915-1909 - T: (423) 524-8461, Fax: (423) 524-8462, E-mail: beckcec@korrnet.org, Internet: www.korrnet.org/beckcec. Exec. Dir.: Avon W. Rollins, Pres.: William V. Powell
Folklore Museum / Library with Exhibitions / Historical Museum - 1975
Local Black history   44512

Blount Mansion, 200 W Hill Av, Knoxville, TN 37902 - T: (865) 525-2375, Fax: (865) 546-5315, E-mail: info@blountmansion.org, Internet: www.blountmansion.org. C.E.O.: C.L. Creech
Local Museum / Historic Site - 1926
Historic house   44513

Confederate Memorial Hall-Bleak House, 3148 Kingston Pike, Knoxville, TN 37919 - T: (423) 522-2371, E-mail: bhpa@korrnet.org. Pres.: Florence E. Hillis
Local Museum - 1959
Historic house   44514

Crescent Bend/Armstrong-Lockett House and William P. Toms Memorial Gardens, 2728 Kingston Pike, Knoxville, TN 37919 - T: (615) 637-3163, Fax: (615) 637-1709, E-mail: tennlaw@awgd.com, Internet: www.korrnet.org/cresbend. Cur.: William Beall
Decorative Arts Museum - 1975
Decorative arts   44515

East Tennessee Discovery Center, 516 N Beaman, Chilhowee Park, Knoxville, TN 37914-0204 - T: (423) 594-1494, Fax: (423) 594-1469, E-mail: etdc@bellsouth.net, Internet: www.kornet.org/etdc. Pres.: Margaret Maddox
Science&Tech Museum / Natural History Museum - 1960
Science Museum with Planetarium/Kama Health Discovery 44516

East Tennessee Historical Society Museum, 600 Market St, Knoxville, TN 37902 - T: (865) 215-8824, Fax: (865) 215-8819, E-mail: eths@east-tennessee-history.org, Internet: www.east-tennessee-history.org. Dir.: Kent Whitworth, Pres.: Edward S. Albers, Assoc. Dir.: Cherel Henderson, Cur.: Lisa Oakley
Local Museum - 1834
Local hist 44517

Ewing Gallery of Art and Architecture, University of Tennessee, Art and Architecture Bldg, 1715 Volunteer Blvd, Knoxville, TN 37996 - T: (865) 974-3200, Fax: (865) 974-3198, E-mail: spangler@utk.edu, Internet: sunsite.utk.edu/ewing_gallery. Dir.: Sam Yates
University Museum / Fine Arts Museum - 1981
Contemporary arts and architecture 44518

Frank H. McClung Museum, University of Tennessee, 1327 Circle Park Dr, Knoxville, TN 37996-3200 - T: (865) 974-2144, Fax: (865) 974-3827, E-mail: museum@utk.edu, Internet: mc-clungmuseum.utk.edu. Dir.: Dr. Jefferson Chapman, Cur.: Elaine A. Evans, Dr. Gary Crites (Paleoethnobotany), Dr. Lynne Sullivan (Archaeology), Dr. Paul Parmalee (Malacology)
University Museum / Local Museum / Natural History Museum / Archaeological Museum - 1961
Local hist, natural hist, SE U.S. archaeology 44519

Knoxville Museum of Art, 1050 World's Fair Park Dr, Knoxville, TN 37916-1653 - T: (865) 525-6101, Fax: (865) 546-3635, E-mail: kma@esper.com, Internet: www.knoxart.org. Chm.: Barbara Apking, Cur.: Stephen C. Wicks
Fine Arts Museum - 1961
Modern and contemporary art in all media, Mexican folk masks, Thorne miniature, paintings, sculpture, photography, works on paper 44520

Mabry-Hazen House, 1711 Dandridge Av, Knoxville, TN 37915 - T: (865) 522-8661, Fax: (865) 522-8471, E-mail: mabryhazen@yahoo.com, Internet: www.korrnet.org/mabry. Pres.: Pat Austin
Local Museum - 1992
Historic house 44521

Marble Springs State Historic Farmstead Governor John Sevier Memorial, 1220 West Gov. John Sevier Hwy, Knoxville, TN 37920 - T: (865) 573-5508, Fax: (865) 573-9768, E-mail: marble@vic.net. Exec. Dir.: Karma S. King, Dir. Maint.: Harry King
Local Museum - 1941
Historic house, home of Tennessee's first governor John Sevier 44522

Ramsey House Museum Plantation, 26l4 Thorngrove Pike, Knoxville, TN 37914 - T: (865) 546-0745, Fax: (865) 546-1851, E-mail: ramhse@aol.com, Internet: www.kornet.org/ramhse. Dir.: Anna McKelvey
Local Museum - 1952
Historic house 44523

Kodiak AK

Alutiiq Museum and Archaeological Repository, 215 Mission Rd, Kodiak, AK 99615 - T: (907) 486-7004, Fax: (907) 486-7048, E-mail: alutiiq2@ptialaska.net, Internet: www.alutiiqmuseum.com. Dir.: Sven Haakanson, Cur.: Amy Steffian, Patrick Saltonstall
Ethnology Museum / Archaeological Museum - 1995
Archaeology 44524

Baranov Museum, Erskine House, 101 Marine Way, Kodiak, AK 99615 - T: (907) 486-5920, Fax: (907) 486-3166, E-mail: baranov@ptialaska.net, Internet: www.ptialaska.net/~baranov. Dir.: David Kaplan, Cur.: Ellen Lester
Local Museum - 1954
Local history, Alexander Baranov (chief manager of Russian American Company), Handwoven grass baskets, Russian American occupation, Kodiak and Aleutian Island hist 44525

Kokomo IN

Elwood Haynes Museum, 1915 S Webster St, Kokomo, IN 46902-2040 - T: (765) 456-7500. Dir.: Kay J. Frazer, Cur.: Mary Dennis
Special Museum - 1967
Home of the inventor Elwood Haynes, Haynes memorabilia, 4 Haynes cars and inventions, exhib. about industrial hist 44526

Howard County Historical Museum, 1200 W Sycamore St, Kokomo, IN 46901 - T: (317) 452-4314, Fax: (765) 452-4581, E-mail: director@howardcountymuseum.org, Internet: www.howardcountymuseum.org. C.E.O.: Kelly Thompson
Historic Site / Local Museum - 1916
Local history 44527

Kotzebue AK

Kotzebue Museum, POB 46, Kotzebue, AK 99752 - T: (907) 442-3747, Fax: (907) 442-3742. C.E.O.: Michael Scott
Local Museum - 1967
Local history 44528

Kure Beach NC

Fort Fisher, 1610 Fort Fisher Blvd, Kure Beach, NC 28449 - T: (910) 458-5538, Fax: (910) 458-0477, E-mail: fisher@ncsl.dcr.state.nc.us, Internet: www.ah.dcr.state.nc/sections/hs/fisher/fisher.htm. Man.: Barbara G. Hoppe
Historical Museum - 1961 44529

Kutztown PA

Pennsylvania German Cultural Heritage Center, c/o Kutztown University, Luckenbill Rd, Kutztown, PA 19530 - T: (610) 683-1589, E-mail: culture@fast.net, Internet: www.kutztown.edu/community/PGCHC. Dir.: Dr. David Valuska
Folklore Museum / Ethnology Museum - 1992
Folk items and art, agriculture, costumes, colonial period 44530

Sharadin Art Gallery, c/o Kutztown University, POB 730, Kutztown, PA 19530-0730 - T: (610) 683-4546, Fax: (610) 683-4547, E-mail: talley@kutztown.edu, Internet: www.kutztown.edu/acad/artgallery. Dir.: Dan R. Talley
Fine Arts Museum / University Museum - 1956
Prints, drawings and paintings 44531

La Conner WA

Museum of Northwest Art, 121 S First St, La Conner, WA 98257 - T: (360) 466-4446, Fax: (360) 466-7431, E-mail: mona@ncia.com, Internet: www.museumofnwart.org. Exec. Dir.: Susan Parke
Fine Arts Museum - 1981
Art 44532

Skagit County Historical Museum, 501 S 4th St, La Conner, WA 98257-0818 - T: (360) 466-3365, Fax: (360) 466-1611, E-mail: museum@co.skagit.wa.us, Internet: www.skagitcounty.net/museum.htm. Dir.: Karen Marshall, Library: Mari C. Anderson-Densmore, Cur.: Patricia A. Doran
Local Museum / Folklore Museum - 1959
Local hist 44533

La Crosse KS

Kansas Barbed Wire Museum, W 1st St, La Crosse, KS 67548 - T: (785) 222-9900, Internet: www.rushcounty.org/barbedwiremuseum. Chm.: Bradley Penka
Historical Museum - 1971
Tools and items 44534

Post Rock Museum, Rush Co Historical Society, 202 W First St, La Crosse, KS 67548-0473 - T: (785) 222-2719, 222-3508. Pres.: James Jecha
Natural History Museum - 1962
Geology, post rock is limestone bedrock used in building, churches, homes 44535

La Crosse WI

Hixon House, 429 N 7th St, La Crosse, WI 54601 - T: (608) 782-1980, Fax: (608) 793-1359, E-mail: lchs@centurytel.net, Internet: www.lchsonline.org. Dir.: Rick Brown, Cur.: Brenda Jordan
Historic Site - 1898
Historic house 44536

Pump House of Regional Arts, 119 King St, La Crosse, WI 54601 - T: (608) 785-1434, Fax: (608) 785-1432, E-mail: info@thepumphouse.org, Internet: www.thepumphouse.org. Exec. Dir.: Jodi Bente
Fine Arts Museum - 1980
Arts 44537

Riverside Museum, 410 E Veterans Memorial Dr, La Crosse, WI 54601 - T: (608) 782-1980, Fax: (608) 793-1359, E-mail: rwbrown_lchs@yahoo.com, Internet: www.lchsonline.org. C.E.O.: Rick Brown, Cur.: Brenda Jordan
Local Museum - 1990
Local hist 44538

Swarthout Memorial Museum, 112 S 9th St, La Crosse, WI 54601 - T: (608) 782-1980, Fax: (608) 793-1359, E-mail: lchs@centurytel.net, Internet: www.lchsonline.org. Dir.: Rick Brown, Cur.: Brenda Jordan
Local Museum - 1898
Local hist 44539

La Fargeville NY

Agricultural Museum at Stone Mills, Rte 180 at Stone Mills, La Fargeville, NY 13656 - T: (315) 658-2353, E-mail: agstonemills@usadatanet.net. Dir.: Maguerite Raineri
Agriculture Museum - 1968 44540

La Grange GA

Chattahoochee Valley Art Museum, 112 Lafayette Pkwy, La Grange, GA 30240 - T: (706) 882-3267, Fax: (706) 882-2878, E-mail: cvam@charter.net. Dir.: Keith Rasmussen
Fine Arts Museum / Decorative Arts Museum - 1963
Decorative arts, paintings, prints, drawings, graphics, sculpture 44541

Lamar Dodd Art Center, c/o La Grange College, 302 Forrest Av, La Grange, GA 30240 - T: (706) 880-8000, Fax: (706) 812-7329, E-mail: doddartc@mentor.lgc.peachnet.edu, Internet: www.lgc.peachnet.edu/academic/art/art_home.htm. Dir.: John Lawrence, Cur.: Debra Jackson Quillen
Fine Arts Museum / University Museum - 1982 44542

La Grange IN

Machan Museum, 405 S Poplar St 4H Fair Grounds, La Grange, IN 46761 - T: (219) 463-2632. Pres.: Robert Lee Yoder
Local Museum - 1966
Local history 44543

La Grange KY

Oldham County History Center, 106 N Second Av, La Grange, KY 40031 - T: (502) 222-0826, Fax: (502) 222-7115, E-mail: ochstryctr@aol.com. Dir.: Anita Fritz
Local Museum 44544

La Grange TX

Fayette Heritage Museum, 855 S Jefferson, La Grange, TX 78945 - T: (409) 968-6418, Fax: (409) 968-5357, E-mail: library@fais.net, Internet: lagrange.fais.net/library/museum.html. Dir.: Kathy Carter
Historical Museum - 1978
Local hist 44545

Nathaniel W. Faison Home and Museum, 232 Clear Lake Dr, La Grange, TX 78945-5330 - T: (979) 242-3566. Pres.: Marjorie Becker
Local Museum - 1960
Local hist 44546

La Habra CA

Children's Museum at La Habra, 301 S Euclid, La Habra, CA 90631 - T: (562) 905-9693, Fax: (562) 905-9698, E-mail: april_morales@lahabracity.com, Internet: www.lhcm.org. Dir.: Kimberly Albarian, Cur.: April Morales
Special Museum - 1977 44547

La Jolla CA

Museum of Contemporary Art San Diego - La Jolla, 700 Prospect St, La Jolla, CA 92037 - T: (858) 454-3541, Fax: (858) 454-6985, E-mail: info@mcasandiego.org, Internet: www.mcasandiego.org. Dir.: Hugh M. Davies, Dep. Dir.: Charles E. Castle, Anne Fawell (Development, Special Projects), Cur.: Toby Kamps, Asst. Cur.: Rachel Teagle, Stephanie Hanor
Fine Arts Museum - 1941 44548

Stuart Collection, University of California, San Diego, 406 University Center, La Jolla, CA 92093, mail addr: 9500 Gilman Dr, La Jolla, CA 92093-0010 - T: (858) 534-2117, Fax: (858) 534-9713, E-mail: mbeebe@ucsd.edu, Internet: stuart-collection.ucsd.edu. Dir.: Mary L. Beebe
Fine Arts Museum / University Museum - 1981 44549

University Art Gallery, University of California, San Diego, 9500 Gilman Dr, La Jolla, CA 92093-0327 - T: (858) 534-0419, 534-2107, Fax: (858) 534-0668, E-mail: uag@ucsd.edu, Internet: www.universityartgallery.ucsd.edu. Dir.: Kathleen Stoughton
Fine Arts Museum / University Museum - 1967
Art gallery 44550

La Junta CO

Bent's Old Fort, 35110 Hwy 194 E, La Junta, CO 81050 - T: (719) 383-5010, Fax: (719) 383-2129, Internet: www.nps.gov/beol. Dir.: Donald C. Hill, Cur.: Nancy J. Russell
Historical Museum - 1963
Living history 44551

Koshare Indian Museum, 115 W 18th, La Junta, CO 81050 - T: (719) 384-4411, Fax: (719) 384-8836, E-mail: koshare@ria.net, Internet: www.koshare.org. Exec. Dir.: Linda Powers
Ethnology Museum - 1949
Indian arts and crafts 44552

La Mirada CA

Biola University Art Gallery, 13800 Biola Av, La Mirada, CA 90639 - T: (562) 903-4807, Fax: (562) 903-4748, E-mail: beckie.eisemann@biola.edu, Internet: www.biola.edu
Public Gallery 44553

La Pointe WI

Madeline Island Historical Museum, Woods Av and Main St, La Pointe, WI 54850 - T: (715) 747-2415, Fax: (715) 747-6985, E-mail: madeline@whs.wisc.edu, Internet: www.madline.wisconsinhistory.org. Dir.: David L. Pamperin, Cur.: Victoria A. Lock
Historical Museum - 1958
Local hist, native american, maritime, 19th c. trades 44554

La Porte IN

La Porte County Historical Society Museum, 809 State St, La Porte, IN 46350-3329 - T: (219) 326-6808 ext 276, Fax: (219) 324-9029, E-mail: lpcohist@csinet.net, Internet: www.lapcohistsoc.org/. Cur.: James Rodgers, Asst. Cur.: Susie Richter
Historical Museum - 1906
Local history 44555

La Porte TX

Battleship Texas, 3527 Battleground Rd, La Porte, TX 77571 - T: (281) 479-2431, Fax: (281) 479-4197, E-mail: barry.ward@tpwd.state.tx.us, Internet: www.tpwd.state.tx.us. Dir.: Barry J. Ward
Historic Site / Military Museum - 1948
Military hist 44556

San Jacinto Museum of History, 1 Monument Circle, La Porte, TX 77571 - T: (281) 479-2421, Fax: (281) 479-6619, E-mail: sjm@sanjacinto-museum.org, Internet: sanjacinto-museum.org. Pres.: George J. Donnelly
Historical Museum - 1938
History 44557

La Puente CA

La Puente Valley Historical Society Museum, 15900 E Main St, La Puente, CA 91744 - T: (626) 369-7220. Pres.: Mildred Deyoung
Historical Museum - 1960 44558

La Veta CO

Francisco Fort Museum, 306 Main St, La Veta, CO 81055 - T: (719) 742-5501, Fax: (719) 742-5501, E-mail: lvcc@ruralwideweb.com, Internet: www.ruralwideweb.com/ivcc.htm. Dir.: Pamela E. Munrde
Local Museum - 1956
Local history 44559

Lac du Flambeau WI

George W. Brown jr. Ojibwe Museum, 603 Peace Pipe, Lac du Flambeau, WI 54538 - T: (715) 588-3333, 588-2139, Fax: (715) 588-2355, E-mail: deanna@ojibwe.com
Folklore Museum - 1988
Cultural history of The Lake Superior Ojibwe 44560

Lackawaxen PA

Zane Grey Museum, Scenic Dr, Lackawaxen, PA 18435 - T: (570) 685-4871, Fax: (570) 685-4874, E-mail: upde_interpretation@nps.gov, Internet: www.nps.gov/upde
Special Museum - 1978 44561

Lackland Air Force Base TX

History and Traditions Museum, 2051 George Av, 37 TRW/MU, Bldg 5206, Lackland Air Force Base, TX 78236-5218 - T: (210) 671-3055, Fax: (210) 671-0347, E-mail: henry.valdez@lackland.af.mil. Dir.: E.A. Valdez
Military Museum - 1956
Military hist 44562

Laclede MO

General John J. Pershing Boyhood Home, POB 141, Laclede, MO 64651 - T: (660) 963-2525, Fax: (660) 963-2520. Dir.: Dr. Douglas Eiken
Historical Museum - 1960
WW I General Pershing 44563

Laconia NH

The Belknap Mill Museum, The Mill Plaza, Laconia, NH 03246 - T: (603) 524-8813, Fax: (603) 528-1228, E-mail: belknap@worldpath.net. Dir.: Mary Rose Boswell, Cur.: Roger Gibbs
Fine Arts Museum / Local Museum - 1970
Art, history 44564

Ladysmith WI

Rusk County Historical Society Museum, W 7891 Old 8 Rd, Ladysmith, WI 54848 - T: (715) 532-5615. Dir./Cur.: Janet Platteter
Local Museum - 1961
Local hist 44565

Lafayette CA

Museum of Vintage Fashion, 1712 Chapparal Ln, Lafayette, CA 94549-1712 - T: (925) 944-1896, E-mail: pattimvf@home.com, Internet: www.museumofvintagefashion.org. Dir.: Patti Parks McClain, Cons.: Lorraine A. Harck (Textiles), Dana Heston
Special Museum / Historical Museum - 1978 44566

Lafayette CO

Lafayette Miners Museum, 108 E Simpson St, Lafayette, CO 80026-2322 - T: (303) 665-7030. Dir.: Glenda L. Chermak
Science&Tech Museum - 1976
Coal mining 44567

Lafayette IN

Art Museum of Greater Lafayette, 102 S 10th St, Lafayette, IN 47905 - T: (765) 742-1128, Fax: (765) 742-1120, E-mail: glma@glmart.org, Internet: www.dcwi.com/~glma. Pres.: Rob Lindsey, Assoc. Dir.: Paige Sharp (Education), Assoc. Dir.: Michael Hathaway (Collections & exhibitions), Cur.: Graeme Reid
Fine Arts Museum - 1909
Art if Indiana 44568

Greater Lafayette Museum of Art → Art Museum of Greater Lafayette

Tippecanoe County Historical Museum, 909 South St, Lafayette, IN 47901 - T: (765) 476-8411, Fax: (765) 476-8414, E-mail: mail@tcha.mus.in.us, Internet: www.tcha.mus.in.us. Dir.: Kevin O'Brien
Local Museum / Historical Museum - 1925
General museum, housed in Moses Fowler Home, nr the site of 1717-91 Fort Ouiatenon, the first fortified European settlement in Indiana 44569

Lafayette LA

Lafayette Museum - Alexandre Mouton House, 1122 Lafayette St, Lafayette, LA 70501 - T: (337) 234-2208, Fax: (337) 234-2208, E-mail: lafayettemuseum@aol.com. Pres.: Romona Mouton
Local Museum - 1954
Local history 44570

Lafayette Natural History Museum, 637 Girard Park Dr, Lafayette, LA 70503 - T: (337) 268-5544, Fax: (337) 268-5464, E-mail: members@lnhm.org, Internet: lnhm.org. Cur.: David Hostetter, Mary Ann Bernard, Cliff Deal
Natural History Museum - 1969
Natural history - planetarium, library 44571

University Art Museum, University of Louisiana at Lafayette, E. Lewis and Girard Park Cr., Lafayette, LA 70504 - T: (337) 482-5326, Fax: (337) 482-5907, E-mail: artmuseum@louisiana.edu, Internet: www.louisiana.edu/uam. Dir.: Gil Carner
Fine Arts Museum - 1968
Art 44572

Lafox IL

Garfield Farm Museum, 3N016 Garfield Rd, Box 403, Lafox, IL 60147 - T: (630) 584-8485, Fax: (630) 584-8522, E-mail: info@garfieldfarm.org, Internet: www.garfieldfarm.org. Dir.: Jerome Martin Johnson
Agriculture Museum - 1977
Historic farm and Inn 44573

Lagrange IN

Machan Museum, 405 S Poplar St, Lagrange, IN 46761 - T: (219) 463-3232
Local Museum - 1966 44574

Laguna Beach CA

Laguna Art Museum, 307 Cliff Dr, Laguna Beach, CA 92651 - T: (949) 494-6531, Fax: (949) 494-1530, E-mail: info@lagunaartmuseum.org, Internet: www.lagunaartmuseum.org. Dir.: Bolton Colburn, Cur.: Tyler Stallings, Janet Blake
Fine Arts Museum - 1918
American art, with focus on California painting 44575

Lahaina HI

Lahaina Restoration Foundation, 120 Dickenson, Lahaina, HI 96761 - T: (808) 661-3262, Fax: (808) 661-9309, E-mail: lrf@hawaii.pp.com, Internet: www.lahainarestoration.org. Dir.: George W. Freeland, Pres.: Bill Royce
Folklore Museum / Open Air Museum - 1962
Historical Houses, Baldwin Home, Masters Reading Rm, Hale Pai Printing House, Wohing Chinese Temple, Hale Paahao Prison, Hale Aloha Church, depicting the life of the Lahaina during the Hawaiian Monarchy (1820-1893) 44576

Laie HI

Polynesian Cultural Center, 55-370 Kamehameha Hwy, Laie, HI 96762 - T: (808) 293-3005, Fax: (808) 293-3022, E-mail: clawsone@polynesia.com
Decorative Arts Museum / Ethnology Museum - 1963
Decorative arts, ethnic material, graphics, paintings, sculpture 44577

Lake Bronson MN

Kittson County History Center Museum, County Rd 28, Lake Bronson, MN 56734 - T: (218) 754-4100, E-mail: history@means.net. Dir.: Cindy Adams
Local Museum / Agriculture Museum - 1973
Regional history 44578

Lake Buena Vista FL

Epcot, Walt Disney World Resort, Lake Buena Vista, FL 32830, mail addr: POB 10000, Lake Buena Vista, FL 32830 - T: (407) 824-4321, Fax: (407) 560-4987, Internet: www.disneyworld.com. C.E.O.: Michael Eisner
Fine Arts Museum - 1971 44579

Lake Charles LA

Children's Museum of Lake Charles, 925 Enterprise Blvd, Lake Charles, LA 70601 - T: (318) 433-9420, Fax: (318) 433-0144, E-mail: dan@child-museum.org, Internet: www.child-museum.org. Dir.: Dan Ellender
Special Museum - 1988 44580

Gibson Barham Gallery, 204 W Sallier St, Lake Charles, LA 70601 - T: (337) 439-3797, Fax: (337) 439-6040
Fine Arts Museum - 1963 44581

Imperial Calcasieu Museum, 204 W Sallier St, Lake Charles, LA 70601 - T: (337) 439-3797, Fax: (337) 439-6040. Exec. Dir.: Elizabeth Allemanlus
Fine Arts Museum / Local Museum - 1963
Local history 44582

Lake City FL

Columbia County Historical Museum, 105 S Hernando St, Lake City, FL 32025 - T: (904) 755-9096, Fax: (904) 755-6605, E-mail: histmusm@isgroup.net. Dir.: John Shoemaker
Local Museum - 1984
Civil war, hist of area 44583

Lake City SC

Browntown Museum, Hwy 341, Lake City, SC 29560, mail addr: 414 Main St, Hemingway, SC 29554 - T: (843) 558-2355, Internet: www.threerivershistsoc.org. Cur.: Nell Morris
Special Museum / Agriculture Museum
Cotton gin, corn crib, smokehouse, farm equip 44584

Lake City SD

Fort Sisseton, 11907 434th Av, Lake City, SD 57247-6142 - T: (605) 448-5701, Fax: (605) 448-5572, E-mail: roylakestp@gfp.state.sd.us
Local Museum - 1972
Local hist 44585

Lake Forest IL

Lake Forest-Lake Bluff Historical Society Museum, 361 E Westminster, Lake Forest, IL 60045 - T: (847) 234-5253, Fax: (847) 234-5236, E-mail: info@lflbhistory.org, Internet: www.lflbhistory.org. Exec. Dir.: Janice Hack
Local Museum - 1972 44586

Lake George NY

Fort William Henry Museum, Canada St, Lake George, NY 12845 - T: (518) 668-5471, Fax: (518) 668-4926, E-mail: d11655@capital.net, Internet: www.fortwilliamhenry.com. Pres.: Robert Flacke, Cur.: Gerald Bradfield
Military Museum - 1952 44587

Lake George Historical Association Museum, Old Country Courthouse, Canada St, Lake George, NY 12845 - T: (518) 668-5044. Pres.: Stephen Miller
Fine Arts Museum / Local Museum / Historical Museum - 1964 44588

Lake Junaluska NC

World Methodist Museum, 575 N Lakeshore Dr, Lake Junaluska, NC 28745 - T: (828) 456-9432, Fax: (828) 456-9433, E-mail: wmc6@juno.com. Dir.: George Freeman, Cur.: Jeanette W. Roberson
Religious Arts Museum - 1881 44589

Lake Linden MI

Houghton County Historical Museum Society, 53150 N Hwy M-26, Lake Linden, MI 49945 - T: (906) 296-4121, Fax: (906) 296-9191, E-mail: mail@houghtonhistory.com, Internet: www.houghtonhistory.net. Pres.: Denise M. Taylor
Local Museum - 1961
Regional history 44590

Lake Norden SD

South Dakota Amateur Baseball Hall of Fame, 519 Main Av, Lake Norden, SD 57248 - T: (605) 785-3553, 785-3884, Fax: (605) 785-3315. Cur.: Rusty Antonen
Special Museum - 1976
Sports 44591

Lake Oswego OR

Oregon Electric Railway Historical Society Museum, 311 N State St, Lake Oswego, OR 97034 - T: (503) 222-2226, Internet: www.trainweb.org/oerhs. Dir.: Greg Bonn
Science&Tech Museum - 1957 44592

Lake Placid NY

John Brown Farm, John Brown Rd, Lake Placid, NY 12946 - T: (518) 523-3900, Fax: (518) 523-4952, E-mail: brendan.mills@oprhp.state.ny.us, Internet: www.nysparks.com. Sc. Staff: Brendon Mills
Agriculture Museum - 1895 44593

Lake Placid-North Elba Historical Society Museum, Averyville Rd, Lake Placid, NY 12946 - T: (518) 523-1608. Pres.: Gordon Pratt
Historical Museum - 1967 44594

Lake Tomahawk WI

Northland Historical Society Museum, 7247 Kelly Dr, Lake Tomahawk, WI 54539 - T: (715) 277-3146. Pres.: Barbara Saving
Local Museum - 1957
Local hist 44595

Lake Waccamaw NC

Lake Waccamaw Depot Museum, 201 Flemington Av, Lake Waccamaw, NC 28450 - T: (910) 646-1992, E-mail: lwdm@ncez.net, Internet: www.lakewaccamaw.com. Chm.: Dr. Eugenia Blake
Historical Museum / Natural History Museum / Science&Tech Museum - 1977 44596

Lake Wales FL

Lake Wales Depot Museum, 325 S Scenic Hwy, Lake Wales, FL 33853 - T: (863) 678-4209, Fax: (863) 678-4299, E-mail: thedepot@cityoflakewales.com, Internet: www.cityoflakewales.com. Dir.: Mimi Reid Hardman, Cur.: Lesley Nash
Local Museum - 1976
Local history 44597

Lake Worth FL

Museum of the City of Lake Worth, 414 Lake Av, Lake Worth, FL 33460 - T: (561) 586-1700, Fax: (561) 586-1651. C.E.O./Cur.: Beverly Mustaine
Local Museum - 1982
Local history 44598

Museum of the Contemporary Art → Palm Beach Institute of Contemporary Art

National Museum of Polo and Hall of Fame, 9011 Lake Worth Rd, Lake Worth, FL 33467 - T: (561) 969-3210, Fax: (561) 964-8299, E-mail: polomuseum@att.net, Internet: www.polomuseum.com. Dir.: George DuPont
Special Museum - 1984
Polo sports hist 44599

Palm Beach Institute of Contemporary Art, 601 Lake Av, Lake Worth, FL 33460 - T: (561) 582-0006, Fax: (561) 582-0504, E-mail: info@palmbeachica.org, Internet: www.palmbeachica.org. Dir.: Dr. Michael Rush
Fine Arts Museum - 1989
Art, housed in 1939 art deco movie theatre 44600

Lakefield MN

Jackson County Historical Museum, 307 N Hwy 86, Lakefield, MN 56150-0238 - T: (507) 662-5505, E-mail: jchs@rconnect.com. Pres.: Sherry Schoewe
Local Museum - 1931
Local history 44601

Lakeland FL

International Sport Aviation Museum, 4175 Medulla Rd, Lakeland, FL 33811 - T: (863) 644-0741, Fax: (863) 648-9264, E-mail: museum@airmuseum.org, Internet: www.airmuseum.org. Pres.: John Burton
Science&Tech Museum - 1989
Aviation 44602

Melvin Art Gallery, Florida Southern College, Dept. of Art, 111 Lake Hollingsworth Dr, Lakeland, FL 33801 - T: (863) 680-4220, Fax: (863) 680-4147, E-mail: shuges@flsouthern.edu, Internet: www.flsouthern.edu
Public Gallery 44603

Polk Museum of Art, 800 E Palmetto, Lakeland, FL 33801-5529 - T: (941) 688-7743, Fax: (941) 688-2611, E-mail: info@polkmuseumofart.org, Internet: www.polkmuseumofart.com. Dir.: Daniel E. Stetson, Pres.: Kristen C. Gunter, Dep. Dir.: Judith M. Barger, Cur.: Todd Behrens
Fine Arts Museum - 1966 44604

Lakeport CA

Lake County Museum, 255 N Main St, Lakeport, CA 95453 - T: (707) 263-4555, Fax: (707) 263-7918, E-mail: museum@co.lake.ca.us, Internet: www.museum.lake.k12.ca.us. Cur.: Donna J. Howard
Historical Museum - 1936 44605

Lakeside MI

Lakeside Studio, 15251 S Lakeshore Rd, Lakeside, MI 49116 - T: (616) 469-1377, Fax: (616) 469-1101, Internet: www.lakesidestudio.com. Exec. Dir.: John Wilson
Public Gallery - 1968
International artists, American, Soviet, Chinese, Dutch work done by artists-in-residence 44606

Lakeview OR

Schminck Memorial Museum, 128 S E St, Lakeview, OR 97630 - T: (541) 947-3134, Fax: (541) 947-3134, E-mail: jenglenn@centurytel.com. Cur.: Sherrain Glenn
Local Museum - 1936 44607

Lakewood CO

Lakewood's Heritage Culture and the Arts Galleries, 797 S Wadsworth Blvd, Lakewood, CO 80226 - T: (303) 987-7850, Fax: (303) 987-7851, E-mail: kriand@lakewood.org. Dir.: Kris Anderson, Cur.: Winifred Ferrill, Elizabeth Nosek
Local Museum / Public Gallery - 1976
20th c Lakewood history 44608

Lakewood NJ

M. Christina Geis Gallery, Georgian Court College, 900 Lakewood Av, Lakewood, NJ 08701-2697 - T: (732) 364-2200 ext 348, Fax: (732) 905-8571, E-mail: velasquez@georgian.edu. Dir.: Dr. Geraldine Velasquez
Fine Arts Museum - 1964 44609

Lakewood OH

Cleveland Artists Foundation at Beck Center for the Arts, 17801 Detroit Av, Lakewood, OH 44107 - T: (216) 227-9507, Fax: (216) 228-6050, E-mail: cshearer@clevelandartists.org, Internet: www.clevelandartists.org. Dir.: Christine Fowler Shearer, Pres.: Leon M. Plevin
Fine Arts Museum - 1984
Contemporary art incl acrylics, collages, etchings, oils, sculpture, watercolors 44610

Oldest Stone House Museum, 14710 Lake Av, Lakewood, OH 44107 - T: (216) 221-7343, Fax: (216) 221-0320, E-mail: lkwdhist@bge.net, Internet: www.lkwdpl.org/histsoc/. Dir.: Mazie M. Adams
Historical Museum / Local Museum - 1952 44611

Lamar MO

Harry S. Truman Birthplace State Historic Site, 1009 Truman Av & 11th St, Lamar, MO 64759 - T: (417) 682-2279, Fax: (417) 682-6304. Dir.: Pam Myers
Historical Museum - 1959 44612

Osage Village Historic Site, 1009 Truman, Lamar, MO 64759 - T: (417) 682-2279, Fax: (417) 682-6304. C.E.O.: Pam Myers
Archaeological Museum - 1984 44613

Lamesa TX

Dal-Paso Museum, 310 S First St, Lamesa, TX 79331 - T: (806) 872-5007, Fax: (806) 872-5700. C.E.O.: Wayne C. Smith
Local Museum - 1988 44614

Lamoni IA

Liberty Hall Historic Center, 1300 W Main St, Lamoni, IA 50140 - T: (515) 784-6133, 784-6408, E-mail: libhall@grm.net, Internet: www.lamonistake.org/libertyhall.html. Pres.: W.B. Spillman, Dir.: A.R. Blair
Local Museum - 1976
Local hist 44615

Lancaster CA

Lancaster Museum/Art Gallery, 44801 W Sierra Hwy, Lancaster, CA 93534 - T: (661) 723-6250, Fax: (661) 948-1322, E-mail: ngurba@cityoflancasterca.org, Internet: www.cityoflancasterca.org/parks/museumgallery.htm. Dir.: Lyle Norton, Cur.: Norma Gurba
Fine Arts Museum / Historical Museum - 1984 44616

Western Hotel Museum, 557 W Lancaster Blvd, Lancaster, CA 93534 - T: (661) 723-6260, Fax: (661) 261-5913, Internet: www.cityoflancasterca.org/parks/westernhotel.htm. Cur.: Norma Gurba
Historical Museum 44617

Lancaster MA

Fifth Meeting House, Town Common, Lancaster, MA 01523 - T: (978) 365-2427, 368-7285, Fax: (978) 368-0194
Religious Arts Museum 44618

Lancaster NH

Lancaster Historical Society Museum, 226 Main St, Lancaster, NH 03584 - T: (603) 788-3004, 788-4629. Pres.: Myra Emerson
Historical Museum - 1964 44619

Lancaster OH

Decorative Arts Center of Ohio, 145 E Main St, Lancaster, OH 43130 - T: (740) 681-1423, Fax: (740) 681-2714, E-mail: harris@decartsohio.org, Internet: www.decartsohio.org. C.E.O.: John Thomas La Porte
Decorative Arts Museum - 1997 44620

The Georgian, 105 E Wheeling St, Lancaster, OH 43130 - T: (740) 654-9923, Fax: (740) 654-9890, E-mail: fairfieldheritage@greenapple.com, Internet: www.fairfieldheritage.org. Dir.: Peggy Smith
Historical Museum / Local Museum - 1976 44621

Sherman House, 137 East Main St, Lancaster, OH 43130 - T: (740) 687-5891, Fax: (740) 654-9890, E-mail: fairfieldheritage@greenapple.com, Internet: www.shermanhouse.com. Dir.: Connie Leitnaker
Local Museum
Furniture, silver, costumes, tools, glass, Indian artifacts, hist Civil War, Sherman family 44622

Lancaster PA

Hands-on House, Children's Museum of Lancaster, 721 Landis Valley Rd, Lancaster, PA 17601-4888 - T: (717) 569-5437, Fax: (717) 581-9283, Internet: www.handsonhouse.org. Exec. Dir.: Lynne Morrison
Natural History Museum / Science&Tech Museum - 1987 44623

Heritage Center of Lancaster County, 13 W King St, Lancaster, PA 17603-3813 - T: (717) 299-6440, Fax: (717) 299-6916, E-mail: heritage@paonline.com, Internet: www.lancasterheritage.com. Dir.: Peter S. Seibert
Fine Arts Museum / Decorative Arts Museum / Local Museum - 1976
History, decorative art 44624

Historic Rock Ford, 881 Rock Ford Rd, Lancaster, PA 17602 - T: (717) 392-7223, Fax: (717) 392-7283, E-mail: hhbecker@rockfordplantation.org, Internet: www.rockfordplantation.org. Exec. Dir.: Heather Hartman Becker
Local Museum - 1958
Local hist 44625

James Buchanan Foundation for the Preservation of Wheatland, 1120 Marietta Av, Lancaster, PA 17603 - T: (717) 392-8721, Fax: (717) 295-8825, E-mail: jbwwheatland@aol.com, Internet: www.wheatland.org. Pres.: Michael J Minney
Historical Museum - 1936
Restored 1828 Federal mansion, residence of President James Buchanan 44626

Lancaster County Museum, 230 N President Av, Lancaster, PA 17603-3125 - T: (717) 392-4633, Fax: (717) 293-2739, E-mail: lchs@ptd.net, Internet: www.lancasterhistory.org. Exec. Dir.: Thomas R. Ryan
Local Museum - 1886
Local hist 44627

Lancaster Museum of Art, 135 N Lime St, Lancaster, PA 17602 - T: (717) 394-3497, Fax: (717) 394-0101, E-mail: lmart@mindspring.com, Internet: www.lancastermuseumart.com. Dir.: Cindi Morrison, Asst. Dir.: Matt Kale
Fine Arts Museum - 1965
Art 44628

Landis Valley Museum, 2451 Kissel Hill Rd, Lancaster, PA 17601 - T: (717) 569-0401 ext 200, Fax: (717) 560-2147, E-mail: stemiller@state.pa.us, Internet: www.landisvalleymuseum.org. Dir.: Stephen Miller, Cur.: Timothy Essig, Bruce Bomberger (Agricultural History), Susan Messimer
Local Museum / Agriculture Museum - 1925
Rural life and culture 44629

The North Museum of Natural History and Science, 400 College Av, Lancaster, PA 17604 - T: (717) 291-3941, Fax: (717) 358-4504, Internet: www.northmuseum.org. Cur.: Dr. Steven Kirsch (Geology, Mineralogy), Allison Eichelberger (Entomology), Shirley Bubb (Ornithology), John Coolidge (Paleontology)
Natural History Museum - 1901
Natural history 44630

Lancaster VA

Mary Ball Washington Museum, 8346 Mary Ball Rd, Lancaster, VA 22503 - T: (804) 462-7280, Fax: (804) 462-6107, E-mail: history@rivnet.net, Internet: www.mbwn.org. C.E.O.: Doris Lackey
Local Museum - 1958
Textiles, furniture, paintings, family and regional memorabilia, folklife, Civil War 44631

Lander WY

Fremont County Pioneer Museum, 630 Lincoln St, Lander, WY 82520 - T: (307) 332-4137, Fax: (307) 332-6498. Dir.: Todd Guenther
Local Museum - 1908
Local hist 44632

Landing NJ

Lake Hopatcong Historical Museum, Hopatcong State Park, Landing, NJ 07850, mail addr: POB 668, Landing, NJ 07850 - T: (973) 398-2616, Fax: (973) 361-8987, E-mail: lhhistory@worldnet.att.net, Internet: www.hopatcong.org/museum. C.E.O.: Marilyn Garrity jr
Local Museum - 1955
Native American, Morris Canal, hist, Lake Hopatcong 44633

Lake Hopatcong Historical Museum, Hopatcong State Park, Landing, NJ 07850 - T: (973) 398-2616, Fax: (973) 361-8987, E-mail: lhhistory@worldnet.att.net, Internet: www.hopatcong.org/museum. C.E.O.: Marilyn Garrity
Historical Museum - 1955 44634

Landisville PA

Amos Herr House, 1756 Nissley Rd, Landisville, PA 17538 - T: (717) 898-8822
Decorative Arts Museum - 1990
Furnishings, farm equip 44635

Langhorne PA

Historic Langhorne Museum, 160 W Maple Av, Langhorne, PA 19047 - T: (215) 757-1888, 757-6158, Fax: (215) 741-5767, E-mail: hla@buxcom.net, Internet: hla.buxcom.net. Cur.: Ruth E. Irwin (Artifacts)
Historical Museum - 1965 44636

Langston OK

Melvin B. Tolson Black Heritage Center, c/o Langston University, POB 907, Langston, OK 73050 - T: (405) 466-2231, Fax: (405) 466-2979. Cur.: Bettye Black
Historical Museum / University Museum - 1959
African American art and artifacts, paintings, photographs 44637

Langtry TX

Judge Roy Bean Visitor Center, Hwy 90, W, Loop 25, Langtry, TX 78871 - T: (915) 291-3340, Fax: (915) 291-3366, E-mail: lytic@dot.state.tx.us, Internet: www.dot.state.tx.us. Head: Vernon N. Billings
Local Museum - 1939
Historic building 44638

Lanham-Seabrook MD

Howard B. Owens Science Center, 9601 Greenbelt Rd, Lanham-Seabrook, MD 20706 - T: (301) 918-8750, Fax: (301) 918-8753, E-mail: owens2@erols.com, Internet: www.pgcpf.org
Natural History Museum - 1978
Science - planetarium 44639

Lansing IL

Lansing Veterans Memorial Museum, Lansing Municipal Airport, Lansing, IL 60438 - T: (708) 895-1321, Fax: (708) 474-0798. Dir.: David Schwolger
Military Museum - 1991 44640

Lansing MI

Carl G. Fenner Nature Center, 2020 E Mt Hope Rd, Lansing, MI 48910 - T: (517) 483-4224, Fax: (517) 377-0012, E-mail: cbratton@ci.lansing.mi.us. Head: Clara Ann Bratton
Natural History Museum - 1959
Natural history 44641

Lansing Art Gallery, 425 S Grand Av, Lansing, MI 48933 - T: (517) 374-6406, Fax: (517) 484-2564, E-mail: lansingartgallery@voyager.com. Dir.: Catherine Babcock
Fine Arts Museum / Public Gallery - 1965
Visual arts 44642

Michigan Historical Museum, 717 W Allegan, Lansing, MI 48918 - T: (517) 373-0515, Fax: (517) 241-4738, E-mail: kwiatkowskip@michigan.gov, Internet: www.michiganhistory.org. Dir.: Phillip C. Kwiatkowski
Local Museum - 1879
Regional history 44643

Museum of Surveying, 220 Museum Dr, Lansing, MI 48933 - T: (517) 484-6605, Fax: (517) 484-3711, E-mail: museumofsurvey@acd.net, Internet: www.surveyhistory.org. C.E.O.: William G. Stark
Historical Museum - 1989
Regional history 44644

R.E. Olds Transportation Museum, 240 Museum Dr, Lansing, MI 48933 - T: (517) 372-0529, Fax: (517) 372-2901, E-mail: deborahh@voyager.net. C.E.O.: Kevin Smith
Science&Tech Museum - 1981
Transport 44645

Laona WI

Camp Five Museum, 5480 Connor Farm Rd, Laona, WI 54541 - T: (715) 674-3414, Fax: (715) 674-7400, Internet: www.camp5museum.org. Dir.: Edward J. Dellin
Science&Tech Museum - 1969
Logging 44646

Laramie WY

The Geological Museum, University of Wyoming, Laramie, WY 82071-3006 - T: (307) 766-2646, Fax: (307) 766-6679, E-mail: uwgeoms@uwyo.edu, Internet: www.uwyo.edu.geomuseum. Dir.: Brent H. Breithaupt
University Museum / Natural History Museum - 1887
Geology 44647

Laramie Plains Museum, 603 Ivinson Av, Laramie, WY 82070-3299 - T: (307) 742-4448, E-mail: laramiemuse@vcn.com, Internet: www.laramiemuseum.org. Dir.: Daniel A. Nelson, Cur.: Carolyn Nelson, Jill Anderson
Local Museum - 1966
Local hist 44648

University of Wyoming Anthropology Museum, Anthropology Bldg, 14th and Ivinson St, Laramie, WY 82071 - T: (307) 766-5136, Fax: (307) 766-2473, E-mail: arrow@uwyo.edu, Internet: www.uwyo.edu/a&s/anth. Dir.: Charles A. Reher
University Museum / Ethnology Museum / Archaeological Museum - 1966
Anthropology 44649

University of Wyoming Art Museum, 2111 Willett Dr, Laramie, WY 82071-3807 - T: (307) 766-6622, Fax: (307) 766-3520, E-mail: uwart@uwyo.edu, Internet: www.uwyo.edu/artmuseum. Dir./Cur.: Susan Moldenhauer, Cur.: Scott Boberg
Fine Arts Museum / University Museum - 1968
Art 44650

Wyoming Territorial Park, 975 Snowy Range Rd, Laramie, WY 82070 - T: (307) 745-3733, Fax: (307) 745-8620, E-mail: prison@lariat.org, Internet: www.wyoprisonpark.org. Dir.: Pam Malone, Cur.: Rita Burleson
Local Museum - 1986
Local hist 44651

Laredo TX

Laredo Children's Museum, c/o Laredo Community College, P-56 Fort Macintosh, Laredo, TX 78040 - T: (956) 725-2299, Fax: (956) 725-7776, E-mail: lcmuseum1@yahoo.com. Pres.: Melissa Cigarroa, C.E.O.: Evelyn Smietana
Special Museum / Historical Museum - 1988 44652

Largo FL

Gulf Coast Museum of Art, 12211 Walshingham Rd, Largo, FL 33778 - T: (727) 518-6933, Fax: (727) 518-1852, E-mail: krollins@gulfcoastmuseum.org, Internet: www.gulfcoastmuseum.org. Dir.: Ken Rollins
Fine Arts Museum / Public Gallery - 1936
20th c American art 44653

Heritage Village - Pinellas County Historical Museum, 11909-125 St N, Largo, FL 33774 - T: (727) 582-2123, Fax: (727) 582-2211, Internet: www.co.pinellas.fl.us/bcc/heritag.htm. Dir.: Jan Loth, Cur.: Donald J. Ivey, Ed.: Ellen Babb
Historical Museum / Open Air Museum - 1961
Living history 44654

Larned KS

Fort Larned, Rte 3, Larned, KS 67550 - T: (316) 285-6911, Fax: (316) 285-3571, E-mail: george_elmore@nps.gov, Internet: www.nps.gov/fols. Dir.: Steve Linderer, Cur.: George Elmore
Historical Museum / Military Museum - 1964
Historic fort on Santa Fe Trail 44655

Santa Fe Trail Museum, Rte 3, Larned, KS 67550 - T: (316) 285-2054, Fax: (316) 285-7491, E-mail: trailctr@larned.net, Internet: www.larned.net/trailctr/. Dir.: Ruth Olson Peters, Cur.: Betsy Crawford-Gore, Beverly Howell
Historical Museum - 1974
Regional history - library 44656

Las Cruces NM

Branigan Cultural Center, 500 N Water, Las Cruces, NM 88001 - T: (505) 541-2155, Fax: (505) 525-3645, E-mail: bcc1@zianet.com, Internet: www.lascruces-culture.org. Dir.: Sharon Bode-Hempton
Fine Arts Museum / Natural History Museum - 1981
Natural hist, art 44657

Las Cruces Museum of Natural History, 700 S Telshor Blvd, Las Cruces, NM 88011 - T: (505) 522-3120, Fax: (505) 522-3744, E-mail: mnh@las-cruces.org, Internet: www.nmsu.edu/museum. Dir.: Kajal Ghoshroy
Natural History Museum - 1988
Chihuahuan desert animals 44658

New Mexico Farm and Ranch Heritage Museum, 4100 Dripping Springs Rd, Las Cruces, NM 88011 - T: (505) 522-4100, Fax: (505) 522-3085, E-mail: cmassey@frh.state.nm.us, Internet: www.frhm.org. Dir.: Mac R. Harris, Cur.: Robert L. Hart
Agriculture Museum / Historical Museum - 1991
Agriculture 44659

New Mexico State University Art Gallery, University Av E. of Solano, Las Cruces, NM 88003-8001 - T: (505) 646-1705, Fax: (505) 646-8036, E-mail: artglry@nmsu.edu, Internet: crl.nmsu.edu/users/retablos/collection/FrontPage.html
Fine Arts Museum / University Museum - 1973 44660

New Mexico State University Museum, Kent Hall, University Av, Las Cruces, NM 88003 - T: (505) 646-3739, Fax: (505) 646-1419, E-mail: estaski@nmsu.edu, Internet: www.nmsu.edu/~museum. Dir.: Edward Staski, Cur.: Dr. Terry Reynolds
University Museum / Ethnology Museum - 1959 44661

Las Vegas NM

City of Las Vegas and Rough Riders Memorial Museum, 727 Grand Av, Las Vegas, NM 87701 - T: (505) 454-1401 ext 283, Fax: (505) 425-7335, Internet: www.arco-iris.com/teddy/roughriders.htm. Dir.: Melanie LaBorwit
Local Museum - 1960
Local history, Spanish-American war 44662

The Fine Arts Gallery, New Mexico Highlands University, Donelly Library, National Av, Las Vegas, NM 87701 - T: (505) 454-3338, Fax: (505) 454-0026, E-mail: gallery@nmhu.edu. Dir.: Bob Read
University Museum / Fine Arts Museum - 1956 44663

Las Vegas NV

Donna Beam Fine Art Gallery, University of Nevada, Las Vegas, 4505 Maryland Pkwy, Las Vegas, NV 89154-5002 - T: (702) 895-3893, Fax: (702) 895-3751, E-mail: schefcij@nevada.edu, Internet: www.unlv.edu/main/museums.html. Dir.: Jerry A. Schefcik, Cur.: Libby Lumpkin
Fine Arts Museum / University Museum - 1962
US works of all media of art (2nd half of 20th c) 44664

Flamingo Gallery, c/o Clark County Library, 1401 E Flamingo Rd, Las Vegas, NV 89119 - T: (702) 733-7810, Fax: (702) 732-7271, Internet: www.lvccld.org. Dir.: Denise Shapiro
Public Gallery - 1970 44665

Guggenheim Hermitage Museum, 3355 Las Vegas Blvd S, Las Vegas, NV 89109 - T: (702) 414-2440, Fax: (702) 414-2442, E-mail: lvvisitorinfo@guggenheim.org, Internet: www.guggenheimlasvegas.org
Fine Arts Museum 44666

Guinness World of Records Museum, 2780 Las Vegas Blvd S, Las Vegas, NV 89109 - T: (702) 792-3766, Fax: (702) 792-0530, E-mail: guinness@wizard.com, Internet: www.guinnessmuseum.com. Cur.: Oli Lewis
Special Museum - 1990 44667

Las Vegas Art Museum, 9600 W Sahara Av, Las Vegas, NV 89117 - T: (702) 360-8000, Fax: (702) 360-8080, E-mail: lvam@earthlink.net. Exec. Dir.: Marianne Lovenz, Cur.: Dr. James Mann
Fine Arts Museum - 1950 44668

Las Vegas International Scouting Museum, 2915 W Charleston, Las Vegas, NV 89102 - T: (702) 878-7268, Fax: (702) 822-2020, E-mail: luismdirector@aol.com. Dir.: J.C. Ellis
Special Museum 44669

Las Vegas Natural History Museum, 900 Las Vegas Blvd N, Las Vegas, NV 89101 - T: (702) 384-3466, Fax: (702) 384-5343, E-mail: lvnathist@aol.com, Internet: www.lvrj.com/communitylink/lvnaturalhistory. C.E.O.: Marilyn Gillespie
Natural History Museum - 1989
Natural history, fossils, animals, prints 44670

Liberace Museum, 1775 E Tropicana, Las Vegas, NV 89119 - T: (702) 798-5595 ext 20, Fax: (702) 798-7386, E-mail: sharris@liberace.org, Internet: liberace.org. Dir.: Sandra L. Harris
Special Museum / Music Museum - 1979 44671

Lied Discovery Children's Museum, 833 Las Vegas Blvd N, Las Vegas, NV 89101 - T: (702) 382-3445, Fax: (702) 382-0592, E-mail: edcm@sprintmail.com. Dir.: Suzanne LeBlanc
Special Museum - 1984 44672

Nevada State Museum, 700 Twin Lakes Dr, Las Vegas, NV 89107 - T: (702) 486-5205, Fax: (702) 486-5172. Dir.: Thomas Dyer (Exhibitions), Cur.: David Millman (Collections), George Austin (Zoology), Barbara Slivac (Education)
Local Museum - 1982
Local hist 44673

UNLV Barrick Museum, 4505 Maryland Pkwy, Las Vegas, NV 89154-4012 - T: (702) 895-3011, Fax: (702) 895-3094, E-mail: barrickmuseum@ccmail.nevada.edu, Internet: hrcweb.nevada.edu/museum. Dir.: Dr. Donald H. Baepler, Cur.: Dr. William Pratt (Invertebrates), Alex Heindl (Herpetology), Aurore Giguet (Exhibits), Dr. John Klicka, Gary Voelker (Ornithology), Asst. Cur.: Kelleen Smith (Ornithology), Asst. Dir.: Sherry Marks
University Museum / Natural History Museum - 1967 44674

Wynn Collection, 3145 Las Vegas Blvd S, Las Vegas, NV 89109 - T: (702) 733-4100
Fine Arts Museum
13 paintings by Steve Wynn 44675

Laurel MD

The Laurel Museum, 817 Main St, Laurel, MD 20707 - T: (301) 725-7975, Fax: (301) 725-7975, E-mail: laurelmuseum@netscape.net, Internet: www.laurelhistory.org. Dir.: Carol Runyon
Local Museum - 1996
Local hist 44676

Montpelier Cultur Arts Center, 12826 Laural-Bowie Rd, Laurel, MD 20708 - T: (301) 953-1993, Fax: (301) 206-9682, E-mail: montpeliermansion@smart.net, Internet: www.smart.net/~parksrec/montpeli.htm. Dir.: Richard Zandler
Decorative Arts Museum - 1979 44677

Montpellier Mansion, Rte 197 and Muirkirk Rd, Laurel, MD 20708 - T: (301) 953-1376, Fax: (301) 699-2544, E-mail: montpeliermansion@pgparks.com, Internet: www.pgparks.com
Decorative Arts Museum - 1976
Art and furnishings 44678

Laurel MS

Lauren Rogers Museum of Art, 565 N Fifth Av, Laurel, MS 39440 - T: (601) 649-6374, Fax: (601) 649-6379, E-mail: lrma@c-gate.net, Internet: www.lrma.org. Dir.: George Bassi, Registrar: Tommie Rodgers
Fine Arts Museum - 1923
19th c European art, 18th c Englisg Georgian silver, 18th-19th c Japanese Ukiyo-e Woodblock prints, 19th-20th c American paintings - library 44679

Laurens IA

Pocahontas County Iowa Historical Society Museum, 272 N Third, Laurens, IA 50554 - T: (712) 845-2577. Cur.: Evelyn Schleushner
Local Museum - 1977
Regional history, photos, medicine 44680

Laurens SC

James Dunklin House, 544 W Main St, Laurens, SC 29360 - T: (864) 984-4735, E-mail: hackster@backroads.net
Decorative Arts Museum - 1972 44681

Laurinburg NC

Indian Museum of the Carolinas, 607 Turnpike Rd, Laurinburg, NC 28352 - T: (910) 276-5880. Dir.: Dr. Margaret Houston
Archaeological Museum - 1969 44682

Lava Hot Springs ID

South Bannock County Historical Center, 110 E Main St, Lava Hot Springs, ID 83246 - T: (208) 776-5254, Fax: (208) 776-5254. Dir.: Ruth Ann Olson, Cur.: Susan Fagnant, Dee Forsythe, Gwendolyn Symons
Local Museum - 1980
Local history 44683

Lawrence KS

Museum of Anthropology, University of Kansas, Lawrence, KS 66045 - T: (913) 864-4245, Fax: (913) 864-5243, Internet: www.ukansas.edu/~kuma. Dir.: Alfred E. Johnson, Cur.: Anta Montet-White, Brad Logan, Mary J. Adair, John Hoopes, Jack Hofman, Robert J. Smith
University Museum / Ethnology Museum - 1975
Anthropology 44684

Natural History Museum, University of Kansas, 1345 Jayhawk Blvd, Lawrence, KS 66045-7561 - T: (785) 864-4540, Fax: (785) 864-5335, E-mail: kunhm@ku.edu, Internet: www.nhm.ku.edu. Dir.: Dr. Leonard Krishtalka, Asst. Dir.: W. Bradley M. Kemp, Jordan Yochim, James Beach, Cur.: Robert Timm, Norman Slade (Mammalogy), Richard O. Prum, Townsend Peterson (Ornithology), James S. Ashe, Michael Engel (Entomology), Roger L. Kaesler (Invertebrate Paleontology), Daphne Fautin (Invertebrate Zoology), Mark Mort, Craig C. Freeman (Botany), Linda Trueb (Herpetology), E.O. Wiley, Walter Dimmick (Ichthyology), Larry Martin (Vertebrate Paleontology), Tom Taylor, Edith Taylor (Paleobotany)
Natural History Museum - 1866
Natural history, zoology, ornitology, icthyology, mammalogy, entomology, paleontology, botany, herpetology - biodiversity research center 44685

Spencer Museum of Art, University of Kansas, 1301 Mississippi St, Lawrence, KS 66045-7500 - T: (785) 864-4710, Fax: (785) 864-3112, E-mail: spencerart@ku.edu, Internet: www.ku.edu/~sma. Dir.: Andrea S. Norris, Cur.: Susan Earle (European and American Arts), Stephen Goddard (Prints, Drawings), John Pultz (Photography), Pat Villeneuve (Education)
Fine Arts Museum / University Museum - 1928
American, European and Asian art, prints, photos, drawings 44686

University of Kansas Ryther Printing Museum, 2425 W 15th St, Lawrence, KS 66049-3903 - T: (785) 864-4341, Fax: (785) 864-7356, E-mail: jgs@ku.edu. Dir.: John G. Sayler
Science&Tech Museum - 1955
Antique printing equipment 44687

Watkins Community Museum of History, 1047 Massachusetts St, Lawrence, KS 66044 - T: (785) 841-4109, E-mail: wcmhist@sunflower.com, Internet: www.ci.lawrence.ks.us/museums/watkins.html. Dir.: Dr. Steve Jansen, Sc. Staff: Judy Sweets (Collections)
Local Museum - 1972
Local history 44688

Lawrence MA

Immigrant City Historical Museum of Lawrence and its People, 6 Essex St, Lawrence, MA 01840 - T: (978) 686-9230, Fax: (978) 975-2154, E-mail: archives@ma.ultranet.com, Internet: www.krhlawrence.com. Exec. Dir.: A. Patricia Jaysane
Local Museum - 1978
City hist, immigrant labor 44689

Lawrenceville GA

Gwinnett Historical Society Museum, 185 Crogan St, Lawrenceville, GA 30045 - T: (770) 822-5174, Fax: (770) 822-5174, 237-5616, E-mail: gwhissoc@bellsouth.net, Internet: www.gwinnetths.org. Pres.: Elaine Roberts
Local Museum / Historical Museum - 1966
Local history 44690

Gwinnett History Museum, 455 Perry St, Lawrenceville, GA 30045 - T: (770) 882-5178, Fax: (770) 237-5612, E-mail: arnoldsa@co.gwinnett.ga.us, Internet: www.gogwinnett.org. Dir.: Sarah Arnold
Local Museum - 1974
County's history 44691

Lawrenceville NJ

Rider University Art Gallery, 2083 Lawrenceville Rd, Lawrenceville, NJ 08648-3099 - T: (609) 896-5168, Fax: (609) 896-5232, E-mail: lnaar@rider.edu, Internet: www.rider.edu. Dir.: Harry I. Naar
Fine Arts Museum - 1970 44692

Lawson MO

Watkins Woolen Mill, 26600 Park Rd N, Lawson, MO 64062 - T: (816) 296-3357, Fax: (816) 580-3784, E-mail: nrwatki@mail.dnr.state.mo.us, Internet: www.mostateparks/wwmill/. Head: Michael D. Beckett
Agriculture Museum / Science&Tech Museum - 1964 44693

Lawtell LA

Matt's Museum, McClelland St and Hwy 190, Lawtell, LA 70550 - T: (337) 543-7223. Dir.: Edvin Matt
Local Museum - 1968
General museum 44694

Lawton OK

Museum of the Great Plains, 601 NW Ferris Av, Lawton, OK 73502 - T: (580) 581-3460, Fax: (580) 581-3458, E-mail: mgp@sirinet.net, Internet: www.museumgreatplains.org. Dir.: John Hernandez, Sc. Staff: Deborah Baroff, Jim Whiteley, Timothy Poteete, Maurianna Johnson, Brian Smith, Joe Anderson (Archaeology)
Local Museum / Historical Museum - 1961 44695

Le Claire IA

Buffalo Bill Museum of Le Claire, Iowa, 200 N River Dr, Le Claire, IA 52753 - T: (319) 289-5580, Fax: (319) 289-4989
Local Museum / Historical Museum - 1957
Indian preservation 44696

Le Roy NY

Le Roy House and Jell-o Gallery, 23 E Main St, Le Roy, NY 14482 - T: (716) 768-7433, Fax: (716) 768-7579, Internet: www.jellomuseum.com. Dir.: Lynne J. Belluscio
Local Museum - 1940 44697

Le Sueur MN

Le Sueur Museum, 709 N Second St, Le Sueur, MN 56058 - T: (612) 357-4488. Pres.: Helen Meyer
Local Museum - 1968
Local history, in first school in Le Sueur 44698

Lead SD

Black Hills Mining Museum, 323 W Main, Lead, SD 57754 - T: (605) 584-1605, E-mail: bhminmus@mato.com, Internet: www.mining-museum.blackhills.com. Dir.: John Meade, Cur.: Donald D. Toms
Science&Tech Museum - 1986 44699

Leadville CO

Healy House and Dexter Cabin, 912 Harrison Av, Leadville, CO 80461 - T: (719) 486-0487, Fax: (719) 486-2557. Dir.: Larry Frank
Historical Museum - 1947 44700

Tabor Opera House Museum, 306-310 Harrison Av, Leadville, CO 80461 - T: (719) 486-1147, Fax: (719) 471-0984, E-mail: sharon@taboroperahouse.net, Internet: www.taboroperahouse.net. C.E.O.: Evelyn E. Furman
Performing Arts Museum - 1955
Historic theater 44701

Leavenworth KS

Leavenworth County Historical Society Museum, 1128 5th Av, Leavenworth, KS 66048-3212 - T: (913) 682-7759, Fax: (913) 682-2089, E-mail: lvcohistsoc@lvworth.com, Internet: leavenworth-net.com/chs. Pres.: Beverley Larque
Local Museum - 1964
Local history 44702

Lebanon OH

Glendower State Memorial, 105 Cincinnati Av, Lebanon, OH 45036 - T: (513) 932-1817, Fax: (513) 932-8560, E-mail: wchs@go-concepts.com
Historic Site - 1944 44703

Warren County Historical Society Museum, 105 S Broadway, Lebanon, OH 45036-1707 - T: (513) 932-1817, Fax: (513) 932-8560, E-mail: wchs@go-concepts.com, Internet: www.wchsmuseum.org. Dir.: Mary Payne, Cur.: Mary Klei
Local Museum - 1940 44704

Lebanon PA

The Stoy Museum of the Lebanon County Historical Society, 924 Cumberland St, Lebanon, PA 17042 - T: (717) 272-1473, Fax: (717) 272-7474, E-mail: staff@lebanonhistory.org, Internet: www.lebanonhistory.org. Pres.: Philip H. Feather
Local Museum - 1898
Local hist 44705

Lebec CA

Fort Tejon, 4201 Fort Tejon Rd, Lebec, CA 93243 - T: (661) 248-6692, Fax: (661) 248-8373, E-mail: ldakatos@frazmtn.com. Head: Donald R. La Katos
Military Museum - 1939 44706

Lecompton KS

Territorial Capital-Lane Museum, 393 N 1900 Rd, Lecompton, KS 66050 - T: (785) 887-6184, Fax: (785) 887-6148, Internet: www.lecomptonkansas.com. Dir.: Paul M. Bahnmaier, Cur.: Arlene Simmons
Historical Museum - 1969
State history 44707

Lee MA

Warehouse Gallery, Council for Creative Projects, 17 Main St, Lee, MA 01238 - T: (413) 243-8030, Fax: (413) 243-8031, E-mail: ccp@ccpexhibits.org, Internet: www.ccpexhibits.org. Dir.: Dr. Gail Gelburd, Asst. Dir.: Joel Meyers, Colleen M. Simo, Michael Vickery
Fine Arts Museum - 1989
Art 44708

Lees Summit MO

Missouri Town 1855, 8010 E Park Rd, Lees Summit, MO 64015 - T: (816) 795-8200 ext 1260, Fax: (816) 795-7938, E-mail: juligor@gw.co.jackson.mo.us, Internet: www.co.jackson.mo.us
Open Air Museum - 1963 44709

Leesburg VA

Loudoun Museum, 14-16 Loudoun St, Leesburg, VA 20175 - T: (703) 777-8331, 777-7427, Fax: (703) 737-8873, E-mail: info@loudounmuseum.org, Internet: www.loudounmuseum.org. Pres.: Art Richmond, Dir.: Douglas Foard
Local Museum - 1967
Local hist 44710

Morven Park Museum, Old Waterford Rd, Leesburg, VA 22075, mail addr: POB 6228, Leesburg, VA 220178-921 - T: (703) 777-6034, Fax: (703) 771-9211, E-mail: myork@morvenpark.org, Internet: www.morvenpark.com
Local Museum - 1955
Carriages, fox hunting, agriculture, folklore 44711

Oatlands Plantation, 20850 Oatlands Plantation Ln, Leesburg, VA 20175 - T: (703) 777-3174, Fax: (703) 777-4427, E-mail: oatlands@erols.com, Internet: www.oatlands.org. Dir.: David Y. Boyce, Assoc. Dir.: Karen Eldridge
Local Museum - 1965
Historic house 44712

Lehi UT

John Hutchings Museum of Natural History, 55 N Center St, Lehi, UT 84043 - T: (801) 768-7180. C.E.O.: Lamar Hutchings
Natural History Museum - 1955
Natural hist 44713

Leland MI

Leelanau Historical Museum, 203 E Cedar St, Leland, MI 49654 - T: (231) 256-7475, Fax: (231) 256-7650, E-mail: info@leelanauhistory.org, Internet: www.leelanauhistory.org. Dir.: R. Mark Livengood, Cur.: Laura J. Quackenbush
Historical Museum - 1957
Local history 44714

Lenhartsville PA

Pennsylvania Dutch Folk Culture Society Museum, Lenhartsville, PA 19534 - T: (610) 867-6705
Folklore Museum - 1965
Folk culture 44715

Lenox MA

Berkshire Scenic Railway Museum, Willow Creek Rd, Lenox, MA 01240 - T: (413) 637-2210, Fax: (518) 392-2225, E-mail: woodworks@taconic.net, Internet: www.RegionNet.com/colberk/berkshirerailway.html
Science&Tech Museum - 1984
1920s-1960s railroad equip, vintage coaches 44716

Lerna IL

Lincoln Log Cabin, 400 S Lincoln Hwy Rd, Lerna, IL 62440 - T: (217) 345-6489, 345-1845, Fax: (217) 345-6472, E-mail: tomandsarah@lincolnlogcabin.org, Internet: www.lincolnlogcabin.org. Man.: Tom Vance, C.E.O.: Maynard Crossland
Historical Museum - 1929
Reconstructed cabin and farm of Thomas and Sara Lincoln on original site 44717

Moore Home, 400 S Lincoln Hwy Rd, Lerna, IL 62440 - T: (217) 345-6489, 345-1845, Fax: (217) 345-6472, E-mail: tomandsarah@lincolnlogcabin.org, Internet: www.lincolnlogcabin.org. Man.: Tom Vance
Historical Museum - 1929
Home of Reuben and Matilda Moore, daughter of Sara Lincoln and stepsister of Abraham Lincoln 44718

Leverett MA

Leverett Historical Museum, N Leverett Rd, Leverett, MA 01054 - T: (413) 548-9082. Pres.: Annette Gibavic
Local Museum - 1963
Local history 44719

Lewes DE

Lewes Historical Society Museum, 110 Shipcarpenter St, Lewes, DE 19958 - T: (302) 645-7670, Fax: (302) 645-2375, E-mail: info@historiclewes.org, Internet: www.historiclewes.org. Dir.: Michael DiPaolo
Local Museum - 1961
Local hist 44720

Lewisburg PA

Edward and Marthann Samek Art Gallery, Bucknell University, Elaine Langone Center, Lewisburg, PA 17837 - T: (570) 577-3792, Fax: (570) 577-3215, E-mail: inthebag@bucknell.edu, Internet: www.bucknell.edu/departments/cgallery/. Dir.: Dan Mills, Op.Mgr.: Cynthia Peltier
Fine Arts Museum / University Museum - 1983
Art 44721

Packwood House Museum, 8 Market St, Lewisburg, PA 17837 - T: (570) 524-0323, Fax: (570) 524-0548, E-mail: packwood@jdweb.com, Internet: www.Packwoodhousemuseum.com. Dir.: Sarah Phinney Kelley
Local Museum - 1976
Local hist 44722

Slifer House, Riverwoods, 1 River Rd, Lewisburg, PA 17837 - T: (570) 524-2245, Fax: (570) 524-2245, E-mail: sliferhs@postoffice.ptd.net, Internet: slifer.albrightcare.org. Dir.: Gary W. Parks
Historic Site - 1976 44723

Union County Museum, Courthouse, Second and Saint Louis Sts, Lewisburg, PA 17837 - T: (570) 524-8666, Fax: (570) 524-8743, E-mail: hstoricl@ptd.net, Internet: www.rootsweb.com. Pres.: Jeannette Lasansky, Dir.: Gary Slear
Local Museum - 1906
History, genealogy, oral traditions 44724

Lewisburg WV

Fort Savannah Museum, 100 E Randolph St, Lewisburg, WV 24901 - T: (304) 645-4010. C.E.O.: Rosalie S. Detch
Military Museum - 1962
Military hist 44725

North House Museum, 301 W Washington St, Lewisburg, WV 24901 - T: (304) 645-3398, Fax: (304) 645-5201, E-mail: info@greenbrier-historical.org, Internet: www.greenbrierhistorical.org. Dir.: Joyce Mott, Pres.: John B. Arbuckle
Local Museum / Historical Museum - 1963
Civil War, Indian artifacts 44726

Lewiston ID

Luna House Museum → Nez Perce County Museum

Nez Perce County Museum, 306 Third St, Lewiston, ID 83501 - T: (208) 743-2535, Fax: (208) 743-2535. Pres.: Richard Riggs
Local Museum - 1960
Local history 44727

Lewiston ME

Bates College Museum of Art, 75 Russell St, Lewiston, ME 04240 - T: (207) 786-6158, Fax: (207) 786-8335, E-mail: museum@bates.edu, Internet: www.bates.edu/acad/museum. Dir.: Genetta McLean, Asst. Cur.: William Low, Coord.: Anthony Shostak (Education)
Fine Arts Museum / University Museum - 1986
Art 44728

Dorothea C. Witham Gallery, 59 Canal St, Lewiston, ME 04240 - T: (207) 782-1369, Fax: (207) 782-5931. Exec. Dir.: J. Michael Patry
Fine Arts Museum - 1993
Photography 44729

Lewiston NY

Niagara Power Project Visitors' Center, 5777 Lewiston Rd, Lewiston, NY 14092 - T: (716) 286-6661, Fax: (716) 286-6091, Internet: nypa.gov/html/vcniager.html. Dir.: Joanne Willmont
Science&Tech Museum 44730

Lewistown IL

Dickson Mounds Museum, 10956 N Dickson Mounds Rd, Lewistown, IL 61542 - T: (309) 547-3721, Fax: (309) 547-3189, E-mail: jfranke@museum.state.il.us, Internet: www.museum.state.il.us/ismsites/dickson/. Dir.: Dr. Judith A. Franke, Asst. Cur.: Alan D. Harn
Archaeological Museum / Historic Site - 1927
Archaeology, American Indian cultures of Illinois 44731

Lewistown MT

Central Montana Historical Association Museum, 408 NE Main St, Lewistown, MT 59457 - T: (406) 538-5436. Pres.: George Simonson
Historical Museum - 1955 44732

Lewistown Art Center, 801 W Broadway, Lewistown, MT 59457 - T: (406) 538-8278, Fax: (406) 538-8278, Internet: www.lewistown2000.com. Dir.: Nancy Hedrick
Fine Arts Museum - 1971
Art work from artists from Central Montana 44733

Lewistown PA

McCoy House, 17 N Main St, Lewistown, PA 17044 - T: (717) 242-1022, 248-4711, Fax: (717) 242-1022, E-mail: mchistory@acsworld.net, Internet: www.mccoyhouse.com. Pres.: Forest K. Fisher
Local Museum - 1921
Historic building 44734

Lexington KY

American Saddlebred Museum, 4093 Iron Works Pike, Lexington, KY 40511 - T: (859) 259-2746, Fax: (859) 255-2909, E-mail: ashm@mis.net, Internet: www.american-saddlebred.com. Exec. Dir.: Tolley Graves
Special Museum - 1962 44735

Ashland - Henry Clay Estate, 120 Sycamore Rd, Lexington, KY 40502 - T: (859) 266-8581, Fax: (859) 268-7266, E-mail: kwillis@henryclay.org, Internet: www.henryclay.org. Exec. Dir.: Kelly B. Willis, Pres.: Robert K. Lewis, Cur.: Eric Brooks
Historical Museum - 1926
1811 estate of Henry Clay, 1857 house of James Clay 44736

Aviation Museum of Kentucky, 4316 Hangar Dr, Blue Grass Airport, Lexington, KY 40510 - T: (859) 231-1219, Fax: (859) 381-8739, E-mail: sparker@aviationky.org, Internet: www.aviationky.org. Exec. Dir.: Steve Parker
Science&Tech Museum - 1995
Kentucky aviation hist, space and exploration 44737

Headley-Whitney Museum, 4435 Old Frankfort Pike, Lexington, KY 40510 - T: (859) 255-6653, Fax: (859) 255-8375, E-mail: dcwachs@headley-whitney.org, Internet: www.headley-whitney.org. Dir.: Diane C. Wachs, Cur.: Travis Robinson
Decorative Arts Museum - 1973
Decorative arts 44738

Hunt-Morgan House, 201 N Mill St, Lexington, KY 40507 - T: (606) 232-3290, Fax: (606) 259-9210, E-mail: bgtrust@mis.net, Internet: www.bluegrasstrust.org. Chm.: Jamie Millard
Local Museum - 1955 44739

International Museum of the Horse, 4089 Iron Works Pkwy, Lexington, KY 40511 - T: (859) 259-4231, 233-4303, Fax: (859) 225-4613, E-mail: khp@mis.net, Internet: www.imh.org. Dir.: Bill Cooke, Cur.: Jenifer Stermer
Fine Arts Museum / Special Museum - 1978 44740

Lexington Children's Museum, 440 W Short St, Lexington, KY 40507 - T: (859) 258-3253, Fax: (859) 258-3255, E-mail: lcmo@prodigy.net, Internet: www.lexingtonchildrensmuseum.com. Dir.: Sara Nees Holcomb
Special Museum - 1990 44741

The Living Arts and Science Center, 362 N Martin Luther King Blvd, Lexington, KY 40508 - T: (606) 252-5222, 255-2284, Fax: (606) 255-7448, E-mail: lasc6898@aol.com, Internet: www.livingarts&science.org. Dir.: Marty Henton, Cur.: Jim Brancaccio
Fine Arts Museum / Ethnology Museum - 1968
Children's art, science 44742

Mary Todd Lincoln House, 578 W Main, Lexington, KY 40507 - T: (859) 233-9999, Fax: (859) 272-9601, E-mail: mtlhouse@iglou.com, Internet: www.mtlhouse.org. Dir.: Kathy Tabb
Decorative Arts Museum - 1968 44743

Morlan Gallery, c/o Transylvania University, Mitchell Fine Arts Ctr, 300 N Broadway, Lexington, KY 40508 - T: (859) 233-8210, Fax: (859) 233-8797, E-mail: nwolsk@mail.transy.edu. Dir.: Nancy Wolsk
Decorative Arts Museum / Natural History Museum - 1978
19th c natural history and portraits, decorative arts 44744

Transylvania Museum, 300 N Broadway, Lexington, KY 40508 - T: (859) 233-8229, Fax: (859) 235-8171, E-mail: jday@transy.edu, Internet: www.transy.edu. Dir.: Dr. James Miller
Historical Museum - 1882
Science, medicine 44745

University of Kentucky Art Museum, Rose and Euclid, Lexington, KY 40506-0241 - T: (859) 257-5716, Fax: (859) 323-1994, E-mail: jrbosw00@uky.edu, Internet: www.uky.edu/ArtMuseum. Dir.: Kathleen Walsh-Piper, Cur.: Rachael Sadinsky, Deborah Borrowdale-Cox
Fine Arts Museum / University Museum - 1976
Art 44746

Waveland Museum, 225 Waveland Museum Ln, Lexington, KY 40515-1601 - T: (859) 272-3611, Fax: (859) 245-4269, E-mail: ron.langdon@mail.state.ky.us, Internet: www.kystateparks.com
Decorative Arts Museum - 1957
Furniture, portraits, China 44747

William S. Webb Museum of Anthropology, c/o University of Kentucky, 211 Lafferty Hall, Lexington, KY 40506-0024 - T: (859) 257-8208, Fax: (859) 323-1968, Internet: www.uky.edu/as/anthropology/museum/museum.htm. Dir.: George M. Crothers
Archaeological Museum / Ethnology Museum / University Museum - 1931
Archaeological and ethnographic materials 44748

Lexington MA

Lexington Historical Society Exhibition, POB 514, Lexington, MA 02420 - T: (781) 862-1703, Fax: (781) 862-4920, E-mail: lexhissc@tiac.net, Internet: www.lexingtonhistory.org. Pres.: Gardner Hayward, Dir.: George S. Comtois
Historical Museum - 1886
Local history, Munroe and Buckman tavern, Hancock-Clarke house, American revolution 44749

Museum of Our National Heritage → National Heritage Museum

National Heritage Museum, Van Gorden-Williams Library and Archives, 33 Marrett Rd, Lexington, MA 02421 - T: (781) 861-6559 ext 100, Fax: (781) 861-9846, E-mail: info@monh.org, Internet: www.monh.org. Dir.: John H. Ott, Dep. Dir.: Hilary Anderson (Collections, Exhibitions), Cur.: Mark Tabbert (Masonic and Fraternal Collections)
Historical Museum - 1971
History 44750

Lexington MO

Battle of Lexington State Historic Site, John Shea Dr, Ext Hwy 13, Lexington, MO 64067 - T: (660) 259-4654, Fax: (660) 259-2378, E-mail: dspblex@mail.dnr.state.mo.us, Internet: www.dnr.state.mo.us. C.E.O.: Janae Fuller
Military Museum / Historical Museum - 1959 44751

Lexington NC

Davidson County Historical Museum, 2 S Main St, Lexington, NC 27292 - T: (336) 242-2035, Fax: (336) 248-4122, E-mail: choffmann@co.davidson.nc.us, Internet: www.co.davidson.nc.us. C.E.O./Cur.: Catherine Matthews Hoffmann
Local Museum - 1976 44752

Davidson County Museum of Art, 220 S Main St, Lexington, NC 27292 - T: (336) 249-2742, Fax: (336) 249-6302, Internet: www.co.davidson.nc.us/arts. Exec. Dir.: Carla Copeland-Burns
Fine Arts Museum - 1968 44753

Lexington NE

Dawson County Historical Museum, 805 N Taft St, Lexington, NE 68850-0369 - T: (308) 324-5340, Fax: (308) 324-5340, E-mail: dawcomus@alltel.net. Pres.: Gail Hall, Dir.: Barbara Vondras
Local Museum - 1958 44754

Lexington OH

Richland County Museum, 51 Church St, Lexington, OH 44904 - T: (419) 884-2230. Pres.: Jeffrey Mandeville
Folklore Museum / Local Museum - 1966 44755

Lexington SC

Lexington County Museum, 231 Fox St, Lexington, SC 29072 - T: (803) 359-8369, Fax: (803) 808-2160. Dir.: Horace E. Harmon
Decorative Arts Museum / Local Museum - 1970
Local hist 44756

Lexington VA

American Work Horse Museum, POB 1051, Lexington, VA 24450 - T: (540) 463-2194, Fax: (540) 464-3507, E-mail: info@horsecenter.org, Internet: www.horsecenter.org. Dir.: Robert Reel
Special Museum - 1971
Horses 44757

Dupont Gallery, Washington and Lee University, Lexington, VA 24450-0303 - T: (540) 463-8861, Fax: (540) 463-8112, E-mail: olsonk@wlu.edu, Internet: www.wlu.edu. Dir.: Kathleen Olson
Public Gallery - 1954 44758

George C. Marshall Museum, VMI Parade Ground, Lexington, VA 24450 - T: (540) 463-7103 ext 225, Fax: (540) 464-5229, E-mail: kemper@marshallfoundation.org, Internet: www.marshallfoundation.org. Dir.: Julie Kemper, Pres.: Albert J. Beveridge
Historical Museum / Military Museum - 1953
Military and political history (20th c) 44759

Lee Chapel and Museum, Washington and Lee University, Lexington, VA 24450 - T: (540) 463-8768, Fax: (540) 463-8741, E-mail: phobbs@wlu.edu, Internet: www.wlu.edu/~chapel. C.E.O.: Patricia A. Hobbs
Historical Museum - 1867
Local hist 44760

The Reeves Center, Washington and Lee University, Lexington, VA 24450 - T: (540) 463-8744, Fax: (540) 463-8741, E-mail: hbailey@wlu.edu. Dir.: Thomas V. Litzenburg
Fine Arts Museum / University Museum - 1982 44761

Rockbridge Historical Society Museum, 101 E Washington St, Lexington, VA 24450 - T: (540) 464-1058, E-mail: rochist@hotmail.com. Pres.: David Reynolds, Dir.: Alice Williams
Local Museum - 1939
Local hist 44762

Virginia Military Institute Museum, Virginia Military Institute, Jackson Memorial Hall, Lexington, VA 24450 - T: (540) 464-7232, Fax: (540) 464-7112, E-mail: gibsonke@vmi.edu, Internet: www.vmi.edu/museum. Dir.: Keith E. Gibson
Military Museum - 1856
Military hist 44763

Liberal KS

Mid-America Air Museum, 2000 W 2nd St, Liberal, KS 67901 - T: (316) 624-5263, Fax: (316) 624-5454, E-mail: liberalcityam@swko.net. Exec. Dir.: Frank Yount
Science&Tech Museum - 1987
Aviation 44764

Liberty MO

Clay County Historical Museum, 14 N Main, Liberty, MO 64068 - T: (816) 781-8062. Cur.: Kevin M. Fisher
Historical Museum - 1965 44765

Historic Liberty Jail Visitors Center, 216 N Main, Liberty, MO 64068 - T: (816) 781-3188, Fax: (816) 781-7311
Religious Arts Museum - 1936
Religious hist 44766

Jesse James Bank Museum, 103 N Water, Liberty, MO 64068 - T: (816) 781-4458, Fax: (816) 628-6676. Head: Elizabeth Gilliam-Beckett
Historical Museum - 1966 44767

Libertyville IL

Libertyville-Mundelein Historical Society Museum, 413 N Milwaukee Av, Libertyville, IL 60048-2280 - T: (847) 362-2330, Fax: (847) 362-0006. Pres.: Jerrold L. Schulkin
Local Museum - 1955
Local history 44768

Ligonier IN

Stone's Tavern Museum, 4946 N State Rd 5 and U.S. 33, Ligonier, IN 46767 - T: (219) 856-2871. Pres.: Dick Hursey
Historical Museum - 1964
Tavern of 1839 44769

Ligonier PA

Fort Ligonier Museum, 216 S Market St, Ligonier, PA 15658-1206 - T: (724) 238-9701, Fax: (724) 238-9732. Dir.: J. Martin West, Cur.: Penelope A. West, Shirley McQuillis Iscrupe
Historical Museum - 1946
History 44770

Lihue HI

Kauai Museum, 4428 Rice St, Lihue, HI 96766 - T: (808) 245-6931, Fax: (808) 245-6864, E-mail: museum@kauaimuseum.org, Internet: www.kauaimuseum.org. Dir.: Carol Lovell, Cur.: Margaret Lovett
Fine Arts Museum / Historical Museum - 1960
History, art 44771

Lima OH

Allen County Museum, 620 W Market St, Lima, OH 45801 - T: (419) 222-9426, Fax: (419) 222-0649, E-mail: acmuseum@bright.net, Internet: www.allencountymuseum.org. Dir.: Patricia F. Smith, Cur.: Anna B. Selfridge, John Carnes, Sarah Rish, Asst. Cur.: Charles Bates
Local Museum - 1908 44772

Artspace-Lima, 65-67 Town Sq, Lima, OH 45802 - T: (419) 222-1721, Fax: (419) 222-6587, E-mail: artspace@worcnet.gen.oh.us. Exec. Dir.: Patricia Good
Public Gallery - 1940 44773

Lincoln IL

Postville Courthouse Museum, 914 Fifth St, Lincoln, IL 62656 - T: (217) 732-8930. Head: Richard Schachtsiek
Historic Site - 1953 44774

Lincoln KS

Lincoln County Historical Society Museum, 214 W Lincoln Av, Lincoln, KS 67455, mail addr: POB 85, Lincoln, KS 67455
Local Museum - 1978
Farm equip, dolls, Indian artifacts, military, F.A. Cooper's paintings, drawings and metal etchings 44775

Lincoln MA

Codman House - The Grange, 36 Codman Rd, Lincoln, MA 01773 - T: (781) 259-8843, Fax: (781) 259-8843, E-mail: ezopes@spnea.org, Internet: www.spnea.org. Head: Crystal Flores
Historical Museum - 1969
1740 Georgian mansion, home of Codman family 44776

DeCordova Museum and Sculpture Park, 51 Sandy Pond Rd, Lincoln, MA 01773 - T: (781) 259-8355, Fax: (781) 259-3650, E-mail: info@decordova.org, Internet: www.decordova.org. Dir.: Paul Master-Karnik, Cur.: Rachel Rosenfield Lafo
Fine Arts Museum / Folklore Museum - 1950
Arts, sculptures, Photography, Paintings 44777

Drumlin Farm, S Great Rd, Lincoln, MA 01773 - T: (781) 259-9500, Fax: (781) 259-7941, E-mail: drumlinfarm@massaudubon.org, Internet: www.massaudubon.org. Dir.: Claudia Thompson
Agriculture Museum - 1955
Living farm 44778

Gropius House, 68 Baker Bridge Rd, Lincoln, MA 01773 - T: (781) 259-8098, (617) 227-3956, Fax: (781) 259-9722, E-mail: gropiushouse@spnea.org, Internet: www.sprea.org. Dir.: Jane Nylander
Historical Museum - 1985
Modern architecture, designed by combining Bauhaus principles with New England building materials 44779

The Thoreau Institute at Walden Woods, 44 Baker Farm, Lincoln, MA 01773 - T: (781) 259-4730, Fax: (781) 259-4730, E-mail: jeff.cramer@walden.org, Internet: www.walden.org. Dir.: Kathi Anderson, Cur.: Jeffrey S. Cramer
Library with Exhibitions - 1991
Regional history, American literature - library 44780

Lincoln NE

Elder Art Gallery, Rogers Center for Fine Arts, c/o Nebraska Wesleyan University, 50th St and Huntington Av, Lincoln, NE 68504 - T: (402) 466-2371, 465-2230, Fax: (402) 465-2179, E-mail: dp@nebrwesleyan.edu. Dir.: Dr. Donald Paoletta
University Museum / Historical Museum / Fine Arts Museum - 1966
Campus coll, prints, paintings and sculpture 44781

Gallery of the Department of Art and Art History, University of Nebraska, 207 Nelle Cochrane Woods Hall, Lincoln, NE 68588-0114 - T: (402) 472-2631, 472-5541, Fax: (402) 472-9746, Internet: www.unl.edu. Dir.: Joseph M. Ruffo
Fine Arts Museum - 1985
Student works 44782

Great Plains Art Collection in the Christlieb Gallery, c/o University of Nebraska-Lincoln, 1155 Q St, Hewit Pl, Lincoln, NE 68588-0250 - T: (402) 472-6220, Fax: (402) 472-2960, E-mail: sgustafson2@unl.edu, Internet: www.unl.edu/plains/gallery. Dir.: James Stubbendieck, Cur.: Sharon Gustafson
Fine Arts Museum / University Museum - 1980 44783

The Lentz Center for Asian Culture, c/o University of Nebraska-Lincoln, 1155 Q St, Lincoln, NE 68588-0252 - T: (402) 472-5841, Fax: (402) 472-8899, E-mail: bbanks@unl.edu. Dir./Cur.: Barbara Chapman Banks
Fine Arts Museum - 1986
Asian art collection, Tibetan ritual and secular art 44784

Lincoln Children's Museum, 1420 P St, Lincoln, NE 68508 - T: (402) 477-0128, Fax: (402) 477-2004, E-mail: lbullcm@navix.net, Internet: www.lincolnchildrensmuseum.org. Dir.: Marilyn R. Gorham
Special Museum - 1989 44785

Museum of American Historical Society of Germans from Russia, 631 D St, Lincoln, NE 68502-1199 - T: (402) 474-3363, Fax: (402) 474-7229, E-mail: ahsgr@aol.com, Internet: www.ahsgr.org
Historical Museum - 1968 44786

Museum of Nebraska History, 131 Centennial Mall N, Lincoln, NE 68508 - T: (402) 471-4754, Fax: (402) 471-3144, E-mail: ednshs@inetnebr.com, Internet: www.nebraskahistory.org. Dir.:

Lawrence J. Sommer, Assoc. Dir.: Brent Carmack, Cur.: John R. Bozell (Anthropology), John Schleicher, Deborah Arenz
Historical Museum - 1878 44787

National Museum of Roller Skating, 4730 South St, Lincoln, NE 68506 - T: (402) 483-7551 ext 16, Fax: (402) 483-1465, E-mail: postmaster@rollerskatingmuseum.com, Internet: www.rollerskatingmuseum.com. Dir.: Deborah L. Wallis
Special Museum - 1980 44788

Nebraska Conference United Methodist Historical Center, 5000 Saint Paul Av, Lincoln, NE 68504-2796 - T: (402) 464-5994, Fax: (402) 464-6203, E-mail: nebrumchc@yahoo.comom, Internet: www.umcneb.org. Dir./Cur.: Maureen Vetter
Religious Arts Museum - 1968 44789

Noyes Art Gallery, 119 S Ninth St, Lincoln, NE 68508 - T: (402) 475-1061, E-mail: rnoyes1348@aol.com, Internet: www.noyesart.com. Dir.: Julia Noyes
Decorative Arts Museum / Fine Arts Museum - 1994 44790

Sheldon Memorial Art Gallery and Sculpture Garden, c/o University of Nebraska-Lincoln, 12th and R Sts, Lincoln, NE 68588-0300 - T: (402) 472-2461, Fax: (402) 472-4258, E-mail: pjacobs@unl.edu, Internet: www.sheldon.unl.edu/. Dir.: Janice Driesbach, Cur.: Daniel Siedell, Karen Janovy
Fine Arts Museum / University Museum - 1963 44791

Thomas P. Kennard House, 1627 H St, Lincoln, NE 68501 - T: (402) 471-4764, Fax: (402) 471-4764, E-mail: museum02@nebraskahistory.org, Internet: www.nebraskahistory.org. C.E.O./Dir.: Larry Sommers
Historical Museum - 1968 44792

University of Nebraska State Museum, 307 Morrill Hall, 14 and U Sts, Lincoln, NE 68588-0338 - T: (402) 472-3779, Fax: (402) 472-8899, E-mail: jestes1@unl.edu, Internet: www.museum.unl.edu. Dir.: Dr. James R. Estes, Asst. Dir.: Dr. Judy Diamond, Cur.: Dr. Michael Voorhies (Parasitology, Vertebrate Paleontology), Dr. Thomas P. Myers (Anthropology), Dr. Margaret R. Bolick (Botany), Dr. Brett C. Ratcliffe (Entomology), Dr. Samuel B. Treves (Geology), Roger K. Pabian, Dr. David K. Watkins (Invertebrate Paleontology), Dr. Robert M. Hunt (Vertebrate Paleontology), Dr. Patricia W. Freeman (Zoology)
University Museum / Natural History Museum - 1871
planetarium, library 44793

University Place Art Center, 2601 N 48th St, Lincoln, NE 68504 - T: (402) 466-8692, Fax: (402) 466-3786, E-mail: info@universityplaceart.com, Internet: www.universityplaceart.com. C.E.O.: James Gustafson
Fine Arts Museum - 1978
Antique and collectible dolls, American prints, paperweights, quilts, buttons, paintings 44794

Lincoln NM

Historic Lincoln, Hwy 380, Lincoln, NM 88338, mail addr: POB 40, Ruidoso Downs, NM 88346 - T: (505) 653-4025, Fax: (505) 653-4627, E-mail: moth@zianet.com, Internet: www.zianet.com/museum. Dir.: Bruce B. Eldredge
Local Museum - 1968
Local Hispanic and Native American culture, county war and Bill the Kid coll, medical instruments, Buffalo Soldiers military 44795

Old Lincoln County Courthouse Museum, Lincoln State Monument, Hwy 380, Lincoln, NM 88338 - T: (505) 653-4372, Fax: (505) 653-4372
Historical Museum - 1937 44796

Lincoln RI

Blackstone Valley Historical Society Museum, 1873 Old Louisquisett Pike, Lincoln, RI 02865 - T: (401) 725-2847
Local Museum - 1958 44797

Flanagan Valley Campus Art Gallery, Louisquisset Pike, Lincoln, RI 02865-4585 - T: (401) 333-7154, Fax: (401) 825-2265, Internet: www.ccri.cc.ri.us. Dir.: Tom Morrissey
Fine Arts Museum - 1974 44798

Lincoln Park MI

Lincoln Park Historical Museum, 1335 Southfield Rd, Lincoln Park, MI 48146 - T: (313) 386-3137, E-mail: citylp@aol.com, Internet: www.downriverarts.com. Cur.: Muriel Lobb
Local Museum - 1972
Local and regional history - library 44799

Lincolnton GA

Elijah Clark Memorial Museum, 2959 McCormick Hwy, Lincolnton, GA 30817 - T: (706) 359-3458, Fax: (706) 359-5856, E-mail: eclark@nu-z.net, Internet: www.gastateparks.com. Cur.: Dorothy Shields
Special Museum - 1961
Replica of the house of Elijah Clark 44800

Lincroft NJ

Monmouth Museum, College Campus, Newman Springs Rd, Lincroft, NJ 07738 - T: (732) 747-2266, Fax: (732) 747-8592, E-mail: monmuseum@netlabs.net, Internet: www.monmouthmuseum.org. Dir.: Dorothy V. Morehouse, Cur.: Marian Kanaga (Education)
Local Museum - 1963
Culture, art, scientific phenomena 44801

Lind WA

Adams County Historical Society Museum, First St, Lind, WA 99341 - T: (509) 677-3393, E-mail: galeirma@ritzcom.net. Dir.: Irma E. Gfeller
Local Museum - 1963 44802

Linden IN

Railway Heritage Network, 207 N Main St, Linden, IN 47955-0061 - T: (765) 339-4896, Fax: (765) 339-4896, E-mail: eutsler@tctc.com. Dir.: David White, Cur.: Therese Eutsler
Science&Tech Museum - 1986
Railroad 44803

Lindenhurst NY

Old Village Hall Museum, 215 S Wellwood Av, Lindenhurst, NY 11757-0296 - T: (516) 957-4385. Dir.: Evelyn M. Ellis, Asst. Dir.: Mary Kollar
Historical Museum - 1958 44804

Lindsay OK

Murray-Lindsay Mansion, POB 282, Lindsay, OK 73052 - T: (405) 756-2121
Local Museum - 1971 44805

Lindsborg KS

Birger Sandzén Memorial Gallery, 401 N First St, Lindsborg, KS 67456-0348 - T: (785) 227-2220, Fax: (785) 227-4170, E-mail: fineart@sandzen.org, Internet: www.sandzen.org. Dir.: Larry L. Griffis
Fine Arts Museum - 1957
Fine art 44806

McPherson County Old Mill Museum, 120 Mill St, Lindsborg, KS 67456 - T: (785) 227-3595, Fax: (785) 227-2810, E-mail: oldmillmuseum@hotmail.com, Internet: www.lindsborg.org/oldmill. Dir.: Lorna Batterson
Historical Museum / Science&Tech Museum - 1959
Local history, mill, genealogy 44807

Mingenback Art Center Gallery, c/o Bethany College, 421 N First St, Lindsborg, KS 67456 - T: (785) 227-3311 ext 8145, Fax: (785) 227-2004, E-mail: tubbsj@bethany.bethanylb.edu, Internet: www.bethanyld.edu/academics. Dir.: Caroline Kahler
Public Gallery
Oil paintings, watercolors, prints, etchings, lithographs, wood engravings, ceramics and sculpture 44808

Linthicum MD

Historical Electronics Museum, 1745 W Nursery Rd, Linthicum, MD 21090 - T: (410) 765-3803, Fax: (410) 765-0240, E-mail: radarmus@erols.com, Internet: www.erols.com/radarmus. Dir.: Katherine Duer Marks
Science&Tech Museum - 1980
Technology 44809

Lisbon OH

Lisbon Historical Society Museum, 117-119 E Washington St, Lisbon, OH 44432 - T: (330) 424-9000, Fax: (330) 424-1861, E-mail: lisbonhs@sky-access.com. Pres.: David Privette, Cur.: Gene Krotky
Local Museum - 1938 44810

Lisle IL

Jurica Nature Museum, Benedictine University, 5700 College Rd, Lisle, IL 60532 - T: (630) 829-6545, Fax: (630) 829-6551, E-mail: tsuchy@ben.edu, Internet: alt.ben.edu/resources/J-Museum/. Cur.: Theodore D. Suchy
University Museum / Natural History Museum - 1970
Natural history 44811

Lisle Station Park, 915-925 Burlington Av, Lisle, IL 60532 - T: (630) 968-0499, Fax: (630) 968-0499, E-mail: ekeating@lisleparkdistrict.org, Internet: www.lisleparkdistrict.org. Dir.: Roy Cripe
Historical Museum / Historic Site / Open Air Museum - 1978 44812

Litchfield CT

Litchfield Historical Society Museum, 7 South St, Litchfield, CT 06759 - T: (860) 567-4501, Fax: (860) 567-3565, E-mail: lhsoc@snet.net, Internet: www.litchfieldhistoricalsociety.org. Dir.: Catherine Keene Fields, Cur.: Judith Livingston
Historical Museum - 1856 44813

White Memorial Conservation Center, 80 Whitehall Rd, Litchfield, CT 06759-0368 - T: (860) 567-0857, E-mail: info@whitememorialcc.org, Internet: www.whitememorialcc.org. Dir.: Keith R. Cudworth
Natural History Museum - 1964 44814

Litchfield MN

Meeker County Museum and G.A.R. Hall, 308 N Marshall, Litchfield, MN 55355 - T: (320) 693-8911. Dir.: Dona Brown
Local Museum - 1961
Regional history 44815

Lithopolis OH

Wagnalls Memorial, 150 E Columbus St, Lithopolis, OH 43136 - T: (614) 833-4767 ext 104, Fax: (614) 837-0781, E-mail: jneff@wagnalls.org, Internet: www.wagnalls.org
Special Museum - 1924
Paintings, poems, Mabel Wagnalls Jones publishing 44816

Little Compton RI

Little Compton Historical Society Museum, 548 West Main Rd, Little Compton, RI 02837 - T: (401) 635-4035, Fax: (401) 635-4035, E-mail: lchistory@yahoo.com, Internet: www.littlecompton.org. Dir.: Carlton C. Brownell
Local Museum - 1937
Antique farming, "Peggotty" artists studio, Portuguese exhibit 44817

Little Falls MN

Charles A. Weyerhaeuser Memorial Museum, 2151 S Lindbergh Dr, Little Falls, MN 56345-0239 - T: (612) 632-4007, Fax: (320) 632-8409, E-mail: mchs@littlefalls.net. Dir.: Jan Warner
Local Museum - 1936
Local history - library 44818

Little Falls NJ

Yogi Berra Museum, c/o Montclair State University, 8 Quarry Rd, Little Falls, NJ 07424 - T: (973) 655-2378, Fax: (973) 655-6894, Internet: www.yogiberramuseum.org. Dir.: Dave Kaplan
Special Museum / University Museum - 1998
Yankees and baseball hist 44819

Little Falls NY

Herkimer Home, 200 State Rte 169, Little Falls, NY 13365 - T: (315) 823-0398, Fax: (315) 823-0587, Internet: www.nysparks.com. Head: Thomas J. Kernan
Historical Museum - 1913 44820

Little Falls Historical Museum, 319 S Ann St, Little Falls, NY 13365 - T: (315) 823-0643, Internet: www.littlefallsny.com/museum/museum.htm. Pres.: Katharine Lyon
Historical Museum - 1962
Local memorabilia, genealogy - library 44821

Little Rock AR

The Arkansas Arts Center, MacArthur Park, 9th and Commerce Sts, Little Rock, AR 72202 - T: (501) 372-4000, Fax: (501) 375-8053, E-mail: center@arkarts.org, Internet: www.arkarts.com. Dir.: Townsend Wolfe, Cur.: Alan B. Dubois (Decorative Arts), Brian Young (Arts)
Fine Arts Museum - 1937
Art, decorative art - children's theater 44822

Arkansas Museum of Science and History - Museum of Discovery, 500 President Clinton Av, Ste 500, Little Rock, AR 72201 - T: (501) 396-7050 ext 200, Fax: (501) 396-7054, E-mail: mod@Aristotle.net, Internet: www.amod.org. Dir.: Bill Bradshaw, Dep. Dir.: Carol Couser (Technology), Diane LaFollette (Programs, Health Education), Kara Rago (Development), Lance Nolley (Exhibits, Facilities), Marci Bynum (Collections, Historical Research)
Historical Museum / Natural History Museum - 1927
History, science 44823

Historic Museum of Arkansas, 200 E Third St, Little Rock, AR 72201 - T: (501) 324-9351, Fax: (501) 324-9345. Dir.: William B. Worthen jr., Cur.: Swannee Bennett
Historical Museum 44824

The Old State House Museum, 300 W Markham St, Little Rock, AR 72201 - T: (501) 324-9685, Fax: (501) 324-9688, E-mail: info@oldstatehouse.com, Internet: www.oldstatehouse.com. Dir.: Bill Gatewood
Historical Museum - 1952
History, built 1833-1842, first state capitol (1836-1911) 44825

University of Arkansas at Little Rock Art Galleries, c/o Dept. of Art, 2801 S University Av, Little Rock, AR 72204-1099 - T: (501) 569-8977, Fax: (501) 569-8775, E-mail: becusham@uair.edu, Internet: www.ualr.edu/artdept. Dir.: Brad Cushman, Cur.: Shannon Dillard Mitchell
Fine Arts Museum / University Museum - 1972 44826

Littleton CO

Colorado Gallery of the Arts, Araphoe Community College, 2500 W College Dr, Littleton, CO 80160 - T: (303) 797-5649, Fax: (303) 797-5935, Internet: www.arapahoe.com
Fine Arts Museum / University Museum - 1979
Art gallery 44827

Littleton Historical Museum, 6028 S Gallup, Littleton, CO 80120 - T: (303) 795-3950, Fax: (303) 730-9818, E-mail: curator@mail.littleton.org, Internet: www.littletongov.org. Dir.: Mary Allman, Cur.: Bill Hastings, Lorena Donohue
Local Museum - 1969
Local history, farming 44828

Livermore IA

Humboldt County Old Settler's Museum, Old Settlers Park, Hwy 222, Livermore, IA 50558 - T: (515) 379-1848, 379-1317, Fax: (515) 379-1472. Pres.: Floyd Raney
Historical Museum / Museum of Classical Antiquities - 1885
Antiques, settlement 44829

Liverpool NY

Sainte Marie among the Iroquois, Onondaga Lake Pkwy, Liverpool, NY 13088 - T: (315) 453-6767, Fax: (315) 453-6762, E-mail: stemarie@nysnet.net, Internet: www.ongov.net/parks. Cur.: Valerie Bell
Open Air Museum - 1933 44830

Salt Museum, Onondaga Lake Park, Liverpool, NY 13088 - T: (315) 453-6767, Fax: (315) 453-6762, E-mail: stemarie@nysnet.net, Internet: www.ongov.net/parks. Dir.: Elaine Wisowaty
Special Museum - 1934 44831

Livingston MT

Livingston Depot Center, 200 W Park, Livingston, MT 59047 - T: (406) 222-2300, Fax: (406) 222-2401. Pres.: John Sullivan, Dir.: Diana L. Seider
Local Museum - 1985
Northern Pacific railroad stn 44832

Yellowstone Gateway Museum of Park County, 118 W Chinook, Livingston, MT 59047 - T: (406) 222-4184, Fax: (406) 222-4184, E-mail: museum@yci.net, Internet: www.avicom.net/parkmuseum/. Dir.: Brian Sparks
Local Museum - 1976
Local and regional history and archaeology, railroads 44833

Livingston TX

Alabama-Coushatta Indian Museum, U.S. Hwy 190, between Livingston and Woodville, Livingston, TX 77351 - T: (409) 563-4391, Fax: (409) 563-4397
Ethnology Museum - 1965
Native American hist 44834

Polk County Memorial Museum, 514 W Mill St, Livingston, TX 77351 - T: (409) 327-8192, Fax: (936) 327-8192, E-mail: museum@livingston.net. C.E.O.: Ray Hill, Cur.: Wanda L. Bobinger
Local Museum - 1963
Local hist 44835

Livingston Manor NY

Catskill Fly Fishing Center and Museum, 1031 Old Rte 17, Livingston Manor, NY 12758 - T: (845) 439-4810, Fax: (845) 439-3387, E-mail: flyfish@catskill.net, Internet: www.cffcm.org. Dir.: Paul N. Dahlie
Special Museum - 1981 44836

Loachapoka AL

Lee County Historical Society Museum, 6500 Stage Rd, Loachapoka, AL 36865 - T: (334) 887-3007. Pres.: Carl Summers
Local Museum - 1968 44837

Lock Haven PA

Heisey Museum, 362 E Water St, Lock Haven, PA 17745 - T: (570) 748-7254, Fax: (570) 748-1590, E-mail: heisey@cub.kcnet.org, Internet: www.kcnet.org/~heisey/. Exec. Dir.: Anne M. McCloskey
Local Museum / Historical Museum - 1921 44838

Piper Aviation Museum, 1 Piper Way, Lock Haven, PA 17745 - T: (570) 748-8283, Fax: (570) 893-8357, E-mail: piper@cub.kcnet.org, Internet: www.kcnet.org/~piper. Cur.: Dr. Ira Masemore
Science&Tech Museum - 1986
Piper aircraft hist 44839

Lockport IL

Illinois and Michigan Canal Museum, 803 S State St, Lockport, IL 60441 - T: (815) 838-5080. Dir.: Rose Bucciferro
Local Museum - 1964
Local history, pioneer settlement 44840

Lockport Gallery, Illinois State Museum, 201 W 10th St, Lockport, IL 60441 - T: (815) 838-7400, Fax: (815) 838-7448, E-mail: jzimmer@museum.state.il.us, Internet: www.museum.state.il.us/ismsites/lockport/. Dir.: Jim L. Zimmer, Asst. Cur.: Geoffrey Bates
Fine Arts Museum / Public Gallery - 1987
Art 44841

Lockport NY

Niagara County Historical Center, 215 Niagara St, Lockport, NY 14094-2605 - T: (716) 434-7433, Fax: (716) 434-3309, Internet: www.niagaracounty.org. Dir.: Melissa L. Dunlap
Local Museum / Historical Museum - 1947
Local history, military, pioneer, Tuscarora trades, Erie Cunnl 44842

Lodi CA

San Joaquin County Historical Museum, 11793 N Micke Grove Rd, Lodi, CA 95241-0030 - T: (209) 331-2055, Fax: (209) 331-2057, E-mail: info@sanjoaquinhistory.org, Internet: www.sanjoaquinhistory.org. Dir.: Michael W. Bennett
Historical Museum / Agriculture Museum - 1966 44843

Logan KS

Dane G. Hansen Memorial Museum, 110 W Main St, Logan, KS 67646 - T: (785) 689-4846, Fax: (785) 689-4892, E-mail: dghansen@ruraltel.net, Internet: www.hansenmuseum.org. Dir.: Lee M. Favre
Fine Arts Museum / Special Museum - 1973
Art 44844

Logan UT

Nora Eccles Harrison Museum of Art, c/o Utah State University, 650 N 1100 E, Logan, UT 84322 - T: (435) 797-1414, Fax: (435) 797-3423, E-mail: Lpier@cc.usu.edu, Internet: www.hass.usu.edu/%7Emuseum. Dir.: Jim Edwards
Fine Arts Museum / University Museum - 1982
Art 44845

Logansport IN

Cass County Historical Society Museum, 1004 E Market St, Logansport, IN 46947 - T: (219) 753-3866, Fax: (219) 722-9267. Cur.: Bruce F. Stuart
Local Museum - 1907
Local history 44846

Loma MT

House of a Thousand Dolls, 106 First St, Loma, MT 59460 - T: (406) 739-4338. C.E.O.: Marion Britton
Decorative Arts Museum - 1979 44847

Lombard IL

Lombard Historical Museum, 23 W Maple, Lombard, IL 60148 - T: (630) 629-1885, Fax: (630) 629-9927, Internet: www.tccafe.com/lhm/lhm.html. Dir.: Joel Van Haaften
Local Museum - 1970
Local hist 44848

Sheldon Peck Museum, 355 E Parkside, Lombard, IL 60148 - T: (630) 629-1885, Fax: (630) 629-9927. Dir.: Joel Van Haaften
Fine Arts Museum - 1999
Reproduction artwork of Sheldon Peck 44849

Lompoc CA

Lompoc Museum, 200 S H St, Lompoc, CA 93436 - T: (805) 736-3888, Fax: (805) 736-2840. Dir.: Dr. Lisa Renken (Anthropology)
Ethnology Museum - 1969 44850

Lompoc Valley Historical Society Museum, 207 N L St, Lompoc, CA 93438 - T: (805) 735-4626. C.E.O.: Dennis Headrick
Historical Museum - 1964
Furnishings, clothing 44851

La Purisima Mission, 2295 Purisima Rd, Lompoc, CA 93436 - T: (805) 733-3713, Fax: (805) 733-2497, E-mail: lapurmis@lapurisima.sbceo.k12.ca.us, Internet: www.lapurismamission.org. Head: Michael Curry
Religious Arts Museum - 1935 44852

London KY

Mountain Life Museum, 998 Levi Jackson Mill Rd, London, KY 40744 - T: (606) 878-8000, Fax: (606) 864-3825, Internet: www.kystateparks.com/agencies/parks/levijack.htm. Dir.: William Meadors
Historical Museum / Ethnology Museum - 1929
History, ethnography 44853

Londonderry NH

The Children's Metamorphosis, 217 Rockingham Rd, Londonderry, NH 03053 - T: (603) 425-2560, Internet: www.discoverthemet.com. Dir.: Betsy Anderson
Special Museum - 1991
Children's museum 44854

Lone Jack MO

Civil War Museum of Lone Jack, Jackson County, 301 S Bynum Rd, Lone Jack, MO 64070 - T: (816) 697-8833. Pres.: Charlotte Remington, Chm.: Loeda Helmig
Military Museum - 1964 44855

Nance Museum, POB 292, Lone Jack, MO 64070 - T: (816) 697-2526, E-mail: pjnmuseum@worldnet.att.net. Dir.: Paul J. Nance
Ethnology Museum - 1981
Traditional Saudi Arabia and Islam outfitted Bedouin tent, jewelry, costume, ethnographic, folk culture - library 44856

Long Beach CA

American Museum of Straw Art, 2324 Snowden Av, Long Beach, CA 90815 - T: (562) 431-3540, Fax: (562) 598-0457, E-mail: curator@strawartmuseum.org, Internet: www.strawartmuseum.org. Cur.: Morgyn Owens-Celli
Decorative Arts Museum / Folklore Museum - 1989
Decorative and folk art 44857

California State University-Long Beach Art Museum, 1250 Bellflower Blvd, Long Beach, CA 90840-1901 - T: (562) 985-5761, Fax: (562) 985-7602, E-mail: uam@csulb.edu, Internet: www.csulb.edu/~uam. Dir.: Constance W. Glenn, Assoc. Dir.: Ilee Kaplan, Cur.: Mary-Kay Lombino, Marina Freeman, Liz Harvey
Fine Arts Museum / University Museum - 1949 44858

Gatov Gallery, 3801 E Willow St, Long Beach, CA 90815 - T: (562) 426-7601, Fax: (562) 424-3915. Dir.: Michael Witenstein
Fine Arts Museum - 1960 44859

Long Beach Museum of Art, 2300 E Ocean Blvd, Long Beach, CA 90803 - T: (562) 439-2119, Fax: (562) 439-3587, Internet: www.lbma.com. Dir.: Harold B. Nelson
Fine Arts Museum - 1950
Southern Californian and European art since 1850, decorative arts, sculpture, ceramics 44860

Museum of Latin American Art, 628 Alamitos Av, Long Beach, CA 90802 - T: (562) 437-1689, Fax: (562) 437-7043, Internet: www.molaa.com. Dir.: Gregorio Luke
Fine Arts Museum - 1996 44861

Queen Mary Museum, 1126 Queens Hwy, Long Beach, CA 90802-6390 - T: (562) 435-3511, Fax: (562) 432-7674, 437-4531, E-mail: queenmry@gte.net, Internet: www.queenmary.com. Pres.: Joseph F. Prevratil, Dir.: Ronald Smith
Special Museum - 1971
Maritime Museum located aboard the Queen Mary, retired British luxury liner 44862

Rancho Los Alamitos, 6400 Bixby Hill Rd, Long Beach, CA 90815 - T: (562) 431-3541, Fax: (562) 430-9694. Dir.: Pamela Seager
Historical Museum - 1970
Decorative arts, furniture, tools, farm implements, Indian artifacts 44863

Rancho Los Cerritos, 4600 Virginia Rd, Long Beach, CA 90807 - T: (562) 570-1755, Fax: (562) 570-1893, E-mail: elcalom@ci.long-beach.ca.us, Internet: www.ci.long-beach.ca.us/park/ranchlc.htm. Dir.: Ellen Calomiris, Cur.: Stephen C. Iverson
Historical Museum - 1955
Furniture, tools, costumes, quilts, coverlets, archaeology 44864

Long Beach WA

World Kite Museum and Hall of Fame, 3rd St NW, Long Beach, WA 98631 - T: (360) 642-4020, Fax: (360) 642-4020, E-mail: info@worldkitemuseum.com, Internet: www.worldkitemuseum.com. Dir.: Kay Buesing
Special Museum - 1988
Japanese kites, other kites used in science, sport and religion 44865

Long Branch NJ

Long Branch Historical Museum, 1260 Ocean Av, Long Branch, NJ 07740 - T: (732) 222-9879. C.E.O. & Pres.: Florence Dinkelspiel
Local Museum - 1953
1879 Saint James Episcopal Chapel, Church of the Presidents, civil war 44866

Long Island City NY

Laguardia and Wagner Archives, 31-10 Thomson Av, Long Island City, NY 11101 - T: (718) 482-5065, Fax: (718) 482-5069, E-mail: richardli@lagcc.cuny.edu, Internet: www.laguardiawagnerarchive.lagcc.cuny.edu. Dir.: Richard K. Lieberman
Local Museum - 1981
New York City housing authority, Queens local hist 44867

Museum for African Art (interim), 36-01 43rd Av, Long Island City, NY 11101 - T: (718) 784-7700, Fax: (718) 784-7718, E-mail: museum@africanart.org, Internet: www.africanart.org. Dir.: Kenita Lloyd, Dep. Dir.: Frank Herreman (Exhibitions, Publications), Tommy Williams (Development), Heidi Holder (Education), Carlyn Mueller (PR, Marketing), Cur.: Laurie Farrell, Alisa McCusker
Ethnology Museum / Fine Arts Museum - 1982 44868

Museum of Modern Art in Queens, 33rd St at Queens Blvd, Long Island City, NY 11101, mail addr: 11 W 53rd St, New York, NY 10019 - T: (212) 708-9400, Fax: (212) 708-9889, E-mail: info@moma.org, Internet: www.moma.org. Dir.: Glenn D. Lowry, Cur.: Peter Galassi (Photography), Deborah Wye (Prints, Illustrated Books), N.N. (Painting, Sculpture), John Elderfield, Terence Riley (Architecture, Design), Mary Lea Bandy (Film, Video), Gary Garrels (Drawings)
Fine Arts Museum - 1929 44869

P.S. 1 Contemporary Art Center, Museum of Modern Art, 22-25 Jackson Av, Long Island City, NY 11101 - T: (718) 784-2084, Fax: (718) 482-9454, E-mail: mail@ps1.org, Internet: www.ps1.org. Dir.: Glenn D. Lowry
Fine Arts Museum - 1971
Contemporary art 44870

Scalamandre Archives, 37-24 24th St, Long Island City, NY 11101 - T: (718) 361-8500, Fax: (718) 361-8311, Internet: www.scalamandre.com
Science&Tech Museum - 1947
Textile coll, wallcoverings and passementerie, carpeting, Scalamandre family and firm 44871

Sculpture Center, 44-19 Purves St, Long Island City, NY 11101 - T: (718) 361-1750, Fax: (718) 786-9336, E-mail: info@sculpture-center.org, Internet: www.sculpture-center.org. Dir.: Mary Ceruti
Fine Arts Museum 44872

Socrates Sculpture Park, Broadway and Vernon Blvds, Long Island City, NY 11106 - T: (718) 956-1819, Fax: (718) 626-1533, Internet: socratess-culpturepark.org. Dir.: Alyson Baker
Fine Arts Museum - 1985
Sculpture garden, contemporary art 44873

Long Lake MN

Western Hennepin County Pioneers Museum, 1953 W Wayzata Blvd, Long Lake, MN 55356 - T: (952) 473-6557, Fax: (952) 473-6557. Cur.: Tammy Allison
Local Museum - 1907
Pioneer museum - archives 44874

Longboat Key FL

Longboat Key Center for the Arts, 6860 Longboat Dr S, Longboat Key, FL 34228 - T: (941) 383-2345, Fax: (941) 383-7915, E-mail: lbkarts@att.net, Internet: www.longboatkeyartscenter.org. Dir.: Beth Cunningham, Asst. Dir.: Carolyn Manning
Fine Arts Museum / Decorative Arts Museum - 1952 44875

Longmeadow MA

Richard Salter Storrs House, 697 Longmeadow St, Longmeadow, MA 01106 - T: (413) 567-3600, E-mail: LCAsearch@aol.com, Internet: www.longmeadow.org. C.E.O.: Phillip Clark, Cur.: Linda C. Abrams
Local Museum - 1899
Local history 44876

Longmont CO

Longmont Museum, 400 Quail Rd, Longmont, CO 80501 - T: (303) 651-8374, Fax: (303) 651-8590, E-mail: martha.clevenger@ci.longmont.co.us, Internet: www.ci.longmont.co.us/museum.htm. Dir.: Martha R. Clevenger, Cur.: Svein Edland, Jill Overlie, Cathey Dunn, Erik Mason
Local Museum - 1940/2002
Regional history 44877

Longview TX

Gregg County Historical Museum, 214 N Fredonia St, Longview, TX 75601 - T: (903) 753-5840, Fax: (903) 753-5854, E-mail: gchm_director@prodigy.net, Internet: www.gregghistorical.org. Exec. Dir.: Nancy McWhorter
Local Museum - 1983
Local hist 44878

Longview Museum of Fine Art, 215 E Tyler St, Longview, TX 75602 - T: (903) 753-8103, Fax: (903) 753-8217, E-mail: director@lmfa.org, Internet: www.lnfa.org. Dir.: Renee Hawkins
Fine Arts Museum - 1970
Art 44879

Longview WA

Lower Columbia College Fine Arts Gallery, 1600 Maple St, Longview, WA 98632 - T: (360) 577-2300, Fax: (360) 577-6620, E-mail: twoods@lcc.ctc.edu, Internet: www.lcc.ctc.edu/events/art-gallery. Dir.: Trudy Woods
Fine Arts Museum / University Museum - 1978
Art 44880

Lookout Mountain TN

Cravens House, Point Park Visitor Center, Lookout Mountain, TN 37350 - T: (423) 821-7786, Fax: (423) 821-5129. C.E.O.: Sam Weddle
Local Museum
Historic house 44881

Lopez Island WA

Lopez Island Historical Museum, 28 Washburn Pl, Lopez Village, Lopez Island, WA 98261 - T: (360) 468-3447, 468-2049, E-mail: lopezmuseum@rockisland.com. Cur.: Nancy McCoy
Historical Museum - 1966
Local hist 44882

Lorain OH

Black River Historical Society of Lorain Museum, 309 W 5th St, Lorain, OH 44052-1611 - T: (440) 245-2563, Fax: (440) 245-3591, E-mail: brhsmoore@centurytel.net, Internet: www.loraincityhistory.org
Local Museum - 1981
Businesses and industries of Lorain 44883

Loretto PA

Southern Alleghenies Museum of Art, Saint Francis University Mall, Loretto, PA 15940 - T: (814) 472-3920, Fax: (814) 472-4131, E-mail: sama@sfcpa.edu, Internet: SAMA-SFC.org. Dir.: Dr. Michael Tomot
Fine Arts Museum - 1975
Visual art 44884

Los Alamos NM

Art Center at Fuller Lodge, 2132 Central Av, Los Alamos, NM 87544 - T: (505) 662-9331, E-mail: artful@losalamos.com, Internet: artful.losalamos.com. Dir.: Gloria Gilmore-House, Asst. Dir.: Craig Carmer
Fine Arts Museum - 1977 44885

Bandelier Site, State Rte 4, Los Alamos, NM 87544, mail addr: HCR 1, Box 1, Ste 15, Los Alamos, NM 87544-9701 - T: (505) 672-3861 ext 517, Fax: (505) 672-9607, E-mail: band-visitor-center@nps.gov, Internet: www.nps.gov/band/
Archaeological Museum - 1916
Archaeology, ethnology of Pueblo Indians of the Pajarito Plateau 44886

Bradbury Science Museum, 15 and Central, Los Alamos, NM 87544 - T: (505) 665-3339, Fax: (505) 665-6932, E-mail: museum@lanl.gov., Internet: bsm.lanl.gov. Dir.: John S. Rhoades
Natural History Museum - 1963 44887

Los Alamos County Historical Museum, Fuller Lodge Cultural Center, 1921 Juniper St, Los Alamos, NM 87544 - T: (505) 662-6272, Fax: (505) 662-6312, E-mail: historicalsociety@losalamos.com, Internet: www.losalamos.com/historicalsociety. Dir.: Hedy Dunn, Pres.: Fred Roensch, Cur.: Marianne Mortenson
Historical Museum - 1968
Manhattan Project history 44888

Los Altos CA

Gallery 9, 143 Main St, Los Altos, CA 94022 - T: (415) 941-7969
Public Gallery - 1970 44889

Los Angeles CA

The American Film Institute, 2021 N Western Av, Los Angeles, CA 90027 - T: (323) 856-7600, Fax: (323) 467-4578, Internet: www.afionline.org. Dir.: Jean Firstenberg, James Hindman
Fine Arts Museum - 1967
Cinematography, film/ TV script coll 44890

Autry Museum of Western Heritage, 4700 Western Heritage Way, Los Angeles, CA 90027-1462 - T: (323) 667-2000, Fax: (323) 660-5721, E-mail: autry@autry-museum.org, Internet: www.autry-museum.org. Dir.: John L. Gray, Cur.: James H. Nottage, Michael Duchemin (History), Asst. Cur.: Michael Fox, Cons.: Linda Strauss
Historical Museum - 1984 44891

Barnsdall Junior Arts Center, 4814 Hollywood Blvd, Los Angeles, CA 90027 - T: (213) 485-4474, Fax: (213) 485-7456, E-mail: jacbac@earthlink.net, Internet: www.culturela.org/communityarts/jac. Dir.: Istiharoh Glasgow
Fine Arts Museum - 1966 44892

California African-American Museum, 600 State Dr, Exposition Park, Los Angeles, CA 90037 - T: (213) 744-7432, Fax: (213) 744-2050, Internet: www.caam.ca.gov. Dir.: Jai Henderson, Cur.: Redell Hearn (History), Mar Hollingworth (Education)
Fine Arts Museum / Historical Museum / Ethnology Museum - 1981
Culture of African-Americans, fine art, sculpture, prints, costume, decorative arts 44893

California Science Center, 700 State Dr, Los Angeles, CA 90037 - T: (213) 744-7400, Fax: (213) 744-2034, E-mail: 4info@cscmail.org, Internet: www.casciencectr.org. Dir.: Jeffrey N. Rudolph, Dep. Dir.: Dr. Diane Perlon (Exhibits), Dr. Dave Combs (Education), Tony Budrovich (Operations), Cur.: Dr. Chuck Kopczak (Ecology), Dr. Kenneth E. Phillips (Aerospace)
Science&Tech Museum - 1880 44894

The Carole and Barry Kaye Museum of Miniatures, 5900 Wilshire Blvd, Los Angeles, CA 90036 - T: (323) 937-6464, 937-7766, Fax: (323) 937-2126, E-mail: carolekaye@aol.com, Internet: www.museumofminiatures.com. C.E.O.: Carole Kaye
Decorative Arts Museum - 1994
Miniatures 44895

Children's Museum of Los Angeles, Hansen Dam Recreation Park, Los Angeles, CA 90012, mail addr: 205 S Broadway, Ste 608, Los Angeles, CA 90012 - T: (213) 687-8800, Fax: (213) 687-0319, E-mail: candace@childrensmuseumla.org, Internet: www.childrensmuseumla.org. Dir.: Candace Barrett
Special Museum - 1979 44896

County of Los Angeles Fire Museum, 1320 N Eastern Av, Los Angeles, CA 90063-3294 - T: (323) 881-2411, Fax: (323) 267-0668. Pres.: Paul Schneider
Historical Museum - 1974
Fire-fighting, historic equipment, helmets, badges 44897

Fine Arts Gallery, c/o California State University Los Angeles, 5151 State University Dr, Los Angeles, CA 90032 - T: (323) 343-4023, Fax: (323) 343-4045. Dir.: Lamont Westmorland
Fine Arts Museum / University Museum - 1954 44898

Fisher Gallery, c/o University of Southern California, 823 Exposition Blvd, Los Angeles, CA 90089-0292 - T: (213) 740-4561, Fax: (213) 740-7676, E-mail: jlavere@bcf.usc.edu, Internet: www.usc.edu/fishergallery. Dir.: Dr. Selma Holo, Assoc. Dir.: Kay Allen, Cur.: Jennifer Jaskowiak, Max Schulz
Fine Arts Museum / University Museum - 1939 44899

Fowler Museum of Cultural History, University of California, Los Angeles, CA 90095-1549 - T: (310) 825-4361, Fax: (310) 206-7007, E-mail: office@fmch.ucla.edu, Internet: www.fmch.ucla.edu. Dir.: Marla C. Berns, Asst. Dir.: David Blair, Patricia Anawalt (Center for Study Regional Dress), Asst.: Beatriz Escandor, Dept. Dir/ Chief Cur.: Mary Nooter Roberts, Roy Hamilton (Southeast Asia and Oceania), Wendy Teeter (Archaeology)
Fine Arts Museum / Decorative Arts Museum / Folklore Museum / Ethnology Museum / Archaeological Museum - 1963 44900

Frederick R. Weisman Art Foundation, 275 N Carolwood Dr, Los Angeles, CA 90077 - T: (310) 277-5321, Fax: (310) 277-5075, Internet: www.weismanfoundation.org. Dir.: Billie Milam Weisman
Fine Arts Museum - 1982
Contemporary art, painting, sculpture, works on paper 44901

Gallery 825, 825 N La Cienega Blvd, Los Angeles, CA 90069 - T: (310) 652-8272, Fax: (310) 652-9251, E-mail: gallery825@laaa.org, Internet: www.laaa.org. Dir.: Ashley Emenegger, Cur.: Sinéad Finnerty
Public Gallery / Fine Arts Museum - 1925 44902

George J. Doizaki Gallery, 244 S San Pedro St, Ste 505, Los Angeles, CA 90012-3895 - T: (213) 628-2725, Fax: (213) 617-8576. Dir.: Robert Hori
Public Gallery - 1980 44903

Grier-Musser Museum, 403 S Bonnie Brae St, Los Angeles, CA 90057 - T: (213) 413-1814, E-mail: griermusser@hotmail.com, Internet: griermusser.losangeles.museum. Dir.: Susana Tejada
Public Gallery - 1984
Postcards of old Los Angeles 44904

Grunwald Center for the Graphic Arts, University of California, Hammer Museum of Art and Cultural Center, 10899 Wilshire Blvd, Los Angeles, CA 90024-4201 - T: (310) 443-7076, Fax: (310) 443-7099, E-mail: cdixon@arts.ucla.edu, Internet: www.hammer.ucla.edu. Dir.: David Rodes, Cur.: Cynthia Burlingham, Asst. Cur.: Carolyn Peter, Cons.: Maureen McGee
Fine Arts Museum / University Museum - 1956
Graphic art 44905

Hammer Museum, University of California Los Angeles, 10899 Wilshire Blvd, Los Angeles, CA 90024 - T: (310) 443-7020, Fax: (310) 443-7099, E-mail: hammerinfo@arts.ucla.edu, Internet: www.hammer.ucla.edu. Dir.: Ann Philbin, Dep. Dir.: Gloria Gerace
Fine Arts Museum / University Museum - 1994
Sculpture garden, paintings, lithographs 44906

Hollywood Bowl Museum, 2301 N Highland Av, Los Angeles, CA 90068 - T: (323) 850-2058, Fax: (323) 850-2066, E-mail: museum@laphil.org, Internet: www.hollywoodbowl.org. Dir.: Dr. Carol Merrill-Mirsky
Music Museum / Performing Arts Museum - 1984
Music and performing arts 44907

Hollywood Guinness World of Records Museum, 6764 Hollywood Blvd, Los Angeles, CA 90028 - T: (323) 463-6433, Fax: (323) 462-3953. Pres.: Spoony Singh
Special Museum - 1991 44908

Hollywood Heritage Museum, 2100 Highland Av, Hollywood, Los Angeles, CA 90068 - T: (323) 874-2276, 874-4005, Fax: (323) 465-5993, Internet: www.hollywoodheritage.org. Dir.: Kay Tornborg, Cur.: Robert Nudelman
Local Museum / Performing Arts Museum - 1982
Film industry 44909

Hollywood Wax Museum, 6767 Hollywood Blvd, Los Angeles, CA 90028 - T: (323) 462-5991, Fax: (323) 462-3953. Cur.: Ken Horn
Decorative Arts Museum - 1965 44910

Holyland Exhibition, 2215 Lake View Av, Los Angeles, CA 90039 - T: (323) 664-3162. Dir.: Betty J. Shepard
Religious Arts Museum - 1924 44911

International Museum of Gay and Lesbian History, 1600 N La Brea Av, Ste 111, Los Angeles, CA 90028 - T: (323) 461-9937, Fax: (323) 461-9938, E-mail: gaymuseum@mac.com, Internet: www.gaymuseum.org. Dir.: Thomas Ryan
Historical Museum - 1996
Social history of gay and lesbian life, gay community 44912

J. Paul Getty Museum, 1200 Getty Center Dr, Ste 1000, Los Angeles, CA 90049-1687 - T: (310) 440-7300, Fax: (310) 440-7751, E-mail: info@getty.edu, Internet: www.getty.edu. Dir.: Deborah Gribbon, Cur.: Marion True (Antiquities), Gillian Wilson (Decorative Arts), Thomas Kren (Manuscripts), W. Naef (Photographs), Scott Schaefer (Paintings), Lee Hendrix (Drawings), Cons.: Brian Considine (Decorative Arts, Sculpture), Mark Leonard (Paintings), Jerry Podany (Antiquities), Marc Harnly (Paper)
Fine Arts Museum - 1953 44913

Japanese American National Museum, 369 E First St, Los Angeles, CA 90012 - T: (213) 625-0414, Fax: (213) 625-1770, Internet: www.janm.org. Dir.: Irene Hirano
Historical Museum / Fine Arts Museum - 1985
History, former 1925 Nishi Hongwanji Buddhist Temple 44914

Jesus Jones and Justice Museum of Art, 7611 S San Pedro St, Los Angeles, CA 90003 - T: (323) 971-9529
Fine Arts Museum 44915

Jose Drudis-Biada Art Gallery, c/o Mount Saint Mary's College, 12001 Chalon Rd, Los Angeles, CA 90049 - T: (310) 476-2237, 954-4361, Fax: (310) 476-9296, E-mail: jbaral@msmc.edu. Dir.: Jody Baral
Fine Arts Museum
Gene Mako coll, recent paintings, works on paper 44916

Korean Museum, 176 S Western Av, Los Angeles, CA 90004 - T: (213) 427-0333
Ethnology Museum / Fine Arts Museum 44917

Laband Art Gallery, c/o Loyola Marymount University, 7900 Loyola Blvd, Los Angeles, CA 90045-8346 - T: (310) 338-2880, Fax: (310) 338-6024, E-mail: gfuglie@lmu.edu, Internet: www.lmu.edu/colleges/cfa/art/laband. Dir.: Gordon L. Fuglie
Fine Arts Museum / University Museum - 1985
Coll o figurative art 44918

Los Angeles Center for Photographic Studies, 6518 Hollywood Blvd, Los Angeles, CA 90028 - T: (323) 466-6232, Fax: (323) 466-3203, E-mail: jbache@calarts.edu, Internet: www.oversight.com/acps. Dir.: Tania Martiniz-Lemke
Fine Arts Museum - 1974 44919

Los Angeles Contemporary Exhibitions, 6522 Hollywood Blvd, Los Angeles, CA 90028-6210 - T: (323) 957-1777, Fax: (323) 957-9025, E-mail: info@artleak.org, Internet: www.artleak.org. Dir.: Irene Tsatsos, Pres.: Frederick S. Reisz
Public Gallery - 1977 44920

Los Angeles County Museum of Art, 5905 Wilshire Blvd, Los Angeles, CA 90036 - T: (323) 857-6000, Fax: (323) 857-4702, E-mail: publicinfo@lacma.org, Internet: www.lacma.org. Dir.: Andrea L. Rich, Cons.: Victoria Blyth-Hill, Cur.: Stephanie Barron, Howard Fox (Modern and Contemporary Art), Stephen A. Markel (Indian and Southeast Asian Art), J. Keith Wilson (Far Eastern Art), Kevin Salatino (Prints, Drawings), Sharon Takeda (Costumes, Textiles), J. Patrice Marandel (European Painting and Sculpture), Bruce Robertson (American Art), Nancy K. Thomas (Ancient and Islamic Art), Wendy Kaplan (Decorative Arts), Robert Sobieszek (Photography), Head: Dorrance Stalvey (Music), Ian Birnie (Film)
Fine Arts Museum - 1910 44921

Los Angeles Craft and Folk Art Museum, 5814 Wilshire Blvd, Los Angeles, CA 90036 - T: (323) 937-4230, Fax: (323) 937-5576. Dir.: Joan Bruin
Folklore Museum / Historical Museum - 1973
Contemporary American crafts and design, international folk art, masks of the worlds 44922

Los Angeles Municipal Art Gallery, 4804 Hollywood Blvd, Los Angeles, CA 90027 - T: (213) 485-4581, Fax: (213) 485-8396, E-mail: cadmag@earthlink.net. Pres.: Thomas McGovern, Dir./ Cur.: Noel Korten
Fine Arts Museum - 1954
Contemporary fineart and design 44923

Los Angeles Museum of the Holocaust, 6006 Wilshire Blvd, Los Angeles, CA 90036 - T: (323) 761-8170, Fax: (323) 761-8174, E-mail: museumgroup@jewishla.org, Internet: www.jewishla.org. Dir.: Marcia Reines Josephy, Rachel Jadoda
Historical Museum - 1978
Art, children's art, personal memorabilia, pre war photos and decorative art 44924

Lummis Home El Alisal, 200 E Av 43, Los Angeles, CA 90031 - T: (323) 222-0546, Fax: (323) 222-0771, E-mail: hssc@socalhistory.org, Internet: www.socalhistory.org. Pres.: Siegfried G. Demke, Exec. Dir.: Thomas F. Andrews
Historical Museum - 1883
Archaeology, ethnology, history, Indian artifacts 44925

MAK Center for Art and Architecture, Pearl M. Mackey Apartment House, 1137-1141 S Cochran Av, Los Angeles, CA 90019 - T: (323) 651-1510, Fax: (323) 651-2340, E-mail: makcenter@earthlink.net, Internet: www.MAK.at. Dir.: Daniela Zyman
Fine Arts Museum - 1994 44926

Mariposa County Gallery, 5009 Fifth Av, Los Angeles, CA 90043 - T: (209) 966-3155, E-mail: info@arts-mariposa.org, Internet: www.arts-mariposa.org
Public Gallery 44927

Museum of African American Art, 4005 Crenshaw Blvd, Los Angeles, CA 90008 - T: (213) 294-7071, Fax: (213) 294-7084. Pres.: Belinda Fontenote-Jamerson
Fine Arts Museum - 1976 44928

Museum of Arts Downtown Los Angeles, 514 S Spring St, Los Angeles, CA 90013 - T: (213) 627-7849
Fine Arts Museum 44929

Museum of Contemporary Art Los Angeles, 250 S Grand Av, California Plaza, Los Angeles, CA 90012 - T: (213) 621-2766, 626-6222, Fax: (213) 620-8674, Internet: www.moca-la.org. Dir.: Richard Koshalek, Jeremy Strick, Cur.: Paul Schimmel, Ann Goldstein, Connie Butler
Fine Arts Museum - 1979 44930

The Museum of Death, 6340 Hollywood Blvd, Los Angeles, CA 90028 - T: (323) 466-8011, Fax: (323) 466-8011, Internet: www.museumofdeath.com. Dir.: Cathee Shultz, James Healy
Special Museum - 1995
Artwork and letters from serial murderers, caskets and coffins, execution devices, mortician tools 44931

Museum of Neon Art, 501 W Olympic Blvd, Los Angeles, CA 90015 - T: (213) 489-9918, Fax: (213) 489-9932, E-mail: info@neonmona.org, Internet: www.museneon.org. Exec. Dir.: Kim Koga
Fine Arts Museum - 1981 44932

Museum of the Korean Cultural Center, 5505 Wilshire Blvd, Los Angeles, CA 90036 - T: (323) 936-7141, Fax: (323) 936-5712, E-mail: info@kccla.org, Internet: www.kccla.org
Ethnology Museum 44933

Natural History Museum of Los Angeles County, 900 Exposition Blvd, Los Angeles, CA 90007 - T: (213) 763-3412, 763-3466, Fax: (213) 743-4843, E-mail: gflorez@nhm.org, Internet: www.nhm.org. Dir.: Dr. Jane G. Pisano, Dep. Dir.: Jural J. Garrett
Natural History Museum - 1910
Ethnology, archaeology, anthropology, botany, ichthyology, entomology, herpetology, paleontology, ornithology, mammalogy, invertebrate zoology, mineralogy 44934

New Image Art, 7906 Santa Monica Blvd, Los Angeles, CA 90046 - T: (323) 654-2192, Fax: (323) 654-2192, E-mail: newimgart@aol.com, Internet: www.newimagartgallery.com. Dir.: Marsea Goldberg
Fine Arts Museum - 1995 44935

Otis Gallery, Otis College of Art and Design, 9045 Lincoln Blvd, Los Angeles, CA 90045 - T: (310) 665-6905, 665-6800, Fax: (310) 665-6908, E-mail: exhibit@otisart.edu, Internet: www.otisart.edu. Dir.: Dr. Anne Ayres
Fine Arts Museum - 1940
Art gallery 44936

Plaza de La Raza, 3450 N Mission Rd, Los Angeles, CA 90031 - T: (323) 223-2475, Fax: (323) 223-1804, E-mail: admin@plazaraza.org, Internet: www.plazaraza.org. C.E.O.: Rose Marie Cano
Fine Arts Museum / Folklore Museum - 1969
Mexican-American folk art, Latino artworks, photos 44937

El Pueblo de Los Angeles Historical Monument, 125 Paseo de la Plaza, Ste 400, Los Angeles, CA 90012 - T: (213) 628-1274, 680-2525, Fax: (213) 485-8238, E-mail: scheng@mailbox.lacity.org, Internet: www.cityofla.org/elp. Dir.: Kory Smith
Historical Museum - 1953
Manuscripts, architectural drawings, slides, archaeology 44938

Self Help Graphics Gallery, 3802 Cesar E Chavez Av, Los Angeles, CA 90063 - T: (323) 264-1259, Fax: (323) 881-6447, Internet: www.selfhelpgraphics.com. Cur.: Cristina Ochoa
Public Gallery - 1972 44939

Side Street Projects, 400 S Main St, Los Angeles, CA 90013 - T: (213) 620-8895, Fax: (213) 620-8896, E-mail: sidest@netcom.com, Internet: www.sidestreet.org. Dir.: Karen Atkinson
Fine Arts Museum - 1991 44940

Simon Wiesenthal Center, 1399 S Roxbury Dr, Los Angeles, CA 90035 - T: (310) 553-9036, Fax: (310) 553-4521, E-mail: information@wiesenthal.net, Internet: www.wiesenthal.com
Historical Museum - 1977 44941

Simon Wiesenthal Center - Museum of Tolerance, 9786 W Pico Blvd, Los Angeles, CA 90035 - T: (310) 553-8403, Fax: (310) 772-7655, E-mail: information@wiesenthal.com, Internet: www.museumoftolerance.com. Dir.: Liebe Geft, Libr.: Adaire Klein
Historical Museum - 1993
Holocaust, Human Rights 44942

Skirball Cultural Center, Hebrew Union College, 2701 N Sepulveda Av, Los Angeles, CA 90049 - T: (310) 440-4500, Fax: (310) 440-4695, E-mail: aburke@skirball.org, Internet: www.skirball.org. Dir.: Adele Burke, Cur.: Grace Cohen Grossman, Barbara Gilbert, Asst. Cur.: Erin Clancey, Tal Gozani
Fine Arts Museum / Historical Museum - 1913 44943

Southern California Chapter Railway and Locomotive Museum, 6006 Wooster Av, Los Angeles, CA 90056-1434
Science&Tech Museum
Railroad 44944

Southwest Museum, 234 Museum Dr, Los Angeles, CA 90065 - T: (213) 221-2164, Fax: (213) 224-8223, E-mail: info@southwestmuseum.org, Internet: www.southwestmuseum.org. Dir.: Dr. Duane H. King, Sen. Cur.: Steve Grate, Asst. Cur.: Amy Simmons, George Kritzman, Byrn Potter
Fine Arts Museum / Decorative Arts Museum / Folklore Museum / Ethnology Museum / Archaeological Museum - 1907
library 44945

SunAmerica Collection, 1 SunAmerica Center, Los Angeles, CA 90067-6022 - T: (310) 772-6000, Fax: (310) 772-6567. Cur.: Joanne Heyler
Fine Arts Museum - 1981 44946

Travel Town Museum, 5200 Zoo Dr, Los Angeles, CA 90027 - T: (213) 662-5874, 485-5520, Fax: (818) 243-0041, E-mail: traveltown@lacity.org, Internet: www.lacity.org/grifmet/tt. Dir.: Linda J. Barth, Asst. Dir.: Thomas W. Breckner
Science&Tech Museum - 1952
Railroad equipment, steam locomotives, wagons 44947

Watts Towers Arts Center, 1727 E 107th St, Los Angeles, CA 90002 - T: (213) 847-4646, 485-1795, Fax: (213) 564-7030, E-mail: cadwattsctr@earthlink.net, Internet: www.wattstowers.net. Dir.: Mark S. Greenfield
Fine Arts Museum - 1975
African art, contemporary art 44948

Weingart Galleries, c/o Occidental College, 1600 Campus Rd, Los Angeles, CA 90041 - T: (323) 259-2714, E-mail: minta@oxy.edu, Internet: www.oxy.edu. Pres.: Linda Lyke
Fine Arts Museum - 1938 44949

Wells Fargo History Museum, 333 S Grand Av, Los Angeles, CA 90071 - T: (213) 253-7166, Fax: (213) 680-2269. Cur.: Melissa Johnson, Juan Colato
Historical Museum - 1982
Banking and express history, gold scales, mining 44950

William Grant Still Art Center, 2520 W View St, Los Angeles, CA 90016 - T: (323) 734-1164
Public Gallery 44951

Zimmer Children's Museum, 6505 Wilshire Blvd, Los Angeles, CA 90048 - T: (323) 761-8991, Fax: (323) 761-8990, E-mail: sherrik@zimmermuseum.org, Internet: www.zimmermuseum.org. Dir.: Sherri Kadovitz, Esther Netter
Historical Museum - 1991
Jewish culture, traditions and history 44952

Los Banos CA

Ralph Milliken Museum, Merced County Park, US Hwy 152, Los Banos, CA 93635, mail addr: POB 2294, Los Banos, CA 93635 - T: (209) 826-5505
Folklore Museum / Historical Museum - 1954
Agriculture, archaeology, military uniforms, Indian artifacts 44953

Los Gatos CA

The Art Museum of Los Gatos and the Nature Museum of Los Gatos, 4 Taut Av, Los Gatos, CA 95030 - T: (408) 354-2646, Fax: (408) 395-7386, E-mail: lgmuseums@aol.com. Dir.: Laura Bajuk, Cur.: Catherine Politopoulos (Natural History)
Fine Arts Museum / Natural History Museum - 1965 44954

Forbes Mill Museum of Regional History, 75 Church St, Los Gatos, CA 95030 - T: (408) 395-7375, Fax: (408) 395-7386, E-mail: lgmuseums@aol.com. Exec. Dir.: Laura Bajuk
Historical Museum - 1965 44955

Lost Creek WV

Watters Smith, Duck Creek Rd, Lost Creek, WV 26385 - T: (304) 745-3081, Fax: (304) 745-3631, E-mail: watterssmith@aol.com. Head: Larry A. Jones
Local Museum / Agriculture Museum - 1964
Local hist 44956

Loudonville OH

Cleo Redd Fisher Museum, 203 E Main St, Loudonville, OH 44842 - T: (419) 994-4050. Cur.: James Sharp
Local Museum - 1973
Local history 44957

Louisa VA

Louisa County Historical Museum, 200 Church Av, Courthouse Sq, Louisa, VA 23093 - T: (703) 967-2794, E-mail: lchs@firstva.com, Internet: www.trevilians.com. Chm.: Pattie Cooke
Local Museum - 1966
Regional history, in 1868 jail 44958

Louisburg NC

Louisburg College Art Gallery, 501 N Main St, Louisburg, NC 27549 - T: (919) 496-2521, Fax: (919) 496-1788, E-mail: hintonwj@yahoo.com, Internet: www.louisburg.edu. Dir.: William Hinton
Fine Arts Museum / University Museum - 1957
American Impressionist art, Primitive art 44959

Louisville KY

Allen R. Hite Art Institute, University of Louisville, Belknap Campus, Louisville, KY 40292 - T: (502) 852-6794, Fax: (502) 852-6791, E-mail: john.begley@louisville.edu, Internet: www.art.louisville.edu. Dir.: Prof. James Grubola
Fine Arts Museum / University Museum - 1946
Art 44960

American Printing House for the Blind, Callahan Museum, 1839 Frankfort Av, Louisville, KY 40206 - T: (502) 895-2405 ext 365, Fax: (502) 899-2363, E-mail: ctobe@aph.org, Internet: www.aph.org. Dir.: Carol B. Tobe
Historical Museum - 1990 44961

Archaeological Museum, Louisville Presbyterian Theological Seminary, 1044 Alta Vista Dr, Louisville, KY 40205-1798 - T: (502) 895-3411, Fax: (502) 895-1096. Cur.: Dr. Eugene March
Archaeological Museum / Religious Arts Museum - 1930
Religion, archaeology 44962

Artswatch, 2337 Frankfort Av, Louisville, KY 40206-2467 - T: (502) 893-9661, Fax: (502) 893-9661, E-mail: admin@frankave.win.net, Internet: www.frankfortave.com. Exec. Dir.: Andy Perry
Public Gallery - 1985 44963

Farmington Historic Home, 3033 Bardstown Rd, Louisville, KY 40205 - T: (502) 452-9920, Fax: (502) 456-1976, E-mail: cjsb@bellsouth.net, Internet: www.historicfarmington.org. Dir.: Carolyn Brooks
Historical Museum - 1958 44964

The Filson Historical Society Museum, 1310 S Third St, Louisville, KY 40208 - T: (502) 635-5083, Fax: (502) 635-5086, E-mail: filson@filsonhistorical.org, Internet: www.filsonhistorical.org. Dir.: Mark V. Wetherington
Local Museum - 1884
Local history 44965

The Joseph A. Callaway Archaeological Museum, Southern Baptist Theological Seminary, 2825 Lexington Rd, Louisville, KY 40280 - T: (502) 897-4011, Fax: (502) 897-4056, E-mail: jdrinkard@sbts.edu, Internet: www.sbts.edu. Cur.: Joel F. Drinkard
Archaeological Museum / Religious Arts Museum - 1961
Biblical archaeology 44966

Kentucky Art and Craft Foundation, 609 W Main St, Louisville, KY 40202 - T: (502) 589-0102, Fax: (502) 589-0154, E-mail: kacf@aye.net, Internet: www.kentuckycrafts.org. Dir.: Mary Miller, Cur.: Brion Clinkingbeard
Decorative Arts Museum / Fine Arts Museum - 1981
Folk art, crafts 44967

Kentucky Derby Museum, 704 Central Av, 1 Churchill Downs, Louisville, KY 40201 - T: (502) 637-1111, Fax: (502) 636-5855, E-mail: info@derbymuseum.org, Internet: www.derbymuseum.org. Dir.: Lynn Ashton, Cur.: Chris Goodlett, Sandy Flaksman
Special Museum - 1985
Thoroughbred racing, equine art, history, science 44968

Locust Grove, 561 Blankenbaker Lane, Louisville, KY 40207 - T: (502) 897-9845, Fax: (502) 897-0103, E-mail: lghh@locustgrove.org, Internet: www.locustgrove.org. Dir.: Julie Parke
Historic Site - 1964
1790 Georgian mansion, home of General George Rogers Clark 44969

Louisville Science Center, 727 W Main St, Louisville, KY 40202 - T: (502) 561-6100, Fax: (502) 561-6145, E-mail: admin@lsclouienet.com, Internet: www.louisvillescience.org. Dir.: Gail R. Becker
Natural History Museum / Science&Tech Museum - 1872
Physical, life and natural science, industrial technology, ethnographic, costumes 44970

Louisville Slugger Museum, 800 W Main St, Louisville, KY 40202 - T: (502) 588-7228, Fax: (502) 585-1179, Internet: www.sluggermuseum.org. Dir.: Bill Williams
Special Museum - 1996
Baseball bats, baseball related artifacts 44971

Louisville Visual Art Museum, 3005 River Rd, Louisville, KY 40207 - T: (502) 896-2146, Fax: (502) 896-2148, E-mail: feedback@louisvillevisualart.org, Internet: www.louisvillevisualart.org. Dir.: John P. Begley, Pres.: Frank F. Weisberg
Fine Arts Museum - 1909
Art gallery 44972

Morris Belknap Gallery, Dario Covi Gallery and SAL Gallery, c/o University of Louisville, Hite Art Institute, Louisville, KY 40292 - T: (502) 852-6794, Fax: (502) 852-6791, Internet: www.louisville.edu. Chm.: James Grubola
University Museum / Fine Arts Museum - 1935
Teaching coll, paintings, drawings, prints 44973

Portland Museum, 2308 Portland Av, Louisville, KY 40212 - T: (502) 776-7678, Fax: (502) 776-9874, E-mail: pmuseum@iglou.com, Internet: www.goportland.org. Dir.: Nathalie Taft Andrews
Local Museum - 1978
Regional history, Beach Grove residence of William Skene 44974

Sons of the American Revolution Museum, 1000 S Fourth St, Louisville, KY 40203 - T: (502) 589-1776, Fax: (502) 589-1671, Internet: www.sar.org. Dir.: William H. Roddis, Cur.: Fletcher L. Elmore
Historical Museum - 1876
National history 44975

Speed Art Museum, 2035 S Third St, Louisville, KY 40208 - T: (502) 634-2700, Fax: (502) 636-2899, E-mail: info@speedmuseum.org, Internet: www.speedmuseum.org. Dir.: Peter Morrin, Cur.: Ruth Cloudman
Fine Arts Museum - 1925
Art 44976

Thomas Edison House, 729-31 E Washington St, Louisville, KY 40202 - T: (502) 585-5247, Fax: (502) 585-5231, E-mail: edisonhouse@edisonhouse.org, Internet: www.edisonhouse.org. Exec. Dir.: Heather Bain
Science&Tech Museum - 1978
Phonographs, kinetoscope and bulbs 44977

Tryart Gallery, Louisville Visual Art Association, 400 W Market St, Louisville, KY 40202 - T: (502) 585-5550, E-mail: lou@louisvillevisualart.org, Internet: www.louisvillevisualart.org
Public Gallery 44978

Louisville MS

American Heritage "Big Red" Fire Museum, 332 N Church Av, Louisville, MS 39339 - T: (662) 773-3421, Fax: (662) 773-7183, Internet: www.taylorbigred.com
Historical Museum - 1989
Early fire equip, hand pumpers, hose reels, horse drawn ladder trucks, Indian artifacts, art 44979

Loveland CO

Loveland Museum and Gallery, 503 N Lincoln, Loveland, CO 80537 - T: (970) 962-2410, 962-2490, Fax: (970) 962-2910, E-mail: isons@ci.loveland.co.us, Internet: www.ci.loveland.co.us. Dir.: Susan P. Ison, Cur.: Janice Currier, Tom Katsimpalis, Jennifer Slichter
Local Museum / Public Gallery - 1937
Local history, art 44980

Loveland OH

Greater Loveland Historical Society Museum, 201 Riverside Dr, Loveland, OH 45140 - T: (513) 683-5692, Fax: (513) 683-5692, E-mail: glhsm@fuse.net, Internet: www.lovelandmuseum.org. Dir.: Janet Beller, Cur.: Jenny Shives
Local Museum - 1975
Local hist 44981

Lowell MA

American Textile History Museum, 491 Dutton St, Lowell, MA 01854-4221 - T: (978) 441-0400, Fax: (978) 441-1412, E-mail: athm@netwayl.mdc.net, Internet: www.athm.org. Dir.: Michael J. Smith, Cur.: Karen Herbaugh (Machinery, Textiles), Cons.: Deirdre Windsor (Textiles)
Historical Museum / Science&Tech Museum - 1960
Textile history, machinery and industry, costumes, clothing - library, archive 44982

Lowell National Historical Park, 67 Kirk St, Lowell, MA 01852 - T: (978) 970-5000, Fax: (978) 275-1762, Internet: www.nps.gov/lowe. Dir.: Patrick C. McCrary, Cur.: Carolyn Goldstein, Historian: Gray Fitzsimons
Local Museum - 1978
Local hist - Labor 44983

Lowell Telecommunications Corporation Museum, 246 Market St, Lowell, MA 01852-0803 - T: (978) 458-5400, Fax: (978) 937-0361, E-mail: info@ltc.org, Internet: valley.uml.edu/ltc
Fine Arts Museum
Paintings, photo, commercial 44984

Middlesex Canal Collection, Center for Lowell History, 40 French St, Lowell, MA 01852 - T: (978) 934-4997, Fax: (978) 934-4995. Dir.: Martha Mayo
Local Museum - 1962
Local history 44985

New England Quilt Museum, 18 Shattuck St, Lowell, MA 01852 - T: (978) 452-4207, Fax: (978) 452-5405, E-mail: nequiltmuseum@erols.com, Internet: www.nequiltmuseum.org. Pres.: Lenore Ouellette, Dir.: Patricia Steuert
Decorative Arts Museum - 1987
Quilts 44986

The Brush Art Gallery and Studios, 256 Market St, Lowell, MA 01852 - T: (978) 459-7819. Exec. Dir.: E. Linda Poras
Fine Arts Museum - 1982 44987

Whistler House Museum of Art, Lowell Art Association, 243 Worthen St, Lowell, MA 01852 - T: (978) 452-7641, Fax: (978) 454-2421, E-mail: mlalley@whistlerhouse.org, Internet: www.whistlerhouse.org. Exec. Dir.: Michael H. Lally, Cur.: Michele Auger
Fine Arts Museum - 1878
Art gallery, birthplace of James A. M. Whistler - Lowell celebrates Kerouac Committee 44988

Lowville NY

Lewis County Historical Society Museum, 7552 S State St, Lowville, NY 13367 - T: (315) 376-8957, E-mail: lcho@northnet.org. Dir.: Lisa Becker
Local Museum - 1930
Archaeology, costumes, family heirlooms, geology, military, technology, local hist 44989

Lubbock TX

Buddy Holly Center, 1801 Av G, Lubbock, TX 79401 - T: (806) 767-2686, Fax: (806) 767-0732, E-mail: cgibbons@mail.ci.lubbock.tx.us
Music Museum / Fine Arts Museum - 1984
Buddy Holly memorabilia, contemporary art 44990

Museum of Texas Tech University, 4th & Indiana St, Lubbock, TX 79409-3191 - T: (806) 742-2442, Fax: (806) 742-1136, E-mail: museum.texastech@ttu.edu, Internet: www.ttu.edu/~museum/. Dir.: Gary Edson, Cur.: Dr. Eileen Johnson (Anthropology), Mei Campbell (Ethnology, Clothing, Textiles), Dr. Robert Baker (Natural Science), Dr. Sankar Chatterjee (Paleontology), Henry B. Crawford (History)
University Museum / Local Museum - 1929
History of Southwestern US, ethnology, natural science, paleontology, fine and contemporary art, Pre-Columbian art coll, archaeology, mammalogy, biodiversity 44991

Science Spectrum, 2579 S Loop 289, Lubbock, TX 79423 - T: (806) 748-1040, Fax: (806) 745-1115, E-mail: spectrum@door.net, Internet: www.sciencespectrum.com. Dir.: Cassandra L. Henry
Science&Tech Museum - 1986
Science 44992

Lubec ME

Roosevelt Campobello, POB 129, Lubec, ME 04652 - T: (506) 752-2922, Fax: (506) 752-6000, E-mail: quirk@fdr.net, Internet: www.fdr.net. Head: Christopher Roosevelt
Historical Museum - 1964
Summer home of Pres. Franklin D. Roosevelt 44993

Lucas OH

Malabar Farm State Park, 4050 Bromfield Rd, Lucas, OH 44843 - T: (419) 892-2784, Fax: (419) 892-3988, E-mail: malabar@richnet.net, Internet: www.malabarfarm.org. C.E.O.: Louis M. Andres
Historical Museum / Agriculture Museum - 1939 44994

Ludington MI

Historic White Pine Village, 1687 S Lakeshore Dr, Ludington, MI 49431 - T: (231) 843-4808, Fax: (231) 843-7089, E-mail: info@historicwhitepinevillage.org, Internet: www.historicwhitepinevillage.org. Dir.: Ronald M. Wood
Open Air Museum / Local Museum - 1937
Local history, reconstructed historical village, 21 bldgs, incl Rose Hawley Museum, Maritime Museum, Abe Nelson Lumbering Museum, Scottville Clown Band's Museum of Music 44995

Ludlow VT

Black River Academy Museum, High St, Ludlow, VT 05149 - T: (802) 228-5050, Fax: (802) 228-7444, E-mail: llt44@ludl.tds.net. Dir.: Georgia Brehm
Local Museum - 1972
Local hist 44996

Lufkin TX

The Museum of East Texas, 503 N Second St, Lufkin, TX 75901 - T: (409) 639-4434, Fax: (409) 639-4435. Dir.: J.P. McDonald, Cur.: Michael Collins, Nancy Wilson (Photographic Coll)
Fine Arts Museum / Historical Museum - 1975
Art, history 44997

Texas Forestry Museum, 1905 Atkinson Dr, Lufkin, TX 75901 - T: (409) 632-9535, 633-6248, Fax: (409) 632-9543, E-mail: info@treetexas.com, Internet: www.treetexas.com. C.E.O.: Carol Riggs
Natural History Museum - 1972 44998

Lumpkin GA

Bedingfield Inn Museum, Cotton St on the Square, Lumpkin, GA 31815 - T: (229) 838-6419, Fax: (229) 838-6134, E-mail: schc@sowega.net, Internet: www.bedingfieldinn.org. Dir.: Vickie Harville
Historical Museum - 1965
1836 Stagecoach Inn , costumes, paintings, decorative art, furnishings 44999

Westville Historic Handicrafts Museum, Martin Luther King Dr, Lumpkin, GA 31815 - T: (229) 838-6310, Fax: (229) 838-4000, E-mail: director@westville.org, Internet: www.westville.org. Dir.: Matthew M. Moye, Cur.: L.M. Moye
Historical Museum / Open Air Museum - 1966
Historic Village 34 buildings and houses c.1850 45000

Lutherville MD

Fire Museum of Maryland, 1301 York Rd, Lutherville, MD 21093 - T: (410) 321-7500, Fax: (410) 769-8433, E-mail: info@firemuseummd.org, Internet: www.firemuseummd.org. Cur.: Stephen G. Heaver
Historical Museum - 1971
Fire fighting 45001

Lynchburg VA

The Anne Spencer Memorial Foundation, 1313 Pierce St, Lynchburg, VA 24501 - T: (804) 845-1313. Chm.: Hugh R. Jones
Local Museum - 1977
Local hist 45002

Daura Gallery, Lynchburg College, 1501 Lakeside Dr, Lynchburg, VA 24501-3199 - T: (804) 544-8100, 544-8343, Fax: (804) 544-8277, E-mail: rothermel@lynchburg.edu, Internet: www.lynchburg.edu/daura. Dir.: Barbara Rothermel
Fine Arts Museum - 1974
Art of Catalan-American Modernis Pierre Daura 45003

Lynchburg Fine Arts Center, 1815 Thomson Dr, Lynchburg, VA 24501 - T: (804) 846-8451, Fax: (804) 846-3806, E-mail: finearts@lynchburg.net, Internet: www.lynchburgbiz.com/fac. Exec. Dir.: Mary Brumbauch
Fine Arts Museum - 1958
Area photography and area art 45004

Lynchburg Museum System, 901 Court St, Lynchburg, VA 24504 - T: (804) 847-1459, Fax: (804) 528-0162, E-mail: museum@ci.lynchburg.va.us, Internet: www.lynchburgmuseum.org. Dir.: Thomas G. Ledford
Historical Museum - 1976
Local hist 45005

Maier Museum of Art, Randolph-Macon Woman's College, 2500 Rivermont Av, Lynchburg, VA 24503 - T: (434) 947-8136, Fax: (434) 947-8726, E-mail: klawson@rmwc.edu, Internet: www.rmwc.edu/maier. Dir.: Karol Lawson, Assoc. Dir.: Ellen Schall Agnew
Fine Arts Museum / University Museum - 1920
Art 45006

Point of Honor, 112 Cabell St, Lynchburg, VA 24504 - T: (804) 847-1459, Fax: (804) 528-0162, E-mail: museum@ci.lynchburg.va.us, Internet: www.pointofhonor.org. Pres.: Karen Buchanan
Local Museum / Folklore Museum - 1976
Historic house 45007

South River Meeting House, 5810 Fort Av, Lynchburg, VA 24502 - T: (804) 239-2548, 239-1688, Fax: (804) 239-6649. Chm.: Jim Garrett
Local Museum - 1757
Historic house 45008

Lynden WA

Lynden Pioneer Museum, 217 W Front St, Lynden, WA 98264 - T: (360) 354-3675, E-mail: troy@lyndenpioneermuseum.com, Internet: www.lyndenpioneermuseum.com. Cur.: Troy Luginbill
Local Museum - 1976
Prehistory and settlement, historic travel and transportation 45009

Lyndon KS

Osage County Historical Society, 631 Topeka Av, Lyndon, KS 66451 - T: (785) 828-3477, E-mail: research@kanza.net, Internet: www.osagechs.org. Dir.: Tammy S. Orear
Local Museum - 1963
Local history, family history, library 45010

Lynn MA

Lynn Museum, 125 Green St, Lynn, MA 01902 - T: (781) 592-2465, Fax: (781) 592-0012, E-mail: lynnmuse@shore.net, Internet: www.lynnmuseum.org. Dir.: Sandra Krein, Cur.: Jennifer Gaudio, Libr.: Diane Shephard
Historical Museum - 1897
Local history, Hyde-Mills house - library 45011

Lyons CO

The Lyons Redstone Museum, 340 High St, Lyons, CO 80540, mail addr: POB 9, Lyons, CO 80540 - T: (303) 823-6692, 823-5271, Fax: (303) 823-8257. Head: LaVern M. Johnson
Local Museum / Historic Site - 1973
Local history 45012

Lyons KS

Coronado-Quivira Museum, 105 W Lyon, Lyons, KS 67554 - T: (316) 257-3941, E-mail: cqmuseum@hotmail.com. Dir.: Janel Cook
Local Museum - 1927
General museum 45013

Lyons NY

Wayne County Historical Society Museum, 21 Butternut St, Lyons, NY 14489 - T: (315) 946-4943, Fax: (315) 946-0069, E-mail: wchs4943@aol.com, Internet: members.aol.com/wchs4943. Dir.: Andrea Evangelist, Cur.: Lisa Williams
Historical Museum - 1946 45014

Lyons Falls NY

Lewis County Historical Society Museum, High St, Lyons Falls, NY 13368 - T: (315) 348-8089, E-mail: histsoc@northnet.org, Internet: web. northnet.org/lewiscountyhistoricalsociety/home. html. Dir.: Lisa Becker
Historical Museum - 1930 45015

Mabel MN

Steam Engine Museum, Steam Engine Park, Mabel, MN 55954 - T: (507) 493-5350. Pres.: Tim Mengis
Science&Tech Museum - 1990
Technology 45016

McAllen TX

McAllen International Museum, 1900 Nolana, McAllen, TX 78504 - T: (956) 682-1564, Fax: (956) 686-1813, E-mail: mim@hiline.net, Internet: www. mcallenmuseum.org. Dir.: John Mueller, Cur.: Vernon Weckbacher
Fine Arts Museum / Science&Tech Museum - 1969
Arts and sciences 45017

McCalla AL

Iron and Steel Museum of Alabama, 12632 Confederate Pkwy, McCalla, AL 35111 - T: (205) 477-5711, Fax: (205) 477-9400, E-mail: tannehillmuseum@att.net, Internet: www. tannehill.org. Dir.: Vicki Gentry
Historical Museum - 1970 45018

McClellanville SC

Hampton Plantation, 1950 Rutledge Rd, McClellanville, SC 29458 - T: (803) 546-9361, Fax: (803) 527-4995, E-mail: hampton_-plantataion_sp@scprt.com, Internet: www. southcarolinaparks.com
Local Museum - 1971
Historic house 45019

McConnells SC

Historic Brattonsville, 1444 Brattonsville Rd, McConnells, SC 29726 - T: (803) 684-2327, Fax: (803) 684-0149, Internet: www.yorkcounty.org. Dir.: Van Shields
Open Air Museum / Historic Site - 1976
Local hist 45020

McCook NE

High Plains Museum, 421 Norris Av, McCook, NE 69001 - T: (308) 345-3661. Dir.: Marilyn Hawkins
Historical Museum - 1969 45021

Senator George Norris State Historic Site, 706 Norris Av, McCook, NE 69001-3142 - T: (308) 345-8484, Fax: (308) 345-8484, E-mail: norris@ mccooknet.com, Internet: www.nebraskahistory.org. Dir.: Lynne Ireland
Historical Museum - 1969 45022

McCutchenville OH

McCutchen Overland Inn, Rte 53 N, McCutchenville, OH 44844 - T: (419) 981-2052. Pres.: Robin Schuster, Cur.: Anna Bea Heilman, Florence Wagner
Local Museum - 1967
Historic house 45023

McDade TX

McDade Museum, Main St, McDade, TX 78650 - T: (512) 273-0044. Pres.: Don Grissom
Local Museum - 1962
Local hist 45024

Macedon NY

Macedon Historical Society Museum, 1185 Macedon Center Rd, Macedon, NY 14502 - T: (716) 388-0629. Pres.: David Taber, Cur.: Blanch Kemp
Historical Museum - 1962 45025

McFarland WI

McFarland Historical Society Museum, 5814 Main St, McFarland, WI 53558 - T: (608) 838-3992, E-mail: bluebee@madtown.net. Chm.: Dale Marsden, Cur.: Harold Muenkel
Local Museum - 1964
Local hist 45026

Machias ME

Burnham Tavern, Hannah Weston Chapter, National Society Daughters of the American Revolution, Main St, Machias, ME 04654 - T: (207) 255-4432, E-mail: valdine@juno.com. Dir.: John R. Atwood, Valdine C. Atwood
Historical Museum - 1910
Tavern from 1770, local hist 45027

Machiasport ME

Gates House, Rte N 92, Machiasport, ME 04655-0301 - T: (207) 255-8461, E-mail: franklf@ nemalne.com. Pres.: Jane C. Armstrong
Historical Museum - 1964 45028

Mackinac Island MI

Fort Mackinac, Mackinac Island, MI 49757 - T: (906) 847-3328, (517) 373-4296, Fax: (906) 847-3815, E-mail: mackinacparks@michigan.gov, Internet: www.mackinacparks.com. Dir.: Carl R. Nold, Deputy Dir.: David A. Armour, Cur.: Steven C. Brisson, Phil Porter, Lynn L. Morand (Archaeology)
Local Museum / Military Museum / Open Air Museum / Historic Site - 1895
Regional history, archaeology 45029

Old Mackinac Pointlightstation, Mackinac Island, MI 49757 - T: (906) 847-3328, (517) 373-4296, Fax: (906) 847-3815, (517) 373-4790, E-mail: mackinacparks@michigan.gov, Internet: www.mackinacparks.com. Dir.: Carl R. Nold, Deputy Dir.: David A. Armour, Cur.: Lynn L. Morand (Archaeology), Steven C. Brisson, Phil Porter
Local Museum - 1895
Archaeology, 1780-1895 Fort Mackinac, 1715-1780 Fort Michilimackinac, colonial time, tourism, transportation, lighthouses, native american - Fort Mackinac 45030

Stuart House City Museum, Market St, Mackinac Island, MI 49757 - T: (906) 847-8181, E-mail: cmim@freeway.net. Dir.: Lewis D. Crusoe, Cur.: Daniel Seeley
Historical Museum / Local Museum - 1930 45031

Mackinaw City MI

Colonial Michilimackinac, 102 W Straits Av, Mackinaw City, MI 49701 - T: (231) 627-5563, Fax: (231) 436-5410, 436-4210, E-mail: mackinacparks@michigan.gov, Internet: www.mackinacparks.com. Dir.: Carl R. Nold, Cur.: Steven C. Brisson, Phil Porter, Lynn L. Morand (Archaeology)
Historic Site / Open Air Museum / Local Museum / Military Museum - 1959
French and British military outpost and fur-trading village 45032

Great Lakes Lighthouse Museum, 100 Dock Dr, Mackinaw City, MI 49701-0712 - T: (231) 436-3333, Fax: (231) 436-7870. C.E.O.: Dr. Sandra Planisek
Special Museum - 1998
Fine art, archeology, lighthouse and maritime artifacts 45033

Historic Mill Creek, Mackinaw City, MI 49701 - T: (231) 436-7301, Fax: (231) 436-5410, 436-4210, E-mail: mackinacparks@michigan.gov, Internet: www.mackinacparks.com. Dir.: Carl R. Nold, Cur.: Phil Porter, Steven C. Brisson, Lynn L. Morand (Archaeology)
Natural History Museum - 1975
18th-c water-powered sawmill 45034

Teysen's Woodland Indian Museum, 300 E Central St, Mackinaw City, MI 49701 - T: (231) 436-7011, 436-7519, Fax: (231) 436-5932. C.E.O.: Kenneth Teysen
Ethnology Museum / Folklore Museum - 1950
Local hist 45035

McKinney TX

Bolin Wildlife Exhibit and Antique Collection, 1028 N McDonald, McKinney, TX 75069 - T: (972) 562-2639. Dir.: Jerry Bolin, Cur.: Tammie Ragsdale
Natural History Museum / Museum of Classical Antiquities - 1980
Natural hist 45036

Collin County Farm Museum, 7117 County Rd 166, McKinney, TX 75070 - T: (972) 548-4793, Fax: (972) 542-2265, E-mail: jlawrence@co.collin. tx.us, Internet: www.co.collin.tx.us. Man.: John Lawrence
Agriculture Museum - 1976
Farming 45037

Heard Natural Science Museum, 1 Nature Pl, McKinney, TX 75069-8840 - T: (972) 562-5566, Fax: (972) 548-9119, E-mail: info@heardmuseum. org, Internet: www.heardmuseum.org. Exec. Dir.: Elizabeth W. Bleiberg, Cur.: Kenneth Steigman
Natural History Museum - 1963
Natural science 45038

McLean TX

McLean-Alanreed Area Museum, 116 Main St, McLean, TX 79057 - T: (806) 779-2731. Cur.: Fayette Belle Barton
Local Museum - 1969
Local hist 45039

McLean VA

CIA Museum, McLean, VA 22101, mail addr: 2430 E St NW, Washington, DC 20505 - T: (703) 482-0623, Fax: (703) 482-1739, Internet: www.cia.gov/cia/ information/tour/cia_museum.html
Special Museum / Historical Museum - 1988 45040

McMinnville OR

Evergreen Aviation Museum, 3685 NE Three Mile Ln, McMinnville, OR 97128 - T: (503) 434-4180, Fax: (503) 434-4058, E-mail: bill.schaub@ sprucegoose.org, Internet: www.sprucegoose.org
Science&Tech Museum - 1992 45041

Macomb IL

Western Illinois University Art Gallery, 1 University circle, Macomb, IL 61455 - T: (309) 298-1587, Fax: (309) 298-2400, E-mail: JR-Graham1@wiu. edu, Internet: www.wiu.edu/artgallery. Cur.: John R. Graham, Pres.: Donald B. Spancer
Fine Arts Museum / University Museum - 1899
Art 45042

Macon GA

Georgia Music Hall of Fame, 200 Martin Luther King Jr Blvd, Macon, GA 31201 - T: (478) 750-8555, Fax: (478) 750-0350, E-mail: info@gamusichall. com, Internet: www.gamusichall.com. C.E.O.: Elizabeth F. Garcia
Music Museum - 1996
Georgia music from pre-colonial to the present 45043

Hay House Museum, 934 Georgia Av, Macon, GA 31201-6708 - T: (478) 742-8155, Fax: (478) 745-4277, E-mail: hayhouse@georgiatrust.org, Internet: www.georgiatrust.org. Dir.: Suzanne Jones Harper
Historical Museum - 1973
Historic House: 1855-59 Italian Renaissance Revival Mansion 45044

Museum of Arts and Sciences, 4182 Forsyth Rd, Macon, GA 31210 - T: (478) 477-3232, Fax: (478) 477-3251, E-mail: info@masmacon.com, Internet: www.masmacon.com. Dir.: Sheila Stewart-Leach
Fine Arts Museum / Science&Tech Museum - 1956
plantearium 45045

Ocmulgee National Monument, 1207 Emery Hwy, Macon, GA 31201 - T: (478) 752-8257 ext 10, Fax: (478) 752-8259, Internet: www.nps.gov/ocmu
Archaeological Museum - 1936
Archaeology, Indian artifacts 45046

Sidney Lanier Cottage, Middle Georgia Historical Society, 935 High St, Macon, GA 31208-3358 - T: (912) 743-3851, Fax: (912) 745-3132, E-mail: sidneylanier@bellsouth.net, Internet: www. sidneylaniercottage.org. Dir.: Katherine C. Oliver, Lucia C. Carr
Historical Museum / Local Museum - 1964
Regional History, birthplace of poet Sidney Lanier - library 45047

Tubman African-American Museum, 340 Walnut St, Macon, GA 31208 - T: (912) 743-8544, Fax: (912) 743-9063, E-mail: cpickard@tubmanmuseum.com, Internet: www.tubmanmuseum.com. Dir.: Carey Pickard
Historical Museum / Folklore Museum - 1982 45048

McPherson KS

McPherson College Gallery, Friendship Hall, 1600 E Euclid, McPherson, KS 67460 - T: (316) 241-0731, Fax: (316) 242-8443, Internet: www.mcpherson. edu. Dir.: Wayne Conyers
Fine Arts Museum - 1960
Oils, original prints, watercolors 45049

McPherson Museum, 1130 E Euclid, McPherson, KS 67460 - T: (620) 241-8464, Fax: (620) 24184644. Dir.: David Flask
Local Museum - 1890
Local history, prehistory, paleontology 45050

Madawaska ME

Tante Blanche Museum, U.S. 1, Madawaska, ME 04756 - T: (207) 728-4518. Pres.: Verna Fortin
Local Museum - 1968
Local hist 45051

Madera CA

Madera County Museum, 210 W Yosemite Av, Madera, CA 93637 - T: (209) 673-0291, Fax: (559) 674-5114, Internet: www.maderahistory.org. Cur.: Dorothy Foust
Local Museum / Historical Museum - 1955 45052

Madison CT

Madison Historical Society Museum, 853 Boston Post Rd, Madison, CT 06443 - T: (203) 245-4567, 421-3050, E-mail: abraid@aol.com, Internet: www. madisonct.com. Dir.: Jane R. Kuhl
Local Museum - 1917 45053

Madison FL

North Florida Community College Art Gallery, Turner Davis Dr, Madison, FL 32340 - T: (850) 973-2288, Fax: (850) 973-2288. Dir.: William F. Gardner jr.
Fine Arts Museum / University Museum - 1975
College Art Gallery 45054

Madison GA

Madison-Morgan Cultural Center Collection, 434 S Main St, Madison, GA 30650 - T: (706) 342-4743, Fax: (706) 342-1154, E-mail: cultural@mail. morgan.public.lib.ga.us, Internet: www.morgan. public.lib.ga.us/madmorg. Exec. Dir.: Tina Lilly
Local Museum - 1976
History of the region, decorative arts, costumes, architectural fragments, tools, household utensils, Civil War 45055

Madison IN

Historic Madison House, 500 West St, Madison, IN 47250 - T: (812) 265-2967, Fax: (812) 273-3941, E-mail: hmihmfi@seidata.com. Pres.: John E. Galvin
Historical Museum / Science&Tech Museum - 1960 45056

Jefferson County Historical Museum, 615 W First St, Madison, IN 47250 - T: (812) 265-2335, Fax: (812) 273-5023, E-mail: jchs@seidata.com, Internet: www.seidata.com/~jchs. Pres.: Robert Wolfschlag
Local Museum - 1850
County history, Madison railroad stn 45057

Lanier Mansion, 511 W 1st St, Madison, IN 47250 - T: (812) 265-3526, Fax: (812) 265-3501, E-mail: lanier1@seidata.com, Internet: www.state. in.us/ism/sites/lanier. Cur.: Link Ludington
Historic Site - 1925
Home of J.F.D. Lanier 45058

Shrewsbury Windle House, 301 W 1st St, Madison, IN 47250 - T: (812) 265-4481. Dir.: Ann S. Windle
Historical Museum - 1948 45059

Madison MN

Lac Qui Parle County Historical Museum, 250 8th Av S, Madison, MN 56256 - T: (612) 598-7678, E-mail: madville@frontiernet.net. Cur.: Lorraine Connor
Local Museum - 1948
Regional history 45060

Madison NJ

Elizabeth P. Korn Gallery, Drew University, Rte 24, Madison, NJ 07940 - T: (973) 408-3000. Dir.: Livio Saganic
Fine Arts Museum / Archaeological Museum - 1968
Ancient Near-East archeaology, different arts 45061

History Center of the United Methodist Church, 36 Madison Av, Madison, NJ 07940 - T: (973) 408-3189, Fax: (973) 408-3909, E-mail: cyrigoye@ drew.edu
Religious Arts Museum - 1885
archives 45062

Museum of Early Trades and Crafts, Main St at Green Village Rd, Madison, NJ 07940 - T: (973) 377-2982, Fax: (973) 377-7358, E-mail: metc@ msn.com, Internet: www.rosenet.org/metc. Dir.: Sheila R. Marines, Cur.: Lori Beth Finkelstein
Historical Museum - 1969 45063

Madison SD

Prairie Village, W Hwy 34, Madison, SD 57042 - T: (605) 256-3644, Fax: (605) 256-9616, Internet: www.prairyvillage.org. Pres.: Mike Tammen
Local Museum / Open Air Museum - 1966
40 restored buildings 45064

Smith-Zimmermann Museum, 221 NE 8th St, Dakota State University Campus, Madison, SD 57042 - T: (605) 256-5308, Fax: (605) 256-5643, E-mail: smith.zimmermann@dsu.edu, Internet: www.smith-zimmermann.dsu.edu. Pres.: Lory Norby
Historical Museum - 1952
History of lake County, Ethnic settlers artifacts, Chautaugua, musical instruments, transportation, farm implements 45065

Madison WI

DeRicci Gallery, c/o Edgewood College, 855 Woodrow, Madison, WI 53711 - T: (608) 257-4861, Fax: (608) 663-3291
Fine Arts Museum - 1965
Local and regional arts 45066

Elvehjem Museum of Art, 800 University Av, Madison, WI 53706-1479 - T: (608) 263-2246, Fax: (608) 263-8188, E-mail: ppowell@lvm.wisc. edu, Internet: www.lvm.wisc.edu. Dir.: Dr. Russell Panczenko, Cur.: Maria Saffiotti Dale (Paintings, Sculpture, Decorative Arts), Anne Lambert (Education), Andrew Stevens (Prints, Drawings)
Fine Arts Museum / University Museum - 1962
Art 45067

Helen Louise Allen Textile Collection, 1300 Linden Dr, University of Wisconsin, Madison, WI 53706 - T: (608) 262-1162, Fax: (608) 262-5335, Internet: sohe.wisc.edu/hlatc. Cur.: Mary Ann Fitzgerald
Special Museum - 1968
Textiles and costume 45068

Madison Art Center, 211 State St, Madison, WI 53703 - T: (574) 257-0158, Fax: (574) 257-5722, E-mail: mac@itis.com, Internet: www. madisonartcenter.org. Dir.: Stephen Fleischman, Cur.: Sara Krajewski, Sheri Castelnuovo
Fine Arts Museum - 1901
Art 45069

Madison Children's Museum, 100 State St, Madison, WI 53703 - T: (608) 256-6445, Fax: (608) 256-3226, E-mail: mcm@kidskiosk.org, Internet: www.kidskiosk.org. C.E.O.: Karen A. Drummer
Special Museum - 1980
Children's museum 45070

State Historical Museum of Wisconsin → Wisconsin Historical Museum

Steep and Brew Gallery, 544 State St, Madison, WI 53703 - T: (608) 256-2902, E-mail: mduerr@madison.k12.wi.us. Dir.: Mark Duerr
Fine Arts Museum - 1985 45071

University of Wisconsin Zoological Museum, 250 North Mills St, Madison, WI 53706 - T: (608) 262-1051, Fax: (608) 262-5395, Internet: www.wisc.edu/zoology/museum/museum.html. Dir.: Dr. John A.W. Kirsch, Cur.: E. Elizabeth Pillaert (Osteology), Dr. John E. Dallman (Paleontology), Dr. John D. Lyons (Fish), Gregory C. Mayer (Herpetology), Registrar: Holly McEntee
University Museum / Natural History Museum - 1887
Vertebrate zoology, osteology 45072

Wisconsin Historical Museum, 30 N Carroll St, Madison, WI 53703-2707 - T: (608) 264-6555, Fax: (608) 264-6575, E-mail: museum@whs.wisc.edu, Internet: www.wisconsinhistory.org/museum. Dir.: Ann Koski (Archaeology), Cur.: Joseph Kapler (Domestic Life), Paul Bourcier, Jennifer Kolb, Scott Roller, Leslie Bellais (Costumes, Textiles), Joan Garland, David Driscoll (Business, Technology), Beth Kowalski, Denise Wiggins, Monica Harrison
Local Museum - 1846
Local hist 45073

The Wisconsin Union Galleries, University of Wisconsin-Madison, 800 Langdon St, Madison, WI 53706 - T: (608) 262-2214, Fax: (608) 262-5487, E-mail: rfrusso@facstaff.wisc.edu, Internet: www.sit.wisc.edu/~wudart/. Dir.: Mark Guthier, Deputy Dir.: Ken Gibson, Cur.: Ralph Russo
Fine Arts Museum - 1928
Art 45074

Wisconsin Veterans Museum Madison, 30 W Mifflin St, Madison, WI 53703 - T: (608) 266-1009, Fax: (608) 264-7615, E-mail: lwolfe@mail.wi.us, Internet: badger.state.wi.us/agencies/dva/museum/wvmmain.html. C.E.O.: Raymond Boland, Cur.: William F. Brewster, Bridgett Zielke
Military Museum - 1901
archive 45075

Mahomet IL

Early American Museum, State Rte 47, Mahomet, IL 61853 - T: (217) 586-2612, Fax: (217) 586-3491, E-mail: early@earlyamericanmuseum.org, Internet: www.earlyamericanmuseum.org. Dir.: Cheryl Kennedy, Cur.: Barbara Oelschlaeger-Garvey
Historical Museum / Agriculture Museum / Decorative Arts Museum - 1967 45076

Mahwah NJ

Art Galleries of Ramapo College, 505 Ramapo Valley Rd, Mahwah, NJ 07430 - T: (201) 684-7587. Dir.: Shalom Gorewitz
Fine Arts Museum - 1979
Haitian art, popular art, prints 45077

Maitland FL

Holocaust Memorial Center of Central Florida, 851 N Maitland Av, Maitland, FL 32751 - T: (407) 628-0555 ext 284, Fax: (407) 628-1079, E-mail: execdir@holocaustedu.org, Internet: www.holocaustedu.org. C.E.O.: Tess Wise, Cur.: Anita Lam
Historical Museum - 1983 45078

Maitland Art Center, 231 W Packwood Av, Maitland, FL 32751-5596 - T: (407) 539-2181, Fax: (407) 539-1198, E-mail: RCmailMAC@aol.com, Internet: www.maitartctr.org. Dir.: James G. Shepp, Cur.: Richard D. Colvin
Fine Arts Museum - 1972
Art 45079

Maitland Historical Museums, Maitland Historical Museum, Telephone Museum, Historic Waterhouse Residence Museum, 820 Lake Lily Dr, Maitland, FL 32751 - T: (47) 6442451, Fax: (407) 644-0057, E-mail: maiths@mpinet.net, Internet: www.ourfrontporch.com/osi/mhs. C.E.O.: Allison Chapman
Local Museum / Science&Tech Museum - 1970
Seminole wars, telephone technology, Maitland and Waterhouse family hist, furnishings, tools and textiles 45080

Makawao HI

Hui No'eau Visual Arts Center, 2841 Baldwin Av, Makawao, HI 96768 - T: (808) 572-6560, Fax: (808) 572-2750, E-mail: info@huinoeau.com, Internet: www.huinoeau.com. Exec. Dir.: Martin Betz
Fine Arts Museum - 1934
Artifacts of Harry and Ethel Baldwin and Francis Cameron 45081

Malden MA

Malden Public Library Art Collection, 36 Salem St, Malden, MA 02148 - T: (781) 324-0218, 388-0800, Fax: (617) 324-4467, E-mail: maldensup@mbln.lib.ma.us, Internet: www.museumca.org/usa/state.html. Head: Dina G. Malgeri
Fine Arts Museum - 1879
Library with special art coll 45082

Malibu CA

Frederick R. Weisman Museum of Art, c/o Pepperdine University Center for the Arts, 24255 Pacific Coast Hwy, Malibu, CA 90263 - T: (310) 506-4851, 506-7257, Fax: (310) 456-4556, 506-4556, E-mail: mzakian@pepperdine.edu, Internet: www.pepperdine.edu/cfa/weismanmuseum.htm. Dir.: Michael Zakian
Fine Arts Museum - 1992
20th c American art 45083

Malibu Lagoon Museum, 23200 Pacific Coast Hwy, Malibu, CA 90265 - T: (310) 456-8432. Pres.: Sandra Mitchell
Historical Museum - 1982
Local history since Chumash Indians - library, botanical garden 45084

Malone NY

House of History, 51 Milwaukee St, Malone, NY 12953 - T: (518) 483-2750. Pres.: Peggy Roulston
Historical Museum - 1903 45085

Malvern AR

The Boyle House - Hot Spring County Museum, 310 E Third St, Malvern, AR 72104 - T: (501) 337-4775. Dir.: Janis West, Cur.: Dorothy Keith
Local Museum - 1981
County history 45086

Malvern PA

Wharton Esherick Museum, 1520 Horseshoe Trail, Malvern, PA 19355, mail addr: POB 595, Paoli, PA 19301-0595 - T: (610) 644-5822, Fax: (610) 644-2244. Exec. Dir.: Robert Leonard, Cur.: Mansfield Bascom
Historical Museum - 1971
Furniture, paintings, prints, sculpture in wood, stone and ceramic, utensils and woodcuts 45087

Mamaroneck NY

Larchmont Historical Society Museum, 740 W Boston Post Rd, Mamaroneck, NY 10543 - T: (914) 381-2239, 834-5136, E-mail: lhs@savvy.net, Internet: members.savvy.net/lhs
Local Museum - 1980
Hist of village and postal district of Larchmont 45088

Mammoth Spring AR

Depot Museum of the Mammoth Spring State Park, Box 36, Mammoth Spring, AR 72554 - T: (501) 625-7364, Fax: (870) 625-3255, E-mail: mammothsprg@arkansas.com, Internet: www.arkansasstateparks.com
Historical Museum - 1971
Local history, Frisco railroad depot, train memorabilia, Frisco Caboose 45089

Manassas VA

Jennie Dean Memorial → Manassas Museum System

Manassas Museum System, 9601 Prince William St, Manassas, VA 20110 - T: (703) 368-1873, Fax: (703) 257-8406, E-mail: info@manassasmuseum.org, Internet: www.manassasmuseum.org. C.E.O.: Melinda Herzog, Cur.: Roxana Adams
Local Museum - 1995
Local hist 45090

Manassas National Battlefield Park, 6511 Sudley Rd, Rte 234, Manassas, VA 20109 - T: (703) 361-1339, Fax: (703) 361-7106, E-mail: mana_superintendent@nps.gov, Internet: www.nps.gov/mana. Sc. Staff: Edmund Raus
Military Museum / Historic Site - 1940
Historic site 45091

Manchester CT

Cheney Homestead, 106 Hartford Rd, Manchester, CT 06040 - T: (860) 643-5588, E-mail: manchesterhistory@juno.com, Internet: www.ci.manchester.ct.us/cheney/historic.htm. C.E.O.: David Smith
Local Museum - 1969 45092

Lutz Children's Museum, 247 S Main St, Manchester, CT 06040 - T: (860) 649-2838, E-mail: reckert@lutzmuseum.org, Internet: www.lutzmuseum.org. Dir.: Bob Eckertn, Cur.: Xavier Stephens (Education), Michaela Tibbits (Animals)
Special Museum - 1953 45093

Manchester MA

Manchester Historical Society Museum, 10 Union St, Manchester, MA 01944 - T: (978) 526-7230, Fax: (978) 526-0060, E-mail: manchester-historical@prodigy.net, Internet: www.manchester-historical.org. Dir.: John Huss, Exec. Dir.: Dorothy Jodice, Cur.: William Walker
Decorative Arts Museum / Local Museum - 1886
Decorative arts, local history 45094

Manchester NH

Alva DeMars Megan Chapel Art Center, Saint Anselm College, 100 Saint Anselm Dr, Manchester, NH 03102 - T: (603) 641-7000, Fax: (603) 641-7116, E-mail: imaclell@anselm.edu, Internet: www.anselm.edu. Dir.: Iain MacLellan
Fine Arts Museum / University Museum - 1967 45095

Chapel Art Center → Alva DeMars Megan Chapel Art Center

Currier Gallery of Art, 201 Myrtle Way, Manchester, NH 03104 - T: (603) 669-6144, Fax: (603) 669-7194, E-mail: hjordan@currier.org, Internet: www.currier.org. Dir.: Susan E. Strickler, Deputy Dir.: Susan Leidy, Cur.: P. Andrew Spahr
Fine Arts Museum - 1929
Architecture, American paintings, drawings, American Indian art, folk art, textiles, woodcarvings, Oriental art, Asian art, porcelain, silver, tapestries, enamels, Baroque art - library 45096

Lawrence L. Lee Scouting Museum, 40 Blondin Rd, Manchester, NH 03109 - T: (603) 627-1492, 669-8919, Fax: (603) 641-6436, E-mail: administrator@scoutingmuseum.org, Internet: www.scoutingmuseum.org. Dir.: Al Lambert, Cur.: Edward Rowan
Folklore Museum - 1969
Scouting 45097

Manchester Historic Association Museum, 129 Amherst St, Manchester, NH 03101 - T: (603) 622-7531, Fax: (603) 622-0822, E-mail: history@manchesterhistoric.org, Internet: www.manchesterhistoric.org. Dir.: Gail Nessell Colglazier, Cur.: Marylou Ashooh Lazos, Eileen O'Brien
Historical Museum - 1896 45098

New Hampshire Institute of Art, 148 Concord St, Manchester, NH 03104 - T: (603) 623-0313, Fax: (603) 641-1832, E-mail: nhiart@gsinet.net, Internet: www.nhia.edu. C.E.O. & Pres.: Andrew Jay Svedlow
Fine Arts Museum - 1898
Arts and science 45099

Manchester VT

The American Museum of Fly Fishing, 3567 Main St, Manchester, VT 05254 - T: (802) 362-3300, Fax: (802) 362-3308, E-mail: amffish@sover.net, Internet: www.amff.com. Dir.: John Price, Cur.: Yoshi Akiyama
Special Museum - 1968
Presidential fishing tackle, fly fishing art 45100

Hildene, 1005 Hildene Rd, Manchester, VT 05254 - T: (802) 362-1788, Fax: (802) 362-1564, E-mail: info@hildene.org, Internet: www.hildene.org. Chm.: Nathaniel A. Boone
Local Museum - 1978
Historic house 45101

Southern Vermont Art Center, West Rd, Manchester, VT 05254 - T: (802) 362-1405, Fax: (802) 362-3274, E-mail: info@svac.org, Internet: www.svac.org. Dir.: Christopher Madkour
Fine Arts Museum / Folklore Museum - 1929
Art 45102

Mangum OK

Old Greer County Museum and Hall of Fame, 222 W Jefferson St, Mangum, OK 73554 - T: (580) 782-2851. Cur.: Joyce Holt
Local Museum - 1972 45103

Manhasset NY

Science Museum of Long Island, Leeds Pond Preserve, 1526 N Plandome Rd, Manhasset, NY 11030 - T: (516) 627-9400 ext 10, Fax: (516) 365-8927, E-mail: smli@compuserve.com, Internet: ourworld.compuserve.com/homepages/smli. Dir.: John Loret
Science&Tech Museum - 1963 45104

Manhattan KS

Goodnow Museum, 2301 Clafin Rd, Manhattan, KS 66502 - T: (785) 565-6490, Fax: (785) 565-6491, Internet: www.kshs.org. Dir.: D. Collins
Historical Museum - 1969
Home of pioneer Kansas educator, Isaac Tichenor Goodnow 45105

Hartford House Museum, 2309 Claflin Rd, Manhattan, KS 66502 - T: (785) 565-6490, Internet: www.co.riley.ks.us. Dir.: D. Cheryl Collins
Historical Museum - 1974
Pre-fabricated house shipped on the Hartford Steamboat to Manhattan, KS 45106

Manhattan Arts Center, 1520 Poyntz Av, Manhattan, KS 66502 - T: (785) 537-4420, Fax: (785) 539-3356, E-mail: director@manhattanarts.org, Internet: www.manhattanarts.org. Dir.: Penny Senften
Fine Arts Museum - 1996
Photograph coll, Grandma Layton drawing, Remington sculpture, Bronco Buster 45107

Marianna Kistler Beach Museum of Art, Kansas State University, 701 Beach Ln, Manhattan, KS 66506 - T: (785) 532-7718, Fax: (785) 532-7498, E-mail: klwalk@ksu.edu, Internet: www.ksu.edu/bma. CEO: Lorne E. Render
Fine Arts Museum / University Museum - 1996
Art of Kansas, American printmaking, works by John Steuart Curry, Thomas Hart Benton and Grant Wood, Gordon Parks, print portfolios 45108

Pioneer Log Cabin, City Park, 11th and Poyntz, Manhattan, KS 66502 - T: (785) 565-6490, Fax: (785) 565-6491, Internet: www.co.riley.ks.us. Dir.: D. Cheryl Collins
Historical Museum - 1914
Farm and shop tools 45109

Riley County Historical Museum, 2309 Claflin Rd, Manhattan, KS 66502 - T: (785) 565-6490, Fax: (785) 565-6491, Internet: www.co.riley.ks.us. Dir.: D. Cheryl Collins
Local Museum - 1914
County history 45110

Wolf House Museum, 630 Fremont, Manhattan, KS 66502 - T: (785) 565-6490, Fax: (785) 565-6491, Internet: www.co.riley.ks.us. Dir.: D. Cheryl Collins, Cur.: Edna Williams
Historical Museum - 1983
1868 boarding house 45111

Manistee MI

Manistee County Historical Museum, 425 River St, Manistee, MI 49660 - T: (231) 723-5531. Dir.: Steve Harold
Local Museum - 1953
Regional history, A.H. Lyman Drug Co 45112

Manistique MI

Imogene Herbert Historical Museum, Pioneer Park, Deer St, Manistique, MI 49854 - T: (906) 341-4680, 341-3650, E-mail: cdixon@up.net. Dir.: Carol Dixon, Cur.: Rebecca Peterson
Local Museum - 1963
Local history 45113

Manitou Springs CO

Miramont Castle Museum, 9 Capitol Hill Av, Manitou Springs, CO 80829 - T: (719) 685-1011. Dir.: Bob Yager
Historical Museum - 1976 45114

Manitowoc WI

Pinecrest Historical Village, 924 Pine Crest Ln, Manitowoc, WI 54221-0574 - T: (920) 684-4445, 684-5110, Fax: (920) 684-0573. Pres.: John Stangel
Local Museum / Open Air Museum - 1970
Local hist 45115

Rahr West Art Museum, 610 N 8th St, Manitowoc, WI 54220 - T: (920) 683-4501, Fax: (920) 683-5047, E-mail: rahrwest@manitowoc.org, Internet: www.rahrwestartmuseum.org. Dir.: Jan Smith, Asst. Dir.: Daniel Juchniewich
Fine Arts Museum - 1950
Art 45116

Wisconsin Maritime Museum, 75 Maritime Dr, Manitowoc, WI 54220-6823 - T: (920) 684-0218, Fax: (920) 684-0219, E-mail: maritime@lakesfield.net, Internet: www.wimaritimemuseum.com. Dir.: Jay C. Martin, Cur.: Bill Thiesen
Historical Museum - 1968
Maritime hist 45117

Mankato KS

Jewell County Historical Museum, 201 N Commercial St, Mankato, KS 66956 - T: (913) 378-3218
Local Museum / Agriculture Museum - 1961
Agriculture 45118

Mankato MN

Blue Earth County Historical Museum, 415 Cherry St, Mankato, MN 56001 - T: (507) 345-5566, E-mail: bechs@juno.com, Internet: www.ic.mankato.mn.us/reg9/bechs. Pres.: Jane Tarjeson, Exec. Dir.: James Lundgreen
Local Museum - 1901
Regional history 45119

Carnegie Art Center, Rotunda and Fireplace Galleries, 120 S Broad St, Mankato, MN 56001 - T: (507) 625-2730
Fine Arts Museum
Regional artists 45120

Helson Hall, Minnesota State University, 136 Mankato Av, Mankato, MN 56002 - T: (507) 389-6412, Internet: www.mankato.msus.edu/dept/artdept. Dir.: Harlan Bloomer
Fine Arts Museum
Drawings, American paintings, prints, crafts, bookplates 45121

Manlius NY

Town of Manlius Museum, 101 Scoville Av, Manlius, NY 13104 - T: (315) 682-6660, Fax: (315) 682-6660. Dir.: Julian Tasick
Local Museum - 1976 45122

Mansfield LA

Mansfield State Historc Site, 15149 Hwy 175, 3 mi SE of Mansfield, Mansfield, LA 71052 - T: (318) 872-1474, (888) 677-6267, Fax: (318) 871-4345, E-mail: mansfield@crt.state.la.us, Internet: www.crt.state.la.us/crt/parks/
Historical Museum / Military Museum - 1957
Civil War Battlefield 45123

Mansfield MO

Laura Ingalls Wilder-Rose Wilder Lane Historic Home and Museum, 3068 Hwy A, Mansfield, MO 65704 - T: (417) 924-3626, Fax: (417) 924-8580, E-mail: liwhone@windo.missouri.org, Internet: www.lauraingallswilderhome.com. C.E.O.: Jean C. Coday
Historical Museum - 1957 45124

Mansfield OH

Mansfield Art Center, 700 Marion Av, Mansfield, OH 44903 - T: (419) 756-1700, Fax: (419) 756-0860, E-mail: allen.56@osu.edu, Internet: www.mansfieldartcenter.com. Dir.: H. Daniel Butts
Fine Arts Museum - 1946 45125

Manteo NC

Fort Raleigh, US 64-264, Manteo, NC 27954 - T: (919) 473-2111, Fax: (919) 473-2595, Internet: www.nps.gov/fora. Head: Robert Raynolds
Natural History Museum - 1941 45126

Roanoke Island Festival Park, Homeport of the Elizabeth II, 1 Festival Park, Manteo, NC 27954 - T: (252) 475-1500, Fax: (252) 475-1507, E-mail: rifp.information@ncmail.net, Internet: www.roanokeisland.com. Dir.: Deloris Harrell
Historical Museum - 1983 45127

Mantorville MN

Dodge County Historical Museum, 615 Main, N, Mantorville, MN 55955 - T: (507) 635-5508, E-mail: dchg@means.net, Internet: www.dodgecohistorical.addr.com. Dir.: Idella M. Conwell
Local Museum - 1876
Regional history, former Episcopal church 45128

Restoration House, 540 Main St, Mantorville, MN 55955 - T: (507) 635-5140
Decorative Arts Museum - 1963
19th-c furniture, dishes, utensils, furnishings 45129

Maple Valley WA

Maple Valley Historical Museum, 23015 SE 216th Way, Maple Valley, WA 98038 - T: (425) 432-3470, Fax: (425) 432-3470, E-mail: pilgrim.dsk-c@worldnet.att.net., Internet: www.maplevalley.com/community/historical. Pres.: Mona Pickering
Local Museum - 1972
Local hist, fire engines 45130

Maquoketa IA

Jackson County Historical Museum, 1212 E Quarry, Fairgrounds, Maquoketa, IA 52060-1245 - T: (319) 652-5020, Fax: (319) 652-5020. Dir.: Toni Kracke
Local Museum / Agriculture Museum - 1964
Local history, agriculture - library 45131

Marathon FL

Crane Point Hammock Museum, 5550 Overseas Hwy, Marathon, FL 33050 - T: (305) 743-7124, 743-3900, Fax: (305) 743-0429, E-mail: tropcranept@aol.com, Internet: www.cranepoint.org. Exec. Dir.: Deanna S. Lloyd
Natural History Museum - 1990 45132

Marble CO

Marble Historical Museum, 412 W Main St, Marble, CO 81623 - T: (970) 963-1710, Fax: (970) 963-8435. C.E.O.: Thomas Williams
Local Museum - 1977
Local history 45133

Marblehead MA

Jeremiah Lee Mansion, 161 Washington St, Marblehead, MA 01945, mail addr: 170 Washington St, Marblehead, MA 01945 - T: (781) 631-1768, Fax: (781) 631-0917
Decorative Arts Museum - 1909
Decorative arts, paintings, maritime and folk art, musical instruments - archives 45134

King Hooper Mansion, 8 Hooper St, Marblehead, MA 01945 - T: (781) 631-2608, Fax: (781) 639-7890, E-mail: maaorg@gis.net, Internet: www.marbleheadarts.org. Exec. Dir.: Dharmena Downey
Fine Arts Museum - 1922 45135

Marblehead Historical Museum and J.O.J. Frost Folk Art Gallery, 170 Washington St, Marblehead, MA 01945 - T: (781) 631-7945, 631-1768, Fax: (781) 631-0917, E-mail: wendy.hubbard2@verizon.net, Internet: www.marbleheadhistory.org. Dir.: Wendy L. Hubbard, Pres.: Richard L. Tuve, Cur.: Judy Anderson
Local Museum / Folklore Museum - 1898
Local history, home of Col. Jeremiah Lee 45136

Marbletown NY

Ulster County Historical Society Museum, Rte 209, Marbletown, NY - T: (914) 338-5614. Dir.: Amanda C. Jones, Pres.: Agnes R. Kelly
Local Museum / Historical Museum - 1930 45137

Marbury MD

Smallwood's Retreat, Smallwood State Park, 2750 Sweden Point Rd, Marbury, MD 20658 - T: (301) 743-7613, Fax: (301) 743-9405, E-mail: park-smallwood@dnr.state.md.us, Internet: www.dnr.state.md.us. Dir.: Roberta Dorsch
Military Museum - 1954
State park museum, 18th c house and kitchen 45138

Marcellus NY

Marcellus Historical Society Museum, 6 Slocombe Av, Marcellus, NY 13108 - T: (315) 673-3112. Pres.: Peg Nolan
Historical Museum - 1960 45139

Marfa TX

Chinati Foundation, 1 Cavalry Row, Marfa, TX 79843 - T: (915) 729-4362, Fax: (915) 729-4597, E-mail: chinati@iglobal.net, Internet: www.chinati.org. Dir.: Marianne Stockebrand, Pres.: Fredericka Hunter
Fine Arts Museum - 1986
Art 45140

Marianna AR

Marianna-Lee County Museum, 67 W Main St, Marianna, AR 72360 - T: (870) 295-2469. Cur.: Suzy Keasler
Local Museum - 1981
Regional history, housed in the Marianna Elks Club 45141

Marietta GA

Cobb County Youth Museum, 649 Cheatham Hill Dr, Marietta, GA 30064 - T: (770) 427-2563, Fax: (770) 427-1060, E-mail: cocoyumu@aol.com, Internet: www.cobbcountyyouthmuseum.org. Dir.: Anita S. Barton
Ethnology Museum - 1964
Youth, jet trainer, canoe, caboose 45142

Cobb Museum of Art, 30 Atlanta St NE, Marietta, GA 30060 - T: (770) 528-1444, Fax: (770) 528-1440, Internet: www.mariettasquare.com. Dir.: Aaron Berger
Fine Arts Museum - 1986
American art (19th-20th c) 45143

Marietta Museum of History, 1 Depot St, Marietta, GA 30060 - T: (770) 528-0430, 528-0431, Fax: (770) 528-0450, E-mail: dcox@city.marietta.ga.us, Internet: www.mariettahistory.org. Exec. Dir.: Dan Cox
Local Museum 45144

Museo Abarth, 1111 Via Bayless, Marietta, GA 30066 - T: (770) 928-1342
Science&Tech Museum - 1989
Abarth engine, model cars, new car brochures, emblems, art work 45145

Root House Museum, Marietta Pkwy and Polk St, Marietta, GA 30060 - T: (770) 426-4982, Fax: (770) 499-9540, E-mail: clhs2@bellsouth.net, Internet: cobblandmarks.com. Dir.: Daryl Barksdale
Local Museum - 1972 45146

Marietta OH

Campus Martius Museum, 601 Second St, Marietta, OH 45750 - T: (740) 373-3750, Fax: (740) 373-3680, E-mail: cmmoriv@ohiohistory.org, Internet: www.ohiohistory.org/places/campus. Dir.: Gary C. Ness
Historical Museum - 1919 45147

The Castle, 418 Fourth St, Marietta, OH 45750 - T: (740) 373-4180, Fax: (740) 373-4233, E-mail: Castle@marietta.edu, Internet: www.mariettacastle.org. Dir.: Lynne Shuman
Local Museum - 1992
Historic house 45148

Grover M. Hermann Fine Arts Center, c/o Marietta College, 215 Fifth St, Marietta, OH 45750 - T: (740) 376-4696, Fax: (740) 376-4529, Internet: www.marietta.edu
Fine Arts Museum - 1965
Contemporary American paintings, sculpture and crafts, African and pre-Columbian art 45149

Harmar Station, 220 Gilman St, Marietta, OH 45750 - T: (740) 374-3424, Fax: (740) 373-7808, E-mail: jmoberg@charter.net, Internet: www.harmarstation.com. C.E.O.: Jack Moberg
Science&Tech Museum - 1996
Engines, cars and accesories, "0" gauge, larger scale toys 45150

Ohio River Museum, 601 Front St, Marietta, OH 45750 - T: (614) 373-3750, Fax: (614) 373-3680, E-mail: Cmmoriv@marietta.edu, Internet: www.ohiohistory.org/places/ohriver. Dir.: Gary C. Ness
Historical Museum - 1941 45151

Marilla NY

Marilla Historical Society Museum, 1810 Two Rod Rd, Marilla, NY 14102 - T: (716) 652-5396. Pres.: Mary Nette
Local Museum - 1960 45152

Marineland FL

Marineland Ocean Museum, 9507 Ocean Shore Blvd, Marineland, FL 32086-9602 - T: (904) 471-1111, Fax: (904) 461-0156, E-mail: mor@aug.com, Internet: www.marineland.com. Dir.: David Internoscia
Historical Museum - 1938 45153

Marinette WI

Marinette County Historical Museum, Stephenson Island, U.S. Hwy 41, Marinette, WI 54143 - T: (715) 732-0831. Pres.: Frank Lauermann
Local Museum - 1962
Local hist 45154

Marion IA

Granger House, 970 Tenth St, Marion, IA 52302-0753 - T: (319) 377-6672, E-mail: grangerhouse@juno.com, Internet: community.marion.ia.us/granger/
Decorative Arts Museum - 1973
Victorian furnishings, wagons 45155

Marion Heritage Center, 590 Tenth St, Marion, IA 52302 - T: (319) 477-6377, E-mail: Marionheritage@juno.com
Local Museum 45156

Marion IL

Williamson County Historical Society Museum, 105 S Van Buren, Marion, IL 62959 - T: (618) 997-5863, E-mail: charla@thewchs.com, Internet: www.thewchs.com. Cur.: Helen Davis
Local Museum - 1976
County history, housed former county jail and sheriff's home 45157

Marion IN

Marion Public Library Museum, Carnegie Bldg, 600 S Washington St, Marion, IN 46953 - T: (765) 668-2900, Fax: (765) 668-2911, Internet: www.marion.lib.in.us. Dir.: Sue Israel
Local Museum - 1884
Local hist 45158

Quilters Hall of Fame, 926 S Washington St, Marion, IN 46953 - T: (765) 674-9602, Fax: (765) 664-9333, E-mail: quilters@comteck.com, Internet: quiltershalloffame.org. Pres.: Hazel Carter
Special Museum - 1979 45159

Marion MA

Cecil Clark Davis Gallery, 80 Pleasant St, Marion, MA 02738 - T: (508) 748-1266, Fax: (508) 748-2759, Internet: www.marionartcenter.org. Dir.: Wendy Bidstrup
Fine Arts Museum - 1957
Cecil Clark Davis (1877-1955), portrait paintings 45160

Marion NC

Historic Carson House, Hwy 70 West of Marion, Marion, NC 28752 - T: (704) 724-4640. Pres.: Nina Greenlee
Historical Museum - 1964 45161

Marion OH

Harding Home and Museum, 380 Mount Vernon Av, Marion, OH 43302 - T: (740) 387-9630, Fax: (740) 387-9630, E-mail: hardinghome@marion.net, Internet: www.ohiohistory.org. C.E.O.: Melinda Gilpin
Historical Museum - 1925 45162

Marion County Historical Society Museum, 169 E Church St, Marion, OH 43302 - T: (740) 387-4255, E-mail: mchist@gte.net, Internet: home1.gte.net/mchist. Dir.: Jane E. Rupp
Local Museum - 1989
County hist, Warren G Harding presidential artifacts 45163

Stengel-True Museum, 504 S State St, Marion, OH 43302 - T: (614) 387-7150. Dir.: J.C. Ballinger
Local Museum - 1973 45164

Marion VA

Smyth County Museum, 105 E Strother St, Marion, VA 24354 - T: (540) 783-7067, 783-7286. Pres.: Brenda Gwyn, Dir.: Joan T. Armstrong
Local Museum - 1961
Local hist 45165

Mariposa CA

California State Mining and Mineral Museum, 5005 Fairgrounds Dr, Mariposa, CA 95338 - T: (209) 742-7625, Fax: (209) 966-3597, E-mail: mineralmuseum@sierratel.com, Internet: www.parks.ca.gov. Dir.: Peggy Ronning
Natural History Museum / Science&Tech Museum - 1988 45166

Marksville LA

Tunica-Biloxi Native American Museum, 150 Melancon Rd, Marksville, LA 71351 - T: (318) 253-8174, Fax: (318) 253-7711, Internet: www.tunica.org. Cur.: Earl J. Barbry jr
Historical Museum - 1989
French and Indian artifacts 45167

Marlboro MA

Peter Rice Homestead, 377 Elm St, Marlboro, MA 01752 - T: (508) 485-4763. Cur.: Richard Wilcox
Local Museum - 1962
Local history 45168

Marlboro NY

Gomez Foundation for Mill House, Mill House Rd, Marlboro, NY 12542 - T: (914) 236-3126, Fax: (914) 236-3365, E-mail: gomezmillhouse@juno.com, Internet: www.gomez.org. Dir.: C.F. William Maurer
Decorative Arts Museum / Local Museum - 1984
Historic house 45169

Marlboro VT

Marlboro Museum, N Main St, Marlboro, VT 05344 - T: (802) 464-0329, Fax: (802) 464-1275, E-mail: dhdaod@sover.net, Internet: www.marlboro.vt.us. Pres.: Alan O. Dann
Local Museum - 1958
Local hist 45170

Marlboro

Southern Vermont Natural History Museum, Rte 9, Marlboro, mail addr: POB 1, Jacksonville, VT 05342 - T: (802) 464-0048, Fax: (802) 464-0017, E-mail: metcalfe@sover.net, Internet: www.vermontmuseum.org. Dir.: Edward C. Metcalfe
Natural History Museum - 1962 45171

Marlinton WV

Pocahontas County Museum, Seneca Trail, Marlinton, WV 24954 - T: (304) 799-4973, Fax: (304) 799-6466. Pres.: Mary Lou Dilley, Cur.: H.L. Sheets
Local Museum - 1962
Local hist 45172

Marquette MI

Marquette County History Museum, 213 N Front St, Marquette, MI 49855 - T: (906) 226-3571, E-mail: fporter@up.net, Internet: www.marquettecohistory.org. Dir.: Frances J. Porter, Cur.: Kaye Hiebel, Joy Bender Hadley
Local Museum - 1918
Local history - library 45173

Northern Michigan University Art Museum, Lee Hall, 1401 Preque Isle Av, Marquette, MI 49855 - T: (906) 227-1481, Fax: (906) 227-2276, E-mail: wfrancis@nmu.edu, Internet: www.nmu.edu/department/admuseum. Dir.: Wayne Francis
Fine Arts Museum
Contemporary prints ans sculpture, Japanese and American illustrations 45174

Marshall AR

Searcy County Museum, Hwy 27, S, Marshall, AR 72650 - T: (870) 448-5786. Pres.: Veda Clemons
Local Museum - 1980
Regional history, Old Searcy County Jail 45175

Marshall IL

Clark County Museum, 4th and Maple Sts, Marshall, IL 62441 - T: (217) 826-6098, E-mail: dalannemiller@hotmail.com. Pres.: Ken Jensen
Local Museum - 1969
Local history 45176

Marshall MI

American Museum of Magic, 107 E Michigan St, Marshall, MI 49068 - T: (616) 781-7674, 781-7666. Head: Elaine H. Lund
Performing Arts Museum - 1978 45177

Honolulu House Museum, 107 N Kalamazoo, Marshall, MI 49068 - T: (616) 781-8544, Fax: (616) 789-0371, E-mail: dircherie@aol.com, Internet: www.marshallhistoricalsociety.org. Dir.: Cherie Riser
Local Museum - 1962 45178

Marshall MN

Lyon County Historical Society Museum, 114 N 3rd St, Marshall, MN 56258 - T: (507) 537-6580, Fax: (507) 537-1699. Dir.: Ellayne Velde-Conyers
Local Museum - 1934
Regional history 45179

Museum of Natural History, Southwest State University, 1501 State St, Marshall, MN 56258 - T: (507) 537-6178, Fax: (507) 537-7154, E-mail: desy@ssu.southwest.msus.edu, Internet: www.southweststate.edu/program. Dir.: Dr. Elizabeth A. Desy
University Museum / Natural History Museum - 1972 45180

Marshall TX

Franks Antique Doll Museum, 211 W Grand Av, Marshall, TX 75670 - T: (903) 935-3065, 935-3070. Head: Clara Franks
Decorative Arts Museum - 1960
Dolls 45181

Harrison County Historical Museum, 707 N Washington, Marshall, TX 75670 - T: (903) 938-2680, Fax: (903) 927-2534, E-mail: museum@shreve.net, Internet: www.cets.sfasu.edu/Harrison/. C.E.O.: Carrol Fletcher
Historical Museum - 1965
Local hist 45182

Michelson Museum of Art, 216 N Bolivar, Marshall, TX 75671 - T: (903) 935-9480, Fax: (903) 935-1974, E-mail: leomich@shreve.net, Internet: www.michelsonmuseum.org. Dir.: Susan Spears
Fine Arts Museum - 1985
Art 45183

Marshalltown IA

Central Iowa Art Museum, Fisher Center, 709 S Center St, Marshalltown, IA 50158 - T: (641) 753-9013, Fax: (641) 753-9013, E-mail: ciaa@marshallnet.com. Dir.: Valerie Busse
Fine Arts Museum / Decorative Arts Museum - 1946
Art, ceramics 45184

Marshall County Museum, 202 E Church St, Marshalltown, IA 50158 - T: (515) 752-6664, E-mail: marshallhistory@adiis.net, Internet: www.marshallnet.com/museum. Pres.: Jeffery Quam, Dir.: Gary L. Cameron
Local Museum - 1908
Local hist 45185

Marshfield WI

New Visions Gallery, 1000 N Oak Av, Marshfield, WI 54449 - T: (715) 387-5562, E-mail: nvisions@tznet.com. Dir.: Ann Waisbrot
Fine Arts Museum / Decorative Arts Museum - 1975
Art 45186

Upham Mansion, 212 W Third, Marshfield, WI 54449 - T: (715) 387-3322
Local Museum - 1952 45187

Marthaville LA

Louisiana Country Music Museum, State Hwy 1221, Marthaville, LA 71450 - T: (318) 472-6255, Fax: (318) 472-6255. C.E.O./Cur.: Marsha Gentry
Music Museum - 1981
Musical instrument-shaped bldg 45188

Martin TN

University Museum, The University of Tennessee at Martin, Martin, TN 38238 - T: (901) 587-7094, Fax: (901) 587-7074, E-mail: museum@utm.edu. Dir.: Richard Saunders
University Museum / Local Museum - 1981
Local hist 45189

Martinsburg WV

Boarman Arts Center, 208 S Queen St, Martinsburg, WV 25401 - T: (304) 263-0224
Fine Arts Museum - 1987
Arts and crafts incl photography, sculpture, oils, acrylics, watercolors by local artisans 45190

General Adam Stephen House, 309 East John St, Martinsburg, WV 25402 - T: (304) 267-4434. Pres.: Martin Keesecker, Cur.: Keith E. Hammersla
Local Museum / Folklore Museum / Decorative Arts Museum - 1959
Historic house 45191

Martinsville VA

Piedmont Arts Museum, 215 Starling Av, Martinsville, VA 24112 - T: (540) 632-3221, Fax: (540) 638-3963, E-mail: PAA@PiedmontArts.org, Internet: www.piedmontarts.org. Dir.: Toy L. Cobbe
Fine Arts Museum - 1961
Arts 45192

Virginia Museum of Natural History, 1001 Douglas Av, Martinsville, VA 24112 - T: (540) 666-8600, Fax: (540) 632-6487, E-mail: spike@vmnh.org, Internet: www.vmnh.org. Dir.: Stephen J. Pike, Cur.: Dr. Elizabeth A. Moore (Colls), Dr. Richard S. Hoffman (Recent Invertebrates), Dr. Lauck W. Ward (Invertebrate Paleontology), Asst. Cur.: Dr. James S. Beard (Earth Sciences), Dr. Nicholas C. Fraser (Vertebrate Paleontology), Dr. Nancy D. Moncrief (Mammalogy)
Natural History Museum - 1984
Natural hist 45193

Marylhurst OR

The Art Gym, Marylhurst University, 17600 Pacific Hwy 43, Marylhurst, OR 97036-0261 - T: (503) 699-6243, Fax: (503) 636-9526, E-mail: artgym@marylhurst.edu, Internet: www.marylhurst.edu/. Dir./Cur.: Terri M. Hopkins
Fine Arts Museum / University Museum - 1980 45194

Marysville OH

Union County Historical Society Museum, 246-254 W Sixth St, Marysville, OH 43040 - T: (937) 644-0568. Pres.: Robert W. Parrott
Local Museum - 1949 45195

Maryville MO

Olive DeLuce Art Gallery, Northwest Missouri State University, 800 University Dr, Maryville, MO 64468 - T: (660) 562-1326, Fax: (660) 562-1346, E-mail: plaber@mail.nwmissouri.edu. Cur.: Philip Laber
Fine Arts Museum
Contemporary 45196

Maryville TN

Fine Arts Center Gallery, Maryville College, 502 E Lamar Alexander Pkwy, Maryville, TN 37804 - T: (865) 981-8000, 981-8150, Fax: (865) 273-8873, E-mail: sowders@maryvillecollege.edu, Internet: www.maryvillecollege.edu. Chm.: Mark Hall
Public Gallery 45197

Sam Houston Historical Schoolhouse, 3650 Old Sam Houston School Rd, Maryville, TN 37804-5644 - T: (423) 983-1550, E-mail: samhoustonschool@aol.com, Internet: www.geocities.com/samhoustonschoolhouse. Pres.: E. Simerly
Local Museum - 1965
Historic House 45198

Mason TX

Mason County Museum, 321 Moody St, Mason, TX 76856 - T: (915) 347-6137
Local Museum - 1965 45199

Mason City IA

Charles H. MacNider Museum, 303 2nd St, SE, Mason City, IA 50401-3666 - T: (641) 421-3666, Fax: (641) 422-9612, E-mail: macnider@macniderart.org, Internet: www.macniderart.org. Dir.: Sheila Perry
Fine Arts Museum - 1964
American art incl. Bil Baird puppets 45200

Mason Neck VA

Gunston Hall Plantation, 10709 Gunston Rd, Mason Neck, VA 22079 - T: (703) 550-9220, Fax: (703) 550-9480, E-mail: Historic@GunstonHall.org, Internet: www.gunstonhall.org. Dir.: Thomas A. Lainhoff, Dep. Dir.: Susan A. Borchardt
Local Museum - 1932
Historic house 45201

Massillon OH

Massillon Museum, 121 Lincoln Way E, Massillon, OH 44646 - T: (330) 833-4061, Fax: (330) 833-2925, Internet: www.massillonmuseum.com. Dir.: John Klassen
Fine Arts Museum / Historical Museum - 1933 45202

Matawan NJ

Burrowes Mansion Museum, 94 Main St, Matawan, NJ 07747 - T: (732) 566-3817, 566-5605
Local Museum - 1976
Local hist 45203

Mattapoisett MA

Mattapoisett Museum and Carriage House, 5 Church St, Mattapoisett, MA 02739 - T: (508) 758-2844, E-mail: mattapoisett.museum@verizon.net. Pres.: Seth F. Mendell, Cur.: Bette Roberts
Local Museum - 1959
Local history, Christian meeting House 45204

Maumee OH

Wolcott House Museum Complex, 1031 River Rd, Maumee, OH 43537 - T: (419) 893-9602, Fax: (419) 893-3108, E-mail: mvhs@accesstoledo.com, Internet: www.maumee.org/wolcott/wolcott.htm. Cur.: Charles Jacobs
Historical Museum - 1961 45205

Mauston WI

The Boorman House, 211 N Union St, Mauston, WI 53948 - T: (608) 462-5931, E-mail: rclarkjco@hotmail.com. Pres.: Nancy McCullick
Local Museum - 1963
Historic house 45206

Maxwell IA

Community Historical Museum, Main St, Maxwell, IA 50161 - T: (515) 385-2376, E-mail: jlengeli@prodigy.net. Pres.: Robert Swanson, Cur.: Jesse Parr, Historian: Mildred McIntosh
Local Museum - 1964
Local history 45207

Maysville KY

Mason County Museum, 215 Sutton St, Maysville, KY 41056 - T: (606) 564-5865, Fax: (606) 564-4372, E-mail: museum@masoncountymuseum.org, Internet: www.masoncountymuseum.org. Dir.: Dawn C. Browning, Cur.: Sue Ellen Grannis (Books, Art and Artifacts)
Fine Arts Museum / Local Museum - 1876
Art, genealogy, local history 45208

Mayville MI

Mayville Area Museum of History and Genealogy, 2124 Ohmer Rd, Mayville, MI 48744 - T: (989) 843-7185, 843-6389. Pres./Dir./Cur.: Frank E. Franzel
Local Museum - 1972
History, genealogy 45209

Mayville ND

Northern Lights Art Gallery, c/o Mayville State University, 330 NE Third St, Mayville, ND 58257 - T: (701) 786-2301 ext 4742, Fax: (701) 786-4748. Dir.: Cynthia Kaldor
University Museum / Fine Arts Museum - 1999 45210

Mayville WI

Mayville Historical Society Museum, 11 N German St, Mayville, WI 53050 - T: (414) 387-2420, Fax: (414) 387-5944, Internet: www.mayvillecity.com. Pres.: Ann Guse
Local Museum - 1968
Local hist 45211

Mazomanie WI

Mazomanie Historical Society Museum, 118 Brodhead St, Mazomanie, WI 53560 - T: (608) 795-2992, 795-4733, Fax: (608) 795-4576, E-mail: robertd@midplains.net, Internet: www.mazoarea.com/ypahist.htm. Pres.: Joan S. Moc, Cur.: Rita Frakes
Historical Museum - 1965
Local hist, tool coll 45212

Meade KS

Meade County Historical Society Museum, 200 E Carthage, Meade, KS 67864 - T: (316) 873-2359, 873-2224. C.E.O.: Leroy Lemaster
Local Museum - 1969
American Indian artifacts 45213

Meadville PA

Baldwin-Reynolds House Museum, 639 Terrace St, Meadville, PA 16335 - T: (814) 724-6080, Fax: (814) 333-8173, E-mail: cchs@ccfls.org, Internet: www.visitcrawford.org. Exec. Dir.: Laura W. Polo, Cur.: Ruth S. Cummings
Historical Museum - 1883
Historic house 45214

Bowman, Megahan and Penelec Galleries, Allegheny College, N Main St, Meadville, PA 16335 - T: (814) 332-4365, Fax: (814) 724-6834, E-mail: rraczka@allegheny.edu, Internet: www.allegheny.edu. Dir.: Robert Raczka
Fine Arts Museum / University Museum - 1970
Contemporary American art 45215

Medford MA

Royall House, 15 George St, Medford, MA 02155 - T: (781) 396-9032, Fax: (781) 395-7766. Pres.: Alan Martoana, Exec. Dir.: Fred J. Schlicher
Historical Museum - 1908
Colonial history, Georgian architecture, American slavery 45216

Tufts University Art Gallery, Aidekman Arts Center, 11 Talbot Av, Medford, MA 02155 - T: (617) 627-3518, Fax: (617) 627-3121, Internet: www.tufts.edu/as/gallery. Dir.: Doug Bell
Fine Arts Museum / University Museum - 1955
Art 45217

Medford NJ

Air Victory Museum, 68 Stacy Haines Rd, Medford, NJ 08055 - T: (609) 267-4488, Fax: (609) 702-1852, Internet: www.airvictorymuseum.org. Pres.: Barbara C. Snyder, Dir.: Ray Pysher
Science&Tech Museum - 1989
Aeronautics 45218

Medford OK

Grant County Museum, Main and Cherokee Sts, Medford, OK 73759 - T: (580) 395-2822, Fax: (580) 395-2343. Pres.: Mariann Smrcka
Local Museum / Historical Museum - 1965 45219

Medford OR

Rogue Gallery and Art Center, 40 S Bartlett, Medford, OR 97501 - T: (541) 772-8118, Fax: (541) 772-0294, E-mail: roguegal@medford.com, Internet: www.roguegallery.org. Dir.: Judy Barnes
Public Gallery / Fine Arts Museum - 1959 45220

Southern Oregon Historical Society Museum, 106 N Central Av, Medford, OR 97501-5926 - T: (541) 773-6536, Fax: (541) 776-7994, E-mail: director@sohs.org, Internet: www.sohs.org. Dir.: Brad Linder, Cur.: Mary Ames Sheret
Historical Museum / Open Air Museum - 1946
library, archive 45221

Media PA

Colonial Pennsylvania Plantation, Ridley Creek State Park, Media, PA 19063 - T: (610) 566-1725. Pres.: David Stitely
Local Museum - 1973
Local hist 45222

Medicine Lodge KS

Carry A. Nation Home Memorial, 211 W Fowler, Medicine Lodge, KS 67104 - T: (316) 886-3553, Fax: (316) 886-5978. C.E.O.: Dorothy Reed
Historical Museum - 1950
1880-1903 home of Carry A. Nation 45223

Medina OH

America's Ice Cream and Dairy Museum, 1050 W Lafayette Rd, Medina, OH 44256 - T: (330) 764-9269, 722-3839, Fax: (330) 722-1326, E-mail: elmfarm934@aol.com. Cur.: Carl T. Abell
Special Museum - 1999
Ice cream, signs, advertising, photos, prints, antique toys, prototype scooper, trucks and bottles, cream separators, butter churns, milk wagon 45224

John Smart House, Medina County Historical Society, 206 N Elmwood St, Medina, OH 44256 - T: (330) 722-1341. Cur.: Thomas D. Hilberg
Local Museum / Historic Site - 1922 45225

Portholes Into the Past, 4450 Poe Rd, Medina, OH 44256 - T: (330) 725-0402, Fax: (330) 722-2439, E-mail: mmishne@nobleknights.com. Pres./Dir.: Merle H. Mishne
Fine Arts Museum / Public Gallery / Historical Museum / Science&Tech Museum - 1984 45226

Meeker CO

White River Museum, 565 Park St, Meeker, CO 81641 - T: (970) 878-9982. Cur.: Ardith Douglass
Folklore Museum / Local Museum - 1956
Regional history 45227

Meeteetse WY

Meeteetse Museums, 1033 Park Av, Meeteetse, WY 82433 - T: (307) 868-2423, Fax: (307) 868-2565, Internet: www.meeteetsewy.com
Local Museum - 1974
Local hist, military from WW 1 to Vietnam War 45228

Melbourne FL

Brevard Museum of Art and Science, 1463-1520 Highland Av, Melbourne, FL 32935, mail addr: POB 360835, Melbourne, FL 32936-0835 - T: (321) 242-0737, Fax: (321) 242-0798, E-mail: artmuseum@mindspring.com, Internet: www.artandscience.org. Dir.: Sheila Stewart-Leach, Jack Lemback, Cur.: Jackie Borsanyi
Fine Arts Museum / Science&Tech Museum - 1978
Art, science 45229

Melrose LA

Melrose Plantation Home Complex, Melrose General Delivery, Melrose, LA 71452 - T: (318) 379-0055, Fax: (318) 379-0055, E-mail: melrose@worldnet.la.net. Cur.: Todd Cooper
Historical Museum / Folklore Museum - 1971
Early Louisiana type plantation, home of Marie Therese Coin-Coin, freed slave who became owner of plantation 45230

Memphis TN

Art Museum of the University of Memphis, 142 Communication & Fine Arts Bldg, Memphis, TN 38152-3200 - T: (901) 678-2224, Fax: (901) 678-5118, E-mail: artmuseum@memphis.edu, Internet: www.amum.org. Dir.: Dr. Leslie Luebbers, Asst. Dir.: Lisa Francisco, Cur.: Patricia Podzorski
Fine Arts Museum - 1981
Fine arts 45231

C.H. Nash Museum-Chucalissa Archaeological Museum, 1987 Indian Village Dr, Memphis, TN 38109 - T: (901) 785-3160, Fax: (901) 785-0519, E-mail: lwweaver@memphis.edu, Internet: cas.memphis.edu/~chucalissa. Dir.: Luella Weaver
University Museum / Ethnology Museum / Archaeological Museum - 1955
Archaeology, Native American Choctaw & Prehistoric Native Mississippian culture 45232

The Children's Museum of Memphis, 2525 Central Av, Memphis, TN 38104 - T: (901) 458-2678, Fax: (901) 458-4033, E-mail: children@cmom.com, Internet: www.cmom.com. Dir.: Judy Caldwell
Special Museum - 1987 45233

Clough-Hanson Gallery, Rhodes College, Clough Hall, 2000 N Pkwy, Memphis, TN 38112 - T: (901) 843-3442, Fax: (901) 843-3727, E-mail: pacini@rhodes.edu, Internet: artslides2.art.rhodes.edu/

gallery.html. Dir./Cur.: Marina Pacini
Fine Arts Museum - 1970
Local, regional and national art, textiles, woodcarvings 45234

The Dixon Gallery and Gardens, 4339 Park Av, Memphis, TN 38117 - T: (901) 761-5250, Fax: (901) 682-0943, E-mail: adm1@dixon.org, Internet: www.dixon.org. Dir.: James J. Kamm, Cur.: Robert W. Torchia, Asst. Cur.: Vivian Kung-Haga
Fine Arts Museum - 1976
Impressionist art - library 45235

Fire Museum of Memphis, 118 Adams Av, Memphis, TN 38103 - T: (901) 320-5650, Fax: (901) 452-8422, E-mail: jim@firemuseum.com, Internet: www.firemuseum.com. C.E.O. & Pres.: Jimmy V. Hamilton, Cur.: Shannon Perry
Special Museum - 1993
Fire fighting 45236

First Tennessee Heritage Collection, 165 Madison Av, Memphis, TN 38103 - T: (901) 523-4382, 523-4291, Fax: (901) 523-4354
Fine Arts Museum - 1979
Engravings, etchings, lithographs, murals, paintings, sculpture, watercolors 45237

Graceland, 3764 Elvis Presley Blvd, Memphis, TN 38116 - T: (901) 332-3322, Fax: (901) 344-3116, E-mail: graceland@memphisonline.com, Internet: www.elvis.com. Pres.: Priscilla Presley, Dir.: Jack Soden
Music Museum - 1982
Mansion occupied by Elvis Presley from 1957 until his death in 1977 45238

Magevney House, 198 Adams, Memphis, TN 38103 - T: (901) 526-4464, Fax: (901) 526-8666. Cur.: Kate Dixon
Local Museum - 1941
Historic house 45239

Mallory-Neely House, 652 Adams Av, Memphis, TN 38105 - T: (901) 523-1484, Fax: (901) 526-8666, Internet: www.memphismuseums.org
Decorative Arts Museum - 1973 45240

Memphis Belle B17 Flying Fortress, 5118 Park Av, Memphis, TN 38117 - T: (901) 412-8071, Fax: (901) 767-4612, E-mail: doctorhar@aol.com, Internet: www.memphisbelle.com
Military Museum - 1967
B-17 aircraft 45241

Memphis Brooks Museum of Art, 1934 Poplar Av, Overton Park, Memphis, TN 38104-2765 - T: (901) 544-6200, Fax: (901) 725-4071, E-mail: brooks@brooksmuseum.org, Internet: www.brooksmuseum.org. Dir.: Kaywin Feldman, Cur.: Dana Holland-Beickert
Fine Arts Museum - 1913
Fine arts, paintings, sculpture, glass, textiles, porcelain - library 45242

Memphis College of Art Gallery, 1930 Poplar Av, Memphis, TN 38104 - T: (901) 726-4085, 272-5100, Fax: (901) 272-5104, E-mail: info@mca.edu, Internet: www.mca.edu. Pres.: Jeffrey D. Nesin
Fine Arts Museum / University Museum - 1936
Art 45243

Memphis Pink Palace Museum, 3050 Central Av, Memphis, TN 38111 - T: (901) 320-6369, 320-6398, Fax: (901) 320-6391, E-mail: more_info@memphismuseums.org, Internet: www.memphismuseums.org. Dir.: Dr. Douglas R. Noble, Pres.: Mary Birks
Historical Museum / Natural History Museum / Science&Tech Museum - 1928
Natural hist, science, cultural hist 45244

Mississippi River Museum at Mud Island River Park, 125 N Front St, Memphis, TN 38103 - T: (901) 576-7241, Fax: (901) 576-6666, E-mail: giuntini@memphis.magibox.net, Internet: www.mudisland.com. Cur.: Trey Giuntini
Local Museum / Natural History Museum - 1978
Natural and cultural hist of the Lower Mississippi River 45245

National Civil Rights Museum, 450 Mulberry St, Memphis, TN 38103 - T: (901) 521-9699, Fax: (901) 521-9740, Internet: www.civilrightsmuseum.org. Pres.: J.R. Hyde, Dir.: Beverly Robertson
Historical Museum
Modern hist 45246

National Ornamental Metal Museum, 374 Metal Museum Dr, Memphis, TN 38106 - T: (901) 774-6380, Fax: (901) 774-6382, E-mail: metal@wspice.com, Internet: www.metalmuseum.org. Dir.: James A. Wallace, Asst. Dir.: Judy Wallace
Decorative Arts Museum - 1976
Historic and contemporary decorative & fine art metalwork, sculptures, jewellery 45247

Peabody Place Museum, 119 S Main St, Memphis, TN 38103 - T: (901) 523-2787
Fine Arts Museum - 1998
Asian art 45248

Mendham NJ

John Ralston Museum, 313 Rte 24, Mendham Rd, Mendham, NJ 07945 - T: (973) 543-6878, Fax: (973) 543-1149, E-mail: pfr14@aol.com, Internet: www.ralstonmuseum.org. Pres.: Tracey Kinsell
Historical Museum - 1964 45249

Mendocino CA

Kelley House Museum, 45007 Albion St, Mendocino, CA 95460 - T: (707) 937-5791, Fax: (707) 937-2156, E-mail: kelleyhs@mcn.org, Internet: www.mendocinohistory.org. Dir.: Katharine Bicknell
Local Museum - 1973
Local hist 45250

Mendocino Art Center Gallery, 45200 Little Lake St, Mendocino, CA 95460 - T: (707) 937-5818, Fax: (707) 937-1764, Internet: www.mendocinoartcenter.org. Dir.: Peggy Templer
Public Gallery - 1959
Graphics, paintings, sculpture 45251

Mendota MN

Sibley Historic Site, 1357 Sibley Memorial Hwy, Mendota, MN 55150, mail addr: POB 50772, Mendota, MN 55150 - T: (651) 452-1596, Fax: (651) 452-1238, E-mail: sibleyhouse@mnhs.org, Internet: www.mnhs.org/sites. Pres.: Marveen Minish
Historical Museum - 1910
Henry Hastings Sibley house, dwelling & trading house, later Minnesota's first state governor's house 45252

Menominee MI

Menominee County Heritage Museum, 904 11th Av, Menominee, MI 49858 - T: (906) 863-9000. Dir./Cur.: William C. King, Cur.: Steven G. Baretow
Local Museum - 1967
Regional history - library, research center 45253

Menomonee Falls WI

Old Falls Village, N 96 W 15791 County Line Rd, Menomonee Falls, WI 53051 - T: (414) 250-5096, Fax: (414) 250-5097, Internet: www.menomoneefalls.us. Dir.: Debra Zindler
Local Museum - 1966
Historic village 45254

Menomonie WI

Furlong Art Gallery, University of Wisconsin-Stout, Department of Art and Design, Menomonie, WI 54751 - T: (715) 232-2261, Fax: (715) 232-1346, E-mail: sorrellm@uwstout.edu, Internet: www.furlonggallery.uwstout.edu. Dir.: M.E. Sorell
Fine Arts Museum / University Museum - 1965
Art 45255

John Furlong Gallery → Furlong Art Gallery

Mentor OH

James A. Garfield National Historic Site, 8095 Mentor Av, Mentor, OH 44060 - T: (440) 255-8722, Fax: (440) 255-8545, E-mail: garfield@wrhs.org, Internet: www.wrhs.org. Dir.: Edith Serkownek
Historic Site - 1936 45256

Lake County Historical Society Museum, 8610 King Memorial Rd, Mentor, OH 44060 - T: (440) -255-8979, Fax: (440) 255-8980. Dir.: Christopher H. Gillcrest
Local Museum - 1936 45257

Mequon WI

Concordia University-Wisconsin Art Gallery, 12800 N Lake Shore Dr, Mequon, WI 53097 - T: (414) 243-5700, Fax: (414) 243-4351, E-mail: gstone@bach.cuw.edu, Internet: www.cuw.edu. Dir.: Jeff Shawhan
Fine Arts Museum / University Museum 45258

Crafts Museum, 11458 N Laguna Dr, Mequon, WI 53092 - T: (262) 242-1571. Dir.: Bob Siegel
Special Museum - 1972
Arts and crafts, wood-carving - woodenshoes, handcarving, ice-harvesting (storage, iceboxes etc.) 45259

Merced CA

Merced County Courthouse Museum, 21st and N Sts, Merced, CA 95340 - T: (209) 723-2401, Fax: (209) 723-8029, E-mail: info@mercedmuseum.org, Internet: www.mercedmuseum.org
Local Museum - 1975
Local history 45260

Mercer PA

Mercer County Museum, 119 S Pitt St, Mercer, PA 16137 - T: (724) 662-3490, Internet: www.pathway.net/mchs. Exec. Dir.: William C. Philson, Pres. & C.E.O.: David M. Miller
Historical Museum - 1946
Local hist 45261

Mercerville NJ

Johnson Atelier, c/o Technical Institute of Sculpture, 60 Ward Av Extension, Mercerville, NJ 08619 - T: (609) 890-7777, Fax: (609) 890-1816, Internet: www.atelier.org. Dir.: Gyuri Hollosy
Fine Arts Museum - 1977 45262

Meriden CT

Meriden Historical Society Museum, 424 W Main St, Meriden, CT 06450 - T: (203) 237-5079. Cur.: Allen Weathers
Historical Museum / Local Museum / Folklore Museum - 1893 45263

Meridian MS

Jimmie Rodgers Museum, 1725 Highland Park Dr, Meridian, MS 39304 - T: (601) 485-1808. Dir.: Jean Bishop, C.E.O.: Todd Adkins
Folklore Museum - 1976 45264

Meridian Museum of Art, 25th Av and Seventh St, Meridian, MS 39301 - T: (601) 693-1501, Fax: (601) 485-3175. Dir.: Terence Heder, Pres.: Bob Bresnahan
Fine Arts Museum - 1969
Drawings, American paintings, prints, sculpture, pottery, photography, decorative art 45265

Merion PA

Barnes Foundation, 300 N Latch's Ln, Merion, PA 19066 - T: (610) 667-0290, Fax: (610) 664-4026, Internet: www.barnesfoundation.org. C.E.O.: Kimberly Camp
Special Museum / Fine Arts Museum / Decorative Arts Museum
American decorative arts, African sculpture, horticulture, Greek, Roman and Egyptian antiquities, paintings, metalwork 45266

Merrill WI

Merrill Historical Museum, 804 E Third St, Merrill, WI 54452 - T: (715) 536-5652, E-mail: merrillhs@aol.com. C.E.O.: Alice F. Krueger
Historical Museum - 1978
Wisconsin hist since 1600s 45267

Merrillan WI

Thunderbird Museum, Hatfield N 9517 Thunderbird Ln, Merrillan, WI 54754-8033 - T: (715) 333-5841, Fax: (715) 333-7214, E-mail: owner@thunderbirdmuseum.com, Internet: www.thunderbirdmuseum.com. Head: Robert Flood, Ellen Flood
Local Museum - 1959
Local hist, Indian Artifacts 45268

Mesa AZ

Arizona Museum For Youth, 35 N Robson, Mesa, AZ 85201 - T: (480) 644-2467/68, Fax: (480) 644-2466, E-mail: azmus4youth@ici.mesa.az.us, Internet: www.ci.mesa.az.us/amfy. Dir.: Barbara Meyerson, Cur.: Rebecca Akins
Fine Arts Museum - 1980
Children fine arts 45269

Galeria Mesa, 155 N Center, Mesa, AZ 85211-1466 - T: (480) 644-2056, Fax: (480) 644-2901, E-mail: schultz@ci.mesa.az.us, Internet: www.mesaarts.com. Cur.: Patty Haberman
Fine Arts Museum - 1981
Contemporary arts and crafts, prints 45270

Mesa Southwest Museum, 53 N Macdonald St, Mesa, AZ 85201 - T: (480) 644-2230, Fax: (480) 644-3424, E-mail: cynthia_diaz@ci.mesa.az.us, Internet: www.ci.mesa.az.us/parksrec/msm/. Dir.: Dr. William Holmes, Cur.: Dr. Robert McCord (Herpetology, Natural Sciences), Dr. Heide-Marie Johnson (Ichthyology), Brian Curtis (Paleontology (Vertebrates)), Douglas Wolfe (Paleontology (Invertebrates)), Leo Langland (Geology), Dr. Larry Marshall (Mammology), Dr. Carlton Moore (Astronomy), Keith Foster (History, Social Sciences), Jerry Howard (Anthropology), Dr. Susan Shaffer (Ethnology), Angelica Docog (Education)
Archaeological Museum / Historical Museum / Natural History Museum - 1977
Paleontology, archaeology, ethnology, history and art 45271

Mesa Verde CO

Mesa Verde National Park Museum, Mesa Verde, CO 81330 - T: (970) 529-4465, Fax: (970) 529-4637, Internet: www.nps.gov/meve. Dir.: Larry Wiese, Cur.: Carolyn Landes
Archaeological Museum - 1917
Archaeology from AD 550-1300, ethnography 45272

Mesilla NM

Gadsden Museum, 1875 Boutz Rd, Mesilla, NM 88046 - T: (505) 526-6293, Internet: www.mnohxy.com/g/gadsdemeu.htm. Cur.: Mary Veitch Alexander
Historical Museum - 1931
Civil war coll, Indian artifacts, clothing, guns 45273

Mesquite TX

Florence Ranch Homestead, 1424 Barnes Bridge Rd, Mesquite, TX 75150 - T: (972) 216-6468, Fax: (972) 216-8109, E-mail: corr@ci.mesquite.tx.us. Exec. Dir.: Charlene Orr
Agriculture Museum - 1987 45274

Metamora IL

Metamora Courthouse, 113 E Partridge, Metamora, IL 61548 - T: (309) 367-4470
Historical Museum - 1845
Courthouse located in the 8th Judicial Circuit that Abraham Lincoln traveled as a circuit lawyer 45275

Metamora IN

Whitewater Canal Historic Site, 19083 Clayborn St, Metamora, IN 47030 - T: (765) 647-6512, Fax: (765) 647-2734, E-mail: wwcshe@bonwell.com. Cur.: Jay Dishman
Science&Tech Museum - 1845 45276

Metlakatla AK

Duncan Cottage Museum, 501 Tait St, Metlakatla, AK 99926 - T: (907) 886-4441 ext 232, Fax: (907) 886-4436, Internet: www.tours.metlakatla.net
Local Museum - 1975 45277

Metropolis IL

Fort Massac, 1308 E 5th St, Metropolis, IL 62960 - T: (618) 524-9321, 524-4712, Fax: (618) 524-9321, E-mail: SMCREE@dnrmail.state.il.us, Internet: www.stateofillinois-dnr-fortmassacstatepark. Dir.: Terry Johnson
Historical Museum - 1908
Located on the site of 1756-1814, Military Post 45278

Mexico MO

American Saddlebred Horse Museum, 501 S Muldrow, Mexico, MO 65265 - T: (573) 581-7155, E-mail: achs@swbell.net, Internet: www.audrain.org. Dir.: Kristine Smiley, Cur.: Jan Nesheim
Historical Museum - 1970 45279

Audrain Historical Museum, Graceland Museum, 501 S Muldrow, Mexico, MO 65265 - T: (573) 581-3910, E-mail: achs@swbell.net, Internet: www.audrain.org. Dir.: Kristine Smiley
Local Museum - 1952 45280

Miami FL

The Art Museum at Florida International University, University Park, PC 110, Miami, FL 33199 - T: (305) 348-2890, Fax: (305) 348-2762, E-mail: artinfo@fiu.edu, Internet: www.artmuseumatfiu.org. Dir.: Dahlia Morgan
Fine Arts Museum / University Museum - 1977
Art 45281

Black Heritage Museum, POB 570327, Miami, FL 33257-0327 - T: (305) 252-3535, Fax: (305) 252-3535, E-mail: blkhermu@bellsouth.net, Internet: gsni.cvom/bhm.htm. Pres.: Pricilla G. Stephens Kruize, Cur.: L.S. Houston
Historical Museum / Folklore Museum - 1987
Books, art, artifacts reated to the Black Heritage around the world 45282

Cuban Museum of Arts and Culture, 1300 SW 12 Av, Miami, FL 33129 - T: (305) 858-8006, Fax: (305) 858-9639, Internet: www.infolatino. Dir.: Louis Jeffery Collette
Fine Arts Museum / Folklore Museum - 1985 45283

Gold Coast Railroad Museum, 12450 SW 152nd St, Miami, FL 33177 - T: (305) 253-0063, Fax: (305) 233-4641, E-mail: gcrm@askchuck.com, Internet: www.goldcoast-railroad.org. Dir.: Connie Greer
Science&Tech Museum - 1957 45284

Historical Museum of Southern Florida, 101 W Flagler St, Miami, FL 33130 - T: (305) 375-1492, Fax: (305) 375-1609, E-mail: hasf@historical-museum.org, Internet: www.historial-museum.org. Dir.: J. Andrew Brian, Cur.: Rebecca A. Smith, Jorge Zamanillo
Historical Museum - 1940 45285

International Art Center, 70 Miracle Mile, Coral Gables, Miami, FL 33134 - T: (305) 567-1750, 471-7383
Public Gallery 45286

Kendall Campus Art Gallery, Miami-Dade Community College, 11011 SW 104th St, Miami, FL 33176-3393 - T: (305) 237-2322, Fax: (305) 237-2901, E-mail: lfontana@kendall.mdcc.edu, Internet: www.kendall.mdcc.edu/. Dir.: Lilia Fontana
Fine Arts Museum / University Museum - 1970
Art gallery 45287

Latin American Art Museum, 2206 SW 8th St, Miami, FL 33135-4914 - T: (305) 644-1127, Fax: (305) 261-6996, E-mail: HispMuseum@aol.com, Internet: www.latinartmuseum.org. C.E.O.: Raul M. Oyuela
Fine Arts Museum - 1991 45288

Miami Art Museum, 101 W Flagler St, Miami, FL 33130 - T: (305) 375-3000, Fax: (305) 375-1725, Internet: www.miamiartmuseum.org. Dir.: Suzanne Delehanty, Asst. Dir.: José Garcia, Cur.: Lorie Mertes, Eva Van Hees, Asst. Cur.: Amy Rosenblum
Fine Arts Museum - 1978
Art 45289

Miami Children's Museum, 701 Arena Blvd, Miami, FL 33136 - T: (305) 373-5439, Fax: (305) 373-5431, E-mail: mcmuseum@bellsouth.net, Internet: www.miamichildrensmuseum.org. Dir.: Deborah Spiegelman, Ass. Dir.: Ilene Primack, Cur.: Suzy Breitner
Special Museum - 1984 45290

Miami Museum of Science, 3280 S Miami Av, Miami, FL 33129 - T: (305) 646-4200, Fax: (305) 646-4300, E-mail: jsatt@miamisci.org, Internet: www.miamisci.org. Dir.: Russell Etling, Ass. Dir.: Jack Horkheimer, Victor Vincent, Brian Mealey (Environmental Sciences), Dr. Rolando Millas (Latin America)
Science&Tech Museum - 1949
Seashells, Entomology collection, Pre-Columbian collection, unique fossile heritage - planetarium 45291

Vizcaya Museum, 3251 S Miami Av, Miami, FL 33129 - T: (305) 250-9133 ext 2221, Fax: (305) 285-2004, Internet: www.vizcayamuseum.com. Dir.: Richard S. Farwell, Cur.: Michele A. McDonald
Decorative Arts Museum / Historical Museum - 1952
Italian Renaissance-styled Villa, formal gardens - gardens 45292

Weeks Air Museum, 14710 SW 128 St, Miami, FL 33196 - T: (305) 233-5197, Fax: (305) 232-4134, Internet: www.weeksairmuseum.com. Dir.: Vincent Tirado
Science&Tech Museum - 1987 45293

Wirtz Gallery, First National Bank of South Miami, 5750 Sunset Dr, Miami, FL 33143 - T: (305) 662-5414, Fax: (305) 662-5413, E-mail: gallery@fnbsm.com, Internet: www.fnbsm.com/wirtz.htm
Public Gallery - 1983 45294

Miami MO

Van Meter State Park, Rte 1, Hwy 122, Miami, MO 65344 - T: (660) 886-7537, Fax: (660) 886-7512, E-mail: vanmeter@mail.dnr.state.mo.us, Internet: www.dnr.state.mo.us/dsp/homedsp.htm
Archaeological Museum - 1932
Missouri Indian village archaeological site 45295

Miami TX

Roberts County Museum, Rte 1, Hwy 60, Miami, TX 79059 - T: (806) 868-3291, Fax: (806) 868-3381. Exec. Dir.: Cecil Gill, Dir.: Katie Underwood
Local Museum - 1979
Local hist 45296

Miami Beach FL

Art Center of South Florida, 924 Lincoln Rd, Miami Beach, FL 33139 - T: (305) 674-8278, Fax: (305) 674-8772, E-mail: info@artcentersf.org, Internet: www.artcentersf.org
Public Gallery 45297

Bass Museum of Art, 2121 Park Av, Miami Beach, FL 33139-1729 - T: (305) 673-7530, Fax: (305) 673-7062, E-mail: info@bassmuseum.org, Internet: www.bassmuseum.org. Dir.: Diane W. Camber
Fine Arts Museum - 1964
Art 45298

Jewish Museum of Florida, 301 Washington Av, Miami Beach, FL 33139-6965 - T: (305) 672-5044 ext 10/18, Fax: (305) 672-5933, E-mail: mzerivitz@jewishmuseum.com, Internet: www.jewishmuseum.com
Historical Museum - 1995
Jewish hist of Florida 45299

The Wolfsonian, Florida International University, 1001 Washington Av, Miami Beach, FL 33139 - T: (305) 531-1001, Fax: (305) 531-2133, Internet: www.wolfsonian.org. Dir.: Kathy Leff, Asst. Dir.: Marianne Lamonaca
Special Museum / Decorative Arts Museum / Historical Museum - 1986
Design, decorative arts, architecture, historic Art Deco District - library 45300

Miami Lakes FL

Jay I. Kislak Foundation, 7900 Miami Lakes Dr W, Miami Lakes, FL 33016 - T: (305) 364-4208, Fax: (305) 894-3209, E-mail: adunkelman@kislak.com, Internet: www.jayikislakfoundation.org. Dir.: Arthur Dunkelman
Fine Arts Museum / Archaeological Museum - 1988 45301

Michigan City IN

John G. Blank Center for the Arts, 312 E Eighth St, Michigan City, IN 46360 - T: (219) 874-4900, Fax: (219) 872-6829, E-mail: jgbartcenter@adsnet.com, Internet: www.blankartcenter.org. Dir.: Lelde Alida Kalmite
Fine Arts Museum - 1977
Art, housed in the Old Michigan City Library, an Beaux Arts structure of Indiana Limestone 45302

Old Lighthouse Museum, Heisman Harbor Rd, Washington Park, Michigan City, IN 46360 - T: (219) 872-6133. Pres.: Fred Devries
Science&Tech Museum - 1973
Maritime history 45303

Middleborough MA

Middleborough Historical Museum, Jackson St, Middleborough, MA 02346 - T: (508) 947-1969. Pres.: Dorothy Thayer
Local Museum - 1960
Local history 45304

Robbins Museum of Archaeology, 17 Jackson St, Middleborough, MA 02346-0700 - T: (508) 947-9005, E-mail: mas@bridgew.edu, Internet: webhost.bridgew.edu/mas. Pres.: Ron Dalton
Archaeological Museum - 1939
Archaeology 45305

Middleburg PA

The Snyder County Historical Society Museum, 30 E Market St, Middleburg, PA 17842 - T: (510) 837-6191, Fax: (510) 837-4282. C.E.O. & Pres.: Teresa J. Berger
Historical Museum - 1898
Local hist 45306

Middlebury VT

The Henry Sheldon Museum of Vermont Histoy, 1 Park St, Middlebury, VT 05753 - T: (802) 388-2117, E-mail: shel-mus@middlebury.edu, Internet: www.henrysheldonmuseum.org. Pres.: Joanne Schneider
Fine Arts Museum / Local Museum - 1882
Art, history, furniture, textiles, documents 45307

The Middlebury College Museum of Art, Center for the Arts, Middlebury, VT 05753-6177 - T: (802) 443-5235, Fax: (802) 443-2069, Internet: www.middlebury.edu/~museum. Dir.: Richard H. Saunders, Assoc. Dir.: Emmie Donadio, Cur.: Sandra Olivo (Education)
Fine Arts Museum / University Museum - 1968
Art 45308

The Sheldon Art Museum → The Henry Sheldon Museum of Vermont Histoy

Vermont Folklife Center, Masonic Hall, 3 Court St, Middlebury, VT 05753 - T: (802) 388-4964, Fax: (802) 388-1844, Internet: www.vermontfolklifecenter.org. Dir.: Jane C. Beck, Assoc. Dir.: Meg Ostrum
Folklore Museum - 1983
Folk art 45309

Vermont State Craft Center at Frog Hollow, 1 Mill St, Middlebury, VT 05753 - T: (802) 388-3177, Fax: (802) 388-5020, E-mail: info@froghollow.org, Internet: www.froghollow.org. Exec. Dir.: William F. Brooks jr.
Historical Museum - 1971 45310

Middlesboro KY

Cumberland Gap National Historical Park, U.S. 25 E, Middlesboro, KY 40965 - T: (606) 248-2817, Fax: (606) 248-7276, Internet: www.nps.gov/cuga. Head: Mark H. Woods
Historical Museum / Archaeological Museum - 1959
History, archaeology 45311

Middleton MA

Lura Watkins Museum, Pleasant St, Middleton, MA 01949 - T: (508) 774-9301, Fax: (978) 777-8675, Internet: www.flintlibrary.org/history.htm. Dir.: Henry Tragent, Public Relations: Carole Smith
Local Museum - 1976
Local history 45312

Middletown CT

Davison Art Center, Wesleyan University, 301 High St, Middletown, CT 06459-0487 - T: (860) 685-2500, Fax: (860) 685-2501, E-mail: swiles@wesleyan.edu, Internet: www.wesleyan.edu/dac. Cur.: Stephanie Wiles
Fine Arts Museum / University Museum - 1952 45313

Ezra and Cecile Zilkha Gallery, c/o Wesleyan University, Center for the Arts, Middletown, CT 06459-0442 - T: (860) 685-2695, Fax: (860) 685-2061, E-mail: parnold@wesleyan.edu, Internet: www.wesleyan.edu/cfa/zilkha. Cur.: Nina Felshin
Fine Arts Museum / University Museum - 1973 45314

Middlesex County Historical Society Museum, 151 Main St, Middletown, CT 06457 - T: (860) 346-0746, Fax: (860) 346-0746, E-mail: middlesexhistory@wesleyan.edu, Internet: www.middlesexhistory.org. Dir.: Dione Longley
Local Museum - 1901 45315

Middletown MD

Middletown Valley Historical Society Museum, 305 W Main St, Middletown, MD 21769 - T: (301) 371-7582, Fax: (301) 371-7582, E-mail: j.dwighthut@juno.com. Pres.: J. Dwight Hutchinson, Lydia C. Hutchinson
Local Museum - 1976
Local hist 45316

Middletown NY

Historical Society of Middletown and the Wallkill Precinct, 25 East Av, Middletown, NY 10940 - T: (914) 342-0941, E-mail: enjine@aol.com. Pres.: Marvin H. Cohen
Historical Museum - 1923 45317

Middletown OH

Middletown Fine Arts Center, AIM Bldg, 130 N Verity Pkwy, Middletown, OH 45042 - T: (513) 424-2417, Fax: (513) 424-1682, E-mail: mfac@siscom.net, Internet: www.middletownfinearts.com. Pres.: Rick Davies
Public Gallery - 1963
library 45318

Middletown VA

Belle Grove Plantation, 336 Belle Grove Rd, Middletown, VA 22645 - T: (540) 869-2028, Fax: (540) 869-9638, E-mail: bellegro@shentel.net, Internet: www.bellegrove.org. Dir.: Elizabeth McClung
Local Museum - 1964
Historic house 45319

Middleville MI

Historic Bowens Mills and Pioneer Park, 200 Old Mill Rd, Middleville, MI 49333 - T: (616) 795-7530, Fax: (616) 795-7530, E-mail: oldmill@iserv.net, Internet: www.bowensmills.com. Dir.: Carleen Sabin, Owen Sabin
Science&Tech Museum - 1978
1864 water-powered grist and cider mill 45320

Midland MI

Arts Midland Galleries, 1801 W Saint Andrews Rd, Midland, MI 48640 - T: (517) 835-7401, Fax: (517) 631-7890, E-mail: winslow@mcfta.org, Internet: www.mcfta.org. Dir.: Bruce B. Winslow
Fine Arts Museum - 1956
Great Lake regional art, local history photographs - art school 45321

Midland County Historical Museum, 1801 W Saint Andrews Rd, Midland, MI 48640 - T: (517) 631-5930. Dir.: Gary F. Skory, Cur.: Emmanuel J. Francisco
Local Museum - 1952
Regional history 45322

Midland NC

Reed Gold Mine, 9621 Reed Mine Rd, Midland, NC 28107 - T: (704) 721-4653, Fax: (704) 721-4657, E-mail: reedmine@dasia.net, Internet: www.itpi.dpi.state.nc.us/reed
Science&Tech Museum - 1971
Mining machinery, coins, steam engines, stamp mill 45323

Midland TX

American Airpower Heritage Museum, 9600 Wright Dr, Midland, TX 79711 - T: (915) 567-3009, Fax: (915) 567-3047, E-mail: director@aahm.org, Internet: www.airpowermuseum.org. Dir.: Tami O'Bannion, Cons.: Jeff Wood
Historical Museum / Military Museum / Science&Tech Museum - 1957
World War II, military aviation 45324

J. Evetts Haley History Center, 1805 W Indiana, Midland, TX 79701 - T: (915) 682-5785, Fax: (915) 685-3512, Internet: www.haleylibrary.com
Local Museum - 1976
Local hist 45325

McCormick Gallery, Midland College, 3600 N Garfield, Midland, TX 79705 - T: (915) 685-4770, Fax: (915) 685-4721, E-mail: mccormickgallery@midland.edu, Internet: www.midland.edu/mccormick. Dir.: J. Don Wallace
Public Gallery 45326

Midland County Historical Museum, 301 W Missouri, Midland, TX 79701 - T: (915) 682-2931, 688-8947. Pres.: Nancy R. McKinley
Local Museum - 1930
Local hist 45327

Museum of the Southwest, 1705 W Missouri Av, Midland, TX 79701-6516 - T: (915) 683-2882, 570-7770, Fax: (915) 570-7077, Internet: www.museumsw.org. Dir.: Thomas Jones, Cur.: J. Winkler, Daniel Holeva
Fine Arts Museum / Local Museum - 1965
Local hist, regional art - Planetarium 45328

The Petroleum Museum, 1500 Interstate 20, Midland, TX 79701 - T: (915) 683-4403, Fax: (915) 683-4509, E-mail: twhite@petroleummuseum.org, Internet: www.petroleummuseum.org. Pres.: Ken Burgess, Dir.: Jane Phares
Historical Museum / Science&Tech Museum - 1967
History, technology - archive 45329

Taylor Brown and Sarah Dorsey House, 213 N Weatherford, Midland, TX 79701, mail addr: 2102 Community Ln, Midland, TX 79701 - T: (915) 682-2931
Decorative Arts Museum - 1899 45330

Midway GA

Fort Morris, 2559 Fort Morris Rd, Midway, GA 31320 - T: (912) 884-5999, Fax: (912) 884-5285, E-mail: ftmorris@clds.net, Internet: www.gastateparks.org. Dir.: Arthur C. Edgar jr.
Military Museum - 1978
Military history 45331

Midway Museum, US-Hwy 17, Midway, GA 31320, mail addr: POB 195, Midway, GA 31320 - T: (912) 884-5837. Cur.: Joann Clark
Local Museum - 1957
Local history 45332

Seabrook Village, 660 Trade Hill Rd, Midway, GA 31320 - T: (912) 884-7008, Fax: (912) 884-7005, E-mail: wallstalk@cld.net, Internet: www.seabrookvillage.org. Cur.: Meredith Devendorf
Folklore Museum
Living hist of an African-American village 45333

Milan OH

Milan Historical Museum, 10 Edison Dr, Milan, OH 44846 - T: (419) 499-2968, Fax: (419) 499-9004, E-mail: museum@milanhist.org, Internet: www.milanhistory.org. Dir.: Ellen Maurer
Local Museum / Decorative Arts Museum - 1930 45334

Thomas Edison Birthplace Museum, 9 Edison Dr, Milan, OH 44846 - T: (419) 499-2135, Fax: (419) 499-3241, E-mail: edisonbp@accnorwalk.com, Internet: www.tomedison.org. Dir.: Robert K.L. Wheeler, Cur.: Laurence J. Russell
Historical Museum - 1947 45335

Miles City MT

Custer County Art Center, Water Plant Rd, Miles City, MT 59301 - T: (406) 232-0635, Fax: (406) 232-0637, E-mail: ccartc@midrivers.com, Internet: www.ccac.milescity.org. Exec. Dir.: Mark Browning
Fine Arts Museum - 1975
Photographic coll, Montana arts 45336

Milford CT

Eells-Stow House, 34 High St, Milford, CT 06460 - T: (203) 874-2664, Fax: (203) 874-5789, E-mail: mhsoc@usa.net, Internet: mhsoc.home.ml.org
Local Museum - 1930 45337

Milford DE

Milford Historical Society Museum, 501 NW Front St, Milford, DE 19963 - T: (302) 422-4222. Pres.: Marvin Shelhouse
Local Museum - 1961
Local hist 45338

Milford Museum, 121 S Walnut St, Milford, DE 19963 - T: (302) 424-1080. Chm.: John Huntzinger
Local Museum - 1983
Local hist 45339

Milford MI

Milford Historical Museum, 124 E Commerce St, Milford, MI 48381 - T: (248) 685-7308. Dir.: Mary Lou Gharrity
Local Museum - 1976
Local hist 45340

Milford NJ

Volendam Windmill Museum, 231 Adamic Hill Rd, Holland Township, Milford, NJ 08848 - T: (908) 995-4365, E-mail: ctbrown@ptd.net. C.E.O.: Charles T. Brown
Historical Museum - 1965 45341

Milford OH

Promont House Museum, 906 Main St, Milford, OH 45150 - T: (513) 831-4704, E-mail: nana00@fuse.net. Pres.: Nancy Storch, Dir.: Tracy Lanham
Historical Museum / Local Museum - 1967 45342

Milford PA

Pike County Museum, 608 Broad St, Milford, PA 18337 - T: (570) 296-8126, E-mail: pchs1@ptd.net. Dir.: Charles Clausen
Local Museum - 1930
Local history 45343

Mill Run PA

Fallingwater - Western Pennsylvania Conservancy, Rte 381 S, Mill Run, PA 15464-0167 - T: (724) 329-8501, Fax: (724) 329-0881, E-mail: fallingwater@paconserve.org, Internet: www.paconserve.org. Dir.: Lynda Waggener
Fine Arts Museum / Decorative Arts Museum - 1963
Historic house designed by Frank Lloyd Wright in 1935, coll of ceramics, decorative arts, furniture, glass, paintings and graphic works by Picasso, Diego Rivera, Japanese prints, sculptures, textiles 45344

Milledgeville GA

Museum and Archives of Georgia Education, Georgia College and State University, 131 S Clarke St, Milledgeville, GA 31061 - T: (478) 445-4391, E-mail: mhargaden@mail.gcsu.edu. Dir.: Mary Hargaden
Historical Museum - 1975
History, education 45345

Millersburg OH

Holmes County Historical Society Museum, 484 Wooster Rd, Millersburg, OH 44654 - T: (330) 674-0022, Fax: (740) 622-4197, E-mail: hchs@valkyrie.net, Internet: www.victorianhouse.org
Local Museum - 1965
Furniture, early medical equip, war mementoes, early law office, pioneer tools 45346

Millersburg PA

Upper Paxton Township Museum, 330 Center St, Millersburg, PA 17061 - T: (717) 692-4084, E-mail: mbghist@epix.net. Dir.: Nancy L. Wert
Local Museum - 1980
Local history 45347

Millersville TN

Beverage Containers Museum, 1055 Ridgecrest Dr, Millersville, TN 37072 - T: (615) 859-5236, Fax: (615) 859-5238, Internet: www.gono.com. Cur.: Tom Bates
Special Museum - 1987
Beverage containers, openers, advertising signs, posters 45348

Milltown NJ

Eureka Fire Museum, 39 Washington Av, Milltown, NJ 08850 - T: (732) 828-7207. Cur.: Edward S. Harto
Historical Museum - 1981
Fighting equip, fire patches, badges and insignia from around the world, uniforms, helmets, hand-drawn fire apparatus 45349

Millville NJ

Museum of American Glass at Wheaton Village, 1501 Glasstown Rd, Millville, NJ 08332 - T: (856) 825-6800, Fax: (856) 825-2410, E-mail: mail@wheatonvillage.org, Internet: www.wheatonvillage.org. Cur.: Gay LeCleire Taylor
Decorative Arts Museum - 1968 45350

Millwood VA

Burwell-Morgan Mill, 15 Tannery Ln, Millwood, VA 22646 - T: (540) 955-2600, Fax: (540) 955-0285, E-mail: ccha@visuallink.com, Internet: www.visuallink.net/ccha. Pres.: Sarah P. Trumbower
Science&Tech Museum - 1964 45351

Milton MA

Blue Hills Trailside Museum, 1904 Canton Av, Milton, MA 02186 - T: (617) 333-0690 ext 0, Fax: (617) 333-0814, E-mail: bluehills@massaudubon.org, Internet: www.massaudubon.org. Dir.: Norman Smith
Natural History Museum - 1959
Natural history, environment 45352

Captain Forbes House Museum, 215 Adams St, Milton, MA 02186 - T: (617) 696-1815, Fax: (617) 696-1815, E-mail: fhm@gis.net, Internet: key-biz.com/ssn/milton/forbes.html. Dir.: Christine M. Sullivan
Historical Museum - 1964 45353

Suffolk Resolves House, 1370 Canton Av, Milton, MA 02186 - T: (617) 333-9700, E-mail: mhs1904@aol.com
Local Museum - 1904
Local history 45354

Milton NH

New Hampshire Farm Museum, Rte 125, Plummer's Ridge, Milton, NH 03851 - T: (603) 652-7840, Fax: (603) 652-7840. Pres.: John Murphy
Agriculture Museum - 1970 45355

Milton VT

Milton Historical Museum, 13 School St, Milton, VT 05468 - T: (802) 893-2340. Dir.: Jane Fitzgerald
Local Museum - 1979 45356

Milton WI

Milton House Museum, 18 S Janesville St, Milton, WI 53563 - T: (608) 868-7772, Fax: (608) 868-1698, E-mail: miltonhouse@miltonhouse.org, Internet: www.miltonhouse.org. Dir.: Deborah Wildes, Asst. Dir.: Sue Schlueter
Historical Museum - 1948
Local hist 45357

Milwaukee WI

America's Black Holocaust Museum, 2233 N Fourth St, Milwaukee, WI 53212 - T: (414) 264-2500, Fax: (414) 264-0112, E-mail: abhmwi@aol.com, Internet: www.blackholocaustmuseum.com. Dir.: Jessie Leonard
Historical Museum - 1988
Slavery, civil rights 45358

Betty Brinn Children's Museum, 929 E Wisconsin Av, Milwaukee, WI 53202 - T: (414) 390-5437, Fax: (414) 291-0906, Internet: www.bbcmkids.org. C.E.O.: Fern Shupeck
Fine Arts Museum / Science&Tech Museum - 1995 45359

Charles Allis Art Museum, 1801 N Prospect Av, Milwaukee, WI 53202 - T: (414) 278-8295, Fax: (414) 278-0335, E-mail: jeniffer.piggins@charlesallimuseum.org, Internet: www.charlesallimuseum.org. Dir.: James D. Temmer, Cur.: Sarah Haberstroh
Fine Arts Museum - 1947
Art 45360

Discovery World - The James Lovell Museum of Science, Economics and Technology, 815 N James Lovell St, Milwaukee, WI 53233 - T: (414) 765-9966, Fax: (414) 765-0311, E-mail: hdq@braintools.org, Internet: www.braintools.org. Dir.: Paul J. Krajniak, Pres.: Michael J. Cudahy
Science&Tech Museum - 1984
Science, economics, technology 45361

Greene Memorial Museum, University of Wisconsin-Milwaukee, 3209 N Maryland Av, Milwaukee, WI 53211 - T: (414) 229-5067, 229-4561, Fax: (414) 229-5452, Internet: www.uwm.edu/dept/gosciences. Cur.: Rod Watkins
Natural History Museum / University Museum - 1913
Geology 45362

Haggerty Museum of Art, 530 N 13th St, Milwaukee, WI 53201-1881 - T: (414) 288-7290, Fax: (414) 288-5415, Internet: www.marquette.etu/haggerty. Dir.: Curtis L. Carter
University Museum / Fine Arts Museum - 1984
Paintings, prints, photography, decorative art, tribal arts, German art 45363

Institute of Visual Arts, University of Wisconsin-Milwaukee, 3253 N Downer Av, Milwaukee, WI 53211 - T: (414) 229-5070, Fax: (414) 229-6785, E-mail: inova@uwm.edu, Internet: www.uwm.edu/soa/inova. Dir.: Peter Doroshenko, Cur.: Marilu Knode
Fine Arts Museum / University Museum - 1982
Art 45364

International Clown Hall of Fame and Research Center, 161 W Wisconsin Av, Ste LL700, Milwaukee, WI 53203 - T: (414) 319-0848, Fax: (414) 319-1070, E-mail: ichof@clownmuseum.org, Internet: www.clownmuseum.org/. Dir.: Kathryn O'Dell, Cur.: Arthur Pedlar
Performing Arts Museum / Special Museum - 1986 45365

Milwaukee Art Museum, 700 N Art Museum Dr, Milwaukee, WI 53202 - T: (414) 224-3200, Fax: (414) 271-7588, E-mail: mam@mam.org, Internet: www.mam.org. Dir.: David Gordon, Dir. of Curatorial Affairs: Brian Ferriso (Contemporary Art), Cur.: Kristin Makholm (Prints, Drawings, Photographs), Laurie Winters (Earlier European Art)
Fine Arts Museum - 1888
Art 45366

Milwaukee County Historical Society Museum, 910 N Old World Third St, Milwaukee, WI 53203 - T: (414) 273-8288, Fax: (414) 273-3268, E-mail: mchs@execpc.com, Internet: www.milwaukeecountyhistsoc.org. Dir.: Robert T. Teske, Cur.: Steven L. Daily, William R. Frick
Local Museum - 1935
Local hist 45367

Milwaukee Public Museum, 800 W Wells St, Milwaukee, WI 53233 - T: (414) 278-2700, Fax: (414) 278-6100, E-mail: jan@mpm.edu, Internet: www.mpm@edu. Pres.: James Krivitz
Natural History Museum - 1882
Natural and human hist 45368

Mitchell Gallery of Flight, c/o Mitchell International Airport, 5300 S Howell Av, Milwaukee, WI 53207-6189 - T: (414) 747-4503, Fax: (414) 747-4525, E-mail: info@mitchellgallery.org, Internet: www.mitchellgallery.org. Dir.: Mark Jung
Science&Tech Museum - 1984 45369

Mount Mary College Costume Museum, 2900 N Menomonee River Pkwy, Milwaukee, WI 53222 - T: (414) 258-4810, Fax: (414) 256-1224, E-mail: gastone@mtmary.edu, Internet: www.mtmary.edu. Cur.: Elizabeth Gaston
University Museum / Special Museum - 1928
Costume 45370

The Patrick and Beatrice Haggerty Museum of Art, 13th and Clybourn, Milwaukee, WI 53233, mail addr: c/o Marquette University, POB 1881, Milwaukee, WI 53201-1881 - T: (414) 288-7290, Fax: (414) 288-5415, E-mail: haggertym@vms.csd.mu.edu, Internet: www.marquette.edu/haggerty. Dir.: Dr. Curtis L. Carter, Asst. Dir.: Lee Coppernoll, Cur.: Annemarie Sawkins
Fine Arts Museum / University Museum - 1984
Art 45371

Union-Art Gallery, University of Wisconsin-Milwaukee, 2200 E Kenwood Blvd, Milwaukee, WI 53201 - T: (414) 229-6310, Fax: (414) 229-6709, E-mail: art_gallery@aux.uwm.edu, Internet: aux.uwm.edu/union/artgal.htm. Head: Steven D. Jaeger
Fine Arts Museum / University Museum - 1972
Art 45372

Villa Terrace Decorative Arts Museum, 2220 N Terrace Av, Milwaukee, WI 53202 - T: (414) 271-3656, Fax: (414) 271-3986, E-mail: jeniffer.piggins@charlesallimuseum.org, Internet: www.villaterracemuseum.org. Exec. Dir.: James D. Temmer, Cur.: Sarah Haberstroh
Decorative Arts Museum - 1967
Decorative arts 45373

Walker's Point Center for the Arts, 911 W National Av, Milwaukee, WI 53204 - T: (414) 672-2787, Fax: (414) 672-5399, E-mail: staff@wpca-milwaukee.org, Internet: www.wpca-milwaukee.org
Public Gallery - 1987 45374

Minburn IA

Voas Museum, 1930 Lexington Rd, Minburn, IA 50167 - T: (515) 465-3577, Fax: (515) 465-3579, E-mail: info@dallas25.org. CEO: Mike Wallace
Natural History Museum - 1991
Rocks, fossils, minerals, rare native elements, quartz specimens 45375

Minden NE

Harold Warp Pioneer Village Foundation, 138 E Hwy 6, Minden, NE 68959-0068 - T: (308) 832-1181, Fax: (308) 832-1181, E-mail: manager@pioneervillage.org, Internet: www.pioneervillage.org. Pres.: Harold G. Warp
Historical Museum - 1953 45376

Kearney County Historical Museum, 530 N Nebraska Av, Minden, NE 68959 - T: (308) 832-1765. Dir.: Wayne Bergsten
Local Museum - 1925 45377

Mineral VA

North Anna Nuclear Information Center, Rte 700, 1022 Haley Dr, Mineral, VA 23117 - T: (804) 771-3200, (540) 894-4394, Fax: (540) 894-0379, Internet: www.dom.com
Science&Tech Museum - 1973
Nuclear energy 45378

Mineral Point WI

Pendarvis, 114 Shake Rag St, Mineral Point, WI 53565 - T: (608) 987-2122, Fax: (608) 987-3738. Dir.: Allen Schroeder, Cur.: Tamara Funk
Local Museum / Folklore Museum - 1971
Historic house 45379

Minneapolis MN

American Swedish Institute, 2600 Park Av, Minneapolis, MN 55407 - T: (612) 871-4907, Fax: (612) 871-8682, E-mail: info@americanswedishinst.org, Internet: www.americanswedishinst.org. Dir.: Bruce N. Karstadt, Cur.: Curt Pederson
Ethnology Museum - 1929
Ethnic museum 45380

The Bakken, Library and Museum of Electricity in Life, 3537 Zenith Av S, Minneapolis, MN 55416-4623 - T: (612) 926-3878, Fax: (612) 927-7265, E-mail: info@thebakken.org, Internet: www.thebakken.org. Dir.: David J. Rhees, Cur.: Beth Murphy (Education), Ellen Kuhfeld (Instruments), Riley Hendrickson (Exhibits)
Historical Museum - 1975
History of electricity in medicine, magnetism, culture 45381

Center for Arts Criticism, 2822 Lyndale Av S, Minneapolis, MN 55408 - T: (612) 874-2818, Fax: (612) 871-6927. Exec. Dir.: Bienvenida Matias
Special Museum / Fine Arts Museum - 1984 45382

Frederick R. Weisman Art Museum, 333 E River Rd, Minneapolis, MN 55455 - T: (612) 625-9494, Fax: (612) 625-9630, Internet: www.weisman.umn.edu. Dir.: Lyndel King
Fine Arts Museum / University Museum - 1934
Paintings, drawings, prints by American artists 45383

Hennepin History Museum, 2303 Third Av S, Minneapolis, MN 55404 - T: (612) 870-1329, Fax: (612) 870-1320, E-mail: hhmuseum@mtn.org, Internet: www.hhmuseum.org. Dir.: Jack Kabrud
Local Museum / Historical Museum - 1938 45384

Humphrey Forum, 301 19 Av S, Minneapolis, MN 55455 - T: (612) 624-5893, Fax: (612) 625-3513, E-mail: ssandell@hhh.umn.edu, Internet: www.umn.edu/humphrey-forum. Dir.: Stephen Sandell
Special Museum - 1989 45385

Intermedia Arts Minnesota, 2822 Lyndale Av S, Minneapolis, MN 55408 - T: (612) 871-4444, Fax: (612) 871-2769, E-mail: allstaff@intermediaarts.org, Internet: www.intermediaarts.org. Dir.: Tom Borrup
Fine Arts Museum 45386

James Ford Bell Museum of Natural History, University of Minnesota, 10 Church St SE, Minneapolis, MN 55455 - T: (612) 624-7083, Fax: (612) 626-7704, E-mail: bellmuse@tc.umn.edu, Internet: www.umn.edu/bellmuse/. Dir.: Scott M. Lanyon, Assoc. Dir.: Karen Lee Davis, Cur.: Anita Cholewa (Vascular Plants), Bob Zink (Ornithology), D. Frank McKinney (Ethology), Elmer C. Birney (Mammalogy), Susan J. Weller (Invertebrate Biology), Kendall W. Corbin (Frozen Tissues), Gordon R. Murdock, Kevin Williams (Education), Donald T. Luce (Exhibits)
Natural History Museum / University Museum - 1872
Frozen tissues, seeds, fossils, mollusks, birds, fishes, mammals, reptiles, amphibians, flowering plants, lichens, mosses, nature art - herbarium 45387

Katherine Nash Gallery, University of Minnesota, 225 19th Av, Lower Concourse, Willey Hall, Minneapolis, MN 55455 - T: (612) 624-6518, Fax: (612) 625-0152, E-mail: nash@tc.umn.edu, Internet: artdept.umn.edu. Dir.: Nicholas Shank
Public Gallery / University Museum - 1973
Ceramics, paintings, prints, sculpture, metalwork, photography 45388

Lutheran Brotherhood Gallery, 625 Fourth Av S, Minneapolis, MN 55415 - T: (612) 340-7000, Fax: (612) 340-8447, E-mail: cic@luthbro.com, Internet: www.luthbro.com. Cur.: Richard L. Hillstrom
Fine Arts Museum / Religious Arts Museum - 1982 45389

Minneapolis College of Art and Design Gallery, 2501 Stevens Av S, Minneapolis, MN 55404 - T: (612) 874-3785, Fax: (612) 874-3704, E-mail: brianszott_@mn.mcad.edu., Internet: www.mcad.edu/admin/gallery/mcadgallery.html. Dir.: Larz Masen
Fine Arts Museum / University Museum - 1886 45390

Minneapolis Institute of Arts, 2400 Third Av S, Minneapolis, MN 55404 - T: (612) 870-3000, 870-3046, Fax: (612) 870-3004, E-mail: miagen@artsmia.org, Internet: www.artsmia.org/mia. Dir.: Patricia J. Grazzini, Cur.: Richard Campbell (Prints, Drawings), Carroll T. Hartwell (Photography), Christopher Monkhouse (Decorative Arts, Sculpture), Robert Jacobsen (Asian Art), Lotus Stack (Textiles), Patrick Noon (Paintings)
Fine Arts Museum - 1915 45391

No Name Exhibitions @ Soap Factory, 110 Fifth Av SE, Minneapolis, MN 55414 - T: (612) 623-9176, E-mail: info@soapfactory.org, Internet: www.soapfactory.org
Public Gallery 45392

The Pillsbury Art Collection, 200 S Sixth St, Minneapolis, MN 55402 - T: (612) 330-4966. Pres.: Paul Walsh
Fine Arts Museum
Contemporary and Western American art, primarily oil paintings, prints and watercolors 45393

Walker Art Center, 725 Vineland Pl, Minneapolis, MN 55403 - T: (612) 375-7622, Fax: (612) 375-7618, E-mail: information@walkerart.org, Internet: www.walkerart.org/. Dir.: Kathy Halbreich, Cur.: Richard Flood, Philippe Vergne, Joan Rothfuss, Philip Bither (Performing Arts), Cis Bierinckx (Film, Video), Asst. Cur.: Siri Engberg
Fine Arts Museum - 1879 45394

Wells Fargo History Museum, Sixth and Marquette Av, Minneapolis, MN 55401 - T: (612) 667-4210, Internet: www.wellsfargohistory.com
Historical Museum 45395

Minot ND

Lillian and Coleman Taube Museum of Art, 2 Main St N, Minot, ND 58702 - T: (701) 838-4445, Fax: (800) 879-6684, E-mail: taube@ndak.net. Dir.: Nancy F. Brown
Fine Arts Museum - 1970
Drawings, folk art, paintings, sculptures by local and national artists 45396

Northwest Art Center, Minot State University, 500 W University Av, Minot, ND 58707 - T: (701) 858-3000, Fax: (701) 858-3894, E-mail: nac@misu.nodak.edu. Dir.: Zoe Spooner
Fine Arts Museum 45397

Ward County Historical Society Museum, North Dakota Fairgrounds, Minot, ND 58702 - T: (701) 839-7330, E-mail: wchs@minto.com, Internet: www.wardcountymuseum.org. C.E.O.: Mark Timbrook
Local Museum - 1951
Local hist 45398

Mishawaka IN

Hannah Lindahl Children's Museum, 1402 S Main St, Mishawaka, IN 46544 - T: (219) 254-4540, Fax: (219) 254-4585, E-mail: hlindahl@michianatoday.com; pmarker@hlcm.org, Internet: www.hlcm.org. Pres.: Eva Jojo, Dir.: Peggy Marker
Ethnology Museum / Local Museum - 1946
Local history 45399

Mission Hills CA

San Fernando Historical Museum, 15151 San Fernando Mission Blvd, Mission Hills, CA 91345 - T: (818) 361-0186, Fax: (818) 361-3276. Dir.: Francis J. Weber, Dep. Dir.: Mary Rose
Local Museum / Historical Museum - 1962 45400

Mississippi State MS

Cobb Institute of Archaeology Museum, POB AR, Mississippi State, MS 39762 - T: (662) 325-3826, Fax: (662) 325-8690, E-mail: jds1@ra.msstate.edu, Internet: www.cobb.msstate.edu. Dir.: Joe Seger, Cur.: John O'Hear (Artifacts)
Archaeological Museum - 1972 45401

Dunn-Seiler Museum, Mississippi State, MS 39762, mail addr: c/o MSU, Dept of Geosciences, POB 5448, Mississippi State, MS 39762 - T: (601) 325-3915, Fax: (601) 325-2907, E-mail: dewey@geosci.msstate.edu, Internet: www.msstate.edu/dept/geosciences/4site/museum. Cur.: Dr. Chris Dawey
Natural History Museum / University Museum - 1947
Mesozoic and Cenozoic palaeontology, Upper Cretaceous lepadomorph barnacles, mineralogy, geology 45402

Missoula MT

Art Museum of Missoula, 335 N Pattee, Missoula, MT 59802 - T: (406) 728-0447, Fax: (406) 543-8691, E-mail: museum@artmissoula.org, Internet: www.artmissoula.org. Dir.: Laura J. Millin, Cur.: Renee Taaffe (Eduction), Stephen Glueckert (Exhibitions)
Fine Arts Museum - 1975
Architecture, ethnology, American Indian, Afo-American, Western art, African art, decorative arts 45403

Gallery of Visual Arts, University of Montana, Missoula, MT 59812 - T: (406) 243-2813, Fax: (406) 243-4968, Internet: www.umt.edu/art/gva.htm
Fine Arts Museum 45404

Historical Museum at Fort Missoula, 322 Fort Missoula, Missoula, MT 59804 - T: (406) 728-3476, Fax: (406) 543-6277, E-mail: ftmslamuseum@montana.com, Internet: www.montana.com/ftmslamuseum. Dir.: Robert M. Brown, Cur.: L. Jane Richards, Tamara King
Local Museum - 1975 45405

Museum of Fine Arts, School of Fine Arts, University of Montana, Missoula, MT 59812 - T: (406) 243-4970, Fax: (406) 243-5726, E-mail: m.mudd@selway.umt.edu, Internet: www.dnr.state.mi.us. Dir.: Margaret Mudd
Fine Arts Museum / University Museum - 1956 45406

Paxson Gallery, University of Montana, Missoula, MT 59812 - T: (406) 243-2019, Fax: (406) 243-4968, Internet: www.umt.edu/partv/famus. Dir.: Margaret Mudd
Fine Arts Museum
Contemporary ceramic sculpture and paintings 45407

Philip L. Wright Zoological Museum, University of Montana, Div. of Biological Sciences, 32 Campus Dr #4824, Missoula, MT 59812 - T: (406) 243-5222, Fax: (406) 243-4184, E-mail: ddyer@selway.umt.edu. Cur.: Dr. Richard Hutto (Ornithology), Dr. Kerry Foresman (Mammalogy), Dr. Andrew Sheldon (Ichthyology), David Dyer (Collections)
University Museum / Natural History Museum - 1909
Research coll - herbarium 45408

Missouri Valley IA

Steamboat Bertrand Museum, DeSoto National Wildlife Refuge, Missouri Valley, IA 51555 - T: (712) 642-4121, Fax: (712) 642-2877, E-mail: r3bertrand@fws.gov, Internet: refuges.fws.gov/nwrsfiles/culturalresources/bertrand/. Cur.: Larry Klimek
Historical Museum - 1969 45409

Mitchell GA

Hamburg State Park Museum, 6071 Hamburg State Park Rd, Mitchell, GA 30820 - T: (912) 552-2393, Fax: (912) 553-1457, E-mail: hamburg@accucomm.net, Internet: www.accucomm.net/~hamburg
Historical Museum / Science&Tech Museum
Industry, 1920 water turbine powered gin and milling complex 45410

Mitchell IN

Spring Mill State Park Pioneer Village and Grissom Memorial, Hwy 60 E, Mitchell, IN 47446 - T: (812) 849-4129, Fax: (812) 849-4004, E-mail: spring@tima.com
Historical Museum / Open Air Museum - 1927
Village life, housed in a Grist Mill, flourishing pioneer village in the 1800s 45411

Virgil I. Grissom State Memorial, POB 376, Mitchell, IN 47446 - T: (812) 849-4129, Fax: (812) 849-4004, Internet: www.dnr.com. Dir.: Gerald J. Pagac
Special Museum - 1971
America's exploration of outer space, second American astronaut 45412

Mitchell SD

Enchanted World Doll Museum, 615 N Main, Mitchell, SD 57301 - T: (605) 996-9896, Fax: (605) 996-0210, E-mail: vala@santel.net. Pres.: Tom Wudel
Decorative Arts Museum - 1977
Dolls 45413

Middle Border Museum of American Indian and Pioneer Life, 1300 E University St, Mitchell, SD 57301 - T: (605) 996-2122, Fax: (605) 996-0323, E-mail: fmb@mitchell.net. Dir.: Chris Hanson
Local Museum / Open Air Museum / Ethnology Museum - 1939
Historic village 45414

Oscar Howe Art Center, 119 W Third Av, Mitchell, SD 57301 - T: (605) 996-4111, Fax: (605) 996-0323, E-mail: fnb@santel.net, Internet: www.oscarhowe.com. Dir.: Joanita Kant Monteith
Fine Arts Museum / Folklore Museum - 1971
Local and regional artists, paintings by Sioux artists 45415

Moab UT

Dan O'Laurie Canyon Country Museum, 118 E Center, Moab, UT 84532 - T: (435) 259-7985. Pres.: Tom Stengel
Local Museum - 1958
Local hist, geology, archaeology 45416

Mobile AL

Bragg-Mitchell Mansion, 1906 Springhill Av, Mobile, AL 36608 - T: (334) 471-6364, Fax: (334) 478-3800, E-mail: ginmckean@aol.com, Internet: www.braggmitchellmansion.com. Dir.: Michael Sullivan
Museum of Classical Antiquities / Local Museum - 1987
Antiques, historic house 45417

Carlen House, 54 Carlen St, Mobile, AL 36606 - T: (334) 208-7569. Dir.: George H. Ewert
Decorative Arts Museum - 1970 45418

Eichold-Heustis Medical Museum of the South → Mobile Medical Museum

Gulf Coast Exploreum, 65 Government St, Mobile, AL 36602 - T: (251) 208-6881, Fax: (251) 208-6889, E-mail: mike@exploreum.net, Internet: www.exploreum.net. Dir.: Michael Sullivan
Science&Tech Museum - 1979 45419

Mobile Medical Museum, 1504 Springhill Av, Mobile, AL 36616-1363 - T: (334) 434-5055, Fax: (334) 434-3752, E-mail: psofeh@aol.com. Dir.: Patsy Starkey
Historical Museum - 1962 45420

Mobile Museum of Art, 4850 Museum Dr, Mobile, AL 36608 - T: (251) 208-5200, Fax: (251) 208-5201, E-mail: schenk@cityofmobile.orgom, Internet: www.mobilemuseumofart.com. Dir.: Joseph B. Schenk, Cur.: Paul W. Richelson, Jill A. Jiminez
Fine Arts Museum - 1964 45421

Museum of Mobile, 111 S Royal St, Mobile, AL 36602-1341 - T: (334) 208-7569, Fax: (334) 208-7686, E-mail: museum@ci.mobile.al.us, Internet: www.museumofmobile.com. Dir.: George H. Ewert, Asst. Dir.: Shelia M. Flanagan, Cur.: Todd A. Kreamer, Dave Morgan
Historical Museum - 1962 45422

Oakleigh House, Historic Mobile Preservation, 300 Oakleigh Pl, Mobile, AL 36604 - T: (334) 432-6161, Fax: (334) 432-8843, E-mail: hmps@bellsouth.net, Internet: www.historicmobile.org. Dir.: Marilyn Culpepper
Historical Museum - 1935
Local history, civil war, period furnishings 45423

Richards-Dar House, 256 N Joachim St, Mobile, AL 36603 - T: (251) 208-7320, Fax: (251) 208-7321. Pres.: James F. Quinn
Historical Museum - 1972
Historic furnishings 45424

USS Alabama Battleship Memorial Park, 2703 Battleship Pkwy, Mobile, AL 36601 - T: (251) 433-2703, Fax: (251) 433-2777, E-mail: ussalbb60@aol.com, Internet: www.ussalabama.com. C.E.O.: Bill Tunnell
Military Museum / Open Air Museum - 1963 45425

Mobridge SD

Klein Museum, 1820 W Grand Crossing, Mobridge, SD 57601 - T: (605) 845-7243, E-mail: kleinmuseum@westriv.com. Dir./Cur.: Diane Kindt
Local Museum - 1975
Local hist, native American beadwork, Sitting Bul pictures 45426

Modesto CA

Great Valley Museum of Natural History, 1100 Stoddard Av, Modesto, CA 95350 - T: (209) 575-6196, Fax: (209) 575-6798, E-mail: lcrawford@yosemite.cc.ca.us, Internet: yosemite.cc.ca.us/community/great-valley. Head: Louise J. Crawford
Natural History Museum - 1973 45427

McHenry Museum, 1402 I St, Modesto, CA 95354 - T: (209) 577-5366, Fax: (209) 491-4313, E-mail: museum@thevision.net, Internet: www.thevision.net/
Local Museum - 1965
Local history, gold mining 45428

Mohall ND

Renville County Historical Society Museum, 504 First St NE, Mohall, ND 58761 - T: (701) 756-6195. Pres.: Dorothy Aalund
Local Museum / Historical Museum - 1978 45429

Moline IL

Deere Museum, One John Deere Pl, Moline, IL 61265 - T: (309) 765-4881, Fax: (309) 765-4088, Internet: www.deere.com. Dir.: James H. Collins
Science&Tech Museum - 1837
Tractors 45430

Rock Island County Historical Museum, 822-11 Av, Moline, IL 61266-0632 - T: (309) 764-8590, Fax: (309) 764-4748, E-mail: richs@netexpress.net, Internet: www.netexpress.net/~richs/. Dir.: Judy Belan
Local Museum - 1905
Local history 45431

Monhegan ME

The Monhegan Museum, 1 Lighthouse Hill, Monhegan, ME 04852 - T: (207) 596-7003. Cur.: Tralice Peck Bracy
Fine Arts Museum / Local Museum / Natural History Museum - 1968
Local history 45432

Monkton MD

Ladew Manor House, 3535 Jarrettsville Pike, Monkton, MD 21111 - T: (410) 557-9570, 557-9466, Fax: (410) 557-7763, Internet: www.ladewgardens.com. C.E.O.: Emily W. Emerick, Jennifer B. Shattuck, Cur.: Hugh J. O'Donovan
Historic Site - 1977
Manor House, English furniture, fox hunting memorabilia and equestrian-inspired paintings 45433

Monmouth IL

Buchanan Center for the Arts, 64 Public Sq, Monmouth, IL 61462 - T: (309) 734-3033, Fax: (309) 734-3554, E-mail: bca@misslink.net. Dir.: Mike A. Difuccia
Fine Arts Museum - 1990 45434

Wyatt Earp Birthplace, 406 S 3rd St and Wyatt Earp Way, Monmouth, IL 61462-1435 - T: (309) 734-6419, Fax: (309) 734-6419, E-mail: wyattearpbirthp@webtv.net, Internet: www.misslink.net/misslink/earp.htm
Local Museum - 1986
Local hist 45435

Monmouth OR

Campbell Hall Gallery, c/o Western Oregon University, 345 Monmouth Av, Monmouth, OR 97361 - T: (503) 838-8000, E-mail: curt@wou.edu, Internet: www.wou.edu. Head: Don Hoskisson
University Museum / Fine Arts Museum
Contemporary Northwestern visual art 45436

Jensen Arctic Museum, Western Oregon University, 590 W Church St, Monmouth, OR 97361 - T: (503) 838-8468, 838-8281, Fax: (503) 838-8289, Internet: www.wou.edu/president/universityadvancement/jensen/. Cur.: Keni Sturgeon
University Museum / Folklore Museum - 1985
Arctic culture 45437

Monroe CT

Monroe Historical Society Museum, Beardsley Homestead, 31 Great Ring Rd, Monroe, CT 06468-0212 - T: (203) 261-1383, Internet: www.monroehistoricsociety.org. Cur.: Michelle Olfra
Local Museum / Historical Museum - 1959 45438

Monroe LA

Biedenharn Museum and Gardens, Emy-Lou Biedenharn Foundation, 2006 Riverside Dr, Monroe, LA 71201 - T: (318) 387-5281, Fax: (318) 387-8253, E-mail: bmuseum@bayou.com, Internet: www.bmuseum.org. Pres.: Murray Biedenharn, Dir.: Ralph Calhoun
Religious Arts Museum / Special Museum - 1971
Bible museum, home of Joseph A. Biedenharn, first bottler of Coca-Cola 45439

Bry Gallery, c/o University of Louisiana at Monroe, 700 University Av, Bry Hall, Monroe, LA 71209-0310 - T: (318) 342-1375, Fax: (318) 342-1369, E-mail: aralexander@uln.edu, Internet: www.uln.edu/art/bryhall.html. Head: Ron J. Alexander
University Museum / Fine Arts Museum - 1931 45440

Masur Museum of Art, 1400 S Grand, Monroe, LA 71202 - T: (318) 329-2237, Fax: (318) 329-2847, E-mail: masur@ci.monroe.la.us, Internet: www.ci.monroe.la.us/mma. Dir.: Suzanne M. Prudhomme
Fine Arts Museum - 1963
Art 45441

Northeast Louisiana Delta African American Heritage Museum, 503 Plum St, Monroe, LA 71202 - T: (318) 323-1167, Fax: (318) 323-1167. Dir.: Nancy T. Johnson
Historical Museum / Folklore Museum - 1994
African art, visual art, furniture 45442

Monroe MI

Monroe County Historical Museum, 126 S Monroe St, Monroe, MI 48161 - T: (734) 240-7780, Fax: (734) 240-7788, E-mail: matthew_switlik@monroemi.org. Dir.: Matthew C. Switlik, Asst. Dir.: Ralph Naveaux, Cur.: James Ryland
Local Museum - 1939
Regional history, Gen. George A. Custer home 45443

Monroe NC

Union County Public Library Union Room, 316 E Windsor St, Monroe, NC 28112 - T: (704) 283-8184, Fax: (704) 282-0657, Internet: www.union.lib.nc.us. Dir.: Dave Eden
Public Gallery 45444

Monroe NY

Museum Village, 1010 Rte 17 M, Monroe, NY 10950 - T: (845) 782-8248, Fax: (845) 782-6432, E-mail: musvil@frontiernet.net, Internet: www.museumvillage.org. C.E.O.: John W. Carnahan
Open Air Museum - 1950 45445

Monroe Township NJ

Stone Museum, 608 Spotswood-Englishtown Rd, Monroe Township, NJ 08831 - T: (732) 521-2232, Fax: (732) 521-3388, E-mail: displayworld@erols.com, Internet: www.thestonemuseum.com. Dir.: Gerald Kleiner
Natural History Museum
Fluorescent rock, rare seashells, minerals, fossils, rare plants 45446

Monroeville AL

Monroe County Heritage Museum, Old Courthouse, Downtown Sq, Monroeville, AL 36461, mail addr: POB 1637, Monroeville, AL 36461 - T: (334) 575-7433, Fax: (334) 575-7934, Internet: www.tokillamockingbird.com. Dir.: Kathy McCoy
Local Museum - 1990
Local hist 45447

Montague MI

Montague Museum, Church and Meade Sts, Montague, MI 49437 - T: (616) 893-8603, Fax: (231) 894-9955, E-mail: cityofmontaque@aol.com. Pres.: Henry E. Roesler
Local Museum - 1964
Local history, former United Methodist Church 45448

Montauk Ny

Montauk Point Lighthouse Museum, 2000 Montauk Hwy, Montauk, Ny 11954 - T: (631) 668-2544 ext 22, Fax: (631) 668-2546, E-mail: tambrosio@montauklighthouse.com, Internet: www.montauklighthouse.com. Exec. Dir.: Thomas J. Ambrosio
Science&Tech Museum - 1987
Fresnel lens, paintings, photographs, maritime, lanterns 45449

Montclair NJ

Montclair Art Museum, 3 S Mountain Av, Montclair, NJ 07042-1747 - T: (973) 746-5555, Fax: (973) 746-9118, E-mail: mail@montclair-art.com, Internet: www.montclair-art.com. Pres.: Nathanial C. Harris, Dir.: Patterson Sims, Cur.: Gail Stavitsky, Tara Belluscio (Education), Twig Johnson (Native American Art)
Fine Arts Museum - 1914
American Indian art, costumes, silver, paintings, drwaings 45450

Montclair Historical Society Museum, 108 Orange Rd, Montclair, NJ 07042 - T: (973) 744-1796, Fax: (973) 783-9419. Pres.: Kathleen Zaracki, C.E.O.: Alice Schatteman, Exec. Dir.: Pamela A. Fosdick, Pres.: Kathleen Zaracki
Local Museum - 1965 45451

Monterey CA

Casa Amesti, 516 Polk St, Monterey, CA 93940 - T: (831) 372-8173, Fax: (831) 372-2808. Pres.: Pam McCollough
Historical Museum / Fine Arts Museum - 1953
Sculpture, various artifacts 45452

Colton Hall Museum, City Hall, Pacific St, Monterey, CA 93940 - T: (831) 646-5640, Fax: (831) 646-3422, E-mail: parttimemuseum@c1.monterey.ca.us, Internet: www.monterey.org/museum. Chm.: Carol Todd
Historical Museum - 1949
Constitutional Convention items 45453

Maritime Museum of Monterey, 5 Custom House Plaza, Monterey, CA 93940 - T: (831) 375-2553, Fax: (831) 655-3054, E-mail: maia@mntmh.org, Internet: www.mntmh.org. Dir.: Shauna Hershfield
Historical Museum - 1970
Maritime artifacts, ship models, paintings, photos 45454

Monterey History and Art Association Museum, 5 Custom House Plaza, Monterey, CA 93940 - T: (831) 372-2608, Fax: (831) 655-3054, E-mail: linda@mntmh.org, Internet: www.mntmh.org. Dir.: Shauna Hershfield
Local Museum - 1931
Local history, paintings, costume, artworks 45455

Monterey Museum of Art, 559 Pacific St, Monterey, CA 93940 - T: (831) 372-5477, Fax: (831) 372-5680, E-mail: mtry_art@mbay.net, Internet: www.monereyart.org. Dir.: Richard W. Gadd, Cur.: Mary Murray
Fine Arts Museum - 1959 45456

Monterey State Historic Park, 20 Custom House Plaza, Monterey, CA 93940 - T: (831) 649-7118, Fax: (831) 647-6236, Internet: www.mbay.net/~mshp. Cur.: Kris N. Quist
Historical Museum / Open Air Museum - 1938 45457

Old Monterey Jail, City Hall, Pacific St, Monterey, CA 93940 - T: (831) 646-5640, Fax: (831) 646-3422, Internet: www.monterey.org/museum. Chm.: Nancy Selfridge
Historical Museum - 1949 45458

San Carlos Cathedral Museum, 500 Church St, Monterey, CA 93940 - T: (831) 373-2628, Fax: (831) 373-0518
Religious Arts Museum
Spanish religious paintings and sculptures 45459

Monterey MA

Bidwell House, Art School Rd, Monterey, MA 01245-0537 - T: (413) 528-6888, Fax: (413) 528-6888, E-mail: museum@bcn.net, Internet: www.bidwellhousemuseum.org. C.E.O.: Candace Thayer
Decorative Arts Museum / Local Museum - 1990
Decorative arts, redware, textiles, furniture, delph, domestic and agricultural tools 45460

Monterey VA

Highland Maple Museum, U.S. 220 S, Monterey, VA 24465 - T: (540) 468-2420, 468-2550, Fax: (540) 468-2551, E-mail: highcc@cfw.com, Internet: www.highlandcounty.org. C.E.O.: Carolyn Pohowsky
Agriculture Museum - 1983
Agriculture 45461

Monterey Park CA

Vincent Price Gallery, c/o East Los Angeles College, 1301 Avenide Nida Csar Chevez Av, Monterey Park, CA 91754 - T: (323) 265-8841, Fax: (323) 265-8763, E-mail: east@laccd.cc.ca.us, Internet: www.lafn.org/education/elac/gallery. Dir.: Thomas Silliman
Fine Arts Museum - 1958
Africa, Peruvian, Mexican artifacts, North Amercian Indian art 45462

Montevideo MN

Chippewa County Historical Society Museum, 151 Pioneer Dr, Montevideo, MN 56265 - T: (320) 269-7636, E-mail: CCHS.June@juno.com, Internet: www.montevideomn.com. Pres.: Dennes Borman
Open Air Museum / Local Museum - 1936 45463

Montezuma KS

Stauth Memorial Museum, 111 N Azetec St, Montezuma, KS 67867 - T: (316) 846-2527, Fax: (316) 846-2810, E-mail: stauthm@ucom.net. Dir.: Kim Legleiter
Local Museum / Decorative Arts Museum - 1996
Decorative art, woodcarvings, sculpture, ivory carvings, musical instruments, weapons, hides, jewelry 45464

Montgomery AL

Alabama History Museum, 624 Washington Av, Montgomery, AL 36130 - T: (334) 242-4363, Fax: (334) 240-3433. Dir.: Edwin C. Bridges
Local Museum - 1901
American Indian art, archaeology, textiles, ceramics, pottery, decorative arts, manuscripts, military art, local history 45465

First White House of the Confederacy, 644 Washington Av, Montgomery, AL 36130 - T: (334) 242-1861. Head: John H. Napier
Historical Museum - 1900
Historic building 45466

Montgomery Museum of Fine Arts, 1 Museum Dr, Montgomery, AL 36117 - T: (334) 244-5700, Fax: (334) 244-5774, E-mail: info@mmfa.org, Internet: www.mmfa.org. Dir.: Mark M. Johnson, Pres.: G. Carl Barker, Cur.: Margaret Lynne Ausfeld, Marisa Pascucci, Tara Sartorius, Irja Thurlow, Tracey Campbell, Megan Masana
Fine Arts Museum - 1930
American paintings and sculptures, Old Master prints, Southern regional art and decorative arts 45467

The Wallace Museum Foundation, 631 S Perry St, Montgomery, AL 36104 - T: (334) 834-1972, Fax: (334) 262-5650, E-mail: info@wallacefoundation.org, Internet: www.wallacefoundation.org. Dir.: Joe Terry
Historical Museum - 1994
Political hist 45468

Montgomery NY

Brick House, Rte 17K, Montgomery, NY 12549 - T: (914) 457-4921, Fax: (914) 457-4906. Cur.: Susan A. Tucker
Historical Museum - 1979 45469

Hill-Hold Museum, 211 Rte 416, Montgomery, NY 12549 - T: (845) 457-4905, Fax: (914) 457-4906, E-mail: stucker@co.orange.ny.us. Dir.: Suasan A. Tucker
Historic Site - 1976 45470

Monticello AR

Drew County Historical Museum, 404 S Main St, Monticello, AR 71655 - T: (870) 367-7446, E-mail: genealogy71655@yahoo.com, Internet: www.arkansasroots.com. Pres.: Connie Mullis
Local Museum - 1970
Regional history, Indian artifacts, textiles, furniture 45471

Monticello IL

Monticello Railway Museum, Interstate 72 at Exit 166, Market St, Monticello, IL 61856 - T: (217) 762-9011, (800) 952-3396, E-mail: mrm@prairienet.org, Internet: www.prairienet.org/mrm/. Pres.: Kent McClure, Donna McClure
Science&Tech Museum - 1966
Railways 45472

Piatt County Museum, 315 W Main, Monticello, IL 61856 - T: (217) 762-4731. C.E.O.: Blanche Stoller
Local Museum - 1965
Local history 45473

Monticello IN

White County Historical Society Museum, 101 S Bluff St, Monticello, IN 47960 - T: (219) 583-3998
Local Museum - 1911
Local history 45474

Montour Falls NY

Schuyler County Historical Society Museum, 108 N Catharine, Montour Falls, NY 14865 - T: (607) 535-9741. Dir.: Bonnie Dilts
Local Museum - 1960 45475

Montpelier OH

Williams County Historical Museum, 619 E Main St, Montpelier, OH 43543 - T: (419) 485-8200. Cur.: Jane McCaskey
Local Museum - 1956 45476

Montpelier VT

T.W. Wood Gallery and Arts Center, Vermont College, Montpelier, VT 05602 - T: (802) 828-8743, Fax: (802) 828-8645, E-mail: woodart@tui.edu. Dir.: Joyce Mandeville
Fine Arts Museum / Public Gallery - 1891
Art 45477

Vermont Historical Society Museum, 109 State St, Pavilion Bldg, Montpelier, VT 05609-0901 - T: (802) 828-2291, Fax: (802) 828-3638, 479-8510, E-mail: vhs@vhs.state.vt.us, Internet: www.vermonthistory.org. Dir.: Gainor B. Davis, Cur.: Jacqueline Calder
Local Museum - 1838
Local hist 45478

The Vermont State House, 115 State St, Montpelier, VT 05633 - T: (802) 828-2228, Fax: (802) 828-2424, Internet: www.leg.state.vt.us. Pres.: Mary Leahy, Cur.: David Schutz
Decorative Arts Museum / Local Museum - 1808
Historic building 45479

Montpelier Station VA

James Madison's Montpelier, 11407 Constitution Hwy, Montpelier Station, VA 22957 - T: (540) 672-2728, Fax: (540) 672-0411, E-mail: education@mmtpelier.org, Internet: www.montpelier.org. Dir.: Kathleen Stiso Mullins
Local Museum - 1984
Historic house, home of President James Madison 45480

Montreat NC

Presbyterian Historical Society Museum, 318 Georgia Terrace, Montreat, NC 28757 - T: (704) 669-7061, Fax: (704) 669-5369, E-mail: pcusadoh@montreat.edu, Internet: www.history.pcusa.org
Religious Arts Museum - 1927 45481

Montrose CO

Montrose County Historical Museum, Main and Rio Grande, Montrose, CO 81402, mail addr: POB 1882, Montrose, CO 81402 - T: (970) 249-6135, E-mail: stepbackintime@montrose.net. Cur.: Marilyn Cox
Local Museum - 1974
Regional history 45482

Ute Indian Museum, 17253 Chipeta Dr, Montrose, CO 81401 - T: (970) 249-3098, Fax: (970) 252-8741, E-mail: cj.brafford@state.co.us. C.E.O.: C.J. Brafford
Ethnology Museum / Historic Site - 1956
Indian history 45483

Montrose PA

Susquehanna County Historical Society, Two Monument Sq, Montrose, PA 18801 - T: (570) 278-1881, Fax: (570) 278-9336, E-mail: suspulib@epix.net, Internet: www.susqcohistsoc.org. Cur.: Elizabeth A. Smith, Asst. Cur.: Debra Adleman
Local Museum - 1890
Local hist 45484

Montville NJ

Montville Township Historical Museum, Taylor Town Rd, Montville, NJ 07045 - T: (973) 334-5604. Pres.: Kathleen Fisher
Historical Museum - 1963 45485

Moorestown NJ

Perkins Center for the Arts, 395 Kings Hwy, Moorestown, NJ 08057 - T: (856) 235-6488, Fax: (856) 235-6624, E-mail: create@perkinscenter.org, Internet: www.perkinscenter.org. Dir.: Alan Willoughby, Asst. Dir.: Denise Creedon
Fine Arts Museum - 1977
Art 45486

Moorhead MN

Clay County Museum, 202 First Av N, Moorhead, MN 56560 - T: (218) 299-5520, Fax: (218) 299-5525, E-mail: lisa.hanson@ci.moorhead.mn.us, Internet: www.info.co.clay.mn.us/history. Dir.: Lisa Hanson
Local Museum / Historical Museum - 1932 45487

Comstock Historic House, 506 8th St, Moorhead, MN 56560 - T: (218) 291-4211, 233-1772. Chm.: Robert J. Loeffler
Local Museum - 1975
Historic house 45488

Heritage Hjemkomst Interpretive Center, 202 First Av N, Moorhead, MN 56561 - T: (218) 299-5511, Fax: (218) 299-5510, E-mail: charlotte.cox@ci.moorhead.mn.us, Internet: www.hjemkomst-center.com. Exec. Dir.: Charlotte Cox
Fine Arts Museum - 1986
Humanities, art, science 45489

Mora MN

Kanabec History Center, 805 W Forest Av, Mora, MN 55051 - T: (320) 679-1665, Fax: (320) 679-1673, E-mail: kanabechhistory@ncis.com, Internet: www.kanabechistory.com. Dir.: Sharon L. Vogt
Historical Museum - 1977 45490

Moraga CA

Hearst Art Gallery, Saint Mary's College, 1928 Saint Mary's Rd, Moraga, CA 94575-5110 - T: (925) 631-4379, Fax: (925) 376-5128, E-mail: cbrewste@stmarys-ca.edu, Internet: www.gaelnet.stmarys-ca.edu/gallery. Head: Carrie Brewster
Fine Arts Museum / University Museum - 1977 45491

Moravia NY

Cayuga-Owasco Lakes Historical Society Museum, 14 W Cayuga, Moravia, NY 13118 - T: (315) 497-3096. Pres.: Sue Stoyell
Local Museum - 1966 45492

Morehead KY

Claypool-Young Art Gallery, c/o Morehead State University, 150 University Blvd, Morehead, KY 40351 - T: (606) 783-2193, E-mail: r.franzi@morehead-st.edu, Internet: www.morehead.edu. Head: Jennifer Reis
University Museum / Fine Arts Museum - 1922
Prints, lithographs 45493

Kentucky Folk Art Center, 102 W First St, Morehead, KY 40351 - T: (606) 783-2204, Fax: (606) 783-5034, E-mail: g.barker@morehead-st.edu, Internet: www.kyfolkart.org. Dir.: Garry Barker, Cur.: Adrian Swain
Folklore Museum - 1985
Folk art 45494

Morehead City NC

Carteret County Museum of History and Art, 1008 Arendell St, Morehead City, NC 28557 - T: (252) 247-7533, Fax: (252) 247-2756, E-mail: historyplace@starfishnet.com, Internet: www.rootsweb.com/~ncchs/
Local Museum - 1971
Local genealogy, Carteret County, pictures 45495

Museum of History and Art, 1008 Arandell St, Morehead City, NC 28557 - T: (252) 247-7533, Fax: (252) 247-7533, E-mail: cchs@clis.com, Internet: www.nccoast.com/museum. Pres.: Les Ewen
Fine Arts Museum / Historical Museum - 1985 45496

Morganton NC

Jailhouse Galleries, Burke Arts Council, 115 E Meeting St, Morganton, NC 28665 - T: (828) 433-7282, Fax: (828) 433-7282, E-mail: burkearts@hci.net, Internet: www.burkearts.hci.net
Fine Arts Museum / Decorative Arts Museum 45497

Morgantown WV

Comer Museum, MRB, Rm 311A, Morgantown, WV 26506-6070 - T: (304) 293-4211, Fax: (304) 293-6751, E-mail: jdean@cemewvu.edu. Interim Dir.: Jim Dean
Science&Tech Museum - 1990 45498

Laura and Paul Mesaros Galleries, POB 6201, Morgantown, WV 26506 - T: (304) 293-4841 ext 3210, Fax: (304) 293-5731, E-mail: kolson@wvu.edu, Internet: www.wvu.edu. Cur.: Kristina Olson
Performing Arts Museum - 1867
Costumes, music, paintings, theatre 45499

West Virginia University Mesaros Galleries, Creative Arts Center, Evansdale Campus, West Virginia University, Morgantown, WV 26506-6111 - T: (304) 293-2140 ext 3210, Fax: (304) 293-5731, E-mail: kolson@wvu.edu, Internet: www.wvu.edu/~ccarts. Dir.: J. Bernard Schultz, Cur.: Kristina Olson, Robert Cobridges (Collection)
University Museum / Fine Arts Museum - 1968 45500

Moriarty NM

Moriarty Historical Museum, 201 Broadway St, Moriarty, NM 87035 - T: (505) 832-4087. Cur.: Joseph McComb
Agriculture Museum - 1981
Ranching area hist 45501

Morrilton AR

Museum of Automobiles, Petit Jean Mountain, 8 Jones Ln, Morrilton, AR 72110 - T: (501) 727-5427, Fax: (501) 727-6482, E-mail: director@museumofautos.com, Internet: www.museumofautos.com. Dir.: Buddy Hoelzeman
Science&Tech Museum - 1964
Antique automobiles 45502

Morris MN

Stevens County Historical Society Museum, 116 W Sixth St, Morris, MN 56267 - T: (320) 589-1719, E-mail: history@info-link.net. Dir.: Randi Hokanson
Historical Museum - 1920 45503

Morristown NJ

Acorn Hall House Museum, 68 Morris Av, Morristown, NJ 07960-4212 - T: (973) 267-3465, Fax: (973) 267-8773, E-mail: acornhall@juno.com, Internet: www.acornhall.org. C.E.O.: Bonnie-Lynn Nadzeika, Cur.: Debra Westmoreland
Historical Museum - 1945 45504

Fosterfields Living Historical Farm, 73 Kahdena Rd, Morristown, NJ 07960 - T: (973) 326-7644, Fax: (973) 631-5023, E-mail: mtexel@morrisparks.net, Internet: www.parks.morris.nj.us. Dir.: Mark Texel, Cur.: Rebecca Hoskins
Agriculture Museum - 1978 45505

Historic Speedwell, 333 Speedwell Av, Morristown, NJ 07960 - T: (973) 540-0211, Fax: (973) 540-0476, E-mail: info@speedwell.org, Internet: www.speedwell.org. Pres.: Jack Kelly
Historical Museum - 1966 45506

Macculloch Hall Historical Museum, 45 Macculloch Av, Morristown, NJ 07960 - T: (973) 538-2404, Fax: (973) 538-9428, E-mail: maccullochhall@aol.com, Internet: www.machall.org. Dir.: David Breslauer, Cur.: Ryan Hyman, Jane Bedula
Local Museum - 1950 45507

The Morris Museum, 6 Normandy Heights Rd, Morristown, NJ 07960 - T: (973) 971-3700, Fax: (973) 538-0154, E-mail: morrismuseum@worldnet.att.net, Internet: www.morrismuseum.org. Exec. Dir.: Steve Miller, Cur.: Erin Dougherty, Jennifer Martin
Local Museum - 1913
American Indian, African and Asian art, paintings, sculpture, anthropology, archaeology, costumes, ceramics, crafts, pottery, primitive and decorative art 45508

Morristown National Historical Park, 30 Washington Pl, Morristown, NJ 07960 - T: (973) 539-2016, Fax: (973) 539-8361, E-mail: Joni_Rowe@nps.gov, Internet: nps.gov/morr
Military Museum / Open Air Museum - 1933 45509

Schuyler-Hamilton House, 5 Olyphant Pl, Morristown, NJ 07960 - T: (973) 267-4039, Fax: (908) 852-1361, E-mail: abren85271@aol.com. C.E.O.: Anita Brennan, Cur.: Phyllis Sanftner, JoAnn Bownan
Decorative Arts Museum - 1923 45510

Morristown NY

Red Barn Museum, 518 River Rd E, Morristown, NY 13669 - T: (315) 375-6390. Pres./Dir.: Lorraine B. Bogardus
Open Air Museum - 1971 45511

Morristown TN

Crockett Tavern Museum, 2002 E Morningside Dr, Morristown, TN 37814 - T: (615) 587-9900. Pres.: Sally B. Bennett
Local Museum - 1958
Local hist 45512

Rose Center Museum, 442 W 2nd N St, Morristown, TN 37816 - T: (423) 581-4330, Fax: (423) 581-4307, E-mail: rosecent@usit.net, Internet: www.rosecenter.org. C.E.O.: Chip Drake
Folklore Museum / Local Museum - 1976
Civic art and culture 45513

Morrisville PA

Pennsbury Manor, 400 Pennsbury Memorial Rd, Morrisville, PA 19067 - T: (215) 946-0400, Fax: (215) 295-2936, E-mail: willpenn17@aol.com, Internet: www.pennsburymanor.org. Dir.: Douglas Miller, Asst. Dir.: Mary Ellyn Kunz, Cur.: Kimberly McCarty
Historic Site - 1939
1683 Pennsbury Manor, residence of William Penn, reconstructed in 1939 45514

Morro Bay CA

Morro Bay State Park Museum of Natural History, State Park Rd, Morro Bay, CA 93442 - T: (805) 772-2694, Fax: (805) 772-7129, E-mail: ndreher@parks.ca.gov, Internet: www.mbspmuseum.org. Cur.: Nancy Dreher
Natural History Museum - 1962
Chumash Indians, birds, mammals 45515

Morton Grove IL

Morton Grove Historical Museum, 6240 Dempster St, Morton Grove, IL 60053 - T: (847) 965-0203, Fax: (847) 965-7484, Internet: nsn.nslsilus.org/mgkhome/parkdist/page7.htm. Cur.: Mary Walsh
Local Museum - 1984
Local memorabilia and artifacts 45516

Moscow ID

The Appaloosa Museum and Heritage Center, 2720 W Pullman Rd, Moscow, ID 83843 - T: (208) 882-5578 ext 279, Fax: (208) 882-8150, E-mail: museum@appaloosa.com, Internet: www.appaloosamuseum.org. Dir.: Stacey Garretson, Pres.: King Rockhill
Historical Museum / Ethnology Museum - 1973
Local history 45517

McConnell Mansion, 110 S Adams, Moscow, ID 83843 - T: (208) 882-1004, Fax: (208) 882-0759, E-mail: lchsoffice@moscow.com, Internet: www.moscow.com/lchs. Dir.: Mary Reed, Cur.: Marilyn Sandmeyer
Historical Museum - 1968
Local history, Governor McConnell - library 45518

Moses Lake WA

Adam East Museum Art Center, 122 W Third, Moses Lake, WA 98837 - T: (509) 766-9395, Fax: (509) 766-9392. Interim Dir.: Terry Mulkey
Fine Arts Museum - 1957
Art 45519

Moses Lake Museum and Art Center, 230 W Third, Moses Lake, WA 98837 - T: (509) 766-9395, Fax: (509) 766-9243, E-mail: museum@moses-lake.com, Internet: www.moses-lake.com. Dir.: Terry Mulkey
Local Museum / Fine Arts Museum - 1957
Native American cultures 45520

Moundsville WV

Grave Creek Mound Historic Site, 801 Jefferson Av, Moundsville, WV 26041 - T: (304) 843-4128, Fax: (304) 843-4131, E-mail: grave.creek@wvculture.org, Internet: www.wvculture.org
Archaeological Museum - 1978
Archaeology of West Virginia 45521

Mount Airy NC

Gertrude Smith House, 708 N Main St, Mount Airy, NC 27030 - T: (336) 786-6856, Fax: (336) 786-9193, E-mail: visitandy@tcia.net, Internet: www.visitmayberry.com
Decorative Arts Museum - 1984
Furniture, artwork 45522

Mount Airy Museum of Regional History, 301 N Main St, Mount Airy, NC 27030 - T: (336) 786-4478, Internet: www.northcarolinamuseum.org
Local Museum 45523

Mount Clemens MI

The Art Center, 125 Macomb Pl, Mount Clemens, MI 48043 - T: (810) 469-8666, Fax: (810) 469-4529. Exec. Dir.: Jo-Anne Wilkie
Public Gallery - 1969
Michigan artists 45524

Crocker House, 15 Union St, Mount Clemens, MI 48043 - T: (810) 465-2488, Internet: www.macombonline.com
Local Museum - 1964
Local history, Crocker House, a Victorian Italianate style house 45525

Michigan Transit Museum, 200 Grand Av, Mount Clemens, MI 48043-5412 - T: (810) 463-1863, Fax: (810) 463-9814, Internet: www.mtmrail.com. Pres.: Timothy D. Backhurst
Science&Tech Museum - 1973
Transport, equipment, Grand Trunk depot railroad Museum 45526

Mount Desert ME

Somesville Museum, 373 Sound Dr, Mount Desert, ME 04660 - T: (207) 276-9323, Fax: (207) 276-4024, E-mail: mdihistory@acadia.net. Dir.: Jaylene Roths
Historical Museum 45527

Sound School House Museum, 373 Sound Dr, Mount Desert, ME 04660 - T: (207) 276-9323, Fax: (207) 276-4024, E-mail: mdihistory@acadia.net. Dir.: Jaylene Roths
Historical Museum 45528

Mount Dora FL

Mount Dora Center for the Arts, 138 E Fifth Av, Mount Dora, FL 32757 - T: (352) 383-0880, Fax: (352) 383-7753, E-mail: mdca@lcia.com. Dir.: Tamara Rejimbal
Folklore Museum - 1985
Folk art 45529

Mount Gilead NC

Town Creek Indian Mound Historic Site, 509 Town Creek Mound Rd, Mount Gilead, NC 27306 - T: (910) 439-6802, Fax: (910) 439-6441, E-mail: towncreek@ncsl.dcr.state.nc.us, Internet: www.ah.dcr.state.nc.us/sections/hs/town/town.htm
Open Air Museum / Historical Museum - 1936 45530

Mount Holly NJ

Historic Burlington County Prison Museum, 128 High St, Mount Holly, NJ 08060 - T: (609) 265-5476, Fax: (609) 265-5797. Pres.: Janet L. Sozio
Historical Museum - 1966 45531

John Woolman Memorial, 99 Branch St, Mount Holly, NJ 08060 - T: (609) 267-3226, Internet: www.woolmancentral.com. Dir.: Jack Walz, Carol Walz
Special Museum - 1915 45532

Mount Olivet KY

Blue Licks Battlefield Museum, Blue Licks Battlefield Park, Hwy 68, Mount Olivet, KY 41064 - T: (859) 289-5507, Fax: (859) 289-5409, E-mail: doug.price@mail.state.ky.us, Internet: www.state.ky.us/agencies/parks/bluelick.htm
Local Museum - 1928
General museum 45533

Mount Pleasant IA

Harlan-Lincoln House, 101 W Broad St, Mount Pleasant, IA 52641 - T: (319) 385-8021, Fax: (319) 385-6324, E-mail: iwcarch@iwc.edu, Internet: www.iwc.edu. Dir.: Lynn Ellsworth
Historical Museum - 1959
Home of U.S. Senator James Harlan (1876-1899) and the summer home of the Robert Todd Lincoln (1876-1899) - Iowa Wesleyan College Archives 45534

Midwest Old Settlers and Threshers Association Museum, 405 E Threshers Rd, Mount Pleasant, IA 52641 - T: (319) 385-8937, Fax: (319) 385-0563, E-mail: admin@oldtreshers.org, Internet: www.oldtreshers.org. Pres.: Earl Reynolds, Cur.: Dr. Mike Kramme (Theatre)
Agriculture Museum / Science&Tech Museum - 1950
Agricultural history, technic 45535

Mount Pleasant MI

Museum of Cultural and Natural History, Central Michigan University, Bellows St, 103 Rowe Hall, Mount Pleasant, MI 48859 - T: (989) 774-3829, Fax: (989) 774-2612, E-mail: lynn.fauver@cmich.edu, Internet: www.museum.cmich.edu/. Dir.: Lynn N. Fauver, Cur.: Tom Hahnenberg, Joyce Salisbury
University Museum / Local Museum - 1970 45536

University Art Gallery, c/o Central Michigan University, Dept. of Art, Wightman 132, Mount Pleasant, MI 48859 - T: (517) 774-3974, 774-3800, E-mail: julia.morrisroe@cmich.edu, Internet: www.ccfa.cmich.edu/uag. Dir.: Julia Morrisroe
Fine Arts Museum 45537

Mount Pleasant OH

Mount Pleasant Historical Society Museum, 342 Union St, Mount Pleasant, OH 43939 - T: (740) 769-2893, Fax: (740) 769-2804, E-mail: kaspenwa@lst.net, Internet: users.lst.net/gudzent. Pres.: Sherry Sawchuk, Cur.: Jim Aspenwall
Local Museum / Historical Museum - 1948 45538

Quaker Yearly Meeting House, 298 Market St, Mount Pleasant, OH 43939 - T: (740) 769-2893, E-mail: gudzent@lst.net, Internet: users.lst.net/gudzent. Man.: Mark Twyford
Religious Arts Museum - 1814 45539

Mount Pleasant SC

Patriots Point Naval and Maritime Museum, 40 Patriots Point Rd, Mount Pleasant, SC 29464 - T: (803) 884-2727, Fax: (803) 881-4232, E-mail: patriotspt@infoave.net, Internet: www.state.sc.us/patpt. Exec. Dir.: David Burnette, Dir.: Steve Ewing (Exhibits, Historian)
Military Museum - 1976
Museum housed in the aircraft carrier USS Yorktown, destroyer USS Laffey, submarine USS Clamagore, Coast Guard cutter Ingham 45540

Mount Prospect IL

Mount Prospect Historical Society Museums, 101 S Maple, Mount Prospect, IL 60056 - T: (847) 392-9006, Fax: (847) 392-8995, E-mail: mphist@aol.com, Internet: www.mphist.org. Dir.: Gavin Kleespies
Historical Museum - 1976
Local history 45541

Mount Pulaski IL

Mount Pulaski Courthouse, 113 S Washington, Mount Pulaski, IL 62548 - T: (217) 792-3919. Head: Richard Schachtsiek
Historical Museum - 1936
Greek Revival County Court House, part of Illinois 8th Judicial Circuit 45542

Mount Vernon IA

Armstrong Gallery → Luce Gallery

Luce Gallery, Cornell College, 600 1st St W, Mount Vernon, IA 52314-1098 - T: (319) 895-4491, Fax: (319) 895-5926, E-mail: scolemann@cornellcollege.edu, Internet: www.cornellcollege.edu. Pres.: Les Garner
Fine Arts Museum / University Museum - 1853
library 45543

Mount Vernon IL

Mitchell Museum at Cedarhurst, Richview Rd, Mount Vernon, IL 62864 - T: (618) 242-1236, Fax: (618) 242-9530, E-mail: mitchell@midwest.net, Internet: www.cedarhurst.org. Cur.: Michael J. Beam, Heather Owens (Craft Fair)
Fine Arts Museum - 1973
Art, sculpture park 45544

Mount Vernon VA

Frank Lloyd Wright's Pope-Leighey House, 9000 Richmond Hwy, Mount Vernon, VA 22309 - T: (703) 780-4000, Fax: (703) 780-8509, E-mail: woodlawn@nthp.org, Internet: www.nthp.org/main/sites/woodlawn.htm. Dir.: Ross G. Randall, Asst. Dir.: Gail Donahue
Local Museum / Fine Arts Museum - 1964 45545

George Washington's Mount Vernon, End of George Washington Pkwy S, Mount Vernon, VA 22121 - T: (703) 780-2000, Fax: (703) 799-8654, E-mail: mvinfo@mountvernon.org, Internet: www.mountvernon.org. Exec. Dir.: James C. Rees
Fine Arts Museum / Historical Museum - 1853
Decorative arts, graphic arts, textiles, archaeology, fine arts, Washington memorabilia 45546

Mountain Lake MN

Heritage Village, County Rd 1, Mountain Lake, MN 56159 - T: (507) 427-2023, Fax: (507) 427-2640, E-mail: pizzamin@prairie.lakes.com. Dir.: R.E Patrick, Cur.: Betty Lou Ratzloff
Historical Museum - 1971 45547

Mountain View AR

Ozark Folk Center, 1032 Park Av, Mountain View, AR 72560 - T: (870) 269-3851, Fax: (870) 269-2909, E-mail: ofc@mvtel.net, Internet: www.ozarkfolkcenter.com. Dir.: John Van Orman
Folklore Museum - 1973
Folk arts and crafts of the Ozark mountain region - library 45548

Mountainair NM

Salinas Pueblo Missions National Monument, Corner of Broadway and Ripley, Mountainair, NM 87036-517 - T: (505) 847-2585, Fax: (505) 847-2441, Internet: www.nps.gov/sapu. Head: Glenn Fulfer
Archaeological Museum - 1909
Prehistoric pithouses c. 800 A.D.; prehistoric Indian ruins c. 1100-1670 A.D.; four Spanish mission ruins c. 1622-1672 45549

Mountainside NJ

Trailside Nature and Science Center, 452 New Providence Rd, Mountainside, NJ 07092 - T: (908) 789-3670, Fax: (908) 789-3270, E-mail: hhoffman@unioncountynj.org. Dir.: Hollace Hoffman, Asst. Dir.: Patricia Bertsch
Natural History Museum - 1941 45550

Mountainville NY

Storm King Art Center, Old Pleasant Hill Rd, Mountainville, NY 10953-0280 - T: (845) 534-3115, Fax: (845) 534-4457, Internet: www.stormking.org. Dir.: David R. Collens, Cur.: Joan Pachner
Fine Arts Museum - 1960 45551

Mulberry FL

Mulberry Phospate Museum, 101 SE 1st St, Mulberry, FL 33860 - T: (863) 425-2823, Fax: (863) 425-0188, E-mail: phaag@gte.net
Archaeological Museum - 1985
Cenozoic fossils 45552

Mullens WV

Twin Falls Museum, Hwy Rte 97, Mullens, WV 25882 - T: (304) 294-4000, Fax: (304) 294-5000, Internet: www.twinfallsresort.com. Head: A. Scott Durham
Local Museum - 1976
Local hist 45553

Mumford NY

Genesee Country Village and Museum, 1410 Flint Hill Rd, Mumford, NY 14511 - T: (585) 538-6822, Fax: (716) 538-2887, E-mail: bpessin@gcv.org, Internet: www.gcv.org. Pres.: Betsy Harrison, Cur.: Dan Barber (Collections), Jill Roberts (Gallery of Wildlife and Sporting Art), Sen. Dir.: Connie Bodner (Programs)
Fine Arts Museum / Historical Museum / Open Air Museum - 1966 45554

Muncie IN

Ball State University Museum of Art, Riversite Av at Warwick, Muncie, IN 47306 - T: (765) 285-5242, Fax: (765) 285-4003, E-mail: ajoyaux@bsu.edu, Internet: www.bsu.edu/artmuseum. Dir.: Alain Joyaux, Cur.: Nancy Huth
Fine Arts Museum / University Museum - 1936
Art 45555

Biology Department Teaching Museum, 2000 University, Muncie, IN 47306 - T: (765) 289-1241, 289-2641, Fax: (765) 285-8804, E-mail: jetaylor@bsu.edu. Chm.: Dr. Carl E. Warnes
University Museum / Natural History Museum - 1918 45556

Muncie Children's Museum, 515 S High St, Muncie, IN 47305 - T: (765) 286-1660, Fax: (765) 286-1662, E-mail: munciemuseum@home.com, Internet: www.muchiechildrensmuseum.com. Dir.: Lenette Freeman
Ethnology Museum - 1977 45557

National Model Aviation Museum, Academie of Model Aeronautics, 5151 E Memorial Dr, Muncie, IN 47302 - T: (765) 287-1256, Fax: (765) 289-4248, E-mail: michaels@modelaircraft.org, Internet: www.modelaircraft.org. Dir.: Joyce Hager, Cur.: Michael Smith
Special Museum - 1936
Aeronautics - Library 45558

Munising MI

Alger County Heritage Center, 1496 Washington St, Munising, MI 49862 - T: (906) 387-4308, Fax: (906) 464-3665. Pres.: Mary Jo Cook
Local Museum - 1966
Local history 45559

Grand Island Trader's Cabin, Washington St, Munising, MI 49862 - T: (906) 387-4308. Pres.: Mark Louma
Historical Museum - 1972
Abraham Williams, 1st white settler in Alger County 45560

Munnsville NY

Fryer Memorial Museum, Williams St, Munnsville, NY 13409 - T: (315) 495-5395, 495-6148. Dir.: Olive S. Boylan
Historical Museum - 1977
Generalogical coll 45561

Munster IN

Northern Indiana Arts Association, 1040 Ridge Rd, Munster, IN 46321 - T: (219) 836-1839, Fax: (219) 836-1863, Internet: www.niaaonline.org. Pres.: Jim Wetzstein
Fine Arts Museum - 1969
Art 45562

Murdo SD

Pioneer Auto Museum, 503 E Fifth St, Murdo, SD 57559, mail addr: POB 76, Murdo, SD 57559 - T: (605) 669-2691, Fax: (605) 669-3217, E-mail: pas@pioneerautoshow.com, Internet: www.

pioneerautoshow.com. Dir.: David A. Geisler, Cur.: John Geisler
Science&Tech Museum - 1953
Transportation 45563

Murfreesboro AR

Crater of Diamonds State Park Museum, Rte 1, Box 364, Murfreesboro, AR 71958 - T: (870) 285-3113, Fax: (870) 285-4169, E-mail: crater@arkansas.com, Internet: www.arkansas.com. Head: Mike Hall
Historic Site / Special Museum - 1972
Diamonds, semi-precious rocks and minerals 45564

Ka-Do-Ha Indian Village Museum, 1010 Caddo Dr, Murfreesboro, AR 71958 - T: (870) 285-3736, E-mail: caddotc@alltel.net, Internet: www.caddotc.com
Ethnology Museum / Archaeological Museum - 1964
Archaeology, on 1,000 A.D. Moundbuilder village and ceremonial center 45565

Murfreesboro NC

Rea Museum, William and Fourth Sts, Murfreesboro, NC 27855 - T: (252) 398-4886, Fax: (252) 398-5871. Dir.: Kay Mitchell
Historical Museum - 1967 45566

Murfreesboro TN

Baldwin Photographic Gallery, Middle Tennessee State University, Learning Resources Center, Murfreesboro, TN 37132 - T: (615) 898-2085, Fax: (615) 898-5682, E-mail: tjimison@mtsu.edu. Cur.: Tom Jimison
Fine Arts Museum / University Museum - 1961 45567

Oaklands Historic House Museum, 900 N Maney Av, Murfreesboro, TN 37130 - T: (615) 893-0022, Fax: (615) 893-0513, E-mail: oaklandsmansion@aol.com. Pres.: Carty Roberts
Local Museum - 1959
Historic house 45568

Stones River National Battlefield, 3501 Old Nashville Hwy, Murfreesboro, TN 37129-3094 - T: (615) 893-9501, Fax: (615) 893-9508, E-mail: stri_information@nps.gov, Internet: www.nps.gov/stri. Dir.: Stuart Johnson
Military Museum / Historic Site - 1927
Military hist 45569

Murphy ID

Owyhee County Historical Museum, POB 67, Murphy, ID 83650 - T: (208) 495-2319. Pres.: James Howard, Dir.: Byron Johnson
Local Museum - 1960
Agriculture, Indian artifacts, geology, mining 45570

Murphy NC

Cherokee County Historical Museum, 87 Peachtree St, Murphy, NC 28906 - T: (828) 837-6792, Fax: (828) 837-6792, E-mail: cchm@webworkz.com, Internet: www.tib.com/cchm
Historical Museum - 1977 45571

Murray KY

University Art Galleries, Murray State University, Price Doyle Fine Arts Center, 15th and Olive Sts, Murray, KY 42071-3342 - T: (270) 762-3052, Fax: (270) 762-3920, E-mail: albert.sperath@murraystate.edu. Dir.: Albert Sperath
Fine Arts Museum / University Museum - 1971
Art 45572

Wrather West Kentucky Museum, Murray State University, Murray, KY 42071-0009 - T: (270) 762-4771, Fax: (270) 762-4485, Internet: www.murraystate.edu. C.E.O.: Kate A. Reeves
Local Museum - 1982
Regional history 45573

Murrells Inlet SC

Brookgreen Gardens, 1931 Brookgreen Gardens Dr, Murrells Inlet, SC 29576 - T: (843) 235-6000, Fax: (843) 237-1014, E-mail: info@brookgreen.org, Internet: www.brookgreen.org. Pres.: Lawrence Henry
Fine Arts Museum - 1931
American sculpture 45574

Muscatine IA

Muscatine Art Center, 1314 Mulberry Av, Muscatine, IA 52761 - T: (319) 263-8282, Fax: (319) 263-4702, E-mail: art@muscanet.com, Internet: www.muscatineartcenter.org. Dir.: Barbara C. Longtin
Fine Arts Museum - 1965
Art, housed in Edwardian style Musser mansion, contemporaray gallery 45575

Muskegon MI

Great Lakes Naval Memorial and Museum, 1346 Bluff St, Muskegon, MI 49441 - T: (231) 755-1230, Fax: (231) 755-5883, E-mail: SS236@aol.com, Internet: www.silversides.org. Asst. Dir.: Cathy J. Morin, Cur.: Robert G. Morin
Historical Museum / Military Museum - 1972
Historic Ship of the WW II, navy sub U.S.S. Silversides, USCGC McLane (WMEC 146) 45576

Hackley & Hume Historic Site, W Webster Av and Sixth St, Muskegon, MI 49440 - T: (616) 722-7578, Fax: (616) 728-4119, E-mail: info@muskegonmuseum.org, Internet: www.muskegonmuseum.org. Dir.: John H. McGarry, Cur.: Lisa M. Barker
Local Museum - 1971
Historic houses 45577

Muskegon County Museum, 430 W Clay, Muskegon, MI 49440 - T: (231) 722-0278, Fax: (231) 728-4119, E-mail: info@muskegonmuseum.org, Internet: www.muskegonmuseum.org. Dir.: John H. McGarry, Asst. Dir.: Diane Szewczyk-Smith, Cur.: Deborah Postema-George, Melinda Johnson, Melissa Welsh, Julia McKee, Kristen Hoeker
Local Museum - 1937
Regional history - children's science museum 45578

Muskegon Museum of Art, 296 W Webster Av, Muskegon, MI 49440 - T: (231) 720-2570, Fax: (231) 720-2585, Internet: www.muskegon.k12.mi.us. Dir.: Susan Talbot-Stanaway, Cur.: J. Houghton
Fine Arts Museum - 1912
Art - library 45579

USS Silversides and Maritime Museum → Great Lakes Naval Memorial and Museum

Muskogee OK

Ataloa Lodge Museum, 2299 Old Bacone Rd, Muskogee, OK 74403-1597 - T: (918) 683-4581 ext 283, Fax: (918) 687-5913, E-mail: jtimothy@bacone.edu, Internet: www.bacone.edu. Dir.: John Timothy
Ethnology Museum / Folklore Museum - 1932 45580

Five Civilized Tribes Museum, Agency Hill, Honor Heights Dr, Muskogee, OK 74401 - T: (918) 683-1701, Fax: (918) 683-3070, E-mail: the5tribes@azalea.net, Internet: www.fivetribes.com. Pres.: Richard Bradley, Dir.: Clara Reekie
Historical Museum / Ethnology Museum / Folklore Museum - 1966
American Indian Museum and Art Gallery 45581

Muskogee War Memorial Park and Military Museum, 3500 Batfish Rd, Muskogee, OK 74401 - T: (918) 682-6294, E-mail: ussbatfish@yahoo.com, Internet: www.geocities.com/ussbatfish. Cur.: Charles Fletcher
Military Museum - 1972
Army, navy, marine and air force, WW 2, Civil War 45582

Thomas-Foreman Home, 1419 W Okmulgee, Muskogee, OK 74401 - T: (918) 682-6938. Pres.: Jerry Marshall
Historical Museum - 1970 45583

Three Rivers Museum, 220 Elgin, Muskogee, OK 74401 - T: (918) 686-6624, Fax: (918) 682-3477, E-mail: 3riversmuseum@mynewroads.com, Internet: www.3riversmuseum.com. Dir.: Linda Moore
Local Museum - 1985
Furnishings, clothing, military, railroad 45584

Myrtle Beach SC

Children's Museum of South Carolina, 2501 N Kings Hwy, Myrtle Beach, SC 29577 - T: (843) 946-9469, Fax: (843) 946-7011, E-mail: cmsc@sccoast.net, Internet: www.cmsckids.org. C.E.O.: Pam Barnhill
Science&Tech Museum / Natural History Museum - 1993 45585

Franklin G. Burroughs-Simeon B. Chapin Art Museum, 3100 S Ocean Blvd, Myrtle Beach, SC 29577 - T: (843) 238-2510, Fax: (843) 238-2910, E-mail: artmuse@sccoast.net. Dir.: Patricia Goodwinl
Fine Arts Museum - 1989
Art 45586

Mystic CT

Mystic Art Association Museum, 9 Water St, Mystic, CT 06355 - T: (860) 536-7601, Fax: (860) 536-0610, E-mail: maa@mystic-art.org, Internet: www.mystic-art.org. Dir.: Joanne K. Newman
Fine Arts Museum / Folklore Museum - 1914 45587

Mystic Seaport, 75 Greenmanville Av, Mystic, CT 06355-0990 - T: (860) 572-0711, Fax: (860) 572-5327, E-mail: info@mysticseaport.org, Internet: www.mysticseaport.org. Dir.: Douglas H. Teeson, Cur.: William Cogar, William Peterson, Mary Anne Stets
Special Museum - 1929 45588

Nacogdoches TX

SFA Galleries, c/o Stephen F. Austin State University, 208 Griffith Fine Arts Bldg, Nacogdoches, TX 75962 - T: (936) 468-1131, Fax: (936) 468-2938, E-mail: eadams@sfasu.edu. Dir.: Eloise Adams
Fine Arts Museum / University Museum 45589

Sterne-Hoya Museum, 211 S Lanana St, Nacogdoches, TX 75961 - T: (936) 560-5426, Fax: (936) 560-5426. Dir.: Lindsey Richardson
Local Museum - 1959
Historic house - library 45590

Stone Fort Museum, Stephen F. Austin State University, Alumni & Griffith Blvds, Nacogdoches, TX 75962, mail addr: POB 6075 (SFASU), Nacogdoches, TX 75962 - T: (936) 468-2408, Fax: (936) 468-7084, E-mail: stonefort@sfasu.edu. Dir.: Dr. James E. Corbin, Cur.: Carolyn Spears
Local Museum / University Museum - 1936
Local hist, Spanish colonial and East Texas prior till 1900 45591

Nageezi NM

Chaco Culture National Historical Park, 1808 Rd 7950, Nageezi, NM 87037 - T: (505) 786-7014 ext 221, Fax: (505) 786-7061, E-mail: chcu@nps.gov, Internet: www.nps.gov/chcu. Cur.: Wendy Bustard, Dabney Ford (Archeology)
Archaeological Museum - 1907 45592

Nambe NM

Liquid Paper Museum, Nambe, NM 87501 - T: (505) 455-3848, Internet: www.gihon.com. Exec. Dir.: Marcia J. Summers
Special Museum - 1980
Manufacturing tools and equip 45593

Nantucket MA

Artists Association of Nantucket Museum, 19 Washington St, Nantucket, MA 02554 - T: (508) 228-0722, 228-0294, Fax: (508) 325-5251, E-mail: aan@nantucket.net, Internet: www.nantucketarts.org. Pres.: Robert Frazer
Fine Arts Museum - 1945
Art gallery 45594

The Coffin School Museum, c/o Egan Institute of Maritime Studies, 4 Winter St, Nantucket, MA 02554 - T: (508) 228-2505, Fax: (508) 228-7069, E-mail: eganinst@nantucket.net. Dir.: Nathaniel Philbrick, Cur.: Margaret Moore
Historical Museum / Fine Arts Museum - 1996
Coffin School memorabilia, portraits and marine paintings, ship models 45595

Hinchman House, Maria Mitchell Association, 7 Milk St, Nantucket, MA 02554 - T: (508) 228-9198, 228-0898, Fax: (508) 228-1031, E-mail: ahunt@mmo.org, Internet: www.mmo.org. Dir.: Kathryn K. Pochman, Asst. Dir.: Vladimir Strelnitski (Astronomy), William T. Maple (National Science), Cur.: Mara Alper
Natural History Museum - 1902
Natural science, astronomy 45596

Mitchell House, Maria Mitchell Association, 4 Vestal St, Nantucket, MA 02554 - T: (508) 228-9198, 228-2896, Fax: (508) 228-1031, E-mail: kpochman@mmo.org, Internet: www.mmo.org. Dir.: Kathryn K. Pochman, Asst. Dir.: Vladimir Strelnitski (Astronomy), William T. Maple (National Science), Cur.: Jascin Leonardo-Finger
Natural History Museum - 1902
Natural science, astronomy, Maria Mitchell's birthplace - Vestal Street and Loines Observatories, aquarium, science library 45597

Nantucket Historical Association Museum, 15 Broad St, Nantucket, MA 02554-1016 - T: (508) 228-1894, Fax: (508) 228-5618, E-mail: nhainfo@nha.org, Internet: www.nha.org. Dir.: Frank D. Milligan, Cur.: Georgen Gilliam
Local Museum - 1894
Local history - library 45598

Nanuet NY

Hudson Valley Children's Museum, Nanuet mall, 75 W Rte 159, Nanuet, NY 10954 - T: (845) 735-9720, Fax: (845) 735-9770, E-mail: HVCM95@worldnet.att.net, Internet: www.HVCM.org. Exec. Dir.: Elizabeth Edgert
Science&Tech Museum / Natural History Museum - 1995 45599

Naperville IL

Naper Settlement Museum, 523 S Webster St, Naperville, IL 60540 - T: (630) 420-6010, 305-5250, Fax: (630) 305-5255, E-mail: grouptours@naperville.il.us, Internet: www.napersettlement.org. Dir.: Peggy Frank, Cur.: Louise Howard, Asst. Cur.: Debbie Grinnell
Open Air Museum - 1969
Historic village 45600

Naples FL

Collier County Museum, 3301 Tamiami Trail E, Naples, FL 34112 - T: (941) 774-8476, Fax: (941) 774-8580, E-mail: mueum@colliergov.net, Internet: www.colliermuseum.com. C.E.O.: Ron D. Jamro
Local Museum - 1978
Local hist and archaeology, steam logging locomotive 45601

Naples Museum of Art, 5833 Pelican Bay Blvd, Naples, FL 34108-2740 - T: (941) 597-1900, Fax: (941) 597-8163, E-mail: museum@naplesphilcenter.org, Internet: www.naplesphilcenter.org. Cur.: Alyce Nash
Public Gallery - 1989 45602

Teddy Bear Museum of Naples, 2511 Pine Ridge Rd, Naples, FL 34109 - T: (941) 598-2711, Fax: (941) 598-9239, E-mail: info@teddymuseum.com, Internet: www.teddymuseum.com. Cur.: George B. Black
Special Museum - 1990 45603

The von Liiebig Art Center, 585 Park St, Naples, FL 34102 - T: (941) 262-6517, Fax: (941) 262-5404, E-mail: info@naplesartcenter.org, Internet: www.naplesartcenter.org. Cur.: Barbara A. Hill
Fine Arts Museum - 1954
Paintings, sculpture, photography, works on paper 45604

Narragansett RI

South County Museum, POB 709, Narragansett, RI 02882 - T: (401) 783-5400, Fax: (401) 783-0506, Internet: www.southcountymuseum.org. Exec. Dir.: L.J. McElroy
Local Museum - 1933
Agriculture, technology, transportation, print shop, Yankee crafts, rural life 45605

Narrowsburg NY

Fort Delaware, Rte 97 N of Port Jervis, Narrowsburg, NY 12764, mail addr: POB 5012, Monticello, NY 12701-5192 - T: (845) 252-6660, Fax: (845) 794-3459, Internet: co.sullivan.ny.us. Dir.: Joanna Szakmary
Historical Museum - 1957 45606

Nashua IA

Chickasaw County Historical Society Museum, Bradford Village, 2729 Cheyenne Av, Nashua, IA 50658 - T: (641) 435-2567, Fax: (641) 435-2567. C.E.O.: Duane Tracy
Local Museum - 1953
Local history 45607

Nashua NH

Nashua Center for Arts, 14 Court St, Nashua, NH 03060 - T: (603) 883-1506, Fax: (603) 882-7705
Public Gallery 45608

Nashville IN

Brown County Art Gallery and Museum, 1 Artist Dr, Nashville, IN 47448 - T: (812) 988-4609, E-mail: brncagal@indiana.edu; brncagal@aol.com, Internet: www.brownco.org; www.geocities.com/brncagal. Pres.: Dr. Emanuel Klein
Fine Arts Museum - 1926
Art gallery 45609

Brown County Historical Society Pioneer Museum, Museum Ln, Nashville, IN 47448 - T: (812) 988-8547, Fax: (812) 988-1901. Pres.: Ed Tratebas
Local Museum / Open Air Museum - 1957
Local history, museum village 45610

T.C. Steele State Historic Site, 4220 T.C. Steele Rd, Nashville, IN 47448 - T: (812) 988-2785, Fax: (812) 988-8457, E-mail: tcsteele@bloomington.in.us, Internet: www.state.in.us/ism/sites/steele. Cur.: Andrea Smith de Tarnowsky
Fine Arts Museum - 1945
C.1907 T.C. Steele home, c.1916 artists studio 45611

Nashville TN

Belle Meade Plantation, 5025 Harding Rd, Nashville, TN 37205 - T: (615) 356-0501, Fax: (615) 356-2336, Internet: www.bellemeadeplantation.com. Exec. Dir.: Norman O.. Burns, Cur.: Janet S. Hasson
Local Museum - 1953
Historic house 45612

Cheekwood Museum of Art, 1200 Forrest Park Dr, Nashville, TN 37205-4242 - T: (615) 356-8000, Fax: (615) 353-0919, E-mail: kwelborn@cheekwood.org, Internet: www.cheekwood.org. Dir.: Dr. John Wetenhall, Cur.: Celia Walker, Asst. Cur.: Rusty Freeman, Terri Smith
Fine Arts Museum - 1960
American art , contemporary art and sculpture, american and english decorative arts - library 45613

Country Music Hall of Fame and Museum, 222 Fifth Av S, Nashville, TN 37203 - T: (615) 416-2001, Fax: (615) 255-2245, Internet: www.countrymusichalloffame.com. Dir.: Kyle Young, Deputy Dir.: Nina Hammontree, Sam Hook, John Knowles, Paul Kingsbury, Diana Johnson, Cur.: Mark Medley
Music Museum - 1964
Country music and historic recording studio 45614

Cumberland Science Museum, 800 Fort Negley Blvd, Nashville, TN 37203 - T: (615) 862-5160, Fax: (615) 862-5178, Internet: www.csmisfun.com. C.E.O.: Ralph J. Schulz, Dir.: B. Matthews (Physical Science)
Natural History Museum / Science&Tech Museum - 1944
Natural science, technology - planetarium 45615

Disciples of Christ Historical Society Museum, 1101 19th Av S, Nashville, TN 37212-2196 - T: (615) 327-1444, Fax: (615) 327-1445, E-mail: dishistsoc@aol.com, Internet: users.aol.com/dishistsoc. Pres.: Peter M. Morgan
Religious Arts Museum - 1941
Religious hist 45616

Fisk University Galleries, Aaron Douglas Gallery and Carl Van Vechten Gallery, 1000 17th Av N, Nashville, TN 37203-3051 - T: (615) 329-8720, Fax: (615) 329-8544, E-mail: galleries@fisk.edu, Internet: www.fisk.edu. C.E.O.: Dr. Carolyn Reid-Wallace
Fine Arts Museum - 1949
African and American art, paintings, drawings, folk art - library 45617

Fort Nashborough, 170 First Av N, Nashville, TN 37201 - T: (615) 862-8400, Fax: (615) 862-5493, E-mail: jackie.jones@nashville.gov, Internet: www.nashville.gov/parks. C.E.O.: James Fyke
Historical Museum - 1780 45618

Frist Center for the Visual Arts, 919 Broadway, Nashville, TN 37203 - T: (615) 244-3340, Fax: (615) 244-3339, Internet: www.fristcenter.org. C.E.O.: Chase Rynd
Fine Arts Museum - 2001
Photographs, sculpture, paintings 45619

Fugitive Art Center, 440 Houston St, Nashville, TN 37203 - T: (615) 256-7067, E-mail: contact@fugitiveart.com, Internet: www.fugitiveart.com. Head: Jack Dingo Ryan
Public Gallery - 1999 45620

Hartzler-Towner Multicultural Museum, 1104 19th Av, Nashville, TN 37212 - T: (615) 340-7481, Fax: (615) 340-7463, E-mail: museum@scarrittbennett.org, Internet: www.scarrittbennett.org. Dir.: Herschell Parker
Decorative Arts Museum / Ethnology Museum - 1992
Anthropology 45621

The Parthenon, 2600 West End Av, Nashville, TN 37203 - T: (615) 862-8431, Fax: (615) 880-2265, E-mail: info@parthenon.org, Internet: www.parthenon.org. Dir.: Wesley M. Paine
Fine Arts Museum - 1897
Cowan coll, paintings, artworks 45622

Ruby Green Contemporary Arts Foundations, 514 Fifth Av S, Nashville, TN 37203 - T: (615) 244-7179
Public Gallery 45623

Tennessee Central Railway Museum, 220 Willow St, Nashville, TN 37210-2159 - T: (615) 244-9001, Fax: (615) 244-2120, E-mail: hultman@nashville.com, Internet: www.tcry.org
Science&Tech Museum - 1990
Rolling stock, Nashville, Chattanooga and St Louis Ry 45624

Tennessee Historical Society Museum, War Memorial Bldg, Nashville, TN 37243-0084 - T: (615) 741-8934, Fax: (615) 741-8937, E-mail: tnhissoc@tennesseehistory.org, Internet: www.tennesseehistory.org. C.E.O.: Ann Toplovich
Historical Museum - 1849 45625

Tennessee State Museum, 505 Deaderick St, Nashville, TN 37243-1120 - T: (615) 741-2692, Fax: (615) 741-7231, E-mail: info@tnmuseum.org, Internet: www.tnmuseum.org. Dir.: Lois S. Riggins-Ezzell, Asst. Dir.: Dan E. Pomeroy (Collections), Patricia Rasbury (Education)
Historical Museum - 1937
State history and art, military history - library 45626

Travellers Rest Historic House Museum, 636 Farrell Pkwy, Nashville, TN 37220 - T: (615) 832-8197, Fax: (615) 832-8169, E-mail: travellersrest@earthlink.net, Internet: www.travellersrestplantation.org. Exec. Dir.: David Currey, Cur.: Desiree Galbreath
Local Museum - 1955
Local hist 45627

Upper Room Chapel Museum, 1908 Grand Av, Nashville, TN 37212 - T: (615) 340-7206, Fax: (615) 340-7293, E-mail: kkimball@upperroom.org, Internet: www.upperroom.org. Dir.: Kathryn A. Kimball
Religious Arts Museum / Fine Arts Museum - 1953
Bibles from 1577, woodcarving of Da Vinci's last supper, furniture, antiquites, religious art, African, Asian, Arfo-American and African Indian art 45628

Vanderbilt University Fine Arts Gallery, Vanderbilt University, 23rd & W End Avs, Nashville, TN 37203 - T: (615) 322-0605, 343-1704, Fax: (615) 343-3786, E-mail: gallery@vanderbilt.edu, Internet: www.vanderbilt.edu/Ans/finearts/gallery.html. Dir.: Joseph S. Mella, Asst. Cur.: Alison G. Melnik
Fine Arts Museum / University Museum - 1961
Asian art, old master print, Italian renaissance painting, Oriental art, rare books - Arts library 45629

Watkins Institute Art Gallery, 100 Powell Pl, Nashville, TN 37204 - T: (615) 383-4848, Fax: (615) 383-4849
Fine Arts Museum
Paintings, graphics and sculpture, etchings 45630

Nassau Bay TX

Arts Alliance Center at Clear Lake, 2000 NASA Rd, Nassau Bay, TX 77058 - T: (281) 335-7777, Fax: (281) 333-8571, Internet: www.taaccl.org. Dir.: Kay Taylor Burnett
Public Gallery - 1997 45631

Natchez MS

Grand Village of the Natchez Indians, 400 Jefferson Davis Blvd, Natchez, MS 39120 - T: (601) 446-6502, Fax: (601) 446-6503, E-mail: gvni@bkbank.com, Internet: mdah.state.ms.us. Dir.: James F. Barnett
Ethnology Museum / Archaeological Museum - 1976
1700-1730 Natchez Indian ceremonial mound center 45632

Rosalie House Museum, 100 Orleans St, Natchez, MS 39120 - T: (601) 445-4555, Fax: (601) 304-1376, E-mail: manager@rosalie.net, Internet: www.rosalie.net. Man.: Cheryl Munyer-Branyan
Historical Museum - 1898
Decorative arts, architecture, family life - historic garden 45633

Natchitoches LA

Bishop Martin Museum, Second and Church Sts, Natchitoches, LA 71457 - T: (318) 352-3422. Dir.: Kenneth J. Roy, Cur.: Kay Fortenberry
Religious Arts Museum - 1839
Immaculate Conception Church and Rectory 45634

Fort Saint Jean Baptiste, 130 Moreau, Natchitoches, LA 71457 - T: (318) 357-3101, Fax: (318) 357-7055, E-mail: ftstjean@crt.state.la.us, Internet: www.crt.state.la.us/crt/parks/ftstjean.html. Cur.: James Prudhomme
Historic Site - 1982
Reconstruction of 1732 fort and several bldgs 45635

Lemee House, 310 Jeffersn St, Natchitoches, LA 71457 - T: (318) 357-7907, Fax: (318) 352-2415
Historical Museum - 1834
Paintings, lamps, 1792 map by French engineer 45636

Naturita CO

Rimrocker Historical Museum of West Montrose County, 411 W Second Av, Naturita, CO 81422, mail addr: POB 913, Nucla, CO 81424 - T: (970) 865-2877, 864-7438, Fax: (970) 864-7564, E-mail: cookib@aol.com. Pres.: Mary Helen de Koevend
Local Museum - 1980
Regional history 45637

Nauvoo IL

Joseph Smith Historic Center, 149 Water St, Nauvoo, IL 62354 - T: (217) 453-2246, Fax: (217) 453-6416, E-mail: jshisctr@nauvoo.net, Internet: www.joseph-smith.com. C.E.O.: Joyce A. Shireman
Historical Museum - 1918
Joseph Smith Homestead, Joseph Smith Red Brick Store, Joseph Smith Mansion House 45638

Nauvoo Historical Society Museum, Nauvoo State Park, Nauvoo, IL 62354 - T: (217) 453-6355, Fax: (217) 453-2512. Pres.: Mary Reed
Local Museum - 1953
Local history 45639

Nazareth PA

Whitefield House Museum, Moravian Historical Society, 214 E Center St, Nazareth, PA 18064 - T: (610) 759-5070, Fax: (610) 759-2461, Internet: www.moravianhistoricalsociety.org. Dir.: Susan M. Dreydoppel, Cur.: Mark A. Turdo
Local Museum / Religious Arts Museum - 1857
Local hist 45640

Nebraska City NE

Arbor Lodge, 2600 Arbor Av, Nebraska City, NE 68410 - T: (402) 873-7222, E-mail: arborlodge@ngpcstate.ne.us. Dir.: Rex Amack
Historical Museum - 1923 45641

Wildwood Center, 420 S Steinhart Park Rd, Nebraska City, NE 68410 - T: (402) 873-6340. Cur.: Richard B. Wearne
Historical Museum - 1967
Victorian frame home, Victorian furnishings 45642

Neenah WI

Bergstrom-Mahler Museum, 165 N Park Av, Neenah, WI 54956 - T: (920) 751-4658, 751-4670, Fax: (920) 751-4755, Internet: www.paperweightmuseum.com. Dir.: Alex D. Vance, Cur.: Jan Smith
Fine Arts Museum / Decorative Arts Museum - 1954
Art 45643

Hiram Smith Octagon House, 343 Smith St, Neenah, WI 54956 - T: (920) 725-4160, E-mail: neenahhistoricalsociety@powernetonline.com
Historical Museum - 1993 45644

Neeses SC

Neeses Farm Museum, 6449 Savannah Hwy, Neeses, SC 29107 - T: (803) 247-5811, Fax: (803) 247-5811. Dir.: Henry Gleaton, Sonja Gleaton
Agriculture Museum - 1976
Native American artifacts, pottery, clothing 45645

Neligh NE

Antelope County Historical Museum, 509 L St, Neligh, NE 68756 - T: (402) 887-4999. Pres.: Alta J. DeCamp
Local Museum - 1965 45646

Neligh Mills, N St and Wylie Dr, Neligh, NE 68756, mail addr: POB 271, Neligh, 68756 - T: (402) 887-4303, Fax: (402) 887-4303, E-mail: mill@bloomnet.com, Internet: www.nebraskahistory.org
Science&Tech Museum - 1971
500-barrel a day flour mill, elevators, plan sifters, purifiers, reel sifters, sackers, water powered turbine 45647

Nelsonville OH

Hocking Valley Museum of Theatrical History, 34 Public Sq, Nelsonville, OH 45764 - T: (740) 753-1924, Fax: (740) 753-2468, E-mail: shirleystuart-soperahouse@yahoo.com. Pres.: Frederick L. Oremus
Performing Arts Museum - 1978 45648

Neodesha KS

Norman No. 1 Oil Well Museum, 106 S First St, Neodesha, KS 66757 - T: (316) 325-5316, Fax: (316) 325-5316. CEO: Irene Gudde
Science&Tech Museum - 1967
Full sized derrick, oil well equip, farming, clown clothing, dolls, standard oil refinery Osage 45649

Neosho MO

Crowder College-Longwell Museum and Camp Crowder Collection, 601 La Clede, Neosho, MO 64850 - T: (417) 451-3223 ext 201, Fax: (417) 451-4280, Internet: www.crowdercollege.net. Dir.: Lori L. Marble
Fine Arts Museum / University Museum - 1970 45650

Neptune NJ

Neptune Township Historical Museum, 25 Neptune Blvd, Neptune, NJ 07754-1125 - T: (732) 988-5200, Fax: (732) 774-1132, E-mail: nept_mus@hotmail.com, Internet: www.neptunpubliclibrary.org. Cur.: Evelyn Stryker Lewis
Historical Museum - 1971
Cherokee based Sand Hill Indians, Antarctic explorer Schlossbach, regional history - library 45651

Nevada MO

Bushwhacker Museum, 231 N Main St, Nevada, MO 64772 - T: (417) 667-9602, Fax: (417) 667-4571, E-mail: info@bushwhacker.org, Internet: www.bushwhacker.org. C.E.O.: Joe C. Kraft
Local Museum / Historical Museum - 1964 45652

Nevada City CA

Firehouse Museum, 214 Main St, Nevada City, CA 95959 - T: (916) 265-5468
Historical Museum - 1947
Relicts of the Donner Party, clothing, furnishings 45653

Miners Foundry Cultural Center, 325 Spring St, Nevada City, CA 95959 - T: (916) 265-5040, Fax: (916) 265-5462, E-mail: mfoundry@news.com. Dir.: Ellen Davis
Science&Tech Museum - 1989
Mining 45654

Nevada County Historical Society Museum, POB 1300, Nevada City, CA 95959 - T: (530) 265-5468, E-mail: jrose@telis.org, Internet: www.nccn.net. Cur.: Glenn Jones (Mining Museum), Ron Sturgell (Video Museum)
Historical Museum - 1945 45655

Transportation Exhibits, First Pioneer Park, Nevada City, CA 95959 - T: (916) 265-5910. Dir.: Doris Foley
Science&Tech Museum
Railroad cars, beer wagons, old vehicles 45656

New Albany IN

Carnegie Center for Art & History, 201 E Spring St, New Albany, IN 47150 - T: (812) 944-7336, Fax: (812) 981-3544. Dir.: Sally Newkirk
Fine Arts Museum / Local Museum - 1971
Local history, art gallery 45657

Conway Fire Museum Aka Vintage Fire Engines, 402 Mount Tabor Rd, New Albany, IN 47150 - T: (812) 941-9901, Fax: (812) 941-9901. CEO: Allen C. Conway
Science&Tech Museum - 1990
Hand and horsedrawn, motorized firefighting equip 45658

Culbertson Mansion, 914 E Main St, New Albany, IN 47150 - T: (812) 944-9600, Fax: (812) 949-6134, E-mail: culbertson@disknet.com, Internet: www.indianamuseum.com. Cur.: Joellen Bye
Historical Museum - 1976
W.S. Culbertson Home, a 25-room Victorian mansion 45659

Floyd County Museum → Carnegie Center for Art & History

New Albany MS

Union County Heritage Museum, 112 Cleveland St, New Albany, MS 38652 - T: (662) 538-0014, Fax: (662) 538-0019, E-mail: uchs@dixie-net.com. Dir.: Betsy Hamilton
Local Museum - 1991
Local history 45660

New Bedford MA

Free Public Library Collection, 613 Plesant St, New Bedford, MA 02740 - T: (508) 991-6279, Fax: (508) 979-1481, Internet: www.ci.new-bedford.ma.us. Dir.: Theresa Coish
Fine Arts Museum - 1852
Paintings, watercolors 45661

New Bedford Whaling Museum, 18 Johnny Cake Hill, New Bedford, MA 02740 - T: (508) 997-0046 ext 10, Fax: (508) 997-0018, E-mail: whaling@ma.ultranet.com, Internet: www.whalingmuseum.org. Exec. Dir.: Anne B. Brengle, Cur.: Michael Jehle, Robert Hauser
Natural History Museum / Local Museum - 1903
Whaling, history 45662

Rotch-Jones-Duff House and Garden Museum, 396 County St, New Bedford, MA 02740 - T: (508) 997-1401, Fax: (508) 997-6846, E-mail: info@rjdmuseum.org, Internet: www.rjdmuseum.org. Dir.: Kate Corkum, Cur.: Everett H. Hoag
Historical Museum - 1984 45663

New Berlin WI

The New Berlin Historical Society Museum, 19765 W National Av, New Berlin, WI 53146 - T: (262) 542-4773. Dir.: Roy Meidenbauer
Historical Museum - 1965
Local hist, 1890's local home, school house room of 1863, 1850's Pioneer log home, carriage barn 45664

New Bern NC

Attmore-Oliver House, 510 Pollock St, New Bern, NC 28560 - T: (252) 638-8558, Fax: (252) 638-5773, E-mail: nbhistoricalsoc@coastalnet.com, Internet: www.hiddencoast.com/historicnewbern. Dir.: Joanne G. Ashton
Historical Museum - 1923 45665

New Bern Firemen's Museum, 408 Hancock St, New Bern, NC 28560 - T: (252) 636-4020, Fax: (252) 636-4087, E-mail: firechief-nb@admin.ci.new-bern.nc.us, Internet: www4.coastalnet.com/newbern/psafepg6.htm. C.E.O.: Robert Aster
Special Museum - 1955 45666

Tryon Palace, 610 Pollock St, New Bern, NC 28562 - T: (252) 514-4900, Fax: (252) 514-4876, E-mail: info@tryonpalace.org, Internet: www.tryonpalace.org. Dir.: Kay P. Williams, Cur.: Hilarie M. Hicks, Nancy E. Richards, Charles P. Mathewes (Gardens), Cons.: Joanna Ruth Harris
Historical Museum - 1945 45667

New Braunfels TX

Children's Museum in New Braunfels, 386 W. San Antonio St, New Braunfels, TX 78130 - T: (830) 620-0939, Fax: (830) 606-0440, E-mail: jbswift@nbchildren.org, Internet: www.nbchildren.org. C.E.O.: Juli Swift
Special Museum - 1986 45668

New Braunfels Conservation Society Museum, 1300 Church Hill, New Braunfels, TX 78131-0933, mail addr: POB 310933, New Braunfels, TX 78131-0933 - T: (210) 629-2943, E-mail: nbcs@axs4u.net, Internet: www.nbconservation.org
Decorative Arts Museum / Local Museum - 1964
Handmade furniture, household items 45669

Sophienburg Museum, 401 W Coll St, New Braunfels, TX 78130 - T: (830) 629-1572, 629-1900, Fax: (830) 629-3906, E-mail: gertxhst@sat.net, Internet: www.new-braunfels.com/sophienburg. Pres.: Anna Lee Hicks, Dir.: Michelle Oatman
Local Museum - 1926
Local hist 45670

New Bremen OH

Bicycle Museum of America, 7 W Monroe St, New Bremen, OH 45869 - T: (419) 629-2311, Fax: (419) 629-3256, E-mail: annette.thompson@crown.com, Internet: www.bicyclemuseum.com. C.E.O.: James F. Dicke
Science&Tech Museum - 1997 45671

New Brighton PA

The Merrick Art Gallery, 1100 5th Av, New Brighton, PA 15066 - T: (724) 846-1130, Fax: (724) 846-0413, Internet: www.themerrick.org. Dir.: Cynthia A. Kundar
Fine Arts Museum - 1880
Art 45672

New Britain CT

Museum of Central Connecticut State University, Art Dept, Samuel S.T. Chen Art Center, New Britain, CT 06050 - T: (860) 832-2633, Fax: (860) 832-2634. Dir.: Dr. Cora Marshall, Mark Strathy
University Museum / Fine Arts Museum / Local Museum - 1965
Anthropology, archaeology, folklore, decorative arts, industry, paintings, graphics, sculpture 45673

New Britain Museum of American Art, 56 Lexington St, New Britain, CT 06052-1412 - T: (860) 229-0257, Fax: (860) 229-3445, E-mail: nbmaa@nbmaa.org, Internet: www.nbmaa.org. Dir.: Laurene Buckley, Douglas Hyland
Fine Arts Museum - 1903 45674

New Britain Youth Museum, 30 High St, New Britain, CT 06051 - T: (860) 225-3020, Fax: (860) 229-4982, E-mail: nbymdwtn@portone.com. Dir.: Deborah Pfeiffenberger
Special Museum - 1956
Circus items, clothing, toys, dolls, farming tools 45675

New Brunswick NJ

Buccleuch Mansion, Buccleuch Park, Easton Av, New Brunswick, NJ 08901 - T: (732) 745-5094, E-mail: skenen@telcordia.com. Cur.: Susan Kenen
Historical Museum / Decorative Arts Museum - 1915 45676

Henry Guest House, 58 Livingston Av, New Brunswick, NJ 08901 - T: (732) 745-5108, Fax: (732) 846-0226. Dir.: Robert Belvin
Historical Museum - 1760 45677

Hungarian Heritage Center Museum → Museum of the American Hungarian Foundation

Jane Voorhees Zimmerli Art Museum, Rutgers State University of New Jersey, 71 Hamilton St, New Brunswick, NJ 08901-1248 - T: (732) 932-7237 ext 610, Fax: (732) 932-8201, E-mail: cate@rci.rutgers.edu, Internet: zimmerlimuseum.rutgers.edu. Dir. & Cur.: Phillip Dennis Cate, Assoc. Dir.: Gregory P. Perry, Cur.: Jeffrey Wechsler, Alla Rosenfeld (Russian and Soviet Art), Dorothea Dietrich (Prints and Drawings), Alfredo Franco (Education), Jane Sharp (Dodge Coll)
Fine Arts Museum / University Museum - 1966
art library 45678

Museum of the American Hungarian Foundation, 300 Somerset St, New Brunswick, NJ 08903 - T: (732) 846-5777, Fax: (732) 249-7033, E-mail: info@ahfoundation.org, Internet: www.ahfoundation.org. Dir.: August J. Molnar, Cur.: Patricia L. Fazekas
Fine Arts Museum / Folklore Museum - 1954 45679

New Canaan CT

New Canaan Historical Society Museum, 13 Oenoke Ridge, New Canaan, CT 06840 - T: (203) 966-1776, Fax: (203) 972-5917, E-mail: newcanaan.historical@snet.net, Internet: www.nchistory.org. Dir.: Janet Lindstrom, Cur.: Laura Einstein, George Cody
Local Museum / Historical Museum - 1889 45680

New Canaan Nature Center, 144 Oenoke Ridge, New Canaan, CT 06840 - T: (203) 966-9577, Fax: (203) 966-6536, Internet: www.newcanaannature.org. Dir.: Dilip A. Das
Natural History Museum - 1960 45681

Silvermine Guild Arts Center, 1037 Silvermine Rd, New Canaan, CT 06840 - T: (203) 966-9700, Fax: (203) 972-7236, E-mail: sgac@silvermineart.org, Internet: www.silvermineart.org. Dir.: Cynthia Clair
Fine Arts Museum - 1922 45682

New Castle DE

New Castle Historical Society Museum, 2 E Fourth St, New Castle, DE 19720 - T: (302) 322-2794, Fax: (302) 322-8923, E-mail: nchistorical@aol.com, Internet: www.newcastlecity.org. Dir.: Bruce Dalleo
Local Museum - 1934
Local hist 45683

New Castle IN

Henry County Historical Museum, 606 S 14th St, New Castle, IN 47362 - T: (765) 529-4028, E-mail: hchisoc@kiva.net, Internet: www.kiva.net/~hchisoc/museum.htm. Cur.: Marianne Hughes
Local Museum / Historical Museum - 1887
Home of Civil War General William Grose 45684

Indiana Basketball Hall of Fame, 408 Trojan Ln, New Castle, IN 47362 - T: (765) 529-1891, Fax: (765) 529-0273, E-mail: mail@hoopshall.com, Internet: www.hoopshall.com. Dir.: Roger Dickinson
Special Museum - 1965 45685

New Castle PA

Hoyt Institute of Fine Arts, 124 E Leasure Av, New Castle, PA 16101 - T: (724) 652-2882, Fax: (724) 657-8786, E-mail: hoyt@lcix.net, Internet: www.hoytartcenter.org. Dir.: Kimberly B. Koller-Jones, Asst. Dir.: Mary Ann Fazzone, Cur.: David Collins
Fine Arts Museum - 1965
Art 45686

New City NY

Rockland County Museum, 20 Zukor Rd, New City, NY 10956 - T: (914) 634-9629, Fax: (914) 634-8690, E-mail: info@rocklandhistory.org, Internet: www.rocklandhistory.org. C.E.O.: Erin L. Martin
Local Museum - 1965 45687

New Glarus WI

Chalet of the Golden Fleece, 618 2nd St, New Glarus, WI 53574 - T: (608) 527-2614, Fax: (608) 527-2062. C.E.O.: Mark Eisenmann
Local Museum - 1955
Historic house 45688

Swiss Historical Village, 612 7th Av, New Glarus, WI 53574 - T: (608) 527-2317, Internet: www.swisshistoricalvillage.com. Pres.: Bradley L. Beal
Local Museum / Open Air Museum - 1938
Historic village 45689

New Gloucester ME

Shaker Museum, 707 Shaker Rd, New Gloucester, ME 04260 - T: (207) 926-4597, E-mail: usshakers@aol.com, Internet: www.shaker.lib.me.us. Dir.: Leonard L. Brooks, Cur.: Michael S. Graham
Historic Site - 1931
Religion, Shaker religious community - library 45690

New Harbor ME

Colonial Pemaquid Historical Site, New Harbor, ME 04554 - T: (207) 677-2423
Archaeological Museum - 1970
Archaeological dig site 45691

New Harmony IN

Historic New Harmony, 506 1/2 Main St, New Harmony, IN 47631 - T: (812) 682-4488, Fax: (812) 682-4313, E-mail: harmony@usi.edu, Internet: www.newharmony.org. Dir.: Connie Weinzapfel, Cur.: Jean Lee
Historic Site - 1973
American history, early natural science, early abolition, early women's movement 45692

New Harmony Gallery of Contemporary Art, University of Southern Indiana, 506 Main St, New Harmony, IN 47631 - T: (812) 682-3156, Fax: (812) 682-3870, E-mail: mhambly@usi.edu, Internet: www.nhgallery.com. Dir.: April Vasher-Dean
Fine Arts Museum - 1975 45693

New Harmony State Historic Site, 410 Main St, New Harmony, IN 47631 - T: (812) 682-3271, Fax: (812) 682-5526, E-mail: newharmonyshs@dynasty.net, Internet: www.ai.org/ism. Dir.: Rachel Perry, Cur.: Jean Graham Lee, Asst. Cur.: Angel Wahnsiedler, Maxine Watson, Diana Zintel
Historical Museum - 1937
Site of two early utopian experiments, the communal societies of New Harmony 45694

New Haven CT

John Slade Ely House, 51 Trumbull St, New Haven, CT 06510 - T: (203) 624-8055, Fax: (203) 624-2306, E-mail: info@clyhouse.org, Internet: www.clyhouse.org. Cur.: Paul Clabby
Fine Arts Museum - 1960
Paintings, sculpture 45695

Knights of Columbus Museum, 1 State St, New Haven, CT 06511-6702 - T: (203) 865-0400, Fax: (203) 865-0351, Internet: www.kofc-supreme-council.org. Dir.: Larry Sowinski, Cur.: Mary Lou Cummings, Archivist: Susan Brosnan
Historical Museum / Association with Coll - 1982
library 45696

New Haven Colony Historical Society Museum, 114 Whitney Av, New Haven, CT 06510 - T: (203) 562-4183, Fax: (203) 562-2002, E-mail: dcarter@nhchs.org, Internet: www.nhchs.org. Dir.: Peter Thomas Lemothe, Cur.: Amy L. Trout
Local Museum - 1862 45697

Peabody Museum of Natural History, Yale University, 170 Whitney Av, New Haven, CT 06520-8118 - T: (203) 432-5050, Fax: (203) 432-9816, E-mail: melanie.brigockas@yale.edu, Internet: www.peabody.yale.edu. Dir.: Richard L. Burger (Anthropology), Sc. Staff: Alison F. Richard (Anthropology), Frank Hole (Anthropology), Andrew Hill (Anthropology), Leo J. Hickey (Paleobotany), Elisabeth Vrba (Vertebrate Zoology), Jacques A. Gauthier (Vertebrate Zoology, Ornitology, Vertebrate Paleontology), Adolf Seilacher (Invertebrate Paleontology), Leo W. Buss (Invertebrates), Jay Ague (Mineraology), Karl K. Turekian (Meteorites, Planetary Science), David F. Musto (Historical Scientific Instruments), Michael Donoghue (Botany), Leonard Munstermann (Entomology), Sean Rice (Invertebrates), David Skelly (Vertebrate Zoology)
University Museum / Natural History Museum - 1866
Anthropology, paleontology, mineralogy, paleobotany, vertebrates, invertebrates, otnitology, entomology, zoology, botany, meteorits, historic scientific instr. 45698

Yale Center for British Art, 1080 Chapel St, New Haven, CT 06520-8280 - T: (203) 432-2850, Fax: (203) 432-4538, E-mail: bacinfo@yale.edu, Internet: www.yale.edu/ycba. Dir.: Constance Clement, Amy Meyers, Ass. Dir.: David Mills, Sen. Cur.: Malcolm Warner (Paintings), Cur.: Elisabeth Fairman (Rare Books and Archives), Scott Wilcox (Prints and Drawings), Asst. Cur.: Julia Alexander (Paintings), Gillian Forrester (Prints and Drawings), Chief Cons.: Theresa Fairbanks
Fine Arts Museum / University Museum - 1977 45699

Yale University Art Gallery, 1111 Chapel St, New Haven, CT 06520 - T: (203) 432-0660, Fax: (203) 432-7159, Internet: www.yale.edu/artgallery. Dir.: Jock Reynolds, Cur.: Suzanne Boorsch (Prints, Drawings and Photographs), Patricia Kane (American Decorative Arts), Helen Cooper (American Painting), Susan Matheson (Ancient Art), Jennifer Gross (European and Contemporary Art), David Sensabaugh (Asian Art)
Fine Arts Museum / University Museum - 1832 45700

Yale University Collection of Musical Instruments, 15 Hillhouse Av, New Haven, CT 06520 - T: (203) 432-0822, Fax: (203) 432-8342, E-mail: musinst@pantheon.yale.edu, Internet: www.yale.edu/musicalinstruments. Dir.: Richard Rephann, Assoc. Cur.: Nicholas Renouf, Asst. Cur.: Susan Thompson
University Museum / Music Museum - 1900 45701

New Haven KY

Kentucky Railway Museum, 136 S Main St, New Haven, KY 40051 - T: (800) 272-0152, (502) 549-5470, Fax: (502) 549-5472, E-mail: kyrail@bardstown.com, Internet: kyrail.org. CEO: John Campbell
Science&Tech Museum - 1954
Railroad engines, steam and diesel, passenger and freight car, blueprints 45702

New Holstein WI

Calumet County Historical Society Museum, 1704 Eisenhower St, New Holstein, WI 53061 - T: (920) 898-1333. Pres.: Ronald Zarling
Local Museum / Agriculture Museum - 1963
Farming 45703

Pioneer Corner Museum, 2103 Main St, New Holstein, WI 53061 - T: (414) 898-5258. Cur.: Wendy Cramer
Local Museum - 1961
Local hist 45704

New Hope PA

Lockhouse-Friends of the Delaware Canal, 145 S Main St, New Hope, PA 18938 - T: (215) 862-2021, Fax: (215) 862-2021, E-mail: fodc@erols.com, Internet: www.fodc.org. Dir.: Susan H. Taylor
Local Museum - 1991 45705

Parry Mansion Museum, 45 S Main St, New Hope, PA 18938 - T: (215) 862-5652, 794-5260, Fax: (215) 862-8227, E-mail: newhope-historicalso@msn.com, Internet: www.parrymansionmuseum.org. Dir.: Scott Magill, Sc. Staff: Terry McNealy, Robert Goodwin
Decorative Arts Museum / Historical Museum - 1966
Decorative arts 45706

New Hyde Park NY

Goudreau Museum of Mathematics in Art and Science, Herricks Community Center, 999 Herricks Rd, New Hyde Park, NY 11040-1353 - T: (516) 747-0777, Fax: (516) 747-0777, E-mail: info@mathmuseum.org, Internet: www.mathmuseum.org. Dir.: Beth J. Deaner
Special Museum - 1980
Mathematics 45707

New Iberia LA

The Shadows-on-the-Teche, 317 E Main St, New Iberia, LA 70560 - T: (337) 369-6446, Fax: (337) 365-5213, E-mail: shadows@shadowsontheteche.org, Internet: www.shadowsontheteche.org. Dir.: Patricia Kahle
Historic Site - 1961
Plantation home 45708

New Ipswich NH

Barrett House, Forest Hall, Main St, New Ipswich, NH 03071 - T: (603) 878-2517, Fax: (617) 227-9204, E-mail: ezopes@spnea.org, Internet: www.spnea.org. Dir.: Elaine Zopes
Historical Museum - 1948 45709

New London CT

Lyman Allyn Museum of Art, 625 Williams St, New London, CT 06320 - T: (860) 443-2545, Fax: (860) 442-1280, Internet: lymanallyn.conncoll.edu. Dir.: Charles A. Shepard
Fine Arts Museum - 1930
American fine arts, decorative arts 45710

New London County Historical Society Museum, 11 Blinman St, New London, CT 06320 - T: (860) 443-1209, Fax: (860) 443-1209, E-mail: nlchsinc@aol.com. Dir.: Alice Sheriff
Local Museum / Historical Museum - 1870 45711

United States Coast Guard Museum, c/o US Coast Guard Academy, 15 Mohegan Av, New London, CT 06320-4195 - T: (860) 444-8511, Fax: (860) 444-8289, E-mail: cherrick@cga.uscg.mil, Internet: www.uscg.mil
Historical Museum - 1967 45712

New London NH

New London Historical Society Museum, Little Sunapee Rd, New London, NH 03257-0965 - T: (603) 526-6564, E-mail: info@newlondonhistoricalsociety.org, Internet: www.nlhs.netx. Pres.: Laurie Lauridsen
Historical Museum - 1954 45713

New London WI

New London Public Museum, 406 S Pearl St, New London, WI 54961 - T: (920) 982-8520, Fax: (920) 982-8617, E-mail: museum@newlondonwi.org, Internet: www.newlondonwi.org. Pres.: Kenneth Renning, Cur.: John Groat
Local Museum - 1917
Local hist 45714

New Madrid MO

Hunter-Dawson State Historic Site, Dawson Rd, Hwy U, New Madrid, MO 63869 - T: (573) 748-5340, Fax: (573) 748-7228, E-mail: dsphunt@mail.dnr.state.mo.us. Head: Michael Comer
Historic Site - 1967 45715

New Market VA

New Market Battlefield State Historical Park, 8895 Collins Dr, New Market, VA 22844 - T: (540) 740-3101, Fax: (540) 740-3033, E-mail: nmjsh@shentel.net, Internet: www.vmi.edu/museum/nm. Dir.: Scott H. Harris, Exec. Dir.: Keith E. Gibson
Historic Site / Military Museum - 1967
Military hist 45716

New Milford CT

New Milford Historical Society Museum, 6 Aspetuck Av, New Milford, CT 06776-0359 - T: (860) 354-3069, Fax: (860) 210-0263, E-mail: nmhistorical@mail.com, Internet: www.nmhistorical.org. Cur.: Delores Dunn, Pamela Edwards
Historical Museum - 1915 45717

New Orleans LA

Academy Gallery, New Orleans Academy of Fine Arts, 5256 Magazine St, New Orleans, LA 70115 - T: (504) 899-8111, Fax: (504) 897-6811, E-mail: noafa@bellsouth.com, Internet: www.noafa.com. Dir.: Dorothy J Coleman
Fine Arts Museum - 1978 45718

Beauregard-Keyes House, 1113 Chartres St, New Orleans, LA 70116 - T: (504) 523-7257, Fax: (504) 523-7257. Dir.: Marion S. Chambon
Historical Museum - 1970
Louisiana raised cottage, home of Gen. P.G.T. Beauregard and Frances Parkinson Keyes 45719

Black Arts National Diaspora, 1530 N Claiborne Av, New Orleans, LA 70116 - T: (504) 949-0807, Fax: (504) 949-6052, E-mail: band@gnofn.org, Internet: www.bandinc.org/. Exec. Dir.: Dr. G. Jeannette Hodge
Fine Arts Museum
Contemporary African art from around the world 45720

Confederate Museum, 929 Camp St, New Orleans, LA 70130 - T: (504) 523-4522, Fax: (504) 523-8595, E-mail: memhall@aol.com, Internet: www.confederatemuseum.com. Cur.: Pat Ricci
Military Museum - 1891
Military, housed in 1890 Memorial Hall 45721

Contemporary Arts Center, 900 Camp St, New Orleans, LA 70130 - T: (504) 528-3805, Fax: (504) 528-3828, E-mail: mshalett@cacno.org, Internet: www.cacno.org. Dir.: Jay Weigel
Fine Arts Museum / Public Gallery - 1976
Art 45722

Fine Arts Gallery, c/o University of New Orleans, 2000 Lake Shore Dr, New Orleans, LA 70148 - T: (504) 280-6493, Fax: (504) 280-7346, E-mail: finearts@uno.edu, Internet: www.uno.edu. Dir.: Doyle Gertjejansen
University Museum / Fine Arts Museum - 1974 45723

Fort Pike, Rte 6, Box 194, New Orleans, LA 70129 - T: (504) 662-5703, Fax: (504) 662-0147, E-mail: fortpike_mgr@crt.state.la.us, Internet: www.crt.state.la.us
Military Museum - 1934
Armaments, dress and battle orders, Louisiana hist 45724

Gallier House, 1118-32 Royal St, New Orleans, LA 70116 - T: (504) 525-5661, Fax: (504) 568-9735, E-mail: hgrimagallier@aol.com, Internet: www.gnofn.org/~hggh. Dir.: Stephen A. Moses, Cur.: Jan Bradford
Local Museum - 1969
Decorative arts 45725

Hermann-Grima House, 820 Saint Louis St, New Orleans, LA 70112 - T: (504) 525-5661, Fax: (504) 568-9735, E-mail: hgrimagallier@aol.com, Internet: www.gnofn.org/~hggh. Dir.: Stephen A. Moses, Cur.: Jan Bradford
Local Museum - 1971
Early example of American influence on New Orleans architecture 45726

The Historic New Orleans Collection, 533 Royal St, New Orleans, LA 70130 - T: (504) 523-4662, Fax: (504) 598-7108, E-mail: hnocinfo@hnoc.org, Internet: www.hnoc.org. Dir.: Priscilla O'Reilly-Lawrence, John H. Lawrence, Cur.: Dr. Alfred Lemmon
Historical Museum - 1966
Hist and culture of Louisiana and Gulf South 45727

Jean Lafitte National Historical Park and Preserve, 365 Canal St, Ste 2400, New Orleans, LA 70130-1142 - T: (504) 589-3882, Fax: (504) 589-3851, E-mail: kathy_lang@nps.gov, Internet: www.nps.gov/jela
Military Museum - 1978
Military, site of decisive battle between American and British forces in War of 1812 45728

Longue Vue House, 7 Bamboo Rd, New Orleans, LA 70124 - T: (504) 488-5488, Fax: (504) 486-7015, Internet: www.longuevue.com. Dir.: Pam O'Brien, Cur.: Lydia H. Schmalz
Fine Arts Museum / Decorative Arts Museum - 1968
Furniture, textile, needlework, wallapers, ceramics, contemporary and modern art - gardens 45729

Louisiana Children's Museum, 420 Julia St, New Orleans, LA 70130 - T: (504) 523-1357, Fax: (504) 529-3666, Internet: www.lcm.org. C.E.O.: Julia W. Bland
Special Museum - 1981 45730

Louisiana State Museum, 751 Chartres St, New Orleans, LA 70116 - T: (800) 568-6968, Fax: (504) 568-4995, E-mail: llovell@crt.state.la.us, Internet: lsm.crt.state.la.us. Dir.: James F. Sefcik, Dep. Dir.: Bob Martin, Cur.: Stephen Teeter (Jazz), Wayne Phillips (Costumes and Textiles), Adrienne Berney (Decorative Arts), Kathryn Page (Maps and Manuscripts), Claudia Kheel-Cox (Visual Arts), Michelle Fontenot (Programs), Greg Lambousy (Collections), Asst. Cur.: Charles Siler
Historical Museum - 1906
History, decorative arts, costume, textiles, maps, manuscripts, aviation 45731

National D-Day Museum, 945 Magazine St, New Orleans, LA 70130 - T: (504) 527-6012, Fax: (504) 527-6088, E-mail: info@ddaymuseum.org, Internet: www.ddaymuseum.org. CEO: Dr. Gordon H. Mueller
Military Museum - 1991
American experience WW 2 45732

New Orleans Artworks Gallery, 727 Magazine St, New Orleans, LA 70130 - T: (504) 529-7279, Fax: (504) 539-5417. Pres.: Geriool Baronne
Decorative Arts Museum / Fine Arts Museum - 1990
Prints, sculpture, etchings and engravings, decorative arts, furniture, glass, metalwork, enamels 45733

New Orleans Fire Department Museum, 1135 Washington Av, New Orleans, LA 70130 - T: (504) 896-4756, 565-7818, Fax: (504) 896-4756, Internet: nofd.com. CEO: Warren E. McDaniels
Historical Museum - 1992 45734

New Orleans Museum of Art, 1 Collins Diboll Circle, New Orleans, LA 70124 - T: (504) 488-2631, Fax: (504) 484-6662, E-mail: webmaster@noma.org, Internet: www.noma.org. Dir.: E. John Bullard, Ass. Dir./Cur.: Steven Maklansky (Photographs), John Keefe (Decorative Arts), Victoria Cooke (Paintings), Lisa Rotonda-McCord (Asian Art), Daniel Piersol (Prints, Drawings), William A. Fagaly (African Art), Registrar: Paul Tarver, Libr.: Norbert Raacke
Fine Arts Museum - 1910
Art, decorative art, paintings, photos 45735

New Orleans Pharmacy Museum, 514 Rue Chartres, New Orleans, LA 70130-2110 - T: (504) 565-8027, Fax: (504) 565-8028, E-mail: nopharmsm@aol.com, Internet: www.pharmacymuseum.org. Dir.: Liz Good, Cur.: Jen Lushear
Historical Museum - 1950
Pharmacy, medicine, Louis Joseph Dufilho, Jr., first licensed pharmacist in the U.S 45736

Newcomb Art Gallery, c/o Newcomb College, Tulane University, Woldenberg Art Center, New Orleans, LA 70118-5698 - T: (504) 865-5328, Fax: (504) 865-5329, E-mail: smain@tulane.edu, Internet: www.newcombartgallery.com. Dir.: Erik Neil, Sen. Cur.: Sally Main
Fine Arts Museum / University Museum - 1886
Art, Newcomb pottery, painting, sculpture, photography 45737

Pitot House Museum, 1440 Moss St, New Orleans, LA 70119 - T: (504) 482-0312, Fax: (504) 482-0363, E-mail: lalndmrk@bellsouth.net, Internet: www.neworleans.com/museum/pitot/. C.E.O. & Pres.: Rick Normand, Chm.: June Rogers, Cur.: Myrna Bergeron
Historical Museum - 1964
1799 French West Indies Plantation style house 45738

Tulane University Art Collection, Tulane University, 7001 Freret St, New Orleans, LA 70118 - T: (504) 865-5685, Fax: (504) 865-5761. Cur.: Joan G. Caldwell
Fine Arts Museum / University Museum - 1980 45739

New Paltz NY

College Art Gallery → Samuel Dorsky Museum of Art

Huguenot Historical Society Museum, 18 Broadhead Av, New Paltz, NY 12561-1403 - T: (845) 255-1660, Fax: (845) 255-0376, E-mail: hhsoffice@hhs-newpaltz.org, Internet: www.hhs-newpaltz.org. Dir.: John H. Braunlein, Asst. Dir.: Stewart A. Crowell, Cur.: Leslie LeFevre-Stratton, Kenneth Shefsiek (Education), Eric Roth (Archives), Admin. Asst.: June L. Heneberry
Local Museum - 1894
History, architecture, decorative arts - archives 45740

Samuel Dorsky Museum of Art, c/o State University of New York New Paltz, 75 S Manheim Blvd, New Paltz, NY 12561 - T: (914) 257-3844, Fax: (914) 257-3854, E-mail: tragern@newpaltz.edu, Internet: www.newpaltz.edu/museum. Dir.: Neil C. Trager, Cur.: Nadine Wasserman, Wayne Lempka (Collections), Preparator: Cynthia Dill
Fine Arts Museum / University Museum - 1963
Regional art, photographs, metals, Asian prints, 20th c works on paper 45741

New Philadelphia OH

Schoenbrunn Village State Memorial, 1984 E High Av, New Philadelphia, OH 44663 - T: (330) 339-3636, Fax: (330) 339-4165, E-mail: schoenbrunn@tusco.net, Internet: www.ohiohistory.org/places/schoenbr/index.html. C.E.O.: Dr. Gary C. Ness
Open Air Museum / Local Museum - 1928 45742

New Port Richey FL

West Pasco Historical Society Museum, 6431 Circle Blvd, New Port Richey, FL 34652 - T: (727) 847-0680, E-mail: wb2ium@att.net. Pres./Cur.: David Prace
Local Museum - 1983
Local history - library 45743

New Providence NJ

Cambria Historical Society Museum, 121 Chanlon Rd, New Providence, NJ 07974 - T: (908) 665-2846. Dir.: Tamika Borden, Cur.: Donald Bruce
Local Museum / Decorative Arts Museum - 1950
China, dolls, furniture, glass, paintings 45744

New Roads LA

Pointe Coupee Museum, 8348 False River Rd, New Roads, LA 70760 - T: (225) 638-7788, Fax: (504) 638-5555. Chm.: Olinde S. Haag
Historical Museum - 1976 45745

New Sweden ME

Lars Noak Blacksmith Shop, Larsson/Ostlund Log Home & One-Room Capitol School, Station Rd, New Sweden, ME 04762 - T: (207) 896-5624, 896-3199, Fax: (207) 896-5624, E-mail: rmhme@mfx.net, Internet: www.aroostok.me.us/newsweden/historical.html. Dir.: Allen Kampe, Linnea Helstrom, Ralph Ostlund
Local Museum / Open Air Museum - 1989
Historic village 45746

New Sweden Historical Museum, 110 Station Rd, New Sweden, ME 04762 - T: (207) 896-3018, 896-5843, Fax: (207) 896-3120. C.E.O.: Gary Dickinson
Local Museum - 1925
Local history 45747

New Ulm MN

Brown County Historical Society Museum, 2 N Broadway, New Ulm, MN 56073-1714 - T: (507) 233-2616, Fax: (507) 354-1068, E-mail: bchs@newulmtel.net, Internet: browncountyhistorymnusa.org. Dir.: Robert Burgess, Cur.: Pam Krzmarzick
Local Museum - 1930 45748

New Wilmington PA

Westminster College Art Gallery, Market St, New Wilmington, PA 16172 - T: (724) 946-7266, Fax: (724) 946-7256, Internet: www.westminster.edu. Dir.: Kathy Koop
Fine Arts Museum - 1854
Drawings, American paintings, prints 45749

New York NW

Czech Center New York, 1109 Madison Av, New York, NW 10028 - T: (212) 288-0830, Fax: (212) 288-0971, E-mail: nycenter@pop.net, Internet: www.czechcenter.com. Dir.: Premysl Pela
Ethnology Museum / Folklore Museum - 1995
Civic art and culture 45750

New York NY

Abigail Adams Smith Museum → Mount Vernon Hotel Museum

Abrons Arts Center, Gallery of Henry Street Settlement, 466 Grand St, New York, NY 10002 - T: (212) 598-0400, Fax: (212) 505-8329, E-mail: sfnarts@aol.com, Internet: www.henrystreetarts.org. Dir.: Jane Delgado, Exec. Dir.: Henry Street Settleman, Daniel Kronenfeld, Admin. Asst.: Amy Blitz, Sc. Staff: Judd Silverman (Urban Youth Theatre), Louis Johnson (Dance), Caroline Stoessinger (Music), Karen Chait (Registrar), Admin. Asst.: Josh Carr, Don Williams, Wanda Egipciaco
Public Gallery - 1893
Contemporary Art - photo gallery 45751

Air Gallery, 40 Wooster St, New York, NY 10013 - T: (212) 966-0799, Fax: (212) 941-7508, E-mail: airinfo@airnyc.org. Dir.: Dena Muller
Fine Arts Museum - 1972 45752

Alternative Museum, 594 Broadway, Ste 402, New York, NY 10012 - T: (212) 966-4444, Fax: (212) 226-2158, E-mail: altmuseum@aol.com, Internet: www.alternativemuseum.org. Dir.: Geno Rodriguez, Asst. Dir.: Jan Rooney, Asst. Cur.: Elisa White
Fine Arts Museum - 1975 45753

American Academy of Arts and Letters Art Museum, 633 W 155 St, New York, NY 10032-7599 - T: (212) 368-5900, Fax: (212) 491-4615. Exec. Dir.: Virginia Dajani, Pres.: Ned Rorem, Exec. Asst.: Rafael Díaz-Tusham (Architecture, Literarture), Staff: Betsey Feeley, Ardith Holmgrain (Music), Kathleen Kienholz (Archivist), Jane Bolster (Publications, Library), Souhad Rafey (Exhibitions, Purchases, Art), Coord.: Richard Rogers
Fine Arts Museum - 1898
Coll of works by Childe Hassam and Eugene Speicher, art painting, sculpture, graphics, music - Archives, library 45754

American Craft Museum, 40 W 53rd St, New York, NY 10019 - T: (212) 956-3535, Fax: (212) 459-0926, E-mail: ursula.neuman@americancraftmuseum.org, Internet: www.americancraftmuseum.org. Dir.: Holly Hotchner, Pres.: Nanette Laitman, Vice Pres.: Patricia Hynes, Chairman: Barbara Tober, Chief. Cur.: David McFadden, Cur.: Ursula Ilse-Neuman, Staff: Marsha Beitchman (Registrar)
Fine Arts Museum / Decorative Arts Museum - 1956
Crafts, design, decorative arts 45755

American Folk Art Museum, 45 W 53rd St, New York, NY 10019 - T: (212) 265-1040, 977-7170 ext 309, Fax: (212) 977-8134, E-mail: info@folkartmuseum.org, Internet: www.folkartmuseum.org. Dir.: Gerard C. Wertkin, Deputy Dir.: Riccardo Salmona, Cur.: Stacy Hollander, Brooke Davis Anderson (Contemporary Center), Elizabeth Warren, Lee Kogan (Folk art Institute, Cur.), Rosemary Gabriel (Publications), Ann-Marie Reilly (Registrar), Judith Gluck Steinberg (Asst. Registrar, Exhebitions)
Folklore Museum - 1961
American 18th-to 20th c folk sculpture and paintings, textile arts, decorative arts, hist 45756

American Irish Historical Society Museum, 991 Fifth Av, New York, NY 10028 - T: (212) 288-2263, Fax: (212) 628-7927, E-mail: amerirish@earthlink.net, Internet: www.aihs.org. Dir.: William Cobert, Pres.: Kevin M. Cahill, Chairman: Hon Hug L. Carey
Historical Museum - 1897
Hist of Irish in America - Library 45757

American Jewish Historical Museum, 15 W 16th St, New York, NY 10001 - T: (212) 294-6160, Fax: (212) 294-6161, E-mail: ajhs@ajhs.org, Internet: www.ajhs.org. Pres.: Kenneth Bielkin, Exec. Dir.: Michael Feldberg, Cur.: Sarah Davis
Folklore Museum / Religious Arts Museum - 1892
Ethnic history - Library 45758

American Museum of Natural History, Central Park W at 79 St, New York, NY 10024 - T: (212) 769-5100, Fax: (212) 496-5018, E-mail: postmaster@amnh.org, Internet: www.amnh.org. Pres.: Ellen V. Futter, Cur.: Dr. Enid Schildkrout (Anthropology), Dr. Charles W. Myers (Herpetology), Dr. Melanie L.J. Stiassny (Ichthyology), Dr. Neil H. Landman (Invertebrates), Dr. Ross D.E. MacPhee (Mammalogy), Dr. Mark A. Norell (Vertebrate Paleontology), Ass. Cur.: Dr. Edmond A. Mathez (Earth and Planetary Sciences), Dr. David Grimaldi (Entomology), Dr. George F. Barrowclough (Ornithology)
Natural History Museum / Historical Museum - 1869
Anthropology, hist buildings, street facades from New York 45759

American Numismatic Society Museum, Broadway at 155 St, New York, NY 10032 - T: (212) 234-3130, Fax: (212) 324-3381, E-mail: info@amnumsoc.org, Internet: www.amnumsoc2.org. Dir.: Ute Wartenberg, Chief Cur.: William E. Metcalf (Roman and Byzantine Coins), Carmen F. Arnold-Biucchi (Creek Coins), Michael L. Bates (Islamic Coins), Alan M. Stahl (Medieval Coins), John M. Kleeberg (Modern Coins), Libr.: Francis D. Campbell
Special Museum - 1858 45760

Americas Society Art Gallery, 680 Park Av, New York, NY 10021 - T: (212) 249-8950, Fax: (212) 249-5868, E-mail: exhibitions@as-coa.org, Internet: www.americas-society.org. Pres.: Alan Stoga, Chm.: David Rockefeller, William Rhodes, Chief Cur.: Gabriel Perez (Visual Arts), Assoc. Cur: Sofia Hernandez (Visual Arts)
Fine Arts Museum - 1967
Temporary exhibitions, coll of Latin American paintings and drawings 45761

Amos Eno Gallery, 59 Franklin St, New York, NY 10012 - T: (212) 226-5342. Dir.: Jane Harris
Fine Arts Museum
Contemporary art 45762

Angel Orensanz Foundation Center for the Arts, 172 Norfolk St, New York, NY 10002 - T: (212) 780-0175, 529-7194, Fax: (212) 529-1864, E-mail: info@orensanz.org, Internet: www.orensanz.org
Fine Arts Museum - 1992
Sculpture 45763

Anne Frank Center USA, 584 Broadway, Ste 408, New York, NY 10012 - T: (212) 431-7993, Fax: (212) 431-8375, E-mail: director@annefrank.com, Internet: www.annefrank.com
Historical Museum 45764

Arsenal Gallery, Arsenal Bldg, Fifth Av at 64th St, New York, NY 10021 - T: (212) 360-8163, Fax: (212) 360-1329, E-mail: Adian.Sas@parks.nyc.gov, Internet: www.nyc.gov/parks. Cur.: Adrian Sas
Natural History Museum
Mixed media-park and nature themes 45765

Arthur A. Houghton Jr. Gallery and the Great Hall Gallery, 7 E 7th St, Foundation Bldg, New York, NY 10003-7120 - T: (212) 353-4155
Fine Arts Museum - 1859
Graphic design, fine arts, painting, sculpture, engineering 45766

Artist's Space, 38 Greene St, New York, NY 10013 - T: (212) 226-3970, Fax: (212) 966-1434, E-mail: artspace@artistsspace.org, Internet: www.artistsspace.org
Public Gallery 45767

Asia Society and Museum, 725 Park Av, New York, NY 10021 - T: (212) 288-6400, Fax: (212) 517-8315, E-mail: pr@asiasoc.org, Internet: www.asiasociety.org. Dir.: Vishakha N. Desai, Pres.: Nicholas Platt, Cur.: Colin McKenzie, Sc. Staff: Amy McEwen (Coll., Registrar)
Fine Arts Museum - 1956
Asian art, Mr. and Mrs. John D. Rockefeller 3rd coll of Asian art 45768

Asian-American Arts Centre, 26 Bowery St, New York, NY 10013 - T: (212) 233-2154, Fax: (212) 766-1287, E-mail: aaac@artspiral.org, Internet: www.artspiral.org. Dir.: Robert Lee, Chairman: Sasha Hohri
Fine Arts Museum / Public Gallery - 1974
Folk art - research library 45769

The AXA Gallery, Equitable Tower, 787 Seventh Av, New York, NY 10019 - T: (212) 554-4731, Fax: (212) 554-2456, E-mail: panistave@axa-financial.com, Internet: www.axa-financial.com/aboutus/gallery.html. Dir.: Pari Stave
Fine Arts Museum / Public Gallery - 1992
19th and 20th century paintings, sculpture and works on paper 45770

The Bard Graduate Center for Studies in the Decorative Arts, Design, and Culture, 18 W 86th St, New York, NY 10024 - T: (212) 501-3000, Fax: (212) 501-3079, E-mail: Mulligan@BGC.bard.edu, Internet: www.bgc.bard.edu. Dir.: Dr. Susan Weber Soros, Dir. Academy: Dr. Andrew Morrall, Sc. Staff: Nina Stritzler-Levine (Dir. Exhibitions), Elena Pinto Simon (Academic Programming), Lorraine Bacalles (Administration), Sarah B. Sherrill (Decorative Arts), Lisa Beth Podos (Public programs)
Decorative Arts Museum / University Museum - 1992
Decorative arts - Library 45771

Black Fashion Museum, 155 W 126th St, New York, NY 10027
Special Museum 45772

The Bohen Foundation, 415 W 13th St, New York, NY 10014 - T: (212) 334-2281, Fax: (212) 334-4178, E-mail: info@bohen.org
Public Gallery 45773

Burden Gallery, Aperture Foundation, 20 E 23 St, New York, NY 10010 - T: (212) 505-5555 ext 325, Fax: (212) 979-7759, E-mail: gallery@aperture.org, Internet: www.aperture.org. Exec. Dir.: Michael E. Hoffman, C.E.O.: Paul Gottlieb, Chm.: Robert Anthoine, Sc. Staff: Sara Wolfe (Gallery, Exhibitions)
Fine Arts Museum - 1952
Prints by (Robert Adams, Nick Waplington, Edward Steichen, Danny Lyon, Timothy O'Sullivan), Paul Strand archive, fine art 45774

Castle Clinton, Battery Park, New York, NY 10004 - T: (212) 344-7220, Fax: (212) 285-6874, E-mail: joe_avery@nps.gov, Internet: www.nps.gov
Historical Museum - 1950 45775

Cathedral of Saint John the Divine Museum, 1047 Amsterdam Av, New York, NY 10025 - T: (212) 316-7490, Fax: (212) 932-7348, E-mail: yost@stjohndivine.org, Internet: www.stjohndivine.org. C.E.O.: Dr. James A. Kowalski
Religious Arts Museum - 1892
Old Master Paintings, decorative arts, silver, tapestries, vestments, religous artifacts 45776

Center for Book Arts, 28 W 27th St, New York, NY 10001 - T: (212) 481-0295, Fax: (212) 481-9853, E-mail: info@centerforbookarts.org, Internet: www.centerforbookarts.org. Dir.: Rorey Golden, Sc. Staff: Sarah Nickels (Public Relations)
Public Gallery - 1974
Contemporary artists and hist books - Library 45777

The Chaim Gross Studio Museum, 526 LaGuardia Pl, New York, NY 10012 - T: (212) 529-4906, Fax: (212) 529-1966, E-mail: grossmuseum@earthlink.net. Pres.: Renee Gross, Vice Pres.: Miriam Gross, Dir./Chief Cur.: April Paul
Fine Arts Museum - 1989
Sculpture, watercolours, drawings, prints 45778

Chancellor Robert R. Livingston Masonic Library and Museum, 71 W 23 St, New York, NY 10010-4171 - T: (212) 337-6620, Fax: (212) 633-2639, E-mail: livmalib@pipeline.com, Internet: www.livmalib.org. Pres.: Paul C. Edwards, Dir.: Thomas M. Savini
Historical Museum / Library with Exhibitions - 1856 45779

The Chase Manhattan Bank Art Collections, 270 Park Av, New York, NY 10017 - T: (212) 270-0667, Fax: (212) 270-0725. Dir.: Manuel Gonzalez, Asst. Cur.: Stacey Gershon
Fine Arts Museum - 1959
17.000 largerly contemporary American works in all media 45780

Children's Museum of Manhattan, 212 W 83rd St, New York, NY 10024 - T: (212) 721-1223, Fax: (212) 721-1127, E-mail: mail@cmom.org, Internet: www.cmom.org. Exec. Dir.: Andrew S. Ackerman, Ass. Dir.: Dana D. Prima, Sc. Staff: Jennifer Kozel (Public Relations)
Special Museum - 1973 45781

Children's Museum of the Arts, 182 Lafayette St, New York, NY 10013 - T: (212) 274-0986, Fax: (212) 274-1776, E-mail: info@cmany.org, Internet: www.cmany.org. Dir.: Evelyn Rosetti
Fine Arts Museum - 1988
Children's art from around the world 45782

China Institute Gallery, 125 E 65 St, New York, NY 10021 - T: (212) 744-8181, Fax: (212) 628-4159, E-mail: gallery@chinainstitute.org, Internet: www.chinainstitute.org. Dir.: Hai Chang Willow, Pres.: Jack Maison, Chairman: H. Christopher Luce
Public Gallery - 1926 45783

The Cloisters, Metropolitan Museum of Art, Fort Tryon Park, 193rd St W at Washington Av, New York, NY 10040 - T: (212) 923-3700, Fax: (212) 928-1146, E-mail: icma@compuserve.com, Internet: www.metmuseum.org. Pres.: Dorothy F. Glass, Cur.: Peter Barnet (Art), Timothy Husband, Julien Chapuis, Cons.: Michele Marincola, Sc. Staff: Anna-Maria Poma Swank (Librarian), Michael Carter (Library Asst.), Keith Glutting (Visitor Service)
Fine Arts Museum / Decorative Arts Museum - 1938
Medieval art 45784

The Collectors Club, 22 E 35 St, New York, NY 10016 - T: (212) 683-0559, Fax: (212) 481-1269, E-mail: collectorsclub@nac.net, Internet: www.collectorsclub.org. Pres.: Thomas C. Mazza
Special Museum - 1896
Medals, stamps, awards, engravings prints, early postal equipment - library 45785

Con Edison Energy Museum (temporary closed), 145 E 14th St, New York, NY 10003 - T: (212) 460-6244
Science&Tech Museum
Age of electricity, Pearl Street dynamo station 45786

Congregation Emanu-el Museum, 1 E 65th St, New York, NY 10021-6596 - T: (212) 744-1400, Fax: (212) 570-0826. Dir.: Reva G. Kirschberg-Grossman, Cur.: Cissy Grossman
Historical Museum
Congregational memorabilia, graphics, Judaica, Paintings 45787

Cooper-Hewitt National Design Museum, 2 E 91st St, New York, NY 10128 - T: (212) 849-8300, Fax: (212) 849-8401, Internet: www.si.edu/ndm. Dir.: Paul Warwick Thompson, Asst. Dir.: Susan Yelavich (Public Projects), Chairman: Kay Allaire, Cur.: Marilyn Symmes (Drawings and Prints), Ellen Lupton (Contemporary Design), Deborah Shinn (Applied Arts, Industrial Design), Gillian Moss (Textiles), Joanne Warner (Wallcoverings), Matilda McQuaid (Textiles), Libr.: Stephen H. Van Dyk
Decorative Arts Museum - 1897
300.000 works representing a span of 300 years 45788

Dahesh Museum of Art, 580 Madison Av, New York, NY 10022 - T: (212) 759-0606, Fax: (212) 759-1235, E-mail: information@daheshmuseum.org, Internet: www.daheshmuseum.org. Dir.: Michael Fahlund, Cur.: Stephen R. Edidin, Lisa Small, Roger Diederen, Jeremy Benjamin, Sc. Staff: Maria Celi (Admin.), Suzanne Yantorno (Exec. Asst.), Jean Rho (Admin. Asst.), Sarah Gianelli (Admin. Asst.), Deborah Block (Education), Lisa Mansfield (Registrar), Richard Feaster (Asst. Registrar)
Fine Arts Museum - 1995
European Art (19th-20th c) 45789

Dan Flavin Art Foundation Temporary Gallery, Dia Art Foundation, 5 Worth St, New York, NY 10013 - T: (212) 431-3033
Public Gallery 45790

Department of Art History & Archaeology Visual Resources Collection, 820-825 Schermerhorn Hall, New York, NY 10027 - T: (212) 854-3044, Fax: (212) 854-7329, Internet: www.mcah.columbia.edu/vrc/htm/index.htm. Cur.: Andrew Gessener, Asst. Cur.: Dorothy Krasowska
Fine Arts Museum
250.000 photographs - Berenson I-Tatti Archive, Dial Iconographic Index, Haseloff Archive, Bartsch Collection, Gaigleres Collection, Arthur Kingsley Porter Collection, Ware Collection, Courtauld Collection, Marburger Index, Windsor Castle, Chatsworth Collection, Millard Meiss Collection 45791

Dia Art Foundation, 535 W 22nd St, New York, NY 10011 - T: (212) 989-5566, Fax: (212) 989-4055, E-mail: info@diaart.org, Internet: www.diaart.org
Fine Arts Museum - 1974 45792

Dia:Chelsea, Dia Art Foundation, 548 W 22nd St, New York, NY 10011 - T: (212) 989-5566, Fax: (212) 989-4055, E-mail: info@diaart.org, Internet: www.diacenter.org. Dir.: Michael Govan, Asst. Dir.: Stephen Dewhurst, Chm.: Leonard Riggio, Vize Chm.: Ann Tenenbaum, Cur.: Lynne Cooke, Sc. Staff: Sara Tucker (Digital Media), Karen Kelly (Publications), Steven Evans (Gallery)
Fine Arts Museum - 1974
Contemporary American/European art 45793

Drawing Center, 35 Wooster St, New York, NY 10013 - T: (212) 219-2166, Fax: (212) 966-2976, E-mail: info@drawingcenter.org, Internet: www.drawingcenter.org. Dir.: Catherine de Zegher, Chairman: Dita Amory, Asst. Dir.: Elizabeth Metcalf, Cur.: Luis Camnitzer, Sc. Staff: Lytle Shaw, Heidi O'Neill (Asst. Cur.), Adam Lehner (Drawings), Meryl Zwanger (Education), Tracey Fugami (Asst. Cur., Registrar)
Fine Arts Museum - 1976
Art hist 45794

Dyckman Farmhouse Museum, 4881 Broadway at 204 St, New York, NY 10034 - T: (212) 304-9422, Fax: (212) 304-9422, E-mail: info@dyckman.org, Internet: www.dyckman.org. Dir.: Allyson Bowen
Historical Museum - 1916 45795

Eldridge Street Project, 12 Eldridge St, New York, NY 10002 - T: (212) 219-0903, Fax: (212) 966-4782, E-mail: eldridge@interport.net, Internet: www.eldridgestreet.org. Dir.: Amy E. Waterman, Chairman: Michael Weinstein, Pres.: Lorinda Ash Ezersky, Sc. Staff: Hanna Griff (Public Programs), Lucien Sonder (Education), Rebecca Faulkner (Program), Delmy Serrano (Admin.)
Folklore Museum / Religious Arts Museum / Historical Museum - 1986
Jewish culture and hist on the Lower East Side 45796

The Ernest W. Michel Historical Judaica Collection, c/o UJA-Federation of New York, 130 E 59 St, New York, NY 10022 - T: (212) 836-1720, Fax: (212) 755-9183. Dir.: Ernest W. Michel, Cur.: Paul Hunter
Ethnology Museum / Historical Museum - 1995
History 45797

Eva and Morris Feld Gallery, American Folk Art Museum, 2 Lincoln Sq, New York, NY 10023-6214 - T: (212) 595-9533, Fax: (212) 977-8134, Internet: www.folkartmuseum.org. Dir.: Gerard C. Wertkin, Deputy Dir.: Riccardo Salmona, Cur.: Stacy Hollander, Brooke Davis Anderson (Contemporary Center), Elizabeth Warren, Lee Kogan
Folklore Museum - 1961 45798

Federal Hall National Memorial, 26 Wall St, New York, NY 10005 - T: (212) 825-6888, Fax: (212) 825-6874, E-mail: joe_avery@nps.gov, Internet: www.nps.gov/feha/
Historical Museum - 1939
Memorabilia of George Washington 45799

Forbes Collection, 60 Fifth Av, New York, NY 10011 - T: (212) 206-5548, E-mail: jgstanley@jgstanley.com, Internet: www.forbes.com/forbescollection
Decorative Arts Museum
Furnishings, decorative accessoires, jewelry, gifts 45800

Fraunces Tavern Museum, 54 Pearl St, New York, NY 10004 - T: (212) 425-1778, Fax: (212) 509-3467, E-mail: publicity@francestavernmuseum.org, Internet: www.francestavernmuseum.org. Dir.: Andrew C. Batten, Chm.: Laurence Simpson, Sc. Staff: Jennifer Eaton (Marketing), Bruc Barraclough (Building), Margaret O'Shaughnessy (Admin.)
Historical Museum - 1907
Decorative arts, textiles, paintings, prints, war memorabilia 45801

Frick Collection, 1 E 70 St, New York, NY 10021 - T: (212) 288-0700, Fax: (212) 628-4417, E-mail: info@frick.org, Internet: www.frick.org. Dir.: Samuel Sachs, Pres.: Helen Clay Chace, Dep., Chief Cur.: Colin B. Bailey, Cur.: Susan Grace Galassi, Deputy Dir.: Robert B. Goldsmith (Admin.), Sc. Staff: Patricia Barnett Diane Farnyk (Librarian), Dennis F. Sweeney (Operations)
Fine Arts Museum / Decorative Arts Museum - 1920
Paintings, sculptures, furniture, decorative art, prints 45802

Gallery at the American Bible Society, 1865 Broadway, New York, NY 10023 - T: (212) 408-875, Fax: (212) 408-1456, E-mail: gallery@americanbible.org, Internet: www.americanbible.org. Pres.: Dr. Eugene B. Habecker, Vice Pres.: Patrick English, Dir. Gallery: Dr. Erna Heller, Cur.: Dr. Patricia Pongracz, Asst. Cur.: Ute Schmid
Religious Arts Museum / Fine Arts Museum - 1816
Art with biblical themes, religious art 45803

Gallery of Prehistoric Paintings, 30 E 81 St, New York, NY 10028 - T: (212) 861-5152. Dir.: Douglas Mazonowicz
Fine Arts Museum - 1975
Primitive art - Library 45804

General Grant National Memorial, Riverside Dr and W 122 St, New York, NY 10027 - T: (212) 666-1640, Fax: (212) 932-9631. Dir.: Joseph T. Avery, Cur.: Judith Muller
Historical Museum - 1897
History 45805

Glove Museum, 304 Fifth Av, New York, NY 10001 - T: (212) 695-0347, Fax: (646) 473-0194, E-mail: glovesla@aol.com. Dir.: Jay G. Ruckel
Special Museum - 1986
Veteran glove maker, antique gloves, vintage clothes, tools 45806

Goethe-Institut New York - Exhibitions, 1014 Fifth Av, New York, NY 10028 - T: (212) 439-8700, Fax: (212) 439-8705, Internet: www.goethe.de/uk/ney/enpausst.htm
Public Gallery 45807

Gracie Mansion, East End Av at 88 St, New York, NY 10128 - T: (212) 570-4741, Fax: (212) 988-4854. Cur.: David L. Reese, Admin.: Jonathan Raiola
Historical Museum / Decorative Arts Museum - 1981 45808

Grey Art Gallery, New York University, 100 Washington Sq E, New York, NY 10003 - T: (212) 998-6780, Fax: (212) 995-4024, E-mail: greygallery@nyu.edu, Internet: www.nyu.edu/greyart. Dir.: Lynn Gumpert, Asst. Dir.: Gwen Stolyarov, Deputy Dir.: Frank Poueymirou, Asst. Deputy Dir.: Jeniffer Bakal, Sc. Staff: Michele Wong (Gallery, Registrar), Preparator: David Colassi, Asst. Preparator: David Colossi
Fine Arts Museum / University Museum - 1975
Paintings, sculpture, graphics, contemporary Asian and Middle East art 45809

Guggenheim Museum Soho, 575 Broadway, New York, NY 10012 - T: (212) 423-3500, Fax: (212) 423-3787, E-mail: publicaffairs@guggenheim.org, Internet: www.guggenheim.org. Dir.: Thomas Krens
Fine Arts Museum / Public Gallery - 1992
Late 19th c and 20th c European and American art, esp. paintings, sculptures, works on paper 45810

Hamilton Grange, 287 Convent Av, New York, NY 10031 - T: (212) 283-5154, 825-8874, Fax: (212) 825-6874, E-mail: joe_avery@nps.gov, Internet: nps.gov. Cur.: Judith Mueller
Agriculture Museum - 1924 45811

Hampden-Booth Theatre Museum, 16 Gramercy Park, New York, NY 10003 - T: (212) 228-1861, Fax: (212) 253-6473, E-mail: hampdenboo@aol.com. Pres.: Robert Winter-Berger, Cur.: Raymond Wemmlinger
Performing Arts Museum - 1888
American and English stage, manuscripts 45812

Hatch-Billops Collections, 491 Broadway, New York, NY 10012 - T: (212) 966-3231, Fax: (212) 966-3231, E-mail: Hatch-Billops@worldnet.att.net. Pres.: Camille Billops
Fine Arts Museum - 1975
Collection of primary and secondary resource materials in the Black Cultural Arts - Owen & Edith Dodson Memorial Collection 45813

Herbert and Eileen Bernard Museum, 1 E 65th St, New York, NY 10021 - T: (212) 744-1400, Fax: (212) 570-0826, E-mail: info@emanuelnyc.org, Internet: www.emanuelnyc.org. Cur.: Elka Deitsch
Decorative Arts Museum / Folklore Museum / Religious Arts Museum - 1948
Judaica, Congregation Emanu-El of the City of New York 45814

Hispanic Society of America, 155th St and Broadway, New York, NY 10032 - T: (212) 926-2234, Fax: (212) 690-0743, E-mail: info@hispanicsociety.org, Internet: www.hispanicsociety.org. Dir.: Mitchell A. Codding, Pres.: Theodore S. Beardsley, Cur.: Gerald J. MacDonald (Modern Books), Patrick Lenaghan (Iconography, Medals), Marcus B. Burke (Paintings), Asst. Cur.: John O'Neill (Manuscripts, Rare Books)
Fine Arts Museum - 1904
Art, sculpture, furniture, ceramics, metalwork, jewellery, textiles, archaeology, costumes, glass 45815

Hunter College Art Galleries, 695 Park Av, New York, NY 10021 - T: (212) 772-4991, Fax: (212) 772-4554, Internet: www.hunter.cuny.edu/artgalleries. Dir.: Sanford Wurmfeld, Cur.: Tracy L. Adler, Jenny Ham (Asst. Cur.), Madelon Galland (Preparator, Registrar),
Fine Arts Museum / University Museum - 1984
American art since 1945 45816

International Center of Photography, 1133 Av of the Americans and 43rd Street, New York, NY 10036 - T: (212) 860-1777, Fax: (212) 360-6490, E-mail: info@icp.org, Internet: www.icp.org. Dir.: Willis Hartshorn, Deputy Dir.: Phillip Block (Programs, Education), Chief Cur.: Brian Wallis, Cur.: Christopher Phillips (Collections), Carol Squiers (Collections), Edward Earle (Digital Media), Ann Doherty (Special Projects), Sc. Staff: Phyllis Levine (Information), Barbara Woytowicz (Registrar), Deidre Donohue (Library), Mack Goode (External Affairs)
Special Museum - 1974
4000 hours of original audio recordings, coll of video taps and films, photographers and photography 45817

Intrepid Sea-Air-Space Museum, W 46th St and 12th Av, New York, NY 10036 - T: (212) 245-0072, Internet: www.intrepidmuseum.org. Pres.: Martin Steel
Science&Tech Museum / Military Museum - 1982
900 ft long aircraft carrier intrepid, Vietnam era destroyer Edson, destroyer escort Slater, guided missile submarine Growler, MIG-21, Scimitar, Etendard, F-14 Super Tomcast, light ship Nantucket 45818

ISE Art Foundation, 555 Broadway, New York, NY 10012 - T: (212) 925-1649, Fax: (212) 226-9362, Internet: www.isefoundation.org/english/ny
Public Gallery - 1984 45819

Japan Society Gallery, 333 E 47 St, New York, NY 10017 - T: (212) 832-1155, Fax: (212) 715-1262, E-mail: amunroe@japansociety.org, Internet: www.japansociety.org. Dir.: Alexandra Munroe, Pres.: William Clark jr., Man.: Eleni Cocordas (Exhibitions)
Fine Arts Museum - 1907
Japanese art 45820

The Jewish Museum, 1109 Fifth Av, New York, NY 10128 - T: (212) 423-3200, Fax: (212) 423-3232, E-mail: jewishmus@aol.com, Internet: www.thejewishmuseum.org. Dir.: Joan Rosenbaum, Chm.: Susan Lytle Lipton, Dep. Dir.: Lynn Thommen (External Affairs), Cur.: Fred Wassermann, Sc. Staff: John L. Vogelstein (Press), Thomas A. Dougherty (Admin.), Ruth Beesch (Exhibitions, Programs), Mary Walling, Susan L. Braunstein (Archaeology, Judaica), Susan Goodman, Norman Kleeblatt (Fine Arts), Vivian Mann (Judaica), Nancy McGary (Collections and Exhibitions), Aviva Weintraub (Media, Public Programms), Grace Rapkin (Marketing), Anne Scher (Communication), Debbie Schwab-Dorfman (Marketing), Jane Rubin (Registrar), Marcia Saft (Visitor Service)
Fine Arts Museum / Historical Museum / Religious Arts Museum - 1904
Judaica collection, ceremonial objects, paintings, drawings, sculpture, prints, textiles, antiquities, photographs, decorativ arts, coins, medals, historic manuscripts, artifacts, broadcast material 45821

John J. Harvey Fireboat Collection, 100 W 72nd St, New York, NY 10023 - Internet: www.fireboat.org
Historical Museum 45822

Judaica Museum of Central Synagogue, 123 E 55 St, New York, NY 10022 - T: (212) 838-5122, Fax: (212) 644-2168, Internet: www.censyn.org. Dir.: Livia Thompson
Folklore Museum / Religious Arts Museum - 1962
Coins, medals, textiles, ritual objects from home and synagoge, sculpture, ephemera, memorabilia, artefacts 45823

Leslie-Lohman Gay Art Foundation, 127b Prince St, New York, NY 10012 - T: (212) 673-7007, Fax: (212) 260-0363, E-mail: lldirector@earthlink.net, Internet: www.leslielohman.org
Public Gallery
Awareness of lesbian, gay, bisexual, transgender and queer art 45824

Lladro Museum, 43 W 57th St, New York, NY 10019 - T: (212) 838-9352
Fine Arts Museum
Porcelain, leather 45825

The Lowe Gallery at Hudson Guild, 441 W 26 St, New York, NY 10001 - T: (212) 760-9800. Dir.: James Furlong
Fine Arts Museum - 1948
Contemporary art 45826

Lower East Side Tenement Museum, 90 Orchard St, New York, NY 10002 - T: (212) 431-0233, Fax: (212) 431-0402, E-mail: lestm@tenement.org, Internet: www.tenement.org. Pres.: Ruth J. Abram, Vice Pres.: Renee Epps (Admin.), Chairman: Richard Kane, Cur.: Steve Long, Public Relations: Katherine Snider
Historical Museum - 1988
Historical immigrant documents, artifacts 45827

Madame Tussaud's Wax Museum, 234 W 42nd St, New York, NY 10036 - T: (800) 246-8872, Fax: (212) 719-9440, E-mail: sarah.sommerfield@madametussaudsny.com, Internet: www.madametussaudsny.com
Fine Arts Museum 45828

Main Gallery of Henry Street Settlement, Abrons Arts Center, 466 Grand St, New York, NY 10002 - T: (212) 598-0400, Fax: (212) 505-8329, Internet: www.henrystreetarts.org. Dir.: Barbara L. Tate
Fine Arts Museum / Public Gallery - 1893 45829

Margaret Thatcher Projects, 529 W 20th St, New York, NY 10011 - T: (212) 675-0222, Internet: www.mtprojects.addr.com
Fine Arts Museum 45830

Marie Walsh Sharpe Art Foundation, Space-Program, 443 Greenwich St, New York, NY 10013 - T: (212) 925-3008, Fax: (719) 635-3018, E-mail: shartpartfdn@qwest.net, Internet: www.shartpartfdn.org
Public Gallery - 1997 45831

Merchant's House Museum, 29 E Fourth St, New York, NY 10003 - T: (212) 777-1089, Fax: (212) 777-1104, E-mail: nyc1832@aol.com, Internet: www.merchantshouse.com. Dir.: Margaret Halsey Gardiner, Pres.: Anne Fairfax, Cur.: Mimi Sherman
Historical Museum - 1936
19th c furniture, decorative arts and textiles 45832

Metropolitan Museum of Art, 1000 Fifth Av, New York, NY 10028-0198 - T: (212) 879-5500, Fax: (212) 570-3879, E-mail: webmaster@metmuseum.org, Internet: www.metmuseum.org. Dir.: Philippe de Montebello, Pres.: David McKinney, Chm.: Morrison H. Heckscher (American Art), James C.Y. Watt (Asian Art), George R. Goldner (Drawings, Prints), Everett Fahy (European Paintings), Ian Wardropper (European Sculpture, Decorative Arts), William S. Lieberman (Modern Art), Hubert von Sonnenburg (Paintings Cons.), Cur.: Alice Cooney Frelinghuysen (American Decorative Arts), Julie Jones (Arts of Africa, Oceania and the Americas), H. Barbara Weinberg (American Painting and Sculpture), Joan Aruz (Ancient Near Eastern Art), Stuart Pyhrr (Arms and Armor), Harold Koda (Costume Institute), Dorothea Arnold (Egyptian Art), Carlos Picon (Greek and Roman Art), Dietrich von Bothmer (Distinguished Research), Daniel Walker (Islamic Art), Laurence B. Kanter (Robert Lehman Coll), Peter Barnet (Medieval Art and the Cloisters), Laurence Libin (Musical Instr), Maria Morris Hambourg (Photographs), Cons.: James H. Frantz (Objects), Majorie Shelley (Paper), Nobuko Kajitani (Textiles)
Fine Arts Museum - 1870
Ancient and modern art of Egypt, Greece, Rome, Near and Far East, Europe, Africa, Oceania, pre-Columbian cultures, USA 45833

Miriam and Ira D. Wallach Art Gallery, 116th St and Broadway, New York, NY 10027 - T: (212) 854-7288, 854-2877, Fax: (212) 854-7800, Internet: www.columbia.edu/cu/wallach. Dir.: Sarah Elliston Weiner
Fine Arts Museum / University Museum - 1986
Art gallery in 1897 Schermerhorn hall 45834

Morris-Jumel Mansion, 65 Jumel Terrace, New York, NY 10032 - T: (212) 923-8008, Fax: (212) 923-8947. Dir.: Kenneth Moss, Pres.: Nancy Goshow, Vice Pres.: James Daly, Cur.: Joanna Pessa
Decorative Arts Museum / Historical Museum - 1904 45835

Mount Vernon Hotel Museum, 421 E 61 St, New York, NY 10021 - T: (212) 838-6878, Fax: (212) 838-7390, E-mail: mvhmuseum@aol.com. Dir.: Amy Northrop Adamo, Pres.: Charlotte Armstrong, Cur.: Lisa Bedell, Sc. Staff: Pat McLaughlin (Education), Rosalind Muggeridge (Public Relations)
Local Museum - 1939/2000
American decorative arts, 18th and 19th c documents and letters 45836

Municipal Art Society, 457 Madison Av, New York, NY 10022 - T: (212) 935-3960, Fax: (212) 753-1816, E-mail: info@mas.org, Internet: www.mas.org. Pres.: Kent Barwick, Vice Pres.: Gloria Troy, Chairman: Frank Emile Sanchis
Fine Arts Museum - 1893
Art 45837

El Museo del Barrio, 1230 Fifth Av, New York, NY 10029 - T: (212) 831-7272, Fax: (212) 831-7927, E-mail: info@elmuseo.org, Internet: www.elmuseo.org. Dir.: Susanna Torruella Leval, Dep. Dir.: Patricia Smalley, Chief Cur.: Fatima Brecht, Cur.: Deborah Cullen, Sc. Staff: Noel Valentin (Registrar)
Fine Arts Museum - 1969
Works on paper, sculptures, prints, paintings, photography, 16 mm films on history, culture and art - junior museum, 510 seat theatre 45838

Museum at the Fashion Institute of Technology, Seventh Av at 27th St, New York, NY 10001-5992 - T: (212) 217-5970, Fax: (212) 217-5978, 217-5800, E-mail: steeleva@fitsuny.edu, Internet: www.fitnyc.suny.edu. Acting Dir./ Chief Cur.: Dr. Valerie Steele, Cur.: Ellen Shanley (Costume), Lynn Felsher (Textiles), Cons.: Anahid Akasheh, Asst. Cons.: Glenn Peterson, Registrar: Deborah Nordon
Special Museum - 1967
Clothing, textiles 45839

Museum of American Financial History, 26 Broadway, New York, NY 10004-1763 - T: (212) 908-4110, 908-4519, Fax: (212) 908-4601, E-mail: krichar@financialhistory.org, Internet: www.financialhistory.org. Exec. Dir.: Brian C. Thompson, Chairman: John E. Herzog, Asst. Dir: Meg Ventrudo (Exhebitions), Kristin Aguillera (Communication)
Historical Museum - 1988
American financial hit from the mid-18th c to present day, stock and bond certificates, books, periodicals 45840

Museum of American Folk Art → American Folk Art Museum

Museum of Chinese in the Americas, 70 Mulberry St, New York, NY 10013 - T: (212) 619-4785, Fax: (212) 619-4720, E-mail: info@moca-nyc.org, Internet: www.moca-nyc.org. Dir.: Fay Chew Matsuda, Pres.: Dr. John K. W. Tchen, Dep. Dir./Cur.: Cynthia Lee, Sc. Staff: Micheal Hew Wing (Program), Lamgen Leon (Operations), Gretchen So (Collections)
Fine Arts Museum / Historical Museum / Folklore Museum - 1980
Chinese history in America 45841

Museum of Jewish Heritage - A Living Memorial to the Holocaust, 18 First Pl, New York, NY 10280 - T: (212) 968-1800, Fax: (212) 968-1369, E-mail: aspilka@mjhnyc.org, Internet: www.mjhnyc.org. Dir.: Dr. David G. Marwell, Cur.: Esther Brumberg (Collections), Dr. Louis Levine (Collections), Jamie Rosenfield (Registrar), Michael Minerva (Operations), Abby R. Spilka (Public Relations)
Historical Museum / Folklore Museum - 1984
Jewish history, 20th-c memorial to the Holocaust 45842

Museum of Modern Art at the Gramercy Theatre, 127 E 23rd St, New York, NY 10001 - T: (212) 777-4900, E-mail: info@moma.org, Internet: www.moma.org. Dir.: Glenn D. Lowry
Fine Arts Museum
Contemporary art 45843

Museum of Sex, 233 Fifth Av, New York, NY 10016 - T: (212) 689-6337, 946-6323, E-mail: info@museumofsex.com, Internet: www.museumofsex.com. Dir.: Daniel Gluck, Cur.: Grady T. Turner
Special Museum - 2002 45844

Museum of Television and Radio, 25 W 52nd St, New York, NY 10019 - T: (212) 621-6600, Fax: (212) 621-6700, Internet: www.mtr.org. Cur.: Ronald Simon, Susan Fisher
Special Museum / Science&Tech Museum - 1975 45845

Museum of the American Piano, 291 Broadway, New York, NY 10007-1814 - T: (212) 246-4646, 406-6060, Fax: (212) 406-5245, E-mail: pianomuseum@pianomuseum.com, Internet: www.museumforpianos.org. Dir.: Kalman Detrich
Music Museum - 1981 45846

Museum of the City of New York, 1220 Fifth Av at 103rd St, New York, NY 10029 - T: (212) 534-1672, Fax: (212) 423-0758, 534-5974, E-mail: mcny@mcny.org, Internet: www.mcny.org. Dir.: Robert R. Macdonald, Deputy Dir.: Evelyn Rossetti (Learning), Cur.: Deborah D. Waters (Decorative Arts), Bob Shamis (Prints, Photographs), Phyllis Magidson (Costumes), Marty Jacobs (Theatre), Andrea Henderson Fahnestock (Paintings, Sculpture)
Local Museum - 1923 45847

Museum Quality Finishes, 307 W 38th St, New York, NY 10018 - T: (212) 465-1077
Fine Arts Museum 45848

National Academy of Design Museum, 1083 Fifth Av, New York, NY 10128 - T: (212) 369-4880, Fax: (212) 360-6795, Internet: www.nationalacademy.com. Dir.: Dr. Annette Blaugrund, Cur.: Dr. David Dearinger, Cons.: Lucie Kinsolving
Fine Arts Museum - 1825 45849

National Arts Club, 15 Gramercy Park S, New York, NY 10003 - T: (212) 475-3424, Fax: (212) 475-3692, Internet: www.nationalartsclub.org. Pres.: Alton James Jr., Chairman: Cheryl Green, Cur.: Carol Lowrey
Fine Arts Museum - 1898
19th and 20th c American painting, sculpture, works on paper, decorative arts 45850

National Museum of Catholic Art and History, 445-447 E 115th St, New York, NY 10029 - T: (212) 828-9700, Fax: (212) 828-8834, E-mail: nmcah@aol.com. Cur.: Leslie Bussis Tait
Religious Arts Museum / Fine Arts Museum - 1995
Old master and contemporary religious paintings, sculpture, prints, liturgical vestments 45851

National Museum of the American Indian, Smithsonian Institution, George Gustav Heye Center, 1 Bowling Green, New York, NY 10004 - T: (212) 514-3700, Fax: (212) 514-3800, Internet: www.nmai.si.edu. Dir.: W. Richard West, Dep. Dir.: Douglas E. Evelyn, Asst. Dir.: Charlotte Heth, Donna A. Scott, Bernstein, James Volkert, Chief Cur.: Mary Jane Lenz
Ethnology Museum / Archaeological Museum / Historical Museum / Decorative Arts Museum / Fine Arts Museum - 1916 45852

Neue Galerie New York, 1048 Fifth Av, New York, NY 10028 - T: (212) 628-6200, Fax: (212) 628-8824, E-mail: museum@neuegalerie.org, Internet: www.neuegalerie.org. Dir.: Gerwald Sonnberger, Renée Price
Fine Arts Museum - 2001
German and Austrian Fine and Decorative Art of the 20th c 45853

Neustadt Museum of Tiffany Art, 124 W 79 St, New York, NY 10024 - T: (212) 875-9693, Fax: (212) 874-0872, E-mail: nmtamuseum@aol.com, Internet: www.neustadtmuseum.org. Pres.: Milton D. Hassol, C.E.O.: Nicholas Cass-Hassol, Sc. Staff: Richard Hanna (Trustee), Sheil Tabakoff (Trustee), David Specter (Trustee), Mary Alice McKay (Trustee)
Fine Arts Museum - 1969
Tiffany lamps, glass and jewels 45854

New Museum of Contemporary Art, 583 Broadway, New York, NY 10012 - T: (212) 219-1222, Fax: (212) 431-5328, E-mail: newmu@newmuseum.org, Internet: www.newmuseum.org. Dir.: Lisa Phillips, Deputy Dir.: Dennis Szakacs, Cur.: Dan Cameron
Fine Arts Museum - 1977 45855

New World Art Center → T.F. Chen Cultural Center

New York City Fire Museum, 278 Spring St, New York, NY 10013 - T: (212) 691-1303, Fax: (212) 924-0430, Internet: www.nycfiremuseum.org. Dir.: Geoff Giglierano
Historical Museum - 1987 45856

New York City Police Museum, 100 Old Slip, New York, NY 10005 - T: (212) 480-3100, Fax: (212) 480-9757, Internet: www.nycpolicemuseum.org. Dir.: Ninfa Segarra, Cur.: Michael Cronin
Historical Museum - 2000 45857

The New York Historical Society Museum, 2 W 77th St, Central Park W, New York, NY 10024 - T: (212) 873-3400, Fax: (212) 874-8706, E-mail: NYHS@interport.net, Internet: www.nyhistory.org. Dir.: Kenneth T. Jackson, Pres.: Paul Gunther, Chm.: Nancy Newcomb, Vice Pres.: Jan Ramirez, Margaret Heilbrunn (Library), Valerie Komor (Print), Rober Del Bagno (Head Exhebitions), Travis Steward (Public Ralations), Nina Nazionale (Public Service, Library), L.J. Krizner (Education), Nicole Wells (Reproductions), Ione Saroyan (Visitor), Steven Jaffe (Public Historien), Kathleen Hulser (Public Historien)
Historical Museum / Local Museum - 1804
Watercolors, paintings, portraits, silver, furniture, Tiffany lamps and glass, ceramics, glass, sculpture, toys, folk art, military and naval hist coll, prints, architectural drawings, rare books, documents, maps, manuscripts 45858

New York Public Library for the Performing Arts, 40 Lincoln Center Plaza, New York, NY 10023-7498 - T: (212) 970-1830, Fax: (212) 873-1870, E-mail: bcohenstratyner@nypl.org, Internet: www.nypl.org. Pres.: Paul Leclerc, Chm.: Samuel Butler, Exec. Dir.: Jaqueline Z. Davis (Art), Sc. Staff: Donald J. Vlack (Design), Robert McGlynn (Illustration), Barbara Cohen-Stratyner (Exhibiton), Robertine Taylor (Theatre), Susan Sommer (Musik), Donald McCormick (Recording), Madeleine Nichols (Dance)
Historical Museum / Performing Arts Museum / Library with Exhibitions / Music Museum - 1965
Prints, letters, manuscripts, photographs, posters, films, video tapes, memorabilia, dance, recordings 45859

New York Studio School of Drawing, Painting and Sculpture Gallery, 8 W Eighth St, New York, NY 10011 - T: (212) 673-6466, Fax: (212) 777-0996, E-mail: library@nyss.org, Internet: www.nyss.org
Public Gallery - 1964
Drawings, paintings, sculptures 45860

Nicholas Roerich Museum, 319 W 107th St, New York, NY 10025-2799 - T: (212) 864-7752, Fax: (212) 864-7704, E-mail: director@roerich.org, Internet: www.roerich.org. Dir.: Daniel Entin
Fine Arts Museum - 1958
Paintings of Tibet, India, Himalaya area by N. Roerich 45861

Pen and Brush Museum, 16 E 10 St, New York, NY 10003 - T: (212) 475-3669, Fax: (212) 475-6018, E-mail: PenBrush99@aol.com. Pres.: Ivece Portiabohn
Fine Arts Museum - 1893
Oil, watercolours, pastel, graphics, sculpture, craft 45862

Pierpont Morgan Library, 29 E 36 St, New York, NY 10016 - T: (212) 685-0610, Fax: (212) 481-3484, E-mail: media@morganlibrary.org, Internet: www.morganlibrary.org. Dir.: Dr. Charles E. Pierce, Deputy Dir.: Brian Regan, Cur.: Robert E. Parks (Literary, Historical Manuscripts), William M. Voelkle (Medieval and Renaissance Manuscripts), Egbert Haverkamp-Begemann (Drawings and Prints), John Bidwell (Printed Books, Bindings), J. Rigbie Turner (Music, Manuscripts and Books), Sidney H. Babcock (Seals, Tablets), Dir. Conservation Center: Margaret Holben Ellis, Cons.: Patricia Reyes, Deborah Evetts
Fine Arts Museum / Library with Exhibitions - 1924
Paintings, art objects, manuscripts, drawings, prints - Gilbert & Sullivan coll 45863

Pratt Manhattan Gallery, 114W 14th St, New York, NY 10011 - T: (718) 647-7778, Fax: (718) 636-3785, E-mail: exhibits@pratt.edu, Internet: www.pratt.edu/exhibitions. Dir.: Loretta Yarlow, Sc. Staff: Niccholas Battins (Registrar), Kathrine Davis (Design)
Fine Arts Museum / University Museum - 1975
Paintings, sculpture, prints, graphics, decorative art 45864

Rose Museum at Carnegie Hall, 154 W 57th St, New York, NY 10019 - T: (212) 903-9629, Fax: (212) 582-5518, E-mail: gfrancesconi@carnegihall.org, Internet: www.carnegiehall.org. Dir.: Gino Francesconi
Performing Arts Museum - 1991 45865

Salmagundi Museum of American Art, 47 Fifth Av, New York, NY 10003 - T: (212) 255-7740, Fax: (212) 229-0172, Internet: www.salmagundi.org. Pres.: Richard Pionk, Chairman: Edward Brennan, Cur.: Thomas Picard, Ruth Reininghaus
Fine Arts Museum / Association with Coll - 1871
Paintings, sculptures, photography - library 45866

Scandinavia House, 58 Park Av, New York, NY 10016 - T: (212) 779-3587
Fine Arts Museum 45867

Schomburg Center for Research in Black Culture, 515 Malcolm X. Blvd, New York, NY 10037-1801 - T: (212) 491-2200, Fax: (212) 491-6760, Internet: www.nypl.org/research/sc/sc.html. Dir.: Howard Dodson, Head: Genette McLaurin (Reference), Victor Smyth (Art, Artifacts), James Briggs Murray (Moving Image, Recorded Sound), Diana Lachatenere (Archives)
Historical Museum / Ethnology Museum - 1925 45868

Sidney Mishkin Gallery of Baruch College, 135 E 22 St, New York, NY 10010 - T: (212) 802-2690, Fax: (212) 802-2693, Internet: www.baruch.cuny.edu/mishikin/gallery.html. Dir.: Sandra Kraskin
Fine Arts Museum / University Museum - 1981
American and European drawings, paintings, photographs, prints and sculptures 45869

Skyscraper Museum, Southern Battery Park City, New York, NY 10280, mail addr: 55 Broad St, New York, NY 10004 - T: (212) 968-1961, Internet: www.skyscraper.org. Dir.: Carol Willis, Chm.: Jed Marcus, Sc. Staff: Kenneth Levine, Laura Lee Pederson (Public Relations)
Special Museum - 1996/2003
Study oh high-rise buildings in past, present and future 45870

Society of Illustrators Museum of American Illustration, 128 E 63 St, New York, NY 10021-7303 - T: (212) 838-2560, Fax: (212) 838-2561, E-mail: society@societyillustrators.org, Internet: www.societyillustrators.org. Dir.: Terrence Brown, Asst. Dir.: Phyllis Harvey
Fine Arts Museum - 1901 45871

Solomon R. Guggenheim Museum, 1071 Fifth Av, New York, NY 10128 - T: (212) 423-3500, Fax: (212) 941-8410, E-mail: visitorinfo@guggenheim.org, Internet: www.guggenheim.org. Dir.: Thomas Krens, Deputy Dir.: Laurie Beckelman, Lisa Dennison, Cur.: John Hanhardt (Film, Media Arts), Julia Brown, Jennifer Blessing, Nancy Spector, Germano Celant (Contemporary Art), Robert Rosenblum, Mark Rosenthal, Carmen Gimenez (20th-C Art), Cons.: Paul Schwartzbaum
Fine Arts Museum - 1937 45872

Sony Wonder Technology Lab, 56th St at Madison Av, New York, NY 10022 - T: (212) 833-8100, Fax: (212) 833-4445, E-mail: stacey-kratz@sonyusa.com, Internet: www.sonywondertechlab.com. Dir.: Courtney White
Science&Tech Museum - 1994
Technology and science 45873

South Street Seaport Museum, 207 Front St, New York, NY 10038 - T: (212) 748-8600, Fax: (212) 748-8725, E-mail: webmaster@southstseaport.org, Internet: www.southstseaport.org. Cur.: Steven Jaffe (Exhibitions), Norman Brouwer (Ships), Barbara Henry (Printing)
Special Museum / Science&Tech Museum - 1967 45874

Spanish Institute, 684 Park Av, New York, NY 10021 - T: (212) 628-0420, Fax: (212) 734-4177, Internet: www.spanishinstitute.org
Public Gallery - 1954
Spanish art 45875

Statue of Liberty National Monument and Ellis Island Immigration Museum, Liberty Island, New York, NY 10004 - T: (212) 363-7772, Fax: (212) 363-8347, E-mail: stli_museum@nps.gov, Internet: www.nps.gov/stli. Dir.: Diane H. Dayson, Chief Cur.: Diana R. Pardue, Cur.: Judith Giuricco (Exhibitions, Media), Geraldine Santoro (Collections), Libr.: Barry Moreno, Jeffrey Dosik, Archivist: George Tselos, Janet Levine (Historic)
Historical Museum / Historic Site - 1924
History, folk art - library, archive 45876

Studio Museum in Harlem, 144 W 125th St, New York, NY 10027 - T: (212) 864-4500, Fax: (212) 864-4800, E-mail: SMHNY@aol.com, Internet: www.studiomuseuminharlem.org. Dir.: Lowery Stokes Sims, Chairman: Raymond J. McGuire, Chief Cur.: Thelma Golden, Asst. Cur.: Christine Y. Kim
Fine Arts Museum - 1967
19th and 20th c African American artists, traditional and contemporary African art, Caribbean art - Archives 45877

Swiss Institute - Contemporary Art, 495 Broadway, New York, NY 10012 - T: (212) 925-2035
Public Gallery 45878

Terrain Gallery, 141 Greene St, New York, NY 10012 - T: (212) 777-4490, Fax: (212) 777-4426, Internet: www.terraingallery.org. Coord.: Marcia Rackow
Public Gallery
Paintings, prints, drawings and photographs with commentary 45879

T.F. Chen Cultural Center, 250 Lafayette St, New York, NY 10012-4075 - T: (212) 966-4363, Fax: (212) 966-5285, E-mail: chen@tfchen.org, Internet: www.tfcheng.org. Pres.: Lucia Chen, Cur.: Julie Chen
Fine Arts Museum - 1996
International contemporary art, neo-iconographic painting 45880

Theodore Roosevelt Birthplace, 28 E 20th St, New York, NY 10003 - T: (212) 260-1616, Fax: (212) 677-3587, E-mail: masithrb@nps.gov, Internet: www.nps.gov/thrb/
Historical Museum - 1923
Theodore Roosevelt memorabilia and hitoric item 45881

Tresure Room Gallery of the Interchurch Center, 475 Riverside Dr, New York, NY 10115 - T: (212) 870-2200, Fax: (212) 870-2440, E-mail: Dennis@interchurch-center.org, Internet: www.interchurch-center.org. Dir.: Mary E. McNamara, Pres.: Sue M. Dennis, Chairman: Randolph Nugent, Cur.: Dorothy Cochran, Ernest Rubinstein (Library)
Library with Exhibitions - 1959 45882

Trinity Museum of the Parish of Trinity Church, Broadway and Wall St, New York, NY 10006 - T: (212) 602-0800, Fax: (212) 602-9648, E-mail: djette@trinitywallstreet.org, Internet: www.trinitywallstreet.org. C.E.O.: Daniel Paul Matthews, Cur.: Jessica Silver, David Jette
Religious Arts Museum - 1966
Books, prints, photographs, paintings, artifacts and religious objects, documents - Archives 45883

Ukrainian Museum, 203 Second Av, New York, NY 10003 - T: (212) 228-0110, Fax: (212) 228-1947, E-mail: info@ukrainianmuseum.org, Internet: www.ukrainianmuseum.org. Dir.: Maria Shust, Pres.: Olha Hnateyko, Admin. Dir.: Daria Bajko
Fine Arts Museum / Folklore Museum / Special Museum - 1976
Fine art, folk art, photographs, documents, fkyers, posters, Ukrain art, culture, architecture and hist, hist of Ukrainian immigration, numismatics and philatelic coll 45884

Visual Arts Museum, 209 E 23 St, New York, NY 10010 - T: (212) 592-2144, Fax: (212) 592-2095, E-mail: fditommaso@adm.schoolofvisualarts.edu, Internet: www.schoolofvisualarts.edu. Dir.: Francis Di Tommaso, Assoc. Dir.: Rachel Gugelberger, Asst. Dir.: Geoffrey Detrani (Exhibitions), Sc. Staff: Collin Mura-Smith (Gallery), Laura Yeffeth (Registrar), Michelle Meier (Admin. Gallery and Museum)
Fine Arts Museum - 1971
Photography, fine art, new media, digital graphic design 45885

Whitney Museum of American Art, 945 Madison Av, New York, NY 10021 - T: (212) 570-3600, Fax: (212) 570-1807, E-mail: feedback@whitney.org, Internet: www.whitney.org. Dir.: Maxwell

Anderson, Chm.: Leonard A. Lauder, Pres.: Joel S. Ehrenkranz, Dep. Dir.: Willard Holmes, Cur.: Barbara Haskell (Prewar American Art), Janie C. Lee (Drawings), Chissie Iles (Film, Video), David Kiehl (Prints), Marla Prather (Prewar American Art), Lawrence R. Rinder (Contemporary Art), Sylvia Wolf (Photography), Sc. Staff: Mary Haus (Communication), Melissa Phillips (Public Programs), Barbar Bantivoglio (External Affairs), Christy Putman (Operations), Eugenie Tsai (Cur. Services), May Castleberry (Librarian), Mary DelMonico (Publications),
Fine Arts Museum - 1930 45886

Yeshiva University Museum, 15 W 16th St, New York, NY 10011 - T: (212) 294-8330, Fax: (212) 294-8335, E-mail: sherskowitz@yum.cjh.edu, Internet: www.yu.edu/museum. Dir.: Sylvia A. Herskowitz, Dep. Dir.: Debra Goldman, Cur.: Rachelle Bradt (Education), Gabriel M. Goldstein, Reba Wulkan, Reba Wulkan (Exhebitions), Bonni-Dara Michaelis (Collections)
Historical Museum / University Museum / Ethnology Museum / Fine Arts Museum - 1973
Jewish ceremonial objects, Jewish hist, ethnography, art and culture 45887

Newark DE

University Gallery, University of Delaware, Main St at N College Av, Newark, DE 19716 - T: (302) 831-8242, Fax: (302) 831-8251, E-mail: bchapp@udel.edu, Internet: www.museum.udel.edu. Dir.: Belena S. Chapp, Cur.: Janet Gardner Broske
Fine Arts Museum / University Museum - 1978
Art 45888

Newark NJ

Aljira Center for Contemporary Art, 100 Washington St, Newark, NJ 07102 - T: (973) 643-6877, Fax: (973) 643-3594, E-mail: aljirainc@aol.com. Exec. Dir.: Victor Davson
Public Gallery - 1983 45889

Junior Museum, Newark Museum, 49 Washington St, Newark, NJ 07101 - T: (973) 596-6605, Fax: (973) 642-0459
Fine Arts Museum - 1926
Children's artwork 45890

New Jersey Historical Society Museum, 52 Park Pl, Newark, NJ 07102 - T: (973) 596-8500, Fax: (973) 596-6957, E-mail: info@jerseyhistory.org, Internet: www.jerseyhistory.org. Dir.: Dr. Sally Yerkovich, Deputy Dir.: Janet Rassweiler, Cur.: Claudia Ocello
Historical Museum / Local Museum - 1845
library 45891

The Newark Museum, 49 Washington St, Newark, NJ 07101-0540 - T: (973) 596-6550, Fax: (973) 642-0459, E-mail: lmcconnell@newarkmuseum.org, Internet: www.newarkmuseum.org. Dir.: Mary Sue Sweeney Price, Cur.: Dr. Susan Auth (Classical), Ulysses G. Dietz (Decorative Arts), Valrae Reynolds (Asian Coll.), Nii Quarcoopome (Africa, The Americas, Pacific), Joseph Jacobs (Painting, Sculpture), Dr. Sule Oygur (Earth Sciences)
Fine Arts Museum / Decorative Arts Museum / Archaeological Museum - 1909
Asian, American, African art, decorative art, Egypt, Greek and Roman Art - planetarium, zoo 45892

Newark OH

Licking County Art Association Gallery, 50 S Secand St, Newark, OH 43055 - T: (740) 349-8031, Fax: (740) 345-3787, E-mail: lcaa@msmisp.com. Pres.: Leah Mitchell, Man.: Vivian DuRant Smith
Fine Arts Museum - 1959 45893

Licking County Historical Museum, Veterans Park, N 6th St, Newark, OH 43058-0785 - T: (740) 345-4898, Fax: (740) 345-2983, E-mail: lchs@alltel.net. Pres.: Scott Walker
Local Museum - 1947
Regional history 45894

Moundbuilders State Memorial and Museum, 99 Cooper Av, Newark, OH 43055 - T: (800) 600-7174, Internet: www.ohiohistory.org/places/moundld/. Head: James Kingery
Ethnology Museum / Archaeological Museum
Prehistoric Indian Art Museum and Historical Site 45895

National Heisey Glass Museum, 169 W Church St, Newark, OH 43055 - T: (740) 345-2932, Fax: (740) 345-9638, E-mail: curator@heiseymuseum.org, Internet: www.heiseymueusm.org. Cur.: Cheri Goldner
Decorative Arts Museum - 1974 45896

Sherwood-Davidson House, Veterans Park, Sixth St, Newark, OH 43058-0785 - T: (740) 345-6525, E-mail: sherwooddavidson@yahoo.com, Internet: www.lickingcountyhistoricalsociety.org. Pres.: Scott Walker
Local Museum / Historical Museum - 1947 45897

Webb House Museum, 303 Granville St, Newark, OH 43055 - T: (740) 345-8540, E-mail: webbhouse@nextek.net, Internet: www.lickingcountyhistoricalsociety.org. Cur.: Mindy Honey Nelson
Historical Museum - 1976 45898

The Works, Ohio Center for History, Art and Technology, 55 S First St, Newark, OH 43055 - T: (740) 349-9277, Fax: (740) 345-7252, Internet: www.attheworks.org. C.E.O.: Marcia W. Downes
Historical Museum / Fine Arts Museum / Science&Tech Museum - 1996 45899

Newark Valley NY

Bement-Billings Farmstead, 9142 Rte 38, Newark Valley, NY 13811 - T: (607) 642-9516, Fax: (607) 642-9516, E-mail: nvhistorical@juno.com, Internet: www.tier.net/nvhistory. Dir.: Harriet Miller
Historical Museum / Historic Site - 1977 45900

Newark Valley Depot Museum, Depot St, Newark Valley, NY 13811 - T: (607) 642-9516, Fax: (607) 642-9516, Internet: www.munex.arme.cornell.edu/nvhs. Dir.: Kim Mayhew
Science&Tech Museum - 1977
Railroad 45901

Newaygo MI

Newaygo County Museum, 85 Water St, Newaygo, MI 49337 - T: (231) 652-9281, Fax: (231) 652-2461, E-mail: bbillerb@newwaygo.net. Pres.: Allen Bradley, C.E.O.: Barb Billerbeck
Local Museum - 1968
Regional history 45902

Newbern VA

Wilderness Road Regional Museum, State Rte 611, 5240 Wilderness Rd, Newbern, VA 24126-0373 - T: (540) 674-4835, Fax: (540) 674-1266, E-mail: wrrm@usit.net, Internet: www.rootsweb/~vapulaski/wrrm/index.htm. Dir.: Ann S. Bailey, Cur.: Sara C. Zimmerman
Local Museum - 1980
Local hist 45903

Newburgh NY

David Crawford House, 189 Montgomery St, Newburgh, NY 12550 - T: (914) 561-2585, Internet: www.newburgh-ny.com. Pres.: Carla Decker
Historical Museum - 1884 45904

Washington's Headquarters, Corner of Liberty and Washington Sts, Newburgh, NY 12551-1476 - T: (914) 562-1195, Internet: www.nysparks.state.ny.us. Sc. Staff: Thomas A. Hughes
Military Museum - 1850 45905

Newbury MA

Coffin House, 14 High Rd, Newbury, MA 01951 - T: (978) 462-2634, Fax: (978) 462-4022, E-mail: ezopes@spnea.org, Internet: www.spnea.org. Dir.: Philip Zea
Historical Museum - 1929
History 45906

Spencer-Peirce-Little Farm, 5 Little's Ln, Newbury, MA 01951 - T: (978) 462-2634, Fax: (978) 462-4022, E-mail: pzea@spnea.org, Internet: www.spnea.org. Pres.: Philip Zea
Local Museum - 1971
Historic house 45907

Newbury Park CA

Stagecoach Inn Museum Complex, 51 S Ventu Park Rd, Newbury Park, CA 91320 - T: (805) 498-9441, Fax: (805) 498-6375, E-mail: stagecoach@toguide.com, Internet: www.toguide.com/stagecoach. Dir.: Sandra Hildebrandt, Cur.: Jackie Pizitz (Education), Miriam Sprankling (History), Cur.: Dr. Thomas Maxwell (Anthropology, Archaeology)
Local Museum - 1967 45908

Newburyport MA

Cushing House Museum, 98 High St, Newburyport, MA 01950 - T: (978) 462-2681, Fax: (978) 462-0134, E-mail: hson@greennet.net, Internet: www.newburyhist.com. Pres.: James Chanler, Audrey Ladd
Local Museum - 1877
Local history 45909

Custom House Maritime Museum, 25 Water St, Newburyport, MA 01950 - T: (978) 462-8681, Fax: (978) 462-8740, E-mail: nms@shore.net. Exec. Dir.: Cari Conway
Historical Museum - 1969
Local maritime hist, boat building 45910

Newcastle TX

Fort Belknap Museum, Farm to Market 61, Newcastle, TX 76372 - T: (940) 549-1856, Internet: www.forttours.com. Dir.: Dr. K.F. Neighbours
Military Museum - 1851
Military hist 45911

Newcastle WY

Anna Miller Museum, 401 Delaware, Newcastle, WY 82701 - T: (307) 746-4188, Fax: (307) 746-4629, E-mail: annamm@trib.com. Dir.: Bobbie Jo Tysdal
Local Museum - 1966
Local hist, Indian artifacts, natural hist, paleontology 45912

Newcomerstown OH

Temperance Tavern, 221 W Canal St, Newcomerstown, OH 43832 - T: (614) 498-7735. Dir.: Barbara Scott
Historical Museum / Local Museum / Historic Site - 1923 45913

USS Radford National Naval Museum, 238 W Canal St, Newcomerstown, OH 43832 - T: (740) 498-4446, Fax: (740) 498-8803, E-mail: vane@sota-oh.com, Internet: www.ussradford446.org. Pres.: Vane S. Scott
Special Museum / Military Museum - 2000
USS Radford DD/DDE 446 - Destroyer, WWII (Korea, Vietnam), 3-D Diorama of Rescue at Kula Gulf 45914

Newell SD

Newell Museum, 108 Third St, Newell, SD 57760 - T: (605) 456-1310, Fax: (605) 456-2587, E-mail: gvelder@myfavoritei.com, Internet: www.sdmuseums.org. Cur.: Linda Velder
Local Museum - 1983
Clothing, Native American artifacts and culture, fossils, antique toys and dolls, musical instruments 45915

Newfield ME

Willowbrook at Newfield, Main St, Newfield, ME 04056 - T: (207) 793-2784, E-mail: director@willowbrookmuseum.org, Internet: www.willowbrookmuseum.org. C.E.O.: D.F. King
Historical Museum - 1970
Regional history 45916

Newfield NJ

Matchbox Road Museum, 17 Pearl St, Newfield, NJ 08344 - T: (800) 976-7623, Fax: (856) 697-0762, Internet: www.mbxroad.com
Special Museum - 1992
27000 miniature Matchbox vehicles 45917

Newhall CA

William S. Hart Museum, National History Museum of Los Angeles County, 24151 San Fernando Rd, Newhall, CA 91321 - T: (661) 254-4584, Fax: (661) 254-6499, E-mail: jashley@nhm.org, Internet: www.hartmuseum.org. Dir.: Dr. Jane Pisano, Pres.: Bill Crowl
Local Museum / Historic Site - 1958
Paintings, sculpture, woodcarvings, Navajo blankets / rugs, furniture, clothing 45918

Newland NC

Avery County Museum, 1829 Schultz Circle, Newland, NC 28657 - T: (828) 733-7111, E-mail: museum@m-y.net. Head: Frank Hamlin
Local Museum / Folklore Museum - 1977 45919

Newport AR

Courthouse Museum, Jacksonport State Park, Newport, AR 72112 - T: (870) 523-2143, Fax: (870) 523-4620, E-mail: jacksonport@arkansas.com, Internet: www.arkansas.com. Dir.: Mark Ballard, Cur.: Donna Bentley
Historical Museum / Local Museum - 1965 45920

Newport OR

Oregon Coast History Center, 545 SW Ninth, Newport, OR 97365 - T: (541) 265-7509, Fax: (541) 265-3992, E-mail: coasthistory@newportnet.com, Internet: www.newportnet.com/coasthistory/home.htm. Cur.: Steve Wyatt
Historical Museum - 1948
Maritime objects, logging, coastal hist 45921

Newport RI

Artillery Company of Newport Military Museum, 23 Clarke St, Newport, RI 02840 - T: (401) 846-8488, Fax: (401) 846-3311, E-mail: info@newportartillery.org, Internet: www.newportartillery.org
Military Museum - 1959
Military hist 45922

Astors' Beechwood-Victorian Living History Museum, 580 Bellevue Av, Newport, RI 02840 - T: (401) 846-3772, Fax: (401) 849-6998, E-mail: linda@astors-beechwood.com, Internet: www.astors-beechwood.com. Exec. Dir.: Sheli Beck Silveria
Historical Museum - 1983 45923

Belcourt Castle, 657 Bellevue Av, Newport, RI 02840-4288 - T: (401) 849-1566, 846-0669, Fax: (401) 846-5345, E-mail: belcourt2001@aol.com, Internet: www.belcourtcastle.com. Exec. Dir.: Harle H. Tinney
Decorative Arts Museum - 1957
Romanesque, Gothic, Renaissance, Louis 14 and Louis 15 and classic revival style interiors, silks, embroideries, Oriental rugs, paintings, porcelains, ancient art 45924

International Tennis Hall of Fame Museum, 194 Bellevue Av, Newport, RI 02840 - T: (401) 849-3990, Fax: (401) 849-8780, E-mail: newport@tennisfame.com, Internet: www.tennisfame.org. Dir.: Ken Yellis
Special Museum - 1954
Sports 45925

The Museum of Newport History, 127 Thames St, Newport, RI 02840 - T: (401) 846-0813, 841-8770, Fax: (401) 846-1853, Internet: www.newporthistorical.org. Dir.: Daniel Snydacker, Cur.: M. Joan Youngken, Ronald Potvin
Historical Museum - 1854
Local hist 45926

Museum of Yachting, Fort Adams State Park, Newport, RI 02840 - T: (401) 847-1018, Fax: (401) 847-8320, E-mail: museum@moy.org, Internet: www.moy.org. Dir.: Patrick L. Muldoon
Special Museum / Science&Tech Museum - 1983
Yachting, sailing 45927

National Museum of American Illustration, Vernon Court, 492 Bellevue Av, Newport, RI 02840 - T: (401) 851-8949, Fax: (401) 851-8974, E-mail: art@americanillustration.org, Internet: www.americanillustration.org. Dir.: Judy Goffman Cutler
Fine Arts Museum - 1998
Works of illustrators 45928

Naval War College Museum, 686 Cushing Rd, Newport, RI 02841-1207 - T: (401) 841-4052, 841-1317, Fax: (401) 841-7689, E-mail: nicolosa@nwc.navy.mil, Internet: www.nwc.navy.mil/museum. Dir.: Anthony S. Nicolosi, Cur.: Robert Cembrola
Military Museum / Historical Museum - 1978
Naval hist 45929

Newport Art Museum, 76 Bellevue Av, Newport, RI 02840 - T: (401) 848-8200, Fax: (401) 848-8205, E-mail: info@newportartmuseum.com, Internet: www.newportartmuseum.com. Dir.: Christine Callahan
Fine Arts Museum - 1912
Drawings, paintings, sculpture, prints, photography 45930

Newport Mansions, 424 Bellevue Av, Newport, RI 02840 - T: (401) 847-1000, Fax: (401) 847-9477, E-mail: jpaduette@newportmansions.org, Internet: www.NewportMansions.org. Pres.: Armin Allen, C.E.O.: Trudy Coxe, Cur.: Paul F. Miller
Local Museum - 1945
Group of 9 mansions 45931

Redwood Library and Athenaeum, 50 Bellevue Av, Newport, RI 02840 - T: (401) 847-0292, Fax: (401) 841-5680, E-mail: redwood@edgenet.net, Internet: www.redwoodlibrary.org. C.E.O.: Cheryl V. Helms, Pres.: Stephen G.W. Walk
Fine Arts Museum - 1747
18th-19th c Anglo-American portraits 45932

Royal Arts Foundation, Belcourt Castle, 657 Bellevue Av, Newport, RI 02840-4280 - T: (401) 846-0669, Fax: (401) 846-5345, E-mail: kevint@belcourt.com, Internet: www.belcourtcastle.com. Dir.: Harle H. Tinney
Decorative Arts Museum / Local Museum - 1957
Historic house, paintings, sculpture, textiles, ceramics 45933

Thames Museum, 77 Long Wharf, Newport, RI 02840 - T: (401) 849-6966, Fax: (401) 849-7144, E-mail: carol@thamesmuseum.org, Internet: www.thamesmuseum.org. Pres.: Jane A. Holdsworth
Natural History Museum - 1948 45934

Newport Beach CA

Orange County Museum of Art, 850 San Clemente Dr, Newport Beach, CA 92660 - T: (949) 759-1122, Fax: (949) 759-5623, E-mail: info@ocma.net, Internet: www.ocma.net. Dir.: Elizabeth Armstrong, Cur.: Irene Hofmann, Sarah Uure
Fine Arts Museum - 1921 45935

Newport News VA

Golf Museum, 1500 Country Club Rd, Newport News, VA 23606 - T: (757) 595-3327, Fax: (757) 596-4807, Internet: www.golfmuseum1932.org
Special Museum - 1932
International golf hist, clubs, balls, tees 45936

The Mariners' Museum, 100 Museum Dr, Newport News, VA 23606 - T: (757) 596-2222, Fax: (757) 591-7311, E-mail: info@mariner.org, Internet: www.mariner.org. Pres.: John B. Hightower, Dir.: Claudia Pennington
Historical Museum / Science&Tech Museum - 1930
Maritime hist 45937

Newsome House Museum, 2803 Oak Av, Newport News, VA 23607 - T: (804) 247-2360, Fax: (804) 928-6754, Internet: www.sightsmag.com. Man.: Katrina M. Boston
Historical Museum - 1991 45938

Peninsula Fine Arts Center, 101 Museum Dr, Newport News, VA 23606 - T: (757) 596-8175, Fax: (757) 596-0807, E-mail: pfac@whro.net, Internet: www.pfac-va.org. Dir.: Lisa C. Swensson, Cur.: Diana Blanchard-Gross
Fine Arts Museum - 1962
Arts 45939

Virginia Living Museum, 524 J. Clyde Morris Blvd, Newport News, VA 23601 - T: (757) 595-1900, Fax: (757) 599-4897, E-mail: webmaster@valivingmuseum.org, Internet: www.valivingmuseum.org. Dir.: Gloria R. Lombardi, David C. Maness (Astronomy), George K. Mathews
Natural History Museum / Special Museum - 1964
Natural hist 45940

The Virginia War Museum, 9285 Warwick Blvd, Huntington Park, Newport News, VA 23607 - T: (757) 247-8523, Fax: (757) 247-8627, Internet: www.warmuseum.org. Cur.: William Barker
Military Museum - 1923
Military hist 45941

Newton IL

Newton Museum, 100 S Vanburen, Newton, IL 62448 - T: (618) 783-8141, 783-3860, Fax: (618) 783-8141, E-mail: newtonpl@pfbnewton.com, Internet: www.pfbnewton.com
Local Museum - 1928
Local history - library 45942

Newton KS

Harvey County Historical Museum, 203 N. Main, Newton, KS 67114 - T: (316) 283-2221, Fax: (316) 283-2221, E-mail: info@hchm.org, Internet: www.hchm.org. Dir.: Roger N. Wilson, Cur.: Jeannine Stults
Historical Museum - 1962
Local history, housed in a Carnegie library bldg 45943

Newton MA

The Jackson Homestead, 527 Washington St, Newton, MA 02158 - T: (617) 552-7238, Fax: (617) 552-7228, E-mail: dolson@ci.newton.ma.us, Internet: www.ci.newton.ma.us/jackson. Dir.: David Olson, Cur.: Susan Abele, Shelia M. Sibley
Historical Museum - 1950
Local history, Jackson Homestead 45944

Newton City Museum → The Jackson Homestead

Newton NC

Catawba County Museum of History, 1 Court Sq, Newton, NC 28658 - T: (828) 465-0383, Fax: (828) 465-9813, E-mail: ccha@twave.net, Internet: www.catabahistory.org. Dir.: Sidney Halma, Asst. Dir.: Steven Mount, Cur.: Alex Floyd
Historical Museum - 1949 45945

Newton NJ

Sussex County Historical Society Museum, 82 Main St, Newton, NJ 07860 - T: (973) 383-6010, Internet: www.sussexcountyhistory.org. Pres.: Robert R. Longcore
Historical Museum - 1904 45946

Newtown PA

Artmobile, Bucks County Community College, Newtown, PA 18940 - T: (215) 968-8432, Fax: (215) 504-8530, E-mail: orlandof@bucks.edu. Dir.: Fran Orlando
Fine Arts Museum / University Museum - 1975 45947

Hicks Art Center, c/o Bucks County Community College, 25 Swamp Rd, Newtown, PA 18940 - T: (215) 968-8425, Fax: (215) 504-8530
Public Gallery - 1970 45948

Newtown Historic Museum, Court St and Centre Av, Newtown, PA 18940 - T: (215) 968-4004, Fax: (215) 968-8925, E-mail: dcnhh@aol.com, Internet: www.newtown.pa.us/historic/nha.html. Cur.: Rick Booream
Historical Museum / Local Museum - 1965
Local history, early 1700s Court Inn 45949

Niagara Falls NY

Niagara Gorge Discovery Center, New York State Parks, Niagara Region, Robert Moses State Pkwy near Main St, Niagara Falls, NY 14303-0132, mail addr: Niagara State Parks, Western Dist, Niagara Region, Niagara Reservation State Park, POB 1132, Niagara Falls, NY 14303-0132 - T: (716) 278-1796, Fax: (716) 278-1747, Internet: www.nysparks.com
Natural History Museum - 1971
Marine invertebrates from middle Silurian and Devonian periods, minerals 45950

Schoellkopf Geological Museum, New York State Parks, Niagara Region, Robert Moses State Pkwy near Main St, Niagara Falls, NY 14303-0132 - T: (716) 278-1780, Fax: (716) 278-1744
Natural History Museum - 1971 45951

Niagara University NY

Castellani Art Museum, Niagara University, NY 14109 - T: (716) 286-8200, Fax: (716) 286-8289, E-mail: cam@niagara.edu, Internet: www.niagara.edu/~cam. Asst. Dir.: Dr. Knapp Olsen, Cur.: Eric Jackson-Forsberg (Collections), Kate Koperski (Folk Arts)
Fine Arts Museum / University Museum - 1973 45952

Niles IL

The Bradford Museum of Collector's Plates, 9333 Milwaukee Av, Niles, IL 60714 - T: (847) 966-2770, Fax: (847) 966-3121
Decorative Arts Museum - 1978
Porcelain, plates 45953

Niles MI

Fort Saint Joseph Museum, 508 E Main St, Niles, MI 49120 - T: (616) 683-4702, Fax: (616) 684-3930, E-mail: cbainbridge@qtm.net, Internet: www.ci.niles.mi.us. Dir.: Carol Bainbridge
Local Museum - 1932
Local history, Henry A. Chapin carriage house 45954

Niles OH

National McKinley Birthplace Memorial, 40 N Main St, Niles, OH 44446 - T: (330) 652-1704, Fax: (330) 652-5788, E-mail: mckinley@oplin.lib.oh.us, Internet: www.mckinley.lib.oh.us. Pres.: Leonard B. Holloway
Historic Site - 1911 45955

Ninety-Six SC

Ninety-Six National Historic Site, 1103 Hwy 248, Ninety-Six, SC 29666 - T: (864) 543-4068, Fax: (864) 543-2058, E-mail: nisiadm@nps.gov, Internet: www.NPS.gov/NISI. Cur.: Eric K. Williams
Local Museum / Open Air Museum - 1976
Local hist 45956

Noank CT

Noank Historical Society Museum, 108 Main Stt, Noank, CT 06340 - T: (860) 536-3021, E-mail: noankhist@snet.net. Cur.: Kenneth O. Hodgson
Local Museum / Historical Museum - 1966 45957

Nobleboro ME

Nobleboro Historical Society Museum, 198 Center St, Nobleboro, ME 04555. Cur.: George F. Dow
Local Museum - 1978
Agriculture, forestry, Indians, sailing vessels, industry 45958

Noblesville IN

Indiana Transportation Museum, 325 Cicero Rd, Noblesville, IN 46061-0083 - T: (317) 773-6000, 776-7881, Fax: (317) 773-5530, E-mail: itm@indy.net, Internet: www.itm.org. C.E.O.: David E. Witcox
Science&Tech Museum - 1960
Rail transportation and technology, 1930 railroad station from Hobbs 45959

Nogales AZ

Pimeria Alta Historical Society Museum, 136 N Grand Av, Nogales, AZ 85621 - T: (520) 287-4621, Fax: (520) 287-5201. Dir.: Patricia Berrones-Molina
Local Museum - 1948 45960

Nome AK

Carrie M. McLain Memorial Museum, 200 E Front St, Nome, AK 99762 - T: (907) 443-6630, Fax: (907) 443-7955, E-mail: museum@ci.nome.ak.us. Dir.: Laura Samuelson, Asst. Dir.: Bev Gelzer
Ethnology Museum / Fine Arts Museum - 1967
Local history, gold rush, Bering Strait Eskimo, aviation, ethnology, dolls, art from 1890-1998 45961

Norfolk CT

Norfolk Historical Museum, 13 Village Green, Norfolk, CT 06058 - T: (203) 542-5761. Pres.: Barry Webber
Local Museum / Historical Museum - 1960 45962

Norfolk VA

The Chrysler Museum of Art, 245 West Olney Rd, Norfolk, VA 23510 - T: (757) 664-6200, Fax: (757) 664-6201, E-mail: museum@chrysler.org, Internet: www.chrysler.org. Dir.: Dr. William Hennessey, Deputy Dir.: Catherine H. Jordan Wass, Cur.: Jefferson Harrison (European Art), Gary E. Baker (Glass), Brooks Johnson (Photography)
Fine Arts Museum - 1933
Art 45963

General Douglas MacArthur Memorial, MacArthur Square, Norfolk, VA 23510 - T: (757) 441-2965, Fax: (757) 441-5389, E-mail: macmem@norfolk.infi.net, Internet: sites.communitylink.org/mac. Dir.: William J. Davis, Cur.: Katherine A. Renfrew
Military Museum / Historical Museum - 1964
Military hist 45964

Hampton Roads Naval Museum, One Waterside Dr, Ste 248, Norfolk, VA 23510-1607 - T: (804) 444-8971, 322-2987, Fax: (804) 445-1867, E-mail: bapoulliot@nsn.cmar.navy.mil, Internet: www.hrnm.navy.mil. Dir.: Elizabeth A. Poulliot, Dennis J. Murphy, Cur.: Joseph M. Judge
Military Museum - 1979
Naval hist 45965

Hermitage Foundation Museum, 7637 N Shore Rd, Norfolk, VA 23505 - T: (757) 423-2052, Fax: (757) 423-1604. Dir.: Philip R. Morrison
Decorative Arts Museum - 1937
Woodcarvings, decorative arts, Chinese bronzes and ceramic tomb figures, lacquer ware, jades, Persian rugs, Spanish and English furniture, paintings, sculpture 45966

Lois E. Woods Museum, c/o Norfolk State University, 2401 Corfew Av, Norfolk, VA 23504 - T: (757) 823-2006, Fax: (757) 823-2005, Internet: www.nsu.edu/resources/woods/index.htm. Dir.: John S. Woods
Fine Arts Museum
African art coll, African-American art 45967

Moses Myers House, 331 Bank St, Norfolk, VA 23510 - T: (757) 664-6283, 664-6255, Fax: (757) 441-2329, E-mail: dbiller@chrysler.org, Internet: www.chrysler.org. Dir.: Dr. William Hennessey
Decorative Arts Museum / Local Museum - 1951
Historic house 45968

Nauticus, Hampton Roads Naval Museum, 1 Waterside Dr, Norfolk, VA 23510 - T: (757) 664-1000, Fax: (757) 623-1287, Internet: www.nauticus.org. Exec. Dir.: Richard C. Conti
Science&Tech Museum / Military Museum - 1994
Commerce and military, USS Wisconsin 45969

Norfolk Historical Society Museum, 810 Front St, Norfolk, VA 23510 - T: (757) 625-1720. C.E.O.: Amy Waters Yarsinske
Local Museum - 1965
Local hist 45970

Old Dominion University Gallery, Visual Arts Bldg, Rm 203, Norfolk, VA 23517 - T: (757) 683-6227, Fax: (757) 683-5923, E-mail: khuntoon@odu.edu, Internet: www.odu.edu/al/artsandletters/gallery/index.html. Dir.: Katherine Huntoon
Fine Arts Museum / University Museum - 1971 45971

Willoughby-Baylor House, 601 E Freemason St, Norfolk, VA 23510 - T: (757) 664-6283, 664-6255, E-mail: dbiller@chrysler.org, Internet: www.chrysler.org. Dir.: Dr. William Hennessey
Decorative Arts Museum / Local Museum - 1962
Historic house 45972

Norman OK

Firehouse Art Center, 444 S Flood, Norman, OK 73069 - T: (405) 329-4523, Fax: (405) 292-9763, E-mail: firehouse@telepath.com. Exec. Dir.: Nancy McClellan
Public Gallery - 1971 45973

Fred Jones Jr. Museum of Art, University of Oklahoma, 410 W Boyd St, Norman, OK 73019 - T: (405) 325-3272, Fax: (405) 325-7696, Internet: www.ou.edu/fjjma. Dir.: Eric M. Lee, Chief Cur.: Gail Kana Anderson, Cur.: Susan G. Baley (Education)
Fine Arts Museum / University Museum - 1936 45974

Norman Cleveland County Historical Museum, 508 N Peters, Norman, OK 73069 - T: (405) 321-0156. Dir.: Gail Cirillo
Historical Museum - 1973 45975

Sam Noble Oklahoma Museum of Natural History, University of Oklahoma, 2401 Chautauqua, Norman, OK 73072-7029 - T: (405) 325-8978, Fax: (405) 325-7699, E-mail: smomnh@ou.edu, Internet: www.snomnh.ou.edu. Cur.: Dr. Michael A. Mares (Mammals), Dr. R.L. Cifelli (Vertebrate Paleontology), Dr. L.J. Vitt (Reptiles), Dr. J.P. Caldwell (Amphibians), Dr. D. Wyckoff (Archeology), Dr. S. Westrop (Invertebrate Paleontology), Dr. B. Matthews, Dr. F. Marsh-Matthews (Ichthyology), Dr. J.K. Braun, Dr. N.J. Czaplewski
University Museum / Natural History Museum - 1899 45976

Norris TN

Museum of Appalachia, Hwy 61, Norris, TN 37828 - T: (865) 494-7680, Fax: (865) 494-8957, E-mail: musofapp@icx.net, Internet: www.museumofappalachia.com. Dir.: John Rice Irwin, Elaine Irwin Meyer
Local Museum / Folklore Museum - 1967
Local hist, folk art 45977

North Adams MA

Mass Moca, 87 Marshall St, North Adams, MA 01247 - T: (413) 664-4481, Fax: (413) 663-8548, E-mail: info@massmoca.org, Internet: www.massmoca.org. C.E.O.: Joseph Thompson
Fine Arts Museum - 1988
Installations of sculpture and paintings 45978

North Andover MA

North Andover Historical Museum, 153 Academy Rd, North Andover, MA 01845 - T: (978) 686-4035, Fax: (978) 686-6616, E-mail: nahistory@juno.com, Internet: www.essexheritage.org/north_andover_hist_soc.htm. Dir.: Carol Majahad
Local Museum - 1913
Local history 45979

Stevens-Coolidge Place, 137 Andover St, North Andover, MA 01845 - T: (978) 682-3580
Decorative Arts Museum - 1962
Chinese porcelain, decorative arts 45980

North Bend OR

Coos County Historical Society Museum, 1220 Sherman, North Bend, OR 97459 - T: (541) 756-6320, Fax: (541) 756-6320, E-mail: museum@ucii.net, Internet: www.coohistory.org. Pres.: Reg Pullen, Dir.: Ann Koppy
Local Museum / Historical Museum - 1891 45981

North Bend WA

Snoqualmie Valley Historical Museum, 320 Bendigo Blvd S, North Bend, WA 98045 - T: (425) 888-3200, Fax: (425) 888-3200, Internet: www.snoqualmie-valleymuseum.org
Local Museum - 1960
Local pioneer artifacts, local Indian hist 45982

North Bennington VT

The Park-McCullough House, Corner of Park & West Sts, North Bennington, VT 05257 - T: (802) 442-5441, Fax: (802) 442-5442, E-mail: thehouse@sover.net, Internet: www.parkmccullough.org. Dir.: Jane Nicholls
Local Museum - 1968
Historic house 45983

North Blenheim NY

Lansing Manor House Museum, NY State Rte 30, North Blenheim, NY 12131 - T: (518) 827-6121, Fax: (607) 588-9466, E-mail: steve.ramsey@nypa.gov, Internet: www.nypa.gov/html/vcblenhe.html. Dir.: Steve Ramsey, Asst. Cur.: Margaret Bailey
Historical Museum - 1977 45984

North Brunswick NJ

New Jersey Museum of Agriculture, College Farm Rd and Rte 1, North Brunswick, NJ 08902 - T: (732) 249-2077, Fax: (732) 247-1035, E-mail: info@agriculturemuseum.org, Internet: www.agriculturemuseum.org. Exec. Dir.: Cynthia A. Goldsmith, Cur.: Coles Roberts, Cyndy Eckhardt, Andrew Jacobson
Agriculture Museum - 1984 45985

North Canton OH

Hoover Historical Center, 1875 Easton St NW, North Canton, OH 44720-3331 - T: (330) 499-0287, 499-9200 ext 3041, Fax: (330) 494-4725, E-mail: ahaines@hoover.com, Internet: www.hoover.com. Dir.: Jackie Love
Science&Tech Museum - 1978
Company history, Hoover family home, evolution of vacuum cleaner, Hoover products for WWII 45986

North Chicago IL

Feet First: The Scholl Story, c/o Finch University, 3333 Green Bay Rd, North Chicago, IL 60064 - T: (312) 280-2904, (847) 578-8417, Fax: (312) 280-2997, Internet: www.finchcms.edu. C.E.O.: Terrence Albright
Historical Museum - 1993
Podiatry 45987

North Conway NH

Conway Scenic Railroad, 38 Norcross Circle, North Conway, NH 03860 - T: (603) 356-5251, Fax: (603) 356-7606, E-mail: info@conwayscenic.com, Internet: www.conwayscenic.com. Pres.: Russell G. Seybold
Science&Tech Museum - 1974
Railroad, wood frame railroad station 45988

Mount Washington Museum, 2936 White Mountain Hwy, North Conway, NH 03860 - T: (603) 356-2137, Fax: (603) 356-0307, E-mail: wdc@mountwashington.org, Internet: www.mountwashington.org. Dir.: Matthew White
Natural History Museum - 1969 45989

Weather Dicovery Center, 2936 White Mountain Hwy, North Conway, NH 03860 - T: (603) 356-2137, Fax: (603) 356-3070, E-mail: wdc@mountwashington.org, Internet: www.mountwashington.org. Dir.: Matthew White
Science&Tech Museum - 2000
Meterology, science, local history 45990

North Dartmouth MA

University Art Gallery, University of Massachusetts-Dartmouth, North Dartmouth, MA 02747 - T: (508) 999-8555, Fax: (508) 999-9279, E-mail: lantonsen@umassd.edu. Dir.: Lasse B. Antonsen
University Museum / Fine Arts Museum - 1987 45991

North East PA

Lake Shore Railway Museum, 31 Wall St, North East, PA 16428-0571 - T: (814) 825-2724. Pres.: Charles W. Farrington
Science&Tech Museum - 1956
Railway 45992

North Easton MA

The Children's Museum in Easton, Sullivan Av, North Easton, MA 02356 - T: (508) 230-3789, Fax: (508) 230-7130, E-mail: ppeterson7@aol.com, Internet: www.childrensmuseumeaston.org. Dir.: Paula Peterson
Historical Museum - 1988
Fire station in town's historical district 45993

North Freedom WI

Mid-Continent Railway Museum, E 8948 Diamond Hill Rd, North Freedom, WI 53951-0055 - T: (608) 522-4261, Fax: (608) 522-4490, E-mail: midcon@baraboo.com, Internet: www.mcrwy.com. Cur.: Donald W. Ginter
Science&Tech Museum - 1959
Railway 45994

North Haven CT

North Haven Historical Society Museum, 27 Broadway, North Haven, CT 06473 - T: (203) 239-7722, Internet: www.northhavenhistoricalsociety.org. Cur.: Barbara Pearsall, Gloria Furnival
Local Museum / Historical Museum - 1957 45995

North Miami FL

Holocaust Documentation and Education Center, 3000 NE 151th St and Biscayne Blvd, North Miami, FL 33181 - T: (305) 919-5690, Fax: (305) 919-5691, E-mail: xholocau@fiu.edu, Internet: holocaust.fiu.edu. Pres.: Harry A. Levy
Historical Museum - 1979
Holocaust oral histories, artifacts, memorabilia 45996

Museum of Contemporary Art, 770 NE 125th St, North Miami, FL 33161 - T: (305) 893-6211, Fax: (305) 891-1472, E-mail: info@mocanomi.org, Internet: www.mocanomi.org. Dir.: Bonnie Clearwater
Fine Arts Museum - 1981
Visual contemporary art 45997

North Miami Beach FL

Ancient Spanish Monastery of Saint Bernard de Clairvaux Cloisters, 16711 W Dixie Hwy, North Miami Beach, FL 33160 - T: (305) 945-1462, Fax: (305) 945-6986, E-mail: monastery@earthlink.net, Internet: www.spanishmonastery.com. Dir.: Dr. Ronald Fox
Fine Arts Museum - 1952
Religious art, reconstruction of monastery, built in 1141 in Segovia Spain, with original stones brought to United States by William Randolph Hearst 45998

North Newton KS

Kauffman Museum, Bethel College, 2801 N Main, North Newton, KS 67117-0531 - T: (316) 283-1612, Fax: (316) 283-2107, E-mail: kauffman@bethelks.edu, Internet: www.bethelks.edu/kauffman.html. Dir.: Rachel K. Pannabecker, Cur.: Charles Regier
University Museum / Local Museum / Natural History Museum - 1941
Cultural and natural history 45999

Mennonite Library and Archives Museum, Bethel College, 300 E 27th St, North Newton, KS 67117 - T: (316) 283-2500, 284-5304, Fax: (316) 284-5286, E-mail: mla@bethelks.edu, Internet: www.bethelks.edu/services/mla. Sc. Staff: John D. Thiesen (Archivist), Barbara A. Thiesen (Library)
Religious Arts Museum - 1938
Religion 46000

North Oxford MA

Clara Barton Birthplace, 68 Clara Barton Rd, North Oxford, MA 01537 - T: (508) 987-5375, Fax: (508) 987-2002. Dir.: Shelley Yeager
Historical Museum - 1921
Historic house 46001

North Plainfield NJ

North Plainfield Exempt Firemen's Museum, 300 Somerset St, North Plainfield, NJ 07060 - T: (908) 757-5720, Fax: (908) 757-7383
Historical Museum - 1904
Antique fire apparatus, helmets 46002

North Platte NE

Buffalo Bill Ranch, 2921 Scouts Rest Ranch Rd, North Platte, NE 69101-8444 - T: (308) 535-8035, Fax: (308) 535-8066, E-mail: bbranch@ns.nque.com, Internet: www.ngpc.state.ne.us
Historical Museum - 1964 46003

Lincoln County Historical Society Museum, 2403 N Buffalo Bill Av, North Platte, NE 68101 - T: (308) 534-5640
Local Museum - 1974
County hist 46004

North Richland Hills TX

Imagisphere Children's Museum, 7624 Grapevine Hwy, North Richland Hills, TX 76180-8314 - T: (817) 589-9000, Fax: (817) 284-7122, E-mail: lauralee@imagisphere.org, Internet: www.imagisphere.org. C.E.O.: Laura Lee Utz
Science&Tech Museum / Natural History Museum - 1993
Science, art, math and music based exhibits 46005

North Salem NH

America's Stonehenge, 105 Haverhill Rd, North Salem, NH 03073, mail addr: POB 84, North Salem, NH 03073 - T: (603) 893-8300, Fax: (603) 893-5889, E-mail: amstonehenge@worldnet.att.net, Internet: www.stonehengeusa.com. C.E.O. & Pres.: Robert E. Stone
Archaeological Museum - 1958
Archaeology on Mystery Hill, site of 4,000 year old archaeo-astronomical site 46006

North Salem NY

Hammond Museum, Deveau Rd off Rte 124, North Salem, NY 10560 - T: (914) 669-5033, Fax: (914) 669-8221, E-mail: gardenprogram@yahoo.com, Internet: www.hammondmuseum.org. Dir.: Abigail Free
Fine Arts Museum / Decorative Arts Museum / Special Museum - 1957 46007

North Tonawanda NY

Herschell Carrousel Factory Museum, 180 Thompson St, North Tonawanda, NY 14120 - T: (716) 693-1885, Fax: (716) 743-9018, E-mail: hcfm@carrouselmuseum.org, Internet: www.carrouselmuseum.org. Dir.: Elizabeth M. Brick
Science&Tech Museum - 1983
Company hist 46008

North Troy VT

Missisquoi Valley Historical Society Museum, Main St, North Troy, VT 05859 - T: (802) 988-2397, E-mail: missisco@hotmail.com. Pres.: Nancy L. Allen
Local Museum - 1976
Local hist 46009

North Wildwood NJ

Hereford Inlet Lighthouse, 11 N Central Av, North Wildwood, NJ 08260 - T: (609) 522-4520, Fax: (609) 523-8590, Internet: www.herefordlighthause.org. Head: Aldo Palombo
Historical Museum - 1982
Maritime hist 46010

North Wilkesboro NC

Wilkes Art Gallery, 800 Elizabeth St, North Wilkesboro, NC 28659 - T: (336) 667-2841, Fax: (336) 667-9564, E-mail: wilkesartgal@wilkes.net, Internet: www.northwilkesboro.com/local. Dir.: Kara Milton-Elmore
Fine Arts Museum / Public Gallery - 1962 46011

North Woburn MA

Rumford Historical Museum, 90 Elm St, North Woburn, MA 01801 - T: (617) 933-0781. Pres.: Leonard Harmon
Historical Museum - 1877
Count Rumford's birthplace 46012

Northampton MA

Calvin Coolidge Memorial Room of the Forbes Library, 20 West St, Northampton, MA 01060 - T: (413) 587-1014, Fax: (413) 587-1015, E-mail: iknox@hge.net, Internet: www.forbeslibrary.org. Cur.: Lu Knox
Historical Museum / Library with Exhibitions - 1920
Presidential life and time 46013

Historic Northampton, 46 Bridge St, Northampton, MA 01060 - T: (413) 584-6011, Fax: (413) 584-7956, E-mail: mailbox@historic-northampton.org, Internet: www.historic-northampton.org. Dir.: Kerry W. Buckley
Historical Museum - 1905
Local history, Parsons house, Isaac Damon house, Shepherd house, Shepherd barn 46014

Smith College Museum of Art, Elm St at Bedford Tce, Northampton, MA 01063 - T: (413) 585-2760, 585-2770, Fax: (413) 585-2782, E-mail: artmuseum@smith.edu, Internet: www.smith.edu/artmuseum. Dir.: Suzannah Fabing, Cur.: Linda Muehlig (Paintings, Sculpture), Nancy Rich (Education), Aprile Gallant (Prints, Drawings, Photographs)
Fine Arts Museum / University Museum - 1920
Paintings, sculptures, drawings, prints, photographs, decorative arts 46015

Words and Pictures Museum, 140 Main St, Northampton, MA 01060 - T: (413) 586-8545, Fax: (413) 586-9855, E-mail: comics@wordsandpictures.org, Internet: www.wordsandpictures.org. Cur.: J. Fiona Russell
Fine Arts Museum - 1991 46016

Northborough MA

Northborough Historical Museum, 50 Main St, Northborough, MA 01532 - T: (508) 393-6298, Internet: www.northboroughhistsoc.org. Pres.: Paul Derosier, Cur.: Ellen Racine
Local Museum - 1906
General museum, housed in Baptist Church 46017

Northeast Harbor ME

Great Harbor Maritime Museum, 125 Main St, Northeast Harbor, ME 04662 - T: (207) 276-5262, Fax: (207) 276-5262, E-mail: ghmmuse@acadia.net
Historical Museum - 1982
Regional boats, harbors, boat builders, arts 46018

Northfield MN

Carleton College Art Gallery, 1 N College St, Northfield, MN 55057 - T: (507) 646-4342, Fax: (507) 646-7042, E-mail: lbradley@carleton.edu, Internet: www.carleton.edu/ARTS/gallery/ART-Gallery_Page.html. Dir.: Laurel Bradley
Fine Arts Museum
American paintings, photography, prints, woodcuts, Asian art, Greek and Roman antiquities 46019

Exhibition of the Norwegian-American Historical Association, 1510 Saint Olaf Av, Northfield, MN 55057-1097 - T: (507) 646-3221, Fax: (507) 646-3734, E-mail: naha@stolaf.edu, Internet: www.naha.stolaf.edu. Dir.: Kim Holland, Cur.: Forrest Brown
Historical Museum - 1925 46020

Northfield Historical Society Museum, 408 Division St, Northfield, MN 55057 - T: (507) 645-9268, E-mail: nhsmuseum@microassist.com, Internet: www.northfieldhistory.org. Dir.: Bruce Colwell
Historical Museum / Local Museum - 1975 46021

Norwegian-American Historical Museum, Saint Olaf College, 1510 Saint Olaf Av, Northfield, MN 55057-1097 - T: (507) 646-3221, Fax: (507) 646-3734, E-mail: naha@stolaf.edu, Internet: www.naha.stolaf.edu. Cur.: Forrest Brown
Historical Museum / Ethnology Museum - 1925
Norwegian-American hist 46022

Steensland Art Museum, Saint Olaf College, 1520 Saint Olaf Av, Northfield, MN 55057 - T: (507) 646-3556, Fax: (507) 646-3776, E-mail: ewaldj@stolaf.edu, Internet: www.stolaf.edu/other/steensland. Dir.: Jill Ewald
Fine Arts Museum - 1976
Prints and paintings, graphics, textiles, religious art, woodcuts, oriental and renaissance art 46023

Northfield OH

Palmer House, 9390 Olde Eight Rd, Northfield, OH 44067 - T: (216) 237-1813, Fax: (330) 467-8322, E-mail: hson@worldnet.att.net, Internet: www.home.att.net/~hson/. C.E.O.: Arch Milani
Local Museum / Historical Museum - 1956 46024

Northfield VT

Norwich University Museum, White Chapel, Norwich University, Northfield, VT 05663 - T: (802) 485-2000, 485-2360, Fax: (802) 485-2580, E-mail: GLORD@Norwich.edu. Cur.: Gary T. Lord
University Museum / Historical Museum - 1819
History 46025

Northport AL

Kentuck Museum and Art Center, 503 Main Av, Northport, AL 35476-4483 - T: (205) 758-1257, Fax: (205) 7581258, E-mail: kentuck@dbtech.net, Internet: www.dbtech.net/kentuck. Dir.: Miah Michaelsen
Local Museum / Fine Arts Museum - 1971 46026

Northport NY

Northport Historical Society Museum, 215 Main St, Northport, NY 11768 - T: (516) 757-9859, Fax: (516) 757-9398, E-mail: info@northporthistorical.org, Internet: www.northporthistorical.org. Dir.: Linda Furey, Cur.: George Wallace
Historical Museum - 1962 46027

Northridge CA

Art Galleries, California State University Northridge, 18111 Nordhoff St, Northridge, CA 91330-8299 - T: (818) 677-2226, 677-2156, Fax: (818) 677-5910, E-mail: art.gallery@csun.edu, Internet: www.csun.edu/artgalleries. Dir.: Louise Lewis
Fine Arts Museum / University Museum - 1972 46028

Northumberland PA

Joseph Priestley House, 472 Priestley Av, Northumberland, PA 17857 - T: (570) 473-9474, Fax: (570) 473-7901, E-mail: mbashore@state.pa.us, Internet: www.phmc.state.pa.us. Pres.: William Vandenheuvel
Historical Museum - 1960
Historic house 46029

Northville MI

Mill Race Historical Village, Griswold St, Northville, MI 48167 - T: (248) 348-1845, Fax: (248) 348-0056
Local Museum - 1972
Victorian furniture, clothing, local hist 46030

Norton MA

Watson Gallery, Wheaton College, E Main St, Norton, MA 02766 - T: (508) 286-3578, Fax: (508) 286-3565, E-mail: amurray@wheatonma.edu, Internet: www.wheatonma.edu/academic/watson/home.html. Dir.: Ann H. Murray
Fine Arts Museum / University Museum - 1960
American and European paintings, prints and drawings 46031

Norwalk CT

Lockwood-Mathews Mansion Museum, 295 West Av, Norwalk, CT 06850 - T: (203) 838-9799, Fax: (203) 838-1434, E-mail: director@lockwoodmathews.org, Internet: www.lockwoodmathews.org. Dir.: Zachary Studenroth
Local Museum / Music Museum - 1966 46032

Musical Box Society International Museum, Lockwood Mathews Mansion, Norwalk, CT 06850 - T: (203) 838-1434, Fax: (310) 377-5240, E-mail: biesboech@aol.com, Internet: www.mbsi.org
Music Museum - 1949 46033

Norwalk OH

Firelands Historical Society Museum, 4 Case Av, Norwalk, OH 44857 - T: (419) 668-6038. Cur.: Marilou Creary
Historical Museum - 1857 46034

Norwich CT

Faith Trumbull Chapter Museum, 42 Rockwell St, Norwich, CT 06360 - T: (860) 887-8737. Cur.: Debra Graskoski
Local Museum / Historical Museum - 1893
American revolution, local history 46035

Leffingwell House Museum, 348 Washington St, Norwich, CT 06360 - T: (860) 889-9440, Fax: (860) 887-4551, Internet: www.visitnewengland.com. Pres.: Annetta Cannon
Decorative Arts Museum - 1901
Norwich silver, antique dolls, Indian artifacts 46036

Slater Memorial Museum, 108 Crescent St, Norwich, CT 06360 - T: (860) 887-2506, 885-0379, Fax: (860) 889-6196, E-mail: tabakoffs@norwichfreeacademy.com, Internet: www.norwichfreeacademy.com. Dir.: Sheila Tabakoff
Fine Arts Museum - 1888
American paintings, graphics, schulpture, Oriental art, costumes, marine, casts, decorative arts, textiles, guns 46037

Norwich NY

Chenango County Historical Society Museum, 45 Rexford St, Norwich, NY 13815 - T: (607) 334-9227, Fax: (607) 334-9227, Internet: www.chenangocounty.org/chencohistso. Pres.: Dale C. Storms
Historical Museum - 1938 46038

Northeast Classic Car Museum, 24 Rexford St, Norwich, NY 13815 - T: (607) 334-2886, Fax: (607) 336-6745, E-mail: kay@classiccarmuseum.org, Internet: www.classiccarmuseum.org. Dir.: Kay Wells Zaia
Science&Tech Museum
Vintage and luxury cars 46039

Norwich OH

National Road/Zane Grey Museum, 8850 E Pike, Norwich, OH 43767 - T: (740) 872-3143, Fax: (740) 872-3510, E-mail: zanegrey@globalco.net, Internet: www.ohiohistory.org. Dir.: Alan King
Science&Tech Museum - 1973 46040

Norwich VT

Montshire Museum of Science, Montshire Rd, Norwich, VT 05055 - T: (802) 649-2200, Fax: (802) 649-3637, E-mail: montshire@montshire.net, Internet: www.montshire.org. Dir.: David Goudy, Assoc. Dir.: Richard Stucker, Cur.: Joan Waltermire
Natural History Museum - 1975 46041

Norwich Historical Society Museum, 37 Church St, Norwich, VT 05055 - T: (802) 649-0124, E-mail: NHS@tpk.net. Pres.: William M. Aldrich
Local Museum - 1951
Local hist 46042

Norwood NY

Norwood Historical Association Museum, POB 163, Norwood, NY 13668-0163. Dir.: Gerald LaComb
Historical Museum - 1968 46043

Notre Dame IN

The Snite Museum of Art, University of Notre Dame, M. Krause Circle, Notre Dame, IN 46556-0368 - T: (219) 631-5466, Fax: (219) 631-8501, E-mail: charles.r.loving.l@nd.edu, Internet: www.nd.edu/~sniteart. Dir.: Charles R. Loving, Cur.: Stephen B. Spiro (Western Arts), Mary Frisk Coffman, Douglas E. Bradley (Ethnographic Arts), Steve Moriarty (Photography), Diana Matthias, Joanne Mack (Native American Art)
Fine Arts Museum / University Museum - 1842
Ethnographic art, photography, design, native American art 46044

Novato CA

Marin Museum of the American Indian, 2200 Novato Blvd, Novato, CA 94947 - T: (415) 897-4064, Fax: (415) 892-7804. Dir.: Shirley Schaufel
Ethnology Museum / Archaeological Museum - 1967
Archaeology, ethnography from Alaska to Peru, native Americans 46045

Novato History Museum, 815 De Long Av, Novato, CA 94945 - T: (415) 897-4320, Fax: (415) 892-9136, E-mail: novatohistory@hotmail.com, Internet: www.ci.novato.com/prcs/museum. Dir.: Greta Brunschwyler
Local Museum - 1976
Local hist - archive 46046

Nowata OK

Nowata County Historical Society Museum, 121 S Pine St, Nowata, OK 74048 - T: (918) 273-1191. Pres.: Raymond Cline
Historical Museum - 1969 46047

Nyack NY

Edward Hopper House, 82 N Broadway, Nyack, NY 10960 - T: (914) 358-0774, E-mail: edwardhopper.house@verizon.net, Internet: www.edwardhopper-houseartcenter.org
Fine Arts Museum - 1971
American Realist painter Edward Hopper 46048

Oak Bluffs MA

Firehouse Gallery, 88 Dukes County Av, Oak Bluffs, MA 02557 - T: (508) 693-9025, E-mail: dreyerc@earthlink.net. Pres.: Chris Dreyer
Public Gallery - 1991 46049

Oak Brook IL

Graue Mill and Museum, York and Spring Rds, Oak Brook, IL 60522-4533 - T: (630) 655-2090, Fax: (630) 920-9721, E-mail: administrator@grauemill.org, Internet: www.grauemill.org. C.E.O.: Warren N. Barr
Local Museum / Science&Tech Museum - 1950
Local history, housed in 1852 restored waterwheel gristmill 46050

Oak Creek WI

Oak Creek Pioneer Village, S 15th Av & E. Forest Hill Av, Oak Creek, WI 53154 - T: (414) 761-2572, Internet: members.aol.com/larryr3670/oc_histr/ochsocie.htm. Pres.: Elroy Honadel, Cur.: Marge Thomas
Local Museum - 1964
Local hist 46051

Oak Park IL

Frank Lloyd Wright Home and Studio, 951 Chicago Av, Oak Park, IL 60302 - T: (708) 848-1976, Fax: (708) 848-1248, E-mail: mercuri@wrightplus.org, Internet: www.wrightplus.org. Pres.: Joan B. Mercuri
Historical Museum - 1974
Residence and Studio of Frank Lloyd Wright 46052

Hemingway Museum, 200 N Oak Park Av, Oak Park, IL 60302 - T: (708) 386-4363, Fax: (708) 386-8506, E-mail: ehfop@theramp.net. CEO: Scott Schwar
Special Museum - 1990
Birthplace and personal artifacts of Ernest Hemingway 46053

Historical Society of Oak Park and River Forest, 217 S Home Av, Oak Park, IL 60302-3101 - T: (708) 848-6755, Fax: (708) 848-0246, E-mail: flipo@enteract.com, Internet: www.oprf.com/ophistory/. Dir.: Frank Lipo, Pres.: Jan Dressel
Public Gallery / Local Museum - 1968
Regional history, Prairie style mansion, photography 46054

Oak Ridge TN

American Museum of Science and Energy, 300 S Tulane Av, Oak Ridge, TN 37830 - T: (865) 576-3200, Fax: (865) 576-6024, E-mail: jcomish@amse.org, Internet: www.amse.org. Dir.: James R. Comish
Science&Tech Museum - 1949
Science, technology, hist of the Manhattan Project 46055

Children's Museum of Oak Ridge, 461 W Outer Dr, Oak Ridge, TN 37830 - T: (423) 482-1074, Fax: (423) 481-4889, Internet: www.newsite.com/cmor. Dir.: Selma Shapiro
Special Museum - 1973 46056

Oak Ridge Art Center, 201 Badger Av, Oak Ridge, TN 37831-3305 - T: (423) 482-1441, Fax: (423) 482-1441. Dir.: Leah Marcum-Estes
Fine Arts Museum - 1952
Mary & Alden coll, contemporary regional art 46057

Oakdale CA

Oakdale Museum, 212 W F St, Oakdale, CA 95361 - T: (209) 847-9229, 847-5822, E-mail: museum@chitons.com, Internet: oakdalemuseum.homestead.com/museum.html. Dir.: Glenn Burghardt
Local Museum - 1985
Local history 46058

Oakland CA

African-American Museum at Oakland, 659 14th St, Oakland, CA 94612 - T: (510) 637-0200, Fax: (510) 637-0204, E-mail: aamlo@juno.com, Internet: www.oaklandlibrary.org. Cur.: Rick Moss
Historical Museum - 1965 46059

Asian Resource Gallery, 310 Eighth St, Oakland, CA 94607 - T: (510) 287-5353, Fax: (510) 763-4143
Fine Arts Museum - 1983 46060

Camron-Stanford House, 1418 Lakeside Dr, Oakland, CA 94612 - T: (510) 444-1876, Fax: (510) 874-7803. Cur.: Wayne Mathes
Fine Arts Museum / Historical Museum - 1971 46061

CCAC Institute, California College of Arts and Crafts, 5212 Broadway, Oakland, CA 94618 - T: (510) 594-3650, Fax: (510) 594-3761, E-mail: institute@ccac.art.edu, Internet: www.ccac-art.edu/institute. Dir.: Ralph Rugoff
Fine Arts Museum - 1907 46062

Creative Growth Art Center, 355 24th St, Oakland, CA 94612 - T: (510) 836-2340, Fax: (510) 836-0769, E-mail: creativg@dnai.com, Internet: www.creativegrowth.org. Dir.: Tom DiMaria
Public Gallery - 1974 46063

Merritt Museum of Anthropology, 12500 Campus Dr, Oakland, CA 94619 - T: (510) 436-2607, 531-4911, Fax: (415) 922-0905, E-mail: 104347.13@compuserve.com. Dir.: Dr. Barbara Joans, Cur.: Leslie Fleming
Ethnology Museum - 1973 46064

Mills College Art Museum, 5000 MacArthur Blvd, Oakland, CA 94613 - T: (510) 430-2164, Fax: (510) 430-3168, E-mail: mcam@mills.edu, Internet: www.mills.edu/mcam. Dir.: Dr. Katherine B. Crum, Stephan Jost
Fine Arts Museum / University Museum - 1925
Asian textiles, Japanese ceramics, old master prints, 19th-20th c prints drawings 46065

Museum of Children's Art, 538 Ninth St, Oakland, CA 94607 - T: (510) 465-8770, Fax: (510) 465-0772, E-mail: hello@mocha.org, Internet: www.mocha.org. Dir.: Mary Marx, Assoc. Dir.: Karen Ransom Lehman
Fine Arts Museum 46066

Oakland Museum of California, 1000 Oak St, Oakland, CA 94607 - T: (510) 238-2200, Fax: (510) 238-2258, E-mail: dmpower@museumca.org, Internet: www.museumca.org. Dir.: Dennis M. Power, Chief Cur.: Philip Linhares (Art), Carey Caldwell (History), Tom Steller (Natural Sciences), Barbara Henry (Education), Cur.: Harvey Jones, Karen Tsujimoto (Art), Drew Johnson (Art Photography), Inez Brooks-Myers (History, Costumes and Textiles), Christopher Richard (Natural Sciences)
Fine Arts Museum / Historical Museum / Library with Exhibitions / Natural History Museum - 1969 46067

Pardee Home Museum, 672 11th St, Oakland, CA 94607 - T: (510) 444-2187, Fax: (510) 444-7120, Internet: www.pardeehome.org. Dir.: David Nicolai
Historical Museum / Historic Site - 1982
Former residence of Governor George Pardee, furniture, ethnography - archive 46068

Pro Arts Gallery, 461 Ninth St, Oakland, CA 94607 - T: (510) 763-4361, Fax: (510) 763-9425, E-mail: proarts@lmi.net, Internet: www.proartsgallery.org. Dir.: Betty Kano
Fine Arts Museum - 1974 46069

Steven H. Oliver Art Center → CCAC Institute

Western Aerospace Museum, 8260 Boeing St, Oakland, CA 94614 - T: (510) 638-7100, Fax: (510) 638-6530, Internet: www.cyberair.com. Dir.: Ben Hance
Science&Tech Museum - 1980
Aerospace 46070

Oakland IA

Nishna Heritage Museum, 123 Main St, Oakland, IA 51560 - T: (712) 482-6802, 482-3075. Dir.: Cena Rattenborg, Cur.: Lloyd Davis
Fine Arts Museum / Local Museum - 1975
Heritage, local history 46071

Oakland MD

Garrett County Historical Museum, 107 S 2nd St, Oakland, MD 21550 - T: (301) 334-3226. Pres.: Robert Boal, Cur.: Charlotte Friend
Local Museum - 1969
Local history 46072

Oakley ID

Oakley Pioneer Museum, 108 W Main, Oakley, ID 83346 - T: (208) 862-3626. Dir.: Becky Clark
Local Museum / Museum of Classical Antiquities - 1967
History, antiques 46073

Oakley KS

Fick Fossil and History Museum, 700 W Third St, Oakley, KS 67748 - T: (785) 672-4839, Fax: (785) 672-3497, E-mail: mullencm@ruraltel.net, Internet: www.oakley-kansas.com/fick. Dir.: Cindy Mullen, Cur.: Lucille Jennings
Historical Museum / Natural History Museum - 1972
Geology, paleontology, history 46074

Oberlin KS

Last Indian Raid Museum, 258 S Penn Av, Oberlin, KS 67749 - T: (913) 475-2712, E-mail: decaturmuseum@nwkansas.com. Cur.: Fonda Farr
Historic Site / Historical Museum - 1958
History, nr the site of 1878 last Indian raid on Kansas soil 46075

Oberlin OH

Allen Memorial Art Museum, Oberlin College, 87 N Main St, Oberlin, OH 44074 - T: (440) 775-8665, Fax: (440) 775-6841, E-mail: leslie.miller@oberlin.edu, Internet: www.oberlin.edu/allenart. Dir.: Dr. Sharon F. Patton, Cur.: Charles Mason (Asian Art), Stephen Borys (Western Art), Sara Hallberg (Education)
University Museum / Fine Arts Museum - 1917 46076

Oberlin Historical and Improvement Organization Museum, 73 1/2 S Professor St, Oberlin, OH 44074 - T: (440) 774-1700, Fax: (440) 774-8061, E-mail: history@oberlinheritage.org, Internet: www.oberlinheritage.org. C.E.O.: Patricia Murphy
Local Museum / Historical Museum - 1964 46077

Ocala FL

Appleton Museum of Art, 4333 NE Silver Springs Blvd, Ocala, FL 34470-5000 - T: (352) 236-7100 ext 0, Fax: (352) 236-2621, E-mail: stalaric@appleton.fsu.edu, Internet: www.appletonmuseum.org. Dir.: Jeffrey J. Spalding
Fine Arts Museum - 1986
European, Pre-Columbian, African, Asian and decorative arts, contemporary art, antiquities 46078

CFCC Webber Center, 3001 SW College Rd, Ocala, FL 34478, mail addr: POB 1388, Ocala, FL 34478-1388 - T: (352) 237-2111 ext 1552, Fax: (352) 873-5886, E-mail: johnsoch@cfcc.cc.fl.us, Internet: www.cfcc.fl.us/exsched.htm. C.E.O.: Dr. Casius Pealer
Decorative Arts Museum - 1995
Folk culture, decorative arts, prints, sculpture 46079

Discovery Science Center of Central Florida, 1211 SE 22nd Rd, Ocala, FL 34471 - T: (352) 401-3900, Fax: (352) 401-3939, E-mail: discover@atlantic.net, Internet: www.ocalafl.org/recreationandp/dsoc.htm. Dir.: Dr. Ellen Gilchrist
Historical Museum / Science&Tech Museum - 1993 46080

Don Garlits Museum of Drag Racing, 13700 SW 16th Av, I-75, Exit 67, Ocala, FL 34473 - T: (352) 245-8661, Fax: (352) 245-6895, E-mail: garlits@pig.net, Internet: www.garlits.com. C.E.O.: Donald G. Garlits
Special Museum - 1976 46081

Silver River Museum, 7189 NE 7th St, Ocala, FL 34470 - T: (352) 236-5401, Fax: (352) 236-7142, E-mail: wingate-e@popmail.firn.edu. Dir.: Guy Marwick
Natural History Museum / Archaeological Museum / Historical Museum - 1991 46082

Occoquan VA

Historic Occoquan, 413 Mill St, Occoquan, VA 22125 - T: (703) 491-7525. Cur.: Nellie K. Curtis
Local Museum - 1969
Local history, Miller's cottage of Grist mill 46083

Ocean City NJ

Ocean City Art Center, 1735 Simpson Av, Ocean City, NJ 08226 - T: (609) 399-7628, Fax: (609) 399-7089, E-mail: ocart@prousa.net, Internet: www.oceancityartcenter.org. Dir.: Eunice Bell
Public Gallery - 1967
Paintings 46084

Ocean City Historical Museum, 1735 Simpson Av, Ocean City, NJ 08226 - T: (609) 399-1801, Fax: (609) 399-0544, E-mail: ocnjhistmuseum@aol.com, Internet: www.ocnjmuseum.org. Dir.: Paul S. Anselm
Historical Museum - 1964 46085

Ocean Grove NJ

Historical Society Museum of Ocean Grove, New Jersey, 50 Pittman Av, Ocean Grove, NJ 07756 - T: (732) 774-1869, Fax: (732) 774-1684, E-mail: info@oceangrovehistory.org, Internet: www.oceangrovehistory.org. Pres.: Philip May
Local Museum - 1969
History of Ocean Grove, history of the camp meeting 46086

Ocean Springs MS

Walter Anderson Museum of Art, 510 Washington Av, Ocean Springs, MS 39564 - T: (228) 872-3164, Fax: (228) 875-4494, E-mail: wama@walterandersonmuseum.org, Internet: www.walterandersonmuseum.org. Dir.: Clayton Bass, Cur.: Dr. Patricia Pinson
Fine Arts Museum - 1991 46087

William M. Colmer Visitor Center, 3500 Park Rd, Davis Bayou Area, Ocean Springs, MS 39564 - T: (228) 875-0823, Fax: (228) 872-2954, Internet: www.nps.gov/guis/
Historical Museum / Natural History Museum - 1970 46088

Oceanside CA

Mission San Luis Rey Museum, 4050 Mission Av, Oceanside, CA 92057 - T: (760) 757-3651, Fax: (760) 757-4613, E-mail: museum@sanluisrey.org, Internet: www.sanluisrey.org. Dir./Cur.: Mary C. Whelan
Historical Museum - 1798
Local hist, decorative and fine arts 46089

Oceanville NJ

The Noyes Museum of Art, Lily Lake Rd, Oceanville, NJ 08231 - T: (609) 652-8848, Fax: (609) 652-6166, E-mail: info@noyesmuseum.org, Internet: www.noyesmuseum.org. Exec. Dir.: Lawrence R. Schmidt
Fine Arts Museum - 1983 46090

Oconto WI

Oconto County Historical Society Museum, 917 Park Av, Oconto, WI 54153 - T: (920) 835-5733, E-mail: dscross@bayland.us, Internet: www.ocontocountyhistsoc.org. Pres.: Peter Stark
Local Museum - 1940
Local hist 46091

Odessa DE

Historic Houses of Odessa, Delaware, Main St, Odessa, DE 19730, mail addr: POB 507, Odessa, DE 19730 - T: (302) 378-4069, Fax: (302) 378-4050, Internet: www.winterthur.org. Dir.: Steven M. Pulinka, Cur.: Deborah Buckson
Local Museum - 1958
Historic house 46092

Odessa TX

The Ellen Noel Art Museum of the Permian Basin, 4909 East University Blvd, Odessa, TX 79762 - T: (915) 368-7222, Fax: (915) 368-9226, E-mail: enam@texasonline.net. Dir.: Marilyn Bassinger
Fine Arts Museum - 1985
Art 46093

The Presidential Museum, 622 N Lee, Odessa, TX 79761 - T: (915) 332-7123, Fax: (915) 498-4021, Internet: www.presidentialmuseum.org. Dir.: Carey F. Behrends, Cur.: Timothy M. Hewitt
Historical Museum - 1965
History 46094

Ogallala NE

Front Street Museum, 519 E First, Ogallala, NE 69153 - T: (308) 284-6000, Fax: (308) 284-0865, E-mail: frontstreet@lakemac.net, Internet: www.negavision.net/frontstreet. C.E.O.: Jan Nielsen
Local Museum - 1964
History 46095

Ogden IA

Hickory Grove Rural School Museum, Don Williams Lake, Ogden, IA 50212 - T: (515) 432-1907, E-mail: bchs@opencominc.com. Dir.: Charles W. Irwin
Local Museum - 1972
Local hist 46096

Ogden UT

Eccles Community Art Center, 2580 Jefferson Av, Ogden, UT 84401 - T: (801) 392-6935, Fax: (801) 392-5295, E-mail: eccles@ogden4arts.org, Internet: www.ogden4arts.org. Dir.: Sandra H. Havas
Fine Arts Museum - 1959
Art 46097

Fort Buenaventura, 2450 A Av, Ogden, UT 84401 - T: (801) 621-4808, 392-5581, Fax: (801) 392-2431
Local Museum - 1980
Replica of 1848 fort located on site of first permanent white settlement in the Great Basin 46098

Myra Powell Art Gallery and Gallery at the Station, Ogden Union Station, Ogden, UT 84401 - T: (801) 629-8444. Exec. Dir.: Bob Geier
Fine Arts Museum - 1979
Painting, sculpture 46099

Ogden Union Station Museums, 25th Wall Av, Union Station, Ogden, UT 84401 - T: (801) 629-8446, Fax: (801) 629-8555, E-mail: bobg@ci.ogden.ut.us, Internet: www.theunionstation.org. Dir.: Bob Geier
Local Museum - 1978
Art, railroads, cars, firearms, natural history 46100

Weber State University Art Gallery, c/o Art Dept, Weber State University, 2001 University Circle, Ogden, UT 84408-2001 - T: (801) 626-7689, Fax: (801) 626-6976. Dir.: H. Barens, Asst. Dir.: Eden Betz
Fine Arts Museum / University Museum - 1960 46101

Ogdensburg NJ

Sterling Hill Mining Museum, 30 Plant St, Ogdensburg, NJ 07439 - T: (973) 209-7212, Fax: (973) 209-8505, E-mail: shm@tapnet.net, Internet: www.sterlinghill.org. Pres.: Richard Hauck
Science&Tech Museum - 1990
Mining 46102

Ogdensburg NY

Frederic Remington Art Museum, 303 Washington St, Ogdensburg, NY 13669 - T: (315) 393-2425, Fax: (315) 393-4464, E-mail: info@fredericremington.org, Internet: www.fredericremington.org. Dir.: Lowell McAllister, Cur.: Laura Foster
Fine Arts Museum / Association with Coll - 1923 46103

Ogunquit ME

Ogunquit Museum of American Art, 543 Shore Rd, Ogunquit, ME 03907-0815 - T: (207) 646-4909, Fax: (207) 646-6903, E-mail: ogunquitmuseum@aol.com. Dir.: Michael Culver
Fine Arts Museum - 1952
American art 46104

Oil City LA

Caddo-Pine Island Oil and Historical Society Museum, 207 S Land Av, Oil City, LA 71061 - T: (318) 995-6845, Fax: (318) 995-6848, E-mail: laoilmuseum@earthlink.net, Internet: www.sec.state.la.us. Pres.: H.D. Farrar
Local Museum - 1965
Local hist 46105

Oil City PA

Venango Museum of Art, Science and Industry, 270 Seneca St, Oil City, PA 16301 - T: (814) 676-2007, Fax: (814) 678-6719, E-mail: venangomuseum@venangomuseum.org. Pres.: Catherine Teig, Dir.: Barbara Perlstein
Fine Arts Museum / Science&Tech Museum - 1961
Art, science, industry 46106

Ojai CA

Ojai Art Center, 113 S Montgomery, Ojai, CA 93023 - T: (805) 646-0117, Fax: (805) 646-0252, E-mail: ojaiartcenter@aol.com. Dir.: Teri Mettala
Public Gallery - 1936 46107

Ojai Valley Museum, 130 W Ojai Av, Ojai, CA 93023 - T: (805) 640-1390, Fax: (805) 640-1342, E-mail: ojaivalleymuseum@aol.com. Dir.: Robin Sim
Local Museum / Natural History Museum - 1966
Local hist, art, cultural and natural hist 46108

Okemah OK

Territory Town USA, Old West Museum, 5 m W of Okemah, on I-40, Okemah, OK 74859 - T: (918) 623-2599. Head: Louise Parsons
Local Museum - 1967
Western relics, Civil War and Native American artefacts 46109

Oklahoma City OK

45th Infantry Division Museum, 2145 NE 36th St, Oklahoma City, OK 73111 - T: (405) 424-5313, Fax: (405) 424-3748, E-mail: curator45th@aol.com, Internet: www.45thdivisionmuseum.com. Cur.: Michael E. Gonzales
Military Museum - 1976 46110

Harn Homestead and 1889er Museum, 313 NE 16th, Oklahoma City, OK 73104 - T: (405) 235-4058, Fax: (405) 235-4041, E-mail: harnhomestead@yahoo.com, Internet: harnhomestead.com. Dir.: Gayle Farley
Historical Museum - 1976 46111

Hulsey Gallery, Oklahoma City University, Norick Art Center, 2501 N Blackwelder, Oklahoma City, OK 73106 - T: (405) 521-5226, Fax: (405) 557-6029, Internet: www.okcu.edu. Dir.: Kirk Niemeyer
Public Gallery 46112

Individual Artists of Oklahoma, 1 N Hudson, Ste 150, Oklahoma City, OK 73102, mail addr: POB 60824, Oklahoma City, OK 73146 - T: (405) 232-6060, Fax: (405) 232-6061, E-mail: iao@telepath.com, Internet: www.iaogallery.org. Dir.: Shirley Blaschke
Fine Arts Museum 46113

Kirkpatrick Science and Air Space Museum at Omniplex, 2100 NE 52nd St, Oklahoma City, OK 73111 - T: (405) 602-6664, Fax: (405) 602-3766, E-mail: omnipr@omniplex.org, Internet: www.omniplex.org. Dir.: Brent Beall
Science&Tech Museum / Natural History Museum - 1958 46114

Melton Art Reference Library Museum, 4300 N Sewell, Oklahoma City, OK 73118 - T: (405) 525-3603, Fax: (405) 525-0396, E-mail: meltonart@aol.com. Dir.: Suzanne Silvester
Library with Exhibitions / Special Museum - 1979 46115

National Cowboy and Western Heritage Museum, 1700 NE 63rd St, Oklahoma City, OK 73111 - T: (405) 478-2250, Fax: (405) 478-4714, E-mail: info@nationalcowboymuseum.org, Internet: www.nationalcowboymuseum.org. Dir.: Chuck Schroeder, Cur.: Ed Muno (Art), Richard Rattenbury (History), Mike Leslie (Ethnology), Don Reeves (Colls)
Historical Museum - 1954 46116

National Softball Hall of Fame and Museum Complex, 2801 NE 50, Oklahoma City, OK 73111 - T: (405) 424-5266, Fax: (405) 424-3855, E-mail: info@softball.org, Internet: www.softball.org. Exec. Dir.: Ron Radigonda, Leiter: Bill Plummer
Special Museum - 1957 46117

Oklahoma City Museum of Art, 415 Couch Dr, Oklahoma City, OK 73102 - T: (405) 236-3100, Fax: (405) 946-7671, E-mail: lspiears@okcmoa.com, Internet: www.okcmoa.com. Dir.: Carolyn Hill, Chief Cur.: Hardy George, Cur.: Brian Hearn (Film), Doris McGranahan (Education), Janice Seline (Exhibitions)
Fine Arts Museum - 1989/2002
Art 46118

Oklahoma Firefighters Museum, 2716 NE 50th, Oklahoma City, OK 73111 - T: (405) 424-3440, Fax: (405) 425-1032, E-mail: osfa@brightok.net, Internet: www.osfa.info. Dir.: Jim Minx, Cur.: Sam Oruch
Special Museum - 1970 46119

Oklahoma Museum of African American Art, 3919 NW 10th St, Oklahoma City, OK 73107 - T: (405) 942-4896
Fine Arts Museum 46120

Oklahoma Museum of History, 2100 N Lincoln Blvd, Oklahoma City, OK 73105 - T: (405) 522-5248, Fax: (405) 521-5402, Internet: www.ok-history.mus.ok.us. Dir.: Dr. Bob Blackburn, Cur.: John Hill (Exhibitions)
Historical Museum - 1893
Historic site - Library, Archives 46121

Overholser Mansion, NW 15th and Hudson, Oklahoma City, OK 73103 - T: (405) 528-8485, E-mail: overholser@ok-history.mus.ok.us. Admin.: W.C. Fullhart
Historical Museum - 1972 46122

State Museum of History → Oklahoma Museum of History

World of Wings Pigeon Center Museum, 2300 NE 63rd, Oklahoma City, OK 73111-8208 - T: (405) 478-5155, Fax: (405) 478-4552, E-mail: jbrown@ionet.net, Internet: www.worldofwings.org
Special Museum - 1973
Paintings, sketches, books, lithographics, WW 1 and 2, European use of pigeons 46123

The World Organization of China Painters, 2641 NW 10th St, Oklahoma City, OK 73107 - T: (405) 521-1234, Fax: (405) 521-1265, E-mail: wocporg@theshop.net, Internet: www.theshop.net/wocporg. Dir.: Patricia Dickerson
Fine Arts Museum / Decorative Arts Museum - 1967
Porcelain 46124

Okmulgee OK

Creek Council House Museum, Town Square, 106 W Sixth, Okmulgee, OK 74447 - T: (918) 756-2324, Fax: (918) 756-3671, E-mail: creekmuseum@prodigy.net. Dir.: David Anderson
Historical Museum / Ethnology Museum - 1923 46125

Okoboji IA

Higgins Museum, 1507 Sanborn Av, Okoboji, IA 51355 - T: (712) 332-5859, Fax: (712) 332-5859. Cur.: Glenn McConnell
Special Museum - 1978
National bank notes from 1863-1935 46126

Olathe KS

Mahaffie Stagecoach Stop and Farm, 1100 Kansas City Rd, Olathe, KS 66061 - T: (913) 782-6972, Fax: (913) 397-5114, E-mail: mahaffie@unicom.net. C.E.O.: Jack L. Tinnell
Historical Museum - 1977
1865 Mahaffie house and stagecoach stop on Santa Fe Trail 46127

Old Bennington VT

Bennington Battle Monument, 15 Monument Circle, Old Bennington, VT 05201 - T: (802) 828-3051, Fax: (802) 447-0550, E-mail: jdumville@dca.state.vt.us, Internet: www.historicvermont.org
Historic Site - 1891
Historic site located near the site of the Bennington Battle of the Revolutionary War 46128

Old Bethpage NY

Old Bethpage Village Restoration, Round Swamp Rd, Old Bethpage, NY 11804 - T: (516) 572-8401, Fax: (516) 572-8413, Internet: www.longislandfair.org. Dir.: James McKenna
Open Air Museum - 1970 46129

Old Bridge Township NJ

Thomas Warne Historical Museum, 4216 Rte 516, Old Bridge Township, NJ 07747 - T: (732) 566-0348, Fax: (732) 566-6943. Cur.: Alvia D. Martin
Local Museum - 1964
Edison phonograph and records sheet music, pottery, carpenter tools, clothing, Indian artifacts, old school books - library 46130

Old Chatham NY

Shaker Museum, 88 Shaker Museum Rd, Old Chatham, NY 12136 - T: (518) 794-9100 ext 100, Fax: (518) 794-8621, E-mail: contact@shakermuseumandlibrary.org, Internet: www.smandl.org. Exec. Dir.: Lili R. Ott, Cur.: Starlyn D'Angelo
Folklore Museum / Historical Museum - 1950 46131

Old Fort NC

Mountain Gateway Museum, Water and Catawba Sts, Old Fort, NC 28762 - T: (828) 668-9259, Fax: (828) 668-0041. Dir.: Sam Gray
Local Museum - 1971 46132

Old Lyme CT

Florence Griswold Museum, 96 Lyme St, Old Lyme, CT 06371 - T: (860) 434-5542, Fax: (860) 434-6259, 434-9778, E-mail: info@flogris.org, Internet: www.flogris.org. Dir.: Jeffrey W. Andersen
Fine Arts Museum / Historical Museum - 1936
American impressionist paintings, decorative arts, toys 46133

Old Shawneetown IL

Shawneetown Historic Site, 280 Washington St, Old Shawneetown, IL 62984-3401 - T: (618) 269-3303
Historical Museum / Open Air Museum - 1917
Historic Building, 1839 4-story Greek Revival Bank 46134

Old Town ME

Old Town Museum, 138 S Main St, Old Town, ME 04468 - T: (207) 827-7256, E-mail: ozmaine@aol.com
Local Museum - 1976
Antique telephones, costumes, glass ceramics 46135

Old Westbury NY

Old Westbury Gardens, 71 Old Westbury Rd, Old Westbury, NY 11568 - T: (516) 333-0048, Fax: (516) 333-6807, Internet: www.oldwestburygardens.org. Pres.: Carol Large
Historical Museum / Decorative Arts Museum - 1959 46136

Olivet MI

Armstrong Collection, Olivet College, Art Department, 320 S Main St, Olivet, MI 49076 - T: (616) 749-7000 ext 7661, Fax: (616) 749-7178, Internet: www.olivet.edu. Dir.: Donald Rowe
Fine Arts Museum
American Indian, Mesopotamian, Philippine and Thailand artifacts, primitive arts, sculpture, modern American prints - library 46137

Olustee FL

Olustee Battlefield, US 90, 2 m E, Olustee, FL 32072, mail addr: POB 40, Olustee, FL 32072 - T: (904) 758-0400, Internet: extlab1.entvem.ufl.edu/olustee
Historic Site / Military Museum - 1909
State historic site, military 46138

Olympia WA

Bigelow House Museum, 918 Glass Av, Olympia, WA 98506 - T: (360) 357-6099, E-mail: annafitz@earthlink.net. Pres.: Annamary Fitzgerald
Local Museum - 1992
Local hist 46139

Evergreen Galleries, Evergreen State College, 2700 Evergreen Pkwy NW, Olympia, WA 98505-0002 - T: (360) 866-6000 ext 6488, Fax: (360) 866-6794, E-mail: alvesb@evergreen.edu, Internet: www.evergreen.edu/user/galleries. Dir.: Peter Ramsey
Fine Arts Museum / University Museum - 1970
Art 46140

Hands on Children's Museum, 106 11th Av SW, Olympia, WA 98501 - T: (360) 956-0818, Fax: (360) 754-8626, E-mail: Prpatty@home.com, Internet: www.hocm.org. Dir.: Patty Belmonte
Science&Tech Museum / Natural History Museum - 1988 46141

Washington State Capital Museum, 211 W 21st Av, Olympia, WA 98501 - T: (360) 753-2580, Fax: (360) 586-8322, E-mail: dvalley@wshs.wa.gov, Internet: www.wshs.com. Dir.: Derek R. Valley, Cur.: Susan Rohrer, Melissa Parr
Local Museum - 1941
Local hist 46142

Omaha NE

Artists' Cooperative Gallery, 405 S 11th St, Omaha, NE 68102 - T: (402) 342-9617. Pres.: Nicholas W. Pella
Fine Arts Museum - 1975
American paintings 46143

Bemis Center for Contemporary Arts, 724 S 12th St, Omaha, NE 68102-3202 - T: (402) 341-7130, Fax: (402) 341-9791, E-mail: bemis@novia.net, Internet: www.bemiscenter.org. Dir.: Ree Schonlau
Fine Arts Museum - 1985
Sculpture, ceramics 46144

Durham Western Heritage Museum, 801 S 10th St, Omaha, NE 68108 - T: (402) 444-5071, Fax: (402) 444-5397, E-mail: info@dwhm.org, Internet: www.dwhm.org. Dir.: Randall Hayes, Cur.: Terry Keane, Janelle Lindberg, Lawrence Lee
Local Museum - 1975 46145

Fine Arts Gallery, Creighton University, 2500 California Plaza, Omaha, NE 68178 - T: (402) 280-2509 ext 2831, Fax: (402) 280-2320, E-mail: bohr@creightonuniversity.edu, Internet: www.creightonuniversity.edu. Dir.: G. Ted Bohr
Fine Arts Museum - 1973
Drawings, graphics, paintings, photography, prints, sculpture 46146

General Crook House Museum, 5730 N 30 St, Omaha, NE 68111-1657 - T: (402) 455-9990, Fax: (402) 453-9448, Internet: www.omahahistory.org. Dir.: Betty J. Davis, Cur.: Patricia Pixley
Local Museum - 1956 46147

Great Plains Black Museum, 2213 Lake St, Omaha, NE 68110 - T: (402) 345-2212, Fax: (402) 345-2256, Internet: members.aol.com/asmith8955/ahist.htm. Pres.: Joyce Young, C.E.O.: Bertha Calloway
Historical Museum - 1975 46148

Joslyn Art Museum, 2200 Dodge St, Omaha, NE 68102-1292 - T: (402) 342-3300, Fax: (402) 342-2376, E-mail: info@joslyn.org, Internet: www.joslyn.org. Dir.: J. Brooks Joyner, Cur.: Marsha V. Gallagher (Material, Culture), Claudia Einecke (European Art), Janet Farber (20th c Art), Sherrie Gauley (Education)
Fine Arts Museum - 1931 46149

El Museo Latino, 4701 S 25th St, Omaha, NE 68107-2728 - T: (402) 731-1137, Fax: (402) 733-7012, E-mail: mgarcia@elmuseolatino.org, Internet: www.elmuseolatino.org. Dir.: Magdalena A. Garcia
Fine Arts Museum / Folklore Museum / Historical Museum - 1993
Latino art and hist 46150

Omaha Center for Contemporary Art, 1116 Jackson St, Omaha, NE 68102 - T: (402) 345-9711. Dir.: Eadwierd Kroy
Fine Arts Museum - 2000 46151

Omaha Children's Museum, 500 S 20th St, Omaha, NE 68102-2508 - T: (402) 342-6164 ext 410, Fax: (402) 342-6165, E-mail: discover@ocm.org, Internet: www.ocm.org. Exec. Dir.: Lindy Hoyer
Special Museum - 1977
Arts, science, humanities 46152

University of Nebraska Art Gallery at Omaha, Fine Arts Bldg, Rm 137, Omaha, NE 68182-0012 - T: (402) 554-2796, Fax: (402) 554-3435, E-mail: n_kelly@unomaha.edu, Internet: www.unomaha.edu. Cur.: Nancy Kelly
Fine Arts Museum / University Museum - 1967
Prints 46153

Onancock VA

Kerr Place, 69 Market St, Onancock, VA 23417 - T: (757) 787-8012, Fax: (757) 787-4271, E-mail: kerr@esva.net, Internet: www.kerrplace.org. Dir.: John H. Verrill
Local Museum - 1957
Local hist 46154

Onchiota NY

Six Nations Indian Museum, County Rte 30, HCR #1, Onchiota, NY 12989 - T: (518) 891-2299, E-mail: redmaple@northnet.org. Dir.: John Fadden
Ethnology Museum - 1954 46155

Oneida NY

Cottage Lawn, 435 Main St, Oneida, NY 13421-0415 - T: (315) 363-4136, Fax: (315) 363-4136. Exec. Dir.: Sydney L. Loftus, Cur.: Michael Martin (Collections)
Historical Museum - 1895 46156

Oneida Community Mansion House, 170 Kenwood Av, Oneida, NY 13421 - T: (315) 363-0745, Fax: (315) 361-4580, E-mail: ocmh@dreamscape.com, Internet: www.oneidacommunity.org. C.E.O.: Bruce M. Moseley
Local Museum - 1987
Furniture, clothing, decorative arts, paintings, works of art on paper 46157

Shakowi Cultural Center, 5 Territory Rd, Oneida, NY 13421-9304 - T: (315) 363-1424, Fax: (315) 363-1843, Internet: www.oneida-nation.org. Dir.: Birdy Birdick
Folklore Museum / Ethnology Museum - 1993
Native Americans, ethnography, beadwork 46158

Oneonta NY

The National Soccer Hall of Fame, 18 Stadium Circle, Oneonta, NY 13820 - T: (607) 432-3351, Fax: (607) 432-8429, E-mail: info@soccerhall.org, Internet: www.soccerhall.org. Pres.: Will Lunn
Special Museum - 1981
Sports hist 46159

Science Discovery Center of Oneonta, State University College, Oneonta, NY 13820-4015 - T: (607) 436-2011, Fax: (607) 436-2654, E-mail: scdisc@oneonta.edu, Internet: www.oneonta.edu/academics/scdisc/index.html. Dir.: Albert J. Read
Science&Tech Museum / Natural History Museum - 1987 46160

The Yager Museum, Hartwick College, West St, Oneonta, NY 13820-4020 - T: (607) 431-4480, Fax: (607) 431-4468, E-mail: museums@hartwick.edu, Internet: www.hartwick.edu/museum. Dir.: Dr. Fiona M. Dejardin (Fine Arts), Cur.: Dr. L. Wilson (Foreman Gallery)
Fine Arts Museum / University Museum / Ethnology Museum / Archaeological Museum / Fine Arts Museum - 1797
Upper Susquehanna Indian artifacts, basketry and pottery 46161

Onset MA

Porter Thermometer Museum, 49 Zarahemla Rd, Onset, MA 02558 - T: (508) 295-5504, Fax: (508) 295-8323, E-mail: thermometerman@aol.com, Internet: members.aol.com/thermometerman/index.html. Dir.: Barbara A. Porter, Cur.: Richard T. Porter
Science&Tech Museum / Historical Museum - 1990
Medical, maritime, antique, weather, souvenir thermometers 46162

Ontario CA

Museum of History and Art, 225 S Euclid Av, Ontario, CA 91761 - T: (909) 983-3198, Fax: (909) 983-8978. Dir.: Theresa Hanley, Sc. Staff: Mary del Moral (History), Cur.: Maricarmen Ruiz-Torres
Local Museum / Fine Arts Museum - 1979
Local history, citrus, social and home life, viticulture, mining, paintings 46163

Ontario NY

Heritage Square Museum, 7147 Ontario Center Rd, Ontario, NY 14519-0462 - E-mail: retoddl@usadata.net.net, Internet: heritagesquaremuseum.org. Cur.: Liz Albright
Local Museum - 1969
Iron ore mining, agriculture, farm machinery 46164

Town of Ontario Historical and Landmark Preservation Society Museum Complex, Heritage Sq, Ontario Center Rd and Brickchurch Rd, Ontario, NY 14519 - T: (315) 524-8928. Cur.: Polly Crombe
Historical Museum / Local Museum - 1969 46165

Ontario OR

Four Rivers Cultural Center, 676 SW 5th Av, Ontario, OR 97914 - T: (541) 889-8191, Fax: (541) 889-7628, E-mail: cfugate@fmtc.com, Internet: www.4rcc.com. Pres.: Ben Plaza, Exec.Dir.: Charlotte Fugate
Local Museum / Folklore Museum - 1987
Local hist 46166

Ontonagon MI

Ontonagon County Historical Society Museum, 422 River St, Ontonagon, MI 49953-0092 - T: (906) 884-6165, Fax: (906) 884-6094, E-mail: ochsmuse@up.net, Internet: www.upbiz.com/mi/ochs.html. Pres.: John Doyle, Cur.: Ruth Ristola
Local Museum - 1957
Regional history 46167

Opelousas LA

Opelousas Museum, 315 N Main St, Opelousas, LA 70570 - T: (337) 948-2589, Fax: (337) 948-2592, E-mail: musdir@hotmail.com, Internet: www.cityofpelousas.com. Dir.: Sue DeVille
Local Museum - 1992
Hist and culture of the Opelousas area 46168

Opelousas Museum of Art, 106 N Union St, Opelousas, LA 70570 - T: (337) 942-4991, Fax: (337) 942-4930, E-mail: omamuseum@aol.com. Dir.: Nan Wier, Cur.: Keith Guidry
Fine Arts Museum - 1997 46169

Oradell NJ

Hiram Blauvelt Art Museum, 705 Kinderkamack Rd, Oradell, NJ 07649 - T: (201) 261-0012, Fax: (201) 391-6418, E-mail: maja218@att.net, Internet: www.blauveltmuszum.com. Dir.: Dr. Marijane Singer
Fine Arts Museum - 1940
Art 46170

Orange TX

Heritage House of Orange County Museum, 905 W Division, Orange, TX 77630 - T: (409) 886-5385, Fax: (409) 886-0917, E-mail: hhmuseum@exp.net, Internet: www.heritagehouseoforange.org. Pres.: Sue Cowling
Historical Museum - 1977
Local hist 46171

Stark Museum of Art, 712 Green Av, Orange, TX 77630 - T: (409) 883-6661, Fax: (409) 883-6361, E-mail: starkmuseum@starkmuseum.org, Internet: www.starkmuseum.org. Dir.: Walter G. Riedel, Cur.: David Hunt, Richard Hunter
Fine Arts Museum - 1974
Art 46172

The W.H. Stark House, 610 W Main St, Orange, TX 77630 - T: (409) 833-3513, Fax: (409) 883-3530, E-mail: starkhouse@exp.net, Internet: www.whstarkhouse.org. C.E.O.: Walter G. Riedel
Local Museum - 1981
Historic house 46173

Orange VA

The James Madison Museum, 129 Caroline St, Orange, VA 22960 - T: (540) 672-1776, Fax: (540) 672-0231, E-mail: info@jamesmadisonmuseum.org, Internet: www.jamesmadisonmuseum.org. Pres.: Margaret Ann Jones
Historical Museum - 1976
Local hist 46174

Orange City IA

Thea G. Korver Visual Art Center, Northwestern College, 101 Seventh St SW, Orange City, IA 51041 - T: (712) 707-7000, E-mail: johnk@nwciowa.edu, Internet: www.nwciowa.edu
Public Gallery - 2003 46175

Orangeburg SC

I.P. Stanback Museum, South Carolina State University, 300 College Str, NE, Orangeburg, SC 29117 - T: (803) 536-7174, 536-8119, Fax: (803) 536-8309, E-mail: fmartin@alphal.scsu.edu, Internet: www.praco.scsu.edu. Pres.: Dr. Leroy Davis, Interim Dir.: Frank Martin
Fine Arts Museum / University Museum - 1980
Art 46176

Orchard Lake MI

Saint Mary's Galeria, 3535 Indian Trail, Orchard Lake, MI 48324 - T: (248) 683-0345. Dir.: Marian Owczarski
Fine Arts Museum - 1963
Former Michigan Military Academy, contemporary Polish paintings and sculpture, Polish printing, folk art, tapestries 46177

Orchard Park NY

Orchard Park Historical Society Museum, S-4287 S Buffalo St, Orchard Park, NY 14127 - T: (716) 662-2185. Dir.: Dennis J. Mill, Cur.: Yasabel Newton Gibson
Historical Museum - 1951 46178

Oregon OH

Oregon-Jerusalem Historical Museum, 1133 Grasser St, Oregon, OH 43616 - T: (419) 691-7561, Fax: (419) 693-7052, E-mail: ojhs@juno.com. Dir.: Kathy M. Clark
Local Museum - 1963
School records, maps, farm equip, musical instruments, office equip, household furniture, Indian artifacts, China, glass, costumes 46179

Oregonia OH

Fort Ancient Museum, 6123 State Rte 350, Exits 32 and 36 off I-71, Oregonia, OH 45054 - T: (513) 932-4421, Fax: (513) 932-4843, E-mail: fancient@your-net.com, Internet: www.ohiohistory.org. Man.: Jack Blosser
Ethnology Museum / Natural History Museum 46180

Orient NY

Museum of Orient and East Marion History, Village Ln, Orient, NY 11957 - T: (631) 323-2480, Fax: (631) 323-3719, E-mail: ohs@southold.org. Dir.: Courtney Burns
Local Museum - 1944
Indian artifacts, marine paintings, whaling and fishing, ship models, navigating instruments, spinning and weaving tools, clothing, furniture, toys, dolls, agricultural tools 46181

Orinda CA

Museum of Robotics, 120 Village Sq, Orinda, CA 94563-2502 - T: (510) 832-6059, 524-1163, Fax: (510) 532-6059 ext 51, E-mail: noeticj@mindspring.com, Internet: www.museumrobotics.org. Dir.: Richard L. Amoroso
Science&Tech Museum - 1987
Technology, robots 46182

Oriskany NY

Oriskany Battlefield, 7801 State Rte 69 W, Oriskany, NY 13424 - T: (315) 768-7224, Fax: (315) 337-3081, E-mail: nancy.demyttenaere@oprhp.state.ny.us, Internet: www.nysparks.com
Military Museum / Open Air Museum - 1927 46183

Orland ME

Orland Historical Museum, Castine Rd, Orland, ME 04472 - T: (207) 469-2476. Pres.: David L. Davis
Local Museum - 1966
Local history 46184

Orlando FL

East Campus Galleries, Valencia Community College, 701 N Econlockhatchee Trail, Orlando, FL 32825 - T: (407) 299-5000 ext 2298, Fax: (407) 249-3943, Internet: www.valencia.cc.fl.us. Pres.: Dr. Sanford Shugart, Cur.: David Walsh
Fine Arts Museum - 1967
Art 46185

Mennello Museum of American Folk Art, 900 E Princeton St, Orlando, FL 32803 - T: (407) 246-4278, Fax: (407) 246-4329, E-mail: cityoforlandoart@mindspring.com, Internet: www.mennellomuseum.com. C.E.O.: Frank Holt
Decorative Arts Museum - 1998
Paintings, folk art on American self-taught artists 46186

Orange County Regional History Center, 65 E Central Blv, Orlando, FL 32801 - T: (407) 836-8517, Fax: (407) 836-8550, E-mail: sara.vanarsdel@ocfl.net, Internet: www.thehistorycenter.org. Dir.: Sara Van Arsdel
Local Museum - 1957
Local Central Florida history 46187

Orlando Museum of Art, 2416 N Mills Av, Orlando, FL 32803-1483 - T: (407) 896-4231, Fax: (407) 896-9920, 894-4314, E-mail: info@omart.org, Internet: www.omart.org. Dir.: Marena Grant Morrisey, Cur.: Susan Rosoff, Hansen Mulford
Fine Arts Museum - 1924
Art 46188

Orlando Science Center, 777 E Princeton St, Orlando, FL 32803 - T: (407) 514-2000, 514-2012, Fax: (407) 514-2001, E-mail: info@osc.org, Internet: www.osc.org. Pres.: Steven Goldman
Science&Tech Museum - 1959
Physical, natural, space and health sciences, applied technology-aerospace, lasers 46189

Terrace Gallery, 900 E Princeton St, Orlando, FL 32803 - T: (407) 246-4279, Fax: (407) 246-4329, E-mail: cityorlandoart@mindspring.com. Cur.: Frank Holt
Fine Arts Museum - 1992 46190

Orleans MA

French Cable Station Museum in Orleans, 41 Rte 28, Orleans, MA 02653 - T: (508) 240-1735, Fax: (508) 240-6099, E-mail: miko@gis.net. Pres.: Gerald Downs
Special Museum - 1972
Atlantic Cable Terminal, communications 46191

Ormond Beach FL

Fred Dana Marsh Museum, 2099 N Beach St, Tomoka State Park, Ormond Beach, FL 32174 - T: (904) 676-4045, 676-4075, Fax: (904) 676-4060, Internet: www.dep.state.pl.us/parks
Open Air Museum / Natural History Museum - 1967
Village of Nocoroco of the 1605, site of British plantation, Mount Oswald, paintings, sculpture, Florida geology and history 46192

Ormond Memorial Art Museum, 78 E Granada Blvd, Ormond Beach, FL 32176 - T: (904) 676-3341, Fax: (904) 676-3244, E-mail: omam78e@aol.com, Internet: www.state.fl.us/ormond. Dir.: Ann Burt
Fine Arts Museum - 1946 46193

Orofino ID

Clearwater Historical Museum, 315 College Av, Orofino, ID 83544 - T: (208) 476-5033, E-mail: chmusuem@clearwater.net, Internet: www.clearwatermuseum.org. Dir.: Bernice Pullen
Local Museum - 1960
Local history, mining, logging, Nez Perce Indians, farming 46194

Orono ME

Hudson Museum, University of Maine, 5476 Maine Center for the Arts, Orono, ME 04469-5746 - T: (207) 581-1901, Fax: (207) 581-1950, E-mail: hudsonmuseum@umit.maine.edu, Internet: www.umaine.edu/hudsonmuseum/. Pres.: Harold Borns
Ethnology Museum / Archaeological Museum - 1986
Anthropology 46195

Museum of Art, University of Maine, 109 Carnegie Hall, Orono, ME 04469 - T: (207) 581-3255, Fax: (207) 581-3083, E-mail: umma@umit.maine.edu, Internet: umma.umecah.maine.edu. Dir.: Wally Mason
Fine Arts Museum / University Museum - 1946
Art, housed in a library of Tusco-Doric (Palladian) design 46196

Oroville CA

Coyote Gallery, 3536 Butte Campus Dr, Oroville, CA 95965 - T: (530) 895-2877, Fax: (530) 895-2346. Dir.: Alan Carrier
Public Gallery - 1981 46197

Oroville Chinese Temple, 1500 Broderick St, Oroville, CA 95965 - T: (530) 538-2415, Fax: (530) 538-2426, Internet: www.oroville-city.com. Dir.: Charles Miller, Cur.: Vorin Dornan
Historical Museum / Religious Arts Museum - 1863 46198

Osage IA

Cedar Valley Memories, 1 1/2 Mile W Hwy 9, Osage, IA 50461 - T: (641) 732-1269
Science&Tech Museum / Local Museum
Steam engines, gas running, agriculture 46199

Mitchell County Historical Museum, N 6th, Osage, IA 50461-8557 - T: (515) 732-4047. Pres.: Lory Mark
Local Museum / Agriculture Museum - 1965
Local history, agriculture, Cedar Valley seminary 46200

Osawatomie KS

John Brown House, 10th and Main Sts, Osawatomie, KS 66064, mail addr: POB 37, Osawatomie, Ks 66064 - T: (913) 755-4384, Fax: (913) 755-4164, E-mail: adaircabin@grapevine.net. CEO: Dr. Ramon Powers
Military Museum - 1854
1856 Battle of Osawatomie, weapons, pictures, antiques, fireplace cooking equip 46201

Osceola NE

Polk County Historical Museum, 561 South St, Osceola, NE 68651 - T: (402) 747-7901. Pres./Dir.: D. Ruth Lux
Local Museum - 1967 46202

Oshkosh NE

Garden County Museum, W First and Av E, Oshkosh, NE 69154-0913 - T: (308) 772-3115. Cur.: Phyllis Chadwick
Local Museum - 1969
Mounted birds, Indian artifacts, pioneer machinery, fossils, local hist of schools 46203

Oshkosh WI

EAA AirVenture Museum, 3000 Poberezny Rd, Oshkosh, WI 54903-3065 - T: (920) 426-4800, Fax: (920) 426-6765, E-mail: museum@eaa.org, Internet: www.airventuremuseum.com. Dir.: Adam. Smith, Cur.: Alan Westby, Cons.: Gordon Selke
Science&Tech Museum - 1963
Aviation 46204

Military Veterans Museum, City Center, # 245, Oshkosh, WI 54901 - T: (920) 426-8615, E-mail: mvm@athnet.net, Internet: www.athnet/~mvm. Dir.: E. Munroe Hjerstedt, Cur.: Euclid Caron
Military Museum - 1985 46205

Oshkosh Public Museum, 1331 Algoma Blvd, Oshkosh, WI 54901 - T: (920) 424-4731, Fax: (920) 424-4738, E-mail: info@publicmuseum.oshkosh.net, Internet: www.publicmuseum.oshkosh.net. Dir.: Bradley Larson, Asst. Dir.: Michael Breza, Cur.: Debra Daubert
Local Museum - 1924
Local hist 46206

Paine Art Center, 1410 Algoma Blvd, Oshkosh, WI 54901-2719 - T: (920) 235-6903, Fax: (920) 235-6303, E-mail: info@paineartcenter.com, Internet: www.paineartcenter.com. Dir.: Aaron Sherer
Fine Arts Museum - 1947
Art Museum 46207

Oskaloosa IA

Nelson Pioneer Farm and Museum, 2294 Oxford Av, Oskaloosa, IA 52577 - T: (515) 672-2989, Internet: www.nelsonpioneer.org. Pres.: Ed Groenendyk, Cur.: Kay Boot
Historical Museum / Agriculture Museum - 1942
Daniel and Margaret Nelson Home, Nelson barn, local history, agriculture 46208

Oskaloosa KS

Old Jefferson Town, 703 Walnut, Hwy 59, Oskaloosa, KS 66066 - T: (785) 863-2070, Internet: www.digitalhistory.com/schools/Oskaloosa/Old_Jeff_Town.html. Cur.: Karen Heady
Local Museum / Open Air Museum - 1966
Seven c.1880 bldgs 46209

Osprey FL

Historic Spanish Point, 337 N Tamiami Trail, Osprey, FL 34229, mail addr: POB 846, Osprey, FL 34229 - T: (941) 966-5214, Fax: (941) 966-1355, E-mail: gcha2@gte.net, Internet: historic-spanishpoint.org. Dir.: Linda W. Mansperger
Historical Museum - 1980
Indian and Pioneer artifacts, shell tools, pottery, textiles 46210

Ossineke MI

Dinosaur Gardens Museum, 11160 U.S. 23 S, Ossineke, MI 49766 - T: (989) 471-5477. Head: Frank A. McCourt
Natural History Museum - 1934
Paleontology 46211

Ossining NY

Ossining Historical Society Museum, 196 Croton Av, Ossining, NY 10562 - T: (914) 941-0001, Fax: (914) 941-0001, E-mail: ohsm@bestweb.net, Internet: www.ossininghistorical.org. Exec. Dir.: Roberta Y. Arminio
Historical Museum / Fine Arts Museum - 1931 46212

Osterville MA

Osterville Historical Museum, 155 W Bay Rd, Osterville, MA 02655 - T: (508) 428-5861, Fax: (508) 428-2241, E-mail: ohs@osterville.org, Internet: www.osterville.org. Pres.: James Eastman
Local Museum - 1931
Local history 46213

Oswego KS

Oswego Historical Museum, 410 Commercial St, Oswego, KS 67356 - T: (620) 795-4500, E-mail: history@oswego.net
Local Museum - 1967
Paintings, photographs, furnishings, personal artifacts 46214

Oswego NY

Fort Ontario, 1 E Fourth St, Oswego, NY 13126 - T: (315) 343-4711, Fax: (315) 343-1430, E-mail: paul.lear@oprhp.state.ny.us, Internet: www.nysparks.com. Sc. Staff: Paul Lear
Military Museum - 1949 46215

Richardson-Bates House Museum, 135 E Third St, Oswego, NY 13126 - T: (315) 343-1342. Dir.: Terrence M. Prior, Cur.: Natalie Siembor
Historical Museum - 1896 46216

Safe Haven, 3651 County Rte 57, Oswego, NY 13126 - T: (315) 343-1971, E-mail: safehavn@juno.com, Internet: www.syracuse.com/safehaven. Pres.: Scott B. Scanlon
Historical Museum
History 46217

Tyler Art Gallery, State University of New York College of Arts and Science, Oswego, NY 13126 - T: (315) 341-2113, Fax: (315) 341-3439, E-mail: kwasigro@oswego.edu, Internet: www.oswego.edu/other_campus/tysleart/index.html. Dir.: David Kwasigroh, Asst. Dir.: Mindy Ostrow
Fine Arts Museum / University Museum
Grant Arnold coll 46218

Ottawa IL

Ottawa Scouting Museum, 1100 Canal St, Ottawa, IL 61350 - T: (815) 431-9353, E-mail: scouter07@hotmail.com. CEO: Mollie Perrot
Special Museum - 1992
Camping gear, uniforms, badges, patches, awards, medals 46219

Ottawa KS

Old Depot Museum, 135 W Tecumseh, Ottawa, KS 66067 - T: (785) 242-1250, Fax: (785) 242-1406, E-mail: history@ott.net, Internet: www.ott.net/~history/. Dir.: Deborah Barker
Historical Museum - 1963
Local manufacturing, furniture, clothing 46220

Ottumwa IA

Airpower Museum, 22001 Bluegrass Rd, Ottumwa, IA 52501-8569 - T: (641) 938-2773, Fax: (641) 938-2084, E-mail: aaaapmhq@pcsia.com, Internet: www.aaa-apm.org
Science&Tech Museum - 1965
Aeronautics 46221

Wapello County Historical Museum, 210 W Main, Ottumwa, IA 52501 - T: (515) 682-8676. Pres.: Edward Kuntz
Local Museum / Ethnology Museum - 1959
Regional history 46222

Overland Park KS

Gallery of Art, Johnson County Community College, 12345 College Blvd, Overland Park, KS 66210 - T: (913) 469-8500, Fax: (913) 469-2348, E-mail: bhartman@jccc.net, Internet: www.jccc.net/gallery. Pres.: Dr. Charles Carlsen, Dir.: Bruce Hartman
Fine Arts Museum / University Museum - 1969
Art gallery, Oppenheimer-Stein sculpture coll 46223

Overton NV

Lost City Museum, 721 S Hwy 169, Overton, NV 89040 - T: (702) 397-2193, Fax: (702) 397-8987, E-mail: lostcity@comnett.net, Internet: www.comnett.net/~lostcity. Cur.: Kathryne Olson
Historical Museum / Local Museum - 1935 46224

Owatonna MN

Owatonna Arts Center, 435 Garden View Ln, West Hills Complex, Owatonna, MN 55060 - T: (507) 451-0533, E-mail: owatonnaartscent@qwest.net. Dir.: Silvan Durben
Fine Arts Museum / Decorative Arts Museum - 1974
Marianne Young costume coll, prints and paintings, sculpture 46225

Owego NY

Tioga County Historical Society Museum, 110 Front St, Owego, NY 13827 - T: (607) 687-2460, Fax: (607) 687-7788, E-mail: tiogamus@clarityconnect.com, Internet: www.tier.net/tiogahistory/. Cur.: Dana Leo
Historical Museum / Local Museum - 1914 46226

Owensboro KY

Anna Eaton Stout Memorial Art Gallery, c/o Brescia University, 717 Frederica, Owensboro, KY 42301 - T: (270) 685-3131, E-mail: maryt@brescia.edu. Dir.: Lance Hunter
Fine Arts Museum / University Museum - 1950 46227

International Bluegrass Music Museum, 101 Daviess St, Owensboro, KY 42303 - T: (270) 926-7891, Fax: (270) 689-9440, E-mail: chuckhayes@bluegrass-museum.org, Internet: www.bluegrass-museum.org. Chm./Pres.: Steves Brechter, Exec. Dir.: Chuck Hayes
Music Museum - 1992
Music hist 46228

Owensboro Area Museum of Science and History, 220 Daviess St, Owensboro, KY 42303 - T: (502) 687-2732, Fax: (502) 687-2738. Dir.: Jeff Jones, Cur.: Kathy Olson
Local Museum - 1966
Local history 46229

Owensboro Museum of Fine Art, 901 Frederica St, Owensboro, KY 42301 - T: (502) 685-3181, Fax: (502) 685-3181, E-mail: omfa@mindspring.com. Dir.: Mary Bryan Hood, Asst. Dir.: Jane Wilson
Fine Arts Museum - 1977
Art, decorative arts 46230

Owls Head ME

Owls Head Transportation Museum, Rte 73, Owls Head, ME 04854 - T: (207) 594-4418, Fax: (207) 594-4410, E-mail: info@ohtm.org, Internet: www.ohtm.org. Dir.: Charles Chiarchiaro
Science&Tech Museum - 1974
Transport 46231

Owosso MI

Curwood Castle, 224 Curwood Castle Dr, Owosso, MI 48867, mail addr: 301 W Main St, Owosso, MI 48867 - T: (989) 725-0511. Cur.: Ivan A. Conger
Special Museum - 1975
Studio of novelist James Oliver Curwood 46232

Michigan State Trust for Railway Preservation, 600 S Oakwood St, Owosso, MI 48867-0665 - T: (989) 725-9464, Fax: (989) 723-1225, E-mail: twelve25@mstrp.com, Internet: www.mstrp.com. Cur.: Steve Knapp
Science&Tech Museum - 1980
Railroad Transportation and technology 46233

The Movie Museum, 318 E Oliver St, Owosso, MI 48867-2351 - T: (989) 725-7621. Pres.: Barbara Moore, C.E.O.: Don Schneider
Special Museum - 1972
Machinery, books, costumes, photos, records 46234

Oxford MA

Oxford Library Museum, 339 Main St, Oxford, MA 01540 - T: (508) 987-6003, Fax: (508) 987-3896, E-mail: tkelley@cwmarsmail.cwmars.org, Internet: www.oxfordma.com. Head: Timothy Kelley
Local Museum - 1903
Local history 46235

Oxford MD

Oxford Museum, Morris and Market Sts, Oxford, MD 21654 - T: (410) 226-5331. Dir.: Lisa Harrington
Local Museum - 1964
Local history 46236

Oxford MI

Northeast Oakland Historical Museum, 1 N Washington St, Oxford, MI 48371 - T: (800) 628-8413, E-mail: mariee1@prodigy.net. Cur.: Marie English
Local Museum - 1971
Local history 46237

Oxford MS

University Gallery, c/o University of Mississippi, Bryandt Hall, Oxford, MS 38677 - T: (662) 232-7193, Fax: (662) 232-5013, E-mail: art@sunset.backbone.oldmiss.edu. Dir.: Margaret Gorove
University Museum / Fine Arts Museum
Student art works 46238

University Museums, c/o University of Mississippi, University Av and Fifth St, Oxford, MS 38677-1848 - T: (662) 915-7073, Fax: (662) 915-7035, E-mail: museums@olemiss.edu, Internet: www.olemiss.edu/depts/u_museum. Man.: William Griffith
University Museum / Fine Arts Museum - 1977
Local history, classical antiquities, folk art of the American South, antique scientific instruments 46239

Oxford NC

Granville County Historical Society Museum, 1 Museum Ln, Oxford, NC 27565 - T: (919) 693-9706, Fax: (919) 692-1030, E-mail: gcmuseum@gloryroad.net. Dir.: Pam Thornton
Local Museum - 1996
Local hist, art, culture, science 46240

Harris Exhibit Hall, 1 Museum Ln, Oxford, NC 27565 - T: (919) 693-9706, Fax: (919) 692-1030, E-mail: gcmuseum@gloryroad.net. Dir.: Pam Thornton
Public Gallery - 1996 46241

Oxford OH

Miami University Art Museum, Patterson Av, Oxford, OH 45056 - T: (513) 529-2232, Fax: (513) 529-6555, E-mail: kretra@muohio.edu, Internet: www.muohio.edu/artmuseum. Dir.: Robert A. Kret, Cur.: Edna Carter Southard, Bonnie N. Mason
Fine Arts Museum / University Museum - 1978 46242

William Holmes McGuffey Museum, 410 E Spring St, Oxford, OH 45056 - T: (513) 529-8380, E-mail: ellisocw@muohio.edu, Internet: www.muohio.edu/artmuseum/. Dir.: Dr. Curtis W. Ellison, Cur.: Beverly Bach
Historical Museum - 1960 46243

Oxnard CA

Carnegie Art Museum, 424 S C St, Oxnard, CA 93030 - T: (805) 385-8157, Fax: (805) 483-3654, Internet: www.vcnet.com/carnart. Dir.: Suzanne Bellah
Fine Arts Museum - 1980 46244

Ventura County Maritime Museum, 2731 S Victoria Av, Oxnard, CA 93035 - T: (805) 984-6260, Fax: (805) 984-5970, E-mail: vcmm@aol.com. Dir.: Mark S. Bacin
Local Museum / Historical Museum - 1991
Maritime and county history, ship models, maritime art 46245

Oxon Hill MD

Oxon Cove Park Museum, 6411 Oxon Hill Rd, Oxon Hill, MD 20745 - T: (301) 839-0211, Fax: (301) 839-1783, Internet: www.nps.gov/nace/oxhi
Agriculture Museum - 1967
Agriculture, farm and farm outbuildings 46246

Oyster Bay NY

Coe Hall, Planting Fields Rd, Oyster Bay, NY 11771-0058 - T: (516) 922-9210, Fax: (516) 922-9226, E-mail: coehall@worldnet.att.net, Internet: www.plantingfields.com. Cur.: Ellen Cone
Historical Museum - 1979 46247

Earle Wightman Museum, 20 Summit St, Oyster Bay, NY 11771 - T: (516) 922-5032, Fax: (516) 922-6892, E-mail: obhistory@aol.com, Internet: members.aol.com/obhistory. Dir.: Thomas A. Kuehhas, Cur.: Richard Kappeler
Historical Museum - 1960
Reichnan coll of early American tools, Theodor Roosevelt coll 46248

Oyster Bay Historical Society Museum → Earle Wightman Museum

Raynham Hall Museum, 20 W Main St, Oyster Bay, NY 11771 - T: (516) 922-6808, Fax: (516) 922-7640, E-mail: raynham-hall-museum@attglobal.net, Internet: www.raynhamhallmuseum.org. Dir.: Andrew C. Batten
Decorative Arts Museum / Historical Museum - 1953 46249

Sagamore Hill National Historic Site, 20 Sagamore Hill Rd, Oyster Bay, NY 11771-1899 - T: (516) 922-4788, Fax: (516) 922-4792, Internet: www.nps.gov/sahi. Cur.: Amy Verone
Historical Museum - 1963 46250

Ozona TX

Crockett County Museum, 404 Eleventh St, Ozona, TX 76943 - T: (915) 392-2837, Fax: (915) 392-5654, E-mail: ccmuseum@hotmail.com. Dir.: P.L. Childress
Local Museum - 1939
Local hist 46251

Pacific Grove CA

Pacific Grove Art Center, 568 Lighthouse Av, Pacific Grove, CA 93950 - T: (831) 375-2208, Fax: (831) 375-2208, E-mail: pgart@mbay.net, Internet: www.pgartcenter.org. Cur.: Robert Gunn
Fine Arts Museum - 1969 46252

Pacific Grove Museum of Natural History, 165 Forest Av, Pacific Grove, CA 93950 - T: (831) 648-5716, Fax: (831) 372-3256, E-mail: pgmuseum@mbay.net, Internet: www.pgmuseum.org. Dir.: Stephen F. Bailey
Natural History Museum - 1881 46253

Pacific Palisades CA

Will Rogers State Historic Park, 1501 Will Rogers State Park Rd, Pacific Palisades, CA 90272 - T: (310) 454-8212, Fax: (310) 459-2031
Historical Museum - 1944
American Indian artifacts, cowboy souvenirs, Western art 46254

Pacifica CA

Sanchez Adobe Historic Site, 1000 Linda Mar Blvd, Pacifica, CA 94044 - T: (650) 359-1462, Fax: (650) 359-1462, E-mail: samhist@aol.com, Internet: www.sanmateocountyhistory.com. Dir.: Mitchell P. Postel, Cur.: Karen Brey
Historical Museum / Local Museum - 1947
Archaeology, furnishings 46255

Paducah KY

Museum of the American Quilter's Society, 215 Jefferson St, Paducah, KY 42002-1540 - T: (270) 442-8856, Fax: (270) 442-5448, E-mail: info@quiltmuseum.org, Internet: www.quiltmuseum.org. Exec. Dir.: Susan Talbot-Stanaway, Cur.: Dorisanna Conner
Fine Arts Museum / Decorative Arts Museum - 1991
Arts and crafts, textiles, quilts 46256

William Clark Market House Museum, 121 S Second St, Market House Sq, Paducah, KY 42001 - T: (270) 443-7759. Exec. Dir.: Penny Baucum-Fields
Local Museum - 1968
History, building was used as a farmers market 46257

Yeiser Art Center, 200 Broadway, Paducah, KY 42001-0732 - T: (270) 442-2453, Fax: (270) 442-2243, E-mail: yacenter@apex.net, Internet: www.yeiser.org. Dir.: Dan Carver
Fine Arts Museum - 1957 46258

Page AZ

John Wesley Powell Memorial Museum, 6 N Lake Powell Blvd, Page, AZ 86040-0547 - T: (928) 645-9496, Fax: (928) 645-3412, E-mail: director@powellmuseum.org, Internet: www.powellmuseum.org. Dir.: Julia P. Betz
Historical Museum - 1969 46259

Pagosa Springs CO

Fred Harman Art Museum, 2560 W Hwy 160, Pagosa Springs, CO 81147 - T: (970) 731-5785, Fax: (970) 731-4832, E-mail: fharman@pagosa.net, Internet: www.harmanartmuseum.com. C.E.O./Cur.: Fred C. Harman
Fine Arts Museum - 1979 46260

Paicines CA

Pinnacles National Monument, 5000 Hwy 146, Paicines, CA 95043 - T: (408) 389-4485 ext 233, Fax: (408) 389-4489, E-mail: pinn-resource_management@nps.gov, Internet: www.nps.gov
Natural History Museum - 1908
Herpetology, entomology, geology, zoology, botany - herbarium 46261

Painesville OH

Indian Museum of Lake County-Ohio, c/o Lake Erie College, 391 W Washington, Painesville, OH 44077 - T: (440) 352-1911. Dir.: Gwen G. King, Asst. Dir.: Ann Dewald
Ethnology Museum / Archaeological Museum - 1980 46262

Painted Post NY

Erwin Museum, 117 W Water St, Painted Post, NY 14870 - T: (607) 962-7021
Local Museum - 1945 46263

Palm Beach FL

Flagler Museum, Cocoanut Row and Whitehall Way, Palm Beach, FL 33480 - T: (561) 655-2833, Fax: (561) 655-2826, E-mail: flagler@emi.net, Internet: www.flagler.org. Dir.: John M. Blades, Cur.: Sandra Barghini
Historical Museum - 1959 46264

The Society of the Four Arts Gallery, 2 Four Arts Plaza, Palm Beach, FL 33480 - T: (561) 655-7227, Fax: (561) 655-7233, E-mail: SFourArts@aol.comts.org, Internet: www.sfourarts.org. Pres.: Ervin S. Duggan, Exec. Vice Pres.: Nancy Mato
Fine Arts Museum - 1936
Art gallery, sculpture garden - library 46265

Palm Coast FL

Florida Agricultural Museum, 1850 Princess Place Rd, Palm Coast, FL 32137 - T: (904) 446-7630, Fax: (904) 446-7631, E-mail: famuseum@pcfl.net, Internet: www.flaglercounty.org/agrimuseum/agri1.htm. C.E.O.: Bruce J. Piatek
Agriculture Museum - 1983
Agriculture 46266

Palm Springs CA

Palm Springs Desert Museum, 101 Museum Dr, Palm Springs, CA 92262 - T: (760) 325-7186, Fax: (760) 327-5069, E-mail: psmuseum@aol.com, Internet: www.psmuseum.org. Dir.: Janice Lyle, Cur.: Katherine Hough (Art), James Cornett (Natural Science)
Fine Arts Museum / Natural History Museum / Performing Arts Museum - 1938 46267

Palmyra NY

Alling Coverlet Museum, 122 William St, Palmyra, NY 14522 - T: (315) 597-6981, Fax: (315) 597-6981, E-mail: bjfhpinc@aol.com, Internet: www.palmyrany.com
Special Museum - 1976
Coverlets, quilts 46268

Hill Cumorah Visitors Center and Historic Sites, 603 State Rte 21 S, Palmyra, NY 14522-9301 - T: (315) 597-5851, Fax: (315) 597-0165, E-mail: rsbcf@redsuspenders.com, Internet: www.canaltown.net/hillcumorah. Dir.: Richard Fox
Religious Arts Museum - 1830
5 historical sites and places of historic significance in connection with the founding of the Church of Jesus Christ of Latter-day Saints 46269

Historic Palmyra, 132 Market St, Palmyra, NY 14522 - T: (315) 597-6981, Fax: (716) 597-4793, E-mail: bjfhpinc@aol.com, Internet: palmyrany.lynet.com. Dir.: Bonnie Hays
Local Museum / Historical Museum - 1967
Local history, military, textiles, Covelelt and quilts coll, naval admirals, W. Churchill's family, mormon hist 46270

Phelps Store Museum, 140 Market St, Palmyra, NY 14522 - T: (315) 597-6981, Fax: (315) 597-4793, E-mail: bjfhpinc@aol.com, Internet: www.palmyrany.com/historicpal/phelps/
Historical Museum - 1964 46271

Palmyra VA

The Old Stone Jail Museum, Court Sq, Palmyra, VA 22963 - T: (804) 842-3378, Fax: (804) 842-3374. C.E.O.: Ellen Miyagawa
Decorative Arts Museum / Local Museum - 1964
Local hist 46272

Palo Alto CA

Palo Alto Art Center, 1313 Newell Rd, Palo Alto, CA 94303 - T: (650) 329-2366, Fax: (650) 326-6165, Internet: www.city.palo-alto.ca.us/palo/city/artsculture/. Dir.: Linda Craighead, Cur.: Signe Mayfield
Fine Arts Museum - 1971 46273

Palo Alto Junior Museum, 1451 Middlefield Rd, Palo Alto, CA 94301 - T: (650) 329-2111, Fax: (650) 473-1965, E-mail: rachel_meyer@city.palo-alto.ca.us, Internet: www.city.palo-alto.ca.us/ross/museum.html. Dir.: Rachel Meyer, Cur.: Jen Dursi, Darin Wacs, Robert Steele
Natural History Museum - 1934
zoo 46274

Pampa TX

White Deer Land Museum, 112-116 S Cuyler, Pampa, TX 79065 - T: (806) 669-8041, Fax: (806) 669-8030, E-mail: museum@pan-tex.net, Internet: www.pan-tex.net. Cur.: Anne Davidson
Local Museum - 1970
Local hist 46275

Pamplin VA

Yesteryear Museum, Rte 1, Box 134 B, Pamplin, VA 23958-9465 - T: (804) 248-5357, E-mail: leemunsick@earthlink.net. C.E.O.: Lee R. Munsick
Music Museum - 1970
Mechanical and automatic music, sound recordings, Edisonia, ragtime, early broadcasting 46276

Panama City FL

The Junior Museum of Bay County, 1731 Jenks Av, Panama City, FL 32405 - T: (850) 769-6129, Fax: (850) 769-6129, E-mail: jrmuseum@knology.net, Internet: www.jrmuseum.org. Dir.: William R. Barton
Ethnology Museum - 1969
Children education 46277

Visual Arts Center of Northwest Florida, 19 E Fourth St, Panama City, FL 32401 - T: (850) 769-4451, Fax: (850) 785-9248, E-mail: vac@visualartscenter.org, Internet: www.visualartscenter.org. Dir.: Kimberly Branscome
Fine Arts Museum / Public Gallery - 1988
Art 46278

Panama City Beach FL

Museum of Man in the Sea, 17314 Panama City Beach Pkwy, Panama City Beach, FL 32413-2020 - T: (904) 235-4101, Fax: (904) 235-4101, E-mail: subraces@panamacity.com, Internet: www.panamacity.cpm/~subraces. Exec. Dir.: Douglas R. Hough
Historical Museum / Historic Site - 1981 46279

Panhandle TX

Carson County Square House Museum, Texas Hwy 207 at Fifth St, Panhandle, TX 79068 - T: (806) 537-3524, Fax: (806) 537-5628, E-mail: shm@squarehousemuseum.org, Internet: www.squarehousemuseum.org. Dir.: Dr. Viola Moore
Local Museum - 1965
Local hist 46280

Paramus NJ

New Jersey Children's Museum, 599 Industrial Av, Valley Hills Pl, Paramus, NJ 07652 - T: (201) 262-2638, Fax: (201) 262-0560, E-mail: esumers@aol.com, Internet: www.njcm.com. Dir.: Anne R. Sumers
Special Museum - 1992 46281

Paris AR

Logan County Museum, 202 N Vine St, Paris, AR 72855 - T: (501) 963-3936. Cur.: Geneva Morton
Local Museum - 1975
History, former Logan County Jail 46282

Paris IL

Bicentennial Art Center and Museum, 132 S Central Av, Paris, IL 61944 - T: (217) 466-8130, Fax: (217) 466-8130, E-mail: bacm@1choice.net. Dir.: Janet M. Messenger, Pres.: Anne J. Johnson
Fine Arts Museum / Public Gallery - 1975 46283

Edgar County Historical Museum, 408 N Main, Paris, IL 61944-1549 - T: (217) 463-5305. Pres.: Theodorsa Day
Local Museum - 1971
Local history, housed in 1872 Arthur House 46284

Paris KY

Hopewell Museum, 800 Pleasant St, Paris, KY 40361 - T: (859) 987-7274, Fax: (859) 987-8107, E-mail: hopemuseum@aol.com. Dir.: Betsy Kephart
Local Museum - 1995
Local hist 46285

Paris TX

Sam Bell Maxey House, 812 S Church St, Paris, TX 75460 - T: (903) 785-5716, Fax: (903) 739-2924, E-mail: maxeyhouse@1starnet.com, Internet: www.maxeyhouse.com. Dir.: Robert Cook
Decorative Arts Museum / Local Museum - 1976
Local hist 46286

Parishville NY

Parishville Museum, Main St, Parishville, NY 13672 - T: (315) 265-7619
Local Museum - 1964 46287

Park City UT

Kimball Art Center, 638 Park Av, Park City, UT 84060 - T: (435) 649-8882, Fax: (435) 649-8889, Internet: www.kimball-art.org. Dir.: Sarah Behrens
Public Gallery - 1976 46288

Park City Museum, 528 Main St, Park City, UT 84060 - T: (435) 649-7457, Fax: (435) 649-7384, E-mail: smorrison@parkcityhistory.org, Internet: www.parkcityhistory.org. Dir.: Sandra Morrison
Local Museum - 1984 46289

Park Hill OK

Murrell Home, 19479 E Murrell Home Rd, Park Hill, OK 74451 - T: (918) 456-2751, Fax: (918) 456-2751, E-mail: murrellhome@intellex.com, Internet: www.ok-history.mus.ok.us
Historical Museum - 1948
Indian artifacts, costumes, pre-Civil War furnishings 46290

Park Rapids MN

North Country Museum of Arts, 301 Court Av, Park Rapids, MN 56470 - T: (218) 732-5237. Cur.: Johanna M. Verbrugghen
Fine Arts Museum - 1977 46291

Park Ridge IL

Wood Library-Museum of Anesthesiology, 520 N Northwest Hwy, Park Ridge, IL 60068-2573 - T: (847) 825-5586, Fax: (847) 825-1692, E-mail: wlm@asahq.org, Internet: www.asahq.org. Cur.: George S. Bause
Historical Museum / Special Museum - 1950
Medicine 46292

Park Ridge NJ

Pascack Historical Society Museum, 19 Ridge Av, Park Ridge, NJ 07656 - T: (201) 573-0307. Pres.: Richard Ross
Local Museum / Historical Museum - 1942 46293

Parker AZ

Colorado River Indian Tribes Museum, Rte 1, Box 23-B, Parker, AZ 85344 - T: (928) 669-9211 ext 1335, Fax: (928) 669-5675, Internet: www.crittourism.rraz.net. Dir.: Betty L. Cornelius
Ethnology Museum - 1970
American Indian - library, archive 46294

Parkersburg WV

The Cultural Center of Fine Arts, 725 Market St, Parkersburg, WV 26101 - T: (304) 485-3859, Fax: (304) 485-3850, E-mail: ekge@earthlink.net, Internet: www.wvfinearts.com. Dir.: Ed Pauley
Fine Arts Museum - 1938
Arts 46295

Parris Island SC

Parris Island Museum, Bldg 111, MCRD, Parris Island, SC 29905-9001 - T: (843) 228-2951, Fax: (843) 228-3065, E-mail: wiser@mcrdpi.usmc.mil, Internet: mcmsmo3.usmc.mil/museum/. Dir.: Dr. Stephen R. Wise
Local Museum - 1976
Ceramics, metal work, uniforms, firearms 46296

Parrish FL

Florida Gulf Coast Railroad Museum, US Hwy 301, Parrish, FL 34219, mail addr: 2146 Ninth St, Sarasota, FL 34237-3404 - T: (941) 766-0906, Fax: (941) 917-0081, E-mail: traininfo@fgcrrm.org, Internet: www.fgcrrm.org. Pres.: James Herron
Science&Tech Museum - 1983
Railroads 46297

Parsippany NJ

Craftsman Farms Foundation, 2352 Rte 10 W, Parsippany, NJ 07950 - T: (973) 540-1165, Fax: (973) 540-1167, E-mail: craftsmanfarms@worldnet.att.net, Internet: www.parsippany.net/craftsmanfarms.html. Dir.: Tommy McPherson, Cur.: Beth Ann McPherson
Historical Museum / Open Air Museum / Agriculture Museum - 1989 46298

Parsons KS

Parsons Historical Society Museum, 401 S 18th St, Parsons, KS 67357 - T: (620) 421-7000
Local Museum - 1969 46299

Pasadena CA

Armory Center for the Arts, 145 N Raymond Av, Pasadena, CA 91103 - T: (626) 792-5101, Fax: (626) 449-0139, Internet: www.armoryarts.org. Dir.: Doris Hausmann
Fine Arts Museum - 1974 46300

Kidspace Children's Museum, 390 S El Molino Av, Pasadena, CA 91101 - T: (626) 449-9144, Fax: (626) 449-9985, Internet: www.kidspacechildrensmuseum.org. Dir.: Carol E. Scott
Special Museum - 1979
Handson, arts, science, humanities 46301

Norton Simon Museum, 411 W Colorado Blvd, Pasadena, CA 91105 - T: (626) 449-6840, Fax: (626) 796-4978, E-mail: art@nortonsimon.org, Internet: www.nortonsimon.org. Dir.: Sara Campbell (Art), Cur.: Gloria Williams, Asst. Cur.: Christine Knoke
Fine Arts Museum - 1924
European paintings and sculpture, Asian sculpture, American art, graphics, old masters paintings 46302

Pacific Asia Museum, 46 N Los Robles Av, Pasadena, CA 91101 - T: (626) 449-2742, Fax: (626) 449-2754, E-mail: PacAsiaMus@aol.com, Internet: pacificasiamuseum.org. Dir.: David Kamansky, Cur.: Meher McArthur (East Asian Art)
Fine Arts Museum / Historical Museum / Folklore Museum - 1971
Ceramics, sculpture, scrolls, screens, woodblock-prints, textiles, folk art, furniture, photos from Asia 46303

Pasadena City College Art Gallery, 1570 E Colorado Blvd, Pasadena, CA 91106 - T: (626) 585-7238, Fax: (626) 585-7914, E-mail: lxmalm@paccd.cc.ca.us, Internet: www.pccd.cc.ca.us. Dir.: Jeff Allen
Fine Arts Museum 46304

Pasadena Historical Museum, 470 W Walnut St, Pasadena, CA 91103-3594 - T: (626) 577-1660, Fax: (626) 577-1662, E-mail: info@pasadenahistory.org, Internet: www.pasadenahistory.org. Exec. Dir.: Richard S. Cohen, Jeanette O'Malley
Local Museum - 1924 46305

Pascagoula MS

Old Spanish Fort and Museum, 4602 Fort St, Pascagoula, MS 39567 - T: (228) 769-1505, Fax: (228) 769-1432, E-mail: lpkhouse@yahoo.com
Historical Museum - 1949 46306

Pasco WA

Franklin County Historical Museum, 305 N 4th Av, Pasco, WA 99301 - T: (509) 547-3714, Fax: (509) 545-2168, E-mail: fchs@bossig.com. Pres.: Rella Reimann, Administrator: Jacque Sonderman
Local Museum - 1982
Local hist 46307

Pateros WA

Fort Okanogan, 1B Otto Rd, Pateros, WA 98846 - T: (509) 923-2473, Fax: (509) 923-2980, Internet: www.parks.wa.gov. Dir.: Cleve Pinnix
Historical Museum - 1965
Indian and pioneer items, basketry, weapons 46308

Paterson NJ

Passaic County Community College Galleries, Broadway Gallery, 1 College Blvd, Paterson, NJ 07505-1179 - T: (973) 684-6555, Fax: (973) 523-6085, E-mail: mgillan@pccc.cc.nj.us, Internet: www.pccc.cc.nj.us/poetry. Dir.: Maria Mazziotti Gillan, Asst. Dir.: Aline Papazian, Cur.: Jane Haw
Fine Arts Museum / University Museum - 1968 46309

Passaic County Historical Society Museum, Lambert Castle, Valley Rd, Paterson, NJ 07503-2932 - T: (973) 247-0085, Fax: (973) 881-9434, E-mail: lambertcastle@yahoo.com, Internet: www.geocities.com/pchslc. Dir.: Andrew F. Shick
Local Museum - 1926
Local history, Koempel Spoon coll, textiles, paintings, decorative art, folk art - library 46310

Paterson Museum, 2 Market St, Paterson, NJ 07501 - T: (973) 881-3874, Fax: (973) 881-3435, Internet: www.thepattersonmuseum.org. Dir.: Giacomo R. DeStefano, Cur.: Bruce Balistrieri (History)
Historical Museum / Natural History Museum / Science&Tech Museum - 1925 46311

Patten ME

Patten Lumberman's Museum, Shin Pond Rd, Patten, ME 04765 - T: (207) 528-2650, Internet: www.mainerec.com/logger.html. Cur.: Marcia Pond-Anderson
Historical Museum / Ethnology Museum - 1959
Logging, lumbering 46312

Patterson LA

Louisiana State Museum, 394 Airport Circle, Patterson, LA 70392 - T: (504) 395-7067, Fax: (504) 395-3179. Dir.: Nicholas Neylon
Science&Tech Museum - 1975
Aviation 46313

Pawhuska OK

Osage County Historical Society Museum, 700 N Lynn Av, Pawhuska, OK 74056 - T: (918) 287-9924. Dir./Cur.: J.B. Smith
Local Museum - 1964 46314

Pawling NY

Gunnison Museum of Natural History, 397 Mizzen Top Rd, Pawling, NY 12564 - T: (914) 855-5099. Cur.: James Mandracchia
Natural History Museum - 1960 46315

John Kane House, 126 East Main St, Pawling, NY 12564 - T: (914) 855-9316
Historical Museum - 1910
George Washington's headquarters in autumn 1778, Lowell Thomas, radio broadcaster 46316

Pawnee City NE

Pawnee City Historical Society Museum, Hwy 50/8 East, Pawnee City, NE 68420 - T: (402) 852-3131, Internet: www.rootsweb.com/~.nepawnee. Pres.: Roy Mullins
Local Museum - 1968 46317

Pawtucket RI

Slater Mill Historic Site, 67 Roosevelt Av, Pawtucket, RI 02860 - T: (401) 725-8638, Fax: (401) 722-3040, E-mail: samslater@aol.com, Internet: www.slatermill.org. Dir.: Jeanne L. Zavada, Cur.: Karen Conopask
Science&Tech Museum / Historic Site - 1921
Hist of textile industry 46318

Paxton IL

Ford County Historical Society Museum, 255 West State St, Paxton, IL 60957 - T: (217) 379-4684, Internet: www.rootsweb.com/~ilford. Pres.: Ed F. Karr
Local Museum - 1967
Local history, housed in County Court House 46319

Paxton MA

Saint Luke's Gallery, Anna Maria College, Moll Art Center, 50 Sunset Ln, Paxton, MA 01612 - T: (508) 849-3300 ext 442, Fax: (508) 849-3408, Internet: www.annamaria.edu. Dir.: Alice Lambert, Elizabeth Killoran
Fine Arts Museum / University Museum - 1968 46320

Peace Dale RI

Museum of Primitive Art and Culture, 1058 Kingstown Rd, Peace Dale, RI 02883 - T: (401) 783-5711. Pres.: Wallace Campbell, Dir.: Sarah Peabody Turnbaugh
Ethnology Museum / Archaeological Museum - 1892
Anthropology 46321

Peaks Island ME

Fifth Maine Regiment Center, 45 Seashore Av, Peaks Island, ME 04108 - T: (207) 766-3330, Fax: (207) 766-3083, E-mail: fifthmaine@juno.com, Internet: fifthmaine.home.att.net. Dir.: Sharon L. McKenna, Cur.: Kim MacIsaac
Military Museum - 1954
Military hist 46322

Pearl River NY

Orangetown Historical Museum, 213 Blue Hill Rd, Pearl River, NY 10965 - T: (845) 735-0429, Fax: (845) 359-8269, E-mail: otownmuseum@fcc.net, Internet: www.orangetown.com/parks/
Local Museum - 1992
archives 46323

Pecos NM

Pecos Park, State Rd 63, 2 mi S of Pecos, Pecos, NM 87552, mail addr: POB 418, Pecos, NM 87552 - T: (505) 757-6414 ext 221, Fax: (505) 757-8460, Internet: www.nps.gov/peco
Archaeological Museum - 1965
Archaeology, A.V. Kidder coll, Mission churches 46324

Pecos TX

West of the Pecos Museum, First at Cedar (U.S. 285), Pecos, TX 79772 - T: (915) 445-5076, Fax: (915) 445-3149, E-mail: wpmuseum@nwol.net. Cur.: Dorenda Zenegas-Millan
Local Museum - 1962
Local hist 46325

Peebles OH

Serpent Mound Museum, 3850 State Rte 73, Peebles, OH 45660 - T: (937) 587-2796, Fax: (937) 587-1116, E-mail: serpent@bright.net, Internet: www.ohiohistory.org
Ethnology Museum - 1900 46326

Peekskill NY

Peekskill Museum, 124 Union Av, Peekskill, NY 10566 - T: (914) 736-0473, Internet: www.peekskillmuseum.org
Local Museum - 1946 46327

Pelham NY

Pelham Art Center, 155 Fifth Av, Pelham, NY 10803 - T: (914) 738-2525, Fax: (914) 738-2686, E-mail: info@pelhamartcenter.org. Pres.: Paisley Kelling, C.E.O.: Lisa Robb
Fine Arts Museum / Folklore Museum - 1975
Art 46328

Pella IA

Pella Historical Village, 507 Franklin, Pella, IA 50219-0145 - T: (515) 628-2409, Fax: (515) 628-9192, E-mail: pellatt@kdsi.net, Internet: www.pellatuliptime.com. Pres.: Merlyn VanderLeest, Dir.: Patsy Sadler
Ethnology Museum / Local Museum - 1965
Ethnography (Dutch), 20 historic buildings 46329

Scholte House Museum, 728 Washington, Pella, IA 50219 - T: (515) 628-3684. Cur.: Shirley J. Rudd
Special Museum - 1982 46330

Pemaquid Point ME

Fishermen's Museum, Lighthouse Park, Pemaquid Point, ME 04554 - T: (207) 677-2494. Dir.: Mary Norton Orrick
Historical Museum - 1972
Old pictures, models of fishing boats 46331

Pembina ND

Pembina State Museum, 805 State Hwy 59, Pembina, ND 58271-0456 - T: (701) 825-6840, Fax: (701) 825-6383, E-mail: mbailey@state.nd.us, Internet: www.discovernd.com/history. Dir.: Merlan E. Paaverud
Historical Museum - 1996
Fur trade, Meti's 46332

Pembroke MA

Pembroke Historical Museum, Center St, Pembroke, MA 02359 - T: (781) 293-9083. Pres.: Denise Hawes, Cur.: Karen E. Proctor
Local Museum - 1950
Local history 46333

Pembroke NC

Native American Resource Center, University of North Carolina at Pembroke, Pembroke, NC 28372 - T: (910) 521-6282, E-mail: stan.knick@uncp.edu, Internet: www.uncp.edu/nativemuseum/. Dir.: Dr. Stanley Knick
University Museum / Ethnology Museum - 1979 46334

Pendleton OR

Umatilla County Historical Society Museum, 108 SW Frazer St, Pendleton, OR 97801 - T: (541) 276-0012, Fax: (541) 276-7989, E-mail: uchs@oregontrail.net, Internet: www.umatillahistory.org. Pres.: Sam Pambrun, Exec. Dir.: Julie Reese
Local Museum - 1974
Local hist 46335

Pendleton SC

Ashtabula Plantation, Hwy 88, Pendleton, SC 29670 - T: (864) 646-7249, Fax: (864) 646-2506, E-mail: pendtour@innova.net, Internet: www.pendleton-district.org
Decorative Arts Museum - 1960 46336

Pendleton District Agricultural Museum, 120 History Ln, Pendleton, SC 29670 - T: (864) 646-3782, Fax: (864) 646-2506, E-mail: pendtour@innova.net, Internet: www.pendleton-district.org. Dir.: Hurley E. Badders, Cur.: Donna K. Roper
Agriculture Museum - 1976
Agriculture 46337

Woodburn Plantation, 130 History Ln, Pendleton, SC 29670 - T: (864) 646-7249
Decorative Arts Museum - 1960 46338

Penn Valley CA

Museum of Ancient and Modern Art, POB 975, Penn Valley, CA 95946 - T: (530) 432-3080, Fax: (530) 272-0184, E-mail: info@mama.org, Internet: www.mama.org. Dir.: Zoe Alowan (Children's Art Academy), Cur.: Dr. Claude Needham (Science and Technology), Jeff Spencer (Antiquities), David Christie (Mathematics and Science), Tim Elston (Interactive Multimedia), Ass. Cur.: Dr. James D. Wrey (Stellar Astronomy), Sc. Staff: Nancy Christie (Conservation (Ancient)), Robbert Trice (Conservation (Modern)), Nancy Burns (Library), Wayne Hoyle (Computer Archive)
Fine Arts Museum - 1981
Art, astromomy, prehistory 46339

Penn Yan NY

Oliver House Museum, 200 Main St, Penn Yan, NY 14527 - T: (315) 536-7318, Fax: (315) 536-7318, E-mail: ycghs@linkny.com, Internet: www.yatespast.com. Exec. Dir.: Idelle Dillon
Local Museum - 1860 46340

Pennsburg PA

Schwenkfelder Library and Heritage Center, 105 Seminary St, Pennsburg, PA 18073-1898 - T: (215) 679-3103, Fax: (215) 679-8175, E-mail: info@schwenkfelder.com, Internet: www.schwenkfelder.com. Exec. Dir.: David W. Luz
Historical Museum - 1913
Local hist 46341

Pensacola FL

Historic Pensacola Village, 120 Church St, Pensacola, FL 32501 - T: (850) 595-5985 ext 103, Fax: (850) 595-5989, E-mail: jdaniels@historicpensacola.org, Internet: www.historicpensacola.org. Dir.: John P. Daniels, Dep. Dir.: Beatrice L. Robertson, Cur.: Lisa Dunbar
Local Museum - 1967
Local history 46342

National Museum of Naval Aviation, 1750 Radford Blvd, Ste C, Pensacola, FL 32508-5402 - T: (904) 452-3604 ext 119, Fax: (904) 452-3296, E-mail: naval.museum@cnet.navy.mil, Internet: www.naval-air.org. Dir.: Robert Rasmussen, Cur.: Robert Macon
Military Museum / Science&Tech Museum - 1963
Naval aviation 46343

Pensacola Historical Museum, 115 E Zaragosa St, Pensacola, FL 32501 - T: (850) 434-1559, Fax: (904) 433-1559, E-mail: phstaff@pcola.gulf.net, Internet: www.penacolahistory.org. Dir.: Sandra L. Johnson
Historical Museum - 1960
History, historic Arbona building 46344

Pensacola Museum of Art, 407 S Jefferson St, Pensacola, FL 32501 - T: (850) 432-6247, Fax: (850) 469-1532, E-mail: info@pensacolamuseumofart.org, Internet: www.pensacolamuseumofart.org. Dir.: Maria V. Butler, Linda P. Nolan, Cur.: Jeffrey Carlson
Fine Arts Museum - 1954
Art Museum, housed in 1908 old city jail 46345

University of West Florida Art Gallery, 11000 University Pkwy, Pensacola, FL 32514 - T: (850) 474-2696, 474-2045, Fax: (850) 474-3247, E-mail: dbond@uwf.edu, Internet: www.uwf.edu/~art. Dir.: Debra Bond, Ass. Dir.: John Markowitz
Fine Arts Museum / Public Gallery / University Museum - 1970 46346

Visual Arts Gallery, 1000 College Blvd, Pensacola, FL 32504 - T: (850) 484-2554, Fax: (850) 484-2564, E-mail: apeterson@pjc.cc.fl.us, Internet: www.pjc.cc.fl.us. Dir.: Allan Peterson
Fine Arts Museum / Decorative Arts Museum / University Museum - 1970 46347

Peoria IL

Heuser Art Center, c/o Bradley University, 1501 W Bradley Av, Peoria, IL 61625 - T: (309) 677-2989, Fax: (309) 677-3642, E-mail: jch@bradley.edu, Internet: www.bradley.edu. Dir.: John Heintzman
Public Gallery / University Museum 46348

Lakeview Museum of Arts and Sciences, 1125 W Lake Av, Peoria, IL 61614-5985 - T: (309) 686-7000, Fax: (309) 686-0280, E-mail: kathleen@lakeview-museum.org, Internet: www.lakeview-museum.org. Dir.: Jim Richerson, Vice Pres.: Kristan H. McKinsey (Collections, Exhibitions)
Fine Arts Museum / Science&Tech Museum - 1965 46349

Peoria Historical Society, 611 SW Washington, Peoria, IL 61602 - T: (309) 674-1921, Fax: (309) 674-1882, Internet: www.peoriahistoricalsociety.org. Dir.: Kathryn Belsley
Historical Museum - 1934
Local history 46350

Wheels O' Time Museum, 11923 N Knoxville Av, Peoria, IL 61612 - T: (309) 243-9020, Fax: (309) 243-5616, E-mail: wotmuseum@aol.com, Internet: www.wheelsotime.org. Pres.: Gary O. Bragg
Science&Tech Museum - 1977
Antique vehicles, clocks, musical devices, tools, toys, farm equipment 46351

Perkasie PA

Pearl S. Buck House, Green Hills Farm, 520 Dublin Rd, Perkasie, PA 18944 - T: (215) 249-0100, Fax: (215) 249-9657, E-mail: info@pearl-s-buck.org, Internet: www.pearl-s-buck.org. Pres.: Sandy Bates, Exec. Dir.: Meredith J. Richardson
Local Museum / Decorative Arts Museum - 1964
Stone farmhouse 46352

Perris CA

Orange Empire Railway Museum, 2201 S A St, Perris, CA 92572-0548 - T: (909) 943-3020, Fax: (909) 943-2676, E-mail: oerm@juno.com, Internet: www.oerm.org. Pres.: Thomas N. Jacobson
Science&Tech Museum - 1956
Railway, historical Santa Fe line from Chicago to San Diego 46353

Perry FL

Forest Capital State Museum, 204 Forest Park Dr, Perry, FL 32348 - T: (850) 584-3227, Fax: (850) 584-3488, E-mail: forestcapital@perry.gulfnet.com, Internet: www.nnyflorida.com
Natural History Museum / Folklore Museum - 1973
Logging, lumber, timber industry, forestry 46354

Perry IA

Forest Park Museum, 1477 K Av, Perry, IA 50220 - T: (515) 465-3577, Fax: (515) 465-3579, E-mail: info@dallas25.org, Internet: www.dallascountyconservation.org. CEO: Mike Wallace
Science&Tech Museum - 1953
Early transportation, farm machinery, tools, railroading, blacksmith shop 46355

Perry OK

Cherokee Strip Museum and Henry S. Johnston Library, 2617 W Fir St, Perry, OK 73077 - T: (580) 336-2405, Fax: (580) 336-2064, E-mail: csmuseum@ionet.net. Cur.: Kaye Bond
Historical Museum - 1965 46356

Perrysburg OH

Fort Meigs State Memorial, State Rte 65, Perrysburg, OH 43551 - T: (419) 874-4121. Dir.: Dr. Larry Nelson
Military Museum - 1975 46357

Perryville KY

Perryville Battlefield Museum, 1825 Battlefield Rd, Perryville, KY 40468-0296 - T: (859) 332-8631, Fax: (859) 332-2440, E-mail: kurtholman@mail.state.ky.us, Internet: www.state.ky.us/agencies/parks/perryvil.html. Head: Kurt Holman
Military Museum - 1965
Civil War hist 46358

Perryville MD

Rodgers Tavern, 259 E Broad St, Perryville, MD 21903 - T: (410) 642-3703, Fax: (410) 642-3641, E-mail: rtavern@iximd.com, Internet: www.Perryvillemd.org. Head: Brenda Price
Local Museum - 1956 46359

Perth Amboy NJ

Kearny Cottage, 63 Catalpa Av, Perth Amboy, NJ 08861 - T: (732) 826-1826, E-mail: writer@ptd.net
Fine Arts Museum / Decorative Arts Museum - 1928
Roger Statuettes furniture, works by local artists 46360

The Royal Governor's Mansion, 149 Kearny Av, Perth Amboy, NJ 08861 - T: (732) 826-5527, E-mail: info@proprietaryhouse.org, Internet: www.proprietaryhouse.org. C.E.O.: Donald J. Peck
Local Museum - 1967
Historic house 46361

Peru IN

Circus City Festival Museum, 154 N Broadway, Peru, IN 46970 - T: (765) 472-3918, Fax: (765) 472-2826, E-mail: perucirc@perucircus.com, Internet: www.perucircus.com. Pres.: Dan Scott, Exec. Vice Pres.: Lowell Maxwell, Vice Pres.: Timothy Bessignano (Museum & exhibits)
Performing Arts Museum - 1959
Circus 46362

Grissom Air Museum, 6500 Hoosier Blvd, Peru, IN 46970 - T: (765) 689-8011, Fax: (765) 688-2956, E-mail: info@grissomairmuseum.com, Internet: www.grissomairmuseum.com. Cur.: John S. Marsh
Military Museum / Science&Tech Museum - 1981
Military hist, aviation 46363

Miami County Museum, 51 N Broadway, Peru, IN 46970 - T: (765) 473-9183, Fax: (317) 473-3880, E-mail: admin@miamicountymuseum.org, Internet: www.miamicountymuseum.org. Dir.: Cinnamon Catlin-Legutko
Local Museum / Ethnology Museum - 1916
County history, circus, Miami Indians, transportation 46364

Peshtigo WI

Peshtigo Fire Museum, 400 Oconto Av, Peshtigo, WI 54157 - T: (715) 582-3244. C.E.O.: Don Hansen, Cur.: Ruth Erickson, Ruth Wiltzius, Arlene Behwke, Jean Hansen, Margaret Wood, Jean Behnke
Local Museum - 1962
Local hist 46365

Petaluma CA

Petaluma Adobe State Historic Park, 3325 Adobe Rd, Petaluma, CA 94954 - T: (707) 762-4871, Fax: (707) 762-4871, E-mail: adobesara@hotmail.com, Internet: www.parks.sonoma.net/adobe
Agriculture Museum - 1951
Ranch life, tools, furnishings 46366

Petaluma Wildlife and Natural Science Museum, 201 Fair St, Petaluma, CA 94952 - T: (707) 778-4787, Fax: (707) 778-4787, E-mail: wildlifemuseum@yahoo.com, Internet: www.sonic.net/~museum. Pres.: George Grossi, Dir./Cur.: Andrea Gates, Marsi Goodwin
Natural History Museum - 1990
Natural science 46367

Peterborough NH

Peterborough Historical Society Museum, 19 Grove St, Peterborough, NH 03458 - T: (603) 924-3235, Fax: (603) 924-3200, E-mail: info@peterboroughhistory.org, Internet: www.peterboroughhistory.org
Local Museum - 1902 46368

Petersburg AK

Clausen Memorial Museum, 203 Fram St, Petersburg, AK 99833 - T: (907) 772-3598, Fax: (907) 772-2698, E-mail: bigfish@clausenmuseum.alaska.net, Internet: www.clausenmuseum.alaska.net. C.E.O.: Sue McCallum
Historical Museum / Local Museum - 1965
Fishing, fish, boats, local history 46369

Petersburg IL

Lincoln's New Salem Historic Site, R.R. 1, Petersburg, IL 62675 - T: (217) 632-4000, Fax: (217) 632-4010, E-mail: newsalem@fgi.net, Internet: www.lincolnsnewsalem.com. Pres.: Carol Jenkins
Local Museum - 1917
New Salem Village, in the 1830s where Lincoln lived as a young man 46370

Petersburg VA

Archibald Graham McIlwaine House, The Petersburg Museums, 425 Cockade Alley, Petersburg, VA 23803 - T: (804) 733-2400, Fax: (804) 863-0837, E-mail: ssavery@techcom.net, Internet: www.petersburg-va.org. Dir.: Suzanne T. Savery, Cur.: Roswitha M. Rash
Local Museum - 1984
Historic house 46371

Centre Hill Mansion, The Petersburg Museums, Centre Hill Center, Petersburg, VA 23803 - T: (804) 733-2400, Fax: (804) 863-0837, E-mail: ssavery@techcom.net, Internet: www.petersburg-va.org. Dir.: Suzanne T. Savery, Cur.: Roswitha M. Rash
Local Museum - 1976
Historic house 46372

Farmers Bank, The Petersburg Museums, 19 Bollingbrook St, Petersburg, VA 23803 - T: (804) 733-2400, Fax: (804) 863-0837, E-mail: ssavery@techcom.net, Internet: www.petersburg-va.org. Dir.: Suzanne T. Savery, Cur.: Roswitha M. Rash
Special Museum - 1974
Banking 46373

Pamplin Park Civil War Site, 6125 Boydton Plank Rd, Petersburg, VA 23803 - T: (804) 861-2408, Fax: (804) 861-2820, E-mail: pamplinpark@mindspring.com, Internet: www.pamplinpark.org. Dir.: A. Wilson Greene, William C. Lazenby, Cur.: Richard Lewis, Sc. Staff: Arthur W. Bergeron (History)
Military Museum - 1994
Military hist 46374

Petersburg Area Art League, 7 Olde St, Petersburg, VA 23803 - T: (804) 861-4611, Fax: (804) 861-3962. Pres.: George Tilarinos
Fine Arts Museum - 1932
Art 46375

The Petersburg Museums, 15 W Bank St, Petersburg, VA 23803 - T: (804) 733-2404, Fax: (804) 863-0837, E-mail: ssavery@techcom.net, Internet: www.petersburg-va.com. Dir.: Suzanne T. Savery, Cur.: Roswitha M. Rash
Local Museum - 1972
Local hist 46376

Petersburg National Battlefield, 1539 Hickory Hill Rd, Petersburg, VA 23803-4721 - T: (804) 732-3531, Fax: (804) 732-0835, Internet: www.nps.gov/pe_info.htm. Sc. Staff: Christopher Calkins (History)
Historic Site / Military Museum - 1926
Military hist 46377

Siege Museum, 15 W Bank St, Petersburg, VA 23803 - T: (804) 733-2404, Fax: (804) 863-0837, E-mail: ssavery@techcom.net, Internet: www.petersburg-va.com. Dir.: Suzanne T. Savery
Military Museum - 1976
Civil war 46378

Trapezium House, The Petersburg Museums, Market St, Petersburg, VA 23803 - T: (804) 733-2400, Fax: (804) 732-9212, E-mail: ssavery@techcom.net, Internet: www.petersburg-va.org. Dir.: Suzanne T. Savery, Cur.: Roswitha M. Rash
Local Museum - 1974
Historic house 46379

Petersham MA

Fisher Museum of Forestry, Harvard University, 326 N Main St, Petersham, MA 01366-0068 - T: (978) 724-3302, Fax: (978) 724-3595, E-mail: jokeefe@fas.harvard.edu, Internet: www.iternet.edu/hfr/mus.html. Dir.: David R. Foster
Natural History Museum / University Museum - 1940
Forest history and ecology 46380

Petersham Historical Museum, 10 N Main St, Petersham, MA 01366 - T: (508) 724-3380. Pres.: James Baird
Local Museum - 1923
Local history 46381

Petoskey MI

Crooked Tree Arts Center, 461 E Mitchell St, Petoskey, MI 49770 - T: (616) 347-4337, Fax: (616) 347-5414, E-mail: dale@crookedtree.org, Internet: www.crookedtree.org. Pres.: Bob Forman, C.E.O./Dir.: Dale Hull, Cur.: Vivi Woodcock
Public Gallery 46382

Little Traverse Historical Museum, 100 Depot Court, Petoskey, MI 49770 - T: (231) 347-2620, Fax: (616) 347-2875, E-mail: mce@freeway.net. Exec. Dir.: Mary Candace Eaton
Local Museum - 1971
Regional history 46383

Virginia M. McCune Community Arts Center, 461 E Mitchell St, Petoskey, MI 49770 - T: (231) 347-4337, Fax: (231) 347-5414, E-mail: ctac@freeway.net, Internet: www.crookedtree.org. Dir.: Dale Hall, Cur.: Judy Landis
Fine Arts Museum - 1981 46384

Pharr TX

Old Clock Museum, 929 E Preston St, Pharr, TX 78577 - T: (210) 787-1923. Man.: Gene Shawn, Barbara Shawn Barber
Science&Tech Museum - 1968
Horology 46385

Philadelphia PA

Academy of Natural Sciences of Philadelphia Museum, 1900 Ben Franklin Pkwy, Philadelphia, PA 19103-1195 - T: (215) 299-1000, Fax: (215) 299-1028, Internet: www.acnatsci.org. Dir.: James Baker, Cur.: Ruth Patrick (Art, Artifacts)
Natural History Museum - 1812
Natural science 46386

The African American Museum in Philadelphia, 701 Arch St, Philadelphia, PA 19106-1557 - T: (215) 574-0380, Fax: (215) 574-3110, E-mail: TRour@AAMPmuseum.org, Internet: www.aampmuseum.org. Pres.: Harrie Harrison
Local Museum - 1976
Intellectural and material cultural of african and american 46387

American Catholic Historical Society Museum, 263 S Fourth St, Philadelphia, PA 19106 - T: (610) 667-2125, Fax: (215) 204-1663, Internet: www.amchs.org. Pres.: Mary Louise Sullivanons, C.E.O.: James P. McCoy
Historical Museum / Religious Arts Museum - 1884
Religious and American hist 46388

American Swedish Historical Museum, 1900 Pattison Av, Philadelphia, PA 19145 - T: (215) 389-1776, Fax: (215) 389-7701, E-mail: ashm@libertynet.org, Internet: www.americanswedish.org. Exec. Dir.: Richard Waldron, Cur.: Margaretha Talerman, Ass. Cur.: Crystal A. Polis
Local Museum / Folklore Museum - 1926
Swedish-American history, art 46389

Artforms Gallery Manuyunk, 106 Levering St, Philadelphia, PA 19127 - T: (215) 483-3030. Dir.: Ronna Cooper
Fine Arts Museum
Paintings, collage prints, ceramic sculpture, wood & stone sculpture & photography 46390

Arthur Ross Gallery, University of Pennsylvania, 220 S 34th St, Philadelphia, PA 19104-6303 - T: (215) 898-4401, Fax: (215) 573-2045, E-mail: arg@pobox.upenn.edu, Internet: www.upenn.edu/arg/. Dir.: Dr. Dilys V. Winegrad
University Museum / Fine Arts Museum - 1983 46391

Athenaeum of Philadelphia, 219 S 6th St, E Washington Sq, Philadelphia, PA 19106 - T: (215) 925-2688, Fax: (215) 925-3755, E-mail: magee@philaathenaeum.org, Internet: www.philaathenaeum.org. Dir.: Dr. Roger W. Moss, Ass. Dir.: Eileen M. Magee, Cur.: Bruce Laverty (Architecture)
Fine Arts Museum / Decorative Arts Museum - 1814
Art coll, manuscripts, architectural drawings, historic design 46392

Atwater Kent Museum - The History Museum of Philadelphia, 15 S 7th St, Philadelphia, PA 19106 - T: (215) 685-4830, Fax: (215) 685-4837, E-mail: akmh@philadephiahistory.org, Internet: www.philadephiahistory.org. Dir.: Viki Sand, Cur.: Jeffrey Ray
Fine Arts Museum / Historical Museum - 1939
History 46393

The Balch Institute for Ethnic Studies, 18 S 7th St, Philadelphia, PA 19106 - T: (215) 925-8090, Fax: (215) 925-8195, E-mail: balchlib@balchinstitute.org, Internet: www.balchinstitute.org. Cur.: Barbara Ward Grubb
Ethnology Museum - 1971
Ethnography 46394

Betsy Ross House, 239 Arch St, Philadelphia, PA 19106 - T: (215) 686-1252, Fax: (215) 686-1256, E-mail: lori@betsyrosshouse.org, Internet: www.betsyrosshouse.org. Exec. Dir.: Lori Dillard Rech
Local Museum - 1898
Historic house, craftman's tools, furnishings - American Flag House 46395

Cedar Grove Mansion, Philadelphia Museum of Art, Fairmount Park, Lansdowne Dr, Philadelphia, PA 19101 - T: (215) 763-8100 ext 4013, Internet: www.philamuseum.org
Decorative Arts Museum 46396

Center for the Visual Arts, Brandywine Workshop, 730 S Broad St, Philadelphia, PA 19146 - T: (215) 546-3675, Fax: (215) 546-2825, E-mail: brandwn@libertynet.org, Internet: www.blackboard.com/brndywne. Dir.: Allan L. Edmunds
Fine Arts Museum - 1972 46397

Cigna Museum and Art Collection, 2 Liberty Pl, 1601 Chestnut St, Philadelphia, PA 19192-2078 - T: (215) 761-4907, Fax: (215) 761-5596, E-mail: melissa.hough@cigna.com. Dir.: Melissa E. Hough, Cur.: Sue M. Levy, Cur. Assoc.: Dinyelle Wertz
Fine Arts Museum / Historical Museum - 1925
Art, history 46398

Civil War Museum, 1805 Pine St, Philadelphia, PA 19103 - T: (215) 735-8196, Fax: (215) 735-3812, Internet: www.libertynet.org/~CWLM. Dir.: John J. Craft, Cur.: Steven J. Wright
Historical Museum - 1888
History 46399

Clay Studio, 139 N Second St, Philadelphia, PA 19106 - T: (215) 925-3453, Fax: (215) 925-7774, Internet: www.theclaystudio.org. Exec. Dir.: James Clark
Decorative Arts Museum - 1974 46400

Cliveden House, 6401 Germantown Av, Philadelphia, PA 19144 - T: (215) 848-1777, Fax: (215) 438-2892, E-mail: chewhouse@aol.com, Internet: www.cliveden.org. Dir.: Kris S. Kepford, Cur.: Phillip Sietz
Local Museum / Historic Site - 1972
Historic house, site of the Battle of Germantown 1777 46401

The Design Center at Philadelphia University, 4200 Henry Av, Philadelphia, PA 19144 - T: (215) 951-2860, Fax: (215) 951-2662, E-mail: thedesigncenter@philau.edu, Internet: www.philau.edu/designcenter. Dir.: Hilary Jay, Ass. Dir.: Amanda Mullin, Cur.: Nancy Packer
Decorative Arts Museum - 1978
Textiles hist, costumes, design 46402

Eastern State Penitentiary Historic Site, 22nd St and Fairmount Av, Philadelphia, PA 19130 - T: (215) 236-3300, Fax: (215) 236-5289, E-mail: e-state@liberty.net.org, Internet: www.easternstate.org. Exec. Dir.: Sara Jane Elk
Historical Museum 46403

Ebenezer Maxwell Mansion, 200 W Tulpehocken St, Philadelphia, PA 19144 - T: (215) 438-1861, Fax: (215) 438-1861. Pres.: Joan Frankel, C.E.O. & Exec. Dir.: Nancy S. Powell
Local Museum - 1975
Local hist 46404

Edgar Allan Poe House, 530-32 N 7th St, Philadelphia, PA 19123 - T: (215) 597-8780, Fax: (215) 597-1901, Internet: www.nps.gov/edal. Man.: Steve Sitarski, Cur.: Doris Fanelli
Special Museum - 1935
Edgar Allan Poe brick house 46405

Elfreth's Alley Museum, 126 Elfreths Alley, Philadelphia, PA 19106 - T: (215) 574-0560, Fax: (215) 922-7869, E-mail: info@elfrethsalley.org, Internet: www.elfrethsalley.org. Exec. Dir.: Beth Richards
Historic Site - 1934
Historic Buildings 46406

Esther M. Klein Art Gallery, University City Science Center, 3600 Market St, Philadelphia, PA 19104 - T: (215) 387-2262, Fax: (215) 382-0056, E-mail: kleinart@libertynet.org, Internet: www.kleinartgallery.org. Dir./Cur.: Dan Schimmel
University Museum / Fine Arts Museum - 1976 46407

The Fabric Workshop and Museum, 1315 Cherry St, Philadelphia, PA 19107 - T: (215) 568-1111, Fax: (215) 568-8211, E-mail: info@fabricworkshopandmuseum.org, Internet: www.fabricworkshopandmuseum.org. Dir.: Marion Boulton Stroud
Fine Arts Museum / Special Museum - 1977
Contemporary art, Studio focusing on fabric and new materials 46408

Fireman's Hall Museum, 147 N 2nd St, Philadelphia, PA 19106-2010 - T: (215) 923-1438, Fax: (215) 923-0479, E-mail: firemusks@aol.com. Dir./Cur.: Kathryn Saldan, Cur.: Henry J. Magee
Historical Museum - 1967
Fire fighting 46409

Fort Mifflin, Fort Mifflin Rd, Philadelphia, PA 19153 - T: (215) 685-4167, Fax: (215) 685-4166. Exec. Dir.: Eilee Young-Vignola
Historical Museum / Military Museum - 1962
Historic 1777 fort 46410

The Franklin Institute, 222 N 20th, Philadelphia, PA 19103-1194 - T: (215) 448-1208, 448-1200, Fax: (215) 448-1081, E-mail: kkirby@fi.edu, Internet: www.fi.edu. Pres. & C.E.O.: Dennis M. Wint
Science&Tech Museum - 1824
Science and technology 46411

Fred Wolf Jr. Gallery, Klein Branch Jewish Community Center, 10100 Jamison Av, Philadelphia, PA 19116 - T: (215) 698-7300, Fax: (215) 673-7447. Dir.: Abby Gilbert
Fine Arts Museum / Decorative Arts Museum - 1975 46412

Germantown Historical Society Museum, 5501 Germantown Av, Philadelphia, PA 19144-2291 - T: (215) 844-0514, Fax: (215) 844-2831, E-mail: ghs@libertynet.org, Internet: www.liberty.org/ghs/. Pres.: Alex B. Humes, C.E.O.: Mary K. Dabney
Historical Museum - 1900
Local hist 46413

The Goldie Paley Gallery, Moore College of Art and Design, 20th St and The Parkway, Philadelphia, PA 19103 - T: (215) 965-4027, Fax: (215) 568-5921, E-mail: mdougherty@moore.edu, Internet: www.thegalleriesatmoore.org. Dir.: Molly Dougherty
Fine Arts Museum - 1948
Art 46414

Grand Army of the Republic Civil War Museum, 4278 Griscom St, Philadelphia, PA 19124-3954 - T: (215) 289-6484, 673-1688, E-mail: garmuslib@aol.com, Internet: suvcw.org/garmus.htm. Dir.: Elmer F. Atkinson
Historical Museum - 1926
Hist of the Civil War 46415

High Wire Gallery, 137 N Second St, Philadelphia, PA 19106 - T: (215) 829-1255, E-mail: malcor@aol.com. Pres.: Jeff Waring
Fine Arts Museum - 1985 46416

Historical Society of Pennsylvania, 1300 Locust St, Philadelphia, PA 19107-5699 - T: (215) 732-6200, Fax: (215) 732-2680, E-mail: pres@hsp.org, Internet: www.hsp.org. Pres.: David Moltke-Hansen
Local Museum / Library with Exhibitions - 1824
Historical Research Center 46417

Independence National Historical Park, 313 Walnut St, Philadelphia, PA 19106 - T: (215) 597-8787, Fax: (215) 597-5556, E-mail: inde_curatiorial@nps.gov, Internet: www.nps.gov/inde. Chief Cur.: Karie Diethorn
Historical Museum / Historic Site - 1948
Local hist 46418

Independence Seaport Museum, Penn's Landing Waterfront, 211 S Columbus Blvd at Walnut St, Philadelphia, PA 19106 - T: (215) 925-5439, Fax: (215) 925-6713, E-mail: seaport@indsm.org, Internet: phillyseaport.org. Dir.: John S. Carter, Ass. Dir.: Paul B. DeOrsay, Cur.: David Beard
Historical Museum - 1961
Maritime hist 46419

Institute of Contemporary Art, University of Pennsylvania, 118 S 36th St, Philadelphia, PA 19104-3289 - T: (215) 898-7108, Fax: (215) 898-5050, E-mail: info@icaphila.org, Internet: www.icaphila.org. Dir.: Claudia Gould, Cur.: Ingrid Schaffner
Fine Arts Museum / University Museum - 1963
Art 46420

John G. Johnson Collection, Philadelphia Museum of Art, Parkway and 26th St, Philadelphia, PA 19101-7646 - T: (215) 684-7646, Fax: (215) 684-7616. Cur.: Joseph Rishel
Fine Arts Museum
Italian renaissance paintings, French 19th c paintings 46421

La Salle University Art Museum, 20th and Olney Av, Philadelphia, PA 19141 - T: (215) 951-1221, 951-1000, Fax: (215) 951-5096, E-mail: wistar@lasalle.edu, Internet: www.lasalle.edu/services/art-mus. Dir.: Daniel Burke, Cur.: Caroline Wistar
Fine Arts Museum / University Museum - 1975
Art 46422

Lemon Hill Mansion, Lemon Hill and Sedgelay Drs, East Fairmount Park, Philadelphia, PA 19130 - T: (215) 646-7084, Fax: (215) 646-8472, Internet: www.lemonhill.org. Pres.: H. Dawson Penniman
Decorative Arts Museum
Decorative arts of Philadelphia 1800 - 1836; local hist 46423

Loudoun Mansion, 4650 Germantown Av, Philadelphia, PA 19144 - T: (215) 686-2067, 677-7830. Pres.: Ursula Reed
Decorative Arts Museum
Historic house 46424

Mario Lanza Museum, c/o Settlement Music School, 712 Montrose St, Philadelphia, PA 19147-3094 - T: (215) 468-3623, Fax: (215) 468-1903, E-mail: nli@mario-lanza-institute.org. Pres.: Mary Galanti Papola
Music Museum - 1962
Music hist 46425

The Masonic Library and Museum of Pennsylvania, Masonic Temple, 1 N Broad St, Philadelphia, PA 19107-2520 - T: (215) 988-1932, Fax: (215) 988-1972, E-mail: gawaldman@pagrandlodge.org, Internet: www.pagrandlodge.org. Dir.: Kenneth W. MCarty, Cur.: Laura L. Libert, Archivist: Joshua M. Silver, Libr.: Glenys A. Waldman, Catherine L. Giaimo
Local Museum
Local hist 46426

Minority Arts Resource Council Studio Art Museum, 1421 W Girard Av, Philadelphia, PA 19130 - T: (215) 236-2688, 236-3977, Fax: (215) 236-4255. C.E.O.: Curtis E. Brown
Fine Arts Museum - 1978
Paintings, drawings, sculptures 46427

Mount Pleasant, Philadelphia Museum of Art, Fairmount Park, Philadelphia, PA 19101 - T: (215) 763-8100 ext 4014, Internet: www.phila.museum.com. Cur.: Jack Lindsey
Decorative Arts Museum
Period furnishings 46428

Muse Art Gallery, 60 N Second St, Philadelphia, PA 19106 - T: (215) 627-5310. Dir.: Sissy Pizzollo
Fine Arts Museum - 1970 46429

The Museum at Drexel University, Chestnut and 32nd Sts, Philadelphia, PA 19104 - T: (215) 895-1749, Fax: (215) 895-6447, Internet: www.drexel.edu. Dir.: Charles Morscheck
University Museum / Fine Arts Museum / Decorative Arts Museum - 1891
Sculpture, European painting, decorative arts and costumes, ceramics, hand printed India cottons, decorative arts of China, Europe, India and Japan 46430

The Museum of Nursing History, Pennsylvania Hospital, 8th and Spruce Sts, Philadelphia, PA 19107 - T: (610) 789-4277. Cur.: Joan T. Large
Historical Museum - 1976
Nursing hist 46431

Mutter Museum, College of Physicians of Philadelphia, 19 S 22nd St, Philadelphia, PA 19103-3097 - T: (215) 563-3737 ext 242, Fax: (215) 561-6477, E-mail: worden@collphyphil.org, Internet: www.collphyphil.org. Dir.: Gretchen Worden
Historical Museum - 1863
Medicine 46432

Naomi Wood Collection at Woodford Mansion, 33rd and Dauphin St, E Fairmont Park, Philadelphia, PA 19132 - T: (215) 229-6115
Natural History Museum - 1926 46433

National Exhibits by Blind Artists, 919 Walnut St, Philadelphia, PA 19107 - T: (215) 627-5930, 683-3213, E-mail: info@nebaart.org, Internet: www.nebaart.org. Pres.: Mary Fediw, Dir.: Vickie Collins
Public Gallery - 1976
Art works by blind and physically handicapped artists 46434

National Liberty Museum, 321 Chestnut St, Philadelphia, PA 19106 - T: (215) 925-2800, Fax: (215) 925-3800, Internet: www.libertymuseum.org. Exec. Dir.: Gwen Borowsky
Fine Arts Museum / Historical Museum - 2000
Glass sculptures, film, artwork 46435

National Museum of American Jewish History, 55 N 5th St, Independence Mall E, Philadelphia, PA 19106-2197 - T: (215) 923-3812, Fax: (215) 923-0763, E-mail: nmajh@nmajh.org, Internet: www.nmajh.org. Pres.: Myles Tannenbaum, Dir.: Dr. Wesley Fisher
Historical Museum / Ethnology Museum / Religious Arts Museum - 1974
Social and ethnic hist 46436

Nexus Foundatoin for Today's Art, 137 N Second St, Philadelphia, PA 19106 - T: (215) 629-1103, E-mail: nexus@libertynet.org. Dir.: John Murphy
Fine Arts Museum - 1975 46437

Painted Bride Art Center Gallery, 230 Vine St, Philadelphia, PA 19106 - T: (215) 925-9914, Fax: (215) 925-7402, E-mail: thebride@onix.com, Internet: www.paintedbride.org. Dir.: Gerry Givnish, Laurel Raczka
Fine Arts Museum - 1968
Contemporary art 46438

The Paley Design Center of Philadelphia University
→ The Design Center at Philadelphia University

Pennsylvania Academy of the Fine Arts Gallery, 118 N Broad St, Philadelphia, PA 19102 - T: (215) 972-7600, Fax: (215) 569-0153, E-mail: pafa@pafa.org, Internet: www.pafa.org. Dir.: Derek Gillman, Assoc. Cur.: Alex Baker
Fine Arts Museum - 1805
American art 46439

Philadelphia Art Alliance, 251 S 18th St, Philadelphia, PA 19103 - T: (215) 545-4305, Fax: (215) 545-0767, E-mail: info@philartalliance.org, Internet: www.philartalliance.org. Pres.: Carole Price Shanis, Exec. Dir.: Sylvia Watts McKinney
Fine Arts Museum - 1915
Art 46440

Philadelphia Mummers Museum, 1100 S Second St, Philadelphia, PA 19147 - T: (215) 336-3050, Fax: (215) 389-5630, E-mail: mummersmus@aol.com, Internet: www.mummers.com. Dir.: Palma B. Lucas, Cur.: Jack Cohen
Decorative Arts Museum / Performing Arts Museum - 1976
Costumes 46441

Philadelphia Museum of Art, 26th St and Benjamin Franklin Pkwy, Philadelphia, PA 19130 - T: (215) 763-8100, Fax: (215) 236-4465, E-mail: pr@philamuseum.org, Internet: www.philamuseum.org. Dir.: Anne d' Harnoncourt, Sen. Cur.: Dean Walker (European Decorative Arts and Sculpture), Innis H. Shoemaker (Prints, Drawings and Photographs), Cur.: Joseph J. Rishel (European Painting Before 1900 and John G. Johnson Collection), Kathryn B. Hiesinger (European Decorative Arts After 1700), Kathleen Foster (American Art), Jack Lindsey (American Decorative Arts), Ann Temkin (20th-Century Art), Felice Fischer (East Asian and Japanese Art), Darielle Mason (Indian and Himalayan Art), Ann B. Percy (Drawings), John Ittmann (Prints), Dilys Blum (Costume and Textiles), Katherine Ware (Photographs), Sen. Cons.: P. Andrew Lins (Decorative Arts and Sculpture), Mark S. Tucker (Paintings), Cons.: David DeMuzio (Furniture), Nancy Ash (Works of Art on Paper)
Fine Arts Museum - 1876
Art 46442

Philadelphia Museum of Judaica-Congregation Rodeph Shalom, 615 N Broad St, Philadelphia, PA 19123 - T: (215) 627-6747, Fax: (215) 627-1313, E-mail: info@rodephshalom.orgg, Internet: www.rodephshalom.org. Dir.: Joan C. Sall
Religious Arts Museum - 1975
Religion, oldest German synagogue in Western hemisphere 46443

Plastic Club, 247 S Camac St, Philadelphia, PA 19107 - T: (215) 545-9324, Internet: plasticc.libertynet.org. Pres.: Elizabeth H. MacDonald
Public Gallery - 1897
Paintings, drawings 46444

Please Touch Museum, 210 N 21st St, Philadelphia, PA 19103 - T: (215) 963-0667, Fax: (215) 963-0424, E-mail: fstone@pleasetouchmuseum.org, Internet: www.pleasetouchmuseum.org. Pres.: Nancy D. Kolb, Cur.: Matthew Rowley
Special Museum - 1976
Children's museum, visual and performing arts, sciences, humanities 46445

Presbyterian Historical Society Museum, 425 Lombard St, Philadelphia, PA 19147 - T: (215) 627-1852, Fax: (215) 627-0509. Dir.: Frederick J. Heuser
Religious Arts Museum - 1852
Religious hist 46446

Print and Picture Collection, c/o Free Library of Philadelphia, 1901 Vine St, Philadelphia, PA 19103 - T: (215) 686-5405, Fax: (215) 563-3628, E-mail: benfordj@library.gov, Internet: www.library.phila.gov. Head: Joseph Benford
Fine Arts Museum - 1954 46447

The Print Center, 1614 Latimer St, Philadelphia, PA 19103 - T: (215) 735-6090, Fax: (215) 735-5511, E-mail: info@printcenter.org, Internet: www.printcenter.org. Dir.: Christine Filippone, Ass. Dir.: Jenna Degen
Public Gallery - 1915
Art 46448

Robert W. Ryerss Museum, Burholme Park, 7370 Central Av, Philadelphia, PA 19111 - T: (215) 745-3061, E-mail: Ryerss@netzero.net. Dir.: Theresa Stuhlman
Historical Museum - 1910
Asian collection 46449

Rodin Museum, Philadelphia Museum of Art, Benjamin Franklin Pkwy at 22nd St, Philadelphia, PA 19130 - T: (215) 763-8100, Fax: (215) 235-0050, Internet: www.rodinmuseum.org. Dir.: Anne d' Harnoncourt, George D. Widener, Cur.: Joseph J. Rishel (European Painting and Sculpture)
Fine Arts Museum - 1926
Art 46450

Rosenbach Museum, 2010 Delancey Pl, Philadelphia, PA 19103 - T: (215) 732-1600, Fax: (215) 545-7529, E-mail: info@rosenbach.org, Internet: www.rosenbach.org. Dir.: Derick Dreher, Libr.: Elizabeth E. Fuller
Special Museum - 1953
Rare books 46451

Rosenwald-Wolf Gallery, University of the Arts, 333 S Broad St, Philadelphia, PA 19102 - T: (215) 717-6480, Fax: (215) 717-6632, E-mail: rwg@uarts.edu, Internet: www.uarts.edu. Pres.: Miguel-Angel Corzo, Dir.: Sid Sachs
Fine Arts Museum / University Museum - 1876
Art 46452

Saint George's United Methodist Church Museum, 235 N Fourth St, Philadelphia, PA 19106 - T: (215) 925-7788
Religious Arts Museum - 1767 46453

Saint Joseph's University Gallery, Boland Hall, 5600 City Line Av, Philadelphia, PA 19131-3195 - T: (610) 660-1840, Fax: (610) 660-2278, E-mail: sfenton@sju.edu, Internet: www.sju.edu. Dir.: Dennis McNelly
Fine Arts Museum / University Museum - 1976 46454

Samuel S. Fleisher Art Memorial, Philadelphia Museum of Art, 709-721 Catharine St, Philadelphia, PA 19147 - T: (215) 922-3456, Fax: (215) 922-5327, Internet: www.fleisher.org. Dir.: Thora E. Jacobson
Fine Arts Museum / Religious Arts Museum - 1898
Religious paintings and sculptures, Portuguese liturgical objects, Russian icons 46455

The Stephen Girard Collection, Girard College, Founder's Hall, 2101 S College Av, Philadelphia, PA 19121 - T: (215) 787-2680, Fax: (215) 787-4404, Internet: www.girardcollege.com. Pres.: Joseph T. Devlin, Cur.: Elizabeth M. Laurent
Historical Museum - 1831
Furniture, decorative arts 46456

Taller Puertorriqueno, 2721 N Fifth St, Philadelphia, PA 19133 - T: (215) 426-3311, Fax: (215) 426-5682. Dir.: Annabella Roige
Fine Arts Museum - 1974 46457

Temple Gallery, Tyler School of Art, Temple University, 45 N Second St, Philadelphia, PA 19106 - T: (215) 925-7379, Fax: (215) 925-7389, E-mail: tylerart@vm.temple.edu. Dir.: Kevin Melchionne
Fine Arts Museum / University Museum - 1985 46458

United States Mint-Philadelphia, 5th and Arch Sts, Philadelphia, PA 19106 - T: (215) 408-0114, Fax: (215) 408-2700, Internet: www.usmint.gov. Head: R.R. Robidoux
Special Museum - 1792
Numismatics 46459

University of Pennsylvania Museum of Archaeology and Anthropology, 33rd and Spruce Sts, Philadelphia, PA 19104-6324 - T: (215) 898-4000, Fax: (215) 898-0657, E-mail: websiters@museum.upenn.edu, Internet: www.upenn.edu/museum/. Dir.: Dr. Jeremy Sabloff, Sc. Staff: Gregory L. Possehl (Asia), Robert Sharer (America), Donald White (Mediterranea), Janet Monge (Physical Anthropology), Erle Leichty (Babylonia), David Silverman (Egypt), Richard Zettler (Near East), Sen. Cons.: Virginia Greene
Ethnology Museum / Archaeological Museum - 1887
Archaeology, anthropology 46460

Vox Populi Gallery, 1315 Cherry St, Philadelphia, PA 19107 - T: (215) 568-5513, Fax: (215) 568-5514, E-mail: vox@op.net, Internet: www.voxpopuligallery.org
Public Gallery - 1988 46461

Wagner Free Institute of Science, 1700 W Montgomery Av, Philadelphia, PA 19121 - T: (215) 763-6529, Fax: (215) 763-1299, Internet: www.wagnerfreeinstitute.org. Dir.: Susan Glassman, Ass. Dir.: David A. Dashiell
Natural History Museum - 1855
Natural hist and science 46462

Woodmere Art Museum, 9201 Germantown Av, Philadelphia, PA 19118 - T: (215) 247-0476, Fax: (215) 247-2387, E-mail: ngreene@woodmereartmuseum.org, Internet: www.woodmereartmuseum.org. Pres.: Joseph Nicholson, Dir./Cur.: Michael W. Schantz
Fine Arts Museum - 1940
Art 46463

Wyck Museum, 6026 Germantown Av, Philadelphia, PA 19144 - T: (215) 848-1690, Fax: (215) 848-1612, E-mail: wyck@libertynet.org, Internet: www.wyck.org. Dir.: John M. Groff, Cur.: Elizabeth Solomon
Historical Museum - 1973
Local hist, furniture, glass, ceramics, metals, textiles 46464

Philip SD

Prairie Homestead, 131 off Interstate Hwy, Philip, SD 57567, mail addr: HCR01, Box 51, Philip, SD 57567 - T: (605) 433-5400, Fax: (605) 433-5434, E-mail: klcrew@gwtc.net, Internet: www.prairiehomestead.com. C.E.O.: Keith Crew
Historic Site / Agriculture Museum / Open Air Museum - 1962
Historic house 46465

West River Museum, Center Av, Philip, SD 57567. Dir.: Arnold Waldon, Ass. Dir.: Bernard O'Connell
Local Museum - 1965
Local hist 46466

Phillips ME

Phillips Historical Society Museum, Pleasant St, Phillips, ME 04966 - T: (207) 639-5013. Pres.: Ken Zieglar, Chief Cur.: Robert J. Beal
Local Museum - 1959
Local history 46467

Phillipsburg KS

Old Fort Bissell, 501 Fort Bissell Av, Phillipsburg, KS 67661 - T: (913) 543-6212, Internet: www.lib.ks.us/towns/phillipsburg/bissell.html. Pres.: Darlene Rumbaugh, Cur.: Eva Maria Hansen
Local Museum - 1961
Local history 46468

Philomath OR

Benton County Historical Museum, 1101 Main St, Philomath, OR 97370 - T: (541) 929-6230, Fax: (541) 929-6261, E-mail: bchm@peak.org, Internet: www.bentonmuseum.org. Dir.: William R. Lewis, Ass. Dir.: Judy Juntunen
Local Museum - 1980 46469

Gallery Gazelle, Oregon State University, 1136 Main St, Philomath, OR 97370 - T: (541) 929-6464
Public Gallery 46470

Phoenix AZ

Arizona Hall of Fame Museum, 1101 W Washington, Phoenix, AZ 85007 - T: (602) 255-2110, Fax: (602) 255-3314, E-mail: hofguide@dlapr.lib.az.us, Internet: www.dlapr.lib.az.us. Dir.: Michael D. Carman
Local Museum - 1986
Local hist 46471

Arizona Mining and Mineral Museum, 1502 W Washington, Phoenix, AZ 85007 - T: (602) 255-3795, Fax: (602) 255-3777, E-mail: susancelestina@hotmail.com, Internet: www.admmr.states.az.us. Dir.: Doug Sawyer, Cur.: Susan Celestina
Natural History Museum / Science&Tech Museum - 1953
Minerals, mining 46472

Arizona Science Center, 600 E Washington, Phoenix, AZ 85004-2394 - T: (602) 716-2007, Fax: (602) 716-2099, E-mail: info@azscience.org, Internet: www.azscience.org. Exec. Dir.: Sheila Grinell
Science&Tech Museum - 1984
Sciences, human body, psxchology, weather, aerospace, geology 46473

Arizona State Capitol Museum, 1700 W Washington, Phoenix, AZ 85007 - T: (602) 542-4675, Fax: (602) 542-4690, E-mail: capmus@lib.az.us, Internet: www.dlapr.lib.az.us. Dir.: Michael D. Carman, Dep. Dir.: Mitchell D. Bowden
Historical Museum - 1974
Restored Capitol Building 46474

Hall of Flame - Museum of Firefighting, 6101 E Van Buren St, Phoenix, AZ 85008-3421 - T: (602) 275-3473, Fax: (602) 275-0896, E-mail: petermolloy@hallofflame.org, Internet: www.hallofflame.org. Dir.: Dr. Peter M. Molloy, Sc. Staff: Donald G. Hale (Restoration)
Historical Museum - 1961
History of fire fighting 46475

Heard Museum, 2301 N Central Av, Phoenix, AZ 85004 - T: (602) 252-8840, Fax: (602) 252-9757, E-mail: postmaster@heard.org, Internet: www.heard.org. Dir.: Frank H. Goodyear jr., Cur.: Diana Pardue (Collections), Margaret Archuleta (Fine Arts)
Fine Arts Museum / Ethnology Museum - 1929
Native cultures, art 46476

Phoenix Art Museum, 1625 N Central Av, Phoenix, AZ 85004-1685 - T: (602) 257-1880, 257-1222, Fax: (602) 253-8662, E-mail: info@phxart.org, Internet: www.phxart.org. Dir.: James K. Ballinger, Cur.: Dr. Claudia Brown (Asian Art Research), Michael Komanecky (European Art), Dr. Beverly Adams (Latin American Art), Brady Roberts (Modern and Contemporary Art), Dr. Janet Baker (Asian Art), Dennita Sewell (Fashion Design)
Fine Arts Museum - 1949
American, European and Asian art, contemporary art 46477

Phoenix Museum of History, 105 N Fifth St, Phoenix, AZ 85004-4404 - T: (602) 253-2734, Fax: (602) 253-2348, E-mail: john@pmoh.org, Internet: www.pmoh.org. Exec. Dir.: John Bircumshaw
Local Museum - 1923
Phoenix history 46478

Pioneer Arizona Living History Museum, 3901 W Pioneer Rd, Phoenix, AZ 85086 - T: (623) 465-1052, Fax: (623) 465-0683, E-mail: plhm@aol.com, Internet: www.pioneer-arizona.com. Exec. Dir.: Juanita Buckley
Historical Museum - 1956
Living history complex 46479

Pueblo Grande Museum, 4619 E Washington, Phoenix, AZ 85034-1909 - T: (602) 495-0901, Fax: (602) 495-5645, E-mail: staff.prl.pueblo.grande@phoenix.gov, Internet: www.pueblogrande.com. Dir.: Roger Lidman, Cur.: Glena Cain (Exhibits), Holly Young (Collections)
Archaeological Museum - 1929
Archaeological site 46480

Pickens SC

Pickens County Museum of Art History, 307 Johnson St, Pickens, SC 29671 - T: (864) 898-5963, Fax: (803) 898-5947, E-mail: picmus@pickens.lib.sc.us, Internet: www.co.pickens.sc.us/cultural_events_new.asp#box. Dir.: C. Allen Coleman, Cur.: Ed L. Bolt
Fine Arts Museum / Local Museum / Historical Museum / Historic Site - 1976
Art, local hist 46481

Pickerington OH

Motorcycle Hall of Fame Museum, 13515 Yarmouth Dr, Pickerington, OH 43147 - T: (614) 856-2222 ext 1234, Fax: (614) 856-2221, E-mail: info@motorcyclemuseum.org, Internet: www.motorcyclemuseum.org. Dir.: Mark Mederski
Science&Tech Museum - 1990
Motorcycles, riding clothing and accesories, related gear, racing 46482

Piedmont SD

Petrified Forest of the Black Hills, 8228 Elk Creek Rd, Piedmont, SD 57769-9520 - T: (605) 787-4560, Fax: (605) 787-6477, E-mail: forest@elkcreek.org, Internet: www.elkcreek.org. Dir./Cur.: Gerald E. Teachout
Natural History Museum - 1929
Geology 46483

Pierre SD

The Museum of the South Dakota State Historical Society, Cultural Heritage Center, 900 Governors Dr, Pierre, SD 57501-2217 - T: (605) 773-3458, Fax: (605) 773-6041, E-mail: david.hartley@state.sd.us, Internet: www.sdhistory.org. Dir.: David B. Hartley, Cur.: Jennifer Littlefield (Collections), Ronette Rumpca (Interpretation)
Historical Museum - 1901
Local hist 46484

South Dakota Discovery Center, 805 W Sioux Av, Pierre, SD 57501 - T: (605) 224-8295, Fax: (605) 224-2865, E-mail: kristiemaher@aol.com. Pres.: Tim Bjork, C.E.O.: Kristie Maher
Science&Tech Museum - 1989
Science 46485

Pilger NE

Stanton County Museum, 345 N Main St, Pilger, NE 68768-0213 - T: (402) 439-2952, E-mail: fullerel@stanton.net
Local Museum - 1965 46486

Pilot Knob MO

Fort Davidson State Historic Site, Hwy 21 and Hwy V, Pilot Knob, MO 63663 - T: (573) 546-3454, Fax: (573) 546-2713. Head: Walter Bush
Military Museum - 1969 46487

Pima AZ

Eastern Arizona Museum, 2 N Main St, Pima, AZ 85543 - T: (520) 485-3032, E-mail: edres@zekes.com. Cur.: Edres Barney
Local Museum / Ethnology Museum - 1963
Local history 46488

Pine Bluff AR

Arts and Science Center for Southeast Arkansas, 701 Main St, Pine Bluff, AR 71601 - T: (870) 536-3375, Fax: (870) 536-3380, E-mail: asc@seark.net, Internet: www.artsandsciencecenter.org. Exec. Dir.: Mary Brock
Fine Arts Museum / Performing Arts Museum - 1968
Arts, culture 46489

Jefferson County Historical Museum, 201 E Fourth St, Pine Bluff, AR 71601 - T: (501) 541-5402, Fax: (501) 541-5405, E-mail: jumuse@ipa.net. Dir.: Sue Trulock
Local Museum - 1980
History of Pine Bluff and Jefferson County 46490

Pine Ridge AR

Lum and Abner Museum and Jot 'Em Down Store, 4562 Hwy 88 W, Pine Ridge, AR 71966 - T: (870) 326-4442, Fax: (870) 326-4442, E-mail: nstucker@alltel.net, Internet: www.lum-abner.com. Dir.: Noah Lon Stucker, Kathryn Moore Stucker
Science&Tech Museum / Historical Museum - 1971
Historic stores on which the Lum and Abner radio program 1931-55 was based, country store, rural life 46491

Pine Ridge SD

The Heritage Center, c/o Red Cloud Indian School, 100 Mission Dr, Pine Ridge, SD 57770 - T: (605) 867-5491, Fax: (605) 867-1209, E-mail: rcheritage@basec.net, Internet: basec.net/rcheritage/. Pres.: Calvin Jumping Bull, Dir.: C.M. Simon
Fine Arts Museum / Ethnology Museum - 1967
Native American art 46492

Pinedale WY

Museum of the Mountain Man, 700 E Hennick, Pinedale, WY 82941 - T: (307) 367-4101, Fax: (307) 367-6768, E-mail: museummtman@wyoming.com, Internet: www.museumofthemountainman.com. Exec. Dir.: Laurie Hartwig
Historical Museum - 1990
History 46493

Pineville NC

James K. Polk Memorial, 308 S Polk St, Pineville, NC 28134 - T: (704) 889-7145, Fax: (704) 889-3057, E-mail: polkmemorial@dasia.net, Internet: www.ah.dcr.state.nc.us/sections/hs/polk/polk.htm
Historical Museum - 1961 46494

Piney Flats TN

Rocky Mount Museum, Rocky Mount Pkwy, 200 Hyder Hill Rd, Piney Flats, TN 37686 - T: (423) 538-7396, Fax: (423) 538-1086, E-mail: rmm@preferred.com, Internet: www.pages.preferred.com/~rmm. Pres.: Myers Massengill, Exec. Dir.: Deborah Montanini
Open Air Museum / Local Museum - 1958
Historical village 46495

Piney Woods MS

Laurence C. Jones Museum, Piney Woods Country Life School, Piney Woods, MS 39148 - T: (601) 845-2214, Fax: (601) 845-2604, Internet: www.pineywoods.org. C.E.O.: Charles H. Beady
Local Museum - 1986
Regional history 46496

Pinson TN

Pinson Mounds State Archaeological Area, 460 Ozier Rd, Pinson, TN 38366 - T: (901) 988-5614, Fax: (901) 424-3909, Internet: www.tnstateparks.com/pinson
Archaeological Museum - 1980
Archaeology 46497

Pipestone MN

Pipestone County Historical Museum, 113 S Hiawatha Av, Pipestone, MN 56164 - T: (507) 825-2563, Fax: (507) 825-2563, E-mail: pipctymu@rconnect.com, Internet: www.pipestoneminnesota.com/Museum. Pres.: Rich Gergen, Dir.: Chris Roelfsema-Hummel
Historical Museum - 1880 46498

Pipestone National Monument, 36 Reservation Av, Pipestone, MN 56164 - T: (507) 825-5464, Fax: (507) 825-5466, E-mail: PIPE_Interpretation@nps.gov, Internet: www.NPS.GOV/PIPE
Historical Museum / Ethnology Museum - 1937 46499

Piqua OH

Piqua Historical Area State Memorial, 9845 N Hardin Rd, Piqua, OH 45356-9707 - T: (937) 773-2522, Fax: (937) 773-4311, E-mail: johnstonfarm@mail2.wesnet.com. Head: Andy Hite
Agriculture Museum - 1972 46500

Piscataway NJ

Cornelius Low House/Middlesex County Museum, 1225 River Rd, Piscataway, NJ - T: (732) 745-4177, 745-4489, Fax: (732) 745-4507, E-mail: info@cultureheritage.org, Internet: www.cultureheritage.org. Exec. Dir.: Anna M. Aschkenes, Cur.: Kenneth M. Helsby, Mark Nonestied
Local Museum - 1979
Local hist 46501

East Jersey Olde Towne, 1050 River Rd and Old Hoes Ln, Piscataway, NJ 08855-0661 - T: (732) 745-3030, 745-4489, Fax: (732) 463-1086, E-mail: info@culturalheritage.org, Internet: www.culturalheritage.org. Pres.: Stanley Bresticker
Local Museum / Open Air Museum - 1971
Historic 18th c village 46502

Pittsburg KS

Crawford County Historical Museum, N of 69 Bypass and W 20th St, Pittsburg, KS 66762-8600 - T: (316) 231-1440. Pres.: Denny Davidson
Local Museum - 1968
Local hist 46503

Pittsburg State University Natural History Museum, c/o PSU Biology Dept, 1701 S Broadway, Heckert-Wells Hall, Pittsburg, KS 66762 - T: (316) 235-4732, Fax: (316) 235-4194, E-mail: sford@pittstate.edu, Internet: pittstate.edu/biol. Cur.: Dr. S.D. Ford (Mammals and Birds), Cur.: Dr. Leon Dinkins (Insects)
Natural History Museum - 1903
Skin and skulls, alcohol specimens, insects 46504

Pittsburg PA

Fort Pitt Museum, Point State Park, Pittsburg, PA 15222, mail addr: 101 Commonwealth Pl, Pittsburgh, PA 15222 - T: (412) 281-9284, Fax: (412) 281-1417, Internet: www.fortpittmuseum.com. Dir.: Chuck Smith
Military Museum - 1964
Military and frontier objects, tools, muskets, cannon, furniture, maps, documents 46505

Pittsburgh PA

The Andy Warhol Museum, 117 Sandusky St, Pittsburgh, PA 15212-5890 - T: (412) 237-8300, Fax: (412) 237-8340, E-mail: warhol@alphaclp.clpgh.org, Internet: www.warhol.org/warhol. Dir.: Thomas Sokolowski, Cur.: Geralyn H. Huxley (Film and Video), Jessica Arcand (Education), Ass. Cur.: Margery King
Fine Arts Museum - 1994
Art, visual arts 46506

Art Institute of Pittsburgh, 420 Blvd of the Allies, Pittsburgh, PA 15233 - T: (412) 471-2473
Public Gallery 46507

Associated Artists of Pittsburgh Gallery, 937 Liberty Av, Pittsburgh, PA 15222 - T: (412) 263-2710, Fax: (412) 471-1765, E-mail: aap@telerama.com. Pres.: Rich Brown, Exec. Dir.: Frances Frederick
Fine Arts Museum - 1910
Art 46508

Car and Carriage Museum, 7227 Reynolds St, Pittsburgh, PA 15208-2923 - T: (412) 371-0600, Fax: (412) 731-9415, E-mail: wsheerer@frickart.org, Internet: www.frickart.org. Dir.: William B. Bodine jr
Science&Tech Museum - 1990 46509

Carnegie Museum of Art, 4400 Forbes Av, Pittsburgh, PA 15213-4080 - T: (412) 622-3131, Fax: (412) 622-3112, Internet: www.cmoa.org. Dir.: Richard Armstrong, Ass. Dir.: Maureen Rolla, Chief Cur.: Sarah Nichols (Decorative Arts), Cur.: Louise Lippincott (Fine Arts), Laura Hoptman (Contemporary Art), Joseph Rosa (Heinz Architectural Center), William D. Judson (Film and Video), Marilyn M. Russell (Education), Chief Cons.: Ellen Baxter
Fine Arts Museum - 1895 46510

Carnegie Museum of Natural History, 4400 Forbes Av, Pittsburgh, PA 15213-4080 - T: (412) 622-3131, Fax: (412) 622-8837, Internet: www.carnegiemuseums.org/cmnh. Dir.: Billie R. DeWalt, Sylvia M. Keller, Cur.: Dr. Mary R. Dawson (Vertebrate Paleontology), Dr. Bradley C. Livezey (Birds), Dr. Frederick H. Utech (Botany), Dr. John R. Wible (Mammals), Dr. James B. Richardson (Anthropology), Ass. Cur.: Dr. John J. Wiens (Amphibians and Reptiles)
Ethnology Museum / Natural History Museum - 1896
Natural hist, anthropology 46511

Carnegie Science Center, 1 Allegheny Av, Pittsburgh, PA 15212-5850 - T: (412) 237-3400, Fax: (412) 237-3309, Internet: www.csc.clpgh.org. Pres.: Ellsworth H. Brown, Dir.: Seddon Bennington, Tom Flaherty (Exhibits), John Radzilowicz (Planetarium and Observatory)
Science&Tech Museum - 1991
Science and technology 46512

Center for American Music, Stephen Foster Memorial, University of Pittsburgh, 4301 Forbes Av, Pittsburgh, PA 15260 - T: (412) 624-4100, Fax: (412) 624-7447, E-mail: amerimus@pitt.edu, Internet: www.pitt.edu/~amerimus. Dir.: Deane L. Root
Music Museum - 1937
American music hist, life and works of Stephen Collins Foster - Research library 46513

Chatham College Art Gallery, Woodland Rd, Pittsburgh, PA 15232 - T: (412) 365-1100, Fax: (412) 365-1505 http://www.chatham.edu. Dir.: Michael Pestel
Fine Arts Museum - 1960 46514

Frame Gallery, c/o Carnegie Mellon University, School of Fine Arts, 5000 Forbes Av, Pittsburgh, PA 15213-3890 - T: (412) 268-2409, Internet: www.art.cfa.cmu.edu. Dir.: David Johnson, Kerry Schneider
Public Gallery / University Museum - 1969 46515

The Frick Art Museum, 7227 Reynolds St, Pittsburgh, PA 15208 - T: (412) 371-0600, Fax: (412) 371-5393, E-mail: info@frickart.org, Internet: www.frickart.org. Dir.: William B. Bodine jr.
Fine Arts Museum - 1970
Art 46516

Henry Clay Frick Estate, 7227 Reynolds St, Pittsburgh, PA 15208 - T: (412) 371-0600, Fax: (412) 241-5393, E-mail: info@frickart.org, Internet: www.frickart.org. Dir.: William B. Bodine jr
Decorative Arts Museum - 1990
Frick family, decorative arts, art, procelain, glass, period furniture, costumes and textiles 46517

Hunt Institute for Botanical Documentation, c/o Carnegie Mellon University, 5000 Forbes Av, Pittsburgh, PA 15213-3890 - T: (412) 268-2434, Fax: (412) 268-5677, Internet: huntbot.andrew.cmu.edu. Dir.: Robert W. Kiger, Cur.: James J. White
Fine Arts Museum / University Museum - 1961
Botanical art and illustration 46518

John P. Barclay Memorial Gallery, c/o Art Institute of Pittsburgh, 420 Blvd of the Allies, Pittsburgh, PA 15219 - T: (412) 263-6600, Internet: www.aip.all.edu. Dir.: Nancy Ruttner
Fine Arts Museum - 1921
Local artists, exhibits 46519

Manchester Craftsmen's Guild, 1815 Metropolitan St, Pittsburgh, PA 15233 - T: (412) 322-1773, Fax: (412) 321-2120. C.E.O.: William Strickland jr.
Decorative Arts Museum - 1968 46520

Mattress Factory Museum, 500 Sampsonia Way, Pittsburgh, PA 15212 - T: (412) 231-3169, Fax: (412) 322-2231, E-mail: info@mattress.org, Internet: www.mattress.org. Dir.: Barbara Luderowski, Cur.: Michael Olijnyk
Fine Arts Museum - 1977
Art 46521

Mellon Financial Corporation's Collection, 1 Mellon Financial Ctr, Pittsburgh, PA 15258 - T: (412) 234-4775, Fax: (412) 234-0831. Dir.: Brian J. Lang
Fine Arts Museum
British drawings and paintings, American historical prints, contemporary works on paper, textiles, photography 46522

Pittsburgh Center for the Arts, 6300 Fifth Av, Pittsburgh, PA 15232 - T: (412) 361-0873, 361-0455, Fax: (412) 361-8338, E-mail: general@pittsburgharts.org, Internet: www.pittsburgharts.org. Dir.: Lourdes Karas, Cur.: Vicky A. Clark
Fine Arts Museum - 1945
Local art 46523

Pittsburgh Children's Museum, 10 Childrens Way, Pittsburgh, PA 15212 - T: (412) 322-5059, Fax: (412) 322-4932, E-mail: info@pittsburghkids.org, Internet: www.pittsburghkids.org. Pres.: Anne V. Lewis, Exec. Dir.: Jane Werner, Dir.: Chris Siefert (Project Mgr.), Dir.: Penny Lodge (Exhibits)
Special Museum - 1980 46524

Senator John Heinz Pittsburgh Regional History Center, Historical Society of Western Pennsylvania, 1212 Smallman St, Pittsburgh, PA 15222 - T: (412) 454-6000, Fax: (412) 454-6031, E-mail: hswp@hswp.org, Internet: www.pghhistory.org
Local Museum - 1879
Urban and regional hist, 20th-century immigrant and ethnic experience, rural life 46525

Silver Eye Center for Photography, 1015 E Carson St, Pittsburgh, PA 15203 - T: (412) 431-1810, Fax: (412) 431-5777, E-mail: info@silvereye.org, Internet: www.silvereye.org. Dir.: Sam Berkovitz
Fine Arts Museum - 1979
Photography as an art 46526

Society for Contemporary Craft Museum, 2100 Smallman St, Pittsburgh, PA 15222 - T: (412) 261-7003, Fax: (412) 261-1941, E-mail: info@contemporarycraft.org, Internet: www.contemporarycraft.org. Dir.: Janet L. McCall, Ass. Dir.: Kate Lydon
Fine Arts Museum / Decorative Arts Museum - 1972
Contemporary crafts in ceramics, glass, wood, metal and fiber 46527

Space 101 Gallery, Brew House Association, 2100 Mary St, Pittsburgh, PA 15203 - T: (412) 381-7767, E-mail: getinfo@brewhouse.org, Internet: www.brewhouse.org
Public Gallery 46528

University Art Gallery, University of Pittsburgh, 104 Frick Fine Arts Bldg, Pittsburgh, PA 15260 - T: (412) 648-2400, Fax: (412) 648-2792, E-mail: jpiller@pitt.edu, Internet: www.pitt.edu/uag. Head: Prof. David G. Wilkins, Programming Dir.: Josienne N. Piller
University Museum / Fine Arts Museum - 1966 46529

Pittsfield MA

Berkshire Artisans, 28 Renne Av, Pittsfield, MA 01201 - T: (413) 499-9348, Fax: (413) 499-9348, E-mail: berkart@taconic.net, Internet: www.berkshireweb.com/artisans/index.html. Pres./Dir.: Daniel M. O'Connell
Fine Arts Museum / Public Gallery - 1976 46530

Berkshire County Historical Society Museum at Arrowhead, 780 Holmes Rd, Pittsfield, MA 01201 - T: (413) 442-1793, Fax: (413) 443-1449, E-mail: melville@berkshire.net, Internet: www.berkshirehistory.org. Exec. Dir.: Susan Eisley
Local Museum / Special Museum - 1962
Regional history, Pittsfield home of author Herman Melville 1850-1863 46531

The Berkshire Museum, 39 South St, Pittsfield, MA 01201 - T: (413) 443-7171 ext 10, Fax: (413) 443-2135, E-mail: pr@berkshiremuseum.org, Internet: www.berkshiremuseum.org. Dir.: Ann Mintz, Cur.: Thomas Smith
Local Museum - 1903
Art, natural science, history - aquarium 46532

Hancock Shaker Village, Rte 20, W Housatonic St, Pittsfield, MA 01202 - T: (413) 443-0188, Fax: (413) 447-9357, E-mail: info@hancockshakervillage.org, Internet: www.hancockshakervillage.org. Dir.: Lawrence J. Yerdon
Historic Site / Open Air Museum - 1960
Historic village, 22 buildings with constructions dating back to 1790 - library, archive 46533

Pittsford NY

Historic Pittsford, 18 Monroe Av, Pittsford, NY 14534 - T: (716) 381-2941. Pres.: Jerry Francis
Local Museum - 1966 46534

Pittsford VT

New England Maple Museum, US Rte 7, Pittsford, VT 05763 - T: (802) 483-9414, Fax: (802) 775-1650, E-mail: info@maplemuseum.com, Internet: www.maplemuseum.com. Dir.: Dona A. Olson
Special Museum - 1977
Maple sugaring, wooden sap buckets, antique sugar tubs, paintings by Vermont artitsts 46535

Pittsford Historical Society Museum, Main St Rte 7, Pittsford, VT 05763 - T: (802) 483-6040, 483-6623, Internet: www.pittsford-historical.org. Pres.: Ann Pelkey, Cur.: Jean S. Davies
Local Museum - 1980
Local hist 46536

Placerville CA

El Dorado County Historical Museum, 104 Placerville Dr, Fairgrounds, Placerville, CA 95667 - T: (530) 621-5865, Fax: (530) 621-6644
Local Museum - 1939
Local hist 46537

Plainfield NJ

Drake House Museum, 602 W Front St, Plainfield, NJ 07060 - T: (908) 755-5831, Fax: (908) 755-0132, Internet: www.drakehouse.org. Pres.: JoAnn Ball
Local Museum - 1921 46538

Plains TX

Tsa Mo Ga Memorial Museum, 1109 Av H, Plains, TX 79355 - T: (806) 456-8855. Dir.: P.W. Saint Romain
Local Museum - 1959
Local hist 46539

Plainview TX

Museum of the Llano Estacado, Wayland University, Plainview, TX 79072 - T: (806) 296-4735. Dir.: Eddie Guffee, Cur.: Patti Guffee
University Museum / Local Museum - 1976
Local hist 46540

Plano TX

Heritage Farmstead Museum, 1900 W 15 St, Plano, TX 75075 - T: (972) 881-0140, Fax: (972) 422-6481, E-mail: museum@airmail.net, Internet: www.heritagefarmstead.org. C.E.O.: Ted H. Peters, Cur.: Lolisa Moores-Franklin
Historical Museum - 1974 46541

Plant City FL

1914 Plant City High School Community Exhibition, 605 N Collins St, Plant City, FL 33566 - T: (813) 757-9226
Local Museum - 1974
Local pioneer family artifacts 46542

Plantation FL

Plantation Historical Museum, 511 N Fig Tree Ln, Plantation, FL 33317 - T: (954) 797-2722, Fax: (954) 797-2717, E-mail: museum511@aol.com, Internet: www.plantation.org. Dir./ Cur.: Shirley Schuler
Local Museum - 1975
Local history 46543

Platteville CO

Fort Vasquez Museum, Colorado Historical Society Regional Museum, 13412 U.S. Hwy 85, Platteville, CO 80651 - T: (970) 785-2832, Fax: (970) 785-9193, E-mail: susan.hoskinson@chs.state.co.us, Internet: www.coloradohistory.org. Dir.: Susan Hoskinson
Historic Site - 1958
Fur trade and Native American, reconstructed adobe fort (1835 trading post) 46544

Platteville WI

The Mining Museum, 405 E Main St, Platteville, WI 53818 - T: (608) 348-3301, Fax: (608) 348-4640, Internet: www.platteville.org. Dir.: Stephen J. Kleefisch, Cur.: Stephanie Saager-Bourret
Science&Tech Museum - 1965
Mining 46545

Rollo Jamison Museum, 405 E Main St, Platteville, WI 53818 - T: (608) 348-3301, Fax: (608) 348-4640, Internet: www.platteville.org. Dir.: Stephen J. Kleefisch, Cur.: Stephanie Saager-Bourret
Historical Museum - 1981
Local hist 46546

Plattsburgh NY

Clinton County Historical Museum, 48 Court St, Plattsburgh, NY 12901 - T: (518) 561-0340, Fax: (518) 561-0340, E-mail: clintoncohist@westelcom.com. Dir./Cur.: John Tomkins
Local Museum - 1973 46547

Kent-Delord House Museum, 17 Cumberland Av, Plattsburgh, NY 12901 - T: (518) 561-1035, Fax: (518) 561-1035, E-mail: director@primelink1.net. Dir.: Gary Worthington
Local Museum - 1924 46548

Plattsburgh Art Museum, State University of New York, 101 Broad St, Plattsburgh, NY 12901 - T: (518) 564-2474, Fax: (518) 564-2473, E-mail: edward.brohel@plattsburgh.edu, Internet: www.plattsburgh.edu/museum. Dir.: Dr. Horace Judson
Fine Arts Museum / University Museum - 1952 46549

Plattsmouth NE

Cass County Historical Society Museum, 646 Main St, Plattsmouth, NE 68048 - T: (402) 296-4770. Pres.: George Miller, Cur.: Margo Prentiss
Local Museum - 1936 46550

Pleasant Hill CA

Diablo Valley College Museum, 321 Golf Club Rd, Pleasant Hill, CA 94523 - T: (925) 685-1230 ext 2303, Fax: (925) 685-1551. Cur.: Audrey Maher-Kamprath
Local Museum - 1960
Anthropology, zoology, mineralogy, scientific instruments 46551

Pleasanton CA

Amador-Livermore Valley Museum, 603 Main St, Pleasanton, CA 94566 - T: (925) 462-2766. Pres.: Lynda Greene
Local Museum - 1972
Local hist 46552

Pleasanton KS

Linn County Museum, Dunlap Park, Pleasanton, KS 66075 - T: (913) 352-8739, Fax: (913) 352-8739. Pres.: Ola May Earnest
Local Museum - 1973
County history 46553

Marais Des Cygnes Memorial Historic Site, Rte 2, Pleasanton, KS 66075 - T: (913) 352-8890, E-mail: minecreek@ckt.net, Internet: www.minecreek.org. Cur.: Russ Corder
Historical Museum
Home of Charles C. Hadsall, used as a fort by John Brown, nr massacre site 46554

Pleasanton TX

Longhorn Museum, 1959 Hwy 97 E, Pleasanton, TX 78064 - T: (830) 569-6313. Dir.: Mary L. Tondre
Historical Museum - 1976 46555

Pleasantville NY

Reader's Digest Art Gallery, Reader's Digest Rd, Pleasantville, NY 10570-7000 - T: (914) 244-5492, Fax: (914) 244-5006, Internet: www.rd.com. Cur.: Marianne Brunson Frisch, Ass. Cur.: Jill DeVonyar-Zansky
Fine Arts Museum 46556

Pleasantville PA

Historic Pithole City, Drake Well Museum, R.D. 1, Pleasantville, PA 16341 - T: (814) 589-7912, 827-2797, Fax: (814) 827-4888, E-mail: bzolli@state.pa.us, Internet: www.drakewell.org. Dir.: Barbara T. Zolli
Open Air Museum - 1975
Oil wells, model of city in 1865 46557

Plymouth IN

Marshall County Historical Museum, 123 N Michigan St, Plymouth, IN 46563 - T: (219) 936-2306, Fax: (219) 936-9306, E-mail: mchistory@mchistoricalsociety.org, Internet: www.mchistoricalsociety.org. Pres.: Peter Trone, Dir.: Linda Rippy
Local Museum - 1957
Local history 46558

Plymouth MA

Howland House, 33 Sandwich St, Plymouth, MA 02360 - T: (508) 746-9590, Fax: (508) 866-5056, E-mail: shawhardin@aol.com
Archaeological Museum - 1897 46559

Mayflower Society Museum, 4 Winslow St, Plymouth, MA 02360 - T: (508) 746-2590. Cur.: Elisabeth L. Hauthaway
Local Museum - 1897 46560

Pilgrim Hall Museum, 75 Court St, Plymouth, MA 02360 - T: (508) 746-1620, Fax: (508) 747-4228, E-mail: pegbaker@ici.net, Internet: www.pilgrimhall.org. C.E.O.: Peggy M. Baker, Cur.: Jane L. Port
Historical Museum / Local Museum - 1820
Local history 46561

Plymoth Plantation Museum, 137 Warren Av, Plymouth, MA 02362 - T: (508) 746-1622, Fax: (508) 746-3407, E-mail: nbrennan@plimoth.org, Internet: www.plimoth.org. Exec. Dir.: Nancy Brennan, Sc. Staff: James W. Baker (History)
Historical Museum - 1947
Outdoor living history 46562

Plymouth Antiquarian Society Museum, 6 Court St, Plymouth, MA 02360 - T: (508) 746-0012, Fax: (508) 746-7908, E-mail: pasm@mindspring.com. Dir.: Donna D. Curtin
Local Museum - 1919
Historic houses: Harlow Fort house, Spooner house, Hedge house, local history 46563

Richard Sparrow House, 42 Summer St, Plymouth, MA 02360 - T: (508) 747-1240, Fax: (508) 746-9521, E-mail: info@sparrowhouse.com, Internet: www.sparrowhouse.com. Pres.: Violet Berry, Dir.: Lois Atherton
Folklore Museum - 1961
Local crafts 46564

Plymouth MI

Plymouth Historical Museum, 155 S Main St, Plymouth, MI 48170 - T: (734) 455-8940, 455-7797, Fax: (734) 455-8571, E-mail: bstew03@aol.com, Internet: www.plymouth.lib.mi.us/~history. Pres.: Dan LeBlond, Dir.: Beth A. Stewart
Historical Museum - 1962
Local history, Petz Abraham Lincoln col 46565

Plymouth NH

Karl Drerup Fine Arts Gallery, Dept of Fine Arts, Plymouth State College, 17 High St, Plymouth, NH 03264 - T: (603) 535-2614, Fax: (603) 535-2938, E-mail: camidon@mail.plymouth.edu, Internet: plymouth.edu/psc/gallery/. Dir.: Catherine Amidon
University Museum / Fine Arts Museum - 1969 46566

Plymouth WI

Bradley Gallery of Art, W 3718 South Dr, Plymouth, WI 53073 - T: (920) 565-2111, Fax: (920) 565-1206, E-mail: presnell.weidnerd@lakeland.edu, Internet: www.lakeland.edu. Dir.: Denise Presnell-Weidner, William Weidner
Public Gallery - 1988 46567

John G. Voigt House, W 5639 Anokijig Ln, Plymouth, WI 53073 - T: (920) 893-0782, Fax: (920) 893-0873. Dir.: Jim Scherer
Local Museum - 1850
Historic house 46568

Plymouth Notch VT

Calvin Coolidge State Historic Site, Plymouth Notch, VT 05056 - T: (802) 672-3773, Fax: (802) 672-3337, E-mail: wjenny@dca.state.vt.us, Internet: www.historicvermont.org
Local Museum - 1951
Early 20th c village, Calvin Coolidge birthplace and homestead 46569

Pocatello ID

Bannock County Historical Museum, 3000 Alvord Loop, Pocatello, ID 83201 - T: (208) 233-0434. Dir.: Mary Lien
Local Museum - 1963
Wrensted, Peake and Larsen colls, railroad, farm equip 46570

Idaho Museum of Natural History, 5th and Dillon, Pocatello, ID 83209 - T: (208) 282-3160, Fax: (208) 282-5893, E-mail: lohserne@isu.edu, Internet: www.isu.edu/departments/museum. Dir.: Dr. E.S. Lohse, Cur.: Dr. William A. Akersten, Sc. Staff: Allen Tedrow (Fossil Preparation)
University Museum / Natural History Museum - 1934
Natural history 46571

John B. Davis Gallery of Fine Art, POB 8004, Pocatello, ID 83209 - T: (208) 236-2361, Fax: (208) 282-4791, E-mail: dialgail@isu.edu, Internet: www.isu.edu/departments/art. Dir.: Amy Jo Johnson
Fine Arts Museum / University Museum - 1956 46572

Point Lookout MO

Ralph Foster Museum, College of the Ozarks, One Cultural Court, Point Lookout, MO 65726 - T: (417) 334-6411 ext 3407, Fax: (417) 335-2618, E-mail: museum@cofo.edu, Internet: www.rfostermuseum.com. Dir.: Annette J. Sain, Cur.: Jeanelle Duzenberry, Cur.: Thomas A. Debo, Gary Ponder
University Museum / Local Museum - 1930
Local history, art, firearms, natural history 46573

Point Marion PA

Friendship Hill National Historic Site, 223 New Geneva Rd, Point Marion, PA 15474 - T: (724) 725-9190, Fax: 7242) 725-1999, E-mail: lawren-dunn@npg.gov, Internet: www.nps.gov/frhi. Cur.: Lawren Dunn
Historic Site - 1978
Local hist 46574

Point Pleasant OH

Grant's Birthplace State Memorial, US 52 and State Rte 232, Point Pleasant, OH 45153 - T: (513) 553-4911. Man.: Loretta Fuhrman
Local Museum 46575

Point Pleasant WV

Point Pleasant Battle Monument State Park → TU-Endie-Wei State Park

TU-Endie-Wei State Park, 1 Main St, Point Pleasant, WV 25550 - T: (304) 675-0869. Head: Stephen Jones
Local Museum / Historic Site - 1901
Historic house and site, where the first battle of the Revolution was fought 46576

West Virginia State Farm Museum, Rte 1, Box 479, Point Pleasant, WV 25550 - T: (304) 675-5737, Fax: (304) 675-5430, E-mail: wvfarmus@ns3.zoomnet.net. Dir.: Lloyd Akers
Agriculture Museum - 1974
Agriculture 46577

Polk City FL

Water Ski Hall of Fame, American Water Ski Educational Foundation, 1251 Holy Cow Rd, Polk City, FL 33868-8200 - T: (863) 324-2472, Fax: (863) 324-3996, E-mail: awsefhalloffame@cs.com, Internet: usawaterski.org. Pres.: Dr. J.D. Morgan, Exec. Dir.: Carole Lowe
Special Museum - 1968 46578

Polson MT

Miracle of America Museum, 58176 Hwy 93, Polson, MT 59860 - T: (406) 883-6804, E-mail: museum@cyberport.net, Internet: www.cyberport.net/museum. Dir.: Mel Adams, Cathleen Wilde, C.E.O.: W. Gilbert Mangels
Historical Museum / Science&Tech Museum - 1985
Ethnology, history, farm machinery, steam engine, fishing, cars, tractors, military vehicles, tranportation 46579

Pomeroy OH

Meigs County Museum, 144 Butternut Av, Pomeroy, OH 45769 - T: (740) 992-3810. Pres.: Margaret Parker
Local Museum - 1960 46580

Ponca City OK

Marland's Grand Home, 1000 E Grand, Ponca City, OK 74601 - T: (580) 767-0427, Internet: www.marlandgrandhome.com. Dir.: Kathy Adams
Historical Museum / Historic Site - 1916 46581

Pioneer Woman Statue and Museum, 701 Monument, Ponca City, OK 74604 - T: (580) 765-6108, Fax: (580) 762-2498, E-mail: piown@ok-history.mus.ok.us, Internet: www.ok.-history.mus.ok.us. Dir.: Jayne Detten
Historical Museum - 1958 46582

Ponce Inlet FL

Ponce DeLeon Inlet Lighthouse, 4931 S Peninsula Dr, Ponce Inlet, FL 32127 - T: (386) 761-1821, Fax: (386) 761-1321, E-mail: lighthouse@ponceinlet.org, Internet: www.ponceinlet.org. Dir.: Ann Caneer, (History)
Historical Museum - 1972 46583

Pontiac MI

Creative Arts Center, 47 Williams St, Pontiac, MI 48341 - T: (248) 333-7849, Fax: (248) 333-7841, E-mail: createpont@aol.com. Dir.: Carol Paster, Cust.: Leon Medlock
Fine Arts Museum / Folklore Museum - 1964
Civic art, culture 46584

Pine Grove Historic Museum, 405 Oakland Av, Pontiac, MI 48342 - T: (248) 338-6732, Fax: (248) 338-6731, E-mail: ocphs@wwnet.net, Internet: www.net/~ocphs/index.html. Pres.: Michael Willis
Historical Museum - 1874
Pine Grove, the Governor Moses Wisner House 46585

Poplar Bluff MO

Margaret Harwell Art Museum, 421 N Main St, Poplar Bluff, MO 63901 - T: (573) 686-8002, Fax: (573) 686-8017, E-mail: tina@mham.org, Internet: www.mham.org. C.E.O.: Tina M. Magill, Chm.: Emily G. Wolpers
Fine Arts Museum - 1981 46586

Port Allen LA

West Baton Rouge Museum, 845 N Jefferson Av, Port Allen, LA 70767 - T: (225) 336-2422, Fax: (225) 336-2448, E-mail: wbrmuseum@inetmail.att.net, Internet: www.westbatonrougemuseum.com. Dir.: Caroline Kennedy, Cur.: Jeannie Giroir Luckett
Historical Museum - 1968
Regional history 46587

Port Angeles WA

The Museum of Clallam County Historical Society, 1st St & Oak St, Federal Bldg, Port Angeles, WA 98362 - T: (360) 452-2662, E-mail: artifact@olypen.com. Exec. Dir.: Kathy Monds
Local Museum - 1948
Local hist 46588

Port Angeles Fine Arts Center, 1203 E Lauridsen Blvd, Port Angeles, WA 98362 - T: (360) 457-3532, 457-0411 ext 4590, Fax: (360) 457-3532, E-mail: pafac@olypen.com, Internet: www.olympus.net/community/pafac. Pres.: Mim Foley, C.E.O.: Jake Seniuk
Fine Arts Museum / Public Gallery - 1986
Art, coll of sculptures, contemporary art of the Northwest 46589

Port Arthur TX

Museum of the Gulf Coast, 700 Procter St, Port Arthur, TX 77640 - T: (409) 982-7000, Fax: (409) 982-9614, E-mail: shannon.hansen@lamarpa.edu, Internet: www.museum.lamarpa.edu. Pres.: Dr. Sam Monroe, Dir.: Shannon Hansen
Local Museum - 1964
Regional history 46590

Port Austin MI

Huron City Museums, 7930 Huron City Rd, Port Austin, MI 48467 - T: (989) 428-4123, Fax: (517) 428-4123, E-mail: huroncity@centurytel.net, Internet: www.wlpf.org. Dir.: Charles A. Scheffner
Local Museum - 1950
Local hist 46591

Port Clinton OH

Ottawa County Historical Museum, 126 W Third St, Port Clinton, OH 43452 - T: (419) 732-2237, E-mail: ochm@thirdplanet.net. Cur.: Vicki Ashton
Historical Museum - 1932 46592

Port Gamble WA

Port Gamble Historic Museum, 3 Rainier Av, Port Gamble, WA 98364 - T: (360) 297-8074, Fax: (360) 297-7455, E-mail: ssmith@orminc.com, Internet: www.ptgamble.com. C.E.O.: Dave Nunes, Cur.: Shana Smith
Historic Site - 1976
Local hist 46593

Port Gibson MS

Grand Gulf Military State Park Museum, Rte 2, 12006 Grand Gulf Rd, Port Gibson, MS 39150 - T: (601) 437-5911, Fax: (601) 437-2929, E-mail: park@grandgulf.state.ms.us, Internet: www.grandgulfpark.state.ms.us. Chm.: Dr. David Headley, C.E.O.: Robert L. Ritchey
Military Museum - 1958 46594

Port Hueneme CA

Civil Engineer Corps and Seabee Museum, Bldg 99, NCBC, 1000 23rd Av, Port Hueneme, CA 93043-4301 - T: (805) 982-5165, Fax: (805) 982-5595, E-mail: museum@cbchue.navfac.navy.mil, Internet: www.ncbc.navy.mil. Dir.: Lara Bickell, George Ward Shannon jr.
Military Museum - 1947
Military hist 46595

Port Huron MI

Jack R. Hennesey Art Galleries, Saint Clair County Community College, 323 Erie St, Port Huron, MI 48061-5015 - T: (810) 989-5709, Fax: (810) 984-2852, E-mail: dkorffstclair.cc.mi.us, Internet: www.stclair.cc.mi.us. Dir.: David Korff
Fine Arts Museum
Paintings, prints, metal and wooden sculpture 46596

Port Huron Museum, 1115 Sixth St, Port Huron, MI 48060 - T: (810) 982-0891, Fax: (810) 982-0053, E-mail: info@phmuseumorg, Internet: www.phmuseum.org. Dir.: Stephen R. Williams, Cur.: T.J. Gaffney
Local Museum - 1967
Local history 46597

Port Jefferson NY

Greater Port Jefferson Museum, 115 Prospect St, Port Jefferson, NY 11777 - T: (516) 473-2665, Internet: www.portjeffhistorical.org
Local Museum - 1967 46598

Port Jervis NY

Minisink Valley Historical Society Museum, 125-133 W Main St, Port Jervis, NY 12771 - T: (914) 856-2375, Fax: (914) 856-1049, E-mail: mvhs1889@magiccarpet.com, Internet: www.minisink.org. Dir.: Peter Osborne
Local Museum - 1889 46599

Port Lavaca TX

Calhoun County Museum, 301 S Ann St, Port Lavaca, TX 77979 - T: (361) 553-4689, E-mail: india@tisd.net. Cur.: George Ann Cormier
Local Museum - 1964 46600

Port Orange FL

Hungarian Folk-Art Museum, 546 Ruth St, Port Orange, FL 32127 - T: (904) 767-4292, Fax: (904) 788-6785. C.E.O.: Dr. Michael J. Horvath, Margaret Pazmandy Horvath
Folklore Museum - 1979 46601

Port Saint Joe FL

Constitution Convention Museum, 200 Allen Memorial Way, Port Saint Joe, FL 32456 - T: (850) 229-8029, Fax: (850) 229-8029, E-mail: anne.harvey@dep.state.fl.us, Internet: www.dep.state.fl.us/parks
Local Museum - 1955
History 46602

Port Sanilac MI

Sanilac County Historical Museum, 228 S Ridge St, Port Sanilac, MI 48469 - T: (810) 622-9946, Fax: (810) 622-9946, E-mail: gened@greatlakes.net. Pres.: Art Schlichting
Historical Museum - 1964
Local history 46603

Port Townsend WA

Centrum Arts and Creative Education, Fort Worden State Park, Port Townsend, WA 98368, mail addr: POB 1158, Port Townsend, WA 98368-0958 - T: (360) 385-3102, Fax: (360) 385-2470, Internet: www.olympus.net/centrum. Exec. Dir.: Carol Shiffman
Fine Arts Museum - 1973
Prints 46604

Jefferson County Historical Society Museum, 540 Water St, Port Townsend, WA 98368 - T: (360) 385-1003, Fax: (360) 385-1042, E-mail: jchsmuseum@olympus.net, Internet: www.jchsmuseum.org. Pres.: Barbara Marseille, Dir.: Dr. Niki R. Clark
Historical Museum - 1951
Northwest Coast history and prehistory 46605

Port Townsend Marine Science Center, Fort Worden State Park, 532 Battery Way, Port Townsend, WA 98368-3431 - T: (360) 385-5582, Fax: (360) 385-7248, E-mail: ptmsc@olympus.net, Internet: www.olympus.net/ptmsc. Dir.: Anne Murphy
Military Museum - 1983
Marine hist 46606

Puget Sound Coast Artillery Museum at Fort Worden, Bldg 201, Fort Worden State Park, Port Townsend, WA 98368 - T: (360) 385-3295, Fax: (360) 385-2328, E-mail: artymus@olypen.com. C.E.O.: Dr. Niki R. Clark
Military Museum - 1976
Military hist 46607

Rothschild House, Franklin St, Port Townsend, WA 98368 - T: (360) 344-4401, Fax: (360) 385-7248, E-mail: jim.farmer@parks.wa.gov, Internet: www.olympus.net/ftworden
Decorative Arts Museum - 1959 46608

Port Washington NY

Polish American Museum, 16 Belleview Av, Port Washington, NY 11050 - T: (516) 883-6542, Fax: (516) 767-1936, E-mail: polishmuseum@aol.com. Cur.: Helena Scuderi
Fine Arts Museum / Decorative Arts Museum / Historical Museum - 1977 46609

Salgo Trust for Education, 95 Middle Neck Rd, Port Washington, NY 11050 - T: (516) 767-3654, Fax: (516) 767-7881, E-mail: thesalgotrust@aol.com. Cur.: Nicolos Salgo
Fine Arts Museum / Decorative Arts Museum - 1994
Hungarian paintings, sculpture and silver, saddles, saddle rugs, French and European furniture and decorations, Chinese art 46610

Sands-Willets House, 336 Port Washington Blvd, Port Washington, NY 11050 - T: (516) 365-9074, E-mail: curator@cowneck.org, Internet: www.cowneck.org. Pres.: Joan Kent, Cur.: Kathy Mullen
Local Museum - 1962 46611

Portage WI

Fort Winnebago Surgeons Quarters, W 8687 St, Hwy 33 E, Portage, WI 53901 - T: (608) 742-2949. C.E.O.: Shirley B. Dalton, Cur.: Rachel Wynn
Local Museum - 1938
Local hist 46612

The Historic Indian Agency House, Hwy 33, Portage, WI 53901-3116 - T: (608) 742-6362
Decorative Arts Museum / Local Museum / Historic Site - 1932
Historic house and site 46613

Portales NM

Blackwater Draw Museum, Eastern New Mexico University, 7 miles north of ENMU campus on Hwy 70, Portales, NM 88130 - T: (505) 562-2202, Fax: (505) 562-2291, E-mail: matthew.hillsman@enmu.edu, Internet: www.enmu.edu. Dir.: Dr. John Montgomery, Cur.: Matthew Hillsman, Sc. Staff: Joanne Dickenson (Archaeology)
Archaeological Museum / University Museum - 1969
1932 America's first multi-cultural, paleoindian archaeological site 46614

Gallery of the Department of Art, Eastern New Mexico University, Portales, NM 88130 - T: (505) 562-2510, Fax: (505) 562-2362, Internet: www.enmu.edu. Dir.: Jim Bryant
Fine Arts Museum / University Museum - 1935
Students artworks 46615

Miles Mineral Museum, Eastern New Mexico University, ENMU Campus, Roosevelt hall, Portales, NM 88130 - T: (505) 562-2651, Fax: (505) 562-2192, E-mail: jim.constantopoulos@enmu.edu, Internet: www.enmu.edu/~constanj/milesmuseum.htm. Dir.: Dr. Jim Constantopoulos
University Museum / Natural History Museum - 1969 46616

Natural History Museum, Eastern New Mexico University, Station 33, Portales, NM 88130 - T: (505) 562-2723, Fax: (505) 562-2192, E-mail: jennifer.frey@enmu.edu, Internet: www.enmu.edu/~gennaroa/museum/naturalhistory.htm. Dir./Cur.: Dr. Jennifer K. Frey (Birds & Mammals), Cur.: Dr. Marvin Lutnesky (Fishes, Reptiles and Amphibians), Dr. Dann Brown (Plants), Dr. Gary Pfaffenberger (Invertebrates)
University Museum / Natural History Museum - 1968 46617

Roosevelt County Museum, Eastern New Mexico University, Portales, NM 88130 - T: (505) 562-1011, Fax: (505) 562-2578. Cur.: Mark Romero
Local Museum - 1934 46618

Porter ME

Parsonsfield-Porter History House, 92 Main St, Porter, ME 04068 - T: (207) 625-4667, 625-7019
Local Museum - 1946
Bridge, local Baptist group 46619

Porterville CA

Porterville Historical Museum, 257 N D St, Porterville, CA 93257 - T: (559) 784-2053, Fax: (559) 784-4009. Pres.: Bill Horst, Cur.: Beverly Faul
Historical Museum - 1965
History 46620

Portland ME

Children's Museum of Maine, 142 Free St, Portland, ME 04101 - T: (207) 828-1234, Fax: (207) 828-5726, Internet: www.childrensmuseumofme.org. Pres.: Harry Pringle, Exec. Dir.: Suzanne Olson
Special Museum - 1976 46621

Danforth Gallery, 34 Danforth St, Portland, ME 04101 - T: (207) 775-6245, Fax: (207) 775-6550, E-mail: info@maineartistspace.org, Internet: www.maineartistspace.org. Dir.: Helen Rivas
Public Gallery - 1986 46622

Institute of Contemporary Art, Maine College of Art, 522 Congress St, Portland, ME 04101 - T: (207) 879-5742 ext 229, Fax: (207) 772-5069, E-mail: ica@meca.edu, Internet: www.meca.edu/ica. Dir.: Mark Bessire
Fine Arts Museum - 1983
Art 46623

Maine Historical Society Museum, 485 Congress St, Portland, ME 04101 - T: (207) 774-1822, Fax: (207) 775-4301, E-mail: info@mainehistory.org, Internet: www.mainehistory.com. Dir.: Richard D'Abate
Local Museum - 1822
Regional history 46624

The Museum of African Tribal Art, 122 Spring St, Portland, ME 04101 - T: (207) 871-7188, Fax: (207) 773-1197, E-mail: africart@maine.rr.com, Internet: www.africantribalmuseum.com. Dir.: Oscar O. Moxeme
Fine Arts Museum - 1998
African art, Sub-Saharan African tribal art 46625

Portland Museum of Art, 7 Congress Sq, Portland, ME 04101 - T: (207) 775-6148, Fax: (207) 773-7324, E-mail: pma@maine.rr.com, Internet: www.portlandmuseum.org. Dir.: Daniel E. O'Leary, Cur.: Jessica Nicoll
Fine Arts Museum - 1882
Maine's largest art museum, prints, drawings, sculpture, photos 46626

Tate House, 1270 Westbrook St, Portland, ME 04102 - T: (207) 774-9781, Fax: (207) 774-6177, E-mail: info@tatehouse.org, Internet: www.tatehouse.org. Pres.: Lynn Glover, Dir.: Kristen Crean
Historical Museum - 1931 46627

Victoria Mansion, 109 Danforth St, Portland, ME 04101 - T: (207) 772-4841, Fax: (207) 772-6290, E-mail: victoria@maine.rr.com, Internet: www.victoriamansion.org. Pres.: Kurt E. Klebe, Dir.: Robert Wolterstorff
Local Museum / Decorative Arts Museum - 1943 46628

Wadsworth-Longfellow House, 485 Congress St, Portland, ME 04101 - T: (207) 774-0427, Fax: (207) 775-4301, E-mail: post@mainehistory.org, Internet: www.mainehistory.org. Dir.: Richard D'Abate, Cur.: Joyce Butler
Special Museum - 1822
Boyhood home of poet Henry Wadsworth Longfellow 46629

Portland OR

American Advertising Museum, 211 NW Fifth Av, Portland, OR 97209 - T: (503) AAM-0000, Fax: (503) 274-2576, E-mail: admuseum@aol.com, Internet: www.admuseum.org. Pres.: Steve Karakas
Special Museum - 1984 46630

Blue Sky, Oregon Center for the Photographic Arts, 1231 NW Hoyt St, Portland, OR 97209 - T: (503) 225-0210. Dir.: Chris Rauschenberg
Public Gallery 46631

Buckley Center Gallery, c/o University of Portland, 5000 N Willamette Blvd, Portland, OR 97203 - T: (503) 283-7258. Dir.: Michael Miller, Mary Margaret Dundore
University Museum / Fine Arts Museum - 1977 46632

Doll Gardner Art GAllery, 8470 SW Oleson Rd, Portland, OR 97223 - T: (503) 246-3351, 244-1379, Internet: www.whuuf.org
Fine Arts Museum - 1970
Paintings, wall sculptures by local artists 46633

Douglas F. Cooley Memorial Art Gallery, c/o Reed College, 3203 SE Woodstock Blvd, Portland, OR 97202-8199 - T: (503) 777-7251, Fax: (503) 788-6691, E-mail: silas.b.cook@reed.edu, Internet: www.reed.edu. Dir.: Silas B. Cook
Fine Arts Museum - 1989
Prints, drawings, paintings, photographs and sculptures 46634

Littman Gallery, Portland State University, 724 SW Harrison St, Portland, OR 97201 - T: (503) 725-5656, Fax: (503) 725-5680, Internet: www.pdx.edu
Fine Arts Museum / University Museum - 1980 46635

North View Gallery, c/o Portland Community College, 12000 SW 49th Av, Portland, OR 97219 - T: (503) 977-4269, Fax: (503) 977-4874. Dir.: Hugh Webb
Fine Arts Museum - 1970
Contemporary Northwestern art 46636

Oregon History Center, 1200 SW Park Av, Portland, OR 97205 - T: (503) 222-1741, Fax: (503) 221-2035, E-mail: orhist@ohs.org, Internet: www.ohs.org. Dir.: Norma Paulus, Marsha Matthews (Artifact Collections), Susan Seyl (Image Collections), Richard Engeman (Manuscripts and Archives Collection)
Historical Museum / Local Museum - 1873 46637

Oregon Museum of Science and Industry, 1945 SE Water Av, Portland, OR 97214 - T: (503) 797-4000, Fax: (503) 797-4500, Internet: www.omsi.edu. Cur.: Judy Margles
Natural History Museum / Science&Tech Museum - 1944 46638

Oregon Sports Hall of Fame and Museum, 321 SW Salmon, Portland, OR 97204 - T: (503) 227-7466, Fax: (503) 227-6925, E-mail: orsports@teleport.com, Internet: www.oregonsportshall.org
Special Museum - 1978 46639

Pittock Mansion, 3229 NW Pittock Dr, Portland, OR 97210 - T: (503) 823-3623, Fax: (503) 823-3619, E-mail: pkdanc@ci.portland.or.us, Internet: www.pittockmansion.com. Pres.: Michael Henley, Dir. & C.E.O.: Daniel T. Crandall
Local Museum / Historic Site - 1965
18th, 19th and early 20th c decorative arts, coll of Thomas Hill paintings 46640

Portland Art Museum, 1219 SW Park Av, Portland, OR 97205 - T: (503) 226-2811, Fax: (503) 226-4842, E-mail: info@pam.org, Internet: www.portlandartmuseum.org. Dir.: John E. Buchanan jr., Cur.: Bruce Guenther (Contemporary and Modern Art), Donald Jenkins (Asian Art), Margaret Bullock (American Art), Bill Mercer (Native American Art), Penelope Hunter-Stiebel (European Art), Pamela Morris (Prints and Drawings), Terry Toedtemeier (Photography), Elizabeth Garrison (Education), Cons.: Elizabeth Chambers
Fine Arts Museum - 1892 46641

Portland Children's Museum Second Generation, 4105 SW Canyon Rd, Portland, OR 97221 - T: (503) 223-6500, Fax: (503) 223-6600, E-mail: rbarton@portlandcm2.org, Internet: www.portlandcm2.org. Exec. Dir.: Margaret Eickmann
Local Museum / Natural History Museum - 1949
Natural hist, paleontology, cultural hist, transportation, toys, dolls, stuffed animals of North America 46642

Portland State University Galleries, 725 SW Harrison, Portland, OR 97207, mail addr: POB 751/SD, Portland, OR 97207 - T: (503) 725-5656, Fax: (503) 725-5680. C.E.O.: Ann Amato
Fine Arts Museum / University Museum
Prints, paintings, sculpture 46643

Washington County Historical Society Museum, 17677 NW Springville Rd, Portland, OR 97229 - T: (503) 645-5353, Fax: (503) 645-5650, E-mail: wchs@teleport.com, Internet: www.washingtoncountymuseum.org
Local Museum - 1956 46644

White Gallery, c/o Portland State University, POB 751, Portland, OR 97207 - T: (503) 725-5656, Fax: (503) 725-5080, Internet: www.pdx.edu
Fine Arts Museum / University Museum - 1970 46645

World Forestry Center, 4033 SW Canyon Rd, Portland, OR 97221 - T: (503) 228-1367, Fax: (503) 228-3624, E-mail: mail@worldforestry.org, Internet: www.worldforestry.org. Pres. & C.E.O.: Glen L. Gilbert, Dir.: Mark Reed
Natural History Museum - 1964 46646

Portsmouth NH

Children's Museum of Portsmouth, 280 Marcy St, Portsmouth, NH 03801 - T: (603) 436-3853, Fax: (603) 436-7706, E-mail: staff@childrens-museum.org, Internet: www.childrens-museum.org. Dir.: Xanthi Gray (Exhibits)
Historical Museum - 1983 46647

Governor John Langdon House, 143 Pleasant St, Portsmouth, NH 03801 - T: (603) 436-3205, Fax: (617) 227-9204, E-mail: ezopes@spnea.org, Internet: www.spnea.org. Dir.: Elaine Zopes
Local Museum - 1947 46648

John Paul Jones House Museum, 43 Middle St, Portsmouth, NH 03802-0728 - T: (603) 436-8420, Fax: (603) 431-9973, E-mail: jpjhouse@seacoastnh.com, Internet: www.johnpauljones.org. Pres.: Maryellen Burke
Local Museum - 1920
Guns, books, china, costumes, documents, furniture, glass, portraits and silver pertaining 46649

MacPheadris/Warner House, 150 Daniel St, Portsmouth, NH 03802-0895 - T: (603) 436-5909, E-mail: bb1798@aol.com, Internet: www.warnerhouse.org. C.E.O.: Dr. Robert L. Barth
Local Museum - 1931 46650

Moffatt-Ladd House, 154 Market St, Portsmouth, NH 03801 - T: (603) 436-8221, Fax: (603) 431-9063, E-mail: moffatt-ladd@juno.com. Pres.: Dr. Barbara McLean Ward
Historic Site - 1911 46651

Portsmouth Athenaeum, 9 Market Sq, Portsmouth, NH 03801 - T: (603) 431-2538, Fax: (603) 431-7180, E-mail: athenaeum@juno.com. Pres.: Eleonore P. Sanderson, C.E.O.: Tom Hardiman
Historical Museum - 1817
Maritinme history, ship models, paintings, portraits - library 46652

Rundlet-May House, 364 Middle St, Portsmouth, NH 03801 - T: (603) 436-3205, Fax: (617) 227-9204, E-mail: pzea@spnea.org, Internet: www.spnea.org. Vice Pres.: Philip Zea
Local Museum - 1971 46653

Strawbery Banke, 454 Court St, Portsmouth, NH 03801, mail addr: POB 300, Portsmouth, NH 03802-0300 - T: (603) 433-1100, Fax: (603) 433-1129, Internet: www.strawberybanke.org. Cur.: John Mayer, Carolyn Roy, Rodney Rowland
Local Museum - 1958 46654

Wentworth-Coolidge Mansion, 375 Little Harbor Rd, Portsmouth, NH 03801 - T: (603) 436-6607, Fax: (603) 436-9889, E-mail: wcc@wcmansion.org, Internet: www.nhpstateparks.org. Dir.: Molly Bolster
Historical Museum - 1954
Home of first British Colonial Governor of New Hampshire 46655

Wentworth Gardner and Tobias Lear Houses, 50 Mechanic St, Portsmouth, NH 03801 - T: (603) 436-4406, Internet: www.seacoastnh.com/wentworth. Pres.: William Manfull
Local Museum / Decorative Arts Museum - 1941
Historic House from 1760, early Georgian architecture 46656

Portsmouth OH

Southern Ohio Museum and Cultural Center, 825 Gallia St, Portsmouth, OH 45662, mail addr: POB 990, Portsmouth, OH 45662 - T: (740) 354-5629, Fax: (740) 354-4090, E-mail: museum82@falcon1.net. Pres.: C. Clayton Johnson, Cur.: Sara Rardin Johnson (Exhibits), Regi Wilkes (Performing Arts)
Fine Arts Museum / Folklore Museum - 1977 46657

Portsmouth RI

Portsmouth Museum, 870 E Main Rd and Union St, Portsmouth, RI 02871 - T: (401) 683-9178. Pres.: Herbert Hall
Local Museum - 1938
Local hist 46658

Portsmouth VA

Children's Museum of Virginia, Portsmouth Museums, 221 High St, Portsmouth, VA 23704 - T: (757) 393-8393, Fax: (757) 393-5228, Internet: www.ci.portsmouth.va.us/childrensmuseumva
Special Museum
Hands-on exhibits 46659

Courthouse Gallery, Portsmouth Museums, 420 High St, Portsmouth, VA 23704 - T: (757) 393-8983, Fax: (757) 393-5228, E-mail: perryn@ci.portsmouth.va.us, Internet: www.ci.portsmouth.va.us. Dir.: Nancy Perry, Cur.: Gayle Paul
Fine Arts Museum - 1974 46660

The Hill House, Portsmouth Historical Association, 221 North St, Portsmouth, VA 23704 - T: (757) 393-0241, Fax: (757) 393-5244. Pres.: Alice C. Hanes
Fine Arts Museum / Historical Museum / Museum of Classical Antiquities - 1957
Local hist, historic house, furnishings 46661

Lancaster Antique Toy and Train Collection, Portsmouth Museums, 420 High St, Portsmouth, VA 23704 - T: (757) 393-8393, Fax: (757) 393-5228, Internet: www.ci.portsmouth.va.us
Special Museum 46662

Lightship Museum and Naval Shipyard Museum, Portsmouth Museums, Water and London Sts, Portsmouth, VA 23704 - T: (757) 393-8741, Fax: (757) 393-5228, Internet: www.ci.portsmouth.va.us. Dir.: Michael Kerekesh
Historical Museum 46663

Portsmouth Museum of Military History, 701 Court St, Portsmouth, VA 23704, mail addr: 626 High St, Portsmouth, VA 23704 - T: (757) 393-2773, Fax: (757) 393-2883
Military Museum - 1998 46664

Portsmouth Naval Shipyard Museum, Portsmouth Museums, 2 High St, Portsmouth, VA 23704 - T: (757) 393-8591, Fax: (757) 393-5228, Internet: www.ci.portsmouth.va.us. Dir.: Alice C. Hanes
Military Museum
Uniforms, cannon balls, models of ships, pieces of the CSS Virginia 46665

Virginia Sports Hall of Fame and Museum, 420 High St, Portsmouth, VA 23704 - T: (757) 393-8031, Fax: (757) 393-5228, E-mail: webbe@ci.portsmouth.va.us, Internet: www.ci.portsmouth.va.us/vasportshall. Pres.: Jimmy Williams, Exec. Dir.: Eddie Webb
Special Museum - 1971
Sports 46666

Visual Arts Center, Tidewater Community College, 340 High St, Portsmouth, VA 23704 - T: (757) 822-6999, Fax: (757) 822-6800, E-mail: tciotta@tc.cc.va.us, Internet: www.tc.cc.va.us
Performing Arts Museum 46667

Poteau OK

Robert S. Kerr Museum, 1507 S McKenna, Poteau, OK 74953 - T: (918) 647-9579, Fax: (918) 647-3952. Cur.: Carol Spindle
Local Museum - 1968 46668

Potsdam NY

Potsdam Public Museum, Civic Center, Potsdam, NY 13676 - T: (315) 265-6910. Dir.: Betsy L. Travis
Local Museum / Decorative Arts Museum - 1940
Decorative arts, local hist 46669

Roland Gibson Gallery, State University of New York College at Potsdam, 44 Pierrepont Av, Potsdam, NY 13676 - T: (315) 267-3290, Fax: (315) 267-4884, Internet: www.potsdam.edu/gibson/gibson.html. Dir.: Romi Seald-Chudzinski, Preparator: Claudette Feffee
Fine Arts Museum / University Museum - 1968 46670

Pottstown PA

Pottsgrove Manor, 100 West King St, Pottstown, PA 19464-6318 - T: (610) 326-4014, Fax: (610) 326-9618, E-mail: pottsgrovemanor@mail.montcopa.org, Internet: www.montcopa.org. Cur./Admin.: William A. Brobst
Local Museum - 1988
Historic house 46671

Pottsville AR

Potts Inn Museum, Town Sq, Pottsville, AR 72801 - T: (501) 968-1877
Local Museum - 1978
1850-1858 home and stage stop of Kirkbride Potts 46672

Poughkeepsie NY

Art Gallery Marist College, 3399 North Rd, Poughkeepsie, NY 12601-1387 - T: (845) 575-3000 ext 2903, Fax: (845) 471-6213, E-mail: donise.english@marist.edu, Internet: marist.edu. Dir.: Donise English
Fine Arts Museum
Paintings, sculptures, photographs, contemporary work 46673

Frances Lehman Loeb Art Center, Vassar College, 124 Raymond Av, Poughkeepsie, NY 12604-0703 - T: (845) 437-5237, Fax: (845) 437-7304, E-mail: jamundy@vassar.edu, Internet: departments.vassar.edu/~fllac/. Dir.: James Mundy, Cur.: Patria Phagan (Prints and Drawings), Joel Smith (Collectons)
Fine Arts Museum - 1864 46674

Locust Grove, Samuel Morse Historic Site, 2683 South Rd, Poughkeepsie, NY 12601 - T: (845) 454-4500 ext 10, Fax: (845) 485-7122, E-mail: locustgrovel@earthlink.net, Internet: www.morsehistoricsite.org. Dir.: Raymond J. Armater
Decorative Arts Museum - 1979
Furniture, China, costumes, dolls, docs, telegraph equip 46675

Mid-Hudson Children's Museum, 75 N Water St, Poughkeepsie, NY 12601 - T: (845) 471-0589, Fax: (845) 471-0415, E-mail: mhcm@vh.net, Internet: www.mhcm.org. Exec. Dir.: Diane Pedevillano
Historical Museum - 1989 46676

Samuel F.B. Morse Historic Site, 370 South Rd, Poughkeepsie, NY 12601 - T: (914) 454-4500, Fax: (914) 485-7122, E-mail: morse-historic-site@worldnet.att.net, Internet: www.morsehistoricsite.org. Pres.: Frances S. Reese, Dir.: Raymond J. Armater
Local Museum - 1979 46677

Poulsbo WA

Suquamish Museum, 15838 Sandy Hook Rd, Poulsbo, WA 98370 - T: (360) 598-3311, 394-5275, Fax: (360) 598-6295, E-mail: suqmuseum@hotmail.com, Internet: www.suquamish.nsn.us. Dir.: Marilyn Jones
Ethnology Museum - 1983
Culture of the Suquamish Tribe and other Puget Sound Tribes 46678

Pound Ridge NY

Pound Ridge Museum, 255 Westchester Av, Pound Ridge, NY 10576 - T: (914) 764-4333, Fax: (914) 764-1778. Pres.: Lise Mayers
Historical Museum / Local Museum - 1970 46679

Powell WY

Northwest Gallery and Sinclair Gallery, Northwest College, 231 W Sixth St, Powell, WY 82435 - T: (307) 754-6111, Fax: (307) 754-6245, E-mail: kelsayd@nwc.cc.wy.us, Internet: www.nwc.cc.wy.us/area/art/index.html
Fine Arts Museum 46680

Powers Lake ND

Burke County Historical Powers Lake Complex, Powers Lake, ND 58773 - T: (701) 546-4491. C.E.O: Larry Tinjum
Local Museum - 1986 46681

Prairie du Chien WI

Fort Crawford Museum, 717 S Beaumont Rd, Prairie du Chien, WI 53821 - T: (608) 326-6960, E-mail: ftcrawford.net, Internet: www.fortcrawford.com. Head: Thomas L. Farrell
Local Museum - 1955
Local hist 46682

Prairie du Chien Museum at Fort Crawford → Fort Crawford Museum

Villa Louis Historic Site, 521 Villa Louis Rd, Prairie du Chien, WI 53821 - T: (608) 326-2721, Fax: (608) 326-5507, E-mail: villalou@pearl.mhtc.net, Internet: www.villalouis.shsw.wisc.edu. Dir.: Michael Douglass
Local Museum - 1936
Local hist 46683

Prairie du Rocher IL

Fort de Chartres Museum, 1350 State Rt 155, Prairie du Rocher, IL 62277 - T: (618) 284-7230, Fax: (618) 284-7230, E-mail: ftdchart@htc.net. Man.: Darrell Duensing
Historic Site / Military Museum - 1913
Original site of the French Fort de Chartes built in 1753 46684

Prairie du Sac WI

Sauk Prairie Area Historical Society Museum, 565 Water St, Prairie du Sac, WI 53578 - T: (608) 643-6406, E-mail: spahs@chorus.net. Pres.: Stephen Dittberner, Cur.: Orie Eilertson
Local Museum - 1961
Local hist 46685

Pratt KS

Pratt County Historical Society Museum, 208 S Ninnescah St, Pratt, KS 67124 - T: (316) 672-7874, Internet: www.pratt.net
Local Museum - 1967
Fossils, Plains Indian artifacts, pioneer period, military, jail 46686

Prattsburgh NY

Narcissa Prentiss House, 7226 Mill Pond Rd, Prattsburgh, NY 14873 - T: (607) 522-4537. C.E.O.: William Willis
Local Museum - 1940 46687

Prescott AZ

Phippen Museum, 4701 Hwy 89 N, Prescott, AZ 86301 - T: (928) 778-1385, Fax: (928) 778-4524, E-mail: phippen@phippenmuseum.org, Internet: www.phippenmuseum.org. Dir.: Deborah Reeder, Sue Willoughby
Fine Arts Museum - 1974
Art of the American West 46688

Sharlot Hall Museum, 415 W Gurley St, Prescott, AZ 86301 - T: (928) 445-3122, Fax: (928) 776-9053, E-mail: sharlot@sharlot.org, Internet: www.sharlot.org. Dir.: Richard Sims, Cur.: Norm Tessman
Local Museum - 1929
Regional history 46689

Smoki Museum, 147 N Arizona St, Prescott, AZ 86304-0224 - T: (928) 445-1230, Fax: (928) 777-0573, E-mail: smoki@futureone.com, Internet: www.smoki.com. Dir.: Paul V. Long jr.
Ethnology Museum - 1935
Anthropology, American Indian art and culture 46690

Presidio TX

Fort Leaton, River Rd FM 170, Presidio, TX 79845 - T: (915) 229-3613, Fax: (915) 229-4814, E-mail: fortleatonshp@brooksdata.net, Internet: tpwd.state.tx.us. C.E.O.: Andrew Sansom
Local Museum - 1977
Local hist, birding, bats, adobe structure maintained, 2 wheel ox-cart 46691

Price UT

College of Eastern Utah Art Gallery, 451 E 400 N, Price, UT 84501 - T: (435) 613-5060, Fax: (435) 637-4102, Internet: www.ceu.edu. Man.: Cliff Bergra, Ass. Dir.: Brent Haddock
Fine Arts Museum / University Museum - 1937
Art 46692

College of Eastern Utah Prehistoric Museum, 155 E Main St, Price, UT 84501 - T: (435) 613-5060, Fax: (435) 637-2514, E-mail: pmiller@ceu.edu, Internet: www.ceu.edu. Dir.: Don Burge, Cur.: Pamela Miller
University Museum / Ethnology Museum / Natural History Museum - 1961
Anthropology, geology 46693

Princess Anne MD

Teackle Mansion, 11736 Mansion St, Princess Anne, MD 21853 - T: (410) 651-2238, E-mail: visitor@teacklemansion.org, Internet: www.teacklemansion.org
Local Museum - 1958
Costumes, decoratives art, furniture, paintings 46694

Princeton IA

Buffalo Bill Cody Homestead, 28050 230th Av, Princeton, IA 52768 - T: (563) 225-2981, Fax: (563) 381-2805, Internet: www.scottcountyiowa.com. C.E.O.: Roger Kean
Local Museum - 1970
Historic house, boyhood home of Buffalo Bill Cody 46695

Princeton IL

Bureau County Historical Society Museum, 109 Park Av W, Princeton, IL 61356-1927 - T: (815) 875-2184. Dir.: Barbara Hansen
Local Museum - 1911
Local history 46696

Princeton KY

Adsmore Museum, 304 N Jefferson St, Princeton, KY 42445 - T: (270) 365-3114, E-mail: ads@ziggycom.net. Cur.: Ardell Jarratt
Historical Museum - 1986
Period furnishings, silver, China, linens, clothing, decorative accessories, photographs, letters, toys 46697

Princeton MO

Casteel-Linn House and Museum, 902 E Oak St, Princeton, MO 64673 - T: (816) 748-3905. Dir.: Joe Dale Linn, Cur.: Nancy Paige Linn
Local Museum - 1982
Local hist 46698

Mercer County Genealogical and Historical Society Museum, 601 Grant, Princeton, MO 64673 - T: (660) 748-3725, Fax: (660) 748-3723, Internet: www.rootsweb/momercer/index.html. Head: Randy Ferguson
Local Museum - 1965 46699

Princeton NJ

Gallery at Bristol-Myers Squibb, POB 4000, Princeton, NJ 08543-4000 - T: (609) 252-4599, Fax: (609) 497-2441. Dir.: Pamela V. Sherin
Public Gallery - 1972 46700

Historic Morven, New Jersey State Museum, 55 Stockton St, Princeton, NJ 08540 - T: (609) 683-4495, Fax: (609) 497-6390, E-mail: morvennj@aol.com, Internet: www.historicmorven.org. Exec. Dir.: Martha Leigh Wolf, Cur.: Pam Ruch
Archaeological Museum
Archaeology 46701

Princeton Museum, 158 Nassau St, Princeton, NJ 08542 - T: (609) 921-6748, Fax: (609) 921-6939, E-mail: gailfstern@aol.com, Internet: www.princetonol.com/groups/histsoc/. C.E.O. & Pres.: Dee Parberg, Dir.: Gail F. Stern, Cur.: Maureen M. Smith
Local Museum - 1938 46702

Princeton University Art Museum, Princeton University, Princeton, NJ 08544-1018 - T: (609) 258-3788, Fax: (609) 258-5949, E-mail: artmuseum@princeton.edu, Internet: www.princetonartmuseum.org. Dir.: Susan M. Taylor, Ass. Dir.: Becky Sender, Ass. Cur.: Michael Padgett (Ancient Art), Betsy Rosasco (Later Western Art), Toby Jurovics (Photography), Cary Y. Liu (Asian Art), Laura Giles (Prints, Drawings), Cons.: Norman Muller
Fine Arts Museum / University Museum - 1882
Ancient Mediterranean, British and American art, Chinese ritual bronze vessels, Far Eastern art, Pre-Columbian and African art - Index of Christian art, library 46703

Princeton University Museum of Natural History (closed until about 2005), Guyot Hall, Princeton University, Princeton, NJ 08544-1003 - T: (609) 258-4102, Fax: (609) 258-1334. Cur.: Elizabeth Horn (Biological Collections)
University Museum / Natural History Museum - 1805 46704

Rockingham, 108 CR 518, Princeton, NJ 08540 - T: (609) 921-8835, Fax: (609) 921-8835, E-mail: peggi@superlink.net, Internet: www.rockingham.net. Cur.: Margaret Carlsen
Historic Site - 1896
1710 Berrien Mansion, Washington's headquarters while Continental Congress was in session in Princeton in 1738 46705

Thomas Clarke House-Princeton Battlefield, 500 Mercer Rd, Princeton, NJ 08540-4810 - T: (609) 921-0074, Fax: (609) 921-0074, E-mail: pbsp@aol.com. Cur.: John K. Mills
Historical Museum / Military Museum - 1976 46706

Prineville OR

A.R. Bowman Memorial Museum, 246 N Main St, Prineville, OR 97754 - T: (541) 447-3715, Fax: (541) 447-3715, E-mail: bowmuse@netscape.net, Internet: www.bowmanmuseum.org. Pres.: William Weberg, Dir.: Gordon Gillespie
Local Museum - 1971 46707

Prividence RI

John Brown House, 52 Power St, Prividence, RI 02906 - T: (401) 331-8575. Cur.: Linda Eppich
Decorative Arts Museum - 1942
Chinese export objects, antique dolls, furniture, portraits, China, glass, pewter and other decorative objects 46708

Proctor VT

Vermont Marble Museum, 52 Main St, Proctor, VT 05765 - T: (800) 427-1396, Fax: (802) 459-2948, E-mail: vmecss@sover.net, Internet: www.vermont-marble.com. Head: Marsha Hemm
Natural History Museum / Science&Tech Museum - 1933
Mining, geology 46709

Wilson Castle, W Proctor Rd, Proctor, VT 05765 - T: (802) 773-3284, Fax: (802) 773-3284. Dir.: Blossom Wilson Davine
Decorative Arts Museum - 1961
European and Oriental objects d'art, stained glass, furniture, antiques 46710

Prospect Park PA

Morton Homestead, 100 Lincoln Av, Prospect Park, PA 19076 - T: (610) 583-7221, Fax: (610) 583-2349, E-mail: erump@state.pa.us. Dir.: Elizabeth Rump
Local Museum - 1939
Local hist 46711

Prosser WA

Benton County Historical Museum, 7th and Paterson, City Park, Prosser, WA 99350 - T: (509) 786-3842
Local Museum - 1968
Indian artifacts, natural hist, guns, dolls, china, handwork, gown coll 46712

Providence RI

Annmary Brown Memorial, 21 Brown St, Providence, RI 02912 - T: (401) 863-1994, E-mail: carol_cramer@brown.edu, Internet: www.brown.edu/facilities/university_library/lihs/amb.html. Man.: Carole Cramer
Fine Arts Museum / University Museum - 1905
Art 46713

Art and Art History Department, Providence College, River Ave and Eaton St, Providence, RI 02918 - T: (401) 865-2401, Fax: (401) 865-2410, E-mail: art@providence.edu, Internet: www.providence.edu/art/art.htm. Chairman: James Janecek
Public Gallery 46714

Betsey Williams Cottage, Roger Williams Park, Providence, RI 02905 - T: (401) 785-9457, Fax: (401) 461-5146, E-mail: museum@musnathist.com. Dir.: Tracey K. Brussat, Cur.: Marilyn Massaro
Historic Site - 1871
Historic house 46715

Culinary Archives and Museum, Johnson and Wales University, 315 Harborside Blvd, Providence, RI 02905 - T: (401) 598-2805, Fax: (401) 598-2807, E-mail: bkuck@jwu.edu, Internet: www.culinary.org. Pres.: John Bowen, Dir.: Barbara Kuck
University Museum / Special Museum - 1989 46716

David Winton Bell Gallery, List Art Center, Brown University, 64 College St, Providence, RI 02912 - T: (401) 863-2932, 863-2929, Fax: (401) 863-9323, Internet: www.brown.edu/bellgallery. Dir.: Jo-Ann Conklin, Cur.: Vesela Sretenovic
Fine Arts Museum / University Museum - 1971
Art 46717

Edward M. Bannister Gallery, Rhode Island College, 600 Mount Pleasant Av, Providence, RI 02908 - T: (401) 456-9765, Fax: (401) 456-9718, E-mail: domalley@ric.edu, Internet: www.ric.edu/bannister. Dir.: Dennis M. O'Malley
Fine Arts Museum - 1978
Visual arts 46718

Governor Henry Lippitt House Museum, 199 Hope St, Providence, RI 02906 - T: (401) 453-0688, Fax: (401) 453-8221, E-mail: sludin@ids.net. C.E.O.: Nicolas Brown, Cur.: Sally Lundin
Local Museum - 1991
Local hist 46719

Governor Stephen Hopkins House, Hopkins and Benefit Sts, Providence, RI 02903 - T: (401) 421-0694. Head: Alice Walsh
Local Museum - 1707
Historic house, 1707 Governor Stephen Hopkins home 46720

Museum of Art, Rhode Island School of Design, 224 Benefit St, Providence, RI 02903-2723 - T: (401) 454-6500, Fax: (401) 454-6556, E-mail: museum@risd.edu, Internet: www.risd.edu/museum.cfm. Dir.: Phillip Johnston, Ass. Dir.: Lora Urbanelli, Cur.: Thomas Michie (Decorative Arts), Maureen O'Brien (Painting and Sculpture), Dr. Georgina Borromeo (Antiquities), Susan Hay (Costume and Textiles), Jan Howard (Prints, Drawings and Photographs), Deborah del Gais Muller (Asian Art), Judith Tannenbaum (Contemporary Art)
Fine Arts Museum / University Museum - 1877
European porcelain, Oriental textiles, ancient Oriental and ethnographic art, modern Latin American art, contempotary graphics 46721

Museum of Natural History, Roger Williams Park, Providence, RI 02905 - T: (401) 785-9457, Fax: (401) 461-5146, E-mail: museum@musnathist.com, Internet: www.osfn.org/museum. Dir.: Tracey Keough, Cur.: Marilyn Massaro
Natural History Museum - 1896
Natural hist - planetarium 46722

Providence Athenaeum, 251 Benefit St, Providence, RI 02903 - T: (401) 421-6970, Fax: (401) 421-2860
Public Gallery
library 46723

Providence Children's Museum, 100 South St, Providence, RI 02903 - T: (401) 273-5437, Fax: (401) 273-1004, E-mail: provcm@childrenmuseum.org, Internet: www.childrenmuseum.org. Pres.: Kathleen Goulding, Dir.: Janice O'Donnell
Special Museum - 1976
Children's museum 46724

Rhode Island Black Heritage Society Museum, 202 Washington St, Providence, RI 02903, mail addr: POB 1656, Providence, RI 02901 - T: (401) 751-3490, Fax: (401) 751-0040, E-mail: blkheritage@netzero.net. Pres.: Walter Stone, Exec. Dir.: Joaquina B. Teixeira
Fine Arts Museum / Historical Museum - 1975
Afro-American history and art 46725

Rhode Island Historical Society Exhibition, Aldrich House, 110 Benevolent St, Providence, RI 02906 - T: (401) 331-8575, Fax: (401) 351-0127. Dir.: Murney Gerlach, Chief Cur.: Linda Eppich, Cur.: Rick Stattler (Manuscripts), Allison Cywin (Graphics)
Local Museum - 1822
Local hist - Historical library of 1874, John Brown House of 1786 46726

Roger Williams National Memorial, 282 N Main St, Providence, RI 02903 - T: (401) 521-7266, Fax: (401) 521-7239, E-mail: rowi_interpretation@nps.gov, Internet: www.nps.gov/rowi. Head: Michael Creasey
Local Museum - 1965
Local hist 46727

Wheeler Gallery, 228 Angell St, Providence, RI 02906 - T: (401) 421-9230. Dir.: Sue Carroll
Fine Arts Museum
Contemporary paintings, sculpture, photography, prints, ceramics, glass, installations 46728

Provincetown MA

Pilgrim Monument and Provincetown Museum, High Pole Hill, Provincetown, MA 02657 - T: (508) 487-1310, Fax: (508) 487-4702, E-mail: cturley@pilgrimmonument.org, Internet: www.pilgrim-monument.org. Pres.: Mark Silva, Cur.: Jeffory Morris
Local Museum - 1892
Local history 46729

Provincetown Art Museum, 460 Commercial St, Provincetown, MA 02657 - T: (508) 487-1750, Fax: (508) 487-4372, E-mail: paam@capecod.net, Internet: www.paam.org. Dir.: Christine McCarthy
Fine Arts Museum - 1914
Art 46730

Provincetown Heritage Museum, 356 Commercial St, Provincetown, MA 02657 - T: (508) 487-7098. Dir.: Dale A. Fanning
Fine Arts Museum / Local Museum - 1976
Local history, housed in Methodist church 46731

Provo UT

B.F. Larsen Gallery, c/o Birgham Young University, Harris Fine Arts Center, Provo, UT 84602 - T: (801) 378-2881, Fax: (801) 378-5964
Fine Arts Museum / University Museum - 1965 46732

Brigham Young University Earth Science Museum, ERTH Bldg, Provo, UT 84602-3300 - T: (801) 378-3939, Fax: (801) 378-7919, E-mail: klstadtman@geology.byu.edu, Internet: www.cpms.byu.edu/esm. Dir./Cur.: Kenneth L. Stadtman
University Museum / Natural History Museum - 1987
Paleontology 46733

Brigham Young University Museum of Art, N Campus Dr, Provo, UT 84602-1400 - T: (801) 378-8256, 378-8257, Fax: (801) 378-8222, E-mail: moasecretary@byu.edu, Internet: www.byu.edu/moa. Dir.: Campbell B. Gray, Ass. Dir.: Ed Lind, Cur.: Dawn Pheysey
Fine Arts Museum / University Museum - 1993
Art 46734

Monte L. Bean Life Science Museum, c/o Brigham Young University, 290 MLBM Bldg, Provo, UT 84602 - T: (801) 378-5052, Fax: (801) 378-3733, E-mail: office@museum.byu.edu, Internet: www.bioag.byu.edu/mlbean. Dir.: Dr. H. Duane Smith, Ass. Dir.: Dr. Douglas C. Cox
Natural History Museum / Science&Tech Museum - 1978
Science 46735

Museum of Peoples and Cultures, c/o Brigham Young University, 700 N 100 E, Allen Hall, Provo, UT 84602 - T: (801) 378-6112, Fax: (801) 378-7123, E-mail: programs@ucs-exch.byn.edu, Internet: fhss.byu.edu/anthro/mopc/main.htm. Dir.: Dr. Marti Lu Allen
Ethnology Museum - 1946
Anthropology, ethnology 46736

Pryor MT

Chief Plenty Coups Museum, Edgar Rd, Pryor, MT 59066 - T: (406) 252-1289, Fax: (406) 252-6668, E-mail: plentycoups@plentycoups.org, Internet: www.plentycoups.org. Dir.: Rich Furber
Ethnology Museum - 1972
Ethnography of Crow Indians, paintings, drawings 46737

Pueblo CO

El Pueblo Museum (temporary location), 119 Central Plaza, Pueblo, CO 81003, mail addr: 324 W 1st St, Pueblo, CO 81003 - T: (719) 583-0453, Fax: (719) 583-0453, Internet: www.coloradohistory.org. Dir.: Deborah Espinosa
Local Museum - 1959
Local history 46738

Pueblo County Historical Society Museum, 217 S Grand Av, Pueblo, CO 81003 - T: (719) 542-1851. Dir.: Patricia Crum
Local Museum - 1986
Edward H. Broadhead Library 46739

Rosemount Museum, 419 W 14th St, Pueblo, CO 81003 - T: (719) 545-5290, Fax: (719) 545-5291, E-mail: rosemnt@usa.net, Internet: www.rosemount.org. Dir.: William T. Henning, Cur.: Martha Valle
Local Museum - 1967
John A. Thatcher residence; Henry Hudson Holly 46740

Sangre de Cristo Arts Center and Buell Children's Museum, 210 N Santa Fe Av, Pueblo, CO 81003 - T: (719) 543-0130, Fax: (719) 543-0134, E-mail: artctr@ris.net, Internet: www.sdc-arts.org. Dir.: Maggie Divelbiss, Cur.: Jenny Cook (Visual Arts), Cur.: Donna Stinchcomb (Children's Museum)
Fine Arts Museum / Special Museum - 1972
Art education 46741

Pulaski VA

Fine Arts Center for New River Valley, 21 W Main St, Pulaski, VA 24301 - T: (540) 980-7363, Fax: (540) 994-5631, E-mail: facnrv@swva.net. Dir.: Michael B. Dowell
Fine Arts Museum / Public Gallery - 1978
Art 46742

Pullman WA

Charles R. Conner Museum, Washington State University, Pullman, WA 99164-4236 - T: (509) 335-3515, Fax: (509) 335-3184, E-mail: crcm@mail.wsu.edu, Internet: www.sci.wsu.edu/cm. Dir.: Dr. Richard E. Johnson
Natural History Museum - 1894
Zoology, natural history 46743

Museum of Anthropology, Department of Anthropology, Washington State University, Pullman, WA 99164-4910 - T: (509) 335-3441, Fax: (509) 335-3999, E-mail: collinsm@wsu.edu. Dir.: William Andrefsky, Ass. Dir.: Mary Collins, Cur.: Joy Mastrogiuseppe
University Museum / Ethnology Museum - 1966
Anthropology 46744

Museum of Art, Washington State University, Pullman, WA 99164-7460 - T: (509) 335-1910, Fax: (509) 335-1908, E-mail: artmuse@wsu.edu, Internet: www.wsu.edu/artmuse. Dir.: Ross Coates, Rob Snyder, Cur.: Roger H.D. Rowley (Collections), Keith Wells
Fine Arts Museum / University Museum - 1973
Art 46745

Punta Gorda FL

Florida Adventure Museum, 260 W Retta Esplanade, Punta Gorda, FL 33950 - T: (941) 639-3777, Fax: (941) 639-3505, E-mail: museum@sunline.net, Internet: www.charlotte-florida.com/museum. Exec. Dir.: Lori Tomlinson
Local Museum - 1969
Local and military history, science 46746

Purchase NY

Neuberger Museum of Art, Purchase College, State University of New York, 735 Anderson Hill Rd, Purchase, NY 10577-1400 - T: (914) 251-6100, Fax: (914) 251-6101, E-mail: neuberger@purchase.edu, Internet: www.neuberger.org. Dir.: Lucinda H. Gedeon, Cur.: Dede Young (Modern and Contemporary art), Christa Clark (African art)
Fine Arts Museum / University Museum - 1974 46747

Put-in-Bay OH

Perry's Victory and International Peace Memorial, 93 Delaware St, Put-in-Bay, OH 43456 - T: (419) 285-2184, Fax: (419) 285-2516, E-mail: pevi_interpretation@nps.gov, Internet: www.nps.gov/pevi/
Historical Museum - 1936
Weapons and equip from the war of 1812, paintings, engravings, lithographs 46748

Putney VT

Putney Historical Society Museum, Town Hall, Putney, VT 05346 - T: (802) 387-5862, E-mail: putneyhs@sover.net. Cur.: Laura Heller, Elaine Dixon
Local Museum / Folklore Museum - 1959
Local hist 46749

Puunene HI

Alexander and Baldwin Sugar Museum, 3957 Hansen Rd, Puunene, HI 96784 - T: (808) 871-8058, Fax: (808) 871-7663, E-mail: sugarmus@maui.net, Internet: www.sugarmuseum.com. Pres.: Stephen Onaga, Exec. Dir.: Gaylord Kubota
Historical Museum / Agriculture Museum - 1980
Agriculture 46750

Puyallup WA

Ezra Meeker Mansion, 312 Spring St, Puyallup, WA 98371 - T: (253) 848-1770, Internet: www.meekermansion.org. Dir.: Dorothy Cardon
Historic Site - 1970
Historic house located at end of the Oregon Trail 46751

Paul H. Karshner Memorial Museum, 309 4th St, Puyallup, WA 98372 - T: (253) 841-8784, Fax: (253) 840-8950, E-mail: reckerson@puyallup.k12.wa.us. Dir.: Rosemary Eckerson, Cur.: Stephen Crowell, Beth Bestrom
Historical Museum - 1930
History 46752

Quantico VA

United States Marine Corps Air-Ground Museum, 2014 Anderson Av, Quantico, VA 22134 - T: (703) 784-2606, Fax: (703) 784-5856. Chief Cur.: Charles A. Wood, Cur.: Kenneth L. Smith-Christmas
Military Museum - 1940
Military hist 46753

Quarryville PA

Robert Fulton Birthplace, 1932 Robert Fulton Hwy, Quarryville, PA 17566 - T: (717) 548-2679, 548-2351, E-mail: slchs@aol.com, Internet: www.rootsweb.com/~paslchs/index.html
Decorative Arts Museum - 1965
Steamboat Clermont builder 46754

Quemado NM

Dia Center for the Arts, Quemado, NM 87829, mail addr: POB 2993, Corrales, NM 87048 - T: (505) 898-3335, Fax: (505) 898-3336, Internet: www.diacenter.org
Fine Arts Museum
Stainless steel poles, land art by Walter De Maria 46755

Quincy CA

Plumas County Museum, 500 Jackson St, Quincy, CA 95971 - T: (530) 283-6320, Fax: (530) 283-6081, E-mail: pcmuseum@psln.com, Internet: www.pluma.s.ca.us. Dir.: Scott J. Lawson, Ass. Dir.: Evelyn Whisman
Local Museum - 1964
Local hist 46756

Quincy FL

Gadsden Arts Center, 13 N Madison, Quincy, FL 32351, mail addr: POB 1945, Quincy, FL 32353 - T: (850) 875-4866, 875-1606, Fax: (850) 627-8606, E-mail: zoe@gadsdenarts.com, Internet: www.gadsdenarts.com. C.E.O.: Zoe C. Golloway
Fine Arts Museum - 1994 46757

Quincy IL

The Gardner Museum of Architecture and Design, 332 Maine St, Quincy, IL 62301 - T: (217) 224-6873, Fax: (217) 224-0006, E-mail: gardnermuseumarchitecture@adams.net, Internet: www.gardnermuseumarchitecture.org. Dir.: Jonathan G. Kesler
Historical Museum / Decorative Arts Museum - 1974
Architecture, design, housed in Richardsonian Romanesque Old Public Library 46758

Quincy and Adams County Museum, 425 S 12th St, Quincy, IL 62301 - T: (217) 222-1835. Pres.: Kathi Kriuacrk, Exec. Dir.: Philip Germann
Historical Museum - 1896
Local history, in home of former Governor of Illinois John Wood, also founder of Quincy 46759

Quincy Art Center, 1515 Jersey St, Quincy, IL 62301 - T: (217) 223-5900, Fax: (217) 223-6950, E-mail: qac@ksni.net, Internet: www.quincynet.com/artcenter. Exec. Dir.: Julie D. Nelson
Fine Arts Museum - 1923 46760

The Quincy Museum, 1601 Maine St, Quincy, IL 62301 - T: (217) 224-7669, Fax: (217) 224-9323. Pres.: Bill Bergman, C.E.O.: Steve Adams
Local Museum / Natural History Museum - 1966
Natural and local history 46761

The Gray Gallery, c/o Quincy University, 1800 College Av, Quincy, IL 62301-2699 - T: (217) 228-5371, Internet: www.quincy.edu. Dir.: Robert Lee Mejer
University Museum / Fine Arts Museum - 1968
Oriental and European prints, student and faculty works, American prints and drawings 46762

Quincy MA

Adams National Historical Park, 135 Adams St, Quincy, MA 02169 - T: (617) 773-1177, 770-1175, Fax: (617) 471-9683, E-mail: adamssuperintendent@nps.gov, Internet: www.nps.gov/adam. Dir.: Marianne Peak, Sc. Staff: Kelly Cobble
Historical Museum - 1927
History 46763

Josiah Quincy House, 20 Muirhead St, Quincy, MA 02170 - T: (617) 227-3956, 471-4508, Fax: (617) 227-9204, E-mail: pzea@spnea.org, Internet: www.spnea.org
Decorative Arts Museum - 1937 46764

Quincy Historical Museum, Adams Academy Bldg, 8 Adams St, Quincy, MA 02169 - T: (617) 773-1144, Fax: (617) 472-4990, E-mail: ghist@ci.quincy.ma.us, Internet: www.ci.quincy.ma.us. Pres.: Joyce Baker, Dir./Cur.: E. Fitzgerald
Local Museum - 1893
Local history - library 46765

Rabun Gap GA

Hambidge Center for the Creative Arts and Sciences, Betty's Creek Rd, Rabun Gap, GA 30568 - T: (706) 746-5718, Fax: (706) 746-9933, E-mail: hambidge@rabun.net, Internet: www.rabun.net/~hambidge. Dir.: Peggy McBride
Decorative Arts Museum / Folklore Museum - 1934
Crafts, folk art 46766

Racine WI

Charles A. Wustum Museum of Fine Arts, 2519 Northwestern Av, Racine, WI 53404 - T: (414) 636-9177, Fax: (414) 636-9231, E-mail: info@wustum.org, Internet: www.wustum.org. Dir.: Bruce W. Pepich
Fine Arts Museum - 1941
Arts 46767

Racine Heritage Museum, 701 S Main St, Racine, WI 53403-1211 - T: (414) 636-3926, Fax: (414) 636-3940, E-mail: inquire@clmail.com, Internet: www.spiritofinnovation.org. Dir.: Christopher Paulson, Cur.: Karen Braun
Historical Museum / Science&Tech Museum - 1960
Southeast Wisconsin industrial and product hist 46768

Radford VA

Radford University Art Museum, 200 Powell Hall, Radford, VA 24142 - T: (540) 831-5475, 831-5754, Fax: (540) 831-6799, E-mail: sarbury@radford.edu, Internet: www.radford.edu/~rumuseum. Dir.: Steve Arbury
Fine Arts Museum / University Museum - 1985
Art 46769

Radium Springs NM

Fort Selden State Monument, Fort Selden Junction 185 and Interstate 25 on Exit 19, Radium Springs, NM 88054 - T: (505) 526-8911, Fax: (505) 647-0421, E-mail: selden@zianet.com, Internet: www.nmculture.org. Head: Nathan Stone
Military Museum - 1973 46770

Raleigh NC

Artspace, 201 E Davie St, Raleigh, NC 27601 - T: (919) 821-2787, Fax: (919) 821-0383, Internet: www.artspace.citysearch.com. Exec. Dir.: Courtney Bailey
Fine Arts Museum - 1986
Fantasy art 46771

Contemporary Art Museum, 336 Fayetteville St, Raleigh, NC 27601 - T: (919) 836-0088, Fax: (919) 836-2239, E-mail: dd@camnc.org, Internet: www.camnc.org. Exec. Dir.: Denise Dickens
Fine Arts Museum - 1983 46772

Exploris, 201 E Hargett St, Raleigh, NC 27601 - T: (919) 834-4040, Fax: (919) 834-3516, E-mail: cschmidt@exploris.org, Internet: www.exploris.org
Special Museum - 1999
Contemporary objects used around the world that relate to sustainable living, global economy, cultural geography and global communication 46773

Mordecai Historic Park, 1 Mimosa St, Raleigh, NC 27604 - T: (919) 834-4844, Fax: (919) 834-7314, E-mail: CapPresInc@aol.com. Pres.: Gary G. Roth
Open Air Museum / Historical Museum - 1972 46774

North Carolina Museum of Art, 2110 Blue Ridge Rd, Raleigh, NC 27607-6494 - T: (919) 839-6262, Fax: (919) 733-8034, E-mail: hmckinney@ncmamail.dcr.state.nc.us, Internet: www.ncartmuseum.org. Dir.: Lawrence J. Wheeler, Assoc. Dir./ Cur.: John W. Coffey (American and Modern Art), Cur.: Rebecca Nagy (African Art), Huston Pascal (Modern Art), Mary Ellen Soles (Ancient Art), David H. Steel (European Art), Dennis P. Weller (European Art), Chief Cons.: David Findley
Fine Arts Museum - 1956 46775

North Carolina Museum of History, 5 E Edenton St, Raleigh, NC 27601-1011 - T: (919) 715-0200, Fax: (919) 733-8655, E-mail: janice.c.williams@ncmail.net, Internet: www.nchistory.org. Dir.: Elizabeth F. Buford, Janice C. Williams, Chief Cur.: Charles LeCount
Historical Museum - 1902 46776

North Carolina Museum of Natural Sciences, 11 W Jones St, Raleigh, NC 27601-1029 - T: (919) 733-7450, Fax: (919) 733-1573, E-mail: museum@naturalscienes.org, Internet: www.naturalsciences.org. Dir.: Dr. Betsy Bennett, Roy G. Campbell (Exhibits), Dr. Stephen Busack (Research and Collections), Cur.: David S. Lee (Birds), Mary K. Clark (Mammals), Dr. Rowland Shelley (Invertebrates), Alvin L. Braswell (Lower Vertebrates), Wayne Starnes (Fishes)
Natural History Museum - 1879 46777

North Carolina State University Gallery of Art and Design, 2610 Cates Av, Raleigh, NC 27695-7306 - T: (919) 515-3503, Fax: (919) 515-6163, E-mail: gallery@ncsu.edu, Internet: www.ncsu.edu/visualarts/. Dir.: Dr. Charlotte V. Brown
University Museum / Fine Arts Museum - 1979
Coll of American, Indian, Asian & pre-Columbian textiles; ceramics, furniture, product design 46778

Raleigh City Museum, Briggs Bldg, 220 Fayetteville St Mall, Raleigh, NC 27601-1310 - T: (919) 832-3775, Fax: (919) 832-3085, E-mail: jkulikowski@raleighcitymuseum.org, Internet: www.raleighcitymuseum.org. Dir.: Jenny Kulikowski
Local Museum - 1993 46779

Frankie G. Weems Gallery & Rotunda Gallery, Meredith College, Gaddy-Hamrick ArtCenter, 3800 Hillsborough St, Raleigh, NC 27607-5298 - T: (919) 760-8465, Fax: (919) 760-2347, E-mail: bankerm@meredith.edu. Dir.: Maureen Banker
Public Gallery
American art, special exhibitions 46780

Ralls TX

Ralls Historical Museum, 801 Main St, Ralls, TX 79357 - T: (806) 253-2425. Pres.: Linda Isbell, Dir.: Rose Pimmins
Local Museum - 1970
Local hist 46781

Ramah NM

El Morro National Monument, Hwy 53, 43 miles west of Grants, Ramah, NM 87321 - T: (505) 783-4226, Fax: (505) 783-4689. Head: P. Eringen
Historical Museum / Archaeological Museum - 1906 46782

Rancho Cucamonga CA

Casa de Rancho Cucamonga → John Rains House

John Rains House, 8810 Hemlock St, Rancho Cucamonga, CA 91730 - T: (909) 989-4970, Fax: (909) 307-0539, E-mail: tbothel@sbcm.sbcounty.gov, Internet: www.co.san-bernardino.ca.us/museum. Dir.: Robert McKernan, Cur.: Dr. Ann Deegan
Local Museum - 1972
Historic house, furnishings, local history 46783

Wignall Museum and Gallery, Chaffey College, 5885 Haven Av, Rancho Cucamonga, CA 91737-3002 - T: (909) 941-2388, Fax: (909) 466-2863, E-mail: wignall@chaffey.cc.ca.us, Internet: 209.129.13.65/wignall. Dir.: Virginia M. Eaton
Fine Arts Museum - 1972 46784

Rancho Mirage CA

Children's Discovery Museum of the Desert, 71-701 Gerald Ford Dr, Rancho Mirage, CA 92270 - T: (760) 321-0602, Fax: (760) 321-1605, E-mail: info@cdmod.org, Internet: www.cdmod.org. Pres.: Betty Barker, Exec. Dir.: LeeAnne Vanderbeck
Special Museum - 1987
Children's Museum 46785

Heartland - The California Museum of the Heart, 39600 Bob Hope Dr, Rancho Mirage, CA 92270 - T: (760) 324-3278, Fax: (760) 346-1867, Internet: www.thehearthospital.com. Dir./Cur.: Adam Rubinstein
Historical Museum - 1988
Heart health 46786

Rancho Palos Verdes CA

Palos Verdes Art Center, 5504 W Crestridge Rd, Rancho Palos Verdes, CA 90275 - T: (310) 541-2479, Fax: (310) 541-9520, E-mail: artcenter@palosverdes.com, Internet: www.pvartcenter.org. Pres.: Jacqueline S. Marks, Dir.: Scott Ward
Fine Arts Museum - 1931
Art 46787

Randleman NC

Saint Paul Museum, 411 High Point St, Randleman, NC 27317 - T: (336) 498-2447. Pres.: Louise Hudson
Local Museum - 1966 46788

Randolph NJ

Historical Museum of Old Randolph, 30 Carrel Rd, Randolph, NJ 07869 - T: (973) 989-7095, E-mail: hsor@juno.com, Internet: www.community.nj.com/cc/hsor. Pres.: Cecile Wilder, Dir.: Linda Pawchuak
Local Museum - 1979
Local history 46789

Randolph VT

Chandler Gallery, Chandler Music Hall and Cultural Center, Main St, Randolph, VT 05060 - T: (802) 728-9878, 728-3840, Fax: (802) 728-4612, E-mail: chandler@quest-net. Pres.: Janet Watton, Dir.: Rebecca B. McMeekin
Fine Arts Museum - 1979
Art 46790

Randolph Historical Society Museum, Salisbury St, Randolph, VT 05060 - T: (802) 728-5398
Local Museum - 1960 46791

Rankin TX

Rankin Museum, 101 W Main St, Rankin, TX 79778 - T: (915) 693-2758, 693-2422, Fax: (915) 693-2303, E-mail: jcpg@yahoo.com, Internet: www.rootsweb.com/~txupton/. Pres.: Judy Greer
Local Museum - 1974
Local hist 46792

Rantoul IL

Octave Chanute Aerospace Museum, 1011 Pacesetter Dr, Rantoul, IL 61866- - T: (217) 893-1613, Fax: (217) 892-5774, E-mail: director@aeromuseum.org, Internet: www.aeromuseum.org. Dir.: James Snyder
Military Museum / Science&Tech Museum - 1992
Fighter, bomber and training aircraft used by USAAF and USAF 46793

Rapid City SD

Dahl Arts Center, 713 Seventh St, Rapid City, SD 57701 - T: (605) 394-4101, Fax: (605) 394-6121, E-mail: rcacaafd@rapidnet.com. Pres.: Carrie Cisle, Exec. Dir.: Don Hotalling
Fine Arts Museum / Performing Arts Museum - 1974
Art 46794

Journey Museum, 222 New York St, Rapid City, SD 57701 - T: (605) 394-6923, 394-2249, Fax: (605) 394-6940, E-mail: journey@journeymuseum.org, Internet: www.journeymuseum.org
Ethnology Museum / Archaeological Museum - 1997
Paleontology, geology, archaeology, history, Native American hist and culture 46795

Minnilusa Pioneer Museum, 222 New York St, Rapid City, SD 57701 - T: (605) 394-6099, Fax: (605) 394-6940, Internet: www.sdsmp.edu/journey/. Dir.: Robert E. Preszler, Cur.: Eileen Howe
Local Museum - 1938
Local hist 46796

Museum of Geology, South Dakota School of Mines and Technology, 501 E St, Rapid City, SD 57701 - T: (605) 394-2467, Fax: (605) 394-6131, E-mail: museum@taz.sdsmt.edu, Internet: www.hpcnet.org/sdsmt/geologymuseum. Dir.: Gale A. Bishop, Cur.: James E. Martin (Paleontology)
University Museum / Natural History Museum - 1885
Natural hist 46797

Sioux Indian Museum, 222 New York St, Rapid City, SD 57701 - T: (605) 394-2381, Fax: (605) 348-6182, Internet: www.journeymuseum.org. Cur.: Paulette Montileaux
Fine Arts Museum / Folklore Museum - 1939
Indian art 46798

Raton NM

Raton Museum, 216 S First St, Raton, NM 87740 - T: (505) 445-8979. C.E.O.: Roger Sanchez
Local Museum / Historical Museum / Military Museum - 1939 46799

Ravenna OH

Portage County Historical Society Museum, 6549 N Chestnut St, Ravenna, OH 44266 - T: (330) 296-3523, E-mail: history@config.com, Internet: www.history.portage.oh.us. Pres.: John Carson
Local Museum - 1951 46800

Ravenswood WV

Washington's Lands Museum and Sayre Log House, Rte 68, Ravenswood, WV 26164 - Fax: 304) 372-7935(, Internet: www.rootsweb.com/~wvjackso/JACK.htm
Local Museum - 1970
Local tools, clothing, Indian artifacts 46801

Rawlins WY

Carbon County Museum, 904 W Walnut St, Rawlins, WY 82301 - T: (307) 328-2740, E-mail: carbonc@wyoming.com. Dir.: Joyce J. Kelley
Local Museum - 1940 46802

Raymond MS

Marie Hull Gallery, Hinds Community College, Raymond, MS 39154 - T: (601) 857-3275, Fax: (601) 857-3392, Internet: www.hinds.cc.ms.us. Dir.: Gayle McCarty
Fine Arts Museum
Prints, sculpture, paintings 46803

Reading MA

Parker Tavern Museum, 103 Washington St, Reading, MA 01867 - T: (781) 944-4030. Pres.: Alan Ulrich
Historical Museum - 1916
Headquarters for Scotch Highlanders prisoners of war during American revolution 46804

Reading OH

Reading Historical Society Museum, 22 W Benson St, Reading, OH 45215 - T: (513) 761-8535. Pres.: Robert Bemmes
Local Museum - 1988
Local hist 46805

Reading PA

Freedman Gallery, Albright College, 1621 N 13th St, Reading, PA 19604 - T: (610) 921-7541, 921-7715, Fax: (610) 921-7768, Internet: www.albright.edu. Dir.: Christopher Youngs
Fine Arts Museum / University Museum - 1976
Art 46806

Historical Society of Berks County Museum, 940 Centre Av, Reading, PA 19601 - T: (610) 375-4375, Fax: (610) 375-4376, E-mail: histsoc@berksweb.com/histsoc. Dir.: Harold E. Yoder
Local Museum - 1869
Local hist 46807

Mid Atlantic Air Museum, 11 Museum Dr, Reading, PA 19605 - T: (610) 372-7333, Fax: (610) 372-1702, E-mail: russ@maam.org, Internet: www.maam.org. Cur.: Linda T. Strine
Science&Tech Museum - 1980
54 aircrafts on aviation 46808

Reading Public Museum and Art Gallery, 500 Museum Rd, Reading, PA 19611-1425 - T: (610) 371-5850, Fax: (610) 371-5632, E-mail: museum@ptd.net, Internet: www.readingpublicmuseum.org. Dir./C.E.O.: Ronald C. Roth
Fine Arts Museum / Natural History Museum / Science&Tech Museum - 1904
Art and science 46809

Reading VT

Reading Historical Society Museum, Main St, Rte 106, Reading, VT 05062 - T: (802) 484-5005. Pres.: Jonathan Springer
Local Museum - 1953
Local hist 46810

Reads Landing MN

Wabasha County Museum, Reads Landing, MN 55968 - T: (507) 282-4027, E-mail: fpass_@rconnect.com. Pres.: Eugene Passe, Cur.: Bessie Hoover
Historical Museum - 1965 46811

Readsboro VT

Readsboro Historical Society Museum, Main St, Readsboro, VT 05350 - T: (802) 423-5432. Pres.: Betty Bolognani
Local Museum - 1972
Local hist 46812

Red Bluff CA

Kelly-Griggs House Museum, 311 Washington St, Red Bluff, CA 96080 - T: (530) 527-1129. Cur.: Robert W. Grootveld
Decorative Arts Museum - 1965
Paintings, Indian artifacts, antique furniture, Victorian costumes 46813

William B. Ide Adobe State Historic Park, 21659 Adobe Rd, Red Bluff, CA 96080 - T: (530) 529-8599, Fax: (530) 529-8598, E-mail: dpetersen@parks.ca.gov, Internet: www.ideadobe.tehama.k12.ca.us. Pres.: Kare Hislop
Local Museum - 1951
1850 adobe cabin, memorial to William B. Ide, president of the California Republic 46814

Red Cloud NE

Webster County Historical Museum, 721 W Fourth Av, Red Cloud, NE 68970 - T: (402) 746-2444. Pres.: Nancy Sherman, Dir.: Helen Mathew
Local Museum - 1965 46815

Willa Cather State Historic Site, 326 N Webster, Red Cloud, NE 68970 - T: (402) 746-2653, Fax: (402) 746-2652, Internet: www.willacather.org. Pres.: John Swift, Exec. Dir.: Steven P. Ryan
Local Museum - 1978 46816

Red Wing MN

Goodhue County Historical Society Museum, 1166 Oak St, Red Wing, MN 55066 - T: (651) 388-6024, Fax: (651) 388-3577, E-mail: goodhuecountyhis@qwest.net, Internet: www.goodhuehistory.mus.mn.us. Dir.: Char Henn, Libr.: Sharon Schroeder
Historical Museum - 1869 46817

Redding CA

Carter House Natural Science Museum, 48 Quartz Hill, Redding, CA 96003 - T: (530) 243-8850, Fax: (530) 243-8898. Pres.: Judith LaLouche
Science&Tech Museum - 1977
Natural science 46818

Redding Museum of Art and History, 56 Quartz Hill Rd, Redding, CA 96003, mail addr: POB 990427, Redding, CA 96099 - T: (530) 243-8801, 225-4155, Fax: (530) 243-8929, Internet: www.turtlebay.org. Dir.: Rob Wilson
Historical Museum / Fine Arts Museum / Natural History Museum - 1963
Ethnographic, historical and fine arts colls, contemporary arts and crafts 46819

Shasta College Museum, 11555 Old Oregon Trail, Redding, CA 96003 - T: (530) 225-4669, 225-4754, Fax: (530) 225-4990, E-mail: dsmith@shastacollege.edu, Internet: www.shastacollege.edu. Cur.: Dottie Smith
Local Museum / University Museum - 1970
Local hist 46820

Redlands CA

Kimberly Crest House, 1325 Prospect Dr, Redlands, CA 92373 - T: (909) 792-2111, Fax: (909) 798-1716, E-mail: kimcrest@empirenet.com, Internet: www.kimberlycrest.org. Dir.: Steven T. Spiller
Decorative Arts Museum / Local Museum - 1981
Historic house 46821

Lincoln Memorial Shrine, 125 W Vine St, Redlands, CA 92373 - T: (909) 798-7632, 798-7636, Fax: (909) 798-7566, E-mail: archives@aksmiley.org, Internet: www.aksmiley.org. Dir.: Jack D. Tompkins, Cur.: Donald McCue
Historical Museum - 1932
History 46822

Peppers Art Gallery, c/o University of Redlands, 1200 E Colton Av, Redlands, CA 92373 - T: (909) 793-2121, Fax: (909) 748-6293
Fine Arts Museum / University Museum
Ethnic art, graphics 46823

San Bernardino County Museum, 2024 Orange Tree Ln, Redlands, CA 92374 - T: (909) 307-2669, Fax: (909) 307-0539, E-mail: sramos@sbcm.sbcounty.gov, Internet: www.sbcountymuseum.org. Dir.: Robert L. McKernan, Dep. Dir.: Laurie Rozko, Cur.: Gerald Braden (Biology), Kathleen Springer, Dr.

Ann Deegan (History), Dr. Adella Schroth (Anthropology), Eric Scott (Paleontology), Chris Sagebiel (Geology)
Natural History Museum - 1959
Local nature 46824

Redmond WA

Marymoor Museum of Eastside History, 6046 W Lake Sammamish Pkwy, Redmond, WA 98073 - T: (206) 885-3684, Fax: (425) 885-3684, E-mail: eastsideheritagemuseum@msn.com, Internet: www.marymoormuseum.org. Pres.: Libby Walgamott, Dir.: Eden R. Toner, Sc. Staff: Barb Williams (Education), Kathryn V. Innes (Collections, Photos)
Local Museum - 1965
Local hist 46825

Redwood City CA

San Mateo County Historical Museum, 777 Hamilton St, Redwood City, CA 94063 - T: (650) 299-0104, Fax: (650) 299-0141, E-mail: samhist@aol.com, Internet: www.sanmateocountyhistory.com. Dir.: Mitchell P. Postel, Cur.: Amie Heath
Historical Museum - 1935
Local hist 46826

Redwood Falls MN

Redwood County Museum, 333965 Laser Av, Redwood Falls, MN 56283 - T: (507) 637-2256, Fax: (507) 637-2828. Cur.: Alice Hunt
Historical Museum - 1949 46827

Reedville VA

Reedville Fishermen's Museum, 504 Main St, Reedville, VA 22539 - T: (804) 453-6529, Fax: (804) 453-7159, E-mail: bunker@crosslink.net, Internet: www.rfmuseum.com. Dir.: Angus Murdoch
Historical Museum - 1986
Fishing industry 46828

Refugio TX

Refugio County Museum, 102 W West St, Refugio, TX 78377 - T: (512) 526-5555, Fax: (512) 526-4943. C.E.O.: Kathleen Campbell
Local Museum - 1983
Local history 46829

Regent ND

Hettinger County Historical Society Museum, 410 1st Av W, Regent, ND 58650 - T: (701) 563-4547. Dir.: Alois Gion
Local Museum / Ethnology Museum - 1962 46830

Rehoboth Beach DE

Rehoboth Art League, 12 Dodds Ln, Rehoboth Beach, DE 19971 - T: (302) 227-8408, Fax: (302) 227-4121, Internet: www.rehobothartleague.org. Dir.: Nancy Alexander
Fine Arts Museum - 1938
Art 46831

Reidsville NC

Chinqua-Penn Plantation, North Carolyna State University, 2138 Wentworth St, Reidsville, NC 27320 - T: (336) 349-4576, Fax: (336) 342-4863, E-mail: charles_leffler@ncsu.edu, Internet: www.chinquapenn.com. Pres.: Judy Burroughs
Ethnology Museum / University Museum - 1966
Antique European furniture, oriental art objects 46832

Reno NV

National Automobile Museum, Harrah Collection, 10 Lake St S, Reno, NV 89501 - T: (775) 333-9300, Fax: (775) 333-9309, E-mail: info@automuseum.org, Internet: www.automuseum.org. Exec. Dir.: Jackie L. Frady
Science&Tech Museum - 1989 46833

Nevada Historical Society Museum, Vevada Department Museums and Library, 1650 N Virginia St, Reno, NV 89503 - T: (702) 688-1191, Fax: (702) 688-2917, Internet: www.dmla.clan.lib.nv.us./docs/museums/reno/his-soc.htm. Dir.: Peter L. Bandurraga, Cur.: Phillip I. Earl (History), Eric N. Moody (Manuscripts), Lee Brumbaugh (Photography)
Historical Museum - 1904
Library 46834

Nevada Museum of Art, 160 W Liberty St, Reno, NV 89501 - T: (775) 329-3333, Fax: (775) 329-1541, E-mail: art@nma.reno.nv.us, Internet: www.nevadaart.org. Dir.: Steven S. High, Cur.: Diane Deming
Fine Arts Museum / Public Gallery - 1931
library 46835

Sheppard Fine Arts Gallery, University of Nevada, Reno, Church Fine Arts Complex, Mail Stop 224, Reno, NV 89557 - T: (775) 784-8015, Fax: (775) 784-6655, E-mail: art@scs.unr.edu, Internet: www.unr.edu. Chm.: Edward Martinez
Fine Arts Museum / University Museum - 1960 46836

Sierra Arts Foundation, 200 Flint St, Reno, NV 89501 - T: (775) 329-2787, Fax: (775) 239-1328, E-mail: jill@aierra-arts.org, Internet: www.sierra-arts.org. Exec. Dir.: Jill Berryman
Public Gallery - 1971
Contemporary works by emerging artists 46837

Wilbur D. May Museum, 1502 Washington St, Reno, NV 89503 - T: (775) 785-5961, Fax: (775) 785-4707. Melva: Howell Strubel, Chm.: Pat Walsh
Local Museum - 1985
Local hist 46838

W.M. Keck Museum, Mackay School of Mines, University of Nevada, Reno, NV 89557 - T: (775) 784-6052, Fax: (702) 784-1766, E-mail: lugaski@mines.unr.edu, Internet: www.mines.unr.edu/museum. Cur.: Dr. Thomas P. Lugaski
University Museum / Natural History Museum - 1908 46839

Rensselaer NY

Crailo State Historic Site, 9 1/2 Riverside Av, Rensselaer, NY 12144 - T: (518) 463-8738, Fax: (518) 463-8738. Head: Donnarae Gordon
Local Museum - 1924 46840

Renton WA

Renton Museum, 235 Mill Av S, Renton, WA 98055-2133 - T: (425) 255-2330, Fax: (425) 255-1570, E-mail: saanderson@ci.renton.wa.us. Dir.: Steve Anderson, Cur.: Rose Mary Greene
Local Museum - 1966
Local hist 46841

Renville MN

Historic Renville Preservation Commission Museum, POB 681, Renville, MN 56284 - T: (612) 329-3545. Pres.: Jane Rice
Historical Museum - 1976 46842

Republic KS

Pawnee Indian Village, Rte 1, Republic, KS 66964 - T: (785) 361-2255, Fax: (785) 361-2255, E-mail: piv@kshs.org, Internet: www.kshs.org. Cur.: Richard Gould, Chairman: Narveen Brzon
Ethnology Museum / Archaeological Museum / Historical Museum - 1967
Archaeology, preserved Pawnee site 46843

Republic MO

General Sweeney's Museum, 5228 S State Hwy ZZ, Republic, MO 65738 - T: (417) 732-1224, Fax: (417) 732-1224, E-mail: tsweeney@alltel.net, Internet: www.civilwarmuseum.com. C.E.O.: Karen Sweeney
Military Museum - 1992
Civil War in the Trans Mississippi 46844

Wilson's Creek National Battlefield, Hwy ZZ & Farm Rd 182, Republic, MO 65738 - T: (417) 732-2662, Fax: (417) 732-1167, Internet: www.nps.gov/wicr. Head: Richard A. Lusardi
Military Museum - 1960 46845

Reston VA

The Greater Reston Arts Center, 11911 Freedom Dr, Reston, VA 20190 - T: (703) 471-9242, Fax: (703) 471-0952, E-mail: graceart@restonart.com, Internet: www.restonart.com. Pres.: James C. Cleveland, C.E.O.: Anne Brown
Fine Arts Museum / Folklore Museum - 1974
Civic art and culture 46846

Rexburg ID

Upper Snake River Valley Historical Museum, 51 N Center, Rexburg, ID 83440 - T: (208) 356-9101, Fax: (208) 356-3379, E-mail: dhc@srv.net. Pres.: David Morris, Dir./Cur.: Louis Clements
Fine Arts Museum / Local Museum - 1965
Local history - library 46847

Rhinebeck NY

Rhinebeck Aerodrome Museum, Stone Church Rd and Norton Rd, Rhinebeck, NY 12572 - T: (845) 752-3200, Fax: (914) 758-6481, E-mail: info@oldrhinebeck.org, Internet: www.oldrhinebeck.org. Pres.: John Costa
Science&Tech Museum - 1977
Aeronautics 46848

Rhinelander WI

Rhinelander Logging Museum, Pioneer Park, Martin Lynch Dr, Rhinelander, WI 54501 - T: (715) 362-2193, 369-5004, Internet: www.ci.rhinelander.wi.us/museum/museum. Pres.: Walt Krause
Folklore Museum / Science&Tech Museum - 1932
Pioneer logging industry 46849

Rialto CA

Rialto Museum, 201-205 N Riverside Av, Rialto, CA 92376 - T: (909) 875-1750, 875-4634. Pres.: Bette Hughbanks
Folklore Museum / Local Museum - 1971
Local hist 46850

Richey MT

Richey Historical Museum, POB 218, Richey, MT 59259 - T: (406) 773-5656. Dir.: Donald Handlos, Chief Cur.: Valerie B. Baldwin Rehbein
Historical Museum - 1973 46851

Richey Historical Society, POB 264, Richey, MT 59259 - T: (406) 773-5615
Local Museum - 1973
Farm tools, clocks, musical instruments, furniture, clothing, machinery, local hist 46852

Richfield Springs NY

Petrified Creatures Museum of Natural History, Rte 20, Richfield Springs, NY 13439 - T: (315) 858-2868, Fax: (315) 858-2868, E-mail: stellapcm@yahoo.com, Internet: www.cooperstownchamber.org. Dir.: Stella C. Mlecz, Ass. Dir.: Sally E. Kennedy
Natural History Museum / Open Air Museum - 1934 46853

Richland WA

Allied Arts Center and Gallery, 89 Lee Blvd, Richland, WA 99352 - T: (509) 943-9815, Fax: (509) 943-4068. Pres.: Marion Goheen
Fine Arts Museum - 1947 46854

Columbia River Exhibition of History, Science and Technology, 95 Lee Blvd, Richland, WA 99352 - T: (509) 943-9000, Fax: (509) 943-1770, E-mail: gwen@crehst.org, Internet: www.crehst.org. Dir.: Gwen I. Leth, Cur.: Connie Estep
Science&Tech Museum - 1963
Science, nuclear hist 46855

Richland Center WI

A.D. German Warehouse, 300 S Church St, Richland Center, WI 53581 - T: (608) 647-2808. Dir.: Harvey W. Glanzer, Bethel I. Caulkins
Fine Arts Museum
Architecture by Lloyd Wright, enginering/architectural models 46856

Richlands NC

Onslow County Museum, 301 S Wilmington St, Richlands, NC 28574 - T: (910) 324-5008, Fax: (910) 324-2897, E-mail: museum@co.onslow.nc.us, Internet: www.co.onslow.nc.us/museum. Dir.: Albert Potts, Ass. Dir.: Lisa Whitman-Grice
Local Museum - 1976 46857

Richmond CA

National Institute of Art and Disabilities, 551 23rd St, Richmond, CA 94804 - T: (510) 620-0290, Fax: (510) 620-0326, E-mail: admin@niadart.org, Internet: www.niadart.org. Dir.: Amanda Cauldwell, Cur.: Rose Kelly
Public Gallery - 1984 46858

Richmond Art Center, 2540 Barrett Av, Richmond, CA 94804 - T: (510) 620-6772/78, Fax: (510) 620-6771, E-mail: admin@therichmondartcenter.org, Internet: www.therichmondartcenter.org. Dir.: Nancy Mizuno Elliott
Public Gallery - 1936 46859

Richmond Museum of History, 400 Nevin Av, Richmond, CA 94802 - T: (510) 235-7387, Fax: (510) 235-4345. Dir.: Kathleen Rupley
Local Museum - 1952
Local hist 46860

Richmond IN

Joseph Moore Museum, Earlham College, Richmond, IN 47374 - T: (765) 983-1303, Fax: (765) 983-1497, E-mail: johni@earlham.edu, Internet: www.earlham.edu. Dir.: Dr. John B. Iverson, Ass. Dir.: Dr. William H. Buskirk, Dr. Leslie Bishop
University Museum / Natural History Museum - 1887
Natural history 46861

Richmond Art Museum, 350 Hub Etchison Pkwy, Richmond, IN 47375 - T: (765) 966-0256, Fax: (765) 973-3738, E-mail: sdingwerth@richmondartmuseum.org, Internet: www.richmondartmuseum.org. Exec. Dir.: Kathleen D. Glynn
Fine Arts Museum - 1898
Art 46862

Wayne County Historical Museum, 1150 N A St, Richmond, IN 47374 - T: (765) 962-5756, Fax: (765) 939-0909, E-mail: micheleb@infocom.com, Internet: www.wchm.org. Dir.: Jan Livingston, Cur.: James Waechter
Local Museum - 1930
General museum, housed in Hicksite Friends Meeting House 46863

Richmond KY

Fort Boonesborough Museum, 4375 Boonesboro Rd, Richmond, KY 40475 - T: (859) 527-3131, Fax: (859) 527-3328, E-mail: phil.gray@mail.state.ky.us, Internet: www.kystateparks.com. Dir.: Lilly Newman (Craft), Cur.: Jerry Raisor
Historical Museum - 1974
History 46864

White Hall Historic Site, 500 White Hall Shrine Rd, Richmond, KY 40475 - T: (856) 623-9178, Fax: (606) 626-8489, E-mail: judy.cook@mail.state.ky.us, Internet: www.state.ky.us/agencies/parks/whthall.htm. C.E.O.: Judith H. cook
Local Museum / Decorative Arts Museum - 1971
Historic house Georgian style bldg, added to in the Italianate style 46865

Richmond ME

CHTJ Southard House Museum, 75 Main St, Richmond, ME 04357 - T: (207) 737-8202, Fax: (207) 737-8772, E-mail: fcmain@ctel.net, Internet: www.southardhousemuseum.com. Pres./Cur.: Carolyn Cooper Case
Local Museum - 1990 46866

Richmond TX

Fort Bend Museum, 500 Houston, Richmond, TX 77469 - T: (281) 342-6478, Fax: (281) 342-2439, E-mail: mmoore@georgeranch.org, Internet: www.fortbendmuseum.org. Dir.: Michael R. Moore, Ass. Dir.: Sue Hanson
Local Museum - 1967
Local hist 46867

Richmond VA

1708 Gallery, 103 E Broad St, Richmond, VA 23219 - T: (804) 643-7829, Fax: (804) 643-7829, E-mail: artgallery1708@mindspring.com, Internet: www.1708gallery.com. Dir.: Peter S. Calvert
Public Gallery - 1978 46868

Agecroft Hall, 4305 Sulgrave Rd, Richmond, VA 23221 - T: (804) 353-4241, Fax: (804) 353-2151, Internet: www.agecrofthall.com. Dir.: Richard W. Moxley, Cur.: Deborah Knott de Arechaga
Local Museum - 1967
Historic house 46869

The American Historical Foundation Museum, 1142 W Grace St, Richmond, VA 23220 - T: (804) 353-1812, Fax: (804) 353-0689. Pres./Cur.: Robert A. Buerlein
Historical Museum / Military Museum - 1982
Military, history 46870

Anderson Gallery, c/o School of the Arts, Virginia Commonwealth University, 907 1/2 W Franklin St, Richmond, VA 23284-2514 - T: (804) 828-1522, Fax: (804) 828-8585, E-mail: jcaperto@atlas.vcu.edu, Internet: www.vcu.edu/artweb/gallery/. Dir.: Ted Potter, Cur.: Amy G. Moorefield
Fine Arts Museum / University Museum - 1969
Art 46871

Artspace, 6 E Broad St, Richmond, VA 23219 - T: (804) 782-8672, Fax: (804) 782-9880, Internet: www.artspacegallery.org. Dir.: Christina Newton
Public Gallery 46872

Beth Ahabah Museum and Archives, 1109 W Franklin St, Richmond, VA 23220 - T: (804) 353-2668, Fax: (804) 358-3451, E-mail: bama@bethahabah.org, Internet: www.bethahabah.org/museum. Pres.: Gail Straus, Dir.: Shirley S. Belkowitz
Historical Museum - 1977
Jewish hist 46873

Children's Museum of Richmond, 2626 W Broad St, Richmond, VA 23220-1904 - T: (804) 474-7000, Fax: (804) 474-7099, E-mail: director@c-mor.org, Internet: www.c.mor.org. Pres.: Nan L. Miller, Exec. Dir.: Nan L. Miller
Special Museum - 1977
Children's museum 46874

Crestar Bank Art Collection, 919 E Main St, Richmond, VA 23219 - T: (804) 782-5000, Fax: (804) 782-5469, Internet: www.suntrust.com
Fine Arts Museum - 1970
Contemporary art 46875

Edgar Allan Poe Museum, 1914-16 E. Main St, Richmond, VA 23223 - T: (804) 648-5523, Fax: (804) 648-8729, E-mail: edgarallanpoemuseum@erols.com, Internet: www.poemuseum.org. Dir.: John P.C. Moon
Local Museum / Special Museum - 1922
Historic house 46876

Folk Art Society of America, 1904 Byrd Av, Richmond, VA 23230 - T: (804) 285-4532, Fax: (804) 285-4532, E-mail: fasa@folkart.org, Internet: www.folkart.org. Pres.: Ann Oppenhimer
Library with Exhibitions - 1987
Folk art 46877

Hand Workshop Art Center, 1812 W Main St, Richmond, VA 23220 - T: (804) 353-0094, Fax: (804) 353-8018. Dir.: Susan Glasser
Fine Arts Museum - 1963 46878

Joel and Lila Harnett Print Study Center, University of Richmond, 28 Westhampton Way, Richmond, VA 23173 - T: (804) 289-8276, Fax: (804) 287-1894, E-mail: rwaller@richmond.edu, Internet: www.arts.richmond.edu
Fine Arts Museum / University Museum - 2001 46879

John Marshall House, 818 E Marshall St, Richmond, VA 23219 - T: (804) 648-7998, Fax: (804) 775-0802, E-mail: jmhapva@aol.com, Internet: apva.org. Exec. Dir.: Elizabeth Kostelny
Local Museum - 1790
Local hist 46880

Lora Robins Gallery of Design from Nature, University of Richmond, 28 Westhampton Way, Richmond, VA 23173 - T: (804) 289-8276, Fax: (804) 287-1894, E-mail: museums@richmond.edu
University Museum / Natural History Museum - 1977
Geology, natural hist 46881

Marsh Art Gallery → University of Richmond Museums

Maymont, 1700 Hampton St, Richmond, VA 23220 - T: (804) 358-7166, Fax: (804) 358-9994, E-mail: info@maymont.org, Internet: www.maymont.org. Dir.: Geoffrey Platt jr., Dep. Dir.: Dale C. Wheary (Historical Collections and Programs), Mark S. Rich (Nature Center and Animals Programs), Shannon Wyatt (Animal Programs), Cur.: Dot Rugus (Carriages)
Decorative Arts Museum / Local Museum / Agriculture Museum - 1925
Historic house 46882

The Museum of the Confederacy, 1201 E Clay St, Richmond, VA 23219-1615 - T: (804) 649-1861, Fax: (804) 644-7150, E-mail: info@moc.org, Internet: www.moc.org. Dir.: Robin Edward Reed, J.A. Barton Campbell, Cur.: Robert Hancock, Rebecca Rose, Sc. Staff: Dr. John M. Coski (History)
Historical Museum - 1896
Confederate military, artefacts, flags, documents 46883

Old Dominion Railway Museum, 102 Hull St, Richmond, VA 23224 - T: (804) 223-6237, Fax: (804) 745-4735, Internet: www.odcnrhs.org. C.E.O.: C. Kevin Frick
Science&Tech Museum - 1990
Railroading hist in Central Virginia, steam, caboose, passenger and freight equip, locomotives and rolling stock 46884

Richmond National Battlefield Park, 3215 E Broad St, Richmond, VA 23223 - T: (804) 226-1981, Fax: (804) 771-8522, Internet: www.nps.gov/rich. Head: Cynthia MacLeod
Military Museum - 1936
Civil War hist 46885

Science Museum of Virginia, 2500 W Broad St, Richmond, VA 23220-2054 - T: (804) 864-1400, Fax: (804) 864-1560, E-mail: smvfeedback@smv.mus.va.us, Internet: www.smv.org. Dir.: Walter R.T. Witschey, Pat Fishback
Science&Tech Museum - 1970
Science, aviation 46886

University of Richmond Museums, 28 Westhampton Way, Richmond, VA 23173 - T: (804) 289-8276, Fax: (804) 287-1894, E-mail: museums@richmond.edu, Internet: www.richmond.edu/cultural/museums. Dir.: Richard Waller
Fine Arts Museum / University Museum - 1830 46887

Valentine Richmond History Center, c/o The Valentine Museum - Richmond History Center, 1015 E Clay St, Richmond, VA 23219-1590 - T: (804) 649-0711, Fax: (804) 643-3510, E-mail: info@richmondhistorycenter.com, Internet: www.richmondhistorycenter.com. Dir.: William J. Martin, Cur.: Colleen Callahan (Costumes and Textiles)
Historical Museum / Decorative Arts Museum - 1892
Urban hist 46888

Virginia Baptist Historical Society Museum, c/o University of Richmond, Boatwright Library, Richmond, VA 23173 - T: (804) 289-8434, Fax: (804) 289-8953, Internet: www.baptistheritage.org. Pres.: Robert F. Woodward, Exec. Dir.: Fred Anderson
Local Museum - 1876
Baptist hist 46889

Virginia Historical Society Museum, 428 North Blvd, Richmond, VA 23220 - T: (804) 358-4901, Fax: (804) 342-2399, E-mail: maribeth@vahistorical.org, Internet: www.vahistorical.org. Dir.: Dr. Charles F. Bryan, Cur.: William Rasmussen (Art), Man.: Tracey Bryan
Historical Museum - 1831
State hist 46890

Virginia Museum of Fine Arts, Blvd & Grove Av, Richmond, VA 23221-2466 - T: (804) 340-1400, Fax: (804) 340-1548, E-mail: webmaster@vmfa.state.va.us, Internet: www.vmfa.state.va.us. Dir.: Dr. Michael Brand, Cur.: Dr. Joseph M. Dye (South Asian and Islamic Art), Dr. David Park Curry (American Art), Richard Woodward (African Art), Malcolm Cormack (European Painting), Kathleen Schrader (European Sculpture, Decorative Arts), Dr. Margaret Ellen Mayo (Ancient Art), John Ravenal (Art after 1900), Cons.: Carol Sawyer (Paintings), Katharine Untch (Objects)
Fine Arts Museum / Folklore Museum - 1934
Art 46891

Wilton House Museum, The National Society of the Colonial Dames of America in the Commonwealth of Virginia, 215 S Wilton Rd, Richmond, VA 23226 - T: (804) 282-5936, Fax: (804) 288-9805, E-mail: wiltonhouse@mindspring.com, Internet: www.wiltonhousemuseum.org. C.E.O.: Sylvia B. Evans
Decorative Arts Museum - 1934
Local hist, decorative arts 46892

Richmond Hill GA

Fort McAllister, 3894 Fort McAllister Rd, Richmond Hill, GA 31324 - T: (912) 727-2339, Fax: (912) 727-3614, E-mail: ftmcallr@g-net.net, Internet: www.fortmcallister.org. Head: Daniel Brown
Military Museum - 1958
1861 Confederate fort 46893

Richmond International Airport VA

Virginia Aviation Museum, 5701 Huntsman Rd, Richmond International Airport, VA 23250-2416 - T: (804) 236-3620, 236-3622, Fax: (804) 236-3623, E-mail: mboehme@smv.org, Internet: www.vam.smv.org. Dir.: Walter R.T. Witschey
Science&Tech Museum - 1987
Aircraft, aviation, WW 2 46894

Ridgecrest CA

Maturango Museum of the Indian Wells Valley, 100 E Las Flores Av, Ridgecrest, CA 93555 - T: (760) 375-6900, Fax: (760) 375-0479, E-mail: matmus@ridgenet.net, Internet: www.maturango.org. Dir.: Jane Burbank, Cur.: Elva Younkin, Bill Mercer (Sylvia Winslow Art Gallery)
Local Museum - 1962
Local hist 46895

Ridgefield CT

Aldrich Museum of Contemporary Art, 258 Main St, Ridgefield, CT 06877 - T: (203) 438-4519, Fax: (203) 438-0198, E-mail: general@aldrichart.org, Internet: www.aldrichart.org. Dir.: Harry Philbrick
Fine Arts Museum - 1964 46896

Keeler Tavern Museum, 132 Main St, Ridgefield, CT 06877 - T: (203) 438-5485, Fax: (203) 438-9953, E-mail: keelertavernmuseum@earthlink.net, Internet: www.keelertavernmuseum.org. Exec. Dir.: Anne Smith, Rosemary Morretta
Historical Museum - 1965
Local hist 46897

Ridgeland MS

Mississippi Crafts Center, Natchez Trace Pky, Ridgeland, MS 39157 - T: (601) 856-7546, Fax: (601) 856-7546. Pres.: Gayle Clark, Dir.: Martha Garrott
Decorative Arts Museum / Folklore Museum - 1975 46898

Ridgewood NJ

Schoolhouse Museum, 650 E Glen Av, Ridgewood, NJ 07450 - T: (201) 652-4584. Pres.: Glenn Corbet, Cur.: D.A. Pangburn
Local Museum - 1949 46899

Rifle CO

Rifle Creek Museum, 337 East Av, Rifle, CO 81650 - T: (970) 625-4862. Dir.: Kim Fazzi
Local Museum - 1967
Local and natural history, Indian artifacts, textiles 46900

Rincon GA

Georgia Salzburger Society Museum, 2980 Ebenezer Rd, Rincon, GA 31326 - T: (912) 754-7001, Fax: (912) 754-7001, E-mail: bgriner@pineland.net, Internet: www.crosswinds.net/~dmabry/salzburger. Pres.: Robert F. Griner
Local Museum - 1925 46901

Ringwood NJ

The Forges and Manor of Ringwood, 1304 Sloatsburg Rd, Ringwood, NJ 07456 - T: (973) 962-2240, Fax: (973) 962-2247, E-mail: ringwood@warwick.net. Cur.: Elbertus Prol
Local Museum - 1935
Local history, industrial history 46902

Rio Hondo TX

Texas Air Museum, 1 Mile E Rio Hondo, Rio Hondo, TX 78583 - T: (956) 748-2112, Fax: (956) 748-3500, Internet: www.texasairmuseum.com. Dir.: John Houston, Cur.: Gilbert Alaniz
Science&Tech Museum - 1986 46903

Ripley OH

Rankin House State Memorial, Liberty Hill, Ripley, OH 45167 - T: (937) 392-4188
Local Museum - 1938 46904

Ripon WI

Little White Schoolhouse, 303 Blackburn St, Ripon, WI 54971 - T: (920) 748-6764, Fax: (920) 748-6784, E-mail: racc@vbl.com, Internet: www.ripon-wi.com. Pres.: Loren Boon, C.E.O.: Ellen C. Sormsen
Historical Museum - 1951
Historic house, Birthplace of Republican Party 46905

Ripon College Art Gallery, 300 Seward St, Ripon, WI 54971 - T: (920) 748-8110, 748-8115, E-mail: kaineu@ripon.edu
Fine Arts Museum - 1965
Paintings, prints, sculpture, multi-media 46906

Ripon Historical Society Museum, 508 Watson St, Ripon, WI 54971 - T: (920) 748-5354
Historical Museum - 1899
Local hist 46907

Rittman OH

Rittman Historical Society Museum, 393 W Sunset Dr, Rittman, OH 44270 - T: (330) 925-7572
Local Museum - 1960 46908

River Edge NJ

Bergen County Historical Society Museum, 1201 Main St, River Edge, NJ 07661 - T: (201) 343-9492, Internet: www.carroll.com/bchs. Cur.: Matt Gebhardt
Local Museum - 1902
China, glass, farm and household tools, paintings, sculptures, toys, quilts, folk art, Wolfkiel pottery, clothing 46909

Steuben House Museum, 1201 Main St, River Edge, NJ 07661 - T: (201) 343-9492, 487-1739, Fax: (201) 498-1696, Internet: www.carroll.com/bchs. Dir.: Kevin Wright, Cur.: Matt Gebhardt
Local Museum - 1902
Artifacts of the Bergen Dutch 1680-1914 46910

River Falls WI

Gallery 101, University of Wisconsin-River Falls, River Falls, WI 54022 - T: (715) 425-3266, Fax: (715) 425-0657, E-mail: michael.a.padgett@uwrf.edu, Internet: www.uwrf.edu. Head: Michael Padgett
Fine Arts Museum - 1973
Art 46911

River Grove IL

Cernan Earth and Space Center, Triton College, 2000 N 5th Av, River Grove, IL 60171 - T: (708) 456-0300 ext 3372, Fax: (708) 583-3153, E-mail: cernan@triton.cc.il.us, Internet: www.triton.cc.il.us/cernan/cernan_home.html. Dir.: Bart Benjamin
Natural History Museum - 1974
Meteorites, space hardware 46912

Riverdale Park MD

Riverdale Mansion, 4811 Riverdale Rd, Riverdale Park, MD 20737 - T: (301) 864-0420, Fax: (301) 927-3498, E-mail: edward.day@pgparks.com, Internet: www.pgparks.com. Dir.: Edward Day, Cur.: Ann Wass (History)
Local Museum - 1949 46913

Riverhead NY

Hallockville Museum Farm, 6038 Sound Av, Riverhead, NY 11901 - T: (516) 298-5292, Fax: (516) 298-5292, E-mail: hallockv@optonline.net. Pres.: James Pim, Exec. Dir.: John Eilertsen
Agriculture Museum - 1975 46914

Railroad Museum of Long Island, 416 Griffling Av, Riverhead, NY 11901 - T: (631) 727-7920, 477-0439, Internet: www.rmli.org
Science&Tech Museum - 1990
Railroading hist of Long Island, HO gauge 46915

Suffolk County Historical Society Museum, 300 W Main St, Riverhead, NY 11901 - T: (631) 727-2881, Fax: (631) 727-3467, E-mail: histsoc@suffolk.lib.ny.us. Pres.: John Sprayue, Dir.: Wallace W. Broege
Local Museum - 1886
Indians, ceramics, decorative arts, whaling, early crafts, trade tools 46916

Riverside CA

California Museum of Photography, 3824 Main St, Riverside, CA 92501 - T: (909) 787-4787, Fax: (909) 787-4797, E-mail: jgreen@citrus.ucr.edu, Internet: www.cmp.ucr.edu. Dir.: Jonathan Green, Cur.: Ted Fisher, Steve Thomas
Fine Arts Museum / University Museum - 1973
Photography 46917

Entomology Research Museum, c/o Department of Entomology, University of California, Riverside, CA 92521-0314 - T: (909) 787-4385, 787-4315, Fax: (909) 787-3086, 787-3681, Internet: insects.ucr.edu/entmus. Dir.: Dr. Timothy D. Paine, Sc. Staff: Serguei V. Triapitsyn, Doug A. Yanega
University Museum / Natural History Museum - 1962
Entomology 46918

March Field Museum, 22550 Van Buren Blvd, Riverside, CA 92518-6463 - T: (909) 697-6600, Fax: (909) 697-6605, E-mail: info@marchfield.org, Internet: www.marchfield.org. Dir.: Bob Miller
Military Museum / Science&Tech Museum - 1979
Military hist 46919

Mission Inn Museum, 3696 Main St, Riverside, CA 92501 - T: (909) 788-9556, Fax: (909) 781-8201, E-mail: missioninnmuseum@pe.net, Internet: www.missioninnmuseum.com. Dir.: John Worden, Ass. Dir.: Allene Archibald
Local Museum
Local hist 46920

Riverside Art Museum, 3425 Mission Inn Av, Riverside, CA 92501 - T: (909) 684-7111, Fax: (909) 684-7332, E-mail: ram@riversideartmuseum.com, Internet: www.riversideartmuseum.com. Dir.: Bobbie Powell
Fine Arts Museum - 1935
Art 46921

Riverside Municipal Museum, 3580 Mission Inn Av, Riverside, CA 92501 - T: (909) 826-5273, Fax: (909) 369-4970, E-mail: resparza@ci.riverside.ca.us, Internet: www.ci.riverside.ca.us/museum. Dir.: Richard R. Esparza, Sen. Cur.: H. Vincent Moses, Education Cur.: Marjorie Mitchell, Cur. of Coll.: Brenda Focht, Cur.: Christopher L. Moser (Anthropology), James Bryant (Natural History)
Local Museum - 1924
Local hist 46922

Sweeney Art Gallery, c/o University of California, Watkins House, 3701 Canyon Crest Dr, Riverside, CA 92521 - T: (909) 787-3755 ext 1465, Fax: (909) 787-3798, E-mail: katherine.warren@ucr.edu, Internet: sweeney.ucr.edu. Dir.: Katherine V. Warren, Cur.: Karen Rapp
University Museum / Fine Arts Museum - 1963 46923

World Museum of Natural History, 4700 Pierce St, Riverside, CA 92515-8247 - T: (909) 785-2209, Fax: (909) 785-2901, 785-2478, E-mail: ballen@lasierra.edu, Internet: www.lasierra.edu/wmnh. Dir.: William M. Allen
Natural History Museum - 1971
Natural history, reptiles, birds, Indian artifacts 46924

Riverton WY

Riverton Museum, 700 E Park Av, Riverton, WY 82501 - T: (307) 856-2665. Dir.: Loren Jost
Local Museum - 1956
Local hist 46925

Robert A. Peck Gallery, Central Wyoming College, 2660 Peck Av, Riverton, WY 82501 - T: (307) 855-2211, Fax: (307) 855-2090, Internet: www.cwc.edu/departments/art
Fine Arts Museum
Local art like paintings, drawings, sculpture 46926

Roanoke VA

Art Museum of Western Virginia, One Market Sq, Roanoke, VA 24011-1436 - T: (540) 342-5760, Fax: (540) 342-5798, E-mail: info@artmuseumroanoke.org, Internet: artmuseumroanoke.org. Dir.: Dr. Judy L. Larson, Cur.: Susannah Koerber
Fine Arts Museum - 1951
Art 46927

Catholic Historical Society of the Roanoke Valley Museum, 400 W Campbell Av, Roanoke, VA 24016 - T: (540) 982-0152, Fax: (540) 982-0152. Pres.: Margaret M. Cochener
Religious Arts Museum - 1983 46928

History Museum of Western Virginia, One Market Sq, Roanoke, VA 24011 - T: (540) 342-5770, Fax: (540) 224-1256, E-mail: history@roanoke.infi.net, Internet: history-museum.org. Pres.: John P. Bradshaw, C.E.O.: D. Kent Chrisman
Historical Museum - 1957
History 46929

Science Museum of Western Virginia, One Market Sq, Roanoke, VA 24011 - T: (540) 342-5710, Fax: (540) 224-1240, E-mail: frontdesk@smwv.org, Internet: www.smwv.org. Pres.: Harry Nickens, Exec. Dir.: Kenneth J. Schutz, Dir.: Leslie Bochenski (Planetarium)
Natural History Museum / Science&Tech Museum - 1970
Science 46930

Virginia Museum of Transportation, 303 Norfolk Av, Roanoke, VA 24016 - T: (540) 342-5670, Fax: (540) 342-6898, E-mail: info@vmt.org, Internet: www.vmt.org. Dir.: Katherine F. Strickland, Cur.: Eric Alexie, Sc. Staff: Darlene Richardson (History)
Science&Tech Museum - 1963
Transportation, trains, automobiles, carriages, aviation equipment 46931

Rochester IN

Fulton County Historical Society Museum, 37 E 375 N, Rochester, IN 46975 - T: (219) 223-4436, E-mail: fchs@rtcol.com, Internet: www.icss.net/~fchs. Dir.: Melinda Clinger, Dep. Dir.: Lola Riddle
Local Museum / Open Air Museum / Historical Museum - 1963
Round Barn, Potawatomi Trail of Death, Reference Room 17 rooms of permanent displays, village with 11 buildings 46932

Rochester MI

Meadow Brook Art Gallery, Oakland University, 209 Wilson Hall, Rochester, MI 48309-4401 - T: (248) 370-3005, Fax: (248) 370-4208, E-mail: goody@oakland.edu, Internet: www.oakland.edu/mbag. Dir.: Dick Goody
Fine Arts Museum / University Museum - 1959
African, Pre-Columbian and Oriental art, furniture 46933

Meadow Brook Hall, Oakland University, Rochester, MI 48309-4401 - T: (248) 370-3140, Fax: (248) 370-4301, E-mail: stobersk@oakland.edu, Internet: www.meadowbrookhall.org. Exec. Dir.: Lisa Baylis
Historical Museum / University Museum - 1971
Paintings, sculpture, prints, drawings, furniture, glass, porcelain, silver, artifacts, photos, films, 46934

Rochester MN

Olmsted County Historical Society Museum, 1195 W Circle Dr SW, Rochester, MN 55902 - T: (507) 282-9447, Fax: (507) 289-5481, E-mail: businessoffice@olmstedhistory.com, Internet: www.olmstedhistory.com. Dir.: John Hunziker, Cur.: Margot Ballard
Historical Museum - 1926
archives 46935

Rochester Art Center, 320 E Center St, Rochester, MN 55904 - T: (507) 282-8629, Fax: (507) 282-7737, E-mail: bjshigaki@juno.com, Internet: www.rochesterusa.com/artcenter. Dir.: Betty Shigaki
Fine Arts Museum - 1946
Contemporary visual arts and crafts 46936

Rochester NY

American Baptist Museum, 1106 S Goodman St, Rochester, NY 14620 - T: (716) 473-1740, E-mail: abhs@crds.edu, Internet: www.crcds.edu/abhs
Religious Arts Museum - 1853
Paintings, books 46937

Baker-Cederberg Museum, Rochester General Hospital, 1425 Portland Av, Rochester, NY 14621-3095 - T: (716) 922-3521, Fax: (716) 922-5292, E-mail: phil.maples@viahealth.org, Internet: www.viahealth.org/archives. Cur.: Philip G. Maples
Science&Tech Museum - 1947
Local history, Company museum 46938

Campbell Whittlesey House, 123 Fitzhugh St, Rochester, NY 14608 - T: (585) 546-7029, Fax: (585) 546-4788, E-mail: info@landmarksociety.org, Internet: www.landmarksociety.org. Dir.: Cindy Boyer
Decorative Arts Museum - 1937
Art, furnishings, decorative arts 46939

Dar-Hervey Ely House, 11 Livingston Park, Rochester, NY 14608 - T: (716) 232-4509. C.E.O.: Alberta Greer
Decorative Arts Museum / Local Museum - 1894 46940

International Museum of Photography and Film, George Eastman House, 900 East Av, Rochester, NY 14607 - T: (716) 271-3361, Fax: (716) 271-3970, Internet: www.eastman.org. Dir.: Anthony Bannon, Sen. Cur.: Paolo Cherchi Usai (Motion Picture Collection), Cur.: Therese Mulligan (Photography Collection), Kathy Connor (George Eastman House), Deirdre Cunningham (Landscape Collection), Todd Gustavson (Technology)
Fine Arts Museum - 1947
Photography, motion pictures 46941

Mercer Gallery, Monroe Community College, 1000 E Henrietta Rd, Rochester, NY 14623 - T: (716) 292-2021, Fax: (716) 292-3120, E-mail: kfarrell@monroecc.edu, Internet: www.monroecc.edu. Dir.: Kathleen Farrell
Fine Arts Museum / University Museum
Art 46942

Rochester Historical Society Museum, 485 East Av, Rochester, NY 14607 - T: (716) 271-2705, Fax: (716) 271-9089, E-mail: asalter@rochesterhistory.org, Internet: www.rochesterhistory.org. Exec. Dir.: Ann C. Salter
Local Museum - 1861 46943

Rochester Museum, 657 East Av, Rochester, NY 14607-2177 - T: (716) 271-4320, Fax: (716) 271-6546, E-mail: katebennett@rmsc.org, Internet: www.rmsc.org. Dir.: Steven Fentress
Historical Museum / Natural History Museum / Science&Tech Museum - 1912 46944

Stone-Tolan House, 2370 East Av, Rochester, NY 14608 - T: (585) 546-7029, Fax: (585) 546-4788, E-mail: info@landmarksociety.org, Internet: www.landmarksociety.org. Dir.: Cindy Boyer
Decorative Arts Museum - 1937
Art, furnishings, decorative arts 46945

Strong Museum, 1 Manhattan Sq, Rochester, NY 14607 - T: (716) 263-2700, Fax: (716) 263-2493, Internet: www.strongmuseum.org. Pres.: G. Rollie Adams
Historical Museum - 1968 46946

Susan B. Anthony House, 17 Madison St, Rochester, NY 14608 - T: (716) 235-6124 ext 10, Fax: (716) 235-6212, E-mail: information@susanbanthonyhouse.org, Internet: susan-banthonyhouse.org. Exec. Dir.: Lorie Barnum
Local Museum - 1946 46947

University of Rochester Memorial Art Gallery, 500 University Av, Rochester, NY 14607 - T: (585) 473-7720 ext 3000, Fax: (585) 473-6266, E-mail: maginfo@mag.rochester.edu, Internet: mag.rochester.edu. Dir.: Grant Holcomb, Ass. Dir.: Kim Hallatt, Cur.: Majorie Searl (American Art), Nancy Norwood (European Art), Marie Via (Exhibitions)
Fine Arts Museum / University Museum / Decorative Arts Museum - 1913 46948

Rochester Hills MI

Rochester Hills Museum at Van Hoosen Farm, 1005 Van Hoosen Rd, Rochester Hills, MI 48306 - T: (248) 656-4663, Fax: (248) 608-8198, E-mail: rhmuseum@rochesterhills.org, Internet: www.rochesterhills.org/museum.htm. Dir.: Patrick McKay
Local Museum / Historical Museum - 1979
Local hist 46949

Rock Hill SC

Museum of York County, 4621 Mount Gallant Rd, Rock Hill, SC 29732-9905 - T: (803) 329-2121, Fax: (803) 329-5249, E-mail: myco@infoave.net, Internet: www.yorkcounty.org. Dir.: W. Van Shields, Cur.: Mary Lynn Norton (Art)
Local Museum - 1950
Local hist, African amimals, art and ethnography, local art, archaeology and natural history 46950

Winthrop University Galleries, Rutledge Bldg, Rock Hill, SC 29733 - T: (803) 323-2126, Fax: (803) 323-2333, E-mail: stanteyt@winthrop.edu, Internet: www.winthrop.edu/vpa. Dir.: Tom Stanley
Fine Arts Museum
Visual arts and design 46951

Rock Island IL

Augustana College Art Gallery, 7th Av and 38th St, Rock Island, IL 61201-2296 - T: (309) 794-7231, 7000, Fax: (309) 794-7678, E-mail: armaurer@augustana.edu, Internet: www2.augustana.edu/resource/gallery. Dir.: Sherry C. Maurer
Fine Arts Museum - 1983
Art 46952

Black Hawk State Historic Site, Hauberg Indian Museum, Illinois Rte 5, Rock Island, IL 61201 - T: (309) 788-9536, Fax: (309) 788-9865, E-mail: hauberg-museum@juno.com. Dir.: Elizabeth Carvey-Stewart
Historic Site / Historical Museum - 1927
1740-1831 site of the main villages of the Sauk and Fox Nations 46953

Colonel Davenport Historical Foundation, Hillman St, Rock Island, Rock Island, IL 61201 - T: (309) 764-6471, 388-9657, E-mail: coldav1833@yahoo.com, Internet: www.davenporthouse.org. Pres.: Susan Wolters
Local Museum - 1978
Local hist 46954

Fryxell Geology Museum, c/o Augustana College, Swenson Hall of Science, Rock Island, IL 61201 - T: (309) 794-7318, Fax: (309) 794-7564, E-mail: glhammer@augustana.edu, Internet: www.augustana.edu. Dir.: William R. Hammer
Natural History Museum - 1929
Geology 46955

Rock Island Arsenal Museum, Attn SMARI-CFS-M, 1 Rock Island Arsenal, Rock Island, IL 61299-5000 - T: (309) 782-5021, Fax: (309) 782-3598, E-mail: leinickek@ria.army.mil, Internet: www.ria.army.mil/. Dir.: Kris G. Leinicke
Military Museum - 1905
Military 46956

Rock Springs WY

Community Fine Arts Center, 400 C St, Rock Springs, WY 82901 - T: (307) 362-6212, Fax: (307) 382-4101, E-mail: cfac@rock.sw1.k12.wy.us, Internet: www.cfa4art.com. Dir.: Debora Thaxton Soule, Ass. Dir.: Jennifer Messer
Fine Arts Museum - 1938
Arts 46957

Rock Springs Historical Museum, 201 B St, Rock Springs, WY 82901 - T: (307) 362-3138, Fax: (307) 352-1516. Pres.: Cyndi Sullivan, Dir.: Bob Nelson (Museum)
Local Museum - 1988
Local hist 46958

Rockford IL

Burpee Museum of Natural History, 737 N Main St, Rockford, IL 61103 - T: (815) 965-3433, Fax: (815) 965-2703, E-mail: info@burpee.org, Internet: www.burpee.org. Pres.: Lewis S.W. Crampton, Dir.: Dr. Wallace A. Steffan, Tom Little
Natural History Museum - 1942
Natural history, new Robert Solem wing 46959

Discovery Center Museum, 711 N Main St, Rockford, IL 61103 - T: (815) 963-6769, Fax: (815) 968-0164, E-mail: webmaster@discoverycentermuseum.org, Internet: www.discoverycentermuseum.org. Pres.: Tom Lasley, Exec. Dir.: Sarah Wolf, Dir.: Jan Aschim
Special Museum - 1981 46960

Midway Village and Museum, 6799 Guilford Rd, Rockford, IL 61107 - T: (815) 397-9112, Fax: (815) 397-9156, E-mail: info@midwayvillage.com, Internet: www.midwayvillage.com. Cur.: Rosalyn Robertson
Open Air Museum - 1970
History Village, 24-building turn-of-the-century complex 46961

Rockford Art Museum, 711 N Main St, Rockford, IL 61103-6999 - T: (815) 968-2787, Fax: (815) 968-0164, E-mail: staff@rockfordartmuseum.com, Internet: www.rockfordartmuseum.org. Dir.: Lorie Langan, Cur.: Joe Houston, Ass. Cur.: Steve Coogan
Fine Arts Museum - 1913
Art 46962

Rockford College Art Gallery/Clark Arts Center, 5050 E State, Rockford, IL 61108 - T: (815) 226-4034, Fax: (815) 394-5167. Dir.: Philip Soosloff
Fine Arts Museum / University Museum - 1847
Art 46963

Tinker Swiss Cottage Museum, 411 Kent St, Rockford, IL 61102 - T: (815) 964-2424, Fax: (815) 964-2466, E-mail: tinker@worldnet.att.net, Internet: www.tinkercottage.com. Pres.: Robert Jakeway, Exec. Dir.: Laura Bachelder
Local Museum / Decorative Arts Museum - 1943
1865 Swiss-style home built by Robert H. Tinker 46964

Rockhill Furnace PA

Railways to Yesterday, Rockhill Trolley Museum, East Broad Top Railroad, State Rte 994, Rockhill Furnace, PA 17249 - T: (610) 965-9028, (814) 447-9576, E-mail: s.gurley@prodigy.net, Internet: www.rockhilltrolley.org. Pres.: Joel Salomon
Science&Tech Museum - 1960
Transportation, specialization in collecting, restoring and maintaining cars that operated in Pennsylvania, trolley cars from Johnstown, Philadelphia, York, Scranton 46965

Rockhill Trolley Museum, Meadow St, Rockhill Furnace, PA 17249 - T: (610) 437-0448, E-mail: sgurley@prodigy.net, Internet: www.rockhilltrolley.org
Science&Tech Museum - 1962
Trolleys from 1899-1947 46966

Rockland ME

Shore Village Museum, 104 Limerock St, Rockland, ME 04841 - T: (207) 594-0311, Fax: (207) 594-9581, E-mail: knb@ime.net, Internet: www.lighthouse.cc/shorevillage. Dir.: Kenneth N. Black, Cur.: Robert Nason Davis (History)
Historical Museum - 1977
Maritime, lighthouse 46967

William A. Farnsworth Art Museum and Wyeth Center, 352 Main St, Rockland, ME 04841-0466 - T: (207) 596-6457, Fax: (207) 596-0509, E-mail: farnsworth@midcoast.com, Internet: www.farnsworthmuseum.org. Dir.: Christopher B. Crosman
Fine Arts Museum - 1948
American art, Louise Nevelson coll - library, Wyeth study center 46968

Rockport MA

Rockport Art Association Museum, 12 Main St, Rockport, MA 01966 - T: (978) 546-6604, Fax: (978) 546-9767, E-mail: raa@sbcglobal.net. Dir.: Carol Linsky
Fine Arts Museum - 1921
Arts 46969

Sandy Bay Historical Museums, 40 King St, Rockport, MA 01966 - T: (508) 546-9533. C.E.O.: Dana V. Woods, Cur.: Cynthia A. Peckham
Local Museum - 1925
Local history, Sewall-Scripture house, old castle 46970

Rockport ME

Center for Maine Contemporary Art, 162 Russell Av, Rockport, ME 04856 - T: (207) 236-2875, Fax: (207) 236-2490, E-mail: info@artsmaine.org, Internet: www.artsmaine.org. Dir.: Sheila Crosby Tasker, Cur.: Bruce Brown
Fine Arts Museum - 1952
Contemporary art 46971

Rockport TX

Fulton Mansion, 317 Fulton Beach Rd, Rockport, TX 78382 - T: (361) 729-0386 ext 26, Fax: (361) 729-6581, E-mail: fmdir@swbell.net, Internet: www.tpwd.state.tx.us/park/fulton/fulton.htm
Decorative Arts Museum - 1983
Period furniture, decorative arts 46972

Texas Maritime Museum, 1202 Navigation Circle, Rockport, TX 78382-2773 - T: (361) 729-1271, Fax: (361) 729-9938, E-mail: klrd@2fords.net, Internet: www.texasmaritimemuseum.org. Pres.: James Mayes, Dir.: Kathy Roberts-Douglass
Historical Museum - 1980
Maritime 46973

Rockton IL

Macktown Living History Site and Whitman Trading Post, Macktown Forest Preserve, Hwy 75 W, Rockton, IL 61072 - T: (815) 877-6100, Fax: (815) 877-6124, E-mail: wcfpd@wcfpd.org, Internet: www.wcfpd.org. Pres.: Ray Ferguson, Marilyn Mohring
Local Museum - 1952
Two-story farm house, home to one of the first white settlers in Winnebago County, 1846 Whitman Trading Post 46974

Rockville MD

Jane L. and Robert H. Weiner Judaic Museum, 6125 Montrose Rd, Rockville, MD 20852 - T: (301) 881-0100, 230-3711, Fax: (301) 881-5512, Internet: www.jccgw.org. C.E.O.: Arnie Sohinki
Fine Arts Museum / Religious Arts Museum - 1925
Judaica 46975

Latvian Museum, 400 Hurley Av, Rockville, MD 20850 - T: (301) 340-1914, Fax: (301) 340-8732, E-mail: alanso@alausa.org. Dir.: Anna Graudina, Cur.: Lilita Bergs
Ethnology Museum / Folklore Museum - 1980
Latvian historic and cultural development from Ice Age to 20th c 46976

Montgomery County Historical Society Museum, 103 W Montgomery Av, Rockville, MD 20850-4212 - T: (301) 340-2825, Fax: (301) 340-2871, E-mail: info@montgomeryhistory.org, Internet: www.montgomeryhistory.org. Pres.: John T. Beatyy, Exec. Dir.: Mary Kay Harper, Cur.: Millicent Gay
Local Museum / Historical Museum - 1944
Beall-Dawson House, 1852 Stonestreet Medical Museum, local history 46977

Rockwell City IA

Calhoun County Museum, 150 W High St, Rockwell City, IA 50579 - T: (712) 297-8139, 297-8585. Cur.: Judy Webb
Local Museum - 1956
Regional history 46978

Rocky Ford CO

Rocky Ford Historical Museum, 1005 Sycamore Av, Rocky Ford, CO 81067 - T: (719) 254-6737. Cur.: Diane Zimmerman
Local Museum - 1940
Local history, sugar produce, farming, military, 1st fire engine, ethnography, minerals and fossils - archives 46979

Rocky Hill CT

Academy Hall Museum of the Rocky Hill Historical Society, 785 Old Main St, Rocky Hill, CT 06067 - T: (860) 563-6704, E-mail: info@rockyhillhistory.org, Internet: www.rockyhillhistory.org. Pres.: Mike Martino
Local Museum - 1962
Local hist, Indian artifacts, clothing, domestics 46980

Rocky Mount NC

Rocky Mount Arts Center, 225 S Church St, Rocky Mount, NC 27803 - T: (252) 972-1163, Fax: (252) 972-1563, E-mail: jackson@ci.rocky-mount.nc.us, Internet: www.ci.rocky-mount.nc.us/artscenter.html. Dir.: Jerry Jackson, Cust.: Raymond Draughn
Fine Arts Museum - 1956 46981

Rocky Mount Children's Museum, 1610 Gay St, Rocky Mount, NC 27804 - T: (919) 972-1167, Fax: (919) 972-1232, E-mail: madrid@ci.rocky-mount.nc.us, Internet: www.ci.rocky-mount.nc.us/museum.html. Dir.: Candy L. Madrid, Cur.: Steve Armstrong
Special Museum - 1952 46982

Roebuck SC

Walnut Grove Plantation, 1200 Otts' Shoals Rd, Roebuck, SC 29376 - T: (864) 576-6546, Fax: (864) 576-4058, E-mail: wannutgrove@mindspring.com, Internet: www.sparklenet.com/historicalassociation. Pres.: Susan Dunlap, C.E.O.: Susan Turpin
Historical Museum - 1961
Historic house 46983

Rogers AR

Daisy International Air Gun Museum → Rogers Daisy Airgun Museum

Rogers Daisy Airgun Museum, 114 S First St, Rogers, AR 72756 - T: (501) 636-1200, Fax: (501) 636-1601, E-mail: info@daisymuseum.com, Internet: www.daisymuseum.com
Science&Tech Museum / Military Museum - 1966
Air guns 46984

Rogers Historical Museum, 322 S Second St, Rogers, AR 72756 - T: (479) 621-1154, Fax: (479) 621-1155, E-mail: museum@rogersarkansas.com, Internet: www.rogersarkansas.com/museum. Dir.: Gaye K. Bland, Ass. Dir.: Allyn Lord
Local Museum / Historical Museum - 1975
Hawkins house, local history 46985

Rogers MN

Ellingson Car Museum, 20950 Rogers Dr, Rogers, MN 55374 - T: (612) 428-7337, Fax: (612) 428-4370, Internet: www.ellingsoncarmuseum.com
Science&Tech Museum - 1994 46986

Rogers City MI

Presque Isle County Historical Museum, 176 W Michigan Av, Rogers City, MI 49779 - T: (517) 734-4121. Cur.: Laural R. Maldonado
Local Museum - 1973
Area hist, maritime, ship model of s/s "Carl D Bradley" 46987

Rogue River OR

Woodville Museum, First and Oak Sts, Rogue River, OR 97537 - T: (541) 582-3088
Public Gallery - 1986 46988

Rohnert Park CA

University Art Gallery, c/o Sonoma State University, 1801 E Cotati Av, Rohnert Park, CA 94928 - T: (707) 664-2295, Fax: (707) 664-4333, 664-2054, E-mail: art.gallery@sonoma.edu, Internet: www.sonoma.edu/artgallery. Dir.: Michael Schwager
Fine Arts Museum / University Museum - 1977
20th c American artworks on paper, Asian art, Garfield coll 46989

Rolla MO

Ed Clark Museum of Missouri Geology, 111 Fairgrounds Rd, Rolla, MO 65401 - T: (573) 368-2100, Fax: (573) 368-2111
Natural History Museum - 1963 46990

Memoryville USA, 2220 N Bishop Av, Rolla, MO 65401 - T: (573) 364-1810, Fax: (573) 364-6975, E-mail: memoryvl@fidnet.com, Internet: www.missouriozarks.org/memory.html
Science&Tech Museum - 1969
Antique and classic automobiles, army truck with machine gun 46991

Rolla Minerals Museum, University of Missouri, 125 McNutt Hall, UMR Campus, Rolla, MO 65401 - T: (573) 341-4616, Fax: (573) 341-6935
University Museum / Natural History Museum - 1870 46992

Rome GA

Chieftains Museum, 501 Riverside Pkwy, Rome, GA 30161 - T: (706) 291-9494, Fax: (706) 291-2410, E-mail: chmuseum@bellsouth.net, Internet: www.chieftainsmuseum.org. Pres.: Ansley Saville
Ethnology Museum / Historical Museum / Archaeological Museum - 1969
Plantation house belonging to Cherokee leader Major Ridge, native American archaeology 46993

Martha Berry Museum, 24 Veterans Memorial Hwy, Rome, GA 30161, mail addr: POB 490189, Mount Berry, GA 30149-0189 - T: (706) 291-1883, Fax: (706) 802-0902, E-mail: oakhill@berry.edu, Internet: www.berry.edu/oakhill
Local Museum - 1972 46994

Rome NY

Erie Canal Village, 5789 New London Rd, RT46/49, Rome, NY 13440 - T: (315) 337-3999, Fax: (315) 339-7595, E-mail: mandm@ntcnet.com, Internet: www.eriecanalvillage.com
Local Museum / Historic Site / Open Air Museum - 1973 46995

Fort Stanwix, 112 E Park St, Rome, NY 13440 - T: (315) 336-2090, Fax: (315) 334-5051, E-mail: michael_caldwell@nps.gov, Internet: www.nps.gov/fost
Local Museum - 1935
Archaeological coll, arms, clothing, glassware and pottery 46996

Rome Art and Community Center, 308 W Bloomfield St, Rome, NY 13440 - T: (315) 336-1040, Fax: (315) 336-1090, E-mail: racc@borg.com, Internet: www.borg.com/~racc. Pres.: Ann Peach Lynch, C.E.O.: Deborah H. O'Shea
Fine Arts Museum - 1967 46997

Rome Historical Society Museum, 200 Church St, Rome, NY 13440 - T: (315) 336-5870, Fax: (315) 336-5912, E-mail: romehist@dreamscape.com. Cur.: Ann Swanson
Local Museum - 1936 46998

Rome City IN

Gene Stratton-Porter House, 1205 Pleasant Point, Rome City, IN 46784, mail addr: Box 639, Rome City, IN 46784 - T: (219) 854-3790, Fax: (219) 854-9102, E-mail: gsporter@kuntrynet.com. Cur.: Margie Sweeney, Ass. Cur.: Martha Swartzlander
Historical Museum 46999

Roosevelt AZ

Tonto National Monument, Hwy 88, Roosevelt, AZ 85545 - T: (928) 467-2241, Fax: (928) 467-2225, E-mail: lee_baiza@nps.gov, Internet: www.nps.gov/tont. Head: Lee Baiza
Archaeological Museum - 1907
Archaeology 47000

Rosanky TX

Central Texas Museum of Automotive History, Hwy 304, Rosanky, TX 78953 - T: (512) 237-2635, Fax: (512) 754-2424, E-mail: dburdick@thermon.com, Internet: www.tourtexas.com/rosanky. Dir.: Richard L. Burdick, Cur.: Kurt McCowan, Sc. Staff: Ray Terry (Restoration)
Science&Tech Museum - 1982
Transportation 47001

Roseau MN

Roseau County Historical Museum, 110 Second Av NE, Roseau, MN 56751 - T: (218) 463-1918, Fax: (218) 463-3795, E-mail: roseau@wiktel.com, Internet: www.angelfire.com/mn/rehistsocmuseum. Dir.: Charleen Haugen
Historical Museum - 1927 47002

Roseburg OR

Douglas County Museum of History and Natural History, 123 Museum Dr, Roseburg, OR 97470 - T: (541) 957-7007, Fax: (541) 957-7017, E-mail: museum@co.douglas.or.us, Internet: www.co.douglas.or.us/museum. Dir.: Stacey B. McLaughlin, Cur.: Jena Mitchell (History), Dennis Ruley (Natural History)
Local Museum / Natural History Museum - 1968 47003

Lane House, 544 SE Douglas Av, Roseburg, OR 97470 - T: (541) 673-4572. Pres.: Jane Clarke
Historical Museum - 1953 47004

Roselle IL

Law Enforcement Museum, POB 72835, Roselle, IL 60172 - T: (847) 795-1547, Fax: (847) 795-2469, E-mail: forgottenheroes@aol.com, Internet: www.forgottenheroes-lema.org. Pres.: Ronald C. Van Raalte
Special Museum - 1989
Law, crime, police deaths 47005

Roselle NJ

Sons of the American Revolution, 101 W Ninth Av, Roselle, NJ 07203-1926 - T: (908) 245-1777
Military Museum - 1889 47006

Rosendale NY

A.J. Snyder Estate, 668 Rte 213, Rosendale, NY 12472-0150 - T: (845) 658-9900, Fax: (845) 658-9277, E-mail: rosendalebuff@aol.com, Internet: www.centuryhouse.org. Pres./Dir.: Dietrich Werner
Historical Museum / Science&Tech Museum - 1988 47007

Roseville OH

Ohio Ceramic Center, 7327 Ceramic Rd NE, Roseville, OH 43777 - T: (740) 697-7021, Fax: (740) 697-0171, E-mail: webmaster@ceramic.22n.com, Internet: www.geocities.com/ceramiccenter
Decorative Arts Museum / Science&Tech Museum - 1970
Develop from Ohio Bluebird potteries to modern ceramic industry 47008

Roslyn NY

Nassau County Museum of Art, 1 Museum Dr, Roslyn, NY 11576 - T: (516) 484-9338, Fax: (516) 484-0710, E-mail: nassaumuseum@yahoo.com, Internet: www.nassaumuseum.org. Dir.: Constance Schwartz, Ass. Dir.: Fernanda Bennett, Cur.: Franklin Hill Perrell
Fine Arts Museum - 1989 47009

Van Nostrand-Starkins House, 221 Main St, Roslyn, NY 11576 - T: (516) 625-4363, Fax: (516) 625-4363, E-mail: roslynlandmarksociety@juno.com. Pres.: Donald Kavanash, Dir.: Catherine M. Tamis
Historical Museum - 1976 47010

Rossville GA

Chief John Ross House, 200 E Lake Av, Rossville, GA 30741 - T: (706) 861-3954
Special Museum / Decorative Arts Museum - 1797
Cherokee alphabet, arrowheads, pictures, letters, furniture, rugs 47011

Roswell GA

Bulloch Hall, 180 Bulloch Av, Roswell, GA 30075 - T: (770) 992-1731, 992-1951, Fax: (770) 587-1840. Dir.: Pam Billingsley
Folklore Museum - 1978
Historic c.1839 Antebellum Greek Revival House and Cottage 47012

Roswell NM

Anderson Museum of Contemporary Art, 409 E College Blvd, Roswell, NM 88202 - T: (505) 623-5600, Fax: (505) 623-5603. Dir.: Donald B. Anderson
Fine Arts Museum - 1994 47013

General Douglas L. McBride Museum, New Mexico Military Institute, 101 West College Blvd, Roswell, NM 88201-8107 - T: (505) 624-8220, Fax: (505) 624-8258, Internet: www.nmmi.cc.nm.us/museum. Dir.: Genee Hardman
Military Museum - 1983
Military 47014

Historical Center for Southeast New Mexico, 200 N Lea Av, Roswell, NM 88201 - T: (505) 622-8333, Fax: (505) 622-8333, E-mail: hssnm@dfn.com, Internet: www.dfn.com/hssnm/. Dir.: Sharon Saskiweicz, Archivist: Elvis Fleming, Cur.: Jean Rockhold
Local Museum / Historical Museum - 1976 47015

Roswell Museum and Art Center, 100 W 11, Roswell, NM 88201 - T: (505) 624-6744 ext 10, Fax: (505) 624-6765, E-mail: rufe@roswellmuseum.org, Internet: www.roswellmuseum.org. Dir.: Laurie J. Rufe, Ass. Dir.: Michael J. Riley, Cur.: Wesley A. Rusnell
Fine Arts Museum / Local Museum - 1937
Regional and Native American fine arts and crafts, graphics, Western history, ethnology, folk art 47016

Round Top TX

Festival-Institute Museum, State Hwy 237, Round Top, TX 78954 - T: (409) 249-3129, Fax: (409) 249-5078, E-mail: lamarl@festivalhill.org, Internet: www.festivalhill.org. Dir.: James Dick, Cur.: Lamar Lentz
Fine Arts Museum / Decorative Arts Museum - 1971
Art 47017

Winedale Historical Center, University of Texas, c/o Austin Center for American History, FM Road 2714, Round Top, TX 78954 - T: (979) 278-3530, Fax: (979) 278-3531, E-mail: g.jaster@mail.utexas.edu, Internet: www.cah.utexas.edu
Local Museum - 1967
Texas-German cultural hist, agricultural hist, American social hist, textiles 47018

Roundup MT

Musselshell Valley Historical Museum, 524 First W Roundup, Roundup, MT 59072 - T: (406) 323-1403, Fax: (406) 323-1518, E-mail: dparrott@midrivers.com. Dir.: Bonnie DeMaio, Ass. Dir.: Shirley Parrott
Local Museum - 1972 47019

Rowe MA

Kemp-McCarthy Memorial Museum, 288 Zoar Rd, Rowe, MA 01367-9774 - T: (413) 339-4700, 339-4729, Fax: (413) 339-4700, E-mail: rowehistorical@netzero.net. Dir.: Alan Bjork
Local Museum - 1963 47020

Rowley MA

Rowley Historical Museum, 233 Main St, Rowley, MA 01969 - T: (508) 948-7483, Internet: www.tiac.net/users/mcmahon. C.E.O.: Edward DesJardins
Local Museum - 1918
Local history 47021

Roxbury MA

Museum of the National Center of Afro-American Artists, 300 Walnut Av, Roxbury, MA 02119 - T: (617) 442-8614, 442-8014, Fax: (617) 445-5525, Internet: www.swift-tourism.com/ncaaa.htm
Fine Arts Museum - 1969
Paintings, prints and graphics by Afro-American artists, African art 47022

Roxbury Historical Museum, 183 Roxbury St, John Eliot Sq, Roxbury, MA 02119 - T: (617) 445-3399, Fax: (617) 445-5883. Dir.: Antonio Menefee
Local Museum - 1901
Local history, Dillaway-Thomas house 47023

Roxbury NY

John Burroughs Memorial, Burroughs Memorial Rd, Roxbury, NY 12474, mail addr: Battlefield SHS, 7801 State Rte 69, Oriskany, NY 13424 - T: (315) 768-7224, Fax: (315) 338-3081, E-mail: nancy.demyttennaere@oprhp.state.ny.us, Internet: www.nysparks.com
Historical Museum - 1964 47024

Royal Oak MI

Wildlife Interpretive Gallery, c/o Detroit Zoological Institute, 8450 W 10 Mile, Royal Oak, MI 48068-0039 - T: (248) 398-0903, Fax: (248) 398-0504. Cur.: Gerry Craig
Fine Arts Museum - 1995
Art coll interpret human's relationship with animals 47025

Royalton VT

Royalton Historical Society Museum, 4184 Rte 14, Royalton, VT 05068 - T: (802) 828-3051, Fax: (802) 828-3206, E-mail: jdumville@gate.dca.state.vt.us. Pres.: John P. Dumville
Local Museum - 1967
Local hist 47026

Rugby ND

Geographical Center Historical Museum, 1 Block E Hwy. US #2 and ND #3, Rugby, ND 58368 - T: (701) 776-6414, Internet: www.artcom.com/museum/. Pres.: Matt Mullally
Local Museum - 1964 47027

Rugby TN

Historic Rugby, State Hwy 52, Rugby, TN 37733 - T: (423) 628-2441, Fax: (423) 628-2266, E-mail: rugbytn@highland.net, Internet: www.historucrugby.htm. Pres.: Gerald Walker, Exec. Dir.: Barbara Stagg
Local Museum - 1966
Historic village 47028

Ruidoso Downs NM

Hubbard Museum of the American West, 841 Hwy 70 W, Ruidoso Downs, NM 88346 - T: (505) 378-4142, Fax: (505) 378-4166, E-mail: moth@zianet.com, Internet: www.hubbardmuseum.com
Natural History Museum / Historical Museum - 1990
Horses 47029

Rushville IL

Schuyler Jail Museum, 200 S Congress St, Rushville, IL 62681 - T: (217) 322-6975. Cur.: Nancy Stauffer
Local Museum - 1968
Local history, housed in Schuyler Jail 47030

Rushville IN

Rush County Historical Society Museum, 619 N Perkins, Rushville, IN 46173 - T: (765) 932-2492, 932-2222
Local Museum - 1922 47031

Russell KS

Deines Cultural Center, 820 N Main St, Russell, KS 67665 - T: (785) 483-3742, Fax: (785) 483-4397, E-mail: deinescenter@russellks.net. Dir.: Nance Selbe
Fine Arts Museum - 1990
Art 47032

Fossil Station Museum, 331 Kansas St, Russell, KS 67665 - T: (913) 483-3637, E-mail: rchs@russellks.net, Internet: www.rchs.russellks.net. Pres.: Connie Wagner
Local Museum / Science&Tech Museum - 1969
Local hist 47033

Gernon House and Blacksmith Shop, 818 N Kansas St, Russell, KS 67665 - T: (913) 483-3637, E-mail: rchs@russellks.net, Internet: www.rchs.russellks.net. Pres.: Jeff McCoy
Local Museum - 1979
Historic buildings 47034

Heym-Oliver House, 503 Kansas St, Russell, KS 67665 - T: (913) 483-3637, E-mail: rchs@russellks.net, Internet: www.rchs.russellks.net. Cur.: Ruby Blake
Ethnology Museum / Historical Museum - 1968 47035

Oil Patch Museum, Interstate 70 and Hwy 281, Russell, KS 67665 - T: (913) 483-6640, E-mail: rchs@russellks.net, Internet: www.rchs.russellks.net. Pres.: Jeff McCoy
Science&Tech Museum - 1973
Industrial oil production 47036

Russell Springs KS

Butterfield Trail Historical Museum, Broadway and Hilts, Russell Springs, KS 67755 - T: (913) 751-4242. Pres.: Jarett Hanemza
Historical Museum - 1964
Local history, housed in the Logan County Courthouse and Jail 47037

Ruston LA

Lincoln Parish Museum, 609 N Vienna St, Ruston, LA 71270 - T: (318) 251-0018, E-mail: lpmuseum@tcainternet.com. C.E.O. & Pres.: William Davis Green
Local Museum - 1975
Local hist 47038

Louisiana Tech Museum, Louisiana Tech University, Ruston, LA 71272 - T: (318) 257-2264, 257-2737, Fax: (318) 257-4735, E-mail: caesar@latech.edu. Dir.: C. Wade Meade, Cur.: J.A. Christian
University Museum / Local Museum - 1982 47039

Rutherford NJ

Meadowlands Museum, 91 Crane Av, Rutherford, NJ 07070 - T: (201) 935-1175, Fax: (201) 935-9791, Internet: www.meadowlandsmuseum.org. Dir.: Jackie Bunker-Lohrenz
Local Museum / Natural History Museum - 1961
Regional rocks and minerals, history 47040

Rutland VT

Chaffee Center for Visual Arts, 16 S Main St, Rutland, VT 05701 - T: (801) 775-0356, Fax: (802) 773-4401. Exec. Dir.: Nicholas Rayburn
Public Gallery - 1961 47041

New England Maple Museum, POB 1615, Rutland, VT 05701 - T: (802) 483-9414, Fax: (802) 775-1650. Pres.: Thomas H. Olson, Dir.: Dona A. Olson
Agriculture Museum - 1977
Local hist 47042

Rye NY

Rye Historical Society Museum, 1 Purchase St, Rye, NY 10580 - T: (914) 967-7588, Internet: www.ryehistoricalsociety.org. Dir.: Catherine Abrams
Local Museum - 1964 47043

Sabetha KS

Albany Historical Museum, 415 Grant, Sabetha, KS 66534 - T: (785) 284-3446, 284-3529. Pres.: Kenny Alderfer
Local Museum - 1965
Local history 47044

Sackets Harbor NY

Sackets Harbor Battlefield State Historic Site, 505 W Washington St, Sackets Harbor, NY 13685 - T: (315) 646-3634, Fax: (315) 646-1203. Head: Stephen R. Wallace, Cur.: Richard West
Military Museum / Open Air Museum - 1933 47045

Saco ME

Saco Museum, York Institute Museum, 371 Main St, Saco, ME 04072 - T: (207) 283-0684, Fax: (207) 283-0754, Internet: www.org/history. Cur.: Lauren Fensterstock
Fine Arts Museum - 1867
Art 47046

Sacramento CA

California State Capitol Museum, State Capitol, Rm B-27, Sacramento, CA 95814 - T: (916) 324-0333, Fax: (916) 445-3628, E-mail: st.capmus@cwo.com, Internet: www.parks.ca.gov. Dir.: Anthony Perez, Cur.: V. Joseph Sgromo
Historical Museum - 1981
History 47047

California State Indian Museum, 2618 K St, Sacramento, CA 95816 - T: (916) 324-0971, 324-8043, Fax: (916) 322-5231, Internet: www.parks.ca.gov. Cur.: Michael S. Tucker
Historical Museum - 1940
California Native American culture and hist 47048

California State Railroad Museum, 111 I St, Sacramento, CA 95814-2265 - T: (916) 445-7387, 323-8075, Fax: (916) 327-5655, E-mail: foundation@californiastaterailroadmuseum.org, Internet: www.californiastaterailroadmuseum.org. Sen. Cur.: Stephen E. Drew
Science&Tech Museum / Historical Museum - 1976
Railroad 47049

Crocker Art Museum, 216 O St, Sacramento, CA 95814 - T: (916) 264-5423, Fax: (916) 264-7372, E-mail: cam@cityofsacramento.org, Internet: www.crockerartmuseum.org. Dir.: Lial A. Jones, Cur.: Scott Shields
Fine Arts Museum - 1885
Drawings, paintings, California art, photography, ceramics 47050

Discovery Museum History Center, 101 I St, Sacramento, CA 95814 - T: (916) 264-7057, Fax: (916) 264-5100, Internet: www.thediscovery.org. Dir.: Evangeline Higginbotham, Cur.: Milita Rios-Samaniego
Historical Museum - 1994
History, science and technology 47051

Governor's Mansion, 1526 H St, Sacramento, CA 95814 - T: (916) 323-3047, Internet: www.cal-parks.ca.gov. Dir.: Janelle Miller
Local Museum / Historical Museum / Historic Site - 1967
Local hist 47052

La Raza-Galeria Posada, 704 O St, Sacramento, CA 95814 - T: (916) 446-5133, Fax: (916) 446-5801, E-mail: marisa@galeriaposada.org, Internet: www.galeriaposada.org. Exec. Dir.: Marisa Gutiérez
Local Museum - 1972 47053

Sutter's Fort, 2701 L St, Sacramento, CA 95816 - T: (916) 445-4422, Fax: (916) 442-8613, E-mail: suttersfortelp@cwo.com, Internet: www.parks.ca.gov. Cur.: Michael S. Tucker
Historical Museum / Historic Site - 1839
Local hist, pre gold rush 47054

Towe Auto Museum, 2200 Front St, Sacramento, CA 95818 - T: (916) 442-6802, Fax: (916) 442-2646, E-mail: info@toweautomuseum.org, Internet: www.toweautomuseum.org. Dir.: Kristin Hartley
Science&Tech Museum / Historical Museum - 1982
Transportation, coll of cars 1900 - 1970s 47055

Wells Fargo History Museum, 400 Capitol Mall, Sacramento, CA 95814 - T: (916) 440-4161, Fax: (916) 492-2931, E-mail: kalnins@wellsfargo.com, Internet: www.wellsfargohistory.com. Cur.: Indulis Kalnins
Historical Museum - 1992 47056

Wells Fargo History Museum Old Sacramento, 1000 Second St, Sacramento, CA 95814 - T: (916) 440-4263, Internet: www.wellsfargohistory.com. Cur.: Denise M. Pranza
Historical Museum - 1984
Company hist 47057

Safety Harbor FL

Safety Harbor Museum of Regional History, 329 Bayshore Blvd S, Safety Harbor, FL 34695 - T: (727) 726-1668, Fax: (727) 725-9938, E-mail: shmuseum@ij.net, Internet: www.safety-harbor-museum.org. Dir.: Batty J. Quibell
Historical Museum / Archaeological Museum - 1970 47058

Safford AZ

Discovery Park, 1651 Discovery Park Blvd, Safford, AZ 85546 - T: (928) 428-6260, Fax: (928) 428-8081, E-mail: discover@discoverypark.com, Internet: www.discoverypark.com. Head: Ed Sawyer
Science&Tech Museum - 1995
Science 47059

Graham County Historical Museum, 808 Eighth Av, Safford, AZ 85546 - T: (928) 348-0470, Fax: (928) 485-0107. Dir.: Raydene Cluff
Local Museum - 1962
Local history 47060

Sag Harbor NY

Sag Harbor Whaling and Historical Museum, 200 Main St, Sag Harbor, NY 11963 - T: (516) 725-0770, Fax: (516) 725-0770, E-mail: mail@sagharborwhalingmuseum.org, Internet: www.sagharborwhalingmuseum.org. Pres.: David H. Cory
Special Museum / Historical Museum - 1936 47061

Saginaw MI

Castle Museum of Saginaw County History, 500 Federal Av, Saginaw, MI 48607 - T: (989) 752-2861, Fax: (989) 752-1533, E-mail: saghist@concentric.net. Exec. Dir.: Charles Hoover
Historical Museum - 1948
Regional history 47062

Saginaw Art Museum, 1126 N Michigan Av, Saginaw, MI 48602 - T: (989) 754-2491, Fax: (989) 754-9387, Internet: www.saginawartmuseum.org. Dir.: Sheila K. Redmann, Cur.: Mary Malocha
Fine Arts Museum - 1947
Art, former residence of Clark L. Ring family, Charles Adams platt designed 47063

Saguache CO

Saguache County Museum, Hwy 285, Saguache, CO 81149 - T: (719) 655-2557, 256-4272, Internet: www.coloradotrails.com. C.E.O.: Evelyn Croft
Local Museum - 1958
Pioneer site, local history 47064

Saint Albans VT

Saint Albans Historical Museum, 9 Church St, Saint Albans, VT 05478 - T: (802) 527-7933. Dir.: Donald J. Miner
Local Museum - 1971
China and glass, furniture, jewelry, quilts, linens, laces, paintings, Central Vermont railway, military, sports, toys, dolls, crafts, X-ray coll 47065

Saint Augustine FL

Castillo de San Marcos Museum, 1 S Castillo Dr, Saint Augustine, FL 32084 - T: (904) 829-6506, Fax: (904) 823-9388, E-mail: casa_administration@nps.gov. Head: Gordon J. Wilson
Historical Museum / Historic Site - 1935
Museum housed in 1672-95 restored Spanish Castillo de San Marcos 47066

Fort Matanzas, 8635 A1A S, Saint Augustine, FL 32080 - T: (904) 471-0116, Fax: (904) 471-7605. Head: Gordon Wilson
Historical Museum - 1935
Site of first European battle for control of New World 47067

Lightner Museum, 75 King St, Saint Augustine, FL 32085-0334 - T: (904) 824-2874, Fax: (904) 824-2712, E-mail: lightner@aug.com, Internet: www.lightnermuseum.org. Dir.: Robert W. Harper, Cur.: James A. Macbeth
Local Museum - 1948
Housed in 1887 Alcazar Hotel 47068

Oldest House Museum Complex, 14 Saint Francis St, Saint Augustine, FL 32084 - T: (904) 824-2872, Fax: (904) 824-2569, E-mail: oldhouse@aug.com, Internet: www.oldcity.com/oldhouse. Exec. Dir.: Taryn Rodriguez-Boette
Historical Museum / Military Museum - 1918
Military, Gonzalez-Alvarez House, Tovar House, Webb Museum of Florida history 47069

Pena-Peck House, 143 St George St, Saint Augustine, FL 32084 - T: (904) 829-5064, Fax: (904) 829-3898, E-mail: mpope@aug.com
Decorative Arts Museum - 1932 47070

Saint Augustine Historical Society Museum, 271 Charlotte St, Saint Augustine, FL 32084 - T: (904) 824-2872, Fax: (909) -824-2569, E-mail: oldhouse@aug.com, Internet: www.oldcity.com/oldhouse. Dir.: Taryn Rodríguez-Boette, Sc. Staff: Reis Libby (Collections), Libr.: Charles A. Tingley
Local Museum - 1883
Local history - library 47071

Saint Augustine Lighthouse and Museum, 81 Lighthouse Av, Saint Augustine, FL 32080 - T: (904) 829-0745, Fax: (904) 808-1248, E-mail: staugl@aug.com, Internet: www.staugustinelighthouse.com. Dir.: Kathy Allen Fleming, Ass. Dir.: Sue Van Vleet
Historical Museum / Historic Site - 1988 47072

Saint Photios Greek Orthodox National Shrine, 41 St George St, Saint Augustine, FL 32085, mail addr: POB 1960, Saint Augustine, FL 32085 - T: (904) 829-8205, Fax: (904) 829-8707, E-mail: stphotios@yahoo.com, Internet: www.stphotios.com. C.E.O.: Nicholas Graff
Religious Arts Museum - 1982
1768 Greek landiing with Minorcans, Italians, Corsicans and Greeks, frescoes, icons 47073

The Spanish Quarter Museum, 29 Saint George St, Saint Augustine, FL 32084 - T: (904) 825-6830, Fax: (904) 825-6874, E-mail: sqmuse@aug.com, Internet: www.historicstaugustine.com. Man.: Charles Dale
Folklore Museum - 1959
Restored village, traditional 18th c life skills 47074

World Golf Hall of Fame, 1 World Golf Pl, Saint Augustine, FL 32082 - T: (904) 940-4000, Fax: (904) 940-4399, Internet: www.wgv.com. Dir.: Jack Peter, Cur.: Andrew Hunold
Special Museum - 1974 47075

Saint Bonaventure NY

F.Donald Kenney Museum and Art Study Wing, Saint Bonaventure University, Saint Bonaventure, NY 14778 - T: (716) 375-2494, Fax: (716) 375-2690, E-mail: bracker@sbu.edu, Internet: www.sbu.edu/qac. Dir.: Barbara Racker, Cur.: Chad Tooker
Fine Arts Museum / University Museum - 1856 47076

Saint Bonaventure Art Collection → F.Donald Kenney Museum and Art Study Wing

Saint Charles IL

Saint Charles Heritage Center, 215 E Main St, Saint Charles, IL 60174 - T: (630) 584-6967, Fax: (630) 584-6077, E-mail: stcmuseum@aol.com, Internet: www.stchistory.www.org. Pres.: Patricia Thayer
Local Museum - 1940
Local hist 47077

Saint Charles MO

First Missouri State Capitol, 200-216 S Main St, Saint Charles, MO 63301 - T: (636) 940-3322, Fax: (636) 940-3324, E-mail: dspfrst@mail.dnr.state.mo.us, Internet: www.dnr.state.mo.us. Head: David Klostermeier
Historical Museum - 1971 47078

Harry D. Hendren Gallery, c/o Lindenwood University, 209 S Kings Hwy, Saint Charles, MO 63301 - T: (636) 949-4862, Fax: (636) 949-4610, E-mail: etillinger@lindenwood.edu, Internet: www.lindenwood.edu
Fine Arts Museum / University Museum - 1969
Contemporary American and European prints 47079

Lewis and Clark Center, 701 Riverside Dr, Saint Charles, MO 63301 - T: (636) 947-3199, Fax: (636) 916-0240, Internet: www.lewisandclarkcenter.org
Special Museum - 1985
Tools, fauna and flora, Indian artifacts 47080

Saint Charles County Museum, 101 S Main St, Saint Charles, MO 63301-2802 - T: (636) 946-9828, E-mail: scchs@mail.win.org, Internet: www.win.org/library/other/historical_society. Dir.: Dr. Daniel T. Brown
Local Museum - 1956 47081

Saint Clairsville OH

Ohio University Art Gallery, 209 Shannon Hall, Saint Clairsville, OH 43950 - T: (614) 695-1720, Internet: www.eastern.ohiou.edu
Public Gallery 47082

Saint Cloud MN

Atwood Memorial Center, Saint Cloud State University, 720 Fourth Av S, Saint Cloud, MN 56301 - T: (320) 255-4636, Fax: (320) 529-1669, Internet: www.stcloudstate.edu/~atwood. Dir.: Janice Courtney
Fine Arts Museum - 1967
Central Minnesota artists 47083

Evelyn Payne Hatcher Museum of Anthropology, 213A Stewart Hall, Saint Cloud State University, Saint Cloud, MN 56301 - T: (320) 255-2294, Fax: (320) 654-5198. Cur.: Richard B. Lane
Ethnology Museum / Archaeological Museum - 1972 47084

Kiehle Gallery, Saint Cloud State University, 720 Fourth Av S, Saint Cloud, MN 56301 - T: (320) 255-4283, Fax: (320) 529-1669, Internet: www.stcloudstate.edu/!utb. Dir.: Joseph Akin
Fine Arts Museum
Paintings, prints, sculpture, photographs 47085

Stearns History Museum, 235 S 33 Av, Saint Cloud, MN 56301-3752 - T: (320) 253-8424, Fax: (320) 253-2172, E-mail: info@stearns-museum.org, Internet: www.stearns-museum.org. Dir.: David F. Ebnet, Cur.: Steven Penick
Historical Museum - 1936 47086

Saint Croix VI

Christiansted National Historic Site, Danish Custom House, Kingswharf-Christiansted, Saint Croix, VI 00821 - T: (809) 773-1460, Fax: (809) 773-5995. Head: Anibal Colon
Local Museum - 1962
Local hist 47087

Saint Francis SD

Buechel Memorial Lakota Museum, Saint Francis Indian Mission, 350 S Oak St, Saint Francis, SD 57572 - T: (605) 747-2745, Fax: (605) 747-5057. Dir.: J. Charmayne Young
Ethnology Museum / Folklore Museum - 1915
Lakota Indian culture 47088

Saint Francisville LA

Audubon State Historic Site, Louisiana State Hwy 965, Saint Francisville, LA 70775 - T: (225) 635-3739, Fax: (225) 784-0578, (888) 677-2838, E-mail: audubon@crt.state.la.us, Internet: www.crt.state.la.us
Fine Arts Museum - 1947
1st Audubon prints, early American lighting devices 47089

Saint George UT

Brigham Young's Winter Home, 67 West 200 North, Saint George, UT 84770 - T: (801) 673-5181, -2517, Fax: (801) 652-9589, E-mail: vcsgeorge@ldschurch.org. Dir.: Roy Wennerholm jr., Cur.: Don Enders (Exhibits and Historic Sites), Richard G. Oman (Art and Artifacts)
Local Museum - 1975
Historic house, Brigham Young winter home 47090

Southwestern Utah Art Gallery, c/o Dixie College, 225 S 700th E, Saint George, UT 84770 - T: (435) 652-7500, Fax: (435) 656-4000, E-mail: starkey@dixie.edu, Internet: www.dixie.edu. Dir.: Brent Hanson
Fine Arts Museum - 1960
Early and contemporary Utah painters 47091

Saint Helena CA

R.L.S. Silverado Museum, 1490 Library Ln, Saint Helena, CA 94574-0409 - T: (707) 963-3757, Fax: (707) 963-0917. Dir.: Edmond Reynolds
Fine Arts Museum - 1968 47092

Saint Helens OR

Columbia County Historical Society Museum, Old County Courthouse, Saint Helens, OR 97051 - T: (503) 397-3868, Fax: (503) 397-7257. Pres.: R.J. Brown
Local Museum - 1969 47093

Saint Ignace MI

Father Marquette National Memorial and Museum, 720 Church St, Saint Ignace, MI 49781 - T: (906) 643-8620, 643-9394, Fax: (906) 643-9329. Head: Wayne Burnett
Religious Arts Museum - 1980
Local hist 47094

Saint Ignatius MT

Flathead Indian Museum, 1 Museum Ln, Saint Ignatius, MT 59865 - T: (406) 745-2951, Fax: (406) 745-2961. Dir.: Jeanine Allard
Ethnology Museum - 1974 47095

Saint James MO

Maramec Museum, The James Foundation, Maramec Spring Park, 21880 Maramec Spring Dr, Saint James, MO 65559 - T: (573) 265-7124, Fax: (573) 265-8770, E-mail: tjf@tigernet.missouri.org. Head: Danny Marshall
Historical Museum / Folklore Museum / Science&Tech Museum - 1971 47096

Saint Johns MI

Clinton County Historical Society Museum, 106 Maple Av, Saint Johns, MI 48879 - T: (517) 224-2894, 224-7402. Dir.: Catherine Rumbaugh
Historical Museum - 1978
Local hist 47097

Saint Johnsbury VT

Fairbanks Museum and Planetarium, 1302 Main St, Saint Johnsbury, VT 05819 - T: (802) 748-2372, Fax: (802) 748-1893, E-mail: info@fairbanksmuseum.org, Internet: www.fairbanksmuseum.org. C.E.O.: Charles C. Browne
Local Museum / Natural History Museum - 1889
Local hist, ethnological coll 47098

Saint Johnsbury Athenaeum, 1171 Main St, Saint Johnsbury, VT 05819 - T: (802) 748-8291, Fax: (802) 748-8086, E-mail: inform@stjathenaeum.org, Internet: www.stjathenaeum.org
Fine Arts Museum - 1873
American landscape paintings of the Hudson River School, sculpture 47099

Saint Johnsville NY

Fort Klock Historic Restoration, Rte 5, Saint Johnsville, NY 13452 - T: (518) 568-7779, E-mail: fortklock@hotmail.com, Internet: www.fortklock.com. Pres.: A. Joyce Berry
Local Museum - 1964 47100

Saint Joseph MI

The Curious Kids' Museum, 415 Lake Blvd, Saint Joseph, MI 49085 - T: (616) 983-2543, Fax: (616) 983-3317, E-mail: ckm@curiouskidsmuseum.org, Internet: www.curiouskidsmuseum.org. Dir.: Bonny Kelly, Pam Muller, Joan Skoda
Science&Tech Museum / Historical Museum - 1988
Science, history, culture, technology 47101

Krasl Art Center, 707 Lake Blvd, Saint Joseph, MI 49085-1398 - T: (616) 983-0271, Fax: (616) 983-0275, E-mail: info@krasl.org, Internet: www.krasl.org. Dir.: Darwin R. Davis, Cur.: Susan Wilczak
Fine Arts Museum - 1963
Sculpture 47102

Saint Joseph MN

Benedicta Arts Center, College of Saint Benedict, 37 S College Av, Saint Joseph, MN 56374 - T: (612) 363-5777, Fax: (612) 363-6097, E-mail: jrule@csbsju.edu. Dir.: Anna M. Thompson
Fine Arts Museum / University Museum - 1963
Contemporary coll of crafts, drawings, paintings, prints and sculpture, East Asian and African colls 47103

Saint Joseph MO

Albrecht-Kemper Museum of Art, 2818 Frederick Av, Saint Joseph, MO 64506 - T: (816) 233-7003, Fax: (816) 233-3413, E-mail: akma@albrecht-kemper.org, Internet: www.albrecht-kemper.org. Dir.: Terry Oldham
Fine Arts Museum - 1914
Paintings, drawings, prints, sculpture 47104

Glore Psychiatric Museum, 3406 Frederick Av, Saint Joseph, MO 64506 - T: (816) 387-2300, Fax: (816) 387-2170, E-mail: glore_museum@mail.dmh.state.mo.us, Internet: www.gloremuseum.org. C.E.O.: Scott Clark
Special Museum - 1967 47105

Jesse James Home Museum, 12 and Penn Sts, Saint Joseph, MO 64502 - T: (816) 232-8206, Fax: (816) 232-3717, E-mail: patee@mail.ponyexpress.net, Internet: www.st.joseph.net/ponyexpress. Dir.: Gary Chilcote, Cur.: Doug Chilcote
Historic Site / Historical Museum - 1939
1879 house where Jesse James was killed in 1882 47106

Patee House Museum, 1202 Penn St, Saint Joseph, MO 64502 - T: (816) 232-8206, Fax: (816) 232-8206, E-mail: patee@mail.ponyexpress.net, Internet: www.stjoseph.net/ponyexpress. Dir.: Gary Chilcote, Cur.: Doug Chilcote
Science&Tech Museum / Historical Museum / Fine Arts Museum - 1964
Pony Express headquarters, trains, cars, fire trucks, antique town 47107

Pony Express Museum, 914 Penn St, Saint Joseph, MO 64503 - T: (816) 279-5059, (800) 530-5940, Fax: (816) 233-9370, Internet: www.ponyexpress.org. Pres.: Richard N. DeShon, Dir.: F. Burns McAndrew
Local Museum - 1959 47108

Saint Joseph Museum, 11th and Charles Sts, Saint Joseph, MO 64502 - T: (816) 232-8471, Fax: (816) 232-8482, E-mail: sjm@stjosephmuseum.org, Internet: www.stjosephmuseum.org. C.E.O. & Dir.: Alberto C. Meloni, Cur.: Carol Wills, Jackie Lewin (History), Marilyn S. Taylor (Ethnology), Robert L. Sipes (Exhibits)
Historical Museum / Ethnology Museum / Natural History Museum - 1927
American Indian art,anthropology, archaeology, ethnology, costumes, Eskimo art, native American art - library 47109

Saint Leonard MD

Jefferson Patterson Museum, 10515 Mackall Rd, Saint Leonard, MD 20685 - T: (410) 586-8500, Fax: (410) 586-0080, E-mail: jppm@dhcd.state.md.us, Internet: www.jefpat.org. Pres.: Patrick W. Furey, Dir.: Michael A. Smolek
Local Museum - 1983
Cultural heritage of people living in the Chesapeake Bay region, archaeology, agriculture, local history 47110

Saint Louis MO

Atrium Gallery, 7638 Forsyth Blvd, Saint Louis, MO 63105 - T: (314) 726-1066, Fax: (314) 726-5444, E-mail: atrium@earthlink.net, Internet: www.atriumgallery.net. Dir.: Carolyn P. Miles
Public Gallery / Folklore Museum - 1986 47111

Boatmen's National Bank Art Collection, 1 Boatmen's Plaza, 800 Market St, Saint Louis, MO 63101 - T: (888) 279-3121
Fine Arts Museum
Political series by Caleb Bingham, transportation series by Oscar E. Berninghause, watercolours 47112

Campbell House Museum, 1508 Locust St, Saint Louis, MO 63103 - T: (314) 421-0325, Fax: (314) 421-0113, E-mail: campbellhousemuseum@worldnet.att.net, Internet: stlouis.missouri.org/501c/chm. Pres.: Janice K. Broderick, C.E.O.: Jeffrey L. Huntington
Decorative Arts Museum / Historical Museum - 1943 47113

Chatillon-DeMenil Mansion, 3352 DeMenil Pl, Saint Louis, MO 63118 - T: (314) 771-5828, Fax: (314) 771-3475, E-mail: demenil@stlouis.missouri.org. Pres.: William Hart, Dir.: Graff Marcia
Local Museum - 1965 47114

City Museum, 701 N 15th St, Saint Louis, MO 63103 - T: (314) 231-2489 ext 110, Fax: (314) 231-1009, E-mail: citymsm@swbell.net, Internet: www.citymuseum.org. C.E.O.: Pat Rich
Local Museum - 1997
Forest, architectural ornaments, glass blowers, weavers, potters and painters 47115

Concordia Historical Institute Museum, 801 DeMun Av, Saint Louis, MO 63105 - T: (314) 505-7900, Fax: (314) 505-7901, E-mail: chi@chi.lcms.org, Internet: chi.lcms.org. Dir.: Martin R. Noland, Ass. Dir.: Mark A. Loest
Religious Arts Museum - 1927
History of American Lutheranism 47116

Contemporary Art Museum of Saint Louis, Forum for Contemporary Art, 3540 Washington Av, Saint Louis, MO 63103 - T: (314) 535-4660, Fax: (314) 535-1226, E-mail: adam.fca@primary.net, Internet: www.forumart.org. Dir.: Elizabeth Wright Millard, Cur.: Mel Watkin
Fine Arts Museum - 1980
Photographs, paintings 47117

Craft Alliance Gallery, 6640 Delmar Blvd, Saint Louis, MO 63130 - T: (314) 725-1177, Fax: (314) 725-2068, E-mail: info@craftalliance.org, Internet: www.craftalliance.org. Dir.: Schuyler Gott Andrews
Fine Arts Museum / Decorative Arts Museum - 1962 47118

The Dinosaur Museum, Science Center, Saint Louis, MO 63110 - T: (314) 289-4400
Natural History Museum - 1991 47119

Eugene Field House and Saint Louis Toy Museum, 634 S Broadway, Saint Louis, MO 63102 - T: (314) 421-4689, Fax: (314) 588-9328, E-mail: efhouse@swbell.org. Pres.: William Piper, Dir.: Frances Kerber Walrond
Local Museum / Decorative Arts Museum - 1936 47120

Gallery 210, University of Missouri Saint Louis, 210 Lucas Hall, Saint Louis, MO 63121 - T: (314) 516-5000, Fax: (314) 516-5816. Dir.: Terry Suhre
Fine Arts Museum - 1972
Contemporary art 47121

General Daniel Bissell House, 10225 Bellefontaine Rd, Saint Louis, MO 63137 - T: (314) 868-0973, 554-5790, Fax: (314) 868-8435, E-mail: jd_magurany@stlouisco.com, Internet: www.st-louiscountyparks.com. Dir.: J.D. Magurany, Cur.: Marc Kollbaum
Historic Site - 1960
Historic house 47122

International Bowling Museum and Hall of Fame, 111 Stadium Plaza, Saint Louis, MO 63102 - T: (314) 231-6340, Fax: (314) 231-4054, E-mail: hofm@bowlingmuseum.com, Internet: www.bowlingmuseum.com. Exec. Dir.: Gerald W. Baltz
Special Museum - 1977 47123

Jefferson Barracks, 533 Grant Rd, Saint Louis, MO 63125-4121 - T: (314) 544-5714, 544-5790, Fax: (314) 638-5009, E-mail: jd_magurany@stlouisco.com, Internet: www.st-louiscountyparks.comw/jb.html. Dir.: J.D. Magurany, Cur.: Marc Kollbaum
Military Museum / Historic Site - 1826
Military post - Gen. Daniel Bissell house, Fort Belle 47124

Jefferson National Expansion Memorial, 11 N Fourth St, Saint Louis, MO 63102 - T: (314) 655-1600, Fax: (314) 655-1639, E-mail: jeff_superintendent@nps.gov, Internet: www.nps.gov/jeff. Dir.: David Grove, Cur.: Kathryn Thomas
Historical Museum - 1935 47125

Laumeier Sculpture Park and Museum, 12580 Rott Rd, Saint Louis, MO 63127 - T: (314) 821-1209, Fax: (314) 821-1248, E-mail: info@laumeier.org, Internet: www.laumeier.org. Dir.: Glen P. Gentele, Cur.: Clara Collins Coleman
Fine Arts Museum - 1976
Contemporary sculpture coll 47126

Magic House-Saint Louis Children's Museum, 516 S Kirkwood Rd, Saint Louis, MO 63122 - T: (314) 822-8900, Fax: (314) 822-8930, Internet: www.magichouse.com. Pres.: Elizabeth Fitzgerald, Chairman: Jerry Kent
Special Museum - 1979 47127

Missouri Historical Society Museum, Lindell and De Baliviere, Saint Louis, MO 63112-0040 - T: (314) 746-4599, Fax: (314) 454-3162, E-mail: info@mohistory.org, Internet: www.mohistory.org. Pres.: Dr. Robert R. Archibald, Dir.: Myron Freedman (Exhibition), Martha Clevenger (Collections and Conservation), Eric Sandweiss (Research)
Historical Museum - 1866 47128

Morton J. May Foundation Gallery, Maryville University, 13550 Conway Rd, Saint Louis, MO 63141 - T: (314) 529-9300, 529-9381, Fax: (314) 529-9940, E-mail: nrice@maryville.edu. Dir.: Nancy N. Rice
Fine Arts Museum / University Museum
American paintings 47129

Museum of Contemporary Religious Art, c/o Saint Louis University, 3700 John E Connelly Pedestrian Mall, Saint Louis, MO 63108 - T: (314) 977-7170, Fax: (314) 977-2999, E-mail: mocra@slu.edu, Internet: mocra.slu.edu. Cur.: Terrence E. Dempsey
Fine Arts Museum / Religious Arts Museum / University Museum - 1993
Art from all religious traditions 47130

Museum of the Dog, 1721 S Mason Rd, Saint Louis, MO 63131 - T: (314) 821-3647, Fax: (314) 821-7381, E-mail: dogarts@aol.com. Exec. Dir.: Barbara Jedda McNab
Fine Arts Museum - 1981
Fine arts 47131

Museum of Transportation, 3015 Barrett Station Rd, Saint Louis, MO 63122 - T: (314) 965-8007, Fax: (314) 965-0242, Internet: www.museumoftransport.org. Pres.: Lee Rottmann, Dir.: James Worton
Science&Tech Museum - 1944 47132

Old Cathedral Museum, 209 Walnut, Saint Louis, MO 63102 - T: (314) 231-3251, Fax: (314) 231-4280, Internet: www.catholic-forum.com/stlouisking/. C.E.O.: Bernard Sandheinrich
Religious Arts Museum - 1970 47133

Saint Louis Art Museum, 1 Fine Arts Dr, Forest Park, Saint Louis, MO 63110-1380 - T: (314) 721-0067, Fax: (314) 721-6172, E-mail: infotech@slam.org, Internet: www.slam.org. Dir.: Brent Benjamin, Cur.: Cornelia Homburg (Modern Art), Steven D. Owyoung (Asian Art), Cara McCarty (Decorative and Design Arts), John Nunley (Arts of Africa, Oceania and the Americas), Judith Mann (Early European Art), Sid Goldstein (Ancient, Islamic), Franesca Consagre (Prints, Photographs)
Fine Arts Museum - 1906
Prints, drawings, photographs, Oceanian, African, Pre-Columbian and American Indian objects, paintings, sculpture, European decorative art, Chinese bronzes and porcelain - Richardson Memorial Library 47134

Saint Louis Artists' Guild Museum, 2 Oak Knoll Park, Saint Louis, MO 63105 - T: (314) 727-6266, Fax: (314) 727-9190, Internet: www.stlouisartistsguild.org. Pres.: Joanne Stremsterfer, C.E.O.: Anne Murphy
Fine Arts Museum - 1886 47135

Saint Louis Science Center Museum, 5050 Oakland Av, Saint Louis, MO 63110 - T: (314) 289-4400, Fax: (314) 289-4420, E-mail: gjasper@slsc.org, Internet: www.slc.org. Pres.: Douglas R. King
Public Gallery / Science&Tech Museum - 1959 47136

Samuel Cupples House, c/o Saint Louis University, 221 N Grand Blvd, Saint Louis, MO 63103 - T: (314) 977-3575, Fax: (314) 977-3581, E-mail: ambrosep2@slu.edu, Internet: www.slu.edu/the-arts/cupples. Exec. Dir.: Pamela E. Ambrose
Fine Arts Museum / University Museum - 1977
American impressionist paintings, Italian and northern renaissance paintings, American sculpture, American and European art glass and furniture 47137

Soldiers' Memorial Military Museum, 1315 Chestnut St, Saint Louis, MO 63103 - T: (314) 622-4550, Fax: (314) 622-4237. Head: Ralph D. Wiechert
Military Museum - 1938 47138

Trova Foundation, 8112 Maryland Av, Saint Louis, MO 63105 - T: (314) 727-2444, Fax: (314) 727-6084. Dir.: Clifford Samuels, Pres.: Philip Samuels
Fine Arts Museum - 1988
Contemporary painting, collage, drawing and sculpture 47139

Washington University Gallery of Art, Forsyth and Skinker Blvds, Saint Louis, MO 63130 - T: (314) 935-5490, Fax: (314) 935-7282, E-mail: Stephanie_Parrish@aismail.wustl.edu, Internet: galleryofart.wustl.edu. Dir.: Dr. Mark S. Weil, Cur.: Sabine Eckmann
Fine Arts Museum / University Museum - 1881
Modern artists incl Miro, Ernst, Picasso, Leger, Moore, old masters, 19th-20th c paintings, sculpture, drawings, prints 47140

Saint Marks FL

San Marcos de Apalache Historic State Park, 148 Old Fort Rd, Saint Marks, FL 32355-0027 - T: (850) 922-6007, Fax: (850) 488-0366, E-mail: sanmarcos@nettally.com, Internet: www.floridastateparks.org. Dir.: Wendy Spencer
Historical Museum / Historic Site - 1964
Second-oldest fortification in Florida 47141

Saint Martinville LA

Longfellow-Evangeline State Historic Site, 1200 N Main St, Saint Martinville, LA 70582 - T: (800) 677-2900, (337) 394-3754, Fax: (337) 394-3553, E-mail: longfellow@crt.state.la.us, Internet: www.lastateparks.com. Cur.: Suzanna Laviolette
Decorative Arts Museum / Fine Arts Museum - 1934
Portraits, textile arts, local craft and folk art, furniture, antiques, religious art, wood carvings, Acadian art 47142

Oliver House Museum, 1200 N Main St, Saint Martinville, LA 70582 - T: (800) 677-2900, Fax: (318) 394-3754, E-mail: longfellow@crt.state.la.usa. Cur.: Suzanna Laviolette
Historical Museum - 1931
History, old plantation house of French and Carribean architecture 47143

Saint Marys OH

Auglaize County Historical Society Museum, 223 S Main St, Saint Marys, OH 45885
Local Museum - 1963
Fort St Marys, Fort Amanda and Fort Barbee artifacts, Indian artifacts, Miami Erie Canal, oil wells, early industry, Civil War 47144

Saint Marys PA

Saint Marys and Benzinger Township Museum, 99 Erie Av, Saint Marys, PA 15857 - T: (814) 834-6525. Dir.: Richard Dornisch, Cur.: Alice Beimel
Local Museum - 1960
Local hist 47145

Saint Mary's City MD

Dwight Frederick Boyden Gallery, Saint Mary's College of Maryland, Montgomery Hall, 18952 Fisher Ln, Saint Mary's City, MD 20686 - T: (240) 895-4246, Fax: (301) 862-0958, E-mail: smglasser@smcm.edu, Internet: www.smcm.edu/academics/gallery/. Dir.: Casey Page
Fine Arts Museum / University Museum - 1839
Art gallery 47146

Historic Saint Mary's City, Rte. 5, Saint Mary's City, MD 20686 - T: (240) 895-4960, Fax: (301) 862-0968, E-mail: hsmc@smcm.edu, Internet: www.stmaryscity.org. C.E.O.: Martin E. Sullivan
Special Museum - 1966
Outdoor living history 47147

Saint Matthews SC

Calhoun County Museum, 303 Butler St, Saint Matthews, SC 29135 - T: (803) 874-3964, Fax: (803) 874-4790, E-mail: calmus@oburg.net. Dir.: Debbie U. Roland
Local Museum - 1954
Local hist 47148

Saint Michaels MD

Chesapeake Bay Maritime Museum, Navy Point, Saint Michaels, MD 21663 - T: (410) 745-2916, Fax: (410) 745-6088, E-mail: letters@cbmm.org, Internet: www.cbmm.org. Pres.: John R. Valliant, Cur.: Ronald E. Lesher
Historical Museum - 1965
Regional maritime history 47149

Saint Paul MN

3M Art Collection, 3M Center, Bldg 225-1S-01, Saint Paul, MN 55144-1000 - T: (651) 733-1110, Fax: (651) 737-4555. Cur.: Charles Thames
Fine Arts Museum - 1974 47150

Alexander Ramsey House, 265 S Exchange St, Saint Paul, MN 55102 - T: (612) 296-8760, Fax: (612) 296-0100, E-mail: ramseyhouse@mnhs.org, Internet: www.mnhs.org. Dir.: Craig Johnson
Local Museum / Decorative Arts Museum - 1964
Late 19th-century upper class Victorian mansion 47151

American Museum of Asmat Art, 3510 Vivian Av, Saint Paul, MN 55126-3852 - T: (651) 287-1132, Fax: (651) 287-1130, E-mail: museum@crosier.org, Internet: www.asmat.org. Dir.: Mary E. Braun
Fine Arts Museum / Ethnology Museum - 1974
Ethnological art 47152

College of Visual Arts and Gallery, 344 Summit Av, Saint Paul, MN 55102 - T: (651) 290-9379, Fax: (651) 224-8854, E-mail: gallery@cva.edu, Internet: www.cva.edu. Dir.: Colleen Mullins
Public Gallery 47153

The Goldstein Museum of Design, c/o University of Minnesota, 244 McNeal Hall, 1985 Buford Av, Saint Paul, MN 55108-6236 - T: (612) 624-7434, Fax: (612) 624-2750, E-mail: dhawebcoordinator@tlcmail.che.umn.edu, Internet: goldstein.che.umn.edu. Dir.: Dr. Lindsay Shen, Cur.: Dr. Marilyn DeLong (Costumes)
Decorative Arts Museum / University Museum - 1976
Historic costumes, 20th c designer garments, decorative arts, furniture, glass, metal, ceramics, textiles 47154

Hamline University Galleries, Dept of Art, Hamline University, 1536 Hewitt Av, Saint Paul, MN 55104 - T: (651) 523-2386, Fax: (651) 523-3066, E-mail: llasansky@gw.hamline.edu, Internet: www.hamline.edu/depts/art. Dir.: Leonardo Lasansky
Fine Arts Museum / University Museum - 1850
Modern works 47155

Historic Fort Snelling, Fort Snelling History Center, Saint Paul, MN 55111 - T: (612) 726-1171, Fax: (612) 725-2429, E-mail: ftsnelling@mnhs.org, Internet: www.mnhs.org/places/sites/hfs
Military Museum / Open Air Museum - 1970
Military hist 47156

James J. Hill House, 240 Summit Av, Saint Paul, MN 55102 - T: (651) 296-8205, Fax: (651) 297-5655, E-mail: hillhouse@mnhs.org, Internet: www.mnhs.org. Head: Craig Johnson
Local Museum - 1978
Historic house 47157

Julian H. Sleeper House, 66 Saint Albans St, S, Saint Paul, MN 55105 - T: (651) 225-1505. C.E.O.: Dr. Seth C. Hawkins
Decorative Arts Museum - 1993
Eastlake-Vernacular House, moved to present site in 1911, President Garfield memorabilia, furniture, pottery 47158

Macalester College Art Gallery, 1600 Grand Av, Saint Paul, MN 55105 - T: (651) 696-6416, Fax: (651) 696-6266, E-mail: gallery@macalester.edu, Internet: www.macalester.edu. Cur.: Devin A. Colman
Fine Arts Museum / Decorative Arts Museum / University Museum - 1964
Regional artists, Asian and British ceramics, African art 47159

Minnesota Air National Guard Exhibition, 670 General Miller Dr, Saint Paul, MN 55111-0598 - T: (612) 713-2523, Fax: (612) 713-2525, E-mail: msp04332@isd.net, Internet: www.mnangmuseum.org. Dir.: Tom Wier
Historical Museum / Science&Tech Museum - 1980
Aircraft, hist of the Minnesota National Guard 47160

Minnesota Children's Museum, 10 W Seventh St, Saint Paul, MN 55102 - T: (651) 225-6001, Fax: (651) 225-6006, E-mail: mcm@mcm.org, Internet: www.mcm.org. Pres.: Carleen Rhodes
Ethnology Museum - 1979 47161

Minnesota Historical Society Museum, 345 Kellogg Blvd W, Saint Paul, MN 55102-1906 - T: (651) 296-6126, (800) 657-3773, Fax: (651) 297-3343, E-mail: fname./name@mnhs.org, Internet: www.mnhs.org. Dir.: Nina M. Archabal, Ass. Dir.: Maureen Otwell
Historical Museum / Historic Site - 1849 47162

Minnesota Museum of American Art, 505 Landmark Center, 75 W Fifth St, Saint Paul, MN 55102-1486 - T: (651) 292-4355, Fax: (651) 292-4340, Internet: www.mmaa.org. Dir.: Bruce Lilly, Cur.: Lin Nelson-Mayson
Fine Arts Museum - 1927
American art, Paul Manship, contemporary art of Upper Midwest, 19th-20th c and native art 47163

Minnesota Transportation Museum, 190 E Pennsylvania Av, Saint Paul, MN 55101-4319 - T: (651) 228-0263, Fax: (651) 228-9412, E-mail: exdir@mtmuseum.org, Internet: www.mtmuseum.org
Science&Tech Museum - 1962
Streetcar, locomotive, truck, Mesaba Electric Railway 47164

Paul Whitney Larson Gallery, 2017 Buford, Saint Paul, MN 55108 - T: (612) 625-0214, Fax: (612) 624-8749, E-mail: hanc0005@gold.tc.umn.edu, Internet: www.spsc.umn.edu/vac/prespective.html
Fine Arts Museum / University Museum - 1979
Contemporary visual arts 47165

Science Museum of Minnesota, 120 Kellogg Blvd W, Saint Paul, MN 55102-1208 - T: (612) 221-9444, Fax: (612) 221-4777, E-mail: postmaster@sci.mus.mn.us, Internet: www.sci.mus.mn.us. Dir.: James L. Peterson, Cur.: Bruce R. Erickson (Paleontology), Dr. Orrin Shane (Anthropology for Archaeology)
Local Museum / Natural History Museum / Science&Tech Museum - 1907 47166

Women's Art Registry of Minnesota Gallery, 550 Rice St, Saint Paul, MN 55103 - T: (651) 292-1188. Dir.: Vicky MacNabb
Fine Arts Museum - 1975 47167

Saint Paul OR

Robert Newell House, DAR Museum, 8089 Champoeg Rd NE, Saint Paul, OR 97137 - T: (503) 266-3944, E-mail: DARcabin@stpaultel.com, Internet: www.ohwy.com/or/r/rnewellhm.htm
Local Museum / Historic Site - 1959 47168

Saint Peter MN

E. St. Julien Cox House, 500 S Washington, Saint Peter, MN 56082 - T: (507) 931-2160, Fax: (507) 931-0172, E-mail: nicolletco@aol.com, Internet: www.nchs.st-peter.mn.us/. Dir.: Mark T. Morrison
Historical Museum - 1971 47169

Treaty Site History Center, 1851 N Minnesota Av, Saint Peter, MN 56082 - T: (507) 931-2160, Fax: (507) 931-0172, E-mail: mmorriso@mnic.net, Internet: www.nchs.st_peter.mn.us/. Dir.: Mark Morris
Historical Museum - 1928 47170

Saint Petersburg FL

Florida Holocaust Museum, 55 Fifth St, Saint Petersburg, FL 33701 - T: (813) 820-0100 ext 221, Fax: (813) 821-8435, E-mail: ldwasser@flholocaustmuseum.org, Internet: www.flholocaustmuseum.org. Dir.: Larry Wasser, Cur.: Stephen M. Goldman
Historical Museum - 1989
History 47171

Florida International Museum, 100 Second St N, Saint Petersburg, FL 33701 - T: (727) 822-3693, 821-1448, Fax: (727) 898-0248, E-mail: floridamuseum@mindspring.com, Internet: www.floridamuseum.org. Pres.: Richard Johnston, Cur.: Vera Espinola
Historical Museum - 1994 47172

Great Explorations, The Pier, 800 2nd Av NE, Saint Petersburg, FL 33701 - T: (727) 821-8992, Fax: (727) 823-7287, E-mail: greatest@greatexplorations.com, Internet: www.greatexplorations.org. Exec. Dir.: Robert B. Patterson
Science&Tech Museum - 1987 47173

Museum of Fine Arts Saint Petersburg, Florida, 255 Beach Dr, NE, Saint Petersburg, FL 33701 - T: (727) 896-2667, Fax: (727) 894-4638, E-mail: jschloder@fine-arts.org, Internet: www.fine-arts.org. Dir.: John E. Schloter, Chief Cur.: Jennifer Hardin
Fine Arts Museum - 1961
Art 47174

Saint Petersburg Museum of History, 335 Second Av NE, Saint Petersburg, FL 33701 - T: (727) 894-1052, Fax: (727) 823-7276, E-mail: mathias@museumofhistoryonline.org, Internet: www.museumofhistoryonline.org. Dir.: Mathias Bergendahl, Cur.: Amy Nolan
Local Museum - 1920
Local history 47175

Salvador Dali Museum, 1000 Third St S, Saint Petersburg, FL 33701 - T: (813) 823-3767, Fax: (813) 894-6068, E-mail: info@salvadordalimuseum.org, Internet: www.salvadordalimuseum.org. Dir.: Marshall Rousseau, Cur.: Joan Kropf, William Jeffet
Fine Arts Museum - 1954 47176

Science Center of Pinellas County, 7701 22nd Av N, Saint Petersburg, FL 33710 - T: (727) 384-0027, Fax: (727) 343-5729, E-mail: scenter5@tampabay.rr.com, Internet: sciencecenterofpinellas.org
Natural History Museum - 1959
Anatomy, anthropology, archaeology, astronomy, botany, entomology, geology, herpetology, marine, medicine, natural hist, paleontology, zoology - aquarium 47177

Saint Simons Island GA

The Arthur J. Moore Methodist Museum, Arthur Moore Dr, Saint Simons Island, GA 31522 - T: (912) 638-4050, Fax: (912) 634-0642, E-mail: methmuse@darientel.net. Dir.: Mary L. Vice
Religious Arts Museum - 1965
Religious, nr Oglethorpe, John and Charles Wesley's activities in 1736 47178

Coastal Center for the Arts, 2012 Demere Rd, Saint Simons Island, GA 31522 - T: (912) 634-0404, Fax: (912) 634-0404, E-mail: coastalart@thebest.net, Internet: www.glynncounty.com/cca. Dir.: Mittie B. Hendrix
Fine Arts Museum - 1947 47179

Fort Frederica, Rte 9, Box 286c, Saint Simons Island, GA 31522 - T: (912) 638-3639, Fax: (912) 638-3639, E-mail: mike_tennent@nps.gov, Internet: www.nps.gov. Head: Mike Tennent
Historical Museum - 1936 47180

The Glynn Art Association, 319 Mallery St, Saint Simons Island, GA 31522 - T: (912) 638-8770, Fax: (912) 634-2787, E-mail: glynnart@earthlink.net, Internet: www.glynnart.org. Dir.: Pat Weaver
Fine Arts Museum - 1948
Primitive painting, pottery 47181

Museum of Coastal History → Saint Simons Island Lighthouse Museum

Saint Simons Island Lighthouse Museum, 101 12th St, Saint Simons Island, GA 31522-0636 - T: (912) 638-4666, Fax: (912) 638-6609, E-mail: ssi1872@bellsouth.net, Internet: www.saintsimonslighthouse.org. Exec. Dir.: Patricia A. Morris
Local Museum / Historical Museum - 1965
History, civil war 47182

Sainte Genevieve MO

Bolduc House Museum, 125 S Main St, Sainte Genevieve, MO 63670 - T: (573) 883-3105, Fax: (573) 883-3359, E-mail: lstange@brick.net. Dir.: Lorraine Stange
Local Museum - 1770 47183

Felix Valle State Historic Site, 198 Merchant St, Sainte Genevieve, MO 63670 - T: (573) 883-7102, Fax: (573) 883-9630, E-mail: dspvalle@mail.dnr.state.mo.us. Head: James Baker
Historic Site - 1970 47184

Sainte Genevieve Museum, Merchant and DuBourg Sts, Sainte Genevieve, MO 63670 - T: (573) 883-3461. Pres.: James Baker, Dir.: Ruby A. Stephens
Local Museum - 1935 47185

Salado TX

Central Texas Area Museum, 1 Main St, Salado, TX 76571 - T: (254) 947) 5232, Fax: (254) 947-5232
Local Museum - 1958
Genealogy, hist, arts and crafts, Scottish folklore, Tonkawa artifacts, antiques 47186

Salamanca NY

Salamanca Rail Museum, 170 Main St, Salamanca, NY 14779-1574 - T: (716) 945-3133, Fax: (716) 945-2034. Cur.: Gerald J. Fordham
Science&Tech Museum - 1980
Telegraph keys, railroad memorabilia, train cars 47187

Seneca-Iroquois National Museum, 794-814 Broad St, Allegany Indian Reservation, Salamanca, NY 14779 - T: (716) 945-1738, Fax: (716) 945-1760, E-mail: senirogm@localnet.com, Internet: www.senecamuseum.org. Dir.: Michele Dean Stock
Ethnology Museum - 1977 47188

Salem IN

Stevens Museum, 307 E Market St, Salem, IN 47167 - T: (812) 883-6495. Pres.: Willie Harlen
Local Museum / Open Air Museum - 1897
Local history, 1824 John Hay birthplace, pionner village - library 47189

Salem MA

Andrew-Safford House, Peabody Essex Museum, 13 Washington Sq W, Salem, MA 01970 - T: (978) 745-9500, E-mail: pem@pem.org, Internet: www.pem.org. Cur.: Dean Lahikainen
Folklore Museum
Early 19th c urban life 47190

Cotting-Smith-Assembly-House, Peabody Essex Museum, Brown St, Salem, MA 01970 - T: (978) 744-2231, Fax: (978) 744-0036, E-mail: pem@pem.org, Internet: www.pem.org. Exec. Dir.: Dan L. Monroe
Historical Museum
Hall for social assemblies 47191

Crowninshield-Bentley House, Peabody Essex Museum, 126 Essex St, Salem, MA 01970 - T: (978) 745-9500, E-mail: pem@pem.org, Internet: www.pem.org. Exec. Dir.: Dan L. Munroe
Decorative Arts Museum
Interior, architecture and furnishing 18th c 47192

Derby-Beebe Summer House, Peabody Essex Museum, 132 Essex St, Salem, MA 01970 - T: (978) 745-9500, E-mail: pem@pem.org, Internet: www.pem.org. Exec. Dir.: Dan L. Monroe
Historical Museum 47193

Gardner-Pingree House, Peabody Essex Museum, 128 Essex St, Salem, MA 01970 - T: (978) 745-9500, E-mail: pem@pem.org, Internet: www.pem.org. Exec. Dir.: Dan L. Monroe
Historical Museum
Federal style of Salem 47194

The House of the Seven Gables, 54 Turner St, Salem, MA 01970 - T: (978) 744-0991, Fax: (978) 741-4350, E-mail: postmaster@7gables.org, Internet: www.7gables.org. Exec. Dir.: Stanley G. Burchfield
Historical Museum / Open Air Museum - 1910
17th, 18th and 19th-century architecture, Nathaniel Hawthorne 47195

John Ward House, Peabody Essex Museum, 132 Essex St, Salem, MA 01970 - T: (978) 745-9500, E-mail: pem@pem.org, Internet: www.pem.org. Exec. Dir.: Dan L. Monroe
Historical Museum 47196

Lyle-Tapley Shoe Shop and Vaughn Doll House, Peabody Essex Museum, 132 Essex St, Salem, MA 01970 - T: (978) 745-9500, E-mail: pem@pem.org, Internet: www.pem.org. Exec. Dir.: Dan L. Monroe
Historical Museum 47197

Peabody Essex Museum, E India Sq, Salem, MA 01970 - T: (800) 745-7550, Fax: (978) 744-6776, E-mail: pem@pem.org, Internet: www.pem.org. Dir.: Dan L. Monroe, Cur.: Dr. Susan Bean (South Asian and Korean Art), John Grimes (Native American Art, African Art and Culture), William Sargent (Asian Export Art), Jane Winchell (Natural History), Dean Lahikainen (American Decorative Arts), Paula Richter (Textiles and Costumes), Dr. Daniel Finamore (Maritime Arts and History), Kimberly Alexander (Architecture), Andrew Maske (Japanese Art), Nancy Berliner (Chinese Art), Clark Worswick (Photographic Collections)
Fine Arts Museum / Local Museum - 1799
Asian, Oceanic, African arts and cultures, native American art and archaeology, maritime arts and history, architecture, decorative arts, natural history - library 47198

Peirce-Nichols House, Peabody Essex Museum, 80 Federal St, Salem, MA 01970 - T: (978) 745-9500, E-mail: pem@pem.org, Internet: www.pem.org. Cur.: Robert Saarnio
Historical Museum 47199

Salem 1630 Pioneer Village, Forest River Park, West Av, Salem, MA 01970 - T: (978) 745-0525, 744-0991, Fax: (978) 741-4350, E-mail: wwalker@7gables.org, Internet: www.7gables.org. Exec. Dir.: Stanley G. Burchfield, Dir.: William Waker
Local Museum / Open Air Museum - 1930
Reproduction of a fishing village 47200

Salem Maritime National Historic Site, 174 Derby St, Salem, MA 01970 - T: (978) 740-1680, Fax: (978) 740-1685, Internet: www.nps.gov/sama. Head: Steve Kesselman, Cur.: David Kayser, Sc. Staff: John Frayler (History)
Historic Site - 1937
Maritime, commerce and World trade 47201

Salem Witch Museum, 19-1/2 Washington Sq N, Salem, MA 01970 - T: (978) 744-1692, Fax: (978) 745-4414, E-mail: facts@salemwitchmuseum.com, Internet: www.salemwitchmuseum.com. Dir.: Patricia MacLeod, C.E.O.: Bruce P. Michaud
Historical Museum - 1971
History 47202

The Stephen Phillips Memorial House, 34 Chestnut St, Salem, MA 01970 - T: (978) 744-0440, Fax: (978) 740-1086, E-mail: info@phillipsmuseum.org, Internet: www.phillipsmuseum.org
Decorative Arts Museum - 1973
Travels, African wood carvings, pottery, porcelain, oriental carpets, cars and carriages 47203

Salem NJ

Salem County Historical Society Museum, 79-83 Market St, Salem, NJ 08079 - T: (856) 935-5004, Fax: (856) 935-0728, E-mail: schs@snip.net, Internet: www.salemcounty.com/schs. Pres.: Ronald E. Magill, Dir./Cur.: James F. Turk
Local Museum - 1884 47204

Salem OH

Salem Historical Society Museum, 208 S Broadway Av, Salem, OH 44460 - T: (330) 337-8514, E-mail: historicalsociety@salemohio.com, Internet: www.salemohio.com/historicalsociety/. Pres.: George W.S. Hays, Dir.: David C. Stratton
Local Museum - 1971 47205

Salem OR

A.C. Gilbert's Discovery Village, 116 Marion St NE, Salem, OR 97301-3437 - T: (503) 371-3631, Fax: (503) 316-3485, E-mail: info@acgilbert.org, Internet: www.acgilbert.org. Exec. Dir.: Pamela Vorachek
Special Museum - 1987 47206

Bush House Museum and Bush Barn Art Center, 600 Mission St SE, Salem, OR 97302 - T: (503) 581-2228, Fax: (503) 371-3342, Internet: www.salemart.org. Dir.: Julie Larson, Cur.: Jenny Hagloch, Paul Porter
Fine Arts Museum / Local Museum - 1919 47207

The Gilbert House Children's Museum → A.C. Gilbert's Discovery Village

Hallie Ford Museum of Art, c/o Willamette University, 700 State St, Salem, OR 97301 - T: (503) 370-6855, Fax: (503) 375-5458, E-mail: museum-art@willamette.edu, Internet: www.willamette.edu/museum_of_art. Dir.: John Olbrantz
Fine Arts Museum / University Museum - 1970 47208

Marion County Historical Society Museum, 260 12th St SE, Salem, OR 97301-4101 - T: (503) 364-2128, Fax: (503) 391-5356, E-mail: mchs@open.org, Internet: www.marionhistory.org. Exec. Dir.: Kyle R. Jansson
Local Museum - 1950 47209

Mission Mill Museum, 1313 Mill St, Salem, OR 97301 - T: (503) 585-7012, Fax: (503) 588-9902, E-mail: missionm@teleport.com, Internet: www.missionmill.org. C.E.O.: Maureen Thomas
Local Museum - 1964
Local hist 47210

Salem VA

Salem Museum, 801 E Main St, Salem, VA 24153 - T: (540) 389-6760, E-mail: info@salemmuseum.org, Internet: www.salemmuseum.org. Pres.: Michael Maxey, Dir.: Mary Hill
Local Museum - 1992 47211

Salida CO

Salida Museum, 406 1/2 W Rainbow Blvd, Salida, CO 81201 - T: (719) 539-4602. Pres.: Judy Micklich
Local Museum - 1954
Local history, Indian artifacts, textiles, mining 47212

Salina KS

Salina Art Center, 242 S Santa Fe, Salina, KS 67402-0743 - T: (785) 827-1431, Fax: (785) 827-0686, E-mail: info@salinaartcenter.org, Internet: www.salinaartcenter.org. Dir.: Wendy Moshier
Fine Arts Museum - 1978
Art 47213

Smoky Hill Museum, 211 W Iron Av, Salina, KS 67401 - T: (785) 309-5776, Fax: (785) 826-7414, E-mail: museum@salina.org, Internet: www.smokyhillmuseum.org. Dir.: Dee Harris, Cur.: Lisa Upshaw (Collection), Sc. Staff: Dorothy Boyle (Registration), Jenny Disney (Education), Susan Dame (Exhibition)
Historical Museum / Local Museum - 1983
History 47214

Salinas CA

Hartnell College Gallery, 156 Homestead Av, Salinas, CA 93901 - T: (831) 755-6700, Fax: (831) 759-6052, E-mail: gsmith@hartnell.cc.ca.us. Dir.: Gary T. Smith
Fine Arts Museum - 1959
Works on paper, Virginia Bacher Haichol artifact coll, Leslie Fenton Netsuke coll 47215

National Steinbeck Center, 1 Main St, Salinas, CA 93901 - T: (831) 796-3833, Fax: (831) 796-3828, E-mail: info@steinbeck.org, Internet: www.steinbeck.org. Dir.: Kim E. Greer
Local Museum / Special Museum / Agriculture Museum - 1983
Literature, local hist, agriculture 47216

Salisbury MD

Salisbury State University Galleries, 1101 Camden Av, Salisbury State University, Salisbury, MD 21801 - T: (410) 543-6271, 543-6000, Fax: (410) 548-3002, E-mail: kabasile@ssu.edu. Dir.: Kenneth A. Basile
Fine Arts Museum / University Museum - 1962
Art 47217

The Ward Museum of Wildfowl Art, Salisbury University, 909 S Schumaker Dr, Salisbury, MD 21804-8743 - T: (410) 742-4988, Fax: (410) 742-3107, E-mail: ward@wardmuseum.org, Internet: www.wardmuseum.org. Dir.: Kenneth A. Basile, Cur.: Dan Brown
Fine Arts Museum - 1976
Art 47218

Salisbury NC

Horizons Unlimited Supplementary Educational Center, 1636 Parkview Circle, Salisbury, NC 28144 - T: (704) 639-3004, Fax: (704) 639-3015, Internet: www.rss.k12.nc.us. Dir.: Cynthia B. Osterhus, Cur.: Lisa Wear (Natural Science), Susan R. Waller (Local and Regional History)
Local Museum / Natural History Museum - 1967 47219

Rowan Museum, 202 N Main St, Salisbury, NC 28144 - T: (704) 633-5946, Fax: (704) 633-9858, E-mail: rowanmuseum@vnet.net, Internet: www.tarheel.net/rowanmuseum. Pres.: Edward Norvell, Dir.: Kaye Brown Hirst
Historical Museum - 1953 47220

Waterworks Visual Arts Center, 123 E Liberty St, Salisbury, NC 28144 - T: (704) 636-1882, Fax: (704) 636-1895, E-mail: waterworks@salisbury.net, Internet: www.waterworks.org. Pres.: J. Foster Owen, Dir.: Denny H. Mecham
Fine Arts Museum / Public Gallery - 1959 47221

Salisbury NH

Salisbury Historical Society Museum, Salisbury Heights, Rte 4, Salisbury, NH 03268 - T: (603) 648-2774. Cur.: Wendy Barrett
Local Museum - 1966 47222

Sallisaw OK

Sequoyah Cabin, Rte 1, Box 141, Sallisaw, OK 74955 - T: (918) 775-2413, Fax: (918) 775-2413, E-mail: SeqCabin@ipa.net. Dir.: Dr. Bob Blackburn, Cur.: Stephen Foster
Local Museum - 1936 47223

Salmon ID

Lemhi County Historical Museum, 210 Main, Salmon, ID 83467 - T: (208) 756-3342, E-mail: lemhimuseum@salmoninternet.com, Internet: www.sacajaweahome.com. Pres.: Hope Benedict
Local Museum - 1963
Local history 47224

Salt Lake City UT

Atrium Gallery, 209 E 500 S, Salt Lake City, UT 84111 - T: (801) 524-8200
Public Gallery 47225

Beehive House, 67 E South Temple, Salt Lake City, UT 84111 - T: (801) 240-2681, Fax: (801) 240-2695. Dir.: McLea, Ass. Dir.: Carol Bitner
Religious Arts Museum - 1961
Historic house, Brigham Young's residence and office 47226

Chase Home Museum of Utah Folk Art, Liberty Park, Salt Lake City, UT 84102 - T: (801) 533-5760, 236-7555, Fax: (801) 533-4202, E-mail: cedison@utah.gov, Internet: www.utahfolkarts.org. Dir.: Carol Edison
Folklore Museum - 1986
Folk art 47227

The Children's Museum of Utah, 840 N 300 West, Salt Lake City, UT 84103 - T: (801) 328-3383, Fax: (801) 328-3384, E-mail: mail@childmuseum.org, Internet: www.childmuseum.org. Chm.: Brent Sloan
Special Museum - 1979 47228

Classic Cars Museum, 355 W 700 South St, Salt Lake City, UT 84101 - T: (801) 322-5509, Fax: (801) 582-6883, E-mail: classiccarsintl@hotmail.com, Internet: www.classiccarsmuseumsales.com. C.E.O.: Stacy Williams
Science&Tech Museum - 1975 47229

Daughters of Utah Pioneers Pioneer Memorial Museum, 300 N Main St, Salt Lake City, UT 84103-1699 - T: (801) 538-1050, Fax: (801) 538-1119, E-mail: dupmuseum@juno.com. Pres.: Mary A. Johnson, Cust.: Edith Menna
Local Museum / Historical Museum - 1901
Pioneer hist 47230

Museum of Church History and Art, 45 N West Temple St, Salt Lake City, UT 84150-3470 - T: (801) 240-2299, Fax: (801) 240-5342, Internet: www.ldchurch.org. Dir.: Glen M. Leonard, Sc. Staff: Robert O. Davis (Art), Donald L. Enders (History), Cur.: Marjorie D. Conder, Mark L. Staker, Cons.: James L. Raines, Blanche Miles
Religious Arts Museum - 1869
Religious art and hist 47231

Salt Lake Art Center, 20 S West Temple, Salt Lake City, UT 84101 - T: (801) 328-4201, Fax: (801) 322-4323, E-mail: allisons@slartcenter.org, Internet: www.slartcenter.org. Dir.: Ric Collier, Ass. Dir.: Allison South
Fine Arts Museum - 1931
Art 47232

This Is The Place Heritage Park, 2601 Sunnyside Av, Salt Lake City, UT 84108 - T: (801) 582-1847, Fax: (801) 583-1869, E-mail: johnz9mart@cs.com, Internet: www.thisistheplace.org. Dir.: Paul Williams, Cur.: Cathy Quinton
Open Air Museum - 1947
Local hist 47233

Utah Museum of Fine Arts, University of Utah, 410 Campus Center Dr, Salt Lake City, UT 84112 - T: (801) 581-7049, Fax: (801) 585-5198, Internet: www.utah.edu/umfa. Dir.: David L. Lee, PR: Isabelle Kalantzes
Fine Arts Museum / University Museum - 1951 47234

Utah Museum of Natural History, c/o University of Utah, 1390 E President's Cir, Salt Lake City, UT 84112 - T: (801) 581-6927, Fax: (801) 585-3684, E-mail: sgeorge@umnh.utah.edu, Internet: www.umnh.utat.edu. Dir.: Sarah B. George, Cur.: Eric Rickart (Vertebrates), Duncan Metcalfe (North American Archaeology), Michael Windham (Herbarium), Laurel Casjens (Collections)
Natural History Museum - 1963
Natural hist 47235

Utah State Historical Society Museum, 300 Rio Grande St, Salt Lake City, UT 84101-1182 - T: (801) 533-3500, Fax: (801) 533-3503, E-mail: ushs@history.state.ut.us, Internet: www.history.state.ut.us. Dir.: Wilson Martin, Cur.: Janet Smoak, Sc. Staff: Craig Fuller (History), Evelyn Seelinger (Archaeology)
Historical Museum - 1897
History 47236

Wheeler Historic Farm, 6351 S 900 E, Salt Lake City, UT 84121 - T: (801) 264-2241, Fax: (801) 264-2213, Internet: www.wheelerfarm.com. Dir.: Vickie Rodman, Cur.: Judson Callaway
Local Museum / Agriculture Museum - 1976
Historic farm representing the initial statehood period and typical of Utah agriculture in 1898 47237

San Andreas CA

Calaveras County Museum, 30 N Main St, San Andreas, CA 95249 - T: (209) 754-3910, Fax: (209) 754-1086. Pres.: David Studley
Local Museum - 1936
County hist, Indian artifacts, gold rush - archives 47238

San Angelo TX

Children's Art Museum, 36 E Twohig St, San Angelo, TX 76903 - T: (915) 659-4391, Fax: (915) 659-2407, E-mail: samfa@airmail.net, Internet: web2.airmail.net/samfa. Dir.: Howard Taylor
Fine Arts Museum / Special Museum - 1994 47239

Helen King Kendall Memorial Art Gallery, c/o San Angelo Art Club, 119 W First St, San Angelo, TX 76903 - T: (915) 653-4405. Pres.: Jean McFerrin
Fine Arts Museum - 1948 47240

Houston Harte University Center, c/o Angelo State University, POB 11027, San Angelo, TX 76909 - T: (915) 942-2062, Fax: (915) 942-2354
Fine Arts Museum / Decorative Arts Museum / University Museum - 1970
Historical artifacts, modern drawings, photography, pottery, weaving 47241

San Angelo Museum of Fine Arts, One Love St, San Angelo, TX 76903 - T: (915) 653-3333, Fax: (915) 659-6800, E-mail: samfa@airmail.net, Internet: web2.airmail.net/samfa. Pres.: Sonny Cleere, Dir.: Howard Taylor
Fine Arts Museum - 1981
Art 47242

San Antonio TX

The Alamo, 300 Alamo Plaza, San Antonio, TX 78205 - T: (210) 225-1391, Fax: (210) 354-3602, E-mail: bbreuer@thealamo.org, Internet: www.thealamo.org. Dir.: Brad Breuer, Cur.: Dr. Bruce Winders
Historic Site / Military Museum / Historical Museum - 1905
Site of the Battle of the Alamo 47243

Art Gallery, University of Texas at San Antonio, 6900 N Loop, San Antonio, TX 78249-0641 - T: (210) 458-4352, Fax: (210) 458-4356, E-mail: rboling@utsa.edu, Internet: www.altamira.arts.utsa.edu. Dir.: Ron Boling
Fine Arts Museum / University Museum - 1982 47244

Bolivar Hall, 418 Villita, San Antonio, TX 78205 - T: (210) 224-5711, Fax: (210) 224-6168, E-mail: conserve@saconservation.org, Internet: www.saconservation.org. Exec. Dir.: Bruce MacDougal
Local Museum - 1971 47245

Buckhorn Museum, 318 E Houston St, San Antonio, TX 78205 - T: (210) 247-4002, Fax: (210) 247-4020, Internet: www.buckhornmuseum.com. Dir.: Dave George
Natural History Museum - 1881
Natural hist 47246

Casa Navarro, 228 S Laredo St, San Antonio, TX 78207 - T: (210) 226-4801, Fax: (210) 226-4801, E-mail: navarro@txdirect.net, Internet: www.tpwd.state.tx.us/park/jose/jose.htm. Chief Cur.: Joanne Avant
Historical Museum - 1964
Furnishings, Hispanic family 47247

Contemporary Art for San Antonio Blue Star Art Space, 116 Blue Star, San Antonio, TX 78204 - T: (210) 227-6960, Fax: (210) 229-9412, Internet: www.bluestarartspace.org. Dir.: Carla Stellwes
Fine Arts Museum - 1986 47248

Coppini Academy of Fine Arts Gallery and Museum, 115 Melrose Pl, San Antonio, TX 78212 - T: (210) 824-8502, Internet: www.coppiniacademy.com. Dir.: Rhonda Coleman
Public Gallery / Local Museum - 1945
Oil paintings, sculpture 47249

Fine Art Gallery at Centro Cultural Aztlan, 803 Castroville Rd, San Antonio, TX 78237 - T: (210) 432-1896, Fax: (210) 432-1899. Exec. Dir.: Malena Gonzalez-Cid
Fine Arts Museum - 1977 47250

Guadalupe Cultural Arts Center, 1300 Guadalupe St, San Antonio, TX 78207 - T: (210) 271-0379, Fax: (210) 271-3480, E-mail: info@guadalupeculturalarts.org, Internet: www.guadalupeculturalarts.org. Dir.: Maria Elena-Torralva
Fine Arts Museum - 1980 47251

Hertzberg Circus Museum (closed) 47252

Institute of Texan Cultures, c/o The University of Texas, 801 S Bowie at Durango Blvd, San Antonio, TX 78205-3296 - T: (210) 458-3296, Fax: (210) 458-2205, E-mail: pburrus@utsa.edu. Exec. Dir.: Rex Ball
Ethnology Museum / University Museum - 1968
Anthropology, ethnology, folk art, Afro-American art 47253

Magic Lantern Castle Museum, 1419 Austin Hwy, San Antonio, TX 78209 - T: (210) 805-0011, Fax: (210) 822-1226, E-mail: castle@magiclanterns.org, Internet: www.magiclanterns.org. C.E.O./Cur.: Jack Judson
Science&Tech Museum - 1991
Magic laterns, glass slides, related materials - library 47254

Marion Koogler McNay Art Museum, 6000 N New Braunfels Av, San Antonio, TX 78209-0069 - T: (210) 824-5368, Fax: (210) 824-0218, E-mail: sbailey@mcnayart.org, Internet: www.mcnayart.org. Dir.: William J. Chiego, Cur.: Linda Hardberger (Tobin Collection of Theater Arts), Lyle Williams (Prints and Drawings)
Fine Arts Museum - 1950
Fine arts 47255

Pioneers, Trail and Texas Rangers Memorial Museum, 3805 Broadway, San Antonio, TX 78209 - T: (210) 661-4238, Fax: (210) 666-5607, E-mail: gccarnes@ktc.com. Cur.: Charles Long
Historical Museum - 1936
Life in early Texas, gun coll, Texas Rangers, saddles, branding irons 47256

Russell Hill Rogers Galleries, Southwest School of Art and Craft, 300 Augusta St, Navarro Campus, San Antonio, TX 78205 - T: (210) 224-1848, Fax: (210) 224-9337, E-mail: info@swschool.org, Internet: www.swschool.org/exhibitions. Dir.: Paula Owen, Assoc. Cur.: Kathy Armstrong-Gillis
Fine Arts Museum - 1965
Contemporary arts and crafts from prominent artists 47257

San Antonio Children's Museum, 305 E Houston St, San Antonio, TX 78205 - T: (210) 212-4453, Fax: (210) 242-1313, E-mail: chris@sakids.org, Internet: www.sakids.org. Pres.: Karen Herrmann, Exec. Dir.: Chris Sinick
Special Museum - 1992 47258

San Antonio Missions Visitor Center, 6701 San Jose Dr, San Antonio, TX 78210 - T: (210) 534-8833, Fax: (210) 534-1106, E-mail: saan_administration@nps.gov, Internet: www.nps.gov/saan
Local Museum - 1978
Anthropology, archaeology, Indian artifacts, Spanish Colonial coll, technology 47259

San Antonio Museum of Art, 200 W Jones Av, San Antonio, TX 78215-1406 - T: (210) 978-8111, Fax: (210) 978-8182, E-mail: director@world-net.net, Internet: www.samuseum.org. Dir.: George W. Neubert, Sen. Cur.: Dr. Marion Oettinger, Cur.: Dr. Gerry Scott (Ancient Art), Martha Blackwelder (Asian Art), George W. Neubert (Contemporary Art)
Fine Arts Museum - 1981
Art 47260

Spanish Governor's Palace, 105 Military Plaza, San Antonio, TX 78205 - T: (210) 224-0601, Fax: (210) 224-0601, E-mail: nward@sanantonio.gov, Internet: www.sanantoniocvb.com/things/attract.htm. Dir.: Malcom Matthew
Historical Museum - 1749
Historic building 47261

Steves Homestead Museum, 509 King William St, San Antonio, TX 78204 - T: (210) 225-5924, Fax: (210) 223-9014, E-mail: dburch@saconservation.org, Internet: www.saconservation.org. Pres.: Jill Souter, Exec. Dir.: Bruce MacDougal
Historical Museum / Historic Site - 1924
Steves Homestead 1876, Wulff House, 1840-1860 Yturri-Edmunds Historic Site 47262

Ursuline Hallway Gallery, Southwest School of Art and Craft, 300 Augusta St, Ursuline Campus, San Antonio, TX 78205 - T: (210) 224-1848, Fax: (210) 224-9337, E-mail: info@swschool.org, Internet: www.swschool.org/exhibitions. Dir.: Paula Owen, Assoc. Cur.: Kathy Armstrong-Gillis
Fine Arts Museum - 1965
Contemporary art by regional artists 47263

Visual Arts Annex Gallery, Guadalupe Cultural Arts Center, 325 S Salado St, San Antonio, TX 78207 - T: (210) 271-0379, E-mail: info@guadalupeculturalarts.org
Public Gallery 47264

Witte Museum, 3801 Broadway, San Antonio, TX 78209 - T: (210) 357-1881, Fax: (210) 357-1882, E-mail: witte@wittemuseum.org, Internet: www.wittemuseum.org. Dir./Cur.: Jim McNutt
Historical Museum - 1926
History 47265

Wooden Nickel Historical Museum, 345 Old Austin Rd, San Antonio, TX 78209 - T: (210) 829-1291, Fax: (210) 832-8965, E-mail: museum@wooden-nickel.net, Internet: www.wooden-nickel.net. C.E.O.: Herb Hornung
Science&Tech Museum - 1998
Printing plates 47266

Yturri-Edmunds Historic Site, 107 King William St, San Antonio, TX 78204-1399 - T: (210) 224-6163, Fax: (210) 224-6168, E-mail: conserve@saconservation.org, Internet: www.saconservation.org. Exec. Dir.: Bruce MacDougal
Historic Site - 1924
Historic houses 47267

San Bernardino CA

Robert V. Fullerton Art Museum, California State University, 5500 University Pkwy, San Bernardino, CA 92407-2397 - T: (909) 880-5493, 880-7373, Fax: (909) 880-7068, E-mail: artmuseum@csusb.edu, Internet: artmuseum.csusb.edu. Dir.: Eva Kirsch
Fine Arts Museum - 1965
Asian and Etruscan ceramics, African sculpture, Egyptian antiquities, contemporary prints, drawings, paintings, sculptures 47268

Sturges Fine Arts Center, 780 North E St, San Bernardino, CA 92413 - T: (909) 885-2816. Pres.: Yolanda Voce
Fine Arts Museum - 1932 47269

San Diego CA

Balboa Park Gallery, San Diego Art Institute, 1439 El Prado, San Diego, CA 92101 - T: (619) 236-0011, Fax: (619) 236-1974, E-mail: admin@sandiego-art.org, Internet: www.sandiego-art.org
Public Gallery 47270

Cabrillo National Monument, 1800 Cabrillo Memorial Dr, Point Loma, San Diego, CA 92106 - T: (619) 557-5450, Fax: (619) 557-5469, Internet: www.nps.gov/cabr
Historical Museum / Historic Site - 1913
Exploration of California coast and San Diego Bay by Juan Rodriguez Cabrillo in 1542, WWII coastal defences 47271

Centro Cultural de la Raza, 2125 Park Blvd, Balboa Park, San Diego, CA 92101 - T: (619) 235-6135, Fax: (619) 595-0034, E-mail: centrocultural@earthlink.com, Internet: www.centroraza.com
Folklore Museum / Fine Arts Museum - 1970
Mexican and Indian culture, contemporary artwork by Chicano artists 47272

Children's Museum, Museo de Los Niños, 200 W Island Av, San Diego, CA 92101 - T: (619) 233-8792, Fax: (619) 233-8796, Internet: www.sdchildrensmuseum.org. Exec. Dir.: Kay Wagner
Special Museum - 1981
Arts, experiances 47273

Command Museum, c/o Marine Corps Recruit Depot, 1600 Henderson Av, Bldg 26, San Diego, CA 92140-5010 - T: (619) 524-6719, Fax: (619) 524-0076, E-mail: mccurtisb@mcrdsdusmc.mil, Internet: www.sdo.usmc.mil/museum.nsf. Dir.: Barbara S. McCurtis
Military Museum - 1987
USMC military equipment, battlefield souvenirs 47274

E.C. Allison Research Center, Department of Geological Sciences, San Diego State University, San Diego, CA 92182-1020 - T: (619) 594-6978, Fax: (619) 594-4372, E-mail: allison.center@geology.sdsu.edu, Internet: www.geology.sdsu.edu. Dir.: Dr. George L. Kennedy

University Museum / Natural History Museum - 1971
Paleontology and Geology Study Collections Museum and Library 47275

Founders Gallery, c/o University of San Diego, 5998 Alcala Park, San Diego, CA 92110 - T: (619) 260-4600, 260-2280, Fax: (619) 260-6875, Internet: www.acusd.edu. Dir.: Dr. Sally Yard
Decorative Arts Museum / Fine Arts Museum / University Museum - 1971
17th-19th c, French tapestries and furniture, South Asian textiles and costumes (19th-20th c), 20th c paintings 47276

Installation Gallery Insite, 964 Fifth Av, San Diego, CA 92101 - T: (619) 544-1482, Fax: (619) 544-1486, E-mail: info@insite2000.org, Internet: www.insite2000.org. Exec. Dir.: Michael Krichman, Ass. Dir.: Danielle Reo
Public Gallery - 1980 47277

Marston House, 3525 Seventh Av, San Diego, CA 92138 - T: (619) 232-6203, Fax: (619) 232-6297, E-mail: lemont@sandiegohistory.org, Internet: www.sandiegohistory.org. Dir.: Robert M. Witty, Cur.: Greg Williams (Photography), Kathy Zygmun (Collections)
Local Museum - 1928
Local hist 47278

Mingei International Museum, 1439 El Prado, Balboa Park, San Diego, CA 92101 - T: (619) 239-0003, Fax: (619) 239-0605, E-mail: mingei@mingei.org, Internet: www.mingei.org. Dir.: Martha W. Longenecker, Ass. Dir.: Rob Sidner
Folklore Museum / Fine Arts Museum / Decorative Arts Museum - 1974
Folk art, craft, design from India, Japan, Indonesia, Mexico, Ethiopia and China, Palesinian costumes, Pre-Columbiana 47279

Mission San Diego de Alcala, 10818 San Diego Mission Rd, San Diego, CA 92108 - T: (619) 283-7319, Fax: (619) 283-7762, Internet: www.missionsandiego.com. Dir./Cur.: Janet Bartel
Religious Arts Museum
First rectory and residence of Fray Junipero Serra, native American baskets, Spanish period, archaeology 47280

Museum of Contemporary Art San Diego - Downtown, 1001 Kettner Blvd, San Diego, CA 92101 - T: (858) 454-3541, Fax: (858) 454-4985, E-mail: info@mcasandiego.org, Internet: www.mcasandiego.org. Dir.: Hugh M. Davies, Pres.: Dr. Charles G. Lochrane
Fine Arts Museum 47281

Museum of Death, 437 19th St, San Diego, CA 92102 - T: (619) 338-8153
Special Museum 47282

Museum of Photographic Arts, 1649 El Prado, Balboa Park, San Diego, CA 92101 - T: (619) 238-7559, Fax: (619) 238-8777, E-mail: info@mopa.org, Internet: www.mopa.org. Dir.: Arthur Ollman, Cur.: Carol McCusker
Fine Arts Museum - 1983
Photographic arts 47283

Old Town San Diego, 4002 Wallace Av, San Diego, CA 92110 - T: (619) 220-5422, Fax: (619) 220-5421, E-mail: oldtown@ixpres.com. Head: Ronilee Clark
Local Museum - 1967
Local hist 47284

Reuben H. Fleet Science Center, 1875 El Prado, Balboa Park, San Diego, CA 92101-1625 - T: (619) 238-1233, Fax: (619) 685-5771, Internet: www.rhfleet.org. Exec. Dir.: Dr. Jeffrey W. Kirsch
Science&Tech Museum - 1973
planetarium 47285

San Diego Aerospace Museum, 2001 Pan American Plaza, Balboa Park, San Diego, CA 92101 - T: (619) 234-8291 ext 10, Fax: (619) 233-4526, E-mail: admin@sdasm.org, Internet: www.aerospacemuseum.org. Exec. Dir.: Bruce Bleakley
Science&Tech Museum - 1961
Aviation, historical aircrafts, engines - library 47286

San Diego Automotive Museum, 2080 Pan American Plaza, Balboa Park, San Diego, CA 92101-1636 - T: (619) 231-2886, Fax: (619) 231-9869, E-mail: sdauto@cts.com, Internet: www.sdautomuseum.org. Exec. Dir.: Art Bishop
Science&Tech Museum - 1987 47287

San Diego Hall of Champions Sports Museum, 2131 Pan America Plaza, Balboa Park, San Diego, CA 92101 - T: (619) 234-2544, Fax: (619) 234-4543, E-mail: bobb@sdhoc.com, Internet: www.sandiegosports.org. Dir.: Bill J. Adams, Cur.: Todd Tobias
Special Museum - 1961
Sports 47288

San Diego Historical Society Museum, 1649 El Prado Casa de Balboa, Balboa Park, San Diego, CA 92101-1621 - T: (619) 232-6203 ext 100, Fax: (619) 232-6297, Internet: www.sandiegohistory.org. Dir.: Robert M. Witty, Cur.: Greg Williams (Photographic Collections), John Panter (Archives)
Local Museum - 1928
Local hist - archives 47289

San Diego Maritime Museum, 1492 N Harbor Dr, San Diego, CA 92101 - T: (619) 234-9153, Fax: (619) 234-8345, E-mail: info@sdmaritime.com, Internet: www.sdmaritime.com. Pres.: William Dysart, Exec. Dir.: Raymond E. Ashley
Science&Tech Museum - 1948
Museum housed in three ships (1863 Star of India, 1898 ferryboat Berkeley, 1904 steam yacht Medea) 47290

San Diego Mesa College Art Gallery and African Art Collection, 7250 Mesa College Dr, San Diego, CA 92111-0103 - T: (619) 388-2829, Fax: (619) 388-5720, E-mail: amoctezu@sdccs.net, Internet: www.sandiegomesacollege.net. Dir.: Allessandra Moctezuma, Asst. Dir.: Pat Vine, Cur.: Barbara W. Blackman (African Art)
Fine Arts Museum 47291

San Diego Model Railroad Museum, 1649 El Prado, San Diego, CA 92101 - T: (619) 696-0199, Fax: (619) 696-0239, E-mail: sdmodrailm@abac.com, Internet: www.sdmodelrailroadm.com. Exec. Dir.: John A. Rotsart
Science&Tech Museum - 1980
Railroad models 47292

San Diego Museum of Art, 1450 El Prado, Balboa Park, San Diego, CA 92101 - T: (619) 232-7931, Fax: (619) 232-9367, E-mail: library2@class.org, Internet: www.samart.org. Dir.: Dr. Don Bacigalupi, Cur.: Caron Smith (Asian Art), Scott Atkinson (American Art), Steven Kern (European Art), Larry Urrutia (California Contemporary Art)
Fine Arts Museum - 1925
Art 47293

San Diego Museum of Man, 1350 El Prado, Balboa Park, San Diego, CA 92101 - T: (619) 239-2001, Fax: (619) 239-2749, E-mail: dsharon@museumofman.org, Internet: www.museumofman.org. Dir.: Dr. Douglas Sharon, Cur.: Javier Guerrero (Southwest Collections), Kenneth Hedges (Ethnology and Archaeology South California), Rose Tyson (Physical Anthropology), Grace Johnson (Ethnology Latin America), Ass. Cur.: Tori Heflin (Physical Anthropology)
Ethnology Museum / Archaeological Museum - 1915
Anthropology 47294

San Diego Natural History Museum, 1788 El Prado, Balboa Park, San Diego, CA 92101 - T: (619) 232-3821 ext 216, Fax: (619) 232-0248, E-mail: mhager@sdnhm.org, Internet: www.sdnhm.org. Dir.: Dr. Michael W. Hager, Cur.: Dr. Jon Rebman (Botany), Dr. Thomas Demere (Paleontology), Dr. Paisley Cato (Collections)
Natural History Museum - 1874
Natural hist 47295

Serra Museum, 2727 Presidio Dr, Presidio Park, San Diego, CA 92103 - T: (619) 297-3258, Fax: (619) 297-3281, E-mail: lemont@sandiegohistory.org, Internet: www.sandiegohistory.org. Dir.: Robert M. Witty, Cur.: Dr. Therese Adams Muranaka
Local Museum - 1928
Local hist 47296

Sushi Performance and Visual Art Museum, 320 11th Av, San Diego, CA 92101 - T: (619) 235-8466, Fax: (619) 235-8552, Internet: www.sushiart.org. Dir.: Vicki Wolf
Fine Arts Museum / Public Gallery - 1980 47297

Timken Museum of Art, 1500 El Prado, Balboa Park, San Diego, CA 92101 - T: (619) 239-5548, Fax: (619) 233-6629, Internet: www.timkenmuseum.org. Dir.: John Petersen
Fine Arts Museum - 1965
European paintings (13th-19th c), American paintings 19th c , gobbelin, tapestries, Russian icons (15th-19th c) 47298

University Art Gallery, San Diego State University, 5500 Campanile Dr, San Diego, CA 92182-4805 - T: (619) 594-5171, 594-4941, Fax: (619) 594-1217, E-mail: artgallery@sdsu.edu, Internet: www.sdsu.edu/artgallery. Dir.: Tina Yapelli
Fine Arts Museum / University Museum - 1977
Contemporary art, Asian sculpture, African and Mexican art 47299

Villa Montezuma Museum, 1925 K St, San Diego, CA 92102 - T: (619) 232-6203, 239-2211, Fax: (619) 232-6297, E-mail: lemont@sandiegohistory.org, Internet: www.sandiegohistory.org. Dir.: Robert M. Witty, Cur.: Greg Williams (Photography), Jennifer Lutsic (Collections)
Local Museum - 1928
Local hist 47300

Wells Fargo History Museum, 2733 San Diego Av, San Diego, CA 92110 - T: (619) 238-3929. Cur.: Allan E. Peterson
Special Museum - 1990
Company hist 47301

San Francisco CA

Adan E. Treganza Anthropology Museum, San Francisco State University, 1600 Holloway Av, San Francisco, CA 94132 - T: (415) 338-2046, Fax: (415) 338-0530, E-mail: yamamoto@sfsu.edu, Internet: www.sfsu.edu/treganza. Dir.: Yoshiko Yamamoto
University Museum / Archaeological Museum / Natural History Museum - 1958
Anthropology 47302

African-American Historical and Cultural Society Collection, Fort Mason Ctr, Bldg C, Rm 165, San Francisco, CA 94123 - T: (415) 441-0640, Fax: (415) 441-2847. Dir.: Vandan Philpatt
Historical Museum / Ethnology Museum - 1955
African artifacts, sculpture, Allensworth, black businesses, Blacks in the west, Haitian art, protest movements 1960s-1970s 47303

American Indian Contemporary Arts, 23 Grant Av, San Francisco, CA 94108 - T: (415) 989-7003, Fax: (415) 989-7025. Dir.: Janeen Antoine
Fine Arts Museum - 1983 47304

Art and Architecture Exhibition Space, 450 Irwin St, San Francisco, CA 94107 - T: (415) 703-9568, Fax: (415) 551-9260, Internet: www.ccac-art.edu. Dir.: Ralph Rugoff
Fine Arts Museum - 1988 47305

Arte Maya Tz'utuhil, POB 40391, San Francisco, CA 94140 - T: (415) 282-7654, E-mail: curator@artemaya.com, Internet: www.artemaya.com
Fine Arts Museum
Oil paintings by Guatemala Indian artists about Mayan life 47306

Artist Gallery, San Francisco Museum of Modern Art, Fort Mason Bldg A, San Francisco, CA 94123 - T: (415) 441-4777, Fax: (415) 441-0614. Dir.: Marian Wintersteen Parmenter
Fine Arts Museum - 1978 47307

Asian Art Museum of San Francisco, Civic Center, 200 Larkin St, San Francisco, CA 94118 - T: (415) 581-3500, 861-2035, Fax: (415) 581-4700, E-mail: pr@asianart.org, Internet: www.asianart.org. Dir.: Dr. Emily J. Sano, Chief Cur.: Forrest McGill (South and Southeast Asian Art), Cur.: Terese Tse Bartholomew (Indian and Himalayan Art), Yoko Woodson (Japanese Art), Kumja Paik Kim (Korean Art), Michael Knight (Chinese Art)
Fine Arts Museum - 1966/2003
Art 47308

Bank of America Galleries, 1 S Van Ness, San Francisco, CA 94103 - T: (415) 241-3678, Fax: (415) 241-5413. Dir.: Bonnie Earls-Solari
Fine Arts Museum 47309

Black Rock Arts Foundation, 3450 Third St, San Francisco, CA 94124 - T: (415) 641-0949, 626-1248, E-mail: info@blackrockarts.org, Internet: www.blackrockarts.org. Dir.: Mark Van Proyen, Douglas Holloway, Will Roger
Public Gallery - 1986 47310

Califonia Palace of the Legion of Honor, Fine Arts Museum of San Francisco, 100 34th Av, San Francisco, CA 94121 - T: (415) 750-3600, Fax: (415) 750-3656, Internet: www.legionofhonor.org. Dir.: Harry S. Parker, Chief Cur.: Dr. Steven A. Nash (European Art), Cur.: Robert Flynn Johnson (Prints and Drawings), Timothy Anglin Burgard (American Arts), Kathleen Berrin (Africa, Oceania and American), Dr. Lynn Federle Orr (European Paintings), Melissa Leventon (Textiles), Renee Dreyfus (Ancient Art and Interpretation), Lee Hunt Miller (European Decorative Arts and Sculpture)
Fine Arts Museum - 1924
Ancient and European arts, sculptures 47311

California Academy of Sciences Museum, Golden Gate Park, San Francisco, CA 94118-4599 - T: (415) 221-5100, Fax: (415) 750-7346, E-mail: llacarrubba@calacademy.org, Internet: www.calacademy.org. Exec. Dir.: J. Patrick Kociolek
Natural History Museum - 1853
Ichthyology, invertebrate zoology, ornithology, mammalogy, botany, entomology, herpetology, athropology, geology, paleontology 47312

Capp Street Project, 525 Second St, San Francisco, CA 94107 - T: (415) 495-7101, Fax: (415) 495-7059. Exec. Dir.: Linda Blumberg
Fine Arts Museum - 1983
Installation art 47313

Cartoon Art Museum, 814 Mission St, San Francisco, CA 94103 - T: (415) 227-8666, Fax: (415) 243-8666, E-mail: office@cartoonart.org, Internet: www.cartoonart.org. Dir.: Rod Gilchrist
Fine Arts Museum - 1984
Cartoons, flat graphics-animation 47314

Center for the Arts at Yerba Buena Gardens → Yerba Buena Center for the Arts

Chinese Culture Center of San Francisco, 750 Kearny St, San Francisco, CA 94108 - T: (415) 986-1822, Fax: (415) 986-2825, E-mail: info@c-c-c.org, Internet: www.c-c-c.org. Dir.: Hon Seng Cheng
Fine Arts Museum / Folklore Museum - 1965
Art 47315

The Exploratorium, 3601 Lyon St, San Francisco, CA 94123 - T: (415) 563-7337, Fax: (415) 561-0307, E-mail: pubinfo@exploratorium.edu, Internet: www.exploratorium.edu. Exec. Dir.: Goery Delacote
Fine Arts Museum / Science&Tech Museum / Ethnology Museum - 1969
Science, art, human perception 47316

The Friends of Photography at the Ansel Adams Center, 650 Mission St, San Francisco, CA 95105 - T: (415) 495-7000, Fax: (415) 495-8517, E-mail: staff@friendsofphotography.org, Internet: www.friendsofphotography.org. Dir.: Deborah Klochko
Fine Arts Museum
Photography 47317

Galeria de la Raza, 2857 24th St, San Francisco, CA 94110 - T: (415) 826-8009, Fax: (415) 826-6235, E-mail: galeria@thecity.sfsu.edu, Internet: thecity.sfsu.edu/~galeria. Dir.: Carolina Ponce de León
Fine Arts Museum - 1970
Chicano/ Latino art and culture 47318

Haas-Lilienthal House, 2007 Franklin St, San Francisco, CA 94109 - T: (415) 441-3000, Fax: (415) 441-3015, E-mail: info@sfheritage.org, Internet: www.sfheritage.org. Head: Christopher Van Raalte
Local Museum - 1973
Historic house 47319

Intersection for the Arts Gallery, 446 Valencia, San Francisco, CA 94103 - T: (415) 626-2787, Fax: (415) 626-1636. Dir.: Deborah Cullinan
Public Gallery - 1965 47320

Japantown Art and Media Collection, 1840 Sutter St, Ste 102, San Francisco, CA 94115 - T: (415) 922-8700, Fax: (415) 922-8700, E-mail: Jtown@sirius.com, Internet: www.janworkshop.com. Exec. Dir.: Dennis Taniguchi
Fine Arts Museum - 1977
Silkscreen posters, art works 47321

The Jewish Museum San Francisco → The Magnes Museum

The Lab, 2948 16th St, San Francisco, CA 94103 - T: (415) 864-8855, Fax: (415) 864-8855, E-mail: info@thelab.org, Internet: www.thelab.org. Dir.: Laura Brun
Fine Arts Museum - 1983 47322

The Magnes Museum, 121 Steuart St, San Francisco, CA 94105 - T: (415) 591-8800, Fax: (415) 591-8815, E-mail: info@magnesmuseum.org, Internet: www.magnesmuseum.org. Dir.: Connie Wolf, Dep. Dir.: Peter Stein (Programs)
Fine Arts Museum / Historical Museum - 1984 47323

The Mexican Museum, Fort Mason Center, Bldg D, Laguna and Marina Blvd, San Francisco, CA 94123 - T: (415) 202-9700, Fax: (415) 441-7683, E-mail: info@mexicanmuseum.org, Internet: www.mexicanmuseum.org. Dir.: Lorraine Garcia-Nakata
Fine Arts Museum / Folklore Museum - 1975
Fine arts 47324

M.H. de Young Memorial Museum, Fine Arts Museums of San Francisco (closed until 2005 for rebuilding), 75 Tea Garden Dr, Golden Gate Park, San Francisco, CA 94118 - T: (415) 750-3600, 750-3615, Fax: (415) 750-7692, Internet: www.thinker.org. Dir.: Harry S. Parker, Chief Cur.: Dr. Steven A. Nash (European Art), Cur.: Robert Flynn Johnson (Prints and Drawings), Timothy Anglin Burgard (American Arts), Kathleen Berrin (Africa, Oceania and American), Dr. Lynn Federle Orr (European Paintings), Melissa Leventon (Textiles), Renee Dreyfus (Ancient Art and Interpretation), Lee Hunt Miller (European Decorative Arts and Sculpture)
Fine Arts Museum - 1894
Fine Arts 47325

Mission Cultural Center for Latino Arts, 2868 Mission St, San Francisco, CA 94110 - T: (415) 821-1155, Fax: (415) 648-0933. Dir.: Jennie Rodriquez
Fine Arts Museum / Folklore Museum - 1977
Civic art 47326

Museo Italoamericano, Fort Mason Center, Bldg C, San Francisco, CA 94123 - T: (415) 673-2200, Fax: (415) 673-2292, E-mail: museo@firstworld.net, Internet: www.museoitaloamericano.org. Dir.: Julie Benbow, Cur.: Robert A. Whyte
Fine Arts Museum / Folklore Museum - 1978
Contemporary Italian, Italian-American art, Italian culture 47327

Museum of Conceptual Art, 657 Howard St, San Francisco, CA 94105 - T: (415) 495-3193, Fax: (415) 495-3793. Dir.: Tom Marioni
Fine Arts Museum - 1970
archives, library 47328

Museum of Craft Folk Art, Fort Mason Center, Bldg A, San Francisco, CA 94123 - T: (415) 775-0990/91, Fax: (415) 775-1861, E-mail: admin@mocfa.org, Internet: www.mocfa.org. Dir.: Miriam de Vriarte, Cur.: Carolyn Kastner
Decorative Arts Museum - 1983
Worldwide tribal, contemporary craft and folk art, outsider art 47329

Museum of Russian Culture, 2450 Sutter St, San Francisco, CA 94115 - T: (415) 921-4082. Dir.: Dmitri G. Brauns, Cur.: Alex Karamzin
Ethnology Museum - 1948
Ethnic hist 47330

The Museum of Vision, c/o Foundation of the American Academy of Ophthalmology, 655 Beach St, Ste 300, San Francisco, CA 94109-1336 - T: (415) 447-0297, 561-8500, Fax: (415) 561-8533, E-mail: tschmitz@aao.org, Internet: www.eyenet.org. Dir.: Licia A. Wells
Special Museum - 1980
Medical hist, medical instruments, ophthalmology, rare books 47331

New Langton Arts, 1246 Folsom St, San Francisco, CA 94103 - T: (415) 626-5416, Fax: (415) 255-1453, E-mail: nla@newlangtonarts.org, Internet: www.newlangtonarts.org. Dir.: Susan Miller
Public Gallery - 1975 47332

Randall Museum, 199 Museum Way, San Francisco, CA 94114 - T: (415) 554-9600, Fax: (415) 554-9609, E-mail: info@randallmuseum.org, Internet: www.randallmuseum.org. Dir.: Amy Dawson, Cur.: John Dillon, Carol Preston (Science), Chris Boettcher (Industrial Arts)
Special Museum - 1937
Children's museum 47333

San Francisco African American Historical and Cultural Society Museum, Fort Mason Center, Bldg C, San Francisco, CA 94123 - T: (415) 441-0640. Head: Vandean Philpott
Folklore Museum / Historical Museum - 1955
African American culture, Haitian art 47334

San Francisco Camerawork, 1246 Folsom St, San Francisco, CA 94103 - T: (415) 863-1001, Fax: (415) 863-1015, E-mail: sfcamera@sfcamerawork.org, Internet: www.sfcamerawork.org. Exec. Dir.: Marnie Gillett
Fine Arts Museum / Public Gallery - 1974
Photography 47335

San Francisco Craft and Folk Art Museum → Museum of Craft Folk Art

San Francisco Fire Department Museum, 655 Presidio Av, San Francisco, CA 94115 - T: (415) 558-3546, 563-4630, Internet: www.sffiremuseum.org. Cur.: Robert Kreuzberger
Special Museum - 1964
Fire museum, specializing in San Francisco history 47336

San Francisco Maritime National Historical Park, Hyde Street Pier, San Francisco, CA 94109 - T: (415) 556-1659, 561-7000, Fax: (415) 556-1624, E-mail: lynn_cullivan@nps.gov, Internet: www.nps.gov/safr. Dir.: William G. Thomas, Cur.: Steve Canright
Historical Museum / Science&Tech Museum - 1951
Maritime hist - historic douments, archives, libraray 47337

San Francisco Museum of Contemporary Hispanic Art, 4178 Mission St, San Francisco, CA 94112 - T: (415) 469-9579, Fax: (925) 469-9481, Internet: www.bohemionews.com/museum.html
Fine Arts Museum - 1987 47338

San Francisco Museum of Modern Art, 151 Third St, San Francisco, CA 94103 - T: (415) 357-4000, Fax: (415) 357-4037, E-mail: conmassistant@sfmoma.org, Internet: www.sfmoma.org. Dir.: Neal Benezra, Cur.: Janet C. Bishop, Madeleine Grynsztejn (Painting and Sculpture), Douglas R. Nickel, Dr. Sandra S. Phillips (Photography), John S. Weber (Education, PR), Benjamin E. Weil (Media Arts), Joseph Rosa (Architecture, Design)
Fine Arts Museum - 1935
Modern art 47339

Southern Exposure Gallery, 401 Alabama St, San Francisco, CA 94110 - T: (415) 863-2141, Fax: (415) 863-1841, E-mail: soex@soex.org, Internet: www.soex.org. Dir.: N. Trisha Lagaso
Public Gallery - 1974 47340

SPC Pioneer Museum, 140 New Montgomery St, San Francisco, CA 94105 - T: (916) 453-6329, Fax: (916) 451-1812. Dir.: Kate Tufrow
Science&Tech Museum - 1968
Telephone hist 47341

Tattoo Art Museum, 841 Columbus Av, San Francisco, CA 94133 - T: (415) 775-4991, Fax: (707) 462-4433, E-mail: lyletutt@pacific.net, Internet: www.lyletuttle.com. Exec. Dir.: Lyle Tuttle
Special Museum - 1974 47342

Telephone Pioneer Communications Museum → SPC Pioneer Museum

Walter and McBean Galleries, San Francisco Art Institute, 800 Chestnut St, San Francisco, CA 94133 - T: (415) 771-7020, 749-4563, Fax: (415) 749-1036, E-mail: exhibitions@sfai.edu, Internet: www.sfai.edu. Head: Ella King Torrey
Fine Arts Museum - 1871
Art 47343

Wells Fargo History Museum, 420 Montgomery St, San Francisco, CA 94163 - T: (415) 396-2619, 396-4157, Fax: (415) 391-8644, E-mail: fontaine@wellsfargo.com, Internet: www.wellsfargohistory.com. Dir.: Charles LaFontaine, Cur.: Anne M. Hall
Historical Museum - 1929
Company history, Wells Fargo Bank's headquarters 47344

Women's Heritage Museum, 870 Market St, #547, San Francisco, CA 94102 - T: (415) 433-3026. Pres.: Elizabeth Colton, Dir.: Jeanne McDonnell
Historical Museum - 1985 47345

Yerba Buena Center for the Arts, 701 Mission St, San Francisco, CA 94103 - T: (415) 978-2700, Fax: (415) 978-9635, E-mail: info@yerbabuenarts.org, Internet: www.yerbabuenaarts.org. Dir.: John Killacky, Cur.: Renny Pritikin (Chief), Loris Bradley (Performing Arts), Rene DeGuzman (Visual Arts), Joel Shepard (Film Video)
Fine Arts Museum / Performing Arts Museum - 1986 47346

San Gabriel CA

San Gabriel Mission Museum, 428 S Mission Dr, San Gabriel, CA 91776 - T: (626) 457-3048, Fax: (626) 282-5308, E-mail: alsgmi@aol.com, Internet: www.sangabrielmission.org. Dir.: Denis Gallo, Cur.: Helen Nelson
Religious Arts Museum
Religious hist 47347

San Jacinto CA

San Jacinto Museum, 181 E Main St, San Jacinto, CA 92583 - T: (909) 654-4952, Fax: (909) 654-9270, Internet: www.ci.san-jacinto.ca.us. Cur.: Phil Brigandi
Local Museum - 1939
Local hist 47348

San Jose CA

Art-Tech, Silicon Valley Institute of Art Technology, 14300 Clayton Rd, San Jose, CA 95127 - T: (408) 929-9969, Fax: (408) 929-3330, E-mail: SVIArttec@aol.com, Internet: www.art-tech.org
Public Gallery
New art forms and media content 47349

Children's Discovery Museum of San Jose, 180 Woz Way, San Jose, CA 95110 - T: (408) 298-5437 ext 0, Fax: (408) 298-6826, E-mail: info@cdm.org, Internet: www.cdm.org. Dir.: Tom Lindsay, Exec. Dir.: Connie Martinez
Special Museum - 1982 47350

History San José, 1650 Senter Rd, San Jose, CA 95112-2599 - T: (408) 287-2290, Fax: (408) 287-2291, E-mail: llennert@historysanjose.org, Internet: www.historysanjose.org. Cur.: Alida Bray
Historical Museum - 1950
Local historic furniture, archaeology, vehicles, textiles, household items 47351

Military Medal Museum, 448 N San Pedro St, San Jose, CA 95110-2232 - T: (408) 298-1100. Cur.: Sara Langton jr.
Military Museum - 1978
Military orders, declarations, medals 47352

Natalie and James Thompson Gallery, San Jose State University, 1 Washington Sq, San Jose, CA 95192-0089 - T: (408) 924-4320, Fax: (408) 924-4326, E-mail: rwmilnes@sjsu.edu, Internet: www.sjsu.edu/depts/art_design. Dir.: Jo Farb Hernández
Public Gallery - 1959 47353

Rosicrucian Egyptian Museum, 1342 Naglee Av, San Jose, CA 95191-0001 - T: (408) 947-3600, Fax: (408) 947-3638, E-mail: director@rcegyptmus.org, Internet: www.rosicrucian.org. Dir.: Julie Scott
Historical Museum / Fine Arts Museum - 1929
Assyrian, Babylonian and Egyptian antiquities, archaeology, paintings, sculpture, graphics, textiles 47354

San Jose Institute of Contemporary Art, 451 S First St, San Jose, CA 95113 - T: (408) 283-8155, Fax: (408) 283-8157, E-mail: info@sjica.org. Dir.: Cathy Kimball
Fine Arts Museum - 1980 47355

San Jose Museum of Art, 110 S Market St, San Jose, CA 95113 - T: (408) 271-6840, Fax: (408) 294-2977, E-mail: info@sjmusart.org, Internet: www.sanjosemuseumofart.org. Dir.: Daniel T. Keegan, Dep. Dir.: Deborah Norberg, Chief Cur.: Susan Landauer
Fine Arts Museum - 1969
Art 47356

San Jose Museum of Quilts and Textiles, 110 Paseo de San Antonio, San Jose, CA 95112-3639 - T: (408) 971-0323 ext 16, Fax: (408) 971-7226, E-mail: jane@sjquiltmuseum.org, Internet: www.sjquiltmuseum.org. Dir.: Jane Przybysz, Robin Treen (Exhibits)
Decorative Arts Museum - 1977
Quilts and textiles 47357

San Jose State University Art Galleries → Natalie and James Thompson Gallery

Youth Science Institute, 16260 Alum Rock Av, San Jose, CA 95127 - T: (408) 258-4322, Fax: (408) 358-3683, E-mail: annedirect@ysi-ca.org, Internet: www.ysi-ca.org. Exec. Dir.: Anne Dunham
Natural History Museum - 1953
Natural hist, mineral and rock coll 47358

San Juan Bautista CA

San Juan Bautista State Historic Park, Second St, Washington and Mariposa Sts, San Juan Bautista, CA 95045-0787 - T: (831) 623-4881, 623-4526, Fax: (831) 623-4612, E-mail: sjbshp@hollinet.com. Cur.: Kris N. Quist
Historical Museum - 1933
Local hist 47359

San Juan Capistrano CA

Mission San Juan Capistrano Museum, 31522 Camino Capistrano, San Juan Capistrano, CA 92675 - T: (949) 234-1300 ext 320, Fax: (949) 443-2061, E-mail: museum@fea.net, Internet: www.missionsjc.com. C.E.O.: Gerald J. Miller
Historic Site - 1980
Local hist, archaeology, native american, period rooms 47360

San Luis Obispo CA

Mission San Luis Obispo de Tolosa, 751 Palm St, San Luis Obispo, CA 93401 - T: (805) 543-6850, 781-8220, Fax: (805) 781-8214, Internet: www.thegrid.net/slomission
Religious Arts Museum
Religious hist 47361

San Luis Obispo Art Center, 1010 Broad St, San Luis Obispo, CA 93406-0813 - T: (805) 543-8562, Fax: (805) 543-4518. Exec. Dir.: Carol Dunn, Cur.: Arne Nybak
Fine Arts Museum - 1952 47362

San Luis Obispo County Historical Museum, 696 Monterey St, San Luis Obispo, CA 93401 - T: (805) 543-0638, Fax: (805) 783-2191, E-mail: slochs@slonet.org, Internet: www.slonet.org/vv/ipslochm/. Pres.: John Schutz
Local Museum - 1956
Local hist 47363

San Marcos CA

Boehm Gallery, 1140 W Mission Rd, San Marcos, CA 92069 - T: (760) 744-1150 ext 2304, Fax: (760) 744-8123, Internet: www.palomar.edu/boehmgallery. Dir.: Vicki Cole
Fine Arts Museum - 1964
Art since 16th c 47364

San Marino CA

California Art Gallery, 1120 Old Mill Rd, San Marino, CA 91108-1840 - T: (626) 449-5458. Exec. Dir.: Jack McQueen
Fine Arts Museum 47365

Huntington Art Collections, 1151 Oxford Rd, San Marino, CA 91108 - T: (626) 405-2140, Fax: (626) 405-0225, E-mail: webmaster@huntington.org, Internet: www.huntington.org. Dir.: John Murdoch, Cur.: Shelley Bennett (British and Continental Art), Amy Meyers (American Art)
Fine Arts Museum - 1919
Art 47366

Old Mill Museum, El Molino Viejo Museo, 1120 Old Mill Rd, San Marino, CA 91108 - T: (626) 449-5450, Fax: (626) 449-1057. Pres.: Warren Weber, Dir.: Jack McQueen
Local Museum
California hist, art 47367

San Martin CA

Wings of History Air Museum, 12777 Murphy Av, San Martin, CA 95046-0495 - T: (408) 683-2290, Fax: (408) 683-2291, E-mail: wohoffice@wingsofhistory.org, Internet: www.wingsofhistory.org. Dir.: Gayle Womack, Sc. Staff: Bill Sadler (Restoration)
Science&Tech Museum - 1983 47368

San Mateo CA

Coyote Point Museum for Environmental Education, 1651 Coyote Point Dr, San Mateo, CA 94401 - T: (650) 342-7755, Fax: (650) 342-7853, Internet: www.coyoteptmuseum.org. Dir.: Gwen Loeb
Natural History Museum - 1953
Natural science 47369

San Miguel CA

Mission San Miguel, 775 Mission St, San Miguel, CA 93451 - T: (805) 467-3256, Fax: (805) 467-2448, Internet: missionsanmiguel.org. Dir.: William Short
Religious Arts Museum
Religion 47370

San Pedro CA

Fort MacArthur Museum, 3601 S Gaffey St, San Pedro, CA 90731 - T: (310) 548-2631, Fax: (310) 241-0847, E-mail: director@ftmac.org, Internet: www.ftmac.org. Dir./Cur.: Stephen R. Nelson
Open Air Museum / Military Museum - 1985 47371

Gallery A and Gallery G, c/o Angels Gate Cultural Center, 3601 S Gaffey St, San Pedro, CA 90733 - T: (310) 519-0936, Fax: (310) 519-8698, E-mail: artatgate@aol.com, Internet: www.angelsgateart.org. Dir.: Robin Hinchliffe
Public Gallery - 1981 47372

Los Angeles Maritime Museum, Berth 84, foot of 6th St, San Pedro, CA 90731 - T: (310) 548-7618, Fax: (310) 832-6537, E-mail: museum@lamaritimemuseum.org, Internet: www.lamaritimemuseum.org. Dir.: William B. Lee, Cur.: Mari Frances Trivelli
Historical Museum - 1980
Maritime, former Los Angeles municipal ferry building, ship building, US Navy 47373

San Rafael CA

Falkirk Cultural Center, 1408 Mission Av, San Rafael, CA 94901 - T: (415) 485-3328, Fax: (415) 485-3404, E-mail: jane.lange@ci.san-rafael.ca.us, Internet: www.falkirkculturalcenter.org. Dir.: Jane Lange, Cur.: Beth Goldberg
Fine Arts Museum / Folklore Museum - 1974
Contemporary arts 47374

Marin History Museum, 1125 B St, San Rafael, CA 94901 - T: (415) 454-8538, Fax: (415) 454-6137, E-mail: infomhm@pacbell.net, Internet: www.marinhistory.org. Dir.: Merry Alberigi
Local Museum - 1935
Local hist, documents, clothing 47375

San Marco Gallery, Dominican University of California, 50 Aacacia Av, San Rafael, CA 94901 - T: (415) 457-4440, Fax: (415) 485-3262, E-mail: satterfield@dominican.edu. Cur.: Foad Satterfield, Coord.: James Fowler (Digital Art)
Public Gallery 47376

San Simeon CA

Hearst Castle, 750 Hearst Castle Rd, San Simeon, CA 93452 - T: (805) 927-2020, Fax: (805) 927-2031, Internet: www.hearstcastle.org. Dir.: Kirk Sturm, Chief Cur.: Hoyt Fields
Local Museum - 1957
Local hist 47377

Sand Springs OK

Sand Springs Cultural and Historical Museum, 6 E Broadway, Sand Springs, OK 74063 - T: (918) 246-2509, Fax: (918) 245-7107, E-mail: jklandis@sandspringsok.org, Internet: www.sandspringsok.org. Dir.: Jamye Landis
Local Museum - 1991 47378

Sandersville GA

Brown House Museum, 268 N Harris St, Sandersville, GA 31082 - T: (478) 552-1965, Fax: (478) 552-2963, Internet: www.rootsweb.com. Dir.: Mary Alice Jordan
Historical Museum 47379

Washington County Museum, 129 Jones St, Sandersville, GA 31082, mail addr: POB 6088, Sandersville, GA 31082 - T: (478) 552-6965. Dir.: Mary Alice Jordan
Local Museum - 1978
Washington County hist 47380

Sandown NH

Sandown Historical Museum, Rte 121-A, Sandown, NH 03873 - T: (603) 887-4520, E-mail: history@sandownnh.com, Internet: www.sandownnh.com/history. Dir.: Paul M. Densen, Cur.: Bertha Deveau
Local Museum - 1977
Local history, railroad stn 47381

Sandpoint ID

Bonner County Historical Museum, 611 S Ella Av, Sandpoint, ID 83864 - T: (208) 263-2344, Fax: (208) 263-2344, E-mail: bchsmuseum@nidlink.com, Internet: www.sandpoint.com/museum. Pres.: Susan Kiebert
Historical Museum - 1972
Local history 47382

Sandusky OH

Follett House Museum, 404 Wayne St, Sandusky, OH 44870 - T: (419) 625-3834, Fax: (419) 625-4574, E-mail: comments@sandusky.lib.oh.us, Internet: www.sandusky.lib.oh.us/
Local Museum - 1902 47383

Museum of Carousel Art and History, W Washington and Jackson Sts, Sandusky, OH 44870 - T: (419) 626-6111, Fax: (419) 626-1297, E-mail: merrygor@aol.com, Internet: www.merrygoroundmuseum.org
Fine Arts Museum / Science&Tech Museum - 1990
Carousel art, tools 47384

Sandwich IL

Sandwich Historical Society Museum, 315 E Railroad, Sandwich, IL 60548 - T: (815) 786-7936. Pres.: Roger Peterson
Local Museum - 1969
Local history, housed in sturdy old structure locally known as the Old Stone Mill 47385

Sandwich MA

Heritage Plantation of Sandwich, 67 Grove St and Pine St, Sandwich, MA 02563 - T: (508) 888-3300, Fax: (508) 888-9535, E-mail: heritage@heritageplantation.org, Internet: www.heritageplantation.org. Exec. Dir.: Glenn Pare, Cur.: Jean Gillis, Jennifer Madden (Collection)
Local Museum - 1969
General museum, military, cars 47386

Old Hoxie House, Rte 130, Water St, Sandwich, MA 02563 - T: (508) 888-1173. Dir./Cur.: Carol McManus
Historical Museum - 1960
Oldest restored house on Cape Cod 47387

Sandwich Glass Museum, 129 Main St, Sandwich, MA 02563 - T: (508) 888-0251, Fax: (508) 888-4941, E-mail: glass@sandwichglassmuseum.org, Internet: www.sandwichglassmuseum.org. Dir.: Bruce A. Courson, Cur.: Nezka Pfeifer
Decorative Arts Museum - 1907
Glass history 47388

Thornton W. Burgess Museum, 4 Water St, Sandwich, MA 02563 - T: (508) 888-4668, Fax: (508) 888-1919, E-mail: tburgess@capecod.net, Internet: www.thorntonburgess.org. Dir.: Jeanne Johnson, Sc. Staff: Russell A. Lovell (History)
Local Museum / Natural History Museum - 1976
History, nature 47389

Yesteryears Doll and Toy Museum, Main and River Sts, Sandwich, MA 02563 - T: (508) 888-1711. Dir.: Diane Costa, Cur.: Eileen Fair
Decorative Arts Museum - 1961
Dolls, toys 47390

Sandy Hook NJ

Fort Hancock Museum, Sandy Hook Unit, Gateway National Recreation Area, Sandy Hook, NJ 07732 - T: (732) 872-5970, Fax: (732) 872-2256, Internet: www.nps.gov./gate. Sc. Staff: Thomas Hoffman (History)
Natural History Museum - 1968 47391

Sandy Spring MD

Sandy Spring Museum, 17901 Bentley Rd, Sandy Spring, MD 20860 - T: (301) 774-0022, Fax: (301) 774-8149, E-mail: dheibein@sandyspringmuseum.org, Internet: www.sandyspringmuseum.org. Dir.: Debbie Heibein
Local Museum / Historical Museum - 1980
Local history, quaker, farming 47392

Sanford FL

Museum of Seminole County History, 300 Bush Blvd, Sanford, FL 32773 - T: (407) 321-2489, Fax: (407) 665-5220, E-mail: kjacobs@co.seminole.fl.us, Internet: www.co.seminole.fl.us. Head: Karen Jacobs
Local Museum - 1983 47393

Sanford Museum, 520 E First St, Sanford, FL 32771 - T: (407) 302-1000, Fax: (407) 330-5666. Cur.: Alicia Clarke
Decorative Arts Museum / Historical Museum / Special Museum - 1957 47394

Sanford NC

House in the Horseshoe, 324 Alston House Rd, Sanford, NC 27330-8713 - T: (910) 947-2051, Fax: (910) 947-2051 (call first), E-mail: horseshoe@ac.net, Internet: www.ah.dcr.state.nc.us/sections/hs/horsesho.htm. Head: Guy Smith
Local Museum - 1972
Furnished house from 1772 47395

Railroad House Historical Museum, 110 Charlotte Av, Sanford, NC 27330 - T: (919) 776-7479
Local Museum - 1962
Local hist, railroad hist, Cole pottery 47396

Sanibel FL

Bailey-Matthews Shell Museum, 3075 Sanibel-Captiva Rd, Sanibel, FL 33957 - T: (941) 395-2233, Fax: (941) 395-6706, E-mail: shell@shellmuseum.org, Internet: www.shellmuseum.org. Dir.: José H. Leal
Natural History Museum - 1986 47397

Sankt Louis MO

Cecille R. Hunt Gallery, Webster University, 8342 Big Bend Blvd, Sankt Louis, MO 63119 - T: (314) 968-7171, E-mail: langtk@websteruniv.edu, Internet: www.webster.edu/dept/finearts/art. Chm.: Tom Lang
Fine Arts Museum - 1950
Local, national and international art in all media 47398

Santa Ana CA

The Bowers Museum of Cultural Art, 2002 N Main St, Santa Ana, CA 92706 - T: (714) 567-3600, 567-3698, Fax: (714) 567-3603, E-mail: pkeller@bowers.org, Internet: www.bowers.org. Pres.: Peter C. Keller, Chief Cur.: Armand Labbe, Cur.: Janet Baker (Asian Art)
Fine Arts Museum - 1936
Art 47399

Old Courthouse Museum, 211 W Santa Ana Blvd, Santa Ana, CA 92701 - T: (714) 834-3703, Fax: (714) 834-2280, E-mail: marshall.duell@pfrd.ocgov.com, Internet: www.ocparks.com. Dir.: Robert Selway, Cur.: Marshall Duell
Local Museum - 1987
County history 47400

Santa Ana College Art Gallery, 1530 W 17th St, Santa Ana, CA 92706 - T: (714) 564-5615, 564-5600, Fax: (714) 564-5629, E-mail: herberg-mayde@rsccd.org, Internet: www.sac.edu. Dir.: Mayde Herberg
Fine Arts Museum / University Museum - 1970 47401

Santa Barbara CA

Santa Barbara Contemporary Arts Forum, Klausner Gallery and Norton Gallery, 653 Paseo Nuevo, Santa Barbara, CA 93101 - T: (805) 966-5373, Fax: (805) 962-1421, Internet: www.sbcas.org. Dir.: Meg Linton
Fine Arts Museum 47402

Santa Barbara Historical Museum, 136 E De la Guerra St, Santa Barbara, CA 93101 - T: (805) 966-1601, Fax: (805) 966-1603, E-mail: ganderjack@sbhistorical.org, Internet: www.santabarbarahistory.org. Dir.: George M. Anderjack, Cur.: David Bisol, Ass. Cur.: Douglas Diller
Local Museum - 1932
Local hist 47403

Santa Barbara Museum of Art, 1130 State St, Santa Barbara, CA 93101-2746 - T: (805) 963-4364, Fax: (805) 966-6840, E-mail: info@sbmuseart.org, Internet: www.sbmuseart.org. Dir.: Robert H. Frankel, Cur.: Diana DuPont (Contemporary Art), Susan Shin-tsu Tai (Asian Art), Karen Sinsheimer (Photography)
Fine Arts Museum - 1941
Art 47404

Santa Barbara Museum of Natural History, 2559 Puesta del Sol Rd, Santa Barbara, CA 93105 - T: (805) 682-4711, Fax: (805) 569-3170, E-mail: info@sbnature2.org, Internet: www.sbnature.org. Dir.: Dr. Karl Hutterer, Cur.: Dr. John R. Johnson (Anthropology), Dr. F.G. Hochberg (Invertebrate Zoology), Paul W. Collins (Vertebrate Zoology)
Natural History Museum - 1916
Natural hist 47405

University Art Museum, University of California Santa Barbara, Santa Barbara, CA 93106-7130 - T: (805) 893-2951, 893-2724, Fax: (805) 893-3013, E-mail: uam@humanitas.ucsb.edu, Internet: uam.ucsb.edu. Dir.: Marla C. Berns, Bonnie G. Kelm, Chief Cur.: Christopher Scoates, Cur.: Kurt Helfrich (Architectural Drawing Collection)
Fine Arts Museum / University Museum - 1959
Paintings, renaissance medals and plaquettes, drawings, graphics, ceramics, sculpture 47406

Santa Clara CA

De Saisset Museum, Santa Clara University, 500 El Camino Real, Santa Clara, CA 95053-0550 - T: (408) 554-4528, Fax: (408) 554-7840, E-mail: rnadel@scu.edu, Internet: www.scu.edu/deSaisset. Dir.: Rebecca M. Schapp, Cur.: Karen Kienzle
Fine Arts Museum / University Museum / Historical Museum - 1955
Art, history 47407

Triton Museum of Art, 1505 Warburton Av, Santa Clara, CA 95050 - T: (408) 247-3754, Fax: (408) 247-3796, E-mail: triton246@aol.com, Internet: www.tritonmuseum.org. Dir.: George Rivera, Ass. Dir.: Beth Bowman, Cur.: Susan Hillhouse
Fine Arts Museum - 1965
Art 47408

Santa Cruz CA

Eloise Pickard Smith Gallery, c/o University of California at Santa Cruz, 1156 High St, Santa Cruz, CA 95064 - T: (831) 459-2953. Dir.: Linda Pope
Fine Arts Museum / University Museum 47409

Mary Porter Sesnon Art Gallery, c/o University of California at Santa Cruz, 1156 High St, Santa Cruz, CA 95064 - T: (831) 459-2314, Fax: (831) 459-3535, E-mail: sesnon@cats.ucsc.edu. Dir.: Shelby Graham
Fine Arts Museum / University Museum - 1974 47410

Museum of Art and History, 705 Front St, Santa Cruz, CA 95060 - T: (831) 429-1964 ext 10, Fax: (831) 429-1954, E-mail: admin@santacruzmah.org, Internet: www.santacruzmah.org. Exec. Dir.: Charles Hilger
Fine Arts Museum / Historical Museum - 1981 47411

Museum of International Children's Art, 765 Cedar St, Santa Cruz, CA 95063 - T: (831) 426-5557, Fax: (831) 426-1161, E-mail: editor@stonesoup.com, Internet: www.stonesoup.com. Pres.: William Rubel
Fine Arts Museum - 1973 47412

Santa Cruz Art League Museum, 526 Broadway, Santa Cruz, CA 95060 - T: (831) 426-5787, Fax: (831) 426-5789, Internet: www.scal.org. Pres.: Stephanie Schriver
Fine Arts Museum - 1919
Pioneer paintings, sculpture 47413

Santa Cruz Museum of Natural History, 1305 E Cliff Dr, Santa Cruz, CA 95062 - T: (831) 420-6115, Fax: (831) 420-6451, E-mail: staff@santacruzmuseum.org, Internet: www.santacruzmuseum.org. Dir.: Greg Moyce, Cur.: Jennifer Lienau
Natural History Museum - 1904
Regional natural hist 47414

Santa Fe NM

American Bicycle and Cycling Museum, POB 8533, Santa Fe, NM 87504 - T: (505) 989-7634, Fax: (505) 989-7634. Dir.: Sandra Vaillancourt
Science&Tech Museum - 1991 47415

Center for Contemporary Arts of Santa Fe, 1050 Old Pecos Trail, Santa Fe, NM 87501 - T: (505) 982-1338, Fax: (505) 982-9854, Internet: www.pla.bart.org. Dir.: Guy Ambrosino, Jerry Barson
Fine Arts Museum - 1985 47416

El Rancho de Las Golondrinas Museum, 334 Los Pinos Rd, Santa Fe, NM 87507 - T: (505) 471-2261, Fax: (505) 471-5623, E-mail: mail@golondrinas.org, Internet: www.golondrinas.org. Dir.: George B. Paloheimo, Cur.: Carla Gomez (Textiles), Julie Anna Lopez (Agriculture), Dr. Donna Pierce (Collection)
Open Air Museum - 1970 47417

Georgia O'Keeffe Museum, 217 Johnson St, Santa Fe, NM 87501 - T: (505) 946-1000, Fax: (505) 946-1091, E-mail: main@okeeffemuseum.org, Internet: www.okeeffemuseum.org. Dir.: George G. King
Fine Arts Museum - 1997
Modern art, paintings 47418

Governor's Gallery, State Capitol Bldg, Rm 400, Santa Fe, NM 87503 - T: (505) 827-3089, Fax: (505) 827-3026, E-mail: gov@gov.state.nm.us, Internet: www.governor.state.nm.us. Dir.: Dr. J. Edson Way, Cur.: Terry Bumpass
Fine Arts Museum - 1973 47419

Indian Arts Research Center, 660 Garcia St, Santa Fe, NM 87505, mail addr: POB 2188, Santa Fe, NM 87504 - T: (505) 954-7205, Fax: (505) 954-7207, E-mail: iarc@sarsf.org, Internet: www.sarweb.org
Fine Arts Museum / Decorative Arts Museum - 1907
Historic and contemporary SW Pueblo Indian pottery, Navajo and Pueblo Indian textiles and jewelry coll, Native American easel paintings, ethnography 47420

Institute of American Indian Arts Museum, 108 Cathedral Pl, 83 Avon Nu Po Rd, Santa Fe, NM 87501 - T: (505) 988-6281, Fax: (505) 988-6273, Internet: www.iaiacad.org. Dir.: Charles Daily, Cur.: Linda Woody Cywink, Ass. Cur.: Tatiana Lomaheftewa-Slock
Ethnology Museum / Fine Arts Museum - 1962 47421

Liquid Paper Correction Fluid Museum, Rte 1, Santa Fe, NM 87501 - T: (505) 455-3848. Pres.: Michael Nesmith, Dir.: Marcia J. Summers
Science&Tech Museum - 1980
Industrial hist 47422

Maria Martinez Museum, Rte 5, Box 315-A, Pueblo of San Ildefonso, Santa Fe, NM 87501 - T: (505) 455-2031, 455-3549
Decorative Arts Museum
Arts and crafts, clothing, painting, pottery 47423

Museum of Fine Arts, 107 W Palace, Santa Fe, NM 87501 - T: (505) 476-5072, Fax: (505) 476-5076, E-mail: mbol@mnn.state.nm.us. Dir.: Marsha C. Bol, Ass. Dir.: Bonnie Anderson, Aline Brandaeur, Cur.: Joseph Traugott (20th Century Art), Dr. Steven A. Yates (Photography), Ellen Zieselman (Education), Terry Bumpass (Governor's Gallery)
Fine Arts Museum - 1917
Art 47424

Museum of Indian Arts and Culture, 708 Camino Lejo, Santa Fe, NM 87505 - T: (505) 476-1250, Fax: (505) 476-1330, E-mail: info@miaclab.org, Internet: www.miaclab.org. Dir.: Duane Anderson, Ass. Dir.: Chris Turnbow, Cur.: Antonio Chavarria (Ethnology), Julia Clifton (Archaeological research coll), John Torres (Archaeology), Ass. Cur.: Dody Fugate, Tony Thibodeau (Archaeology), Valerie Verzuh (Collections)
Fine Arts Museum / Ethnology Museum / Folklore Museum - 1909
Anthropology, ethnology and Indian art 47425

Museum of International Folk Art, 706 Camino Lejo, Santa Fe, NM 87505, mail addr: POB 2087, Santa Fe, NM 87505-2087 - T: (505) 476-1200, Fax: (505) 476-1300, Internet: www.moifa.org. Dir.: Dr. Joyce Ice, Ass. Dir.: Jacqueline Duke, Cur.: Tamara Tjardes (Asian and Mid-Eastern Collections), Robin Farwell-Gavin (Spanish Colonial Collections), Barbara Mauldin (Latin American Folk Art), Dr. Tey Marianna Nunn (Contemporary Hispano and Latino Collections), Annie Carlano (European and American Art Collections), Dr. Barbara Sumberg (Textiles), Renee Jolie (Neutrogena Collections), Libr./ Photo Archivist: Ree Mobley
Folklore Museum - 1953
International folk art 47426

Museum of New Mexico, 113 Lincoln Av, Santa Fe, NM 87501 - T: (505) 476-5060, Fax: (505) 476-5088, E-mail: mnmreg@nm-us.campus.mci.net, Internet: www.museumofnewmexico.org. Dir.: Thomas A. Wilsony, Dep. Dir.: John J. McCarthy, Assoc. Dir.: Dr. Duane Anderson (Anthropology), Dr. Joyce Ice (Folk Art), Phoebe Hackett, Cur.: Aline Brandauer (Contemporary Art), Dr. Steve Yates (Contemporary Photography), Joseph Traugott (20th-Century Art), Charles Bennett (History), Diana Ortega DeSantis (Spanish Colonial History), Dr. Richard Rudisill, Art Olivas (Historic Photography), Louise Stiver (Archaeological Collections), Curtis F. Schaafsma (Anthropological Collections), Robin Farwell-Gavin (Spanish Colonial Folk Art), Barbara Mauldin (Latin American Art), Baldev Ball (Neutrogena), Dr. Tey Marianna Nunn (Hispanic and Latino), Judy Smith (European and American)
Local Museum / Historical Museum - 1909 47427

Museum of Spanish Colonial Art, 750 Camino Lejo, Santa Fe, NM 87505 - T: (505) 982-2226, Fax: (505) 982-4585, E-mail: museum@spanishcolonial.org, Internet: www.spanishcolonial.org. C.E.O.: Stuart A. Ashman
Fine Arts Museum - 1925 47428

Palace of the Governors, Museum of New Mexico, Plaza, Santa Fe, NM 87501, mail addr: POB 2087, Santa Fe, NM 87504-2087 - T: (505) 476-5094, Fax: (505) 476-5104, Internet: www.state.nm.us/moifa. Dir.: Thomas Chavez, Ass. Dir.: Charles Bennett, Cur.: Diana Ortega DeSantis, Pamela Smith, Arthur Olivas, Dr. Richard Rudisill, David H. Snow
Local Museum - 1909
Local hist 47429

San Miguel Mission Church, 401 Old Santa Fe Trail, Santa Fe, NM 87501 - T: (505) 983-3974, Fax: (505) 982-8722, E-mail: sanmiguel1610@yahoo.com
Religious Arts Museum - 1610
Indian art, religious artifacts, pottery 47430

Santa Fe Children's Museum, 1050 Old Pecos Trail, Santa Fe, NM 87501 - T: (505) 989-8359, Fax: (505) 989-7506, E-mail: children@santafehildrensmuseum.org, Internet: www.santafehildrensmuseum.org. Pres.: Peter Wirth, Dir.: Ellen Biderman, Londi Carbajal
Special Museum / Historical Museum - 1985 47431

Santuario de Nuestra Senora de Guadalupe, 100 S Guadalupe St, Santa Fe, NM 87501 - T: (505) 988-2027. Dir.: Emilio I. Ortiz, C.E.O.: Leo Kahn
Religious Arts Museum - 1975 47432

Site Santa Fe, 1606 Paseo de Peralta, Santa Fe, NM 87501 - T: (505) 989-1199, Fax: (505) 989-1188, E-mail: sitesantafe@sitesantafe.org, Internet: www.sitesantafe.org. Dir.: Louis Grachos, Cur.: Nora Kabat
Public Gallery - 1995 47433

Wheelwright Museum of the American Indian, 704 Camino Lejo, Santa Fe, NM 87505 - T: (505) 982-4636, Fax: (505) 989-7386, E-mail: pr@wheelwright.org, Internet: www.wheelwright.org. Dir.: Jonathan Batkin, Cur.: Cheri Falkenstien-Doyle
Folklore Museum / Ethnology Museum - 1937 47434

Santa Fe Springs CA

Hathaway Ranch Museum, 11901 E Florence Av, Santa Fe Springs, CA 90670 - T: (562) 944-7372, Fax: (562) 946-0708. Exec. Dir.: Nadine Hathaway
Agriculture Museum - 1986
American furnishings 19th c, farming 47435

Santa Maria CA

Santa Maria Museum of Flight, 3015 Airpark Dr, Santa Maria, CA 93455 - T: (805) 922-8758, Fax: (805) 922-8958, E-mail: smmof@thegrid.net, Internet: www.smmof.org. Pres.: K.R. Weber
Science&Tech Museum - 1984
Aeronautics 47436

Santa Maria Valley Historical Society Museum, 616 S Broadway, Santa Maria, CA 93454 - T: (805) 922-3130. Cur.: Richard Chenoweth
Local Museum - 1955
Local hist, Indian artifacts, Rancho period 47437

Santa Monica CA

American Museum of Cartoon Art, 2930 Colorado Av, Santa Monica, CA 90404 - T: (310) 828-2919, Fax: (310) 453-3003, E-mail: jeremykay@msn.com, Internet: www.cartoonmuseum.com. Dir./ Cur.: Jeremy Kay
Fine Arts Museum - 1976 47438

California Heritage Museum, 2612 Main St, Santa Monica, CA 90405 - T: (310) 392-8538, Fax: (310) 396-0547, E-mail: calmuseum@earthlink.net. Dir.: Tobi Smith
Historical Museum / Decorative Arts Museum / Fine Arts Museum - 1977
California History, decorative art, folk art 47439

Eighteenth Street Arts Complex, 1639 18th St, Santa Monica, CA 90404 - T: (310) 453-3711, Fax: (310) 453-4347, E-mail: arts18thst@aol.com, Internet: www.artswire.org/arts18st. Dir.: Clayton Campbell, Jan Williamson
Fine Arts Museum 47440

Pete and Susan Barrett Art Gallery, c/o Santa Monica College, 1900 Pico Blvd, Santa Monica, CA 90405 - T: (310) 434-4000, Fax: (310) 434-3646, Internet: www.smc.edu. Chm.: Maurizio Barattuci
Public Gallery - 1973
Southern California prints and drawings 47441

Santa Monica Museum of Art, Bergamot Stn, 2525 Michigan Av, Santa Monica, CA 90404 - T: (310) 586-6488, Fax: (310) 586-6487, E-mail: info@smmoa.org, Internet: www.smmoa.org. Exec. Dir.: Elsa Longhauser
Fine Arts Museum - 1985
Contemporary art, historic former train stn 47442

Santa Paula CA

California Oil Museum, 1001 E Main St, Santa Paula, CA 93060, mail addr: POB 48, Santa Paula, CA 93060 - T: (805) 933-0076, Fax: (805) 933-0096, E-mail: info@oilmuseum.net, Internet: www.oilmuseum.net. Dir.: Mike Nelson, Cur.: John Nichols
Science&Tech Museum - 1950
Oil Industry 47443

Santa Paula Union Oil Museum → California Oil Museum

Santa Rosa CA

Campus Art Gallery, Santa Rosa Junior College, 1501 Mendocino Av, Santa Rosa, CA 95401 - T: (707) 527-4259. Dir.: Deborah Kirklin
Public Gallery / University Museum 47444

Jesse Peter Museum, Santa Rosa Junior College, 1501 Mendocino Av, Santa Rosa, CA 95401 - T: (707) 527-4479, Fax: (707) 524-1861, E-mail: bbenson@santarosa.edu, Internet: www.santarosa.edu/museum. Dir./Cur.: Benjamin Foley Benson
Ethnology Museum - 1932
Native American art 47445

Luther Burbank Home, Santa Rosa and Sonoma Avs, Santa Rosa, CA 95402 - T: (707) 524-5445, Fax: (707) 524-5827, E-mail: burbankhome@lutherburbank.org, Internet: www.lutherburbank.org
Local Museum - 1979
Historic house, furnishings, tools - gardens 47446

Santa Rosa Junior College Art Gallery, 1501 Mendocino Av, Santa Rosa, CA 95401-4395 - T: (707) 527-4298, Fax: (707) 527-4532, Internet: www.santarosa.edu. Dir.: Renata Breth
Fine Arts Museum - 1973 47447

Sonoma County Museum, 425 Seventh St, Santa Rosa, CA 95401 - T: (707) 579-1500, Fax: (707) 579-4849, E-mail: info@sonomacountymuseum.com, Internet: www.sonomacountymuseum.com. Dir.: Natasha Boas, Sc. Staff: Eric Stanley
Local Museum - 1976
Local hist 47448

Sapulpa OK

Sapulpa Historical Museum, 100 E Lee, Sapulpa, OK 74066 - T: (918) 224-4871, Fax: (918) 224-7765, E-mail: saphistoc@juno.com
Local Museum - 1968 47449

Saranac Lake NY

Robert Louis Stevenson Memorial Cottage, 11 Stevenson Ln, Saranac Lake, NY 12983 - T: (518) 891-1462, E-mail: pennypiper@capital.net, Internet: www.penpiper.org. Dir.: Susan Allen, Cur.: John M. Delahant
Special Museum - 1920 47450

Sarasota FL

Art Center Sarasota, 707 N Tamiami Trail, Sarasota, FL 34236-4050 - T: (941) 365-2032, Fax: (941) 366-0585, E-mail: visualartcenter@aol.com, Internet: www.artsarasota.org. Dir.: Lisa-Marie Confessore
Fine Arts Museum / Public Gallery / Association with Coll - 1926 47451

Crowley Museum, 16405 Myakka Rd, Sarasota, FL 34240 - T: (941) 322-1000, Fax: (941) 322-1000, E-mail: crowleymuseum@aol.com, Internet: www.crowleymuseumnaturectr.org. Exec. Dir.: Debbie Dixon
Historical Museum / Natural History Museum - 1974
History, natural history 47452

The John and Mable Ringling Museum of Art, State Art Museum of Florida, 5401 Bay Shore Rd, Sarasota, FL 34243 - T: (941) 359-5700, Fax: (941) 359-5745, E-mail: info@ringling.org, Internet: www.ringling.org. Dir.: John Wetenhall, Cur.: Aaron DeGroft (Chief), Mitchell Merling (Art before 1900), Deborah Walk (Circus Museum), Cons.: Michelle Scalera
Fine Arts Museum / University Museum - 1927
Archaeology, folk culture, costumes and textiles, decorative arts, paintings, photographs, prints, drawings, graphic arts, sculpture, furnishings, botany 47453

Sarasota Classic Car Museum, 5500 N Tamiami Trail, Sarasota, FL 34243 - T: (941) 355-6228, Fax: (941) 358-8065, E-mail: classiccarmuseum@aol.com, Internet: www.sarasotacarmuseum.org. Dir.: John Christian
Science&Tech Museum - 1953
Automobile, horseless carriages, automotive hist, player pianos, organs, Edison's phonographs, music boxes 47454

Selby Gallery, Ringling School of Art and Design, 2700 N Tamiami Trail, Sarasota, FL 34234 - T: (941) 359-7563, Fax: (941) 359-7517, E-mail: selby@ringling.edu, Internet: www.rsad.edu/. Dir.: Kevin Dean, Ass. Dir.: Laura Avery
University Museum - 1986
Library 47455

The Turner Museum, 2846 Golden Poiwciana Palace, Sarasota, FL 34232, mail addr: POB 18133, Sarasota, FL 34276-1133 - T: (941) 924-5622, 378-1885, Fax: (941) 924-5622, 378-1885, E-mail: curator@turnermuseum.org, Internet: www.turnermuseum.org. Pres./Dir.: Douglass J.M. Graham
Fine Arts Museum - 1973
Art of J.M.W. Turner (1775-1851) 47456

Saratoga CA

Montalvo Center for the Arts, 15400 Montalvo Rd, Saratoga, CA 95070 - T: (408) 961-5800, Fax: (408) 961-5850, E-mail: mrowe-shields@villamontalvo.org, Internet: www.villamontalvo.org. Dir.: Elisbeth Challener, Michele Rowe-Shields
Fine Arts Museum - 1930
Paintings, sculpture, decorative art 47457

Saratoga WY

Saratoga Museum, 104 Constitution Av, Saratoga, WY 82331 - T: (307) 326-5511, Internet: members.xoom.com/kaikin/welcome. Dir.: Pat Bensen
Local Museum / Archaeological Museum - 1978
Local hist 47458

Saratoga Springs NY

The Children's Museum at Saratoga, 36 Phila St, Saratoga Springs, NY 12866 - T: (518) 584-5540, Fax: (518) 584-6049, E-mail: cmas@netheaven.com, Internet: www.childrensmuseumatsaratoga.org. Dir.: Ashley Edwards
Special Museum - 1989 47459

National Museum of Dance, 99 S Broadway, Saratoga Springs, NY 12866 - T: (518) 584-2225, Fax: (518) 584-4515, E-mail: info@dancemuseum.org, Internet: www.dancemuseum.org. Dir.: Herbert A. Chesbrough
Performing Arts Museum - 1986 47460

National Museum of Racing and Hall of Fame, 191 Union Av, Saratoga Springs, NY 12866 - T: (518) 584-0400, Fax: (518) 584-4574, E-mail: nmrhof96@race.saratoga.ny.us, Internet: www.racingmuseum.org. Dir.: Peter Hammell, Ass. Dir.: Cathy Maguire
Special Museum - 1950 47461

Saratoga Springs Museum, Casino, Congress Park, Saratoga Springs, NY 12866 - T: (518) 584-6920, Fax: (518) 581-1477, E-mail: historicalsociety@juno.com, Internet: www.saratogahistory.org. Dir.: James D. Parillo, Ass. Dir.: Maryann Fitzgerald, Cur.: Erin Doane
Decorative Arts Museum / Local Museum - 1883 47462

Schick Art Gallery, c/o Skidmore College, Skidmore Campus, 815 N Broadway, Saratoga Springs, NY 12866-1632 - T: (518) 584-5000 ext 2370, Fax: (516) 580-5029, E-mail: damiller@skidmore.edu, Internet: www.skidmorecollege.edu. Dir.: David Miller
Fine Arts Museum / University Museum - 1926 47463

Tang Teaching Museum and Art Gallery, c/o Skidmore College, 815 N Broadway, Saratoga Springs, NY 12866 - T: (518) 580-8080, Fax: (518) 580-5069, Internet: www.skidmore.edu/tang. C.E.O.: Charles Stainback
Fine Arts Museum
Drawings, paintings, prints, sculptures, video, installation art 47464

Saugerties NY

Opus 40 and the Quarryman's Museum, 50 Fite Rd, Saugerties, NY 12477 - T: (914) 246-3400, Fax: (914) 246-1997, Internet: www.opus40.org. C.E.O.: Pat Richards
Fine Arts Museum / Local Museum - 1978 47465

Saugus MA

Saugus Iron Works, 244 Central St, Saugus, MA 01906 - T: (781) 233-0050, Fax: (781) 231-9012, Internet: www.nps.gov/sair. Dir.: Steve Kesselman, Sc. Staff: Carl Salmons-Perez
Science&Tech Museum - 1954
Blast furnace, forge and slitting mill 47466

Sauk Centre MN

Sinclair Lewis Museum, 194 and US 71, Sauk Centre, MN 56378 - T: (320) 352-5201. Pres.: Roberta Olson
Historical Museum - 1960 47467

Saukville WI

Ozaukee County Historical Society Pioneer Village, 4880 Hwy I, Saukville, WI 53080 - T: (262) 377-4510, Fax: (262) 377-4510, Internet: www.co.ozaukee.wi.us/ochs. Pres.: Curtis Grunewald, Cur.: Ruth Renz
Open Air Museum / Local Museum - 1960
Pioneer village 47468

Sault Sainte Marie MI

Sault de Sainte Marie Historical Sites, 501 E Water St, Sault Sainte Marie, MI 49783 - T: (906) 632-3658, Fax: (906) 632-9344, E-mail: valleycamp@sault.com. Pres.: John P. Wellington, Dir.: J.H. Hobaugh
Historical Museum / Science&Tech Museum - 1967
Maritime hist 47469

Saum MN

First Consolidated School in Minnesota, Main St, Saum, MN 56650 - T: (218) 647-8673. C.E.O.: Arnold Wolden
Historical Museum - 1962
1903 original log school, 1912 Saum School 47470

Saunderstown RI

Casey Farm, Route 1A, Saunderstown, RI 02874 - T: (617) 227-3956, Fax: (617) 227-9204, E-mail: ezopes@spnea.org, Internet: www.spnea.org. Dir.: Elaine Zopes
Open Air Museum / Local Museum - 1955
Historic homestead 47471

The Gilbert Stuart Museum, 815 Gilbert Stuart Rd, Saunderstown, RI 02874 - T: (401) 294-3001, Fax: (401) 294-3869, E-mail: deborahethompson@aol.com, Internet: www.gilbertstuartmuseum.org. Cur.: John Thompson, Deborah Thompson
Fine Arts Museum - 1930
Historic house, birthplace of artist Gilbert Stuart 47472

Sausalito CA

Bay Area Discovery Museum, Fort Baker, 557 McReynolds Rd, Sausalito, CA 94965 - T: (415) 487-4398, 289-7276, Fax: (415) 332-9671, E-mail: info@badm.org, Internet: www.badm.org. Pres.: Anne Dickerson Lind, C.E.O.: Lori Fogarty
Special Museum - 1984
Art, nature and science 47473

Headlands Center for the Arts, 944 Fort Barry, Sausalito, CA 94965 - T: (415) 331-2787, Fax: (415) 331-3857, E-mail: staff@headlands.org, Internet: www.headlands.org
Public Gallery 47474

Sautee GA

Sautee-Nacoochee Museum, 283 Hwy 255 N, Sautee, GA 30571 - T: (706) 878-3300, Fax: (706) 878-1395, Internet: www.snca.org. Cur.: Joanna Tinius
Decorative Arts Museum
Paintings, pottery, glass, jewelry 47475

Savannah GA

Archives Museum - Temple Mickve Israel, 20 E Gordon St, Savannah, GA 31401 - T: (912) 233-1547, Fax: (912) 233-3086, E-mail: Rabbelzer@aol.com, Internet: www.mickveisrael.org. Pres.: Joel Greenberg
Religious Arts Museum - 1974
Congregation Mickve Israel Synagogue, oldest Jewish congregation in the South 47476

Davenport House Museum, 324 E State St, Savannah, GA 31401 - T: (912) 236-7938, Fax: (912) 233-7706, E-mail: davenport@g-net.net. Dir.: Stewart. Dohrman
Historical Museum / Historic Site - 1955
Historic House, court inventory, federal furniture, china 47477

Fort Pulaski, US-Hwy 80 E, Savannah, GA 31410 - T: (912) 786-5787, Fax: (912) 786-6023, Internet: www.nps.gov/fopu. Head: John D. Breen
Military Museum - 1924 47478

Georgia Historical Society Museum, 501 Whitaker St, Savannah, GA 31401 - T: (912) 651-2125, Fax: (912) 651-2831, E-mail: ghs@georgiahistory.com, Internet: www.georgiahistory.com. Dir.: Dr. W. Todd Groce
Local Museum - 1839
Regional history 47479

Juliette Gordon Low Birthplace, 10 E Oglethorpe Av, Savannah, GA 31401 - T: (912) 233-4501, Fax: (912) 233-4659, E-mail: birthplace@girlscouts.org, Internet: www.girlscouts.org/birthplace. Dir.: Fran Powell Harold, Cur.: Stephen Bohlin-Davis
Historical Museum - 1956
1818-1821 Wayne-Gordon House 47480

Old Fort Jackson, 1 Fort Jackson Rd, Savannah, GA 31404 - T: (912) 232-3945, Fax: (912) 236-5126, E-mail: fortjackson@chsgeorgia.org, Internet: www.chsgeorgia.org. Exec. Dir.: Scott Smith
Military Museum - 1975
Military 47481

Owens-Thomas House, 124 Abercorn, Savannah, GA 31401 - T: (912) 233-9743, Fax: (912) 233-0102, E-mail: chamberlainc@telfair.org, Internet: www.telfair.org. Dir.: Diane B. Lesko, Cur.: Carola Hunt Chamberlain
Historical Museum - 1951
Original carriage house with slave quarters and walled garden 47482

Savannah College of Art and Design Galleries, 320 E Liberty St, Savannah, GA 31402 - T: (912) 525-4950, Fax: (912) 525-4952, E-mail: info@scad.edu, Internet: www.scad.edu. Dir.: Jeffrey Bilderback
Fine Arts Museum - 1979 47483

Ships of the Sea Maritime Museum, 41 MLK Blvd, Savannah, GA 31401 - T: (912) 232-1511, Fax: (912) 234-7363, E-mail: shipssea@bellsouth.net, Internet: www.shipsofthesea.org. Exec. Dir.: Jeff Fulton
Historical Museum - 1966 47484

Telfair Museum of Art, 121 Barnard St, Savannah, GA 31401 - T: (912) 232-1177, Fax: (912) 232-6954, E-mail: mooreb@telefair.org, Internet: www.telfair.org. Dir.: Diane B. Lesko, Cur.: Harry DeLorme (Education), Hollis K. McCullough (Fine Arts, Exhibitions)
Fine Arts Museum / Science&Tech Museum - 1875 47485

William Scarbrough House, Ships of the Sea Museum, 41 Martin Luther King Blvd, Savannah, GA 31401 - T: (912) 232-1511, Fax: (912) 234-7363, E-mail: shipssea@bellsouth.net, Internet: www.shipsofthesea.org. Dir.: Tony Pizzo, Ass. Dir.: Karl DeVries
Historical Museum - 1966
Maritime history, housed in 1819 Regency style house 47486

Wormsloe State Historic Site, 7601 Skidaway Rd, Savannah, GA 31406 - T: (912) 353-3023, Fax: (912) 353-3023, E-mail: wormsloe@g-net.net, Internet: www.gastateparks.org. Head: Joe H. Thompson
Archaeological Museum - 1973
Ruins of 1739 fortified house 47487

Savannah MO

Andrew County Museum, 202 E Duncan Dr, Savannah, MO 64485-0012 - T: (816) 324-4720, Fax: (816) 324-5271, E-mail: andcomus@ccp.com, Internet: www.artcom.com/museums/. Pres.: Harold Johnson, Dir./Cur.: Patrick S. Clark
Local Museum - 1972 47488

Saxton PA

Captain Phillips' Rangers Memorial, Pennsylvania Hwy 26, Saxton, PA 16678 - T: (717) 787-3602, Fax: (717) 783-1073
Historic Site - 1959
Site of July 16, 1780, Indian massacre of members of Capt. Phillips' militia 47489

Sayville NY

Sayville Historical Society Museum, Edwards St and Collins Av, Sayville, NY 11782 - T: (631) 563-0186, 589-2609
Local Museum - 1944
Local hist 47490

Scarborough ME

Scarborough Historical Museum, 649A U.S. Rte 1, Dunstan, Scarborough, ME 04074 - T: (207) 883-3539. Pres.: Rodney Laughton
Local Museum - 1961
Local history 47491

Scarsdale NY

Scarsdale Historical Society Museum, 937 Post Rd, Scarsdale, NY 10583 - T: (914) 723-1744, Fax: (914) 723-2185, E-mail: history@cloud9.net, Internet: www.scarsdalenet.com/historicalsociety. Exec. Dir.: Penny Brickman, Cur.: Karen Frederick, Kathy Craughwell-Varda
Local Museum - 1973 47492

Weinberg Nature Center, 455 Mamaroneck Rd, Scarsdale, NY 10583 - T: (914) 722-1289, Fax: (914) 723-4784, Internet: www.scarsdale.com/weinberg.asp. Pres.: Lois Weiss, Dir.: Walter D. Terrell
Natural History Museum - 1958 47493

Schaefferstown PA

Historic Schaefferstown, N Market St, Schaefferstown, PA 17088 - T: (717) 949-2444. Pres.: Ed Bixler
Agriculture Museum / Local Museum - 1966
Local hist 47494

Schaumburg IL

Motorola Museum, 1297 E Algonquin Rd, Schaumburg, IL 60196 - T: (847) 576-6400, Fax: (847) 576-6401, E-mail: asd003@email.mot.com. Dir.: Sharon Darling
Science&Tech Museum - 1991 47495

Volkening Heritage Farm at Spring Valley, 1111 E Schaumburg Rd, Schaumburg, IL 60194 - T: (847) 985-2100, Fax: (847) 985-9692, Internet: www.parkfun.com. C.E.O.: Jerry Handlon
Natural History Museum / Agriculture Museum / Historical Museum - 1983
Living history farm, German-American farmlife of the 1880s 47496

Schenectady NY

Schenectady County Historical Society Museum, 32 Washington Av, Schenectady, NY 12305 - T: (518) 374-0263, Fax: (208) 361-5305, E-mail: librarian@schist.org, Internet: www.schist.org. Pres.: William Dimpelfeld
Local Museum - 1905 47497

Schenectady Museum, 15 Nott Terrace Heights, Schenectady, NY 12308 - T: (518) 382-7890, Fax: (518) 382-7893, E-mail: schdymuse@schenectadymuseum.org, Internet: www.schenectadymuseum.org. Dir.: Bart A. Roselli, Ass. Dir.: Randy Roberts
Local Museum - 1934 47498

Schoharie NY

Old Stone Fort Museum Complex, 145 Fort Rd, Schoharie, NY 12157 - T: (518) 295-7192, Fax: (518) 295-7187, E-mail: schosf@telenet.net, Internet: www.schohariehistory.net. Dir.: Carle J. Kopecky, Cur.: Daniel J. Beans
Local Museum / Historical Museum - 1889
Local history, American war for independence - Library, archives 47499

Schoharie Colonial Heritage Association Museum, 1743 Palatine House, Spring St, Schoharie, NY 12157 - T: (518) 295-7505, Fax: (518) 295-6001, E-mail: scha@midtel.net, Internet: www.midtel.net/~scha. Pres.: Judith Warner
Local Museum - 1963 47500

Schwenksville PA

Pennypacker Mills, 5 Haldeman Rd, Schwenksville, PA 19473 - T: (610) 287-9349, Fax: (610) 287-9657, E-mail: pennypackermills@mail.montcopa.org, Internet: www.montcopa.org/culture/history.htm. Dir.: Ella Aderman
Science&Tech Museum - 1981
Historic house 47501

Scituate MA

Scituate Historical Museum, Laidlaw Historical Center, 43 Cudworth Rd, Scituate, MA 02066 - T: (781) 545-1083, Fax: (781) 544-1249, E-mail: history@ziplink.net, Internet: www.scituate-history.org. Pres.: Susan Phippin
Local Museum - 1916
Local history 47502

Scituate Maritime and Irish Mossing Museum, The Driftway, Scituate, MA 02066 - T: (781) 545-1083, Fax: (781) 544-1249, E-mail: history@ziplink.net, Internet: www.scituate-history.org. Cur.: Eugene N. Trainor
Historical Museum - 1997
Maritime hist since the 17th c, North River shipbuilding, coast disasters, Irish mossing, lifesaving services 47503

Scobey MT

Daniels County Museum and Pioneer Town, 7 County Rd, Scobey, MT 59263 - T: (406) 487-5965, Fax: (406) 487-2224, E-mail: papegg@nemontel.net, Internet: www.scobey.org. Pres.: Edgar Richardson, Dir.: Chet Solberg, Lee Cook, Sue Leibrand, Justin Hanson, Mike Stableton, Mary Richardson, Paul Landeraasen
Local Museum - 1965 47504

Scotia CA

Pacific Lumber Company Museum, 125 Main St, Scotia, CA 95565 - T: (707) 764-2222, Fax: (707) 764-4150, Internet: www.palco.com. Dir.: Robert Manne
Historical Museum - 1959
Logging and lumber industry 47505

Scotia NY

Flint House, 421 Reynolds St, Scotia, NY 12302 - T: (518) 377-8799, 374-1071, Fax: (518) 374-0542
Local Museum - 1997
Village hist 47506

Scotia-Glenville Children's Museum, 303 Mohawk Av, Scotia, NY 12302 - T: (518) 346-1764, Fax: (518) 377-6593, E-mail: sgcminfo@crisny.org. Pres.: Dr. Frank B. Strauss, C.E.O.: Nancy Lamb
Special Museum - 1978 47507

Scotland SD

Scotland Heritage Chapel and Museum, 811 6th St, Scotland, SD 57059 - T: (605) 583-2344. Pres.: Betty Woehl, Cur.: Marvin Thum
Local Museum / Religious Arts Museum - 1976
Local and religious hist 47508

Scott AR

Plantation Agriculture Museum, 4815 Hwy 161, Scott, AR 72142 - T: (501) 961-1409, Fax: (501) 961-1579, E-mail: plantationag@arkansas.com, Internet: www.arkansas.com. Dir.: Ben H. Swadley, Cur.: Randy Noah
Agriculture Museum / Local Museum - 1989
Agriculture, local hist 47509

Toltec Mounds Archeological State Park, 490 Toltec Mounds Rd, Scott, AR 72142 - T: (501) 961-9442, Fax: (501) 961-9221, E-mail: toltecmounds@arkansas.com, Internet: www.wwn.cast.vark.edn/~shelly/html/parkin/toltecvisitpg.html. Dir.: Henry Thomason
Archaeological Museum - 1975
Archaeology 47510

Scottdale PA

West Overton Museums, West Overton Village, Scottdale, PA 15683 - T: (724) 887-7910, Fax: (724) 882-5010, E-mail: womuseum@westol.com, Internet: www.fay-west/westoverton.com. Pres.: Susan U. Endersbe, Dir.: Rodney Sturtz
Open Air Museum / Local Museum - 1928
Rural industrial village 47511

Scottsdale AZ

Fleischer Museum, 17207 N Perimeter Dr, Scottsdale, AZ 85255 - T: (480) 585-3108, Fax: (480) 563-6192, E-mail: joan.hoeffel@fleischer.org, Internet: www.fleischer.org. Dir.: Donna H. Fleischer, Ass. Dir.: Joan Hoeffel
Fine Arts Museum - 1990
Art 47512

Rawhide Old West Museum, 23023 N Scottsdale Rd, Scottsdale, AZ 85255 - T: (602) 502-5600, Fax: (602) 502-1301, Internet: www.rawhide.com. Dir.: Victor Ostrow
Local Museum - 1972
Local hist 47513

Scottsdale Museum of Contemporary Art, 7380 E Second St, Scottsdale, AZ 85251 - T: (480) 874-4610, Fax: (480) 874-4699, E-mail: info@sccarts.org, Internet: www.scottsdalearts.org. Dir.: Susan Crane, Cur.: Debra Hopkins, Carolyn Robbins
Fine Arts Museum / Public Gallery - 1975
Contemporary art, architecture, design 47514

Sylvia Plotkin Judaica Museum, 10460 N 56th St, Scottsdale, AZ 85253 - T: (480) 951-0323, Fax: (480) 951-7150, E-mail: museum@templebethisrael.org, Internet: www.sylviaplotkinjudaicamuseum.org. Dir.: Pamela Levin
Religious Arts Museum - 1966
Religious antiques, housed in Temple belonging to oldest Jewish Congregation in the Phoenix area 47515

Scranton PA

The Catlin House Museum, 232 Monroe Av, Scranton, PA 18510 - T: (717) 344-3841, Fax: (717) 344-3815. Pres.: Alan Sweeney, Exec. Dir.: Maryann Moran
Local Museum - 1886
Local hist 47516

Everhart Museum of Natural History, Science and Art, 1901 Mulberry St, Scranton, PA 18510-2390 - T: (570) 346-7186, Fax: (570) 346-0652, E-mail: exdir@everhart.museum.org, Internet: Everhart-museum.org. Dir.: Dr. Michael C. Illuzzi, Ass. Dir.: Julie Orloski, Cur.: Bruce Lanning (Art)
Fine Arts Museum / Natural History Museum / Science&Tech Museum - 1908
Art, science and natural hist 47517

Houdini Museum, 1433 N Main Av, Scranton, PA 18508 - T: (570) 342-5555, E-mail: magicusa@microserve.net, Internet: www.houdini.org. C.E.O.: John Bravo
Performing Arts Museum - 1992
Houdini's life theater, film and artifacts 47518

Marywood University Art Galleries, 2300 Adams Av, Scranton, PA 18509 - T: (717) 348-6278, Fax: (717) 340-6023, E-mail: gallery@marywood.edu, Internet: www.marywood.edu/www2/galleries. Pres.: Mary Reap, Dir.: Sandra Ward Povse
Fine Arts Museum / University Museum - 1924 47519

Pennsylvania Anthracite Heritage Museum, RR 1, Bald Mountain Rd, Scranton, PA 18504 - T: (570) 963-4804, 963-4845, Fax: (570) 963-4194, Internet: www.phmc.state.pa.us. Dir.: Steven Ling, Cur.: Chester Kulesa
Historical Museum - 1975
History 47520

Steamtown National Historic Site, 150 S Washington Av, Scranton, PA 18503 - T: (570) 340-5200, Fax: (570) 340-5309, Internet: www.nps.gov/stea. Dir.: Dr. Harold H. Hagen, Cur.: Ella S. Rayburn
Science&Tech Museum - 1986
Transportation and technology 47521

Seabrook TX

Bay Area Museum, 5000 Nasa Rd I, Seabrook, TX 77586 - T: (281) 326-5950, Fax: (281) 326-5950. Dir.: Joy Smitherman
Local Museum - 1984 47522

Seaford DE

Governor Ross Plantation, 1101 N Pine St, Seaford, DE 19973 - T: (302) 628-9500, Fax: (302) 628-9501. Pres./Dir.: Earl B. Tull
Local Museum - 1977
Local hist, decorative arts 47523

Seaford NY

Seaford Historical Museum, 3890 Waverly Av, Seaford, NY 11783 - T: (516) 826-1150. Pres.: Joshua Soren
Local Museum - 1968 47524

Seagraves TX

Loop Museum and Art Center, 201 Main, Seagraves, TX 79359 - T: (806) 546-2810, Fax: (806) 546-2810. Dir.: Bernell Thompson
Local Museum / Fine Arts Museum - 1974
Barbed wire coll, Indian artifacts, military 47525

Seagrove NC

North Carolina Pottery Center, 250 East Av, Seagrove, NC 27341-0531 - T: (336) 873-8430, Fax: (336) 873-8530, E-mail: ncpc@atomic.net, Internet: www.ncpotterycenter.com. C.E.O.: Joanna Ruth Marsland
Decorative Arts Museum - 1991
North Carolina pottery, southern pottery, tools 47526

Searsport ME

Penobscot Marine Museum, 5 Church St, Searsport, ME 04974-0498 - T: (207) 548-2529, Fax: (207) 548-2520, E-mail: museumoffices@penobscotmarinemuseum.org, Internet: www.penobscotmarinemuseum.org. Dir.: Renny A. Stackpole, Cur.: Kathryn Campbell
Historical Museum - 1936
Maritime hist, 3 sea captain's homes and Town Hall, paintings - Phillips library, Carver gallery 47527

Seattle WA

Blenko Museum of Seattle, 222 Westlake Av N, Seattle, WA 98109 - T: (206) 628-3117, Internet: sherril2.user.msu.edu/blenko/blenko_museum.htm
Fine Arts Museum
Hand-blown designer American glass from the Blenko Company of Milton 47528

Burke Museum of Natural History and Culture, c/o University of Washington, 17th Av NE and NE 45th St, Campus, Seattle, WA 98195 - T: (206) 543-7907, Fax: (206) 685-3039, E-mail: recept@u.washington.edu, Internet: www.burkemuseum.org. Dir.: Dr. George MacDonald, Cur.: Dr. Steve Hawell (Asian Ethnology), Dr. Sievert Rohwer (Birds), Dr. Robin K. Wright (Native American Art), Dr. James Nason (Native American Ethnology), Dr. John M. Rensberger (Vertebrate Paleontology), Dr. Elizabeth Nesbitt (Invertebrate Paleontology), Dr. Ted Pietsch (Fish), Dr. James Kenagy (Mammals), Dr. Scott Edwards (Genetic Resources), Dr. Richard Olmstead (Herbarium)
Ethnology Museum / Natural History Museum / Folklore Museum - 1885
Anthropology, natural hist, art 47529

Center for Wooden Boats, 1010 Valley St, Seattle, WA 98109 - T: (206) 382-2628, Fax: (206) 382-2699, E-mail: cwb@cwb.org, Internet: www.cwb.org. Pres.: Ken Greff, Exec. Dir.: Bob Perkins
Science&Tech Museum - 1978
Boats 47530

Center on Contemporary Art, 1420 11th Av, Seattle, WA 98121-1327 - T: (206) 728-1980, Fax: (206) 728-1980, E-mail: cocoa@cocaseattle.org, Internet: www.cocaseattle.org. Dir.: Steve Tremble
Fine Arts Museum
Contemporary art 47531

The Children's Museum, 305 Harrison St, Seattle, WA 98109 - T: (206) 441-1768, Fax: (206) 448-0910. Dir.: Steve McGraw, Public Relations: Charlotte Beall
Special Museum - 1981
Children's museum 47532

Experience Music Project, 2910 Third Av, Seattle, WA 98121 - T: (206) 770-2700, Fax: (206) 770-2727, Internet: www.emplive.com. C.E.O.: Jody Patton
Music Museum - 1999
Jimi Hendrix, guitar, roots of rock'n'roll, hip-hop, punk, reggae 47533

Frye Art Museum, 704 Terry Av, Seattle, WA 98104 - T: (206) 622-9250, Fax: (206) 223-1707, E-mail: fryeart@aol.com, Internet: www.fryeart.org. Pres.: Richard L. Cleveland, Dir.: Richard V. West, Sc. Staff: Steven Broocks (Education), Debra J. Byrne (Exhebitions), Donna Kovalenko (19th and 20th c American and European paintings)
Fine Arts Museum - 1952
Art 47534

Henry Art Gallery, University of Washington, 15th Av NE and NE 41st St, Seattle, WA 98195, mail addr: Box 351410, Seattle, WA 98195-1410 - T: (206) 543-2280/81, Fax: (206) 685-3123, E-mail: hartg@u.washington.edu, Internet: www.henryart.org. Dir.: Richard Andrews, Cur.: Elizabeth A. Brown, Judy Sourakli (Collections)
Fine Arts Museum / University Museum - 1927
Art 47535

King County Arts Commission Gallery, Smith Tower, Rm 1115, 506 Second Av, Seattle, WA 98104-2311 - T: (206) 296-8671, Fax: (206) 296-8629, E-mail: jimkelly@metrokc.gov, Internet: www.kingcountyarts.org. Dir.: Jim Kelly
Public Gallery - 1967 47536

Klondike Gold Rush National Historical Park, 117 S Main, Seattle, WA 98104 - T: (206) 553-7220, Fax: (206) 553-0614, E-mail: klse_Ranger_-Avtivities@nps.gov, Internet: www.nps.gov/klse. Head: Willie Russell
Historical Museum - 1979
History 47537

Memory Lane Museum at Seattle Goodwill, 1400 S Lane St, Seattle, WA 98144 - T: (206) 329-1000, Fax: (206) 726-1502, E-mail: goodwill@seattlegoodwill.org, Internet: www.seattlegoodwill.org. Pres.: Jill Jones
Local Museum - 1968
Local hist 47538

Museum of Flight, 9404 E Marginal Way S, Seattle, WA 98108 - T: (206) 764-5720, Fax: (206) 764-5707, E-mail: info@museumofflight.org, Internet: www.museumofflight.org. Pres.: Ralph A. Bufano, Cur.: Dennis Parks
Science&Tech Museum / Military Museum / Historical Museum - 1964
Aeronautics 47539

Museum of History and Industry, 2700 24th Av, Seattle, WA 98112 - T: (206) 324-1126, Fax: (206) 324-1346, E-mail: mjh@historymuse-nw.org, Internet: www.seattlehistory.org. Dir.: Leonard Garfield, Cur.: Elizabeth Furlow (Collections)
Historical Museum - 1914
History, industry 47540

Nordic Heritage Museum, 3014 NW 67th St, Seattle, WA 98117 - T: (206) 789-5707, Fax: (206) 789-3271, E-mail: nordic@intelistip.com, Internet: www.nordicmuseum.com. Dir.: Marianne Forssblad, Cur.: Lisa Hill-Festa
Special Museum - 1979
Local hist, nordic hist, nordic american art 47541

Pacific Arts Center, 1500 Lakeview Blvd E, Seattle, WA 98102 - T: (206) 329-2722, Fax: (206) 329-7554. Pres.: Marty Spiegel
Fine Arts Museum - 1983
Art 47542

Pacific Science Center, 200 2nd Av N, Seattle, WA 98109 - T: (206) 443-2001, Fax: (206) 443-3631, E-mail: webmaster@pacsci.org, Internet: www.pacsci.org. Pres.: Lawrence P. Horowitz, Exec. Dir.: George P. Moynihan, Dir.: John D. Warner
Science&Tech Museum - 1962
Science, technology 47543

Sacred Circle Gallery of American Indian Art, United Indians of All Tribes Foundation, Discovery Park, Daybreak Star Art and Cultural Center, Seattle, WA 98101, mail addr: POB 99100, Seattle, WA 98199 - T: (206) 285-4425, Fax: (206) 282-3640, E-mail: info@unitedindians.com, Internet: www.unitedindians.com. Dir.: Steve Charles, Merlee Markishtum
Fine Arts Museum - 1977
Coll of Native American traditional and contemporary artwork and murals, incl works by Nathan Jackson, Robert Montoya, George Morrison, Jimmie Fife and T.C. Cannon, contemporary art 47544

Seattle Art Museum, 100 University St, Seattle, WA 98101-2902 - T: (206) 654-3100, Fax: (206) 654-3135, E-mail: webmaster@seattleartmuseum.org, Internet: www.seattleartmuseum.org. Dir.: Mimi Gardner Gates, Cur.: Lisa Corrin (Modern Art), Barbara Brotherton (Native American Art), Pamela McClusky (Art of Africa and Oceania), Julie Emerson (Decorative Arts), Chiyo Ishikawa (European Painting)
Fine Arts Museum - 1917
Art 47545

Seattle Asian Art Museum, Volunteer Park, 1400 E Prospect, Seattle, WA 98112-3303 - T: (206) 625-8900, Fax: (206) 654-3191, E-mail: webmaster@seattleartmuseum.org, Internet: www.seattleartmuseum.org. Dir.: Mimi Gardner Gates, Cur.: Yukiko Shirahra (Asian Art), Jay Xu (Chinese Art)
Fine Arts Museum - 1917 47546

Shoreline Historical Museum, 749 N 175th St, Seattle, WA 98133 - T: (206) 542-7111, Fax: (206) 542-4645, E-mail: shorelinehistorical@juno.com. Pres.: Stephen Brown
Local Museum - 1976
Local hist 47547

Wing Luke Asian Museum, 407 Seventh Av, Seattle, WA 98104 - T: (206) 623-5124, Fax: (206) 623-4559, E-mail: folks@wingluke.org, Internet: www.wingluke.org. Dir.: Ron Chew
Fine Arts Museum / Ethnology Museum / Historical Museum - 1967
Asian Pacific American hist, art and culture 47548

Sebago ME

The Jones Museum of Glass and Ceramics, 35 Douglas Mountain Rd, Sebago, ME 04029 - T: (207) 787-3370, Fax: (207) 787-2800, Internet: www.jonesmuseum.org. Dir.: John H. Holverson
Decorative Arts Museum - 1978
Glass, ceramics 47549

Sebewaing MI

Luckhard Museum - The Indian Mission, 612 E. Bay St, Sebewaing, MI 48759 - T: (517) 883-2539. Dir.: Jim Bunke
Local Museum / Religious Arts Museum - 1957
Historic house, mission home 47550

Sebring FL

Civilian Conservation Corps Museum, Highlands Hammock State Park, 5931 Hammock Rd, Sebring, FL 33872 - T: (863) 386-6094, Fax: (863) 386-6095, E-mail: hammock@strato.net, Internet: www.dep.state.fl.us/park/central/highlands.html. Head: Peter Anderson
Historical Museum / Natural History Museum - 1994
Housed in 1930s building constructed of heavy native timbers, lumber cut and fabricated 47551

Highlands Museum of the Arts, 351 W Center Av, Sebring, FL 33870 - T: (863) 385-5312, Fax: (863) 385-5336, E-mail: haleague@strato.net, Internet: www.highlandsartleague.com. Dir.: Alice Stroppel
Fine Arts Museum - 1986
Art 47552

Second Mesa AZ

Hopi Cultural Museum, Rte 264, Second Mesa, AZ 86043 - T: (928) 734-6650, Fax: (928) 734-7113. Dir.: Anna Silas
Local Museum / Folklore Museum - 1970 47553

Sedalia MO

Daum Museum of Contemporary Art, c/o State Fair Community College, 3201 W 16th St, Sedalia, MO 65301 - T: (660) 530-5888, Fax: (660) 530-5890, E-mail: info@daummuseum.org, Internet: www.daummuseum.org. Dir.: Douglass Freed
Fine Arts Museum - 2001 47554

Pettis County Historical Society Museum, c/o Sedalia Public Library, 311 W Third St, Sedalia, MO 65301-4399 - T: (660) 826-1314, Fax: (660) 826-0396. Pres.: Rhonda Chalfant
Local Museum - 1943 47555

Sedan KS

Emmett Kelly Historical Museum, 202 E Main, Sedan, KS 67361 - T: (316) 725-3470. Head: Roger Floyd
Local Museum / Performing Arts Museum - 1967
Clowns, history, local history 47556

Sedgwick ME

Sedgwick-Brooklin Historical Museum, Rte 172, Sedgwick, ME 04676 - T: (207) 359-4447. Pres.: John Bishof
Local Museum - 1963
Regional history 47557

Sedona AZ

Sedona Arts Center, Hwy 89a at Art Barn Rd, Sedona, AZ 86336 - T: (928) 282-3809, Fax: (928) 282-1516, E-mail: sac@sedona.net, Internet: www.sedonaartscenter.com. Exec. Dir.: Michael McKitterick
Fine Arts Museum - 1961 47558

Seguin TX

Fiedler Memorial Museum, Texas Lutheran University, Seguin, TX 78155 - T: (830) 372-8038, Fax: (830) 372-8188, Internet: www.txlutheran.edu. Dir.: Evelyn Fiedler Streng
Natural History Museum / Science&Tech Museum - 1973
Geology 47559

Los Nogales Museum, 415 S River, Seguin, TX 78155 - T: (830) 372-2649, E-mail: bj2bt@axs4u.net. Dir.: B.J. Comingore
Local Museum - 1952 47560

Selinsgrove PA

Lore Degenstein Gallery, Susquehanna University, 514 University Av, Selinsgrove, PA 17870-1001 - T: (570) 372-4059, 374-0101, Fax: (570) 372-2775, E-mail: livingst@susqu.edu, Internet: www.susqu.edu/art_gallery. Dir./Cur.: Dr. Valerie Livingston
Fine Arts Museum / University Museum - 1993
Art 47561

Selkirk NY

Bethlehem Historical Association Museum, 1003 River Rd, Selkirk, NY 12158 - T: (518) 767-9432. Pres.: Parker D. Mathusa
Local Museum - 1965 47562

Selma AL

Sturdivant Hall, 713 Mabry St, Selma, AL 36701 - T: (334) 872-5626, E-mail: smuseum@zebra.net. Pres.: Claude Anderson, Cur.: Pat G. Tate, Marie Barker
Local Museum - 1957
Historic house 47563

Senatobia MS

Heritage Museum Foundation of Tate County, POB 375, Senatobia, MS 38668 - T: (601) 562-8559, Fax: (622) 562-5786, E-mail: dperkins@gmi.net. Pres.: Deborah Perkins
Local Museum - 1977
History, agriculture, art, folklore 47564

Seneca SC

World of Energy at Keowee-Toxaway, 7812 Rochester Hwy, Seneca, SC 29672 - T: (864) 885-4600, Fax: (864) 885-4605
Science&Tech Museum - 1969
Energy and electricity 47565

Seneca Falls NY

National Women's Hall of Fame, 76 Fall St, Seneca Falls, NY 13148 - T: (315) 568-8060, Fax: (315) 568-2976, E-mail: womenshall@aol.com, Internet: www.greatwomen.org. Head: Billy Luisi-Potts
Local Museum - 1969 47566

Seneca Falls Historical Society Museum, 55 Cayuga St, Seneca Falls, NY 13148 - T: (315) 568-8412, Fax: (315) 568-8426, E-mail: sfhs@flare.ner, Internet: www.welcome.to/sfhs/. Exec. Dir.: Frances T. Barbieri
Local Museum - 1904 47567

Sequim WA

Museum and Arts Center in the Sequim Dungeness Valley, 175 W Cedar, Sequim, WA 98382 - T: (360) 683-8110, Fax: (360) 681-2353, E-mail: info@sequimmuseum.org, Internet: www.sequimmuseum.org. Exec. Dir.: Dr. Deborah Rambo, Pres.: Layton Carr
Fine Arts Museum / Decorative Arts Museum / Historical Museum - 1992 47568

Setauket NY

Gallery North, 90 N Country Rd, Setauket, NY 11733 - T: (631) 751-2676, Fax: (631) 751-0180, E-mail: gallerynorth@aol.com, Internet: www.gallerynorth.org. Pres.: Elizabeth Goldberg, Dir./Cur.: Collen W. Hanson
Public Gallery - 1965 47569

Three Village Historical Society Museum, 93 N Country Rd, Setauket, NY 11733 - T: (631) 751-3730, Fax: (631) 751-3936, E-mail: TVHistSoc@aol.com, Internet: www.tvhs.org. Dir.: Margaret Conover
Local Museum - 1964 47570

Sewanee TN

The University Gallery of the University of the South, Guerry Hall, Georgia Av, Sewanee, TN 37383-1000 - T: (931) 598-1223, Fax: (931) 598-3335, E-mail: aende@sewanne.edu, Internet: www.sewanee.edu/gallery. Dir.: Arlyn Ende
Fine Arts Museum / University Museum - 1965
Paintings, prints, drawings, graphics, sculpture, photos, furniture, silver, stained glass 47571

Seward AK

Resurrection Bay Historical Society Museum → Seward Museum

Seward Museum, 336 Third Av, Seward, AK 99664 - T: (907) 224-3902. Pres./Dir.: Lee E. Poleske
Local Museum - 1967 47572

Seward NE

Marxhausen Art Gallery, Concordia University, 800 N Columbia Av, Seward, NE 68434 - T: (402) 643-3651, Fax: (402) 643-4073, E-mail: jbockelman@seward.cune.edu, Internet: www.cune.edu. Dir.: James Bockelman
Fine Arts Museum / University Museum - 1951
Contemporary print multiples 47573

Sewickley PA

International Images, 514 Beaver St, Sewickley, PA 15143 - T: (412) 741-3036, Fax: (412) 741-8606, E-mail: intimage@cobweb.net. Pres.: Elena Kornetchuk, Dir.: Charles M. Wiebe
Fine Arts Museum - 1978 47574

Seymour WI

Seymour Community Museum, Depot St, Seymour, WI 54165 - T: (414) 833-2868. Pres.: Rita Gosse
Local Museum - 1976
Local hist 47575

Shady Side MD

Captain Salem Avery House Museum, 1418 EW Shadyside Rd, Shady Side, MD 20764 - T: (410) 867-4486, Fax: (410) 867-4486, E-mail: captainavery@prodigy.net, Internet: www.averyhouse.org. C.E.O.: Janet Surrett
Historical Museum - 1988
Waterman's house 47576

Shaftsbury VT

Shaftsbury Historical Society Museum, Historic 7a, Shaftsbury, VT 05262 - T: (802) 447-7488. C.E.O./Cur.: Robert J. Williams, Pres.: Norman Gronning
Local Museum - 1967
Local hist 47577

Shaker Heights OH

Shaker Historical Society Museum, 16740 S Park Blvd, Shaker Heights, OH 44120 - T: (216) 921-1201, Fax: (216) 921-2615, E-mail: shakhist@wviz.org, Internet: www.cwru.edu/affil/shakhist/shaker.htm. Pres.: Dr. Robert Spurney, Dir.: Cathie Winans
Local Museum - 1947 47578

Sharon MA

Kendall Whaling Museum, 27 Everett St, Sharon, MA 02067 - T: (781) 784-5642, Fax: (781) 784-0451, E-mail: ehazen@kwm.org, Internet: www.kwm.org. Dir.: Stuart M. Frank, Dep. Dir.: Gare B. Reid, Cur.: Michael P. Dyer
Natural History Museum - 1956
History, maritime history, photos 47579

Sharon NH

Sharon Arts Center, 457 Rte 123, Sharon, NH 03458-9014 - T: (603) 924-7256, Fax: (603) 924-6074, E-mail: sharonarts@sharonarts.org, Internet: www.sharonarts.org. Pres.: Elizabeth Rank-Beauchamp, Cur.: Randall Hoel
Fine Arts Museum / Public Gallery - 1947 47580

Sharonville OH

Heritage Village, 11450 Lebanon Pike, Rte 42, Sharonville, OH 45241 - T: (513) 563-9484, Fax: (513) 563-0914, Internet: www.heritagevillagecincinnati.org. Dir.: Bing G. Spitler
Local Museum - 1964 47581

Sharpsburg MD

Antietam National Battlefield, Rte 65 N, Sharpsburg, MD 21782 - T: (301) 432-5124, Fax: (301) 432-4590, E-mail: keith-snyder@nps.gov, Internet: www.nps.gov/anti. Dir.: Terry Carlstrom
Historic Site / Military Museum - 1890
Site of 1862 Civil War Maryland Campaign and battle of Antietam or Sharpsburg 47582

Chesapeake and Ohio Canal Tavern Museum, 16500 Shepherdstown Park, Sharpsburg, MD 21782 - T: (301) 739-4200, Fax: (301) 714-2232, E-mail: doug.stover@nps.gov, Internet: www.nps.gov/choh. Head: Douglas D. Faris
Historical Museum - 1954
Great Falls Tavern, brick railroad station, with operating steam locomotive ride, Ferry Hill slave plantation 47583

Shaw Island WA

Shaw Island Historical Society Museum, Blind Bay Rd, Shaw Island, WA 98286 - T: (360) 468-4068. Cur.: Sherie Christiansen, Marilyn Hoffman
Local Museum - 1966
Local hist 47584

Shawanao WI

Shawano County Museum, 524 N Franklin St, Shawanao, WI 54166 - T: (715) 524-4981
Local Museum - 1940 47585

Shawnee KS

Johnson County Museums, 6305 Lackman Rd, Shawnee, KS 66217 - T: (913) 631-6709, Fax: (913) 631-6359, E-mail: jcmuseum@jocoks.com, Internet: www.digitalhistory.com. Cur.: Anne Marvin
Local Museum - 1967 47586

Old Shawnee Town, 11501 W 57th St, Shawnee, KS 66203 - T: (913) 248-2360, Fax: (913) 248-2363, E-mail: lcasey@cityofshawnee.org, Internet: www.cityofshawnee.org. CEO: Laura Casey
Local Museum - 1966 47587

Shawnee OK

Mabee-Gerrer Museum of Art, 1900 W MacArthur Dr, Shawnee, OK 74801-2499 - T: (405) 878-5300, Fax: (405) 878-5198, E-mail: info@mabeegerrermuseum.org. Pres.: Joi Grissom, Dir.: Debby Williams
Fine Arts Museum - 1917 47588

Sheboygan WI

John Michael Kohler Arts Center, 608 New York Av, Sheboygan, WI 53081 - T: (920) 458-6144, Fax: (920) 458-4473, Internet: www.jmkac.org. Dir.: Ruth Kohler, Cur.: Leslie Umberger
Fine Arts Museum - 1967
Art 47589

Sheboygan County Historical Museum, 3110 Erie Av, Sheboygan, WI 53081 - T: (920) 458-1103, Fax: (920) 458-5152. Pres.: Steve Shaver, Exec. Dir.: Robert Harker
Historical Museum - 1954
Local hist 47590

Sheffield Lake OH

103rd Ohio Volunteer Infantry Memorial, 5501 E Lake Rd, Sheffield Lake, OH 44054 - T: (440) 949-2790. C.E.O.: Darlene Grunaugh, Cur.: Olive Gerber, Ruth Wagner
Military Museum - 1972 47591

Shelburne VT

National Museum of the Morgan Horse, 122 Bostwick Rd, Shelburne, VT 05482 - T: (802) 985-8665, Fax: (802) 985-5242, E-mail: morgans@together.net, Internet: www.morganmuseum.org. Cur.: Kathlyn Robie
Special Museum - 1988
Horses 47592

Shelburne Museum, 5555 Shelburne Rd, Shelburne, VT 05482 - T: (802) 985-3346, Fax: (802) 985-2331, E-mail: info@shelburnemuseum.org, Internet: www.shelburnemuseum.org. Pres.: Hope Alswanis
Local Museum - 1947
Local hist 47593

Shelby MT

Marias Museum of History and Art, 206 12 Av N, Shelby, MT 59474 - T: (406) 434-2551, Fax: (406) 434-5422, E-mail: larrydar@northerntel.net. C.E.O. & Pres.: Larry Munson
Fine Arts Museum / Historical Museum - 1963 47594

Shelby NC

Cleveland County Historical Museum, Court Sq, Shelby, NC 28150 - T: (704) 482-8186, Fax: (704) 482-8186, Internet: www.countrymuseum.com. Pres.: Ginny Hughes, Dir./Cur.: Lamar Wilson
Local Museum - 1976 47595

Shelbyville IN

Louis H. and Lena Firn Grover Museum, 52 W Broadway, Shelbyville, IN 46176 - T: (317) 392-4634, E-mail: grover@shelbynet.net. Pres.: Norman Barnett, C.E.O.: June Barnett
Local Museum - 1980
Local history 47596

Shell Lake WI

Museum of Woodcarving, 539 Hwy 63, Shell Lake, WI 54871 - T: (715) 468-7100. Cur.: Maria McKay
Fine Arts Museum - 1950 47597

Washburn County Historical Society Museum, 102 W Second Av, Shell Lake, WI 54871 - T: (715) 468-2982, E-mail: washburncohhistsoceby@hotmail.com
Local Museum - 1954 47598

Shelter Island NY

Shelter Island Historical Society Museum, 16 S Ferry Rd, Shelter Island, NY 11964 - T: (516) 749-0025, Fax: (516) 749-1825, E-mail: sihissoc@hamptons.com, Internet: www.shelterislandhistsoc.org. Pres.: W.M. Anderson, Dir.: Louise Green
Historical Museum - 1965
archives 47599

Shepherdstown WV

Historic Shepherdstown Museum, 129e German St, Shepherdstown, WV 25443, mail addr: POB 1786, Shepherdstown, WV 25443 - T: (304) 876-0910, Fax: (304) 876-2679, E-mail: hsc86@citilink.net. C.E.O.: Susan Smith
Local Museum - 1983
Local hist 47600

Sheridan AR

Grant County Museum, 521 Shackleford Rd, Sheridan, AR 72150 - T: (870) 942-4496, Fax: (870) 942-4496. Dir.: Elwin L. Goolsby
Local Museum - 1970 47601

Sheridan WY

Trail End State Historic Museum, Colorado-Wyoming Association of Museums, 400 Clarendon Av, Sheridan, WY 82801 - T: (307) 674-4589, Fax: (307) 672-1720, E-mail: cgeorg@state.wy.us, Internet: www.trailend.org. Cur.: Nancy McClure
Historical Museum
History 47602

Sherman TX

Ida Green Gallery, Austin College, 900 N Grande Av, Sherman, TX 75090-4440 - T: (903) 813-2251, Fax: (903) 813-2273, Internet: www.austinc.edu
Public Gallery 47603

Sherwood WI

High Cliff General Store Museum, 7526 N Lower Cliff Rd, Sherwood, WI 54169-0001 - T: (920) 989-1636, E-mail: russjbishop@msn.com, Internet: www.historical-sctyatwebtv.net. Pres.: Russell J. Bishop
Local Museum - 1974
Local hist 47604

Shevlin MN

Clearwater County Historical Museum, Hwy 2 W, Shevlin, MN 56676 - T: (218) 785-2000, Fax: (218) 785-2440, E-mail: cchshist@gvtel.com. C.E.O.: Harry Larson
Local Museum - 1967
Local history 47605

Shiloh TN

Shiloh National Military Park and Cemetery, Hwy 22, 1055 Pittsburg Landing Rd, Shiloh, TN 38376 - T: (731) 689-5275, Fax: (731) 689-5450, E-mail: shil_administration@nps.gov
Military Museum - 1894
Military hist 47606

Shiner TX

Edwin Wolters Memorial Museum, 306 S Av, Shiner, TX 77984 - T: (512) 594-3774, 594-3362, Fax: (512) 594-3566. Cur.: Bernard Siegel
Local Museum - 1963
Local hist 47607

Shippensburg PA

Kauffman Gallery, c/o Shippensburg University, 1871 Old Main Dr, Shippensburg, PA 17257 - T: (717) 477-1530, Fax: (717) 477-4049, E-mail: vhmowe@ship.edu, Internet: www.ship.edu. Dir.: William Q. Hynes
Fine Arts Museum / University Museum - 1972 47608

Shippensburg Historical Society Museum, 52 W King St, Shippensburg, PA 17257 - T: (717) 532-6727, Internet: www.ship.edu/~pegill/shs.html. Cur.: Ed Sheaffer
Local Museum - 1944
Local hist 47609

Shoreview MN

Ramsey Center for Arts, 1071 Highway 96 W, Shoreview, MN 55126 - T: (651) 486-4883, E-mail: info@ramseycfa.org, Internet: www.ramseycfa.org
Public Gallery 47610

Shreveport LA

Ark-La-Tex Antique and Classic Vehicle Museum, 601 Spring St, Shreveport, LA 71101
Science&Tech Museum - 1993 47611

Louisiana State Exhibit Museum, 3015 Greenwood Rd, Shreveport, LA 71109 - T: (318) 632-2020, Fax: (318) 632-2056. Dir.: Forrest Dunn
Historical Museum - 1937
General museum, State hist 47612

Meadows Museum of Art, Centenary College, 2911 Centenary Blvd, Shreveport, LA 71104 - T: (318) 869-5169, Fax: (318) 869-5730, E-mail: ddufilho@centenary.edu, Internet: www.centenary.edu. Dir.: Diane Dufilho, Cur.: Bruce Allen
Fine Arts Museum / University Museum - 1976
Art 47613

Pioneer Heritage Center, LSU Shreveport, 1 University Pl, Shreveport, LA 71115 - T: (318) 797-5332, Fax: (318) 797-5395, E-mail: mplummer@pilot.1sus.edu, Internet: www.lsus.edu. Dir.: Marguerite R. Plummer, Asst. Dir.: Marvin R. Young
Historical Museum - 1977
History Complex 47614

R.S. Barnwell Memorial Garden and Art Center, 601 Clyde Fant Pkwy, Shreveport, LA 71101 - T: (318) 673-7703, Fax: (318) 673-7707, E-mail: jhirscj@ci.shreveport.la.us. Pres.: Barbara White, C.E.O.: Jan Hirsch
Fine Arts Museum / Public Gallery - 1970 47615

The R.W. Norton Art Gallery, 4747 Creswell Av, Shreveport, LA 71106 - T: (318) 865-4201, Fax: (318) 869-0435, E-mail: norton@softdisk.com, Internet: www.softdisk.com/comp/norton. Pres.: Richard W. Norton jr.
Fine Arts Museum - 1946
Art 47616

Sci-Port Discovery Center, 820 Clyde Fant Pkwy, Shreveport, LA 71101 - T: (318) 424-3466, Fax: (318) 222-5592, E-mail: apeek@sciport.org, Internet: www.sciport.org. Pres.: Andre Peek
Science&Tech Museum - 1994
Science 47617

Spring Street Historical Museum, 525 Spring St, Shreveport, LA 71101 - T: (318) 424-0964, Fax: (318) 424-0964, E-mail: sshm@shreve.net, Internet: www.springstreetmuseum.com. Dir.: Debra M. Helton
Local Museum - 1977 47618

Stephens African-American Museum, 2810 Lindlohm, Shreveport, LA 71108 - T: (318) 635-2147, Fax: (318) 636-0504. CEO: Spencer Stephens
Fine Arts Museum
African-American art, paintings, sculptures, prints and drawings 47619

Shrewsbury NJ

Guild of Creative Art, 620 Broad St, Rte 35, Shrewsbury, NJ 07702 - T: (732) 741-1441, E-mail: guildofcreativeart@att.net, Internet: www.guildofcreativeart.com
Public Gallery 47620

Shullsburg WI

Badger Mine and Museum, 279 Estey, Shullsburg, WI 53586 - T: (608) 965-4860. Dir.: Tim Strang
Local Museum - 1964
Local hist 47621

Sibley IA

McCallum Museum, 5th St and 8th Av, Sibley, IA 51249 - T: (712) 754-3882, E-mail: verstoff@heartlandtel.com. Dir.: Jan Stofferan
Local Museum - 1956
Local history 47622

Sibley MO

Fort Osage, 105 Osage St, Sibley, MO 64088 - T: (816) 795-8200 ext 1260, Fax: (816) 795-7938, E-mail: juligor@gw.co.jackson.mo.us, Internet: www.co.jackson.mo.us. Dir.: Bettie Yahn Kramer
Local Museum - 1948 47623

Sidney MT

Mondak Heritage Historical Museum and Art Gallery, 120 Third Av SE, Sidney, MT 59270 - T: (406) 482-3500, Fax: (406) 482-3500, E-mail: mondakheritagecenter@hotmail.com. Dir.: Judith Deitz
Local Museum - 1967 47624

Sidney NE

Fort Sidney Museum and Post Commander's Home, 6th Av and Jackson St, Sidney, NE 69162 - T: (308) 254-2150. Pres.: Thomas LaVerne, Dir.: Joan Olson, Robin Gue, Lloyd Bauer, Lois Heizer, Dorothy Rowe, Terry Christopher
Military Museum - 1954
Military hist 47625

Sidney NY

Sidney Historical Association Museum, 21 Liberty St, Room 218, Sidney, NY 13838 - T: (607) 563-8787. Cur.: Neila C. Hayes
Local Museum - 1945 47626

Siloam Springs AR

Siloam Springs Museum, 112 N Maxwell, Siloam Springs, AR 72761 - T: (501) 524-4011, E-mail: ssmuseum@ipa.net. Dir.: Donald Warden
Historical Museum - 1969
Local history, textiles 47627

Silver City NM

Francis McCray Gallery, Western New Mexico University, 1000 College Av, Silver City, NM 88062 - T: (505) 538-6614, 538-6515, Fax: (505) 538-6619, Internet: www.wnmu.edu. Dir.: Mike Metcalf
Fine Arts Museum / University Museum - 1960
Art 47628

Silver City Museum, 312 W Broadway, Silver City, NM 88061 - T: (505) 538-5921, Fax: (505) 388-1096, E-mail: scmuseum@zianet.com, Internet: www.silvercitymuseum.org. Dir.: Susan Berry, Cur.: Jim Carlson
Local Museum - 1967 47629

Western New Mexico University Museum, Fleming Hall, 10 St, Silver City, NM 88062 - T: (505) 538-6386, Fax: (505) 538-6178, Internet: www.wnmw.edu/univ/museum.htm. Dir.: Dr. Cynthia Ann Bettison, Chm.: Dr. Dale F. Giese
University Museum / Ethnology Museum - 1974 47630

Silver Cliff CO

Silver Cliff Museum, 606 Main St, Silver Cliff, CO 81252 - T: (719) 783-2615, Fax: (719) 783-2615, E-mail: silvercliffttown@piopc.net. C.E.O.: Susan Hutton
Local Museum - 1959
Local history, textiles, silver, paintings, photos 47631

Silver Spring MD

George Meany Memorial Exhibition, 10000 New Hampshire Av, Silver Spring, MD 20903 - T: (301) 431-5451, Fax: (301) 431-0385, E-mail: mmerrill@georgemeany.org, Internet: www.georgemeany.org. Dir.: Michael Merrill
Historical Museum - 1980
American Federation of Labor-Congress of Industrial Organizations (AFL-CIO) 47632

National Capital Trolley Museum, 1313 Bonifant Rd, Silver Spring, MD 20905 - T: (301) 384-6352, Fax: (301) 384-2865, E-mail: nctm@dotrolley.org, Internet: www.dctrolley.org. Dir.: Ken Rucker
Science&Tech Museum - 1959
Electric street cars, postal cards, demonstration railway 47633

Silverton CO

Mayflower Gold Mill, 1 Main St N, Silverton, CO 81433 - T: (970) 387-5838. Head: Beverly Rich
Science&Tech Museum
Local history 47634

San Juan County Historical Museum, 1557 Greene St, Silverton, CO 81433 - T: (970) 387-5838. Head: Beverly Rich
Local Museum - 1964
Local history 47635

Simi CA

R.P. Strathearn Historical Park, 137 Strathearn Pl, Simi, CA 93065 - T: (805) 526-6453, Fax: (805) 526-6462, E-mail: havens1@ix.netcom.com. Dir.: Patricia Havens
Local Museum - 1970
Local hist 47636

Simsbury CT

Simsbury Historical Society Museum, 800 Hopmeadow St, Simsbury, CT 06070 - T: (860) 658-2500, Fax: (860) 658-2500, E-mail: info@simburyhistory.org, Internet: www.simsburyhistory.org. Pres.: Dawn Hutchins Bobyrk
Local Museum - 1911
Local hist 47637

Sioux City IA

Sioux City Art Center, 225 Nebraska St, Sioux City, IA 51101-1712 - T: (712) 279-6272 ext 208, Fax: (712) 255-2921, E-mail: aharris@sioux-city.org, Internet: www.siouxcityartcenter.org. Dir.: Al Harris-Fernandez
Fine Arts Museum - 1914
Art 47638

Sioux City Public Museum, 2901 Jackson St, Sioux City, IA 51104-3697 - T: (712) 279-6174, Fax: (712) 252-5615, E-mail: scpm@sioux-city.org, Internet: www.sioux-city.org/museum. Dir.: Dr. Stephen D. Hansen, Cur.: Grace Linden (History)
Local Museum - 1886
General local history, Peirce mansion, Sergeant Floyd River Museum, Loren D. Callendar gallery 47639

Trinity Heights - Saint Joseph Center-Museum, 2509 33rd St, Sioux City, IA 51105 - T: (712) 239-8670. Exec. Dir.: Bernard F. Cooper
Fine Arts Museum - 1992
Woodcarving 47640

Sioux Falls SD

Battleship South Dakota Memorial, 12th and Kiwanis St, Sioux Falls, SD 57104 - T: (605) 367-7141, 367-7060, Fax: (605) 367-4326. Pres.: David Witte
Military Museum - 1968
Military hist 47641

Delbridge Museum, 805 S Kiwanis Av, Sioux Falls, SD 57104-3714 - T: (605) 367-7003, Fax: (605) 367-8340, E-mail: canderzon@gpzoo.org, Internet: gpzoo.org/. Dir.: Christine Anderson
Natural History Museum - 1957
Natural hist 47642

Eide-Dalrymple Gallery, Augustana College, 29th St and S Grange Av, Sioux Falls, SD 57197 - T: (605) 274-4609, Fax: (605) 274-4368, E-mail: hannus@inst.augie.edu, Internet: www.augie.edu/archlab/al.html. Dir.: L. Adrien Hannus
Fine Arts Museum - 1960
Primitive art, Japanese woodcuts, European prints, New Guinea masks 47643

Jim Savage Art Gallery and Museum, 3301 E 26th St, Village Sq, Sioux Falls, SD 57103 - T: (605) 332-7551, Fax: (605) 332-7551. Dir.: Barb Van Laar
Fine Arts Museum
Woodcarving 47644

Sioux Empire Medical Museum, 1100 S Euclid Av, Sioux Falls, SD 57117-5039 - T: (605) 333-6397. Head: Thenetta Nield
Historical Museum - 1975
Medical hist, regional health care, uniforms, nursing school, hospital life, iron lung 47645

Siouxland Heritage Museums, 200 W 6th St, Sioux Falls, SD 57104-6001 - T: (605) 367-4210, Fax: (605) 367-6004, E-mail: bhoskins@minnehahacounty.org, Internet: www.minnehahacounty.org. Dir.: William J. Hoskins, Cur.: Laura Hortz, April Blazevic, Kevin Gansz
Local Museum - 1926
Local hist 47646

Washington Pavillion of Arts and Science, 301 S Main St, Sioux Falls, SD 57104 - T: (605) 367-7397, Fax: (605) 367-7399, E-mail: info@washingtonpavilion.org, Internet: www.washingtonpavilion.org. Cur.: Sheila Agee
Fine Arts Museum / Folklore Museum / University Museum - 1961
Art 47647

Sisseton SD

Tekakwitha Fine Arts Center, 401 S 8th Av W, Sisseton, SD 57262-0208 - T: (605) 698-7058, Fax: (605) 698-3801. Dir./Cur.: Harold D. Moore
Fine Arts Museum - 1969
Dakotah Sioux art, former dormitory of the Tekakwitha Indian Childrens' home 47648

Sitka AK

Isabel Miller Museum, 330 Harbor Dr, Sitka, AK 99835 - T: (907) 747-6455, Fax: (907) 747-6588, E-mail: sitkahis@ptialaska.net, Internet: www.sitka.org/historicalmuseum. Pres.: Sabra Jenkins
Local Museum - 1957 47649

Sheldon Jackson Museum, 104 College Dr, Sitka, AK 99835 - T: (907) 747-8981, Fax: (907) 747-3004, E-mail: carolyn_young@eed.state.ak.us, Internet: www.museums.state.ak.us. Dir.: Karen R. Crane, Chief Cur.: Bruce Kato
Ethnology Museum - 1888
Alaska native cultures 47650

Sitka National Historical Park, 106 Metlakatla St, Sitka, AK 99835 - T: (907) 747-6281, Fax: (907) 747-5938, E-mail: sitk_administration@nps.gov, Internet: www.nps.gov/sitk. Cur.: Sue Thorsen
Local Museum - 1910
Local hist 47651

Skagway AK

Skagway City Museum, 700 Spring St, Skagway, AK 99840 - T: (907) 983-2420, Fax: (907) 983-3420. Cur.: Judith Munns
Local Museum - 1961
Skagway history - archives 47652

Skowhegan ME

Skowhegan History House, 66 Elm St, Skowhegan, ME 04976 - T: (207) 474-6632, E-mail: skowheganhistoryhouse@hotmail.com. Pres./Cur.: Lee Z. Granville
Historical Museum - 1937 47653

Slidell LA

Slidell Art Center, 444 Erlanger St, Slidell, LA 70458 - T: (504) 646-4375, Fax: (504) 646-4231, E-mail: parsons@gs.verio.net. Dir.: Brian Hammell
Fine Arts Museum - 1989 47654

Smackover AR

Arkansas Museum of Natural Resources, 3853 Smackover Hwy, Smackover, AR 71762 - T: (501) 725-2877, Fax: (501) 725-2161, E-mail: amnr@cei.net, Internet: www.cei.net/~amnr. Dir.: Don Lambert, Cur.: Pam Beasley
Historical Museum / Science&Tech Museum - 1977
History, technology 47655

Smithfield VA

Isle of Wight Courthouse, 130 Main St, Smithfield, VA 23430 - T: (804) 357-3502, Fax: (804) 775-0802, Internet: www.apva.org. Pres.: Peter Knowles, Exec. Dir.: Elizabeth Kostelny
Local Museum - 1750
Historic building 47656

Smithtown NY

Smithtown Historical Society Museum, 5 N Country Rd, Smithtown, NY 11787 - T: (516) 265-6768, Fax: (516) 265-6768, Internet: www.smithtownhistorical.org. Dir.: Carol Ghiorsi-Hart
Local Museum - 1955 47657

Smithville TN

Appalachian Center for Crafts, 1560 Craft Center Dr, Smithville, TN 37166 - T: (615) 597-6801, Fax: (615) 597-6803, E-mail: craftcenter@tntech.edu, Internet: www.craftscenter.tntech.edu. Dir.: Scott Davisson (Crafts Center), Gail S. Looper (Gallery)
Ethnology Museum - 1979 47658

Snohomish WA

Blackman Museum, 118 Av B, Snohomish, WA 98290 - T: (360) 568-5235. Pres.: Windsor Vest
Local Museum - 1969
Local hist 47659

Snoqualmie WA

Northwest Railway Museum, 38625 SE King St, Snoqualmie, WA 98065 - T: (425) 888-3030 ext 201, Fax: (425) 888-9311, E-mail: director@trainmuseum.org, Internet: www.trainmuseum.org. Exec. Dir.: Richard R. Anderson
Science&Tech Museum - 1957
Steam and diesel locomotives, passenger coaches and freight cars, rotary snow plow, cranes, observation cars, kitchen car 47660

Snow Hill MD

Julia A. Purnell Museum, 208 W Market St, Snow Hill, MD 21863 - T: (410) 632-0515, Fax: (410) 632-0515, E-mail: purnellmuseum@dmv.com, Internet: www.purnellmuseum.com. C.E.O.: Mary Saint Hippolyte
Local Museum - 1942
History of American/ Worcester County, folk art, furniture, jewelry, machines, tools 47661

Snyder TX

Scurry County Museum, Western Texas College, 6200 College Av, Snyder, TX 79549 - T: (915) 573-6107, Fax: (915) 573-9321, E-mail: scm@snydertex.com. Dir.: Charlene Akers, Cur.: Sue Goodwin
Local Museum - 1970
Local hist 47662

Socorro NM

New Mexico Bureau of Mines Mineral Museum, New Mexico Tech, 801 Leroy Pl, Socorro, NM 87801 - T: (505) 835-5140, Fax: (505) 835-6333, E-mail: vwlueth@nmt.edu, Internet: geoinfo.nmt.edu. Dir./Cur.: Virgil W. Lueth, Asst. Cur.: Patricia L. Frisch
Natural History Museum - 1926 47663

Sodus Point NY

Sodus Bay Historical Society Museum, 7606 N Ontario St, Sodus Point, NY 14555 - T: (315) 483-4936, Fax: (315) 483-1398, E-mail: sodusbay@ix.netcom.com, Internet: www.peachey.com/soduslight. C.E.O.: Donna P. Jones
Local Museum - 1979
Local hist 47664

Solomons MD

Calvert Marine Museum, 14200 Solomons Island Rd, Solomons, MD 20688 - T: (410) 326-2042, Fax: (410) 326-6691, E-mail: information@calvertmarinemuseum.com, Internet: www.calvertmarinemuseum.com. Dir.: C. Douglass Alves, Cur.: Kenneth Kaumeyer (Estuarine Biology), Stephen J. Godfrey (Paleontology), Richard Dodds (Maritime History)
Historical Museum / Natural History Museum / Special Museum - 1969
Marine, Drum Point Lighthouse on waterfront, seafood packing house 47665

Solvang CA

Old Mission Santa Ines, 1760 Mission Dr, Solvang, CA 93463 - T: (805) 688-4815, Fax: (805) 686-4468, Internet: www.missionsantaines.org
Religious Arts Museum
Religious vestiments, Mexican and Spanish art 47666

Somers NY

Somers Historical Society Museum, Elephant Hotel, Rtes 100 and 202, Somers, NY 10589 - T: (914) 277-4977, Fax: (914) 277-4977, E-mail: oldbet@cloudnine.net. Cur.: Terry Ariano
Historical Museum - 1956
Early American circus 47667

Somers Point NJ

Atlantic County Historical Society Museum, 907 Shore Rd, Somers Point, NJ 08244 - T: (609) 927-5218, Internet: www.aclink.org/achs. Cur.: Allen Pergament, Assist.Cur.: Ruth C. Gold
Local Museum - 1913 47668

Somers Mansion, 1000 Shore Rd, Somers Point, NJ 08244 - T: (609) 927-2212, Fax: (609) 927-1827, E-mail: history54@msn.com. Sc.Staff: Daniel T. Campbell (Hist. Preservation)
Local Museum - 1941 47669

Somerset PA

Somerset Historical Center, 10649 Somerset Pike, Somerset, PA 15501 - T: (814) 445-6077, Fax: (814) 443-6621, E-mail: chfox@state.pa.us, Internet: www.somersetcounty.com/historicalcenter. Dir.: Vernon Berkey, Charles Fox, Cur.: Barbara Black, Educator: Mark Ware
Local Museum - 1969
Local hist 47670

Somerville MA

Somerville Museum, One Westwood Rd, Somerville, MA 02143 - T: (617) 666-9810. Dir.: Regina M. Pisa
Local Museum - 1897
Local history 47671

Somerville NJ

Old Dutch Parsonage, 71 Somerset St, Somerville, NJ 08876 - T: (908) 725-1015. Cur.: Jim Kurzenberger
Local Museum - 1947 47672

Wallace House, 38 Washington Pl, Somerville, NJ 08876 - T: (908) 725-1015. Cur.: Jim Kurzenberger
Decorative Arts Museum / Local Museum - 1947 47673

Somesville ME

Mount Desert Island Historical Museum, 2 Oak Hill Rd, Somesville, ME 04660 - T: (207) 244-5043, Fax: (207) 244-3991, E-mail: jroths@acadia.net. Pres.: Anne Mazlish, Dir.: Jaylene Roths
Local Museum - 1931
Local history 47674

Sonoma CA

Depot Park Museum, 270 First St W, Sonoma, CA 95476 - T: (707) 938-1762, Fax: (707) 938-1762, E-mail: depot@vom.com, Internet: www.vom.com/~depot. Dir.: Diane Smith
Local Museum - 1979 47675

Sonoma State Historic Park, 20 E Spain St, Sonoma, CA 95476 - T: (707) 938-1519, Fax: (707) 938-1406. Cur.: Carol A. Dodge
Local Museum - 1906
Local hist 47676

Sonora TX

Cauthorn Memorial Depot and Sutton County Jail, Oak St, Sonora, TX 76950 - T: (915) 387-2855, Fax: (915) 387-3303
Local Museum / Historical Museum - 1968 47677

South Bend IN

College Football Hall of Fame, 111 S Saint Joseph St, South Bend, IN 46601 - T: (219) 235-9999, Fax: (219) 235-5720, E-mail: hof@collegefootball.org, Internet: www.collegefootball.org
Special Museum - 1978 47678

Copshaholm House Museum and Historic Oliver Gardens, Northern Indiana Center for History, 808 W Washington St, South Bend, IN 46601 - T: (219) 235-9664, Fax: (219) 235-9059, E-mail: director@centerforhistory.org, Internet: www.centerforhistory.org. Cur.: David S. Bainbridge
Local Museum - 1990
Local hist 47679

Northern Indiana Center for History, 808 W Washington, South Bend, IN 46601 - T: (219) 235-9664, Fax: (219) 235-9059, E-mail: director@cenetrforhistory.org, Internet: www.centerforhistory.org. Dir.: Cheryl Taylor Bennett, Ass. Dir.: Kimberly Eveler, Cur.: David S. Bainbridge
Ethnology Museum / Historical Museum - 1994
History, children's interactive museum, Voyages, history of the Saint Joseph River Valley Region, Changing gallery, Carroll gallery, Leighton gallery, traveling 47680

South Bend Regional Museum of Art, 120 S Saint Joseph St, South Bend, IN 46601 - T: (219) 235-9102, Fax: (219) 235-5782, E-mail: sbrma@sbt.infi.net, Internet: www.sbt.infi.net/~sbrma. Dir.: Susan R. Visser, Cur.: William Tourtillotte, Ass. Cur.: Kim Hoffmann, Jason Lahr
Fine Arts Museum - 1947
American art 47681

Studebaker National Museum, 525 S Main St, South Bend, IN 46601 - T: (219) 235-9714, (888) 391-5600, Fax: (219) 235-5522, E-mail: stumuseum@skyenet.net, Internet: www.studebakermuseum.org. Dir.: Ronald Radecki
Science&Tech Museum - 1977
Industry 47682

Worker's Home Museum, Northern Indiana Center for History, 808 W Washington St, South Bend, IN 46601 - T: (219) 235-9664, Fax: (219) 235-9059, E-mail: director@centerforhistory.org, Internet: www.centerforhistory.org. Cur.: David S. Bainbridge
Historical Museum - 1994
History 47683

South Bend WA

Pacific County Historical Museum, 1008 W Robert Bush Dr, South Bend, WA 98586-0039 - T: (360) 875-5224, Fax: (360) 875-5224, E-mail: museum@willapabay.org, Internet: www.pacificcohistory.org. Pres.: Vincent Shaudys, Dir.: Bruce Weilepp
Local Museum - 1970
Local hist 47684

South Berwick ME

Hamilton House, 18 Vaughan's Ln, South Berwick, ME 03908, mail addr: 141 Cambridge St, Boston, ME 03908 - T: (207) 384-2454, (617) 227-3956, Fax: (617) 227-9204, (207) 384-8192, E-mail: ezopes@spnea.org, Internet: www.spnea.org. Dir.: Elaine Zopes
Special Museum - 1949
Personal and decorative objects from Mrs. Tyson 47685

Sarah Orne Jewett House, 5 Portland St, South Berwick, ME 03908 - T: (207) 384-2454, (617) 227-3956, Fax: (617) 227-9204, (207) 384-8192, Internet: www.spnea.org. Head: Andrea Strassner
Special Museum - 1931
Residence of the author Sarah Orne Jewett 47686

South Boston VA

South Boston-Halifax County Museum of Fine Arts and History, 1540 Wilborn Av, South Boston, VA 24592 - T: (804) 572-9200, E-mail: sbhcm@halifax.com, Internet: www2.halifax.com/museum. Cur.: Marjorie Holtman
Local Museum / Fine Arts Museum - 1981
Regional history, art 47687

South Charleston WV

South Charleston Museum, 312 Fourth Av, South Charleston, WV 25303 - T: (304) 744-9711, Fax: (304) 744-8808, E-mail: SCMuseum@aol.com. Dir.: Teresa C. Whitt
Local Museum - 1989 47688

South Chelmsford MA

Chelmsford Historical Society Museum, 40 Byam Rd, South Chelmsford, MA 01824 - T: (978) 256-2311, Internet: www.chelmhist.org. Dir.: Donald Patterschal
Local Museum - 1930
Coll of Chelmsford Glass, clothing, model of country store 47689

South Dartmouth MA

Children's Museum in Dartmouth, 276 Gulf Rd, South Dartmouth, MA 02748 - T: (508) 993-3361, Fax: (508) 993-3332. Pres.: Robert Howland, Dir.: Ronald Mayer
Ethnology Museum / Historical Museum - 1952 47690

South Deerfield MA

Yankee Candle Car Museum, Rte 5, South Deerfield, MA 01373 - T: (413) 665-2020, Fax: (413) 665-2399, Internet: www.yankeecandle.com. Head: Steve Smith
Science&Tech Museum - 1995
Transportation 47691

South Elgin IL

Fox River Trolley Museum, 361 S La Fox St, South Elgin, IL 60177 - T: (630) 665-2581, E-mail: info@foxtrolley.org, Internet: www.foxtrolley.org
Science&Tech Museum - 1958
Cars, diesel locomotives, trolley track 47692

South Hadley MA

Mount Holyoke College Art Museum, Lower Lake Rd, South Hadley, MA 01075-1499 - T: (413) 538-2245, Fax: (413) 538-2144, E-mail: artmuseum@mtholyoke.edu, Internet: www.mtholyoke.edu/go/artmuseum. Dir.: Marianne Doezema, Cur.: Wendy M. Watson
Fine Arts Museum / University Museum - 1875
Art 47693

Skinner Museum of Mount Holyoke College, 35 Woodbridge St, South Hadley, MA 01075 - T: (413) 538-2245, Fax: (413) 538-2144. Cur.: Wendy Watson
Local Museum - 1933
Agriculture, archaeology, geology, glass, hist, bird coll 47694

South Haven MI

Michigan Maritime Museum, 260 Dyckman Av, South Haven, MI 49090 - T: (616) 637-8078, Fax: (616) 637-1594, E-mail: mmmuseum@accn.org, Internet: www.michiganmaritimemuseum.org. Dir.: Dr. Barbara K. Kreuzer, Cur.: Audra Bellmore, Reg.: Judy Schaack, Libr.: Leslie Beil
Historical Museum - 1976
Maritime history - library 47695

South Hero VT

South Hero Bicentennial Museum, Rte 2, South Hero, VT 05486 - T: (802) 372-6615, 672-5552, E-mail: lmjshut@aol.com. Pres./Cur.: Barbara Winch
Local Museum - 1974
Local hist 47696

South Holland IL

South Holland Historical Museum, Box 48, South Holland, IL 60473 - T: (708) 596-2722. Pres.: Bill Paarlberg
Local Museum - 1969
Local history 47697

South Milwaukee WI

South Milwaukee Historical Society Museum, 717 Milwaukee Av, South Milwaukee, WI 53172 - T: (414) 768-8790, 762-8852. C.E.O.: Dean Marlowe, Cur.: Addie Becker
Local Museum - 1972
Local hist 47698

South Natick MA

Historical and Natural History Museum of Natick, 58 Eliot St, South Natick, MA 01760 - T: (508) 647-4841, Fax: (508) 651-7013, E-mail: elliot@ma.ultranet.com, Internet: www.ultranet.com/~elliot/. Pres.: Janice Prescott, Cur.: Anne K. Schaller
Local Museum - 1870
Local history, American Indian artifacts, natural history - library 47699

South Orange NJ

Seton Hall University Museum, 400 South Orange Av, South Orange, NJ 07079 - T: (973) 761-9459, Fax: (973) 275-2368, E-mail: krafther@lanmail.shu.edu, Internet: www.shu.edu. Dir.: Charlotte Nichols
University Museum / Archaeological Museum - 1963
Archaeology 47700

South Pass City WY

South Pass City State Historic Site, 125 South Pass Main St, South Pass City, WY 82520 - T: (307) 332-3684, Fax: (307) 332-3688, E-mail: southpass@onewest.net. Cur.: Scott Goetz
Local Museum - 1967
Local hist 47701

South Saint Paul MN

Dakota County Historical Society Museum, 130 Third Av N, South Saint Paul, MN 55075 - T: (651) 451-6260, Fax: (651) 552-7265, E-mail: dchs@mtn.org, Internet: www.dakotahistory.org. Pres.: Steve Larson, Dir.: Gregory A. Page
Historical Museum - 1939 47702

South Sudbury MA

Longfellow's Wayside Inn Museum, Wayside Inn Rd, South Sudbury, MA 01776 - T: (978) 443-1776;, Fax: (978) 443-8041, E-mail: waysideguy@aol.com, Internet: www.wayside.org. Head: Guy R. LeBlanc
Local Museum - 1716
Local history 47703

South Sutton NH

South Sutton Old Store Museum, 12 Meeting House Hill Rd, South Sutton, NH 03273 - T: (603) 938-5843. Cur.: Peggy Forand
Historical Museum - 1954 47704

South Union KY

Shaker Museum, 850 Shaker Museum Rd, South Union, KY 42283 - T: (502) 542-4167, 542-7734, Fax: (502) 542-7558, E-mail: shakmus@logantele.com, Internet: www.logantele.com/~shakmus/. Dir.: Jerry Wooten, Cur.: Tommy Hines
Historical Museum - 1960
Site of 1807 South Union Shaker village 47705

South Williamsport PA

Peter J. McGovern Little League Baseball Museum, Rte 15, South Williamsport, PA 17701 - T: (570) 326-3607, Fax: (570) 326-2267, E-mail: museum@littleleague.org, Internet: www.littleleague.org. Dir./Cur.: Michael Miller
Special Museum - 1982
Sports, Little League 47706

Southampton NY

Parrish Art Museum, 25 Job's Ln, Southampton, NY 11968 - T: (631) 283-2118 ext 12, Fax: (631) 283-7006, E-mail: fergusone@parrishart.org, Internet: thehamptons.com. Dir.: Trudy C. Kramer, Dep. Dir.: Anke Tom Dieck Jackson, Cur.: Alicia Longwell, Lewis B. Cullman, Dorothy Cullmann, Katherine Crum (Art, Education)
Fine Arts Museum - 1898 47707

Southampton Historical Museum, 177 Meeting House Ln, Southampton, NY 11968 - T: (631) 283-2494, Fax: (631) 283-4540, E-mail: hismusdir@hamptons.com, Internet: www.southamptonhistoricalmuseum.com. C.E.O.: Richard I. Barons
Local Museum - 1898
Local hist, South Fork culture, folk art, Native American, whaling, rural tools, area ethnic hist 47708

Southern Pines NC

Weymouth Woods-Sandhills Nature Preserve Museum, 1024 Fort Bragg Rd, Southern Pines, NC 28387 - T: (919) 692-2167, Fax: (910) 692-8042, E-mail: weymouth@pinehurst.net
Natural History Museum - 1969
Indian artifacts, turpentine industry artifacts, wildlife 47709

Southold NY

Southold Historical Society Museum, Main Rd and Maple Ln, Southold, NY 11971 - T: (516) 765-5500, Fax: (516) 765-5500, E-mail: sohistsoc@aol.com. Pres.: Gerard Gaughran
Local Museum - 1960 47710

Southold Indian Museum, Bayview Rd, Southold, NY 11971 - T: (516) 765-5577, Fax: (516) 765-5577, E-mail: indianmuseum@aol.com. Pres.: Ellen Barcel
Ethnology Museum / Archaeological Museum - 1925 47711

Southwest Harbor ME

Wendell Gilley Museum, Main St and Herrick Rd, Southwest Harbor, ME 04679 - T: (207) 244-7555, Fax: (207) 244-7555, E-mail: gilleymu@acadia.net, Internet: www.wendellgilleymuseum.org. Pres.: Kate Halle Briggs, Dir.: Nina Z. Gormley
Fine Arts Museum / Folklore Museum - 1979
Folk art, woodcarving 47712

Spalding ID

Nez Perce National Historical Park, 39063 US-Hwy 95, Spalding, ID 83540 - T: (208) 843-2261, Fax: (208) 843-2001, E-mail: bob_chenoweth@nps.gov, Internet: www.nps.gov/nepe/. Cur.: Bob Chenoweth
Natural History Museum / Ethnology Museum / Historical Museum - 1965
Prehistoric occupation, Indian ethnographic colls, photos, Dugout canoes, lawyer family coll, 1877 war - archives, research center 47713

Sparta WI

Monroe County Local History Room and Library, 200 W Main St, Sparta, WI 54656 - T: (608) 269-8680, Fax: (608) 269-8921, E-mail: mclhr@centurytel.net, Internet: co.monroe.wi.us. Sc. Staff: Audrey Johnson (History)
Local Museum - 1977 47714

Spartanburg SC

Milliken Gallery, Converse College, 580 E Main St, Spartanburg, SC 29302 - T: (864) 596-9181, Fax: (864) 596-9606, E-mail: mac.boggs@converse.edu, Internet: www.converse.edu. Dir.: Mac Boggs
Fine Arts Museum / University Museum - 1971
Art 47715

Regional Museum of Spartanburg County, 100 E Main St, Spartanburg, SC 29306 - T: (864) 596-3501, Fax: (864) 596-3501, E-mail: regionalmuseum@mindspring.com, Internet: www.spartanarts.org/history. C.E.O.: Susan Turpin, Cur.: Carolyn Creal
Local Museum - 1961
Local hist 47716

The Sandor Teszler Gallery, Wofford College, 429 N Church St, Spartanburg, SC 29303-3663 - T: (864) 597-4300, Fax: (864) 597-4329, E-mail: coburnoh@wofford.edu, Internet: www.sandorteszler.org. Dir.: Oakley H. Coburn
University Museum / Library with Exhibitions
Art, crafts, sciences, social sciences - library 47717

Spartanburg County Museum of Art, 385 S Spring St, Spartanburg, SC 29306 - T: (864) 582-7616, Fax: (864) 948-5353, E-mail: museum@spartanarts.org, Internet: www.sparklenet.com/museumofart. Pres.: Ray Eubanks, Dir.: Theresa Mann
Fine Arts Museum - 1969
Arts 47718

Spartanburg Science Center, 385 S Spring St, Spartanburg, SC 29306 - T: (864) 583-2777, Fax: (864) 948-5353. Exec. Dir.: John F. Green
Natural History Museum / Science&Tech Museum - 1978
Natural hist, science, exotic tortoises, reptiles, fossils, skulls, rocks, minerals, insects, shells, bird nests 47719

University of South Carolina at Spartanburg Art Gallery, 800 University Way, Spartanburg, SC 29303 - T: (864) 503-5838. Dir.: Jane Nodine
University Museum / Fine Arts Museum - 1982 47720

Spearfish SD

Ruddell Gallery, Black Hills State University, 1200 University St, Spearfish, SD 57799 - T: (605) 642-6104 ext 6111, Fax: (605) 642-6105. Dir.: Jim Knutsen
Fine Arts Museum - 1936
Photography, regional, visual artists - library 47721

Spencer NC

North Carolina Transportation Museum, 411 S Salisbury Av, Spencer, NC 28159 - T: (704) 636-2889, Fax: (704) 639-1881, E-mail: nctrans@tarheel.net, Internet: www.nctrans.org. Exec. Dir.: Elizabeth Smith
Science&Tech Museum - 1977
1896 Southern Railway steam primary staging and repair facility complex containing 20 structures, 37 bay roundhouse, turntable and 90,000 feet back shop 47722

Spencerport NY

Ogden Historical Society Museum, 568 Colby St, Spencerport, NY 14559 - T: (716) 352-0660, Fax: (716) 352-5328. Pres.: Ted Rogers
Local Museum - 1958 47723

Spillville IA

Bily Clock Museum and Antonin Dvorak Exhibition, 323 S Main, Spillville, IA 52168 - T: (319) 562-3569, Fax: (319) 562-4373, E-mail: bily@oneota.net, Internet: www.spillville.ia.us
Special Museum - 1923
Clocks 47724

Spiro OK

Spiro Mounds Archaeological Center, Rte 2, Box 339AA, Spiro, OK 74959 - T: (918) 962-2062, Fax: (918) 962-2062, E-mail: spiromds@ipa.net. Head: Dennis Peterson
Archaeological Museum - 1978
Archaeology 47725

Spokane WA

Cheney Cowles Museum → Northwest Museum of Arts and Culture

Children's Museum of Spokane, 110 N Post St, Spokane, WA 99210-0461 - T: (509) 624-5437, Fax: (509) 624-6453, E-mail: cms@childrensmuseum.net, Internet: www.childrensmuseum.net. Exec. Dir.: Don Kardong
Special Museum - 1995 47726

Jundt Art Museum, Gonzaga University, 502 E Boone Av, Spokane, WA 99258-0001 - T: (509) 323-6611, Fax: (509) 323-5525, E-mail: patnode@calvin.gonzaga.edu, Internet: www.gonzaga.edu/jundt/index.html. Dir.: J. Scott Patnode, Ass. Cur.: Paul D. Brekke
Fine Arts Museum / University Museum - 1995
Art 47727

Northwest Museum of Arts and Culture, 2316 First Av W, Spokane, WA 99204 - T: (509) 456-3931, Fax: (509) 363-5303, E-mail: themac@ztc.net, Internet: www.northwestmuseum.org. Dir.: Bruce B. Eldredge, Dep. Dir.: Larry Schoonover (Exhibits, Programs), Maurine Barrett (Operations, Admin.), Joyce M. Cameron (Development, Communication)
Fine Arts Museum / Local Museum - 1916
Local hist 47728

Spotsylvania VA

Spotsylvania Historical Museum, POB 64, Spotsylvania, VA 22553 - T: (540) 582-7167. Pres.: John E. Pruitt, Dir./Cur.: Martha C. Carter
Local Museum - 1962
Local hist 47729

Spring Green WI

The House on the Rock, 5754 Hwy 23, Spring Green, WI 53588 - T: (608) 935-3639, Fax: (608) 935-9472, Internet: www.thehouseontherock.com. Pres.: Susan Donaldson
Local Museum - 1961
Historical house 47730

Spring Valley MN

Methodist Church Museum - a Laura Ingalls Wilder Site, c/o Spring Valley Historical Society, 220 W Courtland St, Spring Valley, MN 55975 - T: (507) 346-7659, Fax: (507) 346-7249, Internet: www.ci.spring-valley.mn.us. Pres.: Donald Larson
Historical Museum - 1956 47731

Springdale AR

Arts Center of the Ozarks, 214 S Main, Springdale, AR 72765 - T: (501) 751-5441, Fax: (501) 927-0308, E-mail: acozarks@swbell.net, Internet: www.nwaonline.net/aco. Dir.: Kathi Blundell
Public Gallery - 1948
Traditional handcrafts, contemporary arts and crafts 47732

Shiloh Museum of Ozark History, 118 W Johnson Av, Springdale, AR 72764 - T: (501) 750-8165, Fax: (501) 750-8171, E-mail: shiloh@springdaleark.org, Internet: www.springdaleark.org/shiloh. Dir.: Bob Besom
Historical Museum - 1965 47733

Springdale PA

Rachel Carson Homestead, 613 Marion Av, Springdale, PA 15144-1242 - T: (724) 274-5459, Fax: (724) 275-1259, Internet: www.rachelcarsonhomestead.org. Exec. Dir.: Vivienne Shaffer
Local Museum - 1975
Historic house 47734

Springdale UT

Zion National Park Museum, Zion Canyon Headquarters, Springdale, UT 84767-1099 - T: (435) 772-3256, Fax: (435) 772-3426, Internet: www.nps.gov/zion. Cur.: Mark Herberger
Historical Museum - 1919
Natural and human hist - archives 47735

Springfield IL

The Dana-Thomas House, 301 E Lawrence Av, Springfield, IL 62703 - T: (217) 782-6773, Fax: (217) 788-9450, E-mail: dthf@warpnet.net, Internet: www.dana-thomas.org. Dir.: Dr. Donald P. Hallmark
Decorative Arts Museum - 1981
Frank Lloyd Wright prairie period house, art glass and furniture, decorative art, social history (20th c) 47736

Illinois State Museum, Spring and Edwards Sts, Springfield, IL 62706-5000 - T: (217) 782-7387, Fax: (217) 782-1254, E-mail: webmaster@museum.state.il.us, Internet: www.museum.state.il.us/. Dir.: Dr. R. Bruce McMillan, Kent Smith (Art), Dr. Judith A. Franke, Cur.: Janice Wass (Decorative Arts), Dr. Eric Grimm (Botany), Dr. Everett D. Cashatt (Zoology), Ass. Cur.: Dr. Richard Toomey (Geology), Dr. H. David Bohlen (Zoology)
Fine Arts Museum / Local Museum / Ethnology Museum / Natural History Museum - 1877
Natural history, anthropology, geology, botany, zoology, decorative art, art 47737

Lincoln Home, 413 S 8th St, Springfield, IL 62701-1905 - T: (217) 492-4241, Fax: (217) 492-4673, E-mail: liho_superintendent@nps.gov, Internet: www.nps.gov/liho. Cur.: Linda Norbut Suits
Historical Museum / Historic Site - 1972
Home of Abraham Lincoln, 16th Pres. of the United States 47738

Lincoln Tomb, Oak Ridge Cemetery, Springfield, IL 62702 - T: (217) 782-2717, Fax: (217) 524-3738
Historic Site - 1874
1874 the tomb of Abraham Lincoln 47739

Old State Capitol, Fifth at Adams Sts, 1 Old Capitol Pl, Springfield, IL 62701 - T: (217) 785-7960, Fax: (217) 557-0282, E-mail: carol-andrews@ihpa.state.il.us
Historical Museum - 1969 47740

The Pearson Museum, 801 N Rutledge, Springfield, IL 62794-9635 - T: (217) 545-8017, 545-4261, Fax: (217) 545-9605, E-mail: bmason@siumed.edu, Internet: www.siumed.edu/medhum/the_pearson_museum/htm. Dir.: Phillip V. Davis, Cur.: Barbara Mason
University Museum / Historical Museum - 1974
Medical hist 47741

Springfield Art Gallery, 700 N Fourth St, Springfield, IL 62702 - T: (217) 523-2631, Fax: (217) 523-3866, E-mail: spiartassc@aol.com, Internet: www.springfieldart.org. Exec. Dir.: Dean Adkins
Fine Arts Museum / Public Gallery - 1913 47742

Vachel Lindsay Home, 603 S Fifth St, Springfield, IL 62703 - T: (217) 524-0901, Fax: (217) 557-0282
Special Museum - 1946
Drawings, letters, manuscripts, books, paintings, sculpture 47743

Springfield KY

Lincoln Homestead, 5079 Lincoln Park Rd, Springfield, KY 40069 - T: (859) 336-7461, Fax: (859) 336-0659, E-mail: gary.feldman@mail.state.ky.us
Historic Site - 1936 47744

Springfield MA

Connecticut Valley Historical Museum, 220 State St, Springfield, MA 01103 - T: (413) 263-6800 ext 304, Fax: (413) 263-6898, E-mail: info@spfldlibmus.org, Internet: www.quadrangle.org. Dir.: Guy McLain
Historical Museum - 1927
Regional history 47745

George Walter Vincent Smith Art Museum, 220 State St, Springfield, MA 01103 - T: (413) 263-6800, Fax: (413) 263-6898, E-mail: info@spfldlibmus.org, Internet: www.quadrangle.org. Pres.: Joseph Carvalho, Dir.: Heather Haskell
Fine Arts Museum / Decorative Arts Museum - 1895
Japanese decorative arts, Chinese cloisonné, Middle Eastern rugs, American paintings of the 19th c 47746

Museum of Fine Arts, 220 State St, Springfield, MA 01103 - T: (413) 263-6800, Fax: (413) 263-6898, E-mail: info@spfldlibmus.org, Internet: www.quadrangle.org. Pres.: Joseph Carvalho, Dir.: Heather Haskell
Fine Arts Museum - 1933
American and European painting, sculptures, decorative art 47747

Naismith Memorial Basketball Hall of Fame, 1150 W Columbus Av, Springfield, MA 01105 - T: (413) 781-6500, Fax: (413) 781-1939, Internet: www.hoophall.com. Dir.: John Doleva, Cur.: Michael Brooslin
Special Museum - 1968
Sports 47748

Springfield Armory Museum, 1 Armory Sq, Springfield, MA 01105-1299 - T: (413) 734-8551, Fax: (413) 747-8062, E-mail: spar_interpretation@nps.gov, Internet: www.nps.gov. Cur.: James D. Roberts
Military Museum - 1870
Military 47749

Springfield Science Museum, 220 State St, Springfield, MA 01103 - T: (413) 263-6800, Fax: (413) 263-6898, E-mail: info@spfldlibmus.org, Internet: www.quadrangle.org. Dir.: David Stier, Cur.: John P. Pretola (Anthropology)
Science&Tech Museum - 1859
African, Native American, minerals 47750

William Blizard Gallery, c/o Springfield College, 263 Alden St, Springfield, MA 01109 - T: (413) 747-3000, 748-0204, Fax: (413) 748-3580. Dir.: Holly Murray
Fine Arts Museum - 1998 47751

Springfield MO

Discovery Center of Springfield, 438 E St Louis, Springfield, MO 65806 - T: (417) 862-9910 ext 0 or ext 700, Fax: (417) 862-6898, E-mail: efox@discoverycenter.org, Internet: discoverycenterof-springfield.org. C.E.O.: Emily Fox
Science&Tech Museum - 1991 47752

History Museum for Springfield-Greene County, 830 Boonville, Springfield, MO 65802 - T: (417) 864-1976, Fax: (417) 864-2019, E-mail: info@historymuseumsgc.org, Internet: www.historymuseumsgc.org. Dir.: Linda Green, Cur.: Shauna Smith, Educator: Linda Loveland
Local Museum / Historical Museum - 1975
Local hist 47753

Springfield Art Museum, 1111 E Brookside Dr, Springfield, MO 65807 - T: (417) 837-5700, Fax: (417) 837-5704, E-mail: watercolourusa@ci.springfield.mo.us, Internet: www.springfieldmogov/egor/art. Dir.: Jerry A. Berger, Asst. Dir.: Faith A. Yorty, Cur.: James M. Beasley
Fine Arts Museum - 1928
Decorative art, drawings, photography, paintings, prints, sculpture - library 47754

Springfield NJ

Springfield Historical Society Museum, 126 Morris Av, Springfield, NJ 07081 - T: (973) 376-4784. Pres.: Margaret Bandrowski
Local Museum - 1954 47755

Springfield OH

Clark County Historical Society Museum, 105 N Thompson Av, Springfield, OH 45504 - T: (937) 324-0657, Fax: (937) 324-1992. Dir.: Roger Steigert, Cur.: Virginia Weygandt
Local Museum - 1897 47756

Springfield Museum of Art, 107 Cliff Park Rd, Springfield, OH 45501 - T: (937) 325-4673, Fax: (937) 325-4674, E-mail: smoa@main-net.com, Internet: www.spfld-museum-of-art.org. Dir.: Mark Chepp, Cur.: Dominique Vasseur
Fine Arts Museum - 1946 47757

Springfield OR

Springfield Museum, 590 Main St, Springfield, OR 97477 - T: (541) 726-3677, Fax: (541) 726-3689, E-mail: kjensen@ci.springfield.or.us, Internet: www.springfieldmuseum.com. Dir.: Kathleen A. Jensen, Cur.: Estelle McCafferty
Local Museum - 1981
Local hist 47758

Springfield VT

Eureka School House, State Rte 11, Springfield, VT 05156 - T: (802) 828-3051, Fax: (802) 828-3206, E-mail: jdumville@dca.state.vt.us, Internet: www.historicvermont.org. Head: John P. Dumville
Local Museum - 1968
Historic house 47759

Miller Art Center, 9 Elm St, Springfield, VT 05156-0313 - T: (802) 885-2415, E-mail: glenshee@excite.com. Dir.: Robert McLaughlin
Local Museum / Fine Arts Museum - 1956
Portraits, pewter, Bennington pottery, paintings, toys, costumes, sculpture, crafts, machine tool industry 47760

Springs PA

Springs Museum, Rte 669, Springs, PA 15562 - T: (814) 662-2625, Fax: (814) 445-2263. Pres.: Joseph Bender
Local Museum - 1957
Local hist 47761

Springville NY

Warner Museum, 98 E Main St, Springville, NY 14141 - T: (716) 592-0094. Cur.: Donald Orton
Local Museum - 1953 47762

Springville UT

Springville Museum of Art, 126 E 400 S, Springville, UT 84663 - T: (801) 489-2727, Fax: (801) 489-2739, E-mail: sharon@admn.shs.nebo.edu, Internet: www.sma.nebo.edu. Dir.: Dr. Vern G. Swanson, Ass. Dir.: Dr. Sharon R. Gray
Fine Arts Museum - 1903
Utah art 47763

Spruce Pine NC

Museum of North Carolina Minerals, Milepost 331, Blue Ridge Pkwy at Hwy 226, Spruce Pine, NC 28777 - T: (704) 765-2761, Fax: (704) 765-0974. Head: Tim Francis
Natural History Museum - 1955 47764

Staatsburg NY

Mills Mansion State Historic Site → Staatsburgh State Historic Museum

Staatsburgh State Historic Museum, Old Post Rd, Staatsburg, NY 12580 - T: (914) 889-8851, Fax: (914) 889-8321, E-mail: melodye.moore@oprhp.state.ny.us. Pres.: Eleanor Williamson
Local Museum - 1938 47765

Stafford County VA

George Washington's Ferry Farm, 268 Kings Hwy, Stafford County, VA 22405 - T: (540) 370-0732, Fax: (540) 371-3398, E-mail: mailroom@kenmore.org, Internet: www.kenmore.org
Historical Museum 47766

Stamford CT

Stamford Historical Society Museum, 1508 High Ridge Rd, Stamford, CT 06903 - T: (203) 322-1565, Fax: (203) 322-1607, E-mail: shsadmin@flvax.ferg.lib.ct.us, Internet: www.stamfordhistory.org. Pres.: Philip E. Norgren
Local Museum / Decorative Arts Museum - 1901
History, decorative arts 47767

Stamford Museum and Nature Center, 39 Scofieldtown Rd, Stamford, CT 06903 - T: (203) 322-1646, Fax: (203) 322-0408, E-mail: smnc@stamfordmuseum.org, Internet: www.stamfordmuseum.org. Dir.: Kenneth Marchione, Sharon Blume, Cur.: Rosa Portell
Fine Arts Museum / Natural History Museum - 1936
Natural hist, art 47768

Whitney Museum of American Art at Champion, 1 Champion Plaza, Stamford, CT 06921 - T: (203) 358-7652, Fax: (203) 358-2975. Cur.: Cynthia Roznoy
Fine Arts Museum - 1981
Art 47769

Standish ME

Marrett House, Rte 25, Standish, ME 04084 - T: (207) 642-3032, (207) 384-2454, Fax: (207) 384-8192, E-mail: pzea@spnea.org, Internet: www.spnea.org
Historical Museum - 1944 47770

Stanfield NC

Reed Gold Mine State Historic Site, 9621 Reed Mine Rd, Stanfield, NC 28163 - T: (704) 721-4653, Fax: (704) 721-4657, E-mail: reedmine@ctc.net, Internet: www.itpi.dpi.state.nc.us/reed. Pres.: Don McNeely
Science&Tech Museum - 1971 47771

Stanford CA

Iris & B. Gerald Cantor Center for Visual Arts at Stanford University, Lomita Dr and Museum Way, Stanford, CA 94305-5060 - T: (650) 723-4177, 725-0462, Fax: (650) 725-0464, Internet: www.stanford.edu/dept/ccva. Dir.: Thomas K. Seligman, Chief Cur.: Bernard Barryte, Cur.: John Listopad (Asian Art), Betsy Fryberger (Prints and Drawings), Hilarie Faberman (Modern and Contemporary Art), Manuel Jordan (Art of the Americas), Patrice Young (Education)
Fine Arts Museum / University Museum - 1885
Art 47772

Stanford KY

William Whitley House, 625 William Whitley Rd, Stanford, KY 40484 - T: (606) 355-2881, Fax: (606) 355-2778, E-mail: jack.bailey@mail.state.ky.us, Internet: www.kystateparks.com/agencies/parks/wmwhitly.htm. Dir.: Jack C. Bailey
Historical Museum - 1938
1792 William Whitley House, the first brick home W of the Alleghenies 47773

Stanford MT

Judith Basin County Museum, 19 Third S, Stanford, MT 59479 - T: (406) 566-2974, 566-2277 ext.123. Pres. & Dir.: Florence E. Harris, Dir.: Oliver Olson, Ruth Hardenbrook, Lorraine Boeck, Mary Mikeson, Cur.: Virginia B. Hayes
Local Museum - 1966 47774

Stanton ND

Knife River Indian Villages National Historic Site, 564 County Rd 37, Stanton, ND 58571 - T: (701) 745-3309, Fax: (701) 745-3708, E-mail: knri_information@nps.gov, Internet: www.nps.gov/knri. Head: Lisa Eckert
Local Museum - 1974
Local hist 47775

Stanton TX

Martin County Historical Museum, 207 E Broadway, Stanton, TX 79782 - T: (915) 756-2722. Pres.: Eugene Byrd, Cur.: Helen Thrailkill
Local Museum - 1969
County hist 47776

Starkville MS

Oktibbeha County Heritage Museum, 206 Fellowship St, Starkville, MS 39759 - T: (601) 323-0211. Head: George Lewis
Historical Museum - 1979 47777

State College PA

Centre County Historical Society Museum, 1001 E College Av, State College, PA 16801 - T: (814) 234-4779, Fax: (814) 234-1694, E-mail: cchs@uplink.net, Internet: centrecountyhistory.org
Local Museum - 1904
Victorian furnishings, clothing, tools, business, hist, Thompson family 47778

Staten Island NY

Alice Austen House Museum, 2 Hylan Blvd, Staten Island, NY 10305 - T: (718) 816-4506, Fax: (718) 815-3959, E-mail: eaausten@aol.com, Internet: www.aliceausten.org. C.E.O.: Carl Rutberg, Dir.: Nancy E. Fiske
Local Museum - 1985
Local hist 47779

Conference House, 7455 Hylan Blvd, Staten Island, NY 10307 - T: (718) 984-6046. Pres.: Madalen Bertolini
Local Museum - 1927 47780

Garibaldi and Meucci Museum, 420 Tompkins Av, Staten Island, NY 10305 - T: (718) 442-1608, Fax: (718) 442-8635, E-mail: gmmuseum@aol.com. Dir.: Anne Alarcon, Cur.: Emily T. Gear
Local Museum - 1956 47781

Historic Richmond Town, 441 Clarke Av, Staten Island, NY 10306 - T: (718) 351-1611, Fax: (718) 351-6057, E-mail: sihs-jfalk@si.rr.com, Internet: www.historicrichmondtown.org. Dir.: John Guild
Historical Museum - 1935
Historic village incl 28 historic buildings from late 17th c to early 20th c 47782

Jacques Marchais Museum of Tibetan Art, 338 Lighthouse Av, Staten Island, NY 10306 - T: (718) 987-3500, Fax: (718) 351-0402, E-mail: jcelli@tibetanmuseum.com, Internet: www.tibetanmuseum.com. Exec. Dir.: Jeanann Celli
Fine Arts Museum / Ethnology Museum / Folklore Museum - 1945 47783

The John A. Noble Collection, 1000 Richmond Terrace, Staten Island, NY 10301 - T: (718) 447-6490, Fax: (718) 447-6056, E-mail: jancol@admin.con2.com, Internet: mcns10.med.nyu.edu/noble/noble.collection.html. C.E.O.: Erin Urban
Fine Arts Museum / Historical Museum - 1986
Art, maritime history 47784

Noble Maritime Collection, 1000 Richmond Tce, Staten Island, NY 10301 - T: (718) 447-6490, Fax: (718) 447-6056, E-mail: erinurban@noblemaritime.org, Internet: www.noblemaritime.org. C.E.O.: Erin Urban
Fine Arts Museum - 1986
Lithographs, paintings, drawings, photographs, marine artifacts 47785

Seguine House, 440 Seguine Av, Staten Island, NY 10307 - T: (718) 967-3542, Fax: (718) 967-5689
Decorative Arts Museum - 1989
Antique furnishings 47786

Snug Harbor Cultural Center, 1000 Richmond Terrace, Staten Island, NY 10301 - T: (718) 448-2500, Fax: (718) 442-8534, E-mail: newhouse@snug-harbor.org. Dir.: Olivia Georgia
Open Air Museum / Folklore Museum / Historic Site / Fine Arts Museum / Performing Arts Museum - 1976 47787

Staten Island Children's Museum, 1000 Richmond Terrace, Staten Island, NY 10301 - T: (718) 273-2060, Fax: (718) 273-2836, E-mail: drosenthal@sichildrenmuseum.org, Internet: www.sichildrenmuseum.org. Exec. Dir.: Dina R. Rosenthal
Special Museum - 1974 47788

Staten Island Ferry Collection (closed) 47789

Staten Island Historical Society Museum, 441 Clarke Av, Staten Island, NY 10306 - T: (718) 351-1611, Fax: (718) 351-6057, Internet: www.historicrichmondtown.org. Dir.: John Guild, Chief Cur.: Maxine Friedman
Local Museum - 1856 47790

Staten Island Institute of Arts and Sciences, 75 Stuyvesant Pl, Staten Island, NY 10301 - T: (718) 727-1135, Fax: (718) 273-5683. Cur.: Bart Bland (Art), Edward Johnson (Science), Patricia Salmon (History)
Fine Arts Museum / Historical Museum / Science&Tech Museum - 1881 47791

Statesboro GA

Georgia Southern University Museum, Rosenwald Bldg, Statesboro, GA 30460 - T: (912) 681-5444, Fax: (912) 681-0729, E-mail: dharvey@gasou.edu, Internet: www2.gasou.edu/musenews. Dir.: Richard Smith, Ass. Dir.: Deborah Harvey, Cur.: Dr. Gale Bishop (Geology), Dr. Richard C. Hulbert (Vertebrate Paleontology), Dr. Frank French (Biology), Dr. Stephen Hale (Anthropology)
University Museum / Natural History Museum - 1980
Natural and cultural history of the Coastal Plain 47792

Statesville NC

Fort Dobbs State Historic Site, US 21, 1 mile off I-40 to SR 1930, West 1 1/2 miles on 1930, Statesville, NC 28677 - T: (704) 873-5866, Fax: (704) 873-5866, E-mail: fortdobbs@statesville.net. Man.: Louise Huston
Military Museum / Open Air Museum - 1969 47793

Iredell Museum of Arts & Heritage, 1335 Museum Rd, Statesville, NC 28625 - T: (704) 873-4734, Fax: (704) 873-4407, E-mail: imuseum@statesville.net, Internet: www.iredellmuseum.com. Exec. Dir.: Mary Bradford
Fine Arts Museum / Natural History Museum / Science&Tech Museum - 1956 47794

Staunton VA

Frontier Culture Museum, 1290 Richmond Rd, Staunton, VA 24401 - T: (540) 332-7850, Fax: (540) 332-9989, E-mail: info@frontiermuseum.state.va.us, Internet: www.frontiermuseum.org
Folklore Museum - 1982
German, Scotch-Irish, English and American folklife and culture 47795

Hunt Gallery, Mary Baldwin College, Market and Vine Sts, Staunton, VA 24401 - T: (540) 887-7196, Fax: (540) 887-7139, E-mail: pryan@mbc.edu, Internet: www.mbc.edu. Dir.: Paul Ryan, Ass. Dir.: Marlena Hobson
Fine Arts Museum / University Museum - 1842
Art gallery 47796

Museum of American Frontier Culture, 1250 Richmond Rd, Staunton, VA 24401 - T: (540) 332-7850, Fax: (540) 332-9989, Internet: www.frontiermuseum.org. Exec. Dir.: John A. Walters
Historical Museum - 1982
European and American folklife and culture, focusing on Germany, England, Northern Ireland, America and immigration & culture 47797

Staunton Augusta Art Center, 1 Gyspy Hill Park, Staunton, VA 24401 - T: (540) 885-2028, Fax: (540) 885-6000, E-mail: saartcenter@aol.com. Exec. Dir.: Margo McGirr
Fine Arts Museum - 1961
Art 47798

Woodrow Wilson Birthplace and Museum, 20 N Coalter St, Staunton, VA 24401 - T: (540) 885-0897, Fax: (540) 886-9874, E-mail: woodrow@cfw.com, Internet: www.woodrowwilson.org. Dir.: Patrick Clarke, Cur.: Edmund Potter
Historical Museum - 1938
Historic house, birthplace of Woodrow Wilson, academic and social life, presidential history 47799

Steeles Tavern VA

Cyrus H. McCormick Memorial Museum, 128 McCormick Farm Circle, Steeles Tavern, VA 24476 - T: (540) 377-2255, Fax: (540) 377-5850, E-mail: steeles@vt.edu. Head: David A. Fiske
Local Museum - 1956
Local hist 47800

Steilacoom WA

Steilacoom Historical Museum, 112 Main St, Steilacoom, WA 98388-0016 - T: (253) 584-4133. Pres.: Harold L. Shellabarger, Sc. Staff: Patricia J. Laughlin (Registrar)
Local Museum - 1970
Local hist 47801

Stephenville TX

Stephenville Museum, 525 E Washington St, Stephenville, TX 76401 - T: (254) 965-5880, E-mail: llohr@our-town.com. Pres.: Betty Heath
Local Museum - 1965
Local hist 47802

Sterling CO

Overland Trail Museum, Junction I-76 and Hwy-6 E, Sterling, CO 80751-0400 - T: (970) 522-3895, Fax: (970) 521-0632, E-mail: hagemeier@sterlingcolo.com, Internet: www.sterlingcolo.com. Cur.: Anna Mae Hagemeier, Ass. Cur.: Cathy Asmus, Lana Tramp, Marilyn Hutt
Local Museum - 1936
Regional history 47803

Sterling IL

Sterling-Rock Falls Historical Society Museum, 1005 E 3rd St, Sterling, IL 61081 - T: (815) 622-6215, E-mail: srfhs@coiinc.com. Pres.: Tim Keller, Cur.: Terence Buckaloo
Local Museum - 1959
Local history - library, archives 47804

Sterling NY

Sterling Historical Society Museum, Rte 104A, Sterling, NY 13156 - T: (315) 947-6461, E-mail: sterlinghistory@lakeontario.net, Internet: www.lakeontario.net/sterlinghistory. C.E.O.: Don H. Richardson
Local Museum - 1976 47805

Steubenville OH

Jefferson County Historical Association Museum, 426 Franklin Av, Steubenville, OH 43952 - T: (740) 283-1133, Internet: www.rootsweb.com/~ohjcha. Pres.: Eleanor Naylor
Local Museum - 1976 47806

Stevens Point WI

The Museum of Natural History, 900 Reserve St, University of Wisconsin, Stevens Point, WI 54481 - T: (715) 346-4224, 346-2858, Fax: (715) 346-4213, E-mail: emarks@uwsp.edu, Internet: www.uwsp.edu/museum/. Cur.: Edward Marks
Natural History Museum / University Museum - 1966
Natural hist 47807

Portage County Museum, 1475 Water St, Stevens Point, WI 54481
Local Museum - 1952
Area domestic liefe, military, local Jewish heritage 47808

Stevenson WA

Columbia George Interpretive Center, 990 SW Rock Creek Dr, Stevenson, WA 98648 - T: (509) 427-8211, Fax: (509) 427-7429, E-mail: info@columbiagorge.org, Internet: www.columbiagorge.org. Dir.: Sharon Tiffany
Local Museum - 1959 47809

Still River MA

Harvard Historical Society Museum, 215 Still River Rd, Still River, MA 01467 - T: (978) 456-8285, E-mail: hhs@ma.ultranet.com, Internet: www.harvard.ma.us. Cur.: Camille Myers Breeze
Local Museum - 1897
Local hist, costumes, furniture, decorative arts 47810

Stillwater MN

Warden's House Museum, 602 N Main St, Stillwater, MN 55082 - T: (612) 439-5956, E-mail: rebecca@wchsmn.org, Internet: www.wchsmn.org. Pres.: Robert Vogel
Historical Museum - 1941 47811

Stillwater NY

Saratoga National Historical Park, 648 Rte 32, Stillwater, NY 12170 - T: (518) 664-9821, Fax: (518) 664-3349, E-mail: sara_info@nps.gov, Internet: www.nps.gov/sara. Dir.: Gina Johnson, Cur.: Christine Robinson
Military Museum / Open Air Museum - 1938
Site of the Battles of Saratoga, Sept. 19 and Oct. 7, 1777 47812

Stillwater OK

Gardiner Art Gallery, 108 Bartlett Center, Oklahoma State University, Stillwater, OK 74078 - T: (405) 744-6016, Fax: (405) 744-5767, Internet: www.okstate.edu/artsci/art/gallery.html. Dir.: Mark White
Fine Arts Museum / University Museum - 1965 47813

National Wrestling Hall of Fame, 405 W Hall of Fame Av, Stillwater, OK 74075 - T: (405) 377-5243, Fax: (405) 377-5244, E-mail: info@wrestlinghalloffame.org, Internet: www.wrestlinghalloffame.org. Pres.: Myron Roderick, Dir.: Tony Linville
Special Museum - 1976 47814

Oklahoma Museum of Higher Education, Old Central, Oregon State University, NE of University and Hester, Stillwater, OK 74078-0705 - T: (405) 744-2828, E-mail: omhe@ok-history.mus.ok.us. Pres.: Linda Jones
Special Museum / University Museum - 1980 47815

Stockbridge MA

Chesterwood Museum, 4 Williamsville Rd, Stockbridge, MA 01262-0827 - T: (413) 298-3579, Fax: (413) 298-3973, E-mail: chesterwood@nthp.org, Internet: www.chesterwood.org. Dir.: Michael W. Panhorst
Historic Site - 1955
Summer estate of Daniel Chester French 47816

Merwin House Tranquility, 14 Main St, Stockbridge, MA 01262 - T: (413) 298-4703, (617) 227-3956, Fax: (617) 227-9204, E-mail: pzea@spnea.org, Internet: www.spnea.org. Vice Pres.: Philip Zea
Decorative Arts Museum / Local Museum - 1966 47817

The Mission House, Main St, Stockbridge, MA 01262 - T: (413) 298-3239, Fax: (413) 298-5239, E-mail: westregion@ttor.org, Internet: www.thetrustees.org. Dir.: Steve McMahon
Religious Arts Museum - 1948
1739 home of Rev. John Sergeant, first missionary to the Stockbridge Indians 47818

Naumkeag House, Prospect Hill, Stockbridge, MA 01262 - T: (413) 298-3239, Fax: (413) 298-5239, E-mail: westregion@ttor.org, Internet: www.thetrustees.org. Dir.: Stephen McMahon
Historical Museum - 1959
Shingle style house, summer home of Joseph Hodges Choate, U.S. Ambassador to the Court of Saint James 47819

Norman Rockwell Museum at Stockbridge, 9 Glendale Rd, Stockbridge, MA 01262 - T: (413) 298-4100, Fax: (413) 298-4142, E-mail: postmaster@nrm.org, Internet: www.nrm.org. Dir.: Laurie Norton Moffatt, Chief Cur.: Maureen Hart Hennessey, Cur.: Linda Szekely (Norman Rockwell Collections), Stephanie Plunkett (Illustration Art)
Fine Arts Museum / Special Museum - 1967
Art, education, art appreciation inspired by Norman Rockwell 47820

Stockbridge Library Historical Room, Library, Stockbridge, MA 01262 - T: (413) 298-5501, E-mail: ballen@cwmars.org, Internet: www.masscat.org. C.E.O.: Rosemary Schneyer, Cur.: Babara Allen
Historical Museum - 1939
Local history 47821

Stockholm ME

Stockholm Historical Society Museum, 280 Main St, Stockholm, ME 04783 - T: (207) 896-5759, E-mail: jhede@mfx.net, Internet: www.aroostok.me.us. Pres.: Albertine Dufour
Local Museum - 1976
Local history 47822

Stockton CA

Children's Museum of Stockton, 402 W Weber Av, Stockton, CA 95203 - T: (209) 465-4386, Fax: (209) 465-4394, E-mail: children@sonnet.com, Internet: www.sonnet.com/usr/children. Dir.: Dorrie Hipschman
Special Museum - 1991 47823

The Haggin Museum, 1201 N Pershing Av, Stockton, CA 95203 - T: (209) 462-4116, 940-6311, Fax: (209) 462-1404, E-mail: info@hagginmuseum.org, Internet: haggingmuseum.org. Dir.: Tod Ruhstaller
Fine Arts Museum / Historical Museum - 1928
French and American art, American, European and Oriental decorative arts, glass, folk art, regional history, Indian artifacts 47824

Jeannette Powell Art Center, c/o University of the Pacific, 3601 Pacific Av, Stockton, CA 95211 - T: (209) 946-2011, Fax: (209) 946-2652, Internet: www.uop.edu. Pres.: Donald DeRosa
Public Gallery / University Museum - 1975 47825

Stockton Springs ME

Fort Knox State Historic Site, 711 Fort Knox Rd, Stockton Springs, ME 04981 - T: (207) 469-7719, Fax: (207) 469-7719. Head: Mike Wilusz
Military Museum / Historic Site - 1943 47826

Stone Mountain GA

Georgia's Stone Mountain Park, Hwy 78, Stone Mountain, GA 30086, mail addr: POB 778, Stone Mountain, GA 30086 - T: (770) 498-5690, Fax: (770) 498-5607, Internet: www.stonemountainpark.org. Head: Curtis Branscome
Local Museum / Natural History Museum - 1958 47827

Stonington CT

Captain Nathaniel B. Palmer House, 40 Palmer St, Stonington, CT 06378 - T: (860) 535-8445, Internet: www.stoningtonhistory.org. Pres.: Michael Davis, Cur.: Constance B. Colon
Local Museum / Special Museum - 1996
Historic house, Antarctica discovery 47828

Old Lighthouse Museum, 7 Water St, Stonington, CT 06378 - T: (860) 535-1440, E-mail: stonlighthouse@netzero.net, Internet: www.stoningtonhistory.org. Pres.: Michael Davis, Cur.: Louise D. Pittaway
Local Museum - 1925
Local hist, paintings - archive 47829

Stony Brook NY

Long Island Museum of American Art, History and Cariages, 1200 Rte 25A, Stony Brook, NY 11790 - T: (631) 751-0066, Fax: (631) 751-0353, E-mail: mail@longislandmuseum.com, Internet: www.longislandmuseum.org. Pres.: Jackie Day, Dep. Dir.: William Ayres (Collections, Interpretation), Cur.: Joshua Ruff (History), Asst. Cur.: Eva Greguski (Art)
Fine Arts Museum / Historical Museum - 1935
American art, hist of transportation 47830

Museum of Long Island Natural Sciences, Earth and Space Sciences Bldg, State University of New York at Stony Brook, Stony Brook, NY 11794-2100 - T: (631) 632-8230, Fax: (631) 632-8240, E-mail: Pamela.Stewart@sunysb.edu, Internet: www.molins.sunysb.edu. Dir.: Pamela Stewart, Cur.: Steven E. Englebright (Geology)
University Museum / Natural History Museum - 1973 47831

Museums at Stony Brook → Long Island Museum of American Art, History and Cariages

University Art Gallery, Staller Center for the Arts, State University of New York at Stony Brook, Stony Brook, NY 11794-5425 - T: (516) 632-7240, Fax: (516) 632-7354, E-mail: rcooper@notes.cc.sunysb.edu. Dir.: Rhonda Cooper
Fine Arts Museum / University Museum - 1975 47832

Stony Point NY

Stony Point Battlefield State Historic Site, Park Rd off US Rte 9W, Stony Point, NY 10980 - T: (914) 786-2521, E-mail: spbattle@ric.lhric.org, Internet: www2.1hric.org/spbattle/spbattle.htm. Head: Julia M. Warger
Military Museum / Open Air Museum - 1897
Site of raid on British stronghold by Brigadier Gen. Anthony Wayne on July 15, 1779 47833

Storm Lake IA

Witter Gallery, 609 Cayuga St, Storm Lake, IA 50588 - T: (712) 732-3400, E-mail: wittergallery@yahoo.com. Dir.: Amanda Kelly
Fine Arts Museum - 1972
Art 47834

Storrs CT

Connecticut State Museum of Natural History, 2019 Hillside Rd, Unit 1023, Storrs, CT 06269-1023 - T: (860) 486-4460, Fax: (860) 486-0827, E-mail: mnhadm05@uconnvm.uconn.edu, Internet: www.mnh.uconn.edu. Dir.: Ellen J. Censky
University Museum / Natural History Museum - 1982
Natural hist 47835

Mansfield Historical Society Museum, 954 Storrs Rd, Storrs, CT 06268 - T: (860) 429-6575, Fax: (860) 429-6575, E-mail: museum@mansfield-history.org, Internet: www.mansfield-history.org. Dir.: Ann Galonska
Local Museum - 1961
Local hist, farming, industry 47836

The William Benton Museum of Art, University of Connecticut, 245 Glenbrook Rd, Storrs, CT 06269-2140 - T: (860) 486-4520, Fax: (860) 486-0234, E-mail: benton@uconn.edu, Internet: www.benton.uconn.edu. Dir.: Salvatore Scalora, Cur.: Thomas P. Bruhn
Fine Arts Museum / University Museum - 1966
Art 47837

Story WY

Fort Phil Kearny, Hwy 87, Story, WY 82842 - T: (307) 684-7629, Fax: (307) 684-7967, E-mail: sreisc@missc.state.wy.us, Internet: www.philkearny.vcn.com. Dir.: John Keck, Cur.: Robert C. Wilson
Military Museum - 1913
Military hist 47838

Stoughton MA

Stoughton Historical Museum, Lucius Clapp Memorial, 6 Park St, Stoughton, MA 02072 - T: (781) 344-5456. Pres.: Elizabeth Leif, Cur.: Edward N. Meserve (History)
Local Museum - 1895
Local history 47839

Stoutsville MO

Mark Twain Birthplace Museum, 37352 Shrine Rd, Stoutsville, MO 65283 - T: (573) 565-3449, Fax: (573) 565-3718, E-mail: dsptwab@mail.dnr.state.mo.us, Internet: www.mostatesports.com/twainsite.htm. Head: John Huffman
Historical Museum - 1960 47840

Stow MA

Randall Library Museum, 19 Crescent St, Stow, MA 01775 - T: (978) 897-8572, Fax: (978) 897-7379, E-mail: stow@mln.lib.ma.us. Dir.: Susan C. Wysk
Local Museum - 1892
Regional history 47841

Stow West 1825 School Museum, Harvard Rd, Stow, MA 01775 - T: (978) 897-7417. Dir.: C.G. Schwarzkopf
Local Museum - 1974
Local hist 47842

Stowe VT

Helen Day Art Center, School St, Stowe, VT 05672 - T: (802) 253-8358, Fax: (802) 253-2703, E-mail: helenday@stowe.nu, Internet: www.helenday.com. Pres.: Ellen Thorndike, C.E.O.: Mickey Myers
Fine Arts Museum - 1981
Art 47843

Strafford VT

Justin Smith Morrill Homestead, 214 Justin Morrill Memorial Hwy, Strafford, VT 05072 - T: (802) 828-3051, Fax: (802) 828-3206, E-mail: jdumville@dca.state.vt.us, Internet: www.historicvermont.org. Head: John P. Dumville
Historic Site - 1969
Historic house, agricultural buildings 47844

Strasburg CO

Comanche Crossing Museum, 56060 E Colfax Av, Strasburg, CO 80136 - T: (303) 622-4690. Cur.: Sandy Miller
Local Museum / Science&Tech Museum - 1969
Regional history, site where the first continuous chain of rails was completed by the Kansas Pacific Railroad, Aug. 15, 1870 47845

Strasburg PA

The National Toy Train Museum, 300 Paradise Lane, Strasburg, PA 17579 - T: (717) 687-8976, 687-8623, Fax: (717) 687-0742, E-mail: toytrain@traincollectors.org, Internet: www.traincollectors.org. Pres.: Newton Derby
Special Museum - 1954
Toy and model trains 47846

Railroad Museum of Pennsylvania, 300 Gap Rd, Strasburg, PA 17579 - T: (717) 687-8629, Fax: (717) 687-0876, E-mail: info@rrmuseumpa.org, Internet: www.rrmuseumpa.org. Dir.: David W. Dunn, Cur.: Bradley Smith
Science&Tech Museum / Historical Museum - 1963
Transportation, passanger and freight locomotives, railcars, PA railroad history - library, archives 47847

Strasburg VA

Museum of American Presidents, 130 N Massanutten St, Strasburg, VA 22657 - T: (540) 465-5999, Fax: (540) 465-8157, E-mail: wayside@shentel.net, Internet: www.waysideofva.com. Dir.: Babs Melton
Historical Museum - 1996
Presidential portraits, signatures and memorabilia 47848

Strasburg Museum, 440 E King St, Strasburg, VA 22657 - T: (540) 465-3428, 465-3175. Pres.: Nicholas Racey
Folklore Museum - 1970
Local hist 47849

Stratford CT

The Stratford Historical Society and Catherine B. Mitchell Museum, 967 Academy Hill, Stratford, CT 06615 - T: (203) 378-0630, Fax: (203) 378-2562, E-mail: judsonhousestfd@aol.com, Internet: www.stratfordhistoricalsociety.com. Cur.: Carol Lovell
Local Museum - 1925
Local hist 47850

Stratford VA

Robert E. Lee Memorial Association, Stratford, VA 22558 - T: (804) 493-8038, Fax: (804) 493-0333, E-mail: shpedu@stratfordhall.org, Internet: www.stratfordhall.org. Pres.: Hugh G. Van der Veer, C.E.O.: Thomas C. Taylor
Historic Site / Historical Museum - 1929
Local hist 47851

Strawberry Point IA

Wilder Memorial Museum, 123 W Mission, Strawberry Point, IA 52076 - T: (563) 933-4615. Cur.: Kay Ryan
Local Museum / Decorative Arts Museum - 1970
Local hist, dolls, antiques, art, tools 47852

Stroudsburg PA

Driebe Freight Station, 537 Ann St, Stroudsburg, PA 18360-2012 - T: (570) 424-1776, Fax: (570) 421-9199, E-mail: mcha@ptd.net, Internet: www.mcha-pa.org. Pres.: William Ramsden, Dir.: Candace McGreevy
Local Museum - 1921
Local hist 47853

Elizabeth D. Walters Library, 900 Main St, Stroudsburg, PA 18360 - T: (570) 421-7703, Fax: (570) 421-9199. Dir.: Candace McGreevy
Decorative Arts Museum
Decorative arts, furniture, Indian artifacts, textiles 47854

Quiet Valley Living Historical Farm, 1000 Turkey Hill Rd, Stroudsburg, PA 18360 - T: (570) 992-6161, Fax: (570) 992-9587, E-mail: qvfarm@ptdprolog.net, Internet: www.quietvalley.org. Head: Alice Wicks, Gary Oiler, Sue Oiler
Agriculture Museum - 1963
Historic farm 47855

Stroud Mansion, 900 Main St, Stroudsburg, PA 18360-1604 - T: (570) 421-7703, Fax: (570) 421-9199, E-mail: mcha@ptd.net, Internet: www.mcha.-pa.org. Pres.: William Ramsden, Exec. Dir.: Candace McGreevy
Local Museum - 1921
Historic house 47856

Stuart FL

Elliott Museum, 825 NE Ocean Blvd, Stuart, FL 34996 - T: (561) 225-1961, Fax: (561) 225-2333, E-mail: hsmc@bellsouth.net, Internet: www.elliottmuseum.good.org. Dir.: Rob Blount
Local Museum - 1961 47857

Gilbert's Bar House of Refuge, 301 SE MacArthur Blvd, Stuart, FL 34996 - T: (561) 225-1961, Fax: (561) 225-2333, E-mail: hsmc@bellsouth.net, Internet: www.goodnature.org/elliotmuseum. Dir.: Tom Prestegard
Historical Museum - 1875 47858

Sturbridge MA

Old Sturbridge Village, 1 Old Sturbridge Village Rd, Sturbridge, MA 01566 - T: (508) 347-3362, Fax: (508) -347-0375, E-mail: osv@osv.org, Internet: www.osv.org. Pres.: Alberta Sebolt George
Open Air Museum / Local Museum - 1946
Re-created rural New England village 47859

Sturgeon Bay WI

Door County Maritime Museum, 120 N Madison Av, Sturgeon Bay, WI 54235 - T: (920) 743-5958, Fax: (920) 743-9483, E-mail: dcmm@itol.com, Internet: www.dcmm.org. Pres.: Dan Austad
Science&Tech Museum - 1969
Maritime hist 47860

Door County Museum, 18 N 4th & Michigan Av, Sturgeon Bay, WI 54235 - T: (414) 743-5809, E-mail: ajinkins@co.door.wi.us. Cur.: Margaret S. Weir
Local Museum - 1939
Local hist 47861

The Farm, 4285 Hwy 57, Sturgeon Bay, WI 54235 - T: (920) 743-6666, Fax: (920) 743-6447, E-mail: thefarm@door.pi.net, Internet: www.thefarmindoorcounty.com. Pres.: Carl Scholz
Agriculture Museum - 1965
Agriculture 47862

Miller Art Museum, 107 S 4th Av, Sturgeon Bay, WI 54235 - T: (920) 746-0707, Fax: (920) 746-0865, E-mail: bmam@dcwis.com, Internet: www.doorcountyarts.com. Dir.: Bonnie Hartmann, Cur.: Deborah Rosenthal
Fine Arts Museum / Public Gallery - 1975
Art 47863

Sturgis SD

Bear Butte State Park Visitors Center, Hwy 79, Sturgis, SD 57785, mail addr: POB 688, Sturgis, SD 57785 - T: (605) 347-5240, Fax: (605) 347-7627, E-mail: bearbutte@gfp.state.sd.us, Internet: www.state.sd.us/gfp/sdparks
Local Museum - 1961
Native American clothing and religious artifacts, archaeological site, geology, military 47864

Stuttgart AR

Stuttgart Agricultural Museum, 921 E Fourth St, Stuttgart, AR 72160 - T: (870) 673-7001, Fax: (870) 673-3959, E-mail: stutagrmus@cpomail.net, Internet: www.aiea.ualr.edu/dina/cities/stuttgart. Dir.: Pat Peacock, Cur.: Sheila Stoner (Collections), Wayne Clow (Restoration-Furniture), Jim Gingerich (Farm Equipment and Furniture)
Folklore Museum / Agriculture Museum - 1972
Science of rice, hay and soybean agriculture, farm family 47865

Sublette KS

The Haskell County Historical Museum, Haskell County Fairgrounds, Sublette, KS 67877 - T: (620) 675-8344, E-mail: museum@pld.com. Dir.: Rosa Kraber
Local Museum - 1983
Rocks and minerals, American Indian artifacts 47866

Suffolk VA

Ruddick's Folly, 510 N Main St, Suffolk, VA 23434 - T: (757) 934-1390, Fax: (757) 934-0411, E-mail: riddicksfolly@prodigy.net, Internet: groups.hamptonroads.com/riddicksfolly. Dir.: Robin K. Rountree
Local Museum - 1978
Riddick family, Suffolk hist, furniture and decorative arts, peanut exhibit, Mills E. Godwin, jr 47867

Suffolk Museum, 118 Bosley Av, Suffolk, VA 23434 - T: (757) 923-2371, Fax: (757) 538-0833, E-mail: nkinzinger@city.suffolk.va.us. Dir.: Nancy Kinzinger
Fine Arts Museum / Public Gallery - 1986
Art 47868

Sugar Grove IL

Air Classic Museum of Aviation, 43 W 264 Rte 30, Sugar Grove, IL 60554 - T: (630) 466-0888. Pres.: Robert Atac
Science&Tech Museum
Planes from the Korean War 2 to Desert Storm, automobiles 47869

Sugarland TX

The Museum of Southern History, 14080 SW Freeway, Sugarland, TX 77478-3553, mail addr: POB 2190, Sugar Land, TX 77487-2190 - T: (281) 269-7171, Fax: (218) 269-7179, E-mail: snoddys@snbtx.com. Dir.: Suzie Snoddy
Historical Museum / Military Museum / Museum of Classical Antiquities - 1978 47870

Suisun City CA

The Western Railway Museum, 5848 State Hwy 12, Suisun City, CA 94585 - T: (707) 374-2978, Fax: (707) 374-6742, Internet: www.wrm.org. Dir.: Loring Jensen
Science&Tech Museum - 1946
Electric railways 47871

Suitland MD

Airmen Memorial Museum, 5211 Auth Rd, Suitland, MD 20746 - T: (301) 899-8386, Fax: (301) 899-8136, E-mail: staff@assahq.org, Internet: www.assahq.org. Exec. Dir.: James D. Staton
Military Museum - 1986
Military 47872

Sullivan's Island SC

Fort Sumter National Monument, 1214 Middle St, Sullivan's Island, SC 29482 - T: (843) 883-3123 ext 22, Fax: (843) 883-3910, E-mail: fosu_ranger_activitie@nps.gov, Internet: www.nps.gov/fosu. Head: Fran Norton
Military Museum - 1948
Military hist 47873

Sulphur LA

Brimstone Museum, 800 Picard Rd, Sulphur, LA 70663 - T: (337) 527-7142, Fax: (337) 527-0860, E-mail: westcal@usunwired.net. Dir.: Glenda Vincent
Local Museum - 1975
Local history 47874

Summersville WV

Carnifex Ferry Battlefield State Park and Museum, State Hwy 129, Summersville, WV 26651 - T: (304) 872-0825, Fax: (304) 872-3820, Internet: wvweb.com/www/carnifax.ferry.html. Head: Mark Mengele
Local Museum
Local hist 47875

Summerville SC

Old Dorchester State Historic Site, 300 State Park Rd, Summerville, SC 29485 - T: (843) 873-1740, Fax: (843) 873-1740, E-mail: old_dorchester_sp@prt.state.sc.us, Internet: www.southcarolinaparks.com. Dir.: John Durst, Sc. Staff: Monica Beck (Archaeology)
Local Museum - 1960
Archaeological site of 18th-century Village of Dorchester 47876

Summit NJ

New Jersey Center for Visual Arts, 68 Elm St, Summit, NJ 07901 - T: (908) 273-9121, Fax: (908) 273-1457, E-mail: njcvaqmycomcast.com, Internet: www.njcva.com. Pres.: Eric Pryor, Chief Cur.: Nancy Cohen, Alice Dillon
Fine Arts Museum - 1933 47877

Sumter SC

South Carolina National Guard Museum, 395 N Pike Rd, Sumter, SC 29150 - T: (803) 806-1107, Fax: (803) 806-1121, E-mail: tng151fa@sc-ngnet.army.mil. Dir.: Roy Pipkin, Cur.: John S. Cato
Military Museum - 1982
Military hist 47878

The Sumter County Museum, 122 N Washington St, Sumter, SC 29150 - T: (803) 775-0908, Fax: (803) 436-5820, E-mail: scmuseum@sumtercountymuseum.com, Internet: www.sumtercountymuseum.com. Dir.: Katherine Richardson
Local Museum - 1976
Local hist 47879

Sumter Gallery of Art, 421 N Main St, Sumter, SC 29151 - T: (803) 775-0543, Fax: (803) 778-2787, E-mail: sumtergallery@sumter.net. Dir.: Priscilla F. Haile
Fine Arts Museum - 1970
Paintings, etchings, drawings by Elizabeth White 47880

Sun Prairie WI

Sun Prairie Historical Museum, 115 E Main St, Sun Prairie, WI 53590 - T: (608) 837-2511, Fax: (608) 825-6879, E-mail: museum@sun-prairie.com, Internet: www.sun-prairie.com. Cur.: Peter Klein, Sc. Staff: Ardin Lapor (History)
Local Museum - 1967
Local hist 47881

Sunbury PA

The Northumberland County Historical Society Museum, The Hunter House, 1150 N Front St, Sunbury, PA 17801 - T: (570) 286-4083, E-mail: nchsmusm@sunlink.net. Pres.: Scott A. Heintzelman, Dir.: Jane DuPree Richardson
Local Museum - 1925
Local hist 47882

Sundance WY

Crook County Museum and Art Gallery, 309 Cleveland St, Sundance, WY 82729 - T: (307) 283-3666, Fax: (307) 283-1192, E-mail: crcogallery@vcm.com, Internet: www.geocities/heartland/park/9867. Dir.: Linda Evans
Fine Arts Museum / Local Museum - 1971
Local hist, art 47883

Sunnyside WA

Sunnyside Historical Museum, 704 S 4th St, Sunnyside, WA 98944 - T: (509) 837-6010, 837-2032, 837-2105, E-mail: ssmuseum@bentonrea.com. Cur.: Don Wade
Local Museum - 1972 47884

Sunnyvale CA

Lace Museum, 552 S Murphy Av, Sunnyvale, CA 94086 - T: (408) 730-4695, Fax: (408) 730-4695, E-mail: sherrigd@thelacemuseum.org, Internet: www.thelacemuseum.org. C.E.O.: Cherie Helm, Eleanore Schwarts
Special Museum - 1980 47885

Sunnyvale Historical Museum, 235 E California Av, Sunnyvale, CA 94086 - T: (408) 749-0220, Fax: (408) 732-4726. Pres.: Janet G. Camp
Local Museum - 1973
Local hist 47886

Sunset TX

Cowboy Museum → Old West Museum

Old West Museum, Hwy 287 at Lawhorn Ln, Sunset, TX 76270 - T: (940) 872-9698, Fax: (940) 872-8504, E-mail: sunsettradingpost@earthlink.net, Internet: www.cowboymuseum.net. Dir.: Jack Glover
Local Museum / Historical Museum - 1956
Local hist, early Texas 47887

Superior MT

Mineral County Museum, Second Av E, Superior, MT 59872 - T: (406) 822-4626, E-mail: mrshezzie@blackfoot.net. C.E.O./Cur.: Cathryn J. Strombo
Local Museum - 1975
Local and natural hist, geology, forest, mining, mullan rd. 47888

Superior WI

Douglas County Historical Society Museum, 1401 Tower Av, Superior, WI 54880 - T: (715) 392-8449, E-mail: doughist@douglascowihistory.org. C.E.O.: Nancy M. Minahan
Local Museum - 1854
Ojibwa Chippewa Indian crafts, Sioux Indian portraits, local hist 47889

Fairlawn Mansion and Museum, 906 E 2nd St, Superior, WI 54880 - T: (715) 394-5712, Fax: (715) 394-2043, Internet: www.visitsuperior.com. Exec. Dir.: Dr. Richard A. Sauers
Decorative Arts Museum - 1963
Pattison Family hist 47890

Old Fire House and Police Museum, 402 23 rd Av, Superior, WI 54880 - T: (715) 394-5712, Fax: (715) 394-2043
Special Museum - 1983
Superior polic & fire dept. hist, Wisconsin fire & police hall of fame 47891

Suquamish WA

Suquamish Museum, Sandy Hook Rd, Suquamish, WA 98392 - T: (360) 394-5275, Fax: (360) 598-6295, E-mail: suamuseum@hotmail.com, Internet: www.suquamish.nsn.us. Dir.: Alexis Barry, Marilyn Jones, Cur.: Charles Sigo
Ethnology Museum - 1983
Indian hist 47892

Surprise AZ

West Valley Art Museum, Sun Cities Museum of Art, 17420 N Av of the Arts, Surprise, AZ 85374 - T: (602) 972-0635, Fax: (602) 972-0456, E-mail: jdavis@wvam.org, Internet: www.wvam.org. Dir.: G. Goldstein, Wallen A. Steffan
Fine Arts Museum - 1980
Art 47893

Surry VA

Bacon's Castle, 465 Bacon's Castle Trail, Surry, VA 23883 - T: (757) 357-5976, 648-1889, Fax: (804) 775-0802, Internet: www.apva.org. Pres.: Martin Kirwan King, Exec. Dir.: Elizabeth Kostelny
Local Museum - 1665
Local hist, oldest brick house in North America 47894

Chippokes Farm and Forestry Museum, 695 Chippokes Park Rd, Surry, VA 23883 - T: (757) 294-3439, Fax: (804) 371-8500, E-mail: cffmuseum@dcr.state.va.us, Internet: www.dcr.state.va.us. Pres.: Frederick M. Quayle
Agriculture Museum / Natural History Museum - 1990 47895

Smith's Fort Plantation, 217 Smith's Fort Ln, Rte 31, Surry, VA 23883 - T: (757) 294-3872. Dir.: Henry Doggatt
Local Museum - 1925
Historic house 47896

Sussex NJ

Space Farms Zoological Park and Museum, Beemerville Rd, Sussex, NJ 07461 - T: (973) 875-3223, Fax: (973) 875-9397, E-mail: fpspace@warwick.net, Internet: www.spacefarms.com. Pres.: Fred Space, C.E.O.: Parker Space
Local Museum / Natural History Museum - 1927 47897

Swampscott MA

Atlantic 1 Museum, 1 Burrill St, Swampscott, MA 01907 - T: (781) 581-5833. Pres.: Rowe Austin, Dir.: Richard Maitland
Historical Museum - 1965
Fire-Fighting 47898

John Humphrey House, 99 Paradise Rd, Swampscott, MA 01907 - T: (781) 599-1297. Pres.: Joseph Balsama
Local Museum - 1921
Local history 47899

Sweet Briar VA

Camp Gallery, Virginia Center for the Creative Arts, Sweet Briar, VA 24595 - T: (804) 946-7236, Fax: (804) 946-7239, E-mail: vcca@vcca.com, Internet: www.vcca.com. Dir.: Suny Monk
Fine Arts Museum - 1971 47900

Sweet Briar College Art Gallery, Sweet Briar College, Sweet Briar, VA 24595 - T: (804) 381-6248, Fax: (804) 381-6173, E-mail: rmlane@sbc.edu, Internet: www.artgallery.sbc.edu/. Dir.: Rebecca Massie Lane
Fine Arts Museum / Public Gallery / University Museum - 1901
Art 47901

Sweet Briar Museum, Sweet Briar College, Sweet Briar, VA 24595 - T: (804) 381-6248, 381-6262, Fax: (804) 381-6173, E-mail: awhitley@sbc.edu, Internet: www.sbc.edu. Dir.: Ann Marshall Whitley
University Museum / Local Museum - 1985
Local hist 47902

Sweetwater TX

City County Pioneer Museum, 610 E Third St, Sweetwater, TX 79556 - T: (915) 235-8547. Dir.: Franzas Cupp
Local Museum - 1968
Local hist 47903

Sylmar CA

Century Gallery, 13000 Sayre St, Sylmar, CA 91342 - T: (818) 362-3220, Fax: (818) 364-7755. Dir.: John Cantley
Public Gallery - 1977 47904

Syracuse NE

Otoe County Museum of Memories, 366 Poplar, Syracuse, NE 68446 - T: (402) 269-3482. Cur.: Rose Garey
Local Museum - 1972 47905

Syracuse NY

Canal Society of New York State Museum, 311 Montgomery St, Syracuse, NY 13202 - T: (315) 478-6551, Fax: (315) 478-0103, E-mail: tgrassox@rochester.rr.com, Internet: www.canalsnys.org
Science&Tech Museum - 1956
Graphics, hist, transportation 47906

Erie Canal Museum, 318 Erie Blvd E, Syracuse, NY 13202 - T: (315) 471-0593, Fax: (315) 471-7220, Internet: www.eriecanalmuseum.org. Exec. Dir.: Nancy Furry, Cur.: Andrew Kitzmann
Local Museum - 1962 47907

Everson Museum of Art, 401 Harrison St, Syracuse, NY 13202 - T: (315) 474-6064, Fax: (315) 474-6943, E-mail: eversonadmin@everson.org, Internet: www.everson.org. Dir.: Sandra Trop, Sen. Cur.: Thomas Piché
Fine Arts Museum - 1896
Ceramics, American painting 47908

Joe and Emily Lowe Art Gallery, Syracuse University, Shaffer Art Bldg, Syracuse, NY 13244-1230 - T: (315) 443-4098, Fax: (315) 443-1303, E-mail: jhart@vpa.syr.edu, Internet: vpa.syr.edu/schools/soad/art.htm. Dir.: Dr. Edward A. Aiken, Dr. Alfred T. Collette (Syracuse University Art Collection), Cur.: David Prince
Fine Arts Museum / University Museum - 1952 47909

Milton J. Rubenstein Museum of Science and Technology, 500 S Franklin St, Syracuse, NY 13202-1245 - T: (315) 425-9068, Fax: (315) 425-9072, Internet: www.most.org. Pres.: Lawrence Leatherman, Exec. Dir.: Stephen A. Karon
Natural History Museum / Science&Tech Museum - 1978 47910

Museum of Automobile History, 321 N Clinton St, Syracuse, NY 13202 - T: (315) 478-2277, Fax: (315) 432-8256, E-mail: info@autolit.com, Internet: www.autolit.com. C.E.O.: Walter Miller
Science&Tech Museum - 1996
Advertising, styling artwork and memorabilia of the hist of trucks, automobiles and motorcycles 47911

Onondaga Historical Association Museum, 321 Montgomery St, Syracuse, NY 13202 - T: (315) 428-1864, Fax: (315) 471-2133, E-mail: tomoha100@hotmail.com, Internet: www.cnyhistory.org. Dir.: Thomas Hunter, Cur.: Vanessa Johnson, Greg Daily, Dennis Connors, Phil McCray
Local Museum - 1862 47912

Syracuse University Art Collection, Sims Hall, Syracuse, NY 13244 - T: (315) 443-4097, Fax: (315) 443-9225, E-mail: djiacono@syr.edu, Internet: sumweb.syr.edu/suart/. Dir.: Dr. Alfred T. Collette, Cur.: David Prince
Fine Arts Museum - 1871
American art 1915-1965, prints, photography 47913

Table Rock NE

Table Rock Historical Society Museum, 414-416 Houston St, Table Rock, NE 68447 - T: (402) 839-4135, Fax: (402) 839-4135, E-mail: fv64137@navix.net. Pres.: Floyd Vrtiska
Local Museum - 1965 47914

Tacoma WA

Camp 6 Logging Museum, 5 Mile Dr, Point Defiance Park, North End of Pearl St, Tacoma, WA 98407 - T: (253) 752-0047, E-mail: camp6museum@harbornet.com, Internet: www.camp-6-museum.org/alcŸY2.html. Dir.: Don Olson
Special Museum - 1964
Logging and lumber industry (buildings, cars and operational logging railroad from logging camps) 47915

Commencement Art Gallery, 902 Commerce, Tacoma, WA 98402-4407 - T: (253) 591-5341, Fax: (253) 591-2002, E-mail: rjones2@ci.tacoma.wa.us, Internet: www.artconduit.net/cag
Fine Arts Museum - 1993
Drawings, paintings, photography, sculpture, ceramics, metalwork 47916

Fort Nisqually Living History Museum, 5400 N Pearl St, Tacoma, WA 98407 - T: (253) 591-5339, Fax: (253) 759-6184, E-mail: fortnisqually@tacomaparks.com, Internet: www.fortnisqually.org. Dir.: Melissa S. McGinnis, Cur.: Doreen Beard-Simpkins
Local Museum / Historic Site - 1937
Local hist 47917

Historic Fort Steilacoom, 9601 Steilacoom Blvd SW, Tacoma, WA 98498-7213 - T: (253) 756-3928, E-mail: fortsteil@yahoo.com, Internet: www.homel.gte.net/5white/fort_steilacoom.html. Pres.: Carol E. Neufeld
Military Museum - 1983
Military hist 47918

James R. Slater Museum of Natural History, University of Puget Sound, Tacoma, WA 98416 - T: (206) 756-3798, Fax: (206) 756-3352, E-mail: dpaulson@ups.edu, Internet: www.ups.edu/biology/museum/museum.htm/. Dir.: Dr. Dennis R. Paulson, Cur.: Dr. Gary Shugart (Collections), Dr. Kathy Ann Miller (Botany), Dr. Peter Wimberger (Ichthyology)
University Museum / Natural History Museum - 1926
Natural hist 47919

Kittredge Art Gallery, University of Puget Sound, 1500 N Lawrence, Tacoma, WA 98416 - T: (253) 879-2806, Fax: (253) 879-3500, E-mail: gbell@ups.edu, Internet: www.ups.edu. Dir.: Greg Bell
University Museum / Fine Arts Museum - 1961
Paintings, drawings, contemporary American ceramics 47920

Museum of Glass, International Center for Contemporary Art, 1801 E Dock St, Tacoma, WA 98402 - T: (253) 396-1768, Fax: (253) 396-1769, E-mail: kmiles@museumofglass.org, Internet: www.museumofglass.org. C.E.O.: Josi Irene Callan
Fine Arts Museum - 1995 47921

Tacoma Art Museum, 1123 Pacific Av, Tacoma, WA 98402 - T: (253) 272-4258, Fax: (253) 627-1898, E-mail: info@tacomaartmuseum.org, Internet: www.tacomaartmuseum.org. Dir.: Janeanne A. Upp, Chief Cur.: Dr. Patricia McDonnell
Fine Arts Museum - 1891
Art 47922

Thomas Handforth Gallery, 1102 Tacoma Av, Tacoma, WA 98402 - T: (253) 591-5666, Fax: (253) 591-5470, E-mail: ddomkoshi@tpl.lib.wa.us, Internet: www.tpl.lib.wa.us. Asst. Dir.: Darrell Matz, Sc. Staff: Gary Reese (Special collections)
Fine Arts Museum / Public Gallery - 1886
Art 47923

Washington State Historical Society Museum, 1911 Pacific Av, Tacoma, WA 98402 - T: (253) 272-3500, Fax: (253) 272-9518, E-mail: dnicandri@wshs.wa.gov, Internet: www.wshs.org. Pres.: David Edwards, Dir.: David L. Nicandri, Sc. Staff: Lynn Anderson (Collections), Edward V. Nolan (Special collections)
Local Museum - 1891
Local hist 47924

Tahlequah OK

Cherokee Heritage Centre, Willis Rd, Tahlequah, OK 74465 - T: (918) 456-6007, Fax: (918) 456-6165, E-mail: info@cherokeeheritage.org, Internet: www.cherokeeheritage.org. Dir.: Mary Ellen Meredith
Historical Museum / Ethnology Museum / Folklore Museum - 1963 47925

Murrell Home, 3 miles S of Tahlequah, 1 mile E of SH 82, Tahlequah, OK 74464 - T: (918) 456-2751, Fax: (918) 456-2751, E-mail: shirleyp@intellex.com. Head: Shirley Pettengill
Local Museum - 1948 47926

Tahoe City CA

Gatekeeper's Museum and Marion Steinbach Indian Basket Museum, 130 W Lake Blvd, Tahoe City, CA 96145 - T: (530) 583-1762, Fax: (530) 583-8992, E-mail: nlths@aol.com, Internet: www.tahoecountry.com/nlths. Dir.: Miriam Biro, Ara Larson
Local Museum - 1969
Local hist, American Indian basketry, archaeology, dolls 47927

Tahoma CA

Ehrman Mansion, Sugarpine Point State Park, Hwy 89, Tahoma, CA 96142, mail addr: POB 266, Tahoma, CA 96142 - T: (916) 525-7982, Fax: (916) 525-0138
Local Museum / Natural History Museum - 1965 47928

Vikingsholm, Emerald Bay State Park, Hwy 89, Tahoma, CA 96142, mail addr: POB 266, Tahoma, CA 96142 - T: (916) 525-7232, Fax: (916) 525-6730. Cur.: Judith K. Polanich
Historic Site - 1953
Furnishings and furniture 47929

Talkeetna AK

Talkeetna Historical Society Museum, First Alley and Village Airstrip, Talkeetna, AK 99676 - T: (907) 733-2487, Fax: (907) 733-2484, E-mail: ths@matnet.com. Cur.: Alice Johannewes
Local Museum - 1972
Local hist 47930

Tallahassee FL

Florida State University Museum of Fine Arts, Fine Arts Bldg, Rm 250, Tallahassee, FL 32306-1140 - T: (850) 644-6836, 644-1254, Fax: (850) 644-7229, E-mail: apcraig@mailer.fsu.edu, Internet: www.fsu.edu/~svad/fsumuseum. Dir.: Allys Palladino-Craig
Fine Arts Museum - 1950
Decorative arts, paintings, photographs, prints, drawings, graphics, sculpture 47931

Knott House Museum, 301 E Park Av, Tallahassee, FL 32301 - T: (850) 922-2459, 245-6400, Fax: (850) 413-7261, E-mail: jmatey@mail.dos.state.fl.us, Internet: www.dos.state.fl.us
Special Museum - 1992 47932

Lake Jackson Mounds Archaeological Park, 3600 Indian Mounds Rd, Tallahassee, FL 32303-2348 - T: (850) 562-0042, 922-6007, Fax: (850) 488-0366, E-mail: lakejackson@nettally.com, Internet: www.floridastateparks.org. Dir.: Wendy Spencer
Historic Site / Archaeological Museum - 1970
Archaeology, 1200-1500 ceremonial center 47933

LeMoyne Art Foundation, 125 N Gadsden St, Tallahassee, FL 32301 - T: (850) 222-8800, Fax: (850) 224-2714, E-mail: art@lemoyne.org, Internet: www.lemoyne.org. Dir.: Marybeth Foss
Fine Arts Museum - 1964
Contemporary art, sculpture 47934

Mary Brogan Museum of Art and Science, 350 S Duval St, Tallahassee, FL 32301 - T: (850) 513-0700 ext 221, 232, Fax: (850) 513-0143, E-mail: cbarber@thebrogan.org, Internet: www.thebrogan.org. Exec. Dir.: Rena Minar
Natural History Museum / Fine Arts Museum - 1990
Visual arts, hands-on science 47935

Museum of Florida History, 500 S Bronough St, Tallahassee, FL 32399-0250 - T: (850) 488-1484, Fax: (850) 921-2503, E-mail: wrichey@mail.dos.state.fl.us, Internet: www.dos.state.fl.us/dhr/museum. Dir.: Jeana Brunson, Cur.: Stephen Oakley
Historical Museum / Archaeological Museum - 1967
History Museum 47936

Riley House Museum of African American History and Culture, 419 E Jefferson St, Tallahassee, FL 32311 - T: (850) 681-7881, Fax: (850) 386-4368, E-mail: rileyhousemuseum@netzero.net, Internet: www.tfn.net/Riley. C.E.O.: Althemese Barnes
Ethnology Museum - 1996
Hist of African Americans 47937

Tallahassee Museum of History and Natural Science, 3945 Museum Dr, Tallahassee, FL 32310-6325 - T: (850) 575-8684, Fax: (850) 574-8243, E-mail: rdaws@tallahasseemuseum.org, Internet: www.tallahasseemuseum.org. Dir.: Russell S. Daws, Cur.: Linda Deaton (Collections and Exhibits), Mike Jones (Animals)
Local Museum / Natural History Museum - 1957 47938

Tampa FL

Children's Museum of Tampa - Kid City, 7550 North Blvd, Tampa, FL 33604 - T: (813) 935-8441, Fax: (813) 915-0063. Dir.: Aharon Yoki
Special Museum - 1987 47939

Contemporary Art Museum, University of South Florida, 4202 E Fowler Av, Tampa, FL 33620 - T: (813) 974-2849, Fax: (813) 974-5130, E-mail: mmiller@arts.usf.edu, Internet: www.usfcam.usf.edu. Dir.: Margaret A. Miller, Ass. Dir.: Alexa Favata, Cur.: Peter Foe, Don Michael Fuller (New Media)
Fine Arts Museum / University Museum - 1968
Contemporary art 47940

Cracker Country Museum, 4800 N Hwy 301, Tampa, FL 33680 - T: (813) 621-7821, Fax: (813) 740-3518, E-mail: ccmuseum@mpinet.net, Internet: www.crackercountry.org. Dir.: Rip Stalvey
Local Museum / Open Air Museum - 1979 47941

Henry B. Plant Museum, 401 W Kennedy Blvd, Tampa, FL 33606 - T: (813) 254-1891, Fax: (813) 258-7272, E-mail: cgandee@ut.edu, Internet: www.plantmuseum.com. Dir.: Cynthia Gandee, Cur.: Susan Carter
Historical Museum / Decorative Arts Museum - 1933
History and Decorative Arts Museum: housed in 1891 Tampa Bay Hotel 47942

Museum of Science and Industry, 4801 E Fowler Av, Tampa, FL 33617-2099 - T: (813) 987-6300, Fax: (813) 987-6310, E-mail: blittlej@mosi.org, Internet: www.mosi.org. Pres.: Wit Ostrenko
Science&Tech Museum - 1962
Science, technology, industry, human hist 47943

Scarfone and Hartley Galleries, University of Tampa, 401 W Kennedy, Tampa, FL 33606 - T: (813) 253-3333, 253-6217, Fax: (813) 258-7211, E-mail: dcowden@ut.edu, Internet: www.ut.edu. Dir.: Dorothy C. Cowden
Fine Arts Museum / University Museum - 1977
Fine Arts 47944

Tampa Bay History Center, 225 S Franklin St, Tampa, FL 33602 - T: (813) 228-0097, Fax: (813) 223-7021, E-mail: thistory@gte.net, Internet: www.tampabayhistorycenter.org. Dir.: Mark Gruetzmacher, Elizabeth L. Dunham, Cur.: Rodney Kite Powell
Historical Museum - 1989
Local hist, militaria, paleoindian archeology, seminole material culture 47945

Tampa Museum of Art, 600 N Ashley Dr, Tampa, FL 33602 - T: (813) 274-8130, Fax: (813) 274-8732, E-mail: tm22@tampagov.net, Internet: www.tampamuseum.com. Dir.: Emily S. Kass, Cur.: Elaine D. Gustafson
Fine Arts Museum - 1979
Contemporary art 47946

Ybor City State Museum, 1818 Ninth Av E, Tampa, FL 33605 - T: (813) 247-6323, Fax: (813) 242-4010, E-mail: director@ybormuseum.org, Internet: www.ybormuseum.org. Dir.: Melinda N. Chavez
Historical Museum / Local Museum - 1980
Ethnically divere immigrants in Ybor City, cigar industry, mutual aid societies 47947

Tamworth NH

Remick Country Doctor Museum and Farm, 58 Cleveland Hill Rd, Tamworth, NH 03886 - T: (603) 323-7591, Fax: (603) 323-8382, E-mail: remick.foundation@rscs.net, Internet: www.remickmuseum.org. Dir.: Robert Cottrell
Local Museum - 1993
Local hist 47948

Taos NM

Governor Bent Museum, 117 Bent St, Taos, NM 87571 - T: (505) 758-2376, Fax: (505) 758-2376, E-mail: gnideon@laplaza.com. C.E.O.: Faye S. Noeding
Historical Museum - 1958 47949

Harwood Museum of Art of the University of New Mexico, 238 Ledoux St, Taos, NM 87571-6004 - T: (505) 758-9826, Fax: (505) 758-1475, E-mail: harwood@unm.edu, Internet: www.harwoodmuseum.org. Dir.: Charles M. Lovell, Cur.: David Witt
Fine Arts Museum / University Museum - 1923 47950

Kit Carson Historic Museums → Taos Historic Museums

Millicent Rogers Museum of Northern New Mexico, 1504 Museum Rd, Taos, NM 87571 - T: (505) 758-2462, Fax: (505) 758-5751, E-mail: mrm@newmex.com, Internet: www.millicentrogers.org. Exec. Dir.: Shelby J. Tisdale, Cur.: Paula Rivera
Fine Arts Museum / Ethnology Museum - 1953 47951

Stables Art Gallery of Taos Art Association, 133 N Pueblo Rd, Taos, NM 87571 - T: (505) 758-2036, Fax: (505) 751-3305, E-mail: taa@taos.newmex.com, Internet: www.taosnet.com/taa/. Exec. Dir.: Betsy Carey
Fine Arts Museum - 1953 47952

Taos Historic Museums, 222 Ledoux St, Taos, NM 87571 - T: (505) 758-0505, Fax: (505) 758-0330, E-mail: thm@taoshistoricmuseums.com, Internet: www.taoshistoricmuseums.com. Dir.: Karen S. Young
Local Museum - 1949
Ernest Blumenschein and Kit Carson home 47953

Tappan NY

Tappantown Historical Society Museum, Box 71, Tappan, NY 10983 - T: (914) 359-1149. Pres.: Peter Schuerholz
Historical Museum - 1965 47954

Tarboro NC

Blount-Bridgers House/ Hobson Pittman Memorial Gallery, 130 Bridgers St, Tarboro, NC 27886 - T: (252) 823-4159, Fax: (252) 823-6190, E-mail: edgecombearts@earthlink.net, Internet: www.edgecombearts.org. Dir.: Meade B. Horne
Fine Arts Museum / Local Museum - 1982
Art 47955

Tarpon Springs FL

Tarpon Springs Cultural Center, 101 S Pinellas Av, Tarpon Springs, FL 34689 - T: (727) 942-5605, Fax: (727) 938-2429, E-mail: jlegath@ci.tarpon-springs.fl.us. Cur.: Judith B. LeGath
Local Museum - 1987
Historical, artistic and ethnographic material 47956

Tarrytown NY

Historic Hudson Valley, 150 White Plains Rd, Tarrytown, NY 10591 - T: (914) 631-8200, Fax: (914) 631-0089, E-mail: mail@hudsonvalley.org, Internet: www.hudsonvalley.org. Cur.: Kathleen E. Johnson
Local Museum - 1951 47957

Lyndhurst, 635 S Broadway, Tarrytown, NY 10591 - T: (914) 631-4481, Fax: (914) 631-5634, E-mail: lyndhurst@nthp.org, Internet: www.lyndhurst.org. Dir.: Susanne Brendel-Pandich, Cur.: Judith Beil
Local Museum - 1964 47958

Tarrytowns Museum, 1 Grove St, Tarrytown, NY 10591 - T: (914) 631-8374. Cur.: Sara Mascia
Local Museum - 1889 47959

Taunton MA

Old Colony Historical Museum, 66 Church Green, Taunton, MA 02780 - T: (508) 822-1622. Dir.: Katheryn P. Viens, Cur.: Jane Emack Cambra
Historical Museum - 1853
History 47960

Tavares FL

Lake County Historical Museum, 317 W Main St, Tavares, FL 32778 - T: (352) 343-9600, Fax: (352) 343-9696, E-mail: dkamp@co.lake.fl.us. Dir.: Dr. Diane D. Kamp
Local Museum - 1965 47961

Taylors Falls MN

Historic W.H.C. Folsom House, 272 W Government Rd, Taylors Falls, MN 55084 - T: (612) 465-3125. Pres.: William W. Scott
Historical Museum - 1968 47962

Taylorsville MS

Watkins Museum, Eureka St, Taylorsville, MS 39168 - T: (601) 785-9816
Local Museum - 1968
Hand printing press, early medical and farm equip, ancient bottle coll, clothing, typewriter 47963

Tazewell VA

Historic Crab Orchard Museum and Pioneer Park, Rte 19 and Rte 460, Tazewell, VA 24651 - T: (540) 988-6755, Fax: (540) 988-9400, E-mail: histcrab@netscope.net, Internet: histcrab.netscope.net. Dir.: Ross Weeks, Cur.: Anne Noel Walker
Folklore Museum / Historical Museum - 1978
Central Appalachian history 47964

Teague TX

Burlington-Rock Island Railroad and Historical Museum, 208 S 3rd Av, Teague, TX 75860 - T: (254) 739-3551, Internet: www.therailroadmuseum.com. Pres.: Sharon Johnson
Science&Tech Museum / Historical Museum - 1969
Railroad 47965

Tecumseh NE

Johnson County Historical Society Museum, Third and Lincoln Sts, Tecumseh, NE 68450 - T: (402) 335-3258. Pres.: John R. Fisher, Boyd Mattox
Local Museum - 1962 47966

Tekamah NE

Burt County Museum, 319 N 13th St, Tekamah, NE 68061 - T: (402) 374-1505. Pres.: Rick Nelsen
Local Museum - 1967 47967

Temecula CA

Temecula Valley Museum, 28314 Mercedes St, Temecula, CA 92590 - T: (909) 676-0021, Fax: (909) 506-6871, E-mail: ottw@cityoftemecula.org, Internet: www.ci.temecula.ca.us/cityhall/commserv/museum/facts.htm. Man.: Wendell Ott
Local Museum - 1985 47968

Tempe AZ

Arizona Historical Society Museum, Central Arizona Division, 1300 N College Av, Tempe, AZ 85281 - T: (480) 929-9499, Fax: (480) 967-5450, E-mail: ahs@ahs.lib.maricopa.gov, Internet: www.tempe.gov/ahs. Dir.: Anne Woosley
Local Museum - 1973
Regional history 47969

Arizona State University Art Museum, 10th St and Mill Av, Nelson Fine Arts Center, Tempe, AZ 85287-2911 - T: (602) 965-2787, Fax: (602) 965-5254, E-mail: asuartmuseum@asu.edu, Internet: asuartmuseum.asu.edu. Dir.: Marilyn Zeitlin, Sen. Cur.: Heather S. Lineberry
Fine Arts Museum / University Museum - 1950
Latin American art, paintings, prints, sculpture, ceramics, crafts, glass 47970

Center for Meteorite Studies, Arizona State University, Tempe, AZ 85287-2504 - T: (480) 965-6511, Fax: (480) 965-2747, E-mail: cmoore@asu.edu, Internet: meteorites.asu.edu. Dir.: Carleton B. Moore
University Museum / Natural History Museum - 1961
Meteorite Museum 47971

Memorial Union Gallery, c/o Arizona State University, Campus, Tempe, AZ 85287 - T: (480) 965-6649, Fax: (480) 727-6212, Internet: www.asu.edu/mu
Public Gallery 47972

Museum of Anthropology, Arizona State University, Tempe, AZ 85287-2402 - T: (480) 965-6213, Fax: (480) 965-7671, E-mail: anthro.museum@asu.edu, Internet: www.asu.edu/museums. Dir.: Dr. John Chance, Cur.: Dulce Aldama (Exhibits), C. Michael Barton (Archaeology and Ethography), Diane Hawkey (Physical Anthropology)
Ethnology Museum / Archaeological Museum / University Museum - 1959
Anthropology, archaeology, ethnography 47973

Tempe Arts Center, Mill Av and First St, Tempe, AZ 85281 - T: (602) 968-0888, Fax: (602) 968-0888. Dir.: Claudia Anderson, Cur.: Patty Haberman
Fine Arts Museum - 1982
Art 47974

Tempe Historical Museum, 809 E Southern Av, Tempe, AZ 85282 - T: (480) 350-5100, Fax: (480) 350-5150, Internet: www.tempe.gov/museum. Dir.: Amy A. Douglass, Cur.: John Akers, Richard Bauer, Chad Phinney, Ann Poulos, Registrar: Kim Gromer
Local Museum - 1972
Local history 47975

Temple TX

Railroad and Heritage Museum, 315 W Av B, Temple, TX 76501 - T: (254) 298-5172, Fax: (254) 298-5171, E-mail: mirving@ci.temple.tx.us, Internet: www.rrdepot.org. Pres.: Fred Springer, Dir.: Mary L. Irving
Historical Museum / Science&Tech Museum - 1973
Transportation, history, Santa Fe, MKT and TX railroads - archives 47976

Slavonic Benevolent Order of the State of Texas Museum, 520 N Main St, Temple, TX 76501 - T: (254) 773-1575, Fax: (254) 774-7447. Dir.: Howard B. Leshikar, Cur.: Dorothy Pechal
Ethnology Museum / Historical Museum - 1971
Czech history, culture and genealogy 47977

Templeton MA

Narragansett Historical Society Museum, 1 Boynton Rd, Templeton, MA 01468 - T: (978) 939-2251. Pres.: Michael Watt
Local Museum - 1928
Regional history 47978

Tenafly NJ

African Art Museum of the S.M.A. Fathers, 23 Bliss Av, Tenafly, NJ 07670 - T: (201) 894-8611, Fax: (201) 541-1280, E-mail: smausa-e@smafathers.org, Internet: www.smafathers.org. Dir.: Robert J. Koenig
Ethnology Museum - 1963 47979

Tenino WA

Tenino Depot Museum, 399 W Park, Tenino, WA 98589 - T: (360) 264-4321
Local Museum - 1974 47980

Tequesta FL

Lighthouse Gallery, 373 Tequesta Dr, Tequesta, FL 33469-3027 - T: (561) 746-3101, Fax: (561) 746-3241, Internet: www.artsforyou.org. Exec. Dir.: Margaret Inserra
Fine Arts Museum - 1965
Drawings, painting-American, photography, sculpture, watercolors, bronzes, ceramics, collages, calligraphy 47981

Terra Alta WV

Americana Museum, 401 Aurora Av, Terra Alta, WV 26764 - T: (304) 789-2361. Dir.: Ruth E. Teets, James W. Teets, Robert G. Teets
Local Museum - 1968
Local hist 47982

Terre Haute IN

Eugene V. Debs Home, 451 N Eighth St, Terre Haute, IN 47807 - T: (812) 232-2163, 237-3443, Fax: (812) 237-8072, E-mail: soking@scifac.indstate.edu, Internet: www.eugenevdebs.com. Dir., Karon Brown
Historical Museum - 1962 47983

Native American Museum, 5170 E Poplar St, Terre Haute, IN 47803 - T: (812) 877-6007, Fax: (812) 232-7313. Cur.: Amanda Smith
Historical Museum / Ethnology Museum - 1994
Indiana history 47984

Paul Dresser Memorial Birthplace, First and Farrington Sts, Terre Haute, IN 47802 - T: (812) 235-9717, Fax: (812) 235-9717, E-mail: vchs@iquest.net, Internet: web.indstate.edulcommunity/uchs/. Exec. Dir.: Marylee Hagan
Historical Museum - 1967 47985

Swope Art Museum, 25 S 7th St, Terre Haute, IN 47807-3692 - T: (812) 238-1676, Fax: (812) 238-1677, E-mail: info@swope.org, Internet: www.swope.org. Dir.: David Vollmer
Fine Arts Museum - 1942
19th-20th c american art 47986

Vigo County Historical Museum, 1411 S 6th St, Terre Haute, IN 47802 - T: (812) 235-9717, Fax: (812) 235-9717, E-mail: vchs@iquest.net, Internet: web.indstate.edu/. Dir.: Marylee Hagan, Ass. Dir.: Barbara Carney
Local Museum - 1958
General museum, brick two story Italianate bldg 47987

Terryville CT

Lock Museum of America, 230 Main St, Terryville, CT 06786 - T: (860) 589-6359, Fax: (860) 589-6359, Internet: www.lockmuseum.com/. Cur.: Thomas F. Hennessy
Science&Tech Museum - 1972
Hist of locks 47988

Teutopolis IL

Teutopolis Monastery Museum, Rte 40 and S. Garrott St, Teutopolis, IL 62467, mail addr: 106 W Water St, Teutopolis, IL 62467 - T: (217) 857-3227, Fax: (217) 857-3227. Pres.: Edward Jansen
Local Museum / Religious Arts Museum - 1975
Local history 47989

Texarkana TX

Ace of Clubs House, 420 Pine St, Texarkana, TX 75501 - T: (903) 793-4831, Fax: (903) 793-7108, E-mail: gcvanderpool@cableone.net, Internet: www.texarkanamuseums.org. Dir.: Guy C. Vanderpool, Cur.: Jamie Simmons, Asst. Cur.: Melissa Nesbitt
Local Museum / Decorative Arts Museum - 1985
Wilbur Smith research library and archives 47990

Texarkana Museums System, 219 N State Line Av, Texarkana, TX 75501 - T: (903) 793-4831, Fax: (903) 793-7108, E-mail: gcvanderpool@cableone.net, Internet: www.texarkanamuseums.org. Exec. Dir.: Guy C. Vanderpool
Local Museum - 1966
Caddo people, regional hist 47991

Texas City TX

The Mainland Museum of Texas City → Texas City Museum

Texas City Museum, 409 Sixth St, Texas City, TX 77592 - T: (409) 643-5799, Fax: (409) 949-9972. Exec. Dir.: Linda Turner
Historical Museum / Science&Tech Museum - 1991
History, industry 47992

Theodore AL

Bellingrath Home, 12401 Bellingrath Gardens Rd, Theodore, AL 36582 - T: (334) 973-2217, Fax: (334) 973-0540, E-mail: bellingrath@juno.com, Internet: www.bellingrath.org. Dir.: Thomas C. McGehee
Decorative Arts Museum - 1932
Porcelain, antique furnishings, silver, crystal - garden 47993

Thermopolis WY

Old West Wax Museum, 119 S 6th, Thermopolis, WY 82443 - T: (307) 864-9396, Fax: (307) 864-9396, E-mail: westwax@westwaxmuseum.com, Internet: www.westwaxmuseum.com. Dir.: Ellen Sue Blakey
Special Museum - 1999
American west figures, maps, clothing, folk hist 47994

Wyoming Dinosaur Center, 110 Carter Ranch Rd, Thermopolis, WY 82443 - T: (307) 864-2997, Fax: (307) 864-5762, E-mail: wdinoc@wyodino.org, Internet: www.wyodino.org. C.E.O.: Burkhart Pohl
Natural History Museum - 1995
Full size mounts of different dinosaurs, geology, prehistoric life on earth 47995

Wyoming Pioneer Home, 141 Pioneer Home Dr, Thermopolis, WY 82443 - T: (307) 864-3151, Fax: (307) 864-2934. Dir.: Ralp Barnes
Local Museum - 1950
Local hist 47996

Thetford VT

Thetford Historical Society Museum, Bicentennial Bldg, 16 Library Rd, Thetford, VT 05074 - T: (802) 785-2068. Pres.: Charles Latham, Cur.: Donald Fifield
Local Museum / Agriculture Museum - 1943
Local hist 47997

Thomaston ME

General Henry Knox Museum, Rte 1 and Rte 131, Thomaston, ME 04861 - T: (207) 354-8062, Fax: (207) 354-3501, E-mail: genknox@midcoast.com, Internet: www.generalknoxmuseum.org. Pres.: Robert A. Smith
Historical Museum - 1931
Montpelier home of Major General Henry Knox 47998

Thomaston Historical Museum, 80 Knox St, Thomaston, ME 04861 - T: (207) 354-2295, 354-8835, E-mail: catsmeow@mint.net, Internet: www.mint.net/thomastonhistoricalsociety. Dir.: Eve Anderson, Cur.: Bertha Styles
Local Museum - 1971
Local history, 1794 Henry Knox farmhouse 47999

Thomasville GA

Lapham-Patterson House, 626 N Dawson St, Thomasville, GA 31792 - T: (912) 225-4004, Fax: (912) 227-2419, E-mail: lphouse@rose.net. Cur.: Cheryl Walters
Historical Museum - 1974
Historic Victorian House c.1884 48000

Pebble Hill Plantation, 1251 US-319 S, Tallahassee Rd, Thomasville, GA 31792 - T: (912) 226-2344, Fax: (912) 227-0095, E-mail: swhite@pebblehill.com, Internet: www.pebblehill.com. Head: Wallace Goodman
Local Museum - 1983
Historic house 48001

Thomasville Cultural Center, 600 E Washington St, Thomasville, GA 31792 - T: (912) 226-0588, Fax: (912) 226-0599, E-mail: tccstaff@rose.net, Internet: www.tccarts.org. Cur.: Gylbert Coker
Fine Arts Museum - 1978
American and European paintings, wildlife art, ceramics 48002

Thousand Oaks CA

Conejo Valley Art Museum, POB 1616, Thousand Oaks, CA 91358 - T: (805) 373-0054, 492-2147, Fax: (805) 492-7677, Internet: www.conejovalleyartmuseum.org. Pres.: Maria E. Dessornes
Fine Arts Museum - 1977 48003

Tiburon CA

Schwartz Collection of Skiing Heritage, 9 Stephens Court, Tiburon, CA 94920 - T: (415) 435-1076, Fax: (415) 435-1076, E-mail: info@picturesnow.com. Dir.: Gary Schwartz, Cur.: Rhoda Valowitz
Special Museum - 1986
Sports 48004

Ticonderoga NY

Fort Ticonderoga, Fort Rd, Ticonderoga, NY 12883 - T: (518) 585-2821, Fax: (518) 585-2210, E-mail: fort@fort-ticonderoga.org, Internet: www.fort-ticonderoga.org. Dir.: Nicholas Westbrook, Cur.: Christopher D. Fox, Ellyn M. Farrar
Military Museum - 1908
Military history (18th c), tourism (19th c) 48005

Tiffin OH

Seneca County Museum, 28 Clay St, Tiffin, OH 44883 - T: (419) 447-5955, Fax: (419) 443-7940. Pres.: Barry Porter, Dir.: Tonia Hoffert
Local Museum - 1942 48006

Tifton GA

Georgia Agrirama, 19th Century Living History Museum, I-75 Exit 20 at 8th St, Tifton, GA 31793 - T: (912) 386-3344, Fax: (912) 386-3386, E-mail: market@ganet.org, Internet: www.ganet.org/agrirama. Exec. Dir.: Kim Littleton
Agriculture Museum / Ethnology Museum - 1972
Agricultural equipment, printing and typesetting equipment, medical and dentist equipment, furnishings 48007

Tillamook OR

Tillamook County Pioneer Museum, 2106 Second St, Tillamook, OR 97141 - T: (503) 842-4553, Fax: (503) 842-4553, E-mail: wjensen@pacifier.com, Internet: www.oregoncoast.com/Piormus.htm. Dir.: M. Wayne Jensen
Local Museum - 1935 48008

Tillamook Naval Air Station Museum, 6030 Hangar Rd, Tillamook, OR 97141 - T: (503) 842-1130, Fax: (503) 842-3054, E-mail: info@tillamookair.com, Internet: www.tillamookair.com. C.E.O.: Larry Schaible
Military Museum - 1994
US war birds, aircraft, WW 2 48009

Tinley Park IL

Tinley Park Historical Society Museum, 6727 W 174 St, Tinley Park, IL 60477 - T: (708) 429-4210, Fax: (708) 444-5099, E-mail: lrtphist@lincolnnet.net, Internet: www.lincolnnet.net/users/lrtphist. Chm.: Brad L. Bettenhausen
Local Museum - 1974 48010

Tishomingo OK

Chickasaw Council House Museum, Court House Sq, Tishomingo, OK 73460 - T: (580) 371-3351. Mgr.: Glenda gavin
Ethnology Museum / Historic Site / Folklore Museum - 1970 48011

Titusville NJ

Howell Living History Farm, 101 Hunter Rd, Titusville, NJ 08560 - T: (609) 737-3299, Fax: (609) 737-6524, E-mail: thefarm@bellatlantic.net, Internet: www.howellfarm.org
Agriculture Museum - 1974
Farm life and farming 48012

Johnson Ferry House Museum, Washington Crossing State Park, 355 Washington Xing Penn Rd, Titusville, NJ 08560-1517 - T: (609) 737-2515, Fax: (609) 737-0627
Local Museum - 1912 48013

Titusville PA

Drake Well Museum, R.D. 3, Titusville, PA 16354-8902 - T: (814) 827-2797, Fax: (814) 827-4888, E-mail: drakewell@usachoice.net, Internet: www.drakewell.org. Pres.: William Dixon, C.E.O.: Brent D. Glass
Local Museum / Science&Tech Museum - 1934
Site of first commercially successful oil well 48014

Tobias NE

Tobias Community Historical Society Museum, Main St, Tobias, NE 68453 - T: (402) 243-2356. Pres.: Judith K. Rada
Local Museum - 1968 48015

Toccoa GA

Traveler's Rest State Historic Site, 8162 Riverdale Rd, Toccoa, GA 30577 - T: (706) 886-2256, E-mail: travelersrest@alltel.net. Man.: Ray Anderson
Historical Museum - 1955
1833 former stagecoach inn 48016

Toledo IA

Tama County Historical Museum, 200 N Broadway, Toledo, IA 52342 - T: (641) 484-6767, E-mail: tracers@pcpartner.net. Pres.: Joyce Wiese
Local Museum - 1942
Local history, housed in a former County Jail 48017

Toledo OH

Blair Museum of Lithophanes, 5403 Elmer Dr, Toledo, OH 43615 - T: (419) 245-1356
Special Museum 48018

Cosi Toledo, 1 Discovery Way, Toledo, OH 43604 - T: (419) 244-2674, Fax: (419) 255-2674, Internet: www.cosi.org. C.E.O.: William H. Booth
Science&Tech Museum / Natural History Museum - 1997 48019

Museum of Science at the Toledo Zoo, 2700 Broadway, Toledo, OH 43609, mail addr: POB 140130, Toledo, OH 43614 - T: (419) 385-5721, Fax: (419) 389-8670, E-mail: andi.norman@toledozoo.org, Internet: www.toledozoo.org. Dir.: William V.A. Dennler, Cur.: Jay F. Hemdal (Fishes), R. Andrew Odum (Herpetology), Robert Webster (Birds), Randy Meyerson (Mammals), Vanessa Neeb (Interpretive Services), Bob Magdich (Education), Head: Bob Harden (Operating), Peter Tolson (Conservation Research), Tim Reichard (Animal Health and Nutrition)
Natural History Museum / Local Museum - 1899 48020

Toledo Museum of Art, 2445 Monroe St, Toledo, OH 43620 - T: (419) 255-8000, Fax: (419) 255-5638, E-mail: informationtoledomuseum.org, Internet: www.toledomuseum.org. Dir.: Dr. Roger M. Berkowitz, Ass. Dir.: Carol Bintz, Cur.: Lawrence W. Nichols (European Painting and Sculpture before 1900), Davira Taragin (19th and 20th-Century Glass), Robert F. Phillips (Modern and Contemporary Painting and Sculpture)
Fine Arts Museum - 1901 48021

Toledo Museum of Science → Museum of Science at the Toledo Zoo

Tolland CT

The Benton Homestead, Metcalf Rd, Tolland, CT 06084 - T: (860) 872-8673. Dir.: Gail W. White
Local Museum - 1969
Historic house 48022

Tolland County Jail and Warden's Home Museum, 52 Tolland Green, Tolland, CT 06084 - T: (860) 875-3544, 870-9599, E-mail: tolland.historical@snet.net, Internet: pages.cthome.net/tollandhistorical. Pres.: Stewart Joslin, Dir.: Mary LaFontaine
Local Museum - 1856
Local hist, farming, Indians 48023

Tomball TX

Tomball Community Museum Center, 510 N Pine St, Tomball, TX 77375 - T: (281) 444-2449. Pres.: Ben Scholl, Dir.: Jean Alexander
Local Museum - 1961
Historic house 48024

Tome NM

Tome Parish Museum, 7 N Church Loop, Tome, NM 87060-0100 - T: (505) 865-7497, Fax: (505) 865-7497. Dir.: Fr. Carl Feil
Religious Arts Museum - 1966
Religion, paintings, santos statues 48025

Toms River NJ

Ocean County Historical Museum, 26 Hadley Av, Toms River, NJ 08754-2191 - T: (732) 341-1880, Fax: (732) 341-4372, E-mail: oceancountyhistory@verizon.net, Internet: www.oceancountyhistory.org. Cur.: Barbara Rivolta
Local Museum - 1950 48026

Tonalea AZ

Navajo National Monument, End of 564 N Rte, Tonalea, AZ 86044-9704 - T: (928) 672-2700, Fax: (928) 672-2703, Internet: www.nps.gov/nava. Head: Irving Francisco
Archaeological Museum - 1909
Archaeology 48027

Tonawanda NY

Tonawandas Museum, 113 Main St, Tonawanda, NY 14150-2129 - T: (716) 694-7406. Exec. Dir.: Jane Penvose
Historical Museum - 1961 48028

Tonkawa OK

A.D. Buck Museum of Natural History and Science, Nothern Oklahoma College, 1220 E Grand, Tonkawa, OK 74653 - T: (405) 628-6200, Fax: (405) 628-6209, E-mail: rackerso@nocaxp.north-ok.edu. Dir.: Rex D. Ackerson
University Museum / Historical Museum / Natural History Museum - 1913 48029

Tonopah NV

Central Nevada Museum, 1900 Logan Field Rd, Tonopah, NV 89049 - T: (702) 482-9676, Fax: (702) 482-5423, E-mail: cnmuseum@citlink.net, Internet: www.tonopahneveda.com
Local Museum - 1981
History of central Nevada, mining hist 48030

Topeka KS

Alice C. Sabatini Gallery, Topeka and Shawnee County Public Library, 1515 W 10th, Topeka, KS 66604-1374 - T: (785) 580-4516, 580-4400, Fax: (785) 580-4496, E-mail: lpeters@tscpl.lib.ks.us, Internet: www.tscpl.org. Dir.: Larry D. Peters (Gallery), David L. Leaman, Dep. Dir.: Robert Banks
Fine Arts Museum / Public Gallery - 1870
American ceramics, prints, paintings, antique/modern glass paperweights, West African cultural objects, wood carving, Chinese pewter, decorative objects - library 48031

Combat Air Museum, Forbes Field, Hangar 602, Topeka, KS 66619 - T: (785) 862-3303, Fax: (785) 862-3304, E-mail: camtopeka@aol.com, Internet: www.combatairmuseum.org. Head: Adam Trupp
Military Museum / Science&Tech Museum - 1976
Topeka Army Air Field, later Forbes AFB, now Forbes Field 48032

Kansas Museum of History, 6425 SW Sixth St, Topeka, KS 66615-1099 - T: (785) 272-8681 ext 401, Fax: (785) 272-8682, E-mail: webmaster@kshs.org, Internet: www.kshs.org. Dir.: Robert J. Keckeisen, Ass. Dir.: Rebecca J. Martin, Cur.: Anne M. Marvin (Fine Art), Blair D. Tarr (Decorative Arts and Domestics), Cons.: Susanne Benda
Decorative Arts Museum / Historical Museum - 1875
History, decorative art 48033

Mulvane Art Museum, 17th and Jewell Sts, Topeka, KS 66621-1150 - T: (785) 231-1124, Fax: (785) 234-2703, E-mail: soppelsa@washburn.edu, Internet: www.washburn.edu/mulvane. Dir.: Edward Barr
Fine Arts Museum / University Museum - 1922
Art 48034

Toppenish WA

Cultural Heritage Center Museum, Confederated Tribes and Bands of the Yakama Indian Nation, 100 Speelyi Loop, Toppenish, WA 98948 - T: (509) 865-2800, Fax: (509) 865-5749, E-mail: marilyn@yakama.com, Internet: www.wolfenet.com/~yingis/hert.html. Chairman: Pamela K. Fabela, Cur.: Marilyn Malatare
Historical Museum / Ethnology Museum - 1980
Indian culture and hist 48035

Toppenish Museum, One S. Elm, Toppenish, WA 98948 - T: (509) 865-4510, Fax: (509) 865-3864. Chairman: Marian Ross
Local Museum - 1989
Local hist 48036

Topsfield MA

Topsfield Historical Museum, 1 Howlett St, Topsfield, MA 01983 - T: (978) 887-9724, E-mail: topshist@tiac.net, Internet: www.tiac.net/users/topshist. Pres.: Norman J. Isler, Cur.: Jean Busch
Historical Museum - 1894
Local history 48037

Torrance CA

El Camino College Art Gallery, 16007 Crenshaw Blvd, Torrance, CA 90506 - T: (310) 660-3010, Fax: (310) 660-3798, Internet: www.elcamino.cc.ca.us/cmart.htm
Fine Arts Museum / University Museum
Prints, sculpture 48038

Torrey UT

Capitol Reef National Park Visitor Center, Capitol Reef National Park, Torrey, UT 84775 - T: (435) 425-3791 ext 111, Fax: (435) 425-3026, E-mail: care_interpretation@nps.gov, Internet: www.nps.gov/care. C.E.O.: Albert J. Hendricks
Natural History Museum - 1968
Natural hist, Native American ethnology 48039

Torrington CT

Torrington Historical Society Museum, 192 Main St, Torrington, CT 06790 - T: (860) 482-8260, E-mail: torringtonhistorical@snet.net. Dir.: Mark McEachern, Cur.: Gail Kruppa
Local Museum - 1944
Local hist 48040

Tougaloo MS

Tougaloo College Art Collection, Tougaloo, MS 39174 - T: (601) 977-7743, Fax: (601) 977-7714, E-mail: art@tougaloo.edu, Internet: www.tougaloo.edu/artcolony. Dir.: Ronald Schnell, Cur.: Bruce O'Hara (Photography)
Fine Arts Museum / University Museum - 1963 48041

Towanda PA

Bradford County Historical Society Museum, 109 Pine St, Towanda, PA 18848 - T: (717) 265-2240, E-mail: bchs@cyber-quest.com. C.E.O.: Henry G. Farley
Local Museum / Historical Museum - 1870
Local hist - Library 48042

French Azilum, R.R. 2, Towanda, PA 18848 - T: (570) 265-3376, Internet: www.frenchazilum.org. Pres.: Pam Emerson, Dir.: Thomas S. Owen
Local Museum - 1954
Historic house, 1793-1803 refuge of the French Royalists 48043

Townsend TN

Cades Cove Open-Air Museum, Great Smoky Mountains National Park, 10042 Campgrounds Dr, Townsend, TN 37882 - T: (865) 436-1256, Fax: (865) 436-1220, E-mail: grsm_smokies_information@nps.gov, Internet: www.nps.gov/grsm
Local Museum / Open Air Museum - 1951
Cable Mill Area and other historic structures typical of Southern Appalachia at turn of the 20th century 48044

Towson MD

Asian Arts and Culture Center, Towson University, Towson, MD 21252 - T: (410) 704-2807, Fax: (410) 704-4032, E-mail: sshieh@towson.edu, Internet: www.towson.edu/tu/asianarts. Dir.: Suewhei Shieh
Fine Arts Museum - 1971
Art 48045

Hampton National Historic Site Museum, 535 Hampton Ln, Towson, MD 21286 - T: (410) 823-1309, Fax: (410) 823-8394, E-mail: laurie_coughlan@nps.gov, Internet: www.nps.gov/hamp. Cur.: Lynne Dakin Hastings
Historical Museum - 1948
Late Georgian Mansion incl slave quarters, agricultural-industrial complex 48046

The Holtzman Art Gallery, c/o Towson University, 8000 York Rd, Towson, MD 21252-0001 - T: (410) 704-2808. Dir.: Prof. Christopher Bartlett
Fine Arts Museum / University Museum - 1973
AfricanAsian arts, contemporary painting and sculpture, Maryland artists coll 48047

Trappe PA

Museum of the Historical Society of Trappe, Collegeville, Perkiomen Valley, 303 Main St, Trappe, PA 19426 - T: (610) 489-7560, Fax: (610) 489-7560. Cur.: John Shetler
Local Museum - 1964
Local hist 48048

Traverse City MI

Con Foster Museum, 181 E Grandview Pkwy, Traverse City, MI 49684 - T: (231) 995-0314, Fax: (231) 946-6750. Pres.: Steve Harold, Exec. Dir.: Ann Hoopfer
Local Museum - 1934
Local history 48049

Dennos Museum Center of Northwestern Michigan College, 1701 E Front St, Traverse City, MI 49686 - T: (231) 995-1055, Fax: (231) 995-1597, E-mail: dmc@nmc.edu, Internet: www.dennosmuseum.org. Dir.: Eugene A. Jenneman
Fine Arts Museum / University Museum - 1991
Art 48050

Trenton MI

Trenton Historical Museum, 306 Saint Joseph, Trenton, MI 48183 - T: (734) 675-2130, Fax: (734) 675-4088. C.E.O.: Tod Davis
Local Museum - 1962
Local history 48051

Trenton NJ

Artworks, c/o Visual Art School of Trenton, 19 Everett Alley, Trenton, NJ 08611 - T: (609) 394-9436, Internet: www.artsworksnj.org. Exec. Dir.: Beth Daly
Fine Arts Museum - 1964 48052

College of New Jersey Art Gallery, Holman Hall, Trenton, NJ 08650-4700 - T: (609) 771-2615, Fax: (609) 771-2633, E-mail: masterjp@tcnj.edu, Internet: www.tcnj.edu/~tcag. Dir.: Prof. Dr. Lois Fichner-Rathus
Fine Arts Museum
Drawings, prints, photography, sculpture, African arts, crafts 48053

The Gallery, Mercer County Community College, 1200 Old Trenton Rd, Trenton, NJ 08690 - T: (609) 586-4800 ext 3589, Internet: www.mccc.edu/gallery. Dir.: Henry Hose
Fine Arts Museum - 1971
Cybis coll, paintings, sculpture, ceramics, Mexican art, folk art - library 48054

The Invention Factory, 650 S Broad St, Trenton, NJ 08611 - T: (609) 396-4214, 396-2002, Fax: (609) 396-0676, E-mail: dcarroll@inventionfactory.com, Internet: www.inventionfactory.com. Exec. Dir.: Daine L. Carroll
Science&Tech Museum
Science, Technology, Industry 48055

New Jersey State House, 125 W State St, Trenton, NJ 08625-0068 - T: (609) 633-2709, Fax: (609) 292-1498, E-mail: phayden@njleg.state.nj.us, Internet: www.njleg.state.nj.us
Historical Museum - 1792
Period furnishings and equip, portraits of former governors and legislative figures 48056

New Jersey State Museum, 205 W State St, Trenton, NJ 08625, mail addr: POB 530, Trenton, NJ 08625-0530 - T: (609) 292-6300, Fax: (609) 599-4098, E-mail: margaret.oreilly@sos.state.nj.us, Internet: www.state.nj.us/state/museum/musidx.html. Dir.: Dr. Helen Shannon, Cur.: Dr. Lorraine Williams (Archaeology and Ethnology), David Parris (Science), Karen Cummins (Education), John Mohr (Exhibits), Ass. Cur.: Karen Flinn, Fran Mollett (Archaeology and Ethnology), Richard Peery (Planetarium), Margaret O'Reilly (Art), Anthony Miskowski, Shirley Albright (Science)
Local Museum / Historical Museum / Fine Arts Museum / Natural History Museum / Ethnology Museum / Archaeological Museum - 1895
Culture, archaeology, ethnology, science, fine and decorative arts 48057

Old Barracks Museum, Barrack St, Trenton, NJ 08608 - T: (609) 396-1776, Fax: (609) 777-4000, E-mail: barracks@voicenet.com, Internet: www.barracks.org. Dir.: Richard Patterson
Military Museum - 1902
American decorative arts (1750-1820), archaeology, tools and household equipment, military artifacts 48058

Trenton City Museum, Cadwalader Park, 319 E State St, Trenton, NJ 08608 - T: (609) 989-3632, Fax: (609) 989-3624, E-mail: bhill@ellarslie.org, Internet: www.ellarslie.org. Dir.: Brian O. Hill
Local Museum - 1971
Ceramics, porcelain 48059

William Trent House, 15 Market St, Trenton, NJ 08611 - T: (609) 989-3027, Fax: (609) 278-7890. Pres.: Derik Sutphin, Dir.: M.M. Pernot
Local Museum - 1939 48060

Trinidad CO

A.R. Mitchell Memorial Museum of Western Art, 150 E Main St, Trinidad, CO 81082 - T: (719) 846-4224, Fax: (719) 846-4002, E-mail: themitch@rmi.net. Dir.: James Baker, Pat Patrich, Cur.: Alan Peterson
Fine Arts Museum - 1979
Western art 48061

Baca House, Trinidad History Museum, 300 E Main, Trinidad, CO 81082 - T: (719) 846-7217, Fax: (719) 845-0117, Internet: www.trinidadco.com/thm. Pres.: Georgianna Contiguglia, Dir.: Paula Manini
Historical Museum - 1870 48062

Bloom Mansion, Trinidad History Museum, 300 E Main, Trinidad, CO 81082 - T: (719) 846-7217, Fax: (719) 845-0117, Internet: www.trinidadco.com/thm. Pres.: Georgianna Contiguglia, Dir.: Paula Manini
Local Museum / Decorative Arts Museum - 1955 48063

Louden-Henritze Archaeology Museum, Trinidad State Junior College, 600 Prospect St, Trinidad, CO 81082 - T: (719) 846-5508, Fax: (719) 846-5667, E-mail: loretta.martin@tsjc.cccoes.edu, Internet: www.tsjc.cccoes.edu/arch_museum/louden1.htm. Dir.: Loretta Martin
University Museum / Archaeological Museum - 1955 48064

Santa Fe Trail Museum, Trinidad History Museum, 300 E Main, Trinidad, CO 81082 - T: (719) 846-7217, Fax: (719) 845-0117, Internet: www.trinidadco.com/thm. Pres.: Georgianna Contiguglia, Dir.: Paula Manini
Historical Museum - 1955 48065

Troutdale OR

Barn Museum and Rail Depot Museum, 726 E Historic Columbia River Hwy, Troutdale, OR 97060 - T: (503) 661-2164, Fax: (503) 674-2995. Cur.: Mary Bryson
Local Museum / Science&Tech Museum - 1968 48066

Troy AL

Pioneer Museum of Alabama, 248 US-231 N, Troy, AL 36081 - T: (334) 566-3597, Fax: (334) 566-3552, E-mail: pioneer@troycable.net, Internet: www.pioneer-museum.org. Dir.: Charlotte Gibson
Local Museum / Agriculture Museum - 1969
Agriculture, local history 48067

Troy MI

Troy Museum and Historic Village, 60 W Wattles Rd, Troy, MI 48098 - T: (248) 524-3570, Fax: (248) 524-3572, E-mail: museum@ci.troy.mi.us. Head: Loraine Campbell
Open Air Museum / Historical Museum - 1927
History Museum 48068

Troy NY

The Arts Center of the Capital Region, 265 River St, Troy, NY 12180 - T: (518) 273-0552, Fax: (518) 273-4591, E-mail: info@theartscenter.cc, Internet: www.artscenteronline.org
Public Gallery 48069

Junior Museum, 105 Eighth St, Troy, NY 12180 - T: (518) 235-2120, Fax: (518) 235-6836, E-mail: info@juniormuseum.org, Internet: www.juniormuseum.org. Exec. Dir.: Timothy S. Allen
Special Museum - 1954
Art hist 48070

Rensselaer County Historical Society Museum, 57 Second St, Troy, NY 12180 - T: (518) 272-7232, Fax: (518) 273-1264, E-mail: info@rchsonline.org, Internet: www.rchsonline.org. Dir.: Donna Hassler, Cur.: Stacy Pomeroy Draper
Local Museum - 1927 48071

Troy OH

Hayner Cultural Center, 301 W Main St, Troy, OH 45373 - T: (937) 339-0457, Fax: (937) 335-6373, E-mail: hayner@tdnpublishing.com, Internet: www.tdn-net.com/hayner
Science&Tech Museum / Historical Museum - 1976
Hayner Distillery and Mary Jane Hayner family 48072

Overfield Tavern Museum, 121 E Water St, Troy, OH 45373 - T: (937) 335-4019. Dir.: Robert Patton, Cur.: Terry Purke, Ass. Cur.: Busser Howell
Local Museum - 1966 48073

Truckee CA

Donner Memorial and Emigrant Trail Museum, 12593 Donner Pass Rd, Truckee, CA 96161 - T: (530) 550-2347, Fax: (530) 582-7893, E-mail: ranger301@jps.net, Internet: www.parks.ca.gov. Cur.: Judith K. Polanich
Historic Site / Historical Museum - 1962 48074

Truth or Consequences NM

Geronimo Springs Museum, 211 Main St, Truth or Consequences, NM 87901 - T: (505) 894-6600, Fax: (505) 894-1244. Pres.: Jim Brannon, Dir.: Ann Welborn
Historical Museum - 1972 48075

Tubac AZ

Tubac Center of the Arts, 9 Plaza Rd, Tubac, AZ 85646-1911 - T: (520) 398-2371, Fax: (520) 398-9511, E-mail: artcntr@flash.net, Internet: www.tubacarts.org. Exec. Dir.: Colleen C. Lester
Fine Arts Museum - 1963 48076

Tuckerton NJ

Barnegat Bay Decoy and Baymen's Museum, 137 W Main St, Tuckerton, NJ 08087 - T: (609) 296-8868, Fax: (609) 296-5810, E-mail: tuckcport@aol.com, Internet: www.tuckertonseaport.org. Pres.: Malcolm J. Robinson, Exec. Dir.: John Gormley
Folklore Museum - 1989
Maritime culture 48077

Tucson AZ

The Aquary Museum, 918 N Plumer, Tucson, AZ 85719-4960 - T: (520) 318-1460. Dir.: Y.Z. Painter-De Monte
Natural History Museum - 1976 48078

Arizona Gallery, 5101 N Oracle Rd, Tucson, AZ 85704 - T: (520) 888-8788
Public Gallery 48079

Arizona Historical Society Museum, Headquarters and Southern Arizona Division, 949 E Second St, Tucson, AZ 85719 - T: (520) 628-5774, Fax: (520) 628-5695, E-mail: lmcbrayer@vms.arizona.edu, Internet: www.w3.arizona.edu/~azhist. Dir.: Tom Peterson
Historical Museum - 1884
History, Spanish colonial time, Mexican culture, weapons, tranportation, ranching, mining 48080

Arizona-Sonora Desert Museum, 2021 N Kinney Rd, Tucson, AZ 85743-8918 - T: (520) 883-1380, Fax: (520) 883-2500, E-mail: rdaley@desertmuseum.org, Internet: www.desertmuseum.org. Dir.: Robert D. Edison
Natural History Museum - 1952
Natural history 48081

Arizona State Museum, University of Arizona, Tucson, AZ 85721-0026 - T: (520) 621-6302, Fax: (520) 621-2976, E-mail: darlene@al.arizona.edu, Internet: www.statemuseum.arizona.edu. Dir.: George J. Gumerman, Cur. Archaeology: Paul Fish, Suzy Fish, E. Charles Adams, Rich Lange, Lynn Teague, Lane Back, John Madsen, Cur. Ethnohistory: Tom Sheridan, Tracy Duvall, Diana Hadley, Cons.: Nancy Odegaard
University Museum / Ethnology Museum / Archaeological Museum - 1893
Anthropology, archaeology, ethnology of the American Southwest and northern Mexico 48082

Center for Creative Photography, University of Arizona, 130 N Olive Rd, Tucson, AZ 85721-0103 - T: (520) 621-7968, Fax: (520) 621-9444, E-mail: oncenter@ccp.library.arizona.edu, Internet: www.creativephotography.org. Dir.: Amy Rulle, Ass. Dir.: Nancy Lutz, Cur.: Trudy Wilner Stack
Fine Arts Museum / Public Gallery / University Museum - 1975
Art - Archives, Library 48083

Degrazia Gallery in the Sun, 6300 N Swan Rd, Tucson, AZ 85718 - T: (520) 299-9192, Fax: (520) 299-1381, E-mail: gallerysun@aol.com, Internet: www.degrazia.org. Pres.: Lorraine Drachman, Dir.: Jon Fowler
Fine Arts Museum - 1977
Art 48084

Dinnerware Contemporary Art Gallery, 135 E Congress St, Tucson, AZ 85701 - T: (520) 792-4503, Fax: (520) 792-1282, E-mail: dinnerware@theriver.com, Internet: www.dinnerwarearts.com. Pres.: Mauricio Toussaint, Exec. Dir.: Barbara McLaughlin
Fine Arts Museum - 1979 48085

Doll Museum, 4940 E Speedway Blvd, Tucson, AZ 85712 - T: (520) 323-0018
Special Museum 48086

Flandrau Science Center, 1601 E University Blvd, Tucson, AZ 85721-0091 - T: (520) 621-7827, Fax: (520) 621-8451, E-mail: marymcox@u.arizona.edu, Internet: www.flandrau.org. Dir.: Alexis Faust
Science&Tech Museum - 1975
Science, astronomy exhibits - planetarium, observatory 48087

The Franklin Museum, 1405 E Kleindale Rd, Tucson, AZ 85719 - T: (520) 326-8038, E-mail: hhff2@aol.com, Internet: www.franklincar.org. Dir.: Bourke A. Runton
Science&Tech Museum - 1992
Franklin vehicles 1904-1934, 25 cars, air cooled motors 1938-1975, H.H Franklin company hist 1892-1936 48088

House of the Redtails Gallery, POB 41625, Tucson, AZ 85717 - T: (520) 805-9601, Internet: www.fountainstudio.com/waldt.html
Public Gallery 48089

International Wildlife Museum, 4800 W Gates Pass Rd, Tucson, AZ 85745 - T: (520) 629-0100, Fax: (520) 618-3561, E-mail: iwm@thewildlifemuseum.org, Internet: www.thewildlifemuseum.org. Dir.: Richard S. White
Natural History Museum - 1988
Natural history dioramas 48090

Pima Air and Space Museum, 6000 E Valencia Rd, Tucson, AZ 85706 - T: (520) 574-0462, Fax: (520) 574-9238, E-mail: pimaair@azstarnet.com, Internet: www.pimaair.org. Exec. Dir.: Edward D. Harrow
Historical Museum / Science&Tech Museum - 1966
Aeronautics, space, Arizona aviation Hall of Fame 48091

Tucson Children's Museum, 200 S Sixth Av, Tucson, AZ 85702-2609 - T: (520) 792-9985, Fax: (520) 792-0639, E-mail: tcm@tucsonchildrensmuseum.org, Internet: www.tucsonchildrenmuseum.org. Dir.: Sheila Saxsburg
Special Museum - 1986 48092

Tucson Museum of Art and Historic Block, 140 N Main Av, Tucson, AZ 85701 - T: (520) 624-2333, Fax: (520) 624-7202, E-mail: info@tucsonarts.com, Internet: www.tucsonarts.com. Dir.: Robert A. Yassin, Cur.: Joanne Stuhr
Fine Arts Museum - 1924
Art 48093

University of Arizona Mineral Museum, Flandrau Science Center, Gould-Simpson Bldg 77, Tucson, AZ 85721 - T: (520) 621-4227, 621-4849, Fax: (520) 621-8451, E-mail: wetmore@geo.arizona.edu, Internet: www.geo.arizona.edu/minmus. Cur.: Dr. Terry Wallace, Shirley Wetmore
University Museum / Natural History Museum - 1891
Mineralogy 48094

University of Arizona Museum of Art, Park and Speedway, Tucson, AZ 85721-0002 - T: (520) 621-5676, Fax: (520) 621-8770, E-mail: azs@u.arizona.edu, Internet: artmuseum.arizona.edu. Dir.: Charles A. Guerin, Cur.: Dr. Peter S. Briggs
Fine Arts Museum / University Museum - 1955
14th-19th c European art, contemporary art 48095

University of Arizona Union Galleries, Student Union Memorial Center, Rm 404, Tucson, AZ 85721 - T: (520) 621-5853, Fax: (520) 621-6930, E-mail: ceagan@u.arizona.edu, Internet: www.arts.arizona.edu/galleries/jg.html. Cur.: Chrissy Lieberman
Public Gallery / University Museum - 1971 48096

Western Archeological and Conservation Center, 1415 N Sixth Av, Tucson, AZ 85705 - T: (520) 670-6501, Fax: (520) 670-6525. Cur.: Gloria J. Fenner, Cons.: Brynn Bender
Local Museum - 1952
Archaeology, ethnography, history, natural science 48097

Womankraft, 388 S Stone Av, Tucson, AZ 85701 - T: (520) 629-9976
Fine Arts Museum - 1974 48098

Tucumcari NM

Tucumcari Historical Research Institute Museum, 416 S Adams, Tucumcari, NM 88401 - T: (505) 461-4201, Fax: (505) 461-2049, E-mail: museum@cityoftucumcari.com. Pres.: Duane Moore
Local Museum - 1958
Local history, folk art, pictures 48099

Tujunga CA

McGroarty Cultural Art Center, 7570 McGroarty Terrace, Tujunga, CA 91042 - T: (818) 352-5285, E-mail: director@mcgroartyarts.org, Internet: www.mcgroartyarts.org
Public Gallery 48100

Tulelake CA

Lava Beds National Monument, Indian Wells Headquarters, Tulelake, CA 96134, mail addr: POB 867, Tulelake, CA 96134 - T: (530) 667-2282, Fax: (530) 667-2737, Internet: www.nps.gov/labe. Head: Craig Dorman
Natural History Museum - 1925
Natural hist 48101

Tulia TX

Swisher County Museum, 127 SW Second St, Tulia, TX 79088 - T: (806) 995-2819. Pres.: Linda Foster, Dir.: Billie Sue Gayler
Local Museum - 1965
Local hist 48102

Tulsa OK

Gershon & Rebecca Fenster Museum of Jewish Art, POB 52188, Tulsa, OK 74152-0188 - T: (918) 299-1366, Fax: (919) 294-8338, E-mail: fenster.museum@ibm.net, Internet: www.jewishmuseum.net. Dir.: Diana Aaronson
Historical Museum / Special Museum / Religious Arts Museum - 1966 48103

Gilcrease Museum, 1400 Gilcrease Museum Rd, Tulsa, OK 74127-2100 - T: (918) 596-2700, Fax: (918) 596-2770, E-mail: gilcreas@ionet.net, Internet: www.gilcrease.org. Dir.: Hilary Kitz, Ass. Dir.: Gary F. Moore, Sen. Cur.: Daniel C. Swan, Sarah Erwin, Cons.: Gayle Clements
Fine Arts Museum / Historical Museum - 1949 48104

Living Museum at Tulsa Zoo, 5701 E 36 St N, Tulsa, OK 74115 - T: (918) 669-6600, Fax: (918) 669-6260, E-mail: tulsazoo@ci.tulsa.ok.us, Internet: www.tulsazoo.org. Dir.: Larry Nunley, Cur.: Kathleen Buck, C. Rippy, Jay Ross (Horticulture), Sc. Staff: Paul Louderback (Zoology), Rusty Grimpe (Education), Asst. Dir.: Stephen Walker
Natural History Museum - 1927 48105

Mac's Antique Car Museum, 1319 E Fourth St, Tulsa, OK 74120 - T: (918) 583-3101, Fax: (918) 583-3108, E-mail: macs@ionet.net. Cur.: D. McGlumphy
Science&Tech Museum - 1991
Antique and classic cars and trucks 48106

Philbrook Museum of Art, 2727 S Rockford Rd, Tulsa, OK 74114-4104 - T: (918) 749-7941, Fax: (918) 743-4230, E-mail: mmanhart@philbrook.org, Internet: www.philbrook.org. Dir.: Marcia Y. Manhart, Christine Knop Kallenberger, Dep. Dir.: G. David Singleton, Cur.: James F. Peck (European and American Art)
Fine Arts Museum - 1938 48107

Tupelo MS

Bank of Mississippi Art Collection, 1 Mississippi Plaza, Tupelo, MS 38802 - T: (662) 680-2000. Pres.: Aubrey B. Patterson jr.
Fine Arts Museum 48108

Natchez Trace Parkway Study Collection, 2680 Natchez Trace Pkwy, Tupelo, MS 38801 - T: (662) 680-4004, Fax: (662) 680-4036, Internet: www.nps.gov/natr. Head: Wendell Simpson
Natural History Museum - 1938 48109

Tupelo Artist Guild Gallery, 211 W Main St, Tupelo, MS 38801 - T: (662) 844-2787, Fax: (662) 844-9751, E-mail: tupeloartgallery@redmagnet.com, Internet: www.tupeloartgallery.com. Exec. Dir.: Tina Lutz
Fine Arts Museum - 1985
Art 48110

Turlock CA

University Art Gallery, c/o California State University Stanislaus, 801 W Monte Vista Av, Turlock, CA 95382 - T: (209) 667-3186, Internet: www.csustan.edu. Dir.: Sophia Isajiw
Fine Arts Museum / University Museum - 1967 48111

Tuscaloosa AL

Alabama Museum of Natural History, Smith Hall, University of Alabama Campus, Tuscaloosa, AL 35487-0340 - T: (205) 348-7550, Fax: (205) 348-9292, Internet: www.museums.ua.edu. C.E.O.: Dr. Richard Diehl
University Museum / Natural History Museum - 1847
Natural hist 48112

Children's Hands-On Museum, 2213 University Blvd, Tuscaloosa, AL 35403 - T: (205) 349-4235, Fax: (205) 349-4276, E-mail: chom@dbtech.net, Internet: www.dbtech.net/chom. Dir.: Kathleen Hughes, Ass. Dir.: Shirley Shirley
Special Museum - 1984 48113

Gorgas House, University of Alabama, Capstone at McCorvy Dr, Tuscaloosa, AL 35487-0266 - T: (205) 348-5906, 348-7551, Fax: (205) 348-9292, E-mail: ftucker@rosie.aalan.ua.edu, Internet: www.ua.edu/gorgasmain.html. Dir.: Dr. Richard Diehl, Cur.: Marion Pearson
Local Museum - 1954
Historic house 48114

The Old Tavern Museum, 500 28th Av, Capitol Park, Tuscaloosa, AL 35401 - T: (205) 758-2238, Fax: (205) 758-8163, E-mail: tcps@dbtech.net, Internet: www.historictuscaloosa.org. Exec. Dir.: Hannah Brown
Local Museum - 1965
Local hist 48115

Paul W. Bryant Museum, 300 Bryant Dr, Tuscaloosa, AL 35487-0385 - T: (205) 348-4668, Fax: (205) 348-8883, E-mail: kgaddy@rosie.aalan.ua.edu, Internet: www.ua.edu/bryant.htm. Dir.: Kenneth Gaddy
Special Museum / University Museum - 1985
Sports, memorabilia of university athletics 48116

Sarah Moody Gallery of Art, University of Alabama, 103 Garland Hall, Tuscaloosa, AL 35487-0270 - T: (205) 348-1890, 348-5967, Fax: (205) 348-0287, E-mail: wdooley@art.as.ua.edu, Internet: www.bama.ua.edu/~artweb/moody.html. Dir.: Bill Dooley
Fine Arts Museum / University Museum - 1967
Primitive art, paintings, drawings, prints, photos, crafts, sculpture 48117

Tuscola IL

Korean War Veterans National Museum, C500 Tuscola Blvd, Tuscola, IL 61953 - T: (217) 253-5813, Fax: (217) 253-9421, E-mail: kwmuseum@theforgottenvictory.org, Internet: www.theforgottenvictory.org
Military Museum - 1997 48118

Tuscumbia AL

Alabama Music Hall of Fame, 617 Hwy 72 W, Tuscumbia, AL 35674 - T: (256) 381-4417, Fax: (256) 381-1031, E-mail: alamhof@hiwaay.net, Internet: www.alamhof.org. Dir.: David A. Johnson, Ass. Dir.: Marcia Weems
Music Museum - 1982
Music 48119

Ivy Green, Birthplace of Helen Keller, 300 W North Commons, Tuscumbia, AL 35674 - T: (256) 383-4066, Fax: (256) 383-4068. Head: Sue Pilkilton
Local Museum - 1952
Historic house 48120

Tennessee Valley Art Association, 511 N Water St, Tuscumbia, AL 35674 - T: (256) 383-0533, Fax: (256) 383-0535, E-mail: tvac@hiwaay.net, Internet: www.tvac.riverartists.com. Dir.: Mary Settle Cooney
Fine Arts Museum / Folklore Museum - 1963
Reynolds coll, festival, fine art, coins, prints 48121

Tuskegee Institute AL

George Washington Carver Museum, 1212 Old Montgomery Rd, Tuskegee Institute, AL 36088-0010 - T: (334) 727-6390, 727-3200, Fax: (334) 727-4597. Head: Brenda B. Caldwell
Historical Museum / Natural History Museum - 1941
History, science 48122

Tuskegee Institute National Historic Site, 1212 Old Montgomery Rd, Tuskegee Institute, AL 36088-0010 - T: (334) 727-6390, Fax: (334) 727-4597, Internet: www.nps.gov/tuin. Head: Brenda B. Caldwell
Historical Museum - 1941
African American hist 48123

Twin Falls ID

Herrett Center for Arts and Science, c/o College of Southern Idaho, 315 Falls Av, Twin Falls, ID 83301 - T: (208) 733-9554 ext 2655, Fax: (208) 736-4712, E-mail: herritt@csi.edu, Internet: www.csi.edu/herrett. Dir.: James C. Woods
University Museum / Ethnology Museum / Natural History Museum - 1952
Anthropology, ethnology, Indian art - Faulkner Planetarium 48124

Twin Falls County Museum, Hwy 30, 3 miles west of hospital, Twin Falls, ID 83301, mail addr: 214 Meadow Ln, Twin Falls, ID 83301 - T: (208) 423-5907. Dir.: Don Dean, Jeanne Dean
Local Museum - 1957
Period clothing, dishes, phonographs, musical instruments, massacre site coll, sewing machines, office machines, farm machinery, gold washer, old picture gallery, mining 48125

Twinsburg OH

Twinsburg Historical Society Museum, 8996 Darrow Rd, Twinsburg, OH 44087 - T: (216) 487-5565, Internet: www.twinsburg.com/historicalsociety/
Local Museum - 1963
Furniture, tools, clothes, toys, local artifacts 48126

Two Harbors MN

Lake County Historical Society Museum, 520 South Av, Two Harbors, MN 55616 - T: (218) 834-4898, Fax: (218) 834-7198, E-mail: lakehrst@lakenet.com, Internet: www.lakecountyhistoricalsociety.org. C.E.O.: Rachelle Malonly
Historical Museum - 1926 48127

Split Rock Lighthouse Historic Site, 3713 Split Rock Lighthouse Rd, Two Harbors, MN 55616 - T: (218) 226-6372, Fax: (218) 226-6373, E-mail: splitrock@mnhs.org, Internet: www.mnhs.org. Dir.: Lee Radzak
Local Museum - 1976
Local hist 48128

Tybee Island GA

Tybee Museum and Tybee Island Light Station, 30 Meddin Dr, Tybee Island, GA 31328 - T: (912) 786-5801, Fax: (912) 786-6538, E-mail: tybeelh@bellsouth.net, Internet: www.tybelllighthouse.org. Dir.: Cullen Chambers
Historical Museum - 1960
History, in old Spanish-American War Coastal Defense Battery, Tybee Island lighthouse and cottages 48129

Tyler TX

Goodman Museum, 624 N Broadway, Tyler, TX 75702 - T: (903) 531-1286, Fax: (903) 531-1372. Cur.: Boyd Sanders
Decorative Arts Museum - 1962
Cradles, china from England and France 48130

Smith County Historical Society Museum, 125 S College Av, Tyler, TX 75702 - T: (903) 592-5561, Fax: (903) 526-0924, E-mail: info@smithcountyhistory.org, Internet: www.smithcountyhistory.org. Pres.: Rendal B. Gilbert
Local Museum - 1959
Local hist 48131

Tyler Museum of Art, 1300 S Mahon Av, Tyler, TX 75701 - T: (903) 595-1001, Fax: (903) 595-1055, E-mail: info@tylermuseum.org, Internet: www.tylermuseum.org. Dir.: Kimberley Bush Tomio
Fine Arts Museum - 1969
Art 48132

Tyringham MA

Santarella Museum and Gardens, 75 Main Rd, Tyringham, MA 01264 - T: (413) 243-3260, Fax: (413) 243-9178, Internet: www.santarella.org. Dir.: Candy Talbert, Michael Atkins
Fine Arts Museum - 1953
Art, former studio of Sir Henry Hudson Kitson 48133

Ukiah CA

Grace Hudson Museum and The Sun House, 431 S Main St, Ukiah, CA 95482 - T: (707) 467-2836, Fax: (707) 467-2835, E-mail: gracehudson@pacific.net, Internet: www.gracehudsonmuseum.org. Dir.: Sherrie Smith-Ferri, Cur.: Marvin Schenck
Local Museum / Fine Arts Museum - 1975
Historic house, art, history, anthropology, Grace Hudson art work, California Indian ethnography, coll about Pomo Indians 48134

Held-Poage Memorial Home, 603 W Perkins St, Ukiah, CA 95482-4726 - T: (707) 462-6969, 462-2039, E-mail: mchs@pacific.net. Dir.: Lila J. Lee
Local Museum - 1970
Local hist 48135

Ulster Park NY

Klyne Esopus Historical Society Museum, 764 Rte 9 W, Ulster Park, NY 12487 - T: (845) 338-8109, E-mail: kehsm@ulster.net. Dir.: Susan B. Wick
Local Museum - 1969
Local and regional hist 48136

Ulysses KS

Grant County Museum, 300 E Oklahoma, Ulysses, KS 67880 - T: (620) 356-3009, Fax: (620) 356-5082, E-mail: ulyksmus@pld.com. Dir.: Ginger Anthony
Local Museum - 1978
Indian artifacts, furnishings, toys, lothing, quilts, local and family hist 48137

Uncasville CT

Tantaquidgeon Indian Museum, Rte 32, 1819 Norwich-New London Rd, Uncasville, CT 06382 - T: (860) 848-9145. Cur.: Gladys Tantaquidgeon
Historical Museum / Ethnology Museum - 1931
Indian hist and culture 48138

Union IL

Illinois Railway Museum, 7000 Olson Rd, Union, IL 60180 - T: (815) 923-4391 ext 404, Fax: (815) 923-2006, Internet: www.irm.org. Pres.: C. Kevin McCabe, C.E.O.: Nick Kallas
Science&Tech Museum - 1953
Railways, housed in Marengo, Illinois rail depot 48139

McHenry County Historical Society Museum, 6422 Main St, Union, IL 60180 - T: (815) 923-2267, Fax: (815) 923-2271, E-mail: info@mchsonline.org, Internet: www.mchsonline.org. C.E.O.: Nancy J. Fike
Local Museum - 1963
Local history 48140

Union KY

Big Bone Lick State Park Museum, 3380 Beaver Rd, Union, KY 41091 - T: (859) 384-3522, Fax: (859) 384-4775, E-mail: john.barker@mail.state.ky.us, Internet: www.state.ky.us/agencies/parks/bigbone.htm
Archaeological Museum - 1971
Mastadon and bison bones 48141

Union ME

Matthews Museum of Maine Heritage, Union Fairgrounds, Union, ME 04862 - T: (207) 785-3321, Fax: (207) 785-3321, E-mail: mitchell@tidewater.net. Dir.: John Crabtree, Cur.: Archie Mitchell, Irene Hawes
Local Museum - 1965
Local history 48142

Union NJ

James Howe Gallery, Kean University, Vaughn Eames Hall, Morris Av, Union, NJ 07083 - T: (908) 737-4000, Fax: (908) 527-2804
Fine Arts Museum / University Museum - 1971
Paintings, prints, sculpture, photographs, design and furniture 48143

Liberty Hall Museum, 1003 Morris Av, Union, NJ 07083 - T: (908) 527-0400, Fax: (908) 352-8915, E-mail: liberty-hall@juno.com, Internet: libertyhallnj.org. C.E.O.: John Kean
Historical Museum - 1968
Livingston and Kean family hist 48144

Union OR

Union County Museum, 333 S Main St, Union, OR 97883 - T: (541) 562-6003, Fax: (541) 562-5196, Internet: www.visitlagrande.com. Dir.: Val Stockhoff, Cur.: Kathleen Almquist
Local Museum - 1969 48145

Union SC

Rose Hill Plantation State Historic Site, 2677 Sardis Rd, Union, SC 29379 - T: (864) 427-5966, Fax: (864) 427-5966, E-mail: rose_hill_-plantation_sp@scprt.com, Internet: www.southcarolinaparks.com
Local Museum - 1960
Local hist 48146

Union County Historical Foundation Museum, American Federal Savings and Loan Bldg, Union, SC 29379. Cur.: Tommy Bishop
Local Museum - 1960
Early American Revolutionary guns, currency, furniture, dolls, China and crystal, pottery, early tools, Confederate War 48147

Union City TN

Dixie Gun Works' Old Car Museum, 1412 W Reelfoot Av, Union City, TN 38261 - T: (731) 885-0561, Fax: (731) 885-0440, E-mail: dixiegun@iswt.com, Internet: www.dixiegun.com
Science&Tech Museum - 1954
American antique automotives, firearms 48148

Union Gap WA

Central Washington Agricultural Museum, 4508 Main St, Union Gap, WA 98903-0008 - T: (509) 457-8735, 248-0432. Pres.: Bob Herber
Agriculture Museum - 1979
Agriculture 48149

University Center MI

Marshall M. Fredericks Sculpture Museum, Saginaw Valley State University, Arbury Arts Center, University Center, MI 48710 - T: (989) 964-7125, Fax: (989) 964-7221, E-mail: ondish@svsu.edu, Internet: www.svsu.edu/mfsm. Dir.: Andrea Ondish
Fine Arts Museum / University Museum - 1988
Sculptures 48150

University Park IL

Nathan Manilow Sculpture Park, c/o Governors State University, Wagner House, University Park, IL 60466 - T: (708) 534-5000, Fax: (708) 534-8959, E-mail: b-goldbe@govst.edu, Internet: www.govst.edu/sculpture. Dir.: Beverly Goldberg
University Museum / Open Air Museum - 1969 48151

University Park PA

The Frost Entomological Museum, c/o Department of Entomology, The Pennsylvania State University, 501 A.S.I. Bldg, University Park, PA 16802 - T: (814) 863-2863, Fax: (814) 865-3048, E-mail: KC_KIM@psu.edu, Internet: www.ento.psu.edu/home/frost. Cur.: Dr. Ke Chung Kim
Natural History Museum - 1968
Natural hist 48152

HUB Robeson Galleries, c/o Pennsylvania State University, 241a HUB-Robeson, University Park, PA 16802 - T: (814) 865-2563, Fax: (814) 863-0812, E-mail: galleries@sa.psu.edu, Internet: www.sa.psu.edu/galleries. Dir.: Ann Shields
University Museum / Public Gallery - 1976 48153

Palmer Museum of Art, The Pennsylvania State University, Curtin Rd, University Park, PA 16802-2507 - T: (814) 865-7672, Fax: (814) 863-8608, E-mail: pjm19@psu.edu, Internet: www.psu.edu/dept/palmermuseum/. Dir.: Jan Keene Muhlert, Cur.: Dr. Leo Mazow (American Art), Charles V. Hallman, Dr. Patrick J. McGrady, Dr. Joyce Robinson
Fine Arts Museum / University Museum - 1972
Art 48154

Upland CA

Cooper Regional History Museum, 217 E A St, Upland, CA 91785-0772 - T: (909) 982-8010, E-mail: info@culturalcenter.org, Internet: www.culturalcenter.org. Dir.: Mary A. Roberts
Local Museum - 1965
Local hist, domestic life, citrus industry 48155

Upland PA

Caleb Pusey House, 15 Race St, Upland, PA 19015 - T: (610) 874-5665, Internet: www.delcohistory.org. Pres.: Harold R. Peden
Local Museum - 1960
Local hist 48156

Upper Marlboro MD

Darnall's Chance, 14800 Gov. Oden Bowie Dr, Upper Marlboro, MD 20772 - T: (301) 952-8010, Fax: (301) 952-1773, E-mail: susan.reidy@pgparks.com, Internet: www.pgparks.com. Dir.: Susan Reidy
Local Museum / Museum of Classical Antiquities - 1988
Darnall and Carroll family home 48157

W. Henry Duvall Tool Museum, Patuxent River Park, 16000 Croom Airport Rd, Upper Marlboro, MD 20772-8395 - T: (301) 627-6074, Fax: (301) 952-9754, E-mail: patuxent@pgparks.com, Internet: www.pgparks.com. Dir.: Greg Lewis
Science&Tech Museum - 1983
Tools 48158

Upper Montclair NJ

Montclair State University Art Galleries, Life Hall, 1 Normal Av, Upper Montclair, NJ 07043 - T: (973) 655-5113, Fax: (973) 655-7665, E-mail: pacel@montclair.edu, Internet: www.montclair.edu/pages/arts. Dir.: Dr. Lorenzo Pace, Ass. Dir.: Teresa Rodriguez
Fine Arts Museum / University Museum - 1973
Contemporary East Indian art, Japanese expressionism in paper - Calcia library 48159

Upper Sandusky OH

Indian Mill Museum State Memorial, 7417 Wyandot County Rd 47, Upper Sandusky, OH 43351 - T: (419) 294-3349, 294-4022
Historic Site - 1967 48160

Wyandot County Historical Society Museum, 130 S Seventh St, Upper Sandusky, OH 43351-0372 - T: (419) 294-3857, E-mail: wchs@udata.com. Cur.: Christie Raber
Local Museum / Historical Museum - 1929 48161

Upton NY

Science Museum, Brookhaven National Laboratory, Upton, NY 11973-5000 - T: (516) 344-2838, Fax: (516) 344-5832, E-mail: jtempel@bnl.gov, Internet: www.bnl.gov. Dir.: Gail Donoghue
Science&Tech Museum - 1977
Science 48162

Urbana IL

Museum of Natural History, University of Illinois at Urbana-Champaign, Natural History Bldg, 1301 W Green St, Urbana, IL 61801 - T: (217) 333-2360, Fax: (217) 244-9419, E-mail: darobbin@uiuc.edu, Internet: www.spurlock.uiuc.edu/. Dir.: Dr. Douglas J. Brewer
University Museum / Natural History Museum - 1870
Natural history 48163

Spurlock Museum, University of Illinois at Urbana-Champaign, 600 S Gregory St, Urbana, IL 61801 - T: (217) 333-2360, Fax: (217) 344-9419, E-mail: ksheahan@uiuc.edu, Internet: www.spurlock.uiuc.edu. Dir.: Dr. Douglas J. Brewer, Cur.: Wayne Pitard (Religious Studies), Norman Whitten (Anthropology), Dan Blake (Natural History), James Dengate (Classics), Kai-Wing Chow (East Asia), Janet Keller, Clark Cunningham (Anthropology)
University Museum / Historical Museum / Natural History Museum - 1911
General Museum 48164

Urbana OH

Champaign County Historical Museum, 809 E Lawn Av, Urbana, OH 43078 - T: (937) 653-6721. Pres.: Chris Callison
Local Museum - 1934 48165

Urbandale IA

Living History Farms Museum, 2600 NW 111th St, Urbandale, IA 50322 - T: (515) 278-5286, Fax: (515) 278-9808, E-mail: lhf@netins.net, Internet: www.livinghistoryfarms.org. Dir.: Rick Finch, C.E.O.: Sandy Yoder
Agriculture Museum - 1967
Agriculture 48166

Utica IL

LaSalle County Historical Society Museum, Mill and Canal Sts, Utica, IL 61373 - T: (815) 667-4861, Fax: (815) 667-5121, E-mail: museum@megsinet.org, Internet: www.lasallecountymuseum.org. Pres.: William Gish, Dir.: Mary C. Toraason
Local Museum - 1967
Local history, housed in 1848 pre-Civil War stone warehouse 48167

Starved Rock State Park, POB 509, Utica, IL 61373 - T: (815) 667-4906, 667-5356, Fax: (815) 667-5354, E-mail: starvedrockvc@ivi.net
Historical Museum - 1911
Former Indian village of Illinois Indians, 1673-1760 French occupation and 1683 French Fort Saint Louis 48168

Utica NY

Children's Museum of History, Natural History and Science at Utica, New York, 311 Main St, Utica, NY 13501 - T: (315) 724-6129, Fax: (315) 724-6120, Internet: www.museum4kids.com. Pres.: Marlene Brown
Special Museum / Natural History Museum - 1963 48169

Munson-Williams-Proctor Arts Institute Museum of Art, 310 Genesee St, Utica, NY 13502 - T: (315) 797-0000 ext 2140, Fax: (315) 797-5608, E-mail: pschweiz@mwpi.edu, Internet: www.mwpai.org/museum. Dir.: Dr. Paul D. Schweizer, Cur.: Mary Murray (20th-Century Art), Anna T. D'Ambrosio (Decorative Arts)
Fine Arts Museum - 1919 48170

Oneida County Historical Society Museum, 1608 Genesee St, Utica, NY 13502-5425 - T: (315) 735-3642, Fax: (315) 732-0806, E-mail: ochs@borg.com, Internet: www.midyork.org/ochs. Pres.: Kevin Marken
Local Museum - 1876 48171

Uvalde TX

Garner Memorial Museum, 333 N Park St, Uvalde, TX 78801 - T: (830) 278-5018, Fax: (830) 279-0512, E-mail: e.salazar@mail.utexas.edu. C.E.O.: Dr. Don Carleton, Cur.: Evangeline Salazar
University Museum / Historical Museum - 1960
Historic house, home of Vice President John N. Garner 48172

Vacaville CA

Vacaville Museum, 213 Buck Av, Vacaville, CA 95688 - T: (707) 447-4513, Fax: (707) 447-2661, E-mail: vacmuseum@aol.com, Internet: www.vacavillemuseum.org. Dir.: Shawn Lum, Ruth Gardner Begell, Cur.: Sabine Goerke-Shrode, Philip Nollar
Local Museum - 1981
Local hist 48173

Vail CO

Colorado Ski Museum and Ski Hall of Fame, 231 S Frontage Rd, Vail, CO 81657 - T: (970) 476-1876, Fax: (970) 476-1879, E-mail: info@skimuseum.net, Internet: www.skimuseum.net. Dir.: Margie J. Plath, Cur.: Pia Reynaldo
Special Museum - 1976
Ski and Snowboard history, Hall of Fame 48174

Vails Gate NY

Edmonston House, c/o National Temple, Rte 94, Vails Gate, NY 12584 - T: (845) 561-5073, Fax: (845) 561-5073, E-mail: swaddell@frontiernet.net, Internet: www.nationaltemplehill.org
Historical Museum - 1933
Period furnishings, American Revolutionary events 48175

Knox's Headquarters State Historic Site, Forge Hill Rd at Rte 94, Vails Gate, NY 12584 - T: (914) 561-5498, Fax: (914) 561-6577, E-mail: Michael.Clark@oprhp.state.ny.us, Internet: www.nysparks.com. C.E.O.: Michael J. Clark
Military Museum - 1922 48176

New Windsor Cantonment State Historic Site and National Purple Heart Hall of Honor, Rte 300 and Temple Hill Rd, Vails Gate, NY 12584 - T: (914) 561-1765, Fax: (914) 561-6577, Internet: www.nysparks.com. Head: Michael J. Clark
Local Museum - 1967 48177

Valdese NC

Museum of Waldensian History, c/o Waldensian Presbyterian Church, Roderet St, Valdese, NC 28690 - T: (704) 874-2531, Fax: (704) 874-0880, E-mail: waldensian@nci.net, Internet: www.waldensianpresbyterian.com. Head: Jewell P. Bounous
Religious Arts Museum - 1955 48178

Valdez AK

The Valdez Museum, 217 Egan Av, Valdez, AK 99686-0008 - T: (907) 835-2764, Fax: (907) 835-5800, E-mail: vldzmuse@alaska.net, Internet: www.alaska.net/~vldzmuse. Dir.: Tabitha Gregory, Cur.: Jerrie Clarke
Local Museum - 1976
Local hist 48179

Valdosta GA

Lowndes County Museum, 305 W Central Av, Valdosta, GA 31601 - T: (229) 247-4780, Fax: (229) 247-2840, E-mail: history@valdostamuseum.org, Internet: www.valdostamuseum.org. C.E.O.: Renate Milner
Local Museum - 1967 48180

Valdosta State University Fine Arts Gallery, College of the Arts, Valdosta, GA 31698-0110 - T: (912) 333-5835, Fax: (912) 245-3799, E-mail: kgmurray@valdosta.edu, Internet: www.valdosta.edu/art. Dir.: Karin G. Murray
Fine Arts Museum / University Museum - 1906 48181

Vale OR

Stonehouse Museum, 255 Main St, Vale, OR 97918 - T: (541) 473-2070
Historical Museum / Local Museum - 1995
Oregon trail, Northern Piautes and Bannock Indians 48182

Valentine NE

Cherry County Historical Society Museum, Main St and Hwy 20, Valentine, NE 69201 - T: (402) 376-2015. Pres.: Pauline Ravenscraft, Cur.: Deane Rathman
Local Museum - 1928 48183

Sawyer's Sandhills Museum, 440 Valentine St, Valentine, NE 69201 - T: (402) 376-3293
Science&Tech Museum / Local Museum - 1958
Antique autos, guns, Indian artifacts, musical instruments, lamps 48184

Vallejo CA

Vallejo Naval and Historical Museum, 734 Marin St, Vallejo, CA 94590 - T: (707) 643-0077, Fax: (707) 643-2443, E-mail: valmuse@pacbell.net, Internet: www.vallejomuseum.org. Dir.: James E. Kern
Local Museum - 1974
Local hist 48185

Valley NE

Valley Community Historical Society Museum, 218 W Alexander St, Valley, NE 68064 - T: (402) 359-2678. Pres.: Dick Allen
Local Museum - 1966 48186

Valley City ND

Barnes County Historical Museum, 315 Central Av N, Valley City, ND 58072 - T: (701) 845-0966, Fax: (701) 845-4755, E-mail: bchistoricalsociety@hotmail.com, Internet: www.cii.vcsu.nodak.edu/cbastian/BC/museum02.html. C.E.O.: Warren Ventsch
Local Museum - 1930 48187

Valley Forge PA

National Center for the American Revolution, POB 122, Valley Forge, PA 19481-0122 - T: (610) 917-3451, Fax: (610) 917-3188, E-mail: vfhs@ix.netcom.com, Internet: www.valleyforgemuseum.org. Dir.: Thomas Daly, Ass. Dir.: Stacey A. Swigart (Collections)
Historic Site / Historical Museum - 1918/2005
History, museum located on the site of Valley Forge encampment area 48188

The Valley Forge Museum → National Center for the American Revolution

Valley Forge National Historical Park, POB 953, Valley Forge, PA 19482-0953 - T: (610) 917-3651, Fax: (610) 917-3188, Internet: www.nps.gov/vafo. Head: Arthur L. Stewart Swigart
Historical Museum / Historic Site - 1893
1777-1778 site of Continental Army winter encampment 48189

Valley Glen CA

Los Angeles Valley College Art Gallery, 5800 Fulton Av, Valley Glen, CA 91401 - T: (818) 781-1200, Internet: www.lavalleycollege.com. Dir.: James Marren
Public Gallery - 1960 48190

Valparaiso FL

Heritage Museum of Northwest Florida, 115 Westview Av, Valparaiso, FL 32580 - T: (850) 678-2615, Fax: (850) 678-4547, E-mail: bmoss@co.okaloosa.fl.us, Internet: www.heritage-museum.org. Dir.: Barbara Lee Moss
Local Museum - 1970
Local history 48191

Valparaiso IN

Brauer Museum of Art, Valparaiso University Center for the Arts, Valparaiso, IN 46383-6349 - T: (219) 464-5365, Fax: (219) 464-5244, Internet: www.valpo.edu/artmuseum. Dir.: Gregg Hertzlieb
Fine Arts Museum / University Museum - 1953
Art 48192

Porter County Old Jail Museum, Old Jail Bldg, 153 Franklin St, Valparaiso, IN 46383 - T: (219) 465-3595, E-mail: hspc@attbi.com, Internet: home.attbi.com/~hspc. Man.: Shirron Soohey, Teresa Schmidt
Local Museum / Special Museum - 1916
Local history, criminology 48193

Van Buren AR

Bob Burns Museum, 813 Main St, Van Buren, AR 72956 - T: (501) 474-2761, Fax: (501) 474-5084, E-mail: vanburen@vanburen.org, Internet: www.vanburen.org. Head: Lance Lanier
Historical Museum - 1994 48194

Van Horn TX

Culberson County Historical Museum, 12 W Broadway, Van Horn, TX 79855 - T: (915) 283-8028. Dir.: Robert Stuckey, Ass. Dir.: Darice McVay
Local Museum - 1975
Local hist 48195

Van Lear KY

Coal Miners' Museum, 78 Miller's Creek Rd, Van Lear, KY 41265 - T: (606) 789-9725, E-mail: coalcamp@yahoo.com, Internet: www.geocities.com/coalcamp
Science&Tech Museum - 1984 48196

Van Wert OH

Wassenberg Art Center, 643 S Washington St, Van Wert, OH 45891 - T: (419) 238-6837, Fax: (419) 238-6828, E-mail: artcentr@bright.net, Internet: www.vanwert.com/wassenberg. Dir.: Michele L. Smith
Fine Arts Museum - 1954
Prints and original art 48197

Vancouver WA

Archer Gallery, Clark College, 1800 E McLoughlin Blvd, MS-13, Vancouver, WA 98663 - T: (360) 992-2370, 992-2246, Fax: (360) 992-2828, E-mail: mhirsch@clark.edu, Internet: www.clark.edu/. Dir.: Marjorie Hirsch
Fine Arts Museum - 1978
Art 48198

Clark County Historical Museum, 1511 Main St, Vancouver, WA 98660 - T: (360) 695-4681, Fax: (360) 695-4034, E-mail: david@cchmuseum.com. Pres.: Ron Hart, Dir.: David Fenton
Historical Museum - 1917
Local hist 48199

Fort Vancouver, 612 E. Reserve St, Vancouver, WA 98661 - T: (360) 696-7655, Fax: (360) 696-7657, E-mail: FOVA_superintendent@nps.gov, Internet: www.nps.gov. Cur.: David K. Hansen
Local Museum - 1948
Local hist 48200

Pearson Air Museum, 1115 E Fifth St, Vancouver, WA 98661 - T: (360) 694-7026, Fax: (360) 694-0824, E-mail: pearson@pacifier.com, Internet: www.pearsonairmuseum.org. Dir.: John Donnelly, Cur.: Tom Clark
Science&Tech Museum - 1987 48201

Vandalia IL

The Little Brick House, 621 St Clair, Vandalia, IL 62471 - T: (618) 283-2371. Cur.: Mary Burtschi
Historical Museum - 1960
1840-1860 James W. Berry property 48202

Vandalia State House, 315 W Gallatin St, Vandalia, IL 62471 - T: (618) 283-1161. Head: Robert Coomer
Historic Site - 1836
1836 Vandalia Statehouse is the oldest Capitol building in the state of Illinois 48203

Varnell GA

Praters Mill, c/o City Hall, Varnell, GA 30756 - T: (706) 694-6455, Fax: (706) 694-8413, E-mail: pratersmill@dalton.net, Internet: www.PratersMill.org
Science&Tech Museum - 1970
Horse-drawn farm implements 48204

Vasa MN

Vasa Lutheran Church Museum, County Rd 7, Vasa, MN 55089 - T: (612) 258-4327. Pres.: Everett Lindquist
Religious Arts Museum - 1930 48205

Vashon WA

Vashon Maury Island Heritage Museum, 10105 SW Bank Rd, Vashon, WA 98070 - T: (206) 463-7808
Local Museum - 1975
Pre-settlement, industry, agriculture 48206

Vaughan MS

Casey Jones Museum, Main St, Vaughan, MS 39179 - T: (601) 673-9864, Fax: (601) 653-6693, E-mail: holmesp@ayrix.net, Internet: www.trainweb.org/caseyjones/home/html
Science&Tech Museum - 1980 48207

Venice CA

Beyond Baroque Art Gallery, 681 Venice Blvd, Venice, CA 90291 - T: (310) 822-3006, Fax: (310) 827-7432, Internet: www.beyondbaroque.org. Dir.: Tosh Berman
Fine Arts Museum
Art gallery 48208

Ventura CA

San Buenaventura Mission Museum, 225 E Main St, Ventura, CA 93001-2622 - T: (805) 643-4318, Fax: (805) 643-7831, E-mail: mission@anacapa.net, Internet: www.anacapa.net/~mission. Dir.: Patrick J. O'Brien
Local Museum
Local hist, Indian artifacts, military, paintings 48209

Ventura College Art Galleries, 4667 Telegraph Rd, Ventura, CA 93003 - T: (805) 648-8974, Fax: (805) 654-6466. Dir.: Sheldon Hocking
Fine Arts Museum - 1970 48210

Ventura County Museum of History and Art, 100 E Main St, Ventura, CA 93001 - T: (805) 653-0323 ext 11, Fax: (805) 653-5267, E-mail: director@vcmha.org, Internet: www.vcmha.org. Dir.: Tim Schiffer, Cur.: Anne Graumlich
Fine Arts Museum / Historical Museum - 1913
Native American, Hispanic and American Settlers periods, contemporary California art, farming 48211

Vergennes VT

The Lake Champlain Maritime Museum, 4472 Basin Harbor Rd, Vergennes, VT 05491 - T: (802) 475-2022, Fax: (802) 475-2953, E-mail: info@lcmm.org, Internet: www.lcmm.org. Dir.: Arthur B. Cohn, Cons.: David Robinson
Archaeological Museum - 1985
Maritime and nautical archaeology 48212

Vermilion OH

Inland Seas Maritime Museum of The Great Lakes Historical Society, 480 Main St, Vermilion, OH 44089 - T: (440) 967-3467, Fax: (440) 967-1519, E-mail: glhs1@inlandseas.org, Internet: www.inlandseas.org. Pres.: Anthony F. Fugaro, Exec. Dir.: Christopher Gillerist
Historical Museum - 1944 48213

Vermillion SD

America's National Music Museum, 414 E Clark St, Vermillion, SD 57069-2390 - T: (605) 677-5306, Fax: (605) 677-5073, E-mail: smm@usd.edu, Internet: www.usd.edu/smm. Dir.: Dr. Andre P. Larson, Cur.: Dr. Margaret Downie Banks, Arian Sheets, Jayson Dobney, Dr. Sabine Klaus, Dr. Deborah Reeves, Cons.: John Koster
Music Museum - 1973
Musical instruments 48214

University Art Galleries, University of South Dakota, Warren M. Lee Center, 414 E Clark, Vermillion, SD 57069 - T: (605) 677-5481, Fax: (605) 677-5988, E-mail: jday@usd.edu, Internet: www.usd.edu/cfa/cfa.html. Dir.: John A. Day
Fine Arts Museum / University Museum - 1976 48215

W.H. Over Museum, 1110 Ratingen St, Vermillion, SD 57069 - T: (605) 677-5228, Internet: www.usd.edu/whover. Pres.: Maxine Johnson, C.E.O.: Dorothy E. Neuhaus
Local Museum / Natural History Museum - 1883
Local hist 48216

Vernal UT

Utah Field House of Natural History State Park, 235 E Main St, Vernal, UT 84078 - T: (435) 789-3799, Fax: (435) 789-4883, E-mail: ufsp@state.ut.us, Internet: www.nr.state.ut.us/parks/www1/utaf.htm. Head: Steven Sroka, Cur.: Sue Ann Bilbey
Natural History Museum - 1946
Natural hist 48217

Vernon TX

Red River Valley Museum, 4600 College Dr W, Vernon, TX 76384 - T: (817) 553-1848, Fax: (817) 553-1849, E-mail: museum@rrvm.org, Internet: www.rrvm.org. Pres.: Ruth Streit, Exec. Dir.: Mary Ann McCuistion
Historical Museum / Science&Tech Museum / Fine Arts Museum - 1963
History, science, fine arts 48218

Vernon VT

Vernon Historical Museum and Pond Road Chapel, 4201 Fort Bridgman Rd, Vernon, VT 05354 - T: (802) 254-8015, Fax: (802) 257-0292. Pres.: Robert E. Johnson
Local Museum - 1968
Local hist 48219

Vernon Hills IL

Cuneo Museum, 1350 N Milwaukee, Vernon Hills, IL 60061 - T: (847) 362-3042, 362-3054, Fax: (847) 362-4130, E-mail: cuneomandg@aol.com. Dir.: James Bert
Fine Arts Museum / Historical Museum - 1991 48220

Vernonia OR

Vernonia Historical Museum, 511 E Bridge St, Vernonia, OR 97064-1406 - T: (503) 429-3713, E-mail: cchsv@vernonia.com
Local Museum
Hist of Nehalem Valley pioneers 48221

Vero Beach FL

Center for the Arts, 3001 Riverside Park Dr, Vero Beach, FL 32963 - T: (772) 231-0707, Fax: (772) 231-0938, E-mail: info@verocfta.org, Internet: www.verocfta.org. Dir.: John Z. Lofgren, Cur.: Kerry Greaves
Fine Arts Museum - 1979
Art audiovisual and film, decorative arts, paintings, photographs, prints, drawings, graphic arts, sculpture 48222

McLarty Treasure Museum, 13180 Hwy A1A, Vero Beach, FL 32963-9400 - T: (561) 589-2147, Fax: (321) 984-4854. Dir.: Ed Perry
Historical Museum / Special Museum - 1970
History, Film, Spanish Shipwreck 48223

Versailles IN

Ripley County Historical Society Museum, Water and Main, Versailles, IN 47023. Dir.: Beatrice Boyd, Cur.: Kathleen Lane
Local Museum - 1930
Local history 48224

Vestal NY

Vestal Museum, 328 Vestal Pkwy E, Vestal, NY 13850 - T: (607) 748-1432, E-mail: vestalhistory@tier.net, Internet: www.tier.net/vestalhistory. Dir.: Jan Roosa, Cur.: Virginia Wood
Local Museum / Science&Tech Museum - 1976 48225

Vevay IN

Switzerland County Historical Society Museum, Main and Market Sts, Vevay, IN 47043 - T: (812) 427-3560, 427-3237. Pres.: Martha Bladen
Local Museum - 1925
General county history 48226

Vicksburg MS

Cairo Museum, 3201 Clay St, Vicksburg, MS 39180 - T: (601) 636-2199, Fax: (601) 638-7329, E-mail: vick_interpretation@nps.gov, Internet: www.nps.gov/vick. Cur.: Elizabeth Joyner
Historical Museum / Military Museum / Natural History Museum - 1980 48227

Cedar Grove Mansion Inn, 2200 Oak St, Vicksburg, MS 39180 - T: (601) 636-1000, Fax: (601) 634-6126, E-mail: info@cedargroveinn.com, Internet: cedargroveinn.com. Dir.: Ted Mackey, Estel Mackey
Historical Museum - 1959 48228

Old Court House Museum-Eva Whitaker Davis Memorial, 1008 Cherry St, Vicksburg, MS 39183 - T: (601) 636-0741, Internet: www.oldcourthouse.org. Dir.: Gordon A. Cotton, Ass. Dir.: Blanche S. Terry
Local Museum - 1947 48229

Vicksburg National Military Park-Cairo Museum, 3201 Clay St, Vicksburg, MS 39180 - T: (601) 636-0583, Fax: (601) 636-9497, Internet: www.nps.gov/vick. Head: William O. Nichols, Cur.: Elizabeth Joyner
Military Museum / Open Air Museum - 1899 48230

Victor NY

Ganondagan State Historic Site, 1488 State Rte 444, Victor, NY 14564 - T: (585) 924-5848, Fax: (585) 742-2353. Man.: Gerald Peter Jemison, Ass. Dir.: John L. Clancy
Historical Museum - 1972 48231

Valentown Museum, Valentown Sq, Victor, NY 14564 - T: (716) 924-4170. Dir.: Lilian Fisher
Local Museum - 1940 48232

Victoria TX

McNamara House Museum, 502 N Liberty, Victoria, TX 77901 - T: (512) 575-8227, Fax: (512) 575-8228, E-mail: vrma@viptx.net, Internet: www.viptx.net/museum/. Pres.: Denise McCue, Dir.: Dinah Mills
Historical Museum - 1959 48233

Nave Museum, 306 W Commercial, Victoria, TX 77901 - T: (512) 575-8227, Fax: (512) 575-8228, E-mail: vrma@viptx.net, Internet: www.viptx.net/museum/. Dir.: Dinah Mills, Cur.: Penelope Sherwood
Fine Arts Museum - 1976
Art 48234

Victorville CA

The Roy Rogers-Dale Evans Museum, 15650 Seneca Rd, Victorville, CA 92392 - T: (760) 243-4548, Fax: (760) 245-2009, E-mail: administrator@royrogers.com, Internet: www.royrogers.com. Pres.: Roy Rogers, Dir.: Cheryl Rogers-Barnett
Special Museum - 1967
Lives and careers of Western entertainers Roy Rogers and Dale Evans 48235

Villanova PA

Villanova University Art Gallery, 800 Lancaster Av, Villanova, PA 19085 - T: (610) 519-4610, Fax: (610) 519-6046, E-mail: maryanne.erwin@villanova.edu, Internet: www.artgallery.villanova.edu. Dir.: Richard G. Canulli
Public Gallery / University Museum 48236

Vinalhaven ME

The Vinalhaven Historical Society Museum, High St, Vinalhaven, ME 04863 - T: (207) 863-4410, E-mail: vhhissoc@midcoast.com, Internet: www.midcoast.com/~vhhissoc. Pres.: Wyman Philbrook
Historical Museum - 1963
Local history 48237

Vincennes IN

George Rogers Clark Park Museum, 401 S Second St, Vincennes, IN 47591 - T: (812) 882-1776, Fax: (812) 882-7270, E-mail: gero_administration.nsp.gov, Internet: www.nps.gov/gero. Dir.: Dale Phillips
Natural History Museum - 1967
American hist, American Revolution, military hist 18th c, frontier hist 18th c 48238

Indiana Territory Capitol, First and Harrison Sts, Vincennes, IN 47591 - T: (812) 882-7472, Fax: (812) 882-0928, Internet: www.state.in.us/ism/sites/vicennes/. Cur.: William V. Menke
Historical Museum - 1949 48239

Michel Brouillet House and Museum, 509 N 1st St, Vincennes, IN 47591 - T: (812) 882-7422. Cur.: Richard Day
Historical Museum - 1975
Furnishings, fur traders exh, Indian weapons, domestic utensils 48240

Old State Bank, 114 N Second St, Vincennes, IN 47591 - T: (812) 882-7472, Fax: (812) 882-0928, Internet: www.state.in.us/ism/sites/vincennes/. Cur.: William V. Menke
Special Museum - 1838 48241

William H. Harrison Museum/ Grouseland, 3 W Scott St, Vincennes, IN 47591 - T: (812) 882-2096, Fax: (812) 882-7626, E-mail: grouseland@wvc.net. Cur.: Dr. E. Joseph Fabyan
Historical Museum / Historic Site - 1911
Local history, William Henry Harrison mansion, Grouseland 48242

Virginia Beach VA

Adam Thoroughgood House, 1636 Parish Rd, Virginia Beach, VA 23455 - T: (757) 664-4000, Fax: (757) 431-3733, E-mail: mreed@vbgov.com. Dir.: Dr. William Hennessey, Dep. Dir.: Catherine H. Jordan Wass
Decorative Arts Museum / Local Museum - 1961
Historic house 48243

Atlantic Wildfowl Heritage Museum, 1113 Atlantic Av, Virginia Beach, VA 23451 - T: (757) 437-8432, Fax: (757) 437-9055, E-mail: atlanticwilfowl@rcn.com, Internet: www.awhm.org. Dir.: Thomas P. Beatty
Fine Arts Museum / Folklore Museum - 1995
Art and artifact concerning wildfowl 48244

Cape Henry Lighthouse, 583 Atlantic Av, Fort Story, Virginia Beach, VA 23459 - T: (757) 422-9421, Internet: www.apva.org. Pres.: Peter Knowles, Exec. Dir.: Elizabeth Kostelny
Local Museum - 1791
Local hist 48245

Contemporary Art Center of Virginia, 2200 Parks Av, Virginia Beach, VA 23451 - T: (757) 425-0000, Fax: (757) 425-8186, E-mail: info@cacv.org, Internet: www.cacv.org. Dir.: Cameron Kitchin, Cur.: Brenda LaBier
Fine Arts Museum - 1952
Art 48246

Francis Land House, 3131 Virginia Beach Blvd, Virginia Beach, VA 23452 - T: (804) 431-4000, Fax: (804) 431-3733, E-mail: mreed@vbgov.com. Head: Joseph J. Owens
Local Museum - 1986
Historic house 48247

Lynnhaven House, Association for the Preservation of Virginia Antiquities, 4405 Wishart Rd, Virginia Beach, VA 23455 - T: (757) 456-0351, 460-1688, Fax: (757) 456-0997, E-mail: ahb@bueche.com, Internet: www.apva.org. Exec. Dir.: Elizabeth Kostelny
Historic Site - 1976
Historic house 48248

Virginia Beach Maritime Museum, 24th St and Atlantic Av, Virginia Beach, VA 23451 - T: (757) 422-1587, Fax: (757) 491-8609, E-mail: FTylerVB2@aol.com, Internet: www.oldcoastguardstation.com. Exec. Dir.: Fielding L. Tyler
Science&Tech Museum - 1981
Maritime hist 48249

Virginia Marine Science Museum, 717 General Booth Blvd, Virginia Beach, VA 23451 - T: (757) 437-4949, Fax: (757) 437-4976, E-mail: fish@vbgov.com, Internet: www.vmsm.com. Dir.: Lynn B. Clements, Cur.: Maylon White, Ass. Cur.: Mark Swingle
Natural History Museum - 1986
Marine science 48250

Virginia City MT

Virginia City Madison County Historical Museum, Wallace St, Virginia City, MT 59755 - T: (406) 843-5500, 843-5484, Fax: (406) 843-5303, E-mail: madsnien@3rivers.net. Cur.: Daryl L. Tichenor
Local Museum - 1958 48251

Virginia City NV

Nevada State Fire Museum and Comstock Firemen's Museum, 125 S C St, Virginia City, NV 89440 - T: (775) 847-0454, Fax: (775) 847-9010, E-mail: mtwain1861@reno.quik.com, Internet: www.comstockfiremuseum.com. Dir.: Michael E. Nevin
Special Museum - 1979
Antique fire Apparatus 48252

Viroqua WI

Vernon County Museum, 410 S Center St, Viroqua, WI 54665 - T: (608) 637-7396, E-mail: vcmuseum@frontiernet.net, Internet: www.frontiernet.net/~vcmuseum. Dir.: Marcia Andrew, Cur.: Judy Mathison
Local Museum - 1942
Local hist 48253

Visalia CA

Tulare County Museum, 27000 S Mooney Blvd, Visalia, CA 93277 - T: (559) 733-6616, Fax: (559) 730-2653. Dir.: Kathy Howell
Local Museum - 1948
Local hist 48254

Vista CA

Antique Gas and Steam Engine Museum, 2040 N Santa Fe Av, Vista, CA 92083 - T: (760) 941-1791, Fax: (760) 941-0690, E-mail: rod@nctimes.net, Internet: www.agsem.com. Dir.: Rod Groenewold
Historical Museum - 1976
Industrial hist 48255

Volga SD

Brookings County Museum, 215 Samara Av, Volga, SD 57071 - T: (605) 627-9149. C.E.O. & Pres.: Lawrence Barnett
Local Museum - 1968
Local hist 48256

Volo IL

Volo Antique Auto Museum and Village, 27582 Volo Village Rd, Volo, IL 60073 - T: (815) 385-3644, Fax: (815) 385-0703, Internet: www.volocars.com. C.E.O.: Greg Grams
Science&Tech Museum / Folklore Museum - 1970
Automobile, village life 48257

Vulcan MI

Iron Mountain Iron Mine, Hwy U.S. 2, Vulcan, MI 49892 - T: (906) 774-7914, E-mail: ironmine@uplogon.com, Internet: www.ironmountainironmine.com. Dir.: Albert H. Carollo, Eugene R. Carollo
Science&Tech Museum - 1956
Mining, Menominee iron range 48258

Wabasso MN

Wabasso Historical Society Museum, South and Maple, Wabasso, MN 56293 - T: (507) 342-5367. Pres.: Armin Dallman
Historical Museum - 1973 48259

Waco TX

Armstrong Browning Library, c/o Baylor University, 710 Speight St, Waco, TX 76798 - T: (254) 710-3566, Fax: (254) 710-3552, E-mail: Kathleen_A_Miller@baylor.edu, Internet: www.browninglibrary.org. Dir.: Mairi C. Rennie, Cur.: Rita Patteson (Manuscripts), Cynthia Burgess (Books and Printed Materials)
University Museum / Library with Exhibitions - 1918
Library of Browningiana 48260

The Art Center of Waco, 1300 College Dr, Waco, TX 76708 - T: (254) 752-4371, Fax: (254) 752-3506, E-mail: info@artcenterwaco.org, Internet: www.artcenterwaco.org. Dir.: Mark A. Tullos
Fine Arts Museum - 1972
Art 48261

Dr Pepper Museum and Free Enterprise Institute, 300 S Fifth St, Waco, TX 76701 - T: (254) 757-1024, Fax: (254) 757-2221, E-mail: dp-info@drpeppermuseum.com, Internet: drpeppermuseum.com. Dir.: Jack McKinney, Cur.: Greg Shuman (Exhibitions)
Science&Tech Museum - 1989 48262

The Earle-Harrison House, 1901 N Fifth St, Waco, TX 76708 - T: (254) 753-2032, Fax: (360) 397-8896, E-mail: earleharrison@texnet.net, Internet: www.earleharrison.com. C.E.O.: Stanley A. Latham
Local Museum - 1956 48263

Martin Museum of Art, c/o Baylor University, Waco, TX 76789-7263 - T: (254) 710-1867, Fax: (254) 710-1566, E-mail: hornik@baylor.edu, Internet: www.baylor.edu/art. Dir.: Dr. Heidi Hornik
Fine Arts Museum / University Museum - 1967
Contemporary painting and sculpture, graphics, prints 48264

Mayborn Museum, c/o Baylor University, 410 S 4th St, Waco, TX 76798 - T: (254) 710-1110, Fax: (254) 710-1173, E-mail: Calvin_Smith@baylor.edu, Internet: diogenes.baylor.edu/WWWproviders/Strecker_Museum/. Dir.: Calvin B. Smith
Natural History Museum - 1893
Natural and cultural hist, science, zoology, herpetology, archaeology, antropology, botany, paleontology, botany, geology, mineralogy, numismatic 48265

Museum of Texas, 715 Columbus, Waco, TX 76702 - T: (254) 753-7395, Fax: (254) 753-2944, E-mail: library@gltexas.org. Cur.: Barbara Mechell
Historical Museum - 1936
History 48266

The Satirical World Art Museum, 201 J.H. Kulgen Hwy, Waco, TX 76706 - T: (888) 413-4064, Fax: (254) 754-0709. Head: Robert Dippel
Fine Arts Museum - 1996
Art 48267

Strecker Museum Complex, S 4th St, Baylor University, Waco, TX 76798 - T: (254) 710-1233, Fax: (254) 710-1173, E-mail: Calvin_Smith@baylor.edu, Internet: diogenes.baylor.edu/WWWproviders/Strecker_Museum/. Dir.: Calvin B. Smith, Cur.: Melinda Herzog
University Museum / Historical Museum / Natural History Museum - 1893
Natural Science, history 48268

Texas Ranger Hall of Fame and Museum, 100 Texas Ranger Trail, Waco, TX 76706 - T: (254) 750-8631, Fax: (254) 750-8629, E-mail: trhf@eramp.net, Internet: www.texasranger.org. Dir.: Byron A. Johnson
Historical Museum - 1968
Texas Ranger hist 48269

Texas Sports Hall of Fame, 1108 S University Parks Dr, Waco, TX 76706 - T: (254) 756-1633, Fax: (254) 756-2384, E-mail: info@hallofame.org, Internet: www.hallofame.org, www.tshof.org. Dir.: Steve Fallon, Cur.: Jay Black
Special Museum - 1989
Sports 48270

Waconia MN

Carver County Historical Society Museum, 555 W First St, Waconia, MN 55387-1203 - T: (612) 442-4234, Fax: (612) 442-3025, E-mail: historical@co.carver.mn.us. Exec. Dir.: Leanne Brown
Historical Museum - 1940 48271

Wadesboro NC

Anson County Historical Society Museum, 206 E Wade St, Wadesboro, NC 28170 - T: (704) 694-6694, Fax: (704) 694-3763, E-mail: achs@vnet.net, Internet: www.users.vnet.net/achs. Dir.: Paul W. Ricketts, Glenda A. Livingston
Local Museum - 1962 48272

Wahoo NE

Saunders County Historical Museum, 240 N Walnut, Wahoo, NE 68066 - T: (402) 443-3090, Internet: www.co.saunders.ne.us/museum.html. Pres.: Kenneth Schoen, Dir./Cur.: Erin Hauser
Historical Museum - 1963 48273

Wahpeton ND

Richland County Historical Museum, Second St and Seventh Av N, Wahpeton, ND 58075 - T: (701) 642-3075. Pres.: Reuben Brownlee
Local Museum - 1946 48274

Wailuku HI

Bailey House Museum, Mauri Historical Society, 2375a Main St, Wailuku, HI 96793 - T: (808) 244-3326, Fax: (808) 242-3920, E-mail: baileyhouse@aloha.net, Internet: www.mauimuseum.org. Exec. Dir.: Cathy Riley
Historical Museum - 1951 48275

Waipahu HI

Hawaii's Plantation Village, 94-695 Waipahu St, Waipahu, HI 96797 - T: (808) 677-0110, Fax: (808) 676-6727
Ethnology Museum - 1973
Ethnic and cultural materials 48276

Waitsfield VT

General Wait House, Rte 100, Waitsfield, VT 05673 - T: (802) 496-3733, Fax: (802) 496-3733
Decorative Arts Museum - 1970 48277

Wakefield KS

Wakefield Museum, 604 Sixth St, Wakefield, KS 67487-0101 - T: (785) 461-5516, E-mail: wakefieldmuseum@oz-online. Cur.: Lorraine Cowell
Local Museum - 1973
Hist of Wakefield, music, textiles, hats, toys, furniture, governor's desk, books, pictures, newspapers 48278

Wakefield MA

Wakefield Historical Museum, Americal Civic Center, 467 Main St, Wakefield, MA 01880 - T: (781) 245-0549, Internet: www.wakefieldma.org. Pres.: Betty Troughton, Cur.: David A. Workman
Local Museum - 1890
Local history 48279

Wakefield RI

Hera Gallery, 327 Main St, Wakefield, RI 02880-0336 - T: (401) 789-1488. Dir.: Katherine Veneman
Public Gallery - 1974 48280

Walden NY

Jacob Walden House, 34 N Montgomery St, Walden, NY 12586 - T: (845) 778-5862. Pres.: Patricia Eisley
Local Museum - 1958 48281

Walhalla ND

Gingras Trading Post, 10534 129 Av NE, Walhalla, ND 58282 - T: (701) 328-1476, Fax: (701) 328-3710, E-mail: rcollin@state.nd.us, Internet: discovernd.com/history
Special Museum - 1956
Fur trade, Antoine Gingras 48282

Walker MN

Walker Wildlife and Indian Artifacts Museum, State Hwy 200, Walker, MN 56484, mail addr: POB 505, Walker, MN 56484 - T: (218) 547-7251
Natural History Museum / Ethnology Museum - 1937
Animals, Indian handicraft, mainly Ojibway/Chibbewa, butterflies, geology, hist, mineralogy 48283

Walla Walla WA

Carnegie Art Center, 109 S Palouse, Walla Walla, WA 99362 - T: (509) 525-4270, E-mail: cac@hscis.net. Dir.: Heidi Thomas
Public Gallery - 1970 48284

Fort Walla Walla Museum, 755 Myra Rd, Walla Walla, WA 99362 - T: (509) 525-7703, Fax: (509) 525-7798, E-mail: info@fortwallawallamuseum.org, Internet: www.fortwallawallamuseum.org. Exec. Dir.: James Payne
Historical Museum - 1968
Pioneer village, agriculture, local hist 48285

Sheehan Gallery at Whitman College, Olin Hall, 814 Isaacs st, Walla Walla, WA 99362 - T: (509) 527-5249, Fax: (509) 527-5039, E-mail: baydenik@whitman.edu, Internet: www.whitman.edu/sheehan. Dir.: Ian Bayden, Sc. Staff: Thomas E. Cronin (Collections)
Fine Arts Museum / University Museum - 1972
Art 48286

Wallace ID

Wallace District Mining Museum, 509 Bank St, Wallace, ID 83873 - T: (208) 556-1592. Pres.: Donald C. Springer, C.E.O.: John Amonson
Science&Tech Museum - 1956 48287

Wallingford CT

Wallingford Historical Society Museum, 180 S Main St, Wallingford, CT 06492 - T: (203) 294-1996. Pres.: Robert N. Beaumont
Local Museum / Historical Museum - 1916
Local hist 48288

Walloomsac NY

Bennington Battlefield Exhibition, Rte 67, Walloomsac, NY 12133, mail addr: POB 163, Long Pond Rd, Grafton, NY 12082 - T: (518) 279-1155, Fax: (518) 279-1902, E-mail: laura.conner@oprhp.state.ny.us
Historical Museum - 1927
1777 Revolutionary War battle site, prints, sculptures 48289

Walnut Creek CA

Bedford Gallery at the Dean Lesher Regional Center for the Arts, 1601 Civic Dr, Walnut Creek, CA 94596 - T: (925) 295-1417, Fax: (925) 295-1486, E-mail: lederer@ci.walnut-creek.ca.us, Internet: www.dlrca.org. Cur.: Carrie Lederer
Fine Arts Museum / Folklore Museum - 1963 48290

Lindsay Wildlife Museum, 1931 First Av, Walnut Creek, CA 94596 - T: (925) 935-1978, Fax: (925) 935-8015, E-mail: webmaster@wildlife-museum.org, Internet: www.wildlife-museum.org. Exec. Dir.: Eunice E. Valentine, Cur.: Suzanne Mahaffay
Natural History Museum - 1955
Natural hist, live native Califonia wildlife 48291

Walnut Grove MN

Laura Ingalls Wilder Museum, 330 Eighth St, Walnut Grove, MN 56180 - T: (507) 859-2358 and 2155, Fax: (507) 859-2933, E-mail: liw@rconnect.com, Internet: www.walnutgrove.org. Dir.: Stanley Gordon
Local Museum - 1975 48292

Walsenburg CO

The Walsenburg Mining Museum and Fort Francisco Museum of La Veta, 112 W Fifth St, Walsenburg, CO 81089 - T: (719) 738-1992, Fax: (719) 738-6218. Dir.: Jeanette Johannessen, Pam Munroe
Science&Tech Museum / Historical Museum - 1987
Mining, history 48293

Walterboro SC

Colleton Museum, 239 N Jeffries Blvd, Walterboro, SC 29488 - T: (803) 549-2303, Fax: (803) 549-7215, E-mail: museum@lowcountry.com. Dir.: Martha Creighton
Local Museum - 1985
Local hist 48294

South Carolina Artisans Center, 334 Wichman St, Walterboro, SC 29488 - T: (843) 549-0011, Fax: (843) 549-7433, E-mail: artisan@lowcountry.com, Internet: www.southcarolinacenter.org. Dir.: Denise P. Simmons
Decorative Arts Museum / Folklore Museum - 1994
Arts and crafts, drawings, ceramics, decorative and folk arts 48295

Waltham MA

Charles River Museum of Industry, 154 Moody St, Waltham, MA 02154 - T: (781) 893-5410, Fax: (781) 891-4536, E-mail: charles_river@msn.com, Internet: www.crmi.org. Pres.: Arthur Nelson, Exec. Dir.: Karen M. LeBlanc
Science&Tech Museum - 1980
Textile, industry, innovation 48296

Gore Place, 52 Gore St, Waltham, MA 02453 - T: (781) 894-2798, Fax: (781) 894-5745, E-mail: info@goreplace.org, Internet: www.goreplace.org. Dir.: Susan Robertson, Cur.: Susanne Olson
Historical Museum - 1935
History 48297

Rose Art Museum, Brandeis University, 415 South St, Waltham, MA 02254-9110 - T: (781) 736-3434, Fax: (781) 736-3439, E-mail: jketner@brandeis.edu, Internet: www.brandeis.edu/rose. Dir.: Joseph D. Ketner
Fine Arts Museum / University Museum - 1961
Art 48298

Waltham Historical Society Museum, 190 Moody St, Waltham, MA 02453-5300 - T: (781) 891-5815, Internet: www.walthamhistoricalsociety.org. Pres.: Joan Sheridan, Cur.: Wayne McCarthy
Local Museum - 1913
Local history, 1813 Francis Cabot Lowell Mill 48299

The Waltham Museum, 196 Charles St, Waltham, MA 02543 - T: (781) 893-8017, E-mail: nancynatick@aol.com, Internet: www.walthammuseum.com. Pres./Dir.: Albert A. Arena
Local Museum - 1971
Local history, 1870 James Baker house 48300

Wamego KS

The Columbian Museum and Art Center, 521 Lincoln Av, Wamego, KS 66547 - T: (785) 456-2029, Fax: (785) 456-9498, E-mail: ctheatre@kansas.net, Internet: www.wamego.com. Exec. Dir.: Barbara Hopper
Fine Arts Museum / Decorative Arts Museum - 1990
Decorative arts 48301

Wapakoneta OH

Neil Armstrong Air and Space Museum, I-75 and Bellefontaine Rd, Wapakoneta, OH 45895 - T: (419) 738-8811, Fax: (419) 738-3361, E-mail: namu@ohiohistory.org, Internet: ohiohistory.org. Dir.: John Zwez
Science&Tech Museum - 1972 48302

Warm Springs GA

Little White House, 401 Little White House Rd, Warm Springs, GA 31830 - T: (706) 655-5870, Fax: (706) 655-5872, E-mail: lwhs@peachnet.campus.mci.net, Internet: www.fdr_littlewhitehouse.org. Head: Frankie Mewborn
Historical Museum - 1946
Georgia home of Pres. Roosevelt, where he died April 12, 1945 48303

Warm Springs OR

The Museum at Warm Springs, 2189 Hwy 26, Warm Springs, OR 97761 - T: (514) 553-3331, Fax: (514) 553-3338, E-mail: museum@madras.net. Exec.Dir.: Carol Leone, Cur.: Natalie Kirk
Ethnology Museum - 1991
Tribal culture, ethnology, archaeology, history, folklore 48304

Warner OK

Wallis Museum at Connors State College, Rte 1, Box 1000, Warner, OK 74469 - T: (918) 463-2931, Fax: (918) 463-6272, E-mail: rmcclur@connors.cc.ok.us, Internet: www.connors.cc.ok.us. C.E.O.: Don Nero, Cur.: Richard McClure
University Museum / Local Museum - 1963 48305

Warner Robins GA

Museum of Aviation at Robins Air Force Base, Hwy 247 and Russell Pkwy, Warner Robins, GA 31099 - T: (478) 923-6600, Fax: (478) 923-8807, E-mail: moaoffice@mindspring.com, Internet: www.museumofaviation.org. Dir.: Wayne W. Schmidt, Cur.: Darwin Edwards
Science&Tech Museum / Military Museum - 1984
Aviation since WWII 48306

Warren ME

Warren Historical Museum, 225 Main St, Warren, ME 04864 - T: (207) 273-2726. Pres.: Dick Ferren, Cur.: Barbara Larson
Local Museum - 1964
Regional history 48307

Warren MI

Ukrainian-American Museum, 26601 Ryan Rd, Warren, MI 48091 - T: (810) 757-8130, 978-9239, Fax: (810) 757-8684. Cur.: Irene Zacharkiw
Military Museum - 1958
Ukrainian military in WW 1, art 48308

Warren MN

Marshall County Historical Society Museum, POB 103, Warren, MN 56762 - T: (218) 745-4803. Pres.: Delvin Potucek, Dir./Cur.: Ethel Thorlacius
Historical Museum - 1920
Antique farm machinery, business, household 48309

Warren OH

John Stark Edwards House, 303 Monroe St NW, Warren, OH 44483 - T: (330) 394-4653. Pres.: David Ambrose, Cur.: Warren Hickman
Local Museum - 1938 48310

National Packard Museum, 1899 Mahoning Av NW, Warren, OH 44483, mail addr: POB 1416, Warren, OH 44482 - T: (330) 394-1899, Fax: (330) 394-7796, E-mail: national@packardmuseum.org, Internet: www.packardmuseum.org. Cur.: Mary Ann Propri
Science&Tech Museum - 1989
Packard motor car, Packard Electric, Ohio Lamp hist 48311

Warren PA

Crary Art Gallery, 511 Market St, Warren, PA 16365 - T: (814) 723-4523. Pres./Cur.: Ann Lesser
Fine Arts Museum - 1977 48312

Warren County Museum, 210 Fourth Av, Warren, PA 16365 - T: (814) 723-1795, E-mail: warrenhistory@kinzua.net, Internet: www.kinzua.net/warrenhistory/. Pres.: John Mangus, Exec. Dir.: Rhonda J. Hoover
Local Museum - 1900
Local hist 48313

Warrensburg MO

Art Center Gallery, Central Missouri State University, 217 Clark St, Warrensburg, MO 64093-5246 - T: (660) 543-4498, Fax: (660) 543-8006, E-mail: gallatin@cmsu1.cmsu.edu, Internet: www.cmsu.edu. Dir.: Morgan Dean Gallatin
Fine Arts Museum - 1984 48314

Central Missouri State University Archives and Museum, James C. Kirkpatrick, Warrensburg, MO 64093-5040 - T: (660) 543-4649. Dir.: John W. Sheets, Ass. Dir.: Vivian Richardson
University Museum / Local Museum / Natural History Museum - 1968 48315

Johnson County Historical Society Museum, 302 N Main St, Warrensburg, MO 64093 - T: (660) 747-6480, Internet: www.digitalhistory.com. Pres.: Clayta Downing
Local Museum - 1920 48316

Warrenton VA

The Old Jail Museum, 10 Waterloo St, Warrenton, VA 20188 - T: (540) 347-5525, E-mail: oldjailmuseum@erols.com. Dir.: Jackie Lee
Local Museum - 1964
Local history, jail 48317

Warsaw NY

Warsaw Historical Museum, 15 Perry Av, Warsaw, NY 14569 - T: (716) 786-5240, E-mail: mhconable@wycol.com. Pres.: Mary Conable
Local Museum - 1938 48318

Warwick MD

Old Bohemia Historical Museum, Bohemia Church Rd, Warwick, MD 21912 - T: (302) 378-5800, Fax: (302) 378-5808, E-mail: office@stjosephmiddletown.com, Internet: www.stjosephmiddletown.com. Pres.: Margaret Matyniak
Local Museum / Religious Arts Museum - 1953
Religious artifacts (liturgical vessels, vestments, prayer books, devotional articles), farm conveyances and tools, historic cemetery 48319

Warwick NY

Pacem in Terris, 96 Covered Bridge Rd, Warwick, NY 10990 - T: (914) 986-4329. Dir.: Dr. Frederick Franck, Dep. Dir.: Claske Berndes
Local Museum - 1972 48320

Town of Warwick Museum, POB 353, Warwick, NY 10990 - T: (914) 986-3236. Pres.: Henry L. Neilsen
Historical Museum - 1906 48321

Warwick RI

Art Department Gallery, Community College of Rhode Island, 400 East Av, Warwick, RI 02886 - T: (401) 825-2220, Fax: (401) 825-1148, Internet: www.ccri.cc.ri.us. Chm.: Nichola Sevigney
Public Gallery - 1972 48322

Warwick Museum of Art, Kentish Artillery Armory, 3259 Post Rd, Warwick, RI 02886 - T: (401) 737-0010, Fax: (401) 737-1796, E-mail: warwickmuseum@hotmail.com. Dir.: Edward McGinley
Fine Arts Museum - 1973
Art 48323

Waseca MN

Farmamerica, County Rds 2 and 17, Waseca, MN 56093 - T: (507) 835-2052, Fax: (507) 835-2053, E-mail: farmamer@mnic.net, Internet: www.farmamerica.org. Exec. Dir.: Kathleen L. Backer
Agriculture Museum - 1978 48324

Waseca County Historical Society Museum, 315 Second Av NE, Waseca, MN 56093 - T: (507) 835-7700, E-mail: director@historical.waseca.mn.us, Internet: www.historical.waseca.mn.us. Pres.: Donald Wynnemer, C.E.O.: Margaret Sinn
Historical Museum - 1938
library, archives 48325

Washburn ND

McLean County Historical Society Museum, 605 Main St, Washburn, ND 58577 - T: (701) 462-3744, E-mail: vmerkel@westriv.com. Pres.: Dan Wieklander
Local Museum - 1967 48326

Washburn WI

Washburn Historical Museum, 1 E Bayfield St, Washburn, WI 54891 - T: (715) 373-5591
Local Museum - 1991
Area hist, industries and people, paintings 48327

Washington AR

Old Washington Museum, 4954 Hwy 278, Washington, AR 71862 - T: (870) 983-2684, 983-2278, Fax: (870) 983-2736, E-mail: oldwashington@arkansas.com, Internet: www.arkansasstateparks.com. Cur.: Glenda Friend
Historical Museum - 1973
History, located in 1824 town 48328

Washington CT

Gunn Memorial Library and Museum, 5 Wykeham Rd, Washington, CT 06793 - T: (860) 868-7756, Fax: (860) 868-7247, E-mail: gunnmus@biblio.org, Internet: www.biblio.org/gunn. Dir.: Jean Chapin, Cur.: Bruce Reinholdt, Ass. Cur.: Suzanne Fateh
Local Museum - 1899
Local hist 48329

Washington DC

AAF Museum, 1735 New York Av NW, Washington, DC 20006-5292 - T: (202) 626-7500, Fax: (202) 879-7764, Internet: www.aaspages.org
Archaeological Museum / Decorative Arts Museum
Archaeology, decorative arts 48330

American Red Cross Museum, 1730 E St NW, Washington, DC 20006 - T: (202) 639-3300, Fax: (202) 628-1362, E-mail: askmuseum@usa.redcross.org, Internet: www.redcross.org. Exec. Dir.: Steven E. Shulman
Historical Museum - 1919
Paintings, decorative arts, uniforms, manuscripts, memorabilia - archives 48331

Anacostia Museum, 1901 Fort Pl SE, Washington, DC 20560-0004 - T: (202) 287-3306, Fax: (202) 287-3183, Internet: www.si.edu. Dir.: Steven C. Newsome, Dep. Dir.: Sharon Reinckens
Fine Arts Museum / Historical Museum - 1967
African American hist and culture 48332

Archives of American Art, Smithsonian Institution, 750 Ninth St NW, Ste 2200, Washington, DC 20560-0937 - T: (202) 275-1950, Fax: (202) 275-1955, E-mail: aaaemref@aaa.si.edu, Internet: www.archivesofamericanart.si.edu. Dir.: Dr. Richard J. Wattenmaker, Ass. Dir.: James B. Byers (Archival Programs), Jody Pettibone (Operations), Dr. Jeanne Baker Driscoll (Development)
Library with Exhibitions - 1954
Letters and diaries of artists and craft persons, critics, works on paper, photographs, recorded interviews 48333

Art Museum of the Americas, 201 18th St NW, Washington, DC 20006 - T: (202) 458-6016/19, Fax: (202) 458-6021, E-mail: fsader@oas.org, Internet: www.oas.org. Dir.: Ana Maria Escallon, Cur.: Maria Leyva (Permanent Collection), Fabian Gonzalas (Temporary Exhibits), Cons.: Lionel Najera
Fine Arts Museum - 1976
Latin American contemporary art 48334

Arthur M. Sackler Gallery, 1050 Independence Av SW, Washington, DC 20560 - T: (202) 357-4880, Fax: (202) 357-4911, Internet: www.si.edu/asia. Dir.: Dr. Milo C. Beach, Dep. Dir.: Dr. Thomas Lentz, Cur.: Louise Cort (Ceramics), Dr. Vidya Dehejia (South and South East Asian Art), Dr. Jenny So (Ancient Chinese Art), Dr. James Ulak (Japanese Art), Ass. Cur.: Jan Stuart (Chinese Art)
Fine Arts Museum / Folklore Museum - 1982
Art 48335

Arts Club of Washington, 2017 I St NW, Washington, DC 20006 - T: (202) 331-7282, Fax: (202) 857-3678, E-mail: artsclub.membership@verizon.net, Internet: www.artsclubofwashington.org. Dir.: Charles Futzel
Historic Site / Fine Arts Museum - 1916 48336

Arts in the Academy, c/o National Academy of Sciences, 2101 Constitution Av NW, Washington, DC 20418 - T: (202) 334-2436, Fax: (202) 334-1210, E-mail: jtomlins@nas.edu. Dir.: Dr. Janis A. Tomlinson
Fine Arts Museum
Science related art 48337

B'nai B'rith Klutznick National Jewish Museum, 2020 K St NW, Washington, DC 20036 - T: (202) 857-6583, Fax: (202) 857-2700, E-mail: museum@bnaibrith.org, Internet: www.bbinet.org. Cur.: Elizabeth Kessin Berman
Fine Arts Museum / Folklore Museum - 1957
Folk art and fine art 48338

Canadian Embassy Art Gallery, 501 Pennsylvania Av NW, Washington, DC 20001 - T: (202) 682-1740, Fax: (202) 682-7791, Internet: www.canadianembassy.org
Public Gallery 48339

Capital Children's Museum, 800 3rd St NE, Washington, DC 20002 - T: (202) 675-4120, Fax: (202) 675-4140, E-mail: information@ccm.org, Internet: www.ccm.org. Pres.: Kathy Dwyer Southern
Special Museum - 1974 48340

Communications and History Museum of Sutton, 17th St and New York Av, Washington, DC 20006 - T: (202) 639-1700, Fax: (202) 639-1768. Pres./ Dir.: David C. Levy, Dep. Dir.: Jack Cowart, Cur.: Terrie Sultan (Contemporary Art), Philip Brookman (Photo and Media Arts), Sarah Cash (American Art), Susan Badder (Education)
Fine Arts Museum / Decorative Arts Museum - 1869 48341

The Corcoran Gallery of Art, 500 17th St and New York Av, Washington, DC 20006 - T: (202) 639-1701, Fax: (202) 639-1768, E-mail: jcowan@corcoran.org, Internet: www.corcoran.org. Dir.: David C. Levy, Cur.: Sarah Cash (American Art), Philip Brookman (Photography and Media Arts), Eric Denker (Prints and Drawings), Terrie Sultan (Contemporary Art)
Fine Arts Museum - 1869
Art 48342

Dadian Gallery, Wesley Theological Seminary Center for the Arts and Religion, 4500 Massachusetts Av NW, Washington, DC 20016 - T: (202) 885-8674, Fax: (202) 885-8683, E-mail: dsokolove@wesleysem.edu, Internet: www.wesleysem.edu/car. Dir.: Catherine Kapinan, Cur.: Deborah Soklove
Fine Arts Museum / Religious Arts Museum - 1989 48343

Daughters of the American Revolution Museum, 1776 D St NW, Washington, DC 20006 - T: (202) 879-3241, Fax: (202) 628-0820, E-mail: museum@dar.org, Internet: www.dar.org. Dir.: Diane L. Dunkley, Cur.: Olive Graffam (Collections), Nancy Tuckhorn (Textiles), Ass. Cur.: Karen Hibbitt
Decorative Arts Museum / Historical Museum - 1890
Decorative arts, history 48344

Decatur House Museum, 748 Jackson Pl NW, Washington, DC 20006 - T: (202) 842-0920, Fax: (202) 842-0030, E-mail: decatur_house@nthp.org, Internet: www.decaturhouse.org. Exec. Dir.: Cynthia B. Malinick
Decorative Arts Museum - 1956
Decorative art, porcellain 48345

Department of the Treasury Museum, 15th and Pennsylvania NW, Washington, DC 20220 - T: (202) 622-1250, Fax: (202) 622-2294, E-mail: richard.cote@do.treas.gov, Internet: www.ustreas.gov/curator. Cur.: Richard Cote
Decorative Arts Museum / Fine Arts Museum / Historical Museum
19th - 20th c furniture, artwork, portraits 48346

Dimock Gallery, c/o George Washington University, 730 21st St NW, Washington, DC 20052 - T: (202) 994-1525, 994-7091, Fax: (202) 994-1632, E-mail: ldmiller@gwu.edu, Internet: www.gwu.edu/~dimock. Dir./Cur.: Lenore D. Miller
Fine Arts Museum / University Museum - 1966
Art 48347

Discovery Creek Children's Museum of Washington DC, 4954 MacArthur Blvd NW, Washington, DC 20007 - T: (202) 364-3111, Fax: (202) 364-3114, E-mail: mail@discoverycreek.org, Internet: www.discoverycreek.org. C.E.O.: Susan M. Seligmann
Special Museum - 1991 48348

District of Columbia Arts Center, 2438 18th St NW, Washington, DC 20009 - T: (202) 462-7833, Fax: (202) 328-7099, E-mail: dcac@dcartscenter.org, Internet: www.dcartscenter.org. Dir.: B. Stanley
Public Gallery - 1989 48349

Dumbarton House, 2715 Que St NW, Washington, DC 20007-3071 - T: (202) 337-2288, Fax: (202) 337-0348, E-mail: pr@dumbartonhouse.org, Internet: www.dumbartonhouse.org. Dir.: William S. Birdseye
Historical Museum - 1891
Historic house 48350

Dumbarton Oaks Collections, Harvard University, 1703 32nd St NW, Washington, DC 20007 - T: (202) 339-6400, Fax: (202) 339-6419, E-mail: dumbartonoaks@doaks.org, Internet: www.doaks.org. Dir.: Edward Keenan, Cur.: Jeffrey Quilter (Pre-Columbian Collection), Susan Boyd (Byzantine Collection)
Fine Arts Museum - 1940
Art 48351

Explorers Hall, National Geographic Society, 1145 17th St NW, Washington, DC 20036 - T: (202) 857-7588, 857-7456, Fax: (202) 857-5864, Internet: www.nationalgeographic.com. Pres.: John M. Fahey, Dir.: Susan E.S. Norton
Natural History Museum / Science&Tech Museum - 1964
Science, geography, expedition equipment 48352

Federal Reserve Board Art Gallery, 20 and C Sts NW, Washington, DC 20551 - T: (202) 452-3000, Fax: (202) 452-5680, Internet: www.federalreserve.gov. Dir.: Mary Anne Goley
Fine Arts Museum - 1975 48353

Fondo Del Sol, Visual Art and Media Center, 2112 R St NW, Washington, DC 20008 - T: (202) 483-2777, Fax: (202) 658-1078. Dir.: W. Marc Zuver
Public Gallery - 1973 48354

Ford's Theatre, Lincoln Museum, 511 10th St NW, Washington, DC 20004 - T: (202) 426-6924, Fax: (202) 426-1845, E-mail: ford's_theatre@nps.gov, Internet: www.nps.gov/foth/index.htm. Dir.: Terry Carlstrom
Performing Arts Museum - 1933
History 48355

Frederick Douglass National Historic Site, 1411 W St SE, Washington, DC 20020 - T: (202) 426-5961, 426-1452, Fax: (202) 426-0880, E-mail: NACE_Frederick_Douglass_NHS@nps.gov, Internet: www.cr.nps.gov/csd/exhibits/douglass. Man.: Kym Elder, Cur.: Cathy Ingram
Historic Site - 1916
History 48356

Freer Gallery of Art, Jefferson Dr at 12th St SW, Washington, DC 20560 - T: (202) 357-4880, Fax: (202) 357-4911, E-mail: arnolje@asia.si.edu, Internet: www.si.edu/asia. Dir.: Dr. Julian Raby, Dep. Dir.: Dr. Thomas Lentz, Chief Cur.: Dr. Vidya Dehejia (South and Southeast Asian Art), Cur.: Dr. James Ulak (Japanese Art), Dr. Jenny So (Ancient Chinese Art), Dr. Linda Merrill (American Art), Louise Cort (Ceramics), Ass. Cur.: Jan Stuart (Chinese Art)
Fine Arts Museum - 1906
Art 48357

Georgetown University Art Collection, 3700 O St NW, Washington, DC 20057-1006 - T: (202) 687-1469, Fax: (202) 687-7501, E-mail: llw@georgetown.edu, Internet: www.library.georgetown.edu/det/speccoll/guac. Dir.: George Martin Barringer, Coord.: Lulen Walker, Sc. Staff: David Alan
Fine Arts Museum / University Museum - 1789
Art 48358

Heurich House Museum, 1307 New Hampshire Av NW, Washington, DC 20036 - T: (202) 785-2068, Fax: (202) 887-5785, E-mail: heurich@ibm.net, Internet: www.hswdc.org. Exec. Dir.: Barbara Franco
Local Museum - 1894
Local hist 48359

Hillwood Museum, Hillwood Museum Foundation, 4155 Linnean Av NW, Washington, DC 20008 - T: (202) 686-8500, Fax: (202) 966-7846, E-mail: admin@hillwoodmuseum.org, Internet: www.hillwoodmuseum.org. Exec. Dir.: Frederick J. Fisher
Decorative Arts Museum - 1976
Decorative art - Library, archives 48360

Hirshhorn Museum and Sculpture Garden, Smithsonian Institution, Seventh St and Independence Av SW, Washington, DC 20560 - T: (202) 357-3091, Fax: (202) 786-2682, E-mail: lawrence_s@hmsg.si.edu, Internet: www.hirshhorn.si.edu. Dir.: Ned Rifkin, Chief Cur.: Kerry Brougher, Chief Cons.: Susan Lake
Fine Arts Museum - 1966
Art 48361

Howard University Gallery of Art, 2455 6th St NW, Washington, DC 20059 - T: (202) 806-7070, Fax: (202) 806-6503, Internet: www.howarduniversity.edu. Dir.: Dr. Tritobia H. Benjamin, Ass. Dir.: Scott Baker
Fine Arts Museum / University Museum - 1928
Art 48362

Howard University Museum, c/o Moorland Spingarn Research Center, 500 Howard Pl NW, Washington, DC 20059 - T: (202) 806-7239, Fax: (202) 806-6405, Internet: www.founders.howard.edu/moorland-spingarn. Dir.: Dr. Thomas C. Battle
University Museum / Historical Museum - 1914
Black hist 48363

Jackson Art Center, Jackson School, 3048 1/2 R St NW, Washington, DC 20007 - T: (202) 342-9778
Public Gallery 48364

The Kreeger Museum, 2401 Foxhall Rd NW, Washington, DC 20007 - T: (202) 337-3050, Fax: (202) 337-3051, E-mail: publicrelations@kreegermuseum.com, Internet: www.kreegermuseum.com. Dir.: Judy A. Greenberg
Fine Arts Museum - 1994
Art 48365

Lillian and Albert Small Jewish Museum, 701 Third St NW, Washington, DC 20001 - T: (202) 789-0900, Fax: (202) 789-0485, E-mail: info@jhsgw.org, Internet: www.jhsgw.org. Exec. Dir.: Laura C. Apelbaum, Pres.: Richard Alper
Religious Arts Museum / Historical Museum - 1975 48366

Marine Corps Art Collection, Bldg 58 Washington Navy Yard, Washington, DC 20374 - T: (202) 433-3840, Fax: (202) 433-7265. Dir.: John W. Ripley
Fine Arts Museum - 1970
Art work by Marines, military music, combat art, historical illustrations, prints cartoons, recruiting posters, sculptures 48367

Mary McLeod Bethune House, 1318 Vermont Av NW, Washington, DC 20005 - T: (202) 673-2402, Fax: (202) 673-2414, Internet: www.nps.gov/mamc. Dir.: Terry Carlstrom
Local Museum - 1979 48368

Meridian International Center - Cafritz Galleries, 1624-30 Crescent Pl NW, Washington, DC 20009 - T: (202) 939-5568, Fax: (202) 319-1306, E-mail: nmatthew@meridian.org, Internet: www.meridan.org. Pres.: Walter L. Cutler, Dir.: Nancy Matthews
Fine Arts Museum / Folklore Museum - 1960
International arts and culture 48369

Museum of Contemporary Art, 1054 31st St NW, Washington, DC 20007 - T: (202) 342-6230
Fine Arts Museum 48370

National Air and Space Museum, Smithsonian Institution, Sixth St and Independence Av SW, Washington, DC 20560 - T: (202) 357-1745, Fax: (202) 357-2426, E-mail: nasm@nasm.si.edu, Internet: www.nasm.si.edu. Dir.: John R. Dailey, Dep. Dir.: Donald Lopez
Science&Tech Museum - 1946
Aeronautics 48371

National Building Museum, 401 F St NW, Washington, DC 20001 - T: (202) 272-2448, Fax: (202) 272-2564, E-mail: jdixon@nbm.org, Internet: www.nbm.org. Pres.: Susan Henshaw Jones
Fine Arts Museum - 1980
Architecture 48372

National Gallery of Art, 6 Constitution Av at Fourth St. NW, Washington, DC 20565 - T: (202) 737-4215, Fax: (202) 842-2356, Internet: www.nga.gov. Pres.: Robert H. Smith, Dir.: Earl A. Powell, Dep. Dir./Chief Cur.: Alan Shestack, Sen. Cur.: Andrew C. Robison, Cur.: Franklin Kelly (American and British Paintings), Arthur Wheelock (Northern Baroque Paintings), John Hand (Northern Renaissance Paintings), David Alan

Brown (Italian Renaissance Paintings), Philip Conisbee (French Paintings), Alison Luchs (Sculpture and Decorative Arts), Jeffrey Weiss (20th-Century Art), Peter Parshall (Old Master Prints), Margaret Morgan Grasselli (Old Master Drawings), Ruth Fine (Modern Prints and Drawings), Sarah Greenough (Photographs), Ruth T. Philbrick (Photographic Archives), Chief Cons.: Ross Merrill
Fine Arts Museum - 1937
Art 48373

National Museum of African Art, Smithsonian Institution, 950 Independence Av SW, Washington, DC 20560-0708 - T: (202) 357-4600, 357-1300, Fax: (202) 357-4879, E-mail: nmafaweb@nmafa.si.edu, Internet: www.si.edu/nmafa. Dir.: Roslyn A. Walker, Ass. Dir.: Patricia Fiske, Chief Cur.: David Binkley, Cur.: Lydia Puccinelli, Bryna Freyer, Ass. Cur.: Andrea Nicolls, Cons.: Stephen Mellor
Fine Arts Museum / Folklore Museum - 1964
Art 48374

National Museum of American Art, Eighth and G Sts NW, Washington, DC 20001 - T: (202) 633-8998, Internet: www.nmaa.si.edu
Fine Arts Museum 48375

National Museum of American History, Smithsonian Institution, 14th St and Constitution Av NW, Washington, DC 20560 - T: (202) 357-2700, Fax: (202) 357-1853, E-mail: infi@si.edu, Internet: americanhistory.si.edu. Dir.: Marc Pachter, Dep. Dir.: Martha Morris
Historical Museum - 1846
American hist 48376

National Museum of American Jewish Military History, 1811 R St NW, Washington, DC 20009 - T: (202) 265-6280, Fax: (202) 462-3192, E-mail: jwv@erols.com, Internet: www.nmajmh.org. Pres.: Edwin Goldwasser, Exec. Dir.: Herb Rosenbleeth
Historical Museum / Military Museum - 1958
American Jewish military hist 48377

National Museum of Health and Medicine, Armed Forces Institute of Pathology, 6900 Georgia Av and Elder St NW, Washington, DC 20307 - T: (202) 782-2200, Fax: (202) 782-3573, E-mail: nmhminfo@afip.osd.mil, Internet: www.natmedmuse.afip.org. Dir.: Adrianne Noe, Cur.: Paul Sledzik (Anatomy), Archie Fobbs (Neuropathology), Alan Hawk (History), Michael Rhode (Archives)
Special Museum - 1862
Medical hist, human anatomy, neuroanatomy, civil war surgery, microscopes, AIDS 48378

National Museum of Natural History, 10th St and Constitution Av NW, Washington, DC 20560 - T: (202) 357-1300, Fax: (202) 357-4779, Internet: nmnh.si.edu. Dir.: Douglas H. Erwin
Natural History Museum - 1846
Natural hist 48379

National Museum of the American Indian, 470 Lenfant Plaza SW, Washington, DC 20024 - T: (202) 357-1300, Internet: www.nnai.si.edu/mall
Historical Museum 48380

National Museum of Women in the Arts, 1250 New York Av NW, Washington, DC 20005 - T: (202) 783-5000, Fax: (202) 393-3235, Internet: www.nmwa.org. Dep. Dir.: Dr. Susan Fisher Sterling (Arts, Programs)
Fine Arts Museum / Folklore Museum - 1981
Art 48381

National Portrait Gallery, 750 Ninth St NW, Ste 8300, Washington, DC 20560-0973 - T: (202) 275-2738, Fax: (202) 275-1887, E-mail: npgweb@npg.si.edu, Internet: www.npg.si.edu. Dir.: Marc Pachter, Dep. Dir.: Carolyn Carr, Cur.: Ellen Miles (Painting and Sculpture), Wendy Wick Reaves (Prints), Ann Schumard (Photographs), Beverly Jones Cox (Exhibitions), Cons.: Cindy Lou Ockershausen
Fine Arts Museum / Historical Museum - 1962
Art 48382

National Postal Museum, Smithsonian Institution, 2 Massachusetts Av NE, Washington, DC 20560-0570 - T: (202) 633-2700, Fax: (202) 633-9393, E-mail: npm@npm.si.edu, Internet: www.si.edu/postal. Dir.: James H. Bruns
Special Museum - 1993
Postal hist 48383

National Society of the Children of the American Revolution Museum, 1776 D St NW, Washington, DC 20006 - T: (202) 638-3153, Fax: (202) 737-3162, E-mail: hq@nscar.org, Internet: www.nscar.org. Head: Joanne Scheifer
Historical Museum - 1895
History 48384

National Trust for Historic Preservation, 1785 Massachusetts Av NW, Washington, DC 20036 - T: (202) 588-6000, Fax: (202) 588-6059. Pres.: Richard Moe
Historical Museum - 1949
Fine and decorative arts, furnishing 48385

The Navy Museum, Washington Navy Yard, 901 M St SE, Washington, DC 20374-5060 - T: (202) 433-4882, Fax: (202) 433-8200, Internet: www.history.navy.mil. Dir.: Kim Nielsen, Cur.: Dr. Edward Furgol
Military Museum - 1961 48386

The Octagon, 1799 New York Av NW, Washington, DC 20006-5292 - T: (202) 638-3221, Fax: (202) 879-7764, E-mail: info@theoctagon.org, Internet: www.theoctagon.org. Cur.: Sherry C. Birk (Collections), Linnea Hamer
Fine Arts Museum / Historic Site - 1942
Architecture 48387

The Old Stone House, 3051 Main St NW, Washington, DC 20007 - T: (202) 426-6851, Fax: (202) 426-0125, E-mail: old_stone_house@nps.gov, Internet: www.nps.gov/rocr. Dir.: Terry Carlstrom
Local Museum - 1950
Historic house 48388

The Phillips Collection, 1600 21st St NW, Washington, DC 20009-1090 - T: (202) 387-2151, Fax: (202) 387-2436, E-mail: webmaster@phillipscollection.org, Internet: www.phillipscollection.org. Dir.: Jay Gates, Cur.: Eliza Rathbone, Elizabeth Hutton Turner, Elsa Mezvinski-Smithgall, Stephen Phillips
Fine Arts Museum - 1918
Art 48389

Renwick Gallery of the Smithsonian American Art Museum, Smithsonian Institution, Pennsylvania Av at 17th St NW, Washington, DC 20006 - T: (202) 357-2700, -2531, Fax: (202) 786-2810, E-mail: info@saam.si.edu, Internet: www.americanart.si.edu. Dir.: Elizabeth Broun
Fine Arts Museum / Decorative Arts Museum - 1972
American craft 48390

Sewall-Belmont House, 144 Constitution Av NE, Washington, DC 20002 - T: (202) 546-1210, Fax: (202) 546-3997, E-mail: info@sewallbelmont.org, Internet: www.sewallbelmont.org. Pres.: Mary Langelan, Exec. Dir.: Angela Gilchrist
Historical Museum - 1929
Women's History Portrait Gallery, residence of Albert Gallatin 1801-1813 and Alice Paul 1929-1972 48391

Smithsoniam American Art Museum (closed until fall 2004), 8th and G Sts NW, Washington, DC 20560-0970 - T: (202) 275-1500, Fax: (202) 275-1715, E-mail: info@saam.si.edu, Internet: AmericanArt.si.edu. Dir.: Dr. Elizabeth Broun, Dep. Dir.: Charles J. Robertson, Chief Cur.: Lynda R. Hartigan, Chief Cons.: Stefano Scafetta
Fine Arts Museum - 1829/1846
Art 48392

Smithsonian Institution, 1000 Jefferson Dr SW, Washington, DC 20560 - T: (202) 357-2700, 633-9126, Fax: (202) 786-2515, E-mail: info@info.si.edu, Internet: www.si.edu. C.E.O.: Lawrence M. Small
Local Museum / Science&Tech Museum / Natural History Museum / Folklore Museum - 1846
Museum, education and research complex: 16 museums and galleries, institutes including: Archives of American Art, Astrophysical Observatory, Environmental Research Center, Tropical Research Institute, Marine Station 48393

Society of the Cincinnati Museum, c/o Anderson House, 2118 Massachusetts Av, Washington, DC 20008-2810 - T: (202) 785-2040, Fax: (202) 293-0729, E-mail: museumoffice@societyofthecincinnati.org, Internet: www.societyofthecincinnati.addr.com. Dir.: Kathleen Betts
Fine Arts Museum / Historical Museum - 1783
History and art 48394

Studio Gallery, 2108 R St NW, Washington, DC 20008 - T: (202) 232-8734, Fax: (202) 232-5894, E-mail: info@studiogallerydc.com, Internet: www.studiogallerydc.com. Dir.: Jana Lyons
Fine Arts Museum - 1964 48395

The Supreme Court of the United States Museum, One First St, NE, Washington, DC 20543 - T: (202) 479-3298, Fax: (202) 479-2926, E-mail: mail76668@pop.net, Internet: www.supremecourtus.gov. Cur.: Catherine Fitts
Historical Museum - 1973
Historic Agency and Building 48396

The Textile Museum, 2320 S St NW, Washington, DC 20008 - T: (202) 667-0441, Fax: (202) 483-0994, E-mail: info@textilemuseum.org, Internet: www.textilemuseum.org. Dir.: Ursula E. McCracken, Cur.: Ann P. Rowe (Western Hemisphere), Carol Bier (Eastern Hemisphere)
Special Museum - 1925
Textiles 48397

Tudor Place Museum, 1644 31st St NW, Washington, DC 20007 - T: (202) 965-0400 ext 100, Fax: (202) 965-0164, E-mail: info@tudorplace.org, Internet: tudorplace.org. Exec. Dir.: Leslie L. Buhler
Historical Museum - 1966
Washington-Custis-Peter memorabilia, furniture, silver, porcelain, sculpture, paintings, textiles, photographs, manuscripts 48398

United States Capitol Visitor Center, Capitol Hill, Washington, DC 20515 - T: (202) 228-1222, 225-6827, Fax: (202) 228-1893, Internet: www.aoc.gov. Cur.: Dr. Barbara A. Wolanin
Fine Arts Museum - 1793
Paintings, sculpture, decorative art, photography 48399

United States Department of the Interior Museum, 1849 C St NW, Washington, DC 20240 - T: (202) 208-4743, Fax: (202) 208-1535, Internet: www.doi.gov/museum. Cur.: Debra Berke
Historical Museum / Ethnology Museum - 1938 48400

United States Holocaust Memorial Museum, 100 Raoul Wallenberg Pl SW, Washington, DC 20024-2150 - T: (202) 488-0400, Fax: (202) 488-2690, E-mail: visitorsmail@ushmm.org, Internet: www.ushmm.org. Dir.: Sara J. Bloomfield, Brewster Chamberlain (Archives), Martin Goldman (Survivor Affairs), Raye Farr (Film and Video), Genya Markon (Photo Archives), Radu Ioanid (National Registry of Holocaust Survivors), Joan Ringelheim (Oral History), Steve Goodell (Exhibitions and Special Projects)
Historical Museum - 1980/1993
History - archives 48401

United States Marine Corps Museum, Marine Corp Historical Center, 1254 Charles Morris St SE, Washington, DC 20374-5040 - T: (202) 433-3534, 433-2484, Fax: (202) 433-7265. Dir.: Michael F. Monigan, Cur.: John T. Dyer, James A. Fairfax
Historical Museum / Military Museum - 1940
Military history 48402

United States Navy Art Gallery, Washington Navy Yard, 805 Kidder Breese SE, Washington, DC 20374-5060 - T: (202) 433-3815, Fax: (202) 433-5635, Internet: www.history.navy.mil. Cur.: Gale Munro
Fine Arts Museum
Graphic arts, paintings, sketches, sculptures 48403

United States Senate Commission on Art Collection, Rm S-411, U.S. Capitol Bldg, Washington, DC 20510-7102 - T: (202) 224-2955, Fax: (202) 224-8799, E-mail: curator@sec.senate.gov, Internet: www.senate.gov/curator/collections.htm. Cur.: Diane K. Skvarla
Fine Arts Museum / Decorative Arts Museum - 1968
Paintings, sculpture, prints, furnishing 48404

Washington Center for Photography, 406 Seventh St NW, Washington, DC 20004 - T: (202) 737-0406, Fax: (202) 737-0419. Pres.: Jerry Smith
Fine Arts Museum - 1986 48405

Washington Dolls House and Toy Museum, 5236 44th St NW, Washington, DC 20015 - T: (202) 244-0024, 363-6400, Fax: (202) 237-1659, Internet: www.dollshousetoymuseum.com. Dir.: Flora Gill Jacobs
Decorative Arts Museum - 1975
Antique Toy ans Dolls 48406

Washington National Cathedral, Cathedral Church of Saint Peter and Saint Paul, Massachusetts and Wisconsin Av, NW, Washington, DC 20016-5098 - T: (202) 537-8991, 537-6200, Fax: (202) 364-6600, E-mail: tours@cathedral.org, Internet: www.cathedral.org/cathedral
Religious Arts Museum - 1893
Gothic design Cathedral, Episcopal Cathedral, structure 48407

Watkins Gallery, American University, 4400 Massachusetts NW Av, Washington, DC 20016 - T: (202) 885-1064, 885-1670, Fax: (202) 885-1132, E-mail: rhaynie@american.edu, Internet: www.american.edu/academic.depts/cas/art/watkins. Dir.: Ron Haynie, Cur.: Jonathan Bucci
Fine Arts Museum / University Museum - 1945
Art 48408

The White House, 1600 Pennsylvania Av NW, Washington, DC 20500 - T: (202) 456-2550, Fax: (202) 456-6820, Internet: www.whitehousehistory.org. Cur.: William G. Allman, Ass. Cur.: Lydia Tederick
Historical Museum - 1792
Hist, politics 48409

Woodrow Wilson House, 2340 S St NW, Washington, DC 20008 - T: (202) 387-4062 ext 14, Fax: (202) 483-1466, E-mail: wilson_house@woodrowwilsonhouse.org, Internet: www.woodrowwilsonhouse.org. Dir.: Frank J. Aucella, Cur.: Meg Nowack
Historical Museum - 1963
Home of President Wilson 48410

Washington GA

Robert Toombs House, 216 E Robert Toombs Av, Washington, GA 30673 - T: (706) 678-2226, Fax: (706) 678-7515, E-mail: toombs@nu-z.net, Internet: web.nu-z.net/~toombs. Man.: Marty Fleming
Natural History Museum - 1974 48411

Washington Historical Museum, 308 E Robert Toombs Av, Washington, GA 30673-2038 - T: (706) 678-2105, Fax: (706) 678-3752
Local Museum - 1959
1836 Barnett-Slaton House, local history 48412

Washington KS

Washington County Historical Society Museum, 206-208 Ballard, Washington, KS 66968 - T: (785) 325-2198
Local Museum - 1982 48413

Washington LA

Washington Museum, 404 N Main St, Washington, LA 70589 - T: (318) 826-3627. Chief Cur.: Malbae Soileau
Local Museum - 1972
Local history 48414

Washington MS

Historic Jefferson College, College and North St, Washington, MS 39190, mail addr: POB 700, Washington, MS 39190 - T: (601) 4422901, Fax: (601) 446-6503, E-mail: hjc@bkbank.com, Internet: mdah.state.ms.us. Dir.: Jim Barnett
Historical Museum - 1971
College uniforms, books, weapons 48415

Washington PA

David Bradford House, 175 S Main St, Washington, PA 15301 - T: (724) 222-3604, E-mail: mthart@pulsenet.com, Internet: www.bradfordhouse.org. C.E.O. & Pres.: Steven Tkach, Mgr.: Myrna Hart
Local Museum - 1960
Historic house 48416

Olin Fine Arts Center, Washington and Jefferson College, 285 E Wheeling St, Washington, PA 15301 - T: (724) 223-6546, Fax: (724) 223-5271, E-mail: htaylor@washjeff.edu, Internet: www.washjeff.edu. Dir.: Ronald F. Sherhofer
Fine Arts Museum / University Museum - 1980 48417

Pennsylvania Trolley Museum, 1 Museum Rd, Washington, PA 15301-6133 - T: (724) 228-9675, Fax: (724) 228-9675, E-mail: ptm@pa-trolley.org, Internet: www.pa-trolley.org. Exec. Dir.: Scott R. Becker
Science&Tech Museum - 1949
Railway 48418

Washington County Historical Society Museum, Le Moyne House, 49 E Maiden St, Washington, PA 15301 - T: (724) 225-6740, Fax: (724) 225-8495, E-mail: infa@wchspa.org, Internet: www.wchspa.org. Cur.: Rebecca Crum
Local Museum - 1900
Le Moyne House, a national historic landmark of the underground railroad incl historic house, doctor's office, gardens, crematory 48419

Washington TX

Barrington Living History Farm, Brazos Park, 23100 Barrington Ln, Washington, TX 77880 - T: (936) 878-2214, Fax: (936) 878-2810, E-mail: wilburt.scaggs@tpwd.state.tx.us, Internet: www.tpwd.state.tx.us/park/parks.htm. Man.: Tom Scaggs
Agriculture Museum - 1936
Historic house, home of Anson Jones, last president of the Republic of Texas 48420

Star of the Republic Museum, Blinn College, 23200 Park Rd 12, Washington, TX 77880 - T: (409) 878-2461, Fax: (936) 878-2462, E-mail: star@acmail.blinncol.edu, Internet: www.starmuseum.org. Dir.: Houston McGaugh, Cur.: Dr. Shawn Carlson
Historical Museum - 1970
Texas hist 1836-1846 48421

Washington Court House OH

Fayette County Museum, 517 Columbus Av, Washington Court House, OH 43160 - T: (740) 335-2953
Local Museum - 1948 48422

Washington Crossing PA

Washington Crossing Historic Park, 1112 River Rd, Washington Crossing, PA 18977 - T: (215) 493-4076, Fax: (215) 493-4820, Internet: www.phmc.state.pa.us. Head: Michael Bertheaud, Cur.: Hilary Krueger
Historical Museum - 1917
Historic Site 48423

Washington Green CT

The Institute For American Indian Studies, 38 Curtis Rd, Washington Green, CT 06793-0260 - T: (860) 868-0518, Fax: (860) 868-1649, E-mail: instituteamer.indian@snet.net, Internet: www.amerindianinstitute.org. Exec. Dir.: Alberto C. Meloni, Sc. Staff: Lucienne Lavin (Archaeology), E. Barrie Kavasch (Ethnobotany)
Ethnology Museum / Archaeological Museum - 1975
American Indian culture and archaeology 48424

Wasilla AK

Dorothy G. Page Museum, 323 Main St, Wasilla, AK 99654 - T: (907) 373-9071, Fax: (907) 373-9072, E-mail: museum@ci.wasilla.ak.us. Dir.: John Cramer
Local Museum - 1966
Local hist 48425

Water Mill NY

Water Mill Museum, 41 Old Mill Rd, Water Mill, NY 11976 - T: (516) 726-4625, Internet: www.watermillmuseum.org. Pres.: Gay Colina
Local Museum - 1942 48426

Waterbury CT

The Mattatuck Museum of the Mattatuck Historical Society, 144 W Main St, Waterbury, CT 06702 - T: (203) 753-0381, Fax: (203) 756-6283, E-mail: info@mattatuckmuseum.org, Internet: www.mattatuckmuseum.org. Dir.: Terry P. Cassidy, Marie Galbraith, Cur.: Ann Smith, Ass. Cur.: Raechel Guest
Fine Arts Museum / Historical Museum - 1877
History and art Temple 48427

Waterbury Center VT

Green Mountain Club, 4711 Waterbury Stowe Rd, Waterbury Center, VT 05677 - T: (802) 244-7037, Fax: (802) 244-5867, E-mail: gmc@sover.net, Internet: www.greenmountainclub.org. Pres.: Rolf Anderson, Exec. Dir.: Ben Rose
Local Museum - 1910 48428

Waterford NY

Waterford Historical Museum, 2 Museum Ln, Waterford, NY 12188 - T: (518) 238-0809, E-mail: whmcc@nycap.rr.com, Internet: www.timesunion.com/communities/whm. Pres.: Dr. Brad L. Utter
Local Museum - 1964 48429

Waterford PA

Fort Leboeuf, 123 High St, Waterford, PA 16441 - T: (814) 732-2575, Fax: (814) 732-2329, E-mail: qolybwx@edinboro.edu
Historical Museum / University Museum - 1929
Period furniture, French occupation 48430

Waterloo IA

Grout Museum of History and Science, 503 South St, Waterloo, IA 50701 - T: (319) 234-6357, Fax: (319) 236-0500, Internet: www.groutmuseumdistrict.org. Dir.: Billie K. Bailey
Historical Museum / Natural History Museum - 1933
History, science 48431

Rensselaer Russell House Museum, 520 W 3rd St, Waterloo, IA 50701 - T: (319) 233-0262, Fax: (319) 236-0500, Internet: www.groutmuseumdistrict.org. Dir.: Billie K. Bailey
Historical Museum - 1861
Historic house built in Italianate architectural style 48432

Science Imaginarium, 322 Wahington St, Waterloo, IA 50701 - T: (319) 233-8708, Fax: (319) 236-0500, Internet: www.groutmuseumdistrict.org. Dir.: Billie K. Bailey, Man.: Alan Sweeney
Natural History Museum - 1993 48433

Snowden House, 306 Washington St, Waterloo, IA 50701 - T: (319) 234-6357, Fax: (319) 236-0500, Internet: www.groutmuseumdistrict.org. Dir.: Billie K. Bailey
Historical Museum - 1933
Summer house of William Snowden, pharmacy 48434

Waterloo Center of the Arts, 225 Commercial St, Waterloo, IA 50701 - T: (319) 291-4490, Fax: (319) 291-4270, E-mail: museum@waterloo-ia.org, Internet: www.waterloo-ia.org/arts. Dir.: Cammie V. Scully, Cur.: Kent Shankle
Fine Arts Museum
Haitian art, Mid-West regional art 48435

Waterloo NY

Memorial Day Museum of Waterloo, 35 E Main St, Waterloo, NY 13165 - T: (315) 539-0533, Fax: (315) 539-7798. Dir.: Judith A. Harrington
Military Museum - 1966 48436

Peter Whitmer Sr. Home and Visitors Center, 1451 Aunkst Rd, Waterloo, NY 13165 - T: (315) 539-2552, Internet: www.ggw.org/hillcumorah. Sc. Staff: Calvin Christiansen
Historic Site - 1980 48437

Terwilliger Museum, 31 E Williams St, Waterloo, NY 13165 - T: (315) 539-0533, Fax: (315) 539-7798, E-mail: ssnyder@lakenet.org, Internet: www.waterloony.com/library.html. Dir.: James T. Hughes
Local Museum / Historical Museum - 1960 48438

Watertown CT

Watertown Historical Society Museum, 22 DeForest St, Watertown, CT 06795-2522 - T: (860) 274-1050, E-mail: aniel922@aol.com. Cur.: Michelle D. Gorski
Local Museum - 1947
Local hist 48439

Watertown MA

Armenian Museum of America, 65 Main St, Watertown, MA 02472 - T: (617) 926-2562, Fax: (617) 926-0175, E-mail: gary@armenianlibraryandmuseum.org, Internet: www.armenianlibraryandmuseum.org. Dir.: Mildred Nahabedian, Cur.: Susan Lind-Sinanian, Gary Lind-Sinanian
Ethnology Museum / Folklore Museum - 1971
Armenian history - Library 48440

Museum on the History of Blindness, c/o Perkins School for the Blind, 175 North Beacon St, Watertown, MA 02472 - T: (617) 972-7250, Fax: (617) 923-8076, E-mail: jan.seymour-ford@perkins.org, Internet: www.perkins.org
Special Museum - 1829
Picture coll, hist of blindness, Nella Braddy Henney coll 48441

Watertown NY

Jefferson County Historical Society Museum, 228 Washington St, Watertown, NY 13601 - T: (315) 782-3491, Fax: (315) 782-2913. Dir.: Fred H. Rollins, Cur.: Elise Chan
Local Museum - 1886 48442

Sci-Tech Center of Northern New York, 154 Stone St, Watertown, NY 13601 - T: (315) 788-1340, Fax: (315) 788-2738, E-mail: scitech@imcnet.net. Exec. Dir.: John Kunz
Science&Tech Museum - 1982
Science and technology 48443

Watertown SD

Codington County Heritage Museum, 27 First Av, Watertown, SD 57201 - T: (605) 886-7335, Fax: (605) 882-4383, E-mail: cchs@dailypost.com, Internet: www.cchsmuseum.org. Exec. Dir.: Tim Hoheisel
Local Museum - 1974
Local hist 48444

Mellette House, 421 Fifth Av, Watertown, SD 57201 - T: (605) 886-4730. Pres.: Prudence K. Calvin
Local Museum - 1943
Historic house, home of Arthur Calvin Mellette, first Governor of South Dakota 48445

Watertown WI

Octagon House, 919 Charles St, Watertown, WI 53094 - T: (920) 261-2796, Internet: www.watertownhistory.org. Pres.: William Jannke, C.E.O.: Linda Werth
Local Museum - 1933
Historic house 48446

Waterville ME

Colby College Museum of Art, 5600 Mayflower Hill, Waterville, ME 04901 - T: (207) 872-3000, 872-3228, Fax: (207) 872-3807, Internet: www.colby.edu/museum. Pres.: William Cotter, Dir.: Hugh J. Gourley
Fine Arts Museum / University Museum - 1959
Art 48447

Redington Museum, 64 Silver St, Waterville, ME 04901 - T: (207) 872-9439, Internet: www.redingtonmuseum.org. Cur.: Donnice Finnemore, Harry Finnemore
Historical Museum - 1903
Local history, residence of Asa Redington 48448

Watervliet NY

The Watervliet Arsenal Museum, Watervliet Arsenal, Rte 32, Watervliet, NY 12189-4050 - T: (518) 266-5805, Fax: (518) 266-5011, E-mail: swantek@wva.army.mill.us, Internet: www.wva.army.mil.us. Dir./Cur.: John E. Swantek
Military Museum - 1975
Military hist 48449

Watford City ND

Pioneer Museum, 104 Park Av W, Watford City, ND 58854 - T: (701) 842-2990. Dir.: Clyde Holman, Cur.: Sylvia Leiseth
Historical Museum - 1968 48450

Watkins Glen NY

International Motor Racing Research Center, 610 S Decatur St, Watkins Glen, NY 14891 - T: (607) 535-9044, Fax: (607) 535-9039, E-mail: research@racingarchives.org, Internet: www.racingarchives.org. Dir.: Michael Rand
Special Museum - 1998
Motorsport, paintings, photographs 48451

Watkinsville GA

Eagle Tavern Museum, 26 N Main St, Watkinsville, GA 30677 - T: (706) 769-5197, Fax: (706) 769-0705, E-mail: eagletavern@aol.com, Internet: www.oconeecounty.com
Special Museum - 1956 48452

Watonga OK

T.B. Ferguson Home, 519 N Weigel, Watonga, OK 73772 - T: (580) 623-5069. Cur.: Mildred Sanders
Local Museum - 1972 48453

Watrous NM

Fort Union National Monument, Rte 161, Watrous, NM 87753 - T: (505) 425-8025, Fax: (505) 454-1155, E-mail: foun_administration@nps.gov, Internet: www.nps.gov/foun/. Head: Dennis Ditmanson
Military Museum - 1956 48454

Watseka IL

Iroquois County Historical Society Museum, 103 West Cherry St, Watseka, IL 60970 - T: (815) 432-2215, E-mail: ichs@localline.com, Internet: www.bdrak.comlichs/museum.html. Pres.: Wayne Hiles
Local Museum - 1967
Local history, housed in Old Iroquois County Courthouse 48455

Watsonville CA

Pajaro Valley Historical Museum, 332 E Beach St, Watsonville, CA 95076 - T: (831) 722-0305, Fax: (831) 722-5501. Pres.: James Dutra
Local Museum - 1940
Local hist, costumes 48456

Wauconda IL

Lake County Discovery Museum, Rte 176, Fairfield Rd, Wauconda, IL 60084 - T: (847) 968-3400, Fax: (847) 526-0024, E-mail: lcmuseum@co.lake.il.us, Internet: www.co.lake.i1.us/forest. Dir.: Janet Gallimore, Cur.: Katherine Hamilton-Smith
Local Museum - 1976
Local and regional history 48457

Wauconda Township Museum, 711 N Main St, Wauconda, IL 60084 - T: (847) 526-9303
Local Museum - 1973
Farm equip, toys, quilts, furnishings, Civil War cavalry equip, fans, cameras, china 48458

Waukegan IL

Haines Museum, 1917 N Sheridan Rd, Bowen Park, Waukegan, IL 60079 - T: (847) 336-1859, 360-4772, Fax: (847) 662-6190, E-mail: haines@waukeganparks.org, Internet: www.waukeganparks.org. Pres.: Peggy Kolber
Local Museum - 1968
Local history 48459

Waukesha WI

Waukesha County Museum, 101 W Main St, Waukesha, WI 53186-4811 - T: (262) 521-2859, Fax: (262) 521-2865, E-mail: exdirector@voyager.net. Dir.: Susan K. Baker, Cur.: Brook Swanson (Collections)
Local Museum - 1911
Local hist - research center 48460

Waupaca WI

Hutchinson House Museum, End of S Main St, South Park, Waupaca, WI 54981 - T: (715) 258-5958, 258-7726, 258-8238. Pres.: Richard Bidwell, Cur.: Linda Pope, Marion Snyder
Local Museum - 1956
Local hist 48461

Waurika OK

Chisholm Trail Historical Museum, US 81 and State Rte 70, Waurika, OK 73573 - T: (405) 228-2166, Fax: (405) 228-3290. Head: Gin Dodson
Local Museum - 1965 48462

Wausau WI

Leigh Yawkey Woodson Art Museum, 700 N 12th St, Wausau, WI 54403-5007 - T: (715) 845-7010, Fax: (715) 845-7103, E-mail: museum@lywam.org, Internet: www.lywam.org. Dir.: Kathy Kelsey Foley, Cur.: Andrew J. McGivern, Jane Weinke
Fine Arts Museum / Decorative Arts Museum - 1973
Art 48463

Marathon County Historical Society Museum, 410 McIndoe St, Wausau, WI 54403 - T: (715) 842-5750, Fax: (715) 848-0576, E-mail: research@marathoncountyhistory.com, Internet: www.marathoncountyhistory.com. Dir.: Mary Jane Hettingg, Cur.: Kathy Anderson
Local Museum - 1952
Local hist 48464

Wauseon OH

Fulton County Historical Museum, 229 Monroe St, Wauseon, OH 43567 - T: (419) 337-7922, E-mail: museum@fulton-net.com, Internet: www.rootsweb.com/~ohfulton/historicalsociety.html. Dir.: Barbara Berry
Local Museum - 1883 48465

Wauwatosa WI

Lowell Damon House, 2107 Wauwatosa Av, Wauwatosa, WI 53213 - T: (414) 273-8288, Fax: (414) 273-3268, E-mail: nchs@prodigy.net, Internet: www.milwaukeecountyhistsoc.org. Pres.: Robert B. Brumder, Exec. Dir.: Robert T. Teske
Local Museum - 1941
Historic house 48466

Waverly TN

World O' Tools Museum, 2431 Hwy 13, Waverly, TN 37185 - T: (931) 296-3218, E-mail: hunterp@usit.net. Cur.: Hunter M. Pilkinton
Science&Tech Museum - 1973
Tools and related items 48467

Waverly VA

Miles B. Carpenter Museum, 201 Hunter St, Waverly, VA 23890 - T: (804) 834-2151, 834-3327. Pres./Cur.: Shirley S. Yancey
Folklore Museum / Agriculture Museum - 1986
Folk art, peanuts 48468

Waxahachie TX

Ellis County Museum, 201 S College St, Waxahachie, TX 75165 - T: (972) 937-0681, Fax: (972) 937-3910, E-mail: ecmuseum@cnbcom.net, Internet: www.rootsweb.com/~txecm. Pres.: Patsy Cornelius, Dir./Cur.: Shannon Simpson
Local Museum - 1967
Local hist 48469

Waxhaw NC

Museum of the Alphabet, Jaars Summer Institute of Linguistics, 6409 Davis Rd, Waxhaw, NC 28173 - T: (704) 843-6066, Fax: (704) 843-6200, E-mail: info@jaars.org, Internet: www.jaars.org. Dir.: LaDonna Mann
Special Museum - 1990
Alphabet 48470

Museum of the Waxhaws and Andrew Jackson Memorial, Hwy 75 E, Waxhaw, NC 28173 - T: (704) 843-1832, Fax: (704) 843-1767, E-mail: mwaxhaw@perigee.net, Internet: www.perigee.net/~mwaxhaw. Dir.: Richard Durschlag
Local Museum / Historical Museum - 1996
Civilian and military related artifacts, President Andrew Jackson 48471

Waycross GA

Okefenokee Heritage Center, 1460 N Augusta Av, Waycross, GA 31503 - T: (912) 285-4260, Fax: (912) 283-2858, E-mail: ohc@acces.net, Internet: www.okeheritage.org. Pres.: T. Henry Clarke, Dir.: Catherine Larkins
Fine Arts Museum / Historical Museum - 1975
History, art 48472

Southern Forest World Museum, 1440 N Augusta Av, Waycross, GA 31503 - T: (912) 285-4056, Fax: (912) 283-2858, Internet: www.okefenokeeswamp.com. Pres.: Earl Smith
Science&Tech Museum / Natural History Museum - 1981
Forestry 48473

Wayland MA

Wayland Historical Museum, 12 Cochituate Rd, Wayland, MA 01778 - T: (508) 358-7959, Internet: j.w.d.home.attbi.com/whs. Pres.: Richard P. Hoyt, Cur.: Joanne Davis
Historical Museum - 1954
General museum 48474

Wayne MI

City of Wayne Historical Museum, 1 Town Sq, Wayne, MI 48184 - T: (734) 722-0113, Fax: (734) 722-5052. Dir.: Virginia Presson
Local Museum - 1966
Local history 48475

Wayne NE

Nordstrand Visual Arts Gallery, Wayne State College, 1111 Main St, Wayne, NE 68787 - T: (402) 375-7000, Fax: (402) 375-7204. Dir.: Prof. Pearl Hansen, Prof. Marlene Mueller
Public Gallery - 1977 48476

Wayne NJ

Ben Shahn Galleries, c/o William Paterson University of New Jersey, 300 Pompton Rd, Wayne, NJ 07470 - T: (973) 720-2654, Fax: (973) 720-3290, E-mail: einreinhofern@wpunj.edu, Internet: www.wpunj.edu. Dir./Cur.: Nancy Einreinhofer
University Museum / Fine Arts Museum - 1969 48477

Dey Mansion, Washington's Headquarters Museum, 199 Totowa Rd, Wayne, NJ 07470 - T: (201) 696-1776, Fax: (973) 696-1365. Dir./Cur.: Raymond Wright
Military Museum - 1934 48478

Van Riper-Hopper House, 533 Berdan Av, Wayne, NJ 07470 - T: (973) 694-7192, Fax: (973) 872-0586, Internet: www.waynetownship.com/. Pres.: Bob Brubaker, Dir./Cur.: Cecilia Paccioretti
Local Museum / Archaeological Museum - 1964 48479

Wayne PA

The Finley House, 113 W Beech Tree Ln, Wayne, PA 19087 - T: (610) 688-2668, 688-4455. Pres.: J. Bennett Hill
Local Museum - 1948
Local hist 48480

Wayne Art Center, 413 Maplewood Ave, Wayne, PA 19087 - T: (610) 688-3553, Fax: (610) 995-0478, E-mail: wayneart@worldnet.att.net, Internet: www.wayneart.com. Dir.: Nancy Campbell
Public Gallery - 1930 48481

Waynesboro PA

Renfrew Museum, 1010 E Main St, Waynesboro, PA 17268 - T: (717) 762-4723, Fax: (717) 762-6384, E-mail: renfrew@innernet.net, Internet: www.renfrewmuseum.com. Cur.: Jeffrey Bliemeister
Decorative Arts Museum - 1973
Decorative arts 48482

Waynesboro VA

Humpback Rocks Mountain Farm Visitor Center, Blue Ridge Pkwy, Mile Post 5.9, Waynesboro, VA 24483 - T: (540) 377-2377, Fax: (540) 377-6758
Local Museum - 1939
Pioneer life, farm implements, tools, household items, toys, firearms 48483

Waynesburg PA

Greene County Historical Museum, 918 Rolling Meadows Rd, Waynesburg, PA 15370 - T: (724) 627-3204, Fax: (724) 627-3204, E-mail: museum@greenepa.net, Internet: www.greenepa.net/~museum/. Pres.: Paul Maytk
Local Museum - 1925
Local hist 48484

Weathersfield VT

Museum of the Weathersfield Historical Society, Weathersfield Center Rd, Weathersfield, VT 05156 - T: (802) 263-5230, 263-5361, Fax: (802) 263-9263, E-mail: efh@sover.net, Internet: www.weathersfield.net. Pres.: Willis Wood
Local Museum - 1951
Local hist 48485

Weaverville CA

J.J. Jackson Memorial Museum, 508 Main St, Weaverville, CA 96093 - T: (530) 623-5211. Dir.: Hal E. Goodyear
Local Museum - 1968
Local hist, mining, Chinese and Indian artifacts 48486

Weaverville Joss House, POB 1217, Weaverville, CA 96093 - T: (530) 623-5284. Cur.: Linda L. Cooper
Local Museum - 1956
Historic house, Taoist temple of worship 48487

Weaverville NC

Zebulon B. Vance Birthplace, 911 Reems Creek Rd, Weaverville, NC 28787 - T: (828) 645-6706, Fax: (828) 645-0936, E-mail: vance@brinet.com, Internet: www.ah.dcr.state.nc.us/sections/vance
Historical Museum - 1961
NC Governor Zebulon B. Vance 48488

Weedsport NY

Hall of Fame and Classic Car Museum, 1 Speedway Dr, Weedsport, NY 13166 - T: (315) 834-6606, Fax: (315) 834-9734, Internet: www.dirtmotorsports.com. Cur.: Romy Caruso
Science&Tech Museum - 1992
Race cars, classic cars 48489

Old Brutus Historical Society Museum, 8943 N Seneca St, Weedsport, NY 13166 - T: (315) 834-9342, E-mail: mriley@baldcom.net. Dir.: Robert W. Ward, Sc. Staff: Jeanne Baker (History)
Local Museum - 1967 48490

Weeping Water NE

Weeping Water Valley Historical Society Museum, 215 W Eldora Av, Weeping Water, NE 68463 - T: (402) 267-6565, E-mail: wd85407@navix.net. Pres./Chm.: Doris Duff
Local Museum - 1969 48491

Weiser ID

Snake River Heritage Center, 2295 Paddock Av, Weiser, ID 83672 - T: (208) 549-0205, Fax: (208) 549-2740
Local Museum - 1962 48492

Snake River Heritage Center, 2295 Paddock Av, Weiser, ID 83672 - T: (208) 549-0205, 549-3834, E-mail: rain01@ruralnetwork.net
Local Museum - 1962
Music, costumes, folklore, glass, geology 48493

Wellesley MA

Crane Collection Gallery, 564 Washington St, Wellesley, MA 02482-6409 - T: (781) 235-1166, Fax: (781) 235-4181, E-mail: cranecolec@aol.com, Internet: www.artnet.com/crane.html
Fine Arts Museum - 1983 48494

Davis Museum, Wellesley College, 106 Central St, Wellesley, MA 02481-8203 - T: (781) 283-2051, Fax: (781) 283-2064, Internet: www.wellesley.edu/DavisMuseum/. Dir.: David Mickenberg, Cur.: Dabney Hailey
Fine Arts Museum / University Museum - 1889
Art 48495

Wellesley Hills MA

Wellesley Historical Society, 229 Washington St, Wellesley Hills, MA 02481 - T: (781) 235-6690, Fax: (781) 235-6690, Internet: www.wellesleyhsoc.com. Pres.: Elizabeth Hunnewell, Exec. Dir.: Laurel Nilsen
Local Museum - 1925
Local history, Dadmun-McNamara house, oldham lace coll , Denton Butterfly and moth coll 48496

Wellfleet MA

Cape Cod National Seashore Museum, 99 Marconi Site Rd, Wellfleet, MA 02667 - T: (508) 255-8925, Fax: (508) 240-3291, E-mail: hope_morrilla@nps.gov, Internet: www.nps.gov/caco
Local Museum - 1961
Local hist, natural hist, archaeology 48497

Wellfleet Historical Society Museum, 266 Main St, Wellfleet, MA 02667 - T: (508) 349-2954, Internet: www.wellfleethistoricalsociety.com. Pres.: Suzanne Albee, Cur.: Joan Hopkins Coughlin
Local Museum - 1953
Local history 48498

Wellington KS

Chisholm Trail Museum, 502 N Washington, Wellington, KS 67152 - T: (316) 326-3820, 326-7466. Pres.: Richard M. Gilfillan
Historical Museum - 1964
History, first hospital in Wellington 48499

Wellington OH

Spirit of '76 Museum, 201 N Main St, Wellington, OH 44090 - T: (440) 647-4367. Pres.: John Perry
Historical Museum - 1968 48500

Wells ME

Wells Auto Museum, 1181 Post Rd, Wells, ME 04090 - T: (207) 646-9064, E-mail: wellsauto@aol.com. Dir.: Jonathan H. Gould
Science&Tech Museum - 1954
Automobile 48501

Wellsville OH

River Museum, 1003 Riverside Av, Wellsville, OH 43968 - E-mail: 1955
Local Museum
Pennsylvania Railroad Cabin Car, Civil War, saber, Indian artifacts, pottery 48502

Wellsville UT

American West Heritage Center, 4025 S Hwy, 89-91, Wellsville, UT 84339 - T: (801) 245-6050, Fax: (801) 245-6052, E-mail: awhc@cc.usu.edu, Internet: www.americanwestcenter.org. C.E.O.: Ronda Thompson
Agriculture Museum / Local Museum - 1979
Historic farm 48503

Ronald V. Jensen Living Historical Farm → American West Heritage Center

Wenatchee WA

Chelan County Public Utility District, Rocky Reach Dam, US 97A Chelau Hwy, Wenatchee, WA 98807, mail addr: POB 1231, Wenatchee, WA 98807-1231 - T: (509) 663-8121, 663-7522, Fax: (509) 664-2874
Local Museum - 1961
History of electricity and Edisonia, geology, anthropology, local Indian history 48504

Gallery '76, 1300 5th St, Wenatchee, WA 98801 - T: (509) 662-1651, Fax: (509) 664-2538, E-mail: gallery76@wucmail.ctc.edu, Internet: www.ctc.edu. Dir.: Rae Dana
Fine Arts Museum - 1976
Art 48505

Rocky Reach Dam, POB 1231, Wenatchee, WA 98807-1231 - T: (509) 663-8121 ext 6624, Fax: (509) 667-3449, Internet: www.chelanpud.org
Fine Arts Museum / Science&Tech Museum - 1963
Paintings, graphics, Indian artifacts, electrical antiques 48506

Wenatchee Valley Museum, North Central Washington Museum, 127 S Mission, Wenatchee, WA 98801 - T: (509) 664-3340, Fax: (509) 664-3356, E-mail: kwilliams@cityofwenatchee.com, Internet: www.museumwsb.wednet.edu. Dir.: Dr. Keith Williams, Cur.: Mark Behler
Local Museum - 1939
Local hist 48507

Wenham MA

Wenham Museum, 132 Main St, Wenham, MA 01984 - T: (978) 468-2377, Fax: (978) 468-1763, E-mail: info@wenhammuseum.org, Internet: www.wenhammuseum.org. Pres.: Elizabeth R. Colt, Exec. Dir.: Emily Stearns
Local Museum - 1921
Social history, dolls, toys, model trains, costumes, textiles, photography 48508

Weslaco TX

Weslaco Bicultural Museum, 515 S Kansas, Weslaco, TX 785-8062 - T: (956) 968-9142, Fax: (956) 968-9142, E-mail: discover@sc200.net, Internet: texasescapes.net
Local Museum - 1971
Local and border hist 48509

West Allis WI

West Allis Historical Society Museum, 8405 West National Av, West Allis, WI 53227-1733 - T: (414) 541-6970. Pres.: John R. Clow
Local Museum - 1966
Local hist 48510

West Barnstable MA

Higgins Art Gallery, c/o Cape Cod Community College, 2240 Iyanough Rd, West Barnstable, MA 02668 - T: (508) 362-2131 ext 4381, Fax: (508) 375-4020, Internet: www.capecod.mass.edu. Dir.: Sarah Ringler
Fine Arts Museum - 1989
Paintings, prints, drawings, graphics, sculpture, mixed media 48511

West Bend WI

Washington County Historical Society Museum, 340 S Fifth Av, West Bend, WI 53095 - T: (414) 335-4678, Fax: (414) 335-4612, E-mail: wchs@historyisfun.com, Internet: www.historyisfun.com. Dir.: Chip Beckford, Cur.: Daniel J. Smith
Local Museum - 1937
Local hist 48512

West Bend Art Museum, 300 S 6th Av, West Bend, WI 53095 - T: (414) 334-9638, Fax: (414) 334-8080, E-mail: officemanager@wbartmuseum.com, Internet: www.wbartmuseum.com. Dir.: Thomas D. Lidtke, Ass. Dir.: Cheryl Ann Parker
Fine Arts Museum - 1961
Wisconsin Art from 1800 - 1950, Carl von Marr coll 48513

West Branch IA

Herbert Hoover National Historic Site, 110 Parkside Dr, West Branch, IA 52358 - T: (319) 643-2541, Fax: (319) 643-5367, E-mail: dan_banta@nps.gov, Internet: www.nps.gov/heho. Dir.: Carol E. Kohan, Sc. Staff: Bill Wilcox (History)
Historic Site - 1965
Birthplace of Herbert Hoover, graves of President and Mrs. Hoover 48514

Herbert Hoover Presidential Library-Museum, 210 Parkside Dr, West Branch, IA 52358 - T: (319) 643-5301, Fax: (319) 643-5825, E-mail: library@hoover.nara.gov, Internet: www.hoover.nara.gov. Dir.: Timoth Walch, Cur.: Maureen Harding, Ass. Cur.: Christine Mouw
Library with Exhibitions - 1962
Presidential library - Archive 48515

West Chester PA

American Helicopter Museum & Education Center, 1220 American Blvd, West Chester, PA 19380 - T: (610) 436-9600, Fax: (610) 436-8642, E-mail: info@helicoptermuseum.org, Internet: www.helicoptermuseum.org. Dir.: Ann Barton Brown, Cur.: John Schneider
Science&Tech Museum - 1993
Aeronautics 48516

Chester County Historical Society Museum, 225 N High St, West Chester, PA 19380 - T: (610) 692-4800, Fax: (610) 692-4357, E-mail: jcarey@chesterhistorical.org, Internet: www.chestercohistorical.org. Pres./Dir.: Roland H. Woodward, Cur.: Ellen Enslow
Local Museum - 1893
Local hist 48517

West Chicago IL

Kruse House Museum, 527 Main St, West Chicago, IL 60185 - T: (630) 231-0564, E-mail: lancey@earthlink.net, Internet: www.krusehousemuseum.eboard.com. Pres.: Lance Conkright
Local Museum - 1976
Local history, housed in 1917 Kruse House 48518

West Chicago City Museum, 132 Main St, West Chicago, IL 60185 - T: (630) 231-3376, 293-2266, Fax: (630) 293-3028, E-mail: museum@westchicago.org, Internet: www.westchicago.org. Dir.: LuAnn Bombard
Local Museum - 1976
Town history 48519

West Columbia TX

Varner-Hogg Plantation, 1702 N 13th St, West Columbia, TX 77486 - T: (979) 345-4656, Fax: (979) 345-4412, E-mail: pat.burris@tpwd.state.tx.us, Internet: www.tpwd.state.tx.us. Exec. Dir.: Andrew Sansom
Decorative Arts Museum - 1958
Decorative arts, archaeology, Sam Houston, Gov James Stephen Hogg 48520

West Fargo ND

Cass County Historical Society Museum, 1351 W Main Av, West Fargo, ND 58078 - T: (701) 282-2822, Fax: (701) 282-7606, E-mail: info@bonanzaville.com, Internet: www.bonanzaville.com. Pres.: Sandra Fuchs, Exec. Dir.: Kathy Anderson
Local Museum - 1954 48521

Red River and Northern Plains Regional Museum, 1351 W Main Av, West Fargo, ND 58078 - T: (701) 282-2822, Fax: (701) 282-7606, E-mail: bonanzaville@fargocity.com, Internet: www.fargocity.com/bonanzaville. Pres.: Sandra Fuchs, C.E.O.: Kathy Anderson
Local Museum / Open Air Museum - 1967 48522

West Frankfort IL

Frankfort Area Historical Museum, 2000 E Saint Louis St, West Frankfort, IL 62896 - T: (618) 932-6159. Cur.: Mavis Wright
Local Museum - 1972
Local history 48523

West Glacier MT

Glacier National Park Museum, Glacier National Park, West Glacier, MT 59936 - T: (406) 888-7936, Fax: (406) 888-7808, E-mail: deirdre-shaw@nps.gov. Cur.: Deirdre Shaw
Natural History Museum / Historical Museum / Archaeological Museum - 1930 48524

West Hartford CT

Joseloff Gallery, University of Hartford, Hartford Art School, Harry Jack Gray Center, 200 Bloomfield Av, West Hartford, CT 06117 - T: (860) 768-4090, Fax: (860) 768-5159, E-mail: zdavis@mail.hartford.edu. Dir.: Zina Davis
Fine Arts Museum / University Museum - 1970 48525

Museum of American Political Life, University of Hartford, 200 Bloomfield Av, West Hartford, CT 06117 - T: (860) 768-4090, Fax: (860) 768-5159, E-mail: zdavis@mail.hartford.edu. Dir.: Zina Davis
Historical Museum - 1989 48526

Noah Webster House - Museum of West Hartford History, 227 S Main St, West Hartford, CT 06107-3430 - T: (860) 521-5362, Fax: (860) 521-4036, E-mail: vfzoe@snet.net, Internet: www.ctstateu.edu/~noahweb/noahwebster.html. Dir.: Vivian F. Zoe
Historical Museum - 1965
Local hist 48527

Saint Joseph College Art Gallery, 1678 Asylum Av, West Hartford, CT 06117 - T: (203) 232-4571, Fax: (203) 231-5754, E-mail: vuccello@sjc.edu, Internet: www.sjc.edu. Pres.: Winifred E. Coleman, Dir.: Vincenza Uccello
Fine Arts Museum / University Museum - 1932 48528

Science Center of Connecticut, 950 Trout Brook Dr, West Hartford, CT 06119 - T: (806) 231-2824, Fax: (806) 232-0705, E-mail: jgoldman@sciencecenterct.org, Internet: www.sciencecenterct.org. Dir.: Ed Forand
Science&Tech Museum - 1927
Science and technology, natural history 48529

West Henrietta NY

New York Museum of Transportation, 6393 E River Rd, West Henrietta, NY 14586 - T: (716) 533-1113, Internet: www.transportation.mus.ny.us/. Pres.: T.H. Strang
Science&Tech Museum - 1974 48530

West Hollywood CA

MAK Center for Art and Architecture, Schindler House, 835 N Kings Rd, West Hollywood, CA 90069-5409 - T: (323) 651-1510, Fax: (323) 651-2340, E-mail: makcenter@earthlink.net, Internet: www.makcenter.com. Dir.: Cara Mullio, Dep. Dir.: LouAnne Greenwald
Fine Arts Museum - 1994 48531

West Lafayette IN

Purdue University Galleries, 1396 Physics Bldg, West Lafayette, IN 47907-1396 - T: (765) 494-3061, Fax: (765) 496-2817, E-mail: gallery@purdue.edu, Internet: www.sla.purdue.edu/galleries. Dir.: Martin Craig, Ass. Dir.: Michael Atwell
Fine Arts Museum / University Museum - 1978
Art gallery 48532

West Liberty OH

Piatt Castles, 10051 Township Rd 47, West Liberty, OH 43357 - T: (937) 465-2821, Fax: (937) 465-7774, E-mail: macochee@logan.net, Internet: www.piattcastles.com. Pres.: Margaret Piatt
Local Museum / Folklore Museum - 1912 48533

West Liberty WV

Women's History Museum, 108 Walnut St, West Liberty, WV 26074 - T: (304) 336-7159, Fax: (304) 336-7893, E-mail: womenshist@earthlink.net, Internet: www.womens-history-museum.com. Dir.: Jeanne Schramm, Cur.: Robert W. Schramm
Historical Museum - 1990
Women's hist 48534

West Newton MA

Chapel Gallery, 60 Highland St W, West Newton, MA 02465 - T: (617) 244-4039, Internet: www.bostonsculptors.com. Dir.: Julie Scaramella
Public Gallery - 1992 48535

West Orange NJ

Edison National Historic Site, Main St at Lakeside Av, West Orange, NJ 07052 - T: (973) 736-0550, Fax: (973) 736-8496, E-mail: edis_superintendent@nps.gov, Internet: www.nps.gov/edis. Head: Maryanne Gerbauckas
Historical Museum - 1956 48536

West Palm Beach FL

Historical Museum of Palm Beach County, 400 N Dixie Hwy, West Palm Beach, FL 33401 - T: (561) 832-4164, Fax: (561) 832-7965. Pres.: Ken Brower, C.E.O.: Kristin H. Gaspari
Local Museum - 1937 48537

Norton Museum of Art, 1451 S Olive Av, West Palm Beach, FL 33401 - T: (561) 832-5196, Fax: (561) 659-4689, E-mail: museum@norton.org, Internet: www.norton.org. Dir.: Christina Orr-Cahall, Chief Cur.: Roger B. Ward (European Art), Cur.: Kevin Sharp (American Art), John Finlay (Chinese Art), Virginia Heckert (Photography)
Fine Arts Museum - 1940
Chinese and contemporary art   48538

Robert and Mary Montgomery Armory Art Center, 1703 Lake Av, West Palm Beach, FL 33401 - T: (561) 832-1776, Fax: (561) 832-0191, E-mail: armory@Bellsouth.net, Internet: www.armoryart.org. C.E.O.: Amelia Ostrosky
Public Gallery - 1987   48539

South Florida Science Museum, 4801 Dreher Trail N, West Palm Beach, FL 33405 - T: (561) 832-1988, 833-5368, Fax: (561) 833-0551, E-mail: rollings@sfsm.org, Internet: www.sfsm.org. Dir.: James R. Rollings, Dep Dir.: Christian Koch (Education)
Science&Tech Museum - 1959   48540

West Park NY

Slabsides, Off John Burroughs Dr, West Park, NY 12493 - T: (212) 769-5169, Fax: (212) 769-5329, E-mail: breslof@amnh.org, Internet: www.research.amnh.org/burroughs. Pres.: Frank Knight
Historical Museum - 1921   48541

West Point NY

Constitution Island Association Museum, POB 41, West Point, NY 10996 - T: (914) 446-8676, E-mail: executivedirector@constitutionisland.org, Internet: www.constitutionisland.org. Dir.: Richard de Koster
Historical Museum - 1916   48542

West Point Museum, United States Military Academy, Bldg 2110, West Point, NY 10996 - T: (845) 938-2203, Fax: (845) 938-7478, Internet: www.usma.edu. Dir.: Michael E. Moss, Cur.: David M. Reel (Art), Edward E. Turner (Armours), Michael J. McAfee (Uniforms and Military History), Richard H. Clark (Design), Cons.: Paul R. Ackermann
Military Museum - 1854   48543

West Saint Paul MN

North Star Scouting Memorabilia, POB 18341, West Saint Paul, MN 55118 - T: (612) 771-9066, E-mail: dickcarroll@juno.com, Internet: www.nssm.org. Dir./Cur.: Richard E. Carroll
Historical Museum - 1976   48544

West Salem WI

Hamlin Garland Homestead, 257 W Garland St, West Salem, WI 54669 - T: (608) 786-1399. Pres.: Errol Kindschy
Local Museum - 1976
Historic house   48545

Palmer/Gullickson Octagon Home, 360 N Leonard, West Salem, WI 54669 - T: (608) 786-1399. Pres.: Errol Kindschy
Local Museum - 1976
Local history   48546

West Sayville NY

Long Island Maritime Museum, 86 West Av, West Sayville, NY 11796 - T: (516) 854-4974, Fax: (516) 854-4979, E-mail: limaritimemuseum@aol.com, Internet: www.limaritime.org. Head: R. Douglas Shaw
Special Museum - 1966   48547

West Springfield MA

Storrowton Village Museum, 1305 Memorial Av, West Springfield, MA 01089 - T: (413) 787-0136, Fax: (413) 787-0166, E-mail: storrow@thebige.com, Internet: www.thebige.com. Dir.: Dennis Picard
Open Air Museum / Historical Museum - 1929
Historic village   48548

West Union IA

Fayette County Historical Museum, 100 N Walnut St, West Union, IA 52175 - T: (319) 422-5797. Pres.: Ruth Brooks, Laura Janssen
Local Museum - 1975
History, genealogy   48549

Westbrook CT

Military Historians Museum, N Main St, Westbrook, CT 06498 - T: (860) 399-9460, E-mail: military-historians@snet.net. Cur.: Frank Young
Military Museum - 1949/2000
Military uniforms   48550

Westbury NY

Town of North Hempstead Museum, 461 Newton St, Westbury, NY 11590 - T: (516) 869-7757, Internet: www.northhempstead.com. Pres.: Dr. George Williams
Historical Museum - 1963   48551

Westerly RI

Hoxie Gallery, Westerly Public Library, 44 Broad St, Westerly, RI 02891 - T: (401) 596-2877, Fax: (401) 596-5600, Internet: seq.clan.lib.ri.us/wes. Dir.: Kathryn T. Taylor
Fine Arts Museum
Local artists   48552

Western Springs IL

Western Springs Museum, 4211 Grand Av, Western Springs, IL 60558 - T: (708) 246-9230. Cur.: Ann Vance
Local Museum - 1967
Local history, housed in a Old Water Tower   48553

Westerville OH

Anti-Saloon League Museum, 126 S State St, Westerville, OH 43081 - T: (614) 882-7277 ext 160, Fax: (614) 882-5369, E-mail: bweinhar@wpl.lib.oh.us
Special Museum - 1990
Publications, fliers, posters, song books   48554

Hanby House, 160 W Main St, Westerville, OH 43081 - T: (614) 895-6017, E-mail: mgale@ee.net. Pres.: Marilyn Gale
Local Museum - 1937   48555

The Ross C. Purdy Museum of Ceramics, 735 Ceramic Pl, Westerville, OH 43081 - T: (614) 890-4700, Fax: (614) 899-6109, E-mail: info@acers.org, Internet: www.acers.org. Dir.: Yvonne Manring
Decorative Arts Museum - 1977
Ceramics   48556

Westfield MA

Jasper Rand Art Museum, 6 Elm St, Westfield, MA 01085 - T: (413) 568-7833, Fax: (413) 568-1558, E-mail: pcramer@exit3.com, Internet: www.ci.westfield.ma.us/athen.thml. Pres.: James A. Rogers, Dir.: Patricia T. Cramer
Fine Arts Museum - 1927
Art gallery   48557

Westfield NJ

Miller-Cory House Museum, 614 Mountain Av, Westfield, NJ 07090 - T: (908) 232-1776, Fax: (908) 232-1740, E-mail: mc@westfieldnj.com, Internet: www.westfieldnj.com. Pres.: Thomas Sherry, C.E.O.: John Petersen
Local Museum - 1972   48558

Westfield NY

McClurg Mansion, Main and Portage Sts, Westfield, NY 14787 - T: (716) 326-2977. Pres.: Roderick A. Nixon, Dir.: Nancy Brown
Local Museum - 1883   48559

Westfield WI

Cochrane-Nelson House → Marquette County Museum

Marquette County Museum, 125 Lawrence St, Westfield, WI 53964. Dir.: Esther Brancel, Cur.: Donald Sprain
Local Museum - 1979
Historic house   48560

Westminster MD

Carroll County Farm Museum, 500 S Center St, Westminster, MD 21157 - T: (410) 848-7775, Fax: (410) 876-8544, E-mail: ccfarm@carr.org, Internet: ccgov.carr.org/farm. Head: Dottie Freeman, Cur.: Victoria Fowler
Public Gallery / Historic Site / Agriculture Museum - 1965   48561

Esther Prangley Rice Gallery, c/o Western Maryland College, Dept. of Art and Art History, Westminster, MD 21157 - T: (410) 857-2595, Fax: (410) 386-4657, E-mail: mlosch@wmdc.edu, Internet: www.wmdc.edu. Dir.: Michael Losch
Ethnology Museum / Fine Arts Museum
Egyptian, African, native American, Asian prints   48562

Historical Society Museum of Carroll County, 210 E Main St, Westminster, MD 21157-5225 - T: (410) 848-6494, Fax: (410) 848-3596, Internet: www.carr.org/hscc. Cur.: Catherine Baty
Local Museum - 1939
Hist and culture, clothing, ceramics and glass, furniture, clocks   48563

Union Mills Homestead and Grist Mill, 3311 Littles Town Pike, Westminster, MD 21158 - T: (410) 848-2288, Fax: (410) 848-2288, E-mail: ejss61@aol.com, Internet: www.carr.org/tourism. Pres.: James M. Shriver, Dir.: Jane S. Sewell
Science&Tech Museum - 1797   48564

Westminster VT

Westminster Historical Society Museum, Main St, Westminster, VT 05158 - T: (802) 387-5778. Pres.: Virginia Lisai, Dir.: Karen Larsen
Local Museum - 1966
Local hist   48565

Weston CT

Coley Homestead and Barn Museum, 104 Weston Rd, Weston, CT 06883 - T: (203) 226-1804, 544-9636, Fax: (203) 227-4268. Pres.: Paul Deysenroth
Local Museum / Agriculture Museum - 1961
Agriculture, handicraft, furnishings - herb garden   48566

Weston MA

Carney Gallery, c/o Regis College Fine Arts Center, 235 Wellesley St, Weston, MA 0293 - T: (781) 768-7034, Fax: (781) 768-7030, Internet: www.regiscollege.edu. Dir.: Rosemary Noon
Fine Arts Museum - 1993
Works of contemporary women artists   48567

Golden Ball Tavern Museum, 662 Boston Post Rd, Weston, MA 02193 - T: (781) 894-1751, Fax: (781) 862-9178, E-mail: joanb5@aol.com, Internet: www.goldenballtavern.org. Pres.: William Wiseman, Dir.: Dr. Joan P. Bines
Local Museum - 1964
Historic house   48568

Museum of the Weston Historical Society, 358 Boston Post Rd, Weston, MA 02493 - T: (781) 237-1447, Fax: (781) 237-1471, E-mail: verandy@aol.com. Pres.: William Martin
Historical Museum - 1963
Local history   48569

Spellman Museum of Stamps and Postal History, Regis College, 235 Wellesley St, Weston, MA 02493 - T: (781) 768-7331, Fax: (781) 768-7332. Exec. Dir.: David W. Gregg, Cur.: George Norton
Special Museum - 1960
Philatelic, postal services   48570

Weston VT

Farrar-Mansur House and Old Mill Museum, Main St, Weston, VT 05161 - T: (802) 824-6781, Fax: (802) 824-4072. Pres.: May Bigelow
Local Museum / Special Museum - 1933
Historic house   48571

Weston WV

Jackson's Mill Historic Area, 160 Jackson Mill Rd, Weston, WV 26452 - T: (304) 287-8206, Fax: (304) 269-3409, E-mail: jmill@wvu.edu, Internet: www.jacksonmill.com. C.E.O.: Dean Hardman, Chm.: Erseline Rumbach
Historic Site - 1968
Local hist, Boyhood home of "Stonewall" Jackson   48572

Westport CT

Westport Historical Museum, 25 Avery Pl, Westport, CT 06880 - T: (203) 222-1424, Fax: (203) 221-0981, E-mail: westporth@snet.net, Internet: www.westporthistory.org. Pres.: Ann E. Sheffer, C.E.O.: Sheila C. O'Neill
Local Museum - 1899
Diorama of historic downtown, costumes - archives   48573

Westport WA

Westport Maritime Museum, 2201 Westhaven Dr, Westport, WA 98595 - T: (360) 268-0078, Fax: (360) 268-0078, E-mail: rwpitzer@techline.com, Internet: www.westportwa.com/museum
Local Museum / Historical Museum - 1985
Local and coast guard hist, shipwrecks, marine mammals   48574

Wethersfield CT

The Webb-Deane-Stevens Museum, 211 Main St, Wethersfield, CT 06109 - T: (860) 529-0612, Fax: (860) 571-8636, E-mail: info@webb-deane-stevens.org, Internet: www.webb-deane-stevens.org. Dir.: Jennifer S. Eifrig, Jane Peake (Education), Cur.: Donna Baron
Local Museum - 1919
Local hist   48575

Wethersfield Museum, 150 Main St, Wethersfield, CT 06109 - T: (860) 529-7656, Fax: (860) 529-9105, E-mail: director@wethhist.org, Internet: www.wethhist.org. Dir.: Brenda Milkofsky
Historical Museum - 1932
Local hist   48576

Wewoka OK

Seminole Nation Museum, 524 S Wewoka Av, Wewoka, OK 74884 - T: (405) 257-5580, Internet: www.wewoka.com/seminole.htm. Dir.: Lewis Johnson, Chief Cur.: Margaret Jane Norman
Folklore Museum / Ethnology Museum / Historical Museum - 1974   48577

Weyauwega WI

Little Red School House Museum, 411 W High St, Weyauwega, WI 54983 - T: (920) 867-2500
Historical Museum - 1970   48578

Wharton TX

Wharton County Historical Museum, 3615 N Richmond Rd, Wharton, TX 77488 - T: (979) 532-2600, Fax: (979) 532-0871, E-mail: marvin@wcnet.net. Pres.: Linda Joy Stovall, C.E.O.: Marvin Albrecht
Local Museum - 1979
Local hist   48579

Wheat Ridge CO

Wheat Ridge Sod House Museum, 4610 Robb St, Wheat Ridge, CO 80033 - T: (303) 421-9111, Fax: (303) 467-2539, E-mail: wrhissoc@aol.com. Pres.: Claudia R. Worth
Historical Museum - 1970
Sod house   48580

Wheaton IL

Billy Graham Center Museum, 500 E College Av, Wheaton, IL 60187 - T: (630) 752-5909, Fax: (630) 752-5916, E-mail: bgcmus@wheaton.edu, Internet: www.wheaton.edu/bgc/museum/. Dir.: James D. Stambaugh
Religious Arts Museum - 1975   48581

Du Page County Historical Museum, 102 E Wesley St, Wheaton, IL 60187 - T: (630) 682-7343, Fax: (630) 682-6549, E-mail: historical.museum@dupageco.org, Internet: www.dupageco.org. Dir.: Susan E. Stob, Sen. Cur.: Steph McGrath, Cur.: Jody Crago, Mary Johnson (Education)
Historical Museum - 1967
County history exhibits with changing costumes and hands-on history for children   48582

The First Division Museum at Cantigny, 1 S 151 Winfield Rd, Wheaton, IL 60187-6097 - T: (630) 260-8185, Fax: (630) 260-9298, E-mail: fdmuseum@tribune.com, Internet: www.rrmtf.org/firstdivision. Dir.: John F. Votaw
Military Museum - 1960
Military hist   48583

Robert R. McCormick Museum at Cantigny, 1 S 151 Winfield Rd, Wheaton, IL 60187 - T: (630) 260-8159, Fax: (630) 260-8160, E-mail: emanyon@tribone.com, Internet: www.cantignypark.com. Dir.: Ellen Manyon
Historical Museum - 1955
Joseph Medill, editor of the Chicago Tribune, Col. Robert R.McCormick (grandson of Medill) editor and publisher of the Chicago Tribune, hisory of journalism   48584

Wheaton History Center, 606 N Main St, Wheaton, IL 60187-4167 - T: (630) 682-9472, Fax: (630) 682-9913, E-mail: wtnhistory@aol.com, Internet: www.wheaton.lib.il.us/whc. Dir.: Alberta Adamson
Local Museum - 1986
Local hist, slavery, underground railroad   48585

Wheaton MN

Traverse County Historical Society Museum, 1201 Broadway, Wheaton, MN 56296 - T: (320) 563-4110, Fax: (302) 563-4823, Internet: www.cityofheaton.com. Pres.: Clarence Juelich
Historical Museum - 1977   48586

Wheeling WV

The Museums of Oglebay Institute, Oglebay Park, Wheeling, WV 26003 - T: (304) 242-7272, Fax: (304) 242-4203, Internet: www.oionline.com. Dir.: Dr. Frederick A. Lambert, Holly H. McCluskey, Asst. Cur.: Travis Zeik
Local Museum - 1930
Local hist   48587

West Virginia Independence Hall, 1528 Market St, Wheeling, WV 26003 - T: (304) 238-1300, Fax: (304) 238-1302, E-mail: gerry.reilly@wvculture.org, Internet: www.wvculture.org. Dir.: Gerry Reilly
Local Museum - 1964
Historic building   48588

West Virginia Northern Community College Alumni Association Museum, 1704 Market St, Wheeling, WV 26003-3699 - T: (304) 233-5900 ext 4265, Fax: (304) 232-0965. Dir.: Zak Witcherly
Local Museum - 1984
Local hist   48589

White Springs FL

Stephen Foster Folk Culture Center, US 41 N, White Springs, FL 32096 - T: (386) 397-2733, Fax: (386) 397.4262, E-mail: martha.j.nelson@dep.state.fl.us, Internet: floridastateparks.org
Folklore Museum - 1939
Paintings, musical instruments, minstrel show material, Stephen Foster's folk songs   48590

White Sulphur Springs MT

Meagher County Historical Association Castle Museum, 310 Second Av SE, White Sulphur Springs, MT 59645 - T: (406) 547-2324
Local Museum - 1967   48591

White Sulphur Springs WV

President's Cottage Museum, 330 W Main St, White Sulphur Springs, WV 24986 - T: (304) 536-1110 ext 7314/7198, Fax: (304) 536-7854, Internet: www.greenbrier.com. Dir.: Ted J. Kleisner, Cur.: Dr. Robert S. Conte
Local Museum - 1932
Local hist 48592

Whiteville NC

North Carolina Museum of Forestry, 415 S Madison St, Whiteville, NC 28472 - T: (910) 914-4185, Fax: (910) 641-0385, E-mail: patricia.l.jones@ncmail.net. Dir.: Harry Warren
Natural History Museum / Agriculture Museum - 2000
NC forest natural hist 48593

Whitewater WI

Crossman Art Gallery, University of Wisconsin Whitewater, Center of the Arts, 800 W Main St, Whitewater, WI 53190 - T: (262) 472-5708, Fax: (262) 472-2808, E-mail: flanagam@uww.edu, Internet: www.uww.edu. Dir.: Michael Flanagam
Public Gallery 48594

Whitewater Historical Museum, 275 N Tratt St, Whitewater, WI 53190 - T: (414) 473-2966. C.E.O.: Dr. Alfred S. Kolmos
Local Museum - 1974
Local hist 48595

Whitingham VT

Whitingham Historical Museum, Stimpson Hill, Whitingham, VT 05361 - T: (802) 368-2448. Pres.: Robert Coombs
Local Museum - 1973
Local hist 48596

Whittier CA

Rio Hondo College Art Gallery, 3600 Workman Mill Rd, Whittier, CA 90601-1699 - T: (310) 908-3428, Fax: (310) 908-3446. Dir.: William Lane
Fine Arts Museum - 1967
Contemporary paintings and graphics 48597

Whittington IL

Illinois Artisans and Visitors Centers, 14967 Gun Creek Trail, Whittington, IL 62897-1000 - T: (618) 629-2220, Fax: (618) 629-2704. Dir.: Ellen Gantner
Decorative Arts Museum - 1990
Craft work of Illinois artisans 48598

Wichita KS

Edwin A. Ulrich Museum of Art, Wichita State University, 1845 Fairmount, Wichita, KS 67260-0046 - T: (316) 978-3664, Fax: (316) 978-3898, E-mail: ulrich@wichita.edu, Internet: www.ulrich.wichita.edu. Dir.: David Butler, Cur.: Elizabeth Dunbar
Fine Arts Museum / University Museum - 1974
Art 48599

Exploration Place, 300 N McLean Blvd, Wichita, KS 67203 - T: (316) 263-3373, Fax: (316) 263-4545, Internet: www.exploration.org. Dir.: Marty Sigwing
Natural History Museum / Science&Tech Museum - 1984 48600

Gallery XII, 412 E Douglas Av, Wichita, KS 67202 - T: (316) 267-5915. Pres.: Brenda Jones
Fine Arts Museum - 1977 48601

Great Plains Transportation Museum, 700 E Douglas, Wichita, KS 67202 - T: (316) 263-0944, Internet: www.gptm.org
Science&Tech Museum - 1983 48602

Indian Center Museum, 650 N Seneca, Wichita, KS 67203 - T: (316) 262-5221, Fax: (316) 262-4216, E-mail: icm@southwind.net, Internet: www.theindiancenter.com/museum.htm. Pres.: Dr. David Hughes, C.E.O.: Shelly Berger
Ethnology Museum / Folklore Museum - 1975
Native American museum, old Indian council grounds 48603

Kansas African American Museum, 601 N Water St, Wichita, KS 67203 - T: (316) 262-7651, Fax: (316) 265-6953. Exec. Dir.: Eric Key
Fine Arts Museum - 1972
Visual art forms of African American life and culture - library 48604

Kansas Aviation Museum, 3350 S George Washington Blvd, Wichita, KS 67210 - T: (316) 683-9242, Fax: (316) 683-0573, E-mail: kam3350@juno.com, Internet: www.saranap.com/kam.html. Exec. Dir.: Bob Knight, Dir.: Donald L. Livengood
Science&Tech Museum - 1991
Aviation 48605

Museum of Decorative Painting and Decorative Arts Collection, 393 N McLean Blvd, Wichita, KS 67203-5968 - T: (316) 269-9300 ext 103, Fax: (316) 269-9191, E-mail: jan@decorativepainters.org, Internet: www.decorativepainters.com. Chairman: Andy B. Jones, Sc. Staff: Kay Blair (Admin.), Jan Vavra (Art collection)
Fine Arts Museum - 1982
Decorative art 48606

Old Cowtown Museum, 1871 Sim Park Dr, Wichita, KS 67203 - T: (316) 264-0671, Fax: (316) 264-2937, E-mail: cowtown@southwind.net, Internet: www.old-cowtown.org. Dir.: JaLayne Wray, Sc. Staff: Vanya Scott (Registrar, Collections)
Local Museum / Open Air Museum - 1952
Open air living history, 1865-1880 era of Wichita and Sedgwick County Kansas 48607

Omnisphere and Science Center, 220 S Main, Wichita, KS 67202 - T: (316) 337-9174. Dir.: Janice McKinney
Science&Tech Museum - 1976
Science 48608

Whittier Fine Arts Gallery, c/o Friends University, 2100 W University St, Wichita, KS 67213 - T: (316) 295-5877, Fax: (316) 295-5656. Cur.: Annie Lowrey
Fine Arts Museum / University Museum - 1963 48609

Wichita Art Museum, 619 Stackman Dr, Wichita, KS 67203 - T: (316) 268-4921, Fax: (316) 268-4980, E-mail: info@wichitaartmuseum.org, Internet: www.wichitaartmuseum.org. Dir.: Charles K. Steiner, Chief Cur.: Stephen Gleissner
Fine Arts Museum - 1935
Art 48610

Wichita Center for the Arts, 9112 E Central, Wichita, KS 67206 - T: (316) 634-2787, Fax: (316) 634-0593, E-mail: arts@wcfta.com, Internet: www.wcfta.com. Exec. Dir.: Howard W. Ellington
Fine Arts Museum - 1920
Arts 48611

Wichita-Sedgwick County Historical Museum, 204 S Main, Wichita, KS 67202 - T: (316) 265-9314, Fax: (316) 265-9319, E-mail: wschm@onemain.com, Internet: www.wscribe.com/history. Pres.: Carolyn Conley, Dir.: Robert A. Puckett
Local Museum - 1939
Local history, old City Hall 48612

Wichita Falls TX

Kell House Museum, 900 Bluff St, Wichita Falls, TX 76301 - T: (940) 723-2712, Fax: (940) 767-5424, E-mail: kellhcurator@aol.com, Internet: www.wichitaheritage.org. Cur.: Ralph Gibson
Historic Site - 1981
Local hist 48613

Wichita Falls Museum and Art Center, 2 Eureka Circle, Wichita Falls, TX 76308 - T: (940) 692-0923, Fax: (940) 696-5358, E-mail: wfmuseum@wf.net, Internet: www.wfmuseum.org. Dir.: Jeff Desborough, Cur.: Janelle Redlaczyk, Margaret Breeze
Fine Arts Museum / Local Museum - 1965
Art, local hist 48614

Wickenburg AZ

Desert Caballeros Western Museum, 21 N Frontier St, Wickenburg, AZ 85390 - T: (520) 684-2272, Fax: (520) 684-5794, E-mail: info@westernmuseum.org, Internet: www.westernmuseum.org. Dir.: Michael J. Ettema
Fine Arts Museum / Historical Museum - 1960
History 48615

Wickliffe KY

Wickliffe Mounds, Museum of Native American Village, 94 Green St, Wickliffe, KY 42087 - T: (270) 335-3681, E-mail: wmounds@brtc.net, Internet: campus.murraystate.edu/org/wmrc/wmrc.htm. Dir.: Kit W. Wesler, Ass. Dir.: Carla Hildebrand
Archaeological Museum - 1932
Archaeology 48616

Wilber NE

Wilber Czech Museum, 102 W Third, Wilber, NE 68465 - T: (402) 821-2183. Dir.: Irma Ourecky
Local Museum / Folklore Museum - 1962
Czechoslovakian cultures, dolls, clothing, pictures 48617

Wilberforce OH

National Afro-American Museum and Cultural Center, 1350 Brush Row Rd, Wilberforce, OH 45384-0578 - T: (937) 376-4944, Fax: (937) 376-2007, E-mail: naamcc@erinet.com, Internet: winslo.ohio.gov/ohswww/places/afroam/. Dir.: Vernon Courtney, Cur.: Dr. Floyd R. Thomas
Historical Museum / Folklore Museum - 1972
African American history 48618

Wild Rose WI

Pioneer Museum, Main St, Wild Rose, WI 54984. Pres.: Rodney Radloff, Cur.: Margaret Walters
Local Museum - 1964
Pioneer hist 48619

Wildwood NJ

Boyer Museum and National Marbles Hall of Fame, 3907 Pacific Av, Wildwood, NJ 08260 - T: (609) 523-0277. Dir.: Robert J. Scully, Sc. Staff: Robert Bright (History)
Local Museum / Historical Museum - 1963 48620

Wilkes-Barre PA

Luzerne County Historical Museum, 69 S Franklin St, Wilkes-Barre, PA 18701 - T: (570) 823-6244, Fax: (570) 823-9011, E-mail: lchs@epix.net, Internet: www.whgs.org. Pres.: William Lewis, C.E.O.: Jesse Teitelbaum
Historical Museum / Natural History Museum - 1858
History, geology 48621

Sordoni Art Gallery, Wilkes University, 150 S River St, Wilkes-Barre, PA 18766 - T: (570) 408-4325, Fax: (570) 408-7733, E-mail: bernier@wilkes.edu, Internet: www.sordorni.wilkes.edu. C.E.O.: Ronald R. Bernier
Fine Arts Museum - 1973
Art 48622

Willcox AZ

Chiricahua Museum, HCR 2, Box 6500, Willcox, AZ 85643 - T: (520) 824-3560, Fax: (520) 824-3421. Cur.: Kathrine Neilsen
Natural History Museum - 1924
Natural history, historical artifacts 48623

Williamsburg VA

Abby Aldrich Rockefeller Folk Art Museum, 307 S England St, Williamsburg, VA 23185 - T: (757) 220-7670, Fax: (757) 565-8915, E-mail: cweekley@cwf.org, Internet: www.colonialwilliamsburg.org. Dir.: Carolyn Weekley, Cur.: Barbara R. Luck
Fine Arts Museum - 1957
Art 48624

Bassett Hall, 522 E Francis St, Williamsburg, VA 23185 - T: (757) 229-1000, Fax: (757) 220-7173, E-mail: lkally@cwf.org, Internet: www.history.org. Dir.: Carolyn Weekley
Local Museum - 1979
Historic house 48625

Carter's Grove Visitor Center, 8797 Pocahontas Trail, Williamsburg, VA 23185 - T: (757) 229-1000, Fax: (757) 220-7173, E-mail: lkelley@cwf.org, Internet: www.history.org. Dir.: Carolyn Weekley
Historical Museum - 1964 48626

Colonial Williamsburg, 134 N Henry St, Williamsburg, VA 23185 - T: (757) 229-1000, Fax: (757) 220-7286, E-mail: shart@cwf.org, Internet: www.colonialwilliamsburg.org. Pres.: Colin Campbell
Local Museum - 1926
Historic town 48627

DeWitt Wallace Decorative Arts Museum, 325 Francis St, Williamsburg, VA 23185, mail addr: 1776, Williamsburg, VA 23187-1776 - T: (757) 220-7984, Fax: (757) 565-8804, E-mail: mcotrill@cwf.org, Internet: www.history.org
Decorative Arts Museum - 1985
English and American decorative arts from 1600-1830 48628

Jamestown Settlement, Jamestown-Yorktown Foundation, Rte 31 S, Williamsburg, VA 23187, mail addr: POB 1607, Williamsburg, VA 23187-1607 - T: (757) 887-1776, 253-4838, Fax: (757) 253-5299, E-mail: jwbailey@jyf.state.va.us, Internet: www.historyisfun.org. Dir.: Philip G. Emerson
Historical Museum / Decorative Arts Museum / Fine Arts Museum - 1957/1976
Furniture, silver, paintings, prints, 18th c revolutionary war artifacts, Powhatan Indians America's first permanent English colony 48629

Muscarelle Museum of Art, College of William and Mary, Williamsburg, VA 23185 - T: (757) 221-2710, Fax: (757) 221-2711, E-mail: bgkelm@wm.edu, Internet: www.wm.edu/muscarelle. Dir.: Bonnie G. Kelm, Cur.: Ann C. Madonia
Fine Arts Museum - 1982
Art 48630

This Century Art Gallery, 219 North Boundary St, Williamsburg, VA 23185 - T: (757) 229-4949, Fax: (757) 258-5624, E-mail: kirbyscorpio@aol.com, Internet: www.thiscenturyartgallery.org. Pres.: Michael Kirby
Fine Arts Museum - 1959
Art 48631

The Twentieth Century Gallery → This Century Art Gallery

Williamsport PA

Thomas T. Taber Museum, 858 W 4th St, Williamsport, PA 17701-5824 - T: (570) 326-3326, Fax: (570) 326-3689, E-mail: lchsmuse@csrlink.net, Internet: www.lycoming.org/lchsmuseum. Pres.: Robert E. Kane, C.E.O., Dir. & Cur.: Sandra B. Rife, Cur.: Scott Sagar
Local Museum / Historical Museum - 1895
Regional hist 48632

Williamstown MA

Chapin Library of Rare Books, Stetson Hall, Williams College, Williamstown, MA 01267 - T: (413) 597-2462, Fax: (413) 597-2929, E-mail: chapin.library@williams.edu, Internet: www.williams.edu/resources/chapin. Cust.: Robert L. Volz
Library with Exhibitions - 1923 48633

Sterling and Francine Clark Art Institute, 225 South St, Williamstown, MA 01267 - T: (413) 458-9545, Fax: (413) 458-2318, E-mail: info@clarkart.edu, Internet: www.clarkart.edu. Dir.: Michael Conforti, Sen. Cur.: Richard Rand, Cur.: Brian Allen (American Paintings), James A. Ganz (Prints, Drawings, Photographs)
Fine Arts Museum - 1950
Decorative art, sculptures, paintings, drawings, prints, photography 48634

Williams College Museum of Art, 15 Lawrence Hall Dr, Ste 2, Williamstown, MA 01267-2566 - T: (413) 597-2037, Fax: (413) 458-9017, E-mail: WCMA@williams.edu, Internet: www.williams.edu/WCMA/. Dir.: Linda Shearer, Cur.: Nancy Mowll Mathews, Deborah Menaker Rothschild
Fine Arts Museum / University Museum - 1926
Art 48635

Williamstown WV

Fenton Glass Museum, 420 Caroline Av, Williamstown, WV 26187 - T: (304) 375-7772, Fax: (304) 375-7833, E-mail: askfenton@fentonartglass.com, Internet: www.fentonartglass.com. Dir.: Dr. Frank M. Fenton
Decorative Arts Museum - 1977 48636

Willimantic CT

Windham Textile and History Museum, 157 Union-Main St, Willimantic, CT 06226 - T: (860) 456-2178, E-mail: millmuseum@hotmail.com, Internet: www.millmuseum.org. Pres.: Charlotte Patros, Dir.: Beverly York
Historical Museum / Science&Tech Museum - 1985 48637

Williston ND

Fort Buford State Historic Site, 15349 39th Ln NW, Williston, ND 58801 - T: (701) 572-9034, Fax: (701) 572-6509, E-mail: ftbuford@dia.net, Internet: www.state.nd.us/hist/. Dir.: Merl Paaverud
Military Museum - 1931 48638

Fort Union Trading Post National Historic Site, 15550 Hwy 1804, Williston, ND 58801 - T: (701) 572-9083, Fax: (701) 572-7321, E-mail: andrey_barnhart@nps.gov, Internet: www.nps.gov/fous. Dir.: Andy Barta, Cur.: Audrey Barnhart, Sc. Staff: Randy Kane (History)
Historical Museum - 1966 48639

Frontier Museum, 6330 2nd Av W, Williston, ND 58801 - T: (701) 572-9751. Pres.: Ruth Robinson
Local Museum - 1958 48640

Willits CA

Mendocino County Museum, 400 E Commercial St, Willits, CA 95490 - T: (707) 459-2736, Fax: (707) 459-7836, E-mail: museum@co.mendocino.ca.us, Internet: www.co.mendocino.ca.us. Cur.: Rebecca Snetselaar
Local Museum - 1972
Local hist 48641

Willmar MN

Kandiyohi County Historical Society Museum, 610 Hwy 71 NE, Willmar, MN 56201 - T: (612) 235-1881, E-mail: kandhist@wecnet.com, Internet: www.freepages.genealogy-rootsweb.com/~kchs/23/index.html. Exec. Dir.: Mona Nelson-Balcer
Historical Museum - 1898 48642

Willow Run Airport MI

Yankee Air Museum, H-2041 A St, Willow Run Airport, MI 48111 - T: (734) 483-4030, Fax: (734) 483-5076, E-mail: yankeeairmuseum@provide.net, Internet: www.yankeeairmuseum.org. Pres.: Jon Stevens
Science&Tech Museum / Military Museum - 1981 48643

Willow St PA

Hans Herr House and Museum, 1849 Hans Herr Dr, Willow St, PA 17584 - T: (717) 464-4438, E-mail: info@hansherr.org, Internet: www.hansherr.org
Historical Museum - 1974
Mennonite rural life, agricultural items 48644

Wilmette IL

Kohl Children's Museum, 165 Green Bay Rd, Wilmette, IL 60091 - T: (847) 512-1300, Fax: (847) 256-5438, E-mail: sturner@kohlchildrensmuseum.org, Internet: www.kohlchildrensmuseum.org. C.E.O.: Sheridan Turner
Ethnology Museum - 1985 48645

Wilmette Historical Museum, 609 Ridge Rd, Wilmette, IL 60091 - T: (847) 853-7666, Fax: (847) 853-7706, E-mail: husseyk@wilmette.com, Internet: www.wilmette.com/museum. Dir.: Kathy Hussey-Arntson
Local Museum - 1947
Local history 48646

Wilmington CA

Banning Residence Museum, 401 E Main St, Wilmington, CA 90744 - T: (310) 548-7777, Fax: (310) 548-2644, Internet: www.banningmuseum.org. Dir.: Michael Sanborn
Local Museum - 1974
Local hist 48647

Drum Barracks Civil War Museum, 1052 Banning Blvd, Wilmington, CA 90744 - T: (310) 548-7509, Fax: (310) 548-2946, E-mail: sogle@raplacity.org, Internet: www.drumbarracks.org. Dir.: Susan F. Ogle
Military Museum / Historical Museum - 1987
Military, civil war, Southern California history - library 48648

Wilmington DE

Delaware Art Museum (until october 2004: Bank One Center on The Riverfront), 800 N Madison St, Wilmington, DE 19801 - T: (302) 571-9590, Fax: (302) 571-0220, E-mail: lmonty@delart.org, Internet: www.delart.org. Dir.: Stephen T. Bruni, Dep. Dir.: James Hanley, Chief Cur.: Nancy Miller Batty
Fine Arts Museum - 1912
American art, English Pre-Raphaelite art 48649

Delaware Museum, 505 Market St, Wilmington, DE 19801 - T: (302) 655-7161, Fax: (302) 655-7844, E-mail: hsd@dca.net, Internet: www.hsd.org. Pres.: Gordon A. Pfeiffer, Dir.: Barbara E. Benson
Local Museum - 1864
Local hist 48650

Delaware Museum of Natural History, 4840 Kennett Pike, Wilmington, DE 19807-0937 - T: (302) 658-9111, Fax: (302) 658-2610, E-mail: ghalfpenny@delmnh.org, Internet: www.delmnh.org. Dir.: Geoff Halfpenny
Natural History Museum - 1957
Natural hist 48651

The Hagley Museum, 298 Buck Rd E, Wilmington, DE 19807-0630 - T: (302) 658-2400, Fax: (302) 658-0568, E-mail: danmuir@udel.edu, Internet: www.hagley.org. Dir.: George L. Vogt, Cur.: Debra Hughes
Historical Museum / Science&Tech Museum - 1952
History, technology 48652

Hendrickson House Museum and Old Swedes Church, 606 Church St, Wilmington, DE 19801 - T: (302) 652-5629, Fax: (302) 652-8615, E-mail: oldswedes@aol.com, Internet: www.oldswedes.org. Pres.: Philip Hoge, C.E.O.: Jo Thompson
Local Museum - 1947
Historic house and nation's oldest church 48653

Nemours Mansion and Gardens, 1600 Rockland Rd, Wilmington, DE 19803 - T: (302) 651-6912, Fax: (302) 651-6933, E-mail: pdietz@nemours.org, Internet: www.nemours.org. Head: Paddy Dietz
Historical Museum / Fine Arts Museum - 1977
Historic house and art coll from the 14th to 19th c 48654

Rockwood Museum, 610 Shipley Rd, Wilmington, DE 19809 - T: (302) 761-4340, Fax: (302) 761-4345, E-mail: pnond@co.new-castle.de.us, Internet: www.rockwood.org
Decorative Arts Museum / Local Museum - 1976
Local hist 48655

Wilmington NC

Battleship North Carolina, Battleship Dr, Eagles Island, Wilmington, NC 28402 - T: (910) 251-5797, Fax: (910) 251-5807, E-mail: ncbb55@aol.com, Internet: www.battleshipnc.com. Dir.: David R. Scheu, Ass. Dir.: Roger Miller
Military Museum - 1961 48656

Bellamy Mansion Museum of History and Design Arts, 503 Market St, Wilmington, NC 28401 - T: (910) 251-3700, Fax: (910) 763-8154, E-mail: correspondence@bellamymansion.org, Internet: www.bellymymansion.org. Dir.: Gene Ayscue
Decorative Arts Museum / Historical Museum / Fine Arts Museum - 1993 48657

Burgwin-Wright Museum, 224 Market St, Wilmington, NC 28401 - T: (910) 762-0570, Fax: (910) 762-8750, E-mail: burgwinw@bellsouth.net, Internet: www.geocities.com/PicketFence/Garden/4354. Dir.: Susan E. Hart
Historical Museum - 1770
Colonial townhome, English and American antiques and works of art (18th-19th c) 48658

Cape Fear Museum, 814 Market St, Wilmington, NC 28401-4731 - T: (910) 342-2415, Fax: (910) 341-4037, E-mail: ssullivan@nhcgov.com, Internet: www.nhcgov.com/cfm. Dir.: Ruth Haas, Cur.: Barbara Rowe, Historian: Eve Carr
Historical Museum / Natural History Museum - 1898 48659

Louise Wells Cameron Art Museum, 3201 S 17th St, Wilmington, NC 28412 - T: (910) 395-5999, Fax: (910) 395-5030, Internet: www.cameronartmuseum.com. Dir.: C. Reynolds Brown
Fine Arts Museum - 1962
NC paintings, sculpture, decorative arts and works on paper 48660

Lower Cape Fear Historical Society Museum, 126 S Third St, Wilmington, NC 28401 - T: (910) 762-0492, Fax: (910) 763-5869, E-mail: latimer@wilmington.net, Internet: www.latimer.wilmington.org. Pres.: Jan Broadfoot, Exec. Dir.: Cathy Myerow
Decorative Arts Museum / Local Museum - 1956 48661

Poplar Grove Historic Plantation, 10200 U.S. Hwy 17 N, Wilmington, NC 28411 - T: (910) 686-4868, Fax: (910) 686-4309, E-mail: pgp@poplargrove.com, Internet: www.poplargrove.com. Pres.: Forrest Lewis, Dir.: Nancy Simon
Local Museum - 1980
Historic house 48662

Saint John's Museum of Art, 114 Orange St, Wilmington, NC 28401 - T: (910) 763-0281, Fax: (910) 341-7981, E-mail: info@stjohnsmuseum.com, Internet: www.stjohnsmuseum.com. Dir.: C. Reynolds Brown, Ass. Dir.: Pamela A. Jobin, Cur.: Anne G. Brennan
Fine Arts Museum - 1962 48663

USS North Carolina Battleship Memorial → Battleship North Carolina

Wilmington Railroad Museum, 501 Nutt St, Wilmington, NC 28401 - T: (910) 763-2634, Fax: (910) 763-2634, Internet: www.wilm.org/railroad. Pres.: Dr. Frank E. Funk, Exec. Dir.: Sadie Ann Hood
Special Museum - 1979
Railroad 48664

Wilmore KY

Student Center Gallery, Asbury College, 1 Macklem Dr, Wilmore, KY 40390 - T: (859) 858-3511 ext 2242, Fax: (606) 858-3921, E-mail: kevin.sparks@asbury.edu. Chm.: Kevin S. Sparks
Public Gallery 48665

Wilson AR

Hampson Museum, 2 Lake Dr, Wilson, AR 72395 - T: (870) 655-8622, E-mail: hampson@arkansas.net. Head: Corinne Fletcher
Archaeological Museum - 1961
Archaeology 48666

Wilson KS

House of Memories Museum, 415 27th St, Wilson, KS 67490-0271 - T: (785) 658-3505, 658-3343. Dir.: Jean T. Kingston
Historical Museum / Decorative Arts Museum - 1986
Czech heritage, trophies, hair wreath, tools, glassware for Czechoslovakia, costumes 48667

Wilson NC

Barton Museum, Whitehead and Gold St, Wilson, NC 27893, mail addr: c/o Barton College, POB 5000, Wilson, NC 27893 - T: (252) 399-6477, Fax: (252) 399-6571, Internet: www.barton.edu. Dir.: Chris Wilson
Fine Arts Museum / University Museum - 1960
Ceramics, recent drawings, painting, prints, sculpture, African masks 48668

Imagination Station Science Museum, 224 E Nash St, Wilson, NC 27893, mail addr: POB 2127, Wilson, NC 27894-2127 - T: (252) 291-5113, Fax: (252) 291-2968, E-mail: mail@imaginescience.org, Internet: www.imaginescience.org. C.E.O.: Jerry Reynolds
Natural History Museum / Science&Tech Museum - 1989 48669

Wilson NY

Wilson Historical Museum, 645 Lake St, Wilson, NY 14172 - T: (716) 751-9331, Fax: (716) 751-6141, E-mail: agaffiliat@aol.com. Cur.: Dorothy Maxfield
Local Museum - 1972 48670

Wilton CT

Weir Farm, 735 Nod Hill Rd, Wilton, CT 06897 - T: (203) 834-1896, Fax: (203) 834-2421, E-mail: wefa_interpretation@nps.gov, Internet: www.nps.gov/wefa
Local Museum - 1990
Art and history 48671

Wilton Historical Museums, 224 Danbury Rd, Wilton, CT 06897 - T: (203) 762-7257, Fax: (203) 762-3297. Dir.: Marilyn Gould
Local Museum - 1938
Local hist 48672

Wilton NH

Frye's Measure Mill, 12 Frye Mill Rd, Wilton, NH 03086 - T: (603) 654-6581, 654-5345, Internet: www.fryesmeasuremill.com. Pres.: Pamela Savage, C.E.O.: Harland Savage
Historical Museum / Science&Tech Museum - 1858
Industry, measure mill, shaker, colonial boxes 48673

Wimberley TX

Pioneer Town, 333 Wayside Dr, Wimberley, TX 78676 - T: (512) 847-3289, Fax: (512) 847-6705. Dir.: Raymond L. Czichos
Local Museum - 1956
Reproduction of c.1880 old West Town 48674

Winchendon MA

Winchendon Historical Museum, 151 Front St, Winchendon, MA 01475 - T: (508) 297-2142, E-mail: historical@trysb.net. Cur.: Shirley Parks, Julia White
Local Museum - 1930
Local history - library 48675

Winchester IN

Randolph County Historical Museum, 416 S Meridian, Winchester, IN 47394 - T: (317) 584-1334. Dir.: Marjorie Birtwhistle
Local Museum - 1968
Clothes, dishes, photos, tools, books, furniture and furnishings 48676

Winchester MA

Arthur Griffin Center for Photographic Art, 67 Shore Rd, Winchester, MA 01890 - T: (781) 729-1158, Fax: (781) 721-2765, E-mail: photos@griffincenter.org, Internet: www.griffincenter.org. Dir.: Maria Lane
Fine Arts Museum - 1992
Photographic art 48677

Winchester TN

Franklin County Old Jail Museum, 400 Dinah Shore Blvd, Winchester, TN 37398 - T: (615) 967-0524. Head: Nancy Hall
Local Museum - 1973
Local hist 48678

Winchester VA

Winchester-Frederick County Historical Society Museum, 1340 S Pleasant Valley Rd, Winchester, VA 22601 - T: (540) 662-6550, Fax: (540) 662-6991, E-mail: wfchs@shentel.net, Internet: www.winchesterhistory.org. Pres.: Robert F. Boxley
Local Museum - 1930
Local hist 48679

Winder GA

Fort Yargo, Georgia Hwy 81, Winder, GA 30680 - T: (770) 867-3489, Fax: (770) 867-7517, Internet: www.gastateparks.org. Head: Paul Bradshaw
Historical Museum / Historic Site - 1954
Restored blockhouse used during the Creek Indian Wars 48680

Windom MN

Cottonwood County Historical Society Museum, 812 Fourth Av, Windom, MN 56101 - T: (507) 831-1134, Fax: (507) 831-2665. Pres.: L. Tjentland, Dir.: Linda Fransen
Historical Museum - 1901 48681

Window Rock AZ

Navajo Nation Museum, Loop Rd, Window Rock, AZ 86515 - T: (520) 871-6673, Fax: (520) 871-4886. Dir.: Geoffrey I. Brown
Historical Museum / Fine Arts Museum - 1961
Anthropology, textiles, pottery, jewelry, Navajo Indian art 48682

Windsor NC

Historic Hope Foundation, 132 Hope House Rd, Windsor, NC 27983 - T: (252) 794-3140, Fax: (252) 794-5583, E-mail: hopeplantation@coastalnet.com, Internet: www.albemarle-nc.com/hope/. Pres.: John C.P. Tyler, Cur.: Tim Hall (Education, Programs)
Decorative Arts Museum / Local Museum - 1965 48683

Windsor NY

Old Stone House Museum, 22 Chestnut St, Windsor, NY 13865 - T: (607) 655-1491. Dir.: Charles L. English, Dep. Dir.: Louella F. English, Sc. Staff: Bernard Osborne (History)
Local Museum - 1970 48684

Windsor VT

American Precision Museum, 196 Main St, Windsor, VT 05089 - T: (802) 674-5781, Fax: (802) 674-2524, E-mail: apm@sover.net, Internet: www.americanprecision.org. Chm.: Gene Cesari
Science&Tech Museum - 1966
Industrial hist, engineering 48685

Old Constitution House, N Main St, Windsor, VT 05089 - T: (802) 672-3773, Fax: (802) 828-3206, E-mail: jdumville@dca.state.vt.us
Historical Museum / Decorative Arts Museum - 1961
Colonial and Civil War periods, pottery, furniture 48686

Windsor Locks CT

New England Air Museum of the Connecticut Aeronautical Historical Association, Bradley International Airport, Windsor Locks, CT 06096 - T: (860) 623-3305, Fax: (860) 627-2820, E-mail: staff@neam.org, Internet: www.neam.org. C.E.O.: Michael P. Speciale
Science&Tech Museum - 1959
Aeronautics, propulsion systems 48687

Winfield IL

Kline Creek Farm, North and Geneva Rds, Winfield, IL 60190, mail addr: POB 5000, Wheaton, IL 60189-5000 - T: (630) 876-5900, Fax: (630) 293-9421, E-mail: forest@dupageforest.com, Internet: www.dupageforest.com
Agriculture Museum - 1989
Farm equip, household furnishings 48688

Winfield KS

The Cowley County Historical Museum, 1011 Mansfield St, Winfield, KS 67156 - T: (316) 221-4811, Fax: (316) 221-0793, Internet: www.cchsm.com. Pres.: Brad Light
Local Museum - 1931
General museum 48689

Winlock WA

John R. Jackson House, Lewis and Clark State Park, Winlock, WA 98596 - T: (360) 864-2643. Dir.: Cleve Pinnix
Local Museum - 1915
Historic house 48690

Winnabow NC

Brunswick Town State Historic Site, 8884 Saint Philips Rd SE, Winnabow, NC 28479 - T: (910) 371-6613, Fax: (910) 383-3806, E-mail: brunswick@vol.com, Internet: www.carolinarosedesigns.com/brunweb. Head: James A. Bartley
Local Museum - 1958 48691

Winnebago MN

Winnebago Area Museum, 18 First Av NE, Winnebago, MN 56098 - T: (507) 893-4660. Pres.: Pete Haight
Historical Museum / Archaeological Museum - 1977 48692

Winnetka IL

Winnetka Historical Museum, 1140 Elm St, Winnetka, IL 60093 - T: (847) 501-6025, Fax: (847) 501-3221, E-mail: winnetkahistory@cs.com, Internet: www.winnetkahistory.com. Dir.: Joan Evanich, Pres.: Vancy Judge, Cur.: Elizabeth Carlson
Local Museum - 1988
Local history 48693

Winnsboro SC

Fairfield County Museum, 231 S Congress St, Winnsboro, SC 29180 - T: (803) 635-9811, E-mail: fairfieldmus@chestertel.com, Internet: www.cmcog.state.sc.us/fcoc/. Dir.: Pelham Lyles
Local Museum - 1963
Local hist 48694

Winona MN

Arches Museum of Pioneer Life, Hwy 14, 9mi W of Winona, Winona, MN 55987 - T: (507) 454-2723, 523-2111, Fax: (507) 454-0006, E-mail: wchs@luminet.net, Internet: www.winonanet.com/digs/wchs. Exec. Dir.: Mark F. Peterson
Agriculture Museum / Local Museum - 1964
Windmill, farm and household, natural hist 48695

Winona County Historical Museum, 160 Johnson St, Winona, MN 55987 - T: (507) 454-2723, Fax: (507) 454-0006, E-mail: wchs@luminet.net, Internet: www.winonanet.com/orgs/wchs. Dir.: Mark F. Peterson, Cur.: Jodi Brom
Historical Museum - 1935 48696

Winslow AZ

Homolovi Ruins State Park, 87 North State Rte, Winslow, AZ 86047 - T: (928) 289-4106, Fax: (928) 289-2021, E-mail: homolovi@pr.state.az.us, Internet: www.pr.state.az.us
Archaeological Museum - 1986
Archaeology 48697

Winston-Salem NC

Charlotte and Philip Hanes Art Gallery, Wake Forest University, Art Dept, Winston-Salem, NC 27109 - T: (336) 758-5855, Fax: (336) 758-6014, E-mail: faccinto@wfu.edu, Internet: www.wfu.edu/Academic-departments/Art/gall_index.html. Dir.: Victor Faccinto, Ass. Dir.: Kathryn McHenry
Fine Arts Museum / University Museum - 1976 48698

Diggs Gallery at Winston-Salem State University, 601 Martin Luther King Jr. Dr, Winston-Salem, NC 27110 - T: (336) 750-2458, 750-2000, Fax: (336) 750-2463. Dir./Cur.: Belinda Tate
Fine Arts Museum / University Museum - 1990
Art 48699

Museum of Anthropology, Wingate Rd, Winston-Salem, NC 27109-7267 - T: (336) 758-5282, Fax: (336) 758-5116, E-mail: moa@wfu.edu, Internet: www.wfu.edu/MOA. Dir.: Dr. Stephen Wittington
University Museum / Ethnology Museum - 1962 48700

Museum of Early Southern Decorative Arts, 924 S Main St, Winston-Salem, NC 27101 - T: (336) 721-7360, Fax: (336) 721-7367, E-mail: webmaster@mesda.org, Internet: www.mesda.org. Vice Pres.: Paula Locklair, Ass. Cur.: Johanna Brown
Decorative Arts Museum - 1965 48701

Old Salem, 600 S Main St, Winston-Salem, NC 27101 - T: (336) 721-7300, Fax: (336) 721-7335, E-mail: webmaster@oldsalem.org, Internet: www.oldsalem.org. Pres.: Paul Reber
Open Air Museum / Local Museum - 1950 48702

Reynolda House, Museum of American Art, 2250 Reynolda Rd, Winston-Salem, NC 27106-1765 - T: (336) 725-5325, Fax: (336) 721-0991, E-mail: reynolda@reynoldahouse.org, Internet: www.reynoldahouse.org. Dir.: John Neff
Fine Arts Museum - 1964 48703

Sciworks, 400 Hanes-Mill Rd, Winston-Salem, NC 27105 - T: (336) 767-6730, Fax: (336) 661-1777, E-mail: bssanford@sciworks.org, Internet: www.sciworks.org. Pres.: Randall Bratton, Exec. Dir.: Dr. Beverly S. Sanford, Dir.: Tom Wilson
Natural History Museum / Science&Tech Museum - 1964 48704

Southeastern Center for Contemporary Art, 750 Marguerite Dr, Winston-Salem, NC 27106 - T: (336) 725-1904, Fax: (336) 722-6059, E-mail: general@secca.org, Internet: www.secca.org. Dir.: Vicki C. Kopf, Cur.: Ron Platt
Fine Arts Museum - 1956 48705

Wake Forest University Fine Arts Gallery, POB 7232, Winston-Salem, NC 27109 - T: (336) 758-5795, Fax: (336) 758-6014, E-mail: faccinto@wfu.edu, Internet: www.wfu.edu/Academic-departments/Art/gall_index.html. Dir.: Victor Faccinto
Public Gallery / University Museum - 1976 48706

Winter Park FL

The Charles Hosmer Morse Museum of American Art, 445 N Park Av, Winter Park, FL 32789 - T: (407) 645-5311, Fax: (407) 647-1284, Internet: www.morsemuseum.org. Dir.: Dr. Laurence J. Ruggiero
Fine Arts Museum - 1942
American art 48707

The George D. and Harriet W. Cornell Fine Arts Museum, Rollins College, 1000 Holt Av, Winter Park, FL 32789-4499 - T: (407) 646-2526, Fax: (407) 646-2524, E-mail: ablumenthal@rollins.edu, Internet: www.rollins.edu/cfam. Dir.: Arthur R. Blumenthal, Cur.: Theo Lotz
Fine Arts Museum / University Museum - 1978
Art 48708

Winterset IA

Birthplace of John Wayne, 224 S 2nd St, Winterset, IA 50273 - T: (515) 462-1044, Fax: (515) 462-3289, E-mail: director@johnwaynebirthplace.org, Internet: www.johnwaynebirthplace.org. Pres.: David Trask, Dir.: Vickie Polk
Historical Museum - 1981
Historic house, birthplace of film star John Wayne 48709

Madison County Historical Society Museum, 815 S 2nd Av, Winterset, IA 50273 - T: (515) 462-2134, E-mail: mchistoricalsociety1@juno.com. C.E.O.: Carol Bass
Local Museum - 1904
Local history 48710

Winterset Art Center, John Wayne Dr, Winterset, IA 50273 - T: (515) 462-3226, 462-4847. Dir.: Don Thomas
Fine Arts Museum - 1958
Art, housed in an Underground Railway stop during the Civil War 48711

Winterthur DE

Winterthur Museum, Rte 52, Winterthur, DE 19735 - T: (302) 888-4600, 448-3883, Fax: (302) 888-4880, Internet: www.winterthur.org. Dir.: Leslie Green Bownan, Chm.: Bruce C. Perkins, Dep. Dir.: Gary Kulik, Pauline K. Eversmann
Decorative Arts Museum / Historical Museum - 1951
Decorative arts, cultural history 48712

Winterville GA

Carter-Coile Country Doctors Museum, 111 Marigold Ln, Winterville, GA 30683, mail addr: POB 306, Winterville, GA 30683 - T: (706) 742-8600, Fax: (706) 742-5476, E-mail: winterville@charter.net, Internet: www.cityofwinterville.com
Historical Museum - 1971
Medicine, office by Dr. Warren Carter and Dr. Frank Coile 48713

Wiscasset ME

The 1811 Old Lincoln County Jail and 1839 Jailer's House Museum, 133 Federal St, Wiscasset, ME 04578 - T: (207) 882-6817, E-mail: lcha@wiscasset.net, Internet: www.lincolncountyhistory.org. Exec. Dir.: Margaret M. Shiels
Local Museum / Folklore Museum - 1954
Regional history 48714

Castle Tucker, Lee St at High St, Wiscasset, ME 04578 - T: (207) 882-1769, Internet: www.spnea.org
Historical Museum - 1974 48715

Maine Art Gallery, Warren St, Wiscasset, ME 04578 - T: (207) 882-7511. Pres.: Maude Olsen, Dir.: Phyllis Wicks
Fine Arts Museum / Public Gallery - 1958
Art gallery 48716

Musical Wonder House, 18 High St, Wiscasset, ME 04578 - T: (207) 882-7163, Fax: (207) 882-6373, E-mail: music@musicalwonderhouse.com, Internet: www.musicalwonderhouse.com/. Pres.: Danilo Konvalinka
Music Museum - 1963
Mechanical musical instr 48717

Nickels-Sortwell House, 121 Main St, Rte US1, Wiscasset, ME 04578 - T: (207) 882-6218, Fax: (617) 227-9204, Internet: www.spnea.org
Historical Museum - 1958 48718

The Old Lincoln County Jail and Museum → The 1811 Old Lincoln County Jail and 1839 Jailer's House Museum

Wisconsin Rapids WI

South Wood County Historical Museum, 540 Third St, Wisconsin Rapids, WI 54494 - T: (715) 423-1580, Fax: (715) 423-6369, E-mail: museum@wctc.net, Internet: www.swch-museum.com. Pres.: J. Marshall Buehler, Dir.: Pam Walker
Local Museum - 1955
Local hist 48719

Wisdom MT

Big Hole National Battlefield, 10 miles W of Wisdom Mount on Hwy 43, Wisdom, MT 59761 - T: (406) 689-3155, Fax: (406) 689-3151, Internet: www.nps.gov/biho. Head: Jon G. James
Military Museum / Open Air Museum / Historic Site - 1910 48720

Wolf Point MT

Wolf Point Area Historical Society Museum, 220 Second Av S, Wolf Point, MT 59201 - T: (406) 653-1912. C.E.O. & Pres.: Alma Hall
Local Museum / Folklore Museum / Agriculture Museum - 1970
Early-day settlers, Assinaboine and Sioux culture, grain farming, livestock ranching 48721

Wolfeboro NH

Clark House Museum Complex, S Main St, Wolfeboro, NH 03894, mail addr: POB 1066, Wolfeboro, NH 03894 - T: (603) 569-4997. Pres.: Dianne Rogers
Local Museum / Historical Museum - 1925
Schoolhouse, firehouse, pre-revolutionary farm house 48722

Libby Museum, 755 n Main St, Wolfeboro, NH 03894 - T: (603) 569-1035, Fax: (603) 569-2246, Internet: www.wolfeboroonline.com/libby. Dir.: Patricia F. Smith
Historical Museum / Natural History Museum - 1912 48723

Wolfeboro Historical Society Museum → Clark House Museum Complex

Wright Museum, 77 Center St, Rte 28, Wolfeboro, NH 03894 - T: (603) 569-1212, Fax: (603) 569-6326, E-mail: wrmuseum@aol.com, Internet: wrightmuseum.org. Pres. & Dir.: David M. Wright, Chm.: Dennis I. Runey
Historical Museum - 1984
History 48724

Womelsdorf PA

Conrad Weiser Homestead, 28 Weiser Rd, Womelsdorf, PA 19567-9718 - T: (610) 589-2934, Fax: (610) 589-9458. Head: James Lewars
Historic Site - 1928
Historic house 48725

Woodbine GA

Woodbine International Fire Museum, 110 Bedell Av, Woodbine, GA 31569-0058 - T: (912) 576-5351. Dir.: Jodie G. Briese
Historical Museum - 1991
Fire fighting equip 48726

Woodbridge CT

Amity and Woodbridge Historical Society Museum, 1907 Litchfield Turnpike, Woodbridge, CT 06525 - T: (203) 387-2823, Internet: woodbridgehistory.org. Dir.: Donald Menzies
Local Museum - 1936
Local hist 48727

Woodbridge NJ

Barron Arts Center and Museum, 582 Rahway Av, Woodbridge, NJ 07095 - T: (732) 634-0413, Fax: (732) 634-8633. Dir.: Stephen J. Kager
Fine Arts Museum - 1977
Arts, crafts and photograph 48728

Woodbury CT

The Glebe House Museum, Hollow Rd, Woodbury, CT 06798 - T: (203) 263-2855, Fax: (203) 263-6726, E-mail: ghmgjg@snet.net, Internet: www.theglebehouse.org. Dir.: Sarah Griswold
Local Museum - 1923
Local hist, American episcopacy 48729

Woodbury KY

Green River Museum, Park St, Woodbury, KY 42261 - T: (270) 526-2133. Cur.: Jerry Martin
Historical Museum - 1982
History 48730

Woodbury NJ

Gloucester County Historical Society Museum, 58 N Broad St, Woodbury, NJ 08096 - T: (856) 848-8531, Fax: (856) 845-0131, E-mail: gchs@net-gate.com, Internet: www.rootsweb.com/njglouce/gchs. Pres.: Dorothy Range
Local Museum - 1903 48731

Woodland CA

Yolo County Historical Museum, 512 Gibson Rd, Woodland, CA 95695 - T: (530) 666-1045. Dir./Cur.: Monika Stengert
Local Museum - 1979
Local history, farming, furnishings - library 48732

Woodland Hills CA

Art Gallery, Pierce College, 6201 Winnetka, Woodland Hills, CA 91371 - T: (818) 719-6498, Fax: (818) 710-2907, E-mail: oliverme@pierce.laccd.edu, Internet: www.piercecollege.com
Public Gallery 48733

Woodruff SC

Thomas Price House, 1200 Oak View Farms Rd, Woodruff, SC 29388 - T: (864) 576-6546, 476-2483, Fax: (864) 576-4058, E-mail: walnutgrove@mindspring.com, Internet: www.spartanarts.org/history/. Pres.: Dr. Jeff Willis, C.E.O. & Exec. Dir.: Susan Turpin
Local Museum - 1972
Historic building 48734

Woods Hole MA

Woods Hole Oceanographic Institution Exhibit Center, 15 School St, Woods Hole, MA 02543 - T: (508) 548-1400, 289-2663, Fax: (508) 457-2034, E-mail: information@whoi.edu, Internet: www.whoi.edu. Dir.: Robert Gagosian
Natural History Museum - 1930
Oceanographic research photographs, data, tools, instruments, vehicles, vessels 48735

Woodside CA

Woodside Store Historic Site, 3300 Tripp Rd, Woodside, CA 94062 - T: (650) 299-0104, Fax: (650) 851-7615, E-mail: samhist@aol.com. Dir.: Mitchell P. Postel
Local Museum - 1954
Local hist 48736

Woodstock CT

Bowen House/ Roseland Cottage, Rte 169, on the Common, Woodstock, CT 06281 - T: (860) 928-4074, Fax: (860) 963-2208, E-mail: prusso@spnea.org, Internet: www.spnea.org. Head: Pam Russo, Dick Russo
Local Museum - 1970
Historic houses, Gothic furniture 48737

Woodstock Historical Society Museum, 523 Rte 169, Woodstock, CT 06281 - T: (860) 928-1035. Pres.: Marilyn Pomeroy
Local Museum - 1967
Local hist, agriculture 48738

Woodstock NY

Center for Photography at Woodstock, 59 Tinker St, Woodstock, NY 12498 - T: (845) 679-7747, Fax: (845) 679-6337, E-mail: info@cpw.org, Internet: www.cpw.org. Dir.: Colleen Kenyon, Kathleen Kenyon, Ass. Dir.: Kate Menconeri, Larry Lewis
Fine Arts Museum - 1977 48739

Woodstock Artists Gallery, 28 Tinker St, Woodstock, NY 12498 - T: (914) 679-2940, Fax: (914) 679-2940 (call first), E-mail: waa@mhv.net, Internet: www.ulster.net/~waa. Dir.: Linda Freaney
Fine Arts Museum - 1920 48740

Woodstock VA

Woodstock Museum of Shenandoah County, 137 W Court St, Woodstock, VA 22664 - T: (540) 459-2542, 984-8035, E-mail: ckn@shentel.com
Local Museum - 1969
Local hist 48741

Woodstock VT

Billings Farm and Museum, River Rd and Rte 12, Woodstock, VT 05091 - T: (802) 457-2355, Fax: (802) 457-4663, E-mail: billingsfarm@valley.net, Internet: www.billingsfarm.org. Dir.: David A. Donath, Ass. Dir.: David A. Miles, David L. Yeatts, Darlyne S. Franzen, Cur.: Robert G. Benz
Open Air Museum / Agriculture Museum / Historic Site - 1976
Local hist 48742

Woodstock Historical Society Museum, 26 Elm St, Woodstock, VT 05091 - T: (802) 457-1822, Fax: (802) 457-2811, E-mail: whs@sover.net. Dir.: Corwin Sharp, Ass. Dir.: Sharon Reed, Cur.: Sherman M. Howe (Photography)
Local Museum - 1943
Local hist 48743

Woodville MS

Rosemont Plantation, Hwy 24 E, Woodville, MS 39669 - T: (601) 888-6809, Fax: (601) 888-3606
Decorative Arts Museum - 1971
Davis furniture, portraits 48744

Wilkinson County Museum, Courthouse Sq, Woodville, MS 39669 - T: (601) 888-3998, Fax: (601) 888-3606, E-mail: wilkmuseum@aol.com. C.E.O.: Ernesto Caldeira
Local Museum / Decorative Arts Museum - 1971
Decorative arts from county plantations and homes, area hist 48745

Woodville TX

Allan Shivers Museum, 302 N Charlton, Woodville, TX 75979 - T: (409) 283-3709, Fax: (409) 283-5258. Dir.: Rosemary Bunch
Local Museum - 1963
Historic house 48746

Heritage Village Museum, Hwy 190 W, Woodville, TX 75979 - T: (409) 283-2272, Fax: (409) 283-2194, E-mail: info@heritage-village.org, Internet: www.heritage-village.org. Dir.: Ofiera Gazzaway
Local Museum
Local hist 48747

Woodward OK

Plains Indians and Pioneers Museum, 2009 Williams Av, Woodward, OK 73801 - T: (580) 256-6136, Fax: (580) 256-2577, E-mail: pipm@swbell.net. Cur.: Louise James
Local Museum - 1966 48748

Wooster OH

The College of Wooster Art Museum, c/o Ebert Art Center, 1220 Beall Av, Wooster, OH 44691 - T: (330) 263-2495, Fax: (330) 263-2633, E-mail: kzurko@acs.wooster.edu, Internet: www.wooster.edu/. Dir.: Kathleen McManus Zurko
Fine Arts Museum / University Museum - 1930 48749

Wayne Center for the Arts, 237 S Walnut St, Wooster, OH 44691 - T: (330) 264-8596, Fax: (330) 264-9314, E-mail: WayneCtr@ssnet.com, Internet: www.wayne-arts.org. Exec. Dir.: Lucy Spurgeon
Public Gallery - 1973 48750

Wayne County Historical Society Museum, 546 E Bowman St, Wooster, OH 44691 - T: (330) 264-8856, Fax: (330) 264-8823, E-mail: host@waynehistorical.org, Internet: www.waynehistorical.org/. Pres.: Greg Long
Local Museum - 1954 48751

Worcester MA

EcoTarium, 222 Harrington Way, Worcester, MA 01604 - T: (508) 929-2700, Fax: (508) 929-2701, E-mail: info@ecotarium.org, Internet: www.ecotarium.org/. Exec. Dir.: Laura H. Myers
Natural History Museum - 1825
Environmental museum 48752

Higgins Armory Museum, 100 Barber Av, Worcester, MA 01606-2444 - T: (508) 853-6015, Fax: (508) 852-7697, E-mail: higgins@higgins.org, Internet: www.higgins.org. Dir.: Kentdur Russell, Cur.: Jeffrey L. Forgeng
Special Museum - 1928
Arms, armor, history, art 48753

Iris and B. Gerald Cantor Art Gallery, College of the Holy Cross, 1 College St, Worcester, MA 01610 - T: (508) 793-3356, Fax: (508) 793-3030, E-mail: cantor@holycross.edu, Internet: www.holycross.edu/departments/cantor/website/cantor.html. Dir.: Roger Hankins
University Museum / Fine Arts Museum - 1983
Art 48754

New England Science Center → EcoTarium

Salisbury Mansion, 40 Highland St, Worcester, MA 01609 - T: (617) 753-8278, Fax: (508) 753-8278, E-mail: worchistmu@aol.com, Internet: www.worcesterhistory.org. Exec. Dir.: William D. Wallace
Local Museum - 1875
Local history, Stephen Salisbury home 48755

Worcester Art Museum, 55 Salisbury St, Worcester, MA 01609-3196 - T: (508) 799-4406 ext 0, Fax: (508) 798-5646, E-mail: information@warcesterart.org, Internet: www.worchesterart.org. Dir.: James A. Welu, Cur.: David Brigham (American Art), James A. Welu (European Art), Louise Virgin (Asian Art), David Acton (Prints, Drawings, Photographs), Cons.: Lawrence Becker
Fine Arts Museum - 1896
American and Asian art, prints, drawings 48756

Worcester Center for Crafts, Krikorian Gallery, 25 Sagamore Rd, Worcester, MA 01605 - T: (508) 753-8183, Fax: (508) 797-5626, E-mail: wcc@worcestercraftcenter.org, Internet: www.worcestercraftcenter.org. Exec. Dir.: Maryon Attwood
Decorative Arts Museum / Public Gallery - 1856
Arts, contemporary American craft 48757

Worcester Historical Museum, 30 Elm St, Worcester, MA 01609 - T: (617) 753-8278, Fax: (508) 753-9070, E-mail: worchistmu@aol.com, Internet: www.worcesterhistory.org. Pres.: James J. Paugh, Exec. Dir.: William D. Wallace
Local Museum - 1875
Local history 48758

Worcester PA

Peter Wentz Farmstead, Shearer Rd, Worcester, PA 19490 - T: (610) 584-5104, Fax: (610) 584-6860, E-mail: peterwentzfarmstead@mail.montcopa.org, Internet: www.montcopa.org. Pres.: Dick Anderl
Historic Site - 1976
Historic building 48759

Worland WY

Washakie Museum, 1115 Obie Sue, Worland, WY 82401 - T: (307) 347-4102, Fax: (307) 347-4865, E-mail: wmuseum@trib.com, Internet: w3.trib.com/~wmuseum. Dir.: Lisa Brahm-Lindberg
Local Museum - 1986
Hist of Big Horn Basin 48760

Worthington MN

Nobles County Art Center Gallery, 407 12 St, Worthington, MN 56187 - T: (507) 376-4431, Fax: (507) 376-3005, E-mail: nchsqfrontiernet.net. Dir.: Alan Swanson
Fine Arts Museum - 1960
International art 48761

Nobles County Historical Society Museum, 407 12 St, Ste 2, Worthington, MN 56187 - T: (507) 376-4431, Fax: (507) 376-3005, E-mail: nchs@frontiernet.net. Pres.: Alan Swanson, Dir.: Roxann L. Polzine
Historical Museum - 1933 48762

Worthington OH

Ohio Railway Museum, 990 Proprietors Rd, Worthington, OH 43085 - T: (614) 885-7345, Internet: www.ohiorailwaymuseum.org. Pres.: Warren W. Hyer
Science&Tech Museum - 1945 48763

Worthington Historical Society Museum, 50 W New England Av, Worthington, OH 43085 - T: (614) 885-1247, Fax: (614) 885-1040, E-mail: worthhsoc@aol.com, Internet: www.worthington.org. Cur.: Jane Trucksis
Historical Museum - 1955 48764

Wray CO

Wray Museum, 205 E Third St, Wray, CO 80758-0161 - T: (970) 332-5063. Dir.: Patricia Welborn
Local Museum / Archaeological Museum - 1969
Local history, archaeology, Paleo Indians, art 48765

Wright-Patterson Air Force Base OH

United States Air Force Museum, 1100 Spaatz St, Wright-Patterson Air Force Base, OH 45433-7102 - T: (937) 255-3286, Fax: (937) 255-3910, E-mail: usaf.museum@wpafb.af.mil, Internet: www.wpafb.af.mil/museum/. Dir.: Charles D. Metcalf, Cur.: Terry Aitken
Military Museum - 1923 48766

Wyandotte MI

Wyandotte Museum, 2610 Biddle Av, Wyandotte, MI 48192 - T: (734) 324-7297, Fax: (734) 324-7283, E-mail: wymuseum@ili.net, Internet: www.angelfire.com/mi/wymuseum. Dir.: Marc Partin
Local Museum - 1958
Local history, Ford-MacNichol home 48767

Wyckoff NJ

James A. McFaul Environmental Center of Bergen County, Crescent Av, Wyckoff, NJ 07481 - T: (201) 891-5571, Fax: (201) 343-7249. Dir.: Wolfgang Albrecht
Natural History Museum - 1967 48768

Wyoming NY

Middlebury Historical Society Museum, 22 S Academy St, Wyoming, NY 14591-9801 - T: (716) 495-6582. Cur.: Mary P. Lester
Local Museum - 1941 48769

Wytheville VA

Rock House Museum, 205 Tazwell St, Wytheville, VA 24382 - T: (540) 223-3330, Fax: (540) 223-3315. Dir.: Francis Emerson
Local Museum - 1970
Local hist 48770

Thomas J. Boyd Museum, 295 Tazwell St, Wytheville, VA 24382 - T: (540) 223-3330, Fax: (540) 223-3315. Dir.: Francis Emerson
Local Museum
Fire truck, farming and mining 48771

Xenia OH

Greene County Historical Society Museum, 74 W Church St, Xenia, OH 45385 - T: (513) 372-4606, Fax: (372) 372-5660, E-mail: gchsxo@aol.com. Pres.: John Balmer
Local Museum - 1929 48772

Yakima WA

Larson Gallery, Yakima Valley Community College, S 16th Ave and Nob Hill Blvd, Yakima, WA 98907-2520 - T: (509) 574-4875, Fax: (509) 574-6826, E-mail: chassen@yvcc.cc.wa.us, Internet: www.yvcc.cc.wa.us/~larson. Dir.: Carol Hassen
Public Gallery - 1949 48773

Yakima Valley Museum, 2105 Tieton Dr, Yakima, WA 98902 - T: (509) 248-0747, Fax: (509) 453-4890, E-mail: info@yakimavalleymuseum.org, Internet: www.yakimavalleymuseum.org. Dir.: John A. Baule, Cur.: Michael Siebol, Andrew Granitto, David Lynx
Local Museum - 1952
Local hist 48774

Yale OK

Jim Thorpe Home, 706 E Boston, Yale, OK 74085 - T: (918) 387-2815, E-mail: jimthorpe@tulsa.net. Cur.: Alice Cussner
Local Museum - 1973 48775

Yankton SD

Bede Art BGallery, Mount Marty College, 1105 W 8th St, Yankton, SD 57078 - T: (605) 668-1011, Fax: (605) 668-1607, E-mail: dkahle@mtmc.edu
Public Gallery 48776

Dakota Territorial Museum, 610 Summit St, Yankton, SD 57078 - T: (605) 665-3898, Fax: (605) 665-6314, E-mail: dtm@willinet.net
Local Museum - 1936
Local hist, paintings, sculpture 48777

Yarmouth ME

Museum of Yarmouth History, Merrill Memorial Library, 215 Main St, Yarmouth, ME 04096 - T: (207) 846-6259, E-mail: yarmouth-history@inetmail.att.net. Dir.: Marilyn J. Hinkley
Local Museum - 1958
Local history 48778

Yarmouth Port MA

Historical Society of Old Yarmouth Museum, 11 Strawberry Ln, Yarmouth Port, MA 02675 - T: (508) 362-3021, E-mail: info@hsoy.org, Internet: www.hsoy.org. Pres.: Basil Dandison, Dir./Cur.: Barbara Milligan Ryan
Decorative Arts Museum / Historical Museum - 1953
Local history 48779

Winslow Crocker House, 250 Main St, Rte 6A, Yarmouth Port, MA 02675 - T: (617) 227-3956, Fax: (617) 227-9204, E-mail: pzea@spnea.org, Internet: www.spnea.org. Vice Pres.: Philip Zea, Jim McGuinness
Local Museum / Decorative Arts Museum - 1935
History 48780

Yates Center KS

Woodson County Historical Museum, 208 W Mary, Yates Center, KS 66783 - T: (316) 625-2371, Fax: (316) 625-2371, E-mail: ical@yatescenterk.net, Internet: skyways.lib.ks.us/kansan/towns/YatesCenter/museum. Pres.: Gary Culbertson, Vice Pres.: Pete Watts, Cur.: Geri Town, Linda Call
Local Museum - 1965
Historic church, country school, log cabin 48781

Yazoo City MS

Yazoo Historical Museum, 332 N Main St, Yazoo City, MS 39194 - T: (601) 746-2273. Pres.: Sam Olden
Historical Museum - 1977 48782

Yellow Springs OH

Glen Helen Ecology Institute Trailside Museum, 505 Corry St, Yellow Springs, OH 45387 - T: (937) 767-7375, Fax: (937) 767-6659. Ass. Dir.: Rick Flood
Natural History Museum - 1951 48783

Noyes and Read Gallery and Herndon Gallery, Antioch College, 795 Livermore St, Yellow Springs, OH 45387 - T: (937) 769-1149. Dir.: Nevin Mercede
Fine Arts Museum - 1972
Painting, photography and video 48784

Yonkers NY

Hudson River Museum of Westchester, 511 Warburton Av, Yonkers, NY 10701-1899 - T: (914) 963-4550, Fax: (914) 963-8558, E-mail: llocke@hrm.org, Internet: www.hrm.org. Dir.: Michael Botwinick, Ass. Dir.: Sue Sanderson, Cur.: Laura L. Vookles
Fine Arts Museum / Local Museum / Folklore Museum - 1919 48785

Philipse Manor Hall, 29 Warburton Av, Yonkers, NY 10701 - T: (914) 965-4027, 965-0473, Fax: (914) 965-6485, E-mail: heather.vaughn@oprhp.state.ny.us
Decorative Arts Museum - 1911
Paintings, photographs, structures, architecture 48786

York ME

Elizabeth Perkins House, POB 312, York, ME 03909 - T: (207) 363-4974, Fax: (207) 363-4021. Exec. Dir.: Scott Stevens
Historical Museum 48787

Jefferds Tavern, Lindsey Rd, York, ME 03909 - T: (207) 363-4974, Fax: (207) 363-4021. Exec. Dir.: Scott Stevens
Historical Museum 48788

John Hancock Warehouse, Lindsey Rd, York, ME 03909 - T: (207) 363-4974, Fax: (207) 363-4021. Exec. Dir.: Scott Stevens
Historical Museum 48789

Old Gaol Museum, POB 312, York, ME 03909 - T: (207) 363-4974, Fax: (207) 363-4021. Exec. Dir.: Scott Stevens, Cur.: Tom Johnson
Historical Museum 48790

Old School House, POB 312, York, ME 03909 - T: (207) 363-4974, Fax: (207) 363-4021, E-mail: oyhs@gwi.org. Exec. Dir.: Scott Stevens
Historical Museum 48791

Old York Historical Museum, 207 York St, York, ME 03909, mail addr: POB 312, York, ME 03909-0312 - T: (207) 363-4974, Fax: (207) 363-4021, E-mail: oyhs@oldyork.org, Internet: www.oldyork.org. Dir.: F. Scott Stevens, Cur.: Thomas B. Johnson
Local Museum - 1984
Historic buildings, local history 48792

York NE

Anna Bemis Palmer Museum, 211 E Seventh St, York, NE 68467 - T: (402) 363-2630, Fax: (402) 363-2601. Dir.: Jim Krejci, Cur.: Ginny L. Driewer
Historical Museum - 1967 48793

York PA

Fire Museum of York County, 757 W Market St, York, PA 17404 - T: (717) 845-1587, Fax: (717) 812-1204, E-mail: chimes@yorkheritage.org, Internet: www.yorkheritage.org. C.E.O. & Pres.: Gayle Petty-Johnson
Historical Museum - 1973
Fire fighting, Royal Fire Stn 6 48794

Industrial and Agricultural Museum, 217 W Princess St, York, PA 17403-2013 - T: (717) 848) 1587, Fax: (717) 812-1204, E-mail: chimes@yorkheritage.org, Internet: www.yorkheritage.org. Cur.: Richard Banz
Historical Museum - 1989
Local industrie, wallpaper and wire cloth manufacturing, defense, physical fitness, refrigeration and air conditioning, automobile manufacturing 48795

York County Museum, 250 E Market St, York, PA 17403 - T: (717) 848-1587, Fax: (717) 812-1204, Internet: www.yorkheritage.org. C.E.O. & Pres.: Gayle Petty-Johnson, Cur.: Richard Banz
Local Museum - 1895
Local hist 48796

York Harbor ME

Sayward-Wheeler House, 9 Barrell Ln Extension, York Harbor, ME 03911 - T: (207) 384-2454, (617) 227-3956, Fax: (617) 227-9204, (207) 384-8182, E-mail: pzea@spnea.org, Internet: www.spnea.org
Decorative Arts Museum - 1977
Queen Anne and Chippendale furniture, portraits, china 48797

Yorktown TX

Yorktown Historical Museum, 144 W Main St, Yorktown, TX 78164 - T: (512) 564-2573, E-mail: muellers219@hotmail.com. Pres.: Shirley Mueller, Cur.: Jay Wilson
Local Museum - 1978
Local hist 48798

Yorktown VA

On the Hill Cultural Arts Center, 121 Alexander Hamilton Blvd, Yorktown, VA 23690 - T: (757) 898-3076. Pres.: Tom Coll
Fine Arts Museum - 1976
Art 48799

Watermen's Museum, 309 Water St, Yorktown, VA 23690 - T: (757) 887-2641, Fax: (757) 888-2089, E-mail: watermens@tni.net, Internet: www.watermens.org. Dir.: George A. Zavodnick
Special Museum - 1980
Seafood industry 48800

Yorktown Visitor Center, Colonial Pkwy and Rte 238, Yorktown, VA 23690 - T: (757) 898-3400, Fax: (757) 898-6346, E-mail: colo_interpretation@nps.gov, Internet: www.nps.gov/colo/
Historical Museum - 1930
17th and 18th-c arms and artifacts 48801

Yorktown Visitor Center Museum, Colonial National Historical Park, Old Rte 238 and Colonial Pkwy, Yorktown, VA 23690 - T: (757) 898-3400, 253-4838, Fax: (757) 898-6346, 253-5299, E-mail: colo_interpretation@nps.gov, Internet: www.nps.gov/colo. Dir.: Alac Gould, Cur.: Richard Raymond
Historic Site / Historical Museum - 1930
Site of the last decisive battle of the American Revolution, America's struggle for independence 48802

Yorktown Heights NY

Yorktown Museum, 1974 Commerce St, Yorktown Heights, NY 10598 - T: (914) 962-2970, Fax: (914) 962-4379, E-mail: staff@yorktownmuseum.org, Internet: www.yorktownmuseum.org. C.E.O.: Linda G. Cooper
Local Museum - 1966 48803

Yosemite National Park CA

The Yosemite Museum, Museum Bldg, Yosemite National Park, CA 95389 - T: (209) 372-0297, Fax: (209) 372-0255, E-mail: yose_museum@nps.gov. Cur.: David M. Forgang, Barbara L. Beroza (Collections), Craig D. Bates (Ethnography), Sc. Staff: Jim Snyder (History)
Local Museum / Ethnology Museum / Natural History Museum - 1915
History, ethnology, natural science, anthropology, archaeology, geology, Indian culture 48804

Youngstown NY

Old Fort Niagara, Fort Niagara State Park, Youngstown, NY 14174 - T: (716) 745-7611, Fax: (716) 745-9141, E-mail: ofn@oldfortniagara.org, Internet: www.oldfortniagara.org. Pres.: Ginger McNally, C.E.O.: Robert L. Emerson
Military Museum / Open Air Museum - 1927 48805

Youngstown OH

Arms Family Museum of Local History, 648 Wick Av, Youngstown, OH 44502 - T: (330) 743-2589, Fax: (330) 743-7210, E-mail: mvhs@mahoninghistory.org, Internet: www.mahoninghistory.org. Dir.: H. William Lawson, Ass. Dir.: Joan M. Reedy, Cur.: Jessica D. Trickett
Local Museum - 1961 48806

Butler Institute of American Art, 524 Wick Av, Youngstown, OH 44502 - T: (330) 743-1711, Fax: (330) 743-9567, E-mail: k_earnhart@butlerart.com, Internet: www.butlerart.com. Dir.: Louis A. Zona, Ass. Dir.: M. Susan Carfano
Fine Arts Museum - 1919 48807

John J. McDonough Museum of Art, 1 Youngstown University Plaza, Youngstown, OH 44555 - T: (330) 742-1400, Fax: (330) 742-1492, E-mail: sbkreism@cc.ysu.edu, Internet: www.ysu.edu
University Museum / Fine Arts Museum - 1991 48808

Yountville CA

Napa Valley Museum, 55 Presidents Circle, Yountville, CA 94599 - T: (707) 944-0500, Fax: (707) 945-0500, E-mail: ericnelson@napavalleymuseum.org, Internet: www.napavalleymuseum.org. Dir.: Eric Nelson, Cur.: Randy Murphy
Fine Arts Museum / Local Museum / Natural History Museum - 1973
Local History, art and natural science 48809

Ypsilanti MI

Ford Gallery and Slide Collection, Eastern Michigan University, Art Dept., 114 Ford Hall, Ypsilanti, MI 48197 - T: (734) 487-1268, Fax: (734) 487-2324, E-mail: art.department@emich.edu, Internet: www.art.acad.emich.edu/. Dir.: Larry Newhouse
Fine Arts Museum 48810

Ypsilanti Historical Museum, 220 N Huron St, Ypsilanti, MI 48197 - T: (734) 482-4990, Fax: (313) 483-7481, Internet: www.ypsilantihistoricalmuseum.org
Local Museum - 1960
Local history 48811

Yreka CA

Klamath National Forest Interpretive Museum, 1312 Fairlane Rd, Yreka, CA 96097 - T: (530) 842-6131, Fax: (530) 842-6327, Internet: llbean.com/parksearch/parks/html/7757gd.htm
Natural History Museum - 1981 48812

Siskiyou County Museum, 910 S Main St, Yreka, CA 96097 - T: (530) 842-3836, Fax: (530) 842-3166, E-mail: hismus@inreach.com. Dir./Cur.: Michael Hendryx
Local Museum - 1950
Local hist, prehistoric marine, fossils, ethnographic Indian and Chinese artifacts 48813

Yuba City CA

Community Memorial Museum of Sutter County, 1333 Butte House Rd, Yuba City, CA 95993 - T: (530) 822-7141, Fax: (530) 822-7291, E-mail: museum@syix.com, Internet: www.syix.com/museum. Dir.: Julie Stark
Historical Museum - 1975
Regional history 48814

Yucaipa CA

Mousley Museum of Natural History, 35308 Panorama Dr, Yucaipa, CA 92399 - T: (909) 790-3163. Dir.: Gregory Maxwell, Cur.: Dr. Ann Deegan, Jolene Redvale
Natural History Museum - 1970
Natural history, minerals, fossils 48815

Yucaipa Adobe, 32183 Kentucky St, Yucaipa, CA 92399 - T: (909) 795-3485, Fax: (909) 307-0539, E-mail: tbothel@sbcm.sbcounty.gov, Internet: www.co.san-bernardino.ca.us/museum. Dir.: Robert McKernan, Cur.: Dr. Ann Deegan
Local Museum - 1958
Local history 48816

Yucca Valley CA

Hi-Desert Nature Museum, 57116 29-Palms Hwy, Yucca Valley, CA 92284 - T: (760) 369-7212, Fax: (760) 369-1605, E-mail: hdnm@hotmail.com, Internet: www.yucca-valley.org. Pres.: Brian Anders, Dir./Cur.: Jim Schooler
Natural History Museum - 1964
Natural history 48817

Yuma AZ

Sarguinetti Century House Museum, 240 S Madison Av, Yuma, AZ 85364 - T: (928) 782-1841, Fax: (928) 783-0680, E-mail: azhistyuma@cybertrails.com, Internet: www.yumalibrary.org. Dir.: Megan Reid, Cur.: Carol Brooks
Historical Museum - 1963
History, housed in 1870s residences 48818

Yuma Territorial Prison Museum, 1 Prison Hill Rd, Yuma, AZ 85364-8792 - T: (928) 783-4771, Fax: (928) 783-7442, E-mail: jmasterson@pr.state.az.us, Internet: www.pr.state.az.us
Historical Museum - 1940 48819

Zanesville OH

Dr. Increase Mathews House, 304 Woodlawn Av, Zanesville, OH 43701 - T: (740) 454-9500. Dir.: Linda Smucker
Local Museum - 1970 48820

Zanesville Art Center, 620 Military Rd, Zanesville, OH 43701 - T: (740) 452-0741, Fax: (740) 452-0797, E-mail: info@zanesvilleartcenter.org, Internet: www.zanesvilleartcenter.org. Pres.: Charles Hunter, Dir.: Philip Alan LaDouceur
Fine Arts Museum - 1936 48821

Zelienople PA

Zelienople Historical Museum, 243 S Main St, Zelienople, PA 16063 - T: (724) 452-9457, E-mail: zeliehistory@fyi.net, Internet: www.fyi/~zhs. C.E.O.: Joyce M. Bessor
Local Museum - 1975
Historic houses - library 48822

Zion IL

Zion Historical Museum, 1300 Shiloh Blvd, Zion, IL 60099 - T: (847) 746-2427, 872-4566. Pres.: Carol Ruesch
Local Museum - 1967
Shiloh House, residence of the founder of the city of Zion 48823

Zionsville IN

Munce Art Center, 205 W Hawthorne St, Zionsville, IN 46077 - T: (317) 873-6862. Exec. Dir.: Edie Kellar Mahaney
Public Gallery - 1981
Fine art class center 48824

P.H. Sullivan Museum and Genealogy Library, 225 W Hawthorn St, Zionsville, IN 46077 - T: (317) 873-4900. Exec. Dir.: Edie Kellar Mahaney
Local Museum / Folklore Museum - 1973
Local history, woman's guild 48825

Zoar OH

Zoar State Memorial, 198 Main St, Zoar, OH 44697 - T: (330) 874-3011, Fax: (330) 874-2936, E-mail: kmfzoar@compuserve.com, Internet: ohiohistory.org/places/zoar
Local Museum / Historical Museum - 1930
Germanic-American folk arts and crafts, tools, furniture, textiles 48826

Zolfo Springs FL

Cracker Trail Museum, 2822 Museum Dr, Zolfo Springs, FL 33890 - T: (863) 735-0119, Fax: (863) 773-0107, E-mail: crckrtrk@strato.net. Cur.: Areca Cotton
Natural History Museum - 1966 48827

Uzbekistan

Afčona

Memorialnyj Muzej Abu Ali Ibn Sina (Abu Ali Ibn Sina Memorial Museum), 705000 Afčona - T: (065) 3545142. Dir.: Kiem Choriev
Special Museum 48828

Andižan

Andižanskij Kraevedčeskij Muzej (Andizhan Regional Museum), Pl Babura, Andižan. Dir.: G.G. Gafurov
Local Museum 48829

Literaturnyj Muzej Andižana (Andizhan Literary Museum), Oktjabrskaja ul 256, Andižan. Dir.: R.A. Tilliabaev
Special Museum 48830

Angren

Angrenskij Kraevedčeskij Muzej (Angren Regional Museum), 69, District 5-1a, Angren. Dir.: L.L. Kerimova
Local Museum 48831

Buchara

Bucharskij Gosudarstvennyj Muzej (Buchara State Museum), Ul Afrasiaba 2, Buchara - T: (065) 2241349, Fax: 2241349, E-mail: robert@bukhara.net. Dir.: Robert V. Almeev
Decorative Arts Museum / Historical Museum / Archaeological Museum / Fine Arts Museum / Natural History Museum - 1922
Textiles, carpets, gold embroidery, decorative arts, coins, seals, manuscripts, armour, photo coll (pre and post Soviet revolution, Soviet era documents, agricultural equipment, pre-revolutionary medical instruments, music, archeology, religion - 10 special museums 48832

Sitorai Mochi-Khosa, Buchara
Decorative Arts Museum 48833

Chiva

Itčan Qala Davlat Muzej Qo'riqxonasi (Itcan-Kala National Reserve Museum), A. Baltaev 41, Chiva - T: (062) 3753169, Fax: 3753169, E-mail: maqsud@tkt.uz, Internet: www.uztour.narod.ru. Dir.: B. Davletov
Local Museum
Local history, architecture 48834

Čirčik

Kraevedčeskij Muzej Čirčika (Circik Regional Museum), ul Sverdlova 14, 702100 Čirčik - T: 63451. Dir.: V. Kolosov
Local Museum 48835

Fergana

Ferganskij Oblastnoj Kraevedčeskij Muzej (Regional Museum Fergana), ul B. Usmanchodžaeva 26, 712000 Fergana - T: (03732) 243191, 243870, Fax: 243191, E-mail: bahodir_hashimov@intal.uz. Dir.: Bahodir Djuraevič Hashimov
Local Museum 48836

Muzej Hamza Hakim-Žade Niazy (Hamza Hakim Žade Niazy Memorial Museum), Hamzaabad, 712000 Fergana der. Shohirmadon - T: (03732) 26681. Dir.: A. Hamzaev
Special Museum / Historical Museum 48837

Jangi-Jul

Dom-muzej Usman Jusupov (Usman Jusupov Memorial Museum), ul Dačnaja 6, Jangi-Jul
Special Museum 48838

Karši

Kaškadarinskij Kraevedčeskij Muzej (Kackadariinsk Regional Museum), ul Kalinina 309, Karši. Dir.: B.R. Artykov
Local Museum 48839

Kattakurgan

Istoriko-Kraevedčeskij Muzej Kattagurgana (Kattakurgan Historical and Regional Museum), Ul Karla Marksa 70, Kattakurgan. Dir.: A. Dzalilov
Historical Museum / Local Museum 48840

Kokand

Dom-muzej Hamza Hakim-zade Niazy (Hamza Hakim-zade Niazy House Museum), ul Matbuot 28, Kokand. Dir.: I. Rahmatulaev
Local Museum 48841

Literaturnyj Muzej G. Guliama iz Fergana (Literary Museum G. Guliam from Fergana), Sovetskaya ul 2, Kokand. Dir.: I. Bekmuradov
Special Museum 48842

Margelan

Yoldosh Oxunboboev Memorial Muzeyi (The Memorial Museum of Yuldash Ahunbabayev), Ozodlik Maydoni 1-uy, Margelan - T: (03732) 333206, 724910, E-mail: muzey_yo@list.ru. Dir.: Alijonov Ganijon
Historical Museum - 1964 48843

Namangan

Kraevedčeskij Muzej Namangana (Namangan Regional Museum), ul Luxemburgovoj 70, Namangan. Dir.: K. Dadabaev
Local Museum 48844

Nukus

Gosudarstvennyj Kraevedčeskij Muzej Karalpakii (Karalpacia State Regional Museum), ul Karla Marksa 2, 742000 Nukus - T: (022) 23751. Dir.: Kalbay Chanazarov
Local Museum 48845

Gosudarstvennyj Muzej Iskusstv Respubliki Karakalpakstan (State Art Museum of Karakalpakstan), pr Doslyk 127, 742000 Nukus - T: (061) 2222556, Fax: 2222556, E-mail: museum@online.ru, Internet: www.webcenter.ru/~museum/. Dir.: Marinika Babanazarova
Fine Arts Museum - 1966
Karakalpak applied art, art of ancient Khorezm, Russian avantgarde of 1910-1930 - library, archive 48846

Karakalpakskij Istoričeskij Muzej (Karakalpak Historical Museum), ul Rachmatova 3, 74200 Nukus
Historical Museum
Uzbek hist, military hist 48847

Samarkand

Gosudarstvennyj Muzej Istorii Kultury i Iskusstva Uzbekistana (Museum of Culture and Art History of Uzbekistan), Pl Registan, 703000 Samarkand - T: (0662) 353896. Dir.: N. Mahmudor
Historical Museum / Fine Arts Museum - 1874
Cultural history, fine art, ceramics, archeology, costumes - library, archive 48848

International Museum of Peace and Solidarity, 56 Mustaqillik St, Central Recreation Park, Samarkand, mail addr: POB 76, 703000 Samarkand - T: (662) 331753, Fax: 331753, E-mail: imps@rol.uz, Internet: www.peace.museum.com. Dir.: Anatoly Ionesov
Special Museum 48849

Kraevedčeskij Muzej (Museum of Local History), ul Kašidov 51, 703000 Samarkand - T: (0662) 330365
Archaeological Museum / Historical Museum - 1981
Archeology 48850

Sadriddin Aini Memorial Museum, ul Registanskaya 7b, 703000 Samarkand - T: (0662) 355153. Dir.: A. Ganiev
Historical Museum - 1964
Literature, history 48851

Ulug-Beg Memorial Museum, Ulug-Beg Observatory, 703000 Samarkand - T: (0662) 350345. Dir.: N. Akramov
Historical Museum - 1964 48852

Taškent

Gosudarstvennyj Muzej Iskusstv (State Museum of Art), ul Proletarskaja 16, 700060 Taškent - T: (071) 2323444. Dir.: D.S. Rusibaev
Fine Arts Museum - 1918
Art, architecture, sculpture, fine arts, graphics, music, theatre, ethnography - library 48853

Historical Museum of Uzbekistan M.T. Oibek, ul Rašidova 3, 700047 Taškent - T: (071) 2391083. Dir.: K.Ch. Inojatov
Historical Museum - 1922
Hist of the Central Asian area, exhibits on the life of Central Asiatic life ranging from primitive communal societies to the present time - library 48854

Literaturnyj Muzej Alisher Navoj (Alisher Navoi State Museum of Literature), Navoi 69, 700011 Taškent - T: (0712) 410275, Fax: 1440061, E-mail: A_navoi@uzsci.net, Internet: www.uzsci.net. Dir.: S.R. Khasanov
Special Museum 48855

Mouhtar Ashrafi Museum, C-1, Dom 15, kv 25, 700000 Taškent - T: (071) 1332384, Fax: 322731. Dir.: G. Hamraeva
Music Museum - 1982
Collection of classic music disks and music hall for concerts, collection of classic Uzbek music instruments 48856

Museum of the History of Termurids, Amir Temur ul 1, 700000 Taškent - T: (071) 21320211, E-mail: wfrd@online.ru. Dir.: Nozim Khabibullaev
Ethnology Museum 48857

Muzej Obščestvennogo Zdorovja Uzbekistana (Uzbekistan Public Health Museum), Ul Kujbyševa 30, 700060 Taškent. Dir.: S. Karimov
Special Museum 48858

Respublikanskij Prirodovedčeskij Muzej (Republican Museum of Nature), ul Salbana 16, 700000 Taškent. Dir.: A. Kajdarov
Natural History Museum 48859

Sergej Borodin Muzej, Ul Ordžonikidze 18, 700000 Taškent - T: (071) 1330932, Fax: 2406264, E-mail: Kalohc@aol-com. Dir.: N. Chebanova
Special Museum - 1978
Coins, books, Sergey Borodin 48860

Tashkent Historical Museum of the People of Uzbekistan, ul Kuibyševa 15, 700047 Taškent - T: (071) 2335733. Dir.: G.R. Rašidov
Historical Museum - 1876 48861

Uzbekistan Art Academy, Šaraf Rašidov Pr 40, 700029 Taškent - T: (0312) 565046, 1525625, Fax: 565046, 1525625, E-mail: acadartu@online.ru, Internet: www.arts-academy.uz
Public Gallery 48862

Uzbekistan Art Academy, Šaraf Rašidov Pr 40, 700029 Taškent - T: (071) 2565046, 2565047, 1525625, Fax: 1525625, E-mail: acadartu@online.ru, Internet: www.arts-academy.uz
Public Gallery 48863

Termiz

Surchondarë Vilojati Archeologija Muzeji (Archeological Museum of Surkhandarya Region), At-Termizi šoch kŭčasi, 732000 Termiz - T: (376) 73017, 40765, Fax: 73017, E-mail: arxeo_muzey@rambler.ru. Dir.: I.T. Botirov
Archaeological Museum - 2002
Archeological collections from Bronce epoch, Early Iron Age, Hellenism, Kushan period, early and developed Midlle Ages, numismatical coll from 2nd c B.C. till 20th c A.C. - library, archives 48864

Vanuatu

Port Vila

Michoutouchkine Pilioko Foundation, Road to Pango, Port Vila, mail addr: POB 224, Port Vila - T: 23053, 27753, Fax: 24224, Internet: www.nicaloi.com.vu. Dir.: A. Pilioko, N. Michoutouchkine
Fine Arts Museum / Ethnology Museum 48865

Vanuatu Cultural Centre and National Museum, Rue Picardie, Port Vila, mail addr: POB 184, Port Vila - T: 22129, Fax: 26590, E-mail: vks@vanuatu.com.vu, Internet: artalpha.anu.edu.au/web/arc/vks/vks.htm. Dir.: Ralph Regenvanu
Ethnology Museum - 1959
Local art and ethnography 48866

Vatican City

Città del Vaticano

Archivio Segreto Vaticano, Cortile del Belvedere, 00120 Città del Vaticano - T: (003906) 69883314, E-mail: asv@asv.va. Head: Sergio Pagano
Library with Exhibitions 48867

Cappelle Sistina, Sala e Gallerie Affrescate, Musei Vaticani, Viale Vaticano, 00120 Città del Vaticano - T: (003906) 69883332. Dir. Gen.: Dr. Francesco Buranelli, Dir.: Dr. Fabrizio Mancinelli
Fine Arts Museum 48868

Collezione d'Arte Religiosa Moderna, Musei Vaticani, Palazzo Apostolico Vaticano, 00120 Città del Vaticano. Cur.: Dr. Arnold Nesselrath
Fine Arts Museum - 1973
Paintings, sculptures, drawings 48869

Galleria degli Arazzi, Musei Vaticani, Viale Vaticano, Palazzo Apostolico Vaticano, 00120 Città del Vaticano
Fine Arts Museum
Tapestry coll 48870

Galleria Lapidaria, Musei Vaticani, Viale Vaticano, Palazzo Apostolico Vaticano, 00120 Città del Vaticano
Museum of Classical Antiquities
Greek, Latin Cristian and Hebrew inscriptions 48871

Monumenti Musei e Gallerie Pontificie, Viale Vaticano, 00120 Città del Vaticano - T: (003906) 69883333, Fax: 69885100, E-mail: musei@scv.va, Internet: www.vatican.va. Dir. Gen.: Dr. Francesco Buranelli, Cur.: Dr. Maurizio Sannibale (Etruscian-Italian Antiquities), Dr. Paolo Liverani (Classical Antiquities), Dr. Giandomenico Spinola (Paleochristian Art), Dr. Giorgio Filippi (Epigraphical Collection), Dep. Dir.: Dr. Arnold Nesselrath (Byzantine, Medieval and Modern Art), Roberto Zagnoli (Ethnology), Cur.: Dr. Micol Forti (18th c and Contemporary Art), Pietro Amato (History), Dr. Anna Maria De Strobel (Byzantine, Medieval and Modern Art), Dr. Ester Maria Console (Ethnology), Coord.: Dr. Lorenzo Nigro (Oriental Antiquities), Dr. Guido Cornini (Photographic archive), Head: Prof. Ulderico Santamaria (Scientific Research), Restaurator: Maurizio De Luca (Painting)
Early 16th c 48872

Museo Chiaramonti e Braccio Nuovo, Musei Vaticani, Palazzo Apostolico Vaticano, 00120 Città del Vaticano - T: (003906) 69883333. Cur.: Dr. Paolo Liverani
Fine Arts Museum
Statues of the Nile, of Demosthenes and of the Augustus 'of Prima Porta', Greek and Roman art 48873

Museo Gregoriano Egizio, Musei Vaticani, Palazzo Apostolico Vaticano, 00120 Città del Vaticano
Museum of Classical Antiquities - 1839
Egyptian antiquities discovered in Rome, Roman imitations of Egyptian statues from Hadrian's villa in Hadrian's Tivoli 48874

Museo Gregoriano Etrusco, Musei Vaticani, Palazzo Apostolico Vaticano, 00120 Città del Vaticano. Cur.: Dr. Maurizio Sannibale
Decorative Arts Museum - 1837
Bronzes, terracottas, jewellery and Greek vases from Etruscan tombs 48875

Museo Gregoriano Profano, Musei Vaticani, Palazzo Apostolico Vaticano, 00120 Città del Vaticano. Cur.: Dr. Paolo Liverani
Fine Arts Museum - 1844
Roman sculptures 48876

Museo Missionario Etnologico, Musei Vaticani, Palazzo Apostolico Lateranese, Piazza San Giovanni 4, 00184 Città del Vaticano. Cur.: Roberto Zagnoli
Ethnology Museum - 1926
Ethnographical coll 48877

Museo Padiglione delle Carozza, Museo Storico (Carriage Museum), Vatican Gardens, 00120 Città del Vaticano. Dir.: Pietro Amato
Science&Tech Museum - 1973
Carriages, berlins and first cars used by the Popes 48878

Museo Pio Clementino, Musei Vaticani, Palazzo Apostolico Vaticano, 00120 Città del Vaticano. Cur.: Dr. Paolo Liverani
Fine Arts Museum
Greek and Roman art 48879

Museo Pio Cristiano, Musei Vaticani, Viale Vaticano, 00120 Città del Vaticano - T: (003906) 69883041, Fax: 69885061, E-mail: secreteria.musei@scv.va. Cur.: Dr. Giandomenico Spinola
Museum of Classical Antiquities - 1854
Large coll of sarcophargi, Latin and Greek inscriptions from Christian cemeteries and basilicas, early Christian art 48880

Museo Profano, Biblioteca Apostolico Vaticano, 00120 Città del Vaticano - T: (003906) 6985051. Cur.: Dr. Giovanni Morello
Fine Arts Museum / Decorative Arts Museum - 1767
Bronze sculptures and minor arts of the classical era 48881

Museo Sacro, Biblioteca Apostolico Vaticano, 00120 Città del Vaticano - T: (003906) 6985051. Dir.: Dr. Giovanni Morello
Religious Arts Museum - 1756 48882

Museo Storico Artistico, Tesoro, Basilica di San Pietro, Capitolo di San Pietro, 00120 Città del Vaticano - T: (003906) 69881840, Fax: 69883465. Dir.: Ennio Francia
Religious Arts Museum
Sacred vestments, silver and goldsmith work 48883

Museo Storico Vaticano (Historical Museum), Palazzo Apostolico Lateranese, Piazza San Giovanni 4, 00184 Città del Vaticano. Dir.: Pietro Amato
Historical Museum - 1973
Arms, uniforms and armour of the pontificial court and Army Court 48884

Pinacoteca Vaticana, Musei Vaticani, Palazzo Apostolico Vaticano, 00120 Città del Vaticano. Cur.: Dr. Arnold Nesselrath
Fine Arts Museum - 1932
Paintings by Giotto, Fra Angelico, Raphael, Leonardo da Vinci, Titian and Caravaggio, the Raphael tapestries 48885

Venezuela

Acarigua

Museo José Antonio Páez, Páez en Curpa, Acarigua 3350
Historical Museum 48886

Aragua

Museo Ornitológico, Vía Ocumare de la Costa, Parque Nacional Rancho Grande, Aragua 2112
Natural History Museum
Ornithology 48887

Barcelona

Galería de Arte de la Escuela Armando Reverón, Calle Páez, Barcelona 6001
Fine Arts Museum 48888

Galería de la Asamblea Legislativa, Av Fuerzas Armadas, Barcelona 6001
Fine Arts Museum 48889

Galería del Museo Anzoátegui, Aeropuerto Internacional José Antonio Anzoátegui, Barcelona 6001
Fine Arts Museum 48890

Galería Municipal de Arte Moderno, Av Estadium, Barcelona 6001
Fine Arts Museum 48891

Museo de Anzoátegui, Calle Juncal 3-45, Barcelona 6001
Local Museum - 1981
17th-19th c painting and sculpture, rgional history, 19th c weapons, docs and furniture - library 48892

Museo El Sol de las Botellas, Peñalver, Barcelona 6001
Fine Arts Museum / Decorative Arts Museum
Painting, metal works, ceramics, graphic design 48893

Barinas

Museo Alberto Arvelo Torrealba, Av Medina Jiménez y Calle 5 de Julio, Barinas 5201
Special Museum - 1981 48894

Barquisimeto

Museo de Barquisimeto, Carrera 15 entre Calles 25 y 26, Barquisimeto 3001 - T: (0251) 310557, 317479, Fax: 310889, E-mail: fundamuseo@cantv.net, Internet: www.geocities.com/Athens/Forum/4330/. Dir.: Francisco Blavia
Local Museum 48895

Boca de Río

Museo del Mar, Universidad de Oriente, Península de Macanao, Boca de Río 6301
University Museum / Historical Museum 48896

Caracas

Casa Natal del Libertador Simón Bolívar (Simón Bolívar's Birthplace), Calle San Jacinto a Traposos, Pl El Venezolano, Caracas - T: (0212) 5412563. Cur.: Josefina de Sandoval
Historical Museum
Murals by Tito Salas depicting the life of Simón Bolívar and the events of the Independence Movement 48897

Centro Cultural Corp Group, c/o Torre Corp Banca, Pl La Castellana, Caracas - T: (0212) 2061149
Public Gallery 48898

Centro de Arte La Cañuela, Av Principal, CC Alto Prado, 1080 Caracas - T: (0212) 9784624, 9781324, E-mail: mcanuela@telecel.net.ve
Fine Arts Museum 48899

Centro de Arte La Estancia, Av Frederico de Miranda, La Floresta, 1060 Caracas - T: (0212) 2080412, Internet: www.pdv.com/estancia
Fine Arts Museum 48900

Colección Ornitológica W.H. Phelps, Blvd de Sabana Grande, Edificio Gran Sabana, Caracas 1050 - T: (0212) 7615631, Fax: 7633695, E-mail: mlentino@reacciun.ve. Dir.: Kathleen D. Phelps, Cur.: Miguel Lentino, Robin Restall (Research), Irving Carreño, Margarita Martínez
Natural History Museum
Ornithology 48901

Galeria de Arte de la UCV, Universidad Central de Venezuela, Adyacente al Aula Magna, Caracas - T: (0212) 619811
Fine Arts Museum 48902

Galería de Arte Nacional, Plaza de los Museos, Los Caobos, Caracas 1050 - T: (0212) 5781818, Fax: 5781661, E-mail: fgan@infoline.wtfe.com, Internet: www.wtfe.com/gan
Public Gallery - 1976
Venezuelan visual art from pre-Hispanic time to the present 48903

Museo Alejandro Otero, Complejo Cultural La Rinconada, Caracas 1010-A - T: (0212) 6820941, 6821841, Fax: 6820023, 6820428, E-mail: museotero@cantv.net. Pres.: Marinelly Bello Morales
Fine Arts Museum 48904

Museo Armando Reverón, Callejón Colón, Av La Playa, Sec Las Quince Letras, Macuto, La Guaira, 1160 Caracas - T: (0212) 4611357
Special Museum 48905

Museo Arte Visuales Alejanoro Otero Mavao → Museo Alejandro Otero

Museo Arturo Michelena, Calle Urapal 82, Altagracia, Caracas 1010 - T: (0212) 8604802, 8623957, E-mail: museomichelena@cantv.net, Internet: www.museomichelena.arts.ve
Fine Arts Museum
19th c home of the printer Arturo Michelena, memorabilia, documents 48906

Museo Audiovisual, Parque Central, Edificio Tacagua Nivel Bolívar, Caracas 1010, mail addr: c/o Academia Nacional de Ciencias y Artes del Cine y la Televisión, Apdo 17030, Caracas - T: (0212) 5721046, 5737757. Dir.: Prof. Oscar Moraña, Sandra Ramón Vilarasau
Science&Tech Museum
Exhibition of technical audiovisual instruments and apparatus used in T.V. radio, and theatre - library, archives 48907

Museo Bolívariano (Bolívar Museum), Calle San Jacinto a Traposos, Pl El Venezolano, Caracas 1010 - T: (0212) 5459828. Dir.: Flor Zambrano de Gentile
Historical Museum - 1911
Personal memorabilia of revolutionary hero Simón Bolívar (1783-1830), portraits, historical paintings of Bolívar contemporaries - library 48908

Museo Cuadra de Bolívar, Calle Piedras a Calle Bárcenas, Caracas 1010
Historical Museum
Murals by Titos Salas depicting the struggle for independence, correspondence and documents by Bolívar 48909

Museo de Arquitectura, Edificio Torre La Primera, Av Francisco de Miranda, Chacao, 1060 Caracas - T: (0212) 2620327, 2622171
Fine Arts Museum 48910

Museo de Arte Colonial, Quinta de Anauco, Av Panteón, Caracas 1011 - T: (0212) 518650, Fax: 518517, E-mail: infoanauco@quintadeanauco.org.ve, Internet: www.quintadeanauco.org.ve. Dir.: Carlos F. Duarte
Fine Arts Museum / Decorative Arts Museum - 1942
Paintings, sculpture, furniture, china of the Venezuelar Colonial period - library 48911

Museo de Arte Contemporáneo de Caracas Sofía Imber, Parque Central, Edificio Anauco Nivel Lecuna, Caracas 1010, mail addr: Apdo 17093, Caracas 1010 - T: (0212) 5738289, 5734602, Fax: 5771883, E-mail: info@maccsi.org.ve, Internet: www.maccsi.org.ve. Dir.: Sofía Imber
Fine Arts Museum / Decorative Arts Museum - 1973
Venezuelan and international works of art, sculpture, painting, arts and crafts, Calder's tapestries, works by Soto and Vasarely - library 48912

Museo de Arte Popular Petare, Calle Guánchez, CC Lino Clemente, Centro Histórico de Petare, Caracas 1073 - T: (0212) 218741, 218335
Folklore Museum 48913

Museo de Bellas Artes de Caracas, Plaza Morelos, Parque Los Caobos, Caracas 1050 - T: (0212) 5710169, Fax: 5712119, E-mail: fmba@reacciun.ve, Internet: www.museodebellasartes.org. Pres.: María Elena Huizi, Cur.: Iris Peruga, Michaelle Ascencio, Tomás Rodríguez, Marco Rodríguez del Camino, Marta Liaño, Julieta González, Milagros González, Enrique Nóbrega
Fine Arts Museum - 1938
Latin American coll of paintings and sculptures, European paintings, coll of prints, drawings and photographs, contemporary sculpture, Chinese ceramics, Egyptian art - library 48914

Museo de Caracas, Esq de Monjas, Alcaldía de Caracas Frente a la Pl Bolívar, Caracas - T: (0212) 5456706
Local Museum 48915

Museo de Ciencias, Pl de los Museos, Parque Los Caobos, Caracas 1010, mail addr: Apdo 5883, Caracas 1010 - T: (0212) 5775094, 5770232, Fax: 5711265, 5732368, E-mail: informacion@museo-de-ciencias.org.ve, Internet: www.museo-de-ciencias.org.ve. Pres.: Sergio Antillano Armas, Sc. Staff: Luis Galindo (Conceptions), Sonia Anzola (Environment)
Natural History Museum / Science&Tech Museum - 1875
Special collections: archaeology, ethnography, herpetology, invertebrates, ichthyology, ornithology, paleontology, physical anthropology, mineralogy, scientific instruments, theriology, toys - library, documentation center 48916

Museo de la Electricidad, Av Sanz, El Marqués, Caracas 1071 - T: (0212) 2088411
Science&Tech Museum 48917

Museo de la Estampa y del Diseño Carlos Cruz Diez, Av Bolívar, entre Calles Sur 11 y Este 8, Paseo Vargas, 1010 Caracas - T: (0212) 57231476, 5716910, E-mail: museocruz-diez@cantv.net
Fine Arts Museum / Decorative Arts Museum 48918

Museo de la Fundación John Boulton, Av Universidad, Torre El Chorro, 1010 Caracas, mail addr: Apdo postal 929, 1010-A Caracas - T: (02) 5644366, Fax: 5631838, E-mail: fjb@reacciun.ve, Internet: www.fundaboulton.org/museo.html
Fine Arts Museum
Paintings, prints, graphics, sculpture, numismatica, decorative arts, Bolivariana 48919

Museo de la Moneda, Edificio Sede del Banco Central de Venezuela, Mezzanina, 1030 Caracas - T: (0212) 8015111
Special Museum 48920

Museo de Los Niños de Caracas, Parque Central, Edificio Tacagua, Nivel Bolívar, Caracas 1010-A - T: (0212) 5734112, 5753022, Fax: 5754302, E-mail: mninos@cantv.net, Internet: www.museodelosninos.org.ve. Dir.: Alicia Pietri de Caldera
Special Museum / Science&Tech Museum 48921

Museo del Beisbol (Museum of Baseball), Bello Campo, 1060 Caracas - T: (0212) 2632063
Special Museum 48922

Museo del Teclado, Parque Central, Edificio Tacagua, Nivel Mezzanina, Caracas 1010 - T: (0212) 5720713, 5729024
Local Museum 48923

Museo del Transporte Guillermo José Schael, Av Francisco de Miranda, Sec Santa Cecilia, Parque del Este, Caracas 1071-009 - T: (0212) 2342234, 2341621, Fax: 2390652, E-mail: teremach@telcel.net.ve. Dir.: Alfredo Schael
Science&Tech Museum - 1970
History of transportation in Venezuela, early motor vehicles, railway history - automobile saloon, aircrafts hangar, carriage saloon, two train stations, library and documental section 48924

Museo Jacobo Borges, Parque del Oeste, Av Sucre, Catia, Estación Gato Negro, Caracas 1030 - T: (0212) 8620427/8101, Fax: 8623821, 8622989, E-mail: mujabo@hotmail.com, Internet: www.museojacoboborges.org.ve. Dir.: Adriana Meneses
Local Museum - 1993 48925

Museo Pedagógico de Historia del Arte, c/o Instituto del Arte, Facultad de Humanidades y Educación, Ciudad Universitaria, Caracas
Fine Arts Museum / University Museum
Paintings, Latin American art 48926

Museo Sacro de Caracas, Calle Torre a Gradillas, La Catedral, Caracas 1010 - T: (0212) 8616562, 8615814
Religious Arts Museum 48927

Sala Cadafe, Av Sanz, Edificio Cadafe, El Marqués, Caracas 1071 - T: (0212) 226256, 208500
Local Museum 48928

Sala Ipostel, Museo de Arte Contemporáneo de Caracas Sofía Imber, Av. José Angel Lamas, Edficio Sede Ipostel, San Martín, 1020 Caracas - T: (0212) 4512495
Fine Arts Museum 48929

Sala Mendoza, Av Andrés Bello, Edificio Las Fundaciones Planta Baja, 1020 Caracas - T: (0212) 5714731, E-mail: salamend@telcel.net.ve
Public Gallery 48930

Catia la Mar

Museo Naval, Escuela Naval de Venezuela, Meseta de Mamo, Catia la Mar, Vargas
Military Museum / Science&Tech Museum - 1965
History, ethnography, technology 48931

Ciudad Bolívar

Casa San Isidro, Av Táchira y calle 5 de Julio, Ciudad Bolívar 8001
Decorative Arts Museum
Local history, first periodical of Venezuela 48932

Museo de Arte Moderno Jesús Soto, Av Germania, Ciudad Bolívar 8001, mail addr: Apdo 211, Ciudad Bolívar 8001-A - T: (0285) 24474, 20518, Fax: 25854, E-mail: museosoto@cantv.net. Pres.: Ivanova Decán Gambús
Fine Arts Museum - 1973
20th c art, mainly by Venezuelan and European artists, Jesús Soto, Constructivism, kinetic art, new realism 48933

Museo de Ciudad Bolívar, Casa del Correo del Orinoco, Ciudad Bolívar 8001
Local Museum
Local history, first periodical of Venezuela 48934

Colonia Tovar

Museo de Historia y Artesanía de la Colonial Tovar, Calle del Museo, Colonia Tovar 1030
Local Museum - 1970
Art, history, natural history, anthropology, ethnography, archaeology, geology 48935

Cumaná

Casa de Andrés Eloy Blanco, Pl Bolívar, Cumaná 5001
Special Museum 48936

Casa Natal de José Antonio Ramos Sucre, Cumaná 5001
Special Museum 48937

Museo Gran Mariscal de Ayacucho, Av Humboldt, Parque Ayacucho, Cumaná 5001
Historical Museum 48938

El Tocuyo

Museo Colonial, El Tocuyo
Local Museum - 1945
Relics relating mainly to the colonial period 48939

Falcón

Museo de Arte Coro y Museo Alberto Henríquez, Balcón Bolívar, Paseo Talavera, Falcón 4101
Fine Arts Museum 48940

Museo de Cerámica y Loza Popular, Balcón de los Arcaya, Calle Zamora, Zona Colonial, Falcón 4101
Decorative Arts Museum 48941

Museo Diocesano Lucas Guillermo Castillo, Calle Zamora, Zona Colonial, Falcón 4101
Religious Arts Museum / Fine Arts Museum 48942

Guanare

Museo de los Llanos, Parque José Antonio Páez, Guanare 3350
Local Museum - 1995
Local history and archaeology, colonial time, cultures - archive 48943

Museo Inés Mercedes Gómez Álvarez, Universidad Ezequiel Zamora, Casco Colonial, Guanare 3350
Historical Museum - 1984 48944

Guayana

Castillos de Guayana la Vieja, Av Manuel Piar, Guayana
Historical Museum
Fortress San Francisco and San Diego de Alcalá 48945

Juangriego

Museo de Arte Popular Venezolano, Tacuantar, Juangriego 6301
Folklore Museum / Decorative Arts Museum 48946

La Asunción

Museo Nueva Cádiz, Calle Independencia, La Asunción 6311
Local Museum
History, ethnography, natural history, archaeology 48947

La Guaira

Casa Natal de José María España, Calle San Francisco 9, La Guaira 1160
Historical Museum
Independence revolution of 1797 48948

Los Teques

Museo J.M. Cruxent, c/o Depto Antropología del Instituto Venezolano de Investigaciones Científicas, Carretera Panamericana, Los Teques 1201 - T: (0212) 5041227, Fax: 5041085, E-mail: svidal@ivic.ivic.ve. Dir.: Silvia M. Vidal
Ethnology Museum / Archaeological Museum - 1959
Archaeology, ethnology 48949

Macuto

Museo Armando Reverón, Callejón Colon, Macuto, Vargas
Historical Museum 48950

Maracaibo

Museo Urdaneta Histórico Militar (Museum of Military History), Maracaibo 4001 - T: (0261) 226778. Dir.: Prof. J.C. Borges Rosales
Military Museum - 1936
Military hist 48951

Maracay

Museo Aeronáutico Colonel Luis Hernan Paredes, Av Las Delicias y Av 19 de Abril, Maracay 2101 - T: (0243) 333812, Fax: 333812. Dir.: Juan C. Flores
Science&Tech Museum - 1963
Aeronautical history 48952

Museo de Antropología e Historia, Fundación Lisandro Alvarado, Blvd La Alcaldía a la Plaza Girardot, Maracay 2101, mail addr: Apdo 4518, Maracay 2101-A - T: (0243) 2472521. Dir.: Henriqueta Peñalver Gómez, Pres. Honoraria: Dr. Adelaida de Díaz Ungría, Sc. Staff: Mary Yamilet Bonilla (Antropología Física), Prof. Delia García de Del Valle (Informatión, Divulgación)
Ethnology Museum / Historical Museum / Archaeological Museum - 1964
Pre-Columbian archeology, Venezuelan ethnology, anthropology, and history, vertebrate paleontology, religious art - library 48953

Museo Mario Abreu, Av 19 de Abril, Complejo Cultural Santos Michelena, Maracay 2107 - T: (0243) 336980, Fax: 338534
Local Museum 48954

Mérida

Museo de Arte Colonial, Av 3, entre Calles 18 y 19, Mérida 5101
Fine Arts Museum 48955

Museo de Arte Moderno, Calle Flamboyán, Santa María, frente a la Plaza Beethoven, Mérida 5101
Fine Arts Museum - 1969
Modern Venezuelan art 48956

Museo del Estado de Mérida, c/o Universidad de Mérida, Mérida 5101
Local Museum
Regional ethnography and history 48957

Nueva Cádiz

Museo Biblioteca Nueva Cádiz y Casa Natal de Juan Bautista Arismendi, Antigua Casa Capitular, Nueva Cádiz 6301
Historical Museum 48958

Pampatar

Museo Biblioteca Rosauro Rosa Acosta, Casa de la Aduana, Pampatar 6301
Decorative Arts Museum
Antiques, books, paintings, sculpture 48959

Píritu

Museo de la Ciudad de Píritu, Esteller, Píritu 3350
Local Museum 48960

Museo de las Muñecas (Doll Museum), Esteller, Píritu 3350
Decorative Arts Museum 48961

Porlamar

Museo de Arte Contemporáneo Francisco Narvárez, Complejo Rómulo Gallegos, Calle Igualdad, Porlamar 6301
Fine Arts Museum - 1981
Sculptures 48962

Puerto Ayacucho

Museo Etnológico de Amazonas, Iglesia, 7101 Puerto Ayacucho
Ethnology Museum - 1984
Cultures of Piaroa, Guahiba, Yanomami, Arawak and Yekuana 48963

Trujillo

Museo Cristóbal Mendoza, Trujillo 3150
Historical Museum 48964

Valencia

Ateneo de Valencia, Av Bolívar Nort, Valencia 2001 - T: (0241) 8580046, 8581962
Fine Arts Museum 48965

Casa Museo Páez, Loc. 99-20, Av Boyacá, Valencia 2001 - T: (0241) 8571272
Local Museum 48966

Museo de Arte e Historia Casa de Los Celis, Av Soublette, Valencia 2001 - T: (0241) 8421245
Historical Museum / Archaeological Museum 48967

Valle del Espíritu Santo

Museo Diocesano, Santuario de Nuestra Señora del Valle, Valle del Espíritu Santo 6301
Religious Arts Museum 48968

Vietnam

Da Nang

National Museum of Cham Sculpture, 2 Tiêû La St, Da Nang - T: (0511) 821951, Fax: 821279
Archaeological Museum - 1915
Champá sculpture and architectural fragments from various periods and places, late 7th-15th c, in Central Vietnam, objects were collected from the temples y Hinduism and Buddhism of Champákinydom 48969

Ha Noi

Air Force Museum, Truong Chinh, Ha Noi
Military Museum 48970

Anti-Aircraft Museum, Truong Chinh, Ha Noi - T: (04) 8522658
Military Museum 48971

Bao Tàng Dân Tôc Hoc Viêt Nam (Vietnam Museum of Ethnology), Nguyen van Huyen St, Cau Giay, Ha Noi - T: (04) 8360350, Fax: 8360351, E-mail: vmel8@hn.vnn.vn. Dir.: Prof. Dr. Hguyen Van Huy
Ethnology Museum 48972

Bao Tàng Quan Doi (Army Museum), 28a Dien Bien Phu, Ha Noi - T: (04) 7334682. Dir.: Ma Luong Le
Military Museum
Military hist 48973

Bien Phong Museum, 2 Tran Hung Dao, Ha Noi - T: (04) 8213835
Local Museum 48974

Exhibition Hall, c/o Ministry of Culture and Information, 29 Hang Bai St, Ha Noi
Public Gallery 48975

Fine Art University Exhibition Hall, 42 Yet Kieu, Hoan Kiem, Ha Noi
Public Gallery 48976

Geology Museum, 6 Pham Ngu Lao, Ha Noi - T: (04) 8266802, 8249112, Fax: 9331496, E-mail: danht-btdc@fpt.vn, Internet: www.idm.gov.vn. Dir.: Prof. Dr. Trinh Danh
Natural History Museum 48977

Ha Noi Museum, 5b Ham Long, Ha Noi - T: (04) 8263982
Local Museum
Local history 48978

Ho Chi Minh Museum, 3 Ngoc Ha, Ba Dinh, Ha Noi - T: (04) 8455525, 8463757, Fax: 7439387. Dir.: Cu Van Chuoc
Special Museum - 1977
Life and work of President Ho Chi Minh 48979

Vien Bao Tang Lich Sa Viet Nam (National Museum of Vietnamese History), 1 Pham Ngu Lao, Ha Noi - T: (04) 8252853, 8242433, Fax: 8252853. Dir.: Phạm Quoc Quan
Historical Museum
Hist of Viet Nam from prehistoric times till 1945 48980

Viet Nam National Fine Arts Museum, 66 Nguyen Thai Hoc, Ha Noi - T: (04) 8231085, 8233084, Fax: 7341427, E-mail: binhtruong451@hn.vnn.vn. Dir.: Prof. Dr. Truong Quoc Binh
Fine Arts Museum - 1966
Folk drawings, modern paintings and sculptures, lacquers and silks, bronzes and stones, ancient ceramics, oil paintings, wood carvings - library, departments of research, propaganda and storage 48981

Viet Nam Revolution Museum, 25 Tong Dan, Ha Noi - T: (04) 8254323, 8254151, Fax: 9342064, E-mail: phammaihung@yahoo.com. Dir.: Prof. Dr. Pham Mai Hung
Military Museum / Historical Museum - 1959
Revolutionary hist of Viet Nam 48982

Viet Nam Women's Museum, 36 Ly Thuong Kiet, Hoan Kiem, Ha Noi - T: (04) 8259935/38. Dir.: Nguyen Thi Nghien
Ethnology Museum 48983

Hai Phong

Bao Tàng Hai Phong (Haiphong Museum), Hai Phong
Local Museum - 1959
Local hist 48984

Ho Chi Minh City

Geological Museum, 2 Nguyen Binh Khiem, Ho Chi Minh City - T: (08) 8294821, 8221156. Dir.: Trinh Van Hong, Dep. Dir.: Tran Huy An
Natural History Museum
Mineralogy, fossils 48985

Ho Chi Minh City Fine Arts Museum, 97a Pho Duc Chinh, Ho Chi Minh City - T: (08) 8294441, Fax: 8213508, E-mail: btmt@hcm.vnn.vn. Dir.: Nguyen Toan Thi
Fine Arts Museum 48986

Ho Chi Minh Museum, 1 Nguyen Tat Thanh, Ho Chi Minh City - T: (08) 8255740, 9402060. Dir.: Nguyen So
Historical Museum 48987

Nan Bo's Southern Women Museum, 202 Vo Thi Sau, Dist 3, Ho Chi Minh City - T: (08) 8298065, 8202690. Dir.: Tran Hong Anh
Ethnology Museum 48988

Revolutionary Museum Ho Chi Minh City, 114 Nam Ky Khoi Nghia, Dist 3, Ho Chi Minh City - T: (08) 8298250, 8299743. Dir.: Pham Van Cong
Historical Museum - 1978
History, revolutionary movement and War of Liberation - library 48989

South-East Armed Force Museum, 247 Hoang Van Thu, Tan Binh, Ho Chi Minh City - T: (08) 8421354, 8229357. Dir.: Phan Oanh
Military Museum 48990

Thong Nhat Palace, 133 Nam Ky Khoi Nighia, Ho Chi Minh City - T: (08) 294991
Fine Arts Museum 48991

Ton Duc Thang Museum, 5 Ton Duc Thang St, Ho Chi Minh City - T: (08) 8295946, 8224887. Dir.: Tran Thi Thuy Phuong
Local Museum 48992

Viet Nam History Museum Ho Chi Minh City, 2 Nguyen Binh Khiem, Dist 1, Ho Chi Minh City - T: (08) 8298146, 8220743. Dir.: Trung Le
Historical Museum 48993

War Remnants Museum, 28 Vo Van Tan, Ho Chi Minh City - T: (08) 9305153, 9306325, 9305587, Fax: 9305153, E-mail: Warrm@cinet.vnnews.com. Dir.: Nguyêñ Quôé Hùng
Historical Museum
Requiem (Photo Coll), Vietnam 35 Years War and Peace, Weapons, hist truths 48994

Hong-Gai

Hong Quang Museum, Hong-Gai
Local Museum
Local history 48995

Hung-Yen

Hung-Yen Museum, Hung-Yen
Local Museum
Local history and archaeology 48996

Lam Dong

Lam Dong Museum, Lam Dong
Local Museum
Modern history of Vietnam, Vietnamese popular arts 48997

Nhatrang

Oceanographic Museum, Institute of Oceanography, 01 Cauda, Nhatrang - T: (058) 590032/36, Fax: 590034, E-mail: haiduong@dng.vnn.vn. Dir.: Dr. Nguyen Tac An
Natural History Museum - 1923
Coll of marine fishes, sea weeds, coelenterates, sponges, polychaetes, crustacean, mollusks, echinoderms, reptiles, sea-birds, sea-mammals etc (about 20 000 specimens of 10 000 species) 48998

Phu Khanh

Phu Khanh Museum, Phu Khanh
Local Museum
Local history before the founding of the Communist Party 48999

Thai Nguyen

Bao Tàng Văn Hóa Các Dân Tôc Viêt Nam (Museum of Cultures of Vietnam's Ethnic Groups), 359 Duong Minh St, Thai Nguyen - T: (0280) 855781, 852182, Fax: 752940, E-mail: mangocdung@yahoo.com, Internet: www.vietnamtourism.com/e_pages/tourist/tourspot/museum/ttm_tn_dantoc.htm. Dir.: Ha Thi Nu
Ethnology Museum - 1960
Cultures of Vietnamese 54 ethnic groups in Viet Nam, clouthes, textiles, musical instruments, tools, things of life, argiculture, houses 49000

Thua Thien Hue

Ho Chi Minh Memorial House, Duong No, Thua Thien Hue 47000
Special Museum 49001

Ho Chi Minh Museum, 06 Le Loi, Thua Thien Hue 47000 - T: (054) 822152, 820250
Special Museum 49002

Thua Thien Hue Museum, 01-23 Thang Tam St, Thua Thien Hue 47000 - T: (054) 822397, 823159. Dir.: Pham Xuân Phuong
Archaeological Museum / Ethnology Museum - 1982
Cham sculptures (10th-11th c), ethnological objects, hist of the old capital 49003

Vinh

Nghe-Tinh Museum, Vinh
Historical Museum
Hist of the Nghe-Tinh 'Soviet' uprising 1930-31 49004

Yemen

Aden

Ethnographical Museum, nr Tanks, Crater, Aden
Ethnology Museum 49005

Military Museum, Sayla Rd, Crater, Aden
Military Museum
Historic weapons 49006

National Museum, Crater, Aden
Archaeological Museum
Archaeological find in an old sultan's palace 49007

The Tanks of Aden, On the Volcanic Slopes, Aden
Science&Tech Museum
18 cisterns from 1st c AD 49008

Al-Mukalla

Al-Mukalla Museum, Al-Mukalla
Folklore Museum
Folk costumes, traditional handicrafts 49009

Sanaa

Military Museum, Tahrir Sq, Sanaa
Military Museum 49010

National Museum, Dar as-Sa'd, nr Tahrir Sq, Sanaa, mail addr: POB 2606, Sanaa - T: (01) 271648. Dir.: Ahmed Naji Sari
Historical Museum / Archaeological Museum / Folklore Museum
South Arabian antiques of the pre-Islamic and Islamic periods, folklore, artefacts of ancient kingdoms of Saba, Ma'in, Ma'rib and Himyar 49011

Seiyun

Seiyun in Wadi Hadhramaut Museum, Seiyun - T: (05) 5402258
Local Museum / Archaeological Museum / Folklore Museum
Housed in a former Sultans palace, handicrafts, folklore items, antiques found in the region   49012

Taizz

Taizz Museum, Taizz
Local Museum
Housed in a former Imams palace, items pertaining to the 1962 Revolution and the events that led up to it   49013

Wadi Baihan

Baihan Al Qasab Museum, Wadi Baihan
Archaeological Museum
Antiques found in the Qataban region dating back to pre-Islamic times   49014

Zambia

Choma

Choma Museum and Crafts Centré, Great North Rd, between Lusaka and Livingstone Rds, Choma, mail addr: POB 630189, Choma - T: (032) 20394, Fax: 20394, E-mail: cmcc@coppernet.zm, Internet: www.catgen.net/cmcc. Dir.: Mwimanji Ndota Chellah
Local Museum - 1987
Material culture of the peoples inhabiting Southern Zambia, ethnographic hist of the Southern Province   49015

Limulunga

Nayuma Museum, POB 96, Limulunga - T: (07) 221421, Fax: 221351. Dir.: Manyando Mukela
Local Museum   49016

Livingstone

Livingstone Museum, National Museum of Zambia, Mosi-oa-Tunya Rd, Livingstone, mail addr: POB 60498, Livingstone - T: (03) 323566, Fax: 324429, E-mail: livmus@zamnet.zm. Dir.: K.V. Katanekwa
Local Museum - 1934
Natural hist, exhibits, general hist, fine arts, relics of Dr Livingstone, archaeology, ethnography, zoology - library   49017

Railway Museum, 140 Chishimba Falls Rd, Livingstone, mail addr: POB 60124, Livingstone - T: (03) 321820, Fax: 324509, E-mail: nhcc@zamnet.zm. Dir.: N.M. Katanekwa, Patrick Lisina Wamulungwe
Science&Tech Museum - 1987
Vintage steam locomotives, wooden passenger carriages, and other memorabialia associated with the site   49018

Victoria Falls Field Museum → Victoria Falls Information Centre

Victoria Falls Information Centre, Mosi-Oa-Tunya Rd, Livingstone, mail addr: POB 60124, Livingstone - T: (03) 323662, Fax: 323653, E-mail: nhccsowe@zamnet.zm. Dir.: N.M. Katanekwa
Local Museum
Displays illustrating formation of the Victoria Falls, Stone Age implements   49019

Lusaka

Lusaka National Museum, Kalima Tower, Lusaka, mail addr: POB 50491, 15101 Lusaka - T: (01) 228805/07, Fax: 223788. Dir.: Dr. Francis B. Musonda
Historical Museum   49020

National Archives of Zambia, Ridgeway, Lusaka, mail addr: POB 50010, Lusaka - T: (01) 250446, Fax: 254080, E-mail: naz@zamnet.zm. Dir.: C. Hamooya
Historical Museum
Stamps and coins, local history, photographs   49021

University of Zambia Library Museums Collection, Great East Rd, Campus, Lusaka, mail addr: POB 32379, Lusaka - T: (01) 250845, Fax: 253952, E-mail: msimui@library.unza.zm, Internet: www.unza.zm/library/special.htm. Dir.: Muyoyeta Simui
Library with Exhibitions - 1969   49022

Mbala

Moto Moto Museum, Lucheche Rd, Mbala, mail addr: POB 420230, Mbala - T: (04) 450243, Fax: 450243, E-mail: motomoto@zamtel.zm. Dir.: Flexon Moono Mizinga
Ethnology Museum / Historical Museum - 1974
Research in ethnography and cultural history, traditional medicine and charms, musical instruments, masks, Bemba girls initiation rite, prehistoric items - library   49023

Ndola

Copperbelt Museum, Buteko Av, Ndola, mail addr: POB 71444, Ndola - T: (02) 617450, 613591, Fax: 617450, E-mail: cbmus@zamnet.zm. Dir.: Stanford Mudenda Siachoono
Science&Tech Museum - 1962
Displays on the copper mining industry, nature and ecology, geology, ethnography   49024

Zimbabwe

Bulawayo

Khami Ruins Site Museum, POB 240, Bulawayo - T: (09) 60045, Fax: 64019, E-mail: monuments@telconet.co.zw. Dir.: Albert Kumirai
Open Air Museum / Archaeological Museum
Ruins of one of Mambo dynasty capitals (15th to early 19th c), archaeological finds from the area   49025

Matopos National Park Site Museums, Bulawayo
Archaeological Museum
Prehistoric rock paintings, Stone Age tools, grave of Cecil Rhodes   49026

National Gallery Bulawayo, 75 Main St, Bulawayo, mail addr: POB 1993, Bulawayo - T: (09) 70721, Fax: 63343, E-mail: sabona@telcenet.co.zw. Dir.: Addelis Sibutha
Fine Arts Museum / Decorative Arts Museum - 1974
Works of contemporary English and South African artists, loan exhibitions, Ndebele and Tonga baskets, Zimbabwean art and craft, works of Zimbabwean and Sadc artists   49027

Natural History Museum of Zimbabwe, Leopold Takawira Av and Park Rd, Bulawayo, mail addr: POB 240, Bulawayo - T: (09) 60045/46, Fax: 64019, E-mail: natmuse@telconet.co.zw. Dir.: Albert Kumirai, Cur.: F.D.P. Cotterill (Mammals), R. Sithole (Entomology), M. Fitzpatrick (Arachnology), A. Msimanga (Ornithology), R.P. Chidavaenzi (Herpetology), D. Munyikwa (Palaeontology), P. Makoni (Ichthyology)
Natural History Museum - 1901
Zoology coll covering Ethiopian region and Southern Africa - library, herbarium   49028

Gweru

Zimbabwe Military Museum, Lobengula Av, Gweru, mail addr: POB 1300, Gweru - T: (054) 22816, Fax: 20321, E-mail: museum@internet.co.zw. Dir.: Tarisai Tsomondo
Military Museum - 1974
Weapons, military vehicles, uniforms, and equipment, aircraft and aviation uniforms and equipment, archaeology, mining, monuments   49029

Harare

Macgregor Museum, Causeway, Harare, mail addr: c/o Geological Survey Department, POB CY210, Harare - T: (04) 726342/3, Fax: 253626, E-mail: zgs@samara.co.zw, Internet: www.zimgeosurv.co.zw. Dir.: T. Hawadi
Natural History Museum - 1940
Eonomic minerals, displays dealing with the Deweras and Umkondo groups, geology of Zimbabwe, great dyke, alkali ring complex rocks   49030

Museum of Human Sciences, Civic Centre, Rotten Row, Causeway, Harare, mail addr: POB CY33, Harare - T: (04) 751797/98, Fax: 774207, E-mail: nmmz@mweb.co.zw. Dir.: Pascall Taruvinska
Ethnology Museum / Archaeological Museum - 1902
National coll of Iron and Stone Age artifacts, rock paintings, ethnographic coll - library   49031

National Gallery of Zimbabwe, 20 Julius Nyerere Way, Harare - T: (04) 704666/67, Fax: 704668, E-mail: ngallery@harare.iafrica.com. Dir.: Prof. George P. Kahari
Fine Arts Museum - 1957
Traditional African art, Zimbabwean stone sculpture (shona sculpture) - library   49032

Queen Victoria Museum, Rotten Row, Causeway, Harare, mail addr: POB 8006, Harare - T: (04) 704831/32, 724915, Fax: 77717. Dir.: Lorraine Margaret Adams
Historical Museum   49033

Inyanga

Nyahokwe Ruins Site Museum, Inyanga
Open Air Museum / Archaeological Museum
Relics of Iron Age, locally found relics of Ziwa culture   49034

Kwekwe

National Mining Museum, POB 512, Kwekwe - T: (055) 23741, Fax: (054) 20321, E-mail: minmus@globalzim.net. Dir.: Josiah Rungano Mhute
Science&Tech Museum - 1984
Mining antiquities, Globe and Phoenix Mining Company founded in 1895, machinery, tools, biographies   49035

Marondera

Children's Library Museum, The Green, Marondera - T: 3356
Special Museum
Objects illustrating man and his implements from the early Stone Age to pioneering days, rocks and minerals, local birds   49036

Masvingo

Great Zimbabwe Site Museum, POB 1060, Masvingo - T: (039) 62080, 65084, Fax: 63310, E-mail: greatzim@africaonline.co.zw. Dir.: Edward Matenga
Archaeological Museum
Zimbabwe Iron Age archaeology, Zimbabwe birds   49037

Mutare

Mutare Museum, Aerodrome Rd, Mutare - T: (020) 63630, 63005, Fax: 61100, E-mail: mutarmus@ecoweb.co.zw. Dir.: Traude Allison Rogers
Local Museum - 1959
Archaeology, history, national coll of transport antiquites and firearms, local flora and fauna   49038

Raylton

National Railways of Zimbabwe Museum, Prospect Av and First St, Raylton, mail addr: POB 945, Bulawayo - T: (09) 322507. Chm.: G.W.T. Tyamzarne
Science&Tech Museum
Former Mashanaland and Bura Rhodesian Railways and National Railways of Zimbabwe, steam locomotives, coaches, and freight cars   49039

Museum Associations

Algeria

Comité National de ICOM de Algérie, c/o Musée National du Bardo, 3 Av F.D. Roosevelt, Alger 16000 - T: (021) 747641, Fax: 742453   49040

Andorra

International Council of Museums, Andorran National Committee, c/o Patrimoni Cultural, Carretera de Bixessarri s/n, Aixovall - T: 844141, Fax: 844343, E-mail: pca.gov@andorra.ad   49041

Angola

ICOM Angola, Rua Major Kanyangulu 77, Luanda, mail addr: c/o Instituto Nacional do Patrimónío Cultural, CP 1267, Luanda - T: (2) 331139, Fax: 332575, E-mail: ipc@snet.co.ao   49042

Argentina

Comisión Nacional de Museos y de Monumentos, Av de Mayo 556, C1084AAN Buenos Aires - T: (011) 43316151   49043

Federación Argentina de Asociaciones de Amigos de Museos, Calle Bolívar 1131, C1066AAW Buenos Aires - T: (011) 43070522, Fax: 43070523, E-mail: fedamimus@fadam.org.ar, Internet: www.fadam.org.ar   49044

ICOM Argentina, Perú 272, Manzana de las Luces, 1piso, C1067 Buenos Aires - T: (011) 43420651, Fax: 43426758, E-mail: icom@aba-conet.com.ar   49045

Australia

Australian Federation of Friends of Museums, The Mint, 10 Macquarie St, Sydney, NSW 2000 - T: (02) 92323466, Fax: 92321699, E-mail: tunnyd@hpb.hht.nsw.gov.au, Internet: www.affm.org.au   49046

Council of Australian Art Museum Directors, c/o National Gallery of Australia, GPOB 1150, Canberra, ACT 2601 - T: (02) 62406400, Fax: 62406529   49047

Council of Australian Museum Directors, c/o Australian War Memorial, GPOB 345, Canberra, ACT 2601 - T: (02) 62434225, Fax: 62434218   49048

Heritage Collections Council, c/o Dept. of Communications, Information Technology and the Arts, GPOB 2154, Canberra, ACT 2601 - T: (02) 62711094, Fax: 62711122, E-mail: hcc.mail@dcita.gov.au   49049

ICOM Asia-Pacific Organization, University of Canberra, Belconnen, ACT 2616 - T: (06) 201-2199, Fax: 201-5999, E-mail: galla@science.can-berra.edu.au   49050

ICOM Australia, POB 270, Subiaco - T: (08) 92679227, Fax: 93814930, E-mail: c.bennet@su-biaco.wa.gov.au   49051

International Committee for University Museums and Collections (UMAC), c/o Peter Stanbury, Vice-chancellor's office, Macquarie University, Macquarie, NSW 2109 - T: (02) 98507431, Fax: 98507565, E-mail: peterstanbury@mq.edu.au, Internet: www.icom.org/umac   49052

Museums Australia, POB 266, Civic Square, ACT 2608 - T: (02 62085044, Fax: 62085015, E-mail: ma@museumsaustralia.org.au, Internet: www.museumsaustralia.org.au   49053

Austria

ICDAD International Committee for Decorative Arts and Design Museums, c/o Dr. E. Schmuttermeier, MAK Wien, Stubenring 5, 1010 Wien - T: (01) 71136234, Fax: 71136388, E-mail: schmutter-meier@mak.at   49054

ICOM Österreichisches Nationalkomitee, c/o Münzkabinett, KHM, Burgring 5, 1010 Wien - T: (01) 52524380, Fax: 52524353, E-mail: guenther.-dembski@khm.at, Internet: www.icom-oesterreich.at   49055

Museumsverband, Verband österreichischer Museen, Galerien, Schau- und Studiensammlungen, Feldegg 1, 4742 Pram - T: (07736) 62610, Fax: 62614, E-mail: olaf.bockhorn@univie.ac.at   49056

MuSiS - Verein zur Unterstützung der Museen und Sammlungen in der Steiermark, Strauchergasse 16, 8020 Graz - T: (0316) 738605, Fax: 738605, E-mail: office@musis.at, Internet: www.musis.at   49057

Oberösterreichischer Musealverein, Gesellschaft für Landeskunde von Oberösterreich, Ursulinenhof, Landstr 31, 4020 Linz - T: (0732) 770218, Fax: 770218, E-mail: ooelandeskunde@aon.at, Internet: www.ooelandeskunde.at   49058

Österreichischer Museumsbund, c/o Kunsthistorisches Museum, Burgring 5, 1010 Wien - T: (01) 52524350, Fax: 52524352, E-mail: elisabeth.herrmann@khm.at, Internet: www.khm.at/static/page1037.html   49059

Verband Österreichischer Privatmuseen, Moor-Hof, 4654 Bad Wimsbach-Neydharting - T: (07245) 5573, Fax: (0732) 77178125   49060

Azerbaijan

ICOM Azerbaijan, c/o State Museum of Azerbaijan Carpets and Applied Art Letif Kerimov, Neftçiler pr 123A, 370005 Baku - T: (012) 930501, 936685, Fax: 930501, E-mail: azcarpetmuseum@a-zeurotel.com; tagiyeva_r@rambler.ru   49061

Bangladesh

ICOM Bangladesh, Shahbagh, Dhaka, mail addr: c/o Bangladesh National Museum, POB 355, Dhaka 1000 - T: (02) 8614441, 9675601, Fax: 8615585, E-mail: jahangirhu@yahoo.com   49062

Barbados

ICOM Barbados, c/o Barbados Museum, 11 Saint Ann's Fort, Garrison, Saint Michael - T: (246) 427-0201, Fax: (246) 429-5946, E-mail: museum@-caribsurf.com, Internet: www.-barbmuse.org.bb   49063

Museums Association of the Caribbean, POB 112, Bridgetown - T: (246) 228-2024, Fax: (246) 228-2024, E-mail: macsecretariat@-caribsurf.com   49064

Belarus

ICOM National Commitee of Belarus, Bogdanoviča ul 15, 220029 Minsk - T: (017) 2347261, Fax: 2347261, E-mail: icombelarus@tut.by   49065

The Association of the State Literary Museums of the Republic of Belarus, Bogdanoviča ul 15, 220029 Minsk - T: (017) 2347261, Fax: 2347261, Internet: nacbibl.org.by/litm/en/lithist.html   49066

Belgium

L' Association Francophone des Musées de Belgique, c/o Musée d'Art Moderne et d'Art Contemporain, 3 Parc de la Boverie, 4020 Liège - T: 043430403, Fax: 043441907, E-mail: mamac@skynet.be, Internet: www.-muse.ucl.ac.be/Icom/AFMB.html   49067

Association Internationale des Musées d'Armes et d'Histoire Militaire (International Association of Museums of Arms and Military History), c/o Musée d'Armes de Liège, Halles du Nord, 4 Rue de la Boucherie, 4000 Liège - T: 042219416/17, Fax: 042219401, E-mail: claude.gaier@mu-seedarmes.be, Internet: www.klm-mra.be/icomam/index.htm   49068

Conseil Bruxellois de Musées, 46 Rue des Bouchers, 1000 Bruxelles - T: 025127780, Fax: 025122066, E-mail: info@brusselsmuseum.be, Internet: www.brusselsmuseums.be   49069

European Collaborative for Science, Industry and Technology Exhibitions, 63 Blvd du Triomphe, 1160 Bruxelles - T: 026475098, Fax: 026475098, E-mail: wststaveloz@ecsite.net, Internet: www-w.ecsite.net   49070

Fédération des Amis des Musées de Belgique (Belgian Federation of Friends of Museums), 9 Rue du Musée, 1000 Bruxelles   49071

Forum Européen des Conseillers et Consultants de Musée (European Museum Advisers Conference), 15 Rue du Paroissien, 1000 Bruxelles - T: 025536843, E-mail: leon.smets@wvc.vlaanderen.be   49072

ICOM - Belgian National Comittee, c/o Musée des Art Contemporains-MAC's, 82 Rue Sainte-Louise, 7301 Hornu - T: 065613851, Fax: 065613891, E-mail: info.macs@grand-hornu.be, Internet: www.mac-s.be   49073

International Association of Custom Museums, c/o Nationaal Museum, Kattendijkdok OK 22, 2000 Antwerpen - T: 032292260, Fax: 032292261, Internet: www.etat.lu/IACM   49074

Musées et Société en Wallonie, 149 Rue des Brasseurs, 5000 Namur - E-mail: vdd@muse.ucl.ac.be, Internet: www.-muse.ucl.ac.be/msw   49075

Vlaamse Museumvereniging, Plaatsnijdersstr 2, 2000 Antwerpen - T: 032160360, Fax: 032570861, E-mail: info@museumvereniging.be, Internet: www.museumvereniging.be/   49076

Benin

ICOM Bénin, c/o Musée Ethnographique, BP 299, Porto-Novo - T: 213566, Fax: 212109   49077

Bolivia

ICOM Bolivia, Casilla de Correo 8083, La Paz - T: (02) 2201250, Fax: 2201250, E-mail: icom@bolivia.com   49078

Bosnia and Herzegovina

ICOM Bosnia-Hercegovina, c/o Zemaljski Musej, Zmaja od Bosne 3ltet, 71000 Sarajevo - T: (033) 668057 I 37, Fax: 668025, E-mail: z.muzej@bih.net.ba   49079

Botswana

ICOM Botswana, c/o Botswana National Herbarium, Private Bag 00114, Gaborone - T: 373860, Fax: 311186, E-mail: turnerq@hotmail.com   49080

Brazil

Comitê Brasileiro do ICOM, Av Independência 867, Porto Alegre 90035-076 - T: (051) 33118200, 33117722, Fax: 3119351, E-mail: icombr@-terra.com.br, Internet: www.icom.org.br   49081

Federaçao de Amigos de Museus do Brasil (Brazilian Federation of Friends of Museums), Rua Horacio Lafer 702, 04538-083 São Paulo - E-mail: msoalmeida@sti.com.br   49082

Bulgaria

Associacija Muzej, c/o Peter Ivanov, 13a ul Gen. Skobelev, 9002 Varna - T: (052) 258263, Fax: 602079, E-mail: asociacia-musei@abv.bg   49083

Bulgarian Museum Chamber, bul Vitoša 2, 1000 Sofia, mail addr: c/o Nacionalen istoričeski muzej, POB 1351, 1000 Sofia - T: (02) 9802258, 9816600, Fax: 980024, E-mail: nim@einet.bg   49084

ICOM Bulgaria, c/o Nacionalen politechničeskij muzej, ul Opälčenska 66, 1303 Sofia - T: (02) 324050, 313004, Fax: 314036, E-mail: bnk_icom@abv.bg   49085

Burkina Faso

ICOM Burkina Faso, c/o Patrimoine Culturel, Ministère des Arts et de la Culture, BP 7007, Ouagadougou 03 - T: 310927, Fax: 316808, E-mail: patrimoine@mcc.gov.bf   49086

Burundi

ICOM Burundi, c/o M Salvator Ntakarutimana, BP 1095, Bujumbura - T: (02) 26822, Fax: 26231   49087

Cambodia

ICOM Cambodia, c/o Vann Molyvann, Ministre d'Etat, Résidence du Conseil des Ministres, Phnom Penh - T: (023) 880623, Fax: 880623, E-mail: apsara.dd-ta@bigpond.com.kh   49088

Cameroon

ICOM Cameroon, c/o Université de Yaoundé I, BP 755, Yaoundé - T: (3) 230614, Fax: 2221873, E-mail: ejm@camnet.cm   49089

Canada

Alberta Museums Association, 9829 103 St, Edmonton, AB T5K 0X9 - T: (780) 424-2626, Fax: (780) 425-1679, E-mail: info@museum-salberta.ab.ca, Internet: www.museum-salberta.ab.ca   49090

Association Museums New Brunswick, 503 Queen St, Fredericton, NB E3B 4Y2 - T: (506) 452-2908, Fax: (506) 459-0481, E-mail: muse@nbnet.nb.ca, Internet: www.amnb.nb.ca   49091

Association of Manitoba Museums, 153 Lombard Av, Ste 206, Winnipeg, MB R3B 0T4 - T: (204) 947-1782, Fax: (204) 942-3749, E-mail: amm@escape.ca, Internet: www.escape.ca/~amm   49092

British Columbia Museums Association, 26 Bastion Sq, Ste 204, Victoria, BC V8W 1H9 - T: (250) 356-5700, Fax: (250) 387-1251, E-mail: bcma@mu-seumsassn.bc.ca, Internet: www.mu-seumsassn.bc.ca/~bcma/   49093

Canadian Art Museum Directors Organization, 280 Metcalfe St, Ste 400, Ottawa, ON K2P 1R7 - T: (613) 567-0099, Fax: (613) 233-5438, E-mail: info@museums.ca   49094

Canadian Federation of Friends of Museums, c/o Art Gallery of Ontario, 317 Dundas St W, Toronto, ON M5T 1G4 - T: (416) 979-6650, Fax: (416) 979-6674, E-mail: cffm_fcam@ago.net   49095

Canadian Museums Association, 280 Metcalfe St, Ste 400, Ottawa, ON K2P 1R7 - T: (613) 567-0099, Fax: (613) 233-5438, E-mail: info@museums.ca, Internet: www.museums.ca   49096

Commonwealth Association of Museums, POB 30192, Chinook Postal Outlet, Calgary, AB T2H 2V9 - T: (403) 938-3190, Fax: (403) 938-3190, E-mail: irvinel@fclc.com, Internet: www.malt-wood.uvic.ca/cam   49097

Community Museums Association of Prince Edward Island, POB 22002, Charlottetown, PE C1A 9S2 - T: (902) 892-8837, Fax: (902) 628-6331, E-mail: cmapei@isn.net   49098

ICFA International Committee for Fine Art Museums, c/o Dr. C. Johnston, National Gallery, 380 Sussex Dr, Ottawa, K1N 9N4 - T: (613) 990-8689, Fax: (613) 990-8689   49099

ICOM Canada, c/o Canadian Museums Association, 280 Metcalfe St, Ste 400, Ottawa, ON K2P 1R7 - T: (613) 567-0099, Fax: (613) 233-5438, E-mail: fcaron@museums.ca, Internet: www.icom.org 49100

Museum Association of Newfoundland and Labrador, One Springdale St, Saint John's, mail addr: POB 5785, Saint John's, NL A1C 5X3 - T: (709) 722-9034, Fax: (709) 722-9035, E-mail: uokshevsky@nf.aibn.com, Internet: manl.nf.ca 49101

Museums Association of Saskatchewan, 1836 Angus St, Regina, SK S4T 1Z4 - T: (306) 780-9279, Fax: (306) 780-9463, E-mail: mas@sask-museums.org, Internet: www.sask-museums.org 49102

Ontario Museum Association, 50 Baldwin St, Toronto, ON M5T 1L4 - T: (416) 348-8672, Fax: (416) 348-0438, E-mail: omachin@planeteer.com, Internet: www.museum-sontario.ca 49103

Organization of Military Museums of Canada, POB 323, Gloucester, ON K1C 1S7 - T: (613) 737-3223, 996-6799, Fax: (613) 737-0821, E-mail: don.carrington@sympatico.ca, Internet: www.ommc.ca 49104

Société des Musées Québécois, CP 8888, Succ Centre-Ville, Montréal, QC H3C 3P8 - T: (514) 987-3264, Fax: (514) 987-3379, E-mail: smq@uqam.ca, Internet: www.musees.quebec.museum 49105

Yukon Historical and Museums Association, 3126 3 Av, Whitehorse, YT Y1A 1E7 - T: (867) 667-4704, Fax: (867) 667-4506, E-mail: yhma@yknet.yk.ca, Internet: www.yukonalaska.com/yhma 49106

Central African Republic

Comitée National de ICOM Centralafrique, Rue des Industries et Av de France, Bangui, mail addr: c/o Musée National Barthélémy Boganda, BP 349, Bangui - T: 615367, 613533, 614568, Fax: 615985, 614568 49107

Chad

ICOM du Tchad, c/o Archives Nationales et du Patrimoine, BP 5394, N'Djamena - T: 524445, Fax: 525538 49108

Chile

Federación Chilena de Amigos de los Museos (Chilean Federation of Friends of Museos), Calle Alameda 651, Santiago de Chile - E-mail: patrimon@ctcinternet.cl 49109

ICOM Chile, c/o Museo de Arte Contemporáneo, Parque Forestal s/n, Santiago de Chile - T: (02) 6380390, Fax: 2712046, E-mail: banados@reuna.cl 49110

China, People's Republic

Chinese Association of Natural Science Museums, c/o Beijing Natural History Museum, 126 Tien Chiao St, 100050 Beijing - T: (010) 754431, Fax: 67011408, E-mail: cansm@btamail.net.cn 49111

Chinese Society of Museums, 29, 4 Jing Shan Qian Jie, 100009 Beijing - T: (010) 85117374, 85117543, Fax: 85117040, 65123119, E-mail: museums@public3.bta.net.cn 49112

ICOM Chinese National Committee, c/o Chinese Society of Museums, Palace Museum, 29, 4 Jing Shan Qian Jie, 100009 Beijing - T: (010) 65132255666, 64005531, Fax: 65123119, E-mail: museums@public3.bta.net.cn 49113

China, Republic

Chinese Association of Museums, 49 Nanhai Rd, Taipei - T: (02) 23610270 ext 108, Fax: 23890718, E-mail: cam@moe.nmh.gov.tw, Internet: www.cam.org.tw 49114

Colombia

Asociación Colombiana de Museos, ACOM, c/o Institutos y Casas de Cultura, Calle 103a No 19-47, Bogotá - T: (01) 6104235, 2367088, Fax: 2186146 49115

Comité Nacional del Consejo Internacional de Museos, ICOM, c/o Museo de Museos Colsubsidiora, Calle 26, No 25-42, Bogotá - T: (01) 3432686, 3432669, Fax: 3432668, E-mail: icomcolombia@yahoo.com 49116

Comoros

ICOM Comores, c/o Ali Mohamed Gou, BP 169, Moroni - T: 744187, 733980, Fax: 744189, 732222, E-mail: cndrs@snpt.km 49117

Congo, Democratic Republic

ICOM République Democratique du Congo, c/o Musées universitaires, Université de Kinshasa, BP 840, Kinshasa XI - E-mail: matshung2002@yahoo.fr 49118

ICOMAC Regional Organization for Central Africa, BP 13933, Kinshasa - T: (012) 60263, 60008, Fax: 43675 49119

Congo, Republic

ICOM Republique Congo, c/o Musée d'Histoire et de la Vie politique nationale, BP 994, Brazzaville - T: 318652, E-mail: jpclabanz@yahoo.fr 49120

Costa Rica

ICOM Costa Rica, c/o Museo de Arte Coatrricense, Apdo 278-1009 Fecosa, San José 1000 - T: 2227155, Fax: 2827247, E-mail: fresent@racsa.co.cr 49121

ICOM Latin America and the Caribbean Regional Organization, c/o Dirección General de Museos, Apdo 10277-1000, San Jose 1000 - T: 2553051, Fax: 2552197, E-mail: lsanroma@terra.e-council.ac.cr 49122

Côte d'Ivoire

ICOM Côté d'Ivoire, c/o Musée National du Costume, BP 311, Grand Bassam - T: 21301370, 21301415, Fax: 20213359, E-mail: barroaminata@yahoo.fr 49123

Croatia

Hrvatski Nacionalni Komitet ICOM, c/o Muzej Grada Zagreba, Opatička 20, 10000 Zagreb - T: (01) 4851361, 4851359, Fax: 4851359, E-mail: muzej-grada-zagreba@mgz.tel.hr 49124

Hrvatsko Muzejsko Društvo, Habdeličeva 2, 10000 Zagreb - T: (01) 14550424, 48511808, Fax: 4851977, E-mail: hmd@hrmud.hr, Internet: www.hrmud.hr 49125

Savez Muzejskih Društva Hrvatske, Mesnička 5, Muzejski Dokum Centar, 10000 Zagreb - T: (01) 426534 49126

Cuba

ICOM Cuba, c/o Conseo Nacional de Patrimonio Cultural, Calle 4, esq 13, Vedado 10400, La Habana - T: (07) 8334193, Fax: 662106, E-mail: patrim@min.cult.cu 49127

Cyprus

Cyprus Federation of Associations of Friends of Museums, 32a Heroes Av, 1105 Lefkosia - E-mail: lana@spidernet.com.cy 49128

ICOM Cyprus, c/o S. Hadjisavvas, Ministry of Communication and Works, Department of Antiquities, Lefkosia - T: (22) 865800, Fax: 303148, E-mail: roctarch@cytanet.com.cy 49129

Czech Republic

Association of Czech Moravian and Silesian Museums, Kostelní 42, 170 00 Praha 7 - T: 220399314, Fax: 220399201, E-mail: amg@volny.cz, Internet: www.cz-museums.cz 49130

Association of Museums and Galleries of Czech Republic, Jindřišská 901/5, 110 00 Praha - T: 224210037, Fax: 224210047, E-mail: amg@vol.cz, Internet: www.cz-museums.cz 49131

Czech Committee of ICOM, c/o Moravské zemské muzeum, Zelný trh 6, 659 37 Brno - T: 542210493, Fax: 542210493, E-mail: icom@mzm.cz, Internet: www.cz-icom.cz 49132

International Association of Agricultural Museums, c/o Dr. Viteclsav Koukal, Valašské Muzeum v Přírodě, Palackého 147, 756 61 Rožnov pod Radhoštěm - T: (0651) 757101, Fax: 654494, E-mail: kou@vmp.cz 49133

Rada Galerii České Republiky (Council of Galleries of the Czech Republic), Husova 19-21, 110 00 Praha 1 - T: 222220218-19, Fax: 222221190 49134

Societas Museologia, c/o Muzeum Tesinska, Hlavní 13, 737 01 Český Těšín - T: 65956795, Fax: 65955060 49135

Denmark

CIDOC International Committee for Documentation, c/o Lene Rold, National Museum, Frederiksholms Kanal 12, 1220 København - T: 33473885, Fax: 33473307, E-mail: lene.rold@natmus.dk 49136

Danish National Council of Museums (closed) 49137

Dansk ICOM, The Danish National Committee of the International Council of Museums, c/o Vivi Jensen, Museet på Koldinghus, PB 91, 6000 Kolding - T: 79301072, Fax: 76338199, E-mail: vj@koldinghus.dk, Internet: denmark.icom.museum 49138

Dansk Kulturhistorisk Museums Forening (Association of Danish Cultural Museums), c/o Nivågårds Malerisamling, Gammel Strandvej 2, 2990 Nivå - T: 49143966, Fax: 49143967, E-mail: info@museek.dk, Internet: www.dkm-mus.dk 49139

Foreningen af Danske Kunstmuseer (Association of Danish Art Museums), c/o Nivågårds Malerisamling, Gammel Strandvej 2, 2990 Nivå - T: 49143966, Fax: 49143967, E-mail: info@museek.dk 49140

Foreningen af Danske Museumsmaend (Association of Danish Museum Curators), c/o Danske Kongers Kronologiske Samling, Rosenborg Slot, Øster Voldg 4a, 1350 København K - T: 33153286, Fax: 33152046, E-mail: jh@dkks.dk 49141

Foreningen af Danske Naturhistoriske Museer, c/o Naturhistorisk Museum, Wilhelm Meyers Allé 210, 8000 Århus C - T: 86129777, Fax: 86130882, E-mail: nm@nathist.dk 49142

Foreningen af Danske Naturvidenskabelige Museer, c/o Fiskeri- og Sofartsmuseet, Tarphagevej, 6710 Esbjerg V - T: 75150666, Fax: 75153057, E-mail: Tougaard@inet.uni-c.dk 49143

Museumstjenesten (Danish Museum Service), Sjørupvej 1, Lysgaard, 8800 Viborg - T: 86666766, Fax: 86667611, E-mail: mtj@museumst-jenesten.com, Internet: www.museumst-jenesten.com 49144

Skandinavisk Museumsforbund, Danske Afdeling, c/o Jens Peter Munk, Reykjaviksg 2, 2300 København S - T: 32961171, Fax: 33667191, E-mail: jemun@btf.kk.dk 49145

Dominican Republic

ICOM République Dominicaine, c/o Arqi Ana Cristina Martínez, Secretaria de Estado de Cultura, Av George Washington, Santo Domingo - T: 6852154, 2214141, Fax: 6865378, E-mail: anacristinamz@yahoo.comnmail.com, Internet: www.cultura.gov.do 49146

Ecuador

ICOM Ecuador, c/o Fredy Olmedo Ron, Banco Central del Ecuador, Las Cumbres, Mz 12 Villa 11, Guayaquil - T: (04) 2852302, Fax: 2852302, E-mail: folmedo@bceg.fin.ec 49147

Egypt

ICOM Arab, Dept. of Egyptology, Faculty of Archaeology, Cairo University, Giza - T: (02) 5678108, Fax: 5675660, E-mail: a_nurelding@hotmail.com 49148

ICOM Egypt, c/o Supreme Council of Antiquities, 4d Fakhri Abdel Nour St, Abbasiya, Cairo - T: (02) 6843627, Fax: 6831117, E-mail: samiaelmallah@hotmail.com 49149

Estonia

Eesti Muuseumiühing Tallinn (Estonian Museum Society in Tallinn), Pikk 70, 10133 Tallinn - T: 6411410, Internet: www.emy.kul.ee 49150

Eesti Muuseumiühing Tartu (Estonian Museum Society in Tartu), Narva mnt 23, 51009 Tartu - T: 7461900, Fax: 7461912, E-mail: heivi.pulleriets@katarina.ee, Internet: www.emy.kul.ee 49151

Estonian Museums Association, c/o Tartu Linnamuuseum, Oru t 2, 2400 Tartu - T: 7422693, E-mail: muuseum@ekm.estnet.ee 49152

ICOM Estonia, c/o Museum of Estonian Architecture, 2 Ahtri St, 10151 Tallinn - T: 6257000, Fax: 6257003, E-mail: karin@arhitektuurimuuseum.ee 49153

Fiji

Pacific Islands Museums Association, c/o Lata Yagona, Government Bldgs, POB 2023, Suva - T: 306227, Fax: 306227, E-mail: pima@is.com.fi, Internet: www.finearts.mcc.edu/pima 49154

Finland

ICAMT International Committee for Architecture and Museums Techniques, c/o Marja-Liisa Pohjanvirta, Finnish Museums Association, Annankatu 16 B 50, 00120 Helsinki - T: (09) 649001, Fax: 608330, E-mail: marja-liisa.pohjanvirta@museoliitto.fi, Internet: www.icom.org/internationals.html#icamt 49155

ICOM Finland, c/o Jari Harju, Helsinki City Museum, PO Box 4300, 00099 Helsinki - T: (09) 1693568, Fax: 1693953, E-mail: jari.harju@hel.fi, Internet: www.museoliitto.fi/icom 49156

International Committee for Museums and Collections of Modern Art, c/o Tuula Arkio, Finnish National Galleries, Kaivokatu 2, 00100 Helsinki - T: (09) 17336253, Fax: 17336227, E-mail: tuula.arkio@fng.fi, Internet: www.cimam.org 49157

Network of European Museum Organisations, c/o Finnish Museums Association, Annankatu 16b 50, 00120 Helsinki - T: (09) 58411730, Fax: 58411750, E-mail: anja@museoliitto.fi, Internet: www.ne-mo.org 49158

Skandinavisk Museumförbund - Skandinaavinen Museoliitto, Finnish Section, c/o Suomen Kansallismuseo, PL 913, 00101 Helsinki - T: (09) 40501, Fax: 4050400, E-mail: kansallis-museo@nba.fi 49159

Suomen Museoliitto (Finnish Museums Association), Annankatu 16 B 50, 00120 Helsinki - T: (09) 58411700, Fax: 58411750, E-mail: museoliitto@-museoliitto.fi, Internet: www.museoliitto.fi 49160

France

Association des Conservateurs et du Personnel Scientifique des Musées de la Ville de Paris, c/o Musée d'Art Moderne, 9 Rue Gaston-de-Saint-Paul, 75116 Paris - T: 0153674000, Fax: 0147233598 49161

Association des Musées Automobiles de France, 6 Pl de la Concorde, 75008 Paris - T: 0143124324, Fax: 0143124343, Internet: www.amaf.asso.fr. Dir.: Dominique Dubarry 49162

Association des Musées et Centres pour le Développement de la Culture Scientifique, Technique et Industrielle, AMCSTI, c/o Carole Grandgirard, 36 Rue Chabot Charny, 21000 Dijon - T: 0380589875, Fax: 0380589858, E-mail: amcsti@u-bourgogne.fr, Internet: ww-w.amcsti.org 49163

Association Européenne des Musées d'Histoire des Sciences Médicales (AEMHSM), c/o Musée d'Histoire de la Médecine, 12 Rue de l'Ecole-de-Médecine, 75006 Paris - T: 0140461693, Fax: 0140461892, E-mail: clin@univ-paris5.fr, Internet: www.aemhsm.org 49164

Association Française des Directeurs de Centres d'Art, Av Conti, Parc Saint-Léger CAC, 58320 Pougues-les-Eaux - T: 0386909660, Fax: 0386909661, E-mail: ptsleger@club-internet.fr, Internet: www.d-c-art.org 49165

Association Française des Musées d'Agriculture et du Patrimoine Rural, AFMA, c/o Musée National des Arts et Traditions Populaires, 6 Av du Mahatma-Gandhi, 75116 Paris - T: 0144176063, Fax: 0144176060, E-mail: jean-francois.charnier@-culture.gouv.fr, Internet: www.afma.asso.fr/main.htm 49166

Association Générale des Conservateurs des Collections Publiques de France, 6 Av du Mahatma Gandhi, 75116 Paris - T: 0144176090, Fax: 0144176060, E-mail: maigret@mnhn.fr 49167

Association Internationale des Musées d'Histoire (International Association of Museums of History), c/o Musée d'Histoire Contemporaine, Hôtel des Invalides, 75007 Paris - T: 0144423150, Fax: 0144189384, E-mail: contact@euroclio.net, Internet: www.euroclio.net 49168

Association Museum and Industries, 21 Rue Beaurepaire, 75010 Paris - T: 0661260875, Fax: 0140226320, E-mail: museum-industries@club-internet.fr, Internet: www.museum-industries.com. Dir.: M. Gilles Muller 49169

Association pour le Respect de l'Intégrité du Patrimoine Artistique, ARIPA, 97 Blvd Rodin, 92130 Issy-les-Moulineaux - E-mail: aripa@wanadoo.fr, Internet: www.aripa-nuances.org 49170

Association pour les Musées de Marseille, c/o Centre de la Vielle Charité, 2 Rue de la Charité, 13002 Marseille - T: 0491145842, 0491562838, Fax: 0491145881, E-mail: ass.musees.marseil-le@wanadoo.fr 49171

Comité National Français de l'ICOM, 13 Rue Molière, 75001 Paris - T: 0142613202, Fax: 0142613202, E-mail: icomfrance@wanadoo.fr, Internet: www.france.icom.museum 49172

Direction de Musées de France, 6 Rue des Pyramides, 75041 Paris Cedex 1 - T: 0140153600, Fax: 0140153625, E-mail: mission-communication.dmf@culture.gouv.fr, Internet: www.culture.gouv.fr 49173

Fédération des Ecomusées et des Musées de Société, 2 Av Arthur Gaulard, 25000 Besançon - T: 0381832255, Fax: 0381810892, E-mail: Info@fems.asso.fr, Internet: www.-fems.asso.fr 49174

Fédération des Maisons d'Ecrivain et des Patrimoines Littéraires, c/o Médiathèque, Blvd Lamarck, BP 18, 18001 Bourges Cedex - T: 0248232250, Fax: 0248245064, E-mail: maison-secrivain@yahoo.com, Internet: www.litterature-lieux.com 49175

Fédération Française des Sociétés d'Amis de Musées, 16-18 Rue de Cambrai, 75019 Paris - T: 0142096610, Fax: 0142094471, E-mail: info@amis-musees.fr, Internet: www.amis-musees.fr 49176

Fédération Internationale des Musées du Jouet et de l'Enfance, c/o Musée du Jouet, 5 Rue du Murgin, 39260 Moirans-en-Montagne - T: 0384423864, Fax: 0384423897 49177

Fédération Mondiale des Sociétés d'Amis de Musées (World Federation of Friends of Museums), c/o FFSAM, Ellen Julia, 16-18 Rue de Cambrai, 75019 Paris - T: 0142093891, Fax: 0142093891, Internet: www.amis-musees.fr/fmam 49178

Fédération Régionale des Amis des Musées du Nord-Pas de Calais, 1 Passage Pierre et Marie Curie, 59140 Dunkerque - T: 0328650532 49179

Groupement des Amis de Musées de la Région Midi-Pyrénées, c/o Musée Ingres, 19 Rue de l'Hôtel de Ville, 82000 Montauban - T: 0563201046, Fax: 0563664134, Internet: www.amis-musees-castres.asso.fr/Arsam.htm 49180

Groupement des Amis des Musées de la Région Centre, c/o Musée des Beaux-Arts, 1 Rue Fernand Rabier, 45000 Orleans - T: 0238817279, Fax: 0238772206, Internet: www.amis-musees.fr/groupements_centre.htm 49181

Groupement des Associations d'Amis de Musées de la Région Bretagne, 9 Lotissement des Dunes, 29920 Nevez - T: 0299870639, E-mail: grsamb.ren-nes@wanadoo.fr 49182

Groupement des Associations d'Amis de Musées de la Région Languedoc-Roussillon, c/o Amis du Musée Fabre, 7 Rue Verrerie Basse, 34000 Montpellier - T: 0467925943 49183

Groupement des Associations d'Amis de Musées de la Région Limousin, c/o Musée Municipal de l'Evêché, Pl de la Cathédrale, 87000 Limoges - T: 0555758099, E-mail: michele.bour-zat@wanadoo.fr 49184

Groupement des Associations des Amis de Musées Région Provence Alpes Côte d'Azur, c/o Claude Guieu, 73 Rue Jean Pezous, 83000 Toulon (Var) - T: 0494928399, E-mail: claude.-guieu@wanadoo.fr 49185

Groupement Régional des Associations d'Amis de Musées de la Région Ile de France, 25 Rue Deparcieux, 75014 Paris - T: 0143202929, Fax: 0143205255, E-mail: villes.et.cine-mas@wanadoo.fr 49186

Groupement Rhône-Alpes des Amis de Musée, c/o Palais Saint-Pierre, 17 Pl des Terreaux, 69001 Lyon - T: 0476470928, Internet: www.amis-musees.fr/groupements_rhone-alpes.htm 49187

ICMAH International Committee for Archaeology and History Museums, c/o Jean-Yves Marin, Musée de Normandie, Logis des Gouverneurs, Château de Caen, 14000 Caen - T: 0231304750, Fax: 0231304769, E-mail: mdn@ville-caen.fr 49188

International Council of Museums ICOM, Maison de l'UNESCO, 1 Rue Miollis, 75732 Paris Cedex 15 - T: 0147340500, Fax: 0143067862, E-mail: secretariat@icom.museum, Internet: ww-w.icom.museum 49189

International Council on Monuments and Sites, 49-51 Rue de la Fédération, 75015 Paris - T: 0145676770, Fax: 0145660622, E-mail: secretariat@icomos.org, Internet: ww-w.icomos.org 49190

International Society of Libraries and Museums of Performing Arts, 58 Rue Richelieu, 75002 Paris - T: 0153012513, Fax: 0153012507, Internet: www.theatrelibrary.org/sibmas/sibmas.html 49191

Réunion des Musées Nationaux, 49 Rue Etienne Marcel, 75039 Paris Cedex 01 - T: 0140134903, Fax: 0140134973, E-mail: beatrice.-foulon@rmn.fr 49192

Germany

Arbeitsgemeinschaft kirchlicher Museen und Schatzkammern, Domerschulstr 2, 97070 Würzburg - T: (0931) 386261, Fax: 3862626, E-mail: kunstreferat@bistum-wuerzburg.de 49193

Association of European Open Air Museums, c/o Westfälisches Freilichtmuseum Hagen, Mäckingerbach, 58091 Hagen, Westfalen - T: (02331) 780710, Fax: 780720, E-mail: wfh-md@freilichtmuseum-hagen.de, Internet: www.frei-lichtmuseum-hagen.de 49194

Bundesverband Museumspädagogik e.V., c/o Dr. H. Kunz-Ott, Landesstelle für nichtstaatliche Museen, Alter Hof 2h, 80331 München - T: (089) 21014027, Fax: 21014040, E-mail: kunz-ott@museumspae-dagogik.org, Internet: www.museumspae-dagogik.org 49195

Deutsche Burgenvereinigung e.V., Marksburg, 56338 Braubach - T: (02627) 536, Fax: 8866, E-mail: info@deutsche-burgen.org, Internet: www.deutsche-burgen.org 49196

Deutscher Museumsbund e.V., Büro Berlin, In der Halde 1, 14195 Berlin - T: (030) 84109517, Fax: 84109519, E-mail: office@museumsbund.de, Internet: www.museumsbund.de 49197

Düsseldorfer Museumsverein e.V., c/o Dr. Spennemann, Deutsche Bank 24, Königsallee 45-47, 40189 Düsseldorf - T: (0211) 8832458, Fax: 883379, E-mail: gert.spen-nemann@db.com 49198

Hessischer Museumsverband e.V., Kölnische Str 44-46, 34117 Kassel - T: (0561) 78896740, Fax: 78896800, E-mail: heidi.schoenewald@mu-seumsverband-hessen.de, Internet: www.mu-seumsverband-hessen.de 49199

ICOFOM International Committee for Museology, c/o Dr. H.K. Vieregg, Bayerische Staatsgemälde-sammlungen, Barer Str 29, 80799 München - T: (089) 23805123, Fax: 23805197, E-mail: vieregg@mpz.bayern.de, Internet: www.icom.org 49200

ICOM International Council of Museums, Deutsches Nationalkomitee, In der Halde 1, 14195 Berlin - T: (030) 69504525, Fax: 69504526, E-mail: icom-deutschland@t-online.de, Internet: www.icom-deutschland.de 49201

International Committee for Museums and Collections of Natural History, c/o Gerhard Winter, Naturmuseum Senckenberg, Senckenberganlage 25, 60325 Frankfurt am Main - T: (069) 7542356, Fax: 7542331, E-mail: gwinter@senckenberg.de, Internet: www.senckenberg.de/icom/nh-board.html 49202

Mülheimer Kunstverein e.V., c/o Kunstmuseum, Viktoriapl 1, 45468 Mülheim an der Ruhr - T: (0208) 4554192, Fax: 4554138 49203

Museumspädagogische Gesellschaft e.V., c/o Museumsdienst Köln, Richartzstr 2-4, 50667 Köln - T: (0221) 22126636, Fax: 22127909, E-mail: museumsdienst@stadt-koeln.de 49204

Museumsverband Baden-Württemberg e.V., c/o Stadtmuseum im Gelben Haus, Hafenmarkt 7, 73728 Esslingen - T: (0711) 35123240, Fax: 35123229, E-mail: museumsverband-bw@web.de 49205

Museumsverband des Landes Brandenburg e.V., Schloßstr 1, 14467 Potsdam - T: (0331) 232790, Fax: 2327920, E-mail: museumverband@t-online.de, Internet: 1ww.museen-brandenburg.de 49206

Museumsverband für Niedersachsen und Bremen e.V., Fössestr 99, 30453 Hannover - T: (0511) 2144983, Fax: 21449844, E-mail: kontakt@mvnb.de, Internet: www.mvnb.de 49207

Museumsverband in Mecklenburg-Vorpommern e.V., Heidberg 15, 18273 Güstrow - T: (03843) 344736, Fax: 344743, E-mail: info@mu-seumsverband-mv.de, Internet: www.mu-seumsverband-mv.de 49208

Museumsverband Sachsen-Anhalt e.V., Käthe-Kollwitz-Str 11, 06406 Bernburg - T: (03471) 628116, Fax: 628983, 628116, E-mail: museums-verbandsachsen-anhalt@t-online.de, Internet: www.mv-sachsen-anhalt.de 49209

Museumsverband Schleswig-Holstein e.V., c/o Museen im Kulturzentrum, Arsenalstr 2-10, 24768 Rendsburg - T: (04331) 331338, Fax: 27687, E-mail: museenrendsburg@web.de, Internet: www.-museumsverband-sh.de 49210

Museumsverband Thüringen e.V., Rittergasse 4, 07545 Gera - T: (0365) 22515, Fax: 2900436, E-mail: museumsverbandthueringen@gmx.de, Internet: www.thueringen.de/museen/ 49211

Museumsverbund Südniedersachsen e.V., Ritterplan 7-8, 37073 Göttingen - T: (0551) 4002883, Fax: 4003135, E-mail: info@mu-seumsverbund.de, Internet: www.mu-seumverbund.de 49212

Rathgen-Forschungslabor, Staatliche Museen zu Berlin - Preußischer Kulturbesitz, Schloßstr 1a, 14059 Berlin - T: (030) 32674910, Fax: 32674912, E-mail: rf@smb.spk-berlin.de, Internet: www.smb.spk-berlin.de. Dir.: Prof. Dr. Josef Riederer, WM: Dr. Christian Goedicke, Boaz Paz, Dr. Achim Unger 49213

Sächsischer Museumsbund e.V., Wilsdruffer Str 2, 01067 Dresden - T: (0351) 4906056, Fax: 4951288 49214

Verband Rheinischer Museen (closed) 49215

Vereinigung Westfälischer Museen, Rothenburg 30, 48143 Münster - T: (0251) 5907256, Fax: 5907210, E-mail: g.dethlefs@lwl.org, Internet: www.-muenster.org/vereinignung-westfaelischer-museen. Geschäftsführer: Dr. Gerd Dethlefs 49216

Ghana

Ghana Museums and Monuments Board, Barnes Rd, Accra, mail addr: POB 3343, Accra - T: (021) 221633/35, 222401, Fax: 234843 49217

Organization of Museums, Monuments and Sites of Africa OMMSA, POB 3343, Accra 49218

Greece

Archaeological Receipts Fund, Aghiou Panépistimiou 57, 105 72 Athinai - T: 2103253901, Fax: 2103242254 49219

Association des Conservateurs d'Antiquités, Ermou 136, 105 53 Athinai - T: 013252214, Fax: 013252214 49220

Department of Byzantine Museums, c/o Ministry of Culture, Bouboulinas Od 20-22, 106 82 Athinai - T: 2103304030, Fax: 2103304009, E-mail: protocol@dbmm.culture.gr, Internet: www.culture.gr 49221

Fédération Hellénique des Amis des Musées (Greek Federation of Associations of Friends of Museums), c/o Mouseio Mpenaki, 1 Odos Koumbaru, 106 74 Athinai 49222

ICOM Grèce, Aghion Assomaton 15, 105 53 Athinai - T: 2103239414, Fax: 2103239414, E-mail: icom@otenet.gr 49223

Greenland

Sammenslutningen af Grønlandske Lokalmuseer (Association of Local Museums in Greenland), Jukkorsuup Aqq 9, 3911 Sisimiut, mail addr: c/o Sisimiut Museum, Postboks 308, 3911 Sisimiut - T: 865087, Fax: 864475, E-mail: sismus@-greennet.gl, Internet: www.museum.gl 49224

Guadeloupe

Musées Départementaux de la Guadeloupe, 24 Rue Peynier, 97110 Pointe-à-Pitre - T: 820804, Fax: 837839 49225

Guatemala

Asociación de Museos de Guatemala, AMG, c/o Museo Universitario de San Carlos, 9a Av 9-79, Zona 1, 01009 Guatemala - T: 2327666, 2320721, Fax: 2320721, E-mail: amg@hotmail.com 49226

ICOM Guatemala, c/o Museo Universitario de San Carlos, 9a Av 9-79, Zona 1, 01009 Guatemala - T: 2327666, 2320721, Fax: 2320721, E-mail: musac@intelnet.net.gt 49227

Haiti

ICOM Comité Haïtien, 3 Rue Baussan, Port-au-Prince, mail addr: c/o Musée d'Art Haïtien, BP 1214, Port-au-Prince - T: 2451509, Fax: 2454535, E-mail: geraldalexis@hotmail.com 49228

Hungary

ICOM Hungary, Szent György tér 2, 1014 Budapest - T: (01) 3559772, 2257821, Fax: 3559175, 2257821, E-mail: cseri@sznm.hu, Internet: ww-w.hungary.icom.museum 49229

Pulszky Society - Hungarian Museums Association, c/o I. Matskási, Magyar Természettudományi Múzeum, Baross ú 13, 1088 Budapest - T: (01) 2661481, Fax: 3171669, E-mail: matskasi@zoo.zoo.nhmus.hu, Internet: www.museum.hu/pulszkytarsasag 49230

Iceland

Association of Icelandic Curators, c/o National Museum of Iceland, Svourgotu 41, 101 Reykjavík - T: 5528967, Fax: 5528967   49231

Icelandic Museums Association, c/o J. Asmundsson, Minjasafn Egilis Olafssonar, Hnjótur, 451 Patreksfjörður - T: 4561569, Fax: 8676344, E-mail: museum@hnjotur.is   49232

ICOM Iceland, c/o Thjóðminjasafn Islands, Lyngás, 210 Garðabaer - T: 5302200, Fax: 5302281, E-mail: lilja@natmus.is, Internet: www.icom.is   49233

Scandinavian Museum Association, Icelandic Section, c/o National Museum of Iceland, Svourgotu 41, 101 Reykjavík - T: 5528967, Fax: 5528967, Internet: www.arbaejarsafn.is   49234

India

Association of Indian Museums, c/o National Museum of Natural History, Barakhambra Rd, Delhi 110001 - T: (011) 3319173   49235

CECA International Committee for Education and Cultural Action of Museums, c/o Ganga S. Rautela, Nehru Science Centre, Dr. E. Moses Rd, Mumbai 400018 - T: (022) 4932668, Fax: 4932668, E-mail: nscm@giasbm01.vsnl.net.in   49236

CIMUSET International Committee for Science and Technology Museums, c/o P.K. Bhaumik, National Science Centre, Bhairon Rd, Pragati Maidan, Gate 1, Delhi 110001 - T: (011) 3371263, 3371945, Fax: 3371263, E-mail: nscd@giasdl01.vsnl.net.in   49237

ICOM India, c/o Indian Museum, 27 Jawaharlal Nehru Rd, Kolkata 700016 - T: (033) 22499979, 22499902, Fax: 22495669, E-mail: imbot@cal2.vsnl.net.in, Internet: india.icom.museum   49238

Indian Association for the Study of Conservation of Cultural Property, c/o National Museum Institute, Janpath, Delhi 110011 - T: (011) 3016098, 3792217, Fax: 3019821, 3011901   49239

Museums Association of India, c/o National Museum, Janpath, Delhi 110011 - T: (011) 383568   49240

National Council of Science Museums, Block GN, Sector V, Bidhan Nagar, Kolkata 700091 - T: (033) 3579347/48, Fax: 3576008, E-mail: ncsmin@giascl01.vsnl.net.in   49241

Iran

ICOM Iran, c/o Iranian Cultural Heritage Organization, 60 Larestan St, Motahhari Av, 15959-3481 Teheran - T: (021) 8898827, Fax: 8898828, E-mail: iranicom_se@yahoo.com   49242

Ireland

ICOM Ireland, c/o National Gallery of Ireland, Elizabeth Coman, Merrion Squ W, Dublin, 2 - T: (01) 6633505, Fax: 6615372, E-mail: lcoman@ngi.ie   49243

Irish Museums Association, 59 Lombard St, Dublin, 8 - T: (01) 4541947, E-mail: karinstierle@utvinternet.com   49244

Israel

Israel National Committee of ICOM, c/o Rishon Le-Zion Museum, POB 7, Rishon Le-Zion 75100 - T: (03) 9565977, Fax: 9565788, E-mail: icom98@netvision.net.il, Internet: www.rakia.com/icom   49245

Museum Association of Israel, c/o Museum of Rishon Le-Zion, POB 7, Rishon Le-Zion 75100 - T: (03) 9565977, Fax: 9565788, E-mail: icom98@netvision.net.il   49246

Italy

Associazione Nazionale dei Musei dei Enti Locali ed Istituzionali, ANMLI, Via Tiziano 323, 25124 Brescia - T: 0302300307, Fax: 0302300307   49247

Associazione Nazionale dei Musei Italiani, Piazza San Marco 49, 00186 Roma - T: 066791343, Fax: 066791343   49248

Associazione Nazionale Musei Scientifici, ANMS, Via G. La Pira 4, 50121 Firenze - T: 0552757460, Fax: 0552737373, E-mail: marcolin@mtsn.tn.it, Internet: www.anms.it   49249

DEMHIST-International Committee for Historic House Museums, c/o ICOM Italia - Museo della Scienza e della Tecnica, Via San Vittore 19-21, 20123 Milano - T: 0248555338, Fax: 0243919840, E-mail: demhist@iol.it, Internet: www.icom-italia.org/demhist_en.htm. Dir.: Rosanna Pavoni   49250

Federazione Italiana delle Associazioni Amici dei Musei (Italian Federation of Associations of Friends of Museums), Via Carducci 8, 50121 Firenze   49251

ICOM Comitato Nazionale Italiano, c/o Museo della Scienza e della Tecnologia, Michela Fasani, Via San Vittore 19-21, 20123 Milano - T: 0248555338, Fax: 0243919840, E-mail: icomit@iol.it, Internet: www.icom-italia.org   49252

International Association of Libraries and Museums of Performing Arts (SIMBAS), c/o Maria Teresa Iovinelli-Biblioteca Burcardo, Via del Sudario 44, 00186 Roma - T: 066819471, Fax: 0668194727, E-mail: biblioteca.burcardo@siae.it, Internet: www.theatrelibrary.org/sibmas/sibmas.html   49253

International Centre for the Study of the Preservation and the Restoration of Cultural Property (ICCROM), Via di San Michele 13, 00153 Roma - T: 06585531, Fax: 0658553349, E-mail: iccrom@iccrom.org, Internet: www.iccrom.org   49254

Jamaica

ICOM Jamaica, c/o Museums of History and Ethnography Institute of Jamaica, 10-16 East St, Kingston - T: (876) 9220622, Fax: 9223795, E-mail: museums@instituteofjamaica.org.jm   49255

Japan

Japanese Association of Museums, Shoyu Kaikan Bldg, 3-3-1 Kasumigaseki, Chiyoda-ku, Tokyo 100-8925 - T: (03) 35917190, Fax: 35917170, E-mail: webmaster@j-muse.or.jp, Internet: www.museum.or.jp/icom-japan/   49256

Japanese Council of Art Museums, c/o Osaka-shiritsu Bijutsukan, 1-82 Chausuyama-cho, Tennoji-ku, Osaka 543-0063 - T: (06) 67766863, Fax: 67766873, E-mail: zenbikai-gi@nifty.com   49257

Japanese National Committee for ICOM, c/o Japanese Association of Museums, Shoyu Kaikan Bldg, 3-3-1 Kasumigaseki, Chiyoda-ku, Tokyo 100-8925 - T: (03) 35917190, Fax: 35917170, E-mail: webmaster@j-muse.or.jp, Internet: www.museum.or.jp/icom-japan/   49258

Nihon Hakubutsukan Kyokai (Japanese Association of Museums), Shoyu Kaikan Bldg, 3-3-1 Kasumigaseki, Chiyoda-ku, Tokyo 100-8925 - T: (03) 35917190, Fax: 35917170, E-mail: webmaster@j-muse.or.jp, Internet: www.j-muse.or.jp   49259

Jordan

ICOM Jordan, Queen Misbah St, 11118 Amman, mail addr: c/o Department of Antiquities, POB 88, 11118 Amman - T: (06) 4644336, Fax: 4615848, E-mail: gbisheh@hotmail.com   49260

Kazakhstan

ICOM Kazakhstan, c/o The A. Kazteev State Museum of Arts, Satpaeva 30a, 480090 Almaty - T: (03272) 478249, Fax: 509567, 478669, E-mail: kazart@nursat.kz   49261

Kenya

ICOM Kenya, c/o National Museum of Kenya, POB 40658, Nairobi - T: (02) 742161, Fax: 741424, E-mail: prnmk@users.africaonline.co.ke   49262

International Confederation, c/o Museum Hill, POB 38706, Nairobi - T: (020) 3748668, Fax: 3748928, E-mail: africom@museums.or.ke, Internet: www.african-museums.org   49263

International Council of African Museums (AFRICOM), POB 38706, 00600 Nairobi - T: (020) 3748668, Fax: 3748928, E-mail: africom@museums.or.ke, Internet: www.african-museums.org. Dir.: Lorna Abungu   49264

Kenya Museum Society, c/o Museum Hill, POB 40658, 00100 Nairobi - T: (020) 3742131 ext 289, E-mail: info@knowkenya.org   49265

Programme for Museum Development in Africa, Old Law Courts Bldg, Nkrumah Rd, Mombasa - T: (011) 2224846   49266

Korea, Republic

Association of Museums in Seoul, 2-57 Sejong-no, Jongno-gu, Seoul 110-050 - T: (02) 3985193/95, Fax: 7237093   49267

ICOM Korea, c/o National Museum of Korea, 1-57 Sejong-no, Jongno-gu, Seoul 110-050 - T: (02) 3985190, Fax: 7350231, E-mail: office@icomkorea.org, Internet: korea.icom.museum   49268

Korean Museum Association, c/o National Museum of Korea, 1-57 Sejong-no, Chongno-gu, Seoul 110-820 - T: (02) 7350230, 3985190, Fax: 7350231, E-mail: kormuseum@dreamwiz.com, Internet: www.museum.or.kr   49269

Korean National Committee for the International Council of Museums (ICOM), c/o National Museum of Korea, 1-57 Sejong-no, Chongno-gu, Seoul 110-820 - T: (02) 7350230, 3985190, Fax: 7350231, E-mail: office@icomkorea.org, Internet: www.icomkorea.org   49270

The Korean Museum Association, c/o National Museum of Korea, 1-57 Sejong-no, Jongno-gu, Seoul 110-050 - T: (02) 3985190, Fax: 7350231, Internet: museum.or.kr   49271

Kyrgyzstan

ICOM Kyrgyzstan, c/o Kyrgyz State Museum of Fine Arts G. Aitiyev, 196 Soviet st, 720000 Biškek - T: (0312) 661623, Fax: 228476, E-mail: erkina2002@mail.ru   49272

Laos

ICOM Lao, Setthathirat Rd, Vientiane, mail addr: c/o Ministry of Information and Culture, Dept. of Museums and Archaeology, POB 122, Vientiane - T: (021) 212423, 212895, Fax: 212408   49273

Latvia

ICOM Latvijas Nacionāla Komiteja, c/o A. Ozola, Tukums Museum, Harmonijas iela 7, Tukums, 3100 - T: (031) 82390, Fax: 22707, E-mail: tukmuz@apollo.lv   49274

Latvian Museum Council, c/o Valsts Makslas Muzejs, 10a K. Valdemara, Rīga, 1010 - T: 7325021, Fax: 7325051, E-mail: vmm@latnet.lv   49275

Latvijas Muzeju Asociācija (Latvian Museums Association), Kalku iela 11a, Rīga, 1050 - T: 7503870, Fax: 7228083, E-mail: muzasoc@acad.latnet.lv, Internet: www.muzeji.lv   49276

State Authority of Museums, Kaļķu eila 11a, Rīga, 1050 - T: 7503870, Fax: 7228083, E-mail: muzejs@com.var.lv   49277

Lebanon

ICOM Liban, Bliss St, Beirut, mail addr: c/o Leila Badre, Musée de l'Université Americaine, BP 11-0236/9, Beirut - T: (01) 340549, Fax: 363235, E-mail: badre@aub.edu.lb, Internet: ddc.aub.edu.lb/project/museum   49278

Libya

ICOM Libyan Arab Jamahiriya, c/o Jamahirya Museum, Es Saray El-Hamara, Tripoli - T: (021) 4449065, Fax: 4440166   49279

Lithuania

ICOM Lietuva (ICOM Lithuania), c/o Vilniaus paveikslu galerija, Vytautas Balciunas, Didžioji 4 - Bokšto 5, 2001 Vilnius - T: (05) 2120841, Fax: 2120841, E-mail: galerija@ldm.lt   49280

Lithuanian Museums Association, Saltoniskiu g 58, 2600 Vilnius - T: (02) 790371, 790918, Fax: 790213, E-mail: muzasoc@takas.lt, Internet: muziejai.mch.mii.lt   49281

Luxembourg

ICOM Luxembourg, c/o Musée National d'Histoire et d'Art, Marché-aux-Poissons, 2345 Luxembourg - T: 4793301, Fax: 479330271, E-mail: musee@jnha.etat.lu, Internet: www.mnha.lu   49282

Macedonia

ICOM F.Y.R. Macedonia, c/o Muzej na Sovremenata Umetnost Skopje, Samoilova b.b., Skopje 1000 - T: (091) 117734,, Fax: 236372, E-mail: icom_mnc@yahoo.com   49283

Muzejsko Društvo na Makedonija, c/o Muzej na Grad Skopje, Mito Hadzi Vasilev bb, 1000 Skopje - T: (02) 54123, 9154123   49284

Madagascar

ICOM Madagascar, 17, rue Dr Villette, Isoraka, mail addr: c/o Musée d'Art et d'Archéologie, BP 564, Antananarivo 101 - T: (20) 2225493, Fax: 2225493, E-mail: vohitra@refer.mg   49285

Malaysia

ICOM Malaysia, c/o National Museum, Dept. of Museums and Antiques, Jalan Damansara, 50566 Kuala Lumpur - T: (03) 22826255, Fax: 22827294, E-mail: janetsm@tm.net.my   49286

Perbadanan Muzium Melaka (Museum Corporation of Meleka), Jalan Kota, Kom. Warisan Melaka, 75000 Melaka - T: (06) 2826526, Fax: 2826745, E-mail: perzim@perpustam.edu.my   49287

Mali

ICOM Mali, Rue du Général Leclerc, mail addr: c/o
Musée National du Mali, BP 159, Bamako -
T: 223486, Fax: 231909, E-mail: musee@a-
fribone.net.ml   49288

ICOM Regional Organization for West Africa, BP
159, Bamako - T: 223489, Fax: 231909,
E-mail: musee@malinet.ml   49289

Malta

Malta National Committee of ICOM, POB 185,
Valletta, CMR 01 - T: 21233034, Fax: 21239915,
E-mail: icom-malta@melitensia.org   49290

Mauritania

ICOM Mauritanie, c/o Musée de Ouadane, BP 1368,
Nouakchott - T: 5256017, Fax: 5255275, 5252802,
E-mail: ouldabidinesidi@hotmail.com   49291

Mauritius

ICOM Mauritius, Chaussée, Port Louis, mail addr: c/o
Mauritius Museums Council, Mauritius Institute, POB
54, Port Louis - T: 2120639, Fax: 2125717,
E-mail: mimuse@intnet.mu   49292

Mexico

**Federación Mexicana de Asociaciones de Amigos
de los Museos** (Mexican Federation of Associations
of Friends of Museums), Calle General Léon 65bis,
11850 México - E-mail: femam@prodigy.net.mx,
Internet: www.femam.org.mx   49293

ICOM México, Santa Veracruz 66, Col Guerrero,
Deleg. Cuauhtémoc, 06300 México - T: (55)
182265, Fax: 104377, E-mail: icommexico@-
solar.sar.net, Internet: www.arts-history.mx/
museos/icom   49294

Monaco

**ICOM - Comité National Monégasque du Conseil
International des Musées**, c/o Musée
Océanographique de Monaco, Av Saint Martin,
98000 Monaco - T: 93153600, Fax: 93505297,
E-mail: nbarcoli@hotmail.com   49295

Mongolia

ICOM Mongolia, c/o O. Norovtseren, Zanabazar
Museum of Fine Arts, Barilgachidyn Talbai 46,
Ulaanbaatar - T: (011) 326060, Fax: 323986,
E-mail: tegshee5@yahoo.com   49296

Morocco

ICOM Maroc, c/o Direction du Patrimoine Culturel, 17
Rue Michlifen, Agdal, 10000 Rabat - T: (037)
671385, Fax: 671397   49297

Namibia

ICOM Namibia, c/o National Art Gallery of Namibia,
POB 994, Windhoek - T: (061) 231160,
Fax: 240930, E-mail: nagn@mweb.com.na   49298

Museums Association of Namibia, MAN, POB 147,
Windhoek - T: (061) 22840, Fax: 222544,
E-mail: silvestj@iway.na   49299

Nepal

ICOM Nepal, Patan Darbar Palace, Kathmandu, mail
addr: c/o Patan Museum, GPO Box 1040,
Kathmandu - T: (01) 521492, Fax: 251479,
E-mail: ptmuseum@mos.com.np   49300

Netherlands

European Association of Open Air Museums, c/o
Nederlands Openluchtmuseum, Postbus 649, 6800
AP Arnhem - T: (026) 3576250, Fax: 3576147,
E-mail: info@openluchtmuseum.nl, Internet: ww-
w.openluchtmuseum.nl   49301

ICOM Netherlands, Museumhuis Bussenschut,
Rapenburgerst 123, 1011 VL Amsterdam, mail addr:
c/o De Nederlandse Museumvereniging, PB 2975,
1000 CZ Amsterdam - T: (020) 5512900,
Fax: 5512901, E-mail: info@museum-
vereniging.nl   49302

**ICOMAM International Committee of Museums and
Collections of Arms and Military History**, c/o Jan
Piet Puype, Koninklijk Nederlands Leger- en
Wapenmuseum, Korte Geer 1, 2611 CA Delft -
T: (015) 2150500, Fax: 2150544,
E-mail: jppuype@hotmail.com,
Internet: www.klm_mra.be/ICOMAM/
index.htm   49303

International Committee for Monetary Museums,
c/o Het Nederlands Muntmuseum, Leidseweg 90,
3500 GK Utrecht - T: (030) 2910482, Fax: 2910467,
E-mail: ICOMON@coins.nl,
Internet: www.icom.org   49304

**International Confederation of Architectural
Museums**, c/o Nederlands Architektuurinstituut,
Museumpark 25, 3015 CB Rotterdam -
E-mail: mwilling@nai.nl, Internet: www.icam-
web.org   49305

De Nederlandse Museumvereniging (Netherlands
Museums Association), Rapenburgerstr 123, 1012
VM Amsterdam, mail addr: Postbus 2975, 1000 CZ
Amsterdam - T: (020) 5512900, Fax: 5512901,
E-mail: info@museumvereniging.nl, Internet: www.-
museumvereniging.nl   49306

Vereniging van Rijksgesubsidieerde Musea
(Association of State Subsidized Museums),
Rapenburgerstr 123, 1011 VL Amsterdam, mail
addr: c/o Museumhuis Bussenschut, Postbus 2975,
1000 CZ Amsterdam - T: (020) 5512900,
Fax: 5512901, E-mail: vrm@netland.nl   49307

New Zealand

ICOM New Zealand, c/o Greg McManus, Rotorua
Museum, Albert Dr, Rotorua 3220 - T: (07) 3494350,
Fax: 3492819, E-mail: greg.mcma-
nus@rdc.govt.nz   49308

Museum Association of Aotearoa New Zealand,
Museums Aotearoa, 104 The Terrace, Wellington
6035, mail addr: POB 10928, Wellington 6035 -
T: (04) 4991313, Fax: 4996313,
E-mail: mail@museums-aotearoa.org.nz,
Internet: www.museums-aotearoa.org.nz   49309

Museum Directors Federation, POB 6401 Te Aro,
Wellington 6015 - T: (04) 3844473,
Fax: 3851198   49310

Niger

ICOM Comité National du Niger, BP 10457, Niamey -
T: 723235, Fax: 722336, 722373,
E-mail: saleytim@yahoo.fr   49311

Nigeria

ICOM Nigeria, Old Residency, Calabar, mail addr: c/o
National Commision for Museums and Monuments,
PMB 1180, Calabar - T: (087) 233476/79,
Fax: 230111   49312

Museums Association of Nigeria, King George V St,
mail addr: c/o National Museum, PMB 12556, Lagos
- T: (01) 2636075   49313

**National Commission for Museums and
Monuments**, Plot 2018, Cotonou Crescent, Wuse
Zone 6, Abuja, mail addr: PMB 171, Garki, Abuja -
T: (09) 5230801, 5238253, Fax: 5238254   49314

Norway

ABM-Utvikling (Norwegian Archive, Library and
Museum Authority), Kronprinsens G 9, 0033 Oslo,
mail addr: Postboks 8145 DEP, 0033 Oslo -
T: 23117500, Fax: 23117501, E-mail: post@abm-
utvikling.no, Internet: www.abm-utvikling.no   49315

**ICLM International Committee for Literary
Museums**, c/o E. Dahl, Edvard Grieg Museum,
Troldhaugen 65, 5040 Paradis - T: 55910710,
Fax: 55911395, E-mail: edah@online.no   49316

**International Committee for Museums and
Collections of Musical Instruments**, c/o C.
Weinheimer, Ringve Museum, Postboks 3064 Lade,
7441 Trondheim - T: 73922411, Fax: 73920422,
E-mail: corinna.weinheimer@ringve.museum.no,
Internet: www.icom.org/cimcim   49317

Norges Museumsforbund, Ullevålsv 11, 0165 Oslo -
T: 22201402, Fax: 22112337, E-mail: museums-
nytt@museumsforbundet.no, Internet: www.mu-
seumsforbundet.no   49318

Norsk ICOM, Ullevålsv 11, 0165 Oslo - T: 22201402,
Fax: 22112337, E-mail: sekr@icom-norway.org,
Internet: www.icom-norway.org   49319

Norske Kunst- og Kulturhistoriske Museer,
Ullevålsv 11, 0165 Oslo - T: 22201402,
Fax: 22112337   49320

Norske Museumspedagogiske, Forening, c/o
Nordlandsmuseet, Prinsensg 116, 8005 Bodø -
T: 08121640   49321

Norske Naturhistoriske Museers, Landsforbund
NNML, c/o Zoologisk Museum, Muséplass 3, 5007
Bergen - T: 55212905, Fax: 55321153,
E-mail: bjarne.meidell@zmb.uib.no, Internet: www.-
toyen.uio.no/nnml/   49322

Norwegian Federation of Friends of Museums,
Postboks 95 Bygdoy, 0211 Oslo -
E-mail: fnm@sol.no   49323

**Skandinavisk Museumsforbund, Norwegian
Section**, Haugar Vestfold Kunstmuseum, 3110
Tønsberg - T: 33307670, Fax: 33307660,
E-mail: einar.wexelsen@vfk.no   49324

Oman

ICOM Oman, c/o Ministry of National Heritage and
Culture, POB 668, Muscat, 113 - T: 602225,
Fax: 602735   49325

Pakistan

The Museums Association of Pakistan, c/o Bait al-
Hikmah, Hamardy University, Sharae Madinat al-
Hikmah, Karachi 74700 - T: (021) 6996001/02,
Fax: 6350574, E-mail: huvc@cyber.net.pk   49326

Panama

**Comisión Nacional de Arqueología y Monumentos
Historicos**, Plaza 5 de Mayo, 662 Panamá City -
T: 621438   49327

ICOM Panamá, Casco Viejo, entre Calle 5ta y 6ta,
Panamá City, mail addr: c/o Museo del Canal
Interoceánico de Panamá, Apdo 1213, Zona 1,
Panamá City - T: 2111994/95, Fax: 2111649/50,
E-mail: pcmuseum@cwpanama.net   49328

Paraguay

Dirección General de Museos de la Nación, Calle
Humaita 673, Asunción - T: (021) 440070   49329

ICOM Paraguay, c/o Centro de Conservación del
Patrimonio Cultural, Almacén Viola, JE O'Leary 1 y
Barranco del Río, Asunción - T: (021) 446829,
Fax: 446829, E-mail: icom@patrimoniocultural-
ccpc.org.py   49330

Peru

ICOM Peru, Jr. Camaná 459, Lima 1 - T: (01)
4602770, Fax: 4602770,
E-mail: acastel@pucp.edu.pe   49331

Philippines

ICOM Philippines, c/o National Museum of the
Philippines, Padre Burgos St, Ermita, 1000 Manila -
T: (02) 5271215, Fax: 5270306,
E-mail: museum@info.com.ph   49332

Museum Volunteers of the Philippines, 4114
Dasmariñas, mail addr: POB 8052, 1222 Makati -
E-mail: MVPhilippines@hotmail.com, Internet: mv-
philippines.hypermart.net   49333

Poland

ICOM Poland, c/o Muzeum Narodowe,
Marcinkowskiego 9, Poznań - T: (061) 8525969,
Fax: 8515898, E-mail: mnp@mnp.art.pl   49334

**Polish Association of Members of the Museum
Professions**, Wawel 5, 31-001 Kraków - T: (012)
4225155, Fax: 4215177   49335

Stowarzyszenie Muzeów na Wolnym Powietrzu
(Association of Open Air Museums), Rynek
Staromiejski 1, Ratusz, 87-100 Toruń   49336

Stowarzyszenie Zwiazek Muzeów Polskich (Polish
Museums Association), ul Krakowska 46, 31-066
Kraków - T: (012) 4305575, 4305563,
Fax: 4306330   49337

Portugal

Associacão Portugesa de Museologia, c/o Panteão
Nacional, Praça B à Travessa Sargento Abílio, Lote
C1, 1500-567 Lisboa - T: 217780687,
Fax: 217780642, E-mail: apom@oninet.pt,
Internet: www.museusportugal.org/apom   49338

Federação de Amigos dos Museus de Portugal,
Calcada do Combro 61, 1200-111 Lisboa -
E-mail: aamportugal@mail.telepac.pt   49339

ICOM Portugal, c/o Ana R. Godinho Carcoso, Museu
Nacional de Arte Antiga, Rua das Janelas Verdes,
1249-017 Lisboa - T: 213912800/07,
Fax: 213973703, E-mail: mnaa@netcabo.pt   49340

Instituto Português de Museus, Palacio Nacional da
Ajuda, Ala Sul, 1349-021 Lisboa - T: 213650800,
Fax: 213647821, E-mail: dd.dsm@ipmuseus.pt,
Internet: www.museus.pt   49341

Qatar

ICOM Qatar, c/o The National Council for Culture, Arts
and Heritage, POB 2777, Doha - T: 4328471,
4437993, Fax: 432871, 4437993,
E-mail: my_taha@yahoo.co.uk   49342

Romania

Asociatia Nationalá a Muzeelor in aer Liber - România, Piaţa Presei Libere 1, 013701 Bucureşti - T: (021) 2244421, Fax: 2244421, E-mail: manuela.-tabacila@cultura.ro 49343

ICOM Romania, c/o Muzeul Judetean de Istorie şi Arheologie Prahova, Str Toma Caragiu 10, 100042 Ploieşti - T: (044) 114437, Fax: 114437 49344

Russia

Associacija Muzeev Rossii (Russian Museums Association), Oktjabrskaja ul 14, 300002 Tula - T: (0872) 779221, 776712, Fax: 393196, 393599, E-mail: assoc@tsu.tula.ru, Internet: www.amr-museum.ru 49345

Museum Council, ul D. Uljanova 19, 117036 Moskva - T: (095) 1251121, Fax: 1260630, E-mail: i_zaitse-va@hotmail.com 49346

Rossijskij Komitet Meždunarodnogo Soveta Muzeev (IKOM Rossii), Volchonka ul 3-4, 119019 Moskva - T: (095) 2036090, Fax: 2038487, E-mail: icom@kremlin.museum.ru, Internet: www.i-comrussia.ru/ 49347

St. Lucia

INTERCOM International Committee for Museums Management, c/o L. Gill, Archaeological and Historical Society, 85 Chaussee Rd, Castries - T: (758) 451-9251, Fax: (758) 451-9324, E-mail: gilll@candw.lc 49348

Senegal

ICOM Comité Sénégalais, c/o Musée Historique de Gorée, BP 206, Dakar - T: 8251990, Fax: 8244918, E-mail: layetoure@hotmail.com 49349

Serbia-Montenegro

Društvo Muzejskih Radnika Vojvodine, Dunavska 35, 21000 Novi Sad - T: 26766 49350

ICOM Nacionalni Komitet Serbia-Montenegro, c/o Galerija Fresaka, Cara Urosa 20, 11000 Beograd - T: (011) 182966, Fax: 183655, E-mail: icom@yubc.net, Internet: www.serbiamon-tenegro.icom.museum 49351

Muzejsko Društvo SR Crne Gore - Cetinje, N. Cerovica bb, 81250 Cetinje - T: (086) 31682, Fax: 31682, E-mail: museums@mu-seumscg.org 49352

Muzejsko Društvo Srbije, c/o Narodni Muzej, Trg Republike 1a, 11000 Beograd - T: (011) 624322 49353

Muzejsko Društvo Srbije, c/o Narodni Muzej, Trg Republike 1, 11000 Beograd - T: (050) 624322 49354

Seychelles

Association of Museums of the Indian Ocean, c/o National Musuem of Seychelles, POB 720, Victoria - T: 321333, Fax: 323183, E-mail: seymus@sey-chelles.net 49355

ICOM Seychelles, c/o National Museum, POB 720, Victoria - T: 321333, Fax: 323183, E-mail: seymus@seychelles.net 49356

Singapore

ICOM Singapore, c/o National Heritage Board, Mita Bldg, 140 Hill St, Singapore 179369 - T: 63323286, 63325593, Fax: 63391941, E-mail: Lim_Siok_-Peng@nhb.gov.sg 49357

Slovakia

ICOM Slovakia, c/o Slovenská Národná Galéria, Riečna 1, 815 13 Bratislava - T: (02) 54430746, Fax: 54433971, E-mail: uz@sng.sk 49358

Zväz muzei na Slovensku (Slovak Museums Association), c/o Slovenské Múzeum Ochrany Prírody a Jaskyniarstva, Školská 4, 031 01 Liptovský Mikuláš - T: (044) 5477210, Fax: 5514381 49359

Slovenia

ICOM Slovenia, c/o Irena Mrušic, Slovene Ethnographic Museum, Metelkova 2, 1000 Ljubljana - T: (01) 4325368, Fax: 4325377, E-mail: irena.marusic@tms.si 49360

ICR International Committee for Regional Museums, c/o I. Zmuc, Mestni Muzej, Gosposka 15, 1000 Ljubljana - T: (01) 2522930, Fax: 2522946 49361

Skupnost Muzejev Slovenije (Museums Association of Slovenia), c/o Taja Cepić, Mestni Muzej, Gosposka 15, 1000 Ljubljana - T: (061) 222930 49362

Slovensko Konservatorsko Društvo (Association of Conservators of Cultural Heritage of Slovenia), Trzaska 4, 1000 Ljubljana - T: (01) 1256079, Fax: 1254198 49363

Slovensko Muzejsko Društvo (Association of Museum Curators of Slovenia), Kongresni Trg 1, 1000 Ljubljana - T: (01) 4213267, Fax: 4213287 49364

South Africa

ICOM South Africa, c/o Johannesburg Art Gallery, POB 23561, Johannesburg 2044 - T: 0117253130, Fax: 0117206000, E-mail: pdube@mj.org.za 49365

Suider-Afrikaanse Museum-Assosiasie (Southern African Museums Association), POB 699, Grahamstown 6140 - T: 0466243087, Fax: 0466243276, E-mail: sama@imaginet.co.za, Internet: sama.museums.org.za 49366

Spain

Amics de los Museos de Cataluña, Palau de la Virreina, La Rambla 99, 08002 Barcelona - T: 933014379, Fax: 933189421, E-mail: amics@a-micsdelsmuseus.org, Internet: www.amics-delsmuseus.org 49367

Amigos de los Museos, La Rambla 99, 08002 Barcelona - T: 933014379 49368

Asociacion de Amigos de los Museos Militares, c/o Museo del Ejercito, Calle Méndez Núñez 1, 28014 Madrid - Fax: 915218078 49369

Asociación Española de Archiveros, Bibliotecarios, Museólogos y Documentalistas, ANABAD, Calle Recoletos 5, 28001 Madrid - T: 915751727, Fax: 915751727 49370

Asociación Española de Museólogos, Av Reyes Católicos 6, 28040 Madrid - T: 915430917, Fax: 915440225, E-mail: aem@museologia.net, Internet: www.museologia.net 49371

Associació del Museo de la Ciència i de la Tècnica i d'Arqueologia Industrial de Catalunya, Rambla d'Egara 270, 08221 Terrassa - T: 937803787, Fax: 937806089, E-mail: associaciomc-t@eic.ictnet.es 49372

European Federation of Associations of Industrial and Technical Heritage, E-FAITH, c/o Museo de la Ciència i de la Tècnica, Rambla d'Egara 270, 08221 Terrassa - T: 937803787, Fax: 937806089, E-mail: associaciomct@eic.ictnet.es, Internet: www.e-faith.org 49373

Federación Española de Asociaciones de Amigos de los Museos, Av Reyes Católicos 6, 28040 Madrid - E-mail: feamamigos@terra.es, Internet: www.friendsdemuseos.org 49374

ICOM Spain, c/o Museo de América, Reyes catolicos 6, 28040 Madrid - T: 915431820, Fax: 915431820, E-mail: info@icom-ce.org, Internet: www.icom-ce.org 49375

International Committee for Museology, c/o Andrea A. García Sastre, Museu Nacional d'Art de Catalunya, Parc de Montjuïc, 08038 Barcelona - T: 936220360, Fax: 936220369, E-mail: wagarcia@correu.gencat.es, Internet: www.umu.se/nordic.museology/icofom.html 49376

Sri Lanka

ICOM Sri Lanka, c/o Dept. of National Museums, POB 854, Colombo 7 - T: (01) 694767, Fax: 695366, E-mail: cnmid@slnet.lk 49377

Swaziland

ICOM Swaziland, c/o National Museum, POB 100, Lobamba H107 - T: (041) 61178/79, Fax: 61875, E-mail: staff@swazimus.org.sz 49378

Sweden

ICOM Sweden, Alsnög 7, 116 41 Stockholm, mail addr: c/o Riksuitställningar, POB 4715, 116 92 Stockholm - T: (08) 6916000, Fax: 6916020, E-mail: mats.widbom@riksutstallningar.se 49379

International Association of Transport and Communication Museums, 262 52 Ängelholm, mail addr: c/o Swedish Railway Museum, Box 407, 801 05 Gävle - T: (026) 144570, Fax: 144598, E-mail: robert.sjoo@jarnvagsmuseum.sese, Internet: iatm.org 49380

MPR International Committee for Museums Marketing and PR, Malmöhusvägen, 201 24 Malmö, mail addr: c/o L. Millinger, Malmö Museer, Box 406, 201 24 Malmö - T: (040) 344404, Fax: 124097, E-mail: lena.millinger@malmo.se, Internet: www.icom.org/internationals.html 49381

Skandinavisk Museumsforbund, Swedish Section, c/o Nordiska Museet, Djurgårdsvägen 6-16, 115 93 Stockholm - Fax: (08) 51954580 49382

Svenska Museiföreningen (Swedish Museums Association), Fridhemsg 68, 112 46 Stockholm - T: (08) 6533988, 6536034, Fax: 6530170, E-mail: info@museiforeningen.se, Internet: www.-museiforeningen.se 49383

Sveriges Museimannaförbund (Swedish Association of Museum Curators), Planiavägen 13, 131 34 Nacka, mail addr: Box 760, 131 24 Nacka - T: (08) 4662400, Fax: 4662413, E-mail: kansli@dik.se, Internet: www.dik.se 49384

Swedish Federation of Friends of Museums, c/o B. Jungner, Storg 57, 115 23 Stockholm - E-mail: birgitta.jungner.safm@telia.com 49385

Switzerland

ICOM Schweiz, Conseil International des Musées - Comité National Suisse, Museumstr 2, 8023 Zürich, mail addr: c/o Schweizerisches Landesmuseum, Geschäftsstelle, Dr. Josef Brülisauer, Postfach 6789, 8023 Zürich - T: 012186588, Fax: 012186589, E-mail: j.bruelisauere@vms-ams.ch 49386

Museumsgesellschaft, Limmatquai 62, 8001 Zürich - T: 012514233, Fax: 012524409, E-mail: info@mug.ch 49387

Verband der Museen der Schweiz, Association des Musées Suisses, Museumstr 2, 8023 Zürich, mail addr: c/o Schweizerisches Landesmuseum, Postfach 6789, 8023 Zürich - T: 012186588, Fax: 012186589, E-mail: contact@vms-ams.ch, Internet: www.vms-ams.ch 49388

Tanzania

ICOM Tanzania, c/o National Museums of Tanzania, POB 511, Dar-es-Salaam - T: (022) 2122030, Fax: 2122840, E-mail: museumh-q@omnisys.co.tz 49389

Thailand

ICOM Thailand, c/o S. Charoenpot, National Museum of H.M. The King's Jubilee, Khlong 5, Pathumthani 12120 - T: (02) 9029833, 9027568, Fax: 9027833, E-mail: somlakc@hotmail.com 49390

Togo

Direction des Musées, Sites et Monuments, BP 12156, Lomé - T: 216807, Fax: 221839, E-mail: musees.togo@rdd.tg 49391

ICOM Togo, 123 Av de la Nouvelle Marché, Lomé, mail addr: c/o Musée National des Sites et Monuments, BP 12156, Lomé - T: (02) 217140, Fax: 2221839, E-mail: musees.togo@rdd.tg 49392

Tunisia

ICOM Tunisia, c/o Institut national du Patrimoine, 4 Pl du Château, 1008 Tunis - T: 71562622, Fax: 71562452 49393

Turkey

ICOM Turkish National Committee, c/o Anitlar ve Müzeler Genel Müdürlügü, Meclis Binasi, 06100 Ulus - T: (0312) 3104960, Fax: 3111417, E-mail: anitlarmuzeler@kultur.gov.tr 49394

Ukraine

ICOM Ukraine, c/o Lviv Art Gallery, ul Stefanika 3, 79000 Lviv - T: (0322) 723009, Fax: 723009, E-mail: dergach@city-adm.lviv.ua 49395

United Kingdom

Alchemy: The Group for Collections Management in Yorkshire and Humberside, c/o Bankfield Museum, Boothtown Rd, Halifax HX3 6HG - T: (01422) 354823, Fax: 349020 49396

Association for British Transport and Engineering Museums, c/o Science Museum, Exhibition Rd, London SW7 2DD - T: (020) 79388234 49397

Association of British Transport and Engineering Museums, 20 Linnell Rd, Rugby CV21 4AN - T: (01788) 542861 49398

Association of Independent Museums, c/o Matthew Tanner, SS Great Britain, Great Western Dockyard, Bristol BS1 9TY - T: (0117) 9260680, Fax: 9255788, E-mail: matthewt@ss-great-britain.com, Internet: www.museums.org.uk/aim 49399

Association of Railway Preservation Societies, 3 Orchard Close, Watford WD1 3DU - T: (01923) 221280, Fax: 241023 49400

AVICOM International Committee for Autovisual and New Technologies Museums, c/o Stephen Done, Museum and Tour Centre, Anfield Rd, Liverpool L4 0TH - T: (0151) 2640160, Fax: 2640149, E-mail: stephen.done@li-verpoolfc.tv 49401

British Association of Friends of Museums, Fonthill Cottages, Lewannick, Launceston PL15 7QE - T: (01566) 782440, Fax: carolbunbury@-waitrose.com, Internet: www.bafm.org.uk 49402

British Aviation Preservation Council, c/o Centre for Lifelong Learning, University of Warwick, Coventry CV4 7AL - T: (01926) 495191, E-mail: bapcchairman@tiscali.co.uk 49403

Campaign for Museums, 35-37 Grosvenor Gardens, London SW1W 0BX - T: (020) 72339796, Fax: 72336770, E-mail: info@campaignformuseums.org.uk, Internet: www.campaignformuseums.org.uk.or 49404

Care of Collections Forum, c/o Falkirk Museums Service, 7-11 Abbotsinch Rd, Grangemouth FK3 9UX - T: (01324) 504689, Fax: 503771, E-mail: carol.whittaker@falkirk.gov.uk 49405

Council for Museums, Archives and Libraries, 16 Queen Anne's Gate, London SW1H 9AA - T: (020) 72731444, Fax: 72731404, E-mail: info@resource.gov.uk, Internet: www.resource.gov.uk 49406

Council of Museums in Wales, The Courtyard, Letty St, Cardiff CF24 4EL - T: (029) 20225432, Fax: 20668516, E-mail: info@cmw.org.uk, Internet: www.cmw.org.uk 49407

Dundee Art Galleries and Museum Association, c/o Frances Towns, 37 Ancrum Dr, Dundee, DD2 2JG - T: (01382) 668720 49408

East Midlands Museums Service, POB 7221, Colston Bassett NG12 3WH - T: (01949) 81734, Fax: 81859, E-mail: emms@emms.org.uk, Internet: www.emms.org.uk 49409

English Heritage, East Midlands Region, 44 Demgate, Northampton NN1 1UH - T: (01604) 735400, Fax: 735401, Internet: www.english-heritage.org.uk 49410

English Heritage North West Region, 3 Chepstow St, Manchester M1 5FW - T: (0161) 2421400, Fax: 2421401, Internet: www.english-heritage.org.uk 49411

European Museum Forum, POB 913, Bristol BS99 5ST - T: (0117) 9238897, Fax: 9732437, E-mail: EuropeanMuseumForum@compuserve.com, Internet: www.europeanmuseumforum.org 49412

Federation of Museums and Galleries in Wales, c/o Ceredigion Museum, Coliseum, Terrace Rd, Aberystwyth SY23 2AQ - T: (01920) 633088, E-mail: museum@ceredigion.gov.uk 49413

Geological Curators' Group, c/o Dr. C. Giles Miller, Dept. of Paleontology, Natural History Museum, Cromwell Rd, London SW7 5BD - T: (020) 79425415, Internet: www.geocurators.org 49414

Group for Costume and Textile Staff in Museums, c/o Ch. Stevens, Museum of Welsh Life, Saint Fagans CF5 6XB - T: (029) 20573420, Fax: 20573490, E-mail: christine.stevens@nmgw.ac.uk 49415

Group for Directors of Museums, c/o Grosvenor Museum, 27 Grosvenor St, Chester CH1 2DD - T: (01244) 402012, Fax: 347587, E-mail: s.matthews@chestercc.gov.uk 49416

Group for Education in Museums, Primrose House, 193 Gillingham Rd, Gillingham, Kent ME7 4EP - T: (01634) 312409, Fax: 312409, E-mail: gemso@blueyonder.co.uk, Internet: www.gem.org.uk/ 49417

ICOM Northern Ireland, c/o Ulster Museum, Robert Heslip, Botanic Gardens, Belfast BT9 5AB - T: (028) 90383015, Fax: 90383013, E-mail: robert.heslip.um@nics.gov.uk 49418

International Committee for Costume Museums, c/o J. Marschner, Royal Ceremonial Dress Collection, Kensington Palace, London W8 4PX - T: (020) 79379561, Fax: 73760198, E-mail: joanna.marschner@hrp.org.uk, Internet: www.kent.edu/museum 49419

International Council of Museums - UK National Committee, c/o H. Hopkins, Council for Museums, Archives and Libraries, 16 Queen Anne's Gate, London SW1H 9AA - T: (020) 72731430, Fax: 72731404, E-mail: henrietta.hopkins@resource.gov.uk 49420

Leicestershire Museums, Arts and Records Service, County Hall, Glenfield LE8 3RA - T: (0116) 2656781, Fax: 2657370, E-mail: hbroughton@leics.gov.uk, Internet: www.leics.gov.uk 1849 49421

London Federation of Museums and Art Galleries, Saint John's Gate, London EC1M 4DA - T: (020) 72536644, Fax: 74908835 49422

mda, Museum Documentation Association, Spectrum Bldg, Michael Young Centre, Purbeck Rd, Cambridge CB2 2PD - T: (01223) 415760, Fax: 415960, E-mail: mda@mda.org.uk, Internet: www.mda.org.uk 49423

Midlands Federation of Museums and Art Galleries, Ironbridge Gorge Museum, Ironbridge, Telford TF8 7AW - T: (01952) 432751, Fax: 432237, E-mail: isabel_churcher@birmingham.gov.uk, Internet: www.bmag.org.uk 49424

MLA West Midland, Regional Council for Museums, Libraries and Archives, Grosvenor House, 14 Bennetts Hill, Birmingham B2 5RS - T: (0121) 6315800, Fax: 6315825, E-mail: info@mlawestmidlands.org.uk, Internet: www.mlawestmidlands.org.uk 49425

Museum Ethnographers Group, c/o Chantal Knowles, National Museums of Scotland, Chambers St, Edinburgh EH1 1JF - T: (0131) 2474065, Fax: 2474070, E-mail: c.knowles@nms.ac.uk, Internet: www.museuethnographers-group.org.uk 49426

Museum Professionals Group, c/o Julie Allsop, Salford Museum and Art Gallery, The Crescent, Salford M5 4WU - T: (0161) 7362649, E-mail: julie.allsop@salford.gov.uk 49427

Museum Trading Association, c/o Everyevent, 41 Britannia Sq, Worcester WR1 3DN - T: (01905) 724734, Fax: 724734, E-mail: mta@everyevent.co.uk, Internet: www.museumstrading.org.uk 49428

Museums and Galleries Disability Association, c/o Hove Museum and Art Gallery, 19 New Church Rd, Hove BN3 4AB - T: (01273) 292828, Fax: 292827, E-mail: abigail.thomas@brighton-hove.gov.uk, Internet: www.magda.org.uk 49429

Museums Association, 24 Calvin St, London E1 6NW - T: (020) 74266970, Fax: 74266961, E-mail: info@museumsassociation.org, Internet: www.museumsassociation.org 49430

Museums in Essex Committee, Essex Record Office, Wharf Rd, Chelmsford CM2 6YT - T: (01245) 244612, 244613, Fax: 244655, E-mail: stephen.lowy@essexcc.gov.uk 49431

Museums North, Northern Federation of Museums and Art Galleries, Sir William Gray House, Clarence Rd, Hartlepool TS24 8BT - T: (01429) 523443, Fax: 523477, E-mail: karenteasdale@beamish.org.uk 49432

Museums Weapons Group, Royal Armouries, Armouries Dr, Leeds LS10 1LT - T: (0113) 2201867, Fax: 2201871, E-mail: grimer@armouries.org.uk 49433

National Heritage: The Museums Action Movement, 9a North St, Clapham, London SW4 0HN - T: (020) 77206789, Fax: 79781815 49434

National Museum Directors' Conference, c/o Imperial War Museum, Lambeth Rd, London SE1 6HZ - T: (020) 74165202, Fax: 74165485, E-mail: nmdc@iwm.org.uk, Internet: www.nationalmuseums.org.uk 49435

National Museums and Galleries of Northern Ireland, c/o Ulster Museum, Botanic Gardens, Belfast BT9 5AB - T: (028) 90383000, Fax: 90383006, Internet: www.ulster-museum.org.uk 49436

North East Museums, Libraries & Archives Council, House of Recovery, Bath Ln, Newcastle-upon-Tyne NE4 5SQ - T: (0191) 2221661, Fax: 2614725, E-mail: nemlac@nemlac.co.uk, Internet: www.nemlac.co.uk 49437

North West Federation of Museums and Art Galleries, Boat Museum, South Pier Rd, Ellesmere Port CH65 4FW - T: (0151) 3555017, Fax: 3554079, E-mail: emma@boatmuseum.fsnet.co.uk, Internet: www.nwfed.org.uk 49438

North Western Federation of Museums and Art Galleries, c/o Museum of Science and Industry in Manchester, Liverpool Rd, Castlefield, Manchester M3 4FP - T: (0161) 8322244 49439

Northern Ireland Museums Council, 66 Donegall Pass, Belfast BT7 1BU - T: (028) 90550215, Fax: 90550216, E-mail: info@nimc.co.uk, Internet: www.nimc.co.uk 49440

Science and Industry Collections Group, Science Museum, Exhibition Rd, London SW7 2DD - T: (020) 79424155, Fax: 79424102, E-mail: j.britton@nmsi.ac.uk, Internet: www.sicg.org.uk 49441

Scottish Museums Council, County House, 20-22 Torphichen St, Edinburgh EH3 8JB - T: (0131) 2297465, Fax: 2292728, E-mail: inform@scottishmuseums.org.uk, Internet: www.scottishmuseums.org.uk 49442

Scottish Museums Federation, c/o Alison Reid, South Lanarkshire Council, Council Offices, Almada St, Hamilton ML3 0AA - T: (01698) 455714, Fax: 454861, E-mail: alison.reid@southlanarkshire.gov.uk 49443

Social History Curators Group, c/o Discovery Museum, Blandford Sq, Newcastle-upon-Tyne NE1 4JA - T: (0191) 2326789, Fax: 2302614, E-mail: enquiry@shcg.org.uk, Internet: www.shcg.org.uk 49444

Society of County Museum Officers, c/o Somerset Museums Service, Castle Green, Taunton TA1 4AA - T: (01823) 320200, Fax: 320229, E-mail: county-museum@somerset.gov.uk, Internet: www.somerset.gov.uk/museums 49445

Society of Decorative Art Curators, c/o Decorative Art Department, National Museums Liverpool, 127 Dale St, Liverpool L69 3LA - T: (0151) 4784261/62, Fax: 4784693, E-mail: pauline.rushton@liverpoolmuseum.org.uk 49446

Society of Museum Archaeologists, c/o Museum of London, London Wall, London EC2Y 5HN - T: (020) 76003699, Fax: 76001058, E-mail: musmda@hants.gov.uk, Internet: www.socmusarch.org.uk 49447

South Eastern Federation of Museums and Art Galleries, 2 Sackville St, Hayes, Bromley BR2 7JT - T: (020) 84622228, E-mail: pwboreham@ukonline.co.uk 49448

South Midlands Museums Federation, c/o Saffron Walden Museum, Museum St, Saffron Walden CB10 1JL - T: (01799) 510333, Fax: 510333, E-mail: cwingfield@uttlesford.gov.uk 49449

South West Museums Council, Creech Castle, Bathpool TA1 2DX - T: (01823) 259696, Fax: 270933, E-mail: general@swmuseums.co.uk, Internet: www.swmuseums.co.uk 49450

South Western Federation of Museums and Art Galleries, c/o Victoria Pirie, East Cliff, Bournemouth BH1 3AA - T: (01202) 451804, E-mail: victoria.pirie@bournemouth.gov.uk 49451

Standing Conference on Archives and Museums, Church House, Ogleforth, York YO1 7JN - T: (01904) 557239, Fax: 557215, E-mail: louiseh@yorkminster.org, Internet: www.hmc.gov.uk/ SCAM 49452

Touring Exhibitions Group, 29 Point Hill, Greenwich, London SE10 8QW - T: (020) 86912660, Fax: 83331987, E-mail: admin@teg-net.org.uk, Internet: www.teg-net.org.uk 49453

University Museums Group, c/o University of Liverpool Art Collections, Liverpool L69 7WY - T: (0151) 7942347, Fax: 7942343, E-mail: artgall@liv.ac.uk 49454

Visual Arts and Galleries Association, The Old School, High St, Witcham, Ely CB6 2LQ - T: (01353) 776356, Fax: 775411, E-mail: admin@vaga.co.uk, Internet: www.vaga.co.uk 1978 49455

Yorkshire and Humberside Federation of Museums and Art Galleries, c/o Carolyn Dalton, Doncaster Museum Service, Chequer Rd, Doncaster DN1 2AE - T: (01302) 734293, Fax: 735409, E-mail: carolyn.dalton@doncaster.gov.uk 49456

Yorkshire Museums Council, Farnley Hall, Hall Ln, Leeds LS12 5HA - T: (0113) 2638909, Fax: 2791479, E-mail: info@yhmc.org.uk, Internet: www.yorkshiremuseums.org.uk 49457

Uruguay

ICOM Uruguay, c/o Sra Siccardi Pisano, Blvd España 2809, 11300 Montevideo - T: (02) 7092804, Fax: 7077062, E-mail: gabysiccardi@yahoo.com 49458

U.S.A.

African American Museums Association, c/o Dr. M.Burroughs, Dusable Museum, 740 E 56th Pl, Chicago, IL 60637 - T: (312) 947-0600, Fax: (312) 947-0677, Internet: www.artnoir.com/aaam.html 49459

Alabama Museums Association, POB 870340, Tuscaloosa, AL 35487 - T: (205) 348-7554, Fax: (205) 348-9292, E-mail: jhall@bama.ua.edu 49460

American Association for Museum Volunteers, c/o Denver Museum of Natural History, 2001 Colorado Blvd, Denver, CO 80205 - T: (303) 370-6419, Fax: (303) 331-6492, E-mail: schristian@dmnh.org 49461

American Association for State and Local History, 1717 Church St, Nashville, TN 37203-2991 - T: (615) 320-3203, Fax: (615) 327-9013, E-mail: history@aaslh.org, Internet: www.aaslh.org 49462

American Association of Museums, 1575 Eye St NW, Ste 400, Washington, DC 20005 - T: (202) 289-1818, Fax: (202) 289-6578, E-mail: marketing@aam-us.org, Internet: www.aam-us.org 49463

American Institute for Conservation of Historic and Artistic Works, 1717 K St NW, Ste 301, Washington, DC 20006 - T: (202) 452-9545, Fax: (202) 452-9328, E-mail: info@aic-faic.org, Internet: www.aic.stanford.edu 49464

Arkansas Museums Association, c/o HRMS, Arkansas State Parks, 1 Capitol Mall, Little Rock, AR 72201 - T: (501) 682-3603, Fax: (501) 682-0081, E-mail: mkbynum@amod.org 49465

Association for Living History, Farm and Agricultural Museums, c/o Judith Sheridan, 8774 Rte 45 NW, North Bloomfield, OH 44450-9701 - T: (440) 685-4410, Fax: (440) 685-4410, E-mail: sheridan@orwell.net, Internet: www.alhfam.org 49466

Association of Art Museum Directors, 41 E 65 St, New York, NY 10021 - T: (212) 249-4423, Fax: (212) 535-5039, E-mail: aamd@amn.org, Internet: www.aamd.org 49467

Association of Children's Museums, 1300 L St NW, Ste 975, Washington, DC 20005 - T: (202) 898-1080, Fax: (202) 898-1086, E-mail: acm@childrensmuseums.org, Internet: www.childrensmuseums.org 49468

Association of College and University Museums and Galleries, c/o Oklahoma Museum of Natural History, 1335 Asp Av, Norman, OK 73019-0606 - T: (405) 325-1009, Fax: (405) 325-7699, E-mail: pbtirrell@ou.edu 49469

Association of Indiana Museums, POB 24428, Indianapolis, IN 46224-0428 - T: (317) 882-5649, Fax: (317) 865-7662, E-mail: wildcat@iquest.net 49470

Association of Midwest Museums, POB 11940, Saint Louis, MO 63112 - T: (314) 454-3110, Fax: (314) 454-3112, E-mail: mmcdirect2@aol.com 49471

Association of Railway Museums, c/o Pennsylvania Trolley Museum, 725 W Chestnut St, Washington, PA 15301-4623 - T: (724) 228-9256, Fax: (724) 228-9675 49472

Association of Science-Museum Directors, c/o San Diego Natural History Museum, 1788 El Prado, San Diego, CA 92101 - T: (619) 232-3821, Fax: (619) 232-0248, E-mail: mhager@sdnhm.org 49473

Association of Science-Technology Centers, 1025 Vermont Av NW, Ste 500, Washington, DC 20005-6310 - T: (202) 783-7200, Fax: (202) 783-7207, E-mail: info@astc.org, Internet: www.astc.org 49474

Association of South Dakota Museums, 200 W Sixth St, Sioux Falls, SD 57102 - T: (605) 367-4210, Fax: (605) 367-6004 49475

Association of Systematics Collections, 1725 K St NW, Ste 601, Washington, DC 20006-1401 - T: (202) 835-9050, Fax: (202) 835-7334, E-mail: general@nscalliance.org, Internet: www.ascoll.org 49476

California Association of Museums, 2002 N Main St, Santa Ana, CA 92706 - T: (714) 542-2611, Fax: (714) 480-0053, E-mail: cam@calmuseums.org, Internet: www.calmuseums.org 49477

Colorado-Wyoming Association of Museums, 400 Clarendon Av, Sheridan, WY 82801 - T: (307) 674-4589, Fax: (307) 672-1720, E-mail: admin@cwamit.org, Internet: www.cwamit.org 49478

Connecticut Museum Association, POB 78, Roxbury, CT 06783 - T: (860) 354-3543 49479

Council for Museum Anthropology, Exthology, University of Arizona, Tucson, AZ 85721 - T: (520) 621-6281, Fax: (520) 621-2976, E-mail: parezo@u.arizona.edu 49480

Council of American Jewish Museums, 12 Eldridge St, New York, NY 10002 - T: (212) 219-0903, Fax: (212) 966-4782, E-mail: aemsy@aol.com 49481

Council of American Maritime Museums, c/o Maine Maritime Museum, 243 Washington St, Bath, ME 04530 - T: (207) 443-1316, Fax: (207) 443-1665, E-mail: wilcox@bathmaine.com 49482

Florida Art Museum Directors Association, 1990 Sand Dollar Ln, Vero Beach, FL 32963 - T: (561) 388-2428, Fax: (561) 388-9313, E-mail: fmda@steds.org 49483

Florida Association of Museums, 1114 Thomasville Rd, Tallahassee, FL 32303, mail addr: POB 10951, Tallahassee, FL 32302-2951 - T: (850) 222-6028, Fax: (850) 222-6112, E-mail: fam@flamuseums.org, Internet: www.flamuseums.org 49484

Georgia Association of Museums and Galleries, c/o Fernbank Science Center, 156 Heaton Park Dr, Atlanta, GA 30307 - T: (404) 378-4311, Fax: (404) 370-1336, E-mail: david.dundee@fernbank.edu 49485

Hawaii Museums Association, POB 4125, Honolulu, HI 96812-4125 - T: (808) 254-4292, Fax: (808) 254-4153, E-mail: dpope@lava.net 49486

ICMS International Committee for Museums Security, c/o W. Faulk, Getty Conservation Institute, 1200 Getty Center Dr, Str 700, Los Angeles, CA 90049-1684 - T: (310) 440-6547, Fax: (310) 440-6979, E-mail: wfaulk@getty.edu 49487

Idaho Association of Museums, c/o Idaho State Historical Museum, 7111 McMullen Rd, Boise, ID 83709 - T: (208) 334-2120, Fax: (208) 334-2775 49488

Illinois Association of Museums, 1 Old State Capitol Plaza, Springfield, IL 62701-1507 - T: (217) 524-7080, Fax: (217) 785-7937, E-mail: mturner@hpa084r1.state.il.us 49489

Institute of Museum and Liberary Services, 1100 Pennsylvania Av, NW, Washington, DC 20506 - T: (202) 606-8539, E-mail: imlsinof@imls.gov, Internet: www.imls.gov 49490

Intermuseum Conservation Association, Allen Art Bldg, Oberlin, OH 44074 - T: (216) 775-7331 49491

International Association of Museum Facility Administrators, 11 W 53rd St, New York, NY 10019, mail addr: POB 1505, Washington, DC 20013-1505 - T: (212) 708-9413, Fax: (212) 333-1169, E-mail: vinnie-magorrian@moma.org, Internet: www.iamfa.org 49492

International Committee for Egyptology in ICOM - CIPEG, c/o Dr. Regine Schulz, Walters Art Museum, 600 N Charles St, Baltimore, MD 21201-5185 - T: (410) 547-9000 ext 255, Fax: (410) 752-4797, E-mail: rschulz@thewalters.org 49493

International Committee for Exhibition Exchange, c/o Anne R. Gossett, Smithsonian Institution, 1100 Jefferson Dr SW, Ste 705, Washington, DC 20560 - T: (202) 633-9220, Fax: (202) 786-2777, E-mail: argossett@intg.si.edu, Internet: www.exhibitionsonline.org/icee 49494

International Committee for Glass Museums, c/o Dr. J.A. Page, Corning Museum of Glass, 1 Glass Centere, Corning, NY 14830-2253 - T: (607) 974-8312, Fax: (607) 974-8473, E-mail: pageja@cmog.org 49495

International Congress of Maritime Museums, c/o Stuart Pames, Connecticut River Museum, 67 Main St, Essex, CT 06426 - T: (860) 767-8269, Fax: (860) 767-7028, E-mail: StuPames@aol.com 49496

International Movement for a New Museology, c/o WAN Museum, POB 1009, Zuni, NM 87327 - T: (505) 782-4403, Fax: (505) 782-2700, E-mail: aamhc@zuni.k12.nm.us 49497

International Museum Theatre Alliance, c/o Museum of Science, Science Park, Boston, MA 02114 - T: (617) 589-0449, Fax: (617) 589-0454, E-mail: imtal@mos.org, Internet: www.mos.org/imtal 49498

Iowa Museum Association, 225 Commercial St, Waterloo, IA 50701 - T: (319) 291-4490, Fax: (319) 291-4270, E-mail: cammie.scully@waterloo-sa.org, Internet: www.iowamuseums.org 49499

Kansas Museums Association, 6425 SW 6th Av, Topeka, KS 66615-1099 - T: (785) 272-8681, Fax: (785) 272-8682, E-mail: starr@kshs.org 49500

Kentucky Association of Museums, POB 9, Murray, KY 42071-0009 - T: (270) 762-3052, Fax: (270) 762-3920 49501

Louisiana Association of Museums, 1609 Moreland Av, Baton Rouge, LA 70808-1173 - T: (225) 383-6800, Fax: (225) 383-6880 49502

Maine Association of Museums, 37 Community Dr, Augusta, ME 04330 - T: (207) 623-8428, Fax: (207) 626-5949 49503

Maryland Association of History Museums, POB 1806, Annapolis, MD 21404-1806 - T: (301) 809-9877, Fax: (301) 809-9878, E-mail: info@mahm.org, Internet: www.mahm.org 49504

Michigan Museums Association, POB 10067, Lansing, MI 48901-0067 - T: (517) 482-4055, Fax: (517) 482-7997, E-mail: ashby.ann@acd.net 49505

Mid-Atlantic Association of Museums, 1 E Chase St, Ste 1124, Baltimore, MD 21202 - T: (410) 223-1194, Fax: (410) 223-2773, E-mail: info@midatlanticmuseums.org, Internet: www.midatlanticmuseums.org 49506

Minnesota Association of Museums, POB 14825, Minneapolis, MN 55414-0825 - T: (612) 624-0089, Fax: (612) 626-7704, E-mail: davis136@tc.umn.edu 49507

Mississippi Museums Association, 640 S Canal St, Box E, Natchez, MS 39120 - T: (601) 446-6502, Fax: (601) 446-6503 49508

Missouri Museums Association, 3218 Gladstone Blvd, Kansas City, MO 64123-1199 - T: (816) 483-8300 49509

Mountain-Plains Museums Association, POB 8321, Durango, CO 81301-0203 - T: (970) 259-7866, E-mail: mpma@frontier.net 49510

Museum Association of Arizona, POB 63902, Phoenix, AZ 85082-3902 - T: (602) 966-9680, E-mail: ann.alger@asu.edu 49511

Museum Association of Montana, c/o Glacier National Park, West Glacier, MT 59936 - T: (406) 888-7936, Fax: (406) 888-7808, E-mail: deirdre_-shaw@nps.gov, Internet: www.montana.edu/~mtmuseum 49512

Museum Association of New York, 265 River St, Troy, NY 12180 - T: (518) 273-3400, Fax: (518) 273-3416, E-mail: info@manyonline.org, Internet: www.manyonline.org 49513

Museum Computer Network, National Office, 1550 S Coast Hwy, S 201, Laguna Beach, CA 92651 - T: (877) MCN-3800, Fax: (949) 376-3456, E-mail: mmisunas@sfmoma.org, Internet: www.mcn.edu 49514

Museum Education Roundtable, 621 Pennsylvania Av SE, Washington, DC 20003 - T: (202) 547-8378, Fax: (202) 547-8344, E-mail: merorg@msn.com, Internet: www.mer-online.org 49515

Museum Trustee Association, 2025 M St NW, Ste 800, Washington, DC 20036-3309 - T: (202) 367-1180, Fax: (202) 367-2180, E-mail: amanda_oehlke@dc.sba.com, Internet: www.mta-hq.org 49516

Museums Alaska, POB 242323, Anchorage, AK 99524 - T: (907) 243-4714, Fax: (907) 243-4714, E-mail: matthews@alaska.net 49517

Nebraska Museums Association, 208 16th St, Aurora, NE 68818-3009 - T: (402) 694-4032, Fax: (402) 694-4035 49518

New England Museum Association, c/o Boston National Historic Park, Charlestown Navy Yard, Boston, MA 02129 - T: (617) 242-2283, Fax: (617) 241-5794 49519

New Jersey Association of Museums, POB 877, Newark, NJ 07101-0877 - T: (888) 356-6526, Fax: (973) 748-6607 49520

New Mexico Association of Museums, POB 5800, Albuquerque, NM 87185-1490 - T: (505) 284-3232, Fax: (505) 284-3244, E-mail: jkwalth@sandia.gov 49521

North Carolina Museums Council, POB 2603, Raleigh, NC 27602 - T: (336) 767-6730, Fax: (336) 661-1777 49522

Northeast Mississippi Museums Association, POB 993, Corinth, MS 38835 - T: (662) 287-3120, E-mail: nemma@tsixrhodes.com 49523

Northern California Association of Museums, California State University, Chico, CA 95929 - T: (916) 898-5861, Fax: (916) 898-6824, E-mail: Kjohnson@savax.csuchico.edu 49524

Ohio Museums Association, 567 E Hudson St, Columbus, OH 43211 - T: (614) 298-2030, Fax: (614) 298-2068, E-mail: ohmuseassn@juno.com 49525

Oklahoma Museums Association, 2100 NE 52nd St, Oklahoma City, OK 73111 - T: (405) 424-7757, Fax: (405) 424-1407, E-mail: oma@ionet.net 49526

Oregon Museums Association, POB 1718, Portland, OR 97207 - T: (503) 823-3623, Fax: (503) 823-3619, E-mail: pkdanc@ci.portland.or.us 49527

Pennsylvania Federation of Museums and Historical Organizations, POB 1026, Harrisburg, PA 17108-1026 - T: (717) 787-3253, Fax: (717) 772-4698, E-mail: phmc.state.pa.us 49528

Rhode Island Museum Network, 58 Walcott St, Pawtucket, RI 02860 49529

Small Museums Association, POB 1425, Clinton, MD 20735 - Internet: www.s-mallmuseum.org 49530

South Carolina Federation of Museums, POB 100107, Columbia, SC 29202 - T: (803) 898-4925, Fax: (803) 898-4969, E-mail: scfm@museum.state.sc.us 49531

Southeastern Museums Conference, 412 N 4th St, Ste 250, Baton Rouge, LA 70821, mail addr: POB 3494, Baton Rouge, LA 70821 - T: (225) 383-5042, Fax: (225) 343-8669, E-mail: SEMCdirect@aol.com, Internet: www.SEMCdirect.net 49532

Tennessee Association of Museums, 200 Hyder Hill, Piney Flats, TN 37686 - T: (615) 538-7396 49533

Texas Association of Museums, 3939 Bee Caves Rd, Bldg A, Ste 1-B, Austin, TX 78746 - T: (512) 328-6812, Fax: (512) 327-9775, E-mail: tam@io.com, Internet: www.io.com/~tam 49534

United States Federation of Friends of Museums, 2 Gittings Av, Baltimore, MD 21212 49535

United States-International Council on Monuments and Sites, 401 F St, Ste 331, Washington, DC 20001 - T: (202) 842-1866, Fax: (202) 842-1861, E-mail: edelage@usicomos.org, Internet: www.u-sicomos.org 49536

Unites States National Committee of the ICOM, c/o American Association of Museums, 1575 Eye St NW, Ste 400, Washington, DC 20005 - T: (202) 218-7681, Fax: (202) 289-6578, E-mail: aam-icom@aam-us.org, Internet: www.aam-us.org/international 49537

Utah Museums Association, POB 2077, Salt Lake City, UT 84110-2077 - T: (435) 654-4092, E-mail: charlotte@utahmuseums.org, Internet: www.utahmuseums.org 49538

Vermont Museum and Gallery Alliance, POB 489, Woodstock, VT 05091 - T: (802) 457-2671 49539

Virginia Association of Museums, 2800 Grove Av, Richmond, VA 23221 - T: (804) 649-8261, Fax: (804) 649-8262, E-mail: mcarlock@va-museums.org, Internet: www.va-museums.org 49540

Volunteer Committees of Art Museum, One Collins Diboll Circle, New Orleans, LA 70179, mail addr: c/o New Orleans Museum of Art, POB 19123, New Orleans, LA 70179-0123 - T: (504) 737-6301, Fax: (504) 738-5103 49541

Washington Museum Association, POB 5817, Factoria Station, Bellevue, WA 98006 - T: (360) 466-3365, Fax: (360) 466-1611, E-mail: wma@harbornet.com 49542

Western Museums Association, 655 Thirteenth St, Ste 301, Oakland, CA 94612, mail addr: POB 13314-578, Oakland, CA 94661 - T: (510) 238-9700, Fax: (510) 238-9701, E-mail: director@-westmuse.org, Internet: www.westmuse.org 49543

Wisconsin Federation of Museums, 700 N 12th St, Wausau, WI 54403 - T: (715) 845-7010, Fax: (715) 845-7103 49544

Uzbekistan

ICOM Uzbekistan, c/o Museum of the History of Termurids, Amir Temur ul 1, 700000 Taškent - T: (071) 21320211, E-mail: unesco@-natcom.org.uz 49545

Venezuela

ICOM Venezuela, c/o Institut for Cultural Heritage, Apdo 17376, Caracas 1014-A - T: (0212) 4836178, Fax: 4837653, E-mail: mtoledo@reacciun.ve 49546

Vietnam

ICOM Viet Nam, c/o Dept. of National Cultural Heritage of Viet Nam, Ministry of Culture and Information, 51-53 Ngo Quyen St, Ha Noi - T: (04) 9437611, Fax: 9439929, E-mail: Nchdvn@hn.vnn.vn 49547

Zambia

ICOM Zambia, c/o Livingstone Museum, POB 60498, Livingstone - T: (03) 324427/28, Fax: 324509, E-mail: livmus@zamnet.zm 49548

Zimbabwe

ICOM Zimbabwe, c/o National History Museum, POB AC 192, Bulawayo - T: (09) 230046, Fax: 234019, E-mail: natmuse@telconet.co.zw 49549

National Museums and Monuments of Zimbabwe, 107 Rotten Row, Harare, mail addr: POB CY 1485, Harare - T: (04) 752876, Fax: 753-085, E-mail: natmus@utande.co.zw, Internet: www.zim-heritage.co.zw 49550

Southern African Development Community Association of Museums and Monuments, c/o National Museums and Monuments of Zimbabwe, POB CY 1485, Harare - T: (04) 752876, Fax: 753-085, E-mail: natmus@baobab.cszim.co.zw 49551

Alphabetical
Index to Museums

100th Bomb Group Memorial Museum, Dickleburgh 38729
The 100th Meridian Museum, Cozad 42686
103rd Ohio Volunteer Infantry Memorial, Sheffield Lake 47591
1078 Gallery, Chico 42369
12 Vancouver Service Battalion Museum, Richmond 06259
150 ans de Couture, Aix-les-Bains 10258
15th Field Artillery Regiment Museum, Vancouver 06664
1708 Gallery, Richmond 46868
1796 Bantry French Armada Exhibition Centre, Bantry 22374
The 1811 Old Lincoln County Jail and 1839 Jailer's House Museum, Wiscasset 48714
1859 Jail-Marshal's Home and Museum, Independence 44199
1866 Battle of Chlum Memorial, Všestary 08729
1890 House-Museum and Center for Victorian Arts, Cortland 42652
19 May Museum, Samsun 37775
19 Mayıs Müzesi, Samsun 37775
19. Sajandi Tartu Linnakodaniku Muuseum, Tartu 09373
1910 Boomtown, Saskatoon 06393
1914 Plant City High School Community Exhibition, Plant City 46542
198 Gallery, London 39563
26 Martyrs Museum, Nagasaki 26542
26th Field Artillery Regiment Museum, Brandon 05115
390th Bomb Group Memorial Air Museum and British Resistance Organisation Museum, Framlingham 39013
3M Art Collection, Saint Paul 47150
4-H Schoolhouse Museum, Clarion 42425
448th Bomb Group Memorial Museum, Seething 40464
45th Infantry Division Museum, Oklahoma City 46110
4711-Museum, Köln 18127
4th Infantry Division Museum, Fort Hood 43397
50er Jahre Erlebnisswelt, Zusmarshausen 20771
75. Yıl Tarsus Culture Center, Mersin 37758
75. Yıl Tarsus Kültür Merkezi, Mersin 37758
82nd Airborne Division War Memorial Museum, Fort Bragg 43371
A. Chaplygin Apartment Museum, Sankt-Peterburg 33450
A. Kolcov Museum, Voronež 33732
A. Kuindgi Apartment Museum, Sankt-Peterburg 33452
A. Kusnetcov Regional Museum of Local History and Nature, Čita 32752
A. Paul Weber-Museum, Ratzeburg 19498
A. Schiiwesch Musée Rural, Binsfeld 27544
A. Sohos Museum, Tinos 21197
A Soldier's Life, Newcastle-upon-Tyne 40032
A Space, Toronto 06558
A.A. Chernov Geological Museum of the Institute of Geology of the Komi Scientific Center of Ural Branch of the Russian Academy of Sciences, Syktyvkar 33572
A.A. Kiselev Museum, Tuapse 33621
A.A. Shogentsukov Memorial Museum, Nalčik 33196
A.A. Vaneev Memorial House Museum, Ermakovskoe 32797
Aabenraa Museum, Aabenraa 08760
AAF Museum, Washington 48330
Aalborg Historiske Museum, Aalborg 08762
Aalholm Automobil Museum, Nysted 09003
Aaltense Oorlogs- en Verzetscollectie 1940-1945, Aalten 28794
Aaragon Museum, Ilupeju 30345
Aardewerkvermuseum Petrus Pegout, Noordbroek 29640
Aargauer Kunsthaus, Aarau 36424
Aaronson House, Zichron Yaakov 22789
Aasiaat Katersugaasiviat Museum, Aasiaat 21228
Aasland Museum Taxidermy, Cranbrook 05286
Aavik's Memorial Museum, Kuressaare 09335
Aavikute Majamuuseum, Kuressaare 09335
A.B. Goldenveyser Museum Apartment, Moskva 33124
Abadan Museum, Abadan 22229
Abai Commemorative Literary Republican Museum, Semey 27092
Abashiri Kyodo Bijutsukan, Abashiri 26083
Abashiri Kyodo Hakubutsukan, Abashiri 26084
Abashiri Municipal Art Museum, Abashiri 26083
Abashiri Municipal Museum, Abashiri 26084
The Abbasid Palace Museum, Baghdad 22341
Abbaye aux Hommes, Caen 10978
Abbaye de Cluny, Cluny 11336
Abbaye de Flaran, Valence-sur-Baise 15052
Abbaye de Saint-Amand de Coly, Saint-Amand-de-Coly 14095
Abbaye Saint-André, Villeneuve-lès-Avignon 15228
Abbe Museum at Downtown, Bar Harbor 41496
Abbe Museum at Sieur de Monts Spring, Bar Harbor 41497
Abbey and Stones Museum, Margam 39909
Abbey House Museum, Leeds 39440
Abbey Museum of Art and Archaeology, Caboolture 00870
Abbey of Bellapais, Girne 08224
Abbey of Flaran, Valence-sur-Baise 15052
Abbey of Pannonhalma Collection, Pannonhalma 21497
Abbey Pumping Station Museum, Leicester 39458
Abbey Visitor Centre, Bury Saint Edmunds 38414
Abbeydale Industrial Hamlet, Sheffield 40481
Abbot Hall Art Gallery, Kendal 39336
Abbot's House, Arbroath 38010
Abbotsford House, Melrose 39931
Abby Aldrich Rockefeller Folk Art Museum, Williamsburg 48624
ABC Architectuurcentrum Haarlem, Haarlem 29321
ABC-Galerie, Ansfelden 01675
Abdeen Palace Museum, Cairo 09252
Abdij Museum, Sint-Truiden 03747
Abegg-Stiftung, Riggisberg 37064
Abel Tasman Kabinet, Lutjegast 29553
Abelardo Díaz Alfaro Pink House, Caguas 32366
Abenteuermuseum Saarbrücken - Sammlung Heinz Rox-Schulz, Saarbrücken 19722
Aberconwy House, Conwy 38626
Aberdeen Art Gallery, Aberdeen 37929
Aberdeen Arts Centre, Aberdeen 37930
Aberdeen Maritime Museum, Aberdeen 37931
Aberdeen University Natural History Museum, Aberdeen 37932
Aberdeen University Natural Philosophy Museum, Aberdeen 37933
Aberdeenshire Farming Museum, Mintlaw 39967
Aberdona Gallery, Alloa 37978
Abergavenny Museum, Abergavenny 37948
Abernethy Museum, Abernethy 37950
Abernethy Nature Heritage Museum, Abernethy 04965
Aberseer Heimathaus, Strobl 02707
Abertillery Museum, Abertillery 37951
Aberystwyth Arts Centre, Aberystwyth 37952
Aberystwyth Yesterday, Aberystwyth 37953
Abgineh Va Sofalineh, Teheran 22287
Abguss Sammlung antiker Plastik, Berlin 15907
Abhai Smarak Panchal Sangrahalaya, Bareilly 21707
Abingdon Museum, Abingdon 37957
Abington Art Center, Jenkintown 44333
Abington Museum, Northampton 40081
Abkar Museum, Teheran 22288
ABM-Utvikling, Oslo 49315
Aboa Vetus - Arkeologis-historiallinen Museo, Turku 10117
Abony Lajos Falumúzeum, Abony 21305
Abony Lajos Village Museum, Abony 21305
Aboriginal Art Museum, Utrecht 29893
Abraham Krinizi Museum, RamatGan 22737
Abraham Lincoln Birthplace, Hodgenville 44046
Abraham Lincoln Museum, Harrogate 43936
Abraham Ojanperän Museo, Liminka 09786
Abraham's Mosterdmakerij, Eenrum 29200
Abramov Memorial and Literature Museum, Verkola 33682
Abramtsevo Estate Museum, Abramcevo 32629
Abri Pataud, Les Eyzies-de-Tayac-Sireuil 12536
Abri Préhistorique de Laugerie Basse, Les Eyzies-de-Tayac-Sireuil 12537
Abrons Arts Center, New York 45751
ABSA Group Museum, Johannesburg 34266
Abteilung Handwerk und dörfliches Leben des Heimatmuseums Neu-Ulm, Neu-Ulm 19006
Abu Ali Ibn Sina Memorial Museum, Afčona 48828
Abu Bakar Royal Museum, Johor Bahru 27624
A.C. Gilbert's Discovery Village, Salem 47206
A.C. White Gallery, Bloemfontein 34181
Academia Brasileira de Arte, São Paulo 04480
Academia Brasileira de Letras, Rio de Janeiro 04313
Academic Museum of Medicine, Poznań 31897
Academician Doncho Kostov House-Museum, Lokorsko 04725
Academician F. Chernyshev Central Scientific-Researching Geological-Prospecting Museum, Sankt-Peterburg 33383
Academisch Historisch Museum van de Universiteit Leiden, Leiden 29517
Academy Art Museum, Easton 43066
The Academy Gallery, Beverly Hills 41675
Academy Gallery, New Orleans 45718
Academy Hall Museum of the Rocky Hill Historical Society, Rocky Hill 46980
Academy of Fine Arts Museum, Kolkata 21896
Academy of Natural Sciences of Philadelphia Museum, Philadelphia 46386
Academy of Sciences Museum of Zoology, Sankt-Peterburg 33495
Academy of Spherical Arts, Toronto 06559
Acadia University Art Gallery, Wolfville 06857
The Accokeek Foundation, Accokeek 41060
Accordeon en Harmonica Museum, Malden 29576
Ace Art, Winnipeg 06817
Ace of Clubs House, Texarkana 47990
Acervo Artístico Cultural dos Palácios do Governo, São Paulo 04481
Acervo Didático de Invertebrados I e II, São Paulo 04482
Acervo Didático de Vertebrados, São Paulo 04483
Achamenian Museum, Shiraz 22280
Acharya Jogesh Chandra Purakirti Bhavan, Bishnupur 21731
Achter de Zuilen, Overveen 29708
Achterhoeks Museum 1940-1945, Hengelo, Gelderland 29397
Ackerbürgermuseum, Reichenbach, Oberlausitz 19545
Ackerbürgermuseum Haus Leck, Grebenstein 17380
Ackland Art Museum, Chapel Hill 42196
Acland Coal Mine Museum, Acland 00697
ACME Art Gallery, Columbus 42585
Acorn Hall House Museum, Morristown 45504
Acropolis Museum, Athinai 20871
Acton Scott Historic Working Farm, Church Stretton 38581
Açude Museum, Rio de Janeiro 04314
A.D. Buck Museum of Natural History and Science, Tonkawa 48029
A.D. German Warehouse, Richland Center 46856
A.D. Sakharov Appartement Museum, Nižnij Novgorod 33216
Adachi Museum of Art, Yasugi 27009
Adalbert-Stifter-Haus, Linz 02225
Adam Chętnik Memorial Kurpic Region Open Air Museum, Nowogród 31832
Adam East Museum Art Center, Moses Lake 45519
Adam Mickiewicz Museum at Śmiełów, Żerków 32217
Adam-Ries-Museum, Annaberg-Buchholz 15496
Adam Thoroughgood House, Virginia Beach 48243
Adam Wodziczko Natural History Museum of Wolin National Park, Międzyzdroje 31804
Ādama Alkšņa Memoriālais Muzejs, Rūjiena 27446
Ādams Alksnis Memorial Museum, Rūjiena 27446
Adams County Historical Museum, Decatur 42835
Adams County Historical Society Museum, Gettysburg 43661
Adams County Historical Society Museum, Lind 44802
Adams County Museum, Brighton 41899
Adams House, Deadwood 42819
Adams Igloo Wildlife Museum, Smithers 06461
Adams Museum, Deadwood 42820
Adams National Historical Park, Quincy 46763
Adams Old Stone Grist Mill, Bellows Falls 41605
Adams State College Luther Bean Museum, Alamosa 41079
Adamson-Eric Museum, Tallinn 09354
Adan E. Treganza Anthropology Museum, San Francisco 47302
Adana Devlet Güzel Sanatlar Galerisi, Adana 37597
Adana Müzesi, Adana 37598
Adana Museum, Adana 37598
Adana State Gallery, Adana 37597
Adare Trinity Museum, Adare 22358
Addington - Ryde House of Heritage, Ryde 01430
Addison Gallery of American Art, Andover 41207
Adelaide Central Gallery, Norwood 01334
Adelaide City Council Civic Collection, Adelaide 00702
Adelaide Gaol, Thebarton 01530
Adelaide House Museum, Alice Springs 00732
Adelaide Hunter Hoodless Homestead, Saint George 06318
Adelaide Lithuanian Museum and Archives, Norwood 01335
Adelaide Masonic Centre Museum, Adelaide 00703
Adelaide River Railway Heritage Precinct, Adelaide River 00718
Adelhausermuseum, Natur- und Völkerkunde, Freiburg im Breisgau 17105
Adena State Memorial, Chillicothe 42378
Adirondack Center Museum, Elizabethtown 43134
Adirondack Museum, Blue Mountain Lake 41758
Adıyaman Müzesi, Adıyaman 37600
Adıyaman Museum, Adıyaman 37600
Adjutant General's Corps Museum, Winchester 40885
Adler Museum of Medicine, Johannesburg 34267
Adlerskij Kraevedčeskij Muzej - Muzej Istorii Adlerskogo Rajona, Soči 33539
Admiral Digby Museum, Digby 05330
Admiral Nimitz National Museum of the Pacific War, Fredericksburg 43531
Adolf-Dietrich-Haus, Berlingen 36538
Ādolfa Alunāna Memoriālais Muzejs, Jelgava 27364
Adsmore Museum, Princeton 46697
Ady Endre Emlékmúzeum, Budapest 21322
Adygean Republican Museum, Majkop 33003
Adygejskij Respublikanskij Kraevedčeskij Muzej, Majkop 33003
A.E. Seaman Mineral Museum, Houghton 44113
Äänekosken Kaupunginmuseo, Äänekoski 09410
Äänekoski Town Museum, Äänekoski 09410
Æbelholt Museum, Hillerød 08872
Ädelfors Gruvmuseum, Holsbybrunn 35963
Die Ägayrischen Gewölbe, Viechtach 20306
Aegean Maritime Museum, Mykonos 21076
Ägyptische Sammlung der Universität/ Museum Schloß Hohentübingen, Tübingen 20220
Ägyptisches Museum der Universität Leipzig - Interim, Leipzig 18382
Ägyptisches Museum und Papyrussammlung, Berlin 15908
Ähtärin Kotiseutumuseo, Ähtäri 09411
Aera Memorial Museum, San Pablo 31441
Ærø Museum, Ærøskøbing 08764
Aero Space Museum of Calgary, Calgary 05159
Aeronautical Museum, Telde 35522
Aeronauticum - Deutsches Luftschiff- und Marinefliegermuseum Nordholz, Nordholz 19123
Aérospatiale, Toulouse 14935
Afdeling Nuttige en Fraaie Handwerken, Uithuizermeeden 29889
Affiche Museum Hoorn, Hoorn 29441
Affresco di Piero della Francesca, Monterchi 24540
Åfjord Bygdetun, Åfjord 30369
Africa Museum, Seoul 27222
Africa-Museum, Tervuren 03772
African-American Historical and Cultural Society Collection, San Francisco 47303
African American Museum, Cleveland 42463
African American Museum, Dallas 42743
African-American Museum at Oakland, Oakland 46059
The African American Museum in Philadelphia, Philadelphia 46387
African American Museums Association, Chicago 49459
African Art Centre, Durban 34223
African Art Museum of Maryland, Columbia 42548
African Art Museum of the S.M.A. Fathers, Tenafly 47979
African Herbalist Shops, Johannesburg 34268
African Heritage Museum, San Juan 32397
African Safari and Veteran Car Museum, Dvůr Králové nad Labem 08336
Africana Museum, Mariannhill 34305
Africana Museum, Monrovia 27498
Afrika Centrum, Cadier en Keer 29050
Afrika Museum, Berg en Dal 28978
Afrika-Museum, Bergen, Kreis Celle 15893
Afrika-Museum, Zug 37424
Afrikaans Language Museum, Paarl 34320
Afrikaans Music Museum, Bloemfontein 34182
Afrikaanse Taalmuseum, Paarl 34320
Afrikahaus Museum und Nold-Namibia-Bibliothek, Sebnitz 19907
Afro-American Cultural Center, Charlotte 42236
Afro-American Historical Society Museum, Jersey City 44338
Afrodisiyas Müzesi, Geyre Köyü Karasu Aydın 37684
Afval-Museum, Zwolle 30082
Afyon Arkeoloji Müzesi, Afyon 37601
Afyon Devlet Güzel Sanatlar Galerisi, Afyon 37602
Afyon Etnografya Müzesi, Afyon 37603
Afyon State Gallery, Afyon 37602
A.G. Malyshkin Memorial Museum, Mokšan 33018
Aga Khan Museum of Islamic Arts, Marawi 31399
Aga Village, Nå 30697
Agassiz-Harrison Historical Museum, Agassiz 04967
Agathonos Monastery Collection, Ypati 21220
Agatunet, Nå 30697
Agawa Bay Exhibition Centre, Wawa 06758
Agder Naturmuseum, Kristiansand 30611
The Age of Steam Railroad Museum, Dallas 42744
Agecroft Hall, Richmond 46869
Agei Saranda Monastery, Spárti 21163
Agensteinhaus und Simmentaler Hausweg, Erlenbach im Simmental 36685
Agfa Photo-Historama, Köln 18128
Agharkar Museum, Allahabad 21688
Agia Lovra Monastery, Kalavryta 20987
Aginskij Okružnoj Kraevedčeskij Muzej im. G. Cybikova, Aginskoe 32630
Agion Panton Church Museum, Metéora 21067
Agios Andreas Monastery Museum, Agios Andreas 20807
Agios Stephanos Monastery, Metéora 21068
Agios Vissarion Monastery, Trikala 21201
Agnes Etherington Art Centre, Kingston 05672
Agnes Gallery, Birmingham 41703
Agnes Jamieson Gallery, Minden 05856
Agnes-Miegel-Haus, Bad Nenndorf 15702
Agora Museum, Athinai 20844
Agrar- und Forstmuseum, Wittenburg 20626
Agrar- und Freilichtmuseum, Crimmitschau 16513
Agrarhistorisches Museum, Schlepzig 19792
Agrarisch en Wagenmuseum, De Waal 29072
Agrarisch Museum Westerhem, Middenbeemster 29598
Agrarmuseum, Greußen 17396
Agrarmuseum Wandlitz, Wandlitz 20390
Agricultural Collection in the Castle of Kačina, Kutná Hora 08440
Agricultural Heritage Museum, Hamilton 30172
Agricultural Implements Museum, Somero 10047
Agricultural Museum, Cairo 09253
Agricultural Museum, Coate 38601
Agricultural Museum, Faisalabad 31017
Agricultural Museum, Jasin 27623
Agricultural Museum, Liuksiala 09791
Agricultural Museum, Miyazaki, Miyazaki-ken 26510
Agricultural Museum, Sipoo 10039
Agricultural Museum, Yangon 28746
Agricultural Museum at Stone Mills, La Fargeville 44540
Agricultural Museum Brook, Dover 38763
Agricultural Museum of Entre Douro e Mino, Vila do Conde 32357
Agricultural Museum of Jeollanam-do, Samho 27219
Agricultural Museum of New Brunswick, Sussex 06521
Agricultural Museum Ohrada, Ohrada 08514
L'Agriculture au Fil du Temps, Maniquerville 12790
L'Agriculture Bressane Musée, Saint-Germain-du-Bois 14238
Agriculture Museum, Imphal 21849
Agropolis Muséum, Montpellier 13118
Agrotechnorama, Ettenhausen 36694
Aguélimuseet, Sala 36171
Agung Rai Museum of Art, Ubud 22212
Ah-Tah-Thi-Ki Museum, Big Cypress Seminole Indian Reservation 41679
Ahlat Açık Hava Müzesi, Ahlat 37604
Ahler Kråm - Volkskundliche Sammlung, Partenstein 19351
Aholan Talomuseo, Keitele 09646
Ahsan Manzil Museum, Dhaka 03082
Ahtausmuseo, Kotka 09699

Åhus Museum, Åhus 35788
A.I. Koslov Museum of Geology and Mineralogy of the Far East State Technical University, Vladivostok 33697
Aichi-ken Bijutsukan, Nagoya, Aichi 26563
Aichi-ken Toji Siryokan, Seto 26739
Aichi Prefectural Ceramics Museum, Seto 26739
Aichi Prefectural Museum of Art, Nagoya, Aichi 26563
Aigantighe Art Museum, Timaru 30264
Aikawa Archaeological Museum, Isesaki 26257
Aikawa Folk Museum and Exhibition Hall of Folk Crafts, Aikawa 26087
Aikawa Kokokan, Isesaki 26257
Aiken County Historical Museum, Aiken 41068
Aiken Thoroughbred Racing Hall of Fame and Museum, Aiken 41069
Ainaži Naval College Museum, Ainaži 27326
Ainažu Jūrskolas Memoriālais Muzejs, Ainaži 27326
Aine Art Museum, Tornio 10113
Aineen Taidemuseo, Tornio 10113
Aineh va Roshananal Museum, Yazd 22334
Ainola, Järvenpää 09571
Ainsley House, Campbell 42070
Ainu Museum, Sapporo 26708
Air Classic Museum of Aviation, Sugar Grove 47869
Air Force Armament Museum, Eglin Air Force Base 43101
Air Force Flight Test Center Museum, Edwards Air Force Base 43096
Air Force Heritage Museum and Air Park, Winnipeg 06818
Air Force Museum, Christchurch 30121
Air Force Museum, Delhi 21762
Air Force Museum, Ha Noi 48970
Air Force Museum, Teheran 22289
Air Gallery, New York 45752
Air Heritage Museum of Santa Barbara/Goleta, Goleta 43719
Air Museum, Carrara San Giorgio 23360
Air Power Park and Museum, Hampton 43894
Air Victory Museum, Medford 45218
Airborne and Special Operations Museum, Fayetteville 43309
Airborne Forces Museum, Aldershot 37965
Airborne Museum Hartenstein, Oosterbeek 29666
Airmen Memorial Museum, Suitland 47872
Airport Gallery 1 & 2, Frankfurt am Main 17030
Airport Museum, Cairo 09254
Airpower Museum, Ottumwa 46221
Aitihasic Puratatva Sangrahalaya, Delhi 21763
Aitonevan Turvemuseo, Kihniö 09663
Aître Saint-Saturnin, Blois 10769
Aiud Museum of History, Aiud 32427
Aiud Natural History Museum, Aiud 32426
Aiwen e Rifat Museum and Art Gallery, Karachi 31027
Aizkraukle History and Art Museum, Aizkraukle 27328
Aizkraukles Vēstures un Mākslas Muzejs, Aizkraukle 27328
A.J. Snyder Estate, Rosendale 47007
Ajax Museum, Amsterdam 28834
Ajtte Museum, Jokkmokk 35981
Ájtte - Svenskt Fjäll- och Samemuseum, Jokkmokk 35982
Ájtte - Swedish Mountain and Sami Museum, Jokkmokk 35982
A.K.A. Gallery, Saskatoon 06394
Akademie der Künste, Berlin 15909
Akademie der Künste, Berlin 15910
Akademisches Kunstmuseum der Universität, Bonn 16225
Akademisches Münzkabinett, Jena 17937
Akadomari-mura Folk Museum, Akadomari 26091
Akama-jingu Treasure House, Shimonoseki 26750
Akanes Folk Museum, Akranes 21618
Akaroa Museum, Akaroa 30092
Akashi Municipal Museum of Astronomy, Akashi 26092
Akashi-shiritsu Tenmon Kagakukan, Akashi 26092
Åkers Hembygdsmuseum, Strängnäs 36300
Akershus Fylkesmuseum, Strømmen 30902
Akershus Regional Museum, Strømmen 30902
Akita Daigaku Kozangakubu Fuzok u Kogyo Hakubutsukan, Akita 26093
Akita-kenritsu Hakubutsukan, Akita 26094
Akita-kenritsu Kindai Bijutsukan, Yokote 27028
Akita Museum of Modern Art, Yokote 27028
Akita Prefectural Art Gallery, Akita 26095
Akita Prefectural Museum, Akita 26094
Akita Senshu Museum of Art, Akita 26096
Akiyoshidai Kagaku Hakubutsukan, Shuuhou 26770
Akiyoshidai Museum of Natural History, Shuuhou 26770
Akko Municipal Museum, Akko 22567
Akpol Museum, Semarang 22186
Akron Art Museum, Akron 41072
Akshaya Kumar Maitreya Museum, Siliguri 22025
Aksum Archaeology Museum, Aksum 09403
Akta Lakota Museum, Chamberlain 42182
Aktion Museum M, Mistelbach an der Zaya 02300
Aktionsforum Praterinsel, München 18822
Aktives Museum Südwestfalen, Siegen 19947
Akureyri Museum, Akureyri 21620
Akwesasne Museum, Hogansburg 44047
Al-Ain Museum, Al-Ain 37915
Ål Bygdemuseum, Ål 30371
A.L. Durov House-Museum, Voronež 33729
A.L. Fetterman Educational Museum, Fort Valley 43466
Al-Karak Museum for Archaeology and Folklore, Al-Karak 27041
Al Kassaba Museum Thafer al Masri Foundation, Nablus 31072
Al Khor Museum, Al Khor 32413
Al Mada'in Museum, Baghdad 22342
Al-Mahatah - Sharjah Aviation Museum, Sharjah 37919
Al-Mansora Museum Dar-ibn-Luqman, Daqahlia 09291
Al Mawsil Museum, Nineveh 22355
Al-Mukalla Museum, Al-Mukalla 49009
Al-Muntaza Palace Museum, Alexandria 09235
Al Shaheed Monument and Museum, Baghdad 22343
Al Sulaimaniya Museum, Sulaimaniya 22357
Al Wakra Museum, AL Wakra 32414
Al Zubara Fort, Doha 32415
Alabama-Coushatta Indian Museum, Livingston 44834
Alabama History Museum, Montgomery 45465
Alabama Mining Museum, Dora 42958
Alabama Museum of Natural History, Tuscaloosa 48112
Alabama Museums Association, Tuscaloosa 49460
Alabama Music Hall of Fame, Tuscumbia 48119
Alacahöyük Arkeoloji Müzesi, Alacahöyük 37607
Alamance Battleground, Burlington 42003
Alamannenmuseum, Weingarten, Württemberg 20478
Alamannenmuseum Ellwangen, Ellwangen 16834
Alambee Auto and Folk Museum, Echuca 01001
The Alamo, San Antonio 47243
Alamo Township Museum-John E. Gray Memorial, Kalamazoo 44376
Alan Macpherson House, Napanee 05963
Åland Art Museum, Mariehamn 09814
Aland Hunting and Fishing Museum, Eckerö 09424
Åland Maritime Museum, Mariehamn 09816
Ålands Jakt och Fiskemuseum, Eckerö 09424
Ålands Konstmuseum, Mariehamn 09814
Ålands Museum, Mariehamn 09815
Ålands Sjöfartsmuseum, Mariehamn 09816
Alapítvány Érc és Ásványbányászati Múzeum, Rudabánya 21519
Alaska Aviation Heritage Museum, Anchorage 41196
Alaska Centennial Center for the Arts, Fairbanks 43257
Alaska Indian Arts, Haines 43869
Alaska Museum of Natural History, Eagle River 43034
Alaska State Museum, Juneau 44368
Alatornion Pitäjämuseo, Tornio 10114
Albadia Museum, Osafia 22726
Albany Civil Rights Movement Museum, Albany 41080
Albany Historical Museum, Sabetha 47044
Albany Institute of History and Art, Albany 41083
Albany Museum, Grahamstown 34249
Albany Museum of Art, Albany 41081
Albany Regional Museum, Albany 41090
Albany Residency Museum, Albany 00721
Albatrossmuseet, Romakloster 36162
Albergo-Museo Atelier sul Mare, Castel di Tusa 23389
Alberni Valley Museum, Port Alberni 06148
Albert Edelfeldt's Atelier Museum, Porvoo 09949
Albert Edelfeltin Ateljeemuseo, Porvoo 09949
Albert Engström-Museerna, Grisslehamn 35931
Albert Kersten GeoCentre, Broken Hill 00845
Albert-König-Museum, Unterlüß 20269
Albert-Schweitzer-Gedenk- und Begegnungsstätte, Weimar, Thüringen 20454
Alberta Art Foundation Collection, Edmonton 05367
Alberta Association of Registered Nurses Museum, Edmonton 05368
Alberta Aviation Museum, Edmonton 05369
Alberta Beach and District Museum, Alberta Beach 04970
Alberta Central Railway Museum, Wetaskiwin 06777
Alberta Forestry Service Museum, Hinton 05599
Alberta Hospital Museum, Ponoka 06145
Alberta Museums Association, Edmonton 49090
Alberta Railway Museum, Edmonton 05370
Alberta Sports Hall of Fame and Museum, Red Deer 06220
Alberta Wheat Pool Grain Museum, Calgary 05160
Albertfalvai Helytörténeti Gyűjtemény és Iskolamúzeum, Budapest 21323
Albertina, Wien 02830
Albertland and Districts Museum, Wellsford 30312
Alberton, Auckland 30101
Alberton Museum, Alberton 04972
Albgaumuseum, Ettlingen 16974
The Albin O. Kuhn Gallery, Baltimore 41447
Albion Academy Historical Museum, Edgerton 43084
Albrecht-Daniel-Thaer-Gedenkstätte-Landesausstellung, Reichenow 19547
Albrecht-Dürer-Gesellschaft, Nürnberg 19132
Albrecht-Dürer-Haus, Nürnberg 19133
Albrecht-Kemper Museum of Art, Saint Joseph 47104
Albrechtsburg, Meißen 18689
Albright-Knox Art Gallery, Buffalo 41981
The Albuquerque Museum of Art and History, Albuquerque 41099
Albury Regional Art Gallery, Albury 00728
Albury Regional Museum, Albury 00729
Alcan Aluminium Corporate Art Collection, Montréal 05886
Alcázar, Sevilla 35471
Alcázar de los Reyes Cristianos, Córdoba 34734
Alcázar de Segovia, Segovia 35460
Alchemy: The Group for Collections Management in Yorkshire and Humberside, Halifax 49396
Aldan Maadyr National Museum of the Republic of Tyva, Kyzyl 32979
Aldborough Roman Town Museum, Boroughbridge 38280
Aldeburgh Museum, Aldeburgh 37962
Alden Historical Society Museum, Alden 41114
Alden House Museum, Duxbury 43027
Alderney Railway - Braye Road Station, Alderney 37963
Alderney Society Museum, Alderney 37964
Aldershot Military Museum and Rushmoor Local History Gallery, Aldershot 37966
Aldfaers Erf Route, Allingawier 28807
Aldheidskeamer Uldrik Bottema, Aldeboarn 28801
Aldrich Museum of Contemporary Art, Ridgefield 46896
Aleko Konstantinov Municipal Historical Museum, Svištov 04879
Aleksandra Rusteiķa Memoriālais Muzejs, Jūrmala 27368
Aleksandrov Literature and Art Museum of Marina and Anastasija Tsvetaeva, Aleksandrov 32635
Aleksandrovskaja Sloboda - Gosudarstvennyj Istoriko-architekturnyj i Chudožestvennyj Muzej-zapovednik, Aleksandrov 32633
Aleksandrovskij Chudožestvennyj Muzej, Aleksandrov 32634
Aleksandrovskij Dvorec - Gosudarstvennyj Muzej Carskoje Selo, Puškin 33334
Aleksandrovskij Literaturno-chudožestvennyj Muzej Mariny i Anastasii Cvetaevych, Aleksandrov 32635
Aleksandrovskij Narodnyj Muzej M.E. Pjatnickogo, Aleksandrovka 32636
Aleksis Kiven Syntymäkoti, Palojoki 09905
Aleksis Kivi's Birth-Place, Palojoki 09905
Ålen Bygdetun, Ålen 30373
Aleppo National Museum, Aleppo 37433
Aleš South Bohemian Gallery, Hluboká nad Vltavou 08351
Ålesunds Museum, Ålesund 30374
Alex Brown Cycle History Museum, Thornhill, Dumfriesshire 40703
Alex Mylonas Museum, Athinai 20845
Alex Robertson Museum, Alonsa 04982
Alex Youck School Museum, Regina 06226
Alexander and Baldwin Sugar Museum, Puunene 46750
Alexander Blok State Museum-Preserve of History and Literature, Solnečnogorsk 33544
Alexander Brest Museum, Jacksonville 44292
Alexander Fleming Laboratory Museum, London 39564
Alexander Graham Bell National Historic Site, Baddeck 05031
Alexander Griboedov State Museum-Preserve of History and Culture, Chmelita 32745
Alexander Keiller Museum, Avebury 38041
Alexander Kuprin Museum, Narovčat 33200
Alexander-Mack-Museum, Bad Berleburg 15607
Alexander McKay Geological Museum, Wellington 30291
Alexander Moutafov House-Museum, Sozopol 04865
Alexander Nevski Cathedral - Crypt - Museum of Old Bulgarian Art, Sofia 04839
Alexander Ramsey House, Saint Paul 47151
Alexander Stamboliiski House-Museum, Sofia 04837
Alexandra Museum, Alexandra 30093
Alexandra Timber Tramway and Museum, Alexandra 00730
Alexandria Archaeology Museum, Alexandria 41120
Alexandria Black History Resource Center, Alexandria 41121
Alexandria Museum of Art, Alexandria 41117
Alexandros Papanastassiou Museum, Levidion 21046
Alexandrovsk Art Museum, Aleksandrov 32634
Alexandrovsk Sloboda - Museum-Preserve of Art, History and Architecture, Aleksandrov 32633
Alexej K. Tolstoy Museum, Krasnyj Rog 32963
Alexej K. Tolstoy Park Museum, Brjansk 32711
Alexej N. Tolstoy Museum-Estate, Samara 33374
Alexej von Jawlensky-Archiv, Locarno 36884
Alexey N. Tolstoy Apartment Museum, Moskva 33129
Alf Lechner Museum, Ingolstadt 17902
Alföldi Galéria, Hódmezővásárhely 21427
The Alfoldy Gallery, Canyon 05195
Alfons Graber-Museum, Steinach 02677
Alford Heritage Centre, Alford, Aberdeenshire 37972
Alford House-Anderson Fine Arts Center, Anderson 41202
Alford Manor House Museum, Alford, Lincolnshire 37974
Alfred East Art Gallery, Kettering 39346
Alfred Ost Museum, Zwijndrecht 03860
Alfred-Vogel-Museum, Teufen 37235
Alfred-Wegener-Gedenkstätte, Zechlinerhütte 20734
Alfrēda Kalniņa Memoriālais Muzejs, Cēsis 27342
Alger County Heritage Center, Munising 45559
Algonquin College Museum, Nepean 05971
Algonquin Culture and Heritage Centre, Golden Lake 05499
Algonquin Park Logging Museum, Whitney 06798
Alice Austen House Museum, Staten Island 47779
Alice C. Sabatini Gallery, Topeka 48031
Alice Springs RSL War Museum, Alice Springs 00733
Alice T. Miner Colonial Collection, Chazy 42268
Alikartano, Numminen 09872
Alikartano Manor, Numminen 09872
Alimentarium, Vevey 37285
Alingsås Museum, Alingsås 35789
Alisgården, Lapinkylä 09758
Alisher Navoi State Museum of Literature, Taškent 48855
Aliwal North Museum and Church Plein Museum, Aliwal North 34171
Aljira Center for Contemporary Art, Newark 45889
All Hallows Undercroft Museum, London 39565
All-Russian Decorative-Applied and Folk Art Museum, Moskva 33183
Allahabad Museum, Allahabad 21689
Allan Shivers Museum, Woodville 48746
Allard Pierson Museum Amsterdam, Amsterdam 28835
Allegan County Historical and Old Jail Museum, Allegan 41141
Allegany County Historical Museum, Cumberland 42724
Allegany County Museum, Belmont 41610
Alleghany Highlands Arts and Crafts Center, Clifton Forge 42490
Allen County-Fort Wayne Historical Society Museum, Fort Wayne 43474
Allen County Historical Museum, Iola 44243
Allen County Museum, Lima 44772
Allen Gallery, Alton 37990
Allen Memorial Art Museum, Oberlin 46076
Allen R. Hite Art Institute, Louisville 44960
Allen Sapp Gallery, North Battleford 06012
Allentown Art Museum, Allentown 41143
Allerhande, Hippolytushoef 29424
Allgäu-Museum, Kempten 18059
Allgäuer Burgenmuseum, Kempten 18060
Allhallows Museum of Lace and Antiquities, Honiton 39259
Alliance and District Museum, Alliance 04977
Allie Griffin Art Gallery, Weyburn 06781
Allied Air Force Museum, Allentown 41144
Allied Arts Center and Gallery, Richland 46854
Alliierten-Museum Berlin, Berlin 15911
Allilujevy House-Museum, Sankt-Peterburg 33448
Alling Coverlet Museum, Palmyra 46268
Allison-Antrim Museum, Greencastle 43800
Allora Historical Museum, Allora 00740
Allschwiler Kunst-Zentrum, Allschwil 36445
Allwood House, Hurstbridge 01114
Alma Firehouse and Mining Museum, Alma 41151
Almaznyj Fond, Moskva 33019
Almond Valley Heritage Centre, Livingston 39533
Almonry Heritage Centre, Evesham 38953
Almviks Tegelbruksmuseum, Västervik 36386
Alne Bank, Gerringong 01050
Alor Gajah Museum, Melaka 27668
Alp-Museum Fasons, Seewis-Dorf 37159
Alpen-Adria-Galerie im Stadthaus, Klagenfurt 02121
Alpenländische Galerie, Kempten 18061
Alpenrail Swiss Model Village and Railway, Claremont, Tasmania 00917
Alpenverein-Museum, Innsbruck 02059
Alpha Museum, Bangalore 21701
Alpin- und Heimatmuseum, Hohe Wand-Stollhof 02038
Alpines Ballonsport-Museum, Mürren 36969
Alpines Museum, Zermatt 37357
Alpines Museum des Deutschen Alpenvereins, München 18823
Alpineum, Luzern 36904
Alpinmuseum, Kempten 18062
Alpinmuseum Dachstein, Ramsau am Dachstein 02481
Alpmuseum Riederalp, Riederalp 37059
Alpsennereimuseum, Hittisau 02033
Als Hjemstavnsmuseum, Hadsund 08852
Alšova Jihočeská Galerie, Hluboká nad Vltavou 08351
Alsters Herrgård, Karlstad 36002
Alstertalmuseum, Hamburg 17526
Alt-Arnstorf-Haus, Arnstorf 15515
Alt-Freden-Sammlung, Freden 17095
Alt-Rothenburger Handwerkerhaus, Rothenburg ob der Tauber 19676
Alt-Segeberger Bürgerhaus, Bad Segeberg 15740
Alt-Stade im Baumhaus, Stade 20021
Alta Museum, Alta 30378
Altai State Regional Studies Museum, Barnaul 32671
Altajskij Gosudarstvennyj Kraevedčeskij Muzej, Barnaul 32671
Altajskij Respublikanskij Kraevedčeskij Muzej im. A.V. Anochina, Gorno-Altajsk 32808
Altdenzlinger Heimethüs mit Otto-Raupp-Stube, Denzlingen 16574
Altdorfer Universitäts-Museum, Altdorf bei Nürnberg 15440
Alte Anton Bruckner-Schule, Windhaag bei Freistadt 03033
Alte Börse, Leipzig 18383
Alte Cuesterey, Essen 16943
Alte Feste, Windhoek 28778
Alte Galerie, Graz 01909
Alte Huf- und Wagenschmiede, Dietmanns 01764
Alte Kirche Friedensdorf, Dautphetal 16554
Alte Marktschmiede, Lasberg 02190
Alte Mühle Schrattenberg, Schrattenberg 02639
Alte Nationalgalerie, Berlin 15912
Alte Oberamtei, Gerabronn 17249
Alte Pinakothek, München 18824
Alte Saline Bad Reichenhall, Bad Reichenhall 15715
Alte Schule mit Clara-Zetkin-Gedächtnisstätte, Königshain-Wiederau 18178
Alte Seifenfabrik, Lauterach 02195
Alte Synagoge, Essen 16944

Alte Synagoge, Hechingen 17655
Alte Wache, Groitzsch bei Pegau 17411
Alte Wassermühlen und Museum Des Bauern Sach und Zeug, Maria Luggau 02267
Das Alte Zollhaus Heimatmuseum, Hitzacker 17770
Alternative Museum, New York 45753
Altertumssammlung der Benediktinerabtei, Engelberg 36681
Altes Amtshaus, Werne 20524
Altes Hafenamt, Dortmund 16656
Altes Haus, Greifenstein 17384
Altes Rathaus, Lüneburg 18554
Altes Rathaus-Potsdam Forum, Potsdam 19431
Altes Rathaus Wilster, Wilster 20603
Altes Residenztheater, München 18825
Altes Schloß Schleißheim, Oekumenische Sammlung Gertrud Weinhold "Das Gottesjahr und seine Feste", Oberschleißheim 19198
Altes Schloß Schleißheim, Sammlung zur Landeskunde Ost- und Westpreußens, Oberschleißheim 19199
Altes Schoß, Abteilung Gemäldegalerie und Kunsthandwerk, Gießen 17278
Altes und Neues Schloß Eremitage, Bayreuth 15839
Altes Zeughaus Landenberg, Sarnen 37122
Altfriesisches Haus, Sylt-Ost 20132
Althorp Museum, Althorp 37989
Altia Oyj, Rajamäki 09975
Altia's Rajamäki Industrial Museum, Rajamäki 09975
Altmärkisches Museum, Stendal 20057
Altmühltaler Mühlenmuseum, Dietfurt 16603
Alton Museum of History and Art, Alton 41157
Altonaer Museum in Hamburg, Hamburg 17527
Altstadtrathaus, Braunschweig 16292
Altun Ha Archaeological Site, Altun Ha 03861
Alūksne Museum of Local Studies and Art, Alūksne 27330
Alūksnes Novadpētniecības un Mākslas Muzejs, Alūksne 27330
Alumni Museum, Catonsville 42141
Alumny Creek School Museum, Grafton 01070
Alupka State Palace and Park Preserve, Alupka 37834
Alushta S.N. Sergeev-Tsensky Literary Museum, Alušta 37835
Aluštinskij Literaturno-Memorialnyj Muzej S.N. Sergeeva-Censkogo, Alušta 37835
Alutiiq Museum and Archaeological Repository, Kodiak 44524
Alva DeMars Megan Chapel Art Center, Manchester 45095
Alvar Aalto Museum, Jyväskylä 09593
Alvdal Museum, Alvdal 30379
Alyth Museum, Alyth 37994
A.M. de Jonghuis, Nieuw Vossemeer 29615
A.M. Gorki House Museum, Moskva 33121
A.M. Gorki Museum, Moskva 33098
Amador-Livermore Valley Museum, Pleasanton 46552
Amagasaki Bunka Art Gallery, Amagasaki 26097
Amagermuseet, Dragør 08795
Amakusa Christian Museum, Hondo 26230
Amakusa Kirishitankan, Hondo 26230
Amalienborg, København 08920
Åmåls Hembygdsmuseum, Åmål 35793
Åmåls Heritage Museum, Åmål 35793
Åmåls Järnvägsmuseum, Åmål 35794
Åmåls Konsthall, Åmål 35795
Amanosan Kongo-ji Treasure House, Kawachi-Nagano 26320
Amarillo Museum of Art, Amarillo 41164
Amasra Müzesi, Amasra 37608
Amasra Museum, Amasra 37608
Amasya Devlet Güzel Sanatlar Galerisi, Amasya 37609
Amasya Müzesi, Amasya 37610
Amasya Museum, Amasya 37610
Amasya State Gallery, Amasya 37609
Amathole Museum, King William's Town 34295
Ambalangoda Mask Museum, Ambalangoda 35742
Amber Museum, Bad Füssing 15647
Ambergris Museum and Cultural Centre, Ambergis Caye 03862
Amberley Working Museum, Amberley 37995
Amelia Douglas Gallery, New Westminster 05982
Amelia Earhart Birthplace Museum, Atchison 41314
Amelia Island Museum of History, Fernandina Beach 43314
Ameliasburgh Historical Museum, Ameliasburgh 04984
American Academy of Arts and Letters Art Museum, New York 45754
American Advertising Museum, Portland 46630
American Airlines C.R. Smith Museum, Fort Worth 43479
American Airpower Heritage Museum, Midland 45324
American Association for Museum Volunteers, Denver 49461
American Association for State and Local History, Nashville 49462
American Association of Museums, Washington 49463
American Baptist Museum, Rochester 46937
American Bicycle and Cycling Museum, Santa Fe 47415
American Catholic Historical Society Museum, Philadelphia 46388
American Classical Music Hall of Fame and Museum, Cincinnati 42397
American Clock and Watch Museum, Bristol 41900
American Cotton Museum, Greenville 43831
American Craft Museum, New York 45755
The American Film Institute, Los Angeles 44890
American Folk Art Museum, New York 45756
American Helicopter Museum & Education Center, West Chester 48516
American Heritage "Big Red" Fire Museum, Louisville 44979
The American Historical Foundation Museum, Richmond 46870
American Independence Museum, Exeter 43251
American Indian Contemporary Arts, San Francisco 47304
American Institute for Conservation of Historic and Artistic Works, Washington 49464
American Irish Historical Society Museum, New York 45757
American Jazz Museum, Kansas City 44394
American Jewish Historical Museum, New York 45758
American Labor Museum, Haledon 43872
American Legation Museum, Tanger 28710
American Maple Museum, Croghan 42705
American Merchant Marine Museum, Kings Point 44490
American Military Museum, Charleston 42207
American Motorcycle Museum, Raalte 29720
American Museum in Britain, Bath 38106
American Museum of Asmat Art, Saint Paul 47152
American Museum of Cartoon Art, Santa Monica 47438
American Museum of Fire Fighting, Hudson 44142
The American Museum of Fly Fishing, Manchester 45100
American Museum of Magic, Marshall 45177
American Museum of Natural History, New York 45759
American Museum of Radio, Bellingham 41601
American Museum of Science and Energy, Oak Ridge 46055
American Museum of Straw Art, Long Beach 44857
American Museum of the Miniature Arts, Dallas 42745
American Museum of the Moving Image, Astoria 41307
American Numismatic Society Museum, New York 45760
American Police Center and Museum, Chicago 42301
American Precision Museum, Windsor 48685
American Printing House for the Blind, Callahan Museum, Louisville 44961
American Quarter Horse Heritage Center and Museum, Amarillo 41165
American Red Cross Museum, Washington 48331
American Royal Museum, Kansas City 44395
American Saddlebred Horse Museum, Mexico 45279
American Saddlebred Museum, Lexington 44735
American Sport Art Museum and Archives, Daphne 42781
American Swedish Historical Museum, Philadelphia 46389
American Swedish Institute, Minneapolis 45380
American Textile History Museum, Lowell 44982
American University of Beirut Archaeological Museum, Beirut 27481
American Visionary Art Museum, Baltimore 41448
American Watchmakers-Clockmakers Institute, Harrison 43928
American West Heritage Center, Wellsville 48503
American Work Horse Museum, Lexington 44757
Americana Manse, Whitney-Halsey Home, Belmont 41611
Americana Museum, El Paso 43111
Americana Museum, Terra Alta 47982
America's Black Holocaust Museum, Milwaukee 45358
America's Ice Cream and Dairy Museum, Medina 45224
America's National Music Museum, Vermillion 48214
Americas Society Art Gallery, New York 45761
America's Stonehenge, North Salem 46006
Amerigo Tot Múzeum, Pécs 21503
Amerika Museum Nederland, Cuijk 29059
The Amerind Foundation, Dragoon 42986
Amerongs Historisch Museum/ Tabaksmuseum, Amerongen 28817
Amersham Museum, Amersham 37998
Amev Verzekeringsmuseum, Utrecht 29894
Amherst County Museum, Amherst 41184
Amherst History Museum, Amherst 41176
Amherst Museum, Amherst 41183
Amics de los Museos de Cataluña, Barcelona 49367
Amida-ji Treasure Storehouse, Hofu 26226
Amigos de los Museos, Barcelona 49368
Amity and Woodbridge Historical Society Museum, Woodbridge 48727
Amon Carter Museum, Fort Worth 43480
Amory Regional Museum, Amory 41186
Amos Anderson Art Museum, Helsinki 09471
Amos Andersonin taidemuseo, Helsinki 09471
Ámos-Anna Collection, Szentendre 21567
Ámos-Anna Gyűjtemény, Szentendre 21567
Amos Eno Gallery, New York 45762
Amos Herr House, Landisville 44635
Amparo Museum, Puebla 28317
Amr Ibrahim Palace, Cairo 09286
Amr Ibrahim Palace, Zamalek 09309
Amreli Archaeological and Art Museum, Amreli 21695
Amrumer Heimatmuseum, Nebel 18983
Het Amsterdams Automuseum, Zwanenburg 30079
Amsterdams Historisch Museum, Amsterdam 28836
Amsterdams Openbaar Vervoer Museum, Amsterdam 28837
Amtshofmuseum, Gernsbach 17255
Amtsrichterhaus, Schwarzenbek 19882
Amtsturm-Museum, Lüchow, Wendland 18547
Amuri Historical Museum, Waiau 30270
Amuri Museum of Workers' Housing, Tampere 10075
Amurin Työläismuseokortteli, Tampere 10075
Amurskij Gorodskoj Kraevedčeskij Muzej, Amursk 32637
Amurskij Oblastnoj Kraevedčeskij Muzej im. G.S. Novikova-Daurskogo, Blagoveščensk 32691
L'Amusette, Mesvin 03627
AMVC-Letterenhuis, Antwerpen 03135
An Dun Transport and Heritage Museum, Ballinahown 22365
An Iodnlann, Isle-of-Tiree 39319
An Lanntair, Stornoway 40614
A.N Radishchev Memorial Museum of Literature, Radiščevo 33346
A.N. Skryabin Museum, Moskva 33082
An Tairbeart Museum, Tarbert 40673
Anacortes Museum, Anacortes 41189
Anacostia Museum, Washington 48332
Anadarko Philomathic Museum, Anadarko 41190
Anadolu Medeniyetleri Müzesi, Ankara 37612
Anaesthetic Museum, London 39566
Anaheim Museum, Anaheim 41194
Anamur Culture Center, Anamur 37611
Anamur Kültür Merkezi, Anamur 37611
Ananda Niketan Kirtishala, Bagnan 21699
Anapskij Archeologičeskij Muzej-zapovednik, Anapa 32639
Anasazi Heritage Center, Dolores 42957
Anasazi State Park, Boulder 41838
Anatomisch Museum, Groningen 29306
Anatomisch Museum, Utrecht 29895
Anatomisch Museum Nijmegen, Nijmegen 29629
Anatomisch Museum van de Rijksuniversiteit Leiden, Leiden 29518
Anatomische Sammlung, Erlangen 16914
Anatomisches Museum, Greifswald 17387
Anatomisches Museum, Innsbruck 02060
Anatomisches Museum Basel, Basel 36494
Anatomy and Pathology Museum, Alexandria 09236
Anatomy Museum, Aberdeen 37934
Anatomy Museum, Chennai 21740
Anatomy Museum, Dunedin 30144
Anatomy Museum, Jakarta 22118
Anatomy Museum, Mumbai 21945
Anchorage Museum of History and Art, Anchorage 41197
Ancien Merv Historical Site, Mary 37817
Ancienne Abbaye de Fontcaude, Cazedarnes 11099
Ancienne Douane, Strasbourg 14804
Ancienne École de Médecine Navale, Rochefort (Charente-Maritime) 13996
Ancienne Mairie-Musée Annexe, Lillebonne 12606
Ancient and Honorable Artillery Company Museum, Boston 41796
Ancient Architecture Museum, Beijing 06940
Ancient Belarusian Culture Museum, Minsk 03120
Ancient City, Samut Prakan 37533
Ancient Coins Museum, Beijing 06941
Ancient Foundry, Chlewiska 31525
Ancient High House, Stafford 40569
Ancient House Museum, Thetford 40694
Ancient Order of Foresters, Southampton 40542
Ancient Orient Museum, Tokyo 26870
Ancient Spanish Monastery of Saint Bernard de Clairvaux Cloisters, North Miami Beach 45998
Ancol Oceanarium Museum, Jakarta 22135
Anders Svors Museet, Hornindal 30563
Anderson County Arts Center, Anderson 41204
Anderson County Historical Museum, Garnett 43627
Anderson County Museum, Anderson 41205
Anderson Gallery, Richmond 46871
Anderson Museum, Cairo 09255
Anderson Museum of Contemporary Art, Roswell 47013
Anderson Park Art Gallery, Invercargill 30184
Andersonville Prison, Andersonville 41206
Andhra Pradesh State Museum, Hyderabad 21842
Andhra Sahitya Parishat Government Museum, Kakinada 21878
Andižanskij Kraevedčeskij Muzej, Andižan 48829
Andizhan Literary Museum, Andižan 48830
Andizhan Regional Museum, Andižan 48829
Andong Folk Museum, Andong 27128
Andover Historical Society Museum, Andover 41208
Andover Museum, Andover 38000
Andøymuseet, Risøyhamn 30793
Andre Garitte Foundation, Berchem 03210
Andrea Robbi-Stiftung, Sils in Engadin 37168
Andréemuseet, Gränna 35927
Andrej Upits' Memorial Apartment, Rīga 27401
Andreja Pumpura Muzejs Lielvārdē, Lielvārde 27376
Andreja Upīša Memoriālmāja, Skrīveri 27452
Andreja Upītša Memoriālais Muzejs, Rīga 27401
Andrejs Pumpurs Museum in Lielvārde, Lielvārde 27376
Andrew and District Local History Museum, Andrew 04994
Andrew Carnegie Birthplace Museum, Dunfermline 38808
Andrew County Museum, Savannah 47488
Andrew J. Blackbird Museum, Harbor Springs 43909
Andrew Johnson National Historic Site, Greeneville 43801
Andrew Logan Museum of Sculpture, Welshpool 40815
Andrew Ross Museum, Kangaroo Ground 01134
Andrew-Safford House, Salem 47190
Andrey Rublev Museum of Ancient Russian Art, Moskva 33024
Andrey Sakharov Museum and Center World, Progress and Human Rights, Moskva 33104
Androscoggin Historical Society Museum, Auburn 41372
Andrøymuseet, Andenes 30386
The Andy Warhol Museum, Pittsburgh 46506
Anfield Museum, Liverpool 39515
Angarskij Gorodskoj Vystavočnyj Zal, Angarsk 32640
Angarskij Muzej Časov, Angarsk 32641
Angarskij Muzej Mineralov, Angarsk 32642
Ånge Zoologiska Museum, Ånge 35802
Angel Kanchev House Museum, Trjavna 04886
Angel Mounds Historic Site, Evansville 43244
Angel Orensanz Foundation Center for the Arts, New York 45763
Angel Row Gallery, Nottingham 40103
Angelburger Kunst- und Kulturhaus, Angelburg 15489
Angelo Roker's Art Centre and Museum, Nassau 03073
Angelos and Angeliki Giallina Gallery, Corfu 20927
Angermuseum, Erfurt 16893
The Angkor Conservation, Siem Reap 04951
Anglesey Heritage Gallery, Llangefni 39550
Anglican Cathedral Museum, Saint John's 06339
Angono National Museum, Angono 31274
Angren Regional Museum, Angren 48831
Angrenskij Kraevedčeskij Muzej, Angren 48831
Angus Folk Museum, Glamis 39036
Anhaltische Gemäldegalerie, Dessau 16576
Anhui Sheng Bo Wu Guan, Hefei 07091
Animal and Fish Museum, Evros 20949
Animal Museum, Amman 27043
Animas Museum, Durango 43014
Anita Gallery, San Antonio 31439
Anıtkabir-Atatürk ve Kurtuluş Müzesi, Ankara 37613
Anjala Manor, Anjalankoski 09414
Anjalan Kartanomuseo, Anjalankoski 09414
Anka Gvozdanović Collection, Zagreb 07841
Ankara Atatürk Culture Center, Ankara 37614
Ankara Atatürk Kültür Merkezi, Ankara 37614
Ankara Devlet Güzel Sanatlar Galerisi, Ankara 37615
Ankara State Gallery, Ankara 37615
Anker's House Museum, Chester-le-Street 38553
Ankkapurha Industrial Museum, Anjalankoski 09415
Ankkapurhan Teollisuusmuseo, Anjalankoski 09415
Ann Arbor Art Center, Ann Arbor 41213
Ann Arbor Hands-On Museum, Ann Arbor 41214
Ann Bryant Art Gallery, East London 34235
Anna Bahr-Mildenburg-Gedenkraum & Hermann Bahr-Gedenkraum, Wien 02831
Anna Bemis Palmer Museum, York 48793
Anna Eaton Stout Memorial Art Gallery, Owensboro 46227
Anna Leonowens Gallery, Halifax 05545
Anna Miller Museum, Newcastle 45912
Annandale National Historic Site, Tillsonburg 06552
Annapolis Valley Macdonald Museum, Middelton 05844
Annas Brigaderes Memoriālais Muzejs, Tērvete 27457
Anne Frank Center USA, New York 45764
Anne Frank Huis, Amsterdam 28838
Anne Grimdalens Minne, Dalen i Telemark 30458
Anne Hathaway's Cottage, Stratford-upon-Avon 40624
Anne Hvides Gård, Svendborg 09083
Anne Murray Centre, Springhill 06481
Anne of Cleves House Museum, Lewes 39483
Anne of Green Gables Museum, Kensington 05657
The Anne Spencer Memorial Foundation, Lynchburg 45002
Anneberg-Samlingerne, Nykøbing Sjælland 09001
Annex Art Centre Gallery, Toronto 06560
Annie E. Woodman Institute, Dover 42972
Annie Riggs Memorial Museum, Fort Stockton 43461
Anniston Museum of Natural History, Anniston 41231
Annmary Brown Memorial, Providence 46713
L'Annonciade, Saint-Tropez 14491
Anoka County Historical and Genealogical Museum, Anoka 41232
Anola and District Museum, Anola 04999
Anoyanakis Collection, Athinai 20846
Anqing Municipal Museum, Anqing 06933
L'Anse aux Meadows National Historic Site, Saint-Lunaire-Griquet 06364
Anshan City Museum, Anshan 06934
Anson County Historical Society Museum, Wadesboro 48272
Antalya Devlet Güzel Sanatlar Galerisi, Antalya 37622
Antalya Müzesi, Antalya 37623
Antalya Museum, Antalya 37623
Antalya State Gallery, Antalya 37622
Antelope County Historical Museum, Neligh 45646
Anten-Gräfsnäs Järnväg, Alingsås 35790
Antenne de l'Imprimerie de la Presse, Louhans 12676
Anthony Henday Museum, Delburne 05318
Anthropological-Ethnological Museum, Athinai 20847
Anthropological Institute and Museum D.N. Anuchin, Moskva 33162
Anthropological Museum, Beijing 06942
Anthropological Museum, Canchipur 21735
Anthropological Museum, Gauhati 21805
Anthropological Museum, Guwahati, Assam 21826

Anthropological Museum of Xiamen University, Xiamen 07289
The Anthropological National Folklore Museum, Amman 27044
Anthropologische Sammlung der Universität Göttingen, Göttingen 17332
Anthropologische Staatssammlung, München 18826
Anthropology Museum, Brisbane 00835
Anthropology Museum, DeKalb 42854
Anthropology Museum, Delhi 21764
Anthropology Museum, Lucknow 21919
Anthropology Museum, Ranchi 22003
Anthropology Museum and Resource Centre, Johannesburg 34269
Anti-Aircraft Defence Museum, Tuusula 10144
Anti-Aircraft Museum, Ha Noi 48971
Anti-Kriegs-Museum, Berlin 15913
Anti-Saloon League Museum, Westerville 48554
Antická Gerulata v Rusovciach, Bratislava 33957
Antico Frantoio, Massa Marittima 24319
Antietam National Battlefield, Sharpsburg 47582
Antifaschistische Mahn- und Gedenkstätte, Lieberose 18462
Antigonish Heritage Museum, Antigonish 05002
Antigua Cárcel de Jaruco, Jaruco 08013
Antigua Casa de los Marqueses de Campo Florido, San Antonio de los Baños 08097
Antiguo Ayuntamiento y Cárcel de Bejucal, Bejucal 07863
Antiguo Recinto del Congreso Nacional, Buenos Aires 00143
Antiken- und Abgußsammlung des Archäologischen Seminars, Marburg 18622
Antikenmuseum Basel und Sammlung Ludwig, Basel 36495
Antikenmuseum der Universität Leipzig, Leipzig 18384
Antikenmuseum und Abgußsammlung des Archäologischen Instituts der Universität Heidelberg, Heidelberg 17662
Antikensammlung, Berlin 15914
Antikensammlung, Bern 36539
Antikensammlung, Kassel 18011
Antikensammlung, Kiel 18071
Antikensammlung der Friedrich-Alexander-Universität Erlangen-Nürnberg, Erlangen 16915
Antikes Wohnmuseum, Weinheim, Bergstraße 20479
Antikmuseet, Göteborg 35909
Den Antikvariske Samling, Ribe 09027
Antiquarian and Landmarks Society Museum, Hartford 43937
Antiquarium, Agropoli 22819
Antiquarium, Ariano Irpino 22928
Antiquarium, Avella 22988
Antiquarium, Borgia 23168
Antiquarium, Boscoreale 23186
Antiquarium, Brescello 23199
Antiquarium, Buccino 23223
Antiquarium, Caldarola 23263
Antiquarium, Castelseprio 23426
Antiquarium, Cesenatico 23509
Antiquarium, Cimitile 23564
Antiquarium, Crotone 23688
Antiquarium, Filadelfia 23812
Antiquarium, Fondi 23903
Antiquarium, Golasecca 24032
Antiquarium, Loreto Aprutino 24217
Antiquarium, Lugnano in Teverina 24237
Antiquarium, Manduria 24277
Antiquarium, Massarosa 24329
Antiquarium, Mergozzo 24361
Antiquarium, Minturno 24429
Antiquarium, Monasterace 24466
Antiquarium, Nonantola 24634
Antiquarium, Numana 24659
Antiquarium, Palazzolo Acreide 24758
Antiquarium, Partinico 24813
Antiquarium, Patti 24816
Antiquarium, Porto Torres 25015
Antiquarium, Prato 25039
Antiquarium, Ravello 25076
Antiquarium, San Marzano sul Sarno 25392
Antiquarium, Santa Flavia 25430
Antiquarium, Santa Maria Capua Vetere 25434
Antiquarium, Sant'Antioco 25455
Antiquarium, Serravalle Scrivia 25550
Antiquarium, Tindari 25705
Antiquarium, Trieste 25809
Antiquarium Cantianense, San Canzian d'Isonzo 25344
Antiquarium Civico, Bagnolo San Vito 23007
Antiquarium Civico, Vazzano 25904
Antiquarium Civico, Vico del Gargano 25998
Antiquarium Comunale, Colleferro 23613
Antiquarium Comunale, Contessa Entellina 23639
Antiquarium Comunale, Milena 24423
Antiquarium Comunale, Monte Romano 24498
Antiquarium Comunale, Roma 25147
Antiquarium Comunale, Sezze 25563
Antiquarium Comunale, Sutri 25658
Antiquarium Comunale, Tiriolo 25707
Antiquarium Comunale N. Pansoni, Cossignano 23671
Antiquarium del Castello Eurialo, Siracusa 25584
Antiquarium del Parco della Forza, Ispica 24107
Antiquarium del Seminario Vescovile, Nola 24630
Antiquarium del Serapeo, Tivoli 25710
Antiquarium del Teatro Greco-Romano, Taormina 25671
Antiquarium del Varignano, Portovenere 25025
Antiquarium delle Grotte di Catullo, Sirmione 25588
Antiquarium di Agrigento Paleocristiana Casa Pace, Agrigento 22814
Antiquarium di Canne, Barletta 23030
Antiquarium di Himera, Termini Imerese 25691
Antiquarium di Megara Hyblaea, Augusta 22985
Antiquarium di Monte Cronio, Sciacca 25527
Antiquarium di Nervia, Ventimiglia 25954
Antiquarium di Poggio Civitate, Murlo 24570
Antiquarium Di Sant'Appiano, Barberino Val d'Elsa 23013
Antiquarium di Tesis, Vivaro 26042
Antiquarium di Villa Romana, Patti 24817
Antiquarium e Archeologica Museo, Cuglieri 23694
Antiquarium e Mosaico Romano, Bevagna 23073
Antiquarium e Zona Archeologica, Lugagnano Val d'Arda 24236
Antiquarium Forense, Roma 25148
Antiquarium Ipogeo dei Volumni, Perugia 24846
Antiquarium Jetino, San Cipirello 25348
Antiquarium Lucio Salvio Quintiano, Ossuccio 24713
Antiquarium Sestinale, Sestino 25553
Antiquarium Tellinum, Teglio 25682
Antiquarium Torre Cimalonga, Scalea 25514
Antiquarium - Villa Maritima, Minori 24428
Antique Auto and Race Car Museum, Bedford 41578
Antique Boat Museum, Clayton 42443
Antique Gas and Steam Engine Museum, Vista 48255
Antiquities Collection, University Museum of Cultural Heritage, Oslo 30769
Antiquities Museum, Alexandria 09237
Antiquities Museum of Tel Aviv-Yafo, Tel Aviv 22745
Antler River Historical Society Museum, Melita 05836
Anton Bruckner-Museum, Ansfelden 01676
Anton Hanak-Museum, Langenzersdorf 02186
Anton-Museum, Zwettl, Niederösterreich 03058
Anton Pieck Museum, Hattem 29351
Anton Van Wouw House, Brooklyn 34196
Anton Wildgans-Haus, Mödling 02308
Antona Austriņa Memoriālais Muzejs, Vecpiebalga 27467
Antonín Dvořák Memorial, Nelahozeves 08495
Antonin Dvořak Memorial House, Vysoká u Příbrami 08732
Antonín Dvořák Museum, Praha 08593
Antonopouleion Archeological Museum, Pylos 21134
Antun Masla Memorial Collection, Dubrovnik 07697
Anyang City Museum, Anyang 06935
Anyang Yin Xu Bo Wu Yuan, Anyang 06935
ANZ Banking Museum, Melbourne 01221
Anza-Borrego Desert Museum, Borrego Springs 41795
Anzac Cottage Museum, Mount Hawthorn 01282
ANZAC Memorial, Sydney 01489
Aomori-kenritsu Kyodokan, Aomori 26099
Aomori Prefectural Museum, Aomori 26099
A.P. Chekhov Apartment Museum, Moskva 33036
A.P. Chekhov Museum Taganrog, Taganrog 33588
Apartment-Museum of G. Krasilnikov, Iževsk 32835
Apeldoorns Museum, Apeldoorn 28924
Aperture Photo Gallery and EMU Art Gallery, Eugene 43220
Apex Museum, Atlanta 41328
Aphrodisias Museum, Geyre Köyü Karasu Aydın 37684
Apolinario Mabini Birthplace Museum, Tanauan 31457
Apolinario Mabini Shrine and Museum, Manila 31367
Apothécairerie de l'Hôtel Dieu-le-Comte, Troyes 15000
Apotheken-Museum, Schiltach 19781
Apothekenmuseum, Hofgeismar 17795
Apothicairerie, Gonesse 11883
Appalachian Center for Crafts, Smithville 47658
Appaloosa Horse Club of Canada Senior Citizens Museum, Claresholm 05254
The Appaloosa Museum and Heritage Center, Moscow 45517
Appartamenti Monumentali, Firenze 23821
Appartment-Museum of E.M. Yaroslavskyj, Jakutsk 32840
Appartment-Museum of Maksim Ammosov, Jakutsk 32841
Appenzeller Brauchtumsmuseum, Urnäsch 37270
Appenzeller Schaukäserei, Stein, Appenzell-Ausserrhoden 37217
Appenzeller Volkskunde-Museum, Stein, Appenzell-Ausserrhoden 37218
Appin Wildlife Museum, Appin 38006
The Apple Trees Museum, Burlington 41995
Appleton Art Center, Appleton 41238
Appleton Museum of Art, Ocala 46078
Appomattox Court House, Appomattox 41242
Apriķu Novada Muzejs, Apriķi 27332
Apsley House, London 39567
Apteekkimuseo, Kouvola 09702
Apteekkimuseo ja Qwensel, Turku 10118
Aptucxet Trading Post Museum, Bourne 41841
Aqualeon Parc de la Natura, Albinyana 34422
Aquaria Vattenmuseum, Stockholm 36230
Aquarium Dubuisson et Musée de Zoologie de l'Université de Liège, Liège 03566
Aquarium-Musée de la Mer, Dinard 11536
Aquarius Wassermuseum, Mülheim an der Ruhr 18813
The Aquary Museum, Tucson 48078
Aquatic Hall of Fame, Winnipeg 06819
Aquatics Museum - Institute of Oceanography and Fisheries, Suez 09306
Aquincumi Múzeum, Budapest 21324
A.R. Bowman Memorial Museum, Prineville 46707
A.R. Mitchell Memorial Museum of Western Art, Trinidad 48061
Arabia Museum-Gallery, Helsinki 09472
Arad Museum, Arad 22571
Arai Local History Museum, Arai 26101
Arai Memorial Museum of Art, Iwanai 26274
Arai-shiritsu Hakubutsukan, Arai 26101
Āraiši Museum Park, Lake Fortress, Drabeši 27350
Āraišu Muzejparks, Ezerpils, Drabeši 27350
Arandjelovac Museum, Arandjelovac 33787
Arany János Múzeum, Nagykőrös 21487
Arany Sas Patika, Budapest 21325
Ararat Gallery, Ararat 00746
Aratoi Wairarapa Museum of Art and History, Masterton 30197
Arbæjarsafn, Reykjavík 21648
Arbeia Roman Fort and Museum, South Shields 40537
Arbeidsgenot, Oudtshoorn 34317
Arbeitsgemeinschaft kirchlicher Museen und Schatzkammern, Würzburg 49193
Arbejder-, Håndværker- og Industrimuseet, Horsens 08894
Arbejdermuseet, København 08921
Arbetets Museum, Norrköping 36115
Arbil Museum, Arbil 22339
Arboga Bryggerimuseum, Arboga 35805
Arboga Museum, Arboga 35806
Årbols Skolmuseum, Åmål 35796
Arbor Lodge, Nebraska City 45641
Arboretum d'Heugleville-sur-Scie, Heugleville-sur-Scie 12023
Arbroath Art Gallery, Arbroath 38011
Arbroath Museum, Arbroath 38012
Arbuthnot Museum, Peterhead 40191
A.R.C. Gallery, Chicago 42302
ARC Gallery, Chicago 42303
Arcade Historical Museum, Arcade 41244
Arcadia Township Historical Museum and Furniture Museum, Arcadia 41245
Arcadia University Art Gallery, Glenside 43694
ARCAM Galerie, Amsterdam 28839
Archaeological and Ethnographic Museum, Diyarbakır 37661
Archaeological and Ethnographic Museum, Edirne 37664
Archaeological and Ethnographic Museum, Eregli 37668
Archaeological and Ethnographic Museum, Łódź 31768
Archaeological and Ethnographical Museum, Corabia 32503
Archaeological and Historical Museum, Ramat Hashofet 22736
Archaeological Collection, Baltimore 41449
Archaeological Collection, Budva 33825
Archaeological Collection, Kibbutz Ruhama 22701
Archaeological Collection, Ljubuški 03916
Archaeological Collection, Metković 07739
Archaeological Collection, Nin 07743
Archaeological Collection, Yehi'am 22783
Archaeological Collection and Lapidarium Dr. Grga Novak, Hvar 07705
Archaeological Collection of the West Bohemian Museum, Plzeň 08542
Archaeological Collection of Youth Village Nitzanim, Doar-Na Evtach 22587
Archaeological Collection Osor, Nerezine 07742
Archaeological Collection, Tohoku University, Sendai 26737
Archaeological Museum, Alacahöyük 37607
Archaeological Museum, Amaravati 21694
Archaeological Museum, Amman 27045
Archaeological Museum, Anuradhapura 35743
Archaeological Museum, Anyang 06936
Archaeological Museum, Bedung 27619
Archaeological Museum, Bijapur 21729
Archaeological Museum, Bodhghaya 21732
Archaeological Museum, Colombo 35745
Archaeological Museum, Dedigama 35753
Archaeological Museum, Delhi 21765
Archaeological Museum, Gdańsk 31568
Archaeological Museum, Gianyar 22100
Archaeological Museum, Gorakhpur 21811
Archaeological Museum, Guntur 21816
Archaeological Museum, Gwalior 21828
Archaeological Museum, Halebidu 21832
Archaeological Museum, Hampi 21833
Archaeological Museum, Hardwar 21835
Archaeological Museum, Jaunpur 21867
Archaeological Museum, Kamalapur 21880
Archaeological Museum, Karachi 31028
Archaeological Museum, Khajuraho 21887
Archaeological Museum, Kibbutz Ein Dor 22682
Archaeological Museum, Kibbutz Gat 22686
Archaeological Museum, Konarak 21915
Archaeological Museum, Lemesos 08207
Archaeological Museum, Louisville 44962
Archaeological Museum, Mahastangarh 03096
Archaeological Museum, Mainamati 03097
Archaeological Museum, Myohaung 28738
Archaeological Museum, Nalanda 21965
Archaeological Museum, Neishaboor 22272
Archaeological Museum, Nesebăr 04742
Archaeological Museum, Old Goa 21969
Archaeological Museum, Pagan 28739
Archaeological Museum, Paharpur 03098
Archaeological Museum, Poznań 31898
Archaeological Museum, Pune 21986
Archaeological Museum, Sanchi 22007
Archaeological Museum, Sarnath 22012
Archaeological Museum, Spanish Town 26081
Archaeological Museum, Swat 31058
Archaeological Museum, Taxila 31059
Archaeological Museum, Tripoli 27504
Archaeological Museum, Udaipur 22043
Archaeological Museum, Vaisali 22052
Archaeological Museum, Varanasi 22055
Archaeological Museum, Varna 04893
Archaeological Museum, Veliko Tărnovo 04910
Archaeological Museum, Wrocław 32173
Archaeological Museum, Zadar 07804
Archaeological Museum Blitar, Blitar 22086
Archaeological Museum Cochin, Kochi 21891
Archaeological Museum Harappa, Harappa 31018
Archaeological Museum in Cracow, Kraków 31693
Archaeological Museum Kediri, Kediri 22144
Archaeological Museum Konarak, Puri 21995
Archaeological Museum Moen-Jo-Daro, Moen-Jo-Daro 31046
Archaeological Museum of Ancient Corinth, Ancient Corinth 20821
Archaeological Museum of Argos, Argos 20832
Archaeological Museum of Baluchistan Quetta, Quetta 31053
Archaeological Museum of Epidaurus, Asklepieion Lygourio 20839
Archaeological Museum of Isthmia, Isthmia 20979
Archaeological Museum of Istria, Pula 07757
Archaeological Museum of Kerameikos, Athinai 20876
The Archaeological Museum of Kfar-Saba, Kfar-Saba 22675
The Archaeological Museum of Meiji University, Tokyo 26887
Archaeological Museum of Nemea, Archaia Nemea 20831
Archaeological Museum of Patiala, Patiala 21975
Archaeological Museum of Piraeus, Piraeus 21120
Archaeological Museum of Shellmounds of Joinville, Joinville 04150
Archaeological Museum of Siteia, Siteia 21158
Archaeological Museum of Thebes, Thebes 21175
Archaeological Museum of Thessaloniki, Thessaloniki 21179
Archaeological Museum Peshawar, Peshawar 31047
Archaeological Museum Red Fort Delhi, Delhi 21766
Archaeological Museum Saidu Sharif, Saidu Sharif 31057
Archaeological Museum Taj Mahal, Agra 21676
Archaeological Museum Umarkot, Umarkot 31060
Archaeological Museums of Chania and Rethymnon, Chania 20915
Archaeological Park, Volterra 26052
Archaeological Preserve Nicopolis ad Istrum, Veliko Tărnovo 04909
Archaeological Receipts Fund, Athinai 49219
Archaeological Resource Centre, York 40958
Archaeological Site Museum, Alampur 21686
Archaeological Site Nimrud (Calah), Nimrud 22354
Archäologie-Museum, Heilbronn 17686
Archäologiemuseum im Fränkischen Freilandmuseum, Bad Windsheim 15775
Archäologisch-Ethnographische Lehr- und Studiensammlung des Instituts für Altamerikanistik und Ethnologie der Universität Bonn, Bonn 16226
Archäologisch-Ökologisches Museum, Albersdorf 15416
Archäologische Ausstellung in der Schule, Nassenfels 18974
Archäologische Gedenkstätte, Klosterneuburg 02139
Archäologische Sammlung, Essen 16945
Archäologische Sammlung der Universität, Freiburg im Breisgau 17106
Archäologische Sammlung der Universität Zürich, Zürich 37369
Archäologische Sammlung des Historischen Museums, Luzern 36905
Archäologische Sammlung Keltenhaus, Taufkirchen, Kreis München 20147
Archäologische Sammlung mit Heimatvertriebenenstube und Kruk-Sammlung, Königsbrunn 18172
Archäologische Sammlung Warmbad-Villach, Villach 02757
Archäologische Staatssammlung München, München 18827
Archaeologische Verzameling der Rijksuniversiteit, Utrecht 29896
Archäologischer Park Cambodunum - APC, Kempten 18063
Archäologischer Park Carnuntum, Petronell 02408
Archäologischer Park Magdalensberg, Pischeldorf, Kärnten 02417
Archäologischer Park mit Museums-Turm, Kellmünz 18053
Archäologischer Park Xanten, Xanten 20727
Archäologisches Freilichtmuseum Oerlinghausen, Oerlinghausen 19231
Archäologisches Landesmuseum, Schleswig 19793
Archäologisches Landesmuseum, Wünsdorf 20690
Archäologisches Landesmuseum Baden-Württemberg, Konstanz 18201
Archäologisches Landesmuseum Mecklenburg-Vorpommern, Groß Raden 17419
Archäologisches Museum, Burgheim 16424
Archäologisches Museum, Donauwörth 16636
Archäologisches Museum, Frankfurt am Main 17031

Archäologisches Museum, Rimpar 19613
Archäologisches Museum Carnuntinum und Amphitheater, Bad Deutsch-Altenburg 01694
Archäologisches Museum der Stadt Kelheim, Kelheim 18049
Archäologisches Museum der Stadt Weißenhorn, Weißenhorn 20500
Archäologisches Museum der Universität Münster, Münster 18932
Archäologisches Museum des Historischen Vereins für Oberfranken, Bayreuth 15840
Archäologisches Museum Essenbach, Essenbach 16965
Archäologisches Museum Gablingen, Gablingen 17186
Archäologisches Museum im Rathaus, Weichering 20423
Archäologisches Museum in der Feldmühle, Rennertshofen 19571
Archäologisches Museum Lavant, Lienz 02219
Archäologisches Museum Neu-Ulm, Neu-Ulm 19007
Archäologisches Pilgermuseum Hemmaberg-Juenna, Globasnitz 01882
Archäologisches Zentrum Hitzacker, Hitzacker 17771
Archaeology and History Museum, Ghogha 31594
Archaeology and Nature Museum of Güzelyurt, Güzelyurt 08228
Archaeology Centre, Bagshot 38056
Archaeology Museum, Allahabad 21690
Archaeology Museum, Chennai 21741
Archaeology Museum, Nsukka 30353
Archaeology Museum, Takayama 26803
Archaeology Museum, Victoria 27707
Archaeology Museum in Cracow, Kraków 31694
Archaeology Museum of Lembah Bujang, Merbok 27677
Archaeology Unit and Transport Museum, Gloucester 39079
Archangelos Mihail İkon Müzesi, Girne 08222
Archangel'skij Gosudarstvennyj Muzej Zodčestva i Narodnogo Iskusstva - Malye Karely, Archangelsk 32646
Archangel'skij Literaturnyj Muzej, Archangelsk 32647
Archangel'skij Oblastnoj Kraevedčeskij Muzej, Archangelsk 32648
Archangel'skij Oblastnoj Muzej Izobrazitelnych Iskusstv, Archangelsk 32649
Archangel'skij Sobor, Moskva 33020
Archbishop's Palace, Trondheim 30937
Archdiocesan Museum, Poznań 31899
Archdiocesan Museum of Manila, Manila 31368
Archelaus Smith Museum, Cape Sable Island 05197
L'Archéodrome de Bourgogne, Meursault 12962
Archeologic Museum of Faro, Faro 32272
Archeologia di Sovana, Sorano 25608
Archeological and Land Study Collection, Alumot 22570
Archeological and Natural History Museum, Brijuni 07684
Archeological and Nature Reserve, Krzemionki koło Ostrowca 31742
Archeological Collection, Agios Kirikos 20809
Archeological Collection, Anafi 20820
Archeological Collection, Apeirathos 20829
Archeological Collection, Astypalaia 20842
Archeological Collection, Dimitsana 20937
Archeological Collection, Drama 20940
Archeological Collection, Edessa 20941
Archeological Collection, Ermoupolis 20947
Archeological Collection, Farsala 20951
Archeological Collection, Feneos 20952
Archeological Collection, Feres 20953
Archeological Collection, Filiatra 20954
Archeological Collection, Folegandros 20959
Archeological Collection, Galaxidi 20960
Archeological Collection, Geraki 20962
Archeological Collection, Grevena 20964
Archeological Collection, Grevena 20965
Archeological Collection, Gythion 20966
Archeological Collection, Ios 20972
Archeological Collection, Istiaia 20980
Archeological Collection, Kardamyli 20994
Archeological Collection, Kastro 21008
Archeological Collection, Kea 21013
Archeological Collection, Kimolos 21019
Archeological Collection, Kos 21029
Archeological Collection, Kozani 21034
Archeological Collection, Liknades 21047
Archeological Collection, Lindos 21049
Archeological Collection, Lixouri 21054
Archeological Collection, Loutra Aidipsou 21055
Archeological Collection, Maroneia 21057
Archeological Collection, Mégara 21062
Archeological Collection, Messinia 21066
Archeological Collection, Mithymna 21072
Archeological Collection, Molyvos 21073
Archeological Collection, Navpaktos 21094
Archeological Collection, Néa Anchialos 21096
Archeological Collection, Neos Skopos 21100
Archeological Collection, Paramythia 21108
Archeological Collection, Platanos 21128
Archeological Collection, Preveza 21133
Archeological Collection, Pythagoreion 21136
Archeological Collection, Serrai 21151
Archeological Collection, Siatista 21153
Archeological Collection, Sifnos 21156
Archeological Collection, Ston 07791
Archeological Collection, Symi 21170
Archeological Collection, Tanagra 21171
Archeological Collection, Tsotili 21205
Archeological Exhibition at Ahmed Bey Mosque, Kjustendil 04705
Archeological Museum, Andros 20822
Archeological Museum, Argostolion 20833
Archeological Museum, Arhaia Olympia 20837
Archeological Museum, Atalanti 20843
Archeological Museum, Bergama 37633
Archeological Museum, Burgas 04631
Archeological Museum, Čerepovec 32729
Archeological Museum, Chaironeia 20912
Archeological Museum, Chalkida 20913
Archeological Museum, Chios 20921
Archeological Museum, Chora 20925
Archeological Museum, Corfu 20928
Archeological Museum, Delos 20935
Archeological Museum, Dion 20939
Archeological Museum, Elefsis 20944
Archeological Museum, Eresos 20945
Archeological Museum, Eretria 20946
Archeological Museum, Florina 20955
Archeological Museum, Iráklion 20974
Archeological Museum, Kabos 20981
Archeological Museum, Kalamata 20982
Archeological Museum, Kalamos 20986
Archeological Museum, Kalymnos 20992
Archeological Museum, Karystos 21003
Archeological Museum, Kastelli Kisamou 21005
Archeological Museum, Kavala 21010
Archeological Museum, Kiato 21014
Archeological Museum, Kilkis 21017
Archeological Museum, Kórinthos 21028
Archeological Museum, Kos 21030
Archeological Museum, Lamia 21039
Archeological Museum, Lárissa 21041
Archeological Museum, Mykonos 21077
Archeological Museum, Myrina 21079
Archeological Museum, Mytilini 21083
Archeological Museum, Naxos 21095
Archeological Museum, Paros 21110
Archeological Museum, Patrai 21113
Archeological Museum, Plaka 21127
Archeological Museum, Plovdiv 04775
Archeological Museum, Polygyros 21130
Archeological Museum, Radnevo 04791
Archeological Museum, Rethymnon 21137
Archeological Museum, Rhodos 21141
Archeological Museum, Salamina 21145
Archeological Museum, Samos 21146
Archeological Museum, Samothráki 21150
Archeological Museum, Septemvri 04810
Archeological Museum, Sicyon 21155
Archeological Museum, Sozopol 04862
Archeological Museum, Spárti 21164
Archeological Museum, Tegea 21172
Archeological Museum, Thassos 21173
Archeological Museum, Thera 21176
Archeological Museum, Thermo 21178
Archeological Museum, Tinos 21198
Archeological Museum, Trichur 22041
Archeological Museum, Vathy 21207
Archeological Museum, Vravrón 21216
Archeological Museum of Agrinion, Agrinion 20811
Archeological Museum of Aiani, Aiani 20813
Archeological Museum of Aigina, Aegina 20803
Archeological Museum of Astros, Astros 20840
Archeological Museum of Delphi, Delphi 20936
Archeological Museum of Durrës, Durrës 00015
Archeological Museum of Ioannina, Ioannina 20967
Archeological Museum of Komotini, Komotini 21023
Archeological Museum of Nafplion, Nafplion 21090
Archeological Museum of Pella, Pella 21116
Archeological Museum of Somothraki, Palaiochora 21105
Archeological Museum of Stavros, Stavros Ithakis 21169
Archeological Museum of Surkhandarya Region, Termiz 48864
Archeological Museum of the Kasan University, Kazan 32885
Archeological Museum of Veroia, Veria 21208
Archeological Museum-Preserve, Anapa 32639
Archeological Museums of Istanbul, İstanbul 37702
Archeological Open Air Museum in Březno u Loun, Louny 08464
Archeological Reserve, Giecz 31591
Archeological Reserve of Old Shumen and Shumen Fortress, Šumen 04869
Archeological Site Avedat, Avedat 22575
Archeologičeska Ekspozicija Kreposta, Silistra 04812
Archeologičeska Ekspozicija v Džamia Achmed Bej, Kjustendil 04705
Archeologičeski Institut s Muzej, Sofia 04827
Archeologičeski Muzej, Burgas 04631
Archeologičeski Muzej, Plovdiv 04775
Archeologičeski Muzej, Radnevo 04791
Archeologičeski Muzej, Septemvri 04810
Archeologičeski Muzej, Sozopol 04862
Archeologičeski Muzej, Varna 04893
Archeologičeski Muzej, Veliko Tărnovo 04910
Archeologičeski Rezervat Starijat Grad Šumen i Šumenska Krepost, Šumen 04869
Archeologičeskij Muzej, Azov 32667
Archeologičeskij Muzej, Čerepovec 32729
Archeologičeskij Muzej Kazanskogo Universiteta, Kazan 32885
Archeologické Múzeum, Bratislava 33958
Archeologické Muzeum, Břeclav 08258
Archeologické Pracoviště, Opava 08518
Archeologické Sbírky, Plzeň 08542
Archeologiemuseum, Stein 29854
Archeologisch Centrum C.W. Bruinvis, Alkmaar 28802
Archeologisch en Paleontologisch Museum Hertogsgemaal, 's-Hertogenbosch 29402
Archeologisch Museum, Harelbeke 03475
Archeologisch Museum, Mechelen 03614
Archeologisch Museum Abdij, Affligem 03127
Archeologisch Museum Haarlem, Haarlem 29322
Archeologisch Museum Van Bogaert-Wauters, Hamme 03472
Archeologisch Museum van de Universiteit, Gent 03433
Archeologisch Openluchtmuseum Eerste Wereldoorlog, Zillebeke 03850
Archeology Department of the Silesian Museum, Opava 08518
Archeology Museum, Shamir 22743
Archeology Museum of Kozani, Kozani 21035
Archeology Museum of the Slovak National Museum, Bratislava 33958
Archeology Museum Oltenița, Oltenița 32558
Archéoscope, Le Mont-Saint-Michel 12453
Archéosite, Aubechies 03190
Archéosite Cathare, Duilhac-sous-Peyrepertuse 11582
Archéosite de la Chapelle Saint-Julien, Martigues 12879
Archéosite de la Préhistoire, Camprieu 11014
Archéosite de la Vallée des Merveilles, Tende 14874
Archéosite de l'Hospice des Pèlerins de St.-Jacques-de-Compostelle, Pons 13796
Archéosite de l'Oppidum Celto-Ligure d'Entremont, Aix-en-Provence 10248
Archéosite du Château et Village Médiéval, Montségur 13151
Archéosite et Exposition de la Cité Militaire Romain de la VIII Légion, Mirebeau-sur-Bèze 12992
Archéosite Gallo-Romain, Lunel 12711
Archéosite Gallo-Romain des Flaviers, Mouzon 13200
Archéosite Gallo-Romain Ruscino, Perpignan 13701
Archeosite Militaire, Verny 15141
Archéosite Préhistorique de Cambous, Viols-en-Laval 15268
Archéosites Gallo-Romains, Fontvieille 11780
Archer County Museum, Archer City 41249
Archer Gallery, Vancouver 48198
Arches Museum of Pioneer Life, Winona 48695
Archibald Graham McIlwaine House, Petersburg 46371
Archibald Historical Museum, La Rivière 05708
Archidiocesan Museum, Katowice 31645
Archidiocesan Museum, Szczecin 32024
Archidiocesan Museum in Cracov, Kraków 31695
Archief en Museum van het Vlaams Leven te Brussel, Bruxelles 03269
Archipelagos Cultural Center, Athinai 20848
Architectur and Ethnographic Museum Talcy, Irkutsk 32812
Architectural Ensemble of the former Spas-Jakovlevsky Monastery, Rostov (Jaroslavskaja obl.) 33354
Architectural Museum Reserve Tsarevets, Veliko Tărnovo 04912
Architecture Foundation, London 39568
Architecture Museum, Bérat 00010
Architektur Forum Zürich, Zürich 37370
Architektur im Ringturm, Wien 02832
Architekturgalerie Luzern, Ausstellungsraum Partikel, Luzern 36906
Architekturmuseum, Basel 36496
Architekturmuseum der Technischen Universität München, München 18828
Architekturmuseum Schwaben, Augsburg 15549
Architekturno-chudožestvennyj Ansambl byvšego Spaso-Jakovlevskogo Monastyrja, Rostov (Jaroslavskaja obl.) 33354
Architekturno-ėtnografičeskij Muzej Angarskaja Derevnja, Bratsk 32702
Architekturno-ėtnografičeskij Muzej Derevjannogo Zodčestva Chochlovka, Perm 33300
Architekturno-etnografski Muzej Etăr, Gabrovo 04665
Architekturno-istoričski Muzej-rezervat, Boženci 04628
Architekturno-muzeen Rezervat Arbanassi, Veliko Tărnovo 04911
Architekturno-muzeen Rezervat Carevec, Veliko Tărnovo 04912
Architekturno-parkov Kompleks Dvorceva, Balčik 04609
Architekturzentrum Wien, Wien 02833
Architektuur Centrum Amsterdam, Amsterdam 28840
Archiv Bürgerbewegung Leipzig e.V., Leipzig 18385
Archiv der deutschen Jugendbewegung, Witzenhausen 20634
Archiv der Universität Wien, Schausammlung, Wien 02834
Archiv für die Waldviertler Urgeschichtsforschung, Horn 02047
Archiv für Philatelie der Museumsstiftung Post und Telekommunikation, Bonn 16227
Archiv und Kollektion Paul Kaiser-Reka, Brandenburg an der Havel 16278
Archiv und Museum des Heimatkreises Leitmeritz, Fulda 17171
Archives et Musée de la Littérature, Bruxelles 03270
Archives Museum - Temple Mickve Israel, Savannah 47476
Archives of American Art, Washington 48333
Archivio Segreto Vaticano, Città del Vaticano 48867
Archivio Storico Fiat, Torino 25729
Archivio Storico-Museo dello Studio-Biblioteca, Bologna 23099
Archivo-Museo Don Alvaro de Bazán, Viso del Marqués 35693
Arcola Museum, Arcola 05004
Arctic Corsair, Kingston-upon-Hull 39375
Ardress House and Farmyard Museum, Annaghmore 38002
Ardrossan Historical Museum, Ardrossan 00749
Ards Art Centre, Newtownards 40073
Aremark Historielag, Aremark 30388
Arend Dieperink Museum, Potgietersrus 34339
Arendal Bymuseum, Arendal 30389
Het Arendonks Heemmuseum, Arendonk 03181
Arents House, Brugge 03246
Arentshuis, Brugge 03246
Argauisch Kantonales Weinbaumuseum, Tegerfelden 37230
Argentine Museum of Sociology, Buenos Aires 00244
Argo Gold Mine and Mill Museum, Idaho Springs 44191
L'Argonaute, Paris 13469
The Argory, Dungannon 38811
Argyll and Sutherland Highlanders Regimental Museum, Stirling 40589
Arhaiologiko Mouseio Thassalonikis, Thessaloniki 21179
Arheološka Zbirka, Budva 33825
Arheološka Zbirka, Metković 07739
Arheološka Zbirka, Nin 07743
Arheološka Zbirka Crne Gore, Podgorica 33886
Arheološka Zbirka i Lapidarij Dr. Grga Novak, Hvar 07705
Arheološka Zbirka Osor, Nerezine 07742
Arheološki Muzej, Prizren 33896
Arheološki Muzej Istre, Pula 07757
Arheološki Muzej u Splitu, Split 07779
Arheološki Muzej Zagreb, Zagreb 07809
Arhitekturni Muzej Ljubljana, Ljubljana 34104
Århus Bymuseum, Århus 08768
Arita Ceramic Museum, Arita 26102
Arita Toji Bijutsukan, Arita 26102
Arithmeum, Bonn 16228
Arizona Gallery, Tucson 48079
Arizona Hall of Fame Museum, Phoenix 46471
Arizona Historical Society Museum, Tempe 47969
Arizona Historical Society Museum, Tucson 48080
Arizona Historical Society Pioneer Museum, Flagstaff 43328
Arizona Mining and Mineral Museum, Phoenix 46472
Arizona Museum For Youth, Mesa 45269
Arizona Science Center, Phoenix 46473
Arizona-Sonora Desert Museum, Tucson 48081
Arizona State Capitol Museum, Phoenix 46474
Arizona State Museum, Tucson 48082
Arizona State University Art Museum, Tempe 47970
Ark-La-Tex Antique and Classic Vehicle Museum, Shreveport 47611
Arkadi Monastery Collection, Rethymnon 21138
Arkaeologisk Museum, Korsør 08963
The Arkansas Arts Center, Little Rock 44822
Arkansas Museum of Natural Resources, Smackover 47655
Arkansas Museum of Science and History - Museum of Discovery, Little Rock 44823
Arkansas Museums Association, Little Rock 49465
Arkansas Post Museum, Gillett 43668
Arkansas Post National Memorial, Gillett 43669
Arkansas State University Art Gallery, Jonesboro 44358
Arkansas State University Museum, Jonesboro 44359
Arken Museum of Modern Art, Ishøj 08906
Arkeologisk Museum i Stavanger, Stavanger 30877
Arkeologiskt Museum Vuollerim 6000 år, Vuollerim 36419
Arkhangelsk Literary Museum, Archangelsk 32647
Arkhangelsk Regional Museum, Archangelsk 32648
Arkhangelsk Regional Museum of Fine Arts, Archangelsk 32649
Arkitekturmuseet, Oslo 30726
Arkitekturmuseet, Stockholm 36231
Arklow Maritime Museum, Arklow 22361
Arkona Lion's Museum, Arkona 05007
Arktisk Museum Nanoq, Jakobstad 09572
The Arkwright Society, Cromford 38674
Arlington Arts Center, Arlington 41263
Arlington Court, Arlington 38014
Arlington Heights Historical Museum, Arlington Heights 41268
Arlington Historical Museum, Arlington 41264
Arlington Historical Society, Arlington 41257
Arlington House - The Robert E. Lee Memorial, Arlington 41265
Arlington Mill Museum, Bibury 38188
Arlington Museum, Birmingham 41704
Arlington Museum of Art, Arlington 41259
Armadale Community Museum, Armadale 38015
Armádní Muzeum Žižkov, Praha 08563
Armagh County Museum, Armagh 38017
Armando Museum, Amersfoort 28819
Armed Forces Museum, Oslo 30733
Armed Forces Museum, Taipei 07343
Armed Forces of the Philippines Museum, Quezon City 31427
Armed Forces Survey Department Museum, Bangkok 37474

Armeemuseum 'Friedrich der Große', Kulmbach 18264
Armémuseum, Stockholm 36232
Armenian Cathedral and Museum, Isfahan 22244
Armenian Museum, Jerusalem 31068
Armenian Museum of America, Watertown 48440
Armeria, Mondavio 24470
Armeria Reale, Torino 25730
Armfelt Museo, Helsinki 09473
Armidale and District Folk Museum, Armidale 00751
Armory Art Gallery, Blacksburg 41726
Armory Center for the Arts, Pasadena 46300
Arms Family Museum of Local History, Youngstown 48806
Armstrong Browning Library, Waco 48260
Armstrong Collection, Olivet 46137
Armstrong-Spallumcheen Museum and Art Gallery, Armstrong 05008
Army Medical Corps Centre Museum, Lucknow 21920
Army Medical Services Museum, Aldershot 37967
Army Museum, Ha Noi 48973
Army Museum, Halifax 05546
Army Museum, Paddington, New South Wales 01350
Army Museum, Stockholm 36232
Army Museum and Fort Copacabana, Rio de Janeiro 04315
Army Museum of Infantry Center, Phachuab Khiri Khan 37524
Army Museum of South Australia, Keswick 01142
Army Museum of Western Australia, Perth 01362
Army Museum Žižkov, Praha 08563
Army Physical Training Corps Museum, Aldershot 37968
Arnhems Oorlogsmuseum 1940-45, Arnhem 28934
Arnol Blackhouse Museum, Arnol 38022
Arnold Schönberg Center, Wien 02835
Arnold Theiler Museum for African Diseases, Onderstepoort 34315
Arnolfini, Bristol 38347
Arnot Art Museum, Elmira 43169
Arnprior and District Museum, Arnprior 05009
Aros Aarhus Kunstmuseum, Århus 08769
Aros Aarhus Museum, Århus 08769
ARP Museum Bahnhof Rolandseck, Remagen 19558
Arquebus Krigshistorisk Museum, Haugesund 30536
Arquivo Histórico e Museu de Canonas Dr. Sezefredo Azambuja Vieira, Canoas 04038
Arran Heritage Museum, Brodick 38372
Arrantzaleen Museoa, Bermeo 34604
Arreton Manor, Arreton 38023
Arrow Rock State Historic Site, Arrow Rock 41271
Arrowmont School of Arts and Crafts Collection, Gatlinburg 43635
Ars Electronica Center, Linz 02226
Ars Nova - Nykytaiteen Museo, Turku 10119
Arsenal Gallery, New York 45765
Arsenal Municipal Gallery, Poznań 31895
Arsenal Museum, London 39569
Arsenal - Museum of the Great Patriotic War, Voronež 33731
Arsenev State Museum of the Primorsky Region, Vladivostok 33709
Arsenik-Schauhütte des Bezirksheimatmuseums Spittal im Pöllatal, Rennweg 02506
Årsunda Viking Museum, Årsunda 35812
Art ab dä Gass, Steckborn 37208
Art and Architecture Exhibition Space, San Francisco 47305
Art and Art History Department, Providence 46714
Art and Culture Center of Hollywood, Hollywood 44060
Art and Design Gallery, Hatfield 39187
Art and Exhibition Complex of the Museum of History and Culture of the Middle Prikamje, Sarapul 33501
Art and Local History Collections, Mackay 01192
Art Association of Harrisburg, Harrisburg 43922
Art Cannon Gallery, Montréal 05887
The Art Center, Bangkok 37475
The Art Center, Mount Clemens 45524
Art Center at Fuller Lodge, Los Alamos 44885
The Art Center Chagall, Ostrava 08528
Art Center Gallery, Warrensburg 48314
Art Center In Hargate, Concord 42604
Art Center of Battle Creek, Battle Creek 41537
Art Center of South Florida, Miami Beach 45297
The Art Center of Waco, Waco 48261
Art Center Sarasota, Sarasota 47451
Art Centr Puškinskaja 10, Sankt-Peterburg 33380
Art Centre, Haifa 22596
Art Collection, Acton 00698
Art Collection, Stirling 40590
Art Collection of the Franciscan Monastery, Hvar 07708
Art Complex Museum, Duxbury 43028
Art Cru Muséum, Bordeaux 10802
Art Cult Center - Tabakmuseum, Wien 02836
Art de l'Enfance, Marcellaz-Albanais 12801
Art Department Gallery, Warwick 48322
Art Exhibition Hall of Bratsk, Bratsk 32703
Art Galleries, Northridge 46028
Art Galleries at UAH, Huntsville 44171
Art Galleries of Ramapo College, Mahwah 45077
Art Gallery, Antalya 37625
Art Gallery, Atlanta 41329
Art Gallery, Balčik 04610
Art Gallery, Blagoevgrad 04625
Art Gallery, Borisoglebsk 32700
Art Gallery, Brooklyn Park 41954
Art Gallery, Chaskovo 04639
Art Gallery, Čirpan 04644
Art Gallery, College Park 42522
The Art Gallery, College Park 42523
The Art Gallery, Decatur 42827
Art Gallery, Dimitrovgrad 04650
Art Gallery, Dobrič 04652
Art Gallery, Drjanovo 04658
The Art Gallery, Durham 43025
Art Gallery, Etobicoke 05417
Art Gallery, Gabrovo 04666
Art Gallery, Gălăbovo 04671
Art Gallery, Haifa 22597
Art Gallery, Havlíčkův Brod 08347
Art Gallery, Herceg-Novi 33840
The Art Gallery, Hillsborough 39243
Art Gallery, Jamestown 44309
Art Gallery, Karlovo 04689
Art Gallery, Kavarna 04694
Art Gallery, Kazanlăk 04697
The Art Gallery, Kuala Lumpur 27637
Art Gallery, Levski 04724
Art Gallery, Loveč 04727
Art Gallery, Mezdra 04736
Art Gallery, Michajlovgrad 04737
Art Gallery, Mostar 03918
Art Gallery, Novi Pazar 04745
Art Gallery, Provadia 04788
Art Gallery, Radnevo 04792
Art Gallery, San Antonio 47244
Art Gallery, Sarajevo 03924
Art Gallery, Silistra 04813
Art Gallery, Skopje 27593
Art Gallery, Sozopol 04863
Art Gallery, Svištov 04877
Art Gallery, Veliko Tărnovo 04913
Art Gallery, Woodland Hills 48733
Art Gallery, Žeravna 04932
Art Gallery and Museum, Bootle 38279
Art Gallery Elena Karamikhailova, Šumen 04870
Art Gallery - House of Puppets of Tatjana Kolinina, Petrozavodsk 33313
Art Gallery Maribor, Maribor 34129
Art Gallery Marist College, Poughkeepsie 46673
Art Gallery of Algoma, Sault Sainte Marie 06410
Art Gallery of Bancroft, Bancroft 05038
Art Gallery of Bishop's University, Lennoxville 05742
Art Gallery of Calgary, Calgary 05161
Art Gallery of Greater Victoria, Victoria 06712
Art Gallery of Hamilton, Hamilton 05567
Art Gallery of Mississauga, Mississauga 05867
Art Gallery of New South Wales, Sydney 01490
Art Gallery of Newfoundland and Labrador, Saint John's 06340
Art Gallery of Northumberland, Cobourg 05262
Art Gallery of Nova Scotia, Halifax 05547
Art Gallery of Ontario, Toronto 06561
Art Gallery of Peel, Brampton 05112
Art Gallery of Peterborough, Peterborough 06116
Art Gallery of Seikado Library, Tokyo 26828
Art Gallery of South Australia, Adelaide 00704
Art Gallery of Southwestern Manitoba, Brandon 05116
Art Gallery of Sudbury, Sudbury 06507
Art Gallery of Swift Current National Exhibition Centre, Swift Current 06524
Art Gallery of the College of Fine and Applied Arts, Khartoum 35763
Art Gallery of the Faculty of Painting, Sculpture and Graphic Art, Bangkok 37476
Art Gallery of the Municipality and Town of Mesolongion, Mesolongion 21064
Art Gallery of the Republic of Srpska Banja Luka, Banja Luka 03909
Art Gallery of the South Okanagan, Penticton 06109
Art Gallery of Western Australia, Perth 01363
Art Gallery of Windsor, Windsor, Ontario 06810
Art Gallery of York University, North York 06029
Art Gallery on the Bastion, Pskov 33330
Art Gallery Rizah Stetić, Brčko 03915
Art Gallery Ruse, Ruse 04802
Art Gallery Varna, Varna 04894
Art Gallery Wozownia, Toruń 32051
Art Gluchowe, Glauchau 17298
Art Guild of Burlington Gallery, Burlington 41996
The Art Gym, Marylhurst 45194
The Art Institute of Boston Main Gallery, Boston 41797
The Art Institute of Chicago, Chicago 42304
Art Institute of Pittsburgh, Pittsburgh 46507
Art Kite Museum für Kunst & Flugobjekte, Detmold 16586
Art League of Houston, Houston 44115
Art League of Manatee County, Bradenton 41860
Art Library, Leeds 39441
Art Museum, Denpasar 22097
Art Museum, Ilulissat 21230
Art Museum, Jakarta 22131
Art Museum, Kokkola 09685
Art Museum, Medan 22160
Art Museum, Padang 22166
Art Museum, Staryj Oskol 33557
Art Museum, Târgu Jiu 32605
Art Museum, Thiruvananthapuram 22033
Art Museum, Tulcea 32617
Art Museum, Valujki 33674
The Art Museum at Florida International University, Miami 45281
Art Museum of Dazu Rock Carvings in Chongqing, Chongqing 07029
Art Museum of Estonia, Tallinn 09358
Art Museum of Greater Lafayette, Lafayette 44568
Art Museum of Kouvola, Kouvola 09703
The Art Museum of Los Gatos and the Nature Museum of Los Gatos, Los Gatos 44954
Art Museum of Missoula, Missoula 45403
Art Museum of Northern Norway, Tromsø 30932
Art Museum of Sochi, Soči 33542
Art Museum of South Texas, Corpus Christi 42643
Art Museum of Southeast Texas, Beaumont 41562
Art Museum of Tartu University, Tartu 09388
Art Museum of the Americas, Washington 48334
Art Museum of the Chinese Univertity of Hong Kong, Hong Kong 07093
Art Museum of The Republic Marij El, Joškar-Ola 32860
Art Museum of the University of Memphis, Memphis 45231
Art Museum of Western Virginia, Roanoke 46927
Art Nouveau House, Varde 09100
Art of Velvet Gallery De Stierenstal, Montfoort 29602
Art Pavilion in Zagreb, Zagreb 07840
Art Pedagocical Museum of Toys, Sergiev Posad 33519
Art Sacré, Eze 11693
The Art Studio, Beaumont 41563
Art-Tech, San Jose 47349
Art Tower Mito, Contemporary Art Center, Mito 26503
Artarmon Galleries, Artarmon 00753
Artas Folklore Museum, Bethlehem 31063
Artbox, Mattersburg 02281
Artcentre Mältinranta, Tampere 10088
Arte Maya Tz'utuhil, San Francisco 47306
Artemis Archery Collection, Oldland 40129
Artemis Collection, Athinai 20849
Artemisia Gallery, Chicago 42305
Artery Gallery of Photography, Kaslo 05645
Artes y Oficios, Monóvar 35126
Artesia Historical Museum and Art Center, Artesia 41272
Artforms Gallery Manuyunk, Philadelphia 46390
Artful Deposit Galleries, Allentown 41142
Arthe, Dinan 11533
Arthur A. Houghton Jr. Gallery and the Great Hall Gallery, New York 45766
Arthur Cottage, Ballymena 38068
Arthur Griffin Center for Photographic Art, Winchester 48677
The Arthur J. Moore Methodist Museum, Saint Simons Island 47178
Arthur M. Sackler Gallery, Washington 48335
Arthur M. Sackler Museum, Cambridge 42037
Arthur Ross Gallery, Philadelphia 46391
Arthurdale Heritage Museum, Arthurdale 41273
Arti et Amicitiae, Amsterdam 28841
Artilleriemuseum Solothurn, Solothurn 37179
Artillery Company of Newport Military Museum, Newport 45922
Artillery Museum of Finland, Hämeenlinna 09447
Artis Geologisch Museum, Amsterdam 28842
Artist Gallery, San Francisco 47307
Artistenmuseum, Marburg 18623
Artists Association of Nantucket Museum, Nantucket 45594
Artists Center and Foundation, Makati 31351
Artists' Cooperative Gallery, Omaha 46143
Artists House Tel Aviv, Tel Aviv 22746
Artist's Space, New York 45767
Artium - Centro Museo Vasco de Arte Contemporáneo, Vitoria-Gasteiz 35694
Artjärven Kotiseutumuseo, Artjärvi 09418
Artjärvi Museum, Artjärvi 09418
Artmedia Art Gallery, Beograd 33793
Artmobile, Newtown 45947
Artothek, Köln 18129
Artothek der Stadt und Regionalbibliothek Erfurt, Erfurt 16894
Artothek der Zentral- und Landesbibliothek Berlin, Berlin 15915
Artothek-Galerie, Wien 02837
Artothek im Bonner Kunstverein, Bonn 16229
Artothek Worpswede, Worpswede 20680
Artothèque Antonin Artaud, Marseille 12844
Artothèque-Sud, Nîmes 13332
Artrain, Ann Arbor 41215
Arts Alliance Center at Clear Lake, Nassau Bay 45631
Arts and Crafts Museum, Bhavnagar 21715
Arts and Science Center for Southeast Arkansas, Pine Bluff 46489
The Arts Center of the Capital Region, Troy 48069
Arts Center of the Ozarks, Springdale 47732
The Arts Centre, Leamington 05739
Arts Centre, Washington, Tyne and Wear 40799
Arts Centre of Christchurch, Christchurch 30122
Arts Club of Washington, Washington 48336
Arts Council of Fayetteville, Fayetteville 43310
Arts Council of Wayne County, Goldsboro 43718
Arts in the Academy, Washington 48337
Arts Midland Galleries, Midland 45321
Arts Project Australia, Northcote 01332
Artsonje Center, Seoul 27223
Artsonje Museum, Gyeongju 27184
Artspace, Auckland 30102
Artspace, Peterborough 06117
Artspace, Raleigh 46771
Artspace, Richmond 46872
Artspace, Woolloomooloo 01617
Artspace-Lima, Lima 44773
Artswatch, Louisville 44963
Artworks, Trenton 48052
Arundel Museum and Heritage Centre, Arundel 38024
Arundel Toy Museum Dolls House, Arundel 38025
Arusha Declaration Museum, Arusha 37452
Arvada Center for the Arts and Humanities, Arvada 41274
Arvidsjaurs Hembygdsmuseum, Arvidsjaur 35813
Arvika Fordonmuseum, Arvika 35815
Arxiu del Monestir, Sant Joan de les Abadesses 35403
Arzamasskij Gosudarstvennyj Literaturno-Memorialnyj Muzej A.P. Gajdara, Arzamas 32655
Arzamasskij Istoriko-chudožestvennyj Muzej, Arzamas 32656
Arzemju Mākslas Muzejs, Rīga 27402
A.S. Golubkina House-Museum, Zarajsk 33745
A.S. Grin House-Museum, Kirov 32917
A.S. Popov Memorial Museum-Laboratory, Kronštadt 32965
A.S. Popov Radio Museum, Ekaterinburg 32780
A.S. Pushkin Memorial Apartment Museum, Moskva 33079
Asa Packer Mansion, Jim Thorpe 44343
Asahi-yaki Pottery Museum, Uji, Kyoto 26988
Asahikawa Youth Science Museum, Asahikawa 26105
Asakura Sculpture Gallery, Tokyo 26829
Åsavallen, Edsbro 35857
Les Ascenceurs du Calal Historique du Centre, Houdeng-Aimeries 03504
Aschan Residence, Heinola 09470
Aschanska Gården, Eksjö 35858
Ascott House, Leighton Buzzard 39473
Asen Zlatarov House-Museum, Chaskovo 04640
Asesepän Paja, Naarva 09854
Ásgrimur Jónsson Gallery, Reykjavík 21663
Ash Lawn-Highland, Charlottesville 42246
Ashburton Aviation Museum, Ashburton 30096
Ashburton Museum, Ashburton 30097
Ashburton Museum, Ashburton 38026
Ashburton Vintage Car Club Museum, Ashburton 30098
Ashby-de-la-Zouch Museum, Ashby-de-la-Zouch 38027
Ashby-Hodge Gallery of American Art, Fayette 43306
Ashcroft Museum, Ashcroft 05011
Ashern Pioneer Museum, Ashern 05012
Asheville Art Museum, Asheville 41275
Ashford Gallery, Dublin 22413
Ashford Museum, Ashford 38028
Ashland - Henry Clay Estate, Lexington 44736
Ashland Historical Museum, Ashland 41288
Ashland Historical Society Museum, Ashland 41299
Ashland Logging Museum, Ashland 41289
Ashland Logging Museum, Ashland 41290
Ashland Railroad Station Museum, Ashland 41292
Ashmolean Museum of Art and Archaeology, Oxford 40141
Ashtabula Arts Center, Ashtabula 41302
Ashtabula County Historical Society Museum, Geneva-on-the-Lake 43646
Ashtabula Plantation, Pendleton 46336
Ashton Court Visitor Centre, Bristol 38348
Ashton Villa, Galveston 43606
Ashwell Village Museum, Ashwell 38036
Ashworths Treasures of the Earth, Home Hill 01108
Asia-Africa Museum, Genève 36724
Asia Society and Museum, New York 45768
Asian-American Arts Centre, New York 45769
Asian Art Museum of San Francisco, San Francisco 47308
Asian Arts and Culture Center, Towson 48045
Asian Center Museum, Quezon City 31428
Asian Civilisations Museum, Singapore 33936
Asian Cultures Museum, Corpus Christi 42644
Asian Galleries, Sydney 01491
Asian Resource Gallery, Oakland 46060
Asiatic Society Museum, Kolkata 21897
Asikkala Museum, Asikkala 09419
Asikkalan Kotiseutumuseo, Asikkala 09419
Aşiyan Müzesi, Bebek 37631
Asiyan Museum, Bebek 37631
Asker Museum, Hvalstad 30574
Askeri Müze ve Kültür Sitesi Komtuanlıği^BE, İstanbul 37691
Askim Museum, Askim 30402
Askon Museo, Lahti 09739
Ásmundarsafn, Reykjavík 21649
Ásmundur Sveinsson Sculpture Museum, Reykjavík 21649
Asociación Colombiana de Museos, Bogotá 49115
Asociacion de Amigos de los Museos Militares, Madrid 49369
Asociación de Museos de Guatemala, Guatemala 49226
Asociación Española de Archiveros, Bibliotecarios, Museólogos y Documentalistas, Madrid 49370
Asociación Española de Museólogos, Madrid 49371
Asociatia Natională a Muzeelor in aer Liber - România, Bucureşti 49343
Aspen Art Museum, Aspen 41305
Aspen Historical Society Museum, Aspen 41306
Aspö-Tosterö Hembygdsmuseum, Strängnäs 36301
Asri Environmental Education Center, Bristol 41903
Assam Forest Museum, Gauhati 21806
Assam Forest Museum, Guwahati 21818
Assam State Museum, Gauhati 21807
Assam State Museum, Guwahati 21819
Åssamuséet, Åtvidaberg 35823
Assiginack Historical Museum and Norisle Heritage Park, Manitowaning 05804

Assiniboia, Regina 06227
Assiniboia and District Historical Society Museum, Assiniboia 05014
Assiniboine Historical Society Museum, Brandon 05117
Associacão Portugesa de Museologia, Lisboa 49338
Associacija Muzeev Rossii, Tula 49345
Associacija Muzej, Varna 49083
Associació del Museo de la Ciència i de la Tècnica i d'Arqueologia Industrial de Catalunya, Terrassa 49372
Associated Artists of Pittsburgh Gallery, Pittsburgh 46508
Association des Conservateurs d'Antiquités, Athinai 49220
Association des Conservateurs et du Personnel Scientifique des Musées de la Ville de Paris, Paris 49161
Association des Musées Automobiles de France, Paris 49162
Association des Musées et Centres pour le Développement de la Culture Scientifique, Technique et Industrielle, Dijon 49163
Association Européenne des Musées d'Histoire des Sciences Médicales (AEMHSM), Paris 49164
Association for British Transport and Engineering Museums, London 49397
Association for Living History, Farm and Agricultural Museums, North Bloomfield 49466
Association Française des Directeurs de Centres d'Art, Pougues-les-Eaux 49165
Association Française des Musées d'Agriculture et du Patrimoine Rural, Paris 49166
L' Association Francophone des Musées de Belgique, Liège 49067
Association Générale des Conservateurs des Collections Publiques de France, Paris 49167
Association Internationale des Musées d'Armes et d'Histoire Militaire, Liège 49068
Association Internationale des Musées d'Histoire, Paris 49168
Association Museum and Industries, Paris 49169
Association Museums New Brunswick, Fredericton 49091
Association of Art Museum Directors, New York 49467
Association of British Transport and Engineering Museums, Rugby 49398
Association of Children's Museums, Washington 49468
Association of College and University Museums and Galleries, Norman 49469
Association of Conservators of Cultural Heritage of Slovenia, Ljubljana 49363
Association of Czech Moravian and Silesian Museums, Praha 49130
Association of Danish Art Museums, Nivå 49140
Association of Danish Cultural Museums, Nivå 49139
Association of Danish Museum Curators, København 49141
Association of European Open Air Museums, Hagen, Westfalen 49194
Association of Icelandic Curators, Reykjavik 49231
Association of Independent Museums, Bristol 49399
Association of Indian Museums, Delhi 49235
Association of Indiana Museums, Indianapolis 49470
Association of Local Museums in Greenland, Sisimiut 49224
Association of Manitoba Museums, Winnipeg 49092
Association of Midwest Museums, Saint Louis 49471
Association of Museum Curators of Slovenia, Ljubljana 49364
Association of Museums and Galleries of Czech Republic, Praha 49131
Association of Museums in Seoul, Seoul 49267
Association of Museums of the Indian Ocean, Victoria 49355
Association of Open Air Museums, Toruń 49336
Association of Railway Museums, Washington 49472
Association of Railway Preservation Societies, Watford 49400
Association of Science-Museum Directors, San Diego 49473
Association of Science-Technology Centers, Washington 49474
Association of South Dakota Museums, Sioux Falls 49475
Association of State Subsidized Museums, Amsterdam 49307
Association of Systematics Collections, Washington 49476
Association Photocenter of the Journalists' Association, Moskva 33165
Association pour le Respect de l'Intégrité du Patrimoine Artistique, Issy-les-Moulineaux 49170
Association pour les Musées de Marseille, Marseille 49171
Associazione Nazionale dei Musei dei Enti Locali ed Istituzionali, Brescia 49247
Associazione Nazionale dei Musei Italiani, Roma 49248
Associazione Nazionale Musei Scientifici, Firenze 49249
Den Ast, Buggenhout 03344
Astan-e-Qods-e Razavi Museums, Mashad 22265
Astley-Cheetham Art Gallery, Stalybridge 40574
Astley Hall Museum and Art Gallery, Chorley 38574
Aston Hall, Birmingham 38209
Aston Manor Transport Museum, Birmingham 38210
Astor House Hotel Museum, Golden 43711
Astors' Beechwood-Victorian Living History Museum, Newport 45923
Astrachanskaja Gosudarstvennaja Kartinnaja Galereja im. B.M. Kustodieva, Astrachan 32658
Astrachanskij Gosudarstvennyj Obedinennyj Istoriko-architekturnyj Muzej-zapovednik, Astrachan 32659
Astrachanskij Kraevedčeskij Muzej, Astrachan 32660
Astrachanskij Kreml, Astrachan 32661
Astrakhan Kremlin, Astrachan 32661
Astrakhan Regional Museum at the Museum-Preserve, Astrachan 32660
Astrakhan State Gallery B.M. Kustodiev, Astrachan 32658
Astrakhan State Historical and Architectural United Museum- Preserve, Astrachan 32659
Astronautics Museum, Beijing 06943
Astronomisch Compensatieuurwerk Kamiel Festraets, Sint-Truiden 03748
Astrup Fearnley Museet for Moderne Kunst, Oslo 30727
Astruptunet, Skei i Jølster 30842
Asuka Historical Museum, Nara National Cultural Properties Research Institute, Asuka 26112
Asuka Shiryokan, Asuka 26112
Asutosh Museum of Indian Art, Kolkata 21898
Asyl der Kunst, Häuslingen 17475
A.T. Bolotov Museum-Estate, Dvorjaninovo 32764
At-Bristol, Bristol 38349
Ataloa Lodge Museum, Muskogee 45580
Atascadero Historical Society Museum, Atascadero 41313
Atatürk and Culture Museum, Eskişehir 37675
Atatürk and Ethnographic Museum, Akşehir 37605
Atatürk Ethnography and Congress Museum, Sivas 37788
Atatürk Evi, Trabzon 37796
Atatürk House, Trabzon 37796
Atatürk Köşkü, Diyarbakır 37659
Atatürk Kongre ve Etnografya Müzesi, Sivas 37788
Atatürk Müzesi, Bursa 37643
Atatürk Müzesi, İzmir 37717
Atatürk Müzesi, Konya 37739
Atatürk Museum, Bursa 37643
Atatürk Museum, Konya 37739
Atatürk Museum, Samsun 37776
Atatürk Revolution Museum, Şişli 37786
Atatürk ve Etnografya Müzesi, Akşehir 37605
Atatürk's House, Diyarbakır 37659
Atatürks Mausoleum and War of Independence Museum, Ankara 37613
Ataürk Müzesi, Şişli 37786
Atchinson, Topeka and Santa Fe Depot, Alden 41113
Atchison County Historical Society Museum, Atchison 41315
Atelier Augarten - Zentrum für zeitgenössische Kunst der Österreichischen Galerie Belvedere, Wien 02838
L'Atelier de Nicolas Schöffer à la Villa des Arts, Paris 13470
Atelier de Taille du Silex, Abilly 10223
Atelier des Bastides, Monpazier 13019
Atelier des Produits Résineux Vidal, Luxey 12717
Atelier d'Estampe Imago, Moncton 05874
Atelier Ernst Hecker, Aue, Sachsen 15542
Atelier Galerie du Manoir de la Caillère, Coutures 11445
Atelier Histoire de Tours, Tours 14968
Atelier Ivan Meštrović, Zagreb 07810
Atelier Kea Homan, Assen 28948
Atelier Ladywood Museum, Ladywood 05716
Atelier Municipal de Passementerie, Lyon 12723
Atelier-Musée de la Soie, Taulignan 14871
Atelier-Musée des Tisserands et de la Charentaise, Varaignes 15086
Atelier-Musée du Bâton Basque, Larressore 12349
Atelier-Musée du Chapeau, Chazelles-sur-Lyon 11262
Atelier Musée du Verre, Trélon 14994
Atelier-Musée du Vitrail et des Métiers d'Art du Verre, Gréoux-les-Bains 11948
Atelier-Musée Livre et Typographie, Grignan 11955
Atelier Na-iem, Gees 29267
Atelier Otto Niemeyer-Holstein, Koserow 18213
Atelier Paul Cézanne, Aix-en-Provence 10249
Atelier Segantini, Maloja 36920
Atelierhaus Philipp Harth, Bayrischzell 15861
Ateliers de l'Abeille, Chavignon 11259
Ateliersammlung Herbert Hiesmayr, Sankt Thomas am Blasenstein 02608
Ateneo Art Gallery, Quezon City 31429
Ateneo de Valencia, Valencia 48965
Ateneo Puertorriqueno Gallery, San Juan 32386
Ateneum Art Museum - Finnish National Gallery, Helsinki 09474
Ateneumin Taidemuseo, Helsinki 09474
Athanassakeion Archeological Museum, Volos 21211
Athelhampton House, Dorchester 38746
Athelstan Museum, Malmesbury 39882
The Athenaeum, Alexandria 41122
Athenaeum of Philadelphia, Philadelphia 46392
Athens University Museum, Athinai 20850
Athlone Castle Museum, Athlone 22362
Athol Murray College of Notre Dame Museum, Wilcox 06799
Atholl Country Life Museum, Blair Atholl 38252
Atikokan Centennial Museum, Atikokan 05017
Atkinson Art Gallery, Southport 40557
The Atlanta College of Art, Atlanta 41330
Atlanta Contemporary Art Center and Nexus Press, Atlanta 41331
The Atlanta Cyclorama, Atlanta 41332
Atlanta History Museum, Atlanta 41333
Atlanta International Museum of Art and Design, Atlanta 41334
Atlanta Museum, Atlanta 41335
Atlantic 1 Museum, Swampscott 47898
Atlantic Canada Aviation Museum, Bedfords 05070
Atlantic City Historical Museum, Atlantic City 41365
Atlantic County Historical Society Museum, Somers Point 47668
Atlantic Salmon Museum on the Miramichi River, Doaktown 05333
Atlantic Statiquarium Marine Museum, Louisbourg 05781
Atlantic Wildfowl Heritage Museum, Virginia Beach 48244
Atlin Historical Museum, Atlin 05019
Atnabrufossen Vannbruksmuseum, Atna 30403
Atom Museum, Haigerloch 17491
Atomium, Bruxelles 03271
Atrium an der Schleuse, Brunsbüttel 16382
Atrium Gallery, Fort Worth 43481
Atrium Gallery, Saint Louis 47111
Atrium Gallery, Salt Lake City 47225
Atsuta-Jingu Museum, Nagoya, Aichi 26564
Attila József Memorial Room, Budapest 21326
Åttingen Hantverk och Lantbruksmuseum, Aneby 35799
Attingham Park, Shrewsbury 40506
attitudes, Genève 36725
Attleboro Area Industrial Museum, Attleboro 41367
Attleboro Museum, Attleboro 41368
Attmore-Oliver House, New Bern 45665
Åtvidabergs Bruks- och Facitmuseum, Åtvidaberg 35824
Atwater Kent Museum - The History Museum of Philadelphia, Philadelphia 46393
Atwell House Gallery, Alfred Cove 00731
Atwell-Wilson Motor Museum, Calne 38440
Atwood Memorial Center, Saint Cloud 47083
Au Glaize Village, Defiance 42853
Au Pays d'Ardenne - Original Museum, Bastogne 03197
Auberlehaus, Trossingen 20217
Auburn-Cord-Duesenberg Museum, Auburn 41370
Auchindrain Museum of Country Life, Inveraray 39292
Auckland Art Gallery - Toi o Tāmaki, Auckland 30103
Auckland Museum and Auckland War Memorial Museum, Auckland 30104
Audi Museum Mobile, Ingolstadt 17903
Audley End House, Saffron Walden 40366
Audorfer Museum im Burgtor, Oberaudorf 19169
Audrain Historical Museum, Graceland Museum, Mexico 45280
Audubon House, Key West 44461
Audubon State Historic Site, Saint Francisville 47089
Auer von Welsbach Museum, Althofen 01666
Auglaize County Historical Society Museum, Saint Marys 47144
Augsburger Puppentheatermuseum Die Kiste, Augsburg 15550
August Deusser-Museum, Zurzach 37429
August-Gottschalk-Haus, Esens 16938
August-Holländer-Museum, Emsdetten 16866
August Horch Museum Zwickau, Zwickau 20774
August Kitzbergi Tubamuuseum, Karksi 09330
August Macke Haus, Bonn 16230
August-Suter-Museum, Eptingen 36684
Augusta Historical Museum, Augusta 00756
Augusta Historical Museum, Augusta 41387
Augusta Museum of History, Augusta 41380
Augustana College Art Gallery, Rock Island 46952
Augustinermuseum, Freiburg im Breisgau 17107
Augustinermuseum, Rattenberg, Inn 02490
Aula Didáctica de Prehistoria de Tito Bustillo, Ribadesella 35320
Aula Didáctica del Castro de Coaña, Coaña 34727
Auld Kirk Museum, Kirkintilloch 39395
Auld Sköll, Fair Isle 38965
Aulestad, Follebu 30501
Auli Mølle, Årnes 30393
Aunt Margaret's Museum of Childhood, Dufresne 05349
Aurelio Sevilla Alvero Library and Museum, Pasay 31410
Aurland Bygdetun og Lensmannsstova, Aurland 30404
Aurnhammer-Sammlung, Treuchtlingen 20199
Aurora Historical Museum, Aurora 41394
Aurora Historical Society Museum, Aurora 41402
Aurora History Museum, Aurora 41393
Aurora Museum, Aurora 05021
Aurora Public Art Commission, Aurora 41395
Aurskog-Høland Bygdetun, Hemnes i Høland 30542
Auschwitz-Birkenau State Museum, Oświęcim 31868
Ausgrabungen Schanzberg bei Gars Thunau, Gars am Kamp 01868
Ausgrabungen Wüstung Hard, Thaya 02727
Ausgrabungsdokumentation 6000 Jahre Wohnberg Oberleis, Ernstbrunn 01821
Ausgrabungsmuseum Esslinger Stadtkirche, Esslingen 16966
Ausgrabungsstätte Schanzberg, Gars am Kamp 01869
Aušros Avenue Mansion, Šiauliai 27525
Aussiedlermuseum im Schüttkasten, Allentsteig 01655
Ausstellung der Kantonalen Schnitzerschule, Brienz, Bern 36585
Ausstellung der Schweizerischen Geigenbauschule, Brienz, Bern 36586
Ausstellung Faszination und Gewalt - Dokumentationszentrum Reichsparteitagsgelände, Nürnberg 19134
Ausstellung Fontane und Hankels Ablage, Zeuthen 20751
Ausstellung Haus Wysburg und Ruine Wysburg, Remptendorf 19563
Ausstellung Heinrich Federer, Sachseln 37080
Ausstellung Historischer Elektromaschinenbau, Leipzig 18386
Ausstellung Hittisauer Lebensbilder aus dem 19. Jahrhundert, Hittisau 02034
Ausstellung Juden in Buttenhausen, Münsingen 18928
Ausstellung Kirche Zillis, Zillis 37361
Ausstellung Max-Kommerell, Münsingen 18929
Ausstellung zur Erd- und Vorgeschichte, Breitscheid, Hessen 16316
Ausstellungen im Bosch-Archiv, Stuttgart 20084
Ausstellungsforum FOE 156, München 18829
AusstellungsHalle, Frankfurt am Main 17032
Ausstellungsräume der Staatlichen Graphischen Sammlung, München 18830
Ausstellungsraum Klingental, Basel 36497
Ausstellungsraum Schloß Büchsenhausen, Innsbruck 02061
Ausstellungssaal Katharinen, Sankt Gallen 37099
Ausstellungszentrum Heft, Hüttenberg 02049
Ausstellungszentrum Heiligenkreuzer Hof, Wien 02839
Ausstellungszentrum im Schloss, Schlettau 19798
Ausstellungszentrum Kloster Cismar, Grömitz 17410
Ausstellungszentrum Kroch-Haus, Leipzig 18387
Ausstellungszentrum Lokschuppen, Rosenheim 19649
Aust-Agder Museet, Arendal 30390
Austefjord Museum, Austefjorden 30405
Austin Children's Museum, Austin 41404
Austin History Center, Austin 41405
Austin Museum of Art, Austin 41406
Austin Nature and Science Center, Austin 41407
Australian Antarctic Division Display, Kingston 01150
Australian Centre for Contemporary Art, Southbank 01464
Australian Centre for Photography, Paddington, New South Wales 01351
Australian Children's Folklore Collection, Melbourne 01222
Australian Electric Transport Museum, Saint Kilda, South Australia 01432
Australian Exhibition Center, Chicago 42306
Australian Federation of Friends of Museums, Sydney 49046
Australian Flying Museum, Archerfield 00748
Australian Freethought Heritage Library, Balwyn 00768
Australian Gallery of Sport and Olympic Museum, Jolimont 01126
Australian Institute of Genealogical Studies, Blackburn 00808
Australian Museum, Sydney 01492
Australian National Maritime Museum, Sydney 01493
Australian Pearling Exhibition, Darwin 00971
Australian Racing Museum, Caulfield 00902
Australian Railway Museum, Melbourne 01223
Australian Stockman's Hall of Fame and Outback Heritage Centre, Longreach 01184
Australian Toy Museum, Collingwood 00939
Australian War Memorial, Campbell 00879
Austråt Slott, Opphaug 30717
Austrått Fort, Brekstad 30450
Austråttborgen, Trondheim 30936
Auto Museum Dr. Carl Benz, Ladenburg 18283
Auto-Museum Fritz B. Busch, Wolfegg 20648
Auto Museum Moncopulli, Osorno 06900
Auto-Sammlung Gut-Hand, Aachen 15369
Auto & Technik Museum, Sinsheim 19968
Auto- und Motorrad-Museum, Öhringen 19225
Auto- und Motorradmuseum, Witzenhausen 20635
Automates Avenue, Falaise 11700
Automatik-Museum, Leipzig 18388
Automaton Museum, Barcelona 34572
Automobil-Museum, Asendorf bei Bruchhausen-Vilsen 15538
Automobil Museum Alte Garage, Rorschach 37071
Automobil-Museum Siegfried Marcus, Stockerau 02698
Automobil- und Motorradmuseum Austria, Mitterndorf an der Fischa 02305
Automobil-Veteranen-Salon, Gundelfingen an der Donau 17461
Automobilhistorisches Museum, Linz 02227
Automobilia, Hebden Bridge 39204
Automobilmuseum, Aspang 01682
Automobilmuseum Dresden, Dresden 16675
Automobilmuseum Stainz, Graz 01910
Automotive Hall of Fame, Dearborn 42822
Automusa, Bergeijk 28979
Automuseum Deventer, Deventer 29142
Automuseum Engstingen, Engstingen 16876
Automuseum E.R. Prihoda, Praha 08564
Automuseum Histo-Mobil, Giethoorn 29279
Automuseum Old Timer, Lo-Reninge 03592
Automuseum Schagen, Schagen 29794
Automuseum Störy, Bockenem 16203
Autotron, Rosmalen 29746
Autoworld, Bruxelles 03272

Autry Museum of Western Heritage, Los Angeles 44891
Auwärter-Museum, Stuttgart 20085
AV Gallery, Limerick 22504
A.V. Sidorov Mineralogical Museum, Irkutsk 32815
Avanersuup Katersugaasivia, Qaanaaq 21236
Aventinus-Museum, Abensberg 15389
Averkin Museum of the Russian Song, Sasovo 33512
Averoff Gallery, Athinai 20851
Averoff Gallery, Metsovon 21070
Averøy Skolemuseum, Averøy 30406
Avery County Museum, Newland 45919
Avery Historical Museum, Smethwick 40531
Avery Research Center for African American History and Culture, Charleston 42208
Avetisians Museum, Erevan 00678
Aviation and Cosmonautical Museum K.E. Tsiolkovsky, Kirov 32921
Aviation Heritage Museum of Western Australia, Bull Creek 00857
Aviation Museum, Praha 08588
Aviation Museum of Kentucky, Lexington 44737
AVICOM International Committee for Autovisual and New Technologies Museums, Liverpool 49401
Avog's Crash Museum, Lievelde 29540
Avon Historical Society Museum, Avon 41428
Avon River Heritage Museum, Hants County 05582
Avoncroft Museum of Historic Buildings, Bromsgrove 38376
Avondale Discovery Farm, Beverley 00800
Avondale House, Rathdrum 22531
Avonlea and District Museum, Avonlea 05025
A.W. Campbell House Museum, Strathroy 06502
A.W.A. Electronic-Communication Museum, Bloomfield 41736
The AXA Gallery, New York 45770
Axbridge Museum, Axbridge 38044
Axe Néo-7 Art Contemporain, Gatineau 05480
Axel Ebbes Konsthall, Trelleborg 36332
Axel Stenross Maritime Museum, Port Lincoln 01383
Axiom Centre for Arts, Cheltenham 38541
Axminster Museum, Axminster 38045
Aya İrini Kilisesi üzesi, İstanbul 37692
Ayala Museum, Vigan 31463
Ayala Museum of Philippine History, Makati 31352
Ayasofya Müzesi, İstanbul 37693
Aycliffe and District Bus Preservation Society, Newton Aycliffe 40064
Aydın Devlet Güzel Sanatlar Galerisi, Aydın 37626
Aydın Müzesi, Aydın 37627
Aydın State Gallery, Aydın 37626
Ayios Dimitrios Crypt Museum, Thessaloniki 21180
Aylmer and District Museum, Aylmer 05026
Aylmer Military Collection, Brading 38303
Aynalıkavak Kasrı, İstanbul 37694
Aynalıkavak Pavillion, İstanbul 37694
Ayrshire Yeomanry Museum, Ayr 38049
Ayscoughfee Hall Museum, Spalding 40562
Ayşe and Ercümend Kalmık Foundation- Museum, Gümüşsuyu 37685
Ayşe ve Ercümend Kalmık Vakfı-Müzesi, Gümüşsuyu 37685
Azadi Museum, Teheran 22290
Azaleen-Museum, Bremen 16317
Azarbayezan Museum, Tabriz 22283
Azerbaijan State Museum of Fine Arts, Baku 03065
Azimio la Arusha Museum, Arusha 37453
Azovskij Kraevedčeskij Muzej, Azov 32668
Aztalan Museum, Jefferson 44326
Aztec Museum and Pioneer Village, Aztec 41429
Aztec Ruins, Aztec 41430
Azumino Mountain Art Museum, Hotaka 26231
B. Bissoondoyal Memorial Centre, Tyack 27742
The B & O Railroad Museum, Baltimore 41450
B & O Railroad Station Museum, Ellicott City 4315502840
Baarle's Museum, Baarle-Hertog 28958
Baba Nyonya Heritage Museum, Melaka 27661
Babe Didrikson Zaharias Museum, Beaumont 41564
Babe Ruth Birthplace & Museum, Baltimore 41451
Babits Mihály Emlékház, Szekszárd 21564
Babls Uhrensammlung, Waffenbrunn 20340
Babol Museum, Babol 22231
Babylon Museum, Babylon 22340
Babylonian Jewry Museum, Or Yehuda 22725
Baca House, Trinidad 48062
Bacău District Museum of History and Archaeology Iulian Anntonescu, Bacău 32433
Bach-Gedenkstätte im Schloß Köthen, Köthen, Anhalt 18189
Bach-Museum, Leipzig 18389
Bachčisaraj State Historical and Cultural Preserve, Bachčisaraj 37836
Bachelor's Club, Tarbolton 40674
Bacher-Museum, Zellerndorf 03052
Bachgau-Museum, Großostheim 17435
Bachhaus Eisenach, Eisenach 16814
Bachkovo Monastery Museum, Bachkovo 04607
Bachkovski Manastir muzej, Bachkovo 04607
Bachmann-Museum Bremervörde, Bremervörde 16346
Backus Heritage Village, Port Rowan 06169
Baclayon Church Museum, Baclayon 31277
Bacon's Castle, Surry 47894
Bad Gasteiner Museum, Bad Gastein 01698
Bad Schwalbacher Kur-Stadt-Apotheken-Museum, Bad Schwalbach 15737
Badè Institute of Biblical Archaeology and Howell Bible Collection, Berkeley 41639
Bademuseum, Bad Elster 15636
Baden-Powell House, London 39570
Badener Puppen- und Spielzeugmuseum, Baden bei Wien 01725
Badger Creek Museum, Cartwright 05213
Badger Mine and Museum, Shullsburg 47621
Badhaus Museum und Galerie, Kulmbach 18265
Badische Landesbibliothek, Karlsruhe 17989
Badischer Kunstverein, Karlsruhe 17990
Badisches Bäckereimuseum und Erstes Deutsches Zuckerbäckermuseum, Kraichtal 18216
Badisches Landesmuseum Karlsruhe, Karlsruhe 17991
Bäckerei- und Dorfgeschichtliches Museum, Bremervörde 16347
Bäckereimuseum, Krummhörn 18253
Bäckereimuseum, Rimpar 19614
Bäckermuseum, Wien 02841
Bärner Heimatstube, Langgöns 18341
Bärnstensmuseet, Höllviken 35957
Bäuerliche Gerätesammlung, Buch bei Jenbach 01755
Bäuerliche Sammlung, Obertilliach 02376
Bäuerliches Gerätemuseum und Venezianer-Gatter, Innervillgraten 02058
Bäuerliches Heimatmuseum der Landtechnik, Geiselhöring 17214
Bäuerliches Museum im Achentaler Heimathaus, Rohrdorf 19642
Bagamoyo Historical Museum, Bagamoyo 37456
Bagatti Valsecchi Museum, Milano 24386
Baghcheh-Jaq Palace, Urmieh 22330
Baghdad Museum, Baghdad 22344
Baghgheh Chogh Palace, Maku 22262
Bagn Bygdesamling, Bagn 30408
Bagpipe Music Museum, Ellicott City 43156
Bagration Regional Museum of Kislyarsk, Kizljar 32932
Bagshaw Museum, Batley 38127
Baguio-Mountain Provinces Museum, Baguio 31282
Bahamas Historical Society Museum, Nassau 03074
Bahamas Museum, Nassau 03075
Bahawalpur Museum, Bhawalpur 31013
Bahawalpur State Museum, Bhawalpur 31014
Bahay Laguna Museum, Liliw 31341
Bahay Tsinoy Museum, Manila 31369
Bahnwärterhaus, Esslingen 16967
Bahrain National Museum, Manama 03078
Baie Verte Peninsula Miners' Museum, Baie Verte 05037
Baierweinmuseum, Bach an der Donau 15583
Baihan Al Qasab Museum, Wadi Baihan 49014
Bailey House Museum, Wailuku 48275
Bailey-Matthews Shell Museum, Sanibel 47397
Baimasi Han Wei Gucheng Display Center, Luoyang 07156
Baird Institute Museum, Cumnock 38686
Bairnsdale Museum, Bairnsdale 00758
Bait Al Zubair, Muscat 31001
Bait Muzna Gallery, Muscat 31002
Baituna al Talhami Museum, Bethlehem 31064
Bajcsy-Zsilinszky Emlékmúzeum, Veszprém 21607
Bajcsy-Zsilinszky Memorial Museum, Veszprém 21607
Bajor Gizi Emlékmúzeum, Budapest 21327
Bajuwarenmuseum Waging am See, Waging 20343
Bak Negara Muzium Matawang, Kuala Lumpur 27638
Bakar Local History Museum, Bakar 07676
Bakelite Museum, Williton 40875
Baker-Cederberg Museum, Rochester 46938
Bakers' Museum, Sopron 21536
Bakersfield Museum of Art, Bakersfield 41439
Baki Urmantshe Museum, Kazan 32894
Bakkemuseet, Frederiksberg 08826
The Bakken, Minneapolis 45381
Bakkerij Museum, Oosterhout 29669
Bakkerijmuseum, Geel 03425
Bakkerijmuseum, Groot-Bijgaarden 03465
Bakkerijmuseum, Huizen 29454
Bakkerijmuseum, Veurne 03811
Bakkerijmuseum De Grenswachter, Luijksgestel 29551
Bakkerijmuseum de Meelzolder, Almelo 28808
Bakonyi Természettudományi Múzeum, Zirc 21617
Bakony Museum of Education, Baku 03066
Bal Sangrahalaya, Lucknow 21921
Bala Like Railway Museum, Bala 38060
Balachninskij Kraevedčeskij Muzej, Balachna 32669
Balai Seni Lukis Negara, Kuala Lumpur 27639
Balance Museum of Heiner Lubja, Mustvee 09339
Balanghai Archeological Site Museum, Butuan 31293
Balassa Bálint Múzeum, Esztergom 21410
Balatoni Múzeum, Keszthely 21453
Balay Negrense Museum, Silay 31447
Balboa Park Gallery, San Diego 47270
The Balch Institute for Ethnic Studies, Philadelphia 46394
Baldomero Aguinaldo House, Kawit 31336
Baldwin County Heritage Museum, Elberta 43126
Baldwin Historical Society Museum, Baldwin 41442
Baldwin Photographic Gallery, Murfreesboro 45567
Baldwin-Reynolds House Museum, Meadville 45214
Balfour Museum of Hampshire Red Cross History, Winchester 40886
Balıkesir Devlet Güzel Sanatlar Galerisi, Balıkesir 37628
Balıkesir State Gallery, Balıkesir 37628
Ball Game Hall, Praha 08590
Ball State University Museum of Art, Muncie 45555
Ballan Shire Historical Museum, Ballan 00760
Ballance House, Glenavy 39073
Ballangen Bygdemuseet, Ballangen 30410
Ballarat Fine Art Gallery, Ballarat 00761
Ballerup Egnsmuseet, Ballerup 08782
Ballinamore Local Museum, Ballinamore 22366
Ballmuseum, Franeker 29260
Ballon- en Luctvaartmuseum Zep/Allon, Lelystad 29529
Ballonmuseum Gersthofen, Gersthofen 17263
Ball's Falls Historical Park, Allanburg 04976
Bally Schuhmuseum, Schönenwerd 37141
Ballybunion Heritage Museum, Ballybunion 22368
Ballycastle Museum, Ballycastle 38065
Ballyheigue Maritime Centre, Ballyheigue 22371
Ballymena Museum, Ballymena 38069
Ballymoney Museum, Ballymoney 38071
Balmoral Grist Mill, Tatamagouche 06534
Balneological Museum, Piešťany 34043
Balneologické Múzeum, Piešťany 34043
Baltimore Civil War Museum, Baltimore 41452
Baltimore County Historical Museum, Cockeysville 42507
Baltimore Maritime Museum, Baltimore 41453
The Baltimore Museum of Art, Baltimore 41454
Baltimore Museum of Industry, Baltimore 41455
Baltimore Public Works Museum, Baltimore 41456
Baltimore Streetcar Museum, Baltimore 41457
Baltimore's Black American Museum, Baltimore 41458
Balvi History and Art Museum, Balvi 27333
Balvu Vēstures un Mākslas Muzejs, Balvi 27333
Balzekas Museum of Lithuanian Culture, Chicago 42307
Bamble Museum, Langesund 30626
Bamburgh Castle, Bamburgh 38073
Bamian Museum, Bamian 00001
Ban Kao Prehistoric Museum, Kanchanaburi 37507
Bananenmuseum, Sierksdorf 19955
Banatski Collection, Vršac 33929
Banbury Museum, Banbury 38075
Banchory Museum, Banchory 38077
Bancroft Mill Engine Trust, Barnoldswick 38089
Bancroft Mineral Museum, Bancroft 05039
Bandaranaike Museum, Colombo 35746
Bandelier Site, Los Alamos 44886
Bandit Museum, Ronda 35339
Banff Museum, Banff 38079
Banff Park Museum, Banff 05041
Bangabandhu Memorial Museum, Dhaka 03083
Bangabandhu Shek Mujibur Rahman Museum, Dhaka 03083
Bangbu City Museum, Bangbu 06937
Bangiya Sahitya Parisad Museum, Kolkata 21899
Bangkok University City Gallery, Bangkok 37477
Bangla Academy Folklore Museum, Dhaka 03084
Bangladesh National Museum, Dhaka 03085
Bangladesh Shamorik Jadughar, Dhaka 03086
Bangladesh Zoological Museum, Dhaka 03086
Bangor Historical Society Museum, Bangor 41492
Bangor Museum and Art Gallery, Bangor, Gwynedd 38081
Bangsbo Museum, Frederikshavn 08828
Bangunan Alat Kebesaran Diraja, Bandar Seri Begawan 04595
Banicke Múzeum, Gelnica 33996
Banicke Múzeum, Rožňava 34052
Bank Leumi Museum, Tel Aviv 22747
Bank Museum of Kansallis-Osake-Pankki, Helsinki 09475
Bank Negara Money Museum, Kuala Lumpur 27638
Bank of America Galleries, San Francisco 47309
Bank of England Museum, London 39571
Bank of Ireland Arts Centre, Dublin 22414
Bank of Japan Currency Museum, Tokyo 26904
Bank of Mississippi Art Collection, Tupelo 48108
Bank of Montreal Museum, Montréal 05888
Bank of Victoria Museum, Yackandandah 01621
Bank One Fort Worth Collection, Fort Worth 43482
Bankfield Museum, Halifax 39149
Banking and Currency Museum, Kadina 01128
Bankmuseet, Stavanger 30878
Banknote and Coin Collection of the National Bank of Hungary, Budapest 21328
Bankside Gallery, London 39572
Banmuseet, Ängelholm 35786
Banner County Historical Museum, Harrisburg 43921
Banning Residence Museum, Wilmington 48647
Bannock County Historical Museum, Pocatello 46570
Bannockburn Heritage Centre, Stirling 40591
Banqueting House, London 39573
Bantock House, Wolverhampton 40915
Bantry House, Bantry 22375
Bányászati Múzeum, Salgótarján 21521
Banys Arabs, Palma de Mallorca 35219
Bao Tàng Dân Tôc Hoc Viêt Nam, Ha Noi 48972
Bao Tàng Hai Phong, Hai Phong 48984
Bao Tàng Quan Doi, Ha Noi 48973
Bao Tàng Văn Hóa Các Dân Tôc Viêt Nam, Thai Nguyen 49000
Bar David Museum, Kibbutz Bar Am 22679
Bar Harbor Historical Society Museum, Bar Harbor 41498
Barabinsk Regional Museum, Barabinsk 32670
Barabinskij Kraevedčeskij Muzej, Barabinsk 32670
De Baracquen Museum voor Bourtanger Bodemvondsten, Bourtange 29009
Barangay Museum, Mandaluyong 31363
Baranov Museum, Kodiak 44525
Barasoain Church Museum, Malolos 31359
Barbados Museum, Saint Michael 03107
Barbara Fritchie House, Frederick 43525
Barbara Hepworth Museum and Sculpture Garden, Saint Ives, Cornwall 40406
Barbarlık Müzesi, Lefkoşa 08234
Barber Institute of Fine Arts, Birmingham 38211
Barberton Museum, Barberton 34174
Barbican Art, London 39574
Barbour's General Store Museum, Saint John 06331
Barcaldine and District Historical Museum, Barcaldine 00769
Barcsay Collection, Szentendre 21568
Barcsay Gyűjtemény, Szentendre 21568
The Bard Graduate Center for Studies in the Decorative Arts, Design, and Culture, New York 45771
Bardeau'sches Kultur- und Ausstellungszentrum, Feldbach 01826
Bardelaere Museum, Lembeke 03558
Bardhaman Science Centre, Bardhaman 21706
Bardu Bygdetun, Salangsdalen 30816
Bārdu Dzimtas Muzejs Rumbiņi, Pociems 27396
Bare Cove Fire Museum, Hingham 44036
Barfüßerkirche, Erfurt 16895
Baripada Museum, Baripada 21708
Barkenhoff Stiftung Worpswede, Worpswede 20681
Barkerville Historic Town, Barkerville 05046
Barkley East Museum, Barkley East 34175
Barleylands Farm Museum, Billericay 38199
Barlow Collection of Chinese Ceramics, Bronzes and Jades, Brighton 38337
Barmouth Sailors' Institute Collection, Barmouth 38084
Barn Museum and Rail Depot Museum, Troutdale 48066
Barnacle Historic State Park, Coconut Grove 42509
Barnard's Mill Art Museum, Glen Rose 43683
Barnegat Bay Decoy and Baymen's Museum, Tuckerton 48077
Barnes County Historical Museum, Valley City 48187
Barnes Foundation, Merion 45266
Barnet Historical Society Museum, Barnet 41507
Barnet Museum, London 39575
Barnsdall Junior Arts Center, Los Angeles 44892
Barnum House Museum, Grafton 05506
Barnum Museum, Bridgeport 41889
Barnwell County Museum, Barnwell 41510
Barockjagdschloß Eckartsau, Eckartsau 01784
Barockmuseum, Reidling 02500
Barockschloß Riegersburg, Riegersburg, Niederösterreich 02513
Baroda Museum and Picture Gallery, Vadodara 22048
Barometer World Museum, Merton 39939
Baroniet Rosendal, Rosendal 30809
Barossa Valley Historical Museum, Tanunda 01516
Barr Colony Heritage Cultural Centre, Lloydminster 05761
Barre Historical Museum, Barre 41511
Barreau Le Maistre Art Gallery, Saint Helier 40399
Barrett House, Forest Hall, New Ipswich 45709
Barrhead and District Centennial Museum, Barrhead 05048
Barrie's Birthplace, Kirriemuir 39399
Barrington Area Historical Museum, Barrington 41512
Barrington Living History Farm, Washington 48420
Barrington Woolen Mill Museum, Barrington 05051
Barron Arts Center and Museum, Woodbridge 48728
Barron County Historical Society's Pioneer Village Museum, Cameron 42068
Bartholomäus-Schmucker-Heimatmuseum, Ruhpolding 19714
Bartholomew County Historical Museum, Columbus 42577
Bartın Culture House, Bartın 37629
Bartın Kültür Evi, Bartın 37629
Bartlesville Area History Museum, Bartlesville 41513
The Bartlett Museum, Amesbury 41174
Bartók Béla Emlékház, Budapest 21329
Bartolomeu Dias Museum Complex, Mossel Bay 34311
Barton County Historical Society Village and Museum, Great Bend 43779
Barton Museum, Bhavnagar 21716
Barton Museum, Wilson 48668
Bartow History Center, Cartersville 42121
Bartow-Pell Mansion Museum, Bronx 41913
Base Borden Military Museum, Borden 05098
Baseball Hall of Fame and Museum, Tokyo 26957
Baseball Hall of Fame of Mexico, Monterrey 28242
Bashkirian State Art Museum, Ufa 33641
Basho Memorial Museum, Ueno 26985
Basho Museum, Tokyo 26830
Basilian Fathers Museum, Mundare 05950
Basilica Collegiata di Santa Maria Assunta, San Gimignano 25360
Basílica de Nuestra Señora del Pilar, Zaragoza 35715
Basilica del Santo Niño Museum, Cebu 31306
Basilica Museum, Schatkamer van de Onze-Lieve-Vrouwbasiliek, Tongeren 03780
Basilika Sipahi Ay. Trias and Kantara Castle, Kantara 08231
Basilique Notre-Dame de Montréal, Montréal 05889
Basilique Royale Saint-Denis, Saint-Denis (Seine-Saint-Denis) 14179
Basin Head Fisheries Museum, Souris 06472
Basin Müzesi Sanat Galerisi, İstanbul 37695
Basing House, Basing 38101
Basingstoke Canal Exhibition, Mytchett 39995

Basis Wien, Wien 02842
Basis Wien, Wien 02843
Baškirskij Respublikanskij Chudožestvennyj Muzej im. M.V. Nesterova, Ufa 33641
Basler Papiermühle, Basel 36498
Basque Museum, Bilbao 34611
Basque Railway Museum, Azpeitia 34514
Basrah Museum, Basrah 22348
Bass Museum of Art, Miami Beach 45298
Bass Museum of Brewing, Burton-upon-Trent 38408
Bassetlaw Museum and Percy Laws Memorial Gallery, Retford 40310
Bassett Hall, Williamsburg 48625
Bassett House Museum, Okanagan Falls 06047
Bastion, Nanaimo 05958
Bastogne Historical Center, Bastogne 03198
Bata Shoe Museum, Toronto 06562
Batavia Depot Museum, Batavia 41520
Batavia-Werf, Lelystad 29530
Batchworth Lock Canal Centre, Rickmansworth 40322
Bate Collection of Historical Instruments, Oxford 40142
Bateman Historical Museum, Bateman 05055
Bateman's, Etchingham 38948
Bateman's Kipling's House, Burwash 38409
Bates College Museum of Art, Lewiston 44728
Bates-Scofield Homestead, Darien 42782
Bath Abbey Heritage Vaults, Bath 38107
Bath Police Museum, Bath 38108
Bath Postal Museum, Bath 38109
Bath Royal Literary and Scientific Institution, Bath 38110
Báthory István Múzeum, Nyírbátor 21491
Bathurst Agricultural Museum, Bathurst 34176
Bathurst and District Historical Museum, Bathurst 00773
Bathurst Regional Art Gallery, Bathurst 00774
Batik Gemi Müzesi, Girne 08223
Batley Art Gallery, Batley 38128
Batman Culture Center, Batman 37630
Batman Kültür Merkezi, Batman 37630
Batoche National Historic Site, Batoche 05059
Batoche National Historic Site, Rosthern 06288
Baton Rouge Gallery, Baton Rouge 41525
Båtsamlingarna på Bassholmen, Uddevalla 36341
Båtsmanskasernen, Karlskrona 35997
Batsto Village, Hammonton 43890
Battle Abbey, Battle 38129
Battle and Farm Museum, Naseby 40002
Battle Museum, Kibbutz Gesher 22687
Battle Museum of Local History, Battle 38130
Battle of Lexington State Historic Site, Lexington 44751
Battle of Pákozd Memorial Site and Museum, Pákozd 21496
Battlefield House Museum, Stoney Creek 06492
Battleford National Historic Site, Battleford 05060
Battles Museums of Rural Life, Girard 43676
Battlesbridge Motorcycle Museum, Battlesbridge 38132
Battleship Cove - Maritime Heritage Museums, Fall River 43281
Battleship North Carolina, Wilmington 48656
Battleship South Dakota Memorial, Sioux Falls 47641
Battleship Texas, La Porte 44556
Baudenkmal Hopfenhaus - Landwirtschaftliche Gerätesammlung - Alt-Seilerei - Ostdeutsche Heimatstube, Aidlingen 15412
Bauern-Technik-Museum, Steyr-Gleink 02691
Bauern- und Handwerker-Museum, Malgersdorf 18608
Bauern- und Heimatmuseum Haigermoos, Sankt Pantaleon 02594
Bauern- und Waldmuseum, Haidmühle 17486
Bauerngerätemuseum des Stadtmuseums, Ingolstadt 17904
Bauernhaus 1809 vor der Industrialisierung, Simonsfeld 02665
Bauernhaus-Museum, Bielefeld 16152
Bauernhaus-Museum, Lindberg 18477
Bauernhaus-Museum, Muttenz 36975
Bauernhaus-Museum, Ruhmannsfelden 19713
Bauernhaus-Museum, Wolfegg 20649
Bauernhausmuseum, Bad Füssing 15646
Bauernhausmuseum, Grafenau, Niederbayern 17367
Bauernhausmuseum Altburg, Calw 16446
Bauernhausmuseum Amerang des Bezirks Oberbayern, Amerang 15481
Bauernhausmuseum des Landkreises Erding, Erding 16890
Bauernhausmuseum Hattingen, Hattingen 17633
Bauernhausmuseum Hohenstein, Württemberg, Hohenstein, Württemberg 17816
Bauernhausmuseum Knechtenhofen, Oberstaufen 19207
Bauernhausmuseum Schniderlihof, Oberried 19195
Bauernhofmuseum, Buchhofen 16388
Bauernhofmuseum Hof, Kirchanschöring 18086
Bauernhofmuseum Jexhof, Schöngeising 19832
Bauernkriegsmuseum, Weinstadt 20482
Bauernkriegsmuseum Kornmarktkirche, Mühlhausen, Thüringen 18805
Bauernmöbelmuseum Propstkeusche, Malta 02259
Bauernmühle-Dorfmuseum, Finkenstein 01838
Bauernmuseum, Schmannewitz 19811
Bauernmuseum, Zahna 20732
Bauernmuseum Althuus, Gurbü 36786
Bauernmuseum Blankensee, Trebbin 20193
Bauernmuseum Großklein, Großklein 01955
Bauernmuseum Guntersdorf, Guntersdorf 01972
Bauernmuseum im Grottenhof, Kaindorf an der Sulm 02094
Bauernmuseum im Holz, Bützberg 36602
Bauernmuseum Inzigkofen, Inzigkofen 17913
Bauernmuseum Landkreis Bamberg, Frensdorf 17127
Bauernmuseum Lanzenkirchen, Lanzenkirchen 02189
Bauernmuseum Liebenau, Liebenau bei Dippoldiswalde 18460
Bauernmuseum mit Kräutergarten, Nitschareuth 19105
Bauernmuseum Mühlhausen, Villingen-Schwenningen 20315
Bauernmuseum Ostdorf, Balingen 15796
Bauernmuseum Osternach, Ort im Innkreis 02385
Bauernmuseum Pfarrscheuer, Bösingen 16220
Bauernmuseum Rothenburg, Rothenburg, Oberlausitz 19684
Bauernmuseum Sollinger-Bauer, Maria Schmolln 02270
Bauernmuseum Spannberg, Spannberg 02667
Bauernmuseum Wittstock, Wittstock bei Prenzlau 20631
Bauernmuseum Zabeltitz, Zabeltitz 20731
Bauernstube, Ellwangen 16835
Baugeschichte der ehemaligen Fürstbischöflichen Residenz Schloß Neuhaus, Paderborn 19332
Baugeschichtliches Archiv der Stadt Zürich, Zürich 37371
Bauhaus-Archiv, Berlin 15916
Bauhaus-Museum, Weimar, Thüringen 20455
Bauska Castle Museum, Bauska 27335
Bauska History and Art Museum, Bauska 27334
Bauskas Novadpētniecības un Mākslas Muzejs, Bauska 27334
Bauskas Pils Muzejs, Bauska 27335
Bautahaugen Samlinger, Hedalen 30541
Bavaria Airways-Museum, Kirchdorf an der Amper 18089
BAWAG Foundation, Wien 02844
Baxter House Museum, Gorham 43730
Baxter Springs Heritage Center and Museum, Baxter Springs 41542
Bay Area Discovery Museum, Sausalito 47473
Bay Area Museum, Seabrook 47522
Bay View Historical Museum, Bay View 41545
Bayanihan Folk Arts Museum, Manila 31370
Baycrafters, Bay Village 41546
Bayerische Staatsbibliothek, München 18831
Bayerische Staatsgemäldesammlungen, München 18832
Bayerisches Armeemuseum, Ingolstadt 17905
Bayerisches Brauereimuseum Kulmbach, Kulmbach 18266
Bayerisches Eisenbahnmuseum, Nördlingen 19107
Bayerisches Moor- und Torfmuseum, Grassau, Chiemgau 17378
Bayerisches Nationalmuseum, München 18833
Bayerisches Schulmuseum, Ichenhausen 17876
Bayerisches Strafvollzugsmuseum, Kaisheim 17972
Bayet Aisha Fahmi (Mogamaa el-Fonoon), Cairo 09256
Bayin Guoleng Zhou Museum, Kuerle 07145
Bayle Museum, Bridlington 38327
Bayou Bend Collection, Houston 44116
Baysgarth House Museum, Barton-upon-Humber 38098
BBC Experience, London 39576
Beachville District Museum, Beachville 05063
Beacon Historical Society Museum, Beacon 41551
The Beacon Whitehaven, Whitehaven 40856
Beaconsfield Historic House, Charlottetown 05224
Beaminster Museum, Beaminster 38134
Beamish, the North of England Open Air Museum, Beamish 38136
Bear Butte State Park Visitors Center, Sturgis 47864
Bear Mountain Trailside Museums Wildlife Center, Bear Mountain 41554
Bear Museum, Petersfield 40192
Beatles Museum, Halle, Saale 17507
Beatrix Potter Gallery, Hawkshead 39198
Beatties Historic Photograph Museum, Dodges Ferry 00983
Beatty Museum, Newport Pagnell 40057
Beau Fort Plantation Home, Bermuda 41653
Beau Village Museum, Saint Victor 06377
Beauchamp Newman Museum, Elizabeth 43131
Beaudesert Museum, Beaudesert 00781
Beaufort Historic Site, Beaufort 41557
Beaufort Museum, Beaufort 41559
Beaufort West Museum, Beaufort West 34177
Beaulieu Abbey Exhibition of Monastic Life, Brockenhurst 38370
Beaulieu Collection, Montréal 05890
Beaumaris Castle, Beaumaris 38137
Beaumaris Gaol and Courthouse, Beaumaris 38138
Beaumont Art League, Beaumont 41565
Beauport-Sleeper-McCann House, Gloucester 43701
Beauregard-Keyes House, New Orleans 45719
Beautiful Plains Museum, Neepawa 05966
Beauvais Heritage Center, Clark 42430
Beauvoir, Biloxi 41693
Beaver Island Historical Museum, Beaver Island 41574
Beaver River Museum, Beaverton 05069
Beaverbrook Art Gallery, Fredericton 05457
Beaverhead County Museum, Dillon 42949
Beccles and District Museum, Beccles 38140
Bechelsdorfer Schulzenhaus, Schönberg, Mecklenburg 19825
Beck Cultural Exchange Center, Knoxville 44512
Beck Isle Museum of Rural Life, Pickering 40201
Becker County Historical Museum, Detroit Lakes 42938
Beckford's Tower and Museum, Bath 38111
Beckoning Hills Museum, Boissevain 05089
Bedale Museum, Bedale 38142
Bede Art BGallery, Yankton 48776
Bede's World, Jarrow 39323
Bedford Central Library Gallery, Bedford 38145
Bedford City/County Museum, Bedford 41583
Bedford Gallery at the Dean Lesher Regional Center for the Arts, Walnut Creek 48290
Bedford Historical Society Museum, Bedford 41581
Bedford Museum, Bedford 38146
Bedfordshire and Hertfordshire Regiment Association Museum Collection, Luton 39843
Bedingfield Inn Museum, Lumpkin 44999
Bedřich Smetana Museum, Praha 08594
Bedrijfsmuseum NUON-ENW Amsterdam, Amsterdam 28843
Beechworth Historic Court House, Beechworth 00782
Beecroft Art Gallery, Southend-on-Sea 40551
Beehive House, Salt Lake City 47226
Beekeeping Museum, Radovljica 34142
Beeldentuin Belling Garde, Bellingwolde 28972
Beenleigh and District Museum, Beenleigh 00787
Be'eri Archaeological Collection, Be'eri 22579
Beeston Castle, Tarporley 40675
Beethoven Emlékmúzeum, Martonvásár 21469
Beethoven Eroicahaus, Wien 02845
Beethoven-Gedenkstätte in Floridsdorf, Wien 02846
Beethoven-Haus, Bonn 16231
Beethoven Heiligenstädter Testament, Wien 02847
Beethoven-Memorial Museum, Martonvásár 21469
Beethoven Pasqualatihaus, Wien 02848
Beethovenhalle, Bonn 16232
Beethovenhaus, Krems 02155
Beethovenhaus " Haus der Neunten", Baden bei Wien 01726
Befreiungshalle Kelheim, Kelheim 18050
Le Befroi et le Musée des Frères Caudron, Rue 14072
Bega Valley Regional Art Gallery, Bega 00789
Begijnhofkerk, Sint-Truiden 03749
Begijnhofmuseum, Dendermonde 03376
Begijnhofmuseum, Herentals 03492
Begijnhofmuseum, Kortrijk 03539
Béguinage d'Anderlecht, Bruxelles 03273
Behnhaus/ Drägerhaus, Lübeck 18533
Het Behouden Blik, Uithuizermeeden 29890
Behringer-Crawford Museum, Covington 42680
Behzad Museum, Teheran 22291
Beiarn Bygdetun, Moldfjord 30689
Beijing Animation Art Museum, Beijing 06944
Beijing Art Museum, Beijing 06945
Beijing Changcheng Hua Ren Huai, Beijing 06946
Beijing Cultural Relic Protection Foundation, Beijing 06947
Beijing Dabaotai Western Han Tomb Museum, Beijing 06948
Beijing Folklorish Museum, Beijing 06949
Beijing Gu Guanxiang Station, Beijing 06950
Beijing Museum, Beijing 06951
Beijing Natural History Museum, Beijing 06952
Beijing Opera Museum, Beijing 06953
Beijing Telephone History Museum, Donghuang 07045
Beit al-Ajaib Museum with House of Wonders Museum, Zanzibar 37468
Beit-Alfa Ancient Synagogue, Kibbutz Chefzi-bah 22680
Beit Hagdudim, Avihail 22576
Beit-Hagefen Art Gallery, Haifa 22598
Beit Hameiri, Zefat 22786
Beit Hankin, Kfar Yehoshua 22677
Beit Ha'Omanim, Jerusalem 22623
Beit Hatefutsoth, Tel Aviv 22748
Beit Lohamei Haghetaot, Lohamei-Hageta'ot 22709
Beit Miriam-Museum, Kibbutz Palmachim 22699
Beit-Shean Museum, Beit Shean 22581
Beit Shturman Museum, Kibbutz Ein Harod 22684
Beiteddine Museum, Shouf 27494
Bekko Museum, Nagasaki 26543
Béla Bartók Memorial Museum, Budapest 21329
Bela County Museum, Metlika 34130
Belair Mansion, Bowie 41843
Belair Stable Museum, Bowie 41844
Belasting en Douane Museum, Rotterdam 29747
Belcarra Eviction Cottage, Castlebar 22387
Belcourt Castle, Newport 45924
Belfast Museum, Christchurch 30123
Belfry, Brugge 03248
Belgian Brewers Museum, Bruxelles 03304
Belgian Federation of Friends of Museums, Bruxelles 49071
Belgorod History and Regional Museum, Belgorod 32676
Belgorodskij Gosudarstvennyj Chudožestvennyj Muzej, Belgorod 32675
Belgorodskij Gosudarstvennyj Istoriko- Kraevedčeskij Muzej, Belgorod 32676
Belgrave Hall and Gardens, Leicester 39459
Belhaven Memorial Museum, Belhaven 41587
Belinskij Rajonnyj Kraevedčeskij Muzej, Belinskij 32678
Belinskyi Regional Museum, Belinskij 32678
Belize Audubon Society, Belize City 03863
Belize Maritime Terminal and Museum, Belize City 03864
Belkhandi Museum, Belkhandi 21711
The Belknap Mill Museum, Laconia 44564
Bell Canada Telephone Historical Collection, Montréal 05891
Bell County Museum, Belton 41618
Bell Homestead, Brantford 05124
Bell Pettigrew Museum, Saint Andrews 40380
Bell Rock Mill Museum, Verona 06710
Bella Coola Museum, Bella Coola 05071
Bellaghy Bawn, Magherafelt 39871
Bellamy Mansion Museum of History and Design Arts, Wilmington 48657
Bellapais Manastiri, Girne 08224
Bellarine Historical Museum, Drysdale 00989
Belle Grove Plantation, Middletown 45319
Belle Meade Plantation, Nashville 45612
Belleville Area Museum, Belleville 41592
Bellevue Art Museum, Bellevue 41597
Bellevue House, Kingston 05673
Bellflower Genealogical and Historical Society Museum, Bellflower 41600
Bellfoundry Museum, Loughborough 39828
Bellingrath Home, Theodore 47993
Bellport-Brookhaven Historical Society Museum, Bellport 41607
Belmont and District Museum, Belmont 05073
Belmont Collection, Throwley 40706
Belmont, Gari Melchers Estate and Memorial Gallery, Fredericksburg 43533
Beloborodov Memorial Museum, Tula 33625
Beloit Historical Society Museum, Beloit 41614
Belokranjski Muzej, Metlika 34130
Belorussian State Museum of the History of the Great Patriotic War, Minsk 03113
Belorusskij Gosudarstvennyj Muzej Istorii Velikoj Otečestvennoj Vojny, Minsk 03113
Beloveżskaja Pušča Muzej, Beloveżskaja Pušča 03110
Belozerskij Istoriko-chudožestvennyj Muzej, Belozersk 32680
Belozerskij Muzej Narodnogo Dekorativno-prikladnogo Iskusstva, Belozersk 32681
Belton House, Grantham 39110
Beltrami County Historical Museum, Bemidji 41621
Bélyegmúzeum, Budapest 21330
Bembridge Maritime Museum and Shipwreck Centre, Bembridge 38162
Bembridge Windmill Museum, Mottistone 39989
Bement-Billings Farmstead, Newark Valley 45900
Bemis Center for Contemporary Arts, Omaha 46144
Ben-Gurion House, Tel Aviv 22749
Ben-Hur Museum, Crawfordsville 42690
Ben Shahn Galleries, Wayne 48477
Ben Uri Gallery, London 39577
Benaki Museum, Athinai 20878
Benalla Costume and Pioneer Museum, Benalla 00792
Benalla Regional Art Gallery, Benalla 00793
Benares Historic House, Mississauga 05868
Benchamabophit National Museum, Bangkok 37478
Bendigo Art Gallery, Bendigo 00794
Benedektinerabtei und Abteimuseum, Seckau 02653
Benedicta Arts Center, Saint Joseph 47103
Benedictine Monastery - Church of the Multiplication of Loaves and Fish Tabgha, Tiberias 22781
Benedikt-Nimser-Haus, Wilhelmsdorf, Württemberg 20591
Benediktinerstift und Stiftssammlungen, Altenburg 01661
The Benedykt Dybowsky Zoological Museum, Lviv 37883
Benga Oral Historic Centre, Dandenong 00966
Bengal Natural History Museum, Darjeeling 21755
Benguet Museum, La Trinidad 31339
Benicia Historical Museum, Benicia 41624
Beningbrough Hall, York 40959
Benjamin and Dr. Edgar R. Cofeld Judaic Museum of Temple Beth Zion, Buffalo 41982
The Benjamin Banneker Museum, Baltimore 41459
Benjamin Franklin House, London 39578
Benjamin Patterson Inn Museum Complex, Corning 42635
Bennett Place State Historic Site, Durham 43017
Bennie Museum, Bathgate 38126
Bennington Battle Monument, Old Bennington 46128
Bennington Battlefield Exhibition, Walloomsac 48289
The Bennington Museum, Bennington 41629
Benson Veteran Cycle Museum, Benson 38166
Bensusan Museum of Photography, Johannesburg 34270
Benton County Historical Museum, Philomath 46469
Benton County Historical Museum, Prosser 46712
The Benton Homestead, Tolland 48022
Bentonville Battleground State Historic Site, Four Oaks 43498
Bent's Old Fort, La Junta 44551
Benxi City Museum, Benxi 06999
Benzie Area Historical Museum, Benzonia 41634
Beobide Lantoki Museoa, Zumaia 35738
Beothuck Village, Grand Falls-Windsor 05511
Beothuk Interpretation Centre, Boyd's Cove 05106
Beppu Daigaku Fuzoku Hakubutsukan, Beppu 26117
Beppu University Museum, Beppu 26117
Berea College Burroughs Geological Museum, Berea 41635
Berea College Doris Ulmann Galleries, Berea 41636
Beredskapsmuseet, Viken 36407

Beregi Múzeum, Vásárosnamény 21605
Berend Lehmann Museum, Halberstadt 17499
Bereznikovskij Istoriko-kraevedčeskij Muzej, Berezniki 32685
Berg-Isel-Museum der Tiroler Kaiserjäger mit Andreas Hofer-Galerie, Innsbruck 02062
Berg-Kragerø Museum, Kragerø 30609
Berg- und Stadtmuseum, Obernkirchen 19188
Bergama Arkeoloji Müzesi, Bergama 37633
Bergartsmuséet, Sandviken 36176
Bergbau- und Greifenstein-Museum, Ehrenfriedersdorf 16794
Bergbau- und Heimatmuseum, Gloggnitz 01883
Bergbau- und Heimatmuseum, Goldkronach 17345
Bergbau- und Heimatmuseum, Jochberg 02089
Bergbau- und Heimatmuseum Paulushof, Essen 16946
Bergbau- und Industriemuseum Ostbayern, Kümmersbruck 18257
Bergbau- und Mineralienmuseum, Oberwolfach 19216
Bergbau- und Stadtmuseum Weilburg, Weilburg 20442
Bergbauernmusem mit Galerie, Frankenfels 01845
Bergbauernmuseum, Alpbach 01656
Bergbauernmuseum, Telfs 02719
Bergbauernmuseum, Wildschönau 03029
Bergbaumuseum, Altenberg, Erzgebirge 15447
Bergbaumuseum, Grünbach am Schneeberg 01965
Bergbaumuseum, Hall in Tirol 01991
Bergbaumuseum, Hausham 17647
Bergbaumuseum, Horgen 36808
Bergbaumuseum, Mühlbach am Hochkönig 02324
Bergbaumuseum, Oelsnitz, Erzgebirge 19227
Bergbaumuseum Achthal, Teisendorf 20153
Bergbaumuseum Graubünden mit Schaubergwerk, Davos Platz 36653
Bergbaumuseum Heilige Barbara, Mürzzuschlag 02327
Bergbaumuseum im Besucherbergwerk Tiefer Stollen, Aalen 15380
Bergbaumuseum Klagenfurt, Klagenfurt 02122
Bergbaumuseum Leogang, Leogang 02212
Bergbaumuseum mit Mineralienschau und Schaubergwerk, Hüttenberg 02050
Bergbaumuseum Peißenberg, Peißenberg 19368
Bergbaumuseum Pöllau, Neumarkt in Steiermark 02352
Bergbaumuseum Schachtanlage Knesebeck, Bad Grund 15654
Bergbaumuseum und Schaustollen, Fohnsdorf 01840
Bergbauschaustollen, Pölfing-Brunn 02429
Bergen Art Museum Lysverket, Bergen 30412
Bergen Art Museum, Rasmus Meyer Collections, Bergen 30413
Bergen Art Museum, Stenersen Collection, Bergen 30414
Bergen County Historical Society Museum, River Edge 46909
Bergen Kunstmuseum, Bergen 30412
Bergen Kunstmuseum - Rasmus Meyers Samlinger, Bergen 30413
Bergen Kunstmuseum - Stenersens Samling, Bergen 30414
Bergen Maritime Museum, Bergen 30417
Bergen Museum, Bergen 30415
Bergen Museum of Art and Science, Hackensack 43857
Bergen Museum of Art and Science, Ho-Ho-Kus 44040
Bergen Museum of Local History, Bergen 41638
Bergen Museum of Technology, Bergen 30418
Bergen Skolemuseum, Bergen 30416
Bergens Sjøfartsmuseum, Bergen 30417
Bergens Tekniske Museum, Bergen 30418
Bergerhaus, Gumpoldskirchen 01971
Bergisches Freilichtmuseum für Ökologie und bäuerlich-handwerkliche Kultur, Lindlar 18481
Bergisches Museum für Bergbau, Handwerk und Gewerbe, Bergisch Gladbach 15896
Bergisches Museum Schloß Burg, Solingen 19983
Bergkerk Deventer, Deventer 29143
Bergkerk Museum, Deventer 29144
Bergkristallmuseum, Saalbach 02530
Bergmännisches Traditionskabinett mit Besucherbergwerk, Breitenbrunn, Erzgebirge 16314
Bergsjö Konsthall, Bergsjö 35831
Bergslagens Motor Museum, Grängesberg 35925
Bergstrom-Mahler Museum, Neenah 45643
Bergsturz-Museum Goldau, Goldau 36768
Bergtheil Museum, Westville 34403
Bergwerksmuseum, Penzberg 19372
Bergwerksmuseum Schacht Mehren, Mehren 18682
Bergwinkelmuseum, Schlüchtern 19804
Berkeley Art Center, Berkeley 41640
Berkeley Art Museum, Berkeley 41641
Berkeley Castle, Berkeley 38167
The Berkeley Costume and Toy Museum, New Ross 22528
Berkeley Plantation, Charles City 42201
Berkshire Artisans, Pittsfield 46530
Berkshire County Historical Society Museum at Arrowhead, Pittsfield 46531
Berkshire Mill Museum, Moora 01269
The Berkshire Museum, Pittsfield 46532
Berkshire Scenic Railway Museum, Lenox 44716
Berkswell Village Museum, Berkswell 38170
Berlevåg Havnemuseum, Berlevåg 30429
Berlin Art and Historical Collections, Berlin 41651
Berlin Historical Society Museum of Local History, Berlin 41652
Berliner Hundemuseum, Ostseebad Binz 19304
Berliner Kinomuseum, Berlin 15917
Berliner Medizinhistorisches Museum der Charité, Berlin 15918
Berliner S-Bahn-Museum, Potsdam 19432
Berlinische Galerie, Berlin 15919
Berlins Gem and Historical Museum, South Nanango 01461
Berman Hall, Jerusalem 22624
Bermuda Historical Society Museum, Hamilton 03881
Bermuda Maritime Museum, Mangrove Bay 03885
Bermuda National Gallery, Hamilton 03882
Bermuda National Trust Museum, Saint George's 03886
Bermuda Natural History Museum, Flatts 03880
Bermuda Society of Arts, Hamilton 03883
Bernadette's Galleries, North Vancouver 06023
Bernadotte Library, Stockholm 36233
Bernadottebiblioteket, Stockholm 36233
Bernandino Jalandoni Ancestral House, Silay 31448
Bernard Historical Museum, Delton 42867
Bernard Price Institute Paleontology Museum, Johannesburg 34271
Bernberg Fashion Museum, Johannesburg 34272
Berndt Museum of Anthropology, Nedlands 01310
Bernice Pauahi Bishop Museum, Honolulu 44072
Bernstein Museum, Bad Füssing 15647
Bernsteinmuseum, Ostseebad Sellin 19318
Berrima District Art Gallery, Bowral 00821
Berrima District Museum, Berrima 00798
Berry Museum, Berry 00799
Bersham Heritage Centre and Ironworks, Wrexham 40939
Das Berta-Hummel-Museum im Hummelhaus, Massing 18663
Berte Museum, Slöinge 36204
Bertha V.B. Lederer Fine Arts Gallery, Geneseo 43638
Berthold-Auerbach-Museum, Horb 17840
Bertram House Museum, Cape Town 34200
Berwick Barracks, Berwick-upon-Tweed 38172
Berwick Borough Museum and Art Gallery, Berwick-upon-Tweed 38173
Berwick Pakenham Historical Museum, Pakenham 01353
Berzeliusmuseet, Stockholm 36234
Bērzgales Pagasta Vēstures Muzejs, Bērzgale 27339
Besættelsessamlingen 1940-45, Grindsted 08843
Besenmuseum & Galerie, Ehingen, Donau 16791
Bessemer Hall of History, Bessemer 41658
Bessie Surtees House, Newcastle-upon-Tyne 40033
Best Friend of Charleston Museum, Charleston 42209
Besucher-Bergwerk Hüttenstollen, Salzhemmendorf 19737
Besucher-Dienste, Berlin 15920
Besucherbergwerk Bad Friedrichshall-Kochendorf, Heilbronn 17687
Besucherbergwerk Finstertal, Asbach bei Schmalkalden 15519
Besucherbergwerk Grube Fortuna, Solms 19988
Besucherbergwerk Grube Gustav, Meißner 18694
Besucherbergwerk Schiefergrube Christine, Willingen, Upland 20598
Besucherbergwerk Vereinigt Zwitterfeld zu Zinnwald, Zinnwald-Georgenfeld 20757
Bet Gordon, Deganya Aleph 22585
Bet Hashomer Museum, Kibbutz Kfar Giladi 22691
Bet Pinhas Museum of Nature, Haifa 22599
Beta Railway Station Historic Museum, Alpha 00741
Beth Ahabah Museum and Archives, Richmond 46873
Beth Tzedec Reuben and Helene Dennis Museum, Toronto 06563
Bethel Historical Society's Regional History Center, Bethel 41661
Bethlehem Historical Association Museum, Selkirk 47562
Bethlehem Museum, Bethlehem 34179
Bethlem Royal Hospital Archives and Museum, Beckenham 38141
Bethune Memorial House, Gravenhurst 05525
Betonzeitschiene, Dresden 16676
Betsey Williams Cottage, Providence 46715
Betsy Ross House, Philadelphia 46395
Bettina und Achim von Arnim Museum, Wiepersdorf bei Jüterbog 20569
Betts House Research Center, Cincinnati 42398
Betty Brinn Children's Museum, Milwaukee 45359
Betuws Fruitteelt Museum, Erichem 29249
Betws-y-coed Motor Museum, Betws-y-coed 38179
Beurs van Berlage Museum, Amsterdam 28844
Beverage Containers Museum, Millersville 45348
Beverley Art Gallery, Beverley 38181
Beverly Art Center, Chicago 42308
Beverly Historical Museum, Beverly 41671
Bewdley Museum, Bewdley 38184
Bewley's Café Museum, Dublin 22415
Bexhill Museum, Bexhill-on-Sea 38186
Bexhill Museum of Costume and Social History, Bexhill-on-Sea 38187
Bexley Historical Society Museum, Bexley 41678
Bexley Museum, London 39579
De Beyerd, Breda 29017
Beyoglu Sanat Merkezi, İstanbul 37696
Beyond Baroque Art Gallery, Venice 48208
Ter Beziens, Kolhorn 29486
Bežigrajska Galerija, Ljubljana 34105
Bežigrajska Galerija 2, Ljubljana 34106
Bezirksgalerie Alsergrund, Wien 02849
Bezirksheimatmuseum, Völkermarkt 02769
Bezirksheimatmuseum mit Zdarsky-Skimuseum, Lilienfeld 02223
Bezirksmuseum, Buchen 16386
Bezirksmuseum Alsergrund, Wien 02850
Bezirksmuseum Brigittenau, Wien 02851
Bezirksmuseum Dachau, Dachau 16522
Bezirksmuseum Döbling, Wien 02852
Bezirksmuseum Donaustadt, Wien 02853
Bezirksmuseum Favoriten, Wien 02854
Bezirksmuseum Floridsdorf, Wien 02855
Bezirksmuseum Hernals, Wien 02856
Bezirksmuseum Hietzing, Wien 02857
Bezirksmuseum Höfli, Zurzach 37430
Bezirksmuseum Innere Stadt, Wien 02858
Bezirksmuseum Josefstadt, Wien 02859
Bezirksmuseum Josefstadt, Wien 02860
Bezirksmuseum Landstraße, Wien 02861
Bezirksmuseum Leopoldstadt, Wien 02862
Bezirksmuseum Margareten, Wien 02863
Bezirksmuseum Mariahilf, Wien 02864
Bezirksmuseum Marzahn-Hellersdorf, Berlin 15921
Bezirksmuseum Meidling mit Galerie, Wien 02865
Bezirksmuseum Neubau, Wien 02866
Bezirksmuseum Ottakring, Wien 02867
Bezirksmuseum Penzing, Wien 02868
Bezirksmuseum Simmering, Wien 02869
Bezirksmuseum Stockerau, Stockerau 02699
Bezirksmuseum Währing, Wien 02870
Bezirksmuseum Wieden, Wien 02871
Bezoekerscentrum Binnenhof, Den Haag 29090
Bezoekerscentrum de Meinweg, Herkenbosch 29400
Bezoekerscentrum Mijl Op Zeven, Ospel 29681
Bezoekerscentrum Oortjespad, Kamerik 29468
B.F. Larsen Gallery, Provo 46732
Bhagalpur Museum, Bhagalpur 21712
Bhagavan Mahavir Government Museum, Cuddapah 21752
Bharat Bhawan Museum, Bhopal 09143
Bharat Itihas Samshodhak Mandal Museum, Pune 21987
Bharat Kala Bhavan, Varanasi 22056
Bharatiya Adim Jati Sevak Sangh Museum, Delhi 21767
Bhirasri Museum of Modern Art, Bangkok 37479
Bhuri Singh Museum, Chamba 21737
Bialik-Museum, Tel Aviv 22750
Białostockie Muzeum WSI, Wasilków 32146
Bibak Museum, Baguio 31283
Bibelgalerie Meersburg, Meersburg 18672
Bibelmuseum, Beuron 16134
Bibelmuseum, Münster 18933
Bibelmuseum Stuttgart, Stuttgart 20086
Bible Lands Museum Jerusalem, Jerusalem 22625
Bible Museum, Tel Aviv 22751
Bible Museum, Trilofo 21203
Bible Museum of the Danubian District of the Hungarian Reformed Church, Budapest 21334
Biblical Arts Center, Dallas 42746
Biblical Museum of Canada, Vancouver 06665
Biblioludothèque, Paris 13471
Biblioteca Antônio Perdigão, Conselheiro Lafaiete 04052
Biblioteca d'Arte, Milano 24369
Biblioteca e Museu Regional Dr. Alípio de Araújo Silva, Rio Preto 04411
Biblioteca Fundaziun Planta Samedan, Samedan 37094
Biblioteca Luis-Angel Arango, Bogotá 07381
Biblioteca Medicea Laurenziana, Firenze 23822
Biblioteca y Museo Histórico Médicos de Valencia, Valencia 35594
Biblioteka, Muzeum i Archiwum Warszawskiego Towarzystwa Muzycznego im. Stanisława Moniuszki, Warszawa 32076
Biblioteka Narodowa, Warszawa 32077
Biblioteka Sejmowa, Warszawa 32078
Biblioteksmuseet, Borås 35838
Bibliotheca Wittockiana-Musée de la Reliure et du Hochet, Woluwe-Saint-Pierre 03844
Bibliothek Otto Schäfer, Schweinfurt 19888
Bibliothèque d'Art ENSAV de la Cambre, Bruxelles 03274
Bibliothèque d'Art et d'Archéologie des Musées d'Art et d'Histoire de la Ville de Genève, Genève 36726
Bibliothèque d'Art et d'Archéologie Jacques Doucet, Paris 13472
Bibliothèque de l'Arsenal, Paris 13473
Bibliothèque d'Histoire de l'Art, Genève 36727
Bibliothèque Marmottan, Boulogne-Billancourt 10834
Bibliothèque Mazarine, Paris 13474
Bibliothèque-Musée, Toulouse 14936
Bibliothèque-Musée de la Comédie-Française, Paris 13475
Bibliothèque-Musée de l'Observatoire, Paris 13476
Bibliothèque-Musée Forney, Paris 13477
Bibliothèque-Musée Valéry-Larbaud, Vichy 15159
Bibliothèque Publique et Universitaire, Genève 36728
Bibliothèque Publique et Universitaire, Salle Rousseau, Neuchâtel 36982
Bibliothèque Royale de Belgique, Bruxelles 03275
Bicentennial Art Center and Museum, Paris 46283
Bicentennial Historical Museum, Cunnamulla 00962
Bickleigh Castle, Bickleigh 38190
Bicycle and Moped Museum, Zoutkamp 30067
Bicycle Culture Center, Tokyo 26863
Bicycle Culture Center, Tokyo 26831
Bicycle Museum, Dresden 16681
Bicycle Museum, Šiauliai 27526
Bicycle Museum Cycle Center, Sakai 26696
Bicycle Museum of America, New Bremen 45671
Bicycle Shop Museum, Osaka 26647
Bidwell House, Monterey 45460
Bidwell Mansion, Chico 42370
Biedenharn Museum and Gardens, Monroe 45439
Bielen-Säge Museum, Unterschächen 37263
Bien Phong Museum, Ha Noi 48974
Bienen- und Wagnereimuseum, Grieskirchen 01942
Bienenkundemuseum, Münstertal 18953
Bienenmuseum, Alberswil 36443
Bienenmuseum, Berlin 15922
Biermuseum, Laa an der Thaya 02172
Bierreclamemuseum, Breda 29018
Biesbosch Museum, Werkendam 29993
Bieszczady National Park Museum, Ustrzyki Dolne 32063
Big Bear Trails Museum, Loon Lake 05778
Big Beaver Nature Centre and Museum, Big Beaver 05077
Big Bell Gu Zhon Museum, Beijing 06954
Big Bone Lick State Park Museum, Union 48141
Big Hole National Battlefield, Wisdom 48720
Big Pit National Mining Museum of Wales, Blaenavon 38250
Big Red Barn Gallery, Clearmont 42451
Big River Memorial Museum, Big River 05078
Big Shell Museum, Tewantin 01524
Big Springs Museum, Caledonia 42032
Big Thunder Gold Mine, Keystone 44474
Big Well, Greensburg 43820
Bigelow House Museum, Olympia 46139
Biggar Gasworks Museum, Biggar 38193
Biggar Museum and Gallery, Biggar 05079
Biggenden Museum, Biggenden 00801
Biggs Museum of American Art, Dover 42967
Bihar Tribal Welfare Research Institute Museum, Ranchi 22004
Bihari Múzeum, Berettyóujfalu 21321
Bijbels Museum, Amsterdam 28845
Bijbels Openluchtmuseum, Heilig Landstichting 29375
Bijenmuseum Hengelhoef, Houthalen 03507
Bijenteeltmuseum De Bankorf, Amen 28816
Bijenteeltmuseum Kalmthout, Kalmthout 03531
Bijlokemuseum, Gent 03434
Bijskij Kraevedčeskij Muzej V.V. Bianki, Bijsk 32687
Bilbao Fine Arts Museum, Bilbao 34609
Bilboko Arte Eder Museoa / Museo de Bellas Artes de Bilbao, Bilbao 34609
Bild- und Tonarchiv, Graz 01911
Bildarchiv Foto Marburg, Marburg 18624
Bildens Hus, Sundsvall 36307
Bilder-Galerie, Ostseebad Binz 19305
Bilder und Zeichen der Frömmigkeit - Sammlung Rudolf Kriss, Straubing 20076
Bilderdijkmuseum, Amsterdam 28846
Bildmuseet, Umeå 36347
Bilecik Devlet Güzel Sanatlar Galerisi, Bilecik 37635
Bilecik State Gallery, Bilecik 37635
Biljarsk Historical, Architectural and Natural Museum Reserve, Biljarsk 32688
Biljarskij Gosudarstvennyj Istoriko-Architekturnyj i Prirodnyj Muzej-Zapovednik, Biljarsk 32688
Bílkova Vila, Praha 08565
Bílkův Dům v Chýnově, Chýnov u Tábora 08323
Billardmuseum, München 18834
Billingham Art Gallery, Billingham 38201
Billings Estate Museum, Ottawa 06065
Billings Farm and Museum, Woodstock 48742
Billnäsin Kirvesmuseo, Pohja 09938
Billy Bishop Heritage Museum, Owen Sound 06087
Billy Graham Center Museum, Wheaton 48581
Bilston Craft Gallery, Wolverhampton 40916
Biltmore Estate, Asheville 41276
Bily Clock Museum and Antonin Dvorak Exhibition, Spillville 47724
Binalong Motor Museum, Binalong 00802
Binchester Roman Fort, Bishop Auckland 38236
Bindereimuseum Hofbräu Kaltenhausen, Hallein 01996
Bingara Museum, Bingara 00803
Bingham Library Trust Art Collection, Cirencester 38582
Binnenschifffahrts-Museum Oderberg, Oderberg, Mark 19221
Binos Collection, Mytilini 21084
Binscarth and District Gordon Orr Memorial Museum, Binscarth 05081
Biodiversity Museum, Dehradun 21758
Biodôme de Montréal, Montréal 05892
Biohistoricum, Neuburg an der Donau 19017
Biola University Art Gallery, La Mirada 44553
Biological Museum, Imphal 21850
Biological Museum, Stockholm 36235
Biological Sciences Collection, Birmingham 38212
Biologiezentrum des Oberösterreichischen Landesmuseums, Linz 02228
Biologiska Museet, Örebro 36133
Biologiska Museet, Södertälje 36210
Biologiska Museet, Stockholm 36235
Biologiska Museet, Uppsala 36350
Biology Department Teaching Museum, Muncie 45556
Biology Museum, Amman 27046
Biology Museum GMU, Yogyakarta 22218
Biology Museum, Saskatoon 06395
Biomedical Museum, Kuala Lumpur 27640
Birbal Sahni Institute of Palaeobotany Museum, Lucknow 21922

Birchills Canal Museum, Walsall 40771
Birchip Local History Museum, Birchip 00804
Bird Museum, Jönköping 35975
Birds of Vermont Museum, Huntington 44163
Birdsville Working Museum, Birdsville 00805
Birdtail Country Museum, Birtle 05082
Birger Sandzén Memorial Gallery, Lindsborg 44806
Birinci Millet Meclisi Müzesi, Ankara 37616
Birjand Museum, Birjand 22234
Birka Vikingastaden, Adelsö 35781
Birkenes Bygdemuseum, Birkeland 30431
Birkenhead Priory and Saint Mary's Tower, Birkenhead 38204
Birkenhead Tramways and Taylor Street Large Object Collections, Birkenhead 38205
Birks Museum, Decatur 42831
Birla Academy of Art and Culture Museum, Kolkata 21900
Birla Industrial and Technological Museum, Kolkata 21901
Birla Museum, Bhopal 21719
Birla Museum, Pilani 21981
Birmingham Bloomfield Art Center, Birmingham 41712
Birmingham Civil Rights Institute Museum, Birmingham 41705
Birmingham Historical Museum, Birmingham 41713
Birmingham Institute of Art and Design, Birmingham 38213
Birmingham Museum and Art Gallery, Birmingham 38214
Birmingham Museum of Art, Birmingham 41706
Birmingham Nature Centre, Birmingham 38215
Birmingham Railway Museum, Birmingham 38216
Birsfelder Museum, Birsfelden 36572
Birth Place of Ferenc Móra, Kiskunfélegyháza 21458
Birthplace of John Wayne, Winterset 48709
Birthplace of Sibelius, Hämeenlinna 09454
Bisbee Mining and Historical Museum, Bisbee 41714
Bischöfliches Diözesanmuseum für christliche Kunst, Münster 18934
Bischöfliches Diözesanmuseum Klagenfurt, Klagenfurt 02123
Bischöfliches Dom- und Diözesanmuseum, Trier 20207
Bischöfliches Dom- und Diözesanmuseum Mainz, Mainz 18598
Biscuit Tin Museum, Duns 38818
Bishnu Museum, Shillong 22016
Bishop Asbury Cottage, West Bromwich 40821
Bishop Bonner's Cottage Museum, East Dereham 38840
Bishop Gallery, Zacatecas 28634
Bishop Hill Colony, Bishop Hill 41716
Bishop Hill Heritage Museum, Bishop Hill 41717
Bishop Martin Museum, Natchitoches 45634
Bishop of Winchester's Palace Site, Witney 40909
Bishops' House Museum, Sheffield 40482
Bishop's Lodge Museum, Hay 01093
The Bishop's Palace, Galveston 43607
Bishop's Stortford Local History Museum, Bishop's Stortford 38239
Bishops Waltham Museum, Bishop's Waltham 38241
Biskupska Pinakoteka, Dubrovnik 07694
Biskupský Dvůr, Brno 08262
Bismarck-Museum, Bad Kissingen 15674
Bismarck-Museum, Friedrichsruh bei Hamburg 17150
Bismarck-Museum, Schönhausen, Elbe 19833
Bistrița-Nasaud District Museum, Bistrița 32440
Bitola Museum and Gallery, Bitola 27584
Bitterne Local History Centre, Southampton 40543
Biwa-ko Bunkakan, Otsu 26681
Bizen Pottery Traditional and Contemporary Art Museum, Bizen 26118
B.J. Hales Museum of Natural History, Brandon 05118
Bjärnums Museum, Bjärnum 35832
Bjarkøy Museum, Bjarkøy 30432
Bjarne Ness Gallery, Fort Ransom 43445
Bjørgan Prestegård, Kvikne 30622
Bjørn West-Museet, Matredal 30669
Bjugn Bygdatun, Bjugn 30436
BKW-Museum, Mühleberg 36961
B.L. Pasternak House Museum, Peredelkino 33297
B.L. Pasternak Memorial Museum, Čistopol 32748
Blaabjerg Egnsmuseum, Nørre Nebel 08991
Blaavandshuk Egnsmuseum, Oksbøl 09016
Black American West Museum and Heritage Center, Denver 42878
Black Arts National Diaspora, New Orleans 45720
Black Country Living Museum, Dudley 38781
Black Creek Pioneer Village, North York 06030
Black Cultural Archives, London 39580
Black Cultural Centre for Nova Scotia, Dartmouth 05303
Black Fashion Museum, New York 45772
Black Hawk State Historic Site, Rock Island 46953
Black Heritage Museum, Miami 45282
Black Hills Mining Museum, Lead 44699
Black Hills Museum of Natural History, Hill City 44022
Black Kettle Museum, Cheyenne 42296
Black Legends of Professional Basketball Museum, Detroit 42915
Black Mountain College Museum and Arts Center, Asheville 41277
Black Nugget Museum, Ladysmith 05714
Black River Academy Museum, Ludlow 44996
Black River Historical Society of Lorain Museum, Lorain 44883
Black Rock Arts Foundation, San Francisco 47310
Black Watch of Canada Regimental Memorial Museum, Montréal 05893
Blackberry Farm-Pioneer Village, Aurora 41396
Blackburn Museum and Art Gallery, Blackburn, Lancashire 38242
Blackgang Sawmill and Saint Catherine's Quay, Blackgang 38245
Blackman Museum, Snohomish 47659
Blackpool Mill, Narberth 40000
Blackridge Community Museum, Blackridge 38247
Blacksmith Shop Museum, Dover-Foxcroft 42976
Blacksmith's Cottage, Bacchus Marsh 00757
Blackstone Valley Historical Society Museum, Lincoln 44797
Blackville Historical Museum, Blackville 05083
Blackwater Draw Museum, Portales 46614
Blackwater Valley Museum, Benburb 38164
Blackwell Street Center for the Arts, Denville 42903
Blackwell - The Arts and Crafts House, Bowness-on-Windermere 38290
Blackwood Gallery, Mississauga 05869
Blagoveščenskij Sobor, Moskva 33021
Blaine County Historical Museum, Hailey 43868
Blaine County Museum, Chinook 42385
Blaine House, Augusta 41388
Blaine Lake Museum, Blaine Lake 05084
Blair Castle, Blair Atholl 38253
Blair House Museum, Kentville 05660
Blair Museum of Lithophanes, Toledo 48018
The Blairs Museum, Aberdeen 37935
Blaise Castle House Museum, Bristol 38350
Blake Museum, Bridgwater 38324
Blakesley Hall, Birmingham 38217
Blakstad Sykehus Museum, Asker 30400
Blanco Family Museum, Angono 31275
Bland District Historical Museum, West Wyalong 01593
Blanden Memorial Art Museum, Fort Dodge 43388
Blandford Forum Museum, Blandford Forum 38255
Blankschmiede Neimke, Dassel 16552
Blasinstrumenten-Sammlung, Zimmerwald 37363
Blaskovich Múzeum, Tápiószele 21591
Blasmusik-Museum, Ratten 02489
Blau-gelbe Viertelsgalerie, Industrieviertel, Bad Fischau 01696
Blau-gelbe Viertelsgalerie, Mostviertel, Weistrach 02805
Blau-gelbe Viertelsgalerie, Weinviertel Weinviertel, Mistelbach an der Zaya 02301
Blaues Schloß, Obernzenn 19191
Blåvand Museum, Blåvand 08784
Blåvand Redningsbådsmuseum, Blåvand 08785
Bleak House, Broadstairs 38365
Bleakhouse Museum, Fogo Island 05430
Bleikeller, Bremen 16318
Blekinge Museum, Karlskrona 35998
Bleloch Museum, Johannesburg 34273
Blenheim Palace, Woodstock 40924
Blenko Museum of Seattle, Seattle 47528
Bletchley Park Exhibition, Bletchley 38259
Blewitt-Harrison-Lee Museum, Columbus 42580
Blicheregnens Museum, Kjellerup 08918
Blichermuseet på Herningsholm, Herning 08865
Blickling Hall, Norwich 40089
Bligh Museum of Pacific Exploration, Bruny Island 00855
Blikmuseum De Blikvanger, Renesse 29726
Blindaž gde podpisan akt o kapituljacii, Kaliningrad 32867
Blindehistorisk Museum, Hellerup 08856
Blinden-Museum, Berlin 15923
Blindenmuseum, Berlin 15924
Blindenmuseum, Hannover 17592
Blists Hill Victorian Town Open Air Museum, Madeley 39870
BLM Bauernhaus-Museum Bortfeld, Wendeburg 20509
Blockhouse Museum, Merrickville 05841
Blodveimuseet, Rognan 30798
Blokkodden Villmarksmuseet, Engerdal 30480
Blokwachterswoning Waterhuizen, Waterhuizen 29986
Bloom Mansion, Trinidad 48063
Bloomfield Academy Museum, Bloomfield 41737
Bloomfield Science Museum Jerusalem, Jerusalem 22626
Bloomington Art Center, Bloomington 41751
Bloomington Historical Museum, Bloomington 41752
Blount-Bridgers House/ Hobson Pittman Memorial Gallery, Tarboro 47955
Blount Mansion, Knoxville 44513
Bloxham Village Museum, Bloxham 38261
Blue Earth County Historical Museum, Mankato 45119
Blue Hills Trailside Museum, Milton 45352
Blue Licks Battlefield Museum, Mount Olivet 45533
Blue Ridge Institute and Museum, Ferrum 43317
Blue Sky, Portland 46631
Bluebell Railway, Uckfield 40743
Blüchermuseum, Kaub 18035
Bluestone Cottage and Museum, Coburg 00933
Bluestone Museum, Hinton 44039
Bluff Maritime Museum, Bluff 30118
B.M. Kustodiev Museum, Ostrovskoe 33277
BMW Museum, München 18835
B'nai B'rith Klutznick National Jewish Museum, Washington 48338
Bo-Kaap Museum, Cape Town 34201
Bø Museum, Bø i Telemark 30438
Boal Mansion Museum, Boalsburg 41762
Boandik Cultural Museum, Beachport 00778
Boarman Arts Center, Martinsburg 45190
Boat Museum, Ellesmere Port 38926
Boatbuilding Museum, Kråkö 09707
Boatmen's National Bank Art Collection, Saint Louis 47112
Boatmuseum Holsmön, Holmön 35961
Bob Burns Museum, Van Buren 48194
Bob Campbell Geology Museum, Clemson 42455
Bob Jones University Museum and Gallery, Greenville 43829
Bob Marley Museum, Kingston 26065
Bobbitt Visual Arts Center, Albion 41096
BOC Museum, London 39581
Boca Raton Historical Society Museum, Boca Raton 41764
Boca Raton Museum of Art, Boca Raton 41765
Bocholter Brouwerij Museum, Bocholt 03220
Bockwindmühle Brehna, Brehna 16310
Bockwindmühlenmuseum, Trebbus 20194
Bodanrück-Bauernmuseum, Allensbach 15432
Bodaskogs Affärs- och Postmuseum, Aneby 35800
Bodelwyddan Castle Museum, Bodelwyddan 38262
Bodenheimer Heimatmuseum, Bodenheim 16207
Bodensee-Naturmuseum, Konstanz 18202
Bodiam Castle, Robertsbridge 40330
Bodie State Historic Park, Bridgeport 41888
Bodmin and Wenford Railway, Bodmin 38263
Bodmin Town Museum, Bodmin 38264
Bodrum Museum of Underwater Archaeology, Bodrum 37637
Bodrum Sualtı Arkeolojisi Müzesi, Bodrum 37637
Böckstein Montanmuseum Hohe Tauern, Böckstein 01742
Böd of Gremista Museum, Lerwick 39478
Boehm Gallery, San Marcos 47364
Boer Tala Zhou Museum and Gallery, Bole 07000
Börde-Heimatmuseum, Lamstedt 18298
Börde-Museum Burg Ummendorf, Ummendorf 20263
Bördenheimatmuseum Heeslingen, Heeslingen 17658
Boerderij Klein Hulze, Almen 28811
Boerderij Museum Duurswold, Slochteren 29831
Boerderijmuseum De Bovenstreek, Oldebroek 29656
Boerderijmuseum De Lebbenbrugge, Borculo 28997
Boerderijmuseum Zelhem, Zelhem 30053
Boerenbondsmuseum, Gemert 29271
Boerenkrijgmuseum, Overmere 03684
Boerenwagenmuseum, Buren, Gelderland 29042
Bofors Industrimuseum, Karlskoga 35993
Bogdan and Varvara Khanenko Museum of Arts, Kyiv 37867
Bognor Regis Museum, Bognor Regis 38268
Bogor Zoological Museum, Bogor 22088
Bogorodickij Dvorec-muzej i Park, Bogorodick 32694
Bogoroditsk Palace-Museum and Park, Bogorodick 32694
Bogstad Gård, Oslo 30728
Bogstad Manor, Oslo 30728
Bogtrykmuseet, Esbjerg 08805
Bogwood Sculpture Artists, Newtowncashel 22529
Bogyoke Aung San Museum, Yangon 28747
The Bohen Foundation, New York 45773
Bohlenständerhaus, Amriswil 36455
Bohol Museum, Tagbilaran 31455
Bohusläns Museum, Uddevalla 36342
Boiler House Steam and Engine Museum, Kurwongbah 01155
Boise Art Museum, Boise 41771
Bokcheon Municipal Museum, Busan 27135
Bokn Bygdemuseet, Bokn 30442
Bolduc House Museum, Sainte Genevieve 47183
Bolesław Prus Museum, Nałęczów 31820
Bolin Wildlife Exhibit and Antique Collection, McKinney 45036
Bolinao National Museum, Bolinao 31289
Bolinas Museum, Bolinas 41775
Bolivar Hall, San Antonio 47245
Bolívar Museum, Caracas 48908
Bolling Hall Museum, Bradford 38294
Bollinger Mill State Historic Site, Burfordville 41993
Bollnäs Konsthallen, Bollnäs 35837
Bolšemuraškinskij Gosudarstvennyj Istoriko-chudožestvennyj Muzej, Bolšoe Muraškino 32697
Bolšoj Dvorec, Lomonosov 32986
Bolton Historical Museum, Bolton 41777
Bolton Library, Cashel 22386
Bolton Museum and Art Gallery, Bolton 38269
Bolton Steam Museum, Bolton 38270
Bolu Culture Center, Bolu 37639
Bolu Devlet Güzel Sanatlar Galerisi, Bolu 37638
Bolu Kültür Merkezi, Bolu 37639
Bolu State Gallery, Bolu 37638
Bomann-Museum Celle, Celle 16452
Bomarsundmuseet i Prästö Lotsstuga, Sund 10059
De Bommelzolder, Zoeterwoude 30065
Bommen Elvemuseum, Vennesla 30984
Bomsholmen Museum, Arendal 30391
Bonavista Museum, Bonavista 05093
Bonavista North Regional Museum, Wesleyville 06770
Bond Store Port of Maryborough Heritage Museum, Maryborough 01214
Bondgate Gallery, Alnwick 37983
Bo'ness and Kinneil Railway, Bo'ness 38274
Bo'ness Heritage Area, Bo'ness 38275
Bonnefantemuseum, Maastricht 29564
Bonner County Historical Museum, Sandpoint 47382
Bonnet House, Fort Lauderdale 43408
Bonnington Arts Centre, Nakusp 05956
Bonsai-Museum, Seeboden 02656
Bonsai Museum Heidelberg, Heidelberg 17663
Bontoc Museum, Bontoc, Ifugao 31291
Bontoc Museum, Bontoc, Mountain Province 31292
Book Art Museum, Wrocław 32186
Book Cultural Museum, Shaoguan 07229
Book Museum, Antigua 21263
Book Museum, Bath 38112
Book Museum, Moskva 33117
Book Museum Prague, Žďár nad Sázavou 08743
Booker T. Washington National Monument, Hardy 43911
Boolarra Historical Museum, Boolarra 00811
Booleroo Steam and Traction Museum, Booleroo Centre 00812
Boomkwekerijmuseum, Boskoop 29007
Boone County Historical Center, Boone 41783
Boone County Historical Society Museum, Belvidere 41619
Boone's Lick Site, Boonesboro 41787
Boonsborough Museum of History, Boonsboro 41788
Boonshoft Museum of Discovery, Dayton 42799
The Boorman House, Mauston 45206
Boot Hill Museum, Dodge City 42954
Booth Museum of Natural History, Brighton 38338
Boothbay Railway Village, Boothbay 41790
Boothbay Region Art Foundation, Boothbay Harbor 41791
Borås Idrottsmuseum, Borås 35839
Borås Konstmuseum, Borås 35840
Borås Museum, Borås 35841
Bordentown Historical Society Museum, Bordentown 41793
Border Ethnographic and Regimental Museum, Caransebeș 32488
Border History Museum, Hexham 39236
Border Museum, Imatra 09566
Border Regiment and King's Own Royal Border Regiment Museum, Carlisle 38487
Borg Verhildersum, Leens 29503
Borgarfjördur County Museum, Borgarnes 21625
Borgarsyssel Museum, Sarpsborg 30829
Borgmuseum, Spøttrup 09078
Borgo e Castello Medioevale, Torino 25731
Borgsjö Hembygdsgård, Erikslund 35868
Borisoglebskij Kraevedčeskij Muzej, Borisoglebsk 32698
Borlach-Museum, Bad Dürrenberg 15631
Bormshuis, Antwerpen 03136
Børnenes Museum, København 08922
Bornholms Kunstmuseum, Gudhjem 08846
Bornholms Museum, Rønne 09037
Borodino State Museum of War and History Museum and Reserve, Borodino 32701
Borosov-Musatov Museum-Estate, Saratov 33507
Borough Museum and Art Gallery, Newcastle-under-Lyme 40031
Boryeong Coal Museum, Boryeong 27133
Boscobel House, Shropshire 40513
Boscobel Restoration, Garrison 43630
Bosmuseum, Amsterdam 28847
Bosmuseum, Hechtel 03486
Bosmuseum, Tessenderlo 03774
Bosmuseum Jan van Ruusbroec, Hoeilaart 03498
Bosmuseum Wildert, Essen 03408
Bosque de Ciência, Manaus 04187
Boston Athenaeum, Boston 41798
Boston Fire Museum, Boston 41799
Boston Guildhall Museum, Boston 38282
Boston National Historical Park, Boston 41800
Boston Public Library Art Collections, Boston 41801
Boston University Art Gallery, Boston 41802
Boswell Museum and Mausoleum, Auchinleck 38038
Boswell Museum of Music, East Springfield 43059
Bosworth Battlefield Visitor Centre and Country Park, Market Bosworth 39914
Botanic Garden Museum, Sapporo 26708
Botanic Gardens Museum, Southport 40558
Botanical Museum, Helsinki 09498
Botanical Museum, Lund 36056
Botanical Museum, Oulu 09895
Botanical Museum, Rawalpindi 31055
Botanical Museum of Harvard University, Cambridge 42038
Botanical Museum of the National Gardens, Athinai 20852
Botanical Museum of the Russian Academy of Sciences, Sankt-Peterburg 33381
Botanical Survey Museum of India, Pune 21988
Botanical Survey of India, Dehradun 21759
Botaničeskij Muzej, Sankt-Peterburg 33381
Botanické Oddělení Národního Muzea, Průhonice 08631
Botanische Staatssammlung München, München 18836
Botanisches Museum, Hamburg 17528
Botanisches Museum Berlin-Dahlem, Berlin 15925
Botanisches Museum der Universität Zürich, Zürich 37372
Botanisk Museum, København 08923
Botaniska Museet, Lund 36056
Botany Department of the National Museum, Průhonice 08631
Botany Museum, Faizabad 21800
Botany Museum, Gorakhpur 21812
Botany Museum, Jaunpur 21868
Botany Museum, Kanpur 21881
Botany Museum, Lucknow 21923
De Botermolen, Keerbergen 03533

Botkyrka Konsthall och Xet-Museet, Tumba 36338
Bøtø Nor Gl. Pumpestation, Væggerløse 09097
Botswana National Museum and Art Gallery, Gaborone 03934
Botwood Heritage Centre, Botwood 05100
Boughton House, Kettering 39347
Boulder City-Hoover Dam Museum, Boulder City 41839
Boulder History Museum, Boulder 41833
Boulevard Arts Center, Chicago 42309
Boulia Stone House Museum, Boulia 00819
Boundary Museum, Grand Forks 05513
Bourbaki-Panorama Luzern, Luzern 36907
Bourgeneuf 1900, Saint-Julien-Chapteuil 14294
Bourne Hall Museum, Ewell 38954
Bournemouth Natural Science Society Museum, Bournemouth 38285
Bournemouth Transport Museum, Christchurch 38575
Bournville Centre for Visual Arts, Birmingham 38218
La Bourrine à Rosalie, Sallertaine 14579
La Bouteillerie, Vallon-Pont-d'Arc 15065
Bouzov castle, Bouzov 08254
Bov Museum, Padborg 09022
Bowden Pioneer Museum, Bowden 05102
Bowdoin College Museum of Art, Brunswick 41971
Bowen House/ Roseland Cottage, Woodstock 48737
Bowers Mansion, Carson City 42117
The Bowers Museum of Cultural Art, Santa Ana 47399
Bowers Science Museum, Cortland 42653
The Bowes Museum, Barnard Castle 38087
Bowes Railway Heritage Museum, Gateshead 39026
Bowhill Collection, Selkirk 40467
Bowie Railroad Station and Huntington Museum, Bowie 41845
Bowling Green State University Fine Arts Center Galleries, Bowling Green 41853
Bowls New Zealand Museum, New Plymouth 30212
Bowman, Megahan and Penelec Galleries, Meadville 45215
Bowmanville Museum, Bowmanville 05103
Bowne House, Flushing 43352
Bowood House and Gardens, Calne 38441
Bowraville Folk Museum, Bowraville 00822
La Box, Bourges 10861
Boxenstopmuseum Auto-Zweirad-Spielzeug, Tübingen 20221
Boxfield Gallery, Stevenage 40582
Boyana Church National Museum, Sofia 04848
Boyer Museum and National Marbles Hall of Fame, Wildwood 48620
Boyertown Museum of Historic Vehicles, Boyertown 41855
The Boyle House - Hot Spring County Museum, Malvern 45086
Boyne Valley Historical Cottage, Ubobo 01557
Boys Town Hall of History & Father Flanagan House, Boys Town 41856
Bozhou City Museum, Bozhou 07001
Brabants Museum Oud Oosterhout, Oosterhout 29670
Bracken Community Museum, Bracken 05110
Bracken Hall Countryside Centre, Baildon 38057
Brački Muzej, Škrip 07777
Bradbury Science Museum, Los Alamos 44887
Bradford Brinton Memorial, Big Horn 41680
Bradford County Historical Society Museum, Towanda 48042
Bradford Historical Society Museum, Bradford 41865
Bradford Industrial Museum and Horses at work, Bradford 38295
The Bradford Museum of Collector's Plates, Niles 45953
Bradford-on-Avon Museum, Bradford-on-Avon 38301
Bradley Gallery of Art, Plymouth 46567
Bradley Museum, Mississauga 05870
Braemar Castle, Braemar 38307
Bräustüberlmuseum, Raab 02468
Bragegården, Vaasa 10157
Bragg-Mitchell Mansion, Mobile 45417
Brahetrolleborg Skolemuseum, Faaborg 08812
Brahmshaus, Baden-Baden 15785
Brahmshaus, Heide, Holstein 17659
Braidwood and Rushbrook Museum, Edinburgh 38870
Braidwood Museum, Braidwood 00829
Brain-Watkins House, Tauranga 30258
Braintree District Museum, Braintree 38308
Braintree Historical Society Museum, Braintree 41867
Braith-Mali-Museum, Biberach an der Riß 16138
Braithwaite Fine Arts Gallery, Cedar City 42146
Bralorne Pioneer Museum, Bralorne 05111
Brāļu Amtmaņu Muzejs, Valle 27465
Brāļu Jurjānu Memoriālais Muzejs Meņģeļi, Ērgļi 27354
Brāļu Kaudzīšu Memoriālais Muzejs, Vecpiebalga 27468
Bramah Tea and Coffee Museum, London 39582
Bramall Hall, Bramhall 38309
Brambuk Living Cultural Centre, Halls Gap 01085
Bramsnæs Museum og Arkiv, Kirke Hyllinge 08917
Branch of the Regional Museum of South-Eastern Moravia in Zlín, Luhačovice 08467
Branchville Railroad Shrine and Museum, Branchville 41868
Brand Library and Art Galleries, Glendale 43687
Brande Museum, Brande 08789
Brandenburgische Kunstsammlungen Cottbus, Cottbus 16500
Brandenburgischer Kunstverein Potsdam e.V., Potsdam 19433
Brandenburgisches Forstmuseum Fürstenberg/Havel, Fürstenberg, Havel 17157
Brandenburgisches Freilichtmuseum Altranft, Altranft 15472
Brandenburgisches Textilmuseum Forst, Forst, Lausitz 17023
Brander Museum, Huntly 39279
Brandon Heritage Museum, Brandon 38310
Brandval Museum, Brandval 30449
Brandweermuseum, Wouwse Plantage 30028
Brandweermuseum en Stormrampmuseum, Borculo 28998
Brandweermuseum Wassenaar, Wassenaar 29982
Brandywine Battlefield, Chadds Ford 42174
Brandywine River Museum, Chadds Ford 42175
Branigan Cultural Center, Las Cruces 44657
Branko Deškovič Art Gallery, Bol 07682
Brant Museum & Archives, Brantford 05125
Brantwood, Coniston 38624
Brasilianische Botschaft, Berlin 15926
Brasilianisches Kulturinstitut, Berlin 15927
Brasilienmuseum im Kloster Bardel, Bad Bentheim 15598
Braşov Country Museum of History, Braşov 32449
Braşov Ethnographical Museum, Braşov 32448
Brass Rubbing Centre, Edinburgh 38871
Bratsk United Museum of the History of the Conquest of the Angara River, Bratsk 32704
Bratskij Chudožestvennyj Vystavočnyj Zal, Bratsk 32703
Bratskij Gorodskoj Objedinennyj Muzej Istorii Osvoenija Angary, Bratsk 32704
Brattle Farm Museum, Staplehurst 40581
Brattleboro Museum and Art Center, Brattleboro 41872
Brauer Museum of Art, Valparaiso 48192
Brauerei-Kontor, Bochum 16192
Brauerei-Museum, Haßfurt 17629
Brauerei-Museum, Nesselwang 18999
Brauerei Museum Bürger-Bräu Hof, Hof, Saale 17791
Braueriechäller Kulturforum, Laufen 36847
Brauereikulturmuseum Gut Riedelsbach, Neureichenau 19057
Brauereimuseum, Aldersbach 15424
Brauereimuseum, Altomünster 15468
Brauereimuseum Bräu im Moos, Tüßling 20235
Brauereimuseum im historischen Kronen-Brauhaus zu Lüneburg, Lüneburg 18555
Brauereimuseum im Stift Göß, Leoben 02207
Brauereimuseum in der Brauerei Franz Xaver Glossner, Neumarkt, Oberpfalz 19045
Brauereimuseum Schöneck, Schöneck, Vogtland 19828
Brauhaus-Galerie, Freistadt, Oberösterreich 01850
Brauhausmuseum, Stadtlauringen 20031
Brauhinia Shire Bicentennial Art Gallery, Springsure 01470
Braumuseum, Wieselburg an der Erlauf 03024
Braunauer Heimatmuseum, Forchheim, Oberfranken 17019
Braunschweigisches Landesmuseum, Braunschweig 16293
Braunschweigisches Landesmuseum, Wolfenbüttel 20651
Braunton and District Museum, Braunton 38311
Bray Heritage Centre and Museum, Bray 22378
Brayshaw Museum Park, Blenheim 30117
Brazilian Federation of Friends of Museums, São Paulo 49082
Brazoria County Historical Museum, Angleton 41210
Brazos Valley Museum of Natural History, Bryan 41974
Brazosport Museum of Natural Science, Brazosport 41873
Brazosport Museum of Natural Science, Clute 42506
Bread & Puppet Museum, Glover 43706
Breadalbane Folklore Centre, Killin 39359
Breamore Countryside Museum, Breamore 38312
Breamore House Museum, Breamore 38313
Brebner Surgical Museum, Johannesburg 34274
Brechin Museum, Brechin 38314
Brecht-Haus Weißensee, Berlin 15928
Brecht-Weigel-Gedenkstätte, Berlin 15929
Brechthaus, Augsburg 15551
Brecknock Museum and Art Gallery, Brecon 38316
Brecon Mountain Railway, Merthyr Tydfil 39936
Breda's Begijnhof Museum, Breda 29019
Breda's Museum, Breda 29020
De Brede, Maasbree 29560
Brede Værk, Kongens Lyngby 08961
Brede Works, Kongens Lyngby 08961
Bredy Farm Old Farming Collection, Bridport 38330
Breendonk Fort National Memorial, Willebroek 03840
Brehm-Gedenkstätte, Renthendorf 19572
Breidablikk, Stavanger 30879
Bremer Rundfunkmuseum, Bremen 16319
Bremerhavener Versorgungs- und Verkehrsmuseum, Bremerhaven 16338
Bremerton Naval Museum, Bremerton 41878
Brenau University Galleries, Gainesville 43588
Brennan and Geraghty's Store Museum, Maryborough 01215
Brennereimuseum Haselünne, Haselünne 17624
Brensbach Museum und Galerie im alten Rathaus, Brensbach 16354
Brentwood Museum, Brentwood 38319
Brenzett Aeronautical Museum, Romney Marsh 40339
Breslaylor Heritage Museum, Paynton 06101
Bressingham Steam Museum, Diss 38733
Brett Whiteley Studio Museum, Surry Hills 01485
Breuberg-Museum, Breuberg 16358
Brevard Museum, Cocoa 42508
Brevard Museum of Art and Science, Melbourne 45229
Brevik Bymuseum, Brevik 30451
Brewarrina Aboriginal Cultural Museum, Brewarrina 00830
Brewery Chapel Museum, Halstead 39158
Brewery Museum, Plzeň 08544
Brewery Museum Arboga, Arboga 35805
Brewery Museum Bocholt, Bocholt 03220
Brewhouse Yard Museum, Nottingham 40104
Briar Herb Factory Museum, Clyde 30135
Bribie Island Community Arts Centre, Bribie Island 00832
Brick House, Montgomery 45469
Brick Store Museum, Kennebunk 44434
Bridewell Museum, Norwich 40090
Bridge Center for Contemporary Art, El Paso 43112
Bridgehampton Historical Society Museum, Bridgehampton 41886
Bridgestone Bijutsukan, Tokyo 26832
Bridgestone Museum of Art, Ishibashi Foundation, Tokyo 26832
Bridgetown Old Gaol Museum, Bridgetown 00833
Bridgnorth Northgate Museum, Bridgnorth 38321
Bridgton Historical Museum, Bridgton 41896
Bridlington Harbour Museum, Bridlington 38328
Bridport Museum, Bridport 38331
Briedes Krogs in the Burtnieki Parish, Burtnieki 27340
Briefmarkenmuseum im Kloster Bardel, Bad Bentheim 15599
Briercrest and District Museum, Briercrest 05132
Brierley Hill Glass Museum, Brierley Hill 38334
Brierly Jigsaw Gallery, Bridgetown 00834
Briged Pasukan Polis Hutan, Kuching 27657
Brigham City Museum-Gallery, Brigham City 41897
Brigham Young University Earth Science Museum, Provo 46733
Brigham Young University Museum of Art, Provo 46734
Brigham Young's Winter Home, Saint George 47090
Brightlingsea Museum, Brightlingsea 38336
Brighton Fishing Museum, Brighton 38339
Brighton Museum and Art Gallery, Brighton 38340
Brillantes Ancestral House, Tayum 31459
Brimstone Museum, Sulphur 47874
Brindley Bank Pumping Station and Museum, Rugeley 40358
Brink 7 Galerij, Yde 30029
Brinkens Museum, Malax 09812
Brisbane City Gallery, Brisbane 00836
Brisbane Tramway Museum, Ferny Grove 01023
Bristol City Museum and Art Gallery, Bristol 38351
Bristol Historical and Preservation Society Museum, Bristol 41904
Bristol Industrial Museum, Bristol 38352
Britannia Heritage Shipyard, Richmond 06260
British Association of Friends of Museums, Launceston 49402
British Aviation Preservation Council, Coventry 49403
British Balloon Museum, Newbury 40029
British Columbia Aviation Museum, Sidney 06448
British Columbia Congenital Heart Museum, Vancouver 06666
British Columbia Farm Machinery and Agricultural Museum, Fort Langley 05440
British Columbia Forest Discovery Centre, Duncan 05352
British Columbia Forest Service Museum, Victoria 06713
British Columbia Golf House Museum, Vancouver 06667
British Columbia Medical Association Museum, Vancouver 06668
British Columbia Mineral Museum, Victoria 06714
British Columbia Museum of Mining, Britannia Beach 05135
British Columbia Museums Association, Victoria 49093
British Columbia Orchard Industry Museum, Kelowna 05650
British Columbia Regiment Museum, Vancouver 06669
British Columbia Sports Hall of Fame and Museum, Vancouver 06670
British Columbia Sugar Museum, Vancouver 06671
British Commercial Vehicle Museum, Leyland 39487
British Cycling Museum, Camelford 38466
British Dental Association Museum, London 39583
British Empire and Commonwealth Museum, Bristol 38353
British Engineerium, Hove 39268
British Film Institute Collections, London 39584
British Golf Museum, Saint Andrews 40381
British in India Museum, Colne 38619
British Lawnmower Museum, Southport 40559
British Library, London 39585
The British Museum, London 39586
British Optical Association Museum, London 39587
British Photographic Museum, Totnes 40722
British Red Cross Museum and Archives, London 39588
British Telecom Museum, Oxford 40143
Brixham Museum, Brixham 38362
Brjanskij Gosudarstvennyj Obedinennyj Kraevedčeskij Muzej, Brjansk 32706
Brjanskij Literaturnyj Muzej, Brjansk 32707
Brjanskij Oblastnoj Chudožestvennyj Muzej, Brjansk 32708
Brno Municipal Museum, Brno 08273
Brno Museum of Technology, Brno 08277
Broadfield House Glass Museum, Kingswinford 39387
Broadview Museum, Broadview 05136
Broadway Magic Experience, Broadway 38368
Broby Hembygdspark, Broby 35847
Brocksden County School Museum, Stratford 06498
Brockville Museum, Brockville 05138
Brodick Castle, Brodick 38373
Brodie Castle, Forres 39007
Brodsworth Hall & Gardens, Doncaster 38740
Bröhan-Museum, Berlin 15930
Broelmuseum, Kortrijk 03540
Broken Hill Regional Art Gallery, Broken Hill 00846
Brome County Historical Society Museum, Knowlton 05703
Bromfield Art Gallery, Boston 41803
Bromfietsmuseum De Peel, Ospel 29682
Bromham Mill and Art Gallery, Bromham 38375
Bromsgrove Museum, Bromsgrove 38377
Bronck Museum, Coxsackie 42685
Brønshøj Museum, Brønshøj 08791
Brontë Parsonage Museum, Haworth 39199
Bronx County Historical Society Museum, Bronx 41914
Bronx Museum of the Arts, Bronx 41915
Brookfield Craft Center, Brookfield 41928
Brookfield Museum, Brookfield 41929
Brookgreen Gardens, Murrells Inlet 45574
Brooking Collection, Dartford 38699
Brookings Arts Council, Brookings 41931
Brookings County Museum, Volga 48256
Brooklands Museum, Weybridge 40840
Brookline Historical Society Museum, Brookline 41934
Brooklyn Arts Council Gallery, Bronx 41916
Brooklyn Children's Museum, Brooklyn 41940
Brooklyn Historical Society Museum, Brooklyn 41953
Brooklyn Museum of Art, Brooklyn 41941
Brooks Academy Museum, Harwich 43954
Brooks and District Museum, Brooks 05139
Brookside Saratoga County Historical Society, Ballston Spa 41445
Broome County Historical Society Museum, Binghamton 41698
Broome Historical Society Museum, Broome 00852
Broomehill Museum, Broomehill 00853
Bror Hjorths Hus, Uppsala 36351
Brot- und Mühlen-Lehrmuseum, Gloggnitz 01884
Brother Kaudzītes Memorial Museum, Vecpiebalga 27468
Brother Rice Museum, Waterford 22552
Broughton House and Garden, Kirkcudbright 39392
Broughty Castle Museum, Dundee 38797
Brouwershuis, Antwerpen 03137
Brouws Museum, Brouwershaven 29031
Broward County Historical Museum, Fort Lauderdale 43409
Brown County Art Gallery and Museum, Nashville 45609
Brown County Historical Society Museum, New Ulm 45748
Brown County Historical Society Pioneer Museum, Nashville 45610
Brown House Museum, Sandersville 47379
Brownella Cottage, Galion 43602
Brownsbank Cottage, Biggar 38194
Brownsville Museum of Fine Art, Brownsville 41965
Browntown Museum, Lake City 44584
Brownvale North Peace Agricultural Museum, Brownvale 05140
Brownville Historical Society Museum, Brownville 41966
Brubacher House Museum, Waterloo 06750
Bruce Castle Museum, London 39589
Bruce County Museum, Southampton 06476
Bruce Mines Museum, Bruce Mines 05141
Brucemore, Cedar Rapids 42156
Bruckbacher Hoarstubn, Weyregg am Attersee 02828
Brucknerzimmer, Kronstorf 02166
Brudavollen Bygdetun, Ørsta 30721
Bruder-Konrad-Museum, Altötting 15462
Die Brücke, Braunschweig 16294
Brücke Museum, Berlin 15931
Brückenhausmuseum, Erfurt 16896
Brueckner Museum, Albion 41097
Brückturm-Museum über der 'Steinernen Brücke', Regensburg 19517
Brüder Grimm-Haus Steinau, Steinau an der Straße 20042
Brüder Grimm-Museum Kassel, Kassel 18012
Brüder-Grimm-Stube, Marburg 18625
Brünner Heimatmuseum, Schwäbisch Gmünd 19860
Brüxer und Komotauer Heimatstuben, Erlangen 16916
Bruggemuseum - Archaeology, Brugge 03247
Bruggemuseum - Archeologie, Brugge 03247
Bruggemuseum - Belfort, Brugge 03248
Bruggemuseum - Brugse Vrije, Brugge 03249
Bruggemuseum - Gruuthuse, Brugge 03250
Bruggemuseum - Onthaalkerk van Onze-Lieve-Vrouw, Brugge 03251
Bruggemuseum - Stadhuis, Brugge 03252
Brugwachterhuis, Dilsen-Stokkem 03390
Brukenthal National Museum, Sibiu 32593
Bruksmuseet i Robertsfors, Robertsfors 36161
Bruksmuseet Smedsgården, Sandviken 36177
Bruksmuseum, Eksjö 35859

Brunei Arts and Handicrafts Training Centre, Bandar Seri Begawan 04600
Brunei Forestry Museum, Sungai Liang 04602
Brunei Gallery, London 39590
Brunei Museum, Bandar Seri Begawan 04598
Brunel Engine House, London 39591
Brunnenmuseum, Bad Vilbel 15758
Brunnenmuseum, Goslar 17347
Brunner Heimathaus mit Rudolf-Steiner-Gedenkstätte, Brunn am Gebirge 01754
Brunner Mine Site, Dobson 30143
Brunnier Art Museum, Ames 41170
Brunskogs Hembygdsgård, Brunskog 35848
Brunswick Railroad Museum, Brunswick 41970
Brunswick Town State Historic Site, Winnabow 48691
Brunswick Valley Museum, Mullumbimby 01288
Brush Country Museum, Cotulla 42670
Brussels Museum of Industry and Labor, Bruxelles 03292
Bruunshåb Gamle Papfabrik, Viborg 09107
Bruxella 1238, Bruxelles 03276
Bry Gallery, Monroe 45440
Bryansk Museum of Fine Arts, Brjansk 32708
Bryansk Museum of Literature, Brjansk 32707
Bryansk State Museum of Local Lore, Brjansk 32706
Bryant Cottage, Bement 41620
Brydone Jack Observatory Museum, Fredericton 05458
Bryggens Museum, Bergen 30419
BSAT Gallery, Newmarket 40049
BT Museum, London 39592
Bu Museum, Utne 30962
Buccleuch Mansion, New Brunswick 45676
Bucerius Kunst Forum, Hamburg 17529
Buchanan Center for the Arts, Monmouth 45434
Buchara State Museum, Buchara 48832
Bucharskij Gosudarstvennyj Muzej, Buchara 48832
Buchdruckmuseum, Rohrbach in Oberösterreich 02523
s'Buchholze Hisli, Schuttertal 19856
Buchholzer Heimatmuseum, Buchholz in der Nordheide 16389
Buchmuseum, Solothurn 37180
Buchmuseum der Sächsischen Landesbibliothek - Staats- und Universitätsbibliothek Dresden, Dresden 16677
Buckfast Abbey, Buckfastleigh 38380
Buckham Fine Arts Project Gallery, Flint 43338
Buckhaven Museum, Buckhaven 38383
Buckhorn Museum, San Antonio 47246
Buckie Drifter Maritime Museum, Buckie 38384
Buckingham Movie Museum, Buckingham 38386
Buckingham Palace, London 39593
Buckinghamshire County Museum, Aylesbury 38046
Buckinghamshire Railway Centre, Quainton 40275
Buckland Abbey, Yelverton 40953
Buckland Heritage Museum, Spruce Home 06483
Buckler's Hard Village Maritime Museum, Buckler's Hard 38388
Buckley Center Gallery, Portland 46632
Buckleys Yesterday's World, Battle 38131
Bucksport Historical Museum, Bucksport 41977
Bucyrus Historical Society Museum, Bucyrus 41978
Budapest History Museum, Budapest 21331
Budapesti Történeti Múzeum, Budapest 21331
Budavári Mátyás Templom Egyházmüvészeti Gyüjteménye, Budapest 21332
Buddelschiff-Museum, Neuharlingersiel 19032
Buddelschiff-Museum, Tangerhütte 20137
Buddelschiff-Museum, Wedel 20413
Buddenbrookhaus, Lübeck 18534
The Buddhist Art Museum, Yangon 28748
Buddhist Art Photo Gallery Banri Namikawa, Hiroshima 26221
Buddhist Museum Koya-San, Koya 26373
Buddle Arts Centre, Wallsend 40768
Buddy Holly Center, Lubbock 44990
Bude-Stratton Museum, Bude 38389
Budenz-Ház, Székesfehérvár 21554
Buderim Pioneer Cottage, Buderim 00856
Budjonny House-Museum, Proletarsk 33329
Buechel Memorial Lakota Museum, Saint Francis 47088
Büchnerhaus, Riedstadt 19601
Büchsenmacher- und Jagdmuseum, Ferlach 01836
Büecheler-Hus, Kloten 36828
Buena Park Historical Society Museum, Buena Park 41979
Bündner Kunstmuseum, Chur 36632
Bündner Natur-Museum, Chur 36633
Bürger- und Bauernmuseum, Hilzingen 17764
Bürgerhaus Grünau, Berlin 15932
Bürgerkorpsmuseum im Kanzlerturm, Eggenburg 01790
Bürgermeister-Müller-Museum, Solnhofen 19992
Bürgerstiftung Kunst für Güglingen, Güglingen 17452
Büro Friedrich, Berlin 15933
Büro Otto Koch, Dessau 16577
Büromaschinen-Museum, Aspang 01683
Büromuseum, Mülheim an der Ruhr 18814
Bürsten- und Heimatmuseum, Schönheide 19834
Büyük Saray Mozaik Müzesi, İstanbul 37697
Buffalo and Erie County Historical Society Museum, Buffalo 41983
Buffalo and Erie County Naval and Military Park, Buffalo 41984
Buffalo Bean Museum, Tompkins 06556
Buffalo Bill Cody Homestead, Princeton 46695
Buffalo Bill Historical Center, Cody 42510
Buffalo Bill Memorial Museum, Golden 43712
Buffalo Bill Museum of Le Claire, Iowa, Le Claire 44696
Buffalo Bill Ranch, North Platte 46003
Buffalo Museum of Science, Buffalo 41985
Buffalo Nations Luxton Museum, Banff 05042
Buffalo Trails Museum, Epping 43197
Buffs Museum, Canterbury 38469
Bugatti Trust, Cheltenham 38542
BuGok Railroad Exhibition Hall, Uiwang 27296
Buguruslanskij Istoriko-kraevedčeskij Muzej, Buguruslan 32712
Building of Bath Museum, Bath 38113
Bujnakskij Istoriko-kraevedčeskij Muzej, Bujnaksk 32713
Bukovac Art Gallery, Cavtat 07688
Bukyoung University Museum, Busan 27136
Bulakan Provincial Museum, Malolos 31361
Bulat Okudshava Memorial House-Museum, Peredelkino 33298
Bulgarian Museum Chamber, Sofia 49084
Bulkley Valley Museum, Smithers 06462
Bullfighting Museum, Valencia 35611
Bulloch Hall, Roswell 47012
Bulwagang Helena Benitez Gallery, Manila 31371
Bunbury Regional Art Galleries, Bunbury 00859
Bunbury Watermill, Bunbury 38393
Bundaberg Arts Centre, Bundaberg 00860
Bundaberg Historical Museum, Bundaberg 00861
Bundaberg Railway Museum, Bundaberg 00862
Bundelkhand Chhatrasal Museum, Banda 21700
Bundesbriefmuseum, Schwyz 37149
Bundesverband Museumspädagogik e.V., München 49195
Bungay Museum, Bungay 38394
Bunin Memorial Literary Museum, Elec 32791
Bunin Museum, Orël 33265
Bunka Gakuen Fukushoku Hakabutsukan, Tokyo 26833
Bunkamura Museum of Art, Tokyo 26834
Bunker d'Hitler, Brûly-de-Pesche 03268
Bunker Hill Museum, Charlestown 42233
Bunker Museet, Frederikshavn 08829
Bunker Museum, Ala-Philaja 09412
Bunker Museum, Kaliningrad 32867
Bunker Museum 1940-1944, Miehikkälä 09826
Bunker of J.W. Stalin, Samara 33366
Bunker Stalina, Samara 33366
Bunnell Street Gallery, Homer 44067
Bunratty Castle and Folkpark, Bunratty 22380
Buque Museo Ex BAP América, Iquitos 31184
Buque-Museo Fragata Presidente Sarmiento, Buenos Aires 00144
Buque Museo Yaraví, Puerto de Puno 31242
Burapha Museum of Art, Chon Buri 37505
La Burbuja-Museo del Niño, Hermosillo 27984
Burchfield-Penney Art Center, Buffalo 41986
Burden Gallery, New York 45774
Burdur Devlet Güzel Sanatlar Galerisi, Burdur 37640
Burdur Müzesi, Burdur 37641
Burdur Museum, Burdur 37641
Burdur State Gallery, Burdur 37640
Bureau County Historical Society Museum, Princeton 46696
Burg Beeskow, Beeskow 15867
Burg Falkenberg, Falkenberg, Oberpfalz 16983
Burg Forchtenstein, Eisenstadt 01803
Burg Gleichen, Wandersleben 20389
Burg Gnandstein, Kohren-Sahlis 18195
Burg Greifenstein, Greifenstein 01937
Burg Hagen, Hagen bei Bremerhaven 17477
Burg Hohenzollern, Bisingen 16172
Burg Kreuzen, Bad Kreuzen 01711
Burg Kreuzenstein, Leobendorf 02211
Burg Kronberg, Kronberg 18246
Burg Lauenstein, Ludwigsstadt 18528
Burg Meersburg, Meersburg 18673
Burg Mildenstein, Leisnig 18426
Burg-Museum, Parsberg 19350
Burg Neuhaus, Wolfsburg 20658
Burg Pappenheim mit Naturmuseum und Historischem Museum, Pappenheim 19347
Burg Prunn, Riedenburg 19595
Burg Rabenstein, Frohnleiten 01856
Burg Stolpen, Stolpen 20069
Burg Trausnitz, Landshut 18308
Burg Trifels, Annweiler 15500
Burg- und Klosteranlage Oybin, Kurort Oybin 18274
Burg- und Mühlenmuseum Pewsum, Krummhörn 18254
Burg- und Schloßmuseum Allstedt, Allstedt 15434
Burg- und Stadtmuseum Königstein, Königstein im Taunus 18181
Burg Vischering, Lüdinghausen 18552
Burg Wernstein, Wernstein am Inn 02824
Burg zu Burghausen, Burghausen, Salzach 16418
Burg Zwernitz, Wonsees 20674
Burgas Museum, Burgas 04632
Burgaski Muzej, Burgas 04632
Burgenkundliche Sammlung im Burgenmuseum, Gossau (Sankt Gallen) 36770
Burgenkundliches Museum des Steirischen Burgenvereins, Bärnbach 01730
Burgenländische Landesgalerie, Eisenstadt 01804
Burgenländisches Brotmuseum, Bad Tatzmannsdorf 01718
Burgenländisches Feuerwehrmuseum, Eisenstadt 01805
Burgenländisches Landesmuseum, Eisenstadt 01806
Burgenländisches Schulmuseum, Lockenhaus 02246
Burgenländisches Steinmuseum, Landsee 02181
Burgenmuseum Eisenberg, Eisenberg, Allgäu 16821
Burger Weeshuis, Zierikzee 30059
Burgersdorp Cultural Historical Museum, Burgersdorp 34197
Burggalerie Laa, Laa an der Thaya 02173
Burghead Museum, Burghead 38396
Burgher's House - Helsinki City Museum, Helsinki 09525
Burghley House, Stamford 40575
Burghofmuseum, Soest 19978
Burgmuseum, Dunaföldvár 21403
Burgmuseum, Güssing 01969
Burgmuseum, Höhr-Grenzhausen 17783
Burgmuseum, Kirschau 18101
Burgmuseum, Lenzen, Elbe 18441
Burgmuseum, Lisberg 18486
Burgmuseum, Ortenberg, Hessen 19269
Burgmuseum, Seebenstein 02655
Burgmuseum, Sulzberg 20127
Burgmuseum, Wolfsegg 20666
Burgmuseum Altnußberg, Geiersthal 17211
Burgmuseum Bad Bodenteich, Bad Bodenteich 15618
Burgmuseum Burg Guttenberg, Haßmersheim 17630
Burgmuseum Clam, Klam 02134
Burgmuseum der Wasserburg Kapellendorf, Kapellendorf 17983
Burgmuseum für Vor- und Frühgeschichte, Deutschlandsberg 01762
Burgmuseum Grünwald, Grünwald 17449
Burgmuseum Marksburg, Braubach 16287
Burgmuseum Reichenstein, Pregarten 02450
Burgmuseum Ruine Dürnstein, Wildbad-Einöd 03028
Burgmuseum Schlossfreiheit, Tangermünde 20138
Burgmuseum Schönfels, Schönfels 19831
Burgmuseum Waldeck, Waldeck, Hessen 20357
Burgruine Münzenberg, Münzenberg 18956
Burgturm Davert, Ascheberg, Westfalen 15535
Burgwin-Wright Museum, Wilmington 48658
Burin Heritage House, Burin 05144
Burjatskij Gosudarstvennyj Objedinennyj Istoričeskij i Architekturno-chudožestvennyj Muzej, Ulan-Udė 33650
Burjatskij Respublikanskij Chudožestvennyj Muzej im. C.S. Sampilova, Ulan-Udė 33651
Burke County Historical Powers Lake Complex, Powers Lake 46681
Burke Museum, Beechworth 00783
Burke Museum of Natural History and Culture, Seattle 47529
Burleson County Historical Museum, Caldwell 42031
Burlington Art Centre, Burlington 05145
Burlington County Historical Society Museum, Burlington 42004
Burlington Historical Museum, Burlington 42000
Burlington Historical Museum, Burlington 42001
Burlington-Rock Island Railroad and Historical Museum, Teague 47965
Burlövs Gamla Prästgård, Arlöv 35811
Burlovs Old Rectory, Arlöv 35811
Burmeister & Wain's Museum, København 08924
Burnaby Art Gallery, Burnaby 05148
Burnaby Village Museum, Burnaby 05149
Burnett House and Myilly Point Heritage Precinct, Darwin 00972
Burnham Museum, Burnham-on-Crouch 38397
Burnham Tavern, Machias 45027
Burnie Regional Art Gallery, Burnie 00863
Burns Cottage Museum, Alloway 37980
Burns House Museum, Mauchline 39925
Burnside Plantation, Bethlehem 41664
Burnt House Museum, Jerusalem 22627
Burntisland Museum, Burntisland 38403
Burøsund Bygdemuseum, Vannareid 30971
Burpee Museum of Natural History, Rockford 46959
Burra Mine Open Air Museum, Burra 00865
Burrell Collection, Glasgow 39039
Burren Centre, Kilfenora 22485
Burritt on the Mountain, Huntsville 44172
Burrowes Mansion Museum, Matawan 45203
Bursa Archaeological Museum, Bursa 37644
Bursa Arkeoloji Müzesi, Bursa 37644
Bursa Devlet Güzel Sanatlar Galerisi, Bursa 37645
Bursa State Gallery, Bursa 37645
Bursa Türk-İslâm Eserleri Müzesi, Bursa 37646
Bursa Turkish and Islamic Art Museum, Bursa 37646
Bursledon Windmill, Bursledon 38404
Burstarfell Local Museum, Vopnafjörður 21675
Burston Strike School, Burston, Diss 38406
Burt County Museum, Tekamah 47967
Burtnieku Pagasta Briedes Krogs, Burtnieki 27340
Burton Agnes Hall, Burton Agnes 38407
The Burton Art Gallery and Museum, Bideford 38191
Burton Constable Hall, Kingston-upon-Hull 39376
Burton Court, Eardisland 38834
Burwell-Morgan Mill, Millwood 45351
Burwell Museum, Burwell 38410
Bury Art Gallery and Museum, Bury, Lancashire 38411
Bury Saint Edmunds Art Gallery, Bury Saint Edmunds 38415
Bury Transport Museum, Bury, Lancashire 38412
Buryatian United Museum of History, Architecture and Art, Ulan-Udė 33650
Busan Museum, Busan 27137
Busan University Museum, Busan 27138
Busan Woman's College Tea-ceremony Museum, Busan 27139
Buscot House, Buscot 38420
Buscot Park House, Faringdon 38977
Bush House Museum and Bush Barn Art Center, Salem 47207
Bushey Museum and Art Gallery, Bushey 38421
Bushman Site Museum, Estcourt 34239
Bushwhacker Museum, Nevada 45652
Bushy Run Battlefield Museum, Jeannette 44320
Bussemakerhuis, Borne 29006
Butcher's Shop from 1920, Roskilde 09045
Bute Museum, Rothesay 40347
Butler County Historical Museum, Allison 41149
Butler County Museum, Hamilton 43883
Butler County Museum and Kansas Oil Museum, El Dorado 43107
Butler Gallery, Kilkenny 22487
Butler Institute of American Art, Youngstown 48807
Butrinti Museum, Butrint 00014
Butte Silver Bow Arts Chateau, Butte 42016
Butter Pat Museum, Bigfork 41686
Butterfield Trail Historical Museum, Russell Springs 47037
Butterfly and Bird Museum, Stockholm 36241
Butuan City Museum, Butuan 31294
Butuan Diocesan Museum, Butuan 31295
Butuan National Museum, Butuan 31296
Buxtehude Museum für Regionalgeschichte und Kunst, Buxtehude 16439
Buxton Museum, North Buxton 06020
Buxton Museum and Art Gallery, Buxton 38427
Buyeo National Museum, Buyeo 27145
Buzău District Museum, Buzău 32477
Buzulukskij Gorodskoj Istoriko-kraevedčeskij Muzej, Buzuluk 32714
Bwlch Farm Stable Museum, Llanelli 39545
By the Bay Museum, Lewisporte 05752
Bydgoszcz Country Educational Museum, Bydgoszcz 31515
Byers-Evans House Museum, Denver 42879
Byfield and District Museum, Byfield 00868
Bygdetunet Jutulheimen, Vågåmo 30967
Byggðasafn, Vestmannaeyjar 21673
Byggðasafn Akraness og Nærsveita, Akranes 21618
Byggðasafn Árnesinga, Eyrarbakki 21631
Byggðasafn Austur-Skaftafellssýslu, Höfn 21638
Byggðasafn Borgarfjardar, Borgarnes 21625
Byggðasafn Dalamanna, Búdardalur 21627
Byggðasafn Dalvíkurbyggdar, Dalvík 21628
Byggðasafn Hafnarfjarðar, Hafnarfjörður 21633
Byggðasafn Húnvetninga og Strandarmanna, Brú 21626
Byggðasafn Rangæinga, Skogar 21670
Byggðasafn Reykjanesbaejar, Reykjanesbaer 21646
Byggðasafn Skagfirdinga, Varmahlid 21672
Byggðasafn Snæfellinga og Hnappdæla, Stykkishólmur 21671
Byggðasafn Vestfjarda, Isafjörður 21641
Byggðasafnid Grenjadarstad, Húsavík 21639
Bygland Museum, Bygland 30455
Bygones at Holkham, Wells-next-the-Sea 40813
Bygones Museum, Claydon 38587
Byland Abbey, Coxwold 38651
Bymodellen, Oslo 30729
Bymuseet, Skjern 09062
Bymuseet Møntergården, Odense 09005
Byron Historical Museum, Byron 42021
Bytown Historical Museum, Ottawa 06066
Byzantine and Christian Museum, Athinai 20853
Byzantine Collection, Chalkida 20914
Byzantine Museum, Paphos 08213
Byzantine Museum, Tinos 21199
Byzantine Museum and Art Galleries, Lefkosia 08194
Byzantine Museum of Antivouniotissa, Corfu 20929
Byzantine Museum of Katapoliani, Paros 21111
Byzantine Museum of the Metropolis of Samos and Ikaria, Samos 21147
C. Grier Beam Truck Museum, Cherryville 42280
Cabanon de Le Corbusier, Roquebrune-Cap-Martin 14024
Cabaret Mechanical Theatre, London 39594
Cabinet d'Art Asiatique, Labarde 12278
Cabinet des Estampes du Musée d'Art et d'Histoire, Genève 36729
Cabinet des Estampes et des Dessins, Liège 03567
Cabinet des Estampes et des Dessins, Strasbourg 14805
Cabinet des Médailles, Bruxelles 03277
Cabinet des Medailles et Antiques, Paris 13478
Cabinet des Monnaies et Médailles, Marseille 12845
Cabinet des Monnais et Médailles du Revest-les-Eaux, Le Revest-les-Eaux 12477
Cabinet Numismatique de la Bibliothèque Nationale et Universitaire de Strasbourg, Strasbourg 14806
Cabinet War Rooms, London 39595
Cable Natural History Museum, Cable 42022
Cabot Historical Society Museum, Cabot 42023
Cabot's Old Indian Pueblo Museum, Desert Hot Springs 42914
Cabri and District Museum, Cabri 05154
Cabrillo National Monument, San Diego 47271
Cachots et Oubliettes au Château, Durtal 11591
Caddo-Pine Island Oil and Historical Society Museum, Oil City 46105
Caddoan Mounds, Cherokee County 42277
Caddy's Diner, Purmerend 29716
Cadeby Experience, Cadeby 38429
Cadeby Light Railway, Cadeby 38430
Cades Cove Open-Air Museum, Townsend 48044
Cadillac Museum, Cadillac 05156

Caernarfon Maritime Museum, Caernarfon 38432
Caerphilly Castle, Caerphilly 38436
Caesarea Museum, Kibbutz Sedot Yam 22703
Café-Museum Zum Puppenhaus, Immenstaad 17894
Cagayan Museum, Tuguegarao 31460
Caguana Indian Ceremonial Park and Museum, Utuado 32410
Cahit Sıtkı Tarancı Culture Museum, Diyarbakır 37660
Cahit Sıtkı Tarancı Müzesi, Diyarbakır 37660
Cahokia Courthouse State Historic Site, Cahokia 42025
Cahokia Mounds State Historic Site, Collinsville 42530
Cahoon Museum of American Art, Cotuit 42668
Caidian District Museum, Wuhan 07279
Cairns Museum, Cairns 00872
Cairns Regional Gallery, Cairns 00873
Cairo Geological Museum, Cairo 09257
Cairo Museum, Vicksburg 48227
Caithness District Museum, Wick 40867
Čajkovskaja Kartinnaja Galereja, Čajkovskij 32715
Čajkovskij Kraevedčeskij Muzej, Čajkovskij 32716
Calala Cottage, Tamworth 01514
Calaveras County Museum, San Andreas 47238
Calbourne Water Mill and Rural Museum, Calbourne 38437
Calcografia, Roma 25149
Calcografia Nacional, Madrid 34989
Calderdale Industrial Museum, Halifax 39150
Calderglen County Park, East Kilbride 38843
Caldicot Castle, Caldicot 38438
Caleb Lothrop House, Cohasset 42513
Caleb Pusey House, Upland 48156
Caledon Museum, Caledon 34198
The Calgach Centre, Derry 38722
Calgary and Edmonton Railway Museum, Edmonton 05371
Calgary Chinese Cultural Centre, Calgary 05162
Calgary Highlanders Museum, Calgary 05163
Calgary Police Service Interpretive Centre, Calgary 05164
Calgary Science Centre, Calgary 05165
Calhoun County Museum, Port Lavaca 46600
Calhoun County Museum, Rockwell City 46978
Calhoun County Museum, Saint Matthews 47148
Calico Museum of Textiles, Ahmedabad 21677
Califonia Palace of the Legion of Honor, San Francisco 47311
California Academy of Sciences Museum, San Francisco 47312
California African-American Museum, Los Angeles 44893
California Art Gallery, San Marino 47365
California Association of Museums, Santa Ana 49477
California Center for the Arts, Escondido 43208
California Heritage Museum, Santa Monica 47439
California Museum of Ancient Art, Beverly Hills 41676
California Museum of Photography, Riverside 46917
California Oil Museum, Santa Paula 47443
California Science Center, Los Angeles 44894
California State Capitol Museum, Sacramento 47047
California State Indian Museum, Sacramento 47048
California State Mining and Mineral Museum, Mariposa 45166
California State Railroad Museum, Sacramento 47049
California State University-Long Beach Art Museum, Long Beach 44858
Call of the Wild Museum, Gaylord 43636
Callahan County Pioneer Museum, Baird 41434
Callander Bay Heritage Museum, Callander 05183
Callanwolde Fine Arts Center, Atlanta 41336
Callendar House, Falkirk 38968
Calleva Museum, Silchester 40517
Calligraphy Museum, Tokyo 26922
Callkins Field Museum, Iowa Falls 44250
Calumet County Historical Society Museum, New Holstein 45703
Calvert Marine Museum, Solomons 47665
Calverton Folk Museum, Calverton 38442
Calvin Coolidge Memorial Room of the Forbes Library, Northampton 46013
Calvin Coolidge State Historic Site, Plymouth Notch 46569
Calvinia Regional Museum, Calvinia 34199
Cámara Santa de la Catedral de Oviedo, Oviedo 35202
Camborne Museum, Camborne 38448
Camborne School of Mines Geological Museum and Art Gallery, Pool 40224
Cambria County Historical Society Museum, Ebensburg 43077
Cambria Historical Society Museum, New Providence 45744
Cambridge and County Folk Museum, Cambridge 38450
Cambridge Galleries, Cambridge 05185
Cambridge Glass Museum, Cambridge 42053
Cambridge Historical Museum, Cambridge 42039
Cambridge Museum, Cambridge 30119
Cambridge Museum, Cambridge 42052
Cambridge Museum of Technology, Cambridge 38451
Cambridge University Collection of Air Photographs, Cambridge 38452
Camden Archives and Museum, Camden 42063
Camden Arts Centre, London 39596
Camden County Historical Society Museum, Camden 42059
Camden Haven Historical Museum, Laurieton 01171
Camden Historical Museum, Camden 00878
Camera Obscura, Edinburgh 38872
Camera Obscura, Hainichen, Sachsen 17495
Cameron Highlanders of Ottawa Regimental Museum, Ottawa 06067
Cameroon Maritime Museum, Douala 04953
Camp 6 Logging Museum, Tacoma 47915
Camp Five Museum, Laona 44646
Camp Floyd, Fairfield 43269
Camp Gallery, Sweet Briar 47900
Camp Hancock, Bismarck 41719
Campaign for Museums, London 49404
Campbell Collections, Durban 34224
Campbell County Rockpile Museum, Gillette 43670
Campbell Hall Gallery, Monmouth 45436
Campbell Historical Museum, Campbell 42071
Campbell House, Toronto 06564
Campbell House Museum, Saint Louis 47113
Campbell River and District Public Art Gallery, Campbell River 05186
Campbell River Museum, Campbell River 05187
Campbell River Optical Maritime Museum, Campbell River 05188
Campbell Whittlesey House, Rochester 46939
Campbellford-Seymour Heritage Centre, Campbellford 05189
Campbelltown City Bicentennial Art Gallery, Campbelltown 00880
Campbeltown Museum, Campbeltown 38468
Camperdown and District Museum, Camperdown 00881
Camperdown Cemetery, Newtown 01320
Campobello Island Museum, Welshpool 06767
Campus Art Gallery, Santa Rosa 47444
Campus Martius Museum, Marietta 45147
CampusGalerie, Bayreuth 15841
Camron-Stanford House, Oakland 46061
Canaan Historical Society Museum, Canaan 42073
Canada Agriculture Museum, Ottawa 06068
Canada Aviation Museum, Ottawa 06069
Canada House Gallery, London 39597
Canada Science and Technology Museum, Ottawa 06070
Canada's Aviation Hall of Fame, Wetaskiwin 06778
Canada's Penitentiary Museum, Kingston 05674
Canada's Sports Hall of Fame, Toronto 06565
Canadian Airborne Forces Museum, Petawawa 06115
Canadian Art Museum Directors Organization, Ottawa 49094
Canadian Automotive Museum, Oshawa 06059
Canadian Baseball Hall of Fame, Toronto 06566
Canadian Centre for Architecture, Montréal 05894
Canadian Clay and Glass Gallery, Waterloo 06751
Canadian County Historical Museum, El Reno 43125
Canadian Embassy Art Gallery, Washington 48339
Canadian Federation of Friends of Museums, Toronto 49095
Canadian Football Hall of Fame and Museum, Hamilton 05568
Canadian Force Base Gagetown Military Museum, Oromocto 06056
Canadian Golf Hall of Fame, Oakville 06037
Canadian Golf Museum, Aylmer 05027
Canadian Lacrosse Hall of Fame, New Westminster 05983
Canadian Military Studies Museum, Limehouse 05754
Canadian Museum of Animal Art, Bolton 05091
Canadian Museum of Contemporary Photography, Ottawa 06071
Canadian Museum of Flight, Langley 05725
Canadian Museum of Health and Medicine, Toronto 06567
Canadian Museum of Nature, Ottawa 06072
Canadian Museum of Rail Travel, Cranbrook 05287
Canadian Museums Association, Ottawa 49096
Canadian Olympic Hall of Fame, Ottawa 06073
Canadian Postal Museum, Gatineau 05483
Canadian Railway Museum, Saint Constant 06313
Canadian Scottish Regiment Museum, Victoria 06715
Canadian Scouting Museum, Ottawa 06074
Canadian Sculpture Centre, Toronto 06568
Canadian Ski Museum, Ottawa 06075
Canadian War Museum, Ottawa 06076
Canadian Warplane Heritage Museum, Mount Hope 05948
Canadian Wildlife and Wilderness Art Museum, Ottawa 06077
Canajoharie Library and Art Gallery, Canajoharie 42074
Çanakkale Devlet Güzel Sanatlar Galerisi, Çanakkale 37648
Çanakkale Martyrs Monument and War Museum, Çanakkale 37650
Çanakkale Müzesi, Çanakkale 37649
Çanakkale Şehitleri Heykeli ve Savaş Müzesi, Çanakkale 37650
Çanakkale State Gallery, Çanakkale 37648
Canal Fulton Heritage Society Museum, Canal Fulton 42075
Canal Museum, Karvion Kanava 09633
Canal Museum, Linlithgow 39505
Canal Museum, Llangollen 39552
Canal Museum, Stoke Bruerne 40602
Canal Society of New York State Museum, Syracuse 47906
Canberra Bicycle Museum, Dickson 00981
Canberra Contemporary Art Space, Braddon 00826
Canberra Museum and Gallery, Canberra 00884
Canberra School of Art Gallery, Acton 00699
Canbulat Tomb and Museum, Gazimağusa 08217
Canbulat Türbe ve Müzesi, Gazimağusa 08217
Canby Depot Museum, Canby 42078
Caney Valley Historical Society Museum, Caney 42079
Cango Caves Interpretive Centre, Oudtshoorn 34318
Cankarjev Dom, Ljubljana 34107
Çankırı 100. Yıl Kültür Merkezi, Çankırı 37652
Çankırı Devlet Güzel Sanatlar Galerisi, Çankırı 37653
Çankırı State Gallery, Çankırı 37653
Cannington Centennial Museum, Cannington 05192
Cannington Manor, Regina 06228
Cannon Falls Area Historical Museum, Cannon Falls 42080
Cannon Hall Museum, Barnsley, South Yorkshire 38090
Cannon Village Visitor Center, Kannapolis 44389
Canolfan Y Plase, Bala 38061
Canolfan Y Plase, Y Bala 40949
Canon City Municipal Museum, Canon City 42081
Canso Museum, Canso 05193
Canterbury Cathedral Archives and Library, Canterbury 38470
Canterbury Heritage Museum, Canterbury 38471
Canterbury Museum, Christchurch 30124
Canterbury Roman Museum, Canterbury 38472
Canterbury Shaker Village, Canterbury 42083
Canton Classic Car Museum, Canton 42088
Canton Historical Museum, Canton 42084
Canton Museum of Art, Canton 42089
Canwood Museum, Canwood 05194
CAP Art Center and Don Sergio Osmeña Memorabilia, Cebu 31307
CAP Art Center and Price Mansion, Tacloban 31451
Cap-de-Bon-Désir, Bergonnes 05075
Caparra Ruins Historical Museum, Guaynabo 32373
CAPC Musée d'Art Contemporain, Bordeaux 10803
Cape Ann Historical Museum, Gloucester 43702
Cape Bonavista Lighthouse, Bonavista 05094
Cape Breton Centre for Heritage and Science, Sydney 06525
Cape Breton Miners' Museum, Glace Bay 05490
Cape Clear Heritage Centre, Skibbereen 22539
Cape Coast Castle Museum, Cape Coast 20791
Cape Cod Museum of Natural History, Brewster 41882
Cape Cod National Seashore Museum, Wellfleet 48497
Cape Fear Museum, Wilmington 48659
Cape Henry Lighthouse, Virginia Beach 48245
Cape May County Historical Museum, Cape May Court House 42098
Cape Museum of Fine Arts, Dennis 42871
Cape Spear National Historic Site, Saint John's 06341
Cape Town Holocaust Centre, Cape Town 34202
Cape Vincent Historical Museum, Cape Vincent 42100
Capella Brancacci, Firenze 23823
Capelle Medicee, Firenze 23824
Ca'Pesaro Galleria Internazionale d'Arte Moderna, Venezia 25912
Capharnaum Ancient Synagogue, Kfar Nahum 22674
Capital Children's Museum, Washington 48340
Capitol Reef National Park Visitor Center, Torrey 48039
Capitola Historical Museum, Capitola Village 42101
Capodistria Museum, Koukouritsa, Evropouli 21033
Capp Street Project, San Francisco 47313
Cappella degli Scrovegni, Padova 24731
Cappelle Sistina, Sala e Gallerie Affrescate, Città del Vaticano 48868
Cappon House Museum, Holland 44052
Captain Charles H. Hurley Library Museum, Buzzards Bay 42020
Captain Cook Birthplace Museum, Middlesbrough 39946
Captain Cook Memorial Museum, Whitby 40850
Captain Cook Schoolroom Museum, Great Ayton 39118
Captain Forbes House Museum, Milton 45353
Captain George Flavel House Museum, Astoria 41308
Captain Nathaniel B. Palmer House, Stonington 47828
Captain Phillips' Rangers Memorial, Saxton 47489
Captain Salem Avery House Museum, Shady Side 47576
Captain's Cottage Museum, Murray Bridge 01290
Car and Carriage Museum, Pittsburgh 46509
Car and Traffic Museum, Kangasala 09617
Car Life Museum, Bonshaw 05097
Caracol Archaeological Site, Caracol 03866
Caramoor Center for Music and the Arts, Katonah 44414
Carberry Plains Museum, Carberry 05200
Carbethon Folk Museum and Pioneer Village, Crows Nest 00955
Carbon County Museum, Rawlins 46802
Carbonear Railway Station, Carbonear 05202
Carboolture Historical Village and Museum, Caboolture 00871
Carcoar Historic Village, Carcoar 00893
Cardiff Castle, Cardiff 38478
Cardigan Heritage Centre, Cardigan 38486
Cardinal Gallery, Annapolis 41225
Cardinal Ó Fiaich Heritage Centre, Cullyhanna 38680
Cardwell Shire Museum, Tully 01552
Care of Collections Forum, Grangemouth 49405
Carew Manor and Dovecote, Beddington 38144
Carey Museum, Hooghly 21839
Ca'Rezzonico Museo del Settecento Veneziano, Venezia 25913
Caribbean Primate Research Center Museum, San Juan 32387
Caricatura Galerie, Kassel 18013
Caricature Museum, Warszawa 32104
Carillon Historical Park, Dayton 42800
Carisbrooke Castle Museum, Newport, Isle of Wight 40053
Carl Eldhs Ateljémuseum, Stockholm 36236
Carl G. Fenner Nature Center, Lansing 44641
Carl-Henning Pedersen og Else Alfelts Museum, Herning 08866
Carl-Hirnbein-Museum, Missen-Wilhams 18750
Carl Jularbo Museum, Avesta 35826
Carl Larsson-Gården, Sundborn 36305
Carl-Lohse-Galerie - Stadtmuseum Bischofswerda, Bischofswerda 16171
Carl-Maria-von-Weber-Museum, Dresden 16678
Carl Michael Ziehrer-Gedenkraum, Wien 02872
Carl Nielsen Museet, Odense 09006
Carl Nielsens Barndomshjem, Årslev 08775
Carl Orff Museum, Dießen am Ammersee 16599
Carl Sandburg Home, Flat Rock 43335
Carl Sandburg State Historic Site, Galesburg 43597
Carl-Schweizer-Museum, Murrhardt 18963
Carlen House, Mobile 45418
Carleton College Art Gallery, Northfield 46019
Carleton University Art Gallery, Ottawa 06078
Carlisle Collection of Miniature Rooms, Nunnington 40119
Carlos Gomes Museum, Campinas 04021
Carlos P. Garcia Memorabilia, Manila 31372
Carlos P. Romulo Collection, Manila 31373
Carlow County Museum, Carlow 22383
Carlsbad Caverns National Park, Carlsbad 42108
Carlsbad Museum and Art Center, Carlsbad 42109
Carlsberg Museum Valby, Valby 09099
Carlson Tower Gallery, Chicago 42310
Carlsro Museum, Kristiinankaupunki 09708
Carlton County Historical Museum and Heritage Center, Cloquet 42502
Carlyle House, Alexandria 41123
Carlyle's House, London 39598
Carman House Museum, Iroquois 05627
Carmarthen Heritage Centre, Carmarthen 38492
Carmarthenshire County Museum, Carmarthen 38493
Carmicheal-Stewart House, New Glasgow 05977
Carnaby Collection of Beetles and Butterflies, Boyup Brook 00825
Carnegie Art Center, Mankato 45120
Carnegie Art Center, Walla Walla 48284
Carnegie Art Museum, Oxnard 46244
Carnegie Center for Art & History, New Albany 45657
Carnegie Historical Museum, Fairfield 43266
Carnegie Museum, Inverurie 39302
Carnegie Museum of Art, Pittsburgh 46510
Carnegie Museum of Natural History, Pittsburgh 46511
Carnegie Science Center, Pittsburgh 46512
Carney Gallery, Weston 48567
Carnifex Ferry Battlefield State Park and Museum, Summersville 47875
Carnton Plantation, Franklin 43521
The Carole and Barry Kaye Museum of Miniatures, Los Angeles 44895
Carolinas Aviation Museum, Charlotte 42237
Carpenter Home Museum, Cle Elum 42446
Carpenter Museum of Antique Outboard Motors, Gilmanton 43672
Carpenter Museum of Antique Outboard Motors, Gilmanton 43673
Carpet Museum, Genemuiden 29274
Carpet Museum, İstanbul 37712
Carpet Museum, Teheran 22296
Carpetbagger Aviation Museum, Harrington 39167
Carpinteria Valley Museum of History, Carpinteria 42112
Carr House, Victoria 06716
Carré d'Art, Nîmes 13333
Le Carré-Scéne Nationale, Château-Gontier 11203
Carrefour du Vitrail, Lavaudieu 12365
Carriage and Harness Museum, Beechworth 00784
Carriage House Museum, Camden 42062
Carriage House Museum, Colorado Springs 42534
Carriage Museum, Città del Vaticano 48878
Carriage Museum, Madrid 35019
Carriage Museum, Saint George's 03887
Carriage Museum of Seville, Sevilla 35486
Carrick Hill Museum, Springfield 01469
Carrie M. McLain Memorial Museum, Nome 45961
Carrie Weedon Natural Science Museum, Galesville 43600
Carrière Souterraine d'Aubigny, Taingy 14849
Carroll County Farm Museum, Westminster 48561
Carroll Reece Museum, Johnson City 44344
Carromato del Max, Mijas 35111
Carry A. Nation Home Memorial, Medicine Lodge 45223
Cars of the Stars Motor Museum, Keswick 39342
Carscadden's Museum, Plenty 06139
Carshalton Water Tower, Carshalton 38498
Carshalton Water Tower, London 39599
Carson County Square House Museum, Panhandle 46280
Carss Cottage Museum, Blakehurst 00810
Cart and Sleigh Museum, Vieremä 10193
Carter-Coile Country Doctors Museum, Winterville 48713
Carter County Museum, Ekalaka 43103
The Carter House, Franklin 43522
Carter House Natural Science Museum, Redding 46818

Carteret County Museum of History and Art, Morehead City 45495
Carter's Grove Visitor Center, Williamsburg 48626
Carton House, Maynooth 22517
Cartoon Art Museum, San Francisco 47314
Cartref Taid, Trevelin 00643
Cartuja de la Asunción, Granada 34863
Cartwright Hall Art Gallery, Bradford 38296
Carver County Historical Society Museum, Waconia 48271
Cary Cottage, Cincinnati 42399
Caryl House, Dover 42970
Casa Adobe de San Rafael, Glendale 43688
Casa Amesti, Monterey 45452
Casa Blanca Museum, San Juan 32392
Casa Buonarroti, Firenze 23825
Casa Contadina, Forenza 23906
Casa da Cultura, Machado 04185
Casa da Memória Arnaldo Estevão de Figueiredo, Campo Grande 04029
Casa da Noal, Treviso 25803
Casa de Andrés Eloy Blanco, Cumaná 48936
Casa de Colón, San Sebastián de La Gomera 35391
Casa de Cora Coralina, Goiás 04113
Casa de Cultura Afrônio Peixoto, Lençóis 04172
Casa de Cultura João Ribeiro, Laranjeiras 04168
Casa de Deodoro, Rio de Janeiro 04316
Casa de Dulce María Loynaz, La Habana 07920
Casa de Hidalgo, Dolores Hidalgo 27891
Casa de José Bonifácio, Rio de Janeiro 04317
Casa de José Jacinto Milanés, Matanzas 08035
Casa de la Constitución de 1814, Apatzingán 27773
Casa de la Cultura, Curuzú Cuatiá 00326
Casa de la Cultura, Enguera 34797
Casa de la Cultura "Augusto Rivera Garces", Bolívar 07435
Casa de la Cultura Benjamín Carrion, Cuenca 09148
Casa de la Libertad, Sucre 03904
Casa de las Ciencias, A Coruña 34746
Casa de las Dueñas, Sevilla 35472
Casa de Lavalleja, Montevideo 40984
Casa de les Roques, Valencia 35595
Casa de los Abuelos, Sonsón 07598
Casa de los Arabes, La Habana 07921
Casa de los Morlanes, Zaragoza 35716
Casa de los Pisas, Granada 34864
Casa de los Tiros, Granada 34865
La Casa de los Tratados, Girón 09165
Casa de Manuel Mujica Láinez, La Cumbre 00377
Casa de Marinos, Aranjuez 34471
Casa de Miguel Failde Pérez, Matanzas 08036
Casa de Oliveira Vianna, Niterói 04224
Casa de Osório, Rio de Janeiro 04318
Casa de Pilatos, Sevilla 35473
Casa de Unidad, Detroit 42916
Casa de Vitorino Ribeiro, Porto 32329
Casa de Zorrilla, Valladolid 35616
Casa del Águila y la Parra, Santillana del Mar 35450
Casa del Arte de la Universidad de Concepción, Concepción 06891
Casa del Boccaccio, Certaldo 23486
Casa del Cordón, Vitoria-Gasteiz 35695
Casa del Escribano Real Don Juan de Vargas, Tunja 07609
Casa del General José Garibaldi, Montevideo 40985
Casa dell'Ariosto, Ferrara 23783
Casa di Carlo Goldoni, Venezia 25914
Casa di Giorgione, Castelfranco Veneto 23400
Casa di Goethe, Roma 25150
Casa di Lazzaro Spallanzani, Scandiano 25516
Casa di Petrarca, Arquà Petrarca 22942
Casa di Pirandello, Agrigento 22815
Casa di Pirandello, Roma 25151
Casa di Xilogravura, Campos de Jordão 04034
Casa do Escultor Ervin Curt Teichmann, Pomerode 04272
Casa dos Sete Candeeiros, Salvador 04419
Casa-Fuerte de Ponce de León, Santo Domingo 09116
Casa Gorordo Museum, Cebu 31308
Casa Grande History Museum, Casa Grande 42127
Casa Grande Ruins, Coolidge 42616
Casa Hidalgo, Segovia 35461
Casa Jesús T. Piñero, Canóvanas 32369
Casa João Turin, Curitiba 04062
Casa Leopardi, Recanati 25085
Casa Loma, Toronto 06569
Casa Luis Barragán, México 28092
Casa Malanca, Brisighella 23214
Casa Manila Museum, Manila 31374
Casa Manuel F. Zárate, Guarraré 31074
Casa Memorială Gheorghe Dima, Brașov 32446
Casa Memorială Vasile Alecsandri, Mireşti 32551
Casa Municipal de Cultura. Sala de Exposiciones, Alcázar de San Juan 34430
Casa Museo 20 de Julio de 1810, Bogotá 07382
Casa Museo A. Gramsci, Ghilarza 24020
Casa Museo A. Uccello, Palazzolo Acreide 24759
Casa Museo Alegre de Sagrera, Terrassa 35523
Casa Museo Almirante Miguel Grau, Piura 31237
Casa Museo Amado Nervo, Tepic 28494
Casa-Museo Antonio Machado, Segovia 35462
Casa Museo Antonio Nariñtildeo y álvarez, Villa de Leyva 07617
Casa-Museo Azorín, Monóvar 35127
Casa Museo Bruzzone, Mar del Plata 00424
Casa Museo Cadete Juan Escutia, Tepic 28495
Casa Museo Carlos Pellicer Cámara, Villahermosa 28604
Casa Museo Coronel Gregorio Méndez Magaña, Jalpa de Méndez 28024
Casa Museo Curros Enríquez, Celanova 34703
Casa Museo de Arrese, Corella 34744
Casa Museo de Bonsor, Mairena del Alcor 35068
Casa Museo de Cervantes, Valladolid 35617
Casa-Museo de Colón, Valladolid 35618
Casa Museo de Doña Emilia Pardo Bazán, A Coruña 34747
Casa-Museo de Lope de Vega, Madrid 34990
Casa Museo de Rafael Alberti, El Puerto de Santa María 35300
Casa-Museo de Unamuno, Salamanca 35357
Casa-Museo de Zúrbaran, Fuente de Cantos 34829
Casa Museo dei Puccini, Pescaglia 24864
Casa Museo del Cima, Conegliano 23637
Casa Museo dell'Alta Valle del Cervo, Rosazza 25279
Casa Museo di A. Oriani, Casola Valsenio 23377
Casa Museo di Dante, Firenze 23826
Casa Museo di Monticello Amiata, Cinigiano 23569
Casa Museo F. Scaglione, Sciacca 25528
Casa Museo Fantoni, Rovetta 25295
Casa Museo Federico García Lorca, Fuente Vaqueros 34831
Casa Museo Fernando Fader, Ischilín 00367
Casa Museo Francesco Baracca, Lugo 24238
Casa Museo G. de Chirico, Roma 25152
Casa Museo G. Mazzarino, Pescina 24879
Casa Museo Gene Byron, Guanajuato 27967
Casa Museo Giovanni Verga, Catania 23444
Casa Museo Ignacio Zuloaga, Zumaia 35739
Casa Museo Ivan Bruschi, Arezzo 22918
Casa-Museo Jorge Eliécer Gaitán, Bogotá 07383
Casa-Museo José Benlliure, Valencia 35596
Casa Museo José Clemente Orozco, Guadalajara 27942
Casa Museo Julián Gayarre, Roncal 35336
Casa Museo La Moreña, La Barca 28041
Casa-Museo La Sebastiana, Valparaíso 06926
Casa-Museo León y Castillo, Telde 35521
Casa Museo Leonardo Valdez Esquer, Etchojoa 27922
Casa Museo López Portillo, Guadalajara 27943
Casa Museo M. Moretti, Cesenatico 23510
Casa Museo Maestro Manuel Altamirano, Tixtla de Guerrero 28516
Casa-Museo Manuel de Falla, Granada 34866
Casa Museo Mario Urteaga, Cajamarca 31125
Casa-Museo Menéndez Pelayo, Santander 35430
Casa Museo Miguel Hernández, Orihuela 35183
Casa Museo Modernista, Novelda 35161
Casa Museo Páez, Valencia 48966
Casa Museo Pavesiano, Santo Stefano Belbo 25464
Casa Museo Piccione d'Avola, Geraci Siculo 24016
Casa Museo Pinazo, Godella 34861
Casa Museo Posada del Moro, Torrecampo 35560
Casa Museo Quinta de Bolívar, Bogotá 07384
Casa Museo R. Bendandi, Faenza 23749
Casa Museo R. Siviero, Firenze 23827
Casa Museo Ricardo Gomez Campuzano, Bogotá 07385
Casa-Museo Rosalía de Castro, Padrón 35208
Casa Museo Sa Domu Antiga, Santadi 25444
Casa Museo Signorini-Corsi, L'Aquila 24142
Casa Museo Silvestre Rodríguez, Nacozari de García 28260
Casa Museo Tito, Ubeda 35582
Casa Museo Tiu Virgiliu, Suni 25652
Casa-Museo Tomás Morales, Moya 35142
Casa Museo V. Cermignani, Giulianova 24029
Casa Museo Valle Inclán, La Poboa do Caramiñal 35277
Casa Museo Vladimir Cora, Acaponeta 27745
Casa-Museo Zenobia-Juan Ramón, Moguer 35115
Casa Museu Abel Salazar da Universidade do Porto, São Mamede de Infesta 32344
Casa Museu Bissaya Barreto, Coimbra 32253
Casa-Museu Castell Gala Dalí, La Pera 35265
Casa-Museu de Almeida Moreira, Viseu 32360
Casa-Museu de Salvador Dalí de Cadaqués, Cadaqués 34643
Casa-Museu del Poeta Verdaguer, Folgueroles 34820
Casa-Museu dos Patudos, Alpiarça 32233
Casa-Museu Dr. Anastácio Gonçalves, Lisboa 32284
Casa-Museu Egas Moniz, Avanca 32238
Casa-Museu Gaudí, Barcelona 34532
Casa Museu Guerra Junqueiro, Porto 32330
Casa-Museu Pare Manyanet, Tremp 35573
Casa-Museu Prat de la Riba, Castellterçol 34696
Casa-Museu Teixeira Lopes, Vila Nova de Gaia 32358
Casa-Museu Teixeira Lopes e Galerias Diego de Macedo, Porto 32331
Casa-Museu Torres Amat, Sallent 35367
Casa Natal de Aquileo Parra, Barichara 07373
Casa Natal de Isabel la Católica, Madrigal de las Altas Torres 35064
Casa Natal de Jesús Montané Oropesa, Nueva Gerona 08054
Casa Natal de José Antonio Ramos Sucre, Cumaná 48937
Casa Natal de José María España, La Guaira 48948
Casa Natal de Legazpi, Zumárraga 35740
Casa Natal de Regino Boti, Guantánamo 07915
Casa Natal de San Ignacio, Azpeitia 34511
Casa Natal de Sant Antoni María Claret, Sallent 35368
Casa Natal de Santa Teresa de Jesús, Avila 34500
Casa Natal de Sarmiento, San Juan 00569
Casa Natal del Libertador Simón Bolívar, Caracas 48897
Casa Natal del Pintor Wifredo Lam, Santa Clara 08117
Casa natale de Santiago Ramón y Cajal, Petilla de Aragón 35267
Casa Natale di A. Rosmini, Rovereto 25290
Casa Natale di G. Verdi, Busseto 23234
Casa Natale di Giosuè Carducci, Pietrasanta 24911
Casa Natale di Pascoli, San Mauro Pascoli 25395
Casa Natale di Pio V, Bosco Marengo 23184
Casa Natale di Raffaello, Urbino 25856
Casa Natale di Toscanini, Parma 24794
Casa Natale di V. Monti, Alfonsine 22852
Casa Natale G. Donizetti, Bergamo 23059
Casa Natale Leonardo da Vinci, Vinci 26024
Casa National de Goya, Fuendetodos 34827
Casa Navarro, San Antonio 47247
Casa-Oficina de António Carneiro, Porto 32332
Casa Pedro Domingo Murillo, La Paz 03893
Casa Real Shrine, Malolos 31360
Casa Rivera, Montevideo 40986
Casa Roche Pombo, Morretes 04214
Casa Romei, Ferrara 23784
Casa Rosada Abelardo Díaz Alfaro, Caguas 32366
Casa San Isidro, Ciudad Bolívar 48932
Casa Santuario de San Pedro Claver, Verdú 35646
Casa Siglo XIX, Chihuahua 27820
Casa y Museo de El Greco, Toledo 35535
Casagwa National Museum, Daraga 31323
Casal Balaguer, Palma de Mallorca 35220
Casal Solleric, Palma de Mallorca 35221
La Casamaures, Saint-Martin-le-Vinoux 14359
Cascina Museo della Civiltà Contadina, Cremona 23677
Casemate, Uffheim 15023
Casemate Museum, Fort Monroe 43431
Caserío de Errecarte, Azpeitia 34512
Casey Farm, Saunderstown 47471
Casey Jones Home and Railroad Museum, Jackson 44287
Casey Jones Museum, Vaughan 48207
Casino dell'Aurora Pallavicini, Roma 25153
Casino Luxembourg - Forum d'Art Contemporain, Luxembourg 27559
Casita del Príncipe, El Pardo 35252
Cason del Buen Retiro, Madrid 34991
Caspar Neher-Gedenkraum, Wien 02873
Cass County Historical Society Museum, Logansport 44846
Cass County Historical Society Museum, Plattsmouth 46550
Cass County Historical Society Museum, West Fargo 48521
Cassia County Museum, Burley 41994
Cassissium, Nuits-Saint-Georges 13375
Cassius Forum Bonn, Bonn 16233
Casteel-Linn House and Museum, Princeton 46698
Castel Beseno, Besenello 23071
Castel Coira, Sluderno 25589
Castel Prösels, Fié 23803
Castel Sant'Elmo, Napoli 24571
Castel Taufers, Campo Tures 23301
Castell Cartoixa Vallparadis, Terrassa 35524
Castell y Waun, Chirk 38571
Castellani Art Museum, Niagara University 45952
Castello D'Albertis, Genova 23977
Castello dei Burattini - Museo Giordano Ferrari, Parma 24795
Castello dei Visconti di San Vito, Somma Lombardo 25597
Castello del Buonconsiglio, Trento 25790
Castello della Manta, Manta 24282
Castello di Donnafugata, Ragusa 25067
Castello di Giulio II, Ostia Antica 24714
Castello di Masnago, Varese 25895
Castello di Montebello, Bellinzona 36526
Castello di Rivoli Museo d'Arte Contemporanea, Rivoli 25131
Castello di Sasso Corbaro, Bellinzona 36527
Castello di Stenico, Stenico 25632
Castello d'Issogne, Issogne 24108
Castello Ducale, Agliè 22810
Castello e Museo Civico F. Baldinucci, Lari 24151
Castello e Museo della Rocca, Roma 25154
Castello e Raccolta Archeologica, Montechiarugolo 24514
Castello Fénis, Fénis 23774
Castello Malaspina, Bobbio 23093
Castello Malaspina, Massa 24313
Castello Pallotta, Caldarola 23264
Castello Principesco, Merano 24350
Castello Reale, Moncalieri 24467
Castello Reale, Racconigi 25062
Castello Reale, Venaria 25910
Castello Reggia di Venaria Reale, Torino 25732
Castillo de Javier, Javier 34927
Castillo de Loarre, Loarre 34980
Castillo de los Tres Reyes del Morro, La Habana 07922
Castillo de San Felipe del Morro, San Juan 32388
Castillo de San Marcos Museum, Saint Augustine 47066
Castillo de Sobroso, Villasobroso 35684
Castillos de Guayana la Vieja, Guayana 48945
Castine Scientific Society Museum, Castine 42136
The Castle, Marietta 45148
Castle Air Museum, Atwater 41369
Castle and Orthodox Church Museum, Olavinlinna 09880
Castle and Regimental Museum, Monmouth 39977
Castle Brand Visitor Centre, Nenagh 22526
Castle Budišov - Moravian Museum Brno, Budišov u Třebíče 08284
Castle Cary and District Museum, Castle Cary 38499
Castle Clinton, New York 45775
Castle Combe Museum, Castle Combe 38500
Castle Coole, Enniskillen 38938
Castle Cornet Military and Maritime Museums, Saint Peter Port 40422
Castle Douglas Art Gallery, Castle Douglas 38502
Castle Fraser, Sauchen 40450
Castle Hill National Historic Park, Placentia 06135
Castle Keep Museum, Newcastle-upon-Tyne 40034
Castle Menzies, Aberfeldy 37946
Castle Military Museum, Cape Town 34203
Castle Museum, Clitheroe 38590
Castle Museum, Colchester 38608
Castle Museum, Esztergom 21414
Castle Museum, Fertőd 21415
Castle Museum, Gonder 09404
Castle Museum, Kwidzyn 31746
Castle Museum, Malbork 31799
Castle Museum, Nagyvázsony 21488
Castle Museum, Niedzica 31823
Castle Museum, Norwich 40091
Castle Museum, Pszczyna 31927
Castle Museum, Siklós 21529
Castle Museum, Simontornya 21530
Castle Museum, Sümeg 21542
Castle Museum, Trakošćan 07792
Castle Museum, Veszprém 21609
Castle Museum, York 40960
Castle Museum in Bolków, Bolków 31509
Castle-Museum in Gołuchów, Gołuchów 31603
Castle Museum of Nagytétény, Budapest 21366
Castle Museum of Saginaw County History, Saginaw 47062
Castle of Saint John, Stranraer 40621
Castle of Znojmo, South Moravian Museum, Znojmo 08758
Castle Park Arts Centre, Frodsham 39018
Castle Point Transport Museum, Canvey Island 38477
Castle Ruin and Folk Monument, Kisnána 21461
Castle Rushen, Castletown 38506
Castle Story, Newark-on-Trent 40018
Castle Tucker, Wiscasset 48715
Castle Ward, Downpatrick 38772
Castle Zvolen of the Slovak National Gallery, Zvolen 34082
Castleford Museum Room, Castleford 38503
Castlemaine Art Gallery and Historical Museum, Castlemaine 00900
Castlemuseum Diosgyőr, Miskolc 21473
Castleton Historical Society Museum, Castleton 42137
Castleton Village Museum, Castleton 38505
Castletown, Celbridge 22391
Castletown Museum, Gerston 39030
Častnyj Muzej Grammofonov i Fonografov, Sankt-Peterburg 33382
Castor and District Museum, Castor 05217
Catacombes, Paris 13479
Catalina Island Museum, Avalon 41426
Catalyst, Widnes 40869
Catawba County Museum of History, Newton 45945
Catawba Science Center, Hickory 44006
Catawissa Railroad Museum, Catawissa 42139
Cater Museum, Billericay 38200
Cathcartston Visitor Centre, Dalmellington 38693
Cathedral Collection, Hvar 07706
Cathedral Museum, Mdina 27697
Cathedral of Saint John the Divine Museum, New York 45776
Cathedral of the Annunciation, Moskva 33021
Cathedral of the Dormition of the Virgin, also Cathedral of the Assumption, Moskva 33182
Cathedral of the Holy Trinity, Sankt-Peterburg 33485
Cathedral Treasure Chamber, Esztergom 21411
Cathedral Treasury, Chichester 38558
Cathedral Treasury, Split 07787
Cathedral Treasury, Trogir 07795
Cathedral Treasury Museum, Carlisle 38488
Cathédrale d'Images, Les Baux-de-Provence 12521
Catholic Historical Society of the Roanoke Valley Museum, Roanoke 46928
Cathrinesminde Teglværksmuseum, Broager 08790
The Catlin House Museum, Scranton 47516
Catlins Historical Museum, Owaka 30224
Cats Museum, Moskva 33119
Catskill Fly Fishing Center and Museum, Livingston Manor 44836
Cattaraugus Area Historical Center, Cattaraugus 42142
Cattle Raisers Museum, Fort Worth 43483
Caudwell's Mill & Craft Centre, Matlock 39920
Causeway School Museum, Bushmills 38423
Cauthorn Memorial Depot and Sutton County Jail, Sonora 47677
Cavalcade of Costume, Blandford Forum 38256
Cavalier Block, Halifax 05548
Cavalry Museum, Lappeenranta 09763
Cavan County Museum, Ballyjamesduff 22372
Cave and Basin National Historic Site, Banff 05043
La Cave aux Sculptures, Dénezé-sous-Doué 11499
Cave des Chartreux, Voiron 15283
Cave Museum of the Rhodopes, Čepelare 04637
Caveau Muséalisé, Cabrières 10970
Caveau-Musée des Jacobines, Santenay 14604

Caveau-Musée Les Vignerons de Roueïre, Quarante 13889
Cavendish Laboratory, Cambridge 38453
Cavernes de l'Abîme à Couvin, Couvin 03363
Caves Muséalisées Byrrh, Thuir 14907
Les Caves Rupestres, Rochecorbon 13994
Cavite City Library Museum, Cavite 31303
Cawdor Castle, Cawdor 38514
Cayuga Museum, Auburn 41373
Cayuga-Owasco Lakes Historical Society Museum, Moravia 45492
Cazenovia College Chapman Art Center Gallery, Cazenovia 42144
CBC Museum, Toronto 06570
CBC Radio Museum, Saint John's 06342
CCA-Centre for Contemporary Arts, Glasgow 39040
CCAC Institute, Oakland 46062
CCC Weeks Gallery, Jamestown 44310
CCNOA, Bruxelles 03278
C.E. Smith Museum of Anthropology, Hayward 43973
Čebelarski Muzej, Radovljica 34142
Čeboksarskij Vystavočnyj Zal, Čeboksary 32717
Cebu Archdiodesan Museum, Cebu 31309
Cebu City Museum, Cebu 31310
Cebu City State College Museum, Cebu 31311
CECA International Committee for Education and Cultural Action of Museums, Mumbai 49236
Cecelia Coker Bell Gallery, Hartsville 43947
Cecil Clark Davis Gallery, Marion 45160
Cecil Higgins Art Gallery, Bedford 38147
Cecille R. Hunt Gallery, Sankt Louis 47398
Cedar Falls Historical Museum, Cedar Falls 42148
Cedar Grove Historical Society Museum, Cedar Grove 42152
Cedar Grove Mansion, Philadelphia 46396
Cedar Grove Mansion Inn, Vicksburg 48228
Cedar Key Historical Society Museum, Cedar Key 42153
Cedar Key State Park Museum, Cedar Key 42154
Cedar Rapids Museum of Art, Cedar Rapids 42157
Cedar Valley Memories, Osage 46199
CEDIAS Musée Social, Paris 13480
Cefn Coed Colliery Museum, Neath 40004
Ceiriog Memorial Institute, Glyn Ceiriog 39086
Celamuse - Porcelain Museum, Seoul 27224
Celbridge Motor Museum, Celbridge 22392
A Celebration of Immigration, London 39600
Celebration of Irish Museum, Carrickmacross 22384
Čeleken Museum, Čeleken 37814
Čelekenskij Muzej, Čeleken 37814
Čeljabinskaja Oblastnaja Kartinnaja Galerija, Čeljabinsk 32724
Čeljabinskij Oblastnoj Kraevedčeskij Muzej, Čeljabinsk 32725
Cementmuseet Slemmestad, Slemmestad 30855
Cemetery Art Museum, Wrocław 32185
Cemetery - Museum, Sankt-Peterburg 33460
Cenacolo del Ghirlandaio, Firenze 23828
Cenacolo di Sant'Apollonia, Firenze 23829
Cenacolo Vinciano, Milano 24370
Centar Savremene Umjetnosti Crne Gore, Podgorica 33887
Centar za Fotografiju, Film i Televiziju, Zagreb 07811
The Centennial Museum at the University of Texas at El Paso, El Paso 43113
Centennial Museum of Canmore, Canmore 05191
Centennial Museum of the Nanaimo Regional General Hospital, Nanaimo 05959
Centennial Park 1910 Logging Museum, Thunder Bay 06544
Centennial Village Museum, Greeley 43783
Center Art Gallery, Grand Rapids 43754
Center for Agricultural Science and Heritage, Indianapolis 44214
Center for American Archeology, Kampsville 44386
Center for American History, Austin 41408
Center for American Music, Stephen Foster Memorial, Pittsburgh 46513
Center for Arts Criticism, Minneapolis 45382
Center for Book Arts, New York 45777
Center for Contemporary Art, Kyïv 37868
Center for Contemporary Art, Rotterdam 29780
Center for Contemporary Art Kitakyushu, Kitakyushu 26342
Center for Contemporary Arts of Santa Fe, Santa Fe 47416
Center for Contemporary Graphic Art and Tyler Graphics Archive Collection, Sukagawa 26776
Center for Contemporary Non Objective Art, Bruxelles 03278
Center for Creative Photography, Tucson 48083
Center for Cultural Arts, Gadsden 43578
Center for Curatorial Studies, Annandale-on-Hudson 41224
Center for Exploratory and Perceptual Art, Buffalo 41987
Center for Intuitive and Outsider Art, Chicago 42311
Center for Maine Contemporary Art, Rockport 46971
Center for Meteorite Studies, Tempe 47971
Center for Photography at Woodstock, Woodstock 48739
Center for Puppetry Arts, Atlanta 41337
Center for the Arts, Vero Beach 48222
Center for the Visual Arts, Denver 42880
Center for the Visual Arts, Philadelphia 46397
Center for Wooden Boats, Seattle 47530
Center Galleries, Detroit 42917
Center of Nautical and Regional Archaeology, Nahshonim 22719
Center on Contemporary Art, Seattle 47531
Centerville Historical Museum, Centerville 42170
Centr Istorii Aviacionnych Dvigatelej im. N.D. Kuznecova, Samara 33367
Centraal Museum, Utrecht 29897
Central Archives for the History of the Jewish People, Jerusalem 22628
Central Art Gallery, Ashton-under-Lyne 38032
Central Australian Aviation Museum, Alice Springs 00734
Central Butte District Museum, Central Butte 05219
Central City Opera House Museum, Central City 42172
Central College Museum, Bangalore 21702
Central Exhibition Hall Manege, Sankt-Peterburg 33389
Central Exhibition Hall of the City, Perm 33301
Central Finland Aviation Museum, Tikkakoski 10106
Central Foundry Museum, Miskolc 21477
Central Hawke's Bay Settlers Museum, Waipawa 30276
Central House of Artists, Moskva 33022
Central Iowa Art Museum, Marshalltown 45184
Central Luzon State University Museum, Muñoz 31403
Central Missouri State University Archives and Museum, Warrensburg 48315
Central Montana Historical Association Museum, Lewistown 44732
Central Museum, Bhopal 21720
Central Museum, Indore 21859
Central Museum, Nagpur 21963
Central Museum of Aviation and Cosmonautics, Moskva 33023
Central Museum of Frontier-Guard Regiments of Russia, Moskva 33025
Central Museum of Labour in Finland, Tampere 10096
Central Museum of Mining, Sopron 21534
Central Museum of Prisoners of War, Opole 31857
Central Museum of Railway Transport, Sankt-Peterburg 33387
Central Museum of Textiles, Łódź 31765
Central Museum of the Armed Forces, Moskva 33028
Central Museum of the Ministry of Interior of Russia, Moskva 33026
Central Museum of the Russian Association of Blind People, Moskva 33029
Central Nation University Museum, Beijing 06955
Central National Herbarium, Haora 21834
Central Naval Museum, Sankt-Peterburg 33388
Central Nevada Museum, Tonopah 48030
Central New Brunswick Woodmen's Museum, Boiestown 05088
Central Sikh Museum, Amritsar 21697
Central State Museum of Kazakhstan, Almaty 27071
Central Texas Area Museum, Salado 47186
Central Texas Museum of Automotive History, Rosanky 47001
Central Washington Agricultural Museum, Union Gap 48149
Centralne Muzeum Jeńców Wojennych w Łambinowicach -Opolu, Opole 31857
Centralne Muzeum Morskie, Gdańsk 31563
Centralne Muzeum Pożarnictwa, Mysłowice 31818
Centralne Muzeum Włókiennictwa, Łódź 31765
Centralnyj Dom Chudožnikov, Moskva 33022
Centralnyj Geologorazvedočnyj Muzej im. Akademika F.N. Černyševa, Sankt-Peterburg 33383
Centralnyj Gosudarstvennyj Muzej Kazachstana, Almaty 27071
Centralnyj Muzej Aviacii i Kosmonavtiki, Moskva 33023
Centralnyj Muzej Drevnerusskoj Kultury i Isskustva im. Andreja Rubleva, Moskva 33024
Centralnyj Muzej Federalnoj Pograničnoj Služby RF, Moskva 33025
Centralnyj Muzej MVD Rossii, Moskva 33026
Centralnyj Muzej Oktjabrskoj Železnoj Dorogi, Sankt-Peterburg 33384
Centralnyj Muzej Pochvovedenija im. V.V. Dokučaeva, Sankt-Peterburg 33385
Centralnyj Muzej Svjazi im. A.S. Popova, Sankt-Peterburg 33386
Centralnyj Muzej Velikoj Otečestvennoj Vojny, Moskva 33027
Centralnyj Muzej Vooružennych Sil, Moskva 33028
Centralnyj Muzej Vserossijskogo Obščestva Slepych, Moskva 33029
Centralnyj Muzej Železnodorožnogo Transporta, Sankt-Peterburg 33387
Centralnyj Voenno-morskoj Muzej, Sankt-Peterburg 33388
Centralnyj Vystavočnyj Zal g. Perm, Perm 33301
Centralnyj Vystavočnyj Zal Manež, Moskva 33030
Centralnyj Vystavočnyj Zal Manež g. Sankt-Peterburga, Sankt-Peterburg 33389
Centre Aeri, Vilanova i la Geltrú 35664
Centre Archéologique Charles-Morel, La Canourgue 12133
Centre Artistique et Médiéval, Richerenches 13964
Centre Artistique Jean-Baffier, Sancoins 14601
Centre Belge de la Bande Dessinée, Bruxelles 03279
Centre Bonastruç ça Porta, Girona 34851
Centre Catherine-de-Saint-Augustin, Bayeux 10614
Centre Commémoratif de l'Holocauste à Montréal, Montréal 05895
Centre County Historical Society Museum, State College 47778
Centre County Library Historical Museum, Bellefonte 41589
Centre Cultural de la Fundació La Caixa, Vic 35649
Centre Culturel de Verdun, Verdun 06704
Centre Culturel des Roches, Rochefort 03701
Centre Culturel et Patrimonial la Poudrière de Windsor, Windsor, Québec 06814
Centre Culturel-Exposition d'Artistes et d'Artisans, Collombey 36640
Centre Culturel Franco-Manitobain, Winnipeg 06820
Centre Culturel Marguerite-Bourgeois, Troyes 15001
Centre d'Art, Baie-Saint-Paul 05035
Centre d'Art, Port-au-Prince 21291
Centre d'Art Contemporain, Avallon 10518
Centre d'Art Contemporain, Besançon 10697
Centre d'Art Contemporain, Bignan 10735
Centre d'Art Contemporain, Bruxelles 03280
Centre d'Art Contemporain, Dijon 11518
Centre d'Art Contemporain, Genève 36730
Centre d'Art Contemporain, Ginals 11867
Centre d'Art Contemporain, Istres 12064
Centre d'Art Contemporain, Lacoux-Hauteville-Lompnes 12294
Centre d'Art Contemporain, Meymac 12968
Centre d'Art Contemporain, Mont-de-Marsan 13026
Centre d'Art Contemporain, Noisiel 13361
Centre d'Art Contemporain, Noyers (Yonne) 13370
Centre d'Art Contemporain, Pau 13664
Centre d'Art Contemporain, Pougues-les-Eaux 13851
Centre d'Art Contemporain, Revin 13958
Centre d'Art Contemporain, Rueil-Malmaison 14073
Centre d'Art Contemporain, Tanlay 14855
Centre d'Art Contemporain Bouvet-Ladubay, Saumur 14642
Centre d'Art Contemporain de Basse-Normandie, Hérouville-Saint-Clair 12015
Centre d'Art Contemporain de Brétigny, Brétigny-sur-Orge 10916
Centre d'Art Contemporain de Castres, Castres 11081
Centre d'Art Contemporain de Vassivière en Limousin, Beaumont-du-Lac 10644
Centre d'Art Contemporain Georges Pompidou, Cajarc 10999
Centre d'Art Contemporain la Synagogue de Delme, Delme 11491
Centre d'Art Contemporain le Quartier, Quimper 13893
Centre d'Art Contemporain Théo Argence, Saint-Priest (Rhône) 14429
Centre d'Art de Cowansville, Cowansville 05283
Centre d'Art de Lévis, Lévis 05750
Centre d'Art de Saint-Georges, Saint-Georges, Quebec 06320
Centre d'Art du Crestet, Crestet 11457
Centre d'Art du Mont-Royal, Montréal 05896
Centre d'Art et de Culture, Soignies 03755
Centre d'Art et de Plaisanterie, Montbéliard 13057
Centre d'Art et d'Exposition Jacques-Henri Lartigue, L'Isle-Adam 12625
Centre d'Art et d'Histoire André Auclair, Cruas 11464
Centre d'Art International, Mulhouse 13206
Centre d'Art Neuchâtel, Neuchâtel 36983
Centre d'Art Nicolas de Staël, Braine-l'Alleud 03235
Centre d'Art Présence Van Gogh, Saint-Rémy-de-Provence 14446
Centre d'Art Sacré, Ille-sur-Têt 12054
Centre d'Art Santa Mònica, Barcelona 34533
Centre d'Art Sébastien, Saint-Cyr-sur-Mer 14173
Centre d'Artistes Vaste et Vague, Carleton 05207
Centre de Cultura Contemporània de Barcelona, Barcelona 34534
Centre de Cultura Sa Nostra, Palma de Mallorca 35222
Centre de Culture Catalane, Perpignan 13702
Centre de Culture scientifique la Rotonde Ecole des Mines, Saint-Étienne 14196
Centre de Documentació i Museu Tèxtil, Terrassa 35525
Centre de Documentation Arabe, Timbuktu 27694
Centre de Documentation Archéologique du Roussillon, Perpignan 13703
Centre de Documentation du Patrimoine, Montpellier 13119
Centre de la Gravure et de l'Image Imprimée de la Communauté Française de Belgique, La Louvière 03546
Centre de la Mémoire d'Oradour, Oradour-sur-Glane 13409
Centre de la Mer, Paris 13481
Centre de la Photographie Genéve, Genève 36731
Centre de la Vieille Charité, Marseille 12846
Centre de Photographie de Lectoure, Lectoure 12501
Centre de Recherches et de Documentation du Sénégal, Saint-Louis 33784
Centre de Recherches et d'Etudes Technologiques des Arts Plastiques, Bruxelles 03281
Centre de Recherches Historiques sur les Maîtres Ebénistes, Paris 13482
Centre de Secours Principal, Tourcoing 14958
Centre d'Edition Contemporaine, Genève 36732
Centre des Arts Contemporains du Québec à Montréal, Montréal 05897
Centre des Arts de Shawinigan, Shawinigan 06429
Centre d'Etudes Archéologiques, Eyguières 11685
Centre d'Études et d'Exposition des Bastides du Rouergue, Sauveterre-de-Rouergue 14655
Centre d'Études Historiques et Archéologiques, Le Barroux 12377
Centre d'Exposition Archéologique de l'Orangerie, Étiolles 11671
Centre d'Exposition Art-Image, Gatineau 05481
Centre d'Exposition d'Amos, Amos 04990
Centre d'Exposition de Keraudan, Landerneau 12316
Centre d'Exposition de Rouyon-Noranda, Rouyn-Noranda 06291
Centre d'Exposition de Saint-Hyacinthe, Saint-Hyacinthe 06321
Centre d'Exposition de Val d'Or, Val d'Or 06658
Centre d'Exposition du Costume, Avallon 10519
Centre d'Exposition Langevin, Grande-Synthe 11906
Centre d'Exposition l'Imagier, Aylmer 05028
Centre d'Exposition Mont-Laurier, Mont-Laurier 05881
Centre d'Exposition Plein Sud, Longueuil 05775
Centre d'Exposition Raymond-Lasnier, Trois-Rivières 06638
Centre d'Exposition sur l'Industrie des Pâtes et Papiers, Trois-Rivières 06639
Centre d'Hébergement, d'Étude sur la Nature et l'Environnement, Allouville-Bellefosse 10294
Centre d'Histoire de la Résistance et de la Déportation, Lyon 12724
Centre d'Histoire de Montréal, Montréal 05898
Centre d'Histoire Locale, Tourcoing 14959
Centre d'Histoire Locale du Canton de Pompey, Pompey 13794
Centre d'Iconographie Genevoise, Genève 36733
Centre d'Interpretació p.n. d'Aigüestortes i Estany de Sant Maurici, Espot 34805
Centre d'Interpretation de la Métabetchouane, Desbiens 05327
Centre d'Interpretation de l'Ardoise, Richmond 06261
Centre d'Interpretation de l'Histoire de Sherbrooke, Sherbrooke, Québec 06439
Centre d'Interprétation des Luys, Brassempouy 10894
Centre d'Interpretation du Parc de l'île-Bonaventure-et-du Rocher-Percé, Percé 06111
Centre d'Interprétation du Patrimoine de Sorel, Sorel-Tracy 06471
Centre du Livre d'Artiste Contemporain, Verderonne , 15127
Centre du Visiteur, Braine-l'Alleud 03236
Centre Européen d'Actions Artistiques Contemporaines, Strasbourg 14807
Centre Européen de la Paix, Souchez 14780
Centre Européen de l'Orgue, Marmoutier 12829
Centre Européen des Métiers d'Art, Givet 11873
Centre for African Studies Collection, Rondebosch 34370
Centre for Art Tapes, Halifax 05549
Centre for Black and African Art and Civilization, Lagos 30350
Centre for Contemporary Art, Warszawa 32080
Centre for Contemporary Photography, Fitzroy 01024
Centre for Experimental Art and Communication, Toronto 06571
Centre for Rocks and Minerals, Jokkmokk 35983
Centre for the Magic Arts, London 39601
Centre for the Study of Greek Traditional Pottery, Athinai 20854
Centre for Visual Arts, Groningen 29307
Centre Franco-Ontarien de Folklore, Sudbury 06508
Centre Hill Mansion, Petersburg 46372
Centre Historique de la Mine, de la Machine à Vapeur et du Chemin de Fer, Oignies 13391
Centre Historique de la Résistance en Drôme et de la Déportation, Romans-sur-Isère 14015
Centre Historique Minier, Lewarde 12574
Centre International d'Art Contemporain de Montréal, Montréal 05899
Centre International d'Art Graphique, Parly 13660
Centre International de l'Automobile, Pantin 13463
Centre Jean-Giono, Manosque 12793
Centre Jeanne d'Arc, Orléans 13428
Centre Minier de Faymoreau, Faymoreau-les-Mines 11710
Centre Missionnaire Sainte-Therèse, Montréal 05900
Centre Muséographique, Québec 06195
Centre National d'Artisanat d'Art, Ouagadougou 04941
Centre National de la Photographie, Paris 13483
Centre National d'Exposition, Jonquière 05634
Centre National Musée Jean-Jaurès, Castres 11082
Centre of Contemporary Art, Christchurch 30125
Centre of Polish Sculpture, Oronsko 31862
Centre Permanent d'Exposition de Poupées Anciennes, Fleury-la-Forêt 11747
Centre Philatélique de Polynésie Française, Papeete 15345
Centre Photographique d'Ile-de-France, Pontault-Combault 13823
Centre pour l'Image Contemporaine Saint-Gervais, Genève 36734
Centre Provincial d'Hébergement Le Caillou, Roisin 03708
Centre Régional d'Art Contemporain, Fontenoy-en-Puisaye 11775
Centre Régional d'Art Contemporain, Montbéliard 13058
Centre Régional d'Art Contemporain, Sète 14729
Centre Régional de la Photographie Nord-Pas-de-Calais, Douchy-les-Mines 11565
Centre Social i Cultural de la Fundació La Caixa, Lleida 34964
Centre Tomi Ungerer, Strasbourg 14808
Centro Agost, Museo de Alfarería, Agost 34408
Centro Ambientale Archeologico, Legnano 24174

Centro Andaluz de Arte Contemporáneo, Sevilla 35474
Centro Andino de Tecnología Tradicional y Cultura de la Comunidades, Ollantaytambo 31233
Centro Arte Contemporanea, Napoli 24572
Centro Atlántico de Arte Moderno, Las Palmas de Gran Canaria 35238
Centro Camuno di Studi Preistorici, Capo di Ponte 23326
Centro Ceremonial de Caguana, San Juan 32389
Centro Cultural Banco do Brasil, Rio de Janeiro 04319
Centro Cultural Corp Group, Caracas 48898
Centro Cultural de la Fundació la Caixa, Barcelona 34535
Centro Cultural de la Raza, San Diego 47272
Centro Cultural España Córdoba, Córdoba 00289
Centro Cultural Isidro Fabela, México 28093
Centro Cultural Paraguayo-Americano, Asunción 31093
Centro Cultural Paraguayo-Argentino, Concepción 31106
Centro Cultural Torre de la Calahorra, Córdoba 34735
Centro Culturale Polivalente, Bagnacavallo 23001
Centro d'Arte Contemporanea Ticino, Bellinzona 36528
Centro d'Arte Verrocchio, Casole d'Elsa 23378
Centro de Arqueologia Annete Laminge Emperaire, Lagoa Santa 04163
Centro de Arte Contemporáneo, Abarca de Campos 34407
Centro de Arte La Cañuela, Caracas 48899
Centro de Arte La Estancia, Caracas 48900
Centro de Arte Moderna da Fundação Calouste Gulbenkian, Lisboa 32285
Centro de Arte Moderno y Contemporáneo Daniel Vázquez Díaz, Nerva 35158
Centro de Arte Visuales, Lima 31197
Centro de Artes Visuales, Asunción 31094
Centro de Artistas Plásticos, Montevideo 40987
Centro de Biologia Marinha, São Sebastião 04546
Centro de Ciencia y Tecnología, Guadalajara 27944
Centro de Desarrollo de las Artes Visuales, La Habana 07923
Centro de Diseño Ambiental, La Habana 07924
Centro de Documentación Musical, Linares 34953
Centro de Educação Ambiental Gralha Azul e Museu de História Natural, Cascavel 04043
Centro de Estudios Árabes y Arqueológicos Ibn Arabi, Murcia 35144
Centro de Estudios Conservacionistas, Guatemala 21266
Centro de Estudios Folklóricos, Guatemala 21267
Centro de Estudos Murilo Mendes, Juiz de Fora 04155
Centro de Exposiciónes de Geologia y Mineria, Buenos Aires 00145
Centro de Exposiciones La Casona de los Olivera, Buenos Aires 00146
Centro de Fotografía, Santa Cruz de Tenerife 35412
Centro de Información e Interpretación del Parque de Pagoeta, Aia 34414
Centro de Interpretación del P.N. de las Hoces del Río Duratón, Sepúlveda 35469
Centro de Interpretación del P.N. del Cañon del Río Lobos, Ucero 35585
Centro de Interpretación del P.N. del Lago de Sanabria, San Martín de Castañeda 35381
Centro de Mesonero Romanos, Madrid 34992
Centro de Pesquisas Folclóricas, Rio de Janeiro 04320
Centro de Pesquisas Paleontológicas da Bacia do Araripe, Crato 04057
Centro del Diseño, Bilbao 34610
Centro di Documentazione Messapica, Oria 24685
Centro di Informazione e Documentazione Arti Visive, Prato 25040
Centro di Scienze Naturali e Raccolta Natura ed Arte, Prato 25041
Centro di Scultura Contemporanea, Cagli 23241
Centro Escolar University Museum and Archives, Manila 31375
Centro Etnográfico Joaquín Díaz, Urueña 35588
Centro Ferroviário de Cultura, Volta Grande 04594
Centro Fotográfico Álvarez Bravo, Oaxaca 28271
Centro Galego de Arte Contemporáneo, Santiago de Compostela 35436
Centro Histórico-Cultural de Enfermagem Ibero-americana, São Paulo 04484
Centro Maggiori, Monte San Giusto 24499
Centro Mundo Aborigen, Córdoba 00290
Centro Municipal de Exposiciones Subste, Montevideo 40988
Centro Museo Universitario di Storia Naturale e della Strumentazione Scientifica, Modena 24433
Centro Nacional de Documentação e Investigação Histórica, Luanda 00094
Centro Nazionale di Studi Alfieriani, Asti 22970
Centro Parque Nacional Picos de Europa - Casa Dago, Cangas de Onis 34672
Centro per l'Arte Contemporanea Luigi Pecci, Prato 25042
Centro Pró-Memória do Club Athlético Paulistano, São Paulo 04485
Centro Pró-Memória Hans Nobiling do Esporte Clube Pinheiros, São Paulo 04486
Centro Regional de Arqueologia Ambiental, Piraju 04265
Centro Regional de Pesquisas Archeológicas Mário Neme, Piraju 04266
Centro Studi I. Silone, Pescina 24880
Centro Studi Naturalistici del Pollino Il Nibbio, Morano Calabro 24561
Centrum Arts and Creative Education, Port Townsend 46604
Centrum Beeldende Kunst, Groningen 29307
Centrum Beeldende Kunst Emmen, Emmen 29229
Centrum Beeldende Kunst Utrecht, Amersfoort 28820
Centrum Kultury i Sztuki Afrykańskiej, Kraków 31681
Centrum Kunstlicht in de Kunst, Eindhoven 29208
Centrum Pamięci Gen. Józefa Hallera, Władysławowo 32158
Centrum Rysunku i Grafiki im. Tadeuza Kulisiewicza, Kalisz 31634
Centrum Rzeźby Polskiej, Oronsko 31862
Centrum Sztuki Studio im S.I. Witkiewicza, Warszawa 32079
Centrum Sztuki Współczesnej, Warszawa 32080
Centrum Sztuki Współczesnej Łaźnia, Gdańsk 31564
Centrum voor de Vlaamse Kunst van de 16de en de 17de Eeuw, Antwerpen 03138
Centrum voor Heiligenbeelden, Kranenburg 29493
Centrum voor Natuur en Landschap, Terschelling-West 29867
Century Gallery, Sylmar 47904
Century Schoolhouse, Toronto 06572
Century Village Museum, Burton 42013
Ceol - Irish Traditional Music Centre, Dublin 22416
Ceramic Centre and Pottery Museum, Tegelen 29864
The Ceramic Collection, Aberystwyth 37954
Ceramics Museum, Bechyně 08243
Ceramics Museum, Tel Aviv 22752
Ceramics Museum, Týnec nad Sázavou 08697
Cercle d'Art, Laval 05732
Čerdynskij Kraevedčeskij Muzej A.S. Puškina, Čerdyn 32728
Cereal Museum, Békéscsaba 21318
Cereal Prairie Pioneer Museum, Cereal 05220
Ceredigion Museum, Aberystwyth 37955
Čerkechskij Muzej Jakutskaja Političeskaja Ssylka, Čerkech 32735
Cerkov Ionna Predteči, Jaroslavl 32846
Cerkov Pokrova v Filjach, Moskva 33031
Cerkov Položenija riz Presvjatoj Bogorodicy, Moskva 33032
Cerkov Roždestva Christova, Jaroslavl 32847
Cerkov Troicy v Nikitnikach, Moskva 33033
Cernan Earth and Space Center, River Grove 46912
Černigiv Mykhailo Kotsiubynsky Literary Museum, Černigiv 37837
Černivci Local Museum, Černivci 37839
Cēsis History Museum, Cēsis 27344
České Centrum Fotografie, Praha 08566
České Muzeum Výtvarných Umění, Praha 08567
České Zdravotnické Muzeum, Praha 08568
Cēsu Izstāžu Nams, Cēsis 27343
Cēsu Vēstures muzejs, Cēsis 27344
CFB Esquimalt Naval Museum and Military Museum, Victoria 06717
CFCC Webber Center, Ocala 46079
Ch. Frenkelis Mansion, Šiauliai 27527
C.H. Moore Homestead, Clinton 42492
C.H. Nash Museum-Chucalissa Archaeological Museum, Memphis 45232
Chaa Creek Natural History Centre, San Ignacio 03870
Chabarovskij Kraevoj Kraevedčeskij Muzej im. N.I. Grodekova, Chabarovsk 32737
Chabarovskij Muzej Archeologii im. A.P. Okladnikova, Chabarovsk 32738
Chabot Museum, Rotterdam 29748
Chácara do Céu Museum, Rio de Janeiro 04321
Chaco Culture National Historical Park, Nageezi 45592
Chadron State College Main Gallery, Chadron 42177
Chaffee Center for Visual Arts, Rutland 47041
Chagall House, Haifa 22600
Chagall Museum, Vitebsk 03123
Chagrin Falls Historical Society Museum, Chagrin Falls 42181
The Chaim Gross Studio Museum, New York 45778
Chaiya National Museum, Surat Thani 37542
Chakasskij Respublikanskij Kraevedčeskij Muzej, Abakan 32627
Chakdara Museum, Chakdara 31015
Châlet de l'Etambeau, Château-d'Oex 36625
Chalet of the Golden Fleece, New Glarus 45688
Chamberlain Museum of Pathology, Birmingham 38219
Chamizal National Memorial, El Paso 43114
Champaign County Historical Museum, Champaign 42186
Champaign County Historical Museum, Urbana 48165
Champignonnière-Musée du Saut aux Loups, Montsoreau 13154
Champion Mill, Champion 42189
Champlain Trail Museum, Pembroke 06106
Champs Chapel Museum, East Hendred 38842
Chamsori Gramophone and Audio Science Museum, Gangneung 27166
Chancellor Robert R. Livingston Masonic Library and Museum, New York 45779
Chandler Gallery, Randolph 46790
Chandler Museum, Chandler 42190
Chandradhari Museum, Darbhanga 21754
Chang Foundation Museum, Taipei 07344
Changji Mulei County Museum, Changji 07006
Changjizhou Museum, Changji 07007
Changning District Revolutionary Display Center, Shanghai 07208
Changqing County Museum, Jinan 07129
Changsha City Museum, Changsha 07009
Changshu City Museum, Changshu 07012
Changshu Engraved Stone Museum, Changshu 07013
Changshu Mausoleum of Fallen Heroes, Changshu 07014
Chania Byzantine and Postbyzantine Collection, Chania 20916
Channel Folk Museum, Lower Snug 01189
Channel Islands Military Museum, Saint Ouen 40418
Channel-Port-aux-Basques Museum, Channel-Port-aux-Basques 05222
Chantharakhasem National Museum, Ayutthaya 37472
Chantry Bagpipe Museum, Morpeth 39987
Chanty-Mansijsk Regional Museum of Nature and Man, Chanty-Mansijsk 32744
Chao Sam Phraya National Museum, Ayutthaya 37473
Chaoyang City Museum, Chaoyang 07016
La Chapeauthèque, Anduze 10338
Chapel Gallery, Bracebridge 05107
Chapel Gallery, North Battleford 06013
Chapel Gallery, West Newton 48535
Chapel Hill Museum, Shag Harbour 06425
Chapelle de Bailly, Saint-Bris-le-Vineux 14133
Chapelle des Indiens, Tadoussac 06532
Chapelle Matisse, Vence 15112
Chapelle-Musée Saint-Nicolas, Vitré 15273
Chapin Library of Rare Books, Williamstown 48633
Chapleau Centennial Museum, Chapleau 05223
Chaplin-Archiv, Frankfurt am Main 17033
Chapman Gallery, Salford 40429
Chapman Historical Museum, Glens Falls 43692
Chapman Museum, Brandon 05119
Chappell Art Gallery, Chappell 42198
Chappell Hill Historical Society Museum, Chappell Hill 42199
Chapter House, London 39602
Chard and District Museum, Chard 38522
Charents Literary Memorial Museum, Erevan 00679
Charkivskij Istoričnij Muzej, Charkiv 37841
Charkovskij Chudožestvennyj Muzej, Charkiv 37842
Charlbury Museum, Charlbury 38525
Charles A. Grignon Mansion, Kaukauna 44418
Charles A. Weyerhaeuser Memorial Museum, Little Falls 44818
Charles A. Wustum Museum of Fine Arts, Racine 46767
Charles Allis Art Museum, Milwaukee 45360
Charles B. Aycock Birthplace, Fremont 43554
Charles B. Goddard Center for Visual and Performing Arts, Ardmore 41251
Charles Carroll House of Annapolis, Annapolis 41226
Charles Dickens Birthplace Museum, Portsmouth 40248
Charles Dickens Centre, Rochester 40334
Charles Ferguson Museum, Mentone 01244
Charles Gates Dawes House, Evanston 43237
Charles H. MacNider Museum, Mason City 45200
Charles H. Scott Gallery, Vancouver 06672
Charles H. Taylor Arts Center, Hampton 43895
Charles H. Wright Museum of African American History, Detroit 42918
The Charles Hosmer Morse Museum of American Art, Winter Park 48707
Charles M. Auampato Discovery Museum, Charleston 42229
Charles R. Conner Museum, Pullman 46743
Charles River Museum of Industry, Waltham 48296
Charles Surt University Art Collection, Wagga Wagga 01568
Charles Towne Landing 1670, Charleston 42210
The Charleston Museum, Charleston 42211
Charleston Trust, Firle 38992
Charlestown Shipwreck and Heritage Centre, Saint Austell 40389
Charleville Historic House Museum, Charlesville 00905
Charlotte and Philip Hanes Art Gallery, Winston-Salem 48698
Charlotte Berlins Museum, Ystad 36420
Charlotte County Museum, Saint Stephen 06373
Charlotte Museum of History and Hezekiah Alexander Homesite, Charlotte 42238
Charney Basset Mill, Wantage 40781
Charney Bassett Mill, Charney Basset 38526
Charnley-Persky House Museum, Chicago 42312
Charnwood Museum, Loughborough 39829
Chartered Insurance Institute's Museum, London 39603
Charterhouse School Museum, Godalming 39087
Chartwell House, Chartwell 38527
Chase and District Museum, Chase 05234
Chase County Museum, Cottonwood Falls 42666
Chase Home Museum of Utah Folk Art, Salt Lake City 47227
The Chase Manhattan Bank Art Collections, New York 45780
Châsse Sainte-Bernadette et Musée, Nevers 13301
Château, Aigle 36437
Château, Arlay 10413
Château, Assier 10448
Château, Belvoir 10680
Château, Castries 11085
Château, Gruyères 36785
Château, Lacave 12292
Château, Larra 12347
Château, Larroque-Toirac 12350
Château, Les Ternes 12558
Château, Moncley-Recologne 13009
Château, Prudhomat 13879
Château, Rousson 14064
Château, Saint-Cirq-Lapopie 14154
Château, Saint-Quintin-sur-Soule 14439
Château, Vogue 15281
Château Beaufief, Mazeray 12906
Château d'Aigremont, Seraing 03730
Château d'Angers, Angers 10341
Château d'Antoine d'Abbadie, Hendaye 12009
Château d'Arcelot, Arceau 10396
Château d'Auvers, Auvers-sur-Oise 10502
Château d'Auzers, Auzers 10516
Château d'Avignon, Saintes-Maries-de-la-Mer 14560
Château d'Azay-le-Ferron, Azay-le-Ferron 10549
Château de Beaumanoir, Quintin 13905
Château de Beloeil, Beloeil 03209
Château de Biron, Monpazier 13020
Château de Bonaguil, Saint-Front-sur-Lemance 14222
Château de Bonneval, Coussac-Bonneval 11441
Château de Bouges, Bouges-le-Château 10831
Château de Bourbilly, Vic-de-Chassenay 15157
Château de Boury-en-Vexin, Boury-en-Vexin 10874
Château de Busca-Naniban, Mansencôme 12797
Château de Castelnou, Castelnou 11079
Château de Cazeneuve, Préchac 13867
Château de Cénévières, Cénévières 11103
Château de Champchevrier, Cléré-les-Pins 11317
Château de Chillon, Territet-Veytaux 37233
Château de Coppet, Coppet 36647
Le Château de Craon, Craon 11449
Château de Crazannes, Crazannes 11451
Château de Deulin, Fronville 03423
Château de Dufau, Coarraze 11338
Château de Fénelon, Sainte-Mondane 14549
Château de Fernelmont, Fernelmont 03416
Château de Fleurac, Rouffignac-Saint-Cernin 14058
Château de Fleurigny, Thorigny-sur-Oreuse 14902
Château de Fougères-sur-Bièvre, Fougères-sur-Bièvre 11795
Château de Fourquevaux, Fourquevaux 11802
Château de Frolois, Frolois 11822
Château de Galard, Terraube 14877
Château de Germolles, Mellecey 12920
Château de Grandson, Grandson 36776
Château de Gratot, Gratot 11925
Château de Guiry-en-Vexin, Guiry-en-Vexin 11975
Château de Hautefort, Hautefort 12000
Château de Jannée, Pessoux 03686
Château de Kergrist, Ploubezre 13766
Château de la Bastie d'Urfé, Saint-Étienne-le-Mollard 14208
Château de la Baume, Prinsuéjols-Marvejols 13874
Château de la Brède, La Brède 12130
Château de la Guerche, La Guerche 12196
Château de la Motte-Tilly, La Motte-Tilly 12211
Château de la Renaissance et Donjon de 1320, Fléville-devant-Nancy 11748
Château de la Roche-Guyon, La Roche-Guyon 12229
Château de Labrède, Labrède 12287
Château de Lacypierre, Saint-Crépin-Carlucet 14164
Château de Langeais, Langeais 12323
Château de l'Angotière, Domjean 11545
Château de Léhélec, Béganne 10666
Château de l'Ermitage, Wavre 03831
Château de l'Hermitage, Condé-sur-l'Escaut 11386
Château de Lichtenberg, Lichtenberg 12584
Château de Losse, Thonac 14892
Château de Lourmarin, Lourmarin 12701
Château de Louvignies, Notre-Dame-de-Louvignies 03662
Château de Luynes, Luynes 12718
Château de Maisons-Laffitte, Maisons-Laffitte 12777
Château de Meillant, Meillant 12916
Château de Messilhac, Raulhac 13915
Château de Meux, Meux 12965
Château de Mogère, Montpellier 13120
Château de Monbazillac, Monbazillac 13007
Château de Montaigut, Camares 11005
Château de Montaner, Montaner 13040
Château de Montignies-sur-Roc, Montignies-sur-Roc 03639
Château de Montméry et son Parc, Ambazac 10299
Château de Montmuran, Les Iffs 12541
Château de Pongamp, Plouguenast 13773
Château de Prades, Lafox 12297
Château de Puymartin, Marquay 12832
Château de Ratilly, Treigny 14991
Château de Reinhardstein, Robertville 03700
Château de Rixensart, Rixensart 03699
Château de Rochambeau, Thoré-la-Rochette 14898
Château de Rochefort-en-Terre, Rochefort-en-Terre 14002
Château de Roquedols, Meyrueis 12970
Château de Rosanbo, Lanvellec 12337
Château de Saint-Aubin-sur-Loire, Saint-Aubin-sur-Loire 14118
Château de Saint-Jean-de-Beauregard, Saint-Jean-de-Beauregard 14274
Château de Simiane, Valréas 15076
Château de Solre-sur-Sambre, Solre-sur-Sambre 03757
Château de Sombreffe, Sombreffe 03758
Château de Sourdis, Gaujacq 11844
Château de Spontin, Yvoir 03849
Château de Sully-sur-Loire, Sully-sur-Loire 14843

Château de Talcy, Marchenoir 12803
Château de Tarascon, Tarascon (Bouches-du-Rhône) 14859
Château de Temniac, Sarlat-la-Canéda 14612
Château de Thoury, Saint-Pourçain-sur-Besbre 14425
Château de Trazegnies, Trazegnies 03798
Château de Vascœuil, Vascœuil 15093
Château de Vaurenard, Gleize 11878
Château de Véves, Celles 03347
Château de Villegongis, Villegongis 15212
Château de Villeneuve, Saint-Germain-Lembron 14246
Château de Villeneuve, Vence 15113
Château de Voltaire/Centre des Monuments Nationaux, Ferney-Voltaire 11719
Le Château d'Eau, Toulouse 14937
Château des Allymes, Ambérieu-en-Bugey 10300
Château des Baux, Les Baux-de-Provence 12522
Château des Ducs d'Epernon, Cadillac 10975
Château des Pêcheurs, La Bussière 12131
Château des Rois Ducs, Sauveterre-la-Lémance 14657
Château des XIVe-XVIIe s, Époisses 11635
Château d'Ételan, Saint-Maurice-d'Ételan 14364
Château d'If, Marseille 12847
Château d'Oiron, Oiron 13393
Château d'Oron, Oron-le-Châtel 37015
Château du Chassan, Faverolles (Cantal) 11708
Château du Clos de Vougeot, Vougeot 15292
Château du Fosteau, Leers-et-Fosteau 03557
Château du Haut-Koenigsbourg, Orschwiller 13439
Château du Lude, Le Lude 12434
Château du Rivau, Lemere 12512
Château du Val Richer, Saint-Ouen-le-Pin 14392
Château du Vert-Bois, Bondues 10791
Château du XVIe s, Ancy-le-Franc 10332
Château d'Ussé, Rigny-Ussé 13968
Château et Musée de Filain-Fort, Filain 11734
Château et Musée de Valangin, Valangin 37275
Château Feodal, Corroy-le-Château 03361
Château Féodal de Beynac, Beynac et Cazenac 10714
Château Ferme, Falaën 03414
Château Fort, Bouillon 03232
Château-Fort de Robert-le-Diable, Moulineaux 13184
Château Franc-Waret, Franc-Waret 03422
Château Le Temple, Valeyrac 15056
Château Les Bories, Antonne-et-Trigonant 10380
Château Logue, Maniwaki 05805
Château Malromé, Saint-André-du-Bois 14107
Château Médiéval de Tancarville, Tancarville 14854
Château Médiéval et Musée Delporte, Thy-le-Château 03777
Château Montauban, Fontvieille 11781
Château-Musée, Aren 10401
Château-Musée, Aulan 10482
Château-Musée, Boën-sur-Lignon 10777
Château-Musée, Boulogne-sur-Mer 10839
Château-Musée, Brissac-Quincé 10937
Château-Musée, Carrouges 11062
Château-Musée, Châteaudun 11213
Château-Musée, Cheverny 11282
Château-Musée, Chitry-les-Mines 11294
Château-Musée, Collonges-lès-Bévy 11355
Château-Musée, Cons-la-Grandville 11398
Château-Musée, Cormatin 11410
Château-Musée, Davayat 11484
Château-Musée, Ferrières (Seine-et-Marne) 11723
Château-Musée, Heudicourt 12022
Château-Musée, La Barben 12119
Château-Musée, Lavardens 12364
Château-Musée, Lavoûte-sur-Loire 12374
Château-Musée, Le Bourg-Saint-Léonard 12385
Château-Musée, Le Plessis-Brion 12465
Château-Musée, Lenoncourt 12513
Château-Musée, Maillebois 12770
Château-Musée, Menthon-Saint-Bernard 12933
Château-Musée, Meung-sur-Loire 12961
Château-Musée, Montmirail 13110
Château-Musée, Pange 13460
Château-Musée, Pirou 13741
Château-Musée, Poudenas 13850
Château-Musée, Roche-la-Molière 13990
Château-Musée, Saint-Vidal 14504
Château-Musée, Tourrette-Levens 14967
Château-Musée, Valprivas 15075
Château-Musée, Vendeuvre 15115
Château-Musée, Villandry 15172
Château-Musée, Virieu-sur-Bourbre 15271
Château-Musée Anjony, Tournemire 14962
Château-Musée d'Andurain, Mauléon-Licharre 12894
Château-Musée d'Anet, Anet 10340
Château-Musée d'Art Populaire et Religieux, Clermont (Haute-Savoie) 11326
Château-Musée d'Aulteribe, Sermentizon 14721
Château-Musée de Bois-Chevalier, Legé 12506
Château-Musée de Bonneville, Chamblac 11143
Château-Musée de Brie, Champagnac-la-Rivière 11150
Château-Musée de Bussy-Rabutin, Bussy-le-Grand 10961
Château-Musée de Buzay, La Jarne 12202
Château-Musée de Cany, Cany-Barville 11031
Château-Musée de Château Dauphin, Pontgibaud 13827
Château-Musée de Chémery, Chémery 11267
Château-Musée de Chenonceau, Chenonceaux 11271
Château-Musée de Combourg, Combourg 11366
Château-Musée de Condé, Condé-en-Brie 11385
Château-Musée de Courson, Courson-Monteloup 11437
Château-Musée de Craon, Haroué 11992
Château-Musée de Culan, Culan 11470
Château-Musée de Dampierre-sur-Boutonne, Aulnay (Charente-Maritime) 10483
Château-Musée de Dieppe, Dieppe 11507
Château-Musée de Filières, Gommerville près Le Havre-Etretat 11881
Château-Musée de Jussy, Jussy-Champagne 12107
Château-Musée de la Batisse, Chanonat 11163
Château-Musée de la Court d'Aron, Saint-Cyr-en-Talmondais 14168
Château-Musée de la Gataudière, Marennes 12819
Château-Musée de la Grange, Manom 12792
Château-Musée de la Nature, Bonnefamille 10795
Château-Musée de la Possonnière, Couture-sur-Loir 11444
Château-Musée de la Roche, Chaptuzat 11169
Château-Musée de la Roche-Racan, Saint-Paterne-Racan 14397
Château-Musée de la Rochelambert, Saint-Paulien 14406
Château-Musée de la Trémolière, Anglards-de-Salers 10351
Château-Musée de Lacassagne, Saint-Avit-Frandat 14119
Château-Musée de Lamartine, Saint-Point 14421
Château-Musée de Lantheuil, Lantheuil 12336
Château-Musée de Maupas, Morogues 13169
Château-Musée de Miromesnil, Tourville-sur-Arques 14979
Château-Musée de Montaigu, Laneuveville-devant-Nancy 12320
Château-Musée de Montal, Saint-Jean-Lespinasse 14290
Château-Musée de Montfleury, Avressieux 10544
Château-Musée de Montgeoffroy, Mazé 12905
Château-Musée de Panloy, Port-d'Envaux 13838
Château-Musée de Pescheray, Le Breil-sur-Merize 12388
Château-Musée de Pont-Chevron, Ouzouer-sur-Trézée 13448
Château-Musée de Préhistoire, Belesta-de-la-Frontière 10669
Château-Musée de Puyguilhem, Villars (Dordogne) 15180
Château-Musée de Ravignan, Perquie 13710
Château-Musée de Ripaille, Thonon-les-Bains 14895
Château-Musée de Selles, Cambrai 11010
Château-Musée de Serrant, Saint-Georges-sur-Loire 14234
Château-Musée de Teillan, Aimargues 10242
Château-Musée de Terre-Neuve, Fontenay-le-Comte 11771
Château-Musée de Vaulaville, Tour-en-Bessin 14955
Château-Musée de Veauce, Ébreuil 11594
Château-Musée de Villeprévost, Tillay-le-Péneux 14913
Château-Musée de Villersexel, Villersexel 15245
Château-Musée de Villesavin, Tour-en-Sologne 14956
Château-Musée de Vollore, Vollore-Ville 15285
Château-Musée des Ducs, Duras 11587
Château-Musée des Effiat, Effiat 11602
Château-Musée des XVIe-XVIIe s, Tanlay 14856
Château-Musée Dillon, Blanquefort 10760
Château-Musée du Fort La Latte, Fréhel 11806
Château-Musée du Grand-Saussay, Ballancourt-sur-Essonne 10571
Château-Musée du Maréchal Lyautey, Thorey-Lyautey 14900
Château-Musée du Moulin, Lassay-sur-Croisne 12352
Château-Musée du Plessis-Bouré, Ecuillé 11600
Château-Musée du Plessis-lès-Tours, La Riche 12225
Château-Musée du Rhône, Tournon-sur-Rhône 14963
Château-Musée du Roussillon, Cahors 10992
Château-Musée du Suscinio, Sarzeau 14628
Château-Musée du Touvet, Le Touvet 12487
Château-Musée du Val, Lanobre 12331
Château-Musée du XVe et XVIIIe Siècle, Commarin 11371
Château-Musée du XVIIe Siècle, Fontaine-Française 11763
Château-Musée d'Urrugne, Urrugne 15029
Château-Musée et Ecuries de Chaumont-sur-Loire, Chaumont-sur-Loire 11252
Château Musée Grimaldi, Cagnes-sur-Mer 10986
Château-Musée la Fayette, Chavaniac-Lafayette 11257
Château-Musée le Denacre, Wimille 15313
Château-Musée Les Martinanches, Saint-Dier-d'Auvergne 14188
Château-Musée Listran, Saint-Vivien-de-Médoc 14508
Château-Musée Mansart, Sagonne 14084
Château-Musée Marguerite de Burgogne, Couches 11418
Château-Musée Municipal, Nemours 13279
Château-Musée Prieuré Lichine, Cantenac 11029
Château-Musée Renaissance, Azay-le-Rideau 10550
Château-Musée Turcan, Ansouis 10367
Château-Musée Verdus et Bardis, Saint-Seurin-de-Cadourne 14473
Château Petit Versailles, Parentignat 13467
Château-Promenade des Parfums, Chilleurs-aux-Bois 11287
Château Royal, Collioure 11348
Château Royal d'Amboise, Amboise 10309
Chatelherault, Ferniegair 38986
Chatham College Art Gallery, Pittsburgh 46514
Chatham Islands Museum, Tuku Rd, Waitangi 30269
Chatham-Kent Museum, Chatham, Ontario 05237
Chatham Railroad Museum, Chatham, Ontario 05238
Chatillon-DeMenil Mansion, Saint Louis 47114
Chatsworth House, Bakewell 38058
Chattahoochee Valley Art Museum, La Grange 44541
Chattanooga African-American Museum, Chattanooga 42258
Chattanooga Regional History Museum, Chattanooga 42259
Chatterley Whitfield Mining Museum, Stoke-on-Trent 40603
Chattishgarh Coin and Papermoney Museum, Katora Talab 21885
Chattishgarh Mudra Sangrahalaya, Katora Talab 21885
Le Chaudron Magique, Brugnac 10942
Cheb Castle, Cheb 08307
Cheb Museum, Cheb 08308
Chebský Hrad, Cheb 08307
Cheddar Man and the Cannibals, Cheddar 38535
Cheddleton Flint Mill, Cheddleton 38536
Chedworth Roman Villa, Yanworth 40950
Chedworth Roman Villa Museum, Cheltenham 38543
Cheekwood Museum of Art, Nashville 45613
Cheesemaking-Museum, Nakkila 09857
Chehel-Sotoon Museum, Qazvin 22273
Chehel-Sotoon Palace Museum, Isfahan 22245
Chehel-Stoun Museum, Ghazvin 22236
Chelan County Historical Museum, Cashmere 42128
Chelan County Public Utility District, Wenatchee 48504
Chelmsford Historical Museum, Chelmsford 42270
Chelmsford Historical Society Museum, South Chelmsford 47689
Chelmsford Museum, Chelmsford 38537
Chelsea Court House Museum, Chelsea 00907
Chelsea Physic Garden, London 39604
Cheltenham Art Gallery and Museum, Cheltenham 38544
Chelyabinsk Regional Picture Gallery, Čeljabinsk 32724
Chemin de Fer-Musée Blonay-Chamby, Lausanne 36851
Chemin de la Soie, Molière-Cavaillac 13004
Le Chemin du Fauvisme, Collioure 11349
Chemung Valley History Museum, Elmira 43170
Chenango County Historical Society Museum, Norwich 46038
Cheney Homestead, Manchester 45092
Chengdu City Museum, Chengdu 07020
Cheongju Early Printing Museum, Cheongju 27148
Cheongju National Museum, Cheongju 27149
Cheongju University Museum, Cheongju 27150
Chepstow Museum, Chepstow 38546
Cheraw Lyceum Museum, Cheraw 42272
Cherokee County Historical Museum, Murphy 45571
Cherokee Heritage Centre, Tahlequah 47925
Cherokee Strip Land Rush Museum, Arkansas City 41256
Cherokee Strip Museum, Alva 41161
Cherokee Strip Museum and Henry S. Johnston Library, Perry 46356
Cherry County Historical Society Museum, Valentine 48183
Cherry Valley Museum, Cherry Valley 42279
Chersonskij Kraevedčeskij Muzej, Cherson 37843
Chertsey Museum, Chertsey 38548
Chesapeake and Ohio Canal Tavern Museum, Sharpsburg 47583
Chesapeake Bay Maritime Museum, Saint Michaels 47149
Chesapeake Beach Railway Museum, Chesapeake Beach 42281
Chesham Town Museum, Chesham 38549
Cheshire County Museum, Keene 44425
Cheshire Military Museum, Chester 38550
Chester Art Guild, Chester 42287
The Chester Beatty Library, Dublin 22417
Chester County Historical Society Museum, West Chester 48517
Chester County Museum, Chester 42286
Chesterfield Historical Society of Verginia Museum, Chesterfield 42291
Chesterfield Museum and Art Gallery, Chesterfield 38554
Chesterholm Museum Roman Vindolanda, Hexham 39237
Chesterwood Museum, Stockbridge 47816
Chestico Museum, Port Hood 06165
Chethams's Hospital and Library, Manchester 39885
Chetopa Historical Museum, Chetopa 42295
Cheviot Museum, Cheviot 30120
Cheyenne Frontier Days Old West Museum, Cheyenne 42297
Chiang Mai Contemporary Art Museum, Chiang Mai 37501
Chiang Saen National Museum, Chiang Rai 37504
Chiba City Museum of Art, Chiba 26120
Chiba-kenritsu Awa Hakubutsukan, Tateyama 26819
Chiba-kenritsu Bijutsukan, Chiba 26121
Chiba-kenritsu Boso Fudoki-No-Oka, Sakae 26694
Chiba-kenritsu Chuo Hakubutsukan, Chiba 26122
Chiba-kenritsu Kazusa Hakubutsukan, Kisarazu 26337
Chiba-kenritsu Sonan Hakubutsukan, Isumi 26260
Chiba Prefectional Awa Museum, Tateyama 26819
Chiba Prefectual Boso Fudoki-No-Oka Museum, Sakae 26694
Chiba Prefectural Accident Museum, Isumi 26260
Chiba Prefectural Kazusa Museum, Kisarazu 26337
Chiba Prefectural Museum of Art, Chiba 26121
Chiba-shi Kasori Kaizuka Hakubutsukan, Chiba 26123
Chiba Sogo Museum of Art, Chiba 26124
The Chicago Academy of Sciences Peggy Notebaert Nature Museum, Chicago 42313
Chicago Architecture Foundation, Chicago 42314
The Chicago Athenaeum - Museum of Architecture and Design, Chicago 42315
Chicago Children's Museum, Chicago 42316
Chicago Cultural Center, Chicago 42317
Chicago Historical Society, Chicago 42318
Chichester District Museum, Chichester 38559
Chichibunomiya Kinen Supohtsu Hakubutsukan, Tokyo 26835
Chickamauga-Chattanooga National Military Park, Fort Oglethorpe 43438
Chickasaw Council House Museum, Tishomingo 48011
Chickasaw County Historical Society Museum, Bradford Village, Nashua 45607
Chico Museum, Chico 42371
Chiddingstone Castle, Chiddingstone 38567
Chido Museum, Tsuruoka 26979
Chief John Ross House, Rossville 47011
Chief Oshkosh Native American Arts, Egg Harbor 43099
Chief Plenty Coups Museum, Pryor 46737
Chiefswood Museum, Ohsweken 06043
Chieftains Museum, Rome 46993
Chiesa di Santa Maria Maddalena de Pazzi, Firenze 23830
Chifley Home, Bathurst 00775
Chihiro Art Museum Azumino, Nagano 26527
Chihiro Art Museum Tokyo, Tokyo 26836
Chikatetsu Hakubutsukan, Tokyo 26837
Chikkyo Art Museum Kasaoka, Kasaoka 26316
Chikubushima Treasure House, Shiga 26747
Chikurin-ji Treasure House, Kochi 26353
Childers Pharmaceutical Museum, Childers 00909
Childhome of Z. Topelius, Uusikaarlepyy 10150
Childhood and Costume Museum, Bridgnorth 38322
Childhood Museum, Alger 00042
Children Art Palace, Islamabad 31022
Children Museum, Čerepovec 32730
Children of Września Regional Museum, Września 32195
Children's Art Museum, San Angelo 47239
Childrens Art Museum, Tako 26815
Children's Art Museum, Warszawa 32127
Children's Creative Art Centre and Gallery, Toruń 32050
Children's Discovery Museum of Central Illinois, Bloomington 41741
Children's Discovery Museum of North San Diego, Carlsbad 42107
Children's Discovery Museum of San Jose, San Jose 47350
Children's Discovery Museum of the Desert, Rancho Mirage 46785
The Children's Discovery Museum of Vermont, Burlington 42007
Children's Hands-On Museum, Tuscaloosa 48113
Children's Health Museum, Charlottesville 42247
Children's Heritage and Science Museum, Amman 27047
Children's Library Museum, Marondera 49036
The Children's Metamorphosis, Londonderry 44854
Children's Museum, Alger 00043
Children's Museum, Amreli 21696
Children's Museum, Bhavnagar 21717
The Children's Museum, Boston 41804
Children's Museum, Detroit 42919
Children's Museum, Holyoke 44065
Childrens Museum, Imphal 21851
Children's Museum, København 08922
Children's Museum, Lucknow 21921
Children's Museum, Muscat 31003
Children's Museum, Quezon City 31430
Children's Museum, San Diego 47273
Children's Museum, San Juan 32400
The Children's Museum, Seattle 47532
Children's Museum, Shanghai 07209
Children's Museum at La Habra, La Habra 44547
The Children's Museum at Saratoga, Saratoga Springs 47459
Children's Museum at Yunker Farm, Fargo 43290
Children's Museum Big Bang, Sakai 26695
Children's Museum in Dartmouth, South Dartmouth 47690
The Children's Museum in Easton, North Easton 45993
Children's Museum in New Braunfels, New Braunfels 45668
Children's Museum of Boca Raton, Boca Raton 41766
The Children's Museum of Cleveland, Cleveland 42464
Children's Museum of Denver, Denver 42881
The Children's Museum of Green Bay, Green Bay 43787
Children's Museum of Helsinki City Museum, Helsinki 09508
Children's Museum of History, Natural History and Science at Utica, New York, Utica 48169
The Children's Museum of Houston, Houston 44117

The Children's Museum of Indianapolis, Indianapolis 44215
The Children's Museum of Kansas City, Kansas City 44391
Children's Museum of Lake Charles, Lake Charles 44580
Children's Museum of Los Angeles, Los Angeles 44896
Children's Museum of Maine, Portland 46621
Children's Museum of Manhattan, New York 45781
The Children's Museum of Memphis, Memphis 45233
Children's Museum of Oak Ridge, Oak Ridge 46056
Children's Museum of Portsmouth, Portsmouth 46647
Children's Museum of Richmond, Richmond 46874
The Children's Museum of Rose Hill Manor Park, Frederick 43526
Children's Museum of South Carolina, Myrtle Beach 45585
Children's Museum of Spokane, Spokane 47726
Children's Museum of Stockton, Stockton 47823
Children's Museum of Tampa - Kid City, Tampa 47939
Children's Museum of the Arts, New York 45782
The Children's Museum of Utah, Salt Lake City 47228
Children's Museum of Virginia, Portsmouth 46659
Children's Own Museum, Toronto 06573
Children's Picture Gallery, Samara 33368
The Children's Science Center, Cape Coral 42094
Childress County Heritage Museum, Childress 42375
Childventure Museum, Fort Washington 43470
Chilean Federation of Friends of Museos, Santiago de Chile 49109
Chillagoe Historical Centre, Chillagoe 00911
Chillida Leku, Hernani 34900
Chilliwack Museum, Chilliwack 05248
Chiltern Athenaeum, Chiltern 00912
Chiltern Motor Museum, Chiltern 00913
Chiltern Open Air Museum, Chalfont Saint Giles 38519
Chimkent Historical and Regional Museum, Čimkent 27078
Chimmey Point Tavern, Addison 41064
Chimneyville Crafts Gallery, Jackson 44277
China Art Gallery, Beijing 06956
China Aviation Museum, Beijing 06957
China Calligraphy Art Museum, Xian 07293
China First History Archive Museum, Beijing 06958
China Great Wall Museum, Beijing 06959
China Institute Gallery, New York 45783
China Jia Wu Zhan Zhen Museum, Weihai 07278
China Museum of Buddhist Literature and Heritage, Beijing 06960
China National Museum, Beijing 06961
China Nationalities Museum of Inner Mongolia, Tongliao 07272
China Palace Museum at the Museum-Preserve, Lomonosov 32989
China Silk Museum, Hangzhou 07080
China Sports Museum, Beijing 06962
China Stamp Museum, Beijing 06963
China Tradition Medicine Museum, Chongqing 07030
China Xiamen Huaqiao Museum, Xiamen 07290
China Yin Xue Museum, Hangzhou 07081
Chinati Foundation, Marfa 45140
Chinchilla and District Historical Society Museum, Chinchilla 00915
Chinese Association of Museums, Taipei 49114
Chinese Association of Natural Science Museums, Beijing 49111
Chinese Culture Center of San Francisco, San Francisco 47315
Chinese House Museum, Echo 43078
Chinese Medicine Museum, Hangzhou 07082
Chinese Museum, Ardebil 22230
Chinese Museum, Melbourne 01224
Chinese Museum of Military Weaponary, Tongzhou 07273
Chinese Pavilion and Japanese Tower, Bruxelles 03340
Chinese Society of Museums, Beijing 49112
Chinikhaneh Museum, Ardebil 22230
Chino City Togariishi Jomon Archaeology Museum, Chino 26127
Chino-shi Togariishi Jomon Kokokan, Chino 26127
Chinqua-Penn Plantation, Reidsville 46832
Chios Museum of Byzantine and Postbyzantine Art, Chios 20922
Chiostro dello Scalzo, Firenze 23831
Chippenham Museum and Heritage Centre, Chippenham 38568
Chippewa County Historical Society Museum, Montevideo 45463
Chippewa Valley Museum, Eau Claire 43074
Chipping Norton Museum of Local History, Chipping Norton 38570
Chippokes Farm and Forestry Museum, Surry 47895
Chiricahua Museum, Willcox 48623
Chirk Castle, Chirk 38571
Chisenhale Gallery, London 39605
Chishaku-in Temple Storehouse, Kyoto 26392
Chisholm Trail Heritage Center Museum, Duncan 43007
Chisholm Trail Historical Museum, Waurika 48462
Chisholm Trail Museum, Kingfisher 44486
Chisholm Trail Museum, Wellington 48499
Chiswick House, London 39606
Chita City Museum, Chita 26129
Chita-shi Rekishi Minzoku Hakubutsukan, Chita 26129
Sri Chitra Art Gallery, Thiruvananthapuram 22034
Chittagong University Museum, Chittagong 03079
Chittenango Landing Canal Boat Museum, Chittenango 42389
Chiverton House Museum, Northampton 01330
Choctaw Museum, Hugo 44147
Chofu City Museum, Chofu 26130
Chofu Museum, Shimonoseki 26751
Chofu-shiritsu Hakabutsukan, Chofu 26130
Chohung Museum of Finance, Seoul 27225
Chojagahara Archaeological Museum, Itoigawa 26265
Chojagahara Kokokan, Itoigawa 26265
Chojin Lama Museum, Ulaanbaatar 28675
Chokoku no Mori Bijutsukan, Hakone 26174
Choma Museum and Crafts Centré, Choma 49015
Chonbuk University Museum, Jeonju 27198
Chongming County Museum, Shanghai 07210
Chongqing Museum, Chongqing 07031
Chongqing Natural Museum, Chongqing 07032
Chonnam University Museum, Gwangju 27181
Choraku Homotsukan, Kamo, Izu 26299
Chorakuji Collection, Kamo, Izu 26299
Chorožskij Istoriko-Kraevedčeskij Muzej, Chorog 37444
Choudomir House-Museum, Kazanlăk 04698
Christ Boelens Jukeboxen Museum, Sint Oedenrode 29823
Christ Church Cathedral Treasury, Oxford 40144
Christ Church Community Museum, Lakefield 05720
Christ Church Picture Gallery, Oxford 40145
Christ the King College Museum, Calbayog 31302
Christchurch Art Gallery Te Puna o Waiwhetu, Christchurch 30126
Christchurch Mansion, Ipswich 39303
Christchurch Tricycle Museum, Christchurch 38576
Christian C. Sanderson Museum, Chadds Ford 42176
Christian Museum, Esztergom 21412
Christian-Wolff-Haus, Halle, Saale 17508
Christianssands Billedgalleri, Kristiansand 30612
Christiansted National Historic Site, Saint Croix 47087
Christmas Museum Gallery, Horsley Park 01111
Christo Botev Memorial House, Kalofer 04686
Christo Danov House-Museum, Plovdiv 04778
Christophs Friseur-Museum, Leipheim 18380
Christos Capralos Museum, Aegina 20804
Christos Capralos Museum, Agrinion 20812
Christos Capralos Museum, Athinai 20855
Christ's Hospital Museum, Horsham 39263
The Chrysler Museum of Art, Norfolk 45963
CHTJ Southard House Museum, Richmond 46866
Chuan Cheng Art Center, Taipei 07345
Chudožestvena Galerija, Balčik 04610
Chudožestvena Galerija, Blagoevgrad 04625
Chudožestvena Galerija, Chaskovo 04639
Chudožestvena Galerija, Čirpan 04644
Chudožestvena Galerija, Drjanovo 04658
Chudožestvena Galerija, Gabrovo 04666
Chudožestvena Galerija, Gălăbovo 04671
Chudožestvena Galerija, Karlovo 04689
Chudožestvena Galerija, Kavarna 04694
Chudožestvena Galerija, Kazanlăk 04697
Chudožestvena Galerija, Levski 04724
Chudožestvena Galerija, Loveč 04727
Chudožestvena Galerija, Mezdra 04736
Chudožestvena Galerija, Michajlovgrad 04737
Chudožestvena Galerija, Pernik 04758
Chudožestvena Galerija, Provadia 04788
Chudožestvena Galerija, Radnevo 04792
Chudožestvena Galerija, Silistra 04813
Chudožestvena Galerija, Sozopol 04863
Chudožestvena Galerija, Svištov 04877
Chudožestvena Galerija, Veliko Tărnovo 04913
Chudožestvena Galerija, Žeravna 04932
Chudožestvena Galerija Darenie Kollekcia Svetlin Russev, Pleven 04763
Chudožestvena Galerija Dobrič, Dobrič 04652
Chudožestvena Galerija Elena Karamichajlova, Šumen 04870
Chudožestvena Galerija Ilija Beškov, Pleven 04764
Chudožestvena Galerija Kiril Petrov, Montana 04740
Chudožestvena Galerija Nikola Marinov, Targovište 04882
Chudožestvena Galerija "Petar Persengiev", Novi Pazar 04745
Chudožestvena Galerija Prof. Ilija Petrov, Razgrad 04796
Chudožestvena Galerija Ruse, Ruse 04802
Chudožestvena Galerija Stanislav Dospevski, Pazardžik 04753
Chudožestvena Galerija Varna, Varna 04894
Chudožestvennaja Galereja - Dom Kukly Tatjany Kalininoj, Petrozavodsk 33313
Chudožestvenno-memorialnyj Muzej K.S. Petrova-Vodkina, Chvalynsk 32746
Chudožestvenno-pedagogičeskij Muzej Igruški - Kulturno-delovoj Centr, Sergiev Posad 33519
Chudožestvenno-vystavočnyj Kompleks, Sarapul 33501
Chudožestvennyj Muzei, Sevastopol 37901
Chudožestvennyj Muzej, Staryj Oskol 33557
Chudožestvennyj Muzej, Valujki 33674
Chudožestvennyj Muzej im. A.N. Radiščeva, Saratov 33504
Chudožestvennyj Muzej im. M.S. Tuganova, Vladikavkaz 33686
Chudžandskij Istoriko-Kraevedčeskij Muzej, Chudžand 37445
Chughtai Museum Trust, Lahore 31033
Chumbhot-Punthip Museum, Bangkok 37480
Chung-Cheng Art Gallery, Jamaica 44303
Chung-Cheng Aviation Museum, Taipei 07346
Chungju Museum, Chungju 27152
Chungnam Telecommunication Museum, Daejeon 27158
Chungnam National University Museum, Daejeon 27159
Church Collection, Oplenac kod Topole 33879
Church Collection, Prčanj 33894
Church Farm Museum, Skegness 40524
Church Farmhouse Museum, London 39607
Church Museum, Laihia 09751
Church Museum Lopud, Lopud 07735
Church of the Deposition of the Robe, Moskva 33032
Church of the Holy Apostles Collection, Parga 21109
Church-Waddel-Brumby House Museum, Athens 41317
Churchill County Museum and Archives, Fallon 43285
Churchill House Museum and Hatton Gallery, Hereford 39223
Churchill Island Agricultural Museum, Newhaven 01319
Chusonji Sankozo, Hiraizumi 26202
Chusonji Temple Treasury, Hiraizumi 26202
Chuvash National Museum, Čeboksary 32719
Chuvash State Art Museum, Čeboksary 32718
Chvalyn Museum of Local History, Nature and Culture, Chvalynsk 32747
Chvalynskij Kraevedčeskij Muzej, Chvalynsk 32747
CIA Museum, McLean 45040
Ciăsa Granda, Stampa 37201
Cider Museum, Hereford 39224
CIDOC International Committee for Documentation, København 49136
Ciências Educação e Artes Luiz de Queiráz, Piracibaba 04264
Ciencias Naturales P. Ignacio Sala, Valencia 35597
Çifte Minareli Medrese Müzesi, Erzurum 37670
Çifte Minareli Medrese Museum, Erzurum 37670
Cigna Museum and Art Collection, Philadelphia 46398
Cimarron Valley Railroad Museum, Cushing 42733
Čimkentskij Istoriko-Kraevedčeskij Muzej, Čimkent 27078
CIMUSET International Committee for Science and Technology Museums, Delhi 49237
Cincinnati Art Museum, Cincinnati 42400
Cincinnati Fire Museum, Cincinnati 42401
Cincinnati Museum Center, Cincinnati 42402
Cinema Museum, London 39608
Cinema Museum, Moskva 33115
La Cinémathèque de Toulouse, Toulouse 14938
Cinémathèque Québécoise - Musée du Cinéma, Montréal 05901
Cinematographic Museum, Kaposvár 21440
Cinematographic Museum, Shkodër 00031
Cineteca Nazionale, Roma 25155
Circik Regional Museum, Čirčik 48835
Circle Craft Gallery, Vancouver 06673
Circuit Géologique des Boves, Arras 10428
Circus City Festival Museum, Peru 46362
Circus Museum, Rapperswil, Sankt Gallen 37042
Circus World Museum, Baraboo 41500
Cirencester Lock-Up, Cirencester 38583
Ciruito Museale Urbano, Cascia 23373
Císařská Konírna, Praha 08569
Čišinski-Gedenkstätte, Panschwitz-Kuckau 19342
Cistercian Museum, Hailes 39145
Cistercian Museum, Wąchock 32066
Cistersian Monastery Museum, Szczyrzyc 32031
The Citadel Archives and Museum, Charleston 42212
Citadel's Artspace, Saint Helens 40396
Cité de la Mer ESTRAN, Dieppe 11508
Cité de l'Énergie, Shawinigan 06430
Cité des Métiers de Tradition, Saint-Laurent-de-la-Plaine 14307
Cité des Sciences et de l'Industrie, Paris 13484
Čitinskij Oblastnoj Chudožestvennyj Muzej, Čita 32750
City and County Museum, Lincoln 39496
City Art Centre, Edinburgh 38873
City Art Gallery, Berkovica 04621
City Art Gallery, Leeds 39442
City Art Gallery, Pernik 04758
City Art Gallery, Wagga Wagga 01569
City Art Museum, Ljubljana 34110
City Art Museum, Wrocław 32188
City County Pioneer Museum, Sweetwater 47903
City Exhibition Hall, Krasnojarsk 32951
City Exhibition Hall of Smolensk, Smolensk 33538
City Exhibition Space, Sydney 01494
City Gallery, Leicester 39460
City Gallery at Chastain, Atlanta 41338
City Gallery East, Atlanta 41339
City Gallery of Bratislava, Bratislava 33963
City Gallery of Fine Arts, Plovdiv 04777
City Gallery Prague, Praha 08577
City Gallery Wellington, Wellington 30292
City Hall Council Chamber Gallery, Charleston 42213
City Hall from Antwerpen, Antwerpen 03174
City History Museum, Szczecin 32027
City Island Nautical Museum, Bronx 41917
City Museum, Ahmedabad 21678
City Museum, Beşiktaş 37634
City Museum, Horažďovice 08358
City Museum, Klobouky u Brna 08415
City Museum, Kosovska Mitrovica 33847
City Museum, Križevci 07730
City Museum, Leeds 39443
City Museum, Makale 09405
City Museum, Radnice u Rokycan 08632
City Museum, Rýmařov 08649
City Museum, Saint Louis 47115
City Museum, Yirgalem 09406
City Museum, Zenica 03932
City Museum Aalst, Aalst 03125
City Museum and Art Gallery, Gloucester 39080
City Museum and Art Gallery, Plymouth 40209
City Museum and Gallery, Hořice v Pokrkonoší 08359
City Museum and Museum of Textiles, Dvůr Králové nad Labem 08337
City Museum and Records Office, Portsmouth 40249
City Museum Bratislava, Bratislava 33970
City Museum in the Oslekov House, Koprivštica 04716
City Museum of Göteborgs, Göteborg 35913
City Museum of Korčula, Korčula 07722
City Museum of Norrköping, Norrköping 36121
City Museum of Performing Arts, Omsk 33254
City Museum of Zagreb, Zagreb 07830
City of Belmont Museum, Belmont 00791
City of Bowie Museums, Bowie 41846
City of Brea Gallery, Brea 41874
City of Gosnells Museum, Gosnells 01068
City of Ketchikan Museum, Ketchikan 44458
City of Las Vegas and Rough Riders Memorial Museum, Las Vegas 44662
City of London Police Museum, London 39609
City of Melbourne Collection, Melbourne 01225
City of Norwich Aviation Museum, Horsham Saint Faith 39266
City of Richmond and Burnley Historical Museum, Richmond, Victoria 01415
City of Saint John Gallery, Saint John 06332
City of Unley Museum, Unley 01561
City of Wayne Historical Museum, Wayne 48475
City of York Museum, York 06872
City Park Radio Museum, Launceston 01167
City Wax Museum, México 28128
Civica Galleria d'Arte Contemporanea, Lissone 24188
Civica Galleria d'Arte Contemporanea F. Scroppo, Torre Pellice 25774
Civica Galleria d'Arte G. Sciortino, Monreale 24479
Civica Galleria d'Arte Moderna, Gallarate 23950
Civica Galleria d'Arte Moderna, Genova 23978
Civica Galleria d'Arte Moderna, Milano 24371
Civica Galleria d'Arte Moderna E. Restivo, Palermo 24763
Civica Galleria d'Arte Villa dei Cedri, Bellinzona 36529
Civica Galleria di Palazzo Rocca, Chiavari 23529
Civica Pinacoteca V. Crivelli, Sant'Elpidio a Mare 25460
Civica Raccolta d'Arte, Medole 24342
Civica Raccolta d'Arte, Roseto degli Abruzzi 25282
Civica Raccolta d'Arte B. Biancolini, Potenza Picena 25029
Civica Raccolta delle Stampe Achille Bertarelli, Milano 24372
Civica Raccolta di Terraglia, Laveno Mombello 24164
Civica Raccolta e Ceramiche Rinascimentali, Camporgiano 23311
Civiche Raccolte Archeologiche e Numismatiche, Milano 24373
Civiche Raccolte d'Arte, Busto Arsizio 23237
Civiche Raccolte d'Arte Applicata, Milano 24374
Civici Musei di Villa Paolina, Viareggio 25984
Civici Musei e Gallerie di Storia ed Arte, Udine 25845
Civico Gabinetto dei Disegni, Milano 24375
Civico Museo, Cairo Montenotte 23257
Civico Museo Antropologico, Balestrate 23010
Civico Museo Archeologico, Acqui Terme 22804
Civico Museo Archeologico, Arsago Seprio 22943
Civico Museo Archeologico, Camogli 23294
Civico Museo Archeologico, Ozieri 24723
Civico Museo Archeologico e di Scienze Naturali Federico Eusebio, Alba 22829
Civico Museo Archeologico L. Barni e Pinacoteca C. Ottone, Vigevano 26006
Civico Museo Bibliografico Musicale, Bologna 23100
Civico Museo Biblioteca dell'Attore del Teatro, Genova 23979
Civico Museo d'Arte Contemporanea, Milano 24376
Civico Museo d'Arte Moderne, Anticoli Corrado 22895
Civico Museo d'Arte Orientale, Trieste 25810
Civico Museo degli Strumenti Musicali, Milano 24377
Civico Museo del Mare, Trieste 25811
Civico Museo del Merletto al Tombolo, Rapallo 25074
Civico Museo del Risorgimento e Sacrario Oberdan, Trieste 25812
Civico Museo della Risiera di San Sabba, Trieste 25813
Civico Museo di Guerra per la Pace Diego de Henriquez, Trieste 25814
Civico Museo di Scienze Naturali, Domodossola 23718
Civico Museo di Storia ed Arte e Orto Lapidario, Trieste 25815
Civico Museo di Storia Naturale della Lombardia, Jerago con Orago 24112
Civico Museo Dianese, Diano Marina 23715
Civico Museo e Antiquarium Comunale, Lanuvio 24139
Civico Museo Flaminio Massetano, Massa Martana 24328
Civico Museo Frignanese, Pavullo nel Frignano 24830
Civico Museo G. Galletti, Domodossola 23719
Civico Museo G.V. Parisi-Valle, Maccagno 24246
Civico Museo Ingauno, Albenga 22831
Civico Museo Insubrico di Storia Naturale, Induno Olona 24097
Civico Museo Morpurgo, Trieste 25816
Civico Museo Naturalistico, Ovada 24722

Civico Museo Naturalistico Ferruccio Lombardi, Stradella 25640
Civico Museo Revoltella e Galleria d'Arte Moderna, Trieste 25817
Civico Museo Sartorio, Trieste 25818
Civico Museo Setificio Monti, Abbadia Lariana 22792
Civico Museo Storico, Palmanova 24783
Civico Museo Storico Archeologico, Savona 25507
Civico Museo Teatrale di Fondazione Carlo Schmidl, Trieste 25819
Civico Studio Museo Francesco Messina, Milano 24378
Civil Engineer Corps and Seabee Museum, Port Hueneme 46595
Civil Guard Museum, Seinäjoki 10030
Civil War Museum, Carrollton 42114
Civil War Museum, Philadelphia 46399
Civil War Museum of Lone Jack, Jackson County, Lone Jack 44855
Civilian Conservation Corps Museum, Sebring 47551
C.L. Alexander Museum, Tumby Bay 01553
Clackmannshire Council Museum, Alloa 37979
Clan Armstrong Museum, Langholm 39421
Clan Cameron Museum, Spean Bridge 40566
Clan Donnachaidh Museum, Pitlochry 40204
Clan Grant Museum, Alness 37982
Clan Gunn Museum, Latheron 39427
Clan Macpherson House and Museum, Newtonmore 40067
Clandestine Immigration and Naval Museum, Haifa 22601
Claphams Clock Museum, Whangarei 30314
Clara Barton Birthplace, North Oxford 46001
Clara Barton Home, Glen Echo 43680
Clara-Zetkin-Museum, Birkenwerder 16167
Clare Ancient House Museum, Clare 38585
Clare Heritage Centre, Corofin 22407
Clare Museum, Ennis 22466
Clare National Trust Museum, Clare 00916
Claremont Museum, Claremont 42421
Claremont Museum, Claremont, Western Australia 00918
Clarencetown and District Historical Museum, Clarencetown 00921
Clarendon House, Nile 01321
Claresholm Museum, Claresholm 05255
Clarin Ancestral House, Loay 31344
Clark Atlanta University Art Galleries, Atlanta 41340
Clark County Historical Museum, Vancouver 48199
Clark County Historical Society Museum, Springfield 47756
Clark County Museum, Henderson 43990
Clark County Museum, Marshall 45176
Clark House Museum Complex, Wolfeboro 48722
Clark Humanities Museum, Claremont 42417
Clarke County Historical Museum, Berryville 41657
Clarke Hall, Wakefield 40759
Clarke House Museum, Chicago 42319
Clarke Memorial Museum, Eureka 43230
Clarke Museum, Orono 06057
Clarkson Historical Museum, Clarkson 42432
Clarksville-Montgomery County Museum-Customs House Museum, Clarksville 42435
Classic Cars Museum, Salt Lake City 47229
Classical and Modern Art Museum, Moskva 33116
Clatteringshaws Forest Wildlife Centre, Clatteringshaws 38586
Claude Crayston Museum, Glenora 05493
Clausen Memorial Museum, Petersburg 46369
Clawson Historical Museum, Clawson 42439
Clay County Historical Museum, Liberty 44765
Clay County Museum, Moorhead 45487
Clay Products Interpretive Centre, Medicine Hat 05830
Clay Studio, Philadelphia 46400
Clay Tobacco Pipe Museum, Broseley 38379
Claydon House, Middle Claydon 39944
Claypool-Young Art Gallery, Morehead 45493
Clayton Collection Museum, Chollerford 38573
Clayton Collection Museum, Humshaugh 39276
Clayton McLain Memorial Museum, Cutknife 05299
Cle Elum Telephone Museum, Cle Elum 42447
Clear Lake Area Historical Museum, Clear Lake 42449
Clearfield County Historical Society Museum, Clearfield 42450
Clearwater County Historical Museum, Shevlin 47605
Clearwater Historical Museum, Orofino 46194
Clegg's Museum of Horse-Drawn Vehicles, Hamiota 05578
Clemens-Sels-Museum, Neuss 19063
Clendening History of Medicine Library and Museum, Kansas City 44392
Cleo Redd Fisher Museum, Loudonville 44957
Clergy House, Alfriston 37975
Clermont State Historic Site, Clermont 42460
Cleve National Trust Museum, Cleve 00925
Clevedon Court, Clevedon 38589
Cleveland Artists Foundation at Beck Center for the Arts, Lakewood 44610
Cleveland Center for Contemporary Art, Cleveland 42465
Cleveland County Historical Museum, Shelby 47595
Cleveland Crafts Centre, Middlesbrough 39947
Cleveland Ironstone Mining Museum, Skinningrove 40526
Cleveland Museum of Art, Cleveland 42466
Cleveland Museum of Natural History, Cleveland 42467
Cleveland Police Museum, Cleveland 42468
Cleveland State University Art Gallery, Cleveland 42469
Clewiston Museum, Clewiston 42487
Cliffe Castle Museum, Keighley 39327
Clifton and District Historical Museum, Clifton 00928
Clifton Community Historical Society, Clifton 42488
Clifton Park Museum, Rotherham 40344
Climax Community Museum, Climax 05257
Clink Prison Museum, London 39610
Clinton Academy Museum, East Hampton 43043
Clinton County Historical Museum, Plattsburgh 46547
Clinton County Historical Society Museum, Saint Johns 47097
Clinton County Museum, Frankfort 43506
Clipper Ship Cutty Sark, London 39611
Clive House Museum, Shrewsbury 40507
Cliveden House, Philadelphia 46401
Cloches de Corneville, Pont-Audemer 13800
Clock Museum, Angarsk 32641
Clock Tower, Saint Albans 40369
Clock Tower, Sapporo 26709
Clock Tower Archive Centre, Youghal 22561
Clocktower Museum, Elsham 38930
The Cloisters, New York 45784
Cloître de Cadouin, Le Buisson-de-Cadouin 12394
Clonalis House, Castlerea 22390
Cloncurry and District Museum, Cloncurry 00929
Clonfert Diocesan Museum, Loughrea 22512
Clonfert Museum, Clonfert 22397
Clos Arqueologic Torre Llauder, Mataró 35098
Clos Arsene Lupin, Etretat 11674
Clothing and Textiles Museum, Winnipeg 06821
Clotworthy Arts Centre, Antrim 38005
Cloud County Historical Museum, Concordia 42607
Clough-Hanson Gallery, Memphis 45234
Clowes Fund Collection, Indianapolis 44216
Cloyne Pioneer Museum, Cloyne 05259
Clun Local History Museum, Clun 38592
Clunes Museum, Clunes 00930
Clyde Historical Museum, Clyde 30136
Clydebank Museum, Clydebank 38593
Clydebuilt, Glasgow 39041
Clymer Museum of Art, Ellensburg 43148
C.M. Bellman Museum, Stockholm 36237
C.M. Booth Collection of Historic Vehicles, Rolvenden 40338
C.M. Russell Museum, Great Falls 43780
C.O. Card Home, Cardston 05205
C.O. Müller-Galerie, Eichstätt 16803
Coal Creek Heritage Village, Korumburra 01153
Coal Miners' Museum, Van Lear 48196
Coal Mining Museum, Zabrze 32199
Coalfields Museum, Collie 00938
Coalport China Museum, Coalport 38597
Coast Artillery Museum, Helsinki 09523
Coastal Center for the Arts, Saint Simons Island 47179
Coastal Discovery Museum, Hilton Head Island 44033
Coastal Heritage Museum, Crystal River 42716
Coastal Museum of Godøy, Godøy 30514
Coasting Hill Pavilion, Lomonosov 32991
Cobalt's Northern Ontario Mining Museum, Cobalt 05261
Cobb and Co Museum, Toowoomba 01539
Cobb County Youth Museum, Marietta 45142
Cobb Institute of Archaeology Museum, Mississippi State 45401
Cobb Museum of Art, Marietta 45143
Cobbaton Combat Collection, Chittlehampton 38572
Cobblestones Museum, Greytown 30171
Cobdogla Irrigation and Steam Museum, Cobdogla 00932
Cobh Museum, Cobh 22399
Cobham Bus Museum, Cobham 38602
Cobra Museum voor Moderne Kunst, Amstelveen 28830
Coburger Puppen-Museum, Coburg 16480
The Coburn Gallery, Ashland 41295
Coca-Cola Memorabilia Museum of Elizabethtown, Elizabethtown 43133
The Coca-Cola Pavillion, Santa Cruz 31442
Cocalico Valley Museum, Ephrata 43194
Cochrane Railway and Pioneer Museum, Cochrane 05263
Cockburn Museum, Edinburgh 38874
Codington County Heritage Museum, Watertown 48444
Codman House - The Grange, Lincoln 44776
Coe Hall, Oyster Bay 46247
Coert Steynbergmuseum, Pretoria 34340
Coffin House, Newbury 45906
The Coffin School Museum, Nantucket 45595
Cogges Manor Farm Museum, Witney 40910
Coggeshall Farm Museum, Bristol 41905
Coggeshall Heritage Centre and Museum, Coggeshall 38607
Cohuna Historical Museum, Cohuna 00934
Coin and Medal Collection of the University of Helsinki, Helsinki 09521
Coin du Miroir, Dijon 11519
Coin Museum, Kerman 22254
Coin Museum, Teheran 22326
Coins Museum, Amman 27048
Cokato Museum and Akerlund Photography Studio, Cokato 42516
Colac Otway Shire Hammerton Bottle Collection, Colac 00935
Colborne Lodge, Toronto 06574
Colburn Gem and Mineral Museum, Asheville 41278
Colby College Museum of Art, Waterville 48447
Colchester Historical Museum, Truro 06648
Colcţia Muzeală a Mănăstirii Lainici, Bumbeşti-Jiu 32475
Cold Spring Harbor Whaling Museum, Cold Spring Harbor 42520
Coldharbour Mill, Uffculme 40745
Coldstream Museum, Coldstream 38616
Coldwater Canadiana Heritage Museum, Coldwater 05264
Cole County Historical Museum, Jefferson City 44327
Cole Harbour Heritage Farm Museum, Cole Harbour 05265
Cole Land Transportation Museum, Bangor 41493
Cole Museum of Zoology, Reading 40294
Coleção Assis Pegado - Museu da Moto, Fortaleza 04097
Coleção de Artes Visuais, São Paulo 04487
Coleção do Palácio do Governo de Campos do Jordão, Campos de Jordão 04035
Coleção Entomológica de Referência, São Paulo 04488
Colecção Maritima do Comandante Ramalho Ortigão, Faro 32270
Colecció Hernández Mora, Mahón 35065
Colección Amazónica, Madrid 34993
Colección Anatomía, Madrid 34994
Colección Arqueológica, Génova 07484
Colección Arqueológica, Pijao 07559
Colección Arqueológica Municipal, Besalú 34605
Colección Benedito, Madrid 34995
Colección Carlos Alberto Pusineri Scala, Asunción 31095
Colección de Anestesioloxia e Reanimación, Santiago de Compostela 35437
Colección de Arqueología, Ciudad Real 34718
Colección de Arqueología y Etnografía Americana, Madrid 34996
Colección de Arte Carmen Rodríguez Acosta, Granada 34867
Colección de Arte y Museo Botero, Bogotá 07386
Colección de Geología, Vilajüiga 35660
Colección de la Biblioteca Musical, Madrid 34997
Colección de la Caja de Ahorros, Valencia 35598
Colección de la Casa de Alba, Epila 34799
Colección de la Casa de Alba, Madrid 34998
Colección de la Facultad de Filosofía y Letras, Madrid 34999
Colección de la Real Academia de la Historia, Madrid 35000
Colección de los Iconos, Torrejón de Ardoz 35562
Colección de los Padres Escolapios, Madrid 35001
Colección de Minerales y Arqueología, Villanueva 07625
Colección de Mineralogía, Madrid 35002
Colección de Numismática, Vitoria-Gasteiz 35696
Colección de Pintura y Recuerdos Históricos del Castell de Balsareny, Balsareny 34525
Colección de Roberto Montenegro, Guadalajara 27945
Colección del Banco de España, Madrid 35003
Colección del Observatorio de Cartuja, Granada 34868
Colección del Poeta Baudilio Montoya, Clarcá 07464
Colección Etnográfica, As Neves (Capela) 35160
Colección Instrumentos Musicales Folklóricos y Cerámica Española, Rupit-Pruit 35344
Colección Krekovic, Palma de Mallorca 35223
Colección Municipal, Granada 34869
Colección Municipal de Arte Contemporáneo, Madrid 35004
Colección Museística de San Mateo, San Mateo 35383
Colección Museográfica Parroquial, Lucena del Cid 34985
Colección Numismática, Bogotá 07387
Colección Ornitológica W.H. Phelps, Caracas 48901
Colección Osuna, Sevilla 35475
Colección Parroquial, Colmenar Viejo 34730
Colección Parroquial, Gascueña 34840
Colección Parroquial, Lietor 34952
Colección Parroquial, Nuevo Baztán 35163
Colección Parroquial, San Mateo 35384
Colección Parroquial, Traiguera 35571
Colección Veri, Marratxinet 35093
Colección Vivot, Palma de Mallorca 35224
Colecciones Biológicas de Referencia, Barcelona 34536
Colecţia de Artă Plastică Fr. Storck şi Cecilia Cecilia Cuţescu Stock, Bucureşti 32451
Colecţia de Istorie a Farmaciei Cluj-Napoca, Cluj-Napoca 32491
Colecţia Etnografică, Poiana Sibiului 32575
Colecţia Etnografică, Răşinari 32579
Colecţia Muzeală de Istorie, Săcueni 32585
Colegiata de Santa María la Mayor, Toro 35556
Colegio de Santa Isabel Museum, Naga 31405
Colegio del Rey The King's College, Alcalá de Henares 34425
Coleham Pumping Station, Shrewsbury 40508
Coleman House Museum, Ainsworth 41070
Coleraine Local History Museum, Coleraine 00937
Coleridge Cottage, Nether Stowey 40010
Colesberg/Kemper Museum, Colesberg 34218
Colesville and Windsor Museum at Saint Luke's Church, Harpursville 43920
Coley Homestead and Barn Museum, Weston 48566
Collecció de la Unió Excursionista de Catalunya, Olesa de Montserrat 35168
Collecció la Magrana, Vilajüiga 35661
Collecció la Porciuncula, L'Arenal 34478
Collecció Marroig, Deià 34767
Collecció Museogràfica d'Arqueologia Local, Riba-Roja de Turia 35317
Collecció Parroquial, Naut Aran 35155
Collecció Parroquial, La Salzadella 35371
Collección Carlos Ferreyros Díaz, Bogotá 07388
Colleccíon de Instrumentos Musicales "Monsenór José Ignacio Perdomo Escobar", Bogotá 07389
Collección del Santo Rosario, Aroche 34485
Collecció d'Autòbils de Salvador Claret Sargatal, Sils 35495
Colleció de la Tossa de Montbui, Santa Margarida de Montbui 35421
Collecció de Sant Andreu de la Barca, Sant Andreu de la Barca 35393
Collecio Thyssen-Bornemisza, Barcelona 34537
Collecíon de Antigüedades, San Andrés de Sotavento 07583
Colleción de Arte y Ciencias Naturales, Ciudad Real 34719
Collecíon Eugenio Fontaneda, Ampudia 34465
Colleción Parroquial, Albocácer 34423
Collecions Municipals del Foment Arqueològic Excursionista Sallentí, Sallent 35369
Collectie A. Veltman, Bussum 29048
Collectie Anderson, Losser 29549
Collectie D.H.G. Bolten, Den Haag 29091
Collectie H.H.F. Salomon, Den Haag 29092
Collectie in het Gemmeentehuis, Brummen 29034
Collection Antonin-Gadal, Ussat-les-Bains 15030
Collection Archéologique, Bram-le-Lauragais 10888
Collection Archéologique, Éclaibes 11598
Collection Archéologique, Garin 11843
Collection Archéologique, Laure-Minervois 12355
Collection Archéologique, Marmoutier 12830
Collection Archéologique, Pringy 13873
Collection Archéologique, Tramont-Emy 14984
Collection Archéologique, Villarzel-Cabardes 15183
Collection Archéologique de la Maison des Fouilles et Maison du Memontois, Malain 12779
Collection Banco de la República, Bogotá 07390
Collection Charles de l'Escalopier, Amiens 10320
Collection d'Affiches de la Période Révolutionnaire, Semur-en-Brionnais 14703
Collection d'Antiquites Nationales, Strasbourg 14809
Collection d'Archéologie, Belmont-Luthézieu 10677
Collection d'Archéologie Biblique USH, Strasbourg 14810
Collection d'Archives et de Peintures sur Jacques Brel, Thionville 14887
Collection d'Art, La Côte-Saint-André 12159
Collection d'Art, Pauillac 13671
Collection d'Art Céramique, Longfosse 12653
Collection d'Art et d'Histoire Religieuse, La Lucerne-d'Outremer 12205
Collection d'Art Religieux Ancien, Prunay-en-Yvelines 13880
Collection d'Arts Décoratifs, Cazaux-Saves 11098
Collection d'Arts Décoratifs, Salers 14569
Collection d'Arts Décoratifs, Villevielle 15253
Collection d'Arts Populaires, Coren-les-Eaux 11408
Collection d'Arts Populaires, Oberdorff 13379
Collection d'Automates, Bellefontaine (Manche) 10673
Collection d'Automates, Gilley 11863
Collection de 2000 ex-voto, Monthermé 13093
Collection de Cloches, Morteau 13172
Collection de Costumes Alsaciens J. Bossert, Strasbourg 14811
Collection de Faïences, Nevers 13302
Collection de la Chapelle Royale Saint-Louis, Dreux 11578
Collection de la Fondation in Memoriam Comtesse Tatiana Zoubov, Genève 36735
Collection de la Guerre de 1870, Le Bourget (Seine-Saint-Denis) 12386
Collection de l'Abbaye de l'Ile Chauvet, Bois-de-Céné 10787
Collection de l'Art Brut, Lausanne 36852
Collection de l'Aventure Automobile, Poissy 13783
Collection de l'Hôtel de Ville, La Rochelle 12236
Collection de Locomotives à Vapeur, Obermodern 13380
Collection de l'Outillage de Tonnellerie, Pauillac 13672
Collection de Machinisme Agricole Fischesser, Wittenheim 15320
Collection de Manuscrits Anciens, Château-Thierry 11209
Collection de Matériel Ancien de Cuvier, Margaux 12822
Collection de Matériel Ferroviaire, Burnhaupt-le-Haut 10959
Collection de Minéraux de l'Université Pierre et Marie Curie, Paris 13485
Collection de Moules de Chapeaux, Montazels 13051
Collection de Parchemins Médiévaux, Cournonterral 11433
Collection de Peintures, Cavaillon 11094
Collection de Peintures, Douai 11557
Collection de Peintures, Issac 12060
Collection de Peintures, Lanildut 12330
Collection de Peintures, Saint-Siffret 14476
Collection de Peintures Héraldiques, Sainte-Julie 14535

Collection de Pipes de Bruyère, Cogolin 11343
Collection de Préhistoire, Retournac 13949
Collection de Sculptures, Peillon 13680
Collection de Sculptures, Viry-Noureuil 15272
Collection de Sous-Bock de Bière, Spezet 14801
Collection de Tapisseries d'Aubusson et des Flandres, Saint-Chamant 14142
Collection de Téléphones Anciens, Saint-Jean-du-Gard 14288
Collection de Tire-Bouchons, Saint-Christophe-des-Bardes 14148
Collection de Tonnellerie, Boersch 10780
Collection de Tonnellerie, Dambach-la-Ville 11481
Collection de Tonnellerie, Saint-Estèphe 14194
Collection de Véhicules de Collection, Eymoutiers 11687
Collection de Vieilles Étiquettes de Grands Crus, Cussac-Fort-Médoc 11472
Collection de Vieux Avions, Habsheim 11983
Collection de Vieux Coffres, Le Quiou-Évran 12475
Collection de Vieux Pressoirs, Paulx 13675
Collection de Voitures Anciennes de S.A.S. Le Prince de Monaco, Monaco 28663
Collection de Voitures Hippomobiles, Blosseville 10776
Collection de Voitures Hippomobiles, Rosières-aux-Salines 14039
Collection Départementale L'Épicerie Ancienne, Castelnau-le-Lez 11073
Collection des Pressoirs des Ducs de Bourgogne, Chenôve 11273
Collection des Serrures Fontaine, Paris 13486
Collection d'Etains, Sierre 37165
Collection d'Étendards, Beynac et Cazenac 10715
Collection d'Histoire Naturelle, Baume-les-Messieurs 10607
Collection d'Histoire Naturelle, La Teste 12265
Collection d'Histoire Naturelle, Le Locle 36887
Collection d'Icônes, Villecroze 15191
Collection Discographique et Bibliographique du Jazz, Villefranche-de-Rouergue 15203
Collection d'Objets, Dions 11538
Collection d'Orgues Mécaniques, Herzeele 12017
Collection d'Outillage Ancien de Tonnellerie, Cussac-Fort-Médoc 11473
Collection d'Outillage Vini-Viticole, Bégadan 10665
Collection d'Outillage Viticole dans la Cave, Saint-Estèphe 14195
Collection du Château d'Attre, Attre 03189
Collection du Château de Canteleu, Canteleu 11027
Collection du Château des Princes, Chimay 03358
Collection du Moulin du Cros, Montagnac-sur-Lède 13035
Collection du Musée Archéologique, Guise 11977
Collection Entomologique, Chaveyriat 11258
Collection Eugène Pesch, Oberkorn 27572
Collection Ferroviaire, Sospel 14775
Collection for Organology, Tachikawa 26781
Collection Frits Lugt, Paris 13487
Collection Gallo-Romaine, La Roquebrussanne 12256
Collection Guido Van Deth, Amsterdam 28848
Collection Historial Cognacq-Jay, Paris 13488
Collection Historique, Assas 10447
Collection Historique, Auch 10468
Collection Historique, Douaumont 11563
Collection Historique, Pennautier 13687
Collection Historique de Fouets, Sorede 14771
Collection Historique de la Marqueterie d'Art Spindler, Boersch 10781
Collection Historique du Café, Les Mages 12543
Collection Historique Maritime, Brest 10906
Collection Internationale d'Épinettes, Sapois-Menaurupt 14606
Collection Jules-Romains, Falicon 11702
Collection Jules Verne, Amiens 10321
Collection Lambert, Avignon 10525
Collection Lapidaire, Gimont 11864
Collection Lapidaire et Historique sur l'Histoire de l'Abbaye de la Grasse, Lagrasse 12299
Collection Maritime, Colmar 11356
Collection Minéralogique, Mizerieux 12997
Collection of Archaeology and Land Study, Nahshonim 22720
Collection of Byzantine and Postbyzantine Art, Kythira 21038
Collection of Icons and Curch Heiröooms at Pyrgos, Thera 21177
Collection of Local History, Budapest 21343
Collection of Martinware Pottery, Southall 40540
Collection of Reitz Foundation, Helsinki 09524
Collection of Religious Art, Šibenik 07773
Collection of the Church of Koimissis tis Theotokou, Panagitsa Pellis 21106
Collection of the Church of Our Lady of Skrpjela, Perast 33882
Collection of the Church of the Evangelistria, Kastron Agiou Georgiou 21009
Collection of the Church of the Pangia, Agiassos 20805
Collection of the Dominican Priory, Stari Grad 07788
Collection of the Evangelismos tis Theotokou, Skiathos 21159
Collection of the Franciscan Monastery, Sinj 07775
Collection of the Franciscan Monastery, Visovac 07802
Collection of the Fraternity of Our Lady of Consolation, Korčula 07724
Collection of the Koroni Monastery, Karditsa 20995
Collection of the Mega Spileon Monastery, Kalavryta 20988
Collection of the Metropolis of Kefallinia, Argostolion 20834
Collection of the Metropolis of Monemvassia and Spárti, Spárti 21165
Collection of the Metropolis of Xanthi, Xanthi 21217
Collection of the Monastery of Agios Andreas, Peratata 21118
Collection of the Monastery of Agios Nikolaos, Apoaika 20830
Collection of the Monastery of Odigitria, Kolymvari 21021
Collection of the Monastery of Saint Ignatios, Kalloni 20991
Collection of the Monastery of Saint John the Divine, Antissa 20828
Collection of the Panagia Tourliani, Ano Mera 20827
Collection of the Proussou Monastery, Karpenission 21001
Collection of the Rendina Monastery, Karditsa 20996
Collection of the Saint John the Divine Monastery, Patmos 21112
Collection of the Tatarna Monastery, Karpenission 21002
Collection of the Worshipful Company of Clockmakers, London 39612
Collection Préhistorique Pagès, Le Moustier 12457
Collection Rare de Tracteurs Viticoles, Savigny-les-Beaune 14669
Collection Républicaine, Urimenil 15028
Collection Schlumpf, Mulhouse 13207
Collection Ski-Montagne, Briançon 10917
Collection sur le Vin et la Gastronomie, Grezels 11952
Collection Vini-Viticole et de Tonnellerie, Zellenberg 15339
Collection Viti-Vinicole, Banyuls-sur-Mer 10579
Collection Viticole, Hautvillers 12004
Collection Viticole, Mardeuil 12817
Collection Viticole, Saint-Hilaire-d'Ozilhan 14262
Collections Archéologiques, Neuville-aux-Bois 13296
Collections Archéologiques, Parmain 13661
Collections Archéologiques et du Tissage, Montchal 13068
Collections Artistiques de l'Université de Liège, Liège 03568
Collections Baur, Genève 36736
Collections Brassicoles, Strasbourg 14812
Collections Claeyssens, Wambrechies 15301
Collections d'Anciens Outils de Tonnellerie, Listrac-Médoc 12632
Collections d'Art et d'Histoire, Clermont (Oise) 11328
Collections d'Arts de la Table, Niderviller 13329
Collections d'Arts Décoratifs du Château de Longpra, Saint-Géoire-en-Valdaine 14229
Collections d'Arts Populaires, Eschau 11642
Collections de la Bibliothèque, La Bernerie-en-Retz 12126
Collections de la Bibliothèque Municipale, Auxerre 10507
Collections de la Bibliothèque Sainte-Geneviève, Paris 13489
Collections de la Cave de la Dive Bouteille, Bourgueil 10870
Collections de la Chapelle du Château-Fort, Lourdes 12684
Collections de la Collégiale Saint-Vincent, Le Mas-d'Agenais 12440
Collections de la Commanderie, Neuilly-sous-Clermont 13289
Collections de la Ferme d'Hier et d'Aujourd'hui, Aviré 10539
Collections de la Fondation Marius-Vazelles, Meymac 12969
Collections de la Fondation Roger-van-Rogger, Bandol 10576
Collections de la Maison de la R.A.T.P., Paris 13490
Collections de la Maison Henri-IV, Saint-Valery-en-Caux 14497
Collections de la Mine Saint-Louis, Sainte-Marie-aux-Mines 14539
Collections de la Salle des Martyrs-Chapelle-Crypte, Paris 13491
Collections de la Serrurerie Dantin, Paris 13492
Collections de la Tour de Bessay, Bessay 10704
Collections de la Tour Eiffel, Paris 13493
Collections de l'Abbaye Bénédictine de Saint-Louis-du-Temple, Vauhallan 15099
Collections de l'Auberge du Cygne, Tôtes 14921
Collections de l'Ecole Nationale Supérieure des Beaux-Arts, Paris 13494
Collections de Molinologie, Fougax-et-Barrineuf 11791
Collections de Papier Peint, Saint-Pandelon 14396
Collections de Sonnailles, Magalas 12760
Collections des Ruchers d'Étretat, Bordeaux-Saint-Clair 10822
Collections d'Histoire Locale, Bourganeuf 10860
Collections d'Histoire Locale, Pont-en-Royans 13809
Collections d'Histoire Naturelle, Asson 10449
Collections d'Objets de Chais et Tonnellerie, Listrac-Médoc 12633
Collections d'Outils de Tonnellerie et d'Appareils Viticoles Anciens, Listrac-Médoc 12634
Collections du Centre d'Instruction Navale de Brest, Brest 10907
Collections du Château, Châteaubriant 11211
Collections du Château, Loches (Indre-et-Loire) 12639
Collections du Château, Xaintrailles 15325
Collections du Château de Born, Saint-Europe-de-Born 14209
Collections du Château de Courances, Courances 11430
Collections du Château de Gizeux, Gizeux 11877
Collections du Château de la Guignardière, Avrillé 10545
Collections du Château de la Thibaudière, Juigné-Béné 12101
Collections du Château de Lantilly, Cervon 11120
Collections du Château de Misnières-en-Bray, Mesnières-en-Bray 12952
Collections du Château de Sury-le-Comtal, Sury-le-Comtal 14847
Collections du Château d'Epernon, Angoulême 10353
Collections du Château des Rohan, Pontivy 13829
Collections du Château du Bouchet, Rosnay 14040
Collections du Château du Breil de Foin, Genneteil 11849
Collections du Château Médiéval des Cars, Les Cars 12531
Collections du Conseil Général, Angers 10342
Collections du Donjon, Bazoges-en-Pareds 10628
Collections du Groupe de Conservation de Vehicules Militaires, Issy-les-Moulineaux 12063
Collections du Haras, La Roche-sur-Yon 12232
Collections du Manoir du Champ-Versant, Bonnebosq 10794
Collections du Moulin, Montfermeil 13080
Collections du Patrimoine, Seyssel 14747
Collections du Relais Louis XIII, Paris 13495
Collections du Restaurant Procope, Paris 13496
Collections du Service Historique de l'Armée de l'Air, Vincennes 15262
Collections François-Fabre, Saugues-en-Gévaudan 14630
Collections Historiques, Andlau 10337
Collections Historiques, Crémieu 11455
Collections Historiques, Marseillan 12841
Collections Historiques, Menou 12931
Collections Historiques, Obernai 13381
Collections Historiques du Château Fort des XIe-XVe s, Montcornet-en-Ardenne 13069
Collections in Situ de l'Unesco, Paris 13497
Collections Internationales de Marionnettes, Charleville-Mézières 11176
Collections Linières, Lille 12595
Collections Littéraires, Kolbsheim 12116
Collections Municipales d'Art et d'Histoire, Condé-sur-l'Escaut 11387
Collections of Cypriot Painting, Sculpture and Graphics, Kolonaki 21020
Collections Universitaires, Grenoble 11937
The Collectors Club, New York 45785
College Art Collections, London 39613
College Football Hall of Fame, South Bend 47678
College Museum, Epsom 38944
College Museum, Lancing 39419
College Museum, Maynooth 22518
College of Art Gallery, Kumasi 20794
College of Eastern Utah Art Gallery, Price 46692
College of Eastern Utah Prehistoric Museum, Price 46693
College of Marin Art Gallery, Kentfield 44448
College of New Jersey Art Gallery, Trenton 48053
College of Textile Technology Museum, Hooghly 21840
College of Visual Arts and Gallery, Saint Paul 47153
The College of Wooster Art Museum, Wooster 48749
College Park Aviation Museum, College Park 42524
Collegio del Cambio - Museo d'Arte, Perugia 24847
Colleton Museum, Walterboro 48294
Collezione A. Checchi, Fucecchio 23940
Collezione Berenson, Firenze 23832
Collezione Borsari, Parma 24796
Collezione Calderara, Ameno 22877
Collezione Civica d'Arte, Pinerolo 24926
Collezione Contini-Bonacossi, Firenze 23833
Collezione d'Arte della Banca Carige, Genova 23980
Collezione d'Arte di Santa Maria di Piazza, Ostra Vetere 24720
Collezione d'Arte Religiosa Moderna, Città del Vaticano 48869
Collezione d'Arte Sacra, Saludecio 25325
Collezione di Carrozze, Maser 24310
Collezione di Ceramiche Mostra Permanente, Fiorano Modenese 23819
Collezione di Farfalle, Guardia Sanframondi 24069
Collezione di Marionette Ferrari, Parma 24797
Collezione di Minerali e Fossili, Semione 37160
Collezione di Violini, Cremona 23678
Collezione Ducati Fratelli Saltarelli, Senigallia 25534
Collezione Entomologica, Sassari 25484
Collezione Etnografica, Forni Avoltri 23921
Collezione Fisica e Medicina, Pavia 24821
Collezione G. Lorenzi, Milano 24379
Collezione Jucker, Milano 24380
Collezione Martini Carissimo, Oria 24686
Collezione Memorie della Comunità, Romano di Lombardia 25275
Collezione Meo-Evoli, Monopoli 24476
Collezione Minici Zotti, Padova 24732
Collezione P. Mariani, Desio 23714
Collezione Permanente del Design Italiano '45-'90, Milano 24381
Collezione Preistorica, Castaneda 36618
Collezione Privata di Attrezzi ed Utensili Contadini, Camerota 23292
Collezione Scaglione, Locri 24198
Collezione Straka-Coppa, Spello 25615
Collezione Tessile de Tela Umbra, Città di Castello 23576
Collezione Titta Ruffo, Pisa 24942
Collezione Wolfson, Genova 23981
Collezioni d'Armi e Ceramiche della Rocca Sforzesca, Imola 24083
Collezioni d'Arte della Cassa di Risparmio, Savona 25508
Collezioni d'Arte e di Storia della Cassa di Risparmio, Bologna 23101
Collezioni degli Istituti di Geologia e di Paleontologia, Milano 24382
Collezioni del Dipartimento di Entomologia e Zoologia Agraria, Portici 25010
Collezioni dell'Istituto Universitario Orientale, Napoli 24573
Collezioni di Presepi del Convento Muri-Gries, Bolzano 23150
Collezioni Egittologiche dell'Università di Pisa, Pisa 24943
Collezioni Naturalistiche del Museo Comunale, Imola 24084
Collezionoe Sarda L. Piloni, Cagliari 23243
Collier County Museum, Naples 45601
Collier Memorial State Park and Logging Museum, Chiloquin 42382
Collin County Farm Museum, McKinney 45037
Collingwood Museum, Collingwood 05267
Collingwood Museum on Americanism, Alexandria 41124
Collins Gallery, Glasgow 39042
Collinsville Depot Museum, Collinsville 42531
Colne Valley Museum, Golcar 39089
Colombo National Museum, Colombo 35747
Colonel Ashley House, Ashley Falls 41301
Colonel Davenport Historical Foundation, Rock Island 46954
Colonel Stephens Railway Museum, Tenterden 40685
Colonel William Jones House, Gentryville 43647
Colonial Burlington Foundation, Burlington 42005
Colonial Cottage Museum, Wellington 30293
Colonial Industrial Quarter, Bethlehem 41665
Colonial Michilimackinac, Mackinaw City 45032
Colonial Pemaquid Historical Site, New Harbor 45691
Colonial Pennsylvania Plantation, Media 45222
Colonial Williamsburg, Williamsburg 48627
Colorado Gallery of the Arts, Littleton 44827
Colorado Historical Society Museum, Denver 42882
Colorado Photographic Arts Center, Denver 42883
Colorado Railroad Museum, Golden 43713
Colorado River Indian Tribes Museum, Parker 46294
Colorado School of Mines Geology Museum, Golden 43714
Colorado Ski Museum and Ski Hall of Fame, Vail 48174
Colorado Springs Fine Arts Center, Colorado Springs 42535
Colorado Springs Museum, Colorado Springs 42536
Colorado University Art Galleries, Boulder 41834
Colorado University Heritage Center, Boulder 41835
Colorado-Wyoming Association of Museums, Sheridan 49478
Colosseum Art Gallery, Haifa 22602
Colour Museum, Bradford 38297
Colter Bay Indian Arts Museum, Colter Bay Village 42544
Colton Area Museum, Colton 42545
Colton Hall Museum, Monterey 45453
Columbia College Art Gallery, Chicago 42320
Columbia County Historical Museum, Lake City 44583
Columbia County Historical Society Museum, Kinderhook 44482
Columbia County Historical Society Museum, Saint Helens 47093
Columbia County Museum, Bloomsburg 41753
Columbia Fire Department Museum, Columbia 42557
Columbia George Interpretive Center, Stevenson 47809
Columbia Museum of Art, Columbia 42558
Columbia River Exhibition of History, Science and Technology, Richland 46855
Columbia River Maritime Museum, Astoria 41309
Columbia State Historic Park, Columbia 42547
The Columbian Museum and Art Center, Wamego 48301
Columbiana-Fairfield Township Museum, Columbiana 42573
Columbus-Belmont Civil War Museum, Columbus 42579
Columbus Cultural Arts Center, Columbus 42586
The Columbus Museum, Columbus 42574
Columbus Museum of Art, Columbus 42587
Columbus Park Museum, Discovery Bay 26063
Colville Lake Museum, Norman Wells 06010
Colzium Museum, Kilsyth 39365
Comanche Crossing Museum, Strasburg 47845
Combat Air Museum, Topeka 48032
Combe Martin Museum, Combe Martin 38620
Combe Mill Beam Engine and Working Museum, Long Hanborough 39821
Comber and District Historical Society Museum, Comber 05268
Comber Pioneer Village, Holland Centre 05602
Comenius Museum, Naarden 29605
Comenius Museum Přerov, Přerov 08622
Comer Museum, Morgantown 45498
Das Comic-Museum, Wiener Neustadt 03014

Comisión Nacional de Arqueología y Monumentos Historicos, Panamá City 49327
Comisión Nacional de Museos y de Monumentos, Buenos Aires 49043
Comitê Brasileiro do ICOM, Porto Alegre 49081
Comité Nacional del Consejo Internacional de Museos, Bogotá 49116
Comité National Français de l'ICOM, Paris 49172
Comitée National de ICOM Centralafrique, Bangui 49107
Comitée National de ICOM de Algérie, Alger 49040
Command Museum, San Diego 47274
Commanda General Store Museum, Commanda 05270
Commander Chr. Christensen's Whaling Museum, Sandefjord 30822
La Commanderie d'Arville, Arville 10443
Commandery Museum, Worcester 40928
Commencement Art Gallery, Tacoma 47916
Commerce Bancshares Fine Art Collection, Kansas City 44396
Commercial and Industrial Museum, Kanpur 21882
Commercial Museum, Gauhati 21808
Commercial Museum, Guwahati 21820
Commissariat House, Saint John's 06343
Commissariat Store Museum, Brisbane 00837
The Commodity Museum of Meiji University, Tokyo 26888
Commonwealth Air Training Plan Museum, Brandon 05120
Commonwealth Association of Museums, Calgary 49097
Commonwealth Institute, London 39614
Commonwealth Museum, Boston 41805
Commonwealth of the Northern Mariana Islands Museum of History and Culture, Saipan 30367
Communications and History Museum of Sutton, Washington 48341
Communications Centre Lokki, Mikkeli 09835
Communications Monument, Seoul 27226
Communications Museum, Tokyo 26931
Community Arts Gallery, Detroit 42920
Community College Art Gallery, Baltimore 41460
Community Fine Arts Center, Rock Springs 46957
Community Historical Museum, Maxwell 45207
Community Historical Museum of Mount Holly, Belmont 41612
Community Memorial Museum of Sutter County, Yuba City 48814
Community Museums Association of Prince Edward Island, Charlottetown 49098
Community of Christ Musuem, Independence 44200
Comox Air Force Museum, Lazo 05737
Complejo Histórico Chivilcoy, Chivilcoy 00275
Complejo Museológico La Estación, Cruz Alta 00325
Complejo Museos Históricos Militares, La Habana 07925
Complesso Museale di Santa Chiara, Napoli 24574
Complex Muzeal de Ştiinţele Naturii, Galaţi 32522
Complexul Monumental Curtea Domnească, Târgovişte 32601
Complexul Muzeal Arad, Arad 32430
Complexul Muzeal Bucovina, Suceava 32600
Complexul Muzeal de Stiinţe ale Naturii Constanţa, Constanţa 32498
Complexul Muzeal de Stiintele Naturii Ion Borcea, Bacău 32432
Complexul Muzeal Goleşti, Goleşti 32528
Complexul Muzeal Măldăreşti, Măldăreşti 32546
Complexul Naţional Muzeal Astra, Sibiu 32591
Compton Castle, Paignton 40158
Compton County Historical Museum, Eaton Corner 05364
Compton Verney Collections, Compton Verney 38622
Computermuseum Aachen, Aachen 15370
Comstock Historic House, Moorhead 45488
Con Edison Energy Museum, New York 45786
Con Foster Museum, Traverse City 48049
Conception Bay Museum, Harbour Grace 05584
Concord Art Association Museum, Concord 42597
Concord Heritage Museum, Concord 00940
Concord Museum, Concord 42598
Concordia Historical Institute Museum, Saint Louis 47116
Concordia University-Wisconsin Art Gallery, Mequon 45258
Conejo Valley Art Museum, Thousand Oaks 48003
Confederate Memorial Hall-Bleak House, Knoxville 44514
Confederate Memorial State Historic Site, Higginsville 44013
Confederate Museum, Crawfordville 42693
Confederate Museum, New Orleans 45721
Confederation Centre Art Gallery and Museum, Charlottetown 05225
Conference House, Staten Island 47780
Confucian Shrine and Chinese Museum, Nagasaki 26544
Congdom Anatomical Museum, Bangkok 37481
Congregation Emanu-el Museum, New York 45787
Coninx Museum, Zürich 37373
Conjunt Monumental de la Esglésias de Sant Pere, Terrassa 35526
Conjunto Arqueológico de Baelo Claudia, Tarifa 35510
Conjunto Arqueológico de Carmona, Carmona 34680
Conjunto Arqueológico de Itálica, Santiponce 35454
Conjunto Arqueológico de Madinat Al Zahra, Córdoba 34736
Conjunto Cultural de Caixa, São Paulo 04489
Conjunto de la Ferrería y Molinos de Agorregi, Aia 34415
Conklin Reed Organ and History Museum, Hanover 43906
Conneaut Railroad Museum, Conneaut 42609
Connecticut Audubon Birdcraft Museum, Fairfield 43263
Connecticut Historical Society Museum, Hartford 43938
Connecticut Museum Association, Roxbury 49479
Connecticut River Museum, Essex 43211
Connecticut State Museum of Natural History, Storrs 47835
Connecticut Trolley Museum, East Windsor 43063
Connecticut Valley Historical Museum, Springfield 47745
Connemara History and Heritage Centre, Clifden 22394
Conner Prairie Living History Museum, Fishers 43324
Connors Museum, Connors 05271
Conrad Mansion Museum, Kalispell 44383
Conrad Weiser Homestead, Womelsdorf 48725
Conseil Bruxellois de Musées, Bruxelles 49069
Conservation Centre Presentation, Liverpool 39516
Conservation Départementale Musées des Pays de l'Ain, Bourg-en-Bresse 10852
Conservation Resource Centre, Glebe 01057
Conservatoire Air et Espace, Mérignac (Gironde) 12944
Conservatoire Alsacien des Instruments de Musique, Guebwiller 11960
Conservatoire Botanique National de Brest, Brest 10908
Conservatoire de la Faune Sauvage de Sologne, Ménestreau-en-Villette 12928
Conservatoire de l'Estuaire de la Gironde, Blaye 10764
Conservatoire de l'outil Maison de Pays des Crètes, Évigny 11679
Conservatoire des Machines de Guerre Médiévales, Tiffauges 14910
Conservatoire d'Outils, Lhuis 12580
Conservatoire du Patrimoine Religieux, Liessies 12585
Conservatoire Maritime Basque, Ciboure 11304
Conservatoire Régional de l'Affiche, Locronan 12643
Conservatoire Rural, Souffrignac 14783
Conservatoire Vinicole, Plassac 13749
Conservatoni du Musée, Gravelines 11927
Conservatorio di Santa Chiara, San Miniato 25397
Le Consortium, Dijon 11520
Constitution Convention Museum, Port Saint Joe 46602
Constitution Island Association Museum, West Point 48542
Constitution Museum, Tabriz 22284
Constitution Square, Danville 42778
Constitutional History Gallery, Bandar Seri Begawan 04596
contact:c4, Berlin 15934
Contemporary Art Center of Fort Worth, Fort Worth 43484
Contemporary Art Center of Virginia, Virginia Beach 48246
Contemporary Art Centre of Montenegro, Podgorica 33887
Contemporary Art Centre of South Australia, Parkside 01355
Contemporary Art for San Antonio Blue Star Art Space, San Antonio 47248
Contemporary Art Gallery, South Yarra 01463
Contemporary Art Gallery, Vancouver 06674
Contemporary Art Museum, Raleigh 46772
Contemporary Art Museum, Tampa 47940
Contemporary Art Museum of Saint Louis, Saint Louis 47117
Contemporary Art Museum of Yerevan, Erevan 00680
Contemporary Art Workshop, Chicago 42321
Contemporary Arts Center, Cincinnati 42403
Contemporary Arts Center, New Orleans 45722
Contemporary Arts Museum, Houston 44118
Contemporary History Museum, Teheran 22292
Contemporary Museum, Baltimore 41461
The Contemporary Museum, Honolulu 44073
The Contemporary Museum at First Hawaiian Center, Honolulu 44074
Convent dels Minims, Santa Maria del Cami 35424
Convent of Saint Agnes of Bohemia, Praha 08584
Convent of Saint George, Praha 08585
Convento de San Antonio el Real, Segovia 35463
Convento de San Plácido, Madrid 35005
Convento dell'ex-Convento di Sant'Onofrio detto di Fuligno, Firenze 23834
Convento y Museo de de las Úrsulas, Salamanca 35358
Conway Fire Museum Aka Vintage Fire Engines, New Albany 45658
Conway Scenic Railroad, North Conway 45988
Conwy Valley Railway Museum, Betws-y-coed 38180
Conzen-Sammlung, Düsseldorf 16719
Cook County Historical Museum, Grand Marais 43751
Cook Inlet Historical Society Museum, Anchorage 41198
Cookeville Art Gallery, Cookeville 42614
Cookeville Depot Museum, Cookeville 42615
Cook's Creek Heritage Museum, Dugald 05350
Cooktown School of Art Gallery, Cooktown 00942
Cookworthy Museum of Rural Life in South Devon, Kingsbridge 39374
Coolspring Power Museum, Coolspring 42617
Cooma Cottage, Yass 01629
Cooper Gallery, Barnsley, South Yorkshire 38091
Cooper-Hewitt National Design Museum, New York 45788
Cooper Regional History Museum, Upland 48155
Cooperative Store Museum, Albany 00722
The Coopersville Area Historical Society Museum, Coopersville 42621
Coop'ren Duikhelm, Giethoorn 29280
Coos Art Museum, Coos Bay 42622
Coos County Historical Society Museum, North Bend 45981
Copenhagen City Museum, København 08933
Copper Cliff Museum, Sudbury 06509
Copper King Mansion, Butte 42017
Copper Mountain Minemuseum, Falun 35883
Copper Museum, Legnica 31754
Copper Village Museum and Arts Center, Anaconda 41188
Copperbelt Museum, Ndola 49024
Coppertown U.S.A., Calumet 42035
Coppini Academy of Fine Arts Gallery and Museum, San Antonio 47249
Copshaholm House Museum and Historic Oliver Gardens, South Bend 47679
Coptic Museum, Cairo 09258
Coquille River Museum, Brandon 41869
Coral Gables Merrick House, Coral Gables 42625
Coral Springs Museum of Art, Coral Springs 42629
Corbridge Roman Site Museum, Corbridge 38631
The Corcoran Gallery of Art, Washington 48342
Cordova Historical Museum, Cordova 42632
Core, Denver 42884
Corfe Castle Museum, Corfe Castle 38632
Corfu Byzantine Collection, Corfu 20930
Corfu Museum of Shells, Kastellanoi Mesis 21004
The Corgi Heritage Centre, Heywood 39239
Corgialenios Historical and Cultural Museum, Argostolion 20835
Corin Maman Ashdod Museum, Ashdod 22572
Corinium Museum, Cirencester 38584
Cork Butter Museum, Cork 22401
Cork Public Museum, Cork 22402
Cornelius Low House/Middlesex County Museum, Piscataway 46501
Cornell Museum, Delray Beach 42863
Cornice Museum of Ornamental Plasterwork, Peebles 40165
Corning Glass Center, Corning 42636
Corning Museum of Glass, Corning 42637
Cornish Mines, Engines and Cornwall Industrial Discovery Centre, Pool 40225
Cornwall Aero Park, Helston 39212
Cornwall Geological Museum, Penzance 40179
Cornwall Historical Museum, Cornwall 42640
Cornwall Iron Furnace, Cornwall 42641
Cornwall Regional Art Gallery, Cornwall 05276
Coromandel School of Mines Museum, Coromandel 30137
Coronach District Museum, Coronach 05279
Coronado National Memorial, Hereford 43997
Coronado-Quivira Museum, Lyons 45013
Corpsmuseum van het Utrechtsch Studenten Corps, Utrecht 29898
Corpus Christi Museum of Science and History, Corpus Christi 42645
Corredor, Gallery of the College of Fine Arts, Quezon City 31431
Corridor Gallery, Glenrothes 39077
Corrie ten Boomhuis, Haarlem 29323
Corrigin Museum, Corrigin 00948
Corris Railway Museum, Machynlleth 39868
Corry Area Historical Society Museum, Corry 42649
Corsham Court, Corsham 38636
Cortijo Bacardi, Málaga 35069
Le Cortil, Falaên 03415
Cortland County Historical Society Museum, Cortland 42654
Çorum Devlet Güzel Sanatlar Galerisi, Çorum 37655
Çorum Müzesi, Çorum 37656
Çorum State Gallery, Çorum 37655
Corvallis Art Center, Corvallis 42656
COSI Columbus, Columbus 42588
Cosi Toledo, Toledo 48019
Cosmocaixa, Alcobendas 34434
Cosmodôme, Laval 05733
Cossit House Museum, Sydney 06526
Costume Museum, Kyoto 26398
Costume Museum of Canada, Dugald 05351
Costume Museum of the Culture School, Tokyo 26833
Cotabato National Museum, Cotabato 31321
Cotehele House, Saint Dominick 40392
Cothey Bottom Heritage Centre, Newport, Isle of Wight 40054
Cotroceni National Museum, Bucureşti 32465
Cotswold Heritage Centre, Northleach 40085
Cotswold Motoring Museum and Toy Collection, Bourton-on-the-Water 38287
Cottage Blundell's, Canberra 00885
Cottage Grove Museum, Cottage Grove 42664
Cottage Lawn, Oneida 46156
Cottage Museum, Lancaster 39411
Cotting-Smith-Assembly-House, Salem 47191
Cotton Museum, Cairo 09259
Cottonlandia Museum, Greenwood 43835
Cottonwood County Historical Society Museum, Windom 48681
Coughton Court, Alcester 37960
Coultershaw Beam Pump, Petworth 40196
Coumantaros Art Gallery of Sparta, Spárti 21166
Council for Museum Anthropology, Tucson 49480
Council for Museums, Archives and Libraries, London 49406
Council of American Jewish Museums, New York 49481
Council of American Maritime Museums, Bath 49482
Council of Australian Art Museum Directors, Canberra 49047
Council of Australian Museum Directors, Canberra 49048
Council of Galleries of the Czech Republic, Praha 49134
Council of Museums in Wales, Cardiff 49407
Count Charles Esterházy Castle and Regional Museum, Pápa 21499
The Country Doctor Museum, Bailey 41432
Country Estate Museum Arkhangelskoe, Archangelskoe 32654
Country Life Museum, Yeovil 40955
Country Museum, Isafjörður 21641
Country Museum, Skogar 21670
Country Museum, Vestmannaeyjar 21673
Country Music Hall of Fame and Museum, Nashville 45614
Countryside Museum, East Budleigh 38837
County Donegal Railway Heritage Centre, Donegal 22411
County Gallery, Namsos 30701
County Museum, Fufeng 07052
County Museum, Sligo 22541
County Museum Dundalk, Dundalk 22463
County Museum of Somogy, Kaposvár 21442
County Museum Technical Centre, Halton 39159
County of Los Angeles Fire Museum, Los Angeles 44897
Courage Shire Horse Centre, Maidenhead 39873
Court Hall Museum, Sittingbourne 40520
Court House and Museum, Pevensey 40199
Court House Museum, Stroud 01481
Courtauld Institute Gallery, London 39615
Courtenay and District Museum and Paleontology Centre, Courtenay 05281
Courthouse Gallery, Portsmouth 46660
Courthouse Museum, Berrien Springs 41654
Courthouse Museum, Exira 43254
Courthouse Museum, Newport 45920
Courthouse Square Museum, Charlotte 42235
Courtney and Lemmerman Galleries, Jersey City 44339
Cousland Smiddy, Cousland 38640
Coutts Memorial Museum of Art, El Dorado 43108
Couven Museum, Aachen 15371
Couvent des Cordeliers, Forcalquier 11784
Coventry Toy Museum, Coventry 38641
Coventry Watch Museum, Coventry 38642
Cowan Vertebrate Museum, Vancouver 06675
Cowboy-Museum Fatsy, Linz 02229
Cowbridge and District Museum, Cowbridge 38648
Cowes Maritime Museum, Cowes 38649
Cowichan Bay Maritime Centre, Cowichan Bay 05284
Cowichan Valley Museum, Duncan 05353
The Cowley County Historical Museum, Winfield 48689
Cowlitz County Historical Museum, Kelso 44430
Cowpens National Battlefield, Chesnee 42282
Cowper and Newton Museum, Olney 40130
Cowra Museums, Cowra 00950
Coyaba Gardens and Awarak Museum, Ocho Rios 26079
Coyote Gallery, Oroville 46197
Coyote Point Museum for Environmental Education, San Mateo 47369
C.P. Nel Museum, Oudtshoorn 34319
Crabble Corn Mill, Dover 38764
Cracker Country Museum, Tampa 47941
Cracker Trail Museum, Zolfo Springs 48827
Craft Alliance Gallery, Saint Louis 47118
Craft Museum of Finland, Jyväskylä 09604
Crafts Council Collection, London 39616
Crafts Galley of the National Museum of Modern Art Tokyo, Tokyo 26940
Crafts Museum, Delhi 21768
Crafts Museum, Mequon 45259
Craftselijke Zadelmakerij Museum, Bellingwolde 28973
Craftsman Farms Foundation, Parsippany 46298
Cragside House, Rothbury 40343
Craig Heritage Park Museum, Parksville 06094
Craigavon Museum, Craigavon 38655
Craigdarroch Castle Historical Museum, Victoria 06718
Crail Museum, Crail 38656
Crailo State Historic Site, Rensselaer 46840
Craiova Art Museum, Craiova 32506
Crakehall Water Mill, Crakehall 38657
Crampton Tower Museum, Broadstairs 38366
Cranbrook Art Museum, Bloomfield Hills 41738
Cranbrook House and Gardens Auxiliary, Bloomfield Hills 41739
Cranbrook Institute of Science, Bloomfield Hills 41740
Cranbrook Museum, Cranbrook 38658
Cranbury Historical and Preservation Society Museum, Cranbury 42688
Crane Collection Gallery, Wellesley 48494
Crane Museum, Dalton 42767
Crane Point Hammock Museum, Marathon 45132
Crary Art Gallery, Warren 48312

Crater of Diamonds State Park Museum, Murfreesboro 45564
Craters of the Moon, Arco 41250
Crathes Castle, Banchory 38078
Craven Museum, Skipton 40527
Cravens House, Lookout Mountain 44881
Crawford Arts Centre, Saint Andrews 40382
Crawford Auto-Aviation Museum, Cleveland 42470
Crawford County Historical Museum, Pittsburg 46503
Crawford Municipal Art Gallery, Cork 22403
Crawford W. Long Museum, Jefferson 44321
Crawfordjohn Heritage Venture, Biggar 38195
Crawley Museum Centre, Crawley 38659
Crazy Mountain Museum, Big Timber 41685
Creamery Museum, Eriksdale 05411
Creatabilitoys! - Museum of Advertising Icons, Coral Gables 42626
Creative Arts Center, Kansas City 44397
Creative Arts Center, Pontiac 46584
Creative Arts Guild, Dalton 42765
Creative Center and Exhibition Hall Fyodor, Sankt-Peterburg 33486
Creative Discovery Museum, Chattanooga 42260
Creative Growth Art Center, Oakland 46063
Creative Spirit Art Centre, Toronto 06575
Creativiteitscentrum Gouden Handen, 's-Heerenberg 29360
Creek Council House Museum, Okmulgee 46125
Creetown Exhibition Centre, Creetown 38661
Creetown Gem Rock Museum, Creetown 38662
Cregneash Folk Village, Cregneash 38663
Cregneash Village Folk Museum, Port Saint Mary 40233
Crescent Arts, Scarborough 40454
Crescent Bend/Armstrong-Lockett House and William P. Toms Memorial Gardens, Knoxville 44515
Crescentia-Gedenkstätte, Kaufbeuren 18036
Creski Muzej, Cres 07691
Cress Gallery of Art, Chattanooga 42261
Crestar Bank Art Collection, Richmond 46875
Crestet-Centre d'Art, Le Crestet 12406
Crestline Shunk Museum, Crestline 42697
Creston and District Museum, Creston 05289
Creswell Crags Museum and Education Centre, Welbeck 40807
Creswick Historical Museum, Creswick 00954
Le Creux de l'Enfer, Centre d'Art Contemporain, Thiers 14885
Crewkerne and District Museum, Crewkerne 38667
Criccieth Castle, Criccieth 38668
Crichton Museum, Dumfries 38786
Cricklade Museum, Cricklade 38669
Crime Museum, Vantaa 10181
Crimean Republics Regional Museum, Simferopol 37904
Criminal Museum, Jakarta 22119
The Criminal Museum of the Meiji University, Tokyo 26886
Criminological Museum of the Altay State University, Barnaul 32674
Criminology Museum, Abbasiya 09231
Cripple Creek District Museum, Cripple Creek 42702
Cripta e Museo di Sant'Anastasio, Asti 22971
Criş County Museum, Oradea 32562
Crkva-Muzej na Oplencu, Oplenac kod Topole 33879
Croatian Heritage Museum, Eastlake 43065
Croatian Historical Museum, Zagreb 07822
Croatian Museum of Literature and Theatre, Zagreb 07831
Croatian Museum of Naive Art, Zagreb 07819
Croatian Museum of Post and Telecommunications, Zagreb 07820
Croatian Natural History Museum, Zagreb 07823
Croatian School Museum, Zagreb 07824
Croatian Sports Museum, Zagreb 07825
Croatian Zoological Museum, Zagreb 07821
Crocker Art Museum, Sacramento 47050
Crocker House, Mount Clemens 45525
Crockett County Museum, Ozona 46251
Crockett Tavern Museum, Morristown 45512
Croft Castle, Leominster 39476
Croft Museum, Somero 10050
Crofter's Museum of Laurinmäki, Janakkala 09578
Crofton Roman Villa, Orpington 40134
Crom Estate, Newtownbutler 40076
Cromarty Courthouse Museum, Cromarty 38670
Cromer Museum, Cromer 38672
Cromford Mill, Cromford 38675
Cromwell Museum, Cromwell 30138
Cromwell Museum, Huntingdon 39277
Cronosaurio, Villa de Leyva 07618
Crook County Museum and Art Gallery, Sundance 47883
Crooked Tree Arts Center, Petoskey 46382
Crosby County Pioneer Memorial Museum, Crosbyton 42709
Crossman Art Gallery, Whitewater 48594
The Crossness Engines, London 39617
Crossroads Museum, Oyen 06092
Crossroads of America, Bethlehem 41663
Crover Folk Museum, Mount Nugent 22522
Crow Canyon Archaeological Center, Cortez 42651
Crow Wing County Historical Museum, Brainerd 41866
Crowder College-Longwell Museum and Camp Crowder Collection, Neosho 45650
Crowley Art Association and Gallery, Crowley 42713
Crowley Museum, Sarasota 47452
Crown Gardens Museum, Dalton 42766
Crown Liquor Saloon, Belfast 38151
Crown Mill, Hämeenlinna 09453
Crown Point State Historic Site, Crown Point 42715
Crowninshield-Bentley House, Salem 47192
Crowsnest Museum, Coleman 05266
Croxteth Hall, Liverpool 39517
Croydon Museum, Croydon 38677
Croydon Natural History and Scientific Society Museum, Croydon 38678
Cruizer Aurora Museum, Sankt-Peterburg 33447
Crusader Church, Abu Ghosh 22562
The Crypt - Town Hall Plate Room, Oxford 40146
Crypte archéologique du Parvis de Notre-Dame, Paris 13498
Crypte Carolingienne de l'Ancienne Abbaye, Flavigny-sur-Ozerain 11743
Cryptoneum, Rostock 19658
Crystal Brook Heritage Centre, Crystal Brook 00959
Crystal City Community Museum, Crystal City 05293
Crystal Kingdom, Coonabarabran 00944
Crystal Lake Falls Historical Museum, Barton 41517
Crystal Mountain - Crystal & Mineral Gallery & Museum, Auckland 30105
Crystal Palace Museum, London 39618
Crystal River State Archaeological Site, Crystal River 42717
C.S. Sampilov Art Museum of the Buryat Republic, Ulan-Udė 33651
Csepel Galéria és Helytörténeti Gyűjtemény, Budapest 21333
Csipkeház, Kiskunhalas 21459
Csók István Képtár, Székesfehérvár 21555
Csolt Monostor Középkori Romkert, Vésztő 21610
Csongrádi Múzeum, Csongrád 21397
Csontváry Múzeum, Pécs 21504
CTS Turner Museum, Elkhart 43139
Cuadros Vivos de la Sabana, Corozal 07466
Cuban Museum of Arts and Culture, Miami 45283
Cubus Kunsthalle, Duisburg 16746
Cuckfield Museum, Cuckfield 38679
Cudrio Kystmuseum, Langesund 30627
Čukotskij Okružnoj Kraevedčeskij Muzej, Anadyr' 32638
Culberson County Historical Museum, Van Horn 48195
Culbertson Mansion, New Albany 45659
Culbertson Museum, Culbertson 42720
Culinair Historisch Museum De Vleer, Appelscha 28929
Culinair Museum, Amersfoort 28821
Culinary Archives and Museum, Providence 46716
Cullman County Museum, Cullman 42722
Culloden Visitor Centre, Inverness 39298
Culross Palace, Culross 38681
Cultural Center Hellenic Cosmos, Athinai 20856
The Cultural Center of Fine Arts, Parkersburg 46295
Cultural Center of the Philippines Museo, Pasay 31411
Cultural Heritage Center, Dallas 42747
Cultural Heritage Center Museum, Toppenish 48035
Cultural History Museum, Búdardalur 21627
Cultural Museum, Kabacan 31333
Cultural Museum, Melaka 27662
Cultural Research Institute, Kolkata 21902
Cultural Rights and Protection/Ute Indian Tribe, Fort Duchesne 43391
Culture Center, Çankırı 37652
Culture Gallery of Naive Artists, Trebnje 34157
Culture House, Reykjavík 21661
Cultureel Centrum van Gogh, Zundert 30074
Cultureel Maçonniek Centrum Prins Frederik, Den Haag 29093
Cultuur-Historisch Museum Sorgdrager, Hollum 29431
Cultuurhistorisch Museum Valkenswaard, Valkenswaard 29922
Cultuurhistorisch Streek- en Handkarrenmuseum De Wemme, Zuidwolde, Drenthe 30071
Cultuurhistorisch Streekmuseum De Acht Zaligheden, Eersel 29202
Culzean Castle and Country Park, Maybole 39927
Cum Museum, Imphal 21852
Cumberland County Historical Society Museum, Greenwich 43834
Cumberland County Museum, Amherst 04986
Cumberland Gap National Historical Park, Middlesboro 45311
Cumberland Heritage Village Museum, Cumberland, Ontario 05295
Cumberland House, Regina 06229
Cumberland Museum, Cumberland, British Columbia 05294
Cumberland Pencil Museum, Keswick 39343
Cumberland Science Museum, Nashville 45615
Cumberland Theatre Arts Gallery, Cumberland 42725
Cumberland Toy and Model Museum, Cockermouth 38603
Cumbernauld Museum, Cumbernauld 38684
Cuming Museum, London 39619
Cummer Museum of Art, Jacksonville 44293
Cunderdin Municipal Museum, Cunderdin 00961
Cuneo Museum, Vernon Hills 48220
Cunningham Dax Collection of Psychiatric Art, Parkville, Victoria 01356
Cupar and District Heritage Museum, Cupar 05296
Cupertino Historical Museum, Cupertino 42729
Cupids Museum, Cupids 05297
Cupola House, Egg Harbor 43100
Curaçao Museum, Curaçao 30088
Curfman Gallery and Duhesa Lounge, Fort Collins 43378
Curiosamuseum Nollée, Izenberge 03524
The Curious Kids' Museum, Saint Joseph 47101
Currahee Military Museum, Virden 06734
Currency Museum of the Bank of Canada, Ottawa 06079
Currier Gallery of Art, Manchester 45096
Curry Historical Society Museum, Gold Beach 43710
Curtis Museum, Alton 37991
Curwood Castle, Owosso 46232
Cusanus-Geburtshaus, Bernkastel-Kues 16126
Cushing House Museum, Newburyport 45909
Cust Museum, Cust 30139
Custer Battlefield Museum, Garryowen 43631
Custer County 1881 Courthouse Museum, Custer 42734
Custer County Art Center, Miles City 45336
Custer County Historical Society Museum, Broken Bow 41911
Custer Museum, Clayton 42441
Custom House Maritime Museum, Newburyport 45910
Custom House Visitor Centre, Dublin 22418
Customs House, Oslo 30755
Customs House Nautical Museum, Robe 01418
Customs Museum, Stockholm 36297
Čuvašskij Gosudarstvennyj Chudožestvennyj Muzej, Čeboksary 32718
Čuvašskij Nacionalnyj Muzej, Čeboksary 32719
Cuyler Manor Museum, Uitenhage 34392
Cuyuna Range Museum, Crosby 42707
CWU Anthropology Department Collection, Ellensburg 43149
Cy Twombly Gallery, Houston 44119
Cyfarthfa Castle Museum and Art Gallery, Merthyr Tydfil 39937
Cygnaeuksen Galleria, Helsinki 09476
Cygnaeus Gallery, Helsinki 09476
Cylburn Nature Museum, Baltimore 41462
Cynon Valley Museum, Aberdare 37928
Cyprus Federation of Associations of Friends of Museums, Lefkosia 49128
Cyprus Folk Art Museum, Lefkosia 08195
Cyprus Historical Museum, Lefkosia 08196
Cyprus Jewellers Museum, Lefkosia 08197
Cyprus Medieval Museum, Lemesos 08208
Cyprus Museum, Lefkosia 08198
Cyprus National Struggle Museum, Lefkosia 08199
Cyprus Olympic Committee Museum, Lefkosia 08200
Cyrus H. McCormick Memorial Museum, Steeles Tavern 47800
Czaar Peterhuisje, Zaandam 30032
Czech Center New York, New York 45750
Czech Center of Photography, Praha 08566
Czech Committee of ICOM, Brno 49132
Czech Museum of Fine Arts, Praha 08567
Czech Private Bicycle Museum, Chotěboř 08316
Czersk Castle, Czersk 31543
Czóbel Béla Múzeum, Szentendre 21569
D-Day Museum and Overlord Embroidery, Portsmouth 40250
D-Day Omaha Musée, Vierville-sur-Mer 15164
D. Ralph Hostetter Museum of Natural History, Harrisonburg 43930
D137, Sankt-Peterburg 33390
D137 The Gallery of Contemporary Art, Sankt-Peterburg 33390
Da Vinci-Museum, Tongerlo 03783
D.A. Wurfel Grain Collection, Pinnaroo 01367
daadgalerie, Berlin 15935
DAAP Galleries, Cincinnati 42404
Dača Šaljapina - Gosudarstvennyj Istoriko-kulturnyj Muzej, Kislovodsk 32927
Dacorum Heritage, Berkhamsted 38169
Dacotah Prairie Museum and Lamont Art Gallery, Aberdeen 41045
Dade Battlefield Historic State Park, Bushnell 42015
Dadian Gallery, Washington 48343
Daegu National Museum, Daegu 27154
Daegu National University of Education Museum, Daegu 27155
Daegwallyeong Museum, Gangneung 27167
Daensmuseum en Archief van de Vlaamse Sociale Strijd, Aalst 03124
DAF Automobiel Museum, Eindhoven 29209
Dagali Museum, Geilo 30510
Dagbladmuseum Abraham Verhoevenhuis, Antwerpen 03139
Dagestan Museum of Fine Arts, Machačkala 32996
Dagestan United Museum of History and Architecture, Machačkala 32995
Dagestanskij Gosudarstvennyj Objedinennyj Istoriko-architekturnyj Muzej, Machačkala 32995
Dagestanskij Muzej Izobrazitelnych Iskusstv, Machačkala 32996
Dagon Grain Museum, Haifa 22603
Dagu Paotai Yi Zhi Museum, Tianjin 07261
Dahe Village Yi Zhi Museum, Zhengzhou 07326
Dahesh Museum of Art, New York 45789
Daheshite Museum, Beirut 27480
Dahl Arts Center, Rapid City 46794
Dahlonega Courthouse Gold Museum, Dahlonega 42739
Daigo Fukuryu Maru Exhibition Hall, Tokyo 26838
Daigo-ji Treasure Hall, Kyoto 26393
Daihoon-ji Treasure House, Kyoto 26394
Daikakuji Temple Treasure House, Kyoto 26395
DaimlerChrysler Contemporary, Berlin 15936
Daimyo Clock Museum, Tokyo 26839
Daimyo Tokei Hakubutsukan, Tokyo 26839
Dairy-Museum, Saukkola 10022
Dairy Museum, Vaasa 10159
Dakota County Historical Society Museum, South Saint Paul 47702
Dakota Dinosaur Museum, Dickinson 42945
Dakota Territorial Museum, Yankton 48777
Dakotaland Museum, Huron 44180
Dakovština Museum, Dakovo 07692
DakshinaChitra Museum, Muttukadu 21956
Dal-Paso Museum, Lamesa 44614
Dalälvarnas Flottningsmuseum, Sandviken 36178
Dalahästmuseum, Dala-Järna 35850
Dalane Folkemuseum, Egersund 30466
Dalarnas Museum, Falun 35882
Dalbeattie Museum, Dalbeattie 38691
Dalby Regional Gallery, Dalby 00964
Dalemain Historic House, Penrith 40175
Dalénmuseet, Stenstorp 36228
Dales Countryside Museum, Hawes 39193
Dalgarven Mill, Kilwinning 39367
Dalhousie Art Gallery, Halifax 05550
Dalian Gallery, Dalian 07034
Dalian Natural History Museum, Dalian 07035
Dalkeith Arts Centre, Dalkeith 38692
Dallam-Hartley XIT Museum, Dalhart 42741
The Dallas Center for Contemporary Art, Dallas 42748
Dallas Historical Society Museum, Dallas 42749
Dallas Holocaust Memorial Center, Dallas 42750
Dallas Museum of Art, Dallas 42751
Dallas Museum of Natural History, Dallas 42752
Dalmeny House, South Queensferry 40534
Dalnavert Museum, Winnipeg 06822
Dalnevostočnyj Chudožestvennyj Muzej, Chabarovsk 32739
Dalnevostočnyj Memorialnyj Dom-muzej V.K. Arsenjeva, Vladivostok 33693
Dals Ironworks Museum, Dalsbruk 09422
Dalton Defenders Museum, Coffeyville 42512
Dalton Gallery, Decatur 42829
Dalvík Local Museum, Dalvík 21628
Daly House Museum, Brandon 05121
Dam Site Museum, Mangla 31045
Damerla Rama Rao Memorial Art Gallery, Rajahmundry 22000
Damjanich János Múzeum, Szolnok 21585
Dampfkornbranntweinbrennerei-Museum, Wildeshausen 20588
Dampflok-Museum, Hermeskeil 17726
Dan Andersson Museum, Ludvika 36051
Dan Flavin Art Foundation Temporary Gallery, New York 45790
Dan Kook University Museum, Seoul 27227
Dan O'Laurie Canyon Country Museum, Moab 45416
Dan Quayle Center and Museum, Huntington 44156
Dan Winters House - Ancestral Home, Loughgall 39833
Dan-yr-Ogof Showcaves Museum, Abercrave 37927
The Dana-Thomas House, Springfield 47736
Danbury Museum, Danbury 42770
Dance Cottage Museum, Ravensthorpe 01408
Dance Museum, La Habana 07965
Dance Museum, Stockholm 36238
Dandong Museum on the War to resist U.S. Aggression and Aid Korea, Dandong 07041
Dane G. Hansen Memorial Museum, Logan 44844
Danford Collection of West African Art and Artefacts, Birmingham 38220
Danforth Gallery, Portland 46622
Danforth Museum of Art, Framingham 43501
Daniel Boone Homestead, Birdsboro 41702
Daniel Owen Museum, Mold 39972
Daniel W. Tantoco jr. Collection, Manila 31376
Daniels County Museum and Pioneer Town, Scobey 47504
Danielson-Kalmari Villa, Vääksy 10165
Danielson-Kalmarin Huvila, Vääksy 10165
Danish Agricultural Museum, Auning 08780
Danish Amber Museum, Oksbøl 09017
The Danish Cultural Institute, Edinburgh 38875
Danish Film Institute, København 08926
Danish Immigrant Museum, Elk Horn 43137
Danish Museum of Books, København 08925
The Danish Museum of Decorative Art, København 08927
Danish Museum of Electricity, Bjerringbro 08783
Danish Museum of Hunting and Forestry, Hørsholm 08899
Danish Museum of the Medias, Odense 09008
Danish Museum Service, Viborg 49144
Danish National Council of Museums, København 49137
Danmarks Bogmuseum, København 08925
Danmarks Cykelmuseum, Ålestrup 08767
Danmarks Fotomuseum, Herning 08867
Danmarks Jernbanemuseum, Odense 09007
Danmarks Keramikmuseum, Middelfart 08984
Danmarks Kloster Museum, Ry 09050
Danmarks Mediemuseum, Odense 09008
Danmarks Tekniske Museum, Helsingør 08860
Dansk Brandværnshistorisk Museum, Næstved 08986
Dansk ICOM, Kolding 49138
Dansk Jagt- og Skovbrugsmuseum, Hørsholm 08899
Dansk Kulturhistorisk Museums Forening, Nivå 49139
Dansk Landbrugsmuseum, Auning 08780
Dansk Veteranflysamling, Skjern 09063
Det Danske Filminstitut, København 08926

Det Danske Hedeselskabs Museum, Viborg 09108
Det Danske Kunstindustrimuseum, København 08927
Dansmuseet, Stockholm 36238
Danvers Historical Society Exhibition, Danvers 42774
Danville Museum of Fine Arts and History, Danville 42780
Dapeng Gucheng Museum, Shenzhen 07238
Dar-es-Salaam National Museum, Dar-es-Salaam 37458
Dar-Hervey Ely House, Rochester 46940
Dar Museum First Ladies of Texas Historic Costumes Collection, Denton 42874
Darbarhall Museum, Junagadh 21876
Darby Houses, Coalbrookdale 38594
Daredevil Hall of Fame, Niagara Falls 05988
Dargaville Museum, Dargaville 30141
Darl At Tifl Museum, Jerusalem 31069
Darlingford School Heritage Museum, Darlingford 05302
Darlington Art Centre, Darlington 38695
Darlington Art Gallery, Darlington 38696
Darlington Province Park Pioneer Home, Bowmanville 05104
Darlington Railway Centre and Museum, Darlington 38697
Darnall's Chance, Upper Marlboro 48157
Daros Exhibitions, Zürich 37374
Darß-Museum, Ostseebad Prerow 19316
Dartford Borough Museum, Dartford 38700
Dartington Crystal Glass Museum, Torrington 40720
Dartmoor District Coach House Museum, Dartmoor 00970
Dartmouth Castle, Dartmouth 38701
Dartmouth Heritage Museum, Dartmouth 05304
Dartmouth Museum, Dartmouth 38702
Darvinovskij Muzej, Moskva 33034
Darwin Museum, Moskva 33034
Dåsettunet, Lyngdal 30659
Dauerausstellung des Missionswerkes, Neuendettelsau 19023
Daugavas Muzejs, Salaspils 27449
Daugavpils Museum of Local Studies and Art, Daugavpils 27347
Daugavpils Muzeja, Daugavpils 27345
Daugavpils Muzeja Izstāžu Zāles, Daugavpils 27346
Daugavpils Novadpētniecības un Mākslas Muzejs, Daugavpils 27347
Daughters of the American Revolution Museum, Washington 48344
Daughters of Utah Pioneers Pioneer Memorial Museum, Salt Lake City 47230
Daum Museum of Contemporary Art, Sedalia 47554
Daura Gallery, Lynchburg 45003
Davao Museum, Davao 31325
Davenport House Museum, Savannah 47477
Davenport Museum of Art, Davenport 42785
Daventry Museum, Daventry 38705
The David and Alfred Smart Museum of Art, Chicago 42322
David Bradford House, Washington 48416
David Conklin Farmhouse, Huntington 44159
David Crawford House, Newburgh 45904
The David Davis Mansion, Bloomington 41742
David Kakabadze Doma, Tbilisi 15358
David Livingstone Centre, Blantyre 38258
David Nichols-Captain John Wilson House, Cohasset 42514
David Palombo Museum, Jerusalem 22629
Davíd Stefánsson Memorial Museum, Akureyri 21619
David Strawn Art Gallery, Jacksonville 44301
David Winton Bell Gallery, Providence 46717
Davids Samling, København 08928
Davidson County Historical Museum, Lexington 44752
Davidson County Museum of Art, Lexington 44753
Davis Art Center, Davis 42791
Davis Art Gallery, Columbia 42550
Davis Museum, Wellesley 48495
Davison Art Center, Middletown 45313
Dawes County Historical Society Museum, Chadron 42178
Dawlish Museum, Dawlish 38706
Dawson City Museum, Dawson City 05311
Dawson County Historical Museum, Lexington 44754
Dawson Creek Art Gallery, Dawson Creek 05313
Dawson Creek Station Museum, Dawson Creek 05314
Dawson Folk Museum, Theodore 01532
Dawson Springs Museum and Art Center, Dawson Springs 42798
Dayi Liu's Manor-House Museum, Chengdu 07021
Daylesford and District Historical Museum, Daylesford 00974
Dayton Art Institute, Dayton 42801
Dayton Historical Depot Society Museum, Dayton 42809
Dayton Visual Arts Center, Dayton 42802
Dazaifu Tenman-gu Hômotsuden, Dazaifu 26132
Dazaifu Tenman-gu Treasure House, Dazaifu 26132
Dazibao, Montréal 05902
DB Museum im Verkehrsmuseum Nürnberg, Nürnberg 19135
DDR-Motorradmuseum, Borna bei Leipzig 16261
De Land Museum of Art, De Land 42813
De Locht - Streekmuseum, Nationaal Asperge- en Champignonmuseum, Horst 29447
De los Viejos Colonos, Bariloche 00135
De Mores State Historic Site, Bismarck 41720
De Morgan Centre, London 39620
De Smet Depot Museum, De Smet 42818
De Valera Library and Museum, Ennis 22467
Deaf Smith County Museum, Hereford 43998
Deal Archaeological Collection, Deal 38707
Deal Castle, Deal 38708
Deal Maritime and Local History Museum, Deal 38709
Dean Castle, Kilmarnock 39361
The Dean Clough Galleries, Halifax 39151
Dean Gallery, Edinburgh 38876
Dean Heritage Museum, Soudley 40532
Dearborn Historical Museum, Dearborn 42823
Death Valley National Park Visitor Center and Museum, Death Valley 42826
DeBolt and District Pioneer Museum, DeBolt 05316
Decatur House Museum, Washington 48345
Decembrists Museum, Moskva 33095
Decorative Art Museum, Isfahan 22246
Decorative Arts Center of Ohio, Lancaster 44620
Decorative Arts Museum of Rhodos, Rhodos 21142
DeCordova Museum and Sculpture Park, Lincoln 44777
Dedham Historical Museum, Dedham 42840
Deep Sea Adventure and Diving Museum, Weymouth 40842
Deer Isle-Stonington Historical Society Museum, Deer Isle 42843
Deere Museum, Moline 45430
Deerfield Beach Historical Society Museum, Deerfield Beach 42851
Defence of Moscow Museum, Moskva 33062
Defence Services Museum, Adelaide 00705
Defence Services Museum, Yangon 28749
Degenhart Paperweight and Glass Museum, Cambridge 42054
Degrazia Gallery in the Sun, Tucson 48084
Deià Museo Arqueológico, Deià 34768
Deichtorhallen Hamburg, Hamburg 17530
Deines Cultural Center, Russell 47032
Deir ez-Zor Museum, Deir ez-Zor 37438
Dejbjerg Jernalder, Skjern 09064
DeKalb Historical Society Museum, Decatur 42830
Dekanatsmuseum, Haus 02009
Dekema State Portrettengalerij, Jelsum 29465
Dekoratīvi Lietišķās Mākslas Muzejs, Rīga 27403
Del Norte County Historical Society Museum, Crescent City 42695
Delano Heritage Park, Delano 42861
Delaware Agricultural Museum, Dover 42968
Delaware and Hudson Canal Museum, High Falls 44014
Delaware Art Museum, Wilmington 48649
Delaware Museum, Wilmington 48650
Delaware Museum of Natural History, Wilmington 48651
Delaware State Museums, Dover 42969
Delbridge Museum, Sioux Falls 47642
Delekovec Local History Collection, Delekovec 07693
Delfina, London 39621
Delgatie Castle, Turriff 40733
Delhi Ontario Tobacco Museum & Heritage Centre, Delhi 05319
Dell Mill, Isle-of-Lewis 39317
Deloraine Museum, Deloraine 05321
Delta Blues Museum, Clarksdale 42431
Delta County Historical Society Museum, Escanaba 43205
Delta County Museum, Delta 42865
Delta Cultural Center, Helena 43981
Delta Mill and Old Stone Mill Museum, Delta 05322
Delta Museum, Delta 05323
DEMHIST-International Committee for Historic House Museums, Milano 49250
Den Hartogh Ford Museum, Hillegom 29415
Denbigh Castle Museum, Denbigh 38713
Denbigh Museum and Gallery, Denbigh 38714
Dene Museum, Fort Good Hope 05439
Dengel-Galerie, Reutte 02510
Denison University Art Gallery, Granville 43772
Deniz Müzesi, İstanbul 37698
Denizli Devlet Güzel Sanatlar Galerisi, Denizli 37657
Denizli State Gallery, Denizli 37657
Denkmalhof Arler, Abtenau 01639
Denkmalhof Gererhof, Annaberg 01673
Denkmalhof Kösslerhäusl, Großarl 01951
Denkmalhof Maurerbauernhof, Zederhaus 03048
Denkmalhof Rauchhaus Möllin, Möllin 18764
Denkmalhof Rauchhaus Mühlgrub, Hof bei Salzburg 02036
Denkmalhof Retschow, Retschow 19573
DenkStätte Weiße Rose am Lichthof der Universität München, München 18837
Denman Island Museum, Denman Island 05325
Denmark Historical Museum, Denmark 00976
Dennison Railroad Depot Museum, Dennison 42872
Dennos Museum Center of Northwestern Michigan College, Traverse City 48050
Denny Ship Model Experiment Tank, Dumbarton 38785
Dental Museum, Edmonton 05372
Dentist Museum, Sunne 36313
Denton County Historical Museum, Denton 42875
Denver Art Museum, Denver 42885
Denver Museum of Miniatures, Dolls and Toys, Denver 42886
Denver Museum of Nature and Science, Denver 42887
Deokpojin Educational Museum, Gimpo 27175
Deosugung Art Museum, Seoul 27228
Départ Musée Ostréophile, Le Château-d'Oléron 12398
Department of Art History & Archaeology Visual Resources Collection, New York 45791
Department of Byzantine Museums, Athinai 49221
Department of Classical Archaeology and Ancient History, Göteborg University, Göteborg 35909
Department of Fine Arts Gallery, Decatur 42828
Department of Geological Sciences Collection, London 39622
Department of Historical Manuscripts, Tokyo 26840
Department of Semitic Studies Collection, Leeds 39444
Department of the Treasury Museum, Washington 48346
Department of Zoology Museum, Kampala 37825
DePaul University Art Gallery, Chicago 42323
DePauw University Anthropology Museum, Greencastle 43798
DePauw University Art Center, Greencastle 43799
Deposit of Cars, La Habana 07926
Depósito del Automóvil, La Habana 07926
Dépôt Archéologique, Gabian 11830
Dépôt Archéologique, Lespugue 12564
Dépôt Archéologique, Saint-Thibéry 14486
Dépôt Archéologique du Fort Vauban, Alès 10284
Dépôt de Fouilles Archéologiques, Mailhac 12768
Dépôt de Fouilles Gallo-Romaines et Préhistoriques de Montmaurin, Montmaurin 13106
Dépôt-Musée Diocésain, Metz 12955
Depot Museum and Fort Sedgwick Museum, Julesburg 44364
Depot Museum Complex, Condon 42608
The Depot Museum Complex, Henderson 43992
Depot Museum of the Mammoth Spring State Park, Mammoth Spring 45089
Depot Park Museum, Sonoma 47675
Depreciation Lands Museum, Allison Park 41150
DePree Art Center and Gallery, Holland 44053
Dept. of Carst and Caves, Museum of Natural History, Wien 02907
Dept. of the History of Music of the Jēkabpils History Museum, Jēkabpils 27361
Derby-Beebe Summer House, Salem 47193
Derby Industrial Museum, Derby 38715
Derby Museum and Art Gallery, Derby 38716
Déri Múzeum, Debrecen 21398
DeRicci Gallery, Madison 45066
Dernier Quartier Général de Napoléon, Genappe 03429
Derrymore House, Bessbrook 38178
Derrynane House, Caherdaniel 22381
Dervish Pasha Mansion Ethnographical Museum, Lefkoşa 08235
Des Moines Art Center, Des Moines 42905
Des Plaines Historical Museum, Des Plaines 42913
Desbrisay Museum and Exhibition Centre, Bridgewater 05130
Deschutes County Historical Society Museum, Bend 41622
Descubre Museo Interactivo de Ciencia y Tecnología, Aguascalientes 27753
Desert Anthropology Museum, Nayin 22271
Desert Caballeros Western Museum, Wickenburg 48615
Desha County Museum, Dumas 43004
The Design Center at Philadelphia University, Philadelphia 46402
Design Center Stuttgart des Landesgewerbeamtes Baden-Württemberg, Stuttgart 20087
Design Centrum České Republiky, Brno 08263
Design Cerntre, Bilbao 34610
The Design Museum, Cape Town 34204
Design Museum, London 39623
Design museum Gent, Gent 03435
Designmuseo, Helsinki 09477
Desmond Castle, Kinsale 22498
Desoto National Memorial, Bradenton 41861
Destillier- und Drogenmuseum, Pernegg 02404
Detlefsen-Museum, Glückstadt 17304
Detroit Artists Market, Detroit 42921
Detroit Focus Gallery, Detroit 42922
Detroit Historical Museum, Detroit 42923
The Detroit Institute of Arts, Detroit 42924
Detroit Repertory Theatre Gallery, Detroit 42925
Detroit Science Center, Detroit 42926
Detskaja Kartinnaja Galereja, Samara 33368
Detskij Muzej, Čerepovec 32730
Detskij Muzej Buratino-Pinokkio, Moskva 33035
Deutsch-Deutsches Museum Mödlareuth, Töpen 20184
Deutsche Arbeitsschutzausstellung, Dortmund 16657
Deutsche Barockgalerie, Augsburg 15552
Deutsche Burgenvereinigung e.V., Braubach 49196
Deutsche Guggenheim, Berlin 15937
Deutsche Mediathek im Filmhaus, Berlin 15938
Deutsche Raumfahrtausstellung, Morgenröthe-Rautenkranz 18789
Das Deutsche Stickmuster-Museum Celle, Celle 16453
Deutscher Museumsbund e.V., Berlin 49197
Deutsches Albert-Schweitzer-Zentrum, Frankfurt am Main 17034
Deutsches Apotheken-Museum im Heidelberger Schloß, Heidelberg 17664
Deutsches Architektur Museum, Frankfurt am Main 17035
Deutsches Automuseum Schloss Langenburg, Langenburg 18329
Deutsches Bauernkriegsmuseum, Böblingen 16210
Deutsches Baumaschinen-Modellmuseum, Weilburg 20443
Deutsches Bergbau-Museum, Bochum 16193
Deutsches Bernsteinmuseum, Ribnitz-Damgarten 19593
Deutsches Bienenmuseum, Weimar, Thüringen 20456
Deutsches Boxsport-Museum, Sagard 19731
Deutsches Buch- und Schriftmuseum der Deutschen Bücherei Leipzig, Leipzig 18390
Deutsches Buchbindermuseum, Mainz 18599
Deutsches Chemie Museum, Merseburg 18712
Deutsches Damast- und Frottiermuseum Großschönau, Großschönau, Sachsen 17440
Deutsches Dampflokomotiv-Museum, Neuenmarkt 19028
Deutsches Drachenmuseum und Stadtmuseum, Furth im Wald 17180
Deutsches Drahtmuseum, Altena 15442
Deutsches Edelsteinmuseum, Idar-Oberstein 17879
Deutsches Eichendorff-Museum, Wangen im Allgäu 20392
Deutsches Elfenbeinmuseum Erbach, Erbach, Odenwald 16887
Deutsches Erdölmuseum Wietze, Wietze 20583
Deutsches Fastnachtmuseum, Kitzingen 18104
Deutsches Feld- und Kleinbahnmuseum, Deinste 16563
Deutsches Feuerwehr-Museum, Fulda 17172
Deutsches Film- und Fototechnik Museum, Deidesheim 16561
Deutsches Filmmuseum, Frankfurt am Main 17036
Deutsches Fleischermuseum, Böblingen 16211
Deutsches Fleischermuseum, Sindelfingen 19962
Deutsches Forum für Figurentheater und Puppenspielkunst, Bochum 16194
Deutsches Freimaurermuseum, Bayreuth 15842
Deutsches Gartenbaumuseum Erfurt, Erfurt 16897
Deutsches Glasmalerei-Museum Linnich, Linnich 18484
Deutsches Glockenmuseum, Greifenstein 17385
Deutsches Goldschmiedehaus, Hanau 17581
Deutsches Harmonikamuseum, Trossingen 20218
Deutsches Hirtenmuseum, Hersbruck 17739
Deutsches Historisches Museum, Berlin 15939
Deutsches Hopfenmuseum, Wolnzach 20672
Deutsches Hugenotten-Museum, Bad Karlshafen 15672
Deutsches Hygiene-Museum, Dresden 16679
Deutsches Jagd- und Fischereimuseum, München 18838
Deutsches Kaltwalzmuseum, Hagen, Westfalen 17478
Deutsches Kartausen-Museum, Buxheim bei Memmingen 16438
Deutsches Kartoffelmuseum Fußgönheim, Fußgönheim 17185
Deutsches Kleingärtnermuseum, Leipzig 18391
Deutsches Klingenmuseum Solingen, Solingen 19984
Deutsches Knopfmuseum, Bärnau 15794
Deutsches Kochbuchmuseum, Dortmund 16658
Deutsches Korbmuseum, Michelau 18727
Deutsches Kunststoff Museum, Düsseldorf 16720
Deutsches Landwirtschaftsmuseum, Stuttgart 20088
Deutsches Landwirtschaftsmuseum Markkleeberg, Markkleeberg 18637
Deutsches Märchen- und Wesersagenmuseum, Bad Oeynhausen 15708
Deutsches Maler- und Lackierer-Museum, Hamburg 17531
Deutsches Medizinhistorisches Museum, Ingolstadt 17906
Deutsches Meeresmuseum, Stralsund 20073
Deutsches Museum, München 18839
Deutsches Museum Bonn, Bonn 16234
Deutsches Museum - Flugwerft Schleißheim, Oberschleißheim 19200
Deutsches Museum für Schulkunst, Hagen, Westfalen 17479
Deutsches Museum - Verkehrszentrum, München 18840
Deutsches Musikautomaten Museum, Bruchsal 16365
Deutsches Orthopädisches Geschichts- und Forschungsmuseum, Frankfurt am Main 17037
Deutsches Panzermuseum Munster, Munster 18958
Deutsches Pferdemuseum, Verden 20301
Deutsches Phonomuseum, Sankt Georgen im Schwarzwald 19749
Deutsches Pinsel- und Bürstenmuseum, Bechhofen 15864
Deutsches Plakat Museum, Essen 16947
Deutsches Porzellanmuseum, Hohenberg an der Eger 17805
Deutsches Röntgen-Museum, Remscheid 19564
Deutsches Salzmuseum - Industriedenkmal Saline Lüneburg, Lüneburg 18556
Deutsches Schaustellermuseum, Lambrecht 18295
Deutsches Schiefermuseum Steinach/Thür., Steinach, Thüringen 20041
Deutsches Schiffahrtsmuseum, Bremerhaven 16339
Deutsches Schloss-und Beschlägemuseum, Velbert 20293
Deutsches Schreibmaschinenmuseum, Bayreuth 15843
Deutsches Schuhmuseum, Hauenstein 17641
Deutsches Schustermuseum, Burgkunstadt 16426
Deutsches Segelflugmuseum mit Modellflug, Gersfeld 17260
Deutsches Sielhafenmuseum in Carolinensiel, Wittmund 20629
Deutsches Skimuseum, Planegg 19410

Deutsches Spiele-Archiv, Marburg 18626
Deutsches Spielemuseum, Chemnitz 16461
Deutsches Spielkartenmuseum, Leinfelden-Echterdingen 18375
Deutsches Spielzeugmuseum, Sonneberg, Thüringen 19997
Deutsches Sport- und Olympia-Museum, Köln 18130
Deutsches Straßenmuseum, Germersheim 17253
Deutsches Tabak- und Zigarrenmuseum, Bünde 16402
Deutsches Tabakpfeifenmuseum, Oberelsbach 19174
Deutsches Tanzarchiv Köln, Köln 18131
Deutsches Tapetenmuseum, Kassel 18014
Deutsches Technikmuseum Berlin, Berlin 15940
Deutsches Textilmuseum Krefeld, Krefeld 18223
Deutsches Theatermuseum, München 18841
Deutsches Uhrenmuseum, Furtwangen im Schwarzwald 17184
Deutsches Verpackungs-Museum, Heidelberg 17665
Deutsches Vogelbauer-Museum, Walsrode 20382
Deutsches Weinbaumuseum, Oppenheim 19261
Deutsches Werbemuseum, Düsseldorf 16721
Deutsches Werkzeugmuseum, Remscheid 19565
Deutsches Zinnfigurenmuseum, Kulmbach 18267
Deutsches Zollmuseum, Hamburg 17532
Deutsches Zweirad- und NSU-Museum, Neckarsulm 18990
Deutschheim State Historic Site, Hermann 44001
Deutschordensmuseum Bad Mergentheim, Bad Mergentheim 15693
DeValera Museum and Bruree Heritage Centre, Bruree 22379
Devil's Coulee Dinosaur Heritage Museum, Warner 06744
Devils Tower Visitor Center, Devils Tower 42939
Devon and Cornwall Constabulary Museum, Exeter 38955
Devon Guild of Craftsmen Gallery, Bovey Tracey 38288
Devonport Gallery and Arts Centre, Devonport 00977
Devonport Maritime Museum, Devonport 00978
Dewa Roman Experience, Chester 38551
Dewa San-Zan History Museum, Haguro 26171
Dewazakura Art Museum, Tendo 26821
Dewberry Valley Museum, Dewberry 05328
Dewey Hotel, Dewey 42940
Dewey Museum, Warminster 40785
DeWitt County Historical Museum, Cuero 42719
DeWitt Historical Society Museum, Ithaca 44270
DeWitt Stetten Jr. Museum of Medical Research, Bethesda 41662
DeWitt Wallace Decorative Arts Museum, Williamsburg 48628
Dewsbury Museum, Dewsbury 38728
Dexter Area Museum, Dexter 42943
Dexter Historical Society Museum, Dexter 42942
Dey Mansion, Wayne 48478
Dezign House, Jefferson 44323
D.H. Lawrence Birthplace Museum, Eastwood 38864
D.H. Lawrence Heritage Centre, Eastwood 38865
Dhaka City Museum, Dhaka 03087
Dhenkanal Science Centre, Dhenkanal 21794
D.I. Mendeleev Museum, Boblovo 32693
D.I. Mendeleev Museum and Archives, Sankt-Peterburg 33429
Dia Art Foundation, New York 45792
Dia:Beacon, Beacon 41552
Dia Center for the Arts, Quemado 46755
Dia:Chelsea, New York 45793
Diablo Valley College Museum, Pleasant Hill 46551
Diamantmuseum, Antwerpen 03140
Diamantmuseum, Grobbendonk 03463
Diamantschleifermuseum, Brücken 16373
Dichter- und Stadtmuseum/ Herwegh-Archiv, Liestal 36876
Dichtermuseum Joseph Maria Lutz, Pfaffenhofen an der Ilm 19381
Dick Institute Museum and Art Gallery, Kilmarnock 39362
The Dickens House Museum, London 39624
Dickens House Museum Broadstairs, Broadstairs 38367
Dickens Museumtheater, Bronkhorst 29030
Dickinson County Heritage Center, Abilene 41048
Dickinson Homestead, Amherst 41177
Dickson Mounds Museum, Lewistown 44731
Dickson Store Museum, Spruce View 06484
Didaktische Ausstellung Urgeschichte, Chur 36634
Didcot Railway Centre, Didcot 38730
Didi Museum, Abuja 30328
Didrichsen Art Museum, Helsinki 09478
Didrichsenin Taidemuseo, Helsinki 09478
Didsbury and District Museum, Didsbury 05329
Dief- en Duifhuisje, Capelle aan den IJssel 29053
Diefenbaker Canada Centre, Saskatoon 06396
Diefenbaker Homestead House, Regina 06230
Diefenbaker House, Prince Albert 06181
Dieter Roth-Museum, Hamburg 17533
Dietrichstein Palace of the The Moravian Museum, Brno 08264
Dietrichsteinský Palác, Brno 08264
Diggs Gallery at Winston-Salem State University, Winston-Salem 48699
Digha Science Centre & National Science Camp, New Digha 21968
Digital Art Lab, Holon 22618
Digital Art Museum, Berlin 15941
Digterhuset, Farsø 08821
Dijecezanski Muzej Zagrebačke Nadbiskupije, Zagreb 07812
De Dijk Te Kijk, Petten 29712
Dikemark Sykehus Museum, Asker 30401
Dillard Mill State Historic Site, Davisville 42797
Dillhäuser Fachwerkhaus im Tiergarten Weilburg, Weilburg 20444
Dimbola Lodge, Freshwater 39017
Dimcho Debelyanov Memorial House, Koprivštica 04712
Dimitâr Blagoev Memorial House, Bankja 04612
Dimitâr Blagoev Memorial House, Sofia 04830
Dimitar Dimov House-Museum, Sofia 04831
Dimitar Peshev House-Museum, Kjustendil 04706
Dimitreion Oikima House, Agios Georgios Nilias 20808
Dimitris Pierides Museum of Contemporary Art, Glyfada 20963
Dimock Gallery, Washington 48347
Dinajpur Museum, Dinajpur 03095
Dingles Steam Village, Lifton 39495
Dingling Museum, Beijing 06964
Dingwall Museum, Dingwall 38731
Dinnerware Contemporary Art Gallery, Tucson 48085
Dinosaur Gardens Museum, Ossineke 46211
Dinosaur Isle, Sandown 40444
Dinosaur Museum, Dorchester 38747
Dinosaur Museum, Malabon 31357
The Dinosaur Museum, Saint Louis 47119
Dinosaur Provincial Park, Patricia 06100
Dinosaur Valley State Park, Glen Rose 43684
Dinosauria - Musée des Dinosaures, Espéraza 11652
Dinosaurier-Freilichtmuseum Münchehagen, Rehburg-Loccum 19539
Dinosaurland, Lyme Regis 39852
Dinsmore Homestead History Museum, Burlington 41999
Diocesan Art Gallery, Dubrovnik 07694
Diocesan Museum, Opole 31858
Diocesan Museum, Płock 31886
Diocesan Museum, Sandomierz 31962
Diocesan Museum, Siedlce 31969
Diocesan Museum, Tarnów 32041
Diocesan Museum Pelpin, Pelplin 31877
Diözesanmuseum, Sankt Pölten 02600
Diözesanmuseum, Bamberg 15804
Diözesanmuseum, Freising 17121
Diözesanmuseum Eisenstadt, Eisenstadt 01807
Diözesanmuseum Graz, Graz 01912
Diözesanmuseum Linz, Linz 02230
Diözesanmuseum Rottenburg, Rottenburg am Neckar 19690
Diözesanmuseum Sankt Afra, Augsburg 15553
Diözesanmuseum Sankt Ulrich, Regensburg 19518
Dionizas Poška Hollowed Trunks, Bijotai 27519
Dionne Homestead Museum, North Bay 06016
Diorama "Battle at the Dnepr", Dnepropetrovsk 37846
Diorama Bethlehem, Einsiedeln 36673
Diorama "Bitva za Dnepr", Dnepropetrovsk 37846
Diorama Kurskaja Bitva - Belgorodskoe Napravlenie, Belgorod 32677
Diorama Saint-Bénilde, Saugues-en-Gévaudan 14631
Dioramenschau Altötting, Altötting 15463
Diósgyőri Vármúzeum, Miskolc 21473
Dipartimento di Storia delle Arti, Pisa 24944
Diplomatic History Museum, Seoul 27229
Diplomatic Record Office of the Ministry of Foreign Affairs, Tokyo 26848
Dirección General de Museos de la Nación, Asunción 49329
Direction de Musées de France, Paris 49173
Direction des Musées, Sites et Monuments, Lomé 49391
Disagården, Uppsala 36352
Dischinger Heimatmuseum, Dischingen 16623
Disciples of Christ Historical Society Museum, Nashville 45616
Discover Houston County Visitors Center-Museum, Crockett 42704
Discovery Center, Fresno 43557
Discovery Center Museum, Rockford 46960
Discovery Center of Idaho, Boise 41772
Discovery Center of Springfield, Springfield 47752
Discovery Center of the Southern Tier, Binghamton 41699
Discovery Center Science Museum, Fort Collins 43379
Discovery Creek Children's Museum of Washington DC, Washington 48348
Discovery Harbour, Penetanguishene 06107
The Discovery Museum, Bridgeport 41890
Discovery Museum, Newcastle-upon-Tyne 40035
Discovery Museum History Center, Sacramento 47051
The Discovery Museums, Acton 41062
Discovery Park, Safford 47059
Discovery Place, Charlotte 42239
Discovery Science Center of Central Florida, Ocala 46080
Discovery World - The James Lovell Museum of Science, Economics and Technology, Milwaukee 45361
Dishman Art Gallery, Beaumont 41566
Diss Museum, Diss 38734
Distillerie du Périgord, Sarlat-la-Canéda 14613
District Archaeological Museum, Dhar 21788
District Art Gallery, Liptovský Mikuláš 34016
District Ethnographic Museum, Elbasan 00017
District Historical Museum, Bérat 00011
District Historical Museum, Fier 00021
District Historical Museum, Përmet 00029
District Historical Museum, Vlorë 00038
District Museum, Apriķi 27332
District Museum, Barpeta 21709
District Museum, Białystok 31489
District Museum, Ciechanów 31537
District Museum, Darrang 21757
District Museum, Gulbarga 21815
District Museum, Guntur 21817
District Museum, Jelenia Góra 31630
District Museum, Konin 31672
District Museum, Krosno 31736
District Museum, Kuldīga 27375
District Museum, Lublin 31793
District Museum, Nowy Sącz 31835
District Museum, Ostrołęka 31864
District Museum, Pillalamari 21982
District Museum, Rzeszów 31960
District Museum, Sandomierz 31965
District Museum, Shimoga 22021
District Museum, Shivpuri 22022
District Museum, Tachov 08674
District Museum, Żyradów 32227
District Museum in Chełm, Chełm 31523
District Museum in Leszno, Leszno 31757
District Museum in Toruń, Toruń 32054
District Museum of History, Galaţi 32524
District Museum Prague-East, Brandýs nad Labem 08255
District of Columbia Arts Center, Washington 48349
District Science Centre, Dharampur 21789
District Science Centre, Purulia 21996
District Science Centre, Tirunelveli 22038
District Six Museum, Cape Town 34205
Ditchling Museum, Ditchling 38735
Dithmarscher Landesmuseum, Meldorf 18695
Dittrick Museum of Medical History, Cleveland 42471
Diverse Works, Houston 44120
Divide County Historical Society Museum, Crosby 42708
Divine Word University Museum, Tacloban 31452
Divisão de Museus, Patrimônio e Arquivo Histórico, Taubaté 04556
División Museo e Investigaciones Históricas de la Policía Federal, Buenos Aires 00147
Divisional Kohima Museum, York 40961
Dixie Gun Works' Old Car Museum, Union City 48148
The Dixon Gallery and Gardens, Memphis 45235
Diyarbakır Arkeoloji ve Etnografi Müzesi, Diyarbakır 37661
Diyarbakır Devlet Güzel Sanatlar Galerisi, Diyarbakır 37662
Diyarbakır State Gallery, Diyarbakır 37662
Djakarta Museum, Jakarta 22105
Djanogly Art Gallery, Nottingham 40105
Djuro Tiljak Memorial Gallery, Komiža 07717
Djurslands Museum - Dansk Fiskerimuseum, Grenå 08841
Djusa Indianmuseum, Dala Husby 35849
DLM - Deutsches Ledermuseum/ Schuhmuseum Offenbach, Offenbach am Main 19239
Dmitrov Kremlin - State Museum Reserve, Dmitrov 32758
Dneprodzerzhinsk History Museum, Dneprodzeržinsk 37845
Dnepropetrovsk State Art Museum, Dnepropetrovsk 37847
Doak House Museum, Greeneville 43802
Dobele Museum of Local Studies, Dobele 27348
Dobeles Novadpētniecības Muzejs, Dobele 27348
Dobergmuseum/Geologisches Museum Ostwestfalen-Lippe, Bünde 16403
Dobó István Vármuzeum, Eger 21406
Dobri Chintulov Memorial House, Sliven 04819
Dobrjanskij Istoriko-kraevedčeskij Muzej, Dobrjanka 32759
Dock Museum, Barrow-in-Furness 38095
Dock- och Textilmuseum, Katrineholm 36004
Dockmuseum, Gärsnäs 35899
documenta Archiv für die Kunst des 20. und 21 Jahrhunderts, Kassel 18015
Doddington Hall, Doddington 38737
Dodengang en Oorlogsmuseum, Diksmuide 03387
Dodge County Historical Museum, Mantorville 45128
Dodge County Historical Society Museum, Beaver Dam 41573
Dodsland Museum, Dodsland 05334
Döderhultar Museum, Oskarshamn 36153
Döderhultarmuseet, Oskarshamn 36153
Dörflihaus-Museum, Springen 37194
Doerner-Institut, München 18842
Dörpmuseum Münkeboe, Südbrookmerland 20118
Doesburgsch Mosterd- en Azijnmuseum, Doesburg 29157
Dofasco Gallery, Dundas 05354
Dog Collar Museum, Maidstone 39875
Dogana d'Arte, Atripalda 22982
Dogra Art Museum, Jammu 21865
Dokken, Hol i Hallingdal 30552
Dokuchaev Central Soil Museum, Sankt-Peterburg 33385
Dokumentation des ehemaligen Heilbades, Bad Pirawarth 01716
Dokumentation Obersalzberg - Orts- und Zeitgeschichte, Berchtesgaden 15884
Dokumentationsraum Georg Matthäus Vischer, Aigen bei Raabs 01649
Dokumentations- und Gedenkstätte, Rostock 19659
Dokumentations- und Informationszentrum Emslandlager (DIZ), Papenburg 19345
Dokumentationsarchiv des österreichischen Widerstandes, Wien 02874
Dokumentationsraum für staufische Geschichte, Göppingen 17315
Dokumentationszentrum Alltagskultur der DDR, Eisenhüttenstadt 16823
Dokumentationszentrum des Landes für die Opfer deutscher Diktaturen, Rostock 19660
Dokumentationszentrum des Landes für die Opfer deutscher Diktaturen, Schwerin 19895
Dokumentationszentrum Prof. Sepp Mayrhuber, Pöchlarn 02420
Dolenjski Muzej Novo Mesto, Novo Mesto 34136
Doll and Bear Museum, Manunda 01208
Doll Gardner Art GAllery, Portland 46633
Doll Museum, Gärsnäs 35899
Doll Museum, Píritu 48961
Doll Museum, Savonlinna 10024
Doll Museum, Tucson 48086
Dollar Museum, Dollar 38738
The Dolly Mixture, Langbank 39420
Dolmabahçe Sarayı Müzesi, İstanbul 37699
Dølmo Bygdetun, Tolga 30923
Dolphin Sailing Barge Museum, Sittingbourne 40521
Dom Eskenów, Toruń 32049
Dom Gerharta Hauptmanna, Jelenia Góra 31629
Dom Jana Matejki, Kraków 31682
Dom Józefa Mehoffera, Kraków 31683
Dom-Museum, Fulda 17173
Dom-Museum Bremen, Bremen 16320
Dom-Museum Hildesheim, Hildesheim 17757
Dom-muzej Akademika E.N. Pavlovskogo, Borisoglebsk 32699
Dom-muzej L.N. Andreeva, Orël 33259
Dom-muzej S.M. Budennogo, Proletarsk 33329
Dom-muzej A.P. Čechova, Moskva 33036
Dom-muzej N.N. Chochrjakova, Kirov 32916
Dom-Muzej T.N. Chrenikova, Elec 32789
Dom-muzej G.V. Čičerina, Tambov 33589
Dom-muzej K.É. Ciolkovskogo, Kaluga 32875
Dom-muzej P.P. Čistjakova, Puškin 33335
Dom-muzej Čudomir, Kazanlâk 04698
Dom-muzej K.I. Čukovskogo, Peredelkino 33296
Dom-muzej M.I. Cvetaevoj, Moskva 33037
Dom-muzej Dekabristov, Kurgan 32970
Dom-muzej F.M. Dostoevskogo, Staraja Russa 33554
Dom-muzej A.L. Durova, Voronež 33729
Dom-muzej A.A. Dydykina, Palech 33279
Dom-muzej Elin Pelin, Bajlovo 04608
Dom-muzej E.M. Jaroslavskogo, Jakutsk 32840
Dom-muzej M.N. Ermolovoj, Moskva 33038
Dom-muzej M.V. Frunze, Samara 33369
Dom-muzej Gannibalov v Petrovskom, Puškinskie Gory 33342
Dom-muzej Generala I.A. Plieva, Vladikavkaz 33687
Dom-muzej N.V. Gogolja, Moskva 33039
Dom-muzej I.I. Golikova, Palech 33280
Dom-muzej M.B. Grekova, Novočerkassk 33232
Dom-muzej A.S. Grina, Kirov 32917
Dom-muzej Hamza Hakim-zade Niazy, Kokand 48841
Dom-muzej im. T.N. Granovskogo, Orël 33260
Dom-muzej Istorii Molodëžnogo Dviženija, Rjazan 33349
Dom-muzej P.D. Korina, Palech 33281
Dom-muzej V.G. Korolenko, Gelendžik 32803
Dom-Muzej I.N. Kramskogo, Ostrogožsk 33275
Dom-muzej P.A. Krasikova, Krasnojarsk 32949
Dom-muzej Pavla Kuznecova, Saratov 33505
Dom-muzej V.I. Lenina, Kazan 32886
Dom-muzej V.I. Lenina, Samara 33370
Dom-muzej M.Ju. Lermontova, Moskva 33040
Dom-muzej N.S. Leskova, Orël 33261
Dom-muzej D.I. Mendeleeva, Boblovo 32693
Dom-muzej M.K. Ammosova, Jakutsk 32841
Dom-muzej N.S. Muchina, Joškar-Ola 32857
Dom-muzej N.S. Muchina, Olikjal 33250
Dom-muzej Narodnogo Chudožnika V.A. Igoševa, Chanty-Mansijsk 32741
Dom-muzej N.A. Nekrasova, Čudovo 32753
Dom-muzej I.S. Nikitina, Voronež 33730
Dom-muzej Osipovych-Vul'f v Trigorskom, Puškinskie Gory 33343
Dom-muzej A.N. Ostrovskogo, Moskva 33041
Dom-muzej B.L. Pasternaka, Peredelkino 33297
Dom-muzej Penjo Penev, Dimitrovgrad 04649
Dom-muzej Petra Pervogo (Petrovskij Domik), Vologda 33721
Dom-muzej M.M. Prišvina, Dunino 32763
Dom-muzej B.I. Prorokova, Ivanovo 32825
Dom-muzej S.V. Rachmaninova, Ivanovka 32824
Dom-Muzej I.E. Repina, Žigulevsk 33747
Dom-muzej F.I. Šaljapina, Moskva 33042
Dom-muzej M.E. Saltykova-Ščedrina, Kirov 32918
Dom-muzej Semji Cvetaevych, Novo-Talicy 33231
Dom-muzej Semji Lopatinych, Stavropol 33560
Dom-muzej Semji Suchanovych, Vladivostok 33694
Dom-muzej Sestër Nevzorovych, Nižnij Novgorod 33205
Dom-muzej Skulptora A.S. Golubkinoj, Zarajsk 33745
Dom-muzej K.S. Stanislavskogo, Moskva 33043
Dom-muzej Tukaevych, Košlauč 32941
Dom-muzej Usman Jusupov, Jangi-Jul 48838
Dom-muzej G.I. Uspenskogo, Sjabrenicy 33524
Dom-muzej V.A. Rusanova, Orël 33262
Dom-muzej Ivan Vazov, Sopot 04861
Dom-muzej Konstantin Veličkov, Pazardžik 04754
Dom-muzej Velimira Chlebnikova, Astrachan 32662

Dom-Muzej V.V. Veresaeva, Tula 33623
Dom-muzej N.M. Zinovjeva, Djagilevo 32757
Dom-Muzej N.N. Žukova, Elec 32790
Dom na Humora i Satirata, Gabrovo 04667
Dom-pametnik na Vrach Buzludža, Kazanlăk 04699
Dom Poėta A.N. Širjaevca - Muzej Krestjanskogo Byta, Žigulevsk 33748
Dom Rodzinny Ojca Świętego Jana Pawła II, Wadowice 32067
Dom und Domschatz Halberstadt, Halberstadt 17500
Dom Uphagena, Gdańsk 31565
Dom Urodzenia Fryderyka Chopina, Warszawa 32081
Domaine Cataraqui, Sillery 06453
Domaine de l'Abbé Saunière, Rennes-le-Château 13944
Domaine de l'Hospitalet, Narbonne 13265
Domaine National de Chambord, Chambord 11146
Domein De Locht, Duffel 03396
Domgrabungsmuseum, Salzburg 02532
Domik Petra I, Sankt-Peterburg 33391
Dominiiklaste Kloostrimuuseum, Tallinn 09355
Dominikanermuseum Rottweil, Rottweil 19695
Dominus Flevit, Jerusalem 22630
Domizil im Berliner Dom, Berlin 15942
Domkammer der Kathedralkirche Sankt Paulus zu Münster, Münster 18935
Dommuseum, Brandenburg an der Havel 16279
Dommuseum, Chur 36635
Dommuseum, Frankfurt am Main 17038
Dommuseum zu Salzburg, Salzburg 02533
Domowniski muzej Dešno, Dissen, Niederlausitz 16625
Domschatz, Trier 20208
Domschatz, Würzburg 20691
Domschatz der Sankt Servatius-Stiftskirche, Quedlinburg 19457
Domschatz Sankt Ursen Kathedrale, Solothurn 37181
Domschatz- und Diözesan-Museum Eichstätt, Eichstätt 16804
Domschatz- und Diözesanmuseum, Passau 19354
Domschatz und Museum des Sankt Petri-Domes, Fritzlar 17152
Domschatzkammer, Aachen 15372
Domschatzkammer, Essen 16948
Domschatzkammer, Köln 18132
Domschatzkammer, Minden, Westfalen 18747
Domschatzkammer Sankt Petri, Bautzen 15834
Domschatzkammer und Diözesanmuseum, Osnabrück 19275
Domschatzmuseum, Regensburg 19519
Domus - Casa del Hombre, A Coruña 34748
Domus Galilaeana, Pisa 24945
Domus Mazziniana, Pisa 24946
DoMuS - Museum und Galerie der Gemeinde Schaan, Schaan 27510
Domus Romana, Aubechies 03191
Domvorhalle, Goslar 17348
Don Bank Museum, North Sydney 01327
Don F. Pratt Museum, Fort Campbell 43376
Don Garlits Museum of Drag Racing, Ocala 46081
Don Harrington Discovery Center, Amarillo 41166
Don River Railway Museum, Devonport 00979
Donald Agricultural Museum, Donald 00984
Donald G. Trayser Memorial Museum, Barnstable 41508
Donalda and District Museum, Donalda 05335
Donation François Mitterrand, Jarnac 12072
Donau-Schiffahrts-Museum-Regensburg, Regensburg 19520
Donauhalle, Donaueschingen 16633
Donazione Putti Biblioteca, Bologna 23102
Donazione Sambo, Trieste 25820
Doncaster Museum and Art Gallery, Doncaster 38741
Doneckij Oblastnoj Kraevedčeskij Muzej, Doneck 37851
Donegal County Museum, Letterkenny 22503
Donegal Historical Society Museum, Rossnowlagh 22537
Donetsk Museum of Art, Doneck 37852
Dong-eui University Museum, Busan 27140
Donga University Museum, Busan 27141
Dongguk University Museum, Seoul 27230
Dongha Museum, Dongen 29166
Dongjin Irrigation Folk Museum, Gimje 27174
Donington Grand Prix Collection, Castle Donington 38501
Donjon-Château Carondolet, Crupet 03364
Donkey Milk House, Key West 44462
Donna Beam Fine Art Gallery, Las Vegas 44664
Dønna Bygdesamling, Dønna 30461
Donnelly Homestead, Lucan 05785
Donnelly River Timber Mill Museum, Donnelly River 00985
Donner Memorial and Emigrant Trail Museum, Truckee 48074
Donskoj Istoriko-kraevedčeskij Muzej, Donskoe 32761
Doon Heritage Crossroads, Kitchener 05695
Door County Maritime Museum, Gills Rock 43671
Door County Maritime Museum, Sturgeon Bay 47860
Door County Museum, Sturgeon Bay 47861
Doozoo Children's Museum, Grand Junction 43747
Doppelkapelle Sankt Crucis, Landsberg bei Halle, Saale 18306
Dorchester Abbey Museum, Dorchester-on-Thames 38754
Dorchester County Historical Society Museum, Cambridge 42050
Dordrechts Museum, Dordrecht 29173
Doreen Young Art Gallery, Great Barrington 43778
Dorf- und Heimatmuseum, Winterbach bei Schorndorf 20614
Dorfmuseum, Bad Alexandersbad 15590
Dorfmuseum, Bennwil 36535
Dorfmuseum, Birmensdorf 36570
Dorfmuseum, Birr 36571
Dorfmuseum, Bönigen 36575
Dorfmuseum, Bottmingen 36580
Dorfmuseum, Ettingen 36695
Dorfmuseum, Feldbrunnen 36698
Dorfmuseum, Fislisbach 36700
Dorfmuseum, Gahlenz 17189
Dorfmuseum, Gontenschwil 36769
Dorfmuseum, Grube, Holstein 17445
Dorfmuseum, Herrnbaumgarten 02025
Dorfmuseum, Hombrechtikon 36807
Dorfmuseum, Hüntwangen 36810
Dorfmuseum, Katzelsdorf, Leitha 02102
Dorfmuseum, Kienberg, Oberbayern 18082
Dorfmuseum, Konolfingen 36831
Dorfmuseum, Langendorf 36845
Dorfmuseum, Nikitsch 02364
Dorfmuseum, Pfaffenweiler 19385
Dorfmuseum, Pöttelsdorf 02434
Dorfmuseum, Rupperswil 37078
Dorfmuseum, Schönbach 19822
Dorfmuseum, Schönwalde am Bungsberg 19837
Dorfmuseum, Schwanden (Glarus) 37147
Dorfmuseum, Therwil 37239
Dorfmuseum, Wiesen 37317
Dorfmuseum, Zeihen 37356
Dorfmuseum, Ziefen 37360
Dorfmuseum Ahnenhaus, Pliezhausen 19417
Dorfmuseum Alter Forsthof, Wetter, Hessen 20549
Dorfmuseum Altkirchen, Altkirchen 15458
Dorfmuseum Bellach, Bellach 36525
Dorfmuseum Buchenberg, Königsfeld im Schwarzwald 18176
Dorfmuseum Daniel-Martin-Haus, Rauschenberg 19504
Dorfmuseum Deckenpfronn, Deckenpfronn 16556
Dorfmuseum Delligsen, Delligsen 16566
Dorfmuseum Dettingen/Iller, Dettingen an der Iller 16594
Dorfmuseum Dietersweiler, Freudenstadt 17128
Dorfmuseum Graberhaus, Strengelbach 37219
Dorfmuseum Günzach, Günzach 17454
Dorfmuseum Hanweiler, Winnenden 20609
Dorfmuseum Hausen im Wiesental, Hausen im Wiesental 17644
Dorfmuseum Haynrode, Haynrode 17652
Dorfmuseum im Greifenhaus, Hausen, Oberfranken 17646
Dorfmuseum Kelter, Marbach am Neckar 18618
Dorfmuseum Kirchbözberg, Unterbözberg 37260
Dorfmuseum Maschwanden, Maschwanden 36929
Dorfmuseum Melihus, Möhlin 36942
Dorfmuseum Mertingen, Mertingen 18715
Dorfmuseum Mönchhof, Mönchhof 02317
Dorfmuseum Ostheim, Nidderau 19090
Dorfmuseum Poppenweiler, Ludwigsburg, Württemberg 18511
Dorfmuseum Roiten, Rappottenstein 02486
Dorfmuseum Schlossweid, Ringgenberg 37065
Dorfmuseum Stove, Stove bei Wismar 20071
Dorfmuseum Tündern, Hameln 17574
Dorfmuseum Weckbach, Weilbach 20441
Dorfmuseum Weinburg, Weinburg 02800
Dorfmuseum Wilsenroth, Dornburg, Westerwald 16649
Dorfmuseum Zeissholz, Zeißholz 20737
Dorfmuseum Zwingendorf, Zwingendorf 03063
Dorfschulmuseum, Ködnitz 18125
Dorfstube Münchholzhausen, Wetzlar 20550
Doric House, Flemington 43337
Dorking and District Museum, Dorking 38755
Dorman Memorial Museum, Middlesbrough 39948
Dornburger Schlösser, Dornburg, Saale 16648
Dorney Court, Windsor 40899
Dorniermuseum im Neuen Schloß, Meersburg 18674
Dornoch Heritage Museum, Dornoch 38758
Dorothea B. Hoover Historical Museum, Joplin 44361
Dorothea C. Witham Gallery, Lewiston 44729
Dorothy G. Page Museum, Wasilla 48425
Dorothy's House Museum, Cambellcroft 05184
Dorpsmuseum de Kleuskes, Liempde 29539
Dorpsmuseum De Kluis, Eext 29203
Dorpsmuseum in de Drie Snoeken, Oud-Gastel 29690
Dorrigo Steam Railway and Museum, Dorrigo 00986
Dorset County Museum, Dorchester 38748
Dorset Teddy Bear Museum, Dorchester 38749
Dorval Art Gallery and Cultural Centre, Dorval 05337
Dory Shop Museum, Shelburne 06434
Doshisha Neesima Memorabilia Room, Kyoto 26396
Dosho-machi Pharmaceutical and Historical Museum, Osaka 26642
Dossin Great Lakes Museum, Detroit 42927
Dostoevsky Literary-Memorial Museum, Sankt-Peterburg 33414
Dotzheimer Museum, Wiesbaden 20570
Doug Kerr Vintage Museum, Oaklands 01340
Douglas County Historical Society Museum, Superior 47889
Douglas County Museum Complex, Armour 41270
Douglas County Museum of History and Natural History, Roseburg 47003
Douglas F. Cooley Memorial Art Gallery, Portland 46634
Douglas Heritage Museum, Douglas, Lanarkshire 38761
Douglas Hyde Gallery, Dublin 22419
Douglass Historical Museum, Douglass 42966
Doumen County Fine Art Calligraphy Society, Zhuhai 07334
Doumen County Museum, Zhuhai 07335
Doune Motor Museum, Doune 38762
Dove Cottage and the Wordsworth Museum, Grasmere 39114
Dover Castle, Dover 38765
Dover Museum, Dover 38766
Dover Old Town Goal, Dover 38767
Dover Transport Museum, Whitfield 40859
Dowd Fine Arts Gallery, Cortland 42655
Dowerin District Museum, Dowerin 00987
Down County Museum, Downpatrick 38773
Down House, Downe 38771
The Downers Grove Park District Museum, Downers Grove 42979
Downey Museum of Art, Downey 42980
Downhill Castle, Castlerock 38504
Downieville Museum, Downieville 42981
Downpatrick Railway Museum, Downpatrick 38774
The Dowse, Hutt City 30180
Dr. Arratta Memorial Museum, Muttaburra 01297
Dr.-Arthur-Lindgens-Jagdmuseum, Schönsee 19836
Dr.-Bauer-Heimatmuseum, Bad Rothenfelde 15720
Dr. Bhau Daji Lad Museum, Mumbai 21946
Dr.-Carl-Haeberlin-Friesen-Museum, Wyk auf Föhr 20726
Dr Daniel W. Kissam House, Huntington 44160
Dr. Eisenbarth- und Heimatmuseum, Oberviechtach 19213
Dr. Engelbert Dollfuß-Museum, Texing 02724
Dr. Francis Medical and Apothecary Museum, Jacksonville 44291
Dr. Giri's Museum, Chennai 21742
Dr. Heins Classic Car Collection, Christchurch 30127
Dr. Henry N. Payne Community Museum, Cow Head 05282
Dr. Hideyo Noguchi Memorial Hall, Inawashiro 26247
Dr. Increase Mathews House, Zanesville 48820
Dr. John Harris Dental Museum, Bainbridge 41433
Dr. Johnson's House, London 39625
Dr. Jose Celso Barbose Museum, Bayamón 32363
Dr. Ljudevit Gaj Museum, Krapina 07727
Dr. Nikola Nezlobinski National Museum, Struga 27595
Dr. Norman Bethune Memorial Hall of Tang Xian, Tang Xian 07260
Dr Pepper Museum and Free Enterprise Institute, Waco 48262
Dr. Raj Bali Pandey Puratatva Sangrahalaya, Deoria 21786
Dr. Samuel D. Harris National Museum of Dentistry, Baltimore 41463
Dr. Sun Yat Sen Memorial House, Macau 07160
D.R. Visual Art Center, Nakorn-Chaisri 37521
Dr. V.L. Watson Allied Arts Centre, Dauphin 05307
Dr. William Robinson Plantation, Clark 42429
Dr. Woods House Museum, Leduc 05741
Draaiorgelmuseum, Assen 28949
Drachenhöhle, Syrau 20134
Drachmanns Hus, Skagen 09054
Dragon- og Frihedsmuseet, Holstebro 08887
Dragoon and Freedom Museum, Holstebro 08887
Dragør Museum, Dragør 08796
Drake House Museum, Plainfield 46538
Drake Well Museum, Titusville 48014
Drammens Museum, Drammen 30462
Drammens Museum for Kunst og Kulturhistorie, Drammen 30463
Drangedal Bygdetun, Drangedal 30464
Dráva Múzeum, Barcs 21316
Drawing Center, New York 45794
Drawings Collection, London 39626
Drayton Hall, Charleston 42214
Drayton Valley Museum, Drayton Valley 05338
Dreamtime Cultural Centre, North Rockhampton 01326
Drechsler- und Metalldrücker-Museum, Wendelstein, Mittelfranken 20510
Dreieich-Museum, Dreieich 16673
Dreikronenhaus, Osnabrück 19276
Drenewydd Museum, Bute Town 38426
Drenthe's Veste Stedelijk Museum, Coevorden 29057
Drents Museum, Assen 28950
De Drentse Glasbloazer, Dalen 29064
Drew County Historical Museum, Monticello 45471
Driebe Freight Station, Stroudsburg 47853
Driels Oudheidkundig Museum, Kerkdriel 29479
Drifting River Museum, Ashville 05013
Drilandmuseum Gronau, Gronau, Westfalen 17414
Drill Hall Gallery, Acton 00700
Driminagh Castle, Dublin 22420
Drjanovski Manastir Muzej, Drjanovo 04659
Drogerie-Museum, Weißenstadt 20502
Drogeriemuseum, Frankfurt am Main 17039
Droitwich Spa Heritage Centre, Droitwich 38776
Dromana and District Museum, Dromana 00988
Droogdok Jan Blanken, Hellevoetsluis 29389
Drostdy Museum, Swellendam 34389
Drostdy Museum, Uitenhage 34393
Droste-Museum, Havixbeck 17651
Droste-Museum, Münster 18936
Droste-Museum im Fürstenhäusle, Meersburg 18675
Drottningholm Slott, Drottningholm 35853
Druckereimuseum, Freienbach 36709
Druckereimuseum, Hatten, Oldenburg 17631
Druckereimuseum, Wildeshausen 20589
Druckmuseum Graz, Graz 01913
Druivenmuseum, Overijse 03682
Drukkerijmuseum Meppel, Meppel 29589
Drum Barracks Civil War Museum, Wilmington 48648
Drum Castle, Drumoak 38780
Drum Museum Taikokan, Tokyo 26841
Drumheller Dinosaur and Fossil Museum, Drumheller 05340
Drumlanrig Castle, Thornhill, Dumfriesshire 40704
Drumlanrig's Tower, Hawick 39194
Drumlin Farm, Lincoln 44778
Drummond Home, Hominy 44070
Drummond Island Historical Museum, Drummond Island 42988
Društvo Muzejskih Radnika Vojvodine, Novi Sad 49350
Druviena Old School, Druviena 27351
Druvienas Vecā Skola, Druviena 27351
Dry Falls Interpretive Center, Coulee City 42672
Dryanovo Monastery Museum, Drjanovo 04659
Dryden and District Museum, Dryden 05346
Du Page County Historical Museum, Wheaton 48582
Du Tam-Tam au Satellite, Angers 10343
Dualchas-Museum Bharraigh Agus Bhatarsaidh, Isle-of-Barra 39314
Dubai Museum, Dubai 37916
De Dubbele Palmboom, Rotterdam 29749
Dubbo Military Museum, Dubbo 00990
Dubbo Museum, Dubbo 00991
Dubbo Regional Gallery, Dubbo 00992
Dublin Castle, Dublin 22421
Dublin Civic Museum, Dublin 22422
Dublin-Laurens Museum, Dublin 42989
Dublin Print Museum, Dublin 22423
Dubrovin Farm Museum, Yisod Hama'ala 22784
Dubuque Museum of Art, Dubuque 42991
Duché d'Uzès, Uzès 15033
Ducheng Museum, Luoyang 07157
Duck Lake Regional Interpretive Centre, Duck Lake 05347
Dudley and Mary Marks Lea Gallery, Findlay 43322
Dudley Museum and Art Gallery, Dudley 38782
Dudmaston House, Quatt 40276
Dülkener Narrenmuseum, Viersen 20313
Dümmer-Museum, Lembruch 18428
Dürstelerhaus, Ottikon (Gossau) 37017
Düsseldorfer Museumsverein e.V., Düsseldorf 49198
Duff Community Heritage Museum, Duff 05348
Dufferin County Museum, Rosemont 06284
Dufferin Historical Museum, Carman 05210
Duftmuseum, Köln 18133
Duggan-Cronin Gallery, Kimberley 34287
Dugger Coal Museum, Dugger 42994
Duke Homestead State Historic Site, Durham 43018
Duke of Cornwall's Light Infantry Museum, Bodmin 38265
Duke University Museum of Art, Durham 43019
Duke University Union Museum and Brown Art Gallery, Durham 43020
Dukelské Múzeum, Svidník 34070
Duksung Women's University Art Museum, Seoul 27231
Duleep Singh Picture Collection, Thetford 40695
Duluth Art Institute, Duluth 42997
Duluth Children's Museum, Duluth 42998
Dulwich Picture Gallery, London 39627
Dům Pánů z Kunštátu, Brno 08265
Dům u Černé Matky Boží, Praha 08570
Dům u Jonáše, Pardubice 08532
Dům u Kamenného Zvonu, Praha 08571
Dům u Zlatého Prstenu, Praha 08572
Dům Umění, České Budějovice 08298
Dům Umění, Znojmo 08755
Dům Umění Města Brna, Brno 08266
Dumbarton House, Washington 48350
Dumbarton Oaks Collections, Washington 48351
Dumfries and Galloway Aviation Museum, Dumfries 38787
Dumfries Museum, Dumfries 38788
DuMont Kunsthalle, Köln 18134
Dunaharaszti-Helytörténeti Emléktár, Dunaharaszti 21404
Dunamelléki Református Egyházkerület Biblia Muzeuma, Budapest 21334
Dunamelléki Református Egyházkerület Ráday Múzeuma, Kecskemét 21445
Dunántúli Református Egyházkerület Tudományos Gyűjteményei Múzeum, Pápa 21498
Dunaskin Open Air Museum, Patna 40163
Dunbar Town House Museum, Dunbar 38793
Dunblane Museum, Dunblane 38796
Duncan Cottage Museum, Metlakatla 45277
The Duncan Gallery of Art, De Land 42814
Duncan-McAshan Visual Arts Center, Ingram 44237
Dundas Historical Society Museum, Dundas 05355
Dundee Art Galleries and Museum Association, Dundee 49408
Dundee City Council Arts and Heritage, Dundee 38798
Dundee Township Historical Society Museum, Dundee 43009
Dundurn Castle, Hamilton 05569
Dundy County Historical Society Museum, Benkelman 41626
Dunedin Fine Arts and Cultural Center, Dunedin 43010
Dunedin Historical Society Museum, Dunedin 43011
Dunedin Public Art Gallery, Dunedin 30145

Dunedin Public Libraries Artprint Collection, Dunedin 30146
Dunfermline Museum, Dunfermline 38809
Dungarvan Museum, Dungarvan 22464
Dungeon and Museum of Namik Kemal, Gazimağusa 08219
Dungog Historical Museum, Dungog 00994
Dunguaire Castle, Kinvara 22500
Dunham Massey Hall, Altrincham 37992
Dunham Tavern Museum, Cleveland 42472
Dunhill Museum, London 39628
Dunimarle Castle, Culross 38682
Dunkeld Cathedral Chapter House Museum, Dunkeld 38814
Dunkers Kulturhus, Helsingborg 35948
Dunklin County Museum, Kennett 44439
Dunlop Art Gallery, Regina 06231
Dunluce House Museum, Kimberley 34288
Dunn-Seiler Museum, Mississippi State 45402
Dunnet Pavilion, Castletown 38507
Dunolly Museum, Dunolly 00995
Dunoon and Cowal Museum, Dunoon 38816
Dunree Military Museum, Inishowen 22480
Dunrobin Castle Museum, Golspie 39091
Duns Area Museum, Duns 38819
Dunster Castle, Dunster 38821
Dunvegan Castle, Dunvegan 38822
Dunwell and Community Museum, Weekes 06761
Dunwich Museum, Dunwich 38823
Dupont Gallery, Lexington 44758
DuPont Historical Museum, DuPont 43013
Durban Art Gallery, Durban 34225
Durban Natural Science Museum, Durban 34226
Durbe Palace, Tukums 27458
Durbes Pils, Tukums 27458
Durham Art Gallery, Durham 05357
Durham Art Guild, Durham 43021
Durham Cathedral Treasures of Saint Cuthbert, Durham 38824
Durham Center Museum, East Durham 43038
Durham Heritage Centre and Museum, Durham 38825
Durham Historic Association Museum, Durham 43026
Durham Light Infantry Museum and Durham Art Gallery, Durham 38826
Durham Western Heritage Museum, Omaha 46145
Durrell Museum, Durrell 05358
Durylin Museum, Korolev 32939
Dusable Museum of African-American History, Chicago 42324
Dutch Dakota Association Exhibition, Schiphol 29807
Dutch Leather and Shoe Museum, Waalwijk 29974
Dutch Period Museum, Colombo 35748
Dutch Resistance Museum, Amsterdam 28912
Dutch Textile Museum, Tilburg 29880
Duwisib Castle, Maltahohe 28761
Duxbury Rural and Historical Society, Duxbury 43029
Dvor Trakošćan, Trakošćan 07792
Dvorec-Muzej Petra I, Sankt-Peterburg 33392
Dvorec-muzej Petra III, Lomonosov 32987
Dvorec Petra I, Strelna 33567
Dwight D. Eisenhower Library-Museum, Abilene 41049
Dwight Frederick Boyden Gallery, Saint Mary's City 47146
Dwór Artusa, Gdańsk 31566
Dwór w Dołędze, Tarnów 32040
Dworek Jana Matejki w Krzesławicach, Kraków 31684
Dworek Wincentego Pola, Oddział Muzeum Lubelskiego w Lublinie, Lublin 31786
Dwyer MacAllister Cottage and Museum, Derrynamuck 22409
Dyckman Farmhouse Museum, New York 45795
Dydykin House-Museum, Palech 33279
Dyer Memorial Library, Abington 41056
Dylan Thomas Boathouse, Laugharne 39429
Dyrøy Bygdemuseum, Tennevoll 30917
Dyvelstens Flottningsmuseum, Forshaga 35892
Džambul Historical and Regional Museum, Džambul 27080
Džambul Literary Memorial Museum, Džambul 27081
Džambulskij Literaturnyj Memorialnyj Muzej, Džambul 27081
Dzeržinsk City Museum, Dzeržinsk 32765
Dzeržinskij Gorodskoj Kraevedčeskij Muzej, Dzeržinsk 32765
Dzezkazgan Historical and Regional Museum, Džezkazgan 27083
Džuro Jakšić Memorial Museum, Srpska Crnja 33916
E. Bindstouw, Viborg 09109
E. de C. Clarke Geological Museum, Crawley 00952
E. St. Julien Cox House, Saint Peter 47169
E-Werk Freiburg, Freiburg im Breisgau 17108
E.A. Boratynskyj Museum, Kazan 32895
EAA AirVenture Museum, Oshkosh 46204
Eagle Historical Society and Museums, Eagle City 43032
Eagle Tavern Museum, Watkinsville 48452
Ealing College Gallery, London 39629
EAM-live-Museum Lippoldsberg, Wahlsburg 20345
EAM-live-Museum Wasserkraftwerk Merkenbach, Dillenburg 16608
EAM-live-Museum Wasserkraftwerk Wülmersen, Kassel 18016
Ear Falls District Museum, Ear Falls 05359
Earist Museum, Manila 31377
The Earle-Harrison House, Waco 48263
Earle Wightman Museum, Oyster Bay 46248
Earls Barton Museum of Local Life, Earls Barton 38835
Early American Museum, Mahomet 45076
Early Christian Mausoleum, Pécs 21513
Earlystreet, Norman Park 01323
Earlyworks Museum Complex, Huntsville 44173
It Earmhus en Oud Friese Greidboerderij, Warten 29981
Earth and Man National Museum, Sofia 04851
Earth Science Museum, Dublin 22424
Earth Science Museum, Rio de Janeiro 04357
Earth Sciences Museum, Waterloo 06752
Easdale Island Folk Museum, Easdale Island 38836
East and Seaport Museum, Greenport 43809
East Anglia Transport Museum, Carlton Colville 38491
East Anglian Film Archive, Norwich 40092
East Anglian Railway Museum, Colchester 38609
East Bohemian Gallery, Pardubice 08532
East Bohemian Gallery, Pardubice 08533
East Bohemian Museum, Pardubice 08534
East Brunswick Museum, East Brunswick 43037
East Campus Galleries, Orlando 46185
East Carlton Steel Heritage Centre, East Carlton 38838
East Coast Museum of Technology, Gisborne 30163
East Coulee School Museum, East Coulee 05360
East Ely Railroad Depot Museum, Ely 43175
East Essex Aviation Society and Museum of the 40's, Saint Osyth 40417
East Ham Nature Reserve, London 39630
East Hampton Historical Society Museum, East Hampton 43044
East Hampton Town Marine Museum, East Hampton 43045
East Hants Historical Museum, Maitland 05801
East Jersey Olde Towne, Piscataway 46502
East Jordan Portside Art and Historical Museum, East Jordan 43052
East Kazakhstan Historical and Regional Museum, Ust-Kamenogorsk 27099
East Lancashire Regiment Museum, Blackburn, Lancashire 38243
East London Museum, East London 34236
East Martello Museum, Key West 44463
East Midlands Museums Service, Colston Bassett 49409
East Poultney Museum, East Poultney 43058
East Riddlesden Hall, Keighley 39328
East Somerset Railway, Shepton Mallet 40492
East Surrey Museum, Caterham 38512
East Tennessee Discovery Center, Knoxville 44516
East Tennessee Historical Society Museum, Knoxville 44517
East Texas Oil Museum at Kilgore College, Kilgore 44479
East Timorese Cultural Centre Museum Collection, Dili 09130
East Troy Electric Railroad Museum, East Troy 43062
East-West Center, Honolulu 44075
Eastbourne Heritage Centre, Eastbourne 38852
Eastchester Historical Society Museum, Bronxville 41927
Eastend Museum, Eastend 05362
Eastend School Museum, Eastend 05363
Eastern Arizona Museum, Pima 46488
Eastern Azarbaijan Province History Museum, Tabriz 22285
Eastern California Museum, Independence 44197
Eastern Edge Art Gallery, Saint John's 06344
Eastern Häme Museum, Hartola 09465
Eastern Kazakhstan Rgional Ethnographical Museum, Ust-Kamenogorsk 27100
The Eastern Museum, Derby 38717
Eastern Oregon Museum on the Old Oregon Trail, Haines 43871
Eastern Shore Art Center, Fairhope 43271
Eastern Southland Gallery, Gore 30166
Eastern State Penitentiary Historic Site, Philadelphia 46403
Eastleigh Museum, Eastleigh 38860
Eastney Beam Engine House, Portsmouth 40251
Eastnor Castle, Ledbury 39439
Easton Farm Park, Easton 38862
Eastwood House, Glasgow 39043
Eaton-Buchan Gallery and Marvin Cone Gallery, Cedar Rapids 42158
Eaved House - Cultural and Art Centre, Lefkoşa 08239
Ebbamåla Bruk, Kyrkhult 36026
Ebbas Hus, Malmö 36072
Ebeltoft Museum, Ebeltoft 08801
Ebenezer Maxwell Mansion, Philadelphia 46404
Ebersdorfer Schulmuseum, Chemnitz 16462
Ebreji Latvijā, Rīga 27404
E.C. Allison Research Center, San Diego 47275
Ec'Art, Betton 10711
Ecce Homo, Jerusalem 22631
Eccles Community Art Center, Ogden 46097
Ecclesiastical Collection, Naoussa 21093
Ecclesiastical Museum, Komotini 21024
Ecclesiastical Museum, Mullingar 22524
Ecclesiastical Museum of Alexandroupolis, Alexandroupolis 20815
Ecclesiastical Museum of the Metropolis of Trikki and Stagoi, Trikala 21202
Echizen-No-Sato Museum, Takefu 26813
Echo Historical Museum, Echo 43079
Echuca Gem Club Collection, Echuca 01002
Echuca Museum, Echuca 01003
Eckley Miners' Village, Eckley 43080
Eco-Musée de la Noix, Castelnaud-la-Chapelle 11075
Éco-Musée du Matériel de la Ferme, Blangy-sur-Bresle 10754
Éco Musée Vivant de Provence, La Gaude 12190
Ecodrome Zwolle, Zwolle 30083
Ecole Dentellière, Bailleul 10568
Ecole du Rang II, Authier 05024
Ecole-Musée de Champagny, Champagny 11154
Ecological Education Centre, Eindhoven 29214
EcoMare, De Koog 29067
Écomusée, Aspres-sur-Buech 10446
Écomusée, Boigneville 10785
Écomusée, Chassagnes 11197
Ecomusée, Etel 11669
Ecomusée Agricole de la Cadole, Brullioles 10944
Ecomusée Agricole du Pays de Fayence, Fayence 11709
Écomusée Castaret-le-Haut, Saint-Gervais-sur-Mare 14248
Ecomusée d'Alsace, Ungersheim 15026
Écomusée d'Alzen, Alzen 10298
Ecomusée d'Arts et Traditions Populaires, Ligny-le-Ribault 12591
Écomusée de Fresnes, Fresnes (Val-de-Marne) 11815
Ecomusée de Hauteluce, Hauteluce 12001
Ecomusée de Keranpercheg, Pont-Aven 13802
Écomusée de la Bourrine du Bois Juquaud, Saint-Hilaire-de-Riez 14261
Ecomusée de la Brenne, Le Blanc 12380
Ecomusée de la Bresse Bourguignonne, Cuiseaux 11469
Ecomusée de la Bresse Bourguignonne, Pierre-de-Bresse 13729
Écomusée de la Cévenne, Saint-Laurent-de-Trèves 14309
Ecomusée de la Communauté, Ciry-le-Noble 11305
Ecomusée de la Communauté Le Creusot Montceau-les-Mines, Le Creusot 12407
Écomusée de la Conservation du Fruit, Turquant 15017
Écomusée de la Courneuve, La Courneuve 12163
Écomusée de la Crau, Saint-Martin-de-Crau 14349
Ecomusée de la Ferme de Kervazegan, Pont-l'Abbé 13811
Écomusée de la Ferme de la Forêt, Saint-Trivier-de-Courtes 14489
Ecomusée de la Ferme de l'Espinousse Prat Alaric, Fraisse-sur-Agout 11803
Écomusée de la Ferme de Roscanvel, Combrit 11367
Ecomusée de la Ferme du Chemin, Madré 12759
Écomusée de la Ferme du Moulin Vanneau, Saints-en-Puisaye 14564
Ecomusée de la Ferme et des Vieux Métiers, Lizio 12638
Écomusée de la Forêt d'Orient, Brienne-la-Vieille 10927
Ecomusée de la Forêt Méditerranéenne, Gardanne 11839
Écomusée de la Forge, Auchy-la-Montagne 10474
Écomusée de la Forge, Menton 12934
Ecomusée de la Gâtine Tourangelle, Rouziers-de-Touraine 14068
Ecomusée de la Grande Lande Marquèze, Sabres 14081
Ecomusée de la Haute-Areuse, Saint-Sulpice, Neuchâtel 37089
Écomusée de la Haute-Beauce, Saint-Evariste 06317
Ecomusée de la Lomagne, Flamarens 11742
Ecomusée de la Lomagne, Miradoux 12987
Ecomusée de la Margeride, Loubaresse 12671
Ecomusée de la Margeride, Ruynes-en-Margeride 14078
Écomusée de la Pêche, Thonon-les-Bains 14896
Écomusée de la Pêche et de la Mer, Capbreton 11033
Ecomusée de la Pomme au Calvados, Le Sap 12480
Écomusée de la région du Viroin, Treignes 03799
Écomusée de la Sainte-Baume, Plan-d'Aups 13747
Ecomusée de la Tradition Basque Jean Vier, Saint-Jean-de-Luz 14279
Écomusée de la Truffe, Sorges 14774
Ecomusée de la Vallee d'Aspe, Accous 10226
Ecomusée de la Vallée de l'Aigre, La Ferté-Villeneuil 12179
Écomusée de la Vallée du Galeizon, Cendras 11102
Écomusée de la Vie en Altitude, Bénévent-et-Charbillac 10682
Écomusée de la Vie Montagnarde, Abries 10225
Ecomusée de la Vigne et du Vin, Gradignan 11895
Écomusée de l'Abeille, Auriac-du-Périgord 10487
Écomusée de l'Abeille, Grateloup 11924
Écomusée de l'Abeille, Le Faou 12412
Écomusée de l'Abeille, Le Vey 12496
Écomusée de l'Agriculture, Aigues-Vives 10238
Ecomusée de l'Agriculture, Charmoille-Provenchère 11185
Ecomusée de l'Agriculture Queyrassine, Arvieux-en-Queyras 10439
Écomusée de l'Apiculture, Montargis 13042
Ecomusée de l'Armagnac, Labastide-d'Armagnac 12279
Ecomusée de l'Ile-de-Groix, Ile-de-Groix 12046
Écomusée de l'Ile-Tudy, Ile-Tudy 12053
Écomusée de l'île d'Ouessant, Ile-d'Ouessant 12051
Ecomusée de Marais Breton Vendéen, La Barre-de-Monts 12121
Ecomusée de Marie Galante, Grand Bourg 21245
Ecomusée de Montjean, Montjean-sur-Loire 13099
Ecomusée de Plein Air du Quercy, Sauliac-sur-Célé 14634
Ecomusée de Saint-Dégan, Brech 10899
Ecomusée de Saint-Joseph, Fargues-sur-Ourbise 11705
Ecomusée de Saint-Nazaire, Saint-Nazaire (Loire-Atlantique) 14380
Ecomusée de Salazie, Salazie 14567
Ecomusée de Savigny-le-Temple, Savigny-le-Temple 14668
Ecomusée Départemental de la Vendée, Les Épesses 12533
Écomusée des Anciennes Carrières de Pierre "Les Capucins", Paris 13499
Ecomusée des Appeaux et de la Faune, Saint-Didier 14183
Ecomusée des Bruneaux, Firminy 11737
Écomusée des Deux-Rives, Valleyfield 06663
Ecomusée des Goémoniers et de l'Algue, Plouguerneau 13774
Ecomusée des Houillères de Lorraine, Freyming-Merlebach 11818
Ecomusée des Monts d'Arrée, Commana 11368
Ecomusée des Monts d'Arrée, Saint-Rivoal 14459
Écomusée des Pays de l'Oise, Beauvais 10653
Écomusée des Vallées du Paillon, Contes 11400
Ecomusée d'Hannonville, Hannonville-sous-les-Côtes 11988
Ecomusée d'Ichkeul, Bizerte 37555
Ecomusée du Bocage, Sains-du-Nord 14090
Écomusée du Bommelaers Wall, Ghyvelde 11858
Écomusée du Château-Fort, Saint-Sylvain-d'Anjou 14483
Écomusée du Chemin de Fer en Vendée, Les Épesses 12534
Écomusée du Cheminot Veynois, Veynes 15150
Écomusée du Cognac, Migron 12977
Ecomusée du Commerce et de l'Artisanat, Rochefort (Charente-Maritime) 13997
Ecomusée du Cuir de la Tannerie Nory, Sainghin-en-Weppes 14089
Écomusée du Domaine de la Petite Couère, Nyoiseau 13377
Écomusée du Haut Pays de la Roya et de la Bevera, Breil-sur-Roya 10901
Écomusée du Haut-Vénéon, Saint-Christophe-en-Oisans 14150
Écomusée du Larzac, Millau 12978
Écomusée du Libournais, Montagne 13036
Écomusée du Liège, Gonfaron 11884
Écomusée du Linge, Montcy-Notre-Dame 13070
Ecomusée du Marais Salant, Loix-en-Ré 12651
Ecomusée du Mont-Lozère, Le Pont-de-Montvert 12470
Écomusée du Montmorillon, Montmorillon 13112
Ecomusée du Moulin de Kerchuz, Saint-Thurien 14488
Écomusée du Moulin de la Sée, Brouains 10940
Écomusée du Moulin Saint-Martin, Cany-Barville 11032
Ecomusée du Pay de la Cerise de Fougerolles, Fougerolles (Haute-Saône) 11796
Ecomusée du Pays de la Roudoule, Puget-Rostang 13884
Ecomusée du Pays de Montfort, Montfort-sur-Meu 13087
Écomusée du Pays de Nied, Gomelange 11880
Ecomusée du Pays de Rennes, Rennes (Ille-et-Vilaine) 13939
Écomusée du Pays des Collines, Lahamaide 03549
Écomusée du Paysan Gascon, Toujouse 14923
Écomusée du Phare de Trezien, Plouarzel 13765
Écomusée du Roannais, Roanne 13984
Ecomusée du Savon, Manosque 12794
Écomusée du Val de Saône, Seurre 14734
Écomusée du Vernon, Savigny-en-Vernon 14667
Écomusée du Verre de Biot, Biot 10738
Ecomusée du Village Breton de Poul-Fetan, Quistinic 13907
Ecomusée Hundisburg, Haldensleben 17505
Ecomusée Industriel de Lochrist-Inzinzac, Lochrist-Inzinzac 12642
Ecomusée la Cité des Abeilles, Saint-Faust 14212
Ecomusée la Ferme du Hameau, Bierre-les-Semur 10728
L'Écomusée la Maison de l'Islandais, Gravelines 11928
Écomusée l'Aubonnière, Chaille-sous-les-Ormeaux 11123
Ecomusée Le Grain de Sel, Châteauneuf-d'Entraunes 11217
Ecomusée Les Outils de la Vigne et du Vin, Saint-Sulpice-de-Faleyrens 14479
Ecomusée Maison Michaud, Chapelle-des-Bois 11167
Ecomusée Picarvie, Saint-Valéry-sur-Somme 14498
Ecomusée Sauvegarde du Vieil Auzon, Auzon 10517
Ecomusée Vivant de la Haie, Châtillon-en-Dunois 11238
Ecomuseo de Guinea, Frontera 34826
Ecomuseo del Habitat Subterráneo de Rojales, Rojales 35331
Ecomuseo della Resistenza, Coazze 23601
Ecomuseo dell'Archeologia Industriale, Schio 25526
Ecomuseo di Archeologia Industriale E. CrumiSre, Villar Pellice 26021
Ecomuseo Los Torres, Lerdo 28056
Ecomuseo - Molino de Zubieta, Zubieta 35736
Ecomuseo Regional Maipú, Maipú 00422
Ecomuseu, Rio de Janeiro 04322

Ecomuseu da Fazenda Boa Vista, Roseira 04414
Ecomuseu de Itaipu, Foz do Iguaçu 04102
Ecomuseu de les Valls d'Aneu, Esterri d'Aneu 34810
Ecomuseu do Rabeirão do Ilha, Florianópolis 04088
Ecomuseum en Archief van de Boomse Baksteen, Boom 03225
Ecomuseum Simplon, Simplon Dorf 37170
Economical Document Collection, Hikone 26192
Economopoulos Collection, Athinai 20857
EcoTarium, Worcester 48752
Ecovillage Centre Africain Reconstitué, Magny-Cours 12763
Écovillage de Lorraine, Ville-sur-Yron 15188
Écovillage Gaulois, Pleumeur-Bodou 13757
Ed Clark Museum of Missouri Geology, Rolla 46990
Eda Skans Museum, Åmotfors 35798
Edams Museum, Edam 29191
Edelfelt-Vallgren Museo, Porvoo 09950
Edelfelt-Vallgren Museum, Porvoo 09950
Edelsteenslijperij de Steenarend, Eindhoven 29210
Eden Camp, Malton 39883
Eden Court Art Gallery, Inverness 39299
Eden Killer Whale Museum, Eden 01006
Eden Valley Museum, Edenbridge 38867
Edgar Allan Poe Cottage, Bronx 41918
Edgar Allan Poe House, Philadelphia 46405
Edgar Allan Poe House and Museum, Baltimore 41464
Edgar Allan Poe Museum, Richmond 46876
Edgar County Historical Museum, Paris 46284
Edge of the Cedars State Park, Blanding 41733
Edgerton and District Museum, Edgerton 05366
Edinburgh Printmakers Workshop and Gallery, Edinburgh 38877
Edinburgh Scout Museum, Edinburgh 38878
Edinburgh Square Heritage and Cultural Centre, Caledonia 05158
Edinburgh University Anatomy Museum, Edinburgh 38879
Edinburgh University Collection of Historic Musical Instruments, Edinburgh 38880
Edinburgh University Natural History Collections, Edinburgh 38881
Edirne Arkoloji ve Etnografi Müzesi, Edirne 37664
Edirne Devlet Güzel Sanatlar Galerisi, Edirne 37665
Edirne State Gallery, Edirne 37665
Edison and Ford Winter Estates, Fort Myers 43434
Edison Community College Gallery of Fine Art, Fort Myers 43435
Edison National Historic Site, West Orange 48536
Edison Plaza Museum, Beaumont 41567
Edisto Island Historic Preservation Society Museum, Edisto Island 43090
Edith Cowan University Museum of Childhood, Claremont, Western Australia 00919
Edith-Ruß-Haus für Medienkunst, Oldenburg, Oldenburg 19253
Edithburgh Museum, Edithburgh 01008
Edmond Historical Society Museum, Edmond 43091
Edmonds Arts Festival Museum, Edmonds 43092
Edmonds South Snohomish County Historical Society Museum, Edmonds 43093
Edmonston House, Vails Gate 48175
Edmonton Art Gallery, Edmonton 05373
Edmonton Public Schools Museum, Edmonton 05374
Edmonton Telephone Historical Centre, Edmonton 05375
Edmund Adler-Galerie, Mannersdorf 02261
Edmund Wright House, Adelaide 00706
Edna Historical Museum, Edna 43094
Edo-Tokyo Museum, Tokyo 26842
Edo-Tokyo Open Air Architectural Museum, Koganei 26362
Edo-Tokyo Tatemono-En, Koganei 26362
Edoardo Villa Museum, Pretoria 34341
Eds MC- och Motormuseum, Ed 35856
Edsel and Eleanor Ford House, Grosse Pointe Shores 43844
Eduard Bargheer-Haus, Hamburg 17534
Eduarda Smiļģa Teātra Muzejs, Rīga 27405
Eduarda Veidenbauma Memoriālais Muzejs, Liepa 27377
Eduards Smiļģis Theatre Museum, Rīga 27405
Educatieve Boerderij en Zijdemuseum de Schans, Oud-Gastel 29691
Education Museum, Cairo 09260
Education Museum, Hyderabad 31019
Educational Science Museum, Kuwait 27305
Eduskuntasalimuseo, Kauhajoki 09636
Edvard Grieg Museum, Paradis 30776
Edventure, Columbia 42559
Edward and Helen Mardigian Museum, Jerusalem 22632
Edward and Marthann Samek Art Gallery, Lewisburg 44721
Edward Dean Museum, Cherry Valley 42278
Edward H. White II Memorial Museum, Brooks Air Force Base 41957
Edward Hopper House, Nyack 46048
Edward M. Bannister Gallery, Providence 46718
Edwards County Historical Museum, Kinsley 44500
Edwards Memorial Museum, Chesterfield 42288
Edwin A. Ulrich Museum of Art, Wichita 48599
Edwin Scharff Museum am Petrusplatz, Neu-Ulm 19008
Edwin Wolters Memorial Museum, Shiner 47607
Edwin Young Collection, Salisbury 40433
Eells-Stow House, Milford 45337
Eemil Halonen Museum and Lapinlahti Art Museum, Lapinlahti 09759
Het Eerste Friese Schaatsmuseum, Hindeloopen 29421
Eerste Nederlandse Opel Automuseum, Tijnje 29876
Eesti Ajaloomuuseum, Tallinn 09356
Eesti Arhitektuurimuuseum, Tallinn 09357
Eesti Kirjandusmuuseum, Tartu 09374
Eesti Kunstimuuseum, Tallinn 09358
Eesti Loodusmuuseum, Tallinn 09359
Eesti Meremuuseum, Tallinn 09360
Eesti Muuseumiühing Tallinn, Tallinn 49150
Eesti Muuseumiühing Tartu, Tartu 49151
Eesti Muuseumraudtee, Haapsalu 09317
Eesti Muuseumraudtee Lavassaare Muuseum, Tallinn 09361
Eesti Piimandusmuuseum, Imavere 09326
Eesti Põllumajandusmuuseum, Tõrvandi 09391
Eesti Postimuuseum, Tartu 09375
Eesti Rahva Muuseum, Tartu 09376
Eesti Spordimuuseum, Tartu 09377
Eesti Tarbekunsti- ja Disainimuuseum, Tallinn 09362
Eesti Teatri- ja Muusikamuuseum, Tallinn 09363
Eesti Tervishoiu Muuseum, Tallinn 09364
Eesti Vabaõhumuuseum, Tallinn 09365
EFA Museum für Deutsche Automobilgeschichte, Amerang 15482
Efes Müzesi, Selçuk 37779
Effigy Mounds Museum, Harpers Ferry 43917
Egawa Museum of Art, Nishinomiya 26605
Egerländer-Elbogner Heimatstuben, Illertissen 17885
Egerland-Museum, Marktredwitz 18652
Egersund Fayancemuseum, Egersund 30467
Egeskov Veteranmuseum, Kværndrup 08966
Egge Museum, Steinkjer 30894
Egge-Museum Altenbeken, Altenbeken 15446
Egged Museum of Passengers Traffic, Holon 22619
Egham Museum, Egham 38922
Egill Olafssons Local Museum, Patreksfjörður 21645
Egnsmuseet Ll. Kolstrupgaard, Aabenraa 08761
Egon Schiele Art Centrum, Český Krumlov 08302
Egon Schiele-Museum, Tulln 02743
Egri Érseki Gyűjteményi Központ Múzeum, Eger 21407
Egypt Centre, Swansea 40657
Egyptian Museum, Cairo 09261
Egyptian National Railways Museum, Cairo 09262
Ehemalige Benediktinerabtei, Seligenstadt 19932
Ehemalige Synagoge Erfelden, Riedstadt 19602
Ehemalige Synagoge mit Ausstellung Juden auf dem Lande- Beispiel Ichenhausen, Ichenhausen 17877
Ehemaliges Benediktinerinnenstift Göß, Leoben 02208
Ehemaliges Jagdschloß Bebenhausen, Tübingen 20222
Ehemaliges Postfuhramt, Berlin 15943
Ehemaliges Schlossvorwerk, Bremervörde 16348
Ehime Bunkakan, Imabari 26243
Ehime Cultural Hall, Imabari 26243
Ehime-kenritsu Bijutsukan, Matsuyama 26483
Ehime-kenritsu Hakubutsukan, Matsuyama 26484
Ehime-kenritsu Rekishi Minzoku Shiryokan, Matsuyama 26485
Ehime Prefectural History and Folklore Museum, Matsuyama 26485
Ehime Prefectural Museum, Matsuyama 26484
Ehm Welk-Haus, Bad Doberan 15624
Ehm-Welk-Literaturmuseum, Angermünde 15491
Ehrensvärd-Museo, Helsinki 09479
Ehrensvärd Museum, Helsinki 09479
Ehrhart Museum, Antwerp 41235
Ehrman Mansion, Tahoma 47928
Ehrwalder Heimatmuseum, Ehrwald 01795
Eicha-Museum, Bergeijk 28980
Eichsfelder Heimatmuseum, Heilbad Heiligenstadt 17684
Eide-Dalrymple Gallery, Sioux Falls 47643
Eidelstedter Heimatmuseum, Hamburg 17535
Eiderstedter Heimatmuseum, Sankt Peter-Ording 19757
Eidsberg og Mysen Historielag, Eidsberg 30471
Eidskog Museum, Eidskog 30472
Eidsvold Historical Complex, Eidsvold 01009
Eidsvoll 1814 - Rikspolitisk Senter, Eidsvoll Verk 30474
Eidsvoll Bygdemuseet, Eidsvoll Verk 30475
Eidsvoll Rural Museum, Eidsvoll Verk 30475
Eifelmuseum, Mayen 18668
Eifelmuseum Blankenheim, Blankenheim, Ahr 16179
Eighteenth Street Arts Complex, Santa Monica 47440
Eikaasgalleriet, Skei i Jølster 30843
Eiktunet Kulturhistorisk Museum, Gjøvik 30513
Eiktunet Museum of Local History, Gjøvik 30513
Eildon Hall Sibbald Memorial Museum, Sutton, Ontario 06522
Eilean Donan Castle Museum, Dornie 38757
Einar Jónsson Museum, Reykjavík 21653
Einari Vuorelan Kirjailijakoti, Keuruu 09660
Einbecker Schreibmaschinenmuseum, Einbeck 16812
Einsiedelei Erzherzog Maximilians des Deutschmeisters, Innsbruck 02063
Einstein-Haus, Bern 36540
Eisei Bunko Museum, Tokyo 26843
Eisenbahn-Museum Lokschuppen Aumühle, Aumühle bei Hamburg 15576
Eisenbahnmuseum, Deutsch Wagram 01758
Eisenbahnmuseum, Eschwege 16935
Eisenbahnmuseum, Falkenberg, Elster 16982
Eisenbahnmuseum, Vienenburg 20311
Eisenbahnmuseum Bayerischer Bahnhof zu Leipzig, Leipzig 18392
Eisenbahnmuseum Bochum-Dahlhausen, Bochum 16195
Eisenbahnmuseum Darmstadt-Kranichstein, Darmstadt 16538
Eisenbahnmuseum Historischer Wasserturm, Bebra 15862
Eisenbahnmuseum Lehmann, Hofheim, Unterfranken 17800
Eisenbahnmuseum Neustadt an der Weinstraße, Neustadt an der Weinstraße 19074
Eisenbahnmuseum - Sammlung Frey, Seifhennersdorf 19927
Eisenbahnmuseum Schwarzenberg, Schwarzenberg, Erzgebirge 19883
Eisenbahnmuseum Strasshof - Das Heizhaus, Strasshof 02706
Eisenbahnmuseum Vienenburg, Bad Zwesten 15781
Eisenerzer Krippenhaus, Eisenerz 01801
Eisenhammer Dorfchemnitz, Dorfchemnitz bei Sayda 16644
Eisenhower Birthplace, Denison 42870
Eisenhower National Historic Site, Gettysburg 43662
Eisenkunstgussmuseum, Büdelsdorf 16396
Eisenkunstgußmuseum, Witzenhausen 20636
Eisenmuseum, Ainring 15414
Eisenmuseum, Murau 02331
Eisenuhren- und Antikuhrenmuseum, Steyr 02682
Eisstockmuseum, Sankt Georgen im Attergau 02568
Eiteljorg Museum of American Indians and Western Art, Indianapolis 44217
Ekaterinburg Museum of Fine Art, Ekaterinburg 32766
Ekaterinburgskij Muzej Izobrazitelnych Iskusstv, Ekaterinburg 32766
Ekaterininskij Dvorec - Gosudarstvennyj Muzej Carskoje Selo, Puškin 33336
Ekehagens Forntidsby, Åsarp 35819
Ekenäs Museum, Ekenäs 09425
Ekenäs Slott, Linköping 36039
Eketahuna and Districts Museum, Eketahuna 30156
Eketorps Borg, Degerhamn 35851
Ekfrid Township Museum, Appin 05003
Ekhof-Theater, Gotha 17357
Ekomuseum Bergslagen, Smedjebacken 36207
Ekomuseum Gränsland och Strømstad Museum, Strømstad 36303
Ekron - The Philistine City and it's Culture, Shiqmim 22744
Eksi Şarkeserleri Müzesi, İstanbul 37700
Eksjö Museum med Albert Engströms Samlingarna, Eksjö 35860
Ėkspozicija "Čelovek. Duša. Duchovnost.", Ivanovo 32826
Ėkspozicija "Ivanovskaja starina", Ivanovo 32827
EKZ-Museum Stromhaus Burenwisen, Glattfelden 36766
El-Barkai Museum, Khartoum 35764
El Camino College Art Gallery, Torrance 48038
El Campo Museum of Natural History, El Campo 43105
El Dorado County Historical Museum, Placerville 46537
El-Ibied Regional Museum, Khartoum 35765
El Monte Historical Society Museum, El Monte 43109
El Morro National Monument, Ramah 46782
El Museo Naval de el Ferrol, Ferrol 34815
El Paso Holocaust Museum, El Paso 43115
El Paso Museum of Art, El Paso 43116
El Paso Museum of History, El Paso 43117
El Pueblo Museum, Pueblo 46738
El Rancho de Las Golondrinas Museum, Santa Fe 47417
Elabuga Regional Museum, Elabuga 32787
Elabuga State Museum-Preserve of History, Architecture and Art, Elabuga 32785
Elabužskij Gosudarstvennyj Istoriko-architekturnyj i Chudožestvennyj Muzej-zapovednik, Elabuga 32785
Eläinmuseo, Helsinki 09480
Elagin Island Palace - Museum of Russian Decorative and Applied Art and Interior Design of the 18th-20th c., Sankt-Peterburg 33393
Elaginoostrovskij Dvorec-Muzej Russkogo Dekorativno -Prikladnogo Iskusstva i Interjera XVIII-XX vv., Sankt-Peterburg 33393
Elazıg Archaeological and Ethnological Museum, Elazıg 37667
Elazıg Arkeoloji ve Etnografi Müzesi, Elazıg 37667
Elbasan Museum, Elbasan 00018
Elbert Hubbard-Roycroft Museum, East Aurora 43035
Elberton Granite Museum, Elberton 43127
Elbow Museum, Elbow 05399
Elbschiffahrtsmuseum mit stadtgeschichtlicher Sammlung, Lauenburg 18350
Elbschloss Bleckede, Bleckede 16184
Elder Art Gallery, Lincoln 44781
Eldnäset Flottningsmuseum, Ånge 35803
Eldon House, London 05763
Eldorado Museum, Eldorado 01010
Eldridge Street Project, New York 45796
Eleanor Barbour Cook Museum of Geology, Chadron 42179
Eleanor Roosevelt National Historic Site, Hyde Park 44186
Eleckij Literaturno-memorialnyj Muzej Pisatelja I.A. Bunina, Elec 32791
Electric Ladyland, Amsterdam 28849
Electric Mountain - Museum of North Wales, Llanberis 39534
Electrical Engineering Museum, Fredericton 05459
The Electrical Industry Museum, Teheran 22293
Electrobroc, Broc 36590
Eleftheriadis Collection, Petra 21119
Eleftherios K. Venizelos Museum, Athinai 20858
Eleker Heimatmuseum, Leimen, Baden 18372
Elektriciteits- en Techniekmuseum, Hoenderloo 29428
Elektrizitätsmuseum, Münchenstein 36963
Elektrizitätszähler-Kabinett, Braunschweig 16295
Elektro Museum, Baden 36483
Elektro-Museum, Hilden 17755
Elektro-Museum Schleswag, Rendsburg 19568
Elektropathologisches Museum, Wien 02875
Elephantine Island's Museum, Aswan 09249
Elfenbein-Museum, Michelstadt 18728
Elfenbeinmuseum, Walldürn 20377
Elfreth's Alley Museum, Philadelphia 46406
The Elgar Birthplace Museum, Lower Broadheath 39835
Elgin Apple Museum, Grabouw 34248
Elgin County Pioneer Museum, Saint Thomas 06374
Elgin Military Museum, Saint Thomas 06375
Elgin Museum, Elgin 38925
Elgin Public Museum, Elgin 43129
Elham Valley Railway Museum, Folkestone 38999
Eli Whitney Museum, Hamden 43876
Eliasu Dzimtas Muzejs Zīlēni, Platone 27395
Elijah Clark Memorial Museum, Lincolnton 44800
Elimäen Kotiseutumuseo ja Koulumuseo, Elimäki 09428
Elimäen Koulumuseo, Elimäki 09429
Elimäki District Museum and Schoolmuseum, Elimäki 09428
Elimäki School Museum, Elimäki 09429
Elin Pelin House-Museum, Bajlovo 04608
Elingaard Museum, Gressvik 30518
Elisabet Ney Museum, Austin 41409
Elisarov Apartment Museum, Sankt-Peterburg 33451
Eliza Cruce Hall Doll Museum, Ardmore 41252
Elizabeth Bay House, Elizabeth Bay 01011
Elizabeth Castle, Saint Helier 40400
Elizabeth D. Walters Library, Stroudsburg 47854
Elizabeth Farm, Rosehill 01424
Elizabeth Myers Mitchell Art Gallery, Annapolis 41227
Elizabeth O'Neill Verner Studio Museum, Charleston 42215
Elizabeth P. Korn Gallery, Madison 45061
Elizabeth Perkins House, York 48787
Elizabeth Rozier Gallery, Jefferson City 44328
Elizabeth Sage Historic Costume Collection, Bloomington 41745
Elizabeth Slocumb Galleries, Johnson City 44345
Elizabethan House Museum, Great Yarmouth 39123
Elk Grove Farmhouse Museum, Elk Grove Village 43136
Elk Lake Heritage Museum, Elk Lake 05401
Elkhart County Historical Museum, Bristol 41902
Ella Sharp Museum, Jackson 44276
The Ellen Noel Art Museum of the Permian Basin, Odessa 46093
Ellen Terry Memorial Museum, Tenterden 40686
Ellenroad Engine House, Milnrow 39959
Ellermeiers Burgmannshof, Hardegsen 17616
Ellerslie Shellfish Museum, Tyne Valley 06654
Elli Riehl-Puppenmuseum, Treffen bei Villach 02739
Ellingson Car Museum, Rogers 46986
Elliot Colliery Winding House, New Tredegar 40017
Elliot Lake Nuclear and Mining Museum, Elliot Lake 05404
Elliott Avedon Museum and Archives of Games, Waterloo 06753
Elliott Museum, Stuart 47857
Ellis County Museum, Waxahachie 48469
Ellisland Farm, Ellisland 38928
Ellsworth County Museum, Ellsworth 43162
Ellwood House Museum, DeKalb 42855
Elman W. Campbell Museum, Newmarket 05987
Elmbridge Museum, Weybridge 40841
Elmhurst Art Museum, Elmhurst 43165
Elmhurst Historical Museum, Elmhurst 43166
Elmira Railway Museum, Elmira 05405
Elmore Progress Association Station Museum, Elmore 01012
Elmuseet, Bjerringbro 08783
Eloaitta, Kaavi 09607
Eloise Pickard Smith Gallery, Santa Cruz 47409
Elrose Heritage Museum, Elrose 05406
Elsenzer Heimatstuben, Eppingen 16878
Elstow Moot Hall, Bedford 38148
Eltham Palace, London 39631
Elvarheim Museum, Åmli 30381
Elvaston Castle Working Estate Museum, Elvaston 38931
Elvehjem Museum of Art, Madison 45067
Elvis History World, Gstatterboden 01966
Elwood Haynes Museum, Kokomo 44526
Ely Museum, Ely 38933
Elztalmuseum - Regionalgeschichte und Orgelbau, Waldkirch 20366
E.M. Pjatnicky Folk Museum, Aleksandrovka 32636
E.M. Violette Museum, Kirksville 44502
Emailmuseum Gertrude Stöhr, Vorchdorf 02774
Emanuel Vigeland Museum, Oslo 30730
Emba Museum of Chinese Modern Art, Ashiya 26110
Embom-Garpom Backstugusittarstuga, Liljendal 09783
Embroiderers Guild Museum, Mile End 01253
Embroiderers' Guild Museum Collection, East Molesey 38847

Embsay Bolton Abbey Steam Railway, Skipton 40528
Emerald Art Gallery, Emerald 01015
Emerald Museum, Emerald 01016
Emerson Gallery, Clinton 42499
Emeryk Hutten-Czapski Museum, Kraków 31700
Emigrantmuseet, Kisa 36008
Emil A. Blackmore Museum of the American Legion, Indianapolis 44218
Emil Cedercreutzin Museo, Harjavalta 09464
Emil Wikström Museo, Valkeakoski 10170
Emīla Dārziņa Muzejs, Jaunpiebalga 27358
Emila Melngaiļa Memoriālais Muzejs, Vidriži 27474
Emile Van Doren Museum, Genk 03430
Emile Verhaeren Museum, Sint-Amands 03734
Emilio Aguinaldo Shrine Museum, Kawit 31337
Emīls Dārziņš Museum, Jaunpiebalga 27358
Emily Carr Arts Centre Museum, Victoria 06719
Emirates Very Special Arts, Sharjah 37920
Emma Kunz-Museum, Würenlos 37352
Emmaville Mining Museum, Emmaville 01017
Emmerich Kálmán-Gedenkraum, Wien 02876
Emmett Kelly Historical Museum, Sedan 47556
Emperor Maximilian of Mexico Museum, Hardegg 02002
Emphiedzhiev House-Museum, Kjustendil 04708
Empire Area Heritage Group - History Museum, Empire 43181
Empire State Aerosciences Museum, Glenville 43697
Emporia State University Geology Museum, Emporia 43182
Emsland-Moormuseum, Geeste 17208
Emslandmuseum Lingen, Lingen 18482
Emslandmuseum Schloß Clemenswerth, Sögel 19974
Emsworth Museum, Emsworth 38936
Emu Park Historical Museum, Emu Park 01018
Enchanted Mansion Doll Museum, Baton Rouge 41526
Enchanted World Doll Museum, Mitchell 45413
End-O-Line Railroad Museum, Currie 42731
End of Steel Heritage Museum, Hines Creek 05598
Endeavour Museum, Cessnock 00904
Enderby and District Museum, Enderby 05408
Endowment of King Petar I Karadjordjevic, Topola 33921
Endre Nemes Múzeum, Pécs 21505
Enebakk Bygdetun, Trysil 30947
Enebakk Museet, Enebakk 30479
Energeia - Museum voor het Industrieel erfgoed Electrabel, Gent 03436
EnergeticA, Museum voor Energietechniek, Amsterdam 28850
Energiemuseum, Fürstenfeldbruck 17160
Enfield Historical Society Museum, Enfield 43188
Enfield Shaker Museum, Enfield 43189
Engadiner Museum, Sankt Moritz 37112
Engelenburg House Art Collection, Pretoria 34342
Engine House, Dunedin 30147
Engine House Project, Chelmsford 38538
Engineering Museum of Catalonia, Barcelona 34547
Englehart and Area Historical Museum, Englehart 05409
English Heritage, East Midlands Region, Northampton 49410
English Heritage North West Region, Manchester 49411
English Heritage South East Region, Guildford 39135
English Heritage South West Region, Bristol 38354
English Heritage West Midlands Region, Birmingham 38221
Engraving Print Village Art Museum, Aikawa 26088
Engsö Slott, Västerås 36378
Engströmsgården, Hult 35967
Enisejskij Kraevedčeskij Muzej, Enisejsk 32796
Enkhuizer Almanak Museum, Enkhuizen 29231
Enköpings Museum, Enköping 35866
Ennejma Ezzahra-Palais du Baron d'Erlanger, Sidi Bou Saïd 37582
Ennsmuseum Kastenreith, Weyer 02826
Enoagrarimuseum, Castelvetrano 23428
Enoch Turner Schoolhouse, Toronto 06576
Enook Galleries, Waterloo 06754
Enoteca Regionale del Monferrato, Vignale Monferrato 26009
Enoteca Regionale Permanente la Serenissima, Gradisca d'Isonzo 24039
Ente Museo Poschiavino, Poschiavo 37030
Entlebucher Heimatmuseum, Schüpfheim 37146
Entomological Museum of Fujikyu, Fujiyoshida 26140
Entomological Society Museum, Cairo 09263
Entomologické Oddělení, Praha 08573
Entomology Research Museum, Riverside 46918
Enviromental Museum, Azpeitia 34513
Environmental Education Center, Basking Ridge 41518
Enwald-Museo, Liperi 09789
Eötvös Loránd Emlékkiállítás, Budapest 21335
Eparchial Church-historical Museum, Samara 33376
Epcot, Lake Buena Vista 44579
Epema-State, Ijsbrechtum 29460
Ephesos-Museum, Wien 02877
Ephesus Museum, Selçuk 37779
Ephraim Foundation Museums, Ephraim 43193
Ephrata Cloister, Ephrata 43195
Épicerie-Musée Klein, Scherwiller 14681
Epigraphical Museum, Athinai 20859
Epigraphy Museum, Tripoli 27505
Epping Forest District Museum, Waltham Abbey 40777
Eptek National Exhibition Centre, Summerside 06514
Epworth Old Rectory, Epworth 38945
Equine Museum, Gwacheon 27179
Equine Museum of Japan, Yokohama 27012
Erbacher Heimatzimmer, Eltville 16841
Erddig Agricultural Museum, Wrexham 40940
Erdgeschichtliches Werksmuseum der ZEAG, Lauffen am Neckar 18355
Erdölmuseum, Neusiedl an der Zaya 02358
Eregli Arkeoloji ve Etnografi Müzesi, Eregli 37668
Eretz-Israel Museum Tel Aviv, Tel Aviv 22753
Erewash Museum, Ilkeston 39286
Erfatal-Museum Hardheim, Hardheim 17617
Eric Thomas Galley Museum, Queenstown 01403
Erica Underwood Gallery, Bentley 00797
Erich Kästner Museum Dresden, Dresden 16680
Erich Mäder-Glasmuseum, Grünenplan 17446
Erich Maria Remarque-Friedenszentrum, Osnabrück 19277
Erichsens Gaard, Rønne 09038
Ericsbergs Slott, Mellösa 36093
Erie Art Museum, Erie 43200
Erie Canal Museum, Syracuse 47907
Erie Canal Village, Rome 46995
Erie History Center, Erie 43201
Eriksbergs Museum, Tranås 36330
Eriksborg Carriage Museum, Ystad 36421
Eriksborg Vagnmuseum, Ystad 36421
Eriksdale Museum, Eriksdale 05412
Erinnerungsstätte Baltringer Haufen Bauernkrieg in Oberschwaben, Mietingen 18736
Erinnerungsstätte für die Freiheitsbewegungen in der deutschen Geschichte, Rastatt 19486
Erith Museum, Erith 38946
Eritrean Archaeological Museum, Asmara 09315
Erkebispegården, Trondheim 30937
Erkel Ferenc Múzeum, Gyula 21423
Erkenbert-Museum, Frankenthal, Pfalz 17029
Erland Lee Museum, Stoney Creek 06493
Erlauftaler Feuerwehrmuseum, Purgstall an der Erlauf 02463
Erlichthof, Rietschen 19611
Ermatinger, Sault Sainte Marie 06411
Ermelova House Museum, Moskva 33038
Ermita de San Antonio de la Florida y Museo Panteón de Goya, Madrid 35006
Ermita de San Baudelio de Berlanga, Caltojar 34663
Erna och Victor Hasselblads Fotografiska Centrum, Göteborg 35910
Ernest and Marion Davis Medical History Museum, Auckland 30106
Ernest Hemingway House Museum, Key West 44464
The Ernest W. Michel Historical Judaica Collection, New York 45797
Ernesta Birznieka-Upīša Muzejs Bisnieki, Zentene 27477
Ernie Pyle House, Dana 42769
Ernst Barlach Haus, Hamburg 17536
Ernst Barlach Museum, Ratzeburg 19499
Ernst Barlach Museum Wedel, Wedel 20414
Ernst Barlach Stiftung Güstrow, Güstrow 17456
Ernst-Bloch-Zentrum, Ludwigshafen am Rhein 18517
Ernst Fuchs-Privatmuseum, Wien 02878
Ernst Glück Museum of the Bible, Alūksne 27331
Ernst-Haeckel-Haus, Jena 17938
Ernst-Moritz-Arndt-Haus, Bonn 16235
Ernst-Moritz-Arndt-Museum, Garz, Rügen 17205
Ernst Múzeum, Budapest 21336
Ernsta Glika Bībeles Muzejs, Alūksne 27331
Erotic Art Museum Hamburg, Hamburg 17537
Erotik-Museum, Berlin 15944
Erotisch Museum, Amsterdam 28851
Errol Station Railway Heritage Centre, Blairgowrie 38254
Ersta Diakonimuseum, Stockholm 36239
Erstes Allgäu-Schwäbisches Dorfschulmuseum, Erkheim 16911
Erstes Bayerisches Schulmuseum, Sulzbach-Rosenberg 20124
Erstes Circusmuseum in Deutschland, Preetz, Holstein 19440
Erstes Deutsches Historic-Actien-Museum, Kürnbach 18261
Erstes Deutsches Motorroller-Museum, Aschaffenburg 15521
Erstes Deutsches Museum für mechanische Musikinstrumente, Rüdesheim am Rhein 19704
Erstes Deutsches Strumpfmuseum, Gelenau, Erzgebirge 17222
Erstes Deutsches Türmermuseum, Vilseck 20324
Erstes Ethnisches Puppenmuseum der Welt, Kreuth 18233
Erstes Imaginäres Museum - Sammlung Günter Dietz, Wasserburg am Inn 20406
Erstes Internationales Wolpertingermuseum, Mittenwald 18753
Erstes Kärntner Handwerksmuseum, Baldramsdorf 01732
Erstes Korkenziehermuseum der Welt, Kreuth 18234
Erstes Nachttopf-Museum der Welt, München 18843
Erstes Niederbayerisches Automobil- und Motorrad-Museum, Adlkofen 15398
Erstes Niederrheinisches Karneval-Museum, Duisburg 16747
Erstes Oberösterreichisches Schnapsmuseum, Sankt Oswald bei Freistadt 02590
Erstes Österreichisches Friedensmuseum und Heimatstube, Wolfsegg 03044
Erstes Österreichisches Funk- und Radiomuseum, Wien 02879
Erstes Österreichisches Museum für Alltagsgeschichte, Neupölla 02356
Erstes Österreichisches Rettungsmuseum, Hohenems 02040
Erstes Österreichisches Tischler-Museum, Pöchlarn 02421
Erstes Osterhasen Museum der Welt, München 18844
Erstes Schutzengel-Museum der Welt, Kreuth 18235
Erstes Südburgenländisches Schnapsbrennereimuseum, Kukmirn 02170
Erstes Tiroler Feuerwehrmuseum, Schwaz 02646
Erstes Tiroler Holzmuseum, Wildschönau 03030
Erstes Tretauto-Museum der Welt, München 18845
Erstes Urgeschichtliches Freilichtmuseum der Steiermark, Kulm bei Weiz 02171
Erstes Waldviertler Webereimuseum, Waidhofen an der Thaya 02782
Erwin Museum, Painted Post 46263
Erwin von Kreibig-Museum, München 18846
Eryldene Heritage House, Gordon 01065
Erzbergbahn- und Wintersportmuseum, Vordernberg 02777
Erzbischöfliches Diözesanmuseum Köln, Köln 18135
Erzbischöfliches Diözesanmuseum und Domschatzkammer, Paderborn 19333
Erzbischöfliches Dom- und Diözesanmuseum, Wien 02880
Erzgebirgische Volkskunst Ausstellung, Grünhainichen 17448
Erzgebirgische Volkskunststube, Bermsgrün 16120
Erzgebirgischer Spielzeugwinkel, Obereisenheim 19173
Erzgebirgisches Freilichtmuseum, Kurort Seiffen 18275
Erzgebirgisches Heimatmuseum Hospital Sankt Johannis, Sayda 19763
Erzgebirgisches Spielzeugmuseum, Kurort Seiffen 18276
Erzgebirgisches Spielzeugmuseum, Liestal 36877
Erzgebirgsmuseum mit Besucherbergwerk, Annaberg-Buchholz 15497
Erzherzog Franz-Ferdinand Museum, Artstetten 01681
Erzherzog Johann-Dokumentationsstätte, Thernberg 02729
Erzincan Culture Center, Erzincan 37669
Erzincan Kültür Merkezi, Erzincan 37669
Erzstollen Silbergründle, Seebach, Baden 19909
Erzurum Archeological and Ethnographical Museum, Erzurum 37671
Erzurum Arkeoloji ve Etnografi Müzesi, Erzurum 37671
Erzurum Culture Center, Erzurum 37672
Erzurum Kültür Merkezi, Erzurum 37672
Erzurum Resim ve Heykel Müzesi, Erzurum 37673
Erzurum State Painting and Sculpture Museum, Erzurum 37673
Esbjerg Art Museum, Esbjerg 08806
Esbjerg Kunstmuseum, Esbjerg 08806
Esbjerg Museum, Esbjerg 08807
Escuela Museo de Bellas Artes General Urquiza, Buenos Aires 00148
Esglesia de Sant Feliu, Xàtiva 35703
Esglesia de Sant Francesc, Palma de Mallorca 35225
Esglesia de Santa María, Elche 34789
Eshvin Literary Museum, Syktyvkar 33571
Esie Museum, Esie 30337
Eskbank House, Lithgow 01180
Eskilstuna Konstmuseum, Eskilstuna 35869
Eskimo Museum, Churchill 05250
Eskişehir Archaeological Museum, Eskişehir 37674
Eskişehir Arkeoloji Müzesi, Eskişehir 37674
Eskişehir Atatürk ve Kültür Müzesi, Eskişehir 37675
Eskişehir Devlet Güzel Sanatlar Galerisi, Eskişehir 37676
Eskişehir State Gallery, Eskişehir 37676
Eskoriatzako Museo Eskola, Eskoriatza 34802
Eslövs Stadsmuseum, Eslöv 35874
Espace Architectural Normand, Crévecœur-en-Auge 11459
Espace Arlaud, Lausanne 36853
Espace Arts Plastiques, Vénissieux 15119
Espace Automobiles Matra, Romorantin-Lanthenay 14019
Espace Bastides, Monflanquin 13014
Espace Cro-Magnon-Musée et Parc, Thonac 14893
Espace Croquet, Condé-sur-Seulles 11388
Espace Culturel Hippolite-Mars, Équeurdreville-Hainneville 11636
Espace d'Art Brut, Brunstatt 10950
Espace d'Art Contemporain, Marseille 12848
Espace d'Art Contemporain Camille-Lambert, Juvisy-sur-Orge 12110
Espace de la Route Romane d'Alsace, Guebwiller 11961
Espace de l'Art Concret, Mouans-Sartoux 13175
Espace des Saveurs, Herve 03496
Espace des Sciences, Rennes (Ille-et-Vilaine) 13940
Espace d'Exposition Minal, Héricourt 12012
Espace du Cheminot, Nîmes 13334
Espace Gallo-Romain, Ath 03187
Espace Géologique "Les Frissons de la Terre", Château-Queyras 11206
Espace Hennessy, Cognac 11341
Espace Horloger de la Vallée de Joux, Le Sentier 37163
Espace Jean-de-Joigny, Joigny (Yonne) 12080
Espace Jean Tinguely - Niki de Saint-Phalle, Fribourg 36711
Espace Joseph Besset, Vanosc 15084
Espace-Jouets, Firminy 11738
Espace Lausannoise d'Art Contemporain, Lausanne 36854
Espace Maritime et Portuaire des Docks Vauban, Le Havre 12423
Espace Minéralogique Minéraux Couleur Nature, Eymoutiers 11688
Espace Mira Phalaina, Montreuil 13140
Espace Muséal, Orcet 13417
Espace Muséal, Rosheim 14038
Espace Muséal, Saint-Bris-le-Vineux 14134
Espace Muséal, Thann 14878
Espace Muséal Arago, Estagel 11660
Espace Muséal Archéologique, Alba-la-Romaine 10268
Espace Muséal de Beaux-Arts, Fontvieille 11782
Espace Muséal de la Maison du Berger, Châtillon-sur-Saône 11240
Espace Muséal de la Maison du Cordonnier, Châtillon-sur-Saône 11241
Espace Muséal de la Route Romane d'Alsace, Neuwiller-les-Saverne 13300
Espace Muséal du Four à Pain, Wasigny 15303
Espace Muséal Les Courtinals, Moureze 13192
Espace Musée, Freissinières 11807
Espace Muséographique, Saint-Goazec 14255
Espace Paul Rebeyrolle, Eymoutiers 11689
Espace Pierre Bonnard, Le Cannet 12395
Espace Pierres Folles, Saint-Jean-des-Vignes 14287
Espace Salvador Dalí, Paris 13500
Espace Verre, Vannes-le-Châtel 15080
Espace Vini-Viticole, Nissan-lez-Ensérune 13347
Espace Virtuel, Chicoutimi 05246
Espaço Cultural da Marinha, Rio de Janeiro 04323
Espaço dos Anjos, Leopoldina 04173
Espaço Lucio Costa, Brasília 03995
Espaço Museu da Vida, Rio de Janeiro 04324
Esperance Museum, Esperance 01020
Espersit Ház, Makó 21467
Espoo City Museum, Espoo 09431
Espoo City Museum, Glims Farmstead Museum, Espoo 09434
Espoon Automuseo, Espoo 09430
Espoon Kaupunginmuseo, Espoo 09431
Esposizione Forte Airolo, Airolo 36441
Essentukskij Gorodskoj Kraevedčeskij Muzej im. V.P. Špakovskogo, Essentuki 32798
Essex Historical Museum, Essex 43212
Essex Police Museum, Chelmsford 38539
Essex Regiment Museum, Chelmsford 38540
Essex Secret Bunker Museum, Mistley 39968
Essex Shipbuilding Museum, Essex 43213
Essig Museum of Entomology, Berkeley 41642
Essley-Noble Museum, Aledo 41115
Estação Ciência / EST CIENC, São Paulo 04490
Estación Enológica, Haro 34897
Estación Experimental de Zonas Áridas, Almería 34452
Estación Ferrocarril Bejucal, Bejucal 07864
Estate Ismaylovo, Moskva 33181
Esterházy-Ausstellung, Eisenstadt 01808
Esterhazy Community Museum, Esterhazy 05413
Esterházy Paláce, Bratislava 33959
Esterházy Palais, Sopron 21531
Esterhazy Palais of the Slovak National Gallery, Bratislava 33959
Esterházy-Palota, Sopron 21531
Estes Park Area Historical Museum, Estes Park 43216
Estes-Winn Antique Automobile Museum, Asheville 41279
Estevan National Exhibition Centre, Art Gallery and Museum, Estevan 05415
Esther M. Klein Art Gallery, Philadelphia 46407
Esther Prangley Rice Gallery, Westminster 48562
The Esther Thomas Atkinson Museum, Hampden-Sydney 43891
Estonian Agricultural Museum, Tõrvandi 09391
Estonian Dairy Museum, Imavere 09326
Estonian Health Care Museum, Tallinn 09364
Estonian History Museum, Tallinn 09356
Estonian Literary Museum, Tartu 09374
Estonian Maritime Museum, Tallinn 09360
Estonian Museum of Applied Art and Design, Tallinn 09362
Estonian Museum of Natural History, Tallinn 09359
Estonian Museum Society in Tallinn, Tallinn 49150
Estonian Museum Society in Tartu, Tartu 49151
Estonian Museums Association, Tartu 49152
Estonian National Defence College Museum, Tartu 09378
Estonian National Museum, Tartu 09376
Estonian Open Air Museum, Tallinn 09365
Estonian Railway Museum, Haapsalu 09317
Estonian Railway Museum Lavassaare, Tallinn 09361
Estonian Sports Museum, Tartu 09377
Estonian Theatre and Music Museum, Tallinn 09363
Estonien Museum of Postal Services, Tartu 09375
Estorick Collection of Modern Italian Art, London 39632
Estudio Museo Ramoneda, Humahuaca 00364
ESWE Technicum, Wiesbaden 20571
E.T.A. Hoffmann-Haus mit Sammlung, Bamberg 15805
Etelä-Karjalan Museo, Lappeenranta 09760
Etelä-Karjalan Taidemuseo, Lappeenranta 09761
Etelä-Pohjanmaan Maakuntamuseo, Seinäjoki 10028
Ethnic Doll and Toy Museum, Canterbury 38473
Ethniki Pinakothiki & Mouseio Alexander Soytzoy, Athinai 20860

Ethnografic and Archeological Museum of the Ufa Scientific Section of the Russian Academy of Sciences, Ufa 33645
Ethnograghic Exhibition, Svištov 04878
Ethnographic and Archeological Collection, Visoko 03930
Ethnographic and Archtectural Museum of Wood Arts and Crafts Hohlovka, Perm 33300
Ethnographic and Archtectural Museum Village at Angara River, Bratsk 32702
Ethnographic Complex, Historical Museum, Vraca 04928
Ethnographic Exhibition Stoyo House, Radomir 04793
Ethnographic Exposition, Pazardžik 04755
Ethnographic Exposition - Vajnory House, Bratislava 33980
Ethnographic Museum, Addis Ababa 09398
Ethnographic Museum, Afyon 37603
Ethnographic Museum, Antalya 37624
Ethnographic Museum, Avgorou 08185
Ethnographic Museum, Bérat 00012
Ethnographic Museum, Durrës 00016
Ethnographic Museum, Gjirokastër 00022
Ethnographic Museum, Guwahati 21821
Ethnographic Museum of Istria, Pazin 07754
Ethnographic Museum of Moldavia, Iași 32535
Ethnographic Museum of the Elbe Region, Přerov 08623
Ethnographic Museum of the Kasan University, Kazan 32887
Ethnographic Museum of the Peoples of the Baykal Region, Ulan-Udė 33652
Ethnographic Museum of the Slovak National Museum, Martin 34022
Ethnographic Museum, University Museum of Cultural Heritage, Oslo 30731
Ethnographic Open Air Museum, Szombathely 21590
Ethnographic Open Air Museum of Ibresi, Ibresi 32810
Ethnographic Open-Air Museum of Latvia, Rīga 27415
Ethnographic Revival Complex, Kavarna 04695
Ethnographical Collection of Jr. József Lele, Szeged 21548
Ethnographical Collection of the Franciscan Monastery, Zaostrog 07842
Ethnographical Collection of the West Bohemian Museum in Pilsen, Plzeň 08543
Ethnographical complex, Kalipetrovo 04685
Ethnographical Department of the Historical Museum, Praha 08605
Ethnographical Historical Museum of Lárissa, Lárissa 21042
Ethnographical House-Museum, Dobrič 04654
Ethnographical Institute of the Moravian Museum, Brno 08267
Ethnographical Museum, Aden 49005
Ethnographical Museum, Ankara 37617
Ethnographical Museum, Berkovica 04620
Ethnographical Museum, Burgas 04633
Ethnographical Museum, Doha 32416
Ethnographical Museum, Elchovo 04662
Ethnographical Museum, Jasenovo 33844
Ethnographical Museum, Khartoum 35766
Ethnographical Museum, Kraków 31701
Ethnographical Museum, Nagyvázsony 21489
Ethnographical Museum, Paphos 08214
Ethnographical Museum, Plovdiv 04776
Ethnographical Museum, Silistra 04814
Ethnographical Museum, Turkmenbashi 37821
Ethnographical Museum, Varna 04895
Ethnographical Museum, Włocławek 32161
Ethnographical Museum, Zagreb 07813
Ethnographical Museum Dunabian Fishing and Boatbuilding, Tutrakan 04891
Ethnographical Museum of Liptov, Liptovský Hrádok 34013
Ethnographical Museum of Transylvania, Cluj-Napoca 32492
Ethnographical Museum Tavrika, Simferopol 37903
Ethnographical Museumof Serbia, Beograd 33794
Ethnographische Sammlung, Fribourg 36712
Ethnographisches Freilichtmuseum, Szenna 21566
Ethnographisches Museum Pöykkölä, Rovaniemi 10000
Ethnographisches Museum Schloss Kittsee, Kittsee 02117
Ethnography and Folk Art Museum, Orăştie 32563
Ethnography Collection, Sopron 21535
Ethnography Museum, Tripoli 27506
Ethnological and Folklore Museum, Chios 20923
Ethnological Collection, Koprivnički 07720
Ethnological Museum, Cairo 09264
Ethnological Museum, Chittagong 03080
Ethnological Museum, Gdańsk 31570
Ethnological Museum, Johannesburg 34275
Ethnological Museum, Pune 21989
Ethnological Museum, Teheran 22294
Ethnological Museum, Teheran 22295
Ethnological Museum, Zamboanga 31469
Ethnological Museum of Pyrsogianni Stonemasons, Konitsa 21027
Ethnologisches Museum, Berlin 15945
Ethnology Museum, Węgorzewo 32148
Etnografi Müzesi, Antalya 37624
Etnografi Museoa, Arcienaga 34476
Ėtnografičeskij Muzej Kazanskogo Universiteta, Kazan 32887
Ėtnografičeskij Muzej Narodov Zabajkalja, Ulan-Udė 33652
Ėtnografičeskij Muzej pod Otkrytym Nebom Torum Maa, Chanty-Mansijsk 32742
Ėtnografičeskij Muzej Tavrika, Simferopol 37903
Etnografické Múzeum, Martin 34022
Etnografické muzeum, Tovačov 08683
Etnografický Ústav, Brno 08267
Etnografisch Museum, Antwerpen 03141
Etnografische Collecties van de Universiteit Gent, Gent 03437
Etnografisk Museum, Oslo 30731
Etnografiska Museet, Stockholm 36240
Etnografski Kompleks na Istoričeski Muzej, Vraca 04928
Etnografska Ekspozicija, Pazardžik 04755
Etnografska Ekspozicija, Svištov 04878
Etnografska Ekspozicija Stojova KäsB3ta, Radomir 04793
Etnografska Zbirka, Koprivnički 07720
Etnografska Zbirka Franjevačkog Samostana, Zaostrog 07842
Etnografska Zbirka i Lapidarij Franjevačke Gimnazije, Visoko 03930
Etnografski Kompleks, Kalipetrovo 04685
Etnografski Kompleks Starijat Dobrič, Dobrič 04653
Etnografski Muzej, Berkovica 04620
Etnografski muzej, Burgas 04633
Etnografski Muzej, Dobrič 04654
Etnografski Muzej, Elchovo 04662
Etnografski Muzej, Plovdiv 04776
Etnografski Muzej, Silistra 04814
Etnografski Muzej, Varna 04895
Etnografski Muzej, Zagreb 07813
Etnografski Muzej Crne Gore, Cetinje 33831
Etnografski Muzej Dunavski Ribolov i Lodkostroenie, Tutrakan 04891
Etnografski Muzej Split, Split 07780
Etnografski Muzej Srbije, Beograd 33794
Etnografski-văzroždenski Kompleks, Kavarna 04695
Etnografya Müzesi, Ankara 37617
Etnološka Muzejska Zbirka, Jasenovo 33844
Etnomuseo dei Monti Lepini, Roccagorga 25138
Eton College Natural History Museum, Eton 38950
Etowah Indian Mounds Historical Site, Cartersville 42122
Etruria Industrial Museum, Stoke-on-Trent 40604
Etzel Museum, Tel Aviv 22754
Eubie Blake National Jazz Museum and Cultural Center, Baltimore 41465
Eugeen Van Mieghem Museum, Antwerpen 03142
Eugene Field House and Saint Louis Toy Museum, Saint Louis 47120
Eugene O'Neill National Historic Site, Danville 42776
Eugene V. Debs Home, Terre Haute 47983
Die Eulenburg, Rinteln 19617
Eulenspiegel Museum, Mölln 18765
Eumundi Museum, Eumundi 01021
Euphrat Museum of Art, Cupertino 42730
Eureka Fire Museum, Milltown 45349
Eureka Museum, Ballarat 00762
Eureka - Parque de la Ciencia, Mendoza 00432
Eureka Pioneer Museum of McPherson County, Eureka 43233
Eureka School House, Springfield 47759
Eureka! The Museum for Children, Halifax 39152
Eurocenter Sächsische Militärgeschichte, Kossa 18214
Europäische Glasmalerei- und Krippenausstellung, Schramberg 19846
Europäischer Skulpturenpark, Willebadessen 20596
Europäisches Brotmuseum, Ebergötzen 16762
Europäisches Industriemuseum für Porzellan und Europäisches Museum für Technische Keramik, Selb 19930
Europäisches Klempner- und Kupferschmiede-Museum, Karlstadt 18008
Europäisches Kulturzentrum Galerie Villa Rolandshof, Remagen 19559
Europäisches Museum für Frieden, Stadtschlaining 02673
Europäisches Spargelmuseum, Schrobenhausen 19851
European Association of Open Air Museums, Arnhem 49301
European Collaborative for Science, Industry and Technology Exhibitions, Bruxelles 49070
European Federation of Associations of Industrial and Technical Heritage, Terrassa 49373
European Folkcraft Museum, Kawakami 26325
European Foundation for Drawing, Meina 24343
European Museum Advisers Conference, Bruxelles 49072
European Museum Forum, Bristol 49412
Europos Parkas, Vilnius 27535
Euskal Arkeologia, Etnografia eta Kondaira Museoa, Bilbao 34611
Eustis Historical Museum, Eustis 43236
Euston Hall, Thetford 40696
Eva and Morris Feld Gallery, New York 45798
Eva Brook Donly Museum, Simcoe 06456
Eva Faschaunerin-Heimatmuseum, Gmünd, Kärnten 01886
Evangélikus Országos Múzeum, Budapest 21337
Evangelisches Diözesanmuseum, Fresach 01852
Evangelisches Diözesanmuseum, Murau 02332
Evangelisches Diözesanmuseum im Burgenland, Stoob 02701
Evangelisches Museum in Wien, Wien 02881
Evangelisches Museum Oberösterreich, Rutzenmoos 02529
Evanston Art Center, Evanston 43238
Evansville Museum of Arts and Science, Evansville 43245
Evelyn Payne Hatcher Museum of Anthropology, Saint Cloud 47084
Ėvenkijskij Okružnoj Kraevedčeskij Muzej, Tura 33635
Evergreen Aviation Museum, McMinnville 45041
Evergreen Firearms Museum, Belmont 05074
Evergreen Galleries, Olympia 46140
Evergreen Historic House, Dartmouth 05305
Evergreen House, Baltimore 41466
Everhart Museum of Natural History, Science and Art, Scranton 47517
Everson Museum of Art, Syracuse 47908
Evje og Hornnes Museum, Evje 30482
Evolutionsmuseet, Uppsala 36353
Evolutionsmuseet, Paleontologi, Uppsala 36354
Evraiko Mouseio tis Ellados, Athinai 20861
Ewelme Cottage, Auckland 30107
Ewha Womens University Museum, Seoul 27232
Ewha Yoja Taehakkyo Pakmulgwan, Seoul 27232
Ewing Gallery of Art and Architecture, Knoxville 44518
Ex Convento de Santo Domingo de Guzman, Oaxtepec 28280
Excell Blacksmith and Engineering Workshop Museum, Tumby Bay 01554
Excelsior House, Jefferson 44324
Excelsior-Lake Minnetonka Historical Museum, Excelsior 43250
Exchange Hotel Civil War Museum, Gordonsville 43729
The Executive Mansion, Frankfort 43507
Exhibit Museum of Natural History, Ann Arbor 41216
Exhibition at the Shipyard, Västanfjärd 10169
Exhibition Center and Gallery, Iževsk 32838
Exhibition Centre, Lisboa 32286
Exhibition Gallery of the Islamic Dáwah Centre, Bandar Seri Begawan 04597
Exhibition Hall, Čeboksary 32717
Exhibition Hall, Čerepovec 32734
Exhibition Hall, Český Těšín 08306
Exhibition Hall, Ha Noi 48975
Exhibition Hall, Jablunkov 08381
Exhibition Hall, Krasnodar 32948
Exhibition Hall, Krasnoturinsk 32962
Exhibition Hall Arsenals of the State Museum of Art, Rīga 27443
Exhibition Hall at the House of Scientists of the Sibirian Section of the Russian Academy of Sciences, Novosibirsk 33245
Exhibition Hall of Daugavpils Museum, Daugavpils 27346
Exhibition Hall of the Artists' Union of Russia, Sankt-Peterburg 33491
Exhibition Hall of the Karelian State Philharmonic, Petrozavodsk 33320
Exhibition Hall of the Kirov Regional Museum, Kirov 32926
Exhibition Hall of the Moscow Artists' Union, Moskva 33185
Exhibition Hall of the Regional Museum, Perm 33309
Exhibition Hall of the Republic Marij El, Joškar-Ola 32862
Exhibition Hall of the Saint-Petersburg Section of the Artists' Union of Russia, Sankt-Peterburg 33492
Exhibition Hall of the State Museum Reserve, Vologda 33725
Exhibition Hall of the Town, Angarsk 32640
Exhibition Hall of the Tver Regional Art Gallery, Tver 33640
Exhibition Hall of the Volgograd Art Museum, Volgograd 33720
Exhibition Hall of Victor and Apollinari Vasnetsov Art Museum, Kirov 32925
Exhibition Hall Rainbow, Čeboksary 32723
Exhibition Hall Rainbow, Samara 33371
Exhibition Hall - Russian Artists of the Government Samara, Žigulevsk 33749
Exhibition Hall Spasskyi Church, Irkutsk 32821
Exhibition Halls in Aksakov's House, Moskva 33184
Exhibition Halls of Liepāja Museum, Liepāja 27379
Exhibition House, Cēsis 27343
Exhibition Ivanovo's Ancient Times, Ivanovo 32827
Exhibition Man-Soul-Mind, Ivanovo 32826
Exhibition of 18th-19th Century Furniture, Čelarevo 33830
Exhibition of the Norwegian-American Historical Association, Northfield 46020
Exhibiton Hall of the Ekaterinburg Culture Association, Ekaterinburg 32784
Exhibtion Centre Ancient Tula of the Kulikovo Field Museum- preserve, Tula 33630
Exhibtion Hall of the Tula Museum of Fine Arts, Tula 33634
Exmouth Museum, Exmouth 38960
Experience Children's Museum, Erie 43202
Experience Music Project, Seattle 47533
Experimentarium, Hellerup 08857
Explora Museum, Frankfurt am Main 17040
Explora Science Center and Children's Museum, Albuquerque 41100
Exploration Place, Wichita 48600
Exploration Station, Boubonnais 41832
Exploration Station, Bourbonnais 41840
Exploratorio, San Isidro 00564
The Exploratorium, San Francisco 47316
Exploratorium - Kindermuseum Stuttgart und Region, Stuttgart 20089
Explorers Hall, Washington 48352
Explorion, Heerlen 29366
Exploris, Raleigh 46773
Expo Haringvliet, Stellendam 29855
Expo-Musée Renault, Boulogne-Billancourt 10835
Expo Rétro Catalane, Estagel 11661
Exposición de Gregorio de Laferrere, Gregorio de Laferrere 00358
Exposición Permanente de Cerámica Indígena, Manizales 07505
Exposición Roberto J. Mouras, Carlos Casares 00264
Expositie 40-45, Blitterswijk 28988
Expositie Versteend Leven, Drouwen 29183
Expositieruimte De Weem, Westeremden 29997
Exposition Apicole Péricard, Beurières 10713
Exposition Archéologique, Cruas 11465
Exposition Archéologique, Servian 14725
Exposition Archéologique de la Maison de la Cour, Givrand 11876
Exposition Archéologique Gallo-Romaine, Mandeure 12788
Exposition Artistique et Viticole, Aigues-Mortes 10235
Exposition Arts et Histoire, Mauvezin (Gers) 12900
Exposition Botanique, Villar-d'Arène 15173
Exposition Caillebotte, Yerres 15327
Exposition d'Archéologie Médiévale, Antignac 10379
Exposition d'Architecture et de Design, Villeurbanne 15248
Exposition d'Armes Anciennes, Olonzac 13402
Exposition d'Art, Nîmes 13335
Exposition d'Art, Saint-Céré 14140
Exposition d'Art Contemporain, Eymoutiers 11690
Exposition d'Art et d'Histoire, Evol 11680
Exposition d'Art et d'Histoire, Pionsat 13740
Exposition d'Art Populaire et Caveau, Caramany 11037
Exposition d'Arts, Saint-Racho 14440
Exposition d'Arts Populaires, Orcières 13419
Exposition de Beaux-Arts, Gramat 11896
Exposition de Coiffes et Dentelles de Bretagne, Guiclan 11972
Exposition de Cristal Berg, Lemberg 12511
Exposition de Faïences, Desvres 11502
Exposition de la Girouette, Le Coudray-Macquard 12403
Exposition de la Préhistoire, Mazières-en-Mauges 12911
Exposition de la Tour de Castellane, Épernay 11623
Exposition de l'Habitat Gallo-Romain, Auch 10469
Exposition de Peintures sur le Thème du Vin, Meursault 12963
Exposition de Tapisseries, Felletin 11716
Exposition des Compagnons du Devoir, Lyon 12725
Exposition des Éditions Tarmeye, Mazet-Saint-Voy 12910
Exposition des Vieux Métiers et Coutumes d'Antan, Labecede-Lauragais 12283
Exposition d'Etains Anciens Arsène Maigne, Gramat 11897
Exposition d'Œuvres de Sculptures, Canville-les-Deux-Églises 11030
Exposition du Château Fort du Fleckenstein, Lembach 12509
Exposition du Cloître des Cordeliers, Tarascon (Bouches-du-Rhône) 14860
Exposition du Compagnonnage, Pont-de-Veyle 13807
Exposition du Cristal, Hartzviller 11993
Exposition du Fort de l'Estissac, Port-Cros 13836
Exposition du Fort Sainte-Agathe, Porquerolles 13834
Exposition du Jouet en Bois, Arvieux-en-Queyras 10440
Exposition du Mémorial Capétien, Bernières-sur-Mer 10694
Exposition du Moulin à Huile, La Cadière-d'Azur 12132
Exposition du Petit Monde de Pagnol, Aubagne 10452
Exposition Ethnographique du Peuple Basque, Isturitz 12066
Exposition Gadal de Préhistoire et d'Archéologie, Tarascon-sur-Ariège 14863
Exposition Géologique du Gouffre de Proumeyssac, Le Bugue 12392
Exposition Historique, Cahors 10993
Exposition Historique, Jarrie 12073
Exposition Historique, Odenas 13385
Exposition Historique de l'Armagnac, Condom 11389
Exposition Historique du Château, La Roche-Maurice 12230
Exposition Historique du Monastère, Sauxillanges 14660
Exposition Historique Sword Beach, Hermanville-sur-Mer 12014
Exposition La Guerre de 100 Ans, Saint-Mesmin 14368
Exposition L'Eau dans tous ses États, Saint-Denis-de-Pile 14177
Exposition Mexico d'Hier et d'Aujourd'hui, Souillac 14784
Exposition Minéralogique, Briançon 10918
Exposition Monastique, Saint-Paulet-de-Caisson 14405
Exposition Muséale A l'Ancienne forge, Merkwiller-Pechelbronn 12946
Exposition Nicolas-Ledoux, Bénouville 10683
Exposition of Asian Art of the National Gallery of Prague, Praha 08574
Exposition of Old Bulgarian Carpets, Kotel 04717
Exposition Permanente, Aigueperse 10234
Exposition Permanente, Coustouge 11442
Exposition Permanente, Lombez 12652

Exposition Permanente, Saint-Julien-en-Beauchene 14298
Exposition Permanente, Sauveterre-de-Guyenne 14654
Exposition Permanente, Thanvillé 14881
Exposition Permanente Cavernicole Les Grandes Canalettes, Villefranche-de-Conflent 15198
Exposition Permanente d'Archéologie, Ainvelle 10244
Exposition Permanente d'Art, Bazens 10626
Exposition Permanente d'Art, Brasparts 10891
Exposition Permanente d'Art, Éguilly 11604
Exposition Permanente d'Art Contemporain, Bonnemazon 10796
Exposition Permanente d'Art et d'Histoire, Venosc 15121
Exposition Permanente d'Arts Plastiques, Brioude 10934
Exposition Permanente d'Attelages de Collection, Sainte-Marie-au-Bosc 14538
Exposition Permanente de Bâtons Traditionnels Basques, Ibarolle-Ibarla 12042
Exposition Permanente de Documents d'Archives, Bruxelles 03282
Exposition Permanente de la Viticulture, Montalba-le-Château 13038
Exposition Permanente de Peintures, Ploudalmézeau 13767
Exposition Permanente de Racines, Cornimont 11411
Exposition Permanente du Lin, Saint-Pierre-le-Vigier 14418
Exposition Permanente Souvenir du Maréchal Lannes, Lectoure 12502
Exposition Permanente sur la Déportation, Charmes 11184
Exposition Permanente sur le Pisé, Boën-sur-Lignon 10778
Exposition Permanente sur les Églises Fortifiées de la Thiérache, Vervins 15146
Exposition Permanente sur l'Histoire de l'Abbaye, Saint-Sauveur-le-Vicomte 14468
Exposition Permanente sur l'Histoire du Rugby, Capendu 11035
Exposition Permanente "Valence à la Croisée des Chemirs", Valence (Drôme) 15050
Exposition Philosophique, Prades 13858
Exposition Préhistorique, Choranche 11301
Exposition Préhistorique, Marseille 12849
Exposition Ruchon Morin, Le Merlerault 12446
Exposition sur la Parfumerie, Eze 11694
Exposition sur la Pierre et la Civilisation du Vin, Saint-Restitut 14456
Exposition sur la Presse Ecrite, Saint-Jean-de-Védas 14285
Exposition sur la Vie Rurale d'Autrefois, Begard 10667
Exposition sur l'Art Cistercien, Bétête 10708
Exposition sur le Sauvetage en Mer au Sémaphore, Ile-de-Molène 12048
Exposition sur l'Énergie Nucléaire, Valence-d'Agen-Golfech 15049
Exposition sur l'Histoire de la Principauté de Salm, Senones 14714
Exposition sur l'Histoire du Textile Choletais, Le Longeron 12431
Exposition Universelle des Vins et Spiritueux, Bandol 10577
Exposition Vie du Bois, Soulages-Bonneval 14792
Exposition Viticole, Ordonnac 13421
Expositions du Château, Pierrefonds 13735
Expositions du Chemin de Fer de Montagne, La Mure 12212
Expositions Pipe et Diamant, Saint-Claude 14158
Expostion Grotte Chauvet Pont d'Arc, Vallon-Pont-d'Arc 15066
Exposure Gallery, Vancouver 06676
Expozee, Lauwersoog 29500
Expozice Asijského Umĕni Národní Galerie v Praze, Praha 08574
Expozice České Lidové Armády, Praha 08575
Expozice Dominikánský Klášter, Jablonné v Podještědí 08379
Expozice Historického Nábytku 16.-19. a Oděvů 19. Století, Turnov 08693
Expozice Josef Hoffmann, Brtnice 08281
Expozice Mladý Gustav Mahler a Jihlava, Jihlava 08389
Expozice Řemesel, Moravské Budějovice 08486
Expozícia Historických Hodín, Bratislava 33960
Expozícia Zbraní a Stredovekého Mestského Opevnenia, Bratislava 33961
Eyam Museum, Eyam 38962
Eyemouth Museum, Eyemouth 38963
Eyhorne Manor Laundry Museum, Hollingbourne 39252
Eyvind Johnson-Stugan, Boden 35834
Ezekiel Harris House, Augusta 41381
Ezra and Cecile Zilkha Gallery, Middletown 45314
Ezra Meeker Mansion, Puyallup 46751
Ėžvinskij Literaturnyj Muzej, Syktyvkar 33571
Faaborg Museum for Fynsk Malerkunst, Faaborg 08813
Fabbrica Casa Museo, Albissola Marina 22840
Fabriano Paper and Watermark Museum, Fabriano 23746
The Fabric Workshop and Museum, Philadelphia 46408
Fabrica, Brighton 38341
Fabricius-Ház, Sopron 21532
Fabricius House, Sopron 21532
Fabrikmuseum der Leonischen Industrie, Roth, Mittelfranken 19672
Fabrikmuseum Johann Nemetz, Wiener Neustadt 03015
Fabrikmuseum Nordwolle, Delmenhorst 16567
Fabyan Villa Museum and Dutch Windmill, Geneva 43640
Das Fachwerk, Bad Salzuflen 15729
Fachwerkbaumuseum im Ständerbau, Quedlinburg 19458
Factory Museum, Eskilstuna 35870
Fächerkabinett, Bielefeld 16153
Fädernegården i Rejpelt, Vörå 10208
Fälschermuseum, Ostseebad Binz 19306
Fængselshistoriske Museum, Horsens 08895
Färberhaus, Oberstaufen 19208
Färbermuseum, Gutau 01976
Fästningsmuseet Karlsborg, Karlsborg 35991
Fågelmuseet, Jönköping 35975
Fågelsjö Gammelgård Bortom åa, Los 36050
Fagus-Gropius-Ausstellung, Alfeld, Leine 15425
Fahl Kro, Hemmet 08864
Fahrradmuseum, Ybbs 03045
Fahrradmuseum der Fahrrad-Veteranen-Freunde-Dresden 1990, Dresden 16681
Fahrradmuseum Zumhaus, Feuchtwangen 16996
Fahrzeugmuseum Marxzell, Marxzell 18660
Fahrzeugmuseum Suhl, Suhl 20121
Fahua Ta Tayuan Museum, Shanghai 07211
Faïences et Emaux, Longwy 12657
Fairbanks Gallery, Corvallis 42657
Fairbanks House, Dedham 42841
Fairbanks Museum and Planetarium, Saint Johnsbury 47098
Fairfax House Museum, York 40962
Fairfax Museum and Visitor Center, Fairfax 43260
Fairfield Art Museum, Fairfield 43267
Fairfield City Museum and Gallery, Smithfield 01455
Fairfield County Museum, Winnsboro 48694
Fairfield Museum, Bothwell 05099
Fairlawn Mansion and Museum, Superior 47890
Fairlynch Museum, Budleigh Salterton 38390
Fairport Historical Museum, Fairport 43275
Fairport Marine Museum, Fairport Harbor 43276
Fairview Museum of History and Art, Fairview 43277
Faith Trumbull Chapter Museum, Norwich 46035
Fakenham Museum of Gas and Local History, Fakenham 38966
Faktoriet, Eskilstuna 35870
Falbygdens Museum, Falköping 35880
Falconer Museum, Forres 39008
Faleide Skulemuseum, Stryn 30904
Falger-Museum, Elbigenalp 01813
Falkenbergs Hembygdsmuseum, Falkenberg 35876
Falkirk Cultural Center, San Rafael 47374
Falkland Palace and Garden, Falkland 38970
Falknereimuseum, Werfen 02821
Fall River County Historical Museum, Hot Springs 44110
Fall River Historical Society Museum, Fall River 43282
Fallingwater - Western Pennsylvania Conservancy, Mill Run 45344
Falmouth Art Gallery, Falmouth 38972
Falmouth Historical Museum, Falmouth 43287
Falstadminnet, Levanger 30638
Falsterbo Museum, Falsterbo 35881
Falumúzeum, Hollókö 21430
Falumúzeum, Isaszeg 21434
Falumúzeum, Törökbálint 21597
Familie Vrouwenhofje - Hofje van Aerden, Leerdam 29505
Familien Ernsts Samlingers Fond, Assens 08778
Familienmuseum Bad Homburg, Bad Homburg v.d.Höhe 15664
Familienmuseum im Altbauernhaus, Göstling an der Ybbs 01900
Familistère de Guise, Guise 11978
Family Museum of Arts and Science, Bettendorf 41670
Family Vault od the Dukes of Courland Exhibition, Jelgava 27366
Famine Museum, Strokestown 22545
Fan Museum, London 39633
Faninadahen Kosas Guahan, Adelup 21255
Fanø Kunstsamling, Fanø 08817
Fanø Museum, Fanø 08818
Fanø Skibsfarts- og Dragtsamling, Fanø 08819
Fanshawe Pioneer Village, London 05764
Faqir Khana Museum, Lahore 31034
Far Eastern Art Museum, Toruń 32055
Far North Regional Museum, Kaitaia 30191
Fargo Air Museum, Fargo 43291
Farleigh Hungerford Castle, Farleigh Hungerford 38978
The Farm, Sturgeon Bay 47862
Farm and Folk Museum, Lanreath 39423
Farm House Museum, Ames 41171
Farm Museum, Naantali 09852
Farm-Museum El Abra, Siguanea 08157
Farmaceutická Expozícia, Bratislava 33962
Farmacevtičeskij Muzej, Moskva 33044
Farmacia Conventuale, Venezia 25915
Farmacia Museo Taquechel, La Habana 07927
Farmācijas Muzejs, Rīga 27406
Farmamerica, Janesville 44317
Farmamerica, Waseca 48324
Farmamuseo Sa Potecaria, Villacidro 26016
Farmer Museum, Novellara 24656
Farmer Museum, Xochitepec 28627
Farmer's Arms Hotel Museum, Euroa 01022
Farmers Bank, Petersburg 46373
Farmers Bank of Rustico, Rustico 06294
Farmer's House, Metulla 22713
The Farmers' Museum, Cooperstown 42618
Farmhouse Museum, Ylijärvi 10215
Farming Through the Ages, Whyte Yarcowie 01599
Farmington Historic Home, Louisville 44964
Farmington Museum, Farmington 43299
Farmland Museum and Denny Abbey, Waterbeach 40802
Farmlife Centre, Thornhill, Central 40702
Farnham Galleries, Indianola 44235
Farnhem Maltings Gallery, Farnham 38980
Farouq Corner Museum, Helwan 09299
Farrar-Mansur House and Old Mill Museum, Weston 48571
Farsh Museum, Teheran 22296
Farshchian Museum, Teheran 22297
Fartygsmuseet, Göteborg 35911
Farums Arkiver og Museer, Farum 08823
Farvergården, Kerteminde 08913
Fashion Museum, Hasselt 03479
Fassbinder- und Weinbaumuseum, Straß im Straßertale 02703
Fastnachtmuseum, Nassereith 02336
Fastnachtmuseum Schloß Langenstein, Orsingen-Nenzingen 19267
Fastnachtsmuseum, Herbstein 17719
Fastnachtsmuseum Fasenickl, Kipfenberg 18084
Faszinosum, Borna bei Leipzig 16262
Father Marquette National Memorial and Museum, Saint Ignace 47094
Father Pandosy Mission, Kelowna 05651
Father Weyland Gallery, Epworth 43198
Faulconer Gallery at Grinnell College, Grinnell 43840
Faulkner County Museum, Conway 42612
Fauske Museum, Fauske 30488
Faust-Museum, Knittlingen 18118
Favell Museum of Western Art and Indian Artifacts, Klamath Falls 44508
Fawick Art Gallery, Berea 41637
Fawley Court Historic House and Museum, Henley-on-Thames 39219
Fayette Art Museum, Fayette 43305
Fayette County Historical Museum, West Union 48549
Fayette County Museum, Washington Court House 48422
Fayette Heritage Museum, La Grange 44545
Fayetteville Museum of Art, Fayetteville 43311
F.Donald Kenney Museum and Art Study Wing, Saint Bonaventure 47076
Featherston Heritage Museum, Featherston 30157
Featherston Memorabilia Museum, Featherston 30158
Federaçao de Amigos de Museus do Brasil, São Paulo 49082
Federaçãon de Amigos dos Museus de Portugal, Lisboa 49339
Federación Argentina de Asociaciones de Amigos de Museos, Buenos Aires 49044
Federación Chilena de Amigos de los Museos, Santiago de Chile 49109
Federación Española de Asociaciones de Amigos de los Museos, Madrid 49374
Federación Mexicana de Asociaciones de Amigos de los Museos, México 49293
Federal Hall National Memorial, New York 45799
Federal Reserve Bank of Boston Collection, Boston 41806
Federal Reserve Board Art Gallery, Washington 48353
Fédération des Amis des Musées de Belgique, Bruxelles 49071
Fédération des Ecomusées et des Musées de Société, Besançon 49174
Fédération des Maisons d'Ecrivain et des Patrimoines Littéraires, Bourges 49175
Fédération Française des Sociétés d'Amis de Musées, Paris 49176
Fédération Hellénique des Amis des Musées, Athinai 49222
Fédération Internationale des Musées du Jouet et de l'Enfance, Moirans-en-Montagne 49177
Fédération Mondiale des Sociétés d'Amis de Musées, Paris 49178
Federation of Art Societies, Singapore , 33937
Federation of Museums and Galleries in Wales, Aberystwyth 49413
Fédération Régionale des Amis des Musées du Nord-Pas de Calais, Dunkerque 49179
Federazione Italiana delle Associazioni Amici dei Musei, Firenze 49251
Federseemuseum Bad Buchau, Bad Buchau 15621
Fedrenes Minne, Hidrasund 30548
Feering and Kelvedon Local History Museum, Kelevedon 39331
Feet First: The Scholl Story, North Chicago 45987
Fehn- und Schiffahrtsmuseum, Rhauderfehn 19583
Fehnmuseum Eiland, Großefehn 17427
Fekete-Ház, Szeged 21547
Fekete Sas Patikamúzeum, Székesfehérvár 21556
Felberturmmuseum, Mittersill 02306
Felbrigg Hall, Norwich 40093
Feld- und Grubenbahnmuseum, Solms 19989
Feld- und Industriebahnmuseum (FIM), Freiland 01848
Feldherrnhalle, München 18847
Feledy-Gyűjtemény - Feledy Ház, Miskolc 21474
Feledy House and Feledy Collection of the Miskolc Gallery of Fine Arts, Miskolc 21474
Felix Jenewein Gallery, Kutná Hora 08437
Felix-Müller-Museum im Zehntspeicher, Neunkirchen am Brand 19051
Felix-Nussbaum-Haus Osnabrück mit Sammlung der Nidersächsischen Sparkassenstiftung, Osnabrück 19278
Felix Valle State Historic Site, Sainte Genevieve 47184
Fell Locomotive Museum, Featherston 30159
Felsberg-Museum, Lautertal, Odenwald 18362
Felsenburg Neurathen, Lohmen, Sachsen 18497
Felsendome Rabenstein, Chemnitz 16463
Felsengarten Sanspareil mit Morgenländischem Bau, Wonsees 20675
Felsenkeller-Labyrinth im Hirschberg - Brauereimuseum, Beilngries 15870
Felsenmeer-Museum, Hemer 17708
Felsenmuseum, Bernstein, Burgenland 01734
Fenelon Falls Museum, Fenelon Falls 05422
Fenghua Xikou Museum, Fenghua 07048
Fengxian Museum, Shanghai 07212
Fenimore Art Museum, Cooperstown 42619
Fenland and West Norfolk Aviation Museum, West Walton 40828
Gershon & Rebecca Fenster Museum of Jewish Art, Tulsa 48103
Fenton Glass Museum, Williamstown 48636
Fenton History Center-Museum and Library, Jamestown 44311
Fenton House, London 39634
Ferdinand Domela Nieuwenhuis Museum, Heerenveen 29362
Ferenc Hopp Museum of Eastern Asiatic Arts, Budapest 21344
Ferenczy Károly Múzeum, Szentendre 21570
Ferens Art Gallery, Kingston-upon-Hull 39377
Ferganskij Oblastnoj Kraevedčeskij Muzej, Fergana 48836
Fergusson Gallery, Perth 40184
Feringa Sach - Ortsgeschichte und heimatkundliche Sammlung, Unterföhring 20268
Fermanagh County Museum at Enniskillen Castle, Enniskillen 38939
Ferme Apicole du Morvan, Rouvray 14067
La Ferme au Fil des Saisons, Amfreville-les-Champs 10319
Ferme aux Abeilles, Saint-Brévin-les-Pins 14129
La Ferme Caussenarde d'Autrefois, Hures-la-Parade 12038
La Ferme des Étoiles, Mauroux 12898
La Ferme Marine-Musée de l'Huître et du Coquillage, Cancale 11015
Ferme-Musée, Sarniguet 14615
Ferme-Musée à Pans de Bois de Sougey, Montrevel-en-Bresse 13145
Ferme-Musée Barret, Pineuilh 13737
Ferme-Musée de Bray, Sommery 14769
Ferme-Musée des Bernant, Rilly-la-Montagne 13971
Ferme-Musée des Frères Perrel, Moudeyres 13177
Ferme-Musée des Sources de la Loire, Sainte-Eulalie 14530
Ferme-Musée du Contentin, Sainte-Mère-Eglise 14547
Ferme-Musée du Léon, Tréflaouenan 14986
Ferme-Musée du Montagnon, Fournets-Luisans 11801
Ferme-Musée lé Moho dé Soyotte, Sainte-Marguerite 14537
Fermes-Musée du Pays Horloger, Grand-Combe-Châteleu 11902
Fernbank Museum of Natural History, Atlanta 41341
Fernbank Science Center, Atlanta 41342
Fernhill House, Belfast 38152
Fernie and District Historical Museum, Fernie 05424
Ferrari Museum, Gotemba 26158
Ferrería de Mirandaola, Legazpia 34944
Ferry Building Gallery, West Vancouver 06773
Ferrymead Heritage Park, Christchurch 30128
Fersman Mineralogical Museum of the Russian Academy of Sciences, Moskva 33084
Festetics-Kastély, Keszthely 21454
Festival-Institute Museum, Round Top 47017
Festivity of Remedios Museum, Remedios 08090
Festung Kniepaß, Unken 02753
Festung Königstein, Königstein, Sächsische Schweiz 18182
Festung Marienberg mit Fürstenbaumuseum, Würzburg 20692
Die Festung Rosenberg - Deutsches Festungsmuseum, Kronach 18242
Festung Wilhelmstein im Steinhuder Meer, Wunstorf 20709
Festungs- und Waffengeschichtliches Museum, Philippsburg 19397
Festungsanlage-Museum Senftenberg, Senftenberg 19938
Festungsmuseum, Salzburg 02534
Festungsmuseum Heldsberg, Sankt Margrethen 37111
Festungsmuseum Reuenthal, Reuenthal 37053
Fethard Park and Folk Museum, Fethard 22470
Fethiye Culture Center, Fethiye 37679
Fethiye Kültür Merkezi, Fethiye 37679
Fethiye Müzesi, Fethiye 37680
Fetlar Interpretive Centre, Fetlar 38988
Fetsund Lenser Fløtingsmuseum, Fetsund 30489

Feuerstätten-Ausstellung im Lausitzer Bergbaumuseum, Hoyerswerda 17846
Feuerwehr-Museum Schloß Waldmannshofen, Creglingen 16508
Feuerwehrmuseum, Adligenswil 36433
Feuerwehrmuseum, Bayreuth 15844
Feuerwehrmuseum, Dietzenbach 16605
Feuerwehrmuseum, Endingen 36680
Feuerwehrmuseum, Kaufbeuren 18037
Feuerwehrmuseum, Kreuzlingen 36834
Feuerwehrmuseum, Lengenfeld, Vogtland 18434
Feuerwehrmuseum, Niederwiesa 19101
Feuerwehrmuseum, Perchtoldsdorf 02397
Feuerwehrmuseum, Rehau 19536
Feuerwehrmuseum, Roding 19625
Feuerwehrmuseum, Salem, Baden 19732
Feuerwehrmuseum, Sankt Florian 02559
Feuerwehrmuseum, Spalt 20006
Feuerwehrmuseum, Stadtprozelten 20034
Feuerwehrmuseum, Steyrermühl 02694
Feuerwehrmuseum, Türnitz 02741
Feuerwehrmuseum, Wasserburg am Inn 20407
Feuerwehrmuseum, Wienerbruck 03022
Feuerwehrmuseum des Landkreises Harburg, Marxen 18659
Feuerwehrmuseum Grethen, Parthenstein 19352
Feuerwehrmuseum Hannover, Hannover 17593
Feuerwehrmuseum Kalmbach, Riedbach 19594
Feuerwehrmuseum Kradolf-Schönenberg, Kradolf 36832
Feuerwehrmuseum Lövenich, Erkelenz 16910
Feuerwehrmuseum Musberg, Leinfelden-Echterdingen 18376
Feuerwehrmuseum Ravensburg, Ravensburg 19506
Feuerwehrmuseum Salzbergen, Salzbergen 19734
Feuerwehrmuseum Schleswig-Holstein, Norderstedt 19117
Feuerwehrmuseum Schröttinghausen, Preußisch Oldendorf 19446
Feuerwehrmuseum Winnenden, Winnenden 20610
Feuerwehrmuseum Zeven, Zeven 20752
Feuerwehrsmuseum, Tumeltsham 02749
F.I. Tyutchev Literary Museum, Ovstug 33278
Fiakermuseum, Wien 02882
Fichtelgebirgsmuseum, Wunsiedel 20708
Fick Fossil and History Museum, Oakley 46074
Fiedler Memorial Museum, Seguin 47559
Field Museum, Chicago 42325
Field Museum of Natural History, Chicago 42326
Fieldcote Museum, Ancaster 04991
Fielding L. Wright Art Center, Cleveland 42462
Fier Archaeological Museum, Fier 00020
Fife Folk Museum, Ceres 38518
Fifth Maine Regiment Center, Peaks Island 46322
Fifth Meeting House, Lancaster 44618
Fifth Parallel Gallery, Regina 06232
Fighter World, Williamtown 01602
Figurencabinett Madamme Lucrezia, Rosegg 02524
Fiji Museum, Suva 09409
Filey Museum, Filey 38990
Filipstads Bergslags Hembygdsgård, Filipstad 35887
Fillmore County Historical Museum, Fountain 43496
Fillmore Historical Museum, Fillmore 43320
Film Center, National Museum of Modern Art Tokyo, Tokyo 26939
Film Forum - Film Archives, Collingswood 42529
Film- och Biografmuseet, Säter 36168
Filmmuseet, Kristianstad 36016
Filmmuseet, Oslo 30732
Filmmuseum, Antwerpen 03143
Filmmuseum, München 18848
Filmmuseum Bendestorf, Bendestorf 15874
Filmmuseum Berlin, Berlin 15946
Filmmuseum Foundation Nederlands, Amsterdam 28852
Filmmuseum Landeshauptstadt Düsseldorf, Düsseldorf 16722
Filmmuseum Potsdam, Potsdam 19434
Filmsammlungen Laxenburg, Laxenburg 02196
The Filson Historical Society Museum, Louisville 44965
Finanzgeschichtliche Sammlung der Bundesfinanzakademie, Brühl, Rheinland 16376
Finch Foundry Working Museum, Okehampton 40125
Finchcocks, Goudhurst 39105
Findlater Museum, Dublin 22425
Fine Art Gallery, Hodonín 08353
Fine Art Gallery, Roudnice nad Labem 08638
Fine Art Gallery at Centro Cultural Aztlan, San Antonio 47250
Fine Art Museum, Astana 27076
Fine Art University Exhibition Hall, Ha Noi 48976
Fine Arts Center for New River Valley, Pulaski 46742
Fine Arts Center Gallery, Maryville 45197
Fine Arts Center of Hot Springs, Hot Springs 44108
Fine Arts Center of Kershaw County, Camden 42064
Fine Arts Collection, Decorah 42838
Fine Arts Collection of the Franciscan Monastery, Orebić 07748
Fine Arts Department Gallery, Cincinnati 42405
Fine Arts Exhibitions, Austin 41410
Fine Arts Gallery, Breckenridge 41875
Fine Arts Gallery, Columbus 42581
Fine Arts Gallery, Cypress 42737
Fine Arts Gallery, Korçë 00024
The Fine Arts Gallery, Las Vegas 44663
Fine Arts Gallery, Los Angeles 44898
Fine Arts Gallery, Luck 37878
Fine Arts Gallery, Náchod 08491
Fine Arts Gallery, New Orleans 45723
Fine Arts Gallery, Omaha 46146
Fine Arts Gallery, Ostrava 08524
Fine Arts Gallery, Tiranë 00033
Fine Arts Museum, Girne 08226
Fine Arts Museum, Sevastopol 37901
Fine Arts Museum, Teheran 22298
Fine Arts Museum, Włocławek 32165
Fine Arts School Museum, Buenos Aires 00148
Fine Piece Museum, Xian 07295
Fingerhutmuseum, Creglingen 16509
Fini's Hoeve, Vriezenveen 29966
Finish Forestareas Museum, Viksjöfors 36410
Finlaggan Centre, Ballygrant 38067
Finlands Svenska Skolmuseum, Munsala 09841
Finlandssvenskt Konstcentrum, Ekenäs 09426
The Finley House, Wayne 48480
Finnetunet, Grue Finnskog 30523
Finney County Kansas Historical Museum, Garden City 43617
Finnish Aviation Museum, Vantaa 10182
Finnish Boxing Museum, Tampere 10087
Finnish Dataprocessing Museum, Jyväskylä 09605
Finnish Folk Instrument Museum, Kaustinen 09643
Finnish Football Museum, Valkeakoski 10173
Finnish Foundry Museum and Högfors Blast Furnace, Karkkila 09628
Finnish Glass Museum, Riihimäki 09995
Finnish Ice Hockey Museum, Tampere 10085
Finnish Museum of Art and Design, Helsinki 09477
Finnish Museum of Horology, Espoo 09438
Finnish Museums Association, Helsinki 49160
Finnish Paint Museum, Kemi 09652
Finnish Railway Museum, Hyvinkää 09556
Finnish School Museum, Tampere 10086
Finnkroken Bygdemuseum, Tromsdalen 30931
Finnskogsmuseet, Viksjöfors 36410
Finspångs Slott, Finspång 35890
Finta Múzeum, Türkeve 21600
Fire Brigade Museum, Budapest 21387
Fire Brigade Museum, Fatih 37678
Fire Brigades Museum, Reigate 40306
Fire Brigadesmens Museum, Wellington 30294
Fire Fighting Museum, Toronto 06577
Fire-Fighting Museum of Latvia, Rīga 27422
Fire Museum, Helsinki 09518
Fire Museum, Kurwongbah 01156
Fire Museum, Kuusankoski 09731
Fire Museum, Lahti 09745
Fire Museum, Minsk 03114
Fire Museum of Maryland, Lutherville 45001
Fire Museum of Memphis, Memphis 45236
Fire Museum of Texas, Beaumont 41568
Fire Museum of York County, York 48794
Fire Police Museum, Sheffield 40483
Fire Power, the Royal Artillery Museum, London 39635
Fire Service Museum, Hethersett 39235
Fire Services Museum of Victoria, East Melbourne 00998
Firearms Technology Museum, Orange 01346
Firefighter Museum, Matanzas 08038
Firefighters' Museum of Nova Scotia and National Exhibition Centre, Yarmouth 06868
Firefighting Museum, Chatham, Ontario 05239
Firehouse Art Center, Norman 45973
Firehouse Art Gallery, Garden City 43618
Firehouse Gallery, Oak Bluffs 46049
Firehouse Museum, Ellicott City 43157
Firehouse Museum, Nevada City 45653
Firelands Historical Society Museum, Norwalk 46034
Firelight Museum, Leongatha 01174
Fireman's Hall Museum, Philadelphia 46409
Firemen's House, La Habana 08002
Firle Place, Firle 38993
Firmenmusemum Novatech, Reutlingen 19575
First Cavalry Division Museum, Fort Hood 43398
First Consolidated School in Minnesota, Saum 47470
The First Division Museum at Cantigny, Wheaton 48583
First Garden City Heritage Museum, Letchworth 39480
First Hussars Citizen Soldiers Museum, London 05765
First Infantry Division Museum, Würzburg 20693
First Michigan Museum of Military History, Holland 44054
First Missouri State Capitol, Saint Charles 47078
First National Bank of Chicago Art Collection, Chicago 42327
First Parish Welfare Museum, Stockholm 36239
First Penny Farthing Museum, Knutsford 39403
First Raadsaal Museum, Bloemfontein 34183
First Tennessee Heritage Collection, Memphis 45237
First Territorial Capitol of Kansas, Fort Riley 43448
First Turkish Grand National Assembly Museum, Ankara 37616
First White House of the Confederacy, Montgomery 45466
Firstsite at the Minories Art Gallery, Colchester 38610
Firth Tower Historical Reserve, Matamata 30202
Fischer- und Webermuseum Steinhude, Steinhude 20053
Fischereimuseum, Neuhausen am Rheinfall 36987
Fischereimuseum, Wassertrüdingen 20411
Fischinger Heimathaus mit Schimuseum, Fischen im Allgäu 17008
Fishbourne Roman Palace and Museum, Chichester 38560
Fisher Gallery, Los Angeles 44899
Fisher Grove Country School, Frankfort 43516
Fisher Museum of Forestry, Petersham 46380
Fisheries Museum of the Atlantic, Lunenburg 05788
Fisherman's Cottage, Tooradin 01538
Fisherman's Life Museum, Halifax 05551
Fisherman's Museum, Musgrave Harbour 05952
Fishermen's Life Museum, Jeddore Oyster Ponds 05632
Fishermen's Museum, Bermeo 34604
Fishermen's Museum, Hastings 39183
Fishermen's Museum, Pemaquid Point 46331
Fishermen's Museum, Port-de-Grave 06159
Fishery Museum, Hel 31614
Fishery Museum, Jastarnia 31624
Fishing and Maritime Museum, Esbjerg 08808
Fishing Museum, Kaskinen 09634
Fishing Museum, Kibbutz Ein Gev 22683
Fishing Museum, Merikarvia 09825
Fishing Museum, Palamós 35211
Fisk University Galleries, Nashville 45617
Fiska- og Náttúrngripasafn Vestmannaeyja, Vestmannaeyjar 21674
Fiskars Museum, Fiskars 09439
Fiskemuséet i Kaskö, Kaskinen 09634
Fiskeri- og Søfartsmuseet, Esbjerg 08808
Fiskerimuseet og Kunstsmie i Sund, Sund i Lofoten 30906
Fiskerimuseet på Hjertøya, Molde 30685
Fiskerimuseum i Måløy, Måløy 30662
Fitchburg Art Museum, Fitchburg 43326
Fitchburg Historical Society Museum, Fitchburg 43327
Fitzwilliam Museum, Cambridge 38454
Five Civilized Tribes Museum, Muskogee 45581
Five Council Museums East Headquarters, Cupar 38687
Fjärilshuset Haga Tradgard, Stockholm 36241
Fjerritslev Bryggeri- og Egnsmuseum, Fjerritslev 08824
Fjordane Forsvarsmuseum, Nordfjordeid 30709
Fjordmuseet, Jyllinge 08909
Fjøsangersamlingene, Fjøsanger 30493
Flachsmuseum Beeck, Wegberg 20419
Flagler Museum, Palm Beach 46264
Flagstaff House Museum of Tea Ware, Hong Kong 07094
Flakkebjerg Skolemuseum, Slagelse 09069
Flambards Victorian Village and Gardens, Helston 39213
Flame!, Carrickfergus 38497
Flamingo Gallery, Las Vegas 44665
Flanagan Valley Campus Art Gallery, Lincoln 44798
Flanders Center, Osaka 26643
Flandrau Science Center, Tucson 48087
Flaske-Peters-Samling, Ærøskøbing 08765
Flat Rock Museum, Flat Rock 05426
Flatanger Bygdemuseum, Flatanger 30494
Flathead Indian Museum, Saint Ignatius 47095
Flaxbourne Settlers Museum, Ward 30288
Flaxman Gallery, Stoke-on-Trent 40605
Fleet Air Arm Museum - Concorde, Yeovilton 40957
Fleet Boston Financial Gallery, Boston 41807
Fleetwood Museum, Fleetwood 38995
Fleischer Museum, Scottsdale 47512
Flekkefjord Museum, Flekkefjord 30495
Fleming Historical Museum, Fleming 43336
Flensburger Schiffahrtsmuseum und Rum-Museum, Flensburg 17011
Flessenscheepjesmuseum, Enkhuizen 29232
Fleur de Lis Heritage Centre, Faversham 38984
Flieger-Flab-Museum, Dübendorf 36666
Fliegermuseum, Altenrhein 36450
Flin Flon Museum, Flin Flon 05428
Flinders University Art Museum, Adelaide 00707
Flint House, Scotia 47506
Flint Institute of Arts, Flint 43339
Flint Ridge State Memorial Museum, Glenford 43690
Flintham Museum, Flintham 38996
Flipje en Jam Museum Tiel, Tiel 29873
Floating Gallery, Winnipeg 06823
Flößer- und Heimatmuseum, Wolfach 20647
Flößer- und Schiffermuseum, Kamp-Bornhofen 17980
Flößerei- und Verkehrsmuseum, Gengenbach 17234
Flößermuseum Unterrodach, Marktrodach 18653
Flood Museum, Johnstown 44352
Floors Castle, Kelso 39333
Flora Twort Gallery, Petersfield 40193
Florence Court House, Enniskillen 38940
Florence Griswold Museum, Old Lyme 46133
Florence Hawley Ellis Museum of Anthropology, Abiquiu 41057
Florence McLeod Hazard Museum, Columbus 42582
Florence Mine Heritage Centre, Egremont 38924
Florence Museum of Art, Science and History, Florence 43348
Florence Nightingale Museum, Aylesbury 38047
Florence Nightingale Museum, London 39636
Florence Price Pioneer Museum, Florence 43346
Florence Ranch Homestead, Mesquite 45274
Florewood State Park, Greenwood 43836
Florianerbahn, Sankt Florian 02560
Florida Adventure Museum, Punta Gorda 46746
Florida Agricultural Museum, Palm Coast 46266
Florida Art Museum Directors Association, Vero Beach 49483
Florida Association of Museums, Tallahassee 49484
Florida Gulf Coast Railroad Museum, Parrish 46297
Florida History Museum, Jupiter 44371
Florida Holocaust Museum, Saint Petersburg 47171
Florida International Museum, Saint Petersburg 47172
The Florida Museum of Hispanic and Latin American Art, Coral Gables 42627
Florida Museum of Natural History, Gainesville 43581
Florida State University Museum of Fine Arts, Tallahassee 47931
Florina Museum of Modern Art, Florina 20956
Florissant Valley Historical Society Museum, Florissant 43349
Floristisches Museum, Perchtoldsdorf 02398
Fløtermuseet, Osen 30724
Flottille en Pertuis, La Flotte-en-Ré 12183
Flottmann-Hallen, Herne 17727
Flour Mill Museum, Sudbury 06510
Flowerdew Hundred Foundation, Hopewell 44099
Floyd County Historical Museum, Charles City 42200
Flughafen Modellschau, Hamburg 17538
Flugmuseum Aviaticum, Wiener Neustadt 03016
Flugpionier-Gustav-Weißkopf-Museum, Leutershausen 18447
Flur-Galerie, Berlin 15947
Fluweelengrot Valkenburg, Valkenburg 29915
Flyhistorisk Museum, Sola 30861
Flynderupgård Museet, Espergærde 08811
Flypast Museum of Australian Army Flying, Oakey 01339
F.M. Dostoevsky Apartment Museum, Moskva 33123
F.M. Dostoevsky House-Museum, Staraja Russa 33554
F.M. Dostoevsky Memorial and Literature Museum, Novokuzneck 33235
F.M. Dostoevsky Museum-Estate in Darovoe, Darovoe 32755
F.M. Dostoevsky Regional Commemorative Literary Museum, Semey 27091
Foam Fotografiemuseum Amsterdam, Amsterdam 28853
Foam Lake Museum, Foam Lake 05429
Focal Point Gallery, Southend-on-Sea 40552
Fochabers Folk Museum, Fochabers 38998
Focke-Museum, Bremen 16321
Föglö Museet, Föglö 09440
Főszékesegyházi Kincstár és Könyvtár, Esztergom 21411
Fogelsangh State, Veenklooster 29931
El Fogon de los Arrieros, Resistencia 00505
Foldalbruket, Kjøllefjord 30596
Folk Art and Photography Galleries, Atlanta 41343
Folk Art Institute, Lefkoşa 08236
Folk Art Museum, Balatonszentgyörgy 21314
Folk Art Museum, Constanța 32500
Folk Art Museum, Girne 08227
Folk Art Museum, Krosno 31737
Folk Art Museum, Lemesos 08209
Folk Art Museum, Moskva 33138
Folk Art Museum, Osiek nad Notecią 31863
Folk Art Museum, Yeroskipos 08216
Folk Art Museum of the Metropolis of Kos, Kos 21031
Folk Art Society of America, Richmond 46877
Folk Craft Museum, Takayama 26801
Folk Historical and Regional Museum of Tatarsk, Tatarsk 33596
Folk Museum, Anuradhapura 35744
Folk Museum, Câtel 38511
Folk Museum, Deloraine 00975
Folk Museum, Eyrarbakki 21631
Folk Museum, Kolbuszowa 31667
Folk Museum, Mbarara 37831
Folk Museum, Mevagissey 39942
Folk Museum, Millom 39955
Folk Museum, Ohrid 27587
Folk Museum, Soroti 37833
Folk Museum of Indian Immigration, Moka 27734
Folk Museum of Meguro-ku, Tokyo 26844
Folk Museum of Ota-ku, Tokyo 26845
Folk Museum of Stranda, Mönsterås 36098
Folkenborg Museum, Mysen 30696
Folkestone Museum and Art Gallery, Folkestone 39000
Folklife Display, Lisnaskea 39511
Folklore and Ethnological Museum of Macedonia and Thrace, Thessaloniki 21181
Folklore Museum, Cairo 09265
Folklore Museum, Karditsa 20997
Folklore Museum, Mysore 21959
Folklore Museum, Pogoniani 21129
Folklore Museum, Thessaloniki 21182
Folklore Museum, Victoria 27708
Folklore Museum, Vitsa 21210
Folklore Museum, Xanthi 21218
Folklore Museum of Avlon, Avlon 20908
Folklore Museum of Florina, Florina 20957
Folklore Museum of Thrace, Komotini 21025
Folkloremuseum Florishof, Oostduinkerke 03665
Folklorish Museum, Nanchang 07175
Folklorish Museum, Wuxi 07285
Folkloristisch Museum, Swalmen 29863
Folldal Bygdetun, Folldal 30499
Folldal Gruver, Folldal 30500
Follett House Museum, Sandusky 47383
Follo Museum, Drøbak 30465
Folsom History Museum, Folsom 43358
Folsom Museum, Folsom 43359
Folterkammer mit Heimatmuseum, Pöggstall 02424
Foltermuseum, Burghausen, Salzach 16419
Foltermuseum, Wien 02883
Fondaçao-Museu Chissano, Matola 28728
Fondatioin Océanographique, Six-Fours-les-Plages 14755

Fondation Beyeler, Riehen 37060
Fondation Cartier pour l'Art Contemporain, Paris 13501
Fondation Carzou, Manosque 12795
Fondation Charles de Gaulle, Colombey-les-Deux-Eglises 11364
Fondation Cziffra, Senlis 14708
Fondation de Jau, Cases-de-Pène 11065
Fondation de l'Automobile Marius-Berliet, Lyon 12726
Fondation de l'Hermitage, Lausanne 36855
Fondation Dosne-Thiers, Paris 13502
Fondation du Château de Maintenon, Maintenon 12774
Fondation Dubuffet, Paris 13503
Fondation Dubuffet, Périgny-sur-Yerres 13691
Fondation et Musée René Carcan, Bruxelles 03283
Fondation François-Brochet, Auxerre 10508
Fondation La Tène, Hauterive 36795
Fondation Le Corbusier, Paris 13504
Fondation L'Estrée, Ropraz 37070
Fondation Louis Moret, Martigny 36923
Fondation Maeght, Saint-Paul (Alpes-Maritimes) 14398
Fondation Martin Bodmer, Cologny 36641
Fondation Neumann, Gingins 36758
Fondation Pierre Gianadda, Martigny 36924
Fondation pour l'Architecture, Bruxelles 03284
Fondation Prouvost, Marcq-en-Barœul 12813
Fondation Rainer Maria Rilke, Sierre 37166
Fondation René Pous, Auterive 10496
Fondation Saner, Studen 37220
Fondation Van-Gogh Arles, Arles 10414
Fondation Vasarely, Aix-en-Provence 10250
Fondazione Antonio Mazzotta, Milano 24383
Fondazione Bandera per l'Arte, Busto Arsizio 23238
Fondazione Europea del Disegno, Meina 24343
Fondazione Galleria Gottardo, Lugano 36897
Fondazione M. Minucci, Vittorio Veneto 26038
Fondazione Magnani Rocca, Mamiano di Traversetolo 24273
Fondazione Museo Glauco Lombardi, Parma 24798
Fondazione Palazz Coronini Cronberg, Gorizia 24033
Fondazione Palazzo Albizzini Collezione Burri, Città di Castello 23577
Fondazione Romano nel Cenacolo di Santo Spirito, Firenze 23835
Fondazione T. Balestra, Longiano 24209
Fondazione Thyssen-Bornemisza, Castagnola 36616
Fonderie de Cloches, Robecourt 13986
Fondo Del Sol, Washington 48354
Fonds Ancien, Avranches 10540
Fonds Ancien de la Bibliothèque Cantonale Jurassienne, Porrentruy 37027
Fonthill Museum of the Bucks County Historical Society, Doylestown 42982
Forbes Collection, New York 45800
Forbes Mill Museum of Regional History, Los Gatos 44955
Forbes Museum, Forbes 01030
Forbes Museum, Tanger 28711
Ford County Historical Society Museum, Paxton 46319
Ford End Watermill, Ivinghoe 39321
Ford Gallery and Slide Collection, Ypsilanti 48810
Ford Green Hall, Stoke-on-Trent 40606
Ford Museum, Dumalag 31327
Forde Abbey, Chard 38523
Ford's Theatre, Washington 48355
Fordyce Joiner's Visitor Centre, Fordyce 39003
Foredown Tower, Portslade-by-Sea 40247
Foreningen af Danske Kunstmuseer, Nivå 49140
Foreningen af Danske Museumsmaend, København 49141
Foreningen af Danske Naturhistoriske Museer, Århus 49142
Foreningen af Danske Naturvidenskabelige Museer, Esbjerg 49143
Forensic Medicine Museum, Bangkok 37482
Forest and Heritage Centre, Geeveston 01047
Forest Capital State Museum, Perry 46354
Forest Department Utilisation Division Museum, Kampala 37826
Forest Entomology Museum, Bangkok 37483
Forest History Center, Grand Rapids 43761
Forest-Lambton Museum, Forest 05431
Forest Lawn Museum, Glendale 43689
Forest Museum, Lycksele 36066
Forest Museum, Peshawar 31048
Forest Museum, Soheul 27293
Forest Museum, Taungdwingyi 28744
Forest Museum in Bojas Palace, Aizpute 27329
Forest Park Museum, Perry 46355
Forest Sandilands Centre and Museum, Winnipeg 06824
Forestburg and District Museum, Forestburg 05432
Forestry Museum, Mora 36101
Forestry Museum, Viitasaari 10198
Forestry Research Institute Malaysia Museum, Kepong 27628
Forge Mill Needle Museum and Bordesley Abbey Visitor Centre, Redditch 40302
Forge-Musée d'Etueffont, Etueffont 11676
Forge Museum, Much Hadham 39991
Forge Museum in Warsaw, Warszawa 32108
The Forges and Manor of Ringwood, Ringwood 46902
Former Governors' Mansion, Bismarck 41721
Former Hong Kong and Shanghai Bank Museum, Nagasaki 26545
Formsammlung der Stadt Braunschweig, Braunschweig 16296
Forncett Industrial Steam Museum, Forncett Saint Mary 39006
Forney Transportation Museum, Denver 42888
Forngården Hembygdsmuseum, Trollhättan 36334
Fornminnesgården, Eksjö 35861
Føroya Fornminnissavn, Tórshavn 09407
Føroya Náttúrugripasavn, Tórshavn 09408
Forrest Museum, Mörsil 36099
Forrester Gallery, Oamaru 30217
Forsand Bygdemuseum, Forsand 30503
Forschungs- und Gedenkstätte Normannenstrasse - Stasi Museum, Berlin 15948
Forschungsarchiv für römische Plastik, Köln 18136
Forssa Natural History Museum, Forssa 09441
Forssan Luonnonhistoriallinen Museo, Forssa 09441
Forst- und Jagdmuseum, Hofgeismar 17796
Forst- und Köhlerhof, Rostock 19661
Forstbotanisches Museum, Tharandt 20170
Forstliche und Jagdkundliche Lehrschau Grillenburg, Grillenburg 17399
Forstmuseum, Reichraming 02499
Forstmuseum Heringen, Heringen, Werra 17722
Forstmuseum im Hochwildpark Karlsberg, Weikersheim 20430
Forsvarsmuseet, Oslo 30733
Forsvarsmuseet på Bornholm, Rønne 09039
Forsvik's Industrial Heritage, Forsvik 35893
Forsviks Industriminnen, Forsvik 35893
Fort Abercrombie Historic Site, Abercrombie 41044
Fort Amherst Heritage Museum, Chatham 38528
Fort Ancient Museum, Oregonia 46180
Fort Anne, Annapolis Royal 04996
Fort Atkinson State Historical Park, Fort Calhoun 43374
Fort Beaufort Historical Museum, Fort Beaufort 34241
Fort Beauséjour National Historic Site, Aulac 05020
Fort Bedford Museum, Bedford 41582
Fort Belknap Museum, Newcastle 45911
Fort Bend Museum, Richmond 46867
Fort Benton Museum of the Upper Missouri, Fort Benton 43367
Fort Bliss Museum, Fort Bliss 43369
Fort Boonesborough Museum, Richmond 46864
Fort Bowie, Bowie 41842
Fort Bridger State Museum, Fort Bridger 43373
Fort Brockhurst, Gosport 39098
Fort Buenaventura, Ogden 46098
Fort Buford State Historic Site, Williston 48638
Fort Calgary, Calgary 05166
Fort Carlton, Regina 06233
Fort Caroline Memorial Museum, Jacksonville 44294
Fort Casey Interpretive Center, Coupeville 42675
Fort Caspar Museum, Casper 42129
Fort-Chambly, Chambly 05221
Fort Charles Maritime Museum, Kingston 26066
Fort Chipewyan Bicentennial Museum, Fort Chipewyan 05434
Fort Christmas, Christmas 42392
Fort Clark Trading Post, Center 42167
Fort Clatsop National Memorial, Astoria 41310
Fort Clinch, Fernandina Beach 43315
Fort Collins Museum, Fort Collins 43380
Fort Columbia House Museum, Chinook 42386
Fort Crawford Museum, Prairie du Chien 46682
Fort Croghan Museum, Burnet 42010
Fort Crook Historical Museum, Fall River Mills 43284
Fort Dalles Museum, The Dalles 42762
Fort d'Aubin-Neufchâteau et son Musée, Neufchâteau 03655
Fort Dauphin Museum, Dauphin 05308
Fort Davidson State Historic Site, Pilot Knob 46487
Fort Davis, Fort Davis 43384
Fort de Chartres Museum, Prairie du Rocher 46684
Fort de Seyne, Seyne-les-Alpes 14741
Fort de Vallorbe, Vallorbe 37277
Fort Delaware, Narrowsburg 45606
Fort Delaware Society Museum, Delaware City 42862
Fort Discovery, Augusta 41382
Fort Dix Museum, Fort Dix 43387
Fort Dobbs State Historic Site, Statesville 47793
Fort Dodge Historical Museum, Fort Dodge 43389
Fort Donelson National Battlefield Museum, Dover 42975
Fort Dorsner, Giromagny 11868
Fort Douglas Military Museum, Fort Douglas 43390
Fort Edmonton Park, Edmonton 05376
Fort Edward, Grand-Pré 05517
Fort Erie Historical Museum, Ridgeway 06268
Fort Erie Railroad Museum, Fort Erie 05435
Le fort et son Musée, Flémalle 03418
Fort Fetterman State Museum, Douglas 42964
Fort Fisher, Kure Beach 44529
Fort Fleur d'Epée, Le Gosier 21246
Fort Frances Museum, Fort Frances 05437
Fort Frederica, Saint Simons Island 47180
Fort Frederick, Big Pool 41681
Fort Garry Horse Regimental Museum, Winnipeg 06825
Fort George, Niagara-on-the-Lake 06000
Fort George and Buckingham House, Saint Paul 06368
Fort George G. Meade Museum, Fort Meade 43426
Fort George Museum, Elk Point 05402
Fort Gibson Historic Site, Fort Gibson 43395
Fort Glanville, Semaphore Park 01446
Fort Grey and Shipwreck Museum, Saint Peter Port 40423
Fort Hancock Museum, Sandy Hook 47391
Fort Harker Museum, Kanopolis 44390
Fort Hartsuff, Burwell 42014
Fort Hays, Hays 43969
Fort Henry, Kingston 05675
Fort Hill Museum, Hillsboro 44026
Fort Hill - The John C. Calhoun House, Clemson 42456
Fort Huachuca Museum, Fort Huachuca 43399
Fort Hunter Mansion, Harrisburg 43923
Fort Inglish, Bonham 41779
Fort Jackson Museum, Fort Jackson 43401
Fort Jesus Museum, Mombasa 27109
Fort Jones Museum, Fort Jones 43405
Fort Kearney Museum, Kearney 44421
Fort Kearny State Historical Park, Kearney 44422
Fort Kijkduin, Castricum 29055
Fort King George Historic Site, Darien 42783
Fort Klock Historic Restoration, Saint Johnsville 47100
Fort Knox State Historic Site, Stockton Springs 47826
Fort La Reine Museum and Pioneer Village, Portage-la-Prairie 06172
Fort Langley National Historic Site, Fort Langley 05441
Fort Laramie, Fort Laramie 43407
Fort Larned, Larned 44655
Fort Laurens State Memorial, Bolivar 41776
Fort Leaton, Presidio 46691
Fort Leavenworth Historical Museum and Post Museum, Fort Leavenworth 43415
Fort Leboeuf, Waterford 48430
Fort l'Ecluse, Leaz 12500
Fort Lee Historic Park and Museum, Fort Lee 43417
Fort Lennox, Saint-Paul-de-Ile-aux-Noix 06370
Fort Lewis Military Museum, Fort Lewis 43422
Fort Ligonier Museum, Ligonier 44770
Fort Loudoun, Chambersburg 42184
Fort McAllister, Richmond Hill 46893
Fort MacArthur Museum, San Pedro 47371
Fort McHenry, Baltimore 41467
Fort McKavett State Historic Park, Fort McKavett 43423
Fort Mackinac, Mackinac Island 45029
Fort Macon, Atlantic Beach 41364
Fort Malden, Amherstburg 04987
Fort Massac, Metropolis 45278
Fort Matanzas, Saint Augustine 47067
Fort Meigs State Memorial, Perrysburg 46357
Fort Mifflin, Philadelphia 46410
Fort Morgan Museum, Fort Morgan 43432
Fort Morgan Museum, Gulf Shores 43852
Fort Morris, Midway 45331
Fort Mountain, Chatsworth 42267
Fort Muséalisé d'Uxegney, Uxegney 15032
Fort Museum, Fort Macleod 05443
Fort Myers Historical Museum, Fort Myers 43436
Fort N5 - Muzej Istorii Velikoj Otečestvennoj Vojny, Kaliningrad 32868
Fort Namutoni, Tsumeb 28774
Fort Napoleon, Oostende 03667
Fort Nashborough, Nashville 45618
Fort Necessity National Battlefield, Farmington 43300
Fort Nelson Heritage Museum, Fort Nelson 05447
Fort Nisqually Living History Museum, Tacoma 47917
Fort No 5 - Museum of the Great Patriotic War, Kaliningrad 32868
Fort Normandeau, Red Deer 06221
Fort-Numéro-Un de la Pointe-de-Lévy, Québec 06196
Fort Okanogan, Pateros 46308
Fort Ontario, Oswego 46215
Fort Osage, Sibley 47623
Fort Ostell Museum, Ponoka 06146
Fort Peck Museum, Fort Peck 43439
Fort Pelley and Livingston Museum, Pelly 06104
Fort Phil Kearny, Story 47838
Fort Pike, New Orleans 45724
Fort Pitt Museum, Pittsburg 46505
Fort Plain Museum, Fort Plain 43443
Fort Point Museum, LaHave 05717
Fort Polk Military Museum, Fort Polk 43444
Fort Pulaski, Savannah 47478
Fort Qu'appelle Museum, Fort Qu'appelle 05448
Fort Queenscliff Museum, Queenscliff 01400
Fort Raleigh, Manteo 45126
Fort Rammekens, Ritthem 29736
Fort Recovery Museum, Fort Recovery 43447
Fort Richardson, Jacksboro 44275
Fort Robinson Museum, Crawford 42689
Fort Rodd Hill Museum, Victoria 06720
Fort Roosevelt Natural Science and History Museum, Hanford 43903
Fort Saint George Museum, Chennai 21743
Fort Saint James National Historic Site, Fort Saint James 05449
Fort Saint Jean Baptiste, Natchitoches 45635
Fort Saint John-North Peace Museum, Fort Saint John 05450
Fort Saint Joseph, Richards Landing 06256
Fort Saint Joseph Museum, Niles 45954
Fort Saint Joseph National Historic Park, Saint Joseph Island 06357
Fort Saint Pierre, Fort Frances 05438
Fort Sam Houston Museum, Fort Sam Houston 43451
Fort San Pedro National Museum, Cebu 31312
Fort Saskatchewan Museum, Fort Saskatchewan 05451
Fort Savannah Museum, Lewisburg 44725
Fort Scott National Historic Site, Fort Scott 43453
Fort Scratchley Museum, Newcastle 01315
Fort Selden State Monument, Radium Springs 46770
Fort Selkirk, Whitehorse 06791
Fort Sidney Museum and Post Commander's Home, Sidney 47625
Fort Sill, Fort Sill 43455
Fort Siloso, Singapore 33938
Fort Sisseton, Lake City 44585
Fort Smith, Fort Smith 43456
Fort Smith Art Center, Fort Smith 43457
Fort Smith Museum of History, Fort Smith 43458
Fort Spokane Visitor Center and Museum, Davenport 42787
Fort Stanwix, Rome 46996
Fort Steele Heritage Town, Fort Steele 05453
Fort Stewart Museum, Fort Stewart 43460
Fort Sumner, Fort Sumner 43463
Fort Sumter National Monument, Sullivan's Island 47873
Fort Tejon, Lebec 44706
Fort Ticonderoga, Ticonderoga 48005
Fort Totten State Historic Museum, Fort Totten 43464
Fort Towson Military Park, Fort Towson 43465
Fort Union National Monument, Watrous 48454
Fort Union Trading Post National Historic Site, Williston 48639
Fort Vancouver, Vancouver 48200
Fort Vasquez Museum, Platteville 46544
Fort Walla Walla Museum, Walla Walla 48285
Fort Walsh, Maple Creek 05809
Fort Ward Museum and Historic Site, Alexandria 41125
Fort Washington, Fort Washington 43469
Fort Washington Museum, Fort Washington 43471
Fort Washita, Durant 43016
Fort Wayne Firefighters Museum, Fort Wayne 43475
Fort Wayne Museum of Art, Fort Wayne 43476
Fort Wellington, Prescott 06179
Fort Whoop-Up Centre, Lethbridge 05745
Fort Widley, Portsmouth 40252
Fort Wilkins Historic Complex, Copper Harbor 42624
Fort William Henry Museum, Lake George 44587
Fort Winnebago Surgeons Quarters, Portage 46612
Fort Worth Museum of Science and History, Fort Worth 43485
Fort Worth Public Library Arts and Humanities, Fort Worth 43486
Fort Yargo, Winder 48680
Fort Zachary Taylor, Key West 44465
Fortaleza de Nuestra Señora de los Angeles de Jagua, Jagua 08011
Fortaleza de San Felipe, Santo Domingo 09117
Forte Rinascimentale, San Leo 25379
Forteresse-Château, Sainte-Suzanne 14552
Forteresse de Mornas, Mornas 13168
Forteresse de Salses, Salses-le-Château 14592
Fortifications-de-Québec, Québec 06197
Fortín San Jerónimo del Boquerón, San Juan 32390
Fortress Museum, Cesena 23502
Fortress Museum, Hanko 09463
Fortress of Louisbourg, Louisbourg 05782
Forts Folle Avoine Historic Park, Danbury 42772
Forty Hall Museum, Enfield 38937
Forum am Deutschen Museum, München 18849
Forum Art Gallery, Sankt-Peterburg 33394
Forum der Schweizer Geschichte, Schwyz 37150
Forum Européen des Conseillers et Consultants de Musée, Bruxelles 49072
Forum Flüh, Flüh 36705
Forum Fränkischer Hof, Bad Rappenau 15714
Forum für Angewandte Kunst im Bayerischen Kunstgewerbeverein e.V., Nürnberg 19136
Forum Gallery, Jamestown 44312
Forum Gießen, Gießen 17279
Forum Hall, Bad Hall 01704
Forum Konkrete Kunst Erfurt, Erfurt 16898
Forum Konkrete Kunst - Peterskirche, Erfurt 16899
Forum Marinum, Turku 10120
Forum Museo, Omegna 24678
Forum Schloßplatz, Aarau 36425
Forwarders' Museum, Prescott 06180
Foshan City Museum, Foshan 07049
Fosnes Bygdemuseum, Jøa 30585
Fossa Magna Museum, Itoigawa 26266
Les Fosses d'Enfer, Saint-Rémy-sur-Orne 14454
Fossesholm Herregård, Vestfossen 30989
Fossielenmuseum, Oostkapelle 29672
Fossil Country Museum, Kemmerer 44431
Fossil Grove, Glasgow 39044
Fossil Museum, Fossil 43494
Fossil Station Museum, Russell 47033
Fossilien- und Heimatmuseum, Messel 18718
Fossilienmuseum im Werkforum Rohrbach Zement, Dotternhausen 16670
Fossilienschauraum, Ernstbrunn 01822
Fossils Museum, Byblos 27489
Fossmotunet - Målselv Bygdemuseum, Moen 30679
Foster and District Historical Society Museum, Foster 01033
Foster Gallery, Eau Claire 43075
Fosterfields Living Historical Farm, Morristown 45505
Fostoria Area Historical Museum, Fostoria 43495
Fota House, Carrigtwohill 22385
Fotevikens Museum, Höllviken 35958
Fotland Bygdemølle, Bryne 30452
Fotland Kraftverk, Bryne 30453
Fotland Power Plant, Bryne 30453
Fotland Village Mill, Bryne 30452
Foto-Museum, Essen 16949

Fotoforum West, Innsbruck 02064
Fotogalerie Alte Feuerwache, Mannheim 18611
Fotogalerie Friedrichshain, Berlin 15949
Fotogalerie Landesbildstelle, Hamburg 17539
Fotografičeskij Muzej Dom Metenkova, Ekaterinburg 32767
Fotograficzny Muzeum Regionalnego w Mielcu, Mielec 31805
Fotografie Forum international, Frankfurt am Main 17041
Fotohistorische Sammlung, Penk 02396
Fotomuséet i Osby, Osby 36152
Fotomuseet Olympia, Falkenberg 35877
Fotomuseum CAMERAMA, Bad Soden am Taunus 15744
Fotomuseum Den Haag, Den Haag 29094
Fotomuseum im Münchner Stadtmuseum, München 18850
Fotomuseum Provincie Antwerpen, Antwerpen 03144
Fotomuseum Winterthur, Winterthur 37327
Fotoplastikon, Warszawa 32082
Fototeca de Cuba, La Habana 07928
Foundation for Photography, Amsterdam 28861
Foundation for Women's Art, London 39637
Founders Gallery, San Diego 47276
Founders Historic Park, Nelson 30209
Founders Room, Raanana 22729
Foundling Museum, London 39638
Foundry Museum, Budapest 21371
Four Rivers Cultural Center, Ontario 46166
Four Solaire, Mont-Louis 13028
Four Wheel Drive Foundation, Clintonville 42501
Fővárosi Képtár, Budapest 21338
Fowler Museum of Cultural History, Los Angeles 44900
Fox Island Historical Society Museum, Fox Island 43499
Fox Lake Historical Museum, Fox Lake 43500
Fox River Trolley Museum, South Elgin 47692
Fox Talbot Museum, Lacock 39408
Foxton Canal Museum, Foxton 39012
Foxton Flax Stripper museum, Foxton 30161
Foxton Museum, Foxton 30162
Foyer Gallery/James Hockey Gallery, Farnham 38981
Foyer Rural, Jupilles 12106
Foyle Valley Railway Museum, Londonderry 39815
Foynes Flying Boat Museum, Foynes 22471
FRAC Limousin, Limoges 12609
Fränkische Galerie, Kronach 18243
Fränkische Hopfenscheune mit heimatkundlicher Sammlung, Neunkirchen am Sand 19053
Fränkische-Schweiz-Museum, Pottenstein 19438
Fränkisches Bauern- und Handwerkermuseum Kirchenburg Mönchsondheim, Iphofen 17914
Fränkisches Brauereimuseum, Bamberg 15806
Fränkisches Freilandmuseum, Bad Windsheim 15776
Fränkisches Freilandmuseum Fladungen, Fladungen 17009
Fränkisches Museum, Feuchtwangen 16997
Fränkisches Spielzeugmuseum, Gößweinstein 17330
Fränkisches Turmuhrenmuseum, Mistelbach 18751
Fraeylemaborg, Slochteren 29832
Frame Gallery, Pittsburgh 46515
Frames Northern Museum, Creighton 05288
Framgi Dadabhoy Alpaiwalle Museum, Mumbai 21947
Framingham Historical Society and Museum, Framingham 43502
Frammuseet, Oslo 30734
Franča Trasuna Muzejs Kolnasāta, Sakstagals 27448
Frances Burke Textile Resource Centre, Melbourne 01226
Frances Lehman Loeb Art Center, Poughkeepsie 46674
Francis Colburn Gallery, Burlington 42008
Francis Land House, Virginia Beach 48247
Francis Ledwidge Cottage and Museum, Slane 22540
Francis McCray Gallery, Silver City 47628
Francis Trasuns Museum Kolnasāta, Sakstagals 27448
Franciscan Monastery, Fojnica 33839
Franciscan Monastery, Ystad 36422
Francisco Fort Museum, La Veta 44559
Die Franckeschen Stiftungen zu Halle, Halle, Saale 17509
Franjevački Samostan, Fojnica 33839
Frank H. McClung Museum, Knoxville 44519
Frank Lloyd Wright Home and Studio, Oak Park 46052
Frank Lloyd Wright's Pope-Leighey House, Mount Vernon 45545
Frank Mills Outdoor Mining Machinery Museum, Silverton 06455
Frank Partridge V.C. Military Museum, Bowraville 00823
Frank Phillips Home, Bartlesville 41514
Frank Slide Interpretive Centre, Crowsnest Pass 05291
Frankenberger Art Gallery, Charleston 42230
Frankenburger Heimatstube, Frankenburg 01844
Frankenmuth Historical Museum, Frankenmuth 43505
Frankenwaldmuseum, Kronach 18244
Frankfort Area Historical Museum, West Frankfort 48523
Frankfurter Äpfelwein-Museum, Frankfurt am Main 17042
Frankfurter Feldbahnmuseum, Frankfurt am Main 17043
Frankfurter Kunstverein e.V., Frankfurt am Main 17044
Frankfurter Sportmuseum, Frankfurt am Main 17045
Franklin County Historical Museum, Pasco 46307
Franklin County Museum, Brookville 41958
Franklin County Old Jail Museum, Winchester 48678
Franklin D. Roosevelt Library-Museum, Hyde Park 44187
Franklin G. Burroughs-Simeon B. Chapin Art Museum, Myrtle Beach 45586
Franklin Historical Society Museum, Franklin 43518
Franklin House, Launceston 01168
The Franklin Institute, Philadelphia 46411
Franklin Mineral Museum, Franklin 43519
Franklin Mint Museum, Franklin Center 43523
The Franklin Museum, Tucson 48088
Franklin Pierce Homestead, Hillsborough 44031
Franks Antique Doll Museum, Marshall 45181
Frankston Primary Old School Museum, Frankston 01034
Frans Hals Museum, Haarlem 29324
Frans Walkate Archief/ SNS Historisch Archief, Kampen 29469
Fransu Cottage, Himanka 09549
Fransu-tupa, Himanka 09549
Franz Jonas-Gedenkraum, Teesdorf 02716
Franz-Liszt-Museum der Stadt Bayreuth, Bayreuth 15845
Franz-Marc-Museum, Kochel am See 18124
Franz Michael Felder-Stube, Schoppernau 02638
Franz Radziwill Haus, Varel 20285
Franz Schmidt Museum, Perchtoldsdorf 02399
Franz Stelzhamer-Geburtshaus, Pramet 02447
Franz Traunfellner-Dokumentation, Pöggstall 02425
Franz von Stuck Geburtshaus Tettenweis, Tettenweis 20163
Franz Winkelmeier-Gedenkraum, Friedburg 01854
Franz Xaver Gruber-Gedächtnishaus, Ach 01640
Franz Xaver Gruber-Museum, Lamprechtshausen 02179
Franz Zeh-Museum, Heidenreichstein 02010
Franzensburg, Laxenburg 02197
Franziskanermuseum, Villingen-Schwenningen 20316
Frasassi- le Grotte, Genga 23974
Fraser-Fort George Regional Museum, Prince George 06186
Fraser Lake Museum, Fraser Lake 05456
Fraserburgh Museum, Fraserburgh 39015
Frau Holle Expreß, Hessisch-Lichtenau 17745
Frauen Museum, Bonn 16236
Frauen Museum Wiesbaden, Wiesbaden 20572
Frauenbad - Zentrum für zeitgenössische Kunst, Baden bei Wien 01727
Fraunces Tavern Museum, New York 45801
Frazer's Museum, Beauval 05067
Fred Dana Marsh Museum, Ormond Beach 46192
Fred Harman Art Museum, Pagosa Springs 46260
Fred Jones Jr. Museum of Art, Norman 45974
Fred Light Museum, Battleford 05061
Fred Wolf Jr. Gallery, Philadelphia 46412
Frederic Chopin Birth House, Warszawa 32081
Frédéric Chopin's House, Sochaczew 31985
Frederic Remington Art Museum, Ogdensburg 46103
Frederick C. Robie House, Chicago 42328
Frederick Chopin Museum, Warszawa 32096
Frederick Douglass National Historic Site, Washington 48356
Frederick Law Olmsted Historic Site, Brookline 41935
Frederick R. Weisman Art Foundation, Los Angeles 44901
Frederick R. Weisman Art Museum, Minneapolis 45383
Frederick R. Weisman Museum of Art, Malibu 45083
Fredericksburg and Spotsylvania National Military Park, Fredericksburg 43534
Fredericksburg Area Museum and Cultural Center, Fredericksburg 43535
Frederikshavn Kunstmuseum- og Exlibrissamling, Frederikshavn 08830
Frederiksværk Bymuseum, Frederiksværk 08833
Fredriksdals Friluftsmuseum, Helsingborg 35949
Fredrikstad Museum, Fredrikstad 30504
Fredy's Mechanisches Musikmuseum, Lichtensteig 36873
Free Public Library Collection, New Bedford 45661
Free State Voortrekker Museum, Winburg 34404
Freeborn County Historical Museum, Albert Lea 41094
Freedman Gallery, Reading 46806
Freeport Arts Center, Freeport 43549
Freeport Historical Society Museum, Freeport 43552
Freer Gallery of Art, Washington 48357
Freestone County Historical Museum, Fairfield 43268
Fregatten Jylland, Ebeltoft 08802
Freiämter Strohmuseum, Wohlen (Aargau) 37348
Freiburger Fasnetmuseum, Freiburg im Breisgau 17109
Freies Deutsches Hochstift/ Frankfurter Goethe-Museum mit Goethe-Haus, Frankfurt am Main 17046
Freiland-Grenzmuseum Sorge, Sorge, Harz 20004
Freilandmuseum Ammerländer Bauernhaus, Bad Zwischenahn 15782
Freilandmuseum Grassemann Naturpark-Infostelle, Warmensteinach 20401
Freilicht- und Heimatmuseum Donaumoos, Karlshuld 17988
Freilichtmuseum, Bad Tatzmannsdorf 01719
Freilichtmuseum, Diesdorf, Altmark 16598
Freilichtmuseum, Stade 20022
Freilichtmuseum Alt Schwerin, Alt Schwerin 15439
Freilichtmuseum am Kiekeberg, Rosengarten, Kreis Harburg 19648
Freilichtmuseum am Rätischen Limes, Rainau 19478
Freilichtmuseum Anzenaumühle, Bad Goisern 01699
Freilichtmuseum Apriacher Stockmühlen, Heiligenblut 02015
Freilichtmuseum Beuren, Beuren bei Nürtingen 16133
Freilichtmuseum des Gebirgskrieges, Kötschach-Mauthen 02149
Freilichtmuseum Domäne Dahlem, Berlin 15950
Freilichtmuseum Dorfstube Ötlingen, Weil am Rhein 20434
Freilichtmuseum Ensemble Gerersdorf, Gerersdorf 01875
Freilichtmuseum Erdöl- und Erdgaslehrpfad, Prottes 02457
Freilichtmuseum Finsterau, Mauth 18666
Freilichtmuseum "Frelsdorfer Brink", Frelsdorf 17126
Freilichtmuseum Fürstenhammer, Lasberg 02191
Freilichtmuseum Glentleiten, Großweil 17443
Freilichtmuseum Hammerschmiede, Bad Wimsbach-Neydharting 01722
Freilichtmuseum Handwerkerhaus Stegwagner, Windhaag bei Freistadt 03034
Freilichtmuseum Hessenpark, Neu-Anspach 19003
Freilichtmuseum Himmelreich, Volders 02770
Freilichtmuseum Historische Volkskunde Kalte Kuchl, Rohr im Gebirge 02519
Freilichtmuseum Katzensteiner Mühle, Weyer 02827
Freilichtmuseum Klausenhof, Herrischried 17736
Freilichtmuseum Klockenhagen, Klockenhagen 18112
Freilichtmuseum Kugelmühle, Seeham 02657
Freilichtmuseum Ledermühle, Sankt Oswald bei Freistadt 02591
Freilichtmuseum Lehde, Lehde bei Lübbenau 18369
Freilichtmuseum Massing, Massing 18664
Freilichtmuseum Mondseer Rauchhaus, Mondsee 02320
Freilichtmuseum Neuhausen ob Eck, Neuhausen ob Eck 19035
Freilichtmuseum Oberlienz, Oberlienz 02369
Freilichtmuseum Ostenfelder Bauernhaus, Husum, Nordsee 17869
Freilichtmuseum Pelmberg, Hellmonsödt 02019
Freilichtmuseum Petronell, Petronell 02409
Freilichtmuseum Rhöner Museumsdorf, Tann, Rhön 20141
Freilichtmuseum Römersteinbruch, Sankt Margarethen 02581
Freilichtmuseum Römervilla in Brederis, Rankweil 02484
Freilichtmuseum Säge Buch, Buch 36595
Freilichtmuseum Sägehammer Hofwies, Windhaag bei Freistadt 03035
Freilichtmuseum Scherzenmühle Weidenberg, Weidenberg 20427
Freilichtmuseum Schwebsingen, Bech-Kleinmacher 27541
Freilichtmuseum Spätbronzezeitlicher Hügelgräber, Siegendorf 02660
Freilichtmuseum Stehrerhof - Dreschmaschinenmuseum, Neukirchen an der Vöckla 02346
Freilichtmuseum Tiroler Bauernhöfe, Kramsach 02152
Freilichtmuseum Venetianersäge, Windhaag bei Freistadt 03036
Freilichtmuseum Vorau, Vorau 02773
Freiligrath Museum, Rüdesheim am Rhein 19705
Freimaurer-Museum, Berlin 15951
Freimaurermuseum der Großen Landesloge der Freimaurer von Deutschland, Sankt Michaelisdonn 19754
Freiraum, Forchtenstein 01841
Frejamuseét, Kil 36006
Fremantle Arts Centre, Fremantle 01035
Fremantle History Museum, Fremantle 01036
Fremantle Prison Precinct, Fremantle 01037
Fremont County Pioneer Museum, Lander 44632
French Art Colony, Gallipolis 43604
French Azilum, Towanda 48043
French Cable Station Museum in Orleans, Orleans 46191
The French Legation Museum, Austin 41411
Frenchman Butte Museum, Frenchman Butte 05470
Fresco Gallery, Beograd 33796
Freshford House Museum, Bloemfontein 34184
Fresno Art Museum, Fresno 43558
Fresno Metropolitan Museum, Fresno 43559
Freud Museum, London 39639
Fri-Art, Fribourg 36713
F.R.I. Museums, Dehradun 21760
Friary Art Gallery, Lichfield 39489
The Frick Art Museum, Pittsburgh 46516
Frick Collection, New York 45802
Fricktaler Museum, Rheinfelden 37054
Fričovo Muzeum, Lázně Bělohrad 08443
Frīdriha Candera Memoriālais Muzejs, Rīga 27407
Friedenshistorisches Museum, Bad Hindelang 15661
Friedensmuseum, Meeder 18670
Friedensmuseum, Remagen 19560
Friedensräume, Lindau, Bodensee 18474
Friedenszimmer im Schloß Altranstädt, Altranstädt 15473
Friedlandstube Hünfeld, Hünfeld 17855
Friedrich-Eckenfelder-Galerie, Balingen 15797
Friedrich-Engels-Haus, Wuppertal 20710
Friedrich-Ludwig-Jahn-Gedenkstätte, Lanz 18342
Friedrich-Ludwig-Jahn-Museum, Freyburg 17130
Friedrich-Rückert-Gedächtnisstätte, Coburg 16481
Friedrich-Wilhelm-Weber-Museum, Bad Driburg 15626
The Friends of Photography at the Ansel Adams Center, San Francisco 47317
Friendship Firehouse, Alexandria 41126
Friendship Hill National Historic Site, Point Marion 46574
Friendship Museum, Darhan 28674
Fries Landbouw Museum, Exmorra 29257
Fries Museum, Leeuwarden 29508
Fries Natuurmuseum, Leeuwarden 29509
Fries Scheepvaart Museum, Sneek 29838
Friesenstube Honkenswarf, Langeneß 18334
Friesisches Heimatmuseum, Niebüll 19092
Frietkotmuseum, Antwerpen 03145
Frigate Suomen Joutsen, Turku 10129
Frigate Unicorn, Dundee 38799
Frihedsmuseet, København 08929
Frilandsmuseet, Kongens Lyngby 08962
Frilandsmuseet i Maribo, Maribo 08980
Friluftmuseet Hallandsgården, Halmstad 35940
Friluftmuseet Skansen, Stockholm 36242
Friluftsmuseet, Jönköping 35976
Friluftsmuseet Gammelgården, Köping 36009
Friluftsmuseet i Apladalen, Värnamo 36376
Friluftsmuseum Färgargården, Norrköping 36116
Frisco Historical Society Museum, Frisco 43564
Frisco Native American Museum and Natural History Center, Frisco 43565
Frisia Museum, Spanbroek 29846
Frist Center for the Visual Arts, Nashville 45619
Fritz-Best-Museum, Kronberg 18247
Fritz Fröhlich-Sammlung im Stift Wilhering, Wilhering 03032
Fritz-Reuter-Literaturmuseum, Reuterstadt Stavenhagen 19574
Fritz-Winter-Haus, Ahlen 15401
Fritz Wotruba-Gedenkraum, Wien 02884
Fritzøe Museum, Larvik 30629
Froaschgass-Museum, Wettenberg 20546
Frobisher Thresherman's Museum, Frobisher 05471
Fröbelmuseum, Keilhau 18048
Frösö Hembygdsmuseum, Frösön 35896
Frövifors Pappersbruksmuseum, Frövi 35897
Frog Museum, Den Haag 29099
Frog Museum, Estavayer-le-Lac 36692
Frogmore House, Windsor 40900
From Holocaust to Revival Museum, Chof Ashkelon 22584
Fromagerie Coumes, Seix 14695
Fromagerie de Démonstration de Gruyères, Pringy 37035
Frome Museum, Frome 39019
Front Gallery, Edmonton 05377
Front Street Museum, Ogallala 46095
Frontenac County Schools Museum, Kingston 05676
Frontier Army Museum, Fort Leavenworth 43416
Frontier Culture Museum, Staunton 47795
Frontier Museum, Williston 48640
Frontier Times Museum, Bandera 41491
Frontier Village Museum, Jamestown 44307
Frontiers of Flight Museum, Dallas 42753
Froschmuseum, Münchenstein 36964
Frøslevlejrens Museum, Padborg 09023
The Frost Entomological Museum, University Park 48152
Frosta Bygdemuseet, Frosta 30506
Frøya Bygdemuseum, Sistranda 30838
Frühmittelaltermuseum Carantana, Rothenthurn 02527
Fruitlands Museums, Harvard 43952
Fruitmarket Gallery, Edinburgh 38882
Fruitteeltmuseum, Kapelle 29475
Frunse House-Museum, Samara 33369
Fry Model Railway, Demesne 22408
Fry Model Railway Museum, Malahide 22515
Fry Public Art Gallery, Saffron Walden 40367
Frye Art Museum, Seattle 47534
The Fryeburg Fair Farm Museum, Fryeburg 43571
Fryer Memorial Museum, Munnsville 45561
Frye's Measure Mill, Wilton 48673
Frysk Letterkundich Museum, Leeuwarden 29510
Fryxell Geology Museum, Rock Island 46955
F.T. Hill Museum, Riverhurst 06274
Fuchu-shi Kyodono-mori, Fuchu 26137
Fünf-Giebel-Haus & Alte Münze, Friedrichstadt 17151
Fürst Pückler Museum - Park und Schloß Branitz, Cottbus 16501
Fürst Thurn und Taxis Marstallmuseum, Regensburg 19521
Fürst Thurn und Taxis Schloßmuseum - Museum Kreuzgang, Regensburg 19522
Fürst Thurn und Taxis Zentralarchiv und Hofbibliothek, Regensburg 19523
Fürstenbergerhof, Zell am Harmersbach 20739
Fürstengruft mit russisch-orthodoxer Kirche, Weimar, Thüringen 20457
Fürstenzimmer im Schloß Kirchheim, Kirchheim unter Teck 18095
Fürstlich Esterházy'sche Sammlungen Burg Forchtenstein, Forchtenstein 01842
Fürstlich Fürstenbergisches Schloßmuseum, Donaueschingen 16634
Fürstlich Hohenzollernsche Sammlungen, Sigmaringen 19956
Fürstlich Leiningensche Sammlungen - Heimatmuseum, Amorbach 15485
Fürstlich Ysenburg- und Büdingensches Schloßmuseum, Büdingen 16397

Fürstliches Residenzschloß, Detmold 16587
Fürstliches Schloß mit Gemäldegalerie, Mausoleum, Bückeburg 16392
Fuerte de la Punta del Sauce, La Carlota 00376
Fugger-Museum, Babenhausen, Schwaben 15582
Fuggerei-Museum, Augsburg 15554
Fugitive Art Center, Nashville 45620
Fuglsøcentret, Knebel 08919
Fuhlrott-Museum, Wuppertal 20711
Fujairah Museum, Fujairah 37918
Fuji Art Museum, Fujinomiya 26139
Fuji Visitor Center, Kawaguchiko 26323
Fujian Province Museum, Fuzhou 07056
Fujii Bijutsu Mingeikan, Takayama 26801
Fujii Saisei-kai Yurinkan, Kyoto 26397
Fujita Museum of Art, Osaka 26644
Fujita Vente, Tokyo 26846
Fukagawa Edo Museum of Television, Tokyo 26874
Fukui City Natural Science Museum, Fukui 26141
Fukui Fujita Art Museum, Fukui 26142
Fukui Fujita Bijutsukan, Fukui 26142
Fukui-ken Togeikan, Miyazaki, Fukui 26508
Fukui-kenritsu Bijutsukan, Fukui 26143
Fukui-kenritsu Hakubutsukan, Fukui 26144
Fukui Prefectural Ceramics Museum, Miyazaki, Fukui 26508
Fukui Prefectural Fine Arts Museum, Fukui 26143
Fukui Prefectural Museum, Fukui 26144
Fukuoka Art Museum, Fukuoka 26146
Fukuoka City Museum, Fukuoka 26147
Fukuoka-kenritsu Bijutsukan, Fukuoka 26145
Fukuoka Prefectural Museum of Art, Fukuoka 26145
Fukuoka-shi Bijutsukan, Fukuoka 26146
Fukuoka-shi Hakubutsukan, Fukuoka 26147
Fukushima Cultural Center, Fukushima 26148
Fukushima-ken Bunka Center, Fukushima 26148
Fukushima-kenritsu Bijutsukan, Fukushima 26149
Fukushima-kenritsu Hakubutsukan, Aizuwakamatsu 26090
Fukushima Museum, Aizuwakamatsu 26090
Fukushima Prefectural Museum of Art, Fukushima 26149
Fukuyama Auto and Clock Museum, Fukuyama 26150
Fukuyama-Jo Castle Museum, Fukuyama 26151
Fukuyama Museum of Art, Fukuyama 26152
Fukuzawa Memorial Hall, Nakatsu 26574
Fuller Museum of Art, Brockton 41909
Fullerton Museum Center, Fullerton 43572
Fulton County Historical Museum, Wauseon 48465
Fulton County Historical Society Museum, Rochester 46932
Fulton County Museum, Groversville 43849
Fulton Mansion, Rockport 46972
Fultz House Museum, Lower Sackville 05784
Funabashi Hakubutsukan, Funabashi 26154
Funabashi Municipal Museum, Funabashi 26154
Fundação Casa de Jorge Amado, Salvador 04420
Fundação Clóuis Salgado - Palácio das Artes, Belo Horizonte 03979
Fundação Cultural Ema Gordon Klabin, São Paulo 04491
Fundação Eva Klabin Rappaport, Rio de Janeiro 04325
Fundação Hansen Bahia, Cachoeira 04013
Fundação Maria Luisa e Oscar Americano, São Paulo 04492
Fundação Memorial da América Latina, São Paulo 04493
Fundação Museu do Zebu Edilson Lamartine Mendes, Uberaba 04574
Fundação Nacional Pró-Memória, Rio de Janeiro 04326
Fundaçao Oscar Niemeyer, Rio de Janeiro 04327
Fundação Ricardo do Espírito Santo Silva, Lisboa 32287
Fundació Antoni Tàpies, Barcelona 34538
Fundació Barceló, Palma de Mallorca 35226
Fundació Emili Vilá, Llagostera 34960
Fundació Joan Miró, Barcelona 34539
Fundació la Caixa en las Islas Baleares, Palma de Mallorca 35227
Fundació Pilar i Joan Miró, Palma de Mallorca 35228
Fundació Pública Institut d'Estudis Ilerdencs, Lleida 34965
Fundación Alfredo L. Palacios, Buenos Aires 00149
Fundación Archivo Gráfico y Museo Histórico de la Ciudad de San Francisco y la Región, San Francisco 00560
Fundación Banco Francés, Buenos Aires 00150
Fundación César Manrique, Teguise 35519
Fundación Cultural Otero Pedrayo, Trasalba-Amoeiro 35572
Fundación de Fomento a las Artes, La Paz 03894
Fundación Federico Jorge Klemm, Buenos Aires 00151
Fundación Folch, Barcelona 34540
Fundación Juan March, Madrid 35007
Fundación Municipal de Cultura Luis Ortega Brú, San Roque 35390
Fundacion Museo de la Caricatura Severo Vaccaro, Buenos Aires 00152
Fundacion Privada Espai Guinovart, Agramunt 34409
Fundación Solar Rietti, Buenos Aires 00153
Fundación Yannick y Ben Jakober, Alcúdia 34439
Fundy Geological Museum, Parrsboro 06095
Fune no Kagakukan, Tokyo 26847
Funen Village, Odense 09010
Funnefoss Industriarbeidermuseum, Årnes 30394
Fur Museum, Fur 08835
Fureai Minatokan, Osaka 26645
Furlong Art Gallery, Menomonie 45255
Furnas-Gosper Historical Society Museum, Arapahoe 41243
Furneaux Museum, Flinders Island 01028
Furness Abbey, Barrow-in-Furness 38096
Furniture Collection, Duchcov 08335
Furniture Industry Museum Virserum, Virserum 36412
Furniture Museum, Markušovce 34021
Furniture Museum, Tokyo 26865
Fursdon House, Cadbury 38428
Furthmühle, Egenhofen 16785
Fushun City Museum, Fushun 07053
Fusiliers London Volunteers' Museum, London 39640
Fusiliers' Museum Lancashire, Bury, Lancashire 38413
Fusiliers Museum of Northumberland, Alnwick 37984
Fusions Gallery, Fortitude Valley 01031
Futtsu Oceanographic Museum of Chiba Prefecture, Kimitsu 26334
Fuxin City Museum, Fuxin 07054
Fuyang Museum, Fuyang 07055
Fuzhou City Hualin Si, Fuzhou 07057
Fuzoku Hakubutsukan, Kyoto 26398
Fyns Kunstmuseum, Odense 09009
Den Fynske Landsby, Odense 09010
Fyresdal Bygdemuseet, Fyresdal 30507
Fyresdal Open Air Museum, Fyresdal 30507
Fyvie Castle, Fyvie 39020
G. Tsybikov Regional Museum of Aginskoe, Aginskoe 32630
GAA Museum, Dublin 22426
Gabdulla Tukaj Museum, Kazan 32896
Gabinet Numizmatyczny Mennicy Państwowej, Warszawa 32083
Gabinet Prof. K. Sosnowskiego, Ośrodek Muzealny KTG, Kraków 31685
Gabinet Rycin Biblioteki Uniwersyteckiej w Warszawie, Warszawa 32084
Gabinet Rycin Polskiej Akademii Umiejętności w Krakowie, Kraków 31686
Gabinete de Antigüedades, Madrid 35008
Gabinete de Física Experimental Mentora Alsina, Barcelona 34541
Gabinete Numismático de Cataluña, Barcelona 34542
Gabinetto dei Disegni e delle Stampe, Bologna 23103
Gabinetto delle Stampe, Roma 25156
Gabinetto Disegni e Stampe degli Uffizi, Firenze 23836
Gabinetto Disegni e Stampe-Dipartimento di Storia delle Arti dell'Università di Pisa, Pisa 24947
Gabinetto Fotografico, Firenze 23837
Gabinetto Geologico e Botanico Piccinini, Pergola 24841
Gabinetto Nazionale delle Stampe, Roma 25157
Gabinetto Stampe e Disegni, Venezia 25916
Gablonzer Archiv Museum, Kaufbeuren 18038
Gabonamúzeum, Békéscsaba 21318
Gacheon Museum, Incheon 27190
Gadebuscher Galerie am Schlossberg, Gadebusch 17187
Gadsby's Tavern Museum, Alexandria 41127
Gadsden Arts Center, Quincy 46757
Gadsden Museum, Mesilla 45273
Gadsden Museum of Fine Arts, Gadsden 43579
Gaelic College of Celtic Arts and Crafts, English Town 05410
Gällersta Forngård, Örebro 36134
Gärtner- und Häckermuseum, Bamberg 15807
Gäubodenmuseum, Straubing 20077
Gage County Historical Museum, Beatrice 41555
Gaidu un Skautu Muzejs, Ogre 27390
Gaildorfer Stadtmuseum im Alten Schloß, Gaildorf 17192
Gailtaler Heimatmuseum-Sammlung Georg Essl, Hermagor 02023
Gaimusho, Gaiko Shiryokan, Tokyo 26848
Gaineswood, Demopolis 42869
Gainsborough Old Hall, Gainsborough 39021
Gainsborough's House, Sudbury, Suffolk 40642
Gairloch Heritage Museum, Gairloch 39022
Gakki Hakubutsukan, Tokyo 26849
Gakkigaku Shiryôkan, Tachikawa 26781
Galarie du Centre, Saint-Lambert 06358
Galashiels Museum, Galashiels 39023
Galchon Mask Museum, Goseong 27178
Galena-Jo Daviess County Historical Museum, Galena 43593
Galena Mining and Historical Museum, Galena 43596
Galereja Forum, Sankt-Peterburg 33394
Galereja Le Vall, Novosibirsk 33239
Galereja-masterskaja Chudožnika G.S. Rajševa, Chanty-Mansijsk 32743
Galereja na Bastionnoj, Pskov 33330
Galereja Novyj Passaž, Sankt-Peterburg 33395
Galereja Odoevskogo, Ekaterinburg 32768
Galereja Riza, Sergiev Posad 33520
Galereja Sovremennogo Iskusstva Arka, Vladivostok 33695
Galereja Sovremennogo Iskusstva Artétaž, Vladivostok 33696
Galereja Zarubežnogo Iskusstva im. Professora M.F. Gabyševa, Jakutsk 32842
Galeri Suav ve Küsav, İstanbul 37701
Galeria Bałucka, Łódź 31766
Galería Bienes Culturales, Victoria de las Tunas 08169
La Galería de Arte, La Habana 07929
Galería de Arte de la Escuela Armando Reverón, Barcelona 48888
Galería de Arte de la UCV, Caracas 48902
Galería de Arte de Tabasco, Villahermosa 28605
Galeria de Arte do Instituto de Artes da Universidade Federal do Rio Grande do Sul, Porto Alegre 04273
Galería de Arte Iztapalapa, México 28094
Galería de Arte Jaguar Despertado, Villahermosa 28606
Galería de Arte Moderna, Sucre 03905
Galería de Arte Nacional, Caracas 48903
Galeria de Arte Prof. Sylvio Vasconcellos, Belo Horizonte 03980
Galeria de Arte UNICAMP, Campinas 04022
Galería de Arte Universal, Santiago de Cuba 08128
Galería de Cinemateca, Montevideo 40989
Galería de Escuela Nacional de Artes Plásticas, México 28095
Galeria de Exposições Temporárias da CMMP, Macau 07161
Galería de Historia o Museo del Caracol, México 28096
Galería de la Asamblea Legislativa, Barcelona 48889
Galería de la Escuela de Diseño y Artesanias del Instituto Nacional de Bellas Artes, México 28097
Galería de la Escuela Nacional de Artes Plásticas, México 28098
Galería de la Raza, San Francisco 47318
Galería del Museo Anzoátegui, Barcelona 48890
Galería del Sur, México 28099
Galería Dr. Miguel Angel Gómez Ventura, Villahermosa 28607
Galería Episcopal, Zacatecas 28634
Galeria Erotica-Museum für erotische Kunst, Köln 18137
Galería Facultad de Bellas Artes, San José 07651
Galeria i Ośrodek Plastycznej Twórczości Dziecka, Toruń 32050
Galería IFAL, México 28100
Galéria J. Jakobyha, Košice 34004
Galería José María Velasco, México 28101
Galería la Capella de l'Antic, Barcelona 34543
Galería Los Oficios, La Habana 07930
Gáleria Marie Medvedckej, Tvrdošín 34076
Galería Mesa, Mesa 45270
Galéria Mesta Bratislavy, Bratislava 33963
Galeria Mexicana de Diseño, México 28102
Galeria Międzynarodowego Centrum Kultury, Kraków 31687
Galeria Miejeska Arsenał, Poznań 31895
Galería Monumento Histórico Nacional a la Bandera, Rosario 00524
Galería Municipal de Arte Moderno, Barcelona 48891
Galería Nacional, San Juan 32391
Galería Nacional de Arte, Tegucigalpa 21302
Galería Nacional de Bellas Artes, Santo Domingo 09118
Galería Nacional y Museo de los Niños, San José 07652
Galeria Okręgowe, Biała Podlaska 31483
Galeria Okręgowe, Chełm 31522
Galería Oriente, Santiago de Cuba 08129
Galería Pocitos, Montevideo 40990
Galeria Słowiańska przy Parafii Prawosławnej, Kraków 31688
Galeria Sztuki Dawna Synagoga, Nowy Sącz 31834
Galeria Sztuki im. W. i J. Kulczyckich, Zakopane 32204
Galeria Sztuki Polskiej XIX w. w Sukiennicach, Kraków 31689
Galeria Sztuki Wozownia, Toruń 32051
Galeria Sztuki Współczesnej, Szczecin 32023
Galería Teatro Nacional Enrique Echandi y Joaquín García Monge, San José 07653
Galería Universitaria Artistos, México 28103
Galeria Virtual da Casa das Rosas, São Paulo 04494
Galeria Władysława Hasiora, Zakopane 32205
Galeria Zamek w Reszlu, Reszel 31946
Galerías Pacífico de Centro Cultural Borges, Buenos Aires 00154
Galerie 100, Berlin 15952
Galerie 37. Kunst im Museum der Weltkulturen, Frankfurt am Main 17047
Galerie 5020, Salzburg 02535
Galerie a Muzeum Litoměřické Diecéze, Litoměřice 08455
Galerie Albstadt, Albstadt 15417
Galerie Alte Reichsvogtei, Schweinfurt 19889
Galerie Alte Schule, Ahrensbök 15406
Galerie Alte Schule, Vils 02764
Galerie Alte Schule Wittstedt, Bramstedt 16275
Galerie Altes Rathaus, Worpswede 20682
Galerie am Dom, Wetzlar 20551
Galerie am Domhof, Zwickau 20775
Galerie am Graben, Augsburg 15555
Galerie am Kamp, Teterow 20160
Galerie Am Markt, Bad Saulgau 15731
Galerie am Markt, Hofgeismar 17797
Galerie am Prater, Berlin 15953
Galerie am Schloß, Senftenberg 19939
Galerie an der Bleiche, Ludwigslust 18524
Galerie Anna Paulownahuis, Soest 29841
Galerie Antonína Chittussiho, Ronov nad Doubravou 08637
Galerie Arcus, Berlin 15954
Galerie art one, Zürich 37375
Galerie Beaubourg, Vence 15114
Galerie Benedikta Rejta v Lounech, Louny 08465
Galerie Bezirksamt Mitte, Berlin 15955
Galerie Biebertal, Biebertal 16146
Galerie Blau-gelbe Zwettel, Waldviertel, Zwettl, Niederösterreich 03059
Galerie Bodenseekreis im Landratsamt, Friedrichshafen 17147
Galerie Bodenseekreis im Roten Haus, Meersburg 18676
Galerie Bovary, Ry 14079
Galerie Capazza, Nançay 13234
Galerie Colline, Edmundston 05395
Galerie Contact, Böblingen 16212
Galerie Daguerre, Paris 13505
Galerie d'Art, Moncton 05875
Galerie d'Art, Montréal 05903
Galerie d'Art Contemporain, Chamalières 11135
Galerie d'Art Contemporain, La Seyne-sur-Mer 12260
Galerie d'Art Contemporain, Menton 12935
Galerie d'Art Contemporain, Sarlat-la-Canéda 14614
Galerie d'Art Contemporain Am Tunnel, Luxembourg 27560
Galerie d'Art de Créteil, Créteil 11458
Galerie d'Art de Matane, Matane 05821
Galerie d'Art d'Esch, Esch-sur-Alzette 27555
Galerie d'Art du Centre Culturel, Sherbrooke, Québec 06440
Galerie d'Art du Château, Bettembourg 27543
Galerie d'Art du Parc, Trois-Rivières 06640
Galerie d'Art l'Union-Vie, Drummondville 05343
Galerie d'Art Moderne, Passavant-la-Rochère 13663
Galerie d'Art Municipale, Baixas 10570
Galerie d'Art Municipale, Oberkorn 27573
Galerie d'Art Municipale, Rumelange 27574
Galerie d'Art Stewart Hall, Pointe-Claire 06144
Galerie de Carbonnier, Castillonnès 11080
Galerie de Catalans Illustres, Barcelona 34544
Galerie de Lange, Emmen 29230
Galerie de l'École d'Art, Marseille 12850
Galerie de l'École la Chaufferie, Strasbourg 14813
Galerie de l'École Nationale des Beaux-Arts, Nancy 13237
Galerie de l'École Régionale des Beaux-Arts, Nantes 13249
Galerie de l'UQAM, Québec 06198
Galerie de Minéralogie, Paris 13506
Galerie de Nesle - Exposition, Paris 13507
La Galerie de Noisy, Noisy-le-Sec 13362
Galerie de Paléobotanique, Paris 13508
Galerie de Pouzauges, Pouzauges 13855
Galerie der Bezirksbibliothek Rheinhausen, Duisburg 16748
Galerie der Freien Akademie Feldkirchen, Feldkirchen in Kärnten 01834
Galerie der Hochschule für Graphik und Buchkunst, Leipzig 18393
Galerie der Jenaoptik, Jena 17939
Galerie der Mitte, Linz 02231
Galerie der Sammlung Berthold-Sames, Oberaudorf 19170
Galerie der Stadt, Bad Wimpfen 15768
Galerie der Stadt Backnang, Backnang 15585
Galerie der Stadt Fellbach, Fellbach 16990
Galerie der Stadt Plochingen, Plochingen 19418
Galerie der Stadt Remscheid, Remscheid 19566
Galerie der Stadt Salzburg im Mirabellgarten, Salzburg 02536
Galerie der Stadt Schwaz, Schwaz 02647
Galerie der Stadt Sindelfingen, Sindelfingen 19963
Galerie der Stadt Stuttgart, Stuttgart 20090
Galerie der Stadt Traun, Traun 02736
Galerie der Stadt Tuttlingen, Tuttlingen 20236
Galerie der Stadt Vöcklabruck, Vöcklabruck 02766
Galerie der Stadt Waiblingen Kameralamt, Waiblingen 20348
Galerie der Stadt Wels, Wels 02811
Galerie der Stadt Wendlingen am Neckar, Wendlingen am Neckar 20512
Galerie des Beaux-Arts, Bordeaux 10804
Galerie des Bildungshauses Sodalitas, Tainach 02710
Galerie des Dames, Chenonceaux 11272
Galerie des Estampes, Rouen 14045
Galerie des Jenaer Kunstvereins, Jena 17940
Galerie des Kultur- und Festspielhauses Wittenberge, Wittenberge 20624
Galerie des Kunstvereins Neustadt an der Weinstraße, Neustadt an der Weinstraße 19075
Galerie des Landkreises Rügen, Putbus 19455
Galerie des Marburger Kunstvereins, Marburg 18627
Galerie des Polnischen Instituts Düsseldorf, Düsseldorf 16723
Galerie des Transports, Marseille 12851
Galerie d'Exposition d'Art et d'Histoire, Villaries 15179
Galerie d'Exposition de la Direction des Musées, Rabat 28703
Galerie d'Exposition sur la Bourse, Paris 13509
Galerie Dominion, Montréal 05904
Galerie Dorée du Comte de Toulouse, Paris 13510
Galerie du Bastion, Antibes 10370
Galerie du Château, Nice 13308
Galerie du Conseil Général du Bas-Rhin, Strasbourg 14814
Galerie du Musée Montebello, Trouville-sur-Mer 14998
Galerie du Vitrail, Amiens 10322
Galerie Elizabeth LeFort, Cheticamp 05243
Galerie Europeenne de la Forêt et du Bois, Dompierre (Orne) 11547
Galerie Felixe Jeneweina, Kutná Hora 08437
Galerie Fernand Léger - Le Crédac, Ivry-sur-Seine 12067
Galerie Fototreppe 42, Hanau 17582

Galerie Freihausgasse, Villach 02758
Galerie für Zeitgenössische Kunst Leipzig, Leipzig 18394
Galerie Georges-Goguen, Moncton 05876
Galerie Gersag Emmen, Emmenbrücke 36679
Galerie Gmünd, Gmünd, Kärnten 01887
Galerie Goethe 53, München 18851
Galerie Grünstraße, Berlin 15956
Galerie Günther Frey, Radenthein 02473
Galerie Handwerk, München 18852
Galerie Hans Steger, Zeulenroda 20749
Galerie Haus 23, Cottbus 16502
Galerie Haus Dacheröden, Erfurt 16900
Galerie Hausruck, Altenhof am Hausruck 01663
Galerie Heimatverein Zierow e.V., Zierow 20756
Galerie Hinter dem Rathaus, Wismar 20617
Galerie Hlavního Města Prahy, Praha 08576
Galerie Hlavního Města Prahy, Praha 08577
Galerie im 44er Haus, Leonding 02214
Galerie im Adalbert Stifter-Haus, Linz 02232
Galerie im Alten Rathaus, Prien 19449
Galerie im Amtshaus, Bad Wurzach 15779
Galerie im Bildhauerhaus und Skulpturenwanderweg, Einöde 01799
Galerie im Bürger- und Gemeindezentrum Hofstetten-Grünau, Hofstetten-Grünau 02037
Galerie im Bürgerhaus, Haigerloch 17492
Galerie im Bürgerhaus, Neunkirchen, Saar 19055
Galerie im Bürgerspital, Drosendorf an der Thaya 01773
Galerie im Coudrayhaus, Bad Berka 15605
Galerie im Cranach-Haus, Lutherstadt Wittenberg 18574
Galerie im Ermelerspeicher, Schwedt 19886
Galerie im Fontanehaus, Berlin 15957
Galerie im Franck-Haus, Marktheidenfeld 18645
Galerie im Gemeinschaftshaus, Berlin 15958
Galerie im Hörsaalbau, Leipzig 18395
Galerie im Kehrwiederturm, Hildesheim 17758
Galerie im Körnerpark, Berlin 15959
Galerie im Körnerpark, Berlin 15960
Galerie im Kreishaus, Wetzlar 20552
Galerie im Kulturhaus Spandau, Berlin 15961
Galerie im Kunsthaus Erfurt, Erfurt 16901
Galerie im Malzhaus, Plauen 19411
Galerie im Nachtwächterhaus, Poysdorf 02440
Galerie im Polnischen Institut, Leipzig 18396
Galerie im Prediger, Schwäbisch Gmünd 19861
Galerie im Rathaus, Bad Aussee 01690
Galerie im Rathaus Köpenick, Berlin 15962
Galerie im Saalbau, Berlin 15963
Galerie im Schloß Porcia, Spittal an der Drau 02669
Galerie im Stadtmuseum, Jena 17941
Galerie im Stadtturm, Gmünd, Kärnten 01888
Galerie im Taxispalais, Innsbruck 02065
Galerie im Teisenhoferhof der Malschule Motiv Wachau, Weißenkirchen in der Wachau 02803
Galerie im Theater am Saumarkt, Feldkirch 01829
Galerie im Tor, Emmendingen 16852
Galerie im Traklhaus, Salzburg 02537
Galerie im Troadkasten, Pram 02444
Galerie im Turm, Berlin 15964
Galerie im Volkspark, Halle, Saale 17510
Galerie im Willy-Brandt-Haus, Berlin 15965
Die Galerie in der Alten Schule, Berlin 15966
Galerie in der Brotfabrik, Berlin 15967
Galerie in der Hauptschule, Ulrichsberg 02751
Galerie Inkatt, Bremen 16322
Galerie Jamborův Dům, Tišnov 08681
Galerie K & S, Berlin 15968
Galerie Křižovníků, Praha 08578
Galerie Kulturzentrum Lerchhaus, Eibiswald 01797
Galerie Kunst der Gegenwart, Salzburg 02538
Galerie Kunstbrücke Osteuropa, Berlin 15969
Galerie Kunsthoken der Stadt Quedlinburg, Quedlinburg 19459
Galerie Kunstlade, Zittau 20760
Galerie Landesbank Baden-Württemberg, Stuttgart 20091
Galerie L'Aquarium, Valenciennes 15053
Galerie Le Carré, Bayonne 10620
Galerie l'Industrielle-Alliance, Montréal 05905
Galerie Loisel Grafik, Pörtschach am Wörther See 02433
Galerie Ludvika Kuby, Březnice 08260
Galerie M, Berlin 15970
Galerie Malovaný Dům, Třebíč 08686
Galerie Marktschlößchen, Halle, Saale 17511
Galerie Města Blanska, Blansko 08250
Galerie Montcalm, Gatineau 05482
Galerie Münsterland, Emsdetten 16867
Galerie Municipale, Vitry-sur-Seine 15276
Galerie Municipale au Palais Montcalm, Québec 06199
Galerie Municipale d'Art Contemporain Julio-Gonzalez, Arcueil 10398
Galerie Municipale Renoir, Nice 13309
Galerie-Musée de l'Auberge Champenoise, Moussy 13193
Galerie-Musée Le Petit Chapitre, Fosses-la Ville 03421
Galerie N, Dahn 16532
Galerie Nationale de la Tapisserie et de l'Art Textile, Beauvais 10654
Galerie Nationale du Jeu de Paume, Paris 13511
Galerie Neue Meister, Dresden 16682
Galerie Numero 16, Noordbroek 29641
Galerie Palais Walderdorff, Trier 20209
Galerie Palette Röderhaus, Wuppertal 20712
Galerie Parterre, Berlin 15971
La Galerie Passage, Tallinn 09366
Galerie Peters-Barenbrock im Haus Elisabeth von Eicken, Ostseebad Ahrenshoop 19300
Galerie Port-Maurice, Saint-Léonard 06363
Galerie Portyč, Písek 08539
Galerie Profil, Cham 16457
Galerie Rudolfinum, Praha 08579
Galerie Sala Terrena, Mödling 02309
Galerie Sankt Georg, Gardelegen 17197
Galerie Sans Nom, Moncton 05877
Galerie Schloß Lamberg, Steyr 02683
Galerie Schloß Rimsingen, Breisach am Rhein 16311
Galerie Skell, Schmiedeberg, Osterzgebirge 19812
Galerie Stephanie Hollenstein, Lustenau 02257
Galerie Stift Eberndorf, Eberndorf 01783
Galerie Taisei, Tokyo 26850
Galerie Terra Viva, Saint-Quentin-la-Poterie 14438
Galerie Theodor von Hörmann, Imst 02054
Galerie Umění, Ostrov nad Ohří 08530
Galerie Umění Karlovy Vary, Karlovy Vary 08400
Galerie und Weinmuseum Schloß Gamlitz, Gamlitz 01867
Galerie Výtvarného Umění, Havlíčkův Brod 08347
Galerie Výtvarného Umění, Hodonín 08353
Galerie Výtvarného Umění, Náchod 08491
Galerie Výtvarného Umění, Ostrava 08524
Galerie Výtvarného Umění, Roudnice nad Labem 08638
Galerie Weberhaus, Weiz 02810
Galerie zum alten Ötztal, Oetz 02383
Galeriehaus, Nürnberg 19137
Galeries de Paléontologie et d'Anatomie Comparée, Paris 13512
Galeries du Panthéon Bouddhique du Japon et de la Chine, Paris 13513
Galeries Nationales du Grand Palais, Paris 13514
Galerieverein Leonberg e.V., Leonberg, Württemberg 18442
Galerija Antuna Augustinčića, Klanjec 07715
Galerija Benko Horvat, Zagreb 07814
Galerija Božidar Jakac, Kostanjevica na Krki 34098
Galerija Centralnog Kluba Vojske Jugolavije, Beograd 33795
Galerija Freska, Beograd 33796
Galerija Hlebine-Muzejska Zbirka, Hlebine 07704
Galerija Jerolim, Stari Grad 07789
Galerija Klovićevi Dvori, Zagreb 07815
Galerija Lazar Vozarević, Sremska Mitrovica 33912
Galerija Likovnih Samorastnikov, Trebnje 34157
Galerija Likovnih Umjetnosti Republike Srpske Banja Luka, Banja Luka 03909
Galerija Matice Srpske, Novi Sad 33869
Galerija Mestne Hiše, Kranj 34099
Galerija Milan Konjović, Sombor 33909
Galerija Milene Pavlović Barilli, Požarevac 33891
Galerija Murska Sobota, Murska Sobota 34133
Galerija Naivnih Slikara, Kovačica 33850
Galerija Portreta Tuzla, Tuzla 03928
Galerija Reprodukcija i Umetničkih Dela, Beograd 33797
Galerija Samoukih Likovnih Umetnika Svetozarevo, Svetozarevo 33919
Galerija Sebastian, Dubrovnik 07695
Galerija Slika, Motovun 07740
Galerija Slika Save Sumanovića, Sid 33904
Galerija Sopoćanska Vidjenja, Novi Pazar 33867
Galerija Srpske Akademije Nauka i Umetnosti, Beograd 33798
Galerija Suvremene Umjetnosti, Zagreb 07816
Galerija Umjetnina, Split 07781
Galerija Umjetnina Narodnog Muzeja Zadar, Zadar 07805
Galerija Zavjetnih Slika Brodova, Dubrovnik 07696
Galerije Sivčeva Hiša, Radovljica 34143
Galesburg Civic Art Center, Galesburg 43598
Galion Historical Museum, Galion 43603
Galle National Museum, Galle 35754
Gallen-Kallela Museum, Espoo 09432
Galleri 21, Norberg 36113
Galleri Espolin, Kabelvåg 30586
Galleri Svalbard, Longyearbyen 30654
Galleria Accademia Albertina di Belle Arti, Torino 25733
Galleria Alberoni, Piacenza 24887
Galleria Civica, Valdagno 25870
Galleria Civica Anna e Luigi Parmiggiani, Reggio Emilia 25094
Galleria Civica d'Arte Contemporanea, Caltagirone 23270
Galleria Civica d'Arte Contemporanea, Suzzara 25663
Galleria Civica d'Arte Contemporanea, Termoli 25693
Galleria Civica d'Arte Moderna, Santhià 25463
Galleria Civica d'Arte Moderna, Spoleto 25622
Galleria Civica d'Arte Moderna e Contemporanea, Torino 25734
Galleria Civica d'Arte Moderna e Contemporanea, Verona 25967
Galleria Colonna, Roma 25158
Galleria Comunale d'Arte, Cagliari 23244
Galleria Comunale d'Arte, Lecco 24169
Galleria Comunale d'Arte Contemporanea, Arezzo 22919
Galleria Comunale d'Arte Moderna, Bologna 23104
Galleria Comunale d'Arte Moderna, Verucchio 25977
Galleria Comunale d'Arte Moderna e Contemporanea, Roma 25159
Galleria Comunale d'Arte Risorgimento, Imola 24085
Galleria Comunale S. Croce, Cattolica 23456
Galleria Corsini, Firenze 23838
Galleria d'Arte Contemporanea, Ascoli Piceno 22949
Galleria d'Arte Contemporanea, Assisi 22961
Galleria d'Arte Contemporanea L. Spazzapan, Gradisca d'Isonzo 24040
Galleria d'Arte Contemporanea V. Stoppioni, Santa Sofia 25443
Galleria d'Arte dell'Opera Bevilacqua la Masa, Venezia 25917
Galleria d'Arte Moderna, Firenze 23839
Galleria d'Arte Moderna, Udine 25846
Galleria d'Arte Moderna A. Discovolo, Bonassola 23159
Galleria d'Arte Moderna Arnoldo Bonzagni, Cento 23472
Galleria d'Arte Moderna Carlo Rizzarda, Feltre 23771
Galleria d'Arte Moderna Comunale, San Severino Marche 25411
Galleria d'Arte Moderna e Contemporanea, Bergamo 23060
Galleria d'Arte Moderna e Contemporanea R. Guttuso, Bagheria 22998
Galleria d'Arte Moderna F. Montanari, Moncalvo 24468
Galleria d'Arte Moderna Giannoni, Novara 24644
Galleria d'Arte Moderna Moretti, Civitanova Marche 23593
Galleria d'Arte Moderna O. Marchesi, Copparo 23643
Galleria d'Arte Moderna Ricci-Oddi, Piacenza 24888
Galleria d'Arte Rocca Sforzesca, Imola 24086
Galleria d'Arte Sacra dei Contemporanei, Milano 24384
Galleria degli Arazzi, Città del Vaticano 48870
Galleria degli ex Voto del Santuario, Livorno 24190
Galleria degli Uffizi, Firenze 23840
Galleria del Costume, Firenze 23841
Galleria del Maggio, Villa Minozzo 26014
Galleria dell'Accademia, Firenze 23842
Galleria dell'Accademia di Belle Arti, Napoli 24575
Galleria dell'Accademia Nazionale di San Luca, Roma 25160
Galleria dell'Accademia Tadini, Lovere 24223
Galleria dello Spedale degli Innocenti, Firenze 23843
Galleria di Palazzo Bianco, Genova 23982
Galleria di Palazzo degli Alberti, Prato 25043
Galleria di Palazzo Rosso, Genova 23983
Galleria Doria Pamphilj, Roma 25161
Galleria e Mostra del Presepe nel Mondo, Santuario di Montevergine 25468
Galleria Estense, Modena 24434
Galleria Ferrari, Maranello 24293
Galleria G. Pedriali, Forlì 23907
Galleria Giorgio Franchetti alla Ca' d'Oro, Venezia 25918
Galleria Lapidaria, Città del Vaticano 48871
Galleria M. Rizzi, Sestri Levante 25561
Galleria Municipale, Francavilla al Mare 23930
Galleria Nazionale, Parma 24799
Galleria Nazionale d'Arte Antica, Trieste 25821
Galleria Nazionale d'Arte Antica Palazzo Barberini, Roma 25162
Galleria Nazionale d'Arte Antica Palazzo Corsini, Roma 25163
Galleria Nazionale d'Arte Moderna-Arte Contemporanea, Roma 25164
Galleria Nazionale delle Marche, Urbino 25857
Galleria Nazionale dell'Umbria, Perugia 24848
Galleria Nazionale di Arte Moderna e Contemporanea, San Marino 33759
Galleria Nazionale di Palazzo Spinola, Genova 23984
Galleria Palatina, Firenze 23844
Galleria Palazzo Cini, Venezia 25919
Galleria Pallavicini, Roma 25165
Galleria Pinacotheca, Jyväskylä 09594
Galleria Regionale d'Arte Moderna e Contemporanea, Sassoferrato 25493
Galleria Regionale della Sicilia, Palermo 24764
Galleria Regionale di Palazzo Bellomo, Siracusa 25585
Galleria Rinaldo Carnielo, Firenze 23845
Galleria Sabauda, Torino 25735
Galleria Spada, Roma 25166
Galleria Storica del Lloyd Triestino, Trieste 25822
Gallerie dell'Accademia, Venezia 25920
Gallerie di Palazzo Leoni Montanari, Vicenza 25992
The Galleries, Woking 40913
Galleries of Justice, Nottingham 40106
The Gallery, Gateshead 39027
The Gallery, Luton 39844
The Gallery, Trenton 48054
Gallery 101, River Falls 46911
Gallery 101.Galerie 101, Ottawa 06080
Gallery 181, Ames 41172
Gallery 2, Chicago 42329
Gallery 210, Saint Louis 47121
Gallery 400, Chicago 42330
Gallery 44, Toronto 06578
Gallery 57, Cambridge 42040
Gallery '76, Wenatchee 48505
Gallery 825, Los Angeles 44902
Gallery 9, Los Altos 44889
Gallery A and Gallery G, San Pedro 47372
Gallery Abarth, Yamanakako 27006
Gallery and Museum of the Diocese of Litomerice, Litoměřice 08455
Gallery Arcturus, Toronto 06579
Gallery at Bristol-Myers Squibb, Princeton 46700
Gallery at the American Bible Society, New York 45803
Gallery at the Wharf, Coupeville 42676
The Gallery at UTA, Arlington 41260
Gallery Connexion, Fredericton 05460
Gallery Gazelle, Philomath 46470
Gallery II, Bradford 38298
Gallery II, Kalamazoo 44377
Gallery III, Makati 31353
Gallery Lambton, Sarnia 06391
Gallery Le Vall, Novosibirsk 33239
Gallery North, Setauket 47569
Gallery of Antonín Chittussi, Ronov nad Doubravou 08637
Gallery of Art, Cedar Falls 42149
Gallery of Art, Dickinson 42946
Gallery of Art, Overland Park 46223
Gallery of British Columbia Ceramics, Vancouver 06677
Gallery of Contemporary Art, Colorado Springs 42537
The Gallery of Contemporary Art, Fairfield 43262
Gallery of Contemporary Art Arca, Vladivostok 33695
Gallery of Contemporary Art Artetage, Vladivostok 33696
Gallery of Costume, Manchester 39886
Gallery of Fine Arts, Split 07781
Gallery of Fine Arts Koroška, Slovenj Gradec 34149
Gallery of Florina Artists, Florina 20958
Gallery of Horyu-ji Treasures, Tokyo 26851
Gallery of Local Art, Novi Sad 33876
Gallery of Modern Art, Glasgow 39045
Gallery of Modern Art, Zagreb 07829
Gallery of Modern Greek Art of Kalamata, Kalamata 20983
Gallery of Murska Sobota, Murska Sobota 34133
Gallery of Musical Instruments, Delhi 21769
Gallery of Naive Art, Kovačica 33850
Gallery of Naive Art, Zlatar 07843
Gallery of Prehistoric Paintings, New York 45804
Gallery of Sailor's Votive Paintings, Dubrovnik 07696
Gallery of Šariš, Prešov 34048
Gallery of Szombathely, Szombathely 21589
Gallery of the Department of Art, Portales 46615
Gallery of the Department of Art and Art History, Lincoln 44782
Gallery of the Faculty of Architecture, Bangkok 37484
Gallery of the Knights of the Cross, Praha 08578
Gallery of the Municipality of Patras, Patrai 21114
Gallery of the Royal Scottish Academy, Edinburgh 38883
Gallery of the Serbian Academy of Sciences and Arts, Beograd 33798
Gallery of the Society for Epirot Studies, Ioannina 20968
Gallery of the Society for Macedonian Studies, Thessaloniki 21183
Gallery of Traditional Japanese Toys, Takayama 26809
Gallery of Traditional Ornamental Art, Minsk 03115
Gallery of Visual Arts, Missoula 45404
Gallery Oldham, Oldham 40128
Gallery on the Roof, Regina 06234
Gallery One, Ellensburg 43150
Gallery One One One, Winnipeg 06826
Gallery Pinacotheca of the Jyväskylä University Museum, Section of Cultural History, Jyväskylä 09594
Gallery Sculpturama, Bornem 03227
Gallery Slav Epoch of Alfons Mucha on Castle Moravsky Krumlov, Moravský Krumlov 08488
Gallery Stratford, Stratford 06499
Gallery-Studio of the Painter G. Rayshev, Chanty-Mansijsk 32743
Gallery West, Alexandria 41128
Gallery XII, Wichita 48601
Gallier House, New Orleans 45725
Gallo-Romeins Museum, Tongeren 03781
Galloway House and Village, Fond du Lac 43360
Galloway Station Museum, Edson 05397
Galtebosamlingen, Spydeberg 30872
Galveston Arts Center, Galveston 43608
Galveston County Historical Museum, Galveston 43609
Galway Arts Centre, Galway 22472
Galway City Museum, Galway 22474
Gambia National Museum, Banjul 15352
Game and Fisheries Museum, Entebbe 37822
Gamla Bankgården, Vrigstad 36418
Gamla Brukets Muséer, Munkfors 36108
Gamla Krukmakarverkstaden, Arvika 35816
Gamla Linköping, Linköping 36040
Gamla Skeninge, Skänninge 36190
Gamle Bergen Museum, Bergen 30420
Den Gamle By, Århus 08770
Den Gamle Gaard, Faaborg 08814
Gamle Hvam Museum, Årnes 30395
Gamle Kvernes Bygdemuseum, Averøy 30407
Gamlehaugen, Paradis 30777
Gammel Estrup Jyllands Herregårdsmuseum, Auning 08781
Gammelgården Friluftsmuseet, Bengtfors 35829
Gammelgruva, Løkken Verk 30648
Gamvik Museum 71N, Gamvik 30508
Gan-Song Art Museum, Seoul 27233
Gananoque Museum, Gananoque 05473
Gandahus, Vals 37281
Gandhi Centenary Museum, Karimnagar 21884
Gandhi Memorial Museum, Madurai 21934
Gandhi Museum, Bhavnagar 21718
Gandhi Museum, Lucknow 21924
Gandhi Museum, Sevagram 22015

Gandhi National Memorial, Pune 21990
Gandhi Sangrahalaya, Patna 21977
Gandhi Smarak Sangrahalaya, Ahmedabad 21679
Gandhi Smarak Sangrahalaya, Barrackpore 21710
Gandhi Smarak Sangrahalaya, Sevagram 22015
Ganga Government Museum, Bikaner 21730
Gangidori Art Gallery, Joetsu 26280
Gangidori Bijutsukan, Joetsu 26280
Gangneung Municipal Museum, Gangneung 27168
Gangwon Folk Museum, Cheongil 27147
Ganondagan State Historic Site, Victor 48231
Gansu Provincial Museum, Lanzhou 07147
Garda Museum, Dublin 22427
Garden County Museum, Oshkosh 46203
Garden Museum, Przemyśl 31920
Garden of Fine Art Kyoto, Kyoto 26399
Garden of Roman Ruins, Szentendre 21574
Garden of the Gulf Museum, Montague 05883
Garden Park Farm Museum, Alberta Beach 04971
Gardiner Art Gallery, Stillwater 47813
Gardner Arts Centre, Falmer 38971
Gardner House Museum, Albion 41098
Gardner Museum, Gardner 43623
The Gardner Museum of Architecture and Design, Quincy 46758
Gardner-Pingree House, Salem 47194
Gárdonyi Géza Emlékmúzeum, Eger 21408
Gårdsmuséet, Åre 35807
Garfield Farm Museum, Lafox 44573
Garibaldi and Meucci Museum, Staten Island 47781
Garlogie Mill Power House Museum, Garlogie 39025
Garnavillo Historical Museum, Garnavillo 43626
Garner Memorial Museum, Uvalde 48172
Garnisionsmuseum Graz, Graz 01914
Garnisionsmuseum Nürnberg, Nürnberg 19138
Garnisonsmuseet, Boden 35835
Gäröströms Industrimuseum, Gnosjö 35906
Garrett County Historical Museum, Oakland 46072
Garrett Historical Museum, Garrett 43629
Garrison Gallery, Historical and Military Museum, Millers Point 01256
Garst Museum, Greenville 43827
De Garstkamp, Overasselt 29706
Gartenkunst-Museum Schloss Fantasie, Eckersdorf 16778
Garter Lane Arts Centre, Waterford 22553
Garverimuseet, Simrishamn 36185
Garverimuseet, Volda 30998
Gas Museum, Kodaira 26358
Gas Science Center, Tokyo 26852
Gas Science Museum, Takaishi 26788
Gascoyne Junction Museum, Gascoyne Junction 01041
Gaseum, Essen 16950
Gaspesian British Heritage Village, New Richmond 05980
Gass Forest Museum, Coimbatore 21750
Gaston County Museum of Art and History, Dallas 42742
Gasu no Kagakukan, Takaishi 26788
Gasu no Kagakukan, Tokyo 26852
Gatchina Regional Museum at Prioratsky Palace, Gatčina 32800
Gatčinskij Kraevedčeskij Muzej - Prioratskij Dvorec, Gatčina 32800
Gatčinskij Literaturno-memorialnyj Muzej-usadba P.E. Ščerbova, Gatčina 32801
Gatekeeper's Museum and Marion Steinbach Indian Basket Museum, Tahoe City 47927
Gately House, East London 34237
Gates House, Machiasport 45028
Gates Mills Historical Society Museum, Gates Mills 43634
Gateway to the Panhandle, Gate 43633
Gatov Gallery, Long Beach 44859
Gaudete, Museum voor Volksdevotie, Boxtel 29012
Gaudnek-Museum, Altomünster 15469
Gauermann-Museum, Miesenbach 02297
Gauhati Medical College Museum, Gauhati 21809
Gavilan Community College Art Gallery, Gilroy 43674
Gaviolizaal, Helmond 29393
Gavrilo Princip Memorial Museum, Bosansko Grahova 03914
Gawharah Museum, Cairo 09281
Gawharah Palace Museum, Cairo 09285
Gawler Museum, Gawler 01042
Gawsworth Hall, Macclesfield 39863
Gay 90's Mansion Museum, Barnesville 41506
Gaya Museum, Gaya 21810
Gayndah Museum, Gayndah 01043
Gayo Museum, Takengon 22207
Gaz Factory Museum, Nižnij Novgorod 33212
Gaziantep Archaeological Museum, Gaziantep 37681
Gaziantep Arkeoloji Müzesi, Gaziantep 37681
Gaziantep Devlet Güzel Sanatlar Galerisi, Gaziantep 37682
Gaziantep Etnografi Müzesi, Gaziantep 37683
Gaziantep State Gallery, Gaziantep 37682
Gazirah Museum, Cairo 09266
Gdańsk Photography Gallery, Gdańsk 31567
Gdańska Galeria Fotografii, Gdańsk 31567
Gebirgsjägermuseum, Sonthofen 20000
Gebrüder-Lachner-Museum, Rain am Lech 19476
Geburtshaus des heiligen Konrad von Parzham, Bad Griesbach im Rottal 15652
Geburtshaus Levi Strauss Museum Jeans und Kult, Buttenheim 16435
Gedächtnisstätte Mida Huber, Landsee 02182
Gedächtnisstätte von Scheidt-Saalfeld, Bad Bergzabern 15602
Geddes Historic District Village, Geddes 43637
Gede Museum and National Monument, Watamu 27115
Gedenk- und Dokumentationsstätte Opfer politischer Gewaltherrschaft, Frankfurt/Oder 17081
Gedenkräume, Wien 02885
Gedenkräume im Schloß Hartheim, Alkoven 01654
Gedenkraum 1945, Hochwolkersdorf 02035
Gedenkstätte Bergen-Belsen, Lohheide 18496
Gedenkstätte Breitenau, Guxhagen 17468
Gedenkstätte Buchenwald, Weimar, Thüringen 20458
Gedenkstätte der Luftfahrt, Stölln 20065
Gedenkstätte Deutscher Widerstand, Berlin 15972
Gedenkstätte Ehemalige Synagoge, Adelsheim 15396
Gedenkstätte Erfurter Parteitag 1891, Erfurt 16902
Gedenkstätte für C.G. Salzmann und J.C.F. GuthsMuths, Schnepfenthal 19819
Gedenkstätte für die Opfer politischer Gewaltherrschaft 1945-1989, Magdeburg 18580
Gedenkstätte Goldener Löwe, Eisenach 16815
Gedenkstätte Großbeeren 1813, Großbeeren 17424
Gedenkstätte Hadamar, Hadamar 17472
Gedenkstätte in der JVA Wolfenbüttel, Wolfenbüttel 20652
Gedenkstätte Münchner Platz Dresden, Dresden 16683
Gedenkstätte Museum in der Runden Ecke, Leipzig 18397
Gedenkstätte/Museum Seelower Höhen, Seelow 19919
Gedenkstätte Plötzensee für die Opfer des Nationalsozialismus, Berlin 15973
Gedenkstätte Synagoge, Dornum 16651
Gedenkstätte und Museum Sachsenhausen, Oranienburg 19264
Ģederta Eliasa Jelgavas Vēstures un Mākslas Muzejs, Jelgava 27365
Ģederts Eliass Jelgava History and Art Museum, Jelgava 27365
Het Gedistilleerd Museum, Schiedam 29800
GEDOK Künstlerinnenforum, Karlsruhe 17992
Geelong Gallery, Geelong 01044
Geelong Heritage Centre, Geelong 01045
Geelong Naval and Maritime Museum, North Geelong 01325
Geels & Co. Koffie- en Theemuseum, Amsterdam 28854
Geelvinck Hinlopen Huis, Amsterdam 28855
Geeson Brothers Motor Cycle Museum, South Witham 40539
Geevor Tin Mining Museum, Pendeen 40171
Geffrye Museum, London 39641
Geidai Bijutsukan, Tokyo 26853
Geigenbau-Museum, Bubenreuth 16385
Geigenbaumuseum, Mittenwald 18754
Geiseltalmuseum der Martin-Luther-Universität, Halle, Saale 17512
Gekkeikan Okura Kinenkan, Kyoto 26400
Das Gelbe Haus, Flirns Dorf 36704
Gelbgießerei und Nadelmuseum in der Historischen Fabrikanlage Barendorf, Iserlohn 17920
Gelders Geologisch Museum, Velp 29936
Gelders Schuttersmuseum, Didam 29148
Gelderse Smalspoor Museum, Erlecom 29250
Geldgeschichtliches Museum, Köln 18138
Geldmuseum der Deutschen Bundesbank, Frankfurt am Main 17048
Gelendžikskij Istoriko-kraevedčeskij Muzej, Gelendžik 32804
Gellert-Museum, Hainichen, Sachsen 17496
Gemäldegalerie, Berlin 15974
Gemäldegalerie Alte Meister, Dresden 16684
Gemäldegalerie Alte Meister, Kassel 18017
Gemäldegalerie Dachau, Dachau 16523
Gemäldegalerie der Akademie der Bildenden Künste, Wien 02886
Gemäldesammlung, Erlangen 16917
Gemeentegrot Valkenburg, Valkenburg 29916
Gemeentelijk Archaeologisch Museum, Grobbendonk 03464
Gemeentelijk Archeologisch Museum, Aardenburg 28797
Gemeentelijk Expositiecentrum Aemstelle, Amstelveen 28831
Gemeentelijk Heemkundig Museum, Hoeilaart 03499
Gemeentelijk Heemkundig Museum, Rijkevorsel 03697
Gemeentelijk Historisch Museum Ouder-Amstel, Ouderkerk aan de Amstel 29699
Gemeentelijk Museum, Melle 03623
Gemeentelijk Museum Gustaaf de Smet, Deurle 03380
Gemeentelijk Museum 't Oude Slot, Veldhoven 29934
Gemeentelijk Museum 't Oude Slot, Veldhoven 29935
Gemeentelijk Streekmuseum De Veste, Sint-Stevens-Woluwe 03746
Gemeentelijke Expositieruimte Kampen, Kampen 29470
Gemeentelijke Oudheidkamer, Ermelo 29251
Gemeentelijke Oudheidkamer, Geldrop 29268
Gemeentemuseum, Maassluis 29562
Gemeentemuseum, Temse 03768
Gemeentemuseum, Weesp 29990
Gemeentemuseum De Tiendschuur, Weert 29988
Gemeentemuseum Den Haag, Den Haag 29095
Gemeentemuseum Elburg, Elburg 29222
Gemeentemuseum Helmond, Helmond 29394
Gemeentemuseum Het Hannemahuis, Harlingen 29345
Gemeentemuseum Het Markiezenhof, Bergen op Zoom 28983
Gemeentemuseum 't Behouden Huijs, Terschelling-West 29868
Gemeentemuseum 't Sterkenhuis, Bergen, Noord-Holland 28981
Gemeentemuseum voor Religieuze Kunst Jacob van Horne, Weert 29989
Gemeinde-Heimatmuseum Harsum, Harsum 17621
Gemeinde- und Forstmuseum, Oftersheim 19244
Gemeindegalerie, Wiener Neudorf 03013
Gemeindemuseum, Krauchthal 36833
Gemeindemuseum, Regensdorf 37048
Gemeindemuseum, Schweiggers 02652
Gemeindemuseum Absam, Absam 01637
Gemeindemuseum im Historischen Rathaus, Seeheim-Jugenheim 19918
Gemeindemuseum Rothus, Oberriet 37002
Gemersko-Malohontské Múzeum, Rimavská Sobota 34051
Gemstone Gallery, Kemi 09648
Genadendal Museum, Genadendal 34243
Genç Culture Center, Bingöl 37636
Genç Kültür Merkezi, Bingöl 37636
Gencor Art Gallery, Auckland Park 34172
Gene Fornby, Örnsköldsvik 36142
Gene Stratton-Porter House, Rome City 46999
Generaal Maczek Museum, Breda 29021
General Adam Stephen House, Martinsburg 45191
General Crook House Museum, Omaha 46147
General Daniel Bissell House, Saint Louis 47122
General Douglas L. McBride Museum, Roswell 47014
General Douglas MacArthur Memorial, Norfolk 45964
General George C. Marshall Museum, Zwijndrecht 30081
General Grant National Memorial, New York 45805
General Henry Knox Museum, Thomaston 47998
General Jacob Brown Historical Museum, Brownville 41968
General John J. Pershing Boyhood Home, Laclede 44563
General Lewis B. Hershey Museum, Angola 41211
General Patton Memorial Museum, Chiriaco Summit 42387
General Patton Memorial Museum, Ettelbruck 27557
General Pliyev House Museum, Vladikavkaz 33687
General Sterling Price Museum, Keytesville 44478
General Sweeney's Museum, Republic 46844
General Wait House, Waitsfield 48277
Generali Foundation, Wien 02887
Genesee Country Village and Museum, Mumford 45554
Genia Schreiber University Art Gallery, Ramat Aviv 22730
Genossenschaft Pro Sagi, Samstagern 37097
Gentilhaus, Aschaffenburg 15522
Geo Inn, Oosterbeek 29667
Geo Milev Memorial House, Stara Zagora 04866
Geochang Museum, Geochang 27171
Geoffrey Kaye Museum of Anaesthetic History, Melbourne 01227
Geographical Center Historical Museum, Rugby 47027
Geographical Collection of Hungary, Érd 21409
Geographical Museum of Slovenia, Ljubljana 34124
Geography Museum, Faizabad 21801
Geoje Museum, Geoje 27172
Geologian museo, Helsinki 09481
Geologian Tutkimuskeskuksen Kivimuseo, Espoo 09433
Geological Curators' Group, London 49414
Geological Museum, Čeljabinsk 32727
Geological Museum, Dublin 22428
Geological Museum, Guwahati 21822
Geological Museum, Helsinki 09481
Geological Museum, Ho Chi Minh City 48985
Geological Museum, Johannesburg 34276
Geological Museum, Khartoum 35767
Geological Museum, København 08930
The Geological Museum, Laramie 44647
Geological Museum, Lucknow 21925
Geological Museum, Mizpe Ramon 22716
Geological Museum, Oulu 09894
Geological Museum, Riyadh 33771
Geological Museum, Teheran 22299
Geological Museum, Varanasi 22057
Geological Museum and Art Gallery, Redruth 40303
Geological Museum of Central Siberia, Krasnojarsk 32955
The Geological Museum of China, Beijing 06965
Geological Museum of North Wales, Wrexham 40941
Geological Museum of the Finnish Museum of Natural History, Helsinki 09502
Geological Museum of the Institute of Geology, Erevan 00681
Geological Museum of the Joint Stock Company Polar Uralgeology, Vorkuta 33727
Geological Museum of the Polish Geological Institute, Warszawa 32098
Geological Museum, University of Wrocław, Wrocław 32177
Geological Museum Volgageology, Nižnij Novgorod 33221
Geological Survey and Mines Museum, Entebbe 37823
Geological Survey Museum, Dhaka 03088
Geological Survey Museum, East Perth 01000
Geological Survey Museum, Ipoh 27621
Geological Survey Museum, Windhoek 28779
Geological Survey of Finland, Mineralogical Museum, Espoo 09433
Geologičeskij Muzej, Vorkuta 33727
Geologičeskij Muzej im. A.A. Černova, Syktyvkar 33572
Geologisch-Mineralogische Ausstellung der Eidgenössischen Technischen Hochschule Zürich, Zürich 37376
Geologisch Museum Hofland, Laren, Noord-Holland 29498
Geologisch-Paläontologisches Museum, Münster 18937
Geologisch-Paläontologisches Museum der Universität Hamburg, Hamburg 17540
Geologisch Streek-Museum de Ijsselvallei, Olst 29660
Geologische Landessammlung von Vorpommern, Greifswald 17388
Geologische Sammlung Schloß Kapfenstein, Kapfenstein 02097
Geologisches Freilichtmuseum, Gmünd, Niederösterreich 01891
Geologisches Museum der DSK-Saar, Saarbrücken 19723
Geologisches Museum München, München 18853
Geologisches und Mineralogisches Museum der Christian-Albrechts-Universität, Kiel 18072
Geologisk Museum, København 08930
Geologisk Museum, Oslo 30735
Geologo-mineralogičeskij Muzej, Kazan 32888
Geologo-mineralogičeskij Muzej im. A.I. Kozlova, Vladivostok 33697
Geology and Geophysics Museum, Roorkee 22005
Geology Department Museum, Aberdeen 37936
Geology Education Museum, Durban 34227
Geology Museum, Amman 27049
Geology Museum, Auckland 30108
Geology Museum, Ha Noi 48977
Geology Museum, Huntington 44164
Geology Museum, Kampala 37827
Geology Museum, Kingston 26067
Geology Museum, Legon 20798
Geology Museum, Lucknow 21926
Geology Museum of the University of Otago, Dunedin 30148
Geology Museum of the University of Stellenbosch, Stellenbosch 34380
GeoMuseum der Universität, Köln 18139
Georg Elser Gedenkstätte, Königsbronn 18170
Georg-Kolbe-Museum, Berlin 15975
Georg-Kramann-Heimatmuseum, Nordwalde 19126
Georg-Meistermann-Museum, Wittlich 20628
Georg Papendicks Faschings- und Karnevalsordenmuseum, Bad Reichenhall 15716
Georg Rendl-Museum, Sankt Georgen bei Salzburg 02566
Georg Trakl-Forschungs- und Gedenkstätte, Salzburg 02539
George A. Spiva Center for the Arts, Joplin 44362
The George Adams Gallery, Melbourne 01228
George B. Dorr Museum of Natural History, Bar Harbor 41499
George Bush Presidential Library and Museum, College Station 42525
George C. Marshall Museum, Lexington 44759
The George D. and Harriet W. Cornell Fine Arts Museum, Winter Park 48708
George Eliot Hospital Museum, Nuneaton 40117
George Fraser Gallery, Auckland 30109
George I. Ashby Memorial Museum, Copper Center 42623
George J. Doizaki Gallery, Los Angeles 44903
George Johnston Tlingit Indian Museum, Teslin 06540
George Meany Memorial Exhibition, Silver Spring 47632
George Museum, George 34244
George Paton Gallery, Victoria 01567
George R. Gardiner Museum of Ceramic Art, Toronto 06580
George Rogers Clark Park Museum, Vincennes 48238
George Taylor House, Catasauqua 42138
George W. Brown jr. Ojibwe Museum, Lac du Flambeau 44560
George W. Somerville Historical Library, Chillicothe 42376
George Walter Vincent Smith Art Museum, Springfield 47746
George Washington Birthplace National Monument, Colonial Beach 42532
George Washington Carver House, Diamond 42944
George Washington Carver Museum, Tuskegee Institute 48122
George Washington Masonic National Memorial, Alexandria 41129
George Washington's Ferry Farm, Stafford County 47766
George Washington's Headquarters, Cumberland 42726
George Washington's Mount Vernon, Mount Vernon 45546
Georgetown College Gallery, Georgetown 43651
Georgetown Museum, Columbus 42584
Georgetown University Art Collection, Washington 48358
Georgi Benkovski Memorial House, Koprivštica 04713
Georgi Dimitrov Memorial House, Kovačevci 04721
Georgi Dimitrov National Museum, Sofia 04849
Georgi Velchev Art Museum, Varna 04898

Georgia Agrirama, Tifton 48007
Georgia Association of Museums and Galleries, Atlanta 49485
Georgia Capitol Museum, Atlanta 41344
Georgia Historical Society Museum, Savannah 47479
Georgia Mountains History Museum, Gainesville 43589
Georgia Museum of Art, Athens 41318
Georgia Museum of Natural History, Athens 41319
Georgia Music Hall of Fame, Macon 45043
Georgia O'Keeffe Museum, Santa Fe 47418
Georgia Salzburger Society Museum, Rincon 46901
Georgia Southern University Museum, Statesboro 47792
Georgia State University Art Gallery, Atlanta 41345
Georgia Veterans Memorial Museum, Cordele 42631
The Georgian, Lancaster 44621
Georgian House, Bristol 38355
The Georgian House, Edinburgh 38884
Georgian State Art Museum, Tbilisi 15359
Georgian State Museum of Oriental Art, Tbilisi 15360
Georgian State Picture Gallery, Tbilisi 15361
Georgian Theatre Royal Museum, Richmond, North Yorkshire 40315
Georgia's Stone Mountain Park, Stone Mountain 47827
Georgikon Agrarmuseum, Keszthely 21455
Georgikon Majormúzeum, Keszthely 21455
Georgina Pioneer Museum, Keswick 05665
Georgiou Collection, Lindos 21050
Geosammlung der Technischen Universität Clausthal, Clausthal-Zellerfeld 16475
Geoscience Museum, Pretoria 34343
Geowissenschaftliche Sammlungen, Freiberg, Sachsen 17099
Gerätemuseum des Coburger Landes, Ahorn, Kreis Coburg 15405
Gerätesammlung Georg Bauer, Stadtlauringen 20032
Gerätesammlung Koch, Königsberg in Bayern 18169
Gerald E. Eddy Discovery Center, Chelsea 42271
Gerald R. Ford Library Museum, Grand Rapids 43755
Geraldton Regional Art Gallery, Geraldton 01048
Geralka Rural Farm, Spalding 01467
Gerbereimuseum, Marktschellenberg 18654
Gerbermuseum, Bretten 16355
Gereedschap Museum Mensert, Delft 29076
Gerhard-Marcks-Haus, Bremen 16323
Gerhart-Hauptmann-Haus, Düsseldorf 16724
Gerhart-Hauptmann-Haus, Kloster, Hiddensee 18113
Gerhart-Hauptmann-Museum, Erkner 16912
Gerhart Hauptmann's House, Jelenia Góra 31629
Germa Museum, Germa 27501
German Museum of Shoe, Hauenstein 17641
German Occupation Museum, Forest 39004
German Underground Hospital, Saint Lawrence 40411
Germanisches Nationalmuseum, Nürnberg 19139
Germantown Historical Society Museum, Philadelphia 46413
Gernon House and Blacksmith Shop, Russell 47034
Geroldsecker-Museum im Storchenturm, Lahr, Schwarzwald 18289
Geronimo Berenguer de los Reyes jr. Museum, Cavite 31304
Geronimo Springs Museum, Truth or Consequences 48075
Gerringong and District Museum, Gerringong 01051
Gerrit Valk's Bakkerij- en Ijsmuseum, Hellendoorn 29384
Gertrude Contemporary Art Spaces, Fitzroy 01025
Gertrude Herbert Institute of Art, Augusta 41383
Gertrude Posel Gallery, Johannesburg 34277
Gertrude Smith House, Mount Airy 45522
Gervais Wheels Museum, Alida 04974
Geschichte auf Rädern, Melle 18697
Geschichtlich-heimatkundliche Sammlung, Aschheim 15537
Geschichtliches Museum Enns-Donauwinkel, Sankt Valentin 02609
Geschied- en Oudheidkundig Museum 't Freulekeshuus, Venray 29941
Geschiedkundig Museum Mesen, Mesen 03626
Gesellschaft der Musikfreunde in Wien, Wien 02888
Gesellschaft für Aktuelle Kunst, Bremen 16324
Gesenkschmiede Lubenbach, Zella-Mehlis 20744
Gesterby Manor, Kirkkonummi 09672
Gesterbyn Kartano - Kirkkonummen Kunnan Museoalue, Kirkkonummi 09672
Gestütsmuseum Offenhausen, Gomadingen 17346
Gettysburg National Military Park, Gettysburg 43663
Geumho Museum of Art, Seoul 27234
Gevangenismuseum Veenhuizen, Veenhuizen 29930
Gewerbe-Museum, Spaichingen 20005
Gewerbemuseum, Winterthur 37328
Gewerbemuseum der LGA im Germanischen Nationalmuseum, Nürnberg 19140
Geymüller Schlössel, Wien 02889
Géza Gárdonyi Memorial Museum, Eger 21408
Ggantija Prehistoric Temples, Xaghra 27714
Ghalib Museum, Delhi 21770
Ghana Armed Forces Museum, Kumasi 20795
Ghana Museums and Monuments Board, Accra 49217
Ghana National Museum, Accra 20788
Ghar Dalam Cave and Museum, Birzebbuga 27695
Gharb Folklore Museum, Gharb 27696
Ghazni Museum, Ghazni 00002
Gheorghe Dima Memorial House, Braşov 32446
Gherla History Museum, Gherla 32526
Ghetto Fighters' House Museum, Lohamei-Hageta'ot 22709
Ghoochan Museum, Ghoochan 22238
G.I. Katsigras Museum, Lárissa 21043
G.I. Nevelskyj Museum of the History of the Far East Sea Academy, Vladivostok 33705
G.I. Uspensky House-Museum, Sjabrenicy 33524
GianFu Classic Art Museum, Beijing 06966
Giant's Castle, Marazion 39907
Giant's Causeway and Bushmills Railway, Bushmills 38424
Giants Causeway Visitor Centre, Bushmills 38425
Giardino di Boboli, Firenze 23846
Giardino Storico e Villa Garzoni, Pescia 24874
Gibbes Museum of Art, Charleston 42216
Gibbs Farm Museum, Falcon Heights 43278
Gibbs Museum of Pioneer and Dakotah Life, Falcon Heights 43279
Gibraltar Museum, Gibraltar 20802
Gibran Museum, Bsharri 27488
Gibson Barham Gallery, Lake Charles 44581
Gibson Gallery, London 05766
Gibson House, North York 06031
Gibson House Museum, Boston 41808
Gidan Makama Museum, Kano 30349
Gifu-ken Bijutsukan, Gifu 26157
Gifu-ken Hakubutsukan, Seki 26729
Gifu-ken Toji Shiryokan, Tajimi 26787
Gifu Prefectural Ceramics Museum, Tajimi 26787
Gifu Prefectural Museum, Seki 26729
Gig Harbor Peninsula Historical Society Museum, Gig Harbor 43667
Gila County Historical Museum, Globe 43700
Gilbert Collection, London 39642
Gilbert House, Atlanta 41346
The Gilbert Stuart Museum, Saunderstown 47472
Gilbert White's House and the Oates Museum, Selborne 40465
Gilbert's Bar House of Refuge, Stuart 47858
Gilcrease Museum, Tulsa 48104
Gilde-Museum, Oldenburg in Holstein 19250
Gildehaus Bardowick, Bardowick 15823
Het Gildenhuys, Blokzijl 28990
Gildeskål Bygdesamling, Gildeskål 30511
Gilgandra Museum, Gilgandra 01052
Gillam Community Museum, Gillam 05487
Gilleleje Museum, Gilleleje 08836
Gillesgården, Pohja 09939
Gillespie Museum of Minerals, De Land 42815
Gillingham Library Gallery, Gillingham, Kent 39032
Gillingham Museum, Gillingham, Dorset 39031
Gilman Garrison House, Exeter 43252
Gilman Museum, Hellertown 43985
Gilman Town Hall Museum, Issaquah 44269
Gilmore-CCCA Museum, Hickory Corners 44009
Gilpin History Museum, Central City 42173
Gilroy Historical Museum, Gilroy 43675
Gilstrap Heritage Centre, Newark-on-Trent 40019
Gingras Trading Post, Walhalla 48282
Ginny Williams Family Foundation, Denver 42889
Gipfelmuseum, Ehrwald 01796
Gippsland Art Gallery Sale, Sale 01437
Gippsland Heritage Park, Moe 01262
Gipsformerei, Berlin 15976
Gipsmuseum Oberwiesen, Schleitheim 37135
Gipsoteca, Lucca 24225
Gipsoteca Canoviana e Casa del Canova, Possagno 25027
Gipsoteca del Castello Normanno Svevo, Bari 23019
Gipsoteca F. Jerace, Catanzaro 23451
Gipsoteca Istituto d'Arte, Firenze 23847
Gipsoteca M. Guerrisi, Palmi 24784
Girne Kalesi, Girne 08225
Gisborne Steam Park, Gisborne 01053
Gislöfs Smidesmuseum, Simrishamn 36186
Gitstappermolen, Vlodrop 29957
Giustina Gallery, Corvallis 42658
Give-Egnens Museum, Give 08837
Giza Zoological Museum, Giza 09294
Gizi Bajor Memorial and Theatre Museum, Budapest 21327
Gjenreisningsmuseet, Hammerfest 30531
Gjesdal Bygdemuseum, Ålgård 30376
Gjirokastër Museum, Gjirokastër 00023
G.K. Zhukov Museum, Ulaanbaatar 28676
Glacier National Park Museum, West Glacier 48524
Gladstone and District Museum, Gladstone 05491
Gladstone Court Museum, Biggar 38196
Gladstone Gaol, Gladstone, South Australia 01056
Gladstone Maritime Museum, Gladstone, Queensland 01054
Gladstone Regional Art Gallery and Museum, Gladstone, Queensland 01055
Gladstone Working Pottery Museum, Stoke-on-Trent 40607
Gläsermuseum, Gerersdorf 01876
Glamis Castle, Glamis 39037
Glandford Shell Museum, Glandford 39038
Glanmore National Historic Site of Canada, Belleville 05072
Glanum, Saint-Rémy-de-Provence 14447
Glas-Museum Marienhütte und Teufelsmoor-Museum und Teufelsmoor-Galerie, Gnarrenburg 17306
Glas- und Keramikmuseum, Großalmerode 17423
Glasbruksmuseet i Surte, Surte 36316
Glasgow Art Gallery and Museum, Glasgow 39046
Glasgow Print Studio, Glasgow 39047
Glasgow School of Art - Mackintosh Collection, Glasgow 39048
Glashaus-Derneburg, Holle 17822
Glashütte, Bad Reichenhall 15717
Glashüttenmuseum des Erzgebirges, Neuhausen, Sachsen 19036
Glasmuseet Ebeltoft, Ebeltoft 08803
Glasmuseum, Frauenau 17088
Glasmuseum, Hergiswil, Nidwalden 36801
Glasmuseum, Immenhausen 17893
Glasmuseum, Warmensteinach 20402
Glasmuseum Alter Hof Herding, Coesfeld 16489
Glasmuseum Boffzen, Boffzen 16221
Glasmuseum Grünenplan, Grünenplan 17447
Glasmuseum Hadamar, Hadamar 17473
Glasmuseum Rheinbach, Rheinbach 19589
Glasmuseum Steina, Bad Sachsa 15721
Glasmuseum Weisswasser, Weisswasser 20503
Glasmuseum Wertheim, Wertheim 20531
Glasmuseum Zalto, Nagelberg 02335
Glass Gallery and Main Gallery, El Paso 43118
The Glass Museum, Dunkirk 43012
Glass Museum, Harrachov v Krkonoších 08343
Glass Museum, Kamenický Šenov 08399
Glass Museum, Nový Bor 08507
Glass Museum, Tel Aviv 22755
Glass Museum Železný Brod, Železný Brod 08748
Glasschmelzofenbau-Hütte mit Glasausstellung, Plößberg 19420
Glassware and Ceramic Museum of Iran, Teheran 22287
Glastonbury Abbey Museum, Glastonbury 39070
Glastonbury Lake Village Museum, Glastonbury 39071
Glastonbury Museum, Glastonbury 43678
Glauberg-Museum, Glauburg 17297
Glazovskij Kraevedčeskij Muzej, Glazov 32805
Glebe House and Gallery, Church Hill 22393
The Glebe House Museum, Woodbury 48729
Gledswood Farm Museum and Homestead, Catherine Fields 00901
Das Gleimhaus, Halberstadt 17501
Glen Eira City Gallery, Caulfield 00903
Glen Ewen Community Antique Centre, Glen Ewen 05492
Glen Helen Ecology Institute Trailside Museum, Yellow Springs 48783
Glenbow Museum, Calgary 05167
Glencairn Museum, Bryn Athyn 41976
Glencoe and North Lorn Folk Museum, Glencoe 39074
Glencolmcille Folk Village Museum, Glencolmcille 22477
Glendon Gallery, North York 06032
Glendower State Memorial, Lebanon 44703
Glenesk Folk Museum, Brechin 38315
Glenesk Folk Museum, Glenesk 39075
Glenfarclas Distillery Museum, Ballindalloch 38064
Glenfiddich Distillery Museum, Dufftown 38784
Glenfinnan Station Museum, Fort William 39010
Glengarry Pioneer Museum, Dunvegan, Ontario 05356
Glengarry Sports Hall of Fame, Maxville 05826
Glenhyrst Art Gallery of Brant, Brantford 05126
Glenluce Motor Museum, Glenluce 39076
Glenn H. Curtiss Museum, Hammondsport 43888
Glenn House, Cape Girardeau 42095
Glenreagh Memorial Museum, Glenreagh 01060
Glensheen Historic Estate, Duluth 42999
Glentworth Museum, Glentworth 05494
Glenview Area Historical Museum, Glenview 43695
Glessner House Museum, Chicago 42331
Gletschergarten, Luzern 36908
Glichenstein Museum, Zefat 22787
Glimmingehus, Hammenhög 35943
Glims Talomuseo, Espoo 09434
Global Arts Link, Ipswich 01122
Global Health Odyssey, Atlanta 41347
Globenmuseum der Österreichischen Nationalbibliothek, Wien 02890
Glocken-Museum, Siegen 19948
Glockenmuseum, Apolda 15507
Glockenmuseum, Laucha, Unstrut 18345
Glockenmuseum der Glockengiesserei, Innsbruck 02066
Glockenschmiede, Ruhpolding 19715
Gloddfa Ganol Slate Mine, Blaenau Ffestiniog 38248
Glomdalsmuseet, Elverum 30477
Glommersträsks Hembygdsmuseum, Glommersträsk 35905
Glore Psychiatric Museum, Saint Joseph 47105
Gloria Maris Schelpengalerie, Giethoorn 29281
Glossop Heritage Centre, Glossop 39078
Gloucester County Historical Society Museum, Woodbury 48731
Gloucester Folk Museum, Gloucester 01061
Gloucester Folk Museum, Gloucester 39081
Gloucester Lodge Museum, Yanchep 01623
Gloucester Museum, Gloucester 05495
Gloucester Prison Museum, Gloucester 39082
Gloucester School Museum, Gloucester 01062
Gloucestershire Warwickshire Railway, Toddington 40714
Glove Museum, New York 45806
Glud Museum, Horsens 08896
Glücksspielmuseum, Saxon 37127
Glyndor Gallery and Wave Hill House Gallery, Bronx 41919
The Glynn Art Association, Saint Simons Island 47181
Glynn Vivian Art Gallery, Swansea 40658
Glyptothèque, Zagreb 07817
G.N. Jha Kendriya Sanskrit Vidyapeetha, Allahabad 21691
G.N. Prosritelev and G.K. Prave Regional Museum, Stavropol 33563
Gnadenhutten Historical Park and Museum, Gnadenhutten 43707
Gneisenau-Gedenkstätte, Gneisenaustadt Schildau 17308
Goa Science Centre, Panaji 21972
Gobabis Museum, Gobabis 28754
Goclette La Recouvrance, Brest 10909
Godalming Museum, Godalming 39088
Godøy Kystmuseum, Godøy 30514
Godwin and Ternbach Museum, Flushing 43353
Göcsejer-Museum, Zalaegerszeg 21614
Göcseji Falumúzeum, Zalaegerszeg 21613
Göcseji Múzeum, Zalaegerszeg 21614
Göltzschtalgalerie-Nicolaikirche, Auerbach, Vogtland 15545
Goemanszorg - Streek- en Landbouwmuseum, Dreischor 29180
Göreme Açıkhava Müzesi, Nevşehir 37766
Göreme Open Air Museum, Nevşehir 37766
Görög-Római Szobormásolatok Múzeuma, Tata 21592
Göschenhaus / Seume-Gedenkstätte, Grimma 17400
Gösta Serlachiuksen Taidemuseo, Mänttä 09810
Gösta Serlachius Museum of Fine Arts, Mänttä 09810
Göteborg Museum of Art, Göteborg 35912
Göteborgs Konstmuseum, Göteborg 35912
Göteborgs Stadsmuseum, Göteborg 35913
Goethe-Gedenkstätte, Jena 17942
Goethe-Gedenkstätte im Amtshaus, Ilmenau 17890
Goethe Institut, Budapest 21339
Goethe-Institut New York - Exhibitions, New York 45807
Goethe-Institut Sydney, Woollahra 01616
Goethe-Museum Düsseldorf, Düsseldorf 16725
Goethe-Museum Stützerbach mit Museum zur Geschichte des technischen Glases, Stützerbach 20081
Goethe-Stube, Bad Berka 15606
Goethe- und Schiller-Archiv, Weimar, Thüringen 20459
Goethes Gartenhaus 2, Bad Sulza 15752
Goethes Gartenhaus - Goethe-Nationalmuseum, Weimar, Thüringen 20460
Goethes Wohnhaus mit Goethe-Nationalmuseum, Weimar, Thüringen 20461
Goetz/Fleischack Museum, Potchefstroom 34334
Gol Bygdemuseet, Gol 30515
Golan Archaeological Museum, Qatzrin 22728
Gold Coast City Art Gallery, Surfers Paradise 01484
Gold Coast Railroad Museum, Miami 45284
Gold Museum, Ballarat 00763
Gold Prospector Museum, Tankavaara 10099
Gold Treasury Museum, Melbourne 01229
Gold- und Silberschmiedemuseum, Mülsen-Sankt-Jakob 18821
Gold- und Silberschmiedemuseum, Wien 02891
Goldberg-Museum, Riesbürg 19610
Golden and District Museum, Golden 05498
Golden Ball Tavern Museum, Weston 48568
Golden Bay Museum and Gallery, Golden Bay 30165
Golden City Paddle Steamer Museum, Ballarat 00764
Golden Dragon Museum, Bendigo 00795
Golden Hind Museum, Brixham 38363
Golden Hinde Educational Museum, London 39643
Golden Key Museum, Karlovy Vary 08403
Golden Spike National Historic Site, Brigham City 41898
Goldenes Dachl-Maximilianeum, Innsbruck 02067
The Goldie Paley Gallery, Philadelphia 46414
Goldmarkgedenkhaus Deutschkreutz, Deutschkreutz 01761
Goldsmiths' Hall, London 39644
Goldsmith's House Museum, La Habana 07943
The Goldstein Museum of Design, Saint Paul 47154
Goldstream Region Museum, Victoria 06721
Golestan Palace Museum, Teheran 22300
Golf Australia House, Melbourne 01230
Golf Museum, Far Hills 43288
Golf Museum, Newport News 45936
Goliad State Historical Park, Goliad 43722
Golikov House-Museum, Palech 33280
Het Gols-Station, Winterswijk 30013
Gomez Foundation for Mill House, Marlboro 45169
Gomshall Gallery, Gomshall 39093
Gongju Folk Drama Museum, Gongju 27176
Gongju National Museum, Gongju 27177
Gonias Monastery, Kolymvari 21022
Gonzales Memorial Museum, Gonzales 43724
Gonzen-Museum, Sargans 37117
Goochland County Museum, Goochland 43725
Goochland County Museum, Goochland 43726
Goodhue County Historical Society Museum, Red Wing 46817
Goodman Museum, Tyler 48130
Goodnow Museum, Manhattan 45105
Goodsoil Historical Museum, Goodsoil 05500
Goodwood House, Chichester 38561
Goois Museum, Hilversum 29419
Goold Catholic Museum, East Melbourne 00999
Goole Museum and Art Gallery, Goole 39094
Goolwa National Trust Museum, Goolwa 01063
Goors Historisch Museum, Goor 29289
Gorcums Museum, Gorinchem 29291
Gordion Müzesi, Ankara 37618
Gordion Museum, Ankara 37618
Gordon Brown Collection, Ravenshead 40288
Gordon Highlanders Museum, Aberdeen 37937
Gordon Museum, London 39645
Gordon Snelgrove Art Gallery, Saskatoon 06397
Gore Airforce Museum, Gore 30167

Gore Historical Museum and Hokonui Heritage Research Centre, Gore 30168
Gore Place, Waltham 48297
Gorenjski Muzej Kranj, Kranj 34100
Gorgan Museum, Gorgan 22239
Gorgas House, Tuscaloosa 48114
Goriški Muzej, Nova Gorica 34135
Gorj District Museum, Târgu Jiu 32607
Gorj Museum of Folk Architecture, Bumbeşti-Jiu 32476
Gorki Memorial Museum, Kazan 32892
Gorman House Arts Centre, Braddon 00827
Górnośląski Park Etnograficzny, Chorzów 31533
Gornyj Muzej, Sankt-Peterburg 33396
Gorodec Regional Museum, Gorodec 32809
Gorodeckij Kraevedčeskij Muzej, Gorodec 32809
Gorodskoj Kraevedčeskij Muzej, Elec 32792
Gorodskoj Muzej Boevoj Slavy, Kaluga 32876
Gorodskoj Muzej Iskusstvo Omska, Omsk 33253
Gorodskoj Muzej Teatralnogo Iskusstva, Omsk 33254
Gorodskoj Vystavočnyj Zal, Petrozavodsk 33314
Gorrotxategi Konfiteri Museoa, Tolosa 35549
Gorsium Roman Ruin, Székesfehérvár 21557
Gorsium Szabadtéri Múzeum, Székesfehérvár 21557
Goschenhoppen Folklife Museum, Green Lane 43793
Goshen Historical Society Museum, Goshen 43732
Goslarer Museum, Goslar 17349
Goslarer Zinnfiguren-Museum, Goslar 17350
Gospel Music Hall of Fame and Museum, Detroit 42928
Gosport Museum, Gosport 39099
Goss and Crested China Centre, Horndean 39260
Gosudarstvennyj Istoriko-architekturnyj i Chudožestvennyj Muzej-zapovednik Drevnij Derbent, Derbent 32756
Gosudarstvennaja Kollekcija Unikalnych Muzykalnych Instrumentov, Moskva 33045
Gosudarstvennaja Tretjakovskaja Galerja, Moskva 33046
Gosudarstvennaja Tretjakovskaja Galerja na Krymskom Valu, Moskva 33047
Gosudarstvennyj Biologičeskij Muzej im. K.A. Timirjazeva, Moskva 33048
Gosudarstvennyj Borodinskij Voenno-istoričeskij Muzej-zapovednik, Borodino 32701
Gosudarstvennyj Centralnyj Muzej Musykal'noj Kultury im. M.I. Glinki, Moskva 33049
Gosudarstvennyj Centralnyj Muzej Sovremennoj Istorii Rossii, Moskva 33050
Gosudarstvennyj Centralnyj Teatralnyj Muzej im. Bachrušina, Moskva 33051
Gosudarstvennyj Chudožestvenno-architekturnyj Dvorcovo-parkovyj Muzej-zapovednik Oranienbaum, Lomonosov 32988
Gosudarstvennyj Chudožestvenno-architekturnyj Dvorcovo-parkovyj Muzej-zapovednik Pavlovsk, Pavlovsk 33285
Gosudarstvennyj Chudožestvennyj Istoriko-architekturnyj i prirodno-landšaftnyj Muzej-zapovednik Kolomenskoe, Moskva 33052
Gosudarstvennyj Chudožestvennyj Muzej Altajskogo Kraja, Barnaul 32672
Gosudarstvennyj Dom-muzej P.I. Čajkovskogo, Klin 32933
Gosudarstvennyj Ėrmitaž, Sankt-Peterburg 33397
Gosudarstvennyj Geologičeskij Muzej im V.I. Vernadskogo, Moskva 33053
Gosudarstvennyj Istoričeskij Muzej, Moskva 33054
Gosudarstvennyj Istoričeskij Zapovednik Gorki Leninskie, Gorki Leninskie 32807
Gosudarstvennyj Istoriko-architekturnyj, Chudožestvennyj i Landšaftnyj Muzej-Zapovednik Caricyno, Moskva 33055
Gosudarstvennyj Istoriko-architekturnyj i Etnografičeskij Muzej-zapovednik Kiži, Kiži 32931
Gosudarstvennyj Istoriko-architekturnyj i Etnografičeskij Muzej-zapovednik Kiži, Petrozavodsk 33315
Gosudarstvennyj Istoriko-architekturnyj i Prirodno-landšaftnyj Muzej Zapovednik Izborsk, Izborsk 32834
Gosudarstvennyj Istoriko-Architekturnyj i Prirodnyj Muzej-Zapovednik Monrepo, Vyborg 33741
Gosudarstvennyj Istoriko-chudožestvennyj Dvorcovo-parkovyj Muzej-zapovednik Gatčina, Gatčina 32802
Gosudarstvennyj Istoriko-ėtnografičeskij i Architekturnyj Muzej-zapovednik Staraja Sarepta, Volgograd 33714
Gosudarstvennyj Istoriko-ėtnografičeskij Muzej-zapovednik Šušenskoe, Šušenskoe 33569
Gosudarstvennyj Istoriko-kulturnyj i Prirodnyj Muzej-zapovednik A.S. Griboedova - Chmelita, Chmelita 32745
Gosudarstvennyj Istoriko-kulturnyj Muzej-zapovednik "Moskovskij Kreml", Moskva 33056
Gosudarstvennyj Istoriko-literaturnyj i Prirodnyj Muzej-zapovednik A.A. Bloka, Solnečnogorsk 33544
Gosudarstvennyj Istoriko-literaturnyj Muzej-Zapovednik A.S. Puškina s usadbami Vjazemy i Zacharovo, Bolšie Vjazemy 32696
Gosudarstvennyj Istoriko-memorialnyj Sankt-Peterburgskij Muzej Smolnyj, Sankt-Peterburg 33398
Gosudarstvennyj Istoriko-memorialnyj Zapovednik Rodina V.I. Lenina, Uljanovsk 33656
Gosudarstvennyj Kraevedčeskij Muzej Karalpakii, Nukus 48845
Gosudarstvennyj Literaturno-memorialnyj Muzej Anny Achmatovoj v Fontannom Dome, Sankt-Peterburg 33399
Gosudarstvennyj Literaturno-memorialnyj Muzej N.A. Dobroljubova, Nižnij Novgorod 33206
Gosudarstvennyj Literaturno-memorialnyj Muzej im. M.Ju. Lermontova, Pjatigorsk 33321
Gosudarstvennyj Literaturno-memorialnyj Muzej N. Ostrovskogo, Soči 33540
Gosudarstvennyj Literaturno-memorialnyj Muzej A.N. Radiščeva, Radiščevo 33346
Gosudarstvennyj Literaturno-memorialnyj Muzej-zapovednik A.P. Čechova, Melichovo 33009
Gosudarstvennyj Literaturno-memorialnyj Muzej-zapovednik N.A. Nekrasova "Karabicha", Karabicha 32883
Gosudarstvennyj Literaturnyj Muzej, Moskva 33057
Gosudarstvennyj Literaturnyj Muzej A.M. Gorkogo, Nižnij Novgorod 33207
Gosudarstvennyj Literaturnyj Muzej im. I.S. Turgeneva, Orël 33263
Gosudarstvennyj Memorialnyj Dom-muzej Bulata Okudžavy, Peredelkino 33298
Gosudarstvennyj Memorialnyj Dom-muzej N.A. Rimskogo-Korsakova, Tichvin 33599
Gosudarstvennyj Memorialnyj i Prirodnyj Muzej-zapovednik A.N. Ostrovskogo - Ščelykovo, Ščelykovo 33513
Gosudarstvennyj Memorialnyj i Prirodnyj Muzej-zapovednik I.S. Turgeneva 'Spasskoe Lutovinovo', Spasskoe-Lutovinovo 33550
Gosudarstvennyj Memorial'nyj Istoriko-chudožestvennyj i Prirodnyj Muzej-zapovednik V.D. Polenova, Strachovo 33566
Gosudarstvennyj Memorialnyj Muzej im. A.V. Suvorova, Sankt-Peterburg 33400
Gosudarstvennyj Memorialnyj Muzej Oborony i Blokady Leningrada, Sankt-Peterburg 33401
Gosudarstvennyj Memorialnyj Muzej-usadba V.G. Belinskogo, Belinskij 32679
Gosudarstvennyj Moskovskij Muzej Naivnogo Iskusstva, Moskva 33058
Gosudarstvennyj Muzej Detskich Teatrov, Moskva 33059
Gosudarstvennyj Muzej K.A. Fedina, Saratov 33506
Gosudarstvennyj Muzej Iskusstv, Taškent 48853
Gosudarstvennyj Muzej Iskusstv Respubliki Karakalpakstan, Nukus 48846
Gosudarstvennyj Muzej Istorii Aviacii, Sankt-Peterburg 33402
Gosudarstvennyj Muzej Istorii i Kultury Belarusa, Minsk 03116
Gosudarstvennyj Muzej Istorii Kosmonavtiki im. K.Ė. Ciolkovskogo, Kaluga 32877
Gosudarstvennyj Muzej Istorii Kultury i Iskusstva Uzbekistana, Samarkand 48848
Gosudarstvennyj Muzej Istorii Religii, Sankt-Peterburg 33403
Gosudarstvennyj Muzej Istorii Sankt-Peterburga - Petropavlovskij Sobor, Sankt-Peterburg 33404
Gosudarstvennyj Muzej Izobrazitelnogo Iskusstva Rossijskogo Severa, Archangelsk 32650
Gosudarstvennyj Muzej Izobrazitelnych Iskusstv Respubliki Kalmykija, Ėlista 32793
Gosudarstvennyj Muzej A.I. Kuprina, Narovčat 33200
Gosudarstvennyj Muzej V.V. Majakovskogo, Moskva 33060
Gosudarstvennyj Muzej-masterskaja Skulptora A.S. Golubkinoj, Moskva 33061
Gosudarstvennyj Muzej Narodnogo Obrazovanija Gruzii, Tbilisi 15362
Gosudarstvennyj Muzej Oborony Moskvy, Moskva 33062
Gosudarstvennyj Muzej Palechskogo Iskusstva, Palech 33282
Gosudarstvennyj Muzej-panorama Stalingradskaja Bitva, Volgograd 33715
Gosudarstvennyj Muzej Političeskoj Istorii Rossii, Sankt-Peterburg 33405
Gosudarstvennyj Muzej A.S. Puškina, Moskva 33063
Gosudarstvennyj Muzej-Reservat Mangyšlaka Sokroviśča-Zapovedniki Mangyšlaka i Ustyrta, Ševčenko 27094
Gosudarstvennyj Muzej-Reservat Pamjatniki Drevnego Taraza, Džambul 27082
Gosudarstvennyj Muzej Vadima Sidura, Moskva 33064
Gosudarstvennyj Muzej L.N. Tolstogo, Moskva 33065
Gosudarstvennyj Muzej L.N. Tolstogo, Moskva 33066
Gosudarstvennyj Muzej L.N. Tolstogo "Jasnaja Poljana", Jasnaja Poljana (Tula) 32856
Gosudarstvennyj Muzej-usadba Archangelskoe, Archangelskoe 32654
Gosudarstvennyj Muzej-usadba P.I. Čajkovskogo, Votkinsk 33737
Gosudarstvennyj Muzej-zapovednik S.A. Esenina, Konstantinovo 32937
Gosudarstvennyj Muzej Zapovednik Petergof, Sankt-Peterburg 33406
Gosudarstvennyj Muzej-zapovednik M.A. Šolochova, Vešenskaja 33683
Gosudarstvennyj Muzej Životnovodstva im Akademika E.F. Liskuna, Moskva 33067
Gosudarstvennyj Nacionalnyj Muzej Ust-Ordynskogo Burjatskogo Avtonomnogo Okruga, Ust-Ordynsk 33672
Gosudarstvennyj Naučno-issledovatelskij Muzej Architektury im. A.V. Ščuseva, Moskva 33068
Gosudarstvennyj Okružnoj Muzej Prirody i Čeloveka Goroda Chanty-Mansijsk, Chanty-Mansijsk 32744
Gosudarstvennyj Russkij Muzej, Sankt-Peterburg 33407
Gosudarstvennyj Russkij Muzej, Sankt-Peterburg 33408
Gosudarstvennyj Severnyj Morskoj Muzej, Archangelsk 32651
Gosudarstvennyj Vladimiro-Suzdalskij Istoriko-architekturnyj i Chudožestvennyj Muzej-zapovednik, Vladimir 33692
Gosudarstvennyj Voenno-istoričeskij i Prirodnyj Muzej-zapovednik Kulikovo Pole, Tula 33624
Gosudarstvennyj Voenno-istoričeskij Muzej-zapovednik Prochorovskoe Pole, Prochorovka 33328
Gosudarstvennyj Vystavočnyj Zal Zamoskvorec^Bie, Moskva 33069
Gothaer Haus der Versicherungsgeschichte, Gotha 17358
Gothaer Kunstforum, Köln 18140
Gothenburg Radio Museum, Göteborg 35918
Gotischer Freskenraum, Ostermiething 02388
Gotisches Haus, Berlin 15977
Gotisches Haus, Wörlitz 20641
Gotlands Fornsal med Fenomenalen, Visby 36413
Gotlands Konstmuseum, Visby 36414
Gotland's Museum of Natural History, Visby 36415
Gotlands Naturmuseum, Visby 36415
Gotoh Bijutsukan, Tokyo 26854
The Gotoh Museum, Tokyo 26854
Gottfried-August-Bürger-Museum, Molmerswende 18784
Gottfried-Keller-Zentrum, Glattfelden 36767
Gotthelf-Stube, Lützelflüh 36895
Gottlieb Daimler-Gedächtnisstätte, Stuttgart 20092
Gottlieb-Häußler-Heimatmuseum, Filderstadt 17001
Goudreau Museum of Mathematics in Art and Science, New Hyde Park 45707
Gouds Poppentheater en Museum, Gouda 29293
Goulandris Collection, Athinai 20862
Goulandris Natural History Museum, Kifissia 21015
Goulburn Regional Art Gallery, Goulburn 01069
Gounaropoulos Museum of Zografou, Zografou 21224
Gouriotis Collection, Lárissa 21044
Gouverneur Historical Association Museum, Gouverneur 43735
Het Gouverneurshuis, Heusden 29414
Govan and District Museum, Govan 05504
Government Art Collection, London 39646
Government Central Museum, Jaipur, Rajasthan 21862
Government Educational Museum, Bulandshahar 21733
Government Educational Museum, Deoria 21787
Government Educational Museum, Etawah 21799
Government House, Sydney 01495
Government House Museum and Heritage Property, Regina 06235
Government Industrial and Commercial Museum, Kolkata 21903
Government J.T.C. Museum, Faizabad 21802
Government Museum, Ajmer 21684
Government Museum, Alwar 21693
Government Museum, Bharatpur 21714
Government Museum, Chennai 21744
Government Museum, Hassan 21838
Government Museum, Jodhpur 21874
Government Museum, Kodagu 21893
Government Museum, Mathura 21940
Government Museum, Mount Abu 21944
Government Museum, Pudukottai 21985
Government Museum, Thiruvananthapuram 22035
Government Museum, Udaipur 22044
Government Museum and Art Gallery, Chandigarh 21738
Government Museum Jhalawar, Jhalawar 21871
Government Museum Vellore, Vellore 22059
Governmental Educational Museum, Muzaffarnagar 21957
Governor Bent Museum, Taos 47949
Governor General's Foot Guards Regimental Museum, Ottawa 06081
Governor Henry Lippitt House Museum, Providence 46719
Governor John Langdon House, Portsmouth 46648
Governor Printz Park, Essington 43214
Governor Ross Plantation, Seaford 47523
Governor Seay Mansion, Kingfisher 44487
Governor Stephen Hopkins House, Providence 46720
Governor's Gallery, Santa Fe 47419
Governor's Mansion, Columbia 42560
Governor's Mansion, Sacramento 47052
Govett-Brewster Art Gallery, New Plymouth 30213
Gower Heritage Centre, Gower 39106
Gowganda and Area Museum, Gowganda 05505
Gozo Cathedral Museum, Victoria 27709
Graaf-Reinet Museum, Graaff-Reinet 34246
Grabkapelle Württemberg, Stuttgart 20093
Gråbo Minnenas Museum, Karlskoga 35994
Grabungsmuseum, Langenburg 18330
Grabungsmuseum Kirchhof, Coburg 16482
Grace Campbell Gallery, Prince Albert 06182
Grace Darling Museum, Bamburgh 38074
Grace Hudson Museum and The Sun House, Ukiah 48134
Grace Museum, Abilene 41053
Gracefield Arts Centre, Dumfries 38789
Graceland, Memphis 45238
Gracie Mansion, New York 45808
Gradska Chudožestvena Galerija, Berkovica 04621
Gradska Chudožestvena Galerija, Plovdiv 04777
Gradska Chudožestvena Galerija Petko Čurčuliev, Dimitrovgrad 04650
Gradski Archeologičeski Muzej, Chisar 04642
Gradski Archeologičeski Muzej, Nesebăr 04742
Gradski Archeologičeski Muzej, Sandanski 04809
Gradski Istoričeski Muzej, Asenovgrad 04604
Gradski Istoričeski Muzej, Balčik 04611
Gradski Istoričeski Muzej, Botevgrad 04627
Gradski Istoričeski Muzej, Čirpan 04645
Gradski Istoričeski Muzej, Dalgopol 04647
Gradski Istoričeski Muzej, Jeravna 04683
Gradski Istoričeski Muzej, Karnobat 04692
Gradski Istoričeski Muzej, Kavarna 04696
Gradski Istoričeski Muzej, Klisura 04711
Gradski Istoričeski Muzej, Lom 04726
Gradski Istoričeski Muzej, Melnik 04734
Gradski Istoričeski Muzej, Nova Zagora 04744
Gradski Istoričeski Muzej, Orjachovo 04749
Gradski Istoričeski Muzej, Panagjurište 04750
Gradski Istoričeski Muzej, Peruštica 04760
Gradski Istoričeski Muzej, Samakov 04808
Gradski Istoričeski Muzej, Sevlievo 04811
Gradski Istoričeski Muzej, Sozopol 04864
Gradski Istoričeski Muzej, Teteven 04884
Gradski Istoričeski Muzej Aleko Konstantinov, Svištov 04879
Gradski Istoričeski Muzej Iskra, Kazanlăk 04700
Gradski Muzej, Bjelovar 07681
Gradski Muzej, Foča 33838
Gradski Muzej, Kosovska Mitrovica 33847
Gradski Muzej, Križevci 07730
Gradski Muzej, Požega 07756
Gradski Muzej, Sremski Karlovci 33915
Gradski Muzej i Galerija, Bečej 33791
Gradski Muzej Karlovac, Karlovac 07713
Gradski Muzej Makarska, Makarska 07736
Gradski Muzej Siska, Sisak 07776
Gradski Muzej Sombor, Sombor 33910
Gradski Muzej Varaždin, Varaždin 07797
Gradski Muzej - Városi Muzeum, Subotica 33918
Gradski Muzej Virovitica, Virovitica 07801
Gradski Muzej Vršac, Vršac 33928
Gräfliche Sammlungen und Afrikanisches Jagdmuseum, Erbach, Odenwald 16888
Graeme Park/Keith Mansion, Horsham 44107
Grängesbergsbanornas Järnvägsmuseum, Grängesberg 35926
Graf Harrach'sche Familiensammlung, Rohrau 02520
Graf-Luxburg-Museum, Bad Bocklet 15615
De Grafelijke Torenmolen, Zeddam 30047
Grafička Zbirka Nacionalne i Sveučilišne Knjižnice, Zagreb 07818
Grafik Museum Stiftung Schreiner, Bad Steben 15750
Grafikens Hus, Mariefred 36083
Grafikmuseum, Korsberga 36014
Grafisch Historisch Centrum - Drukkerijmuseum, Etten Leur 29253
Grafisch Musem-Atelier in den Groenen Zonck, Wouw 30027
Grafisch Museum Groningen, Groningen 29308
Grafisch Museum Zutphen, Zutphen 30075
Grafische Sammlung, Nürnberg 19141
Grafschafter Museum im Moerser Schloß, Moers 18776
Grafschaftsmuseum, Wertheim 20532
Grafton Museum, Grafton 43737
Grafton Regional Gallery, Grafton 01071
Graham County Historical Museum, Safford 47060
Grain Store Museum, Vihti 10196
Grainger Museum, Parkville, Victoria 01357
Grains Industry Museum, Cabanatuan 31299
Grammophonmuseum, Bad Urach 15755
Gramophone Records Museum, Cape Coast 20792
Grampian Police Museum, Aberdeen 37938
Grampian Transport Museum, Alford, Aberdeenshire 37973
Granary Museum, Renko 09991
Grand Army of the Republic Civil War Museum, Philadelphia 46415
Grand Army of the Republic Memorial and Veteran's Military Museum, Aurora 41397
Grand Canyon National Park Museum Collection, Grand Canyon 43740
Grand Coteau Heritage and Cultural Centre, Shaunavon 06428
Grand County Museum, Hot Sulphur Springs 44112
Grand Encampment Museum, Encampment 43186
Grand Falls Museum, Grand Falls 05510
Grand Forks Art Gallery, Grand Forks 05514
Grand Forks County Historical Society Museum, Grand Forks 43741
Grand Gulf Military State Park Museum, Port Gibson 46594
Grand Island Trader's Cabin, Munising 45560
Grand Lake Area Historical Museum, Grand Lake 43750
The Grand Lodge of Scotland Museum, Edinburgh 38885
Grand Manan Museum, Grand Manan 05516
Grand Mound History Center, International Falls 44239
Grand Portage, Grand Marais 43752
Grand-Pré National Historic Site of Canada, Grand-Pré 05518
Grand Prix Museum, Macau 07162
Grand Rapids Art Museum, Grand Rapids 43756

Grand Rapids Children's Museum, Grand Rapids 43757
Grand River Historical Society Museum, Chillicothe 42377
Grand Shaft, Dover 38768
Grand Village of the Natchez Indians, Natchez 45632
Grande Museo, Fabriano 23745
Grande Prairie Museum, Grande Prairie 05519
Grangärde Hembygdsgården, Grangärde 35929
La Grange Béranger, Beblenheim 10658
Grange-Conservatoire de l'Othain, Grand-Failly 11903
Grange Museum of Community History, London 39647
Grangemouth Museum, Grangemouth 39108
Granger Homestead Society Museum, Canandaigua 42076
Granger House, Marion 45155
Granitabbaumuseum, Königshain 18177
Granma Memorial, La Habana 07931
Granösunds Fiskeläge, Södra Vallgrund 10044
Grans Lantbruksmuseum, Öjebyn 36132
Grant County Historical Museum, Canyon City 42093
Grant County Historical Museum, Elbow Lake 43128
Grant County Historical Museum, Ephrata 43196
Grant County Museum, Elgin 43130
Grant County Museum, Hyannis 44185
Grant County Museum, Medford 45219
Grant County Museum, Sheridan 47601
Grant County Museum, Ulysses 48137
Grant-Humphreys Mansion, Denver 42890
Grant-Kohrs Ranch National Historic Site, Deer Lodge 42845
Grant Medical College Museum, Mumbai 21948
Grant Museum of Zoology and Comparative Anatomy, London 39648
Grantham Museum, Grantham 39111
Granton Centre, Edinburgh 38886
Grantown Museum, Grantown-on-Spey 39113
Grant's Birthplace State Memorial, Point Pleasant 46575
Grants Pass Museum of Art, Grants Pass 43767
Granville County Historical Society Museum, Oxford 46240
Granville Historical Museum, Granville 43773
Granvin Bygdamuseum, Granvin 30516
Grapevine Museum, Chiltern 00914
Graphic and Cartographical Collections of the Jagiellonian Library, Kraków 31724
Graphikmuseum Pablo Picasso Münster, Münster 18938
Graphische Sammlung, Augsburg 15556
Graphische Sammlung, Kassel 18018
Graphische Sammlung am Kunsthistorischen Institut der Universität Tübingen, Tübingen 20223
Graphische Sammlung der Eidgenössischen Technischen Hochschule, Zürich 37377
Graphische Sammlung der Universität, Erlangen 16918
Graphothek Berlin, Berlin 15978
Graslitzer Gedenk- und Informationsraum, Aschaffenburg 15523
Grassagården Miljömuseum, Strängnäs 36302
Grasselmühle, Reichenthal 02497
Grassimuseum Leipzig, Leipzig 18398
Graue Mill and Museum, Oak Brook 46050
Grave Creek Mound Historic Site, Moundsville 45521
Gravelbourg and District Museum, Gravelbourg 05524
Gravensteen Museum voor Gerechtsvoorwerpen, Gent 03438
Graves Art Gallery, Sheffield 40484
Gravesham Museum, Gravesend, Kent 39116
Gray's Printing Press, Strabane 40619
Grays School of Art Gallery and Museum, Aberdeen 37939
Grazer Kunstverein, Graz 01915
Grazer Stadtmuseum, Graz 01916
Great Bardfield Cage, Great Bardfield 39119
Great Bardfield Cottage Museum, Great Bardfield 39120
Great Barn Museum of Wiltshire Rural Life, Avebury 38042
Great Basin Museum, Delta 42866
Great Basin National Park, Baker 41436
Great Blacks in Wax Museum, Baltimore 41468
Great Brak River Museum, Great Brak River 34255
Great Central Railway Museum, Loughborough 39830
Great Cobar Heritage Centre, Cobar 00931
Great Explorations, Saint Petersburg 47173
Great Fish River Museum, Cradock 34220
Great Harbor Maritime Museum, Northeast Harbor 46018
Great Lakes Historical Museum, Tuncurry 01556
Great Lakes Lighthouse Museum, Mackinaw City 45033
Great Lakes Naval Memorial and Museum, Muskegon 45576
Great Lakes Science Center, Cleveland 42473
Great Laxey Wheel and Mines Trail, Laxey 39432
Great Orme Tramway, Llandudno 39540
Great Palace at the Museum-Preserve, Lomonosov 32986
Great Patriotic War Museum, Moskva 33027
Great Plains Art Collection in the Christlieb Gallery, Lincoln 44783
Great Plains Black Museum, Omaha 46148
Great Plains Transportation Museum, Wichita 48602
Great Sandhills Museum, Sceptre 06415
Great Valley Museum of Natural History, Modesto 45427
Great War Flying Museum, Cheltenham 05242
Great Yarmouth Museums, Great Yarmouth 39124
Great Zimbabwe Site Museum, Masvingo 49037
Greater Harvard Area Historical Society, Harvard 43951
Greater Hazleton Historical Society Museum, Hazleton 43978
Greater Loveland Historical Society Museum, Loveland 44981
Greater Manchester Police Museum, Manchester 39887
Greater Port Jefferson Museum, Port Jefferson 46598
The Greater Reston Arts Center, Reston 46846
Greater Sudbury Heritage Museum, Sudbury 06511
Greater Vernon Museum, Vernon, British Colombia 06706
Greb Jagd-Museum, Busswil (Thurgau) 36610
Greco-Roman Museum, Alexandria 09238
Greek Federation of Associations of Friends of Museums, Athinai 49222
Greek Orthodox Museum, Jerusalem 22633
Green Bay Packer Hall of Fame, Green Bay 43788
Green Dragon Museum, Stockton-on-Tees 40599
Green Gables House, Charlottetown 05226
Green Hill Center for North Carolina Art, Greensboro 43811
Green Howards Museum, Richmond, North Yorkshire 40316
Green Mountain Club, Waterbury Center 48428
Green Palace Museum, Teheran 22301
Green Park Shipbuilding Museum and Yeo House, Port Hill 06164
Green River Museum, Woodbury 48730
Greenaway Gallery, Camberwell, Victoria 00876
Greenbelt Museum, Greenbelt 43796
Greene County Historical Museum, Waynesburg 48484
Greene County Historical Society Museum, Xenia 48772
Greene Memorial Museum, Milwaukee 45362
Greenfield Historical Society Museum, Greenfield 43808
Greenfield Museum, Greenfield 43807
Greenfield Valley Museum, Greenfield 39128
Greenhill Covenanter's House, Biggar 38197
Greenland National Museum and Archives, Nuuk 21234
Green's Mill and Science Centre, Nottingham 40107
Greensboro Artists' League Gallery, Greensboro 43812
Greensboro Historical Museum, Greensboro 43813
Greenspond Court House, Greenspond 05527
Greensward Gallery, Corvallis 42659
Greentown Glass Museum, Greentown 43822
Greenville County Museum of Art, Greenville 43830
Greenville Museum of Art, Greenville 43825
Greenwich Heritage Centre, London 39649
Greenwich Local History Centre, London 39650
Greenwich Theatre Art Gallery, London 39651
Greenwood County Historical Society Museum, Eureka 43232
Greenwood Great House Museum, Greenwood 26064
Greenwood Military Aviation Museum, Greenwood, Nova Scotia 05529
Greenwood Museum, Greenwood, British Columbia 05528
Gregg County Historical Museum, Longview 44878
Gregor Mendel Memorial, Brno 08268
Greifensteiner Burgmuseum, Greifenstein 17386
Grekiskt Kulturcentrum, Stockholm 36243
Grenada National Museum, Saint George's 21244
Grenen Kunstmuseum, Skagen 09055
Grenfell and District History Museum, Grenfell 01074
Grenfell Community Museum, Grenfell 05530
Grenfell House Museum, Saint Anthony 06305
Grenjadarstadur Folk Museum, Húsavík 21639
Grenslandmuseum, Dinxperlo 29156
Grenzland-Museum Bad Sachsa, Bad Sachsa 15722
Grenzland- und Trenckmuseum, Waldmünchen 20371
Grenzlandheimatstuben des Heimatkreises Marienbad, Neualbenreuth 19011
Grenzlandmuseum, Schnackenburg 19814
Grenzlandmuseum Eichsfeld, Teistungen 20154
Grenzlandmuseum Raabs an der Thaya, Raabs an der Thaya 02470
Grenzlandmuseum Swinmark, Schnega 19818
Grenzmuseum Philippsthal (Werra), Philippsthal, Werra 19399
Grenzmuseum Schifflersgrund, Asbach-Sickenberg 15520
Grenzwald-Destillation Museum, Crottendorf 16516
Gresham History Museum, Gresham 43838
Greve Museum, Greve 08842
Grevenbroek Museum, Hamont-Achel 03473
Grey Art Gallery, New York 45809
Grey County Museum, Owen Sound 06088
Greybull Museum, Greybull 43839
Greyhound Hall of Fame, Abilene 41050
Greytown Museum, Greytown 34257
Grier-Musser Museum, Los Angeles 44904
Grietje Tump Museum, Landsmeer 29496
Griffith Artworks, Nathan 01309
Griffith Pioneer Park Museum, Griffith 01075
Griffith Regional Art Gallery, Griffith 01076
Griffiths Sea Shell Museum and Marine Display, Lakes Entrance 01161
Grillparzer-Gedenkzimmer, Wien 02892
Grimsby Museum, Grimsby 05531
Grimsby Public Art Gallery, Grimsby 05532
Grindheim Bygdemuseum, Kollungtveit 30599
Grindsted Museum, Grindsted 08844
Grinnell College Art Gallery, Grinnell 43841
Grinnell Historical Museum, Grinnell 43842
Grinter Place, Kansas City 44393
Gripes Modeltheatremuseum, Nyköping 36126
Gripsholms Slott, Mariefred 36084
Grissom Air Museum, Peru 46363
Grist Mill, Keremeos 05662
Grizzly Bear Prairie Museum, Wanham 06743
Groam House Museum, Rosemarkie 40341
Grocer's Shop of Roskilde Museum, Roskilde 09044
Gród Piastowski w Gieczu, Giecz 31591
Grødaland Bygdetun, Nærbø 30698
Grodnenski Gosudarstvennyj Istoričeskij Muzej, Grodno 03111
Grodno State Historical Museum, Grodno 03111
De Groene Schuur, Culemborg 29061
Grönegau-Museum, Melle 18698
Groeninge Museum, Brugge 03253
Groeningeabdij, Kortrijk 03541
Groeningemuseum, Brugge 03253
Grönsöö Slott, Enköping 35867
Gróf Esterházy Károly Kastély és Tájmúzeum, Pápa 21499
Grong Bygdamuseum, Grong 30521
Groninger Museum, Groningen 29309
Groninger Schaatsmuseum, Sappemeer 29791
Groot Constantia Manor House and Wine Museum, Constantia 34219
Groot Kasteel van Loppem, Loppem 03598
Grootfontein Museum Das Alte Fort, Grootfontein 28755
Grootmoeders Keukenmuseum, Nijmegen 29630
Gropius House, Lincoln 44779
Grosse Ile Historical Museum, Grosse Ile 43843
Große Kunstschau, Worpswede 20683
Großer Wappensaal im Landhaus, Klagenfurt 02124
Großherzoglich-Hessische Porzellansammlung, Darmstadt 16539
Großmitterberger Troadkasten, Laussa 02194
Grosvenor Lodge, London 05767
Grosvenor Museum, Chester 38552
Groton Historical Museum, Groton 43846
Grotte de Rouffignac, Rouffignac-Saint-Cernin 14059
Grotte du Chien, Chamalières 11136
Grotte et Parc Préhistoriques, Foissac 11751
Grotte Préhistorique Ornée, Miers 12976
Grottes de Vallorbe, Vallorbe 37278
Grottes Préhistoriques, Soyons 14798
Grottes Préhistoriques de Sare-Lezea, Sare 14608
Grotto Museum, Aggetelek 21306
Groudle Glen Railway, Onchan 40133
Groundbirch Museum, Groundbirch 05535
Grounds For Sculpture, Hamilton 43878
Group for Costume and Textile Staff in Museums, Saint Fagans 49415
Group for Directors of Museums, Chester 49416
Group for Education in Museums, Gillingham, Kent 49417
Groupement des Amis de Musées de la Région Midi-Pyrénées, Montauban 49180
Groupement des Amis des Musées de la Région Centre, Orleans 49181
Groupement des Associations d'Amis de Musées de la Région Bretagne, Nevez 49182
Groupement des Associations d'Amis de Musées de la Région Languedoc-Roussillon, Montpellier 49183
Groupement des Associations d'Amis de Musées de la Région Limousin, Limoges 49184
Groupement des Associations des Amis de Musées Région Provence Alpes Côte d'Azur, Toulon (Var) 49185
Groupement Régional des Associations d'Amis de Musées de la Région Ile de France, Paris 49186
Groupement Rhône-Alpes des Amis de Musée, Lyon 49187
Grout Museum of History and Science, Waterloo 48431
Grove Rural Life Museum, Ramsey, Isle of Man 40280
Grover Cleveland Birthplace, Caldwell 42029
Grover M. Hermann Fine Arts Center, Marietta 45149
Grovewood Gallery, Asheville 41280
Grubb Shaft Gold and Heritage Museum, Beaconsfield 00780
Grube Alte Hoffnung Erbstolln, Mittweida 18757
Grubenmann-Sammlung, Teufen 37236
Grünauer Wassersportmuseum, Berlin 15979
Grünes Gewölbe, Dresden 16685
Grüttert Uhrenmuseum Bremen, Bremen 16325
Gruetunet Museum, Kirkenær i Solør 30593
Grumman Memorial Park, Calverton 42036
Grundtvigs Mindestuer i Udby, Lundby 08978
Grundy Art Gallery, Blackpool 38246
Grunt Gallery, Vancouver 06678
Grunwald Center for the Graphic Arts, Los Angeles 44905
Gruuthuse, Brugge 03250
Gruvmuseet, Sala 36172
Grytøy Bygdetun, Lundenes 30658
G.S. Novikov-Daurskiy Regional Museum of the Amur Region, Blagoveščensk 32691
Gschlößl Leithaprodersdorf-Freilichtanlage, Leithaprodersdorf 02203
Gsellmanns Weltmaschine, Edelsbach bei Feldbach 01785
GSIS Gallery, Pasay 31412
Guadalupe Cultural Arts Center, San Antonio 47251
Guam Museum, Agana 21256
Guangdong Art Gallery, Guangzhou 07060
Guangdong Folk Arts and Crafts Museum, Guangzhou 07061
Guangdong Museum, Guangzhou 07062
Guangxi Natural Museum, Nanning 07189
Guangxi Provincial Museum, Guilin 07073
Guangzhou Art Gallery, Guangzhou 07063
Guangzhou Lu Xun Museum, Guangzhou 07064
Guangzhou Liwan District Museum, Guangzhou 07065
Guangzhou Lu Xun Museum, Guangzhou 07066
Guangzhou Museum, Guangzhou 07067
Guard House and Soldiers Barracks, Fredericton 05461
Guard Ship 'Red Pennant' of 1911, Vladivostok 33710
Guardhouse Museum, Tattershall 40676
The Guards Museum, London 39652
Gudbrandsdal Krigsminnesamling, Kvam 30621
Guelph Civic Museum, Guelph 05536
Günter Grass-Kulturstiftung Hansestadt Lübeck, Lübeck 18535
Guernsey County Museum, Cambridge 42055
Guernsey Museum and Art Gallery, Saint Peter Port 40424
Güzel Sanatlar Müzesi, Girne 08226
Güzelyurt Müzesi, Güzelyurt 08228
Guggenheim Hermitage Museum, Las Vegas 44666
Guggenheim Museum Bilbao, Bilbao 34612
Guggenheim Museum Soho, New York 45810
Guide Heritage Centre, London 39653
Guido Gezelle Museum, Brugge 03254
Guido Gezellemuseum, Brugge 03254
Guild Gallery, Bristol 38356
Guild Hall Museum, East Hampton 43046
Guild of Creative Art, Shrewsbury 47620
Guildford Cathedral Treasury, Guildford 39136
Guildford House Gallery, Guildford 39137
Guildford Museum, Guildford 39138
Guildhall, Bath 38114
Guildhall, Beverley 38182
Guildhall, Exeter 38956
Guildhall, Leicester 39461
Guildhall, Thaxted 40693
Guildhall Art Gallery, London 39654
Guildhall Gallery, Winchester 40887
Guildhall Museum, Carlisle 38489
Guildhall Museum, Chichester 38562
Guildhall Museum, Rochester 40335
Guildhall Museum, Sandwich 40446
Guilford College Art Gallery, Greensboro 43814
Guilford Courthouse National Military Park, Greensboro 43815
Guilin City Museum, Guilin 07074
Guinness Archives, London 39655
Guinness Museum of World Records, Niagara Falls 05989
Guinness Storehouse, Dublin 22429
Guinness World of Records Museum, Las Vegas 44667
Guitar Museo Ex Teresa Arte Actual, México 28104
Guizhou Provincial Museum, Guiyang 07077
Gukgiwon Taekwondo Museum, Seoul 27235
Gulbenes Vēstures un Mākslas Muzejs, Gulbene 27357
Gulf Beach Art Center, Indian Rocks Beach 44209
Gulf Coast Exploreum, Mobile 45419
Gulf Coast Museum of Art, Largo 44653
Gulf Museum, Port-aux-Basques 06153
Gulf of Georgia Cannery, Richmond 06262
Gulf Station Historic Farm, Yarra Glen 01626
Gullhaugen Setermuseum, Venabygd 30983
Gulli Skoletun, Andebu 30385
Gumanitarnyj Centr-muzej Tvorčestva Autsajderov, Moskva 33070
Gumbez Manace Literary Ethnographic Museum, Taš-Aryk 27315
Gumeracha and District History Centre, Gumeracha 01078
Gunarsa Museum, Klungkung 22148
Gundagai Historical Museum, Gundagai 01079
Gunderson House, Kenyon 44450
Gunma-kenritsu Kindai Bijutsukan, Takasaki 26798
Gunma Prefectural Museum of History, Takasaki 26799
Gunn Memorial Library and Museum, Washington 48329
Gunnebo House and Gardens, Mölndal 36096
Gunnebo Slott och Trädgårdar, Mölndal 36096
Gunnersbury Park Museum, London 39656
Gunnison County Pioneer and Historical Museum, Gunnison 43853
Gunnison Museum of Natural History, Pawling 46315
Gunston Hall Plantation, Mason Neck 45201
Guovdageainnu Gilisillju, Kautokeino 30592
Guriev Historical and Regional Museum, Guriev 27084
Gurievskij Istoriko-Kraevedčeskij Muzej, Guriev 27084
Gurkha Museum, Winchester 40888
Gurusaday Museum, Kolkata 21904
Gush Ezyon Museum, Gush Ezyon 22594
Gustaf-Dalman-Institut für biblische Landes- und Altertumskunde, Greifswald 17389
Gustafson Gallery, Fort Collins 43381
Gustav-Adolf-Gedenkstätte, Lützen 18564
Gustav-Adolf-Museum, Geleithaus, Weißenfels 20497
Gustav-Freytag-Archiv und Museum, Wangen im Allgäu 20393
Gustav-Freytag-Gedenkstätte, Gotha 17359
Gustav III.'s Antikmuseum, Stockholm 36244
Gustav III's Museum of Antiquities, Stockholm 36244

Gustav III.'s Paviljong, Solna 36218
Gustav Jeeninga Museum of Bible and Near Eastern Studies, Anderson 41203
Gustav-Lübcke Museum, Hamm, Westfalen 17576
Gustav-Wolf-Kunstgalerie, Östringen 19233
Gustavsbergs Porslinmuseum, Gustavsberg 35932
Gut Seekamp der Hans Kock-Stiftung, Kiel 18073
Gutao Wenming Museum, Beijing 06967
Gutenberg-Gedenkstätte, Eltville 16842
Gutenberg Museum, Fribourg 36714
Gutenberg-Museum, Mainz 18600
Gutshaus Steglitz, Berlin 15980
Guwahati Medical Museum, Guwahati 21823
Guy Lombardo Museum, London 05768
Guyana Museum, Georgetown 21290
G.V. Tchitcherin House-Museum, Tambov 33589
Gwalia Historical Museum, Leonora 01175
Gwangju Municipal Folk Museum, Gwangju 27182
Gwangju National Museum, Gwangju 27183
Gwili Steam Railway, Bronwydd 38378
Gwinnett Historical Society Museum, Lawrenceville 44690
Gwinnett History Museum, Lawrenceville 44691
Gwynedd Education and Culture, Caernarfon 38433
Gyemyung University Museum, Daegu 27156
Gyeongbo Museum of Paleontology, Namjeong 27214
Gyeongbuk National University Museum, Daegu 27157
Gyeonggi Provincial Museum, Yongin 27299
Gyeongju National Museum, Gyeongju 27185
Gyeongju University Museum, Gyeongju 27186
Gympie and District Historical and Gold Mining Museum, Gympie 01082
Györ Diocese Library and Treasure Chamber, Győr 21419
Györ Egyházmegyei Könyvtár es Kincstár, Győr 21419
Gyoërffy István Nagykun Múzeum, Karcag 21444
Gyokudo Art Museum, Ome 26634
Gyokusenji Collection, Kamo, Izu 26300
Gyokusenji Homotsukan, Kamo, Izu 26300
It Gysbert Japicxhûs Museum, Bolsward 28994
Gyula Derkovits Galéria, Budapest 21340
Gyula Hincz Memorial Museum and Exhibition Building, Vác 21601
H. B. Lamb Early Transport Buggy Museum, Camperdown 00882
H. Earl Clack Museum, Havre 43964
Hå Bygdemuseum, Varhaug 30975
Hå Gamle Prestegard, Varhaug 30976
Ha Noi Museum, Ha Noi 48978
Haager Heimatstuben, Haag am Hausruck 01981
Haags Historisch Museum, Den Haag 29096
Haags Openbaar Vervoer Museum, Den Haag 29097
Haardplatenmuseum Klarenbeek, Klarenbeek 29482
Haas Gallery of Art, Bloomsburg 41754
Haas-Lilienthal House, San Francisco 47319
Haastrup Folkemindesamling, Faaborg 08815
Habitat Ancien, Montagnac-la-Crempse 13034
Habitation Troglodytique Seigneuriale, Turquant 15018
Hachiga Folk Art Gallery, Takayama 26802
Hachiga Minzoku Bijutsukan, Takayama 26802
Hachijo Municipal Museum, Hachijo 26161
Hachinohe City Museum of Art, Hachinohe 26162
Hachioji City Museum, Hachioji 26164
Hachioji-shi Hakubutsukan, Hachioji 26164
Hachiro Yuasa Memorial Museum, Mitaka 26498
Hacı Ömer Sabancı Culture Center, Adana 37599
Hacı Ömer Sabancı Kültür Merkezi, Adana 37599
Haçıbektaş Müzesi, Nevşehir 37767
Hacienda Buena Vista, Ponce 32377
Hacienda El Paraíso, El Cerrito 07473
Hackettstown Historical Society Museum, Hackettstown 43859
Hackley & Hume Historic Site, Muskegon 45577
Hackney Museum, London 39657
Hadaka no Taisho Kinenkan, Kyoto 26401
Haddo House, Methlick 39941
Haddonfield Museum, Haddonfield 43860
Hadeland Bergverksmuseum, Grua 30522
Hadeland Folkemuseum, Jaren 30581
Hadeland Glassverks Museum, Jevnaker 30583
Haden Hall, Cradley Heath 38653
Haden Hill House, Cradley Heath 38654
Haderslev Museum, Haderslev 08849
Hadiqat al-Asmak Museum, Zamalek 09308
Hadjidimou Collection, Athinai 20863
Hadley Farm Museum, Hadley 43862
Hadsund Egns Museum, Hadsund 08853
Hadtörténeti Múzeum, Budapest 21341
Haegang Ceramics Museum, Icheon 27187
Hægebostad Bygdemuseum, Tingvatn 30920
Hägnan Friluftsmuseet i Gammelstad, Gammelstad 35902
Hägnan Open Air Museum, Gammelstad 35902
Haeju Historical Museum, Haeju 27116
Häkkilän Museo, Toholampi 10110
Hälleforsnäs Gjuterimuseum, Hälleforsnäs 35934
Hälleviks Fiskemuseum, Sölvesborg 36214
Hällisch-Fränkisches Museum, Schwäbisch Hall 19864
Hällristningsmuseet vid Brunnssalongen, Norrköping 36117
Hälsinglands Museum, Hudiksvall 35965
Häme Castle, Hämeenlinna 09448
Häme Museum, Tampere 10076
Hämeen Linna, Hämeenlinna 09448
Hämeen Museo, Tampere 10076
Hämeenkyrö Museum, Hämeenkyrö 09444
Hämeenkyrön Kotiseutumuseo, Hämeenkyrö 09444
Hämeenlinna Art Museum, Hämeenlinna 09451
Hämeenlinna Historical Museum, Hämeenlinna 09449
Hämeenlinna Telephone Museum, Hämeenlinna 09450
Hämeenlinnan Kaupungin Historiallinen Museo, Hämeenlinna 09449
Hämeenlinnan Puhelinmuseo, Hämeenlinna 09450
Hämeenlinnan Taidemuseo, Hämeenlinna 09451
Händel-Haus, Halle, Saale 17513
Haenel-Pancera-Familienmuseum, Bad Ischl 01705
Härjedalens Fjällmuseum, Funäsdalen 35898
Härkätien Museo, Renko 09991
Härtsfeld-Museum, Neresheim 18994
Härtsfeldbahn-Museum, Neresheim 18995
Haffenreffer Museum of Anthropology, Bristol 41906
Haffmuseum Ueckermünde, Ueckermünde 20247
Hafnarborg Art Gallery, Hafnarfjörður 21634
Hafnarfjörður Museum, Hafnarfjörður 21633
Hafnarhúsið, Reykjavík 21650
Haft Tappeh Museum, Haft Tappeh 22241
Hagadorn House Museum, Almond 41153
Hagan, Eggedal 30468
Hagedoorns Plaatse, Epe 29246
Haggerty Museum of Art, Milwaukee 45363
The Haggin Museum, Stockton 47824
Haghna Museum, Tel Aviv 22756
Hagi Municipal Museum, Hagi 26168
Hagia Sophia Museum, İstanbul 37693
Hagley Hall, Hagley 39144
The Hagley Museum, Wilmington 48652
Hahndorf Academy Public Art Gallery and Museum, Hahndorf 01083
Hahns Peak Area Historical Museum, Clark 42428
Hahoedong Mask Museum, Andong 27129
Hahs Museum, Hattiesburg 43957
Haida Gwaii Museum at Qay'llnagaay, Skidegate 06460
Haidhausen-Museum, München 18854
Haifa City Museum, Haifa 22604
Haifa Museum of Art, Haifa 22605
Haig Colliery Mining Museum, Whitehaven 40857
Haileybury Heritage Museum, Haileybury 05541
Hailsham Heritage Centre, Hailsham 39146
Hailuodon Kotiseutumuseo Kniivilä, Hailuoto 09457
Hailuoto Museum Kniivilä, Hailuoto 09457
Haimatmuseum Ginsheim-Gustavsburg, Ginsheim-Gustavsburg 17290
Haimatmuseum Großenlüder, Großenlüder 17430
Hainan Museum, Haikou 07079
Haines Museum, Waukegan 48459
Haiphong Museum, Hai Phong 48984
Hajdusági Múzeum, Hajdúböszörmény 21425
Hakasalmen Huvila, Helsinki 09482
Hakasalmi Villa - Helsinki City Museum, Helsinki 09482
Hakhamaneshi Museum, Shiraz 22280
Hakodate City Museum, Hakodate 26172
Hakodate-shiritsu Hakubutsukan, Hakodate 26172
Hakone-Jinja Homotsuden, Hakone 26175
Hakone Museum of Art, Hakone 26176
Hakone Open-Air Museum, Hakone 26174
Hakone Shrine Treasure House, Hakone 26175
Hakone Souunzan Bijutsukan, Hakone 26176
Håkon's Hall and The Rosenkrantz Tower, Bergen 30421
Håkonshallen og Rosenkrantztårnet, Bergen 30421
Hakuba Bijutsukan, Hakuba 26178
Hakuba Museum of Art, Hakuba 26178
Hakubutsukan Meiji-Mura, Inuyama 26249
Hakutsuru Fine Art Museum, Kobe 26345
Halden Historiske Samlinger, Halden 30524
Haldensvassdragets Kanalmuseum, Ørje 30719
Haldimand County Museum, Cayuga 05218
Hale Farm and Village, Bath 41524
Hale School Museum, Wembley Downs 01590
Halesworth and District Museum, Halesworth 39148
Halfa Museum, Wadi Halfa 35775
Hali Logging Camp Museum, Virrat 10202
Haliburton Highlands Museum, Haliburton 05543
Haliburton House Museum, Windsor, Nova Scotia 06808
Halifax Citadel, Halifax 05552
Halifax Historical Museum, Daytona Beach 42810
Halifax Police Museum, Halifax 05553
Halikko Local Museum, Halikko 09458
Halikkon Museo, Halikko 09458
Halin Metsäkämppämuseo, Virrat 10202
Halk Sanatları Müzesi, Girne 08227
Hall-I'Th'-Wood Museum, Bolton 38271
Hall of Art, Budapest 21365
Hall of Fame and Classic Car Museum, Weedsport 48489
Hall of Fame for Great Americans, Bronx 41920
Hall of Flame - Museum of Firefighting, Phoenix 46475
Hallaton Museum, Hallaton 39157
La Halle aux Oiseaux, Marseillan 12842
Halle für Kunst e.V., Lüneburg 18557
Halle Saint-Pierre Museum, Paris 13515
De Hallen, Haarlem 29325
Hallen für neue Kunst, Schaffhausen 37130
Haller Feuerwehrmuseum, Schwäbisch Hall 19865
Hallerbosmuseum, Halle 03467
Hallertauer Heimat- und Hopfenmuseum, Mainburg 18594
Hallertauer Hopfen- und Heimatmuseum, Geisenfeld 17216
Hallie Ford Museum of Art, Salem 47208
Hallingdal Folkemuseum, Nesbyen 30707
Halliwell's House Museum, Selkirk 40468
Hallockville Museum Farm, Riverhead 46914
Hall's Croft, Stratford-upon-Avon 40625
Hallwylska Museet, Stockholm 36245
Halmens Hus, Bengtsfors 35830
Halosenniemi Museo, Tuusula 10143
Halsey Gallery, Charleston 42217
Haltdalen Bygdetun, Haltdalen 30526
Halton Region Museum, Milton 05852
Ham House, Richmond, Surrey 40318
Hama National Museum, Hama 37439
Hamaland-Museum und Westmünsterländische Hofanlage, Vreden 20335
Hamamatsu City Museum, Hamamatsu 26180
Hamamatsu City Museum of Art, Hamamatsu 26179
Hamamatsu-shiritsu Hakubutsukan, Hamamatsu 26180
Hamarøy Bygdetun, Harmarøy 30532
Hambacher Schloss, Neustadt an der Weinstraße 19076
Hambidge Center for the Creative Arts and Sciences, Rabun Gap 46766
Hamburg State Park Museum, Mitchell 45410
Hamburger Bahnhof - Museum für Gegenwart Berlin, Berlin 15981
Hamburger Kunsthalle, Hamburg 17541
Hamburger Schulmuseum, Hamburg 17542
Hameau du Fromage, Cléron 11330
Hameau en Beaujolais, Romanèche-Thorins 14012
Hamhung Historical Museum, Hamhung 27117
Hamilton Art Gallery, Hamilton, Victoria 01088
The Hamilton Children's Museum, Hamilton 05570
Hamilton Grange, New York 45811
Hamilton Heritage Museum, Hamilton, Tasmania 01087
Hamilton House, South Berwick 47685
Hamilton Hume Museum, Yass 01630
Hamilton Library and Two Mile House, Carlisle 42104
Hamilton Low Parks Museum, Hamilton 39160
Hamilton Military Museum, Hamilton 05571
Hamilton Museum of Steam and Technology, Hamilton 05572
Hamilton Psychiatric Hospital Museum & St. Joseph's Mountain Site, Hamilton 05573
Hamilton van Wogener Museum, Clifton 42489
Hamilton's Gallery, London 39658
Hamina Town Museum, Hamina 09459
Haminan Kaupunginmuseo, Hamina 09459
Hamiota Pioneer Club Museum, Hamiota 05579
Hamizgaga Museum, Kibbutz Nachsholim 22697
Hamlin Garland Homestead, West Salem 48545
Hamline University Galleries, Saint Paul 47155
Hammaslääketieteen Museo, Helsinki 09483
Hammer Museum, Los Angeles 44906
Hammer- und Waffenschmiede-Museum Hexenagger, Altmannstein 15459
Hammerichs Hus, Ærøskøbing 08766
Hammerschmiede und Stockerhof, Neuburg an der Kammel 19020
Hammond Castle Museum, Gloucester 43703
Hammond-Harwood House Museum, Annapolis 41228
Hammond Historical Museum, Hammond 43886
Hammond Museum, North Salem 46007
Hampden-Booth Theatre Museum, New York 45812
Hampshire Farm Museum, Botley, Hampshire 38283
Hampson Museum, Wilson 48666
Hampstead Museum, London 39659
Hampton County Historical Museum, Hampton 43893
Hampton Court Palace, East Molesey 38848
Hampton National Historic Site Museum, Towson 48046
Hampton Plantation, McClellanville 45019
Hampton-Preston Mansion, Columbia 42561
Hampton Roads Naval Museum, Norfolk 45965
Hampton University Museum, Hampton 43896
Hamptonne Country Life Museum, Saint Lawrence 40412
Hamura Local Museum, Hamura 26181
Hamura-shiritsu Hakubutsukan, Hamura 26181
Hamza Hakim-zade Niazy House Museum, Kokand 48841
Hamza Hakim Žade Niazy Memorial Museum, Fergana 48837
Han Kuk Art Museum, Yongin 27300
Hana Cultural Center, Hana, Maui 43900
Hana Senesh House, Kibbutz Sedot Yam 22704
Hanauer Museum, Kehl 18047
Hanbat Education Museum, Daejeon 27160
Hanbury Hall, Droitwich 38777
Hanby House, Westerville 48555
Hanch Hall, Lichfield 39490
Hancock County Historical Museum, Carthage 42125
Hancock Historical Museum, Findlay 43323
Hancock Historical Society Museum, Hancock 43901
Hancock House, Hancock's Bridge 43902
Hancock Museum, Newcastle-upon-Tyne 40036
Hancock Shaker Village, Pittsfield 46533
Hand Workshop Art Center, Richmond 46878
Handel House Museum, London 39660
Handels- og Søfartsmuseet paa Kronborg, Helsingør 08861
Hands on Children's Museum, Olympia 46141
Hands on History, Kingston-upon-Hull 39378
Hands-on House, Lancaster 44623
Hands On! Regional Museum, Johnson City 44346
Handschriftenabteilung der Landes-, Universitäts- und Murhardschen Bibliothek, Kassel 18019
Handschriftenabteilung der Universitätsbibliothek, Würzburg 20694
Handsworth Saint Mary's Museum, Sheffield 40485
Handweaving Museum and Arts Center, Clayton 42444
Handweberei Henni Jaensch-Zeymer, Geltow 17232
Handwerk & Gewerbe Museum, Krauschwitz 18220
Handwerker Gallery of Art, Ithaca 44271
Handwerker- und Heimatstube, Gernsbach 17256
Handwerkerstuben, Feuchtwangen 16998
Handwerksmuseum, Deggendorf 16559
Handwerksmuseum am Mühlenberg, Suhlendorf 20123
Handwerksmuseum Dingwerth, Verl 20305
Handwerksmuseum Groß-Gerau, Gross-Gerau 17415
Handwerksmuseum Ovelgönne, Ovelgönne 19331
Handwerksmuseum Rattenberg, Rattenberg, Inn 02491
Handwerksmuseum und Friseurmuseum, Berlin 15982
Hanf-Museum, Berlin 15983
Hanford Mills Museum, East Meredith 43057
Hangar-7, Salzburg 02540
Hangguk Minsok-chon, Kihung 27203
Hangon Rintamamuseo, Karjaa 09625
Haniel Museum, Duisburg 16749
Hanita Museum, Kibbutz Hanita 22689
Hank Snow Country Music Centre, Liverpool 05758
Hankasalmen Kotiseutumuseo, Hankasalmi 09461
Hankasalmi Local History Museum, Hankasalmi 09461
Hanko Front Museum, Hanko 09462
Hanko Museo, Hanko 09463
Hanley House, Clayton 42442
Hanlim Museum, Daejeon 27161
Hanna Pioneer Museum, Hanna 05581
Hannah Lindahl Children's Museum, Mishawaka 45399
Hannans North Tourist Mine, Kalgoorlie 01132
Hannes Hus og Fonden Gamle Sønderho, Fanø 08820
Hannoversches Straßenbahn-Museum, Sehnde 19926
Hanns Schell-Collection, Graz 01917
Hanover Historical Society Museum, Hanover 43908
Hanover House, Clemson 42457
Hanover Museum, Montego Bay 26078
Hanrieder-Gedenkraum, Putzleinsdorf 02467
Hanriis Hus, Duved 35855
Hans-Böckler-Geburtshaus, Trautskirchen 20192
Hans Christian Andersen Museum, Odense 09011
Hans Christian Andersens Barndomshjem, Odense 09012
Hans Erni Museum, Luzern 36909
Hans-Fallada-Gedenkstätte, Berkenbrück bei Fürstenwalde 15906
Hans-Fallada-Haus, Feldberg, Mecklenburg 16987
Hans-Grade-Museum, Borkheide 16259
Hans Herr House and Museum, Willow St 48644
Hans Maurachar-Museum, Graz 01918
Hans Nielsens Hauges Minne, Rolvsøy 30802
Hans-Thoma-Gedächtnisstätte und Vortaunusmuseum, Oberursel 19212
Hans-Thoma-Museum, Bernau, Baden 16121
Hans Trudel-Haus Stiftung, Baden 36484
Hans van Riessen Museum, Vledderveen 29952
Hanságí Múzeum, Mosonmagyaróvár 21484
Hanseatic Booth or The Pier House, Symbister 40669
Det Hanseatiske Museum og Schøtstuene, Bergen 30422
Hansjakobmuseum im Freihof, Haslach 17626
Hansong Womens College Museum, Seoul 27236
Hantverks- och Sjörfartsmuseét på Norra Berget, Sundsvall 36308
Hantverksloftet, Simrishamn 36187
Hantverksmuseet, Ängelholm 35787
Hanwon Art Museum, Seoul 27237
Har-Ber Village, Grove 43847
Hara Bijutsukan, Tokyo 26855
Hara Castle Memorial Hall, Minamiarima 26490
Hara Museum ARC, Shibukawa 26744
Hara Museum of Contemporary Art, Tokyo 26855
Haras National, Gelos 11845
Haras National, Strasbourg 14815
Harbor Branch Oceanographic Institution, Fort Pierce 43440
Harbor Defense Museum of New York City, Brooklyn 41942
Harborough Museum, Market Harborough 39915
Harbour Gallery, Mississauga 05871
Harbour Life Exhibition, Bridport 38332
Harbour Museum, Londonderry 39816
Harcerskie Muzeum Etnograficzne przy Szkole Podstawowej nr 11 w Katowicach, Katowice 31644
Hardanger Folkemuseum, Lofthus 30647
Hardanger Folkemuseum, Utne 30963
Hardin County Historical Museum, Kenton 44449
Harding Home and Museum, Marion 45162
Harding Museum, Franklin 43520
Hardom Sädesmagasin och Stenkulla Torp, Loviisa 09798
Hardwick Hall, Chesterfield 38555
Hardwick Historical Museum, Hardwick 43910
Hardy's Cottage, Higher Bockhampton 39242
Haremere Hall, Etchingham 38949
Harestanes Countryside Visitor Centre, Ancrum 37999
Harewood House, Harewood 39161
Hariphunchai National Museum, Lampun 37512
Hariya Razna and Ahmed Urabi Museum, Zaqaziq 09310
Harjamäen Sairaalamuseo, Siilinjärvi 10035

Harjukosken Vesimylly, Mikkeli 09829
Harjumaa Muuseum, Keila 09332
Harlan-Lincoln House, Mount Pleasant 45534
Harlech Castle, Harlech 39162
Harlekinäum-Lachmuseum, Wiesbaden 20573
Harley Gallery, Welbeck 40808
Harlinger Aardewerk Museum, Harlingen 29346
Harlow Carr Museum of Gardening, Harrogate 39168
Harlow Gallery, Hallowell 43874
Harlow Museum, Harlow 39163
Harmar Station, Marietta 45150
Harmonium-Art-Museum, Schelle 03725
Harmonium-Museum, Hennef 17710
Harmonium-Museum, Liestal 36878
Harn Homestead and 1889er Museum, Oklahoma City 46111
Harness Racing Museum and Hall of Fame, Goshen 43733
Harney County Historical Museum, Burns 42011
Harold Warp Pioneer Village Foundation, Minden 45376
Harper City Historical Museum, Harper 43916
Harpers Ferry National Historical Park, Harpers Ferry 43918
Harriet Beecher Stowe Center, Hartford 43939
Harris Art Gallery, James M. Lykes Maritime Gallery and Hutchings Gallery, Galveston 43610
Harris Exhibit Hall, Oxford 46241
Harris Heritage and Museum, Harris 05585
Harris Museum and Art Gallery, Preston 40266
Harrison County Historical Museum, Marshall 45182
Harrison Gray Otis House, Boston 41809
Harrison House, Branford 41870
Harrow Museum, Harrow 39173
Harry D. Hendren Gallery, Saint Charles 47079
Harry J. Music Museum, Kingston 26068
Harry Oppenheimer Diamond Museum, Ramat Gan 22731
Harry S. Truman Birthplace State Historic Site, Lamar 44612
Harry S. Truman Home, Independence 44201
Harry S. Truman Library Museum, Independence 44202
Harry S. Truman Little White House Museum, Key West 44466
Harry S. Truman Office and Courtroom, Independence 44203
Harry S. Washbrook Museum, Edam 05365
Harry's Truman Farm Home, Grandview 43763
Hart-Cam Museum, Hartney 05588
Hart House, Toronto 06581
Hartenbos Museum, Hartenbos 34259
Hartford House Museum, Manhattan 45106
Hartham Park - Underground Quarry Museum, Corsham 38637
Hartland Quay Museum, Bideford 38192
Hartland Quay Museum, Hartland 39174
Hartlepool Art Gallery, Hartlepool 39175
Hartmanin Mökki, Oripää 09886
Hartnell College Gallery, Salinas 47215
Hartsville Museum, Hartsville 43948
Hartung's Auto and License Plate Museum, Glenview 43696
Hartzler-Towner Multicultural Museum, Nashville 45621
Harvard Historical Society Collection, Harvard 43953
Harvard Historical Society Museum, Still River 47810
Harvard House, Stratford-upon-Avon 40626
Harvard Museum of Natural History, Cambridge 42041
Harvard University Art Museums, Cambridge 42042
Harvard University Semitic Museum, Cambridge 42043
Harvery Art Gallery, Harvey 01090
Harvey County Historical Museum, Newton 45943
Harvey Grant Heritage Centre Community Museum, Springdale 06480
Harvey House Museum, Florence 43347
Harvey's Wine Museum, Bristol 38357
Harwich Maritime Museum and Harwich Lifeboat Museum, Harwich 39179
Harwich Redoubt Fort, Harwich 39180
Harwood Museum of Art of the University of New Mexico, Taos 47950
Haryana Prantiya Puratatva Sangrahalaya, Jhajjar 21870
Harzer Roller-Kanarien-Museum, Sankt Andreasberg 19744
Harzmuseum, Wernigerode 20525
Hasegawa Art Museum, Tokyo 26856
Hasegawa Bijutsukan, Tokyo 26856
Haselünner Heimathäuser, Haselünne 17625
Hasenmuseum, Bubikon 36593
The Hash Marihuana Hemp Museum, Amsterdam 28856
Hashimoto Kansetsu Memorial Museum, Kyoto 26402
Hasičské Muzeum, Přibyslav 08626
The Haskell County Historical Museum, Sublette 47866
Haslemere Educational Museum, Haslemere 39182
Haslev Museum, Haslev 08855
Hassett's Uralla Military Museum, Uralla 01562
Hastings Museum, Hastings 43956
Hastings Museum and Art Gallery, Hastings 39184
Hastings-Western Port Historical Museum, Hastings 01091
Hat-Making Museum, Nový Jičín 08509
Hat Works, Museum of Hatting, Stockport 40596
Hatakeyama Collection, Tokyo 26857
Hatay Culture Center, Antakya, Hatay 37621
Hatay Devlet Güzel Sanatlar Galerisi, Hatay 37686
Hatay Kültür Merkezi, Antakya, Hatay 37621
Hatay Müzesi, Hatay 37687
Hatay Museum, Hatay 37687
Hatay State Gallery, Hatay 37686
Hatch-Billops Collections, New York 45813
Hathaway Ranch Museum, Santa Fe Springs 47435
Hatton-Eielson Museum, Hatton 43959
Hatton Gallery, Fort Collins 43382
Hatton Gallery, Newcastle-upon-Tyne 40037
Hauchs Physiske Cabinet, Sorø 09075
Haugar Vestfold Kunstmuseum, Tønsberg 30925
Haugesund Art Gallery, Haugesund 30537
Haugesund Billedgalleri, Haugesund 30537
Hauho Museum, Hauho 09466
Hauhon Esinemuseo, Hauho 09466
Haukipudas School Museum, Haukipudas 09467
Haukiputaan Koulumuseo, Haukipudas 09467
Hauptstaatsarchiv Stuttgart, Stuttgart 20094
Haus am Kleistpark, Berlin 15984
Haus am Lützowplatz, Berlin 15985
Haus am Waldsee, Berlin 15986
Haus der Donauschwaben, Sindelfingen 19964
Haus der Fotografie, Hannover 17594
Haus der Fotografie - Dr. Robert-Gerlich-Museum, Burghausen, Salzach 16420
Haus der Heimat, Olbernhau 19248
Haus der Heimat Freital, Freital 17124
Haus der Kulturen der Welt, Berlin 15987
Haus der Kunst, München 18855
Haus der Kunst, Nürnbrecht 19130
Haus der Landbrandenburg Lottogesellschaft, Potsdam 19435
Haus der Natur, Eichendorf 16800
Haus der Natur, Willingen, Upland 20599
Haus der Naturfreunde, Duisburg 16750
Haus der Ortsgeschichte, Schwäbisch Hall 19866
Haus der Ost- und Westpreußen, Oberschleißheim 19201
Haus der Seidenkultur, Krefeld 18224
Haus der Stadtgeschichte, Donauwörth 16637
Haus der Stadtgeschichte, Offenbach am Main 19240
Haus der Völker, Schwaz 02648
Haus des Gastes mit heimatkundlicher Sammlung, Gößweinstein 17331
Haus des Moores, Heidenreichstein 02011
Haus des Waldes, Köln 18141
Haus Esters, Krefeld 18225
Haus für Relief und Halbfiguren von Hans Josephsohn, Giornico 36760
Haus Giersch - Museum Regionaler Kunst, Frankfurt am Main 17049
Haus Kickelhain, Mosbach, Baden 18793
Haus Konstruktiv, Zürich 37378
Haus Mährisch-Schönberg, Bad Hersfeld 15659
Haus Opherdicke, Holzwickede 17834
Haus Rottels, Neuss 19064
Haus Tannenbusch, Dormagen 16645
Haus Völker und Kulturen - Ethnologisches Museum, Sankt Augustin 19746
Haus Westland, Mönchengladbach 18770
Haus Wittgenstein, Wien 02893
Haus zum Kiel, Zürich 37379
Haus zum Kirschgarten, Basel 36499
Haus zum Palmbaum - Bachausstellung Arnstadt, Arnstadt 15513
Haus zum Stockfisch - Stadtmuseum, Erfurt 16903
Haus zum Torggel, Berneck 36555
Hausenhäusl, Reit im Winkl 19554
Hausjärven Kotiseutumuseo, Hausjärvi 09468
Hausjärvi Museum, Hausjärvi 09468
Hausmühle, Steinbach am Attersee 02678
Hausmuseum Kloster Kreuzlingen, Kreuzlingen 36835
Hauteville House, Saint Peter Port 40425
Havant Museum, Havant 39189
Havayeda Museum, Holon 22620
Havelkovo Muzeum, Loštice 08462
Havelock Museum, Havelock 30175
Het Havenmuseum, Rotterdam 29750
Haverford Township Historical Society Museum, Havertown 43963
Haverhill and District Local History Centre, Haverhill 39192
Haverhill Historical Museum, Haverhill 43961
Haverhill Public Library Special Collections, Haverhill 43962
Havesdonckhoeve, Bornem 03228
De Havilland Aircraft Heritage Centre, Saint Albans 40370
Havråtunet, Lonevåg 30652
Havre de Grace Decoy Museum, Havre de Grace 43965
Hawaii Children's Discovery Center, Honolulu 44076
Hawaii Maritime Center, Honolulu 44077
Hawaii Museums Association, Honolulu 49486
Hawaii Pacific University Gallery, Honolulu 44078
Hawaii's Plantation Village, Waipahu 48276
Hawick Museum, Hawick 39195
Hawke House, Bordertown 00815
Hawker Museum, Hawker, South Australia 01092
Hawke's Bay Museum, Napier 30207
Hawkesbury Museum, Windsor 01605
Hawkeye Log Cabin, Burlington 41997
Hawks Inn, Delafield 42859
Hawks Tower State Park, Ansted 41233
Haworth Art Gallery, Accrington 37959
Hawthorns Urban Wildlife Centre, Southampton 40544
Hay Gaol Museum, Hay 01094
Hay House Museum, Macon 45044
Hayashibara Bijutsukan, Okayama 26624
Hayashibara Museum of Art, Okayama 26624
Haydn-Geburtshaus, Rohrau 02521
Haydn-Gedenkstätte mit Brahms-Gedenkraum, Wien 02894
Haydn-Haus Eisenstadt, Eisenstadt 01809
Hayloft Gallery, Armagh 38018
Hayner Cultural Center, Troy 48072
Haynes Motor Museum, Sparkford 40565
Haystack Mountain School of Crafts Gallery, Deer Isle 42844
Hayward Gallery, London 39661
Hazama Inosuke Museum of Art, Kaga 26286
Hazor Museum, Ayelet-Hashahar 22577
Hazrati Museum, Semnan 22278
HAZU Print Room, Zagreb 07826
Head-Smashed-In Buffalo Jump, Fort Macleod 05444
Headland Historical Museum, Nambucca Heads 01298
Headlands Center for the Arts, Sausalito 47474
Headley-Whitney Museum, Lexington 44738
Headlund Museum, Hugo 44146
Headquarters Museum, Mikkeli 09833
Healdton Oil Museum, Healdton 43979
Health Adventure, Asheville 41281
Health Museum, Hyderabad 21843
Health Museum, Yangon 28750
Health Museum of Cleveland, Cleveland 42474
Health Science Museum, Hiroshima 26210
Healy House and Dexter Cabin, Leadville 44700
Heaman's Antique Autorama, Carman 05211
Heard Museum, Phoenix 46476
Heard Natural Science Museum, McKinney 45038
Hearst Art Gallery, Moraga 45491
Hearst Castle, San Simeon 47377
Heart of West Texas Museum, Colorado City 42533
Hearthstone Historic House Museum, Appleton 41239
Heartland - The California Museum of the Heart, Rancho Mirage 46786
Heart's Content Cable Station, Heart's Content 05593
Heatherbank Museum of Social Work, Glasgow 39049
Heatherslaw Mill, Cornhill-on-Tweed 38633
Heaton Hall, Manchester 39888
Heaven Farm Museum, Uckfield 40744
Hebbel-Museum, Wesselburen 20539
Hebei Museum, Shijiazhuang 07246
Hebei Provincial Museum, Wuhan 07280
Hebezeug-Museum, Witten 20620
Hebrew Union College-Jewish Institute of Religion Skirball Museum, Cincinnati 42406
Hebrew University Collections of Natural History, Jerusalem 22634
Heckington Windmill, Heckington 39205
Heckscher Museum of Art, Huntington 44161
Hecla Island Heritage Home Museum, Riverton 06277
Heddal Bygdetun, Notodden 30714
Heddon Museum, Dowagiac 42977
Hedmarksmuseet og Domkirkeodden, Hamar 30528
Hedon Museum, Hedon 39207
Hedrum Bygdetun, Larvik 30630
Heemerf De Schutsboom, Goirle 29288
Heemkamer Barthold Van Hessel, Aarle Rixtel 28798
Heemkundemuseum Beek, Beek 28966
Heemkundemuseum Paulus Van Daesdonck, Ulvenhout 29891
Heemkundig Museum, Asse 03186
Heemkundig Museum, Borgerhout 03226
Heemkundig Museum, Bree 03242
Heemkundig Museum, Ommeren 29663
Heemkundig Museum, Tervuren 03773
Heemkundig Museum, Wilrijk 03843
Heemkundig Museum, Zolder 03854
Heemkundig Museum Boekhoute, Boekhoute 03222
Heemkundig Museum Gerard Meeusen, Essen 03409
Heemkundig Museum Sincfala, Knokke 03535
Heemkundig Museum Slag van Lafelt, Vlijtingen 03820
Heemkundig Museum Tempelhof, Beerse 03206
Heemkundig Museum vat het Gaverdomein, Deerlijk 03373
Heemkundig Museum Wetteren, Wetteren 03837
Heemkundig Museum Wissekerke, Kruibeke 03544
Heemkundig Streekmuseum Jan Uten Houte, Etten Leur 29254
Heemmuseum Bystervelt, Schelle 03726
Heemmuseum De Kaeck, Wommelgem 03845
Heemmuseum de Zuiderkempen, Westerlo 03836
Heemmuseum Die Swane, Heist-op-den-Berg 03488
Heemmuseum Eeklo, Eeklo 03402
Heemschuur Maasland, Heesch 29370
Heeresgeschichtliches Museum im Arsenal, Wien 02895
Heffel Gallery, Vancouver 06679
Hegau-Museum, Singen, Hohentwiel 19966
Hegelhaus, Stuttgart 20095
Hegmataneh Museum, Samedan 22276
Hegyridéki Helytörténeti Gyûjtemény & Kortárs Galéria, Budapest 21342
De Heibergske Samlinger - Sogn Folkemuseum, Kaupanger 30591
Heide Museum of Modern Art, Bulleen 00858
Heide Museum of Modern Art, Melbourne 01231
Heidegalerie, Wels 02812
Heidelberg Motor Museum, Heidelberg 34260
Heidelberger Kunstverein, Heidelberg 17666
Heidemuseum Dat ole Huus, Bispingen 16173
Heidemuseum Rischmannshof Walsrode, Walsrode 20383
Heidi Weber-Museum, Zürich 37380
Heijo Palace Site Museum, Nara 26575
Heijokyuseki Shiryokan, Nara 26575
Heikintupa, Pohjaslahti 09940
Heikki's Cabin, Pohjaslahti 09940
Heiliggeistkirche, Landshut 18309
Heilongjiang Province Nation Museum, Harbin 07089
Heimat-Jagdmuseum, Prigglitz 02455
Heimat-Museum, Millstatt 02298
Heimat Museum Amöneburg, Amöneburg 15484
Heimat-Museum Maintal, Maintal 18597
Heimat-Naturmuseum Untere Havel, Havelberg 17649
Heimat- und Bauernmuseum, Bruck, Oberpfalz 16371
Heimat- und Bergbaumuseum, Lugau, Erzgebirge 18566
Heimat- und Bergbaumuseum, Nentershausen, Hessen 18993
Heimat- und Bienenzuchtmuseum, Orth an der Donau 02386
Heimat und Bildhauer Kern Museum, Forchtenberg 17021
Heimat- und Brauereimuseum, Pleinfeld 19414
Heimat- und Braunkohlemuseum, Steinberg, Oberpfalz 20046
Heimat- und Buddelmuseum, Osten 19289
Heimat- und Dorfmuseum Pfaffenwiesbach, Wehrheim 20421
Heimat- und Feuerwehrmuseum, Schauenstein 19766
Heimat- und Flößermuseum Calmbach, Bad Wildbad 15761
Heimat- und Grimmelshausenmuseum, Oberkirch 19180
Heimat- und Hafnermuseum, Heidenheim, Mittelfranken 17683
Heimat- und Handfeuerwaffenmuseum, Kemnath 18056
Heimat-und Handwerkermuseum, Leutershausen 18448
Heimat- und Handwerks Museum Stolberg, Stolberg, Rheinland 20068
Heimat- und Heringsfängermuseum Heimsen, Petershagen, Weser 19378
Heimat- und Humboldtmuseum, Eibau 16796
Heimat- und Industriemuseum, Kolbermoor 18199
Heimat- und Industriemuseum, Wackersdorf 20336
Heimat- und Keramikmuseum, Kandern 17982
Heimat- und Krippenmuseum, Zirl 03054
Heimat- und Landlermuseum, Bad Goisern 01700
Heimat- und Miedermuseum Heubach, Heubach, Württemberg 17748
Heimat- und Montanmuseum in Schloß Oberkindberg, Kindberg 02108
Heimat- und Naturkunde-Museum Wanne-Eickel, Herne 17728
Heimat- und Palitzsch-Museum Prohlis, Dresden 16686
Heimat- und Pfarrmuseum, Wildalpen 03026
Heimat- und Posamentermuseum Sissach, Sissach 37177
Heimat- und Rebbaumuseum, Spiez 37192
Heimat- und Schiffahrtsmuseum, Heinsen 17698
Heimat- und Schmiedemuseum, Widdern 20563
Heimat- und Ski-Museum, Braunlage 16291
Heimat- und Torfmuseum, Gröbenzell 17407
Heimat- und Uhrenmuseum, Villingen-Schwenningen 20317
Heimat- und Wallfahrtsmuseum, Xanten 20728
Heimatdiele Kutenholz, Kutenholz 18278
Heimatecke am Seifenbach, Beierfeld 15868
Heimatgeschichtliche Sammlung des Kirchspiels, Schwabstedt 19859
Heimatgeschichtliches Museum, Modautal 18760
Heimathaus, Nesselwang 19000
Heimathaus Alte Mühle, Schladen 19788
Heimathaus Aying, Aying 15581
Heimathaus Beandhaus, Sankt Johann am Walde 02573
Heimathaus Bevergern, Hörstel 17788
Heimathaus De Theeshof, Schneverdingen 19820
Heimathaus der Stadt Lauingen, Lauingen 18357
Heimathaus der Stadt Warendorf, Warendorf 20400
Heimathaus des Heimatvereins Haslach, Haslach 02004
Heimathaus des Rupertiwinkels und Heimatstube der Sudetendeutschen, Tittmoning 20182
Heimathaus Dingden, Hamminkeln 17580
Heimathaus Ebensee, Ebensee 01780
Heimathaus Fahringer, Pürgg 02460
Heimathaus Gallneukirchen, Gallneukirchen 01864
Heimathaus Greven Worth, Selsingen 19936
Heimathaus-Handwerkermuseum, Scheidegg 19770
Heimathaus im alten Zollhaus, Kobersdorf 02144
Heimathaus Julbach, Julbach 02093
Heimathaus Königswiesen, Königswiesen 02147
Heimathaus Litzelsdorf, Litzelsdorf 02245
Heimathaus Mehedorf, Bremervörde 16349
Heimathaus mit Photographiemuseum, Mariazell 02274
Heimathaus Mörbisch, Mörbisch 02318
Heimathaus Neuchl-Anwesen, Hohenschäftlarn 17812
Heimathaus Neufelden, Neufelden 02342
Heimathaus Neukirchen, Neukirchen bei Altmünster 02347
Heimathaus Obernberg am Inn, Obernberg am Inn 02371
Heimathaus Ollershof, Munster 18959
Heimathaus Pfarrkirchen, Pfarrkirchen 19386
Heimathaus Pregarten, Pregarten 02451
Heimathaus Raab, Raab 02469

Heimathaus Richard Eichinger und Steinmuseum, Enzenkirchen 01820
Heimathaus Sankt Georgen an der Gusen, Sankt Georgen an der Gusen 02564
Heimathaus Sankt Peter im Sulmtal, Sankt Peter im Sulmtal 02599
Heimathaus Schalchen, Schalchen 02624
Heimathaus Schörfling, Schörfling am Attersee 02637
Heimathaus Schwanenstadt, Schwanenstadt 02642
Heimathaus Sittensen, Sittensen 19973
Heimathaus Sonthofen, Sonthofen 20001
Heimathaus Spitalskirche/Bürgerspital, Bad Leonfelden 01712
Heimathaus Steinbach am Attersee, Steinbach am Attersee 02679
Heimathaus Stinatz, Stinatz 02697
Heimathaus Ulrichsberg, Ulrichsberg 02752
Heimathaus und Stadtmuseum, Perg 02403
Heimathaus Vöcklabruck, Vöcklabruck 02767
Heimathaus Waidhofen, Waidhofen an der Thaya 02783
Heimathaus Wartenberg an der Krems, Wartberg an der Krems 02793
Heimathaus Wendelstein, Wendelstein, Mittelfranken 20511
Heimathaus Wenigzell, Wenigzell 02820
Heimathausanlage Schafstall, Bremervörde 16350
Heimathof Emsbüren, Emsbüren 16865
Heimatkabinett Westerholt, Herten 17740
Heimatkundehaus und Münzkabinett, Sankt Marien 02582
Heimatkundesammlung Inzersdorf, Herzogenburg 02026
Heimatkundliche Sammlung, Elzach 16844
Heimatkundliche Sammlung, Heideck 17661
Heimatkundliche Sammlung, Heroldsbach 17732
Heimatkundliche Sammlung, Isen 17919
Heimatkundliche Sammlung, Lich 18453
Heimatkundliche Sammlung, Pfronten 19392
Heimatkundliche Sammlung, Richterswil 37056
Heimatkundliche Sammlung, Uznach 37274
Heimatkundliche Sammlung Bergendorf, Holzheim bei Rain, Lech 17828
Heimatkundliche Sammlung Burg Rheinfels, Sankt Goar 19750
Heimatkundliche Sammlung des Heimatdienstes Hindelang, Bad Hindelang 15662
Heimatkundliche Sammlung Strick, Bad Mitterndorf 01715
Heimatkundliche Sammlung und Ausstellung, Hermannsburg 17724
Heimatkundliche Schulsammlung, Hollingstedt bei Schleswig 17826
Heimatkundliches Museum, Friedeburg, Ostfriesland 17140
Heimatkundliches Museum Medaria, Matrei in Osttirol 02280
Heimatkundliches Museum Wetzlhäusl, Sankt Gilgen 02569
Heimatmuseum, Adelsdorf 15394
Heimatmuseum, Aesch, Basel-Land 36434
Heimatmuseum, Aidlingen 15413
Heimatmuseum, Aken 15415
Heimatmuseum, Allendorf, Lumda 15431
Heimatmuseum, Allensbach 15433
Heimatmuseum, Angermünde 15492
Heimatmuseum, Arneburg 15511
Heimatmuseum, Arnoldstein 01680
Heimatmuseum, Attiswil 36474
Heimatmuseum, Bad Großpertholz 01702
Heimatmuseum, Bad Neustadt an der Saale 15705
Heimatmuseum, Bad Orb 15712
Heimatmuseum, Bad Radkersburg 01717
Heimatmuseum, Bad Rodach 15719
Heimatmuseum, Bad Schandau 15733
Heimatmuseum, Belgern 15872
Heimatmuseum, Bernau bei Berlin 16123
Heimatmuseum, Bernhardsthal 01733
Heimatmuseum, Bezau 01736
Heimatmuseum, Blindheim 16187
Heimatmuseum, Brugg 36591
Heimatmuseum, Buttstädt 16436
Heimatmuseum, Camburg 16450
Heimatmuseum, Dahlen, Sachsen 16529
Heimatmuseum, Deutschneudorf 16595
Heimatmuseum, Dietenhofen 16602
Heimatmuseum, Dömitz 16629
Heimatmuseum, Donzhausen 36663
Heimatmuseum, Eibelstadt 16797
Heimatmuseum, Elsenfeld 16839
Heimatmuseum, Eltmann 16840
Heimatmuseum, Ergoldsbach 16908
Heimatmuseum, Falkensee 16984
Heimatmuseum, Falkenstein, Vogtland 16986
Heimatmuseum, Frankenberg, Sachsen 17027
Heimatmuseum, Friedland bei Neubrandenburg 17142
Heimatmuseum, Fügen 01858
Heimatmuseum, Gaaden 01862
Heimatmuseum, Gablitz 01863
Heimatmuseum, Gerstungen 17264
Heimatmuseum, Gleisdorf 01880
Heimatmuseum, Gnas 01898
Heimatmuseum, Grabow, Mecklenburg 17366
Heimatmuseum, Grafenwörth 01906
Heimatmuseum, Gressenberg 01939
Heimatmuseum, Greußen 17397
Heimatmuseum, Grindelwald 36781
Heimatmuseum, Groß-Enzersdorf 01946
Heimatmuseum, Großröhrsdorf, Oberlausitz 17437
Heimatmuseum, Großzschepa 17444
Heimatmuseum, Grüningen 36782
Heimatmuseum, Hadersdorf 01984
Heimatmuseum, Haimhausen 17493
Heimatmuseum, Hallau 36790
Heimatmuseum, Haynsburg 17653
Heimatmuseum, Herbrechtingen 17717
Heimatmuseum, Hergensweiler 17721
Heimatmuseum, Höpfingen 17787
Heimatmuseum, Holzgau 02046
Heimatmuseum, Immenstaad 17895
Heimatmuseum, Kals am Großglockner 02095
Heimatmuseum, Karlstein am Main 18010
Heimatmuseum, Kematen an der Ybbs 02106
Heimatmuseum, Kirchbach 02109
Heimatmuseum, Kirchdorf auf Poel 18090
Heimatmuseum, Kirchham 02113
Heimatmuseum, Kirchschlag 02114
Heimatmuseum, Kölleda 18126
Heimatmuseum, Krieglach 02164
Heimatmuseum, Kuchl 02168
Heimatmuseum, Küssnacht am Rigi 36841
Heimatmuseum, Langenlois 02183
Heimatmuseum, Langenzersdorf 02187
Heimatmuseum, Lengenfeld, Vogtland 18435
Heimatmuseum, Leupahn 18446
Heimatmuseum, Litschau 02244
Heimatmuseum, Lommatzsch 18502
Heimatmuseum, Luckenwalde 18509
Heimatmuseum, Mank 02260
Heimatmuseum, Marchegg 02263
Heimatmuseum, Markranstädt 18641
Heimatmuseum, Mautern in Steiermark 02284
Heimatmuseum, Mering 18710
Heimatmuseum, Möckmühl 18762
Heimatmuseum, Moosburg an der Isar 18788
Heimatmuseum, Mügeln bei Oschatz 18799
Heimatmuseum, Mülheim an der Ruhr 18815
Heimatmuseum, Müllrose 18820
Heimatmuseum, Mureck 02334
Heimatmuseum, Neckargerach 18989
Heimatmuseum, Nellingen 18992
Heimatmuseum, Neukirch, Lausitz 19038
Heimatmuseum, Neustadt in Sachsen 19082
Heimatmuseum, Niederleis 02359
Heimatmuseum, Niederndorf 02361
Heimatmuseum, Oberhofen 02368
Heimatmuseum, Oberndorf am Neckar 19185
Heimatmuseum, Obertrum am See 02378
Heimatmuseum, Oberweningen 37004
Heimatmuseum, Oederan 19222
Heimatmuseum, Osterwieck 19297
Heimatmuseum, Perleberg 19376
Heimatmuseum, Pfaffstätten 02412
Heimatmuseum, Pfunds 02413
Heimatmuseum, Polling, Kreis Weilheim 19426
Heimatmuseum, Pressbaum 02453
Heimatmuseum, Prieros 19451
Heimatmuseum, Purkersdorf 02466
Heimatmuseum, Radeburg 19472
Heimatmuseum, Radstadt 02474
Heimatmuseum, Rattenberg 19497
Heimatmuseum, Reichenau an der Pulsnitz 19541
Heimatmuseum, Reinach (Basel-Land) 37052
Heimatmuseum, Reuland 03695
Heimatmuseum, Rietz 02516
Heimatmuseum, Rötha 19636
Heimatmuseum, Rothrist 37073
Heimatmuseum, Ruhla 19709
Heimatmuseum, Sandhausen 19741
Heimatmuseum, Sankt Koloman 02578
Heimatmuseum, Scharfenberg bei Meißen 19764
Heimatmuseum, Scheibbs 02629
Heimatmuseum, Schöneiche bei Berlin 19830
Heimatmuseum, Schrems 02640
Heimatmuseum, Schwarzenberg in Vorarlberg 02645
Heimatmuseum, Siget 02661
Heimatmuseum, Sohland 19982
Heimatmuseum, Sternberg 20061
Heimatmuseum, Strausberg 20078
Heimatmuseum, Tarrenz 02714
Heimatmuseum, Taufkirchen an der Pram 02715
Heimatmuseum, Teesdorf 02717
Heimatmuseum, Telfs 02720
Heimatmuseum, Thaya 02728
Heimatmuseum, Traismauer 02732
Heimatmuseum, Treuenbrietzen 20202
Heimatmuseum, Trofaiach 02740
Heimatmuseum, Wald, Zürich 37299
Heimatmuseum, Waltensburg 37304
Heimatmuseum, Wartberg im Mürztal 02794
Heimatmuseum, Weisendorf 20487
Heimatmuseum, Weissach im Tal 20489
Heimatmuseum, Wiesenbach, Baden 20577
Heimatmuseum, Wilsdruff 20602
Heimatmuseum, Wörgl 03041
Heimatmuseum Aarburg, Aarburg 36430
Heimatmuseum Achental, Achenkirch 01642
Heimatmuseum Adelboden, Adelboden 36432
Heimatmuseum Adlhoch-Haus, Altdorf, Niederbayern 15441
Heimatmuseum Aflenz, Aflenz 01646
Heimatmuseum Ahlem, Hannover 17595
Heimatmuseum Ahlen, Ahlen 15402
Heimatmuseum Ahrbergen, Giesen 17276
Heimatmuseum Aichach, Aichach 15408
Heimatmuseum Alberschwende, Alberschwende 01653
Heimatmuseum Algermissen, Algermissen 15430
Heimatmuseum Allschwil, Allschwil 36446
Heimatmuseum Alt-Falkenstein, Balsthal 36492
Heimatmuseum Alte Weberstube, Niedercunnersdorf 19096
Heimatmuseum Altenmarkt, Yspertal 03047
Heimatmuseum Alter Pfarrhof, Raisting 19479
Heimatmuseum Altes Rathaus, Angelburg 15490
Heimatmuseum Altes Rathaus, Böhl-Iggelheim 16215
Heimatmuseum Altes Schulhaus, Böhl-Iggelheim 16216
Heimatmuseum Altlichtenwarth, Absdorf 01638
Heimatmuseum Altmannstein, Altmannstein 15460
Heimatmuseum am Kobernaußerwald, Lohnsburg am Kobernaußerwald 02250
Heimatmuseum am Pfäffikersee, Pfäffikon (Zürich) 37021
Heimatmuseum Amt Blankenstein, Gladenbach 17293
Heimatmuseum Arnold Bärtschi, Dulliken 36667
Heimatmuseum Aschen, Diepholz 16597
Heimatmuseum Auetal, Auetal 15547
Heimatmuseum Bad Aibling, Bad Aibling 15589
Heimatmuseum Bad Eilsen, Bad Eilsen 15635
Heimatmuseum Bad Endbach, Bad Endbach 15639
Heimatmuseum Bad König, Bad König 15676
Heimatmuseum Bad Laer, Bad Laer 15686
Heimatmuseum Bad Lauterberg, Bad Lauterberg 15689
Heimatmuseum Bad Münder, Bad Münder 15695
Heimatmuseum Bad Oldesloe, Bad Oldesloe 15711
Heimatmuseum Balingen, Balingen 15798
Heimatmuseum Bammental, Bammental 15820
Heimatmuseum Battenberg-Laisa, Battenberg, Eder 15829
Heimatmuseum Baunach, Baunach 15831
Heimatmuseum Beratzhausen, Beratzhausen 15882
Heimatmuseum Berching mit Ritter-v.-Gluck-Archiv, Berching 15883
Heimatmuseum Bergen-Enkheim, Frankfurt am Main 17050
Heimatmuseum Berkatal, Berkatal 15904
Heimatmuseum Berkatal, Berkatal 15905
Heimatmuseum Betzenstein, Betzenstein 16132
Heimatmuseum Beuel, Bonn 16237
Heimatmuseum Beutelsbach, Weinstadt 20483
Heimatmuseum Biebesheim, Biebesheim 16148
Heimatmuseum Biebesheim, Biebesheim 16149
Heimatmuseum Biebrich, Wiesbaden 20574
Heimatmuseum Bislich, Wesel 20534
Heimatmuseum Blankenau, Hosenfeld 17844
Heimatmuseum Blaubeuren, Blaubeuren 16180
Heimatmuseum Bleicherode, Bleicherode 16185
Heimatmuseum Bockwindmühle, Lebusa 18364
Heimatmuseum Bodenfelde, Bodenfelde 16205
Heimatmuseum Börgerende-Rethwisch, Börgerende 16219
Heimatmuseum Boizenburg, Boizenburg 16224
Heimatmuseum Borgloh, Hilter 17763
Heimatmuseum Boxberg, Boxberg, Baden 16267
Heimatmuseum Brackenheim, Brackenheim 16269
Heimatmuseum Breckerfeld, Breckerfeld 16308
Heimatmuseum Brigachtal, Brigachtal 16360
Heimatmuseum Brüssow, Brüssow 16381
Heimatmuseum Brunsbüttel, Brunsbüttel 16383
Heimatmuseum Bucheggberg, Buchegg 36596
Heimatmuseum Buchenau, Dautphetal 16555
Heimatmuseum Buchenberg, Buchenberg bei Kempten 16387
Heimatmuseum Buchloe, Buchloe 16390
Heimatmuseum Büddenstedt, Büddenstedt 16395
Heimatmuseum Büderich, Wesel 20535
Heimatmuseum Bühl, Baden, Bühl, Baden 16399
Heimatmuseum Bürgeln, Cölbe 16488
Heimatmuseum Burg Stargard, Burg Stargard 16413
Heimatmuseum Burgau, Burgau, Schwaben 16414
Heimatmuseum Calau, Calau 16441
Heimatmuseum Carl Swoboda, Schirgiswalde 19784
Heimatmuseum Charlottenburg-Wilmersdorf, Berlin 15988
Heimatmuseum Crumstadt, Riedstadt 19603
Heimatmuseum Dachwig, Dachwig 16527
Heimatmuseum Dahme, Mark, Dahme, Mark 16531
Heimatmuseum Davos, Davos 36652
Heimatmuseum Debstedt, Langen bei Bremerhaven 18320
Heimatmuseum der Albert-Edelmann-Stiftung, Ebnat-Kappel 36669
Heimatmuseum der Deutschen aus Bessarabien, Stuttgart 20096
Heimatmuseum der Gemeinde Dossenheim, Dossenheim 16669
Heimatmuseum der Gemeinde Weißenkirchen, Perschling 02405
Heimatmuseum der Insel Hiddensee, Kloster, Hiddensee 18114
Heimatmuseum der Marktgemeinde Wiggensbach, Wiggensbach 20584
Heimatmuseum der Stadt Bad Tölz, Bad Tölz 15754
Heimatmuseum der Stadt Gernsheim, Gernsheim 17257
Heimatmuseum der Stadt Herrnhut, Herrnhut 17737
Heimatmuseum der Stadt Hückeswagen, Hückeswagen 17851
Heimatmuseum der Stadt Ketzin, Ketzin 18067
Heimatmuseum der Stadt Marsberg, Marsberg 18658
Heimatmuseum der Stadt Murau, Murau 02333
Heimatmuseum der Stadt Neunkirchen, Neunkirchen, Niederösterreich 02354
Heimatmuseum der Stadt Northeim, Northeim 19127
Heimatmuseum der Stadt Rerik, Ostseebad Rerik 19317
Heimatmuseum der Stadt Rheinau in Freistett, Rheinau 19588
Heimatmuseum der Stadt Vohenstrauß, Vohenstrauß 20330
Heimatmuseum der Talschaft Lauterbrunnen, Lauterbrunnen 36868
Heimatmuseum des Heimatkreises Scheiflingertal, Scheifling 02631
Heimatmuseum des Landkreises Regensburg, Altenthann 15456
Heimatmuseum des Nordböhmischen Niederlandes, Böblingen 16213
Heimatmuseum Dietzenbach, Dietzenbach 16606
Heimatmuseum Dirlewang, Dirlewang 16622
Heimatmuseum Dölzig, Schkeuditz 19785
Heimatmuseum Dohna, Dohna 16631
Heimatmuseum Dornstetten, Dornstetten 16650
Heimatmuseum Duderstadt, Duderstadt 16716
Heimatmuseum Durmersheim, Durmersheim 16759
Heimatmuseum Dykhus, Borkum 16260
Heimatmuseum Ebenhausen, Oerlenbach 19230
Heimatmuseum Ebermannstadt, Ebermannstadt 16764
Heimatmuseum Ebern, Ebern 16765
Heimatmuseum Ebersbach in der Humboldt-Baude, Ebersbach, Sachsen 16768
Heimatmuseum Echzell, Echzell 16774
Heimatmuseum Egg, Egg 01789
Heimatmuseum Eggenstein-Leopoldshafen, Eggenstein-Leopoldshafen 16789
Heimatmuseum Eisenbach, Obernburg 19182
Heimatmuseum Elgg, Elgg 36678
Heimatmuseum Ellrich, Ellrich 16832
Heimatmuseum Elsbethen, Elsbethen-Glasenstein 01814
Heimatmuseum Elze, Elze 16845
Heimatmuseum Emskirchen, Emskirchen 16869
Heimatmuseum Epfenbach, Epfenbach 16877
Heimatmuseum Erbenheim, Wiesbaden 20575
Heimatmuseum Eriskirch, Eriskirch 16909
Heimatmuseum Eschenburg, Eschenburg 16932
Heimatmuseum Eschwege, Eschwege 16936
Heimatmuseum Eversberg e.V., Meschede 18716
Heimatmuseum Feuerwehrzeugstätte, Neumarkt am Wallersee 02349
Heimatmuseum Finsterbergen, Finsterbergen 17004
Heimatmuseum Flacht, Weissach, Württemberg 20490
Heimatmuseum Freiamt, Freiamt 17097
Heimatmuseum Freigericht, Freigericht 17119
Heimatmuseum Freudenstadt, Freudenstadt 17129
Heimatmuseum Freudenthal, Memmingen 18704
Heimatmuseum Friedewald, Friedewald, Hessen 17141
Heimatmuseum Friedrichsdorf-Seulberg, Friedrichsdorf, Taunus 17144
Heimatmuseum Friedrichshain, Berlin 15989
Heimatmuseum Fronfeste, Limbach-Oberfrohna 18468
Heimatmuseum für Stadt und Kreis Gelnhausen, Gelnhausen 17223
Heimatmuseum für Stadt- und Landkreis, Kirchheimbolanden 18098
Heimatmuseum Gadebusch, Gadebusch 17188
Heimatmuseum Gadernheim, Lautertal, Odenwald 18363
Heimatmuseum Garbenheim, Wetzlar 20553
Heimatmuseum Garbsen, Garbsen 17195
Heimatmuseum Geisa, Geisa 17213
Heimatmuseum Geislingen, Geislingen an der Steige 17218
Heimatmuseum Gemünden, Weilrod 20452
Heimatmuseum Gensungen, Felsberg 16993
Heimatmuseum Geretsried, Geretsried 17250
Heimatmuseum Gersau, Gersau 36757
Heimatmuseum Gersfeld, Gersfeld 17261
Heimatmuseum Giesen, Giesen 17277
Heimatmuseum Glonn, Glonn 17302
Heimatmuseum Görwihl, Görwihl 17328
Heimatmuseum Gößnitz, Gößnitz, Thüringen 17329
Heimatmuseum Graben-Neudorf, Graben-Neudorf 17364
Heimatmuseum Grächen, Grächen 36772
Heimatmuseum Grafenau Schloß Dätzingen, Grafenau, Württemberg 17370
Heimatmuseum Grafing, Grafing bei München 17375
Heimatmuseum Grafling, Grafling 17376
Heimatmuseum Grafschaft Hoya, Hoya 17845
Heimatmuseum Grahhof, Ramsau am Dachstein 02482
Heimatmuseum Gransee, Gransee 17377
Heimatmuseum Greene, Kreiensen 18230
Heimatmuseum Greversdorf, Geversdorf 17272
Heimatmuseum Grimmen "Im Mühlentor", Grimmen 17406
Heimatmuseum Gröbming, Gröbming 01944
Heimatmuseum Grötzingen, Aichtal 15410
Heimatmuseum Großengersdorf, Großengersdorf 01952
Heimatmuseum Großes Walsertal, Sonntag 02666
Heimatmuseum Großschönau, Großschönau 01963
Heimatmuseum Großseelheim, Kirchhain 18092
Heimatmuseum Günzburg, Günzburg 17455
Heimatmuseum Guntramsdorf, Guntramsdorf 01973
Heimatmuseum Hähnlein, Alsbach-Hähnlein 15436
Heimatmuseum Haiger, Haiger 17487
Heimatmuseum Haiterbach, Haiterbach 17498

Heimatmuseum Hallstadt, Hallstadt 17525
Heimatmuseum Haus Morgensonne, Ostseebad Zingst 19319
Heimatmuseum Hebertsfelden, Hebertsfelden 17654
Heimatmuseum Heidelsheim, Bruchsal 16366
Heimatmuseum Heiligenhafen, Heiligenhafen 17694
Heimatmuseum Heinrich Zoller, Wittelshofen 20619
Heimatmuseum Heuchelheim-Kinzenbach, Heuchelheim, Kreis Gießen 17750
Heimatmuseum Heusenstamm, Heusenstamm 17751
Heimatmuseum Hochzeitshaus, Homberg, Efze 17835
Heimatmuseum Höchstädt an der Donau, Höchstädt an der Donau 17779
Heimatmuseum Hoheneggelsen, Söhlde 19975
Heimatmuseum Hohenroda, Hohenroda 17811
Heimatmuseum Hohenschönhausen, Berlin 15990
Heimatmuseum Hohenwestedt, Hohenwestedt 17818
Heimatmuseum Holzgerlingen, Holzgerlingen 17827
Heimatmuseum Hornburg, Hornburg, Kreis Wolfenbüttel 17843
Heimatmuseum Hossingen, Meßstetten 18720
Heimatmuseum Hüttenberg, Hüttenberg 17862
Heimatmuseum Hus tu Löwenberg, Löwenberg 18492
Heimatmuseum Ihringen, Ihringen 17883
Heimatmuseum im alten Bruderhaus und in der Dechanathofscheune, Altenmarkt im Pongau 01664
Heimatmuseum im Alten Kloster, Erbendorf 16889
Heimatmuseum im alten Marktturm, Fischamend 01839
Heimatmuseum im Alten Pfarrhaus, Hagen am Teutoburger Wald 17476
Heimatmuseum im Alten Rathaus, Bruchköbel 16363
Heimatmuseum im Amonhaus, Lunz 02256
Heimatmuseum im Berchtoldshof, Uhingen 20255
Heimatmuseum im Fünfeckigen Turm, Neckarbischofsheim 18985
Heimatmuseum im Hartmannhaus, Marktoberdorf 18648
Heimatmuseum im Herrenhaaus, Burghaun 16417
Heimatmuseum im Hintermeierhaus, Donauwörth 16638
Heimatmuseum im Neuen Spielhaus, Bruchköbel 16364
Heimatmuseum im Oberen Torturm, Lauchheim 18347
Heimatmuseum im Schelfenhaus, Volkach 20332
Heimatmuseum im Schloß, Zörbig 20766
Heimatmuseum im Schloß zu Werdorf, Aßlar 15539
Heimatmuseum im Unteren Turm, Leutershausen 18449
Heimatmuseum im Vogteigebäude, Hüttlingen 17863
Heimatmuseum im Wachtturm, Geyer 17273
Heimatmuseum im Weserrenaissance Schloß, Bevern, Kreis Holzminden 16135
Heimatmuseum im Wolfschneider-Hof, Taufkirchen, Kreis München 20148
Heimatmuseum in der ehemaligen Schule Hüllhorst, Hüllhorst 17854
Heimatmuseum in der Scheune, Mössingen 18780
Heimatmuseum in der Windmühle Gettorf, Gettorf 17271
Heimatmuseum Ingersleben/Neudietendorf, Ingersleben 17901
Heimatmuseum Ittersbach, Karlsbad 17986
Heimatmuseum Kalchofengut, Unken 02754
Heimatmuseum Karlsdorf, Karlsdorf-Neuthard 17987
Heimatmuseum Kastl, Kastl bei Amberg 18034
Heimatmuseum Kaumberg, Kaumberg 02103
Heimatmuseum Kaunertal, Kaunertal 02104
Heimatmuseum Kautzen, Kautzen 02105
Heimatmuseum Kefenrod, Kefenrod 18046
Heimatmuseum Keltern, Keltern 18055
Heimatmuseum Kirberg, Hünfelden 17859
Heimatmuseum Kirchhain, Kirchhain 18093
Heimatmuseum Kirchheim, Heidelberg 17667
Heimatmuseum Kirchheim, Schwaben, Kirchheim, Schwaben 18094
Heimatmuseum Klösterle, Schönau im Schwarzwald 19821
Heimatmuseum Klosterlangheim, Lichtenfels, Bayern 18455
Heimatmuseum Klus, Klus 36829
Heimatmuseum Königsdorf, Königsdorf, Oberbayern 18175
Heimatmuseum Köpenick, Berlin 15991
Heimatmuseum Kösching, Kösching 18187
Heimatmuseum Kohbauernhaus, Köstendorf 02148
Heimatmuseum Kornburg, Nürnberg 19142
Heimatmuseum Kraiburg am Inn, Kraiburg am Inn 18215
Heimatmuseum Kreuzlingen, Kreuzlingen 36836
Heimatmuseum Ladbergen, Ladbergen 18281
Heimatmuseum Lahnau-Waldgirmes, Lahnau 18286
Heimatmuseum Lampertheim, Lampertheim 18296
Heimatmuseum Lamspringe, Lamspringe 18297
Heimatmuseum Landau, Landau an der Isar 18299
Heimatmuseum Langelsheim, Langelsheim 18317
Heimatmuseum Langenau, Langenau, Württemberg 18326
Heimatmuseum Langenseifen, Bad Schwalbach 15738
Heimatmuseum Langenselbold, Langenselbold 18337
Heimatmuseum Langenzenn, Langenzenn 18338
Heimatmuseum Laubach, Laubach, Hessen 18344
Heimatmuseum Lauda-Königshofen, Lauda-Königshofen 18348
Heimatmuseum Lauenau, Lauenau 18349
Heimatmuseum Leeheim, Riedstadt 19604
Heimatmuseum Leer, Leer 18366
Heimatmuseum Leingarten Altes Rathaus Schluchtern, Leingarten 18378
Heimatmuseum Leipheim, Leipheim 18381
Heimatmuseum Lembach, Lembach 02204
Heimatmuseum Lenggries, Lenggries 18438
Heimatmuseum Lengsdorf, Bonn 16238
Heimatmuseum Lette, Coesfeld 16490
Heimatmuseum Leuk Stadt, Leuk Stadt 36872
Heimatmuseum Leutershausen, Leutershausen 18450
Heimatmuseum Lichtenberg, Berlin 15992
Heimatmuseum Lilienthal, Lilienthal 18464
Heimatmuseum Lölling, Lölling 02248
Heimatmuseum Lorch, Lorch, Württemberg 18504
Heimatmuseum Losenstein, Losenstein 02254
Heimatmuseum Luditzer Kreis, Bad Sooden-Allendorf 15746
Heimatmuseum Lübbecke, Lübbecke 18531
Heimatmuseum Lügde, Lügde 18553
Heimatmuseum Lütgendortmund, Dortmund 16659
Heimatmuseum Magstadt, Magstadt 18590
Heimatmuseum Markt Piesting, Markt Piesting 02277
Heimatmuseum Marktl, Marktl, Inn 18647
Heimatmuseum Marner Skatklub von 1873, Marne 18657
Heimatmuseum Maßbach, Maßbach 18662
Heimatmuseum Meerane, Meerane 18671
Heimatmuseum Meerholz, Gelnhausen 17224
Heimatmuseum Mehrstetten, Mehrstetten 18683
Heimatmuseum Meinhard, Meinhard 18684
Heimatmuseum Mellrichstadt, Mellrichstadt 18700
Heimatmuseum Melsungen, Melsungen 18702
Heimatmuseum-Menton, Teningen 20159
Heimatmuseum Merkendorf, Merkendorf, Mittelfranken 18711
Heimatmuseum Michelbacher Schlößchen, Alzenau 15476
Heimatmuseum Michelhausen, Michelhausen 02295
Heimatmuseum Miesbach, Miesbach 18735
Heimatmuseum Mindelheim, Mindelheim 18741
Heimatmuseum mit Hugo-Geißler-Saal, Tuttlingen 20237
Heimatmuseum mit ostdeutscher Heimatstube, Hanerau-Hademarschen 17589
Heimatmuseum mit Raimund von Montecuccoli-Gedenkraum, Hafnerbach 01987
Heimatmuseum Mitterfels, Mitterfels 18755
Heimatmuseum Moringen, Moringen 18790
Heimatmuseum Münchingen, Korntal-Münchingen 18211
Heimatmuseum Münsingen, Münsingen 18930
Heimatmuseum Nauheim, Nauheim 18977
Heimatmuseum Naumburg, Naumburg, Hessen 18978
Heimatmuseum Naunheim, Wetzlar 20554
Heimatmuseum Neu-Ulm-Pfuhl, Neu-Ulm 19009
Heimatmuseum Neuenwalde, Langen bei Bremerhaven 18321
Heimatmuseum Neukirchen, Neukirchen, Knüllgebirge 19041
Heimatmuseum Neunkirchen, Neunkirchen bei Mosbach 19054
Heimatmuseum Neureichenau, Neureichenau 19058
Heimatmuseum Neuried, Neuried, Ortenaukreis 19059
Heimatmuseum Neustadt an der Aisch, Neustadt an der Aisch 19071
Heimatmuseum Neustadtgödens, Sande, Kreis Friesland 19740
Heimatmuseum Nidda, Nidda 19089
Heimatmuseum Nied, Frankfurt am Main 17051
Heimatmuseum Niederaichbach, Niederaichbach 19095
Heimatmuseum Niemes und Prachatitz, Ingolstadt 17907
Heimatmuseum Nüdlingen, Nüdlingen 19129
Heimatmuseum Nürnberg, Nürnberg 19143
Heimatmuseum Nutli-Hüschi, Klosters 36827
Heimatmuseum Obbornhofen, Hungen 17868
Heimatmuseum Obdach, Obdach 02366
Heimatmuseum Oberbichl, Prägarten 02443
Heimatmuseum Oberderdingen, Oberderdingen 19172
Heimatmuseum Obere Mühle, Loßburg 18507
Heimatmuseum Obergünzburg mit Südseesammlung, Obergünzburg 19175
Heimatmuseum Oberndorf am Lech, Oberndorf am Lech 19184
Heimatmuseum Obernfeld, Obernfeld 19187
Heimatmuseum Oberstdorf, Oberstdorf 19210
Heimatmuseum Ochsenfurt, Ochsenfurt 19217
Heimatmuseum Oettingen, Oettingen 19236
Heimatmuseum Ole Schüne, Drakenburg 16671
Heimatmuseum Oltingen-Wenslingen-Anwil, Oltingen 37012
Heimatmuseum Osterhofen, Osterhofen 19293
Heimatmuseum Pabneukirchen, Pabneukirchen 02391
Heimatmuseum Pankow, Berlin 15993
Heimatmuseum Papenburg, Papenburg 19346
Heimatmuseum Peldemühle, Wittmund 20630
Heimatmuseum Persenbeug-Gottsdorf, Persenbeug 02406
Heimatmuseum Pfaffenhausen, Pfaffenhausen 19380
Heimatmuseum Pfarrscheuer, Römerstein 19633
Heimatmuseum Philippsburg, Philippsburg 19398
Heimatmuseum Postbauer-Heng, Postbauer-Heng 19429
Heimatmuseum Prättigau, Grüsch 36784
Heimatmuseum Pressath, Pressath 19444
Heimatmuseum Prestegg, Altstätten 36452
Heimatmuseum Prien, Prien 19450
Heimatmuseum Pulkau, Pulkau 02461
Heimatmuseum Rabenstein, Rabenstein an der Pielach 02472
Heimatmuseum Rain am Lech, Rain am Lech 19477
Heimatmuseum Rapperswil, Rapperswil, Sankt Gallen 37043
Heimatmuseum Rauchkate, Zetel 20747
Heimatmuseum Rauchstubenhaus Edelschachen, Anger 01672
Heimatmuseum Raunheim, Raunheim 19503
Heimatmuseum Rauschenberg, Rauschenberg 19505
Heimatmuseum Rechnitz, Rechnitz 02494
Heimatmuseum Reiderland, Weener 20417
Heimatmuseum Reilingen, Reilingen 19549
Heimatmuseum Reinheim, Reinheim 19553
Heimatmuseum Reinickendorf, Berlin 15994
Heimatmuseum Reischenau, Dinkelscherben 16618
Heimatmuseum Reiterhaus, Neusalza-Spremberg 19062
Heimatmuseum Reith, Reith im Alpbachtal 02505
Heimatmuseum Reutlingen, Reutlingen 19576
Heimatmuseum Rheinwald, Splügen 37196
Heimatmuseum Rhüden, Seesen 19922
Heimatmuseum Riedlingen, Riedlingen 19600
Heimatmuseum Rieneck, Rieneck 19608
Heimatmuseum Rodenberg, Rodenberg, Deister 19622
Heimatmuseum Rodenstein, Fränkisch-Crumbach 17024
Heimatmuseum Rodewald, Rodewald 19623
Heimatmuseum Römstedthaus, Bergen, Kreis Celle 15894
Heimatmuseum Rötz, Rötz 19638
Heimatmuseum Ronnenberg, Ronnenberg 19645
Heimatmuseum Roßwein, Roßwein 19657
Heimatmuseum Rotenburg, Rotenburg, Wümme 19671
Heimatmuseum Rother Hof, Pottendorf 02436
Heimatmuseum Rothmühle, Rannersdorf 02485
Heimatmuseum Runder Turm, Sigmaringen 19957
Heimatmuseum Sankt Egidien, Sankt Egidien 19748
Heimatmuseum Sankt Laurentius, Dahlenburg 16530
Heimatmuseum Sankt Martin am Wöllmißberg, Sankt Martin am Wollmißberg 02586
Heimatmuseum Schanfigg, Arosa 36469
Heimatmuseum Scheeßel, Scheeßel 19768
Heimatmuseum Schermbeck, Schermbeck 19774
Heimatmuseum Schifferstadt, Schifferstadt 19777
Heimatmuseum Schinznach-Dorf, Schinznach Dorf 37134
Heimatmuseum Schliersee, Schliersee 19802
Heimatmuseum Schlitz, Schlitz 19803
Heimatmuseum Schloß Adelsheim, Berchtesgaden 15885
Heimatmuseum Schloß Brenz, Sontheim an der Brenz 19999
Heimatmuseum Schloß Fels, Fels 01835
Heimatmuseum Schloß Hochhaus, Vorchdorf 02775
Heimatmuseum Schloß Pragstein, Mauthausen 02288
Heimatmuseum Schloß Schönebeck, Bremen 16326
Heimatmuseum Schloß Tenneberg, Waltershausen 20386
Heimatmuseum Schloss Wildeck, Zschopau 20769
Heimatmuseum Schloß Wolkenstein, Wolkenstein 20670
Heimatmuseum Schnaittach, Schnaittach 19815
Heimatmuseum Schönau, Günselsdorf 01968
Heimatmuseum Schöneck, Schöneck, Vogtland 19829
Heimatmuseum Schöningen, Schöningen 19835
Heimatmuseum Schulte-Wessels, Neuenhaus 19025
Heimatmuseum Schwalmtal, Niederrhein, Schwalmtal, Niederrhein 19872
Heimatmuseum Schwanfeld, Schwanfeld 19875
Heimatmuseum Schwanheim, Frankfurt am Main 17052
Heimatmuseum Schwarza, Schwarza, Suhl 19879
Heimatmuseum Schwarzbubenland, Dornach 36664
Heimatmuseum Seeg, Seeg 19916
Heimatmuseum Seehof, Buonas 36604
Heimatmuseum Seelze, Seelze 19920
Heimatmuseum Seon, Seon 37164
Heimatmuseum Seßlach, Seßlach 19941
Heimatmuseum Siebenlehn, Siebenlehn 19942
Heimatmuseum Siegbach, Siegbach 19943
Heimatmuseum Simbach am Inn, Simbach am Inn 19959
Heimatmuseum Spangenberg, Spangenberg 20008
Heimatmuseum Spittel, Büren an der Aare 36599
Heimatmuseum Sprendlingen, Sprendlingen 20017
Heimatmuseum Spycher, Rickenbach (Luzern) 37058
Heimatmuseum Stade, Stade 20023
Heimatmuseum Stadt Bernstadt an der Eigen, Bernstadt auf dem Eigen 16130
Heimatmuseum Stadt Nagold-Steinhaus, Nagold 18971
Heimatmuseum Stadt Starnberg, Starnberg 20036
Heimatmuseum Stadt Teltow, Teltow 20157
Heimatmuseum Stadt und Landkreis Neudek im Erzgebirge, Augsburg 15557
Heimatmuseum Stadtilm, Stadtilm 20030
Heimatmuseum Stadtsteinach, Stadtsteinach 20035
Heimatmuseum Staufenberg, Staufenberg, Hessen 20039
Heimatmuseum Stein, Stein am Rhein 37213
Heimatmuseum Steinach, Steinbach, Taunus 20045
Heimatmuseum Steinbach, Baden-Baden 15786
Heimatmuseum Steinfischbach, Waldems 20358
Heimatmuseum Steinwiesen, Steinwiesen 20055
Heimatmuseum Steyregg, Steyregg 02693
Heimatmuseum Stockstadt am Main, Stockstadt am Main 20063
Heimatmuseum Strasburg, Strasburg 20075
Heimatmuseum Straub, Gruibingen 17450
Heimatmuseum Stromberg, Stromberg 20079
Heimatmuseum Strümpfelbach, Weinstadt 20484
Heimatmuseum Suhr, Suhr 37222
Heimatmuseum Tambach-Dietharz, Tambach-Dietharz 20136
Heimatmuseum Tannheimer Tal, Tannheim 02713
Heimatmuseum Tempelhof, Berlin 15995
Heimatmuseum Tiergarten, Berlin 15996
Heimatmuseum Todtmoos, Todtmoos 20183
Heimatmuseum - Traktoren- und Landmaschinenmuseum, Großengottern 17428
Heimatmuseum Trebur, Trebur 20197
Heimatmuseum Treptow, Berlin 15997
Heimatmuseum Trimmis, Trimmis 37254
Heimatmuseum Trubschachen, Trubschachen 37255
Heimatmuseum Uelzen mit Gläsersammlung Röver, Uelzen 20248
Heimatmuseum Uetze, Uetze 20251
Heimatmuseum und Archiv des Heimatvereins für den Bezirk Steglitz, Berlin 15998
Heimatmuseum und Buchdruckerstube, Beromünster 36557
Heimatmuseum und Dokumentationszentrum zur Deutschen Nachkriegsgeschichte, Wanfried 20391
Heimatmuseum und Galerie Neue Diele, Jork 17961
Heimatmuseum und Gedenkstätte Bützow, Bützow 16409
Heimatmuseum und Hedwig Courths-Mahler Archiv, Nebra 18984
Heimatmuseum und Karl-August-Forster-Bienenmuseum, Illertissen 17886
Heimatmuseum und Keltenhaus, Ligist 02222
Heimatmuseum und Klöpferhaus, Eibiswald 01798
Heimatmuseum und Klosterruine, Arendsee, Altmark 15510
Heimatmuseum und Naturalienkabinett, Waldenburg, Sachsen 20360
Heimatmuseum und Pfeifenmuseum, Sankt Aegyd am Neuwalde 02556
Heimatmuseum und Schiele Museum, Neulengbach 02348
Heimatmuseum und Stadtarchiv, Flörsheim am Main 17015
Heimatmuseum und Textil-Schauwerkstatt, Greiz 17392
Heimatmuseum Unterboihingen, Wendlingen am Neckar 20513
Heimatmuseum Unterengadin, Scuol 37153
Heimatmuseum Untergrombach, Bruchsal 16367
Heimatmuseum Usingen, Usingen 20278
Heimatmuseum Usseln, Willingen, Upland 20600
Heimatmuseum Varel, Varel 20286
Heimatmuseum Velburg, Velburg 20296
Heimatmuseum Viernheim, Viernheim 20312
Heimatmuseum Vietze, Höhbeck 17782
Heimatmuseum Vilsbiburg - Kröninger Hafnermuseum, Vilsbiburg 20322
Heimatmuseum Vogtturm, Zell am See 03050
Heimatmuseum Vollmers Mühle, Seebach, Baden 19910
Heimatmuseum Wächtersbach, Wächtersbach 20338
Heimatmuseum Waidhofen, Waidhofen an der Thaya 02784
Heimatmuseum Waidhofen an der Ybbs, Waidhofen an der Ybbs 02786
Heimatmuseum Waldaschaff, Waldaschaff 20352
Heimatmuseum Waldbrunn, Waldbrunn, Westerwald 20355
Heimatmuseum Waldthurn, Waldthurn 20374
Heimatmuseum Walldorf, Mörfelden-Walldorf 18774
Heimatmuseum Waltrop, Waltrop 20387
Heimatmuseum Wandsbek, Hamburg 17543
Heimatmuseum Wanna, Wanna 20398
Heimatmuseum Warnemünde, Rostock 19662
Heimatmuseum Wedding, Berlin 15999
Heimatmuseum Wedel, Wedel 20415
Heimatmuseum Weener, Weener 20418
Heimatmuseum Weesen, Weesen 37308
Heimatmuseum Wehlen, Stadt Wehlen 20028
Heimatmuseum Weiler, Schorndorf, Württemberg 19843
Heimatmuseum Weitenung, Bühl, Baden 16400
Heimatmuseum Wemding, Wemding 20508
Heimatmuseum Weng im Innkreis, Weng im Innkreis 02819
Heimatmuseum Wennigsen, Wennigsen 20514
Heimatmuseum Wertach, Wertach 20530
Heimatmuseum Wertingen, Wertingen 20533
Heimatmuseum Westerhausen, Westerhausen 20541
Heimatmuseum Wettenberg, Wettenberg 20547
Heimatmuseum Wiedenbrück, Rheda-Wiedenbrück 19584
Heimatmuseum Wiedensahl, Wiedensahl 20564
Heimatmuseum Wiedlisbach, Wiedlisbach 37315
Heimatmuseum Windeck, Windeck 20605
Heimatmuseum Windischgarsten, Windischgarsten 03040
Heimatmuseum Windmühle Reken, Reken 19556
Heimatmuseum Winterberg im Böhmerwald, Freyung 17133
Heimatmuseum Wippra, Wippra 20616
Heimatmuseum Wißmar, Wettenberg 20548
Heimatmuseum Witten, Witten 20621

Heimatmuseum Wolfratshausen, Wolfratshausen 20657
Heimatmuseum Wolfskehlen, Riedstadt 19605
Heimatmuseum Wommelshausen, Bad Endbach 15640
Heimatmuseum Worben, Worben 37351
Heimatmuseum Zarrentin, Zarrentin, Mecklenburg 20733
Heimatmuseum Zehlendorf, Berlin 16000
Heimatmuseum Zorge, Zorge 20767
Heimatmuseum Zusmarshausen, Zusmarshausen 20772
Heimatscheune, Zschepplin 20768
Heimatstube, Altenstadt an der Waldnaab 15454
Heimatstube Adlergebirge, Waldkraiburg 20368
Heimatstube Alfeld, Alfeld, Leine 15426
Heimatstube Alten, Dessau 16578
Heimatstube Altenau, Altenau, Harz 15445
Heimatstube Altenbrak, Altenbrak 15449
Heimatstube Am Grevendiek, Sprockhövel 20020
Heimatstube Ansprung, Zöblitz 20764
Heimatstube Arenborn, Oberweser 19215
Heimatstube Bad Brambach, Bad Brambach 15619
Heimatstube Badenhausen, Badenhausen 15793
Heimatstube Bliedersdorf, Bliedersdorf 16186
Heimatstube Bredenbeck, Wennigsen 20515
Heimatstube Bühlau, Bühlau 16401
Heimatstube Calbe, Calbe 16443
Heimatstube Crostau, Crostau 16515
Heimatstube Cumlosen, Cumlosen 16517
Heimatstube Demnitz, Demnitz bei Fürstenwalde 16572
Heimatstube der Deutsch-Reichenauer, Haslach 02005
Heimatstube der Stadt Saaz, Roth, Mittelfranken 19673
Heimatstube Dreetz, Dreetz bei Neustadt, Dosse 16672
Heimatstube Eime, Eime 16811
Heimatstube Elbingerode, Elbingerode, Harz 16828
Heimatstube Endersbach, Weinstadt 20485
Heimatstube Feldberg, Feldberg, Mecklenburg 16988
Heimatstube Fischbach, Niedereschach 19097
Heimatstube Frauenwald, Frauenwald 17091
Heimatstube Freest, Freest 17096
Heimatstube Freiwaldau-Bieletal, Kirchheim unter Teck 18096
Heimatstube Fröndenberg, Fröndenberg 17155
Heimatstube für Volkskunst, Podelwitz 19425
Heimatstube Gräfenhain/ Nauendorf, Georgenthal 17240
Heimatstube Groß Nemerow, Groß Nemerow 17418
Heimatstube Großbodungen, Großbodungen 17425
Heimatstube Großraming, Großraming 01959
Heimatstube Gutenberg, Oberostendorf 19193
Heimatstube Hänigsen, Uetze 20252
Heimatstube Haiger, Haiger 17488
Heimatstube Heynitz, Heynitz 17752
Heimatstube Hinternah, Hinternah 17766
Heimatstube Hohenhameln, Hohenhameln 17807
Heimatstube Hohenzieritz, Hohenzieritz 17819
Heimatstube im "Spieker Anno 1754", Tarmstedt 20144
Heimatstube Langenaubach, Haiger 17489
Heimatstube Lichtenstadt, Zirndorf 20758
Heimatstube Mühlbach mit Philipp-Neubrand-Gedächtnisstube, Eppingen 16879
Heimatstube Mühlhausen, Villingen-Schwenningen 20318
Heimatstube Münstedt, Lahstedt 18291
Heimatstube Neuhaus-Schiernitz, Neuhaus-Schierschnitz 19034
Heimatstube Neunheilingen, Neunheilingen 19050
Heimatstube Offenbach, Mittenaar 18752
Heimatstube Podersam-Jechnitz, Kronach 18245
Heimatstube Röckwitz, Röckwitz 19627
Heimatstube Röhrnbach-Kaltenbach, Röhrnbach 19632
Heimatstube Rohrbach, Eppingen 16880
Heimatstube Rothenklempenow, Rothenklempenow 19687
Heimatstube Ruhland, Ruhland 19712
Heimatstube Sankt Martin am Tennengebirge, Sankt Martin am Tennengebirge 02585
Heimatstube Schlesien, Kaufbeuren 18039
Heimatstube Schönwalde, Schönwalde bei Tangerhütte 19838
Heimatstube Schwarzenberg am Böhmerwald, Schwarzenberg am Böhmerwald 02643
Heimatstube Seeheilbad Graal-Müritz, Seeheilbad Graal-Müritz 19917
Heimatstube Sperenberg, Sperenberg 20010
Heimatstube Stadt und Landkreis Saaz, Georgensgmünd 17238
Heimatstube Tribsees, Tribsees 20204
Heimatstube Trochtelfingen, Bopfingen 16252
Heimatstube Untere Baranya, Gingen 17288
Heimatstube Usedom, Usedom 20276
Heimatstube Wahrenbrück, Wahrenbrück 20347
Heimatstube Wehrstedt, Bad Salzdetfurth 15726
Heimatstube Wendhausen, Schellerten 19773
Heimatstube Werben, Werben, Altmark 20516
Heimatstube Wiesenburg, Wiesenburg, Mark 20578
Heimatstube Wiesental, Waghäusel 20341
Heimatstube Wilthen, Wilthen 20604
Heimatstuben, Ellrich 16833
Heimatstuben, Langelsheim 18318
Heimatstuben, Volkmarsen 20334
Heimatstuben, Waldbronn 20353
Heimatstuben der Csávolyer im Beinsteiner Torturm, Waiblingen 20349
Heimatstuben der Stadt, Titisee-Neustadt 20180
Heimatstuben im Arresturm, Spalt 20007
Heimatstuben im Oberen Tor, Scheinfeld 19771
Heimatstuben Schlesien, Vilsbiburg 20323
Heimatstuben Weipert und Erzgebirgsschau, Gunzenhausen 17463
Heimatvertriebenen-Stuben, Traun 02737
Heimilisiðnardarsafnid Halldórustofa, Blönduós 21624
Heimschneidermuseum, Großwallstadt 17442
Heimtali Koduloomuuseum, Heimtali 09322
Heine-Haus, Hamburg 17544
Heineken Experience, Amsterdam 28857
Heino Lubja Kaalumuuseum, Mustvee 09339
Heinola Town Museum, Heinola 09469
Heinolan Kaupunginmuseo, Heinola 09469
Heinrich-Blickle-Museum, Sammlung gußeiserner Ofenplatten, Rosenfeld 19647
Heinrich-Büssing-Haus, Wolfsburg 20659
Heinrich Harrer-Museum, Hüttenberg 02051
Heinrich-Heine-Institut-Museum, Düsseldorf 16726
Heinrich-Hoffmann-Museum, Frankfurt am Main 17053
Heinrich-Mayer-Haus Elektromuseum, Esslingen 16968
Heinrich-Schliemann-Gedenkstätte, Neubukow 19014
Heinrich-Schliemann-Museum, Ankershagen 15493
Heinrich-Schütz-Haus, Bad Köstritz 15680
Heinrich-Schütz-Haus Weißenfels, Weißenfels 20498
Heinrich-Sohnrey-Archiv und Gedächtnisstätte, Mautturm, Jühnder Schloß, Jühnde 17963
Heinrich Suso Waldeck und Hans Schnopfhagen-Gedenkraum, Sankt Veit im Mühlkreis 02616
Heinrich Vogeler Stiftung Haus im Schluh, Worpswede 20684
Heinz Nixdorf MuseumsForum, Paderborn 19334
Heirloom Doll Museum, Airlie Beach 00720
Heisey Museum, Lock Haven 44838
Heizungsmuseum der Buderus Heiztechnik, Lollar 18501
Heizungsmuseum Wien, Wien 02896
De Heksenwaag, Oudewater 29702
Held Joan Museum, Carlton South 00894
Held-Poage Memorial Home, Ukiah 48135
Helen Day Art Center, Stowe 47843
Helen E. Copeland Gallery, Bozeman 41857
Helen King Kendall Memorial Art Gallery, San Angelo 47240
Helen Louise Allen Textile Collection, Madison 45068
Helena Rubinstein Pavillon for Contemporary Art, Tel Aviv 22757
Helena Thompson Museum, Workington 40934
Helensville and District Pioneer Museum, Helensville 30178
Helfštýn Hrad, Týn nad Bečvou 08695
Helge Ands Kyrkoruin, Visby 36416
The Helicopter Museum, Weston-super-Mare 40834
Heliloojate Kappide Majamuuseum, Suure-Jaani 09352
Helinä Rautavaaran museo, Espoo 09435
Hellenic Antiquities Museum, Melbourne 01232
Hellenic Children's Museum, Athinai 20864
Hellenic Folklore Research Centre, Athinai 20865
Hellenic Maritime Museum, Piraeus 21124
Hellenic Museum and Cultural Center, Chicago 42332
Hellenic Theatre Museum and Study Center, Athinai 20866
Hellen's House, Much Marcle 39992
Hellweg-Museum der Stadt Unna, Unna 20264
Helmcken House Pioneer Doctor's Residence, Victoria 06722
Helme Kihelkonnamuuseum, Helme 09323
Helmeringhausen Museum, Helmeringhausen 28756
Helmhaus, Zürich 37381
Helms-Museum, Hamburg 17545
Helmshore Textile Museums, Helmshore 39211
Helmstedter Freundeskreis für Paramentik und christliche Kunst, Helmstedt 17702
Helsingborgs Idrottsmuseum, Helsingborg 35950
Helsingborgs Skolmuseum, Helsingborg 35951
Helsingborgs Slott, Helsingborg 35952
Helsinge Hembygdsmuseum, Vantaa 10179
Helsingin Automuseo, Helsinki 09484
Helsingin Diakonissalaitoksen Museo, Helsinki 09485
Helsingin Kaupungin Taidemuseo, Mejlahti, Helsinki 09486
Helsingin Kaupungin Taidemuseo, Tennispalatsi, Helsinki 09487
Helsingin Kaupunginmuseo, Helsinki 09488
Helsingin Taidehalli, Helsinki 09489
Helsingin Väestönsuojelumuseo, Helsinki 09490
Helsingin Yliopistomuseo, Helsinki 09491
Helsingin Yliopistomuseo - Eläinlääketieteen Historian Museo, Helsinki 09492
Helsingin Yliopiston Lääketieteen Historian Laitos ja Museo, Helsinki 09493
Helsingin Yliopiston Maatalousmuseo, Helsinki 09494
Helsingør Bymuseum, Helsingør 08862
Helsinki Car Museum, Helsinki 09484
Helsinki City Art Museum, Helsinki 09486
Helsinki City Art Museum, Helsinki 09487
Helsinki City Museum, Helsinki 09488
Helsinki Deaconess Institute Museum, Helsinki 09485
Helsinki Parish Museum, Vantaa 10179
Helsinki University Museum, Helsinki 09491
Helsinki University Museum - Museum of the History of Veterinary Medicine, Helsinki 09492
Helson Hall, Mankato 45121
Helston Folk Museum, Helston 39214
Heltborg Museum, Hurup Thy 08904
Helvetia Museum, Helvetia 43986
Helwan Corner Museum, Helwan 09299
Helytörténeti Gyűjtemény, Budapest 21343
Helytörténeti Múzeum, Pápa 21500
Hembygdsgården, Bjurholm 35833
Hembygdsgården i Kristvalla, Nybro 36125
Hembygdsgården Labbas, Storby 10056
Hembygdsgården Rots Skans, Älvdalen 35784
Hembygdsmuseet i Korsberga, Korsberga 36015
Hemingway Museum, Oak Park 46053
Hemne Bygdemuseum, Kyrksæterøra 30624
Hemnes Museum, Bjerka 30433
Hemsedal Bygdatun, Hemsedal 30543
Henan Provincial Museum, Zhengzhou 07327
Henderson State University Museum, Arkadelphia 41255
Hendrickson House Museum and Old Swedes Church, Wilmington 48653
Henfield Museum, Henfield 39218
Hengistburgmuseum, Hengsberg 02020
Henie Onstad Kunstsenter, Høvikodden 30571
Henneberg-Museum, Münnerstadt 18927
Hennebergisches Museum, Kloster Veßra 18115
Hennepin History Museum, Minneapolis 45384
Henri-Arnaud-Haus - Waldensermuseum, Ötisheim 19235
Henrik Ibsen Museum, Skien 30845
Henry Art Gallery, Seattle 47535
Henry B. Plant Museum, Tampa 47942
Henry Blogg Lifeboat Museum, Cromer 38673
Henry Clay Frick Estate, Pittsburgh 46517
Henry County Historical Museum, New Castle 45684
Henry County Museum and Cultural Arts Center, Clinton 42495
Henry-Dunant-Museum, Heiden 36797
Henry Ford Estate, Dearborn 42824
Henry Ford Museum and Greenfield Village, Dearborn 42825
Henry Guest House, New Brunswick 45677
Henry H. Blommel Historic Automotive Data Collection, Connersville 42610
Henry Kendall Cottage and Historical Museum, Gosford 01067
Henry Lawson Centre, Gulgong 01077
Henry Moore Institute, Leeds 39445
Henry S. Reuss Ice Age Visitor Center, Campbellsport 42072
The Henry Sheldon Museum of Vermont Histoy, Middlebury 45307
Henry van de Velde Museum, Chemnitz 16464
Henry Whitfield State Historical Museum, Guilford 43851
Henryk Sienkiewicz Museum, Oblęgorek 31841
Henryk Tomaszewski Toy Museum, Karpacz 31641
Heptonstall Museum, Heptonstall 39222
Her Majesty Customs and Excise National Museum, Liverpool 39518
Her Majesty Tower of London, London 39662
Hera Gallery, Wakefield 48280
Heraldic Museum, Dublin 22430
Heras Institute of Indian History and Culture, Mumbai 21949
Herat Museum, Herat 00003
Herbarium, Cambridge 38455
Herbarium, University of Turku, Turku 10121
Herbert and Eileen Bernard Museum, New York 45814
Herbert Art Gallery and Museum, Coventry 38643
Herbert E. Clark Collection of Near Eastern Antiquities, Jerusalem 22635
Herbert F. Johnson Museum of Art, Ithaca 44272
Herbert Hoover National Historic Site, West Branch 48514
Herbert Hoover Presidential Library-Museum, West Branch 48515
Herberta Dorbes Muzejs Senču Putekļi, Ventspils 27470
Herberts Dorbe Memorial Museum Senču Putekļi (The Dust of Ancestors), Ventspils 27470
Herborner Heimatmuseum, Herborn, Hessen 17715
Herdenkingsbordenmuseum, Lochem 29544
Herdla Museum, Herdla 30544
Hereford City Museum and Art Gallery, Hereford 39225
Hereford Inlet Lighthouse, North Wildwood 46010
Herefordshire Light Infantry Regimental Museum, Hereford 39226
Herendi Porcelánművészeti, Herend 21426
Herfurthsche Haus, Hainichen, Sachsen 17497
Herinneringscentrum Kamp Westerbork, Hooghalen 29439
Heriot-Watt University Museum and Archive, Edinburgh 38887
Heritage Art Center, Quezon City 31432
The Heritage Center, Pine Ridge 46492
Heritage Center of Lancaster County, Lancaster 44624
Heritage Centre of Saint Louis Convent, Monaghan 22520
Heritage Collection Catherina Brand, Ladybrand 34300
Heritage Collections Council, Canberra 49049
Heritage Conservancy, Doylestown 42983
Heritage Discover Center, Johnstown 44353
Heritage Farm & Village, North Battleford 06014
Heritage Farmstead Museum, Plano 46541
Heritage Hall Museum and Archives, Freeman 43548
Heritage Hazenmore, Hazenmore 05592
Heritage Hill Museum, Dandenong 00967
Heritage Hill State Park, Green Bay 43789
Heritage Hjemkomst Interpretive Center, Moorhead 45489
Heritage House Museum, Smiths Falls 06465
Heritage House of Orange County Museum, Orange 46171
Heritage Library and Museum, Anchorage 41199
Heritage Motor Centre, Gaydon 39029
The Heritage Museum, Astoria 41311
Heritage Museum, Baltimore 41469
Heritage Museum, Buenos Aires 00202
Heritage Museum, Idaho Springs 44192
Heritage Museum, Kuah 27633
Heritage Museum, Langruth 05726
Heritage Museum and Potton House, Big Spring 41683
The Heritage Museum at Falfurrias, Falfurrias 43280
Heritage Museum Foundation of Tate County, Senatobia 47564
The Heritage Museum of Fine Arts for Youth, Detroit 42929
Heritage Museum of Northwest Florida, Valparaiso 48191
Heritage Park, Fort McMurray 05445
Heritage Park Folk Museum, Saint Phillip 03108
Heritage Park - Historical Village, Calgary 05168
Heritage Park Museum, Terrace 06539
Heritage Plantation of Sandwich, Sandwich 47386
Heritage Royal Mail Collection, London 39663
The Heritage Society Museum, Houston 44121
Heritage Square Museum, Ontario 46164
Heritage Village, Mountain Lake 45547
Heritage Village, Sharonville 47581
Heritage Village Museum, Woodville 48747
Heritage Village - Pinellas County Historical Museum, Largo 44654
Heritage Walk Museum, Escondido 43209
Heritage World Centre, Dungannon 38812
Herkimer County Historical Society Museum, Herkimer 44000
Herkimer Home, Little Falls 44820
Herkomer-Museum am Mutterturm, Landsberg am Lech 18303
Herman de Cuyper Museum, Willebroek 03841
Herman Ottó Múzeum, Miskolc 21475
Herman Ottó Múzeum, Miskolc 21476
Herman Teirlinckhuis, Beersel 03207
Hermann-Allmers-Haus, Sandstedt 19742
Hermann Broch-Museum, Teesdorf 02718
Hermann-Grima House, New Orleans 45726
Hermann-Grochtmann-Museum Datteln, Datteln 16553
Hermann-Hesse-Höri-Museum, Gaienhofen 17190
Hermann-Hesse-Museum, Calw 16447
Hermann Hesse Museum, Hiroshima 26211
Hermann-Köhl-Museum, Pfaffenhofen an der Roth 19384
Hermann-Oberth-Raumfahrt-Museum, Feucht 16994
The Hermitage, Ho-Ho-Kus 44041
Hermitage Foundation Museum, Norfolk 45966
Hermitage Gatehouse Museum, Ancaster 04992
The Hermitage - Home of President Andrew Jackson, Hermitage 44003
Hermitage Rooms, London 39664
Herne Bay Museum and Gallery, Herne Bay 39232
Herning Kunstmuseum, Herning 08868
Herning Museum, Herning 08869
Heron Corn Mill and Museum of Papermaking, Beetham 38150
Herons Reef Historic Gold Diggings, Fryerstown 01040
Herøy Bygdesamling, Herøy 30545
Herøy Kystmuseum, Herøy 30546
Herøy Kystmuseum, Herøy 30547
Herregården Museum, Larvik 30631
Herrenhaus Altenhof, Altenhof 15453
Herrenhausen-Museum, Hannover 17596
Herreshoff Marine Museum/America's Cup Hall of Fame, Bristol 41907
Herrett Center for Arts and Science, Twin Falls 48124
Herring Era Museum of Iceland, Siglufjörður 21669
Herrliberger-Sammlung, Maur 36931
Herron Gallery, Indianapolis 44219
Herschell Carrousel Factory Museum, North Tonawanda 46008
Hershey Museum, Hershey 44004
Hertford Museum, Hertford 39234
Herttoniemen Museo, Helsinki 09495
Herttoniemi Museum, Helsinki 09495
Hertzberg Circus Museum, San Antonio 47252
Hervey Bay Historical Society Museum, Hervey Bay 01096
Herzen Memorial House Museum, Moskva 33075
Herzliya Museum of Contemporary Art, Herzliya 22616
Herzog Anton Ulrich-Museum, Braunschweig 16297
Herzog August Bibliothek, Wolfenbüttel 20653
Herzogschloss, Celle 16454
Herz'sche Heimatstiftung Hilgerhof, Pittenhart 19409
Hessaby Museum, Teheran 22302
Hessische Landes- und Hochschulbibliothek, Darmstadt 16540
Hessischer Museumsverband e.V., Kassel 49199
Hessisches Braunkohle Bergbaumuseum, Borken, Hessen 16257
Hessisches Forst-Kulturhistorisches Museum, Biebergemünd 16145

Hessisches Kutschen- und Wagenmuseum, Lohfelden 18495
Hessisches Landesmuseum Darmstadt, Darmstadt 16541
Hessisches Puppenmuseum, Hanau 17583
Hester Rupert Art Museum, Graaff-Reinet 34247
Hetjens-Museum, Düsseldorf 16727
Hettinger County Historical Society Museum, Regent 46830
Heuneburgmuseum, Herbertingen 17714
Heureka - The Finnish Science Centre, Vantaa 10180
Heurich House Museum, Washington 48359
Heuser Art Center, Peoria 46348
Heuson-Museum im Rathaus, Büdingen 16398
Heussenstamm Stiftung, Frankfurt am Main 17054
Hever Castle and Gardens, Edenbridge 38868
Hevosajoneuvomuseo Ameriikka, Vieremä 10193
Hexenbürgermeisterhaus, Lemgo 18429
Hexenmuseum, Riegersburg, Steiermark 02515
Hexenmuseum, Ringelai 19616
Hexenturm, Vicosoprano 37292
Heym-Oliver House, Russell 47035
Heyward-Washington House, Charleston 42218
Hezlett House, Coleraine 38618
HfG-Archiv, Ulm 20257
H.G. Albee Memorial Museum, Estherville 43218
H.H. Maharaja Jayaji Rao Scindia Museum, Gwalior 21829
Hi-Desert Nature Museum, Yucca Valley 48817
Hibbing Historical Museum, Hibbing 44005
Hibel Museum of Art - Jupiter, Jupiter 44372
Hickories Museum, Elyria 43177
Hickory Grove Rural School Museum, Ogden 46096
Hickory Museum of Art, Hickory 44007
Hicks Art Center, Newtown 45948
Hicksville Gregory Museum, Hicksville 44010
Hida Folk Village, Takayama 26804
Hida Minzoku Kokokan, Takayama 26803
Hida Minzoku-mura, Takayama 26804
Hida Takayama Bijutsukan, Takayama 26805
Hida Takayama Museum, Takayama 26806
Hida Takayama Museum of Art, Takayama 26805
Hida Takayama Shunkei Kaikan, Takayama 26807
Hidalgo County Historical Museum, Edinburg 43088
Hidalgo Pumphouse Heritage, Hidalgo 44011
Hidde Nijland Museum, Hindeloopen 29422
Hiddenite Center, Hiddenite 44012
Hieizan Natural History Museum, Kyoto 26403
Hiekan Taidemuseo, Tampere 10077
Hiekka Art Museum, Tampere 10077
Hierapolis Archeological Museum, Denizli 37658
Hierapolis Arkeoloji Müzesi, Denizli 37658
Higashi-Hiroshima City Museum of Art, Higashi-Hiroshima 26187
Higashi-Hiroshima-shiritsu Bijutsukan, Higashi-Hiroshima 26187
Higashi-Murayama Municipal Museum of Provincial History, Higashi-Murayama 26188
Higashi-Osaka Municipal Local Museum, Higashi-Osaka 26189
Higashi-Osaka-shiritsu Kyodo Hakubutsukan, Higashi-Osaka 26189
Higashi-yamate District Historic Preservation Center, Nagasaki 26546
Higgins Armory Museum, Worcester 48753
Higgins Art Gallery, West Barnstable 48511
Higgins Museum, Okoboji 46126
High Cliff General Store Museum, Sherwood 47604
High Desert Museum, Bend 41623
High Museum of Art, Atlanta 41348
High Plains Heritage Center, Great Falls 43781
High Plains Museum, Goodland 43727
High Plains Museum, McCook 45021
High Point Museum, High Point 44015
High Prairie and District Museum, High Prairie 05594
High Wire Gallery, Philadelphia 46416
Highland Folk Museum, Kingussie 39388
Highland Folk Museum, Newtonmore 40068
Highland House Museum, Hillsboro 44027
Highland Maple Museum, Monterey 45461
Highland Museum of Childhood, Strathpeffer 40633
Highland Park Historical Museum, Highland Park 44020
Highland Pioneers Museum, Baddeck 05032
Highland Village Living History Museum, Iona 05625
Highlands, Fort Washington 43472
Highlands Museum and Discovery Center, Ashland 41287
Highlands Museum of the Arts, Sebring 47552
Highwic, Auckland 30110
Hiihtomuseo, Lahti 09740
Hiiumaa Muuseum, Kärdla 09328
Hikone Castle Collection, Hikone 26193
Hildene, Manchester 45101
Hill Aerospace Museum, Hill Air Force Base 44021
Hill Country Museum, Kerrville 44455
Hill Cumorah Visitors Center and Historic Sites, Palmyra 46269
Hill-Hold Museum, Montgomery 45470
Hill House, Helensburgh 39208
The Hill House, Portsmouth 46661
Hill of Tarvit Mansion House, Cupar 38688
Hill-Stead Museum, Farmington 43295
Hill Top, Sawrey 40451
Hill Tribes Museum, Bangkok 37485
Hillary House and Koffler Museum of Medicine, Aurora 05022
Hillcrest Museum, Souris 06473
Hillel Jewish Student Center Gallery, Cincinnati 42407
Hilleshuis Museum, Rotterdam 29751
Hillforest House Museum, Aurora 41400
Hillsboro Area Historical Society Museum, Hillsboro 44029
Hillsboro Museum, Hillsboro 44024
Hillsborough Railway Museum, Hillsborough 05596
Hillview Museum, Bagenalstown 22364
Hillwood Art Museum, Brookville 41959
Hillwood Museum, Washington 48360
Hilprecht-Sammlung Vorderasiatischer Altertümer der Friedrich-Schiller-Universität Jena, Jena 17943
Himachal State Museum, Shimla 22020
Himangan Kotiseutumuseo, Himanka 09550
Himanka Museum, Himanka 09550
Himeji City Museum of Art, Himeji 26195
Himezaki Lighthouse Museum, Ryotsu 26686
Himley Hall, Himley 39245
Himmel och Hav, Norrköping 36118
Hinchingbrooke House, Huntingdon 39278
Hinchman House, Nantucket 45596
Hinckley and District Museum, Hinckley 39246
Hinckley Fire Museum, Hinckley 44035
Hinckley Foundation Museum, Ithaca 44273
Hincz Gyula Állandó Gyüjtemény, Vác 21601
Hindi Sangrahalaya, Allahabad 21692
Hindley Museum, Hindley 39247
Hinsdale Historical Society Museum, Hinsdale 44038
Hinterglasmuseum, Sandl 02555
Hinterlandmuseum Schloss Biedenkopf, Biedenkopf 16150
Hipp-Halle, Gmunden 01894
Hippo Regius Museum, Annaba 00048
Hippological Museum, Slatiňany 08656
Hippologické Muzeum, Slatiňany 08656
Hirado Castle Donjon, Hirado 26198
Hirado Kanko Historical Museum, Hirado 26199
Hirado Kanko Shiryôkan, Hirado 26199
Hiraide Archaeological Museum, Shiojiri 26758
Hiraizumi Museum, Hiraizumi 26203
Hirakata Gotenyama Art Center, Hirakata 26205
Hirakawa-go Open Air Museum, Shirakawa 26763
Hiram Blauvelt Art Museum, Oradell 46170
Hiram Smith Octagon House, Neenah 45644
Hirano-go Folk Museum, Osaka 26646
Hirano Hakabutsukan, Osaka 26647
Hirano Image Library, Osaka 26648
Hirano Soundscape Museum, Yamatokoriyama 27007
Hirata Folk Art Museum, Takayama 26808
Hirata Kinenkan, Takayama 26808
Hiratsuka Bijutsukan, Hiratsuka 26207
Hiratsuka City Museum, Hiratsuka 26208
Hiratsuka Museum of Art, Hiratsuka 26207
Hiratsuka-shi Hakubutsukan, Hiratsuka 26208
Hirosaki City Museum, Hirosaki 26209
Hirosaki-shiritsu Hakubutsukan, Hirosaki 26209
Hiroshima Bijutsukan, Hiroshima 26212
Hiroshima Castle, Hiroshima 26213
Hiroshima Children's Museum, Hiroshima 26214
Hiroshima City Museum of Contemporary Art, Hiroshima 26218
Hiroshima City Museum of Traditional Provincial Industry, Hiroshima 26215
Hiroshima Heiwa Kinen Shiryokan, Hiroshima 26216
Hiroshima-kenritsu Bijutsukan, Hiroshima 26217
Hiroshima Museum of Art, Hiroshima 26212
Hiroshima Peace Memorial Museum, Hiroshima 26216
Hiroshima Prefectural Art Museum, Hiroshima 26217
Hiroshima-shi Gendai Bijutsukan, Hiroshima 26218
Hirschbacher Bauernmöbelmuseum, Hirschbach 02030
Hirschberger Heimatstuben, Alfeld, Leine 15427
Den Hirschsprungske Samling, København 08931
Hirschwirtscheuer-Museum für die Künstlerfamilie Sommer, Künzelsau 18258
Hirsel Homestead Museum, Coldstream 38617
Hirshhorn Museum and Sculpture Garden, Washington 48361
Hirsmäen Museoalue, Valkeala 10174
Hiscock House, Trinity 06633
Hispanic Society of America, New York 45815
HistoRail Limousin du Chemin de Fer, Saint-Léonard-de-Noblat 14322
Historial de la Grande Guerre, Péronne 13698
Historial de la Médaille Miraculeuse, Lourdes 12685
Historial/Musée de Cire, La Chaise-Dieu 12137
Historiallinen Museo ja Näyttelyhalli, Kokkola 09681
Historic Allaire Village, Allaire 41140
Historic and Ethnic Instrument Collection, Nedlands 01311
Historic Annapolis Foundation, Annapolis 41229
Historic Atlas Coal Mine, East Coulee 05361
Historic Babcock Mill, Odessa 06042
Historic Bath State Historic Site, Bath 41523
Historic Bethany, Bethany 41659
Historic Bowens Mills and Pioneer Park, Middleville 45320
Historic Brattonsville, McConnells 45020
Historic Burlington County Prison Museum, Mount Holly 45531
Historic Camden Revolutionary War Site, Camden 42065
Historic Carson House, Marion 45161
Historic Charleston Foundation, Charleston 42219
Historic Charlton Park Village and Museum, Hastings 43955
Historic Cherry Hill, Albany 41084
Historic Columbia Foundation, Columbia 42562
Historic Columbus Foundation, Columbus 42575
Historic Crab Orchard Museum and Pioneer Park, Tazewell 47964
Historic Cragfont, Castalian Springs 42134
Historic Daniel Boone Home and Boonesfield Village, Defiance 42852
Historic Deerfield, Deerfield 42849
Historic Dockyard Chatham, Chatham 38529
Historic Edenton State Historic Site, Edenton 43081
Historic-Ethnographical Collection, Oświęcim 31869
Historic Fallsington, Fallsington 43286
Historic Ferryland Museum, Ferryland 05425
Historic Fort Snelling, Saint Paul 47156
Historic Fort Steilacoom, Tacoma 47918
Historic Fort Stockton, Fort Stockton 43462
Historic Fort York, Toronto 06582
Historic Gardner's Basin, Atlantic City 41366
Historic General Dodge House, Council Bluffs 42673
Historic Georgetown, Georgetown 43648
Historic Governors' Mansion, Cheyenne 42298
Historic Halifax, Halifax 43873
Historic Hat Creek Ranch, Cache Creek 05155
Historic Hermann Museum, Hermann 44002
Historic Hope Foundation, Windsor 48683
Historic Houses of Odessa, Delaware, Odessa 46092
Historic Hudson Valley, Tarrytown 47957
The Historic Indian Agency House, Portage 46613
Historic Jefferson College, Washington 48415
Historic Kenmore, Fredericksburg 43536
Historic Landmarks Foundation of Indiana, Indianapolis 44220
Historic Langhorne Museum, Langhorne 44636
Historic Latta Plantation, Huntersville 44152
Historic Liberty Jail Visitors Center, Liberty 44766
Historic Lincoln, Lincoln 44795
Historic London Town, Edgewater 43085
Historic Lyme Village, Bellevue 41595
Historic Madison House, Madison 45056
Historic Mann House, Concord 42603
Historic Markerville Creamery, Markerville 05815
Historic Michie Tavern, Charlottesville 42248
Historic Mill Creek, Mackinaw City 45034
Historic Morven, Princeton 46701
Historic Museum of Arkansas, Little Rock 44824
Historic New Harmony, New Harmony 45692
The Historic New Orleans Collection, New Orleans 45727
Historic Newton Home, Decatur 42836
Historic Northampton, Northampton 46014
Historic Occoquan, Occoquan 46083
Historic O'Keefe Ranch, Vernon, British Columbia 06707
Historic Palmyra, Palmyra 46270
Historic Pensacola Village, Pensacola 46342
Historic Pithole City, Pleasantville 46557
Historic Pittsford, Pittsford 46534
Historic Preservation Association of Bourbon County, Fort Scott 43454
Historic Renville Preservation Commission Museum, Renville 46842
Historic Resources Centre, Annan 38003
Historic Richmond Town, Staten Island 47782
Historic Rock Ford, Lancaster 44625
Historic Rosedale, Charlotte 42240
Historic Rugby, Rugby 47028
Historic Saint Mary's City, Saint Mary's City 47147
Historic Sauder Village, Archbold 41248
Historic Schaefferstown, Schaefferstown 47494
Historic Scotland, Edinburgh 38888
Historic Shepherdstown Museum, Shepherdstown 47600
Historic Smithfield, Blacksburg 41727
Historic Spanish Point, Osprey 46210
Historic Speedwell, Morristown 45506
Historic Stagville, Bahama 41431
Historic Stewart Farmhouse, Surrey 06518
Historic Wax Museum, Buenos Aires 00209
Historic W.H.C. Folsom House, Taylors Falls 47962
Historic White Pine Village, Ludington 44995
Historic Yale Museum, Yale 06867
Historical Agriculture Collection, Wadowice 32069
Historical and Architectural Museum Red Hill, Kemerovo 32911
Historical and Art Museum, Uglič 33649
Historical and Cultural Museum and Nature Park of the Republic Karatchaevo-Tcherkessiya, Čerkessk 32736
Historical and Cultural Museum Shalyapin's Estate, Kislovodsk 32927
Historical and Ethnographical Museum, Mary 37818
Historical and Ethnographical Museum, Turkmenabat 37820
Historical and Ethnological Museum, Beiuş 32438
Historical and Ethnological Museum of Cappadocia, Kavala 21011
Historical and Ethnological Museum of Patras, Patrai 21115
Historical and Ethnological Museum of the Mani, Kranae 21037
Historical and Folk Art Museum of Gavalohori, Chania 20917
Historical and Folklore Museum, Kalamata 20984
Historical and Genealogical Society of Indiana County, Indiana 44210
Historical and Memorial Museum Complex Bobriki, Donskij 32760
Historical and Military Museum of Kamtchatka Region, Petropavlovsk-Kamčatskij 33311
Historical and Natural History Museum of Natick, South Natick 47699
Historical and Regional Museum, Arkalyk 27075
Historical and Regional Museum, Temirtau 27097
Historical and Regional Museum Donskoe, Donskoe 32761
Historical and Regional Museum of Bujnaksk, Bujnaksk 32713
Historical and Regional Museum of Gelendzhik, Gelendžik 32804
Historical, Architectural and Archeological Museum-Reserve, Staraja Ladoga 33553
Historical, Architectural and Artistic Museum-Reserve, Velikij Ustjug 33681
Historical, Architectural and Artistic Museum Reserve of Ples, Ples 33325
Historical, Architectural and Nature Museum-Reserve Monrepo, Vyborg 33741
Historical, Architecture and Art Museum of Zvenigorod, Zvenigorod 33751
Historical Archive and University Museum of Ljubljana, Ljubljana 34125
Historical Center for Southeast New Mexico, Roswell 47015
Historical Collection Electronical Engineering, Delft 29077
Historical Collection of Furnishings 16th-19th c and Costumes 19th c, Turnov 08693
Historical Electronics Museum, Linthicum 44809
Historical Estate Boat of Peter I, the Great, Veskovo 33684
Historical-Ethnographical Museum, Chojnice 31528
Historical-ethnographical Museum House of Galsky, Čerepovec 32731
Historical, Folk Art and Natural History Museum of Kozani, Kozani 21036
Historical Goverment House, Takayama 26811
Historical Memorial Museum of the Family Fadeevy-Hahn-Blavatsky, Dnepropetrovsk 37849
Historical Memorial State Preserve Homeplace of V.I. Lenin, Uljanovsk 33656
Historical Museum, Batak 04616
Historical Museum, Białystok 31486
Historical Museum, Blagoevgrad 04626
Historical Museum, Bracigovo 04629
Historical Museum, Città del Vaticano 48884
Historical Museum, Dnepropetrovsk 37848
Historical Museum, Drjanovo 04660
Historical Museum, Gabrovo 04668
Historical Museum, Jerusalem 22636
Historical Museum, Kruševo 27586
Historical Museum, Lund 36057
Historical Museum, Mahébourg 27733
Historical Museum, Razgrad 04797
Historical Museum, Slavkov u Brna 08657
Historical Museum, Tutrakan 04892
Historical Museum and Pioneer Village, Sundre 06516
Historical Museum at Fort Missoula, Missoula 45405
The Historical Museum at Saint Gertrude, Cottonwood 42665
Historical Museum by V. Tarnovsky, Černigiv 37838
Historical Museum in Wrocław, Wrocław 32178
Historical Museum Memorial of Victory, Krasnojarsk 37865
Historical Museum of Anthiros, Karditsa 20998
Historical Museum of Arta, Arta 20838
Historical Museum of Azogire, Azogire 20909
Historical Museum of Bay County, Bay City 41543
Historical Museum of Cecil County, Elkton 43147
Historical Museum of Crete, Iráklion 20975
Historical Museum of Frederick County, Frederick 43527
Historical Museum of Hokkaido, Sapporo 26712
Historical Museum of Old Randolph, Randolph 46789
Historical Museum of Palm Beach County, West Palm Beach 48537
Historical Museum of Portitsa, Karditsa 20999
Historical Museum of Private Schools at the Foreign Settlement, Nagasaki 26547
Historical Museum of Saint James-Assiniboia, Winnipeg 06827
Historical Museum of Sciences Carlos J. Finlay, La Habana 07971
Historical Museum of Serbia, Beograd 33799
Historical Museum of Sofia, Sofia 04860
Historical Museum of Southern Florida, Miami 45285
Historical Museum of Talbot County, Easton 43067
Historical Museum of Tarnobrzeg, Tarnobrzeg 32039
Historical Museum of the city of Cracow - Pomorska Branch, Kraków 31708
Historical Museum of the Construction of the Nurek Hydroelectric Factory, Nurek 37449
Historical Museum of the D.R. Barker Library, Fredonia 43545
Historical Museum of the Moscow Metro, Moskva 33108
Historical Museum of the National Museum in Prague, Praha 08580
Historical Museum of the National Resistance of Rentina, Agrapha, Karditsa 21000
Historical Museum of the Old City of Warsaw, Warszawa 32101
Historical Museum of Uzbekistan M.T. Oibek, Taškent 48854
Historical Society Museum, Hudson 44144
Historical Society Museum of Carroll County, Westminster 48563
Historical Society Museum of Ocean Grove, New Jersey, Ocean Grove 46086
Historical Society Museum of the Town of Greenwich, Greenwich 43832

Historical Society of Berks County Museum, Reading 46807
Historical Society of Bloomfield Museum, Bloomfield 41734
Historical Society of Kent County Museum, Chestertown 42292
Historical Society of Middletown and the Wallkill Precinct, Middletown 45317
Historical Society of Oak Park and River Forest, Oak Park 46054
Historical Society of Old Yarmouth Museum, Yarmouth Port 48779
Historical Society of Pennsylvania, Philadelphia 46417
Historical Society of Saint Kilda, Saint Kilda, Victoria 01433
Historical Society of Santuit and Cotuit, Cotuit 42669
Historical Transport Museum, Chlumec u Ústi nad Labem 08312
Historical Village and Pioneer Museum, Willingdon 06806
Historical Woolscour Blackall, Blackall 00807
Historické Múzeum, Bratislava 33964
Historické Muzeum, Praha 08580
Historické Muzeum, Slavkov u Brna 08657
Historicum, Sargans 37118
Historiekamer Hardenberg, Hardenberg 29340
Historiengewölbe, Rothenburg ob der Tauber 19677
Historisch Documentatiecentrum voor het Nederlands Protestantisme 1800-Heden, Amsterdam 28858
Historisch Museum, Capelle aan den IJssel 29054
Historisch Museum Arnhem, Arnhem 28935
Historisch Museum de Bevelanden, Goes 29286
Historisch Museum de Scheper, Eibergen 29207
Historisch Museum De Tien Malen, Putten 29718
Historisch Museum Den Briel, Brielle 29028
Historisch Museum Deventer, Deventer 29145
Historisch Museum Ede, Ede 29192
Historisch Museum Grenadiers en Jagers, Arnhem 28936
Historisch Museum Haarlemmermeer, Hoofddorp 29436
Historisch Museum Hedel, Hedel 29356
Historisch Museum Het Kleine Veenlo, Veenendaal 29928
Historisch Museum Het Palthe Huis, Oldenzaal 29657
Historisch Museum Oald Hengel, Hengelo, Overijssel 29398
Historisch Museum Piet Dorenbosch, Boxtel 29013
Historisch Museum Rotterdam Het Schielandshuis, Rotterdam 29752
Historisch Museum Ter Aar, Ter Aar 28796
Historisch Museum Tweestromenland, Beneden Leeuwen 28975
Historisch Museum Warsenhoeck, Nieuwegein 29619
Historisch Museum Wolfheze, Wolfheze 30017
Historisch Museum Zuid-Kennemerland, Haarlem 29326
Historisch Muzeum Hazerswoude, Hazerswoude Dorp 29355
Historisch Openluchtmuseum Eindhoven, Eindhoven 29211
Historisch Pijp en Tabaksmuseum, Sint-Niklaas 03739
Historisch-Technisches Informationszentrum, Peenemünde 19362
Historische Apothekenausstellung, Bremervörde 16351
Historische Arztpraxis, Burgstädt 16430
Historische Ausstellung Krupp, Essen 16951
Historische Bibliothek, Quedlinburg 19460
Historische Expositie Klederdracht en Visserijmuseum, Bunschoten Spakenburg 29038
Historische Fahrzeugsammlung, Simmelsdorf 19960
Historische Fraunhofer-Glashütte, Benediktbeuern 15877
Historische Gebirgsmühle mit Bastelkunstwerken, Fischbachau 17006
Historische Genie Verzameling, Vught 29970
Historische Gesellenherberge, Blankenburg, Harz 16176
Historische Hammerschmiede, Blaubeuren 16181
Historische Handwerkerstuben, Gingst 17289
Historische Höhler, Gera 17243
Historische Käsküche, Wiggensbach 20585
Historische Kuranlagen und Goethe-Theater Bad Lauchstädt, Bad Lauchstädt 15688
Historische Lehrsammlung der Feuerwehr Köln, Köln 18142
Historische Lochgefängnisse im Alten Rathaus, Nürnberg 19144
Historische Ochsentretanlage im Brunnenhausmuseum, Schillingsfürst 19778
Historische Ortssammlung, Reigoldswil 37050
Historische Räume des Stadtschlosses, Fulda 17174
Historische Sammlung Bethel, Bielefeld 16154
Historische Sammlung Eltville, Eltville 16843
Historische Sammlung im Zeitturm, Mellingen 36937
Historische Sammlung Schloß Hegi, Winterthur 37329
Historische Sammlungen im Gesundheitspark, Bad Gottleuba 15651
Historische Schlosserei Pelzer, Jena 17944
Historische Silbergruben - Schaubergwerk und Museum, Oberzeiring 02381
Historische Spinnerei Gartetal, Gleichen 17300
Historische Turmstuben, Winnenden 20611
Historische Verzameling Aan- en Afvoertroepen, Stroe 29859
Historische Verzameling Intendance, Bussum 29049
Historische Verzameling Korps Nationale Reserve, Harskamp 29347
Historische Verzameling Luchtdoelartillerie, Ede 29193
Historische Verzameling Militair Geneeskundige Dienst, Loosdrecht 29545
Historische Verzameling Regiment van Heutsz, Arnhem 28937
Historische Weberei, Braunsdorf 16307
Historische Wehranlage, Mühlhausen, Thüringen 18806
Historischer Ausstellungsraum im Heizkraftwerk Moabit, Berlin 16001
Historischer Eisenhammer, Roth, Mittelfranken 19674
Historischer Handblaudruck Wagner, Bad Leonfelden 01713
Historischer Kunstbunker, Nürnberg 19145
Historischer Saal der Fischerzunft, Würzburg 20695
Historischer Schieferbergbau Lehesten, Lehesten, Thüringer Wald 18370
Historischer Straßenbahnhof Leipzig-Möckern, Leipzig 18399
Historisches Archiv der Stadt Köln, Köln 18143
Historisches Bergamt Bad Wildungen-Bergfreiheit, Bad Wildungen 15762
Historisches Binz Museum, Ostseebad Binz 19307
Historisches Erzbergwerk im Silberbergwerk Bodenmais, Bodenmais 16208
Historisches Feuerwehrmuseum Lüchow-Dannenberg, Dannenberg, Elbe 16535
Historisches Heimatmuseum, Östringen 19234
Historisches Kabinett Burgruine Eckartsburg, Eckartsberga 16775
Historisches Kabinett - Sammlung für Bergbaukunde, Modellsammlung, Winkler-Gedenkstätte und Karzer, Freiberg, Sachsen 17100
Historisches Käsereimuseum, Altusried 15474
Historisches Museum Aargau, Lenzburg 36870
Historisches Museum am Hohen Ufer, Hannover 17597
Historisches Museum am Strom - Hildegard von Bingen, Bingen am Rhein 16164
Historisches Museum Arbon, Arbon 36465
Historisches Museum Aurich, Aurich 15578
Historisches Museum Bamberg, Bamberg 15808
Historisches Museum Basel, Basel 36500
Historisches Museum Bayreuth, Bayreuth 15846
Historisches Museum Bern, Bern 36541
Historisches Museum Bielefeld, Bielefeld 16155
Historisches Museum Blumenstein, Solothurn 37182
Historisches Museum Bremerhaven, Bremerhaven 16340
Historisches Museum der Pfalz, Speyer 20011
Historisches Museum der Stadt Baden, Baden 36485
Historisches Museum des Kantons Thurgau, Frauenfeld 36706
Historisches Museum Frankfurt am Main, Frankfurt am Main 17055
Historisches Museum Hanau, Hanau 17584
Historisches Museum Heiden, Heiden 36798
Historisches Museum im Marstall, Paderborn 19335
Historisches Museum im Spital, Dinkelsbühl 16615
Historisches Museum Luzern, Luzern 36910
Historisches Museum Murten, Murten 36974
Historisches Museum Obwalden, Sarnen 37123
Historisches Museum Olten, Olten 37008
Historisches Museum Regensburg, Regensburg 19524
Historisches Museum Saar, Saarbrücken 19724
Historisches Museum Sankt Gallen, Sankt Gallen 37100
Historisches Museum Schloß Bad Urach, Bad Urach 15756
Historisches Museum Schloß Gifhorn, Gifhorn 17285
Historisches Museum Uri, Altdorf, Uri 36447
Historisches Museum Verden, Verden 20302
Historisches Museum Wiedlisbach, Wiedlisbach 37316
Historisches Rathaus, Krempe 18231
Historisches Schmucksteinbergwerk Silberschacht, Bach an der Donau 15584
Historisches Schuhmuseum, Landsberg am Lech 18304
Historisches Silberbergwerk "Hella-Glücksstollen", Neubulach 19015
Historisches Silbererzbergwerk Grube Samson und Heimatmuseum, Sankt Andreasberg 19745
Historisches Stadtmuseum, Burghausen, Salzach 16421
Historisches Stadtmuseum Innsbruck, Innsbruck 02068
Historisches Straßenbahn-Depot Sankt Peter, Nürnberg 19146
Historisches Waffenmuseum im Zeughaus, Überlingen 20243
Historisches Zentrum, Wuppertal 20713
Historisk Museum, Oslo 30736
Historisk Museum, Slangerup 09072
Historiska Museet, Lund 36057
Historiska Museet, Stockholm 36246
Historium de Sedan, Sedan 14689
History and Archaeology Museum, Tulcea 32619
History and Architecture Museum Fortress of Kuznetsk, Novokuzneck 33234
History and Art Museum, Gulbene 27357
History and Art Museum, Krāslava 27374
History and Art Museum Jurino, Jurino 32863
History and Legendary Museum, Kuah 27634
History and Natural History Museum, Alger 00040
History and Regional Museum, Vsevoložsk 33740
History and Regional Museum of Kronstadt, Kronštadt 32964
History and Regional Museum of the Komi Republic, Syktyvkar 33573
History and Traditions Museum, Lackland Air Force Base 44562
History Center of the United Methodist Church, Madison 45062
History House, Armadale, Western Australia 00750
History House, Portland 01390
History Museum, Ahmednagar 21683
History Museum, Bansko 04613
History Museum, Bratislava 33964
History Museum, Burgas 04634
History Museum, Čiprovci 04643
History Museum, Dimitrovgrad 04651
History Museum, Goce Delčev 04674
History Museum, Gorna Orjachovica 04675
History Museum, Grahamstown 34250
History Museum, Ichtiman 04678
History Museum, Isperich 04679
History Museum, Jēkabpils 27362
History Museum, Omurtag 04746
History Museum, Pavlikeni 04752
History Museum, Petrič 04761
History Museum, Pomorie 04783
History Museum, Popovo 04784
History Museum, Pravec 04787
History Museum, Provadia 04789
History Museum, Razlog 04798
History Museum, Svištov 04880
History Museum, Târgu Jiu 32606
History Museum, Velingrad 04922
History Museum for Springfield-Greene County, Springfield 47753
History Museum Landing of the Russian Army at Svishtov, Svištov 04881
History Museum of Joshkar-Ola, Joškar-Ola 32859
History Museum of Latvia, Rīga 27428
History Museum of Moldavia, Iaşi 32533
History Museum of Neamţ County, Piatra-Neamţ 32568
History Museum of Saint Paul, Saint Paul 06369
History Museum of the Romanian Jews, Bucureşti 32456
History Museum of the Taiping Heavenly Kingdom in Nanjing, Nanjing 07176
History Museum of Western Virginia, Roanoke 46929
History Museum-Palace in Dukla, Dukla 31558
History of Contraception Museum, Toronto 06583
History of Grudziądz, Grudziądz 31610
History of Medicine Collections, Durham 43022
History of Transportation, Moose Jaw 05933
History San José, San Jose 47351
History Shop, Wigan 40870
Hitachi City Local Museum, Hitachi 26224
Hitachi Kyodo Hakubutsukan, Hitachi 26224
Hitchin Museum and Art Gallery, Hitchin 39248
Hiwa Museum for Natural History, Hiwa 26225
Hiwan Homestead Museum, Evergreen 43249
Hixon House, La Crosse 44536
Hiyas ng Bulakan Museum, Malolos 31361
H.J. van de Kamp Museum, Sint Oedenrode 29824
Hjedding Mejerimuseum, Ølgod 09018
Hjemmevaernsmuseet, Holstebro 08888
Hjerl Hedes Frilandsmuseum, Vinderup 09113
HM Prison Service Museum, Rugby 40354
HMAS Castlemaine - Museum Ship, Williamstown 01600
HMCS Haida, Toronto 06584
HMCS Sackville, Halifax 05554
HMS Belfast, London 39665
HMS Buffalo, Glenelg 01059
HMS Ganges Association Museum, Ipswich 39304
HMS Trincomalee, Hartlepool 39176
HMS Victory, Portsmouth 40253
HMS Warrior 1860, Portsmouth 40254
Ho-Am Art Museum, Yongin 27301
Ho Chi Minh City Fine Arts Museum, Ho Chi Minh City 48986
Ho Chi Minh Memorial House, Thua Thien Hue 49001
Ho Chi Minh Museum, Ha Noi 48979
Ho Chi Minh Museum, Ho Chi Minh City 48987
Ho Chi Minh Museum, Thua Thien Hue 49002
Ho Phrakèo, Vientiane 27319
Hoard Historical Museum, Fort Atkinson 43365
Hobart Heritage Museum, Hobart 01097
Hobart Historical Society Museum, Hobart 44042
Hobbies Museum of Fretwork, Dereham 38721
Hobby- och Leksaksmuseum, Stockholm 36247
Hobro Museum, Hobro 08879
Hochburg-Museum, Emmendingen 16853
Hochheimer Kunstsammlung, Hochheim am Main 17773
Hochofen-Museum Bundschuh, Thomatal 02730
Hochofenmuseum Radwerk IV, Vordernberg 02778
Hochrheinmuseum, Bad Säckingen 15723
Hochschul-und Landesbibliothek, Fulda 17175
Hochstift Meissen, Meißen 18690
Hockaday Museum of Arts, Kalispell 44384
Hockey Hall of Fame, Toronto 06585
Hocking Valley Museum of Theatrical History, Nelsonville 45648
Hodgeville Community Museum, Hodgeville 05600
Höbarth- und Madermuseum der Stadt Horn, Horn 02048
Höganäs Museum och Konsthall, Höganäs 35956
Högarps Bymuseum, Vetlanda 36402
Höhlenkundemuseum Dechenhöhle, Iserlohn 17921
Höhlenmuseum, Frasdorf 17087
Höhlenmuseum, Obertraun 02377
Höhlenmuseum, Sundlauenen 37224
Höhlenmuseum Eisensteinhöhle, Bad Fischau 01697
Höhlenmuseum in der Lurgrotte, Peggau 02395
Höhlenmuseum Kubacher Kristallhöhle und Freilicht-Steinemuseum, Weilburg 20445
Hölderlinturm, Tübingen 20224
Hörby Museum, Hörby 35959
Hof Haina mit Heimatmuseum, Biebertal 16147
Hof van Hessen, Huissen 29453
Hoffmann-von-Fallersleben-Museum, Wolfsburg 20660
Hofgarten an der Residenz, München 18856
Hofinge's Rahmenmuseum, Innsbruck 02069
Hofjagd- und Rüstkammer des Kunsthistorischen Museums, Wien 02897
Hofje Van Gratie, Delft 29078
Hofmarkmuseum, Eggenfelden 16786
Hofmarkmuseum Schloß Eggersberg, Riedenburg 19596
Hofstra Museum, Hempstead 43987
Hofu Tenmangu History Hall, Hofu 26227
Hofwyl-Broadfield Plantation, Brunswick 41969
Hogarth's House, London 39666
Hogia PC-Museum, Stenungsund 36229
Hohberger Bienenmuseum, Hohberg 17802
Hohenhof, Hagen, Westfalen 17480
Hohenlohe-Museum, Neuenstein, Württemberg 19029
Hohenloher Freilandmuseum, Schwäbisch Hall 19867
Hohenloher Kunstverein e.V., Langenburg 18331
Hohenloher Urweltmuseum, Waldenburg, Württemberg 20361
Hohenzollerisches Landesmuseum, Hechingen 17656
Hohhaus-Museum, Lauterbach, Hessen 18361
Hoiles-Davis Museum, Greenville 43823
Højer Mølle- og Marskmuseum, Højer 08883
Hokkaido Asahikawa Museum of Art, Asahikawa 26106
Hokkaido Bungakukan, Sapporo 26710
Hokkaido Daigaku Nogakubu Hakubutsukan, Sapporo 26711
Hokkaido Hakodate Museum of Art, Hakodate 26173
Hokkaido Kaitaku Kinenkan, Sapporo 26712
Hokkaido Migishi Kotaro Museum of Art, Sapporo 26715
Hokkaido Museum of Literature, Sapporo 26713
Hokkaido Museum of Modern Art, Sapporo 26714
Hokkaido Obihiro Museum of Art, Obihiro 26611
Hokkaidoritsu Asahikawa Bijutsukan, Asahikawa 26106
Hokkaidoritsu Hakodate Bijutsukan, Hakodate 26173
Hokkaidoritsu Kindai Bijutsukan, Sapporo 26714
Hokkaidoritsu Migishi Kotaro Bijutsukan, Sapporo 26715
Hokkaidoritsu Obihiro Bijutsukan, Obihiro 26611
Hokodate Museum of Art, Hokodate 26229
Hokuetsu Art Museum, Nakajo 26573
Hokuetsu Bijutsukan, Nakajo 26573
Hokumouken Kita-mi Bunka, Kita-mi 26339
Hol Bygdemuseum, Hol i Hallingdal 30553
Holburne Museum of Art, Bath 38115
Holden Gallery, Manchester 39889
Holden Historical Society Museum, Holden 05601
Holdhus Skulemuseum, Eikelandsosen 30476
Holländer-Windmühle, Stove bei Wismar 20072
Holland Area Arts Council, Holland 44055
Holland Experience, Amsterdam 28859
Holland Historical Society Museum, Holland 44058
Holland Land Office Museum, Batavia 41521
Holland Museum, Holland 44056
Het Hollands Kaasmuseum, Alkmaar 28803
De Hollandsche Schouwburg, Amsterdam 28860
Hollenberg Pony Express Station Museum, Hanover 43905
Holler Heimatmuseum, Holle 17823
Hollola Local History Museum, Hollola 09551
Hollolan Kotiseutumuseo, Hollola 09551
Hollufgård - Arkeologi og Landskab, Odense 09013
Hollycombe Steam Collection, Liphook 39509
Hollytrees Museum, Colchester 38611
Hollywood Bowl Museum, Los Angeles 44907
Hollywood Guinness World of Records Museum, Los Angeles 44908
Hollywood Heritage Museum, Los Angeles 44909
Hollywood Wax Museum, Los Angeles 44910
Holmes County Historical Society Museum, Millersburg 45346
Holmestova, Frekhaug 30505
Holmestrand Museum, Holmestrand 30554
Holmgrens Volkswagenmuseum, Pålsboda 36155
Holmöns Båtmuseum, Holmön 35961
Holmsbu Billedgalleri, Holmsbu 30556
Holocaust Documentation and Education Center, North Miami 45996
Holocaust Memorial Center of Central Florida, Maitland 45078
Holocaust Museum, Chełmno 31524
Holocaust Museum Houston, Houston 44122
Holocaust Museum of Treblinka, Kosów Lacki 31677
Hølonda Skimuseum of Bygdasamling, Gåsbakken 30509
Holowood - Holographiemuseum Bamberg, Bamberg 15809
Holst Birthplace Museum, Cheltenham 38545
Holstebro Kunstmuseum, Holstebro 08889
Holstebro Museum, Holstebro 08890
Holstentor-Museum, Lübeck 18536

Holsworthy Museum, Holsworthy 39255
Holt Skolemuseum, Tvedestrand 30951
Holter Museum of Art, Helena 43983
The Holtzman Art Gallery, Towson 48047
Holy Defense Museum, Kerman 22251
Holyhead Maritime Museum, Holyhead 39257
Holyland Exhibition, Los Angeles 44911
Holzgerätemuseum, Schlüchtern 19805
Holzknechtmuseum im Salzkammergut, Bad Goisern 01701
Holzknechtmuseum Ruhpolding, Ruhpolding 19716
Holzknechtmuseum Trübenbach im Naturpark Ötscher-Tormäuer, Wienerbruck 03023
Holzschnitt-Museum Klaus Herzer, Mössingen 18781
Holztechnisches Museum, Rosenheim 19650
Holztriftanlage Mendlingtal, Göstling an der Ybbs 01901
Holzwurm-Museum, Quedlinburg 19461
Home Knowledge Museum, Nové Zámky 34039
Home of Franklin D. Roosevelt, Hyde Park 44188
Home of History, Rotterdam 29753
Home of Stone, Dodge City 42955
Home Sweet Home Museum, East Hampton 43047
Homer Watson House and Gallery, Kitchener 05696
Homerville Museum, Homer 44069
Homestead Antique Museum, Drumheller 05341
Homestead Museum, Biggar 05080
Homestead National Monument of America, Beatrice 41556
Homestead Park Pioneer Museum, Port Augusta 01379
Homewood House Museum, Baltimore 41470
Homma Museum of Art, Sakata 26703
Homolovi Ruins State Park, Winslow 48697
Homs Museum, Homs 37440
Honarhaye Moaser Tehran, Teheran 22303
Honarhaye Tazini - Rakibkhaneh, Isfahan 22246
Honda Collection Hall, Suzuka 26780
Honda Museum, Kanazawa 26305
Hondenmuseum, Eindhoven 29212
Honeybee Science Center, Tokyo 26858
Honeywood Heritage Centre, London 39667
Hong-ik University Museum, Seoul 27238
Hong Kong Heritage Museum, Hong Kong 07095
Hong Kong Museum of Art, Hong Kong 07096
Hong Kong Museum of History, Hong Kong 07097
The Hong Kong Racing Museum, Hong Kong 07098
Hong Kong Railway Museum, Hong Kong 07099
Hong Kong Science Museum, Hong Kong 07100
Hong Kong Space Museum, Hong Kong 07101
Hong Kong Visual Arts Centre, Hong Kong 07102
Hong Quang Museum, Hong-Gai 48995
Hongsan Museum, Seoul 27239
Honolulu Academy of Arts Museum, Honolulu 44079
Honolulu House Museum, Marshall 45178
Honouring Hall of Juárez, Guelatao de Juárez 27980
Hontza Natur Zientzien Museoa, Durango 34781
Hoo-Hoo International Forestry Museum, Gurdon 43854
Hood Museum of Art, Hanover 43907
Hood River County Historical Museum, Hood River 44095
Hooge Crater Museum, Zillebeke 03851
Hoosier Salon Gallery, Indianapolis 44221
Hooton Park Exhibition Centre, Ellesmere Port 38927
Hoover Historical Center, North Canton 45986
Hop Farm, Paddock Wood 40155
Hope Cottage, Kingscote 01149
Hope Historical Society Museum, Hope 44097
Hope Lodge and Mather Mill, Fort Washington 43473
Hope Museum, Hope 05603
Hope Water Powered Saw Mill, Peterborough 06118
Hopetoun House, South Queensferry 40535
Hopewell Culture National Historic Park, Chillicothe 42379
Hopewell Furnace National Historic Site, Elverson 43174
Hopewell Museum, Hopewell 44098
Hopewell Museum, Paris 46285
Hopfen Erlebnis Hof, Altmannstein 15461
Hopi Cultural Museum, Second Mesa 47553
Hôpital Notre-Dame de la Rose, Lessines 03561
Hopmuseum De Stadsschaal, Poperinge 03687
Hopp Ferenc Kelet-Ázsiai Müvészeti Múzeum, Budapest 21344
Hopsewee Plantation, Georgetown 43653
Horace Greeley House, Chappaqua 42197
Horácka Galerie, Nové Město na Moravě 08502
Horácké Muzeum, Nové Město na Moravě 08503
Horaiji-san Shizenkagaku Hakubutsukan, Hourai 26233
Horatio Colony House Museum, Keene 44426
Hordamuseet, Fana 30485
Horehronské Múzeum, Brezno 33982
Horim Museum, Seoul 27240
Horizons Unlimited Supplementary Educational Center, Salisbury 47219
Hornby Museum, Hornby 44104
Hornické Muzeum OKD, Ostrava 08525
Hornické Muzeum Příbram, Příbram 08625
Hornický Skanzen důl Mayrau, Vinařice u Kladna 08719
Horniman Museum, London 39668
Hornsbury Mill, Chard 38524
Hornsea Museum of Village Life, Hornsea 39261
Horog Historical and Regional Museum, Chorog 37444
Horology Museum, Šternberk 08662
Hororata Historic Museum, Darfield 30140
Horry County Museum, Conway 42613
Horse-Breeding Museum, Moskva 33118
Horsemanship Museum of Takekoma Shrine, Natori 26591
Horsens Kunstmuseum, Horsens 08897
Horsens Museum, Horsens 08898
Horsens Museum of Modern Art, Horsens 08897
Horseshoe Bend National Military Park, Daviston 42796
Horsforth Village Museum, Leeds 39446
Horsham Arts Centre, Horsham 39264
Horsham Historical Museum, Horsham 01109
Horsham Museum, Horsham 39265
Horsham Regional Art Gallery, Horsham 01110
Hørsholm Egns Museum, Hørsholm 08900
Horst-Janssen-Museum, Oldenburg, Oldenburg 19254
Horster Motorrad-Museum, Gelsenkirchen 17227
Horta-Lambeaux Pavilion, Bruxelles 03285
Horten Bilmuseum, Horten 30564
Hortobágyi Pásztormúzeum, Hortobágy 21433
Horyuji Daihozoden Treasure Museum, Ikoma 26240
Horyuji Kondo Hekiga Mosha Tenjikan, Nagakute 26525
Horyuji Temple, Ikoma 26240
Hoskins House, Burlington 42006
Hospital and Medical Care Museum, Deventer 29147
Hospital de los Venerables, Sevilla 35476
Hospital Museum, Jyväskylä 09602
Hospital Museum, Kellokoski 09647
Hospital Museum, Lahti 09749
Hospital Museum, Turku 10123
Hospital-Santuario de Nuestra Señora de la Caridad, Illescas 34916
Hospitals and Clinics Medical Museum, Iowa City 44245
Hospitalsmuseet, Vadstena 36367
Hosyokan Byodoin Museum, Uji, Kyoto 26989
Hotel and Restaurant Museum, Helsinki 09496
Hotel de Paris Museum, Georgetown 43649
Hôtel Groslot, Orléans 13429
Hotel-Museum Arthur Merghelynck, Ieper 03514
Hotelli- ja Ravintolamuseo, Helsinki 09496
Hotelmuseum, Flims Waldhaus 36703
Hotmuseum, Filzmoos 01837
Hotoko Ninomiya Jinja Homotsuden, Odawara 26612
Hou Wang Chinese Temple and Museum, Atherton 00754
Houdini Museum, Scranton 47518
Houghton County Historical Museum Society, Lake Linden 44590
Houghton Hall Soldier Museum, Houghton 39267
Housatonic Museum of Art, Bridgeport 41891
House in the Horseshoe, Sanford 47395
House Mill, London 39669
House Museum and Memorial House of Yordan Yovkov, Dobrič 04656
House-Museum f the conductor N.S. Golovanov, Moskva 33122
House Museum of Karl Ristikivi, Tartu 09380
House Museum of Oskar Luts, Tartu 09381
House-Museum of the Academician E.N. Pavlovsky, Borisoglebsk 32699
House-Museum of the Decembrists, Kurgan 32970
House-Museum of the Hannibal Family, Puškinskie Gory 33342
House Museum of the History of Youth Movement, Rjazan 33349
House-Museum of the Lopatin Family, Stavropol 33560
House-Museum of the Nevsorovy Sisters, Nižnij Novgorod 33205
House-Museum of the Painter V.A. Igoshev, Chanty-Mansijsk 32741
House-Museum of the Poet Shirjaevts - Museum of Farmers' Life, Žigulevsk 33748
House-Museum of the Sukhanov Family, Vladivostok 33694
House-Museum of the Tsvetaeva Family, Novo-Talicy 33231
House-Museum of V. Veresaev, Tula 33623
House-Museum Peter the Great, Vologda 33721
House-Museum Rayna Knyaginya, Panagjurište 04751
House of a Thousand Dolls, Loma 44847
House of Arts, South Moravian Museum, Znojmo 08755
House of Bottles, Kinglake 01148
House of Bottles and Bottle Museum, Tewantin 01525
House of Cards, Hämeenlinna 09452
House of Dun, Montrose 39981
House of Hadjigeorgakis Kornesios, Lefkosia 08201
House of History, Malone 45085
House of Humour and Satire, Gabrovo 04667
House of International Dolls, Fredericton 05462
The House of Lords, Dublin 22431
House of Manannan, Peel 40167
House of Memories, Latchford 05731
House of Memories Museum, Wilson 48667
House of Music-Parma, Parma 24800
House of Nobility, Stockholm 36276
House of Roses, Deadwood 42821
House of Straw, Bengtsfors 35830
House of Technology, Luleå 36055
House of the Binns, Linlithgow 39506
House of the Martyrs Museum, La Habana 07945
House of the Redtails Gallery, Tucson 48089
House of the Scribe, Almog 22569
The House of the Seven Gables, Salem 47195
House of the Templarknights, Caudebec-en-Caux 11087
House of Wickersham, Juneau 44369
House on Crutches Museum, Bishop's Castle 38238
House on the Hill Museums Adventure, Stansted Mountfitchet 40578
The House on the Rock, Spring Green 47730
Houseboatmuseum, Amsterdam 28916
Household Cavalry Museum, Windsor 40901
Housesteads Roman Fort and Museum, Hexham 39238
Houston Fire Museum, Houston 44123
Houston Harte University Center, San Angelo 47241
Houston Museum of Decorative Arts, Chattanooga 42262
Houston Museum of Natural Science, Houston 44124
Houston Police Museum, Houston 44125
Høvåg Museum, Høvåg 30569
Hovden Jernvinnemuseum, Bykle 30456
Hove Museum and Art Gallery, Hove 39269
Hovercraft Museum, Gosport 39100
Howard B. Owens Science Center, Lanham-Seabrook 44639
Howard County Center of African American Culture, Columbia 42549
Howard County Historical Museum, Kokomo 44527
Howard County Historical Society Museum, Ellicott City 43158
Howard-Dickinson House Museum, Henderson 43993
Howard Gardens Gallery, Cardiff 38479
Howard House of Artifacts, Old Perlican 06048
Howard Steamboat Museum, Jeffersonville 44330
Howard University Gallery of Art, Washington 48362
Howard University Museum, Washington 48363
Howard W. Cannon Aviation Museum, Henderson 43991
Howell Harris Museum, Brecon 38317
Howell Historical Society & Committee Museum, Howell 44139
Howell Living History Farm, Titusville 48012
Howick Historical Village, Pakuranga 30228
Howick Museum, Howick 34264
Howland House, Plymouth 46559
Hoxie Gallery, Westerly 48552
Hoyt Institute of Fine Arts, New Castle 45686
Hoyt Sherman Place, Des Moines 42906
Hozat Culture Center, Hozat 37688
Hozat Kültür Merkezi, Hozat 37688
H.R. MacMillan Space Centre, Vancouver 06680
Hrad Roštejn, Telč 08675
Hrdlička's Museum of Man, Praha 08581
Hrdličkovo Muzeum Člověka, Praha 08581
Hristo Smirenski Memorial House, Sofia 04829
Hrvatski Muzej Naivne Umjetnosti, Zagreb 07819
Hrvatski Muzej Pošte i Telekomunikacija, Zagreb 07820
Hrvatski Nacionalni Komitet ICOM, Zagreb 49124
Hrvatski Narodni Zoološki Muzej, Zagreb 07821
Hrvatski Povijesni Muzej, Zagreb 07822
Hrvatski Prirodoslovni Muzej, Zagreb 07823
Hrvatski Školski Muzej, Zagreb 07824
Hrvatski Sportski Muzej, Zagreb 07825
Hrvatsko Muzejsko Društvo, Zagreb 49125
HTS-Museum, Rødovre 09035
Huanghe Museum, Zhengzhou 07328
Huangshan City Museum, Huangshan 07116
Huangshi Municipal Museum, Huangshi 07117
Huanki Cultural Centre, Alofi 30365
HUB Robeson Galleries, University Park 48153
Hubbard Museum of the American West, Ruidoso Downs 47029
Hubbardton Battlefield Museum, Hubbardton 44141
Hubbell Trading Post, Ganado 43616
Huberte Goote Gallery, Zug 37425
Hubschraubermuseum, Bückeburg 16393
Huddersfield Art Gallery, Huddersfield 39272
Huddleston Farmhouse Inn Museum, Cambridge City 42056
Hudetz-Turm, Wiesent 20580
Hudiksvalls Bruksminnen, Hudiksvall 35966
Hudobná Expozícia - Rodný Dom J.N. Hummela, Bratislava 33965
Hudobné Múzeum, Bratislava 33966
Hudson Bay Museum, Hudson Bay 05606
Hudson Museum, Orono 46195
Hudson River Maritime Museum, Kingston 44493
Hudson River Museum of Westchester, Yonkers 48785
Hudson Valley Children's Museum, Nanuet 45599
Hudson's Hope Museum, Hudson's Hope 05607
Huebmer-Gedächtnisstätte, Naßwald 02337
Hülser Heimatstuben, Krefeld 18226
Huerta de San Vicente, Granada 34870
Hürten-Heimatmuseum, Bad Münstereifel 15697
Hütten- und Technikmuseum Ilsenburg, Ilsenburg 17892
Hüttenberger Heimatmuseum, Linden, Hessen 18478
Hüttenmuseum Thale, Thale 20166
Hufschmiede Museum Frehrking, Neustadt am Rübenberge 19068
Hufschmiedemuseum, Engelhartszell 01816
Hufthamartunet, Storebø 30901
Hugenotten-Museum, Berlin 16002
Hugenotten-Museum und Heimatmuseum, Stutensee 20083
The Hugh Lane Municipal Gallery of Modern Art, Dublin 22432
Hugh Miller's Cottage, Cromarty 38671
Hughenden Manor, High Wycombe 39240
Hughes Fine Arts Center, Grand Forks 43742
Hugo Thimig-Gedenkraum, Wien 02898
Hugo Wolf-Haus, Perchtoldsdorf 02400
Huguenot Historical Society Museum, New Paltz 45740
Huguenot Memorial Museum, Franschhoek 34242
Huhehot City Museum, Huhehot 07118
Hui No'eau Visual Arts Center, Makawao 45081
Huichang County Museum, Huichang 07120
't Huijs Dever, Lisse 29542
Huis de Lalaing, Oudenaarde 03676
Huis Hellemans, Edegem 03401
Huis Marseille, Amsterdam 28861
Huis Singraven, Denekamp 29138
Het Huis van Alijn, Gent 03439
Het Huis Van Alijn, Tournai 03788
Huis Verwolde, Laren, Gelderland 29497
Huis Zypendaal, Arnhem 28938
Huittisten Museo, Huittinen 09552
Huize Betje Wolff, Middenbeemster 29599
Huize Keizer, Denekamp 29139
Huize Nijenstede, Hardenberg 29341
Huizer Klederdrachtmuseum, Huizen 29455
Huizer Museum Het Schoutenhuis, Huizen 29456
Huldigungssaal und Rathaus, Goslar 17351
Huldreheimen, Bykle 30457
Huleh Valley Regional Prehistoric Museum, Kibbutz Maayan Baruch 22696
Hulihee Palace, Kailua-Kona 44374
Hull and East Riding Museum, Kingston-upon-Hull 39379
Hull Lifesaving Museum, Hull 44149
Hull Maritime Museum, Kingston-upon-Hull 39380
Hull University Art Collection, Kingston-upon-Hull 39381
Hulsey Gallery, Oklahoma City 46112
Huludao City Museum, Huludao 07121
Humačka Arheološko Zbirka, Ljubuški 03916
Human Science Museum, Tokai University, Shimizu 26749
Humber-Bay of Islands Museum, Corner Brook 05273
Humber Estuary Discovery Centre, Cleethorpes 38588
Humbert Collection, Münster 18939
Humboldt and District Museum and Gallery, Humboldt 05608
Humboldt County Historical Association Museum, Dakota City 42740
Humboldt County Historical Association Museum, Humboldt 44150
Humboldt County Old Settler's Museum, Livermore 44829
Humboldt Historical Museum, Humboldt 44151
Humboldt-Museum Schloß Tegel, Berlin 16003
Humboldt State University Natural History Museum, Arcata 41246
Humpback Rocks Mountain Farm Visitor Center, Waynesboro 48483
Humphrey Forum, Minneapolis 45385
Hunan Provincial Museum, Changsha 07010
Hunan Revolutionary Cemetery, Changsha 07011
Hundemuseum, Berlin 16004
Hundsmarktmühle, Thalgau 02726
Hung-Yen Museum, Hung-Yen 48996
Hungarian Chemical Museum, Várpalota 21604
Hungarian Folk-Art Museum, Port Orange 46601
Hungarian Museum of Architecture, Budapest 21356
Hungarian Museum of Commerce and Catering Trade, Budapest 21358
Hungarian Museum of Electrical Engineering, Budapest 21355
Hungarian Museum of Naive Arts, Kecskemét 21451
Hungarian Museum of Water Administration and Environmental Protection, Esztergom 21413
Hungarian National Gallery, Budapest 21360
Hungarian National Museum, Budapest 21361
Hungarian Natural History Museum, Budapest 21362
Hungarian Open Air Museum, Szentendre 21575
Hungarian Orthodoxy Museum, Miskolc 21478
Hungarian Theatre Museum and Institute, Budapest 21375
Hungary-German Museum, Tata 21594
Hunsrück-Museum, Simmern, Hunsrück 19961
Hunt Gallery, Staunton 47796
Hunt Institute for Botanical Documentation, Pittsburgh 46518
Hunt-Morgan House, Lexington 44739
The Hunt Museum, Limerick 22505
Hunter College Art Galleries, New York 45816
Hunter-Dawson State Historic Site, New Madrid 45715
Hunter House, East Kilbride 38844
Hunter Museum of American Art, Chattanooga 42263
Hunter Valley Museum of Rural Life, Scone 01444
Hunter West Gallery, Peterborough 06119
Hunterdon Museum of Art, Clinton 42497
Hunterian Art Gallery, Glasgow 39050
Hunterian Museum, Glasgow 39051
Hunterian Museum, London 39670
Hunterian Museum, Zoology Section, Glasgow 39052
Hunters Hill Historical Museum, Sydney 01496
Hunting Museum of Finland, Riihimäki 09996
Huntingdon County Museum, Huntingdon 44153
Huntington Art Collections, San Marino 47366
Huntington Beach Art Center, Huntington Beach 44168
Huntington Beach International Surfing Museum, Huntington Beach 44169
Huntington County Historical Society Museum, Huntington 44157

Huntington Historical Society Museum, Huntington 44162
Huntington Museum of Art, Huntington 44165
Huntington Railroad Museum, Huntington 44166
Huntly and Districts Historical Museum, Huntly 01112
Huntly House Museum, Edinburgh 38889
Huntsville Museum of Art, Huntsville 44174
Huon Valley Apple and Heritage Museum, Huonville 01113
Hurdal Bygdetun, Hurdal 30573
Hurley Patentee Manor, Hurley 44177
Huron City Museums, Port Austin 46591
Huron County Museum, Goderich 05497
Huronia Museum, Midland 05846
Hurricane Valley Heritage Park Museum, Hurricane 44181
Hurtigrutemuseet, Stokmarknes 30898
Hurworth Cottage, New Plymouth 30214
Hus-Museum, Konstanz 18203
Husarmuseum, Eksjö 35862
Húsavík Museum, Húsavík 21640
Huseby Bruk, Grimslöv 35930
Húsipari Múzeum, Budapest 21345
Husitské Muzeum v Táboře, Tábor 08673
Huskvarna Stadsmuseum, Huskvarna 35969
Hussite Museum in Tabor, Tábor 08673
Hussite Museum - Weis' House, Veselí nad Lužnicí 08716
Husslik-Heimatmuseum, Pöls 02432
Hutchinson County Museum, Borger 41794
Hutchinson House Museum, Waupaca 48461
Huttermuseum, Erdweg 16892
Huygens Museum Hofwijck, Voorburg 29961
Hvar Heritage Museum, Hvar 07707
Hvitträsk, Kirkkonummi 09673
Hwa Kang Museum, Taipei 07347
Hwajeong Museum, Seoul 27241
Hyde Art Gallery, El Cajon 43104
Hyde Collection Art Museum, Glens Falls 43693
Hyde Hall, East Springfield 43060
Hyde Park Art Center, Chicago 42333
Hyde Park Barracks Museum, Sydney 01497
Hyderabad Museum, Hyderabad 31020
Hydro Industripark-Museum, Porsgrunn 30779
Hydrobiological Museum, Alexandria 09239
Hyeonchungsa Shrine, Asan 27131
Hylténs Industrimuseum, Gnosjö 35907
Hyman and Sons General Store, Gaspé 05477
Hymers Museum, Kakabeka Falls 05637
Hyogo Ceramics Museum, Kobe 26346
Hyogo-ken Togeikan, Kobe 26346
Hyogo-kenritsu Bijutsukan, Kobe 26347
Hyogo-kenritsu Rekishi Hakubutsukan, Himeji 26196
Hyogo Prefectural Museum of Art, Kobe 26347
Hyogo Prefectural Museum of History, Himeji 26196
Hypocaust, Saint Albans 40371
Hyrax Hill Museum, Hyrax Hill 27102
Hythe Local History Room, Hythe, Kent 39283
The Ian Potter Art Museum, Melbourne 01233
Iaşi Natural History Museum, Iaşi 32534
Ibara Municipal Denchu Art Museum, Ibara 26234
Ibaraki Daigaku Izura Bijutsu Bunka Kenkyujo, Kitaibaraki 26340
Ibaraki-ken Kindai Bijutsukan, Mito 26500
Ibaraki-ken Rekishikan, Mito 26501
Ibaraki Museum of Modern Art, Mito 26500
Ibaraki Prefectural History Museum, Mito 26501
Ibaraki University Izura Institut of Arts and Culture, Kitaibaraki 26340
IBRA Collection, Cardiff 38480
Ibrahim Hussein Foundation Museum, Pulau Langkawi 27680
Ibresinskij Ėtnografičeskij Muzej pod Otkryrym Nebom, Ibresi 32810
Ibsen-museet, Oslo 30737
Ibsenhuset og Grimstad Bymuseet, Grimstad 30519
ICAMT International Committee for Architecture and Museums Techniques, Helsinki 49155
ICDAD International Committee for Decorative Arts and Design Museums, Wien 49054
Icebreaker Angara, Irkutsk 32819
Icebreaker Baykal, Angarsk 32643
Icelandic Institute of Natural History, Reykjavík 21658
Icelandic Institute of Natural History, Akureyri Division, Akureyri 21621
Icelandic Maritime Museum, Hafnarfjörður 21637
Icelandic Museums Association, Patreksfjörður 49232
Icelandic Postal Museum, Hafnarfjörður 21636
Iceni Village and Museums, Cockley Cley 38606
ICFA International Committee for Fine Art Museums, Ottawa 49099
Ichijo-ji Treasure House, Kasai 26314
Ichikawa Municipal Museum, Ichikawa 26236
Ickworth House, Horringer 39262
ICLM International Committee for Literary Museums, Paradis 49316
ICMAH International Committee for Archaeology and History Museums, Caen 49188
ICMS International Committee for Museums Security, Los Angeles 49487
ICOFOM International Committee for Museology, München 49200
ICOM Angola, Luanda 49042
ICOM Arab, Giza 49148
ICOM Argentina, Buenos Aires 49045
ICOM Asia-Pacific Organization, Belconnen 49050
ICOM Australia, Subiaco 49051
ICOM Azerbaijan, Baku 49061
ICOM Bangladesh, Dhaka 49062
ICOM Barbados, Saint Michael 49063
ICOM - Belgian National Comittee, Hornu 49073
ICOM Bénin, Porto-Novo 49077
ICOM Bolivia, La Paz 49078
ICOM Bosnia-Hercegovina, Sarajevo 49079
ICOM Botswana, Gaborone 49080
ICOM Bulgaria, Sofia 49085
ICOM Burkina Faso, Ouagadougou 49086
ICOM Burundi, Bujumbura 49087
ICOM Cambodia, Phnom Penh 49088
ICOM Cameroon, Yaoundé 49089
ICOM Canada, Ottawa 49100
ICOM Chile, Santiago de Chile 49110
ICOM Chinese National Committee, Beijing 49113
ICOM Comitato Nazionale Italiano, Milano 49252
ICOM Comité Haïtien, Port-au-Prince 49228
ICOM Comité National du Niger, Niamey 49311
ICOM - Comité National Monégasque du Conseil International des Musées, Monaco 49295
ICOM Comité Sénégalais, Dakar 49349
ICOM Comores, Moroni 49117
ICOM Costa Rica, San José 49121
ICOM Côté d'Ivoire, Grand Bassam 49123
ICOM Cuba, La Habana 49127
ICOM Cyprus, Lefkosia 49129
ICOM du Tchad, N'Djamena 49108
ICOM Ecuador, Guayaquil 49147
ICOM Egypt, Cairo 49149
ICOM Estonia, Tallinn 49153
ICOM Finland, Helsinki 49156
ICOM F.Y.R. Macedonia, Skopje 49283
ICOM Grèce, Athinai 49223
ICOM Guatemala, Guatemala 49227
ICOM Hungary, Budapest 49229
ICOM Iceland, Garðabaer 49233
ICOM India, Kolkata 49238
ICOM International Council of Museums, Deutsches Nationalkomitee, Berlin 49201
ICOM Iran, Teheran 49242
ICOM Ireland, Dublin 49243
ICOM Jamaica, Kingston 49255
ICOM Jordan, Amman 49260
ICOM Kazakhstan, Almaty 49261
ICOM Kenya, Nairobi 49262
ICOM Korea, Seoul 49268
ICOM Kyrgyzstan, Biškek 49272
ICOM Lao, Vientiane 49273
ICOM Latin America and the Caribbean Regional Organization, San Jose 49122
ICOM Latvijas Nacionālā Komiteja, Tukums 49274
ICOM Liban, Beirut 49278
ICOM Libyan Arab Jamahiriya, Tripoli 49279
ICOM Lietuva, Vilnius 49280
ICOM Lithuania, Vilnius 49280
ICOM Luxembourg, Luxembourg 49282
ICOM Madagascar, Antananarivo 49285
ICOM Malaysia, Kuala Lumpur 49286
ICOM Mali, Bamako 49288
ICOM Maroc, Rabat 49297
ICOM Mauritanie, Nouakchott 49291
ICOM Mauritius, Port Louis 49292
ICOM México, México 49294
ICOM Mongolia, Ulaanbaatar 49296
ICOM Nacionalni Komitet Serbia-Montenegro, Beograd 49351
ICOM Namibia, Windhoek 49298
ICOM National Commitee of Belarus, Minsk 49065
ICOM Nepal, Kathmandu 49300
ICOM Netherlands, Amsterdam 49302
ICOM New Zealand, Rotorua 49308
ICOM Nigeria, Calabar 49312
ICOM Northern Ireland, Belfast 49418
ICOM Österreichisches Nationalkomitee, Wien 49055
ICOM Oman, Muscat 49325
ICOM Panamá, Panamá City 49328
ICOM Paraguay, Asunción 49330
ICOM Peru, Lima 49331
ICOM Philippines, Manila 49332
ICOM Poland, Poznań 49334
ICOM Portugal, Lisboa 49340
ICOM Qatar, Doha 49342
ICOM Regional Organization for West Africa, Bamako 49289
ICOM República Dominicaine, Santo Domingo 49146
ICOM Republique Congo, Brazzaville 49120
ICOM République Democratique du Congo, Kinshasa 49118
ICOM Romania, Ploieşti 49344
ICOM Schweiz, Zürich 49386
ICOM Seychelles, Victoria 49356
ICOM Singapore, Singapore 49357
ICOM Slovakia, Bratislava 49358
ICOM Slovenia, Ljubljana 49360
ICOM South Africa, Johannesburg 49365
ICOM Spain, Madrid 49375
ICOM Sri Lanka, Colombo 49377
ICOM Swaziland, Lobamba 49378
ICOM Sweden, Stockholm 49379
ICOM Tanzania, Dar-es-Salaam 49389
ICOM Thailand, Pathumthani 49390
ICOM Togo, Lomé 49392
ICOM Tunisia, Tunis 49393
ICOM Turkish National Committee, Ulus 49394
ICOM Ukraine, Lviv 49395
ICOM Uruguay, Montevideo 49458
ICOM Uzbekistan, Taškent 49545
ICOM Venezuela, Caracas 49546
ICOM Viet Nam, Ha Noi 49547
ICOM Zambia, Livingstone 49548
ICOM Zimbabwe, Bulawayo 49549
ICOMAC Regional Organization for Central Africa, Kinshasa 49119
ICOMAM International Committee of Museums and Collections of Arms and Military History, Delft 49303
Icon Museum, Girne 08222
Icon Museum of Iskele, İskele 08230
Iconografisch Bureau, Den Haag 29098
ICR International Committee for Regional Museums, Ljubljana 49361
ID Galerie, Helmond 29395
Ida Aalbergin Lapsuudenkoti, Leppäkoski 09778
Ida Aalberg's CXhildhood Home, Leppäkoski 09778
Ida Green Gallery, Sherman 47603
Idaho Association of Museums, Boise 49488
Idaho Museum of Mining and Geology, Boise 41773
Idaho Museum of Natural History, Pocatello 46571
Idaho State Historical Museum, Boise 41774
Idemitsu Bijutsukan, Tokyo 26859
Idemitsu Museum of Arts, Tokyo 26859
Idnakar - Historical and Cultural Museum-Preserve, Glazov 32806
Idojiri Archaeological Museum, Fujimi 26138
Idojiri Kokokan, Fujimi 26138
Idrija Municipal Museum, Idrija 34091
Idrottsmuseet, Malmö 36073
Idstedt-Gedächtnishalle, Idstedt 17881
I.E. Repin House-Museum, Žigulevsk 33747
I.E. Repin Museum-Estate, Repino 33347
ifa-Galerie Berlin, Berlin 16005
ifa-Galerie Bonn, Bonn 16239
ifa-Galerie Stuttgart, Stuttgart 20097
Ifield Watermill, Crawley 38660
Iga Art and Industry Institute, Ueno 26986
Iga-Ryu Ninja Yashiki, Ueno 26987
Igarskij Kraevedčeskij Kompleks Muzej Večnoj Merzloty, Igarka 32811
Iggesunds Bruksmuseum, Iggesund 35971
Iglesia ni Cristo Museum and Gallery, Quezon City 31433
Ignace Heritage Centre, Ignace 05612
Ignaz J. Pleyel Museum, Großweikersdorf 01964
Igor Talkov Museum, Moskva 33105
Ii Art Museum, Hikone 26194
Iida City and Art Museum, Iida 26237
Iida-shi Bijutsu Hakubutsukan, Iida 26237
Iisakin Jussin Tupa, Kauhava 09638
Iisakin Jussi's Cabin, Kauhava 09638
Iisaku Muuseum, Iisaku 09325
Iittala Glass Museum, Iittala 09559
Iittalan Tehtaan Museo, Iittala 09559
IJzertoren-Museum Oorlog-Vrede-Vlaamse Ontvoogding, Diksmuide 03388
Ike Taiga Museum of Art, Kyoto 26404
Ikeda 20-seiki Bijutsukan, Ito 26263
Ikeda Museum of 20th Century Art, Ito 26263
Ikomayama Uchu Kagakukan, Ikoma 26241
Ikon Gallery, Birmingham 38222
Ikonen-Museum, Recklinghausen 19512
Ikonen-Museum der Stadt Frankfurt am Main, Frankfurt am Main 17056
Ikonenmuseum, Autenried 15580
Ikonenmuseum Schloß Autenried, Ichenhausen 17878
Ikuno Kobutsukan, Ikuno, Hyogo 26242
Ikuno Mineral Museum, Ikuno, Hyogo 26242
Il Mauriziano, Reggio Emilia 25095
Ilana Goor Museum, Tel Aviv 22758
Ilchester Museum, Ilchester 39284
Ilfracombe Museum, Ilfracombe 01117
Ilfracombe Museum, Ilfracombe 39285
Ilias Lalaounis Jewelry Museum, Athinai 20867
Iligan Museum, Iligan 31328
Ilijanum Museum of Naive Art, Sid 33905
Ilja Čavčavadze Memorial Museum, Tbilisi 15363
Illawarra Museum, Wollongong 01609
Illingworth Kerr Gallery, Calgary 05169
Illinois and Michigan Canal Museum, Lockport 44840
Illinois Art Gallery, Chicago 42334
Illinois Artisans and Visitors Centers, Whittington 48598
Illinois Association of Museums, Springfield 49489
Illinois Citizen Soldier Museum, Galesburg 43599
Illinois Railway Museum, Union 48139
Illinois State Museum, Springfield 47737
Illusoria-Land, Ittigen 36818
Ilmajoen Museo, Ilmajoki 09561
Ilmajoki Museum, Ilmajoki 09561
Ilmatorjuntamuseo, Tuusula 10144
Ilmavoimien Viestikoulun Perinnehuone, Tikkakoski 10105
Ilocaniana Cultural Museum, Magsingal 31349
Iloniemen Pajamuseo, Kuusjoki 09734
Ilulissat Katersugaasiviat, Ilulissat 21229
Ilulissat Town Museum, Ilulissat 21229
Ilwaco Heritage Museum, Ilwaco 44196
Ilyo Voivoda House-Museum, Kjustendil 04707
Im Kinsky-Museum, Wien 02899
Imabari City Kono Shiniichi Memorial Culture Hall, Imabari 26244
Imagina-Museo Interactivo Puebla, Puebla 28316
The Imaginarium, Anchorage 41200
Imaginarium Hands-On Museum, Fort Myers 43437
Imagination Station Science Museum, Wilson 48669
Imagisphere Children's Museum, North Richland Hills 46005
Imaizumi Museum, Shiozawa 26759
Imari Municipal Folk History Museum, Imari 26245
Imari-shi Rekishi Minzoku Shiryokan, Imari 26245
Imatra Art Gallery, Imatra 09564
Imatra Museum of Cultural History, Imatra 09563
Imatran Kulttuurihistoriallinen Kaupunginmuseo, Imatra 09563
Imatran Taidemuseo, Imatra 09564
Imhoff Art Gallery, Saint Walburg 06379
Imhoff-Stollwerck-Museum, Köln 18144
Imker- und Heimatmuseum, Wassertrüdingen 20412
Imkereiausstellung Einst-Jetzt, Reidling 02501
Imkereigeschichtliche und bienenkundliche Sammlungen, Celle 16455
Imkereimuseum, Pöggstall 02426
Imkereimuseum, Pramet 02448
Imkereimuseum Grüningen, Wetzikon 37312
Imkerijmuseum Poppendamme, Grijpskerke 29301
Immigrant City Historical Museum of Lawrence and its People, Lawrence 44689
Immigrant-institutets Museum, Borås 35842
Immigration Museum, Melbourne 01234
Immingham Museum, Immingham 39289
Imogene Herbert Historical Museum, Manistique 45113
Imperato Collection of West African Artifacts, Chanute 42192
Imperial and District Museum, Imperial 05614
Imperial Calcasieu Museum, Lake Charles 44582
Imperial Stables, Praha 08569
Imperial War Museum, London 39671
Imperial War Museum Duxford, Cambridge 38456
Imperial War Museum North, Manchester 39890
Impossible Microworld Museum, Bath 38116
Impressions Gallery of Photography, York 40963
Imura Art Museum, Kyoto 26405
In Buri National Museum, Sing Buri 37536
In de Gecroonde Duijvekater, Zaandam 30033
In de Zevende Hemel, Apeldoorn 28925
In Flanders Fields Museum, Ieper 03515
I.N. Kramskoy House-Museum, Ostrogožsk 33275
inatura- Erlebnis Naturschau Dornbirn, Dornbirn 01769
Inazawa City Oguiss Memorial Art Museum, Inazawa 26248
Incheon Metroploitan City Museum, Incheon 27191
Independence Hall, Tel Aviv 22759
Independence Hall of Korea, Cheonan 27146
Independence Historical Museum, Independence 44198
Independence National Historical Park, Philadelphia 46418
Independence Seaport Museum, Philadelphia 46419
Independence Visitors Center, Independence 44204
Inderøy Museums- og Historielag, Inderøy 30576
India Arts Museum, Chennai 21745
Indian Arts Research Center, Santa Fe 47420
Indian Association for the Study of Conservation of Cultural Property, Delhi 49239
Indian Center Museum, Wichita 48603
Indian City U.S.A., Anadarko 41191
Indian Head Museum, Indian Head 05616
Indian Hill Historical Society Museum, Cincinnati 42408
Indian King Tavern Museum, Haddonfield 43861
Indian Mill Museum State Memorial, Upper Sandusky 48160
Indian Museum, Kolkata 21905
Indian Museum, Lemmer 29535
Indian Museum of Lake County-Ohio, Painesville 46262
Indian Museum of North America, Crazy Horse 42694
Indian Museum of the Carolinas, Laurinburg 44682
Indian Pueblo Cultural Center, Albuquerque 41101
Indian Springs State Park Museum, Flovilla 43351
Indian Temple Mound Museum, Fort Walton Beach 43467
Indian War Memorial Museum, Delhi 21771
Indiana Basketball Hall of Fame, New Castle 45685
Indiana Historical Society Museum, Indianapolis 44222
Indiana Medical History Museum, Indianapolis 44223
Indiana State Museum, Indianapolis 44224
Indiana Territory Capitol, Vincennes 48239
Indiana Transportation Museum, Noblesville 45959
Indiana University Art Museum, Bloomington 41746
Indiana War Memorials Museum, Indianapolis 44225
Indianapolis Art Center, Indianapolis 44226
Indianapolis Motor Speedway Hall of Fame Museum, Indianapolis 44227
Indianapolis Museum of Art, Indianapolis 44228
Indianapolis Museum of Art - Columbus Gallery, Columbus 42578
Indigo Resist Dyeing Museum, Pápa 21501
Indira Gandhi National Centre for the Arts, Delhi 21772
Individual Artists of Oklahoma, Oklahoma City 46113
Indo-Cuban Bani Museum, Banes 07854
Indre Sør-Troms Distriktsmuseum, Tennevoll 30918
Industrial and Agricultural Museum, York 48795
Industrial and Commercial Museum, Lahore 31035
Industrial Heritage Complex, Smiths Falls 06466
Industrial Museum, Nottingham 40108
Industrie Museum Lauf, Lauf an der Pegnitz 18352
Industrie- und Filmmuseum Wolfen, Wolfen 20650
Industrie- und Vorgeschichtemuseum, Wattens 02795
Industrieel Museum, Sas van Gent 29792
Industrieel Smalspoor Museum, Erica 29248
Industriemuseum, Limbach-Oberfrohna 18469
Industriemuseum Brandenburg, Brandenburg an der Havel 16280
Industriemuseum Chemnitz, Chemnitz 16465
Industriemuseum Elmshorn, Elmshorn 16838

Industriemuseum Lohne, Lohne, Oldenburg 18498
Industrieviertel-Museum, Wiener Neustadt 03017
Industrimuseet, Kopperå 30608
Industrimuséet C.W. Thorstensons Mekaniska Verkstad, Åmål 35797
Industrion Museum for Industry and Society, Kerkrade 29480
Infantierie Museum, Harskamp 29348
Infantry and Small Arms School Corps Weapons Collection, Warminster 40786
Infantry Museum, Mikkeli 09830
Infirmary Museum, Saint Ronan's Church Museum and Columba Centre, Isle-of-Iona 39315
Informationsstelle des Naturparks Fichtelgebirge, Zell, Oberfranken 20742
Informationszentrum am Wasserstraßenkreuz Minden, Minden, Westfalen 18748
Informationszentrum Schloss Paffendorf, Bergheim, Erft 15895
Infozentrum und Elektromuseum, Ansbach 15501
Ingatestone Hall, Ingatestone 39290
Ingeborgmuseet, Tangen 30916
Ingebrigt Vik's Museum, Øystese 30775
Ingersoll Cheese Factory Museum, Ingersoll 05617
Inglewood District Historical Museum, Inglewood 01119
Ingrow Loco Museum, Keighley 39329
Ingurugiro Etxea, Azpeitia 34513
Ingušskij Gosudarstvennyj Muzej Kraevedenija im. T.Ch. Malsagova, Nazran 33203
Inland Seas Maritime Museum of The Great Lakes Historical Society, Vermilion 48213
Inland-Water Ecological Laboratory Collection, Jerusalem 22637
Inn-Galerie, Kufstein 02169
Inn-Museum, Rosenheim 19651
Inner Mongolia Museum, Huhehot 07119
Innisfail and District Historical Museum, Innisfail 01120
Innisfail and District Historical Museum, Innisfail 05619
Inniskeen Folk Museum, Inniskeen 22482
Innisville and District Museum, Innisville 05620
Innovatum Kunskapens Hus, Trollhättan 36335
Inns of Court and City Yeomanry Museum, London 39672
Innviertler Freilichtmuseum Brunnbauerhof, Andorf 01671
Inpa Coleções Zoológicas, Manaus 04188
Inquisitor's Palace, Vittoriosa 27712
Insectarium de Montréal, Montréal 05906
Insects Museum, Amman 27050
Inselmuseum, Pellworm 19371
Inselmuseum im Alten Leuchtturm, Wangerooge 20397
Inselmuseum Spiekeroog, Spiekeroog 20014
Insho-Domoto Museum of Fine Arts, Kyoto 26406
Insights - El Paso Science Center, El Paso 43119
Inspire - Hands-on Science Centre, Norwich 40094
Installation Gallery Insite, San Diego 47277
Institut d'Art Contemporain, Villeurbanne 15249
Institut de France, Saint-Jean-Cap-Ferrat 14270
Institut et Musée Voltaire, Genève 36737
Institut Français d'Architecture, Paris 13516
Institut für moderne Kunst, Nürnberg 19147
Institut für Museumskunde, Berlin 16006
Institut für Neue Technische Form, Darmstadt 16542
Institut für Vogelforschung -Vogelwarte Helgoland, Wilhelmshaven 20593
Institut für Wissenschafts- und Technikgeschichte, Kustodie, Freiberg, Sachsen 17101
Institut Tessin, Paris 13517
Institut und Museum für Geologie und Paläontologie, Tübingen 20225
Institut Zeileis, Gallspach 01865
Institute and Museum of the History of Science, Firenze 23848
The Institute For American Indian Studies, Washington Green 48424
Institute for Jewish Studies Gallery, Jerusalem 22638
Institute Menezes Braganza, Panaji 21973
Institute of African Studies Teaching Museum, Legon 20799
Institute of American Indian Arts Museum, Santa Fe 47421
Institute of Archaeology and Museum Studies, Jos 30346
Institute of Archaeology with Museum, Sofia 04827
Institute of Arts and Crafts, Dhaka 03089
Institute of Contemporary Art, Boston 41810
Institute of Contemporary Art, Philadelphia 46420
Institute of Contemporary Art, Portland 46623
Institute of Contemporary Arts, London 39673
Institute of Geological and Nuclear Sciences, Hutt City 30181
Institute of Jamaica, Kingston 26069
Institute of Meteoritics Meteorite Museum, Albuquerque 41102
Institute of Museum and Liberary Services, Washington 49490
Institute of Nature Study, Tokyo 26860
Institute of Texan Cultures, San Antonio 47253
Institute of Visual Arts, Milwaukee 45364
Instituto Amatller de Arte Hispánico, Barcelona 34545
Instituto Cultural Cabañas, Guadalajara 27946
Instituto de Artes Gráficas de Oaxaca, Oaxaca 28272
Instituto de Investigaciones Arqueológicas y Museo Prof. Mariano Gambier, Albardón 00109
Instituto de Valencia de Don Juan, Madrid 35009
Instituto Geográfico Agustín Codazzi, Bogotá 07391
Instituto Gómez-Moreno de la Fundación Rodríguez-Acosta, Granada 34871
Instituto Mexicano Norteamericano de Jalisco, Guadalajara 27947
Instituto Moreira Sales, São Paulo 04495
Instituto Moreira Salles, Belo Horizonte 03981
Instituto Moreira Salles, Poços de Caldas 04270
Instituto Moreira Salles, Rio de Janeiro 04328
Instituto Português de Museus, Lisboa 49341
Instituto Português do Património Arquitectónico e Arqueológico, Lisboa 32288
Instituto Regional de Ucayali, Pucallpa 31240
Instituts- und Studiensammlung des Instituts für Ur- und Frühgeschichte, Wien 02900
Insurance Museum, Kraków 31721
Inter Art - Sonsbeek Art and Design, Arnhem 28939
Inter Oceans Museum, Saint-Barthélemy 21250
Intercisa Múzeum, Dunaújváros 21405
INTERCOM International Committee for Museums Management, Castries 49348
Interlaken Historical Society Museum, Interlaken 44238
Intermedia Arts Minnesota, Minneapolis 45386
Intermuseum Conservation Association, Oberlin 49491
Internasjonale Barnekunstmuseet, Oslo 30738
Internationaal Exlibriscentrum, Sint-Niklaas 03740
Internationaal Museum 1939-1945, Uithuizen 29886
International Art Center, Miami 45286
International Association of Agricultural Museums, Rožnov pod Radhoštěm 49133
International Association of Custom Museums, Antwerpen 49074
International Association of Libraries and Museums of Performing Arts (SIMBAS), Roma 49253
International Association of Museum Facility Administrators, New York 49492
International Association of Museums of Arms and Military History, Liège 49068
International Association of Museums of History, Paris 49168
International Association of Transport and Communication Museums, Ängelholm 49380
International Bluegrass Music Museum, Owensboro 46228
International Bottle Museum, Sonkajärvi 10052
International Bowling Museum and Hall of Fame, Saint Louis 47123
International Center of Graphic Arts, Ljubljana 34109
International Center of Photography, New York 45817
International Centre for the Study of the Preservation and the Restoration of Cultural Property (ICCROM), Roma 49254
International Centre - Museum of N.K. Roerich, Moskva 33083
International Clown Hall of Fame and Research Center, Milwaukee 45365
International Coffee Cup Museum, Posio 09957
International Committee for Costume Museums, London 49419
International Committee for Egyptology in ICOM - CIPEG, Baltimore 49493
International Committee for Exhibition Exchange, Washington 49494
International Committee for Glass Museums, Corning 49495
International Committee for Monetary Museums, Utrecht 49304
International Committee for Museology, Barcelona 49376
International Committee for Museums and Collections of Modern Art, Helsinki 49157
International Committee for Museums and Collections of Musical Instruments, Trondheim 49317
International Committee for Museums and Collections of Natural History, Frankfurt am Main 49202
International Committee for University Museums and Collections (UMAC), Macquarie 49052
International Confederation, Nairobi 49263
International Confederation of Architectural Museums, Rotterdam 49305
International Congress of Maritime Museums, Essex 49496
International Council of African Museums (AFRICOM), Nairobi 49264
International Council of Museums, Andorran National Committee, Aixovall 49041
International Council of Museums ICOM, Paris 49189
International Council of Museums - UK National Committee, London 49420
International Council on Monuments and Sites, Paris 49190
International Crane Foundation Museum, Baraboo 41501
International Cultural Center for Youth in Jerusalem, Jerusalem 22639
International Fox Museum, Summerside 06515
International Hippocratic Foundation of Kos, Kos 21032
International Ice Hockey Federation Museum, Kingston 05677
International Images, Sewickley 47574
International Institute of Metropolitan Detroit, Detroit 42930
International Jewish Sports Hall of Fame, Netanya 22722
International Motor Racing Research Center, Watkins Glen 48451
International Movement for a New Museology, Zuni 49497
International Museum Centre of the Arsenev State Museum of the Primorsky Region, Vladivostok 33701
International Museum of Art, El Paso 43120
International Museum of Cartoon Art, Boca Raton 41767
International Museum of Children's Art, Oslo 30739
International Museum of Cultures, Dallas 42754
International Museum of Gay and Lesbian History, Los Angeles 44912
International Museum of Naive Art of Brazil, Rio de Janeiro 04387
International Museum of Peace and Solidarity, Samarkand 48849
International Museum of Photography and Film, Rochester 46941
International Museum of Surgical Science, Chicago 42335
International Museum of the Horse, Lexington 44740
International Museum of Wine Labels, Aigle 36439
International Museum Theatre Alliance, Boston 49498
International Red Cross and Red Crescent Museum, Genève 36748
International Sculpture Center, Hamilton 43879
International Society of Libraries and Museums of Performing Arts, Paris 49191
International Sport Aviation Museum, Lakeland 44602
International Swimming Hall of Fame, Fort Lauderdale 43410
International Tennis Hall of Fame Museum, Newport 45925
International Wildlife Museum, Tucson 48090
International Women's Air and Space Museum, Cleveland 42475
Internationale Jugendbibliothek, München 18857
Internationale Puppenausstellung, Sankt Wolfgang im Salzkammergut 02619
Internationale Spitzensammlung, Nordhalben 19119
Internationale Tage Boehringer Ingelheim, Ingelheim am Rhein 17899
Internationales Esperanto-Museum der Österreichischen Nationalbibliothek, Wien 02901
Internationales FIS Wintersport- und Heimatmuseum, Mürzzuschlag 02328
Internationales Haus der Photographie, Hamburg 17546
Internationales Keramik-Museum, Weiden, Oberpfalz 20425
Internationales Luftfahrtmuseum, Villingen-Schwenningen 20319
Internationales Muschelmuseum, Wangerland 20396
Internationales Radiomuseum, Bad Laasphe 15685
Internationales Wind- und Wassermühlenmuseum, Gifhorn 17286
Internationales Zeitungsmuseum der Stadt Aachen, Aachen 15373
Interoceanic Canal Museum of Panamá, Panamá City 31087
Intersection for the Arts Gallery, San Francisco 47320
Intrepid Sea-Air-Space Museum, New York 45818
The Invention Factory, Trenton 48055
Inveraray Bell Tower, Inveraray 39293
Inveraray Castle, Inveraray 39294
Inveraray Jail, Inveraray 39295
Inveraray Maritime Museum, Inveraray 39296
Inverkeithing Museum, Inverkeithing 39297
Inverness Miners Museum, Inverness 05623
Inverness Museum and Art Gallery, Inverness 39300
Inženernyj (Michailovskij) Zamok, Sankt-Peterburg 33409
Ioannidis Collection, Lindos 21051
Ioannina Museum, Ioannina 20969
Iolani Palace, Honolulu 44080
Iona Heritage Centre, Isle-of-Iona 39316
Ionad Arann Heritage Centre, Aran Islands 22359
Ionad Dualchais Nis, Ness 40009
Ionnina Byzantine Museum, Ioannina 20970
Iosco County Historical Museum, East Tawas 43061
Iowa Aviation Museum, Greenfield 43804
Iowa Masonic Library and Museum, Cedar Rapids 42159
Iowa Museum Association, Waterloo 49499
Iowa Railroad Historical Museum, Boone 41784
I.P. Pavlov Apartment Museum at the I.P. Pavlov Physiological Institut of the Russian Academy of Sciences, Sankt-Peterburg 33420
I.P. Stanback Museum, Orangeburg 46176
Iparművészeti Múzeum, Budapest 21346
Ipogeo dei Volumni, Ponte San Giovanni 24993
Ippuku Museum of Art, Asahi 26104
Ipswich Historical Society Museum, Ipswich 44251
Ipswich Museum, Ipswich 39305
Ipswich Transport Museum, Ipswich 39306
Iqbal Museum, Lahore 31036
Iquest Children's Museum, Bellevue 41598
Iraan Museum, Iraan 44253
Iran Bastan Museum, Teheran 22304
Iranian National Museum of Water, Teheran 22305
Iraq Natural History Research Centre and Museum, Baghdad 22345
Iraqi Museum, Baghdad 22346
Irbid Archaeological Museum, Irbid 27062
Irchester Narrow Gauge Railway Museum, Wellingborough 40810
Iredell Museum of Arts & Heritage, Statesville 47794
Ireland House Museum, Burlington 05146
Ireland's Historic Science Centre, Birr 22377
Irene Cullis Gallery, Greensboro 43816
Iris and B. Gerald Cantor Art Gallery, Worcester 48754
Iris & B. Gerald Cantor Center for Visual Arts at Stanford University, Stanford 47772
Irish Agricultural Museum, Wexford 22558
Irish American Heritage Museum, East Durham 43039
Irish Architectural Archive, Dublin 22433
Irish Horse Museum, Tully 22551
Irish Jewish Museum, Dublin 22434
Irish Labour History Society Museum, Dublin 22435
Irish Linen Centre and Lisburn Museum, Lisburn 39510
Irish Museum of Modern Art, Dublin 22436
Irish Museums Association, Dublin 49244
Irish Music Hall of Fame, Dublin 22437
Irish Palatine Association Museum, Rathkeale 22533
Irkutskij Architekturno-ėtnografičeskij Muzej Talcy, Irkutsk 32812
Irkutskij Oblastnoj Chudožestvennyj Muzej im. V.P. Sukačeva, Irkutsk 32813
Irkutskij Oblastnoj Kraevedčeskij Muzej, Irkutsk 32814
Irma Stern Museum of the University of Cape Town, Rosebank 34372
Iron and Steel Museum of Alabama, McCalla 45018
Iron County Museum, Caspian 42132
Iron Creek Museum, Lougheed 05780
Iron Forging Museum, Kropa 34102
Iron Garden, Bridgetown 03103
Iron Mill Complex, Aia 34415
Iron Mission Museum, Cedar City 42147
Iron Mountain Iron Mine, Vulcan 48258
Ironbridge Gorge Museum, Ironbridge 39308
Ironbridge Tollhouse, Ironbridge 39309
Ironwood Area Historical Museum, Ironwood 44255
Ironworld Discovery Center, Chisholm 42388
Iroquois County Historical Society Museum, Watseka 48455
Iroquois Falls Pioneer Museum, Iroquois Falls 05628
Iroquois Indian Museum, Howes Cave 44140
Irrseer Heimathaus, Zell am Moos 03049
Irvine Burns Club Museum, Irvine 39311
Irvine Fine Arts Center, Irvine 44256
Irvine Museum, Irvine 44257
Irving Arts Center, Irving 44259
Irving Arts Center, Irving 44260
Irving E. and Ray Kanner Heritage Museum, North York 06033
Irving House Historic Centre and New Westminster Museum, New Westminster 05984
I.S. Klyuchnikov-Palantai Memorial Museum, Joškar-Ola 32858
I.S. Nikitin House-Museum, Voronež 33730
I.S. Shemanovsky Museum of the Jamalo-Nenetsk Autonomous Region, Salechard 33364
I.S. Turgenev State Literary Museum, Orël 33263
Isaac Farrar Mansion, Bangor 41494
Isaak Kaplan Old Yishuv Coourt Museum, Jerusalem 22640
Isaakevskij Sobor - Memorialnyj Muzej-pamjatnik, Sankt-Peterburg 33410
Isabel Miller Museum, Sitka 47649
Isabella Stewart Gardner Museum, Boston 41811
Isahakians Museum, Erevan 00682
Isanti County Museum, Cambridge 42051
Ischua Valley Historical Society, Franklinville 43524
ISE Art Foundation, New York 45819
Isenbaye Art Gallery and Cultural Troupe, Oshogbo 30356
Isergebirgs Museum Neugablonz, Kaufbeuren 18040
Isetan Bijutsukan, Tokyo 26861
Isetan Museum of Art, Tokyo 26861
Isfara Historical and Regional Museum, Isfara 37447
Ishavsmuseet Aarvak, Brandal 30448
Ishibashi Museum of Art and Asian Gallery, Kurume 26388
Ishii Chawan Bijutsukan, Hagi 26169
Ishikawa-kenritsu Bijutsukan, Kanazawa 26306
Ishikawa-kenritsu Dento Sangyo Kogeikan, Kanazawa 26307
Ishikawa-kenritsu Kyodo Shiryokan, Kanazawa 26308
Ishikawa-kenritsu Rekishi Hakubutsukan, Kanazawa 26309
Ishikawa Prefectural Art Museum, Kanazawa 26306
Ishikawa Prefectural History Museum, Kanazawa 26309
Ishikawa Prefectural Museum, Kanazawa 26308
Ishikawa Prefectural Museum of Traditional Products and Crafts, Kanazawa 26307
Ishikawa Takuboku Memorial Museum, Tamayama 26818
Ishinomaki Culture Center, Ishinomaki 26259
Isinger Dorfmuseum - Alte Kelter, Tübingen 20226
Isis District Historical Complex, Childers 00910
İskele İon Müzesi, İskele 08230
Iskitimskij Kraevedčeskij Muzej, Iskitim 32822
Isla Center for the Arts at the University of Guam, Mangilao 21258
Islamabad Museum, Islamabad 31023
Islamia College Museum, Peshawar 31049
Islamic Museum, Abbasiya 09232
Islamic Museum, Amman 27051
Islamic Museum, Cairo 09267
Islamic Museum, Jerusalem 22641
Islamic Museum, Jerusalem 31070
Islamic Museum, Teheran 22306
Islamic Museum, Tripoli 27507
Island County Historical Society Museum, Coupeville 42677

Island Mountain Arts Public Gallery, Wells 06765
Islandic Phallological Museum, Reykjavik 21662
Isle La Motte Historical Society Museum, Isle La Motte 44265
Isle of Wight Courthouse, Smithfield 47656
Isle of Wight Steam Railway and Isle of Wight Railway Heritage Museum, Havenstreet 39190
Isle of Wight Wax Works, Brading 38304
Isleford Historical Museum, Isleford 44266
Isles of Scilly Museum, Saint Mary's 40415
Islesboro Historical Museum, Islesboro 44267
Islington Education Artefacts Library, London 39674
Islington Museum, London 39675
Islip Art Museum, East Islip 43051
Ismailia Museum, Ismailia 09300
Isokyrö Local History Museum, Isokyrö 09570
Isonkyrön Kotiseutumuseo, Isokyrö 09570
İsparta Devlet Güzel Sanatlar Galerisi, İsparta 37689
Isparta State Gallery, İsparta 37689
Israel Bible Museum, Zefat 22788
Israel Children's Museum, Holon 22621
Israel Defense Forces History Museum, Tel Aviv 22760
Israel Goor Theater Archive and Museum, Jerusalem 22642
Israel Museum, Jerusalem, Jerusalem 22643
Israel National Committee of ICOM, Rishon Le-Zion 49245
Israel Oil Industry Museum, Haifa 22606
Israel Railway Museum, Haifa 22607
Israel Theater Museum, Tel Aviv 22761
Israeli Air Force Museum, Hatzerim 22615
Israeli Museum of Photography, Tel-Hai 22778
Istana Batu, Kota Bharu 27629
İstanbul Arkeoloji Müzeleri, İstanbul 37702
İstanbul Büyükşehir Belediyesi Karikatür ve Mizah Müzesi, Fatih 37677
İstanbul Devlet Güzel Sanatlar Galerisi, İstanbul 37703
İstanbul Divan Edebiyatı Müzesi, İstanbul 37704
Istanbul Fortress Museum, Bebek 37632
İstanbul Hisarlar Müzesi, Bebek 37632
İstanbul Museum of Caricature and Humour, Fatih 37677
İstanbul Ottoman Poetry Museum, İstanbul 37704
İstanbul State Gallery, İstanbul 37703
Istituto della Cultura Arbereshe Giuseppe Gangale, Caraffa 23340
Istituto di Fotografia Alpina Vittorio Sella, Biella 23078
Istituto e Museo di Storia della Scienza, Firenze 23848
Istituto Italiano dei Castelli ONLUS, Roma 25167
Istituto Italiano di Paleontologia Umana, Roma 25168
Istituto per la Storia della Resistenza e della Societa Contemporanea nelle Province di Biella e Vercelli, Borgosesia 23176
Istoki, Belozersk 32682
Istoričeskaja Usadba Botik Petra I, Veskovo 33684
Istoričeski Muzej, Bansko 04613
Istoričeski Muzej, Batak 04616
Istoričeski Muzej, Blagoevgrad 04626
Istoričeski Muzej, Bracigovo 04629
Istoričeski Muzej, Burgas 04634
Istoričeski Muzej, Čiprovci 04643
Istoričeski Muzej, Dimitrovgrad 04651
Istoričeski Muzej, Dobrič 04655
Istoričeski Muzej, Drjanovo 04660
Istoričeski Muzej, Gabrovo 04668
Istoričeski Muzej, Goce Delčev 04674
Istoričeski Muzej, Gorna Orjachovica 04675
Istoričeski Muzej, Ichtiman 04678
Istoričeski Muzej, Isperich 04679
Istoričeski Muzej, Karlovo 04690
Istoričeski Muzej, Loveč 04728
Istoričeski Muzej, Omurtag 04746
Istoričeski Muzej, Pavlikeni 04752
Istoričeski Muzej, Petrič 04761
Istoričeski Muzej, Pomorie 04783
Istoričeski Muzej, Popovo 04784
Istoričeski Muzej, Pravec 04787
Istoričeski Muzej, Provadia 04789
Istoričeski Muzej, Razgrad 04797
Istoričeski Muzej, Razlog 04798
Istoričeski Muzej, Svištov 04880
Istoričeski Muzej, Velingrad 04922
Istoričeski Muzej Belogradčik, Belogradčik 04617
Istoričeski Muzej Krastata Kazarma, Vidin 04923
Istoričeski Muzej - Preminavane na Ruskite Vojski pri Svištov, Svištov 04881
Istoričeski Muzej Silistra, Silistra 04815
Istoričeski Muzej Targovište, Targovište 04883
Istoričeskij Muzej, Dnepropetrovsk 37848
Istoričeskij Muzej, Kyïv 37869
Istoričeskij Muzej, Tutrakan 04892
Istorijski Muzej Srbije, Beograd 33799
Istoriko-Architekturnyj, Chudožestvennyj i Archeologičeskij Muzej "Zarajskij Kreml", Zarajsk 33746
Istoriko-Architekturnyj i Chudožestvennyj Muzej Ivangorodskaja Krepost, Ivangorod 32823
Istoriko-architekturnyj Muzej Kuzneckaja Krepost', Novokuzneck 33234
Istoriko-chudožestvennyj Muzej, Uglič 33649
Istoriko-ėtnografičeskij Muzej Usadba Galskich, Čerepovec 32731
Istoriko-Kraevedčeskij Muzej, Arkalyk 27075
Istoriko-Kraevedčeskij Muzej, Ivanovo 32828
Istoriko-Kraevedčeskij Muzej, Karaganda 27085
Istoriko-Kraevedčeskij Muzej, Temirtau 27097
Istoriko-Kraevedceskij Muzej, Tokmok 27316
Istoriko-Kraevedčeskij Muzej Džezkazgana, Džezkazgan 27083
Istoriko-kraevedčeskij Muzej g. Kronštadta, Kronštadt 32964
Istoriko-Kraevedčeskij Muzej Kattagurgana, Kattakurgan 48840
Istoriko-Kraevedčeskij Muzej Kokčetava, Kokčetav 27086
Istoriko-Kraevedčeskij Muzej Kzyl-Orda, Kzyl-Orda 27087
Istoriko-Kraevedčeskij Muzej Mangyšlaka, Ševčenko 27095
Istoriko-Kraevedčeskij Muzej Ura Tjube, Ura-Tjube 37451
Istoriko-Kraevedčeskij Muzej Vostočnogo Kazachstana, Petropavlovsk 27090
Istoriko-kulturnyj Muzej-zapovednik Idnakar, Glazov 32806
Istoriko-literaturnyj Muzej I.A. Gončarova, Uljanovsk 33657
Istoriko-memorialnyj i Architurno-chudožestvennyj Muzej, Tichvin 33600
Istoriko-memorialnyj Kompleks Gerojam Stalingradskoj Bitvy na Mamaevom Kurgane, Volgograd 33716
Istoriko-memorialnyj Muzej M.V. Lomonosova, Lomonosovo 32992
Istoriko-memorialnyj Muzej Semji Fadeevyh-Chan-Blavackij, Dnepropetrovsk 37849
Istoriko-memorial'nyj Muzejnyj Kompleks Bobriki, Donskij 32760
Istoriski Muzej, Kruševo 27586
István Dobó Castle Museum, Eger 21406
Itabashi Art Museum, Tokyo 26862
Itabashi Kuritsu Bijutsukan, Tokyo 26862
Itä-Hämeen Museo, Hartola 09465
Ital Reding-Haus, Schwyz 37151
Italian Federation of Associations of Friends of Museums, Firenze 49251
Italian Historical Museum, Carlton South 00895
Itami City Museum, Itami 26262
Itami City Museum of Art, Itami 26261
Itami-shiritsu Bijutsukan, Itami 26261
Itami-shiritsu Hakubutsukan, Itami 26262
Itasca Heritage Center Museum, Grand Rapids 43762
Itcan-Kala National Reserve Museum, Chiva 48834
Itčan Qala Davlat Muzej Qo'riqxonasi, Chiva 48834
İtfaiye Müzesi, Fatih 37678
Itimuseum, Buenos Aires 00155
Itsukaichi Folk Museum, Itsukaichi 26270
Itsukushima-jinja Homotsukan, Hatsukaichi 26184
Itsukushima Shrine Treasury, Hatsukaichi 26184
Itsuo Bijutsukan, Ikeda 26239
Itsuoh Art Museum, Ikeda 26239
Itsutsubashikan, Sendai 26730
Ittinger Museum, Warth 37306
Ituna Cultural and Historical Museum, Ituna 05630
Iupui Cultural Arts Gallery, Indianapolis 44229
I.V. Tsvetaev Art Museum, Moskva 33180
IVAM Centre Julio González, Valencia 35599
Ivan Dougherty Gallery, Paddington, New South Wales 01352
Ivan Franko Museum, Winnipeg 06828
Ivan Meštrović Gallery, Split 07782
Ivan Meštrović Memorial Gallery, Vrpolje 07803
Ivan Vazov Memorial House, Berkovica 04622
Ivan Vazov Memorial House, Sofia 04833
Ivan Vazov Museum, Sopot 04861
Ivano-Frankovsk Local Museum, Ivano-Frankovsk 37854
Ivanovo Art Museum, Ivanovo 32829
Ivanovskij Oblastnoj Chudožestvennyj Muzej, Ivanovo 32829
Ivar Aasen-tunet, Hovdebygda 30570
Ivar Lo-Museet, Stockholm 36248
Ivé Múzeum Obchodu, Bratislava 33967
Iveland og Vegusdal Bygdemuseum, Vatnestrom 30979
I.V.K. Rajwade Sanshodhan Mandal Museum, Dhule 21795
Ivy Green, Tuscumbia 48120
Iwaki City Art Museum, Iwaki 26271
Iwakuni Municipal Museum, Iwakuni 26272
Iwalewa Haus, Bayreuth 15847
Iwasaki Museum, Yokohama 27013
Iwasaki Museum of Art, Ibusuki 26235
Iwata Senshinkan, Inuyama 26250
Iwata-shi Kyu Mitsukegakko, Iwata, Shizuoka 26275
Iwate-kenritsu Hakubutsukan, Morioka 26515
Iwate Museum of Art, Morioka 26516
Iwate Prefectural Museum, Morioka 26515
Ixchel Museum of Indigenous Textiles and Clothing, Guatemala 21270
Iyoboya Salmon Museum, Murakami 26520
Izaak Walton's Cottage, Shallowford 40479
Izba Muzealna im. Antoniego Krajewskiego, Lanckorona 31747
Izba Regionalna Polskiego Towarzystwa Turystyczno-Krajoznawczego, Sulejów 32005
Izložba na Stari Kotlenski Kilimi, Kotel 04717
Izložbena Dvorana Sv. Mihovila, Korčula 07721
Izmir Archaeological Museum, İzmir 37718
İzmir Arkeoloji Müzesi, İzmir 37718
İzmir Resim ve Heykel Müzesi, İzmir 37719
İzmir State Painting and Sculpture Museum, İzmir 37719
Iznik Müzesi, Iznik 37720
Iznik Museum, Iznik 37720
Izstāžu Zāle, Madona 27383
Izumo Taisha Shrine Treasure, Taisha 26784
Izumo Taisha Treasure House, Izumo 26279
J. Evetts Haley History Center, Midland 45325
J. F. Schreiber-Museum, Esslingen 16969
J. Łukasiewicz Regional Museum, Gorlice 31605
J. Paul Getty Museum, Los Angeles 44913
J. Wayne Stark University Center Galleries, College Station 42526
Jabatan Muzium Sabah, Kota Kinabalu 27631
Jabotinsky Museum, Tel Aviv 22762
Jacek Malczewski Muzeum, Radom 31938
Jachthuis Sint-Hubertus, Hoenderloo 29429
Jacinto Courthouse, Corinth 42633
Jack Heath Art Gallery, Pietermaritzburg 34325
Jack London State Historic Park, Glen Ellen 43681
Jack Lynn Memorial Museum, Horsefly 05605
Jack Miner Museum, Kingsville 05689
Jack R. Hennesey Art Galleries, Port Huron 46596
Jack S. Blanton Museum of Art, Austin 41412
Jackfield Tile Museum, Jackfield 39322
Jackson Art Center, Washington 48364
Jackson County Historical Museum, Lakefield 44601
Jackson County Historical Museum, Maquoketa 45131
Jackson County Historical Society Museum, Black River Falls 41724
Jackson Hall Gallery, Frankfort 43508
Jackson Hole Historical Museum, Jackson 44289
The Jackson Homestead, Newton 45944
Jackson-Washabaugh Historical Museum, Kadoka 44373
Jackson's Mill Historic Area, Weston 48572
Jacksonville Fire Museum, Jacksonville 44295
Jacksonville Museum of Modern Art, Jacksonville 44296
Jacob Breda Bullmuseet, Rendalen 30788
Jacob Kelley House Museum, Hartsville 43949
Jacob Walden House, Walden 48281
Jacquard-Stübli, Pratteln 37032
Jacqueline Casey Hudgens Center for the Arts, Duluth 42995
Jacques Marchais Museum of Tibetan Art, Staten Island 47783
Jacques van Mourik Ruim, Mook 29603
Jägerndorfer Heimatstuben, Ansbach 15502
Jægerspris Slot, Jægerspris 08907
Jael Stichting Mystic Museum, Dronten 29182
Jämtlands Flyg och Lottamuseum, Östersund 36145
Jämtlands Läns Museum, Östersund 36146
Jærmuseet, Nærbø 30699
Järnvägs- och Industrimuseum, Hagfors 35938
Järnvägsmuseet, Kristianstad 36017
Järvamaa Muuseum, Paide 09345
Jaffna National Museum, Jaffna 35756
Jaffrey Civic Center, Jaffrey 44302
Jagd- und Falknereimuseum, Riedenburg 19597
Jagd- und Fischereimuseum, Adelsdorf 15395
Jagd- und Fischereimuseum Schloss Tambach, Weitramsdorf 20505
Jagd- und Forstmuseum, Feistritz am Wechsel 01825
Jagd- und Naturkunde Museum, Niederstetten 19098
Jagd- und Naturkundemuseum, Brüggen, Niederrhein 16374
Jagd- und Schloßmuseum Spangenberg, Spangenberg 20009
Jagdhaus Gabelbach, Ilmenau 17891
Jagdkundemuseum, Dischingen 16624
Jagdmuseum, Buschow 16432
Jagdmuseum Brandhof, Gollrad 01905
Jagdmuseum Wulff, Dedelstorf 16558
Jagdschau im Jagdschloss Springe, Springe 20018
Jagdschloß Granitz, Ostseebad Binz 19308
Jagdschloß Grunewald, Berlin 16007
Jagdschloß Nienover, Bodenfelde 16206
Jagdschloß Paulinzella, Rottenbach 19689
Jagdschloss Letzlingen, Letzlingen 18444
Jagiellonian University Museum, Kraków 31722
Jaguar Daimler Heritage Trust, Allesley 37977
Jail Museum, Horsens 08895
Jail Training School Museum, Lucknow 21927
Jailhouse Galleries, Morganton 45497
Jakarta History Museum, Jakarta 22106
Jakob-Grünenwald-Gedächtnisstätte, Ebersbach an der Fils 16766
Jakob-Philipp-Hackert Ausstellung, Prenzlau 19442
Jakobstads Museum, Jakobstad 09573
Jaktvårdsmuseum, Eksjö 35863
Jakutskij Gosudarstvennyj Muzej Istorii i Kultury Narodov Severa im. Jaroslavskogo, Jakutsk 32843
Jalasjärven Museo, Jalasjarvi 09577
Jalkaväkimuseo, Mikkeli 09830
Jalokivi Galleria, Kemi 09648
Jamaica Center for Arts, Jamaica 44304
Jamaica Folk Museum, Kingston 26070
Jamaican People's Museum of Craft and Technology, Spanish Town 26082
Jamalo-Neneckij Okružnoj Kraevedčeskij Muzej im. I.S. Šemanovskogo, Salechard 33364
James A. Garfield National Historic Site, Mentor 45256
James A. McFaul Environmental Center of Bergen County, Wyckoff 48768
James A. Michener Art Museum, Doylestown 42984
James and Meryl Hearst Center for the Arts, Cedar Falls 42150
James Buchanan Foundation for the Preservation of Wheatland, Lancaster 44626
James Cook Historical Museum, Cooktown 00943
James Dunklin House, Laurens 44681
James E. Lewis Museum of Art, Baltimore 41471
James Ford Bell Museum of Natural History, Minneapolis 45387
James Gilbert Rugby Football Museum, Rugby 40355
James Hall Museum of Transport, Johannesburg 34278
James Hogg Exhibition, Selkirk 40469
James House Museum, Bridgetown 05128
James Howe Gallery, Union 48143
James H.W. Thompson House, Bangkok 37486
James J. Hill House, Saint Paul 47157
James J. O'Mara Pharmacy Museum, Saint John's 06345
James Joyce Centre, Dublin 22438
James Joyce Museum, Dublin 22439
James K. Polk Ancestral Home, Columbia 42570
James K. Polk Memorial, Pineville 46494
James-Krüss-Turm, München 18858
The James Madison Museum, Orange 46174
James Madison's Montpelier, Montpelier Station 45480
James Mitchell Museum, Galway 22473
James Mitchell Varnum House and Museum, East Greenwich 43040
James Monroe Museum and Memorial Library, Fredericksburg 43537
James Paterson Museum, Moniaive 39975
James R. Slater Museum of Natural History, Tacoma 47919
James W. Dillon House Museum, Dillon 42951
James Whitcomb Riley Birthplace and Museum, Greenfield 43805
Jamestown Museum, Jamestown 01123
Jamestown Museum, Jamestown 44314
Jamestown Settlement, Williamsburg 48629
Jamestown Visitor Center Museum, Jamestown 44316
Jamieson Museum, Moosomin 05937
Jamtli Historieland, Östersund 36147
Jan Amos Comenius Pedagogical Museum, Praha 08611
Jan Dzierżoń Museum, Kluczbork 31665
Jan Karlsgarden, Sund 10060
Jan Kochanowski Muzeum, Czarnolas 31541
Jan Van Riebeeckhuis, Culemborg 29062
Jan Vissermuseum, Helmond 29396
Jāņa Akuratera Muzejs, Rīga 27408
Jāņa Jaunsudrabiņa Muzejs Riekstiņi, Neretas Pagasts 27389
Jaņa Rozentāla un Rūdolfa Blaumaņa Muzejs, Rīga 27409
Jāņa Zābera Memoriālais Muzejs, Meirāni 27388
Janaček Museum, Brno 08275
Janco-Dada Museum, Ein Hod 22590
Jane Addams' Hull-House Museum, Chicago 42336
Jane Austen's House, Chawton 38533
Jane L. and Robert H. Weiner Judaic Museum, Rockville 46975
Jane Neville-Rolfe Gallery, Alpha 00742
Jane Voorhees Zimmerli Art Museum, New Brunswick 45678
Jane Welsh Carlyle's House, Haddington 39142
Janet Turner Print Museum, Chico 42372
Janggigot Lighthouse Museum, Pohang 27217
Jāņis Akurāters Museum, Rīga 27408
Janis Rozentals and Rudolfs Blaumanis Museum, Rīga 27409
Jannis Spyropoulos Museum, Ekali 20942
Janošík Prison Museum, Liptovský Mikuláš 34014
Jansen Collection, Pretoria 34344
Jantyik Mátyás Múzeum, Békés 21317
Janus Pannonius Múzeum Igazgatòsàga, Pécs 21506
Janus Pannonius Múzeum Természettudományi Osztálya, Pécs 21507
Japan Amateur Art Museum, Ogi 26616
Japan Calligraphy Art Museum, Tokyo 26907
Japan-China Peace Negotiations Memorial Hall, Shimonoseki 26752
Japan Folk Art Museum, Osaka 26649
Japan Folk Crafts Museum, Tokyo 26906
The Japan Folk Crafts Museum, Osaka, Suita 26775
Japan Footwear Museum, Fukuyama 26153
Japan Society Gallery, New York 45820
Japan Toy Museum, Tokyo 26903
Japan Wood-block Prints Museum, Matsumoto 26479
Japane Open Air Folk House Museum, Kawasaki 26329
Japanese American National Museum, Los Angeles 44914
Japanese Association of Museums, Tokyo 49259
Japanese Association of Museums, Tokyo 49256
Japanese Council of Art Museums, Tokyo 49257
Japanese Cultural Center of Hawaii, Honolulu 44081
Japanese National Committee for ICOM, Tokyo 49258
Japanese Rural Toy Museum, Kurashiki 26380
Japanese Ski Memorial Museum, Joetsu 26281
Japanese Sword Museum, Tokyo 26935
Japanisches Kulturinstitut, Köln 18145
Japantown Art and Media Collection, San Francisco 47321
Jarash Archaeological Museum, Jarash 27064
Jardim-Museu Agrícola Tropical, Lisboa 32289
Le Jardin aux Papillons, Vannes (Morbihan) 15081
Jardin de Sculptures et d'Agrumes du Palais, Menton 12936
Le Jardin des Papillons, Paris 13518
Le Jardin Ferroviaire, Chatte 11245

Jaroslavl Fine Art Museum - Governor's House, Jaroslavl 32848
Jaroslavl Historical and Architectural Museum-Preserve, Jaroslavl 32849
Jaroslavl History Museum, Jaroslavl 32853
Jaroslavl Museum of Combat Fame, Jaroslavl 32850
Jaroslavskij Chudožestvennyj Muzej - Gubernatorskij Dom, Jaroslavl 32848
Jaroslavskij Istoriko-architekturnyj i Chudožestvennyj Muzej-zapovednik, Jaroslavl 32849
Jaroslavskij Muzej Boevoj Slavy, Jaroslavl 32850
Jarrell Plantation Georgia, Juliette 44365
Jartunet, Åsgreina 30399
Jasin Museum, Melaka 27669
Jasna Góra Treasury, Częstochowa 31548
Jasper Cultural and Historical Centre, Maple Creek 05810
Jasper Rand Art Museum, Westfield 48557
Jasper-Yellowhead Museum and Archives, Jasper 05631
Jász Múzeum, Jászberény 21435
Jaunmokas Palace Museum, Tukums 27459
Jaunmoku Pils Muzejs, Tukums 27459
Jaunpils Museum, Jaunpils 27359
Jaunpils Muzejs, Jaunpils 27359
J.A.V. David Museum, Killarney 05666
Javaherat, Teheran 22307
Jawaharlal Nehru State Museum, Itanagar 21860
Jay I. Kislak Foundation, Miami Lakes 45301
Sri Jayachamarajendra Art Gallery, Mysore 21960
Jazep Vitol Memorial Museum, Gaujiena 27356
Jāzepa Vītola Memoriālais Muzejs, Gaujiena 27356
Jazz & Art Galerie, Gelsenkirchen 17228
Jazz Museum, Kolbäck 36012
Jazzens Museum, Kolbäck 36012
Jazzothèque, Nice 13310
J.B. Wallis Museum of Entomology, Winnipeg 06829
JCII Camera Museum, Tokyo 26902
J.E. Reeves Home and Museum, Dover 42973
Jean Giraudoux' Birthplace, Bellac 10671
Jean Lafitte National Historical Park and Preserve, New Orleans 45728
Jean P. Haydon Museum, Pago Pago 00082
Jean-Paul-Museum der Stadt Bayreuth, Bayreuth 15848
Jean Paul Slusser Gallery, Ann Arbor 41217
Jean-Paul-Zimmer in der Rollwenzelei, Bayreuth 15849
Jean-Pierre Pescatore Collection Villa Vauban, Luxembourg 27561
Jeannette Powell Art Center, Stockton 47825
Jedburgh Castle Jail Museum, Jedburgh 39324
Jeff Matthews Memorial Museum, Galax 43592
Jefferds Tavern, York 48788
Jefferson Barracks, Saint Louis 47124
Jefferson County Historical Association Museum, Steubenville 47806
Jefferson County Historical Museum, Madison 45057
Jefferson County Historical Museum, Pine Bluff 46490
Jefferson County Historical Society Museum, Port Townsend 46605
Jefferson County Historical Society Museum, Watertown 48442
Jefferson Historical Museum, Jefferson 44325
Jefferson National Expansion Memorial, Saint Louis 47125
Jefferson Patterson Museum, Saint Leonard 47110
Jefferson Telephone Museum, Jefferson 44322
Jehangir Art Gallery, Mumbai 21950
Jeju-do Folklore and Natural History Museum, Jeju 27194
Jeju Education Museum, Jeju 27195
Jeju Folklore Museum, Jeju 27196
Jeju National University Museum, Jeju 27197
Jēkabpils Vēstures Muzeja Brīvdabas Nodaļa, Jēkabpils 27360
Jēkabpils Vēstures Muzeja Mūzikas Vēstures Nodaļa, Jēkabpils 27361
Jēkabpils Vēstures Muzejs, Jēkabpils 27362
Jekyll Island Museum, Jekyll Island 44331
Jelly van den Bosch Museum, Roden 29739
Jemez State Monument, Jemez Springs 44332
Jenbacher Museum, Jenbach 02086
Jenisch Haus, Hamburg 17547
Jenle Museum, Roslev 09047
Jenner Museum, Berkeley 38168
Jennings-Brown House Female Academy, Bennettsville 41627
Jenny-Marx-Haus, Salzwedel 19738
Jenő Kerényi Memorial Museum, Szentendre 21571
Jens Nielsens & Olivia Holm-Møller Museet, Holstebro 08891
Jens Søndergaard Museet, Lemvig 08971
Jensen Arctic Museum, Monmouth 45437
Jeonju Municipal Museum, Jeonju 27199
Jeonju National Museum, Jeonju 27200
Jeremiah Lee Mansion, Marblehead 45134
Jericho Historical Society Museum, Jericho Corners 44335
Jerilderie Doll World Museum, Jerilderie 01125
Jerome County Historical Society, Jerome 44337
Jerome K. Jerome Birthplace Museum, Walsall 40772
Jerome State Historic Park, Jerome 44336
Jersey Battle of Flowers Museum, Saint Ouen 40419
Jersey City Museum, Jersey City 44340
Jersey Heritage Trust, Saint Dominick 40393
Jersey Motor Museum, Saint Peter 40420
Jersey Museum, Saint Helier 40401
Jersey Photographic Museum, Saint Helier 40402
Jerusalem Artists House, Jerusalem 22623
Jerusalem Artists' House, Jerusalem 22644
Jerusalemhaus mit Verwaltung der Städtischen Sammlungen Wetzlar, Wetzlar 20555
Jerzy Dunin-Borkowski Museum, Krośniewice 31734
Jesse Besser Museum, Alpena 41154
Jesse James Bank Museum, Liberty 44767
Jesse James Farm and Museum, Kearney 44420
Jesse James Home Museum, Saint Joseph 47106
Jesse Peter Museum, Santa Rosa 47445
Jesuitenkolleg, Mindelheim 18742
Jesus Jones and Justice Museum of Art, Los Angeles 44915
Jevrejski Istorijski Muzej, Beograd 33800
Jewel Tower, London 39676
Jewell County Historical Museum, Mankato 45118
Jewett Hall Gallery, Augusta 41389
Jewish Battalions Museum, Ahivil 22566
Jewish Historical Museum, Beograd 33800
Jewish Holocaust Centre, Elsternwick 01013
Jewish Institute for the Arts, Boca Raton 41768
Jewish Legions Museum W.W. I, Avihail 22576
Jewish Museum, London 39677
The Jewish Museum, New York 45821
Jewish Museum, Sarajevo 03921
Jewish Museum Finchley, London 39678
Jewish Museum in Prague, Praha 08620
Jewish Museum in Stockholm, Stockholm 36249
Jewish Museum of Australia, Saint Kilda, Victoria 01434
Jewish Museum of Buenos Aires Dr. Salvador Kibrick, Buenos Aires 00221
Jewish Museum of Deportation and Resistance, Mechelen 03615
Jewish Museum of Florida, Miami Beach 45299
Jewish Museum of Greece, Athinai 20861
Jewish Museum of Maryland, Baltimore 41472
Jewish Museum of Thessaloniki, Thessaloniki 21184
Jewish National Fund House, Tel Aviv 22763
Jewry Wall Museum, Leicester 39462
Jews in Latvia, Rīga 27404
Jeypore Branch Museum, Jaipur, Orissa 21861
J.F. Willumsens Museum, Frederikssund 08832
Jfj. Lele J. Néprajzi Gyűjteménye, Szeged 21548
JFK Special Warfare Museum, Fort Bragg 43372
Jhalawar Archaeology Museum, Jhalawar 21872
Jiading District Museum, Shanghai 07213
Jian City Museum, Jian 07122
Jiangmen Museum, Jiangmen 07123
Jiangnan Gongyuan History Display Center, Nanjing 07177
Jiangning County Museum, Nanjing 07178
Jiangyin City Museum, Jiangyin 07124
Jiaonan City Museum, Jiaonan 07126
Jiaozhuang Hu Didao Station, Beijing 06968
Jihočeské Muzeum v Českých Budějovicích, České Budějovice 08299
Jihomoravské Muzeum ve Znojmě, Znojmo 08756
Jikjiseongbo Museum, Gimcheon 27173
Jilin City Wenmiao Museum, Jilin 07127
Jilin Museum, Changchun 07002
Jilin Natural Museum, Changchun 07003
Jilin Revolutionary Museum, Changchun 07004
Jim Clark Room, Duns 38820
Jim Gatchell Museum, Buffalo 41991
Jim Savage Art Gallery and Museum, Sioux Falls 47644
Jim Thorpe Home, Yale 48775
Jimmie Rodgers Museum, Meridian 45264
The Jimmy Stewart Museum, Indiana 44211
Jimo City Museum, Jimo 07128
Jin Contemporary Shi Museum, Shenyang 07233
Jinan City Museum, Jinan 07130
Jinan Revolutionary Mausoleum of Fallen Heroes, Jinan 07131
Jingdezhen Porcelain Museum, Jingdezhen 07138
Jingu Agricultural Museum, Ise 26254
Jingu Museum of Antiquities, Ise 26253
Jingu Nogyokan, Ise 26254
Jinju National Museum, Jinju 27202
Jinshan Museum, Shanghai 07214
Jinze Xuan Art Center, Shenzhen 07239
Jinzhou District Museum, Dalian 07036
Jitensha Bunka, Tokyo 26863
Jitensha Hakubutsukan Saikuru Senta, Sakai 26696
Jixian Display Center, Jixian 07142
Jizdárna Pražskeho Hradu, Praha 08582
J.J. Jackson Memorial Museum, Weaverville 48486
J.K. MacCarthy Museum, Goroka 31091
J.L. Runebergin Koti, Porvoo 09951
J.L. Runeberg's Home, Porvoo 09951
J.L. Shellshear Museum of Comparative Anatomy and Physical Anthropology, Sydney 01498
J.M. Davis Arms and Historical Museum, Claremore 42422
Jødisk Museum, Trondheim 30938
Jodrell Bank Science Centre and Arboretum, Macclesfield 39864
Joe and Emily Lowe Art Gallery, Syracuse 47909
Joe Weatherly Museum, Darlington 42784
Joel and Lila Harnett Print Study Center, Richmond 46879
Jönköping County Museum, Jönköping 35977
Jönköpings Läns Museum, Jönköping 35977
Joensuu Art Museum, Joensuu 09580
Joensuun Taidemuseo, Joensuu 09580
Jörg-Metzler-Stube, Ravenstein 19510
Joetsu Municipal Museum, Joetsu 26282
Joetsu-shiritsu Hakubutsukan, Joetsu 26282
Johan Nygaardsvold Museum, Hommelvik 30559
Johann-Baptist-Graser-Schulmuseum, Bayreuth 15850
Johann-David-Köhler-Haus, Colditz 16492
Johann-Friedrich-Böttger und die Geschichte der Porzellanmanufaktur Meissen, Schleiz 19790
Johann-Friedrich-Danneil-Museum, Salzwedel 19739
Johann Jacobs Museum, Zürich 37382
Johann Köleri Muuseum, Vastemõisa 09393
Johann Michael Haydn-Gedenkstätte, Salzburg 02541
Johann Ulrich Steiger-Freilichtmuseum, Zurzach 37431
Johanna Museet, Skurup 36202
Johanna-Spyri-Museum im Alten Schulhaus, Hirzel 36805
Johannes Brahms-Museum, Mürzzuschlag 02329
Johannes Jørgensens Mindestuer, Svendborg 09084
Johannes Larsen Museet, Kerteminde 08914
Johannes Linnankosken Nuoruudenkoti, Askola 09421
Johannes Linnankoski's Childhood Home, Askola 09421
Johannes-Molzahn-Centrum für Documentation und Publication, Kassel 18020
Johannes Stegmann Art Gallery, Bloemfontein 34185
Johannesburg Art Gallery, Johannesburg 34279
Johanniter-Museum, Krautheim, Jagst 18221
Johanniter- und Maltesermuseum, Heitersheim 17699
John A. Hermann jr. Memorial Art Museum, Bellevue 41596
John A. Logan College Museum, Carterville 42124
The John A. Noble Collection, Staten Island 47784
John Abbott II House, Hamilton 43880
The John and Mable Ringling Museum of Art, Sarasota 47453
John B. Davis Gallery of Fine Art, Pocatello 46572
John Brown Farm, Lake Placid 44593
John Brown House, Osawatomie 46201
John Brown House, Prividence 46708
John Brown Wax Museum, Harpers Ferry 43919
John Buchan Centre, Tweedoale 40737
John Bunyan Museum, Bedford 38149
John Burroughs Memorial, Roxbury 47024
John Creasey Museum, Salisbury 40434
John Day Fossil Beds National Monument, Kimberly 44481
John Deere House, Dixon 42952
John Dony Field Centre, Bushmead 38422
John E. and Walter D. Webb Museum of Vintage Fashion, Island Falls 44264
John E. Conner Museum, Kingsville 44499
John E. Weatherhead Gallery, Fort Wayne 43477
John Elliott Classics Museum, Hobart 01098
John F. Kennedy Presidential Library-Museum, Boston 41812
John Fisher Memorial Museum, Kingston 05678
John Fitzgerald Kennedy House, Brookline 41936
John G. Blank Center for the Arts, Michigan City 45302
John G. Diefenbaker Replica Law Office, Wakaw 06740
John G. Johnson Collection, Philadelphia 46421
John G. Neihardt Center, Bancroft 41490
John G. Voigt House, Plymouth 46568
John Gershom-Parkington Collection of Timekeeping Instruments, Bury Saint Edmunds 38416
John Gorrie Museum, Apalachicola 41236
John Greenleaf Whittier Home, Amesbury 41175
John H. Vanderpoel Art Gallery, Chicago 42337
John Hancock Warehouse, York 48789
John Hansard Gallery, Southampton 40545
The John Harris/Simon Cameron Mansion, Harrisburg 43924
John Hastie Museum, Strathaven 40632
John Humphrey House, Swampscott 47899
John Hutchings Museum of Natural History, Lehi 44713
John J. Harvey Fireboat Collection, New York 45822
John J. McDonough Museum of Art, Youngstown 48808
John James Audubon Museum, Henderson 43988
John Jarrold Printing Museum, Norwich 40095
John Jay French House, Beaumont 41569
John Jay Homestead, Katonah 44415
John Kane House, Pawling 46316
John King Workshop Museum, Pinxton 40203
John Knox's House, Edinburgh 38890
John McDouall Stuart Museum, Dysart 38832
John Mariani Art Gallery, Greeley 43784
John Marshall House, Richmond 46880
John Maxine Belger Center, Kansas City 44398
John Michael Kohler Arts Center, Sheboygan 47589
John Moore Countryside Museum, Tewkesbury 40690
John Muir's Birthplace, Dunbar 38794
John P. Barclay Memorial Gallery, Pittsburgh 46519
John Paul Jones Birthplace Museum, Arbigland 38008
John Paul Jones House Museum, Portsmouth 46649
The John Q. Adams Center for the History of Otolaryngology - Head and Neck Surgery, Alexandria 41130
John R. Jackson House, Winlock 48690
John R. Park Homestead, Harrow 05587
John Rains House, Rancho Cucamonga 46783
John Ralston Museum, Mendham 45249
John Rivers Communications Museum, Charleston 42220
John Rylands Library, Manchester 39891
John S. Barry Historical Society Museum, Constantine 42611
John Sinclair Railway Collection, Killingworth 39360
John Slade Ely House, New Haven 45695
John Smart House, Medina 45225
The John Southern Gallery, Dobwalls 38736
John Stark Edwards House, Warren 48310
John Strong Mansion, Addison 41065
John Sydnor's 1847 Powhatan House, Galveston 43611
John-Wagener-Haus Sievern, Langen bei Bremerhaven 18322
John Ward House, Salem 47196
John Weaver Sculpture Museum, Hope 05604
John Wesley Powell Memorial Museum, Page 46259
John Woolman Memorial, Mount Holly 45532
John Wornall House Museum, Independence 44205
The Johns Hopkins University Archaeological Collection, Baltimore 41473
Johnson Atelier, Mercerville 45262
Johnson Collection of Photographs, Movies and Memorabilia, Chanute 42193
Johnson County Historical Society Museum, Coralville 42630
Johnson County Historical Society Museum, Tecumseh 47966
Johnson County Historical Society Museum, Warrensburg 48316
Johnson County History Museum, Franklin 43517
Johnson County Museums, Shawnee 47586
Johnson Ferry House Museum, Titusville 48013
Johnson Hall, Johnstown 44350
Johnson Heritage Post, Grand Marais 43753
Johnson-Humrickhouse Museum, Coshocton 42662
Johnstown Historical Society Museum, Johnstown 44351
Jókai Memorial Room, Budapest 21347
Jókai Mór Emlékmúzeum, Balatonfüred 21311
Jokioinen Parsonage Museum, Jokioinen 09584
Jokioinen Railway Museum and Narrow Gauge Museum, Jokioinen 09582
Jokioisten Museorautatie ja Kapearaidemuseo, Jokioinen 09582
Jokioisten Naulamuseo, Jokioinen 09583
Jokioisten Pappilamuseo, Jokioinen 09584
Jokkmokks Stencenter, Jokkmokk 35983
Joliet Area Historical Museum, Joliet 44355
Jølstramuseet, Vassenden 30978
Jonathan Hager House and Museum, Hagerstown 43865
Jones Center for Contemporary Art, Austin 41413
The Jones Museum of Glass and Ceramics, Sebago 47549
Jonesborough-Washington County History Museum, Jonesborough 44360
Jonson Gallery, Albuquerque 41103
Joods Historisch Museum, Amsterdam 28862
Joods Museum van Deportatie en Verzet, Mechelen 03615
Joodse Schooltje, Leek 29501
Joongang University Museum, Seoul 27242
Jopie Huisman Museum, Workum 30021
Jordan Archaeological Museum, Amman 27052
Jordan Folklore Museum, Amman 27053
Jordan Historical Museum of the Twenty, Jordan 05635
Jordan Museum of Popular Tradition, Amman 27054
Jordan National Gallery of Fine Arts, Amman 27055
Jordan Natural History Museum, Irbid 27063
Jorge B. Vargas Museum and Filipiana Research Center, Quezon City 31434
Jorge Barlin National Monument, Baao 31276
Joroinen Local Arts and Crafts Museum, Joroinen 09585
Joroisten Kotiseutumuseo, Joroinen 09585
Jorvik Museum, York 40964
Jos National Museum and Museum of Traditional Nigerian Architecture, Jos 30347
Jósa András Múzeum, Nyíregyháza 21492
Jose Drudis-Biada Art Gallery, Los Angeles 44916
Jose P. Laurel Memorial Museum, Manila 31378
José P. Laurel Monument Museum, Santo Tomas 31444
José Rizal Shrine Museum, Calamba 31301
José Rizal Shrine Museum, Dapitan 31322
José Rizal Shrine Museum, Manila 31379
Josef-Haubrich-Kunsthalle, Köln 18146
Josef Kainz-Gedenkraum, Wien 02902
Josef Suk Memorial, Křečovice 08432
Josef Weinheber-Museum, Kirchstetten 02115
Josefine-Weihrauch-Heimatmuseum, Neudenau 19021
Joseloff Gallery, West Hartford 48525
Joseph A. Cain Memorial Art Gallery, Corpus Christi 42646
The Joseph A. Callaway Archaeological Museum, Louisville 44966
Joseph A. Driscoll Art Gallery, Brockton 41910
Joseph A. Tallman Museum, Cherokee 42273
Joseph Brant Museum, Burlington 05147
Joseph D. Carrier Art Gallery, Toronto 06586
Joseph Manigault House, Charleston 42221
Joseph Misson-Gedenkstätte, Mühlbach am Mannhartsberg 02325
Joseph Moore Museum, Richmond 46861
Joseph Parry's Cottage, Merthyr Tydfil 39938
Joseph Priestley House, Northumberland 46029
Joseph Schneider Haus, Kitchener 05697
Joseph Smith Historic Center, Nauvoo 45638

Josiah Quincy House, Quincy 46764
Joslowitzer Heimatstube, Zwingendorf 03064
Joslyn Art Museum, Omaha 46149
Jost House Museum, Sydney 06527
Jottos Museum-Workshop, Erevan 00683
Jourdan-Bachman Pioneer Farm, Austin 41414
Journey Museum, Rapid City 46795
Journey's End Cottage and Laishley House, Auckland 30111
Joutsa Museum, Joutsa 09586
Joutsan Kotiseutumuseo, Joutsa 09586
The Joyo Geibun Center, Mito 26502
Józef Czechowicz Museum, Lublin 31792
Jozef Gregor Tajovský Memorial House, Tajov 34072
Jozef I. Kraszewski Museum, Poznań 31914
Józef Kraszewski Museum, Romanów 31952
Józef Wybicki Memorial Museum, Nowy Karczma 31833
József Attila Emlékmúzeum, Balatonszárszó 21312
József Attila Múzeum, Makó 21468
J.T. Wilson Museum of Human Anatomy, Sydney 01499
J.U. Polimski Muzej, Berane 33822
Juan Luna Shrine Museum, Badoc 31281
The Judah P. Benjamin Confederate Memorial at Gamble Plantation, Ellenton 43153
Judaica Museum of Central Synagogue, New York 45823
Judaica Museum of the Hebrew Home for the Aged at Riverdale, Bronx 41921
Judenbad, Friedberg, Hessen 17138
Judge Roy Bean Visitor Center, Langtry 44638
The Judge's Lodging, Presteigne 40265
Judges' Lodgings, Lancaster 39412
Judiska Museet i Stockholm, Stockholm 36249
Judith Basin County Museum, Stanford 47774
Jüdische Galerie Berlin, Berlin 16008
Jüdische Gedenkstätte und ehemalige Synagoge, Wallhausen, Württemberg 20381
Jüdisches Kulturmuseum, Augsburg 15558
Jüdisches Kulturmuseum und Synagoge, Veitshöchheim 20291
Jüdisches Kulturzentrum, Fulda 17176
Jüdisches Museum, Frankfurt am Main 17057
Jüdisches Museum, Göppingen 17316
Jüdisches Museum, München 18859
Jüdisches Museum Berlin, Berlin 16009
Jüdisches Museum der Schweiz, Basel 36501
Jüdisches Museum der Stadt Wien, Wien 02903
Jüdisches Museum Emmendingen, Emmendingen 16854
Jüdisches Museum Franken in Fürth, Fürth, Bayern 17165
Jüdisches Museum Franken in Schnaittach, Schnaittach 19816
Jüdisches Museum Georgensgmünd, Georgensgmünd 17239
Jüdisches Museum Hohenems, Hohenems 02041
Jüdisches Museum im Raschi-Haus, Worms 20677
Jüdisches Museum Rendsburg und Dr.-Bamberger-Haus, Rendsburg 19569
Jugendhuset, Varde 09100
Jugendkunstschule Pankow, Berlin 16010
Jugendmuseum Schöneberg, Berlin 16011
Jugendstilmuseum Reissenweber, Brühl, Baden 16375
Jugoslovenska Galerija Reprodukcija Umetnickih Dela, Beograd 33801
Jugoslovenska Galerija Umetnickih Dela, Beograd 33802
Juhani Ahon Museo, Iisalmi 09557
Juice and Vinegar Museum, Doesburg 29157
The Jukebox Collection, Sissach 37178
Jukkasjärvi Museet, Jukkasjärvi 35984
Julia A. Purnell Museum, Snow Hill 47661
Julia C. Butridge Gallery, Austin 41415
Julian H. Sleeper House, Saint Paul 47158
Juliette Gordon Low Birthplace, Savannah 47480
Julistemuseo, Lahti 09741
Julita Sveriges Lantbruksmuseums, Julita 35985
Julius Gordon Africana Centre, Riversdale 34368
Jumalon Museum and Art Gallery, Cebu 31313
Juming Museum, Taipei 07348
Junagadh Museum, Junagadh 21877
Junction City Historical Society Museum, Junction City 44367
Junction Cottage, Pontypool 40220
Jundt Art Museum, Spokane 47727
Juneau-Douglas City Museum, Juneau 44370
Junee Historical Museum, Junee 01127
Junge Kunst, Wolfsburg 20661
Das Junge Museum, Bottrop 16264
Jungmun Folklore Museum, Seogwipo 27220
Jungsteinzeitliche Grabhügel, Sarmenstorf 37121
Juniata College Museum of Art, Huntingdon 44154
Junior Museum, Newark 45890
Junior Museum, Troy 48070
The Junior Museum of Bay County, Panama City 46277
JuniorMuseum im Ethnologischen Museum, Berlin 16012
Junkerhaus, Lemgo 18430
Jura-Bauernhof-Museum, Hitzhofen 17772
Jura-Museum, Eichstätt 16805
Jurica Nature Museum, Lisle 44811
Jurinskij Istoriko-chudožestvennyj Muzej, Jurino 32863
Jurjeveckij Kraevedčeskij Muzej, Jurjevec 32864
Jurmala City Museum, Jūrmala 27369
Jūrmalas Pilsētas Muzejs, Jūrmala 27369
Jussi Björlingmuseet, Borlänge 35845
Justice and Police Museum, Sydney 01500
Justin Smith Morrill Homestead, Strafford 47844
Justina M. Barnicke Gallery, Hart House, Toronto 06587
Justinus-Kerner-Haus, Weinsberg 20481
Justinus Mulle-Museum, Sankt Veit an der Glan 02611
Jusupovskij Dvorec, Sankt-Peterburg 33411
Jute Museum, Kolkata 21906
Jutulheimen Bygdemuseum, Vaagaa 30965
Juuan Pitäjänmuseo, Juuka 09589
Juvan Museo, Juva 09591
J.V. Snellman Home Museum, Kuopio 09718
J.V. Snellmanin Kotimuseo, Kuopio 09718
J.W. Parmely Historical Home Museum, Ipswich 44252
Jysk Automobilmuseum, Gjern 08838
Jyväskylä Art Museum, Jyväskylä 09597
Jyväskylä School Museum, Jyväskylä 09595
Jyväskylä University Museum - Section of Cultural History, Jyväskylä 09599
Jyväskylä University Museum - Section of Natural History, Jyväskylä 09598
Jyväskylän Lyseon Museo, Jyväskylä 09595
Jyväskylän Näkövammaisten Koulun Museo, Jyväskylä 09596
Jyväskylän Taidemuseo, Jyväskylä 09597
Jyväskylän Yliopiston Museo - Keski-Suomen Luontomuseo, Jyväskylä 09598
Jyväskylän Yliopiston Museo - Kultuurihistoriallinen Osasto, Jyväskylä 09599
K & K-Museum, Türnitz 0274232890
K20 Kunstsammlung am Grabbeplatz, Düsseldorf 16728
K21 Kunstsammlung im Ständehaus, Düsseldorf 16729
Ka-Do-Ha Indian Village Museum, Murfreesboro 45565
K.A. Timiryazev Apartment Museum, Moskva 33128
K.A. Timiryazev State Museum of Biology, Moskva 33048
Kaarinan Koulumuseo, Littoinen 09790
Kaarlela Local History Museum, Kokkola 09682
Kaarlelan Kotiseutumuseo, Kokkola 09682
Kaasboerderijmuseum de Weistaar, Maarsbergen 29555
Kaasmuseum Bodegraven, Bodegraven 28991
Kaaswaag Gouda, Gouda 29294
Kaatsmuseum, Franeker 29260
Kaatza Station Museum, Lake Cowichan 05719
Kaban ng Hiyas ng Lungsod ng Mandaluyong, Mandaluyong 31364
Kabardino-Balkarian Art Museum, Nalčik 33193
Kabardino-Balkarskij Gosudarstvennyj Muzej Izobrazitelnych Iskusstv, Nalčik 33193
Kabarnet Museum, Kabarnet 27103
Kabayan National Museum, Kabayan 31334
Kabinet Grafike HAZU, Zagreb 07826
De Kabinetten van de Vleeshal, Middelburg 29591
Kabul Museum, Kabul 00004
Kachchh Museum, Bhuj 21728
Kachelmuseum De Drie Kronen, Boekel 28992
Kackadariinsk Regional Museum, Karši 48839
Kadina Heritage Museum, Kadina 01129
Kadman Numismatic Pavilion, Tel Aviv 22764
Kärntner Bauernmöbelsammlung, Maria Saal 02268
Kärntner Freilichtmuseum, Maria Saal 02269
Kärsämäen Kotiseutumuseo, Kärsämäki 09609
Käsewelt Schleedorf, Schleedorf 02633
Käthe-Kollwitz-Museum Berlin, Berlin 16013
Käthe Kollwitz Museum Köln, Köln 18147
Käthe Kruse-Poppenmuseum, Den Helder 29133
Käthe-Kruse-Puppen-Museum, Donauwörth 16639
Kaffeekannenmuseum, Schöppenstedt 19839
Kagaku Gijutsukan, Tokyo 26864
Kagawa-ken Bunka Kaikan, Takamatsu 26789
Kagawa Prefecture Cultural Center, Takamatsu 26789
Kagoshima Cultural Center, Kagoshima 26287
Kagoshima-ken Bunka Center, Kagoshima 26287
Kagoshima-kenritsu Hakubutsukan, Kagoshima 26288
Kagoshima Prefectural Museum, Kagoshima 26288
Kagu no Hakubutsukan, Tokyo 26865
Kahitsukan - Kyoto Museum of Contemporary Art, Kyoto 26407
Kahramanmaraş Culture Center, Kahramanmaraş 37723
Kahramanmaraş Devlet Güzel Sanatlar Galerisi, Kahramanmaraş 37722
Kahramanmaraş Kültür Merkezi, Kahramanmaraş 37723
Kahramanmaraş Müzesi, Kahramanmaraş 37724
Kahramanmaraş Museum, Kahramanmaraş 37724
Kahramanmaraş State Gallery, Kahramanmaraş 37722
Kahutara Canoes and Taxidermy Museum, Featherston 30160
Kaieji Buddhist Temple Site Museum, Sennan 26738
Kaifeng Municipal Museum, Kaifeng 07143
Kaikohe Pioneer Village and Museum, Kaikohe 30189
Kaikoura District Museum, Kaikoura 30190
Kainuun Museo, Kajaani 09610
Kaisendo Museum, Kaminoyama 26297
Kaiser Franz-Josef-Museum für Handwerk und Volkskunst, Baden bei Wien 01728
Kaiser Wilhelm Museum, Krefeld 18227
Kaiserappartements, Sisi Museum und Silberkammer, Wien 02904
Kaiserburg Nürnberg, Nürnberg 19148
Kaiserdom-Museum, Königslutter 18179
Kaisergruft, Wien 02905
Kaiserliche Hofburg zu Innsbruck, Innsbruck 02070
Kaiserliches Hofmobiliendepot, Wien 02906
Kaiserpfalz mit Sankt Ulrichskapelle, Goslar 17352
Kaiserpfalz Salzburg, Bad Neustadt an der Saale 15706
Kaiserpfalzruine, Gelnhausen 17225
Kaisersaal Schwarzburg, Schwarzburg 19881
Kaiserstühler Heimatmuseum, Endingen 16871
Kaiserstühler Weinbaumuseum, Vogtsburg 20329
Kaiservilla, Bad Ischl 01706
Kaitseväe Ühendatud Õppeasutuste Muuseum, Tartu 09378
Kaivolan Museo, Laitila 09753
Kajaani Art Museum, Kajaani 09611
Kajaanin Taidemuseo, Kajaani 09611
Kaji Aso Studio Gallery Nature and Temptation, Boston 41813
Kajuma Nasyri Museum, Kazan 32899
Kake Tribal Heritage Foundation, Kake 44375
Kakh-e-Rejat Va Ebrat & Mellat, Teheran 22308
Kakurin-ji Treasure House, Kakogawa 26292
Kala Art Institute, Berkeley 41643
Kalahari-Oranje Museum, Upington 34395
Kalajoen Kalastusmuseo, Kalajoki 09613
Kalajoen Kotiseutumuseo, Kalajoki 09614
Kalajoki Fishing Museum, Kalajoki 09613
Kalamazoo Aviation History Museum, Kalamazoo 44378
Kalamazoo Institute of Arts, Kalamazoo 44379
Kalamazoo Valley Museum, Kalamazoo 44380
Kalamunda History Village, Kalamunda 01130
Kalan Torppa, Kauhava 09639
Kalannin Kotiseutumuseo, Kalanti 09615
Kalanti Local History Museum, Kalanti 09615
Kalantiaw Shrine Museum, Batan 31286
Kalaupapa Historical Park, Kalaupapa 44381
Kaleidoscope, Kansas City 44399
Kaleko Mill, Faaborg 08816
Kaleko Mølle, Faaborg 08816
Kali-Bergbaumuseum Volpriehausen, Uslar 20279
Kalinčeva Kăšta, Trjavna 04885
Kalincheva House, Trjavna 04885
Kaliningrad Amber Museum, Kaliningrad 32872
Kaliningradskaja Oblastnaja Chudožestvennaja Galereja, Kaliningrad 32869
Kaliningradskij Oblastnoj Istoriko-chudožestvennyj Muzej, Kaliningrad 32870
Kaliningradskij Oblastnoj Kraevedčeskij Muzej, Kaliningrad 32871
Kalix Flottningsmuseum, Kalix 35986
Kalkaska County Historical Museum, Kalkaska 44385
Kallenaution Kievari, Korkeakoski 09691
Kallioniemi, Taivalkoski 10069
Kallmann-Museum, Ismaning 17927
Kalluntalo Museum, Laukaa 09770
Kalmar Art Museum, Kalmar 35987
Kalmar Castle, Kalmar 35990
Kalmar Konstmuseum, Kalmar 35987
Kalmar Läns Museum, Kalmar 35988
Kalmar Sjöfartsmuseum, Kalmar 35989
Kalmar Slott, Kalmar 35990
Kalmyckij Respublikanskij Kraevedčeskij Muzej im. Prof. N.N. Palmova, Ėlista 32794
Kalncempji Parish Museum of Local Studies - Ates Mill, Kalncempji 27373
Kalncempju Pagasta Novadpētniecības Muzejs Ates Dzirnavās, Kalncempji 27373
Kaluga Regional Art Museum, Kaluga 32878
Kaluga Regional Museum, Kaluga 32879
Kalundborg og Omegns Museum, Kalundborg 08911
Kalužskij Oblastnoj Chudožestvennyj Muzej, Kaluga 32878
Kalužskij Oblastnoj Kraevedčeskij Muzej, Kaluga 32879
Kalvolan Kunnan Kotiseutumuseo, Iittala 09560
Kamada Local Museum, Sakaide 26701
Kamakura Kokuhokan, Kamakura 26293
Kamakura Treasure Museum, Kamakura 26293
Kamakuragu Homotsu Chinretsujo, Kamakura 26294
Kamčatskij Oblastnoj Kraevedčeskij Muzej, Petropavlovsk-Kamčatskij 33310
Kamčatskij Voenno-istoričeskij Muzej, Petropavlovsk-Kamčatskij 33311
Kamenný Dům, Kutná Hora 08438
Kamera- und Fotomuseum Leipzig, Leipzig 18400
Kamernyj Šaljapinskij Zal, Kazan 32889
Kami no Hakubutsukan, Tokyo 26866
Kamienica Hipolitów, Kraków 31690
Kamienica Szołayskich, Kraków 31691
Kamiina Museum, Ina 26246
Kaminski House Museum, Georgetown 43654
Kamiya Bijutsukan, Handa 26183
Kamiya Museum of Art, Handa 26183
Kamloops Art Gallery, Kamloops 05638
Kamloops Museum, Kamloops 05639
Kammerhofgalerie der Stadt Gmunden, Gmunden 01895
Kammerhofmuseum Ausseerland, Bad Aussee 01691
Kammerhofmuseum der Stadt Gmunden, Gmunden 01896
Kamnik Museum, Kamnik 34093
Kamniški Muzej, Kamnik 34093
Kamper Tabaksmuseum, Kampen 29471
Kamphaeng Phet National Museum, Kamphaeng Phet 37506
Kamsack and District Museum, Kamsack 05643
Kamthieng House, Bangkok 37487
Kanabec History Center, Mora 45490
Kanagawa-kenritsu Kanazawabunko Museum, Yokohama 27014
Kanagawa Kenritsu Kindai Bijutsukan, Hayama 26185
Kanagawa-kenritsu Rekishi Hakabutsukan, Yokohama 27015
Kanagawa Prefectural Gallery, Yokohama 27016
Kanagawa Prefectural Kanazawabunko-Museum, Yokohama 27014
Kanagawa Prefectural Museum of Cultural History, Yokohama 27015
Kanai History and Folk Museum, Kanai 26303
Kanai-machi Hakabutsukan, Kanai 26303
Kanal- och Sjöfartsmuseet, Motala 36105
Kanalmuseet, Trollhättan 36336
Kanalmuseet Skantzen, Hallstahammar 35939
Kanazawa-shiritsu Nakamura Kinen Bijutsukan, Kanazawa 26310
Kandahar Museum, Kandahar 00007
Kandeloos Museum, Kojoor 22260
Kandelous Museum, Kandelous 22248
Kandiyohi County Historical Society Museum, Willmar 48642
Kandos Bicentennial Industrial Museum, Kandos 01133
Kandy National Museum, Kandy 35757
Kanebo Museum of Textiles, Osaka 26650
Kang Weon Folk Museums, Chunchon 27151
Kang Xicao Museum, Beijing 06969
Kangasalan Museo, Kangasala 09616
Kangaslammin Koti- ja Koulumuseo, Kangaslampi 09618
Kangaslampi Home and School Museum, Kangaslampi 09618
Kangasniemen Museo, Kangasniemi 09619
Kangasniemi Museum, Kangasniemi 09619
Kanizsai Dorottya Múzeum, Mohács 21482
Kankaanpään Kaupunginmuseo, Niinisalo 09862
Kankakee County Historical Society Museum, Kankakee 44388
Kannada Research Institute Museum, Dharwar 21793
Kannonkosken Kotiseutukokoelma, Kannonkoski 09621
Kannuksen Museo, Kannus 09622
Kansainvälinen Kahvikuppimuseo, Posio 09957
Kansainvälinen Pullomuseo, Sonkajärvi 10052
Kansallis-Osake-Pankin Rahanäyttely, Helsinki 09497
Kansallispukukeskus, Jyväskylä 09600
Kansas African American Museum, Wichita 48604
Kansas Aviation Museum, Wichita 48605
Kansas Barbed Wire Museum, La Crosse 44534
Kansas City Museum/Science City at Union Station, Kansas City 44400
Kansas Cosmosphere and Space Center, Hutchinson 44183
Kansas Health Museum, Halstead 43875
Kansas Museum of History, Topeka 48033
Kansas Museums Association, Topeka 49500
The Kansas Teachers' Hall of Fame, Dodge City 42956
Kanshin-ji Reihokan, Kawachi-Nagano 26321
Kanshin-ji Treasure House, Kawachi-Nagano 26321
Kant- en Textielcentrum, Diest 03385
Kanta Museum Argungu, Argungu 30331
Kantcentrum, Brugge 03255
Het Kantenhuis, Amsterdam 28863
Kantmuseum, Olsene 03663
Kantmuseum, Uithuizen 29887
Kantonales Fischereimuseum Mettlen, Netstal 36980
Kantonales Museum Altes Zeughaus, Solothurn 37183
Kanuma Municipal Art Museum of Kawakami Sumio, Kanuma 26312
Kanzeon-ji Treasure House, Dazaifu 26133
Kao Chong, Trang 37544
Kao Luang, Nakhon Si Thammarat 37518
Kao Ta Phet, Sukhothai 37538
Kao Yai, Saraburi 37535
Kapenguria Museum, Kapenguria 27104
Kaperdalen Samemuseum, Senja 30836
Kapilavastu Museum, Taulihawa 28793
Kapitän Tadsen Museum, Langeneß 18335
Kapiteinshuis Pekela, Nieuwe Pekela 29618
Kapiti Coast Museum Waikanae, Wellington 30295
Kaplanstöckl, Hohenzell 02043
Kaple Sv. Kříže, Praha 08583
Kaposvar Historic Site, Esterhazy 05414
Kapucijnenmuseum, 's-Hertogenbosch 29403
Kapunda Museum, Kapunda 01135
Kapuzinerturm, Radstadt 02475
Karačaevo-Čerkesskij Istoriko-kul'turnyj i Prirodnyj Muzej-Zapovednik, Čerkessk 32736
Karacolskij Istoričeskij Kraevedčeskij Muzej, Karacol 27311
Karaganda Historical and Regional Museum, Karaganda 27085
Karakalpak Historical Museum, Nukus 48847
Karakalpakskij Istoričeskij Muzej, Nukus 48847
Karaliichev House-Museum, Sofia 04828
Karalpacia State Regional Museum, Nukus 48845
Karaman Müzesi, Karaman 37725
Karaman Museum, Karaman 37725
Karamea Centennial Museum, Karamea 30192
Karamzin Public Library Museum, Uljanovsk 33660
Karasek-Museum, Seifhennersdorf 19928

Karatepe Açıkhava Müzesi, Kadirli 37721
Karatepe Open Air Museum, Kadirli 37721
Karby Gård Konstcentrum, Täby 36319
Kardamyla Cultural Centre of Michael and Stamatia Xylas, Ano Kardamyla 20826
Karden-und Heimatmuseum, Katsdorf 02101
Kare Shelley Railroad Museum, Boone 41785
Karelian Farmhouse, Imatra 09565
Karelian Museum of Fine Arts, Petrozavodsk 33318
Karelian State Regional Museum, Petrozavodsk 33316
Karelskij Gosudarstvennyj Kraevedčeskij Muzej, Petrozavodsk 33316
Karen Blixen Museet, Rungsted Kyst 09049
Karen Blixen Museum, Nairobi 27110
Karepa Kalame Talumuuseum, Vihula 09394
Karepe Fishermen Museum, Vihula 09394
Kareum - Gamla Bilsalongen, Sparreholm 36224
Kargopol State Museum of History, Architecture and Art, Kargopol 32884
Kargopolskij Gosudarstvennyj Istoriko-Architekturnyj i Chudožestvennyj Muzej, Kargopol 32884
Karhula Glass Museum, Karhula 09623
Karhulan Lasimuseo, Karhula 09623
Kariandusi Prehistoric Site Museum, Gilgil 27101
Karijoen Kotiseutumuseo, Karijoki 09624
Karikatur und Cartoon Museum Basel, Basel 36502
Karikaturmuseum Krems, Krems 02156
Karjaan Museo, Karjaa 09626
Karjalainen Kotitalo, Imatra 09565
Karjalan Kotiseutumuseo, Mynämäki 09847
Karkkila Högforsin Työläismuseo, Karkkila 09627
Karkkila Worker's Museum, Karkkila 09627
Karl Drerup Fine Arts Gallery, Plymouth 46566
Karl Ernst Osthaus-Museum der Stadt Hagen, Hagen, Westfalen 17481
Karl Ernst von Baeri Muuseum, Tartu 09379
Karl Heinrich Waggerl-Haus, Wagrain 02781
Karl-Marx-Haus, Trier 20210
Karl-May-Haus, Hohenstein-Ernstthal 17813
Karl-May-Museum, Radebeul 19469
Karl Ristikivi Majamuuseum, Tartu 09380
Karl-Seckinger-Ausstellung, Karlsruhe 17993
Karl-Wagenplast-Museum, Schwaigern 19870
Kārļa Skalbes Muzejs, Vecpiebalga 27469
Kārļa Ulmaņa Pikšas, Bērze 27338
Karlebo Museum, Kokkedal 08958
Karlinger-Schmiede, Unterweißenbach 02756
Karlovac Municipal Museum, Karlovac 07713
Karlovarské Muzeum, Karlovy Vary 08401
Karlovské Muzeum, Velké Karlovice 08711
Karlovy Vary Art Gallery, Karlovy Vary 08400
Karlshamns Museum, Karlshamn 35992
Karlskoga Konsthall, Karlskoga 35995
Karmøy Fiskerimuseum, Vedavågen 30980
Karmsund Folkemuseum, Haugesund 30538
Karnataka Government Museum and Venkatappa Art Gallery, Bangalore 21703
Karnevalmuseum, Mönchengladbach 18771
Karol Plicka Múzeum, Blatnica 33955
Karpatendeutsches Museum, Karlsruhe 17994
Karrasburg Museum Coswig, Coswig bei Dresden 16499
Karrenmuseum, Essen 03410
Kars Culture Center, Kars 37727
Kars Devlet Güzel Sanatlar Galerisi, Kars 37726
Kars Kültür Merkezi, Kars 37727
Kars Müzesi, Kars 37728
Kars Museum, Kars 37728
Kars State Gallery, Kars 37726
Karst- und Höhlenkundliche Abteilung, Wien 02907
Karstmuseum Heimkehle, Uftrungen 20254
Karstulan Kotiseutumuseo, Karstula 09629
Kartäusermuseum Tückelhausen, Ochsenfurt 19218
Kartause Aggsbach, Aggsbach Dorf 01648
Kartause Gaming, Gaming 01866
Karthaus-Prüll Museen des Bezirksklinikums Regensburg, Regensburg 19525
Kartinnaja Galereja A.A. Plastova, Uljanovsk 33658
Kartinnaja Galereja K. Vasiljeva, Kazan 32890
Kartinnaja Galereja Pejzažej P.M. Grečiškina, Stavropol 33561
Kartinnaja Galereja Respubliki Adygeja, Majkop 33004
Kartinnaja Galerija im. P.I. Šolochova, Borisoglebsk 32700
Das Kartoffelmuseum, München 18860
Karttulan Kotiseutumuseo, Karttula 09630
Kartynna Galereya, Luck 37878
Karvian Museo, Karvia 09632
Karyes-Protaton, Agion Oros 20806
Kashima-jingu Treasure House, Kashima, Ibaraki 26318
Kashubian Museum, Kartuzy 31643
Kaškadarinskij Kraevedčeskij Muzej, Karši 48839
Kaskines Collection, Lindos 21052
Kaskö Hembygdsmuseum, Kaskinen 09635
Kasori Shell Mounds Site Museum, Chiba 26123
Kass Galéria, Szeged 21549
Kass Gallery, Szeged 21549
Kassák Museum, Budapest 21348
Kassuth Lajos Memorial Museum, Monok 21483
Kăšta-muzej Akademik Dončo Kostov, Lokorsko 04725
Kăšta-muzej Aleksandăr Mutafov, Sozopol 04865
Kăšta-muzej Angel Kănčev, Trjavna 04886
Kăšta-muzej Angel Karalijčev, Sofia 04828
Kăšta-muzej Asen Razcvetnikov, Draganovo 04657
Kăšta-muzej Asen Zlatarov, Chaskovo 04640
Kăšta-muzej Bojan Chonos, Vidin 04924
Kăšta-muzej Canko Cerkovski, Bjala Čerkva 04624
Kăšta-muzej Chadži Dimităr, Sliven 04818
Kăšta-muzej Christo Botev, Kalofer 04686
Kăšta-muzej Christo G. Danov, Plovdiv 04778
Kăšta-muzej Christo i Ivan Michailovi, Michajlovgrad 04738
Kăšta-muzej Christo Smirnenski, Sofia 04829
Kăšta-muzej Dimcho Debeljanov, Koprivštica 04712
Kašta-muzej Dimităr Blagoev, Bankja 04612
Kăšta-muzej Dimităr Blagoev, Sofia 04830
Kăšta-muzej Dimităr Dimov, Sofia 04831
Kăšta-muzej Dimitar Pešev, Kjustendil 04706
Kăšta-muzej Dimităr Poljanov, Karnobat 04693
Kăšta-muzej Dobri Čintulov, Sliven 04819
Kăšta-muzej Dobri Voinikov, Šumen 04871
Kăšta-muzej Došo Mihajlov, Babuk 04606
Kăšta-muzej Emilijan Stanev, Veliko Tărnovo 04914
Kăšta-muzej Ěrdan Ěovkov, Žeravna 04933
Kăšta-muzej Geo Milev, Stara Zagora 04866
Kăšta-muzej Georgi Benkovski, Koprivštica 04713
Kăšta-muzej Georgi Damianovo, Georgi Damianovo 04673
Kăšta-muzej Georgi Dimitrov, Kovačevci 04721
Kăšta-muzej Iljo Vojvoda, Kjustendil 04707
Kăšta-muzej Ivan Lazarov, Sofia 04832
Kašta-muzej Ivan Vazov, Berkovica 04622
Kăšta-muzej Ivan Vazov, Sofia 04833
Kăšta-muzej Lamartine, Plovdiv 04779
Kăšta-muzej Ljuben Karavelov, Koprivštica 04714
Kăšta-muzej Mitko Palauzov, Gabrovo 04669
Kăšta-muzej na Slivenskija Bit ot 19 Vek, Sliven 04820
Kăšta-muzej Neofit Rilski, Bansko 04614
Kăšta-muzej Nikola Ěnkov Vapcarov, Bansko 04615
Kăšta-muzej Nikola P. Karadžchata, Bradvari 04630
Kăšta-muzej Nikola Parapunov, Razlog 04799
Kăšta-muzej Nikola Vapcarov, Sofia 04834
Kăšta-muzej Panaět Chitov, Sliven 04821
Kăšta-muzej Panaět Volov, Šumen 04872
Kăšta-muzej Pančo Vladigerov, Šumen 04873
Kăšta-muzej Pejo Javorov, Sofia 04835
Kăšta-muzej Pejo K. Javorov, Čirpan 04646
Kăšta-muzej Petko i Pencho Slavejkovi, Sofia 04836
Kăšta-muzej Rajna Knjaginja, Panagjurište 04751
Kăšta-muzej Rusi Čorbadži, Žeravna 04934
Kăšta-muzej s Dom-pametnik Jordan Jovkov, Dobrič 04656
Kăšta-muzej Sava Filaretov, Žeravna 04935
Kăšta-muzej Slavejkovi, Trjavna 04887
Kăšta-muzej Stanislav Dospevski, Pazardžik 04756
Kăšta-muzej Stojan i Vladimir Zaimovi, Pleven 04765
Kăšta-muzej Svetoslav Obretenov, Provadia 04790
Kăšta-muzej Todor Kableškov, Koprivštica 04715
Kăšta-muzej Vasil Kolarov, Šumen 04874
Kăšta-muzej Zachari Stojanov, Medven 04733
Kăšta-muzej Zachari Stojanov, Ruse 04803
Kastamonu Devlet Güzel Sanatlar Galerisi, Kastamonu 37729
Kastamonu State Gallery, Kastamonu 37729
Kasteel Achtendries, Gent 03440
Kasteel Amerongen, Amerongen 28818
Kasteel Ammersoyen, Ammerzoden 28829
Kasteel Beauvoorde, Wulveringem 03847
Kasteel Cannenburch, Vaassen 29914
Kasteel De Doornenburg, Doornenburg 29169
Kasteel de Haar, Haarzuilens 29333
Kasteel Doorwerth, Doorwerth 29170
Kasteel Duivenvoorde, Voorschoten 29963
Kasteel Groeneveld, Baarn 28959
Kasteel Heeswijk, Heeswijk-Dinther 29372
Kasteel Heeze - Collectie H.N.C. Baron Van Tuyll Van Serooskerken Van Heeze en Leende, Heeze 29374
Kasteel Hernen, Hernen 29401
Kasteel Het Hijenhuis, Heino 29382
Kasteel Hoensbroek, Hoensbroek 29430
Kasteel Huis Doorn, Doorn 29167
Kasteel Middachten, De Steeg 29071
Kasteel-Museum Sypesteyn, Loosdrecht 29546
Kasteel Ooidonk, Deinze 03374
Kasteel Radboud, Medemblik 29582
Kasteel Rosendael, Rozendaal 29783
Kasteel van Beersel, Beersel 03208
Kasteel van Bornem, Bornem 03229
Kasteel van Gaasbeek, Gaasbeek 03424
Kasteel van Horst, Sint-Pieters-Rode 03745
Kasteel van Leeuwergem, Zottegem 03856
Kasteel van Wijnendale, Torhout 03784
Kasteelmuseum Slot van Laarne, Laarne 03548
Kasteelruïne Valkenburg, Valkenburg 29917
Kasteeltoren Ijsselstein, Ijsselstein 29461
Kaštel Town Museum, Kaštel Lukšić 07714
Kaštela Gradski Muzej, Kaštel Lukšić 07714
Kastélymúzeum, Fertőd 21415
The Kasteyev State Museum of Arts of the Republic of Kazakhstan, Almaty 27072
Kastleholm Castle, Sund 10061
Kastoria Byzantine Museum, Kastoria 21007
Kastrupgaardsamlingen, Kastrup 08912
Kasuga Shrine Treasure House, Nara 26576
Kasuga Taisha, Nara 26576
Kasvimuseo, Helsinki 09498
Kasvimuseo, Turku 10121
Katamatite Museum, Katamatite 01136
Katanning Historical Museum, Katanning 01137
The Kate Chopin House and Bayou Folk Museum, Cloutierville 42505
Katedralna Zbirka, Hvar 07706
Kateri Galleries, Auriesville 41392
Katharina-Luther-Stube, Torgau 20185
Katharinas Puppenhaus, Pleystein 19415
Katherine Mansfield Birthplace, Wellington 30296
Katherine Museum, Katherine 01138
Katherine Nash Gallery, Minneapolis 45388
Kathmandu - Hot Spring in the Art Museum, Yuzawa 27034
Kathree Häusle, Dettenhausen 16592
Katina Paxinou Museum, Athinai 20868
Katona József Múzeum, Kecskemét 21446
Katona József Múzeum, Kecskemét 21447
Katona József Múzeum, Kecskemét 21448
Katonah Museum of Art, Katonah 44416
Katori-jingu Treasure House, Sawara 26726
Katrineholms Hembygdsmuseet, Kristineholm 36021
Katschtaler Heimatmuseum, Rennweg 02507
Katsushika Hokusai Art Museum, Tsuwano 26980
Katsushika Hokusai Bijutsukan, Tsuwano 26980
Katsushika-ku Kyoiku Shiryokan, Tokyo 26867
Kattakurgan Historical and Regional Museum, Kattakurgan 48840
Katten Kabinet, Amsterdam 28864
Kattlunds Museigård, Havdhem 35946
Katumuseo, Helsinki 09499
Katwijks Museum, Katwijk aan Zee 29477
Katzenmuseum, Traunstein 20188
Kauai Children's Discovery Museum, Kapaa 44413
Kauai Museum, Lihue 44771
Kauffman Gallery, Shippensburg 47608
Kauffman Museum, North Newton 45999
Kaufmannsmuseum des Heimatvereins Haslach, Haslach 02006
Kauhajoen Museo, Kauhajoki 09637
Kauhavanmuseo, Kauhava 09640
Kaulbachatelier, Ohlstadt 19245
Kaunislehdon Talomuseo, Hyrynsalmi 09555
Kaunislehto Farmhouse, Hyrynsalmi 09555
Kauppila House, Humppila 09553
Kauppilan perinnetalo, Humppila 09553
Kauppilan Umpipiha, Laitila 09754
Kauppilanmäen Museo, Valkeakoski 10171
The Kauri Museum, Matakohe 30201
Kaurila School Museum, Tohmajärvi 10108
Kaurilan Koulumuseo, Tohmajärvi 10108
Kaustisen Kotiseutumuseo, Kaustinen 09642
Kauttua Factory Museum, Kauttua 09644
Kauttuan Tehtaan Museo, Kauttua 09644
Kavalierhaus Gifhorn- Museum für bürgerliche Wohnkultur, Gifhorn 17287
Kaw Mission, Council Grove 42674
Kawaguchi-ko Motor Museum, Narusawa 26589
Kawaguchi Tibetan Collection, Sendai 26731
Kawaguchiko Bijutsukan, Kawaguchiko 26324
Kawaguchiko Museum of Art, Kawaguchiko 26324
Kawai Kanjiro's House, Kyoto 26408
Kawamura Memorial Museum of Art, Sakura 26705
Kawanabe Kyosai Memorial Museum, Warabi 26999
Kawartha Settlers' Village, Bobcaygeon 05087
Kawasaki Citizen Museum, Kawasaki 26328
Kawasaki Municipal Industrial and Cultural Museum, Kawasaki 26327
Kawasaki-shi Shimin Hakubutsukan, Kawasaki 26328
Kawasaki-shiritsu Nihon Minkaen, Kawasaki 26329
Kawhia Regional Museum Gallery, Kawhia 30193
Kayseri Archaeological Museum, Kayseri 37732
Kayseri Arkeoloji Müzesi, Kayseri 37732
Kayseri Devlet Güzel Sanatlar Galerisi, Kayseri 37733
Kayseri State Gallery, Kayseri 37733
Kazanlăshka Roza, Kazanlăk 04701
Kazantzakis Museum, Iráklion 20976
Kazemattenmuseum, Oosterend 29668
Kazemattenmuseum Kornwerderzand, Kornwerderzand 29491
Kazimierz Pułaski Museum, Warka-Winiary 32075
Kazuaki Iwasaki Space Art Gallery, Ito 26264
Kazuo County Museum, Chaoyang 07017
KBCC Art Gallery, Brooklyn 41943
KdF-Museum, Ostseebad Binz 19309
K.E. Kivirikon Lintu- ja Nisäkäskokoelma, Helsinki 09500
Kealley's Gemstone Museum, Nannup 01299
Kearney Area Children's Museum, Kearney 44423
Kearney County Historical Museum, Minden 45377
Kearney Mansion Museum, Fresno 43560
Kearny Cottage, Perth Amboy 46360
Keats House, London 39679
Keats-Shelley House, Roma 25169
Kebon Binatang Taman Sari, Bandung 22070
Kecskeméti Képtár és Tóth Menyhért Emlékmúzeum, Kecskemét 21449
Kedah Royal Museum, Alor Setar 27616
Kedah State Art Gallery, Alor Setar 27617
Kedah State Museum, Alor Setar 27618
Keeler Tavern Museum, Ridgefield 46897
Keetmanshoop Museum, Keetmanshoop 28757
Kegworth Museum, Kegworth 39326
Kei Fujiwara Art Museum, Bizen 26119
Keighley and Worth Valley Railway Museum, Haworth 39200
Keikyän Kotiseutumuseo, Keikyä 09645
Keillor House Museum, Dorchester 05336
Keir Memorial Museum, Kensington 05658
Keitele-Museo, Suolahti 10064
Keith Harding's World of Mechanical Music, Northleach 40086
Keith National Trust Museum, Keith 01139
Kékfestő Múzeum, Pápa 21501
Keladi Museum, Keladi 21886
Kelantan State Museum, Kota Bharu 27630
Kelham Island Museum, Sheffield 40486
Kell House Museum, Wichita Falls 48613
Kellergedenkstätte Krippen, Bad Schandau 15734
Kellermuseum, Falkenstein 01823
Kellermuseum Das Preßhaus, Großkrut 01958
Kellerviertel Heiligenbrunn, Heiligenbrunn 02017
Kelley House Museum, Mendocino 45250
Kellie Castle, Pittenweem 40207
Kelliher and District Heritage Museum, Kelliher 05649
Kellogg Historical Society Museum, Kellogg 44428
Kellokosken Sairaalan Museo, Kellokoski 09647
Kellross Heritage Museum, Leross 05743
Kelly Gallery, Glasgow 39053
Kelly-Griggs House Museum, Red Bluff 46813
Kelmscott Manor, Kelmscott 39332
Kelnhof-Museum, Bräunlingen 16270
Kelowna Art Gallery, Kelowna 05652
Kelowna Museum, Kelowna 05653
Kelsey Museum of Ancient Archaeology, Ann Arbor 41218
Kelso House, Kent 44445
Kelso Museum and Turret Gallery, Kelso 39334
Kelsterbacher Museum für Porzellan, Kelsterbach 18054
Keltenmuseum, Hallein 01997
Keltenmuseum Gracarca, Sankt Kanzian 02577
Keltenmuseum Hochdorf/Enz, Eberdingen 16760
Kelter- und Weinbaumuseum, Niederstetten 19099
Keltisch-Römisches Museum, Manching 18610
Kelton House Museum, Columbus 42589
Kelvedon Hatch Secret Nuclear Bunker, Kelvedon Hatch 39335
Kemajuan Kraftangan Malaysia, Rawang 27683
Kemerer Museum of Decorative Arts, Bethlehem 41666
Kemerovo Museum of Fine Art, Kemerovo 32913
Kemerovskij Istoriko-architekturnyj Muzej Krasnaja Gorka, Kemerovo 32911
Kemerovskij Oblastnoj Kraevedčeskij Muzej, Kemerovo 32912
Kemerovskij Oblastnoj Muzej Izobrazitelnych Iskusstv, Kemerovo 32913
Kemi Art Museum, Kemi 09650
Kemijärven Kotiseutumuseo, Kemijärvi 09653
Kemin Museo, Kemi 09649
Kemin Museum, Kemi 09649
Kemin Taidemuseo, Kemi 09650
Kemin Työläismuseo, Kemi 09651
Keminmaan Museo, Keminmaa 09654
Kemp-McCarthy Memorial Museum, Rowe 47020
Kempeleen Kotiseutumuseo, Kempele 09655
Kemper Museum of Contemporary Art, Kansas City 44401
Kempisch Museum, Brecht 03240
Kempsey Historical and Cultural Museum, Kempsey 01141
Ken Domon Museum of Photography, Sakata 26704
Kendal Museum, Kendal 39337
Kendall Campus Art Gallery, Miami 45287
The Kendall College Mitchell Museum of the American Indian, Evanston 43239
Kendall Gallery, Grand Rapids 43758
Kendall Whaling Museum, Sharon 47579
Kenderdine Art Gallery, Saskatoon 06398
Kenilworth Historical Society Museum, Kenilworth 44432
Kenji Igarashi Memorial Museum, Tokyo 26868
Kenmin Hall Art Museum Toyama, Toyama 26968
Kennebunkport Historical Museum, Kennebunkport 44435
Kennedy-Douglass Center for the Arts, Florence 43343
Kennedy House, Selkirk 06418
Kennedy Museum of Art, Athens 41324
Kennesaw Civil War Museum, Kennesaw 44437
Kennesaw Mountain National Battlefield Park, Kennesaw 44438
Kennet and Avon Canal Trust Museum, Devizes 38725
Keno City Mining Museum, Keno City 05655
Kenosha County Museum, Kenosha 44440
Kenosha Public Museum, Kenosha 44441
Kenritsu Kagakukan Joetsu, Joetsu 26283
Kent and East Sussex Railway, Tenterden 40687
Kent and Sharpshooters Yeomanry Museum, Edenbridge 38869
Kent Art Association, Kent 44443
Kent Battle of Britain Museum, Hawkinge 39197
Kent Campus Museum and Gallery, Jacksonville 44297
Kent-Delord House Museum, Plattsburgh 46548
Kent Police Museum, Chatham 38530
Kent State University Art Galleries, Kent 44446
Kent State University Museum, Kent 44447
Kentuck Museum and Art Center, Northport 46026
Kentucky Art and Craft Foundation, Louisville 44967
Kentucky Association of Museums, Murray 49501
Kentucky Derby Museum, Louisville 44968
Kentucky Folk Art Center, Morehead 45494
Kentucky Historical Society Museum, Frankfort 43509
Kentucky Military History Museum, Frankfort 43510
The Kentucky Museum, Bowling Green 41849
Kentucky New State Capitol, Frankfort 43511
Kentucky Railway Museum, New Haven 45702
Kenwood, London 39680
Kenya Museum Society, Nairobi 49265
Keokuk Art Center, Keokuk 44451
Keokuk River Museum, Keokuk 44452
Képcsarnok - Gulácsy Lajos Terem, Szeged 21550
Kepler-Gedächtnishaus, Regensburg 19526

Keplermuseum, Weil der Stadt 20439
Képzőművészek Gulácsy Lajos, Budapest 21349
Keramiekcentrum Tiendschuur, Tegelen 29864
Keramik-Museum, Bürgel 16406
Keramik-Museum, Triengen 37253
Keramik-Museum Berlin, Berlin 16014
Keramik Museum Mettlach, Mettlach 18724
Keramikmuseum, Frechen 17092
Keramikmuseum Schloss Obernzell, Obernzell 19190
Keramikmuseum Staufen, Staufen 20037
Keramikmuseum Westerwald, Höhr-Grenzhausen 17784
Keramisch Museum Goedewaagen, Nieuw Buinen 29613
Kerava Art Museum, Kerava 09657
Keravan Museo, Kerava 09656
Keravan Taidemuseo, Kerava 09657
Kerbyville Museum, Kerby 36014
Kerch Museum of Culture and History, Kerč 37860
Kerčskij Gosudarstvennyj Istoriko-Kulturnyj Zapovednik, Kerč 37860
Kerényi Jenő Emlékmúzeum, Szentendre 21571
Keresztény Múzeum, Esztergom 21412
Kerkmuseum, Sint-Niklaas 03741
Kerkmuseum Janum, Janum 29464
Kerkonkosken Myllymuseo, Rautalampi 09986
Kermis- en Circusmuseum Steenwijk, Steenwijk 29851
Kern County Museum, Bakersfield 41440
Kernstock-Museum, Bruck an der Lafnitz 01751
Kërpeeva Kašta, Kotel 04718
Kerr Place, Onancock 46154
Kerrobert and District Museum, Kerrobert 05664
The Kerry Bog Village Museum, Glenbeigh 22476
Kerry County Museum, Tralee 22547
Kershaw County Historical Society Museum, Camden 42066
Kertemende Egnens Museer, Kerteminde 08915
Kesälahden Museo, Kesälahti 09659
Keski-Suomen Ilmailumuseo, Tikkakoski 10106
Keski-Suomen Museo, Jyväskylä 09601
Keski-Suomen Sairaanhoitopiirin Sairaalamuseo, Jyväskylä 09602
Keski-Suomen Tieliikennemuseo, Kintaus 09671
Keskisuomalaisen Museo, Jyväskylä 09603
Kestner Gesellschaft, Hannover 17598
Kestner-Museum, Hannover 17599
Keswick Museum and Art Gallery, Keswick 39344
Ketterer-Haus-Museum, Biberach, Baden 16142
Kettle River Museum, Midway 05848
Kettle's Yard, Cambridge 38457
Kettumäen Ulkomuseo ja Kotiseututalo, Kuusankoski 09730
Kettumäki Local History Museum, Kuusankoski 09730
Keuruu Open Air Museum, Keuruu 09661
Keuruun Kotiseutumuseo, Keuruu 09661
Keuruun Museo, Keuruu 09662
Kev Rohrlach Technology and Heritage Museum, Tanunda 01517
Kew Bridge Steam Museum, Kew 39349
Kew Historical Museum, Kew 01143
Kew Palace Museum of the Royal Botanic Gardens, Kew 39350
Kewaunee County Historical Museum, Kewaunee 44460
Keweenaw County Historical Society Museum, Eagle Harbor 43033
Key West Lighthouse Museum, Key West 44467
Key West Museum of Art and History, Key West 44468
Keystone Area Museum, Keystone 44475
Keystone Pioneer Museum, Roblin 06279
Kgosi Bathoen II (Segopotso) Museum, Kanye 03936
K.H. Renlund Museum, Kokkola 09683
K.H. Renlundin Museo, Kokkola 09683
Khachatrians Museum, Erevan 00684
Khadzhi Dimitâr Memorial House, Sliven 04818
Khajana Buildings Museum, Hyderabad 21844
Khalifa's House Museum, Omdurman 35773
Khalif's House Museum, Khartoum 35768
Khalkhal Museum, Khalkhal 22256
Khama III Memorial Museum, Serowe 03939
Khami Ruins Site Museum, Bulawayo 49025
Kharkiv Art Museum, Charkiv 37842
Kharkiv Historical Museum, Charkiv 37843
Kherson Local Museum, Cherson 37841
Khiching Museum, Khiching 21889
Khmelnitski Regional Museum, Chmelnickij 37844
Khodshents Historical and Regional Museum, Chudžand 37445
Khokhryakov House-Museum, Kirov 32916
Khon Kaen National Museum, Khon Kaen 37508
Khorasan Natural History Museum, Mashad 22266
Khoy Museum, Khoy 22259
K.I. Tchukovsky House-Museum, Peredelkino 33296
Kiangan National Museum, Kiangan 31338
Kiasma Museum of Contemporary Art, Helsinki 09501
Kiasma Nykytaiteen Museo, Helsinki 09501
Kibbutz Art Museum, Tel Aviv 22765
Kibbutz Negba Museum, Kibbutz Negba 22698
Kibi Archaeological Collection, Soja 26771
Kibo Art Gallery, Marangu 37462
Kidderminster Railway Museum, Kidderminster 39352
Kidspace Children's Museum, Pasadena 46301
Kidwelly Industrial Museum, Kidwelly 39354
Kiehle Gallery, Saint Cloud 47085
't Kiekhuus, Wolvega 30018
Kieler Stadt- und Schiffahrtsmuseum, Kiel 18074
Kierlinger Heimatmuseum, Kierling 02107

Kiev Lesya Ukrainka State Literature Museum, Kyïv 37870
Kiev Museum of Russian Art, Kyïv 37871
Kiev-Pechersky National Museum, Kyïv 37872
Kiev State Historical Museum, Kyïv 37869
Kiev Taras Shevchenko National Museum, Kyïv 37873
Kihniön Museo, Kihniö 09664
Kii Fudoki-No-Oka Museum, Wakayama 26996
Kiihtelysvaaran Museo, Kiihtelysvaara 09665
Kiikalan Kotiseutumuseo, Kiikala 09666
Kiikoisten Kotiseutumuseo, Kiikoinen 09667
Kiimingin Museo, Kiiminki 09668
Kijk en Luister Museum, Bennekom 28976
Kijk- en Luistermuseum, Bant 28962
KiK - Kultur im Kloster, Klostermarienberg 02138
Kikinda National Museum, Kikinda 33845
Kikkermuseum, Den Haag 29099
Kikuchi-Rekishikan, Kikuchi 26333
Kikusui Handicraft Museum, Kawanishi 26326
Kilby Historic Store and Farm, Harrison Mills 05586
Kildonan Museum, Kildonan 39356
Kilens Hembygdsgård, Sideby 10031
Kilkee Heritage Gallery, Kilkee 22486
Kilkivan Historical Museum, Kilkivan 01145
Killarney Centennial Museum, Killarney 05667
Killhope, the North of England Lead Mining Museum, Weardale 40804
Kilmainham Gaol and Museum, Dublin 22440
Kilmallock Museum, Kilmallock 22494
Kilmaurs Historical Society Museum, Kilmaurs 39364
Kilmore Quay Maritime Museum, Kilmore Quay 22495
Kilmore Quay Maritime Museum, Wexford 22559
Kilsyth's Heritage, Kilsyth 39366
Kilwinning Abbey Tower, Kilwinning 39368
Kimba and Gawler Ranges Historical Society Museum, Kimba 01146
Kimball Art Center, Park City 46288
Kimball House Museum, Battle Creek 41538
Kimbell Art Museum, Fort Worth 43487
Kimberley Heritage Museum, Kimberley 05668
Kimberley Mine Museum, Kimberley 34289
Kimberly Crest House, Redlands 46821
Kimble County Historical Museum, Junction 44366
Kimchi Field Museum, Seoul 27243
Kimo Bruks Museum and Gallery, Oravais 09882
Kina Slott, Drottningholm 35854
Kincaid Museum, Kincaid 05669
Kinder-Akademie Fulda Werkraummuseum, Fulda 17177
Kinder-Knürstl-Museum, Götzis 01902
Kinder- und Jugendgalerie Sonnensegel, Brandenburg an der Havel 16281
Kinder- und Jugendmuseum München, München 18861
Kindergarten Museum, Helsinki 09509
Kindergartenmuseum, Bruchsal 16368
Kinderkunsthal Villa Zebra, Rotterdam 29754
Kindermuseum, Frankfurt am Main 17058
Kindermuseum, Karlsruhe 17995
Kindermuseum, Wuppertal 20714
Kindermuseum Hamburg, Hamburg 17548
Kindermuseum Zoom, Wien 02908
Kindersley Plains Museum, Kindersley 05670
Kinderwagenmuseum, Nieuwolda 29625
Kinderwagens van toen, Dwingeloo 29185
Kinderweltmuseum, Vöcklamarkt 02768
Kindheitsmuseum, Marburg 18628
Kindheitsmuseum, Schönberg, Holstein 19823
Kinenkan Mikasa, Yokosuka 27026
King County Arts Commission Gallery, Seattle 47536
King Hooper Mansion, Marblehead 45135
King Island Historical Museum, Currie 00963
King John's Castle, Limerick 22506
King Kamehameha V - Judiciary History Center, Honolulu 44082
King Manor, Jamaica 44305
King Matthias Museum, Visegrád 21611
King Saud University Museum, Riyadh 33772
King Seaman School Museum, River Herbert 06273
King Sejong The Great Memorial Exhibition, Seoul 27244
King Township Historical Museum, King City 05671
Kingaroy Art Gallery, Kingaroy 01147
Kingman County Historical Museum, Kingman 44489
Kingman Museum of Natural History, Battle Creek 41539
Kingman Tavern Historical Museum, Cummington 42727
Kings County Museum, Hampton 05580
Kings County Museum, Kentville 05661
Kings Landing Historical Settlement, Prince William 06191
King's Lynn Arts Centre, King's Lynn 39369
King's Lynn Museum, King's Lynn 39370
King's Mill Visitor Centre, Wrexham 40942
Kings Mountain National Military Park, Blacksburg 41725
King's Own Royal Regiment Museum, Lancaster 39413
King's Own Scottish Borderers Regimental Museum, Berwick-upon-Tweed 38174
King's Own Yorkshire Light Infantry Regimental Museum, Doncaster 38742
The King's Royal Hussars Museum, Winchester 40889
Kings Weston Roman Villa, Bristol 38358
Kingsbury Watermill Museum, Saint Albans 40072
Kingsgate Gallery, London 39681
Kingsland Homestead, Flushing 43354
Kingsley Plantation, Jacksonville 44298

Kingston Archaeological Centre, Kingston 05679
Kingston Fire Department Museum, Kingston 05680
Kingston Mills Blockhouse, Elgin 05400
Kingston Museum, Kingston-upon-Thames 39385
Kingston Pioneer Museum, Kingston 01151
Kinistino District Pioneer Museum, Kinistino 05691
Kinizsi Vármúzeum, Nagyvázsony 21488
Kinlough Folk Museum, Kinlough 22497
Kinneil Museum and Roman Fortlet, Bo'ness 38276
Kinney Pioneer Museum, Clear Lake 42448
Kinnulan Kotiseutumuseo, Kinnula 09670
Kinreizuka Archaeological Collection, Kisaradu 26336
Kinross Museum, Kinross 33990
Kinsale Regional Museum, Kinsale 22499
Kipling District Historical Society Museum, Kipling 05692
Kipp Gallery, Indiana 44212
Ķirbizi Forest Museum, Viļķene 27476
Ķirbižu Meža Muzejs, Viļķene 27476
Kirche am Hohenzollernplatz, Berlin 16015
Kirchengeschichtliches Museum in der Pfalzkapelle, Bad Wimpfen 15769
Kirchenhäusl, Sankt Oswald bei Freistadt 02592
Kirchenmuseum, Ernen 36688
Kirchenmuseum, Marienhafe 18635
Kirchenmuseum in der Pfarrei, Gengenbach 17235
Kirchenschatz, Bremgarten (Aargau) 36584
Kirchenschatz, Glarus 36763
Kirchenschatz des Chorherrenstiftes, Beromünster 36558
Kirchenschatz im Sankt Fridolinsmünster, Bad Säckingen 15724
Kirchenschatz-Museum, Baden 36486
Kirchenschatz-Museum Sankt Martin, Altdorf, Uri 36448
Kirchenschatz Sankt Pelagius Kirche, Bischofszell 36573
Kirchner Museum Davos, Davos Platz 36654
Kırıkkale Culture Center, Kırıkkale 37734
Kırıkkale Kültür Merkezi, Kırıkkale 37734
Kiril Petrov Art Gallery, Montana 04740
Kirillo-Beloserskiy Historical, Architectural and Artistic Museum-Reserve, Kirillov 32915
Kirillo-Belozerskij Istoriko-Architekturnyj i Chudožestvennyj Muzej-Zapovednik, Kirillov 32915
Kirkaldy Testing Museum, London 39682
Kirkcaldy Museum and Art Gallery, Kirkcaldy 39391
Kirkham House, Paignton 40159
Kirkkomuseo, Mikkeli 09831
Kirkland Fine Arts Center-Perkinson Gallery, Decatur 42832
Kirkleatham Museum, Redcar 40300
Kirklees Collection of Photographs, Huddersfield 39273
Kirkpatrick Science and Air Space Museum at Omniplex, Oklahoma City 46114
Kirkuk Museum, Kirkuk 22350
Kirms-Krackow-Haus, Weimar, Thüringen 20462
Kirov Regional Museum, Kirov 32920
Kirovograd Regional Museum of Local History, Art and Nature, Kirovograd 37861
Kirovskij Oblastnoj Chudožestvennyj Muzej im. Viktora i Apollinarija Vasnecovych, Kirov 32919
Kirovskij Oblastnoj Kraevedčeskij Muzej, Kirov 32920
Kirpilä Art Collection, Helsinki 09539
Kirriemuir Gateway to the Glens Museum, Kerriemuir 39341
Kırşehir Culture Center, Kırşehir 37736
Kırşehir Devlet Güzel Sanatlar Galerisi, Kırşehir 37735
Kırşehir Kültür Merkezi, Kırşehir 37736
Kırşehir State Gallery, Kırşehir 37735
Kirsten Flagstad Museum, Hamar 30529
Kirsten Kjærs Museum, Frøstrup 30834
Kirsti, Home of a Seaman Museum, Rauma 09980
Kirsti Rauman Museo, Rauma 09980
Kirtland Temple Historic Center, Kirtland 44504
Kis Géza Ormánság Múzeum, Sellye 21528
Kiscelli Múzeum, Budapest 21350
Kisfaludy Emlékmúzeum, Sümeg 21541
Kisfaludy-Memory-Museum, Sümeg 21541
Kiskon Kotiseutumuseo, Kisko 09674
Kiskun Múzeum, Kiskunfélegyháza 21457
Kislovodsk Historical Museum Fortress, Kislovodsk 32928
Kislovodskij Istoriko-kraevedčeskij Muzej Krepost', Kislovodsk 32928
Kiss Pál Múzeum, Tiszafüred 21596
Kistefos-museet, Jevnaker 30584
Kisumu Museum, Kisumu 27105
Kit Carson Historical Society Museum, Kit Carson 44506
KIT Kindermuseum, Amsterdam 28865
KIT Tropenmuseum, Amsterdam 28866
Kitajski Dvorec-muzej, Lomonosov 32989
Kitakamakura Museum, Kamakura 26295
Kitakami Municipal Museum, Kitakami 26341
Kitakyushu Municipal Museum of Art, Kitakyushu 26343
Kitakyushu-shiritsu Bijutsukan, Kitakyushu 26343
Kitale Museum, Kitale 27106
Kitami Regional Centre of Science, History and Art, Kita-mi 26339
Kitamura Museums, Kyoto 26409
Kitano Bijutsukan, Nagano 26528
Kitano Museum of Art, Nagano 26528
Kitano Temman-gu Treasure House, Kyoto 26410
Kitazawa Bijutsukan, Suwa 26778
Kitazawa Museum of Art, Suwa 26778

Kitchener-Waterloo Art Gallery, Kitchener 05698
Kite Museum, Melaka 27671
Kite Museum, Tokyo 26930
Kiteen Kotiseutumuseo, Kitee 09675
Kithur Rani Channamma Memorial Museum, Kittur 21890
Kitimat Centennial Museum, Kitimat 05700
Kitsap Museum, Bremerton 41879
Kitsos Makris Folk Art Center, Volos 21212
Kitte no Hakubutsukan, Tokyo 26869
Kittelsenhuset, Kragerø 30610
Kittery Historical and Naval Museum, Kittery 44507
Kittilän Kotiseutumuseo, Kittilä 09676
Kittilbu Utmarksmuseum, Østre Gausdal 30773
Kittredge Art Gallery, Tacoma 47920
Kittson County History Center Museum, Lake Bronson 44578
Kitwanga Fort, Queen Charlotte 06213
Kiuruveden Kotiseutumuseo, Kiuruvesi 09677
Kivikauden Kylä, Saarijärvi 10011
Kivimuseo, Helsinki 09502
Kivimuseo, Tampere 10078
Kiwanis Van Slyke Museum Foundation, Caldwell 42027
Kiyoharu Shirakaba Museum, Nagasaka 26541
Kiyosato Museum of Photographic Arts, Takane 26794
Kiyose-shi Kyodo Hakubutsukan, Kiyose 26344
Kizljarskij Kraevedčeskij Muzej im. P.I. Bagrationa, Kizljar 32932
Kizyl-Arvat Museum, Kizyl-Arvat 37816
Kjarvalsstaðir, Reykjavík 21651
Kjerringgav Gamle Handelssted, Bodø 30439
K.L. Chetagurov North-Ossetian Museum of Literature, Vladikavkaz 33691
Klaavola Museo, Tuusula 10145
Klæbu Bygdemuseum, Klæbu 30597
Kläppgården Hembygdsmuseum, Harads 35945
Klamath County Museum, Klamath Falls 44509
Klamath National Forest Interpretive Museum, Yreka 48812
Klapka György Múzeum, Komáron 21464
Klášter Sv. Anežky České, Praha 08584
Klašter Sv. Jiří, Praha 08585
Klaus-Groth-Museum und Neue Museumsinsel Lüttenheid, Heide, Holstein 17660
Klein Museum, Mobridge 45426
Klein Saab Museum of Oude Bolneus, Woerden 30015
Die Kleine Galerie, Wien 02909
Kleine Humboldt-Galerie, Berlin 16016
Das kleine Spielzeugmuseum, Baden-Baden 15787
Kleines Guß-Museum, Selfkant 19931
Kleines Heimatmuseum Windmühle, Werdum 20520
Kleines Kirchengeschichtsmuseum Sankt Gumbertus, Illesheim 17887
Kleines Museum am Hafen, Romanshorn 37068
Kleines Museum - Kinder der Welt, Frankfurt/Oder 17082
Kleines Plakatmuseum, Bayreuth 15851
Kleines Stuck-Museum, Freiburg im Breisgau 17710
Kleist-Museum, Frankfurt/Oder 17083
Klemettimuseo, Kuortane 09724
Klemm Gallery, Adrian 41066
Klepp Bygdemuseum, Kleppe 30598
Klepper Museum, Rosenheim 19652
Klerksdorp Museum, Klerksdorp 34297
Klettgau-Museum, Waldshut-Tiengen 20373
Klevfos Industrimuseum, Ådalsbruk 30368
Klickitat County Historical Society Museum, Goldendale 43716
Kline Creek Farm, Winfield 48688
Klingspor-Museum, Offenbach am Main 19241
Klinskoe Muzejnoe Obedinenie, Klin 32934
Kloboučnické Muzeum, Nový Jičín 08509
Klöppelmuseum und Heimatkundliche Sammlung, Abenberg 15387
Klokkengieterij Museum, Heiligerlee 29376
Klokkengieterijmuseum, Vries 29965
Klokkenmuseum, Frederiksoord 29262
Klokkenmuseum, Hechtel 03487
Klokkenmuseum van de Sint-Martinusbasiliek, Halle 03468
Klokkergården Bygdetun Lyngdal Misjonsmuseum, Lyngdal 30660
Klompenmuseum De Platijn, Best 28984
Klompenmuseum Gebr. Wietzes, Eelde 29197
Klompenmuseum 't Oale Ambacht, Goor 29290
Klompenmuseum 't Schöpke Enter, Enter 29243
De Klophoek, Beilen 28970
Klondike Gold Rush National Historical Park, Seattle 47537
Klondike National Historic Sites, Dawson City 05312
Klopfermühle mit Mühlenmuseum, Lengenfeld, Vogtland 18436
Klopstock Museum, Quedlinburg 19462
Kloster Altenberg, Solms 19990
Kloster Ebstorf, Ebstorf 16772
Kloster Irsee, Irsee 17917
Kloster Isenhagen, Hankensbüttel 17590
Kloster-Kunstsammlung, Preetz, Holstein 19441
Kloster Lüne, Lüneburg 18558
Kloster Mariensee, Neustadt am Rübenberge 19069
Kloster Medingen, Bad Bevensen 15613
Kloster-Museum, Sankt Märgen 19753
Kloster Sankt Marienberg, Helmstedt 17703
Kloster Seeon, Seeon 19921
Kloster Walsrode, Walsrode 20384
Kloster Wienhausen, Wienhausen 20568
Kloster zum Heiligen Kreuz, Rostock 19663

Klosteranlage mit Klostermuseum, Maulbronn 18665
Klosterbräu Brauereimuseum, Irsee 17918
Klostergalerie, Zehdenick 20735
Klosterkirche Blaubeuren, Blaubeuren 16182
Klosterlund Museum og Naturcenter, Engesvang 08804
Klostermühlenmuseum, Thierhaupten 20172
Klostermuseum, Müstair 36970
Klostermuseum, Muri (Aargau) 36972
Klostermuseum, Roggenburg 19640
Klostermuseum der Benediktiner-Abtei, Ottobeuren 19327
Klostermuseum der Sankt Josefskongregation, Ursberg 20274
Klostermuseum Disentis, Disentis 36662
Klostermuseum Heggbach, Maselheim 18661
Klostermuseum Hirsau, Calw 16448
Klostermuseum in der Pfarrkirche Sankt Magnus, Bad Schussenried 15735
Klostermuseum Jerichow, Jerichow 17954
Klostermuseum Sankt Georgen, Stein am Rhein 37214
Klostersammlung der Benediktinerabtei, Michaelbeuern 02293
Klostertal-Museum, Dalaas 01757
Klostertunet, Halsnøy Kloster 30525
Kluane Museum of Natural History, Burwash Landing 05153
Kluuvin Galleria - Glogalleriet, Helsinki 09503
Klyne Esopus Historical Society Museum, Ulster Park 48136
Klyutchevsky Museum, Penza 33289
Kmetty Múzeum, Szentendre 21572
Knappogue Castle, Quin 22530
Knaresborough Castle and Old Courthouse Museum, Knaresborough 39400
Knauf-Museum, Iphofen 17915
Knebworth House, Knebworth 39402
Kneehill Historical Museum, Three Hills 06543
Kner Nyomdaipari Múzeum, Gyomaendrőd 21418
Kner Printing Industry Museum, Gyomaendrőd 21418
Knežev Dvor, Cavtat 07689
Knife River Indian Villages National Historic Site, Stanton 47775
Knight Museum of High Plains Heritage, Alliance 41148
Knights of Columbus Museum, New Haven 45696
Knock Folk Museum, Knock 22502
Knockreer House, Killarney 22490
Knole, Sevenoaks 40474
Knott House Museum, Tallahassee 47932
Knox County Historical Society Museum, Edina 43087
Knox County Museum, Benjamin 41625
Knox County Museum, Knoxville 44511
Knox's Headquarters State Historic Site, Vails Gate 48176
Knoxville Museum of Art, Knoxville 44520
Knud Rasmussens Hus, Hundested 08903
Knudaheio - Garborgheimen, Undheim 30959
Knutsford Heritage Centre, Knutsford 39404
Knysna Museum, Knysna 34298
K.O. Braun Museum, Ludwigshafen am Rhein 18518
Koan Collection, Hadano 26167
Kobarid Museum, Kobarid 34094
Kobariški Muzej, Kobarid 34094
Kobe City Museum, Kobe 26350
Kobe Fashion Museum, Kobe 26348
Kobe Maritime Museum, Kobe 26349
Kobe-shiritsu Hakubutsukan, Kobe 26350
København Museum for Moderne Kunst, København 08932
Københavns Bymuseum, København 08933
Kobrinski Voenno-istoričeski Muzej im. A.V. Suvorova, Kobrin 03112
Kocaeli Devlet Güzel Sanatlar Galerisi, Kocaeli 37737
Kocaeli Sabancı Culture House, Kocaeli 37738
Kocaeli Sabancı Kültür Sitesi, Kocaeli 37738
Kocaeli State Gallery, Kocaeli 37737
Kochi-ken Kaitokukan, Kochi 26354
Kochi-kenritsu Bijutsukan, Kochi 26355
Kochi Prefectural Kaito Hall, Kochi 26354
Kodai Orient Hakubutsukan, Tokyo 26870
Kodai Yuzenen, Kyoto 26411
Kodak Gallery Hiroshima, Hiroshima 26219
Kodály Zoltán Emlékmúzeum, Budapest 21351
Kodisjoen Kotiseutumuseo, Kodisjoki 09678
Köhlereimuseum, Hasselfelde 17628
Kölner Weinmuseum, Köln 18148
Kölnischer Kunstverein, Köln 18149
Kölnisches Stadtmuseum, Köln 18150
König Ludwig II.-Museum, Herrenchiemsee 17733
Königshaus am Schachen und Alpengarten, Garmisch-Partenkirchen 17201
Königspesel, Hooge 17838
Königspfalz Freilichtmuseum, Tilleda 20177
Köpings Museum, Köping 36010
Het Koetshuis, Den Haag 29100
Köyliö Croft-Museum, Tuiskula 10116
Köyliön Torpparimuseo, Tuiskula 10116
Középkori O-Zsinagóga, Sopron 21533
Közlekedési Múzeum, Budapest 21352
Központi Bányászati Múzeum, Sopron 21534
Központi Kohászati Múzeum, Miskolc 21477
Koffie- en Theemuseum, Amsterdam 28867
Koffie- en Winkelmuseum, Pieterburen 29713
Koffiebanderij De Gulden Tas, Bree 03243
Koffler Gallery, Toronto 06588
Kofukuji Kokuhokan, Nara 26577
Kofukuji National Treasure House, Nara 26577
Køge Museum, Køge 08956
Kohán Múzeum, Gyula 21424
Kohl Children's Museum, Wilmette 48645
Kohtla Kaevanduspark-muuseum, Ida 09324
Kohtla Oil Shale Mining Museum, Ida 09324
Koizumi Yakumo Kinenkan, Matsue 26470
Kokcetav Historical and Regional Museum, Kokčetav 27086
Koke'e Natural History Museum, Kauai 44417
Kokemäen Maatalousmuseo, Kokemäki 09679
Kokemäen Ulkomuseo, Kokemäki 09680
Kokemäki Agricultural Museum, Kokemäki 09679
Kokemäki Open Air Museum, Kokemäki 09680
Kokubunji Cultural Exhibition Center, Kokubunji 26365
Kokubunji Municipal Archaeological Gallery, Kokubunji 26366
Kokubunji-shi Bunkazai Hozonkan, Kokubunji 26366
Kokugakuin University Archaeological Collection, Tokyo 26871
Kokuritsu Kagaku Hakubutsukan, Tokyo 26872
Kokuritsu Kokusai Bijutsukan, Suita 26773
Kokuritsu Minzokugaku Hakubutsukan, Minpaku, Suita 26774
Kokuritsu Rekishi Minzoku Hakubutsukan, Sakura 26706
Kokuritsu Seiyo Bijutsukan, Tokyo 26873
Kolarin Kunnan Kotiseutumuseo, Sieppijärvi 10032
Kolbenheyer-Archiv und Gedenkstätte, Geretsried 17251
Koldo Mitxelena Kulturunea Erakustaret, Donostia-San Sebastián 34774
Kolhapur Museum, Kolhapur 21895
Kolín Regional Museum, Kolín 08417
Kolju Ficheto Museum, Drjanovo 04661
Kolmanskop Museum, Kolmanskop 28758
Kolomoki Mounds State Park Museum, Blakely 41732
Kolomya State Museum of Folk Art, Kolomija 37863
Kolpings- und Handwerksmuseum im Faltertor, Dettelbach 16591
Komagata Jukichi Bijutsu Kinenkan, Nagaoka 26531
Komagata Jukichi Memorial Art Museum, Nagaoka 26531
Komatsu City Museum, Komatsu 26368
Komatsu Hitoshi Art Museum, Kyoto 26412
Komatsu Shiritsu Hakubutsukan, Komatsu 26368
Kombolois Museum, Nafplion 21091
Komi-Permjackij Okružnoj Kraevedčeskij Muzej im. Subbotina-Permjaka, Kudymkar 32968
Komi-Permyatsk Regional Museum, Kudymkar 32968
Komi Respublikanskij Istoriko-Kraevedčeskij Muzej, Syktyvkar 33573
Kommandør Chr. Christensen's Hvalfangst Museum, Sandefjord 30822
Kommunale Galerie, Berlin 16017
Kommunale Galerie, Darmstadt 16543
Kommunale Galerie Gelsenkirchen, Gelsenkirchen 17229
Kommunale Galerie im Leinwandhaus, Frankfurt am Main 17059
Komoka Railway Museum, Komoka 05704
Komperon Kotiseutumuseo, Viinijärvi 10197
Kompleksi Monumental i Lidhjes Shqiptare të Prizrenit, Prizren 33897
Komponierstube Gustav Mahlers, Steinbach am Attersee 02680
Økomuseum Grenseland, Sarpsborg 30830
Kon-Tiki Museum, Oslo 30740
Kondo Yuzo Memorial Museum, Kyoto 26413
Konfeksjonsmuseet, Molde 30686
Den Kongelige Mønt- og Medaillesamling, København 08934
Den Kongelige Mynts Museum, Kongsberg 30601
Kongenhus Mindeparks Museum, Viborg 09110
Konginkankaan Kotiseutumuseo, Konginkangas 09687
Kongosho-ji Treasure House, Ise 26255
Kongsberg Arms and Industry Collection, Kongsberg 30603
Kongsberg Ski Museum, Kongsberg 30602
Kongsberg Våpenfabrikks Museum, Kongsberg 30603
Kongsvinger Festningsmuseum, Kongsvinger 30606
Koninklijk Museum voor Schone Kunsten Antwerpen, Antwerpen 03146
Koninklijk Nederlands Leger- en Wapenmuseum, Delft 29079
Koninklijk Oudheidkundig Genootschap, Amsterdam 28868
Koninklijk Paleis te Amsterdam, Amsterdam 28869
Het Koninklijk Penningkabinet, Leiden 29519
Koninklijk Tehuis voor Oud-Militairen en Museum Bronbeek, Arnhem 28940
Koninklijke Hoofdgilde Sint-Sebastiaan, Brugge 03256
Koninklijke Maatschappij voor Dierkunde van Antwerpen, Antwerpen 03147
Konjušenny Muzej -Muzej Avtomobil'nogo Transporta, Sankt-Peterburg 33412
Konneveden Kotiseutumuseo, Konnevesi 09688
Konradsburg Ermsleben, Ermsleben 16929
Konstandoglou Collection, Athinai 20869
Konstantin Fedin Museum, Saratov 33506
Konstantin Palace, Sankt-Peterburg 33413
Konstantin Velichkov House-Museum, Pazardžik 04754
Konstantinovskij Dvorec, Sankt-Peterburg 33413
Konstmuseum, Lund 36058
Konstmuseum Gösta Werner och Havet, Simrishamn 36188
Konstmuseum Gösta Werner och Rådhusets Konsthall, Örnsköldsvik 36143
Konstsamlingarna, Uppsala 36355
Kontiolahden Museo, Kontiolahti 09689
Konventmuseum der Barmherzigen Brüder, Wien 02910
Konya Devlet Güzel Sanatlar Galerisi, Konya 37740
Konya Ethnographic Museum, Konya 37741
Konya Etnografi Müzesi, Konya 37741
Konya Müzesi, Konya 37742
Konya Museum, Konya 37742
Konya State Gallery, Konya 37740
Koochiching County Historical Society Museum, International Falls 44240
Kook Museum, Jerusalem 22645
Kookmin College Museum, Seoul 27245
Koopmans-De Wet House Museum, Cape Town 34206
Koorda Museum, Koorda 01152
Koornmarktspoort, Kampen 29472
Kootenai Brown Pioneer Village, Pincher Creek 06133
Kootenay Gallery of Art, History and Science, Castlegar 05214
Kópavogur Art Museum, Kópavogur 21642
Koper Regional Museum, Koper 34097
Kopermolen, Vaals 29913
Koperslagersmuseum Van der Beele, Horst 29448
Kopiergerätemuseum, Wien 02911
Kopparberget Gruvmuseum, Falun 35883
Het Koptisch Museum, Ruinerwold 29785
Korablinskij Kraevedčeskij Muzej, Korablino 32938
Korallen- und Heimatmuseum, Nattheim 18975
Korbmacher-Museum, Malsfeld 18609
Korçë Museum, Korçë 00025
Korea Maritime University Museum, Busan 27142
Korea University Museum, Seoul 27252
Korea University Museum, Seoul 27246
Korea War Memorial, Seoul 27247
Korean Agricultural Museum, Seoul 27248
Korean Art Gallery, Pyongyang 27119
Korean Central Ethnographic Museum, Pyongyang 27120
Korean Central Historical Museum, Pyongyang 27121
Korean Folk Village, Kihung 27203
Korean Furniture Museum, Seoul 27249
Korean Magazine Museum, Seoul 27250
Korean Museum, Los Angeles 44917
Korean Museum Association, Seoul 49269
Korean Museum of Contemporary Clothing, Seoul 27251
Korean National Committee for the International Council of Museums (ICOM), Seoul 49270
Korean Revolutionary Museum, Pyongyang 27122
Korean Ski Museum, Ganseong 27170
Korean War Veterans National Museum, Tuscola 48118
Korekawa Archaeological Museum, Hachinohe 26163
Koren en Pel Molen De Eendracht, Anjum 28921
Koren en Pelmolen De Noordstar, Noordbroek 29642
Korenmolen de Hoop, Hellendoorn 29385
Korenmolen de Hoop, Klarenbeek 29483
Korenmolen de Phenix, Nes 29610
Korenmolen de Zandhaas, Santpoort 29789
Koreshan Historic Site, Estero 43215
Korin Memorial House Museum, Moskva 33076
Koriyama City Museum of Art, Koriyama 26371
Kornel Makuszyński Museum, Zakopane 32208
Kornhaus Georgenthal-Klosterruinen, Georgenthal 17241
Kornhaus-Museum, Weiler-Simmerberg 20447
Kornhausforum, Bern 36542
Kornschütte, Luzern 36911
Koroška Galerija Likovnih Umetnosti, Slovenj Gradec 34149
Koroški Muzej Ravne na Koroškem, Ravne na Koroškem 34144
Korpilahden Kotiseutumuseo, Korpilahti 09692
Korppoon Kotiseutumuseo, Korppoo 09693
Korsnäs Hembygdsmuseum, Korsnäs 09694
Korsør By- og Overfartsmuseum, Korsør 08964
Kortárs Művészeti Múzeum - Ludwig Múzeum Budapest, Budapest 21353
Kortedala Museum, Göteborg 35914
Kortelisy Historical Museum, Kortelisy 37864
Kortesjärven Museo, Kortesjärvi 09696
Kortright Centre Museum, Woodbridge 06861
Korttien Talo, Hämeenlinna 09452
Korvenkylän Nuorisoseuran Museo, Muhniemi 09837
Korvensuun Museo, Mynämäki 09848
Korvensuun Voimalaitos- ja Konepajamuseo, Mynämäki 09849
Koryo Museum of Art, Kyoto 26414
Koryo Taehakyo Pakmulgwan, Seoul 27252
Koryu-ji Reihoden, Kyoto 26415
Koryu-ji Temple Treasure House, Kyoto 26415
Kosanji Temple Museum, Toyota, Hiroshima 26975
Koschatmuseum, Klagenfurt 02125
Kosciuszko-Museum, Solothurn 37184
Kosetsu Bijutsukan, Kobe 26351
Kosetsu Museum of Art, Kobe 26351
Koshare Indian Museum, La Junta 44552
Kosken Kotiseutumuseo, Koski 09697
Koskenniskan Mylly- ja Kievarimuseo, Tuupovaara 10141
Kossuth Lajos Emlékmúzeuma, Monok 21483
Kossuth Múzeum, Cegléd 21395
Kostede Museum für Überlebenskunst, Kamen 17976
Kostroma City Gallery of Arts, Kostroma 32944
Kostroma Historical and Architectural Museum-Preserve, Kostroma 32942
Kostroma Museum of Fine Arts, Kostroma 32943
Kostromskoj Gosudarstvennyj Istoriko-architekturnyj Muzej-zapovednik, Kostroma 32942
Kostromskoj Gosudarstvennyj Obedinennyj Chudožestvennyj Muzej, Kostroma 32943
Kostüm-Museum im neuen Schloß Schleißheim, Oberschleißheim 19202
Kostuummuseum De Gouden Leeuw, Noordhorn 29644
Koszta József Múzeum, Szentes 21579
Kotel Enlighteners Museum and Rakovski Pantheon, Kotel 04719
Kotiseutumuseo, Jurva 09588
Kotiseutumuseo Lukkarin Puustelli, Loppi 09797
Kotiseutumuseo Muina, Rauma 09981
Kotiseutumuseo Pellava ja Sahti Lammin Ajokalumuseo, Lammi 09757
Kotiseututalo, Noormarkku 09867
Kotkaniemi - Presidentti P.E. Svinhufvudin koti, Luumäki 09803
Kotkaniemi - The Home of President P.E. Svinhufvud, Luumäki 09803
Koto-ku Fukagawa Edo Siryokan, Tokyo 26874
Kotohira-gu Museum, Kotohira 26372
Kotsu Hakubutsukan, Tokyo 26875
Kotsu Kagaku Hakubutsukan, Osaka 26651
Kotula's Timber House, Havířov 08344
Kotulova Dřevěnka, Havířov 08344
Kotzebue Museum, Kotzebue 44528
Koulumuseo, Helsinki 09504
Kourion Museum, Episkopi 08186
Kouseiroudoushou Sangyo Anzen Gijutsukan, Tokyo 26876
Kouvolan Taidemuseo, Kouvola 09703
Kovács Margit Kerámiagyűjtemény, Szentendre 21573
Kovács Margit Múzeum, Győr 21420
Kovalenko Art Museum, Krasnodar 32946
Kovjoki Museo, Uusikaarlepyy 10149
Koyama Keizo Art Museum, Komoro 26370
Koyasan Reihokan, Koya 26373
Koyunoglu Müzesi, Konya 37743
Koyunoglu Museum, Konya 37743
Kozu Kobunka Museum, Kyoto 26416
Kräutermuseum - Naturpark Jauerling Wachau, Maria Laach am Jauerling 02266
Kraevaja Detskaja Kartinnaja Galereja, Vladivostok 33698
Kraevedčeskij Muzej, Samarkand 48850
Kraevedčeskij Muzej, Žytomyr 37914
Kraevedčeskij Muzej Čirčika, Čirčik 48835
Kraevedčeskij Muzej Evrejskoj Avtonomnoj Oblasti, Birobidžan 32689
Kraevedčeskij Muzej g. Lomonosova, Lomonosov 32990
Kraevedčeskij Muzej g. Puškina, Puškin 33337
Kraevedčeskij Muzej g. Puškino, Puškino 33341
Kraevedčeskij Muzej Namangana, Namangan 48844
Kraevedčeskij Muzej Novgorodskogo Rajona, Velikij Novgorod 33677
Kraevoj Muzej Istorii Literatury, Iskusstva i Kultury Altaja, Barnaul 32673
Kraftwerkmuseum Löntsch, Netstal 36981
Krahuletz-Museum, Eggenburg 01791
Krajanské Múzeum MS Bratislava, Bratislava 33968
Krajská Galerie, Hradec Králové 08367
Krajská Galerie Výtvarného Umeni ve Zlíně, Zlín 08750
Krajské Muzeum Cheb, Cheb 08308
Krajské Muzeum Sokolov, Sokolov 08660
Kråkö Båtbyggarmuseum, Kråkö 09707
Kråksundet notnaust Sjøbruksmuseum, Tustna 30950
Kralingsmuseum, Rotterdam 29755
Kraljevo Public Museum, Kraljevo 33855
Královsky Letohradek, Praha 08586
Krambuvika Bygdemuseum, Tennevoll 30919
Das Kranichhaus, Otterndorf 19322
Krankenhaus-Museum am Zentralkrankenhaus Bremen-Ost, Bremen 16327
Krankenhausmuseum, Nürnberg 19149
Krannert Art Museum, Champaign 42187
Krasl Art Center, Saint Joseph 47102
Krāslavas Vēstures un Mākslas Muzejs, Krāslava 27374
Krasnodarskij Chudožestvennyj Muzej im. F.A. Kovalenko, Krasnodar 32946
Krasnodarskij Gosudarstvennyj Istoriko-archeologičeskij Muzej-zapovednik, Krasnodar 32947
Krasnodarskij Vystavočnyj Zal, Krasnodar 32948
Krasnojarsk Regional Museum, Krasnojarsk 32952
Krasnojarskij Chudožestvennyj Muzej im. V.I. Surikova, Krasnojarsk 32950
Krasnojarskij Gorodskoj Vystavočnyj Zal, Krasnojarsk 32951
Krasnojarskij Istoričeskij Muzej Memorial Pobedy, Krasnojarsk 37865
Krasnojarskij Kraevoj Kraevedčeskij Muzej, Krasnojarsk 32952
Krasnojarskij Kulturno-istoričeskij Muzejnyj Kompleks, Krasnojarsk 32953
Krasnokamsk Picture Gallery, Krasnokamsk 32958
Krasnokamskaja Kartinnaja Galereja, Krasnokamsk 32958
Krasnokamskij Kraevedčeskij Muzej, Krasnokamsk 32959
Krasnoturinsk Regional Museum, Krasnoturinsk 32960
Krasnoturinskij Kraevedčeskij Muzej, Krasnoturinsk 32960

Kraszewski-Museum, Dresden 16687
The Kreeger Museum, Washington 48365
Kreis-Heimatmuseum, Bad Frankenhausen 15642
Kreis- und Heimatmuseum, Bogen 16222
Kreis- und Stadtmuseum, Dieburg 16596
Kreis- und Universitätsmuseum Helmstedt, Helmstedt 17704
Kreisagrarmuseum, Dorf Mecklenburg 16643
Kreisgalerie, Dahn 16533
Kreisgalerie, Mellrichstadt 18701
Kreisheimatmuseum, Demmin 16571
Kreisheimatmuseum, Frankenberg, Eder 17025
Kreisheimatmuseum, Grimma 17401
Kreisheimatmuseum Striediecks Hof, Bünde 16404
Kreisheimatmuseum Weißes Haus, Rotenburg an der Fulda 19670
Kreisheimatstube, Ellzee 16837
Kreisheimatstuben Riederau, Dießen am Ammersee 16600
Kreismuseum, Neuwied 19085
Kreismuseum, Oschersleben 19274
Kreismuseum, Osterburg 19290
Kreismuseum, Rathenow 19493
Kreismuseum Bad Liebenwerda, Bad Liebenwerda 15692
Kreismuseum Bitterfeld, Bitterfeld 16175
Kreismuseum der Heimatvertriebenen, Seligenstadt 19933
Kreismuseum Finsterwalde, Finsterwalde 17005
Kreismuseum Geilenkirchen, Geilenkirchen 17212
Kreismuseum Gräfenhainichen, Oranienbaum 19262
Kreismuseum Heinsberg, Heinsberg 17697
Kreismuseum Herzogtum Lauenburg, Ratzeburg 19500
Kreismuseum Jerichower Land, Genthin 17237
Kreismuseum Lodron-Haus, Mühldorf am Inn 18803
Kreismuseum Oranienburg, Oranienburg 19265
Kreismuseum Peine mit Kreisarchiv, Peine 19366
Kreismuseum Prinzeßhof, Itzehoe 17934
Kreismuseum Schönebeck, Schönebeck, Elbe 19827
Kreismuseum Syke, Syke 20131
Kreismuseum Walderbach, Walderbach 20363
Kreismuseum Wewelsburg, Büren, Westfalen 16405
Kreismuseum Wittenberg, Prettin 19445
Kreismuseum Zons, Dormagen 16646
Krell'sche Schmiede, Wernigerode 20526
Kresge Art Museum, East Lansing 43053
Kreuzberg Museum, Berlin 16018
Kreuzstadelmuseum, Mogersdorf 02319
Kriminal- und Foltermuseum Henke, Brandenburg an der Havel 16282
Kriminalmuseum der Kantonspolizei Zürich, Zürich 37383
Krippenmuseum, Glattbach 17296
Krippenmuseum, Telgte 20155
Krippensammlung, Großraming 01960
Krippenstube-Heimatstube, Plößberg 19421
Krišjāņa Barona Muzejs, Rīga 27410
Krišjānis Barons Museum, Rīga 27410
Kristall-Museum, Obergesteln 36996
Kristalle und Edle Steine Turracher Höhe, Ebene Reichenau 01779
Kristallgrotte, Guttannen 36787
Kristallmuseum, Guttannen 36788
Kristallmuseum, Viechtach 20307
Kristallmuseum Riedenburg, Riedenburg 19598
Kristalmuseum 't Los Hoes, Borculo 28999
Kristianhus Motormuseum, Vik i Sogn 30992
Kristiansand Kanonmuseum, Kristiansand 30613
Kristinehamn Museum of Art, Kristinehamn 36019
Kristinehamns Konstmuseum, Kristinehamn 36019
Kristinehamns Museum, Kristinehamn 36020
Kristjan Raud Museum, Tallinn 09367
Krkonošské Muzeum, Jilemnice 08392
Krkonošské Muzeum, Paseky nad Jizerou 08535
Krkonošské Muzeum, Vrchlabí 08725
Krøderbanen, Krøderen 30620
Kröller-Müller Museum, Otterlo 29686
Kröpeliner Heimatstube, Kröpelin 18241
Kröpeliner Tor, Rostock 19664
Kronberger Haus, Frankfurt am Main 17060
Kronbloms Kök, Örebro 36135
Kronborg Castle, Helsingør 08863
Kronborg Slot, Helsingør 08863
Kronobergs Lantbruksmuseum, Alvesta 35792
Krookilan Kotiseutualue, Raisio 09974
Krshishevskij and Starkov Memorial Museum, Minusinsk 33014
Krudttaarnsmuseet, Frederikshavn 08831
Krüge-Museum, Creußen 16512
Krügersches Haus, Geesthacht 17209
Kruger Museum, Pretoria 34345
Kruidentuin de Groene Kruidhof, Elburg 29223
Kruiermuseum, Balen 03195
Kruse House Museum, West Chicago 48518
Kruševac Regional Museum, Kruševac 33857
Krylov Museum of the Tula Museum of Fine Arts, Tula 33626
Krymski Respublikanskij Kraevedčeskij Muzej, Simferopol 37904
Krypta 182, Bergisch Gladbach 15897
Krypte en Schatkamer van de O.L.V. Basiliek, Halle 03469
Kryptemuseum onder de Sint-Hermeskerk, Ronse 03711
Krzysztof Kawenczynski Muzeum, Trzcianne 32058
K.S. Stanislavsky House Museum, Moskva 33043
Ksan Historical Village and Museum, Hazelton 05590
Kuala Lumpur Craft Museum, Kuala Lumpur 27641
Kubalu School Museum, Dundaga 27352
Kubalu Skolas Muzejs, Dundaga 27352
Kubin-Haus, Wernstein am Inn 02825
Kubinyi Ferenc Múzeum, Szécsény 21546
Kuboso Memorial Museum of Arts, Izumi 26276
Kubus Hannover, Hannover 17600
Kuddnäs Z. Topeliusksen Lapsuudenkoti, Uusikaarlepyy 10150
Kügelgenhaus, Dresden 16688
Künstlerbahnhof Ebernburg, Bad Münster 15696
Künstlerforum Bonn, Bonn 16240
Künstlergarten Alfred Kurz, Lichtenau 02218
Künstlerhaus Bethanien, Berlin 16019
Künstlerhaus Exter, Übersee 20246
Künstlerhaus Graz, Graz 01919
Künstlerhaus Hooksiel, Hooksiel 17839
Künstlerhaus Lenz, Gladenbach 17294
Künstlerhaus Marktoberdorf, Marktoberdorf 18649
Künstlerhaus mit Galerie, Göttingen 17333
Künstlerhaus Schloß Balmoral, Bad Ems 15637
Künstlerhaus Walter Helm, Aschaffenburg 15524
Künstlerhaus Wien, Wien 02912
Küppers Historisches Biermuseum, Köln 18151
Kürbismühlenmuseum, Preding 02449
Küsten-Museum der Stadt Wilhelmshaven, Wilhelmshaven 20594
Küstenmuseum, Juist 17968
Kütahya Devlet Güzel Sanatlar Galerisi, Kütahya 37748
Kütahya Müzesi, Kütahya 37749
Kütahya Museum, Kütahya 37749
Kütahya State Gallery, Kütahya 37748
Kufa Gallery, London 39683
Kuhlmann King Historical House and Museum, Boerne 41770
Kuhmalahden Kotiseutumuseo, Kuhmalahti 09712
Kuhmoisten Kotiseutumuseo, Kuhmoinen 09715
Kuivaniemen Kotiseutumuseo, Kuivaniemi 09716
K.u.k. Hausmuseum, Weyregg am Attersee 02829
Kukje Gallery, Seoul 27253
Kukkola Fiskemuseum, Haparanda 35944
Kuknip Minsok Pakmulgwan, Seoul 27254
Kuldīgas Novada Muzejs, Kuldīga 27375
Kulikovo Field - Museum-preserve of Military History and Nature, Tula 33624
Kuljab Historical and Regional Museum, Kuljab 37448
Kuljabskij Istoriko-Kraevedčeskij Muzej, Kuljab 37448
Kulla Gunnarstorps Mölla, Helsingborg 35953
Kullaan Kotiseutumuseo, Kullaa 09717
Kullängsstugan, Askersund 35821
Kultamuseo Tankavaara, Tankavaara 10099
Kulttuurien Museo, Helsinki 09505
Kultur Bahnhof Eller, Düsseldorf 16730
Kultur-Gut-Museum, Aigen-Schlägl 01651
Kultur-Historisches Museum Grenchen, Grenchen 36778
Kultur- und Kommunikationszentrum Lagerhalle Osnabrück, Osnabrück 19279
Kultur- und Militärmuseum, Grafenwöhr 17374
Kultur- und Stadthistorisches Museum Duisburg, Duisburg 16751
Kulturama, Zürich 37384
Kulturamt Mitte, Berlin 16020
Kulturamt Neukölln, Berlin 16021
Kulturbunker Mülheim, Köln 18152
Kulturelles Forum im Freiherr-vom-Stein-Haus, Langenfeld 18336
Kulturen i Lund, Lund 36059
Kulturerbe Hallstatt, Hallstatt 02000
Kulturforum Alte Post, Neuss 19065
Kulturforum Burgkloster, Lübeck 18537
Kulturgården på Lassfolk, Lillby 09785
Kulturgeschichtliches Museum Bügeleisenhaus, Hattingen 17634
Kulturgeschichtliches Museum Osnabrück, Osnabrück 19280
Kulturhaus der Otto-Hellmeier-Stiftung, Raisting 19480
Kulturhistorische Sammlung, Frankenmarkt 01846
Kulturhistorische Sammlung, Graz 01920
Kulturhistorische Sammlung, Iphofen 17916
Kulturhistorisches Museum Barockhaus, Görlitz 17323
Kulturhistorisches Museum der Hansestadt Stralsund, Stralsund 20074
Kulturhistorisches Museum Franziskanerkloster, Zittau 20761
Kulturhistorisches Museum Kaisertrutz/Reichenbacher Turm, Görlitz 17324
Kulturhistorisches Museum Magdeburg, Magdeburg 18581
Kulturhistorisches Museum Prenzlau im Dominikanerkloster, Prenzlau 19443
Kulturhistorisches Museum Schloss Köthen, Köthen, Anhalt 18190
Kulturhistorisches Museum Schloß Merseburg, Merseburg 18713
Kulturhistorisk Museum, Randers 09025
Kulturhistoriska Museet, Lund 36060
Kulturhistoriska Museet i Bunge, Farösund 35884
De Kulturhistoriske Samlinger, Bergen 30423
Kulturhuset, Stockholm 36250
Kulturinstitut in der Italienischen Botschaft, Berlin 16022
Kulturmühle Lützelflüh, Lützelflüh 36896
Kulturni Centar Ivan Napotnik, Velenje 34161
Kulturno Prosvetni Centar Bela Crkva-Muzejska Jedinica, Bela Crkva 33792
Kulturno-vystavočnyj Centr Raduga, Samara 33371
Kulturno-vystavočnyj Centr Raduga, Uljanovsk 33659
Kulturnyj Centr Kazan, Kazan 32891
Kulturnyj Centr-muzej V.S. Vysockogo, Moskva 33071
Kulturspeicher im Schamuhn Museum, Uelzen 20249
Kulturzentrum der Aktion Lebensqualität, München 18862
Kulturzentrum Hans-Reiffenstuel-Haus, Pfarrkirchen 19387
Kulturzentrum Kolvenburg, Billerbeck 16163
Kulturzentrum Ostpreußen, Ellingen, Bayern 16830
Kulturzentrum Schloß Bonndorf, Bonndorf im Schwarzwald 16251
Kulturzentrum Sinsteden des Kreises Neuss, Rommerskirchen 19643
Kuma Museum of Art, Kuma 26374
Kumagai Morikazu Museum, Tokyo 26877
Kumamoto Castle, Kumamoto 26375
Kumamoto City Museum, Kumamoto 26378
Kumamoto International Folk Art Museum, Kumamoto 26376
Kumamoto-kenritsu Bijutsukan, Kumamoto 26377
Kumamoto Prefectural Museum of Art, Kumamoto 26377
Kumamoto-shiritsu Hakubutsukan, Kumamoto 26378
Kumano Nachi Taisha Treasure House, Nachikatsuura 26524
Kumaya Art Museum, Hagi 26170
Kumaya Bijutsukan, Hagi 26170
Kume Bijutsukan, Tokyo 26878
Kume Museum of Art, Tokyo 26878
Kumrovec Memorial Park, Kumrovec 07731
Kunaicho Sannomaru Shozokan, Tokyo 26879
Kunewälder Heimatstube, Leimen, Baden 18373
Kungajaktmuseet, Vargön 36400
Kungl. Myntkabinettet, Stockholm 36251
Kungliga Akademien för de Fria Konsterna, Stockholm 36252
Kungsstugan och Cajsa Wargs Hus, Örebro 36136
Kungsudden Local Museum, Kungsör 36025
Kungurskij Kraevedčeskij Muzej, Kungur 32969
Kunisaki History and Folklore Museum, Kunisaki 26379
Kunisaki-machi Rekishi Minzoku Shiryokan, Kunisaki 26379
Kunja-Urgench Historical Site Museum, Keneurgench 37815
Kunozan Toshogu Museum, Shizuoka 26764
Kunst Archiv Darmstadt, Darmstadt 16544
Kunst auf der Zugspitze, Garmisch-Partenkirchen 17202
Kunst aus Nordrhein-Westfalen, Aachen 15374
Kunst im Alten Schützenhaus, Zofingen 37365
Kunst in der Klinik, Bad Krozingen 15683
Kunst-Kabinett Usedom, Benz 15881
Kunst-Museum Ahlen, Ahlen 15403
Kunst Raum Goethestraße, Linz 02233
Kunst Raum Riehen, Riehen 37061
Kunst- und Ausstellungshalle der Bundesrepublik Deutschland Bonn, Bonn 16241
Kunst- und Heimathaus, Paderborn 19336
Kunst- und Heimatmuseum, Lorch, Rheingau 18503
Kunst und Museum, Hollfeld 17824
Kunst- und Museumsbibliothek, Köln 18153
Kunstakademiets Bibliotek, København 08935
Kunstamt Tempelhof-Schöneberg, Berlin 16023
Kunstausstellung des Rothenburger Künstlerbundes, Rothenburg ob der Tauber 19678
Kunstausstellung Stift Herzogenburg, Herzogenburg 02027
Kunstbank, Berlin 16024
Kunstbibliothek, Berlin 16025
Kunstbunker Tumulka, München 18863
Kunstcentrum De Waagh, Oldenzaal 29658
Kunstcentrum Pand Paulus, Schiedam 29801
Kunstenaarscentrum De Fabriek, Eindhoven 29213
Kunstfabrik am Flutgraben, Berlin 16026
Kunstforum Arabellapark, München 18864
Kunstforum Bâloise, Basel 36503
Kunstforum Ebendorf, Wien 02913
Kunstforum in der Grundkreditbank, Berlin 16027
Kunstforum Ostdeutsche Galerie, Regensburg 19527
Kunstgewerbemuseum, Berlin 16028
Kunstgewerbemuseum, Dresden 16689
Kunstgußmuseum Hirzenhain, Hirzenhain 17768
Kunstgußmuseum Lauchhammer, Lauchhammer 18346
Kunsthal Rotterdam, Rotterdam 29756
Kunsthal Sint-Pietersabdij, Gent 03441
Kunsthalle am Goetheplatz, Weimar, Thüringen 20463
Kunsthalle Barmen, Wuppertal 20715
Kunsthalle Basel, Basel 36504
Kunsthalle Bern, Bern 36543
Kunsthalle Bielefeld, Bielefeld 16156
Kunsthalle Bremen, Bremen 16328
Kunsthalle Bremerhaven, Bremerhaven 16341
Kunsthalle Darmstadt, Darmstadt 16545
Kunsthalle der Hypo-Kulturstiftung, München 18865
Kunsthalle Dominikanerkirche, Osnabrück 19281
Kunsthalle Dresden im Art'otel Dresden, Dresden 16690
Kunsthalle Düsseldorf, Düsseldorf 16731
Kunsthalle Erfurt im Haus zum Roten Ochsen, Erfurt 16904
Kunsthalle Faust, Hannover 17601
Kunsthalle Fridericianum, Kassel 18021
Kunsthalle Gießen, Gießen 17280
Kunsthalle Göppingen, Göppingen 17317
Kunsthalle Helsinki, Helsinki 09489
Kunsthalle im Schloss, Isny 17929
Kunsthalle in Emden, Emden 16847
Kunsthalle Jesuitenkirche, Aschaffenburg 15525
Kunsthalle Koblenz, Koblenz 18119
Kunsthalle Krems, Krems 02157
Kunsthalle Leoben, Leoben 02209
Kunsthalle Lingen, Lingen 18483
Kunsthalle Loppen, Loppem 03599
Kunsthalle Mannheim, Mannheim 18612
Kunsthalle Neumarkt, Neumarkt, Oberpfalz 19046
Kunsthalle Nürnberg, Nürnberg 19150
Kunsthalle Palazzo, Liestal 36879
Kunsthalle Prisma, Arbon 36466
Kunsthalle Rostock, Rostock 19665
Kunsthalle Sankt Gallen, Sankt Gallen 37101
Kunsthalle Sankt Moritz, Sankt Moritz 37113
Kunsthalle Sparkasse Leipzig, Leipzig 18401
Kunsthalle Steyr, Steyr 02684
Kunsthalle Tirol, Hall in Tirol 01992
Kunsthalle Tübingen, Tübingen 20227
Kunsthalle Vierseithof, Luckenwalde 18510
Kunsthalle Wien, Wien 02914
Kunsthalle Wien, Projekt Space, Wien 02915
Kunsthalle Wil, Wil 37319
Kunsthalle Wilhelmshaven, Wilhelmshaven 20595
Kunsthalle Winterthur, Winterthur 37330
Kunsthalle Würth, Schwäbisch Hall 19868
Kunsthalle Ziegelhütte, Appenzell 36461
Kunsthalle zu Kiel der Christian-Albrechts-Universität, Kiel 18075
Kunsthalle Zürich, Zürich 37385
Kunsthallen, København 08936
Kunsthallen Brandts Klaedefabrik, Odense 09014
Kunsthandwerk und Plastik Sammlung, Kassel 18022
Kunsthaus, Grenchen 36779
Kunsthaus Apolda Avantgarde, Apolda 15508
Kunsthaus Baselland, Muttenz 36976
Kunsthaus Bregenz, Bregenz 01745
Kunsthaus Centre PasquArt, Biel, Kanton Bern 36563
Kunsthaus Dresden, Dresden 16691
Kunsthaus Essen, Essen 16952
Kunsthaus Glarus, Glarus 36764
Kunsthaus Graz, Graz 01921
Kunsthaus Hamburg, Hamburg 17549
Kunsthaus Hohenlockstedt, Hohenlockstedt 17809
Kunsthaus in Stade, Stade 20024
Kunsthaus Kannen, Münster 18940
Kunsthaus Kaufbeuren, Kaufbeuren 18041
Kunsthaus Kloster Gravenhorst, Hörstel 17789
Kunsthaus Meyenburg, Nordhausen 19120
Kunsthaus Mürzzuschlag, Mürzzuschlag 02330
Kunsthaus Nürnberg, Nürnberg 19151
Kunsthaus Stadt Bocholt, Bocholt 16188
Kunsthaus Zürich, Zürich 37386
Kunsthaus Zug, Zug 37426
KunstHausWien, Wien 02916
Kunsthistorisches Museum, Seckau 02654
Kunsthistorisches Museum im Palais Harrach, Wien 02917
Kunsthistorisches Museum Wien, Wien 02918
Kunsthof Zürich, Zürich 37387
Kunstigalerii, Narva 09340
Kunstindustrimuseet, Oslo 30741
Kunstkammer der Pfarrkirche Sankt Georg, Bocholt 16189
Kunstkammer des Innsbrucker Servitenklöster, Innsbruck 02071
Kunstkaten Ahrenshoop, Ostseebad Ahrenshoop 19301
Kunstkeller Annaberg, Annaberg-Buchholz 15498
Kunstmuseet Køge Skitsesamling, Køge 08957
Kunstmuseum, Mülheim an der Ruhr 18816
Kunstmuseum, Sankt Gallen 37102
Kunstmuseum, Solothurn 37185
Kunstmuseum Basel, Basel 36505
Kunstmuseum Bayreuth mit Tabakhistorischer Sammlung, Bayreuth 15852
Kunstmuseum Bern, Bern 36544
Kunstmuseum Bonn, Bonn 16242
Kunstmuseum Celle mit Sammlung Robert Simon, Celle 16456
Kunstmuseum des Kantons Thurgau, Warth 37307
Kunstmuseum Dr. Krupp, Weinbach 20477
Kunstmuseum Heidenheim, Heidenheim an der Brenz 17679
Kunstmuseum Hohenkarpfen, Hausen ob Verena 17645
Kunstmuseum Kloster Unser Lieben Frauen, Magdeburg 18582
Kunstmuseum Liechtenstein, Vaduz 27514
Kunstmuseum Luzern, Luzern 36912
Kunstmuseum Nörvenich, Nörvenich 19111
Kunstmuseum Olten, Olten 37009
Kunstmuseum Thun, Thun 37240
Kunstmuseum Winterthur, Winterthur 37331
Kunstmuseum Wolfsburg, Wolfsburg 20662
Kunstpanorama im Bourbaki, Luzern 36913
Kunstpaviljoen, Nieuw Roden 29614
Kunstpavillon, München 18866
Kunstraum Aarau, Aarau 36426
Kunstraum Alter Wiehrebahnhof, Freiburg im Breisgau 17111
Kunstraum Baden, Baden 36487
Kunstraum Berlin, Berlin 16029
Kunstraum Bruxelles, Bruxelles 03286
Kunstraum Burgdorf, Burgdorf 36605
Kunstraum Dornbirn, Dornbirn 01770
Kunstraum Düsseldorf, Düsseldorf 16732
Kunstraum Eching, Eching 16773
Kunstraum Farmsen, Hamburg 17550

Kunstraum Fuhrwerkswaage, Köln 18154
Kunstraum Innsbruck, Innsbruck 02072
Kunstraum Klosterkirche, Traunstein 20189
Kunstraum Kreuzberg/Bethanien, Berlin 16030
Kunstraum München, München 18867
Kunstraum neue Kunst, Hannover 17602
Kunstraum Neuruppin, Neuruppin 19060
Kunstraum Notkirche, Essen 16953
Kunstraum Sankt Virgil, Salzburg 02542
Kunstsammlung der Universität Göttingen, Göttingen 17334
Kunstsammlung des Benediktinerstifts Seitenstetten, Seitenstetten 02658
Kunstsammlung des Herzoglichen Georgianums, München 18868
Kunstsammlung im Schloß Rheinstein, Trechtingshausen 20198
Kunstsammlung Lorenzkapelle Rottweil, Rottweil 19696
Kunstsammlung Neubrandenburg, Neubrandenburg 19012
Kunstsammlung Robert Spreng, Reiden 37049
Kunstsammlung Sankt Nicolai-Kirche, Kalkar 17974
Kunstsammlung Villa Schüpbach, Steffisburg 37211
Kunstsammlung Volpinum, Wien 02919
Kunstsammlungen, Schwerin 19896
Kunstsammlungen Chemnitz, Chemnitz 16466
Kunstsammlungen der Ruhr-Universität Bochum, Bochum 16196
Kunstsammlungen der Stadt Limburg, Limburg an der Lahn 18470
Kunstsammlungen der Veste Coburg, Coburg 16483
Kunstsammlungen des Stiftes Kremsmünster, Kremsmünster 02161
Kunstsammlungen Palais Schwarzenberg, Wien 02920
Kunstsammlungen und Graphische Sammlung, Furth bei Göttweig 01861
Kunstsammlungen Zwickau, Zwickau 20776
Kunstschacht Katernberg, Essen 16954
Kunststätte Bossard, Jesteburg 17955
Kunststätte Kuenburg, Payerbach 02393
Kunststiftung Baden-Württemberg, Stuttgart 20098
Kunststiftung Poll, Berlin 16031
Kunststube, Drosendorf an der Thaya 01774
't Kunstuus, Heinkenszand 29380
Kunstverein Bad Salzdetfurth, Bad Salzdetfurth 15727
Kunstverein Braunschweig e.V., Braunschweig 16298
Kunstverein Friedrichstadt, Berlin 16032
Kunstverein für die Rheinlande und Westfalen, Düsseldorf 16733
Kunstverein Gelderland, Geldern 17221
Kunstverein Grafschaft Bentheim, Neuenhaus 19026
Kunstverein Hannover, Hannover 17603
Kunstverein Heilbronn, Heilbronn 17688
Kunstverein Hof, Hof, Saale 17792
Kunstverein in Hamburg e.V, Hamburg 17551
Kunstverein Ingolstadt, Ingolstadt 17908
Kunstverein Kärnten, Klagenfurt 02126
Kunstverein Köln rechtsrheinisch e.V., Köln 18155
Kunstverein Konstanz e.V., Konstanz 18204
Kunstverein München, München 18869
Kunstverein Passau- Sankt Anna-Kapelle, Passau 19355
Kunstverein Ruhr e.V., Essen 16955
Kunstverein Schwerte, Schwerte 19902
Kunstverein Speyer, Speyer 20012
Kunstverein Springhornhof e.V., Neuenkirchen, Lüneburger Heide 19027
Kunstverein Talstrasse, Halle, Saale 17514
Kunstverein Weiden, Weiden, Oberpfalz 20426
Kunstverein zu Frechen e.V., Frechen 17093
Kunstvereniging Diepenheim, Diepenheim 29149
Kunstwerk, Köln 18156
Kuntsi Art Collection, Vaasa 10158
Kuntsin Taidekokoelma, Vaasa 10158
Kuny Domokos Múzeum, Tata 21593
Kuokkalan Museoraitti, Lempäälä 09774
Kuon-ji Treasure House, Minobu 26492
Kuopio Art Museum, Kuopio 09721
Kuopio Natural History Museum, Kuopio 09720
Kuopion Korttelimuseo, Kuopio 09719
Kuopion Luonnontieteellinen Museo, Kuopio 09720
Kuopion Taidemuseo, Kuopio 09721
Kupferberg-Museum, Mainz 18601
Kupferschmiede-Museum, Tangermünde 20139
Kupferstich-Kabinett, Dresden 16692
Kupferstichkabinett, Basel 36506
Kupferstichkabinett, Wien 02921
Kupferstichkabinett - Sammlung der Zeichnungen und Druckgraphik, Berlin 16033
Kur-und Stadtmuseum, Bad Ems 15638
Kura Gallery, Wellington 30297
Kuralan Kylämäki, Turku 10122
Kuramayama Museum, Kyoto 26417
Kurashiki Archaeological Museum, Kurashiki 26381
Kurashiki City Art Museum, Kurashiki 26382
Kurashiki Mingeikan, Kurashiki 26383
Kurashiki Museum of Folkcraft, Kurashiki 26383
Kurayoshi Museum, Kurayoshi 26386
The Kurdish Museum, Brooklyn 41944
Kure Bijutsukan, Kure 26387
Kure Museum of Art, Kure 26387
Kurfürstliches Gärtnerhaus, Bonn 16243
Kurgan Regional Art Museum, Kurgan 32971
Kurgan Regional Museum, Kurgan 32972
Kurganskij Oblastnoj Chudožestvennyj Muzej, Kurgan 32971
Kurganskij Oblastnoj Kraevedčeskij Muzej, Kurgan 32972
Kurikan Museo, Kurikka 09726
Kurikka Museum, Kurikka 09726
Kurita Bijutsukan, Ashikaga 26108
Kurita Museum, Ashikaga 26108
Kurmuseum, Bad Tatzmannsdorf 01720
Kurmuseum Bad Wildungen, Bad Wildungen 15763
Kurmuseum des Österreichischen Moorforschungsinstituts, Bad Wimsbach-Neydharting 01723
Kurnikova Hiša, Tržič 34158
Kuroda Kinenshitsu, Tokyo 26880
Kuroda Memorial Hall, Tokyo 26880
Kurpfälzisches Museum der Stadt Heidelberg, Heidelberg 17668
Kursk Art Gallery, Kursk 32973
Kursk State Museum of Archeology, Kursk 32975
Kursk State Regional Museum, Kursk 32974
Kurskaja Kartinnaja Galerija im. A.A. Denejki, Kursk 32973
Kurskij Gosudarstvennyj Oblastnoj Kraevedčeskij Muzej, Kursk 32974
Kurskij Gosudarstvennyj Oblastnoj Muzej Archeologii, Kursk 32975
Kurt-Tucholsky-Gedenkstätte, Rheinsberg 19591
Kurtuluş Savaşı ve Cumhuriyet Müzeleri, Ankara 37619
Kurukshetra Panorama & Science Centre, Kurukshetra 21918
Kurun Ulkomuseo, Kuru 09727
Kurzemes Hercogu Kapenes, Jelgava 27366
Kuser Farm Mansion, Hamilton 43881
Kushiro Art Museum, Kushiro 26390
Kushiro City Museum, Kushiro 26391
Kustavin Kotiseutumuseo, Kustavi 09728
Kutaisi State Museum of History and Ethnography, Kutaisi 15356
Kutaisskij Gosudarstvennyj Muzej Istorii i Etnografii, Kutaisi 15356
Kutná Hora Regional Museum, Kutná Hora 08439
Kutschen-, Schlitten- und Wagenmuseum Rottach-Egern, Rottach-Egern 19688
Kutschen- und Heimatmuseum, Sillian 02664
Kutschen- und Schlittenmuseum, Großraming 01961
Kutschenmuseum, Augustusburg 15571
Kutschenmuseum, Basel 36507
Kutschenmuseum, Gaildorf 17193
Kutschenmuseum, Laa an der Thaya 02174
Kutschenmuseum, Ludwigslust 18525
Kutschenmuseum Hessisches Landgestüt, Dillenburg 16609
Kutschensammlung, Eigeltingen 16809
Kutschensammlung Robert Sallmann, Amriswil 36456
Kutuzov's Hut and Battle of Borodino Panorama, Moskva 33145
Kuurojen Museo, Helsinki 09506
Kuusamon Kotiseutumuseo, Kuusamo 09729
Kuusisto Manor, Kuusisto 09733
Kuusiston Kartano, Kuusisto 09733
Kuwait National Museum, Kuwait 27306
Kuybyshev Republican Memorial Museum, Kzyl-Orda 27088
K.V. Ivanov Literary Museum, Čeboksary 32720
Kvæfjord Museum, Harstad 30533
Kvæven Bygdetun, Tjørhom 30922
Kvam Bygdemuseum, Norheimsund 30712
Kvarken Boat Museum, Malax 09813
Kvarkens Båtmuseum, Malax 09813
Kvarnbacken Prylmuseum, Sandviken 36179
Kvarnbackmuseet i Harrström, Korsnäs 09695
Kvevlax Hembygdsmuseum, Kvevlax 09735
Kvikmyndasafn Islands, Hafnarfjörður 21635
Kvindemuseet i Danmark, Århus 08771
Kviteseid Bygdetun, Kviteseid 30623
KW Institute for Contemporary Art, Berlin 16034
Kwa Muhle Museum, Durban 34228
Kwagiulth Museum, Quathiaski Cove 06194
Kwangdong College Museum, Gangneung 27169
Kweichow Provincial Museum, Kueiyang 07144
Kwinitsa Station Railway Museum, Prince Rupert 06188
KX., Hamburg 17552
Kyffhäuser-Denkmal, Bad Frankenhausen 15643
Kyle and Carrick District Library and Museum, Ayr 38050
Kymenlaakson maakuntamuseo, Kotka 09700
Kyneton Museum, Kyneton 01157
Kyngston House Museum, Saint Albans 40373
Kynologisches Museum, Wien 02922
Kyodo Gangu-kan, Takayama 26809
Kyösti- ja Kalervo Kallion Museo, Nivala 09864
Kyongju University Museum, Kyongju 27207
Kyongnam College Museum, Masan 27209
Kyorpeev's House, Kotel 04718
Kyoto Arashiyama Music Box Museum, Kyoto 26418
Kyoto City Archaeological Museum, Kyoto 26419
Kyoto City Youth Science Center, Kyoto 26431
Kyoto Daigaku Bungakubu Hakubutsukan, Kyoto 26420
Kyoto Daigaku Sougou Hakubutsukan, Kyoto 26421
Kyoto-fu Kyoto Bunka Hakubutsukan, Kyoto 26422
Kyoto Gion Oil Lamp Museum, Kyoto 26423
Kyoto Kokuritsu Hakubutsukan, Kyoto 26424
Kyoto Kokuritsu Kindai Bijutsukan, Kyoto 26425
Kyoto Mingei Kan, Kyoto 26426
Kyoto Municipal Museum of Art, Kyoto 26430
Kyoto Museum for World Peace, Kyoto 26427
Kyoto Museum of Traditional Crafts - Fureaikan, Kyoto 26428
Kyoto National Museum, Kyoto 26424
Kyoto Prefectural Museum, Kyoto 26429
Kyoto-shi Bijutsukan, Kyoto 26430
Kyoto-shi Seishonen Kagaku, Kyoto 26431
Kyoto University Museum, Kyoto 26421
Kyoto Yuzen Bunka Kaikan, Kyoto 26432
Kyrenia Castle, Girne 08225
Kyrgyz State Museum of Fine Arts G. Aitiyev, Biškek 27307
Kyriazopoulos Collection, Thessaloniki 21185
Kyrou Collection, Athinai 20870
Kystmuseet Hvaler, Vesterøy 30988
Kystmuseet i Nord-Trøndelag, Rørvik 30807
Kystmuseet i Øygarden, Rong 30804
Kystmuseet i Sogn og Fjordane, Florø 30497
Kystmuseet i Sør-Trøndelag, Hitra 30549
Kysuce Galéria, Oščadnica 34040
Kysucke Múzeum, Čadca 33984
Kyu Aoyama Bettei, Otaru 26678
Kyunghee University Museum, Seoul 27255
Kyungsung Museum, Busan 27143
Kyusei Atami Art Museum, Atami 26114
Kyushu Ceramic Museum, Arita 26103
Kyushu Historical Museum, Dazaifu 26134
Kyushu Rekishi Shiryokan, Dazaifu 26134
Kyyjärven Kotiseutumuseo, Kyyjärvi 09736
KZ-Gedenk- und Begegnungsstätte, Ladelund 18282
KZ-Gedenkstätte - Dachau, Dachau 16524
KZ-Gedenkstätte Flossenbürg, Flossenbürg 17017
KZ-Gedenkstätte Husum-Schwesing, Schwesing 19904
KZ-Gedenkstätte Mauthausen, Mauthausen 02289
KZ-Gedenkstätte Mittelbau-Dora, Nordhausen 19121
KZ-Gedenkstätte Neuengamme, Hamburg 17553
KZ-Gedenkstätte und Zeitgeschichte-Museum Ebensee, Ebensee 01781
Kzyl-Orda Historical and Regional Museum, Kzyl-Orda 27087
L. Lange's Ovnmuseum, Svendborg 09085
L. Laptsy Museum-Appartment, Salechard 33365
L. Novomeský Múzeum, Senica 34057
La Hougue Bie Museum, Saint Helier 40403
L.A. Mayer Museum for Islamic Art, Jerusalem 22646
La Para Municipal Historical Museum, La Para 00382
La Raza-Galeria Posada, Sacramento 47053
La Salle University Art Museum, Philadelphia 46422
La Trobe University Art Museum, Melbourne 01235
The Lab, San Francisco 47322
Laband Art Gallery, Los Angeles 44918
Laboratário de Ensino de Ciências, Ribeirão Preto 04309
Laboratório de Anatomia e Identificação de Madeiras, Manaus 04189
Laboratório de Demonstração do Instituto de Fisica, São Paulo 04496
Labour Union Art Museum, Reykjavík 21652
Labour Union Museum, Amsterdam 28886
Labrador Heritage Museum, Happy Valley 05583
Labrador Straits Museum, L'Anse-au-Loup 05001
Labråten, Hvalstad 30575
Labyrinth Kindermuseum Berlin, Berlin 16035
Lac Cardinal Regional Pioneer Village Museum, Grimshaw 05534
Lac La Hache Museum, Barkerville 05047
Lac LaRonge Museum, LaRonge 05728
L.A.C. Lieu d'Art Contemporain, Sigean 14750
Lac Qui Parle County Historical Museum, Madison 45060
Lac Sainte-Anne and District Pioneer Museum, Sangudo 06390
Lace House, Kiskunhalas 21459
Lace House Museum, Black Hawk 41723
Lace Museum, Prachatice 08561
Lace Museum, Sunnyvale 47885
Lace museum, Vamberk 08708
Lacey Historical Society Museum, Forked River 43363
Lackham Museum of Agriculture and Rural Life, Lacock 39409
Lacquerware Museum, Chiapa de Corzo 27818
Lacquerware Museum, Pagan 28740
The Lacrosse Museum and National Hall of Fame, Baltimore 41474
Laczkó Dezsoē Múzeum, Veszprém 21608
Ladbyskibsmuseet, Kerteminde 08916
Ladew House Museum, Monkton 45433
Lady Denman Maritime Museum, Huskisson 01116
Lady Franklin Gallery, Lenah Valley 01173
Lady Lever Art Gallery, Port Sunlight 40235
Lady Waterford Gallery, Berwick-upon-Tweed 38175
Lady Wilson Museum, Dharampur 21790
Ladysmith Railway Museum, Ladysmith 05715
Läänemaa Muuseum, Haapsalu 09318
Lääninkivalteri Aschanin Talo, Heinola 09470
Läckö Slott, Lidköping 36033
Lähetysmuseo, Helsinki 09507
Lände, Kressbronn am Bodensee 18232
Ländliches Heimatmuseum, Lahntal 18288
Längelmäen Kirkkomuseo, Längelmäki 09737
Längelmäen Pellavamuseo, Länkipohja 09738
Länsmuseet Gävleborg, Gävle 35900
Länsmuseet Halmstad, Halmstad 35941
Länsmuseet Västernorrland, Härnösand 35935
Länsmuseet Varberg, Varberg 36395
Læsø Museum, Læsø 08967
Lafayette College Art Gallery, Easton 43068
Lafayette Miners Museum, Lafayette 44567
Lafayette Museum - Alexandre Mouton House, Lafayette 44570
Lafayette Natural History Museum, Lafayette 44571
Lafcadio Hearn Memorial Museum, Matsue 26470
Lagan Lookout Centre, Belfast 38153
Laganland Bilmuseum, Lagan 36027
Lågdalsmuseet, Kongsberg 30604
Laguardia and Wagner Archives, Long Island City 44867
Laguna Art Museum, Laguna Beach 44575
Lahaina Restoration Foundation, Lahaina 44576
LaHave Islands Marine Museum, LaHave 05718
Lahden Historiallinen Museo, Lahti 09742
Lahden Kaupunginmuseo, Lahti 09743
Lahden Taidemuseo, Lahti 09744
Lahore Fort Museum, Lahore 31037
Lahore Museum, Lahore 31038
Lahti Art Museum, Lahti 09744
Lahti City Museum, Lahti 09743
Lahti Historical Museum, Lahti 09742
Lahti Poster Museum, Lahti 09741
Laidhay Croft Museum, Dunbeath 38795
Laidley District Historical Village, Laidley 01158
Laihian Kirkkomuseo, Laihia 09751
Laihian Museo, Laihia 09752
Laing Art Gallery, Newcastle-upon-Tyne 40038
Laing Museum, Newburgh 40027
Lajos Vajda Memorial Museum, Szentendre 21578
Lake Broadwater Natural History Museum, Dalby 00965
The Lake Champlain Maritime Museum, Vergennes 48212
Lake Country Museum, Okanagan 06046
Lake County Discovery Museum, Wauconda 48457
Lake County Historical Museum, Tavares 47961
Lake County Historical Society Museum, Kirtland Hills 44505
Lake County Historical Society Museum, Mentor 45257
Lake County Historical Society Museum, Two Harbors 48127
Lake County Museum, Lakeport 44605
Lake District Museum of Southern Ostrobothnia - Väinö's House, Vasikka-Aho 10189
Lake Erie Nature and Science Center, Bay Village 41547
Lake Forest-Lake Bluff Historical Society Museum, Lake Forest 44586
Lake George Historical Association Museum, Lake George 44588
Lake Guernsey Museum, Guernsey 43850
Lake Hopatcong Historical Museum, Landing 44633
Lake Hopatcong Historical Museum, Landing 44634
Lake Jackson Mounds Archaeological Park, Tallahassee 47933
Lake Macquarie City Art Gallery, Booragul 00814
Lake Malawi Museum, Mangochi 27612
Lake Meredith Aquatic and Wildlife Museum, Fritch 43566
Lake of the Red Cedars Museum, Cedar Lake 42155
Lake of the Woods County Museum, Baudette 41541
Lake of the Woods Museum, Kenora 05656
Lake Placid-North Elba Historical Society Museum, Lake Placid 44594
Lake Saint Louis Historical Society Museum, Montréal 05907
Lake Shore Railway Museum, North East 45992
Lake Superior Maritime Visitors Center, Duluth 43000
Lake Superior Railroad Museum, Duluth 43001
Lake Tabourie Museum, Lake Tabourie 01160
Lake Taupo Museum and Art Gallery, Taupo 30257
Lake Waccamaw Depot Museum, Lake Waccamaw 44596
Lake Wales Depot Museum, Lake Wales 44597
Lakeland Motor Museum, Grange-over-Sands 39107
Lakes District Museum, Arrowtown 30095
Lakes District Museum, Burns Lake 05152
Lakeside Museum, Bulyea 05142
Lakeside Studio, Lakeside 44606
Lakeview Museum of Arts and Sciences, Peoria 46349
Lakewood's Heritage Culture and the Arts Galleries, Lakewood 44608
Lalbagh Fort Museum, Dhaka 03090
Lam Dong Museum, Lam Dong 48997
Lamanai Archaeological Site, Lamanai 03867
Lamar Dodd Art Center, La Grange 44542
Lamartine Memorial House, Plovdiv 04779
Lambing Flat Museum, Young 01634
Lambropoulos Collection, Polygyros 21131
Lambton Heritage Museum, Grand Bend 05509
The Lamont Gallery, Exeter 43253
Lampenmuseum, Geel 03426
Lampenmuseum, Wezemaal 03839
Lampi-Museo, Liminka 09787
Lampi Museum, Liminka 09787
Lamu Museum, Lamu 27107
Lan Sang, Tak 37543
Lanark Museum, Lanark 39410
Lancaster Antique Toy and Train Collection, Portsmouth 46662
Lancaster City Museum, Lancaster 39414
Lancaster County Museum, Lancaster 44627
Lancaster Historical Society Museum, Lancaster 44619
Lancaster Maritime Museum, Lancaster 39415
Lancaster Museum/Art Gallery, Lancaster 44616
Lancaster Museum of Art, Lancaster 44628
Lancefield Court House Museum, Lancefield 01162
Lancer Centennial Museum, Lancer 05723
Land- en Tuinbouwmuseum, Etten-Leur 29255

Land of the Beardies History House Museum, Glen Innes 01058
Land Surveying Museum, Helsinki 09512
Het Land van Strijen, Strijen 29858
Het Land van Thorn/ Panorama Thorn, Thorn 29870
Landbouw- en Juttersmuseum Swartwoude, Buren, Friesland 29041
Landbouwmuseum Erve Niehof, Diepenheim 29150
Landbouwmuseum Leiedal, Bissegem 03218
Landbrugs- og Interiørmuseet, Farsø 08822
Landbrugsmuseet Melstedgård, Gudhjem 08847
Landbrugsmuseet Skarregaard, Nykøbing Mors 08998
Landbruksmuseet for Møre og Romsdal, Vikebukt 30993
Landes-Feuerwehrmuseum, Stendal 20058
Landesbergbaumuseum Baden-Württemberg, Sulzburg 20128
Landesbibliothek Oldenburg, Oldenburg, Oldenburg 19255
Landesgalerie Oberösterreich, Linz 02234
Landesgeschichtliche Sammlung der Schleswig-Holsteinischen Landesbibliothek, Kiel 18076
Landeskirchliches Museum, Ludwigsburg, Württemberg 18512
Landesmuseum für Kunst und Kulturgeschichte, Schleswig 19794
Landesmuseum für Kunst und Kulturgeschichte Oldenburg, Oldenburg, Oldenburg 19256
Landesmuseum für Natur und Mensch, Oldenburg, Oldenburg 19257
Landesmuseum für schaumburg-lippische Geschichte, Landes- und Volkskunde, Bückeburg 16394
Landesmuseum für Technik und Arbeit in Mannheim, Mannheim 18613
Landesmuseum für Vorgeschichte, Dresden 16693
Landesmuseum für Vorgeschichte Sachsen-Anhalt, Halle, Saale 17515
Landesmuseum Joanneum, Graz 01922
Landesmuseum Kärnten, Klagenfurt 02127
Landesmuseum Koblenz, Koblenz 18120
Landesmuseum Mainz, Mainz 18602
Landesmuseum Schloß Tirol, Tirolo di Merano 25708
Landesrabbiner Dr. I.E. Lichtigfeld-Museum, Michelstadt 18729
Landesschau Äthiopien, Neulingen, Enzkreis 19043
Landeszeughaus, Graz 01923
Landis Valley Museum, Lancaster 44629
Landlmuseum Sulzbürg, Mühlhausen, Oberpfalz 18804
Landlord's Manor House Museum, Dayi 07043
Landmark Forest Heritage Park, Carrbridge 38496
Landmark Park, Dothan 42960
Landmaschinenmuseum - Sammlung Speer, Rimbach bei Eggenfelden 19612
Lands Museum, Dokka 30460
Landscapes of the Holy Land Park, Tel Aviv 22766
Landschaftsinformationszentrum (LIZ) Hessisches Kegelspiel Rasdorf, Rasdorf 19485
Landschaftsmuseum, Seligenstadt 19934
Landschaftsmuseum Angeln, Langballig 18316
Landschaftsmuseum der Dübener Heide, Bad Düben 15629
Landschaftsmuseum der Kulmregion, Pischelsdorf in Steiermark 02418
Landschaftsmuseum im Schloß Trautenfels, Trautenfels 02738
Landschaftsmuseum Obermain, Kulmbach 18268
Landschaftsmuseum Schönhengstgau, Göppingen 17318
Landschaftsmuseum Westerwald, Hachenburg 17471
Landschloss Pirna-Zuschendorf-Botanische Sammlungen, Pirna 19405
Landschulmuseum Göldenitz, Göldenitz bei Rostock 17314
Landskrona Konsthall, Landskrona 36028
Landskrona Museum, Landskrona 36029
Landstingsmuseet, Örebro 36137
Landtechnik-Museum Gut Steinhof, Braunschweig 16299
Landtechnikmuseum, Leiben 02201
Landtechnisches Museum Burgenland, Sankt Michael im Burgenland 02589
Landwirtschaftliches Museum und Pfarrer Franz Engel-Museum, Prinzendorf 02456
Landwirtschaftliches Museum Wetzlar, Wetzlar 20556
Landwirtschafts- und Heimatmuseum, Karben 17985
Landwirtschaftsmuseum, Rhede, Ems 19587
Landwirtschaftsmuseum, Weil am Rhein 20435
Landwirtschaftsmuseum Hof Espe, Bad Berleburg 15608
Landwirtschaftsmuseum Lüneburger Heide, Suderburg 20117
Landwirtschaftsmuseum Schloss Ehrental, Klagenfurt 02128
Lane Community College Art Gallery, Eugene 43221
Lane County Historical Museum, Dighton 42947
Lane County Historical Museum, Eugene 43222
Lane House, Roseburg 47004
The Lane Place, Crawfordsville 42691
Lanesfield School, Edgerton 43083
Lang Pioneer Village, Keene 05648
Lang Water Powered Grist Mill, Peterborough 06120
Långbans Gruvby, Filipstad 35888
Langbeinmuseum, Hirschhorn, Neckar 17767
Långelanda Tingshus, Årjäng 35808
Langelands Museum, Rudkøbing 09048
Langham and District Heritage Village Museum, Langham 05724
Langham Cultural Centre Galleries, Kaslo 05646
Långholmen Prison Museum, Stockholm 36253
Långholmens Fängelsemuseum, Stockholm 36253
Langi Morgala Museum, Ararat 00747
Langingkoski Imperial Fishing Lodge, Kotka 09701
Langlade County Historical Society Museum, Antigo 41234
Langley Centennial Museum and National Exhibition Centre, Fort Langley 05442
Langsdorfer Heimatmuseum, Lich 18454
Langton Matravers Museum, Langton Matravers 39422
Lanhydrock, Bodmin 38266
Lanier Mansion, Madison 45058
Lanier Museum of Natural History, Buford 41992
Lanigan and District Heritage Centre, Lanigan 05727
Lanman Museum, Framlingham 39014
Lanna Museum, Lampang 37509
Lansing Art Gallery, Lansing 44642
Lansing Manor House Museum, North Blenheim 45984
Lansing Veterans Memorial Museum, Lansing 44640
Lantbruksmuseum, Ingatorp 35972
Lanzhou City Museum, Lanzhou 07148
Laoag Museum, Vigan 31464
Lapham-Patterson House, Thomasville 48000
Lapidaire Gallo-Romain, Quimper 13894
Lapidari Museum, Lefkoşa 08240
Lapidarij - Klaustar Samostana Sv. Domenika, Trogir 07793
Lapidario Civico, Gradisca d'Isonzo 24041
Lapidario Comunale, Osimo 24707
Lapidarium, Berlin 16036
Lapidarium, Neustadt am Main 19067
Lapidarium, Sankt Gallen 37103
Lapidarium - Historische Grenzsteinsammlung, Niederstetten 19100
Lapidarium of Roman Age Cathedral Museum, Pécs 21515
Lapin Maakuntamuseo, Rovaniemi 10001
Lapin Metsämuseo, Rovaniemi 10002
Lapin Tl. Kotiseutumuseo, Lappi 09766
Lapinlahden Taidemuseo ja Eemil Halosen Museo, Lapinlahti 09759
Lapland Forestry Museum, Rovaniemi 10002
Lappa Valley Steam Railway, Newquay 40059
Lappstaden, Arvidsjaur 35814
Lapworth Museum of Geology, Birmingham 38223
Laquer Ware Museum, Takayama 26807
Laramie Plains Museum, Laramie 44648
Larchmont Historical Society Museum, Mamaroneck 45088
Larco Archaeological Museum, Lima 31200
Lårdal Bygdemuseum, Høydalsmo 30572
Lårdal Rural Museum, Høydalsmo 30572
Laredo Children's Museum, Laredo 44652
Largs Museum, Largs 39425
Lark Lane Motor Museum, Liverpool 39519
Larnaca District Archaeological Museum, Larnaka 08189
Larnaca District Museum, Larnaka 08190
Larne Museum, Larne 39426
Larrybane and Carrick-A-Rede, Ballycastle 38066
Lars Noak Blacksmith Shop, Larsson/Ostlund Log Home & One-Room Capitol School, New Sweden 45746
Larsmo Hembygdsmuseum, Larsmo 09769
Larson Gallery, Yakima 48773
Larvik Maritime Museum, Larvik 30632
Larvik Sjøfartsmuseum, Larvik 30632
Larz Anderson Auto Museum, Brookline 41937
Las Cruces Museum of Natural History, Las Cruces 44658
Las Vegas Art Museum, Las Vegas 44668
Las Vegas International Scouting Museum, Las Vegas 44669
Las Vegas Natural History Museum, Las Vegas 44670
LaSalle County Historical Society Museum, Utica 48167
Lasarettimuseo, Turku 10123
Lascaux II, Montignac 13094
Lashburn Centennial Museum, Lashburn 05730
Lashenden Air Warfare Museum, Headcorn 39202
Laško Museum Collection, Laško 34103
Lassaner Mühle, Lassan 18343
Lassen Museum Waikiki, Honolulu 44083
Last Indian Raid Museum, Oberlin 46075
Lastenmuseo, Helsinki 09508
Lastentarhamuseo, Helsinki 09509
Laténium, Hauterive 36796
Latgale Culture and History Museum, Rēzekne 27400
Latgales Kultūtvēstures Muzejs, Rēzekne 27400
Latin American Art Museum, Miami 45288
Latin American Cultural Center Museum, Koyang 27205
Latitude 53, Edmonton 05378
Latrobe Bicycle Race Club Museum, Latrobe 01165
Latrobe Court House Museum, Latrobe 01166
Latrobe Regional Gallery, Morwell 01279
Lattelekom Muzejs, Rīga 27411
Latvia Museum of the History of Chemistry, Rīga 27418
Latvia University Museum of Botany, Rīga 27423
Latvia University Museum of Geology, Rīga 27424
Latvia University Museum of Zoology, Rīga 27427
Latvian Architecture Museum, Rīga 27413
Latvian Centre for Contemporary Art, Rīga 27412
Latvian History Museum, Toronto 06589
Latvian Museum, Rockville 46976
Latvian Museum, Wayville 01588
Latvian Museum Council, Rīga 49275
Latvian Museum of Culture Dauderi, Rīga 27419
Latvian Museum of the History of Apiculture, Bebri 27336
Latvian Museums Association, Rīga 49276
Latvian Photography Museum, Rīga 27416
Latvian War Museum, Rīga 27417
Latvijas Arhitektūras Muzejs, Rīga 27413
Latvijas Biškopības Vēstures Muzejs, Bebri 27336
Latvijas Dabas Muzejs, Rīga 27414
Latvijas Etnogrāfiskais Brīvdabas Muzejs, Rīga 27415
Latvijas Fotogrāfijas Muzejs, Rīga 27416
Latvijas Kara Muzejs, Rīga 27417
Latvijas Ķīmijas Vēstures Muzejs, Rīga 27418
Latvijas Kultūras Muzejs Dauderi, Rīga 27419
Latvijas Lauksaimniecības Universitātes Muzejs, Jelgava 27367
Latvijas Muzeju Asociācija, Rīga 49276
Latvijas Okupācijas Muzejs, Rīga 27420
Latvijas Republikas Meliorācijas un Zemkopības Muzejs, Mālpils 27387
Latvijas Sporta Muzejs, Rīga 27421
Latvijas Ugunsdzēsības Muzejs, Rīga 27422
Latvijas Universitātes Botānikas Muzejs, Rīga 27423
Latvijas Universitātes Ģeologijas Muzejs, Rīga 27424
Latvijas Universitātes Skaitļošanas Tehnikas un Informatikās Muzejs, Rīga 27425
Latvijas Universitātes Vēstures Muzejs, Rīga 27426
Latvijas Universitātes Zoologijas Muzejs, Rīga 27427
Latvijas Vēstures Muzejs, Rīga 27428
Laudal Museum, Marnardal 30667
Lauder Museum, Amityville 41185
Lauderdale House, London 39684
Laufener Stiftsschatz, Laufen, Salzach 18354
Lauksaimniecības Tehnikas Muzejs Kalēji, Talsi 27455
Laumeier Sculpture Park and Museum, Saint Louis 47126
Launceston Steam Railway, Launceston 39430
Laura and Paul Mesaros Galleries, Morgantown 45499
Laura Ingalls Wilder Museum, Burr Oak 42012
Laura Ingalls Wilder Museum, Walnut Grove 48292
Laura Ingalls Wilder-Rose Wilder Lane Historic Home and Museum, Mansfield 45124
Laura Secord Homestead, Niagara Falls 05990
Laure A. Sprague Art Gallery, Joliet 44356
Laurel and Hardy Museum, Ulverston 40748
The Laurel Museum, Laurel 44676
Lauren Rogers Museum of Art, Laurel 44679
Laurence C. Jones Museum, Piney Woods 46496
Laurent Hubert Musée, Orbey 13415
Lauri Viidan Museo, Tampere 10079
Laurier House, Ottawa 06082
Laurinmäen Torpparimuseo, Janakkala 09578
Lauriston Castle, Edinburgh 38891
Lausitzer Bergbaumuseum Knappenrode, Hoyerswerda 17847
Lava Beds National Monument, Tulelake 48101
Lavanttaler Heimatmuseum, Eitweg 01812
Lavanttaler Heimatmuseum, Wolfsberg, Kärnten 03042
Lavanttaler Obstbaumuseum, Sankt Paul 02596
Lavian Kotiseutumuseo, Lavia 09771
Le Lavoir de Mougins, Mougins 13178
Law Enforcement Museum, Roselle 47005
Law Uk Folk Museum, Hong Kong 07103
Lawn, Lincoln 39497
Lawn Heritage Museum, Lamaline 05721
Lawrence County Gray House Museum, Ironton 44254
Lawrence County Historical Museum, Bedford 41579
Lawrence Hall of Science, Berkeley 41644
Lawrence House Museum, Launceston 39431
Lawrence House Museum, Maitland 05802
Lawrence L. Lee Scouting Museum, Manchester 45097
Lawrence Wilson Art Gallery, Crawley 00953
Laws Railroad Museum, Bishop 41715
Lawton Gallery, Green Bay 43790
Laxfield and District Museum, Laxfield 39434
Layland Museum, Cleburne 42454
Laznia Centre for Contemporary Art, Gdańsk 31564
L.C. Bates Museum, Hinckley 44034
L.D. Brinkman Art Foundation, Kerrville 44456
LDM-Múzeum Andreja Sládkoviča Krupina, Krupina 34009
Le Roy House and Jell-o Gallery, Le Roy 44697
Le Sueur Museum, Le Sueur 44698
Lea County Cowboy Hall of Fame and Western Heritage Center, Hobbs 44043
Leadhills Miners' Library Museum, Leadhills 39435
Leaf Rapids National Exhibition Centre, Leaf Rapids 05738
Leaming's Run Garden and Colonial Farm, Cape May Court House 42099
Leamington Spa Art Gallery and Museum, Leamington Spa 39436
Leanin' Tree Museum of Western Art, Boulder 41836
Learmonth Museum, Learmonth 01172
Leaseholdermuseum, Kiikoinen 09667
Leather Museum, Swakopmund 28771
Leatherhead Museum of Local History, Leatherhead 39437
Leavenworth County Historical Society Museum, Leavenworth 44702
Lebell Residence, Kristiinankaupunki 09709
Lebende Galerie, Graz 01924
Lebendes Textilmuseum, Groß Siegharts 01949
Lebendiges Museum, Bad Wildungen 15764
Lebzelterei- und Wachsziehereimuseum, Pfaffenhofen an der Ilm 19382
Lechfeldmuseum, Königsbrunn 18173
Lechflößermuseum, Lechbruck am See 18365
Ledaal Museum, Stavanger 30880
Lee Chapel and Museum, Lexington 44760
Lee County Historical Society Museum, Loachapoka 44837
Lee-Fendall House, Alexandria 41131
Leeds Industrial Museum, Leeds 39447
Leeds Metropolitan University Gallery, Leeds 39448
Leedy-Voulke's Art Center, Kansas City 44402
Leek Art Gallery, Leek 39457
Leelanau Historical Museum, Leland 44714
Lefferts Homestead, Brooklyn 41945
Leffingwell House Museum, Norwich 46036
Left Bank Art Gallery, Greymouth 30169
Lefteris Kanakakis Gallery, Rethymnon 21139
Legaspi City Museum, Legaspi 31340
Legends of the Game Baseball Museum, Arlington 41261
Legislative Building Art Galleries, Regina 06236
Lehár-Schlößl, Wien 02923
Lehár-Villa, Bad Ischl 01707
Lehigh County Historical Society Museum, Allentown 41145
Lehigh University Art Galleries/Museum, Bethlehem 41667
Lehman College Art Gallery, Bronx 41922
Lehr- und Schaubergwerk Frisch Glück, Johanngeorgenstadt 17960
Lehr- und Schaubergwerk Herkules Frisch Glück, Beierfeld 15869
Lehtimäen Museo, Lehtimäki 09772
Lei Cheng Uk Han Tomb Museum, Hong Kong 07104
Leib'sches Haus, Abteilung Stadtgeschichte und Volkskunde, Gießen 17281
Leica Galerija Praha, Praha 08587
Leica Gallery Prague, Praha 08587
Leica Stammbaum und Museum, Solms 19991
Leicestershire CCC Museum, Leicester 39463
Leicestershire Museums, Arts and Records Service, Glenfield 49421
Leigh Heritage Centre, Leigh-on-Sea 39472
Leigh Yawkey Woodson Art Museum, Wausau 48463
Leighton Buzzard Railway, Leighton Buzzard 39474
Leighton Foundation Collection, Calgary 05170
Leighton Hall, Carnforth 38494
Leighton House Museum, London 39685
Leimarel Museum and Research Centre, Imphal 21853
Leinen- und Spitzenmuseum Haigerseelbach, Haiger 17490
Leineweber-Museum, Rheda-Wiedenbrück 19585
Leirfjord Bygdesamlinger, Leirfjord 30633
Leirvika Bygdesamling, Foldereid 30498
Leitch Collieries, Crowsnest Pass 05292
Leith Hall, Huntly 39280
Leitheimer Schloß-Museum, Kaisheim 17973
Leithenmühle, Windhaag bei Freistadt 03037
Lejre Forsøgscenter, Lejre 08970
Leka Bygdemuseum, Leka 30634
Leksaksmuseet, Stockholm 36254
Leksbergs Skolmuseum, Mariestad 36089
Leksvik Bygdesamling, Leksvik 30636
Lembaga Muzium Negeri, Pulau Pinang 27681
Lemee House, Natchitoches 45636
Lemhi County Historical Museum, Salmon 47224
Lemin Kotiseutumuseo, Lemi 09773
Lemon Hill Mansion, Philadelphia 46423
LeMoyne Art Foundation, Tallahassee 47934
Lemun Kotiseutumuseo, Lemu 09777
Lemvig Museum Vesterhus, Lemvig 08972
Lenbachmuseum, Schrobenhausen 19852
Lenin House-Museum, Kazan 32886
Lenin-Museo, Tampere 10080
Lenin Museum, Moskva 33130
Lenin Museum, Tampere 10080
Lennox and Addington County Museum and Archives, Napanee 05964
Lennoxlove House, Haddington 39143
L'Enrajolada Casa-Museu Santacana, Martorell 35094
Lentos Kunstmuseum Linz, Linz 02235
The Lentz Center for Asian Culture, Lincoln 44784
Lenvik Bygdemuseet, Finnsnes 30490
Lenziemill Archive Store, Cumbernauld 38685
Leominster Folk Museum, Leominster 39477
Leon Apacible Historical Landmark Museum, Taal 31449
Leon Wyczółkowski Regional Museum, Bydgoszcz 31514
Leona Paegles Memoriālais Muzejs, Vidriži 27475
Leonard & Bina Ellen Art Gallery, Montréal 05908
Leonhardi-Museum, Dresden 16694
Leonhardi-Museum Aigen, Bad Füssing 15648
Leopold Figl-Museum, Michelhausen 02296
Leopold-Hoesch-Museum Düren, Düren 16717
Leopold Museum, Wien 02924
Lepikon Torppa, Pielavesi 09927
Leppävirran Kotiseutumuseo, Leppävirta 09779
Leppävirta Local History Museum, Leppävirta 09779
Lepramuseet Sant Jørgens Hospital, Bergen 30424
Leptis Magna Museum, Leptis Magna 27502
Lermontov Apartment Museum, Moskva 33040
Lermontov State Literary Memorial Museum, Pjatigorsk 33321
Lermontov State Museum-Estate Tarkhany, Lermontovo 32980

Lermontovskij Gosudarstvennyj Muzej-zapovednik Tarchany, Lermontovo 32980
Leroy and District Heritage Museum, Leroy 05744
Lesbian Herstory Educational Foundation, Brooklyn 41946
Lesja Bygdatun, Lesja 30637
Lesjöforsmuseum, Lesjöfors 36030
Leslie Hill Open Farm, Ballymoney 38072
Leslie-Lohman Gay Art Foundation, New York 45824
Lesnícke a Drevárske Múzeum, Zvolen 34081
Lesnické, Myslivecké a Rybářské Muzeum, Hluboká nad Vltavou 08352
Lesotho National Museum, Maseru 27495
Lessing-Museum, Kamenz 17978
Lester-Garland Premises, Trinity 06634
Lestijärven Kotiseutumuseo, Lestijärvi 09780
Lesueur County Historical Museum, Elysian 43179
Letecké Muzeum, Praha 08588
Lethbridge Community College Gallery, Lethbridge 05746
Letterkundig Museum en Kinderboekenmuseum, Den Haag 29101
Lettl-Atrium, Augsburg 15559
Lev Tolstoy Museum-Estate Nikolskoe-Vjasemskoe, Nikol'skoe-Vjazemskoe 33204
Levanger Museum, Levanger 30639
Levende Grafisk Museum, Skjeberg 30850
Leventis Municipal Museum of Nicosia, Lefkosia 08202
Levere Memorial Temple, Evanston 43240
Leverett Historical Museum, Leverett 44719
Levi Coffin House, Fountain City 43497
Levine Museum of the New South, Charlotte 42241
Levitan Memorial House-Museum, Ples 33323
Lewes Castle and Barbican House Museum, Lewes 39484
Lewes Historical Society Museum, Lewes 44720
Lewis and Clark Center, Saint Charles 47080
Lewis Collection, Cambridge 38458
Lewis County Historical Museum, Chehalis 42269
Lewis County Historical Society Museum, Lowville 44989
Lewis County Historical Society Museum, Lyons Falls 45015
Lewis Elton Gallery, Guildford 39139
Lewis, James and Nellie Stratton Gallery, Columbia 42551
Lewis Textile Museum, Blackburn, Lancashire 38244
Lewisham Local Studies Centre, London 39686
Lewistown Art Center, Lewistown 44733
Lexington Children's Museum, Lexington 44741
Lexington County Museum, Lexington 44756
Lexington Historical Society Exhibition, Lexington 44749
Lgovskij Gosudarstvennyj Kraevedčeskij Muzej, Lgov 32981
Lgovskij Literaturno-memorialnyj Muzej A.P. Gajdara, Lgov 32982
Lgovskij Literaturno-memorialnyj Muzej N.N. Aseeva, Lgov 32983
Li Xian Jun Former Residence, Nanjing 07179
Li Zong Ren Display Center, Guilin 07075
Liane and Danny Taran Gallery, Montréal 05909
Liangzhu Cultural Museum, Hangzhou 07083
Liao-Jin Dynasty City Walls Museum, Beijing 06970
Liao Jincheng Yuan, Beijing 06970
Liaoning Art Gallery, Shenyang 07234
Liaoning Museum, Shenyang 07235
Liaoning Provincial Museum, Chinchow 07028
Liaoyang City Museum, Liaoyang 07150
Libby Museum, Wolfeboro 48723
Liberace Museum, Las Vegas 44671
Liberty County Museum, Chester 42283
Liberty Hall, Frankfort 43512
Liberty Hall Historic Center, Lamoni 44615
Liberty Hall Museum, Union 48144
Liberty Memorial Museum of World War One, Kansas City 44403
Liberty of Bruges, Brugge 03249
Liberty Village Arts Center and Gallery, Chester 42284
Libertyville-Mundelein Historical Society Museum, Libertyville 44768
Library and Collection of the Worshipful Company of Clockmakers, London 39687
Library Drawings Collection, London 39688
Library Museum, Borås 35838
Library, Museum and Archives of the Stanisław Moniuszko Warsaw Musical Society, Warszawa 32076
Library of the Greek Orthodox Patriarchate of Alexandria and All Africa, Alexandria 09240
Libreria Sansoviniana, Venezia 25921
Licheng District Museum, Jinan 07132
Lichfield Heritage Centre, Lichfield 39491
Lichtdruck-Kunst Leipzig e.V., Leipzig 18402
Lichtdruck-Werkstatt-Museum, Dresden 16695
Lichtenburg Museums and Art Gallery, Lichtenburg 34301
Lichtentaler Pfarrmuseum, Wien 02925
Licking County Art Association Gallery, Newark 45893
Licking County Historical Museum, Newark 45894
Lidköpings Konsthall, Lidköping 36034
Liebenberger Schloß Museum, Liebenberg 18461
Liebermann House, Nahariya 22717
Liebermann-Villa, Berlin 16037
Liebig-Museum, Gießen 17282
Liechtenstein Museum, Wien 02926
Liechtenstein Schloss Wilfersdorf, Wilfersdorf 03031
Liechtensteinische Landesbibliothek, Vaduz 27515
Liechtensteinisches Landesmuseum, Vaduz 27516
Lied Discovery Children's Museum, Las Vegas 44672
Liedenpohjan Museo, Virrat 10203
Liedon Vanhalinna, Vanhalinna 10178
Liemers Museum, Zevenaar 30055
Liepāja History and Art Museum, Liepāja 27380
Liepājas Muzeja, Liepāja 27378
Liepājas Muzeja Izstāžu Zāles, Liepāja 27379
Liepājas Vēstures un Mākslas Muzejs, Liepāja 27380
Lier Bygdetun, Tranby 30928
Lierne museer, Nordli 30710
Lietuvos Dailes Muziejus, Vilnius 27536
Lietuvos Nacionalinis Muziejus, Vilnius 27537
Lieu d'Art Contemporain, Colomiers 11365
Lieu Historique National de Côteau-du-Lac, Côteau-du-Lac 05280
Lieu Historique National de Sir Wilfrid Laurier, Ville des Laurentides 06733
Lieu Historique National des Forges du Saint-Maurice, Trois-Rivières 06641
Lieu Historique National du Canada de la Bataille-de-la-Ristigouche, Pointe-à-la-Croix 06141
Lieu Historique National du Commerce de la Fourrure, Lachine 05711
Lieu Historique National du Manoir-Papineau, Montebello 05884
Lieutenant General Ashton Armoury Museum, Victoria 06723
Lifeboat House, Margate 39910
Lifeboat Museum, Barmouth 38085
Light Factory, Charlotte 42242
Light Infantry Museum, Winchester 40890
Light Square Gallery, Adelaide 00708
Lighthouse Gallery, Tequesta 47981
Lighthouse Keepers Cottage, Carnarvon 00899
Lighthouse Poole Centre for the Arts, Poole 40226
Lightner Museum, Saint Augustine 47068
Lightship Museum and Naval Shipyard Museum, Portsmouth 46663
Ligthing and Refrigerator Museum, Nový Jičín 08510
Likion Ton Ellinidon Collection, Rethymnon 21140
Lilienhof, Lilienthal 18465
Liljendal Hembygdsmuseum, Liljendal 09784
Liljevalch's Art Gallery, Stockholm 36255
Liljevalchs Konsthall, Stockholm 36255
Lille Heddinge Rytterskole, Rødvig Stevns 09036
Lillehammer Art Museum, Lillehammer 30640
Lillehammer Kunstmuseum, Lillehammer 30640
Lillesand By-og Sjøfartsmuseum, Lillesand 30644
Lillesand Town and Maritime Museum, Lillesand 30644
Lillian and Albert Small Jewish Museum, Washington 48366
Lillian and Coleman Taube Museum of Art, Minot 45396
Lillian Stevenson Nursing Archives Museum, Saint John's 06346
Lillie Art Gallery, Milngavie 39958
Lilliput Antique Doll and Toy Museum, Brading 38305
Lillooet District Museum, Lillooet 05753
Lima Hembygdsgård, Lima 36036
Limassol District Museum, Lemesos 08210
Limassol Municipal Art Gallery, Lemesos 08211
Limbaži Museum, Limbaži 27381
Limbažu Muzejs, Limbaži 27381
Limberlost State Historic Site, Geneva 43641
Limburgs Miniatuurmuseum, Sint Geertruid 29820
Limburgs Museum, Venlo 29939
Limburgs Openluchtmuseum Eynderhoof, Nederweert Eind 29608
Limerick City Gallery of Art, Limerick 22507
Limerick Museum, Limerick 22508
Limesmuseum, Tulln 02744
Limesmuseum Aalen, Aalen 15381
Limestone Mine Museum, Lohja 09793
Limfjordsmuseet, Løgstør 08975
Limhamns Museum, Malmö 36074
Limingan Kotiseutumuseo, Liminka 09788
Lin San Zhi Art Display Center, Zhujiang 07337
Linan Museum, Hangzhou 07084
Lincoln Cathedral Treasury, Lincoln 39498
Lincoln Children's Museum, Lincoln 44785
Lincoln County Historical Museum, Davenport 42788
Lincoln County Historical Society Museum, Lincoln 44775
Lincoln County Historical Society Museum, North Platte 46004
Lincoln County Historical Society Museum of Pioneer History, Chandler 42191
Lincoln County Pioneer Museum, Hendricks 43995
Lincoln Home, Springfield 47738
Lincoln Homestead, Springfield 47744
Lincoln Log Cabin, Lerna 44717
Lincoln Memorial Shrine, Redlands 46822
The Lincoln Museum, Fort Wayne 43478
Lincoln Parish Museum, Ruston 47038
Lincoln Park Historical Museum, Lincoln Park 44799
The Lincoln-Tallman Restorations, Janesville 44318
Lincoln Tomb, Springfield 47739
Lincoln Train Museum, Gettysburg 43664
Lincoln's New Salem Historic Site, Petersburg 46370
Lincolnshire Road Transport Museum, Lincoln 39499
Lindås Skulemuseum, Isdalstø 30579
Linden-Museum Stuttgart, Stuttgart 20099
Linden - Saint Kilda Centre for Contemporary Arts, Saint Kilda, Victoria 01435
Lindenau-Museum, Altenburg, Thüringen 15450
Lindenfelser Museum, Lindenfels 18480
Lindesbergsmuseum, Lindesberg 36038
Lindesnes Bygdemuseum, Sør-Audnedal 30864
Lindfield Parvise Museum, Haywards Heath 39201
Lindholm Høje Museet, Nørresundby 08992
Lindigtmühle am Lindenvorwerk, Kohren-Sahlis 18196
Lindisfarne Priory, Holy Island 39256
Lindisfarne Wine and Spirit Museum, Berwick-upon-Tweed 38176
Lindsay Gallery, Lindsay 05755
Lindsay Wildlife Museum, Walnut Creek 48291
Linen Museum, Länkipohja 09738
Lingnan Hua Pai Memorial Hall, Guangzhou 07068
Lingtong Exhibition, Changzhou 07015
Lingyuan City Museum, Lingyuan 07151
Linley Sambourne House, London 39689
Linlithgow Palace, Linlithgow 39507
Linlithgow Story, Linlithgow 39508
Linn County Historical Museum and Moyer House, Brownsville 41964
Linn County Historical Society Museum, Cedar Rapids 42160
Linn County Museum, Pleasanton 46553
Linnaeus Museum, Uppsala 36356
Linnan Museo ja Ortodoksinen Kirkkomuseo, Olavinlinna 09880
Linnanmäen Museo, Helsinki 09510
Linnémuseet, Uppsala 36356
Linnenschmidt'sche Vormals Landesherrliche Mühle zu Venne, Ostercappeln 19292
Linnés Hammarby, Uppsala 36357
Linnés Råshult, Älmhult 35782
Linnoitus- ja Kotiseutumuseo, Luumäki 09804
Linton and District Museum, Linton 01177
Lintong County Museum, Xian 07294
LinzGenesis, Linz 02236
Lion Dance Ceremony Exhibition Hall, Takayama 26810
Lion Salt Works, Northwich 40087
Lionel Wendt Art Gallery, Colombo 35749
Lipeckij Oblastnoj Kraevedčeskij Muzej, Lipeck 32984
Lipetsk Regional Museum, Lipeck 32984
Lipica Museum, Szilvásvárad 21583
Lipicai Múzeum, Szilvásvárad 21583
Lipizzaner Museum, Wien 02927
Lippische Landesbibliothek, Detmold 16588
Lippisches Landesmuseum, Detmold 16589
LIPS Slotenmuseum, Dordrecht 29174
Liptovské Múzeum, Ružomberok 34053
Liquid Paper Correction Fluid Museum, Santa Fe 47422
Liquid Paper Museum, Nambe 45593
Lisbon Historical Society Museum, Lisbon 44810
Liselund Gamle Slot, Borre 08788
Lishui County Museum, Nanjing 07180
Lishui County Museum, Zaicheng 07323
Liskun State Museum of Cattle Breeding, Moskva 33067
Lisle Station Park, Lisle 44812
Lismore Regional Art Gallery, Lismore 01178
Lista Museum, Vanse 30972
Listasafn Así, Àsmundarsalur, Reykjavík 21652
Listasafn Einars Jónssonar, Reykjavík 21653
Listasafn Kópavogs - Gerðasafn, Kópavogur 21642
Listasafn Sigurjóns Ólafssonar, Reykjavík 21654
Listasafn Íslands, Reykjavík 21655
Liszt Ferenc Emlékmúzeum és Kutatóközpont, Budapest 21354
Liszt Ferenc Memorial Museum and Research Centre, Budapest 21354
Liszthaus - Goethe-Nationalmuseum, Weimar, Thüringen 20464
Lisztmuseum, Raiding 02477
Lit Sing Kwang Chinese Temple, Innisfail 01121
Litaraturny muzej Janki Kupaly, Minsk 03117
Litcham Village Museum, Litcham 39512
Litchfield Historical Society Museum, Litchfield 44813
Literair Museum, Hasselt 03480
Literárna Expozícia - Múzeum Janka Jesenského, Bratislava 33969
Literary Documentation Centre H.B. Yasin, Jakarta 22107
Literary History Museum, Minsk 03118
Literary Memorial House-Museum of Sulejman Stalsky, Ašaga-Stalsk 32657
Literary Memorial Museum of A.S. Pushkin and P.I. Chaikovski, Kamenka 37858
Literary Memorial Museum of Ivan Franko, Lviv 37884
Literary-Memorial Museum of Lesya Ukrayinka, Kolodjažne 37862
Literary Memorial Museum of N.A. Ostrovski, Šepetovka 37900
Literary Museum, Abakumcevo 32628
Literary Museum, Ulaanbaatar 28684
Literary Museum G. Guliam from Fergana, Kokand 48842
Literary Museum of the Institute of Russian Literature of the Russian Academy of Sciences, Sankt-Peterburg 33416
Literatur- und Heimatmuseum Altaussee, Altaussee 01659
Literaturarchiv Sulzbach-Rosenberg, Sulzbach-Rosenberg 20125
Literature and Art Museum of Marina Tsvetaeva, Usen-Ivanovskoe 33670
Literature and Memorial Museum N.N. Aseev, Lgov 32983
Literature and Memorial Museum of A.P. Gaydar, Lgov 32982
Literature Museum of Naltchik, Nalčik 33194
Literature, Theatre and Music Museum, Rīga 27429
Literaturhaus, Magdeburg 18583
Literaturhaus München, München 18870
Literaturium / Micro Hall Art Center, Edewecht 16781
Literaturmuseum Brecht-Weigel-Haus, Buckow, Märkische Schweiz 16391
Literaturmuseum im Baumbachhaus, Meiningen 18685
Literaturmuseum Theodor Storm, Heilbad Heiligenstadt 17685
Literaturno-chudožestvennyj Muzej M. Cvetaevoj, Usen-Ivanovskoe 33670
Literaturno-chudožestvennyj Muzej-usadba Prijutino, Vsevoložsk 33739
Literaturno-Memoralnyj Muzej N.A Ostrovskogo, Šepetovka 37900
Literaturno-memorialny Muzei A.S. Puškina i P.I. Čajkovskogo, Kamenka 37858
Literaturno-memorialny Muzej Ivana Franko, Lviv 37884
Literaturno-Memorialny Muzej Lesi Ukrayinky, Kolodjažne 37862
Literaturno-memorialnyj Dom-Muzej D.N. Mamina-Sibirjaka, Ekaterinburg 32769
Literaturno-memorial'nyj Dom-Muzej F.M. Rešetnikova, Ekaterinburg 32770
Literaturno-memorialnyj Dom-muzej Sulejmana Stalskogo, Ašaga-Stalsk 32657
Literaturno-memorialnyj Muzej F.M. Dostoevskogo, Novokuzneck 33235
Literaturno-memorialnyj Muzej F.M. Dostoevskogo, Sankt-Peterburg 33414
Literaturno-memorialnyj Muzej Vasilija Erošenko, Staryj Oskol 33558
Literaturno-memorialnyj Muzej F.A. Abramova, Verkola 33682
Literaturno-memorialnyj Muzej im. A.M. Gorkogo, Kazan 32892
Literaturno-memorialnyj Muzej M. Gorkogo, Samara 33372
Literaturno-memorialnyj Muzej Stancionnyj Smotritel, Vyra 33743
Literaturno-memorialnyj Muzej M.M. Zoščenko, Sankt-Peterburg 33415
Literaturno-teatralnyj Muzej N.M. Djakonova, Syktyvkar 33574
Literaturnyj Muzej, Krasnojarsk 32954
Literaturnyj Muzej, Penza 33286
Literaturnyj Muzej Abakumcevo, Abakumcevo 32628
Literaturnyj Muzej Alisher Navoj, Taškent 48855
Literaturnyj Muzej Andižana, Andižan 48830
Literaturnyj Muzej-centr K.G. Paustovskogo, Moskva 33072
Literaturnyj Muzej Goroda Nalčik, Nalčik 33194
Literaturnyj Muzej G. Guliama iz Fergana, Kokand 48842
Literaturnyj Muzej im. K.V. Ivanova, Čeboksary 32720
Literaturnyj Muzej Instituta Russkoj Literatury, Sankt-Peterburg 33416
Literaturnyj Muzej F.I. Tjutčeva, Ovstug 33278
Lithographiesteinarchiv und druckhistorische Werkstätte, München 18871
Lithuanian Art Museum, Vilnius 27536
The Lithuanian Museum, Chicago 42338
Lithuanian Museum-Archives of Canada, Mississauga 05872
Lithuanian Museums Association, Vilnius 49281
Lithuanian State Museum, Vilnius 27538
Little Bighorn Battlefield Museum, Crow Agency 42712
The Little Brick House, Vandalia 48202
Little Carpathian Museum in Pezinok, Pezinok 34041
Little Cavern, Biebelnheim 16144
Little Compton Historical Society Museum, Little Compton 44817
Little Current-Howland Centennial Museum, Sheguiandah 06433
Little Falls Historical Museum, Little Falls 44821
Little Gallery, Prince Albert 06183
Little Holland House, London 39690
Little Houses, Dunkeld 38815
Little Moreton Hall, Congleton 38623
Little Museum, Tewkesbury 40691
Little Norway, Blue Mounds 41757
Little Prairie Heritage Museum, Chetwynd 05245
Little Red School House Museum, Weyauwega 48578
Little Red Schoolhouse-Living Library, Beloit 41613
Little School Museum, Lockeport 05762
Little Sweets Museum, Osaka 26652
Little Traverse Historical Museum, Petoskey 46383
Little White House, Warm Springs 48303
Little White Schoolhouse, Ripon 46905
Little White Schoolhouse, Truro 06649
Little World Museum of Man, Inuyama 26251
Little World - Museum of Miniature Puppets, Semipalatinsk 33517
Littlehampton Museum, Littlehampton 39514
Littleton Historical Museum, Littleton 44828
Littman Gallery, Portland 46635
Liuhe County Display Center, Liucheng 07154
Liuksialan Maatalousmuseo, Liuksiala 09791
Liverpool Museum, Liverpool 39520
Liverpool Scottish Regimental Museum, Liverpool 39521
Livesey Museum for Children, London 39691
Living Art Museum, Reykjavík 21660
The Living Arts and Science Center, Lexington 44742
Living History Farms Museum, Urbandale 48166

Living Museum at Tulsa Zoo, Tulsa 48105
Living Prairie Museum, Winnipeg 06830
Living Word National Bible Museum, Aledo 41116
Livingston County Historical Society Museum, Geneseo 43639
Livingston Depot Center, Livingston 44832
Livingstone and Stanley Memorial, Tabora 37467
Livingstone Museum, Livingstone 49017
Livonijas Ordeņa Pils Tornis, Tukums 27460
Livrustkammaren, Stockholm 36256
Lizauli Cultural Village, Lizauli 28759
Lizzadro Museum of Lapidary Art, Elmhurst 43167
Ljósmyndasafn Reykjavíkur Grófarhús, Reykjavík 21656
Ljungbergmuseet, Ljungby 36043
Ljungby Gamla Torg Hembygdsmuseum, Ljungby 36044
Ljusdalsbygdens Museum, Ljusdal 36045
Ljusterö Hembygdsmuseum, Ljusterö 36046
LKAB Gruvmuseum, Kiruna 36007
Lladro Museum, New York 45825
Llanberis Lake Railway, Llanberis 39535
Llancaiach Fawr Living History Museum, Nelson 40007
Llandudno Museum and Art Gallery, Llandudno 39541
Llangollen Motor Museum, Llangollen 39553
Llangollen Railway, Llangollen 39554
Llanidloes Museum, Llanidloes 39556
Llanyrafon Farm, Cwmbran 38689
Llechwedd Slate Caverns, Blaenau Ffestiniog 38249
Lleyn Historical and Maritime Museum, Nefyn 40006
La Llonja, Palma de Mallorca 35229
Lloyd George Museum and Highgate, Llanystumdwy 39559
Lloyd's Nelson Collection, London 39692
Llywernog Silver-Lead Mine Museum, Ponterwyd 40219
L.N. Andreev House Museum, Orël 33259
L.N. Tolstoy Country Estate Museum, Moskva 33157
L.N. Tolstoy State Museum, Moskva 33065
L.N. Tolstoy State Museum, Moskva 33066
L.N. Tolstoy State Museum, Stancija Lev Tolstoj 33552
Lobaumuseum, Wien 02928
Lobdengau-Museum, Ladenburg 18284
Lobkovicky Palác, Praha 08589
Lobkovicz Palace, Praha 08589
Local and Maritime Museum, Newhaven 40045
Local Antiquities Museum, Chitradurga 21749
Local History and Ethnography Museum, Brad 32443
Local History Collection, Aberfoyle Park 00696
Local History Collection, Szigetszentmiklós 21581
Local History Museum, Buzsák 21394
Local History Museum, Krivoj Rog 37866
Local History Museum, Mezőkövesd 21471
Local History Museum in Pöytyä, Pöytyä 09936
Local History Museum of Sárkös, Decs 21401
Local Museum, Aleksinac 33786
Local Museum, Ashkelon 22574
Local Museum, Bhanpura 21713
Local Museum, Bileća 03913
Local Museum, Bileća 33823
Local Museum, Brú 21626
Local Museum, Dakovo 07692
Local Museum, Danilovgrad 33835
Local Museum, Doboj 33837
Local Museum, Höfn 21638
Local Museum, Isaszeg 21434
Local Museum, Jalta 37855
Local Museum, Jaša Tomić 33843
Local Museum, Kibbutz Maabarot 22695
Local Museum, Kibbutz Sasa 22702
Local Museum, Našice 07741
Local Museum, Nikšić 33864
Local Museum, Ogulin 07747
Local Museum, Otočac 07752
Local Museum, Pljevlja 33885
Local Museum, Považská Bystrica 34047
Local Museum, Prijedor 03920
Local Museum, Ruma 33901
Local Museum, Skiptvet 30849
Local Museum, Stykkishólmur 21671
Local Museum, Törökbálint 21597
Local Museum, Travnik 03926
Local Museum, Trebinje 33922
Local Museum, Ulcinj 33924
Local Museum, Visoko 03931
Local Museum of Amursk, Amursk 32637
Local Museum of History and Culture, Lugansk 37881
Local Museum of Perniö, Perniö 09920
Local Museum Ozalj, Ozalj 07753
Local Museum Poreč, Poreč 07755
Local Museum Zemun, Zemun 33931
Local Studies Collection, Marrickville 01213
Localbahnmuseum, Innsbruck 02073
Localbahnmuseum Bayerisch Eisenstein, Bayerisch Eisenstein 15838
Loch Ness 2000 Exhibition, Drumnadrochit 38778
Lochwinnoch Community Museum, Lochwinnoch 39561
Lock Museum of America, Terryville 47988
Lockehaven Schoolhouse Museum, Enfield 43190
Lockerbie Street Home of James Whitcomb Riley, Indianapolis 44230
Locke's Distillery Museum, Kilbeggan 22484
Lockhouse-Friends of the Delaware Canal, New Hope 45705
Lockport Gallery, Lockport 44841
Lockwood-Mathews Mansion Museum, Norwalk 46032
Locust Grove, Louisville 44969
Locust Grove, Poughkeepsie 46675
Locust Lawn and Terwilliger House, Gardiner 43621
Łódź Archidiocesan Museum, Łódź 31769
Lödöse Museum, Lödöse 36048
Löfstad Slott Museum, Norrköping 36119
Löhe-Zeit-Museum, Neuendettelsau 19024
Lönnströmin Taidemuseo, Rauma 09982
Lötschentaler Museum, Kippel 36826
Lövångers Sockenmuseum, Lövånger 36049
Löwen-Drogerie und Museum, Oelsnitz, Vogtland 19229
Lofoten Krigsminnemuseum, Svolvær 30911
Lofotmuseet, Kabelvåg 30587
Log Cabin Museum, Murray Harbour 05951
Log Cabin Village, Fort Worth 43488
The Log Farm, Nepean 05972
Logan Art Gallery, Logan 01183
Logan County Historical Society Museum, Bellefontaine 41588
Logan County Museum, Paris 46282
Logan Museum of Anthropology, Beloit 41615
Lohgerber-, Stadt- und Kreismuseum, Dippoldiswalde 16620
Lohilammen Museo, Sammatti 10019
Lohjan Museo, Lohja 09792
Lohrbacher Heimatstuben, Mosbach, Baden 18794
Lohtajan Kotiseutumuseo, Lohtaja 09794
Loimaan Kotiseutumuseo, Loimaa 09795
Lois E. Woods Museum, Norfolk 45967
Lok Virsa Museum, Islamabad 31024
Løkken Museum, Løkken 08977
Lolland-Falsters Stiftsmuseum, Maribo 08981
Lolland-Falsters Traktor- og Motormuseum, Eskildstrup 08810
Lom Bygdamuseum, Lom 30650
Lomakovskij Muzej Starinnych Avtomobilei i Motociklov, Moskva 33073
Lombard Historical Museum, Lombard 44848
Lommedalsbanen, Rykkinn 30812
Lompoc Museum, Lompoc 44850
Lompoc Valley Historical Society Museum, Lompoc 44851
Lon C. Hill Home, Harlingen 43913
London Borough of Bromley Museum, Orpington 40135
London Brass Rubbing Centre, London 39693
The London Brass Rubbing Centre in Washington D.C., Gaithersburg 43591
London Canal Museum, London 39694
London Federation of Museums and Art Galleries, London 49422
London Fire Brigade Museum, London 39695
London Institute Gallery, London 39696
London Irish Rifles Regimental Museum, London 39697
London Motorcycle Museum, Greenford 39129
London Museum of Archaeology, London 05769
London Regional Children's Museum, London 05770
London Scottish Regimental Museum, London 39698
London Sewing Machine Museum, London 39699
London Toy and Model Museum, London 39700
Londonderry Mines Museum, Londonderry 05774
London's Transport Museum, London 39701
Lone Star Flight Museum/Texas Aviation Hall of Fame, Galveston 43612
Long Beach Museum of Art, Long Beach 44860
Long Branch Historical Museum, Long Branch 44866
Long Eaton Town Hall, Long Eaton 39820
Long Island Children's Museum, Garden City 43619
Long Island Culture History Museum, Commack 42594
Long Island Maritime Museum, West Sayville 48547
Long Island Museum of American Art, History and Cariages, Stony Brook 47830
Long Island Museum of Science and Technology, Garden City 43620
Long Shop Museum, Leiston 39475
Long Warehouse, Coalbrookdale 38595
Longboat Key Center for the Arts, Longboat Key 44875
Longdale Craft Centre and Museum, Ravenshead 40289
Longfellow-Evangeline State Historic Site, Saint Martinville 47142
Longfellow National Historic Site, Cambridge 42044
Longfellow's Wayside Inn Museum, South Sudbury 47703
Longgang Ke Jia Folklorish Museum, Shenzhen 07240
Longhorn Museum, Pleasanton 46555
Longhua Mausoleum of Fallen Heroes, Shanghai 07215
Longleat House, Warminster 40787
Longmont Museum, Longmont 44877
Longquanyi District Museum, Chengdu 07022
Longreach Power House Museum, Longreach 01185
Longstreet Farm, Holmdel 44062
Longue Vue House, New Orleans 45729
Longview Museum of Fine Art, Longview 44879
Longwood Center for the Visual Arts, Farmville 43304
Longyear Museum, Chestnut Hill 42293
La Lonja, Zaragoza 35717
Look Out Discovery Centre, Bracknell 38292
Loop Museum and Art Center, Seagraves 47525
Loosduins Museum De Korenschuur, Den Haag 29102
Lopdell House Gallery, Auckland 30112
Lopez Island Historical Museum, Lopez Island 44882
Lopez Memorial Museum, Pasig 31420
Lora Robins Gallery of Design from Nature, Richmond 46881
Loránd Eötvös Collection, Budapest 21335
Lord Howe Island Museum, Lord Howe Island 01187
Lord Selkirk Settlement, Charlottetown 05227
Lord Strathcona's Horse Museum, Calgary 05171
Lore Degenstein Gallery, Selinsgrove 47561
Lørenskog Bygdemuseum, Skårer 30840
Lorenzo State Historic Site, Cazenovia 42145
Lorn Museum, Ledaig 39438
Lorne Scots Regimental Museum, Brampton 05113
Los Alamos County Historical Museum, Los Alamos 44888
Los Angeles Center for Photographic Studies, Los Angeles 44919
Los Angeles Contemporary Exhibitions, Los Angeles 44920
Los Angeles County Museum of Art, Los Angeles 44921
Los Angeles Craft and Folk Art Museum, Los Angeles 44922
Los Angeles Maritime Museum, San Pedro 47373
Los Angeles Municipal Art Gallery, Los Angeles 44923
Los Angeles Museum of the Holocaust, Los Angeles 44924
Los Angeles Valley College Art Gallery, Valley Glen 48190
Los Nogales Museum, Seguin 47560
Loseley House, Guildford 39140
Loški Muzej, Škofja Loka 34148
Lossiemouth Fisheries and Community Museum, Lossiemouth 39826
Lost City Museum, Overton 46224
Lostwithiel Museum, Lostwithiel 39827
Løten Bankmuseum, Løten 30656
Lotherton Hall, Aberford 37947
Lothringer 13, München 18872
Lottan Torppa, Lokalahti 09796
Lotte World Folk Museum, Seoul 27256
Lou Holtz and Upper Ohio Valley Hall of Fame, East Liverpool 43055
Louden-Henritze Archaeology Museum, Trinidad 48064
Loudoun Mansion, Philadelphia 46424
Loudoun Museum, Leesburg 44710
Louhisaaren Kartanolinna, Askainen 09420
Louhisaari Manor, Askainen 09420
Louis Couperus Museum, Den Haag 29103
Louis E. May Museum, Fremont 43555
Louis H. and Lena Firn Grover Museum, Shelbyville 47596
Louis Spohr-Gedenk- und Forschungsstätte, Kassel 18023
Louis Tussaud Wax Museum, København 08937
Louis Tussaud's Waxworks Museum, Niagara Falls 05991
Louisa County Historical Museum, Louisa 44958
Louisburg College Art Gallery, Louisburg 44959
Louise Wells Cameron Art Museum, Wilmington 48660
Louisiana Arts and Science Center, Baton Rouge 41527
Louisiana Association of Museums, Baton Rouge 49502
Louisiana Children's Museum, New Orleans 45730
Louisiana Country Music Museum, Marthaville 45188
Louisiana Museum of Modern Art, Humlebæk 08902
Louisiana Naval War Memorial U.S.S. Kidd, Baton Rouge 41528
Louisiana Old State Capitol, Center for Political and Governmental History, Baton Rouge 41529
Louisiana State Exhibit Museum, Shreveport 47612
Louisiana State Museum, New Orleans 45731
Louisiana State Museum, Patterson 46313
Louisiana State University Museum of Art, Baton Rouge 41530
Louisiana Tech Museum, Ruston 47039
Louisville Science Center, Louisville 44970
Louisville Slugger Museum, Louisville 44971
Louisville Visual Art Museum, Louisville 44972
Lounais-Hämeen Museo, Forssa 09442
Louth Museum, Louth 39834
Louwman Collection - Het National Automobilmuseum, Raamsdonksveer 29722
Lovački Muzej, Zagreb 07827
Loveland Museum and Gallery, Loveland 44980
Lovely Lane Museum, Baltimore 41475
Loviisa Town Museum, Loviisa 09799
Loviisan Kaupungin Museo, Loviisa 09799
Lovriner Stube, Donauwörth 16640
Lowe Art Museum, Coral Gables 42628
The Lowe Gallery at Hudson Guild, New York 45826
Lowell Damon House, Wauwatosa 48466
Lowell National Historical Park, Lowell 44983
Lowell Telecommunications Corporation Museum, Lowell 44984
Lower Cape Fear Historical Society Museum, Wilmington 48661
Lower Columbia College Fine Arts Gallery, Longview 44880
Lower Danube Museum, Călăraşi 32479
Lower East Side Tenement Museum, New York 45827
Lower Fort Garry, Selkirk 06419
Lower Methil Heritage Centre, Lower Methil 39836
Lowestoft and East Suffolk Maritime Museum, Lowestoft 39838
Lowestoft Museum, Lowestoft 39839
Lowewood Museum, Hoddesdon 39251
Lowndes County Museum, Valdosta 48180
The Lowry Gallery, Salford 40430
Loxton District Historical Village, Loxton 01190
Loyal Edmonton Regiment Military Museum, Edmonton 05379
Loyalist Cultural Centre, Bath 05056
Loyalist House Museum, Saint John 06333
Lu Xun Museum In Shaoxing, Shaoxing 07232
Lublin Archidiocesan Museum, Lublin 31787
Lubovňa Castle Museum, Stará Lubovňa 34065
Lubovnianske Múzeum - Hrad, Stará Lubovňa 34065
Lubovniansky Skanzen, Stará Lubovňa 34066
Lubuskie Muzeum Wojskowe w Zielonej Górze z/s w Drzonowie, Letnica 31758
Luce Gallery, Mount Vernon 45543
Luchou Museum, Luchou 07155
Luchtvaart Museum Texel, De Cocksdorp 29066
Luchtvaart Museum Twenthe, Enschede 29236
Luckhard Museum - The Indian Mission, Sebewaing 47550
Lucy Craft Laney Museum of Black History, Augusta 41384
Lucy Maud Montgomery Birthplace, Charlottetown 05228
Luda Bērziņa Memoriālais Muzejs, Jūrmala 27370
Ludlow Museum, Ludlow 39842
Ludovit Fulla Gallery of the Slovak National Gallery, Ružomberok 34054
Ludvika Gammelgård och Gruvmuseum, Ludvika 36052
Ludvika Old Homestead and Museum of Mining, Ludvika 36052
Ludwig-Doerfler-Galerie, Schillingsfürst 19779
Ludwig-Forum für Internationale Kunst, Aachen 15375
Ludwig Galerie Schloß Oberhausen, Oberhausen, Rheinland 19177
Ludwig-Gebhard-Museum, Tiefenbach, Oberpfalz 20175
Ludwig-Harms-Haus, Hermannsburg 17725
Ludwig Museum Budapest - Museum of Contemporary Art, Budapest 21353
Ludwig Museum im Deutschherrenhaus, Koblenz 18121
Ludwig-Roselius-Museum für Ur- und Frühgeschichte, Worpswede 20685
Ludwig-Thoma-Haus, Tegernsee 20149
Ludwig Wittgenstein-Dauerausstellung, Kirchberg am Wechsel 02111
Ludza Museum of Local Studies, Ludza 27382
Ludzas Novadpētniecības Muzejs, Ludza 27382
Lüderitz Museum, Lüderitz 28760
Lügenmuseum Schloß Gantikow, Gantikow 17194
Lüzinyan Evi, Lefkoşa 08237
Luftfahrt-Museum Laatzen-Hannover, Laatzen 18279
Luftfahrt- und Technik-Museumspark, Merseburg 18714
Luftfahrtausstellung im Alten Straßenbahndepot, Brandenburg an der Havel 16283
Luftfahrttechnisches Museum, Rothenburg, Oberlausitz 19685
Luftwaffenmuseum der Bundeswehr, Berlin 16038
Lugouqiao Display Center, Beijing 06971
Luigi Cattaneo Anatomical Wax Model Museum, Bologna 23118
Luis E. Peña G. Collection, Santiago de Chile 06907
Luis Muñoz Rivera Museum, Barranquitas 32362
Luisenhütte, Balve 15803
Lullingstone Roman Villa, Eynsford 38964
Lum and Abner Museum and Jot 'Em Down Store, Pine Ridge 46491
Lummis Home El Alisal, Los Angeles 44925
Lumsden Heritage Museum, Lumsden 05786
Luna Mimbres Museum, Deming 42868
Lunacharski Apartment Museum, Moskva 33125
Lund Bygdemuseum, Moi 30684
Lundar Museum, Lundar 05787
Lunds Konsthall, Lund 36061
Lunds Universitets Antikmuseum, Lund 36062
Lundströmska Gården, Sigtuna 36182
Lundy's Lane Historical Museum, Niagara Falls 05992
Lunenburg Art Gallery, Lunenburg 05789
Lungauer Heimatmuseum Tamsweg, Tamsweg 02711
Lungauer Landschaftsmuseum, Mauterndorf 02286
Lunt Roman Fort, Baginton 38054
Luonnonhistoriallinen Museo, Porvoo 09952
Luonnontieteellinen Museo, Helsinki 09511
Luontomuseo, Kokkola 09684
Luontotalo Arkki, Pori 09943
Luopioinen Museum, Luopioinen 09801
Luopioisten Museo, Luopioinen 09801
Luopioisten Torpparimuseo, Luopioinen 09802
Luostarinmäen Käsityöläismuseo, Turku 10124
Luostarinmäki Handicraft Museum, Turku 10124
Luotsitupa, Uusikaupunki 10153
Luoyang City Folklorish Museum, Luoyang 07158
Luoyang City Museum, Luoyang 07159
Lura Watkins Museum, Middleton 45312
Lurens, Loviisa 09800
Lusaka National Museum, Lusaka 49020
Luseland and Districts Museum, Luseland 05790
Lushun Museum, Dalian 07037
Lushun Snakes Dao Natural Museum, Dalian 07038
Lushun Su Jun Mausoleum of Fallen Heroes, Dalian 07039
Lusignan House, Lefkoşa 08237
Lusto-Suomen-metsämuseo ja metsätietokeskus, Punkaharju 09962

Lusto - The Finnish Forest Museum, Punkaharju 09962
Luther Burbank Home, Santa Rosa 47446
Luther-Stube Mansfeld, Mansfeld, Südharz 18617
Lutheran Brotherhood Gallery, Minneapolis 45389
Lutheran Church Museum, Budapest 21337
Lutherhaus, Eisenach 16816
Lutherhaus Wittenberg, Lutherstadt Wittenberg 18575
Lutherkirche und Lutherzimmer im Dorfgemeinschaftshaus, Möhra 18763
Luton Museum and Art Gallery, Luton 39845
Lutz Children's Museum, Manchester 45093
Lutz Mountain Meeting House, Moncton 05878
Luusuan Kylämuseo, Luusua 09805
Luvian Kotiseutumuseo, Luvia 09806
Luxor Museum of Ancient Art, Al-Uqsur 09234
Luzerne County Historical Museum, Wilkes-Barre 48621
Lviv Art Gallery, Lviv 37885
Lviv Historical Museum, Lviv 37886
The Lyceum - Alexandria's History Museum, Alexandria 41132
Lyceum Museum, Puškin 33339
Lydd Town Museum, Lydd 39850
Lydia Koidulu Memoriaalmuuseum, Pärnu 09343
Lydiard House, Swindon 40662
Lyle-Tapley Shoe Shop and Vaughn Doll House, Salem 47197
Lyly Signal Depot Museum, Lyly 09807
Lylyn Viestivarikon Museo, Lyly 09807
Lyman Allyn Museum of Art, New London 45710
Lyman House Memorial Museum, Hilo 44032
Lyme Hall, Disley 38732
Lyme Regis Philpot Museum, Lyme Regis 39853
Lyn and Exmoor Museum, Lynton 39856
Lynchburg Fine Arts Center, Lynchburg 45004
Lynchburg Museum System, Lynchburg 45005
Lynden Pioneer Museum, Lynden 45009
Lyndhurst, Tarrytown 47958
Lyndon B. Johnson National Historical Park, Johnson City 44349
Lyndon Baines Johnson Museum, Austin 41416
Lyndon House Art Center, Athens 41320
Lynn Canyon Ecology Centre, North Vancouver 06024
Lynn Lake Mining Town Museum, Lynn Lake 05791
Lynn Museum, Lynn 45011
Lynnhaven House, Virginia Beach 48248
Lynnwood Arts Centre, Simcoe 06457
Lyon County Historical Society Museum, Marshall 45179
Lyon County Museum, Emporia 43183
Lyonel-Feininger-Galerie, Quedlinburg 19463
The Lyons Redstone Museum, Lyons 45012
Lyth Arts Centre, Lyth 39857
Lytham Hall, Lytham Saint Anne's 39858
Lytham Heritage Centre, Lytham Saint Anne's 39859
Lytham Lifeboat Museum, Lytham Saint Anne's 39860
Lytham Windmill Museum, Lytham Saint Anne's 39861
Lyttelton Historical Museum, Christchurch 30129
Lytton Museum, Lytton 05792
Lyuben Karavelov Memorial House, Koprivštica 04714
M. Christina Geis Gallery, Lakewood 44609
M. Gorky Memorial Museum, Samara 33372
M. Sarians Museum, Erevan 00685
Maanmittausmuseo, Helsinki 09512
Maarten van Rossum Museum, Zaltbommel 30044
Maas- en Scheepvaartmuseum, Maasbracht 29559
Maas en Waals Museum 1939-1945, Winssen 30011
Maatilamuseo Luhdinsola, Naantali 09852
Mabee-Gerrer Museum of Art, Shawnee 47588
Mabel Larson Fine Arts Gallery, Clarksville 42436
Måbødalen Kulturlandskapsmuseum, Eidfjord 30470
Mabry-Hazen House, Knoxville 44521
Macalester College Art Gallery, Saint Paul 47159
McAllen International Museum, McAllen 45017
McAllister House Museum, Colorado Springs 42538
Macau Museum of Art, Macau 07163
Macau Wine Museum, Macau 07164
Macaulay Heritage Park, Picton 06127
Macaulay Museum of Dental History, Charleston 42222
MacBride Museum, Whitehorse 06792
McCaig Museum, Oban 40123
MacCallum More Museum, Chase City 42255
McCallum Museum, Sibley 47622
McCallum's Museum, Dauphin 05309
McClelland Gallery, Langwarrin 01164
Macclesfield Silk Museum, Macclesfield 39865
McClurg Mansion, Westfield 48559
McCollum-Chidester House Museum, Camden 42057
McCone County Museum, Circle 42414
McConnell Mansion, Moscow 45518
McCord and District Museum, McCord 05794
McCord Museum, Montréal 05910
McCormick Gallery, Midland 45326
McCoy House, Lewistown 44734
McCrae Homestead Museum, McCrae 01191
McCrae House, Guelph 05537
McCrossin's Mill Museum, Uralla 01563
Macculloch Hall Historical Museum, Morristown 45507
McCulloch House Museum and Hector Exhibit Centre, Pictou 06129
McCutchen Overland Inn, McCutchenville 45023
McDade Museum, McDade 45024
Macdonald Stewart Art Centre, Guelph 05538
Das McDonald's Junior-Tüten & Pin Museum, Wiener Neustadt 03018
McDougall Mill Museum, Renfrew 06251
McDowell House and Apothecary Shop, Danville 42779
Macedon Historical Society Museum, Macedon 45025
Macedonian Museum of Contemporary Art, Thessaloniki 21186
Macedonian Museum of Natural History, Skopje 27592
McFaddin-Ward House, Beaumont 41570
McFarland Historical Society Museum, McFarland 45026
McFarland House, Niagara Falls 05993
McGillis Pioneer Home, Saint Victor 06378
Macgregor Museum, Harare 49030
McGregor Museum and Duggan Cronin Gallery, Kimberley 34290
McGroarty Cultural Art Center, Tujunga 48100
Machan Museum, La Grange 44543
Machan Museum, Lagrange 44574
McHenry County Historical Society Museum, Union 48140
McHenry Museum, Modesto 45428
Machida City Museum of Graphic Arts, Machida 26464
Machida-shiritsu Hakubutsukan Machida City Museum, Machida 26463
Machida-shiritsu Kokusai Hanga Bijutsukan, Machida 26464
MACHmit! Museum für Kinder, Berlin 16039
McIntosh County Historical Society Museum, Ashley 41300
McIntosh Gallery, London 05771
McIntyre Street Gallery, Regina 06237
McKays Museum, Bowsman 05105
McKechnie Institute, Girvan 39034
Mackenzie and District Museum, Mackenzie 05795
MacKenzie Art Gallery, Regina 06238
MacKenzie Heritage Printery Museum, Queenston 06214
Mackenzie House, Toronto 06590
Mackenzie King Estate, Ottawa 06083
McKinley Museum and McKinley National Memorial, Canton 42090
McKissick Museum, Columbia 42563
Macklin and District Museum, Macklin 05796
Macktown Living History Site and Whitman Trading Post, Rockton 46974
MacLaren Art Centre, Barrie 05049
McLarty Treasure Museum, Vero Beach 48223
Maclaurin Art Gallery, Ayr 38051
McLean-Alanreed Area Museum, McLean 45039
McLean County Arts Center, Bloomington 41743
McLean County Historical Society Museum, Washburn 48326
McLean County Museum of History, Bloomington 41744
McLean Mill, Port Alberni 06149
McLean Museum and Art Gallery, Greenock 39131
Macleay Museum, Sydney 01501
McLellan Galleries, Glasgow 39054
McLurg Museum, Wilkie 06800
McManus Galleries, Dundee 38800
McMaster Museum of Art, Hamilton 05574
McMichael Canadian Art Collection, Kleinburg 05702
McMinn County Living Heritage Museum, Athens 41327
McMullen Museum of Art, Chestnut Hill 42294
McNamara House Museum, Victoria 48233
Macon County Museum Complex, Decatur 42833
MacPheadris/Warner House, Portsmouth 46650
McPherson College Gallery, McPherson 45049
McPherson County Old Mill Museum, Lindsborg 44807
McPherson Museum, McPherson 45050
MacPherson's Mill and Farm Homestead, New Glasgow 05978
MacRobert Gallery, Stirling 40592
Macroom Museum, Macroom 22514
Macrorie House Museum, Pietermaritzburg 34326
Macrorie Museum, Macrorie 05797
Mac's Antique Car Museum, Tulsa 48106
MacSwiney Memorial Museum, Kilmurry 22496
McWane Center, Birmingham 41707
Madaba Archaeology Museum, Ajloun 27040
Madam Brett Homestead, Beacon 41553
Madame Tussaud's, London 39702
Madame Tussaud's Amsterdam, Amsterdam 28870
Madame Tussaud's Wax Museum, New York 45828
Madang Museum, Yomba 31092
Madara Nacionalen Istoriko-archeologičeski Rezervat, Madara 04731
La Madeleine, Tursac 15020
Madeline Island Historical Museum, La Pointe 44554
Madera County Museum, Madera 45052
Madhavan Nair Foundation, Edapally 21796
Madhya Pradesh Tribal Research and Development Institute, Bhopal 21721
Madison Art Center, Madison 45069
Madison Children's Museum, Madison 45070
Madison County Historical Museum, Edwardsville 43097
Madison County Historical Society Museum, Winterset 48710
Madison Historical Society Museum, Madison 45053
Madison-Morgan Cultural Center Collection, Madison 45055
Madona Museum of Local Studies and Art, Madona 27383
Madona Museum of Local Studies and Art, Madona 27384
Madonas Novadpētniecības un Mākslas Muzejs, Madona 27384
Madonna House Pioneer Museum, Combermere 05269
Madras Christian College Museum, Chennai 21746
Madres Dominicanas - Monasterio Sancti Spiritus, Toro 35557
Madurodam, Den Haag 29104
Maeght Musée, Paris 13519
Mährisch-Schlesisches Heimatmuseum, Klosterneuburg 02140
Maejima Memorial Museum, Joetsu 26284
Mälsåkers Slott, Stallarholmen 36226
Mäntsälän Kotiseutumuseo, Mäntsälä 09808
Mäntyharju Museum, Mäntyharju 09811
Mäntyharjun Museo, Mäntyharju 09811
Märchenhain Gföhl, Gföhl 01877
Märchenhaus und Heimatmuseum Ottenschlag, Ottenschlag 02390
Märchenofen, Neu-Ulm 19010
Märkisches Museum, Berlin 16040
Märkisches Museum, Witten 20622
Märkisches Ziegelei-Museum Glindow, Glindow 17301
Märklin-Museum, Göppingen 17319
Maffeischächte der Grube Auerbach-Nitzlbuch, Auerbach, Oberpfalz 15544
Maffra Sugarbeet Museum, Maffra 01195
Mafikeng Museum, Mafikeng 34304
Magadanskij Oblastnoj Kraevedčeskij Muzej, Magadan 32999
Magan Sangrahalaya Samiti, Wardha 22061
Magasin - Centre National d'Art Contemporain, Grenoble 11938
Magasin-Musée de la Coutellerie Traditionnelle, Laguiole 12300
Magdalen Museum, Wainfleet 40758
Magdeburger Museen, Magdeburg 18584
Magdeburská Kasárna, Terezín 08679
Magersfontein Battlefields Museum, Kimberley 34291
Magevney House, Memphis 45239
Magic House-Saint Louis Children's Museum, Saint Louis 47127
Magic Lantern Castle Museum, San Antonio 47254
La Magnanerie du Coudray, Le Coudray-Macquard 12404
Magnanerie Muséalisée de la Roque, Molezon 13003
The Magnes Museum, Berkeley 41645
The Magnes Museum, San Francisco 47323
Magnetawan Historical Museum, Magnetawan 05798
Magnitogorsk Picture Gallery, Magnitogorsk 33001
Magnitogorsk Regional Museum, Magnitogorsk 33002
Magnitogorskaja Kartinnaja Galereja, Magnitogorsk 33001
Magnitogorskij Kraevedčeskij Muzej, Magnitogorsk 33002
Magnolia Grove-Historic House Museum, Greensboro 43810
Magnolia Manor Museum, Cairo 42026
Magnolia Mound Plantation, Baton Rouge 41531
Magnolia Plantation, Charleston 42223
Magnus Dagestad Museet, Voss 31000
Magoffin Home, El Paso 43121
Magsingal National Museum, Magsingal 31350
Magyar Elektrotechnikai Múzeum, Budapest 21355
Magyar Építészeti Múzeum, Budapest 21356
Magyar Földrajzi Gyűjtemény, Érd 21409
Magyar Fotográfiai Múzeum, Kecskemét 21450
Magyar Képzőművészek és Iparművészek Szövetsége, Budapest 21357
Magyar Kereskedelmi és Vendéglátóipari Múzeum, Budapest 21358
Magyar Környezetvédelmi és Vízügyi Múzeum, Esztergom 21413
Magyar Mezőgazdasági Múzeum, Budapest 21359
Magyar Naiv Művészek Múzeuma, Kecskemét 21451
Magyar Nemzeti Galéria, Budapest 21360
Magyar Nemzeti Múzeum, Budapest 21361
Magyar Olajipari Múzeum, Zalaegerszeg 21615
Magyar Ortodox Múzeum, Miskolc 21478
Magyar Természettudományi Múzeum, Budapest 21362
Magyar Vegyészeti Múzeum, Várpalota 21604
Maha Al Saqqa Center - Palestinian Folk Museum, Bethlehem 31065
Maha Wirawong National Museum, Nakhon Ratchasima 37517
Mahaffie Stagecoach Stop and Farm, Olathe 46127
Mahakoshal Art Gallery, Raipur, Madhya Pradesh 21999
Mahant Ghasidas Memorial Museum, Raipur, Karnataka 21998
Maharaja Banaras Vidya Mandir Museum, Varanasi 22058
Maharaja Fate Singh Museum, Vadodara 22049
Maharaja Sawai Man Singh II Museum, Jaipur, Rajasthan 21863
Mahatma Gandhi Hindi Sangrahalaya, Kalpi 21879
Mahatma Gandhi Memorial College Museum, Udupi 22046
Mahatma Gandhi Museum, Mangalore 21938
Mahatma Gandhi Museum, Verulam 34397
Mahatma Phule Vastu Sangrahalaya, Pune 21991
Mahn- und Gedenkstätte Düsseldorf, Düsseldorf 16734
Mahn- und Gedenkstätte Isenschnibber-Feldscheune, Gardelegen 17198
Mahn- und Gedenkstätte Ravensbrück, Fürstenberg, Havel 17158
Mahn- und Gedenkstätte Steinwache, Dortmund 16660
Mahn- und Gedenkstätte Wernigerode, Wernigerode 20527
Mahn- und Gedenkstätten Wöbbelin, Wöbbelin 20640
Mahogany Inn, Mahogany Creek 01196
Mahtra Talurahvamuuseum, Juuru 09327
Maidstone Library Gallery, Maidstone 39876
Maidstone Museum and Bentlif Art Gallery, Maidstone 39877
Maier Museum of Art, Lynchburg 45006
Maihaugen, Lillehammer 30641
Mail and Telecommunication Museum, Gdańsk 31574
Maimana Museum, Maimana 00008
Main Art Gallery, Fullerton 43573
Main Centre Heritage Museum, Main Centre 05800
Main Gallery of Henry Street Settlement, New York 45829
Main Line Art Center, Haverford 43960
Maine Art Gallery, Wiscasset 48716
Maine Association of Museums, Augusta 49503
Maine Historical Society Museum, Portland 46624
Maine Maritime Museum, Bath 41522
Maine State Museum, Augusta 41390
Mainfränkisches Museum Würzburg, Würzburg 20696
Maironis Lithuanian Literature Museum, Kaunas 27520
Maisel's Brauerei- und Büttnerei-Museum, Bayreuth 15853
Maison A.-Ravier, Morestel 13156
Maison André-Benjamin-Papineau, Laval 05734
Maison-Atelier Foujita, Villiers-le-Bacle 15255
Maison Berckheim du Parc Anglais de Schoppenwihr, Ostheim 13444
Maison Buttin-de Loës, Grandvaux 36777
La Maison Couleur du Temps, Venas 15111
Maison Creole Eureka, Moka 27735
Maison d'Abraham Mazel à Falguières, Mialet 12974
Maison d'Auguste Comte, Paris 13520
La Maison d'Aure, Sailhan 14086
Maison de Balzac, Paris 13521
Maison de Boua Kang Bung, Luang Prabang 27317
La Maison de celle qui peint, Roquevaire 14029
Maison de Géologie de Haute-Alsace, Sentheim 14716
Maison de Gergovie, La Roche-Blanche 12228
Maison de la Baie, Courtils 11440
Maison de la Baie du Mont Saint-Michel, Vains 15041
Maison de la Broderie, Villers-Outréaux 15243
Maison de la Canne, Les Trois-Ilets 27725
La Maison de la Chicorée, Orchies 13418
Maison de la Dentelle, Urçay 15027
Maison de la Dernière Cartouche, Bazeilles 10625
La Maison de la Dordogne Quercynoise, Souillac 14785
Maison de la Faïence, Badonviller 10556
Maison de la Faïence, Desvres 11503
Maison de la Faune, Murat (Cantal) 13219
Maison de la Fonderie, Vrigne-aux-Bois 15295
Maison de la Forêt, Bon-Secours 03223
Maison de la Forêt de Miers, Pleaux 13752
La Maison de la Forêt et du Bois, Saint-Martin-en-Bresse 14356
Maison de la Lentille du Berry, Chouday 11302
Maison de la Loire, Montlouis-sur-Loire 13101
Maison de la Magie Robert-Houdin, Blois 10770
Maison de la Manufacture d'Armes Blanches, Klingenthal 12115
Maison de la Mariée, Saint-Joachim 14292
Maison de la Mer, Courseulles-sur-Mer 11434
Maison de la Metallurgie et de l'Industrie de Liège, Liège 03569
Maison de la Meunerie, Nieul-sur-l'Autise 13331
Maison de la Miniature, Saint-Galmier 14223
Maison de la Montagne et du Canigou, Casteil 11069
Maison de la Musique Mécanique, Mirecourt 12993
Maison de la Nature, Eze 11695
Maison de la Nature, Paris 13522
Maison de la Nature et de l'Oiseau, Neuville-sur-Ailette 13298
Maison de la Négritude et des Droits de l'Homme, Champagney 11152
Maison de la Pierre de Volvic, Volvic 15287
Maison de la Pierre et du Ciment, Montalieu-Vercieu 13039
Maison de la Pisciculture, Sizun 14757
Maison de la Pomme et de la Poire, Barenton 10589
Maison de la Poste, Montréal 05911
Maison de la Réserve Naturelle du Lac de Remoray, Labergement-Sainte-Marie 12284
Maison de la Résistance, Chasseneuil-sur-Bonnieure 11199
Maison de la Rivière, Châteauneuf-sur-Sarthe 11222
Maison de la Rivière, de l'Eau et de la Pêche, Sizun 14758
Maison de la Rivière et du Pêcheur, Saint-Georges-de-Montaigu 14231
Maison de la Sainte-Victoire, Saint-Antonin-sur-Bayon 14114
Maison de la Science, Liège 03570
Maison de la Terre Cuite, Les Rairies 12547
Maison de la Thiérache, Liart 12581
Maison de la Vallée d'Ossau, Laruns 12351

Maison de la Vie Rurale, Frizon 11821
Maison de la Vigne, Essoyes 11659
Maison de l'Abbé Grégoire, Embermenil 11613
Maison de l'Abeille et du Miel, Riez 13965
Maison de l'Air, Paris 13523
Maison de l'Amandier, Saint-Rémy-de-Provence 14448
Maison de l'Araire, Yzeron 15336
Maison de l'Archéologie des Vosges du Nord, Niederbronn-les-Bains 13330
Maison de l'Argile, Aubagne 10453
La Maison de l'Eau, Mallièvre 12786
Maison de l'Eau et de la Pêche, Besse-en-Chandesse 10705
Maison de l'Eau et de la Pêche, Neuvic (Corrèze) 13292
Maison de l'Eclusier, Saint-Malo-de-Guersac 14339
Maison de l'Energie, Eguzon 11605
Maison de l'Environnement et de la Chasse, Sault (Vaucluse) 14638
Maison de l'Espace Vert, Nancy 13238
Maison de l'Etain, Villedieu-les-Poêles 15192
Maison de l'Éventail, Bèze 10717
Maison de l'Histoire de la Terre de Gorze, Gorze 11890
Maison de l'Industrie - Exposition Permanente, Saint-Berthevin 14123
Maison de l'Olivier, Le Val 12489
Maison de Louis Pasteur, Arbois 10389
La Maison de l'Ours, Saint-Lary-Soulan 14304
Maison de l'Outil et de la Pensée Ouvrière, Troyes 15002
Maison de Nostradamus, Salon-de-Provence 14587
Maison de Pays, Bage-le-Chatel 10557
Maison de Pays, Mornant 13167
Maison de Pays, Pont-sur-Sambre 13820
Maison de Pays, Sainte-Marie-aux-Mines 14540
Maison de Pays, Seuilly 14732
Maison de Pays, Tourzel-Ronzieres 14980
Maison de Pays du Haut Verdon, Beanvezer 10630
Maison de Pays du Haut-Verdon, Beauvezer 10656
Maison de Robert Schuman, Scy-Chazelles 14685
Maison de Sainte Marie-Madeleine-Postel, Barfleur 10590
La Maison de Van Gogh, Auvers-sur-Oise 10503
Maison de Victor Hugo, Paris 13524
Maison d'Elsa Triolet et Louis Aragon, Saint-Arnoult-en-Yvelines 14116
Maison Départementale de l'Innovation, Clermont-Ferrand 11319
Maison d'Erasme, Bruxelles 03287
Maison des Abeilles, Brignoles 10930
Maison des Amis du Blanc, Le Blanc 12381
Maison des Ancêtres de Bossuet, Seurre 14735
Maison des Archers, Quimperlé 13902
Maison des Arts, Malakoff 12780
Maison des Arts, Tunis 37591
Maison des Arts et du Vin, La Réole 12221
Maison des Arts et Tradition Populaires de la Landes Médocaine, Carcans 11040
Maison des Arts Ruraux, Saint-Germain-de-Marencennes 14237
Maison des Beaux-Arts, Rablay-sur-Layon 13908
Maison des Chapais, Saint-Denis 06314
Maison des Châteaux Forts, Obersteinbach 13384
Maison des Cinq Sens, Paris 13525
Maison des Compagnons du Devoir du Tour de France, Strasbourg 14816
Maison des Deux Marines, Briare 10922
Maison des Esclaves, Gorée 33781
Maison des Etangs, Saint-Viâtre 14502
Maison des Fortifications, Maubeuge 12889
Maison des Fromages d'Auvergne, Egliseneuve-d'Entraigues 11603
Maison des Jardies-Musée Léon Gambetta, Sèvres 14738
Maison des Johnnies, Roscoff 14032
Maison des Liqueurs de l'Auzonnet, Saint-Florent (Gard) 14215
Maison des Marais, Marchesieux 12804
Maison des Minéraux, Crozon 11463
Maison des Paludiers, Saille 14087
Maison des Papillons, Saint-Tropez 14492
Maison des Pilhaoueriens, Loqueffret 12663
Maison des Rochers, Graufthal 11926
Maison des Sirènes et des Siréniens, Castellane 11071
Maison des Sports Bretons, Berrien 10695
Maison des Traditions, La Chapelle-des-Marais 12146
Maison des Traditions Agricoles et Artisanales, Avallon 10520
Maison des Traditions Rurales, Saint-Martin-la-Sauveté 14357
La Maison des Vieux Métiers, Maillezais 12771
Maison d'Histoire Locale, Cocheren 11339
Maison d'Histoire Locale, L'Hôpital 12579
Maison Dieu, Faversham 38985
Maison Dieu, Ospringe 40136
Maison dite de la Duchesse Anne, Morlaix 13162
Maison d'Offwiller, Offwiller 13388
Maison d'Ossau, Arudy 10438
Maison du Bison d'Europe, Sainte-Eulalie 14531
La Maison du Blé et du Pain, Echallens 36670
Maison du Buronnier, Laveissière 12369
Maison du Calvet, Montréal 05912
La Maison du Cerf, Ligny-le-Ribault 12592
Maison du Chanoine, Treigny 14992
Maison du Cheval, Corlay 11409
Maison du Comté, Poligny 13789
Maison du Folklore de Saintonge, Saintes 14554
Maison du Gabardan, Gabarret 11829
Maison du Kochersberg, Truchtersheim 15011
La Maison du Lac, Les Salles-sur-Verdon 12557
Maison du Lac, Saint-Philbert-de-Grand-Lieu 14410
Maison du Lauzeron, Champclause 11155
Maison du Lin, Routot 14066
Maison du Littoral, Perros-Guirec 13712
Maison du Livre, de l'Image et du Son, Villeurbanne 15250
Maison du Luthier-Musée, Jenzat 12079
Maison du Miel, Volvic 15288
Maison du Pain d'Alsace, Sélestat 14697
Maison du Parc, Sorèze 14773
Maison du Parc et des 4 Montagnes, Autrans 10497
Maison du Parc National des Ecrins, Vallouise 15070
Maison du Parc Naturel du Vercors, Chichilianne 11285
Maison du Parc Naturel Régional de Camargue, Saintes-Maries-de-la-Mer 14561
Maison du Parc Naturel Régional de Lorraine, Bisping 10745
Maison du Parc Naturel Régional de Maine-Normandie, Carrouges 11063
Maison du Parc Naturel Régional des Ballons des Vosges, Munster 13218
Maison du Parc Naturel Régional des Vosges du Nord, La Petite-Pierre 12217
Maison du Parc Naturel Régional du Haut-Languedoc, Roquebrun 14023
Maison du Parc Naturel Régional du Luberon, Apt 10385
Maison du Patrimoine, Blanquefort 10761
Maison du Patrimoine, Carhaix-Plouguer 11049
Maison du Patrimoine, La Garde 12185
Maison du Patrimoine, Lampaul-Guimiliau 12314
Maison du Patrimoine, Le Crès 12405
Maison du Patrimoine, Le Relecq-Kerhuon 12476
Maison du Patrimoine, Lesterps 12566
Maison du Patrimoine, Marsannay-la-Côte 12840
Maison du Patrimoine, Matour 12888
Maison du Patrimoine, Montlieu-la-Garde 13100
Maison du Patrimoine, Villard-de-Lans 15178
Maison du Patrimoine, Wimmenau 15315
Maison du Patrimoine de Saint-Chef, Saint-Chef 14144
Maison du Patrimoine d'Oloron et du Haut Béarn, Oloron-Sainte-Marie 13404
Maison du Patrimoine Maritime, Camaret-sur-Mer 11006
Maison du Pays des Étangs, Tarquimpol 14870
Maison du Pays Roussillonnais, Roussillon (Isère) 14063
Maison du Pays Welche, Fréland 11813
La Maison du Père Mousset, Vrigny 15296
Maison du Platin, La Flotte-en-Ré 12184
Maison du Portal, Levens 12569
Maison du Protestantisme, Nîmes 13336
Maison du Recteur et de la Paroisse, Loqueffret 12664
Maison du Rhône, Givors 11875
Maison du Roi, Bruxelles 03288
Maison du Sabot Neufchâtelois, Neufchâtel-en-Saosnois 13286
Maison du Saint-Curé, Ars-sur-Formans 10434
Maison du Saint-Nectaire, Saint-Nectaire 14381
Maison du Sauvetage, Grand-Fort-Philippe 11904
Maison du Seigle, Menessaire 12927
Maison du Spectacle La Bellone, Bruxelles 03289
Maison du Terroir, Saint-Martin-Lacaussade 14358
Maison du Tourisme et du Vin de Pauillac, Pauillac 13673
Maison du Val de Villé, Albé 10271
Maison du Vieil Alby, Albi 10274
Maison du Vieux-Zinal, Zinal 37364
Maison du Vin, Tilburg 29877
Maison Dumulon, Rouyn-Noranda 06292
Maison et Atelier de Jean-François Millet, Barbizon 10585
Maison et la Tour de Mélusine, Vouvant 15293
Maison Européenne de la Photo, Paris 13526
Maison-Forte Musée, Bazincourt-sur-Saulx 10627
Maison Francis Jammes, Orthez 13442
Maison Guillaume de Rubroek, Rubrouck 14071
Maison Hamel-Bruneau, Sainte-Foy 06383
Maison Hansi, Riquewihr 13975
Maison Henri IV, Cahors 10994
Maison J.A. Vachon, Sainte-Marie 06385
Maison Jacques Prévert, Omonville-la-Petite 13406
Maison Jean-Giono, Manosque 12796
Maison Jean-Vilar, Avignon 10526
Maison Jeanne d'Arc, Orléans 13430
Maison Lamontagne, Rimouski 06271
Maison Lansyer, Loches (Indre-et-Loire) 12640
Maison Levanneur, Chatou 11244
Maison Littéraire de Victor Hugo, Bièvres 10731
Maison Louis-Hippolyte Lafontaine, Boucherville 05101
Maison Maillou, Québec 06200
Maison Marie Henry, Clohars-Carnoët 11335
Maison Médard-Bourgault, Saint-Jean-Port-Joli 06327
Maison-Musée de Charles Maurras, Martigues 12880
Maison-Musée de Jeanne Jugan, Cancale 11016
Maison-Musée de Kerlard, Ile-de-Groix 12047
Maison-Musée de la Nature, Marcillé-Robert 12811
Maison-Musée de la Vie d'Autrefois et des Métiers, La Pesse 12216
Maison-Musée des Arômes, Montguers 13091
Maison-Musée des Charcot, Neuilly-sur-Seine 13290
Maison-Musée des Sciences, Lettres et Arts de Cholet et de sa Région, Cholet 11297
Maison-Musée du Parc Naturel Régional du Haut-Jura, Lajoux 12307
Maison-Musée du Paysan, Touvois 14982
Maison-Musée du Sabotier, La Chapelle-des-Marais 12147
Maison-Musée du Vigneron de Champagne, Saint-Imoges 14268
Maison-Musée Ted Jacobs, Les Cerqueux-sous-Passavent 12532
Maison-Musée Vivant des Papillons Exotiques, Hunawihr 12035
Maison Natale-Bibliothèque du Président Gaston-Doumergue, Aigues-Vives 10239
Maison Natale de Claude Gellée, Chamagne 11134
Maison Natale de Jean Giraudoux, Bellac 10671
Maison Natale de Jeanne d'Arc et Centre d'Interprètation, Domremy-la-Pucelle 11551
Maison Natale de la Religieuse Sophie Barat, Joigny (Yonne) 12081
Maison Natale de Saint-Vincent-de-Paul, Saint-Vincent-de-Paul 14505
Maison Natale du Brave Crillon, Murs 13225
Maison Natale du Maréchal Foch, Tarbes 14865
Maison Natale du Père Brothier, La Ferté-Saint-Cyr 12176
Maison natale Sainte Therese, Alençon 10279
Maison Nationale Bonaparte, Ajaccio 10262
Maison Nationale de la Pêche et de l'Eau, Ornans 13437
Maison Rurale de l'Outre-Forêt, Kutzenhausen 12117
Maison Saint-Dominique, Fanjeaux 11703
Maison-Souvenir de George Sand, Nohant-Vic 13354
Maison Stendhal, Grenoble 11939
Maison Tavel, Genève 36738
Maison Tournaisienne, Tournai 03789
Maison Traditionnelle de la Boucherie, Limoges 12610
Maison Vauban, Saint-Léger-Vauban 14321
Maison Vincent Van Gogh, Cuesmes 03365
Maison Visinand, Montreux 36946
Les Maisons de Bouteilles, Cap-Egmont 05196
Maitland Art Center, Maitland 45079
Maitland City Art Gallery, Maitland 01198
Maitland Historical Museums, Maitland 45080
Maitland Museum, Maitland, South Australia 01199
Majdanpek Mining Collection, Majdanpek 33860
The Major General Frederick Funston Boyhood Home and Museum, Iola 44244
Major John Bradford House, Kingston 44492
MAK Center for Art and Architecture, Los Angeles 44926
MAK Center for Art and Architecture, West Hollywood 48531
MAK - Österreichisches Museum für angewandte Kunst, Wien 02929
Makarenko Museum, Moskva 33132
Makasiinimuseo, Polvijärvi 09941
Makati Museum, Makati 31354
Makedonsko Archeološko Društvo - Zavod i Muzej Prilep, Prilep 27588
Makerere Art Gallery, Kampala 37828
Makonde Art Museum, Bammental 15821
Maksim Bogdanovich Literature Museum, Minsk 03119
Mala Galerija, Ljubljana 34108
Malabar Farm State Park, Lucas 44994
Malacañan Palace Presidential Museum, Manila 31380
Malacca Museums Corporation, Malacca 27660
Malacological Museum, Makarska 07737
Malahide Castle, Malahide 22516
Malakološki Muzej, Makarska 07737
Malatya Devlet Güzel Sanatlar Galerisi, Malatya 37750
Malatya Müzesi, Malatya 37751
Malatya Museum, Malatya 37751
Malatya Sabancı Culture Center, Malatya 37752
Malatya Sabancı Kültür Merkezi, Malatya 37752
Malatya State Gallery, Malatya 37750
Malay Ethnographic Museum, Kuala Lumpur 27642
Malay Technology Museum, Bandar Seri Begawan 04599
Malaysian Aboriginal Museum, Melaka 27676
Malaysian Youth Museum, Melaka 27663
Malazgirt Culture Center, Malazgirt 37753
Malazgirt Kültür Merkezi, Malazgirt 37753
Malda Museum, Malda 21936
Malden Public Library Art Collection, Malden 45082
Maldon and District Agricultural and Domestic Museum, Goldhanger 39090
Maldon District Museum, Maldon 39880
Maldon Museum, Maldon 01200
Malé Máslovické Muzeum Másla, Vodochody 08723
Malek Museum, Teheran 22309
Måleriyrkets Museum, Stockholm 36257
Malermuseum Wetzikon, Wetzikon 37313
Malerstübchen Willingshausen, Willingshausen 20601
Malibu Lagoon Museum, Malibu 45084
Målilla Hembygdspark, Målilla 36067
Målilla Motormuseum, Målilla 36068
Målilla Sanatoriums Museum, Målilla 36069
Malki Museum, Banning 41495
Mall Galleries, London 39703
Malla Bleikvasslis Samlinger, Bleikvasslia 30437
Mallaig Heritage Centre, Mallaig 39881
Mallala and Districts Historical Museum, Mallala 01201
Mallalieu Motor Museum, Christ Church 03104
Mallawy Museum, Mallawy 09301
Mallory-Neely House, Memphis 45240
La Malmaison, Cannes 11023
Malmö Konsthall, Malmö 36075
Malmö Konstmuseum, Malmö 36076
Malmö Museer, Malmö 36077
Malmska Gården, Jakobstad 09574
Malojaroslaveckaja Gorodskaja Kartinnaja Galereja, Malojaroslavec 33005
Malojaroslaveckij Istoriko-kraevedčeskij Muzej, Malojaroslavec 33006
Malojaroslaveckij Muzej Voennoj Istorii 1812 Goda, Malojaroslavec 33007
Malojaroslaveckij Muzejno-vystavočnyj Centr, Malojaroslavec 33008
Malokarpatské Múzeum v Pezinku, Pezinok 34041
Malouinière-Musée, Saint-Malo (Ille-et-Vilaine) 14340
Maloyaroslavets City Art Gallery, Malojaroslavec 33005
Maloyaroslavets Exhibition Center, Malojaroslavec 33008
Maloyaroslavets Historical Museum, Malojaroslavec 33006
Maloyaroslavets Museum of History of the War of 1812, Malojaroslavec 33007
Målselv Bygdemuseum, Moen 30680
Malta National Committee of ICOM, Valletta 49290
Malteser-Museum Mailberg, Mailberg 02258
Malton Museum, Malton 39884
Maltwood Art Museum and Gallery, Victoria 06724
Malungs Hembygdsgård, Malung 36082
Malura-Museum, Unterdießen 20267
Malvern Museum, Great Malvern 39122
Mamco, Genève 36739
Mamie Doud Eisenhower Birthplace, Boone 41786
Mammoth Site of Hot Springs, Hot Springs 44111
Man and His Health Museum, Varna 04896
Man and His Work Center in Memory of S. Avitsur, Tel Aviv 22767
Man and Telecommunication Museum, Edmonton 05380
Man and the Living World Museum, Ramat Gan 22732
Man From Snowy River Folk Museum, Corryong 00949
Man in the Galilee Museum, Kibbutz Ginosar 22688
MAN Museum, Augsburg 15560
Manassas Museum System, Manassas 45090
Manassas National Battlefield Park, Manassas 45091
Manastirli Palace and Nilometer, Cairo 09268
Manastirski Muzej, Cetinje 33832
Manatee Village Historical Park Museum, Bradenton 41862
Manchester Art Gallery, Manchester 39892
Manchester Craftsmen's Guild, Pittsburgh 46520
Manchester Historic Association Museum, Manchester 45098
Manchester Historical Society Museum, Manchester 45094
Manchester Jewish Museum, Manchester 39893
Manchester Museum, Manchester 39894
Manchester Museum of Transport, Manchester 39895
Manchester United Museum and Tour Centre, Manchester 39896
Manchester University Medical School Museum, Manchester 39897
Mandal Bymuseum, Mandal 30663
Mandal og Opplands Folkemuseum, Mandal 30664
Mander and Mitchenson Theatre Collection, London 39704
Mandurah Community Museum, Mandurah 01204
Mané-Katz Museum, Haifa 22608
Maneesi Sotamuseo, Helsinki 09513
Manež Exhibition Hall, Moskva 33030
Mangapps Farm Railway Museum, Burnham-on-Crouch 38398
Manggha Centrum Sztuki i Techniki Japońskiej, Kraków 31692
Mångkulturellt Centrum, Tumba 36339
Mangyslak Historical and Regional Museum, Ševčenko 27095
Mangyslak State Park Museum Sites and Monuments of Mangyslak and Ustyrt, Ševčenko 27094
Manhattan Arts Center, Manhattan 45107
Manhyia Museum, Kumasi 20796
Manial Palace Museum, Cairo 09269
Maniitsup Katersugaasivia, Maniitsoq 21231
Manila Police Department Museum and Gallery, Manila 31381
Manilla Historical Royce Cottage Museum, Manilla 01205
Maniototo Early Settlers Museum, Naseby 30208
Manipur State Museum, Imphal 21854
Manipur University Museum, Canchipur 21736
Manisa Arkeoloji Müzesi, Manisa 37754
Manisa Devlet Güzel Sanatlar Galerisi, Manisa 37755
Manisa Müzesi, Manisa 37756
Manisa Museum, Manisa 37756
Manisa Salihli Culture Center, Salihli/Manisa 37774
Manisa Salihli Kültür Merkezi, Salihli/Manisa 37774
Manisa State Art Gallery, Manisa 37755
Manistee County Historical Museum, Manistee 45112
Manitoba Agricultural Hall of Fame, Brandon 05122
Manitoba Agricultural Museum, Austin 05023
Manitoba Amateur Radio Museum, Brandon 05123
Manitoba Automobile Museum, Elkhorn 05403
Manitoba Children's Museum, Winnipeg 06831

Manitoba Electrical Museum, Winnipeg 06832
Manitoba Museum of Man and Nature, Winnipeg 06833
Manitoba Sports Hall of Fame and Museum, Winnipeg 06834
Manitou Pioneer Museum, Neilburg 05969
Manitoulin Historical Society Museum, Gore Bay 05502
Manjimup Timber Museum, Manjimup 01206
Manjusha Museum, Dharmasthala 21791
Manly Art Gallery and Museum, Manly 01207
Mann-Simons Cottage, Columbia 42564
Manneken-Pis-Museum, Geraardsbergen 03457
Mannenzaal van het Sint Pieters en Bloklands Gasthuis, Amersfoort 28822
Mannerheim Museo, Helsinki 09514
Manning Regional Art Gallery, Taree 01520
Manno Art Museum, Osaka 26653
Manoir Automobile, Lohéac 12649
Manoir de Kernault, Mellac 12919
Manoir de la Ville de Martigny, Martigny 36925
Manoir de Veygoux, Scénomusée des Combrailles, Charbonnières-les-Varennes 11173
Manoir du Huis Bois-Maison P.N.R. du Boulonnais, Le Wast 12499
Manoir Leboutillier, Anse-au-Griffon 05000
Manoir Mauvide-Jenest, Saint-Jean 06325
Manoir-Musée de Villers, Saint-Pierre-de-Manneville 14415
Manor Cottage Heritage Centre, Southwick 40560
Manor Farm, Bursledon 38405
Manor House, Donington-le-Heath 38745
Manor House, Sandford Orcas 40441
The Manor House in Łopuszna, Łopuszna 31781
Manor House Museum, Kettering 39348
Manor House Museum and Art Gallery, Ilkley 39287
Manor Museum, Manor 05806
Manos Faltaits Museum, Euboea 20948
Mansfeld-Museum Hettstedt, Hettstedt, Sachsen-Anhalt 17747
Mansfelder Bergwerksbahn e.V., Benndorf 15878
Mansfeldgalerie im Kulturhaus, Lutherstadt Eisleben 18569
Mansfield Art Center, Mansfield 45125
Mansfield Costume Study Centre, Colchester 38612
Mansfield Historical Society Museum, Storrs 47836
Mansfield Museum and Art Gallery, Mansfield 39906
Mansfield State Historc Site, Mansfield 45123
Manship House Museum, Jackson 44278
Mansion House, Warkworth 30289
Manuel L. Quezon Memorial Shrine Museum, Quezon City 31435
Manuel Lepe Museum Gallery, Puerto Vallarta 28350
Manuscript Museum, Alexandria 09241
Manx Museum, Douglas, Isle of Man 38760
Manyara Museum, Manyara 37461
Manzoni Villa, Lecco 24170
Mao Dun Former Residence, Beijing 06972
Maple Ridge Art Gallery, Maple Ridge 05812
Maple Ridge Museum, Maple Ridge 05813
Maple Sugar Museum, Art Gallery and Pioneer Home, Sundridge 06517
Maple Syrup Museum, Saint Jacobs 06323
Maple Valley Historical Museum, Maple Valley 45130
Mappa Mundi and Chained Library, Hereford 39227
Mapungubwe Museum, Pretoria 34346
Maragheh Museum, Maragheh 22263
Marais Des Cygnes Memorial Historic Site, Pleasanton 46554
Maramec Museum, Saint James 47096
Maramureş District Museum, Baia Mare 32435
Maras Icon Museum, Gazimağusa 08218
Maraş Ikon Müzesi, Gazimağusa 08218
Maratha History Museum, Pune 21992
Marathon County Historical Society Museum, Wausau 48464
Mårbacka Manor, Östra Ämtervik 36149
Marble Hill House, Twickenham 40738
Marble Historical Museum, Marble 45133
Marble Mountain Community Museum, West Bay 06771
Marble Palace Art Gallery and Zoo, Kolkata 21907
Marble Springs State Historic Farmstead Governor John Sevier Memorial, Knoxville 44522
Marblehead Historical Museum and J.O.J. Frost Folk Art Gallery, Marblehead 45136
Marburger Universitätsmuseum für Kunst und Kulturgeschichte, Marburg 18629
Marc Chagall Kunsthuis, Amsterdam 28871
Marcela M. Agoncillo Historical Museum, Taal 31450
Marcella Sembrich Opera Museum, Bolton Landing 41778
Marcellus Historical Society Museum, Marcellus 45139
Marcelo H. del Pilar Museum, Malolos 31362
March and District Museum, March 39908
March Field Museum, Riverside 46919
March-Museum, Vorderthal 37296
Marchfeldmuseum, Weikendorf 02798
Marcos Museum, Batac 31285
Mardi Gras Museum, Biloxi 41694
Mardin Müzesi, Mardin 37757
Mardin Museum, Mardin 37757
Mardom-shenasi-ye Kavir, Nayin 22271
Mareeba District Rodeo Museum, Mareeba 01210
Mareeba Heritage Museum, Mareeba 01211
Margam County Park, Port Talbot 40237
Margaree Salmon Museum, North East Margaree 06021
Margaret Fort Trahern Gallery, Clarksville 42437
Margaret Harvey Gallery, Saint Albans 40374
Margaret Harwell Art Museum, Poplar Bluff 46586
Margaret Hutchinson Compton Gallery, Cambridge 42045
Margaret Laurence Home, Neepawa 05967
The Margaret Mitchell House and Museum, Atlanta 41349
Margaret Thatcher Projects, New York 45830
Margarete-Steiff-Museum, Giengen an der Brenz 17274
Margaretha Museum, Laag Keppel 29495
Margate Caves, Margate 39911
Margret-Knoop-Schellbach-Museum, Körle 18186
Margrove - South Cleveland Heritage Centre, Boosbeck 38278
Marguerite d'Youville Museum, Montréal 05913
Maria de Lisitzin Fine Art and Historical Museum, Porvoo 09953
Maria Martinez Museum, Santa Fe 47423
Mariager Museum, Mariager 08979
Marian and Religious Museum, Brooklyn 41947
Marianna Kistler Beach Museum of Art, Manhattan 45108
Marianna-Lee County Museum, Marianna 45141
Mariano Rodríguez Gallery, La Habana 07932
Mariánské Lázně Municipal Museum, Mariánské Lázně 08472
Marias Museum of History and Art, Shelby 47594
Maribor National Liberation Museum, Maribor 34126
Marie Curie Museum, Warszawa 32113
Marie Hull Gallery, Raymond 46803
Marie Rawdon Museum, Matjiesfontein 34306
Marie Tak van Poortvliet Museum, Domburg 29165
Marie Walsh Sharpe Art Foundation, New York 45831
Mariefreds Hembygdsmuseum, Mariefred 36085
Marienglashöhle Friedrichroda, Friedrichroda 17143
Mariestads Industrimuseum, Mariestad 36090
Marietta House Museum, Glenn Dale 43691
Marietta Museum of History, Marietta 45144
Marika Kotopouli Museum, Zografou 21225
Marilla Historical Society Museum, Marilla 45152
Marin History Museum, San Rafael 47375
Marin Museum of the American Indian, Novato 46045
Marine Biology Collection, Novi Dojran 33866
Marine Corps Art Collection, Washington 48367
Marine-Ehrenmal und Technisches Museum U 995, Laboe 18280
Marine Museum at Fall River, Fall River 43283
Marine-Museum Limburg, Limburg an der Lahn 18471
Marine Museum of Manitoba, Selkirk 06420
Marine Museum of the Great Lakes, Kingston 05681
Marine Museum of Upper Canada, Toronto 06591
Marine Science Museum, Tokai University, Shizuoka 26769
Marine Sciences Museum, Mayagüez 32376
Marine Transportation Museum, Ogi 26617
Marineland Ocean Museum, Marineland 45153
Marinemuseet, Horten 30565
Marinemuseum, Den Helder 29134
The Mariners' Museum, Newport News 45937
Mariners' Park Museum, Milford 05850
Marinette County Historical Museum, Marinette 45154
Mariniersmuseum, Rotterdam 29757
Marinmuseum, Karlskrona 35999
Mario Lanza Museum, Philadelphia 46425
Marion County Historical Society Museum, Marion 45163
Marion County Historical Society Museum, Salem 47209
Marion Heritage Center, Marion 45156
Marion Koogler McNay Art Museum, San Antonio 47255
Marion Public Library Museum, Marion 45158
Marion Scott Gallery, Vancouver 06681
Marionettmuseet, Stockholm 36258
Mariposa County Gallery, Los Angeles 44927
Marischal Museum, Aberdeen 37940
Maritiem en Jutters Museum, Oudeschild 29701
Maritiem Museum Rotterdam, Rotterdam 29758
Maritime and Historical Museum of Croatian Littoral, Rijeka 07763
Maritime and Industrial Museum, Swansea 40659
Maritime and Metalwork Museum, Reykjavík 21666
Maritime and Seafood Industry Museum, Biloxi 41695
Maritime Archaeology Museum, Melaka 27664
Maritime Collections at Troense, Svendborg 09086
Maritime Command Museum, Halifax 05555
Maritime Heritage Exhibition, Yarmouth 40951
Maritime Institute of the Åbo Academy, Turku 10128
Maritime Museum, Amsterdam 28888
Maritime Museum, Cohasset 42515
The Maritime Museum, Dublin 22441
Maritime Museum, Dubrovnik 07700
Maritime Museum, Eyrarbakki 21632
Maritime Museum, Göteborg 35920
Maritime Museum, Jakarta 22114
Maritime Museum, Kristiinankaupunki 09710
Maritime Museum, Low Head 01188
Maritime Museum, Melaka 27665
Maritime Museum, Oskarshamn 36154
Maritime Museum, Piran 34138
Maritime Museum, Port Victoria 01388
Maritime Museum, Ramsgate 40281
Maritime Museum, Singapore 33939
Maritime Museum, Szczecin 32028
Maritime Museum, Vaasa 10164
Maritime Museum, Vittoriosa 27713
Maritime Museum, Zadar 07807
Maritime Museum for East Anglia, Great Yarmouth 39125
Maritime Museum Montenegro, Kotor 33848
Maritime Museum of Andros, Andros 20823
Maritime Museum of British Columbia, Victoria 06725
Maritime Museum of Finland, Helsinki 09532
Maritime Museum of Macau, Macau 07165
Maritime Museum of Monterey, Monterey 45454
Maritime Museum of Porsgrunn, Porsgrunn 30781
Maritime Museum of Tasmania, Hobart 01099
Maritime Museum of the Atlantic, Halifax 05556
Maritime Museum of Thera (Santorini), Oia 21101
Maritime Museum of Townsville, Townsville 01545
Maritime Museum Zierikzee, Zierikzee 30060
Maritime Tradition Museum, Piraeus 21121
Marjorie Kinnan Rawlings Historic State Park, Cross Creek 42710
Mark Hall Cycle Museum, Harlow 39164
Mark Twain Birthplace Museum, Stoutsville 47840
Mark Twain Home and Museum, Hannibal 43904
Mark Twain House, Hartford 43940
Markarydsortens Hembygdsmuseum, Markaryd 36092
Marker Museum, Marken 29580
Market Gallery, Toronto 06592
Market Lavington Village Museum, Market Lavington 39917
Markfield Beam Engine and Museum, London 39705
Markgräfler Museum Müllheim, Müllheim, Baden 18819
Markgräfliches Opernhaus, Bayreuth 15854
Markgrafenmuseum Ansbach, Ansbach 15503
Markham Museum and Historic Village, Markham 05816
Marko Vovchok Memorial Museum, Nalčik 33195
Marks-Hirshfeld Museum of Medical History, Herston 01095
Markt Einersheimer Heimatstuben, Markt Einersheim 18642
Markt- und Schaustellermuseum, Essen 16956
Marland's Grand Home, Ponca City 46581
Marlboro County Historical Museum, Bennettsville 41628
Marlboro Museum, Marlboro 45170
Marlipins Museum, Shoreham-by-Sea 40503
Marmormuseum, Adnet 01645
Marnardal Museum, Marnardal 30668
Marquerite-Bourgeoys Museum, Montréal 05925
Marquette County History Museum, Marquette 45173
Marquette County Museum, Westfield 48560
Marquisat de Pont-Croix, Pont-Croix 13805
Marrett House, Standish 47770
Marringhurst Pioneer Park Museum, Pilot Mound 06131
Marshall County Historical Museum, Holly Springs 44059
Marshall County Historical Museum, Plymouth 46558
Marshall County Historical Society Museum, Warren 48309
Marshall County Museum, Marshalltown 45185
Marshall M. Fredericks Sculpture Museum, University Center 48150
Marstal Maritime Museum, Marstal 08983
Marstal Søfartsmuseum, Marstal 08983
Marstallmuseum, München 18873
Marston House, San Diego 47278
Mart Saare Majamuuseum, Suure-Jaani 09353
Marten River Logging Museum, Marten River 05817
Martha Berry Museum, Rome 46994
Martha's Vineyard Historical Society Exhibition, Edgartown 43082
Martin and Osa Johnson Safari Museum, Chanute 42194
Martin Art Gallery, Allentown 41146
Martin Benka Múzeum, Martin 34023
Martin County Historical Museum, Stanton 47776
The Martin D'Arcy Museum of Art, Chicago 42339
Martin-Gropius-Bau, Berlin 16041
Martin-Lauterburg-Stiftung, Schloss Jegenstorf, Bern 36545
Martin Luther King jr. Center for Nonviolent Social Change, Atlanta 41350
Martin Luther King jr. National Historic Site and Preservation District, Atlanta 41351
Martin Luthers Geburtshaus, Lutherstadt Eisleben 18570
Martin Luthers Sterbehaus, Lutherstadt Eisleben 18571
Martin Museum of Art, Waco 48264
Martin Van Buren Historic Site, Kinderhook 44483
Martin-von-Wagner-Museum der Universität Würzburg, Würzburg 20697
Martinustoren, Losser 29550
Marton Historic Village Museum, Marton 30196
Marttilan Kirkkomuseo, Marttila 09819
Marttilan Kotiseutumuseo, Marttila 09820
Martyn Ferenc Gyüjtemény, Pécs 21508
Martyrologiczny Punkt Upamiętnienia - Rotunda, Zamość 32211
Martyr's Memorial at Sports City, Amman 27056
Martyrs' Shrine, Midland 05847
Marugame Bijutsukan, Marugame 26466
Marugame Genichiro-Inokuma, Marugame 26467
Marugame Museum of Art, Marugame 26466
Maruzian Museum, Szczytno 32032
Marvin Newton House, Brookfield 41930
Marvol Museum, Kuilsriver 34299
Marwen Foundation, Chicago 42340
Marxhausen Art Gallery, Seward 47573
Mary and Leigh Block Museum of Art, Evanston 43241
Mary Arden's House and the Countryside Museum, Stratford-upon-Avon 40627
Mary Ball Washington Museum, Lancaster 44631
Mary Brogan Museum of Art and Science, Tallahassee 47935
Mary MacKillop Pilgrimage Centre, Fitzroy 01026
Mary Mackillop Place Museum, North Sydney 01328
Mary McLeod Bethune House, Washington 48368
Mary March Regional Museum and Logging Exhibition, Grand Falls-Windsor 05512
Mary Moffat Museum, Griquatown 34258
Mary Porter Sesnon Art Gallery, Santa Cruz 47410
Mary Queen of Scots' House, Jedburgh 39325
Mary Rose Museum, Portsmouth 40255
Mary Todd Lincoln House, Lexington 44743
Mary Washington College Galleries, Fredericksburg 43538
Mary Washington House, Fredericksburg 43539
Maryfield Museum, Maryfield 05818
Maryhill Museum of Art, Goldendale 43717
Maryland Art Place, Baltimore 41476
Maryland Association of History Museums, Annapolis 49504
Maryland Historical Society Museum, Baltimore 41477
Maryland Institute Museum, Baltimore 41478
Maryland Science Center, Baltimore 41479
Marymoor Museum of Eastside History, Redmond 46825
Maryport Maritime Museum, Maryport 39918
Marystown Museum, Marystown 05819
Marywood University Art Galleries, Scranton 47519
Masaki Art Museum, Osaka 26654
Masao Koga Museum, Tokyo 26881
Masaryk-Museum, Hodonín 08354
Masarykovo Muzeum, Hodonín 08354
Maschenmuseum, Albstadt 15418
Mashiko Ceramics Museum, Mashiko 26468
Mashiko Sankokan, Mashiko 26468
Masia Museu Can Magarola, Alella 34443
Maskun Museo, Masku 09821
Mason County Museum, Mason 45199
Mason County Museum, Maysville 45208
The Masonic Library and Museum of Pennsylvania, Philadelphia 46426
Masonic Temple, Hobart 01100
Masonry Museum Vånevik and Näset, Påskallavik 36156
Måsøy Museum, Havøysund 30540
Mass Moca, North Adams 45978
Massachusetts Historical Society Museum, Boston 41814
Massacre Rocks State Park Museum, American Falls 41169
Massey Area Museum, Massey 05820
Massillon Museum, Massillon 45202
Massnes Villmarksmuseum, Bjordal 30434
Massua-Educational Museum on the Holocaust, Tel Yitzhak 22780
The Masterworks Foundation Collection, Hamilton 03884
Masur Museum of Art, Monroe 45441
Matagorda County Museum, Bay City 41544
Match Museum, Jönköping 35979
Matchbox Road Museum, Newfield 45917
Matchboxmuseum Latent, Prinsenbeek 29715
Matches Museum, Bystrzyca Kłodzka 31518
Matchimawas National Museum, Songkhla 37537
Matenadaran, Erevan 00686
Mathematikum, Gießen 17283
Mathematisch-Physikalischer Salon, Dresden 16696
Matheson Museum, Gainesville 43582
Mathias Ham House, Dubuque 42992
Matilda Roslin-Kalliolan Kirjailijakoti, Merikarvia 09824
Matopos National Park Site Museums, Bulawayo 49026
Mátra Múzeum, Gyöngyös 21417
Matrica Museum and Archeological Park, Százhalombatta 21545
Matrica Múzeum, Százhalombatta 21545
Matsqui Sumas Abbotsford Museum, Abbotsford 04964
Matsudo Museum, Matsodo 26469
Matsumoto City Museum, Matsumoto 26477
Matsumoto Folk Arts Museum, Matsumoto 26476
Matsumoto-shiritsu Hakubutsukan, Matsumoto 26477
Matsunaga Memorial Hall, Odawara 26613
Matsuoka Museum of Art, Tokyo 26882
Matsura History Museum, Hirado 26200
Matsushima Kanrantei Museum, Matsushima 26481
Matsushita Art Museum, Aira 26089
Matsuura Shiryo Hakubutsukan, Hirado 26200
Matsuyama Municipal Shiki Kinen Museum, Matsuyama 26486
Mattancherry Palace Museum, Kochi 21892
Mattapoisett Museum and Carriage House, Mattapoisett 45204
The Mattatuck Museum of the Mattatuck Historical Society, Waterbury 48427
Mattawa and District Museum, Mattawa 05824
Matthews Museum of Maine Heritage, Union 48142
Matthias Church of Buda Castle Ecclesiastical Art Collection, Budapest 21332
Mattisrud Småbruksmuseum, Løten 30657

Mattress Factory Museum, Pittsburgh 46521
Matt's Museum, Lawtell 44694
Mattye Reed African Heritage Center, Greensboro 43817
Maturango Museum of the Indian Wells Valley, Ridgecrest 46895
Mátyás Király Múzeum, Visegrád 21611
Matyó Múzeum, Mezőkövesd 21471
Maud Railway Museum, Maud 39926
Maude I. Kerns Art Center, Eugene 43223
Mauermuseum - Museum Haus am Checkpoint Charlie, Berlin 16042
Mauersberger-Museum, Großrückerswalde 17439
Maurermuseum und Dachdeckermuseum, Langenlois 02184
Mauritianum, Altenburg, Thüringen 15451
Mauritius Postal Museum, Port Louis 27738
Mauritshuis, Den Haag 29105
Mausefallen-Museum, Neroth 18996
Mausefallen- und Galerie der Stillen Örtchen, Güntersberge 17453
Mausoleum of Struggle and Martyrdom, Warszawa 32085
Mauzoleum Walki i Męczeństwa 1939-1945, Warszawa 32085
Max-Ernst-Kabinett, Brühl, Rheinland 16377
Max Euwe Centrum, Amsterdam 28872
Max-Klinger-Gedenkstätte, Naumburg, Saale 18979
Max-Reger-Gedächtniszimmer, Brand, Oberpfalz 16277
Maxhütten-Museum, Bergen, Chiemgau 15891
Maxim-Gorki-Gedächtnisstätte, Seebad Heringsdorf 19913
Maximilianmuseum, Augsburg 15561
Maximiliansanlagen mit Friedensengel, München 18874
Maxwell Museum of Anthropology, Albuquerque 41104
Maxwelton House Museum, Moniaive 39976
May Museum and Park, Farmville 43303
May Natural History Museum and Museum of Space Exploration, Colorado Springs 42539
Mayborn Museum, Waco 48265
Mayflower Gold Mill, Silverton 47634
Mayflower Society Museum, Plymouth 46560
Mayibuye Centre Collection, Bellville 34178
Maymont, Richmond 46882
Mayne Island Museum, Mayne Island 05827
Mayville Area Museum of History and Genealogy, Mayville 45209
Mayville Historical Society Museum, Mayville 45211
Mazar-i-Sharif Museum, Mazar-i-Sharif 00009
Mazar Islamic Museum, Al-Mazar 27042
Mazomanie Historical Society Museum, Mazomanie 45212
Mazot-Musée de Plan-Cerisier, Martigny 36926
Mazovian Museum in Płock, Płock 31887
Mazzini-Gedenkstätte, Grenchen 36780
M.B. Grekov House-Museum, Novočerkassk 33232
M.C. Mehta Gallery, Ahmedabad 21680
MC-Museum Gyllene Hjulet, Surahammar 36314
MCC Museum, London 39706
mda, Cambridge 49423
Mead Art Museum, Amherst 41178
Mead Gallery, Coventry 38644
Meade County Historical Society Museum, Meade 45213
Meadow Brook Art Gallery, Rochester 46933
Meadow Brook Hall, Rochester 46934
Meadow Farm Museum, Glen Allen 43679
Meadow Garden Museum, Augusta 41385
Meadow Lake Museum, Meadow Lake 05828
Meadowcroft Museum of Rural Life, Avella 41427
Meadowlands Museum, Rutherford 47040
Meadows Museum, Dallas 42755
Meadows Museum of Art, Shreveport 47613
Meaford Museum, Meaford 05829
Meagher County Historical Association Castle Museum, White Sulphur Springs 48591
Meanskinisht Museum, Kitwanga 05701
Measham Museum, Measham 39928
Meath Archaeological and Historical Museum, Trim 22548
Mechanical Music and Doll Collection, Chichester 38563
Mechanical Music Museum and Bygones, Cotton 38639
Mechanische Schau-Werkstätte, Rehau 19537
Mechanisches Musikmuseum, Sursee 37225
Mecklenburgisches Volkskundemuseum Schwerin, Schwerin 19897
Mecosta County Historical Museum, Big Rapids 41682
Mecseki Banyászati Múzeum, Pécs 21509
Médaillier Municipal, Bordeaux 10805
Medal Art Museum, Wrocław 32187
Medal of Honor Museum of Military History, Chattanooga 42264
Medelhavsmuseet, Stockholm 36259
Medeltidsmuseet, Stockholm 36260
Medgyessy Múzeum, Debrecen 21399
Medical College Museum, Vadodara 22050
Medical History Museum, Göteborg 35915
Medical History Museum, Hobart 01101
Medical History Museum, Melbourne 01236
Medical Museum, Amman 27057
Medicine and Pioneers Museum, Menahimiya 22711
Medicine Hat Museum and Art Gallery, Medicine Hat 05831
Medicinhistoriska Museet, Göteborg 35915
Medicinhistoriska Museet, Linköping 36041
Medicinhistoriska Museet, Lund 36063
Medicinhistoriska Museet, Vänersborg 36372
Medicinhistoriska Museet Eugenia, Stockholm 36261
Medicinsk-Historisk Museum, København 08938
Medieval Old Synagogue, Sopron 21533
Medisch Farmaceutisch Museum de Griffioen, Delft 29080
Medizin- und Pharmaziehistorische Sammlung Kiel der Christian-Albrechts-Universität, Kiel 18077
Medizinhistorische Sammlung der Ruhr-Universität Bochum, Bochum 16197
Medizinhistorische Sammlungen, Chemnitz 16467
Medizinhistorisches Museum, Wien 02930
Medizinhistorisches Museum, Zürich 37388
Međnarodni Grafični Likovni Centar, Ljubljana 34109
Medrese Müzesi, Akşehir 37606
Medway Heritage Centre, Chatham 38531
Medway Towns Gallery, Rochester 40336
Meeker County Museum and G.A.R. Hall, Litchfield 44815
Meeker Home Museum, Greeley 43785
Sri Meenakshi Sundaresvara Temple Museum, Madurai 21935
Meerhemmuseum, Gent 03442
Meerrettichmuseum, Baiersdorf 15795
Meeteetse Museums, Meeteetse 45228
Meezkeret-Batia Museum, Meezkeret-Batia 22710
Megginch Castle, Errol 38947
Meghalaya State Museum, Shillong 22017
Megisti Museum, Kastellorizo 21006
Meguro Gajoen Bijutsukan, Tokyo 26883
Meguro Gajoen Museum of Art, Tokyo 26883
Meguro Kiseichukan, Tokyo 26884
Meguro Museum of Art, Tokyo 26885
Meguro Parasitological Museum, Tokyo 26884
Mehrangarh Museum, Jodhpur 21875
Meierimuseet, Ås 30396
Meierische Museumboerderij, Heeswijk-Dinther 29373
Meigle Museum of Sculptured Stones, Meigle 39929
Meigs County Museum, Pomeroy 46580
Meijerimuseo, Saukkola 10022
Meiji-Daigaku Keiji Hakubutsukan, Tokyo 26886
Meiji-Daigaku Kouko Hakubutsukan, Tokyo 26887
Meiji-Daigaku Shouhin Hakubutsukan, Tokyo 26888
Meiji Jingu Homotsuden, Tokyo 26889
Meiji Memorial Picture Gallery, Tokyo 26890
Meiji Shrine Museum, Tokyo 26889
Meiji the Great Memorial Hall of Tama, Tama 26816
Meininger Museen, Meiningen 18686
Meir Dizengoff Museum, Tel Aviv 22768
Meißener Porzellan-Sammlung Stiftung Ernst Schneider, Oberschleißheim 19203
Meißner Porzellan-Kabinett, Bad Soden 15743
Mejerimuseet vid Korsholms Lantbruksskolor, Vaasa 10159
Mekaanisen Musiikin Museo, Varkaus 10185
Mel Fisher Maritime Heritage Museum, Key West 44469
Melaka Govenor's Museum, Melaka 27675
Melanchthonhaus Bretten, Bretten 16356
Melanchthonhaus Wittenberg, Lutherstadt Wittenberg 18576
Melbourne Clocks Museum, Hampton 01089
Melbourne Hall, Melbourne 39930
Melbourne Museum, Carlton South 00896
Melbourne Museum of Printing, Footscray 01029
Melbourne Tank Museum, Narre Warren North 01306
Melbourne's Living Museum of the West, Maribyrnong 01212
Meldal Bygdemuseum, Meldal 30672
Melford Hall, Long Melford 39823
Melfort and District Museum, Melfort 05835
Melicharovo Městské Muzeum, Unhošt 08700
Mellat Museum, Teheran 22310
Mellemværftet, Kristiansund 30617
Mellerstain House, Gordon 39096
Mellette House, Watertown 48445
Melli Museum, Teheran 22311
Melliläin Museoriihi, Mellilä 09822
Mellon Financial Corporation's Collection, Pittsburgh 46522
Melnikov Memorial House-Museum, Sarapul 33502
Meløy Bygdemuseum, Ørnes 30720
Meløy Local Museum, Ørnes 30720
Melrose Abbey Museum, Melrose 39932
Melrose Courthouse Museum, Melrose 01243
Melrose House, Pretoria 34347
Melrose Plantation Home Complex, Melrose 45230
Melton Art Reference Library Museum, Oklahoma City 46115
Melton Carnegie Museum, Melton Mowbray 39933
Melville Discovery Centre, Applecross 00744
Melville Heritage Museum, Melville 05838
Melville Railway Museum, Melville 05839
Melvin Art Gallery, Lakeland 44603
Melvin B. Tolson Black Heritage Center, Langston 44637
Mem-Erie Historical Museum, Erie 43199
Memling Museum - St John's Hospital, Brugge 03257
Memlingmuseum Sint Janshospitaal, Brugge 03257
Memme-Taadi Kamber, Karksi 09331
Mémoire de la Nationale 7, Piolenc 13738
Mémoire de Saumon, Saint-Louis-la-Chaussée 14329
Mémoire du Rhin, Saint-Louis-la-Chaussée 14330
Mémoires de Grande-Synthe, Grande-Synthe 11907
Les Mémoires d'Obersoultzach, Obersoultzbach 13383
Memorial and Literature Museum of A.P. Bondin, Ekaterinburg 32771
Mémorial Caen-Normandie, Caen 10979
Memorial Centre of Jozef Haller, Władysławowo 32158
Memorial Coplex Voroshilov Battery, Vladivostok 33700
Memorial Day Museum of Waterloo, Waterloo 48436
Mémorial de l'Algérie Française, Port-Vendres 13846
Memorial de Sergipe, Aracaju 03950
Mémorial de Vendée, Saint-Sulpice-le-Verdon 14481
Mémorial des Guerres en Indochine, Fréjus 11808
Mémorial des Soldats de La Nouvelle France, Le Château-d'Oléron 12399
Mémorial d'Évocation Vaudois et Huguenot, La Roque-d'Anthéron 12254
Memorial di Imigração Ucraniana, Curitiba 04063
Memorial do Imigrante, São Paulo 04497
Mémorial du Maréchal Leclerc de Hauteclocque et de la Libération de Paris et Musée Jean Moulin, Paris 13527
Memorial Goethe, Sessenheim 14727
Memorial Guard Submarine S-56 from 1939, Vladivostok 33699
Memorial Hall Museum, Deerfield 42850
Memorial Hall of the Zunyi Conference, Zunyi 07341
Memorial Historical Complex to the Heroes of the Stalingrad Battle on Mamaev Hill, Volgograd 33716
Memorial House Moseum of S.T. Aksakov, Ufa 33642
Memorial House-Museum of A. Uchtomskij, Rybinsk 33360
Memorial House-Museum of D. Mamin-Sibiryak, Ekaterinburg 32769
Memorial House-Museum of F. Reshetnikov, Ekaterinburg 32770
Memorial House-Museum of G.V. Plekhanov, Lipeck 32985
Memorial House-Museum of I.I. Shishkin, Elabuga 32786
Memorial House-Museum of I.M. Vinogradov, Velikie Luki 33675
Memorial House-Museum of L.V. Sobinov, Jaroslavl 32851
Memorial House Museum of Mashit Gafuri, Ufa 33643
Memorial House-Museum of N.G. Slavyanov, Perm 33302
Memorial House-Museum of P. Bazhov, Ekaterinburg 32772
Memorial House-Museum of the Ulyanov Family, Astrachan 32663
Memorial House-Museum of V.K. Arsenyev, Vladivostok 33693
Memorial House of Adalbert Stifter, Horní Planá 08361
Memorial House of Bedřich Smetana, Jabkenice 08377
Memorial House of Božena Němcová, Červený Kostelec 08293
Memorial House of Dimitar Polyanov, Karnobat 04693
Memorial House of František Palacký, Hodslavice 08355
Memorial House of Jan Hus, Husinec 08375
Memorial House of Javornickij, Dnepropetrovsk 37850
Memorial House of Josef Mánes, Čechy pod Košířem 08290
Memorial House of Karel Čapek, Stará Huť u Dobříše 08661
Memorial House of Karel J. Erben, Miletin 08477
Memorial House of Karel V. Rais, Lázně Bělohrad 08444
Memorial House of King Jiří z Poděbrad and Lapidarium, Poděbrady 08550
Memorial House of Leoš Janáček, Hukvaldy 08373
Memorial House of Mikuláš Aleš, Mirotice 08479
Memorial House of Petr Bezruč, Museum Prostejov, Kostelec na Hané 08422
Memorial House of Rippl-Rónai, Kaposvár 21441
Memorial House of Svatopluk Čech, Ostředek 08529
Memorial House of Václav Beneš Třebízský and of Svatopluk Čech, Liten 08454
Memorial JK, Brasília 03996
Memorial Karel Havlíček Borovský, Havlíčkův Brod 08348
Memorial Library and Art Gallery, Saskatoon 06399
Memorial Literature Museum Estate A.P. Chekhov, Melichovo 33009
Memorial Literature Museum of N.A. Dobrolyubov, Nižnij Novgorod 33206
Mémorial Musée Privé de Souvenirs de la Grande Guerre 14-18, Essigny-le-Grand 11657
Memorial Museum, Ada 41063
Memorial Museum, Yogyakarta 22219
Memorial Museum Apartment of Rimsky-Korsakov, Sankt-Peterburg 33421
Memorial Museum B.P. Hasdeu, Câmpina 32480
Memorial Museum Illegal Printery of the Perm Committee of the Russian Social Democratic Labour Party of 1906, Perm 33303
Memorial Museum Ion Creangă's Cottage, Iaşi 32537
Memorial Museum King Tribhuvan, Kathmandu 28787
Memorial Museum M.V. Frunse, Ivanovo 32830
Memorial Museum of Alia Moldagulova, Aktöbe 27070
Memorial Museum of A.S. Popov, Sankt-Peterburg 33422
Memorial Museum of A.S. Popov - the Inventor of the Radio, Krasnoturinsk 32961
Memorial Museum of Cosmonautics, Moskva 33078
Memorial Museum of France Prešeren, Kranj 34101
Memorial Museum of Hostages, Begunje na Gorenjskem 34084
Memorial Museum of Karim Khakimov, Ufa 33644
Memorial Museum of the Academy Members A.E. and B.A. Arbusov, Kazan 32893
Memorial Museum of the Kanto Earthquake Disaster, Tokyo 26891
Memorial Museum of the Mexican Academy of Language, México 28161
Memorial Museum of the Peasant Movement Institute by Comrade Mao Zedong, Guangzhou 07069
Memorial Museum of the War of Liberation, Pyongyang 27123
Memorial Museum-preserve of V.D. Polenov, Strachovo 33566
Memorial Museum Saint Isaacs Cathedral, Sankt-Peterburg 33410
Memorial Museum The Grave of T.G. Shevchenko, Kanev 37859
Memorial Museum The October 21st, Kragujevac 33854
Memorial of Jan Amos Comenius, Bílá Třemešná 08248
Memorial of Otakar Štáfl, Havlíčkův Brod 08349
Memorial Pengisytiharan Kemerdekaan, Melaka 27666
Memorial Piskarevskoye Cemetery - Museum, Sankt-Peterburg 33476
Memorial Pontes de Miranda da Justiça do Trabalho em Alagoas, Maceió 04177
Memorial Room, Antonin 31472
Memorial Studio Museum of the Sculptor S.T. Konenkov, Moskva 33081
Memorial Sultan Tidore Museum, Tidore 09134
Memorial Tancredo Neves, São João Del Rei 04466
Memorial Union Art Gallery, Corvallis 42660
Memorial Union Art Gallery, Davis 42792
Memorial Union Gallery, Fargo 43292
Memorial Union Gallery, Tempe 47972
Memorial War Museum, Bathurst 05057
Memorialen Kompleks Balova Shuma, Gavril Genovo 04672
Memorialmuseum Friedrich Fröbel, Oberweißbach 19214
Memorialnaja Gvardejskaja Krasnoznamënnaja Podvodnaja Lodka S-56 1939 g., Vladivostok 33699
Memorialnaja Muzej-kvartira N.A. Nekrasova, Sankt-Peterburg 33417
Memorialno-chudožestvennyj Dom-muzej Vladimira Aleksandroviča Serova, Ėmmaus 32795
Memorialno-literaturnyj Muzej A.P. Bondina, Ekaterinburg 32771
Memorialnyj Chudožestvennyj Muzej Valentina Aleksandroviča Serova v Domotkanovo, Krasnaja Nov' 32945
Memorialnyj Dom-muzej Akademika S.P. Koroleva, Moskva 33074
Memorialnyj Dom-muzej Akademika A.A. Uchtomskogo, Rybinsk 33360
Memorialnyj Dom-muzej Akademika I.M. Vinogradova, Velikie Luki 33675
Memorialnyj Dom-muzej S.T. Aksakova, Ufa 33642
Memorialnyj Dom-Muzej M.V. Biškek, Biškek 27308
Memorialnyj Dom-muzej Gercena, Moskva 33075
Memorialnyj Dom-muzej I.I. Levitana, Ples 33323
Memorialnyj Dom-muzej P.D. Korina, Moskva 33076
Memorialnyj Dom-muzej Marko Vovčok, Nalčik 33195
Memorialnyj Dom-muzej Mažita Gafuri, Ufa 33643
Memorialnyj Dom-muzej im. N.G. Slavjanova, Perm 33302
Memorialnyj Dom-muzej G.V. Plechanova, Lipeck 32985
Memorialnyj Dom-muzej Podpolnaja Tipografija Permskogo Komiteta RSDRP 1906 g., Perm 33303
Memorialnyj Dom-muzej I.P. Požalostina, Solotča 33545
Memorialnyj Dom-Muzej P.P. Bažova, Ekaterinburg 32772
Memorialnyj Dom-Muzej I.I. Šiškina, Elabuga 32786
Memorialnyj Dom-muzej L.V. Sobinova, Jaroslavl 32851
Memorialnyj Dom-muzej Uljanovych, Astrachan 32663
Memorialnyj Dom-muzej A.A. Vaneeva, Ermakovskoe 32797
Memorialnyj Dom-muzej Viktora i Apolinarija Vasnecovych, Rjabovo 33348
Memorialnyj Dom-muzej V.M. Vaznecova, Moskva 33077
Memorialnyj Dom-muzej N.E. Žukovskogo, Orechovo 33258
Memorialnyj Istoriko-biografičeskij Dom-muzej Akademika N.V. Melnikova, Sarapul 33502
Memorialnyj Kompleks G. Tukaja, Novyj Kyrlaj 33249
Memorialnyj Kompleks 'Vorošilovskaja Batareja', Vladivostok 33700
Memorialnyj Literaturnyj Muzej F.M. Dostoevskogo, Semey 27091
Memorialnyj Muzej Abu Ali Ibn Sina, Afčona 48828
Memorialnyj Muzej Akademikov A.E. i B.A. Arbuzovych, Kazan 32893
Memorialnyj Muzej-dača A.S. Puškina, Puškin 33338
Memorialnyj Muzej Jurija Gagarina, Gagarin 32799
Memorialnyj Muzej-kabinet M.V. Frunze, Ivanovo 32830

Memorialnyj Muzej Karima Chakimova, Ufa 33644
Memorialnyj Muzej I.S. Ključnikova-Palantaja, Joškar-Ola 32858
Memorialnyj Muzej Kosmonavtiki, Moskva 33078
Memorialnyj Muzej-kvartira A.A. Šogencukova, Nalčik 33196
Memorialnyj Muzej-kvartira Aktërov Samojlovych, Sankt-Peterburg 33418
Memorialnyj Muzej-Kvartira S.M. Kirova, Vladikavkaz 33688
Memorialnyj Muzej-kvartira P.K. Kozlova, Sankt-Peterburg 33419
Memorialnyj Muzej-kvartira G.M. Kržižanovskogo i V.V. Starkova, Minusinsk 33014
Memorialnyj Muzej-kvartira I.P. Pavlova, Sankt-Peterburg 33420
Memorialnyj Muzej-kvartira A.S. Puškina, Moskva 33079
Memorialnyj Muzej-kvartira Rimskogo-Korsakova, Sankt-Peterburg 33421
Memorialnyj Muzej-kvartira M.S. Spiridonova, Čeboksary 32721
Memorialnyj Muzej-kvartira Vadima Alekseeviča Kozina, Magadan 33000
Memorialnyj Muzej-kvartira A.M. Vasnecova, Moskva 33080
Memorialnyj Muzej-laboratorija A.S. Popova, Kronštadt 32965
Memorialnyj Muzej Licej, Puškin 33339
Memorialnyj Muzej A.G. Malyškina, Mokšan 33018
Memorialnyj Muzej-Masterskaja Skulptora S.T. Konenkova, Moskva 33081
Memorialnyj Muzej Alii Moldagulovoj, Geroiny Sovetskogo Sojuza, Aktöbe 27070
Memorial'nyj Muzej N.I. Beloborodova, Tula 33625
Memorialnyj Muzej B.L. Pasternaka, Čistopol 32748
Memorialnyj Muzej A.S. Popova, Sankt-Peterburg 33422
Memorialnyj Muzej A.S. Popova - Izobretatelja Radio, Krasnoturinsk 32961
Memorialnyj Muzej N.M. Prževalskogo, Prževalsk 27313
Memorialnyj Muzej A.N. Skrjabina, Moskva 33082
Memorialnyj Muzej-usadba Akademika I.P. Pavlova, Rjazan 33350
Memorialnyj Muzej-usadba Chudožnika N.A. Jarošenko, Kislovodsk 32929
Memorialnyj Muzej-usadba M.P. Musorgskogo, Naumovo 33202
Memorialnyj Muzej-zapovednik N.A. Rimskogo-Korsakova Ljubensk-Večaša, Pljussa 33326
Memorialship Mikasa, Yokosuka 27026
Memorialul Ipotești-Centrul Național de Studii Mihai Eminescu, Ipotești 32542
Memorijalna Galerija Djure Tiljka, Komiža 07717
Memorijalna Galerija Veliša Lekovića, Bar 33789
Memorijalna Zbirka Antuna Masle, Dubrovnik 07697
Memorijalna Zbirka Eugena Kumičića, Brseč 07685
Memorijalni Muzej Džuro Jakšić, Srpska Crnja 33916
Memorijalni Muzej Gavrila Principa u Obljaju, Bosansko Grahova 03914
Memorijalni Muzej u Goši, Smederevska Palanka 33907
Memorijalni Muzeji Bela Crkva i Stolice, Krupanj 33856
Memorijalnyj Dom-muzej Javornickogo, Dnepropetrovsk 37850
Memory Hall of the Military School of Montaña, Jaca 34921
Memory Lane Museum at Seattle Goodwill, Seattle 47538
Memory Museum, Kyoto 26444
Memoryville USA, Rolla 46991
Memphis Belle B17 Flying Fortress, Memphis 45241
Memphis Brooks Museum of Art, Memphis 45242
Memphis College of Art Gallery, Memphis 45243
Memphis Pink Palace Museum, Memphis 45244
Menard Art Museum, Komaki 26367
Mencendorfa Nams, Riga 27430
Menczer Museum of Medicine and Dentistry, Hartford 43941
Mendel Art Gallery, Saskatoon 06400
Mendelianum - Památnik Gregora Mendela, Brno 08268
Mendelssohn-Haus, Leipzig 18403
Mendocino Art Center Gallery, Mendocino 45251
Mendocino County Museum, Willits 48641
The Menil Collection, Houston 44126
Menin Gate of the Brno City Museum, Brno 08269
Měninská Brána, Brno 08269
Mennello Museum of American Folk Art, Orlando 46186
Mennonite Heritage Center, Harleysville 43912
Mennonite Heritage Museum, Goessel 43709
Mennonite Heritage Museum, Rosthern 06289
Mennonite Heritage Village, Steinbach 06488
Mennonite Library and Archives Museum, North Newton 46000
Menominee County Heritage Museum, Menominee 45253
Mentalvårdsmuseet Säter, Säter 36169
Mentlhof-Bergbauernmuseum, Heiligenblut 02016
Mentor Graham Museum, Blunt 41761
Mentougou Museum, Beijing 06973
Mentzendorff's House, Riga 27430
Meopham Windmill, Meopham 39934
Meppeler Expositie Centrum, Meppel 29590
Meråker Bygdemuseum, Meråker 30673
Merano Arte, Merano 24351
Mercati Dr. Traiano, Roma 25170
Mercator Graventoren-Watermolen, Rupelmonde 03717
Mercator Museum, Sint-Niklaas 03742
Merced County Courthouse Museum, Merced 45260
Mercedes-Benz Museum, Stuttgart 20100
Mercer Art Gallery, Harrogate 39169
Mercer County Genealogical and Historical Society Museum, Princeton 46699
Mercer County Historical Museum, Celina 42165
Mercer County Museum, Mercer 45261
Mercer Gallery, Rochester 46942
Mercer Museum of the Bucks County Historical Society, Doylestown 42985
Mercer Union - Centre for Contemporary Visual Art, Toronto 06593
Merchant Adventurers' Hall, York 40965
Merchant's House Museum, New York 45832
Merchant's House Museum, Plymouth 40210
Mercosur Itinerant Contemporary Art Museum, Buenos Aires 00155
Mercury Bay and District Museum, Whitianga 30317
Merdøgård, Arendal 30392
Mere Museum, Mere 39935
Meredith Gallery, Baltimore 41480
Meriden Historical Society Museum, Meriden 45263
Meridian International Center - Cafritz Galleries, Washington 48369
Meridian Museum of Art, Meridian 45265
Merijärven Kotiseutumuseo, Merijärvi 09823
Merikarvian Kalastusmuseo, Merikarvia 09825
Merimbun Heritage Park, Tutong 04603
Merimiehen Koti, Uusikaupunki 10154
Merimiehenkotimuseo, Oulu 09890
Meritalo Museum, Salo 10018
Meritalon Museo, Salo 10018
Meriwether Lewis Dredge Museum, Brownville 41967
Meriwether Lewis National Monument, Hohenwald 44048
Merkelbach-Museum, Höhr-Grenzhausen 17785
Merklappenmuseum, Dieteren 29153
Meroogal House, Nowra 01336
Merowe Museum, Merowe 35772
Merredin Military Museum, Merredin 01248
Merredin Railway Station Museum, Merredin 01249
The Merrick Art Gallery, New Brighton 45672
Merrill Historical Museum, Merrill 45267
Merrill Museum, Carrollton 42113
Merritt Museum of Anthropology, Oakland 46064
Merriwa Colonial Museum, Merriwa 01250
Mersea Island Museum, West Mersea 40827
Merseyside Maritime Museum, Liverpool 39522
Mersin Culture Center, Mersin 37759
Mersin Kültür Merkezi, Mersin 37759
Meru Museum, Meru 27108
Les Merveilles de la Mer, Jdeidet El-Metn 27491
Mervyn Quinlan Museum, Benenden 38165
Merwin House Tranquility, Stockbridge 47817
Mesa Southwest Museum, Mesa 45271
Mesa Verde National Park Museum, Mesa Verde 45272
Meshkin Shahr Museum, Meshkin Shahr 22269
Mesnil aux Abeille, Beautheil 10652
Mesolithic Museum, Abinger Common 37958
Messerermuseum, Steinbach an der Steyr 02681
Messina Museum, Messina 34307
Messner Mountain Museum Dolomites, Cibiana di Cadore 23559
Messner Mountain Museum Juval, Castelbello 23392
Mestna Galerija, Šoštanj 34152
Mestna Galerija Ljubljana, Ljubljana 34110
Mestni Muzej Idrija, Idrija 34091
Mestni Muzej Ljubljana, Ljubljana 34111
Městská Galerie, Polička 08554
Městské a Textilni Muzeum, Dvůr Králové nad Labem 08337
Mestské Etnografické Múzeum, Smižany 34059
Městské Muzeum, Aš 08242
Městské Muzeum, Bílovec 08249
Městské Muzeum, Budyně nad Ohří 08285
Městské Muzeum, Bystřice nad Pernštejnem 08286
Městské Muzeum, Čáslav 08288
Městské Muzeum, Čelákovice 08292
Městské Muzeum, Česká Třebová 08297
Městské Muzeum, Chotěboř 08315
Městské Muzeum, Chrast u Chrudimě 08317
Městské Muzeum, Chrastava 08318
Městské Muzeum, Dačice 08324
Městské Muzeum, Dobruška 08329
Městské Muzeum, Františkovy Lázně 08338
Městské Muzeum, Frenštát pod Radhoštěm 08339
Městské Muzeum, Holešov 08356
Městské Muzeum, Horažďovice 08358
Městské Múzeum, Ilava 34000
Městské Muzeum, Jesenice u Rakovnika 08385
Městské Muzeum, Klobouky u Brna 08415
Městské Muzeum, Kožlany 08426
Městské Muzeum, Králíky 08428
Městské Muzeum, Lanškroun 08442
Městské Muzeum, Ledeč nad Sázavou 08445
Městské Muzeum, Letohrad 08447
Městské Muzeum, Mnichovo Hradiště 08483
Městské Muzeum, Moravská Třebová 08485
Městské Muzeum, Moravský Krumlov 08487
Městské Muzeum, Nejdek 08494
Městské Muzeum, Nepomuk 08497
Městské Muzeum, Nové Město nad Metují 08504
Městské Muzeum, Nové Strašecí 08506
Městské Muzeum, Nový Bydžov 08508
Městské Muzeum, Počátky 08548
Městské Muzeum, Polička 08555
Městské Muzeum, Přelouč 08621
Meštské Muzeum, Přibyslav 08627
Městské Muzeum, Protivín 08630
Městské Muzeum, Radnice u Rokycan 08632
Městské Muzeum, Rýmařov 08649
Městské Múzeum, Sabinov 34055
Městské Muzeum, Sadská 08650
Městské Muzeum, Sedlčany 08651
Městské Muzeum, Skuteč 08653
Městské Muzeum, Slapanice 08655
Městské Muzeum, Strážnice 08665
Městské Muzeum, Stříbro 08666
Městské Muzeum, Úpice 08701
Městské Muzeum, Valašské Klobouky 08705
Městské Muzeum, Velká Bíteš 08709
Městské Muzeum, Veselí nad Moravou 08717
Městské Muzeum, Vimperk 08718
Městské Muzeum, Volyně 08724
Městské Muzeum, Žamberk 08737
Městské Muzeum, Zbiroh 08740
Městské Múzeum, Zlaté Moravce 34080
Městské Muzeum a Galerie, Břeclav 08259
Městské Muzeum a Galerie, Hlinsko v Čechách 08350
Městské Muzeum a Galerie, Hořice v Pokrkonoší 08359
Městské Muzeum a Galerie, Lomnice nad Popelkou 08461
Městské Muzeum a Galerie, Svitavy 08671
Městské Muzeum a Galerie, Vodňany 08722
Městské Muzeum a Galerie J. Karse, Velvary 08715
Městské Muzeum a Galerie Otakara Spaniela a Josefa Wágnera, Jaroměř 08383
Městské Muzeum a Galerie T.F. Simona, Železnice 08746
Městské Muzeum a Památnik Jakuba Jana Ryby, Rožmitál pod Třemšínem 08641
Městské Muzeum Antonína Sovy, Pacov 08531
Městské Múzeum Filakovo, Filakovo 33993
Městské Muzeum Klenotnice, Nová Paka 08500
Městské Múzeum L. Štúra, Uhrovec 34077
Městské Múzeum Michala Tillnera, Malacky 34020
Městské Múzeum Poltár, Poltár 34044
Městské Múzeum Rajec, Rajec 34050
Mestské Múzeum v Bratislave, Bratislava 33970
Městské Muzeum v Mariánských Lázních, Mariánské Lázně 08472
Městské Muzeum v Železném Brodě, Železný Brod 08747
Městské Vlastivědné Mudruňkovo Muzeum, Říčany u Prahy 08634
Městské Vrbasovo Muzeum, Ždánice 08742
Mesuroscope, Douai 11558
Metallmuseum, Tullnerbach-Lawies 02748
Metals Museum, Sendai 26733
Metamora Courthouse, Metamora 45275
Metamorphosis Church Museum, Metéora 21069
Metchosin School Museum, Victoria 06726
Metenkov House - Museum of Photography, Ekaterinburg 32767
Meteorkrater-Museum, Steinheim am Albuch 20049
Meteorological Museum of the Main Observatory, Sankt-Peterburg 33457
Methil Heritage Centre, Methil 39940
Methodist Church Museum - a Laura Ingalls Wilder Site, Spring Valley 47731
Les Métiers d'Antan, Monêtier-les-Bains 13013
Métiers d'Art Sant Roch, Céret 11107
Les Métiers du Champagne, Épernay 11624
Metro Arts, Brisbane 00838
Metrological Coll of the Central Office of Measures, Warszawa 32114
Metrological Collection - Central Office of Measures, Warszawa 32144
Metrònom, Barcelona 34546
Metropole Gallery, Folkestone 39001
Metropolit Chambers - Museum of Ancient Russian Art, Jaroslavl 32852
Metropolitan Museum of Art, New York 45833
Metropolitan Museum of Manila, Manila 31382
Metropolitan Police Historical Museum, London 39707
Metropolitan Toronto Police Museum and Discovery Centre, Toronto 06594
Metsämuseo, Helsinki 09515
Mevlâna Müzesi, Konya 37744
Mevlâna Rumi Museum, Konya 37744
Mevlevi Tekke Müzesi, Lefkoşa 08238
Mexic-Arte Museum, Austin 41417
Mexican Federation of Associations of Friends of Museums, México 49293
Mexican Fine Arts Center Museum, Chicago 42341
The Mexican Museum, San Francisco 47324
Meyerhold Museum of Scenic Performance, Penza 33292
Meža Muzejs Boju Pilī, Aizpute 27329
Meždunarodnyj Centr-Muzej im. N.K. Rericha, Moskva 33083
Meždunarodnyj Muzejno-vystavočnyj Centr, Vladivostok 33701
M.F. Gabyshin Gallery of Foreign Art, Jakutsk 32842
M.H. de Young Memorial Museum, San Francisco 47325
Mhiripiri Gallery, Edina 43086
M.I. Glinka Museum Estate, Novospasskoe 33246
M.I. Glinka State Central Museum of Music, Moskva 33049
Miami Art Museum, Miami 45289
Miami Children's Museum, Miami 45290
Miami County Museum, Peru 46364
Miami Museum, Miami 05843
Miami Museum of Science, Miami 45291
Miami University Art Museum, Oxford 46242
Miandoab Museum, Urmieh 22331
Mianposhteh Palace Museum, Bandar-Anzali 22232
Miasskij Kraevedčeskij Muzej, Miass 33010
Michael Bruce Cottage Museum, Kinnesswood 39389
Michael C. Carlos Museum, Atlanta 41352
Michael C. Rockefeller Arts Center Gallery, Fredonia 43546
Michael Davitt National Memorial Museum, Straide 22544
Michael-Ende-Museum, München 18875
Michael Faraday's Laboratory and Museum, London 39708
Michael og Anna Anchers Hus og Saxilds Gaard, Skagen 09056
Michael Pacher-Haus, Sankt Wolfgang im Salzkammergut 02620
Michaelis Collection, Cape Town 34207
Michajlovskij Istoričeskij Muzej, Michajlov 33011
Michajlovskoe - Gosudarstvennyj Memorialnyj Istoriko-literaturnyj i Prirodno-landšaftnyj Muzej-Zapovednik A.S. Puškina, Puškinskie Gory 33344
Michel Brouillet House and Museum, Vincennes 48240
Michelham Priory, Hailsham 39147
Michelson Museum of Art, Marshall 45183
Michigan Chapter Gallery, Detroit 42931
Michigan Historical Museum, Lansing 44643
Michigan Maritime Museum, South Haven 47695
Michigan Museums Association, Lansing 49505
Michigan Sports Hall of Fame, Detroit 42932
Michigan State Trust for Railway Preservation, Owosso 46233
Michigan State University Museum, East Lansing 43054
Michigan Transit Museum, Mount Clemens 45526
Michoutouchkine Pilioko Foundation, Port Vila 48865
Mico INAFCA Museum, Kingston 26071
Micovna, Praha 08590
Micro-Musée de la Lessive, Seyne-les-Alpes 14742
Micro-Musée de l'École, Seyne-les-Alpes 14743
Micro-Musée de l'Ex-Colonie Pénitentiaire, Mettray 12954
Micro-Musée du Château-Fort, Saint-Saturnin-de-Lenne 14463
Micro-Musée du Tailleur, Seyne-les-Alpes 14744
Micromusée, La Trinité 27723
Micromusée Archéologique, Padirac 13450
Micromusée de la Légion Etrangère, Douzillac 11572
Micromusée de la Maison de Retraîte Jeanne Pierretée Carnot, Nolay 13363
Micromusée de Marcel Proust, Cabourg 10967
Micromusée du Village Ardéchois, Pailhares 13451
Micromusée Goethe, Sessenheim 14728
Micromusée Républicain, Villars-les-Blamont 15181
Mid-America Air Museum, Liberal 44764
Mid-America Science Museum, Hot Springs 44109
Mid Atlantic Air Museum, Reading 46808
Mid-Atlantic Association of Museums, Baltimore 49506
Mid-Atlantic Center for the Arts, Cape May 42097
Mid-Continent Railway Museum, North Freedom 45994
Mid Hampshire Railway Museum, Alresford 37987
Mid-Hudson Children's Museum, Poughkeepsie 46676
Mid-Richmond Historical Museum, Coraki 00945
Middelfart Museum, Middelfart 08985
Middendorpshuis, Den Ham 29131
Middle Border Museum of American Indian and Pioneer Life, Mitchell 45414
Middle Eastern Culture Centre in Japan, Mitaka 26499
Middle Lake Museum, Middle Lake 05845
Middleborough Historical Museum, Middleborough 45304
The Middlebury College Museum of Art, Middlebury 45308
Middlebury Historical Society Museum, Wyoming 48769
Middlesbrough Art Gallery, Middlesbrough 39949
Middlesex Canal Collection, Lowell 44985
Middlesex County Historical Society Museum, Middletown 45315
Middleton Place Foundation, Charleston 42224
Middleton Top Engine House, Middleton-by-Wirksworth 39951
Middletown Fine Arts Center, Middletown 45318
Middletown Valley Historical Society Museum, Middletown 45316
Middleville Museum, Lanark 05722
Midland Air Museum, Baginton 38055
Midland County Historical Museum, Midland 45322
Midland County Historical Museum, Midland 45327
Midland Motor Museum, Bridgnorth 38323
Midland Railway Centre, Ripley, Derbyshire 40325
Midland Warplane Museum, Warwick 40790
Midlands Art Centre, Birmingham 38224
Midlands Federation of Museums and Art Galleries, Telford 49424
Midorikawa Yoishi Shashin Bijutsukan, Okayama 26625
Midsomer Norton and District Museum, Radstock 40277
Midtown Art Center, Houston 44127

Midtsønderjyllands Museum, Gram 08840
Midttunet, Skei i Jølster 30844
Midway Museum, Midway 45332
Midway Village and Museum, Rockford 46961
Midwest Museum of American Art, Elkhart 43140
Midwest Old Settlers and Threshers Association Museum, Mount Pleasant 45535
Mie-kenritsu Bijutsukan, Tsu 26976
Mie-kenritsu Hakubutsukan, Tsu 26977
Mie Prefectural Art Museum, Tsu 26976
Mie Prefectural Museum, Tsu 26977
Miegunyah Pioneer Women's Memorial House Museum, Bowen Hills 00820
Miejska Galeria Sztuki, Łódź 31767
Miele-Museum, Gütersloh 17459
Miellerie des Gorges de la Loire, Roche-la-Molière 13991
Miervalda Ķemera Muzejs, Jūrmala 27371
Mies-Pilsner-Heimatmuseum, Dinkelsbühl 16616
Mies van der Rohe Haus, Berlin 16043
Mieszkanie-Pracownia Kazimiery Iłłakowiczówny, Poznań 31896
Migration Museum, Adelaide 00709
Migros Museum für Gegenwartskunst, Zürich 37389
Miguel Malvar Museum, Santo Tomas 31445
Mihály Babits Memorial Museum, Szekszárd 21564
Mihály Zichy Memorial Museum, Zala 21612
Mihkli Talumuuseum, Kihelkonna 09333
Miho Museum, Shigaraki 26748
Mikailov Historical Museum, Michajlov 33011
Mikhailovskoe - State Preserve of A.S. Pushkin, Puškinskie Gory 33344
Mikkeli Art Museum, Mikkeli 09832
Mikkelin Taidemuseo, Mikkeli 09832
Mikumi Museum, Mikumi 37463
Milam County Historical Museum, Cameron 42067
Milan Historical Museum, Milan 45334
Milano Model and Toy Museum, Elmhurst 43168
Milas Culture Center, Milas 37760
Milas Kültür Merkezi, Milas 37760
Milas Müzesi, Milas 37761
Milas Museum, Milas 37761
Milchwirtschaftliches Museum, Kiesen 36824
Milden Community Museum, Milden 05849
Mildenhall and District Museum, Mildenhall, Suffolk 39952
Mildred M. Mahoney Silver Jubilee Dolls' House Gallery, Fort Erie 05436
Mildura Arts Centre, Mildura 01252
Miles and District Historical Village Museum, Miles 01254
Miles B. Carpenter Museum, Waverly 48468
Miles Mineral Museum, Portales 46616
Milestones: Hampshire's Living History Museum, Basingstoke 38102
Milevské Muzeum, Milevsko 08478
Milford Haven Museum, Milford Haven 39953
Milford Historical Museum, Milford 45340
Milford Historical Society Museum, Milford 45338
Milford Museum, Milford 45339
Mili Weber-Haus, Sankt Moritz 37114
Milieu Educatie Centrum, Eindhoven 29214
Milieucentrum De Grote Rivieren, Heerewaarden 29364
Militär- und Jagdgeschichtliche Sammlung, Bad Wildungen 15765
Militärgeschichtliche Ortssammlung, Schnifis 02636
Militärgeschichtliches Museum, Ardagger 01677
Militärhistorisches Museum der Bundeswehr, Dresden 16697
Militair Historisch Museum De Veteraan, Eefde 29196
Militaire Luchtvaart Museum, Soesterberg 29843
Militarial Musée Mémorial pour la Paix, Boissezon 10788
Military Academy Museum, Seoul 27257
Military Aviation Museum, Tangmere 40672
Military Communications and Electronics Museum, Kingston 05682
Military Heritage Museum, Lewes 39485
Military Heritage Tours, Longford 22510
Military Historians Museum, Westbrook 48550
Military-Historical Museum of Artillery, Engineer and Signal Corps, Sankt-Peterburg 33487
Military Historical Museum of the Pacific Fleat, Vladivostok 33712
Military History Museum War of Liberation 1877-1878, Bjala 04623
Military Marine Museum, Bandar-Anzali 22233
Military Medal Museum, San Jose 47352
Military Medical Museum, Sankt-Peterburg 33488
Military Museum, Aden 49006
Military Museum, Białystok 31488
Military Museum, Cairo 09270
Military Museum, El-Alamein 09292
Military Museum, Kingston 26072
Military Museum, Macau 07166
Military Museum, Sanaa 49010
Military Museum, Teheran 22312
Military Museum, Ulaanbaatar 28677
Military Museum and Cultural Centre Command, İstanbul 37691
Military Museum - City Armoury, Wrocław 32179
Military Museum Fort, Bloemfontein 34186
Military Museum Manege, Helsinki 09513
Military Museum of Belgrade, Beograd 33819
Military Museum of Devon and Dorset, Dorchester 38750
Military Museum of Finland, Helsinki 09529
Military Museum of Southern New England, Danbury 42771
Military Technical Museum, Krhanice 08433
Military Vehicle Museum, Newcastle-upon-Tyne 40039
Military Veterans Museum, Oshkosh 46205
Militia History Museum, Sankt-Peterburg 33438
Miljømuseet Dokken, Haugesund 30539
Mill Green Museum and Mill, Hatfield 39188
Mill Grove, The Audubon Wildlife Sanctuary, Audubon 41379
Mill House Cider Museum and Dorset Collection of Clocks, Owermoigne 40140
Mill Museum, Juuka 09590
Mill-Museum, Rautalampi 09986
Mill Museum, Sappee 10021
Mill Museum, Värtsilä 10168
Mill of the Castle, Amsterdam 28873
Mill Race Historical Village, Northville 46030
Mill Trail Visitor Centre, Alva 37993
Millard Fillmore House, East Aurora 43036
Millenium Underground Museum, Budapest 21363
Millennium Galleries, Sheffield 40487
Millenniumi Földalatti Vasúti Múzeum, Budapest 21363
Miller Art Center, Springfield 47760
Miller Art Museum, Sturgeon Bay 47863
Miller Bakehouse Museum, Palmyra 01354
Miller-Cory House Museum, Westfield 48558
Miller House Museum, Hagerstown 43866
Miller Museum of Geology, Kingston 05683
Millesgården, Lidingö 36032
Millet and District Museum, Millet 05851
Millgate Museum, Newark-on-Trent 40020
Millicent National Trust Museum, Millicent 01257
Millicent Rogers Museum of Northern New Mexico, Taos 47951
Milliken Gallery, Spartanburg 47715
Millmount Museum and Tower, Drogheda 22412
Mills College Art Museum, Oakland 46065
Mills County Museum, Glenwood 43698
Mills Observatory Museum, Dundee 38801
Millstreet Local Museum, Millstreet 22519
Millwall FC Museum, London 39709
Milne Bay Military Museum, Toowoomba 01540
Milner House, Chatham, Ontario 05240
Milton Blacksmith Shop Museum, Milton 05853
Milton Historical Museum, Milton 45356
Milton House Museum, Milton 45357
Milton J. Rubenstein Museum of Science and Technology, Syracuse 47910
Milton Keynes Gallery, Milton Keynes 39961
Milton Keynes Museum, Milton Keynes 39962
Milton's Cottage, Chalfont Saint Giles 38520
Milwaukee Art Museum, Milwaukee 45366
Milwaukee County Historical Society Museum, Milwaukee 45367
Milwaukee Public Museum, Milwaukee 45368
Minami-yamate District Historic Preservation Center, Nagasaki 26548
Mind and Matter Gallery, White Rock 06789
Mindener Museum für Geschichte, Landes- und Volkskunde, Minden, Westfalen 18749
Mine d'Argent Saint-Barthélemy, Sainte-Marie-aux-Mines 14541
La Mine-Image, La Motte-d'Aveillans 12210
Mine Témoin d'Alès, Alès 10285
Minera Lead Mines, Minera 39965
Mineral and Gem Geological Museum, Parrsboro 06096
Mineral and Lapidary Museum of Henderson County, Hendersonville 43994
Mineral County Museum, Superior 47888
Mineral Museum, Butte 42018
Mineral- och Gruvmuseet, Holsbybrunn 35964
Mineral Resources Divisional Museum, Dodoma 37460
Mineralenexpositie De Siersteen, Oostwold, Leek 29675
Mineralien-Fossilien-Bergbau, Langenlois 02185
Mineralien-Fossilien-Museum, Neckartenzlingen 18991
Mineralien-Kabinett der TU Braunschweig, Braunschweig 16300
Mineralien Museum, Seedorf (Uri) 37156
Mineralien-Museum Andreas Gabrys, Lam 18294
Mineralien-Sammlung, Hohenwarth 17817
Mineralien- und Heimatmuseum, Pleystein 19416
Mineralienmuseum Essen, Essen 16957
Mineralienmuseum Pforzheim-Dillweißenstein, Pforzheim 19388
Mineraliensammlung, Lauingen 18358
Mineralienschau, Afritz 01647
Mineralienschau, Vohenstrauß 20331
Mineralinemuseum, Einsiedeln 36674
Mineralogical Collection, Stari Trg 33917
Mineralogical Museum of Ecole des Mines d'Alès, Alès 10288
Mineralogical Museum of Harvard University, Cambridge 42046
Mineralogical Museum of Kamarzia, Attica 20907
Mineralogical Museum of Lavrion, Lavrion 21045
Mineralogical Museum of the Institute of Geological Sciences, Wrocław 32180
Mineralogičeskij Muzej, Apatity 32644
Mineralogičeskij Muzej im. A.E. Fersmana Rossijskoj Akademii Nauk, Moskva 33084
Mineralogičeskij Muzej im. A.V. Sidorova, Irkutsk 32815
Mineralogisch-Geologisch Museum, Delft 29081
Mineralogisch-Geologische Gesteins-Sammlung, Schwarzenfeld 19885
Mineralogisch Museum, Grou 29318
Mineralogisch Museum, Merksem 03624
Mineralogisch-Petrografische Sammlungen der Eidgenössischen Technischen Hochschule, Zürich 37390
Mineralogisch-petrographische Sammlung der Universität Leipzig, Leipzig 18404
Mineralogische Sammlung, Erlangen 16919
Mineralogische Schau- und Lehrsammlung, Tübingen 20228
Mineralogisches Museum der Philipps-Universität Marburg, Marburg 18630
Mineralogisches Museum der Universität, Würzburg 20698
Mineralogisches Museum der Universität Bonn, Bonn 16244
Mineralogisches Museum der Universität Hamburg, Hamburg 17554
Mineralogisches Museum (Kristalle und Gesteine), Münster 18941
Mineralogy Museum, Bangkok 37488
Mineralogy Museum Baia Mare, Baia Mare 32434
Mineralogy Museum of the Geological Institute of the Kola Scientific Center of the Russian Academy of Sciences, Apatity 32644
Mineralogy, Petrography and Volcanology Museum, Catania 23445
Mineraloška Zbirka Rudnika Trepča, Stari Trg 33917
Mineraloško-Petrografski Muzej, Zagreb 07828
Mineralovodskij Kraevedčeskij Muzej, Mineral'nye Vody 33012
Miners Foundry Cultural Center, Nevada City 45654
Mines d'Asphalte de la Presta, Travers 37251
Mines de Sel de Bex, Bex 36560
Ming Shu Wangling Museum, Chengdu 07023
Mingcheng Yuan Shi Museum, Nanjing 07181
Mingei International Museum, San Diego 47279
Mingenback Art Center Gallery, Lindsborg 44808
Mingenew Museum, Mingenew 01258
Minhauzena Muzejs, Dunte 27353
Mini-Château, Amboise 10310
Mini-Musée de l'Aviation, Mèze 12971
Mini-Musée de l'Ossuaire, Pleyben 13759
Mini Musée des Miniatures, Sospel 14776
Mini-Musée Ferroviaire, La Seyne-sur-Mer 12261
Mini-Musée Historique, Rodemack 14005
Miniature English Village and Brass Rubbing Centre, Flaxton 01027
Miniaturpark Klein-Erzgebirge, Oederan 19223
Miniatuur Walcheren, Middelburg 29592
Miniatuurstad, Antwerpen 03148
Minimundus, Klagenfurt 02129
Minimuseum, Groningen 29310
Mining and Iron Works Museum, Złoty Stok 32223
Mining Industry House, Braddon 00828
Mining Museum, Bogatynia 31503
Mining Museum, Gelnica 33996
Mining Museum, Nowa Ruda 31826
Mining Museum, Ostrava 08525
Mining Museum, Outokumpu 09900
Mining Museum, Pécs 21509
Mining Museum, Petroşani 32564
The Mining Museum, Platteville 46545
Mining Museum, Příbram 08625
Mining Museum, Rožňava 34052
Mining Museum, Sala 36172
Mining Museum, Salgótarján 21521
Mining Museum, Sankt-Peterburg 33396
Mining Skansen Museum Queen Louise, Zabrze 32201
Miniota Municipal Museum, Miniota 05858
Minischeepvaartmuseum, Ouwerkerk 29704
Minisink Valley Historical Society Museum, Port Jervis 46599
Minjasafn Austurlands, Egilsstadir 21629
Minjasafn Egils Ólafssonar, Patreksfjörður 21645
Minjasafnid Burstarfelli, Vopnafjörður 21675
Minjasafnida á Akureyri, Akureyri 21620
Minlaton National Trust Museum, Minlaton 01259
Minneapolis College of Art and Design Gallery, Minneapolis 45390
Minneapolis Institute of Arts, Minneapolis 45391
Minnedosa and District Museum, Minnedosa 05859
Minnesota Air National Guard Exhibition, Saint Paul 47160
Minnesota Association of Museums, Minneapolis 49507
Minnesota Children's Museum, Saint Paul 47161
Minnesota Historical Society Museum, Saint Paul 47162
Minnesota Museum of American Art, Saint Paul 47163
Minnesota Pioneer Park Museum, Annandale 41223
Minnesota Transportation Museum, Saint Paul 47164
Minnilusa Pioneer Museum, Rapid City 46796
Minobusan Homotsukan, Minobu 26492
Minolta Photo Space Hiroshima, Hiroshima 26220
Minority Arts Resource Council Studio Art Museum, Philadelphia 46427
Minowa Museum, Minowa 26493
Minster Abbey, Minster 39966
Minster Abbey Gatehouse Museum, Sheerness 40480
Mint Museum, Osaka 26655
Mint Museum of Art, Charlotte 42243
Mint Museum of Craft and Design, Charlotte 42244
Minto Museum, Minto 05860
Minton Museum, Stoke-on-Trent 40608
Minusinskaja Chudožestvennaja Kartinnaja Galereja, Minusinsk 33015
Minusinskij Regionalnyj Kraevedčeskij Muzej im. N.M. Martjanova, Minusinsk 33016
Minute Man National Historical Park, Concord 42599
Mir-Emad Calligraphy Museum, Teheran 22313
Miracle of America Museum, Polson 46579
Miramar Zeemuseum, Vledder 29949
Miramichi Natural History Museum, Miramichi 05861
Miramon Kutxaespacio de la Ciencia, Donostia-San Sebastián 34775
Miramont Castle Museum, Manitou Springs 45114
Mirasaka Peace Museum of Art, Mirasaka 26494
Mirehouse, Keswick 39345
Mireuksa Temple Museum, Iksan 27188
Miriam and Ira D. Wallach Art Gallery, New York 45834
Mirror and District Museum, Mirror 05863
Miryang Municipal Museum, Miryang 27211
Mise en Valeur du Site Archéologique, Barzan 10597
Mishima Taisha Treasure House, Mishima 26496
Mishkan Le'Omanut, Ein Harod 22589
Misijné Múzeum Nitra, Nitra 34034
Misjonsmuseet, Stavanger 30881
Misjonsmuseet på Fjellhaug, Oslo 30742
Miskolc Gallery of Fine Arts - Rákóczi House, Miskolc 21479
Miskolci Galéria - Rákóczi-ház, Miskolc 21479
Misora Hibari Memorial House, Kyoto 26433
Missiemuseum Steyl, Steijl 29853
Mission and Folklore Museum, Polanica Zdrój 31891
Mission Bell Museum, Coweta 42684
Mission Cultural Center for Latino Arts, San Francisco 47326
Mission Gallery, Swansea 40660
The Mission House, Stockbridge 47818
Mission Houses Museum, Honolulu 44084
Mission Inn Museum, Riverside 46920
Mission Mill Museum, Salem 47210
Mission Museum, Czerna 31542
Mission Museum, Helsinki 09507
Mission Museum, Krosno 31735
Mission Museum, Mission 05865
Mission San Carlos Borromeo del Rio Carmelo, Carmel 42110
Mission San Diego de Alcala, San Diego 47280
Mission San Juan Capistrano Museum, San Juan Capistrano 47360
Mission San Luis Obispo de Tolosa, San Luis Obispo 47361
Mission San Luis Rey Museum, Oceanside 46089
Mission San Miguel, San Miguel 47370
Missionary Museum, King William's Town 34296
Missionary Museum of the N.G. Kerk, Stellenbosch 34381
Missions-Ethnographisches Museum St. Gabriel, Mödling 02310
Missions-Museum der Pallottiner Limburg, Limburg an der Lahn 18472
Missionsmuséet, Vårgårda 36397
Missionsmuseum, Sankt Ottilien 19756
Missionsmuseum, Schwarzach am Main 19880
Missionsmuseum Bug, Bamberg 15810
Missionsmuseum der Mariannhiller Missionare, Würzburg 20699
Missionsmuseum der Spiritaner Knechtsteden, Dormagen 16647
Missionsmuseum des päpstlichen Missionswerks der Kinder in Deutschland, Aachen 15376
Missisquoi Museum, Stanbridge East 06486
Missisquoi Valley Historical Society Museum, North Troy 46009
Mississagi Strait Lighthouse Museum, Meldrum 05833
Mississippi Baptist Historical Commission Museum, Clinton 42496
Mississippi County Historical Society Museum, Charleston 42206
Mississippi Crafts Center, Ridgeland 46898
Mississippi Governor's Mansion, Jackson 44279
Mississippi Museum of Art, Jackson 44280
Mississippi Museum of Natural Science, Jackson 44281
Mississippi Museums Association, Natchez 49508
Mississippi Petrified Forest Museum, Flora 43341
Mississippi River Museum, Dubuque 42993
Mississippi River Museum at Mud Island River Park, Memphis 45245
Mississippi University for Women Museum, Columbus 42583
Mississippi Valley Textile Museum, Almonte 04979
Mississippi Agriculture and Forestry/National Agricultural Aviation Museum, Jackson 44282
Missouri Historical Society Museum, Saint Louis 47128
Missouri Museums Association, Kansas City 49509
Missouri State Museum, Jefferson City 44329
Missouri Town 1855, Lees Summit 44709
Místní Muzeum, Kopidlno 08419
Místní Muzeum, Libáň 08448
Místní Muzeum, Městec Králové 08474
Místní Muzeum, Mladá Vožice 08482
Místní Muzeum, Netolice 08498
Místní Muzeum, Netvořice 08499
MIT-List Visual Arts Center, Cambridge 42047
The MIT Museum, Cambridge 42048
Mitchell County Historical Museum, Osage 46200
Mitchell Gallery of Flight, Milwaukee 45369

Mitchell House, Nantucket 45597
Mitchell Museum at Cedarhurst, Mount Vernon 45544
Mitchell Museum of the American Indian, Evanston 43242
Mitko Palauzov Memorial House, Gabrovo 04669
Mito Geijutsukan Gendai Bijutsu Center, Mito 26503
Mitropoličji Palaty - Muzej Drevnerusskogo Iskusstva, Jaroslavl 32852
Mitsubishi Automobile Gallery, Okazaki 26630
Mitsuke School Historical Site, Iwata, Shizuoka 26275
Mitsukuni and Nariaki Tokugawa Memorial Collection, Mito 26504
Mittamuseo, Virrat 10204
Mittelalterliches Foltermuseum, Rüdesheim am Rhein 19706
Mittelalterliches Kriminalmuseum, Rothenburg ob der Tauber 19679
Mittelmoselmuseum im Barockhaus Böcking, Traben-Trarbach 20187
Mittelrhein-Museum, Koblenz 18122
Mittelschwäbisches Heimatmuseum Krumbach, Krumbach, Schwaben 18251
Mitzpe Revivim Museum, Kibbutz Revivim 22700
Miyagi-ken Bijutsukan, Sendai 26732
Miyagi Michio Memorial Hall, Tokyo 26892
Miyagi Prefecture Museum of Art, Sendai 26732
Miyakonojo City Museum of Art, Miyakonojo 26507
Miyandoab Museum, Miyandoab 22270
Miyazaki-ken Sogo Hakubutsukan, Miyazaki, Miyazaki-ken 26511
Miyazaki-kenritsu Bijutsukan, Miyazaki, Miyazaki-ken 26512
Miyazaki Prefectural Art Museum, Miyazaki, Miyazaki-ken 26512
Miyazaki Prefectural Museum of Nature and History, Miyazaki, Miyazaki-ken 26511
Mizel Museum of Judaica, Denver 42891
Mizuhomachi Kyodo Shiryokan, Mizuho 26513
Mizunami Fossil Museum, Mizunami 26514
Mizunami-shi Kaseki Hakubutsukan, Mizunami 26514
Mizuno Old Ceramics House, Miyazaki, Fukui 26509
Mjellby Konstmuseum, Halmstad 35942
Mjölby Hembygdsgård, Mjölby 36094
M.K. Čiurlionis National Museum of Art, Kaunas 27521
MLA West Midland, Birmingham 49425
M.M. Prishvin House-Museum, Dunino 32763
M.M. Soshchenko Literary Memorial Museum, Sankt-Peterburg 33415
MOA Bijutsukan, Atami 26115
MOA Museum of Art, Atami 26115
Moanalua Gardens Foundation, Honolulu 44085
Moat Park Heritage Centre, Biggar 38198
Moaven Al- Molk Museum, Kermanshah 22255
Mobach Keramiek Museum, Utrecht 29899
Mobile Die Cast Toy Museum, Vianden 27577
Mobile Medical Museum, Mobile 45420
Mobile Museum of Art, Mobile 45421
Mobile Städtische Galerie im Museum Folkwang, Essen 16958
Mobiles Kindermuseum im Freizeitheim Vahrenwald, Hannover 17604
Mobilia, Kangasala 09617
Mobius Gallery, Boston 41815
MoCHA, London 39710
Mockbeggar Plantation, Bonavista 05095
Modalen Skulemuseum, Modalen 30677
Model House Gallery, Llantrisant 39557
Model Railway Museum, Matlock 39921
Modelbouwmuseum, Wassenaar 29983
Modellbahnmuseum-Muggendorf, Wiesenttal 20581
Modemuseum, München 18876
Modemuseum Provincie Antwerpen, Antwerpen 03149
Modern Art Museum of Bucaramanga, Bucaramanga 07437
Modern Art Museum of Fort Worth, Fort Worth 43489
Modern Art Oxford, Oxford 40147
Modern Hungarian Gallery I, Pécs 21510
Modern Hungarian Gallery II, Pécs 21511
Modern Magyar Képtár I, Pécs 21510
Modern Magyar Képtár II, Pécs 21511
Modern Museum, Stockholm 36262
Modern Transportation Museum, Osaka 26651
Moderna Galerija, Ljubljana 34112
Moderna Galerija, Podgorica 33888
Moderna Galerija, Zagreb 07829
Moderna Galerija Rijeka - Muzej Moderne i Suvremene Umjetnosti, Rijeka 07760
Moderna Museet, Stockholm 36262
Moderne Galerie im Weinstadtmuseum Krems, Krems 02158
Modesammlung, Wien 02931
Modest P. Musorgski Memorial Estate Museum, Naumovo 33202
Modoc County Historical Museum, Alturas 41159
Moe Historical Museum, Moe 01263
Möbelindustrimuseum i Virserum, Virserum 36412
Mödlinger Stadtverkehrsmuseum, Mödling 02311
Möhkö Ironworks Museum, Möhkö 09836
Möhkön Ruukki, Möhkö 09836
Möllner Museum Historisches Rathaus, Mölln 18766
Mölndals Museum, Mölndal 36097
Mönchehaus-Museum für moderne Kunst Goslar, Goslar 17353
Mönchguter Museen im Ostseebad Göhren, Göhren, Rügen 17313
Mörfelden Museum, Mörfelden-Walldorf 18775
Mörikehaus Ochsenwang, Bissingen an der Teck 16174
Mörsbacher Museum, Mörsbach 18779
Moervarststede, Wachtebeke 03822
Moesgård Museum, Højbjerg 08880
Möwe Bay Museum, Möwe Bay 28762
Moffat Museum, Moffat 39970
Moffatt-Ladd House, Portsmouth 46651
Mohave Museum of History and Arts, Kingman 44488
Moheda Skolmuseum, Moheda 36100
Mohonk Preserve, Gardiner 43622
Moira Furnace, Moira 39971
Mõisaküla Muuseum, Mõisaküla 09338
Moisburger Mühlenmuseum, Moisburg 18782
Mok Am Museum of Art, Koyang 27206
Moka Buddhist Museum, Gangcheon 27164
Mokichi Saito Museum, Kaminoyama 26298
Mokuzo-gan Gallery, Odawara 26614
Mola- het Provinciaal Molenmuseum, Wachtebeke 03823
Moldovan State Art Museum, Chişinău 28658
Molen-, Bakkerij- en Stoommuseum, Essen 03411
Molen De Vriendschap, Weesp 29991
Molen van Frans Expositie, Mander (Tubbergen) 29577
Molen van Sloten, Amsterdam 28873
Molenmuseum, Koog aan de Zaan 29489
Molenmuseum, Lommel 03595
Molenmuseum, Sint-Amands 03735
Molenmuseum de Assumburg, Nieuw Vossemeer 29616
Molenmuseum De Valk, Leiden 29520
Molenmuseum De Wachter, Zuidlaren 30070
Molerhiisli, Hausach 17642
Molermuseet, Nykøbing Mors 08999
Moli d'en Gaspar, Lluchmajor 34979
Molino-Museo Gregorio Prieto, Valdepeñas 35590
Molkerei-Museum, Bernbeuren 16124
Molly Brown House Museum, Denver 42892
Molnár C. Pál Müteremmuzeum, Budapest 21364
Molong Historical Museum, Molong 01264
Mølsteds Museum, Dragør 08797
Molteno Museum, Molteno 34309
Moltke-Gedächtnisstätte, Parchim 19348
Moluks Historisch Museum, Utrecht 29900
Molwitz-Stube, Mitterteich 18756
Momoyama Art Museum, Kyoto 26434
Mompesson House, Salisbury 40435
Mon State Museum, Mawlamyine 28736
Mona Vale Aero Nautical Museum, Mona Vale 01265
Monacensia-Literaturarchiv und Bibliothek, München 18877
Monaco Modern Art Museum, Monaco 28664
Monaghan County Museum, Monaghan 22521
Monarch Historical Museum, Williamtown 01603
Monash Gallery of Art, Wheelers Hill 01596
Monash University Museum of Art, Clayton 00923
Monasterio de Dominicas, Quejana 35304
Monasterio de la Cartuja, Sevilla 35477
Monasterio de la Encarnación, Madrid 35010
Monasterio de la Encarnación, Osuna 35195
Monasterio de la Santa Cruz, Sahagún 35355
Monasterio de las Descalzas Reales, Madrid 35011
Monasterio de las Huelgas de Burgos, Burgos 34628
Monasterio de Nuestra Señora de Guadelupe, Guadelupe 34887
Monasterio de Nuestra Señora de la Piedad, Casalarreina 34688
Monasterio de San Juan de los Reyes, Toledo 35536
Monasterio de San Lorenzo de El Escorial, San Lorenzo de El Escorial 35380
Monasterio de San Millán de Suso, San Millán de Suso 35386
Monasterio de San Pedro, San Pedro de Cardeña 35388
Monasterio de San Pedro de Cardeña, Castrillo del Val 34697
Monasterio de Sant Cugat, Sant Cugat del Vallès 35397
Monasterio de Santa Catalina, Arequipa 31112
Monasterio de Santa Clara, Zafra 35710
Monasterio de Santa Clara de Tordesillas, Tordesillas 35552
Monasterio de Santa María, Ripoll 35324
Monasterio de Santa María, Santa María de Huerta 35422
Monasterio de Santa María, Sobrado 35500
Monasterio de Santa María de la Rábida, Palos de la Frontera 35245
Monasterio de Santa María la Real, Nájera 35153
Monasterio de Santa María San Salvador, Cañas 34666
Monasterio de Santes Creus, Santes Creus 35435
Monasterio de Santo Domingo el Antiguo, Toledo 35537
Monasterio San Juan de Duero, Soria 35505
Monasterio Santo Espíritu, Gilet 34850
Monasterium De Wijngaard, Brugge 03258
Monastery Collection, Raška 33900
Monastery Museum, Cetinje 33832
Monastery of Saint Catherine, Gebel Katherîna 09293
Monastery of the Archangel Michael Panormitis, Chora 20926
Monastery of the Evangelistria, Skopelos 21160
Monastery of the Panagia Xenia, Almyros 20816
Monastery of the Taxiarchs, Aigion 20814
Monastery of the Zoodochos Pigi or Agia, Batsi 20910
Moncton Museum, Moncton 05879
Moncur Gallery, Boissevain 05090
Mondak Heritage Historical Museum and Art Gallery, Sidney 47624
Le Monde de Belibaste, Villerouge-Termenès 15241
Le Monde des Abeilles, Villeneuve-de-Berg 15223
Mondriaanhuis - Museum voor Constructieve en Concrete Kunst, Amersfoort 28823
Monemvasia Archeological Collection, Monemvasia 21074
Monestir de Cura, Randa 35308
Money Museum, Kingston 26073
Money Museum, Teheran 22314
Mongolian National Modern Art Gallery, Ulaanbaatar 28678
Mongolian Theatre Museum, Ulaanbaatar 28679
The Monhegan Museum, Monhegan 45432
Mõniste Muuseum, Kuutsi 09337
Monks' Dormitory Museum, Durham 38827
Monkwearmouth Station Museum, Sunderland 40644
Monmouth County Historical Museum, Freehold 43547
Monmouth Museum, Lincroft 44801
Monocacy National Battlefield, Frederick 43528
Monroe County Heritage Museum, Monroeville 45447
Monroe County Historical Museum, Monroe 45443
Monroe County Historical Society, Bloomington 41747
Monroe County Local History Room and Library, Sparta 47714
Monroe Historical Society Museum, Monroe 45438
Mons Breidvik Galleries, Norheimsund 30713
Møns Museum, Stege 09079
Monsignor Hawes Priest House Museum, Mullewa 01286
Monsignor Yatco Ecclesiastical Museum, Batangas 31287
Mont De Lancey Historical Museum, Wandin 01575
Mont Orgueil Castle, Gorey 39097
Montafoner Heimatmuseum Schruns, Schruns 02641
Montafoner Tourismusmuseum Gaschurn, Gaschurn 01872
Montagu Museum, Montagu 34310
Montague Museum, Montague 45448
Montalvo Center for the Arts, Saratoga 47457
Montana Auto Museum, Deer Lodge 42846
Montana Historical Society Museum, Helena 43984
Montanmuseum, Gußwerk 01975
Montanmuseum, Hieflau 02028
Montauk, Clermont 42459
Montauk Point Lighthouse Museum, Montauk 45449
Montclair Art Museum, Montclair 45450
Montclair Historical Society Museum, Montclair 45451
Montclair State University Art Galleries, Upper Montclair 48159
Monte L. Bean Life Science Museum, Provo 46735
Monterey History and Art Association Museum, Monterey 45455
Monterey Museum of Art, Monterey 45456
Monterey State Historic Park, Monterey 45457
Monteverdi Car Collection, Binningen 36568
Montfort-Museum, Tettnang 20164
Montgomery County Historical Society Center, Dayton 42803
Montgomery County Historical Society Museum, Rockville 46977
Montgomery Museum and Lewis Miller Regional Art Center, Christiansburg 42391
Montgomery Museum of Fine Arts, Montgomery 45467
Montgomery's Inn, Etobicoke 05418
Monticello, Home of Thomas Jefferson, Charlottesville 42249
Monticello Railway Museum, Monticello 45472
Montpelier Cultur Arts Center, Laurel 44677
Montpellier Mansion, Laurel 44678
Montréal Museum of Fine Arts, Montréal 05918
Montrose Air Station Museum, Montrose 39982
Montrose County Historical Museum, Montrose 45482
Montrose Museum and Art Gallery, Montrose 39983
Montshire Museum of Science, Norwich 46041
Montville Township Historical Museum, Montville 45485
Monumen Nasional, Jakarta 22108
Monument Lefebvre, Memramcook 05840
Monument of Života'e's Tragedy, Havířov 08346
Monumental Complex of the Prizren Albanian League, Prizren 33897
Monumenti Antichi, Medioevali e Moderni, Roma 25171
Monumenti Musei e Gallerie Pontificie, Città del Vaticano 48872
Monumento a Cristo Rey, Belalcázar 07379
Monumento Arqueológico de Chavín, Huari 31176
Moody County Museum, Flandreau 43334
Moody Mansion Museum, Galveston 43613
Sree Moolam Shastyabdapurti Memorial Institute, Thiruvananthapuram 22036
Moominvallay Collection of Tampere Art Museum, Tampere 10093
Moonah Arts Centre, Moonah 01266
Moonta Mines Museum, Moonta 01267
Moonta National Trust Museum, Moonta 01268
Moor- und Fehnmuseum, Barßel 15827
Moorabbin Air Museum, Cheltenham 00908
Moorabbin Air Museum, Moorabbin 01270
Moore County Historical Museum, Dumas 43005
Moore Home, Lerna 44718
Moore Museum, Mooretown 05932
Mooreichensammlung Johann Weber, Göppingen 17320
Moores Creek National Battlefield, Currie 42732
Moormuseum Moordorf, Südbrookmerland 20119
Mooroopna Hospital, Mooroopna 01271
Moose Factory Centennial Museum, Kirkland Lake 05693
Moose Jaw Museum and Art Gallery, Moose Jaw 05934
Moosehorn Heritage Museum, Moosehorn 05936
Mór Wosinsky County Museum, Szekszárd 21565
Móra Ferenc Emlékház, Kiskunfélegyháza 21458
Móra Ferenc Múzeum, Szeged 21551
Moran Open-air Museum, Namyangju 27216
Morat-Institut für Kunst und Kunstwissenschaft, Freiburg im Breisgau 17112
Moravian Gallery Brno, Brno 08271
Moravian Gallery Brno, Brno 08270
Moravian Museum, Pudsey 40272
Moravian Museum of Bethlehem, Bethlehem 41668
Moravian Museum - The House of the Lords of Kunštát, Brno 08265
Moravská Galerie Brno - Místodrzitelsky Palác, Brno 08270
Moravská Galerie Brno - Pražákův Palác, Brno 08271
Moravské Zemské Muzeum, Brno 08272
Morawa Old Police Station Museum, Morawa 01272
Mordecai Historic Park, Raleigh 46774
Morden and District Museum, Morden 05939
Mordialloc Historical Society Museum, Mentone 01245
Mordovian Museum of Fine Arts, Saransk 33496
Mordovskij Muzej Izobrazitelnych Isskustv im. S.D. Ėrzi, Saransk 33496
Mordovskij Respublikanskij Kraevedčeskij Muzej, Saransk 33497
Moree Plains Gallery, Moree 01273
Moreton's Harbour Museum, Moreton's Harbour 05941
Morgan Row Museum, Harrodsburg 43932
Mori Art Museum, Tokyo 26893
Mori Bijitsukan, Tokyo 26893
Mori Hokokai Hakubutsukan, Hofu 26228
Mori Museum, Hofu 26228
Moriarty Historical Museum, Moriarty 45501
Morija Museum, Morija 27496
The Morikami Museum and Japanese Gardens, Delray Beach 42864
Morioka City Local Hall, Morioka 26517
Morioka Hashimoto Museum of Art, Morioka 26518
Morishita Art Museum, Hinase 26197
Morishita Bijutsukan, Hinase 26197
Morlan Gallery, Lexington 44744
Morley Gallery, London 39711
Mormon Visitors Center, Independence 44206
Morningside Nature Center, Gainesville 43583
Mornington Peninsula Arts Centre, Mornington 01276
Morphett's Enginehouse Museum, Burra 00866
Morrin Museum, Morrinsville 30204
Morris and District Centennial Museum, Morris 05943
Morris and Helen Belkin Art Gallery, Vancouver 06682
Morris Belknap Gallery, Dario Covi Gallery and SAL Gallery, Louisville 44973
Morris-Butler House Museum, Indianapolis 44231
Morris Graves Museum of Art, Eureka 43231
Morris-Jumel Mansion, New York 45835
The Morris Museum, Morristown 45508
Morris Museum of Art, Augusta 41386
Morrison Museum of the Country School, Islay 05629
Morristown National Historical Park, Morristown 45509
Morro Bay State Park Museum of Natural History, Morro Bay 45515
Morrow Mountain State Park Museum, Albemarle 41092
Morse Museum, Morse 05945
Morskoj Muzej, Petrozavodsk 33317
Morskoj Muzej-Akvarium, Vladivostok 33702
Morslands Historiske Museum, Nykøbing Mors 09000
Morton Grove Historical Museum, Morton Grove 45516
Morton Homestead, Prospect Park 46711
Morton House Museum, Benton Harbor 41633
Morton J. May Foundation Gallery, Saint Louis 47129
Morton Museum of Cooke County, Gainesville 43590
Morven Historical Museum, Morven 01278
Morven Park Museum, Leesburg 44711
Morwellham Quay Historic Port & Copper Mine, Tavistock 40680
Mosaic Gallery, Amman 27058
Mosaïque Gallo-Romaine, Amou 10329
Moschakeion, Moschato 21075
Moscow Archaeology Museum, Moskva 33091
Moscow Art Academic Theatre Museum, Moskva 33135
Moscow House of Photography, Moskva 33086
Moscow Kremlin State Museum-Preserve of History and Culture, Moskva 33056
Moscow Museum-Estate Ostankino, Moskva 33090
Moscow State Esenin Museum, Moskva 33087
Moscow State Museum of Naive Art, Moskva 33058
Moser Glass Museum, Karlovy Vary 08402
Moses Lake Museum and Art Center, Moses Lake 45520
Moses Myers House, Norfolk 45968
Moskovskaja Gosudarstvennaja Kartinnaja Galereja A. Šilova, Moskva 33085
Moskovskij Dom Fotografii, Moskva 33086
Moskovskij Gosudarstvennyj Muzej S.A. Esenina, Moskva 33087

Moskovskij Gosudarstvennyj Vystavočnyj Zal Malyi Manež, Moskva 33088
Moskovskij Literaturnyj Muzej-Centr K.G. Paustovskogo, Moskva 33089
Moskovskij Muzej-usad'ba Ostankino, Moskva 33090
Moskvitch Factory Museum, Moskva 33159
Moss Mansion Museum, Billings 41688
Moss-Thorns Gallery of Arts, Hays 43970
Mossbank and District Museum, Mossbank 05946
Mosses Pottery, Bennettsbridge 22376
Mostmuseum, Neumarkt im Mühlkreis 02351
Mostmuseum, Sankt Leonhard am Forst 02580
Mostmuseum und Heimathaus, Sankt Marienkirchen an der Polsenz 02583
Mostra Archeologica G. Venturini, San Felice sul Panaro 25357
Mostra Cabriniana, Codogno 23604
Mostra Cartografica, Mendatica 24347
Mostra Culturale di Apicoltura, Porto Marghera 25013
Mostra degli Antichi Mestieri di Calabria, Tropea 25839
Mostra dei Pupi Siciliani, Caltagirone 23271
Mostra della Civiltà Contadina, Lavello 24163
Mostra della Civiltà Contadina, Massa Marittima 24320
Mostra della Civiltà Contadina e Pastorale, Avezzano 22992
Mostra della Giudaica e Raccolta di Minerali, Laino Borgo 24128
Mostra di Cimeli del Risorgimento, Salemi 25315
Mostra di Palazzo Farnese, Piacenza 24889
Mostra Etnografica Museo Contadino della Piana, Capannori 23323
Mostra Mineraria Permanente, Sutri 25659
Mostra Nazionale di Pittura Contemporanea, Marsala 24304
Mostra Permanenta P. Mariani, Bordighera 23163
Mostra Permanente del Costume Arbereshe, Vaccarizzo Albanese 25864
Mostra Permanente del Presepio, Muggia 24568
Mostra Permanente della Biblioteca Estense, Modena 24435
Mostra Permanente della Ceramica, San Lorenzello 25382
Mostra Permanente della Civiltà Contadina, Montefoscoli 24528
Mostra Permanente della Cultura Materiale, Levanto 24182
Mostra Permanente della Resistenza, Lugo 24239
Mostra Permanente della Resistenzo, Massa Marittima 24321
Mostra Permanente della Tradizione Mineraria, Tarvisio 25675
Mostra Permanente di Paleontologia, Terni 25694
Mostra Permanente di Xilografie di Pietro Parigi, Firenze 23849
Mostra Permanente Le Carrozze d'Epoca, Roma 25172
Mostviertelmuseum Haag, Haag, Niederösterreich 01982
Mostviertler Bauernmuseum, Amstetten 01669
Mosul Museum, Mosul 22351
Mosvik Museum, Mosvik 30695
Motala Museum, Motala 36106
Motherwell Heritage Centre, Motherwell 39988
Motherwell Homestead, Abernethy 04966
Moto Moto Museum, Mbala 49023
Motoori Norinaga Memorial Hall, Matsusaka 26480
Motor Car Museum of Japan, Futatsunashi 26155
Motor Museum, Filching 38989
Motor Museum, Ramsgate 40282
Motor-Sport-Museum Hockenheimring, Hockenheim 17775
The Motorboat Museum, Basildon 38099
Motorcycle Hall of Fame Museum, Pickerington 46482
Motorcycle Haven, Adelaide River 00719
Motormuseet, Strømmen 30903
Motorola Museum, Schaumburg 47495
Motorrad-Museum, Augustusburg 15572
Motorrad Museum, Ibbenbüren 17874
Motorrad-Museum Krems-Egelsee, Krems 02159
Motorrad-Veteranen- und Technikmuseum, Großschönau, Sachsen 17441
Motorradmuseum, Gossau (Sankt Gallen) 36771
Motorradmuseum, Michelstadt 18730
Motorradmuseum, Neunkirchen, Niederösterreich 02355
Motorradmuseum, Sulz 02709
Motown Historical Museum, Detroit 42933
Motsu-ji Storage House, Hiraizumi 26204
Motts Military Museum, Groveport 43848
Motueka District Museum, Motueka 30205
Moudy Exhibition Hall, Fort Worth 43490
Mouhtar Ashrafi Museum, Taškent 48856
Moulagensammlung des Universitätsspitals und der Universität Zürich, Zürich 37391
Mouldsworth Motor Museum, Mouldsworth 39990
Moulin à Huile, Opio 13408
Moulin à Mer de Traou-Meur-Écomusée, Pleudaniel 13754
Moulin à Musique Mécanique, Mormoiron 13165
Le Moulin à Papier de Brousses, Brousses-et-Villaret 10941
Moulin à Papier Vallis-Clausa, Fontaine-de-Vaucluse 11757
Moulin à Vent de 1802, Boeschepe 10782
Moulin à Vent Gaillardin, Chapelon 11168
Moulin-Bateau La Sainte-Catherine, Cahors 10995
Moulin de Beaumont, Beaumont 05065
Moulin de la Croix, Saint-Thomas-de-Conac 14487
Moulin Doisy, Denain 11493
Moulin Fleming, LaSalle 05729
Moulin Légaré, Saint-Eustache 06315
Moulin Maître Marcel, Sainte-Agathe-en-Donzy 14514
Moulin-Musée de la Brosserie, Saint-Félix 14213
Moulin-Musée de La Roche, La Possonnière 12220
Moulin-Musée de Vauboyen, Bièvres 10732
Moulin-Musée Le Rotrou, Vaas 15036
Les Moulins, Sagy 14085
Moulins à Huile, Gordes 11885
Moulins Souterrains du Col-des-Roches, Le Locle 36888
Moundbuilders State Memorial and Museum, Newark 45895
Mount Airy Museum of Regional History, Mount Airy 45523
Mount Bruce Pioneer Museum, Masterton 30198
Mount Clare Museum House, Baltimore 41481
Mount Desert Island Historical Museum, Somesville 47674
Mount Dora Center for the Arts, Mount Dora 45529
Mount Edgcumbe House, Cremyll 38664
Mount Holyoke College Art Museum, South Hadley 47693
Mount Horaiji Natural History Museum, Hourai 26233
Mount Ikoma Space Science Museum, Ikoma 26241
Mount Laura Homestead Museum, Whyalla Norrie 01598
Mount Mary College Costume Museum, Milwaukee 45370
Mount Morgan Historical Museum, Mount Morgan 01283
Mount Pleasant, Philadelphia 46428
Mount Pleasant Historical Society Museum, Mount Pleasant 45538
Mount Prospect Historical Society Museums, Mount Prospect 45541
Mount Pulaski Courthouse, Mount Pulaski 45542
Mount Royal College Gallery, Calgary 05172
Mount Rushmore National Memorial, Keystone 44476
Mount Saint Vincent University Art Gallery, Halifax 05557
Mount Stewart House, Newtownards 40074
Mount Vernon Hotel Museum, New York 45836
Mount Vernon Museum of Incandescent Lighting, Baltimore 41482
Mount Victoria and District Historical Museum, Mount Victoria 01284
Mount Wachusett Community College Art Galleries, Gardner 43624
Mount Washington Museum, North Conway 45989
Mountain Farm Museum, Cherokee 42275
Mountain Gateway Museum, Old Fort 46132
Mountain Heritage Center, Cullowhee 42723
Mountain Life Museum, London 44853
Mountain Mills Museum, Saint Catharines 06309
Mountain-Plains Museums Association, Durango 49510
Mountain Resort Museum, Chengde 07018
Mountain View Doukhobor Museum, Grand Forks 05515
Mountain View Gallery, Port Moody 06166
Mountain View Museum, Olds 06049
Mountaineering Museum, Darjeeling 21756
Mountbatten Exhibition, Romsey 40340
Mounted Branch Museum, East Molesey 38849
Mountfitchet Castle and Norman Village, Stansted Mountfitchet 40579
Mouseio Akropoleos, Athinai 20871
Mouseio Ellinikis Laïkis Technis, Athinai 20872
Mouseio Ethnikon Archaiologikon, Athinai 20873
Mouseio Isrorias tis Ellinikis Endymasias, Athinai 20874
Mouseio Istorias Laografias Aharnon, Athinai 20875
Mouseio Kerameikos, Athinai 20876
Mouseio Kompologiou, Nafplion 21091
Mouseio Laikon Organon, Athinai 20877
Mouseio Mpenaki, Athinai 20878
Mouseio Trenon, Athinai 20879
Mouseio Vorre, Paiania 21104
Mouseion Goulandri Fysikis Istorias, Kifissia 21015
Mousley Museum of Natural History, Yucaipa 48815
Moussa Castle Museum, Beiteddine 27486
The Movie Museum, Owosso 46234
Movieland Wax Museum of the Stars, Niagara Falls 05994
Moviemento-Art-Galerie, Linz 02237
Moyse's Hall Museum, Bury Saint Edmunds 38417
Mozart Figarohaus, Wien 02932
Mozart-Gedenkstätte im Bezirksgericht, Sankt Gilgen 02570
Mozart Wohnhaus, Salzburg 02543
Mozarthaus, Augsburg 15562
Mozarts Geburtshaus, Salzburg 02544
Mozimúzeum, Kaposvár 21440
MPG Town Gallery, Odiongan 31408
MPR International Committee for Museums Marketing and PR, Malmö 49381
Mramornyj Dvorec, Sankt-Peterburg 33423
Mrštík Brothers Memorial House, Diváky 08327
M.S. Spiridonov Memorial Museum-Apartment, Čeboksary 32721
M.S. Tuganov Museum of Fine Art, Vladikavkaz 33686
MSC Forsyth Center Galleries, College Station 42527
Mtengatenga Postal Museum, Namaka 27614
Much Wenlock Museum, Much Wenlock 39993
The Muchnic Gallery, Atchison 41316
Muckenthaler Cultural Center Gallery, Fullerton 43574
Muckleburgh Collection, Weybourne 40839
Muckross House Gardens and Traditional Farms, Killarney 22491
Műcsarnok, Budapest 21365
Mudac-Musée de Design et d'Arts Appliqués Contemporains, Lausanne 36856
Mudanya Armistice Museum, Mudanya 37762
Mudanya Mutareke Evi Müzesi, Mudanya 37762
Mudgee Colonial Inn Museum, Mudgee 01285
Die Mühle, Eberswalde 16770
Mühle Oberneuland, Bremen 16329
Mühlen- und Landwirtschaftsmuseum, Jever 17956
Mühlen- und Landwirtschaftsmuseum, Westfehmarn 20543
Das Mühlendorf, Ottenhöfen 19321
Mühlenfachmuseum, Aurich 15579
Mühlenhof-Freilichtmuseum Münster, Münster 18942
Mühlenmuseum, Pfullingen 19393
Mühlenmuseum, Sontra 20002
Mühlenmuseum, Woldegk 20646
Mühlenmuseum Brüglingen, Münchenstein 36965
Mühlenmuseum Haren (Ems), Haren 17618
Mühlenmuseum Katzbrui, Apfeltrach 15506
Mühlenmuseum Mitling-Mark mit Sammlung Omas Küche, Westoverledingen 20544
Mühlerama, Zürich 37392
Mühlviertler Keramikwerkstätte Hafnerhaus, Leopoldschlag 02216
Mühlviertler Kulturgütermuseum, Sankt Johann am Wimberg 02574
Mühlviertler Schlossmuseum Freistadt, Freistadt, Oberösterreich 01851
Mühlviertler Vogelkundeweg, Gutau 01977
Mühlviertler Waldhaus, Windhaag bei Freistadt 03038
Mülheimer Kunstverein e.V., Mülheim an der Ruhr 49203
Muenchausen's Museum, Dunte 27353
Münchhausen-Museum, Bodenwerder 16209
Münchner Feuerwehrmuseum, München 18878
Münchner Puppenmuseum, München 18879
Münchner Stadtmuseum, München 18880
Münchner Tiermuseum, München 18881
Münter-Haus, Murnau 18961
Münzensammlung, Graz 01925
Münzkabinett, Berlin 16044
Münzkabinett, Dresden 16698
Münzkabinett, Sankt Veit an der Glan 02612
Münzkabinett der Preussag AG, Hannover 17605
Münzkabinett im Stadtarchiv Mainz, Mainz 18603
Münzkabinett und Antikensammlung der Stadt Winterthur, Winterthur 37332
Münzkabinett und Archäologische Lehrsammlung der Universität Rostock, Rostock 19666
Münzprägestätte - Alte Münze, Hall in Tirol 01993
Müritz-Museum, Waren 20399
Muestra Arqueológica, Armenia 07370
Muestra Arqueológica, Montenegro 07529
Muestra Arqueológica, Quimbaya 07573
Muestra Arqueológica Colección Rosmary, Colosó 07465
Muestrario Arqueológico de Amazonas, Chachapoyas 31141
Mughal Museum, Lahore 31039
Muğla Culture Center, Muğla 37764
Muğla Devlet Güzel Sanatlar Galerisi, Muğla 37763
Muğla Kültür Merkezi, Muğla 37764
Muğla State Gallery, Muğla 37763
Muhoksen Kotiseutumuseo, Muhos 09838
Muiderslot, Muiden 29604
Mukaishima Marine Biological Station, Mukaishima 26519
Mukhtar Museum, Cairo 09271
Mukti Juddha Museum, Dhaka 03091
Mulberry Phospate Museum, Mulberry 45552
Mulford House and Farm, East Hampton 43048
Mulgi Külamuuseum, Halliste 09320
Mulgrave Settlers Museum, Gordonvale 01066
Mull Museum, Tobermory 40713
Mullach Ban Folk Museum, Mullach Ban 39994
Mullingar Military Museum, Mullingar 22525
Multatuli Museum, Amsterdam 28874
Multi Colour Museum, Middelburg 29593
Multian Kotiseutumuseo, Multia 09839
Multicultural Heritage Centre, Stony Plain 06494
Mulvane Art Museum, Topeka 48034
Munakata Prints Museum, Kamakura 26296
Munakata Shiko Kinenkan, Aomori 26100
Munakata Taisha Shinpōkan, Genkai 26156
Muncaster Castle, Ravenglass 40285
Muncaster Watermill, Ravenglass 40286
Munce Art Center, Zionsville 48824
Munch-museet, Oslo 30743
Munch's house, Åsgårdstrand 30398
Munchs Hus, Åsgårdstrand 30398
Muncie Children's Museum, Muncie 45557
El Mundode Muñecas, Icod de los Vinos 34912
Mundubbera and District Historical Museum, Mundubbera 01289
Mundulla National Trust Museum, Bordertown 00816
Municipal and Open Air Museum, Reykjavík 21648
Municipal Archaeological Museum, Mojokerto 22161
Municipal Archaeological Museum, Sandanski 04809
Municipal Archeological Museum, Chisar 04642
Municipal Art Gallery, Thessaloniki 21187
Municipal Art Gallery of Xanthi, Xanthi 21219
Municipal Art Society, New York 45837
Municipal d'Arts Plastiques, Choisy-le-Roi 11295
Municipal Gallery, Orosháza 21495
Municipal Gallery, Székesfehérvár 21562
Municipal Gallery of Athens, Athinai 20880
Municipal Gallery of Corfu, Corfu 20931
Municipal Gallery of Herakleion, Iráklion 20977
Municipal Gallery of Lamia, Lamia 21040
Municipal Gallery of Livadia, Livadia 21053
Municipal Gallery of Piraeus, Piraeus 21122
Municipal Gallery of Rhodes, Rhodos 21143
Municipal Gallery of Samos, Samos 21148
Municipal Gallery of Volos, Volos 21213
Municipal Historical Museum, Asenovgrad 04604
Municipal Historical Museum, Balčik 04611
Municipal Historical Museum, Belogradčik 04617
Municipal Historical Museum, Dalgopol 04647
Municipal Historical Museum, Jeravna 04683
Municipal Historical Museum, Karlovo 04690
Municipal Historical Museum, Karnobat 04692
Municipal Historical Museum, Kavarna 04696
Municipal Historical Museum, Klisura 04711
Municipal Historical Museum, Lom 04726
Municipal Historical Museum, Melnik 04734
Municipal Historical Museum, Orjachovo 04749
Municipal Historical Museum, Panagjurište 04750
Municipal Historical Museum, Peruštica 04760
Municipal Historical Museum, Samakov 04808
Municipal Historical Museum, Sevlievo 04811
Municipal Historical Museum, Sozopol 04864
Municipal Historical Museum, Teteven 04884
Municipal History Museum, Botevgrad 04627
Municipal History Museum, Čirpan 04645
Municipal History Museum, Etropole 04664
Municipal History Museum, Kazanlăk 04700
Municipal History Museum, Nova Zagora 04744
Municipal Museum, Alexandria 09242
Municipal Museum, Baoji 06939
Municipal Museum, Chojnów 31530
Municipal Museum, Chotěboř 08315
Municipal Museum, Dimona 22586
Municipal Museum, Foča 33838
Municipal Museum, Jiuquan 07141
Municipal Museum, Kőszeg 21466
Municipal Museum, Letohrad 08447
Municipal Museum, Sremski Karlovci 33915
Municipal Museum, Subotica 33918
Municipal Museum, Žamberk 08737
Municipal Museum and Gallery, Bečej 33791
Municipal Museum and Gallery Breclav, Břeclav 08259
Municipal Museum Gwalior, Gwalior 21830
Municipal Museum of Amsterdam, Amsterdam 28902
Municipal Museum of Guantanamo - Old Prison, Guantánamo 07918
Municipal Museum of Kavala, Kavala 21012
Municipal Museum of Železný Brod, Železný Brod 08747
Municipal Museum Roermond, Roermond 29743
Municipal Picture Gallery, Budapest 21338
Municipality Museum, Hebron 31067
Municipalnaja Chudožestvennaja Galereja g. Kostromy, Kostroma 32944
Municipalnyj Objedinennyj Muzej Pisatelej Urala, Ekaterinburg 32773
Municipialnyj Muzej Anna Achmatova - Serebrjannyj vek, Sankt-Peterburg 33424
Munkácsy Mihály Múzeum, Békéscsaba 21319
Munnuisten Museo, Mynämäki 09850
Munsala Hembygdsmuseum, Munsala 09842
Munsin Museum, Masan 27210
Munson-Williams-Proctor Arts Institute Museum of Art, Utica 48170
Munster Literature Centre, Cork 22404
Munt- en Penningkabinet van de Provincie Limburg, Tongeren 03782
Munt- en Penningkabinet van de Spaar- en Voorschotbank, Surhuisterveen 29860
Munting Museo Ng Namayan, Mandaluyong 31365
Muonion Kotiseutumuseo, Muonio 09843
Murakami Folk Museum, Murakami 26521
Murauchi Art Museum, Hachioji 26165
Murchison Falls National Park Museum, Murchison Falls 37832
Murchison Museum, Murchison 30206
Murchison Settlement Museum, Mullewa 01287
Mures District Art Museum, Tårgu Mureş 32609
Mures District Museum of Ethnography and Folk Art, Tårgu Mureş 32610
Mures District Museum of Natural History, Tårgu Mureş 32611
Murgtal-Museum, Forbach 17018
Murie Museum, Kelly 44429
Murilla Shire Art Gallery, Miles 01255
Murmansk Regional Art Museum, Murmansk 33188
Murmansk Regional Museum, Murmansk 33189
Murmanskij Oblastnoj Chudožestvennyj Muzej, Murmansk 33188
Murmanskij Oblastnoj Kraevedčeskij Muzej, Murmansk 33189
Murney Tower Museum, Kingston 05684
Muroran-shi Seishonen Kagakukan, Muroran 26522
Muroran Youth Science Museum, Muroran 26522
Murray-Lindsay Mansion, Lindsay 44805
Murray's Motorcycle Museum, Laxey 39433
Murray's Museum of History, Neepawa 05968
Murrell Home, Park Hill 46290
Murrell Home, Tahlequah 47926
Murrumburrah-Harden Historical Museum, Murrumburrah 01291
Murrurundi Museum, Murrurundi 01292

Murtoa Water Tower - Concordia Collage Museum, Murtoa 01293
Murtovaara Farmhouse, Valtimo 10175
Murtovaaran Talomuseo, Valtimo 10175
Musa Dshalil Museum-Appartment, Kazan 32902
Músaem Cathrach Na Gaillimhe, Galway 22474
Músaem Corca Dhuibhne, Ballyferriter 22370
Musafir-Khana, Cairo 09272
Musashimurayama City Rekishi Minzoku Shiryo-kan, Musashimurayama 26523
Musashino Museum, Kodaira 26359
Muscarelle Museum of Art, Williamsburg 48630
Muscat Gate Museum, Muscat 31004
Muscatine Art Center, Muscatine 45575
Muschel- und Schneckenmuseum, Norden 19112
Muschelkalkmuseum Hagdorn, Ingelfingen 17898
Muse Art Gallery, Philadelphia 46429
Museactron, Maaseik 03602
Museal Complex of Natural Sciences, Bacău 32432
Museam na Oileran, Aran Islands 22360
Musée, Hautvillers 12005
Musée, Kampong Thom 04948
Musée, Le Landeron 36844
Musée, Moyen 13203
Musée, Quiberon 13892
Musée 1900, Arpaillargues-et-Aureillac 10423
Musée 2ème Guerre Mondiale, Ambleteuse 10306
Musée 39-45, Roscoff 14033
Musée 40-44, Monceau-Imbrechies 03631
Musée à Flot, Bordeaux 10806
Musée à Flot, Cherbourg 11275
Musée à Flot de l'Escorteur d'Escadre, Nantes 13250
Musée à Flot du Galion, Plouharnel 13777
Musée à la Ferme de Rome, Bézu-la-Forêt 10723
Musée à la Mémoire des Combattants et de Victimes de Guerre, Mâcon 12756
Musée a la Recherche du Temps Perdu, Bricquebec 10924
Musée À la Rencontre des Vieux Métiers, Bouray-sur-Juine 10842
Musée Abbaye d'Airvault, Airvault 10247
Musée-Abbaye de Charroux, Charroux 11190
Musée-Abbaye Saint-Germain, Auxerre 10509
Musée Abbé Deletoille, Fruges 11824
Musée Abbé-Jules-Lemire, Vieux-Berquin 15166
Musée-Académie, Beaumes-de-Venise 10642
Le Musée Acadien, Caraquet 05198
Musée Acadien, Cheticamp 05244
Musée Acadien, Gloucester 05496
Musée Acadien, Miscouche 05864
Musée Acadien, Moncton 05880
Musée Acadien de Pubnico-Ouest, West Pubnico 06772
Musée Acadien du Québec, Bonaventure 05092
Musée Accous-Fermiers Basco-Béarnais, Accous 10227
Musée Adam Mickiewicz, Paris 13528
Musée Adolphe Hardy, Dison 03393
Musée Adolphe-Pégoud, Montferrat 13082
Musée Adrien-Mentienne, Bry-sur-Marne 10952
Musée Adzak, Paris 13529
Musée Aéronautique, La Baule-Escoublac 12125
Musée Aérorétro, Albon 10277
Musée Africain, Ile-d'Aix 12044
Musée Africain, Lyon 12727
Musée Africain de Namur, Namur 03644
Musée Agathois, Agde 10228
Musée Agricole, Coffrane 36639
Musée Agricole, Villy-le-Maréchal 15260
Musée Agricole Bras de Brosne, Marles-sur-Canche 12826
Musée Agricole de la Haute Hesbaye, Liernu 03589
Musée Agricole Départemental Marcel-Mouilleseaux, Botans 10826
Musée Agricole des Ruralies, Prahecq 13863
Musée Agricole du Château de Didonne, Semussac 14704
Musée Agricole du Verdus, Freyssenet 11820
Musée Agricole et Viticole, Richelieu 13961
Musée Agricole-Ferme des Aïeux, Plélo 13753
Musée Agricole Paysan, Vallon-Pont-d'Arc 15067
Musée Agricole Vivant, Bissey-la-Pierre 10746
Musée Agro-Pastoral d'Aussois, Aussois 10495
Musée Airborne, Sainte-Mère-Eglise 14548
Musée Al Mathaf El Lubnani, Beiteddine 27487
Musée Alain-Fournier et Jacques-Rivière, La Chapelle-d'Angillon 12144
Musée Albert André, Bagnols-sur-Cèze 10565
Musée Albert Schweitzer, Gunsbach Village 11981
Musée Albert Schweitzer, Kaysersberg 12111
Musée Alésia, Alise-Sainte-Reine 10290
Musée Alexandre Dumas, Villers-Cotterêts 15242
Musée Alexandre-Louis Martin, Carnières 03346
Musée Alexis Forel, Morges 36950
Musée Alfred Bonnot, Chelles 11266
Musée Alice Taverne, Ambierle 10305
Musée Alphonse Daudet, Fontvieille 11783
Musée Alphonse-Daudet, Saint-Alban-Auriolles 14091
Musée Alpin, Chamonix-Mont-Blanc 11148
Musée Alpin d'Anzère, Anzère 36460
Musée Alsacien, Haguenau 11985
Musée Alsacien, Strasbourg 14817
Musée America-Gold Beach, Ver-sur-Mer 15125
Musée Amora, Dijon 11521
Musée Amphoralis, Sallèles-d'Aude 14576
Musée Anatole-Le-Braz, Saint-Brieuc 14131
Musée André Abbal, Carbonne 11039
Musée André-Dhôtel, Attigny 10451
Musée André Dunoyer-de-Ségonzac, Boussy-Saint-Antoine 10877
Musée André-Marie-Ampère, Poleymieux-au-Mont-d'Or 13788
Musée Angladon, Avignon 10527
Musée Animalier, Ville-sous-Anjou 15185
Musée Animé des Arts et Traditions Populaires, Serralongue 14722
Musée Animé du Tissage, Arles-sur-Tech 10419
Musée Animé du Vin et de la Tonnellerie, Chinon 11288
Musée Anne de Beaujeu, Moulins (Allier) 13185
Musée Annexe de Youkounkoun, Youkounkoun 21287
Musée Antoine Brun, Sainte-Consorce 14525
Musée Antoine Lécuyer, Saint-Quentin (Aisne) 14434
Musée Antoine Vivenel, Compiègne 11375
Musée Antoine Wiertz, Bruxelles 03290
Musée Août-1944, Falaise 11701
Musée Apicole, Le Mesnil-sous-Jumièges 12447
Musée Apicole, Nedde 13278
Musée-Aquariophile, Dunkerque 11584
Musée-Aquarium du Laboratoire Arago, Banyuls-sur-Mer 10580
Musée-Aquarium Marin du Roc, Granville 11909
Musée Archéologique, Aigues-Mortes 10236
Musée Archéologique, Andilly-en-Bassigny 10336
Musée Archéologique, Auzances 10515
Musée Archeologique, Azé 10552
Musée Archéologique, Bagnols-en-Forêt 10564
Musée Archéologique, Banassac 10575
Musée Archéologique, Bezouce 10722
Musée Archéologique, Bray-sur-Seine 10897
Musée Archéologique, Brignon 10932
Musée Archéologique, Brumath 10946
Musée Archéologique, Champagnole 11153
Musée Archéologique, Charleroi 03349
Musée Archéologique, Châteaurenard (Loiret) 11225
Musée Archéologique, Châtelais 11229
Musée Archéologique, Chirac 11292
Musée Archéologique, Corseul 11414
Musée Archéologique, Couffy 11422
Musée Archéologique, Cutry 11478
Musée Archéologique, Delme 11492
Musée Archéologique, Dijon 11522
Musée Archéologique, Eauze 11593
Musée Archéologique, Eloyes 11611
Musée Archéologique, Ensisheim 11614
Musée Archéologique, Entrains-sur-Nohain 11617
Musée Archéologique, Escolives-Sainte-Camille 11644
Musée Archéologique, Ferrière-Poussarou 11721
Musée Archéologique, Fontaine-Française 11764
Musée Archéologique, Gafsa 37561
Musée Archéologique, Gouzeaucourt 11894
Musée Archéologique, Jonzac 12088
Musée Archéologique, Jujurieux 12102
Musée Archéologique, Kassba 28696
Musée Archéologique, La Villeneuve-au-Châtelot 12273
Musée Archeologique, L'Aigle 12302
Musée Archéologique, Laissac 12306
Musée Archéologique, Larache 28697
Musée Archéologique, Le Bouchon-sur-Saulx 12383
Musée Archéologique, Le Thoureil 12485
Musée Archéologique, Lectoure 12503
Musée Archéologique, Loupiac 12681
Musée Archéologique, Magalas 12761
Musée Archéologique, Martizay 12882
Musée Archéologique, Marvejols 12884
Musée Archéologique, Monségur 13022
Musée Archéologique, Montbard 13052
Musée Archéologique, Montseret 13153
Musée Archéologique, Mormoiron 13166
Musée Archéologique, Murol 13222
Musée Archéologique, Nages-et-Solorgues 13233
Musée Archéologique, Namur 03645
Musée Archéologique, Nîmes 13337
Musée Archéologique, Palaja 13455
Musée Archéologique, Panossas 13462
Musée Archéologique, Petit-Bersac 13718
Musée Archéologique, Peyriac-de-Mer 13720
Musée Archéologique, Pithiviers-le-Vieil 13742
Musée Archéologique, Pons 13797
Musée Archéologique, Port-des-Barques 13839
Musée Archéologique, Prades 13859
Musée Archéologique, Prunoy 13883
Musée Archéologique, Quarante 13890
Musée Archéologique, Rabat 28704
Musée Archéologique, Rochefort (Charente-Maritime) 13998
Musée Archéologique, Saint-Bonnet-de-Joux 14125
Musée Archéologique, Saint-Gilles-du-Gard 14252
Musée Archéologique, Saint-Macaire 14334
Musée Archéologique, Saint-Martin-de-Bromes 14348
Musée Archéologique, Saint-Pal-de-Mons 14394
Musée Archéologique, Saint-Paulien 14407
Musée Archéologique, Sainte-Agnès 14515
Musée Archéologique, Sainte-Bazeille 14520
Musée Archéologique, Saintes 14555
Musée Archéologique, Saumane-de-Vaucluse 14641
Musée Archéologique, Saverne 14661
Musée Archéologique, Sceaux-du-Gatinais 14679
Musée Archéologique, Sollières-Sardières 14764
Musée Archéologique, Soulosse-sous-Saint-Élophe 14794
Musée Archéologique, Soyons 14799
Musée Archéologique, Strasbourg 14818
Musée Archéologique, Suippes 14842
Musée Archéologique, Tarare 14858
Musée Archéologique, Tétouan 28714
Musée Archéologique, Therouanne 14882
Musée Archéologique, Vachères 15037
Musée Archéologique, Vaison-la-Romaine 15043
Musée Archéologique, Vienne-en-Val 15162
Musée Archéologique, Villeneuve-d'Ascq 15216
Musée Archéologique Armand Viré, Luzech 12721
Musée Archéologique Blasimon, Blasimon 10763
Musée Archéologique d'Argentomagus, Saint-Marcel (Indre) 14344
Musée Archéologique de Djemila, Sétif 00070
Musée Archéologique de la Basse-Meuse, Oupeye 03681
Musée Archéologique de la Porte du Croux, Nevers 13303
Musée Archéologique de la Région de Breteuil, Breteuil 10915
Musée Archéologique de l'Institut Catholique, Toulouse 14939
Musée Archéologique de l'Université Americaine, Beirut 27481
Musée Archéologique de Makthar, Makthar 37570
Musée Archéologique de Rom-Sainte-Soline, Rom 14011
Musée Archéologique de Sfax, Sfax 37579
Musée Archéologique de Site, Liffol-le-Grand 12586
Musée Archéologique de Thésée-la-Romaine, Thésée-la-Romaine 14883
Musée Archéologique de Touraine, Tours 14969
Musée Archéologique de Viuz-Faverges, Faverges 11707
Musée Archéologique Départemental, Jublains 12099
Musée Archéologique Départemental, Saint-Bertrand-de-Comminges 14124
Musée Archéologique Départemental du Val-d'Oise, Guiry-en-Vexin 11976
Musée Archeologique du Cap Bon, Nabeul 37576
Musée Archéologique du Château Féodal, Bressieux 10904
Musée Archéologique du Gâtinais, Montargis 13043
Musée Archéologique du Théâtre de Guelma, Guelma 00065
Musée Archéologique d'Uxellodunun, Vayrac 15104
Musée Archéologique - Eglise Saint-Laurent, Grenoble 11940
Musée Archéologique en Plein Air, Magnac-Laval 12762
Musée Archéologique et d'Art Populaire, Saint-Goussaud 14256
Musée Archéologique et de Paléontologie, Minerve 12984
Musée Archéologique et d'Histoire Locale, Saint-Emilion 14192
Musée Archéologique et d'Histoire Locale, Saint-Prix 14432
Musée Archéologique et Historique, Clichy 11333
Musée Archéologique et Historique, Loupian 12683
Musée Archéologique et Historique, Proupiary 13877
Musée Archéologique et Historique Cantonal de Gimont, Gimont 11865
Musée Archéologique et Historique de la Vigne, Guebwiller 11962
Musée Archéologique et Historique du Comte de Logne, Vieuxville 03814
Musée Archéologique et Historique Municipal, Ermont 11638
Musée Archéologique et Lapidaire, Aix-les-Bains 10259
Musée Archéologique et Lapidaire, Blois 10771
Musée Archéologique et Minéralogique, Olonzac 13403
Musée Archéologique et Minéralogique, Saint-Antonin-Noble-Val 14111
Musée Archéologique et Missionnaire, Saxon-Sion 14677
Musée Archéologique Forez-Jarez, Saint-Étienne 14197
Musée Archéologique Gallo-Romain, Jonvelle 12086
Musée Archéologique Gallo-Romain, Revel-Tourdan 13955
Musée Archéologique Henri-Prades, Lattes 12353
Musée Archéologique - Hôtel de Sade, Saint-Rémy-de-Provence 14449
Musée Archéologique Hôtel Dieu, Cavaillon 11095
Musée Archéologique Jean Régnier, Mont-Saint-Vincent 13033
Musée Archéologique Le Cloitre, Elne 11608
Musée Archéologique Léon Alègre, Bagnols-sur-Cèze 10566
Musée Archéologique Ludna, Saint-Georges-de-Reneins 14232
Musée Archéologique Mariste de Puylata, Lyon 12728
Musée Archéologique Municipal, Pelissanne 13681
Musée Archéologique Municipal de Fréjus, Fréjus 11809
Musée Archéologique Parat, Arcy-sur-Cure 10399
Musée Archéologique Régional d'Orp-le-Grand, Orp-le-Grand 03675
Musée Archeologique René Galloux, Montrichard 13147
Musée Archéologique Géologique et Ethnologique des Vans, Les Vans 12559
Musée Architectural, Charnat 11186
Musée-Archives de Saint-Pierre, Saint-Pierre 33756
Musée Ardeche d'Autrefois, Thueyts 14905
Musée Ardoisien, Saint-Julien-Mont-Denis 14300
Musée Ariana, Genève 36740
Musée Aristide-Maillol, Banyuls-sur-Mer 10581
Musée Armand Charnay, Charlieu 11180
Musée Arménien de France, Paris 13530
Musée Arouane, Wendake 06769
Musée Art du Chocolat, Lisle-sur-Tarn 12630
Musée Art et Culture, Lescar 12561
Musée Art et Histoire, Penne-d'Agenais 13688
Musée Art Paysan, Villeneuve-de-Berg 15224
Musée Arteum, Châteauneuf-le-Rouge 11219
Musée Arthur Batut, Labruguiere 12288
Musée Arthur Bonnet, Saint-Jean-d'Angély 14272
Musée Arthur-Le-Duc, Torigni-sur-Vire 14919
Musée Arthur Rimbaud, Charleville-Mézières 11177
Musée Artisanal Animé, Les Loges-Marchis 12542
Musée Artisanal et Rural d'Arts, Ars 10433
Musée Arts d'Afrique et d'Asie, Vichy 15160
Musée Arts et Histoire, Bormes-les-Mimosas 10823
Musée-Atelier Calixa-Lavellée, Calixa-Lavallée 05182
Musée Atelier d'Automates, Lusigny-sur-Barse 12713
Musée-Atelier de Fresques, Blain 10752
Musée-Atelier de la Cristallerie des Papes, Fontaine-de-Vaucluse 11758
Musée-Atelier de Poterie, Neuvic-sur-l'Isle 13295
Musée-Atelier de Poupées Francépoque, Nances-Lac d'Aiguebelette 13235
Musée Atelier de Soldats de Plomb, Senonches 14712
Musée-Atelier du Cuivre, Villedieu-les-Poêles 15193
Musée-Atelier du Cuivre et de l'Argent, Paris 13531
Musée-Atelier Werner-Lichtner-Aix, Sérignan-du-Comtat 14718
Musée Atger, Montpellier 13121
Musée Athois, Ath 03188
Musée Au fil du papier, Pont-à-Mousson 13799
Musée Au Filament Rouge, Perrefitte 37019
Musée Aubois d'Histoire de l'Éducation, Troyes 15003
Musée Auguste Rodin, Paris 13532
Musée Augustin-Bernard, Bourbon-l'Archambault 10847
Musée Auto Moto Vélo, Châtellerault 11232
Musée Auto-Retro, Trooz 03801
Musée Automobile, Genève 36741
Musée Automobile, Saint-Germain-Laval 14243
Musée Automobile, Saint-Jacques 06324
Musée Automobile de la Sarthe, Le Mans 12435
Musée Automobile des Voitures des Chéfs d'Etat, Sauvigny-Le-Bois 14659
Musée aux Dominicaines, Pont-l'Évêque 13814
Musée Baccarat, Baccarat 10554
Musée Baccarat, Paris 13533
Musée Baillet-Latour, Latour 03555
Musée Bajén-Vega, Monesties 13011
Musée Balzac, Saché 14082
Musée Bamilike, Dschang 04955
Musée Barbey d'Aurévilly, Saint-Sauveur-le-Vicomte 14469
Musée Barbier-Mueller, Genève 36742
Musée Baron Gérard, Bayeux 10615
Musée Baron Martin, Gray 11933
Musée Baroncelli, Saintes-Maries-de-la-Mer 14562
Musée Barrois, Bar-le-Duc 10583
Musée Barthélemy-Thimonnier de la Machine à Coudre et du Cycle, Amplepuis 10330
Musée Bartholdi, Colmar 11357
Musée-Base V 3 de Mimoyecques, Landrethun-le-Nord 12319
Musée Basque et de l'Histoire de Bayonne, Bayonne 10621
Musée Bastien Lepage, Montmédy 13107
Musée Bastion Saint-André, Antibes 10371
Musée Baud, L'Auberson 36476
Musée Baudy, Giverny 11870
Musée Bayard et de la Chevalerie, Pontcharra 13824
Musée Béarnais, Pau 13665
Musée Beauceron du Grand Breau, Tivernon 14917
Musée Beaulne, Coaticook 05260
Musée Benoist, Le Gavre 12417
Musée Benoît de Puydt, Bailleul 10569
Musée Bernadette, Lourdes 12686
Musée Bernadotte, Pau 13666
Musée Bernard Buffet, Paris 13534
Musée Bernard Buffet, Shizuoka 26765
Musée Bernard d'Agesci, Niort 13343
Musée Bernard Palissy, Lacapelle-Biron 12289
Musée Bert Flint, Agadir 28691
Musée Bert Flint, Marrakech 28698
Musée-Bibliothèque A.-Albert, Briançon 10919
Musée-Bibliothèque de l'Histoire du Protestantisme, Joigny (Yonne) 12082
Musée-Bibliothèque François Pétrarque, Fontaine-de-Vaucluse 11759
Musée-Bibliothèque Humaniste, Sélestat 14698
Musée-Bibliothèque Pierre-André Benoît, Alès 10286
Musée Bigouden, Pont-l'Abbé 13812
Musée Bigourdan du Vieux Moulin, Bagnères-de-Bigorre 10559
Musée Bijoux de Braque, Saint-Dié-des-Vosges 14185
Musée Biochet-Brechot, Caudebec-en-Caux 11087
Musée Boleslaw Biegas, Paris 13535
Musée Bon-Pasteur, Québec 06201
Musée Bonaparte, Auxonne 10513
Musée Bonaventure Fieullien, Regniowez 13922
Musée Bonnat, Bayonne 10622
Musée Bonnevallais, Bonneval 10797
Musée Bossuet, Meaux 12912
Musée Botanique, Conakry 21280
Musée Botanique de Wakombo, M'Baiki 06880
Musée Bouchard, Paris 13536
Musée Boucher-de-Perthes, Abbeville 10222

Musée Bouilhet-Christofle, Paris 13537
Musée Bourbonnais, Moulins (Allier) 13186
Musée Bourbonnais de Vesse à Bellerive, Bellerive-sur-Allier 10674
Musée Bourdelle, Paris 13538
Musée Bourgeon-Jallieu, Bourgoin-Jallieu 10869
Musée Bourguignon Perrin de Puycousin, Tournus 14964
Musée Bourvil, Yvetot 15331
Musée Bres Marcel, Saint-Léger-près-Troyes 14319
Musée Breton, Quimper 13895
Musée Briard et de la Crypte Mérovingienne, Jouarre 12091
Musée Bruno Danvin, Saint-Pol-sur-Ternoise 14422
Musée Bruxellois de la Gueuze, Bruxelles 03291
Musée Bruxellois de l'Industrie et du Travail, Bruxelles 03292
Musée Buffon, Montbard 13053
Musée-Cabinet Lafaille, La Rochelle 12237
Musée Cachot, Lourdes 12687
Musée Calbet, Grisolles 11958
Musée Calvet, Avignon 10528
Musée Calvin, Noyon 13372
Musée Camille Lemonnier, Bruxelles 03293
Musée Campagnard Agricole, Fillières 11735
Musée Campagnard du Haut-Beaujolais, Saint-Christophe-la-Montagne 14151
Musée Campanaire, L'Isle-Jourdain 12627
Musée Campanaire Bollée, Saint-Jean-de-Braye 14276
Musée Campredon, L'Isle-sur-la-Sorgue 12628
Musée Canadien de la Poste, Gatineau 05483
Musée Canadien des Civilisations, Gatineau 05484
Musée Cantini, Marseille 12852
Musée Cantonal d'Archéologie, Sion 37171
Musée Cantonal d'Archéologie et d'Histoire, Lausanne 36857
Musée Cantonal de Géologie, Lausanne 36858
Musée Cantonal de Zoologie, Lausanne 36859
Musée Cantonal des Beaux-Arts, Sion 37172
Musée Cantonal des Beaux-Arts de Lausanne, Lausanne 36860
Musée Cantonal d'Histoire, Sion 37173
Musée Cantonal d'Histoire Militaire, Saint-Maurice 37087
Musée Cantonal d'Histoire Naturelle, Sion 37174
Musée Cappon, Marans 12799
Musée Cappuis-Fähndrich, Develier 36658
Musée Carcéral Souterrain, Villefranche-de-Conflent 15199
Musée Carnavalet - Histoire de Paris, Paris 13539
Musée Casa Catalana de la Cultura, Céret 11108
Musée Casa De Les Alberes, Argelès-sur-Mer 10403
Musée Casimir Delavigne, Pressagny-l'Orgueilleux 13870
Musée Castral, Wintzenheim 15316
Musée Catalan des Arts et Traditions Populaires, Perpignan 13704
Musée Catalan d'Histoire, Salses-le-Château 14593
Musée Caverne du Dragon, Oulches-la-Vallée-Foulon 13447
Musée Cavernicole, Blanot 10759
Musée Cavernicole, Prignac-et-Marcamps 13872
Musée Cavernicole de la Grotte de Balme, La Balme-les-Grottes 12118
Musée Cavernicole de la Grotte de la Vache, Alliat 10293
Musée Cavernicole de la Grotte de Thais, Saint-Nazaire-en-Royans 14379
Musée Cavernicole de la Grotte des Planches, Arbois 10390
Musée Cavernicole de la Grotte d'Osselle, Roset-Fluans 14036
Musée Cavernicole de Marquay, Marquay 12833
Musée C.C. Olsommer, Veyras 37291
Musée Célestin-Freinet, Bonnut 10800
Musée Celte - Gallo Romain, Seltz 14700
Musée-Centre Charles-Péguy, Orléans 13431
Musée Centre Culturel, Vichy 15161
Musée-Centre d'Arts Plastiques Chanot, Clamart 11309
Musée-Centre de Documentation Alfred Desmasures, Hirson 12027
Musée Centre de l'Alchimie, Tiffauges 14911
Musée-Centre de l'Imaginaire Arthurien, Concoret 11383
Musée Centre Jean Rostand, Pouydesseaux 13854
Musée Centre National Jean Moulin, Bordeaux 10807
Musée Cernuschi, Paris 13540
Musée Césaire Phisalix, Mouthier-Haute-Pierre 13196
Musée César-Filhol, Annonay 10366
Musée Cévenol, Le Vigan (Gard) 12497
Musée-Chalutier Le Kifanlo, Les Sables-d'Olonne 12552
Musée Champenois de l'Imprimerie, Épernay 11625
Musée Champollion, Figeac 11731
Musée-Chapelle Bellini, Cannes 11024
Musée-Chapelle Saint-Blaise-des-Simples, Milly-la-Forêt 12981
Musée-Chapelle Sainte-Thècle, Seguret 14692
Musée Charbonneau-Lassay, Loudun 12674
Musée Charles Cros, Fabrezan 11698
Musée Charles-de-Bruyères, Remiremont 13936
Musée Charles de Gaulle, Lille 12596
Musée Charles Léandre, Domfront 11544
Musée Charles-Louis-Philippe, Cérilly 11111
Musée Charles Milcendeau-Jean Yole, Soullans 14793
Musée Charles-Portal, Cordes 11406
Musée Charles-VII, Mehun-sur-Yèvre 12915
Musée Charlier, Bruxelles 03294
Musée-Château, Grignan 11956
Musée-Château, La Ferté-Saint-Aubin 12174
Musée-Château, Le Plessis-Macé 12466
Musée-Château, Malesherbes 12783
Musée-Château, Montmort-Lucy 13115
Musée-Château, Montreuil-Bellay 13141
Musée-Château, Senonches 14713
Musée Château Abbaye de Cassan, Roujan 14062
Musée Château d'Aigremont, Awirs 03192
Musée Château d'Annecy et Observatoire Régional des Lacs Alpins, Annecy 10361
Musée-Château de Bourdeilles, Bourdeilles 10851
Musée-Château de Fontaine-Henry, Fontaine-Henry 11765
Musée-Château de Haute-Goulaine, Haute-Goulaine 11998
Musée-Château de la Garnache, La Garnache 12188
Musée-Château de la Pioline, Aix-en-Provence 10251
Musée-Château de La Verrerie, Oizon 13396
Musée-Château de Pommard, Pommard 13792
Musée-Château de Raguin, Chazé-sur-Argos 11261
Musée-Château de Rochebrune, Etagnac 11664
Musée-Château de Saint-Germain-de-Livet, Saint-Germain-de-Livet 14236
Musée-Château de Saint-Ouen, Saint-Ouen 14389
Musée-Château des Adhémar, Montélimar 13073
Musée-Château des Evêques de Monistrol, Monistrol-sur-Loire 13016
Musée Château des Princes de Ligne et Musée Lapidaire, Antoing 03132
Musée-Château des Roures, La Bastide-de-Virac 12122
Musée-Château d'Espéran, Saint-Gilles-du-Gard 14253
Musée Château du Bucheneck, Soultz-Haut-Rhin 14795
Musée-Château du Moine Sacristain, Aurec-sur-Loire 10486
Musée-Château du Riau, Villeneuve-sur-Allier 15234
Musée-Château Saint-Brisson, Saint-Brisson-sur-Loire 14136
Musée Chaussures Humeau, La Salle-et-Chapelle-Aubry 12257
Musée Chemtou, Jendouba 37564
Musée Chintreuil, Pont-de-Vaux 13806
Musée Christian-Dior, Granville 11910
Musée Ciotaden, La Ciotat 12156
Musée Claude Bernard, Saint-Julien-en-Beaujolais 14299
Musée Claude Chappe, Brûlon 10945
Musée Claude Debussy, Saint-Germain-en-Laye 14240
Musée Claude Monet, Giverny 11871
Musée Claude Nicolas Ledoux Saline Royale, Arc-et-Senans 10394
Musée Clément Ader, Muret 13221
Musée Cognacq-Jay, Paris 13541
Musée Cointreau, Saint-Barthélemy-d'Anjou 14121
Musée Colette, Saint-Sauveur-en-Puisaye 14467
Musée Collection Ferroviaire, Miramas 12988
Musée Colombophile, Bouvignies 10879
Musée Colombophile du Mont-Valérien, Suresnes 14844
Musée Communal, Bouvignes 03234
Musée Communal, Clérac 11316
Musée Communal, Xhoris 03848
Musée Communal d'Archéologie, d'Art et d'Histoire, Nivelles 03661
Musée Communal de Folklore Léon Maes, Mouscron 03641
Musée Communal de Huy, Huy 03511
Musée Communal de la Pierre de Sprimont, Sprimont 03763
Musée Communal de la Résistance et de la Déportation, Vénissieux 15120
Musée Communal de la Ville de Braine-le-Comte, Braine-le-Comte 03239
Musée Communal de Woluwe-Saint-Lambert, Bruxelles 03295
Musée Communal des Naufragés, Ile-de-Molène 12049
Musée Communal des Traditions Populaires Locales, Cussac-Fort-Médoc 11474
Musée Communal du Comte de Jette, Bruxelles 03296
Musée Communal Georges Mulpas, Elouges 03403
Musée Communal Herstalien d'Archéologie et de Folklore, Herstal 03495
Musée Communal Robert Tatin, Cossé-le-Vivien 11417
Musée Comtadin, Carpentras 11055
Musée Comtois, Besançon 10698
Musée Condé, Chantilly 11164
Musée Conrad-et-Marcel-Schlumberger, Crèvecœur-en-Auge 11460
Musée Conservatoire, Mauriac 12896
Musée-Conservatoire d'Arts et Traditions Populaires, Villefagnan 15197
Musée-Conservatoire de la Dentelle, Luxeuil-les-Bains 12714
Musée-Conservatoire de la Savonnerie Marius-Fabre, Salon-de-Provence 14588
Musée Conservatoire de la Vie Agricole et Rurale, Hétomesnil 12020
Musée Conservatoire de la Vie Agricole et Rurale d'Autrefois, Gimont 11866
Musée Conservatoire de l'Agriculture, Chartres 11192
Musée-Conservatoire de l'Outil, Brecy-Brières 10900
Musée-Conservatoire des Productions Fruitières, Saint-Jean-d'Arvey 14273
Musée Conservatoire du Matériel Agricole, Droyes 11581
Musée-Conservatoire du Patrimoine, La Garde-Freinet 12187
Musée-Conservatoire du Pneu, Clermont-Ferrand 11320
Musée Conservatoire Ethnologique de Haute-Provence, Mane 12789
Musée-Conservatoire International de la Plaisance, Bordeaux 10808
Musée Conservatoire Maritime et Rural, Narbonne 13266
Musée-Conservatoire Nationale de la Typographie, Paris 13542
Musée Constantin Meunier, Bruxelles 03297
Musée Corneille, Rouen 14046
Musée Créatif du Tissage, Louhossoa 12679
Musée Crozatier, Le Puy-en-Velay 12473
Musée Curie, Paris 13543
Musée Curtius, Liège 03571
Musée da Guine Portugesa, Bissau 21288
Musée d'Abeche, Abeche 06882
Musée d'Allard, Montbrison 13062
Musée d'Allauch, Allauch 10291
Musée d'Anatomie Delmas-Orfila-Rouvière, Paris 13544
Musée d'Anatomie Lesbres-Tagand de l'Ecole Vétérinaire de Lyon, Marcy-l'Étoile 12815
Musée d'Anatomie Normale, Strasbourg 14819
Musée d'Anatomie Pathologique, Strasbourg 14820
Musée d'Andernos, Andernos-les-Bains 10334
Musée d'Ansembourg, Liège 03572
Musée d'Anthropologie, Kinshasa 07634
Musée d'Anthropologie Préhistorique, Monaco 28665
Musée Dapper, Paris 13545
Musée d'Aquitaine, Bordeaux 10809
Musée Dar Ayed, Ksar Hellal 37567
Musée Dar Bourguiba, Tunis 37592
Musée Dar-Chraiet, Tozeur 37589
Musée Dar-El-Annabi, Sidi Bou Saïd 37583
Musée Dar-Hammamet, Hammamet 37562
Musée Dar-Si-Said, Marrakech 28699
Musée d'Archéologie, Battambang 04946
Musée d'Archéologie, Béjaïa 00049
Musée d'Archéologie, Capdenac 11034
Musée d'Archéologie, Carignan 11051
Musée d'Archéologie, Dakar 33776
Musée d'Archéologie, Houffalize 03506
Musée d'Archéologie, Izernore 12068
Musée d'Archéologie, Le Pègue 12461
Musée d'Archéologie, Séverac-le-Château 14737
Musée d'Archéologie, Tournai 03790
Musée d'Archéologie Bargoin, Clermont-Ferrand 11321
Musée d'Archéologie de l'Université du Québec à Trois-Rivières, Trois-Rivières 06642
Musée d'Archéologie, du Costume, d'Art et Traditions Populaires, Saint-Jean-de-Maurienne 14282
Musée d'Archéologie du Jura, Lons-le-Saunier 12660
Musée d'Archéologie et de Géologie, Rougemont 14060
Musée d'Archéologie et de Sciences Naturelles, Douai 11559
Musée d'Archéologie et d'Ethnologie, Villeneuve (Alpes-de-Haute-Provence) 15215
Musée d'Archéologie et d'Histoire Locale, Denain 11494
Musée d'Archéologie et Folklore, Verviers 03808
Musée d'Archéologie Imaginaire, Saint-Laurent-du-Pont 14313
Musée d'Archéologie Industrielle, Tournai 03791
Musée d'Archéologie Méditerranéenne, Marseille 12853
Musée d'Archéologie Précolombienne et de Préhistoire de la Martinique, Fort-de-France 27721
Musée d'Archéologie Préhistorique de l'Université de Liège, Liège 03573
Musée d'Archéologie Sublacustre, Sanguinet 14602
Musée d'Archéologie Tricastin, Saint-Paul-Trois-Châteaux 14404
Musée d'Archéologieque, Saint-Ciers-sur-Gironde 14152
Musée d'Archéologique, Saint-Raphaël 14442
Musée d'Archéologique, d'Arts et d'Folklorique Al-Kaçabah, Tanger 28712
Musée d'Archéologique Municipal, Martres-Tolosane 12883
Musée d'Architecture - La Loge, Bruxelles 03298
Musée d'Arenberg, Rebecq 03693
Musée d'Argonne, Varennes-en-Argonne 15089
Musée d'Armes Anciennes, La Cluse-et-Mijoux 12157
Musée d'Armes-Citadelle de Dinant, Dinant 03391
Musée d'Armes de Liège, Liège 03574
Musée d'Armes du Bordj Nord, Fèz 28694
Musée d'Armes et d'Historie Militaire, Tournai 03792
Musée d'Armes et Objets Anciens, Sonvilier 37190
Musée d'Arromanches, Arromanches-les-Bains 10432
Musée d'Art, Toulon (Var) 14926
Musée d'Art Africain, Dakar 33777
Musée d'Art Africain Religieux, Gentinnes 03455
Musée d'Art Américain, Giverny 11872
Musée d'Art Ancien, Bruxelles 03299
Musée d'Art Ancien, Montpeyroux 13135
Musée d'Art Brut, Beauchastel 10633
Musée d'Art Contemporain, Chef-du-Pont 11264
Musée d'Art Contemporain, Marseille 12854
Musée d'Art Contemporain de la Brenne, Concremiers 11384
Musée d'Art Contemporain de Lyon, Lyon 12729
Musée d'Art Contemporain de Montréal, Montréal 05914
Musée d'Art Contemporain du Château de Veauce, Veauce 15105
Musée d'Art Contemporain en Plein Air le Cyclop, Milly-la-Forêt 12982
Musée d'Art Contemporain et d'Histoire Locale, Chaumont (Yonne) 11253
Musée d'Art Contemporain et Moderne, Belmont-sur-Lausanne 36533
Musée d'Art Contemporain - FAE, Pully 37037
Musée d'Art de Joliette, Joliette 05633
Musée d'Art de Mont-Saint-Hilaire, Mont-Saint-Hilaire 05882
Musée d'Art de Saint-Laurent, Saint-Laurent 06360
Musée d'Art Differencie, Liège 03575
Musée d'Art et d'Archéologie, Aire-sur-Adour 10246
Musée d'Art et d'Archéologie, Aurillac 10490
Musée d'Art et d'Archéologie, Château-Gontier 11204
Musée d'Art et d'Archéologie, Cruzy 11467
Musée d'Art et d'Archéologie, Hyères 12041
Musée d'Art et d'Archéologie, Laon 12339
Musée d'Art et d'Archéologie, Senlis 14709
Musée d'Art et d'Archéologie, Soulac-sur-Mer 14790
Musée d'Art et d'Archéologie de l'Université d'Antananarivo, Antananarivo 27600
Musée d'Art et d'Artisanat, Corsavy 11412
Musée d'Art et de Folklore Régional, Fessy 11728
Musée d'Art et de Nature, Commana 11369
Musée d'Art et de Tradition Populaire, Bazoges-en-Pareds 10629
Musée d'Art et de Traditions Populaires André Abet, Saint-Laurent-de-Cerdans 14305
Musée d'Art et des Traditions Populaires, Sizun 14759
Musée d'Art et d'Histoire, Belfort 10670
Musée d'Art et d'Histoire, Bergues 10691
Musée d'Art et d'Histoire, Bulgnéville 10956
Musée d'Art et d'Histoire, Château-sur-Allier 11208
Musée d'Art et d'Histoire, Chaumont (Haute-Marne) 11249
Musée d'Art et d'Histoire, Cholet 11298
Musée d'Art et d'Histoire, Dreux 11579
Musée d'Art et d'Histoire, Eymet 11686
Musée d'Art et d'Histoire, Firmi 11736
Musée d'Art et d'Histoire, Fribourg 36715
Musée d'Art et d'Histoire, Frontignan 11823
Musée d'Art et d'Histoire, Genève 36743
Musée d'Art et d'Histoire, Grézolles 11954
Musée d'Art et d'Histoire, Kaysersberg 12112
Musée d'Art et d'Histoire, Lay-Saint-Christophe 12375
Musée d'Art et d'Histoire, Ligny-en-Barrois 12590
Musée d'Art et d'Histoire, Livry-Gargan 12637
Musée d'Art et d'Histoire, Meudon 12959
Musée d'Art et d'Histoire, Montferrer 13083
Musée d'Art et d'Histoire, Mouthiers-sur-Boëme 13197
Musée d'Art et d'Histoire, Narbonne 13267
Musée d'Art et d'Histoire, Nice 13311
Musée d'Art et d'Histoire, Oisy-le-Verger 13395
Musée d'Art et d'Histoire, Pezens 13725
Musée d'Art et d'Histoire, Poissy 13784
Musée d'Art et d'Histoire, Ravel 13916
Musée d'Art et d'Histoire, Rochefort (Charente-Maritime) 13999
Musée d'Art et d'Histoire, Rueil-Malmaison 14074
Musée d'Art et d'Histoire, Saint-Antonin-Noble-Val 14112
Musée d'Art et d'Histoire, Saint-Denis (Seine-Saint-Denis) 14180
Musée d'Art et d'Histoire, Saint-Julien-du-Sault 14297
Musée d'Art et d'Histoire, Schirmeck 14683
Musée d'Art et d'Histoire, Thorens-Glières 14899
Musée d'Art et d'Histoire, Villefranche-sur-Mer 15206
Musée d'Art et d'Histoire, Villespassans 15247
Musée d'Art et d'Histoire Alfred-Douët, Saint-Flour (Cantal) 14218
Musée d'Art et d'Histoire de Baugé, Baugé 10605
Musée d'Art et d'Histoire de la Chapelle Notre-Dame, Luz-Saint-Sauveur 12719
Musée d'Art et d'Histoire de Langres, Langres 12326
Musée d'Art et d'Histoire de Lisieux, Lisieux 12621
Musée d'Art et d'Histoire de Provence, Grasse 11917
Musée d'Art et d'Histoire de Puisaye, Villiers-Saint-Benoît 15257
Musée d'Art et d'Histoire de Toul, Toul 14924
Musée d'Art et d'Histoire des Côtes d'Armor, Saint-Brieuc 14132
Musée d'Art et d'Histoire du Chinonais, Chinon 11289
Musée d'Art et d'Histoire du Judaïsme, Paris 13546
Musée d'Art et d'Histoire du Vieux Pérouges, Pérouges 13700
Musée d'Art et d'Histoire Louis Senlecq, L'Isle-Adam 12626
Musée d'Art et d'Histoire Neuchâtel, Neuchâtel 36984
Musée d'Art et d'Histoire Roger Rodière, Montreuil-sur-Mer 13144
Musée d'Art et d'Histoire Romain Rolland, Clamecy 11311
Musée d'Art et d'Industrie, Quintin 13906
Musée d'Art et d'Industrie, Saint-Étienne 14198
Musée d'Art et d'Industrie - La Piscine, Roubaix 14044
Musée d'Art et Historique, Montbéliard 13059

Musée d'Art et Tradition Populaire, Lamballe 12310
Musée d'Art et Traditions Populaires, Binic 10737
Musée d'Art et Traditions Populaires, Nancy 13239
Musée d'Art et Traditions Populaires, Sidi Boulbaba 37585
Musée d'Art Haïtien, Port-au-Prince 21292
Musée d'Art Islamique, Marrakech 28700
Musée d'Art Islamique du Ribat, Monastir 37575
Musée d'Art Islamique Raqqada, Kairouan 37565
Musée d'Art Juif, Paris 13547
Musée d'Art Juif J.C.-Katz, Colmar 11358
Musée d'Art Militaire, Vincey 15266
Musée d'Art Moderne, Bruxelles 03300
Musée d'Art Moderne, Saint-Étienne 14199
Musée d'Art Moderne, Troyes 15004
Musée d'Art Moderne de la Ville de Paris, Paris 13548
Musée d'Art Moderne des Templiers, Collioure 11350
Musée d'Art Moderne et Contemporain, Strasbourg 14821
Musée d'Art Moderne et Contemporain, Toulouse 14940
Musée d'Art Moderne et d'Art Contemporain, Liège 03576
Musée d'Art Moderne et d'Art Contemporain, Nice 13312
Musée d'Art Moderne Grand-Duc Jean, Luxembourg 27562
Musée d'Art Moderne Jean Peské, Collioure 11351
Musée d'Art Moderne Lille Métropole, Villeneuve-d'Ascq 15217
Musée d'Art Moderne Méditerranéen, Cagnes-sur-Mer 10987
Musée d'Art Moderne Richard Anacréon, Granville 11911
Musée d'Art Naïf, Lasne-Chapelle-Saint-Lambert 03553
Musée d'Art Naif, Nice 13313
Musée d'Art Nègre, Yaoundé 04961
Musée d'Art Néo-Byzantin, Montréal 05915
Musée d'Art Oriental Asiatica, Biarritz 10724
Musée d'Art Polonais, Montrésor 13139
Musée d'Art Populaire, Le Monastier-sur-Gazeille 12450
Musée d'Art Populaire, Sauveterre-de-Rouergue 14656
Musée d'Art Populaire Africain, Besançon 10699
Musée d'Art Populaire des Mangettes, Saint-Étienne-du-Bois 14206
Museé d'Art Populaire du Hauran, Bosra 37434
Musée d'Art Populaire Marocain, Tétouan 28715
Musée d'Art Populaire Régional, Nantes 13251
Musée d'Art Religieux, Blois 10772
Musée d'Art Religieux, Marsal 12838
Musée d'Art Religieux, Vermand 15135
Musée d'Art Religieux, Wellington, Prince Edward Island 06764
Musée d'Art Religieux et d'Art Mosan, Liège 03577
Musée d'Art Religieux, Verdelais 15126
Musée d'Art Roger Quilliot, Clermont-Ferrand 11322
Musée d'Art Rustique, Vianden 27576
Musée d'Art Sacré, Bergerac 10687
Musée d'Art Sacré, Bourbon-l'Archambault 10848
Musée d'Art Sacré, Dijon 11523
Musée d'Art Sacré, Entrevaux 11620
Musée d'Art Sacré, Gramat 11898
Musée d'Art Sacré, Hambye 11987
Musée d'Art Sacré, Le Monêtier-les-Bains 12452
Musée d'Art Sacré, Le Val 12490
Musée d'Art Sacré, Paris 13549
Musée d'Art Sacré, Saint-Cirq-Lapopie 14155
Musée d'Art Sacré, Saint-Michel-l'Observatoire 14374
Musée d'Art Sacré, Senez 14707
Musée d'Art Sacré, Viviers (Ardèche) 15278
Musée d'Art Sacré à la Cathédrale Russe de 1912, Nice 13314
Musée d'Art Sacré Copte et Byzantin Scete, Le Revest-les-Eaux 12478
Musée d'Art Sacré de Fourvière, Lyon 12730
Musée d'Art Sacré de la Cathédrale Saint-Siffrein, Carpentras 11056
Musée d'Art Sacré de Loukine, Arsonval 10435
Musée d'Art Sacré du Gard, Pont-Saint-Esprit 13817
Musée d'Art Sacré - Francis Poulenc, Rocamadour 13987
Musée d'Art Sacré Occidental, Le Revest-les-Eaux 12479
Musée d'Art Singulièr Raymond Reynaud, Sénas 14706
Musée d'Arte Sacré, Lorgues 12665
Musée d'Artillerie, Caudeval 11089
Musée d'Artisanat Monuments en Allumettes et Sciences Naturelles, Fontet 11779
Musée d'Arts Africains, Langonnet 12325
Musée d'Arts et de Traditions Populaires, Amélie-les-Bains-Palalda 10317
Musée d'Arts et de Traditions Populaires, Augirein 10481
Musée d'Arts et de Traditions Populaires, Aurice 10488
Musée d'Arts et de Traditions Populaires, Bonifacio 10792
Musée d'Arts et de Traditions Populaires, Cervione 11119
Musée d'Arts et de Traditions Populaires, Lavaufranche 12367
Musée d'Arts et de Traditions Populaires, Le Passage 12460
Musée d'Arts et de Traditions Populaires, Mussidan 13227
Musée d'Arts et de Traditions Populaires, Oisly 13394
Musée d'Arts et de Traditions Populaires, Palinges 13458
Musée d'Arts et de Traditions Populaires, Poncé-sur-le-Loir 13795
Musée d'Arts et de Traditions Populaires, Saint-Paul-de-Fenouillet 14400
Musée d'Arts et d'Histoire, Hesdin 12018
Musée d'Arts et d'Histoire, Sainte-Maure-de-Touraine 14543
Musée d'Arts et d'Histoire de la Poterne, Preuilly-sur-Claise 13871
Musée d'Arts et d'Histoire du Donjon, Niort 13344
Musée d'Arts et Traditions Populaires, Cancale 11017
Musée d'Arts et Traditions Populaires, La Guérinière 12197
Musée d'Arts et Traditions Populaires, Marmoutier 12831
Musée d'Arts et Traditions Populaires, Montmaur 13105
Musée d'Arts et Traditions Populaires, Saint-Romain-Lachalm 14462
Musée d'Arts et Traditions Populaires, Sainte-Cathérine-de-Fierbois 14521
Musée d'Arts et Traditions Populaires, Troo 14997
Musée d'Arts et Traditions Populaires, Yssingeaux 15329
Musée d'Arts et Traditions Populaires de Castellane et du Moyen Verdon, Castellane 11072
Musée d'Arts et Traditions Populaires Paul Reclus, Domme 11546
Musée d'Arts et Traditions Rurales, Saint-Alban-Auriolles 14092
Musée d'Arts Populaires, Asco 10445
Musée d'Arts Populaires, Briançonnet 10921
Musée d'Arts Populaires, Dieue-sur-Meuse 11509
Musée d'Arts Populaires, Fources 11799
Musée d'Arts Populaires, Gramat 11899
Musée d'Arts Populaires, Laroque-des-Albères 12345
Musée d'Arts Populaires de l'Argonne, Braux-Sainte-Cohière 10896
Musée d'Arts Populaires de Lille-Sud, Lille 12597
Musée d'Arts Régionaux, Jard-sur-Mer 12070
Musée d'Assier, Feurs 11729
Musée Daubigny, Auvers-sur-Oise 10504
Musée Dauphinois, Grenoble 11941
Musée d'Automates, Courtilles 11439
Musée d'Automobiles en Miniature - Den Dinky, Vianden 27577
Musée David et Alice Van Buuren, Bruxelles 03301
Musée d'Aylmer, Aylmer 05029
Musée de Bagnes, Le Châble 36620
Musée de Baie Comeau, Baie Comeau 05034
Musée de Basse-Navarre et des Chemins de Saint-Jacques, Saint-Palais (Pyrénées-Atlantiques) 14395
Musée de Béjaïa, Béjaïa 00050
Musée de Bible et Terre Sainte, Paris 13550
Musée de Bibracte, Saint-Léger-sous-Beuvray 14320
Musée de Biot, Biot 10739
Musée de Boîtes à Musique et Automates, Sainte-Croix 37090
Musée de Bonoua, Bonoua 07669
Musée de Borda, Dax 11486
Musée de Botanique, Lausanne 36861
Musée de Bouteilles Anciennes et Originales, Saint-Christophe-des-Bardes 14149
Musée de Bouxwiller et du Pays de Hanau, Bouxwiller 10880
Musée de Bretagne, Rennes (Ille-et-Vilaine) 13941
Musée de Brou, Bourg-en-Bresse 10853
Musée de Butemo, Butemo 07631
Musée de Cahors Henri-Martin, Cahors 10996
Musée de Calligraphie et Epigraphie Arabe, Damascus 37435
Musée de Carouge, Carouge 36613
Musée de Cerdagne, Sainte-Léocadie 14536
Musée de Cerdagne d'Eyne, Eyne 11692
Musée de Cervières, Cervières 11118
Musée de Charlevoix, Pointe-au-Pic 06143
Musée de Charroux et de son Canton, Charroux-d'Allier 11191
Musée de Château Guillaume, Lignac 12587
Musée de Châtillon-Coligny, Châtillon-Coligny 11237
Musée de Chauny, Chauny 11254
Musée de Cherchell, Cherchell 00055
Musée de Cherves en Mirebalais, Cherves-Mirebeau 11280
Musée de Chine, Bruxelles 03302
Musée de Circonscription Archéologique, Sétif 00071
Musée de Cire, Waterloo 03828
Musée de Cire de l'Historial, Sainte-Anne-d'Auray 14518
Musée de Cire et Salle de Documents Historiques, Perros-Guirec 13713
Musée de Cire-Historial de la Haute-Auvergne, Aurillac 10491
Musée de Cires, Monaco 28666
Musée de Cognac, Cognac 11342
Musée de Cohennoz, Cohennoz 11346
Musée de Constantine, Constantine 00057
Musée de Cosne, Cosne-Cours-sur-Loire 11416
Musée de Cotonou, Cotonou 03873
Musée de Cox, Cox 11448
Musée de Dar-El-Jamaï, Meknès 28701
Musée de Diamare, Maroua 04958
Musée de Djemila, Djemila 00060
Musée de Dol, Dol-de-Bretagne 11540
Musée de Domaine de Lacroix-Laval, Marcy-l'Étoile 12816
Musée de Figurines Végétales, Basse-Pointe 27720
Musée de Folklore, Nismes 03658
Musée de Folklore de la Chée, Heiltz-le-Maurupt 12008
Musée de Folklore et d'Histoire Armand Pellegrin, Opheylissem 03673
Musée de Folklore Flamand Jeanne-Devos, Wormhout 15322
Musée de France de Berck-sur-Mer, Berck-sur-Mer 10686
Musée de Géologie, Lozanne 12707
Musée de Géologie, Saint-Avit-Senieur 14120
Musée de Géologie, Sainte-Foy 06384
Musée de Géologie Botanique, La Bourboule 12128
Musée de Géologie et du Marbre, Seix 14696
Musée de Germigny et Grange Germignonne, Germigny-des-Prés 11854
Musée de Glozel, Ferrières-sur-Sichon 11724
Musée de Grenoble, Grenoble 11942
Musée de Groesbeeck de Croix, Namur 03646
Musée de Hottemme, Durbuy 03397
Musée de Jean Chouan, Saint-Ouen-des-Toits 14390
Musée de Jouet et da la Poupée Ancienne, L'Isle-sur-la-Sorgue 12629
Musée de Jouques, Jouques 12094
Musée de Jules Gounon-Loubens, Loubens-Lauragais 12672
Musée de Kabgayi, Kabgayi 33753
Musée de Kamouraska, Kamouraska 05642
Musée de Kerhinet, Saint-Lyphard 14333
Musée de la Bande Dessinée, Angoulême 10354
Musée de la Banderette, Travers 37252
Musée de la Banque Nationale de Belgique, Bruxelles 03303
Musée de la Barrique, Moulis-en-Médoc 13190
Musée de la Base Secrète de V 2, Eperlecques 11622
Musée de la Basilique et des Thermes Romains, Arlon 03182
Musée de la Bataille, Fontenoy-en-Puisaye 11776
Musée de la Bataille, Rocroi 14004
Musée de la Bataille de Leipzig, Boue 10830
Musée de la Bataille de Tilly sur Seulles 1944, Tilly-sur-Seulles 14914
Musée de la Bataille des Ardennes, Wiltz 27582
Musée de la Bataille du 6 Août 1870, Woerth 15321
Musée de la Bataille Mai-Juin 1940, Semuy 14705
Musée de la Batellerie, Conflans-Sainte-Honorine 11392
Musée de la Batellerie, Offendorf 13386
Musée de la Batellerie de l'Ouest, Redon 13919
Musée de la Batellerie et du Plan Incliné, Saint-Louis-Arzviller 14328
Musée de la Batellerie et du Vieux Chinon, Chinon 11290
Musée de la Batterie de Merville, Merville 12950
Musée de la Beate, Marlhes 12827
Musée de la Bécane à Grand-Père, Sault-lès-Rethel 14637
Musée de la Bendrologie, Manéga 04939
Musée de la Bière, Armentières 10420
Musée de la Bière, Stenay 14803
Musée de la Blanchardière, Flers 11744
Musée de la Blanchisserie, Grezieu-la-Varenne 11953
Musée de la Blanchisserie Artisanale Joseph-Gladel, Craponne (Rhône) 11450
Musée de la Bohème, Yviers 15335
Musée de la Boisselleries, Bois-d'Amont 10786
Musée de la Boite à Biscuits, Opheylissem 03674
Musée de la Bonneterie, Troyes 15005
Musée de la Bonneterie et du Negoce de la Toile, Quevaucamps 03690
Musée de la Boulangerie, Bonnieux 10799
Musée de la Boulangerie Rurale, La Haye-de-Routot 12199
Musée de La Bouteille, Saint-Emilion 14193
Musée de la Brasserie, Bruxelles 03304
Musée de la Brasserie, Saint-Dizier 14190
Musée de la Bresse, Saint-Cyr-sur-Menton 14172
Musée de la Broderie, Fontenoy-le-Château 11778
Musée de la Cabane des Bangards, Thann 14879
Musée de la Cadillac, Saint-Michel-sur-Loire 14376
Musée de la Camargue, Arles 10415
Musée de la Caricature, La Cassagne 12134
Musée de la Casse, Orcières 13420
Musée de la Castre, Cannes 11025
Musée de la Cavalerie, Saumur 14643
Musée de la Cave, Damery 11482
Musée de la Cave des Champagnes de Castellane, Épernay 11626
Musée de la Céramique, Digoin 11516
Musée de la Céramique, Lezoux 12576
Musée de la Céramique, Rouen 14047
Musée de la Céramique d'Andenne, Andenne 03129
Musée de la Céramique et de l'Ivoire, Commercy 11373
Musée de la Céramique Saint-Jean-l'Aigle, Longwy 12658
Musée de la Cervoise, du Gruyt et des Bières Medièvales, Anthisnes 03131
Musée de la Chalosse, Montfort-en-Chalosse 13085
Musée de la Chapellerie, Espéraza 11653
Musée de la Chapellerie, Le Somail 12482
Musée de la Charronnerie, Brienne-la-Vieille 10928
Musée de la Chartreuse et Fondation Bugatti, Molsheim 13005
Musée de la Chasse, Boutenac 10878
Musée de la Chasse, Chambord 11147
Musée de la Chasse, de la Vénerie et de la Protection de la Nature, Lavaux-Sainte-Anne 03556
Musée de la Chasse et de la Nature, Foix 11752
Musée de la Chasse et de la Nature, Paris 13551
Musée de la Chasse et de la Venerie, Villiers-le-Duc 15256
Musée de la Châtaigne, Pied-de-Borne 13728
Musée de la Châtaigneraie, Joyeuse 12098
Musée de la Chaumière, Audierne 10477
Musée de la Chemiserie et de l'Elégance Masculine, Argenton-sur-Creuse 10408
Musée de la Chimie, Jarrie 12074
Musée de la Chouannerie et des Guerres de l'Ouest, Plouharnel 13778
Musée de la Cigarette, Dijon 11524
Musée de la Citadelle, Bitche 10747
Musée de la Citadelle, Sisteron 14753
Musée de la Citadelle Militaire, Verdun (Meuse) 15129
Musée de la Civilisation, Québec 06202
Musée de la Civilisation de la Vigne et du Vin, Gigondas 11862
Musée de la Civilisation Gallo-Romaine, Lyon 12731
Musée de la Cloche, Sévrier 14740
Musée de la Cloches et de Sonnailles, Hérépian 12011
Musée de la Cochonnaille, Tourzel-Ronzieres 14981
Musée de la Coiffe, Blesle 10767
Musée de la Coiffe et Broderies de Touraine, Rochecorbon 13995
Musée de la Coiffe et du Costume Oléronnais, Le Grand-Village-Plage 12419
Musée de la Comédie, Preignac 13868
Musée de la Commanderie, Viaprès-le-Petit 15155
Musée de la Communication en Alsace, Riquewihr 13976
Musée de la Compagnie des Indes, Port-Louis 13842
Musée de la Compagnie Nationale du Rhône, Lyon 12732
Musée de la Compagnie Royale des Anciens Arquebusiers de Visé, Visé 03818
Musée de la Comtesse de Ségur, Aube 10456
Musée de la Conciergerie, Paris 13552
Musée de la Confiture, Pau 13667
Musée de la Confrérie de l'Immaculée-Conception, Bastia 10601
Musée de la Confrérie des Vignerons, Vevey 37286
Musée de la Conscription, Strasbourg 14822
Musée de la Conserverie Le Gall, Loctudy 12645
Musée de la Construction Navale, Noirmoutier-en-l'Ile 13357
Musée de la Contrefaçon, Paris 13553
Musée de la Corbillière, Mer 12941
Musée de la Cordonnerie, Alby-sur-Chéran 10278
Musée de la Correrie, Saint-Pierre-de-Chartreuse 14411
Musée de la Corse, Corte 11415
Musée de la Course Landaise, Bascons 10598
Musée de la Course Landaise, Pomarez 13790
Musée de la Coutellerie, Nogent-en-Bassigny 13350
Musée de la Coutellerie, Thiers 14886
Musée de la Création Franche, Bègles 10668
Musée de la Crèche, Chaumont (Haute-Marne) 11250
Musée de la Crèche Provençale, Cavaillon 11096
Musée de la Crêpe Dentelle des Crêpes Bretonnes, Quimper 13896
Musée de la Cristallerie, Saint-Louis-les-Bitche 14331
Musée de la Cristallière, Charmeil 11183
Musée de la Cuisine, Drummondville 05344
Musée de la Curiosité et de la Magie, Paris 13554
Musée de la Dame aux Camélias, Gacé 11831
Musée de la Dentelle, Caudry 11091
Musée de la Dentelle, Chamalières-sur-Loire 11138
Musée de la Dentelle, Marche-en-Famenne 03608
Musée de la Dentelle, Mirecourt 12994
Musée de la Dentelle à la Main, Arlanc-en-Livradois 10412
Musée de la Dentelle au Point d'Alençon, Alençon 10280
Musée de la Dentelle du Puy-la-Galerie, Le Puy-en-Velay 12474
Musée de la Déportation, Labourse 12286
Musée de la Déportation et de la Résistance, Tarbes 14866
Musée de la Diligence, Riquewihr 13977
Musée de la Distillerie, Pontarlier 13821
Musée de la Distillerie Combier, Saumur 14644
Musée de la Douane et des Frontières, Hestrud 12019
Musée de la Fabuloserie, Dicy 11505
Musée de la Faculté de Médecine, Strasbourg 14823
Musée de la Faïence, Forges-les-Eaux 11786
Musée de la Faïence, Longfosse 12654
Musée de la Faïence, Marseille 12855
Musée de la Faïence, Montereau-Fault-Yonne 13076
Musée de la Faïence et des Arts de la Table, Samadet 14594
Musée de la Faïence Jules Verlingue, Quimper 13897
Musée de la Faïencerie de Gien, Gien 11859
Musée de la Faïencerie de Quimper H.-B. Henriot, Quimper 13898
Musée de la Famille, Chasselay 11198
Musée de la Faucillonnaie, Vitré 15274
Musée de la Faune, La Chapelle-d'Abondance 12143
Musée de la Faune, Lanhélin 12329
Musée de la Faune Alpine, Servoz 14726
Musée de la Faux, Pont-Salomon 13819
Musée de la Fédération Nationale de Spéléologie, Revel 13953

Musée de la Ferme d'Antan, Jugon-lès-Lacs 12100
Musée de la Ferme d'Antan, Ploudiry 13768
Musée de la Ferme de la Claison, Saint-Étienne-du-Bois 14207
Musée de la Ferme et des Vieux Métiers, Bosquentin 10825
Musée de la Ferme Miniature, Briec-de-l'Odet 10926
Musée de la Ferronnerie et des Métiers Annexes, Francheville 11804
Musée de la Fève et de la Crèche, Blain 10753
Musée de la Figurine, Toulon (Var) 14927
Musée de la Figurine Historique, Charre 11189
Musée de la Figurine Historique, Compiègne 11376
Musée de la Figurine Historique, La Grande-Fosse 12193
Musée de la Figurine Historique et du Jouet Ancien, Le Val 12491
Musée de la Filature, Angoustrine-Villeneuve 10359
Musée de la Flore et de la Faune du Haut Bugey, Hotonnes 12032
Musée de la Foire, Saint-Ghislain 03718
Musée de la Folie Marco, Barr 10593
Musée de la Fontaine et de l'Eau, Genval 03456
Musée de la Forêt, Saugues-en-Gévaudan 14632
Musée de la Forêt, Spa 03760
Musée de la Forêt Ardennaise, Renwez 13946
Musée de la Forge, Berlise 10692
Musée de la Forge, Ittre 03520
Musée de la Forge et des Sapeurs-Pompiers, Saint-Germain-l'Herm 14247
Musée de la Fortification, Auxonne 10514
Musée de la Fortification Cuirassée, Villey-le-Sec 15254
Musée de la Fraise et du Patrimoine, Plougastel-Daoulas 13770
Musée de la Fraise et du Terror Wépionnais, Wépion 03834
Musée de la Franc-Maçonnerie, Paris 13555
Musée de la France Protestante de l'Ouest, Monsireigne 13023
Musée de la Ganterie et de la Peau, Millau 12979
Musée de la Gaspésie, Gaspé 05478
Musée de la Gendarmerie, Melun 12922
Musée de la Gendarmerie, Toamasina 27608
Musée de la Géologie, Blangy-sur-Bresle 10755
Musée de la Glace, Mazaugues 12904
Musée de La Glacerie, La Glacerie 12191
Musée de la Goubaudière, Cholet 11299
Musée de la Grande Forge, Buffon 10953
Musée de la Grange aux Outils, Chens-sur-Léman 11274
Musée de la Grosse Forge, Aube 10457
Musée de la Grosse Horloge, La Rochelle 12238
Musée de la Grotte de Cougnac, Payrignac 13677
Musée de la Grotte des Huguenots, Vallon-Pont-d'Arc 15068
Musée de la Guerre, Calais 11002
Musée de la Guerre 1939-45, Pourrain 13853
Musée de la Guerre au Moyen Age, Castelnaud-la-Chapelle 11076
Musée de la Guerre de 1870, Gravelotte 11930
Musée de la Guerre de Vendée, Les Sables-d'Olonne 12553
Musée de la Halte du Pèlerin, Larressingle 12348
Musée de la Hardt, Fessenheim 11727
Musée de la Haute-Auvergne, Saint-Flour (Cantal) 14219
Musée de la Haute Sûre, Martelange 03613
Musée de la Houille Blanche et de ses Industries, Lancey 12315
Musée de la Kasbah, Rabat 28705
Musée de la la Faune des Pyrénées, Nébias 13277
Musée de la Laine, Saint-Hernin 14258
Musée de la Laine, Verviers 03809
Musée de la Lauze, Annoisin-Châtelans 10365
Musée de la Lavande, Cabrières-d'Avignon 10971
Musée de la Lavande, Montguers 13092
Musée de la Lavande, Saint-Remèze 14443
Musée de la Légion Étrangère, Aubagne 10454
Musée de la Liberation, Aywaille 03193
Musée de la Libération, Cherbourg 11276
Musée de la Libération 15 Août 1944, Le Muy 12458
Musée de la Libération de la Normandie, Surrain 14846
Musée de la Liberté, Quineville 13903
Musée de la Ligne Koningshooikt-Wavre, Chaumont 03357
Musée de la Ligne Maginot, Bambiderstroff 10574
Musée de la Ligne Maginot, Entrange 11618
Musée de la Ligne Maginot, Hatten 11995
Musée de la Ligne Maginot, Hunspach 12037
Musée de la Ligne Maginot, La Ferté-sur-Chiers 12177
Musée de la Ligne Maginot, Lembach 12510
Musée de la Ligne Maginot, Longuyon 12656
Musée de la Ligne Maginot Alpine, Sainte-Agnès 14516
Musée de la Ligne Maginot des Alpes, Sospel 14777
Musée de la Ligne Maginot Immerhof, Hettange-Grande 12021
Musée de la Lunette, Morez 13158
Musée de la Lutherie et de l'Archèterie Françaises, Mirecourt 12995
Musée de la Machine à Vapeur, Arc-en-Barrois 10393
Musée de la Machine Agricole, Le Bocasse 12382
Musée de la Machine Agricole, Saint-Loup 14332
Musée de la Machine Agricole, Vroncourt 15297
Musée de la Machine Agricole et à Vapeur, Ambert 10302
Musée de la Machine de Guerre, Espalion 11646
Musée de la Maille, Riorges 13974
Musée de la Main, Lausanne 36862
Musée de la Mairie de Crécy, Crécy-la-Chapelle 11452
Musée de la Maison de Retraite, Couilly-Pont-aux-Dames 11423
Musée de la Maison de Tartarin, Tarascon (Bouches-du-Rhône) 14861
Musée de la Maison Sauvagnarde, Sauvain 14652
Musée de la Maison s'Kleenderfel, Weyersheim 15312
Musée de la Maison Traditionelle du Queyras, Saint-Véran 14500
Musée de la Marine, Etaples 11666
Musée de la Marine, Grasse 11918
Musée de la Marine, Saint-Brévin-les-Pins 14130
Musée de la Marine, Saint-Laurent-de-la-Salanque 14308
Musée de la Marine de la Seine, Caudebec-en-Caux 11088
Musée de la Marine de Loire, Châteauneuf-sur-Loire 11221
Musée de la Marine et de l'Économie de Marseille, Marseille 12856
Musée de la Médecine, Bruxelles 03305
Musée de la Médecine Légale, Strasbourg 14824
Musée de la Mémoire de la Vigne et du Vin, Saint-Pierre-de-Mézoargues 14416
Musée de la Mémoire des Murs et d'Archéologie Locale, Verneuil-en-Halatte 15139
Musée de la Mémoire du Royans, Rochechinard 13992
Musée de la Mémoire et de la Paix, Clerval 11332
Musée de la Mémoire Paysanne, Estissac 11662
Musée de la Mer, Biarritz 10725
Musée de la Mer, Cannes 11026
Musée de la Mer, Gorée 33782
Musée de la Mer, Havre-Aubert 05589
Musée de la Mer, Iles-de-la-Madeleine 05613
Musée de la Mer, Le Grau-du-Roi 12421
Musée de la Mer, Nosy-Bé 27607
Musée de la Mer, Paimpol 13452
Musée de la Mer de Rimouski, Pointe-au-Père 06142
Musée de la Mer des Faluns, Doué-la-Fontaine 11566
Musée de la Mer OCEAM, Les Sables-d'Olonne 12554
Musée de la Métallurgie, Bogny-sur-Meuse 10783
Musée de la Météorite, L'Aigle 12303
Musée de la Météorologie, Valleraugues 15062
Musée de la Meunerie, Bannegon 10578
Musée de la Meunerie, Beaumont-sur-Sarthe 10646
Musée de la Meunerie, Braine-le-Château 03238
Musée de la Meunerie, Challain-la-Potherie 11125
Musée de la Meunerie, Courtelevant 11438
Musée de la Meunerie, Huisseau-sur-Mauves 12034
Musée de la Meunerie, Le Breuil 12389
Musée de la Meunerie, Saint-Michel-Mont-Mercure 14375
Musée de la Meunerie et de la Boulangerie, Angrie 10360
Musée de la Mine, Brassac-les-Mines 10892
Musée de la Mine, Champagnac-les-Mines 11151
Musée de la Mine, Gréasque 11936
Musée de la Mine, Houdeng-Aimeries 03505
Musée de la Mine, La Machine 12206
Musée de la Mine, Nœux-les-Mines 13349
Musée de la Mine, Saint-Étienne 14200
Musée de la Mine, Villar-Saint-Pancrace 15176
Musée de la Mine de Cap Garonne, Le Pradet 12472
Musée de la Mine de Cuivre et de Soufre, Saint-Pierre-de-la-Palud 14413
Musée de la Mine et de Meunerie-Moulin de Marcy, Le Molay-Littry 12449
Musée de la Mine et des Hommes, Blanzy 10762
Musée de la Mine et des Techniques Minières, Giromagny 11869
Musée de la Mine Lucien-Mazars, Aubin 10465
Musée de la Mine Marcel Maulini, Ronchamp 14022
Musée de la Mine, Musée de la Clouterie, Musée du Gazomètre, Fontaine-l'Evêque 03420
Musée de la Mine - Tissage, Villars (Loire) 15182
Musée de la Miniature, Saint-Sauves-d'Auvergne 14465
Musée de la Mode, Marseille 12857
Musée de la Mode et du Textile, Paris 13556
Musée de la Mode Retrovée, Digoin 11517
Musée de la Moineaudière, Xonrupt-Longemer 15326
Musée de la Monnaie, Paris 13557
Musée de la Montagne et de la Forêt, La Haut-du-Them 12198
Musée de la Montagne Saint-Pierre, Lanaye 03550
Musée de la Mosaïque et des Émaux, Briare 10923
Musée de la Mosaique Gallo-Romaine, Sorde-l'Abbaye 14770
Musée de la Moto, Marseille 12858
Musée de la Moto, Savigny-les-Beaune 14670
Musée de la Motocyclette, Entrevaux 11621
Musée de la Musique, Anduze 10339
Musée de la Musique, Paris 13558
Musée de la Musique de Ouagadougou, Ouagadougou 04942
Musée de la Musique Mécanique, Crillon-le-Brave 11461
Musée de la Musique Mécanique, Les Gets 12539
Musée de la Mytiliculture, Esnandes 11645
Musée de la Mytiliculture, Pénestin 13684
Musée de la Nacre et de la Tabletterie, Méru 12948
Musée de la Naissance de l'Aviation Suisse, Avenches 36480
Musée de la Nativité, Lourdes 12688
Musée de la Nature, Albaret-Sainte-Marie 10270
Musée de la Nature, Ettelbruck 27558
Musée de la Nature, Sivry 03754
Musée de la Nature et de la Chasse, Thuir 14908
Musée de la Navigation Fluviale/ Ascenseur à Bateaux, Arques (Pas-de-Calais) 10427
Musée de la Pailletterie, Amilly 10326
Musée de la Papeterie, Puymoyen 13888
Musée de la Papeterie Canson et Montgolfier, Davézieux 11485
Musée de la Parfumerie, Bastia 10602
Musée de la Parfumerie, Paris 13559
Musée de la Parfumerie Fragonard, Grasse 11919
Musée de la Parfumerie Fragonard, Paris 13560
Musée de la Parfumerie Galimard, Grasse 11920
Musée de la Parfumerie Molinard, Grasse 11921
Musée de la Parole, Bastogne 03199
Musée de la Paysannerie, Baguer-Morvan 10567
Musée de la Pêche, Beauchastel 10634
Musée de la Pêche, Concarneau 11380
Musée de la Pêche et de la Nature, Levallois-Perret 12568
Musée de la Pelote Basque, Saint-Étienne-de-Baigorry 14202
Musée de la Pelote Basque, Sare 14609
Musée de la Percée d'Avranches, Avranches 10541
Musée de la Perle, Papeete 15346
Musée de la Petite Bergère, Bartres 10596
Musée de la Petite Gare, Olonne-sur-Mer 13400
Musée de la Pétrification, Savonnières 14676
Musée de la Pharmacie, Montpellier 13122
Musée de la Pharmacie, Tence 14873
Musée de la Pharmacie Albert Ciurana, Montpellier 13123
Musée de la Photographie, Charleroi 03350
Musée de la Photographie, Mougins 13179
Musée de la Photographie, Port Louis 27739
Musée de la Pierre, Antoing 03133
Musée de la Pierre, Muno 03643
Musée de la Pierre, Trambly 14983
Musée de la Pierre, Vézelay 15152
Musée de la Pierre à Fusil, Luçay-le-Male 12709
Musée de la Pierre à Fusil, Meusnes 12964
Musée de la Pierre et du Marbre, Basècles 03196
Musée de la Pierre et Site des Carrières, Maffle 03605
Musée de la Pierre Philosophale, Issoire 12061
Musée de la Pince, Montecheroux 13072
Musée de la Planète Métal, Hagondange 11984
Musée de la Plongée, Espalion 11647
Musée de la Poche de Colmar, Turckheim 15016
Musée de la Pointe Saint-Mathieu, Plougonvelin 13771
Musée de la Poire Tapée, Rivarennes 13981
Musée de la Pomme, Bourg-Saint-Maurice 10855
Musée de la Pomme et du Cidre, Pleudihen-sur-Rance 13755
Musée de la Pomme et du Cidre, Vaudeurs 15098
Musée de la Pomme et du Cidre et des Métiers Traditionnels, Rosay 14031
Musée de la Porcelaine, Saint-Yrieix-la-Perche 14511
Musée de la Porte, Tubize 03802
Musée de la Porte de Bourgogne, Mouzon 13201
Musée de la Porte de Hal, Bruxelles 03306
Musée de la Porte de Thann, Cernay 11115
Musée de la Poste, Amélie-les-Bains-Palalda 10318
Musée de la Poste, Paris 13561
Musée de la Poste, Prunelli-di-Fium'Orbu 13881
Musée de la Poste, Saint-Flour (Cantal) 14220
Musée de la Poste des Pays de Loire, Nantes 13252
Musée de la Poste et des Techniques de Communication de Basse-Normandie, Caen 10980
Musée de la Poste et des Voyages, Amboise 10311
Musée de la Poterie, Nospelt 27571
Musée de la Poterie, Saint-Jean-de-Fos 14278
Musée de la Poterie, Vallauris 15059
Musée de la Poterie de Grès, Betschdorf 10710
Musée de la Poterie du Sartre, Saint-Alban-Auriolles 14093
Musée de la Poterie et de la Céramique, Sadirac 14083
Musée de la Poudrerie Nationale, Vaujours 15100
Musée de la Poupée, Aubeterre-sur-Dronne 10460
Musée de la Poupée, Le Beausset 12378
Musée de la Poupée, Montbrison 13063
Musée de la Poupée, Paris 13562
Musée de la Poupée Ancienne, Cerisiers 11112
Musée de la Poupée et des Jouets Anciens, Guérande 11965
Musée de la Préhistoire, Coux-et-Bigaroque 11446
Musée de la Préhistoire, Gesves 03460
Musée de la Préhistoire, Jemeppe-sur-Sambre 03529
Musée de la Préhistoire, Le Mas-d'Azil 12442
Musée de la Préhistoire, Saint-Flovier 14221
Musée de la Préhistoire, Saint-Porchaire 14424
Musée de la Préhistoire, Solesmes 14763
Musée de la Préhistoire Charentaise, La Rochefoucauld 12234
Musée de la Préhistoire du Vercors, Vassieux-en-Vercors 15094
Musée de la Préhistoire en Wallonie, Flémalle 03419
Musée de la Préhistoire L'Age des Garrigues, Viols-le-Fort 15269
Musée de la Préhistoire-Le Cairn, Saint-Hilaire-la-Forêt 14265
Musée de la Préhistoire/Paléontologie, Peyzac-le-Moustier 13723
Musée de la Préhistorique, Mozet 03642
Musée de la Première Guerre Mondiale, Villeneuve-les-Convers 15230
Musée de la Princerie, Verdun (Meuse) 15130
Musée de la Principauté de Stavelot-Malmedy, Stavelot 03764
Musée de la Protohistoire, Beynac et Cazenac 10716
Musée de la Protohistoire, Saint-Martin-de-Fressengeas 14350
Musée de la Prune et du Pruneau, Lafitte-sur-Lot 12296
Musée de la Publicité, Paris 13563
Musée de la Radio, Cornol 36649
Musée de la Radio et du Phonographe, Lanobre 12332
Musée de la Radio Galletti, Saint-Maurice-de-Rotherens 14363
Musée de la Radio Les Années 30, Saint-Victor-sur-Arlanc 14503
Musée de la Radiodiffusion et Télévision Belge, Bruxelles 03307
Musée de la Reddition, Reims 13925
Musée de la Régence, Ensisheim 11615
Musée de la Reine Bérengère, Le Mans 12436
Musée de la Reliure, Beaumesnil 10643
Musée de la Réparation Navale, Marseille 12859
Musée de la Reproduction du Son, Saint-Fargeau 14210
Musée de la Résistance, Auch 10470
Musée de la Résistance, Cabanès (Aveyron) 10965
Musée de la Résistance, Limoges 12611
Musée de la Résistance, Mussy-sur-Seine 13228
Musée de la Résistance, Saint-Connan 14163
Musée de la Résistance, Sospel 14778
Musée de la Résistance, Varennes-Vauzelles 15090
Musée de la Résistance Bretonne, Saint-Marcel (Morbihan) 14345
Musée de la Résistance, de l'Internement et de la Déportation, Chamalières 11137
Musée de la Résistance du Mont Mouchet, Auvers (Haute-Loire) 10501
Musée de la Résistance en Morvan, Saint-Brisson (Nièvre) 14135
Musée de la Résistance en Vercors, Vassieux-en-Vercors 15095
Musée de la Résistance en Zone Interdite, Denain 11495
Musée de la Résistance et de la Bataille du 19 Juin 1940, Chargé 11175
Musée de la Résistance et de la Déportation, Agen 10230
Musée de la Résistance et de la Déportation, Besançon 10700
Musée de la Résistance et de la Déportation, Castelnau-le-Lez 11074
Musée de la Résistance et de la Déportation, Grenoble 11943
Musée de la Résistance et de la Déportation, Montauban 13046
Musée de la Résistance et de la Déportation en Picardie, Fargniers 11704
Musée de la Résistance et Déportation, Blois 10773
Musée de la Résistance et des Anciens Combattants, Floing 11749
Musée de la Résistance Henri-Queuille, Neuvic (Corrèze) 13293
Musée de la Résistance Nationale, Champigny-sur-Marne 11157
Musée de la Révolution Française, Vizille 15280
Musée de la Rose et des Arts, Les Rosiers-sur-Loire 12549
Musée de la Roue Tourne, La Mothe-Achard 12209
Musée de la Route, Mons 03632
Musée de la Rubanerie Cominoise, Comines 03360
Musée de la Sahla, Audun-le-Tiche 10480
Musée de la Schlitte, Barr 10594
Musée de la Schlitte et des Métiers du Bois, Muhlbach-sur-Munster 13205
Musée de la Science-Fiction, de l'Utopie et des Voyages Extraordinaires, Yverdon-les-Bains 37353
Musée de la Scierie Ariel-Vincent, Sainte-Croix-aux-Mines 14526
Musée de la Seconde Guerre Mondiale, Digne-les-Bains 11511
Musée de la Seconde Guerre Mondiale, Tourcoing 14960
Musée de la Seconde Guerre Mondiale Roger Bellon, Conlie 11393
Musée de la Sénatorie, Guéret 11967
Musée de la Serrure, Paris 13564
Musée de la Société Archéologique de Corseul, Plancoët 13748
Musée de la Société Archéologique et Historique de la Charente, Angoulême 10355
Musée de la Société de l'Histoire du Protestantisme Français, Paris 13565
Musée de la Société d'Histoire et d'Archéologie, Briord 10933
Musée de la Soie, Jujurieux 12103
Musée de la Soie, Monoblet 13018
Musée de la Soierie, Charlieu 11181
Musée de La Source, Valignat 15057
Musée de la Station Biologique, Roscoff 14034
Musée de la Straize, Gy-en-Sologne 11982
Musée de la Symbolique Militaire, Vincennes 15263
Musée de la Taillanderie, Nans-sous-Sainte-Anne 13248
Musée de la Taille de Pierre, Saint-Antoine-l'Abbaye 14109

Musée de la Tapisserie et des Arts du Tissu, Tournai 03793
Musée de la Tapisserie, Enghien 03405
Musée de la Tapisserie Contemporaine, Angers 10344
Musée de la Tapisserie de Bayeux, Bayeux 10616
Musée de la Targette, Neuville-Saint-Vaast 13297
Musée de la Terre, Rambervillers 13909
Musée de la Terre Ardèchoise, Privas 13876
Musée de la Terre et du Bois, Saint-George 37084
Musée de la Thiérache, Vervins 15147
Musée de la Toinette, Murat-le-Quaire 13220
Musée de la Tonnellerie, Chécy 11263
Musée de la Tonnellerie, Generac 11847
Musée de la Tonnellerie, Narbonne 13268
Musée de la Tonnellerie Animée, Vergèze 15134
Musée de la Tonnellerie et du Vin, Aloxe-Corton 10296
Musée de la Tour, Antibes 10372
Musée de la Tour, Coucy-le-Château-Auffrique 11420
Musée de la Tour aux Puces, Thionville 14888
Musée de la Tour Carelot, Avensan 10522
Musée de la Tour Carrée, Rosans 14030
Musée de la Tour de l'Abbaye, Jouarre 12092
Musée de la Tour de l'Orle d'Or, Semur-en-Auxois 14701
Musée de la Tour des Echevins, Luxeuil-les-Bains 12715
Musée de la Tour d'Honneur, Lesparre-Médoc 12563
Musée de la Tour du Brau, Les Baux-de-Provence 12523
Musée de la Tour du Moulin, Marcigny 12810
Musée de la Tour Romaine, Arlon 03183
Musée de la Tour Salamandre, Beaumont 03202
Musée de la Tradition Champenoise, Épernay 11627
Musée de la Tradition de la Brigade des Sapeurs-Pompiers de Paris, Paris 13566
Musée de la Tradition de la Brigade des Sapeurs-Pompiers de Paris, Paris 13567
Musée de la T.S.F., Charleville-Mézières 11178
Musée de la Tuilerie, Malbrans 12782
Musée de la Vallée de la Creuse, Eguzon 11606
Musée de la Vallée de la Gueule, Neu-Moresnet 03654
Musée de la Vallée de l'Ubaye, Barcelonnette 10587
Musée de la Vallée du Lot, Villeneuve-sur-Lot 15235
Musée de la Vallée et de la Faïencerie, Rarecourt 13913
Musée de la Vannerie, Cadenet 10974
Musée de la Vannerie, Remilly-sur-Lozon 13935
Musée de la Vannerie, Villaines-les-Rochers 15169
Musée de la Vannerie et de l'Artisant, Vallabrègues 15058
Musée de la Vannerie L'Osarium, Le Mayet-en-Montagne 12443
Musée de la Vénerie et des Spahis, Senlis 14710
Musée de la Verrerie, Blangy-sur-Bresle 10756
Musée de la Verrerie, Saint-Galmier 14224
Musée de la Verrerie, Veauche 15106
Musée de la Vie, Bidon 10727
Musée de la Vie Artisanale, Ham-sur-Heure 03471
Musée de la Vie Bourguignonne Perrin-de-Puycousin, Dijon 11525
Musée de la Vie d'Autrefois, Marchin 03611
Musée de la Vie d'Autrefois, Vandré 15079
Musée de la Vie d'Autrefois, Vivoin 15279
Musée de la Vie en Bassin Minier, Escaudain 11641
Musée de la Vie Lensoise, Lens 03559
Musée de la Vie Locale et de la Coutellerie, Gembloux 03428
Musée de la Vie Monastique, Saint-Hilaire-du-Harcouët 14263
Musée de la Vie Paysanne, Dampicourt 03372
Musée de la Vie Populaire, Soumagne 03759
Musée de la Vie Réginal des Rièzes et des Sarts, Cul-des-Sarts 03367
Musée de la Vie Régionale, Cerfontaine 03348
Musée de la Vie Romantique, Paris 13568
Musée de la Vie Rural, Monflanquin 13015
Musée de la Vie Rurale, Chasteix 11200
Musée de la Vie Rurale, Desaignes 11501
Musée de la Vie Rurale, Mont-Saint-Jean 13031
Musée de La Vie Rurale, Saint-Quentin-Fallavier 14436
Musée de la Vie Rurale, Steenwerck 14802
Musée de la Vie Rurale, Tusson 15022
Musée de la Vie Rurale Condruze, Nandrin 03653
Musée de la Vie Rurale d'Huissignies, Huissignies 03509
Musée de la Vie Rurale en Wallonie, Saint-Hubert 03719
Musée de la Vie Rurale et Forestière, Saint-Michel-en-Thiérache 14372
Musée de la Vie Rurale Li Vîle Grègne, Erezée 03407
Musée de la Vie Wallonne, Liège 03578
Musée de La Vieille École, Pernes-les-Fontaines 13695
Musée de la Vieille Forge, Denazé 11497
Musée de la Vieille Pharmacie, Moutiers-Saint-Jean 13198
Musée de la Vigne, Boën-sur-Lignon 10779
Musée de la Vigne, Gleize 11879
Musée de la Vigne, Gornac 11889
Musée de la Vigne, Salles-Arbuissonnas-en-Beaujolais 14582
Musée de la Vigne, Verzenay 15148
Musée de la Vigne Benoit-Raclet, Romanèche-Thorins 14013
Musée de la Vigne et de la Vie Rurale, Plauzat 13751
Musée de la Vigne et du Terroir, Saint-Pourçain-sur-Sioule 14427
Musée de la Vigne et du Vin, Aigle 36438
Musée de la Vigne et du Vin, Ansouis 10368
Musée de la Vigne et du Vin, Aubière 10461
Musée de la Vigne et du Vin, Buzet-sur-Baise 10964
Musée de la Vigne et du Vin, Cérons 11117
Musée de la Vigne et du Vin, Curtil-Vergy 11471
Musée de la Vigne et du Vin, Gruissan 11959
Musée de la Vigne et du Vin, Igé 12043
Musée de la Vigne et du Vin, Le Mesnil-sur-Oger 12448
Musée de la Vigne et du Vin, Lézignan-Corbières 12575
Musée de la Vigne et du Vin, Lods 12648
Musée de la Vigne et du Vin, Loupiac 12682
Musée de la Vigne et du Vin, Mareau-aux-Près 12818
Musée de la Vigne et du Vin, Onzain 13407
Musée de la Vigne et du Vin, Pierreclos 13730
Musée de la Vigne et du Vin, Prayssas 13866
Musée de la Vigne et du Vin, Vaux-en-Beaujolais 15102
Musée de la Vigne et du Vin d'Anjou, Saint-Lambert-du-Lattay 14303
Musée de la Vigne et du Vin de Franche-Comté, Arbois 10391
Musée de la Vilaine Maritime, La Roche-Bernard 12227
Musée de la Villa Romaine de Pully, Pully 37038
Musée de la Ville de Saint-Quentin-en-Yvelines, Montigny-le-Bretonneux 13097
Musée de la Ville de Saverne, Saverne 14662
Musée de la Ville de Strasbourg, Strasbourg 14825
Musée de la Ville d'Eaux, Spa 03761
Musée de la Viscose, Échirolles 11596
Musée de la Viticulture, Barizey 10592
Musée de la Viticulture, Durban-Corbières 11589
Musée de la Viticulture, Lhomme 12578
Musée de la Viticulture, Mirepeisset 12996
Musée de la Viticulture, Montlouis-sur-Loire 13102
Musée de la Viticulture, Santenay 14605
Musée de la Viticulture et des Arts Populaires, Portel-des-Corbières 13847
Musée de la Viticulture et Renaissance du Vignoble, Contz-les-Bains 11401
Musée de la Voie Étroite et des Chemins de Fer de Montagne, Saint-Georges-de-Commiers 14230
Musée de la Voie Sacrée, Souilly 14789
Musée de la Voiture à Cheval, Les Épesses 12535
Musée de la Voiture de Course, Savigny-les-Beaune 14671
Musée de la Voiture Hippomobile et de la Citadelle de Bourg, Bourg-sur-Gironde 10858
Musée de la Volaille de Bresse, Romenay 14017
Musée de l'Abbaye, Echternach 27552
Musée de l'Abbaye, Lacaune 12290
Musée de l'Abbaye de Bourgueil, Bourgueil 10871
Musée de l'Abbaye de Clairvaux, Ville-sous-la-Ferté 15186
Musée de l'Abbaye de Port-Royal, Magny-lès-Hameaux 12765
Musée de l'Abbaye d'Orval, Villers-devant-Orval 03815
Musée de l'Abbaye Romane, La Sauve-Majeure 12258
Musée de l'Abbaye Saint-Vigor, Cérisy-la-Forêt 11113
Musée de l'Abbaye Sainte-Croix, Les Sables-d'Olonne 12555
Musée de l'Abeille, Bedoues 10664
Musée de l'Abeille, Château-Richer 05235
Musée de l'Abeille, Québec 06203
Musée de l'Abeille, Tilff 03779
Musée de l'Abeille et de la Cire, Toulouse 14941
Musée de l'Abeille et du Braconnage, Salbris 14568
Musée de l'Abri, Hatten 11996
Musée de l'Absinthe, Auvers-sur-Oise 10505
Musée de l'Academie de la Val d'Isère, Moutiers (Savoie) 13199
Musée de l'Accordéon, Montmagny 05885
Musée de Lachine, Lachine 05712
Musée de l'Affiche de la Carte Postale et de l'Art Graphique, Toulouse 14942
Musée de l'Agriculture Catalane, Saint-Michel-de-Llotes 14369
Musée de l'Agriculture de Montagne, Saint-Paul-sur-Ubaye 14403
Musée de l'Air et de l'Espace, Le Bourget (Seine-Saint-Denis) 12387
Musée de l'Alambic, Quimper 13899
Musée de l'Alambic, Saint-Desirat 14182
Musée de l'Alambic Louis Roque, Souillac 14786
Musée de l'Albanais, Rumilly 14077
Musée de l'Algérie Française, Perpignan 13705
Musée de l'Alta Rocca, Lévie 12572
Musée de l'Amérique Française, Québec 06204
Musée de l'Amour et des ses Traditions, Oger 13389
Musée de l'Ancien Collège des Jésuites, Reims 13926
Musée de l'Ancien Havre, Le Havre 12424
Musée de l'Ancienne Abbaye de Landévennec, Landévennec 12317
Musée de l'Ancienne Cathédrale, Noyon 13373
Musée de l'Ancienne Chartreuse de la Verne, Collobrières 11352
Musée de l'Apéritif Noilly-Prat, Marseillan 12843
Musée de l'Arc de Triomphe, Paris 13569
Musée de l'Archéologie, Céret 11109
Musée de l'Archerie Traditionnelle, Ayssenes 10547
Musée de l'Archiconfrérie Notre-Dame de la Miséricorde, Pellevoisin 13683
Musée de l'Ardenne, Charleville-Mézières 11179
Musée de l'Ardoise, Fumay 11826
Musée de l'Ardoise, Renazé 13938
Musée de l'Ardoise, Trélazé 14993
Musée de l'Areuse, Boudry 36581
Musée de l'Argonne, Sainte-Menehould 14546
Musée de l'Arles et Provence Antiques, Arles 10416
Musée de l'Armagnac, Condom 11390
Musée de l'Arme Blanche et Conservatoire de l'Épée, Monistrol-sur-Loire 13017
Musée de l'Armée, Alger 00041
Musée de l'Armée, Paris 13570
Musée de l'Armée des Alpes, Sospel 14779
Musée de l'Armée Russe, Paris 13571
Musée de l'Art Africain, Sailly 14088
Musée de l'Art Campanaire, Labergement-Sainte-Marie 12285
Musée de l'Art Culinaire, Villeneuve-Loubet 15232
Musée de l'Art Forain et de la Musique Mécanique, Conflans-en-Jarnisy 11391
Musée de l'Art Wallon, Liège 03579
Musée de l'Artillerie, Draguignan 11575
Musée de l'Artisanat et des Traditions Rurales, Brebotte 10898
Musée de l'Artisanat Rural Ancien, Tigy 14912
Musée de l'Assistance Publique, Bruxelles 03308
Musée de l'Assistance Publique-Hôpitaux de Paris, Paris 13572
Musée de l'Association des Marches Folkloriques de l'Entre-Sambre-et-Meuse, Gerpinnes 03459
Musée de l'Atelier de Rosa-Bonheur, Thomery 14891
Musée de l'Atelier de Saintonge, Pont-l'Abbé-d'Arnoult 13813
Musée de l'Attelage, Marquillies 12834
Musée de l'Attelage et du Cheval, Sérignan (Hérault) 14720
Musée de l'Audiovisuel, Montarcher 13041
Musée de l'Auditoire, Joinville (Haute-Marne) 12084
Musée de l'Auditoire, Sainte-Suzanne 14553
Musée de l'Auld Alliance Franco-Écossaise, Aubigny-sur-Nère 10463
Musée de l'Automate et de la Robotique, Souillac 14787
Musée de l'Automobile, Grenoble 11944
Musée de l'Automobile, Martigny 36927
Musée de l'Automobile, Muriaux 36973
Musée de l'Automobile, Orgon 13424
Musée de l'Automobile, Plan-les-Ouates 37024
Musée de l'Automobile, Valençay 15047
Musée de l'Automobile, Velaine-en-Haye 15108
Musée de l'Automobile Ancienne, Buis-sur-Damville 10955
Musée de l'Automobile de Vendée, Talmont-Saint-Hilaire 14850
Musée de l'Automobile Française, Reims 13927
Musée de l'Automobile La Belle Époque, Pont-l'Évêque 13815
Musée de l'Automobile Miniature, Fontenay-sur-Mer 11774
Musée de l'Automobile Miniature et des Poupées Anciennes, Nointel (Oise) 13355
Musée de l'Automobile Sportive, Sanary-sur-Mer 14599
Musée de l'Automobiliste, Mougins 13180
Musée de l'Avallonnais, Avallon 10521
Musée de l'Aventure Industrielle, Apt 10386
Musée de l'Aviation, Savigny-les-Beaune 14672
Musée de l'Aviation Charles-Noetinger, Perpignan 13706
Musée de l'Aviation Légère de l'Armée de Terre, Dax 11487
Musée de l'Eau, Pont-en-Royans 13810
Musée de l'Eau de Vie et des Vieux Métiers, Valognes 15071
Musée de l'Échevinage, Saintes 14556
Musée de l'Eclairage, Dinant 03392
Musée de l'Éclairage, Liège 03580
Musée de l'École, Bourges 10862
Musée de l'Ecole, Bruxelles 03309
Musée de l'École, Carcassonne 11042
Musée de l'Ecole, Chartres 11193
Musée de l'École, Châtelus (Allier) 11234
Musée de l'Ecole, Echery 11595
Musée de l'École, Saint-Étienne-de-Tinée 14203
Musée de l'Ecole, Villeneuve-d'Ascq 15218
Musée de l'Ecole 1900, Saint-Martin-des-Olmes 14354
Musée de l'Ecole Biblique et Archéologique Française, Jerusalem 31071
Musée de l'École d'Autrefois, Pontis 13828
Musée de l'Ecole de Nancy, Nancy 13240
Musée de l'Ecole et de la Mine, Harnes 11990
Musée de l'École Nationale d'Art Décoratif, Aubusson 10466
Musée de l'Ecole Navale, Lanvéoc-Poulmic 12338
Musée de l'Ecole Rurale, Trégarvan 14987
Musée de l'École Rurale d'Auvergne, Messeix 12953
Musée de l'Ecologie des Rives de l'Adour, Orist 13427
Musée de l'Église de Lorris, Lorris 12669
Musée de l'Eglise Notre-Dame, Montréal 05916
Musée de l'Elysée, Lausanne 36863
Musée de l'Empéri, Salon-de-Provence 14589
Musée de l'Enfance, Alger 00042
Musée de l'Entité de Walcourt, Walcourt 03824
Musée de l'Ephèbe, Agde 10229
Musée de l'Epicerie et des Commerces, Lignerolles 12589
Musée de l'Escrime Charles Debeur, Bruxelles 03310
Musée de l'Espace, Kourou 15342
Musée de l'Estérel, Les Adrets-de-l'Estérel 12515
Musée de l'Établissement des Constructions Navales de Ruelle, Ruelle 14076
Musée de l'Etang de Thau, Bouzigues 10882
Musée de l'Evéché, Sion 37175
Musée de l'Evêché, Verdun (Meuse) 15131
Musée de l'Eventail, Paris 13573
Musée de l'Evolution du Style Plantagenêt, Angers 10345
Musée de l'Habitat rural en Pays d'Aigues, La Tour-d'Aigues 12267
Musée de l'Habitat Rural Passé et des Traditions, La Garnache 12189
Musée de l'Heure et du Feu, Villerest 15240
Musée de l'Histoire de France, Paris 13574
Musée de l'Histoire de France à travers son Armée, Montet et Bouxal 13079
Musée de l'Histoire de la Forêt d'Ardenne, Saint-Hubert 03720
Musée de l'Histoire de la Médecine, Vandœuvre-les-Nancy 15078
Musée de l'Histoire de la Médecine de Toulouse, Toulouse 14943
Musée de l'Histoire de la Poterie, Bouconville-Vauclair 10829
Musée de l'Histoire de la Poterie, La Chapelle-des-Pots 12148
Musée de l'Histoire de l'Emigration Percheronne au Canada, Tourouvre 14966
Musée de l'Histoire des Bastides et de l'Evolution de l'Habitat, Bassoues 10600
Musée de l'Histoire du Costume, Scey-sur-Saône-et-Saint-Albin 14680
Musée de l'Histoire du Fer, Jarville 12075
Musée de l'Histoire et de la Vie Salmiennes, Vielsalm 03812
Musée de l'Histoire Vivante Parc Montreau, Montreuil (Seine-Saint-Denis) 13143
Musée de l'Histore Estudiantine, Assens 36473
Musée de l'Historire de Montpellier, Montpellier 13124
Musée de l'Historire de Rosny, Rosny-sous-Bois 14041
Musée de l'Holographie, Paris 13575
Musée de l'Homme, Paris 13576
Musée de l'Homme de Néandertal, La Chapelle-aux-Saints 12141
Musée de l'homme et de l'Industrie, Le Creusot 12408
Musée de l'Homme et de sa Montagne, Sainte-Croix-Vallée-Française 14527
Musée de l'Hôpital, Yssingeaux 15330
Musée de L'Hôpital Général de Dijon, Dijon 11526
Musée de l'Hôpital Psychiatrique, Brumath 10947
Musée de l'Horlogerie, Pesmes 13715
Musée de l'Horlogerie, Saint-Nicolas-d'Aliermont 14383
Musée de l'Horlogerie Ancienne, Fougères (Ille-et-Vilaine) 11792
Musée de l'Horlogerie du Haut-Doubs, Morteau 13173
Musée de l'Horlogerie et de l'Emaillerie, Genève 36744
Musée de l'Horlogerie et du Décolletage, Cluses 11337
Musée de l'Hospice Comtesse, Lille 12598
Musée de l'Hospice Saint-Roch, Issoudun 12062
Musée de l'Hôspital, La Rochefoucauld 12235
Musée de l'Hôtel Bellevue, Bruxelles 03311
Musée de l'Hôtel de Barral, Soissons 14761
Musée de l'Hôtel de Berny, Amiens 10323
Musée de l'Hôtel de Vermandois, Senlis 14711
Musée de l'Hôtel de Ville, Hondschoote 12028
Musée de l'Hôtel-Dieu, Beaune 10647
Musée de l'Hôtel-Dieu, Mantes-la-Jolie 12798
Musée de l'Hôtel-Dieu, Porrentruy 37028
Musée de l'Hôtel Sandelin, Saint-Omer 14386
Musée de l'Huître, Marennes 12820
Musée de Lignan et du Canton de Créon, Lignan-de-Bordeaux 12588
Musée de l'Iguanodon, Bernissart 03216
Musée de l'Ile de France, Sceaux 14678
Musée de l'Image Populaire, Pfaffenhoffen 13726
Musée de l'Imagerie Publicitaire sur le Chocolat, Pontlevoy 13830
Musée de l'Images, Épinal 11632
Musée de l'Impression sur Etoffes, Mulhouse 13208
Musée de l'Imprimerie, Billom 10736
Musée de l'Imprimerie, Bordeaux 10810
Musée de l'Imprimerie, Bruxelles 03312
Musée de l'Imprimerie, Nantes 13253
Musée de l'Imprimerie de Lyon, Lyon 12733
Musée de l'Industrie Régionale de la Chaussure, Saint-André-de-la-Marche 14105
Musée de l'Infanterie, Montpellier 13125
Musée de l'Insigne et de la Symbolique Militaire, Vincennes 15264
Musée de l'Insolite, Cabrerets 10968
Musée de l'Insolite, Font-Romeu-Odeillo-Via 11755
Musée de l'Insolite, Loriol-sur-Drôme 12667
Musée de l'Institut de Géologie et de Géoscience de Rennes, Rennes (Ille-et-Vilaine) 13942
Musée de l'Institut d'Égyptologie, Strasbourg 14826
Musée de l'Institut du Monde Arabe, Paris 13577
Musée de l'Invasion Aéroportée, Bénouville 10684
Musée de l'île d'Oleron Aliénor d'Aquitaine, Saint-Pierre-d'Oléron 14417

Musée de l'Océanie, Saint-Symphorien-sur-Coise 14485
Musée de Lodève, Lodève 12647
Musée de l'Œuvre, Avignon 10529
Musée de l'Œuvre de la Madeleine, Vézelay 15153
Musée de l'Oeuvre Notre-Dame, Strasbourg 14827
Musée de l'Olivette, Sorede 14772
Musée de l'Olivier, Les Baux-de-Provence 12524
Musée de l'Olivier, Nyons 13378
Musée de l'Opéra National de Paris, Paris 13578
Musée de l'Opinel, Saint-Jean-de-Maurienne 14283
Musée de l'Optique, Biesheim 10729
Musée de l'Optométrie, Bures-sur-Yvette 10958
Musée de l'Or, Jumilhac-le-Grand 12104
Musée de l'Oratoire Saint-Joseph, Montréal 05917
Musée de l'Ordre de la Libération, Paris 13579
Musée de l'Ordre de Malte, Bardonnex 36493
Musée de l'Orfevrerie Boilhet-Christofle, Saint-Denis (Seine-Saint-Denis) 14181
Musée de l'Orfevrerie de la Communaute Française, Seneffe 03729
Musée de l'Ostrévant, Bouchain 10827
Musée de Lourdes, Lourdes 12689
Musée de l'Outil, Espezel 11654
Musée de l'Outil, Turquant 15019
Musée de l'Outil à Bois, Peaugres 13678
Musée de l'Outil à la Ferme, Juvigné 12108
Musée de l'Outil et de la Vie au Village, Saint-Privat-des-Près 14430
Musée de l'Outil et des Métiers, Tinténiac 14916
Musée de l'Outil et des Vieux Métiers, La Celle-Guenand 12135
Musée de l'Outil et du Balnéaire Romain, Wy-Dit-Joli-Village 15324
Musée de l'Outillage Agricole et Viticole du Château Aney, Cussac-Fort-Médoc 11475
Musée de l'Outillage Artisanal Rural et Bourguignon, Cruzille-en-Mâconnais 11466
Musée de l'Outillage et des Techniques Traditionnelles de la Taille de Pierre, Coucouron 11419
Musée de Louvain-la-Neuve, Louvain-la-Neuve 03600
Musée de Luluabourg, Luluabourg 07640
Musée de l'Uniforme Legionnaire, Puyloubier 13887
Musée de l'Uniforme Militaire Français et du Vieux Bourbon, Bourbon-Lancy 10843
Musée de l'Union Compagnonnique des Devoirs Unis, Nantes 13254
Musée de l'Université de Fianarantsoa, Fianarantsoa 27606
Musée de l'Université de Tuléar, Tuléar 27610
Musée de l'Uranium, Lachaux 12293
Musée de Machines Agricoles Miniatures, Guerlesquin 11970
Musée de Mahdia, Mahdia 37569
Musée de Maison-Alfort, Maisons-Alfort 12775
Musée de Maquettes, Vallon-en-Sully 15064
Musée de Marine, Faranui 15343
Musée de Maroua, Maroua 04959
Musée de Matériel Agricole, Saint-Laurent-des-Autels 14310
Musée de Matériel Viticole, Saint-Laurent-des-Autels 14311
Musée de Matière Médicale, Paris 13580
Musée de Mayombe, Kinshasa 07635
Musée de Mbandaka, Mbandaka 07642
Musée de Megève, Megève 12913
Musée de Melun, Melun 12923
Musée de Miellerie, Saint-Saturnin-les-Avignon 14464
Musée de Minéralogie, Strasbourg 14828
Musée de Minéralogie de l'Ecole des Mines de Paris, Paris 13581
Musée de Minéralogie et de Géologie, Bruxelles 03313
Musée de Miniatures, Brantôme 10889
Musée de Mobilier Breton, Saint-Vougay 14509
Musée de Modèles Réduits, La Rochelle 12239
Musée de Modélisme, Savigny-les-Beaune 14673
Musée de Montmartre, Paris 13582
Musée de Monuments d'Allumettes et d'Artisanat, La Réole 12222
Musée de Morlaix et Maison du 9 Grand Rue, Morlaix 13163
Musée de Moulages, Strasbourg 14829
Musée de Musiques, L'Auberson 36477
Musée de Natitingou, Natitingou 03874
Musée de Nogent, Nogent-sur-Marne 13352
Musée de Normandie, Caen 10981
Musée de Notre-Dame-de-Paris, Paris 13583
Musée de Ouadane, Nouakchott 27730
Musée de Paléontologie, La Voulte-sur-Rhône 12275
Musée de Paléontologie, Menat 12924
Musée de Paléontologie, Villers-sur-Mer 15244
Musée de Paléontologie, Villeurbanne 15251
Musée de Paléontologie Christian Guth, Chilhac 11286
Musée de Paléontologie Humaine de Terra Amata, Nice 13315
Musée de Palmyra, Palmyra 37441
Musée de Payerne et Abbatiale, Payerne 37018
Musée de Pays de Seine-et-Marne, Saint-Cyr-sur-Morin 14175
Musée de Peinture, Rodilhan 14009
Musée de Peinture Contemporaine, Vars 15091
Musée de Peinture J. Drevon, Saint-Jean-de-Bournay 14275
Musée de Peinture Louis-Français, Plombières-les-Bains 13761
Musée de Peinture Mario Prassinos, Saint-Rémy-de-Provence 14450
Musée de Peintures Contemporaines Hors du Temps, Pierrefeu (Alpes-Maritimes) 13732
Musée de Peintures de Monsieur Paul Ricard, Le Brusc 12391
Musée de Peyne, Laurède 12356
Musée de Pharmacie Dusquenoy, Illkirch-Graffenstaden 12057
Musée de Picardie, Amiens 10324
Musée de Pierre Corneille, Le Petit-Couronne 12462
Musée de Plein Air, Parakou 03876
Musée de Plein Air, Saint-Vallier-de-Thiey 14499
Musée de Plein Air, Seurre 14736
Musée de Plein Air de Rothéneuf, Rothéneuf 14043
Musée de Plein Air des Maisons Comtoises, Nancray 13236
Musée de Plein Air du Quercy Cuzals, Cahors 10997
Musée de Plein de Cherchell, Cherchell 00056
Musée de Pont-Aven, Pont-Aven 13803
Musée de Pontarlier, Pontarlier 13822
Musée de Préhistoire, Aurignac 10489
Musée de Préhistoire, Avrillé 10546
Musée de Préhistoire, Bedeilhac 10663
Musée de Préhistoire, Coulmiers 11426
Musée de Préhistoire, Echternach 27553
Musée de Préhistoire, Kinshasa 07636
Musée de Préhistoire Amédée Lemozi, Cabrerets 10969
Musée de Préhistoire des Gorges du Verdon, Quinson 13904
Musée de Préhistoire d'île-de-France, Nemours 13280
Musée de Préhistoire et d'Art Populaire, Violay 15267
Musée de Préhistoire James Miln-Zacharie le Rouzic, Carnac 11053
Musée de Préhistoire Libanaise, Beirut 27482
Musée de Préhistoire Mésolitique L. Coulonges, Sauveterre-la-Lémance 14658
Musée de Préhistoire Régionale, Menton 12937
Musée de Provins et du Provinois, Provins 13878
Musée de Pully, Pully 37039
Musée de Radio France, Paris 13584
Musée de Région Auguste Chabaud, Graveson 11931
Musée de Rome, Caen 10982
Musée de Rouget de Lisle, Lons-le-Saunier 12661
Musée de Royan, Royan 14069
Musée de Saint-Boniface, Saint-Boniface 06307
Musée de Saint-Gengoux-le-Royal, Saint-Gengoux-le-National 14228
Musée de Saint-Gervais, Saint-Gervais-sur-Mare 14249
Musée de Saint-Martin, Saint-Martin 21252
Musée de Saint-Maurin, Saint-Maurin 14366
Musée de Saint-Paul, Saint-Paul (Alpes-Maritimes) 14399
Musée de Saint-Pierre-Jolys, Saint-Pierre-Jolys 06372
Musée de Sainte-Anne, Sainte-Anne-de-Beaupré 06382
Musée de Sainte-Sigolène, Sainte-Sigolène 14551
Musée de Salon et de la Crau, Salon-de-Provence 14590
Musée de Sarreguemines, Sarreguemines 14623
Musée de Sciences Naturelles, Vevey 37287
Musée de Sétif, Sétif 00072
Musée de Sismologie et Magnétisme Terrestre, Strasbourg 14830
Musée de Site, Digne-les-Bains 11512
Musée de Site Le Bazacle, Toulouse 14944
Musée de Skikda, Skikda 00074
Musée de Sologne, Cheverny 11283
Musée de Sologne, Romorantin-Lanthenay 14020
Musée de Sonis, Bataille du 2 Décembre 1870, Loigny-la-Bataille 12650
Musée de Soueida, Soueida 37442
Musée de Sousse, Sousse 37586
Musée de Souvigny, Souvigny 14797
Musée de Spéléologie, Fontaine-de-Vaucluse 11760
Musée de Spéléologie, Villefranche-de-Conflent 15200
Musée de Statues d'Enfants, Les Mages 12544
Musée de Sucy, Sucy-en-Brie 14840
Musée de Suresnes René-Sordes, Suresnes 14845
Musée de Surréalisme, Vaux-le-Pénil 15103
Musée de Tabarka, Tabarka 37587
Musée de Tahiti et des Iles-Te Fare Iamanaha, Punaauia 15348
Musée de Tauroentum, Saint-Cyr-les-Lecques 14171
Musée de Tautavel-Centre Européen de la Préhistoire, Tautavel 14872
Musée de Tazoult, Tazoult 00075
Musée de Temouchent, Ain Temouchent 00039
Musée de Tessé, Le Mans 12437
Musée de Tiemcen, Tiemcen 00077
Musée de Tigran, Champvoux 11161
Musée de Timgad, Timgad 00078
Musée de Tipasa, Tipasa 00079
Musée de Tipaza, Tipaza 00080
Musée de Tissage, Chauffailles 11246
Musée de Tlemcen, Tlemcen 00081
Musée de Tourisme et d'Artisanat, Lys-Saint-Georges 12755
Musée de Traditions Populaires et d'Archéologie, Chauvigny 11255
Musée de Uahuka, Uahuka 15349
Musée de Vavoua, Vavoua 07673
Musée de Ventabren, Ventabren 15123
Musée de Verrières-le-Buisson, Verrières-le-Buisson 15142
Musée de Vieux-la-Romaine, Vieux-la-Romaine 15167
Musée de Vieux Sallèles, Sallèles-d'Aude 14577
Musée de Voitures Anciennes et Sellerie, Menetou-Salon 12929
Musée de Voitures Hippomobiles Anciennes, Tour-en-Sologne 14957
Musée de Vulliod Saint-Germain, Pézenas 13724
Musée de Waterloo, Waterloo 03829
Musée de Zoologie Auguste Lameere, Bruxelles 03314
Musée d'Eben, Eben-Emael 03398
Musée d'Egyptologie, Villeneuve-d'Ascq 15219
Musée d'El-Oued, El-Oued 00063
Musée Delphinal, Beauvoir-en-Royans 10657
Musée Delta, Athis-Mons 10450
Musée d'Enfidaville, Enfidaville 37560
Musée d'Ennery, Paris 13585
Musée Denoix, Brive-la-Gaillarde 10938
Musée Dentaire de Lyon, Lyon 12734
Musée d'Entrecasteaux, Entrecasteaux 11619
Musée Départemantal des Sapeurs-Pompiers de l'Orne, Bagnoles-de-l'Orne 10563
Musée Départemental Albert-Kahn, Boulogne-Billancourt 10836
Musée Départemental Alexandre Franconie, Cayenne 15340
Musée Départemental Breton, Quimper 13900
Musée Départemental d'Archéologie, Montrozier 13150
Musée Départemental d'Art Ancien et Contemporain, Épinal 11633
Musée Départemental d'Art Contemporain de Rochechouart, Rochechouart 13993
Musée Départemental d'Art Religieux, Sées 14691
Musée Départemental d'Art Religieux Contemporain, Saint-Pierre-de-Chartreuse 14412
Musée Départemental de Flandre, Cassel 11067
Musée Départemental de la Préhistoire, Le Grand-Pressigny 12418
Musée Départemental de la Résistance, Le Teil 12483
Musée Departemental de la Résistance et de la Déportation, Forges-les-Eaux 11787
Musée Départemental de la Résistance et de la Déportation, Lorris 12670
Musée Départemental de la Résistance et de la Déportation, Manneville-sur-Risle 12791
Musée Départemental de la Résistance et de la Déportation, Tulle 15012
Musée Départemental de la Résistance et de la Déportation de l'Ain et du Haut-Jura, Nantua 13264
Musée Départemental de la Résistance et de la Déportation Jean Philippe, Toulouse 14945
Musée Départemental de la Tapisserie, Aubusson 10467
Musée Départemental de la Vigne et des Pressoirs, Champlitte 11158
Musée Départemental de l'Abbaye de Saint-Riquier, Saint-Riquier 14457
Musée Départemental de l'École Publique, Chevregny 11284
Musée Départemental de l'École Publique, Saint-Clar-de-Lomagne 14157
Musée Départemental de l'Éducation, Saint-Ouen-l'Aumône 14391
Musée Départemental de l'Oise, Beauvais 10655
Musée Départemental de Préhistoire, Solutré-Pouilly 14767
Musée Départemental de Préhistoire Corse, Sartène 14626
Musée Départemental de Saint-Antoine, Saint-Antoine-l'Abbaye 14110
Musée Départemental del'Ariège, Foix 11753
Musée Départemental des Antiquités de la Seine-Maritime, Rouen 14048
Musée Départemental des Arts et Traditions Populaires de la Haute-Loire et du Massif Central, Saint-Didier-en-Velay 14184
Musée Départemental des Arts et Traditions Populaires du Perche, Saint-Cyr-la-Rosière 14169
Musée Départemental des Hautes-Alpes, Gap 11838
Musée Départemental des Sapeurs-Pompiers du Val-d'Oise, Osny 13443
Musée Départemental Dobrée, Nantes 13255
Musée Departemental du Textile, Lavelanet 12370
Musée Départemental Georges-de-La-Tour, Vic-sur-Seille 15158
Musée Départemental Hébert, La Tronche 12270
Musée Départemental Ignon-Fabre, Mende 12925
Musée Départemental Jérôme-Carcopino, Aléria 10283
Musée Départemental Maurice-Denis, Saint-Germain-en-Laye 14241
Musée Départemental Stéphane Mallarmé, Vulaines-sur-Seine 15298
Musée des Abénakis, Odanak 06041
Musée des Affiches Léonetto-Cappiello, Épernay 11628
Musée des Alambics, Saint-Romain-de-Benet 14460
Musée des Alpilles, Saint-Rémy-de-Provence 14451
Musée des Amis de Castrum Vetus, Châteauneuf-les-Martigues 11220
Musée des Amis de Montmélian, Montmélian 13108
Musée des Amis de Thann, Thann 14880
Musée des Amis du Vieux Corbie, Corbie 11404
Musée des Amis du Vieux Crozet, Le Crozet 12410
Musée des Amis du Vieux Donzère, Donzère 11553
Musée des Amis du Vieux Guérigny, Guérigny 11969
Musée des Amis du Vieux Lormont, Lormont 12668
Musée des Amis du Vieux Montrichard, Montrichard 13148
Musée des Amis du Vieux Nolay, Nolay 13364
Musée des Amis du Vieux Saint-Étienne, Saint-Étienne 14201
Musée des Amoureux, Werentzhouse 15310
Musée des Anciennes Industries, Sedan 14690
Musée des Anciens Canadiens, Saint-Jean-Port-Joli 06328
Musée des Anciens Combattants, Carcans 11041
Musée des Anciens Outils Agricoles, Saint-Mathurin 14361
Musée des Années 30, Boulogne-Billancourt 10837
Musée des Antiquités de Volubilis, Moulay Driss 28702
Musée des Antiquités Nationales, Saint-Germain-en-Laye 14242
Musée des Archives, Saint-Hubert 03721
Musée des Archives, Villeneuve-la-Comptal 15225
Musée des Archives de l'Etat à Namur, Namur 03647
Musée des Archives Départementales de l'Aveyron, Rodez 14006
Musée des Armes, Tulle 15013
Musée des Arômes de Provence, Saint-Rémy-de-Provence 14452
Musée des Arômes et du Parfum, Graveson 11932
Musée des Arts Africains, Océaniens, Amérindiens, Marseille 12860
Musée des Arts Anciens du Namurois, Namur 03648
Musée des Arts Asiatiques, Nice 13316
Musée des Arts Contemporains de la Communauté Française, Hornu 03503
Musée des Arts Décoratifs, Bordeaux 10811
Musée des Arts décoratifs, Lyon 12735
Musée des Arts Décoratifs, Marseille 12861
Musée des Arts Décoratifs, Paris 13586
Musée des Arts Décoratifs, Saumur 14645
Musée des Arts Décoratifs, Strasbourg 14831
Musée des Arts Décoratifs et de la Modernité, Gourdon (Alpes-Maritimes) 11892
Musée des Arts Décoratifs Sabatier d'Espeyran, Montpellier 13126
Musée des Arts et de l'Enfance, Fécamp 11711
Musée des Arts et des Sciences, Sainte-Croix 37091
Musée des Arts et des Traditions Bamboun, Foumban 04956
Musée des Arts et Metiers, Paris 13587
Musée des Arts et Métiers de la Vigne et du Vin, Moulis-en-Médoc 13191
Musée des Arts et Tradition Apicoles, Fontan 11770
Musée des Arts et Traditions, Tozeur 37590
Musée des Arts et Traditions Béarnaises, Salies-de-Béarn 14571
Musée des Arts et Traditions de la Haute-Vézère, Treignac 14990
Musée des Arts et Traditions Populaires, Auxi-le-Château 10512
Musée des Arts et Traditions Populaires, Baume-les-Messieurs 10608
Musée des Arts et Traditions Populaires, Bressuire 10905
Musée des Arts et Traditions Populaires, Cherves-Mirebeau 11281
Musée des Arts et Traditions Populaires, Djerba 37558
Musée des Arts et Traditions Populaires, Esse 11655
Musée des Arts et Traditions Populaires, Gaillac 11833
Musée des Arts et Traditions Populaires, La Petite-Pierre 12218
Musée des Arts et Traditions Populaires, Laval-Roquecezière 12363
Musée des Arts et Traditions Populaires, Le Sel-de-Bretagne 12481
Musée des Arts et Traditions Populaires, Locronan 12644
Musée des Arts et Traditions Populaires, Marignane 12823
Musée des Arts et Traditions Populaires, Monbazillac 13008
Musée des Arts et Traditions Populaires, Montendre-les-Pins 13075
Musée des Arts et Traditions Populaires, Montmorin 13114
Musée des Arts et Traditions Populaires, Revel-Tourdan 13956
Musée des Arts et Traditions Populaires, Saint-Arnoult-en-Yvelines 14117
Musée des Arts et Traditions Populaires, Saint-Esprit 27726
Musée des Arts et Traditions Populaires, Valbonne 15045
Musée des Arts et Traditions Populaires, Wattrelos 15308
Musée des Arts et Traditions Populaires Dar Ben Abdallah, Tunis 37593
Musée des Arts et Traditions Populaires de la Haute-Loire, Lavaudieu 12366
Musée des Arts et Traditions Populaires de la Vallée de la Cère, Arpajon-sur-Cère 10425
Musée des Arts et Traditions Populaires de Moyenne Provence, Draguignan 11576
Musée des Arts et Traditions Populaires et des Arts Appliqués, Moissac 13001
Musée des Arts Populaires, Reillanne 13924
Musée des Arts Populaires et Traditions, Casbah 00053

Musée des Arts Populaires et Traditions, Sfax 37580
Musée des Arts Traditionnels, Tétouan 28716
Musée des Ateliers de l'Art du Fer, Livarot 12636
Musée des Attelages de la Belle Epoque, Saint-Martin-du-Lac 14355
Musée des Attelages de la Belle Epoque, Souillac 14788
Musée des Attelages, de la Carrosserie et du Charronnage, Vonnas 15291
Musée des Augustines de l'Hôpital Général de Québec, Québec 06205
Musée des Augustins, Toulouse 14946
Musée des Automates, La Rochelle 12240
Musée des Automates, Neuilly-sur-Seine 13291
Musée des Automates, Saint-Pourçain-sur-Besbre 14426
Musée des Automates, Sauclières 14629
Musée des Automates et Maison Enchantée, Amboise 10312
Musée des Avelines, Saint-Cloud 14161
Musée des Ballons, Balleroy 10572
Musée des Batailles, Montesquieu-des-Albères 13077
Musée des Bateliers de la Dordogne, Port-Sainte-Foy 13845
Musée des Beaux-Arts, Agen 10231
Musée des Beaux-Arts, Angers 10346
Musée des Beaux-Arts, Angoulême 10356
Musée des Beaux-Arts, Arras 10429
Musée des Beaux-Arts, Beaune 10648
Musée des Beaux Arts, Beirut 27483
Musée des Beaux-Arts, Béziers 10718
Musée des Beaux-Arts, Blois 10774
Musée des Beaux-Arts, Brest 10910
Musée des Beaux-Arts, Caen 10983
Musée des Beaux-Arts, Carcassonne 11043
Musée des Beaux-Arts, Chambéry 11139
Musée des Beaux-Arts, La Chaux-de-Fonds 36627
Musée des Beaux-Arts, Dijon 11527
Musée des Beaux-Arts, Dole 11541
Musée des Beaux-Arts, Gaillac 11834
Musée des Beaux-Arts, Kinshasa 07637
Musée des Beaux-Arts, La Ferté-Macé 12169
Musée des Beaux-Arts, La Rochelle 12241
Musée des Beaux-Arts, Lille 12599
Musée des Beaux-Arts, Le Locle 36889
Musée des Beaux-Arts, Lyon 12736
Musée des Beaux-Arts, Marseille 12862
Musée des Beaux-Arts, Menton 12938
Musée des Beaux-Arts, Mirande 12990
Musée des Beaux-Arts, Montbard 13054
Musée des Beaux-Arts, Mulhouse 13209
Musée des Beaux-Arts, Nancy 13241
Musée des Beaux-Arts, Nantes 13256
Musée des Beaux-Arts, Nîmes 13338
Musée des Beaux-Arts, Orléans 13432
Musée des Beaux-Arts, Pau 13668
Musée des Beaux-Arts, Quimper 13901
Musée des Beaux-Arts, Reims 13928
Musée des Beaux-Arts, Rouen 14049
Musée des Beaux-Arts, Saintes 14557
Musée des Beaux-Arts, Strasbourg 14832
Musée des Beaux-Arts, Tarbes 14867
Musée des Beaux-Arts, Tourcoing 14961
Musée des Beaux-Arts, Tours 14970
Musée des Beaux-Arts, Valenciennes 15054
Musée des Beaux-Arts, Vannes (Morbihan) 15082
Musée des Beaux-Arts, Villeneuve-sur-Yonne 15237
Musée des Beaux-Arts Charleroi, Charleroi 03351
Musée des Beaux-Arts de Bordeaux, Bordeaux 10812
Musée des Beaux-Arts de Dunkerque, Dunkerque 11585
Musée des Beaux-Arts de la Ville de Mons, Mons 03633
Musée des Beaux-Arts de Montréal, Montréal 05918
Musée des Beaux-Arts de Sherbrooke, Sherbrooke, Québec 06441
Musée des Beaux-Arts de Tournai, Tournai 03794
Musée des Beaux-Arts Denys Puech, Rodez 14007
Musée des Beaux-Arts et Arts Décoratifs Raymond Ritter, Morlanne 13164
Musée des Beaux-Arts et Céramique, Verviers 03810
Musée des Beaux-Arts et d'Archéologie, Besançon 10701
Musée des Beaux-Arts et d'Archéologie, Libourne 12582
Musée des Beaux-Arts et d'Archéologie, Rennes (Ille-et-Vilaine) 13943
Musée des Beaux-Arts et d'Archéologie, Vienne (Isère) 15163
Musée des Beaux-Arts et d'Archeologie Joseph Déchelette, Roanne 13985
Musée des Beaux-Arts et de la Dentelle, Alençon 10281
Musée des Beaux-Arts et de la Dentelle, Calais 11003
Musée des Beaux-Arts et d'Histoire, Saint-Lô 14326
Musée des Beaux-Arts Jules Chéret, Nice 13317
Musée des Bêtises de Cambrai, Cambrai 11011
Musée des Blindés, Saumur 14646
Musée des Bois Jolis, Felleries 11715
Musée des Bois Sculptes, Cancale 11018
Musée des Bories, Gordes 11886
Musée des Bujoliers, Saint-Cezaire 14141
Musée des Calèches, Apremont-sur-Allier 10384
Musée des Camions de Brasserie, Romedenne 03710
Musée des Canadiens Nord-Bourguignons, Sainte-Colombe-sur-Seine 14523
Musée des Canonniers Sédentaires de Lille, Lille 12600
Musée des Carrosses, Versailles 15143
Musée des Caves de la Cantrie, Saint-Fiacre-sur-Maine 14214
Musée des Champs, Saint-Ségal 14470
Musée des Charmettes, Chambéry 11140
Musée des Chartrons, Bordeaux 10813
Musée des Chasseurs à Pied, Charleroi 03352
Musée des Chasseurs Alpins, Villefranche-sur-Mer 15207
Musée des Châteaux Forts, Scherwiller 14682
Musée des Chemins de Fer Belges, Bruxelles 03315
Musée des Civilisations, Saint-Just-Saint-Rambert 14302
Musée des Civilisations de Côte d'Ivoire, Abidjan 07666
Musée des Civilisations de L'Europe et de la Méditerranée, Marseille 12863
Musée des Coiffes, Fresnay-sur-Sarthe 11814
Musée des Coiffes d'Anjou, Les Ponts-de-Cé 12546
Musée des Collections Historiques de la Préfecture de Police, Paris 13588
Musée des Commerces Anciens, Doué-la-Fontaine 11567
Musée des Contenants Vinaires, Pouzols-Minérvois 13856
Musée des Corbières, Sigean 14751
Musée des Costumes, Carcassonne 11044
Musée des Couronnes de Mariées, Vacheresse-les-Basses 15038
Musée des Cultures Guyanaises, Cayenne 15341
Musée des Cultures Légumières et ses Réserves, La Courneuve 12164
Musée des Cultures Taurines, Nîmes 13339
Musée des Curiosités Horlogères, Puidoux 37036
Musée des Débuts de l'Aviation, Douzy 11573
Musée des Demineurs, Lepuix 12514
Musée des Démineurs, Saint-Maurice-sur-Moselle 14365
Musée des Distilleries Limougeaudes, Limoges 12612
Musée des Docks Romains, Marseille 12864
Musée des Eaux de Vie, Fougerolles (Haute-Saône) 11797
Musée des Eaux de Vie, Lapoutroie 12341
Musée des Egouts de Paris, Paris 13589
Musée des Empreintes et Traditions, Cogolin 11344
Le Musée des Enfants- Het Kindermuseum, Bruxelles 03316
Musée des Engins de Travaux Publics, Mallemort 12785
Musée des Enrôles de Force, Dudelange 27550
Musée des Épaves Sous-Marines, Commes 11374
Musée des Équipages, Maincy 12773
Musée des Évolutions, Bousies 10875
Musée des Fagnes, Roly 03709
Musée des Faïences Anciennes de la Tour d'Aigues, La Tour-d'Aigues 12268
Musée des Faïences de Varages, Varages 15085
Musée des Faïences E. Tessier et de Faïencerie d'Art de Malicorne, Malicorne-sur-Sarthe 12784
Musée des Feuillardiers, Chalus 11133
Musée des Flûtes du Monde, Bollène 10790
Musée des Fontaines Salées, Saint-Père-sous-Vezelay 14409
Musée des Fossiles, Montceau-les-Mines 13066
Musée des Francs et de la Famenne, Marche-en-Famenne 03609
Musée des Glacières, Strasbourg 14833
Musée des Glaciers, Lourtier 36893
Musée des Goemoniers, Plouguerneau 13775
Musée des Grenouilles, Estavayer-le-Lac 36692
Musée des Grottes Préhistoriques de Gargas, Aventignan 10523
Musée des Guerres de Vendée, Le Pin-en-Mauges 12464
Musée des Guerres de Vendée, Saint-Florent-le-Vieil 14216
Musée des Haudères, Les Haudères 36793
Musée des Hospices Civils de Lyon, Lyon 12737
Musée des Illustres, Lectoure 12504
Musée des Instruments de Musique, Bruxelles 03317
Musée des Instruments de Musique, L'Aigle 12304
Musée des Instruments de Musique à Vent, La Couture-Boussey 12165
Musée des Ivoires, Yvetot 15332
Musée des Jacobins, Auch 10471
Musée des Jacobins, Saint-Sever (Landes) 14474
Musée des Jallouli, Sfax 37581
Musée des Jasseries des Monts du Forez, Saint-Anthème 14108
Musée des Liqueurs Cherry-Rocher, La Côte-Saint-André 12160
Musée des Machines Agricoles Anciennes, Montigny-le-Gannelon 13098
Musée des Machines Agricoles Anciennes, Orainville 13410
Musée des Maisons d'Autrefois, Brennilis 10903
Musée des Majorettes, Saint-Quentin-Fallavier 14437
Musée des Maladies de la Peau, Paris 13590
Musée des Manufactures de Dentelles, Retournac 13950
Musée des Maquettes, Forges-les-Eaux 11788
Musée des Maquettes, Saint-Privat-des-Près 14431
Musée des Marais Salants, Batz-sur-Mer 10604
Musée des Mariniers, Chouzé-sur-Loire 11303
Musée des Mariniers du Rhône, Serrières 14724
Musée des Materiaux du Centre de Recherche sur les Monuments Historiques, Paris 13591
Musée des Médailles et Vieux Courseulles, Courseulles-sur-Mer 11435
Musée des Merveilles, Tende 14875
Musée des Métiers de France, Argent-sur-Sauldre 10405
Musée des Métiers et des Légendes de la Forêt d'Orléans, Loury 12702
Musée des Métiers et Traditions Paysannes, Argy 10411
Musée des Métiers Ruraux, Eternoz 11670
Musée des Minéraux et de la Faune des Alpes, Le Bourg-d'Oisans 12384
Musée des Minéraux et des Fossiles, Rougemont 37074
Musée des Minéraux et Fossiles des Ardennes, Bogny-sur-Meuse 10784
Musée des Mines d'Argent des Gorges du Fournel, L'Argentière-la-Bessée 12344
Musée des Mines de Fer de Lorraine, Neufchef 13287
Musée des Miniatures Pompiers-Cirque, Le Mayet-en-Montagne 12444
Musée des Missions, Plouguerneau 13776
Musée des Moulages, Lyon 12738
Musée des Moulages, Montpellier 13127
Musée des Moulins, Villeneuve-d'Ascq 15220
Musée des Musiques Populaires, Montluçon 13103
Musée des Oiseaux, Douzens 11571
Musée des Ostensions et de la Religon Populaire, Esse 11656
Musée des Oudaïa, Rabat 28706
Musée des Outil d'Hier, Chauvirey-le-Vieil 11256
Musée des Outils du Terroir Normand, Caugé 11092
Musée des Papes, Grand-Anse 05507
Musée des Papillons, Fuveau 11828
Musée des Papillons, Saint-Chély-d'Apcher 14145
Musée des Parachutistes, Pau 13669
Musée des Patenôtriers, Brain-sur-Allonnes 10885
Musée des Peintres de l'Ecole de Murol, Murol 13223
Musée des Peintres du Pays, Saint-Cyprien 14166
Musée des Pénitents, Villar-Saint-Pancrace 15177
Musée des Pénitents Blancs, Marsac-en-Livradois 12836
Musée des Petits Hommes en Pyrénées, Arreau 10430
Musée des Petits Métiers de la Ferme, Wervicq-Sud 15311
Musée des Petits Meubles Bretons, Plozevet 13781
Musée des Pioneers, Saint-André-Avelin 06301
Musée des Plans-Reliefs, Paris 13592
Musée des Plantes Médicinales et de la Pharmacie, Bruxelles 03318
Musée des Pompiers, Fontainebleau 11767
Musée des Pompiers, Wasquehal 15304
Musée des Postes et Telecommunications, Luxembourg 27563
Musée des Poupées, Josselin 12090
Musée des Poupées d'Antan, Maisons-lès-Chaource 12778
Musée des Poupées Pascalines, Commana 11370
Musée des Rangers, Grandcamp-Maisy 11905
Musée des Records, La Tour-Blanche 12266
Musée des Religions, Nicolet 06005
Musée des Réserves Naturelles de la Haute-Savoie, Sallanches 14575
Musée des Roulottes Anciennes, Saintes-Maries-de-la-Mer 14563
Musée des Santons Animés, Maussane-les-Alpilles 12899
Musée des Santons des Baux, Les Baux-de-Provence 12525
Musée des Sapeurs-Pompiers, Saverne 14663
Musée des Sapeurs-Pompiers de France, Montville 13155
Musée des Sapeurs-Pompiers du Grand Lyon, Lyon 12739
Musée des Sciences, Laval (Mayenne) 12359
Musée des Sciences Naturelles, Orléans 13433
Musée des Sciences Naturelles, Vaudreuil 06701
Musée des Soeurs de Sainte-Anne, Lachine 05713
Musée des Soeurs Grises de Montréal, Montréal 05919
Musée des Sous-Stations R.A.T.P., Paris 13593
Musée des Souvenirs Napoléoniens et des Archives du Palais, Monaco 28667
Musée des Spahis, La Horgne 12201
Musée des Suisses dans le Monde, Pregny-Chambésy 37034
Musée des Tanneurs, Montargis 13044
Musée des Tanneurs et des Ciriers, Maringues 12824
Musée des Tapisseries, Aix-en-Provence 10252
Musée des Techniques Faïencières, Sarreguemines 14624
Musée des Techniques Fromagères, Saint-Pierre-sur-Dives 14419
Musée des Télécommunications, Perros-Guirec 13714
Musée des Télécommunications et de la Poste, Bordeaux 10814
Musée des Télécommunications Rhône-Alpes, Lyon 12740
Musée des Télécoms, Pleumeur-Bodou 13758
Musée des Téléphones de Genève, Plan-les-Ouates 37025
Musée des Temps Barbares, Marle 12825
Musée des Terre-Neuvas et de la Pêche, Fécamp 11712
Musée des Timbres et des Monnaies, Monaco 28668
Musée des Tisserands Mayennais, Ambrières-les-Vallées 10316
Musée des Tissus, Lyon 12741
Musée des Toiles Peintes, Colombier 36643
Musée des Tourneurs, Aiguines 10241
Musée des Tradition de l'île, Noirmoutier-en-l'Ile 13358
Musée des Traditions Agricoles du Ségala, Pradinas 13862
Musée des Traditions Bugistes, Saint-Rambert-en-Bugey 14441
Musée des Traditions Comtadines, Pernes-les-Fontaines 13696
Musée des Traditions du Ban-de-la-Roche, Neuviller-la-Roche 13299
Musée des Traditions du Vieux Dirinon, Dirinon 11539
Musée des Traditions et Arts Normands, Martainville-Epreville 12876
Musée des Traditions et Arts Populaires, Gréoux-les-Bains 11949
Musée des Traditions et Arts Populaires, Meylan 12967
Musée des Traditions et des Arts Catalans, Corsavy 11413
Musée des Traditions et des Barques du Léman, Saint-Gingolph 37085
Musée des Traditions Locales, Plounéour-Trez 13779
Musée des Traditions Locales, Sainte-Maxime 14544
Musée des Traditions Populaires, Collonges-la-Rouge 11353
Musée des Traditions Populaires, Olonne-sur-Mer 13401
Musée des Traditions Populaires, Saint-Gilles-du-Gard 14254
Musée des Traditions Populaires, Saint-Hilaire-en-Lignière 14264
Musée des Traditions Populaires Cap Al Campestre, Lherm 12577
Musée des Traditions Populaires de la Frasse, Araches-les-Carroz 10388
Musée des Traditions Populaires Marius Audin, Beaujeu 10639
Musée des Traditions Religieuses de la Haute-Loire, La Séauve-sur-Semène 12259
Musée des Traditions Rousselandes, Les Rousses 12550
Musée des Traditions Stéphanoises, Saint-Étienne-de-Tinée 14204
Musée des Traditions Vésubiennes, Saint-Martin-Vésubie 14360
Musée des Traditions Vigneronnes, Vongnes 15290
Musée des Trains et des Transports Miniatures, Savigné-sur-Lathan 14665
Musée des Trains-Jouets, Eymoutiers 11691
Musée des Trains Miniatures, Lyon 12742
Musée des Tramway et Autobus, Luxembourg 27564
Musée des Tramways à Vapeur et des Chemins de Fer Secondaires Français, Butry-sur-Oise 10963
Musée des Transports, Bavinchove 10612
Musée des Transports, Pithiviers-le-Vieil 13743
Musée des Transports, du Tourisme et des Communications, Toulouse 14947
Musée des Transports en Commun du Pays de Liège, Liège 03581
Musée des Transports Urbains, Colombes 11362
Musée des Trois-Guerres, Saint-Ame 14102
Musée des Trophées de Chasse, La Chapelle-Glain 12149
Musée des Troupes de Marine, Fréjus 11810
Musée des Troupes de Montagne, Grenoble 11945
Musée des Ursulines, Mâcon 12757
Musée des Ursulines, Québec 06206
Musée des Ursulines, Trois-Rivières 06643
Musée des Ustensiles de Cuisine Anciens, Saint-Denis-la-Chevasse 14178
Musée des Vallées Cévenoles, Saint-Jean-du-Gard 14289
Musée des Vieilles Automobiles, Canet-en-Roussillon 11019
Musée des Vieilles Landes, Lit-et-Mixe 12635
Musée des Vieilles Pierres, Chazay-d'Azergues 11260
Musée des Vieux-Commerces, Yvetot 15333
Musée des Vieux Métiers, Ardes-sur-Couze 10400
Musée des Vieux Métiers, Melgven 12918
Musée des Vieux Métiers, Saissac 14566
Musée des Vieux Métiers et des Eaux-de-vie, Dabo 11479
Musée des Vieux Métiers et des Traditions Populaires, Sainte-Croix-Volvestre 14528
Musée des Vieux Métiers et du Travail, Sarzay 14627
Musée des Vieux Métiers Vivants, Azannes-et-Soumazannes 10548
Musée des Vieux Outils Noël-Morard, Caromb 11054
Musée des Vieux Tacots, Les Riceys 12548
Musée des Vieux Tracteurs, Sainte-Geneviève (Meurthe-et-Moselle) 14534
Musée des Vins de Touraine, Tours 14971
Musée des Vins et Spiritueux, Bendol 10681
Musée des Voitures Anciennes, Landivisiau 12318
Musée des XVIes Jeux Olympiques d'Hiver, Albertville 10272
Musée Despiau Wlérick, Mont-de-Marsan 13027
Musée d'Estavayer, Estavayer-le-Lac 36693
Musée d'Ethnographie, Conches 36646
Musée d'Ethnographie, Genève 36745
Musée d'Ethnographie, Le Mans 12438
Musée d'Ethnographie, Neuchâtel 36985
Musée d'Ethnographie Corse, Bastia 10603
Musée d'Ethnographie de l'Université de Bordeaux II, Bordeaux 10815
Musée d'Ethnographie et d'Histoire de Conflans, Albertville 10273
Musée d'Evreux, Evreux 11681

Musée d'Exposition des Fouilles Archéologiques, Javols 12077
Musée d'Eysses, Villeneuve-sur-Lot 15236
Musée d'Hippone, Annaba 00048
Musée d'Histoire, La Chaux-de-Fonds 36628
Musée d'Histoire, La Neuveville 36989
Musée d'Histoire, Ouidah 03875
Musée d'Histoire 1939-1945 L'Appel de la Liberté, Fontaine-de-Vaucluse 11761
Musée d'Histoire Contemporaine, Paris 13594
Musée d'Histoire de la Médecine, Paris 13595
Musée d'Histoire de la Médecine et de la Pharmacie, Lyon 12743
Musée d'Histoire de la Ville de Luxembourg, Luxembourg 27565
Musée d'Histoire de la Ville et d'Ethnographie du Pays Malouin, Saint-Malo (Ille-et-Vilaine) 14341
Musée d'Histoire de Marseille, Marseille 12865
Musée d'Histoire des Sciences, Genève 36746
Musée d'Histoire d'Orainville, Orainville 13411
Musée d'Histoire du 20e Siècle, Estivareilles 11663
Musée d'Histoire et d'Archéologie, La Sarre 05709
Musée d'Histoire et d'Archéologie, Seclin 14687
Musée d'Histoire et d'Archéologie, Vannes (Morbihan) 15083
Musée d'Histoire et d'Archéologie, Warneton 03827
Musée d'Histoire et d'Archéologie de Die et du Diois, Die 11506
Musée d'Histoire et d'Archéologie de la Chartreuse, Molsheim 13006
Musée d'Histoire et d'Archéologie des Baux de Provence, Les Baux-de-Provence 12526
Musée d'Histoire et d'Archéologie René Bauberot, Châteauponsac 11223
Musée d'Histoire et d'Art, Mirande 12991
Musée d'Histoire et d'Arts Populaires, Pellafol 13682
Musée d'Histoire et de la Nature, Jougne 12093
Musée d'Histoire et de Traditions Populaires, Azincourt 10553
Musée d'Histoire et de Traditions Populaires, Gaspé 05479
Musée d'Histoire et des Arts Décoratifs, Tournai 03795
Musée d'Histoire et d'Ethnographie, Aneho 37546
Musée d'Histoire et Traditions Populaires, L'Oudon-Notre-Dame-de-Fresnay 12673
Musée d'Histoire Local, Maubourguet 12891
Musée d'Histoire Locale, Cagnes-sur-Mer 10988
Musée d'Histoire locale, Deuil-La Barre 11504
Musée d'Histoire Locale, Mouans-Sartoux 13176
Musée d'Histoire Locale, Orschwiller 13440
Musée d'Histoire Locale, Saint-Paul-de-Vence 14402
Musée d'Histoire Locale, Saint-Renan 14455
Musée d'Histoire Locale, Savigny-sous-Mâlain 14675
Musée d'Histoire Locale, Viarmes 15156
Musée d'Histoire locale et des Traditions, Fréjus 11811
Musée d'Histoire Locale et des Vieux Mètiers, Saint-Ciers-sur-Gironde 14153
Musée d'Histoire Locale, Patrimoine Historique, Arts et Traditions Populaires, Olargues 13397
Musée d'Histoire Maritime, Le Conquet 12402
Musée d'Histoire Médiévale, Châtel-sur-Moselle 11228
Musée d'Histoire Militaire à Bandera, Ajaccio 10263
Musée d'Histoire Militaire A. Henriot, Montréjeau 13138
Musée d'Histoire Naturell, Auxerre 10510
Musée d'Histoire Naturelle, Aix-en-Provence 10253
Musée d'Histoire Naturelle, Amiens 10325
Musée d'Histoire Naturelle, Amnéville-les-Thermes 10327
Musée d'Histoire Naturelle, Angers 10347
Musée d'Histoire Naturelle, Besançon 10702
Musée d'Histoire Naturelle, Chambéry 11141
Musée d'Histoire Naturelle, Champeaux 11156
Musée d'Histoire Naturelle, La Chaux-de-Fonds 36629
Musée d'Histoire Naturelle, Dijon 11528
Musée d'Histoire Naturelle, Eloyes 11612
Musée d'Histoire Naturelle, Fribourg 36716
Musée d'Histoire Naturelle, Gray 11934
Musée d'Histoire Naturelle, La Rochelle 12242
Musée d'Histoire Naturelle, Nantes 13257
Musée d'Histoire Naturelle, Perpignan 13707
Musée d'Histoire Naturelle, Rouen 14050
Musée d'Histoire Naturelle, Saint-Léger-les-Mélèzes 14318
Musée d'Histoire Naturelle, Saint-Michel (Gers) 14373
Musée d'Histoire Naturelle de Mons, Mons 03634
Musée d'Histoire Naturelle de Toulon, Toulon (Var) 14928
Musée d'Histoire Naturelle et de Géologie, Lille 12601
Musée d'Histoire Naturelle et de la Préhistoire, Nîmes 13340
Musée d'Histoire Naturelle et d'Ethnographie, Colmar 11359
Musée d'Histoire Naturelle et d'Histoire Locale, Elbeuf 11607
Musée d'Histoire Naturelle et Vivarium, Tournai 03796
Musée d'Histoire Naturelle Gabriel-Foucher, Bourges 10863
Musée d'Histoire Naturelle Philadelphe Thomas, Gaillac 11835
Musée d'Histoire Paul Mirat, Sauveterre-de-Béarn 14653
Musée d'Histoire Urbaine de Bergerac, Bergerac 10688
Musée d'Histore Naturelle Victor-Brun, Montauban 13047
Musée d'Homme, Porto-Novo 03877
Musée d'Horlogerie du Locle, Le Locle 36890
Musée d'Huez et de l'Oisans, L'Alpe-d'Huez 12309
Musée Dicks, Vianden 27578
Musée d'Iconographie Historique, Onoz 03664
Musee d'Ifri, Ifri 00066
Musée d'Initiation à la Nature de Normandie, Caen 10984
Musée d'Initiation à la Préhistoire, Tamnies 14853
Musée d'Institut National de Archéologique d'El-Jem, El-Jem 37559
Musée d'Instruments Anciens et d'Archives au Conservatoire de Musique, Luxembourg 27566
Musée d'Intérêt National du Tabac, Bergerac 10689
Musée Diocésain d'Art Religieux, Bayeux 10617
Musée Diocésain d'Art Sacré, Moulins (Allier) 13187
Musée Diocésain et Trésor de la Cathédrale Saint-Aubain, Namur 03649
Musée Diocésan d'Art Religieux, Lille 12602
Musée-Diorama du Pèlerinage du 19 Mars, Espaly-Saint-Marcel 11650
Musée d'Istres, Istres 12065
Musée d'Ixelles, Bruxelles 03319
Musée d'Izieu Mémorial des Enfants Juifs Exterminés, Izieu 12069
Musée d'Métiers et traditions du Pays d'Olliergues, Olliergues 13399
Musée Dobrée, Nantes 13258
Musée Docteur Joseph Fau, Conques 11395
Musée Domaine de Gourjade, Castres 11083
Musée Domaine de Samara, La Chaussée-Tirancourt 12154
Musée Don Bosco, Duekoue 07670
Musée Donation Suzy-Solidor, Cagnes-sur-Mer 10989
Musée Donjon, Ballon 10573
Musée d'Orange, Orange 13412
Musée d'Orbe, Orbe 37013
Musée d'Orbigny-Bernon, La Rochelle 12243
Musée d'Orgues de Kermesse, Bruxelles 03320
Musée d'Orsay, Paris 13596
Musée d'Orstom, Antananarivo 27601
Musée Doubrère, Marciac 12807
Musée d'Ourthe-Ambléve, Comblain-au-Pont 03359
Musée d'Outil, Champoulet 11160
Musée d'Outillage Agricole Miniature, Caden 10973
Musée d'Outillage Paysan, Jonvelle 12087
Musée du 11 Septembre 1709, Bavay 10610
Musée du 18 Novembre 1939, Téboursouk 37588
Musée du Bailles, Nismes 03659
Musée du Bain Rituel Juif, Bischheim 10742
Musée du Barreau de Paris, Paris 13597
Musée du Bas Saint-Laurent, Rivière-du-Loup 06278
Musée du Bassin Houiller Lorrain, Petite-Rosselle 13719
Musée du Bateau, Douarnenez 11561
Musée du Bateau-Lavoir Le Saint-Julien, Laval (Mayenne) 12360
Musée du Batha, Fèz 28695
Musée du Béret, Nay 13276
Musée du Berry, Bourges 10864
Musée du Biterrois, Béziers 10719
Musée du Bizarre, Lavilledieu 12373
Musée du Blé au Pain, Pierreclos 13731
Musée du Blé et du Pain, Verdun-sur-le-Doubs 15132
Musée du Bocage Normand, Saint-Lô 14327
Musée du Bois, Aubonne 36478
Musée du Bois, Saint-Amant-Roche-Savine-Fournols 14100
Musée du Bois, Seyssel 14748
Musée du Bois de Maredret-Galerie A la Fontaine, Maredret 03612
Musée du Bois et de la Forêt, La Chaise-Dieu 12138
Musée du Bois et de l'Outil, Montgobert 13090
Musée du Bonbon Haribo, Uzès 15034
Musée du Bonsaï, Châtenay-Malabry 11235
Musée du Bouchardais, L'Ile-Bouchard 12593
Musée du Bouton, Ambleville 10308
Musée du Breuil, Bourbon-Lancy 10844
Musée du Breuil de Saint-Germain, Langres 12327
Musée du Bronze d'Inverness, Inverness 05624
Musée du Bûcheron, Grandes-Piles 05521
Musée du Bugey-Valmorey, Lochieu 12641
Musée du Buron, Saint-Germain-du-Teil 14239
Musée du Café Gondrée, Bénouville 10685
Musée du Calvados et des Métiers Anciens de Pont-l'Évêque, Pont-l'Évêque 13816
Musée du Calvaire de Pontchateau, Pontchâteau 13825
Musée du Camembert, Vimoutiers 15261
Musée du Camp d'Internement, Le Vernet 12495
Musée du Canal, Cleden-Poher 11315
Musée du Canal, Ecuisses 11601
Musée du Canal de Berry, Audes-Reugny 10476
Musée du Canal du Duc de Berry, Dun-sur-Auron 11583
Musée du Canal du Midi, Revel 13954
Musée du Capitellu, Ajaccio 10264
Musée du Cardinal-Verdier, La Croix-Barrez 12167
Musée du Carmel, Libourne 12583
Musée du Cartonnage et de l'Imprimerie, Valréas 15077
Musée du Casque de Combat, Saint-Vincent-sur-Jabron 14506
Musée du Centenaire, Bischwiller 10743
Musée du Centre Culturel, Blangy-sur-Bresle 10757
Musée du Centre de Recherches sur les Monuments Historiques, Paris 13598
Musée du Chablais, Thonon-les-Bains 14897
Musée du Champignon, Saumur 14647
Musée du Charroi Rural, Salmiech 14586
Musée du Châtaignier, Marrons et Champignons, Villefranche-du-Périgord 15205
Musée du Château, Aubenas 10458
Musée du Château, Baugé 10606
Musée du Château, Dinan 11534
Musée du Château, Flers 11745
Musée du Château, Fougères (Ille-et-Vilaine) 11793
Musée du Château, Laas 12276
Musée du Château, Noirmoutier-en-l'Ile 13359
Musée du Château, Roquebrune-Cap-Martin 14025
Musée du Château, Siorac-en-Périgord 14752
Musée du Château de Cassaigne, Cassaigne 11066
Musée du Château de Dourdan, Dourdan 11569
Musée du Château de Flaugergues, Montpellier 13128
Musée du Château de Franchimont, Theux 03775
Musée du Château de la Louviere, Montluçon 13104
Musée du Château de Lunéville, Lunéville 12712
Musée du Château de Pontécoulant, Pontécoulant 13826
Musée du Château de Vincennes, Vincennes 15265
Musée du Château de Vitré, Vitré 15275
Musée du Château des Comtes de Marchin, Modave 03628
Musée du Château des Ducs de Wurtemberg, Montbéliard 13060
Musée du Château d'Henri IV, Nérac 13281
Musée du Château d'Oigny-en-Valois, Oigny-en-Valois 13392
Musée du Château du Marais, Le Val-Saint-Germain 12493
Musée du Château du Prince Noir, Arcizans-Avant 10397
Musée du Château et des Anciennes Écuries, Montbard 13055
Musée du Château-Fort, Ecaussinnes-Lalaing 03400
Musée du Château Fort-Liberia, Villefranche-de-Conflent 15201
Musée du Château Paul Pastre, Marsillargues 12873
Musée du Château Ramezay, Montréal 05920
Musée du Château Saint-Jean, Nogent-le-Rotrou 13351
Musée du Châtillonnais, Châtillon-sur-Seine 11243
Musée du Chemin de Fer, Apremont-la-Forêt 10383
Musée du Chemin de Fer Miniature, Clécy 11313
Musée du Cheminot, Ambérieu-en-Bugey 10301
Musée du Cheval, Gondrecourt-le-Château 11882
Musée du Cheval, La Ferté-Saint-Aubin 12175
Musée du Cheval, La Sarraz 37125
Musée du Cheval, Saumur 14648
Musée du Cheval, de la Vie Rurale et du Tabac, Thuillies 03776
Musée du Cheval en 1900, Cussac-Fort-Médoc 11476
Musée du Cheval et de l'Attelage, Obernai 13382
Musée du Chien, Villeneuve-les-Convers 15231
Musée du Cidre, Montaure 13049
Musée du Cidre, Saint-Jean-des-Champs 14286
Musée du Cidre Breton, Argol 10409
Musée du Cidre du Pays d'Othe, Eaux-Puiseaux 11592
Musée du Cinéma, Bruxelles 03321
Musée du Cinéma, Nismes 03660
Musée du Cinéma Amateur, Montesquieu-des-Albères 13078
Musée du Cinéma Henri Langlois, Paris 13599
Musée du Cinquantenaire, Bruxelles 03322
Musée du Circuit de Spa-Francorchamps, Stavelot 03765
Musée du Cirque, Vatan 15096
Musée du Cirque, Wasquehal 15305
Musée du Clocher, Haute-Rivoire 11999
Musée du Cloître, Tulle 15014
Musée du Cloître Notre-Dame en Vaux, Châlons-en-Champagne 11128
Musée du Clos-Lucé, Amboise 10313
Musée du Collège Bourget, Rigaud 06270
Musée du College de Lévis, Lévis 05751
Musée du Colombier, Alès 10287
Musée du Commerce International et de la Vie Quotidienne des Armateurs, Négociants et Corsaires, Troissereux 14996
Musée du Commissariat de l'Armée de Terre, Montpellier 13129
Musée du Compagnonnage, Bordeaux 10816
Musée du Compagnonnage, Paris 13600
Musée du Compagnonnage, Tours 14972
Musée du Compagnonnage du Tour de France, Fumel 11827
Musée du Coquillage, Le Lavandou 12430
Musée du Coquillage, Papara 15344
Musée du Corps de la Cavalerie Française 1940, Jandrain-Jandrenouille 03527
Musée du Costume, Château-Chinon 11201
Musée du Costume, Le Portel 12471
Musée du Costume Breton, Sainte-Anne-d'Auray 14519
Musée du Costume Civils, La Chapelle-Caro 12142
Musée du Costume Comtadin, Pernes-les-Fontaines 13697
Musée du Costume Comtois, Montgesoye 13089
Musée du Costume et de la Dentelle, Bruxelles 03323
Musée du Costume Provençal, Solliès-Ville 14765
Musée du Costume Savoyard, Bourg-Saint-Maurice 10856
Musée du Costume Trégor-Goëlo, Paimpol 13453
Musée du Coticule, Vielsalm 03813
Musée du Crest-Cherel, Ugine 15024
Musée du Crime, Bruxelles 03324
Musée du Cristal, Bayel 10613
Musée du Cristal, Vallerysthal-Troisfontaines 15063
Musée du Cuir et de la Tannerie, Château-Renault 11207
Musée du Cuir et du Parchemin, Levroux 12573
Musée du Cuivre, Cerdon 11104
Musée du Cwarmê, Malmedy 03606
Musée du Débarquement à Utah Beach, Sainte-Marie-du-Mont 14542
Musée du Débarquement en Provence, Toulon (Var) 14929
Musée du Désert, Mialet 12975
Musée du Dessin et de l'Estampe Originale, Gravelines 11929
Musée du Docteur Faure, Aix-les-Bains 10260
Musée du Dolder, Riquewihr 13978
Musée du Donjon, Rouen 14051
Musée du Donjon de la Toque, Huriel 12039
Musée du Faouët, Le Faouët 12413
Musée du Fer, Reichshoffen 13923
Musée du Fer à Repasser, Longwy 12659
Musée du Fer Blanc Ancien et Moderne, Saint-Arcons-d'Allier 14115
Musée du Fer et de la Métallurgie Ancienne, Saint-Hubert 03722
Musée du Fer et des Traditions Catalanes, Prades 13860
Musée du Fer et du Chemin de Fer, Vallorbe 37279
Musée du Fer et du Fil, Dompierre (Orne) 11548
Musée du Feu Adjudant-Chef Gérard, Châlons-en-Champagne 11129
Musée du Feutre, Mouzon 13202
Musée du Fil de Soie, Vierzon 15165
Musée du Fil D.M.C., Mulhouse 13210
Musée du Fjord, La Baie 05705
Musée du Flacon à Parfum, La Rochelle 12244
Musée du Florentinois, Saint-Florentin 14217
Musée du Florival, Guebwiller 11963
Musée du Foie Gras, Frespech 11817
Musée du Foie Gras, Roquettes 14028
Musée du Foie Gras et des Traditions Populaires, Samatan 14595
Musée du Folklore, Ittre 03521
Musée du Folklore, Moulins (Allier) 13188
Musée du Folklore, Sainte-Enimie 14529
Musée du Folklore et de la Vie Montoise, Mons 03635
Musée du Football en France - Musée du Sport, Paris 13601
Musée du Fort de Huy, Huy 03512
Musée du Fort de la Pompelle, Reims 13929
Musée du Fort de Vaux, Vaux-devant-Damloup 15101
Musée du Fort d'Embourg, Embourg 03404
Musée du Fort Saint-Jean, Saint-Jean 06326
Musée du Fort Vauban, Ambleteuse 10307
Musée du Frère André, Montréal 05921
Musée du Fromage, Laye 12376
Musée du Fromage, Saint-Marcellin 14346
Musée du Fromage de la Chèvrerie, Noirmoutier-en-l'Ile 13360
Musée du Gabarier, Saint-Simon (Charente) 14477
Musée du Gemmail, Lourdes 12690
Musée du Gemmail, Tours 14973
Musée du Général Thys, Dalhem 03368
Musée du Grand-Lens, Lens 36869
Musée du Grand Saint-Bernard, Le Grand-Saint-Bernard 36775
Musée du Granit, Bécon-les-Granits 10660
Musée du Granit, Saint-Michel-de-Montjoie 14370
Musée du Graveur Oscar Roty, Jargeau 12071
Musée du Grenier du Roy Louis XIII, Villemur-sur-Tarn 15214
Musée du Grès, Saint-Amand-en-Puisaye 14096
Musée du Groupe Jovinien de Résistance Bayard, Joigny (Yonne) 12083
Musée du Guesclin, Châteauneuf-de-Randon 11216
Musée du Hard Rock Café, Paris 13602
Musée du Haut-Richelieu, Saint-Jean-sur-Richelieu 06330
Musée du Haut-Rouergue, Laguiole 12301
Musée du Haut-Val-d'Arly, Megève 12914
Musée du Jeu de l'Oie, Rambouillet 13910
Musée du Jouet, Bruxelles 03325
Musée du Jouet, Canet-en-Roussillon 11020
Musée du Jouet, Clervaux 27546
Musée du Jouet, Moirans-en-Montagne 12999
Musée du Jouet, Poissy 13785
Musée du Jouet Ancien "Atlantrain", Saint-Just-Luzac 14301
Musée du Jouet Ancien Automobile, Rocamadour 13988
Musée du Jouet Automobile, Argence 10404
Musée du Jouet et de l'Enfant, Ferrières 03417
Musée du Jouet et des Petits Trains, Colmar 11360
Musée du Jus de Fruit, Saint-Andiol 14104
Musée du Lac de Paladru, Charavines 11170
Musée du Lac Léman, Nernier 13283
Musée du Lait, Belvedere 10678
Musée du Lait, Montebourg 13071
Musée du Lait et des Traditions, Saint-Étienne-de-Tinée 14205
Musée du Lapidaire, Lamoura 12313
Musée du Lavage et du Repassage, Verneuil-en-Bourbonnais 15138
Musée du Lavandin, Carennac 11048
Musée du Léman, Nyon 36993
Musée du Léon, Lesneven 12562

Musée du Liège, Maureillas-las-Illas 12895
Musée du Liège et du Bouchon, Mezin 12973
Musée du Littoral et de des Fours à Chaux, Regnéville-sur-Mer 13920
Musée du Livre, Langres 12328
Musée du Livre, de la Pierre et du Verre, Conches-en-Ouche 11381
Musée du Livre et Cabinets de Donations de la Bibliothèque Royale de Belgique, Bruxelles 03326
Musée du Loup, Le Cloître-Saint-Thégonnec 12401
Musée du Louvre, Paris 13603
Musée du Luxembourg, Paris 13604
Musée du Lycée Militaire de Saint-Cyr, Saint-Cyr-l'École 14170
Musée du Lydia, Port-Barcarès 13835
Musée du Machinisme Agricole, Bourbon-Lancy 10845
Musée du Machinisme Agricole, Le Bersac 12379
Musée du Machinisme Agricole, Neuvic (Corrèze) 13294
Musée du Machinisme Agricole, Prissac 13875
Musée du Machinisme Agricole, Revest-Saint-Martin 13957
Musée du Machinisme Agricole, Saint-Amans 14099
Musée du Machinisme Agricole, Saint-Antonin-Noble-Val 14113
Musée du Machinisme Agricole, Tullins-Fures 15015
Musée du Machinisme Agricole et du Cheval de Trait de 1830 à nos Jours, Juvigny-sous-Andaine 12109
Musée du Maïs, Laas 12277
Musée du Maïs, Morlaas 13160
Musée du Malgré-Tout, Treignes 03800
Musée du Manoir, Saussey 14651
Musée du Manoir d'Argentelles, Villebadin 15189
Musée du Marbre et de la Pierre Bleue, Bellignies 10675
Musée du Maréchal Lannes, Mareuil-sur-Belle 12821
Musée du Maréchal Murat, Labastide-Murat 12282
Musée du Marineland, Antibes 10373
Musée du Mas de la Pyramide, Saint-Rémy-de-Provence 14453
Musée du Matériel Agricole, La Villeneuve-les-Convers 12274
Musée du Mémorial du Martyr Juif Inconnu, Paris 13605
Musée du Mémorial National de la Déportation, Natzwiller 13273
Musée du Meuble Normand, Villedieu-les-Poêles 15194
Musée du Miel, Lobbes 03593
Musée du Miel et de l'Abeille, Gramont 11900
Musée du Mineur, Ensisheim 11616
Musée du Mineur, La Grand-Combe 12192
Musée du Modèle Réduit, Varces 15088
Musée du Monde Rural, Rettel 13951
Musée du Monde Souterrain, Han-sur-Lesse 03474
Musée du Monde Souterrain et Historique de la Spéléologie Française, Saint-Remèze 14444
Musée du Mont Corbier, Saint-Jean-de-Maurienne 14284
Musée du Mont-de-Piété et de la Condition des Soies, Avignon 10530
Musée du Mont-Repais, La Caquerelle 36612
Musée du Mont Riant, Alger 00043
Musée du Moteur, Saumur 14649
Musée du Moulin, Saint-Jean-Saint-Nicolas 14291
Musée du Moulin, Wissant 15318
Musée du Moulin à Eau, Eschviller 11643
Musée du Moulin à Eau et de la Boulangerie, Harzé 03478
Musée du Moulin à Marée, Trégastel 14988
Musée du Moulin de Boly, Lourdes 12691
Musée du Moulin de la Roue, Crémeaux 11454
Musée du Moulin Roupeyrac, Durenque 11590
Musée du Mouton et de la Bergerie Nationale, Rambouillet 13911
Musée du Mouvement National, Tunis 37594
Musée du Moyen Âge et de la Chevalerie, Figeac 11732
Musée du Mur de l'Atlantique, Audinghen 10479
Musée du Mur de l'Atlantique, Ouistreham 13445
Musée du Navigateur Flottant, Saint-Joseph-de-Sorel 06356
Musée du Nord de la Vendée, Montaigu (Vendée) 13037
Musée Du Nougat Arnaud Soubeyran, Montélimar 13074
Musée du Nouveau Monde, La Rochelle 12245
Musée du Noyonnais, Noyon 13374
Musée du Pain, Uhlwiller 15025
Musée du Pain Bouilli et du Four Communal, Villar-d'Arène 15174
Musée du Pain d'Épices d'Alsace et des Douceurs, Gertwiller 11855
Musée du Palais, Foumban 04957
Musée du Palais de la Reine, Antananarivo 27602
Musée du Palais des Evêques, Saint-Lizier 14325
Musée du Palais du Dey, Casbah 00054
Musée du Palais Royal, Phnom Penh 04949
Musée du Panache Gascon, Termes-d'Armagnac 14876
Musée du Panorama de la Vie de Sainte-Bernadette, Lourdes 12692
Musée du Panthéon National Haïtien, Port-au-Prince 21293
Musée du Papier Chiffon, Muzillac 13231
Musée du Papier Le Nil, Angoulême 10357
Musée du Papier Peint, Rixheim 13983
Musée du Papillon, Orgerus 13422
Musée du Para, Orléans 13434
Musée du Parc, Richelieu 13962
Musée du Parchemin et de l'Enluminure, Duras 11588
Musée du Parchemin et du Sceau, Saint-Omer 14387
Musée du Passé Agricole de Beauvechain, Beauvechain 03204
Musée du Pastel, Magrin 12767
Musée du Pastis, Aubagne 10455
Musée du Patrimoine, Néris-les-Bains 13282
Musée du Patrimoine, Roquebrune-sur-Argens 14026
Musée du Patrimoine, Six-Fours-les-Plages 14756
Musée du Patrimoine de l'Isle Crémieu, Hières-sur-Amby 12024
Musée du Patrimoine des Pères de Bétharram, Lestelle-Bétharram 12565
Musée du Patrimoine du Canton de Giat, Voingt 15282
Musée du Patrimoine et de la Dentelle, Chantilly 11165
Musée du Patrimoine et des Pratiques Locales, Jouy (Eure-et-Loir) 12097
Musée du Patrimoine Montagnard, Nages 13232
Musée du Patrimoine Pontois, Pons 13798
Musée du Patrimoine Religieux et des Croyances Populaires, Moustey 13194
Musée du Patrimoine Rural, Dompierre (Orne) 11549
Musée du Pays Brayaud, Châtelguyon 11230
Musée du Pays Brignolais, Brignoles 10931
Musée du Pays d'Albe, Sarralbe 14616
Musée du Pays de Caux, Yvetot 15334
Musée du Pays de France, Villieurs-le-Bel 15259
Musée du Pays de Luchon, Bagnères-de-Luchon 10562
Musée du Pays de Retz, Bourgneuf-en-Retz 10868
Musée du Pays de Sarrebourg, Sarrebourg 14622
Musée du Pays de Thônes, Thônes 14894
Musée du Pays du Der, Sainte-Rémy-en-Bouzemont 14550
Musée du Pays et du Vignoble de Reuilly, Reuilly (Indre) 13952
Musée du Pays et Val de Charmey, Charmey (Gruyère) 36624
Musée du Pays Rabastinois, Monesties 13012
Musée du Pays Vaurais, Lavaur 12368
Musée du Peigne et de la Plasturgie, Oyonnax 13449
Musée du Peintre Gustave Stoskopf, Brumath 10948
Musée du Père Jean-Marie de la Mennais, Ploërmel 13760
Musée du Père Noël, Lans-en-Vercors 12333
Musée du Perigord, Périgueux 13692
Musée du Petit Bateau et des Aventures de la Mer, Canet-en-Roussillon 11021
Musée du Petit Lourdes, Lourdes 12693
Musée du Petit-Palais, Avignon 10531
Musée du Pétrole, Merkwiller-Pechelbronn 12947
Musée du Pétrole, Parentis-en-Born 13468
Musée du Peuple Haïtien, Port-au-Prince 21294
Musée du Phare de Cordouan, Le Verdon-sur-Mer 12494
Musée du Phonographe et de la Musique Mécanique, Sainte-Maxime 14545
Musée du Phonographe et de Musique Mécanique, Limoges 12613
Musée du Pilori, Niort 13345
Musée du Poète Racan, Aubigné-Racan 10462
Musée du Poids Lourd et des Véhicules Anciens, Mondoubleau 13010
Musée du Poitier Gallo-Romain, Blicquy 03219
Musée du Pousse-Rapière, Saint-Puy 14433
Musée du Premier Empire, Fixin 11740
Musée du Président Jacques Chirac, 10221
Musée du Présidial, Castelnaudary 11078
Musée du Prieuré, Charolles 11187
Musée du Prieuré, Harfleur 11989
Musée du Prieuré, Perrecy-les-Forges 13711
Musée du Prieuré de Graville, Le Havre 12425
Musée du Prophète Djouman Mihin, Vavoua 07674
Musée du Protestantisme Dauphinois, Le Poët-Laval 12467
Musée du Protestantisme en Haut Languedoc, Ferrières (Tarn) 11725
Musée du Quercorb, Puivert 13885
Musée du Radar Allemand, Douvres-la-Délivrande 11570
Musée du Rail, Cajarc 11000
Musée du Rail, Dinan 11535
Musée du Ranquet, Clermont-Ferrand 11323
Musée du Regiment GG.FF., Firenze 23850
Musée du Regourdou, Montignac 13095
Musée du Rethélois e du Porcien, Rethel 13947
Musée du Revermont, Treffort-Cuisiat 14985
Musée du Rhum, Sainte-Marie 27729
Musée du Rhum, Sainte-Rose 21253
Musée du Roi de Cuba, Mushenge 07643
Musée du Rouergue, Espalion 11648
Musée du Rouergue Arts Métiers, Salles-la-Source 14585
Musée du Roussard, Sarge-sur-Braye 14611
Musée du Roy Soleil, Mont-Louis 13029
Musée du Royal 22e Régiment, Québec 06207
Musée du Sabot, Buironfosse 10954
Musée du Sabot, La Haye-de-Routot 12200
Musée du Sabot, Porcheresse 03689
Musée du Sabotier, Le Brugeron 12390
Musée du Sabotier, Soucht 14782
Musée du Safran, Boynes 10884
Musée du Santon, Generagues 11848
Musée du Santon, Le Val 12492
Musée du Santon, Marseille 12866
Musée du Santon, Pierrefeu-du-Var 13733
Musée du Santon et des Traditions de Provence, Fontaine-de-Vaucluse 11762
Musée du Santons, Gréoux-les-Bains 11950
Musée du Sapeur-Pompier, Bouzigues 10883
Musée du Sapeur-Pompier, Mulhouse 13211
Musée du Sapeur Pompier, Saint-Hippolyte-du-Fort 14266
Musée du Sapeurs-Pompiers, Ille-sur-Têt 12055
Musée du Saut du Tarn, Saint-Juéry 14293
Musée du Savignéen, Savigné-sur-Lathan 14666
Musée du Sceau Alsacien, La Petite-Pierre 12219
Musée du Schlittage et de la Forêt, Le Hohwald 12429
Musée du Scribe, Saint-Christol-lès-Alès 14147
Musée du Second-Empire, Bitche 10748
Musée du Sel, Marsal 12839
Musée du Sel, Salies-de-Béarn 14572
Musée du Séminaire, Consolation-Maisonettes 11399
Musée du Séminaire de Saint-Hyacinthe, Saint-Hyacinthe 06322
Musée du Séminaire de Sherbrooke, Sherbrooke, Québec 06442
Musée du Septennat de François Mitterrand, Château-Chinon 11202
Musée du Service de Santé des Armées, Paris 13606
Musée du Silex, Eben-Emael 03399
Musée du Site Balnéaire, Dinard 11537
Musée du Site de l'outil au Moutier-d'Ahun, Ahun 10233
Musée du Ski, Besse-en-Chandesse 10706
Musée du Ski, Briançon 10920
Musée du Ski et du Bobsleigh, Les Rousses 12551
Musée du Souvenier, Seillans 14694
Musée du Souvenir, Guer 11964
Musée du Souvenir, Soulac-sur-Mer 14791
Musée du Souvenir 1914-1918, Ablain-Saint-Nazaire 10224
Musée du Souvenir-Arts et Traditions Mullem-William, Cheminon 11268
Musée du Souvenir du Génie, Angers 10348
Musée du Souvenir du Prytanée Militaire, La Flèche 12180
Musée du Souvenir Général Estienne, Berry-au-Bac 10696
Musée du Souvenir Leersois, Leers 12505
Musée du Souvenir Militaire de Lyon, Lyon 12744
Musée du Souvenir Militaire de Thiérache, Martigny 12878
Musée du Souvenir Pierre de Bourdeille, Saint-Crépin-de-Richemont 14165
Musée du Suaire et du Pèlerinage, Cadouin 10976
Musée du Tacot, Cléron 11331
Musée du Tapis d'Art, Clermont-Ferrand 11324
Musée du Téléphone, Nancy 13242
Musée du Téléphone Narbonne, Narbonne 13269
Musée du Temple de Minerve, Tebessa 00076
Musée du Temps, Besançon 10703
Musée du Temps des Baigneurs, Cordemais 11405
Musée du Temps et de l'Art Religieux, Ceillac 11100
Musée du Temps Passé, Sainte-Agnès 14517
Musée du Temps qui Passe, Carquefou 11061
Musée du Terrain d'Aviation de Conde-Vraux, Vraux 15294
Musée du Terroir, Villeneuve-d'Ascq 15221
Musée du Terroir Bressan, Montpont 13136
Musée du Terroir de Peille, Peille 13679
Musée du Terroir des Clots, Mizoën-en-Oisans 12998
Musée du Terroir et de la Volaille, Romenay 14018
Musée du Terroir Hérissonnais, Hérisson 12013
Musée du Terroir Marseillais, Marseille 12867
Musée du Terroir Saint-Dalmas, Valdeblore 15046
Musée du Terroire, Conches-en-Ouche 11382
Musée du Textile, Cholet 11300
Musée du Textile des Vosges, Ventron 15124
Musée du Textile et de la Vie Sociale, Fourmies 11800
Musée du Textile et du Peigne en Corne, Lavelanet 12371
Musée du Textilen, La Labastide-Rouairoux 12203
Musée du Thé, Paris 13607
Musée du Théâtre, Couilly-Pont-aux-Dames 11424
Musée du Théâtre de Toone, Bruxelles 03327
Musée du Théâtre Forain et Musée Archéologique, Artenay 10436
Musée du Théâtre Royal de Toone, Bruxelles 03328
Musée du Tire-Bouchon, Ménerbes 12926
Musée du Tissage et de la Soierie, Bussières 10960
Le Musée du Tisserand Dauphinois, La Batie-Montgascon 12123
Musée du Touquet, Le Touquet-Paris-Plage 12486
Musée du Tour Automatique et d'Histoire de Moutier, Moutier 36959
Musée du Tour de France, Arvieux-en-Queyras 10441
Musée du Train, Clairac 11307
Musée du Train à Vapeur, Sainte-Foy-l'Argentière 14533
Musée du Train et de la Miniature, Saint-Sauves-d'Auvergne 14466
Musée du Train et des Equipages Militaires, Tours 14974
Musée du Train et du Jouet, Arpaillargues-et-Aureillac 10424
Musée du Transport Urbain Bruxellois, Bruxelles 03329
Musée du Travail Charles-Peyre, Montfermeil 13081
Musée du Trégor, Guimaec 11973
Musée du Tribunal Révolutionnaire, Tinchebray 14915
Musée du Trièves, Mens 12932
Musée du Trompe L'Oeil, Béziers 10720
Musée du Trophée des Alpes, La Turbie 12271
Musée du Val-de-Cher, Selles-sur-Cher 14699
Musée du Val-du-Grâce, Paris 13608
Musée du Valois, Vez 15151
Musée du Valois et de l'Archerie, Crépy-en-Valois 11456
Musée du Vélo, Carpiquet 11060
Musée du Vélo, Fenneviller 11718
Musée du Vélo, Labastide-d'Armagnac 12280
Musée du Vélo, Periers 13690
Musée du Vélocipède, Cadouin 10977
Musée du Veneur, Céré-la-Ronde 11106
Musée du Ver à Soie, Montreuil-Bellay 13142
Musée du Verre, Blaye-les-Mines 10765
Musée du Verre, Liège 03582
Musée du Verre, Sars-Poteries 14625
Musée du Verre Art et Technique, Charleroi 03353
Musée du Verre chez Val-Saint-Lambert Château, Seraing 03731
Musée du Verrier, Saint-Prex 37088
Musée du Vieaux Château, Bricquebec 10925
Musée du Vieil Aix, Aix-en-Provence 10254
Musée du Vieil Argenteuil, Argenteuil 10407
Musée du Vieil Auvillar, Auvillar 10506
Musée du Vieil Eygalières, Eygalières 11684
Musée du Vieux-Baulmes, Baulmes 36523
Musée du Vieux-Bex, Bex 36561
Musée du Vieux Biarritz, Biarritz 10726
Musée du Vieux Bourg, Mimizan 12983
Musée du Vieux Brest, Brest 10911
Musée du Vieux-Château, Laval (Mayenne) 12361
Musée du Vieux-Cimetière, Soignies 03756
Musée du Vieux Clairac, Clairac 11308
Musée du Vieux Courseulles, Courseulles-sur-Mer 11436
Musée du Vieux Figeac, Figeac 11733
Musée du Vieux Fort de Bertheaume, Plougonvelin 13772
Musée du Vieux Granville, Granville 11912
Musée du Vieux Honfleur, Honfleur 12029
Musée du Vieux Lambesc, Lambesc 12312
Musée du Vieux L'Arbresle, L'Arbresle 12342
Musée du Vieux Marseille, Marseille 12868
Musée du Vieux Mazeres, Mazères (Ariège) 12907
Musée du Vieux Merville, Merville 12951
Musée du Vieux-Monthey, Monthey 36945
Musée du Vieux Montpellier, Montpellier 13130
Musée du Vieux-Montreux, Montreux 36947
Musée du Vieux-Moudon, Moudon 36957
Musée du Vieux Moulin, Villar-Loubière 15175
Musée du Vieux Moulin à Vent, Maves 12902
Musée du Vieux Moulin à Vent, Vensac 15122
Musée du Vieux Moulin de Pierre, Hauville 12006
Musée du Vieux Nîmes, Nîmes 13341
Musée du Vieux Nimy, Mons 03636
Musée du Vieux-Pays, Le Châble 36621
Musée du Vieux Pays, Dieulouard 11510
Musée du Vieux-Pays d'Enhaut, Château-d'Oex 36626
Musée du Vieux Pérouges, Meximieux 12966
Musée du Vieux-Phare, Matane 05822
Musée du Vieux Pommiers, Pommiers (Loire) 13793
Musée du Vieux Pressoir et de la Vigne, Coulanges-la-Vineuse 11425
Musée du Vieux-Saxon, Saxon 37128
Musée du Vieux Toulon, Toulon (Var) 14930
Musée du Vieux Toulouse, Toulouse 14948
Musée du Vieux-Tréport, Le Tréport 12488
Musée du Vieux Vélo, Trois-Fontaines 14995
Musée du Vieux Warcq, Warcq 15302
Musée du Vigneron, Chaumont-le-Bois 11251
Musée du Vigneron, Wuenheim 15323
Musée du Vigneron Paul Coulon et Fils, Rasteau 13914
Musée du Vignoble et des Vins d'Alsace, Kientzheim 12113
Musée du Vignoble Montluçonnais, Domérat 11543
Musée du Vignoble Nantais, Le Pallet 12459
Musée du Village, Moknine 37574
Musée du Village, Saint-Sorlin-d'Arves 14478
Musée du Vin, Brem-sur-Mer 10902
Musée du Vin, Châteauneuf-du-Pape 11218
Musée du Vin, Cheignieu-la-Balme 11265
Musée du Vin, Ehnen 27554
Musée du Vin, Nangy 13247
Musée du Vin, Paris 13609
Musée du Vin, Saint-Hilaire-de-Loulay 14260
Musée du Vin dans l'Art, Pauillac 13674
Musée du Vin de Bourgogne, Beaune 10649
Musée du Vin de Bourgogne, Beaune 10650
Musée du Vin de Cahors et de la Table Lotoise, Cahors 10998
Musée du Vin de Champagne Piper-Heidsieck, Reims 13930
Musée du Vin de la Batellerie et de la Tonnellerie, Bergerac 10690
Musée du Vin et de la Mirabelle, Bruley 10943
Musée du Vin et de la Tonnellerie, Clermont-Soubiran 11329
Musée du Vin et du Pèlerinage de Saint-Jacques de Compostelle, Pomerol 13791
Musée du Vitrail, Gordes 11887
Musée du Vitrail, Mont-Louis 13030
Musée du Vivarais Protestant, Pranles 13864
Musée du Zinc, Montpellier 13131
Musée Ducal, Bouillon 03233
Musée Duhamel du Monceau, Pithiviers-le-Vieil 13744
Musée d'Unterlinden, Colmar 11361

Musée Duplessis, Carpentras 11057
Musée Dupuytren, Paris 13610
Musée d'Utique, Utique 37596
Musée d'Uxellodunum, Martel 12877
Musée Dynamique, Dakar 33778
Musée d'Yverdon-les-Bains et sa Région, Yverdon-les-Bains 37354
Musée E. Chenon, Château-Meillant 11205
Musée E.-Villard, La Mure 12213
Musée Eclaté d'Arts et de Traditions Populaires, Cardaillac 11047
Musée Éclaté de la Sidérurgie en Bourgogne du Nord, Sainte-Colombe-sur-Seine 14524
Musée-Ecole de Broderie, Cilaos 32418
Musée-Ecole de la Perrine, Laval (Mayenne) 12362
Musée-École du Grand Meaulnes, Épineuil-le-Fleuriel 11634
Musée Écologique Vanier, Laval 05735
Musée-Écurie de l'Insolite, Palau-del-Vidre 13456
Musée EDF Electropolis, Mulhouse 13212
Musée Edgar Melik, Cabriès 10972
Musée Edgard Clerc, Le Moule 21247
Musée Edith Piaf, Paris 13611
Musée Edmond Rostand, Cambo-les-Bains 11009
Musée Edouard Barthe, Montblanc 13061
Musée Edouard Branly, Paris 13612
Musée Edouard Mahé, Retiers 13948
Musée Éducatif de la Préhistoire, Saintes 14558
Musée Éducatif de Préhistoire et de Géologie, Villeneuve-la-Comtesse 15226
Musée Éducatif d'Entomologie de Levens, Levens 12570
Musée Emile Aubry, Béjaïa 00051
Musée Emile Chéron, Châteaumeillant 11215
Musée Émile-Guillaumin, Ygrande 15328
Musée Émile-Jean, Villiers-sur-Marne 15258
Musée Émile Verhaeren, Honnelles 03501
Musée Emile Villez, Guines 11974
Musée Emir Abdelkader, Miliana 00067
Musée Emmanuel de la Villéon, Fougères (Ille-et-Vilaine) 11794
Musée en Herbe, Paris 13613
Musée en Piconrue, Bastogne 03200
Musée en Plein Air de Sculptures Contemporaines, Étiolles 11672
Musée en Plein Air du Sart-Tilman, Liège 03583
Musée Entomologique, Saint-Quentin (Aisne) 14435
Musée Ernest Cognacq, Saint-Martin-de-Ré 14351
Musée Ernest Renan, Tréguier 14989
Musée Espace Bérenger Saunière, Rennes-le-Château 13945
Musée Espéranto a Gray, Gray 11935
Musée Estève, Bourges 10865
Musée et Atelier d'Art Animalier, La Chapelle-Thouarault 12151
Musée et Centre de Transmission de la Culture Daniel Weetaluktuk, Inukjuak 05621
Musée et Exposition Archéologiques, Luzy 12722
Musée et Parc Archéologiques de Montauban, Buzenol 03345
Musée et Pavillon Flaubert, Croisset 11462
Musée et Salon Permanent de l'Automobile de Sport Prestige et Collection, Chauffailles 11247
Musée et Site Archéologiques de Nice-Cimiez, Nice 13318
Musée et Sites Archéologiques de Saint-Romain-en-Gal-Vienne, Saint-Romain-en-Gal 14461
Musée et Temple des Bastides, Labastide-d'Armagnac 12281
Musée et Trésor de l'Hospice, Bourg-Saint-Pierre 36582
Musée et Villa Gallo-Romain, Plassac 13750
Musée Ethnographique, Chefchaouen 28692
Musée Ethnographique, Porto-Novo 03878
Musée Ethnographique, Tétouan 28717
Musée Ethnographique de l'Olivier, Cagnes-sur-Mer 10990
Musée Ethnographique de Site, Sare 14610
Musée Ethnographique du Donjon, Niort 13346
Musée Ethnographique Regional, Bouar 06879
Musée Ethnologique Intercommunal du Vermandois, Vermand 15136
Musée Ethnolopique Provincial, Tshikappa 07644
Musée Etienne-Jules Marey, Beaune 10651
Musée Etival dans le Temps, Etival-Clairefontaine 11673
Musée Eugène Boudin, Honfleur 12030
Musée Eugène Burnand, Moudon 36958
Musée Eugène Farcot, Sainville 14565
Musée Eugène le Roy et Vieux Métiers, Montignac 13096
Musée Européen de Sculptures Contemporaines en Plein Air, Launstroff 12354
Musée Eve-Lavallière, Thuillières 14906
Musée-Expo de la Grange aux Abeilles, Giffaumont-Champaubert 11861
Musée Expo Forêt, Gérardmer 11852
Musée Exposition La Voiture à Travers les Âges, Chamblanc 11144
Musée Extraordinaire Georges-Mazoyer, Ansouis 10369
Musée Fabre, Montpellier 13132
Musée Fantastique de la Bête de Gévaudan, Saugues-en-Gévaudan 14633
Musée Fayet, Béziers 10721
Musée Féerie des Coquillages, Granville 11913
Musée Fenaille, Rodez 14008
Musée-Ferme Conservatoire Bigourdane, Péré 13689
Musée-Ferme d'Antan, Saint-Fargeau 14211
Musée Ferme d'Autrefois et Matériel Artisanal, Thourie 14904
Musée-Ferme des Castors du Chili, Arzacq-Arraziguet 10444
Musée-Ferme Georges-Ville, Paris 13614
Musée Fernandèl, Carry-le-Rouet 11064
Musée Ferroviaire, Bize-Minervois 10751
Musée Ferroviaire, Connerré 11394
Musée Ferroviaire, Longueville 12655
Musée Ferroviaire, Saint-Sulpice (Loir-et-Cher) 14482
Musée Ferroviaire de Saint-Géry, Saint-Géry 14250
Musée Ferroviaire et des Vieilles Gares, Guîtres 11979
Musée Ferroviaire La Lorraine en Périgord, Excideuil 11683
Musée Fesch, Ajaccio 10265
Musée Flaubert et d'Histoire de la Médecine, Rouen 14052
Musée Flottant-Architecture Navale, Audierne 10478
Musée Folklorique de Ghardaïa, Ghardaïa 00064
Musée Folklorique et Viticole à Possen, Bech-Kleinmacher 27542
Musée-Fondation Alexandra David-Néel, Digne-les-Bains 11513
Musée-Fondation Arp, Clamart 11310
Musée-Fondation Bemberg, Toulouse 14949
Musée-Fondation Louis-Jou, Les Baux-de-Provence 12527
Musée Fondation Musée Volti, Villefranche-sur-Mer 15208
Musée Fondation Royale d'Albanie, La Chapelle-d'Angillon 12145
Musée Fort de Sucy, Sucy-en-Brie 14841
Musée Fort Lagarde, Prats-de-Mollo-la-Preste 13865
Musée Fougou, Montpellier 13133
Musée Fragonard de l'Ecole Nationale Vétérinaire d'Alfort, Maisons-Alfort 12776
Musée Français - 1e Armée Française Mai 1940, Cortil-Noirmont 03362
Musée Français de la Brasserie, Saint-Nicolas-de-Port 14385
Musée Français de la Photographie, Bièvres 10733
Musée Français de la Spéléologie, Courniou-les-Grottes 11432
Musée Français de Spéléologie, Gagny 11832
Musée Français des Phares et Balises, Ile-d'Ouessant 12052
Musée Français du Chemin de Fer, Mulhouse 13213
Musée Francis Jammes, Hasparren 11994
Musée Francisque Mandet, Riom 13972
Musée Franco-Américain, Sommepy-Tahure 14768
Musée Franco-Tchécolosvaque, Darney 11483
Musée François Desnoyer, Saint-Cyprien 14167
Musée François-Flori "Ricordi Vividi Antichi Niulinchi", Calacuccia 11001
Musée François Guiguet, Corbelin 11402
Musée François Mauriac, Saint-Maixant (Gironde) 14338
Musée François-Mauriac, Vemars 15110
Musée François Pilote, La Pocatière 05707
Musée François-Pompon, Saulieu 14636
Musée Frédéric-Japy, Beaucourt 10636
Musée Frédéric Mistral, Maillane 12769
Musée Friry, Remiremont 13937
Musée Fromages et Patrimoine, Ambert 10303
Musée Funéraire du Château, Lourdes 12694
Musée G.-Delage, Seguret 14693
Musée Gadagne, Lyon 12745
Musée-Galerie Alexis et Gustave-Adolf Mossa, Nice 13319
Musée-Galerie de la Mine de Fer de Framont, Grandfontaine (Bas-Rhin) 11908
Musée Galerie Honoré Camos, Bargemon 10591
Musée-Galerie Numismatique, La Rochelle 12246
Musée-Galerie Raoul-Dufy, Nice 13320
Musée Gallé-Juillet, Creil 11453
Musée Galliéra, Paris 13615
Musée Gallo-Romain, Berneau 03215
Musée Gallo-Romain, Biesheim 10730
Musée Gallo-Romain, Périgueux 13693
Musée Gallo-Romain, Rumes 03715
Musée Gallo-Romain, Saint-Méard 14367
Musée Gallo-Romain d'Aoste, Aoste 10382
Musée Gallo-Romain de Tauroentum, Saint-Cyr-sur-Mer 14174
Musée Gallo-Romain d'Octodure, Martigny 36928
Musée Gantner, La Chapelle-sous-Chaux 12150
Musée Gardanne Autrefois, Gardanne 11840
Musée Garinet, Châlons-en-Champagne 11130
Musée Garret, Vesoul 15149
Musée Gaspar, Arlon 03184
Musée Gaston Fébus, Mauvezin (Hautes-Pyrénées) 12901
Musée Gaston Grégor, Salles-d'Angles 14584
Musée Gatien-Bonnet, Lagny-sur-Marne 12298
Musée Gauguin, Le Carbet 27724
Musée Gay-Lussac, Saint-Léonard-de-Noblat 14323
Musée General Leclerc, Alençon 10282
Musée Géo Charles, Échirolles 11597
Musée Géologique, Conakry 21281
Musée Géologique, Dakar 33779
Musée Géologique, La Charguia 37568
Musée Géologique, Olargues 13398
Musée Geologique, Vernet-les-Bains 15137
Musée Géologique du Rwanda, Kigali 33754
Musée Géologique et Paléontologique, Langé 12321
Musée Géologique Fossiles Préhistoire, Neuil 13288
Musée Geologique Sengier-Cousin, Jadotville 07632
Musée Géologique ULP, Strasbourg 14834
Musée George Sand et de la Vallée Noire, La Châtre 12153
Musée Georges Borias, Uzès 15035
Musée Georges Clemenceau, Paris 13616
Musée Georges-Labit, Toulouse 14950
Musée Georgette-Lemaire, Angoulême 10358
Musée Gilles-Villeneuve, Berthierville 05076
Musée Girodet, Montargis 13045
Musée Girouxville, Girouxville 05489
Musée Gletton, Vaiges 15040
Musée Goetz-Boumeester, Villefranche-sur-Mer 15209
Musée Gorsline, Bussy-le-Grand 10962
Musée Goya, Castres 11084
Musée Granet, Aix-en-Provence 10255
Musée Grétry, Liège 03584
Musée Greuze, Tournus 14965
Musée Grévin, Dijon 11529
Musée Grévin, Paris 13617
Musée Grévin, Saint-Jean-de-Luz 14280
Musée Grévin de la Provence, Salon-de-Provence 14591
Musée Grévin de Lourdes, Lourdes 12695
Musée Grobet-Labadié, Marseille 12869
Musée Grotte de Limousis, Limousis 12618
Musée Gruérien, Bulle 36603
Musée Guerre et Paix en Ardennes, Novion-Porcien 13368
Musée Guillaume Apollinaire, Stavelot 03766
Musée Guillion, Romanèche-Thorins 14014
Musée Gustave Moreau, Paris 13618
Musée Gyger, Vallorbe 37280
Musée-Hameau de Sculptures XIXe s, Fransèches 11805
Musée Hardy, Clécy 11314
Musée Harmas Jean-Henri Fabre, Sérignan-du-Comtat 14719
Musée Haut Savoyard de la Résistance, Bonneville 10798
Musée Haviland, Limoges 12614
Musée Hector Berlioz, La Côte-Saint-André 12161
Musée Henri-Barre, Thouars 14903
Musée Henri Boez, Maubeuge 12890
Musée Henri Chapu, Le Mée-sur-Seine 12445
Musée Henri Dupuis, Saint-Omer 14388
Musée Henri-Giron, Le Vigan (Lot) 12498
Musée Henri IV, Saint-Sulpice-de-Faleyrens 14480
Musée Henri Malartre, Rochetaillée-sur-Saône 14003
Musée Henri-Mathieu, Bruyères 10951
Musée Henri Ughetto, Lyon 12746
Musée Henry Clews, Mandelieu 12787
Musée Henry de Monfreid, Ingrandes (Indre) 12058
Musée Héritage, Saint-Albert 06300
Musée Hermès, Paris 13619
Musée Historial, Mazères (Gironde) 12908
Musée Historial, Port-Joinville 13840
Musée Historial du Vieux Pessac, Pessac 13716
Musée Historie Locale, Marchiennes 12806
Musée Historique, Abomey 03871
Musée Historique, Antananarivo 27603
Musée Historique, Bapaume 10582
Musée Historique, Basse-Rentgen 10599
Musée Historique, Bessé-sur-Braye 10707
Musée Historique, Bort-les-Orgues 10824
Musée Historique, Bourail 30090
Musée Historique, Carhaix-Plouguer 11050
Musée Historique, Cellettes 11101
Musée Historique, Cérisy-la-Forêt 11114
Musée Historique, Chalençon 11124
Musée Historique, Châtillon-sur-Saône 11242
Musée Historique, Clervaux 27547
Musée Historique, Elne 11609
Musée Historique, Fénetrange 11717
Musée Historique, Fondremand 11754
Musée Historique, Gourdon (Alpes-Maritimes) 11893
Musée Historique, Haguenau 11986
Musée Historique, La Couvertoirade 12166
Musée Historique, Laroquebrou 12346
Musée Historique, Le Chambon-sur-Lignon 12397
Musée Historique, Mont-Saint-Michel 13032
Musée Historique, Mulhouse 13214
Musée Historique, Paris 13620
Musée Historique, Peyrusse-le-Roc 13722
Musée Historique, Plomelin 13763
Musée Historique, Strasbourg 14835
Musée Historique 1814, Essises 11658
Musée Historique Charles Le Moyne, Longueuil 05776
Musée Historique d'Abomey, Abomey 03872
Musée Historique de Gorée, Dakar 33780
Musée Historique de Gorée, Gorée 33783
Musée Historique de Graffiti Anciens, Marsilly 12874
Musée Historique de la Citadelle, Belle-Ile-en-Mer 10672
Musée Historique de la Faïence, Moustiers-Sainte-Marie 13195
Musée Historique de la Laub, Bischwiller 10744
Musée Historique de la Ligne Maginot Aquatique, Sarralbe 14617
Musée Historique de la Médecine Scientifique et des Pratiques Populaires, Beauchastel 10635
Musée Historique de la Poterie, Wismes 15317
Musée Historique de la Réformation, Genève 36747
Musée Historique de la Tour de la Chaîne, La Rochelle 12247
Musée Historique de Lausanne, Lausanne 36864
Musée Historique de l'Hydraviation, Biscarrosse 10741
Musée Historique de l'Ile-de-Sein, Ile-de-Sein 12050
Musée Historique de Saint-Gilles-les-Hauts, Saint-Paul 32423
Musée Historique de Saint-Pierre, Saint-Pierre 27727
Musée Historique de Troyes et de la Champagne, Troyes 15006
Musée Historique de Verfeil, Verfeil 15133
Musée Historique de Vevey, Vevey 37288
Musée Historique de Villèle, Saint-Gilles-les-Hauts 32422
Musée Historique des Incorporés de Force et de Tambow, Amnéville-les-Thermes 10328
Musée Historique du Bailliage de Rouffach, Rouffach 14057
Musée Historique du Centre-Var, Le Luc 12432
Musée Historique du Château, Langoiran 12324
Musée Historique du Cidre, Melleray-la-Vallée 12921
Musée Historique du Cloître, Salles-Arbuissonnas-en-Beaujolais 14583
Musée Historique du Domaine National, Saint-Cloud 14162
Musée Historique du Groupe Lorraine, Reims 13931
Musée Historique du Madawaska, Edmundston 05396
Musée Historique du Papier, Ambert 10304
Musée Historique du Papier, Couze-et-Saint-Front 11447
Musée Historique du Papier, Saint-Jean-de-Côle 14277
Musée Historique du Port, La Rochelle 12248
Musée Historique et Archéologique, Montségur 13152
Musée Historique et Archéologique de l'Orléanais, Orléans 13435
Musée Historique et de la Pêche, Talmont-sur-Gironde 14852
Musée Historique et des Porcelaines, Nyon 36994
Musée Historique et Diorama 1914-1918, Souchez 14781
Musée Historique et Erckmann-Chatrian, Phalsbourg 13727
Musée Historique et Lapidaire, Isle-Aumont 12059
Musée Historique et Lapidaire, Morlaas 13161
Musée Historique et Logis Thiphaine, Le Mont-Saint-Michel 12454
Musée Historique et Militaire, Brest 10912
Musée Historique et Militaire, Freyming-Merlebach 11819
Musée Historique et Militaire, Huningue 12036
Musée Historique et Préhistorique Van den Steen, Jehay-Amay 03528
Musée Historique Valdec-de Lessart, Portets 13849
Musée Hofer-Bury, Lavérune 12372
Musée Horlogerie Automates Yves Cupillard, Morteau 13174
Musée Horreum Romain, Narbonne 13270
Musée Horta, Bruxelles 03330
Musée Hospitalier, Charlieu 11182
Musée Hospitalier - Apothicairerie, Bourg-en-Bresse 10854
Musée Hospitalier et Apothicairerie, Louhans 12677
Musée-Hôtel Bertrand, Châteauroux (Indre) 11227
Musée-Hôtel de Beaumont, Valognes 15072
Musée Hôtel de la Dentelle, Brioude 10935
Musée-Hôtel Granval-Caligny, Valognes 15073
Musée Hôtel Lallemand, Bourges 10866
Musée-Hôtel Le Vergeur, Reims 13932
Musée Humoristique Albert Dubout, Palavas-les-Flots 13457
Musée Huperel de l'Histoire Cathare, Minerve 12985
Musée Hyacinthe Rigaud, Perpignan 13708
Musée Hydrogéologique, Chaudfontaine 03356
Musée Ianchelevici, La Louvière 03547
Musée Impérial de la Miniature, Les Barils 12520
Musée in Situ des Bains Romains, Aix-les-Bains 10261
Musée Industriel Corderie Vallois, Notre-Dame-de-Bondeville 13365
Musée Industriel du Val-de-Travers, Fleurier 36702
Musée Industriel et d'Ethnologie, Lille 12603
Musée Ingres, Montauban 13048
Musée Intercommunal d'Histoire et d'Archéologie, Louvres 12705
Musée International d'Arts Modestes, Sète 14730
Musée International de Akum, Bamenda 04952
Musée International de la Chasse, Gien 11860
Musée International de la Chaussure, Romans-sur-Isère 14016
Musée International de la Croix-Rouge et du Croissant-Rouge, Genève 36748
Musée International de la Faune, Argelès-Gazost 10402
Musée International de la Faune, Québriac 13891
Musée International de la Marionnette, Bruxelles 03331
Musée International de la Parfumerie, Grasse 11922
Musée International de l'Automobile, Le Grand-Saconnex 36774
Musée International de l'Etiquette, Aigle 36439
Musée International de Mobilier Miniature, Vendeuvre 15116
Musée International des Hussards, Tarbes 14868
Musée International des Polices et des Gendarmeries, Charvieu-Chavagneux 11196
Musée International d'Horlogerie, La Chaux-de-Fonds 36630
Musée International du Carnaval et du Masque, Binche 03217
Musée International du Coquillage, Saint-Barthélemy 21250
Musée International du Long Cours Cap Hornier, Saint-Malo (Ille-et-Vilaine) 14342

Musée International du Menu Gastronomique, Nointel (Oise) 13356
Musée International du Trans-Manche, Escalles 11640
Musée International, Pétanque et Boules, Saint-Bonnet-le-Château 14126
Musée Isérables, Isérables 36815
Musée Ivan-Tourguéniev, Bougival 10832
Musée J. Armand Bombardier, Valcourt 06661
Musée J.-E.-Blanche, Offranville 13387
Musée J.-F. Leyraud, La Roche-sur-le-Buis 12231
Musée Jacquaire, Ferrières (Tarn) 11726
Musée Jacquemart-André, Fontaine-Chaalis 11756
Musée Jacquemart-André, Paris 13621
Musée Jacques Warminski, Saint-Georges-des-Sept-Voies 14233
Musée Jadis Allevard, Allevard-les-Bains 10292
Musée-Jardin, Granville 11914
Musée-Jardin d'Art Contemporain, Bitche 10749
Musée-Jardin Paul-Landowski, Boulogne-Billancourt 10838
Musée J.B. Mathon et André Durand, Neufchâtel-en-Bray 13285
Musée Jean-Aicard, La Garde 12186
Musée Jean Aicard, Solliès-Ville 14766
Musée Jean-Boudou et Lucien-Girma, Saint-Laurent-d'Olt 14312
Musée Jean-Charles Cazin, Samer 14596
Musée Jean-Claude Colin, Saint-Bonnet-le-Troncy 14127
Musée Jean Cocteau, Menton 12939
Musée Jean de la Fontaine, Château-Thierry 11210
Musée Jean Farkas, Baden 10555
Musée Jean-Gabin, Mériel 12943
Musée Jean-Henri Fabre, Saint-Léons 14324
Musée Jean-Honoré Fragonard, Grasse 11923
Musée Jean-Hotte, Saint-Eustache 06316
Musée Jean-Jacques Rousseau, Genève 36749
Musée Jean-Jacques Rousseau, Montmorency 13111
Musée Jean-Jacques Rousseau, Môtiers 36954
Musée Jean-Lurçat, Angers 10349
Musée Jean Lurçat, Saint-Laurent-les-Tours 14315
Musée Jean Macé, Beblenheim 10659
Musée Jean-Marie Souplet, Engis 03406
Musée Jean-Mermoz, Aubenton 10459
Musée Jean-Moulin, Paris 13622
Musée Jean-Philippe-Marchand, Marsais 12837
Musée Jean-Racine, La Ferté-Milon 12172
Musée Jean Tua, Genève 36750
Musée Jeanne d'Aboville, La Fère 12168
Musée Jeanne d'Arc, Chinon 11291
Musée Jeanne-d'Arc, Rouen 14053
Musée Jeanne d'Arc, Sainte-Cathérine-de-Fierbois 14522
Musée Jehanne d'Hier et d'Aujourd'hui, Domremy-la-Pucelle 11552
Musée Jenisch, Vevey 37289
Musée Joachim du Bellay, Liré 12620
Musée Johannique, Vaucouleurs 15097
Musée Joseph Abeilhe, Marciac 12808
Musée Joseph Denais, Beaufort-en-Vallée 10637
Musée Joseph Durand, Saint-Clément-des-Baleines 14159
Musée Joseph Lhoménède, Frugières-le-Pin 11825
Musée Joseph-Vaylet, Espalion 11649
Musée Jourdain, Morez 13159
Musée Judéo-Alsacien, Bouxwiller 10881
Musée Juif Comtadin, Cavaillon 11097
Musée Juin 1944, L'Aigle 12305
Musée Jules Desbois, Parçay-les-Pins 13466
Musée Jules Destrée, Charleroi 03354
Musée Jules Romains, Saint-Julien-Chapteuil 14295
Musée Jules Verne, Nantes 13259
Musée Jungle des Papillons Vivants, Antibes 10374
Musée Jurassien d'Art et d'Histoire, Delémont 36657
Musée Jurassien des Arts, Moutier 36960
Musée Jurassien des Sciences Naturelles, Porrentruy 37029
Musée Juste Pour Rire, Montréal 05922
Musée K. Raphaël, Vavoua 07675
Musée Kateri Tekakwitha, Kahnawake 05636
Musée Kaysone Phomvihane, Vientiane 27320
Musée Kio-Warini, Loretteville 05779
Musée Kwok-On, Paris 13623
Musée La Diana, Montbrison 13064
Musée la Faïencerie, Ancy-le-Franc 10333
Musée La Ferme Forézienne, Saint-Bonnet-les-Oules 14128
Musée la Magie des Automates, Lans-en-Vercors 12334
Musée La Main et l'Outil, Pannes 13461
Musée La Maison du Passé, Royat-les-Bains 14070
Musée la Maison du Pêcheur et "Le Hope", Saint-Gilles-Croix-de-Vie 14251
Musée la Muse, Mérindol 12945
Musée la Percée du Bocage 1944, Saint-Martin-des-Besaces 14353
Musée La Sagne, La Sagne 37083
Musée la Vie des Jouets, Mauleon 12893
Musée la Villa Aurélienne, Fréjus 11812
Musée Labasso, Bangassou 06877
Musée l'Abeille Vivante, Le Faouët 12414
Musée Labenche d'Art et d'Histoire, Brive-la-Gaillarde 10939
Musée Lacordaire, Recey-sur-Ource 13918
Musée Lacoune, Lacaune 12291
Musée Laennec, Nantes 13260
Musée Lamartine, Mâcon 12758
Musée Lambinet, Versailles 15144
Musée Lamothe-Cadillac, Saint-Nicolas-de-la-Grave 14384
Musée Langlois, Beaumont-en-Auge 10645
Musée Languédocien, Montpellier 13134
Musée Laperouse, Albi 10275
Musée Lapidaire, Avignon 10532
Musée Lapidaire, Baume-les-Messieurs 10609
Musée Lapidaire, Cabasse 10966
Musée Lapidaire, Carpentras 11058
Musée Lapidaire, Lalouret-Laffiteau 12308
Musée Lapidaire, Léhon 12507
Musée Lapidaire, Narbonne 13271
Musée Lapidaire, Riez 13966
Musée Lapidaire, Saint-Germain-Laval 14244
Musée Lapidaire, Saint-Guilhem-le-Désert 14257
Musée Lapidaire, Villeveyrac 15252
Musée Lapidaire de la Cité, Carcassonne 11045
Musée Lapidaire de l'Abbaye, Savigny (Rhône) 14674
Musée Lapidaire de l'Abbaye Saint-Pierre, Maillezais 12772
Musée Lapidaire de Mozac, Mozac 13204
Musée Lapidaire du Cloître de l'Ancienne Cathédrale, Vaison-la-Romaine 15044
Musée Lapidaire Municipal, Saint-Sever (Landes) 14475
Musée Lapidaire Paléochrétien, Toulx-Sainte-Croix 14954
Musée L'Art en Marche Hauterives Art Brut, Neuve Invention, Hauterives 12002
Musée L'Art en Marche Lapalisse Art Brut, Lapalisse 12340
Musée Laurier, Victoriaville 06731
Musée Lautrecois, Lautrec 12358
Musée Le Chafaud, Percé 06112
Musée Le Corbusier, Pessac 13717
Musée "Le Grenier de l'Histoire", Lèves 12571
Musée Le Jacquemart, Langeac 12322
Musée Le Libertaire, Fontenay-les-Briis 11773
Musée Le Masque en Liberté, Nibelle 13306
Musée Le Minerve, Yzeures-sur-Creuse 15337
Musée Le Mont-Saint-Michel, Le Mont-Saint-Michel 12455
Musée Le Palais des Naïfs, Bages (Pyrénées-Orientales) 10558
Musée Le Petit Louvre, La Pacaudière 12215
Musée le Petit Mont-Saint-Michel, Saint-Marcan 14343
Musée Le Pionnier, Saint-Malo 06365
Musée Le Secq des Tournelles - Musée de la Ferronnerie, Rouen 14054
Musée le Soum, Saint-Véran 14501
Musée le Temple du Soleil, Saint-Michel-en-l'Herm 14371
Musée Leblanc-Duvernoy, Auxerre 10511
Musée Leclerc Briant, Épernay 11629
Musée Lecoq, Clermont-Ferrand 11325
Musée Lella Hadria, Midoun 37573
Musée Lénine, Paris 13624
Musée Léon de Smet, Deurle 03381
Musée Léon Dierx, Saint-Denis 32420
Musée Léon Marès, Lovagny 12706
Musée Léon Perrin, Môtiers 36955
Musée Les Amis de l'Outil, Bièvres 10734
Musée Les Ateliers du Bois, Vadencourt 15039
Musée les Retrouvailles, Saint-Jean-Port-Joli 06329
Musée les Sources d'Hercule, Deneuvre 11498
Musée les Thermes d'Antonin, Carthage 37556
Musée Libertador du Général San Martin, Boulogne-sur-Mer 10840
Musée Ligier Richier, Saint-Mihiel 14377
Musée Lillet, Podensac 13782
Musée Littéraire Victor Hugo, Vianden 27579
Musée Local, Aumont-Aubrac 10484
Musée Local, Brandenbourg 27545
Musée Local, Lansargues 12335
Musée Local, Weiler-la-Tour 27581
Musée Local d'Art, Eze 11696
Musée Lombard, Doullens 11568
Musée Longines, Saint-Imier 37086
Musée Lorrain, Nancy 13243
Musée Louis-Braille, Coupvray 11429
Musée Louis-Cornu, Wassigny 15306
Musée Louis-Hemon, Peribonka 06113
Musée Louis Jou, Les Baux-de-Provence 12528
Musée Louis-Jourdan, Saint-Paul-de-Varax 14401
Musée Louis-Lacrocq, Guéret 11968
Musée Louis Pasteur, Strasbourg 14836
Musée Louis Pergaud, Belmont 10676
Musée Louis-Philippe, Eu 11677
Musée Louis-Vouland, Avignon 10533
Musée Louise Cottin, Vigneulles-lès-Hattonchâtel 15168
Musée Louise Weiss, Saverne 14664
Musée Lucien Roy, Beure 10712
Musée Luxembourgeois, Arlon 03185
Musée Maçonnique de la Grande Loge de France, Paris 13625
Musée Mado Robin, Yzeures-sur-Creuse 15338
Musée Magie des Abeilles, Villechauve 15190
Musée Magnanerie, Vallon-Pont-d'Arc 15069
Musée Magnelli, Vallauris 15060
Musée Magnin, Dijon 11530
Musée Maillol, Paris 13626
Musée Mainssieux, Voiron 15284
Musée Mairie, Le Pont-de-Beauvoisin 12468
Musée-Maison d'Art Contemporain Chaillioux, Fresnes (Val-de-Marne) 11816
Musée-Maison de Chateaubriand, Châtenay-Malabry 11236
Musée Maison de Clemenceau, Saint-Vincent-sur-Jard 14507
Musée Maison de George Sand, Gargilesse-Dampierre 11842
Musée Maison de la Baleine, Luc-sur-Mer 12708
Musée Maison de la Brique, Saint-Martin-d'Aubigny 14347
Musée Maison de la Dame de Brassempouy, Brassempouy 10895
Musée-Maison de la Nature, Samer 14597
Musée-Maison de la Nature et de l'Estuaire de l'Orne, Sallenelles 14578
Musée Maison de la Soie, Saint-Hippolyte-du-Fort 14267
Musée-Maison de la Vie Rurale, La Flocellière 12181
Musée-Maison de l'Armateur, Le Havre 12426
Musée-Maison de l'Aspre, Thuir 14909
Musée-Maison de l'Erdre, Nantes 13261
Musée Maison de l'Huître, Gujan-Mestras 11980
Musée-Maison de Sainte-Thérèse, Lisieux 12622
Musée-Maison d'Ecole, Montceau-les-Mines 13067
Musée Maison Déodat Roché, Arques (Aude) 10426
Musée-Maison des Amis de la Forêt, Mervent 12949
Musée-Maison des Arts des Hauts-Cantons, Bédarieux 10661
Musée-Maison des Canuts, Lyon 12747
Musée-Maison des Dentelles et du Point d'Argentan, Argentan 10406
Musée-Maison des Milelli, Ajaccio 10266
Musée-Maison des Pierreux, Massangis 12886
Musée Maison des Templiers, Salers 14570
Musée-Maison des Tresses et des Lacets, La Terrasse-sur-Dorlay 12264
Musée-Maison des Vanniers, Feytiat 11730
Musée-Maison du Café, Vieux-Habitants 21254
Musée-Maison du Canal, Fegreac 11714
Musée-Maison du Jardinier, Gétigné 11857
Musée-Maison du Pain, Commeny 11372
Musée-Maison du Parc National et de la Vallée, Luz-Saint-Sauveur 12720
Musée-Maison du Parc National et du Val d'Azun, Arrens-Marsous 10431
Musée-Maison du Parc Naturel Régional de la Montagne de Reims, Pourcy 13852
Musée Maison du Pays, Moisdon-la-Rivière 13000
Musée-Maison du Pêcheur, La Chevrolière 12155
Musée-Maison du Petit Poitou, Chaillé-les-Marais 11122
Musée Maison du Potier, Le Fuilet 12416
Musée-Maison du Saumon et de la Rivière, Brioude 10936
Musée-Maison du Terroir, Châteauponsac 11224
Musée-Maison du Verre, Meisenthal 12917
Musée-Maison Lohobiague dite Maison Louis XIV, Saint-Jean-de-Luz 14281
Musée-Maison Marcel Proust, Illiers-Combray 12056
Musée Maison Mathelin, Bastogne 03201
Musée-Maison Natale de Jean de Lattre de Tassigny, Mouilleron-en-Pareds 13182
Musée-Maison Natale de Saint-Henri-Dorie, Talmont-Saint-Hilaire 14851
Musée-Maison Natale du Maréchal Jourdan, Limoges 12615
Musée-Maison Natale Gustave Courbet, Ornans 13438
Musée-Maison Paternelle de Bernadette, Lourdes 12696
Musée Maison Robert-Doisneau, Gentilly 11850
Musée Maison Saint-Gabriel, Montréal 05923
Musée Malraux, Le Havre 12427
Musée M'Am Jeanne, Fontenoy-en-Puisaye 11777
Musée Manoir de Kerazan, Loctudy 12646
Musée-Manoir de la Touche, Nantes 13262
Musée Manoir de Vains, Vains 15042
Musée-Manoir des Évêques de Lisieux, Deauville 11488
Musée-Manoir des Sciences, Réaumur 13917
Musée Maraîchin, Sallertaine 14580
Musée Marc-Aurèle Fortin, Montréal 05924
Musée Marc Deydier, Cucuron 11468
Musée Marc Leclerc, La Ménitré 12207
Musée Marcel Cachin, Choisy-le-Roi 11296
Musée Marcel Collet, Loverval 03601
Musée Marcel de Marcheville, Romorantin-Lanthenay 14021
Musée Marcel-Lenoir, Montricoux 13149
Musée Marcel Sahut, Volvic 15289
Musée Marchiennois d'Histoire et d'Archéologie Industrielle, Marchienne-au-Pont 03610
Musée Maréchal Joffre, Rivesaltes 13982
Musée Marguerite-Audoux, Aubigny-sur-Nère 10464
Musée Marguerite Bourgeoys, Montréal 05925
Musée Marguerite-de-Bourgogne, Tonnerre 14918
Musée Marguerite-Yourcenar, Saint-Jans-Cappel 14269
Musée Marial de Beauraing, Beauraing 03203
Musée Marie Laurencin, Chino 26128
Musée Marie-Rose Durocher, Longueuil 05777
Musée Marin, Port-Navalo 13844
Musée-Marinarium du Haut Lavédan, Pierrefitte-Nestalas 13734
Musée Marine-et-Montagne, Mons (Var) 13021
Musée Maritime, Camaret-sur-Mer 11007
Musée Maritime, Carantec 11038
Musée Maritime, Le Mont-Saint-Michel 12456
Musée Maritime à Flot France I, La Rochelle 12249
Musée Maritime Chantereyne, Cherbourg 11277
Musée Maritime de l'Ile de Tatihou, Saint-Vaast-la-Hougue 14494
Musée Maritime de l'île de Tatihou, Saint-Vaast-la-Hougue 14495
Musée Maritime de Regnéville, Regnéville-sur-Mer 13921
Musée Maritime du Québec, L'Islet 05757
Musée Maritime, Fluvial et Portuaire, Rouen 14055
Musée Maritime Islais, Port-Joinville 13841
Musée Maritime La Rochelle, La Rochelle 12250
Musée Maritime l'Esvale et Ostréicole, La Tremblade 12269
Musée Marius Barbeau, Saint-Joseph-de-Beauce 06355
Musée Marmottan Claude Monet, Paris 13627
Musée Marsa El-Kharez, El-Kala 00061
Musée Marsil, Saint-Lambert 06359
Musée Martin Duby, Auriol 10493
Musée Massey, Tarbes 14869
Musée Matheysin, La Mure 12214
Musée Mathurin Méheut, Lamballe 12311
Musée Matisse, Le Cateau-Cambrésis 12396
Musée Matisse, Nice 13321
Musée Maurice Beaumont, Luxeuil-les-Bains 12716
Musée Maurice Carême, Bruxelles 03332
Musée Maurice-Dufresne, Azay-le-Rideau 10551
Musée Maurice et Eugénie de Guérin, Andillac 10335
Musée Maurice Genevoix, Saint-Denis-de-l'Hôtel 14176
Musée Maurice Gottlob, Mougins 13181
Musée Maurice Poignant, Bourg-sur-Gironde 10859
Musée Maurice Ravel, Montfort-l'Amaury 13086
Musée Maurice-Sabourin, Bouillé-Courdault 10833
Musée Maxime Mabilleau des Vins Effervescents, Saumur 14650
Musée Médiéval, Brain-sur-Allonnes 10886
Musée Medieval, Serralongue 14723
Musée Médiumnique Fernand Desmoulin, Brantôme 10890
Musée Mémoire de la Vie Rurale, Saint-Beauzely 14122
Musée Mémoires du Moyen Âge, Carcassonne 11046
Musée Mémorial 1914-1918, Wattwiller 15309
Musée Memorial Alain, Mortagne-au-Perche 13170
Musée-Mémorial de la Bataille de l'Atlantique, Camaret-sur-Mer 11008
Musée Mémorial de la Bataille de Normandie, Bayeux 10618
Musée Mémorial de la Bataille de Verdun, Fleury-devant-Douaumont 11746
Musée Mémorial de la Ligne Maginot du Rhin, Marckolsheim 12812
Musée-Mémorial de la Résistance et de la Déportation, Metz 12956
Musée Mémorial du Général de Gaulle, Bayeux 10619
Musée-Mémorial du Linge, Orbey 13416
Musée-Mémorial National du Débarquement en Provence (1944), Toulon (Var) 14931
Musée Memorial Omaha Beach, Saint-Laurent-sur-Mer 14316
Musée Mer et Désert, Villerville 15246
Musée Michel Braibant, Montolieu 13117
Musée Militaire, Bordeaux 10817
Musée Militaire, Cambrai 11012
Musée Militaire, Clères 11318
Musée Militaire, Colombier 36644
Musée Militaire, Mer 12942
Musée Militaire, Veckring 15107
Musée Militaire, Villeneuve-Loubet 15233
Musée Militaire de Bure, Bure-Tressange 10957
Musée Militaire de Thiaucourt, Thiaucourt 14884
Musée Militaire des Gloires et Souvenirs du Périgord, Périgueux 13694
Musée Militaire du 12e Régiment Blindé du Canada, Trois-Rivières 06644
Musée Militaire du Fort, Douaumont 11564
Musée Militaire du Souvenir, Dompierre-sur-Mer 11550
Musée Militaire Faller, Mars-la-Tour 12835
Musée Militaire Genevois, Cologny 36642
Musée Militaire Ligne Mareth, Mareth 37572
Musée Militaire National, Manouba 37571
Musée Militaire Vaudois, Morges 36951
Musée Mine, Cagnac-les-Mines 10985
Musée Minéralogique, Nîmes 13342
Musée Minéralogique d'Asbestos, Asbestos 05010
Musée Minéralogique de la Société Industrielle, Mulhouse 13215
Musée Minéralogique de l'École des Mines d'Alès, Alès 10288
Musée Minéralogique du Dolon, Chanas 11162
Musée Minéralogique du Morvan, La Grande-Verrière 12194
Musée Minéralogique et Minier de Thetford Mines, Thetford Mines 06542
Musée Minéralogique et Paléontologique, Saint-Pierre-de-la-Palud 14414
Musée Minéralogique et Paléontologique de Guerledan, Saint-Gelven 14227
Musée Miniatures et Poupées, Gréoux-les-Bains 11951
Musée Missionaire, Goult 11891
Musée Missionnaire, Pontmain 13831
Musée Mistorique, Jaulny 12076
Musée Mnemosina, Prunelli-di-Fium'Orbu 13882
Musée Moissan, Paris 13628
Musée Mondial du Rugby, Avignonet-Lauragais 10537
Musée Mondial du Sable, Le Château-d'Olonne 12400
Musée Monetaire Cantonal, Lausanne 36865
Musée Monsieur Pigneau de Behaine, Origny-en-Thiérache 13426

Musée Montagnard, Les Houches 12540
Musée Montagnard du Lavedan, Aucun 10475
Musée Montebello, Trouville-sur-Mer 14999
Musée Montenot Agricole et Archéologique, Genay 11846
Musée Moralès, Port-de-Bouc 13837
Musée Morice Lipsi, Rosey 14037
Musée Moto du Douhet, Le Douhet 12411
Musée-Moulin à Eau, Chenillé-Changé 11270
Musée-Moulin à Vent de Rairé, Sallertaine 14581
Musée Moulin Cézanne, Le Tholonet 12484
Musée-Moulin de Guerin, Saint-Julien-Chapteuil 14296
Musée Moulin de Maupertuis, Donzy 11554
Musée-Moulin de Pierre, Artenay 10437
Musée-Moulin du Pape Malaval, Tornac 14920
Musée Municipal, Amboise 10314
Musée Municipal, Barentin 10588
Musée Municipal, Bernay 10693
Musée Municipal, Bourbonne-les-Bains 10849
Musée Municipal, Châlons-en-Champagne 11131
Musée Municipal, Chartres 11194
Musée Municipal, Châtellerault 11233
Musée Municipal, Conques 11396
Musée Municipal, Coutances 11443
Musée Municipal, Cusset 11477
Musée Municipal, Diekirch 27548
Musée Municipal, Digne-les-Bains 11514
Musée Municipal, Dudelange 27551
Musée Municipal, Ferrette 11720
Musée Municipal, Forcalquier 11785
Musée Municipal, Gerberoy 11853
Musée Municipal, Hazebrouck 12007
Musée Municipal, Hennezel-Clairey 12010
Musée Municipal, La Charité-sur-Loire 12152
Musée Municipal, La Réole 12223
Musée Municipal, La Roche-sur-Yon 12233
Musée Municipal, Le Monastier-sur-Gazeille 12451
Musée Municipal, Lillebonne 12607
Musée Municipal, Lons-le-Saunier 12662
Musée Municipal, Louhans 12678
Musée Municipal, Mauriac 12897
Musée Municipal, Mazan 12903
Musée Municipal, Nuits-Saint-Georges 13376
Musée Municipal, Pierrelatte 13736
Musée Municipal, Ribeauvillé 13959
Musée Municipal, Richelieu 13963
Musée Municipal, Saint-Amand-les-Eaux 14097
Musée Municipal, Saint-Calais 14137
Musée Municipal, Saint-Dié-des-Vosges 14186
Musée Municipal, Saint-Dizier 14191
Musée Municipal, Saint-Germain-Laval 14245
Musée Municipal, Semur-en-Auxois 14702
Musée Municipal, Villandraut 15170
Musée Municipal, Ville-d'Avray 15184
Musée Municipal, Vire 15270
Musée Municipal A. Canel, Pont-Audemer 13801
Musée Municipal A. Danicourt, Péronne 13699
Musée Municipal A.G. Poulain, Vernon 15140
Musée Municipal Albert Marzelles, Marmande 12828
Musée Municipal Ancienne Abbaye Saint-Léger, Soissons 14762
Musée Municipal Apt, Apt 10387
Musée Municipal Auguste Grasset, Varzy 15092
Musée Municipal Auguste Jacquet, Beaucaire 10631
Musée Municipal Bar-sur-Seine, Bar-sur-Seine 10584
Musée Municipal Bourbon-Lancy, Bourbon-Lancy 10846
Musée Municipal Châteaubriant, Châteaubriant 11212
Musée Municipal d'Archéologie, Roquefort-sur-Soulzon 14027
Musée Municipal d'Archéologie et du Vin de Champagne, Épernay 11630
Musée Municipal d'Archéologique, Murviel-les-Montpellier 13226
Musée Municipal d'Art et d'Histoire, Colombes 11363
Musée Municipal d'Art Moderne, Céret 11110
Musée Municipal d'Art Naïf, Nantillé 13263
Musée Municipal d'Art Naïf, Noyers (Yonne) 13371
Musée Municipal d'Arts Asiatiques, Toulon (Var) 14932
Musée Municipal d'Avranches, Avranches 10542
Musée Municipal de Cambrai, Cambrai 11013
Musée Municipal de Civray, Civray 11306
Musée Municipal de Draguignan, Draguignan 11577
Musée Municipal de la Chartreuse, Douai 11560
Musée Municipal de la Poterie, La Chapelle-aux-Pots 12140
Musée Municipal de la Toile de Jouy, Jouy-en-Josas 12096
Musée Municipal de la Vie Sauvage, Le Bugue 12393
Musée Municipal de l'École de Barbizon - Auberge Ganne, Barbizon 10586
Musée Municipal de l'Évêché, Limoges 12616
Musée Municipal de Louviers, Louviers 12704
Musée Municipal de Millau, Millau 12980
Musée Municipal de Mokolo, Mokolo 04960
Musée Municipal de Montmorillon, Montmorillon 13113
Musée Municipal de Moret, Moret-sur-Loing 13157
Musée Municipal de Pithiviers, Pithiviers-le-Vieil 13745
Musée Municipal de Préhistoire, Fismes 11739
Musée Municipal de Préhistoire, Les Matelles 12545
Musée Municipal de Préhistoire Régionale, Saint-Pons-de-Thomières 14423
Musée Municipal de Saint-Barthélemy, Saint-Barthélemy 21251
Musée Municipal de Saint-Gaudens, Saint-Gaudens 14226
Musée Municipal de Saint-Maur, La Varenne-Saint-Hilaire 12272
Musée Municipal de Sault, Sault (Vaucluse) 14639
Musée Municipal de Vendôme, Vendôme 15117
Musée Municipal Département Jouet, La Ferté-Macé 12170
Musée Municipal d'Ernée, Ernée 11639
Musée Municipal des Beaux-Arts, Valence (Drôme) 15051
Musée Municipal des Beaux Arts et d'Histoire Naturelle, Châteaudun 11214
Musée Municipal des Capucins, Coulommiers 11427
Musée Municipal des Fossiles, Tourtour 14978
Musée Municipal d'Étampes, Etampes 11665
Musée Municipal d'Histoire et d'Archéologie, Harnes 11991
Musée Municipal d'Orbec, Orbec 13414
Musée Municipal du Château, Gannat 11836
Musée Municipal du Peigne, Ezy-sur-Eure 11697
Musée Municipal du Présidial, Bazas 10624
Musée Municipal Frédéric Blandin, Nevers 13304
Musée Municipal Gautron du Coudray, Marzy 12885
Musée Municipal Georges Turpin, Parthenay 13662
Musée Municipal Joseph-Jacquiot, Montgeron 13088
Musée Municipal Max Claudet, Salins-les-Bains 14573
Musée Municipal Méditerranéen de Cassis, Cassis 11068
Musée Municipal Nicolas Poussin, Les Andelys 12516
Musée Municipal Paul Lafran, Saint-Chamas 14143
Musée Municipal Robert Dubois-Corneau, Brunoy 10949
Musée Municipal Saint-John-Perse, Pointe-à-Pitre 21248
Musée Municipal Saraleguinea, Guéthary 11971
Musée Municipal Urbain-Cabrol, Villefranche-de-Rouergue 15204
Musée Municipal Vendôme, Naveil 13275
Musée Municipale, Mont-de-Lans 13025
Musée Municipale, Villefranche-de-Lonchat 15202
Musée Nader, Port-au-Prince 21295
Musée Namesokanjik, Lac Mégantic 05710
Musée Napoleon, Ligny 03590
Musée Napoléon Ier et Tresors des Eglises, Brienne-le-Château 10929
Musée Napoléonien, Ajaccio 10267
Musée Napoléonien, Ile-d'Aix 12045
Musée Napoléonien d'Art et d'Histoire Militaire, Fontainebleau 11768
Musée Napoléonien du Château de Grosbois, Boissy-Saint-Léger 10789
Musée Natiocional des Deux Victoires, Mouilleron-en-Pareds 13183
Musée National, Beirut 27484
Musée National, Moroni 07630
Musée National, N'Djamena 06883
Musée National, Porto-Novo 03879
Musée National Adrien Dubouché, Limoges 12617
Musée National Ahmed Zabana - Demaeght Museum, Oran 00068
Musée National Auguste Rodin, Meudon 12960
Musée National Barthélémy Boganda, Bangui 06878
Musée National Cirta, Constantine 00058
Musée National d'Archéologie de Sétif, Sétif 00073
Musée National d'Art Brassicole et Musée de la Tannerie, Wiltz 27583
Musée National d'Art Moderne, Paris 13629
Musée National de Burkina Faso, Ouagadougou 04943
Musée National de Carthage, Carthage 37557
Musée National de Céramique, Sèvres 14739
Musée National de Conakry, Conakry 21282
Musée National de Géologie, Antananarivo 27604
Musée National de Gitega, Gitega 04945
Musée National de Guinée, Conakry 21283
Musée National de Kananga, Kananga 07633
Musée National de la Céramique, Safi 28709
Musée National de la Coopération Franco-Américaine, Blérancourt 10766
Musée National de la Légion d'Honneur et des Ordres de Chevalerie, Paris 13630
Musée National de la Marine, Brest 10913
Musée National de la Marine, Paris 13631
Musée National de la Marine, Port-Louis 13843
Musée National de la Marine, Rochefort (Charente-Maritime) 14000
Musée National de la Marine, Saint-Tropez 14493
Musée National de la Marine, Toulon (Var) 14933
Musée National de la Renaissance, Ecouen 11599
Musée National de la Résistance, Bruxelles 03333
Musée National de la Résistance, Esch-sur-Alzette 27556
Musée National de la Voiture et du Tourisme, Compiègne 11377
Musée National de l'Éducation, Rouen 14056
Musée National de l'Orangerie, Paris 13632
Musée National de Lubumbashi, Lumumbashi 07641
Musée National de Monaco, Monaco 28669
Musée National de Nouakchott, Nouakchott 27731
Musée National de Phnom Penh, Phnom Penh 04950
Musée National de Préhistoire, Les Eyzies-de-Tayac-Sireuil 12538
Musée National de Préhistoire et d'Ethnographie du Bardo, Alger 00044
Musée National de Sarh, Sarh 06885
Musée National de Yaoundé, Yaoundé 04962
Musée National d'Enéerune, Nissan-lez-Ensérune 13348
Musée National des Antiquités, Alger 00045
Musée National des Arts Asiatiques Guimet, Paris 13633
Musée National des Arts d'Afrique et d'Océanie, Paris 13634
Musée National des Arts et Traditions, Libreville 15350
Musée National des Arts et Traditions Populaires, Paris 13635
Musée National des Beaux-Arts d'Alger, Alger 00046
Musée National des Beaux-Arts du Québec, Québec 06208
Musée National des Chantiers de Jeunesse, Châtelguyon 11231
Musée National des Châteaux de Malmaison et de Bois-Préau, Rueil-Malmaison 14075
Musée National des Châteaux de Versailles et de Trianon, Versailles 15145
Musée National des Douanes, Bordeaux 10818
Musée National des Ecoles Préparatoires de l'Armée de Terre, Autun 10498
Musée National des Granges de Port Royal, Magny-lès-Hameaux 12766
Musée National des Mines Fer Luxembourgeoisie, Rumelange 27575
Musée National des Monuments Français, Paris 13636
Musée National d'Histoire et d'Art, Luxembourg 27567
Musée National d'Histoire Militaire, Diekirch 27549
Musée National d'Histoire Naturelle, Luxembourg 27568
Musée National du Bardo, Bardo 37553
Musée National du Château de Compiègne - Musée du Second Empire, Compiègne 11378
Musée National du Château de Fontainebleau, Fontainebleau 11769
Musée National du Château de Pau, Pau 13670
Musée National du Congo, Brazzaville 07645
Musée National du Costume, Grand Bassam 07671
Musée National du Djihad, Alger 00047
Musée National du Foie Gras, Thiviers 14890
Musée National du Gabon, Libreville 15351
Musée National du Mali, Bamako 27691
Musée National du Marbre, Rance 03692
Musée National du Moudjahid, El Madania 00062
Musée National du Moyen Age, Paris 13637
Musée National du Niger, Niamey 30324
Musée National du Papier, Malmedy 03607
Musée National du Rwanda, Butare 33752
Musée National du Scoutisme en France, Thorey-Lyautey 14901
Musée National du Sport, Paris 13638
Musée National du Togo, Lomé 37549
Musée National Ernest Hébert, Paris 13639
Musée National Eugène Delacroix, Paris 13640
Musée National Fernand Léger, Biot 10740
Musée National Jean-Jacques Henner, Paris 13641
Musée National Lao, Vientiane 27321
Musée National Message Biblique Marc Chagall, Nice 13322
Musée National Nasserdine Dinet, Bou Saada 00052
Musée National Picasso La Guerre et la Paix, Vallauris 15061
Musée National Suisse, Prangins 37031
Musée National Suisse de l'Audiovisuel, Montreux 36948
Musée Naval, Monaco 28670
Musée Naval de Nice, Nice 13323
Musée Naval de Sarcelles, Sarcelles 14607
Musée Naval et Napoléonien, Antibes 10375
Musée Naval Fort Balaguier, La Seyne-sur-Mer 12262
Musée N'Djamena, N'Djamena 06884
Musée Nicéphore Niépce, Chalon-sur-Saône 11126
Musée Nicholas Ibrahim Sursock, Beirut 27485
Musée Nissim de Camondo, Paris 13642
Musée No.4 Commando, Ouistreham 13446
Musée Notre Dame, Le Folgoët 12415
Musée Notre-Dame, Lourdes 12697
Musée Notre Dame de la Pierre, Sarrance 14619
Musée Numismatique J. Puig, Perpignan 13709
Musée Nungesser et Coli, Etretat 11675
Musée Oberlin, Waldersbach 15299
Musée-Observatoire de la Vallée d'Anjou, Saint-Mathurin-sur-Loire 14362
Musée Océanien de Cuet, Montrevel-en-Bresse 13146
Musée Océanographique, Arcachon 10395
Musée Océanographique, Bonifacio 10793
Musée Océanographique, Kingersheim 12114
Musée Océanographique, L'Ile-Rousse 12594
Musée Océanographique/Aquariophilie, Saint-Macaire 14335
Musée Océanographique Dar-El-Hout de Salammbô, Salammbô 37577
Musée Océanographique de l'Odet, Ergué-Gabéric 11637
Musée Océanographique de Monaco, Monaco 28671
Musée Olivier-de-Serres, Mirabel (Ardèche) 12986
Musée Ollier, Les Vans 12560
Musée Olympique Lausanne, Lausanne 36866
Musée Organistrum et des Vielles à Roues du Périgord Noir, Belvès 10679
Musée Ornithologique Charles Payraudeau, La Chaize-le-Vicomte 12139
Musée Ostréicole, Bourcefranc-le-Chapus 10850
Musée Ostréicole, Étaules 11668
Musée Ostréicole, Saint-Trojan-les-Bains 14490
Musée P. Dubois-A. Boucher, Nogent-sur-Seine 13353
Musée P.-J. Redouté et de l'Illustration Botanique, Saint-Hubert 03723
Musée Pablo Casals, Prades 13861
Musée Paderewski, Morges 36952
Musée Palais Lascaris, Nice 13324
Musée Palaisien du Hurepoix, Palaiseau 13454
Musée Paléo-Écologique, Marchamp 12802
Musée Paléochrétien de Saint-Seurin, Bordeaux 10819
Musée Paléontologique, Aguessac 10232
Musée Paléontologique du Gouffre de la Face, Larche 12343
Musée-Palombière, Le Mas-d'Agenais 12441
Musée Parc de la Droséra, Jeansagnière 12078
Musée Passé Simple, Pleudihen-sur-Rance 13756
Musée Pasteur, Dole 11542
Musée Pasteur, Paris 13643
Musée Pasteur, Calmette et Guérin, Lille 12604
Musée Pastoral le Monde Paysan d'Autrefois, Saint-Pé-de-Bigorre 14408
Musée Patrimoine et Traditions, Montferrier 13084
Musée Paul Arbaud, Aix-en-Provence 10256
Musée Paul Charnoz, Paray-le-Monial 13465
Musée Paul Dini, Villefranche-sur-Saône 15211
Musée Paul Dupuy, Toulouse 14951
Musée Paul-Emile Victor, Prémanon 13869
Musée Paul Gauguin, Papeete 15347
Musée Paul Gauguin, Pont-Aven 13804
Musée Paul Géradin, Jodoigne 03530
Musée Paul-José Gosselin, Saint-Vaast-la-Hougue 14496
Musée Paul Raymond, Pont-Saint-Esprit 13818
Musée Paul Valéry, Sète 14731
Musée Paul Voivenel, Capoulet-Junac 11036
Musée Paysan, Clion-sur-Seugne 11334
Musée Paysan, Le Grand-Village-Plage 12420
Musée Paysan de Bourgogne Nivernaise, La Celle-sur-Loire 12136
Musée Paysan de la Save, Espaon 11651
Musée Paysan du Moulin Neuf, Saint-Diéry 14189
Musée Paysan du Sundgau, Oltingue 13405
Musée Paysan et Artisanal, La Chaux-de-Fonds 36631
Musée Pédagogique de Circonscription, Sarre-Union 14620
Musée Percheron, Mortagne-au-Perche 13171
Musée Petiet, Limoux 12619
Musée Peugeot, Sochaux 14760
Musée Peynet, Antibes 10376
Musée Picasso, Antibes 10377
Musée Picasso, Paris 13644
Musée Pierre-Bayle, Carla-Bayle 11052
Musée Pierre Borrione, Aime-en-Tarentaise 10243
Musée Pierre Boucher, Trois-Rivières 06645
Musée Pierre de Luxembourg, Villeneuve-lès-Avignon 15229
Musée Pierre Fauchard, Paris 13645
Musée Pierre-Gaudin, Puteaux 13886
Musée Pierre-Loti, Rochefort (Charente-Maritime) 14001
Musée Pierre Marly, Paris 13646
Musée Pierre Mondanel, Pont-du-Château 13808
Musée Pierre Noël, Saint-Dié-des-Vosges 14187
Musée Pierre Tauziac, Montcaret 13065
Musée Pierre-Vigne, Boucieu-le-Roi 10828
Musée Pigeard, Magny-en-Vexin 12764
Musée Pillon, Chaumont-en-Vexin 11248
Musée Pincé, Angers 10350
Musée Pissarro, Pontoise 13832
Musée-Placard d'Erik Satie, Paris 13647
Musée Place-Royale, Québec 06209
Musée Pobe Mengao, Mengao 04940
Musée Pointe des Chênes, Sainte-Anne 06381
Musée Pol Mara, Gordes 11888
Musée Pontois, Le Pont-de-Beauvoisin 12469
Musée Populaire des Arts et Métiers, Noyant 13369
Musée Portuaire, Dunkerque 11586
Musée Postal, Bruxelles 03334
Musée Postal, Rabat 28707
Musée Postal, Tunis 37595
Musée Postal d'Aquitaine, Saint-Macaire 14336
Musée Postal du Lot, Peyrilles 13721
Musée Poveal, Battambang 04947
Musée-Préau des Accoules, Marseille 12870
Musée Préfectoral de Boké, Boké 21279
Musée Préfectoral de Kissidougou, Kissidougou 21284
Musée Préfectoral de Koundara, Koundara 21285
Musée Préfectoral de N'Zerekore, N'Zerekore 21286
Musée Préhistorique, Marsoulas 12875
Musée Préhistorique Charles Nardin, Sainte-Foy-la-Grande 14532
Musée Préhistorique du Tumulus de Barnenez, Plouezoch 13769
Musée Préhistorique et de Peinture, Montaut 13050
Musée Préhistorique Finistérien, Penmarch 13685
Musée Privé de la Documentation Ferroviaire-Mupdofer, Bruxelles 03335
Musée Privé Saint-Jean l'Aigle, Herserange 12016
Musée-Promenade Marly-le-Roi, Louveciennes 12703
Musée Protestant de la Grange de Wassy, Wassy 15307
Musée Provençal des Transports Urbains et Régionaux, La Barque 12120
Musée Provençal et Folklorique, Taradeau 14857
Musée Provençal et Folklorique Taradeau, Les Arcs 12518

Musée Provincial de Douala, Douala 04954
Musée Provincial de la Forêt, Namur 03650
Musée Provincial du Houet, Bobo-Dioulasso 04936
Musée Provincial du Poni, Gaoua 04937
Musée Provincial du Sanmatenga, Kaya 04938
Musée Provincial Félicien Rops, Namur 03651
Musée Pyrénéen, Lourdes 12698
Musée Pyrénéen de Niaux, Niaux 13305
Musée Québécois de Culture Populaire, Trois-Rivières 06646
Musée Quentovic, Etaples 11667
Musée Rabelais, Seuilly 14733
Musée Raimu, Cogolin 11345
Musée Rambolitrain, Rambouillet 13912
Musée Raoul Dastrac, Aiguillon 10240
Musée Rath, Genève 36751
Musée Raymond Lafage, Lisle-sur-Tarn 12631
Musée Raymond Peynet, Brassac-les-Mines 10893
Musée Raymond Poincaré, Sampigny 14598
Musée Raymond Rochette, Saint-Sernin-du-Bois 14471
Musée Réattu, Arles 10417
Musée Regards sur le Passé, Hourtin 12033
Musée Régimentaire les Fusiliers de Sherbrooke, Sherbrooke, Québec 06443
Musée Regional, Kisangani 07639
Musée Régional André Grenard Matsoua, Kinkala 07646
Musée Régional Bieth d'Abengourou, Abengourou 07665
Musée Régional Charles Combes, Bingerville 07667
Musée Regional d'Argenteuil, Saint-André-d'Argenteuil 06302
Musée Régional d'Armes, Mutzig 13229
Musée Régional d'Arts et de Traditions Populaires, Grimaud 11957
Musée Régional d'Auvergne, Riom 13973
Musée Regional de Beyla, Beyla 21278
Musée Régional de Bondoukou, Bondoukou 07668
Musée Régional de Fouras, Fouras 11798
Musée Régional de Géologie Pierre Vetter, Decazeville 11490
Musée Régional de Kara, Kara 37548
Musée Régional de la Côte-Nord, Sept-Iles 06422
Musée Régional de la Poterie bas Normande, Ger 11851
Musée Régional de la Résistance et de la Déportation, Thionville 14889
Musée Regional de la Vigne et du Vin, Montmélian 13109
Musée Régional de l'Air, Marcé 12800
Musée Régional de l'Alsace Bossue, Sarre-Union 14621
Musée Régional de l'Orléanais, Beaugency 10638
Musée Régional de Préhistoire, Orgnac-l'Aven 13423
Musée Régional de Rimouski, Rimouski 06272
Musée Régional de Sikasso, Sikasso 27693
Musée Régional de Sokadé, Sokadé 37550
Musée Régional de Vaudreuil-Soulanges, Vaudreuil 06702
Musée Régional de Zinder, Zinder 30325
Musée Régional des Arts de la Table, Arnay-le-Duc 10421
Musée Régional des Arts et Traditions Populaires, Kef 37566
Musée Régional des Mines et des Arts de Malartic, Malartic 05803
Musée Régional des Savanes, Dapaong 37547
Musée Régional des Télécommunications en Flandres, Marcq-en-Barœul 12814
Musée Régional d'Ethnologie du Nord/Pas-de-Calais, Béthune 10709
Musée Régional d'Histoire et d'Archéologie, Visé 03819
Musée Régional d'Histoire et d'Artisanat du Val-de-Travers, Môtiers 36956
Musée Régional d'Histoire et d'Ethnographie, Fort-de-France 27722
Musée Régional du Cerel, Toamasina 27609
Musée Régional du Chemin de Fer, Rosny-sous-Bois 14042
Musée Régional du Chemin de Fer Nord-Pas-de-Calais, Denain 11496
Musée Régional du Cidre et du Calvados, Valognes 15074
Musée Régional du Machinisme Agricole, La Ferté-Milon 12173
Musée Régional du Sahel, Gao 27692
Musée Régional du Timbre et de la Philatélie, Le Luc 12433
Musée Régional du Vieux-Coppet, Coppet 36648
Musée Régional Dupuy-Méstreau, Saintes 14559
Musée Régional Ex-Dixième Riaom, Thiès 33785
Musée Régional Ma-Loango Diosso, Pointe-Noire 07647
Musée Régional Peleforo Gbon Coulibaly, Korhogo 07672
Musée Religieux d'Art Franciscain, Nice 13325
Musée Religieux Franco-Canadien, Tours 14975
Musée Religieux Saint-Louis Marie Grignion-de-Montfort, Saint-Laurent-sur-Sèvre 14317
Musée Remenber 39-45, Léhon 12508
Musée Remise aux Outils Champenois, Dormans-en-Champagne 11555
Musée Renaudot, Loudun 12675
Musée René Davoine, Charolles 11188
Musée René Louis Cadou, Louisfert 12680
Musée Renoir, Cagnes-sur-Mer 10991
Musée Républicain, Touet-sur-Var 14922
Musée Requien, Avignon 10534
Musée Rétromobile Drouais, Dreux 11580
Musée Ribauri, Lasne-Chapelle-Saint-Lambert 03554
Musée Rignault, Saint-Cirq-Lapopie 14156
Musée Riquet et du Canal du Midi, Avignonet-Lauragais 10538
Musée Rochelais d'Histoire Protestante, La Rochelle 12251
Musée Rodava, Rêves 03696
Musée Rodriguez Huguette, Saint-Macaire 14337
Musée Roger Thières, Payrac 13676
Musée Rolin, Autun 10499
Musée Romain, Avenches 36481
Musée Romain, Caudeval 11090
Musée Romain, Lausanne 36867
Musée Romain, Nyon 36995
Musée Romand de la Machine Agricole, Gingins 36759
Musée Ronsard, La Riche 12226
Musée Roux, Villefranche-sur-Mer 15210
Musée Royal de l'Armée et d'Histoire Militaire, Bruxelles 03336
Musée Royal de Mariemont, Morlanwelz-Mariemont 03640
Musée Royaume de l'Horloge, Villedieu-les-Poêles 15195
Musée Roybet Fould, Courbevoie 11431
Musée Rude, Dijon 11531
Musée Rupert-de-Chièvres, Poitiers 13786
Musée Rural, Auris-en-Oisans 10494
Musée Rural, Doyet 11574
Musée Rural, Foucherans 11790
Musée Rural, Saint-André-d'Embrun 14106
Musée Rural, Usson-en-Forez 15031
Musée Rural Berry-Marche, Boussac 10876
Musée Rural d'Arts et Traditions Populaires La Combà, autrafé, La Combe-de-Lancey 12158
Musée Rural de la Sologne Bourbonnaise, Beaulon 10641
Musée Rural des Art Populaires, Laduz 12295
Musée Rural du Bois, Coupiac 11428
Musée Rural du Porzay, Plomodiern 13764
Musée Rural du Porzay, Saint-Nic-Pontrez 14382
Musée Rural Jurassien, Les Genevez 36756
Musée Ruzo, Territet-Montreux 37232
Musée Saharien de Ouargla, Ouargla 00069
Musée Saint-Brieux, Saint-Brieux 06308
Musée Saint-Étienne, Honfleur 12031
Musée Saint-François-Régis, La Louvesc 12204
Musée Saint-Georges, Saint-Georges, Manitoba 06319
Musée Saint-Jacques, Moissac 13002
Musée Saint-Jean, Anneyron 10364
Musée Saint-Jean, La Rochette (Savoie) 12253
Musée Saint-Joachim, La Broquerie 05706
Musée Saint-Joseph, Saint-Joseph 06354
Musée Saint-Loup, Troyes 15007
Musée Saint-Martin, Tours 14976
Musée Saint-Raymond, Toulouse 14952
Musée Saint-Remi, Reims 13933
Musée Saint-Rémy, Cuesmes 03366
Musée Saint-Sauveur Nibelle Autrefois, Nibelle 13307
Musée Saint-Simon, La Ferté-Vidame 12178
Musée Saint-Vic, Saint-Amand-Montrond 14098
Musée Sainte-Catherine-Laboure, Fain-les-Moutiers 11699
Musée Sainte-Croix, Poitiers 13787
Musée Sainte-Jeanne-Antide-Thouret, Sancey-le-Long 14600
Musée Sainte-Marie, Church Point 05249
Musée Salésien, Annecy 10362
Musée Salies, Bagnères-de-Bigorre 10560
Musée Salle Documentaire, Coucy-le-Château-Auffrique 11421
Musée Santons du Monde, Clermont-l'Hérault 11327
Musée Sarret de Grozon, Arbois 10392
Musée Savoisien, Chambéry 11142
Musée Sbeïtla, Sbeïtla 37578
Musée Schiller-Goethe, Châlons-en-Champagne 11132
Musée Schœlcher, Pointe-à-Pitre 21249
Musée Scientifique de Boukoko, M'Baïki 06881
Musée Scolaire, Rittershoffen 13980
Musée Scolaire, Rosenwiller 14035
Musée Scolaire de Hautepierre, Strasbourg 14837
Musée Scolaire Freinet, Saales 14080
Musée Scout Baden-Powell, Sisteron 14754
Musée Serret, Saint-Amarin 14101
Musée Sherlock Holmes, Lucens 36894
Musée Sidi Bou Saïd, Sidi Bou Saïd 37584
Musée Sidi Med Ben Abdellah, Essaouira 28693
Musée Sidi Zitouni, Houmt Souk 37563
Musée Simon-Segal, Aups 10485
Musée Site Départemental d'Archéologie de Bavay, Bavay 10611
Musée Skolig al Louarn, Plouvien 13780
Musée Sobirats, Carpentras 11059
Musée Sonvilier, Sonvilier 37191
Musée Souleïado Charles Demery, Tarascon (Bouches-du-Rhône) 14862
Musée Sous-Glaciaire, La Grave 12195
Musée Sous Marin Pays Lorient, Lorient 12666
Musée Souterrain de l'Outillage Ancien, Chacé 11121
Musée Spadois du Cheval, Spa 03762
Musée Spectacle de Musiques du Monde, Montoire-sur-le-Loir 13116
Musée Stendhal, Grenoble 11946
Musée Sterna de l'Armée et des Trois Guerres, Seynod 14746
Musée Stewart au Fort de lle Sainte-Hélène, Montréal 05926
Musée Suffren et du Vieux Saint-Cannat, Saint-Cannat 14138
Musée Suisse, Zürich 37393
Musée Suisse de la Figurine Historique, Morges 36953
Musée Suisse de la Machine à Coudre, Fribourg 36717
Musée Suisse de la Marionette, Fribourg 36718
Musée Suisse de la Mode, Yverdon-les-Bains 37355
Musée Suisse de l'Appareil Photographique, Vevey 37290
Musée Suisse de l'Audiovisuel - Audiorama, Territet-Veytaux 37234
Musée Suisse de l'Orgue, Roche 37066
Musée Suisse de Spéléologie, Chamoson 36623
Musée Suisse du Jeu, La Tour-de-Peilz 37249
Musée Suisse du Sel, Aigle 36440
Musée Suisse du Vitrail, Romont 37069
Musée Sundgauvien, Altkirch 10297
Musée sur l'Archéologie et l'Histoire du Pays d'Ancenis, Ancenis 10331
Musée sur l'Artillerie, la Cavalerie et l'Infanterie, Seclin 14688
Musée sur l'Ordre de Malte, Compesières 36645
Musée Talleyrand, Saint-Chéron 14146
Musée Tancrède, Hauteville-la-Guicharde 12003
Musée Tavet-Delacour, Pontoise 13833
Musée Tchantchès - Musée de la République Libre d'Outre-Meuse, Liège 03585
Musée Terrasse, Viverols 15277
Musée Territorial de Nouvelle-Calédonien, Nouméa 30091
Musée Terrus, Elne 11610
Musée Textile de Haute-Alsace, Husseren-Wesserling 12040
Musée Théophile Jouglet, Anzin 10381
Musée Thimonnier-Doyen, Saint-Germain-au-Mont-d'Or 14235
Musée Thomas-Henry, Cherbourg 11278
Musée Toffoli, Charenton-le-Pont 11174
Musée Toulouse-Lautrec, Albi 10276
Musée Toulouse-Lautrec, Naucelle 13274
Musée Tour de la Lanterne, La Rochelle 12252
Musée Tour Saint-Michel, Guérande 11966
Musée Tradition et Modernité, Verbier 37283
Musée Traditions et Vie, Châtillon-sur-Chalaronne 11239
Musée Traditions Verrieres, Eu 11678
Musée-Trésor d'Église, Joncels 12085
Musée Trésor d'Église, Metz 12957
Musée-Trésor d'Eglise de la Cathédrale Sainte-Croix, Orléans 13436
Musée Trio et du Vieil Outil Hastière, Hastière 03485
Musée Troglodytique, Louresse 12700
Musée Troglodytique de la Fosse, Dénezé-sous-Doué 11500
Musée Une Halte sur le Chemin de Saint-Jacques, Borce 10801
Musée Urbain Tony Garnier, Lyon 12748
Musée Utrillo-Valadon, Sannois 14603
Musée Valaisan de la Vigne et du Vin, Sierre 37167
Musée Valentin Haüy, Paris 13648
Musée Valery Stuyver, Seraing-le-Château 03732
Musée Van Œveren, Bourgueil 10872
Musée Vauban, Neuf-Brisach 13284
Musée Vauban et de la Fortification dans les Alpes, Mont-Dauphin 13024
Musée Vendéen, Fontenay-le-Comte 11772
Musée Verlaine, Juniville 12105
Musée Vert, Le Mans 12439
Musée Victor Aubert, Maule 12892
Musée Victor-Hugo, Villequier 15239
Musée Vigneron, Orschwiller 13441
Musée Vigneron, Vendres 15118
Musée Villa Tamaris Pacha, La Seyne-sur-Mer 12263
Musée-Village des Automates, Saint-Cannat 14139
Musée-Village Gallo-Romain de Chênehutte-les-Tuffeaux, Chênehutte-Trêves-Cunault 11269
Musée Villageois d'Orgon, Orgon 13425
Musée Villeneuvien, Villeneuve-sur-Yonne 15238
Musée Villien, Avesnes-sur-Helpe 10524
Musée Vini-Viticole, Barr 10595
Musée Vini-Viticole, Chambolle-Musigny 11145
Musée Vini-Viticole, Gertwiller 11856
Musée Vini-Viticole, Volnay 15286
Musée Vini-Viticole Gallo-Romain, Beaucaire 10632
Musée Vinicole, Villandraut 15171
Musée Vissoie, Vissoie 37294
Musée Viticole, Bourgueil 10873
Musée Viticole, Cerdon 11105
Musée Viticole, Saint-Yzans-de-Médoc 14512
Musée Viticole, Verdigny 15128
Musée Viticole Charles-Bernard, Fixin 11741
Musée Vivant de Bujumbura, Bujumbura 04944
Musée Vivant de la Forge, Seyne-les-Alpes 14745
Musée Vivant de la Gare Rurale d'Autrefois, Saint-Hilaire-de-Chaléons 14259
Musée Vivant de la Laine et du Mouton, Saint-Pierreville 14420
Musée Vivant de la Métairie de Crampet, Mazères (Gironde) 12909
Musée Vivant de la Meunerie, Cales 11004
Musée Vivant de la Meunerie, Wimille 15314
Musée Vivant de la Mine, Auchel 10473
Musée Vivant de la Moisson, Rochehaut 03702
Musée Vivant de la Passementerie, Jonzieux 12089
Musée Vivant de la Plante Aquatique, Limal 03591
Musée Vivant de la Polyculture, Lucey 12710
Musée Vivant de l'Abeille, Corbeny 11403
Musée Vivant de l'Abeille, Valensole 15055
Musée Vivant de l'Apiculture du Ban-de-la-Roche, Waldersbach 15300
Musée Vivant de l'Apiculture Gâtinaise, Châteaurenard (Loiret) 11226
Musée Vivant de l'Arbre, Fontaine-les-Coteaux 11766
Musée Vivant de l'Aviation, Cerny 11116
Musée Vivant de l'Enfance, Sauliac-sur-Célé 14635
Musée Vivant de l'Impression, Ribeauvillé 13960
Musée Vivant de l'Oie, Collonges-la-Rouge 11354
Musée Vivant Denon, Chalon-sur-Saône 11127
Musée Vivant des Vieux Métiers, Argol 10410
Musée Vivant d'Histoire Naturelle, Nancy 13244
Musée Vivant du Cheval, Chantilly 11166
Musée Vivant du Cheval de Trait et de l'Attelage, Pradelles 13857
Musée Vivant du Cinéma, Lyon 12749
Musée Vivant du Parchemin et de l'Enluminure, Miramont-de-Guyenne 12989
Musée Vivant du Textile - Écomusée du Moulinage, Chirols 11293
Musée Vivant et Historique du Train Historique du Lac de Rillé, Rillé 13969
Musée Vivant Européen du Cirque, Piolenc 13739
Musée Vivant Médiéval, Murol 13224
Musée Vosgien de la Brasserie, Ville-sur-Illon 15187
Musée Vulcanologique Franck-Arnold-Perret, Saint-Pierre 27728
Musée Wagon de l'Armistice, Compiègne 11379
Musée Wellington, Waterloo 03830
Musée Westercamp, Wissembourg 15319
Musée Yan' Dargent, Saint-Servais 14472
Musée Yani Faux, Orbais-l'Abbaye 13413
Musée Yves-Brayer, Cordes 11407
Musée Yves Brayer, Les Baux-de-Provence 12529
Musée Zadkine, Les Arques 12519
Musée Zadkine, Paris 13649
Musée Zervos, Vézelay 15154
Musée Ziem, Martigues 12881
Musée Zoologique de l'Université Louis Pasteur et de la Ville de Strasbourg, Strasbourg 14838
Muséem d'Histoire Naturelle, Marseille 12871
Museen Alte Bischofsburg, Wittstock, Dosse 20632
Museen der Stadt Bad Kösen, Bad Kösen 15679
Museen für Kunst und Kulturgeschichte der Hansestadt Lübeck - Verwaltung, Lübeck 18538
Museen im Alten Rathaus, Pirmasens 19401
Museen im Kulturzentrum, Rendsburg 19570
Museen im Rathaus, Perchtoldsdorf 02401
Museen im Wehrturm, Perchtoldsdorf 02402
Museerne i Fredericia, Fredericia 08825
Musées de la Cour d'Or, Metz 12958
Musées de La Poëslerie et de la Dentelle, Villedieu-les-Poêles 15196
Musées de la Réole, La Réole 12224
Musées de l'Horlogerie Pater, Langueville 03552
Musées de Sens, Sens 14715
Musées Départementaux Albert Demard, Champlitte 11159
Musées Départementaux de la Guadeloupe, Pointe-à-Pitre 49225
Musées des Colombiers Cauchois, Oherville 13390
Musées des Technique et Cultures Comtoises, Salins-les-Bains 14574
Musées et Société en Wallonie, Namur 49075
Musées Gaumais, Virton 03817
Musées Royaux d'Art et d'Histoire, Bruxelles 03337
Musées Universitaire, Kinshasa 07638
Museet Ett Hem, Turku 10125
Museet Færgegaarden, Jægerspris 08908
Museet for Dansk Bladtegning, København 08939
Museet for Fotokunst, Odense 09015
Museet for Holbæk og Omegn, Holbæk 08884
Museet for Religiøs Kunst og Bodil Kaalund Samlingerne, Lemvig 08973
Museet for Samtidskunst, Oslo 30744
Museet for Samtidskunst, Roskilde 09040
Museet for Thy og Vester Hanherred, Thisted 09091
Museet for Varde By og Omegn, Varde 09101
Museet Holmen, Løgumkloster 08976
Museet i Mælandsgården, Skudeneshavn 30853
Museet Kvarnen, Filipstad 35889
Museet Kystens Arv, Stadsbygd 30874
Museet Malmahed, Malmköping 36070
Museet Näktergalen, Vimmerby 36411
Museet på Gudhjem Station, Gudhjem 08848
Museet på Koldinghus, Kolding 08959
Museet på Sønderborg Slot, Sønderborg 09074
Museet på Sønderskov, Brørup 08792
Museet Psykiatrisk Hospital i Århus, Risskov 09034
Museet Tikøb Frysehus, Tikøb 09092
Museet ved Sct. Ansgar Kirke, København 08940
Museet ved Trelleborg, Slagelse 09070
Musehum.BL, Liestal 36880
Musei Anatomici, Modena 24436
Musei Capitolini, Roma 25173
Musei Civici, Lecco 24171
Musei Civici, Pavia 24822
Musei Civici, Reggio Emilia 25096
Musei Civici agli Eremitani, Padova 24733
Musei Civici e Pinacoteca L. Sturzo, Caltagirone 23272
Musei Civici - Museo della Città, Monza 24558
Musei Civici Veneziani, Venezia 25922
Musei del Castello Scaligero, Malcesine 24267
Musei della Civiltà Contadina del Friuli Imperiale, Aiello del Friuli 22821

Musei della Cultura Popolare Radana, San Benedetto Po 25337
Musei, Gallerie, Gabinetto Stampe e Archivio Fotografico, Roma 25174
Musei Provinciali di Gorizia, Gorizia 24034
Musei Sistini del Piceno, San Benedetto del Tronto 25332
Museifartyget Pommern, Mariehamn 09817
Museion - Museo d'Arte Moderna e Contemporanea, Bolzano 23151
Museisällskapet Jädraås-Tallås Järnväg, Jädraås 35973
Museispårvägen Malmköping, Malmköping 36071
Museo 13 de Marzo, Pinar del Río 08070
Museo 9 de Abril, Santa Clara 08118
Museo A. Binda, Cittiglio 23586
Museo A. Cassioli, Asciano 22946
Museo A. Colocci, Jesi 24113
Museo A. e C. Gaffoglio, Rapallo 25075
Museo a la Bandera y Santuario de la Patria, Iguala de la Independencia 28011
Museo A. Lia, La Spezia 24121
Museo A. Murer, Falcade 23759
Museo A. Ricci dei Minerali Elbani, Rio nell'Elba 25121
Museo Abarth, Marietta 45145
Museo Abel Santamaría, La Habana 07933
Museo Abel Santamaría, Santa Clara 08119
Museo Abraham González, Vicente Guerrero 28598
Museo Acacia, La Habana 07934
Museo Academia de Historia Leonardo Tascón, Buga 07440
Museo Activo del Pago de los Arroyos, Rosario 00525
Museo Ada e Giuseppe Marchetti, Fumone 23943
Museo Adolfo López Mateos, Atizapán de Zaragoza 27781
Museo Aeronáutico, Baradero 00133
Museo Aeronáutico, Montevideo 40991
Museo Aeronautico, Padova 24734
Museo Aeronautico Caproni di Taliedo, Roma 25175
Museo Aeronautico Caproni di Taliedo, Vizzola Ticino 26043
Museo Aeronáutico Colonel Luis Hernan Paredes, Maracay 48952
Museo Aeronáutico Torreón de Gando, Telde 35522
Museo Aeronautico y del Espacio, Quito 09193
Museo Aerospaziale Monte di Apollo, Perugia 24849
Museo Africano, Roma 25176
Museo Africano, Verona 25968
Museo Africano Mundo Negro, Madrid 35012
Museo Afro Antillano, Panamá City 31076
Museo Agrario Tropicale, Firenze 23851
Museo Agrarista de Tzurúmutaro, Pátzcuaro 28306
Museo Agricolo, Ronco Briantino 25277
Museo Agricolo Brunnenburg, Tirolo di Merano 25709
Museo Agricolo della Civiltà Contadina L. Carminati, San Giuliano Milanese 25376
Museo Agricolo e del Vino Ricci Curbastro, Capriolo 23337
Museo Agricolo e Museo dell'Arte Conciaria, Castelfranco Veneto 23401
Museo Agro-Forestale San Matteo, Erice 23738
Museo Agro-Pastorale dell'Area Ellenofona, Bova Marina 23189
Museo Agrumario, Reggio Calabria 25089
Museo al Aire Libre, Buenos Aires 00156
Museo Alberto Arvelo Torrealba, Barinas 48894
Museo Alcázar de Colón, Santo Domingo 09119
Museo Aldrovandiano, Bologna 23105
Museo Alejandro Galvis, Tona 07606
Museo Alejandro Otero, Caracas 48904
Museo Alejo Carpentier, Camagüey 07873
Museo Alessandro Minuziano, San Severo 25415
Museo Alessi, Enna 23732
Museo Alfieriano, Asti 22972
Museo Alfonsiano, Pagani 24754
Museo Alfredo Ramírez de Arellano & Rosello, San Germán 32384
Museo All'Aperto di Storia dell'Agricultura, Sassari 25485
Museo Almacén El Recreo, Chivilcoy 00276
Museo Almafuerte, La Plata 00385
Museo Alpino Duca degli Abruzzi, Courmayeur 23674
Museo Alta Valle Scrivia, Valbrevenna 25869
Museo Altar de la Patria, Ixcateopan de Cuauhtémoc 28014
Museo Alternativo Remo Brindisi, Comacchio 23620
Museo Alto Bierzo, Bembibre 34598
Museo Amano, Lima 31198
Museo Ambientale del W.W.F., Orbetello 24682
Museo Ambientalistico Madonita, Polizzi Generoso 24980
Museo Ambiente Cubano, Gibara 07909
Museo Amedeo Bocchi, Parma 24801
Museo Americanista, Lomas de Zamora 00409
Museo Americanistico Federico Lunardi, Genova 23985
Museo Amparo, Puebla 28317
Museo Anatomia Veterinaria, Napoli 24576
Museo Anatomico, Pisa 24948
Museo Anatomico, Siena 25568
Museo Anatómico, Valladolid 35619
Museo Anatomico G. Tumiati, Ferrara 23785
Museo Andrés Avelino Cáceres, Lima 31199
Museo Andrés Cué, Amancio 07849
Museo Anenecuilco, Ayala 27785
Museo Angel Barrios, Granada 34872
Museo Angel Orensanz y Artes de Serralbo, Sabiñánigo 35350
Museo Antártico, Montevideo 40992
Museo Antica Miniera di Talco Brunetta, Cantoira 23319
Museo Antiguo Colegio de San Ildefonso, México 28105
Museo Antiguo Cuartel de Caballería del Ejército Español, Camagüey 07874
Museo Antiguo Palacio de la Medicina Mexicana, México 28106
Museo Antimperialista, Nueva Gerona 08055
Museo Antiquarium Archeologico, Falerone 23760
Museo Antiquarium Etrusco, Colle di Val d'Elsa 23608
Museo Antón, Candás 34667
Museo Antoniano, Padova 24735
Museo Antonio Lussich, Punta Ballena 41034
Museo Antonio Maceo, San Pedro 08107
Museo Antonio Martínez, La Roda 35328
Museo Antonio Raimondi, La Merced 31194
Museo Antonio Ricaurte, Villa de Leyva 07619
Museo Antonio Rodríguez Luna, Montoro 35138
Museo Antrológico, Cereté 07461
Museo Antropología e Historia, Victoria 28601
Museo Antropologia e Historia Valle de Sula, San Pedro Sula 21301
Museo Antropológico, Ibagué 07496
Museo Antropológico, Sucre 03906
Museo Antropológico de Antofagasta, Antofagasta 06887
Museo Antropológico de Iquique, Iquique 06896
Museo Antropológico de Tunja, Tunja 07610
Museo Antropológico del Banco Central, Guayaquil 09168
Museo Antropológico Montané, La Habana 07935
Museo Antropológico Reina T. de Araúz, Panamá City 31077
Museo Antropológico Shuar, Quito 09194
Museo Antropológico Tairona, Santa Marta 07585
Museo Antzetik Ta Jtelum, Zinacantán 28656
Museo Anzoátegui, Pamplona 07541
Museo Aperos de Labranza, Lerdo 28057
Museo Apistico, Bologna 23106
Museo Apistico Didattico, Bregnano 23196
Museo A.R. Giorgi, Reggiolo 25101
Museo Archeologica, Savignone 25503
Museo Archeologico, Acqualagna 22799
Museo Archeologico, Amelia 22875
Museo Archeologico, Arborea 22911
Museo Archeologico, Artena 22944
Museo Archeologico, Bonorva 23161
Museo Archeologico, Caltanissetta 23274
Museo Archeologico, Camaiore 23279
Museo Archeologico, Carassai 23342
Museo Archeologico, Castello di Godego 23413
Museo Archeologico, Castiglione della Pescaia 23432
Museo Archeologico, Cavriana 23463
Museo Archeologico, Cecina e Marina 23464
Museo Archeologico, Cesena 23497
Museo Archeologico, Dorgali 23721
Museo Archeologico, Enna 23733
Museo Archeologico, Faenza 23750
Museo Archeologico, Fermo 23777
Museo Archeologico, Follonica 23898
Museo Archeologico, Frosinone 23939
Museo Archeologico, Gropello Cairoli 24053
Museo Archeologico, Isola della Scala 24106
Museo Archeologico, Lentini 24177
Museo Archeologico, Marianopoli 24299
Museo Archeologico, Milano 24385
Museo Archeologico, Molfetta 24457
Museo Archeologico, Monopoli 24477
Museo Archeologico, Ostiglia 24717
Museo Archeologico, Palazzuolo sul Senio 24761
Museo Archeologico, Pontecagnano 24994
Museo Archeologico, Povegliano Veronese 25031
Museo Archeologico, Priverno 25054
Museo Archeologico, Pula 25056
Museo Archeologico, Rocca di Mezzo 25135
Museo Archeologico, San Gimignano 25361
Museo Archeologico, San Miniato 25398
Museo Archeologico, Santa Severina 25441
Museo Archeologico, Santadi 25445
Museo Archeologico, Santorso 25466
Museo Archeologico, Scansano 25517
Museo Archeologico, Teramo 25687
Museo Archeologico, Varallo Pombia 25890
Museo Archeologico, Venafro 25909
Museo Archeologico, Ventotene 25957
Museo Archeologico, Veroli 25964
Museo Archeologico, Villasimius 26022
Museo Archeologico al Teatro Romano, Verona 25969
Museo Archeologico Antiquarium Arborense, Oristano 24692
Museo Archeologico Antonio Santarelli, Forlì 23908
Museo Archeologico Aquaria, Soncino 25599
Museo Archeologico Attrezzato e Cattedrale di San Zeno, Pistoia 24955
Museo Archeologico B. Antonucci, Pietrasanta 24912
Museo Archeologico Baglio Anselmi, Marsala 24305
Museo Archeologico Civico, Forlimpopoli 23918
Museo Archeologico Comprensoriale, Teti 25703
Museo Archeologico Comunale, Vicchio 25989
Museo Archeologico Comunale di Artimino, Carmignano 23349
Museo Archeologico dei Campi Flegrei, Bacoli 22996
Museo Archeologico del Finale, Finale Ligure 23818
Museo Archeologico del Territorio, Cupra Marittima 23699
Museo Archeologico del Territorio - Antiquarium Suasanum, San Lorenzo in Campo 25383
Museo Archeologico del Territorio di Populonia, Piombino 24935
Museo Archeologico della Badia, Licata 24183
Museo Archeologico della Lucania Occidentale, Padula 24753
Museo Archeologico della Sabbia, Gavardo 23964
Museo Archeologico dell'Abruzzo, Crecchio 23675
Museo Archeologico dell'Agro Nocerino, Nocera Inferiore 24627
Museo Archeologico dell'Alto Adige, Bolzano 23152
Museo Archeologico dell'Alto Canavese, Cuorgnè 23698
Museo Archeologico dell'Antica, Alife 22858
Museo Archeologico dell'Antica Calatia, Maddaloni 24256
Museo Archeologico dell'Antica Capua, Santa Maria Capua Vetere 25435
Museo Archeologico dell'Arte della Lana, Arpino 22939
Museo Archeologico di Casteggio, Casteggio 23385
Museo Archeologico di Morgantina, Aidone 22820
Museo Archeologico di Naxos, Giardini Naxos 24021
Museo Archeologico di Sepino, Sepino 25541
Museo Archeologico di Vallecamonica, Cividate Camuno 23590
Museo Archeologico di Villa Sulcis, Carbonia 23344
Museo Archeologico e Antiquarium, Sala Consilina 25314
Museo Archeologico e Antiquarium Nazionale, Formia 23920
Museo Archeologico e d'Arte della Maremma, Grosseto 24056
Museo Archeologico e della Ceramica, Montelupo Fiorentino 24533
Museo Archeologico e della Collegiata, Casole d'Elsa 23379
Museo Archeologico e della via Flaminia, Cagli 23242
Museo Archeologico e Paleontologico, Asti 22973
Museo Archeologico e Paleontologico di Farneta, Cortona 23662
Museo Archeologico e Pinacoteca, Piacenza 24890
Museo Archeologico e Pinacoteca Comunale, Foligno 23897
Museo Archeologico e Storico Aristico, Bra 23192
Museo Archeologico ed Etnografico, Ittireddu 24110
Museo Archeologico Eoliano, Lipari 24187
Museo Archeologico Etneo, Adrano 22807
Museo Archeologico Etnografico, Paulilatino 24820
Museo Archeologico F. Milizia, Oria 24687
Museo Archeologico G. Allevi, Offida 24669
Museo Archeologico G. Cilnio Mecenate, Arezzo 22920
Museo Archeologico G. Moretti, San Severino Marche 25412
Museo Archeologico G. Rambotti, Desenzano del Garda 23711
Museo Archeologico Girolamo Rossi, Ventimiglia 25955
Museo Archeologico Ibleo, Ragusa 25068
Museo Archeologico Isidoro Falchi, Vetulonia 25982
Museo Archeologico Iulium Carnicum, Zuglio 26061
Museo Archeologico Lametino, Lamezia Terme 24131
Museo Archeologico Liutprando, San Giovanni in Persiceto 25372
Museo Archeologico Lomellino, Gamboló 23956
Museo Archeologico Lomellino, Garlasco 23961
Museo Archeologico Lucus Feroniae, Capena 23325
Museo Archeologico Luigi Donini, San Lazzaro di Savena 25377
Museo Archeologico Medievale, Attimis 22983
Museo Archeologico Michele Janora, Irsina 24098
Museo Archeologico Nazionale, Adria 22808
Museo Archeologico Nazionale, Aquileia 22907
Museo Archeologico Nazionale, Cagliari 23245
Museo Archeologico Nazionale, Campli 23299
Museo Archeologico Nazionale, Capaccio 23322
Museo Archeologico Nazionale, Cassino 23382
Museo Archeologico Nazionale, Chieti 23544
Museo Archeologico Nazionale, Chiusi Città 23555
Museo Archeologico Nazionale, Cividale del Friuli 23588
Museo Archeologico Nazionale, Crotone 23689
Museo Archeologico Nazionale, Eboli 23726
Museo Archeologico Nazionale, Firenze 23852
Museo Archeologico Nazionale, Gioia del Colle 24027
Museo Archeologico Nazionale, Manfredonia 24280
Museo Archeologico Nazionale, Mantova 24283
Museo Archeologico Nazionale, Metaponto 24367
Museo Archeologico Nazionale, Napoli 24577
Museo Archeologico Nazionale, Parma 24802
Museo Archeologico Nazionale, Quarto d'Altino 25059
Museo Archeologico Nazionale, Sperlonga 25617
Museo Archeologico Nazionale, Spoleto 25623
Museo Archeologico Nazionale, Taranto 25672
Museo Archeologico Nazionale, Venezia 25923
Museo Archeologico Nazionale, Venosa 25953
Museo Archeologico Nazionale, Viterbo 26032
Museo Archeologico Nazionale del Melfese, Melfi 24345
Museo Archeologico Nazionale della Sibaritide, Cassano allo Jonio 23380
Museo Archeologico Nazionale delle Marche, Ancona 22881
Museo Archeologico Nazionale dell'Umbria, Perugia 24850
Museo Archeologico Nazionale di Cosa, Orbetello 24683
Museo Archeologico Nazionale di Luni, Ortonovo 24702
Museo Archeologico Nazionale di Metaponto, Bernalda 23067
Museo Archeologico Nazionale di Palestrina, Palestrina 24780
Museo Archeologico Nazionale e Antiquarium Statale, Locri 24199
Museo Archeologico Nazionale Etrusco, Cerveteri 23491
Museo Archeologico Nazionale Etrusco, Siena 25569
Museo Archeologico Nazionale Etrusco, Tuscania 25844
Museo Archeologico Oliveriano, Pesaro 24857
Museo Archeologico per la Preistoria e Protostoria del Tigullio, Chiavari 23530
Museo Archeologico Provinciale, Bari 23020
Museo Archeologico Provinciale, Potenza 25028
Museo Archeologico Provinciale, Salerno 25317
Museo Archeologico Provinciale F. Ribezzo, Brindisi 23212
Museo Archeologico Regionale, Agrigento 22816
Museo Archeologico Regionale, Aosta 22900
Museo Archeologico Regionale, Gela 23970
Museo Archeologico Regionale, Santa Croce Camerina 25429
Museo Archeologico Regionale A. Salinas, Palermo 24765
Museo Archeologico Regionale Paolo Orsi, Siracusa 25586
Museo Archeologico Remo Fumagalli, Novara 24645
Museo Archeologico San Giovanni in Compito, Savignano sul Rubicone 25502
Museo Archeologico Sentinate, Sassoferrato 25494
Museo Archeologico Statale, Altamura 22861
Museo Archeologico Statale, Arcevia 22913
Museo Archeologico Statale, Ascoli Piceno 22950
Museo Archeologico Statale, Cingoli 23565
Museo Archeologico Statale, Teano 25678
Museo Archeologico Statale, Urbisaglia 25862
Museo Archeologico Statale V. Capialbi, Vibo Valentia 25987
Museo Archeologico Statale V. Laviola, Amendolara 22876
Museo Archeologico Tifernum Mataurense, Sant'Angelo in Vado 25449
Museo Archeologico Villa Abbas, Sardara 25472
Museo-Archivio di Fotografia Storica, Roma 25177
Museo Archivio Sacrario di Storia Patria, Bagheria 22999
Museo-Archivo de Falset y Comarca, Falset 34812
Museo Arciprestal, Morella 35140
Museo Arcivescovile, Ravenna 25079
Museo Areneo de Estudios Históricos de Nueva Pompeya, Buenos Aires 00157
Museo Argentino de Ciencias Naturales Bernardino Rivadavia, Buenos Aires 00158
Museo Argentino de Motos Antiguas, Mendoza 00433
Museo Armando Reverón, Caracas 48905
Museo Armando Reverón, Macuto 48950
Museo Armería 9 de Abril, La Habana 07936
Museo Arqueològic Municipal Cal Guimerà, El Vendrell 35644
Museo Arqueológica de Mongua, Mongua 07527
Museo Arqueológical Rafael Larco Herrera, Lima 31200
Museo Arqueológico, Aguilares 00108
Museo Arqueológico, Alcalá de Henares 34426
Museo Arqueológico, Almuñécar 34456
Museo Arqueológico, Aranzazu 07368
Museo Arqueológico, Cacabelos 34640
Museo Arqueológico, La Carolina 34682
Museo Arqueológico, Cartago 07459
Museo Arqueológico, Cuenca 09149
Museo Arqueológico, Curumaní 07470
Museo Arqueológico, Gata de Gorgos 34841
Museo Arqueológico, Granada 30321
Museo Arqueológico, Gualeguaychú 00360
Museo Arqueológico, Inzá 07499
Museo Arqueológico, La Tebaida 07503
Museo Arqueológico, Manizales 07506
Museo Arqueológico, Nerja 35157
Museo Arqueológico, Novelda 35162
Museo Arqueológico, Oiba 07538
Museo Arqueológico, Osuna 35196
Museo Arqueológico, Paéz 07539
Museo Arqueológico, Pasca 07545
Museo Arqueológico, Puerto Berrío 07569
Museo Arqueológico, Puerto de la Cruz 35298
Museo Arqueológico, Sagunto 35354
Museo Arqueológico, Salamina 07581
Museo Arqueológico, Santa Cruz de Tenerife 35413
Museo Arqueológico, Sogamoso 07597
Museo Arqueológico, Tafí del Valle 00626
Museo Arqueológico Adán Quiroga, San Fernando del Valle de Catamarca 00555
Museo Arqueológico Alejandro Pezzia Aseretto, La Angostura 31191
Museo Arqueológico Alto Maestrazgo, Benasal 34601
Museo Arqueológico Atahualpa, Ibarra 09179
Museo Arqueológico Calima, Calima 07454
Museo Arqueologico Carlos Aiiercado, Esmeraldas 09163
Museo Arqueológico Casa de Madame Augustín, Santa Marta 07586
Museo Arqueológico Casa del Marqués de San Jorge, Bogotá 07392
Museo Arqueológico Chiametlán, Rosario 28360
Museo Arqueológico Chimica, El Copey 07476
Museo Arqueológico Comarcal, Gandía 34835
Museo Arqueológico Comarcal, Orihuela 35184

Museo Arqueológico, Costumbrista y Naturalista, Güimar 34891
Museo Arqueológico Cuicuilco, México 28107
Museo Arqueológico de Ancash, Huaraz 31174
Museo Arqueológico de Apaxco, Apaxco 27775
Museo Arqueológico de Asturias, Oviedo 35203
Museo Arqueológico de Baza, Baza 34593
Museo Arqueológico de Cajamarca y Museo Médico, Cajamarca 31126
Museo Arqueológico de Campeche, Campeche 27795
Museo Arqueológico de Cancún, Cancún 27803
Museo Arqueológico de Chasicó, Chasicó 00273
Museo Arqueológico de Ciudad Guzmán, Guzmán 27981
Museo Arqueológico de Comayagua, Comayagua 21298
Museo Arqueológico de Comitán, Comitán de Domínguez 27848
Museo Arqueológico de Guacarí, Guacarí 07486
Museo Arqueológico de la Ciudad, Emiliano Zapata 27908
Museo Arqueológico de la Costa Grande, Zihuatanejo 28654
Museo Arqueológico de la Plana Baja, Burriana 34637
Museo Arqueológico de La Serena, La Serena 06898
Museo Arqueológico de la Universidad Nacional del Altiplano, Pucara 31241
Museo Arqueológico de Lagos de Moreno, Lagos de Moreno 28047
Museo Arqueológico de Martins Sarmento, Guimarães 32277
Museo Arqueológico de Mazatlán, Mazatlán 28076
Museo Arqueológico de Muzo, Muzo 07531
Museo Arqueológico de Nextlalpan, Nextlalpan 28266
Museo Arqueológico de Puerto Esperanza, Puerto Esperanza 00490
Museo Arqueológico de Salta, Salta 00537
Museo Arqueológico de Tepeapulco, Tepeapulco 28487
Museo Arqueológico de Tilcara, Tilcara 00635
Museo Arqueológico de Tizatlán, Tizatlán 28518
Museo Arqueológico de Tonalá, Tonalá, Chiapas 28552
Museo Arqueológico de Tula Jorge R. Acosta, Tula de Allende 28565
Museo Arqueológico de Úbeda, Ubeda 35583
Museo Arqueológico de Venustiano Carranza, Venustiano Carranza 28592
Museo Arqueológico de Xochimilco, México 28108
Museo Arqueológico d'Eivissa i Formentera, Eivissa 34785
Museo Arqueologico del Banco Central de Bahia, Bahia de Caráculez 09139
Museo Arqueológico del Centro de Estudios Histórico Sociales Julio Espejo Nuñez, Jauja 31189
Museo Arqueológico del Cerro de la Estrella, México 28109
Museo Arqueológico del Cesar, Valledupar 07616
Museo Arqueológico del Huila, Neiva 07533
Museo Arqueológico del Instituto de Arqueología y Etnología, Mendoza 00434
Museo Arqueológico del Sinú, Tierralta 07605
Museo Arqueológico del Soconusco, Tapachula 28455
Museo Arqueológico Dr. Román Piña Chan, Tenango del Valle 28477
Museo Arqueológico e Histórico de Andahuaylas, Andahuaylas 31111
Museo Arqueológico Etnológico Municipal, Guardamar de Segura 34889
Museo Arqueológico Frederico Galvez Durand, Huancayo 31168
Museo Arqueológico Guamuhaya, Trinidad 08159
Museo Arqueológico Horacio Urteaga, Cajamarca 31127
Museo Arqueológico I.B. Niguel de Mañara, San José de la Rinconada 35377
Museo Arqueológico José Casinelli, Santa Inés 31248
Museo Arqueologico José María Morante de la Universidad Nacional de San Augustín de Arequipa, Arequipa 31113
Museo Arqueológico Juan Sepúlveda y Museo Eduardo Ruiz, Uruapán 28578
Museo Arqueológico Julio César Cubillos, Cali 07444
Museo Arqueológico Julio César Cubillos, San Agustín 07582
Museo Arqueológico La Bagatela, Villa del Rosario 07623
Museo Arqueológico La Merced, Cali 07445
Museo Arqueológico Luis G. Urbina, México 28110
Museo Arqueológico Marco Fidel Micolta, Guamo 07491
Museo Arqueológico Mesoamericano, Tijuana 28510
Museo Arqueológico Monográfico de Cástulo Linares, Linares 34954
Museo Arqueológico Municipal, Alcúdia 34440
Museo Arqueológico Municipal, Caravaca de la Cruz 34676
Museo Arqueológico Municipal, Cartagena 34684
Museo Arqueológico Municipal, Crevillente 34758
Museo Arqueológico Municipal, Dénia 34771
Museo Arqueológico Municipal, Doña Mencia 34773
Museo Arqueológico Municipal, Elda 34794
Museo Arqueológico Municipal, Jerez de la Frontera 34928
Museo Arqueológico Municipal, Lorca 34982
Museo Arqueológico Municipal, Marchena 35088
Museo Arqueológico Municipal, Puente Genil 35297
Museo Arqueológico Municipal, Santaella 35429
Museo Arqueológico Municipal Alejandro Ramos Folqués, Elche 34790
Museo Arqueológico Municipal Camilo Visedo Molto, Alcoi 34435
Museo Arqueológico Municipal Cayetano Mergelina, Yecla 35708
Museo Arqueológico Municipal de Obulco, Porcuna 35286
Museo Arqueológico Municipal José María Soler, Villena 35685
Museo Arqueológico Municipal Precolombino, Benalmádena 34600
Museo Arqueológico Municipal y Museo Municipal Miguel Justino Ramírez, Piura 31238
Museo Arqueológico Nacional, Madrid 35013
Museo Arqueológico Nacional Brüning, Lambayeque 31195
Museo Arqueológico Padre Martín Recio, Estepa 34808
Museo Arqueológico Pío P. Díaz, Cachi 00255
Museo Arqueológico Poblado de la Hoya, Laguardia 34934
Museo Arqueológico Provincial, Badajoz 34516
Museo Arqueológico Provincial, Cehegín 34702
Museo Arqueológico Provincial, Huesca 34907
Museo Arqueológico Provincial, Ourense 35198
Museo Arqueológico Provincial, San Salvador de Jujuy 00595
Museo Arqueológico Provincial, Sevilla 35478
Museo Arqueológico Provincial Andalgalá, Andalgalá 00114
Museo Arqueológico Provincial Condor Huasi (interim), Belén 00138
Museo Arqueologico Provincial de Orense, Orense 35182
Museo Arqueológico Provincial-MARQ, Alicante 34446
Museo Arqueológico Regional Anibal Montes, Río Segundo 00521
Museo Arqueológico Regional de Ancash, Ancash 31110
Museo Arqueológico Regional Guane, Floridablanca 07481
Museo Arqueológico Regional Inca Huasi, La Rioja 00395
Museo Arqueológico R.P. Gustavo Le Paige S.J., San Pedro de Atacama 06906
Museo Arqueológico San Miguel de Azapa, Arica 06889
Museo Arqueológico y Colonial, Fuerte Quemado 00350
Museo Arqueológico y de Historia Natural, Santo Domingo de Silos 35457
Museo Arqueológico y Etnográfico, Vélez Rubio 35642
Museo Arqueológico y Etnográfico Soler Blasco, Jávea 34926
Museo Arqueológico y Etnológico Córdoba, Córdoba 34737
Museo Arqueológico y Etnológico de Granada, Granada 34873
Museo Arqueológico y Paleontológico de Guane, Barichara 07374
Museo Arqueológico y Paleontológico Municipal, Rojales 35332
Museo Arqueológico y Termas Romanas, Caldes de Montbui 34655
Museo Arqueoloógico y Etnográfico, Ibarra 09180
Museo Arquidiocesano, Santiago de Cuba 08130
Museo Arquidiocesano de Arte Religioso, Pamplona 07542
Museo Arquidiocesano de Arte Religioso de Popayán, Popayán 07561
Museo Arquitectura de Trinidad, Trinidad 08160
Museo Art Nouveau y Art Deco, Salamanca 35359
Museo Artes Decorativo, Gibara 07910
Museo Artes Plásticas, Pinar del Río 08071
Museo Artes y Costumbres Populares Alto Guadalquivir, Cazorla 34701
Museo Artesanal de Gualaceo, Gualaceo 09166
Museo Arti e Mestieri di un Tempo, Cisterna d'Asti 23573
Museo Arti e Tradizioni Popolari del Gargano Giovanni Tancredi, Monte Sant'Angelo 24502
Museo Artístico de Roncesvalles, Roncesvalles 35337
Museo Artistico della Bambola, Suvereto 25661
Museo Artistico Industriale F. Palizzi, Napoli 24578
Museo Arturo Michelena, Caracas 48906
Museo Astronomico Copernicano, Roma 25178
Museo Astronomico e Geofisico, Modena 24437
Museo Atelier Antonio Ortiz Echagüe, Carro Quemado 00266
Museo Audiovisual, Caracas 48907
Museo Augustín Landívar, Cuenca 09150
Museo Augusto Righi, Montese 24546
Museo Aurelio Castelli, Siena 25570
Museo Aurelio Espinosa Polit, Cotocollao 09147
Museo Aurelio Espinoza Pólit, Quito 09195
Museo Aurelio Marena, Bitonto 23091
Museo Austral de Pintura Primitiva Moderna Naif, Esquel 00345
Museo Auto d'Ecopa, San Marino 33760
Museo Azuayo del Folklore, Cuenca 09151
Museo Badia di San Gemolo, Valganna 25876
Museo Bagatti Valsecchi, Milano 24386
Museo Bahía de los Angeles, Ensenada 27912
Museo Balaa Xte Guech Gulal, Teotitlán del Valle 28484
Museo Balear Ciencies Naturals, Sóller 35501
Museo Balmes, Vic 35650
Museo Balseros del Mar del Sur, Salango 09225
Museo Baluarte de Santiago, Veracruz 28593
Museo Banco Central de Reserva del Perú, Lima 31201
Museo Banco del Pacifico, Guayaquil 09169
Museo Bandini, Fiesole 23805
Museo Bardini, Firenze 23853
Museo Baroffio e del Santuario del Sacro Monte sopra Varese, Varese 25896
Museo Barovier e Toso, Venezia 25924
Museo Barracco, Roma 25179
Museo Barrau, Santa Eulària des Riu 35417
Museo Beata P. Morosini, Albino 22836
Museo Beato Angelico, Vicchio 25990
Museo Beato Angelo, Acri 22805
Museo Belgraniano, La Plata 00386
Museo Belisario Porras, Panamá City 31078
Museo Bellapart, Santo Domingo 09120
Museo Bello Piñeio, Ferrol 34816
Museo Benedettino Nonantolano e Diocesano di Arte Sacra, Nonantola 24635
Museo Benigno Malo, Cuenca 09152
Museo Benito Hortiz, Sancti-Spíritus 08108
Museo Benito Juárez, La Habana 07937
Museo Benito Juárez, José Azueta 28034
Museo Berenziano, Cremona 23679
Museo Bernabé de las Casas, Mina 28218
Museo Bernardino Caballero, Asunción 31096
Museo Bernardo de Muro, Tempio Pausania 25683
Museo Bernardo Martínez Villegas, Bácum 27789
Museo Bernardo Samper Sordo, Bogotá 07393
Museo Bersano delle Contadinerie e Stampe antiche del Vino, Nizza Monferrato 24624
Museo B.Gigli, Recanati 25086
Museo Biblioteca Comunale, Etroubles 23744
Museo, Biblioteca e Archivio, Bassano del Grappa 23037
Museo Biblioteca La Casona, Tudanca 35577
Museo Biblioteca Municipal Cesar Fernández Navarro, Santa Fé 00601
Museo Biblioteca Nueva Cádiz y Casa Natal de Juan Bautista Arismendi, Nueva Cádiz 48958
Museo Biblioteca Palacio Postal, México 28111
Museo Biblioteca Palafoxiana, Puebla 28318
Museo Biblioteca Pape, Monclova 28224
Museo Biblioteca Rosauro Rosa Acosta, Pampatar 48959
Museo Bicknell, Bordighera 23164
Museo Bicocchi, Pomarance 24983
Museo Bodoniano, Parma 24803
Museo Bolívariano, Caracas 48908
Museo Bolivariano de Arte Contemporáneo, Santa Marta 07587
Museo Bologna-Buonsignori, Siena 25571
Museo Boncompagni Ludovisi per le Arti Decorative, Roma 25180
Museo Borromeo, Isola Bella 24104
Museo Botanico, Buenos Aires 00159
Museo Botánico, Córdoba 00291
Museo Botánico, Montevideo 40993
Museo Botánico, Tuxtla Gutiérrez 28569
Museo Botanico Cesare Bicchi, Lucca 24226
Museo Botanico della Lessinia, Fumane 23942
Museo Bottacin, Padova 24736
Museo Bottega della Tarsia Lignea, Sorrento 25610
Museo Brandolini e Giol, Oderzo 24664
Museo Brembano di Scienze Naturali, San Pellegrino Terme 25405
Museo C. Nivola, Orani 24681
Museo Ca' la Ghironda, Bologna 23107
Museo Cabrera, Ica 31180
Museo Cabriniano, Sant'Angelo Lodigiano 25450
Museo Cacique Balata, La Cumbre 00378
Museo Calabozo de Hidalgo, Chihuahua 27821
Museo Calabrese di Etnografia e Folklore R. Corso, Palmi 24785
Museo Camillo Leone, Vercelli 25959
Museo Camilo Egas del Banco Central, Quito 09196
Museo Camón Aznar, Zaragoza 35718
Museo Campagna G. Bruno, Campagna 23296
Museo Campamento Irritila, San Pedro 28419
Museo Camuno e Biblioteca Civica, Breno 23197
Museo Canario, Las Palmas de Gran Canaria 35239
Museo Canonica, Roma 25181
Museo Canonicale, Verona 25970
Museo Cantábrico, Comillas 34732
Museo Cantonale d'Arte, Lugano 36898
Museo Cantonale di Storia Naturale, Lugano 36899
Museo Capilla Alfonsina, México 28112
Museo Capitán Juan de Zevallos, Valle Hermoso 00653
Museo Capitolare, Assisi 22962
Museo Capitolare, Atri 22980
Museo Capitolare, Cagliari 23246
Museo Capitolare, Ortona 24699
Museo Capitolare delle Antichità Corfiniesi, Corfinio 23650
Museo Capitolare di Arte Sacra, Gravina di Puglia 24049
Museo Capitolare di San Lorenzo, Perugia 24851
Museo Cappella San Severo, Napoli 24579
Museo Cappuccini Emiliani, Reggio Emilia 25097
Museo Capuaniano, Mineo 24427
Museo Cardenal Crisanto Luque, Tenjo 07604
Museo Carducci - Biblioteca e Casa, Bologna 23108
Museo Carlo Venturini, Massa Lombarda 24317
Museo Carlos Emilio Grijalva, Tulcán 09228
Museo Carlos Maside, Sada 35352
Museo Carlos Torres Barraza, Valentín Gómez Farías 28580
Museo Carnico delle Arti Popolari Michele Gortani, Tolmezzo 25725
Museo Carozzi, Seriate 25543
Museo Casa Alejandro de Humboldt, La Habana 07938
Museo Casa Blanca, San Juan 32392
Museo Casa Busoni, Empoli 23728
Museo Casa Cautiño, Guayama 32372
Museo Casa Clautana E. Borsatti, Claut 23599
Museo Casa Colonial, Pamplona 07543
Museo Casa Cultural "Alfonso López Pumarejo", Honda 07494
Museo Casa de Africa, La Habana 07939
Museo Casa de Agustín Arrieta, Puebla 28319
Museo Casa de Asia, La Habana 07940
Museo Casa de Benalcazar, Quito 09197
Museo Casa de Bernardo A. Houssay, Buenos Aires 00160
Museo Casa de Bolívar, Bucaramanga 07436
Museo Casa de Carmen Montilla, La Habana 07941
Museo Casa de Carranza, Cuatrocienegas 27868
Museo Casa de Carranza, México 28113
Museo Casa de Colón, Las Palmas de Gran Canaria 35240
Museo Casa de Cultura de Ixtlán, Ixtlán del Río 28019
Museo Casa de Dulcinea, El Toboso 35534
Museo Casa de Hidalgo La Francia Chiquita, San Felipe 28383
Museo Casa de la Bola, México 28114
Museo Casa de la Cultura, Montemorelos 28228
Museo Casa de la Cultura de Barichara, Barichara 07375
Museo Casa de la Cultura de Cuacutecuta, Cuacutecuta 07467
Museo Casa de la Cultura de Pensilvania, Pensilvania 07555
Museo Casa de la Cultura "Luis Camacho Rueda", Socorro 07596
Museo Casa de la Moneda, Mariquita 07511
Museo Casa de la Obrapía, La Habana 07942
Museo Casa de la Orfebrería, La Habana 07943
Museo Casa de la Plomada, Vallecillo 28586
Museo Casa de la Poesía, La Habana 07944
Museo Casa de la Tecnología, Monterrey 28229
Museo Casa de la Troya, Santiago de Compostela 35438
Museo Casa de León Trotsky, México 28115
Museo Casa de los Mártires, La Habana 07945
Museo Casa de Morelos, Ecatepec de Morelos 27902
Museo Casa de Morelos, Morelia 28243
Museo Casa de Policarpa Salavarrieta, Guaduas 07488
Museo Casa de Puerto Rico y Sala del Tabaco, La Habana 07946
Museo Casa de Ramón López Velarde, Jerez de García Salinas 28029
Museo Casa de Ricardo Rojas, Buenos Aires 00161
Museo Casa de Sais Montes de Oca Hermanos, Pinar del Río 08072
Museo Casa de Sucre, Quito 09198
Museo Casa de Yrurtia, Buenos Aires 00162
Museo Casa de Zela, Tacna 31253
Museo Casa del Agua, Tehuacán 28472
Museo Casa del Alfeñique, Puebla 28320
Museo Casa del Deán, Puebla 28321
Museo Casa del Diego, Celaya 27808
Museo Casa del Dr. Mora, Comonfort 27851
Museo Casa del Duca, Venezia 25925
Museo Casa del Fundador Ponzalo Suárez Rendón, Tunja 07611
Museo Casa del General Alvaro Obregón, Huatabampo 27998
Museo Casa del Libertador Simón Bolívar, La Habana 07947
Museo Casa del Maestro José Márquez Figueroa, Puebla 28322
Museo Casa del Marques de Aguayo y Museo Municipal, Mazapil Zacatecas 28075
Museo Casa del Padre, Orselina 37016
Museo Casa Diego Rivera, Guanajuato 27968
Museo Casa Dr. Belisario Domínguez, Comitán de Domínguez 27849
Museo Casa Estudio Diego Rivera y Frida Kahlo, México 28116
Museo Casa Francisco Villa, Hidalgo del Parral 27991
Museo Casa Fundación Oswaldo Guayasamín, La Habana 07948
Museo Casa Galimberti, Cuneo 23695
Museo Casa José Lezama Lima, La Habana 07949
Museo Casa Mata, Matamoros 28073
Museo Casa Maya, Cancún 27804
Museo Casa Mosquera, Popayán 07562
Museo Casa Murillo, Sevilla 35479
Museo Casa Natal de Antonio Maceo, Santiago de Cuba 08131
Museo Casa Natal de Calixto Garcia, Holguín 08003
Museo Casa Natal de Camilo Cienfuegos, La Habana 07950
Museo Casa Natal de Carlos Manuel de Céspedes, Bayamo 07858
Museo Casa Natal de Celia Sanchez Manduley, Media Luna 08045
Museo Casa Natal de Cervantes, Alcalá de Henares 34427
Museo Casa Natal de Frank País, Santiago de Cuba 08132
Museo Casa Natal de Hermanos Ameijeiras, Pueblo Viejo 08083

Museo Casa Natal de Ignacio Agramonte, Camagüey 07875
Museo Casa Natal de José María Heredia, Santiago de Cuba 08133
Museo Casa Natal de José Martí, La Habana 07951
Museo Casa Natal de Morelos, Morelia 28244
Museo Casa Natal de Pedro Martínez Brito, Ciego de Avila 07886
Museo Casa Natal de Serafín Sánchez, Sancti-Spíritus 08109
Museo Casa Natal General Santander, Villa del Rosario 07624
Museo Casa Natal Juan Manuel Márquez, La Habana 07952
Museo Casa Natale di Giotto, Vicchio 25991
Museo Casa Natale di San Pio X, Riese Pio X 25109
Museo Casa Natale di Tiziano Vecellio, Pieve di Cadore 24914
Museo Casa Natale G. D'Annunzio, Pescara 24866
Museo Casa Natale Giacomo Puccini, Lucca 24227
Museo Casa Negret, Popayán 07563
Museo Casa Padilla, San Miguel de Tucumán 00580
Museo Casa Paoli, Ponce 32378
Museo Casa Pascoli, Barga 23017
Museo Casa Rafael Núñez, Cartagena 07455
Museo Casa Roig, Humacao 32375
Museo Casa Rossini, Pesaro 24858
Museo Casa Ruth Lechuga, México 28117
Museo Casa Studio F. Melani, Pistoia 24956
Museo Casa Walser, Macugnaga 24253
Museo Casabianca, Malo 24270
Museo Casartelli, Como 23626
Museo Casita Blanca de Agustín Lara, Boca del Río 27793
Museo Castello Masegra, Sondrio 25602
Museo Castillo de la Fortaleza de Ansite, Santa Lucía 35420
Museo Castillo El Macho, Peñiscola 35264
Museo Castillo Serrallés, Ponce 32379
Museo Catedral, Palma de Mallorca 35230
Museo Catedral de La Plata, La Plata 00387
Museo Catedralicio, Almería 34453
Museo Catedralicio, Badajoz 34517
Museo Catedralicio, Baeza 34522
Museo Catedralicio, Burgo de Osma 34627
Museo Catedralicio, Burgos 34629
Museo Catedralicio, Cádiz 34646
Museo Catedralicio, Ciudad Real 34720
Museo Catedralicio, Ciudad Rodrigo 34724
Museo Catedralicio, Cuenca 34762
Museo Catedralicio, Eivissa 34786
Museo Catedralicio, Granada 34874
Museo Catedralicio, Guadix 34888
Museo Catedralicio, Jaén 34922
Museo Catedralicio, León 34946
Museo Catedralicio, Lleida 34966
Museo Catedralicio, Málaga 35070
Museo Catedralicio, Murcia 35145
Museo Catedralicio, Palencia 35213
Museo Catedralicio, Salamanca 35360
Museo Catedralicio, Santo Domingo de la Calzada 35456
Museo Catedralicio, Segovia 35464
Museo Catedralicio, Sigüenza 35493
Museo Catedralicio, Tortosa 35568
Museo Catedralicio, Zamora 35712
Museo Catedralicio de La Seo de Zaragoza, Zaragoza 35719
Museo Catedralicio-Diocesano, León 34947
Museo Catedralicio Diocesano, Pamplona 35247
Museo Catedralicio-Diocesano, Valencia 35600
Museo Catedralico y Giralda, Sevilla 35480
Museo Católica de Santa María, Cercado 31139
Museo Católico Peninsular, Mérida 28079
Museo Cavour, Santena 25462
Museo Cemento Rezola, Donostia-San Sebastián 34776
Museo Centrale del Risorgimento, Roma 25182
Museo Centrale dell'Istituto Storico della Resistenza, Imperia 24093
Museo Centro Cultural Pachamama, Amaicha del Valle 00113
Museo Centro de Cultura Mayo de El Júpare Blas Mazo, Huatabampo 27999
Museo Centro de la Imagen, México 28118
Museo Centro Studi A.G. Barrili, Carcare 23346
Museo Centro Taurino Potosino, San Luis Potosí 28398
Museo Ceramoteca, Salamanca 28363
Museo Cerlogne, Saint Nicolas 25310
Museo Cerralbo, Madrid 35014
Museo Cerro de la Campana, Santiago Suchilquitongo 28439
Museo Cerro de los Huizaches, San Pablo Huixtepec 28418
Museo Cervi, Gattatico 23963
Museo Chairama, Santa Marta 07588
Museo Charcas, Sucre 03907
Museo Chavin de Huantar, Martínez 00431
Museo Chiaramonti e Braccio Nuovo, Città del Vaticano 48873
Museo Chihuahuense de Arte Contemporáneo, Chihuahua 27822
Museo Chileno de Arte Precolombino, Santiago de Chile 06908
Museo Chorro de Maita, Yaguajay 08178
Museo Christiano, Cividale del Friuli 23589
Museo Ciénaga de San Pedro, Madera 28065
Museo Ciencias Naturales, Nueva Gerona 08056
Museo Ciencias Naturales Carlos de la Torre, Sancti-Spíritus 08110
Museo Ciudades del Mundo, La Habana 07953
Museo Civico, Aci Castello 22797
Museo Civico, Agrigento 22817
Museo Civico, Airola 22822
Museo Civico, Alatri 22827
Museo Civico, Amalfi 22869
Museo Civico, Andreis 22887
Museo Civico, Apice 22904
Museo Civico, Argenta 22925
Museo Civico, Ariano Irpino 22929
Museo Civico, Asolo 22959
Museo Civico, Atina 22978
Museo Civico, Avola 22995
Museo Civico, Baranello 23011
Museo Civico, Bardonecchia 23015
Museo Civico, Barga 23018
Museo Civico, Belluno 23048
Museo Civico, Biella 23079
Museo Civico, Bisacquino 23085
Museo Civico, Bojano 23096
Museo Civico, Bojano 23097
Museo Civico, Bolzano 23153
Museo Civico, Borgo Velino 23174
Museo Civico, Bormio 23179
Museo Civico, Busseto 23235
Museo Civico, Cabras 23240
Museo Civico, Caldarola 23265
Museo Civico, Campagnano di Roma 23297
Museo Civico, Campochiaro 23306
Museo Civico, Canneto sull'Oglio 23314
Museo Civico, Canneto sull'Oglio 23315
Museo Civico, Caprino Veronese 23336
Museo Civico, Casale Monferrato 23364
Museo Civico, Casamicciola Terme 23371
Museo Civico, Castel Bolognese 23386
Museo Civico, Castelleone 23410
Museo Civico, Castelnovo Bariano 23416
Museo Civico, Castelnuovo Scrivia 23423
Museo Civico, Castelraimondo 23424
Museo Civico, Castroreale 23439
Museo Civico, Centuripe 23475
Museo Civico, Cerchio 23478
Museo Civico, Champdepaz 23517
Museo Civico, Cittadella 23583
Museo Civico, Collelongo 23614
Museo Civico, Conversano 23641
Museo Civico, Cori 23651
Museo Civico, Cosenza 23665
Museo Civico, Crema 23676
Museo Civico, Crotone 23690
Museo Civico, Cuneo 23696
Museo Civico, Erba 23735
Museo Civico, Feltre 23772
Museo Civico, Ferentino 23776
Museo Civico, Finale Emilia 23815
Museo Civico, Foggia 23892
Museo Civico, Fondi 23904
Museo Civico, Fornovo San Giovanni 23923
Museo Civico, Fratta Polesine 23935
Museo Civico, Fucecchio 23941
Museo Civico, Gangi 23958
Museo Civico, Gibellina 24023
Museo Civico, Guardiagrele 24070
Museo Civico, Iesi 24079
Museo Civico, Larciano 24150
Museo Civico, Larino 24152
Museo Civico, Licata 24184
Museo Civico, Lodi 24201
Museo Civico, Lucignano 24234
Museo Civico, Luino 24241
Museo Civico, Maddaloni 24257
Museo Civico, Magliano Sabina 24260
Museo Civico, Manerbio 24279
Museo Civico, Mattinata 24336
Museo Civico, Mazara del Vallo 24337
Museo Civico, Medicina 24341
Museo Civico, Mirandola 24431
Museo Civico, Monsampolo del Tronto 24482
Museo Civico, Montelparo 24532
Museo Civico, Nocera Umbra 24628
Museo Civico, Noto 24640
Museo Civico, Osimo 24708
Museo Civico, Patrica 24815
Museo Civico, Pegognaga 24833
Museo Civico, Pescia 24875
Museo Civico, Piedimonte 24906
Museo Civico, Pieve di Cento 24919
Museo Civico, Pistoia 24957
Museo Civico, Pizzighettone 24968
Museo Civico, Pontecorvo 24997
Museo Civico, Putignano 25057
Museo Civico, Ragogna 25066
Museo Civico, Recanati 25087
Museo Civico, Rende 25103
Museo Civico, Rieti 25110
Museo Civico, Riva del Garda 25130
Museo Civico, Rovereto 25291
Museo Civico, Salemi 25316
Museo Civico, San Bonifacio 25340
Museo Civico, San Cesario di Lecce 25346
Museo Civico, San Ferdinando di Puglia 25358
Museo Civico, San Gimignano 25362
Museo Civico, San Severo 25416
Museo Civico, Sanremo 25425
Museo Civico, Sansepolcro 25427
Museo Civico, Santa Giusta 25431
Museo Civico, Sesto Calende 25555
Museo Civico, Siena 25572
Museo Civico, Susa 25654
Museo Civico, Taverna 25677
Museo Civico, Terrasini 25700
Museo Civico, Tolfa 25724
Museo Civico, Trevignano Romano 25802
Museo Civico, Trinitapoli 25833
Museo Civico, Troia 25837
Museo Civico, Vasanello 25902
Museo Civico, Viterbo 26033
Museo Civico A. Giacomelli, Montagnana 24489
Museo Civico A. Klitsche de la Grange, Allumiere 22859
Museo Civico A. Parazzi, Viadana 25983
Museo Civico A. Tubino, Masone 24312
Museo Civico A.E. Baruffaldi, Badia Polesine 22997
Museo Civico Ala Ponzone, Cremona 23680
Museo Civico Albano, Albano Laziale 22830
Museo Civico Alta Val Brembana, Valtorta 25888
Museo Civico Antiquarium, Nettuno 24616
Museo Civico Antiquarium Platina, Piadena 24895
Museo Civico Antonino Olmo e Gipsoteca, Savigliano 25499
Museo Civico Antonio Cordici, Erice 23739
Museo Civico Archeologica e Quadreria, Monterubbiano 24545
Museo Civico Archeologico, Angera 22889
Museo Civico Archeologico, Anzio 22898
Museo Civico Archeologico, Arona 22936
Museo Civico Archeologico, Barbarano Romano 23012
Museo Civico Archeologico, Bene Vagienna 23052
Museo Civico Archeologico, Bergamo 23061
Museo Civico Archeologico, Bologna 23109
Museo Civico Archeologico, Camerino 23283
Museo Civico Archeologico, Canosa di Puglia 23317
Museo Civico Archeologico, Casalmaggiore 23366
Museo Civico Archeologico, Castelfranco Emilia 23398
Museo Civico Archeologico, Castelleone di Suasa 23411
Museo Civico Archeologico, Castro dei Volsci 23438
Museo Civico Archeologico, Castrovillari 23441
Museo Civico Archeologico, Cavaion Veronese 23459
Museo Civico Archeologico, Cologna Veneta 23618
Museo Civico Archeologico, Concordia Sagittaria 23636
Museo Civico Archeologico, Fiesole 23806
Museo Civico Archeologico, Gazzo Veronese 23969
Museo Civico Archeologico, Gottolengo 24037
Museo Civico Archeologico, Grotte di Castro 24063
Museo Civico Archeologico, Latronico 24161
Museo Civico Archeologico, Marciana 24295
Museo Civico Archeologico, Massa Marittima 24322
Museo Civico Archeologico, Mel 24344
Museo Civico Archeologico, Mondragone 24474
Museo Civico Archeologico, Montalto Marche 24493
Museo Civico Archeologico, Nepi 24614
Museo Civico Archeologico, Nicotera 24620
Museo Civico Archeologico, Norma 24637
Museo Civico Archeologico, Padria 24752
Museo Civico Archeologico, Pitigliano 24963
Museo Civico Archeologico, Portoferraio 25017
Museo Civico Archeologico, Ramacca 25070
Museo Civico Archeologico, Remedello 25102
Museo Civico Archeologico, Roccagloriosa 25137
Museo Civico Archeologico, Rosignano Marittimo 25284
Museo Civico Archeologico, Rutigliano 25304
Museo Civico Archeologico, Salò 25323
Museo Civico Archeologico, Santa Marinella 25440
Museo Civico Archeologico, Sarteano 25481
Museo Civico Archeologico, Tolentino 25717
Museo Civico Archeologico, Treia 25788
Museo Civico Archeologico, Verucchio 25978
Museo Civico Archeologico Arsenio Crespellani, Bazzano 23044
Museo Civico Archeologico C. Cellini, Ripatransone 25122
Museo Civico Archeologico della Val Tenesi, Manerba del Garda 24278
Museo Civico Archeologico di Fregellae, Ceprano 23477
Museo Civico Archeologico e Paleobotanico, Perfugas 24840
Museo Civico Archeologico e Pinacoteca, Chiomonte 23551
Museo Civico Archeologico Eno Bellis, Oderzo 24665
Museo Civico Archeologico Etnologico, Modena 24438
Museo Civico Archeologico F Saverio Majellaro, Bisceglie 23086
Museo Civico Archeologico Genna Maria, Villanovaforru 26020
Museo Civico Archeologico Goffredo Bellini, Asola 22958
Museo Civico Archeologico L. Fantini, Monterenzio 24542
Museo Civico Archeologico M. Petrone, Vieste 26004
Museo Civico Archeologico O. Nardini, Velletri 25905
Museo Civico Archeologico P. Giovio, Como 23627
Museo Civico Archeologico Paleoambientale, Budrio 23224
Museo Civico Archeologico 'Romualdi', Notaresco 24639
Museo Civico Archeologico Sa Domu Nosta, Senorbì 25540
Museo Civico Archeologico Trebula Mutesca, Monteleone Sabino 24530
Museo Civico Archeologico U. Granafei, Mesagne 24362
Museo Civico Arecheologico delle Acque, Chianciano Terme 23522
Museo Civico Aufidenate, Castel di Sangro 23388
Museo Civico Aufidenate De Nino, Alfedena 22851
Museo Civico B. Romano, Termini Imerese 25692
Museo Civico Belliniano, Catania 23446
Museo Civico Borbonico, Salle 25322
Museo Civico C. G. Nicastro, Bovino 23191
Museo Civico C. Verri, Biassono 23077
Museo Civico Casa Cavassa, Saluzzo 25326
Museo Civico Castel Nuovo, Napoli 24580
Museo Civico Castello Ursino, Catania 23447
Museo Civico Chiusa, Chiusa 23552
Museo Civico Craveri di Storia Naturale, Bra 23193
Museo Civico D. dal Lago, Valdagno 25871
Museo Civico d'Arte, Modena 24439
Museo Civico d'Arte, Pordenone 25007
Museo Civico d'Arte Antica, Torino 25736
Museo Civico d'Arte Contemporanea, Albissola Marina 22841
Museo Civico d'Arte Contemporanea U. Apollonio, San Martino di Lupari 25389
Museo Civico d'Arte Industriale e Galleria Davia Bargellini, Bologna 23110
Museo Civico dei Villaggi Scomparsi, Villa Estense 26013
Museo Civico del Castello, Conegliano 23638
Museo Civico del Marmo, Carrara 23357
Museo Civico del Risorgimemto, Bologna 23111
Museo Civico del Risorgimento, Modena 24440
Museo Civico del Sigillo, La Spezia 24122
Museo Civico del Territorio, San Daniele del Friuli 25354
Museo Civico della Carta, Cairate 23256
Museo Civico della Ceramica, Nove 24654
Museo Civico della Cultura Materiale, Roseto degli Abruzzi 25283
Museo Civico della Laguna Sud, Chioggia 23550
Museo Civico della Media Valle del Liri, Sora 25606
Museo Civico della Navigazione Fluviale, Battaglia Terme 23043
Museo Civico della Torre, Treviglio 25801
Museo Civico della Val Fiorentina Vittorino Cazzetta, Selva di Cadore 25531
Museo Civico delle Armi L. Marzoli, Brescia 23201
Museo Civico delle Arti e Tradizioni Popolari, Micigliano 24368
Museo Civico delle Centuriazioni Romane Padovana, Borgoricco 23175
Museo Civico delle Ceramiche, Santo Stefano di Camastra 25465
Museo Civico delle Scienze, Pordenone 25008
Museo Civico di Archeologia Ligure, Genova 23986
Museo Civico di Arona, Arona 22937
Museo Civico di Arte Contadina, Romagnese 25273
Museo Civico di Arte Moderna, Mombercelli 24465
Museo Civico di Belle Arti, Lugano 36900
Museo Civico di Belriguardo, Voghiera 26046
Museo Civico di Merano - Stadtmuseum Meran, Merano 24352
Museo Civico di Numismatica, Etnografia e Arti Orientali, Torino 25737
Museo Civico di Palazzo Te, Mantova 24284
Museo Civico di Paleontologia, Empoli 23729
Museo Civico di Paleontologia e Archeologia, Ugento 25851
Museo Civico di Paleontologia e Paletnologia, Borgosesia 23177
Museo Civico di San Francesco, Montefalco 24517
Museo Civico di San Francesco, Montone 24556
Museo Civico di Santa Maria della Consolazione, Altomonte 22864
Museo Civico di Schifanoia, Ferrara 23786
Museo Civico di Scienze Naturali, Faenza 23751
Museo Civico di Scienze Naturali, Lovere 24224
Museo Civico di Scienze Naturali, Voghera 26044
Museo Civico di Scienze Naturali E. Caffi, Bergamo 23062
Museo Civico di Scienze Naturali ed Archeologia della Valdinievole, Pescia 24876
Museo Civico di Storia Naturale, Carmagnola 23348
Museo Civico di Storia Naturale, Casalnuovo Monterotaro 23368
Museo Civico di Storia Naturale, Chies d'Alpago 23542
Museo Civico di Storia Naturale, Cittanova 23585
Museo Civico di Storia Naturale, Crocetta del Montello 23686
Museo Civico di Storia Naturale, Ferrara 23787
Museo Civico di Storia Naturale, Milano 24387
Museo Civico di Storia Naturale, Morbegno 24563
Museo Civico di Storia Naturale, Taino 25668
Museo Civico di Storia Naturale, Trieste 25823
Museo Civico di Storia Naturale, Venezia 25926
Museo Civico di Storia Naturale, Verona 25971
Museo Civico di Storia Naturale del Liceo Glassico N. Machiavelli, Lucca 24228
Museo Civico di Storia Naturale del Salento, Calimera 23269
Museo Civico di Storia Naturale Giacomo Doria, Genova 23987
Museo Civico di Vignola, Vignola 26010
Museo Civico di Villa Rathgeb, Abano Terme 22790
Museo Civico di Zoologia, Roma 25183
Museo Civico Didattico di Scienze Naturali, Pinerolo 24927
Museo Civico Didattico Gian Andrea Irico, Trino 25834

Museo Civico Diocesano, Tropea 25840
Museo Civico Diocesano G. B. Leopardi, Penne 24837
Museo Civico Diocesano La Castellina, Norcia 24636
Museo Civico Don Queirolo, Vado Ligure 25865
Museo Civico e Antiquarium, Latina 24158
Museo Civico e Archeologico, Locarno 36885
Museo Civico E. Barba, Gallipoli 23955
Museo Civico e d'Arte Sacra, Colle di Val d'Elsa 23609
Museo Civico e della Ceramica, Cerreto Sannita 23485
Museo Civico e Diocesano d' Arte Sacra, Montalcino 24491
Museo Civico e Foro Romano, Assisi 22963
Museo Civico E. Nardi, Poggio Mirteto 24977
Museo Civico e Pinacoteca, Fano 23762
Museo Civico e Pinacoteca, Sassoferrato 25495
Museo Civico e Pinacoteca, Urbania 25853
Museo Civico e Pinacoteca A. Vernarecci, Fossombrone 23928
Museo Civico e Pinacoteca Basilio Cascella, Pescara 24867
Museo Civico e Pinacoteca E. Lancerotto, Noale 24625
Museo Civico e Pinacoteca P.F. Crociani, Montepulciano 24538
Museo Civico e Risorgimentale Don Giovanni Verità, Modigliana 24453
Museo Civico e Teatro e Serbatoio Romano, Falerone 23761
Museo Civico Etno-Antropologico, Petralia Sottana 24883
Museo Civico Etnografico, Atri 22981
Museo Civico Etnografico, Casale di Scodosia 23363
Museo Civico Etnografico, Stanghella 25629
Museo Civico Etnografico C.G. Franchini, Oleggio 24674
Museo Civico Etnografico La Lessinia, Bosco Chiesanuova 23183
Museo Civico Etnografico M.G. Fontana, Sappada 25469
Museo Civico F. Bodini, Gemonio 23973
Museo Civico F. de Rocco, San Vito al Tagliamento 25418
Museo Civico F. L. Belgiorno, Modica 24451
Museo Civico F. Rittatore Von Willer, Farnese 23765
Museo Civico Fedrigo, Sona 25598
Museo Civico Filippo Meli, Ciminna 23563
Museo Civico Fossili, Besano 23070
Museo Civico G. Sutermeister, Legnano 24175
Museo Civico G. Ugonia, Brisighella 23215
Museo Civico G. Zannato, Montecchio Maggiore 24512
Museo Civico Gaetano Filangieri, Napoli 24581
Museo Civico-Galleria di Palazzo Pretorio, Prato 25044
Museo Civico G.B. Adriani, Cherasco 23520
Museo Civico Geo-Speleologico, Garessio 23960
Museo Civico Geologia e Etnografia, Predazzo 25051
Museo Civico Giacomo Rodolfo, Carignano 23347
Museo Civico Giovanni Fattori, Livorno 24191
Museo Civico Giulio Ferrari, Carpi 23353
Museo Civico Gonzaga, Novellara 24655
Museo Civico Guiseppe Fiorelli, Lucera 24233
Museo Civico Il Correggio, Correggio 23656
Museo Civico L. Mallé, Dronero 23725
Museo Civico Luigi Bailo, Treviso 25804
Museo Civico Luigi Dalla Laita, Ala 22823
Museo Civico M. Trucco, Albisola Superiore 22839
Museo Civico Mambrini, Galeata 23949
Museo Civico Marinaro Gio-Bono Ferrari, Camogli 23295
Museo Civico Marinaro U. Mursia, Milano 24388
Museo Civico Medievale, Bologna 23112
Museo Civico Messapico, Alezio 22850
Museo Civico Naturalistico, Maserada sul Piave 24311
Museo Civico Naturalistico dei Monti Prenestini, Capranica Prenestina 23331
Museo Civico Naturalistico Severo Sini, Villa d'Almè 26012
Museo Civico Orientale S. Cardu, Cagliari 23247
Museo Civico Ornitologico, Lonato 24206
Museo Civico Ornitologico e di Scienze Naturali Luigi Scanagatta, Varenna 25894
Museo Civico P. A. Garda, Ivrea 24111
Museo Civico P. Mortara, Canneto sull'Oglio 23316
Museo Civico P. Rosario, Ascoli Satriano 22956
Museo Civico Padre Michele Jacobelli, Casalvieri 23369
Museo Civico Paleontologico, Macerata Feltria 24252
Museo Civico per la Preistoria del Monte Cetona, Cetona 23514
Museo Civico Pietro Lotti, Ischia di Castro 24099
Museo Civico-Pinacoteca, Vicenza 25993
Museo Civico Pio Capponi, Terracina 25699
Museo Civico Polivalente, Mistretta 24432
Museo Civico Preistorico, Pofi 24972
Museo Civico Rocca Flea, Gualdo Tadino 24066
Museo Civico Rogadeo, Bitonto 23092
Museo Civico Speleo-Archeologico, Nuoro 24660
Museo Civico Storico Archeologico, Leno 24176
Museo Civico Storico Artistico, Antrodoco 22896
Museo Civico Storico ed Etnografico, Primaluna 25053
Museo Civico Storico-Etnografico, Ripatransone 25123
Museo Civico U. Formentini, La Spezia 24123
Museo Civicodi Scienze Naturali, Randazzo 25072
Museo Civicodi Storia Naturale, Stazzano 25630
Museo Civiltà Lavoro Contadino e Artigiano, Pagnacco 24755
Museo Clarisse Coulombie de Goyaud, Ituzaingó 00369
Museo Clemente Rospigliosi, Pistoia 24958
Museo Coahuila y Texas, Monclova 28225
Museo Colombiano de Informática, Bogotá 07394
Museo Colonial, El Tocuyo 48939
Museo Colonial de Acolman, Acolman 27751
Museo Colonial del Conde de Sierra Gorda, Santander Jiménez 28436
Museo Colonial e Histórico, Luján 00413
Museo Coltzin, Culiacán 27881
Museo Comandancia La Plata, Santo Domingo 08152
Museo Comarcal, Zalduondo 35711
Museo Comarcal da Fonsagrada, La Fonsagrada 34821
Museo Comarcal Durán y Sanpere, Cervera 34706
Museo Comarcal Reus, Reus 35312
Museo Come Eravamo, Borgamanero 23165
Museo Comercial, Hellín 34898
Museo Comité Olímpico, México 28119
Museo Communale Antiquarium, Atena Lucana 22977
Museo Comparativo de Biología Marina, Viña del Mar 06930
Museo Complesso della Collegiata, Castiglione Olona 23436
Museo Comunal de Chañar Ladeado, Chañar Ladeado 00271
Museo Comunal Pedro Bargero, Emilio Bunge 00340
Museo Comunal Regional de San Guillermo, San Guillermo 00563
Museo Comunale, Montaione 24490
Museo Comunale, Monte San Savino 24501
Museo Comunale, Nova Ponente 24641
Museo Comunale, Paria a Mare 24793
Museo Comunale, Roggiano Gravina 25144
Museo Comunale, Vico Equense 26000
Museo Comunale A. Mendola, Favara 23770
Museo Comunale Archeologico, Viddalba 26003
Museo Comunale d'Arte Moderna di Ascona, Ascona 36470
Museo Comunale della Ceramica, Cutrofiano 23705
Museo Comunale della Manifattura Chini, Borgo San Lorenzo 23172
Museo Comunale della Valle dei Nuraghi, Torralba 25768
Museo Comunale della Valle del Sarno, Sarno 25476
Museo Comunale E. Durio, Civiasco 23587
Museo Comunale La Malaria e la sua Storia, Pontinia 25001
Museo Comunale Storico, Acquaviva delle Fonti 22802
Museo Comunale Trappeto Maratea, Vico del Gargano 25999
Museo Comunidad Las Terrazas, San Cristobal 08101
Museo Comunitario, Mineral del Monte 28220
Museo Comunitario, Puente de Ixtla 28346
Museo Comunitario Altagracia de Arauz, Ensenada 27913
Museo Comunitario Amuzgo de Xochistlahuaca, Xochistlahuaca 28625
Museo Comunitario Colonia Vicente Guerrero, Colonia Vicente Guerrero 27843
Museo Comunitario Concuemitl, Cuencamé 27872
Museo Comunitario Coronela Amelia La Güera Robles, Xochipala 28624
Museo Comunitario Crónica y Arte Agropecuario de la Sierra Gorda, Landa de Matamoros 28050
Museo Comunitario Cuarenta Casas, Valentín Gómez Farías 28581
Museo Comunitario de Antropología e Historia, Apatzingán 27774
Museo Comunitario de Atoyac, Atoyac 27783
Museo Comunitario de Carrillo Puerto, Alvaro Obregón 27769
Museo Comunitario de Ciudad Lerdo, Lerdo 28058
Museo Comunitario de Estación Coahuila, Mexicali 28087
Museo Comunitario de Historia de San José de Gracia, San José de Gracia 28387
Museo Comunitario de Huitzapula, Huitzapula 28007
Museo Comunitario de Ixtlahuacán, Ixtlahuacán 28018
Museo Comunitario de la Ballena, La Paz 28042
Museo Comunitario de la Sal, Armería 27780
Museo Comunitario de Las Varas, Compostela 27852
Museo Comunitario de Pejelagartero, Huimanguillo 28005
Museo Comunitario de Pipillola, Españita 27921
Museo Comunitario de San Andrés Mixquic, México 28120
Museo Comunitario de San Nicolás Zoyatlán, San Nicolás Zoyatlán 28416
Museo Comunitario de Santa Eulalia, Santa Euralia 28433
Museo Comunitario de Santa Martha, Mulegé 28257
Museo Comunitario de Tototepec, Tototepec 28564
Museo Comunitario de Villa Regina, Villa Regina 00673
Museo Comunitario de Xalisco, Xalisco 28619
Museo Comunitario de Xolalpan, Ixtacamaxtitlán 28016
Museo Comunitario del Valle de Guadalupe, Ensenada 27914
Museo Comunitario el Asalto a las Tierras, Mexicali 28088
Museo Comunitario El Rosario, El Rosario 27907
Museo Comunitario Felipe Carrillo Puerto, Motul 28255
Museo Comunitario Francisco I. Madero, Francisco I. Madero, Coahuila 27924
Museo Comunitario General Francisco Villa, Durango 27894
Museo Comunitario Hicupa, Tehuacán 28473
Museo Comunitario Hitalulu, San Martín Huamelulpan 28408
Museo Comunitario Huitza Chilin, San Pedro 28420
Museo Comunitario Iluikatlachiyalistli, Yahualica 28628
Museo Comunitario Ismael Girón González, Pánuco, Zacatecas 28302
Museo Comunitario Itzmal Kauil, Izamal 28020
Museo Comunitario Ji, Ocosingo 28284
Museo Comunitario Jna Niingui, San Miguel Tequixtepec 28413
Museo Comunitario Joyonaque, Tuxtla Gutiérrez 28570
Museo Comunitario Juan García Aldama de la Comunidad Cucapá, El Mayor Indígena 27905
Museo Comunitario Kumkuy Ys Untzi, Copainalá 27855
Museo Comunitario Maika, Poanas 28315
Museo Comunitario Note Ujía, Santa María Asunción Tlaxiaco 28434
Museo Comunitario Nu-kuiñe, Cuquila 27887
Museo Comunitario Raramuri, Guachochi 27939
Museo Comunitario Rubén Jaramillo, Tlaquiltenango 28531
Museo Comunitario Serafín Olarte, Papantla 28303
Museo Comunitario Shan-Dany, Santa Ana del Valle 28426
Museo Comunitario sin Paredes Colonia Orizaba, Mexicali 28089
Museo Comunitario Snuuvico, San Juan Mixtepec Juxtlahuaca 28396
Museo Comunitario Tejamen, Nuevo Ideal 28270
Museo Comunitario Tzakualli, Zacualpan 28645
Museo Comunitario Unidad Indígena Emiliano Zapata, Hueyapan de Ocampo 28003
Museo Comunitario Unión y Progreso, Cuatrocienegas 27869
Museo Comunitario Xiximes, Gómez Palacio 27935
Museo Comunitario Xolalpan Calli, Hueyapan 28002
Museo Comunitario Ya Nfädi Yu Nohño Los Conocimientos de los Otomies, Tolimán 28539
Museo Comunitario Yucu-Iti, Santa María Yucu-Iti 28435
Museo Comunitario Ze Acatl Topiltzin Quetzalcoatl, Tepoztlán 28501
Museo Concha Ferrant, La Habana 07954
Museo Conchiliologico e della Carta Moneta, Bellaria Igea Marina 23047
Museo Contadino, Lana 24133
Museo Contadino, Montalto Pavese 24495
Museo Contadino, Varese Ligure 25900
Museo Contadino della Bassa Pavese, San Cristina e Bissone 25353
Museo Contalpa de Nombre de Dios, Nombre de Dios 28269
Museo Contemporáneo al Aire Libre, Aracena 34470
Museo Contisuyo, Moquegua 31229
Museo Convento de San Diego, Quito 09199
Museo Convento del Desierto de la Candelaria, Ráquira 07574
Museo Convento Santo Ecce Homo, Sutamarchán 07603
Museo Conventual, Medina de Pomar 35101
Museo Conventual de Santa Paula, Sevilla 35481
Museo Cooperativo Eldorado, Eldorado 00337
Museo Coronel Félix Luque Plata, Guayaquil 09170
Museo Correale di Terranova, Sorrento 25611
Museo Correr, Venezia 25927
Museo Costumbres Populares Pedro Antonio de Alarcón, Capileira 34675
Museo Costumbristá, La Paz 03895
Museo Costumbrista de Sonora, Alamos 27765
Museo Coyug-Curá, Pigüé 00476
Museo Creadores, San Fernando 28384
Museo Criollo de los Corrales, Buenos Aires 00163
Museo Cristero Ing. Efrén Quezada, Encarnación de Díaz, Jalisco 27911
Museo Cristero Señor Cura Cristóbal Magallanes, Totatiche 28561
Museo Cristóbal Mendoza, Trujillo 48964
Museo Cruz Herrera, La Línea de la Concepción 34955
Museo Cuadra de Bolívar, Caracas 48909
Museo Cuartel de Emiliano Zapata, Tlaltizapán 28526
Museo Cuartel Zapatista, México 28121
Museo Cultura Antigua Ribera del Bernesga, Cuadros 34761
Museo Cultura e Musica Popolare dei Peloritani, Messina 24363
Museo Cultura y Tradición de Jalcomulco, Jalcomulco 28022
Museo Cultural del Instituto Geografico Militar, Quito 09200
Museo Cultural Ijidio Guaranga, Guaranga 09167
Museo D. Agostinelli, Roma 25184
Museo D. Chalonge, Erice 23740
Museo da Citania de Santa Tegra, La Guardia 34890
Museo da Terra de Melide, Melide 35107
Museo Dantesco, Ravenna 25080
Museo d'Arte, Giulianova 24030
Museo d'Arte, Tenero 37231
Museo d'Arte Antica, Milano 24389
Museo d'Arte C. Barbella, Chieti 23545
Museo d'Arte Contemporanea, Torino 25738
Museo d'Arte Contemporanea D. Formaggio, Teolo 25686
Museo d'Arte Contemporanea di Villa Croce, Genova 23988
Museo d'Arte d'Ammobigliamento, Stupinigi 25645
Museo d'Arte e Ammobiliamento, Nichelino 24619
Museo d'Arte e Storia Antica Ebraica, Casale Monferrato 23365
Museo d'Arte G. Bargellini, Pieve di Cento 24920
Museo d'Arte Mendrisio, Mendrisio 36938
Museo d'Arte Moderna, Brescia 23202
Museo d'Arte Moderna, Gazoldo degli Ippoliti 23967
Museo d'Arte Moderna, Lugano 36901
Museo d'Arte Moderna, Tertenịa 25702
Museo d'Arte Moderna e Contemporanea, Ferrara 23788
Museo d'Arte Moderna e Contemporanea di Trento e Rovereto, Trento 25791
Museo d'Arte Moderna L. Répaci, Palmi 24786
Museo d'Arte Moderna M. Rimoldi, Cortina d'Ampezzo 23660
Museo d'Arte Moderna Pagani, Castellanza 23405
Museo d'Arte Nuoro, Nuoro 24661
Museo d'Arte Orientale, Venezia 25928
Museo d'Arte Orientale Edoardo Chiossone, Genova 23989
Museo d'Arte P. Pini, Milano 24390
Museo d'Arte Pietro Cavoti, Galatina 23948
Museo d'Arte Preistorica, Pinerolo 24928
Museo d'Arte S. Pertini, Savona 25509
Museo d'Arte Sacra, Asciano 22947
Museo d'Arte Sacra, Baiardo 23008
Museo d'Arte Sacra, Camaiore 23280
Museo d'Arte Sacra, Chiaramonte Gulfi 23524
Museo d'Arte Sacra, Colle di Val d'Elsa 23610
Museo d'Arte Sacra, Faenza 23752
Museo d'Arte Sacra, Gradoli 24044
Museo d'Arte Sacra, Montespertoli 24549
Museo d'Arte Sacra, Ponzone 25003
Museo d'Arte Sacra, San Casciano in Val di Pesa 25345
Museo d'Arte Sacra, San Gimignano 25363
Museo d'Arte Sacra, San Giovanni in Persiceto 25373
Museo d'Arte Sacra, San Leo 25380
Museo d'Arte Sacra, Tavarnelle Val di Pesa 25676
Museo d'Arte Sacra, Viterbo 26034
Museo d'Arte Sacra Cardinale Agnifili, Rocca di Mezzo 25136
Museo d'Arte Sacra della Insigne Collegiata di San Lorenzo, Montevarchi 24550
Museo d'Arte Sacra della Marsica, Celano 23469
Museo d'Arte Sacra della Santa Maria Assunta, Gallarate 23951
Museo d'Arte Sacra della Val d'Arbia, Buonconvento 23229
Museo d'Arte Sacra L. Acquarone, Lucinasco 24235
Museo d'Arte Sacra San Marco, Mombaroccio 24462
Museo d'Arte Sacro San Martino, Alzano Lombardo 22868
Museo d'Arti e Mestieri Antichi, Montelupone 24534
Museo das Mariñas, Betanzos 34607
Museo das Peregrinacións, Santiago de Compostela 35439
Museo David Paltán, San Gabriel 09227
Museo David Paltan, Tulcán 09229
Museo David Ramírez Lavoignet, Misantla 28221
Museo de Abancay, Abancay 31109
Museo de Academia de San Carlos, México 28122
Museo de Acaponeta, Acaponeta 27746
Museo de Aduanas y Puerto, Buenos Aires 00164
Museo de Aeronáutica y Astronáutica, Madrid 35015
Museo de Aguascalientes, Aguascalientes 27754
Museo de Ahumada, Villa Ahumada y Anexas 28603
Museo de Akil Uyotoch Cah, Akil 27764
Museo de Albacete, Albacete 34419
Museo de Alfarería Tradicional Vasca, Elosu 34796
Museo de Almería, Almería 34454
Museo de Ambiente Histórico Cubano, Santiago de Cuba 08134
Museo de Ameca, Vetagrande 28596
Museo de América, Madrid 35016
Museo de Anatomía, México 28123
Museo de Animales Venenosos, Buenos Aires 00165
Museo de Antioquia, Medellín 07514
Museo de Antofagasta, Antofagasta 06888
Museo de Antropología, Barranquilla 07377
Museo de Antropología, Córdoba 00292
Museo de Antropología, Ibarra 09181
Museo de Antropología, Tecolotlán 28467
Museo de Antropología de Tenerife - Casa de Carta, La Laguna 34936
Museo de Antropología de Xalapa, Xalapa 28615
Museo de Antropología e Historia, Maracay 48953
Museo de Antropología e Historia de Allende, Allende 27767
Museo de Antropología e Historia de Santiago Papasquiaro, Santiago Papasquiaro 28438
Museo de Antropología e Historia Natural Los Desmochados, Casilda 00267
Museo de Antropología y Ciencias Naturales, Concordia 00287
Museo de Anzoátegui, Barcelona 48892
Museo de Armas, Montevideo 40994
Museo de Armas de la Nación, Buenos Aires 00166
Museo de Armería de Alava, Vitoria-Gasteiz 35697
Museo de Arqueología, Acapulco de Juárez 27748
Museo de Arqueología, La Habana 07955

Museo de Arqueología, Ixtepec 28017
Museo de Arqueología, Siete Aguas 35492
Museo de Arqueología, Vallada 35615
Museo de Arqueología Colonial Rodolfo I. Bravo, Cafayate 00256
Museo de Arqueología de Alava, Vitoria-Gasteiz 35698
Museo de Arqueología de Córdoba, Córdoba 27856
Museo de Arqueología de la Universidad Nacional de Trujillo, Trujillo 31260
Museo de Arqueología de la Universidad Nacional de Tucumán, San Miguel de Tucumán 00581
Museo de Arqueología de León, León 28053
Museo de Arqueología de Occidente de México, Guadalajara 27948
Museo de Arqueología e Historia Natural de Yungay, Yungay 31271
Museo de Arqueología El Chamizal, Juárez 28036
Museo de Arqueología Josefina Ramos de Cox del Instituto Riva-Agüero, Lima 31202
Museo de Arqueología Nabor Rosales Araiza, Tolimán 28540
Museo de Arqueología Samuel Humberto Espinoza Lozano, Huaytará 31177
Museo de Arqueología y Antropología, Lima 31203
Museo de Arqueología y Etnografía, Sinarcas 35496
Museo de Arquitectura, Caracas 48910
Museo de Arquitectura Leopoldo Rother, Bogotá 07395
Museo de Arte Abstracto Español, Cuenca 34763
Museo de Arte Abstracto Manuel Felguérez, Zacatecas 28635
Museo de Arte Alberto Mena Caamaño, Quito 09201
Museo de Arte Alvar y Carmen T. de Carrillo Gil, México 28124
Museo de Arte Americano de Maldonado, Maldonado 40980
Museo de Arte colonial, Antigua 21260
Museo de Arte Colonial, Bogotá 07396
Museo de Arte Colonial, Caracas 48911
Museo de Arte Colonial, Mérida 48955
Museo de Arte Colonial, Morelia 28245
Museo de Arte Colonial, Quito 09202
Museo de Arte Colonial de la Habana, La Habana 07956
Museo de Arte Colonial de Palacio Valle Iznaga, Sancti-Spíritus 08111
Museo de Arte Colonial de San Francisco, Santiago de Chile 06909
Museo de Arte Colonial Pedro de Osma, Lima 31204
Museo de Arte Contemporáneo, Bahía Blanca 00125
Museo de Arte Contemporáneo, Bogotá 07397
Museo de Arte Contemporáneo, Cusco 31152
Museo de Arte Contemporáneo, Elche 34791
Museo de Arte Contemporáneo, Montevideo 40995
Museo de Arte Contemporáneo, Panamá City 31079
Museo de Arte Contemporáneo, Santiago de Chile 06910
Museo de Arte Contemporaneo, Sevilla 35482
Museo de Arte Contemporáneo, Toledo 35538
Museo de Arte Contemporaneo, Valdivia 06924
Museo de Arte Contemporáneo Alfredo Zalce, Morelia 28246
Museo de Arte Contemporáneo Ángel Zárraga, Durango 27895
Museo de Arte Contemporáneo Ateneo de Yucatán, Mérida 28080
Museo de Arte Contemporáneo de Caracas Sofía Imber, Caracas 48912
Museo de Arte Contemporáneo de Chihuahua, Chihuahua 27823
Museo de Arte Contemporáneo de Monterrey, Monterrey 28230
Museo de Arte Contemporáneo de Oaxaca, Oaxaca 28273
Museo de Arte Contemporáneo de Puerto Rico, San Juan 32393
Museo de Arte Contemporáneo Fra Angélico, La Plata 00388
Museo de Arte Contemporáneo Francisco Narvárez, Porlamar 48962
Museo de Arte Contemporáneo José María Moreno Galván, Sevilla 35483
Museo de Arte Contemporáneo Moderno de Ibagué, Ibagué 07497
Museo de Arte Contemporáneo Número 8, Aguascalientes 27755
Museo de Arte Contemporáneo Pajar de Agustín, Valle de Hecho 35635
Museo de Arte Coro y Museo Alberto Henríquez, Falcón 48940
Museo de Arte Costarricense, San José 07654
Museo de Arte de Caguas, Caguas 32367
Museo de Arte de Lima, Lima 31205
Museo de Arte de Matanzas, Matanzas 08037
Museo de Arte de Mazatlán, Mazatlán 28077
Museo de Arte de Orizaba y del Estado de Veracruz, Orizaba 28290
Museo de Arte de Pereira, Pereira 07557
Museo de Arte de Ponce, Ponce 32380
Museo de Arte de Puerto Rico, San Juan 32394
Museo de Arte de Querétaro, Querétaro 28352
Museo de Arte de Sinaloa, Culiacán 27882
Museo de Arte e Historia, Durango 34782
Museo de Arte e Historia, Lima 31206
Museo de Arte e Historia Casa de Los Celis, Valencia 48967
Museo de Arte e Historia de la Ciudad "Jorge y Elisa", Cuacutecuta 07468
Museo de Arte e História de Los Toldos, Los Toldos 00411
Museo de Arte Eduardo A. Minnicelli, Río Gallegos 00513
Museo de Arte en Ciudad Juárez, Juárez 28037
Museo de Arte Español, Buenos Aires 00167
Museo de Arte Francisco Oller, Bayamón 32364
Museo de Arte Gauchesco La Recova, San Antonio de Areco 00547
Museo de Arte Gráficas Juan Pablos, México 28125
Museo de Arte Guillermo Ceniceros, Durango 27896
Museo de Arte Habana, La Habana 07957
Museo de Arte Hispanoamericano Isaac Fernández Blanco, Buenos Aires 00168
Museo de Arte, Historia y Cultura Casa Alonso, Vega Baja 32411
Museo de Arte Industrial, Montevideo 40996
Museo de Arte Italiano, Lima 31207
Museo de Arte José Luis Bello y González, Puebla 28323
Museo de Arte José Luis Bello y Zetina, Puebla 28324
Museo de Arte Latinoamericano de Buenos Aires, Buenos Aires 00169
Museo de Arte Moderno, Buenos Aires 00170
Museo de Arte Moderno, Cuenca 09153
Museo de Arte Moderno, Mérida 48956
Museo de Arte Moderno, México 28126
Museo de Arte Moderno, Santo Domingo 09121
Museo de Arte Moderno de Barranquilla, Barranquilla 07378
Museo de Arte Moderno de Bogotá, Bogotá 07398
Museo de Arte Moderno de Bogotá II, Bogotá 07399
Museo de Arte Moderno de Bucaramanga, Bucaramanga 07437
Museo de Arte Moderno de Cartagena, Cartagena 07456
Museo de Arte Moderno de Durango, Gómez Palacio 27936
Museo de Arte Moderno de la Ciudad de Buenos Aires, Buenos Aires 00171
Museo de Arte Moderno de Medellín, Medellín 07515
Museo de Arte Moderno del Estado de México, Toluca 28541
Museo de Arte Moderno Jesús Soto, Ciudad Bolívar 48933
Museo de Arte Moderno La Tertulia, Cali 07446
Museo de Arte Moderno Ramírez Villamizar, Pamplona 07544
Museo de Arte Olga Costa, Guanajuato 27969
Museo de Arte Oriental, Avila 34501
Museo de Arte Popular Americano, Santiago de Chile 06911
Museo de Arte Popular de la Universidad, Puebla 28325
Museo de Arte Popular de la Universidad Nacional San Cristóbal de Huamanga, Humanga 31179
Museo de Arte Popular de Quinua, Quinua 31244
Museo de Arte Popular de San Bartolo de Coyotepec, San Baltazar Chichicapan 28375
Museo de Arte Popular del Instituto Riva-Agüero, Lima 31208
Museo de Arte Popular Petare, Caracas 48913
Museo de Arte Popular Poblano y Museo de Artesanías, Puebla 28326
Museo de Arte Popular Tlajomulco, Tlajomulco de Zúñiga 28523
Museo de Arte Popular Venezolano, Juangriego 48946
Museo de Arte Prehispánico, Mascota 28071
Museo de Arte Prehispánico Carlos Pellicer, Tepoztlán 28502
Museo de Arte Prehispánico de México Rufino Tamayo, Oaxaca 28274
Museo de Arte Religioso, La Habana 07958
Museo de Arte Religioso, Huaquechula 27997
Museo de Arte Religioso, Parita 31089
Museo de Arte Religioso Colonial, Comayagua 21299
Museo de Arte Religioso Colonial, Panamá City 31080
Museo de Arte Religioso Concepción, Riobamba 09221
Museo de Arte Religioso Convento de San Francisco, Cajamarca 31128
Museo de Arte Religioso de Girón, Girón 07485
Museo de Arte Religioso de la Catedral, Lima 31209
Museo de Arte Religioso de la Catedral de San Nicolás, Rionegro 07577
Museo de Arte Religioso de Monguí, Monguí 07528
Museo de Arte Religioso de Piura, Piura 31239
Museo de Arte Religioso de Santa Mónica, Puebla 28327
Museo de Arte Religioso Ex Convento Franciscano, Huejotzingo 28000
Museo de Arte Religioso Juan de Tejeda, Córdoba 00293
Museo de Arte Religioso Julio Franco Arango, Duitama 07471
Museo de Arte Religioso la Concepción, Baños 09141
Museo de Arte Religioso Porta Coeli, San Juan 32395
Museo de Arte Religioso Presbítero Antonio María Franco, Supía 07602
Museo de Arte Religioso Santo Domingo de Porta Coeli, San Germán 32385
Museo de Arte Religioso Tiberio de J. Salazar y Herrera, Sonsón 07599
Museo de Arte Religioso y Colonial, Cali 07447
Museo de Arte Sacro, Calatayud 34653
Museo de Arte Sacro, Castrojeriz 34699
Museo de Arte Sacro, Chihuahua 27824
Museo de Arte Sacro, Huete 34909
Museo de Arte Sacro, Monforte de Lemos 35123
Museo de Arte Sacro, Osuna 35197
Museo de Arte Sacro, Santiago de Compostela 35440
Museo de Arte Sacro Antiguo, Villanueva de Lorenzana 35681
Museo de Arte Sacro de la Colegiata de Iria Flavia, Padrón 35209
Museo de Arte Sacro de La Rioja, La Rioja 00396
Museo de Arte Sacro de Santa Clara, Allariz 34448
Museo de Arte Sacro de Santa María do Campo, A Coruña 34749
Museo de Arte Sacro de Santiago de Galdar, Galdar 34832
Museo de Arte Sacro San Francisco, Salta 00538
Museo de Arte Universidad Nacional de Colombia, Bogotá 07400
Museo de Arte Virreinal de Taxco, Taxco de Alarcón 28457
Museo de Arte y Artesanía de Linares, Linares 06899
Museo de Arte y Diseño Contemporáneo, San José 07655
Museo de Arte y Tradiciones Populares, Bogotá 07401
Museo de Artes Decorativas de Palacio Salcines, Guantánamo 07916
Museo de Artes e Industrias Populares, Pátzcuaro 28307
Museo de Artes Gráficas, Bogotá 07402
Museo de Artes Plásticas, Madonado 40978
Museo de Artes Plásticas Eduardo Sívori, Buenos Aires 00172
Museo de Artes Populares, Tepic 28496
Museo de Artes Visuales Aramara, Tepic 28497
Museo de Artes y Artesanías Enrique Estrada Bello, Santo Tomé 00620
Museo de Artes y Costumbres Populares, Bornos 34622
Museo de Artes y Costumbres Populares, Combarro 34731
Museo de Artes y Costumbres Populares, Jaén 34923
Museo de Artes y Costumbres Populares, Piedrafita de El Cebrero 35270
Museo de Artes y Costumbres Populares, Ribadavia 35318
Museo de Artes y Costumbres Populares, Sevilla 35484
Museo de Artes y Costumbres Populares. Unicaja, Málaga 35071
Museo de Artes y Tradiciones Populares, Espinal 07477
Museo de Artes y Tradiciones Populares, Madrid 35017
Museo de Artes y Tradiciones Populares de Ráquira, Ráquira 07575
Museo de Artes y Tradiciones Populares de Tlaxcala, Tlaxcala 28532
Museo de Artesanía Iberoamericana, La Orotava 35193
Museo de Artesanias Cefa, Quito 09203
Museo de Artesanías del Mundo, Silvia 07592
Museo de Artesanías Tradicionales Folklóricas, Corrientes 00319
Museo de Atoyac, Atoyac de Alvarez 27784
Museo de Autos y del Transporte Humberto Lobo Villarreal, Monterrey 28231
Museo de Avila, Avila 34502
Museo de Ayutla, Ayutla de los Libres 27786
Museo de Bahía de Cochinos, Playa Girón 08081
Museo de Baracoa, Baracoa 07855
Museo de Barquisimeto, Barquisimeto 48895
Museo de Batopilas, Francisco I. Madero, Coahuila 27925
Museo de Belas Artes da Coruña, A Coruña 34750
Museo de Bellas Artes, Badajoz 34518
Museo de Bellas Artes, Córdoba 34738
Museo de Bellas Artes, Lincoln 00407
Museo de Bellas Artes, Luján 00414
Museo de Bellas Artes, Mahón 35066
Museo de Bellas Artes, Valencia 35601
Museo de Bellas Artes, Viña del Mar 06931
Museo de Bellas Artes Agustin Araujo, Treinta y Tres 41043
Museo de Bellas Artes Bonaerense, La Plata 00389
Museo de Bellas Artes Ceferino Carnacini, Villa Ballester 00659
Museo de Bellas Artes Claudio León Sempere, Burzaco 00254
Museo de Bellas Artes de Alava, Vitoria-Gasteiz 35699
Museo de Bellas Artes de Asturias, Oviedo 35204
Museo de Bellas Artes de Caracas, Caracas 48914
Museo de Bellas Artes de Castellón, Castellón de la Plana 34693
Museo de Bellas Artes de Coronel Pringles, Coronel Pringles 00317
Museo de Bellas Artes de Granada, Granada 34875
Museo de Bellas Artes de la Boca, Buenos Aires 00173
Museo de Bellas Artes de Santander, Santander 35431
Museo de Bellas Artes de Sevilla, Sevilla 35485
Museo de Bellas Artes de Toluca, Toluca 28542
Museo de Bellas Artes Departamental de San José, San José de Mayo 41041
Museo de Bellas Artes Domingo Faustino Sarmiento, Mercedes 00442
Museo de Bellas Artes Dr. Juan Ramón Vidal, Corrientes 00320
Museo de Bellas Artes Franklin Rawson, San Juan 00570
Museo de Bellas Artes Juan Yapari, Posadas 00481
Museo de Bellas Artes Laureano Brizuela, San Fernando del Valle de Catamarca 00556
Museo de Bellas Artes Octavio de la Colina, La Rioja 00397
Museo de Bermejillo, Bermejillo 27792
Museo de Betancuria, Betancuria 34606
Museo de Bomberos, Madrid 35018
Museo de Bordados Paso Blanco, Lorca 34983
Museo de Buenos Aires, Tacotalpa 28448
Museo de Burgos, Burgos 34630
Museo de Cáceres, Cáceres 34641
Museo de Cádiz, Cádiz 34647
Museo de Calcos y Esculturas Compardas, Buenos Aires 00174
Museo de Campeche, Campeche 27796
Museo de Caracas, Caracas 48915
Museo de Carruajes, Madrid 35019
Museo de Carruajes de Sevilla, Sevilla 35486
Museo de Casa Popenoe, Antigua 21261
Museo de Caza Benito Albarrán, Zapopan 28647
Museo de Centro Cultural Recoleta, Buenos Aires 00175
Museo de Cera, Guadalajara 27949
Museo de Cera, Madrid 35020
Museo de Cera de la Ciudad de México, México 28127
Museo de Cera de la Villa, México 28128
Museo de Cera de Tijuana, Tijuana 28511
Museo de Cerámica Contemporánea Luis García Romo, Las Navas de la Concepción 35156
Museo de Cerámica de la Cartuja, Salteras 35370
Museo de Cerámica Nacional, Chinchilla 34713
Museo de Cerámica Ruiz de Luna, Talavera de la Reina 35508
Museo de Cerámica y Bellas Artes Julián de la Herreria, Asunción 31097
Museo de Cerámica y Loza Popular, Falcón 48941
Museo de Chilecito, Chilecito 00274
Museo de Chusis de Sechura, Sechura 31249
Museo de Ciencia, Cuernavaca 27873
Museo de Ciencia y Técnica, Buenos Aires 00176
Museo de Ciencia y Tecnología del Estado de Veracruz, Xalapa 28616
Museo de Ciencias, Caracas 48916
Museo de Ciencias, Huánuco 31171
Museo de Ciencias Antropológicas y Naturales, Santiago del Estero 00616
Museo de Ciencias de Ensenada, Ensenada 27915
Museo de Ciencias Explora, León 28054
Museo de Ciencias Morfológicas, Rosario 00526
Museo de Ciencias Naturales, Asunción 31098
Museo de Ciencias Naturales, Cusco 31153
Museo de Ciencias Naturales, Onda 35177
Museo de Ciencias Naturales, Pamplona 35248
Museo de Ciencias Naturales, Panamá City 31081
Museo de Ciencias Naturales, Pontevedra 35283
Museo de Ciencias Naturales, Salta 00539
Museo de Ciencias Naturales, Toluca 28543
Museo de Ciencias Naturales, Utrera 35589
Museo de Ciencias Naturales, Villafranca del Bierzo 35679
Museo de Ciencias Naturales, La Virgen del Camino 35692
Museo de Ciencias Naturales Augusto G. Schulz, Resistencia 00506
Museo de Ciencias Naturales Bartolomé Mitre, Córdoba 00294
Museo de Ciencias Naturales Carlos de la Torre, Holguín 08004
Museo de Ciencias Naturales de Alava, Vitoria-Gasteiz 35700
Museo de Ciencias Naturales de Oberá, Oberá 00460
Museo de Ciencias Naturales de Tenerife, Santa Cruz de Tenerife 35414
Museo de Ciencias Naturales del Colegio de San José, Medellín 07516
Museo de Ciencias Naturales del Departamento San Cristóbal, San Cristóbal 00554
Museo de Ciencias Naturales Dr. Amado Bonpland, Corrientes 00321
Museo de Ciencias Naturales e Historia, Posadas 00482
Museo de Ciencias Naturales Federico Carlos Lehmann, Cali 07448
Museo de Ciencias Naturales Luma, Tanti 00631
Museo de Ciencias Naturales Rvdo. P. Antonio Scasso, San Nicolás de los Arroyos 00589
Museo de Ciencias Naturales Tomás Romay, Santiago de Cuba 08135
Museo de Ciencias Naturales y Antropológicas Juan Cornelio Moyano, Mendoza 00435
Museo de Ciencias Naturales y Antropológicas Prof. Antonio Serrano, Paraná 00465
Museo de Ciencias Naturales y Misional del Colegio San José, Esperanza 00342
Museo de Ciencias y Antropología, Cartago 07460
Museo de Ciudad Bolívar, Ciudad Bolívar 48934
Museo de Ciudad Real, Ciudad Real 34721
Museo de Ciudades Hermanas, Guadalajara 27950
Museo de Coamo, Coamo 32371
Museo de Cochoapa, Ometepec 28289
Museo de Cocula es El Mariachi, Cocula 27834
Museo de Colexiata do Sar, Santiago de Compostela 35441
Museo de Colón, Colón 27841
Museo de Conkal, Conkal 27854
Museo de Cosautlán de Carvajal, Cosautlán de Carvajal 27861

Museo de Coscomatepec, Coscomatepec de Bravo 27862
Museo de Cuajinicuilapa, Cuajinicuilapa 27866
Museo de Cuenca, Cuenca 34764
Museo de Cultura Popular Angel Gil Hermidas, Villahermosa 28608
Museo de Cultura Popular Costa Rica, Heredia 07649
Museo de Cultura Populares del Estado de México, Toluca 28544
Museo de Culturas Populares, Durango 27897
Museo de Culturas Populares de Chiapas, San Cristóbal de las Casas 28377
Museo de Culturas Populares de San Luis Potosí, San Luis Potosí 28399
Museo de Culturas Populares e Indígenas, Obregón 28281
Museo de Culturas Populares e Indígenas de Sonora, Hermosillo 27985
Museo de Descubrimiento, Montevideo 40997
Museo de Dibujo Castillo de Larrés, Sabiñánigo 35351
Museo de Ejército Oriental, Holguín 08005
Museo de El Pueblito, Corregidora 27859
Museo de Emiliano Zapata, Emiliano Zapata 27909
Museo de Escuela de Educación Técnica Número 1, Dolores 00329
Museo de Escultura al Aire Libre, Leganés 34943
Museo de Escultura Novarro Santafe, Villena 35686
Museo de Escultura Octavio Vicent, Jijona 34930
Museo de Esculturas Luis Perlotti, Buenos Aires 00177
Museo de Etnografía, Quito 09204
Museo de Etnohistoria de Suyo, Suyo 31252
Museo de Farmacia, Burgos 34631
Museo de Farmacia, Llivia 34975
Museo de Farmacia, Peñaranda de Duero 35263
Museo de Farmacia Militar, Madrid 35021
Museo de Ferrocarriles en Miniatura Werner Dura, La Falda 00379
Museo de Filatelia de Oaxaca, Oaxaca 28275
Museo de Filigrana de Cobre, La Esperanza 31192
Museo de Firmat, Firmat 00348
Museo de Física de la Universidad Nacional de La Plata, La Plata 00390
Museo de Física Recreativa, Puebla 28328
Museo de Fósiles y Minerales, Igea 34913
Museo de Frank País, Holguín 08006
Museo de Gendarmería Nacional, Buenos Aires 00178
Museo de General Zaragoza, General Zaragoza 27933
Museo de Geología, Manizales 07507
Museo de Geología de la UNAM, México 28129
Museo de Geología del IPN, México 28130
Museo de Geología Dr. Jenaro González Reyna, Morelia 28247
Museo de Geología y Paleontología, Neuquén 00458
Museo de Geología y Suelos, Armenia 07371
Museo de Gomellano, Gumiel de Hizán 34896
Museo de Granjita Siboney, Santiago de Cuba 08136
Museo de Guadalajara, Guadalajara 34885
Museo de Guadalupe, Guadalupe 27962
Museo de Guamúchil de Salvador Alvarado, Guamúchil 27966
Museo de Heráldica Alavesa, Mendoza 35109
Museo de Herrera, Panamá City 31082
Museo de Historia de Ciencias Naturales, Chuquimarca 31148
Museo de Historia de Ensenada, Ensenada 27916
Museo de Historia de Higueras, Higueras 27992
Museo de Historia de la Medicina, Bogotá 07403
Museo de Historia de la Medicina y de la Cirugía Vincente A. Risolía, Buenos Aires 00179
Museo de Historia de la Minería de Santa Rosalía, Mulegé 28258
Museo de Historia de Lampazos de Naranjo y las Armas Nacionales, Lampazos de Naranjo 28049
Museo de Historia de Linares, Linares 28062
Museo de Historia de Panamá, Panamá City 31083
Museo de Historia de Tabasco, Villahermosa 28609
Museo de Historia de Tenerife y Archivo Insular, La Laguna 34937
Museo de História del Deporte, La Habana 07959
Museo de Historia del Transporte, Guadalupe 27963
Museo de Historia Económica, Bogotá 07404
Museo de Historia Mexicana, Monterrey 28232
Museo de Historia Natural, Alta Suiza 07365
Museo de Historia Natural, Bogotá 07405
Museo de Historia Natural, Bucaramanga 07438
Museo de Historia Natural, Guatemala 21268
Museo de Historia Natural, La Paz 28043
Museo de Historia Natural, Manizales 07508
Museo de Historia Natural, Mérida 28081
Museo de Historia Natural, México 28131
Museo de Historia Natural, Panamá City 31084
Museo de Historia Natural, Pereira 07558
Museo de Historia Natural, Popayán 07564
Museo de Historia Natural, Puebla 28329
Museo de Historia Natural, Santiago de Compostela 35442
Museo de História Natural, Tunja 07612
Museo de Historia Natural, Villahermosa 28610
Museo de Historia Natural, Zapotlán del Rey 28651
Museo de Historia Natural Alfredo Dugès, Guanajuato 27970
Museo de Historia Natural de Concepción, Concepción 06892
Museo de Historia Natural de El Salvador, San Salvador 09312
Museo de Historia Natural de la Universidad Antenor Orrego, Trujillo 31261
Museo de Historia Natural de San Pedro Nolasco, Santiago de Chile 06912
Museo de Historia Natural de Valparaíso, Valparaíso 06927
Museo de Historia Natural del Ateneo Fuente, Saltillo 28365
Museo de Historia Natural del Paraquay, Asunción 31099
Museo de Historia Natural Dr. Manuel M. Villada, Toluca 28545
Museo de Historia Natural Dr. Manuel Martínez Solórzano, Morelia 28248
Museo de Historia Natural Dr. Ricardo S. Vadell, Suipacha 00624
Museo de Historia Natural Felipe Poey, La Habana 07960
Museo de Historia Natural Javier Prado, Lima 31210
Museo de Historia Natural José Vilet Brullet, Mexquitic 28214
Museo de Historia Natural Regional, Lerdo 28059
Museo de Historia Natural Valle de la Prehistoria, Santiago de Cuba 08137
Museo de Historia Natural Víctor Vaca Aguinaga, Lambayeque 31196
Museo de Historia Reginal San Lorenzo y Galería del Libertador General San Martín, San Lorenzo 00575
Museo de Historia Regional de Pánuco, Pánuco, Veracruz 28301
Museo de Historia Regional de Sabinas Hidalgo, Sabinas Hidalgo 28362
Museo de Historia Regional de Tristán Suárez, Trisán Suárez 00646
Museo de Historia Republicana, Tegucigalpa 21303
Museo de Historia y Artesanía de la Colonial Tovar, Colonia Tovar 48935
Museo de História y Ciencias Naturales, Lobería 00408
Museo de Historia y Cultura Casa Pedrilla, Cáceres 34642
Museo de Histórico, Tunja 07613
Museo de Hostotipaquillo, Hostotipaquillo 27993
Museo de Hualpén, Concepción 06893
Museo de Huelva, Huelva 34906
Museo de Imáges de la Semana Santa en Popayán, Popayán 07565
Museo de Insectos de la Universidad de Costa Rica, San José 07656
Museo de Instituto Antártico Argentino, Buenos Aires 00180
Museo de Instituto Magnasco, Gualeguaychú 00361
Museo de Instituto Nacional de Estudios de Teatro, Buenos Aires 00181
Museo de Instrumentos Musicales, Buenos Aires 00182
Museo de Instrumentos Musicales Pablo Traversari, Quito 09205
Museo de Intendencia, Madrid 35022
Museo de Jaén, Jaén 34924
Museo de Jala, Jala 28021
Museo de Jamapa, Jamapa 28026
Museo de la Academia de Infantería, Toledo 35539
Museo de la Acuarela del Estado de México, Toluca 28546
Museo de la Administración Federal de Ingresos Públicos, Buenos Aires 00183
Museo de la Alhambra, Granada 34876
Museo de la Amistad México-Cuba, Tuxpan de Rodríguez Cano 28567
Museo de la Antigua Estación Ferroviaria, Teocelo 28480
Museo de la Artesanía Tradicional Juan Alfonso Carrizo, La Plata 00391
Museo de la Asegurada, Alicante 34447
Museo de la Aviación Naval, Bahía Blanca 00126
Museo de la Basílica de Guadalupe, México 28132
Museo de la Basílica Nuestra Señora de la Candelaria, Candelaria 34668
Museo de la Batalla de Vitoria, Vitoria-Gasteiz 35701
Museo de la Caña de Azúcar, El Cerrito 07474
Museo de la Canción Yucateca, Mérida 28082
Museo de la Caricatura, México 28133
Museo de la Casa de Acuerdo de San Nicolás, San Nicolás de los Arroyos 00590
Museo de la Casa de Cultura de Tepeapulco, Tepeapulco Hidalgo 28489
Museo de la Casa de Cultura de Zacapú, Zacapu 28633
Museo de la Casa de Gobierno, San Miguel de Tucumán 00582
Museo de la Casa de la Cultura, Pinchote 07560
Museo de la Casa de la Cultura, San Luis Potosí 28400
Museo de la Casa de la Cultura Ecuatoriana, Quito 09206
Museo de la Casa de la Cultura Martín Gamarra, Gamarra 07482
Museo de la Casa de la Independencia, Asunción 31100
Museo de la Casa de la Música Mexicana, México 28134
Museo de la Casa de las Artesanías del Estado de Chihuahua, Bocoyna 27794
Museo de la Casa del Risco, México 28135
Museo de la Casa del Teatro, Buenos Aires 00184
Museo de la Casa Histórica de la Independencia Nacional, San Miguel de Tucumán 00583
Museo de la Casa Nacional de la Moneda, Potosí 03903
Museo de la Casa Rosada, Buenos Aires 00185
Museo de la Catedral, Cusco 31154
Museo de la Catedral, Trujillo 31262
Museo de la Catedral de Santiago de Compostela, Santiago de Compostela 35443
Museo de La Cerería, Tlayacapan 28536
Museo de la Charrería, México 28136
Museo de la Ciencia y el Cosmos, La Laguna 34938
Museo de la Ciencia y el Juego, Bogotá 07406
Museo de la Ciudad, Buenos Aires 00186
Museo de la Ciudad, Campeche 27797
Museo de la Ciudad, Guadalajara 27951
Museo de la Ciudad, Mérida 28083
Museo de la Ciudad, Paraná 00466
Museo de la Ciudad, Quito 09207
Museo de la Ciudad, Salta 00540
Museo de la Ciudad, Tecate 28466
Museo de la Ciudad, Victoria 00656
Museo de la Ciudad, Vinaròs 35691
Museo de la Ciudad de Chetumal, Chetumal 27816
Museo de la Ciudad de Colón, Colón 00280
Museo de la Ciudad de Córdoba, Córdoba 27857
Museo de la Ciudad de Irapuato, Irapuato 28013
Museo de la Ciudad de La Habana, La Habana 07961
Museo de la Ciudad de León, León 28055
Museo de la Ciudad de México, México 28137
Museo de la Ciudad de Píritu, Píritu 48960
Museo de la Ciudad de Querétaro, Querétaro 28353
Museo de la Ciudad de San Francisco, San Francisco 00561
Museo de la Ciudad de Santiago de Compostela, Santiago de Compostela 35444
Museo de la Ciudad de Sombrerete, Sombrerete 28446
Museo de la Ciudad de Tepatitlan de Morelos, Tepatitlán de Morelos 28485
Museo de la Ciudad de Veracruz, Veracruz 28594
Museo de la Ciudad Tuxtlán, Tuxtla Gutiérrez 28571
Museo de la Clandestinidad, Nueva Gerona 08057
Museo de la Colegiata, Belmonte 34597
Museo de la Colegiata, Medinaceli 35105
Museo de la Colegiata de la Coruña, A Coruña 34751
Museo de la Colegiata de Santa Juliana y Claustro, Santillana del Mar 35451
Museo de la Colegiata San Luis, Villagarcía de Campos Valladolid 35680
Museo de la Colonia Siete de Marzo, Juan Aldama 28035
Museo de la Colonización, Esperanza 00343
Museo de la Comisión Provincial de Monumentos, León 34948
Museo de la Comunidad de Agua Blanca, Puerto López 09192
Museo de la Comunidad de Chordeleg, Chordeleg 09145
Museo de la Constitución, Guáimaro 07912
Museo de la Coria, Trujillo 35576
Museo de la Cueva del Señor del Calvario, México 28138
Museo de la Cultura de Albán, Albán 07363
Museo de la Cultura Huasteca, Tampico 28453
Museo de la Cultura José Arens Berg, Sullana 31251
Museo de la Cultura Maya, Chetumal 27817
Museo de la Cultura Potosina, San Luis Potosí 28401
Museo de la Dirección Nacional del Antártico, Buenos Aires 00187
Museo de la Diversidad Biológica y Cultural del Pacífico, Quibdó 07572
Museo de la E.E.M. Número 3, Dolores 00330
Museo de la Electricidad, Caracas 48917
Museo de la Electricidad, Lima 31211
Museo de la Encarnación, Corella 34745
Museo de la Energía, Embalse 00339
Museo de la Escuela General de Policía, Madrid 35023
Museo de la Escuela Normal Alejandro Carbo, Córdoba 00295
Museo de la Escultura Mexica Eusebio Dávalos, Acatitlán 27749
Museo de la Estampa, Cuitzeo 27880
Museo de la Estampa del Estado de México, Toluca 28547
Museo de la Estampa y del Diseño Carlos Cruz Diez, Caracas 48918
Museo de la Evangelización, Huejotzingo 28001
Museo de la Fabrica nacional de Moneda y Timbre, Madrid 35024
Museo de la Facultad de Ciencias Naturales y del Instituto Miguel Lillo, San Miguel de Tucumán 00584
Museo de la Familia Dominicana Siglo XIX, Santo Domingo 09122
Museo de la Farmacia Dra. D'Alessio Bonino, Buenos Aires 00188
Museo de la Farmacia Hispana, Madrid 35025
Museo de la Fauna, Aguascalientes 27756
Museo de la Fauna de Veracruz, Xalapa 28617
Museo de la Fauna y Ciencias Naturales, Monterrey 28233
Museo de la Ferrería de La Pradera, Subachoque 07601
Museo de la Fotografía, Pachuca 28293
Museo de la Fotografía, Rafaela 00497
Museo de la Fuerza de Aviación Naval, Callao 31131
Museo de la Fuerza de Submarinos, Callao 31132
Museo de la Fundación Duque de Lerma, Toledo 35540
Museo de la Fundación Guayasamin, Quito 09208
Museo de la Fundación John Boulton, Caracas 48919
Museo de la Gaita, Gijón 34845
Museo de la Gráfica de la Historia Social de Taxco Siglo XX, Taxco de Alarcón 28458
Museo de la Guardia Civil, Madrid 35026
Museo de la Guerra de Castas, Felipe Carrillo Puerto 27923
Museo de la Guerra Hispano-Cubano-Norteamericana, Santiago de Cuba 08138
Museo de la Historia de la Cultura José de Obaldia, David 31073
Museo de la Historia de Ponce, Ponce 32381
Museo de la Historia y la Tradición, Panamá City 31085
Museo de La Huaxteca, Amatlán de los Reyes 27770
Museo de la Huerta de Almoradi, Almoradi 34455
Museo de la Iglesia, Oviedo 35205
Museo de la Iglesia de la Compañía de Jesús, Ica 31181
Museo de la Iglesia de San Pedro, Chucuito 31144
Museo de la Iguana, Tecomán 28469
Museo de La Imagen, Vista Alegre 08177
Museo de la Independencia, Dolores Hidalgo 27892
Museo de la Indumentaria Mexicana Luis Márquez Romay, México 28139
Museo de la Industria Azucarera, Abel Santamaría 07845
Museo de la Inmaculada Concepción, Cuenca 09154
Museo de la Insurgencia, Rincón de Romos 28358
Museo de la Isla de Cozumel, Cozumel 27865
Museo de la Labranza, Francisco I. Madero, Hidalgo 27928
Museo de la Lealtad Republicana, Chihuahua 27825
Museo de la Lucha Clandestina, Nueva Gerona 08058
Museo de la Lucha Clandestina, Santiago de Cuba 08139
Museo de la Lucha Estudiantil Jesús Suárez Gayol, Camagüey 07876
Museo de la Lucha Obrera, Cananea 27801
Museo de la Luz, México 28140
Museo de la Máquina Agrícola, Esperanza 00344
Museo de la Máscara, Morelia 28249
Museo de la Medicine, Cuenca 09155
Museo de la Memoria, Cuacutecuta 07469
Museo de la Memoria, Tlaxcala 28533
Museo de la Minería, San Juan de Guadalupe 28391
Museo de la Minería del Estado de México, El Oro 27906
Museo de la Minería José de la Borda, Taxco de Alarcón 28459
Museo de la Minería y de la Industria de Asturias, El Entrego 34798
Museo de la Moneda, Caracas 48920
Museo de la Muerte, San Juan del Río 28392
Museo de la Música Alejandro García Caturla, Santa Clara 08120
Museo de la Música Grabada, Zapotlanejo 28652
Museo de la Música Rodrigo Prats, Santa Clara 08121
Museo de la Nacionalidad, Panamá City 31086
Museo de la Naturaleza de Cantabria, Cabezón de la Sal 34638
Museo de la No Intervención Fuerte de Loreto, Puebla 28330
Museo de la Paeria, Lleida 34967
Museo de la Palabra, Villa Adelina 00658
Museo de la Parroquia de Gámbita, Gámbita 07483
Museo de la Partitura Historica, Rosario 00527
Museo de la Patagonia Dr. Francisco P. Moreno, Bariloche 00136
Museo de la Pintura Mural y Museo Manuel Gamio, Teotihuacán 28481
Museo de la Piratería, Santiago de Cuba 08140
Museo de La Plata, La Plata 00392
Museo de la Platería, Taxco de Alarcón 28460
Museo de la Pluma, México 28141
Museo de la Policía del Chaco, Resistencia 00507
Museo de la Policía Federal Argentina, Buenos Aires 00189
Museo de la Policía Preventiva de la Ciudad de México, México 28142
Museo de la Provincia de Granma, Bayamo 07859
Museo de la Provincia El Dorado, El Dorado 31164
Museo de la Psicología Experimental Argentina Horacio G. Piñero, Buenos Aires 00190
Museo de la Purísima Concepción, Celaya 27809
Museo de La Quemada, Guadalupe 27964
Museo de la Radiodifusión, Puebla 28331
Museo de la Real Academia de Bellas Artes de la Purísima Concepción, Valladolid 35620
Museo de la Real Academia de Bellas Artes de San Fernando, Madrid 35027
Museo de la Real Capilla, Arenas de San Pedro 34479
Museo de la Real Colegiata, Roncesvalles 35338
Museo de la Real Plaza de Toros de Sevilla, Sevilla 35487
Museo de la Recoleta, Yanahuara 31270
Museo de la Reconquista, Orihuela 35185
Museo de la Reconquista, Tigre 00632
Museo de la Región de Ansenuza Aníbal Montes, Miramar 00448
Museo de la Reincorporación, Tacna 31254
Museo de la Resistencia Indígena, Ixcateopan de Cuauhtémoc 28015
Museo de la Revolución, La Habana 07962
Museo de la Revolución, Nueva Gerona 08059
Museo de la Revolución, Puebla 28332
Museo de la Revolución de San Pedro, San Pedro 28421
Museo de la Rioja, Logroño 34981
Museo de la Sal, Zipaquirá 07628
Museo de la Salle, Dasmariñas 31324

Museo de la Santa Iglesia Catedral, Avila 34503
Museo de la Secretaria de Hacienda y Credito Publico Antiguo Palacio del Arzobispado, México 28143
Museo de la Selva Juan Forster, Miramar 00449
Museo de la Sep, México 28144
Museo de la Sidra Copa de Oro, San Andrés Cholula 28374
Museo de la Sociedad Amigos de Laguardia, Laguardia 34935
Museo de la Soledad, Oaxaca 28276
Museo de la Solidaridad Salvador Allende, Santiago de Chile 06913
Museo de la Técnica de Euskadi, Barakaldo 34529
Museo de la Tortuga, Aquila 27778
Museo de la Universidad Nacional Hermilio Valdizán, Huánuco 31172
Museo de la Vera Cruz, Caravaca de la Cruz 34677
Museo de la Vid y el Vino Juan Carcelén, Jumilla 34931
Museo de la Vida Animal Herpetario, Puebla 28333
Museo de la Vida Rural, L'Espluga de Francolí 34804
Museo de la Villa de Ahome, Ahome 27760
Museo de Laca, Chiapa de Corzo 27818
Museo de Lagos de Moreno, Lagos de Moreno 28048
Museo de Las Americas, Denver 42893
Museo de Las Américas, San Juan 32396
Museo de las Artes, Guadalajara 27952
Museo de las Artes Populares Cidap, Cuenca 09156
Museo de las Artes Populares de Jalisco, Guadalajara 27953
Museo de las Atarazanas, Santo Domingo 09123
Museo de las Aves de México, Saltillo 28366
Museo de las Californias, Los Cabos 28064
Museo de las Californias, Tijuana 28512
Museo de las Casas Reales, Santo Domingo 09124
Muséo de Las Conceptas, Cuenca 09157
Museo de las Culturas, Cotacahi 09146
Museo de las Culturas, Saltillo 28367
Museo de las Culturas Aborígenes, Cuenca 09158
Museo de las Culturas Afromestizas, Cuajinicuilapa 27867
Museo de las Culturas de la Huasteca Potosina Tamuantzán, Valles 28587
Museo de las Culturas de Oaxaca, Oaxaca 28277
Museo de las Culturas de Occidente, Colima 27836
Museo de las Culturas del Norte, Monte Verde 28227
Museo de las Culturas Prehispánicas, Puerto Vallarta 28348
Museo de las Culturas Prehispánicas de Durango, Durango 27898
Museo de las Encartaciones, Sopuerta 35504
Museo de las Estelas Mayas, Campeche 27798
Museo de las Excavaciones de Torralba, Ambrona 34461
Museo de las Leyendas, Guanajuato 27971
Museo de las Luchas Obreras, Manzanillo 08031
Museo de las Madres Benedictinas, Sahagún 35356
Museo de las Miniaturas Poblanas, Palmar de Bravo 28299
Museo de las Misiones Jesuitas, Loreto 28063
Museo de las Momias, Guanajuato 27972
Museo de las Muñecas, Píritu 48961
Museo de las Parrandas de Remedios, Remedios 08090
Museo de las Pinturas Rupestres de San Ignacio, Pueblo de San Ignacio 28345
Museo de las Reales Atarazanas, Valencia 35602
Museo de las Revoluciones Mariano Jiménez, San Luis Potosí 28402
Museo de las Telecomunicaciones, Madrid 35028
Museo de las Telecomunicationes, México 28145
Museo de las Termas Públicas de Caesaraugusta, Zaragoza 35720
Museo de las Tradiciones Potosinas, San Luis Potosí 28403
Museo de l'Enginyeria de Catalunya, Barcelona 34547
Museo de León, León 34949
Museo de Lluc, Escorca 34801
Museo de los Altos de Chiapas, San Cristóbal de las Casas 28378
Museo de los Andes, Socha 07595
Museo de los Asentamientos, Federación 00347
Museo de los Bomberos, Guayaquil 09171
Museo de los Bomberos, Matanzas 08038
Museo de los Caminos, Astorga 34495
Museo de los Combates contra los Bandidos, Trinidad 08161
Museo de los Combatientes del Morro de Arica, Lima 31212
Museo de los Concilios y de la Cultura Visigoda, Toledo 35541
Museo de los Condestables de Castilla, Medina de Pomar 35102
Museo de los Corporales, Daroca 34766
Museo de los Corrales Viejos de Parque de los Patricios, Buenos Aires 00191
Museo de los Llanos, Guanare 48943
Museo de los Metales, Cuenca 09159
Museo de los Niños, Bogotá 07407
Museo de los Niños Abasto, Buenos Aires 00192
Museo de los Niños Barrilete, Córdoba 00296
Museo de Los Niños de Caracas, Caracas 48921
Museo de los Orishas, La Habana 07963
Museo de los Pioneros, Río Gallegos 00514
Museo de los Reyes Católicos, Granada 34877
Museo de Málaga, Málaga 35072
Museo de Málaga, Málaga 35073
Museo de Manacor, Manacor 35078
Museo de Maní y Museo del Convento San Miguel Arcángel, Maní 28067
Museo de Marionetas, Bogotá 07408
Museo de Medicina Legal y Ciencas Forenses, Bogotá 07409
Museo de Medicina Maya, San Cristóbal de las Casas 28379
Museo de Medicina Tradicional y Herbolaria, Cuernavaca 27874
Museo de Medicina Tropical Carlos J. Finlay, La Habana 07964
Museo de Medios de Comunicación, Resistencia 00508
Museo de Menorca, Mahón 35067
Museo de Mercedes, Mercedes 40983
Museo de Metrología, Tres Cantos 35574
Museo de Mexticacan, Mexticacán 28215
Museo de Mier y Noriega, Mier y Noriega 28217
Museo de Minerales del Instituto Geofísico, Bogotá 07410
Museo de Minerales y Fósiles, Zumárraga 35741
Museo de Mineralogía, Guanajuato 27973
Museo de Mineralogía, Pachuca 28294
Museo de Mineralogía Dr Miguel Romero Sánchez, Tehuacán 28474
Museo de Mineralogía y Geología Dr. Alfredo Stelzner, Córdoba 00297
Museo de Mineralogía y Geología Ing. Luis Silva Ruelas, Morelia 28250
Museo de Minería de la Compañía Real del Monte, Pachuca 28295
Museo de Minería e Historia de Cosala, Cosalá 27860
Museo de Miniaturas, Huaraz 31175
Museo de Mitos y Leyendas, Tafí del Valle 00627
Museo de Momias de Celaya, Celaya 27810
Museo de Monseñor Ramón Ibarra y González, Puebla 28334
Museo de Motivos Argentinos José Hernández, Buenos Aires 00193
Museo de Murcia, Murcia 35146
Museo de Murcia, Murcia 35147
Museo de Museos Colsubsidio, Bogotá 07411
Museo de Navajas y Curiosidades del Mundo, Puebla 28335
Museo de Navarra, Pamplona 35249
Museo de Nosa Señora da Antiga, Monforte de Lemos 35124
Museo de Nuestra Raíz Africana, San Juan 32397
Museo de Nuestra Señora del Rosario, Talpa de Allende 28452
Museo de Numismática, San José 07657
Museo de Numismática del Estado de México, Toluca 28548
Museo de Odontología, México 28146
Museo de Oro del Perú y Armas del Mundo, Lima 31213
Museo de Oro Precolombino, San José 07658
Museo de Oxolotán, Tacotalpa 28449
Museo de Palencia, Palencia 35214
Museo de Paleontología, Delicias 27889
Museo de Paleontología de Guadalajara, Guadalajara 27954
Museo de Paleontología de la Preparatoria, Apaxtla de Castrejón 27776
Museo de Paleontología de Rincón Gallardo, General Cepeda 27932
Museo de Paleontología Eliseo Palacios Aguilera, Tuxtla Gutiérrez 28572
Museo de Paracho, Paracho 28305
Museo de Patología, Buenos Aires 00194
Museo de Pericos, Culiacán 27883
Museo de Piedra y Artesanía Canaria, Ingenio 34917
Museo de Pintura, Sant Pol de Mar 35406
Museo de Piria, Piriápolis 41033
Museo de Pontevedra, Pontevedra 35284
Museo de Prehistoria e Arqueoloxia de Vilalba, Vilalba 35662
Museo de Prehistoria y Servicio de Investigación Prehistórica, Valencia 35603
Museo de Pungarabato, Pungarabato 28351
Museo de Ra Regoles, Cortina d'Ampezzo 23661
Museo de Relojes, A Coruña 34752
Museo de Reproducciones Artísticas, Bilbao 34613
Museo de Reproducciones de El Greco, Yecla 35709
Museo de Rocas, Yaiza 35707
Museo de Ruiz, Ruiz 28361
Museo de SADAIC Vincente López y Planes, Buenos Aires 00195
Museo de Salamanca, Salamanca 35361
Museo de San Antolín, Tordesillas 35553
Museo de San Esteban Tetelpa, Zacatepec de Hidalgo 28643
Museo de San Isidro, Madrid 35029
Museo de San Jerónimo, Cusco 31155
Museo de San José María de Yermo y Parres, Puebla 28336
Museo de San Juan, San Juan 32398
Museo de San Juan Raya, Zapotitlán Salinas 28650
Museo de San Juan Tlacotenco, San Juan Tlacotenco 28397
Museo de San Lorenzo Tenochtitlán, Texistepec 28509
Museo de San Miguel, Tlaxiaco 28535
Museo de San Pablo, San Pablo Huitzo 28417
Museo de San Pedro, Navolato 28265
Museo de San Pedro, San Pedro Lagunillas 28423
Museo de Santa Clara, Bogotá 07412
Museo de Santa Cruz, Toledo 35542
Museo de Santa Monica, Panay 31409
Museo de Santiago de los Caballeros, Antigua 21262
Museo de Sayula Juan Rulfo, Sayula 28443
Museo de Segóbriga, Saelices 35353
Museo de Segovia, Segovia 35465
Museo de Semana Santa, Hellín 34899
Museo de Semana Santa, Orihuela 35186
Museo de Semana Santa, Zamora 35713
Museo de Semana Santa Baena, Baena 34521
Museo de Semana Santa Escultor José Noguera Valverde, Callosa de Segura 34660
Museo de Sitio Arqueologico el Mongote Real Alto, Guayaquil 09172
Museo de Sitio Arqueológico Kuntur Wasi, San Pablo 31247
Museo de Sitio Boca de Potrerillos, Mina 28219
Museo de Sitio Casa de Juárez, Oaxaca 28278
Museo de Sitio Castillo de Teayo, Castillo de Teayo 27807
Museo de Sitio Complejo Arqueológico de Sillustani, Atuncolla 31119
Museo de Sitio de Cacaxtla, Nativitas 28262
Museo de Sitio de Cempoala, Cempoala 27811
Museo de Sitio de Chalcatzingo, Chalcatzingo 27813
Museo de Sitio de Chan Chan, Trujillo 31263
Museo de Sitio de Chichen Itza, Timun 28515
Museo de Sitio de Chinchero, Urubamba 31266
Museo de Sitio de Cholula, San Pedro Cholula 28422
Museo de Sitio de Coatetelco, Coatetelco 27833
Museo de Sitio de Comalcalco, Comalcalco 27847
Museo de Sitio de El Tajín, Papantla 28304
Museo de Sitio de El Zapotal, Ignacio de la Llave 28010
Museo de Sitio de Higueras, Vega de Alatorre 28590
Museo de Sitio de Ingapirca, Azogues 09138
Museo de Sitio de la Pampa Galeras, Quinua 31245
Museo de Sitio de La Venta, Huimanguillo 28006
Museo de Sitio de la Zona Arqueológica de Tzintzuntzan, Tzintzuntzan 28577
Museo de Sitio de Monte Albán, Oaxaca 28279
Museo de Sitio de Narihualá, Catacaos 31138
Museo de Sitio de Ocuilan, Ocuilan 28288
Museo de Sitio de Pachacamac, Lima 31214
Museo de Sitio de Palenque Alberto Ruz Lhuillier, Palenque 28298
Museo de Sitio de Paracas Julio C. Tello, Pisco 31236
Museo de Sitio de Pomona, Tenosique de Pino Suárez 28479
Museo de Sitio de Puruchuco, Lima 31215
Museo de Sitio de Querétaro, Querétaro 28354
Museo de Sitio de San Isidro, Tembladera 31259
Museo de Sitio de San Lorenzo Tenochtitlán, Tenochtitlán 28478
Museo de Sitio de San Miguel Ixtapan, San Miguel Ixtapan 28412
Museo de Sitio de Sipán, Zaña 31272
Museo de Sitio de Tenayuca, Tlalnepantla 28524
Museo de Sitio de Teotihuacán, Teotihuacán 28482
Museo de Sitio de Toniná, Ocosingo 28285
Museo de Sitio de Tres Zapotes, Santiago Tuxtla 28440
Museo de Sitio de Túcume, Campo 31136
Museo de Sitio de Uxmal, Santa Elena 28432
Museo de Sitio de Wari, Wari 31267
Museo de Sitio de Xochicalco, Xochicalco 28623
Museo de Sitio de Xochitecatl, Nativitas 28263
Museo de Sitio Degollado Jalisco, Degollado 27888
Museo de Sitio del Campo de la Alianza, Tacna 31255
Museo de Sitio del Claustro de Sor Juana, México 28147
Museo de Sitio del Rumicucho, San Antonio 09226
Museo de Sitio El Algarrobal, El Algarrobal 31163
Museo de Sitio El Torreoncito, Torreón 28555
Museo de Sitio Huaca El Dragón, La Esperanza 31193
Museo de Sitio Ocotelulco, Totolac 28562
Museo de Sitio Polyforum Siqueiros, México 28148
Museo de Sitio San Agustín, Juárez 28038
Museo de Sitio Talavera, México 28149
Museo de Sitio Tecpan, México 28150
Museo de Sitio Wari, Ayacucho 31121
Museo de Sitio Wari Willca, Huancayo 31169
Museo de Siyasa, Cieza 34716
Museo de Suelos, Iquitos 31185
Museo de Susticacán, Susticacán 28447
Museo de Tabar, Tabar - Urraul Bajo 35507
Museo de Tacuichamona, Culiacán 27884
Museo de Tahdziú, Tahdziú 28450
Museo de Tapalpa, Tapalpa 28456
Museo de Tapices, Oncala 35176
Museo de Tarlac, Tarlac 31458
Museo de Taximaroa, Hidalgo 27990
Museo de Tecnología Aeronáutica y Espacial, Córdoba 00298
Museo de Telecomunicaciones, Buenos Aires 00196
Museo de Telefonía, Delicias 27890
Museo de Tepeticpa, Tepeticpa 28491
Museo de Terra Santa, Santiago de Compostela 35445
Museo de Texcalyacac, Texcalyacac 28507
Museo de Tlahualilo, Tlahualilo de Zaragoza 28521
Museo de Tlalancaleca, San Matías Tlalancaleca 28409
Museo de Tlapa, Tlapa de Comonfort 28527
Museo de Tlayacapan, Tlayacapan 28537
Museo de Todos los Santos, La Paz 28044
Museo de Totolapan, Totolapan 28563
Museo de Tradiciones Populares de Aguadas, Aguadas 07361
Museo de Trajes Regionales de Colombia, Bogotá 07413
Museo de Transportes, Luján 00415
Museo de Tudela, Tudela 35578
Museo de Tultitlán, Tultitlán de Mariano Escobedo 28566
Museo de Ulia, Montemayor 35134
Museo de Urología, Buenos Aires 00197
Museo de Valladolid, Valladolid 35621
Museo de Velardeña, Velardeña 28591
Museo de Xiutetelco, Xiutetelco 28622
Museo de Xochitepec, Xochitepec 28626
Museo de Xolalpancalli, Zacapoaxtla 28632
Museo de Yautepec, Yautepec 28629
Museo de Zamora, Zamora 35714
Museo de Zaragoza, Zaragoza 35721
Museo de Zaragoza, Zaragoza 35722
Museo de Zaragoza, Zaragoza 35723
Museo de Zaragoza, Zaragoza 35724
Museo de Zoología, Córdoba 00299
Museo de Zoología Alfonso L. Herrera, México 28151
Museo de Zoología Juan Ormea, Trujillo 31264
Museo de Zurbarán, Marchena 35089
Museo degli Affreschi G.B. Cavalcaselle, Verona 25972
Museo degli Alpini, Bassano del Grappa 23038
Museo degli Alpini, Savignone 25504
Museo degli Arazzi delle Madrice, Marsala 24306
Museo degli Argenti, Ariano Irpino 22930
Museo degli Argenti, Firenze 23854
Museo degli Argenti Contemporanei, Sartirana Lomellina 25482
Museo degli Arredi Sacri, Castel Sant'Elia 23390
Museo degli Attrezzi Agricoli, Susa 25653
Museo degli Attrezzi Agricoli Ferretti Florindo, Sefro 25529
Museo degli Ex Voto, Viterbo 26035
Museo degli Indios dell'Amazonia, Assisi 22964
Museo degli Insetti, Bisegna 23088
Museo degli Scavi, Piuro 24965
Museo degli Strumenti della Riproduzione del Suono, Roma 25185
Museo degli Strumenti Musica Populare Sardi, Tadasuni 25664
Museo degli Strumenti Musicali, Cesena 23498
Museo degli Strumenti Musicali Meccanici, Savio 25505
Museo degli Strumenti Musicali Meccanici, Sestola 25559
Museo degli Studenti e della Goliardia, Bologna 23113
Museo degli Usi e Costumi della Gente di Romagna, Santarcangelo di Romagna 25457
Museo degli Usi e Costumi della Gente Trentina, San Michele all'Adige 25396
Museo degli Usi e Costumi della Valle di Goima, Zoldo Alto 26059
Museo degli Usi e Costumi delle Genti dell'Etna, Giarre 24022
Museo dei Bambini Explora, Roma 25186
Museo dei Benedettini, Pontida 25000
Museo dei Bozzetti, Pietrasanta 24913
Museo dei Bronzi Dorati, Pergola 24842
Museo dei Burattini, Mantova 24285
Museo dei Burattini e delle Figure, Cervia 23492
Museo dei Cappuccini, Bassano del Grappa 23039
Museo dei Combattenti, Soncino 25600
Museo dei Costumi della Partita a Scacchi, Marostica 24303
Museo dei Cuchi, Roana 25133
Museo dei Damaschi, Lorsica 24221
Museo dei Ferri Battuti e Galleria d'Arte Moderna Carlo Rizzarda, Feltre 23773
Museo dei Ferri Chirurgici, Pistoia 24959
Museo dei Ferri Taglienti, Scarperia 25520
Museo dei Fossili, Meride 36940
Museo dei Fossili, Vestenanova 25981
Museo dei Fossili, Zogno 26056
Museo dei Fossili Don Giuseppe Mattiacci, Serra San Quirico 25545
Museo dei Fossili e dei Minerali, Smerillo 25591
Museo dei Fossili e di Storia Naturale, Montefalcone Appennino 24518
Museo dei Fossili e Minerali del Monte Nerone, Apecchio 22903
Museo dei Fossili e Mostra dei Funghi, Pioraco 24939
Museo dei Grandi Fiumi, Rovigo 25297
Museo dei Legni Processionali, Petriolo 24885
Museo dei Magli, Ponte Nossa 24992
Museo dei Minerali e della Miniera, Oltre il Colle 24677
Museo dei Minerali Elbani, Rio Marina 25120
Museo dei Navigli, Milano 24391
Museo dei Parati Sacri, Montemarano 24536
Museo dei Reperti Bellici e Storici della Guerra 1915-1918, Capovalle 23330
Museo dei Reperti della Civiltà Contadina, Alberobello 22835
Museo dei Soldati del Montello, Nervesa della Battaglia 24615
Museo dei Soldatino e della Figurina Storica, Calenzano 23266
Museo dei Tasso e della Storia Postale, Camerata Cornello 23282
Museo dei Trasporti, Ranco 25071
Museo dei Trombini di Lessinia, San Bortolo 25341
Museo dei Vigili Urbani, Cosenza 23666
Museo del Agua y del Suelo, Viedma 00657
Museo del Aire, Madrid 35030
Museo del Alcázar, Toledo 35543
Museo del Almudín, Xàtiva 35704

Museo del Ámbar de Chiapas, San Cristóbal de las Casas 28380
Museo del Ambiente Histórico Cubano, Santiago de Cuba 08141
Museo del Area Fundacional, Mendoza 00436
Museo del Ateneo de Bellas Artes, Sucre 03908
Museo del Automóvil, Buenos Aires 00198
Museo del Automóvil, Luján 00416
Museo del Automóvil, México 28152
Museo del Automóvil, Montevideo 40998
Museo del Automóvil Club Argentino, Buenos Aires 00199
Museo del Automóvil de Santa Teresita, Santa Teresita 00615
Museo del Automóvil Puebla, Puebla 28337
Museo del Automovilismo Juan Manuel Fangio, Balcarce 00130
Museo del Azulejo, Montevideo 40999
Museo del Azulejo, Onda 35178
Museo del Azulejo Francés, Madonado 40979
Museo del Banco Central, Cuenca 09160
Museo del Banco Central, Loja 09185
Museo del Banco Central, Riobamba 09222
Museo del Banco Central de Manta, Manta 09188
Museo del Banco Provincia de Córdoba, Córdoba 00300
Museo del Bandolero, Ronda 35339
Museo del Baroffio e del Sacro Monte, Gallarate 23952
El Museo del Barrio, New York 45838
Museo del Barro, Asunción 31101
Museo del Battistero, Albenga 22832
Museo del Beisbol, Caracas 48922
Museo del Bigallo, Firenze 23855
Museo del Bijou, Casalmaggiore 23367
Museo del Biroccio Marchigiano e Museo Beltrami, Filottrano 23813
Museo del Blat y de la Pagesia, Cervera 34707
Museo del Borgo, Amato 22874
Museo del Bosco, Sovicille 25614
Museo del Botijo, Villena 35687
Museo del Bracciante Artigiano, Berra 23068
Museo del Brigante, Sonnino 25604
Museo del Café, San Cristóbal de las Casas 28381
Museo del Calzado, Elda 34795
Museo del Calzado El Borceguí, México 28153
Museo del Calzado y Ciencias Naturales, Arnedo 34484
Museo del Camino Real de Hecelchakan, Hecelchakán 27983
Museo del Camoscio, Opi 24680
Museo del Campesino, Xochitepec 28627
Museo del Camposanto Vecchio e dell'Opera, Pisa 24949
Museo del Canal Interoceanico de Panamá, Panamá City 31087
Museo del Cañamo, Callosa de Segura 34661
Museo del Canasto Cafetero y Muestra Arqueológica de la Cultura Quimbaya, Filandia 07478
Museo del Capoluogo, Castelbellino 23391
Museo del Cappello, Alessandria 22847
Museo del Cappello, Montappone 24496
Museo del Capriolo, Bisegna 23089
Museo del Capriolo, San Donato Val di Comino 25356
Museo del Carajo, Cali 07449
Museo del Carbón, Lenguazaque 07504
Museo del Carmen, México 28154
Museo del Carmen, Villa de Leyva 07620
Museo del Carmen de Maipú, Santiago de Chile 06914
Museo del Carnaval, Santiago de Cuba 08142
Museo del Carro y la Labranza, Tomelloso 35550
Museo del Carruaje El Tacu, Villa General Belgrano 00668
Museo del Cartel José P.H. Hernández, Río Grande 32382
Museo del Casin, Bagni di Lucca 23003
Museo del Castagno, Pescaglia 24865
Museo del Castello, Fumone 23944
Museo del Castello Colleoni Porto, Thiene 25704
Museo del Castello di Porciano, Stia 25633
Museo del Castello di San Giusto e Lapidario Tergestino, Trieste 25824
Museo del Castello di Sarre, Sarre 25477
Museo del Castello e della Città, Piombino 24936
Museo del Castello Scaligero, Torri del Benaco 25776
Museo del Castillo de Odna, Onda 35179
Museo del Castillo de Peralada, Peralada 35266
Museo del Cattedrale, Ferrara 23789
Museo del Cavallo Giocattolo, Grandate 24046
Museo del Cenacolo di Andrea del Sarto a San Salvi, Firenze 23856
Museo del Cenedese, Vittorio Veneto 26039
Museo del Centro Caprense Ignazio Cerio, Capri 23334
Museo del Centro Cultural de Villasarracino, Villasarracino 35683
Museo del Centro Cultural Joaquín Arcadio Pagaza, Valle de Bravo 28583
Museo del Centro Cultural La Cantera, Jonacatepec 28032
Museo del Centro Cultural Patio de los Ángeles, Guadalajara 27955
Museo del Centro Cultural Sor Juana Inés de la Cruz, Tepetlixpa 28492
Museo del Centro Cultural Universitario Quinta Gameros, Chihuahua 27826
Museo del Centro Cultural Zacualpan, Comala 27844
Museo del Centro de Estudios de la Revolución Mexicana, Jiquilpan 28031
Museo del Centro de Historia de Tuluá, Tuluá 07607
Museo del Centro de Investigación Arqueológica de Ancón, Lima 31216
Museo del Centro Histórico, San Juan del Río 28393
Museo del Centro Studi, Albissola Marina 22842
Museo del Cervo Sardo, Sinnai 25583
Museo del Chiodo, Forno di Zoldo 23922
Museo del Chocolate, Astorga 34496
Museo del Cielo, Villa Carlos Paz 00661
Museo del Cine, Durango 27899
Museo del Cine Pablo C. Ducrós Hicken, Buenos Aires 00200
Museo del Cine y la Fotografía, Puebla 28338
Museo del Cinema, Milano 24392
Museo del Cioccolato, Norma 24638
Museo del Círculo de Bellas Artes, Pozoblanco 35289
Museo del Círculo de Estudios Ferroviarios del Uruguay, Montevideo 41000
Museo del Cobre, Bogotá 07414
Museo del Colegio Costa y Llobera, Port de Pollença 35288
Museo del Colegio Médico de Santiago, Santiago de Compostela 35446
Museo del Colegio Nacional Amauta, Chupaca 31146
Museo del Colegio Nacional Justo José de Urquiza, Paraná 00467
Museo del Colegio Nacional Pedro Vicente Maldonado, Riobamba 09223
Museo del Colegio Padres Franciscanos, Ontinyent 35180
Museo del Colegio Stella Maris, Atacames 09137
Museo del Collezionista d'Arte, Milano 24393
Museo del Coltello Sardo, Arbus 22912
Museo del Combattente, Modena 24441
Museo del Conservatorio die Napoli, Napoli 24582
Museo del Convento de La Merced, Mantas 31228
Museo del Convento de los Descalzos, Lima 31217
Museo del Convento de San Esteban, Salamanca 35362
Museo del Convento de San Francisco, Lima 31218
Museo del Convento de Santa Catalina, Cusco 31156
Museo del Convento de Santa Clara, Carrión de Los Condes 34683
Museo del Convento de Santa Clara, Salamanca 35363
Museo del Convento de Santo Domingo, Cusco 31157
Museo del Convento di San Francesco, Susa 25655
Museo del Corallo, Ravello 25077
Museo del Corallo, Torre del Greco 25771
Museo del Costume Arbereshe, Frascineto 23934
Museo del Costume e della Tradizione Nostra Gente, Guardiagrele 24071
Museo del Costume Farnesiano, Gradoli 24045
Museo del Costume R. Piraino, Palermo 24766
Museo del Costume Tradizionale, Grosio 24054
Museo del Cuale, Puerto Vallarta 28349
Museo del Danza, La Habana 07965
Museo del Deporte, Cienfuegos 07890
Museo del Deporte, Holguín 08007
Museo del Deporte, Pabellón de Arteaga 28292
Museo del Deporte Pierre de Coubertin, La Falda 00380
Museo del Desierto, Saltillo 28368
Museo del Disco, Zipacón 07627
Museo del Doctor Olavide, Madrid 35031
Museo del Duomo, Città di Castello 23578
Museo del Duomo, Fidenza 23801
Museo del Duomo, Guardiagrele 24072
Museo del Duomo, Massa 24314
Museo del Duomo, Milano 24394
Museo del Duomo, Ravello 25078
Museo del Duomo, Udine 25847
Museo del Duomo, Valenza 25874
Museo del Ejército, Madrid 35032
Museo del Ejército y Fuerza Aérea Bethlemitas, México 28155
Museo del Ejército y Fuerza Aérea Mexicanos Cuartel Colorado, Guadalajara 27956
Museo del Ejidatario, Guasave 27979
Museo del Emigrante, Teguise 35520
Museo del Estado, Morelia 28251
Museo del Estado de Mérida, Mérida 48957
Museo del Este, Monte Caseros 00452
Museo del Ex Convento de Culhuacán, México 28156
Museo del Falegname T. Sana-Onlus, Almenno San Bartolomeo 22860
Museo del Ferro e della Ghisa, Follonica 23899
Museo del Ferrocarril, Aguascalientes 27757
Museo del Ferrocarril, Guadalajara 27957
Museo del Ferrocarril, Monterrey 28234
Museo del Ferrocarril, Torreón 28556
Museo del Ferrocarril de Madrid, Madrid 35033
Museo del Festero, Villena 35688
Museo del Fin del Mundo, Ushuaia 00649
Museo del Fiore, Acquapendente 22800
Museo del Folklore e delle Tradizioni Popolari, Caltanissetta 23275
Museo del Foro Caesaraugusta, Zaragoza 35725
Museo del Foro d'Augusto, Roma 25187
Museo del Fossile del Monte Baldo, Brentonico 23198
Museo del Foto Gabinetto die Fisica, Urbino 25858
Museo del Frer, Chiaverano 23537
Museo del Fuerte de San Felipe, Bacalar 27788
Museo del Fuerte de San Juan de Ulúa, Veracruz 28595
Museo del Fungo e di Scienze Naturali, Boves 23190
Museo del Gaucho y de la Moneda, Montevideo 41001
Museo del General Toribio Ortega, Coyame 27863
Museo del Giocattolo, Palermo 24767
Museo del Giocattolo, Sezze 25564
Museo del Gioco del Pallone a Bracciale e Tamburello, Santarcangelo di Romagna 25458
Museo del Grabado Español Contemporáneo, Marbella 35086
Museo del Grano, Cerignola 23481
Museo del Hombre, Tegucigalpa 21304
Museo del Hombre Dominicano, Santo Domingo 09125
Museo del Hombre en el Universo, Sopó 07600
Museo del Hombre y su Entorno, Caleta Olivia 00257
Museo del Humor, San Antonio de los Baños 08098
Museo del Indio, Los Toldos 00412
Museo del Indio de Puerto Rico, San Juan 32399
Museo del Indio y del Gaucho, Tacuarembó 41042
Museo del Instituto Americano del Arte, Cusco 31158
Museo del Instituto de Investigaciones Antropológicas, México 28157
Museo del Instituto Nacional de Cultura, Arequipa 31114
Museo del Int. Presepio in Miniatura Guido Colitti, Campobasso 23303
Museo del Istmo, La Línea de la Concepción 34956
Museo del Jade, San José 07659
Museo del Jazz G. Dagnino, Genova 23990
Museo del Juguete Tradicional Mexicano, San Francisco de los Romo 28385
Museo del Lago Gutiérrez, Bariloche 00137
Museo del las Comunicaciones de Mar del Plata, Mar del Plata 00425
Museo del Lavoro, Castelmagno 23414
Museo del Lavoro, Follonica 23900
Museo del Lavoro Contadino, Brisighella 23216
Museo del Lavoro Contadino, Campobello di Mazara 23305
Museo del Lavoro e della Civiltà Rurale, Palaia 24756
Museo del Lavoro e della Tradizioni Popolari della Versilia Storica, Seravezza 25542
Museo del Lavoro Povero e della Civiltà Contadina, Livraga 24196
Museo del Lazio Meridionale, Anagni 22879
Museo del Legno, Cantù 23320
Museo del Libro, Madrid 35034
Museo del Libro, San Javier 00566
Museo del Libro Antiguo, Antigua 21263
Museo del Limari, Ovalle 06902
Museo del Lino, Pescarolo 24871
Museo del Litoral Boliviano, La Paz 03896
Museo del Lupo Appenninico, Civitella Alfedena 23597
Museo del Maglio, Breganze 23195
Museo del Malcantone, Curio 36651
Museo del Mantecado, Estepa 34809
Museo del Mar, Boca de Río 48896
Museo del Mar, Cádiz 34648
Museo del Mar, La Barra 40977
Museo del Mar, Mazatlán 28078
Museo del Mar, San Pedro del Pinatar 35389
Museo del Mar, Santa Pola 35428
Museo del Mar El Rodadero, Santa Marta 07589
Museo del Mar Mundo Marino, Santa Marta 07590
Museo del Mare, Furci Siculo 23945
Museo del Mare, Ischia Ponte 24100
Museo del Mare, Nard 24609
Museo del Mare, Pesaro 24859
Museo del Mare, Piombino 24937
Museo del Mare, Pizzo 24969
Museo del Mare, Pollica 24982
Museo del Mare e della Costa M. Zei, Sabaudia 25306
Museo del Médico, Santa Fé 00602
Museo del Medioevo e del Rinascimento, Sorano 25609
Museo del Melonero, Villaconejos 35674
Museo del Menù, Bolgheri 23098
Museo del Merletto, Offida 24670
Museo del Merletto, Venezia 25929
Museo del Milagroso, Buga 07441
Museo del Modellismo Storico, Voghiera 26047
Museo del Molino de Papel, México 28158
Museo del Monasterio de San Joaquín y Santa Ana, Valladolid 35622
Museo del Monasterio de Santa Isabel, Valladolid 35623
Museo del Monasterio de Santa María de la Vid, La Vid 35653
Museo del Monasterio de Tulebras, Tulebras 35581
Museo del Monastero della Beata Filippa Mareri, Petrella Salto 24884
Museo del Mondo Contadino, Savoca 25506
Museo del Motociclo, Rimini 25114
Museo del Motociclo Moto Guzzi, Mondello del Lario 24473
Museo del Mundo, Buenos Aires 00201
Museo del Niño, Albacete 34420
Museo del Niño, San Juan 32400
Museo del Niño, Santa Ana del Valle 28427
Museo del Niño Globo mi Ciudad Pequeña, Guadalajara 27958
Museo del Niño Papalote, México 28159
Museo del Observatorio Astronómico Nacional, Madrid 35035
Museo del Opera Omnia R. Musa e Pinacoteca Parmigiani, Bedonia 23045
Museo del Oppidum de Iruña, Iruña de Oca 34919
Museo del Origen, Santiago Ixcuintla 28437
Museo del Oro, Bogotá 07415
Museo del Oro, Ipiales 07501
Museo del Oro Calima, Cali 07450
Museo del Oro Nariño, Pasto 07546
Museo del Oro Quimbaya, Armenia 07372
Museo del Oro Quimbaya, Manizales 07509
Museo del Oro y Metales Preciosos, La Paz 03897
Museo del Paesaggio, Castelnuovo Berardenga 23418
Museo del Paesaggio, Pallanza 24782
Museo del Paesaggio e Museo Storico Artistico, Verbania Pallanza 25958
Museo del Paesaggio Storico dell'Appennino, Firenzuola 23887
Museo del Palacio de Bellas Artes, México 28160
Museo del Palacio Nacional, Guatemala 21269
Museo del Palazzo del Podestà e Gipsoteca Libero Andreotti, Pescia 24877
Museo del Pane, Sant'Angelo Lodigiano 25451
Museo del Papiro, Siracusa 25587
Museo del Parco Nazionale Gran Paradiso, Noasca 24626
Museo del Parque Abel Santamaría Cuadrado, Santiago de Cuba 08143
Museo del Parque Nacional Los Alerces, Villa Futalaufquen 00667
Museo del Pasado Cuyano, Mendoza 00437
Museo del Patriarca, Valencia 35604
Museo del Patrimonio Histórico, Buenos Aires 00202
Museo del Patrimonio Industriale, Bologna 23114
Museo del Patrimonium, Sutri 25660
Museo del Periodismo Bonaerense, Capilla del Señor 00261
Museo del Periodismo y las Artes Gráficas, Guadalajara 27959
Museo del Pianoforte Antico, Ala 22824
Museo del Piccolo Regio, Torino 25739
Museo del Po, Monticelli d'Ongina 24553
Museo del Po e Young Museum, Revere 25105
Museo del Policía, Monterrey 28235
Museo del Presepe, Modena 24442
Museo del Presepio, Dalmine 23708
Museo del Presepio Tipologico Internazionale, Roma 25188
Museo del Primer Supremo Tribunal de Justicia de la Nación, Ario de Rosales 27779
Museo del Profumo, Milano 24395
Museo del Pueblo, Guanajuato 27974
Museo del Pueblo, Piranė 00478
Museo del Pueblo-Hospital, Quiroga 28356
Museo del Pueblo Maya Dzibilchaltún, Chablekal 27812
Museo del Puerto de Ingeniero White, Ingeniero White 00366
Museo del Real Seminario de Bergara, Bergara 34603
Museo del Recuerdo de la Academia Mexicana de la Lengua, México 28161
Museo del Reggimento "Giovani Fascisti", Ponti sul Mincio 24999
Museo del Regio Esercito Italiano, Orta 24696
Museo del Retablo, Burgos 34632
Museo del Retrato Hablado, México 28162
Museo del Río Magdalena, Honda 07495
Museo del Risorgimento, Brescia 23203
Museo del Risorgimento, Castelfidardo 23394
Museo del Risorgimento, Genova 23991
Museo del Risorgimento, Imola 24087
Museo del Risorgimento, Lucca 24229
Museo del Risorgimento, Massa Marittima 24323
Museo del Risorgimento, Piacenza 24891
Museo del Risorgimento, Santa Maria Capua Vetere 25436
Museo del Risorgimento, Solferino 25596
Museo del Risorgimento, Villafranca 26017
Museo del Risorgimento Aurelio Saffi, Forlì 23909
Museo del Risorgimento Duca d'Aosta, Sanluri 25423
Museo del Risorgimento e della Resistenza, Ferrara 23790
Museo del Risorgimento e della Resistenza, Vicenza 25994
Museo del Risorgimento e Raccolte Storiche, Milano 24396
Museo del Risorgimento F. Tanara, Langhirano 24137
Museo del Risorgimento L. Musini, Fidenza 23802
Museo del Risorgimento Vittorio Emanuele Orlando, Palermo 24768
Museo del Risorgmento e Resistenza R. Giusti, Mantova 24286
Museo del Ron, Santiago de Cuba 08144
Museo del Ron Havana Club, La Habana 07966
Museo del Rubinetto e della sua Tecnologia, San Maurizio D'Opaglio 25393
Museo del Sacrario, Asiago 22957
Museo del Sacro dell'Alta Val Trebbia, Montebruno 24506
Museo del Sacromonte, Granada 34878
Museo del Sale, Paceco 24727
Museo del Samán, Guacarí 07487
Museo del Sannio, Benevento 23053
Museo del Santuario de la Virgen de Agua Santa, Baños 09142
Museo del Santuario del SS. Crocifisso, Borgo a Buggiano 23169
Museo del Santuario di Crea, Serralunga di Crea 25546
Museo del Santuario di Montevergine, Mercogliano 24360
Museo del Santuario di Santa Maria Santissima della Fontenuova, Monsummano Terme 24485

Museo del Seminario Conciliar de Nueva Caceres, Naga 31406
Museo del Seminario Diocesano, Burgos 34633
Museo del Sidecar, Cingoli 23566
Museo del Siglo XIX, Bogotá 07416
Museo del Sottosuolo P. Parenzan, Latiano 24155
Museo del Sovrano Ordine Militare dei Cavalieri di Malta, Roma 25189
Museo del Sud-Ovest Americano, Cuveglio 23707
Museo del Tabaco Herminio, Caguas 32368
Museo del Tamburo Parlante, Montone 24557
Museo del Tango Roberto Firpo, Salto 00544
Museo del Tasso, Roma 25190
Museo del Teatro, Almagro 34451
Museo del Teatro, Cesena 23499
Museo del Teatro, Faenza 23753
Museo del Teatro, Spoleto 25624
Museo del Teatro Argentina, Roma 25191
Museo del Teatro Colón, Buenos Aires 00203
Museo del Teatro dell'Aquila, Fermo 23778
Museo del Teatro G. Borgatti, Cento 23473
Museo del Teatro Municipale, Piacenza 24892
Museo del Teatro Romagnolo, Forlì 23910
Museo del Teatro y la Música de Córdoba Cristobal de Aguilar, Córdoba 00301
Museo del Teclado, Caracas 48923
Museo del Tejido Sedero Valenciano, Valencia 35605
Museo del Templo Mayor, México 28163
Museo del Tequila, Tequila 28504
Museo del Territorio, Finale Emilia 23816
Museo del Territorio, Foggia 23893
Museo del Territorio, Longiano 24210
Museo del Territorio, Riccione 25108
Museo del Territorio, San Severino Marche 25413
Museo del Territorio Biellese, Biella 23080
Museo del Territorio dell'Alta Valle dell'Aulella, Casola in Lunigiana 23376
Museo del Territorio F.R. Fazio, Roccapalumba 25141
Museo del Tesoro, Lodi 24202
Museo del Tesoro del Duomo, Berceto 23057
Museo del Tesoro del Duomo, Monza 24559
Museo del Tesoro del Duomo, Rieti 25111
Museo del Tesoro del Duomo, Veroli 25965
Museo del Tesoro della Cattedrale, Anagni 22880
Museo del Tesoro della Cattedrale, Aosta 22901
Museo del Tesoro della Cattedrale, Savona 25510
Museo del Tesoro della Cattedrale di San Lorenzo, Genova 23992
Museo del Tesoro Santuario della Misericordia, Savona 25511
Museo del Tessile, Chieri 23538
Museo del Tessile e della Tradizione Industriale, Busto Arsizio 23239
Museo del Tessuto, Prato 25045
Museo del Traje, La Rioja 00398
Museo del Traje en Tabasco, Villahermosa 28611
Museo del Transporte, Garza García 27929
Museo del Transporte Guillermo José Schael, Caracas 48924
Museo del Transporte Terrestre, Santiago de Cuba 08145
Museo del Trattore Agricolo, Senago 25533
Museo del Tricolore, Reggio Emilia 25098
Museo del Turismo dell'Alta Pusteria, Villabassa 26015
Museo del Vajont, Longarone 24208
Museo del Valle de Tehuacán, Tehuacán 28475
Museo del Valle de Xico, Valle de Chalco 28584
Museo del Vetro, Venezia 25930
Museo del Vicino Oriente, Roma 25192
Museo del Vidrio, Monterrey 28236
Museo del Vidrio, San Ildefonso 35375
Museo del Villaggio, Chiusa 23553
Museo del Vino, Caldaro 23262
Museo del Vino, Torgiano 25726
Museo del Vino, Vilafranca del Penedès 35658
Museo del Vino, Villafamés 35677
Museo del Vino e della Donna, Ciliverghe 23562
Museo del Virrey Ezpeleta, Guaduas 07489
Museo Deleddiano, Nuoro 24662
Museo della Accademia Ligustica di Belle Arti, Genova 23993
Museo della Antica Civiltà Locale, Bronte 23217
Museo della Badia Benedettina, Cava dei Tirreni 23458
Museo della Badia di San Salvatore, Vaiano 25867
Museo della Barca Lariana, Pianello del Lario 24898
Museo della Basilica, Gandino 23957
Museo della Basilica, Grotte di Castro 24064
Museo della Basilica, Santa Maria degli Angeli 25437
Museo della Basilica di San Marco, Venezia 25931
Museo della Basilica di San Michele Arcangelo, Monte Sant'Angelo 24503
Museo della Basilica di San Nicola, Bari 23021
Museo della Basilica di San Pancrazio, Roma 25193
Museo della Basilica di San Venanzio, Camerino 23284
Museo della Basilica di Santa Maria del Colle, Pescocostanzo 24881
Museo della Basilica di Santa Maria della Passione, Milano 24397
Museo della Basilica Patriarcale S. Maria degli Angeli, Assisi 22965
Museo della Battaglia, San Martino della Battaglia 25388
Museo della Battaglia, Vittorio Veneto 26040
Museo della Battaglia del Senio, Alfonsine 22853
Museo della Battaglia di Marengo, Alessandria 22848
Museo della Battaglia di Marengo, Spinetta Marengo 25621
Museo della Battaglia di San Martino, Desenzano del Garda 23712
Museo della Biblioteca Maldotti, Guastalla 24073
Museo della Bilancia, Campogalliano 23307
Museo della Bonifica, Argenta 22926
Museo della Bonifica, San Donà di Piave 25355
Museo della Calzatura, Sant'Elpidio a Mare 25461
Museo della Calzatura d'Autore di Rossimoda, Strà 25638
Museo della Calzatura P. Bertolini, Vigevano 26007
Museo della Canape e della Vita Contadina, Bentivoglio 23055
Museo della Canzone e della Riproduzione Sonora, Vallecrosia 25881
Museo della Carrozza, Macerata 24247
Museo della Carta, Amalfi 22870
Museo della Carta e della Filigrana, Fabriano 23746
Museo della Carta e della Filigrana, Pioraco 24940
Museo della Cartolina S. Nuvoli, Isera 24102
Museo della Casa Carnica, Prato Carnico 25050
Museo della Casa Carsica, Monrupino 24481
Museo della Casa Contadina, Bolognetta 23147
Museo della Casa Contadina, Corciano 23646
Museo della Casa Fiorentina Antica, Firenze 23857
Museo della Casa Trevigiana, Treviso 25805
Museo della Casina delle Civette, Roma 25194
Museo della Cattedrale, Bari 23022
Museo della Cattedrale, Barletta 23031
Museo della Cattedrale, Chiusi Città 23556
Museo della Cattedrale, Fossano 23926
Museo della Cattedrale, Monopoli 24478
Museo della Centuriazione, Cesena 23500
Museo della Ceramica, Ascoli Piceno 22951
Museo della Ceramica, Bassano del Grappa 23040
Museo della Ceramica, Castellamonte 23403
Museo della Ceramica, Fiorano Modenese 23820
Museo della Ceramica, Patti 24818
Museo della Ceramica, Salerno 25318
Museo della Ceramica, Vietri 26005
Museo della Ceramica A. Ribezzi, Latiano 24156
Museo della Ceramica del Castello, Salerno 25319
Museo della Ceramica di Castelli, Castelli 23412
Museo della Certosa, Certosa di Pavia 23488
Museo della Certosa, Serra San Bruno 25544
Museo della Chiesa di San Francesco, Mercatello sul Metauro 24357
Museo della Chiesa di San Lorenzo, Portovenere 25026
Museo della Città, Ancona 22882
Museo della Città, Aquino 22910
Museo della Città, Rimini 25115
Museo della Città, Udine 25848
Museo della Città e del Territorio, Monsummano Terme 24486
Museo della Civiltà Contadina, Acri 22806
Museo della Civiltà Contadina, Aliano 22856
Museo della Civiltà Contadina, Amandola 22872
Museo della Civiltà Contadina, Andrate 22886
Museo della Civiltà Contadina, Ateleta 22976
Museo della Civiltà Contadina, Barolo 23034
Museo della Civiltà Contadina, Bastiglia 23042
Museo della Civiltà Contadina, Bentivoglio 23056
Museo della Civiltà Contadina, Borghi 23166
Museo della Civiltà Contadina, Borgo San Lorenzo 23173
Museo della Civiltà Contadina, Calvisano 23278
Museo della Civiltà Contadina, Castelfranco Emilia 23399
Museo della Civiltà Contadina, Castelnovo no' Monti 23417
Museo della Civiltà Contadina, Cavenago d'Adda 23462
Museo della Civiltà Contadina, Cervia 23493
Museo della Civiltà Contadina, Copparo 23644
Museo della Civiltà Contadina, Curtatone 23703
Museo della Civiltà Contadina, Fabriano 23747
Museo della Civiltà Contadina, Figline Valdarno 23810
Museo della Civiltà Contadina, Filottrano 23814
Museo della Civiltà Contadina, Guardia Piemontese 24068
Museo della Civiltà Contadina, Loret Aprutino 24213
Museo della Civiltà Contadina, Maierato 24262
Museo della Civiltà Contadina, Mairano 24265
Museo della Civiltà Contadina, Moio della Civitella 24456
Museo della Civiltà Contadina, Mombaroccio 24463
Museo della Civiltà Contadina, Montechiaro d'Acqui 24513
Museo della Civiltà Contadina, Montefiore dell'Aso 24523
Museo della Civiltà Contadina, Novellara 24656
Museo della Civiltà Contadina, Perdifumo 24839
Museo della Civiltà Contadina, Roscigno 25280
Museo della Civiltà Contadina, San Nicola La Strada 25401
Museo della Civiltà Contadina, Sappada 25470
Museo della Civiltà Contadina, Sassocorvaro 25491
Museo della Civiltà Contadina, Serrastretta 25549
Museo della Civiltà Contadina, Sesto Fiorentino 25556
Museo della Civiltà Contadina, Seui 25562
Museo della Civiltà Contadina, Spinetoli 25620
Museo della Civiltà Contadina, Teggiano 25679
Museo della Civiltà Contadina, Todi 25713
Museo della Civiltà Contadina, Torre Pallavicina 25773
Museo della Civiltà Contadina, Verdello 25961
Museo della Civiltà Contadina, Zibello 26055
Museo della Civiltà Contadina A. Marsiano, Niscemi 24622
Museo della Civiltà Contadina D. Bianco, Sammichele di Bari 25330
Museo della Civiltà Contadina del Cilento, Montecorice 24516
Museo della Civiltà Contadina del Mendrisiotto, Stabio 37198
Museo della Civiltà Contadina dell'Alto Monferrato e della Bassa Langa, Castagnole delle Lanze 23384
Museo della Civiltà Contadina e Artigianale d'Enza, Montecchio Emilia 24511
Museo della Civilta Contadina e della Canapa G. Romagnoli, Argelato 22924
Museo della Civiltà Contadina e Tradizioni Popolari, Tuglie 25842
Museo della Civiltà Contadina ed Artigiana, Monterosso Calabro 24543
Museo della Civiltà Contadina ed Artigiana, Ripatransone 25124
Museo della Civilta Contadina Friulana, Farra d'Isonzo 23766
Museo della Civiltà Contadina in Val Vibrata, Controguerra 23640
Museo della Civiltà Contadina L. Rubat, Piscina 24954
Museo della Civiltà Contadina Masseria Lupoli, Crispiano 23685
Museo della Civiltà Contadina nell'Area, Montefalcone di Val Fortore 24519
Museo della Civiltà Contadina Valle dell'Aniene, Roviano 25296
Museo della Civiltà del Lavoro, Campiglia Marittima 23298
Museo della Civiltà Locale, Buseto Palizzolo 23233
Museo della Civiltà Locale, Trevi 25799
Museo della Civiltà Messapica, Poggiardo 24973
Museo della Civiltà Montanara, Sestola 25560
Museo della Civiltà Romana, Roma 25195
Museo della Civiltà Rupestre, Zungri 26062
Museo della Civiltà Rurale, Altamura 22862
Museo della Civiltà Rurale del Vicentino, Malo 24271
Museo della Civiltà Salinara, Cervia 23494
Museo della Civiltà Solandra, Malé 24268
Museo della Civiltà Valligiana, Bardi 23014
Museo della Civitella, Chieti 23546
Museo della Collegiata, Castell'Arquato 23406
Museo della Collegiata, Chianciano Terme 23523
Museo della Collegiata, San Candido 25342
Museo della Collegiata di Santa Andrea, Empoli 23730
Museo della Collegiata di Santa Maria a Mare, Maiori 24264
Museo della Collezione Gambarotta, Piozzo 24941
Museo della Comunità Ebraica, Venezia 25932
Museo della Comunità Ebraica Carlo e Vera Wagner, Trieste 25825
Museo della Confraternita della Misericordia, Anghiari 22891
Museo della Congregazione Mechitarista dei Padri Armeni, Venezia 25933
Museo della Corte, Porto Viro 25016
Museo della Croce Rossa Italiana, Campomorone 23308
Museo della Cultura Alpina del Comelico, Comelico Superiore 23624
Museo della Cultura Arbereshe, San Paolo Albanese 25403
Museo della Cultura Marinara, Tortoreto Lido 25780
Museo della Cultura Mezzadrile, Morro d'Alba 24566
Museo della Cultura Popolare, Grosseto 24057
Museo della Cultura Popolare e Contadina, Carrega Ligure 23361
Museo della Donna, Angrogna 22893
Museo della Donna E. Ortner, Merano 24353
Museo della Esposizione Permanente, Milano 24398
Museo della Farmacia Picciola, Trieste 25826
Museo della Figurina, Modena 24443
Museo della Figurina di Gesso e dell'Emigrazione, Coreglia Antelminelli 23649
Museo della Filigrana, Campo Ligure 23300
Museo della Flora, Fauna e Mineralogia, Auronzo di Cadore 22987
Museo della Fondazione Giovanni Scaramangà di Altomonte, Trieste 25827
Museo della Fondazione Horne, Firenze 23858
Museo della Fondazione Mandralisca, Cefalù 23466
Museo della Fondazione Querini Stampalia, Venezia 25934
Museo della Fondazione Ugo da Como, Lonato 24207
Museo della Fotografia Storica e Contemporanea, Torino 25740
Museo della Frutticoltura Adofo Bonvicini, Massa Lombarda 24318
Museo della Gente dell'Appennino Pistoiese, Cutigliano 23704
Museo della Gente Senza Storia, Altavilla Irpina 22863
Museo della Geotermia, Pomarance 24984
Museo della Grancia, Serre di Rapiano 25552
Museo della Guerra, Castel del Rio 23387
Museo della Guerra, Gardone Riviera 23959
Museo della Guerra Adamellina, Spiazzo 25618
Museo della Guerra Bianca, Temù 25685
Museo della Guerra Bianca, Vermiglio 25962
Museo della Linea Gotica, Montefiore Conca 24521
Museo della Liquirizia, Rossano 25287
Museo della Liuteria, Arpino 22940
Museo della Macchina da Scrivere P. Mitterhofer, Parcines 24792
Museo della Magnifica Comunità di Cadore, Pieve di Cadore 24915
Museo della Mail Art, Montecarotto 24508
Museo della Marineria dell'Alto e Medio Adriatico, Cesenatico 23511
Museo della Marionetta, Torino 25741
Museo della Miniera, Cesena 23501
Museo della Miniera, Massa Marittima 24324
Museo della Miniera, Prata di Pordenone 25038
Museo della Miniera, Schilpario 25524
Museo della Miniera Aurifera della Guia, Macugnaga 24254
Museo della Miniera di Zolfo di Cabernardi, Sassoferrato 25496
Museo della Misericordia, San Miniato 25399
Museo della Montagna, Macugnaga 24255
Museo della Nave Romana, Comacchio 23621
Museo della Nostra Terra, Pieve Torina 24923
Museo della Paglia e dell'Intreccio D. Michalacci, Signa 25581
Museo della Pesca, Caslano 36614
Museo della Pesca, Magione 24259
Museo della Pesca e delle Civiltà Marinara, San Benedetto del Tronto 25333
Museo della Pietà Popolare, Molfetta 24458
Museo della Pietra Serena, Firenzuola 23888
Museo della Pievania, Corciano 23647
Museo della Pieve, Sant'Ambrogio di Valpolicella 25448
Museo della Pieve di San Pietro, Prato 25046
Museo della Pieve di Staggia, Poggibonsi 24975
Museo della Pipa, Gavirate 23966
Museo della Plastica, Pont Canavese 24988
Museo della Preistoria, Celano 23470
Museo della Preistoria della Tuscia, Valentano 25873
Museo della Propositura di San Pietro, Montecatini Val di Nievole 24510
Museo della Regina, Cattolica 23457
Museo della Repubblica Partigiana, Montefiorino 24525
Museo della Resistenza e del '900, Imola 24088
Museo della Resistenza e della Civiltà Contadina, Pietrabruna 24909
Museo della Resistenza e del Folclore Valsabbino, Pertica Bassa 24844
Museo della Rocca, Cesena 23502
Museo della Rocca, Dozza 23723
Museo della Sanità e dell'Assistenza, Bologna 23115
Museo della Santa, Bologna 23116
Museo della SAT, Trento 25792
Museo della Scuola, Bolzano 23154
Museo della Scuola, Pramollo 25036
Museo della Scuola Grande del Carmini, Venezia 25935
Museo della Seta Abegg, Garlate 23962
Museo della Sindone, Torino 25742
Museo della Società di Esecutori di Pie Disposizioni, Siena 25573
Museo della Società di Studi Patri, Gallarate 23953
Museo della Società Geografica Italiana, Roma 25196
Museo della Società Storia del Novese, Novi Ligure 24657
Museo della Specola, Bologna 23117
Museo della Stampa, Jesi 24114
Museo della Stampa, Soncino 25601
Museo della Tarsia, Rolo 25146
Museo della Tecnica e del Lavoro MV Agusta, Samarate 25328
Museo della Tecnica e del Lavoro MV Augusta, Trequanda 25798
Museo della Tecnologia Contadina, Santu Lussurgiu 25467
Museo della Terza Armata, Padova 24737
Museo della Tipografia, Città di Castello 23579
Museo della Tonnara, Milazzo 24421
Museo della Tonnara, Stintino 25637
Museo della Torre, Albino 22837
Museo della Val Codera, Novate Mezzola 24653
Museo della Val d'Agri, Sant'Arcangelo 25456
Museo della Val Gardena, Ortisei 24698
Museo della Val Venosta, Sluderno 25590
Museo della Valchiavenna, Chiavenna 23535
Museo della Valle, Cavargna 23461
Museo della Valle Cannobina, Gurro 24078
Museo della Valle Intelvi, Lanzo d'Intelvi 24140
Museo della Via Ostiense, Roma 25197
Museo della Vicaria di San Lorenzo, Zogno 26057
Museo della Villa Bettoni, Bogliaco 23095
Museo della Vita, Castelmagno 23415
Museo della Vita Contadina, Castelnuovo Don Bosco 23421
Museo della Vita Contadina in Romagnolo, Russi 25302
Museo della Vita e del Lavoro della Maremma Settentrionale, Cecina e Marina 23465
Museo della Vita e delle Tradizioni Popolari Sarde, Nuoro 24663
Museo della Vite e del Vino, Carmignano 23350
Museo della Vite e del Vino, Rufina 25301
Museo della Viticoltura, Prarostino 25037
Museo della Xilografia, Carpi 23354
Museo della Zampogna, Scapoli 25518
Museo della Zisa, Palermo 24769
Museo dell'Abazzia di San Colombano, Bobbio 23094
Museo dell'Abbazia, Casamari-Veroli 23370
Museo dell'Abbazia, Castiglione a Casauria 23431
Museo dell'Abbazia, San Benedetto Po 25338
Museo dell'Abbazia di Farfa, Fara Sabina 23764
Museo dell'Abbazia di San Nilo, Grottaferrata 24060

Museo dell'Abbazia di Santa Maria in Sylvis, Sesto al Reghena 25554
Museo dell'Accademia d'Arte C. Scalabrino, Montecatini Terme 24509
Museo dell'Accademia di Belle Arti, Perugia 24852
Museo dell'Accademia di Sant'Anselmo, Aosta 22902
Museo dell'Accademia Etrusca, Cortona 23663
Museo dell'Accademia Ligustica di Belle Arti, Genova 23994
Museo dell'Accademia Nazionale Virgiliana, Mantova 24287
Museo dell'Aeronautica G. Caproni, Trento 25793
Museo dell'Agricoltura e del Mondo Rurale, San Martino in Rio 25390
Museo dell'Agricoltura Meridionale, San Tammaro 25417
Museo dell'Agro Falisco, Civita Castellana 23592
Museo dell'Agro Veientano, Formello 23919
Museo dell'Alta Val Venosta, Curon Venosta 23702
Museo dell'Alto Medioevo, Roma 25198
Museo dell'Apicoltura, Renon 25104
Museo dell'Apicultura, Abbiategrasso 22794
Museo dell'Arciconfraternita, Tolentino 25718
Museo dell'Arciconfraternita dei Genovesi, Cagliari 23248
Museo dell'Ardesia, Cicagna 23560
Museo dell'Arredo Contemporaneo, Russi 25303
Museo dell'Arte Classica, Sezione di Archeologia, Roma 25199
Museo dell'Arte Contadina, Marciana 24296
Museo dell'Arte del Cappello, Ghiffa 24019
Museo dell'Arte del Vino, Staffolo 25628
Museo dell'Arte della Seta, Catanzaro 23452
Museo dell'Arte della Tornitura del Legno, Pettenasco 24886
Museo dell'Arte e della Tecnologia Confetteria, Sulmona 25647
Museo dell'Arte Mineraria, Iglesias 24081
Museo dell'Arte Sacra, Aldino 22846
Museo dell'Arte Serica e Laterizia, Malo 24272
Museo dell'Arte Votiva, Cesena 23503
Museo dell'Artigianato Tessile e della Seta, Reggio Calabria 25090
Museo dell'Attore Napoletano, Napoli 24583
Museo dell'Automobile, San Martino in Rio 25391
Museo dell'Automobile Carlo Biscaretti di Ruffia, Torino 25743
Museo dell'Automobile e della Tecnica, Farra d'Isonzo 23767
Museo dell'Automobile L. Bonfanti, Romano d'Ezzelino 25274
Museo dell'Aviazione, Rimini 25116
Museo dell'Avifauna Appenninica, Sarnano 25473
Museo delle Anime dei Defunti, Roma 25200
Museo delle Armi, Terni 25695
Museo delle Armi Antiche, Martinsicuro 24308
Museo delle Armi Antiche, Offagna 24667
Museo delle Armi Antiche, San Marino 33761
Museo delle Armi Antiche e Fortezza Medievale, Acquaviva Picena 22803
Museo delle Armi, Armature e Strumenti di Tortura, Ischia Ponte 24101
Museo delle Armi e del Martello, Sarnano 25474
Museo delle Armi e delle Uniformi, Urbisaglia 25863
Museo delle Armi Moderne, San Marino 33762
Museo delle Arti e delle Tradizioni, Treviso 25806
Museo delle Arti e delle Tradizioni di Puglia, Latiano 24157
Museo delle Arti e delle Tradizioni Popolari, Canepina 23312
Museo delle Arti e delle Tradizioni Popolari, Sassoferrato 25497
Museo delle Arti e Tradizioni Popolari, Civitanova Marche 23594
Museo delle Arti e Tradizioni Popolari, Correggio 23657
Museo delle Bilance e dei Pesi, Monterchi 24541
Museo delle Carrozze, Catanzaro 23453
Museo delle Carrozze, Firenze 23859
Museo delle Carrozze, Napoli 24584
Museo delle Carrozze, Trani 25782
Museo delle Carrozze dell'Ottocento, Verona 25973
Museo delle Centuriazioni, Granze 24047
Museo delle Ceramiche, Forlì 23911
Museo delle Ceramiche, Tolentino 25719
Museo delle Ceramiche Abruzzesi, Loreto Aprutino 24218
Museo delle Cere, Roma 25201
Museo delle Cere Anatomiche Luigi Cattaneo, Bologna 23118
Museo delle Cere - Strumenti di Tortura, San Marino 33763
Museo delle Civiltà Contadina, San Pellegrino in Alpe 25404
Museo delle Contadinerie, Costigliole d'Asti 23672
Museo delle Cripte, Poggiardo 24974
Museo delle Culture Extraeuropee, Castagnola 36617
Museo delle Culture Extraeuropee Dinz Rialto, Rimini 25117
Museo delle Curiosità, San Marino 33764
Museo delle Due Guerre Mondiali, Loro Piceno 24220
Museo delle Erbe, Teggiano 25680
Museo delle Erbe, Veroli 25966
Museo delle Ferrovie, Monserrato 24484
Museo delle Ferrovie in Sardegna, Cagliari 23249
Museo delle Genti d'Abruzzo, Pescara 24868
Museo delle Genti di Montagna, Palazzuolo sul Senio 24762
Museo delle Grigne, Esino Lario 23742
Museo delle Guerre, Grassobbio 24048
Museo delle Icone, Peccioli 24832
Museo delle Marionette, Campomorone 23309
Museo delle Miniere, Valle Aurina 25879
Museo delle Mummie, Ferentillo 23775
Museo delle Mura, Roma 25202
Museo delle Navi e Antiche Carte Geografiche, Bologna 23119
Museo delle Navi Romane, Fiumicino 23889
Museo delle Navi Romane, Nemi 24613
Museo delle Origini, Roma 25203
Museo delle Palafitte, Molina di Ledro 24461
Museo delle Pentole nella Storia, Rozzano 25299
Museo delle Porcellane, Firenze 23860
Museo delle Rimembranze, Cosenza 23667
Museo delle Scienze della Terra e del Lavoro Contadino, Piandimeleto 24896
Museo delle Sinopie, Pisa 24950
Museo delle Statue Menhir, Laconi 24127
Museo delle Statue - Stele Lunigianesi, Pontremoli 25002
Museo delle Tavolette di Biccherna, Siena 25574
Museo delle Terme, Bagni di Lucca 23004
Museo delle Terre Marchigiane, San Lorenzo in Campo 25384
Museo delle Tradizioni Agroalimentari della Sardegna, Siddi 25566
Museo delle Tradizioni ed Arti Contadine, Picciano 24904
Museo delle Tradizioni Locali, Zoppè di Cadore 26060
Museo delle Tradizioni Popolari, Città di Castello 23580
Museo delle Tradizioni Popolari, Offida 24671
Museo delle Tradizioni Popolari, San Vito di Cadore 25420
Museo delle Trame Mediterranee, Gibellina 24024
Museo delle Truppe Alpine Mario Balocco, Biella 23081
Museo delle Valli, Comacchio 23622
Museo delle Valli d'Argenta, Argenta 22927
Museo delle Valli Valdesi, Torre Pellice 25775
Museo dell'Emigrante Casa Giannini, Favale di Malvaro 23769
Museo dell'Emigrazione G.B. Scalabrini, Francavilla Angitola 23931
Museo dell'Energia Elettrica, Brescia 23204
Museo dell'Enoteca Regionale Piemontese, Grinzane Cavour 24052
Museo dell'Homo Salvadego, Cosio Valtellino 23670
Museo dell'Illustrazione, Ferrara 23791
Museo dell'Immagine, Cesena 23504
Museo dell'Informazione, Senigallia 25535
Museo dell'Ingegno e della Tecnologia Preindustriale, Colorno 23619
Museo dell'Intreccio Mediterraneo, Castelsardo 23425
Museo dell'Istituto di Anatomia Patologica, Padova 24738
Museo dell'Istituto di Patologia del Libro, Roma 25204
Museo dell'IstitutoCentral di Patologia, Roma 25205
Museo dello Sbarco, Anzio 22899
Museo dello Sbarco Alleato, Nettuno 24617
Museo dello Scalpellino Povese, Pove del Grappa 25030
Museo dello Scarpone e della Scarpa Sportiva, Montebelluna 24504
Museo dello Sfilato Siciliano, Chiaramonte Gulfi 23525
Museo dello Spazzacamino, Santa Maria Maggiore 25438
Museo dello Studio, Bologna 23120
Museo dell'Occhiale, Pieve di Cadore 24916
Museo dell'Olio, Cisano 23572
Museo dell'Olio in Sabina, Castelnuovo di Farfa 23420
Museo dell'Olivo, Imperia 24094
Museo dell'Olivo e dell'Olio, Torgiano 25727
Museo dell'Ombrello e del Parasole, Gignese 24026
Museo dell'Opera, Borgo a Buggiano 23170
Museo dell'Opera del Duomo, Orvieto 24704
Museo dell'Opera del Duomo, Perugia 24853
Museo dell'Opera del Duomo, Prato 25047
Museo dell'Opera del Santuario, Tolentino 25720
Museo dell'Opera di Santa Croce, Firenze 23861
Museo dell'Opera di Santa Maria del Fiore, Firenze 23862
Museo dell'Opera di Santa Niccolao, Buggiano 23227
Museo dell'Opera Metropolitana, Siena 25575
Museo dell'Opificio delle Pietre Dure, Firenze 23863
Museo dell'Orologio da Torre G.B. Bergallo, Tovo San Giacomo 25781
Museo dell'Orso, Villavallelonga 26023
Museo dell'Osservatorio, Monte Porzio Catone 24497
Museo dell'Osservatorio Astronomico di Capodimonte, Napoli 24585
Museo dell'Uomo, Serrapetrona 25548
Museo dell'Uomo, Susegana 25657
Museo dell'Uomo e dell'Ambiente, Terra del Sole 25698
Museo dell'Utensileria, Lanzo Torinese 24141
Museo Demantropologico, Cervaro 23490
Museo Demoantropologico, Pastena 24814
Museo Demologico dell'Economia, del Lavoro e della Storia Sociale Silana, San Giovanni in Fiore 25370
Musée Départemental A. Demard, Le-Haut-du-Them-Château-Lambert 12422
Museo Depero, Rovereto 25292
Museo des Origenes, La Habana 07967
Museo di Anatomia, Camerino 23285
Museo di Anatomia Comparata, Bologna 23121
Museo di Anatomia Comparata Battista Grassi, Roma 25206
Museo di Anatomia Patologica, Roma 25207
Museo di Anatomia Patologica C. Taruffi, Bologna 23122
Museo di Anatomia Patologica Veterinaria, Ozzano dell'Emilia 24724
Museo di Anatomia Umana, Napoli 24586
Museo di Anatomia Umana, Torino 25744
Museo di Anatomia Umana Normale, Bologna 23123
Museo di Anatomia Umana Normale, Parma 24804
Museo di Anatomia Veterinaria, Napoli 24587
Museo di Antichita, Torino 25745
Museo di Antichità Etrusche e Italiche, Roma 25208
Museo di Antonio da Sangallo il Giovane, Montefiascone 24520
Museo di Antropologia, Bologna 23124
Museo di Antropologia, Napoli 24588
Museo di Antropologia Criminale, Torino 25746
Museo di Antropologia ed Etnografia, Padova 24739
Museo di Antropologia ed Etnografia, Torino 25747
Museo di Antropologia ed Etnologia, Firenze 23864
Museo di Antropologia G. Sergi, Roma 25209
Museo di Apicoltura Guido Fregonese, Piavon di Oderze 24899
Museo di Archeologia, Pavia 24823
Museo di Archeologia Sacra e Profana, Roma 25210
Museo di Archeologia Urbana e dei Commerc Antichi, Lanciano 24135
Museo di Architettura, Ferrara 23792
Museo di Architettura Militare, Bologna 23125
Museo di Arte Cinese ed Etnografico, Parma 24805
Museo di Arte Contadina, Montegallo 24529
Museo di Arte Contemporanea, Stia 25634
Museo di Arte Contemporanea e del Novecento, Monsummano Terme 24487
Museo di Arte e Giacimenti Minerari, Latina 24159
Museo di Arte e Storia delle Miniere, Massa Marittima 24325
Museo di Arte e Tradizione Contadina, Olevano di Lomellina 24676
Museo di Arte Medioevale e Moderna, Arezzo 22921
Museo di Arte Moderna e Contemporanea di Trento e Rovereto, Rovereto 25293
Museo di Arte Religiosa, Oleggio 24675
Museo di Arte Sacra, Agnone 22811
Museo di Arte Sacra, Bientina 23083
Museo di Arte Sacra, Castrovillari 23442
Museo di Arte Sacra, Longiano 24211
Museo di Arte Sacra, Sabbioneta 25307
Museo di Arte Sacra, Saracena 25471
Museo di Arte Sacra, Suvereto 25662
Museo di Arte Sacra, Vibo Valentia 25988
Museo di Arte Sacra del Castello, Genga 23975
Museo di Arte Sacra Diocesano, Ripatransone 25125
Museo di Arte Sacra San Giuseppe, Rogliano 25145
Museo di Arti Decorative della Fondazione Pietro Accorsi, Torino 25748
Museo di Auto e Moto d'Epoca, Vigolzone 26011
Museo di Bevagna, Bevagna 23074
Museo di Biologia Marina, Fano 23763
Museo di Biologia Marina, Porto Cesareo 25012
Museo di Biologia Marina, Taranto 25673
Museo di Blenio, Lottigna 36892
Museo di Botanica, Firenze 23865
Museo di Capodimonte, Napoli 24589
Museo di Casa Vasari, Arezzo 22922
Museo di Castelgrande, Bellinzona 36530
Museo di Castelvecchio, Verona 25974
Museo di Chimica, Roma 25211
Museo di Cimeli Storico Militari, Chiaramonte Gulfi 23526
Museo di Civiltà Contadina, Castelnuovo Calcea 23419
Museo di Civiltà Preclassiche della Murgia Meridionale, Ostuni 24721
Museo di Collodi e Pinocchio, Pescia 24878
Museo di Criminologia Medievale, San Gimignano 25364
Museo di Criminologico, Roma 25212
Museo di Cultura Contadina, Oriolo 24690
Museo di Cultura Contadina dell'Alta Val Trebbia, Montebruno 24507
Museo di Cultura Popolare, Egna 23727
Museo di Dipinti Sacri Ponte dei Greci, Venezia 25936
Museo di Ecologia e Storia Naturale, Marano sul Panaro 24294
Museo di Etnografico e Antropologia Giovanni Podenzana, La Spezia 24124
Museo di Etnomedicina, Piazzola sul Brenta 24903
Museo di Etnomedicina A. Scarpa, Genova 23995
Museo di Etnopreistoria, Napoli 24590
Museo di Fisica, Bologna 23126
Museo di Fisica-Dipartimento di Scienze Fisiche, Napoli 24591
Museo di Fossili, Ronca 25276
Museo di Geologia, Camerino 23286
Museo di Geologia, Napoli 24592
Museo di Geologia, Roma 25213
Museo di Geologia e Paleontologia, Firenze 23866
Museo di Geologia e Paleontologia, Padova 24740
Museo di Geologia e Paleontologia, Pavia 24824
Museo di Geologia e Paleontologia, Torino 25749
Museo di Informatica e Storia del Calcolo, Pennabilli 24834
Museo di Leventina, Giornico 36761
Museo di Merceologia, Roma 25214
Museo di Milano, Milano 24399
Museo di Minerali e Fossili, Montefiore Conca 24522
Museo di Mineralogia, Massa Marittima 24326
Museo di Mineralogia, Palermo 24770
Museo di Mineralogia, Roma 25215
Museo di Mineralogia, di Petrologia e Geologia, Modena 24444
Museo di Mineralogia e Paleontologia, Finale Emilia 23817
Museo di Mineralogia e Paleontologia, Saint Vincent 25312
Museo di Mineralogia e Petrografia, Parma 24806
Museo di Mineralogia e Petrografia, Pavia 24825
Museo di Mineralogia e Petrografia L. Bombicci, Bologna 23127
Museo di Mineralogia e Petrologia, Padova 24741
Museo di Mineralogia L. De Prunner, Cagliari 23250
Museo di Muggia e del Territorio, Muggia 24569
Museo di Nostra Signora di Bonaria, Cagliari 23251
Museo di Palazzo Altieri, Oriolo Romano 24691
Museo di Palazzo d'Arco, Mantova 24288
Museo di Palazzo De Vio, Gaeta 23946
Museo di Palazzo della Penna, Perugia 24854
Museo di Palazzo Ducale, Mantova 24289
Museo di Palazzo Fortuny, Venezia 25937
Museo di Palazzo Gamilli, Nocera Umbra 24629
Museo di Palazzo Mirto, Palermo 24771
Museo di Palazzo Mocenigo, Venezia 25938
Museo di Palazzo Pepoli Campogrande, Bologna 23128
Museo di Palazzo Piccolomini, Pienza 24907
Museo di Palazzo Pretorio, Certaldo 23487
Museo di Palazzo Reale, Napoli 24593
Museo di Palazzo Reale Genova, Genova 23996
Museo di Palazzo Strozzi, Firenze 23867
Museo di Palazzo Vecchio, Firenze 23868
Museo di Paleobotanica ed Etnobotanica dell'Orto Botanico, Napoli 24594
Museo di Paleontologia, Milano 24400
Museo di Paleontologia, Modena 24445
Museo di Paleontologia, Napoli 24595
Museo di Paleontologia, Roma 25216
Museo di Paleontologia dell'Accademia Federiciana, Catania 23448
Museo di Paleontologia e di Mineralogia, Valdagno 25872
Museo di Paleontologia e Mineralogia, Campomorone 23310
Museo di Paleontologia e Paletnologia, Maglie 24261
Museo di Paleontologia e Speleologia E.A. Martel, Carbonia 23345
Museo di Paleontologia G. Buriani, San Benedetto del Tronto 25334
Museo di Paletnologia, Polignano a Mare 24979
Museo di Pantelleria, Pantelleria 24789
Museo di Peppone e Don Camillo, Brescello 23200
Museo di Pittura Murale, Prato 25048
Museo di Prali e della Val Germanasca, Prali 25034
Museo di Preistoria e del Mare, Trapani 25784
Museo di Preistoria e Protostoria della Valle del Fiume Fiora, Manciano 24275
Museo di Preistorico e Paleontologico, Sant'Anna d'Alfaedo 25454
Museo di Rievocazione Storica, Mondavio 24471
Museo di Rocca Fregoso, Sant'Agata Feltria 25447
Museo di Rodoretto, Prali 25035
Museo di Roma, Roma 25217
Museo di Roma in Trastevere, Roma 25218
Museo di San Domenico, Bologna 23129
Museo di San Francesco, Aversa 22991
Museo di San Francesco, Montella 24531
Museo di San Giuseppe, Bologna 23130
Museo di San Marco, Firenze 23869
Museo di San Mercuriale, Forlì 23912
Museo di San Michele, Sagrado 25309
Museo di San Petronio, Bologna 23131
Museo di San Pietro, Assisi 22966
Museo di Santa Cecilia, San Lazzaro di Savena 25378
Museo di Santa Chiara, Camerino 23287
Museo di Santa Maria degli Angioli, Lugano 36902
Museo di Santa Maria delle Grazie, San Giovanni Valdarno 25375
Museo di Santa Maria di Castello, Genova 23997
Museo di Santa Restituta, Lacco Ameno 24126
Museo di Sant'Agostino, Genova 23998
Museo di Sant'Antonino, Piacenza 24893
Museo di Santo Stefano, Bologna 23132
Museo di Scienza della Terra, San Gemini 25359
Museo di Scienza della Terra, Bari 23023
Museo di Scienze Archeologiche e d'Arte, Padova 24742
Museo di Scienze della Terra U. Baroli, Crodo 23687
Museo di Scienze Naturale e Umane, L'Aquila 24143
Museo di Scienze Naturali, Belvi 23051
Museo di Scienze Naturali, Bolzano 23155
Museo di Scienze Naturali, Brescia 23205
Museo di Scienze Naturali, Camerino 23288
Museo di Scienze Naturali, Cesena 23505
Museo di Scienze Naturali, Città della Pieve 23574
Museo di Scienze Naturali, Malnate 24269
Museo di Scienze Naturali, Pavia 24826
Museo di Scienze Naturali, Rosignano Marittimo 25285
Museo di Scienze Naturali del Collegio, Lodi 24203
Museo di Scienze Naturali Don Bosco, Alassio 22826
Museo di Scienze Naturali L. Paolucci, Offagna 24668
Museo di Scienze Naturali Tommaso Salvadori, Fermo 23779
Museo di Sculture Iperspaziali, Bomarzo 23157

Museo di Speleologia, Borgo Grotta Gigante 23171
Museo di Speleologia e Carsismo A. Parolini, Valstagna 25886
Museo di Speleologia Vincenzo Rivera, L'Aquila 24144
Museo di Stato, San Marino 33765
Museo di Storia Contemporanea, Milano 24401
Museo di Storia, d'Arte e d'Antichità Don Florindo Piolo, Serravalle Sesia 25551
Museo di Storia della Fisica, Padova 24743
Museo di Storia della Fotografia Fratelli Alinari, Firenze 23870
Museo di Storia della Medicina, Roma 25219
Museo di Storia dell'Agricoltura, Cesena 23506
Museo di Storia dell'Agricoltura, Urbania 25854
Museo di Storia dell'Agricoltura e della Pastorizia, Morano Calabro 24562
Museo di Storia delle Mezzadria, Senigallia 25536
Museo di Storia e Arte, Gorizia 24035
Museo di Storia e Civiltà, Medesano 24340
Museo di Storia e Cultura Contadina, Genova 23999
Museo di Storia e Cultura della Val del Biois, Vallada Agordina 25878
Museo di Storia Locale, Velturno 25908
Museo di Storia Naturale, Cremona 23681
Museo di Storia Naturale, Follonica 23901
Museo di Storia Naturale, Genova 24000
Museo di Storia Naturale, Macerata 24248
Museo di Storia Naturale, Merate 24356
Museo di Storia Naturale, Parma 24807
Museo di Storia Naturale, Parma 24808
Museo di Storia Naturale, Perugia 24855
Museo di Storia Naturale, Piacenza 24894
Museo di Storia Naturale, Senna Lodigiana 25539
Museo di Storia Naturale, Stroncone 25644
Museo di Storia Naturale, Sulmona 25648
Museo di Storia Naturale A. Orsini, Ascoli Piceno 22952
Museo di Storia Naturale A. Stoppani, Venegono Inferiore 25911
Museo di Storia Naturale Aquilegia, Assemini 22960
Museo di Storia Naturale del Cilento, Laureana Cilento 24162
Museo di Storia Naturale della Lunigiana, Aulla 22986
Museo di Storia Naturale della Maremma, Grosseto 24058
Museo di Storia Naturale dell'Accademia dei Fisocritici, Siena 25576
Museo di Storia Naturale Don Bosco, Torino 25750
Museo di Storia Naturale e del Territorio, Calci 23260
Museo di Storia Naturale e dell'Uomo, Carrara 23358
Museo di Storia Naturale Faraggiana-Ferrandi, Novara 24646
Museo di Storia Naturale S. Ferrari, Bedonia 23046
Museo di Storia Naturale - Sez Mineralogia, Firenze 23871
Museo di Storia Naturale - Sez Zoologica La Specola, Firenze 23872
Museo di Storia Naturali e Archeologia, Montebelluna 24505
Museo di Storia Quarnese, Quarna Sotto 25058
Museo di Strumenti del Conservatorio Statale di Musica Giuseppe Verdi, Torino 25751
Museo di Torcello, Venezia 25939
Museo di Tradizioni Popolari e del Costume d'Epoca, San Pietro Avellana 25407
Museo di Val Verzasca, Sonogno 37189
Museo di Vallemaggia, Giumaglio 36762
Museo di Valmaggia, Cevio 36619
Museo di Villa Beatice d'Este, Cinto Euganeo 23570
Museo di Villa Cagnola, Gazzada 23968
Museo di Villa Carlotta, Tremezzo 25789
Museo di Villa Faraggiana, Albissola Marina 22843
Museo di Vita Artigiana e Contadina, Scarperia 25521
Museo di Vita Cappuccina, Genova 24001
Museo di Vita Quotidiana e Lavoro in Villa, Orgiano 24684
Museo di Zoologia, Bari 23024
Museo di Zoologia, Bologna 23133
Museo di Zoologia, Modena 24446
Museo di Zoologia, Napoli 24596
Museo di Zoologia, Roma 25220
Museo di Zoologia e Mineralogia, Siddi 25567
Museo di Zoologia Pietro Doderlein, Palermo 24772
Museo di Zoologico, Catania 23449
Museo di Zoologico e di Anatomia, Torino 25752
Museo Diacesano, Enna 23734
Museo Diaz-Caneja de Arte Contemporaneo, Palencia 35215
Museo Didáctico Antonini, Nasca 31231
Museo Didáctico Artiguista, Maldonado 40981
Museo Didáctico de Prehistoria, Alba de Tormes 34417
Museo Didattico, Morimondo 24565
Museo Didattico, Niscemi 24623
Museo Didattico, Tivoli 25711
Museo Didattico Archeologico, Laterza 24154
Museo Didattico d'Arte e Vita Preistorica, Capo di Ponte 23327
Museo Didattico del Mare, Napoli 24597
Museo Didattico della Riserva Regionale Incisioni Rupestri, Ceto 23513
Museo Didattico della Scuola Medica Salernitana, Salerno 25320
Museo Didattico della Seta, Como 23628
Museo Didattico delle Maioliche, Grottaglie 24061
Museo Didattico Giuseppe Pellizza, Volpedo 26048
Museo Didattico Zoologico, Oria 24688
Museo Diefenbach, Capri 23335
Museo Diego Aragona Pignatelli Cortes, Napoli 24598
Museo Diego Rivera Anahuacalli, México 28164
Museo Diffuso, Pennabilli 24835
Museo Dillmann S. Bullock, Angol 06886
Museo d'Interesse Locale, Crespadoro 23684
Museo Diocesà, Tarragona 35511
Museo Diocesano, Acerenza 22795
Museo Diocesano, Agrigento 22818
Museo Diocesano, Albenga 22833
Museo Diocesano, Ancona 22883
Museo Diocesano, Andria 22888
Museo Diocesano, Ariano Irpino 22931
Museo Diocesano, Ascoli Piceno 22953
Museo Diocesano, Bari 23025
Museo Diocesano, Benevento 23054
Museo Diocesano, Bisceglie 23087
Museo Diocesano, Brugnato 23219
Museo Diocesano, Capua 23338
Museo Diocesano, Cassano allo Jonio 23381
Museo Diocesano, Castelvecchio Subequo 23427
Museo Diocesano, Catanzaro 23454
Museo Diocesano, Ciudad Real 34722
Museo Diocesano, Córdoba 34739
Museo Diocesano, Cortona 23664
Museo Diocesano, Empoli 23731
Museo Diocesano, Fermo 23780
Museo Diocesano, Gaeta 23947
Museo Diocesano, Gerace 24015
Museo Diocesano, Gubbio 24074
Museo Diocesano, Imola 24089
Museo Diocesano, Jaca 34920
Museo Diocesano, Jesi 24115
Museo Diocesano, Lamezia Terme 24132
Museo Diocesano, Lanciano 24136
Museo Diocesano, Lanusei 24138
Museo Diocesano, Lleida 34968
Museo Diocesano, Lugo 34986
Museo Diocesano, Mantova 24290
Museo Diocesano, Mazara del Vallo 24338
Museo Diocesano, Melfi 24346
Museo Diocesano, Milano 24402
Museo Diocesano, Nola 24631
Museo Diocesano, Osimo 24709
Museo Diocesano, Ourense 35199
Museo Diocesano, Palencia 35216
Museo Diocesano, Piazza Armerina 24900
Museo Diocesano, Pienza 24908
Museo Diocesano, Pistoia 24960
Museo Diocesano, Pitigliano 24964
Museo Diocesano, Pordenone 25009
Museo Diocesano, Recanati 25088
Museo Diocesano, Salamanca 35364
Museo Diocesano, Salerno 25321
Museo Diocesano, San Miniato 25400
Museo Diocesano, Santa Lucia del Mela 25432
Museo Diocesano, Sant'Agata de'Goti 25446
Museo Diocesano, Sarzana 25483
Museo Diocesano, Sassari 25486
Museo Diocesano, Spoleto 25625
Museo Diocesano, Squillace 25627
Museo Diocesano, Sulmona 25649
Museo Diocesano, Trani 25783
Museo Diocesano, Tudela 35579
Museo Diocesano, Urbania 25855
Museo Diocesano, Valle del Espíritu Santo 48968
Museo Diocesano, Vallo della Lucania 25882
Museo Diocesano, Velletri 25906
Museo Diocesano A. Bernareggi, Bergamo 23063
Museo Diocesano Albani, Urbino 25859
Museo Diocesano Antonio Bergamaschi, Pennabilli 24836
Museo Diocesano-Catedralicio, Astorga 34497
Museo Diocesano-Catedralicio, Barbastro 34530
Museo Diocesano-Catedralicio, Cuenca 34765
Museo Diocesano-Catedralicio, Ourense 35200
Museo Diocesano-Catedralicio, Segorbe 35458
Museo Diocesano-Catedralicio, Valladolid 35624
Museo Diocesano Catedralicio de Arte Sacro, Orihuela 35187
Museo Diocesano d'Arte Sacra, Alghero 22854
Museo Diocesano d'Arte Sacra, Brescia 23206
Museo Diocesano d'Arte Sacra, Caltanissetta 23276
Museo Diocesano d'Arte Sacra, Grosseto 24059
Museo Diocesano d'Arte Sacra, Nicotera 24621
Museo Diocesano d'Arte Sacra, Orte 24697
Museo Diocesano d'Arte Sacra, Pinerolo 24929
Museo Diocesano d'Arte Sacra, Piteglio 24962
Museo Diocesano d'Arte Sacra, Rossano 25288
Museo Diocesano d'Arte Sacra, Scaria 25519
Museo Diocesano d'Arte Sacra, Treviso 25807
Museo Diocesano d'Arte Sacra, Trivento 25836
Museo Diocesano d'Arte Sacra A. Luciani, Vittorio Veneto 26041
Museo Diocesano d'Arte Sacra Santa Apollonia, Venezia 25940
Museo Diocesano de Albarracín, Albarracín 34421
Museo Diocesano de Arte Antiguo, Sigüenza 35494
Museo Diocesano de Arte Religioso Nuestra Señora del Cisne, Loja 09186
Museo Diocesano de Arte Sacro, Bilbao 34614
Museo Diocesano de Arte Sacro, Moguer 35116
Museo Diocesano de Arte Sacro, Las Palmas de Gran Canaria 35241
Museo Diocesano de Arte Sacro, Teruel 35529
Museo Diocesano de Huesca, Huesca 34908
Museo Diocesano de San Sebastián, Donostia-San Sebastián 34777
Museo Diocesano della Basilica del Crocefisso, Amalfi 22871
Museo Diocesano dell'Arredo Sacro, Bertinoro 23069
Museo Diocesano di Arte Sacra, Chiavari 23531
Museo Diocesano di Arte Sacra, Genova 24002
Museo Diocesano di Arte Sacra, Lodi 24204
Museo Diocesano di Arte Sacra, Palermo 24773
Museo Diocesano di Arte Sacra, Santa Severina 25442
Museo Diocesano di Arte Sacra, Sarsina 25479
Museo Diocesano di Arte Sacra, Susa 25656
Museo Diocesano di Arte Sacra, Volterra 26051
Museo Diocesano di Arte Sacra del Duomo, Arezzo 22923
Museo Diocesano di Arte Sacra di Italo Bolano, Marina di Campo 24301
Museo Diocesano di Arte Sacra San Gregorio Barbarigo, Padova 24744
Museo Diocesano di Santo Stefano, Firenze 23873
Museo Diocesano e Catedralicio de Mondoñedo, Mondoñedo 35121
Museo Diocesano e Collezione dei Presepi, Bressanone 23211
Museo Diocesano e Gallerie del Tiepolo, Udine 25849
Museo Diocesano e Oratorio di San Bernardino, Siena 25577
Museo Diocesano e Tesoro della Cattedrale, Troia 25838
Museo Diocesano Inercomunale di Arte Sacra, Castignano 23437
Museo Diocesano Inercomunale di Arte Sacra, Rotella 25289
Museo Diocesano Intercomunale di Arte Sacra, Comunanza 23635
Museo Diocesano Intercomunale di Arte Sacra, Grottammare 24062
Museo Diocesano Intercomunale di Arte Sacra, Monteprandone 24537
Museo Diocesano Intercomunale di Arte Sacra, Ripatransone 25126
Museo Diocesano Lucas Guillermo Castillo, Falcón 48942
Museo Diocesano Regina Coeli, Santillana del Mar 35452
Museo Diocesano San Pietro, Teggiano 25681
Museo Diocesano Teatino, Chieti 23547
Museo Diocesano Tridentino, Trento 25794
Museo División del Norte, Canutillo 27805
Museo División del Norte, Lerdo 28060
Museo do Humor, Fene 34814
Museo do Mosteiro de San Paio de Antealtares, Santiago de Compostela 35447
Museo do Moucho, Cerceda 34705
Museo do Pobo Galego, Santiago de Compostela 35448
Museo Doctor Francia, Yaguarón 31108
Museo Documental, Guernica y Luno 34892
Museo Documentario della Città, Gradisca d'Isonzo 24042
Museo Doganale Svizzero, Gandria 36722
Museo Dolomythos di San Candido, San Candido 25343
Museo Dolores Olmedo Patiño, México 28165
Museo Domenicani, Taggia 25665
Museo Don Pio Palla, Leonessa 24178
Museo Doña Rosario, Santiago de Cuba 08146
Museo Donazione Luxoro, Genova 24003
Museo Donazione U. Mastroianni, Arpino 22941
Museo Donizettiano, Bergamo 23064
Museo Dr. Atl, Pihuamo 28311
Museo Dr. José Gómez Panaco, Balancán 27790
Museo Duca di Martina, Napoli 24599
Museo Ducati, Bologna 23134
Museo Dupré, Fiesole 23807
Museo e Archivio Capitolare, Assisi 22967
Museo E. Bernardi, Padova 24745
Museo e Biblioteca della Resistenza, Sansepolcro 25428
Museo e Centro Culturale Marco Scacchi, Gallese 23954
Museo e Certosa di San Martino, Napoli 24600
Museo e Chiostri Monumentali di Santa Maria Novella, Firenze 23874
Museo E. Galessi, Montevarchi 24551
Museo E. Leandro, San Cesario di Lecce 25347
Museo e Pinacoteca, Barletta 23032
Museo e Pinacoteca Civica, Alessandria 22849
Museo e Pinacoteca Civici, Vasto 25903
Museo e Pinacoteca Comunali, Gubbio 24075
Museo e Pinacoteca della Basilica di San Paolo, Roma 25221
Museo e Pinacoteca della Città, Todi 25714
Museo e Pinacoteca della Comunità di Fiemme, Cavalese 23460
Museo e Pinacoteca delle Arti Epizephiri, Locri 24200
Museo e Pinacoteca Diocesana, Camerino 23289
Museo e Pinacoteca Nazionale di Palazzo Mansi, Lucca 24230
Museo e Pinacoteca S. Gentili, San Ginesio 25368
Museo E. Renzi, Coriano 23652
Museo E. Treccani, Milano 24403
Museo e Villaggio Africano, Basella di Urgnano 23036
Museo Ebraica di Roma, Roma 25222
Museo Ebraico, Asti 22974
Museo Ebraico, Bologna 23135
Museo Ebraico, Ferrara 23793
Museo Ebraico, Firenze 23875
Museo Ebraico, Livorno 24192
Museo Ebraico, Merano 24354
Museo Ebraico, Soragna 25607
Museo Ebraico, Venezia 25941
Museo Ecclesiastico, Caorle 23321
Museo Ecuatoriano de Ciencias Naturales, Quito 09209
Museo Eduardo Carranza, Villavicencio 07626
Museo-Eerola, Tuulos 10140
Museo Efrain Martínez Zambrano, Popayán 07566
Museo Egipcio, Montevideo 41002
Museo Egizio, Torino 25753
Museo El Cañón, Puerto Boniato 08084
Museo El Castillo Diego Echavarría, Medellín 07517
Museo El Centenario, Garza García 27930
Museo El Chapulín, Saltillo 28369
Museo El Hombre y la Naturaleza, San Juan 00571
Museo El Hurón Azul, La Habana 07968
Museo El Jonotal, Playa Vicente, Veracruz 28313
Museo El Minero, Santa Bárbara 28429
Museo El Pariancito, San Luis Potosí 28404
Museo El Piñero, Nueva Gerona 08060
Museo El Polvorín, Monclova 28226
Museo El Reencuentro, Darregueira 00327
Museo El Remate, Comala 27845
Museo El Sol de las Botellas, Barcelona 48893
Museo Elder, Las Palmas de Gran Canaria 35242
Museo Elías Nandino, Cocula 27835
Museo Elisarion, Minusio 36941
Museo elle Arti e Tradizioni Contadine, Roccasecca dei Volsci 25142
Museo elle Genti delle Valli di Lanzo, Ceres 23479
Museo Emidiano, Agnone 22812
Museo Emilia Ortiz, Tepic 28498
Museo Emilio Greco, Catania 23450
Museo Emilio Greco, Orvieto 24705
Museo Enologico Grasso, Milazzo 24422
Museo Entomológco Mariposas del Mundo, San Miguel 00579
Museo Epper, Ascona 36471
Museo Erbario, Roma 25223
Museo Eritreo Bottego, Parma 24809
Museo Ermita de Santa Elena, Irún 34918
Museo Ernest Hemingway, San Francisco de Paula 08103
Museo Ernesto Laroche, Montevideo 41003
Museo Escolar Agrícola de Pusol, Elche 34792
Museo Escolar de Ciencias Naturales Carlos A. Merti, San Antonio de Areco 00548
Museo Escolar de Sitio de la Matamba, Jamapa 28027
Museo Escolar María Goretti, Pasto 07547
Museo Escolar y Comunitario de Acamalín, Xico 28620
Museo Escultórico de Geles Cabrera, México 28166
Museo Español de Arte Contemporaneo, Madrid 35036
Museo Específico de Ceuta, Ceuta 34711
Museo Específico de la Academia de Artillería, Segovia 35466
Museo Específico de la Academia de Caballería, Valladolid 35625
Museo Específico de la Academia de Ingenieros, Hoyo de Manzanares 34905
Museo Específico de la Academia General Militar, Zaragoza 35726
Museo Específico de la Brigada Paracaidista, Alcalá de Henares 34428
Museo Específico de la Legión, Ceuta 34712
Museo Estatal de Culturas Populares, Monterrey 28237
Museo Estatal de Patología, Puebla 28339
Museo Estudio Diego Rivera, México 28167
Museo Ethnográfico, Florencia 07479
Museo Ethnográfico de las Obras Misionales Pontificias, Buenos Aires 00204
Museo Ethnohistórico, Soatá 07594
Museo Etiopico G. Massaia, Frascati 23932
Museo Etnico-Agricolo-Pastorale ed Artigiano, Alcamo 22844
Museo Etnico Arbereshe, Civita 23591
Museo Étnico de los Seris, Hermosillo 27986
Museo Étnico de los Yaquis, Obregón 28282
Museo Etnico della Civiltà Salentina Agrilandi Museum, Brindisi 23213
Museo Etno-Antropologico, Calatafimi 23259
Museo Etno-Antropologico, San Cipirello 25349
Museo Etno-Antropologico, San Mauro Castelverde 25394
Museo Etno-Antropologico, Scaletta Zanclea 25515
Museo Etno-Antropologico della Terra di Zabut, Sambuca di Sicilia 25329
Museo Etno-Antropologico della Valle del Belice, Gibellina 24025
Museo Etno-Antropologico delle Madonie, Geraci Siculo 24017
Museo Etnobotánico, Tuluá 07608
Museo Etnográfico, Albán 07364
Museo Etnográfico, Alcubilla del Marqués 34438
Museo Etnografico, Aprica 22906
Museo Etnografico, Aritzo 22934
Museo Etnográfico, Arteta 34492
Museo Etnográfico, Atauta 34499
Museo Etnografico, Bomba 23158
Museo Etnográfico, Cajamarca 31129
Museo Etnográfico, Camporrobles 34664
Museo Etnográfico, Castrojeriz 34700
Museo Etnografico, Collinas 23616
Museo Etnografico, Faeto 23758
Museo Etnografico, Fossalta di Portogruaro 23924
Museo Etnografico, Fratta Polesine 23936
Museo Etnográfico, Grado 34862
Museo Etnográfico, Grandas de Salime 34882

Museo Etnográfico, Inzá 07500
Museo Etnografico, Lusevera 24244
Museo Etnográfico, Madruga 08023
Museo Etnografico, Malborghetto Valbruna 24266
Museo Etnografico, Montodine 24555
Museo Etnografico, Novalesa 24643
Museo Etnografico, Novara di Sicilia 24652
Museo Etnografico, Oneta 24679
Museo Etnografico, Ortonovo 24703
Museo Etnografico, Ossimo Superiore 24712
Museo Etnografico, Parma 24810
Museo Etnografico, Ponte in Valtellina 24990
Museo Etnográfico, Quintana Redonda 35306
Museo Etnografico, Roccalbegna 25139
Museo Etnográfico, Rollamienta 35334
Museo Etnográfico, Romanillos de Medinaceli 35335
Museo Etnográfico, Santa Lucía 08127
Museo Etnográfico, Schilpario 25525
Museo Etnográfico, Torreandaluz 35558
Museo Etnografico, Trebisacce 25787
Museo Etnográfico, Tuxtla Gutiérrez 28573
Museo Etnografico Africo, Bari 23026
Museo Etnográfico Andrés Barbero, Asunción 31102
Museo Etnografico Antico Mulino ad Acqua Licheri, Fluminimaggiore 23890
Museo Etnografico Archeologico, Palau 24757
Museo Etnografico Cerginolano, Cerignola 23482
Museo Etnografico Civiltà Contadina, Forlì 23913
Museo Etnografico Comunale, Premana 25052
Museo Etnografico Coumboscuro della Civiltà Provenzale in Italia, Sancto Lucìa de Coumboscuro 25422
Museo Etnográfico da Limia, Vilar de Santos 35669
Museo Etnográfico de Amurrio Felix Murga, Amurrio 34466
Museo Etnográfico de Azuaga de la Sierra y la Campiña, Azuaga 34515
Museo Etnográfico de Cantabria, Muriedas 35151
Museo Etnográfico de Colombia, Bogotá 07417
Museo Etnográfico de la Universidad de La Guajira, Riohacha 07576
Museo Etnográfico de los Valles de Campoo, Canduela 34669
Museo Etnográfico de Oyón-Oion, Oyón 35207
Museo Etnografico dei Cimbri, Selva di Progno 25532
Museo Etnografico del Cansiglio Servadei, Tambre 25669
Museo Etnografico del Carretto Siciliano, Terrasini 25701
Museo Etnografico del Cologio Nacional Mejía, Quito 09210
Museo Etnografico del Coumboscuro, Monterosso Grana 24544
Museo Etnografico del Ferro, Bienno 23082
Museo Etnografico del Pinerolese e Museo del Legno, Pinerolo 24930
Museo Etnografico del Ponente Ligure, Cervo 23495
Museo Etnográfico del Pueblo de Asturias, Gijón 34846
Museo Etnografico della Civiltà Contadina, Marianopoli 24300
Museo Etnografico della Cultura Contadina, Morigerati 24564
Museo Etnografico della Lunigiana, Villafranca in Lunigiana 26018
Museo Etnografico della Piana del Dragone, Volturara Irpina 26054
Museo Etnografico della Provincia die Belluno, Cesiomaggiore 23512
Museo Etnografico della Trinità, Botticino 23187
Museo Etnografico della Val Varatella, Toirano 25715
Museo Etnografico della Valle, Ultimo 25852
Museo Etnografico della Valle Brembana, Zogno 26058
Museo Etnografico dell'Alta Valle Seriana, Ardesio 22916
Museo Etnografico dell'Etna, Linguaglossa 24186
Museo Etnografico di Servola, Trieste 25828
Museo Etnografico di Sorrentini, Patti 24819
Museo Etnografico Don Luigi Pellegrini, Castiglione di Garfagnana 23435
Museo Etnográfico e da Historia de San Paio de Narla, San Paio de Narla-Friol 35387
Museo Etnografico e del Folklore Valsesiano, Borgosesia 23178
Museo Etnografico e della Cultura Materiale, Aquilonia 22909
Museo Etnografico e della Stregoneria, Triora 25835
Museo Etnografico e di Scienze Naturali, Torino 25754
Museo Etnografico e Tradizioni Contadine Borgo Antico, Torricella Sicura 25778
Museo Etnográfico Extremeño González Santana, Olivenza 35171
Museo Etnografico Francesco Bande, Sassari 25487
Museo Etnografico G. Carpani, Lizzano in Belvedere 24197
Museo Etnografico Galluras, Luras 24243
Museo Etnográfico Huichol Wixarica, Zapopan 28648
Museo Etnografico I Zuf, Vione 26027
Museo Etnografico Il Cicle della Vita, Quartu Sant'Elena 25060
Museo Etnográfico Juán B. Ambrosetti, Buenos Aires 00205
Museo Etnografico La Steiva, Piverone 24967
Museo Etnográfico Leones Ildefonso Fierro, León 34950
Museo Etnográfico Liste, Oseira 35194
Museo Etnográfico Madre Laura, Medellín 07518
Museo Etnográfico Miguel Angel Builes, Medellín 07519
Museo Etnográfico Municipal Dámaso Arce, Olavarría 00461
Museo Etnográfico Piedad Isla, Cervera de Pisuerga 34708
Museo Etnografico Romagnolo Benedetto Pergoli, Forlì 23914
Museo Etnográfico Rural, Valderrueda 35593
Museo Etnográfico Rural y Comarcal, Prioro 35296
Museo Etnografico San Domu de is Ainas, Armungia 22935
Museo Etnográfico Santa Rosa de Ocopa, Concepción 31149
Museo Etnografico Siciliano Giuseppe Pitrè, Palermo 24774
Museo Etnográfico Sotelo Blanco, Santiago de Compostela 35449
Museo Etnografico sulla Lavorazione del Legno, San Vito di Leguzzano 25421
Museo Etnográfico Textil Pérez Enciso, Plasencia 35273
Museo Etnografico Tiranese, Madonna di Tirano 24258
Museo Etnografico Tiranese, Tirano 25706
Museo Etnografico U. Ferrandi, Novara 24647
Museo Etnográfico Vallivo, Val Masino 25868
Museo Etnográfico y Archivo Histórico Enrique Squirru, Azul 00124
Museo Etnográfico y Colonial Juan de Garay, Santa Fé 00603
Museo Etnohistórico de Ayabacara, Ayabacara 31120
Museo Etnológico, Barca 34531
Museo Etnológico, Bejís 34595
Museo Etnológico, Bielsa 34608
Museo Etnológico, Boltaña 34621
Museo Etnológico, San Juan de Plan 35379
Museo Etnológico, Sechura 31250
Museo Etnológico Aljibes de Gasparito, Rojales 35333
Museo Etnológico Casa Mazo, Valle de Hecho 35636
Museo Etnológico de Amazonas, Puerto Ayacucho 48963
Museo Etnológico de la Diputación, Castellón de la Plana 34694
Museo Etnológico de Morella y del Meastrazgo, Morella 35141
Museo Etnológico de Navarra Julio Caro Baroja, Ayegui 34508
Museo Etnologico della Apuane, Massa 24315
Museo Etnológico Misional C.M.F., Santa Isabel 09314
Museo Etnologico Missionario, Castelnuovo Don Bosco 23422
Museo Etnológico Popular, Fuensanta 34828
Museo Etnolólogico Anselmo Buil, Blecua 34618
Museo Etnomusicale I Gigli di Nola, Nola 24632
Museo Etrusco, Asciano 22948
Museo Etrusco, Chiusi Città 23557
Museo Etrusco, San Gimignano 25365
Museo Etrusco Gasparri, Piombino 24938
Museo Etrusco Gasparri, Populonia 25006
Museo Etrusco M. Guarnacci, Volterra 26052
Museo Etrusco Ranuccio Bianchi Bandinelli, Colle di Val d'Elsa 23611
Museo Ettore Pomarici Santomasi, Gravina di Puglia 24050
Museo Evaristo Valle, Gijón 34847
Museo Evocativo y de Bellas Artes Osvaldo Gasparini, San Antonio de Areco 00549
Museo Ex Convento Agustino de San Pablo, Yuriria 28631
Museo Ex Convento Agustino Siglo XVI, México 28168
Museo Ex-Convento de San Juan Bautista, Tlayacapan 28538
Museo Ex Convento del Carmen, Guadalajara 27960
Museo Ex Hacienda San Gabriel de Barrera, Guanajuato 27975
Museo Ex Templo de San Agustín, Zacatecas 28636
Museo Ex Voto di Santa Maria della Portella, Cervara di Roma 23489
Museo Ex Votos Sr. de la Misericordia, Tepatitlán de Morelos 28486
Museo Exposición El Hombre, Bogotá 07418
Museo Extremeño e Iberoamericano de Arte Contemporáneo, Badajoz 34519
Museo F. Assetto, Frontino 23937
Museo F. Renzi, Borghi 23167
Museo F. Renzi, San Giovanni in Galilea 25371
Museo F.A. Marcucci, Ascoli Piceno 22954
Museo Fallero, Valencia 35606
Museo Farallón Dillon, Ballenita 09140
Museo Farmacéutico, Matanzas 08039
Museo Farmacobotánica, Buenos Aires 00206
Museo Faryluk, Aristóbulo del Valle 00118
Museo Felisa Rincón de Gautier, San Juan 32401
Museo Félix de Jesús, México 28169
Museo Fernán Félix de Amador, Luján 00417
Museo Fernando García, Canelones 40976
Museo Ferrocarrilero, Empalme 27910
Museo Ferrovario, Trieste 25829
Museo Ferroviario, Alcázar de San Juan 34431
Museo Ferroviario, Cuneo 23697
Museo Ferroviario, Tacna 31256
Museo Ferroviario de Gualeguaychú, Gualeguaychú 00362
Museo Ferroviario del Verbano, Luino 24242
Museo Ferroviario Piemontese, Savigliano 25500
Museo Ferroviaro, Bogotá 07419
Museo Ferrucciano, Gavinana 23965
Museo Ferrucciano, San Marcello Pistoiese 25385
Museo Filatélico del Banco de la República, Medellín 07520
Museo Filemón Gutiérrez Ramírez, Ameca 27771
Museo Filipe Santiago Gutiérrez, Toluca 28549
Museo Fin de la Tierra, Francisco I. Madero, Coahuila 27926
Museo Finca El Abra, Siguanea 08157
Museo Fiorentino di Preistoria, Firenze 23876
Museo Fioroni, Legnago 24173
Museo Fittile, Ripatransone 25127
Museo Florencio de la Fuente, Huete 34910
Museo Florencio Molina Campos, Moreno 00454
Museo Florentino Ameghino, Bolívar 00141
Museo Folklórico, La Rioja 00399
Museo Folklórico Araucano de Cañete Juan A. Ríos M., Cañete 06890
Museo Folklórico Provincial, San Miguel de Tucumán 00585
Museo Folklórico Regional de Humahuaca, Humahuaca 00365
Museo Fomento Cultural Banamex, México 28170
Museo Fondazione C. Faina e Museo Civico Palazzo Faina, Orvieto 24706
Museo Fondazione Famiglia Piccolo di Calanovella, Capo d'Orlando 23329
Museo-Fondazione P. Conti, Fiesole 23808
Museo Forestal de la Policía Ecológica, Jesús María 31190
Museo Forestale C. Siemoni, Poppi 25004
Museo Fortaleza de San Carlos de la Cabaña, La Habana 07969
Museo Fotográfico, Calarcá 07443
Museo Fotográfico de Nanchital, Nanchital de Lázaro Cárdenas del Río 28261
Museo Fournier de Naipes de Alava, Vitoria-Gasteiz 35702
Museo Fragua Martiana, La Habana 07970
Museo Francescano, Roma 25224
Museo Francescano Padre Aurelio Menin, Chiampo 23521
Museo Francescano - Raccolta d'Arte, Gubbio 24076
Museo Francesco Borgogna, Vercelli 25960
Museo Francesco Cilea, Palmi 24787
Museo Francisco Campos, Guayaquil 09173
Museo Francisco Goitia, Zacatecas 28637
Museo Francisco Huerta Rendón en la Casona Universitaria, Guayaquil 09174
Museo Francisco Javier Sauza, Tequila 28505
Museo Francisco José de Caldas, Bogotá 07420
El Museo Francisco Oller y Diego Rivera, Buffalo 41988
Museo Francisco Sarabia, Lerdo 28061
Museo Franco Azzinari, Altomonte 22865
Museo Franco Lázaro, Chiapa de Corzo 27819
Museo Franz Mayer, México 28171
Museo Fray Bernardo Padilla, Acámbaro 27743
Museo Frey Pedro Bedón, Ibarra 09182
Museo Frida Kahlo, México 28172
Museo Frissel de Arte Zapoteca, Santa Ana del Valle 28428
Museo Friulano di Storia Naturale, Udine 25850
Museo Fuentes de Loreto y Guadelupe, Palmar de Bravo 28300
Museo Fuerte Conde de Mirasol de Vieques, Vieques 32412
Museo Fuerte de la Loma, Victoria de las Tunas 08170
Museo Fuerte Independencia, Tandil 00629
Museo Fundación Estero Beach, Ensenada 27917
Museo Fundación Naum Komp, Buenos Aires 00207
Museo G. Arcucci, Ariano Irpino 22932
Museo G. Filangieri, San Potito Sannitico 25408
Museo G. Manzù, Ardea 22915
Museo G. Marconi, Pontecchio Marconi 24996
Museo G. Scarabelli, Imola 24090
Museo G. Spontini, Maiolati Spontini 24263
Museo G. Whitaker, Marsala 24307
Museo Gabriel García Márquez, Aracataca 07367
Museo Gabriel Mateus, Sabanagrande 07580
Museo Gabriela Mistral de Vicuña, Vicuña 06929
Museo Galego do Xoguete, Allariz 34449
Museo Galería Manuel Lepe, Puerto Vallarta 28350
Museo Galleria di Villa Borghese, Roma 25225
Museo Garibaldino, Caprera 23332
Museo Garibaldino, Genova 24004
Museo Garibaldino della Campagna dell'Agro Romano per la Liberazione di Roma 1867, Mentana 24349
Museo Gauchesco Ricardo Güiraldes, San Antonio de Areco 00550
Museo G.B. Filippa, Rimella 25113
Museo G.D. Cassini, Perinaldo 24843
Museo Gemológico, Bogotá 07421
Museo General, Yanahuanca 31269
Museo General Belgrano, Buenos Aires 00208
Museo General de Arequito, Arequito 00117
Museo General Francisco Villa, San Juan del Río 28394
Museo General Ignacio Zaragoza, Puebla 28340
Museo General Lavalle, General Pinto 00356
Museo General Porfirio Rubio, Landa de Matamoros 28051
Museo Geo-Paleontologico, Ferrara 23794
Museo Geográfico Einstein, San Juan 00572
Museo Geologico, Castell'Arquato 23407
Museo Geológico, Laspaules 34940
Museo Geológico de la Universidad Nacional de Ingeniería del Perú, Lima 31219
Museo Geológico del Seminario, Barcelona 34548
Museo Geológico del Uruguay, Montevideo 41004
Museo Geologico e Paleontologico G. Capellini, Bologna 23136
Museo Geologico G.G. Gemmellaro, Palermo 24775
Museo Geológico José Royo y Gómez, Bogotá 07422
Museo Geológico Marino Arce Herrera, Bucaramanga 07439
Museo Geológico Petrolero, Neiva 07534
Museo Geominero, Madrid 35037
Museo Geopaleontologico Alto Aventino, Arielli 22933
Museo Geopaleontologico Cava Bomba, Cinto Euganeo 23571
Museo Geopaleontologico dei Fossili della Lessinia, Velo Veronese 25907
Museo Geopaleontologico del Castello, Lerici 24179
Museo Geopaleontologico Naturalistico Antropico e Ornitologico Brancaleoni, Piobbico 24934
Museo Germán Guglielmetti, Benito Juárez 00139
Museo Gianmaria da Tusa, Cefalù 23467
Museo Giannettino Luxoro, Genova 24005
Museo Gianni Visentin, Carpané di San Nazario 23351
Museo Giovanni Antonio Sanna, Sassari 25488
Museo Giovanni Boldini, Ferrara 23795
Museo Gli Orsanti, Compiano 23633
Museo Gonzalo Carrasco, Otumba 28291
Museo Gráfico de la Mujer Guerrenese, Chilpancingo 27829
Museo Gran Casino, Bayamo 07860
Museo Gran Mariscal de Ayacucho, Cumaná 48938
Museo Gregoriano Egizio, Città del Vaticano 48874
Museo Gregoriano Etrusco, Città del Vaticano 48875
Museo Gregoriano Profano, Città del Vaticano 48876
Museo Gregorio Aguilar Barea, Chontales 30320
Museo Gregorio Prieto, Valdepeñas 35591
Museo Guillermo Perez Chiriboga del Banco Central, Quito 09211
Museo Guillermo Spratling, Taxco de Alarcón 28461
Museo Gustavo de Maeztu, Estella 34807
Museo Hacienda San Pedro, General Zuazua 27934
Museo Hans Multscher e Museo Civico, Vipiteno 26028
Museo Hendrik Christian Andersen, Roma 25226
Museo Herbario de la Facultad de Ciencias, México 28173
Museo Hermanas Giralt, Cienfuegos 07891
Museo Hermann Hesse, Montagnola 36944
Museo Hermanos López Rayón, Tlalpujahua 28525
Museo Hermanos Nacif Weiss, Rivadavia 00522
Museo Hermenegildo Galeana, Tecpan de Galeana 28470
Museo Hermila Domínguez de Castellanos, Comitán de Domínguez 27850
Museo Hidalgo, Salamanca 28364
Museo Hidráulico del Sistema de Drenaje Profundo, México 28174
Museo Hidráulico los Molinos del Río Segura, Murcia 35148
Museo Historia de las Ciencias Carlos J. Finlay, La Habana 07971
Museo Historia del Ferrocarril de Antioquia, Medellín 07521
Museo Historia Municipal, Antilla 07851
Museo Historiador Hernández Galiano, Tostado 00638
Museo Histórica Ex Convento de Tepoztlán, Tepoztlán 28503
Museo Histórico, El Carmen de Bolívar 07472
Museo Histórico, Pinar del Río 08073
Museo Histórico, Riobamba 09224
Museo Historico, San Antonio de los Baños 08099
Museo Histórico, Zapala 00676
Museo Histórico Andrés Avelino Cáceres, Ayacucho 31122
Museo Histórico Andrés Avelino Cáceres, Huamanga 31165
Museo Histórico Anton García de Bonilla, Ocaña 07537
Museo Histórico Arqueológico, A Coruña 34753
Museo Histórico Arqueológico Guillermo Magrassi, Mar del Plata 00426
Museo Histórico, Arqueológico y de Arte Pedro Balduín, San Pedro de Jujuy 00593
Museo Histórico Bae Calderon, Guayaquil 09175
Museo Histórico BBVA, Bilbao 34615
Museo Histórico Casa de la Convención de Rionegro, Rionegro 07578
Museo Historico Casa de los Tratados, Cuenca 09161
Museo Histórico, Colonial y de Bellas Artes y Museo de Ciencias Naturales Regional Mesopotámico, Mercedes 00443
Museo Histórico Comunal, Villa Trinidad 00674
Museo Histórico Comunal de San Genaro Norte, San Genaro Norte 00562
Museo Histórico Comunal y de la Colonización Judía Rabino Aaron H. Goldman, Moisés Ville 00451
Museo Histórico Conventual San Carlos, San Lorenzo 00576
Museo Histórico Cultural Juan Santamaría, Alajuela 07648
Museo Histórico de 26 de Julio, Santiago de Cuba 08147
Museo Histórico de Acapulco, Acapulco 27747
Museo Histórico de Antioquia, Medellín 07522
Museo Histórico de Arenaza, Arenaza 00116
Museo Histórico de Arrecifes, Arrecifes 00120
Museo Histórico de Arte, Morón 00456
Museo Histórico de Ayotzinapa, Tixtla de Guerrero 28517
Museo Histórico de Cañuelas, Cañuelas 00260

Museo Histórico de Cartagena Casa de la Inquisición, Cartagena 07457
Museo Histórico de Cera, Buenos Aires 00209
Museo Histórico de Chacamarka, Chacamarka 31140
Museo Historico de Ciego de Avila, Ciego de Avila 07887
Museo Histórico de Corrientes Manuel Cabral de Mayo y Alpoín, Corrientes 00322
Museo Histórico de Entre Ríos Martiniano Leguizamón, Paraná 00468
Museo Histórico de Guachinango, Guachinango 27938
Museo Histórico de Guatraché, Guatraché 00363
Museo Histórico de la Casa de la Cultura, Ambalema 07366
Museo Histórico de la Ciudad, Torreón 28557
Museo Histórico de la Ciudad, Valencia 35607
Museo Histórico de la Ciudad de Buenos Aires Brigadier-General Cornelio de Saavedra, Buenos Aires 00210
Museo Histórico de la Colonia San Carlos, San Carlos Centro 00553
Museo Histórico de la Dirección General Impositiva, Buenos Aires 00211
Museo Histórico de la Educación Tecnológica en México, Chilpancingo 27830
Museo Histórico de la Honorable Cámara de Diputados de la Nación, Buenos Aires 00212
Museo Histórico de la Iglesia, Buenos Aires 00213
Museo Histórico de la Policía de la Provincia de Misiones, Posadas 00483
Museo Histórico de la Policía National, Bogotá 07423
Museo Histórico de la Prefectura Naval Argentina, Tigre 00633
Museo Histórico de la Provincia, Santiago del Estero 00617
Museo Histórico de la Provincia de Catamarca, San Fernando del Valle de Catamarca 00557
Museo Histórico de la Revolución Mexicana, Chihuahua 27827
Museo Histórico de La Rioja, La Rioja 00400
Museo Histórico de la Sierra Gorda, Jalpan 28025
Museo Histórico de Laborde, Laborde 00401
Museo Histórico de Múzquiz, Múzquiz 28259
Museo Histórico de Navarro, Navarro 00457
Museo Histórico de Osorno, Osorno 06901
Museo Histórico de Palma Soriano, Palma Soriano 08064
Museo Histórico de Ranchos, Ranchos 00501
Museo Histórico de Requena y su Comarca, Requena 35311
Museo Histórico de Reynosa, Reynosa 28357
Museo Histórico de San Francisco, Santa Fé 00604
Museo Histórico de San Miguel de Allende, San Miguel de Allende 28410
Museo Histórico de San Nicolás de los Garza, San Nicolás de los Garza 28415
Museo Historico del Norte, Salta 00541
Museo Histórico del Oriente de Morelos, Cuautla 27870
Museo Histórico del Regimiento de Granaderos a Caballo General San Martín, Buenos Aires 00214
Museo Histórico del Transporte Carlos Hillner Decoud, Quilmes 00494
Museo Historico Dr. Rafael Angel Calderón Guardia, San José 07660
Museo Histórico Etnológico, Llosa de Ranes 34978
Museo Histórico Ex Aduana de Ciudad Juárez, Juárez 28039
Museo Histórico Ferroviario Escribano Alfredo Rueda, Rueda 00534
Museo Histórico Franciscano, San Salvador de Jujuy 00596
Museo Histórico Fuerte Barragan, Ensenada 00341
Museo Histórico Fuerte de San José el Alto, Campeche 27799
Museo Histórico General Julio de Vedia, 9 de Julio 00106
Museo Histórico Hipólito Unanue, Ayacucho 31123
Museo Histórico José Hernández-Chacra Pueyrredón, Villa Ballester 00660
Museo Histórico Judío y del Holocausto Tuvie Maizel, México 28175
Museo Histórico La Casona de Santa Rosa, Liberia 07650
Museo Histórico La Gallareta Forestal, La Gallareta 00381
Museo Histórico Local, Cañete de las Torres 34671
Museo Histórico Local, Fuente Tojar 34830
Museo Histórico Local, Montoro 35139
Museo Histórico Manuel A. Moreira, Laboulaye 00402
Museo Histórico Mexicano de Cananea, Cananea 27802
Museo Histórico Militar, Asunción 31103
Museo Histórico Militar Real Felipe, Callao 31133
Museo Histórico Minero Don Felipe de Borbón y Grecia, Madrid 35038
Museo Historico Municipal, Bahía Blanca 00127
Museo Histórico Municipal, Cádiz 34649
Museo Histórico Municipal, Ocotlán 28286
Museo Histórico Municipal, Salto 41038
Museo Histórico Municipal, San Fernando 35373
Museo Histórico Municipal, Taxco de Alarcón 28462
Museo Histórico Municipal Alfredo E. Múlgura, General Belgrano 00353
Museo Histórico Municipal Andrés A. Roverano, Santo Tomé 00621
Museo Histórico Municipal Brigadier General Juan Martín de Pueyrredón, San Isidro 00565
Museo Histórico Municipal de Armstrong, Armstrong 00119
Museo Histórico Municipal de Cañada de Gómez, Cañada de Gómez 00259
Museo Histórico Municipal de Écija, Ecija 34783
Museo Histórico Municipal de Guanabacoa, Guanabaoa 07913
Museo Histórico Municipal de Luque, Luque 00420
Museo Histórico Municipal de Pergamino, Pergamino 00472
Museo Histórico Municipal de Regla, Regla 08089
Museo Histórico Municipal de Villa Gesell, Villa Gesell 00669
Museo Histórico Municipal General Levalle, General Levalle 00354
Museo Histórico Municipal Guillermo Zegarra Meneses, Arequipa 31115
Museo Histórico Municipal Hércules J. Rabagliati, Ramallo 00500
Museo Histórico Municipal Juan Lavalle, Baradero 00134
Museo Histórico Municipal La Para, La Para 00382
Museo Histórico Municipal Monte Grande, Monte Grande 00453
Museo Histórico Municipal Víctor E. Míguez, Mercedes 00444
Museo Histórico Municipal Villa Clara, Villa Clara 00663
Museo Histórico Municipal Villa del Rosario, Villa del Rosario 00666
Museo Histórico Municipal y Colección de Arte Precolombino Arminio Weiss, Rafaela 00498
Museo Historico Munipal, Montilla 35137
Museo Histórico Nacional, Buenos Aires 00215
Museo Histórico Nacional, Santiago de Chile 06915
Museo Histórico Nacional Casa del Virrey Liniers, Alta Gracia 00111
Museo Histórico Nacional del Cabildo de Buenos Aires y de la Revolucion de Mayo, Buenos Aires 00216
Museo Histórico Nacional Luis A. de Herrera, Montevideo 41005
Museo Histórico Naval, Cienfuegos 07892
Museo Histórico Naval Central, México 28176
Museo Histórico Policial de La Plata, La Plata 00393
Museo Historico Provincial, Cienfuegos 07893
Museo Histórico Provincial, Sancti-Spíritus 08112
Museo Histórico Provincial Agustín V. Gnecco, San Juan 00573
Museo Histórico Provincial Brig. Estanislao López, Santa Fé 00605
Museo Histórico Provincial Colonel Manuel José Olascoaga, Chos Malal 00278
Museo Histórico Provincial de Guantánamo, Guantánamo 07917
Museo Histórico Provincial de Rosario Dr. Julio Marc, Rosario 00528
Museo Histórico Provincial Marqués de Sobremonte, Córdoba 00302
Museo Histórico Regional, Alpachiri 00110
Museo Histórico Regional, Gualeguay 00359
Museo Histórico Regional - Casa Garcilaso Cusco, Cusco 31159
Museo Histórico Regional de Ayacucho, Ayacucho 00123
Museo Histórico Regional de Gaiman, Gaiman 00351
Museo Histórico Regional de la Colonia San José, San José 00567
Museo Histórico Regional De la Isla, Isla del Cerrito 00368
Museo Histórico Regional de Magallanes, Punta Arenas 06904
Museo Histórico Regional de Río Cuarto, Río Cuarto 00511
Museo Histórico Regional de Tacna, Tacna 31257
Museo Histórico Regional de Urdinarrain, Urdinarrain 00648
Museo Histórico Regional de Villa La Angostura, Villa La Angostura 00670
Museo Histórico Regional Ex Cuartel de la Compañía Fija, Ensenada 27918
Museo Histórico Regional Gabriel Campomar Cervera, Salliqueló 00536
Museo Histórico Regional Ichoalay, Resistencia 00509
Museo Histórico Regional Municipal de Magdalena, Magdalena 00421
Museo Histórico Regional Pablo Argilaga, Santo Tomé 00622
Museo Histórico Regional Padre Francisco Cremasco, Villa Concepción del Tío 00664
Museo Histórico San Ignacio de Loyola, San José 00568
Museo Histórico Sanmartíniano, Mendoza 00438
Museo Histórico Sarmiento, Buenos Aires 00217
Museo Histórico y Antropológico de la Universidad Austral de Chile, Valdivia 06925
Museo Histórico y Arqueológico, Belén de Umbría 07380
Museo Histórico y Arqueológico, Charalá 07462
Museo Histórico y de la Tradiciones Populares de la Boca, Buenos Aires 00218
Museo Histórico y Natural de Lavalle, Lavalle Villa Tulumaya 00406
Museo Histórico y Regional Pico Truncado, Pico Truncado 00475
Museo Histórico y Tradicional de Barracas al Sud, Avellaneda 00121
Museo Históricos del Banco de la Provincia de Buenos Aires, Buenos Aires 00219
Museo Hotel Marquetá, Mariquita 07512
Museo Houssay de Historia de la Ciencia y Técnologia, Buenos Aires 00220
Museo Huehuetla-tolli, Comala 27846
Museo Hunucmá de Sisal, Hunucmá 28008
Museo I Luoghi del Lavoro Contadino, Buscemi 23232
Museo I. Mormino, Palermo 24776
Museo I. Nievo, Fossalta di Portogruaro 23925
Museo I. Salvini, Cocquio Trevisago 23602
Museo Iberoamericano de Arte Moderno de Popayán, Popayán 07567
Museo Ibleo delle Arti e Tradizioni Popolari S.A. Guastella, Modica 24452
Museo Iconográfico, Itaugua 31107
Museo Iconográfico del Quijote, Guanajuato 27976
Museo Ideale Leonardo Da Vinci, Vinci 26025
Museo Iglesia del Salvador, Oña 35175
Museo Ignacio Zuloaga, Pedraza de la Sierra 35259
Museo Igneológico del Cuerpo Ofical de Bomberos, Bogotá 07424
Museo Il Giardino dell'Arte, Portoferraio 25018
Museo Illichiano, Castell'Arquato 23408
Museo Iloilo, Iloilo 31329
Museo Immaginario, Domodossola 23720
Museo in Erba, Bellinzona 36531
Museo In Situ, Sulmona 25650
Museo Inca de la Universidad Nacional San Antonio Abad, Cusco 31160
Museo Independencia, Córdoba 00303
Museo Indiano, Bologna 23137
Museo Indígena de Colombia Ethnia, Bogotá 07425
Museo Indígena de Guatavita, Guatavita 07492
Museo Indígena Regional Enin, Mitú 07525
Museo Indigenista, Esquel 00346
Museo Indigeno, San José 07661
Museo Industrial de Santa Catarina El Blanqueo, Santa Catarina 28430
Museo Inés Mercedes Gómez Álvarez, Guanare 48944
Museo Instituto Cultural México Israel, México 28177
Museo Insular de la Palma, Santa Cruz de la Palma 35411
Museo Inter-étnico de la Amazonía, Florencia 07480
Museo Interactivo de Ciencia, Tecnología y Medio Ambiente Sol del Niño, Mexicali 28090
Museo Interactivo de Ciencias, Granada 34879
Museo Interactivo de Ciencias, Paraná 00469
Museo Interactivo de Ciencias Naturales, Ituzaingó 00370
Museo Interactivo del Centro de Ciencias de Sinaloa, Culiacán 27885
Museo Interactivo del Medio Ambiente, México 28178
Museo Interactivo El Rehilete, Pachuca 28296
Museo Interactivo La Avispa, Chilpancingo 27831
Museo Interattivo delle Scienze, Foggia 23894
Museo Internacional de Arte Contemporáneo, Arrecife 34487
Museo Internacional de Arte Naïf, Jaén 34925
Museo Internazionale del Folklore e Civiltà Contadina, Atina 22979
Museo Internazionale del Presepio, Morrovalle 24567
Museo Internazionale della Campana, Agnone 22813
Museo Internazionale della Caricatura, Tolentino 25721
Museo Internazionale della Croce Rossa, Castiglione delle Stiviere 23433
Museo Internazionale della Fisarmonica, Castelfidardo 23395
Museo Internazionale delle Ceramiche, Faenza 23754
Museo Internazionale delle Marionette A. Pasqualino, Palermo 24777
Museo Internazionale dell'Etichetta, Cupramontana 23701
Museo Internazionale dell'Immagine Postale, Belvedere Ostrense 23050
Museo Internazionale di Burattini e Marionette, L'Aquila 24145
Museo Interparroquial de Alaejos, Alaejos 34416
Museo Irineo Germán, Azoyú 27787
Museo Irpino, Avellino 22989
Museo Irureta, Tilcara 00636
Museo Isabel Rubio, Isabel Rubio 08010
Museo Isidro Fabela, Atlacomulco 27782
Museo It Akean, Kalibo 31335
Museo Italgas, Torino 25755
Museo Italiano della Ghisa, Longiano 24212
Museo Italoamericano, San Francisco 47327
Museo Ittico, Pescara 24869
Museo Ittico Augusto Capriotti, San Benedetto del Tronto 25335
Museo Ixchel del Traje Indigena, Guatemala 21270
Museo Jacinto Higueras, Santisteban del Puerto 35455
Museo Jacinto Jijón y Caamaño, Quito 09212
Museo Jacobo Borges, Caracas 48925
Museo Jarocho Salvador Ferrando, Tlacotalpan 28520
Museo Jesuítico de Sitio, Yapeyú 00675
Museo Jesuitico Nacional de Jesus María, Córdoba 00304
Museo Jesútico Nacional de Jesús María, Jesús María 00371
Museo J.M. Cruxent, Los Teques 48949
Museo Jorge Eliécer Gaitán, Puerto Gaitán 07570
Museo Jorge Pasquini López, San Salvador de Jujuy 00597
Museo José Antonio Páez, Acarigua 48886
Museo José Celso Barbosa, Bazamón 32365
Museo José de Jesús Almaza, Xicoténcatl 28621
Museo José Fernando Ramírez, Durango 27900
Museo José Guadalupe Posada, Aguascalientes 27758
Museo José Luis Cuevas, Colima 27837
Museo José Luis Cuevas, México 28179
Museo José Manuel Estrada, Suipacha 00625
Museo José María Luis Mora, Ocoyoacac 28287
Museo José María Morelos y Pavón, Cuautla 27871
Museo José María Velasco, Toluca 28550
Museo José Martí, La Habana 07972
Museo José Natividad Correa Toca Teapa, Teapa 28464
Museo José Serra Farré, La Riba 35316
Museo José y Tomás Chávez Morado, Silao 28445
Museo Jovellanos, Gijón 34848
Museo Juan Carlos Iramaín, San Miguel de Tucumán 00586
Museo Juan Lorenzo Lucero, Pasto 07548
Museo Juan Manuel Blanes, Montevideo 41006
Museo Juan Pablo Duarte, Santo Domingo 09126
Museo Juan Zorrilla de San Martín, Montevideo 41007
Museo Juárez del Jardín Borda, Cuernavaca 27875
Museo Juárez e Historia de Mapimí y Ojuela, Mapimí 28070
Museo Juarista de Congregación Hidalgo, Entronque Congregación Hidalgo 27919
Museo Jubanguana, Santa Fe de la Janguana 07584
Museo Judío de Buenos Aires Dr. Salvador Kibrick, Buenos Aires 00221
Museo Julio Romero de Torres, Córdoba 34740
Museo Kan Pepen, Teabo 28463
Museo Kartell, Noviglio 24658
Museo Ken Damy di Fotografia Contemporanea, Brescia 23207
Museo L. Ceselli, Subiaco 25646
Museo L. Garaventa, Chiavari 23532
Museo L. Minguzzi, Milano 24404
Museo la Antigua Casa del Agua, Hunucmá 28009
Museo La Casa del Libro, San Juan 32402
Museo La Chole, Petatlán 28309
Museo La Cinacina, San Antonio de Areco 00551
Museo La Flor de Jimulco, Torreón 28558
Museo La Fudina, Comelico Superiore 23625
Museo La Isabelica, Santiago de Cuba 08148
Museo La Pesca, Benito Juárez 27791
Museo La Vieja Estación, María Teresa 00430
Museo La Vigía, Matanzas 08040
Museo-Laboratorio, Vernio 25963
Museo Laboratorio del Tessile, Soveria Mannelli 25613
Museo Laboratorio di Archeologia, Monsampolo del Tronto 24483
Museo Laboratorio di Arte Contemporanea, Roma 25227
Museo Ladino di Fassa, Pozza di Fassa 25032
Museo Ladino-Fodom, Livinallongo del Col di Lana 24189
Museo Laguna del Caimán, Tlahualilo de Zaragoza 28522
Museo Lapidario, Ferrara 23796
Museo Lapidario, Urbino 25860
Museo Lapidario del Duomo, Novara 24648
Museo Lapidario del Duomo di Sant' Eufemia, Grado 24043
Museo Lapidario e del Tesoro del Duomo, Modena 24447
Museo Lapidario Estense, Modena 24448
Museo Lapidario Maffeiano, Verona 25975
Museo Lapidario Marsicano, Avezzano 22993
Museo Lara, Ronda 35340
El Museo Latino, Omaha 46150
Museo Lázaro Galdiano, Madrid 35039
Museo Legislativo los Sentimientos de la Nación, México 28180
Museo Leonardiano, Vinci 26026
Museo Leoniano, Carpineto Romano 23356
Museo Lítico de Pukara, Pukara 31243
Museo Local de Acámbaro, Dolores Hidalgo 27893
Museo Local de Antropología e Historia de Compostela, Compostela 27853
Museo Local de Valle de Santiago, Valle de Santiago 28585
Museo Local Tuxteco, Santiago Tuxtla 28441
Museo Locale, Termeno 25690
Museo Lodovico Pogliaghi, Varese 25897
Museo Lombardo di Storia dell'Agricoltura, Sant'Angelo Lodigiano 25452
Museo López Claro, Santa Fé 00606
Museo Lorenzo Coullaut-Valera, Marchena 35090
Museo Loringiano, Málaga 35074
Museo Los Amantes de Sumpa, Guayaquil 09176
Museo Luciano Rosero, Pasto 07549
Museo Lucio Balderas Márquez, Landa de Matamoros 28052
Museo Luigi Varoli, Cotignola 23673
Museo Luis A. Calvo, Agua de Dios 07360
Museo Luis Alberto Acuña, Villa de Leyva 07621
Museo Luis Donaldo Colosio, Francisco I. Madero, Coahuila 27927
Museo M. Antonioni, Ferrara 23797
Museo Maestro Alfonso Zambrano, Pasto 07550
Museo Malacologico, Erice 23741
Museo Malacologico delle Argille, Cutrofiano 23706
Museo Malacologico Piceno, Cupra Marittima 23700
Museo Malvinas Argentinas, Río Gallegos 00515
Museo Manuel de Falla, Alta Gracia 00112
Museo Manuel Ojinaga, Manuel Ojinaga 28068
Museo Manuela Sáenz, Quito 09213
Museo Manzoniano, Lesa 24180
Museo Manzoniano, Milano 24405
Museo Marceliano Santa María, Burgos 34634

Museo Marcelo López del Instituto Hellen Keller, Córdoba 00305
Museo Marcha del Pueblo Combatiente, La Habana 07973
Museo Marchigiano del Risorgimento G. e D. Spadoni, Macerata 24249
Museo Marciano, Venezia 25942
Museo Marcos Redondo, Pozoblanco 35290
Museo María Augusta Urrutia, Quito 09214
Museo Mariano, La Habana 07974
Museo Mariano Acosta, Ibarra 09183
Museo Mariano Matamoros, Jantetelco 28028
Museo Maridiaz, Pasto 07551
Museo Marinaro Tommasino-Andreatta, San Colombano Certenoli 25351
Museo Marino d'Arte Sacra Contemporanea, Comacchio 23623
Museo Marino de Tecolutla, Tecolutla 28468
Museo Marino Marini, Firenze 23877
Museo Marino Marini, Milano 24406
Museo Marino Marini, Pistoia 24961
Museo Mario Abreu, Maracay 48954
Museo Mario Praz, Roma 25228
Museo Marítimo de Asturias, Luanco 34984
Museo Marítimo de Ushuaia y Presidio, Ushuaia 00650
Museo Marítimo del Cantábrico, Santander 35432
Museo Marítimo-Ecológico Malvín, Montevideo 41008
Museo Marítimo Torre del Oro, Sevilla 35488
Museo Marítimo y Naval de la Patagonia Austral, Río Gallegos 00516
Museo Marsiliano, Bologna 23138
Museo Martín Gusinde, Puerto Williams 06903
Museo Martin Perez, Montevideo 41009
Museo Martínez de Compañon, Tambogrande 31258
Museo Martini di Storia dell'Enologia, Chieri 23539
Museo Martini di Storia dell'Enologia, Pessione 24882
Museo Mascagnano, Livorno 24193
Museo Maschera, Folklore e Civiltà Contadina, Acerra 22796
Museo Massó, Bueu 34625
Museo Maurice Minkowski, Buenos Aires 00222
Museo Máximo Gómez, La Habana 07975
Museo Medardo Burbano, Pasto 07552
Museo Medardo Rosso, Barzio 23035
Museo Mediceo della Petraia e Giardino, Firenze 23878
Museo Melezet, Bardonecchia 23016
Museo Melia Cayo Coco y Museo Tryp Colonial, Cayo Coco 07884
Museo Memoria Coronel Leoncio Prado, Callao 31134
Museo Memorial 12 de Septiembre, La Habana 07976
Museo Memorial 26 de Julio, Victoria de las Tunas 08171
Museo Memorial Antonio Guiteras Holmes, Pinar del Río 08074
Museo Memorial El Morrillo, Matanzas 08041
Museo Memorial Ernesto Che Guevara, Santa Clara 08122
Museo Memorial José Martí, La Habana 07977
Museo Memorial La Demajagua, Manzanillo 08032
Museo Memorial Los Malagones, Moncada 08050
Museo Memorial Mártires de Barbados, Victoria de las Tunas 08172
Museo Memorial Vicente García, Victoria de las Tunas 08173
Museo Memorias de Yucundé, San Pedro y San Pablo Teposcolula 28424
Museo Memorie Pollentine, Pollenza 24981
Museo Mercantile, Bolzano 23156
Museo Mercedes Sierra de Pérez El Chico, Bogotá 07426
Museo Meteorológico Nacional Dr. Benjamín A. Gould, Córdoba 00306
Museo Metropolitano, Buenos Aires 00223
Museo Metropolitano de Monterrey, Monterrey 28238
Museo Mexitlán, Tijuana 28513
Museo Michelangelo, Caprese 23333
Museo Michoacano de las Artesanías, Morelia 28252
Museo Miguel Álvarez del Toro, Tuxtla Gutiérrez 28574
Museo Militar de Colombia, Bogotá 07427
Museo Militar de Menorca, Es Castell 34689
Museo Militar Regional, A Coruña 34754
Museo Militar Regional, Palma de Mallorca 35231
Museo Militar Regional de Burgos, Burgos 34635
Museo Militar Regional de Canarias, Santa Cruz de Tenerife 35415
Museo Militar Regional de Sevilla, San Fernando 35374
Museo Mille Voci e Mille Suoni, Bologna 23139
Museo Mineralogico, Bortigiadas 23181
Museo Mineralogico, La Paz 03898
Museo Mineralogico, Valle Aurina 25880
Museo Mineralógico, Valverde del Camino 35640
Museo Mineralogico Campano, Vico Equense 26001
Museo Mineralogico e Naturalistico, Bormio 23180
Museo Mineralogico e Paleontologico delle Zolfare, Caltanissetta 23277
Museo Mineralogico Permanente, Carro 23362
Museo Mineralógico Prof. Manuel Tellechea, Mendoza 00439
Museo Mineralógico Salón Tulio Ospina, Medellín 07523
Museo Mineralogico Sardo, Iglesias 24082
Museo Mineralógico y Antropológico, Ibagué 07498
Museo Minerario Alpino, Cogne 23607
Museo Minero, Gallarta 34834
Museo Minero, La Unión 35587
Museo Minero de la Comarca de Riotinto, Riotinto 35323
Museo Minero Ferrería de San Blas, Sabero 35349
Museo Minimo, Corigliano Calabro 23653
Museo Miniscalchi Erizzo, Verona 25976
Museo Mirador de Quistococha, Iquitos 31186
Museo Miscellaneo Galbiati, Brugherio 23218
Museo Misional de Nuestra Señora de Regla, Chipiona 34715
Museo Missionario, Loreto 24214
Museo Missionario, Padova 24746
Museo Missionario Cinese e di Storia Naturale, Lecce 24165
Museo Missionario delle Grazie, Rimini 25118
Museo Missionario Etnologico, Città del Vaticano 48877
Museo Missionario Francescano, Fiesole 23809
Museo Mitre, Buenos Aires 00224
Museo Moesano, San Vittore 37098
Museo Mohicca, Mohicca 28223
Museo Molino Nant Fach, Trevelin 00644
Museo Molino Papelero de Capellades, Capellades 34674
Museo Monasterio Santa María La Real de Vileña, Villarcayo 35682
Museo Monográfico Aquis Querquernis, Bande 34526
Museo Monográfico Celsa. Centro de Investigación, Velilla de Ebro 35643
Museo Monográfico de Clunia, Peñalba de Castro 35262
Museo Monográfico de la Alcudia, Elche 34793
Museo Monográfico de la Villa Romana de la Olmeda, Saldaña 35366
Museo Monográfico de Tiermes, Montejo de Tiermes 35133
Museo Monográfico del Azafrán, Monreal del Campo 35128
Museo Monográfico del Castro de Viladonga, Castro de Rei 34698
Museo Monográfico del Cigarralejo, Mula 35143
Museo Monográfico y Necrópolis Púnica de Puig des Molins, Eivissa 34787
Museo Mons Juan Sinforiano Bogarin, Asunción 31104
Museo Monseñor José Fagnano, Río Grande 00519
Museo Montemartini, Roma 25229
Museo Monumento al Deportato, Carpi 23355
Museo Morandi - Collezioni Comunali d'Arte, Bologna 23140
Museo Morando Bolognini, Sant'Angelo Lodigiano 25453
Museo Morelos, Carácuaro 27806
Museo Multidisciplinario del Colegio La Salle, Lima 31220
Museo Mundocaña, Cali 07451
Museo Mundocaña, Palmira 07540
Museo Municipal, Alcázar de San Juan 34432
Museo Municipal, Algeciras 34445
Museo Municipal, Alzira 34460
Museo Municipal, Amposta 34463
Museo Municipal, Antequera 34468
Museo Municipal, Aroche 34486
Museo Municipal, Ayllón 34509
Museo Municipal, Cabra 34639
Museo Municipal, Calatayud 34654
Museo Municipal, Carmona 34681
Museo Municipal, Ciego de Avila 07888
Museo Municipal, Consuegra 34733
Museo Municipal, Forcall 34822
Museo Municipal, Holguín 08008
Museo Municipal, Iquitos 31187
Museo Municipal, Jérica 34929
Museo Municipal, Medina de Rioseco 35103
Museo Municipal, Melilla 35108
Museo Municipal, Mier 28216
Museo Municipal, Nerva 35159
Museo Municipal, Orce 35181
Museo Municipal, Ourense 35201
Museo Municipal, Palma del Río 35237
Museo Municipal, Pavias 35258
Museo Municipal, Pizarra 35272
Museo Municipal, Ponteareas 35282
Museo Municipal, El Puerto de Santa María 35301
Museo Municipal, Reus 35313
Museo Municipal, Sancti-Spíritus 08113
Museo Municipal, Tárrega 35517
Museo Municipal, Valdepeñas 35592
Museo Municipal, Vélez-Málaga 35641
Museo Municipal, Zuheros 35737
Museo Municipal Alex Urquiola, El Salvador 08095
Museo Municipal Barão de Santo Angelo, Rio Pardo 04409
Museo Municipal Cabildo de Montevideo, Montevideo 41010
Museo Municipal Carmen Funes, Plaza Huincul 00479
Museo Municipal Casa de Alfaro, Montecristi 09189
Museo Municipal C.I.P.A.S., Salto 00545
Museo Municipal de 10 de Octubre, La Habana 07978
Museo Municipal de Abreus, Abreus 07846
Museo Municipal de Aguada de Pasajeros, Aguada de Pasajeros 07847
Museo Municipal de Alto Songo y La Maya, Alto Songo 07848
Museo Municipal de Amancio, Amancio 07850
Museo Municipal de Arqueología y Etnología, Segorbe 35459
Museo Municipal de Arqueología y Etnología, La Vila Joiosa 35656
Museo Municipal de Arte, Rauch 00502
Museo Municipal de Arte Angel María de Rosa, Junín 00373
Museo Municipal de Arte Decorativo Firma y Odilo Estévez, Rosario 00529
Museo Municipal de Arte Juan Carlos Castagnino, Mar del Plata 00427
Museo Municipal de Arte Moderno, Cuenca 09162
Museo Municipal de Arte Moderno de Mendoza, Mendoza 00440
Museo Municipal de Artes Plásticas, Avellaneda 00122
Museo Municipal de Artes Plásticas, Olavarría 00462
Museo Municipal de Artes Plásticas, Rivera 41036
Museo Municipal de Artes Plásticas Pompeo Boggio, Chivilcoy 00277
Museo Municipal de Artes Visuales, Concordia 00288
Museo Municipal de Artes Visuales, Quilmes 00495
Museo Municipal de Artes Visuales, Santa Fé 00607
Museo Municipal de Arucas, Arucas 34493
Museo Municipal de Báguano, Báguano 07852
Museo Municipal de Bahía Honda, Bahía Honda 07853
Museo Municipal de Baraguá, Baraguá 07856
Museo Municipal de Bartolomé Masó, Bartolomé Masó 07857
Museo Municipal de Bayamo, Bayamo 07861
Museo Municipal de Bellas Artes, Bahía Blanca 00128
Museo Municipal de Bellas Artes, Godoy Cruz 00357
Museo Municipal de Bellas Artes, La Calera 00375
Museo Municipal de Bellas Artes, La Paz 00383
Museo Municipal de Bellas Artes, Pergamino 00473
Museo Municipal de Bellas Artes, San Nicolás de los Arroyos 00591
Museo Municipal de Bellas Artes, Santa Cruz de Tenerife 35416
Museo Municipal de Bellas Artes, Tandil 00630
Museo Municipal de Bellas Artes, Xàtiva 35705
Museo Municipal de Bellas Artes de Campana, Campana 00258
Museo Municipal de Bellas Artes de Valparaíso, Valparaíso 06928
Museo Municipal de Bellas Artes Dr. Genaro Perez, Córdoba 00307
Museo Municipal de Bellas Artes Dr. Genaro Pérez, Río Cuarto 00512
Museo Municipal de Bellas Artes Dr. Urbano Poggi, Rafaela 00499
Museo Municipal de Bellas Artes Juan B. Castagnino, Rosario 00530
Museo Municipal de Bellas Artes Juan Manuel Blanes, Montevideo 41011
Museo Municipal de Bellas Artes Lucas Braulio Areco, Posadas 00484
Museo Municipal de Bellas Artes Prof. Amelio Ronco Ceruti, Metán 00446
Museo Municipal de Bolivia, Bolivia 07865
Museo Municipal de Boyeros, La Habana 07979
Museo Municipal de Buey Arriba, Buey Arriba 07866
Museo Municipal de Cabaiguán, Cabaiguán 07867
Museo Municipal de Cabana, Cabana 31124
Museo Municipal de Cacomun, Cacomun 07868
Museo Municipal de Caibarién, Caibarién 07869
Museo Municipal de Caimanera, Caimanera 07870
Museo Municipal de Calahorra, Calahorra 34650
Museo Municipal de Calasparra, Calasparra 34652
Museo Municipal de Calimete, Calimete 07872
Museo Municipal de Camajuaní Hermanos Vidal Caro, Camajuaní 07878
Museo Municipal de Campechuela, Campechuela 07879
Museo Municipal de Candelaria, Candelaria 07880
Museo Municipal de Carlos Manuel de Céspedes, Carlos Manuel de Céspedes 07882
Museo Municipal de Cauto Cristo, Cauto Cristo 07883
Museo Municipal de Cerámica, Paterna 35257
Museo Municipal de Chambas, Chambas 07885
Museo Municipal de Chincha, Chincha Alta 31143
Museo Municipal de Ciencias, Bahía Blanca 00129
Museo Municipal de Ciencias Naturales, El Real de la Jara 35309
Museo Municipal de Ciencias Naturales Carlos Ameghino, Mercedes 00445
Museo Municipal de Ciencias Naturales Carlos Darwin, Punta Alta 00493
Museo Municipal de Ciencias Naturales Lorenzo Scaglia, Mar del Plata 00428
Museo Municipal de Cifuentes, Cifuentes 07894
Museo Municipal de Ciro Redondo, Ciro Redondo 07895
Museo Municipal de Colón José R. Zulueta, Colón 07897
Museo Municipal de Consolación del Sur, Consolación del Sur 07898
Museo Municipal de Contramaestre, Contramaestre 07899
Museo Municipal de Corralillo, Corralillo 07900
Museo Municipal de Cruces, Cruces 07901
Museo Municipal de Cueto, Cueto 07903
Museo Municipal de Cumanayagua, Cumanayagua 07904
Museo Municipal de El Trébol, El Trébol 00336
Museo Municipal de Eldorado, Eldorado 00338
Museo Municipal de Esmeralda, Esmeralda 07905
Museo Municipal de Etnografía, Villadiego 35675
Museo Municipal de Etnología, Castellón de la Plana 34695
Museo Municipal de Florencia, Florencia 07906
Museo Municipal de Florida, Florida 07907
Museo Municipal de Fomento, Fomento 07908
Museo Municipal de Gibara, Gibara 07911
Museo Municipal de Guamá, La Plata 08080
Museo Municipal de Guane, Guane 07914
Museo Municipal de Guantánamo - Antigua Cárcel, Guantánamo 07918
Museo Municipal de Guayaquil, Guayaquil 09177
Museo Municipal de Guisa, Guisa 07919
Museo Municipal de Habana del Este, La Habana 07980
Museo Municipal de Historia, Necolí 07532
Museo Municipal de Historia del Arte, Montevideo 41012
Museo Municipal de Historia Malitzín de Huiloapan, Huiloapan de Cuauhtémoc 28004
Museo Municipal de Historia Natural, General Alvear 00352
Museo Municipal de Historia Natural, San Rafael 00594
Museo Municipal de Historia y Arqueología, González 27937
Museo Municipal de Historia y Arqueología, Rivera 41037
Museo Municipal de Huaytará, Huaytará 31178
Museo Municipal de Imías, Playitas y Cajobabo, Cajobabo 07871
Museo Municipal de Jagüey Grande, Jagüey Grande 08012
Museo Municipal de Jesús Menéndez, Jesús Menéndez 08015
Museo Municipal de Jiguaní, Jiguaní 08016
Museo Municipal de Jovellanos Domingo Mujica, Jovellanos 08019
Museo Municipal de la Ciudad de Carcarañá, Carcarañá 00262
Museo Municipal de la Ciudad de Rosario, Rosario 00531
Museo Municipal de la Ciudadela, Ciudadela de Menorca 34725
Museo Municipal de la Construcción, Montevideo 41013
Museo Municipal de la Lisa, La Habana 07981
Museo Municipal de La Sierpe, La Sierpe 08156
Museo Municipal de La Yaya, La Yaya 08182
Museo Municipal de Lajas, Lajas 08020
Museo Municipal de Lomas de Zamora, Lomas de Zamora 00410
Museo Municipal de Los Arabos Clotilde García, Los Arabos 08021
Museo Municipal de Los Palacios, Los Palacios 08022
Museo Municipal de Madrid, Madrid 35040
Museo Municipal de Maisí, Maisí 08024
Museo Municipal de Majagua, Majagua 08025
Museo Municipal de Majibacoa, Majibacoa 08026
Museo Municipal de Manatí Jesús Suárez Gayol, Manatí 08027
Museo Municipal de Manicaragua, Manicaragua 08028
Museo Municipal de Mantua, Mantua 08029
Museo Municipal de Manuel Tames, Manuel Tames 08030
Museo Municipal de Manzanillo, Manzanillo 08033
Museo Municipal de Marianao, La Habana 07982
Museo Municipal de Martí, Martí 08034
Museo Municipal de Mayarí, Mayarí 08044
Museo Municipal de Media Luna, Media Luna 08046
Museo Municipal de Minas, Minas 08047
Museo Municipal de Minas de Matahambre, Minas de Matahambre 08048
Museo Municipal de Moa, Moa 08049
Museo Municipal de Morón, Morón 08051
Museo Municipal de Najasa, Sibanicú 08154
Museo Municipal de Nazca y Casa Museo María Reiche, Nazca 31232
Museo Municipal de Niceto Pérez, Niceto Pérez 08052
Museo Municipal de Niquero, Niquero 08053
Museo Municipal de Nuevitas, Nuevitas 08063
Museo Municipal de Palma Soriano, Palma Soriano 08065
Museo Municipal de Pedro Betancourt, Pedro Betancourt 08067
Museo Municipal de Perico, Perico 08068
Museo Municipal de Pilón, Pilón 08069
Museo Municipal de Pintura, Villadiego 35676
Museo Municipal de Placetas, Placetas 08079
Museo Municipal de Poblado de Jimaguayú, Jimaguayú 08017
Museo Municipal de Porteña, Porteña 00480
Museo Municipal de Prehistoria, Gandía 34836
Museo Municipal de Primero de Enero, Primero de Enero 08082
Museo Municipal de Quemado de Güines, Quemado de Güines 08086
Museo Municipal de Rafael Freyre, Rafael Freyre 08087
Museo Municipal de Ranchuelo, Ranchuelo 08088
Museo Municipal de Río Cauto, Río Cauto 08091
Museo Municipal de Rodas, Rodas 08092
Museo Municipal de Sagua de Tánamo, Sagua de Tánamo 08093
Museo Municipal de Sagua la Grande, Sagua la Grande 08094
Museo Municipal de San Cristobal, San Cristobal 08102
Museo Municipal de San Juan y Martínez, San Juan y Martínez 08104
Museo Municipal de San Luis 29 de Abril, San Luis 08105

Museo Municipal de San Miguel del Padrón, La Habana 07983
Museo Municipal de San Telmo, Donostia-San Sebastián 34778
Museo Municipal de Sandino, Sandino 08116
Museo Municipal de Santa Cruz del Sur, Santa Cruz del Sur 08126
Museo Municipal de Santo Domingo, Santo Domingo 08153
Museo Municipal de Sibanicú, Sibanicú 08155
Museo Municipal de Sierra de Cubitas, Cubitas 07902
Museo Municipal de Taguasco, Taguasco 08158
Museo Municipal de Trinidad, Trinidad 08162
Museo Municipal de Unión de Reyes Juan G. Gómez, Unión de Reyes 08164
Museo Municipal de Urbano Noris, Urbano Noris 08165
Museo Municipal de Varadero, Varadero 08166
Museo Municipal de Vedado, La Habana 07984
Museo Municipal de Venezuela, Venezuela 08167
Museo Municipal de Vertientes, Vertientes 08168
Museo Municipal de Vigo Quiñones de León, Vigo 35655
Museo Municipal de Viñales Adela Azcuy Labrador, Pinar del Río 08075
Museo Municipal de Yaguajay, Yaguajay 08179
Museo Municipal de Yara, Yara 08180
Museo Municipal de Yateras, Yateras 08181
Museo Municipal del Cerro, La Habana 07985
Museo Municipal del Deporte, San Fernando del Valle de Catamarca 00558
Museo Municipal del III Frente, Santiago de Cuba 08149
Museo Municipal Dr. Rodolfo Doval Fermi, Sastre 00623
Museo Municipal Dreyer, Dreyer 31162
Museo Municipal Eduard Camps Cava, Guissona 34895
Museo Municipal Elisa Cendrero, Ciudad Real 34723
Museo Municipal Emilio Daudinot, San Antonio del Sur 08100
Museo Municipal Etnológico de la Huerta, Alcantarilla 34429
Museo Municipal Fernando García Grave de Peralta, Puerto Padre 08085
Museo Municipal Forte de San Damián, Ribadeo 35319
Museo Municipal Francisco Javier Balmaseda, Santa Clara 08123
Museo Municipal Histórico Fotográfico de Quilmes, Quilmes 00496
Museo Municipal Histórico Regional Almirante Brown, Bernal 00140
Museo Municipal Histórico Regional Santiago Lischetti, Villa Constitución 00665
Museo Municipal Ignacio Balvidares, Puan 00487
Museo Municipal IV Centenario, Pinos 28312
Museo Municipal Jatibonico, Jatibonico 08014
Museo Municipal Jerónimo Molina, Jumilla 34932
Museo Municipal Jesús González Herrera, Matamoros 28074
Museo Municipal Jesús H. Salgado, Teloloapan 28476
Museo Municipal José A. Mulazzi, Tres Arroyos 00641
Museo Municipal José Manuel Maciel, Coronda 00315
Museo Municipal José Reyes Meza, Altamira 27768
Museo Municipal Juan M. Ameijeiras, El Salvador 08096
Museo Municipal Lino Enea Spilimbergo, Unquillo 00647
Museo Municipal Los Guachimontones y Museo de Arquitectura Prehispánica, Teuchitlán 28506
Museo Municipal Manuel Torres, Marín 35092
Museo Municipal Mariano Benlliure, Crevillente 34759
Museo Municipal Mateo Hernández, Béjar 34594
Museo Municipal Nueva Gerona, Nueva Gerona 08061
Museo Municipal Paula Florido, 25 de Mayo 00105
Museo Municipal Precolombino y Colonial, Montevideo 41014
Museo Municipal Primeros Pobladores, San Martín de los Andes 00578
Museo Municipal Punta Hermengo, Miramar 00450
Museo Municipal Quetzalpapalotl, Teotihuacán 28483
Museo Municipal Ramón María Aller Ulloa, Lalín 34939
Museo Municipal Roberto Rojas Tamayo, Colombia 07896
Museo Municipal Rosendo Arteaga, Jobabo Dos 08018
Museo Municipal Sala Dámaso Navarro, Petrer 35269
Museo Municipal Taurino, Córdoba 34741
Museo Municipal Ulpiano Checa, Colmenar de Oreja 34729
Museo Municipal Victorio Macho, Palencia 35217
Museo Municpal Dr. Santos F. Tosticarelli, Casilda 00268
Museo Mural Diego Rivera, México 28181
Museo Mural Homenaje a Benito Juárez, México 28182
Museo Muratoriano, Modena 24449
Museo Musicale d'Abruzzo, Ortona 24700
Museo Na-Bolom, San Cristóbal de las Casas 28382
Museo Nacional Casa Guillermo Valencia, Popayán 07568
Museo Nacional Centro de Arte Reina Sofía, Madrid 35041
Museo Nacional David J. Guzmán, San Salvador 09313
Museo Nacional de Aeronáutica, Buenos Aires 00225
Museo Nacional de Agricultura, Texcoco de Mora 28508
Museo Nacional de Antropología, Bogotá 07428
Museo Nacional de Antropología, Madrid 35042
Museo Nacional de Antropología, México 28183
Museo Nacional de Antropología, Montevideo 41015
Museo Nacional de Antropología, Arqueología e Historia del Perú, Lima 31221
Museo Nacional de Arqueología, La Paz 03899
Museo Nacional de Arqueología Marítima, Cartagena 34685
Museo Nacional de Arqueología y Etnología, Guatemala 21271
Museo Nacional de Arquitectura, Madrid 35043
Museo Nacional de Arquitectura, México 28184
Museo Nacional de Arte, La Paz 03900
Museo Nacional de Arte, México 28185
Museo Nacional de Arte Decorativo, Buenos Aires 00226
Museo Nacional de Arte Fantástico, Córdoba 27858
Museo Nacional de Arte Hispanomusulmán, Granada 34880
Museo Nacional de Arte Moderno, Guatemala 21272
Museo Nacional de Arte Oriental, Buenos Aires 00227
Museo Nacional de Arte Popular, Mérida 28084
Museo Nacional de Arte Romano, Mérida 35110
Museo Nacional de Artes Decorativas, La Habana 07986
Museo Nacional de Artes Decorativas, Madrid 35044
Museo Nacional de Artes Decorativas de Santa Clara, Santa Clara 08124
Museo Nacional de Artes e Industrias Populares, México 28186
Museo Nacional de Artes Visuales, Montevideo 41016
Museo Nacional de Bellas Artes, Buenos Aires 00228
Museo Nacional de Bellas Artes, La Habana 07987
Museo Nacional de Bellas Artes, Montevideo 41017
Museo Nacional de Bellas Artes de Santiago de Chile, Santiago de Chile 06916
Museo Nacional de Bellas Artes y Antigüedades, Asunción 31105
Museo Nacional de Camilo Cienfuegos, Sancti-Spíritus 08114
Museo Nacional de Caza, Riofrío 35321
Museo Nacional de Cerámica y de las Artes Suntuarias González Martí, Valencia 35608
Museo Nacional de Ciencias Naturales, Madrid 35045
Museo Nacional de Colombia, Bogotá 07429
Museo Nacional de Costa Rica, San José 07662
Museo Nacional de Culturas Populares, México 28187
Museo Nacional de Escultura, Valladolid 35626
Museo Nacional de Etnografía y Folklore, La Paz 03901
Museo Nacional de Ferrocarriles Mexicanos, Puebla 28341
Museo Nacional de Historia, Guatemala 21273
Museo Nacional de Historia, México 28188
Museo Nacional de Historia Colonial, Omoa 21300
Museo Nacional de Historia de la Medicina Eduardo Estrella, Quito 09215
Museo Nacional de Historia Natural, La Habana 07988
Museo Nacional de Historia Natural, Santiago de Chile 06917
Museo Nacional de Historia Natural y Antropología, Montevideo 41018
Museo Nacional de la Acuarela, México 28189
Museo Nacional de la Alfabetización, La Habana 07989
Museo Nacional de la Cerámica, La Habana 07990
Museo Nacional de la Cerámica, Tonalá, Jalisco 28553
Museo Nacional de la Ciencia y la Tecnología, Madrid 35046
Museo Nacional de la Cultura Peruana, Lima 31222
Museo Nacional de la Dirección Regional del Banco Central del Ecuador, Quito 09216
Museo Nacional de la Estampa, México 28190
Museo Nacional de la Histórico del Traje, Buenos Aires 00229
Museo Nacional de la Máscara, San Luis Potosí 28405
Museo Nacional de la Música, La Habana 07991
Museo Nacional de la Revolución, México 28191
Museo Nacional de las Culturas, México 28192
Museo Nacional de las Intervenciones, México 28193
Museo Nacional de las Telecomunicaciones, Bogotá 07430
Museo Nacional de los Ferrocarriles Mexicanos, México 28194
Museo Nacional de Nicaragua, Managua 30322
Museo Nacional de Panamá, Panamá City 31088
Museo Nacional de Reproducciones Artísticas, Madrid 35047
Museo Nacional de San Carlos, México 28195
Museo Nacional de Virreinato, Tepotzotlán 28500
Museo Nacional del Cobre, Salvador Escalante 28373
Museo Nacional del Grabado, Buenos Aires 00230
Museo Nacional del Hombre, Buenos Aires 00231
Museo Nacional del Ministerio del Interior, La Habana 07992
Museo Nacional del Petróleo, Comodoro Rivadavia 00282
Museo Nacional del Petróleo Samuel Schneider Uribe, Barrancabermeja 07376
Museo Nacional del Prado, Madrid 35048
Museo Nacional del Sombrero, Aguadas 07362
Museo Nacional del Títere, Huamantla 27994
Museo Nacional Justo José de Urquiza, Concepción del Uruguay 00285
Museo Nacional Mariano, Chiquinquira 07463
Museo Nacional Tihuanacu, La Paz 03902
Museo Nacional y Centro de Estudios Históricos Ferroviarios, Buenos Aires 00232
Museo Nacional y Centro de Investigación de Altamira, Santillana del Mar 35453
Museo Nacional y Zoológico La Aurora, Guatemala 21274
Museo Nahim Isaias, Guayaquil 09178
Museo Nájerillense, Nájera 35154
Museo Napoleónico, La Habana 07993
Museo Napoleonico, Rivoli Veronese 25132
Museo Napoleonico, Roma 25230
Museo Napoleonico, Tolentino 25722
Museo Napoleonico G. Antonelli, Arcole 22914
Museo Natural, Pensilvania 07556
Museo Natural de Historia y Geografía, Santo Domingo 09127
Museo Natural Dr. Carlos A. Marelli, Colón 00281
Museo Naturali e Appennino, Revi nel Lazio 25106
Museo Naturalistica-Archeologico, Vicenza 25995
Museo Naturalistico, Champdepraz 23518
Museo Naturalistico, Chieri 23540
Museo Naturalistico, L'Aquila 24146
Museo Naturalistico, Lesina 24181
Museo Naturalistico, Pescasseroli 24872
Museo Naturalistico, Picinisco 24905
Museo Naturalistico, Portoferraio 25019
Museo Naturalistico Archeologico M. Locati, Lama dei Peligni 24130
Museo naturalistico del Frignano, Pavullo nel Frignano 24831
Museo Naturalistico del Lago, Montepulciano 24539
Museo Naturalistico del Parco, San Romano di Garfagnana 25409
Museo Naturalistico della Riserva Naturale Orientata di Onferno, Gemmano 23971
Museo Naturalistico della Vallata del Bidente, Bagno di Romagna 23006
Museo Naturalistico e della Civiltà Contadina, Berceto 23058
Museo Naturalistico F. Minà Palumbo, Castelbuono 23393
Museo Naturalistico G. Zanardo, Tambre 25670
Museo Naturalistico Libero Gatti, Copanello 23642
Museo Naturalistico Missionario, Chiusa Pesio 23554
Museo Naturalistico N. De Leone, Penne 24838
Museo Naturalistico O. Perini, Borca di Cadore 23162
Museo Naturalistico P. Barrasso, Caramanico Terme 23341
Museo Naucalpan de la Cultura Tlatilca, Naucalpan de Juárez 28264
Museo Naval, Catia la Mar 48931
Museo Naval, Madrid 35049
Museo Naval, Montevideo 41019
Museo Naval de Cartagena, Cartagena 34686
Museo Naval de Ilo, Ilo 31183
Museo Naval de la Nación, Tigre 00634
Museo Naval de Viña del Mar, Viña del Mar 06932
Museo Naval del Perú, Callao 31135
Museo Naval del Puerto de la Cruz, Puerto de la Cruz 35299
Museo Naval Puerto Belgrano, Puerto Belgrano 00488
Museo Navale, Genova 24006
Museo Navale, Napoli 24601
Museo Navale Archeologico N. Lamboglia, La Maddalena 24117
Museo Navale Didattico, Milano 24407
Museo Navale Internazionale del Ponente Ligure, Imperia 24095
Museo Navale O. Zibetti, Caravaggio 23343
Museo Navale Romano, Albenga 22834
Museo Nazionale, Ravenna 25081
Museo Nazionale, Reggio Calabria 25091
Museo Nazionale Archeologico, Chieti 23548
Museo Nazionale Archeologico, Civitavecchia 23596
Museo Nazionale Archeologico, Ferrara 23798
Museo Nazionale Archeologico, Sarsina 25480
Museo Nazionale Archeologico, Tarquinia 25674
Museo Nazionale Archeologico di Egnazia, Fasano-Savelletri 23768
Museo Nazionale Archeologico di Vulci, Canino 23313
Museo Nazionale Atestino, Este 23743
Museo Nazionale Cagliari, Cagliari 23252
Museo Nazionale Concordiese, Portogruaro 25023
Museo Nazionale d'Abruzzo, L'Aquila 24147
Museo Nazionale d'Arte Medievale e Moderna, Matera 24334
Museo Nazionale d'Arte Orientale, Roma 25231
Museo Nazionale degli Strumenti Musicali, Roma 25232
Museo Nazionale degli Strumenti per il Calcolo, Pisa 24951
Museo Nazionale del Bargello, Firenze 23879
Museo Nazionale del Cinema, Torino 25756
Museo Nazionale del Cinema, Torino 25757
Museo Nazionale del Palazzo di Venezia, Roma 25233
Museo Nazionale del Risorgimento Italiano, Torino 25758
Museo Nazionale del San Gottardo, Airolo 36442
Museo Nazionale della Attività Subacquee, Marina di Ravenna 24302
Museo Nazionale della Certosa, Calci 23261
Museo Nazionale della Fotografia, Brescia 23208
Museo Nazionale della Montagna Duca degli Abruzzi, Torino 25759
Museo Nazionale della Residenza Napoleonica, Portoferraio 25020
Museo Nazionale della Residenza Napoleonica dei Mulini, Portoferraio 25021
Museo Nazionale della Scienza e della Tecnica Leonardo da Vinci, Milano 24408
Museo Nazionale della Siritide, Policoro 24978
Museo Nazionale dell'Agro Picentino, Pontecagnano 24995
Museo Nazionale dell'Alta Val d'Agri, Grumento Nova 24065
Museo Nazionale dell'Antartide F. Ippolito, Genova 24007
Museo Nazionale dell'Arma della Cavalleria, Pinerolo 24931
Museo Nazionale delle Arti e Tradizioni Popolari, Roma 25234
Museo Nazionale delle Arti Naïves C. Zavattini, Luzzara 24245
Museo Nazionale delle Paste Alimentari, Roma 25235
Museo Nazionale dell'Età Neoclassica in Romagna, Faenza 23755
Museo Nazionale di Canossa N. Campanini, Ciano d'Enza 23558
Museo Nazionale di Casa Giusti, Monsummano Terme 24488
Museo Nazionale di Castel Sant'Angelo, Roma 25236
Museo Nazionale di Palazzo Reale, Pisa 24952
Museo Nazionale di San Matteo, Pisa 24953
Museo Nazionale di Santa Maria delle Monanche e Paleolitico, Isernia 24103
Museo Nazionale di Villa Guinigi, Lucca 24231
Museo Nazionale Domenico Ridola, Matera 24335
Museo Nazionale Etrusco di Villa Giulia, Roma 25237
Museo Nazionale Etrusco Pompeo Aria, Marzabotto 24309
Museo Nazionale Ferroviario, Napoli 24602
Museo Nazionale Garibaldino, La Maddalena 24118
Museo Nazionale Jatta, Ruvo di Puglia 25305
Museo Nazionale Preistorico ed Etnografico Luigi Pigorini, Roma 25238
Museo Nazionale Romano-Terme di Diocleziano, Roma 25239
Museo Negrense, Bacolod 31278
Museo Néstor, Las Palmas de Gran Canaria 35243
Museo Nezahualcóyotl Acomiztli, Nezahualcóyotl 28267
Museo ng Bangko Sentral ng Pilipinas, Manila 31383
Museo ng Batangas, Lipa 31342
Museo ng Buhay Pilipino, Pasay 31413
Museo ng Kalinangang Pilipino, Manila 31384
Museo ng Kalinangang Pilipino, Pasay 31414
Museo ng Katipunan, Lipa 31343
Museo ng Makati, Makati 31354
Museo ng Manila, Manila 31385
Museo ng Rebolusyon, San Juan 31440
Museo Ñiace, Tepelmeme de Morelos 28490
Museo Nicanor Piñole, Gijón 34849
Museo Ñico Lopez, Bayamo 07862
Museo Nicola Antonio Manfroce, Palmi 24788
Museo Niño Minero, Vetagrande 28597
Museo Norace, Rosignano Marittimo 25286
Museo Norawa, Guachochi 27940
Museo Normanno-Bizantino, San Marco d'Alunzio 25386
Museo Novarese d'Arte e Storia R. Fumagalli, Novara 24649
Museo Nuestra Señora de Carrodilla, Luján de Cuyo 00418
Museo Nuestro Pueblo y Museo Etnográfico de Tecpatán, Tecpatán 28471
Museo Nueva Cádiz, La Asunción 48947
Museo Numantino, Soria 35506
Museo Numismático, La Habana 07994
Museo Numismático del Banco Continental, Arequipa 31116
Museo Numismático del Banco Nacíonal, Buenos Aires 00233
Museo Numismático del Banco Wiese, Lima 31223
Museo Numismatico della Zecca, Roma 25240
Museo Numismático Dr. José Evaristo Uriburu, Buenos Aires 00234
Museo Nuovo - Museo del Conservatori, Roma 25241
Museo Obispo Fray José Antonio de San Alberto, Córdoba 00308
Museo Obispo Vellosillo, Ayllón 34510
Museo Ocarina e degli Strumenti in Terracotta, Budrio 23225
Museo Ochoa, Valencia 35609
Museo Odontológico Dr. Jorge E. Dunster, Corrientes 00323
Museo O'Higginiano y de Bellas Artes de Talca, Talca 06922
Museo Omar Huerta Escalante, Jonuta 28033
Museo Omero, Ancona 22884
Museo Oncativo, Oncativo 00463
Museo Onsernonese, Loco 36891
Museo Ora Ton, Chamula 27814
Museo Oraziano, Licenza 24185
Museo Orazio Comes, Portici 25011
Museo Organologico Didattico, Cremona 23682
Museo Organológico Folklórico Musical, Bogotá 07431
Museo Oriental, Valladolid 35627
Museo Orientale, Tagliacozzo 25666
Museo Orlando Binaghi, Moreno 00455
Museo Ornitológico, Aragua 48887
Museo Ornitologico, Poppi 25005
Museo Ornitologico, San Gimignano 25366

Museo Ornitologico C. Beni, Stia 25635
Museo Ornitologico e di Scienze Naturali, Ravenna 25082
Museo Ornitologico Naturalistico S. Bambini, Pietralunga 24910
Museo Ornitológico Patagónico, El Bolsón 00334
Museo Ornitologico U. Foschi, Forlì 23915
Museo Orve, Chaupimascos 31142
Museo Oscar Fernandez Morera, Sancti-Spíritus 08115
Museo Oscar María de Rojas, Cárdenas 07881
Museo Ossenvanza, Bologna 23141
Museo Ostetrico, Bologna 23142
Museo Ostetrico, Padova 24747
Museo Ostiense, Ostia Antica 24715
Museo Ostiense, Scavi di Ostia, Roma 25242
Museo Othoniano, San Luis Potosí 28406
Museo P. Calderini, Varallo Sesia 25891
Museo P. Canonica, Roma 25243
Museo P. Vagliasindi, Randazzo 25073
Museo Pablo Bush Romero, Puerto Aventura 28347
Museo Pablo Casals, San Juan 32403
Museo Pablo Gargallo, Zaragoza 35727
Museo Pablo Serrano, Zaragoza 35728
Museo Padiglione delle Carozza, Città del Vaticano 48878
Museo Padre Coll, Buenos Aires 00235
Museo Paisa, Caicedonia 07442
Museo Palacio de Don Pedro I, Astudillo 34498
Museo-Palacio de Fuensalida, Toledo 35544
Museo Palacio de la Canal, San Miguel de Allende 28411
Museo-Palacio del Emperador Carlos V, Cuacos de Yuste 34760
Museo Palatino, Roma 25244
Museo Palatino, Roma 25245
Museo Palazzina Storica, Peschiera del Garda 24873
Museo Palenteológico de la Laguna, Torreón 28559
Museo Paleocristiano, Aquileia 22908
Museo Paleomarino, Reggio Calabria 25092
Museo Paleontologico, Amandola 22873
Museo Paleontologico, Bova 23188
Museo Paleontologico, Fluminimaggiore 23891
Museo Paleontologico, L'Aquila 24148
Museo Paleontológico, Mariquita 07513
Museo Paleontológico, Miño de Medinaceli 35113
Museo Paleontologico, Mondaino 24469
Museo Paleontologico, Monfalcone 24475
Museo Paleontologico, Montevarchi 24552
Museo Paleontológico, Pinar del Río 08076
Museo Paleontológico, Villa de Leyva 07622
Museo Paleontologico, Zaragoza 35729
Museo Paleontologico Archeologico V. Caccia, San Colombano al Lambro 25350
Museo Paleontológico, Arqueológico e Histórico de la Ciudad de Deán Funes, Deán Funes 00328
Museo Paleontológico Egidio Feruglio, Trelew 00639
Museo Paleontologico M. Gortani, Portogruaro 25024
Museo Paleontológico Municipal, Valencia 35610
Museo Paleontologico Parmense, Parma 24811
Museo Paleontologico S. Lai, Ceriale 23480
Museo Paleontológico y Petrolero Astra, Comodoro Rivadavia 00283
Museo Paleoveneto, Pieve di Cadore 24917
Museo Pambata, Manila 31386
Museo Pampeano de Chascomús, Chascomús 00272
Museo Pampeano del Pergamino, Pergamino 00474
Museo Pantaleón Panduro, Tlaquepaque 28529
Museo Parigino a Roma, Roma 25246
Museo Parma Gemma, Casarza Ligure 23372
Museo Parque de Esculturas, Montevideo 41020
Museo Parque de la Cristianía, Chapala 27815
Museo Parrocchiale, Bionaz 23084
Museo Parrocchiale, Campo Tures 23302
Museo Parrocchiale, Castell'Arquato 23409
Museo Parrocchiale, Challand Saint Victor 23515
Museo Parrocchiale, Chambave 23516
Museo Parrocchiale, Champorcher 23519
Museo Parrocchiale, Fié 23804
Museo Parrocchiale, Gressoney Saint Jean 24051
Museo Parrocchiale, La Salle 24120
Museo Parrocchiale, Mogliano Marche 24454
Museo Parrocchiale, Ornavasso 24694
Museo Parrocchiale, Ponte Buggianese 24989
Museo Parrocchiale, Saint Vincent 25313
Museo Parrocchiale, San Marco d'Alunzio 25387
Museo Parrocchiale, Sarre 25478
Museo Parrocchiale, Valgrisenche 25877
Museo Parrocchiale, Valtournenche 25889
Museo Parrocchiale d'Arte Sacra, Dozza 23724
Museo Parrocchiale del Santuario del Santissimo Crocifisso, Buggiano 23228
Museo Parrocchiale della Chiesa Collegiata, Mercatello sul Metauro 24358
Museo Parrocchiale della Propositura di San Martino, Lastra a Signa 24153
Museo Parrocchiale di Arte Sacra, Ponte in Valtellina 24991
Museo Parrocchiale di Arte Sacra, Valstrona 25887
Museo Parrocchiale e Museo P. Mascagni, Bagnara di Romagna 23002
Museo Parrocchiale Madonna dei Raccomandati, Gessopalena 24018
Museo Parrocchiale San Giacomo, Massignano 24331
Museo Parrocchiale San Pietro Martire, Venezia 25943
Museo Parroquial, La Almunia de Doña Godina 34457
Museo Parroquial, Alquezar 34458
Museo Parroquial, Barco de Avila 34592
Museo Parroquial, Benabarre 34599
Museo Parroquial, Bocairente 34619
Museo Parroquial, Celanova 34704
Museo Parroquial, Cervera de Pisuerga 34709
Museo Parroquial, Ecija 34784
Museo Parroquial, Espejo 34803
Museo Parroquial, Ezcaray 34811
Museo Parroquial, Hondarribia 34902
Museo Parroquial, Madrid 35050
Museo Parroquial, Medina de Rioseco 35104
Museo Parroquial, Miranda del Castañar 35114
Museo Parroquial, Paradas 35251
Museo Parroquial, Pastrana 35256
Museo Parroquial, Roda de Isábena 35329
Museo Parroquial, San Sebastián del Oeste 28425
Museo Parroquial, Santa Gadea del Cid 35419
Museo Parroquial, Santa María del Campo 35425
Museo Parroquial, Segovia 35467
Museo Parroquial Colegiata de San Miguel, Aguilar de Campoo 34413
Museo Parroquial de Arte Religioso, Turmequé 07615
Museo Parroquial de Arte Sacro y Etnología, Anso 34467
Museo Parroquial de Monterroso, Monterroso 35135
Museo Parroquial de San Cosme y San Damián, Covarrubias 34757
Museo Parroquial de San Félix, Girona 34852
Museo Parroquial de San Martiño de Mondoñedo, Foz 34824
Museo Parroquial de San Martiño de Mondoñedo, San Martiño de Mondoñedo-Foz 35382
Museo Parroquial de Santa Eulalia, Paredes de Nava 35254
Museo Parroquial de Zurbarán, Marchena 35091
Museo Parroquial San Pedro, Cisneros 34717
Museo Parroquial Santa María del Salvador, Chinchilla 34714
Museo Parroquial Santa María La Real, Xunqueira de Ambia 35706
Museo Participativo de Ciencias, Buenos Aires 00236
Museo Particular Los Abuelos, Franck 00349
Museo Partigiano, Carpasio 23352
Museo Partigiano Alfredo Di Dio, Ornavasso 24695
Museo Patio del Moro, Guaduas 07490
Museo Patio Herreriano, Valladolid 35628
Museo Patria Chica de Mohamed Diaz, Realicó 00504
Museo Pavese di Scienze Naturali, Pavia 24827
Museo Pecharromán, Pasarón de la Vera 35255
Museo Pedagógico Carlos Stuardo Ortiz, Santiago de Chile 06918
Museo Pedagógico Ciencias Naturales Jesús María Hernando, Valladolid 35629
Museo Pedagógico de Arte Infantil, Madrid 35051
Museo Pedagógico de Historia del Arte, Caracas 48926
Museo Pedagógico José Pedro Varela, Montevideo 41021
Museo Pedrin Troya, San Nicolás de Bari 08106
Museo Pedro Ara, Córdoba 00309
Museo Pedro Coronel, Zacatecas 28638
Museo Pedro Luro, Dolores 00331
Museo Penitenciario Argentino, Buenos Aires 00237
Museo Peñón Blanco, Peñón Blanco 28308
Museo per la Matematica - Giardino di Archimede, Priverno 25055
Museo per la Storia dell'Università di Pavia, Pavia 24828
Museo per l'Arte e l'Archeologia del Vastese, Gissi 24028
Museo Pérez Comendador-Leroux, Hérvas 34901
Museo Pérez Galdós, Las Palmas de Gran Canaria 35244
Museo Perrando, Sassello 25490
Museo Petatlán, Petatlán 28310
Museo Peten Ak, Valladolid 28582
Museo Petrográfico del Servicio Nacional de Geología y Minería, Quito 09217
Museo Picasso, Buitrago del Lozoya 34626
Museo Piersanti, Matelica 24332
Museo Pietro Canonica, Stresa 25641
Museo Pietro della Vedova, Rima San Giuseppe 25112
Museo Pietro Micca e dell'Assedio, Torino 25760
Museo-Pinacoteca, Visso 26031
Museo Pinacoteca A. Salvucci, Molfetta 24459
Museo-Pinacoteca Comunale, Mogliano Marche 24455
Museo-Pinacoteca de Arte Contemporáneo, Zarzuela del Monte 35734
Museo Pinacoteca dell'Arte dei Bambini, Smerillo 25592
Museo - Pinacoteca San Francesco, San Marino 33766
Museo Pinacoteca Santa Casa, Loreto 24215
Museo Pio Clementino, Città del Vaticano 48879
Museo Pio Collivadino, Banfield 00132
Museo Pio Cristiano, Città del Vaticano 48880
Museo Pío del Río Ortega, Valladolid 35630
Museo Pio IX, Senigallia 25537
Museo Pio X, Salzano 25327
Museo Planetario, Garza García 27931
Museo Plaza de Revolución General Antonio Maceo, Santiago de Cuba 08150
Museo Plebano, Agno 36436
Museo Polare Etnografico Silvio Zavatti, Fermo 23781
Museo Poldi Pezzoli, Milano 24409
Museo Policial, Avila 34504
Museo Polifacético Regional Vottero, Laguna Larga 00403
Museo Polivalente, Chiaramonte Gulfi 23527
Museo Polivalente, Vittoria 26036
Museo Polivalente de Palmira, Palmira 08066
Museo Pomposiano, Codigoro 23603
Museo Ponchielliano, Paderno Ponchielli 24730
Museo Popol Vuh, Guatemala 21275
Museo Popoli e Culture, Milano 24410
Museo Popular de Arte Contemporáneo, Villafamés 35678
Museo Porfirio Corona Covarrubias, El Grullo, Jalisco 27904
Museo Posta de Yatasto, Metán 00447
Museo Postal Cubano, La Habana 07995
Museo Postal Eduardo Santos, Bogotá 07432
Museo Postal y Filatélico del Perú, Lima 31224
Museo Postal y Telegráfico, Madrid 35052
Museo Postal y Telegráfico Doctor Ramon J. Carcano, Buenos Aires 00238
Museo Postale e Telegrafico della Mitteleuropa, Trieste 25830
Museo Postale, Filatelico-Numismatico, San Marino 33767
Museo Prehistórico de Tepexpan, Tepexpan 28493
Museo Preistorico, Paceco 24728
Museo Preistorico Balzi Rossi, Ventimiglia 25956
Museo Preistorico dell'Isolino, Biandronno 23076
Museo Preistorico e Archeologico A.C. Blanc, Viareggio 25985
Museo Preistorico e Lapidario, Verucchio 25979
Museo Preistorico N. Lamboglia e Val Varatello, Toirano 25716
Museo Presidente José Evaristo Uriburu, Salta 00542
Museo Presidio Modelo, Nueva Gerona 08062
Museo Privado de Arqueología Regional Julio Gironde, Carmen de Patagonés 00265
Museo Prof. Arturo Reyes Viramontes, Jalpa 28023
Museo Prof. Dr. Juan Augusto Olsacher, Zapala 00677
Museo Prof. Moisés Sáenz Garza, Apodaca 27777
Museo Prof. Ricardo Vega Noriega, San Ignacio 28386
Museo Profano, Città del Vaticano 48881
Museo Provincial, Ciego de Avila 07889
Museo Provincial, Lugo 34987
Museo Provincial, Teruel 35530
Museo Provincial Arqueológico Eric Boman, Santa María de Catamarca 00611
Museo Provincial de Arqueología Wagner, Santiago del Estero 00618
Museo Provincial de Artes de La Pampa, Santa Rosa 00612
Museo Provincial de Bellas Artes, Corrientes 00324
Museo Provincial de Bellas Artes, Salta 00543
Museo Provincial de Bellas Artes Dr. Pedro E. Martínez, Paraná 00470
Museo Provincial de Bellas Artes Emiliano Guiñazu - Casa de Fader, Luján de Cuyo 00419
Museo Provincial de Bellas Artes Emilio A. Caraffa, Córdoba 00310
Museo Provincial de Bellas Artes Ramón Gómez Cornet, Santiago del Estero 00619
Museo Provincial de Bellas Artes Rosa Galisteo de Rodríguez, Santa Fé 00608
Museo Provincial de Bellas Artes Timoteo Eduardo Navarro, San Miguel de Tucumán 00587
Museo Provincial de Ciencias Naturales Dr. Angelo Gallardo, Rosario 00532
Museo Provincial de Ciencias Naturales Florentino Ameghino, Santa Fé 00609
Museo Provincial de Ciencias Naturales y Oceanográfico, Puerto Madryn 00491
Museo Provincial de Historia Natural de La Pampa, Santa Rosa 00613
Museo Provincial de Holguín La Periquera, Holguín 08009
Museo Provincial de la Historia de Pinar del Río, Pinar del Río 08077
Museo Provincial de Matanzas, Matanzas 08042
Museo Provincial de Villa Clara y Museo Municipal, Santa Clara 08125
Museo Provincial do Mar, San Ciprian-Concello de Cervo 35372
Museo Provincial Don Emilio Bacardí Moreau, Santiago de Cuba 08151
Museo Provincial Dora Ochoa de Masramón, San Luis 00577
Museo Provincial General Vicente García, Victoria de las Tunas 08174
Museo Provincial Ignacio Agramonte, La Vigía 08176
Museo Provincial José María Morante, Arequipa 31117
Museo Provincial Mario Brozoski, Puerto Deseado 00489
Museo Provincial y Parroquial, Piña de Campos 35271
Museo Provinciale, Catanzaro 23455
Museo Provinciale, Chieti 23549
Museo Provinciale Campano, Capua 23339
Museo Provinciale d'Arte Contempranea, Crotone 23691
Museo Provinciale della Caccia e della Pesca, Racines 25064
Museo Provinciale della Vita Contadina, San Vito al Tagliamento 25419
Museo Provinciale delle Miniere, Racines 25065
Museo Provinciale delle Miniere, Vipiteno 26029
Museo Provinciale delle Tradizioni Popolari Abbazia Cerrate, Lecce 24166
Museo Provinciale di Storia Naturale, Foggia 23895
Museo Provinciale di Storia Naturale, Livorno 24194
Museo Provinciale Sigismondo Castromediano, Lecce 24167
Museo Pucciniano, Torre del Lago Puccini 25772
Museo Pueblo de Luis, Trelew 00640
Museo Puertorriqueño del Deportes, Salinas 32383
Museo Quattroruote, Rozzano 25300
Museo Quevedo Zornoza, Zipaquirá 07629
Museo Quezaltenango, Quezaltenango 21277
Museo Quinta Amalia Simoni, Camagüey 07877
Museo Quinta Casa de Juan Montalvo, Ambato 09135
Museo Quinta de San Pedro Alejandrino, Santa Marta 07591
Museo Quinta Juan Leon Mera, Ambato 09136
Museo R. Campelli, Pieveboviglìana 24925
Museo R. Cassolo, Mede 24339
Museo R. Cuneo, Savona 25512
Museo R. De Cesare, Spinazzola 25619
Museo Rabelo, La Habana 07996
Museo-Raccolta di Fisica, Bari 23027
Museo Radiofónico de la Ciudad de Boulogne, Boulogne 00142
Museo Rafael Coronel, Zacatecas 28639
Museo Rafael Escriña, Santa Clara de Saguier 00600
Museo Raíces, Jesús María 07502
Museo Raíces de Satevó, Satevó 28442
Museo Ralli, Marbella 35087
Museo Ralli, Punta del Este 41035
Museo Ralli, Santiago de Chile 06919
Museo Ramón Gaya, Murcia 35149
Museo Ramón López Velarde, México 28196
Museo Ramón Pérez Fernández, Rivadavia 00523
Museo Ramos Generales, Villa María 00671
Museo Ratti dei Vini d'Alba, La Morra 24119
Museo Rauzi, Palmira 00464
Museo Rayo, Roldanillo 07579
Museo Real Colegiata de San Isidoro, León 34951
Museo Recoleto, Quezon City 31436
Museo Regional, Chichicastenango 21264
Museo Regional, San Juan Bautista Tuxtepec 28389
Museo Regional Amazónico, Iquitos 31188
Museo Regional Aníbal Cambas, Posadas 00485
Museo Regional Carlos Funes Derieul, Coronel Dorrego 00316
Museo Regional Castelli, Castelli 00269
Museo Regional Cayetano Alberto Silva, Venado Tuerto 00654
Museo Regional Comunitario Altepepialcalli, México 28197
Museo Regional Cuauhnáhuac, Cuernavaca 27876
Museo Regional Daniel Hernández Morillo, Huancavelica 31167
Museo Regional de Acambay, Acambay 27744
Museo Regional de Actopán, Actopán 27752
Museo Regional de Aldama, Aldama 27766
Museo Regional de Antropología, Resistencia 00510
Museo Regional de Antropología Carlos Pellicer Cámara, Villahermosa 28612
Museo Regional de Antropología e Historia de Baja California Sur, La Paz 28045
Museo Regional de Antropología J. Jesús Figueroa Torres, Sayula 28444
Museo Regional de Arqueología, Huamanga 31166
Museo Regional de Arqueología de Junín, Chupaca 31147
Museo Regional de Arqueología de Tuxpan, Tuxpan de Rodríguez Cano 28568
Museo Regional de Arqueología Maya, Ciudad de Copán 21297
Museo Regional de Arte e Historia, Jerez de García Salinas 28030
Museo Regional de Arte Popular La Huatápera, Uruapán 28579
Museo Regional de Atacama, Copiapó 06895
Museo Regional de Campeche, Campeche 27800
Museo Regional de Casma Max Uhle, Casma 31137
Museo Regional de Chiapas, Tuxtla Gutiérrez 28575
Museo Regional de Ciencias Naturales Tomás Santa Coloma, Tres Arroyos 00642
Museo Regional de Cinco Saltos, Cinco Saltos 00279
Museo Regional de Claromecó, Balneario Claromecó 00131
Museo Regional de Cuetzalan, Cuetzalán 27879
Museo Regional de Durango y Museo del Niño, Durango 27901
Museo Regional de Guadalajara, Guadalajara 27961
Museo Regional de Guanajuato Alhóndiga de Granaditas, Guanajuato 27977
Museo Regional de Guerrero, Chilpancingo 27832
Museo Regional de Hidalgo, Pachuca 28297
Museo Regional de Historia, Hermosillo 27987
Museo Regional de Historia de Aguascalientes, Aguascalientes 27759
Museo Regional de Historia de Colima, Colima 27838
Museo Regional de Historia de Tamaulipas, Victoria 28602
Museo Regional de Ica María Reiche Gross Newman, Ica 31182
Museo Regional de Iguala, Iguala de la Independencia 28012
Museo Regional de Iquique, Iquique 06897
Museo Regional de la Araucania, Temuco 06923
Museo Regional de la Cerámica, Tlaquepaque 28530
Museo Regional de la Ciudad de La Paz, La Paz 00384
Museo Regional de la Laguna, Torreón 28560
Museo Regional de las Culturas Occidente, Guzmán 27982
Museo Regional de Mascota, Mascota 28072
Museo Regional de Nayarit, Tepic 28499
Museo Regional de Nuevo León, Monterrey 28239
Museo Regional de Pigüé, Pigüé 00477

Museo Regional de Pintura José Antonio Terry, Tilcara 00637
Museo Regional de Prehistoria y Arqueología de Cantabria, Santander 35433
Museo Regional de Puebla, Puebla 28342
Museo Regional de Querétaro, Querétaro 28355
Museo Regional de Río Verde, Río Verde 28359
Museo Regional de Sacanta, Sacanta 00535
Museo Regional de San Carlos, San Carlos 41039
Museo Regional de San Martín, Moyobamba 31230
Museo Regional de Sinaloa, Culiacán 27886
Museo Regional de Sonora, Hermosillo 27988
Museo Regional de Telecomunicaciones Tomás Guzmán Cantú, La Paz 28046
Museo Regional de Tierra Caliente, Coyuca de Catalán 27864
Museo Regional de Tlaxcala, Tlaxcala 28534
Museo Regional de Yucatán, Mérida 28085
Museo Regional del Valle del Fuerte, Ahome 27761
Museo Regional Doctor Leonardo Oliva, Ahualulco de Mercado 27762
Museo Regional Dr. Adolfo Alsina, Carhué 00263
Museo Regional Dr. Federico Escalada, Río Mayo 00520
Museo Regional Dr. José Luro, Pedro Luro 00471
Museo Regional El Fuerte, El Fuerte 27903
Museo Regional Francisco Mazzoni, Maldonado 40982
Museo Regional Guayupe de Puerto Santander, Puerto Santander 07571
Museo Regional Histórico y de Ciencias Naturales, Coronel Pringles 00318
Museo Regional Huasteco, Valles 28588
Museo Regional José G. Brochero, Santa Rosa de Río Primero 00614
Museo Regional Las Varillas, Las Varillas 00405
Museo Regional Lázaro Cárdenas, Tlapehuala 28528
Museo Regional Luciano Márquez, Zacatlán 28644
Museo Regional Malargüe, Malargüe 00423
Museo Regional Maracó, General Pico 00355
Museo Regional Michoacano, Morelia 28253
Museo Regional Municipal de El Calafate, El Calafate 00335
Museo Regional Particular Epifanio Saravia, Santa Catalina 00599
Museo Regional Patagónico, Comodoro Rivadavia 00284
Museo Regional Potosino, San Luis Potosí 28407
Museo Regional Provincial Padre Manuel Jesús Molina, Río Gallegos 00517
Museo Regional Rescate de Raíces, Ahualulco de Mercado 27763
Museo Regional Rincón de Vida, Villa Mirasol 00672
Museo Regional Rufino Muñiz Torres, Ocampo 28283
Museo Regional Rumi Mayu (Río de Piedra), Sanagasta 00598
Museo Regional Salesiano de Rawson, Rawson 00503
Museo Regional Salesiano Maggiorino Borgatello, Punta Arenas 06905
Museo Regional Trevelin, Trevelin 00645
Museo Regional Valcheta, Valcheta 00652
Museo Regional Valparaíso, Valparaíso 28589
Museo Regional y de Arte Marino, Puerto San Julián 00492
Museo Regionale, Messina 24364
Museo Regionale A. Pepoli, Trapani 25785
Museo Regionale della Centovalli e del Pedemonte, Intragna 36814
Museo Regionale della Ceramica, Caltagirone 23273
Museo Regionale della Ceramica, Deruta 23709
Museo Regionale di Camarina, Ragusa 25069
Museo Regionale di Scienze Naturali, Saint Pierre 25311
Museo Regionale di Scienze Naturali, Torino 25761
Museo Religioso de Guatavita, Guatavita 07493
Museo Religioso Santa Domingo, Bolivar 09144
Museo Religioso y Colonial de San Francisco, Cali 07452
Museo Renacimiento Indígena, Huamuxtitlán 27996
Museo Renato Brozzi, Traversetolo 25786
Museo Retrospectivo de Farmacia y Medicina, El Masnou 35096
Museo Richard Ginori della Manifattura di Doccia, Sesto Fiorentino 25557
Museo Ripley, México 28198
Museo Risorgimentale, Montichiari 24554
Museo Risorgimentale, Pieve di Cadore 24918
Museo Rivarossi dei Treni in Miniatura, Como 23629
Museo Roberto M. Arata, Buenos Aires 00239
Museo Roberto Noble, Buenos Aires 00240
Museo Roca, Buenos Aires 00241
Museo Rocsen, Nono 00459
Museo Rodolfo Valentino, Castellaneta 23404
Museo Rognoni Salvaneschi, Novara 24650
Museo Romano, Tortona 25779
Museo Romántico, Madrid 35053
Museo Romántico, Montevideo 41022
Museo Romántico, Trinidad 08163
Museo Rómulo Raggio, Vicente López 00655
Museo Ron Arehucas, Arucas 34494
Museo Rosendo Mejica, Iloilo 31330
Museo Rosminiano, Stresa 25642
Museo Rubén Herrera, Saltillo 28370
Museo Rudolf Stolz, Sesto in Pusteria 25558
Museo Runa de Antropología, Tafí del Valle 00628
Museo Rural, Pozorrubio de Santiago 35291
Museo Rural de la Posta de Sinsacate, Jesús María 00372
Museo S. Fancello, Dorgali 23722
Museo Sa Domu De Donna Nassia, Lotzorai 24222
Museo Sac-be, Yaxcabá 28630
Museo Sacrario delle Bandiere, Roma 25247
Museo Sacrario Galileo Ferraris, Livorno Ferraris 24195
Museo Sacro, Città del Vaticano 48882
Museo Sacro, Pompei 24985
Museo Sacro de Caracas, Caracas 48927
Museo Sacro de la Catedral, San Miguel de Tucumán 00588
Museo Sacro - Tesoro di Sant'Ambrogio, Milano 24411
Museo Sala, San Juan Bautista Tuxtepec 28390
Museo Sala de Arte, Tijuana 28514
Museo Sala de Arte Moderno, Juchitán de Zaragoza 28040
Museo Sala de Arte Público David Alfaro Siqueiros, México 28199
Museo Sala de Exposición Banco Central de Esmeraldas, Esmeraldas 09164
Museo-Sala de los Símbolos Patrios, Hermosillo 27989
Museo Salesiano, Huancayo 31170
Museo Salesiano Ceferino Namuncura, Córdoba 00311
Museo Salvatore Ferragamo, Firenze 23880
Museo Salzillo, Murcia 35150
Museo San Antonio de Padua, Córdoba 00312
Museo San Francisco, Teruel 35531
Museo San Giuseppe da Copertino, Osimo 24710
Museo San Gregorio de Polanco, San Gregorio de Polanco 41040
Museo San José el Mogote, San José el Mogote 28388
Museo San Juan de la Cruz, Ubeda 35584
Museo San Juan de Letrán, Chucuito 31145
Museo San Juan en la Historia, San Juan del Río 28395
Museo San Miguel del Padrón, La Habana 07997
Museo San Miguel Teotongo, México 28200
Museo San Nicolò, Militello in Val di Catania 24425
Museo San Roque, Buenos Aires 00242
Museo Santa Barbara, Mammola 24274
Museo Santa Clara la Real, Tunja 07614
Museo Sant'Andrea, Clusone 23600
Museo-Santuario de San Pedro Claver, Cartagena 07458
Museo Santuario Nuestra Señora Natividad del Guayco, La Magdalena 09187
Museo Santuarios Andinos de la Universidad Católica de Santa María, Arequipa 31118
Museo Sardo di Antropologia ed Etnografia, Cagliari 23253
Museo Sardo di Geologia e Paleontologia D. Lovisato, Cagliari 23254
Museo Schaferrer, Oxapampa 31234
Museo Scientifico L. Guidi, Pesaro 24860
Museo Scout-Guía, Madrid 35054
Museo Scuola Odin-Bertot, Angrogna 22894
Museo Sefardí, Toledo 35545
Museo Selinuntino, Castelvetrano 23429
Museo Sella e Mosca, Alghero 22855
Museo Senador Domingo Faustino Sarmiento, Buenos Aires 00243
Museo Senen Mexic, Acatlán de Osorio 27750
Museo Serfín de Indumentaria Indígena, México 28201
Museo Servando Cabrera Moreno, La Habana 07998
Museo Severino Pose, Montevideo 41023
Museo Siciliano delle Tradizioni Religiose, San Salvatore di Fitalia 25410
Museo Siderúrgico de Colombia, Nobsa 07535
Museo Silvanus G. Morley y de las Estelas, El Petén 21265
Museo Silvestre Vargas, Tecalitlán 28465
Museo Simón Bolívar, Bolívar 34620
Museo Sinagoga de Santa María la Blanca, Toledo 35546
Museo Sistino Vescovile, Montalto Marche 24494
Museo Sito Arqueológico Guayabo de Turrialba, Turrialba 07664
Museo Social Argentino de Universidad, Buenos Aires 00244
Museo Sol y Mar, Matanzas 08043
Museo Soldati della Battaglia, San Biagio di Callalta 25339
Museo Sor María de Jesús de Agreda, Agreda 34411
Museo Sorolla, Madrid 35055
Museo Soumaya, México 28202
Museo Speleopaleontologico, Genga 23976
Museo Speologico, Sgonico 25565
Museo Sperimentale d'Arte Contemporanea Muspac, L'Aquila 24149
Museo Statale, Anghiari 22892
Museo Statale, Mileto 24424
Museo Staur s di Arte Sacra Contemporanea, Isola del Gran Sasso 24105
Museo Stibbert, Firenze 23881
Museo Storia Memoria, Sossano 25612
Museo Storico, Lugano 36903
Museo Storico, Montese 24547
Museo Storico, Voghera 26045
Museo Storico-Aeronautica Militare, Bracciano 23194
Museo Storico Alfa Romeo, Arese 22917
Museo Storico Aloisiano, Castiglione delle Stiviere 23434
Museo Storico Alpino, Antrodoco 22897
Museo Storico Archeologico, Cicagna 23561
Museo Storico Archeologico, Segni 25530
Museo Storico Archeologico del Territorio, Bagni di Lucca 23005
Museo Storico Archeologico dell'Antica Nola, Nola 24633
Museo Storico Archeologico G. Gabetti, Dogliani 23716
Museo Storico Artistico, Cassino 23383
Museo Storico Artistico, Città del Vaticano 48883
Museo Storico Badogliano, Bari 23028
Museo Storico C. Levi, Aliano 22857
Museo Storico C. Musazzi, Parabiago 24790
Museo Storico Cappuccino, Camerino 23290
Museo Storico Civico Cuggionese, Cuggiono 23693
Museo Storico D. Foschi, Forlì 23916
Museo Storico degli Spaghetti, Pontedassio 24998
Museo Storico degli Truppe Alpini, Trento 25795
Museo Storico dei Bersaglieri, Roma 25248
Museo Storico dei Granatieri di Sardegna, Roma 25249
Museo Storico dei Vigili del Fuoco, Mantova 24291
Museo Storico del Castello di Miramare, Trieste 25831
Museo Storico del Combattente, Paderno Dugnano 24729
Museo Storico del Forte, Osoppo 24711
Museo Storico del Mutuo Soccorso, Pinerolo 24932
Museo Storico del Nastro Azzurro, Salò 25324
Museo Storico del Risorgimento della Società Economica, Chiavari 23533
Museo Storico del Soldatino M. Massacesi, Bologna 23143
Museo Storico del Teatro Argentina, Roma 25250
Museo Storico del Trotto, Civitanova Marche 23595
Museo Storico del Vetro e della Bottiglia J.F. Mariani, Montalcino 24492
Museo Storico dela Caccia e del Territorio, Cerreto Guidi 23484
Museo Storico della Brigata Sassari, Sassari 25489
Museo Storico della Città, Bergamo 23065
Museo Storico della Didattica, Roma 25251
Museo Storico della Fanteria, Roma 25252
Museo Storico della Filarmonica Sestrese, Genova 24008
Museo Storico della Guardia di Finanza, Roma 25253
Museo Storico della Guerra 1915-1918, Roana 25134
Museo Storico della Liberazione di Roma, Roma 25254
Museo Storico della Linea Gotica, Auditore 22984
Museo Storico della Motorizzazione Militare, Roma 25255
Museo Storico della Resistenza S. Maneschi, Neviano degli Arduini 24618
Museo Storico della Resistenza, Stazzema 25631
Museo Storico della Tappezzeria, Bologna 23144
Museo Storico dell'Arma dei Carabinieri, Roma 25256
Museo Storico dell'Arma del Genio, Roma 25257
Museo Storico dell'Arte Sanitaria, Roma 25258
Museo Storico delle Armi, Civitella del Tronto 23598
Museo Storico delle Poste e Telecomunicazioni, Roma 25259
Museo Storico delle Saline, Margherita di Savoia 24297
Museo Storico dell'Oro Italiano, Silvano d'Orba 25582
Museo Storico di Architettura Militare, Roma 25260
Museo Storico Dittico Alto Livenza, Sacile 25308
Museo Storico e Topografico, Firenze 23882
Museo Storico Etnografico, Bruscoli 23222
Museo Storico Etnografico, Sampeyre 25331
Museo Storico-Etnografico, Sanluri 25424
Museo Storico Etnografico della Bassa Valsesia, Romagnano Sesia 25272
Museo Storico Etnografico delle Alpi Liguri, Mendatica 24348
Museo Storico Etnografico Naturalistico, Chiesa in Valmalenco 23543
Museo Storico G. Garibaldi, Como 23630
Museo Storico in Trento Onlus, Trento 25796
Museo Storico Italiano della Guerra, Rovereto 25294
Museo Storico Italo-Ungherese, Vittoria 26037
Museo Storico Lisotti Maria, Gradara 24038
Museo Storico Michele Ghislieri, Vicoforte 26002
Museo Storico Militare, Comun Nuovo 23634
Museo Storico Militare e Sacrario die Redipuglia, Fogliano Redipuglia 23896
Museo Storico Militare Umberto I, Turate 25843
Museo Storico Minerario, Perticara 24845
Museo Storico Minerario di Perticara, Novafeltria 24642
Museo Storico Multimediale B. d'Alviano, Alviano 22867
Museo Storico Navale, Venezia 25944
Museo Storico Nazionale di Artiglieria, Torino 25762
Museo Storico Novarese Aldo Rossini, Novara 24651
Museo Storico Perugina, Perugia 24856
Museo Storico Vaticano, Città del Vaticano 48884
Museo Stradivariano, Cremona 23683
Museo Strumenti Musicali, Ravenna 25083
Museo Sudtirolese della Frutticoltura, Lana 24134
Museo Sveviano, Trieste 25832
Museo T. Nuvolari, Mantova 24292
Museo Taller de Escultura, Victoria de las Tunas 08175
Museo Taller del Moro, Toledo 35547
Museo Taller Luis Nishizawa, Toluca 28551
Museo Tamayo Arte Contemporáneo, México 28203
Museo Taminango de Artes y Tradiciones Populares de Nariño, Pasto 07553
Museo Tarike, Chihuahua 27828
Museo Taurino, Cali 07453
Museo Taurino, Huamantla 27995
Museo Taurino, La Línea de la Concepción 34957
Museo Taurino, Madrid 35056
Museo Taurino, Salamanca 35365
Museo Taurino, Valencia 35611
Museo Taurino Conde de Colombi, Alcalá de Guadaira 34424
Museo Taurino de Bogotá, Bogotá 07433
Museo Taurino de la Plaza de Acho, Lima 31225
Museo Taurino de la Real Maestranza de Caballería de Ronda, Ronda 35341
Museo Taurino de Mijas, Mijas 35112
Museo Taurino José Vega, Gerena 34844
Museo Taurino Municipal, Antequera 34469
Museo Teatrale alla Scala, Milano 24412
Museo Teatrale del Burcardo, Roma 25261
Museo Teatro La Casa de los Títeres, Monterrey 28240
Museo Tecnico Navale, La Spezia 24125
Museo Técnico Pedagógico de la Región de Pasco, San Juan 31246
Museo Tecnologia, Cultura e Civiltà Contadina, Guardia Lombardi 24067
Museo Tecnológico Aeroespacial, Las Higueras 00404
Museo Tecnológico de la Comisión Federal de Electricidad, México 28204
Museo Tecnológico Ingeniero Eduardo Latzina, Buenos Aires 00245
Museo Telefónico Victoria, México 28205
Museo Templete de los Heros Nacionales, Quito 09218
Museo Tenderi, Masaya 30323
Museo Teniente José Azuela, Zihuatanejo 28655
Museo Teodoro Ramos Blanco, La Habana 07999
Museo Tepeapulco, Tepeapulco 28488
Museo Teresiano, Alba de Tormes 34418
Museo Teresiano, Avila 34505
Museo Teresiano Monasterio de la Encarnación, Avila 34506
Museo Territoriale del Lago di Bolsena, Bolsena 23148
Museo Territoriale dell'Agro Foronovano, Torri in Sabina 25777
Museo Tesoro Basilica di San Francesco, Assisi 22968
Museo-Tesoro Catedralicio, Córdoba 34742
Museo-Tesoro Catedralicio, Lugo 34988
Museo-Tesoro Catedralicio, Plasencia 35274
Museo-Tesoro Catedralicio, Toledo 35548
Museo-Tesoro Catedralicio y Diocesano, Calahorra 34651
Museo-Tesoro de la Basílica de la Macarena, Sevilla 35489
Museo-Tesoro de la Cofradía de la Expiración, Málaga 35075
Museo Tesoro de la Santina, Cangas de Onis 34673
Museo-Tesoro de la Santina, Covadonga 34756
Museo Tesoro del Tempio della Beata Vergine, Reggio Emilia 25099
Museo-Tesoro del Templo del Cristo del Gran Poder, Sevilla 35490
Museo Tesoro della Collegiata di San Lorenzo, Chiavenna 23536
Museo-Tesoro Parroquial, Arcos de la Frontera 34477
Museo Tesoro Parroquial, Lebrija 34942
Museo-Tesoro Parroquial de Santiago, Orihuela 35188
Museo Tetetzontlilco, Tizayuca 28519
Museo Textil La Trinidad, Santa Cruz Tlaxcala 28431
Museo Thermalia, Caldes de Montbui 34656
Museo Thyssen-Bornemisza, Madrid 35057
Museo Timoteo L. Hernández, Villaldama 28614
Museo Tipologico del Presepe, Macerata 24250
Museo Tlallán, Tala 28451
Museo Tohue, Vicente Guerrero, Durango 28600
Museo Toma de Zacatecas o Cerro de la Bufa, Zacatecas 28640
Museo Tomaskitla, Epazoyucan 27920
Museo Tomochic, Vicente Guerrero 28599
Museo Tonallán, Tonalá, Jalisco 28554
Museo Tonatiuh, Zempoala 28653
Museo Torlonia, Roma 25262
Museo Tornambe de la Universidad Nacional de San Juan, San Juan 00574
Museo Torre di Porta Romana, Gubbio 24077
Museo Torres García, Montevideo 41024
Museo Torricelliano, Faenza 23756
Museo Toti dal Monte, Pieve di Soligo 24922
Museo Towi, Guachochi 27941
Museo Tradicional Ik Al Ojov, Zinacantán 28657
Museo Tradicionalista El Rancho, Chacabuco 00270
Museo Transumanza e Costume Abruzzese Molisano, Sulmona 25651
Museo Tribunal de la Santa Inquisición y del Congreso, Lima 31226
Museo Tridentino di Scienze Naturali, Trento 25797
Museo Túenl Casa Parker, Angangueo 27772
Museo Tuscolano, Frascati 23933
Museo U Gumbu, Cervo 23496
Museo Ucraniano, Apóstoles 00115
Museo Universitario, Cochabamba 03892
Museo Universitario, Medellín 07524
Museo Universitario, Mexicali 28091
Museo Universitario, Pasto 07554
Museo Universitario Alejandro Rangel Hidalgo, Nogueras 28268
Museo Universitario Antigua Casa de los Muñecos, Puebla 28343

Museo Universitario Contemporáneo de Arte, México 28206
Museo Universitario de Arqueología de Manzanillo, Manzanillo 28069
Museo Universitario de Artes, Mendoza 00441
Museo Universitario de Artes Populares, Colima 27839
Museo Universitario de Ciencias, Zacatecas 28641
Museo Universitario de Ciencias y Artes, Roma, México 28207
Museo Universitario de Paleontología, México 28208
Museo Universitario de San Carlos, Guatemala 21276
Museo Universitario del Chopo, México 28209
Museo Universitario Florentino y Carlos Ameghino, Rosario 00533
Museo Universitario Lariab de Historia Antigua de la Huaxteca, Tamuín 28454
Museo Universitario Pio López Martínez, Cayey 32370
Museo Universitario y Museo de Anatomía General, Yanacancha 31268
Museo Univérsitas, El Cerrito 07475
Museo Urdaneta Histórico Militar, Maracaibo 48951
Museo Usina Vieja, San Antonio de Areco 00552
Museo V. Venturi, Loro Ciuffenna 24219
Museo Valdese, Rorà 25278
Museo Valdese della Balziglia, Massello 24330
Museo Valenciano de Historia Natural, Valencia 35612
Museo Valenzuela, Valenzuela 31462
Museo Vallerano Bregagliotto, Stampa 37202
Museo Vallivo, Valfurva 25875
Museo Valtellinese di Storia e Arte, Sondrio 25603
Museo Vanvitelliano, Caserta 23374
Museo Vasariano di San Croce, Bosco Marengo 23185
Museo Vasco de Gastronomía, Laudio 34941
Museo Vasco de Historia de las Ciencias y de la Medicina, Leioa 34945
Museo Vasco del Ferrocarril, Azpeitia 34514
Museo Vásquez Fuller, Otavalo 09190
Museo Vela, Ligornetto 36882
Museo Vesuviano G. B. Alfano, Pompei 24986
Museo V.G. Rossi, Santa Margherita Ligure 25433
El Museo Viajero, Buenos Aires 00246
Museo Víctor Alejandro Jaramillo, Ibarra 09184
Museo Víctor Manuel, La Habana 08000
Museo Vilal Visconti Venosta, Grosio 24055
Museo Villa dei Cedri, Bellinzona 36532
Museo Villa Medicea, Poggio a Caiano 24976
Museo Villa Urania-Antiche Maioliche di Castelli, Pescara 24870
Museo Villa Urpo, Siivikkala 10036
Museo Virgen de la Portería, Avila 34507
Museo Virgen de Zapopan, Zapopan 28649
Museo Virgiliano, Virgilio 26030
Museo Virreinal de Zinacantepec, San Miguel Zinacantepec 28414
Museo Virtual de Artes el País, Montevideo 41025
Museo Vitaliano Zuccardi, Sincelejo 07593
Museo Vivo della Scienza, Napoli 24603
Museo Vostell-Malpartida de Cáceres, Malpartida de Cáceres 35077
Museo V.S. Breda, Padova 24748
Museo Vulcanologico dell'Osservatorio Vesuviano, Ercolano 23736
Museo Wakuatay, Playas de Rosarito 28314
Museo Weilbauer, Quito 09219
Museo Wifredo Lam, La Habana 08001
Museo Wilhelm Schmid, Brè sopra Lugano 36583
Museo Xochiltepec, Magdalena 28066
Museo Xólotl, San Bartolo Tenayuca 28376
Museo Xul Solar, Buenos Aires 00247
Museo y Archivo Dardo Rocha, La Plata 00394
Museo y Archivo Histórico de San Nicolás, San Nicolás de los Arroyos 00592
Museo y Archivo Histórico Diocesano, Tui 35580
Museo y Archivo Histórico Localista Almirante Guillermo Brown, Adrogué 00107
Museo y Artesanía el Molino, Agüimes 34412
Museo y Biblioteca Blanco Acevedo, Montevideo 41026
Museo y Biblioteca de la Literature Porteña, Buenos Aires 00248
Museo y Biblioteca Leoncio Prado, Huánuco 31173
Museo y Centro Cultural AGADU, Montevideo 41027
Museo y Centro Cultural Victoria Ocampo, Mar del Plata 00429
Museo y Centro Estudios Históricos de la Facultad de Odontología, Buenos Aires 00249
Museo y Jardin Botánico Profesor Atilio Lombardo, Montevideo 41028
Museo y Monumento Histórico Las Bóvedas, Uspallata 00651
Museo y Parque Arqueológico de Obando, Obando 07536
Museo y Parque Historico de Caparra, San Juan 32404
Museo y Parque Libres del Sur, Dolores 00332
Museo y Parque Nacional, Montenegro 07530
Museo Yacimiento Romano, Cartagena 34687
Museo Yoloxúchitl, Cuernavaca 27877
Museo Zabaleta, Quesada 35305
Museo Zacatecano, Zacatecas 28642
Museo Zambiano, Castelfidardo 23396
Museo Zoloxúchitl, Zacualpan 28646
Museo Zoologico, Padova 24749
Museo Zoologico Cambria, Messina 24365
Museo Zoológico César Domìnguez Flores, Tuxtla Gutiérrez 28576
Museo Zoológico Dámaso A. Larrañaga, Montevideo 41029
Museo Zoologico degli Vertebrati, Avellino 22990
Museo Zoologico dell'Istituto Nazionale per la Fauna Selvatica, Ozzano dell'Emilia 24725
Museo Zoologico G. Scarpa, Treviso 25808
Museo Zucchi Collection, Milano 24413
Museo Zuloaga, Segovia 35468
Museo Zumalacárregui, Ormaiztegi 35191
Museoalus Sigyn, Turku 10126
Museokeskus Vapriikki, Tampere 10081
Museokylä Kalluntalo, Laukaa 09770
Museon, Den Haag 29106
Museon Arlaten, Arles 10418
Museonder, Otterlo 29687
Muséoparc de Découverte des Tourbières et du Cezallier, Saint-Alyre-ès-Montagne 14094
Muséoparc de la Ferme de l'Aurochs, Menétrux-en-Joux 12930
Muséoparc de la Préhistoire, Saint-Vrain 14510
Muséoparc du Soleil et du Cosmos, Les Angles 12517
Muséoparc La Petite Ferme Provençale, Antibes 10378
Museos Arqueológico, Portoviejo 09191
Museos de la Universidad Nacional de Cajamarca, Cajamarca 31130
Museos del Gaucho y de la Moneda, Montevideo 41030
Museos Integrales de Antofagasta de la Sierra y Laguna Blanca, San Fernando del Valle de Catamarca 00559
Muséosite Cavernicole de la Grotte de la Madeleine, Saint-Remèze 14445
Muséosite de la Citadelle Vivante de Bitche, Bitche 10750
Muséosite de l'Amphithéâtre Gallo-Romain, Lillebonne 12608
Muséosite du Volcan à Ciel Ouvert, Saint-Ours-les-Roches 14393
Muséosite Gallo-Romain, Pithiviers-le-Vieil 13746
Museotalo Warpunen, Anjalankoski 09416
Muséotrain Animé, Massangis 12887
Museu Académico de Coimbra, Coimbra 32254
Museu Aeroespacial, Rio de Janeiro 04329
Museu Afro-Brasileiro, Salvador 04421
Museu Afro Brasileiro de Sergipe, Laranjeiras 04169
Museu Alfredo Andersen, Curitiba 04064
Museu Alfredo Varela, Jaguarão 04143
Museu Amsterdam Sauer de Pedras Preciosas, Rio de Janeiro 04330
Museu Anchieta Ciencias Naturais, Porto Alegre 04274
Museu Angelo Agostini / Casa de Cultura Laura Alvim, Rio de Janeiro 04331
Museu Aníbal Ribeiro Filho, Paranaguá 04244
Museu Anjos Teixeira, Sintra 32349
Museu Antoniano, Lisboa 32290
Museu Antonino, Faro 32271
Museu Antonio Granemann de Souza, Curitibanos 04079
Museu Antonio Lago, Rio de Janeiro 04332
Museu Antonio Parreiras, Niterói 04225
Museu Antropológico, Coimbra 32255
Museu Antropológico, Goiânia 04108
Museu Antropológico Caldas Júnior, Santo Antônio da Patrulha 04452
Museu Antropológico Diretor Pestana, Ijuí 04127
Museu Antropológico do Instituto Superior de Cultura Brasileira, Rio de Janeiro 04333
Museu Antropológico do Rio Grande do Sul, Porto Alegre 04275
Museu Arquediocesano Dom Joaquim, Brusque 04012
Museu Arqueològic, Ponts 35285
Museu Arqueològic Comarcal, Banyoles 34527
Museu Arqueològic de l'Esquerda, Roda de Ter 35330
Museu Arqueològic i Paleontològic, Baldomar 34524
Museu Arqueològic i Paleontològic, Moià 35117
Museu Arqueològic Municipal, Els Prats de Rei 35294
Museu Arqueològic Municipal, La Vall d'Uixo 35614
Museu Arqueológico, Lagoa Santa 04164
Museu Arqueológico, Lisboa 32291
Museu Arqueològic, Oliva 35169
Museu Arqueológico de Sambaqui Joinville, Joinville 04150
Museu Arqueológico de São Miguel de Odrinhas, Sintra 32350
Museu Arqueológico e Etnológico António Tomás Pires, Elvas 32267
Museu Arqueológico e Lapidar do Infante D. Henrique, Faro 32272
Museu Arquidiocesano de Mariana, Mariana 04196
Museu Arquivo Histórico da Santa Casa, Belém 03970
Museu Arquivo Histórico Florense, Flores da Cunha 04087
Museu-Arxiu Arbocenc, L'Arboç 34474
Museu Arxiu Comarcal, Moià 35118
Museu-Arxiu de Santa María de Mataró, Mataró 35099
Museu Arxiu de Vilassar de Dalt, Vilassar de Dalt 35671
Museu-Arxiu Municipal, Tortosa 35569
Museu-Arxiu Municipal de Calella, Calella 34659
Museu-Arxiu Parroquial, Canet de Mar 34670
Museu Arxiu Parroquial, Montesa 35136
Museu-Arxiu Tomàs Balvey i Bas, Cardedeu 34678
Museu Banespa, São Paulo 04498
Museu Barão de Mauá, Mauá 04201
Museu Bi Moreira, Lavras 04170
Museu-Biblioteca da Fundacão de Casa de Bragança, Vila Viçosa 32359
Museu Biblioteca Fundació Mauri, La Garriga 34839
Museu Botânico Dr. João Barbosa Rodrigues, São Paulo 04499
Museu Calmon Barreto, Araxá 03956
Museu Calouste Gulbenkian, Lisboa 32292
Museu Câmara Cascudo, Natal 04218
Museu Capela Santa Luzia, Vitória 04590
Museu Capitular, Lleida 34969
Museu Capitular de la Catedral de Girona, Girona 34853
Museu Carlos Costa Pinto, Salvador 04422
Museu Carlos Reis, Torres Novas 32355
Museu Carmen Miranda, Rio de Janeiro 04334
Museu Carpológico do Jardim Botânico do Rio de Janeiro, Rio de Janeiro 04335
Museu Casa Alphonsus de Guimaraens, Mariana 04197
Museu Casa Cel. Joaquim Lacerda, Lapa 04166
Museu Casa da Hera, Vassouras 04582
Museu Casa d'Areny-Plandolit, Ordino 00085
Museu Casa de Benjamin Constant, Rio de Janeiro 04336
Museu Casa de Portinari, Brodowski 04011
Museu Casa de Rui Barbosa, Rio de Janeiro 04337
Museu Casa de Rui Barbosa, Salvador 04423
Museu Casa do Anhanguera, Santana de Parnaíba 04448
Museu Casa do Pontal, Rio de Janeiro 04338
Museu Casa do Sertão, Feira de Santana 04085
Museu Casa dos Contos, Ouro Preto 04234
Museu Casa Fritz Alt, Joinville 04151
Museu Casa Guignard, Ouro Preto 04235
Museu Casa Guimarães Rosa, Cordisburgo 04054
Museu Casa Pedro Américo, Areia 03960
Museu Casa Rull, Sispony 00087
Museu-Casa Verdaguer, Vallvidrera 35639
Museu Castro Alves, Salvador 04424
Museu Cau Ferrat, Sitges 35497
Museu Central das Forças Armadas, Luanda 00095
Museu Cerdà, Puigcerdà 35303
Museu Ceroplástico Augusto Esteves, São Paulo 04500
Museu Civico-Religioso Padre Cicero, Juazeiro do Norte 04154
Museu Clarà, Barcelona 34549
Museu Claretiano, Vic 35651
Museu Codorniú, Sant Sadurní d'Anoia 35408
Museu Comajoan Fauna del Montseny, Santa María de Palautordera 35423
Museu Comarcal, Tárrega 35518
Museu Comarcal de Berga, Berga 34602
Museu Comarcal de la Conca de Barberà, Montblanc 35129
Museu Comarcal de la Garrotxa, Olot 35172
Museu Comarcal de l'Anoia, Igualada 34914
Museu Comarcal de Manresa, Manresa 35082
Museu Comarcal Salvador Vilaseca, Reus 35314
Museu Comendador Ananias Arruda, Baturit 03969
Museu Comendador Jos' Dias de Andrade, Arceburgo 03959
Museu Comercial e Arqueológico do Sindicato dos Empregados, Maceió 04178
Museu Comunitário, Ipumirim 04128
Museu Comunitário, Itapiranga 04135
Museu Condes de Castro Guimarães, Cascais 32249
Museu Corina Novelino, Sacramento 04417
Museu Coritiba Football Club, Curitiba 04065
Museu Cosme Bauça, Felanitx 34813
Museu Criminal, São Paulo 04501
Museu D. João VI, Rio de Janeiro 04339
Museu D. Lopo de Almeida, Abrantes 32229
Museu da Abolição, Recife 04295
Museu da Agua da Epal, Lisboa 32293
Museu da Arte Brasileira, Maceió 04179
Museu da Arte Pierre Chalita, Maceió 04180
Museu da Associação Nacional dos Veteranos, São João Del Rei 04467
Museu da Bacia do Paraná, Maringá 04199
Museu da Borracha, Rio Branco 04311
Museu da Brigada Militar, Porto Alegre 04276
Museu da Cachaça, Paty do Alferes 04250
Museu da Casa Brasileira, São Paulo 04502
Museu da Casa da Cultura de Teresina, Teresina 04563
Museu da Cerâmica de Sacavém, Loures 32317
Museu da Cidade, Campinas 04023
Museu da Cidade, Lisboa 32294
Museu da Cidade, São Paulo 04503
Museu da Cidade de Recife, Recife 04296
Museu da Companhia Independente do Palácio Guanabara, Rio de Janeiro 04340
Museu da Companhia Paulista, Jundiá 04161
Museu da Cultura e Arte Popular, João Pessoa 04148
Museu da Curia Metropolitana, Porto Alegre 04277
Museu da Educação e do Brinquedo, São Paulo 04504
Museu da Eletricidade, Rio de Janeiro 04341
Museu da Energia, Itu 04138
Museu da Escola de Engenharia, Rio de Janeiro 04342
Museu da Escola de Minas Gerais, Belo Horizonte 03982
Museu da Escola Naval, Rio de Janeiro 04343
Museu da Escravatura, Luanda 00096
Museu da Estrada de Ferro Madeira-Mamoré, Porto Velho 04291
Museu da Estrada de Ferro Sorocabana, Sorocaba 04553
Museu da Faculdade de Direito, São Paulo 04505
Museu da Faculdade de Odontologia, Araraquara 03954
Museu da Família Colonial, Blumenau 03991
Museu da Farmáciada Santa Casa da Misericórdia do Rio de Janeiro, Rio de Janeiro 04344
Museu da Fauna, Rio de Janeiro 04345
Museu da Fazenda Federal, Rio de Janeiro 04346
Museu da Força Expedicionária Brasileira, Rio de Janeiro 04347
Museu da Fundação Nacional de Saúde, Brasília 03997
Museu da Gravura, Curitiba 04066
Museu da Gravura Brasileira, Bagé 03963
Museu da Imagem, Campinas 04024
Museu da Imagem, Franca 04103
Museu da Imagem e do Som, Campo Grande 04030
Museu da Imagem e do Som, Rio de Janeiro 04348
Museu da Imagem e do Som de Alagoas, Maceió 04181
Museu da Imagem e do Som de Campinas, Campinas 04025
Museu da Imagem e do Som de Campos, Campos dos Goitacazes 04036
Museu da Imagem e do Som de Cascavel, Cascavel 04044
Museu da Imagem e do Som de Curitiba, Curitiba 04067
Museu da Imagem e do Som de e da Imprensa da Bahia, Salvador 04425
Museu da Imagem e do Som de Goiás, Goiás 04114
Museu da Imagem e do Som de Piracicaba, São Paulo 04506
Museu da Imagem e do Som de Resende, Resende 04307
Museu da Imagem e do Som de Santa Catarina, Florianópolis 04089
Museu da Imagem e do Som de São Paulo, São Paulo 04507
Museu da Imagem e do Som de Taubaté, Taubaté 04557
Museu da Imagem e do Som do Ceará, Fortaleza 04098
Museu da Imagem e do Som do Pará, Belém 03971
Museu da Imagem e do Som do Paraná, Curitiba 04068
Museu da Imigração, Santa Bárbara d'Oeste 04440
Museu da Imprensa, Brasília 03998
Museu da Inconfidência, Ouro Preto 04236
Museu da Liga dos Combatentes da Grande Guerra, Lisboa 32295
Museu da Limpeza Urbana - Casa de Banhos de Dom João VI, Rio de Janeiro 04349
Museu da Literatura, São Paulo 04508
Museu da Loucura, Barbacena 03966
Museu da Música Portuguesa, Estoril 32268
Museu DA Pessoa, São Paulo 04509
Museu da Polícia Civil, Rio de Janeiro 04350
Museu da Polícia Militar de Pernambuco, Recife 04297
Museu da Porcelana Senhor Adelino dos Santos Gouveia, Pedreira 04253
Museu da Quinta das Cruzes, Funchal 32274
Museu da Rainha Dona Leonor, Beja 32242
Museu da Regiao Flâviense, Chaves 32252
Museu da República, Rio de Janeiro 04351
Museu da Revolução, Maputo 28720
Museu da Santa Casa da Misericórdia, Coimbra 32256
Museu da Secção de Tecnologia do Serviço Florestal, Rio de Janeiro 04352
Museu da Terra e da Vida, Mafra 04186
Museu da Universidade Federal do Pará, Belém 03972
Museu da Venrável Ordem Terceira de São Francisco da Penitência, Rio de Janeiro 04353
Museu Darder d'Història Natural, Banyoles 34528
Museu d'Arqueologia de Catalunya, Barcelona 34550
Museu d'Arqueologia de Catalunya, Olèrdola 35167
Museu d'Arqueologia de Catalunya-Empúries, L'Escala 34800
Museu d'Arqueologia de Catalunya Girona, Girona 34854
Museu d'Arqueologia de Catalunya Ullastret, Ullastret 35586
Museu d'Arqueològia Submarina, Pals 35246
Museu d'Arquitectura de la Real Càtedra Gaudí, Barcelona 34551
Museu d'Art, Cadaqués 34644
Museu d'Art, Girona 34855
Museu d'Art Casa Turull, Sabadell 35345
Museu d'Art Contemporani, Pego 35260
Museu d'Art Contemporani, Valldemosa 35632
Museu d'Art Contemporani de Barcelona, Barcelona 34552
Museu d'Art Contemporani de Mallorca, Sa Pobla 35276
Museu d'Art Contemporani d'Eivissa, Eivissa 34788
Museu d'Art Espanyol Contemporani, Palma de Mallorca 35232
Museu d'Art Frederic Marès, Montblanc 35130
Museu d'Art Matern, Sant Vicenç dels Horts 35409
Museu d'Art Modern, Tarragona 35512
Museu d'Art Modern del MNAC, Barcelona 34553
Museu d'Art Modern 'Jaume Morera, Lleida 34970
Museu d'Art Popular, Horta de Sant Joan 34903

Museu das Alfaias da Paróquia da Cachoeira, Cachoeira 04014
Museu das Armas, Lapa 04167
Museu das Bandeiras, Goiás 04115
Museu das Comunicações, Lisboa 32296
Museu das Monções, Porto Feliz 04289
Museu das Reduções, Ouro Preto 04237
Museu de Alberto Sampaio, Guimarães 32278
Museu de Anatomia Humana Prof. Dr. Alfonso Bovera, São Paulo 04510
Museu de Anatomia Veterinária Prof. Dr. Plínio Pinto e Silva, São Paulo 04511
Museu de Angra do Heroísmo, Angra do Heroísmo 32237
Museu de Antropologia do Vale do Paraíba, Jacareí 04142
Museu de Armas Ferreira da Cunha, Petrópolis 04262
Museu de Armas Major Lara Ribas, Florianópolis 04090
Museu de Arqueologia e Artes Populares, Paranaguá 04245
Museu de Arqueologia e Etnologia, Salvador 04426
Museu de Arqueologia e Etnologia da Universidade de São Paulo, São Paulo 04512
Museu de Arte, Belém 03973
Museu de Arte, Goiânia 04109
Museu de Arte, Joinville 04152
Museu de Arte, Londrina 04174
Museu de Arte Assis Chateaubriand, Campina Grande 04020
Museu de Arte Brasileira, São Paulo 04513
Museu de Arte Contemporâea, Jataí 04145
Museu de Arte Contemporânea, Feira de Santana 04086
Museu de Arte Contemporânea da Universidade de São Paulo, São Paulo 04514
Museu de Arte Contemporânea de Niterói, Niterói 04226
Museu de Arte Contemporânea de Pernambuco, Olinda 04231
Museu de Arte Contemporônea, Curitiba 04069
Museu de Arte da Bahia, Salvador 04427
Museu de Arte da Pampulha, Belo Horizonte 03983
Museu de Arte da Universidade Fedral do Ceará, Fortaleza 04099
Museu de Arte de Santa Catarina, Florianópolis 04091
Museu de Arte de São Paulo Assis Chateaubriand, São Paulo 04515
Museu de Arte do Paranà, Curitiba 04070
Museu de Arte do Rio Grande do Sul Aldo Malagoli, Porto Alegre 04278
Museu de Arte e Cultura Canjira, Itaobim 04134
Museu de Arte e Cultura Popular Coordenação de Cultura, Cuiabá 04059
Museu de Arte e História, Natal 04219
Museu de Arte e História Racioppi, Belo Horizonte 03984
Museu de Arte e Histórico, Jaboticabal 04141
Museu de Arte Mágica e Ilusionismo João Peixoto dos Santos, São Paulo 04516
Museu de Arte Moderna, Resende 04308
Museu de Arte Moderna da Bahia, Salvador 04428
Museu de Arte Moderna de São Paulo, São Paulo 04517
Museu de Arte Moderna do Rio de Janeiro, Rio de Janeiro 04354
Museu de Arte Popular, Lisboa 32297
Museu de Arte Popular da Fortaleza dos Reis Magos, Natal 04220
Museu de Arte Religiosa, Vitória 04591
Museu de Arte Sacra, Rio de Janeiro 04355
Museu de Arte Sacra, Salvador 04429
Museu de Arte Sacra, São Cristóvão 04459
Museu de Arte Sacra, São João Del Rei 04468
Museu de Arte Sacra, São Luís 04476
Museu de Arte Sacra, São Paulo 04518
Museu de Arte Sacra, São Sebastião 04547
Museu de Arte Sacra, Taubaté 04558
Museu de Arte Sacra da Catedral-Basílica, Salvador 04430
Museu de Arte Sacra da Universidade, Coimbra 32257
Museu de Arte sacra de Angra dos Reis, Angra dos Reis 03945
Museu de Arte Sacra de Boa Morte, Goiás 04116
Museu de Arte Sacra de Iguape, Iguape 04126
Museu de Arte Sacra de Santos, Santos 04453
Museu de Arte Sacra do Carmo / Paróquia do Pilar, Ouro Preto 04238
Museu de Arte Sacra do Estado de Alagoas, Marechal Deodoro 04195
Museu de Arte Sacra do Pará, Belém 03974
Museu de Arte Sacra Dom Ranulfo, Maceió 04182
Museu de Arte Sacra Padre Roberto Barbalho, Recife 04298
Museu de Artes Plásticas, Taubaté 04559
Museu de Artes Plásticas Quirino da Silva, Mococa 04204
Museu de Artes Sacras Iria Josepha da Silva, Mococa 04205
Museu de Artes Visuais, São Luís 04477
Museu de Artes Visuais Ruth Schneider, Passo Fundo 04246
Museu de Astronomia e Ciências Afins, Rio de Janeiro 04356
Museu de Aveiro, Aveiro 32239
Museu de Azambuja, Azambuja 32240
Museu de Badalona, Badalona 34520
Museu de Belas-Artes, Cataguases 04046
Museu de Bellvís, Bellvís 34596
Museu de Biodiversidade do Cerrado, Uberlândia 04575
Museu de Biologia Prof. Mello Leitão, Santa Teresa 04447
Museu de Bonecos e Ventrílocos, São Paulo 04519
Museu de Carlos Machado, Ponta Delgada 32327
Museu de Carrosses Fúnebres, Barcelona 34554
Museu de Cartão, São Paulo 04520
Museu de Cera, Barcelona 34555
Museu de Cera, Binissalem 34617
Museu de Ceràmica, Barcelona 34556
Museu de Ceràmica de Manises, Manises 35080
Museu de Ciência e Técnica da Escola de Minas, Ouro Preto 04239
Museu de Ciência e Tecnologia, Salvador 04431
Museu de Ciências da Terra - DNPM, Rio de Janeiro 04357
Museu de Ciências Naturais, Guarapuava 04120
Museu de Ciências Naturais, Porto Alegre 04279
Museu de Ciências Naturais, Recife 04299
Museu de Ciências Naturais, Triunfo 04569
Museu de Ciências Naturais PUC Minas, Belo Horizonte 03985
Museu de Ciències Naturals, Lleida 34971
Museu de Ciències Naturals de Barcelona, Barcelona 34557
Museu de Comunicação Social Hipólito José da Costa, Porto Alegre 04280
Museu de Corrente, Corrente 04056
Museu de Coses del Poble, Collbató 34728
Museu de Curiositats Marineres, Vilanova i la Geltrú 35665
Museu de Documentos Especiais, Praia 06876
Museu de Esportes Mané Garrincha, Rio de Janeiro 04358
Museu de Etnografia do Lobito, Lobito 00093
Museu de Etnografia e História, Porto 32333
Museu de Evora, Evora 32269
Museu de Ex-votos do Senhor do Bonfim, Salvador 04432
Museu de Farmácia, São Paulo 04521
Museu de Física, Coimbra 32258
Museu de Folclore Édison Carneiro, Rio de Janeiro 04359
Museu de Folclore Saul Martins, Vespasiano 04584
Museu de Francisco Tavares Proença Júnior, Castelo Branco 32251
Museu de Gavà, Gavà 34842
Museu de Gelida, Gelida 34843
Museu de Geociências, São Paulo 04522
Museu de Geociências da Universidade de Brasília, Brasília 03999
Museu de Geologia, Barcelona 34558
Museu de Geologia, Maringá 04200
Museu de Geologia, Porto Alegre 04281
Museu de Geologia, Sant Celoni 35395
Museu de Geológia, Paleontológia e Mineralógia, Luanda 00097
Museu de Geologia Valenti Masachs, Manresa 35083
Museu de Granollers, Granollers 34883
Museu de Granollers-Ciències Naturals, Granollers 34884
Museu de Grão Vasco, Viseu 32361
Museu de Historia da Ocupação Colonial e da Resistencia, Maputo 28721
Museu de História e Ciências Naturais, Além Paraiba 03941
Museu de História Natural, Belo Horizonte 03986
Museu de História Natural, Campinas 04026
Museu de História Natural, Coimbra 32259
Museu de História Natural, Crato 04058
Museu de História Natural, Maputo 28722
Museu de História Natural, Porto 32334
Museu de História Natural Prof. Antonio Pergola, Atibaia 03962
Museu de Homem do Norte, Manaus 04190
Museu de Homem Sergipano, Aracaju 03951
Museu de Imagem e do Som de Pernambuco, Recife 04300
Museu de Images do Inconsciente, Rio de Janeiro 04360
Museu de Índio, Uberlândia 04576
Museu de Instrumentos de Cálculo Numérico, São Carlos 04458
Museu de José Malhoa, Caldas da Rainha 32246
Museu de la Catedral, Barcelona 34559
Museu de la Ciencia de la Fundació la Caixa, Barcelona 34560
Museu de la Ciència i de la Tècnica de Catalunya, Terrassa 35527
Museu de la Ciutat, Valls 35638
Museu de la Farmàcia Catalana, Barcelona 34561
Museu de la Fauna Ibero-Balear, Costitx 34755
Museu de la Festa, Casal de Sant Jordi, Alcoi 34436
Museu de la Fusta, Areu 34482
Museu de la Música, Barcelona 34562
Museu de la Noguera, Balaguer 34523
Museu de la Pedra i de l'Estable, Guimerà 34893
Museu de la Pesca, Palamós 35211
Museu de la Piel, Igualada 34915
Museu de la Vall de Lord, Sant Lorenç de Morunys 35405
Museu de la Vila, Vilar-Rodona 35670
Museu de l'Acordió, Arsèguel 34488
Museu de l'Adet, Torelló 35554
Museu de l'Aigua Col·lecció Gavarró, Vilanova del Camí 35663
Museu de Lamego, Lamego 32282
Museu de l'Aquarella, Llança 34962
Museu de l'Automòbil, Barcelona 34563
Museu de Leiria, Leiria 32283
Museu de l'Empordà, Figueres 34817
Museu de les Arts Decoratives, Barcelona 34564
Museu de les Arts Escèniques, Barcelona 34565
Museu de les Arts Gràfiques, Barcelona 34566
Museu de l'Estampació de Premià de Mar, Premià de Mar 35295
Museu de L'Hospitalet de Llobregat, L'Hospitalet de Llobregat 34904
Museu de l'Institut de Criminologia, Barcelona 34567
Museu de l'Institut Paleontològic Miquel Crusafont, Sabadell 35346
Museu de l'Instituto Botánico, Barcelona 34568
Museu de Llaberia, Tivissa 35533
Museu de Llavaneres, Sant Andreu de Llavaneres 35394
Museu de Lloret de Mar, Lloret de Mar 34977
Museu de Lluis Salvador d'Austria, Deià 34769
Museu de Malacologia Cau del Cargol, Vilassar de Dalt 35672
Museu de Mallorca, Palma de Mallorca 35233
Museu de Marinha, Lisboa 32298
Museu de Mataró, Mataró 35100
Museu de Medallística Enrique Giner, Nules 35164
Museu de Medicina, Curitiba 04071
Museu de Minerais e Rochas, Uberlândia 04577
Museu de Mineralogia, Congonhas 04050
Museu de Mineralogia Luiz Englert, Porto Alegre 04282
Museu de Montgrí i del Baix Ter, Torroella de Montgrí 35566
Museu de Montserrat, Monistrol de Montserrat 35125
Museu de Nampula, Nampula 28729
Museu de Nossa Senhora da Glória do Outeiro, Rio de Janeiro 04361
Museu de Odontologia Dr. Solon de Miranda Galvão, Natal 04221
Museu de Odontologia Professor Salles Cunha, Rio de Janeiro 04362
Museu de Olaria, Barcelos 32241
Museu de Ornitologia, Goiânia 04110
Museu de Ovar, Ovar 32325
Museu de Paleontologia, Monte Alto 04208
Museu de Patologia do Instituto Oswaldo Cruz, Rio de Janeiro 04363
Museu de Pedras Ramis Bucair, Cuiabá 04060
Museu de Pesca, Santos 04454
Museu de Poblet, Monestir de Poblet 35122
Museu de Polícia Militar, São Paulo 04523
Museu de Pré-História Professora Márcia Angelina Alves, Perdizes 04259
Museu de Prehistòria i de les Cultures de València, Valencia 35613
Museu de Relógio Prof. Dimas de Melo Pimenta, São Paulo 04524
Museu de Rocafort, El Pont de Vilomara i Rocafort 35281
Museu de Roque Gameiro, Minde 32320
Museu de Rua Alto Paraná Ontem e Hoje, Alto Paran 03942
Museu de Rubí, Rubí 35342
Museu de Sal de Josep Arnau, Cardona 34679
Museu de Sant Joan de Mediona, Mediona 35106
Museu de Sant Pol de Mar, Sant Pol de Mar 35407
Museu de Santo André, Santo André 04451
Museu de São Roque, Lisboa 32299
Museu de Saúde Pública Emílio Ribas, São Paulo 04525
Museu de Serralves, Porto 32335
Museu de Sertão, Petrolina 04261
Museu de Setúbal - Convento de Jesus - Galeria de Arte Quinhentista, Setúbal 32346
Museu de Telecomunicações, Rio de Janeiro 04364
Museu de Torrebesses, Torrebesses 35559
Museu de Torrellebreta, Malla 35076
Museu de Torroja, Torroja del Priorat 35567
Museu de Tradições do Nordeste, Brasília 04000
Museu de Valldoreix, Sant Cugat del Vallès 35398
Museu de Valores, Rio de Janeiro 04365
Museu de Valores do Banco Central do Brasil, Brasília 04001
Museu de Venâncio Aires, Venâncio Aires 04583
Museu de Vilafranca-Museu del Vi, Vilafranca del Penedès 35659
Museu de Zoologia, São Paulo 04526
Museu d'Eines Antigues, Torregrossa 35561
Museu d'Eines del Camp Masia de Can Deu, Sabadell 35347
Museu d'Eines del Pagès, Sant Climent de Llobregat 35396
Museu del Bast, Llaberia-Tivissa 34959
Museu del Blat, Taradell 35509
Museu d'El Bruc, El Bruc 34624
Museu del Calcat Antic, Barcelona 34569
Museu del Camp, Vilabella 35657
Museu del Càntir, Argentona 34483
Museu del Ferrocarril, Vilanova i la Geltrú 35666
Museu del Joguet de Catalunya, Figueres 34818
Museu del Monestir de Santa María de L'Estany, L'Estany 34806
Museu del Montsec, Artesa de Segre 34491
Museu del Montsià, Amposta 34464
Museu del Pagès, Castelldans 34691
Museu del Pagès, Linyola 34958
Museu del Pagès, Torroella de Fluvià 35565
Museu del Pastor, Fornells de la Muntanya 34823
Museu del Perfum, Barcelona 34570
Museu del Prat, El Prat de Llobregat 35292
Museu del Temple Expiatori de la Sagrada Familia, Barcelona 34571
Museu del Vidre, Algaida 34444
Museu del Volcans, Olot 35173
Museu dels Autòmats, Barcelona 34572
Museu dels Raiers, El Pont de Claverol 35280
Museu des Comunicações Marechal Rondon, Ji-Paran 04147
Museu d'Etnografia d'Eivissa, Santa Eulària des Riu 35418
Museu d'Etnologia el Conreu de l'Arros, Pego 35261
Museu d'Història, Sabadell 35348
Museu d'Història Casa Castellarnau, Tarragona 35513
Museu d'Història de la Ciudad, Sant Feliu de Guíxols 35400
Museu d'Història de la Ciutat, Barcelona 34573
Museu d'Història de la Ciutat, Girona 34856
Museu d'Historia de Nules, Nules 35165
Museu d'Historia de Tarragona Pretori Romà, Tarragona 35514
Museu di Arte Contemporânea, Americana 03943
Museu Diocesà de Barcelona, Barcelona 34574
Museu Diocesà de Girona, Girona 34857
Museu Diocesà de Mallorca, Palma de Mallorca 35234
Museu Diocesa de Menorca, Ciudadela de Menorca 34726
Museu Diocesá d'Urgell, La Seu d'Urgell 35470
Museu Diocesà i Comarcal, Solsona 35502
Museu Diocesà i Comarcal, Solsona 35503
Museu Diocesano de Arte Sacra, Funchal 32275
Museu do Ar, Alverca do Ribatejo 32234
Museu do Automóvel, Arte & História, São Francisco de Paula 04461
Museu do Banco de Crédito Real de Minas Gerais, Juiz de Fora 04156
Museu do Bonde, Rio de Janeiro 04366
Museu do Brinquedo, São Paulo 04527
Museu do Café, Luanda 00098
Museu do Café Cel. Francisco Schmidt, Ribeirão Preto 04310
Museu do Cangaço, Triunfo 04570
Museu do Caramulo, Caramulo 32247
Museu do Carnaval, Rio de Janeiro 04367
Museu do Carnaval Hilton Silva, Florianópolis 04092
Museu do Carro Eléctrico, Porto 32336
Museu do Ceará, Fortaleza 04100
Museu do Chiado, Lisboa 32300
Museu do Círio de Nazaré, Betém 03990
Museu do Colégio Mauá, Santa Cruz do Sul 04441
Museu do Colono, Santa Leopoldina 04442
Museu do Congo, Carmona 00090
Museu do Diamante, Diamantina 04080
Museu do Dundu, Chitato 00091
Museu do Estado da Bahia, Salvador 04433
Museu do Estado de Pernambuco, Recife 04301
Museu do Estado do Pará, Belém 03975
Museu do Eucalipto, Rio Claro 04312
Museu do Expedicionário, Curitiba 04072
Museu do Gás, Rio de Janeiro 04368
Museu do Homem, Curitiba 04073
Museu do Homem do Nordeste, Recife 04302
Museu do Índio, Florianópolis 04093
Museu do Índio, Lagoa Seca 04165
Museu do Índio, Manaus 04191
Museu do Indio, Rio de Janeiro 04369
Museu do Instituto Arqueológico, Histórico e Geográfico Pernam Bucano, Recife 04303
Museu do Instituto Butantan, São Paulo 04528
Museu do Instituto de Antropologia Câmara Cascudo, Natal 04222
Museu do Instituto Geografico e Historico da Bahia, Salvador 04434
Museu do Instituto Histórico, Carpina 04042
Museu do Instituto Histórico e Geográfico Brasileiro, Rio de Janeiro 04370
Museu do Instituto Histórico e Geográfico de Alagoas, Maceió 04183
Museu do Instituto Histórico e Geográfico do Rio Grande do Norte, Natal 04223
Museu do Instituto Oceanográfico, São Paulo 04529
Museu do Jardim Botânico, Rio de Janeiro 04371
Museu do Mamulengo, Olinda 04232
Museu do Mar - Rei D. Carlos, Cascais 32250
Museu do Minstério do Trabalho, Brasília 04002
Museu do Monumento Nacional aos Mortos da Segunda Guerra Mundial, Rio de Janeiro 04372
Museu do Ouro, Sabará 04416
Museu do Piauí, Teresina 04564
Museu do Pio XII, Novo Hamburgo 04230
Museu do Pioneiro, Malange 00102
Museu do Porto de Belém, Belém 03976
Museu do Porto do Rio, Rio de Janeiro 04373
Museu do Primeiro Reinado, Rio de Janeiro 04374
Museu do Rádio, Juiz de Fora 04157
Museu do Reino do Koongo, Mbanza Koongo 00103
Museu do Santuário de Nossa Senhora da Abadia, Amares 32236
Museu do Seridó, Caicó 04017
Museu do Sol, Penápolis 04256
Museu do STF, Brasília 04003
Museu do Superior Tribunal de Justiça, Brasília 04004
Museu do Telephone, Rio de Janeiro 04375
Museu do Theatro Municipal, São Paulo 04530
Museu do Trem, Rio de Janeiro 04376
Museu do Trem, São Leopoldo 04474
Museu do Trem da Cidade de Recife, Recife 04304

Museu do Tribunal de Justiça do Estado de São Paulo, São Paulo 04531
Museu do Tropeiro, Castro 04045
Museu do Vaqueiro, Morada Nova 04213
Museu do Vinho, Videira 04588
Museu Dom Avelar Brandão Vilela, Teresina 04565
Museu Dom Diogo de Souza, Bagé 03964
Museu Dom Inocencio, Campanha 04019
Museu Dom João VI, Rio de Janeiro 04377
Museu Dom José, Sobral 04552
Museu Dom Vital, Recife 04305
Museu dos Baleeiros, Lajes do Pico 32281
Museu dos Inhamuns, Tauá 04555
Museu dos Teatros do Rio de Janeiro, Rio de Janeiro 04378
Museu dos Transportes, Coimbra 32260
Museu dos Transportes Públicos Gaetano Ferolla, São Paulo 04532
Museu Dr. José Faibes Lubianca, Porto Alegre 04283
Museu e Arquivo Histórico, Itu 04139
Museu e Arquivo Histórico do Centro Cultural Banco do Brasil, Rio de Janeiro 04379
Museu e Arquivo Histórico Municipal, Guapor 04119
Museu e Arquivo Municipal, Bom Jesus 03993
Museu e Arquivo Público Municipal de Campo Belo, Campo Belo 04028
Museu e Biblioteca do Instituto Geográfico e Histórico do Amazonas, Manaus 04192
Museu e Biblioteca Pública Pelotense, Pelotas 04255
Museu e Laboratório Mineralógico e Geológico, Lisboa 32301
Museu Ecologia, Nanuque 04215
Museu Educativo Gama d'Eça, Santa Maria 04444
Museu Egipci de Barcelona, Barcelona 34575
Museu Els Cups, Montbrió del Camp 35131
Museu Eng. António de Almeida, Porto 32337
Museu Enric Monjó, Vilassar de Mar 35673
Museu Episcopal de Vic, Vic 35652
Museu-Escola Esacro do Estado da Paraiba, João Pessoa 04149
Museu Estadual do Carvão, Arroio dos Ratos 03961
Museu Etnogràfic Andino-Amazònic, Barcelona 34576
Museu Etnogràfic de Ripoll, Ripoll 35325
Museu Etnografic Municipal, Moncada 35120
Museu Etnografic Municipal, Torrella 35563
Museu Etnográfico da Sociedade de Geografia de Lisboa, Lisboa 32302
Museu Etnográfico e Arqueológico do Dr. Joaquim Manso, Nazaré 32321
Museu Etnografico Nacional, Bissau 21289
Museu Etnològic de Barcelona, Barcelona 34577
Museu Etnològic de Dénia, Dénia 34772
Museu Etnologic de Guadalest, Guadalest 34886
Museu Etnologic de Muro, Muro 35152
Museu Etnològic del Montseny La Gabella, Arbúcies 34475
Museu Etnologic d'Era Val d'Aran, Vielha 35654
Museu Etnològic i Arqueològic, Juneda 34933
Museu Etnologic Moli del Dalt, Sant Lluis 35404
Museu Eugênio Teixeira Leal, Salvador 04435
Museu Farmàcia de l'Hospital de Santa Catarina, Girona 34858
Museu Farroupilha, Triunfo 04571
Museu Fazenda, Nanuque 04216
Museu Ferreira de Almeida, Nampula 28730
Museu Ferroviário de Pires do Rio, Pires do Rio 04269
Museu Florestal Octávio Vecchi, São Paulo 04533
Museu Folclorico da Divisão de Discoteca e Biblioteca de Música de São Paulo, São Paulo 04534
Museu Frederic Marès, Barcelona 34578
Museu Frei Galvão, Guaratinguetá 04122
Museu Futbol Club Barcelona President Núñez, Barcelona 34579
Museu Gabinet Postal, Barcelona 34580
Museu Geológico, Lisboa 32303
Museu Geológico da Bahia, Salvador 04436
Museu Geológico Valdemar Lefèvre, São Paulo 04535
Museu Getúlio Vargas, São Borja 04456
Museu Goiano Zoroastro Artiaga, Goiânia 04111
Museu Guido Straube, Curitiba 04074
Museu Gustavo Barroso, Fortaleza 04101
Museu H. Stern, Rio de Janeiro 04380
Museu Henriqueta Catharino, Salvador 04437
Museu Hipólito Cabaço, Alenquer 32232
Museu Histórico da Cidade, Brasília 04005
Museu Històric de la Seu, Manresa 35084
Museu Històric Municipal, Riudoms 35327
Museu Historic Municipal de Ca l'Arra, Barcelona 34581
Museu Historic Municipal de Polinyà, Polinyà 35278
Museu Histórico, Cambé 04018
Museu Histórico, Divinópolis 04081
Museu Histórico, Igarassu 04124
Museu Histórico, Lavras 04171
Museu Histórico, Londrina 04175
Museu Histórico, Nova Ponte 04228
Museu Histórico, Pará de Minas 04243
Museu Histórico, Rio Pomba 04410
Museu Histórico, São Francisco do Sul 04462
Museu Histórico, São Paulo 04536
Museu Histórico, Sertanópolis 04550
Museu Histórico, Siqueira Campos 04551
Museu Histórico Abílio Barreto, Belo Horizonte 03987
Museu Histórico Aurélio Dolabella, Santa Luzia 04443
Museu Histórico Bárbara Heliodora, São Gonçalo do Sapucaí 04465
Museu Histórico Beato José de Anchieta, Pedreira 04254
Museu Histórico Casa do Imigrante, Bento Gonçalves 03989
Museu Histórico Corália Venites Maluf, Sacramento 04418
Museu Histórico Cultural, Rio do Sul 04407
Museu Histórico da Cidade do Rio de Janeiro, Rio de Janeiro 04381
Museu Histórico da Imigração Japonesa no Brasil, São Paulo 04537
Museu Histórico da Universidade Federal, Viçoasa 04586
Museu Histórico de Araxá - Don Beja, Araxá 03957
Museu Histórico de Brejo Madre de Deus, Brejo Madre de Deus 04010
Museu Histórico de Jataí Francisco Honório de Campos, Jataí 04146
Museu Histórico de Sergipe, São Cristóvão 04460
Museu Histórico de Witmarsum, Palmeira 04242
Museu Histórico Desembargador Edmundo Mercer Júnior, Tibagi 04568
Museu Histórico do Corpo de Bombeiros Militar do Estado do Rio de Janeiro, Rio de Janeiro 04382
Museu Histórico do Exército e Forte de Copacabana, Rio de Janeiro 04383
Museu Histórico do Piauí, Teresina 04566
Museu Histórico do Senado Federal, Brasília 04006
Museu Histórico Dona Mariana Joaquina da Costa, Vespasiano 04585
Museu Histórico Dr. Sellmann Nazareth, São José do Rio Preto 04471
Museu Histórico e Artístico, Quitandinha 04293
Museu Histórico e Artístico do Maranhão, São Luís 04478
Museu Histórico e de Artes, Santana do Ipanema 04449
Museu Histórico e de Ordem Geral Plínio Travassos dos Santos, Rebeirão Preto 04294
Museu Histórico e Diplomático do Itamaraty, Rio de Janeiro 04384
Museu Histórico e Geográfico de Monte Sião, Monte Sião 04211
Museu Histórico e Geográfico de Poços de Caldas, Poços de Caldas 04271
Museu Histórico e Geral da Cidade de São Vicente, São Vicente 04549
Museu Histórico e Pedagógico, Mococa 04206
Museu Histórico e Pedagógico Conselheiro Rodrigues Alves, Guaratinguetá 04123
Museu Histórico e Pedagógico Dr. Washington Luís, Batatais 03968
Museu Histórico e Pedagógico Fernão Dias Paes, Penápolis 04257
Museu Histórico e Pedagógico Marechal Cândido Rondon, Araçatuba 03953
Museu Histórico e Pedagógico Monteiro Lobato, Taubaté 04560
Museu Histórico e Pedagógico Pe. Manoel da Nóbrega, São Manuel 04479
Museu Histórico e Pedagógico Prof. Lourenço Filho, Porto Ferreira 04290
Museu Histórico e Pedagógico Zequinha de Abreu, Santa Rita do Passa Quatro 04446
Museu Histórico Farroupilha, Piratini 04268
Museu Histórico Kiyoshi Takano, Ura 04580
Museu Histórico Militar, Maputo 28723
Museu Histórico Muncipal José Chiachiri, Franca 04104
Museu Histórico Municipal, Carangola 04039
Museu Histórico Municipal, Dois Irmãos 04082
Museu Histórico Municipal, Montenegro 04212
Museu Histórico Municipal, Telêmaco Borba 04562
Museu Histórico Municipal e da Imigração Italiana Oswaldo Samuel Massei, São Caetano do Sul 04457
Museu Histórico Municipal Tuany Toledo, Pouso Alegre 04292
Museu Histórico Nacional, Rio de Janeiro 04385
Museu Histórico Pedagógico Conselheiro Dr. João da Silva Carrão, Americana 03944
Museu Histórico Pedagógico Índia Vanuíre, Tupã 04572
Museu Histórico Prof. Carlos de Silva Lacaz, São Paulo 04538
Museu Histórico Professor Jos' Alexandre Vieira, Palmas 04241
Museu Histórico Regional, Apucarana 03948
Museu Histórico Regional, Itambacuri 04132
Museu Histórico Regional, Passo Fundo 04247
Museu Histórico Tenente Coronel PM Augusto de Almeida Garrett, Curitiba 04075
Museu Histórico Visconde de São Leopoldo, São Leopoldo 04475
Museu Homo Sapiens, Nanuque 04217
Museu i Centre d'Estudis de l'Esport Dr. Melcior Colet, Barcelona 34582
Museu i Centre d'Estudis Fray Juniper Serra, Petra 35268
Museu I Fons Artistic, Porreres 35287
Museu i Necròpolis Paleocristians, Tarragona 35515
Museu Imperial, Petrópolis 04263
Museu Inaldo de Lyra Neves-Manta, Rio de Janeiro 04386
Museu Instrumental, Lisboa 32304
Museu Integrado de Roraima, Boa Vista 03992
Museu Internacional de Arte Naïf do Brasil, Rio de Janeiro 04387
Museu Jaguaribano, Aracati 03952
Museu João Pedro Nunes, São Gabriel 04464
Museu Joaquim José Felizardo, Porto Alegre 04284
Museu José Bonifácio, São Paulo 04539
Museu Julio de Castilhos, Porto Alegre 04285
Museu la Granja, Espai Cultural, Santa Perpètua de Mogoda 35427
Museu Lasar Segall, São Paulo 04540
Museu Leprológico, Curitiba 04076
Museu Local Arqueològic, Artesa de Lleida 34490
Museu Local d'Artesania Terrissaire, Verdú 35647
Museu Luso-Hebraico de Albraão Zacuto, Tomar 32353
Museu Maçônico Mário Verçosa, Manaus 04193
Museu Malinverni Filho, Lages 04162
Museu Manolo Hugué, Caldes de Montbui 34657
Museu Marès de la Punta, Arenys de Mar 34480
Museu Mariano Procópio, Juiz de Fora 04158
Museu Maricel de Mar, Sitges 35498
Museu Marítim de Barcelona, Barcelona 34583
Museu Mazzaropi, Taubaté 04561
Museu Memória do Bixiga, São Paulo 04541
Museu Meridional, Porto Alegre 04286
Museu Metropolitano de Arte, Curitiba 04077
Museu Militar, Barcelona 34584
Museu Militar, Coimbra 32261
Museu Militar de Lisboa, Lisboa 32305
Museu Militar do Forte do Brum, Recife 04306
Museu Mineiro, Belo Horizonte 03988
Museu Mineralógico da Escola de Minas, Ouro Preto 04240
Museu Mineralógico e Geológico, Coimbra 32262
Museu Moacir Andrade, Manaus 04194
Museu Mollfulleda de Mineralogía, Arenys de Mar 34481
Museu Monàstic, Vallbona de les Monges 35631
Museu Monografic de Pol Lèntia, Alcúdia 34441
Museu Monogràfic del Castell de Llinars, Llinars del Vallés 34973
Museu Monográfico de Conimbriga, Condeixa-a-Nova 32266
Museu Monstruário de Manica, Manica 28719
Museu Muncipal de Victor Graeff, Victor Graeff 04587
Museu Municipal, Alcochete 32231
Museu Municipal, Alcover 34437
Museu Municipal, Barbacena 03967
Museu Municipal, Cachoeira do Sul 04016
Museu Municipal, Caxias do Sul 04048
Museu Municipal, Conquista 04051
Museu Municipal, Garibaldi 04107
Museu Municipal, Guimerà 34894
Museu Municipal, Itambaracá 04133
Museu Municipal, Llagostera 34961
Museu Municipal, Llivia 34976
Museu Municipal, Manlleu 35081
Museu Municipal, Missal 04203
Museu Municipal, Molins de Rei 35119
Museu Municipal, Nova Lisboa 00104
Museu Municipal, Palafrugell 35210
Museu Municipal, Paulínia 04251
Museu Municipal, Pedras Grandes 04252
Museu Municipal, Pinhel 32326
Museu Municipal, Rafelcofer 35307
Museu Municipal, Riudecanyes 35326
Museu Municipal, Rolândia 04412
Museu Municipal, Rosário de Oeste 04413
Museu Municipal, Sant Feliu de Guíxols 35401
Museu Municipal, São João Del Rei 04469
Museu Municipal, Tona 35551
Museu Municipal, Torrente 35564
Museu Municipal, Tossa de Mar 35570
Museu Municipal, Uberlândia 04578
Museu Municipal, Visconde do Rio Branco 04589
Museu Municipal Abade Pedrosa, Santo Tirso 32343
Museu Municipal Adão Wolski, Contenda 04053
Museu Municipal Adolfo Eurich, Turvo 04573
Museu Municipal Alípio Vaz, Cataguases 04047
Museu Municipal Amadeo de Souza-Cardoso, Amarante 32235
Museu Municipal Atílio Rocco, São José dos Pinhais 04473
Museu Municipal Can Xifreda, Sant Feliu de Codines 35399
Museu Municipal Capitão Henrique Jos' Barbosa, Canguçu 04037
Museu Municipal d'Agramunt, Agramunt 34410
Museu Municipal David Canabarro, Sant'Anna do Livramento 04450
Museu Municipal de Antônio Prado, Antônio Prado 03946
Museu Municipal de Arqueologia, Monte Alto 04209
Museu Municipal de Arqueologia, Silves 32348
Museu Municipal de Arte e História, Nova Era 04227
Museu Municipal de Costums, Oropesa del Mar 35192
Museu Municipal de la Pagesia, Castellbisbal 34690
Museu Municipal de Nàutica, El Masnou 35097
Museu Municipal de Óbidos, Óbidos 32322
Museu Municipal de Pallejà, Pallejà 35218
Museu Municipal de Pollença, Pollença 35279
Museu Municipal de Portalegre, Portalegre 32328
Museu Municipal de Santarém, Santarém 32341
Museu Municipal de São José dos Campos, São José dos Campos 04472
Museu Municipal de Viana do Castelo, Viana do Castelo 32356
Museu Municipal Deolindo Mendes Pereira, Campo Mourão 04033
Museu Municipal do Folclore, Penápolis 04258
Museu Municipal do Funchal (História Natural), Funchal 32276
Museu Municipal do Seixal Núcleo Sede, Seixal 32345
Museu Municipal Domingos Battistel, Nova Prata 04229
Museu Municipal Dr. José Formosinho, Lagos 32280
Museu Municipal Dr. Santos Rocha, Figueira da Foz 32273
Museu Municipal Elisabeth Aytai, Monte Mor 04210
Museu Municipal Embaixador Hélio A. Scarabôtolo, Marília 04198
Museu Municipal Francisco Manoel Franco, Itaúna 04137
Museu Municipal Francisco Veloso, Cunha 04061
Museu Municipal Guilleries, Sant Hilari Sacalm 35402
Museu Municipal Joan Pal i Gras, Llinars del Vallés 34974
Museu Municipal Joaquim de Bastos Bandeira, Perdões 04260
Museu Municipal Josep Aragay, Breda 34623
Museu Municipal Karl Ramminger, Mondaí 04207
Museu Municipal Les Maleses, Montcada i Reixac 35132
Museu Municipal Miquel Soldevila, Prats de Lluçanès 35293
Museu Municipal Napoleão Joele, São Sebastião de Paraíso 04548
Museu Municipal Oswaldo Russomano, Bragança Paulista 03994
Museu Municipal Padre Antônio Ribeiro Pinto, Urucânia 04581
Museu Municipal Pedro Laragnoit, Miracatu 04202
Museu Municipal Pedro Nunes, Alcácer do Sal 32230
Museu Municipal Polinucleado de Tomae, Tomar 32354
Museu Municipal Prof. Hugo Daros, Gramado 04118
Museu Municipal Quinta do Conventinho, Loures 32318
Museu Municipal Vicenç Ros, Martorell 35095
Museu Municipal Visconde de Guarapuava, Guarapuava 04121
Museu Municipal Wenceslau Braz, Itajubá 04130
Museu Municipal Wülson Jehovah Lütz Farias, Frederico Westphalen 04106
Museu Nacional, Rio de Janeiro 04388
Museu Nacional, São Tomé 33770
Museu Nacional Arqueològic de Tarragona, Tarragona 35516
Museu Nacional da Ciência e da Técnica, Coimbra 32263
Museu Nacional da Moeda, Maputo 28724
Museu Nacional d'Art de Catalunya, Barcelona 34585
Museu Nacional de Antropologia, Luanda 00099
Museu Nacional de Arqueologia, Benguela 00088
Museu Nacional de Arqueologia, Lisboa 32306
Museu Nacional de Arte, Maputo 28725
Museu Nacional de Arte Antiga, Lisboa 32307
Museu Nacional de Belas Artes, Rio de Janeiro 04389
Museu Nacional de Etnologia, Lisboa 32308
Museu Nacional de Geologia, Maputo 28726
Museu Nacional de História Natural, Lisboa 32309
Museu Nacional de História Natural, Luanda 00100
Museu Nacional de Imigração e Colonização, Joinville 04153
Museu Nacional de l'Automòbil, Encamp 00083
Museu Nacional de Machado de Castro, Coimbra 32264
Museu Nacional de Soares dos Reis, Porto 32338
Museu Nacional do Mar - Embarações Brasileiras, São Francisco do Sul 04463
Museu Nacional do Teatro, Lisboa 32310
Museu Nacional do Traje, Lisboa 32311
Museu Nacional dos Coches, Lisboa 32312
Museu Naval de Amazônia, Belém 03977
Museu Naval e Oceanográfico, Rio de Janeiro 04390
Museu Navio Comandante Bauru, Rio de Janeiro 04391
Museu Nossa Senhora Aparecida, Aparecida 03947
Museu Numismático e Filatélico, Rio de Janeiro 04392
Museu Numismático Português, Lisboa 32313
Museu O Mundo Ovo de Eli Heil, Florianópolis 04094
Museu Oceanográfico, Setúbal 32347
Museu Oceanográfico do Valo do Itajaí, Itajaí 04129
Museu Oceanográfico Prof. Eliézer de C. Rios, Rio Grande 04408
Museu Oswaldo Aranha, Alegrete 03940
Museu Padre Joseph Cornellius Maria Demam, Coronel Fabriciano 04055
Museu Padre Júlio Maria, Russas 04415
Museu Palácio Nacional da Ajuda, Lisboa 32314
Museu Paleontologic Juna Cano Forner, San Mateo 35385
Museu Paraense Emílio Goeldi, Belém 03978
Museu Paranaense, Curitiba 04078
Museu Paroquial de Óbidos, Óbidos 32323
Museu Parque Malwee, Jaraguá do Sul 04144
Museu Parraquial, Campos 34665
Museu Parroquial, Altafulla 34459
Museu Parroquial, Calonge de Mar 34662
Museu Parroquial, Castellò d'Empúries 34692
Museu Parroquial, Deià 34770
Museu Parroquial, Llanera de Ranes 34963
Museu Parroquial, Santa Pau 35426
Museu Parroquial, Vinaixa 35690
Museu Parroquial Palau Solitar, Palau de Plegamans 35212
Museu Parroquiali, Vimbodí 35689
Museu Particular de Armas de Arlindo Pedro Zatti, Porto Alegre 04287
Museu Patríco Corrêa da Câmara, Bagé 03965
Museu Pau Casals, El Vendrell 35645

Museu Paulista da Universidade de São Paulo, São Paulo 04542
Museu Paulo Firpo, Dom Pedrito 04083
Museu Paulo Machado de Carvalho, São Paulo 04543
Museu Pedro Ludovico, Goiânia 04112
Museu Perrot Moore d'Art Grafic Europeu, Cadaqués 34645
Museu Picasso, Barcelona 34586
Museu Pinacoteca, Igarassu 04125
Museu-Poblat Ibèric, Tornabous 35555
Museu Postal d'Andorra, Ordino 00086
Museu Postal e Telegráfico da ECT, Brasília 04007
Museu Professor Hugo Machiado da Silveira, Patrocínio 04249
Museu Rafael Bordalo Pinheiro, Lisboa 32315
Museu Regional, Vitória da Conquista 04593
Museu Regional Abade de Baçal, Bragança 32245
Museu Regional D. Bosco, Campo Grande 04031
Museu Regional da Fauna e Flora do Itatiaia, Itatiaia 04136
Museu Regional da Huila, Lumbango 00101
Museu Regional d'Artá, Artá 34489
Museu Regional de Arqueologia D. Diogo de Sousa, Braga 32243
Museu Regional de Cabinda, Cabinda 00089
Museu Regional de Olinda, Olinda 04233
Museu Regional de São João Del Rei, São João Del Rei 04470
Museu Regional do Alto Uruguai, Erechim 04084
Museu Regional do Planalto Central, Huambo 00092
Museu Regional Olívio Otto, Carazinho 04041
Museu Republicano Convenção de Itu, Itu 04140
Museu Restauraçao, Lisboa 32316
Museu Rocaguinarda, Oristà 35190
Museu Romàntic Can Llopis, Sitges 35499
Museu Romantic Can Papiol, Vilanova i la Geltrú 35667
Museu Romàntic Delger, Caldes de Montbui 34658
Museu Romântico da Quinta da Macieirinha, Porto 32339
Museu Rural e do Vinho do Concelho, Cartaxo 32248
Museu Sacro da Igreja de São Sebastião, Araxá 03958
Museu Sacro São José de Ribamar, Aquiraz 03949
Museu Salles Cunha, Rio de Janeiro 04393
Museu São João Batista, Caratinga 04040
Museu São Norberto, Pirapora do Bom Jesus 04267
Museu Sargento Edésio de Carvalho, Sousa 04554
Museu Sentronà, Tiana 35532
Museu Sitio Arqueológico Casa dos Pilões, Rio de Janeiro 04394
Museu Solar Monjardim, Vitória 04592
Museu Taurí de la Monumental, Barcelona 34587
Museu Teatro, Rio de Janeiro 04395
Museu Técnico-Científico do Instituto Oscar Freire, São Paulo 04544
Museu Tempostal, Salvador 04438
Museu Teresa Bernardes Adami de Carvalho, Sant Antônio do Monte 04439
Museu Territorial do Amapá, Macapá 04176
Museu Textil i d'Indumentaria, Barcelona 34588
Museu Théo Brandão de Antropologia de Folclore, Maceió 04184
Museu Theodormiro Carneiro Santiago, Itajubá 04131
Museu Tinguí-Cuera, Araucária 03955
Museu Torre Balldovina, Santa Coloma de Gramenet 35410
Museu-Tresor Parroquial, Olot 35174
Museu-Tresor Parroquial, Verdú 35648
Museu Universitário, Campinas 04027
Museu Universitário de Arte, Uberlândia 04579
Museu Universitário Gama Filho, Rio de Janeiro 04396
Museu Universitário Professor Oswaldo Rodrigues Cabral, Florianópolis 04095
Museu Valencia del Joguet, Ibi 34911
Museu Vallhonrat, Rubí 35343
Museu Víctor Balaguer, Vilanova i la Geltrú 35668
Museu Victor Bersani, Santa Maria 04445
Museu Victor Meirelles, Florianópolis 04096
Museu Viladomat d'Escultura, Escaldes-Engordany 00084
Museu Villa-Lobos, Rio de Janeiro 04397
Museu Vivo da Memória Candanga, Brasília 04008
Museu von Martius, Teresópolis 04567
Museu Zé Didor, Campo Maior 04032
Museu Zoobotânico Augusto Ruschi, Passo Fundo 04248
Museu Zoológico, Coimbra 32265
Museum, Bagheria 23000
Museum, Coswig, Anhalt 16498
The Museum, Greenwood 43837
Museum, Mühlacker 18801
The Museum, Newton Stewart 40065
Museum, Waldheim 20364
Museum, Zofingen 37366
Museum 15, Wien 02933
Museum 1806, Cospeda 16497
Museum 1915-1918, Kötschach-Mauthen 02150
Museum 1940-1945, Dordrecht 29175
Museum 3. Dimension, Dinkelsbühl 16617
Museum '40-'45, Slochteren 29833
Museum Abdij Mariënlof, Kerniel 03534
Museum Abdij van Egmond, Egmond Binnen 29206
Museum Abdijkerk, Thorn 29871
Museum Abodiacum, Denklingen 16573
Museum Abri Satriamandala, Jakarta 22109
Museum Abtei Liesborn, Wadersloh 20337
Museum Adam Malik, Jakarta 22110
Museum Adorf, Adorf, Vogtland 15399
Museum Affandi - Museum Seni, Yogyakarta 22216
Museum Africa, Johannesburg 34280
Museum Agios Nikolaos, Agios Nikolaos 20810
Muséum Agricole et Industriel de Stella Matutina, Piton-Saint-Leu 32419
Museum Aguntum, Dölsach 01768
Museum Ald Slot, Wergea 29992
Museum Alpin, Pontresina 37026
Museum Alte Brettersäge, Rappottenstein 02487
Museum Alte Kirche, Reken 19557
Museum Alte Lateinschule Großenhain, Großenhain, Sachsen 17429
Museum "Alte Münze", Stolberg, Harz 20066
Museum Alte Pfefferküchlerei, Weißenberg 20491
Museum Alte Post, Pirmasens 19402
Museum Alte Schmiede, Wien 02934
Museum Alte Textilfabrik, Weitra 02807
Museum Altes Bad Pfäfers, Bad Ragaz 36482
Museum Altes Bürgerhaus, Stolberg, Harz 20067
Museum Altes Gymnasium, Schweinfurt 19890
Museum Altes Land, Jork 17962
Museum Altes Rathaus, Gerolzhofen 17259
Museum Altomünster, Altomünster 15470
Museum Alzey, Alzey 15477
Museum am Burghof, Lörrach 18490
Museum am Dannewerk, Dannewerk 16537
Museum am Lindenbühl, Mühlhausen, Thüringen 18807
Museum am Lindenplatz, Weil am Rhein 20436
Museum am Markt, Schiltach 19782
Museum am Markt / Schubarts Museum, Aalen 15382
Museum am Mühlturm, Isny 17930
Museum am Odenwaldlimes, Elztal 16846
Museum am Ostwall, Dortmund 16661
Museum am Schölerberg, Osnabrück 19282
Museum am Thie, Göttingen 17335
Museum Amandinhuis, Herk-de-Stad 03494
Museum Amden, Amden 36454
Museum Amelinghausen, Amelinghausen 15480
Museum Amstelkring, Amsterdam 28875
Museum Amtspforte Stadthagen, Stadthagen 20029
Museum an der Krukenburg, Bad Karlshafen 15673
Museum Anatomicum, Marburg 18631
Museum Anatomicum, Riga 27431
Museum Anatomy FK UI, Jakarta 22111
Museum, Ancient Synagogue and Necropolis, Beit Shearim 22582
Museum and Archive of Town History Admiral William Brown, Adrogué 00107
Museum and Archives of Georgia Education, Milledgeville 45345
Museum and Art Gallery, Burdwan 21734
Museum and Art Gallery, Forfar 39005
Museum and Art Gallery, Hooghly 21841
Museum and Art Gallery, Letchworth 39481
Museum and Art Gallery, Minden 27678
Museum and Art Gallery, Newport, Gwent 40051
Museum and Art Gallery, Nuneaton 40118
Museum and Art Gallery, Pulau Pinang 27681
Museum and Art Gallery, Shah Alam 27686
Museum and Art Gallery Leicester, Leicester 39464
Museum and Art Gallery of the Northern Territory, Darwin 00973
Museum and Arts Center in the Sequim Dungeness Valley, Sequim 47568
Museum and Exhibition Center, Dal'negorsk 32754
Museum and Exhibition Center, Ivanovo 32833
Museum and Exhibition Center - Diorama, Kirov 32923
Museum and Exhibition Center - Kremlin of Volokolamsk, Volokolamsk 33726
Museum and Gallery of Northern Pilsen Region, Kralovice 08429
Museum and Institute of the Roerich Family, Sankt-Peterburg 33437
Museum and Institute of Zoology of the Polish Academy of Science, Warszawa 32102
Museum and Regional Art Gallery, Jičín 08388
Museum Anna Nordlander, Skellefteå 36196
Museum Anna Paulowna, Breezand 29025
Museum-Appartement of A. Tvardovsky in Smolensk, Smolensk 33528
Museum Appenzell, Appenzell 36462
Museum-Aquarium de Nancy, Nancy 13245
Museum-Aquarium of the Pacific Research Institute of Fisherie and Oceanography, Vladivostok 33702
Museum Arbeitswelt Steyr, Steyr 02685
The Museum Archaeological Institute of Kashihara, Kashihara 26317
Museum-Armoury, Liw 31764
Museum Arnold Vander Haeghen, Gent 03443
Museum-Art Collection of the National Bank, Athinai 20881
Museum Artha Suaka, Jakarta 22112
Museum Åsättra, Ljusterö 36047
Museum Asia Africa, Bandung 22071
Museum Asimbojo, Bima 22085
Museum Asmat, Jakarta 22113
Museum Aspern-Essling 1809, Wien 02935
Museum Asserajah El Hasyimiah Palace, Bengkalis 22082
Museum Association of Aotearoa New Zealand, Wellington 49309
Museum Association of Arizona, Phoenix 49511
Museum Association of Israel, Rishon Le-Zion 49246
Museum Association of Montana, West Glacier 49512
Museum Association of New York, Troy 49513
Museum Association of Newfoundland and Labrador, Saint John's 49101
Museum Astros, Astros 20841
The Museum at Drexel University, Philadelphia 46430
Museum at Mountain Home, Johnson City 44347
Museum at the Fashion Institute of Technology, New York 45839
Museum at the Site of the First National Congress of the Communist Party of China, Shanghai 07216
The Museum at Warm Springs, Warm Springs 48304
Museum Auerbach, Auerbach, Vogtland 15546
Museum auf Abruf, Wien 02936
Museum auf dem Burghof, Springe 20019
Museum auf der Burg, Raron 37045
Museum auf der Osterburg, Weida 20424
Museum Bad Abbach, Bad Abbach 15588
Museum Bad Arolsen, Bad Arolsen 15591
Museum Bad Füssing, Bad Füssing 15649
Museum Baden, Solingen 19985
Museum Bärengasse, Zürich 37394
Museum Bahari, Jakarta 22114
Museum Bakkerij Mendels, Middelstum 29597
Museum Balanga, Palangkaraya 22167
Museum Bangga & Lore, Poso 22180
Museum Barockschloß Rammenau, Rammenau 19481
Museum Barsinghausen, Barsinghausen 15826
Museum Batara Guru, Palopo 22171
Museum Batara Guru, Pare-Pare 22173
Museum Batik, Pekalongan 22174
Museum Batik, Yogyakarta 22217
Museum Battle of the Silver Helmets, Halen 03466
Museum Bayerisches Vogtland, Hof, Saale 17793
Museum Bebinghehoes, Exloo 29256
Museum Beeckestijn, Velsen Zuid 29937
Museum Beelden aan Zee, Den Haag 29107
Museum - Begegnung der Kulturen, Krenglbach 02163
Museum bei der Kaiserpfalz, Ingelheim am Rhein 17900
Museum beim Markt - Angewandte Kunst seit 1900, Karlsruhe 17996
Museum beim Solenhofer Aktien-Verein, Maxberg 18667
Museum Bellerive, Zürich 37395
Museum Bergér, Eichstätt 16806
Museum Berlin-Karlshorst, Berlin 16045
Museum Berliner Arbeiterleben, Berlin 16046
Museum Bernhard Brühl, Landsberg bei Halle, Saale 18307
Museum Bevrijdende Vleugels, Best 28985
Museum Bickel, Walenstadt 37300
Museum Bickenbach, Bickenbach, Bergstraße 16143
Museum Biologi UGM, Yogyakarta 22218
Museum Bischofsheim, Bischofsheim bei Rüsselsheim 16170
Museum Bischofszell, Bischofszell 36574
Museum Blaafarveværket, Åmot i Modum 30382
Museum Blauer Anger, Bergen, Chiemgau 15892
Museum Blindenwerkstatt Otto Weidt, Berlin 16047
Museum Bochum, Bochum 16198
Museum Boerhaave, Leiden 29521
Museum Boijmans Van Beuningen, Rotterdam 29759
Museum Bragegården, Vaasa 10157
Museum Bramberg "Wilhelmgut", Bramberg 01743
Museum Brawijaya, Malang 22153
Museum Bredius, Den Haag 29108
Museum Brigade en Garde Prinses Irene, Oirschot 29653
Museum Briner und Kern, Winterthur 37333
Museum Broeker Veiling, Broek op Langedijk 29029
Museum Bruder Klaus, Sachseln 37081
Museum Brückenkopf, Jülich 17964
Museum Bürgstadt, Bürgstadt 16407
Museum Bundo Kandung, Bukittinggi 22092
Museum Buren en Oranje, Buren, Gelderland 29043
Museum Burg Abenberg, Abenberg 15388
Museum Burg Bederkesa, Bad Bederkesa 15595
Museum Burg Brome, Brome 16361
Museum Burg Eisenhardt, Belzig 15873
Museum Burg Falkenstein, Pansfelde 19344
Museum Burg Frankenberg, Aachen 15377
Museum Burg Freyenstein, Freyenstein 17132
Museum Burg Golling, Golling an der Salzach 01904
Museum Burg Heidenreichstein, Heidenreichstein 02012
Museum Burg Hohnstein, Hohnstein 17820
Museum Burg Kriebstein, Kriebstein 18239
Museum Burg Linn, Krefeld 18228
Museum Burg Mylau, Mylau 18966
Museum Burg Posterstein, Posterstein 19430
Museum Burg Pottenstein, Pottenstein 19439
Museum Burg Querfurt, Querfurt 19465
Museum Burg Ramsdorf, Velen 20297
Museum Burg Ranis, Ranis 19483
Museum Burg Ronneburg, Ronneburg, Hessen 19644
Museum Burg Scharfenstein, Scharfenstein 19765
Museum Burg Stein, Hartenstein bei Zwickau 17622
Museum Burg Stickhausen, Detern 16585
Museum Burghalde, Lenzburg 36871
Museum Buurt Spoorweg, Haaksbergen 29320
Museum Caledon River, Smithfield 34378
Museum California Center for the Arts Escondido, Escondido 43210
Museum Camera, Braunschweig 16301
Museum Çanakkale, Çanakkale 37649
Museum Casa Anatta, Casa Selma und Klarwelt der Seligen, Ascona 36472
Museum de Casteelse Poort, Wageningen 29975
Museum Castle Red Rock, Častá 33985
Museum Catharijneconvent, Utrecht 29901
Museum Centre Vapriikki, Tampere 10081
Museum Ceuclum, Cuijk 29060
Museum Cheann A'Loch, Ballallan 38062
Museum Chill Donnan, Kildonan 39357
Museum Chora, Amorgos 20819
Museum Chornhuus, Gränichen 36773
Museum Chris Van Niekerk, Boshof 34194
Museum-Church of the Decembrists, Čita 32751
Museum Chuvash School of Simbirsk - Appartement-Museum of I. Jakovlev, Uljanovsk 33665
Museum Classisal Secondary School, Uljanovsk 33666
Museum Collection, Imotski 07709
Museum Collection, Knić 33846
Museum Collection and Old Pharmacy of the Friars Minor, Dubrovnik 07698
Museum Collection Co-operative printing-house Rabotnik, Veliko Tărnovo 04915
Museum Collection First Socialist Meeting, Veliko Tărnovo 04916
Museum Collection of the Capuchin Monastery, Karlobag 07712
Museum Collection of the Dimitrij Tucović National Library, Čajetina 33829
Museum Collection of the Dominican Monastery, Bol 07683
Museum Collection of the Franciscan Monastery, Imotski 07710
Museum Collection of the Old Orthodox Church, Sarajevo 03923
Museum Complex Izmailovo, Moskva 33156
Museum Computer Network, Laguna Beach 49514
Museum Connection Die, Cape Town 34208
Museum Constant Permeke, Jabbeke 03526
Museum Corporation of Meleka, Melaka 49287
Museum Corps de Logis, Düsseldorf 16735
Museum Çorum, Çorum 37656
Museum Council, Moskva 49346
Museum Daerah Bangkalan, Bangkalan 22077
Museum Daerah Blambangan, Banyuwangi 22081
Museum Daerah Sumenep, Sumenep 22197
Museum Dara Yuanti, Sintang 22193
Museum de 5000 Morgen, Hoogeveen 29437
Museum De Bres, Ruisbroek, Antwerpen 03714
Museum de Burghse Schoole, Burgh-Haamstede 29045
Museum De Cateraars, Groningen 29311
Museum De Cruquius, Cruquius 29058
Museum De Doornboom, Hilvarenbeek 29416
Museum de Géologie Provençale, La Roque-d'Anthéron 12255
Museum de Gevangenpoort, Den Haag 29109
Museum De Ghulden Roos, Roosendaal 29745
Museum De Goudse Glazen - Sint Janskerk, Gouda 29295
Museum De Grutterswinkel, Leeuwarden 29511
Museum De Helpoort, Maastricht 29565
Museum de Historische Drukkerij, Maastricht 29566
Museum De Kijkuit, Merksem 03625
Museum De Kluis, Boekel 28993
Museum De Koloniehof, Frederiksoord 29263
Museum de Koperen Knop, Hardinxveld-Giessendam 29343
Museum de Maurits 1940-1945, Doesburg 29158
Museum De Moriaan, Gouda 29296
Museum De Paviljoens, Almere 28813
Museum De Roode Tooren, Doesburg 29159
Museum De Schilpen, Maasland 29561
Museum de Speeltoren, Monnickendam 29601
Museum de Stratemakerstoren, Nijmegen 29631
Museum de Striid tsjin it Wetter, Wommels 30020
Museum de Timmerwerf, De Lier 29068
Museum de Trije Gritenijen, Grou 29319
Museum de Valkhof, Hellendoorn 29386
Museum de Verzamelaar, Zuidhorn 30069
Museum De Vier Quartieren, Oirschot 29654
Museum De Wieger, Deurne 29141
Museum de Zwarte Tulp, Lisse 29543
Museum Delfzijl, Delfzijl 29088
Museum der Anthropologie, Zürich 37396
Museum der Arbeit, Hamburg 17555
Museum der Barbarossastadt Gelnhausen, Gelnhausen 17226
Museum der bildenden Künste Leipzig, Leipzig 18405
Museum der Brotkultur, Ulm 20258
Museum der Cistercienserinnen-Abtei Lichtenthal, Baden-Baden 15788
Museum der Deutschen Binnenschifffahrt Duisburg-Ruhrort, Duisburg 16752
Museum der Deutschen Spielzeugindustrie, Neustadt bei Coburg 19080
Museum der deutschen Sprachinselorte bei Brünn, Erbach, Donau 16885
Museum der Dinge-Werkbundarchiv, Berlin 16048
Museum der Donauschwaben, Herbrechtingen 17718
Museum der Elbinsel Wilhelmsburg, Hamburg 17556
Museum der Freiwilligen Feuerwehr, Laxenburg 02198
Museum der Gewerkschaft Agrar-Nahrung-Genuß, Wien 02937
Museum der Göttinger Chemie, Göttingen 17336
Museum der Grafschaft, Barmstedt 15825
Museum der Grafschaft Mark, Altena 15443
Museum der Granitindustrie, Bischheim-Häslich 16168
Museum der Heimatvertriebenen, Wels 02813
Museum der heimischen Tierwelt, Nabburg 18967

Museum der Hermann-Lietz-Schule, Spiekeroog 20015
Museum der historischen Waschtechnik, Ostbevern 19288
Museum der Katakombenstichting, Valkenburg, Limburg 29918
Museum der Klosterruine mit Lapidarium, Rüeggisberg 37075
Museum der Kommunikations- und Bürogeschichte, Bamberg 15811
Museum der Kulturen Basel, Basel 36508
Museum der Landschaft Hasli, Meiringen 36934
Museum der Marktgemeinde Sankt Johann in Tirol, Sankt Johann in Tirol 02576
Museum der Mechitharisten-Congregation, Wien 02938
Museum der Natur, Gotha 17360
Museum der Natur und Umwelt Cottbus, Cottbus 16503
Museum der RaumKunst aus Renaissance, Barock und Rokoko, Berlin 16049
Museum der Schwalm, Schwalmstadt 19871
Museum der Schweizer Kapuzinerprovinz, Sursee 37226
Museum der Seefahrt, Geiselhöring 17215
Museum der Staatlichen Porzellan-Manufaktur Meissen, Meißen 18691
Museum der Stadt Alfeld (Leine), Alfeld, Leine 15428
Museum der Stadt Aue, Aue, Sachsen 15543
Museum der Stadt Bad Berleburg, Bad Berleburg 15609
Museum der Stadt Bad Gandersheim, Bad Gandersheim 15650
Museum der Stadt Bad Ischl, Bad Ischl 01708
Museum der Stadt Bad Neuenahr-Ahrweiler, Bad Neuenahr-Ahrweiler 15703
Museum der Stadt Bad Staffelstein, Bad Staffelstein, Oberfranken 15748
Museum der Stadt Bensheim, Bensheim 15880
Museum der Stadt Bludenz, Bludenz 01741
Museum der Stadt Boppard, Boppard 16255
Museum der Stadt Borna, Borna bei Leipzig 16263
Museum der Stadt Butzbach im Solms-Braunfelser Hof, Butzbach 16437
Museum der Stadt Calw, Calw 16449
Museum der Stadt Dommitzsch, Dommitzsch 16632
Museum der Stadt Dorsten, Dorsten 16653
Museum der Stadt Ehingen, Ehingen, Donau 16792
Museum der Stadt Eschborn, Eschborn 16931
Museum der Stadt Ettlingen, Ettlingen 16975
Museum der Stadt Fürstenfeld, Fürstenfeld 01859
Museum der Stadt Füssen, Füssen 17168
Museum der Stadt Gladbeck, Gladbeck 17291
Museum der Stadt Gmünd, Gmünd, Kärnten 01889
Museum der Stadt Güstrow, Güstrow 17457
Museum der Stadt Hagenow, Hagenow 17485
Museum der Stadt Kapfenberg, Kapfenberg 02096
Museum der Stadt Köflach, Köflach 02146
Museum der Stadt Korneuburg, Korneuburg 02151
Museum der Stadt Kraichtal, Kraichtal 18217
Museum der Stadt Lahnstein im Hexenturm, Lahnstein 18287
Museum der Stadt Lahr, Lahr, Schwarzwald 18290
Museum der Stadt Langen, Langen in Hessen 18323
Museum der Stadt Lauffen am Neckar, Lauffen am Neckar 18356
Museum der Stadt Lennestadt, Lennestadt 18440
Museum der Stadt Leoben, Leoben 02210
Museum der Stadt Lienz, Lienz 02220
Museum der Stadt Ludwigsfelde, Ludwigsfelde 18516
Museum der Stadt Lünen, Lünen 18562
Museum der Stadt Miltenberg und Porzellansammlung Kreis Dux, Miltenberg 18740
Museum der Stadt Mittweida "Alte Pfarrhäuser", Mittweida 18758
Museum der Stadt Nauen, Nauen 18976
Museum der Stadt Neu-Isenburg Haus zum Löwen, Neu-Isenburg 19004
Museum der Stadt Neustadt an der Weinstraße, Neustadt an der Weinstraße 19077
Museum der Stadt Neustrelitz, Neustrelitz 19083
Museum der Stadt Neutraubling - Ortsgeschichtliche Dokumentation, Neutraubling 19084
Museum der Stadt Parchim, Parchim 19349
Museum der Stadt Pasewalk und Künstlergedenkstätte Paul Holz, Pasewalk 19353
Museum der Stadt Pegau, Pegau 19364
Museum der Stadt Poysdorf, Poysdorf 02441
Museum der Stadt Ratingen, Ratingen 19494
Museum der Stadt Rüsselsheim, Rüsselsheim 19708
Museum der Stadt Schkeuditz, Schkeuditz 19786
Museum der Stadt Schopfheim, Schopfheim 19842
Museum der Stadt Schwartau, Bad Schwartau 15739
Museum der Stadt Schwaz, Schwaz 02649
Museum der Stadt Sinsheim, Sinsheim 19969
Museum der Stadt Steyr, Steyr 02686
Museum der Stadt Troisdorf, Troisdorf 20216
Museum der Stadt Villach, Villach 02759
Museum der Stadt Vils, Vils 02765
Museum der Stadt Waiblingen, Waiblingen 20350
Museum der Stadt Weinheim, Weinheim, Bergstraße 20480
Museum der Stadt Wolgast, Wolgast 20667
Museum der Stadt Worms, Worms 20678
Museum der Stadt Zerbst mit Sammlung Katharina II., Zerbst 20746
Museum der Stadtwerke, Pirmasens 19403
Museum der Trauerarbeitsplätze, Klagenfurt 02130
Museum der Wahrnehmung, Graz 01926
Museum der Weltkulturen, Frankfurt am Main 17061
Museum der Westlausitz Kamenz, Kamenz 17979
Museum der Winterthur-Versicherungen, Winterthur 37334
Museum Dermbach, Dermbach 16575
Museum des Augustiner-Chorherrenstifts, Reichersberg 02498
Museum des Blindenwesens, Wien 02939
Museum des Chorherrenstifts Klosterneuburg, Klosterneuburg 02141
Museum des ehemaligen Kreises Stuhm/Westpr., Bremervörde 16352
Museum des Haager Landes, Haag, Oberbayern 17469
Museum des Handwerks Bremerhaven-Wesermünde in Bederkesa, Bad Bederkesa 15596
Museum des Heimatkundlichen Vereins, Scheßlitz 19775
Museum des Historischen Vereins Freising, Freising 17122
Museum des Instituts für gerichtliche Medizin, Wien 02940
Museum des Kreises Plön mit norddeutscher Glassammlung, Plön 19419
Museum des Landes Glarus, Näfels 36978
Museum des Nötscher Kreises, Nötsch im Gailtal 02365
Museum des Oberbergischen Kreises, Nümbrecht 19131
Museum des Ohrekreises, Wolmirstedt 20671
Museum des Sciences naturelles de Belgique, Bruxelles 03338
Museum des Todesmarsches im Belower Wald, Wittstock, Dosse 20633
Museum des Vereins für Heimatkunde im Landkreis Birkenfeld, Birkenfeld, Nahe 16166
Museum des Veterinäramtes, Wien 02941
Muséum des Volcans, Aurillac 10492
Museum des Wiener Männergesang-Vereins, Wien 02942
Museum des Zisterzienserstifts mit Margret Bilger-Galerie, Schlierbach 02635
Museum Dewantara Kirti Griya, Yogyakarta 22219
Museum Dharma Wiratama, Yogyakarta 22220
Muséum d'Histoire Naturelle, Autun 10500
Muséum d'Histoire Naturelle, Bagnères-de-Bigorre 10561
Museum d'Histoire Naturelle, Blois 10775
Muséum d'Histoire Naturelle, Chartres 11195
Muséum d'Histoire-Naturelle, Cherbourg 11279
Muséum d'Histoire Naturelle, Genève 36752
Muséum d'Histoire Naturelle, Gras 11916
Muséum d'Histoire Naturelle, Grenoble 11947
Muséum d'Histoire Naturelle, Le Havre 12428
Muséum d'Histoire Naturelle, Lyon 12750
Muséum d'Histoire Naturelle, Neuchâtel 36986
Muséum d'Histoire Naturelle, Nice 13326
Muséum d'Histoire Naturelle, Saint-Denis 32421
Muséum d'Histoire Naturelle, Troyes 15008
Muséum d'Histoire Naturelle de Bordeaux, Bordeaux 10820
Muséum d'Histoire Naturelle de la Ville de Bayonne, Bayonne 10623
Muséum d'Histoire Naturelle de Toulouse, Toulouse 14953
Muséum d'Histoire Naturelle de Tours, Tours 14977
Museum Dhondt-Dhaenens, Deurle 03382
Museum-Didactic Centre of Wielkopolski National Park, Mosina 31812
Museum Diergeneeskunde, Utrecht 29902
Museum Dingolfing-Herzogsburg, Dingolfing 16614
Museum-Diorama "Orel Offensive Operation in 1943", Orël 33264
Museum Diponegoro, Magelang 22150
Museum Directors Federation, Wellington 49310
Museum Dirgantara Mandala, Yogyakarta 22221
Museum Documentation Centre, Zagreb 07835
Museum Dom Benoît, Notre-Dame-de-Lourdes 06036
Museum Dorestad, Wijk bij Duurstede 30004
Museum Dorf, Wittenbach 37345
Museum Dorpsbehoud Papendrecht, Papendrecht 29710
Museum Dr. Guislain, Gent 03444
Muséum du Conte de Fées, La Bourboule 12129
Muséum du Coquillage, Les Sables-d'Olonne 12556
Museum du Parc Tsimbazaza, Antananarivo 27605
Museum Duin en Bosch, Castricum 29056
Museum Echt, Echt 29190
Museum Eckernförde, Eckernförde 16776
Museum Education for Letchworth Museum and Hitchin Museum, Hitchin 39249
Museum Education Roundtable, Washington 49515
Museum een Eeuw Landelijk Leven, Torhout 03785
Museum ehemalige Klöppelschule Tiefenbach, Tiefenbach, Oberpfalz 20176
Museum Eisenhüttenwerk Peitz, Peitz 19370
Museum Elisabeth Weeshuis, Culemborg 29063
Museum en oud Kempisch Dorp, Heist-op-den-Berg 03489
Museum Enschedé, Haarlem 29327
Museum Ensorhuis, Oostende 03668
Museum Ephraim-Palais, Berlin 16050
Museum Erwin Rehmann, Laufenburg 36849
Museum Erzgebirgische Volkskunst "Buntes Holz" im Postgut am Altmarkt, Hohenstein-Ernstthal 17814
Museum-estate of Lev Tolstoy "Yasnaya Polyana", Jasnaja Poljana (Tula) 32856
Museum-Estate of Literature and Art Priyutino, Vsevoložsk 33739
Museum-Estate of N.A. Durova, Elabuga 32788
Museum-Estate of N.K. Roerich, Izvara 32839
Museum-Estate of the Poet Dmitry Venevitinov, Novoživotinnoe 33248
Museum-Estate of the Writer S.T. Aksakov, Aksakovo 32632
Museum-Estate Ostafjevo "Russian Parnas", Ostafjevo 33274
Museum-Estate Tvardovsky in Zagorye, Zagorje 33744
Museum Ethnografic Park in Wdzydze, Wdzydze Kiszewskie 32147
Museum Ethnographers Group, Edinburgh 49426
Museum Ethnography Gaziantep, Gaziantep 37683
Museum Europäischer Kulturen, Berlin 16051
Museum Expressiver Realismus, Kißlegg 18102
Museum Fahrzeug-Technik-Luftfahrt, Bad Ischl 01709
Museum Falak-ol-Aflak, Khorram-Abaad 22257
Museum Falsters Minder, Nykøbing Falster 08996
Museum Félix de Boeck, Drogenbos 03395
Museum Festung Dresden - Kasematten, Dresden 16699
Museum Fethiye, Fethiye 37680
Museum 't Fiskershúske, Moddergat 29600
Museum Flavia Solva, Wagna 02780
Museum Flederwisch, Furth im Wald 17181
Museum Flehite Amersfoort, Amersfoort 28824
Museum för Utombordsmotorer, Varberg 36396
Museum Folkwang Essen, Essen 16959
Museum for African Art, Long Island City 44868
Museum for Beduin Culture, Kibbutz Lahav 22694
Museum for Children, Manila 31386
Museum for Contemporary Art, Gent 03452
Museum for History of Medicine, Gent 03446
Museum for Textiles, Toronto 06595
Museum for the Blind, Berlin 15924
Museum for the Victims of Political Repression, Ulaanbaatar 28680
Museum for Zone-Redningskorpsets, Holbæk 08885
Museum Ford and Bulgaria, Sofia 04838
Museum Fort Kijkduin, Den Helder 29135
Museum Forum der Völker, Werl 20521
Museum Franz Gertsch, Burgdorf 36606
Museum Franz Schubert und sein Freundeskreis, Atzenbrugg 01688
Museum Freriks, Winterswijk 30014
Museum Frerikshuus, Aalten 28795
Museum Freudenthaler Glassammlung, Weißenkirchen im Attergau 02802
Museum-Freundschaften, Ostseebad Binz 19310
Museum Friedrichshagener Dichterkreis, Berlin 16052
Museum Friesenheim, Ludwigshafen am Rhein 18519
Museum für Abgüsse Klassischer Bildwerke, München 18882
Museum für aktuelle Kunst, Groß-Umstadt 17421
Museum für Angewandte Kunst, Frankfurt am Main 17062
Museum für Angewandte Kunst, Gera 17244
Museum für Angewandte Kunst, Köln 18157
Museum für Antike Schiffahrt des Römisch-Germanischen Zentralmuseums, Mainz 18604
Museum für Archäologie, Frauenfeld 36707
Museum für Archäologie und Volkskunde, Kösching 18188
Museum für Astronomie und Technikgeschichte, Kassel 18024
Museum für bäuerliche Arbeitsgeräte, Imst 02055
Museum für bäuerliche Arbeitsgeräte des Bezirks Oberfranken, Bayreuth 15855
Museum für bäuerliche und sakrale Kunst, Ruhpolding 19717
Museum für bäuerliches Handwerk und Kultur, Wilhelmsdorf, Württemberg 20592
Museum für Bergedorf und die Vierlande, Hamburg 17557
Museum für bergmännische Volkskunst Schneeberg, Schneeberg, Erzgebirge 19817
Museum für Beschirrung und Besattelung, Hufbeschlag und Veterinär-Orthopädie, Wien 02943
Museum für bildende Kunst im Landkreis Neu-Ulm, Nersingen 18997
Museum für Billard- und Kaffeehauskultur, Wien 02944
Museum für Blasmusikinstrumente, Kürnbach 18262
Museum für Brauereigeschichte, Burghausen, Salzach 16422
Museum für das Fürstentum Lüneburg, Lüneburg 18559
Museum für die Archäologie des Eiszeitalters, Neuwied 19086
Museum für Druck, Mosbach, Baden 18795
Museum für Druckkunst, Leipzig 18406
Museum für Eisenkunstguß, Hirzenhain 17769
Museum für Energiegeschichte(n), Hannover 17606
Museum für Europäische Gartenkunst, Düsseldorf 16736
Museum für Forst- und Jagdwirtschaft, Groß Schönebeck 17420
Museum für Fotokopie, Mülheim an der Ruhr 18817
Museum für Frühgeschichte des Landes Niederösterreich, Traismauer 02733
Museum für Frühislamische Kunst, Bamberg 15812
Museum für Gegenwartskunst, Basel 36509
Museum für Gegenwartskunst Siegen, Siegen 19949
Museum für Geologie und Paläontologie am Geowissenschaftlichen Zentrum der Universität Göttingen, Göttingen 17337
Museum für Gestaltung Basel, Basel 36510
Museum für Gestaltung Zürich, Zürich 37397
Museum für Glaskunst, Lauscha 18360
Museum für Hamburgische Geschichte, Hamburg 17558
Museum für Haustierkunde Julius Kühn, Halle, Saale 17516
Museum für historische Wehrtechnik, Röthenbach an der Pegnitz 19637
Museum für Höchster Geschichte, Frankfurt am Main 17063
Museum für Höhlenkunde, Laichingen 18292
Museum für Holographie, Esens 16939
Museum für Holographie und neue Medien, Pulheim 19453
Museum für Holzhandwerke, Sinzig, Rhein 19972
Museum für Indische Kunst, Berlin 16053
Museum für Industrie- und Technikgeschichte, Frankfurt am Main 17064
Museum für islamische Fliesen und Keramik, Tegernsee 20150
Museum für Islamische Kunst, Berlin 16054
Museum für Jagdtier- und Vogelkunde des Erzgebirges, Augustusburg 15573
Museum für Kaffeetechnik, Emmerich 16859
Museum für Kartographie, Gotha 17361
Museum für klösterliche Kultur, Bad Wurzach 15780
Museum für Kloster- und Heimatgeschichte, Harsefeld 17620
Museum für Kommunikation, Bern 36546
Museum für Kommunikation Berlin, Berlin 16055
Museum für Kommunikation Frankfurt, Frankfurt am Main 17065
Museum für Kommunikation Hamburg, Hamburg 17559
Museum für Kommunikation Nürnberg im Verkehrsmuseum, Nürnberg 19152
Museum für konkrete Kunst, Ingolstadt 17909
Museum für Kunst in Steatit, Frankfurt am Main 17066
Museum für Kunst und Gewerbe Hamburg, Hamburg 17560
Museum für Kunst und Kulturgeschichte der Stadt Dortmund, Dortmund 16662
Museum für Kutschen, Chaisen, Karren, Heidenheim an der Brenz 17680
Museum für Lackkunst, Münster 18943
Museum für ländliches Kulturgut, Landwirtschaft, Forsten und Jagd, Ulrichstein 20262
Museum für Landtechnik und Landarbeit, Emmerthal 16863
Museum für landwirtschaftliche Geräte, Grafenwörth 01907
Museum für Literatur am Oberrhein, Karlsruhe 17997
Museum für Luftfahrt und Technik, Wernigerode 20528
Museum für Magie und Hexenverfolgung, Penzlin bei Waren 19374
Museum für mechanische Musik und Volkskunst, Haslach 02007
Museum für Medizin-Meteorologie, Zwettl, Niederösterreich 03060
Museum für Militär- und Zeitgeschichte, Kolitzheim 18200
Museum für Mineralogie und Geologie, Dresden 16700
Museum für moderne Kunst, Cremlingen 16511
Museum für Moderne Kunst Frankfurt am Main, Frankfurt am Main 17067
Museum für Modernes Glas, Rödental 19628
Museum für Mühlenbautechnik, Syrau 20135
Museum für Musikautomaten, Seewen 37158
Museum für Naive Kunst, Bönnigheim 16217
Museum für Natur und Umwelt, Lübeck 18539
Museum für Naturkunde, Chemnitz 16468
Museum für Naturkunde, Dortmund 16663
Museum für Naturkunde, Düsseldorf 16737
Museum für Naturkunde, Magdeburg 18585
Museum für Naturkunde der Humboldt-Universität zu Berlin, Berlin 16056
Museum für Naturkunde der Stadt Gera, Gera 17245
Museum für Naturkunde des Zittauer Landes, Zittau 20762
Museum für Naturkunde und Völkerkunde Julius Riemer, Lutherstadt Wittenberg 18577
Museum für Naturkunde und Vorgeschichte, Dessau 16579
Museum für Neue Kunst, Freiburg im Breisgau 17113
Museum für Neue Kunst, Karlsruhe 17998
Museum für Niederrheinische Sakralkunst, Kempen 18057
Museum für Nummernschilder, Verkehrs- und Zulassungsgeschichte, Großolbersdorf 17434
Museum für Österreichische Zeitgeschichte, Scharnstein 02626
Museum für Ostasiatische Kunst, Berlin 16057
Museum für Ostasiatische Kunst, Köln 18158
Museum für Outsiderkunst, Schleswig 19795
Museum für Photographie, Braunschweig 16302
Museum für Puppentheater, Lübeck 18540
Museum für Rechtsgeschichte, Pöggstall 02427
Museum für Regionalgeschichte und Volkskunde, Gotha 17362
Museum für Sächsische Fahrzeuge, Chemnitz 16469
Museum für Sächsische Volkskunst, Dresden 16701
Museum für Sakrale Kunst und Liturgie, Heidelberg 17669
Museum für schlesische Landeskunde im Haus Schlesien, Königswinter 18183
Museum für Schnitzkunst und Kulturgeschichte, Oberammergau 19168

Museum für Seenotrettungsgeräte, Neuharlingersiel 19033
Museum für Sepulkralkultur, Kassel 18025
Museum für Sozialkunde und Geschichte des Möbels, Gleisdorf 01881
Museum für Stadtgeschichte, Alpirsbach 15435
Museum für Stadtgeschichte, Breisach am Rhein 16312
Museum für Stadtgeschichte, Freiburg im Breisgau 17114
Museum für Stadtgeschichte, Neuenburg am Rhein 19022
Museum für Stadtgeschichte Dessau, Dessau 16580
Museum für Stadtgeschichte im Adam-und-Eva-Haus, Paderborn 19337
Museum für Stadtgeschichte und Volkskunde, Heppenheim 17712
Museum für Thüringer Volkskunde Erfurt, Erfurt 16905
Museum für Tierkunde, Dresden 16702
Museum für Uhren und mechanische Musikinstrumente, Oberhofen am Thunersee 36998
Museum für Uhren und Schmuck, Frankfurt am Main 17068
Museum für Unterwasserarchäologie, Saßnitz 19761
Museum für Ur- und Frühgeschichte, Eichstätt 16807
Museum für Ur- und Frühgeschichte, Freiburg im Breisgau 17115
Museum für Ur- und Frühgeschichte, Stillfried 02696
Museum für Ur- und Frühgeschichte, Wieselburg an der Erlauf 03025
Museum für Ur- und Frühgeschichte Thüringens, Weimar, Thüringen 20465
Museum für Urgeschichte, Koblach 02145
Museum für Urgeschichte des Landes Niederösterreich, Asparn an der Zaya 01685
Museum für Urgeschichte(n), Zug 37427
Museum für verfolgte Kunst-Israel, Ashdod 22573
Museum für Verkehr und Technik, Berlin 16058
Museum für visuelle Kommunikation, Köln 18159
Museum für Völkerkunde, Burgdorf 36607
Museum für Völkerkunde, Wien 02945
Museum für Völkerkunde, Witzenhausen 20637
Museum für Völkerkunde der Universität Kiel, Kiel 18078
Museum für Völkerkunde Hamburg, Hamburg 17561
Museum für Völkerkunde zu Leipzig/ Grassimuseum, Leipzig 18407
Museum für Volkskultur in Württemberg, Waldenbuch 20359
Museum für Volkskultur Spittal an der Drau, Spittal an der Drau 02670
Museum für Volkskunst, Meßstetten 18721
Museum für Vor- und Frühgeschichte, Berlin 16059
Museum für Vor- und Frühgeschichte, Gunzenhausen 17464
Museum für Vor- und Frühgeschichte, Langenau, Württemberg 18327
Museum für Vor- und Frühgeschichte, Saarbrücken 19725
Museum für Vor- und Frühgeschichte sowie Stadtgeschichte, Egeln 16784
Museum für Waage und Gewicht, Balingen 15799
Museum für Waffentechink, Ausrüstung, Auszeichnungswesen, Vilshofen 20325
Museum für Wattenfischerei, Wremen 20687
Museum für Weinbau und Stadtgeschichte, Edenkoben 16779
Museum für Weinkultur, Deidesheim 16562
Museum für Wohnkultur des Historismus und des Jugendstils, Hilterfingen 36803
Museum für Zeitgenössische Glasmalerei, Langen in Hessen 18324
Museum für zeitgenössische Metallplastik, Sankt Pantaleon 02595
Museum Furthmühle, Pram 02445
Museum G. Frey des Entomologischen Instituts, Tutzing 20240
Museum & Galerie Rob Mohlman, Venhuizen 29938
Museum Galgenhaus, Berlin 16060
Museum Garching an der Alz, Garching an der Alz 17196
Museum Gasteiger-Haus, Utting 20281
Museum Gayo, Aceh Tengah 22062
Museum Gedong Kirtya, Singaraja 22192
Museum Gedung Arca, Gianyar 22100
Museum Gedung Joang '45, Jakarta 22115
Museum-Gemaal de Hoogte, Nieuwolda 29626
Museum Geologi, Bandung 22072
Museum Geologie/Paläontologie, Heidelberg 17670
Museum Georg Schäfer, Schweinfurt 19891
Museum Gesigt van't Dok, Hellevoetsluis 29390
Museum Gevaert-Minne, Sint-Martens-Latem 03738
Museum Geyerhammer, Scharnstein 02627
Museum GGZ-Drenthe, Assen 28951
Museum Goa Bala Lompoa, Sungguminasa 22198
Museum Goch, Goch 17309
Museum Godshuis Belle, Ieper 03516
Museum Göltzsch, Rodewisch 19624
Museum Goldener Steig, Waldkirchen, Niederbayern 20367
Museum Gottfried Silbermann, Frauenstein 17090
Museum Graphia, Urbino 25861
Museum Grootseminarie, Brugge 03259
Museum Grossauheim, Hanau 17585
Museum Großklein, Großklein 01956
Museum Großkrotzenburg, Großkrotzenburg 17433
Museum Gülden Creutz, Worbis 20676
Museum Gula, Klaten 22147
Museum Gunnar-Wester-Haus, Schweinfurt 19892
Museum Gustavianum, Uppsala 36358
Museum Hacibektaş, Nevşehir 37767
Museum Haldensleben, Haldensleben 17506
Museum Halle, Halle, Westfalen 17524
Museum Hameln, Hameln 17575
Museum Haus Cajeth, Heidelberg 17671
Museum Haus Lange, Krefeld 18229
Museum Haus Löwenberg, Gengenbach 17236
Museum Haus Ludwig für Kunstausstellungen, Saarlouis 19729
Museum Haus Martfeld, Schwelm 19894
Museum Havezate Mensinge, Roden 29740
Museum Headquarter of V.K. Bluecher, Tjumen 33608
Museum Headquarters of the Russian Army 1877-1878, Pordim 04785
Museum Hedendaagse Grafiek en Glaskunst, Vledder 29950
Museum Heimathaus Irmintraut, Ottersberg 19325
Museum Heimathaus Münsterland, Telgte 20156
Museum Heineanum, Halberstadt 17502
Museum Helferhaus, Backnang 15586
Museum Henriette Polak, Zutphen 30076
Museum Heraldiek Benelux, Temse 03769
Museum Herbarium Bogoriensis, Bogor 22087
Museum - Herberg de Ar, Westerbork 29995
Museum Herisau, Herisau 36802
Museum Herzogsburg, Braunau am Inn 01744
Museum Hessenstube, Baunatal 15832
Museum Het Alaam, Genk 03431
Museum het Catharina Gasthuis, Gouda 29297
Museum Het Groot Graffel, Warnsveld 29979
Museum Het Oude Raadhuis, Megen 29587
Museum Het Paleis, Den Haag 29110
Museum Het Petershuis, Gennep 29275
Museum Het Prinsenhof, Delft 29082
Museum Het Rembrandthuis, Amsterdam 28876
Museum Het Schip, Amsterdam 28877
Museum het Tramstation, Schipluiden 29809
Museum Het Valkhof, Nijmegen 29632
Museum Het Verscholen Dorp, Vierhouten 29944
Museum Heylshof, Worms 20679
Museum Historische Verzameling Nederlandse Politie, Zaandam 30034
Museum Höxter-Corvey, Höxter 17790
Museum Hoffmann'sche Sammlung, Kohren-Sahlis 18197
Museum Hofmühle, Immenstadt 17896
Museum Hohenau an der March, Hohenau an der March 02039
Museum Hohenzollern in Franken, Kulmbach 18269
Museum Hraček, Praha 08591
Museum HSF, Zwolle 30084
Museum Huelsmann, Bielefeld 16157
Museum Hüsli- Sammlung Schwarzwälder Volkskunst, Grafenhausen 17371
MUseum Huize Bareldonk, Berlare 03213
Museum Humanum, Waldkirchen 02790
Museum Huta Bolon Simanindo, Pematangsiantar 22176
Museum Huta Bolon Simanindo, Samosir 22183
Museum Huthaus Einigkeit, Brand-Erbisdorf 16276
Museum Huthaus Zinnwald, Altenberg, Erzgebirge 15448
Museum Ianchelevici, Goudriaan 29300
Museum Idar-Oberstein, Idar-Oberstein 17880
Museum Illingen, Illingen 17888
Museum Ilz, Ilz 02053
Museum im Adler, Benningen 15879
Museum im alten Brauhaus, Homberg, Ohm 17836
Museum im Alten Rathaus, Bad Brückenau 15620
Museum im Alten Rathaus, Mönchberg 18769
Museum im Alten Rathaus, Neckargemünd 18987
Museum im Alten Rathaus, Schmitten 19813
Museum im Alten Rathaus, Waghäusel 20342
Museum im Alten Schloß, Altensteig 15455
Museum im Alten Schloß, Neckarbischofsheim 18986
Museum im Ammes Haus, Hatzfeld 17640
Museum im Amtshausschüpfla, Erlangen 16920
Museum im Astorhaus, Walldorf, Baden 20376
Museum im Ballhaus, Imst 02056
Museum im Bellpark, Kriens 36839
Museum im Bierlinghaus, Bad Bayersoien 15594
Museum im Blaahaus am Unteren Römerweg, Kiefersfelden 18070
Museum im Bock, Leutkirch im Allgäu 18451
Museum im Boyneburgischen Schloß, Sontra 20003
Museum Im Dorf, Reutlingen 19577
Museum im Dorf, Wittlingen 20627
Museum im ehemaligen Augustiner-Chorherrenstift, Herrenchiemsee 17734
Museum im Franck-Haus, Marktheidenfeld 18646
Museum im 'Fressenden Haus' - Burgkasten Weißenstein, Regen 19515
Museum im Frey-Haus, Brandenburg an der Havel 16284
Museum im Fürstenstöckl, Ebenau 01778
Museum im Goetz-Haus, Leipzig 18408
Museum im Goldschmiedehaus, Ahlen 15404
Museum im Gotischen Haus, Bad Homburg v.d.Höhe 15665
Museum im Greuterhof, Islikon 36816
Museum im Grünen Haus der Marktgemeinde Reutte, Reutte 02511
Museum im Heimathaus, Traunstein 20190
Museum im Herrenhaus, Hausach 17643
Museum im Hof, Sankt Pölten 02601
Museum im Hollerhaus, Dietfurt 16604
Museum im Jost-Sigristen-Haus, Ernen 36689
Museum im Kirchhoferhaus, Sankt Gallen 37104
Museum im Klösterle, Peiting 19369
Museum im Kloster Grafschaft, Schmallenberg 19810
Museum im Kloster - Museum des Landkreises Osnabrück, Bersenbrück 16131
Museum im Koffer, Nürnberg 19153
Museum im Kornhaus, Rorschach 37072
Museum im Kräuterkasten, Albstadt 15419
Museum im Kreuzgang, Landshut 18310
Museum im Kulturspeicher, Würzburg 20700
Museum im Lagerhaus, Sankt Gallen 37105
Museum im Ledererhaus, Purgstall an der Erlauf 02464
Museum im Malhaus, Wasserburg, Bodensee 20410
Museum im Markgrafen-Schloss, Emmendingen 16855
Museum im Marstall, Winsen, Luhe 20613
Museum im Mesnerhaus, Pfaffenhofen an der Ilm 19383
Museum im Pflegschloss, Schrobenhausen 19853
Museum im Prediger, Schwäbisch Gmünd 19862
Museum im Rathaus Möhringen, Tuttlingen 20238
Museum im Ritterhaus, Offenburg 19242
Museum im Ritterhaus, Osterode am Harz 19296
Museum im Römerbad, Heidenheim an der Brenz 17681
Museum im Schäferhaus, Wahlsburg 20346
Museum im Schafhof Bayerns Landwirtschaft seit 1800, Freising 17123
Museum im Schlößle, Freiberg am Neckar 17098
Museum im Schloß, Frohburg 17156
Museum im Schloss, Fürstenberg, Weser 17159
Museum im Schloß Bad Pyrmont, Bad Pyrmont 15713
Museum im Schloß Lützen, Lützen 18565
Museum im Schloß Wolfenbüttel, Wolfenbüttel 20654
Museum im SchmidtHaus, Nabburg 18968
Museum im Schottenstift, Wien 02946
Museum im Schulhaus, Niederrohrdorf 36991
Museum im Seelhaus, Bopfingen 16253
Museum im Stadtpark, Grevenbroich 17398
Museum im Stadtturm, Groitzsch bei Pegau 17412
Museum im Stasi-Bunker, Machern 18579
Museum im Steinhaus, Bad Wimpfen 15770
Museum im Steintor, Anklam 15494
Museum im Steintorturm, Brandenburg an der Havel 16285
Museum im Stockalperschloß, Brig 36588
Museum im Strumpferhaus, Oberstaufen 19209
Museum im Tabor, Feldbach 01827
Museum im Thomas Legler-Haus, Diesbach 36659
Museum im Troadkostn zu Giem, Feldbach 01828
Museum im Tuchmacherhaus, Thammhausen 20169
Museum im Turmhof, Steckborn 37209
Museum im Umweltschutz-Informationszentrum Oberfranken mit Kinder-Erlebnis-Museum, Bayreuth 15856
Museum im Vorderen Schloss, Mühlheim an der Donau 18812
Museum im Wasserwerk, Berlin 16061
Museum im Wittelsbacher Schloss Friedberg, Friedberg, Bayern 17137
Museum im Zendenrathaus, Ernen 36690
Museum im Zeughaus, Innsbruck 02074
Museum im Zeughaus, Vechta 20290
Museum im Zwinger, Goslar 17354
Museum in Biskupin, Gĺsawa 31597
Museum in Bruntál, Bruntál 08282
Museum in Commemoration of Pēteris Upītis, Dobele 27349
Museum in de Stiftkerk, Thorn 29872
Museum in de Veenen, Vinkeveen 29945
Museum in den Halven Maen, Rockanje 29737
Museum in der Adler-Apotheke, Eberswalde 16771
Museum in der Alten Schule, Efringen-Kirchen 16783
Museum in der Burg, Bad Driburg 15627
Museum in der Burg, Coppenbrügge 16495
Museum in der Burg Zug, Zug 37428
Museum in der Fronfeste, Neumarkt am Wallersee 02350
Museum in der Gaststätte Scherrerwirt, Markt Piesting 02278
Museum in der Kaiserpfalz, Paderborn 19338
Museum in der Majolika-Manufaktur, Karlsruhe 17999
Museum in der Präparandenschule, Höchberg 17777
Museum in der Remise, Bad Harzburg 15656
Museum in der Scheuergasse, Zwingenberg, Bergstraße 20783
Museum in der Wegscheid, Ternberg 02722
Museum in Kochi Park, Kochi 26356
Museum in Memory of Lu Xun, Beijing 06974
Museum in Progress, Wien 02947
Museum in Schweizer Hof, Bretten 16357
Museum in 't Houtenhuis, De Rijp 29069
Museum in The Bled Castle, Bled 34085
Museum in the Clouds, Cibiana di Cadore 23559
Museum in the Community, Hurricane 44182
The Museum in the Park, Stroud 40639
Museum in the World of Fairy Tales, Smolensk 33532
Museum Indonesia, Jakarta 22116
Museum Industrieforum, Steyr 02687
Museum Industriekultur, Osnabrück 19283
Museum Industriekultur mit Motorradmuseum, Nürnberg 19154
Museum Innviertler Volkskundehaus und Galerie der Stadt Ried, Ried im Innkreis 02512
Museum Insel Hombroich, Neuss 19066
Museum Internationales Baum Archiv, Winterthur 37335
Museum Istana Mangkunegaran, Surakarta 22202
Museum Istana Sultan Ternate, Maluku Utara 09133
Museum Istana Sultan Ternate, North Malaku 22164
Museum Istant Siak Sri Indapura, Bengkalis 22083
Museum It Kokelhûs van Jan en Sjut, Earnewald 29189
Museum Jacobs van den Hof, Amersfoort 28825
Museum Jagd und Wild auf Burg Falkenstein, Falkenstein, Oberpfalz 16985
Museum Jagdschloß Kranichstein, Darmstadt 16546
Museum Jakob Smits, Mol 03629
Museum Jamu Nyonya Menir, Semarang 22187
Museum Jan Boon, De Rijp 29070
Museum Jan Cunen, Oss 29684
Museum Jan Heestershuis, Schijndel 29805
Museum Jan Lont, Hippolytushoef 29425
Museum Jan van der Togt, Amstelveen 28832
Museum Jannink, Enschede 29237
Museum Jean Tinguely, Basel 36511
Museum Jerusalem Panorama Kreuzigung Christi, Altötting 15464
Museum Joang '45, Medan 22157
Museum Joang '45, Surabaya 22199
Museum Jordanbad, Eppingen 16881
Museum Josephine Baker, Castelnaud-la-Chapelle 11077
Museum Joure, Joure 29466
Museum Judengasse, Frankfurt am Main 17069
Museum Judenplatz Wien, Wien 02948
Museum Kaiser Franz Joseph I. und die Jagd, Neuberg an der Mürz 02340
Museum Kalimantan Tengah, Palangkaraya 22168
Museum Kalt-Heiß, Deckenpfronn 16557
Museum Kameleon Dorp en Museum Hans Brinker, Terherne 29865
Museum Kaprun, Kaprun 02098
Museum Kartause Astheim, Volkach 20333
Museum Kartini, Jepara 22143
Museum Kartini Rembang, Rembang 22182
Museum Kasper, Norrtälje 36122
Museum Kasteel Wijchen, Wijchen 30002
Museum Katendrecht, Rotterdam 29760
Museum Katharinenhof mit Mühlenturm und Stadtscheune, Kranenburg, Niederrhein 18219
Museum Kebangkitan Nasional, Jakarta 22117
Museum Kebudayaan dan Kemajuan Asmat, Irian Jaya 22103
Museum Kebun Binatgang Semarang, Semarang 22188
Museum Kebun Raya Bogor, Bogor 22088
Museum Kedokteran, Jakarta 22118
Museum Kellinghusen, Kellinghusen 18052
Museum Kempenland, Eindhoven 29215
Museum Kempenland, Lommel 03596
Museum Kendil Riau, Tanjung Pandan 22209
Museum Kennemerland, Beverwijk 28986
Museum Kepolisian Negara Republik Indonesia, Jakarta 22119
Museum Kereta, Ambarawa 22065
Museum Kerkschat Sint-Katharinakerk, Maaseik 03603
Museum Khan, Hadera 22595
Museum Kinderwereld, Roden 29741
Museum Kindheit und Jugend, Berlin 16062
Museum Kirche zum Heiligen Kreuz, Zittau 20763
Museum Kitzbühel, Kitzbühel 02118
Museum Kleines Klingental, Basel 36512
Museum Kleines Schloß, Blankenburg, Harz 16177
Museum Klingelbeutel, Gaukönigshofen 17207
Museum Klösterli, Ettiswil 36696
Museum de Klompenmaker, Keijenborg 29478
Museum Kloster Asbach, Rotthalmünster 19694
Museum Kloster Bentlage, Rheine 19590
Museum Kloster Hude, Hude, Oldenburg 17850
Museum Kloster Ter Apel, Ter Apel 28922
Museum Kloster Zeven, Zeven 20753
Museum Kloster Zinna, Kloster Zinna 18116
Museum Knoblauchhaus, Berlin 16063
Museum Knochenstampfe, Zwönitz 20784
Museum Kölner Karnevalsorden, Köln 18160
Museum Komodo, Jakarta 22120
Museum Komplex of the Tomsk Polytechnical University, Tomsk 33614
Museum Kranenburgh, Bergen, Noord-Holland 28982
Museum Kraton Kasepuhan, Cirebon 22095
Museum Kraton Yogyakarta, Yogyakarta 22222
Museum Kremayr, Ybbsitz 03046
Museum Kriminal-Mabak, Jakarta 22121
Museum Kronstadt Fortress, Kronštadt 32966
Museum Kruijsenhuis, Oirschot 29655
Museum Krupka, Krupka 08436
Museum Kuenburggewölbe, Werfen 02822
Museum Künstlerkolonie, Darmstadt 16547
Museum Küppersmühle, Duisburg 16753
Museum Kulturgeschichte der Hand, Wolnzach 20673
Museum Kunst-Kultur-Kellerromantik, Schleinbach 02634
Museum Kunst Palast mit Sammlung Kunstakademie und Glasmuseum Hentrich, Düsseldorf 16738
Museum Der Kunststall, Dahlem 16528
Museum Kura Hulanda, Curaçao 30089
Museum Kurhaus Kleve, Kleve 18107
Museum Kutschen-Wagen-Karren, Gescher 17265
Museum La Diligence, Heerlen 29367
Museum La Pawowoi, Watampone 22215
Museum La Truaisch, Sedrun 37155
Museum Lambert Van Meerten, Delft 29083
Museum Lammert Boerma, Borgercompagnie 29005

Museum Langenargen/ Bodensee, Langenargen 18325
Museum Langenthal, Langenthal 36846
Museum Langes Tannen, Uetersen 20250
Museum Langmatt, Baden 36488
Museum Laufental, Laufen 36848
Museum Lauriacum, Enns 01818
Museum Laxenburg, Laxenburg 02199
Museum Le Mayeur, Sanur 22184
Museum Leben am Meer, Esens 16940
Museum Lettergieten 1983, Westzaan 29998
Museum Leuchtenburg, Seitenroda 19929
Museum-Library of National Languages, Penza 33287
Museum Lidice, Lidice 08453
Museum Lindengut, Winterthur 37336
Museum Lindwurm, Stein am Rhein 37215
Museum Liner Appenzell, Appenzell 36463
Museum Lionardo da Vinci Ideale, Karlskrona 36000
Museum Löffingen, Löffingen 18489
Museum Löwenburg, Ederswiler 36671
Museum Loka Budaya, Jayapura 22141
Museum London, London 05772
Museum Ludwig, Köln 18161
Museum Ludwig in der Halle Kalk, Köln 18162
Museum Maagdenhuis, Antwerpen 03150
Museum Maarssen, Maarssen 29557
Museum Malerwinkelhaus, Marktbreit 18644
Museum Malikusaleh, Aceh Utara 22064
Museum Mandala Bakti, Semarang 22189
Museum Mandala Wangsit Siliwangi, Bandung 22073
Museum Manggala Wanabakti, Jakarta 22122
Museum Mannersdorf, Mannersdorf 02262
Museum Mayer van den Bergh, Antwerpen 03151
Museum mechanischer Musikinstrumente, Königslutter 18180
Museum Meerenberg, Bloemendaal 28989
Museum Meermanno-Westreenianum, Den Haag 29111
Museum Megalopolis, Megalopolis 21061
Museum Meiji-Mura, Inuyama 26249
Museum Menkemaborg, Uithuizen 29888
Museum Mensch und Natur, München 18883
Museum Menshikov Palace - State Hermitage Museum, Sankt-Peterburg 33433
Museum Mesdag, Den Haag 29112
Museum Meteorological Station of Simbirsk, Uljanovsk 33662
Museum Militer, Jakarta 22123
Museum Mini Korem, Sintang 22194
Museum Mistra, Mystras 21082
Museum Mobil, Bandung 22074
Museum Modern Art, Hünfeld 17856
Museum Moderner Kunst Kärnten, Klagenfurt 02131
Museum Moderner Kunst Stiftung Ludwig Wien, Wien 02949
Museum Moderner Kunst - Stiftung Wörlen, Passau 19356
Museum Modest Huys, Zulte 03859
Museum Mödling, Mödling 02312
Museum-Monument Spas na Krovi, Sankt-Peterburg 33462
Museum Moorseer Mühle, Nordenham 19114
Museum Morsbroich, Leverkusen 18452
Museum MPU Tantular, Surabaya 22200
Museum Münster, Münster 36968
Museum Municipal, Beira 28718
Museum Musica, Stadskanaal 29847
Museum Nagele, Nagele 29607
Museum Nan Eilean, Sgoil Lionacleit, Benbecula 38163
Museum Nan Eilean, Steornabhagh, Stornoway 40615
Museum Nanning Hendrik Bulthuis, Leeuwarden 29512
Museum Nasional, Jakarta 22124
Muséum National d'Histoire Naturelle, Paris 13650
Museum National d'Histoire Naturelle, Rabat 28708
Muséum National d'Histoire Naturelle du Val Rameh, Menton 12940
Museum Natur und Mensch, Greding 17381
Museum Nature of the Sea and its Protection, Institute of Ocean Biology of the Far Eastern Dept. of the Russian Academy of Sciences, Vladivostok 33707
Museum near the Ming Tombs, Changping 07008
Museum Necca and New England Center for Contemporary Art, Brooklyn 41939
Museum-Necropol of the Demidov Family and Exhibition Hall Tula Metal, Tula 33627
Museum Nederlandse Cavalerie, Amersfoort 28826
Museum Negeri Bali, Denpasar 22096
Museum Negeri Jambi, Jambi 22140
Museum Negeri Java Tengah, Semarang 22190
Museum Negeri Jawa Barat, Bandung 22075
Museum Negeri Kalimantan Barat, Pontianak 22179
Museum Negeri Kalimantan Timur Mulawarman, Tenggarong 22211
Museum Negeri Lampung, Bandarlampung 22069
Museum Negeri Nusa Tenggara Barat, Mataram 22156
Museum Negeri of Aceh, Banda Aceh 22068
Museum Negeri of Bengkulu, Bengkulu 22084
Museum Negeri of Central Sulawesi, Palu 22172
Museum Negeri of Irian Jaya, Jayapura 22142
Museum Negeri of La Galigo, Ujungpanang 22214
Museum Negeri of Lambung Mangkurat, Banjarbaru 22079
Museum Negeri Propinsi Nusa Tenggara Timur, Kupang 22149
Museum Negeri Propinsi Sumatera Selatan Balaputra Dewa, Palembang 22169
Museum Negeri Sulawesi Tenggara, Kendari 22146
Museum Negeri Sulawesi Utara, Manado 22154
Museum Negeri Sumatera Barat, Padang 22165
Museum Negeri Sumatera Utara, Medan 22158
Museum Negeri Timor-Timur, Dili 09131
Museum Nekara, Selayar 22185
Museum Neue Mühle, Erfurt 16906
Museum Neuhaus, Biel, Kanton Bern 36564
Museum Neukirchen-Vluyn, Neukirchen-Vluyn 19042
Museum Neukölln, Berlin 16064
Museum Neuruppin, Neuruppin 19061
Museum Nicolaihaus, Berlin 16065
Museum Nienburg, Nienburg, Weser 19102
Museum Niesky, Niesky 19104
Museum Nikolaikirche, Berlin 16066
Museum No 1, Richmond, Surrey 40319
Museum Nordenham, Nordenham 19115
Museum NordJura, Weismain 20488
Museum Nostalgie der 50er Jahre, Burgpreppach 16428
Museum Nusantara, Delft 29084
Museum Ober-Ramstadt, Ober-Ramstadt 19167
Museum Oberes Donautal, Fridingen 17136
Museum Oculorum, Buenos Aires 00250
Museum Oedenhof, Wittenbach 37346
Museum of Aboriginal Affairs, Gombak 27620
Museum of Acre, Acre 22563
Museum of Actors and Theater Producers Brothers Amtmaŋi, Valle 27465
Museum of African American Art, Los Angeles 44928
Museum of African Arts, Beograd 33803
The Museum of African Tribal Art, Portland 46625
Museum of Afro-American History, Boston 41816
Museum of Afro-American History, Brookline 41938
Museum of Alpine Farming, Bohinjska Bistrica 34086
Museum of Alpine Farming, Bohinjsko Jezero 34087
Museum of Alpine Farming, Srednja Vas v Bohinju 34154
Museum of A.M. Gorky's Childhood - Kashirin's House, Nižnij Novgorod 33209
Museum of Amana History, Amana 41163
Museum of Ambleside, Ambleside 37996
Museum of American Architecture and Decorative Arts, Houston 44128
Museum of American Financial History, New York 45840
Museum of American Frontier Culture, Staunton 47797
Museum of American Glass at Wheaton Village, Millville 45350
Museum of American Historical Society of Germans from Russia, Lincoln 44786
Museum of American Political Life, West Hartford 48526
Museum of American Presidents, Strasburg 47848
Museum of Anatolian Civilisations, Ankara 37612
Museum of Anatomy, Glasgow 39055
Museum of Anatomy of the Department of Anatomy, Athinai 20882
Museum of Ancient and Modern Art, Penn Valley 46339
Museum of Ancient Artifacts, Chicago 42342
Museum of Ancient Culture, Kilmartin 39363
Museum of Ancient Mazovian Metallurgy, Pruszków 31918
Museum of Ancient Metallurgy, Nowa Słupia 31828
Museum of Andrej Kmet, Martin 34025
Museum of Andrey Tarkovsky, Jurjevec 32866
Museum of Andrzej Strug, Warszawa 32088
Museum of Anhui Province, Hefei 07091
Museum of Animal Husbandary and Veterinary, Guwahati 21824
Museum of Anthracite Mining, Ashland 41298
Museum of Anthropology, Ann Arbor 41219
Museum of Anthropology, Chico 42373
Museum of Anthropology, Columbia 42552
Museum of Anthropology, Denver 42894
Museum of Anthropology, Fullerton 43575
Museum of Anthropology, Highland Heights 44018
Museum of Anthropology, Lawrence 44684
Museum of Anthropology, Pullman 46744
Museum of Anthropology, Tempe 47973
Museum of Anthropology, Vancouver 06683
Museum of Anthropology, Winston-Salem 48700
Museum of Anthropology and Archaeology, Pretoria 34348
Museum of Anthropology and Natural Sciences, Concordia 00287
Museum of Antique Armour Helmets and Swords, Kyoto 26435
Museum of Antiquities, Alnwick 37985
Museum of Antiquities, Jamnagar 21866
Museum of Antiquities, Newcastle-upon-Tyne 40040
Museum of Antiquities, Saskatoon 06401
Museum of Antiquities, Tanger 28712
Museum of Appalachia, Norris 45977
Museum of Applied Art, Beograd 33810
Museum of Applied Art, Sankt-Peterburg 33431
Museum of Applied Arts, Budapest 21346
Museum of Applied Arts, Poznań 31911
Museum of Aqaba Antiquities, Aqaba 27061
Museum of Archaeological Site Moenjodaro, Dokri 31016
Museum of Archaeology, Durham 38828
Museum of Archaeology, La Habana 07955
Museum of Archaeology, Legon 20800
Museum of Archaeology, Vadodara 22051
Museum of Archaeology Adamclisi, Adamclisi 32424
Museum of Archaeology and Ethnography of the Far East State University, Vladivostok 33703
Museum of Archaeology and Ethnography of the Syktyvkar State University, Syktyvkar 33576
Museum of Archaeology and Ethnology, Burnaby 05150
Museum of Archaeology and History, Dublin 22442
Museum of Archaeology and History, Turku 10117
Museum of Archaeology, Classics and Oriental Studies, Liverpool 39523
Museum of Archaeology, Ethnography and Ecology of Siberia, Kemerovo State University, Kemerovo 32914
Museum of Archaeology of the Institute of Language, Literature and History of the Komi Science Center of the Ural Division of the Russian Academy of Sciences, Syktyvkar 33575
Museum of Architecture, Samara 33373
Museum of Architecture, Wrocław 32175
Museum of Architecture and Archaeology Tower of Burana, Čujsk 27310
Museum of Architecture and of the Architectural Development of Siberia, Novosibirsk 33241
Museum of Arms and City Fortification, Bratislava 33961
Museum of Army Flying, Middle Wallop 39945
Museum of Army Transport, Beverley 38183
Museum of Art, Ein Harod 22589
Museum of Art, Fort Lauderdale 43411
Museum of Art, Orono 46196
Museum of Art, Providence 46721
Museum of Art, Pullman 46745
Museum of Art and Archaeology, Columbia 42553
Museum of Art and Archaeology, Dharwad 21792
Museum of Art and Archaeology, Mysore 21961
Museum of Art and History, Santa Cruz 47411
Museum of Art, Ehime, Matsuyama 26483
Museum of Art in Łódź, Łódź 31777
Museum of Art, Kochi, Kochi 26355
Museum of Arthropoda, Pune 21993
Museum of Arts and Crafts, Bratislava 33975
Museum of Arts and Crafts, Lucknow 21928
Museum of Arts and Crafts, Zagreb 07834
The Museum of Arts and Sciences, Daytona Beach 42811
Museum of Arts and Sciences, Macon 45045
Museum of Arts Downtown Los Angeles, Los Angeles 44929
Museum of Asian Art, Corfu 20932
Museum of Asian Art, Kuala Lumpur 27648
Museum of Audio Visual Technology, Wellington 30298
Museum of Automobile History, Syracuse 47911
Museum of Automobile Transport, Kursk 32976
Museum of Automobiles, Morrilton 45502
Museum of Aviation, Krumovo 04723
Museum of Aviation, Paraparaumu 30233
Museum of Aviation at Robins Air Force Base, Warner Robins 48306
Museum of Bad Art, Dedham 42842
Museum of Banknotes of the Ionian Bank, Corfu 20933
Museum of Barbarism, Lefkoşa 08234
Museum of Barnstaple and North Devon, Barnstaple 38093
Museum of Baseball, Caracas 48922
Museum of Bath at Work, Bath 38117
Museum of Beauty, Melaka 27670
Museum of Bedřich Hrozný, Lysá nad Labem 08468
Museum of Belize, Belize City 03865
Museum of Berkshire Aviation, Woodley 40923
Museum of Bērzgale Parish History, Bērzgale 27339
Museum of Bohemian Karst Beroun, Branch Žebrák, Žebrák 08745
Museum of Bohemian Karst in Beroun, Beroun 08247
Museum of Bosnian Serb Republic, Banja Luka 03910
Museum of Božena Němcová, Česká Skalice 08295
Museum of Bread, Sankt-Peterburg 33480
Museum of British Road Transport, Coventry 38645
The Museum of Broadcast Communications, Chicago 42343
Museum of Bronx History, Bronx 41923
Museum of Brushs, Bankeryd 35828
Museum of Bryansk Forest, Brjansk 32710
Museum of Bucarest, Bucureşti 32461
Museum of Buffalo and Horse-Breeding, Šumen 04875
Museum of Bulgarian National Revival and the National Liberation Struggles, Elena 04663
Museum of Byzantine Culture, Thessaloniki 21188
Museum of Cannock Chase, Hednesford 39206
Museum of Cape Breton Heritage, North East Margaree 06022
Museum of Carlsbad Porcelain, Březová u Karlových Var 08261
Museum of Carousel Art and History, Sandusky 47384
Museum of Carriages, Studénka 08667
Museum of Cars, Lagan 36027
Museum of Casts and Archeological Collection, Thessaloniki 21189
Museum of Central Australia, Alice Springs 00735
Museum of Central Bohemia, Roztoky u Prahy 08643
Museum of Central Connecticut State University, New Britain 45673
Museum of Central Finland, Jyväskylä 09601
Museum of Central Kalimantan, Palangkaraya 22168
Museum of Central Pomerania, Słupsk 31980
Museum of Central Slovakia, Banská Bystrica 33950
Museum of Ceramics, Bolesławiec 31507
Museum of Ceramics, East Liverpool 43056
Museum of Childhood, Boscombe 38281
Museum of Childhood, Dublin 22443
Museum of Childhood, Edinburgh 38892
Museum of Childhood, Masterton 30199
Museum of Childhood, Sudbury, Derbyshire 40641
Museum of Childhood, Toronto 06596
Museum of Childhood at Bethnal Green, London 39712
Museum of Childhood Memories, Beaumaris 38139
Museum of Children's Art, Oakland 46066
Museum of Chinese in the Americas, New York 45841
Museum of Chodsko, Domažlice 08332
Museum of Chungju National University, Chungju 27153
Museum of Church History and Art, Salt Lake City 47231
The Museum of Clallam County Historical Society, Port Angeles 46588
Museum of Classical Antiquities, Lund 36062
Museum of Classical Archaeology, Adelaide 00710
Museum of Classical Archaeology, Cambridge 38459
Museum of Classical Art, Hostinné 08364
Museum of Classical Balinese Painting, Klungkung 22148
Museum of Clock and Watch Making, Prescot 40263
Museum of Clocks and Handicrafts, Warszawa 32123
Museum of Coast and Anti-Aircraft Artillery, Green Point 34256
Museum of Combat Fame, Kaluga 32876
Museum of Communication, Bo'ness 38277
Museum of Communication, Den Haag 29115
Museum of Comparativ Anatomy, Roma 25206
Museum of Computing Technique and Computer Science, Rīga 27425
Museum of Conceptual Art, San Francisco 47328
Museum of Connecticut History, Hartford 43942
Museum of Contemporary Art, Andros 20824
Museum of Contemporary Art, Beograd 33812
Museum of Contemporary Art, Chicago 42344
Museum of Contemporary Art, Fort Collins 43383
Museum of Contemporary Art, Gdańsk 31580
Museum of Contemporary Art, Marugame 26467
Museum of Contemporary Art, North Miami 45997
Museum of Contemporary Art, Novi Sad 33872
Museum of Contemporary Art, Roskilde 09040
Museum of Contemporary Art, Teheran 22303
Museum of Contemporary Art, Turku 10119
Museum of Contemporary Art, Washington 48370
Museum of Contemporary Art, Wrocław 32189
Museum of Contemporary Art Denver, Denver 42895
Museum of Contemporary Art Los Angeles, Los Angeles 44930
Museum of Contemporary Art of Antwerp, Antwerpen 03156
Museum of Contemporary Art of the Jewish Autonomous Region, Birobidžan 32690
Museum of Contemporary Art San Diego - Downtown, San Diego 47281
Museum of Contemporary Art San Diego - La Jolla, La Jolla 44548
Museum of Contemporary Art Sapporo, Sapporo 26716
Museum of Contemporary Art Sydney, Sydney 01502
Museum of Contemporary Art, Tokyo, Tokyo 26945
Museum of Contemporary Articrafts, Teheran 22315
Museum of Contemporary Canadian Art, North York 06034
Museum of Contemporary Greek Painters, Amfissa 20818
The Museum of Contemporary Photography, Chicago 42345
Museum of Contemporary Religious Art, Saint Louis 47130
Museum of Contemporary Sculpture, Tokyo 26894
Museum of Cosmetology, Chicago 42346
Museum of Costume, Bath 38118
Museum of Costume, New Abbey 40011
Museum of Costume and Textiles, Nottingham 40109
Museum of Country Life, Castlebar 22388
Museum of Craft Folk Art, San Francisco 47329
Museum of Crafts, Ånge 35804
Museum of Cres, Cres 07691
Museum of Cretan Ethnology, Vori 21215
Museum of Croatian Archaeological Monuments, Split 07784
Museum of Cuban Historical Background, Santiago de Cuba 08134
Museum of Cultural and Natural History, Mount Pleasant 45536
Museum of Cultural History, Lund 36060
Museum of Cultural History, Požarevac 33892
Museum of Culture and Art History of Uzbekistan, Samarkand 48848
Museum of Cultures, Helsinki 09505
Museum of Cultures of Vietnam's Ethnic Groups, Thai Nguyen 49000
Museum of Cumania Minor, Kiskunfélegyháza 21457
Museum of Cycladic and Ancient Greek Art, Athinai 20883
Museum of Czech Garnet, Třebenice 08685
Museum of Czech Health Sciences, Praha 08568
Museum of Czech Literature, Praha 08609
Museum of Czech Music, Praha 08595
Museum of Czech Porcelain, Klášterec nad Ohří 08411
Museum of Dacian and Roman Civilisation, Deva 32511
Museum of Daejeon History, Daejeon 27162

Museum of Danish Cartoon Art, København 08939
Museum of Danish Resistance 1940-1945, København 08929
Museum of Dartmoor Life, Okehampton 40126
Museum of Datong, Datong 07042
The Museum of Death, Los Angeles 44931
Museum of Death, San Diego 47282
Museum of Decorative and Applied Art of the Ural, Čeljabinsk 32726
Museum of Decorative and Applied Folk Art, Belozersk 32681
Museum of Decorative Applied Arts, Rīga 27403
Museum of Decorative Art, Chicago 42347
Museum of Decorative Arts, Athinai 20884
Museum of Decorative Arts and Design in Oslo, Oslo 30741
Museum of Decorative Arts and History, Dublin 22444
Museum of Decorative Arts in Prague, Praha 08617
Museum of Decorative Painting and Decorative Arts Collection, Wichita 48606
Museum of Delphic Celebrations of Angelos and Eva Sikellianou, Athinai 20885
Museum of Dentistry, Liverpool 39524
Museum of Development of Moscow Power Supply, Moskva 33111
Museum of Dionysios Solomos and Eminent Zakynthians, Zakynthos 21221
Museum of Discovery and Science, Fort Lauderdale 43412
Museum of Divine Treasures, Genkai 26156
Museum of Dobruška, Dobruška 08329
Museum of Dolls and Costumes, Hatanpää Mansion, Tampere 10082
Museum of Domestic Design and Architecture MODA, Barnet 38088
Museum of Dr. Sun Yat-Sen, Zhongshan 07331
Museum of Early Southern Decorative Arts, Winston-Salem 48701
Museum of Early Trades and Crafts, Madison 45063
Museum of Earth Science of the M.V. Lomonosov Moscow State University, Moskva 33160
Museum of Earth Science of the Polish Academy of Sciences, Warszawa 32137
Museum of East Anglian Life, Stowmarket 40618
Museum of East Asian Art, Bath 38119
The Museum of East Texas, Lufkin 44997
Museum of Eastern Bohemia in Hradec Kralove, Hradec Králové 08368
Museum of Eastern Slovakia, Košice 34006
Museum of Education, Beograd 33815
Museum of Education, Elbasan 00019
Museum of Education, Korçë 00026
Museum of Education in Flanders, Ieper 03518
Museum of Electricity, Christchurch 38577
Museum of English Rural Life, Reading 40295
Museum of Engravings and Graphic Arts, Athinai 20886
Museum of Entertainment, Whaplode 40848
Museum of Epirot Folk Art, Metsovon 21071
Museum of Estonian Architecture, Tallinn 09357
Museum of Ethnographic Costumes on Dolls, Moskva 33097
Museum of Ethnography, Budapest 21367
Museum of Ethnography, Stockholm 36240
Museum of Ethnography and Folklore, Tel Aviv 22769
Museum of Ethnology and Folk Art, Ratnapura 35758
Museum of Eton Life, Eton 38951
Museum of Evolution, Uppsala 36353
Museum of Evolution of the Palaeobiological Institute of the Polish Academy of Sciences, Warszawa 32094
Museum of Evolution, Paleontology, Uppsala 36354
Museum of Exploration, Survey and Land Settlement, Adelaide 00711
Museum of Far Eastern Antiquities, Stockholm 36271
Museum of Farming Equipment Kalēji (The Blacksmiths), Talsi 27455
Museum of Farming Life, Ellon 38929
Museum of Farnham, Farnham 38982
Museum of Fiber Science and Technology, Tokyo University of Agriculture and Technology, Koganei 26364
Museum of Filipino Life, Pasay 31413
Museum of Fine Art, Lugansk 37882
Museum of Fine Art, Novokuzneck 33236
The Museum of Fine Art, Gifu, Gifu 26157
Museum of Fine Art of the Republic Udmurtiya, Iževsk 32837
Museum of Fine Arts, Beijing 06975
Museum of Fine Arts, Boston 41817
Museum of Fine Arts, Budapest 21383
Museum of Fine Arts, Chandigarh 21739
Museum of Fine Arts, Gent 03448
Museum of Fine Arts, Hobart 01102
The Museum of Fine Arts, Houston 44129
Museum of Fine Arts, Komsomolsk-na-Amure 32935
Museum of Fine Arts, Missoula 45406
Museum of Fine Arts, Nanchang 07171
Museum of Fine Arts, Rostov-na-Donu 33356
Museum of Fine Arts, Santa Fe 47424
Museum of Fine Arts, Springfield 47747
Museum of Fine Arts, Tbilisi 15364
Museum of Fine Arts and Cultural Center, Alexandria 09243
Museum of Fine Arts Saint Petersburg, Florida, Saint Petersburg 47174
Museum of Finnish Architecture, Helsinki 09533
Museum of Finnish Tourism, Imatra 09567
Museum of Fire, Edinburgh 38893
Museum of First Romanian School of Braşov, Braşov 32450
Museum of Fishing, Santos 04454
Museum of Flight, North Berwick 40077
Museum of Flight, Seattle 47539
Museum of Florida History, Tallahassee 47936
Museum of Folk Architecture, Sanok 31966
Museum of Folk Architecture - Ethnographic Park in Olsztynek, Olsztynek 31853
Museum of Folk Art, Uljanovsk 33663
Museum of Folk Craft and Applied Arts, Trojan 04890
Museum of Folk Culture and Art, Poznań 31902
Museum of Folk Education, Penza 33290
Museum of Folk Education in the Simbirsk Government in the 70th and 80th of the 19th Century, Uljanovsk 33664
Museum of Folk Graphics, Moskva 33139
Museum of Folk Musical Instruments, Szydłowiec 32038
Museum of Folklore, Brugge 03264
Museum of Foreign Art, Rīga 27402
Museum of Forestry, Antol 33946
Museum of Forestry, Hunting and Fisheries, Hluboká nad Vltavou 08352
Museum of Freemasonry, London 39713
Museum of Frontier Guards, Moskva 33147
Museum of Fulham Palace, London 39714
Museum of Garden History, London 39715
Museum of Gems and Minerals, Ratnapura 35759
Museum of Geologic Collection, Kielce 31663
Museum of Geology, Edmonton 05381
Museum of Geology, Rapid City 46797
Museum of Geology of the Institute of Geological Sciences of the Polish Academy of Sciences, Kraków 31703
Museum of Geology, Oil and Gas, Tjumen 33603
Museum of Glass, Tacoma 47921
Museum of Glass and Jewellry, Jablonec nad Nisou 08378
Museum of Gorica, Nova Gorica 34135
Museum of Greek Folk Art, Athinai 20872
Museum of Greek Musical Instruments, Thessaloniki 21190
Museum of Greek Popular Musical Instruments, Athinai 20877
Museum of Guides and Scouts, Ogre 27390
Museum of Gujarat Vidyasabha, Ahmedabad 21681
Museum of Handicraft, Architecture and Allday Life, Kaluga 32881
Museum of Harjamäki Mental Hospital, Siilinjärvi 10035
Museum of Harlow, Harlow 39165
Museum of Hartlepool, Hartlepool 39177
Museum of Health and Medical Science, Houston 44130
Museum of Health Care, Kingston 05685
Museum of Herzegovina, Mostar 03917
Museum of Highlands, Telč 08676
Museum of Highlands, Třešť 08690
Museum of Highlands Jihlava, Jihlava 08390
Museum of Historic Clocks, Bratislava 33960
Museum of Historical Agricultural Engineering, Wageningen 29976
Museum of Historical Archaeology, Kingston 26074
Museum of Historical Geology and Geological Survey of Pakistan, Quetta 31054
Museum of Historical Philips Products, Eindhoven 29216
Museum of History, Dobrič 04655
Museum of History, Jambol 04681
Museum of History and Art, Belozersk 32680
Museum of History and Art, Kaliningrad 32870
Museum of History and Art, Morehead City 45496
Museum of History and Art, Ontario 46163
Museum of History and Art, Serpuchov 33522
Museum of History and Art, Tichvin 33600
Museum of History and Culture of the Moscow Quarter, Nižnij Novgorod 33210
Museum of History and Culture of Votkinsk, Votkinsk 33738
Museum of History and Ethnography Negeri, Melaka 27667
Museum of History and Industry, Seattle 47540
Museum of History, Anthropology and Art, San Juan 32405
Museum of History of Katowice, Katowice 31646
Museum of History of Orenburg, Orenburg 33269
Museum of History of Riga and Navigation, Rīga 27441
Museum of History of the City of Cracow, Jewish Department, Kraków 31699
Museum of History of the City of Gdańsk, Gdańsk 31571
Museum of History of the City of Łódź, Łódź 31770
Museum of History of the County Nógrád, Salgótarján 21523
Museum of History of the Prioksky Quarter, Nižnij Novgorod 33214
Museum of History of the University of Latvia, Rīga 27426
Museum of History of Varna, Varna 04903
Museum of History Silistra, Silistra 04815
Museum of Holography, Chicago 42348
Museum of Home Décor, Kežmarok 34001
Museum of Horyuji Mural Paintings, Nagakute 26525
Museum of Human Sciences, Harare 49031
Museum of Hungarian Agriculture, Budapest 21359
Museum of Hungarian Aluminium Industry, Székesfehérvár 21558
Museum of Hunting, Zagreb 07827
Museum of Hunting and Fishing, Moskva 33144
Museum of Hunting and Horsemanship, Warszawa 32111
Museum of Hunting of the Irkutsk Agricultural Academy, Irkutsk 32820
Museum of Hygiene, Cairo 09273
Museum of Icons, Varna 04901
Museum of Icons and Art Objects, Gangtok 21804
Museum of Icons of the National Revival, Radomir 04794
Museum of Images from the Unconscious, Rio de Janeiro 04360
Museum of Independence, Warszawa 32116
Museum of Independent Telephony, Abilene 41051
Museum of Indian Arts and Culture, Santa Fe 47425
Museum of Indian Culture, Allentown 41147
Museum of Industrial Worker's Dwellings, Imatra 09568
Museum of Industry, Stellarton 06489
Museum of Industry, Tokyo 26934
Museum of Industry and Technic, Wałbrzych 32072
Museum of Inhaca Island, Maputo 28727
Museum of Installation, London 39716
Museum of Instruments, London 39717
Museum of Interial Manor, Ożarów 31872
Museum of International Ceramic Art Denmark, Middelfart 08984
Museum of International Children's Art, Santa Cruz 47412
Museum of International Folk Art, Santa Fe 47426
Museum of International Friendship, Beijing 06976
Museum of International Friendship, Saransk 33499
Museum of Irish Transport, Killarney 22492
Museum of Iron and Darby Furnace, Coalbrookdale 38596
Museum of Iron Ore Mining, Częstochowa 31546
Museum of Ironwork, Komárov u Horovic 08418
Museum of Islamic Art, Cairo 09274
Museum of Island History, Newport, Isle of Wight 40055
Museum of Islay Life, Port Charlotte 40231
Museum of Israeli Art, Ramat Gan 22733
Museum of Istrian History, Pula 07758
Museum of Ivanovo Calico, Ivanovo 32831
Museum of Japanese Sword Fittings, Tokyo 26895
Museum of Jewish Art, Jerusalem 22647
Museum of Jewish Culture, Bratislava 33976
Museum of Jewish Heritage - A Living Memorial to the Holocaust, New York 45842
Museum of Jewish Religion and History, Budapest 21376
Museum of Jindřich Jindřich, Domažlice 08333
Museum of J.V. Sládek, Zbiroh 08741
Museum of Kainuu, Kajaani 09610
Museum of Kārlis Ulmanis Pikšas, Bērze 27338
Museum of Karlovy Vary, Karlovy Vary 08401
Museum of Kashubian and Pomeranian Literature and Music, Wejherowo 32149
Museum of Kazakh Popular Musical Instruments, Almaty 27073
Museum of Kent Life, Sandling 40443
Museum of Kerala History, Edapally 21797
Museum of Kerman, Kerman 22252
Museum of Kežmarok, Kežmarok 34002
Museum of Kilims and Flatweaves, İstanbul 37714
Museum of Komotini, Komotini 21026
Museum of Korea Indigenous Straw and Plant, Seoul 27258
Museum of Korean Buddhist Art, Seoul 27259
Museum of Korean Commercial History, Yongin 27302
Museum of Korean Embroidery, Seoul 27260
Museum of Korean Traditional Music, Seoul 27261
Museum of Krkonoše Region, Jilemnice 08392
Museum of Kyoto, Kyoto 26422
Museum of Lakeland Life, Kendal 39338
Museum of Lancashire, Preston 40267
Museum of Land Reclamation and Agriculture of the Latvian Republic, Mālpils 27387
Museum of Landscape Painting, Ples 33324
Museum of Latin American Art, Long Beach 44861
Museum of Lead Mining, Wanlockhead 40780
Museum of Lighting, Edinburgh 38894
Museum of Lillydale, Lilydale 01176
Museum of Lincolnshire Life, Lincoln 39500
Museum of Literary Life in the Jaroslavl Region, Jaroslavl 32854
Museum of Literature, Melaka 27673
Museum of Literature, Warszawa 32110
Museum of Literature and Music, Banská Bystrica 33947
Museum of Literature and the Art Theatre and Gallery MAK, Sarajevo 03922
Museum of Liverpool Life, Liverpool 39525
Museum of Local Crafts and Industries, Burnley 38399
Museum of Local History, Hastings 39185
Museum of Local History, Samarkand 48850
Museum of Local History and Gallery of Contemporary Art, Budapest 21342
Museum of Local History and Industry, Llandrindod Wells 39537
Museum of Local History and Nature, Ekaterinburg 32782
Museum of Local Life, Worcester 40929
Museum of London, London 39718
Museum of Long Island Natural Sciences, Stony Brook 47831
Museum of Lower Silesian Weaving, Kamienna Góra 31637
Museum of Macao, Macau 07167
Museum of Macedonia - Archaeological, Ethnological and Historical, Skopje 27590
Museum of Malawi, Blantyre 27611
Museum of Man in the Sea, Panama City Beach 46279
Museum of Mankind, London 39719
Museum of Manuscripts and Calligraphy, İstanbul 37711
Museum of Marine Life of Cyprus, Aghia Napa 08183
Museum of Maritime Science, Tokyo 26847
Museum of Maroccan Arts, Tanger 28713
Museum of Martsial Mineral Water, Petrozavodsk 33319
Museum of Martyrdom, Bielsk Podlaski 31491
Museum of Martyrdom, Poznań 31907
Museum of Maryland History, Baltimore 41483
Museum of Masharov's House, Tjumen 33602
Museum of Masovien Village, Sierpc 31975
Museum of Meat Industry, Budapest 21345
Museum of Mechanical Music, Varkaus 10185
Museum of Medical Equipment, Bangkok 37489
Museum of Medical History, Bruxelles 03305
Museum of Medical History, Linköping 36041
Museum of Medical History, Seltjarnarnes 21668
Museum of Medical History, Shanghai 07217
Museum of Medical History, Vänersborg 36372
Museum of Medical Sciences, Hong Kong 07105
Museum of Medieval Stockholm, Stockholm 36288
Museum of Mediterranean and Near Eastern Antiquities, Stockholm 36259
Museum of Mental Health Services, Toronto 06597
Museum of Methodism, London 39720
Museum of Migrating People, Bronx 41924
Museum of Military and Naval History, San Juan 32406
Museum of Military History, Budapest 21341
Museum of Military History, Gorna Studena 04676
Museum of Military History, Maracaibo 48951
Museum of Military Intelligence, Chicksands 38566
Museum of Military Medicine, Lahti 09750
Museum of Mineralogy and Geology Dr. Alfredo Stelzner, Córdoba 00297
Museum of Mineralogy, Petrology and Geology, Zografou 21226
Museum of Mining and Balneology in Jáchymov, Jáchymov 08382
Museum of Mining and Metallurgy, Bor 33824
Museum of Mining of Metals and Minerals, Rudabánya 21519
Museum of Mobile, Mobile 45422
Museum of Modern and Contemporary Art, Aalborg 08763
Museum of Modern and Contemporary Fine Arts, Sosnovyj Bor 33549
Museum of Modern Art, Arnhem 28941
Museum of Modern Art, Cairo 09275
Museum of Modern Art, Dubrovnik 07702
Museum of Modern Art, Ljubljana 34112
The Museum of Modern Art, Machynlleth 39869
Museum of Modern Art, Niepołomice 31824
Museum of Modern Art, Radom 31939
Museum of Modern Art, Szczecin 32023
Museum of Modern Art at the Gramercy Theatre, New York 45843
Museum of Modern Art Gunma, Takasaki 26798
Museum of Modern Art in Queens, Long Island City 44869
Museum of Modern Art Ostend, Oostende 03669
Museum of Modern Art, Saitama, Saitama 26693
Museum of Modern Art, Shiga, Otsu 26683
The Museum of Modern Art, Toyama, Toyama 26969
Museum of Modern Art Wakayama, Wakayama 26998
Museum of Modern History and Culture of North Osetiya, Vladikavkaz 33689
Museum of Modern Japanese Literature, Tokyo 26905
Museum of Mohamed Mahmoud Khalil and his wife, Giza 09295
Museum of Mongolian Ethnography, Ulaanbaatar 28681
Museum of Montaneus Banat, Reşiţa 32581
Museum of Mosaics, Devnja 04648
The Museum of Museums, Waregem 03826
Museum of Music and the Theatre, Kislovodsk 32930
Museum of Music Boxes and Automata, Sainte-Croix 37090
Museum of Music History, Budapest 21392
Museum of Musical Instruments, Sankt-Peterburg 33459
Museum of Musical Instruments, Musashino Academia Musicae, Tokyo 26849
Museum of Nahariya, Nahariya 22718
Museum of NaJu Pears, Naju 27213
Museum of National Antiquities, Stockholm 36285
Museum of National Antiquities, Stockholm 36246
Museum of National Culture, Kazan 32903
Museum of National History, Humenné 33999
Museum of National History and Archaeology, Constanţa 32501
Museum of Nativity, Třeběchovice pod Orebem 08684
Museum of Natural History, Dublin 22445
Museum of Natural History, Eugene 43224
Museum of Natural History, Jerusalem 22648
Museum of Natural History, Los Baños 31345
Museum of Natural History, Marshall 45180
Museum of Natural History, Neskaupstadur 21644
Museum of Natural History, Providence 46722

The Museum of Natural History, Stevens Point 47807
Museum of Natural History, Urbana 48163
Museum of Natural History, Vestmannaeyjar 21674
Museum of Natural History and Archaeology, Trondheim 30946
Museum of Natural History and Forest, Smołdzino 31981
Museum of Natural History and Historical Photography, Polygyros 21132
Museum of Natural History of the Łódź University, Łódź 31775
Museum of Natural History, Wrocław University, Wrocław 32184
Museum of Natural Science, Baton Rouge 41532
Museum of Natural Sciences, Bruxelles 03338
Museum of Natural Sciences, Saskatoon 06402
Museum of Natural Sciences, Tiranë 00035
Museum of Nature, Čerepovec 32732
Museum of Nature, Kazimierz Dolny 31650
Museum of Nature, Smolensk 33533
The Museum of Naval Firepower, Gosport 39101
Museum of Nebraska Art, Kearney 44424
Museum of Nebraska History, Lincoln 44787
Museum of Neon Art, Los Angeles 44932
Museum of Net Manufacture, Dorset 38759
Museum of New Hampshire History, Concord 42605
Museum of New Mexico, Santa Fe 47427
The Museum of Newport History, Newport 45926
Museum of Ningxia Autonomous Region of the Hui Nationality, Yinchuan 07319
Museum of Nógrád County, Balassagyarmat 21310
Museum of Nonconformist Art, Sankt-Peterburg 33461
Museum of North Carolina Minerals, Spruce Pine 47764
Museum of North Craven Life, Settle 40473
Museum of North Idaho, Coeur d'Alene 42511
Museum of Northern Arizona, Flagstaff 43329
Museum of Northern British Columbia, Prince Rupert 06189
Museum of Northern History at the Sir Harry Oakes Château, Kirkland Lake 05694
Museum of Northwest Art, La Conner 44532
Museum of Northwest Colorado, Craig 42687
Museum of Nottingham Lace, Nottingham 40110
The Museum of Nursing, Camperdown 00883
The Museum of Nursing History, Philadelphia 46431
Museum of Odontology, Helsinki 09483
Museum of Old Silesian Trade, Świdnica 32014
Museum of One Picture, Penza 33295
Museum of Ore-Mining and Mining Construction, Madan 04730
Museum of Orient and East Marion History, Orient 46181
Museum of Oriental Ceramics Osaka, Osaka 26671
Museum of Oriental Manuscripts, Prizren 33898
Museum of Our Lady of the Poetterie, Brugge 03260
The Museum of Outdoor Arts, Englewood 43191
Museum of Oxford, Oxford 40148
Museum of Painting and Sculpture, İstanbul 37705
Museum of Palace Interior, Choroszcz 31532
Museum of Palekh Art, Palech 33282
Museum of Paleontology, Berkeley 41646
Museum of Palestinian Popular Heritage, Al-Bireh 31061
Museum of Partisan Struggle, Polichno 31893
Museum of Pathology, Sydney 01503
Museum of Patrons and Benefactors of Russia, Moskva 33133
Museum of Pedagogics, Kaunas 27522
Museum of Peoples and Cultures, Provo 46736
Museum of Persecuted Art-Israel, Ashdod 22573
Museum of Petroleum Industry in Bóbrka, Chorkówka 31531
Museum of Pharmacy, Bratislava 33962
Museum of Pharmacy, Rīga 27406
Museum of Pharmacy, Collegium Medicum at the Jagiellonian University, Kraków 31702
Museum of Philippine Art, Manila 31387
Museum of Philippine Humanities, Manila 31384
Museum of Philippine Humanities, Pasay 31414
Museum of Philippine Political History, Manila 31388
Museum of Philippine Traditional Cultures, Pasay 31416
Museum of Photographic Art, Odense 09015
Museum of Photographic Arts, San Diego 47283
Museum of Physical Education and Sports, Budapest 21385
Museum of Pioneer Settlement, Kibbutz Yifat 22706
Museum of Piping, Glasgow 39056
Museum of Piracy, Santiago de Cuba 08140
Museum of Police Techniques, Solna 36220
Museum of Polish Military Health Services, Łódź 31774
Museum of Post and Telecomunication Mokhaberat, Teheran 22316
Museum of Postindependence Athens, Athinai 20887
Museum of Pottery and Ceramics, Kostelec nad Černými lesy 08423
Museum of Precious Stones of the Baykal Region, Sljudjanka 33527
Museum of Prehistory, Jerusalem 22649
Museum of Prehistory, Shaar Hagolan 22742
Museum of Primitive Art and Culture, Peace Dale 46321
Museum of Primitive Methodism, Englesea Brook, Crewe 38665
Museum of Printing History, Houston 44131
Museum of Private Collections, Moskva 33131
Museum of Psalms, Jerusalem 22650
Museum of Public Health, Sankt-Peterburg 33469
Museum of Puppetry, Chrudim 08320
Museum of Puppets, Monterrey 28240
Museum of Puppets and Children Books Wonderland, Ekaterinburg 32777
Museum of Radio and Technology, Huntington 44167
Museum of Rail and Truck, Ängelholm 35786
Museum of Rail Travel, Keighley 39330
Museum of Railway Technics, Sankt-Peterburg 33470
Museum of Rape Making, Älvängen 35783
Museum of Reading, Reading 40296
Museum of Recent History Celje, Celje 34089
Museum of Reconstruction, Hammerfest 30531
Museum of Regional and Mediterranean Archaeology, Nir-David 22723
Museum of Regional History of San Lorenzo and Gallery of the Liberator General San Martín, San Lorenzo 00575
Museum of Religious Art, Haarlem 29329
Museum of Religious Art, La Habana 07958
Museum of Religious History, Ulaanbaatar 28682
Museum of Richmond, Richmond, Surrey 40320
Museum of Robotics, Orinda 46182
Museum of Roman Antiquities, Rabat 27700
Museum of Romanian Literature, Iaşi 32536
Museum of Romanticism, Opinogóra 31855
Museum of Rovinj's Heritage, Rovinj 07766
Museum of Rugby, Twickenham 40739
Museum of Rural Industry, Sticklepath 40588
Museum of Rural Life, Denton 42873
Museum of Russian Culture, San Francisco 47330
Museum of Sacred Art, Macau 07168
Museum of Sacred Icons, Athinai 20888
Museum of Saint Albans, Saint Albans 40375
Museum of Samoa, Apia 33757
Museum of Science, Boston 41818
Museum of Science and History of Jacksonville, Jacksonville 44299
Museum of Science and Industry, Chicago 42349
Museum of Science and Industry, Tampa 47943
Museum of Science and Industry in Manchester, Manchester 39898
Museum of Science and Technology, Accra 20789
Museum of Science and Technology, Beograd 33807
Museum of Science and Technology, Pretoria 34349
Museum of Science at the Toledo Zoo, Toledo 48020
Museum of Scotland, Edinburgh 38895
Museum of Scottish Country Life, East Kilbride 38845
Museum of Scottish Lighthouses, Fraserburgh 39016
Museum of Sculpture, Sankt-Peterburg 33465
Museum of Sculpture and Figurines of Loukia Georganti, Athinai 20889
Museum of Sculptures of S.T. Konenkov, Smolensk 33529
Museum of Sea Industry, Varna 04899
Museum of Seminole County History, Sanford 47393
Museum of Sex, New York 45844
Museum of Shanxi Province, Taiyuan 07257
Museum of Shells of the Greek Seas, Néa Moudiana 21099
Museum of Shipbuilding, Beograd 33811
Museum of Shops, Eastbourne 38853
Museum of Shrouds, Torino 25742
Museum of Silesia Opole, Opole 31859
Museum of Site, Most I, Hong Kong 07106
Museum of Site, Most II, Hong Kong 07107
Museum of Sketches, Lund 36064
Museum of Škofja Loka, Škofja Loka 34148
Museum of Slavonia Osijek, Osijek 07750
Museum of Smuggling History, Ventnor 40755
Museum of South East Alberta, Etzikom 05419
Museum of South-Eastern Moravia, Zlín 08751
Museum of South Somerset, Yeovil 40956
Museum of South Yorkshire Life, Doncaster 38743
Museum of South Zealand, Vordingborg 09115
Museum of Southern African Rock Art, Johannesburg 34281
Museum of Southern History, Jacksonville 44300
The Museum of Southern History, Sugarland 47870
Museum of Southwestern Biology, Albuquerque 41105
Museum of Spanish Abstract Art, Cuenca 34763
Museum of Spanish Colonial Art, Santa Fe 47428
Museum of Special Educational System, Levoča 34011
Museum of Speed, Pendine 40173
Museum of Spiš, Spišská Nová Ves 34064
Museum of Sport and Tourism, Łódź 31776
Museum of Sports, Cienfuegos 07890
Museum of Sports, Malmö 36073
Museum of Sports and Tourism, Warszawa 32126
Museum of Sports History, La Habana 07959
Museum of Srem, Sremska Mitrovica 33913
Museum of St. Petersburg Railway Line, Lahti 09746
Museum of Stefan Żeromski's School Years, Kielce 31657
Museum of Stone Masonry, Akşehir 37606
Museum of Strife for Independence, Kraków 31697
Museum of Study and Conquest of the European North, Apatity 32645
Museum of Surveying, Lansing 44644
Museum of Sussex Archaeology, Lewes 39486
Museum of Swedish Shoe Industry, Kumla 36022
Museum of Sydney, Sydney 01504
Museum of Tatra National Park, Tatranská Lomnica 34073
Museum of Taxes, Jerusalem 22651
Museum of Technology, Helsinki 09541
Museum of Technology in Warsaw, Warszawa 32129
Museum of Telecommunications, Néa Kifissia 21097
Museum of Telecommunications, Rīga 27411
Museum of Television and Radio, Beverly Hills 41677
Museum of Television and Radio, New York 45845
Museum of Texas, Waco 48266
Museum of Texas Tech University, Lubbock 44991
Museum of Textile Industry, Budapest 21386
Museum of Textile Industry, Sliven 04822
Museum of the 10th Pavilion of the Warszaw Citadel, Warszawa 32136
Museum of the 16th Winter Olympic Games, Albertville 10272
Museum of the 19th Century Tartu Citizens, Tartu 09373
Museum of the 40's, Point Clear Bay 40215
Museum of the Academy of Mining and Metallurgy, Kraków 31704
Museum of the Agricultural College and Research Institute, Coimbatore 21751
Museum of the Air Force, Madrid 35030
Museum of the Albemarle, Elizabeth City 43132
Museum of the Alphabet, Waxhaw 48470
Museum of the Altaj Republic named after A.V. Anochin, Gorno-Altajsk 32808
Museum of the American Hungarian Foundation, New Brunswick 45679
Museum of the American Numismatic Association, Colorado Springs 42540
Museum of the American Piano, New York 45846
Museum of the American Quilter's Society, Paducah 46256
Museum of the Archdiocese, Wrocław 32174
Museum of the Archeology of Prikamsk Region, Perm 33305
Museum of the Archipelago, Lappoby-Åland 09767
Museum of the Armed October Rebellion, Voronež 33733
Museum of the Artist Morozov, Ivanovo 32832
Museum of the Artistic Culture of the Russian North, Archangelsk 32650
Museum of the Association of Sports Dynamo Moscow, Moskva 33142
Museum of the Aviation in the North, Archangelsk 32652
Museum of the Banat, Timişoara 32614
Museum of the Bārda Family Rumbiņi, Pociems 27396
Museum of the Battle of Grunwald, Stębark 32000
Museum of the Battle of Legnica, Legnickie Pole 31755
Museum of the Bedford Historical Society, Bedford 41580
Museum of the Benua Family, Sankt-Peterburg 33464
Museum of the Berkeley Springs, Berkeley Springs 41650
Museum of the Beskid Mountains, Wisła 32156
Museum of the Big Bend, Alpine 41155
Museum of the Black Eagle Pharmacy, Székesfehérvár 21556
Museum of the Blind - Typhlology, Zagreb 07839
Museum of the Bohemian Paradise, Turnov 08694
Museum of the Bulgarian National Revival, Varna 04900
Museum of the Cape Fear Historical Complex, Fayetteville 43312
Museum of the Čapek Brothers, Malé Svatoňovice 08470
Museum of the Cariboo Chilcotin, Williams Lake 06802
Museum of the Castle Basin, Baranów Sandomierski 31475
Museum of the Central Bank of the Philippines, Manila 31383
Museum of the Central Marine Fisheries Research Station, Mandapam Camp 21937
Museum of the Centre of Europe, Vilnius 27535
Museum of the Chado Research Center, Kyoto 26436
Museum of the Cherokee Indian, Cherokee 42276
Museum of the Cherokee Strip, Enid 43192
Museum of the Chinese People's Revolutionary Military Affairs, Beijing 06977
Museum of the Church of Saint Peter and Paul, Tjumen 33601
Museum of the City of Athens, Athinai 20890
Museum of The City of Gdynia, Gdynia 31586
Museum of the City of Havana, La Habana 07961
Museum of the City of Lake Worth, Lake Worth 44598
Museum of the City of Manila, Manila 31385
Museum of the City of New York, New York 45847
Museum of the City of Podgorica, Podgorica 33889
Museum of the City of Skopje, Skopje 27589
Museum of the City of Split, Split 07783
Museum of the College of Engineering, Chennai 21747
The Museum of the Confederacy, Richmond 46883
Museum of the Conspirativ Flat of the Russian Social Democratic Party of 1904-1906, Uljanovsk 33661
Museum of the Cracow Salt Mines, Wieliczka 32153
Museum of the Croup of Beverlo, Leopoldsburg 03560
Museum of the Cultural Palace of National Minorities, Beijing 06978
Museum of the Culture of Astrakhan, Astrachan 32666
Museum of the Culture of Carpatian Germans, Bratislava 33971
Museum of the Culture of Hungarians in Slovakia, Bratislava 33972
Museum of the Cumbraes, Millport 39956
Museum of the Czech Countryside, Kačina 08396
Museum of the Deaf, Helsinki 09506
Museum of the Decembrists, Minusinsk 33017
Museum of the Decembrists - House of the Volkonskyjs, Irkutsk 32817
Museum of the Decembrists - House of Trubetskoy, Irkutsk 32816
Museum of the Diplomatic Corps, Vologda 33722
Museum of the Dobrzyń Region, Golub-Dobrzyń 31602
Museum of the Dog, Saint Louis 47131
Museum of the Dolenjsko Region, Novo Mesto 34136
Museum of The Duke of Wellington's Regiment, Halifax 39153
Museum of the Dutch Clock, Zaandam 30035
Museum of the Education of the Komi Region at the Syktyvkar State University, Syktyvkar 33577
Museum of the Elbe Region, Poděbrady 08551
Museum of the Eliasi Family Zīlēni, Platone 27395
Museum of the Estonian Swedes, Haapsalu 09319
Museum of the Evenks, Tura 33635
Museum of the Faculty of Agriculture, Sapporo 26711
Museum of the Faculty of Arts, Alexandria 09244
Museum of the Făgăras County, Făgăraş 32518
Museum of the former Residence of Comrade Mao Zedong at Shaoshan, Shaoshan 07231
Museum of the former Residence of Premier Zhou En-Lai, Huaian 07115
Museum of the Franciscan Convent, Jerusalem 22652
Museum of the Franciscan Monastery, Rovinj 07765
Museum of the Fur Trade, Chadron 42180
Museum of the Galician People, Santiago de Compostela 35448
Museum of the Geological Sciences, Blacksburg 41728
Museum of the George and Nefeli Giabra Pierides Collection, Lefkosia 08203
Museum of the Glory of the Fighters, Astrachan 32664
Museum of the Great Plains, Lawton 44695
Museum of the Grove of the Village Shrine, Osaka 26656
Museum of the Guangxi Province, Nanning 07190
Museum of the Gulf Coast, Port Arthur 46590
Museum of the Highwood, High River 05595
Museum of the Historical Society of Trappe, Collegeville, Perkiomen Valley, Trappe 48048
Museum of the History and Art of the Holy City of Missolonghi, Mesolongion 21065
Museum of the History and Culture of the Middle Prikamje, Sarapul 33503
Museum of the History of Adler District of Sochi, Soči 33539
Museum of the History of Aksay, Aksaj 32631
Museum of the History of Architecture and Industrial Technology of the Ural Region, Ekaterinburg 32774
Museum of the History of Azerbaijan, Baku 03067
Museum of the History of Buzuluk, Buzuluk 32714
Museum of the History of Children's Games and Books, Myrina 21080
Museum of the History of Communication of the Tatarian Republic, Kazan 32898
Museum of the History of Cypriot Coinage, Lefkosia 08204
Museum of the History of Dagestan Fishing Industry, Machačkala 32997
Museum of the History of Department of Internal Affairs of the Kaluga Region, Kaluga 32880
Museum of the History of Development of Norilsk Industrial Region, Norilsk 33229
Museum of the History of Education, Leeds 39449
Museum of the History of Ekaterinburg, Ekaterinburg 32775
Museum of the History of Folk Arts and Crafts, Nižnij Novgorod 33211
Museum of the History of Houses in the 19th and 20th Centuries, Tjumen 33605
Museum of the History of Irkutsk, Irkutsk 32818
Museum of the History of Kasan University, Kazan 32897
Museum of the History of Lublin, Lublin 31790
Museum of the History of Medicine, Astrachan 32665
Museum of the History of Medicine, Cairo 09276
Museum of the History of Medicine, Varna 04902
Museum of the History of Moscow, Moskva 33109
Museum of the History of Moscow District Military Regiments, Moskva 33112
Museum of the History of Political Banishment, Bratsk 32705
Museum of the History of Political Banishment in Yakutia, Jakutsk 32844
Museum of the History of Printing, Sankt-Peterburg 33439
Museum of the History of Revolution, Lhasa 07149
Museum of the History of Schlüsselburg, Šlisselburg 33525
Museum of the History of Science, Oxford 40149
Museum of the History of Science, Sydney 01505
Museum of the History of Sochi, Soči 33541
Museum of the History of Stavropol, Stavropol 33562
Museum of the History of Tel Aviv-Yafo, Tel Aviv 22770
Museum of the History of Termurids, Taškent 48857
Museum of the History of the Blind, Hellerup 08856
Museum of the History of the City of Poznań, Poznań 31904
Museum of the History of the District, Belozersk 32683

Museum of the History of the Herzen State Pedagogical University of Russia, Sankt-Peterburg 33443
Museum of the History of the Perm Region, Perm 33306
Museum of the History of the Poltical Police of Russia, Sankt-Peterburg 33441
Museum of the History of the Revolutionary-Democratic Movement of the 1880-1890 Years, Sankt-Peterburg 33442
Museum of the History of the Saams of the Kola peninsula, Lovozero 32993
Museum of the History of the Salt Industry, Zigong 07340
Museum of the History of the Television Factory V.I. Lenin, Nižnij Novgorod 33213
Museum of the History of the Theatres of Dagestan, Machačkala 32998
Museum of the History of the VEF Stock Company, Rīga 27442
Museum of the History of Tiberias and the Lake Kinnereth, Tiberias 22782
Museum of the History of Tjumen, Tjumen 33606
Museum of the History of Tourism, Sankt-Peterburg 33445
Museum of the Holmesdale Natural History Club, Reigate 40307
Museum of the Holy Land, Santiago de Compostela 35445
Museum of the Holy Trinity Church of Ethiopia, Addis Ababa 09399
The Museum of the Home, Pembroke 40169
Museum of the Hudson Highlands, Cornwall-on-Hudson 42642
Museum of the Hungarian Culture & Danubian Region, Komárno 34003
Museum of the Hungarian Petroleum Industry, Zalaegerszeg 21615
Museum of the Hussite, Žlutice 08754
Museum of the Imperial Collections, Tokyo 26879
Museum of the Imperial Palace of Manchu State, Changchun 07005
Museum of the Institute of African Studies, Ibadan 30339
Museum of the Institute of African Studies, Oshogbo 30357
Museum of the Institute of History and Philology, Academia Sinica, Taipei 07349
Museum of the Institute of Ocean Biology of the Far Eastern Dept. of the Russian Academy of Sciences, Vladivostok 33704
Museum of the Iron Age, Andover 38001
Museum of the Isles, Armadale 38016
Museum of the Japan Monkey Centre, Inuyama 26252
Museum of the Jewellery Quarter, Birmingham 38225
Museum of the Jewish Historical Institute, Warszawa 32138
Museum of the Jimmy Carter Library, Atlanta 41353
Museum of the Kalisz Region, Kalisz 31635
Museum of the Kampinoska Forest, Kampinos 31639
Museum of the Kazan Chemical Secondary School, Kazan 32900
Museum of the King Saint Stephen, Székesfehérvár 21561
Museum of the Kirov Works, Sankt-Peterburg 33446
Museum of the Kłodzko Region, Kłodzko 31664
Museum of the Korean Cultural Center, Los Angeles 44933
Museum of the Kórnik Library, Kórnik 31673
Museum of the Krapina Prehistoric Man, Krapina 07728
Museum of the Krkonoše Mounts, Vrchlabí 08725
Museum of the Krotoszyn Region, Krotoszyn 31738
Museum of the Kujawy and Ziemia Dobrzyńska, Włocławek 32163
Museum of the Kyoto University Faculty of Letters, Kyoto 26420
Museum of the Latvia Agriculture University, Jelgava 27367
Museum of the Liangshan Autonomous Prefecture of the Yi Nationality, Xichang 07309
Museum of the Liberation of Pleven 1877, Pleven 04767
Museum of the Light Infantry, Charleroi 03352
Museum of the Linxia Autonomous Region, Linxia 07152
Museum of the Literary Life of the Ural in the 19th Century, Ekaterinburg 32779
Museum of the Llano Estacado, Plainview 46540
Museum of the Lubusz Region, Zielona Góra 32220
Museum of the Manchesters, Ashton-under-Lyne 38033
Museum of the Marsh of the Village Fighter, La Habana 07973
Museum of the Martyrdom of Allied Prisoners of War, Żagań 32202
Museum of the Mausoleum of King Nanyue, Guangzhou 07070
Museum of the Medical College, Mysore 21962
Museum of the Merchant Marine, Piraeus 21123
Museum of the Metropolis of Messinia, Kalamata 20985
Museum of the Mexican Army and Air Force at Barrack Colorado, Guadalajara 27956
Museum of the Mid-Suffolk Light Railway, Wetheringsett 40838
Museum of the Middle Otava Area, Strakonice 08663
Museum of the Ministry of Internal Affairs, Sofia 04841
Museum of the Mologa Region, Rybinsk 33361
Museum of the Moravian Heights, Nové Město na Moravě 08503
Museum of the Mordovian Culture, Saransk 33500
Museum of the Mountain Man, Pinedale 46493
Museum of the Moving Images, London 39721
Museum of the Mussorgsky State Academic Opera and Ballet Theatre, Sankt-Peterburg 33435
Museum of the Nagasaki Heavy Industries, Nagasaki 26549
Museum of the National Academy of Art, Sofia 04840
Museum of the National Bank of Belgium, Bruxelles 03303
Museum of the National Center of Afro-American Artists, Boston 41819
Museum of the National Center of Afro-American Artists, Roxbury 47022
Museum of the National Opera, Sofia 04843
Museum of the National Palace, Guatemala 21269
Museum of the National Park of the Losiny Island, Moskva 33102
Museum of the Nature of Buryatya, Ulan-Udė 33655
Museum of the Nenetsk Autonomous Region, Narjan-Mar 33198
Museum of the Nizhni Novgorod' Intelligentsia, Nižnij Novgorod 33219
Museum of the North American Indian Travelling College, Cornwall 05277
Museum of the Northamptonshire Regiment, Northampton 40082
Museum of the Northern Great Plains, Fort Benton 43368
Museum of the Norwegian Knitting Industry, Salhus 30817
Museum of the Oaş Land, Negreşti-Oaş 32556
Museum of the Occupation of Latvia (1940 - 1991), Rīga 27420
Museum of the Ocean Fleat, Moskva 33134
Museum of the Old Poland Basin, Sielpia 31971
Museum of the Olive and Greek Olive Oil, Spárti 21167
Museum of the Olomučany ceramics, Olomučany 08517
Museum of the Opole Countryside, Opole 31860
Museum of the Order of Saint John, London 39722
Museum of the Origin of the Polish State, Gniezno 31600
Museum of the Paper Industry, Duszniki Zdrój 31559
Museum of the Peasant Revolts, Gornja Stubica 07703
Museum of the People's Assambly, Cairo 09277
Museum of the Percy Tenantry Volunteers 1798-1814, Alnwick 37986
Museum of the Petrozavod Works, Sankt-Peterburg 33428
Museum of the Plains Indian, Browning 41960
Museum of the Poet S. Orlov, Belozersk 32684
Museum of the Police of the Slovak Republic, Bratislava 33973
Museum of the Polish Tourist Association, Grodzisk Mazowiecki 31609
Museum of the Považie Region, Žilina 34079
Museum of the Poznań Army, Poznań 31900
Museum of the Poznań-Citadel, Poznań 31912
Museum of the Presidential Center of Culture of the Republic of Kazakhstan, Astana 27077
Museum of the Puck Region, Puck 31929
Museum of the Rebellion of Warsaw, Warszawa 32120
Museum of the Red Cross Organisation of Russia, Moskva 33141
Museum of the Red River, Idabel 44190
Museum of the Reformed College and Ecclesiastical Art, Debrecen 21400
Museum of the Regiments, Calgary 05173
Museum of the Region of Podlasie, Siedlce 31970
Museum of the Region of Pyzdry, Pyzdry 31935
Museum of the region of the Upper Hron, Brezno 33982
Museum of the Region Wallacxhia in Vsetin, Vsetín 08730
Museum of the Revolution, La Habana 07962
Museum of the Revolution, Moskva 33149
Museum of the Revolution, Nanchang 07172
Museum of the Revolution, Yanan 07313
Museum of the River Fleet of the Volga State Academy of Naval Transport, Nižnij Novgorod 33220
Museum of the Rockies, Bozeman 41858
Museum of the Romanaţi, Caracal 32486
Museum of the Rose, Kazanlăk 04701
Museum of the Royal College of Physicians, London 39723
Museum of the Royal College of Surgeons of Edinburgh, Edinburgh 38896
Museum of the Royal Houses, Santo Domingo 09124
Museum of the Royal Leicestershire Regiment, Leicester 39465
Museum of the Royal Military School of Music, Twickenham 40740
Museum of the Royal National Lifeboat Institution, Eastbourne 38854
Museum of the Royal Pharmaceutical Society of Great Britain, London 39724
Museum of the Royal Regiment of Canada, Toronto 06598
Museum of the Royal Thai Air Force, Bangkok 37490
Museum of The Royal Westminster Regiment Historical Society, New Westminster 05985
Museum of the Russian Academy of Art, Sankt-Peterburg 33463
Museum of the Sacrifice of the People of Kalavryta, Kalavryta 20989
Museum of the Sarvajanik Wachanalaya, Nasik 21967
Museum of the Sculpture Studio, Victoria de las Tunas 08175
Museum of the Sea Fleet of the Far East Sea Shippery, Vladivostok 33706
Museum of the September Uprising, Michajlovgrad 04739
Museum of the Serbian Orthodox Church, Beograd 33813
Museum of the Serbian Orthodox Church, Dubrovnik 07699
Museum of the Shwenawdaw Pagoda, Bago 28731
Museum of the Silesian Piasts, Brzeg 31511
Museum of the Slovak National Councils, Myjava 34032
Museum of the Slovakian National Uprising, Banská Bystrica 33948
Museum of the Slovakian Village, Martin 34024
Museum of the Slovenian Revolution, Slovenj Gradec 34150
The Museum of the South Dakota State Historical Society, Pierre 46484
Museum of the Southern Jewish Experience, Jackson 44283
Museum of the Southwest, Midland 45328
Museum of the State Academic Maly Theatre, Moskva 33100
Museum of the Statesman Eleftherios Venizelos and the Corresponding Historical Period, Athinai 20891
Museum of the Struggle against Bandits, Trinidad 08161
Museum of the Struggle for National Liberation, Tiranë 00034
Museum of the Students Struggle, Camagüey 07876
Museum of the Sugar Industry, Abel Santamaría 07845
Museum of the Thirties, Boulogne-Billancourt 10837
Museum of the Tkachev Brothers, Brjansk 32709
Museum of the Town, Penza 33288
Museum of the Transdanubian Reformed Church District, Pápa 21498
Museum of the Tujia and Miao Autonomous Prefecture in Western Hunan, Jishou 07140
Museum of the Turkish Revolution 1839, İstanbul 37707
Museum of the Twentieth Century, Hoorn 29442
Museum of the Underground Prisoners-Acre, Acre 22564
Museum of the University of Connecticut Health Center, Farmington 43296
Museum of the Ural State Technical University, Ekaterinburg 32781
Museum of the Walewski Family in Tubadzin, Wróblew 32172
Museum of the Waxhaws and Andrew Jackson Memorial, Waxhaw 48471
Museum of the Weathersfield Historical Society, Weathersfield 48485
Museum of the Welsh Woollen Industry, Llandysul 39543
Museum of the Western Jesuit Missions, Hazelwood 43977
Museum of the Western Prairie, Altus 41160
Museum of the Weston Historical Society, Weston 48569
Museum of the White Mountains of Samaria, Chania 20918
Museum of the Worcestershire Regiment, Worcester 40930
Museum of the Work of Outsiders, Moskva 33070
Museum of the World Ocean, Kaliningrad 32873
Museum of the Writer A.P. Bibik, Mineral'nye Vody 33013
Museum of the Writers of Orël, Orël 33266
Museum of the Young Defenders of the Homeland, Kursk 32977
Museum of the Yugoslav Cinema, Beograd 33806
Museum of the Zawkrzańska Region, Mława 31810
Museum of Theatre Art of Serbia, Beograd 33809
Museum of Theatre Puppets by A.A. Veselov, Voronež 33734
Museum of Theatrical, Musical and Cinematographic Art of Ukraine, Kyïv 37874
Museum of Tools, Delft 29076
Museum of Tourism and History of Teberda, Teberda 33597
Museum of Town Construction and Everyday Life of Taganrog, Taganrog 33583
Museum of Town Council, Tjumen 33604
Museum of Town History, Pécs 21516
Museum of Town Life Style, Ruse 04804
Museum of Trade and Industry, Warszawa 32122
Museum of Trademen's Life, Ekaterinburg 32778
Museum of Traditional Custumes, Alor Gajah 27615
Museum of Traditional Toys, San Francisco de los Romo 28385
Museum of Transport, Glasgow 39057
Museum of Transport and Technology, Auckland 30113
Museum of Transportation, Saint Louis 47132
Museum of Transportation and Rural Industries, Boyanup 00824
Museum of Tropical Queensland, Townsville 01546
Museum of Tropinin and His Contemporaries, Moskva 33154
Museum of Tuchola Wood, Tuchola 32059
Museum of Turkish and Islamic Art, Edirne 37666
Museum of Turkish and Islamic Art, İstanbul 37710
Museum of Turkish tiles and wood-and-metal-work, İstanbul 37713
Museum of Turopolja, Velika Gorica 07799
Museum of Ukrainian Arts and Culture, Edmonton 05382
Museum of Ukrainian-Ruthenian Culture, Svidník 34071
Museum of Underground Struggle, Nueva Gerona 08058
Museum of Unearthed Artifacts, Nagasaki 26550
Museum of Velká Bíteš, Velká Bíteš 08709
Museum of Vertebrate Zoology, Berkeley 41647
Museum of Veterinary, Guwahati 21825
Museum of Victorian Reed Organs and Harmoniums, Shipley 40501
Museum of Victorian Whitby, Whitby 40851
Museum of Vintage Fashion, Lafayette 44566
The Museum of Vision, San Francisco 47331
Museum of Visual Art, Galaţi 32523
Museum of Visual Impairment, Jiris 09579
Museum of Visual Science and Optometry, Waterloo 06755
Museum of Vítkovice, Ostrava 08526
Museum of Vladimir Dal, Moskva 33094
Museum of Volynian Orthodox Icons, Luck 37879
Museum of Vyatsk Folk Arts and Crafts, Kirov 32922
Museum of Waldensian History, Valdese 48178
Museum of Warsaw Gaswork, Warszawa 32097
Museum of Waxen Figures, Sankt-Peterburg 33468
Museum of Wellington, City and Sea, Wellington 30299
Museum of Welsh Life, Saint Fagans 40395
Museum of Western Australian Sport, Claremont, Western Australia 00920
Museum of Western Colorado, Grand Junction 43748
Museum of Western Kashubia, Bytów 31520
Museum of Wine and Viticulture, Aigle 36438
Museum of Witchcraft, Cornwall 38634
Museum of Wonders, Imbil 01118
Museum of Wood Carving and Icon Paintings, Trjavna 04888
Museum of Woodcarving, Shell Lake 47597
Museum of Woodwork and Ornamental Turning, Ashburton 30099
Museum of Worcester Porcelain, Worcester 40931
Museum of Work, Norrköping 36115
Museum of Workers' Struggles, Manzanillo 08031
Museum of Works by Theophilos, Mytilini 21085
Museum of Works by Theophilos, Varia Lesbos 21206
Museum of Wschowa Region, Wschowa 32196
Museum of Yachting, Newport 45927
Museum of Yarmouth History, Yarmouth 48778
Museum of Yarmukian, Kibbutz Shaar Hagolan 22705
Museum of Ylä-Savo, Iisalmi 09558
Museum of York County, Rock Hill 46950
Museum of Yorkshire Dales Lead Mining, Earby 38833
Museum of Yugoslav History, Beograd 33805
Museum of Zoology, Amherst 41179
Museum of Zoology, Ann Arbor 41220
Museum of Zoology, Edmonton 05383
Museum of Zoology, Lund 36065
Museum of Zoology of the A.I. Herzen State Pedagogical University, Sankt-Peterburg 33494
Museum of Zoology of the Sankt-Petersburg State University, Sankt-Peterburg 33493
Museum Okręgowe im. Stanisława Staszica, Piła 31880
Museum Omega, Biel, Kanton Bern 36565
Museum on the History of Blindness, Watertown 48441
Museum on the Mound, Edinburgh 38897
Museum on the Seam, Jerusalem 22653
Museum onder de N.H. Kerk, Elst 29228
Museum Onze-Lieve-Vrouw ter Potterie, Brugge 03260
Museum Oorlog en Vrede, Breda 29022
Museum Orvelte, Orvelte 29680
Museum Oskar Reinhart am Stadtgarten, Winterthur 37337
Museum Osterzgebirgsgalerie im Schloß, Dippoldiswalde 16621
Museum Otto Ludwig, Eisfeld 16827
Museum Otzberg, Otzberg 19330
Museum Oud-Asperen, Asperen 28946
Museum Oud Overschie, Rotterdam 29761
Museum Oud-Rijnsburg, Rijnsburg 29732
Museum Oud Soest, Soest 29842
Museum Oud Vriezenveen, Vriezenveen 29967
Museum Oud Westdorpe, Westdorpe 29994
Museum Oude Boekdrukkunst, Almen 28812
Museum Pachten, Dillingen, Saar 16613
Museum Palace of Peter the Great, Sankt-Peterburg 33392
Museum Palagan, Ambarawa 22066
Museum Palthehof, Nieuwleusen 29624
Museum Pancacsila Sakti, Jakarta 22125
Museum Pangeran Diponegoro, Yogyakarta 22223
Museum Papageorgiou, Limenaria 21048
Museum Papiermühle Homburg, Triefenstein 20205
Museum Passeier - Andreas Hofer, San Leonardo in Passiria 25381
Museum Pater Valentinus Paquay-Heilig Paterke, Hasselt 03481
Museum Paul Delvaux, Sint-Idesbald 03737

Museum Paul Tétar Van Elven, Delft 29085
Museum Pemda Balige, Balige 22067
Museum Pemirintah Daerah Grobogan, Purwodadi Grobogan 22181
Museum Pendidikan Islam, Yogyakarta 22224
Museum Perjuangan, Bogor 22089
Museum Perjuangan, Yogyakarta 22225
Museum Perjuangan Bukit Barisan, Medan 22159
Museum Pers, Surakarta 22203
Museum Pers Antara, Jakarta 22126
Museum Petersberg, Petersberg bei Halle, Saale 19377
Museum Pfleggerichtshaus, Abfaltersbach 01636
Museum Pfleggerichtshaus, Anras 01674
Museum Plagiarius, Berlin 16067
Museum Plantin-Moretus, Antwerpen 03152
Museum Pos & Giro, Bandung 22076
Museum Prabu Geusan Ulun, Sumedang 22196
Museum Preserve Kremlin of Kazan, Kazan 32906
Museum Presidency, Bloemfontein 34187
Museum Professionals Group, Salford 49427
Museum Pugung Ulago Sembah, Donggala 22099
Museum Pura Mangkunegara, Surakarta 22204
Museum Purbakala Mojokerto, Mojokerto 22161
Museum Purbakala Trowulan, Mojokerto 22162
Museum Puri Lukisan, Ubud 22213
Museum Quality Finishes, New York 45848
Museum Quintana - Archäologie in Künzing, Künzing 18260
Museum Raabe-Haus, Eschershausen 16933
Museum Rade am Schloß Reinbek, Reinbek 19550
Museum Radio-Wereld, Diever 29154
Museum Radya Pustaka, Surakarta 22205
Museum Raesfeld, Raesfeld 19474
Museum Ratna Wartha, Gianyar 22101
Museum Regiunal, Savognin 37126
Museum Regiunal Surselva Casa Carniec, Ilanz 36813
Museum Reich der Kristalle, München 18884
Museum Reichenau, Reichenau, Baden 19542
Museum Reichenfels, Hohenleuben 17808
Museum Rekor Indonesia, Srondol 22195
Museum Rekor Indonesia Jamu Jago, Semarang 22191
Museum Reksa Artha, Jakarta 22127
Museum Rietberg Zürich, Zürich 37398
Museum Rijn- en Binnenvaart, Antwerpen 03153
Museum Rijswijk Het Tollenshuis, Rijswijk, Zuid-Holland 29735
Museum Roemervilla, Bad Neuenahr-Ahrweiler 15704
Museum Römervilla, Grenzach-Wyhlen 17395
Museum Römische Villa Nennig, Perl 19375
Museum Rolf Werner, Seebad Bansin 19912
Museum Rufferdinge, Landen 03551
Museum Ruman Bolon, Pematang 22175
Museum Rupelklei, Terhagen 03770
Museum Sacrum, Tiel 29874
Museum Saet en Cruyt, Andijk 28919
Museum Saigerhütte Olbernhau- Kupferhammer, Olbernhau 19249
Museum Salzbütte, Huttwil 36811
Museum Sankt Blasien, Sankt Blasien 19747
Museum Sankt Ingbert, Sankt Ingbert 19751
Museum Sankt Wendel, Sankt Wendel 19758
Museum Sarganserland, Sargans 37119
Museum Sasmita Loka, Yogyakarta 22226
Museum Sasmita Loka A. Yani, Jakarta 22128
Museum Satria Mandala, Jakarta 22129
Museum Scheveningen, Den Haag 29113
Museum Schietkamp-Harskamp, Harskamp 29349
Museum Schloß Bernburg, Bernburg 16125
Museum Schloß Burgk, Burgk 16425
Museum Schloss Colditz, Colditz 16493
Museum Schloß Delitzsch, Delitzsch 16564
Museum Schloß Ehrenstein, Ohrdruf 19246
Museum Schloß Erla, Sankt Valentin 02610
Museum Schloss Fasanerie, Eichenzell 16802
Museum Schloss Friedrichsfelde, Berlin 16068
Museum Schloß Glücksburg, Römhild 19634
Museum Schloss Hardenberg, Velbert 20294
Museum Schloss Hellenstein, Heidenheim an der Brenz 17682
Museum Schloss Herzberg, Herzberg am Harz 17742
Museum Schloß Hohenlimburg, Hagen, Westfalen 17482
Museum Schloß Hundshaupten, Egloffstein 16790
Museum Schloß Klippenstein, Radeberg 19468
Museum Schloß Kuckuckstein, Liebstadt 18463
Museum Schloss Kyburg, Kyburg 36842
Museum Schloss Lembeck, Dorsten 16654
Museum Schloss Lichtenberg, Fischbachtal 17007
Museum Schloss Luisium, Dessau 16581
Museum Schloß Molsdorf, Molsdorf 18785
Museum Schloss Moritzburg, Moritzburg 18791
Museum Schloß Moritzburg, Zeitz, Elster 20738
Museum Schloss Moyland, Bedburg-Hau 15866
Museum Schloss Netzschkau, Netzschkau 19002
Museum Schloß Neu-Augustusburg, Weißenfels 20499
Museum Schloss Neuenburg, Freyburg 17131
Museum Schloss Oberschwappach, Knetzgau 18117
Museum Schloß Pöllau, Pöllau 02430
Museum Schloß Ratibor, Roth, Mittelfranken 19675
Museum Schloß Rochlitz, Rochlitz 19620
Museum Schloß Rochsburg, Lunzenau 18568
Museum Schloß Schwarzenberg, Schwarzenberg, Erzgebirge 19884
Museum Schloß Steinheim, Hanau 17586
Museum Schloss Waldegg, Feldbrunnen 36699
Museum Schloß Weesenstein, Müglitztal 18800
Museum Schloß Wetzdorf, Glaubendorf 01879
Museum Schloß Wilhelmsburg, Schmalkalden 19808
Museum Schmelzra, Scuol 37154
Museum Schnütgen, Köln 18163
Museum Schöngrabern, Hollabrunn 02044
Museum Schokland, Ens 29235
Museum Schwab, Biel, Kanton Bern 36566
Museum Schwarzes Ross, Hilpoltstein 17762
Museum Schweizer Hotellerie und Tourismus, Zürich 37399
Museum Science and Technology, Jakarta 22130
Museum Sejarah Mesjid Banten, Bogor 22090
Museum Seni, Denpasar 22097
Museum Seni, Jakarta 22131
Museum Seni, Medan 22160
Museum Seni, Padang 22166
Museum Seni Rupa dan Keramik, Jakarta 22132
Museum Sensenwerk, Deutschfeistritz 01760
Museum Sepakat Segenap, Aceh Tenggara 22063
Museum Seyitgazi, Seyitgazi 37780
Museum-Ship, Krasnojarsk 32956
Museum Ship Dar Pomorza, Gdańsk 31581
Museum Ship Dar Pomorza, Gdynia 31590
Museum Ship Sigyn, Turku 10126
Museum Ship Sołdek, Gdańsk 31582
Museum Simalungun, Pematangsiantar 22177
Museum Sint Bernardushof, Aduard 28800
Museum Sint Sellian, Sellingen 29816
Museum Siwa Lima, Ambon 09129
Museum Skänninge Rådhus, Skänninge 36191
Museum Slag bij Heiligerlee, Heiligerlee 29377
Museum Slag der Zilveren Helmen, Halen 03466
Museum Slager, 's-Hertogenbosch 29404
Museum Smallingerland, Drachten 29179
Museum Smidt van Gelder, Antwerpen 03154
Museum Smolensk Region in the Years of the Great Patriotic War, Smolensk 33530
Museum Soltau, Soltau 19993
Museum Sono Budoyo, Yogyakarta 22227
Museum Sonyine Malige, Halmahera Tengah 09132
Museum Spaans Gouvernement, Maastricht 29567
Museum Spasskiy Church, Tjumen 33607
Museum Specken, Bad Zwischenahn 15783
Museum SPUR Cham, Cham 16458
Museum Stad Appingedam, Appingedam 28931
Museum Stadt Bad Hersfeld, Bad Hersfeld 15660
Museum Stadt Königsberg, Duisburg 16754
Museum Stammertal, Unterstammheim 37267
Museum Stapelen, Boxtel 29014
Museum Stedhûs Sleat, Sloten 29835
Museum Steinarbeiterhaus, Hohburg 17803
Museum Steinmetzhaus, Eggenburg 01792
Museum Stellingwerff-Waerdenhof, Hasselt 03482
Museum Stemmler, Schaffhausen 37131
Museum Stichting van het Rotterdamsche Tramweg Maatschappij, Ouddorp 29693
Museum Stift Admont, Admont 01643
Museum Stift Börstel, Berge bei Quakenbrück 15890
Museum Stoffels Säge-Mühle, Hohenems 02042
Museum Stoomdepot, Rotterdam 29762
Museum Stoomgemaal Winschoten, Winschoten 30008
The Museum Studio and Arts Centre, Nairobi 27111
Museum Suaka Budaya, Surakarta 22206
Museum Subak Bali, Kediri 22145
Museum Sudirman, Magelang 22151
Museum Sulawesi Tengah, Palu 22172
Museum Sumpah Pemuda, Jakarta 22133
Museum Suriname, Amsterdam 28878
Museum Sursilvan, Trun 37256
Museum Swaensteyn, Voorburg 29962
Museum Synagoge Gröbzig, Gröbzig 17408
Museum Synthese, München 18885
Museum 't Coopmanshûs, Franeker 29261
Museum 't Gevang, Doetinchem 29161
Museum 't Kniphof, Essen 03412
Museum 't Nieuwhuys Hoegaarden, Hoegaarden 03497
Museum 't Schilderhuis, Driebergen-Rijsenburg 29181
Museum Takstil, Jakarta 22134
Museum Taman Laut Ancol, Jakarta 22135
Museum Taman Prasati, Jakarta 22136
Museum Taruna Akbari Udarat, Magelang 22152
Museum Tegernseer Tal, Tegernsee 20151
Museum-Telefonzentrale, Magden 36919
Muséum Testut, Lyon 12751
Museum Theo Jans, Klarenbeek 29484
Museum Theo Kerg, Schriesheim 19850
Museum Thonet, Frankenberg, Eder 17026
Museum Tni A.L. Loka Jala Carana, Surabaya 22201
Museum Ton Schulten, Ootmarsum 29676
Museum Trading Association, Worcester 49428
Museum Transgariep, Philippolis 34323
Museum Tre Kronor, Stockholm 36263
Museum - Treasures from the National Archives, Kew 39351
Museum Trustee Association, Washington 49516
Museum Tugu Nasional, Jakarta 22137
Museum Tysmans, Houthalen 03508
Museum und Archiv der Stadt Gronau (Leine), Gronau, Leine 17413
Museum und Besucherbergwerk, Goslar 17355
Museum und Besucherbergwerk der Graphit Kropfmühl AG, Hauzenberg 17648
Museum und Galerie der Stadt, Schwabmünchen 19858
Museum und Kunstsammlung Schloß Hinterglauchau, Glauchau 17299
Museum und Schatzkammer des Deutschen Ordens, Wien 02950
Museum und Stiftung Anton Geiselhart, Münsingen 18931
Museum und Studienstätte Schloss Nöthnitz, Bannewitz 15822
Museum U.P.T. Balitung, Tanjungpandan 22210
Museum Uranbergbau, Schlema 19791
Museum Uslar, Uslar 20280
Museum Valkenheide, Maarsbergen 29556
Museum Van Bommel Van Dam, Venlo 29940
Museum van de Abdij van Roosenberg, Waasmunster 03821
Museum van de Boerenkrijg, Berlare 03214
Museum van de Kanselarij der Nederlandse Orden, Apeldoorn 28926
Museum van de Koninklijke Marechaussee, Buren, Gelderland 29044
Museum van de Kruisbooggilde Sint-Joris, Brugge 03261
Museum van de Onze-Lieve-Vrouwkerk, Brugge 03262
Museum van de Sint-Jakobskerk, Antwerpen 03155
Museum van de Stichting Bisdom van Vliet, Haastrecht 29334
Museum van de Twintigste Eeuw, Hoorn 29442
Museum van de Willebroekse Vaart, Willebroek 03842
Museum van Deinze en de Leiestreek, Deinze 03375
Museum van Egmond, Egmond aan Zee 29204
Museum Van Gerwen-Lemmens, Valkenswaard 29923
Museum van Hedendaagse Kantwerken, Sint-Truiden 03750
Museum van Hedendaagse Kunst Antwerpen, Antwerpen 03156
Museum Van Hemessen, Woubrugge 30025
Museum van het Abtenhuis, Geraardsbergen 03458
Museum van het Ambacht, Den Haag 29114
Museum van het Groot Begijnhof, Sint-Amandsberg 03736
Museum van het Heilig Bloed, Brugge 03263
Museum van het Kamp van Beverlo, Leopoldsburg 03560
Museum van het Nederlandse Uurwerk, Zaandam 30035
Museum van het Vlaams Studentenleven, Leuven 03562
Museum van Knipkunst, Westerbork 29996
Museum van Lien, Fijnaart 29259
Museum Van Loon, Amsterdam 28879
Museum van Zwerfstenen in de Rosmolen, Zeddam 30048
Museum Veeteelt en K.I., Beers bij Cuyk 28969
Museum Veluwezoom, Doorwerth 29171
Museum Verbindingsdienst, Ede 29194
Museum "Vermessen in Bayern - von der Messlatte zur Antenne", München 18886
Museum Victoria, Carlton South 00897
Museum Viechtach, Viechtach 20308
Museum Villa Haiss, Zell am Harmersbach 20740
Museum Villa Rot - Kunstsammlung Hoenes-Stiftung, Burgrieden 16429
Museum Villa Rustica, Möckenlohe 18761
Museum Villa Sarabodis, Gerolstein 17258
Museum Villa Stahmer, Georgsmarienhütte 17242
Museum Villa Stuck, München 18887
Museum Village, Monroe 45445
Museum Vlaamse Minderbroeders, Sint-Truiden 03751
Museum Vleeshuis, Antwerpen 03157
Museum Vliegbasis Deelen, Deelen 29074
Museum Volunteers of the Philippines, Dasmariñas 49333
Museum von Abgüssen und Originalsammlung, Innsbruck 02075
Museum voor Anesthesie Verantare, Antwerpen 03158
Museum voor Communicatie, Den Haag 29115
Museum voor de Geschiedenis van de Wetenschappen, Gent 03445
Museum voor de Oudere Technieken, Grimbergen 03462
Museum voor Figuratieve Kunst de Buitenplaats, Eelde 29198
Museum voor Folklore, Zottegem 03857
Museum voor Geschiedenis van de Geneeskunde, Gent 03446
Museum voor Hedendaagse Kunst, 's-Hertogenbosch 29405
Museum voor Heem- en Oudheidkunde, Kontich 03538
Museum voor Heem- en Volkskunde, Wenduine 03833
Museum voor Heemkunde Almelo, Almelo 28809
Museum voor het Kruideniersbedrijf, Utrecht 29903
Museum voor het Radiozendamateurisme Jan Corver, Budel 29035
Museum voor Industriele Archeologie en Textiel, Gent 03447
Museum voor Keramiek Pablo Rueda Lara, Rotterdam 29763
Museum voor Kerkelijke Kunst, Workum 30022
Museum voor Kerkelijke Kunst Sint-Carolus, Antwerpen 03159
Museum voor Klederdracht en Oud Speelgoed, Warnsveld 29980
Museum voor Moderne Kunst, Arnhem 28941
Museum voor Moderne Kunst Oostende (PMMK), Oostende 03669
Museum voor Naaldkunst, Wedde 29987
Museum voor Natuur- en Wildbeheer, Doorwerth 29172
Museum voor Plaatselijke Geschiedenis, Nieuwpoort 03657
Museum voor Religieuze Kunst, Uden 29884
Museum voor Schone Kunsten, Oostende 03670
Museum voor Schone Kunsten Gent, Gent 03448
Museum voor Torhouts Aardewerk, Torhout 03786
Museum voor Valse Kunst, Vledder 29951
Museum voor Volkskunde, Brugge 03264
Museum voor Volkskunde, Dendermonde 03377
Museum voor Vrede en Geweldloosheid, Amsterdam 28880
Museum Voswinckelshof, Dinslaken 16619
Museum Vrolik, Amsterdam 28881
Museum Waemena, Irian Jaya 22104
Museum Wald und Umwelt, Ebersberg 16769
Museum Waldhof, Bielefeld 16158
Museum Wanua Paksinanta, Manado 22155
Museum Wasseralfingen, Aalen 15383
Museum Wasseramt, Halten 36792
Museum Wasserburg, Wasserburg am Inn 20408
Museum Wasserburg Anholt, Isselburg 17933
Museum Wateringhuis, Lommel 03597
Museum Watersnood 1953, Ouwerkerk 29705
Museum Wattens, Wattens 02796
Museum Wayang, Jakarta 22138
Museum Wierdenland, Ezinge 29258
Museum Wiesbaden, Wiesbaden 20576
Museum Wildberg, Wildberg, Württemberg 20586
Museum Willem van Haren, Heerenveen 29363
Museum Willet-Holthuysen, Amsterdam 28882
Museum Wolfhalden, Wolfhalden 37349
Museum Wolfram von Eschenbach, Wolframs-Eschenbach 20656
Museum Woning voor antieke Horlogerie, Mechelen 03616
Museum World of Water of Saint-Petersburg, Sankt-Peterburg 33458
Museum Würth, Künzelsau 18259
Museum Wurzen mit Ringelnatzsammlung, Wurzen 20720
Museum Wustrow, Wustrow, Niedersachsen 20724
Museum Wuyts-Van Campen en Baron Caroly, Lier 03586
Museum Yadnya, Tangawi 22208
The Museum Yamato Bunkakan, Nara 26578
Museum Yerseke, Yerseke 30030
Museum Yogya Kembali, Yogyakarta 22228
Museum Zahal, Hakirya 22614
Museum Zeitreise Mensch, Cortaccia 23659
Museum Zella-Mehlis, Zella-Mehlis 20745
Museum Ziegelei Lage, Lage, Lippe 18285
Museum Zitadelle, Jülich 17965
Museum zu Allerheiligen, Schaffhausen 37132
Museum zum Anfassen, Ostseebad Binz 19311
Museum Zum Arabischen Coffe Baum, Leipzig 18409
Museum zum Schiff, Laufenburg 36850
Museum zur brandenburg-preußischen Geschichte/ Zinnfigurenmuseum, Gusow 17466
Museum zur Geschichte der Juden in Kreis und Stadt Heilbronn, Obersulm 19211
Museum zur Geschichte Hohenheims, Stuttgart 20101
Museum zur Geschichte von Christen und Juden, Laupheim 18359
Museum zur Kloster- und Stadtgeschichte, Steinheim an der Murr 20050
Museum zur Ronmühle, Schötz 37144
Museum Zwaantje Hans Stockman's Hof, Schoonebeek 29811
Museumboerderij, Leens 29504
Museumboerderij, Paasloo 29709
Museumboerderij, Staphorst 29850
Museumboerderij de Karstenhoeve, Ruinerwold 29786
Museumboerderij de Tip, Herveld 29412
Museumboerderij de Zwemkolk, Markelo 29578
Museumboerderij Erve Hofman, Hellendoorn 29387
Museumboerderij Eungs Schöppe, Markelo 29579
Museumboerderij Gilde Koat, Zeddam 30049
Museumboerderij New Greenwich Village, Zuidwolde, Drenthe 30072
Museumboerderij Scholten, Den Ham 29132
Museumboerderij Tante Jaantje, Callantsoog 29052
Museumboerderij Vreeburg, Schagen 29795
Museumboerderij Wendezoele, Ambt-Delden 28815
Museumboerderij Westfrisia, Hoogwoud 29440
Museumbrouwerij de Hemel, Nijmegen 29633
Museumbrouwerij De Roos, Hilvarenbeek 29417
Museumgemaal Caners, 's- Hertogenbosch 29406
Museumhaven Zeeland, Zierikzee 30061
'T Museumke, Handel 29338
Museumkelder Derlon, Maastricht 29568
Museumkerk Sint Pieter, Rekem 03694
Museummolen, Schermerhorn 29799
Museummolen de Nieuwe Palmboom, Schiedam 29802
Museummolen Jan Pol, Dalen 29065
Museumproject AZG, Groningen 29312
Museums Abashirikangoku, Abashiri 26085
Museums Alaska, Anchorage 49517
Museums and Galleries Disability Association, Hove 49429
Museums and Study Collection, London 39725
Museums Association, London 49430
Museums Association of India, Delhi 49240
Museums Association of Namibia, Windhoek 49299
Museums Association of Nigeria, Lagos 49313

The Museums Association of Pakistan, Karachi 49326
Museums Association of Saskatchewan, Regina 49102
Museums Association of Slovenia, Ljubljana 49362
Museums Association of the Caribbean, Bridgetown 49064
Museums Australia, Civic Square 49053
Museums Collection of the Nationbal Ossoliński Institute, Wrocław 32193
Museums-Everten Johanne Dan, Ribe 09028
Museums-Gutshof Sonnekalb, Kleinheringen 18106
Museums in Essex Committee, Chelmsford 49431
Museums North, Hartlepool 49432
Museums of Coins and Medals, Kremnica 34007
Museums of Farum, Farum 08823
Museums of Filipinana and Rizaliana, Sampaloc 31438
The Museums of Oglebay Institute, Wheeling 48587
Museums of South Lanarkshire, Ferniegair 38987
Museums of the Perm State University, Perm 33304
Museums of the Turkish Independence War and Turkish Republic, Ankara 37619
Museums Weapons Group, Leeds 49433
Museumsanlage Kulturstiftung Landkreis Osterholz, Osterholz-Scharmbeck 19294
Museumsbahn Steyrtal, Steyr 02688
Museumsberg Flensburg, Flensburg 17012
Museumsbibliothek, Lutherstadt Eisleben 18572
Museumsboerderij Oud Noordwijk, Noordwijk, Zuid-Holland 29645
Museumscenter Hanstholm, Hanstholm 08854
Museumschip Mercuur, Den Haag 29116
Museumsdorf Bayerischer Wald, Tittling 20181
Museumsdorf Cloppenburg, Cloppenburg 16479
Museumsdorf Düppel, Berlin 16069
Museumsdorf Krumbach, Krumbach 02167
Museumsdorf und Technisches Denkmal, Baruth, Mark 15828
Museumsdorf Volksdorf mit Spiekerhus, Hamburg 17562
Museumseisenbahn Payerbach-Hirschwang, Hirschwang 02031
Museumseisenbahn Schwalm-Knüll, Fritzlar 17153
Museumsfeuerschiff Amrumbank/Deutsche Bucht, Emden 16848
Museumsfriedhof Tirol, Kramsach 02153
Museumsgalerie, Altomünster 15471
Museumsgalerie Allerheiligenkirche, Mühlhausen, Thüringen 18808
Museumsgården, Læsø 08968
Museumsgesellschaft, Zürich 49387
Museumshäuschen, Krebes 18222
Museumshof, Bad Oeynhausen 15709
Museumshof, Rahden 19475
Museumshof, Roßtal 19656
Museumshof am Sonnenlück, Erkner 16913
Museumshof auf dem Braem, Gescher 17266
Museumshof Emmerstedt, Helmstedt 17705
Museumshof-Galerie, Oldenburg in Holstein 19251
Museumshof Historischer Moorhof Augustendorf, Gnarrenburg 17307
Museumshof Lerchennest - Friedrich-der-Große-Museum, Sinsheim 19970
Museumskirche Sankt Katharinen, Lübeck 18541
Museumsland Donauland Strudengau, Mitterkirchen 02303
Museumslandschaft Deilbachtal, Essen 16960
Museumslogger AE7 Stadt Emden, Emden 16849
Museumsmühle Hasbergen, Delmenhorst 16568
Museumsmühle mit heimatkundlicher Sammlung, Varel 20287
Museumspädagogische Beratung, Kassel 18026
Museumspädagogische Gesellschaft e.V., Köln 49204
Museumspark, Rüdersdorf bei Berlin 19703
Museumspoorlijn Star, Stadskanaal 29848
Museumsscheune, Bremervörde 16353
Museumsscheune Fränkische Schweiz, Hollfeld 17825
Museumsschiff FMS Gera, Bremerhaven 16342
Museumsschiff Mannheim des Landesmuseums für Technik und Arbeit, Mannheim 18614
Museumsschiff STÖR, Holzminden 17830
Museumsstadl, Bernried, Niederbayern 16127
Museumsstiftung Post und Telekommunikation, Bonn 16245
Museumsstube, Eisgarn 01811
Museumsstube Obermeiser, Calden 16444
Museumstjenesten, Viborg 49144
Museumstoomtram Hoorn-Medemblik, Hoorn 29443
Museumsverband, Pram 49056
Museumsverband Baden-Württemberg e.V., Esslingen 49205
Museumsverband des Landes Brandenburg e.V., Potsdam 49206
Museumsverband für Niedersachsen und Bremen e.V., Hannover 49207
Museumsverband in Mecklenburg-Vorpommern e.V., Güstrow 49208
Museumsverband Sachsen-Anhalt e.V., Bernburg 49209
Museumsverband Schleswig-Holstein e.V., Rendsburg 49210
Museumsverband Thüringen e.V., Gera 49211
Museumsverbund Südniedersachsen e.V., Göttingen 49212
Die Museumswelt, Wiener Neustadt 03019
Museumszentrum Lorsch, Lorsch 18505
Museumszentrum-Rehau, Rehau 19538
Museumwerf 't Kromhout, Amsterdam 28883
Museumwinkel Albert Heijn, Zaandam 30036
Museumwoning de Kiefhoek, Rotterdam 29764
Museun of Japanese Steel, Yasugi 27010
Museus de História Natural e Etnologia Indígena, Juiz de Fora 04159
Muséyé Chay-e Lahijan, Lahijan 22261
Muséyé Honarha-ye Melli, Teheran 22317
Muséyé Kerman, Kerman 22252
Muséyé Mardom Shenassi, Teheran 22318
Mushakoji Saneatsu Memorial Hall, Chofu 26131
Music and Time - Private Museum of John Mostoslavsky, Jaroslavl 32855
Music Box of Zami Museum, Metula 22712
The Music House, Acme 41061
Music-Memorial Museum of Igor Strawinsky, Ustyloog 37908
Music Museum, La Habana 07991
Music Museum, Riga 27432
Music Museum of the Slovak National Museum, Bratislava 33966
Musica Kremsmünster, Kremsmünster 02162
Musical Box Society International Museum, Norwalk 46033
Musical Instruments Museum, Jerusalem 22654
Musical Museum, London 39726
Musical Museum of Macedonia, Thessaloniki 21191
Musical Wonder House, Wiscasset 48717
Musicological Department of the Silesian Museum, Opava 08519
Mus'ign, Bad Essen 15641
Mus'ign - Anthologie Quartett Designmuseum, Preußisch Oldendorf 19447
Musik- und Wintersportmuseum, Klingenthal 18111
Musikhistorische Sammlung Jehle, Albstadt 15420
Musikhistorisk Museum og Carl Claudius' Samling, København 08941
Musikinstrumenten-Ausstellung des Händel-Hauses, Halle, Saale 17517
Musikinstrumenten-Museum, Berlin 16070
Musikinstrumenten-Museum, Markneukirchen 18640
Musikinstrumenten-Museum der Universität Leipzig (Interim), Leipzig 18410
Musikinstrumenten- und Puppenmuseum, Goslar 17356
Musikinstrumentenmuseum, München 18888
Musikinstrumentenmuseum, Sankt Gilgen 02571
Musikinstrumentenmuseum Lißberg, Ortenberg, Hessen 19270
Musikinstrumentensammlung, Erlangen 16921
Musikinstrumentensammlung der Universität, Göttingen 17338
Musikinstrumentensammlung Hans und Hede Grumbt Wasserburg Haus Kemnade, Hattingen 17635
Musikmuseet, Stockholm 36264
Musikmuseum, Basel 36513
MuSiS - Verein zur Unterstützung der Museen und Sammlungen in der Steiermark, Graz 49057
Muskegon County Museum, Muskegon 45578
Muskegon Museum of Art, Muskegon 45579
Muskogee War Memorial Park and Military Museum, Muskogee 45582
Muskoka Heritage Place, Huntsville 05610
Muskoka Lakes Museum, Port Carling 06155
Musquodoboit Railway Museum, Musquodoboit Harbour 05953
Musselshell Valley Historical Museum, Roundup 47019
Mustafa Kamil Museum, Cairo 09278
Mustansiriya School Collections, Baghdad 22347
Mustard Shop Museum, Norwich 40096
Musteum of the History of Literature, Art and Culture in Altay Region, Barnaul 32673
Mustiala Agricultural Museum, Mustiala 09844
Mustialan Maataloushistoriallinen Museo, Mustiala 09844
Muswellbrook Regional Arts Centre, Muswellbrook 01295
Mutare Museum, Mutare 49038
MUTEC Museo Pinacoteca Comunale, Barletta 23033
Mutsen en Poffermuseum Sint-Paulusgasthuis, Sint Oedenrode 29825
Muttart Art Gallery, Calgary 05174
Mutter Museum, Philadelphia 46432
Mutua Museum, Imphal 21855
Muurla Arts and Crafts Museum, Muurla 09845
Muurlan Kotiseutumuseo, Muurla 09845
Muuruveden Kotiseutumuseo, Muuruvesi 09846
Muzeal Conacul Bellu, Urlaţi 32622
Muzeal de Istorie, Târgovişte 32602
Muzeen Kat Kooperativna Pečatnica Rabotnik, Veliko Tărnovo 04915
Muzeen Kat Parva Socialističeska Sbirka, Veliko Tărnovo 04916
Muzei Permskogo Gosudarstvennogo Universiteta, Perm 33304
Muzej, Novoselica 37891
Muzej, Pliska 04773
Muzej 700 let - Landskrona, Nevskoe Ustje, Nienšanc, Sankt-Peterburg 33425
Muzej A Muzy ne Molčali, Sankt-Peterburg 33426
Muzej A.A. Kiseleva, Tuapse 33621
Muzej Afričke Umetnosti-Zbirka Vede i Dr. Zdravka Pečara, Beograd 33803
Muzej Aleksandăr Stambolijski, Slavovica 04817
Muzej Aleksandăr Stambolijski, Sofia 04837
Muzej Alpinizma, Turizma i Istorii Kurorta Teberda, Teberda 33597
Muzej Antropologii i Etnografii im. Petra Velikogo (Kunstkamera), Sankt-Peterburg 33427
Muzej AO Petrozavod, Sankt-Peterburg 33428
Muzej Archeologii, Syktyvkar 33575
Muzej Archeologii i Ėtnografii, Syktyvkar 33576
Muzej Archeologii i Ėtnografii, Ufa 33645
Muzej Archeologii i Ėtnografii, Vladivostok 33703
Muzej Archeologii Moskvy, Moskva 33091
Muzej Archeologii Prikamja, Perm 33305
Muzej 'Archeologija, Ėtnografija i Ėkologija Sibiri' Kemerovskogo Gosudarstvennogo Universiteta, Kemerovo 32914
Muzej Architektury Byta Narodov Nižegorodskogo Povolžja, Nižnij Novgorod 33208
Muzej Architektury i Archeologii Vez Burana, Čujsk 27310
Muzej Architektury i Stroitelstva, Samara 33373
Muzej-Archiv D.I. Mendeleeva, Sankt-Peterburg 33429
Muzej Arsenal - Muzej Velikoj Otečestvennoj Vojny, Voronež 33731
Muzej Aviacii Severa, Archangelsk 32652
Muzej Avtografov imeni Imperatora Nikolaja Vtorogo, Novosibirsk 33240
Muzej Avtomobilnogo Transporta, Kursk 32976
Muzej Baki Urmanče, Kazan 32894
Muzej Belišće, Belišće 07678
Muzej Boevogo i Trudovogo Podviga 1941-1945, Saransk 33498
Muzej Boevoj Slavy, Astrachan 32664
Muzej E.A. Boratynskogo, Kazan 32895
Muzej Bratjev Tkačevych, Brjansk 32709
Muzej Brdovec, Savski Marof 07768
Muzej Brjanskij Les, Brjansk 32710
Muzej Budva, Budva 33826
Muzej V.I. Čapaeva, Čeboksary 32722
Muzej Carskoselskaja Kollekcija, Puškin 33340
Muzej Cerkov Dekabristov, Čita 32751
Muzej Cerkov Petra i Pavla, Tjumen 33601
Muzej Cetinjske Krajine, Sinj 07774
Muzej Chrama Christa Spasitelja, Moskva 33092
Muzej Cirkovogo Iskusstva, Sankt-Peterburg 33430
Muzej-čitalnja N.V. Fëdorova, Moskva 33093
Muzej-čitalnja na Nacionalnych Jazykach, Penza 33287
Muzej Čovek i negovoto Zdrave, Varna 04896
Muzej V.I. Dalja, Moskva 33094
Muzej Dekabristov, Minusinsk 33017
Muzej Dekabristov, Moskva 33095
Muzej Dekabristov - Dom Trubeckogo, Irkutsk 32816
Muzej Dekabristov - Dom Volkonskich, Irkutsk 32817
Muzej Dekorativno-prikladnogo Iskusstva, Sankt-Peterburg 33431
Muzej Dekorativno-prikladnogo Iskusstva Urala, Čeljabinsk 32726
Muzej Derevjannogo Zodčestva Malye Karely, Archangelsk 32653
Muzej Detskogo Tvorčestva, Sankt-Peterburg 33432
Muzej Detstva A.M. Gorkogo - Domik Kaširina, Nižnij Novgorod 33209
Muzej-Diorama Orlovskaja Nastupatelnaja Operacija, Orël 33264
Muzej Diplomatičeskogo Korpusa, Vologda 33722
Muzej Dom Mašarova, Tjumen 33602
Muzej Dominikanskog Samostana, Bol 07683
Muzej Družba na Narodite ot 1944 g., Varna 04897
Muzej A.A. Durova, Taganrog 33582
Muzej Durylina S.N., Korolev 32939
Muzej Dvorec A.D. Menšikova, Sankt-Peterburg 33433
Muzej Ekslibrisa, Moskva 33096
Muzej Emfiedžieva Kăšta, Kjustendil 04708
Muzej Etnografičeskogo Kostjuma na Kuklach, Moskva 33097
Muzej Ėtnografii, Istorii i Kultury Narodov Baškortostana, Ufa 33646
Muzej-Filial Nadi Ruševoj, Kyzyl 32978
Muzej Ford i Bălgarija, Sofia 04838
Muzej Franjevačkog Samostana, Rovinj 07765
Muzej Franjevačkog Samostana Košljun, Punat 07759
Muzej Gabdulla Tukaja, Kazan 32896
Muzej-Galerija Kavadarci, Kavadarci 27585
Muzej Geologii, Čeljabinsk 32727
Muzej Geologii Centralnoj Sibirii, Krasnojarsk 32955
Muzej Geologii, Nefti i Gaza, Tjumen 33603
Muzej Georgi Velčev, Varna 04898
Muzej Glavna Kvartira na Ruskata Armija 1877-1878, Pordim 04785
Muzej A.M. Gorkogo, Moskva 33098
Muzej Goroda Jurjevca, Jurjevec 32865
Muzej Goroda Penzy, Penza 33288
Muzej Gorodskaja Duma, Tjumen 33604
Muzej Gosudarstvennogo Akademičeskogo Bolšogo Teatra Rossii, Moskva 33099
Muzej Gosudarstvennogo Akademičeskogo Malogo Teatra, Moskva 33100
Muzej Gosudarstvennogo Akademičeskogo Marijnskogo Teatra Opery i Baleta, Sankt-Peterburg 33434
Muzej Gosudarstvennogo Akademičeskogo Teatra Opery i Baleta imeni Mussorgskogo, Sankt-Peterburg 33435
Muzej Gosudarstvennogo Centralnogo Teatra Kukol pod Rukovodstvom Narodnogo Artista S.V. Obrazcova, Moskva 33101
Muzej Gosudarstvennogo Prirodnogo Nacionalnogo Parka Losinogo Ostrova, Moskva 33102
Muzej Grada, Šibenik 07772
Muzej Grada Beograda, Beograd 33804
Muzej Grada Koprivnice, Koprivnica 07718
Muzej Grada Novog Sada, Novi Sad 33870
Muzej Grada Perasta, Perast 33881
Muzej Grada Rijeke, Rijeka 07761
Muzej Grada Splita, Split 07783
Muzej Grada Trogira, Trogir 07794
Muzej Grada Zagreba, Zagreb 07830
Muzej Grada Zenice, Zenica 03932
Muzej Gradostroitelstva i Byta Taganroga, Taganrog 33583
Muzej Grebnych Vidov Sporta, Moskva 33103
Muzej Hamza Hakim-Žade Niazy, Fergana 48837
Muzej Hercegovine, Mostar 03917
Muzej Hrvatske Književnosti i Kazališne Umjetnosti, Zagreb 07831
Muzej Hrvatskih Arheoloških Spomenika, Split 07784
Muzej Hvarske Baštine, Hvar 07707
Muzej i Galerija Bitola, Bitola 27584
Muzej i Obščestvennyj Centr Mir, Progress, Prava Čeloveka im. Andreja Sacharova, Moskva 33104
Muzej I.A. Bunina, Orël 33265
Muzej Igora Stravinskogo, Ustyloog 37908
Muzej Igorja Talkova, Moskva 33105
Muzej im. S.M. Kirova, Sankt-Peterburg 33436
Muzej im. B.M. Kustodieva, Ostrovskoe 33277
Muzej im. N.A. Ostrovskogo, Moskva 33106
Muzej-institut Semji Rerichov, Sankt-Peterburg 33437
Muzej Instituta Biologii Morja, Vladivostok 33704
Muzej Internacionalnoj Družby, Saransk 33499
Muzej Iskusstva Narodov Vostoka, Moskva 33107
Muzej Istične Bosně, Tuzla 03929
Muzej Istorii Aksaja, Aksaj 32631
Muzej Istorii Architektury i Architekturnogo Obrazovanija Sibiri, Novosibirsk 33241
Muzej Istorii Architektury i Promyšlennoj Techniki Urala, Ekaterinburg 32774
Muzej Istorii Burjatii im. M.N. Changalova, Ulan-Udė 33653
Muzej Istorii Dal'nevostočnoj Morskoj Akademii im. G.I. Nevel'skogo, Vladivostok 33705
Muzej Istorii Doma XIX-XX vekov, Tjumen 33605
Muzej Istorii Ekaterinburga, Ekaterinburg 32775
Muzej Istorii g. Stavropolja, Stavropol 33562
Muzej Istorii Goroda Irkutska, Irkutsk 32818
Muzej Istorii Goroda Joškar-Oly, Joškar-Ola 32859
Muzej Istorii Goroda-Kurorta Soči, Soči 33541
Muzej Istorii Goroda Naberežnye Čelny, Naberežnye Čelny 33192
Muzej Istorii Goroda Šlisselburga, Šlisselburg 33525
Muzej Istorii Goroda Tjumeni, Tjumen 33606
Muzej Istorii i Kultury Goroda Votkinska, Votkinsk 33738
Muzej Istorii i Kultury Moskovskogo Rajona, Nižnij Novgorod 33210
Muzej Istorii i Kultury Srednego Prikamja, Sarapul 33503
Muzej Istorii Izučenija i Osvoenija Evropejskogo Severa, Apatity 32645
Muzej Istorii Jaroslavlja, Jaroslavl 32853
Muzej Istorii Kamnereznogo i Juvelirnogo Iskusstva, Ekaterinburg 32776
Muzej Istorii Kazanskogo Universiteta, Kazan 32897
Muzej Istorii Kolskich Saamov, Lovozero 32993
Muzej Istorii Kraja, Belozersk 32683
Muzej Istorii Milicii, Sankt-Peterburg 33438
Muzej Istorii Moskovskogo Metropolitena, Moskva 33108
Muzej Istorii Moskvy, Moskva 33109
Muzej Istorii Narodnych Chudožestvennych Promyslov, Nižnij Novgorod 33211
Muzej Istorii OAO Gaz, Nižnij Novgorod 33212
Muzej Istorii OAO Nižegorodskij Televizionnyj Zavod im. V.I. Lenina, Nižnij Novgorod 33213
Muzej Istorii Orenburga, Orenburg 33269
Muzej Istorii Osvoenija i Razvitija Norilskogo Promyšlennogo Rajona, Norilsk 33229
Muzej Istorii Otečestvennogo Predprinimatelstva, Moskva 33110
Muzej Istorii Pečati Sankt-Peterburga, Sankt-Peterburg 33439
Muzej Istorii Permskogo Rajona, Perm 33306
Muzej Istorii Peterburgskoj Konservatorii, Sankt-Peterburg 33440
Muzej Istorii Političeskoj Polcii Rossii - Gorochovaja 2, Sankt-Peterburg 33441
Muzej Istorii Političeskoj Ssylki, Bratsk 32705
Muzej Istorii Politssylki v Jakutii, Jakutsk 32844
Muzej Istorii Poljarnych Olimpiad, Murmansk 33190
Muzej Istorii Priokskogo Rajona, Nižnij Novgorod 33214
Muzej Istorii Prosveščenija Komi Kraja, Syktyvkar 33577
Muzej Istorii Razvitija Mediciny, Astrachan 32665
Muzej Istorii Razvitija Mosenergo, Moskva 33111
Muzej Istorii Revoljucionno-demokratičeskogo Dviženija 1880-1890 gg, Sankt-Peterburg 33442
Muzej Istorii Rossijskogo Gosudarstvennogo Pedagogičeskogo Universiteta im A.I. Gercena, Sankt-Peterburg 33443
Muzej Istorii Rybnoj Promyšlennosti Dagestana, Machačkala 32997
Muzej Istorii Sankt-Peterburgskogo Universiteta, Sankt-Peterburg 33444
Muzej Istorii Svjazi Respubliki Tatarstan, Kazan 32898
Muzej Istorii Teatrov Dagestana, Machačkala 32998
Muzej Istorii Turizma, Sankt-Peterburg 33445
Muzej Istorii UVD Kalužskoj Oblasti, Kaluga 32880
Muzej Istorii Vojsk Moskovskogo Voennogo Okruga, Moskva 33112
Muzej Istorije Jugoslavije, Beograd 33805
Muzej Ivanovskogo Sitca, Ivanovo 32831

Muzej Izobrazitel'nych Iskusstv, Ašgabat 37811
Muzej Izobrazitelnych Iskusstv, Astana 27076
Muzej Izobrazitelnych Iskusstv, Komsomolsk-na-Amure 32935
Muzej Izobrazitelnych Iskusstv, Rostov-na-Donu 33356
Muzej Izobrazitelnych Iskusstv im. A.S. Puškina, Moskva 33113
Muzej Izobrazitelnych Iskusstv Karelii, Petrozavodsk 33318
Muzej Izobrazitelnyh Iskusstv Respubliki Marij Ėl, Joškar-Ola 32860
Muzej Jantarja, Kaliningrad 32872
Muzej Jesenice, Jesenice 34092
Muzej Jevreja Bosne i Hercegovine, Sarajevo 03921
Muzej Jovana Jovanovića-Zmaja, Sremska Kamenica 33911
Muzej Jugoslavenska Kinoteka, Beograd 33806
Muzej Junye Zaščitniki Rodiny, Kursk 32977
Muzej K. Ė. Ciolkovskogo, Aviacii i Kosmonavtiki, Kirov 32921
Muzej Kajuma Nasyri, Kazan 32899
Muzej Käkrinsko Chanče, Käkrina 04684
Muzej Karamzinskaja Obščestvennaja Biblioteka, Uljanovsk 33660
Muzej Kazanskoj Chimičeskoj Školy, Kazan 32900
Muzej Keramiki i Usadba Kuskovo XVIII Veka, Moskva 33114
Muzej Kino, Moskva 33115
Muzej Kirovskogo Zavoda, Sankt-Peterburg 33446
Muzej Kizyl-Arvata, Kizyl-Arvat 37816
Muzej Klassičeskogo i Sovremennogo Iskusstva, Moskva 33116
Muzej Kliničke Psihijatrijske Bolnice Vrapče, Zagreb 07832
Muzej V.O. Ključevskogo, Penza 33289
Muzej Knigi, Moskva 33117
Muzej Kninske Krajine, Knin 07716
Muzej Književnosti i Pozorišne Umjetnosti Bosne i Hercegovine i Galerija MAK, Sarajevo 03922
Muzej A. Kolcova, Voronež 33732
Muzej Kolju Fičeto, Drjanovo 04661
Muzej Konevodstva, Moskva 33118
Muzej Konspiritavnaja Kvartira Simbirskoj Gruppy RSDRP 1904-1906, Uljanovsk 33661
Muzej Korčula, Korčula 07722
Muzej Košek, Moskva 33119
Muzej Kosova, Priština 33895
Muzej Kraevedenija, Jalta 37855
Muzej Kraevedenija g. Elabuga, Elabuga 32787
Muzej Krajine Negotin, Negotin 33862
Muzej Krapinskog Pračovjeka, Krapina 07728
Muzej Krejsera Avrora, Sankt-Peterburg 33447
Muzej-krepost Baba Vida, Vidin 04925
Muzej Krestovosdviženskaja Cerkov, Palech 33283
Muzej Kriminalistiki, Barnaul 32674
Muzej-kripta Aleksandăr Nevski, Sofia 04839
Muzej Kronštadtskaja Krepost, Kronštadt 32966
Muzej Kronštadtskogo Morskogo Zavoda, Kronštadt 32967
Muzej Kruticke Podvore, Moskva 33120
Muzej Krylova, Tula 33626
Muzej Kukol i Detskoj Knigi Strana Čudes, Ekaterinburg 32777
Muzej Kulturne Istorije, Požarevac 33892
Muzej Kultury Astrachani, Astrachan 32666
Muzej Kupečeskogo Byta, Ekaterinburg 32778
Muzej-kvartira Alliluevych, Sankt-Peterburg 33448
Muzej-kvartira A.M. Gorkogo, Moskva 33121
Muzej-kvartira I.I. Brodskogo, Sankt-Peterburg 33449
Muzej-kvartira A.S. Čaplygina, Sankt-Peterburg 33450
Muzej-kvartira M.I. Cvetaevoj v Bolševo, Korolev 32940
Muzej-kvartira Dirižëra N.S. Golovanov, Moskva 33122
Muzej-kvartira F.M. Dostoevskogo, Moskva 33123
Muzej-kvartira Elizarovych, Sankt-Peterburg 33451
Muzej-kvartira S.B. Goldenvejzera, Moskva 33124
Muzej-kvartira A.M. Gorkogo, Nižnij Novgorod 33215
Muzej-kvartira G.D. Krasilnikova, Iževsk 32835
Muzej-kvartira A.I. Kuindži, Sankt-Peterburg 33452
Muzej-kvartira L. Lapcuja, Salechard 33365
Muzej-kvartira Lunačarskogo, Moskva 33125
Muzej-kvartira V.S. Mejercholda, Moskva 33126
Muzej-kvartira Naziba Žiganova, Kazan 32901
Muzej-kvartira V.I. Nemiroviča-Dančenko, Moskva 33127
Muzej-kvartira A. Puškina, Sankt-Peterburg 33453
Muzej-kvartira A.D. Sacharova, Nižnij Novgorod 33216
Muzej-kvartira F.I. Šaljapina, Sankt-Peterburg 33454
Muzej-kvartira T.G. Ševčenko, Sankt-Peterburg 33455
Muzej-kvartira Ju.P. Spegalskogo, Pskov 33331
Muzej-kvartira K.A. Timirjazeva, Moskva 33128
Muzej-kvartira A.N. Tolstogo, Moskva 33129
Muzej-kvartira A.T. Tvardovskij v Smolenske, Smolensk 33528
Muzej-kvartita Musa Džalilja, Kazan 32902
Muzej Lavka Čechovych, Taganrog 33584
Muzej-ledokol Angara, Irkutsk 32819
Muzej-ledokol Bajkal, Angarsk 32643
Muzej V.I. Lenina, Moskva 33130
Muzej Ličnych Kollekcij, Moskva 33131
Muzej Literaturnaja Žizn' Urala XIX Veka, Ekaterinburg 32779
Muzej Literaturnoj Žizni Jaroslavskogo Kraja, Jaroslavl 32854
Muzej Literatury Burjatii im. Choca Namsaraeva, Ulan-Udė 33654
Muzej Ljudske Revolucije Slovenj Gradec, Slovenj Gradec 34150
Muzej Ljudske Revolucije Trbovlje, Trbovlje 34156
Muzej M.V. Lomonosova, Sankt-Peterburg 33456
Muzej A.S. Makarenko, Moskva 33132
Muzej Marcialnye Vody, Petrozavodsk 33319
Muzej Mecenatov i Blagotvoritelej Rossii, Moskva 33133
Muzej Medjimurja, Čakovec 07687
Muzej Meteorologii Glavnoj Geofizičeskoj Observatorii im. A.I. Voejkova, Sankt-Peterburg 33457
Muzej Meterologičeskaja Stancija Simbirska, Uljanovsk 33662
Muzej Miniaturnych Kukol Malenkij Mir, Semipalatinsk 33517
Muzej Mir Vody Sankt-Peterburga, Sankt-Peterburg 33458
Muzej Mirovogo Okeana, Kaliningrad 32873
Muzej Mologskogo Kraja, Rybinsk 33361
Muzej Mordovskoj Kultury, Saransk 33500
Muzej Morskogo Flota, Moskva 33134
Muzej Morskogo Flota Dal'nevostočnogo Morskogo Parochodstva, Vladivostok 33706
Muzej Moskovskogo Chudožestvennogo Akademičeskogo Teatra, Moskva 33135
Muzej Moskovskoj Konservatorii, Moskva 33136
Muzej Moslavine, Kutina 07733
Muzej Muzykalnoj i Teatralnoj Kultury na Kavkazskich Mineralnyh Vodach, Kislovodsk 32930
Muzej Muzykalnych Instrumentov, Sankt-Peterburg 33459
Muzej na Aviacijata, Krumovo 04723
Muzej na Bivolarstvoto i Konevădstvoto, Šumen 04875
Muzej na Blejskem Gradu, Bled 34085
Muzej na Chudožestvenata Akademija, Sofia 04840
Muzej na Chudožestvenite Zanajati i Priložnite Izkustva, Trojan 04890
Muzej na Grad Skopje, Skopje 27589
Muzej na Gradskij Bit Oslekova Kăšta, Koprivština 04716
Muzej na Gradskija Bit, Ruse 04804
Muzej na Ikonata v Carkvata Sv. Nikolai, Pleven 04766
Muzej na Kotlenskite Vazroždenci i Panteon na Georgi S. Rakovski, Kotel 04719
Muzej na Makedonija - Arceološki, Etnološki i Istoriski, Skopje 27590
Muzej na Ministerstvoto na Vnatrešnite raboti, Sofia 04841
Muzej na Morskoto Stopanstvo, Varna 04899
Muzej na Mozaikite, Devnja 04648
Muzej na Naroden Teatar Ivan Vazov, Sofia 04842
Muzej na Narodnata Opera, Sofia 04843
Muzej na Poklonnoj, Moskva 33137
Muzej na Rezbarskoto i Zografsko Izkustvo, Trjavna 04888
Muzej na Rodopskija Karst, Čepelare 04637
Muzej na Rudodobiva i Minnoto Delo, Madan 04730
Muzej na Septemvrijskoto Văstanie, Michajlovgrad 04739
Muzej na Sovremenata Umetnost Skopje, Skopje 27591
Muzej na Tekstilnata Industrija, Sliven 04822
Muzej na Tetovskiot Kraj, Tetovo 27598
Muzej na Văzraždaneto, Varna 04900
Muzej na Văzroždeneto i Nacionalno-osvoboditelnite Borbi, Elena 04663
Muzej na Văzroždenskata Ikona, Varna 04901
Muzej Nacionalnoj Kultury, Kazan 32903
Muzej Naivne Umetnosti, Sid 33905
Muzej Narodne Osvobodilve, Maribor 34126
Muzej Narodnogo Chudožnika Rossii A.I. Morozova, Ivanovo 32832
Muzej Narodnogo Derevjannogo Zodčestva Vitoslavlicy, Velikij Novgorod 33678
Muzej Narodnogo Iskusstva, Moskva 33138
Muzej Narodnogo Obrazovanija Oblasti, Penza 33290
Muzej Narodnogo Tvorčestva, Penza 33291
Muzej Narodnogo Tvorčestva, Uljanovsk 33663
Muzej Narodnoj Grafiki, Moskva 33139
Muzej Narodnoje Obrazovanie Simbirskoj Gubernii v 70-80 gody 19 veka, Uljanovsk 33664
Muzej Narodnych Muzykalnych Instrumentov Kazachstana, Almaty 27073
Muzej Nauke i Tehnike, Beograd 33807
Muzej Nekropol' Demidovych i Vystavočnyj Zal Tulskij Metall, Tula 33627
Muzej-nekropol Literatorskie Mostki, Sankt-Peterburg 33460
Muzej N.G. Rubinstejna, Moskva 33140
Muzej Nikole Tesle, Beograd 33808
Muzej Nižegorodskaja Radiolaboratorija, Nižnij Novgorod 33217
Muzej Nižegorodskij Ostrog, Nižnij Novgorod 33218
Muzej Nižegorodskoj Intelligencii, Nižnij Novgorod 33219
Muzej Nonkonformistskogo Iskusstva, Sankt-Peterburg 33461
Muzej Novejše Zgodovine Celje, Celje 34089
Muzej Novejše Zgodovine Slovenije, Ljubljana 34113
Muzej Obščestva Krasnogo Kresta Rossii, Moskva 33141
Muzej Obščestva Sporta Dinamo-Moskva, Moskva 33142
Muzej Obščestvennogo Pitanija, Moskva 33143
Muzej Obščestvennogo Zdorovja Uzbekistana, Taškent 48858
Muzej Ochotovedenija, Irkutsk 32820
Muzej Ochoty i Rybolovstva, Moskva 33144
Muzej Oktjabrskogo Vooružennogo Vosstanija, Voronež 33733
Muzej Orijentalnih Rukopisa, Prizren 33898
Muzej Osvoboždenieto na Pleven 1877, Pleven 04767
Muzej-Pamjatnik Chram Voskresenija Christova (Spas na Krovi), Sankt-Peterburg 33462
Muzej-panorama Borodinskaja Bitva, Moskva 33145
Muzej Parka Iskusstv na Krymskoj Naberežnoj, Moskva 33146
Muzej-Parochod Svjatitel Nikolaj, Krasnojarsk 32956
Muzej Pejzaža, Ples 33324
Muzej Pisatelej-orlovcev, Orël 33266
Muzej Pisatelja A.P. Bibika, Mineral'nye Vody 33013
Muzej po Istorii Stroitelstva Gidroelektričeskogo Zavoda v Nurke, Nurek 37449
Muzej Podviga Ivana Susanina, Susanino 33568
Muzej Poėta S. Orlova, Belozersk 32684
Muzej Pograničnoj Ochrany, Moskva 33147
Muzej Ponišavlja Pirot, Pirot 33884
Muzej Pozorišne Umetnosti Srbije, Beograd 33809
Muzej Prezidentskogo Centra Kultury Respubliki Kazachstan, Astana 27077
Muzej Prigorja, Sesvete 07771
Muzej Primenjene Umetnosti, Beograd 33810
Muzej Priroda Morja i eë Ochrana, Vladivostok 33707
Muzej Prirody, Čerepovec 32732
Muzej Prirody Burjatii, Ulan-Udė 33655
Muzej S.S. Prokofjeva, Moskva 33148
Muzej A.S. Puškina, Toržok 33619
Muzej A.S. Puškina v Bernove, Bernov 32686
Muzej Radio im. A.S. Popova, Ekaterinburg 32780
Muzej Radničkog Pokreta i Narodne Revolucije, Novi Sad 33871
Muzej Radničkog Pokreta i NOB za Slavoniju i Baranju, Slavonski Brod 07778
Muzej Rafail Popov, Madara 04732
Muzej Ras, Novi Pazar 33868
Muzej Rečnog Brodarstva, Beograd 33811
Muzej Rečnogo Flota, Nižnij Novgorod 33220
Muzej Remesla, Architektury i Byta, Kaluga 32881
Muzej Republike Srpske, Banja Luka 03910
Muzej Revoljucii, Moskva 33149
Muzej Revoljucionnogo Dvizenija, Altanbulag 28673
Muzej-riznica Stare Srpske Pravoslavne Crkve, Sarajevo 03923
Muzej Rossijskoj Akademii Chudožestv, Sankt-Peterburg 33463
Muzej Rudarstva i Metalurgije, Bor 33824
Muzej Rumănski Voin, Pordim 04786
Muzej Russko-Armjanskoj Družby, Rostov-na-Donu 33357
Muzej Russkoj Pesni im. A. Averkina, Sasovo 33512
Muzej Salicha Sajdaševa, Kazan 32904
Muzej M.E. Saltykova-Ščedrina, Tver 33636
Muzej Šamocvety Bajkala, Sljudjanka 33527
Muzej Šarifa Kamala, Kazan 32905
Muzej Savremene Likovne Umetnosti, Novi Sad 33872
Muzej Savremene Umetnosti, Beograd 33812
Muzej Sceničeskogo Iskusstva im. V.Ė. Mejercholda, Penza 33292
Muzej Seljackih Buna, Gornja Stubica 07703
Muzej Semejstvo Obretenovi, Ruse 04805
Muzej Semji Benua, Sankt-Peterburg 33464
Muzej Simbirskaja Čuvašskaja Škola - Kvartira I.Ja. Jakovleva, Uljanovsk 33665
Muzej Simbirskaja Klassičeskaja Gimnazija, Uljanovsk 33666
Muzej Skulptury, Sankt-Peterburg 33465
Muzej Skulptury S.T. Konenkova, Smolensk 33529
Muzej Slavonije Osijek, Osijek 07750
Muzej Slivenski Zatvor, Sliven 04823
Muzej Smolenščina v Gody Velikoj Otečestvennoj Vojny 1941 -1945, Smolensk 33530
Muzej Smolenskij Len, Smolensk 33531
Muzej Snovidenij Zigmunda Frejda, Sankt-Peterburg 33466
Muzej Sovremennogo Iskusstva Evrejskoj Avtonomnoj Oblasti, Birobidžan 32690
Muzej Sovremennogo Izobrazitelnogo Iskusstva im. A.A. Plastova, Uljanovsk 33667
Muzej Sovremennoj Istorii i Kultury Severnoj Osetii, Vladikavkaz 33689
Muzej Spasskaja Cerkov, Tjumen 33607
Muzej Sporta v Lužnikach, Moskva 33150
Muzej Srema, Sremska Mitrovica 33913
Muzej Srpske Pravoslavne Crkve, Beograd 33813
Muzej Srpske Pravoslavne Crkve, Dubrovnik 07699
Muzej Štab-kvartira V.K. Bljuchera, Tjumen 33608
Muzej Stara Livnica, Kragujevac 33851
Muzej Staražytna Belaruskaj Kultury, Minsk 03120
Muzej Staryj Anglijskij Dvor, Moskva 33151
Muzej-studija Radioteatra, Moskva 33152
Muzej A.V. Suvorova, Velikij Novgorod 33679
Muzej Suvremene Umjetnosti, Zagreb 07833
Muzej Svjazi Amurskoj Oblasti, Blagoveščensk 32692
Muzej S.I. Taneeva v Djutkovo, Zvenigorod 33750
Muzej Andreja Tarkovskogo, Jurjevec 32866
Muzej Teatra, Sankt-Peterburg 33467
Muzej Teatra Operetty, Moskva 33153
Muzej Teatralnoj Kukly A.A Veselova, Voronež 33734
Muzej A.K. Tolstogo, Krasnyj Rog 32963
Muzej L.N. Tolstogo na stancii Lev Tolstoj, Stancija Lev Tolstoj 33552
Muzej Tomaža Godca, Bohinjska Bistrica 34086
Muzej Tropinina i Moskovskich Chudožnikov Ego Vremeni, Moskva 33154
Muzej Tul'skie Samovary, Tula 33628
Muzej Tul'skij Kreml', Tula 33629
Muzej Turopolja, Velika Gorica 07799
Muzej Tverskogo Byta, Tver 33637
Muzej u Arandjelovcu, Arandjelovac 33787
Muzej u Smederevu, Smederevo 33906
Muzej Uezdnogo Goroda, Čistopol 32749
Muzej Ulcinj, Ulcinj 33923
Muzej Unikalnych Kukol, Moskva 33155
Muzej Uralskogo Gosudarstvennogo Techničeskogo Universiteta, Ekaterinburg 32781
Muzej-usadba A.T. Bolotova, Dvorjaninovo 32764
Muzej-usadba V.E. Borsova-Musatova, Saratov 33507
Muzej-usadba N.G. Černyševskogo, Saratov 33508
Muzej- Usadba F.M. Dostoevskogo Darovoe, Darovoe 32755
Muzej-usadba N.A. Durovoj, Elabuga 32788
Muzej-usadba M.I. Glinki, Novospasskoe 33246
Muzej-usadba im. N.K. Rericha, Izvara 32839
Muzej-usadba Izmajlovo, Moskva 33156
Muzej-usadba L.N. Tolstogo Nikol'skoe Vjazemskoe, Nikol'skoe-Vjazemskoe 33204
Muzej-usadba "Muranovo" im. F.I. Tjutčeva, Lugovskoe 32994
Muzej-usadba Ostafjevo "Russkij Parnas", Ostafjevo 33274
Muzej-usadba poėta D. Venevitinova, Novoživotinnoe 33248
Muzej-usadba I.E. Repina, Repino 33347
Muzej-usadba Roždestveno, Roždestveno 33359
Muzej-usadba V.I. Surikova, Krasnojarsk 32957
Muzej-usadba A.V. Suvorova, Končanskoe-Suvorovskoe 32936
Muzej-usadba A.N. Tolstogo, Samara 33374
Muzej-Usadba L.N. Tolstogo v Chamovnikach, Moskva 33157
Muzej-usadba A.T. Tvardovskij na Chutore Zagorje, Zagorje 33744
Muzej V Mire Skazok, Smolensk 33532
Muzej Vasil Levski, Karlovo 04691
Muzej Vasil Levski, Loveč 04729
Muzej Văzraždane i Učreditelno Săbranie, Veliko Tărnovo 04917
Muzej Văzroždenski Ikoni, Radomir 04794
Muzej Velenje, Velenje 34162
Muzej Vereščaginych, Čerepovec 32733
Muzej Vjatskie Narodnye Chudožestvennye Promysly, Kirov 32922
Muzej Vladimira Raevskogo, Bogoslovka 32695
Muzej Vody, Moskva 33158
Muzej Vojniško Văstanie 1918, Radomir 04795
Muzej Volynskoj Ikony, Luck 37879
Muzej Voskovych Figur, Sankt-Peterburg 33468
Muzej za Istorija na Medicinata, Varna 04902
Muzej za Istorija na Varna, Varna 04903
Muzej za Umjetnost i Obrt, Zagreb 07834
Muzej-zapovednik Abramcevo, Abramcevo 32629
Muzej-zapovednik Dmitrovskij Kreml, Dmitrov 32758
Muzej-zapovednik Kazanskij Kreml, Kazan 32906
Muzej-zapovednik Pisatelja S.T. Aksakova, Aksakovo 32632
Muzej Zavoda Crvena Zastava, Kragujevac 33852
Muzej Zavoda Moskvič, Moskva 33159
Muzej Zdravoochranenija, Sankt-Peterburg 33469
Muzej Železnodorožnoj Techniki, Sankt-Peterburg 33470
Muzej Zemlevedenija Moskovskogo Gosudarstvennogo Universiteta M.V. Lomonosova, Moskva 33160
Muzeji i Galerije Podgorica, Podgorica 33889
Muzeji Radovljiške Občine, Begunje na Gorenjskem 34084
Muzeji Radovljiške Občine, Kropa 34102
Muzejno-vystavočnyj Centr, Dal'negorsk 32754
Muzejno-vystavočnyj Centr, Ivanovo 32833
Muzejno-vystavočnyj Centr - Diorama, Kirov 32923
Muzejno-vystavočnyj Centr Ego, Sankt-Peterburg 33471
Muzejno-vystavočnyj Centr Tul'skie Drevnosti, Tula 33630
Muzejno-vystavočnyj Kompleks, Moskva 33161
Muzejno-vystavočnyj Kompleks Volokolamskij Kreml, Volokolamsk 33726
Muzejnyj Kompleks Tomskogo Politechničeskogo Universiteta, Tomsk 33614
Muzejska Zbirka, Imotski 07709
Muzejska Zbirka, Knić 33846
Muzejska Zbirka, Rogoška Slatina 34147
Muzejska Zbirka Franjevačkog Samostana, Imotski 07710
Muzejska Zbirka Jastrebarsko, Jastrebarsko 07711
Muzejska Zbirka Kapucinskog Samostana, Karlobag 07712
Muzejska Zbirka Krapina i Okolica, Krapina 07729
Muzejska Zbirka Laško, Laško 34103
Muzejska Zbirka NOB, Zagorje 34166
Muzejska Zbirka pri Narodnoj Biblioteki Dimitrije Tucović, Čajetina 33829
Muzejski Dokumentacijski Centar, Zagreb 07835
Muzejsko Društvo na Makedonija, Skopje 49284
Muzejsko Društvo SR Crne Gore - Cetinje, Cetinje 49352
Muzejsko Društvo Srbije, Beograd 49353
Muzejsko Društvo Srbije, Beograd 49354
Muzeu Historik Fier, Fier 00021
Muzeu i Filmit Shkodër, Shkodër 00031
Muzeu i Shkencave Natyrore, Tiranë 00035

Muzeul Arheologic Adamclisi, Adamclisi 32424
Muzeul Arheologic Sarmizegetusa, Sarmizegetusa 32586
Muzeul Arhitecturii Populare din Gorj, Bumbeşti-Jiu 32476
Muzeul Arta lemnului, Câmpulung Moldovenesc 32484
Muzeul Banatului, Timişoara 32614
Muzeul Banatului Montan, Reşiţa 32581
Muzeul Brăilei, Brăila 32444
Muzeul Bran, Bran 32445
Muzeul Breslelor, Tîrgu Secuiesc 32615
Muzeul Câmpiei Băileştitor, Băileşti 32436
Muzeul Castelul Corvinestilor, Hunedoara 32530
Muzeul Civilizaţiei Dacice şi Romăne, Deva 32511
Muzeul Colecţiilor de Artă, Bucureşti 32452
Muzeul Cornel Medrea, Bucureşti 32453
Muzeul Curtea Veche, Bucureşti 32454
Muzeul de Arheologie, Săveni 32588
Muzeul de Arheologie Callatis Mangalia, Mangalia 32547
Muzeul de Arheologie Olteniţa, Olteniţa 32558
Muzeul de Arheologie şi Etnografie, Corabia 32503
Muzeul de Artă, Braşov 32447
Muzeul de Artă, Drobeta-Turnu Severin 32515
Muzeul de Artă, Iaşi 32532
Muzeul de Artă, Medgidia 32548
Muzeul de Artă, Târgovişte 32603
Muzeul de Artă, Târgu Jiu 32605
Muzeul de Artă, Tulcea 32617
Muzeul de Artă Constanţa, Constanţa 32499
Muzeul de Artă Craiova, Craiova 32506
Muzeul de Artă Dinu şi Sevasta Vintilă, Topalu 32616
Muzeul de Artă Piatra-Neamţ, Piatra-Neamţ 32565
Muzeul de Artă Populară, Constanţa 32500
Muzeul de Artă Populară, Ploieşti 32570
Muzeul de Artă Populară Prof. Dr. Nicolae Minovici, Bucureşti 32455
Muzeul de Artă Populară şi Etnografie, Tulcea 32618
Muzeul de Artă şi Artă Populară, Calafat 32478
Muzeul de Artă Vizuală, Galaţi 32523
Muzeul de Etnografie Braşov, Braşov 32448
Muzeul de Etnografie Piatra-Neamţ, Piatra-Neamţ 32566
Muzeul de Etnografie şi a Regimentului de Graniţă, Caransebeş 32488
Muzeul de Etnografie şi Artă Populară, Reghin 32580
Muzeul de Etnografie şi Artă Populară Orăştie, Orăştie 32563
Muzeul de Istorie, Bicaz 32439
Muzeul de Istorie, Oneşti 32559
Muzeul de Istorie, Târgu Jiu 32606
Muzeul de Istorie a Evreilor din România, Bucureşti 32456
Muzeul de Istorie al Moldovei, Iaşi 32533
Muzeul de Istorie Augustin Bunea, Blaj 32441
Muzeul de Istorie, Etnografie şi Artă Plastică, Lugoj 32544
Muzeul de Istorie Gherla, Gherla 32526
Muzeul de Istorie Locală şi Etnografie, Brad 32443
Muzeul de Istorie Naţională şi Archeologie, Constanţa 32501
Muzeul de Istorie Naturală din Sibiu, Sibiu 32592
Muzeul de Istorie Naturală Iaşi, Iaşi 32534
Muzeul de Istorie şi Arheologie, Tulcea 32619
Muzeul de Istorie şi Artă Roman, Roman 32582
Muzeul de Istorie şi Etnografie, Târgu Neamţ 32612
Muzeul de Istorie Sighişoara, Sighişoara 32595
Muzeul de Istorie Turda, Turda 32621
Muzeul de Istorie Valea Hârtibaciului, Agnita 32425
Muzeul de Mineralogie Baia Mare, Baia Mare 32434
Muzeul de Ştiinte Naturale, Piatra-Neamţ 32567
Muzeul de Ştiinţele Naturii, Dorohoi 32513
Muzeul de Ştiinţele Naturii, Focşani 32520
Muzeul de Stiinţele Naturii, Roman 32583
Muzeul de Ştiinţele Naturii Aiud, Aiud 32426
Muzeul de Şttiinte Naturale, Tulcea 32620
Muzeul Doftana, Doftana 32512
Muzeul Dunării de Jos, Călăraşi 32479
Muzeul Etnografic, Vatra Dornei 32625
Muzeul Etnografic al Moldovei, Iaşi 32535
Muzeul Etnografic al Transilvaniei, Cluj-Napoca 32492
Muzeul Etnografic Ioan Tugui, Câmpulung Moldovenesc 32485
Muzeul Etnografic Lupşa, Lupşa 32545
Muzeul Etnografic Tehnici Populare Bucovinene, Rădăuţi 32576
Muzeul Grăniceresc Năsăudean, Năsăud 32553
Muzeul Haáz Rezsö, Odorheiu Secuiesc 32557
Muzeul Hrandt Avakian, Bucureşti 32457
Muzeul în Aer Liber, Negreşti-Oaş 32555
Muzeul Judeţean Alexandru Ştefulescu, Târgu Jiu 32607
Muzeul Judeţean Argeş, Piteşti 32569
Muzeul Judeţean Bistriţa-Năsăud, Bistriţa 32440
Muzeul Judeţean Botoşani, Botoşani 32442
Muzeul Judeţean Buzău, Buzău 32477
Muzeul Judeţean de Artă, Ploieşti 32571
Muzeul Judeţean de Etnografie, Slatina 32597
Muzeul Judeţean de Istorie, Galaţi 32524
Muzeul Judeţean de Istorie, Piatra-Neamţ 32568
Muzeul Judeţean de Istorie Braşov, Braşov 32449
Muzeul Judeţean de Istorie şi Arheologie Iulian Antonescu Bacău, Bacău 32433
Muzeul Judeţean de Istorie şi Arheologie Prahova, Ploieşti 32572
Muzeul Judeţean de Istorie şi Artă, Slatina 32598
Muzeul Judeţean de Istorie şi Artă Zalău, Zalău 32626
Muzeul Judeţean de Istorie Teleorman, Alexandria 32429
Muzeul Judeţean de Ştiinţele Naturii Prahova, Ploieşti 32573
Muzeul Judeţean Ialomiţa, Slobozia 32599
Muzeul Judeţean Maramureş, Baia Mare 32435
Muzeul Judeţean Mureş, Târgu Mureş 32608
Muzeul Judeţean Mureş-Secţia de Artă, Târgu Mureş 32609
Muzeul Judeţean Mureş-Secţia de Etnografie şi Artă Populară, Târgu Mureş 32610
Muzeul Judeţean Mureş-Secţia de St^Biinţele Naturii, Târgu Mureş 32611
Muzeul Judeţean Satu Mare, Satu Mare 32587
Muzeul Judeţean Ştefan cel Mare, Vaslui 32624
Muzeul Judeţean Teohari Antonescu, Giurgiu 32527
Muzeul Judeţean Vâlcea, Râmnicu Vâlcea 32578
Muzeul K.H. Zambaccian, Bucureşti 32458
Muzeul Literaturii Române, Iaşi 32536
Muzeul Maramureşului, Sighetu Marmaţiei 32594
Muzeul Marinei Române, Constanţa 32502
Muzeul Memorial Ady Endre, Oradea 32560
Muzeul Memorial Avram Iancu, Avram Iancu 32431
Muzeul Memorial Bojdeuca Ion Creangă, Iaşi 32537
Muzeul Memorial Emil Isac, Cluj-Napoca 32493
Muzeul Memorial George Coşbuc, Coşbuc 32505
Muzeul Memorial George Enescu, Dorohoi 32514
Muzeul Memorial Gheorghe M. Tattarascu, Bucureşti 32459
Muzeul Memorial Iosif Vulcan, Oradea 32561
Muzeul Memorial Liviu Rebreanu, Năsăud 32554
Muzeul Memorial Nicolae Grigorescu, Câmpina 32481
Muzeul Memorial Octavian Goga, Ciucea 32490
Muzeul Memorial Petőfi Sándor, Coltau 32497
Muzeul Mihai Eminescu, Iaşi 32538
Muzeul Militar Naţional, Bucureşti 32460
Muzeul Mineritului, Petroşani 32564
Muzeul Municipal, Huşi 32531
Muzeul Municipal, Râmnicu Sărat 32577
Muzeul Municipal Câmpulung, Câmpulung 32482
Muzeul Municipal Câmpulung-Secţia de Etnografie şi, Câmpulung 32483
Muzeul Municipal Curtea de Argeş, Curtea de Argeş 32509
Muzeul Municipal de Istorie, Roşiorii de Vede 32584
Muzeul Municipal Dej ş Galeria de Artă, Dej 32510
Muzeul Municipal Ioan Raica Sebeş, Sebeş 32589
Muzeul Municipal Medias, Mediaş 32549
Muzeul Municipiului Bucureşti, Bucureşti 32461
Muzeul National al Literaturii Române, Bucureşti 32462
Muzeul Naţional al Petrolului, Ploieşti 32574
Muzeul Naţional al Pompierilor, Bucureşti 32463
Muzeul Naţional al Satului, Bucureşti 32464
Muzeul Naţional al Unirii, Alba Iulia 32428
Muzeul Naţional Brukenthal, Sibiu 32593
Muzeul Naţional Cotroceni, Bucureşti 32465
Muzeul Naţional de Artă al României, Bucureşti 32466
Muzeul Naţional de Artă Cluj-Napoca, Cluj-Napoca 32494
Muzeul National de Arte Plastice, Chişinău 28658
Muzeul National de Etnografie si Istorie Naturala, Chişinău 28659
Muzeul National de Istorie a Moldovei, Chişinău 28660
Muzeul Naţional de Istorie a României, Bucureşti 32467
Muzeul Naţional de Istorie a Transilvaniei, Cluj-Napoca 32495
Muzeul Naţional de Istorie Naturala Grigore Antipa, Bucureşti 32468
Muzeul Naţional George Enescu, Bucureşti 32469
Muzeul Naţional Peleş, Sinaia 32596
Muzeul National Secuisec, Sfântu Gheorghe 32590
Muzeul Nicolae Iorga, Vălenii de Munte 32623
Muzeul Obiceiurilor Populare din Bucovina, Gura Humorului 32529
Muzeul Olteniei, Craiova 32507
Muzeul Orăşanesc Fălticeni, Fălticeni 32519
Muzeul Orăşenecs de Istorie şi Etnografie, Beiuş 32438
Muzeul Orăşenesc, Carei 32489
Muzeul Orăşenesc, Lipova 32543
Muzeul Orăşenesc, Tecuci 32613
Muzeul Orăşenesc de Istorie, Aiud 32427
Muzeul Orăşenesc Molnar Istvan, Cristuru Secuiesc 32508
Muzeul Pedagogic Republican, Chişinău 28661
Muzeul Primei Şcoli Româneşti din Scheii Braşovului, Braşov 32450
Muzeul Regiunii Porţilor de Fier, Drobeta-Turnu Severin 32516
Muzeul Romanaţiului, Caracal 32486
Muzeul Romanaţiului Secţia de Artă Plastică, Caracal 32487
Muzeul Sătesc, Cornu 32504
Muzeul Secuiesc al Ciucului, Miercurea-Ciuc 32550
Muzeul Ştiinţei şi Tehnicii Ştefan Procopiu, Iaşi 32539
Muzeul Tăranului Român, Bucureşti 32470
Muzeul Ţării Crişurilor, Oradea 32562
Muzeul Ţării Oaşului, Negreşti-Oaş 32556
Muzeul Tarisznyás Márton, Gheorghieni 32525
Muzeul Taru Făgărasului, Făgăraş 32518
Muzeul Teatrului, Iaşi 32540
Muzeul Teatrului Naţional, Bucureşti 32471
Muzeul Tehnic Prof. Ing. Dimitrie Leonida, Bucureşti 32472
Muzeul Theodor Aman, Bucureşti 32473
Muzeul Theodor Pallady, Bucureşti 32474
Muzeul Tiparului şi al Cąrtii Vechi Româneşti, Târgovişte 32604
Muzeul Unirii, Iaşi 32541
Muzeul Vasile Pârvan, Bârlad 32437
Muzeul Vrancei, Focşani 32521
Muzeul Zoologic al Universităţii Babeş-Bolyai, Cluj-Napoca 32496
Múzeum, Bardejovské Kúpele 33953
Muzeum, Bzenec 08287
Muzeum, Koszalin 31678
Muzeum, Litvínov 08460
Muzeum, Zábřeh na Moravě 08736
Muzeum 1 Pułku Strzelców Podhalańskich Armii Krajowej, Szczawa 32021
Muzeum 24 Pułku Ułanów, Kraśnik 31730
Muzeum 600-lecia Jasnej Góry, Częstochowa 31544
Muzeum 7 Pułku Ułanów Lubelskich, Mińsk Mazowiecki 31808
Múzeum a Galéria Hont Šahy, Šahy 34056
Muzeum a Galerie, Hranice 08370
Muzeum a Galerie Severního Plzeňska, Kralovice 08429
Muzeum a Pojizerská Galerie, Semily 08652
Muzeum Adwokatury Polskiej, Warszawa 32086
Muzeum Afrykanistyczne im. Dr. Bogdana Szczygła, Olkusz 31848
Muzeum Akademii Medyczney, Poznań 31897
Muzeum Akademii Sztuk Pięknych, Warszawa 32087
Muzeum Aloise Jiráska, Hronov 08371
Muzeum Aloise Jiráska a Mikoláše Alše, Praha 08592
Múzeum Andreja Kmeťa, Martin 34025
Muzeum Andrzeja Struga, Warszawa 32088
Muzeum Antického Umění, Hostinné 08364
Muzeum Antonína Dvořáka, Praha 08593
Muzeum Archeologiczne, Gdańsk 31568
Muzeum Archeologiczne, Gniew 31598
Muzeum Archeologiczne, Poznań 31898
Muzeum Archeologiczne, Wrocław 32173
Muzeum Archeologiczne i Etnograficzne, Łódź 31768
Muzeum Archeologiczne Środkowego Nadodrza, Świdnica 32013
Muzeum Archeologiczne w Biskupinie, Gąsawa 31562
Muzeum Archeologiczne w Krakowie, Kraków 31693
Muzeum Archeologiczne w Krakowie, Oddział w Nowej Hucie, Kraków 31694
Muzeum Archeologiczno-Historyczne, Głogów 31594
Muzeum Archidiecezjalne, Katowice 31645
Muzeum Archidiecezjalne, Poznań 31899
Muzeum Archidiecezjalne, Przemyśl 31920
Muzeum Archidiecezjalne, Szczecin 32024
Muzeum Archidiecezjalne, Wrocław 32174
Muzeum Archidiecezjalne Lubelskie, Lublin 31787
Muzeum Archidiecezjalne w Krakowie, Kraków 31695
Muzeum Archidiecezjalne w Oliwie, Gdańsk 31569
Muzeum Archidiecezji Łódzkiej, Łódź 31769
Muzeum Archidiecezji Warszawskiej, Warszawa 32089
Muzeum Architektury, Wrocław 32175
Muzeum Armii Krajowej, Kraków 31696
Muzeum Armii Poznań, Poznań 31900
Muzeum Azji i Pacyfiku, Warszawa 32090
Múzeum Bábkarských Kultúr a Hračiek Hrad Modrý Kameň, Modrý Kameň 34031
Múzeum Bábkarských Kutúr a Hračiek Hrad Modrý Kameň, expozícia Dolná Strhová, Dolná Strehová 33988
Muzeum Bedřicha Hrozného, Lysá nad Labem 08468
Muzeum Bedřicha Smetany, Praha 08594
Muzeum Beskidzkie im. A. Podżorskiego, Wisła 32156
Muzeum Beskyd Frýdek-Místek, Frýdek-Místek 08340
Muzeum Betlémů, Karlštejn 08404
Muzeum Biblioteki Kórnickiej, Kórnik 31673
Muzeum Biblioteki Publicznej Warszawa-Bielany, Warszawa 32091
Muzeum Bicyklů, Rokycany 08635
Muzeum Biograficzne Władysława Orkana, Poręba Wielka 31894
Muzeum Bitwy Grunwaldzkiej, Stębark 32000
Muzeum Bitwy Legnickiej, Legnickie Pole 31755
Muzeum Blansko, Blansko 08251
Muzeum Bolesława Prusa, Bolesława 31505
Muzeum Bolesława Prusa, Nałęczów 31820
Muzeum Borów Tucholskich, Tuchola 32059
Muzeum Boskovicka, Boskovice 08253
Muzeum Boženy Němcové, Česká Skalice 08295
Muzeum Bratří Čapků, Malé Svatoňovice 08470
Muzeum Broni Pancernej, Poznań 31901
Muzeum Bučovice, Bučovice 08283
Muzeum Budownictwa Ludowego, Sanok 31966
Muzeum Budownictwa i Techniki Wiejskiej, Bogdaniec 31504
Muzeum Budownictwa Ludowego - Park Etnograficzny w Olsztynku, Olsztynek 31853
Muzeum Byłego Obozu Zagłady w Chełmnie nad Narem, Chełmno 31524
Muzeum Byłego Obozu Zagłady w Sobiborze, Sobibór 31982
Muzeum Cechu Rzemiosł Skórzanych im. Jana Kilińskiego, Warszawa 32092
Muzeum Ceramiki, Bolesławiec 31507
Muzeum Ceramiki Kaszubskiej Neclów, Chmielno 31526
Múzeum Červený Kameň, Častá 33985
Múzeum Červený Kláštor, Červený Kláštor 33986
Muzeum České Hudby, Praha 08595
Muzeum Českého granátu, Třebenice 08685
Muzeum Českého Krasu v Berouně, Beroun 08247
Muzeum Českého Krasu v Berouně - pobačka muzeum v Žebráku, Žebrák 08745
Muzeum Českého Porcelánu, Klášterec nad Ohří 08411
Muzeum Českého Ráje, Turnov 08694
Muzeum Chodska, Domažlice 08332
Muzeum Cystersów, Wąchock 32066
Muzeum Częstochowskie, Częstochowa 31545
Muzeum Czynu Niepodległościowego, Kraków 31697
Muzeum Czynu Partyzanckiego, Polichno 31893
Muzeum Czynu Powstańczego, Leśnica 31756
Muzeum Czynu Zbrojnego Pracowników Huty im. Tadeusza Sendzimira, Kraków 31698
Muzeum Dawnego Kupiectwa, Świdnica 32014
Muzeum Diecezjalne, Płock 31886
Muzeum Diecezjalne, Siedlce 31969
Muzeum Diecezjalne, Tarnów 32041
Muzeum Diecezjalne Sztuki Kościelnej, Sandomierz 31962
Muzeum Diecezjalne Sztuki Religijnej, Lublin 31788
Muzeum Diecezjalne w Opolu, Opole 31858
Muzeum Diecezji Pelpińskiej, Pelplin 31877
Muzeum Dom Urbańczyka, Chrzanów 31535
Muzeum Dom Wincentego Witosa, Wierzchosławice 32155
Muzeum Dr. Aleše Hrdličky, Humpolec 08374
Muzeum Dr. Bohuslava Horáka, Dobřiv 08328
Muzeum Dr. Bohuslava Horáka, Rokycany 08636
Muzeum Drukarstwa Warszawskiego, Warszawa 32093
Muzeum-Dworek Wincentego Pola, Lublin 31789
Muzeum Dworek Zabytkowy, Stryszów 32002
Muzeum Dworu Polskiego, Plochocin 31885
Muzeum Dzieje i Kultura Żydów, Kraków 31699
Muzeum Emeryka Hutten-Czapskiego, Kraków 31700
Muzeum Emila Zegadłowicza, Wadowice 32068
Muzeum Energetyki Jeleniogórskiej, Szklarska Poręba 32033
Muzeum Etnograficzne, Poznań 31902
Muzeum Etnograficzne, Toruń 32052
Muzeum Etnograficzne, Włocławek 32161
Muzeum Etnograficzne, Wrocław 32176
Muzeum Etnograficzne im. Franciszka Kotuli, Rzeszów 31959
Muzeum Etnograficzne im. Seweryna Udzieli, Kraków 31701
Muzeum Etnograficzne w Oliwie, Gdańsk 31570
Muzeum Etnograficzne w Zielonej Górze z Siedzibą w Ochli, Ochla 31842
Muzeum Etnograficzny, Tarnów 32042
Muzeum Ewolucji Instytutu Paleobiologii PAN, Warszawa 32094
Muzeum Farmacji, Kraków 31702
Muzeum Farmacji, Warszawa 32095
Muzeum Feliksa Nowowiejskiego, Barczewo 31476
Múzeum Ferdiša Kostku, Stupava 34067
Muzeum Filumenistyczne, Bystrzyca Kłodzka 31518
Muzeum Fojtství, Kopřivnice 08420
Muzeum-Fort VII, Oddział Muzeum Historii Ruchu Robotniczego w Poznaniu, Poznań 31903
Muzeum - Františkánský klaster, Kadaň 08397
Muzeum Fryderyka Chopina, Warszawa 32096
Muzeum Fryderyka Chopina w Żelazowej Woli, Sochaczew 31985
Muzeum G. Casanovy, Duchcov 08334
Muzeum Gazownictwa, Paczków 31874
Muzeum Gazownictwa, Sobótka 31983
Muzeum Gazownictwa przy Gazowni Warszawskiej, Warszawa 32097
Muzeum Geologiczne, Kraków 31703
Muzeum Geologiczne, Kraków 31704
Muzeum Geologiczne, Wrocław 32177
Muzeum Geologiczne Obszaru Górnośląskiego Instytutu Geologicznego, Sosnowiec 31990
Muzeum Geologiczne Państwowego Instytutu Geologicznego, Warszawa 32098
Muzeum Geologiczne Uniwersytetu Szczecińskiego, Szczecin 32025
Muzeum Geologii Złóż im. Czesława Poborskiego, Gliwice 31592
Muzeum Górnictwa i Hutnictwa Kopalina Złota, Złoty Stok 32223
Muzeum Górnictwa i Hutnictwa Rud Żelaza, Częstochowa 31546
Muzeum Górnictwa Podziemnego, Nowa Ruda 31826
Muzeum Górnictwa Węglowego, Zabrze 32199
Muzeum Górnicze, Bogatynia 31503
Muzeum Górnośląskie, Bytom 31519
Muzeum Gross-Rosen, Wałbrzych 32071
Muzeum Henryka Sienkiewicza, Wola Okrzejska 32168
Muzeum Henryka Sienkiewicza w Oblęgorku, Oblęgorek 31841
Muzeum Historických Motocyklů, Kašperské Hory 08406
Muzeum Historii Fotografii, Kraków 31705
Muzeum Historii Fotografii im. Prof. Władisława Bogackiego, Kraków 31706
Muzeum Historii Katowic, Katowice 31646
Muzeum Historii Medycyny i Farmacji, Szczecin 32026
Muzeum Historii Miasta, Szczecin 32027
Muzeum Historii Miasta, Zduńska Wola 32216
Muzeum Historii Miasta Łodzi, Łódź 31770
Muzeum Historii Miasta Lublina, Lublin 31790
Muzeum Historii Miasta Poznania, Poznań 31904
Muzeum Historii Młynarstwa i Wodnych Urządzeń Przemysłu Wiejskiego w Jaraczu, Jaracz 31620

Muzeum Historii Polskiego Rucha Ludowego, Piaseczno koło Gniewa 31878
Muzeum Historii Polskiego Ruchu Ludowego, Warszawa 32099
Muzeum Historii Polskiego Ruchu Ludowego w Warszawie, Oddział w Sandomierzu, Sandomierz 31963
Muzeum Historii Przemysłu, Opatówek 31854
Muzeum Historii Włocławka, Włocławek 32162
Muzeum Historii Żdów Polskich, Warszawa 32100
Muzeum Historyczne, Białystok 31486
Muzeum Historyczne, Przasnysz 31919
Muzeum Historyczne Miasta Gdańska, Gdańsk 31571
Muzeum Historyczne Miasta Krakowa, Kraków 31707
Muzeum Historyczne Miasta Krakowa - Oddział Pomorska, Kraków 31708
Muzeum Historyczne Miasta Starego Warszawy, Warszawa 32101
Muzeum Historyczne Miasta Tarnobrzega, Tarnobrzeg 32039
Muzeum Historyczne - Pałac w Dukli, Dukla 31558
Muzeum Historyczne w Sanoku, Sanok 31967
Muzeum Historyczne w Wrocławiu, Wrocław 32178
Muzeum Historycznego Miasta Krakowa, Kraków 31690
Muzeum Historyczno-Archeologiczne, Ostrowiec Świętokrzyski 31866
Muzeum Historyczno-Etnograficzne, Chojnice 31528
Muzeum Hlavního Města Prahy, Praha 08596
Muzeum Hodin, Šternberk 08662
Muzeum Hrnčířství a Keramiky, Kostelec nad Černými lesy 08423
Muzeum Husitství, Žlutice 08754
Muzeum Hymnu Narodowego, Nowy Karczma 31833
Muzeum i Instytut Zoologi PAN, Warszawa 32102
Muzeum Ignacego Jana Paderewskiego i Wychodźstwa Polskiego w Ameryce, Warszawa 32103
Muzeum im. Adama Mickiewicza w Śmiełowie, Żerków 32217
Muzeum im. Aleksandra Świętochowskiego, Gołotczyzna 31601
Muzeum im. Anny i Jarosława Iwaszkiewiczów w Stawisku, Podkowa Leśna 31890
Muzeum im. Edmunda Bojanowskiego w Grabonogu, Grabonóg 31608
Muzeum im. Jana Dzierzona, Kluczbork 31665
Muzeum im. Jana Kasprowicza, Inowrocław 31617
Muzeum im. Jana Nikodema Jaronia, Olesno 31847
Muzeum im. Jerzego Dunin-Borkowskiego, Krośniewice 31734
Muzeum im. J.G. Herdera w Morągu, Morąg 31811
Muzeum im. Kazimierza Pułaskiego, Warka-Winiary 32075
Muzeum im. Michąla Kajki w Ogródku, Ogródek 31844
Muzeum im. Nałkowskich, Wołomin 32170
Muzeum im. Orła Białego, Skarżysko-Kamienna 31976
Muzeum im. Oskara Kolberga, Przysucha 31924
Muzeum im. prof. Władysława Szafera, Ojców 31845
Muzeum im. Stanisława Noakowskiego, Nieszawa 31825
Muzeum im. Stanisława Staszica, Hrubieszów 31615
Muzeum im. Wiktora Stachowiaka, Trzcianka 32057
Muzeum im. Władysława Orkana, Rabka 31936
Muzeum im. Władysława St. Reymonta, Lipce Reymonotowskie 31763
Muzeum im. Wojciecha Kętrzyńskiego, Kętrzyn 31655
Muzeum Instrumentów Muzycznych, Poznań 31905
Muzeum Inżynierii Miejskiej, Kraków 31709
Muzeum Jáchymovského Hornictví a Lázeňství, Jáchymov 08382
Muzeum Jana Ámoše Komenského, Uherský Brod 08699
Muzeum Jana Cybisa, Głogówek 31595
Muzeum Jana Kasprowicza, Zakopane 32206
Múzeum Janka Krála, Liptovský Mikuláš 34015
Muzeum Jihovýchodní Moravy, Zlín 08751
Muzeum Jindřicha Jindřicha, Domažlice 08333
Muzeum Jindřicha Simona Baara, Klenčí pod Čerchovem 08413
Muzeum Jindřicho Hradecka, Jindřichův Hradec 08394
Muzeum Josefa Dobrovského a pamětní síň Jaroslava Kvapila, Chudenice 08322
Muzeum Józefa Ignacego Kraszewskiego, Romanów 31952
Muzeum Juliana Fałata, Oddział Muzeum Okręgowego w Bielsku-Białej, Bystra 31517
Muzeum Kamieni Szlachetnych, Polanica Zdrój 31892
Muzeum Kamienica Łozińskich, Kraków 31710
Muzeum Kamienica Orsettich w Jarosławiu, Jarosław 31622
Muzeum Karkonoskie, Jelenia Góra 31630
Muzeum Karola Szymanowskiego, Zakopane 32207
Muzeum Karykatury, Warszawa 32104
Muzeum-Kaszubski Park Etnograficzny w Wdzydzach Kiszewskich, Wdzydze Kiszewskie 32147
Muzeum Kaszubskie, Kartuzy 31643
Muzeum Kaszubskie, Kościerzyna 31675
Muzeum Katedralne Jana Pawła II, Kraków 31711
Muzeum Katolickiego Uniwersytetu Lubelskiego im. Ks. Władzińskiego, Lublin 31791
Muzeum Katyńskie, Warszawa 32105
Muzeum Keramiky, Bechyně 08243
Muzeum Kinematografii, Łódź 31771
Muzeum Klasztorne OO Cystersów, Szczyrzyc 32031
Muzeum Klimkovice, Klimkovice 08414
Muzeum Knihy, Žďár nad Sázavou 08743
Muzeum Kolei Wąskotorowej, Sochaczew 31986
Muzeum Kolei Wąskotorowej w Wenecji, Wenecja 32150
Muzeum Kolejnictwa, Warszawa 32106
Muzeum Kolekcji im. Jana Pawła II, Warszawa 32107
Muzeum Komenského v Přerově, Přerov 08622
Muzeum Kornela Makuszyńskiego, Zakopane 32208
Muzeum Kościuszkowskie Dworek Zacisze, Miechów 31800
Muzeum Kouřimska, Kouřim 08424
Muzeum Kowalstwa w Warszawie, Warszawa 32108
Muzeum Krajky, Prachatice 08561
Muzeum Krajky, Vamberk 08708
Muzeum Kralupy, Kralupy nad Vltavou 08430
Muzeum Krnov, Krnov 08434
Múzeum Krompachy, Krompachy 34008
Muzeum Krupka, Krupka 08436
Muzeum Książąt Czartoryskich, Kraków 31712
Muzeum Książki Artystycznej, Łódź 31772
Múzeum Kultúry Karpatských Nemcov, Bratislava 33971
Muzeum Kultury Łemkowskiej w Zyndranowej, Tylawa 32062
Muzeum Kultury Ludowej, Kolbuszowa 31667
Muzeum Kultury Ludowej, Osiek nad Notecią 31863
Muzeum Kultury Ludowej, Węgorzewo 32148
Múzeum Kultúry Maďarov na Slovensku, Bratislava 33972
Muzeum Kultury Szlacheckiej, Łopuszna 31781
Muzeum Lachów Sądeckich im. Zofii i Stanisława Chrząstowskich, Podegrodzie 31889
Muzeum Lasu i Drewna przy Lesnym Zakładzie Doświadczalnym SGGW, Rogów 31949
Muzeum Lat Szkolnych Stefana Żeromskiego, Kielce 31657
Muzeum Latarnia Morska, Władysławowo 32159
Muzeum Łazienki Krolewskie, Warszawa 32109
Muzeum Lidových Staveb, Kouřim 08425
Muzeum Literackie Henryka Sienkiewicza, Poznań 31906
Muzeum Literackie im. Józefa Czechowicza, Lublin 31792
Muzeum Literatury im. Adama Mickiewicza, Warszawa 32110
Muzeum Literatury im. Jarosława Iwaszkiewicza, Sandomierz 31964
Muzeum Litovel, Litovel 08459
Muzeum Lotnictwa Polskiego, Kraków 31713
Muzeum Loutkářských Kultur, Chrudim 08320
Muzeum Łowiectwa i Jeździectwa, Warszawa 32111
Muzeum Lubelskie, Lublin 31793
Múzeum Ľudovíta Štúra, Modra 34030
Muzeum Ludowych Instrumentów Muzycznych, Szydłowiec 32038
Múzeum Madarskej Kultúry a Podunajska, Komárno 34003
Muzeum Małego Miasta, Bieżuń 31496
Muzeum Marie Gardavské, Kojetín 08416
Muzeum Marii Dąbrowskiej, Warszawa 32112
Muzeum Marii Konopnickiej, Suwałki 32009
Muzeum Marii Konopnickiej w Żarnowcu, Jedlicze 31627
Muzeum Marii Skłodowskiej-Curie, Warszawa 32113
Muzeum Martyrologiczne w Żabikowie, Luboń 31797
Muzeum Martyrologii, Bielsk Podlaski 31491
Muzeum Martyrologii Alianckich Jeńców Wojennych, Żagań 32202
Muzeum Martyrologii i Walki Radogoszcz, Łódź 31773
Muzeum Martyrologii Pod Zegarem, Lublin 31794
Muzeum Martyrologii (Sonnenburg), Słońsk 31978
Muzeum Martyrologii Wielkopolan w Forcie VII, Poznań 31907
Muzeum Marynarki Wojennej, Gdynia 31585
Muzeum Mazowieckie w Płocku, Płock 31887
Muzeum Mazowsza Zachodniego, Żyradów 32226
Muzeum Mazurskie, Szczytno 32032
Muzeum Města Brna, Brno 08273
Muzeum Města Ústí nad Labem, Ústí nad Labem 08703
Muzeum Miar - Zbiory Metrologiczne Glównego Urzędu Miar, Warszawa 32114
Muzeum Miasta Gdyni, Gdynia 31586
Muzeum Miasta i Rzeki Warty, Warta 32145
Muzeum Miasta Jaworzna, Jaworzno 31626
Muzeum Miasta Kołobrzegu, Kołobrzeg 31669
Muzeum Miasta Ostrowa Wielkopolskiego, Ostrów Wielkopolski 31865
Muzeum Miasta Pabianice, Pabianice 31873
Muzeum Miasta Zgierza, Zgierz 32218
Múzeum Michala Greisigera, Spišská Béla 34061
Muzeum Miedzi, Legnica 31754
Muzeum Miejskie, Nowa Sól 31829
Muzeum Miejskie, Świętochłowice 32016
Muzeum Miejskie, Wyszków 32197
Muzeum Miejskie, Zabrze 32200
Muzeum Miejskie im. Maksymiliana Chroboka, Ruda Śląska 31953
Muzeum Mikołaja Kopernika, Frombork 31561
Muzeum Mikołaja Kopernika, Toruń 32053
Muzeum Militariów Arsenał Miejski, Wrocław 32179
Muzeum Mineralogiczne, Szklarska Poręba 32034
Muzeum Mineralogiczne, Wrocław 32180
Muzeum Mineralogicznego Uniwersytetu Wrocławskiego, Wrocław 32181
Muzeum Misyjne, Czerna 31542
Muzeum Misyjne, Krosno 31735
Muzeum Misyjne Misjonarzy Oblatów MN, Święty Krzyż 32017
Muzeum Misyjno-Etnograficzne, Pieniężno 31879
Muzeum Mladaboleslavska, Mladá Boleslav 08480
Muzeum Młynarstwa Powietrznego, Bęsia 31482
Muzeum Mohelnice, Mohelnice 08484
Muzeum Morskie, Szczecin 32028
Muzeum Motocyklů, Lesná u Znojma 08446
Muzeum Motoryzacji, Otrębusy 31870
Muzeum Motoryzacji Automobilklubu Wielkopolski, Poznań 31908
Muzeum Nadwiślański Park Etnograficzny, Babice 31474
Muzeum Nadwiślańskie, Kazimierz Dolny 31649
Muzeum Narodowe, Gdańsk 31572
Muzeum Narodowe, Szczecin 32029
Muzeum Narodowe, Biblioteka Czartoryskich, Kraków 31714
Muzeum Narodowe Rolnictwa i Przemysłu Rolno-Spożywczego, Uzarzewo 32064
Muzeum Narodowe Rolnictwa i Przemysłu Rolno-Spożywczego w Szreniawie, Komorniki 31671
Muzeum Narodowe w Kielcach, Kielce 31658
Muzeum Narodowe w Krakowie, Kraków 31715
Muzeum Narodowe w Poznaniu, Poznań 31909
Muzeum Narodowe w Poznaniu, Oddział w Rogalinie, Rogalin 31947
Muzeum Narodowe w Warszawie, Warszawa 32115
Muzeum Narodowe we Wrocławiu, Wrocław 32182
Muzeum Narodowe Ziemi Przemyskiej, Przemyśl 31921
Muzeum Niepodległości, Warszawa 32116
Muzeum Nikifora, Krynica 31740
Muzeum Oceanograficzne Mir, Gdynia 31587
Muzeum Oddział im. Albina Makowskiego, Chojnice 31529
Muzeum Odona Bujwida, Kraków 31716
Muzeum of A. Dvořák, Zlonice 08753
Muzeum of Sport Education and Sport, Praha 08597
Muzeum Okręgowe, Bielsko-Biała 31494
Muzeum Okręgowe, Ciechanów 31537
Muzeum Okręgowe, Konin 31672
Muzeum Okręgowe, Krosno 31736
Muzeum Okręgowe, Nowy Sącz 31835
Muzeum Okręgowe, Ostrołęka 31864
Muzeum Okręgowe, Piotrków Trybunalski 31883
Muzeum Okręgowe, Rzeszów 31960
Muzeum Okręgowe, Sandomierz 31965
Muzeum Okręgowe, Sieradz 31973
Muzeum Okręgowe, Suwałki 32010
Muzeum Okręgowe, Tarnów 32043
Muzeum Okręgowe, Zaborów 32198
Muzeum Okręgowe, Zamość 32212
Muzeum Okregowe, Żyradów 32227
Muzeum Okręgowe im. Leona Wyczółkowskiego, Bydgoszcz 31514
Muzeum Okręgowe w Chełmie, Chełm 31523
Muzeum Okręgowe w Lesznie, Leszno 31757
Muzeum Okręgowe w Toruniu, Toruń 32054
Muzeum Okręgowe Zabytków Techniki, Tarnów 32044
Muzeum Okręgowe Ziemi Kaliskiej, Kalisz 31635
Muzeum Okręt Błyskawica, Gdynia 31588
Muzeum Olomučanské Keramiky, Olomučany 08517
Muzeum Oręża Polskiego, Kołobrzeg 31670
Muzeum Orlických Hor, Rychnov nad Kněžnou 08647
Muzeum Oświatowe, Puławy 31931
Muzeum Oświaty w Bydgoszczy, Bydgoszcz 31515
Muzeum Pałac w Wilanowie, Warszawa 32117
Muzeum Pamiątek po Janie Matejce "Koryznówka", Nowy Wiśnicz 31839
Muzeum Pamięci Narodowej, Kraków 31717
Muzeum Pamięci Narodowej lata 1939 -1956, Kielce 31659
Muzeum Papiernictwa, Duszniki Zdrój 31559
Muzeum Parafialne, Bobowa 31500
Muzeum Parafialne, Dobra 31554
Muzeum Parafialne, Grybów 31613
Muzeum Parafialne, Iwkowa 31619
Muzeum Parafialne, Krynica 31741
Muzeum Parafialne, Pakość 31875
Muzeum Parafialne, Rzepiennik Strzyżewski 31958
Muzeum Parafialne, Tropie 32056
Muzeum Parafialne, Widawa 32151
Muzeum Parafialne, Złota 32221
Muzeum Parafialne im. Jana Wnęka w Odporyszowie, Odporyszów 31843
Muzeum Parafialne im. Ks. Edwarda Nitki, Paszyn 31876
Muzeum Pedagogiczne, Gdańsk 31573
Muzeum Piastów Śląskich, Brzeg 31511
Muzeum Pienińskie im. Józefa Szalaya, Szczawnica 32022
Muzeum Pierwszych Piastów na Lednicy, Lednogóra 31752
Muzeum Piśmiennictwa i Muzyki Kaszubsko-Pomorskiej, Wejherowo 32149
Muzeum Plakatu w Wilanowie, Warszawa 32118
Muzeum Początków Państwa Polskiego, Gniezno 31600
Muzeum Poczty i Telekomunikacji, Wrocław 32183
Muzeum Poczty i Telekomunikacji Oddział w Gdańsku, Gdańsk 31574
Muzeum Podhalańskie PTTK, Nowy Targ 31837
Muzeum Podkrkonoší, Trutnov 08692
Muzeum Pojezierza Łęczyńsko-Włodawskiego, Włodawa 32166
Múzeum Polície Slovenskej Republiky, Bratislava 33973
Muzeum Politechniki Warszawskiej, Warszawa 32119
Muzeum Polná, Polná 08558
Muzeum Północno-Mazowiecke, Łomża 31780
Muzeum Polskiej Wojskowej Służby Zdrowia, Łódź 31774
Muzeum Południowego Podlasia, Biała Podlaska 31484
Muzeum Pomorza Środkowego, Słupsk 31980
Muzeum Porcelánu Pirkenhammer, Březová u Karlových Var 08261
Muzeum Powstania Chochołowskiego, Chochołów 31527
Muzeum Powstania Warszawskiego, Warszawa 32120
Muzeum Pożarnictwa, Alwernia 31471
Muzeum Pożarnictwa, Lidzbark 31760
Muzeum Pożarnictwa Ziemi Olkuskiej, Olkusz 31849
Muzeum Pożarnicze, Dział Muzeum w Przeworsku, Przeworsk 31922
Muzeum-Pracownia Literacka Arkadego Fiedlera, Puszczykowo 31934
Muzeum Prawa i Prawników Polskich, Katowice 31647
Muzeum Prof. Josepha Wittiga, Nowa Ruda 31827
Muzeum Prostějovska, Prostějov 08629
Muzeum Prowincji oo Bernardynów, Leżajsk 31759
Muzeum Prywatne Diabła Polskiego Przedpiekle, Warszawa 32121
Muzeum Przemysłu, Warszawa 32122
Muzeum Przemysłu i Techniki, Wałbrzych 32072
Muzeum Przemysłu Naftowego w Bóbrce, Chorkówka 31531
Muzeum przy Zakładach Metalowych im. Hipolita Cegielskiego, Poznań 31910
Muzeum Przyrodnicze, Jelenia Góra 31631
Muzeum Przyrodnicze, Kazimierz Dolny 31650
Muzeum Przyrodnicze, Władysławowo 32160
Muzeum Przyrodnicze Babiogórskiego Parku Narodowego, Zawoja 32214
Muzeum Przyrodnicze Bieszczadzkiego Parku Narodowego, Ustrzyki Dolne 32063
Muzeum Przyrodnicze Instytutu Systematyki i Ewolucji Zwierząt, Kraków 31718
Muzeum Przyrodnicze Karkonoskiego Parku Narodowego, Jelenia Góra 31632
Muzeum Przyrodnicze Uniwersytetu Łódzkiego, Łódź 31775
Muzeum Przyrodnicze Uniwersytetu Wrocławskiego, Wrocław 32184
Muzeum Przyrodnicze Wolińskiego Parku Narodowego im. Prof. Adama Wodziczki, Międzyzdroje 31804
Muzeum Przyrodniczo-Leśne, Białowieża 31485
Muzeum Przyrodniczo-Leśne Słowińskiego Parku Narodowego, Smołdzino 31981
Muzeum Przyrodniczo-Leśne Świętokrzyskiego Parku Narodowego, Święty Krzyż 32018
Muzeum Puszczy Kampinoskiej, Kampinos 31639
Muzeum Reformacji Polskiej, Mikołajki 31807
Muzeum Regionalne, Barlinek 31478
Muzeum Regionalne, Bełchatów 31481
Muzeum Regionalne, Biecz 31490
Muzeum Regionalne, Biłgoraj 31497
Muzeum Regionalne, Brodnica 31510
Muzeum Regionalne, Brzeziny 31512
Muzeum Regionalne, Cedynia 31521
Muzeum Regionalne, Chojnów 31530
Muzeum Regionalne, Człuchów 31549
Muzeum Regionalne, Głogówek 31596
Muzeum Regionalne, Iłża 31616
Muzeum Regionalne, Jarocin 31621
Muzeum Regionalne, Jasło 31623
Muzeum Regionalne, Jawor 31625
Muzeum Regionalne, Kościan 31674
Muzeum Regionalne, Kozienice 31680
Muzeum Regionalne, Kraśnik 31731
Muzeum Regionalne, Krasnystaw 31733
Muzeum Regionalne, Kutno 31745
Muzeum Regionalne, Łęczna 31750
Muzeum Regionalne, Lubań 31784
Muzeum Regionalne, Lubartów 31785
Muzeum Regionalne, Łuków 31798
Muzeum Regionalne, Miechów 31801
Muzeum Regionalne, Międzychód 31802
Muzeum Regionalne, Mielec 31806
Muzeum Regionalne, Myślibórz 31817
Muzeum Regionalne, Nowe Miasto nad Pilicą 31831
Muzeum Regionalne, Ojców 31846
Muzeum Regionalne, Opoczno 31856
Muzeum Regionalne, Ostrzeszów 31867
Muzeum Regionalne, Pińczów 31882
Muzeum Regionalne, Pszczew 31925
Muzeum Regionalne, Pułtusk 31933
Muzeum Regionalne, Pyzdry 31935
Muzeum Regionalne, Radomsko 31941
Muzeum Regionalne, Radzyn Chełmiński 31942
Muzeum Regionalne, Siedlce 31970
Muzeum Regionalne, Sławków 31977
Muzeum Regionalne, Słupca 31979
Muzeum Regionalne, Środa Śląska 31993
Muzeum Regionalne, Sucha Beskidzka 32004
Muzeum Regionalne, Szczecinek 32030
Muzeum Regionalne, Szydłów 32037
Muzeum Regionalne, Wągrowiec 32070
Muzeum Regionalne, Wiślica 32157
Muzeum Regionalne, Wronki 32194
Muzeum Regionalne Dom Grecki, Myślenice 31816
Muzeum Regionalne im. Adama Fastnachta, Brzozów 31513
Muzeum Regionalne im. Albina Nowickiego, Ryn 31956
Muzeum Regionalne im. Andrzeja Kaube, Wolin 32169

Muzeum Regionalne im. Antoniego Minkiewicza, Olkusz 31850
Muzeum Regionalne im. Dzieci Wrzesińskich, Września 32195
Muzeum Regionalne im. Janusza Petera, Tomaszów Lubelski 32047
Muzeum Regionalne im. Marcina Rożka, Wolsztyn 32171
Muzeum Regionalne im. Seweryna Udzieli, Stary Sącz 31999
Muzeum Regionalne im. Władysława Kowalskiego, Dobczyce 31553
Muzeum Regionalne im Wojciechy Dutkiewicz, Rogoźno 31951
Muzeum Regionalne Polskiego Towarzystwa Turystyczno-Krajoznawczego, Grodzisk Mazowiecki 31609
Muzeum Regionalne PTTK, Golub-Dobrzyń 31602
Muzeum Regionalne PTTK, Kępno 31653
Muzeum Regionalne PTTK, Muszyna 31815
Muzeum Regionalne PTTK, Puławy 31932
Muzeum Regionalne PTTK, Starachowice 31996
Muzeum Regionalne PTTK i Urzędu Gminy, Iwanowice 31618
Muzeum Regionalne PTTK im. Hieronima Ławinczaka, Krotoszyn 31738
Muzeum Regionalne PTTK im. J. Łukasiewicza, Gorlice 31605
Muzeum Regionalne PTTK w Zagórzu Śląskim Zamek Grodno, Zagórze Śląskie 32203
Muzeum Regionalne Siemiatycki Ośrodek Kultury, Siemiatycze 31972
Muzeum Regionalne w Stęszewie, Stęszew 32001
Muzeum Regionalne w Świebodzinie, Świebodzin 32015
Muzeum Regionalne w Zagórzu Śląskim, Zamek Grodno, Jugowice 31633
Muzeum Regionalne Ziemi Limanowskiej, Limanowa 31762
Muzeum Regionalne Ziemi Sadowieńskiej, Sadowne 31961
Muzeum Regionalne Ziemi Zbąszyńskiej PTTK, Zbąszyń 32215
Muzeum Regionu Valšsko ve Vsetině - Zámek Vsetín, Vsetín 08730
Muzeum Rekordů a Kuriozit, Pelhřimov 08536
Muzeum Rolnictwa im. Ks. Krzysztofa Kluka, Ciechanowiec 31538
Muzeum Romantyzmu, Opinogóra 31855
Muzeum Ruchu Rewolucyjnego, Oddział Muzeum Okręgowego w Białymstoku, Białystok 31487
Muzeum Rumburk, Rumburk 08646
Muzeum Rybackie, Jastarnia 31624
Muzeum Rybołówstwa, Hel 31614
Muzeum Rybołówstwa Morskiego, Świnoujście 32019
Muzeum Rzemiosł Artystycznych i Precyzyjnych, Warszawa 32123
Muzeum Rzemiosł Ludowych w Biłgoraju, Biłgoraj 31498
Muzeum Rzemiosła, Krosno 31737
Muzeum Rzemiosła Tkackiego, Turek 32060
Muzeum Rzeźby im. Xawerego Dunikowskiego Królikarnia, Warszawa 32124
Muzeum s Historickou Expozicí, Hostinné 08365
Múzeum Samuela Jurkovia Sobotište, Sobotište 34060
Muzeum Sejmu, Warszawa 32125
Muzeum Skansen, Pszczyna 31926
Muzeum Skansen Kolejnictwa, Kościerzyna 31676
Muzeum Skla, Harrachov v Krkonoších 08343
Muzeum Skla a Bižuterie, Jablonec nad Nisou 08378
Muzeum J.V. Sládka, Zbiroh 08741
Muzeum Śląska Cieszyńskiego w Cieszynie, Cieszyn 31540
Muzeum Śląska Opolskiego, Opole 31859
Muzeum Śląskie, Katowice 31648
Muzeum Ślężańskie im. Stanisława Dunajewskiego, Sobótka 31984
Múzeum Slovenského Národného Povstania, Banská Bystrica 33948
Múzeum Slovenských Národných Rád, Myjava 34032
Muzeum Sopotu, Sopot 31988
Múzeum Spiša, Spišská Nová Ves 34064
Muzeum Społeczne, Strzyżów 32003
Muzeum Sportu i Turystyki, Łódź 31776
Muzeum Sportu i Turystyki, Warszawa 32126
Muzeum Sportu i Turystyki Regionu Karkonoszy, Karpacz 31640
Muzeum Sportu i Turystyki Ziemi Gdańskiej, Gdańsk 31575
Muzeum Správy Krnap, Vrchlabí 08726
Muzeum Sprzętu Gospodarstwa Domowego, Ziębice 32219
Muzeum Śremskie, Śrem 31992
Muzeum Środowiska Przyrodniczego i Łowiectwa, Uzarzewo 32065
Muzeum Stanisława Staszica, Piła 31881
Muzeum Stanisława Wyspiańskiego, Kraków 31719
Muzeum Starożytnego Hutnictwa Mazowieckiego, Pruszków 31918
Muzeum Starożytnego Hutnictwa Świętokrzyskiego im. prof. M. Radwana, Nowa Słupia 31828
Muzeum Stefana Żeromskiego, Bolesława 31506
Muzeum Stefana Żeromskiego, Nałęczów 31821
Muzeum Středního Pootaví, Strakonice 08663
Muzeum Strojíren Poldi, Kladno 08409
Muzeum Šumavy, Kašperské Hory 08407
Muzeum Šumavy, Sušice 08669
Muzeum Svitidel a Chladičů, Nový Jičín 08510
Muzeum Sztuk Użytkowych, Poznań 31911
Muzeum Sztuki Cmentarnej, Wrocław 32185
Muzeum Sztuki Dziecka, Warszawa 32127
Muzeum Sztuki Książki, Wrocław 32186
Muzeum Sztuki Medalierskiej, Wrocław 32187
Muzeum Sztuki Mieszczańskiej, Wrocław 32188
Muzeum Sztuki Nowoczesnem, Niepołomice 31824
Muzeum Sztuki Sakralnej, Bardo 31477
Muzeum Sztuki w Łodzi, Łódź 31777
Muzeum Sztuki Współczesnej, Radom 31939
Muzeum Sztuki Współczesnej, Wrocław 32189
Muzeum Sztuki Złotniczej, Kazimierz Dolny 31651
Múzeum Tatranského Národného Parku, Tatranská Lomnica 34073
Muzeum Tatrzańskie im. Tytusa Chałubińskiego, Zakopane 32209
Muzeum Teatralne, Kraków 31720
Muzeum Teatralne, Warszawa 32128
Muzeum Technik Ceramicznych, Koło 31668
Muzeum Techniki w Warzawie, Warszawa 32129
Muzeum Techniki Włókienniczej, Bielsko-Biała 31495
Muzeum Telč, Telč 08676
Múzeum Telesnej Kultúry VSR, Bratislava 33974
Muzeum Tělovýchovy a Sportu, Praha 08597
Muzeum Těšínska, Český Těšín 08305
Muzeum Těšínska, Havířov 08345
Muzeum T.G. Masaryk's House, Čejkovice 08291
Muzeum Tkactwa Dolnośląskiego, Kamienna Góra 31637
Muzeum Tradycji i Perspektyw Huty im. B. Bieruta, Częstochowa 31547
Muzeum Tradycji Niepodległościowych, Łódź 31778
Muzeum Třešť', Třešť 08690
Muzeum Třineckých Železáren, Třinec 08691
Muzeum Twierdza Wisłoujście, Gdańsk 31576
Muzeum Týn nad Vltavou, Týn nad Vltavou 08696
Muzeum Tynecké Keramiky, Týnec nad Sázavou 08697
Muzeum Ubezpieczeń, Kraków 31721
Múzeum Ukrajinsko-Rusínskej Kultúry, Svidník 34071
Múzeum Umeleckých Remesiel, Bratislava 33975
Muzeum Umění, Benešov 08246
Muzeum Umění Olomouc, Olomouc 08515
Muzeum Uniwersytetu Jagiellońskiego - Collegium Maius, Kraków 31722
Muzeum Uniwersytetu Warszawskiego, Warszawa 32130
Muzeum Uniwersytetu Wrocławskiego, Wrocław 32190
Muzeum Úsov, Úsov 08702
Muzeum Uzbrojenia - Cytadela Poznańska, Poznań 31912
Muzeum v Bruntále, Bruntál 08282
Múzeum v Kežmarku, Kežmarok 34002
Muzeum ve Štramberku, Štramberk 08664
Muzeum Velké Meziříčí, Velké Meziříčí 08713
Múzeum vo Svätý Antone, Svätý Anton 34068
Muzeum Voskových Figurín České Historie, Praha 08598
Muzeum Voskových Figurín České Historie, Praha 08599
Muzeum Východních Čech v Hradci Králové, Hradec Králové 08368
Muzeum Vyškovska, Vyškov 08731
Muzeum Vysočiny Jihlava, Jihlava 08390
Muzeum w Bielsku Podlaskim, Bielsk Podlaski 31492
Muzeum w Biskupinie, Gąsawa 31597
Muzeum w Bochni im. Prof. Stanisława Fischera, Bochnia 31501
Muzeum w Chorzowie, Chorzów 31534
Muzeum w Chrzanowie, Chrzanów 31536
Muzeum w Darłowie, Darłowo 31550
Muzeum w Elblągu, Elbląg 31560
Muzeum w Gliwicach, Gliwice 31593
Muzeum w Gorzowie Wielkopolskim, Gorzów Wielkopolski 31606
Muzeum w Gostyniu, Gostyń 31607
Muzeum w Grudziądzu, Grudziądz 31611
Muzeum w Grudziądzul w Klasztorna, Grudziądz 31612
Muzeum w Kętach, Kęty 31656
Muzeum w Kwidzynie, Kwidzyn 31746
Muzeum w Lęborku, Lębork 31749
Muzeum w Łęczycy, Łęczyca 31751
Muzeum w Łowiczu, Łowicz 31782
Muzeum w Lubaczowie, Lubaczów 31783
Muzeum w Międzyrzeczu, Międzyrzecz 31803
Muzeum w Nysie, Nysa 31840
Muzeum w Oporowie, Oporów 31861
Muzeum w Przeworsku, Przeworsk 31923
Muzeum w Raciborzu, Racibórz 31937
Muzeum w Rybniku, Rybnik 31955
Muzeum w Sosnowcu, Sosnowiec 31991
Muzeum w Stargardzie, Stargard 31997
Muzeum w Szklarskiej Porębie Hoffmanna, Szklarska Poręba 32035
Muzeum w Tarnowskich Górach, Tarnowskie Góry 32045
Muzeum w Tomaszowie Mazowieckim, Tomaszów Mazowiecki 32048
Muzeum w Tykocinie, Tykocin 32061
Muzeum w Wałbrzychu, Wałbrzych 32073
Muzeum w Wodzisławiu Śląskim, Wodzisław Śląski 32167
Muzeum w Żywcu, Żywiec 32228
Muzeum Walewskich w Tubądzinie, Wróblew 32172
Muzeum Walk o Wał Pomorski przy Miejsko-Gminnym Ośrodku Kultury, Mirosławiec 31809
Muzeum Walki i Męczeństwa w Treblince, Kosów Lacki 31677
Muzeum Warmii i Mazur, Olsztyn 31852
Muzeum Warmińskie, Lidzbark Warmiński 31761
Muzeum Westerplatte Sucharskiego, Gdańsk 31577
Muzeum Weterynarii, Ciechanowiec 31539
Muzeum Wiedzy o Środowisku, Poznań 31913
Muzeum Więzienia Pawiak, Warszawa 32131
Muzeum Wikliniarstwa i Chmielarstwa, Nowy Tomyśl 31838
Muzeum Wikliny, Olkusz 31851
Muzeum Wisły, Tczew 32046
Muzeum Władysława Broniewskiego, Warszawa 32132
Muzeum Wnętrz Dworskich, Ożarów 31872
Muzeum Wnętrz Pałacowych w Choroszczy, Choroszcz 31532
Muzeum Wnętrz Zabytkowych, Dębno 31552
Muzeum Wojsk Inżynieryjnych, Wrocław 32191
Muzeum Wojska, Białystok 31488
Muzeum Wojska Polskiego, Warszawa 32133
Muzeum Wojska Polskiego Galeria Sztuki, Warszawa 32134
Muzeum Woli, Warszawa 32135
Muzeum Wsi Kieleckiej, Kielce 31660
Muzeum Wsi Lubelskiej, Lublin 31795
Muzeum Wsi Mazowieckiej, Sierpc 31975
Muzeum Wsi Opolskiej, Opole 31860
Muzeum Wsi Radomskiej, Radom 31940
Muzeum Wsi Słowińskiej w Klukach, Kluki 31666
Muzeum X Pawilonu Cytadeli Warszawskiej, Warszawa 32136
Muzeum Zabawek ze Zbiorow Henryka Tomaszewskiego, Karpacz 31641
Muzeum Zabawkarstwa, Kielce 31661
Muzeum Zachodnio-Kaszubskie, Bytów 31520
Muzeum Zagłębia, Będzin 31480
Muzeum Zagłębia Staropolskiego w Sielpi, Sielpia 31971
Muzeum Zakładowe im. St. Staszica Kieleckiej Fabryki Pomp "Białogon", Kielce 31662
Muzeum Zamek, Baranów Sandomierski 31475
Muzeum-Zamek Górków, Szamotuły 32020
Muzeum-Zamek w Bolkowie, Bolków 31509
Muzeum-Zamek w Gołuchowie, Gołuchów 31603
Muzeum Zamek w Łańcucie, Łańcut 31748
Muzeum Zamkowe, Pszczyna 31927
Muzeum Zamkowe w Malborku, Malbork 31799
Muzeum Zamku w Niedzicy, Niedzica 31823
Muzeum Zamoyskich w Kozłówce, Kamionka 31638
Muzeum Zbiorów Geologicznych, Kielce 31663
Muzeum-Zbiory Ludoznawcze im. Stefana i Tadeusza Szymańskich, Zakopane 32210
Muzeum Zbrojownia, Liw 31764
Múzeum Ždiarsky dom Ždiar, Ždiar 34078
Muzeum Zegarów Wieżowych, Gdańsk 31578
Múzeum Židovskej Kultúry, Bratislava 33976
Muzeum Ziemi Augustowskiej, Augustów 31473
Muzeum Ziemi Dobrzyńskiej, Rypin 31957
Muzeum Ziemi Kępińskiej, Kępno 31654
Muzeum Ziemi Kłodzkiej, Kłodzko 31664
Muzeum Ziemi Kociewskiej, Starogard Gdański 31998
Muzeum Ziemi Krajeńskiej, Nakło nad Notecią 31819
Muzeum Ziemi Krotoszyńskiej, Krotoszyn 31739
Muzeum Ziemi Krzeszowickiej, Krzeszowice 31743
Muzeum Ziemi Kujawskiej i Dobrzyńskiej, Włocławek 32163
Muzeum Ziemi Lubawskiej, Nowe Miasto Lubawskie 31830
Muzeum Ziemi Lubuskiej, Zielona Góra 32220
Muzeum Ziemi Mrągowskiej, Mrągowo 31813
Muzeum Ziemi Otwockiej, Otwock 31871
Muzeum Ziemi Pałuckiej, Żnin 32224
Muzeum Ziemi Piskiej, Oddział Muzem Okręgowego w Suwałkach, Pisz 31884
Muzeum Ziemi Polskiej Akademii Nauk, Warszawa 32137
Muzeum Ziemi Prudnickiej, Prudnik 31917
Muzeum Ziemi Puckiej, Puck 31929
Muzeum Ziemi Rawickiej, Rawicz 31945
Muzeum Ziemi Rawskiej, Rawa Mazowiecka 31944
Muzeum Ziemi Sochaczewskiej, Sochaczew 31987
Muzeum Ziemi Średzkiej Dwór w Koszutach, Koszuty 31679
Muzeum Ziemi Sulmierzyckiej im. S.F. Klonowica, Sulmierzyce 32006
Muzeum Ziemi Wałeckiej, Wałcz 32074
Muzeum Ziemi Wieluńskiej, Wieluń 32154
Muzeum Ziemi Wschowskiej, Wschowa 32196
Muzeum Ziemi Zaborskiej i Galeria Sztuki Ludowej, Wiele 32152
Muzeum Ziemi Zawkrzańskiej, Mława 31810
Muzeum Ziemi Złotowskiej, Złotów 32222
Muzeum Zoologiczne Instytutu Zoologii Uniwersytetu Jagiellońskiego, Kraków 31723
Muzeum Żup Krakowskich, Wieliczka 32153
Muzeum Żuraw, Gdańsk 31579
Muzeum Żydowskiego Instytutu Historycznego w Polsce, Warszawa 32138
Muziekinformatie- en documentatiecentrum Ton Stolk, Vlaardingen 29946
Muziekinstrumenten-Museum, Peer 03685
Muziekinstrumentenmakersmuseum, Tilburg 29878
Muzikologické Pracoviště, Opava 08519
Muzium Alor Gajah, Melaka 27668
Muzium Angkatan Tentera, Kuala Lumpur 27643
Muzium Arkeologi, Merbok 27677
Muzium Brunei, Bandar Seri Begawan 04598
Muzium dan Galeri Seni, Minden 27678
Muzium Darul Ridzwan, Ipoh 27622
Muzium Diraja Abu Bakar, Johor Bahru 27624
Muzium Jasin, Melaka 27669
Muzium Kecantikan, Melaka 27670
Muzium Layang Layang, Melaka 27671
Muzium Negara, Kuala Lumpur 27644
Muzium Negeri Kedah, Alor Setar 27618
Muzium Negeri Kelantan, Kota Bharu 27630
Muzium Negeri Perlis, Kangar 27625
Muzium Negeri Sarawak, Kuching 27658
Muzium Negeri Selangor, Shah Alam 27687
Muzium Negeri Sembilan, Seremban 27684
Muzium Negeri Trengganu, Kuala Terengganu 27656
Muzium Numismatik Maybank, Kuala Lumpur 27645
Muzium Perak, Taiping 27689
Muzium Polis Diraja Malaysia, Kuala Lumpur 27646
Muzium Rakyat, Melaka 27672
Muzium Sastera, Melaka 27673
Muzium Sejarah National, Kuala Lumpur 27647
Muzium Seni Asia, Kuala Lumpur 27648
Muzium Teknologi Melayu, Bandar Seri Begawan 04599
Muzium Tentera Laut Diraja Malaysia, Melaka 27674
Muzium Tuan Yang Terutama Melaka, Melaka 27675
Muzj Istorii Rossijskich Voennych Učilišč, Sankt-Peterburg 33472
Muzyka i Vremja - Častnyj Muzej Džona Mostoslavskogo, Jaroslavl 32855
M.V. Biškek Memorial Museum, Biškek 27308
M.V. Lomonosov Memorial Museum, Lomonosovo 32992
M.V. Lomonosov Museum, Sankt-Peterburg 33456
My Old Kentucky Home, Bardstown 41503
M.Y. Williams Planet Earth Museum, Vancouver 06684
Myers Museum, Eton 38952
Mykonos Folklore Museum, Mykonos 21078
Myllarheimen, Rauland 30787
Myllykolu, Birthplace of F.E. Sillanpää, Hämeenkyrö 09445
Myllykolu, F.E. Sillanpään Syntymäkoti, Hämeenkyrö 09445
Myllymuseo, Juuka 09590
Myllysaaren Museo, Valkeakoski 10172
Myntkabinett, Oslo 30745
Myntsafn Sedlabanka og Thjódminjasafns, Reykjavík 21657
Myôhôin Homotsukan, Kyoto 26437
Myohyang-san Museum, Hyangsan 27118
Myong Ji University Museum, Seoul 27262
Myra Powell Art Gallery and Gallery at the Station, Ogden 46099
Myrbergsgården, Vörå 10209
Myreton Motor Museum, Aberlady 37949
Myrskylän Kotiseutumuseo, Myrskylä 09851
Myrtleville House Museum, Brantford 05127
Mysore Silk Museum, Bangalore 21704
Mystic Art Association Museum, Mystic 45587
Mystic Seaport, Mystic 45588
Mzuzu Regional Museum, Mzuzu 27613
N. Hadjikyriakos-Ghikas Gallery, Athinai 20892
N. Ostrovskyj Memorial Museum of Literature, Soči 33540
N.A. Nekrasov Apartment Museum, Sankt-Peterburg 33417
N.A. Nekrasov House-Museum, Čudovo 32753
N.A. Nekrasov Memorial Museum Preserve of Literature, Karabicha 32883
N.A. Ostrovski Museum, Moskva 33106
N.A. Yaroshenko Memorial Estate Museum, Kislovodsk 32929
Naaimachine Museum, Dordrecht 29176
Naaimachinemuseum, Nieuweschans 29621
Naantali Museum, Naantali 09853
Naantalin Museo, Naantali 09853
NAB Gallery, Chicago 42350
Nábytek jako umění a řemeslo, Duchcov 08335
Nábytkové Múzeum, Markušovce 34021
Nachttopf-Museum, Kreuth 18236
Nacionalen Archeologičeski Rezervat Kabile, Jambol 04680
Nacionalen Čărkoven Istoriko-archeologičeski Muzej, Sofia 04844
Nacionalen Etnografski Muzej, Sofia 04845
Nacionalen Istoričeski Muzej, Sofia 04846
Nacionalen Istoriko-archeologičeski Rezervat i Muzej Veliki Preslav, Veliki Preslav 04908
Nacionalen Istoriko-archeologičeski Rezervat Pliska, Pliska 04774
Nacionalen Literaturen Muzej, Sofia 04847
Nacionalen Muzej Bojanska Crkva, Sofia 04848
Nacionalen Muzej Georgi Dimitrov, Sofia 04849
Nacionalen Muzej na Bălgarskata Architektura, Veliko Tărnovo 04918
Nacionalen Muzej na Fizičeskata Kultura i Sport, Sofia 04850
Nacionalen Muzej na Obrazovanieto, Gabrovo 04670
Nacionalen Muzej na Transporta i Săobščenijata, Ruse 04806
Nacionalen Muzej Parachod Radecki, Kozloduj 04722
Nacionalen Muzej Rilski Manastir, Rilski Manastir 04800
Nacionalen Muzej Roženski Manastir, Rožen 04801
Nacionalen Muzej Zemjata i Chorata, Sofia 04851
Nacionalen Park-muzej Samuilova krepost, Petrič 04702
Nacionalen Park-muzej Šipka-Buzludža, Kazanlăk 04702
Nacionalen Politechničeski Muzej, Sofia 04852
Nacionalen Prirodonaučen Muzej, Sofia 04853

Nacionalen Selskostopanski Muzej, Sofia 04854
Nacionalen Voenno-morski Muzej, Varna 04904
Nacionalen Voennoistoričeski Muzej, Sofia 04855
Nacionalna Chudožestvena Galerija, Sofia 04856
Nacionalna Galerija za Čuždestranno Izkustvo, Sofia 04857
Nacionalna Galerija za Dekorativni Izkustva, Sofia 04858
Nacionalna Izložba na Narodnite Chudožestveni Zanajati i Priložni Izkustva, Orešak 04747
Nacionalnaja Galereja Respubliki Komi, Syktyvkar 33578
Nacionalnij Muzej u Lvovi, Lviv 37887
Nacionalnyj Chudožestvennyj Muzej Respubliki Belarus, Minsk 03121
Nacionalnyj Chudožestvennyj Muzej Respubliki Sacha (Jakutija), Jakutsk 32845
Nacionalnyj Muzej Kabardino-Balkarskoj Respubliki, Nalčik 33197
Nacionalnyj Muzej Respubliki Baškortostan, Ufa 33647
Nacionalnyj Muzej Respubliki Komi, Syktyvkar 33579
Nacionalnyj Muzej Respubliki Marij Ėl im. T. Evseeva, Joškar-Ola 32861
Nacionalnyj Muzej Respubliki Tatarstan, Kazan 32907
Nacionalnyj Muzej Udmurtskoj Respubliki im. K. Gerda, Iževsk 32836
Nádasdi Ferenc Múzeum, Sárvár 21527
Nader Mausoleum, Mashad 22267
Nadlerhaus, Hundshübel 17867
Nähmaschinen-Museum, Steckborn 37210
Nähmaschinen-Museum Gebr. Mey, Albstadt 15421
Näkövammaismuseo, Jiris 09579
Närpes Hembygdsmuseum, Närpes 09855
Næs Jernverksmuseum, Tvedestrand 30952
Næstved Museum, Næstved 08987
Nafplion Folklore Museum, Nafplion 21092
Naftagas Collection, Novi Sad 33877
Nagano-ken Shinano Bijutsukan, Nagano 26529
Nagano Prefectural Shinano Art Museum, Nagano 26529
Nagaoka City Industrial Exhibition Hall, Nagaoka 26535
Nagaoka Cog Museum, Nagaoka 26532
Nagaoka Local History Museum, Nagaoka 26534
Nagaoka Municipal Science Museum, Nagaoka 26533
Nagaoka-shiritsu Hakabutsukan, Nagaoka 26534
Nagaoka-shiritsu Kogyo Hakurankai, Nagaoka 26535
Nagasaki Atomic Bomb Museum, Nagasaki 26551
Nagasaki City Museum of History and Folklore, Nagasaki 26552
Nagasaki-kenritsu Bijutsu Hakubutsukan, Nagasaki 26553
Nagasaki-kenritsu Hakubutsukan, Nagasaki 26554
Nagasaki Kite Museum, Nagasaki 26555
Nagasaki Municipal Museum, Nagasaki 26557
Nagasaki Municipal Museum of Woodblock Prints, Nagasaki 26559
Nagasaki Prefectural Art Museum, Nagasaki 26553
Nagasaki Prefectural Museum, Nagasaki 26554
Nagasaki Science Museum, Nagasaki 26556
Nagasaki-shiritsu Hakabutsukan, Nagasaki 26557
Nagasaki-shiritsu Nyokodo Nagai Kinenkan, Nagasaki 26558
Nagasaki-shiritsu Ukiyo-e Bijutsukan, Nagasaki 26559
Nagashima Museum, Kagoshima 26289
Nagatoro Kyukokan, Chichibu 26125
Nagelschmiede, Sulz, Aargau 37223
Nagi Museum, Cairo 09279
Nagoya-Boston Museum of Fine Arts, Nagoya, Aichi 26565
Nagoya Castle Treasure House, Nagoya, Aichi 26566
Nagoya City Art Museum, Nagoya, Aichi 26568
Nagoya City Hideyoshi and Kiyomasa Memorial Museum, Nagoya, Aichi 26567
Nagoya City Museum, Nagoya, Aichi 26569
Nagoya City Science Museum, Nagoya, Aichi 26570
Nagoya-shi Bijutsukan, Nagoya, Aichi 26568
Nagoya-shi Hakubutsukan, Nagoya, Aichi 26569
Nagoya-shi Kagakukan, Nagoya, Aichi 26570
Nagu hembyggdsmuseum/Nauvon Kotiseutumuseo, Nauvo 09859
Nagy István Képtár, Baja 21308
Nagytétényi Kastélymúzeum, Budapest 21366
Nahkl Fort Museum, Nahkl 31009
Nahsholim Museum, Hof Dor 22617
Nahum Gutman's Museum, Tel Aviv 22771
Naicam Museum, Naicam 05954
Nail Museum in Jokioinen, Jokioinen 09583
Nairn Fishertown Museum, Nairn 39996
Nairn Museum, Nairn 39997
Naismith Memorial Basketball Hall of Fame, Springfield 47748
Naito Kinen Kusuri Hakubutsukan, Kawashima, Gifu 26331
Naito Museum of Pharmaceutical Science and Industry, Kawashima, Gifu 26331
Nakagawa Photo Gallery, Kyoto 26438
Nakambale Museum, Ondangwa 28766
Nakamoura Kenichi Museum of Art, Koganei 26363
Nakamura Memorial Art Museum, Kanazawa 26310
Nakano Historical Museum, Tokyo 26896
Nakayama Archaeological Museum, Matsumoto 26478
Nakhon Si Thammarat National Museum, Nakhon Si Thammarat 37519
Nakkilan Kotiseutumuseo, Nakkila 09857
Nakusp Museum, Nakusp 05957
Nam Nao, Petchabun 37523
Namangan Regional Museum, Namangan 48844
Namık Kemal Zindanı ve Müzesi, Gazimağusa 08219
Namikawa Banri Bukkyo Bijutsu Shashin Gallery, Hiroshima 26221
Namjin Art Museum, Imhoe 27189
Namsaraev Museum of the Literature of Buryatya, Ulan-Udė 33654
Namsdalsmuseet, Namsos 30700
Namsskogan Bygdatun, Namsskogan 30702
Nan Bo's Southern Women Museum, Ho Chi Minh City 48988
Nan Yue Wang Palace Museum, Guangzhou 07071
Nanaimo Art Gallery and Exhibition Centre, Nanaimo 05960
Nanaimo District Museum, Nanaimo 05961
Nanban Bunkakan, Osaka 26657
Nance Museum, Lone Jack 44856
Nanchang City Museum, Nanchang 07173
Nancy Island Historic Site, Wasaga Beach 06745
Nandan Museum-Vichittra and Art Gallery, Santiniketan 22010
Nandewar Historical Museum, Barraba 00770
Nanhai Museum, Foshan 07050
Naniwa-no Umino Jikukan, Osaka 26658
Nanji Guan, Qingdao 07201
Nanjing Folklorish Museum, Nanjing 07182
Nanjing International Culture and Arts Exchange Center, Nanjing 07183
Nanjing Museum, Nanjing 07184
Nanjingdi Zhen Science Museum, Nanjing 07185
Nanjingdi Zhi Museum, Nanjing 07186
Nankai Broadcasting Sun Park Museum of Art, Matsuyama 26487
Nankang County Museum, Ganzhou 07058
Nanning City Museum, Nanning 07191
Nanortalik Local Museum, Nanortalik 21232
Nanortallip Katersugaasivia, Nanortalik 21232
Nansong Guanyao Museum, Hangzhou 07085
Nansong Qian Currency Museum, Hangzhou 07086
Nantgarw China Works Museum, Nantgarw 39998
Nanton Lancaster Air Museum, Nanton 05962
Nantong Museum, Nantong 07193
Nantucket Historical Association Museum, Nantucket 45598
Nantwich Museum, Nantwich 39999
Nanyang City Museum, Nanyang 07194
Nanyang Hanhua Guan, Nanyang 07194
Naomi Wood Collection at Woodford Mansion, Philadelphia 46433
Napa Valley Museum, Yountville 48809
Naper Settlement Museum, Naperville 45600
Naples Museum of Art, Naples 45602
Napoleon Museum, Salenstein 37092
Napoleon- und Heimatmuseum, Deutsch Wagram 01759
Napoleonic Society of America, Clearwater 42452
Napotnikova Galerija, Šoštanj 34153
Náprstek Museum of Asian, African and American Culture, Praha 08600
Náprstek Museum of Asian, African and American Cultures, Liběchov 08449
Náprstkovo Muzeum Asijských, Afrických a Amerických Kultur, Praha 08600
Nara City Museum of Photography, Nara 26579
Nara-kenritsu Bijutsukan, Nara 26580
Nara-kenritsu Kashihara Kokogaku Kenkyujo Fuzoku Hakubutsukan, Kashihara 26317
Nara-kenritsu Minzoku Hakubutsukan, Yamatokoriyama 27008
Nara Kokuritsu Hakubutsukan, Nara 26581
Nara National Museum, Nara 26581
Nara Prefectural Museum of Art, Nara 26580
Nara Prefectural Museum of Folk Culture, Yamatokoriyama 27008
Naracoorte Art Gallery, Naracoorte 01300
Naracoorte Museum, Naracoorte 01301
Naramata Museum, Naramata 05965
Narcissa Prentiss House, Prattsburgh 46687
Narembeen Historical Museum, Narembeen 01302
Naritasan History Museum, Narita 26587
Naroden Muzej, Ohrid 27587
Naroden Muzej, Veles 27599
Naroden Muzej Dr. Nikola Nezlobinski, Struga 27595
Narodna Galerija, Ljubljana 34114
Národní Dům na Smíchově, Praha 08601
Národní Kulturní Památník - Valy, Mikulčice 08475
Narodni Muzej, Bački Petrovac 33788
Narodni Muzej, Beograd 33814
Narodni Muzej, Kragujevac 33853
Narodni Muzej, Leskovac 33859
Narodni Muzej, Pančevo 33880
Narodni Muzej, Požarevac 33893
Narodni Muzej, Smederevska Palanka 33908
Narodni Muzej, Štip 27594
Narodni Muzej, Užice 33925
Narodni Muzej, Vranje 33927
Narodni Muzej, Zadar 07806
Narodni Muzej, Zaječar 33930
Narodni Muzej, Zrenjanin 33932
Narodni Muzej Čačak, Čačak 33827
Narodni Muzej Crne Gore, Cetinje 33833
Narodni Muzej Kikinda, Kikinda 33845
Narodni Muzej Kraljevo, Kraljevo 33855
Narodni Muzej Kruševac, Kruševac 33857
Narodni Muzej Labin, Labin 07734
Narodni Muzej Niš, Niš 33865
Narodni Muzej Sabac, Sabac 33902
Narodni Muzej Slovenije, Ljubljana 34115
Narodni Muzej Toplice, Prokuplje 33899
Narodni Muzej Valjevo, Valjevo 33926
Národní Muzeum, Praha 08602
Národní Technické Muzeum, Praha 08603
Národní Zemědělské Muzeum, Praha 08604
Národní Zemědělské Muzeum Praha, Kačina 08396
Národní Zemědělské Muzeum, Úsek Valtice, Valtice 08707
Narodnyj Geologičeskij Muzej Volgageologija, Nižnij Novgorod 33221
Narodnyj Istoriko-kraevedčeskij Muzej Tatarska, Tatarsk 33596
Národopisné Múzeum Liptova, Liptovský Hrádok 34013
Národopisné Muzeum Plzeňska, Plzeň 08543
Národopisné Muzeum Třebíz, Třebíz 08688
Národopisné Oddělení, Praha 08605
Narok Museum, Narok 27113
Narooma Lighthouse Museum, Narooma 01303
Narovčatskij Rajonnyj Kraevedčeskij Muzej, Narovčat 33201
Narrabri Old Gaol Heritage Centre, Narrabri 01304
Narragansett Historical Society Museum, Templeton 47978
Narrenschopf, Bad Dürrheim 15632
Narrogin Gallery, Narrogin 01307
Narrogin Old Courthouse Museum, Narrogin 01308
Narrow Gauge Railway Museum, Sochaczew 31986
Narrow Gauge Railway Museum, Tywyn 40742
Narryna Heritage Museum, Battery Point 00777
Narsaq Museum, Narsaq 21233
Narukawa Art Museum, Hakone 26177
Narukawa Bijutsukan, Hakone 26177
Narva Gunsmith's Shop, Naarva 09854
Narva Muuseum, Narva 09341
Narwhal Inuit Art Gallery, London 39727
NASA Lewis Research Center's Visitor Center, Cleveland 42476
Nash's House and New Place, Stratford-upon-Avon 40628
Nashua Center for Arts, Nashua 45608
Nasionale Afrikaanse Letterkundige Museum en Navorsingsentrum, Bloemfontein 34188
Nasiriya Museum, Nasiriya 22353
Nasjonalgalleriet, Oslo 30746
Nassau County Museum of Art, Roslyn 47009
Nassau Public Library and Museum, Nassau 03076
Nastolan Kotiseutumuseo, Nastola 09858
Nata-dera Homotsukan, Komatsu 26369
Nata-dera Treasure House, Komatsu 26369
Natal Museum, Pietermaritzburg 34327
Natale Labia Museum, Muizenberg 34312
Natalie and James Thompson Gallery, San Jose 47353
Natchez Trace Parkway Study Collection, Tupelo 48109
Nathan Denison House, Forty Fort 43493
Nathan Manilow Sculpture Park, University Park 48151
Nathaniel W. Faison Home and Museum, La Grange 44546
Nation Museum, Beijing 06979
Nationaal Ambulance- en Eerste Hulpmuseum, Winschoten 30009
Nationaal Archief, Den Haag 29117
Het Nationaal Autominiaturen Museum, Asperen 28947
Nationaal Baggermuseum, Sliedrecht 29829
Nationaal Beiaardmuseum, Asten 28954
Nationaal Bevrijdingsmuseum 1944-1945, Groesbeek 29305
Nationaal Borstelmuseum, Izegem 03522
Nationaal Brandweermuseum, Hellevoetsluis 29391
Nationaal Brilmuseum Amsterdam, Amsterdam 28884
Nationaal Coöperatie Museum, Schiedam 29803
Nationaal Fietsmuseum Velorama, Nijmegen 29634
Nationaal Glasmuseum, Leerdam 29506
Nationaal Historisch Orgelmuseum Elburg, Elburg 29224
Nationaal houtambachtenmuseum De Wimpe, Herenthout 03493
Nationaal Hunebedden Infocentrum, Borger 29004
Nationaal Jenevermuseum, Hasselt 03483
Nationaal Landschapskundig Museum, Dordrecht 29177
Nationaal Likeur- en Frisdrankenmuseum Isidorus Jonkers, Hilvarenbeek 29418
Nationaal Luchtvaart Museum Aviodome, Schiphol 29808
Nationaal Modelspoor Museum, Sneek 29839
Nationaal Monument Kamp Vught, Vught 29971
Nationaal Museum en Archief van Douane en Accijnzen, Antwerpen 03160
Nationaal Museum Historisch Landbouwtechniek, Wageningen 29976
Nationaal Museum van de Speelkaart, Turnhout 03803
Nationaal Museum van Speelklok tot Pierement, Utrecht 29904
Nationaal Museum Verpleging en Verzorging, Zetten 30054
Nationaal Natuurhistorisch Museum Naturalis, Leiden 29522
Nationaal Oorlogs- en Verzetsmuseum, Overloon 29707
Nationaal Reddingmuseum Dorus Rijkers, Den Helder 29136
Nationaal Rijtuigmuseum, Leek 29502
Nationaal Ruimtevaart Museum, Lelystad 29531
Nationaal Schaakmuseum, Den Haag 29118
Nationaal Scheephistorisch Centrum, Leylstad 29538
Nationaal Scheepvaartmuseum, Antwerpen 03161
Nationaal Schoeiselmuseum, Izegem 03523
Nationaal Schoolmuseum, Rotterdam 29765
Nationaal Scoutsmuseum, Leuven 03563
Nationaal Sleepvaartmuseum, Maassluis 29563
Nationaal Smalspoormuseum - Stoomtrein Valkenburgse Meer, Valkenburg, Zuid-Holland 29921
Nationaal Spaarpottenmuseum, Amsterdam 28885
Nationaal Tinnen Figuren Museum, Ommen 29661
Nationaal Vakbondsmuseum De Burcht, Amsterdam 28886
Nationaal Visserijmuseum van Oostduinkerke, Oostduinkerke 03666
Nationaal Vlas-, Kant- en Linnenmuseum, Kortrijk 03542
Nationaal Vlechtmuseum, Noordwolde 29647
Nationaal Volkssportmuseum voor de Vinkensport, Hulste 03510
Nationaal Wielermuseum, Roeselare 03703
National 1798 Visitor Centre, Enniscorthy 22468
National Academy of Design Museum, New York 45849
National Afro-American Museum and Cultural Center, Wilberforce 48618
The National Agricultural Center and Hall of Fame, Bonner Springs 41781
National Agricultural Museum, Sofia 04854
National Air and Space Museum, Washington 48371
National Aivazovsky Picture Gallery, Feodosija 37853
National Apple Museum, Biglerville 41687
National Archaeological Museum, Athinai 20873
National Archaeological Museum, Lisboa 32306
National Archaeological Museum, Napoli 24577
National Archaeological Reserve Cabyle, Jambol 04680
National Archives of Zambia, Lusaka 49021
National Army Museum, Camberley 38443
National Army Museum, London 39728
National Army Museum Sandhurst Departments, Sandhurst, Berkshire 40442
National Art Gallery, Colombo 35750
National Art Gallery, Dhaka 03092
National Art Gallery, Islamabad 31025
National Art Gallery, Kuala Lumpur 27639
National Art Gallery, Minsk 03122
National Art Gallery, Sofia 04856
National Art Gallery of Armenia, Erevan 00687
National Art Gallery of Namibia, Windhoek 28780
National Art Museum of Sport, Indianapolis 44232
National Art Museum of the Republic of Belarus, Minsk 03121
National Art Museum of Ukraine, Kyïv 37875
National Arts Club, New York 45850
National Arts Education Archive, Wakefield 40760
National Arts Museum, Teheran 22317
National Astra Museum, Sibiu 32591
National Atomic Museum, Albuquerque 41106
National Automobile Museum, Reno 46833
National Automobile Museum of Tasmania, Launceston 01169
National Automotive and Truck Museum of the United States, Auburn 41371
National Aviation Museum Avidome, Schiphol 29808
National Baseball Hall of Fame and Museum, Cooperstown 42620
National Bicycle Museum Velorama, Nijmegen 29634
National Border Patrol Museum and Memorial Library, El Paso 43122
National Building Museum, Washington 48372
National Canal Museum, Easton 43069
National Capital Trolley Museum, Silver Spring 47633
National Carriage Museum, Leek 29502
National Center for American Western Art, Kerrville 44457
National Center for the American Revolution, Valley Forge 48188
National Ceramics Museum, Safi 28709
National Children's Museum, Delhi 21773
National Children's Theatres Museum, Moskva 33059
National Civil Rights Museum, Memphis 45246
National Coal Mining Museum for England, Wakefield 40761
National Commission for Museums and Monuments, Abuja 49314
National Copper Museum, Salvador Escalante 28373
National Coracle Centre, Cenarth 38517
National Corvette Museum, Bowling Green 41850
National Costume Center of Finland, Jyväskylä 09600
National Council of Science Museums, Kolkata 49241
National Cowboy and Western Heritage Museum, Oklahoma City 46116
National Cowgirl Museum and Hall of Fame, Fort Worth 43491
National Cryptologic Museum, Fort Meade 43427
National Cultural History Museum, Pretoria 34350
National Customs Museum, Bordeaux 10818
National Cycle Collection, Llandrindod Wells 39538
National Czech and Slovak Museum, Cedar Rapids 42161
National D-Day Museum, New Orleans 45732
National Dairy Museum, Ashurst 38035
National Dinosaur Museum, Gungahlin 01080
National Doukhobour Heritage Village, Verigin 06705
National Dragonfly Biomuseum, Ashton, Oundle 38031

National Educational Museum and Library, Budapest 21374
National English Literary Museum, Grahamstown 34251
National Ethnographical Museum of the Bulgarian Academy of Sciences, Sofia 04845
National Exhibition of Folk Artistic Crafts and Applied Arts, Orešak 04747
National Exhibits by Blind Artists, Philadelphia 46434
National Fairground Museum, Northampton 40083
National Farm Toy Museum, Dyersville 43030
National Film Archive of Iceland Collection, Hafnarfjörður 21635
National Fine Arts Gallery, Santo Domingo 09118
National Fine Arts Museum, Rio de Janeiro 04389
National Fire Fighters' Museum, Bucureşti 32463
National Firearms Museum, Fairfax 43261
National Fishing Heritage Centre, Grimsby 39133
National Folk Museum, Seoul 27254
National Folk Museum, Seoul 27263
National Folk Museum of Lesbos, Mytilini 21086
National Football Museum, Canton 42091
National Football Museum, Preston 40268
National Fresh Water Fishing Hall of Fame, Hayward 43976
National Frontier Trails Center, Independence 44207
National Gallery, London 39729
National Gallery Bulawayo, Bulawayo 49027
National Gallery for Decorative Arts, Sofia 04858
National Gallery for Foreign Art, Sofia 04857
National Gallery in Prague, Praha 08615
National Gallery, National Museum of Art, Oslo 30746
National Gallery of Art, Washington 48373
National Gallery of Australia, Canberra 00886
National Gallery of Canada, Ottawa 06084
National Gallery of Corfu, Skripero 21161
National Gallery of Iceland, Reykjavík 21655
National Gallery of Ireland, Dublin 22446
National Gallery of Jamaica, Kingston 26075
National Gallery of Modern Art, Delhi 21774
National Gallery of Scotland, Edinburgh 38898
National Gallery of Slovenia, Ljubljana 34114
National Gallery of Victoria, Melbourne 01237
National Gallery of Zimbabwe, Harare 49032
National Gandhi Museum and Library, Delhi 21775
The National Gas Museum, Leicester 39466
National Geological Museum, Maputo 28726
National Glass Centre, Sunderland 40645
National Glass Museum, Leerdam 29506
National Hall of Fame for Famous American Indians, Anadarko 41192
National Handicraft Museum, Rawang 27683
National Hearing Aid Museum, London 39730
National Heisey Glass Museum, Newark 45896
National Heritage Museum, Lexington 44750
National Heritage: The Museums Action Movement, London 49434
National Historic Oregon Trail Interpretive Center, Baker City 41437
National Historical and Archeological Reserve Madara, Madara 04731
National Historical and Archeological Reserve Pliska, Pliska 04774
National Historical-Archaeological Reserve and Museum Veliki Preslav, Veliki Preslav 04908
National Historical Memory Park, Opusztaszer 21493
National Historical Museum, Athinai 20893
National Historical Museum, Montevideo 40986
National Historical Museum, Tiranë 00036
National History Museum, Campinas 04026
National History Museum, Kuala Lumpur 27647
National Horseracing Museum, Newmarket 40050
National Infantry Museum, Fort Benning 43366
National Institute of Art and Disabilities, Richmond 46858
National Institute of Industrial Safety Museum, Tokyo 26876
National Inventors Hall of Fame, Akron 41073
National Jesuit Museum Jesus Mary, Jesús María 00371
National Jewelry Treasury of Iran, Teheran 22307
National Liberty Museum, Philadelphia 46435
National Library, Valletta 27701
National Library, Warszawa 32077
National Literary and Memorial Museum-Complex of Sabit Mukanov and Gabit Musrepov, Almaty 27074
National McKinley Birthplace Memorial, Niles 45955
National Maritime Museum, Alexandria 09245
National Maritime Museum, Antwerpen 03161
National Maritime Museum, Galle 35755
National Maritime Museum, Haifa 22609
National Maritime Museum, London 39731
National Maritime Museum, Mokpo 27212
National Maritime Museum Cornwell, Falmouth 38973
National Maritime Museum of Ireland, Dun Laoghaire 22462
National memorial, Kielce 31659
National Military Museum, Bucureşti 32460
National Mining Museum, Kwekwe 49035
National Model Aviation Museum, Muncie 45558
National Monument, Jakarta 22108
National Motor Museum, Birdwood 00806
National Motor Museum, Brockenhurst 38371
National Motor Racing Museum, Bathurst 00776
National Motorcycle Museum, Bickenhill 38189
National Motorcycle Museum, Mitchell 01261
National Museum, Aden 49007
National Museum, Bački Petrovac 33788
National Museum, Bangkok 37491
National Museum, Beograd 33814
National Museum, Gdańsk 31572
National Museum, Kragujevac 33853
National Museum, Kuala Lumpur 27644
National Museum, Leskovac 33859
National Museum, Luang Prabang 27318
National Museum, Malé 27690
National Museum, Monrovia 27499
National Museum, Nagara Pathama 37515
National Museum, Oshogbo 30358
National Museum, Pančevo 33880
National Museum, Požarevac 33893
National Museum, Poznań 31909
National Museum, Praha 08602
National Museum, Riyadh 33773
National Museum, Sanaa 49011
National Museum, Sarajevo 03925
National Museum, Smederevska Palanka 33908
National Museum, Štip 27594
National Museum, Szczecin 32029
National Museum, Teheran 22311
National Museum, Teheran 22319
National Museum, Tórshavn 09407
National Museum, Užice 33925
National Museum, Valjevo 33926
National Museum, Veles 27599
National Museum, Victoria 33934
National Museum, Vranje 33927
National Museum, Zadar 07806
National Museum, Zrenjanin 33932
National Museum, Abuja, Abuja 30329
National Museum and Art Gallery of Trinidad and Tobago, Port-of-Spain 37552
National Museum and Gallery, Cardiff 38481
National Museum at Ruwi, Muscat 31005
National Museum Bauchi, Bauchi 30333
National Museum Benin, Benin City 30334
National Museum Bloemfontein, Bloemfontein 34189
National Museum Chiang Mai, Chiang Mai 37503
National Museum, Department of Entomology, Praha 08573
National Museum Directors' Conference, London 49435
National Museum Esie, Esie 30338
National Museum for Civilization, Cairo 09280
National Museum for Footwear, Izegem 03523
National Museum for Trading, Riyadh 33774
National Museum George Enescu, Bucureşti 32469
National Museum Ibadan, Ibadan 30340
National Museum Ile-Ife, Ife 30342
National Museum in Cracow, Kraków 31715
National Museum in Kielce, Kielce 31658
National Museum in Lviv, Lviv 37887
National Museum in Warsaw, Warszawa 32115
National Museum in Wroclaw, Wrocław 32182
National Museum Kaduna, Kaduna 30348
National Museum, Lagos, Onikan 30354
National Museum Makurdi, Makurdi 30351
National Museum Minna, Minna 30352
National Museum Nairobi, Nairobi 27112
National Museum of African Art, Washington 48374
National Museum of Agriculture, Praha 08604
National Museum of Agriculture, Valtice 08707
National Museum of Agriculture and Food Industry, Komorniki 31671
National Museum of American Art, Washington 48375
National Museum of American History, Washington 48376
National Museum of American Illustration, Newport 45928
National Museum of American Jewish History, Philadelphia 46436
National Museum of American Jewish Military History, Washington 48377
National Museum of Antiquities, Leiden 29524
National Museum of Archaeology, Tiranë 00037
National Museum of Archaeology, Valletta 27702
National Museum of Archeology and Ethnology, Guatemala 21271
National Museum of Art and History, Yangon 28751
National Museum of Art of Romania, Bucureşti 32466
National Museum of Art, Osaka, Suita 26773
National Museum of Australia, Canberra 00887
National Museum of Australian Pottery, Wodonga 01608
National Museum of Bashkortostan, Ufa 33647
National Museum of Bhutan, Paro 03891
National Museum of Brushware, Izegem 03522
National Museum of Bulgarian Architecture, Veliko Tărnovo 04918
National Museum of Cacak, Čačak 33827
National Museum of Calabar, Calabar 30335
National Museum of Catholic Art and History, New York 45851
National Museum of Ceramic Art and Glass, Baltimore 41484
National Museum of Ceramics, Leeuwarden 29514
National Museum of Cham Sculpture, Da Nang 48969
National Museum of Chinese History, Beijing 06980
National Museum of Civil War Medicine, Frederick 43529
National Museum of Colonial History, Aba 30326
The National Museum of Communications, Irving 44261
National Museum of Contemporary Art, Athinai 20894
National Museum of Contemporary Art, Gwacheon 27180
National Museum of Contemporary Art, Oslo 30744
National Museum of Contemporary History, Ljubljana 34113
National Museum of Damascus, Damascus 37436
National Museum of Dance, Saratoga Springs 47460
National Museum of Decorative Arts, Trondheim 30939
National Museum of Denmark, København 08943
National Museum of Ecclesiastical History and Archaeology, Sofia 04844
National Museum of Education, Gabrovo 04670
National Museum of Enugu, Enugu 30336
National Museum of Ethiopia, Addis Ababa 09400
National Museum of Ethnography and Natural History, Chişinău 28659
National Museum of Ethnology, Leiden 29525
National Museum of Ethnology, Minpaku, Suita 26774
National Museum of Fine Arts, La Habana 07987
National Museum of Fine Arts, Stockholm 36265
National Museum of Fine Arts, Valletta 27703
National Museum of Fine Arts of the Saha Republic (Yakutia), Jakutsk 32845
National Museum of Finland, Helsinki 09531
National Museum of Funeral History, Houston 44132
National Museum of Gardening, Helston 39215
National Museum of Health and Medicine, Washington 48378
National Museum of History, Sofia 04846
National Museum of History, Taipei 07350
National Museum of Iceland, Reykjanik 21647
National Museum of Ilorin, Ilorin 30344
National Museum of India, Delhi 21776
National Museum of Japanese History, Sakura 26706
National Museum of Kashan, Kashan 22250
National Museum of Korea, Seoul 27264
National Museum of Labour History, Manchester 39899
National Museum of Literature, Sofia 04847
National Museum of Lithuania, Vilnius 27537
National Museum of Man, Bhopal 21722
National Museum of Mandalay, Mandalay 28733
National Museum of Maritime History, Varna 04904
National Museum of Medieval Art, Korçë 00027
National Museum of Military History, Sofia 04855
National Museum of Modern Art, Guatemala 21272
National Museum of Modern Art Kyoto, Kyoto 26425
The National Museum of Modern Art, Tokyo, Tokyo 26938
National Museum of Modern Chinese Literature, Beijing 06981
National Museum of Mongolian History, Ulaanbaatar 28683
National Museum of Music, Beijing 06982
National Museum of Namibia, Windhoek 28781
National Museum of Natural Histories, Luanda 00100
National Museum of Natural History, Colombo 35751
National Museum of Natural History, Delhi 21777
National Museum of Natural History, La Habana 07988
National Museum of Natural History, Mdina 27698
National Museum of Natural History, Washington 48379
National Museum of Natural Sciences, Sofia 04853
National Museum of Naval Aviation, Pensacola 46343
National Museum of Nepal, Kathmandu 28788
National Museum of Pakistan, Karachi 31029
National Museum of Pasta Food, Roma 25235
National Museum of Photography, Film and Television, Bradford 38299
National Museum of Polo and Hall of Fame, Lake Worth 44599
National Museum of Port Harcourt, Port Harcourt 30361
National Museum of Racing and Hall of Fame, Saratoga Springs 47461
National Museum of Roller Skating, Lincoln 44788
National Museum of Science and Technology, Budapest 21373
National Museum of Science and Technology, Lahore 31040
National Museum of Science and Technology, Stockholm 36293
National Museum of Science, Planning and Technology, Haifa 22610
National Museum of Slovenia, Ljubljana 34115
National Museum of Sport, Sofia 04850
National Museum of the American Indian, New York 45852
National Museum of the American Indian, Washington 48380
National Museum of the History and Culture of Belarus, Minsk 03116
National Museum of the Imo State, Owerri 30359
National Museum of the Kabardino-Balkarian Republic, Nalčik 33197
National Museum of the Komi Republic, Syktyvkar 33579
National Museum of the Morgan Horse, Shelburne 47592
National Museum of the Ogun State, Abeokuta 30327
National Museum of the Ondo State, Akure 30330
National Museum of the Philippines, Manila 31390
National Museum of the Republic of Tajikistan, Dušanbe 37446
National Museum of the Republic Udmurtiya, Iževsk 32836
National Museum of the Romanian Literature, Bucureşti 32462
National Museum of the Tatarian Republic, Kazan 32907
National Museum of the Ust-Ordynsk Buryat Autonomous Region, Ust-Ordynsk 33672
National Museum of Transport and Communication, Ruse 04806
National Museum of Turkmenistan, Ašgabat 37812
National Museum of Vietnamese History, Ha Noi 48980
National Museum of Watercolours, México 28189
The National Museum of Western Art, Tokyo 26873
National Museum of Wildlife Art, Jackson 44290
National Museum of Women in the Arts, Washington 48381
National Museum of Woodcarving, Custer 42735
National Museum of Workers' Halls, Riihimäki 09997
National Museum of World Cultures, Göteborg 35922
National Museum Oron, Oron 30355
National Museum Uyo, Uyo 30364
National Museums and Galleries of Northern Ireland, Belfast 49436
National Museums and Monuments of Zimbabwe, Harare 49550
National Museums of Scotland, Edinburgh 38899
National Music Museum, Bloemfontein 34190
National New York Central Railroad Museum, Elkhart 43141
National Oil Museum, Ploieşti 32574
National Ornamental Metal Museum, Memphis 45247
National Packard Museum, Warren 48311
National Palace Museum, Taipei 07351
National Park-Museum Samuil-Castle, Petrič 04762
National Park Museum Shipka-Budloudzha, Kazanlăk 04702
National Philatelic Museum, Delhi 21778
National Picture Gallery and Alexander Soutzos Museum, Athinai 20860
National Pioneer Women's Hall of Fame, Alice Springs 00736
National Police Museum and Ancient Police Museum, Cairo 09281
National Polytechnical Museum, Sofia 04852
National Portrait Gallery, London 39732
National Portrait Gallery, Montacute 39979
National Portrait Gallery, Washington 48382
National Postal Museum, Washington 48383
National Preserve of Tauric Chersonesos, Sevastopol 37902
National Print Museum, Dublin 22447
National Rail Museum, Delhi 21779
National Railroad Museum, Green Bay 43791
National Railroad Museum and Hall of Fame, Hamlet 43885
National Railway Museum, Port Adelaide 01373
National Railway Museum, York 40966
National Railways of Zimbabwe Museum, Raylton 49039
National Revival and Constituent Assembly, Veliko Tărnovo 04917
National Road/Zane Grey Museum, Norwich 46040
National Route 66 Museum and Old Town Museum, Elk City 43135
National Science Centre, Delhi 21780
National Science Museum, Tokyo 26872
National Science Museum of Korea, Daejeon 27163
National Scout Museum of New Zealand, Kaiapoi 30188
National Scouting Museum, Irving 44262
National Soaring Museum, Elmira 43171
The National Soccer Hall of Fame, Oneonta 46159
National Society of the Children of the American Revolution Museum, Washington 48384
National Softball Hall of Fame and Museum Complex, Oklahoma City 46117
National Space Centre, Leicester 39467
National Space Museum, Lelystad 29531
National Sportsmuseum, Patiala 21976
National Sprint Car Hall of Fame and Museum, Knoxville 44510
National Steinbeck Center, Salinas 47216
National Taiwan Art Gallery, Taipei 07352
National Taiwan Science Education Center, Taipei 07353
National Technical Museum, Praha 08603
National Theater Museum, Ljubljana 34120
National Theatre Museum, Bloemfontein 34191
The National Time Museum, Chicago 42351
National Tobacco Museum, Wervik 03835
The National Toy Train Museum, Strasburg 47846
National Tramway Museum, Matlock 39922
National Transport Museum, Dublin 22448
National Treasure of the Rengeoin Temple, Kyoto 26452
National Trust for Historic Preservation, Washington 48385
National Trust Museum, Balaklava 00759
National Trust Museum, Streaky Bay 01480
National Viceroyalty Museum, Tepotzotlán 28500
National Vietnam Veterans Art Museum, Chicago 42352
National Village Museum, Bucureşti 32464
National Vintage Wireless and Television Museum, Harwich 39181
National Wallace Monument, Stirling 40593
National War- and Resistance Museum, Overloon 29707
National War Museum of Scotland, Edinburgh 38900
National War Museum of Umauhia, Umuahia 30363
National Warplane Museum, Horseheads 44105
National Watch and Clock Museum, Columbia 42555
National Waterways Museum, Gloucester 39083

National Wireless Museum, Seaview 40463
National Women's Hall of Fame, Seneca Falls 47566
National Wool Museum, Geelong 01046
National Wrestling Hall of Fame, Stillwater 47814
National Yiddish Book Center, Amherst 41180
Det Nationale Fotomuseum, København 08942
La Nationale Galerie d'Art Alyssa, Bardo 37554
Nationalgalerie Friedrichswerdersche Kirche - Schinkelmuseum, Berlin 16071
Det Nationalhistoriske Museum på Frederiksborg, Hillerød 08873
Nationalmuseet, København 08943
Nationalmuseum, Stockholm 36265
Nationalpark-Haus, Butjadingen 16434
Nationalparkhaus, Berchtesgaden 15886
Nationalparkhaus, Zernez 37359
Nationalparkmuseum, Mittersill 02307
Native American Exhibit, Fonda 43361
Native American Heritage Museum at Highland Mission, Highland 44017
Native American Museum, Terre Haute 47984
Native American Resource Center, Pembroke 46334
Native Museum, San José 07661
Natsagdorj Museum, Ulaanbaatar 28684
Náttúrufræðaistofnun Islands, Akureyrarsetur, Akureyri 21621
Natturufrædistofa Kopavogs, Kópavogur 21643
Náttúrufræðlistofnun Íslands, Reykjavík 21658
Náttúrugripasafnid i Neskaupstad, Neskaupstadur 21644
Natur-Museum Luzern, Luzern 36914
Natur-Museum mit Bauerngarten, Goldberg, Mecklenburg 17344
Natur- und Heimatmuseum Vellberg, Vellberg 20298
Natural History and Ethnological Native Museums, Juiz de Fora 04159
Natural History Department, Hitchin 39250
Natural History Museum, Århus 08772
Natural History Museum, Bangor, Gwynedd 38082
Natural History Museum, Belfast 38154
Natural History Museum, Belogradčik 04619
Natural History Museum, Beograd 33816
Natural History Museum, Bratislava 33977
Natural History Museum, Colchester 38613
Natural History Museum, Gorgan 22240
Natural History Museum, Hamedan 22242
Natural History Museum, Helsinki 09511
Natural History Museum, Ife 30343
Natural History Museum, Ilam 22243
Natural History Museum, Isfahan 22247
Natural History Museum, Jelenia Góra 31631
Natural History Museum, Karachi 31030
Natural History Museum, Kathmandu 28789
Natural History Museum, Khorram-Abaad 22258
Natural History Museum, Kingston 26076
Natural History Museum, Kotel 04720
Natural History Museum, Lahore 31041
Natural History Museum, Las Cuevas 03868
Natural History Museum, Lawrence 44685
Natural History Museum, London 39733
Natural History Museum, Medani 35771
Natural History Museum, Nottingham 40111
Natural History Museum, Oslo 30747
Natural History Museum, Port Louis 27740
Natural History Museum, Port Sudan 35774
Natural History Museum, Portales 46617
Natural History Museum, Portsmouth 40256
Natural History Museum, Porvoo 09952
Natural History Museum, Rijeka 07764
Natural History Museum, Teheran 22320
Natural History Museum, Tring 40727
Natural History Museum, Tripoli 27508
Natural History Museum, Ulaanbaatar 28685
Natural History Museum, Urmieh 22332
Natural History Museum, Yangon 28752
Natural History Museum, Yazd 22335
Natural History Museum and Institute, Chiba, Chiba 26122
Natural History Museum Complex, Constanța 32498
Natural History Museum of Amarousio, Amarousio 20817
Natural History Museum of Babia Góra National Park, Zawoja 32214
Natural History Museum of Bakony Mountains, Zirc 21617
Natural History Museum of Bombay Natural History Society, Mumbai 21951
Natural History Museum of Cephalonia and Ithaca, Argostolion 20836
Natural History Museum of Elassona, Elassona 20943
Natural History Museum of Kópavogur, Kópavogur 21643
Natural History Museum of Latvia, Rīga 27414
Natural History Museum of Liberia, Monrovia 27500
Natural History Museum of Los Angeles County, Los Angeles 44934
Natural History Museum of Montenegro, Podgorica 33890
Natural History Museum of Oeta, Ipati 20973
Natural History Museum of the Aegean, Samos 21149
Natural History Museum of the National Museum, Praha 08613
Natural History Museum of the University of Basrah, Basrah 22349
Natural History Museum of Tilos, Tilos 21196
Natural History Museum of Zimbabwe, Bulawayo 49028
Natural History Society and Folk Museum, Bacup 38053
Natural Science Center of Greensboro, Greensboro 43818
Natural Science Dept. of the Silesian Museum, Opava 08521
Natural Science Museum, Marawi 31400
Natural Science Museum, Plovdiv 04782
Natural Science Museum, Split 07785
Natural Science Museum, Tulcea 32620
Natural Science Museum, Victoria 27710
Natural Science Museum of the Institute of Systematics and Evolution, Kraków 31718
Natural Sciences Museum, Burgas 04636
Natural Sciences Museum, Černi Osăm 04638
Natural Sciences Museum, Hulata 22622
Natural Sciences Museum, Varna 04906
Natural Sciences Museum Complex, Galați 32522
Naturama Aargau, Aarau 36427
Nature en Provence, Riez 13967
Nature Hall The Ark, Pori 09943
Nature in Art, Gloucester 39084
Nature Museum, Charlotte 42245
Nature Museum, Kokkola 09684
Nature Museum at Grafton, Grafton 43738
Nature-Study and Folk Art Museum of Loutra Almopias, Loutraki 21056
Naturens Hus, Stockholm 36266
Natureum Niederelbe, Balje 15801
Naturhistorisches Museum, Admont 01644
Naturhistorisches Museum, Heiden 36799
Naturhistorisches Museum, Heilbronn 17689
Naturhistorisches Museum, Mainz 18605
Naturhistorisches Museum, Nürnberg 19155
Naturhistorisches Museum, Wien 02951
Naturhistorisches Museum Basel, Basel 36514
Naturhistorisches Museum der Burgergemeinde Bern, Bern 36547
Naturhistorisches Museum Schloss Bertholdsburg, Schleusingen 19799
Naturhistorisk Museum, Århus 08772
Naturhistoriska Museet, Malmö 36078
Naturhistoriska Museet i Göteborg, Göteborg 35916
Naturhistoriska Riksmuseet, Stockholm 36267
Naturhistoriske Samlinger, Bergen 30425
Naturkunde-Museum, Bielefeld 16159
Naturkunde-Museum, Coburg 16484
Naturkunde-Museum Bamberg, Bamberg 15813
Naturkunde-Museum K.-W. Donsbach, Herborn, Hessen 17716
Naturkunde- und Feuerwehrmuseum, Dobersberg 01765
Naturkundemuseum, Altdorf, Uri 36449
Naturkundemuseum, Reutlingen 19578
Naturkundemuseum Erfurt, Erfurt 16907
Naturkundemuseum Freiberg, Freiberg, Sachsen 17102
Naturkundemuseum Haus der Natur, Salzburg 02545
Naturkundemuseum im Marstall, Paderborn 19339
Naturkundemuseum im Ottoneum, Kassel 18027
Naturkundemuseum im Tierpark, Hamm, Westfalen 17577
Naturkundemuseum Leipzig, Leipzig 18411
Naturkundemuseum Ludwigslust, Ludwigslust 18526
Naturkundemuseum Niebüll, Niebüll 19093
Naturkundemuseum Ostbayern, Regensburg 19528
Naturkundliche Sammlung, Altusried 15475
Naturkundliche Sammlung, Königsbrunn 18174
Naturkundliches Bildungszentrum, Ulm 20259
Naturkundliches Museum, Wiesenfelden 20579
Naturkundliches Museum in der Harmonie, Schweinfurt 19893
Naturkundliches Museum und Schulungsstätte "Alte Schmiede", Handeloh 17588
Naturmuseum, Neuberg an der Mürz 02341
Naturmuseum, Sankt Gallen 37106
Naturmuseum der Stadt Augsburg, Augsburg 15563
Naturmuseum Lüneburg, Lüneburg 18560
Naturmuseum Olten, Olten 37010
Naturmuseum Solothurn, Solothurn 37186
Naturschutzausstellung der Naturschutzstation, Neschwitz 18998
Naturum Stendörren, Nyköping 36127
Naturwissenschaftliche Sammlung, Stans 37204
Naturwissenschaftliche Sammlungen, Berlin 16072
Naturwissenschaftliche Sammlungen, Innsbruck 02076
Naturwissenschaftliche Sammlungen der Stadt Winterthur, Winterthur 37338
Naturwissenschaftliche Sammlungen des Kantons Glarus, Engi 36683
Naturwissenschaftliches Museum, Aschaffenburg 15526
Naturwissenschaftliches Museum der Stadt Flensburg, Flensburg 17013
Naturwissenschaftliches Museum Duisburg, Duisburg 16755
Naturzentrum Nordfriesland, Bredstedt 16309
Natuur Historisch Museum en Heemkunde Centrum, Meerssen 29586
Natuurdiorama Holterberg, Holten 29433
Natuurhistorisch en Volkenkundig Museum, Oudenbosch 29697
Natuurhistorisch Museum, Antwerpen 03162
Natuurhistorisch Museum Boekenbergpark, Antwerpen 03163
Natuurhistorisch Museum de Peel, Asten 28955
Natuurhistorisch Museum het Diorama, Nunspeet 29650
Natuurhistorisch Museum Maastricht, Maastricht 29569
Natuurmuseum Ameland, Nes 29611
Natuurmuseum Brabant, Tilburg 29879
Natuurmuseum de Wielewaal, Lopik 29547
Natuurmuseum Dokkum, Dokkum 29163
Natuurmuseum E. Heimans, Zaandam 30037
Natuurmuseum Enschede, Enschede 29238
Natuurmuseum Groningen, Groningen 29313
Natuurmuseum het Drents-Friese Woud, Wateren 29985
Natuurmuseum Mar en Klif, Oudemirdum 29696
Natuurmuseum Nijmegen, Nijmegen 29635
Natuurmuseum Rotterdam, Rotterdam 29766
Natuurpunt Museum, Turnhout 03804
Natuurwetenschappelijk Museum, Antwerpen 03164
Naučno-issledovatelskij Institut i Muzej Antropologii im. D.N. Anučina, Moskva 33162
Naučno-memorialnyj Muzej N.E. Žukovskogo, Moskva 33163
Naučnyj Morskoj Muzej, Kaliningrad 32874
Naumann-Museum, Köthen, Anhalt 18191
Naumkeag House, Stockbridge 47819
Nausicaa, Boulogne-sur-Mer 10841
Nautelankosken Museo, Lieto 09782
Nautical Museum, Castletown 38508
Nautical Museum of Crete, Chania 20919
Nautical Museum of Galaxidi, Galaxidi 20961
Nauticus, Norfolk 45969
Nautikon Mouseiontis Ellados, Piraeus 21124
Nauvoo Historical Society Museum, Nauvoo 45639
Navajo Nation Museum, Window Rock 48682
Navajo National Monument, Tonalea 48027
Naval Academy Museum, Jinhae 27201
Naval and Maritime Museum, Ballina 00766
Naval Museum, Cienfuegos 07892
Naval Museum, İstanbul 37698
Naval Museum, Karlskrona 35999
Naval Museum, Rio de Janeiro 04390
Naval Museum of Alberta, Calgary 05175
Naval Museum of the North Fleet, Murmansk 33191
Naval Undersea Museum, Keyport 44473
Naval War College Museum, Newport 45929
Navan Centre, Armagh 38019
Navarro County Historical Society Museum, Corsicana 42650
Nave Museum, Victoria 48234
Naviscope Alsace, Strasbourg 14839
Navy Museum, Gdynia 31585
The Navy Museum, Washington 48386
Nayong Pilipino Museum, Pasay 31415
Nayuma Museum, Limulunga 49016
Nazib Shiganov Museum-Appartement, Kazan 32901
NBS-Múzeum Mincí a Medailí, Kremnica 34007
N.D. Kusnetsov Centre for the History of Aeromotors, Samara 33367
N.E. Zhukovsky Memorial House-Museum, Orechovo 33258
N.E. Zhukovsky Memorial Museum, Moskva 33163
Néa Moni Collection, Chios 20924
Neanderthal Museum, Mettmann 18725
Neath Museum, Neath 40005
Nebraska Conference United Methodist Historical Center, Lincoln 44789
Nebraska Museums Association, Aurora 49518
Nebraska Prairie Museum, Holdrege 44051
Neckarschiffahrts-Museum und Weinbau, Stadt- und Industriegeschichte, Heilbronn 17690
Nécropole de Louis Cauvin, Gareoult 11841
The Ned Shed Museum, Meldrum Bay 05834
Nederlands Architektuurinstituut, Rotterdam 29767
Nederlands Artillerie Museum, 't Harde 29339
Nederlands Bakkerijmuseum Het Warme Land, Hattem 29352
Nederlands Baksteen en Dakpanmuseum de Panoven, Zevenaar 30056
Nederlands Biermuseum de Boom, Alkmaar 28804
Nederlands Centrum voor Handwerken, Breda 29023
Nederlands Drogisterij Museum, Maarssen 29558
Nederlands Economisch Penningkabinet, Rotterdam 29768
Nederlands Foto Instituut, Rotterdam 29769
Nederlands Goud-, Zilver- en Klokkenmuseum, Schoonhoven 29812
Nederlands Graanmuseum/Olie- en Korenmolen Woldzigt, Roderwolde 29742
Nederlands Instituut voor Mediakunst - Montevideo, Amsterdam 28887
Nederlands Kachelmuseum, Alkmaar 28805
Nederlands Kansspelmuseum, Den Haag 29119
Nederlands Leder- en Schoenenmuseum, Waalwijk 29974
Nederlands Militair Kustverdedigingsmuseum, Hoek van Holland 29427
Het Nederlands Muntmuseum, Utrecht 29905
Nederlands Museum van Knipkunst, Schoonhoven 29813
Nederlands Museum voor Glas en Glastechniek, Hoogeveen 29438
Nederlands Openluchtmuseum, Arnhem 28942
Nederlands Parfumflessenmuseum, Winkel 30007
Nederlands Politie Museum, Apeldoorn 28927
Nederlands Scheepvaartmuseum, Amsterdam 28888
Nederlands Spoorwegmuseum, Utrecht 29906
Het Nederlands Sportmuseum Olympion, Lelystad 29532
Nederlands Steendrukmuseum, Valkenswaard 29924
Nederlands Stoommachinemuseum, Medemblik 29583
Nederlands Strijkijzer-Museum, Noordbroek 29643
Nederlands Tegelmuseum, Otterlo 29688
Nederlands Textielmuseum, Tilburg 29880
Het Nederlands Vestingmuseum, Naarden 29606
Nederlands Waterleidingmuseum, Utrecht 29907
Nederlands Wijnmuseum, Arnhem 28943
Nederlands Zouavenmuseum, Oudenbosch 29698
De Nederlandse Museumvereniging, Amsterdam 49306
Nedervetil Hembygdsgård, Nedervetil 09860
Neeses Farm Museum, Neeses 45645
Nef des Jouets, Soultz-Haut-Rhin 14796
Negev Museum, Be'ersheva 22580
Negotin National Museum, Negotin 33862
Negri Sembilan State Museum, Seremban 27684
Negri Sembilan State Museum, Seremban 27685
The Negros Museum, Bacolod 31279
Nehru Children's Museum, Kolkata 21908
Nehru Memorial Museum and Library, Delhi 21781
Nehru Science Centre, Mumbai 21952
Neidhart Fresken, Wien 02952
Neil Armstrong Air and Space Museum, Wapakoneta 48302
Neill-Cochran Museum House, Austin 41418
Neill Museum, Fort Davis 43385
Neiraku Museum, Nara 26582
Neisser Haus - Heimathaus und Archiv, Hildesheim 17759
Neka Museum and Gallery, Gianyar 22102
Neligh Mills, Neligh 45647
Nelimarkka Museo . Etelä-Pohjanmaan Aluetaidemuseo ja Nelimarkka-resedenssi, Alajärvi 09413
Nelimarkka Museum, Regional Art Museum of Southern Ostrobothnia, Alajärvi 09413
Nels Berggran Museum, Imperial 05615
The Nelson-Atkins Museum of Art, Kansas City 44404
Nelson Mandela Metropolitan Art Museum, Port Elizabeth 34332
Nelson Monument, Edinburgh 38901
Nelson Museum, Nelson 05970
Nelson Museum and Local History Centre, Monmouth 39978
Nelson Pioneer Farm and Museum, Oskaloosa 46208
Nelson Provincial Museum, Nelson 30210
Nelson Tower, Forres 39009
Német Nemzetiségi Muzeum, Tata 21594
NEMO, Amsterdam 28889
Nemours Mansion and Gardens, Wilmington 48654
Nemzeti Történeti Emlékpark, Opusztaszer 21493
Nenagh District Heritage Centre, Nenagh 22527
Nene Valley Railway, Stibbington 40587
Neneckij Okružnoj Kraevedčeskij Muzej, Narjan-Mar 33198
Nenthead Mines Heritage Centre, Nenthead 40008
Neofit Rilski House Museum, Bansko 04614
Neot Kedumim, Lod 22708
Nepean Historical Museum, Sorrento 01456
Nepean Museum, Nepean 05973
Népművészeti Tájház, Balatonszentgyörgy 21314
Néprajzi Gyűjtemény, Sopron 21535
Néprajzi Kiállítás, Pécs 21512
Néprajzi Múzeum, Budapest 21367
Néprajzi Múzeum, Nagyvázsony 21489
Neptune Township Historical Museum, Neptune 45651
Ner Hole Museum, Åndalsnes 30383
Nergal Gate Museum, Mosul 22352
Nerima Art Museum, Tokyo 26897
Nerima Bijutsukan, Tokyo 26897
Nerima Home Town Museum, Tokyo 26898
Nes Lensemuseum, Skiptvet 30848
Nesch-Museet, Ål 30372
Nesna Bygdemuseum, Nesna 30708
Ness Historical Society Museum, Port-of-Ness 40232
Nesstofusafn, Seltjarnarnes 21668
Netaji Museum, Kolkata 21909
Netherland Inn House Museum, Kingsport 44491
Netherlands Museums Association, Amsterdam 49306
Network of European Museum Organisations, Helsinki 49158
Neuberger Museum of Art, Purchase 46747
Neuberin-Museum, Reichenbach, Vogtland 19546
Neubistritzer Heimatstube, Reingers 02504
Neue Galerie, Dachau 16525
Neue Galerie, Graz 01927
Neue Galerie im Höhmann-Haus, Augsburg 15564
Neue Galerie New York, New York 45853
Neue Galerie Oberschöneweide der Karl-Hofer-Gesellschaft, Berlin 16073
Neue Galerie, Staatliche und Städtische Kunstsammlungen, Kassel 18028
Neue Gesellschaft für bildende Kunst e.V., Berlin 16074
Neue Nationalgalerie, Berlin 16075
Neue Pinakothek, München 18889
Neue Residenz, Bamberg 15814
Neue Sächsische Galerie, Chemnitz 16470
Die Neue Sammlung, München 18890
Neue Sammlung, Passau 19357
Neue Städtische Galerie Lüdenscheid, Lüdenscheid 18548
Neuer Berliner Kunstverein, Berlin 16076
Neuer Sächsischer Kunstverein, Dresden 16703
Neues Kunsthaus Ahrenshoop, Ostseebad Ahrenshoop 19302
Neues Kunstquartier Berlin, Berlin 16077
Neues Museum, Hollabrunn 02045
Neues Museum, Nürnberg 19156
Neues Museum Schwechat, Schwechat 02651

Neues Museum Weimar, Weimar, Thüringen 20466
Neues Museum Weserburg Bremen, Bremen 16330
Neues Schloß Bayreuth, Bayreuth 15857
Neues Schloß Herrenchiemsee, Herrenchiemsee 17735
Neues Schloß Meersburg, Meersburg 18677
Neues Schloß Schleißheim, Oberschleißheim 19204
Neues Schloß, Schloßmuseum, Tettnang 20165
Neues Schloß und Instrumentenmuseum, Kißlegg 18103
Neues Schloss Wallerstein, Wallerstein 20380
Neues Stadtmuseum Landsberg am Lech, Landsberg am Lech 18305
Neugablonzer Industrie- und Schmuckmuseum im Isergebirgs-Museum, Kaufbeuren 18042
Das Neumann Haus Museum, Laidley 01159
Neustadt Museum of Tiffany Art, New York 45854
Neustädter Rathaus, Hanau 17587
Neuwerk Kunsthalle, Konstanz 18205
Nevada County Historical Society Museum, Nevada City 45655
Nevada Historical Society Museum, Reno 46834
Nevada Museum of Art, Reno 46835
Nevada State Fire Museum and Comstock Firemen's Museum, Virginia City 48252
Nevada State Museum, Carson City 42118
Nevada State Museum, Las Vegas 44673
Nevada State Railroad Museum, Carson City 42119
Neversink Valley Area Museum, Cuddebackville 42718
Neville Blakey Museum of Locks, Keys and Safes, Brierfield 38333
Neville Public Museum of Brown County, Green Bay 43792
Nevşehir Archaeological and Ethnographic Museum, Nevşehir 37768
Nevşehir Arkeoloji ve Etnografya Müzesi, Nevşehir 37768
Nevşehir Culture Center, Nevşehir 37770
Nevşehir Devlet Güzel Sanatlar Galerisi, Nevşehir 37769
Nevşehir Kültür Merkezi, Nevşehir 37770
Nevşehir State Gallery, Nevşehir 37769
New Art Centre, East Winterslow 38851
The New Art Gallery Walsall, Walsall 40773
New Bedford Whaling Museum, New Bedford 45662
The New Berlin Historical Society Museum, New Berlin 45664
New Bern Firemen's Museum, New Bern 45666
New Braunfels Conservation Society Museum, New Braunfels 45669
New Britain Museum of American Art, New Britain 45674
New Britain Youth Museum, New Britain 45675
New Britain Youth Museum at Hungerford Park, Kensington 44442
New Brunswick College of Craft and Design Gallery, Fredericton 05463
New Brunswick Healthcare Museum, Fredericton 05464
New Brunswick Mining and Mineral Interpretation Centre, Petit-Rocher 06124
New Brunswick Museum, Saint John 06334
New Brunswick Sports Hall of Fame, Fredericton 05465
New Canaan Historical Society Museum, New Canaan 45680
New Canaan Nature Center, New Canaan 45681
New Castle Historical Society Museum, New Castle 45683
New Denmark Memorial Museum, New Denmark 05974
New Echota, Calhoun 42033
New England Air Museum of the Connecticut Aeronautical Historical Association, Windsor Locks 48687
New England Brass and Iron Lace Foundry Museum, Uralla 01564
New England Carousel Museum, Bristol 41901
New England College Gallery, Henniker 43996
New England Fire and History Museum, Brewster 41883
New England Maple Museum, Pittsford 46535
New England Maple Museum, Rutland 47042
New England Museum Association, Boston 49519
New England Quilt Museum, Lowell 44986
New England Regional Art Museum, Armidale 00752
New England Ski Museum, Franconia 43504
New England Wireless and Steam Museum, East Greenwich 43041
New Forest Museum and Visitor Centre, Lyndhurst 39855
New Hall, Dymchurch 38831
New Hall Women's Art Collection, Cambridge 38460
New Hampshire Antiquarian Society Museum, Hopkinton 44101
New Hampshire Farm Museum, Milton 45355
New Hampshire Institute of Art, Manchester 45099
New Harmony Gallery of Contemporary Art, New Harmony 45693
New Harmony State Historic Site, New Harmony 45694
New Haven Colony Historical Society Museum, New Haven 45697
New History of Veliko Tărnovo, Veliko Tărnovo 04919
New Iceland Heritage Museum, Gimli 05488
New Image Art, Los Angeles 44935
New International Cultural Center, Antwerpen 03165
New Jersey Association of Museums, Newark 49520
New Jersey Center for Visual Arts, Summit 47877
New Jersey Children's Museum, Paramus 46281
New Jersey Historical Society Museum, Newark 45891
New Jersey Museum of Agriculture, North Brunswick 45985
New Jersey Naval Museum, Hackensack 43858
New Jersey State House, Trenton 48056
New Jersey State Museum, Trenton 48057
New Lanark World Heritage Village, New Lanark 40012
New Langton Arts, San Francisco 47332
New London County Historical Society Museum, New London 45711
New London Historical Society Museum, New London 45713
New London Public Museum, New London 45714
New Market Battlefield State Historical Park, New Market 45716
New Mexico Association of Museums, Albuquerque 49521
New Mexico Bureau of Mines Mineral Museum, Socorro 47663
New Mexico Farm and Ranch Heritage Museum, Las Cruces 44659
New Mexico Museum of Natural History and Science, Albuquerque 41107
New Mexico Museum of Space History, Alamogordo 41077
New Mexico State University Art Gallery, Las Cruces 44660
New Mexico State University Museum, Las Cruces 44661
New Mexico Wing-Commemorative Air Force, Hobbs 44044
New Milford Historical Society Museum, New Milford 45717
New Mills Heritage and Information Centre, New Mills 40013
New Museum of Contemporary Art, New York 45855
New Museum of European and Eastern Art, Athinai 20895
New Norcia Museum and Art Gallery, New Norcia 01314
New Orleans Artworks Gallery, New Orleans 45733
New Orleans Fire Department Museum, New Orleans 45734
New Orleans Museum of Art, New Orleans 45735
New Orleans Pharmacy Museum, New Orleans 45736
New Otani Art Museum, Tokyo 26899
New South Wales Lancers Memorial Museum, Parramatta 01358
New Sweden Farmstead Museum, Bridgeton 41893
New Sweden Historical Museum, New Sweden 45747
New Tretyakov Gallery on Krymsky Val, Moskva 33047
New Virgin Nunnery, Moskva 33164
New Visions Gallery, Marshfield 45186
New Windsor Cantonment State Historic Site and National Purple Heart Hall of Honor, Vails Gate 48177
New York City Fire Museum, New York 45856
New York City Police Museum, New York 45857
New York Hall of Science, Flushing 43355
The New York Historical Society Museum, New York 45858
New York Museum of Transportation, West Henrietta 48530
New York Public Library for the Performing Arts, New York 45859
New York State Museum, Albany 41085
New York Studio School of Drawing, Painting and Sculpture Gallery, New York 45860
New York Transit Museum, Brooklyn 41948
New Zealand Academy of Fine Arts Gallery, Wellington 30300
New Zealand Centre for Photography, Wellington 30301
New Zealand Cricket Museum, Wellington 30302
New Zealand Fighter Pilots Museum, Wanaka 30284
New Zealand Fleet Air Arm Museum, Auckland 30114
New Zealand Marine Studies Centre, Dunedin 30149
New Zealand National Maritime Museum, Auckland 30115
New Zealand Police Museum, Porirua 30239
New Zealand Portrait Gallery, Wellington 30303
New Zealands Rugby Museum, Palmerston North 30229
New Zone Virtual Gallery, Eugene 43225
Newark Air Museum, Newark-on-Trent 40021
The Newark Museum, Newark 45892
Newark Museum, Newark-on-Trent 40022
Newark Town Treasures and Art Gallery, Newark-on-Trent 40023
Newark Valley Depot Museum, Newark Valley 45901
Newarke Houses Museum, Leicester 39468
Newaygo County Museum, Newaygo 45902
Newbridge House, Donabate 22410
Newburn Hall Motor Museum, Newburn 40028
Newby Hall, Ripon 40327
Newcastle Region Art Gallery, Newcastle 01316
Newcastle Region Maritime Museum, Newcastle 01317
Newcastle Regional Museum, Newcastle 01318
Newcomb Art Gallery, New Orleans 45737
Newcomen Engine House, Dartmouth 38703
Newell Museum, Newell 45915
Newham Grange Leisure Farm Museum, Middlesbrough 39950
Newham Heritage Centre, London 39734
Newhaven Fort, Newhaven 40046
Newhaven Heritage Museum, Edinburgh 38902
Newlyn Art Gallery, Penzance 40180
Newman House, Dublin 22449
Newport Art Museum, Newport 45930
Newport Mansions, Newport 45931
Newport Pagnell Historical Society Museum, Newport Pagnell 40058
Newport Roman Villa, Newport, Isle of Wight 40056
Newport State Park, Ellison Bay 43161
Newry and Mourne Arts Centre and Museum, Newry 40061
Newry Museum, Newry 40062
The Newseum, Arlington 41266
Newsome House Museum, Newport News 45938
Newspaper Kkeskisuomalainen's Museum, Jyväskylä 09603
Newsstand Museum, Osaka 26659
Newstead Abbey, Ravenshead 40290
Newton Abbot Town and Great Western Railway Museum, Newton Abbot 40063
Newton Museum, Newton 45942
Newtown Historic Museum, Newtown 45949
Newtown Textile Museum, Newtown, Powys 40069
Nexø Museum, Nexø 08988
Nexus Foundatoin for Today's Art, Philadelphia 46437
Nez Perce County Museum, Lewiston 44727
Nez Perce National Historical Park, Spalding 47713
Nezu Bijutsukan, Tokyo 26900
Nezu Museum of Fine Arts, Tokyo 26900
N.G. Chernyshevski Museum-Estate, Saratov 33508
N.G. Poletaev Regional Museum of Tuapse, Tuapse 33622
Nghe-Tinh Museum, Vinh 49004
Ngurdoto Gate Museum, Arusha 37454
Nhabe Museum, Nhabe 03938
NHK Broadcasting Museum, Tokyo 26901
NHK Hoso Hakubutsukan, Tokyo 26901
Niagara Apothecary, Niagara-on-the-Lake 06001
Niagara County Historical Center, Lockport 44842
Niagara Falls Art Gallery - Kurlek Collection, Niagara Falls 05995
Niagara Fire Museum, Niagara-on-the-Lake 06002
Niagara Gorge Discovery Center, Niagara Falls 45950
Niagara Historical Museum, Niagara-on-the-Lake 06003
Niagara Power Project Visitors' Center, Lewiston 44730
Niavaran Palace, Teheran 22321
Nichido Bijutsukan, Kasama 26315
Nichido Museum of Art, Kasama 26315
Nicholas Roerich Museum, New York 45861
Nichols House Museum, Boston 41820
Nicholson Museum, Sydney 01506
Nici Self Museum, Centennial 42166
Nickels-Sortwell House, Wiscasset 48718
The Nickle Arts Museum, Calgary 05176
Nicola Valley Museum, Merritt 05842
Nicolas Denys Museum, Saint Peters 06371
Nicolaus Copernicus Museum, Frombork 31561
Nicolaus-Schmidt-Künzel-Gedenkstätte, Tanna bei Schleiz 20143
Nicolaysen Art Museum, Casper 42130
Nicosia Municipal Arts Centre, Lefkosia 08205
Nidderdale Museum, Harrogate 39170
Nidwaldner Museum, Stans 37205
Niederbayerisches Feuerwehrmuseum, Eggenfelden 16787
Niederbayerisches Landwirtschaftsmuseum, Regen 19516
Niederbayerisches Vorgeschichtsmuseum, Landau an der Isar 18300
Niederbergisches Museum Wülfrath, Wülfrath 20688
Niederebersdorfer Heimat- und Archivstuben, Tutzing 20241
Niederlausitz-Museum und Karl-Liebknecht-Gedenkstätte, Luckau, Niederlausitz 18508
Niederlausitzer Apothekenmuseum, Cottbus 16504
Niederlausitzer Heidemuseum, Spremberg 20016
Niederösterreichisches Dokumentationszentrum für Moderne Kunst, Sankt Pölten 02602
Niederösterreichisches Feuerwehrmuseum, Tulln 02745
Niederösterreichisches Freilichtmuseum, Haag, Niederösterreich 01983
Niederösterreichisches Landesjagdmuseum und Afrikamuseum, Marchegg 02264
Niederösterreichisches Landesmuseum, Sankt Pölten 02603
Niederösterreichisches Museum für Volkskultur, Groß Schweinbarth 01948
Niederösterreichisches Schulmuseum, Asparn an der Zaya 01686
Niederrheinisches Freilichtmuseum, Grefrath 17383
Niederrheinisches Motorradmuseum, Moers 18777
Niederrheinisches Museum für Volkskunde und Kulturgeschichte, Kevelaer 18068
Niedersächsisches Bergbaumuseum, Langelsheim 18319
Niedersächsisches Deichmuseum, Dorum 16668
Niedersächsisches Kleinbahn-Museum Bruchhausen-Vilsen, Bruchhausen-Vilsen 16362
Niedersächsisches Kutschenmuseum, Lilienthal 18466
Niedersächsisches Landesmuseum Hannover, Hannover 17607
Niedersächsisches Münzkabinett der Deutschen Bank, Hannover 17608
Niedersächsisches Museum für Kali- und Salzbergbau, Ronnenberg 19646
Nielstrup Museum, Hadsten 08851
Niemeyer Tabaksmuseum, Groningen 29314
Nietzsche-Archiv, Weimar, Thüringen 20467
Nietzsche-Haus, Naumburg, Saale 18980
Nietzsche-Haus, Sils in Engadin 37169
Nieuw Land Poldermuseum, Lelystad 29533
Nieuwe Republiek Museums - Vryheid, Vryheid 34400
De Nieuwe Toren, Kampen 29473
NIFCA - Nordic Institute for Contemporary Art, Helsinki 09516
Nigde Müzesi, Nigde 37771
Nigde Museum, Nigde 37771
Niguliste Muuseum, Tallinn 09368
Nihon Camera Hakubutsukan, Tokyo 26902
Nihon Gangu Shiryokan, Tokyo 26903
Nihon Ginko Kin'yu Kenkyujo Kahei Hakubutsukan, Tokyo 26904
Nihon Hakubutsukan Kyokai, Tokyo 49259
Nihon Kindai Bungakukan, Tokyo 26905
Nihon Kinzoku Gakkai Fuzoku Kinzoku Hakubutsukan, Sendai 26733
Nihon Mingeikan, Tokyo 26906
Nihon Minka Shuraku Hakubutsukan, Toyonaka 26973
Nihon Monki Senta Hakubutsukan, Inuyama 26252
Nihon Shodo Bijutsukan, Tokyo 26907
Nihon Ukiyo-e Hakubutsukan, Matsumoto 26479
Niigata City Aizu Yaichi Memorial Museum, Niigata 26594
Niigata City Art Museum, Niigata 26595
Niigata City Folk Museum, Niigata 26592
Niigata-kenritsu Kindai Bijutsukan, Nagaoka 26536
Niigata-kenritsu Rekishi Hakubutsukan, Nagaoka 26537
Niigata Prefectural Museum of History, Nagaoka 26537
Niigata Prefectural Museum of Modern Art, Nagaoka 26536
Niigata Science Museum, Niigata 26593
Niigata-shiritsu Aizu Yaichi Kinenkan, Niigata 26594
Niigata-shiritsu Bijutsukan, Niigata 26595
Niimi Museum of Art, Niimi 26601
Niitsu House, Niigata 26596
Nijmeegs Volkenkundig Museum, Nijmegen 29636
Nikko Futarasan Jinja Hakubutsukan, Nikko 26602
Nikko Futarasan Shrine Museum, Nikko 26602
Nikko Toshogu Treasure Museum, Nikko 26603
Nikodem Jaroń Regional Museum, Olesno 31847
Nikola Parapunov Memorial House, Razlog 04799
Nikola Tesla Museum, Beograd 33808
Nikola Vaptsarov Memorial House, Sofia 04834
Nikolaevsk Local Museum, Nikolaev 37890
Nikolaos Perantinos Museum of Sculpture, Athinai 20896
Nikolaus Matz Bibliothek (Kirchenbibliothek), Michelstadt 18731
Nikon Gallery, Hiroshima 26222
Nikopolis ad Istrum-Antičen grad, Nikjup 04743
Nikos Nikolaides Theatrical Archives, Lemesos 08212
Nikou Collection, Mytilini 21087
Nikšićki Muzej, Nikšić 33863
Nils Aas Kunstverksted, Inderøy 30577
Nilsiän Kotiseutumuseo, Nilsiä 09863
Nimbin Museum, Nimbin 01322
Ninart Centro de Cultura, México 28210
Ninety-Six National Historic Site, Ninety-Six 45956
Ningbo Baoguo Si Display Center, Ningbo 07195
Ningbo Museum, Ningbo 07196
Ningyo no Ie, Kyoto 26439
Ninja Museum of Igaryu, Ueno 26987
Ninna-ji Temple Treasure House, Kyoto 26440
Nipawin and District Living Forestry Museum, Nipawin 06006
Nipigon Museum, Nipigon 06007
Nipissing Township Museum, Nipissing 06008
Nippon Kokeshi Museum, Naruko 26588
Nishijin Textile Center, Kyoto 26441
Nishimura Museum, Iwakuni 26273
Nishna Heritage Museum, Oakland 46071
Niu Art Museum, DeKalb 42856
Nivågårds Malerisamling, Nivå 08989
Nivala Museum Katvala, Nivala 09865
Nivalan Museo Katvala, Nivala 09865
Nizami Ganjavi, Baku 03068
Nizami Ganjavi State Museum of Azerbaijan Literature, Baku 03068
Nižegorodskij Chudožestvennyj Muzej, Nižnij Novgorod 33222
Nižegorodskij Gosudarstvennyj Istoriko-architekturnyj Muzej-zapovednik, Nižnij Novgorod 33223
Nižegorodskij Kreml s Archangelskim Soborom, Nižnij Novgorod 33224
Nizhni Novgorod Art Museum, Nižnij Novgorod 33222
Nizhni Novgorod Kremlin with Archangel Cathedral, Nižnij Novgorod 33224
Nizhni Novgorod State Reserve Museum of History and Architecture, Nižnij Novgorod 33223
Nizhny Tagil Museum-Reserve of Mining and Metallurgy in the Middle Urals, Nižnij Tagil 33228
Nizhny Tagil Town Museum of Fine Arts, Nižnij Tagil 33227
Nižnetagilskij Municipalnyj Muzej Izobrazitelnych Iskusstv, Nižnij Tagil 33227
Nižnetagilskij Muzej-Zapovednik Gornozavodskogo Dela Srednego Urala, Nižnij Tagil 33228
Njegošev Muzej, Cetinje 33834
Njegoš's Museum, Cetinje 33834

Njudungs Hembygdsmuseum, Vetlanda 36403
N.M. Djakonov Literary and Theater Museum, Syktyvkar 33574
N.M. Przevalsky Regional Museum, Prževalsk 27313
NMI-Museum IJkwezen, Delft 29086
N.N. Shukov House-Museum, Elec 32790
No Kaiga Art Museum, Kyoto 26442
No Man's Land Historical Museum, Goodwell 43728
No Name Exhibitions @ Soap Factory, Minneapolis 45392
Noah Webster House - Museum of West Hartford History, West Hartford 48527
Noank Historical Society Museum, Noank 45957
Nobel Museum, Stockholm 36268
Nobelmuseet och Bofors Industrimuseum, Karlskoga 35996
Noble Maritime Collection, Staten Island 47785
Nobleboro Historical Society Museum, Nobleboro 45958
Nobles County Art Center Gallery, Worthington 48761
Nobles County Historical Society Museum, Worthington 48762
Nobynäs Säteri, Aneby 35801
Nogata Municipal Coal Museum, Nogata 26609
Nogata-shi Sekitan Kinenkan, Nogata 26609
Nógrádi Megyei Múzeum, Salgótarján 21522
Nógrádi Történeti Múzeum, Salgótarján 21523
Noh Theater Museum of Sado, Ryotsu 26688
Le Noir Forge, Arichat 05006
Noirmont Command Bunker, Saint Brelade 40391
Nokia Local History Museum and Museum of Workers' Homes, Nokia 09866
Nokian Kotiseutumuseo, Nokia 09866
Nokomis and District Museum, Nokomis 06009
Nolan Gallery, Tharwa 01529
Nolde-Museum, Neukirchen bei Niebüll 19039
Nolhaga Slotts Konsthall, Alingsås 35791
Nolhin Torppa, Laitila 09755
Nomikos Collection, Pyrgos 21135
Nomura Art Museum, Kyoto 26443
Nonnahûs, Akureyri 21622
Nonthaburi Natural History Museum, Nonthaburi 37522
Noord-Hollands Motoren Museum, Nieuwe Niedorp 29617
Noordbrabants Museum, 's-Hertogenbosch 29407
Noordelijk Busmuseum, Winschoten 30010
Noordelijk Scheepvaartmuseum, Groningen 29315
Het Noorderhuis, Zaandam 30038
De Noordwester, Vlieland 29954
Noosa Regional Art Gallery, Tewantin 01526
Noosa Shire Museum, Pomona 01372
Nor West Bend Museum, Morgan 01274
Nor' Wester and Loyalist Museum, Williamstown 06805
Nora Barnacle House Museum, Galway 22475
Nora Eccles Harrison Museum of Art, Logan 44845
Nora Museum, Gyttorp 35933
Norchard Railway Centre, Lydney 39851
Nord-Jarlsbergmuseene, Holmestrand 30555
Nord-Troms Museum, Sørkjosen 30866
Nord-Trøndelag Fylkesgalleri, Namsos 30701
Nordamerika Native Museum, Zürich 37400
Norddal Museum, Valldal 30970
Norddeutsches Auto- und Motorrad-Museum, Bad Oeynhausen 15710
Norddeutsches Spielzeugmuseum, Soltau 19994
Norddeutsches Vogelmuseum, Osterholz-Scharmbeck 19295
Nordenfjeldske Kunstindustrimuseum, Trondheim 30939
Nordens Ark, Hunnebostrand 35968
Norderneyer Fischerhausmuseum, Norderney 19116
Nordfjord Folkemuseum, Sandane 30820
Nordfriesisches Museum Ludwig-Nissen-Haus, Husum, Nordsee 17870
Nordfyns Museum, Bogense 08787
Nordhallands Hembygdsförening, Kungsbacka 36023
Nordhannoversches Bauernhaus-Museum, Isernhagen 17926
Nordic Heritage Museum, Seattle 47541
Nordic House, Reykjavík 21659
Nordica Homestead Museum, Farmington 43298
Nordico - Museum der Stadt Linz, Linz 02238
Nordische Botschaften Gemeinschaftshaus, Berlin 16078
Nordiska Akvarellmuseet, Skärhamn 36192
Nordiska Museet, Stockholm 36269
Nordiska Travmuseet i Årjäng, Årjäng 35809
Nordjyllands Kunstmuseum, Aalborg 08763
Nordkappmuseet, Honningsvåg 30562
Nordland Red Cross War Museum, Narvik 30704
Nordland Røde Kors Krigsminnemuseum, Narvik 30704
Nordlandsmuseet, Bodø 30440
Nordli Bygdemuseum, Nordli 30711
Nordmøre Museum, Kristiansund 30618
Nordnorsk Fartøyvernsenter og Båtmuseum, Gratangen 30517
Nordnorsk Kunstmuseum, Tromsø 30932
Nordpfälzer Heimatmuseum, Rockenhausen 19621
Nordre Husan, Alvdal 30380
Nordseemuseum, Bremerhaven 16343
Nordsjaellandsk Folkemuseum, Hillerød 08874
Nordsjøfartmuseet, Tælavåg 30914
Nordsømuseet, Hirtshals 08876
Nordstrand Visual Arts Gallery, Wayne 48476
Nordvärmlands Jakt och Fiskemuseum, Sysslebäck 36318
Nordwestdeutsches Schulmuseum Friesland, Zetel 20748
Nore og Uvdal Bygdetun, Uvdal i Numedal 30964
Norfolk and Suffolk Aviation Museum, Flixton 38997
Norfolk Historical Museum, Norfolk 45962
Norfolk Historical Society Museum, Norfolk 45970
Norfolk Island Museum, Kingston 30366
Norges Birøkterlags Museet, Billingstad 30430
Norges Fiskerimuseet, Bergen 30426
Norges Hjemmefrontmuseum, Oslo 30748
Norges Museumsforbund, Oslo 49318
Norges Olympiske Museum, Lillehammer 30642
Nørholm, Homborsund 30557
Norilsk Art Gallery, Norilsk 33230
Norilskaja Chudožestvennaja Galereja, Norilsk 33230
Norman Cleveland County Historical Museum, Norman 45975
Norman No. 1 Oil Well Museum, Neodesha 45649
Norman R. Eppink Art Gallery, Emporia 43184
Norman Rockwell Museum at Stockbridge, Stockbridge 47820
Norman Wells Historical Centre, Norman Wells 06011
Normanby Hall, Scunthorpe 40458
Normanby Park Farming Museum, Scunthorpe 40459
Normanton Church Museum, Oakham 40120
Normisist Folk Inventions Museum, Butuan 31297
Norræna Húsid, Reykjavík 21659
Norrbottens Järnvägsmuseum, Luleå 36053
Norrbottens Museum, Luleå 36054
Norrbyskärs Museum, Hörnefors 35960
Norris Museum, Saint Ives, Cambridgeshire 40405
Norrköping Museum of Art, Norrköping 36120
Norrköpings Konstmuseum, Norrköping 36120
Norrköpings Stadsmuseum, Norrköping 36121
Norrtälje Konsthall, Norrtälje 36123
Norseman Historical and Geological Collection, Norseman 01324
Norsewood Pioneer Cottage Museum, Norsewood 30216
Norsk Barnemuseum, Stavanger 30882
Norsk Bergverksmuseum, Kongsberg 30605
Norsk Bremuseum, Fjærland 30491
Norsk Emballasje Museum, Oslo 30749
Norsk Farmasihistorisk Museum, Oslo 30750
Norsk Fiskeindustrimuseum, Melbu 30670
Norsk Fiskerværsmuseet, Sørvågen 30869
Norsk Fjellmuseum, Lom 30651
Norsk Folkemuseum, Oslo 30751
Norsk Grafisk Museum, Stavanger 30883
Norsk Hagebruks Museum, Grimstad 30520
Norsk Hermetikkmuseum, Stavanger 30884
Norsk Husflidsmuseum, Moen 30681
Norsk ICOM, Oslo 49319
Norsk Industriarbeidermuseet, Rjukan 30795
Norsk Jernbanemuseum, Hamar 30530
Norsk Kartmuseum, Hønefoss 30560
Norsk Kjøretøyhistorisk Museum, Lillehammer 30643
Norsk Klippfiskmuseum, Kristiansund 30619
Norsk Landbruksmuseum, Ås 30397
Norsk Luftfartsmuseum, Bodø 30441
Norsk Museum for Fotografi - Preus Fotomuseum, Horten 30566
Norsk Oljemuseum, Stavanger 30885
Norsk Reiselivsmuseum, Balestrand 30409
Norsk Seminmuseum, Stange 30876
Norsk Sjøfartsmuseum, Oslo 30752
Norsk Skogbruksmuseum, Elverum 30478
Norsk Speidermuseum, Oslo 30753
Norsk Teknisk Museum, Oslo 30754
Norsk Telemuseum - Kristiansand, Kristiansand 30614
Norsk Telemuseum - Lødingen, Lødingen 30646
Norsk Telemuseum - Sørvågen, Sørvågen 30870
Norsk Telemuseum - Stavanger, Stavanger 30886
Norsk Telemuseum - Trondheim, Trondheim 30940
Norsk Tindemuseum, Åndalsnes 30384
Norsk Tollmuseum, Oslo 30755
Norsk Trikotasjemuseum, Salhus 30817
Norsk Utvandrermuseum, Ottestad 30774
Norsk Vasskraft- og Industristadmuseum, Tyssedal 30958
Norsk Vegmuseum, Fåberg 30483
Norsk Veterinærmedisinsk Museum, Oslo 30756
Norske Grenselosers Museum, Bjørkelangen 30435
Norske Kunst- og Kulturhistoriske Museer, Oslo 49320
Norske Museumspedagogiske, Bodø 49321
Norske Naturhistoriske Museers, Bergen 49322
North American Black Historical Museum, Amherstburg 04988
North Andover Historical Museum, North Andover 45979
North Anna Nuclear Information Center, Mineral 45378
North Atlantic Aviation Museum, Gander 05474
North Ayrshire Museum, Saltcoats 40439
North Bay and Area Museum, North Bay 06017
North Bengal Science Centre, Siliguri 22026
North Berwick Museum, North Berwick 40078
North Bohemian Museum Liberec, Liberec 08451
North Bohemian Museum of Art Litoměřice, Litoměřice 08457
North Carolina Central University Art Museum, Durham 43023
North Carolina Maritime Museum, Beaufort 41558
North Carolina Museum of Art, Raleigh 46775
North Carolina Museum of Forestry, Whiteville 48593
North Carolina Museum of History, Raleigh 46776
North Carolina Museum of Life and Science, Durham 43024
North Carolina Museum of Natural Sciences, Raleigh 46777
North Carolina Museums Council, Raleigh 49522
North Carolina Pottery Center, Seagrove 47526
North Carolina State University Gallery of Art and Design, Raleigh 46778
North Carolina Transportation Museum, Spencer 47722
North Carr Lightship, Dundee 38802
North Castle Historical Society Museum, Armonk 41269
North Cornwall Museum and Gallery, Camelford 38467
North Country Museum of Arts, Park Rapids 46291
North Dakota Museum of Art, Grand Forks 43743
North Devon Maritime Museum, Appledore, Devon 38007
North Down Heritage Centre, Bangor, County Down 38080
North East Aircraft Museum, Sunderland 40646
North East Museums, Newcastle-upon-Tyne 49437
North Florida Community College Art Gallery, Madison 45054
North Hastings Heritage Museum, Bancroft 05040
North Haven Historical Society Museum, North Haven 45995
North Hertfordshire Museums, Letchworth 39482
North Highland Community Museum, Dingwall 05331
North Hills Museum, Granville Ferry 05523
North House Museum, Lewisburg 44726
North Huron District Museum, Wingham 06815
North Karelian Museum, Joensuu 09581
North Kerry Museum, Ballyduff 22369
North Lanark Regional Museum, Almonte 04980
North Lee County Historic Center and Santa Fe Depot Museum Complex, Fort Madison 43425
North Leverton Windmill, North Leverton 40079
North Lincolnshire Museum, Scunthorpe 40460
The North Museum of Natural History and Science, Lancaster 44630
North Naval Museum, Archangelsk 32651
North Norfolk Railway Museum, Sheringham 40497
North Norwegian Vessel Preservation Center and Boatmuseum, Gratangen 30517
North-Osetian Museum of History, Architecture and Literature, Vladikavkaz 33690
North Otago Museum, Oamaru 30218
North Pacific Cannery Village Museum, Port Edward 06161
North Plainfield Exempt Firemen's Museum, North Plainfield 46002
North Platte Valley Museum, Gering 43656
North Sea Museum, Hirtshals 08876
The North Shore Arts Association, Gloucester 43704
North Somerset Museum, Weston-super-Mare 40835
North Star Mining Museum, Grass Valley 43776
North Star Scouting Memorabilia, West Saint Paul 48544
North Stradbroke Island Historical Museum, Dunwich 00996
North Sumatera Government Museum, Medan 22158
North Thompson Museum, Barriere 05050
North Vancouver Museum, North Vancouver 06025
North View Gallery, Portland 46636
North Weald Airfield Museum and Memorial, Epping 38943
North West Federation of Museums and Art Galleries, Ellesmere Port 49438
North West Film Archive, Manchester 39900
North West Sound Archive, Clitheroe 38591
North Western Agricultural Museum, Warracknabeal 01579
North Western Federation of Museums and Art Galleries, Manchester 49439
North Wind Undersea Institute, Bronx 41925
North Woolwich Old Station Museum, London 39735
North Yorkshire Moors Railway, Pickering 40202
Northampton and Lamport Railway, Chapel Brampton 38521
Northampton County Historical and Genealogical Society Museum, Easton 43070
Northampton Museum and Art Gallery, Northampton 40084
Northborough Historical Museum, Northborough 46017
Northcliffe Pioneer Museum, Northcliffe 01331
Northcote Pottery, Thornbury 01533
Northcutt Steele Gallery, Billings 41689
Northeast Classic Car Museum, Norwich 46039
Northeast Louisiana Delta African American Heritage Museum, Monroe 45442
Northeast Martyrs Memorial Hall, Harbin 07090
Northeast Mississippi Museum, Corinth 42634
Northeast Mississippi Museums Association, Corinth 49523
Northeast Oakland Historical Museum, Oxford 46237
Northeastern Illinois University Art Gallery, Chicago 42353
Northeastern Montana Threshers and Antique Association Museum, Culbertson 42721
Northeastern Nevada Museum, Elko 43146
Northern Arizona University Art Museum and Galleries, Flagstaff 43330
Northern California Association of Museums, Chico 49524
Northern Culture Museum, Yokogoshi 27011
Northern Galleries, Aberdeen 41046
Northern Gallery for Contemporary Art, Sunderland 40647
Northern Gateway Museum, Denare Beach 05324
Northern Illinois University Art Gallery in Chicago, Chicago 42354
Northern Illinois University Art Museum, DeKalb 42857
Northern Indiana Arts Association, Munster 45562
Northern Indiana Center for History, South Bend 47680
Northern Ireland Museums Council, Belfast 49440
Northern Kentucky University Art Galleries, Highland Heights 44019
Northern Life Museum and National Exhibition Centre, Fort Smith 05452
Northern Lights Art Gallery, Mayville 45210
Northern Lights Military Museum, Goose Bay 05501
Northern Michigan University Art Museum, Marquette 45174
Northern Ostrobothnia Museum, Oulu 09897
Northern Ostrobothnia Museum - SailorS Home, Oulu 09890
Northfield Farm Museum, New Pitsligo 40015
Northfield Historical Society Museum, Northfield 46021
Northland Historical Society Museum, Lake Tomahawk 44595
Northland Viking Centre, Auckengill 38039
Northport Historical Society Museum, Northport 46027
The Northumberland County Historical Society Museum, Sunbury 47882
Northumberland Fisheries Museum, Pictou 06130
Northwest Art Center, Minot 45397
Northwest Gallery and Sinclair Gallery, Powell 46680
Northwest Museum of Arts and Culture, Spokane 47728
Northwest Railway Museum, Snoqualmie 47660
Northwestern National Exhibition Centre, Hazelton 05591
Northwestern Oklahoma State University Museum, Alva 41162
Northwestern Ontario Sports Hall of Fame, Thunder Bay 06545
Norton Conyers, Near Ripon 40003
Norton Museum of Art, West Palm Beach 48538
Norton Priory Museum, Runcorn 40359
Norton Simon Museum, Pasadena 46302
Norway's Resistance Museum, Oslo 30748
Norwegian-American Historical Museum, Northfield 46022
Norwegian Archive, Library and Museum Authority, Oslo 49315
Norwegian Aviation Museum, Bodø 30441
Norwegian Beekeepers Association Museum, Billingstad 30430
The Norwegian Canning Museum, Stavanger 30884
Norwegian Center for Constitutional History, Eidsvoll Verk 30474
Norwegian Federation of Friends of Museums, Oslo 49323
Norwegian Fishing Village Museum, Sørvågen 30869
Norwegian Forestry Museum, Elverum 30478
Norwegian Industrial Workers' Museum, Rjukan 30795
Norwegian Map Museum, Hønefoss 30560
Norwegian Maritime Museum, Oslo 30752
Norwegian Mining Museum, Kongsberg 30605
Norwegian Mountain Museum, Lom 30651
Norwegian Museum of Agriculture, Ås 30397
The Norwegian Museum of Architecture, Oslo 30726
Norwegian Museum of Hydropower and Industry, Tyssedal 30958
Norwegian Museum of Science and Technology, Oslo 30754
The Norwegian Museum of Veterinary History, Oslo 30756
Norwegian Railway Museum, Hamar 30530
Norwegian Road Museum, Fåberg 30483
Norwich and District Museum, Norwich 06035
Norwich Gallery, Norwich 40097
Norwich Historical Society Museum, Norwich 46042
Norwich University Museum, Northfield 46025
Norwood Historical Association Museum, Norwood 46043
Norwood Museum, Holm 39253
Nose Creek Valley Museum, Airdrie 04969
Nostalgie auf Rädern - Fahrzeugmuseum, Großklein 01957
Nostalgie Museum, Brandenburg an der Havel 16286
Nostalgie-Museum, Wörth an der Donau 20644
Nostalgiebahnen in Kärnten, Ebental, Kärnten 01782
Nostalgisches Musikparadies, Oberhasli 36997
Nostell Priory, Wakefield 40762
Nøstetangen Museum, Hokksund 30551
De Notelaer, Hingene 29423
Notgeld-Sammlung 1918/20, Bad Wimsbach-Neydharting 01724
Nothe Fort Museum of Coastal Defence, Weymouth 40843
Notojima Glass Art Museum, Notojima 26610
Notranjska Museum, Postojna 34139
Notranjski Muzej Postojna, Postojna 34139
Notre Dame of Jolo College Museum, Jolo 31331
Nottingham Castle, Nottingham 40112
Nottingham Transport Heritage Centre, Ruddington 40350
Nottingham University Museum, Nottingham 40113
Nousiaisten Kotiseutumuseo, Nousiainen 09868

Nova Istoria na Veliko Tărnovo, Veliko Tărnovo 04919
Nova Scotia Centre for Craft and Design, Halifax 05558
Nova Scotia Museum, Halifax 05559
Nova Scotia Museum of Natural History, Halifax 05560
Novalis-Museum, Wiederstedt 20566
Novato History Museum, Novato 46046
Novgorod State Museum Reservation, Velikij Novgorod 33680
Novgorodskij Gosudarstvennyj Muzej-zapovednik, Velikij Novgorod 33680
Novi Sad City Museum, Novi Sad 33870
Novi Vinodolski Regional Museum, Novi Vinodolski 07746
Novočerkasskij Muzej Istorii Donskich Kazakov, Novočerkassk 33233
Novocherkassk Museum of the History of the Don Cossacks, Novočerkassk 33233
Novodevičij Monastyr, Moskva 33164
Novohradská Galéria, Lučenec 34018
Novohradské Múzeum, Filakovo 33994
Novohradské Múzeum, Lučenec 34019
Novokuzneckij Chudožestvennyj Muzej, Novokuzneck 33236
Novokuzneckij Kraevedeskij Muzej, Novokuzneck 33237
Novorossijskij Gosudarstvennyj Istoričeskij Muzej Zapovednik, Novorossijsk 33238
Novorossiysk State Historical Preserve, Novorossijsk 33238
Novosibirsk Museum of the Nature, Novosibirsk 33243
Novosibirsk Picture Gallery, Novosibirsk 33242
Novosibirsk Regional Museum, Novosibirsk 33244
Novosibirskaja Kartinnaja Galereja, Novosibirsk 33242
Novosibirskij Muzej Prirody, Novosibirsk 33243
Novosibirskij Oblastnoj Kraevedčeskij Muzej, Novosibirsk 33244
Novotroick History Museum, Novotroick 33247
Novotroickij Istoriko-kraevedčeskij Muzej, Novotroick 33247
Novum Forum, Neumarkt in Steiermark 02353
Nowata County Historical Society Museum, Nowata 46047
Nowra Museum, Nowra 01337
Noyes and Read Gallery and Herndon Gallery, Yellow Springs 48784
Noyes Art Gallery, Lincoln 44790
The Noyes Museum of Art, Oceanville 46090
NRW-Forum Kultur und Wirtschaft, Düsseldorf 16739
N.S. Leskov House Museum, Orël 33261
N.S. Muchin Appartment Museum, Joškar-Ola 32857
N.S. Muchin Museum-Apartment, Olikjal 33250
NTT InterCommunication Center, Tokyo 26908
Nuantta Sunakkutaangit Musuem, Iqaluit 05626
Nubien Museum, Aswan 09250
Núcleo Museológico do Santuário do Senhor Jesus da Pedra, Óbidos 32324
Nuijamaa Museum, Lappeenranta 09762
Nuijamaan Museo, Lappeenranta 09762
Nukarin Koulumuseo, Nukari 09870
Nukke- ja Pukumuseo - Hatanpää Mansion, Tampere 10082
Nukkemuseo Suruton, Savonlinna 10024
Nukumuuseum, Tallinn 09369
Number 1 Royal Crescent Museum, Bath 38120
Numismatic Museum, Kathmandu 28790
Numismatic Museum, Reykjavík 21657
Numismatic Museum, Athens, Athinai 20897
Nummen Kotiseutumuseo, Nummi 09871
Nunatta Katersugaasivia Allagaateqarfialu, Nuuk 21234
Nundah and Districts Historical Museum, Nundah 01338
Nuova-Icona, Venezia 25945
Nuovo Museo Provinciale Sannitico, Campobasso 23304
Nurmeksen Museo, Nurmes 09873
Nurmon Museo, Nurmo 09875
NUS Museum, Singapore 33940
Nussknackermuseum, Neuhausen, Sachsen 19037
Nutcote Museum, Neutral Bay 01313
Nutimik Lake Museum, Seven Sisters Falls 06423
Nutzfahrzeugmuseum, Hartmannsdorf 17623
Nuutajärvi Glass Museum, Nuutajärvi 09876
N.V. Fedorov Library-Museum, Moskva 33093
N.V. Gogol House Museum - City Library - Culture Centre, Moskva 33039
N.V. Gogol Literary Memorial Museum, Velikie Soročintsy 37910
NVA-Museum, Ostseebad Binz 19312
Ny Ålesund By- og Gruvemuseum, Ny-Ålesund 30715
Ny Carlsberg Glyptotek, København 08944
N.Y. Vaptsarov Memorial House, Bansko 04615
Nyahokwe Ruins Site Museum, Inyanga 49034
Nyborg og Omegns Museer, Nyborg 08995
Nykarleby Museum, Uusikaarlepyy 10151
Nylander Museum, Caribou 42103
Nýlistasafnið, Reykjavík 21660
Nyman House and Pharmacy Museum, Tohmajärvi 10109
Nymphenburger Porzellan-Sammlung Bäuml, München 18891
Nynäs Slott, Västerljung 36385
Nynäshamns Järnvägsmuseum, Nynäshamn 36130
Nyoirin-ji Treasure House, Yoshino 27032
Nyokodo Nagasaki Municipal Longtime Memorial Museum, Nagasaki 26558
Nyozezo Private Museum, Nagaoka 26538
Nyslotts Landskapsmuseum, Nyslott 09877
Nyströmska Gården, Köping 36011
NZH Vervoers Museum, Haarlem 29328
O Art Museum, Tokyo 26909
O. Henry Home and Museum, Austin 41419
O Museu do Marajó, Cachoeira do Arari 04015
Oak Creek Pioneer Village, Oak Creek 46051
Oak Hall, Niagara Falls 05996
Oak House Museum, West Bromwich 40822
Oak Ridge Art Center, Oak Ridge 46057
Oakdale Museum, Oakdale 46058
Oakham Castle, Oakham 40121
Oakland Museum of California, Oakland 46067
Oaklands Historic House Museum, Murfreesboro 45568
Oakleigh and District Museum, Oakleigh 01341
Oakleigh House, Mobile 45423
Oakley Pioneer Museum, Oakley 46073
Oaks House Museum, Jackson 44284
Oakville Galleries, Centennial, Oakville 06038
Oakville Galleries, Gairloch, Oakville 06039
Oakville Museum at Erchless Estate, Oakville 06040
Oakwell Hall Country Park, Birstall 38235
Het Oale Meestershuus, Slagharen 29828
Oale Smederie, Hellendoorn 29388
Oatlands Plantation, Leesburg 44712
Ob Luang, Chiang Mai 37502
Obalne Galerije - Galerija Loža, Koper 34096
Obalne Galerije - Mestna Galerija, Piran 34137
Obec Architektů, Brno 08274
Obecní Dům, Praha 08606
Obelisk Museum, Al-Matariyya 09233
Oberburg Giebichenstein, Halle, Saale 17518
Oberfränkisches Bauernhofmuseum, Zell, Oberfranken 20743
Oberfränkisches Textilmuseum, Helmbrechts 17701
Oberharzer Bergwerksmuseum, Clausthal-Zellerfeld 16476
Oberhausmuseum Passau, Passau 19358
Oberkärntner Brauchtums- und Maskenmuseum, Oberdrauburg 02367
Oberlausitzer Sechsstädtebund- und Handwerksmuseum Löbau, Löbau 18488
Oberlin College Gallery, Cleveland 42477
Oberlin Historical and Improvement Organization Museum, Oberlin 46077
Obermühle Hochburg-Ach, Ach 01641
Obermühlviertler Denkmalhof Unterkagerer, Auberg 01689
Oberösterreichische Fotogalerie, Linz 02239
Oberösterreichischer Musealverein, Linz 49058
Oberösterreichischer Steingarten, Vorchdorf 02776
Oberösterreichisches Freilichtmuseum Sumerauerhof, Sankt Florian 02561
Oberösterreichisches Jagdmuseum, Sankt Florian 02562
Oberösterreichisches Landesmuseum - Außenstelle Linz-Haag, Linz 02240
Oberösterreichisches Schiffahrtsmuseum, Grein an der Donau 01938
Oberpfälzer Fischereimuseum, Tirschenreuth 20178
Oberpfälzer Flußspat-Besucherbergwerk Reichhart-Schacht, Stulln 20082
Oberpfälzer Freilandmuseum Neusath-Perschen, Nabburg 18969
Oberpfälzer Handwerksmuseum, Rötz 19639
Oberpfälzer Künstlerhaus-Kebbel-Villa, Schwandorf 19873
Oberpfälzer Volkskundemuseum, Burglengenfeld 16427
Oberrheinische Narrenschau, Kenzingen 18066
Oberrheinisches Bäder- und Heimatmuseum Bad Bellingen, Bad Bellingen 15597
Oberrheinisches Tabakmuseum, Mahlberg 18591
Oberschlesisches Landesmuseum, Ratingen 19495
Oberschwäbische Galerie Kloster Heiligkreuztal, Altheim bei Riedlingen 15457
Oberschwäbisches Museumsdorf Kreisfreilichtmuseum Kürnbach, Bad Schussenried 15736
Obersimmentaler Heimatmuseum, Zweisimmen 37432
Oberweißbacher Bergbahn, Mellenbach-Glasbach 18699
Obir-Tropfsteinhöhlen, Bad Eisenkappel 01695
Objedinenie Fotocentr Sojuza Žurnalistov, Moskva 33165
Oblasten Istoričeski Muzej, Jambol 04681
Oblastná Galéria P.M. Bohúňa, Liptovský Mikuláš 34016
Oblastnaja Kartinnaja Galereja Obraz, Kaluga 32882
Oblastní Galerie, Liberec 08450
Oblastní Galerie Vysočiny v Jihlavě, Jihlava 08391
Oblastnoj Chudožestvennyj Muzej, Petropavlovsk-Kamčatskij 33312
Oblastnoj Kraevedčeskij Muzej, Ekaterinburg 32782
Oblastnoj Kraevedčeskij Muzej im A.A. Kuznecova, Čita 32752
Oblastnoj Muzejnyj Centr, Sankt-Peterburg 33473
Obrazárna Pražského Hradu, Praha 08607
Obrazcov Central State Puppet Theater Museum, Moskva 33101
Obščinski Istoričeski Muzej, Etropole 04664
Observatoriemuseet, Stockholm 36270
Observatory Museum, Grahamstown 34252
Observatory Museum, Stockholm 36270
Obstbaumuseum, Werder, Havel 20518
Obstmuseum, Sörup 19977
Obuda Local Museum, Budapest 21368
Óbudai Helytörténeti Gyűjtemény, Budapest 21368
Óbudai Pincegaléria, Budapest 21369
Óbudai Társaskör Galéria, Budapest 21370
Obuvnické Muzeum, Zlín 08752
OCAD Gallery, Toronto 06599
Occupation Tapestry Gallery and Maritime Museum, Saint Helier 40404
Ocean City Art Center, Ocean City 46084
Ocean City Historical Museum, Ocean City 46085
Ocean County Historical Museum, Toms River 48026
Oceania Design, Wellington 30304
Oceanographic Museum, Nhatrang 48998
Océanopolis, Brest 10914
Océarium du Croisic, Le Croisic 12409
Ocmulgee National Monument, Macon 45046
Oconto County Historical Society Museum, Oconto 46091
The Octagon, Washington 48387
The Octagon Center for the Arts, Ames 41173
The Octagon House, Hudson 44145
Octagon House, Watertown 48446
Octave Chanute Aerospace Museum, Rantoul 46793
October Railway Central Museum, Sankt-Peterburg 33384
Odalstunet Gårdsmuseum, Skarnes 30841
Odapark, Venray 29942
Odawara Castle Museum, Odawara 26615
Odawara Crustacea Museum, Tokyo 26910
Odděleni Oblastni Muzeum Jihovýchodní Moravy, Napajedla 08493
Oddělení Oblastního Muzea Jihovychodní Moravy, Zlín, Luhačovice 08467
Oddelenie Technické Múzeum Košice, Spišská Béla 34062
Oddentunet, Os i Østerdalen 30722
Odder Museum, Odder 09004
Oddział Literacki im. Marii Dąbrowskiej w Russowie, Russów 31954
Oddział Sztuki Współczesnej, Gdańsk 31580
Oddział Zbiorów Graficznych i Kartograficznych, Kraków 31724
O'Dell Inn, Annapolis Royal 04997
Odense City Museum, Odense 09005
Odenwälder Freilandmuseum, Walldürn 20378
Odenwald- & Spielzeugmuseum, Michelstadt 18732
Oderlandmuseum, Bad Freienwalde 15645
Odessa Archaeological Museum, Odessa 37892
Odessa Fine Arts Museum, Odessa 37893
Odessa Local History Museum, Odessa 37894
Odessa State Museum of European and Oriental Art, Odessa 37895
Odigia Ikonen-Museum, Den Haag 29120
Odinani Museum, Awka 30332
Odoevsky Gallery, Ekaterinburg 32768
Odontological Museum, London 39736
Odontology Museum Prof. Salles Cunha, Rio de Janeiro 04362
Odsherreds Kulturhistoriske Museum, Højby 08882
Odsherreds Kunstmuseum, Asnæs 08776
Odsherreds Museum, Asnæs 08777
Odsherreds Museum, Nykøbing Sjælland 09002
Ödenburger Heimatmuseum, Bad Wimpfen 15771
Öffentliche Bibliothek der Universität Basel, Basel 36515
Öjskogsparkens Museiområde, Närpes 09856
Ölands Forngård, Borgholm 35844
Öle-Museum, Münsingen 36967
Ölmühle Michelau, Rudersberg 19699
Önningeby Museum, Mariehamn 09818
Önningebymuseet, Mariehamn 09818
Öntödei Múzeum, Budapest 21371
Örebro County Museum, Örebro 36139
Örebro Konsthallen, Örebro 36138
Örebro Läns Museum, Örebro 36139
Oerka Irene Verbeek Museum, Raard 29723
Örnsköldsviks Museum, Örnsköldsvik 36144
Oertijdmuseum De Groene Poort, Boxtel 29015
Őslénytani Telep, Rudabánya 21520
Östereichisches Brückenbaumuseum, Edelsbach bei Feldbach 01786
Östergötlands Länsmuseum, Linköping 36042
Österlens Museum, Simrishamn 36189
Österreichische Galerie Belvedere, Halbturn 01990
Österreichische Galerie Belvedere, Wien 02953
Österreichische Galerie Belvedere, Wien 02954
Das Österreichische Motorradmuseum, Eggenburg 01793
Österreichische Nationalbibliothek, Wien 02955
Österreichischer Museumsbund, Wien 49059
Österreichisches Circus- und Clown-Museum, Wien 02956
Österreichisches Donau- und Fischereimuseum, Orth an der Donau 02387
Österreichisches Felsbildermuseum, Spital am Pyhrn 02668
Österreichisches Filmmuseum Wien, Wien 02957
Österreichisches Forstmuseum Silvanum, Großreifling 01962
Österreichisches Freilichtmuseum Stübing, Stübing bei Graz 02708
Österreichisches Freimaurermuseum, Rosenau Schloß 02525
Österreichisches Gartenbaumuseum, Wien 02958
Österreichisches Gesellschafts- und Wirtschaftsmuseum, Wien 02959
Österreichisches Getreidemuseum, Wels 02814
Österreichisches Ikonenmuseum, Potzneusiedl 02438
Österreichisches Jüdisches Museum, Eisenstadt 01810
Österreichisches Kriminalmuseum, Scharnstein 02628
Österreichisches Luftfahrtmuseum, Feldkirchen bei Graz 01833
Österreichisches Museum für Volkskunde, Wien 02960
Österreichisches Olympia- und Sportmuseum, Wien 02961
Österreichisches Pfahlbaummuseum und Museum Mondseeland, Mondsee 02321
Österreichisches Schloß und Schlüsselmuseum, Graz 01928
Österreichisches Spiele Museum, Leopoldsdorf im Marchfelde 02217
Österreichisches Sprachinselmuseum, Wien 02962
Österreichisches Straßenbahn- und Lokalbahnbetriebsmuseum, Mariazell 02275
Österreichisches Theatermuseum, Wien 02963
Österreichisches Tonbandmuseum, Wien 02964
Österreichisches Wandermuseum, Alpl 01657
Österreichisches Werbemuseum, Wien 02965
Österreichisches Zuckermuseum, Tulln 02746
Östersund City Museum, Östersund 36148
Östra Södermanlands Museijärnväg, Mariefred 36086
Oeteldonks Gemintemuzejum, 's-Hertogenbosch 29408
Ötztaler Freilichtmuseum, Längenfeld 02176
Övermark Hembygdsmuseum, Övermark 09879
Övertorneå Hembygdsmuseum, Övertorneå 36151
O'Fallon Historical Museum, Baker 41435
Ofen- und Keramikmuseum Velten, Velten 20300
Ofenplattensammlung der Schwäbische Hüttenwerke, Aalen 15384
Oficina Museu da Universidade Estácio de Sá, Rio de Janeiro 04398
Ofoten Museum, Narvik 30705
Ogarako Folk Museum, Misawa 26495
Ogden Historical Society Museum, Spencerport 47723
Ogden House, Fairfield 43264
Ogden Union Station Museums, Ogden 46100
Oglethorpe University Museum of Art, Atlanta 41354
Ogni Moskvy - Muzej Istorii Gorodskogo Osveščenija, Moskva 33166
Ogniwo Polish Museum, Winnipeg 06835
Ogre History and Art Museum, Ogre 27391
Ogres Vēstures un Mākslas Muzejs, Ogre 27391
Ogunquit Museum of American Art, Ogunquit 46104
Ohara Bijutsukan, Kurashiki 26384
Ohara Museum of Art, Kurashiki 26384
Ohio Ceramic Center, Roseville 47008
Ohio Historical Society Museum, Columbus 42590
Ohio Museums Association, Columbus 49525
Ohio Railway Museum, Worthington 48763
Ohio River Museum, Marietta 45151
Ohio University Art Gallery, Saint Clairsville 47082
The Ohr-O'Keefe Museum of Art, Biloxi 41696
Ohsabanan museijärnväg, Växjö 36388
The Ohsha'joh Museum of Art, Hiroshima 26223
Oil and Gas Exhibition Centre, Qurm 31010
Oil Museum of Canada, Oil Springs 06045
Oil Patch Museum, Russell 47036
Oil Sands Discovery Centre, Fort McMurray 05446
Oinoussian Maritime Museum, Oinoussai 21102
Oisu Tehnikumi Muuseum, Halliste 09321
Oita-kenritsu Geijutsu Kaikan, Oita 26622
Oita Prefectural Art Hall, Oita 26622
Ojai Art Center, Ojai 46107
Ojai Valley Museum, Ojai 46108
Ojāra Vācieša Memoriālais Muzejs, Rīga 27433
Ojeblikket, København 08945
Okains Bay Maori and Colonial Museum, Okains Bay 30219
Okanoyama Museum of Art, Nishiwaki 26608
Okaukuejo Museum, Okaukuejo 28763
Okawa Bijutsukan, Kiryu 26335
Okawa Museum of Art, Kiryu 26335
Okaya Sericultural, Equipment and Literature and Silk Museum, Okaya 26623
Okayama Astronomy Museum, Kamogata 26302
Okayama-Kenritsu Bijutsukan, Okayama 26626
Okayama-kenritsu Hakubutsukan, Okayama 26627
Okayama-kenritsu Kibiji Local Museum, Soja 26772
Okayama Orient Museum, Okayama 26628
Okayama Prefectural Museum, Okayama 26627
Okayama Prefectural Museum of Art, Okayama 26626
Okayama-shiritsu Oriento Bijutsukan, Okayama 26628
Okayama Tenmon Hakubutsukan, Kamogata 26302
Okefenokee Heritage Center, Waycross 48472
Okeresztény Mauzóleum, Pécs 21513
Okinawa-kenritsu Hakubutsukan, Naha 26572
Okinawa Prefectural Museum, Naha 26572
Okkupasjonsmuseet, Eidsvoll 30473
Okladnikov Museum of Archaeology of Khabarovsk, Chabarovsk 32738
Oklahoma City Museum of Art, Oklahoma City 46118
Oklahoma Firefighters Museum, Oklahoma City 46119
Oklahoma Forest Heritage Center Forestry Museum, Broken Bow 41912
Oklahoman Museum of African American Art, Oklahoma City 46120
Oklahoma Museum of Higher Education, Stillwater 47815
Oklahoma Museum of History, Oklahoma City 46121

Oklahoma Museums Association, Oklahoma City 49526
Oklahoma Route 66 Museum, Clinton 42500
Oklahoma Territorial Museum, Guthrie 43855
Okražen Istoričeski Muzej, Chaskovo 04641
Okražen Istoričeski Muzej, Montana 04741
Okražen Istoričeski Muzej, Pernik 04759
Okražen Istoričeski Muzej, Plovdiv 04780
Okražen Istoričeski Muzej, Sliven 04824
Okražen Istoričeski Muzej, Smoljan 04826
Okražen Istoričeski Muzej, Veliko Tărnovo 04920
Okražen Istoričeski Muzej, Vidin 04926
Okražen Istoričeski Muzej, Vraca 04929
Okražen Muzej na Văzraždaneto i Nacionalno-osvoboditelnite Borbi, Plovdiv 04781
Okražna Chudožestvena Galerija, Burgas 04635
Okražna Chudožestvena Galerija, Kardžali 04687
Okražna Chudožestvena Galerija, Pleven 04768
Okražna Chudožestvena Galerija, Stara Zagora 04867
Okražna Chudožestvena Galerija, Vidin 04927
Okražna Chudožestvena Galerija, Vraca 04930
Okražna Chudožestvena Galerija Dimităr Dobrovič, Sliven 04825
Okražna Chudožestvena Galerija Georgi Papazov, Jambol 04682
Okražna Chudožestvena Galerija Vladimir Dimitrov-Majstora, Kjustendil 04709
Okręgowe Muzeum Techniki Drogowej i Mostowej Okręgu Lubelskiego przy Zarządzie Dróg w Zamościu, Zamość 32213
Okresné Vlastivedné Múzeum, Humenné 33999
Okresní Muzeum, Benátky nad Jizerou 08245
Okresní Muzeum, Blovice 08252
Okresní Muzeum, Chomutov 08314
Okresní Muzeum, Děčín 08326
Okresní Muzeum, Hořovice 08362
Okresní Muzeum, Ivančice 08376
Okresní Muzeum, Litoměřice 08456
Okresni Muzeum, Louny 08466
Okresní Muzeum, Mělník 08473
Okresni Muzeum, Most 08489
Okresní Muzeum, Pelhřimov 08537
Okresní Muzeum, Rakovník 08633
Okresní Muzeum, Tachov 08674
Okresní Muzeum, Vlašim 08721
Okresní Muzeum a Galerie, Jičín 08388
Okresní Muzeum Kroměřížska, Kroměříž 08435
Okresní Muzeum Praha-východ, Brandýs nad Labem 08255
Okresni Muzeum v Kutné Hoře - Hradek, Kutná Hora 08439
Okresni Vlastivědné Muzeum, Český Krumlov 08303
Okresni Vlastivědné Muzeum, Nový Jičín 08511
Okresní Vlastivědné Muzeum, Šumperk 08668
Okresní Vlastivědné Muzeum a Galerie, Česká Lípa 08294
Okresní Vlastivědné Muzeum Nový Jičín, Příbor 08624
Øksnes Bygdemuseum, Alsvåg 30377
Oktibbeha County Heritage Museum, Starkville 47777
Oku Archaeological Collection, Oku 26631
Oku Kokokan, Oku 26631
Okubank Group Museum, Helsinki 09517
Okukiyotsu Electric Power Museum, Yuzawa 27035
Okupatsioonimuuseum, Tallinn 09370
Okura Shukokan Museum, Tokyo 26911
Okutama Kyodo Shiryokan, Okutama 26632
Okyo and Rosetsu Art Museum, Kushimoto 26389
Olaf-Gulbransson-Museum, Tegernsee 20152
Olana State Historic Site, Hudson 44143
Olav Bjaaland Museum, Morgedal 30690
Olav Holmegaards Samlinger, Mandal 30665
Olavinlinna Castle, Olavinlinna 09881
Old Aircraft Museum, Arnemuiden 28932
Old Arts Gallery, Pretoria 34351
Old Atwood House Museum, Chatham 42256
Old Bank of New Brunswick Museum, Riverside-Albert 06276
Old Barracks Heritage Centre, Cahersiveen 22382
Old Barracks Museum, Trenton 48058
Old Bell Museum, Montgomery 39980
Old Bergen Museum, Bergen 30420
Old Bethpage Village Restoration, Old Bethpage 46129
Old Blythewood, Pinjarra 01366
Old Bohemia Historical Museum, Warwick 48319
Old Borroloola Police Station Museum, Borroloola 00817
Old Bridge House Museum, Dumfries 38790
Old Brown's Mill School, Chambersburg 42185
Old Brutus Historical Society Museum, Weedsport 48490
The Old Byre Heritage Centre, Dervaig 38724
Old Cable Station Museum, Apollo Bay 00743
Old Canberra Tram Company Museum, Dickson 00982
Old Capitol Museum of Mississippi History, Jackson 44285
Old Carleton County Court House, Woodstock 06863
Old Carriages Museum, Roma 25172
Old Castle Jevišovice - Moravian Museum Brno, Jevišovice 08387
Old Castle Museum, Baldwin City 41443
Old Cathedral Museum, Saint Louis 47133
Old City Hall and Prison of Bejucal, Bejucal 07863
Old City Park - The Historical Village of Dallas, Dallas 42756
Old Clock Museum, Pharr 46385
Old Colony Historical Museum, Taunton 47960
Old Constitution House, Windsor 48686
Old Conway Homestead Museum and Mary Meeker Cramer Museum, Camden 42058
Old Council Chambers Museum, Cleve 00926
Old Council Chambers Museum, Norton Summit 01333
Old Court House, Croydon 00957
Old Court House Museum, Durban 34229
Old Court House Museum, Guysborough 05539
Old Court House Museum-Eva Whitaker Davis Memorial, Vicksburg 48229
Old Courthouse Heritage Museum, Inverness 44242
Old Courthouse Museum, Santa Ana 47400
Old Courtyard Museum, Kibbutz Ein Shemer 22685
Old Cowtown Museum, Wichita 48607
Old Crofton School Museum, Crofton 05290
Old Crown Court and Shire Hall, Dorchester 38751
Old Depot Museum, Ottawa 46220
Old Derbent - Museum-Preserve of History, Architecture and Art, Derbent 32756
Old Dominion Railway Museum, Richmond 46884
Old Dominion University Gallery, Norfolk 45971
Old Dorchester State Historic Site, Summerville 47876
Old Dubbo Gaol, Dubbo 00993
Old Dutch Parsonage, Somerville 47672
Old Economy Village Museum, Ambridge 41168
Old English Court Museum, Moskva 33151
Old Exchange and Provost Dungeon, Charleston 42225
Old Falls Village, Menomonee Falls 45254
Old Fire House and Police Museum, Superior 47891
Old Firehouse Museum, Greenville 43824
Old Forge, Hellendoorn 29388
Old Fort Bissell, Phillipsburg 46468
Old Fort Erie, Niagara Falls 05997
Old Fort Garland, Fort Garland 43394
Old Fort Harrod Museum, Harrodsburg 43933
Old Fort Harrod State Park Mansion Museum, Harrodsburg 43934
Old Fort House Museum, Fort Edward 43392
Old Fort Jackson, Savannah 47481
Old Fort Johnson, Fort Johnson 43404
Old Fort Lauderdale Museum of History, Fort Lauderdale 43413
Old Fort Meade Museum, Fort Meade 43428
Old Fort Niagara, Youngstown 48805
Old Fort Number 4 Associates, Charlestown 42234
Old Fort Western, Augusta 41391
Old Fort William Historical Park, Thunder Bay 06546
Old Foundry Museum, Kragujevac 33851
Old Gala House, Galashiels 39024
Old Gaol and Courthouse, York 01632
Old Gaol Museum, Albany 00723
Old Gaol Museum, Buckingham 38387
Old Gaol Museum, York 48790
Old George's Authentic Collectibles, Whitewood 06796
Old Government House, Belair 00790
Old Government House, Brisbane 00839
Old Government House, Fredericton 05466
The Old Governor's Mansion, Frankfort 43513
Old Grammar School, Castletown 38509
Old Greer County Museum and Hall of Fame, Mangum 45103
The Old Guard Museum, Fort Myer 43433
Old Guildhall Museum, Looe 39825
Old Haa, Yell 40952
Old Harbour Museum, Hermanus 34262
Old Hastings Mill Store Museum, Vancouver 06685
Old Highercombe Museum, Tea Tree Gully 01522
Old House, Hereford 39228
Old House Museum, Bakewell 38059
Old House Museum, Durban 34230
Old House of Keys, Castletown 38510
Old House of the Marquises of Campo Florido, San Antonio de los Baños 08097
Old Hoxie House, Sandwich 47387
Old Iron County Courthouse Museum, Hurley 44178
The Old Jail Art Center, Albany 41091
Old Jail House, Croydon 00958
Old Jail Museum, Albion 41095
The Old Jail Museum, Crawfordsville 42692
The Old Jail Museum, Warrenton 48317
The Old Jameson Distillery, Dublin 22450
Old Jefferson Town, Oskaloosa 46209
Old Kuopio Museum, Kuopio 09719
Old Lifeboat Museum, Poole 40227
Old Lighthouse Museum, Michigan City 45303
Old Lighthouse Museum, Stonington 47829
Old Lincoln County Courthouse Museum, Lincoln 44796
Old Log Jail and Chapel Museums, Greenfield 43806
Old Mackinac Pointlightstation, Mackinac Island 45030
The Old Manse, Concord 42600
Old Market House, Galena 43594
Old Meeting House Museum, Barrington 05052
Old Melbourne Gaol and Penal Museum, Melbourne 01238
Old Merchant's House and Row 111 Houses, Great Yarmouth 39126
Old Mill Museum, Cimarron 42395
Old Mill Museum, San Marino 47367
Old Mission Santa Ines, Solvang 47666
Old Monterey Jail, Monterey 45458
Old Mornington Post Office Museum, Mornington 01277
Old Museum Arts Centre, Belfast 38155
Old Newcastle Gaol Museum, Toodyay 01537
Old Operating Theatre, Museum and Herb Garret, London 39737
Old Ordinary Museum, Hingham 44037
Old Parliament House, Canberra 00888
Old Police Station Museum Brookton, Brookton 00851
Old Post Office Museum, Turriff 40734
The Old Prison, Victoria 27711
Old Prison Museum, Deer Lodge 42847
Old Prison of Jaruco, Jaruco 08013
Old Railway Station Museum, Northam 01329
Old Rectory Museum, Loughborough 39831
Old Royal Palace, Praha 08614
Old Saint Edward's Anglican Church, Clementsport 05256
Old Saint Ferdinand's Shrine, Florissant 43350
Old Salem, Winston-Salem 48702
Old Sarepta- State Museum-Preserve of History, Ethnography and Architecture, Volgograd 33714
Old School House, York 48791
Old School House Arts Centre, Qualicum Beach 06193
Old School Museum, Merimbula 01247
Old Schoolhouse Museum, Ballintubber 22367
Old Schwamb Mill, Arlington 41258
Old Shawnee Town, Shawnee 47587
Old Slavonic Ringwall - National Cultural Monument, Mikulčice 08475
Old South Meeting House, Boston 41821
Old Spanish Fort and Museum, Pascagoula 46306
Old Speech Room Gallery, London 39738
Old Springsure Hospital Museum, Springsure 01471
Old State Bank, Vincennes 48241
Old State Capitol, Springfield 47740
Old State House, Boston 41822
Old State House, Hartford 43943
The Old State House Museum, Little Rock 44825
Old Steeple, Dundee 38803
Old Stone Fort Museum Complex, Schoharie 47499
The Old Stone House, Washington 48388
The Old Stone House Museum, Brownington 41962
Old Stone House Museum, Windsor 48684
The Old Stone Jail Museum, Palmyra 46272
Old Sturbridge Village, Sturbridge 47859
The Old Tavern Museum, Tuscaloosa 48115
Old Timers Traeger Museum, Alice Springs 00737
The Old Town, Århus 08770
Old Town Hall, Hemel Hempstead 39217
Old Town Hall Museum, Fifield 43319
Old Town Hall Museum, Margate 39912
Old Town Museum, Old Town 46135
Old Town San Diego, San Diego 47284
Old Toy Show, Lincoln 39501
Old Trail Museum, Choteau 42390
Old Village Hall Museum, Lindenhurst 44804
Old Ware House Gallery, Maryborough 01216
Old Washington Museum, Washington 48328
Old West Museum, Sunset 47887
Old West Wax Museum, Thermopolis 47994
Old Westbury Gardens, Old Westbury 46136
Old Wool and Grain Store Museum, Beachport 00779
Old World Wisconsin, Eagle 43031
Old York Historical Museum, York 48792
Old Zhi Display Center, Xing Si Army, Nanchang 07174
Olde Colonial Courthouse, Barnstable 41509
'T Olde Ras, Doesburg 29160
Oldenburg-Museum, Unna 20265
Oldenburger Fahrradmuseum, Oldenburg, Oldenburg 19258
The Oldest House Museum, Key West 44470
Oldest House Museum Complex, Saint Augustine 47069
Oldest Stone House Museum, Lakewood 44611
Oldham County History Center, La Grange 44544
Oldman River Cultural Centre, Brocket 05137
Oldtimer-Museum, Arbon 36467
Oldtimer Museum, Rheinfelden 37055
Oldtimercentrum Select, Joure 29467
Oldtimermuseum, Ardagger 01678
Oldtimermuseum De Rijke, Oostvoorne 29674
Oldtimermuseum De Ronkel, Kloosterburen 29485
Oldtimermuseum im Schloß, Blindenmarkt 01740
Dat ole Hus, Aukrug 15574
Ole Rømer Museet, Taastrup 09090
Olfactorium de Coëx, Coëx 11340
Ølgod Museum, Ølgod 09019
Oliemolen de Zoeker, Zaandam 30039
Oliemolen Het Pink, Koog aan de Zaan 29490
Oliewenhuis Art Museum, Bloemfontein 34192
Olin Art Gallery, Gambier 43615
Olin Fine Arts Center, Washington 48417
Olive DeLuce Art Gallery, Maryville 45196
Olive Hyde Art Gallery, Fremont 43553
Olive Schreiner House, Cradock 34221
Oliver Cromwell's House, Ely 38934
Oliver House Museum, Penn Yan 46340
Oliver House Museum, Saint Martinville 47143
Oliver Kelley Farm, Elk River 43138
Oliver Tucker Historic Museum, Beverly 41672
Olkijoen Rauhanpirtti, Pattijoki 09914
Olle Olsson-Huset, Solna 36219
Olmstead Place State Park, Ellensburg 43151
Olmsted County Historical Society Museum, Rochester 46935
Olofsfors Bruksmuseum, Nordmaling 36114
Olomouc Museum of Art, Olomouc 08515
Oloneckaja Kartinnaja Galereja, Olonec 33251
Oloneckij Nacionalnyj Muzej Karelov-Livvikov im. N.T.Prilukin, Olonec 33252
Olorgesailie Prehistoric Site Museum, Olorgesailie 27114
Olustee Battlefield, Olustee 46138
Olustvere Muuseum, Olustvere 09342
Olympic Hall of Fame and Museum, Calgary 05177
Olympic Museum, Wellington 30305
Oma-Freese-Huus, Dornum 16652
Omachi Alpine Museum, Omachi 26633
Omaha Center for Contemporary Art, Omaha 46151
Omaha Children's Museum, Omaha 46152
Oman Natural History Museum, Muscat 31006
Omani-French Museum Bait Fransa, Muscat 31007
Omaruru Museum, Omaruru 28764
Ombalantu Baobab Tree, Ombalantu 28765
Ome Municipal Museum, Ome 26636
Ome Municipal Museum of Art, Ome 26635
Ome-shiritsu Bijutsukan, Ome 26635
Ome-shiritsu Hakubutsukan, Ome 26636
Omi Natural History Museum, Omi 26637
Omi Shrine Clock Museum, Otsu 26682
Omnisphere and Science Center, Wichita 48608
Omoide Museum, Kyoto 26444
Omroepmuseum en Smalfilmmuseum, Hilversum 29420
Omsk Fine Art Museum Mikhail Vrubel, Omsk 33257
Omsk Literature Museum F.M. Dostoevsky, Omsk 33256
Omskij Gosudarstvennyj Istoriko-kraevedčeskij Muzej, Omsk 33255
Omskij Gosudarstvennyj Literaturnyj Muzej im. F.M. Dostoevskogo, Omsk 33256
Omskij Oblastnoj Muzej Izobrazitelnych Iskusstv im. M.A. Vrubelja, Omsk 33257
On the Hill Cultural Arts Center, Yorktown 48799
Ondergronds Museum, Kanne 03532
Onderstepoort Veterinary History Museum, Onderstepoort 34316
Onderwijsmuseum Educatorium, Ootmarsum 29677
Oneida Community Mansion House, Oneida 46157
Oneida County Historical Society Museum, Utica 48171
Oneida Nation Museum, De Pere 42816
Ongaonga Old School Museum, Ongaonga 30220
Ongerup and Needilup District Museum, Ongerup 01344
Onggi Folk Museum and Institute, Seoul 27265
Onomichi City Museum of Art, Onomichi 26641
Onomichi Shiritsu Bijutsukan, Onomichi 26641
Onondaga Historical Association Museum, Syracuse 47912
Ons Museum, Giessenburg 29277
Ons Museum, Wintelre 30012
Onslow County Museum, Richlands 46857
Onslow Goods Shed Museum, Onslow 01345
Ontario Agricultural Museum, Milton 05854
Ontario County Historical Society Museum, Canandaigua 42077
Ontario Museum Association, Toronto 49103
Ontario Police College Museum, Aylmer 05030
Ontario Science Centre, Toronto 06600
De Ontdekhoek Kindermuseum, Rotterdam 29770
Ontmoetingscentrum de Veldkei, Expositie, Havelte 29354
Ontonagon County Historical Society Museum, Ontonagon 46167
Onufri Iconographic Museum, Berat 00013
Onyang Folk Museum, Asan 27132
Onyang Minsok Pakmulgwan, Asan 27132
Oorlogs- en Verzetsmuseum Johannes Post, Ridderkerk 29730
Oorlogsmuseum, Bloemfontein 34193
Oorlogsmuseum Bezinning 1940-1945, Borculo 29000
Oorlogsverzetsmuseum Rotterdam, Rotterdam 29771
Oost-Indisch Huis, Amsterdam 28890
Oostends Historisch Museum De Plate, Oostende 03671
Opal and Gem Museum, Ballina 00767
Opatska Riznica Sv. Marka, Korčula 07723
Općinski Muzej, Mali Lošinj 07738
Opelousas Museum, Opelousas 46168
Opelousas Museum of Art, Opelousas 46169
Open-Air Dept. of the Jēkabpils History Museum, Jēkabpils 27360
Open Air Museum, Ahlat 37604
Open Air Museum, Buenos Aires 00156
Open-Air-Museum, Karlskrona 36001
Open Air Museum, Kihniö 09664
Open Air Museum, Kongens Lyngby 08962
Open Air Museum, Stará Lubovňa 34066
Open Air Museum, Szalafő 21543
Open Air Museum, Székesfehérvár 21559
Open Air Museum, Villa Carlos Paz 00661
Open Air Museum for Archeology, Mrówki 31814
Open Air Museum Italo Bolano, Portoferraio 25018
Open-Air Museum of Ethnography, Gabrovo 04665
Open Air Museum of Old Japanese Farmhouses, Toyonaka 26973
Open Air Museum of Sculpture Middelheim, Antwerpen 03166
Open Air Museum of Sóstó, Sóstógyógyfürdő 21540
Open Air Museum of Szymbark and branch in Bartnem, Sękowa 31968
Open Air Museum of the Oaş Land, Negreşti-Oaş 32555
Open Air Museum of Water Supply, Szolnok 21586
Open Air Museum Old Dobrich, Dobrič 04653
Open-Air Water-Power Museum, Dimitsana 20938
Open Eye Photography Gallery, Liverpool 39526

Open Haven Museum, Amsterdam 28891
Open Museum, Migdal-Tefen 22715
Open Museum, Omer 22724
Open Space Gallery, Victoria 06727
Openbaar Vervoer Museum, Borculo 29001
Openbaar Vervoer Museum, Rotterdam 29772
Openlucht Laagveenderij Museum Damshûs, Nij Beets 29627
Openluchtmuseum De Duinhuisjes, Rockanje 29738
Openluchtmuseum Ellert en Brammert, Schoonoord 29815
Openluchtmuseum Erve Kots, Lievelde 29541
Openluchtmuseum Het Hoogeland, Warffum 29978
Openluchtmuseum Nieuw Amsterdam, Nieuw Amsterdam 35776
Openluchtmuseum Ootmarsum, Ootmarsum 29678
Openluchtmuseum voor Beeldhouwkunst Middelheim, Antwerpen 03166
Operetta Theatre Museum, Moskva 33153
Opie's Museum of Memories, Wigan 40871
Oplenova Hiša, Srednja Vas v Bohinju 34154
Opotiki Museum, Opotiki 30221
Oppdal Bygdemuseum, Oppdal 30716
Oppenheimers Konsthall, Eldsberga 35865
Opštinski Muzej, Sremska Mitrovica 33914
Optisches Museum, Oberkochen 19181
Optisches Museum der Ernst-Abbe-Stiftung Jena, Jena 17945
Opus 40 and the Quarryman's Museum, Saugerties 47465
Orang Asli Museum, Melaka 27676
Orange County Historical Museum, Hillsborough 44030
Orange County Museum of Art, Newport Beach 45935
Orange County Regional History Center, Orlando 46187
Orange Empire Railway Museum, Perris 46353
Orange Regional Gallery, Orange 01347
Orangedale Railway Museum, Orangedale 06053
Orangerie, Gera 17246
Orangerie, 's-Hertogenbosch 29409
Orangerie Benrath, Düsseldorf 16740
Orangerie im Englischen Garten, München 18892
Orangerie und Schloßpark Belvedere, Weimar, Thüringen 20468
Orangetown Historical Museum, Pearl River 46323
Oranien-Nassau-Museum Oranienstein, Diez 16607
Oranje Museum, Baarn 28960
Orava Gallery, Dolný Kubín 33989
Orava Gallery, Námestovo 34033
Orava Gallery, Tvrdošín 34076
Oravská Galéria, Dolný Kubín 33989
Oravská Galéria, Námestovo 34033
Oravské Múzeum Pavla Országha Hviezdoslava, Dolný Kubín 33990
Orawski Park Etnograficzny, Zubrzyca Górna 32225
Orcas Island Historical Museum, Eastsound 43071
Orchard Gallery, Londonderry 39817
Orchard House - Home of the Alcotts, Concord 42601
Orchard Park Historical Society Museum, Orchard Park 46178
Ordenmuseum, Neuffen 19030
Ordensmuseum Abtei Kamp, Kamp-Lintfort 17981
Order of Saint John Museum, Christchurch 30130
Ordrupgaard, Charlottenlund 08793
Ordsall Hall Museum, Salford 40431
Ordu Devlet Güzel Sanatlar Galerisi, Ordu 37772
Ordu State Gallery, Ordu 37772
Ore-Petrographic Museum, Moskva 33167
Orebić Maritime Museum, Orebić 07749
Øregaard-Museum, Hellerup 08858
Oregon Air and Space Museum, Eugene 43226
Oregon Coast History Center, Newport 45921
Oregon Electric Railway Historical Society Museum, Lake Oswego 44592
Oregon History Center, Portland 46637
Oregon-Jerusalem Historical Museum, Oregon 46179
Oregon Military Museum, Clackamas 42416
Oregon Museum of Science and Industry, Portland 46638
Oregon Museums Association, Portland 49527
Oregon Sports Hall of Fame and Museum, Portland 46639
Oregon Trail Museum, Gering 43657
Oregon Trail Regional Museum, Baker City 41438
Orel Regional Museum of Fine Art, Orël 33268
Orenburg Museum of Fine Arts, Orenburg 33271
Orenburg Regional Museum, Orenburg 33270
Orenburgskij Oblastnoj Kraevedčeskij Muzej, Orenburg 33270
Orenburgskij Oblastnoj Muzej Izobrazitelnych Iskusstv, Orenburg 33271
Organ Historical Trust of Australia, Camberwell, Victoria 00877
Organization of Military Museums of Canada, Gloucester 49104
Organization of Museums, Monuments and Sites of Africa OMMSA, Accra 49218
Orgel-Art-Museum Rhein-Nahe, Windesheim 20606
Orgelbaumuseum, Ostheim vor der Rhön 19299
Orgelmuseet i Fläckebo, Salbohed 36175
Orgelmuseum Altes Schloß, Valley 20284
Orgelmuseum Borgentreich, Borgentreich 16256
Orgelmuseum Kelheim, Kelheim 18051
Oriamu Museum, Izumiotsu 26278
Oriel Davies Gallery, Newtown, Powys 40070
Oriel Gallery, Mold 39973
Oriel Mostyn Gallery, Llandudno 39542
Oriel Ynys Môn, Llangefni 39550
Oriental Institute Museum, Chicago 42355
Oriental Kazakh Regional Historical Museum, Petropavlovsk 27090
Oriental Museum, Durham 38829
Oriental Museum for Carpets, Riyadh 33775
Orientalisches Münzkabinett Jena, Jena 17946
Orientteppich-Museum, Hannover 17609
Original-Dorfschmiede Ehlen, Habichtswald 17470
Original- und Abgußsammlung der Universität Trier, Trier 20211
Orillia Museum of Art and History, Orillia 06054
Orimattila Local History Museum, Orimattila 09884
Orimattilan Kotiseutumuseo, Orimattila 09884
Orimattilan Taidemuseo, Orimattila 09885
Orimattilas Art Museum, Orimattila 09885
Orinasukan, Kyoto 26445
Oripään Museo, Oripää 09887
Oriskany Battlefield, Oriskany 46183
Orissa State Museum, Bhubaneshwar 21726
Oriveden Paltanmäen Museo, Orivesi 09888
Orivesi Paltanmäki Museum, Orivesi 09888
Orkdal Bygdemuseum, Svorkmo 30912
Orkdal Bygdetun, Fannrem 30487
Orkney Farm and Folk Museum, Birsay 38234
Orkney Farm and Folk Museum, Harray 39166
Orkney Museum, Kirkwall 39397
Orkney Wireless Museum, Kirkwall 39398
Orland Historical Museum, Orland 46184
Orlando Brown House, Frankfort 43514
Orlando Museum of Art, Orlando 46188
Orlando Science Center, Orlando 46189
Orleans House Gallery, Twickenham 40741
Orlická Galerie, Rychnov nad Kněžnou 08648
Orlické Muzeum, Choceň 08313
Orlogsmuseet, København 08946
Orlovskij Oblastnoj Kraevedčeskij Muzej, Orël 33267
Orlovskij Oblastnoj Muzej Izobrazitelnych Iskusstv, Orël 33268
Ormeau Baths Gallery, Belfast 38156
Ormond Memorial Art Museum, Ormond Beach 46193
Ornithology and Entomology Museum, Cairo 09282
Ornunga Museum, Vårgårda 36398
Oroville Chinese Temple, Oroville 46198
Orskij Istoriko-kraevedčeskij Muzej, Orsk 33272
Országos Aluminiumipari Múzeum, Székesfehérvár 21558
Országos Geológia Múzeum, Budapest 21372
Országos Műszaki Múzeum, Budapest 21373
Országos Pedagógiai Könyvtár és Múzeum, Budapest 21374
Országos Színháztörténeti Múzeum és Intézet, Budapest 21375
Országos Zsidó Vallási és Történeti Gyűjtemény, Budapest 21376
Orthodox Church in Bartne, Bartne 31479
Orthodox Church Museum of Finland, Kuopio 09722
Orto Botanico, Palermo 24778
Orto Botanico Hanbury, Genova 24009
Ortodoksinen Kirkkomuseo, Kuopio 09722
Orton Geological Museum, Columbus 42591
Orts- und Weinbaumuseum, Neftenbach 36979
Orts- und Wohnmuseum, Marthalen 36922
Ortsgeschichtliche Sammlung, Bovenden 16266
Ortsgeschichtliche Sammlung, Oberrieden 37001
Ortsgeschichtliche Sammlung Rebstein, Rebstein 37046
Ortsgeschichtliches Museum, Siegenburg 19952
Ortskundliche Sammlung Bargteheide, Bargteheide 15824
Ortskundliches Museum Jois, Jois 02091
Ortsmuseum, Amriswil 36457
Ortsmuseum, Andwil 36459
Ortsmuseum, Bergün 36536
Ortsmuseum, Binningen 36569
Ortsmuseum, Bülach 36598
Ortsmuseum, Bütschwil 36601
Ortsmuseum, Häggenschwil 36789
Ortsmuseum, Jona 36821
Ortsmuseum, Kaltbrunn 36822
Ortsmuseum, Laax 36843
Ortsmuseum, Liesberg 36875
Ortsmuseum, Meilen 36933
Ortsmuseum, Merenschwand 36939
Ortsmuseum, Nürensdorf 36992
Ortsmuseum, Oftringen 37007
Ortsmuseum, Rafz 37040
Ortsmuseum, Roggwil 37067
Ortsmuseum, Rüti, Zürich 37077
Ortsmuseum, Sankt Stephan 37116
Ortsmuseum, Schänis 37129
Ortsmuseum, Thalwil 37237
Ortsmuseum, Unterengstringen 37261
Ortsmuseum, Untersiggenthal 37266
Ortsmuseum, Vaz 37282
Ortsmuseum, Vnà 37295
Ortsmuseum, Wängi 37298
Ortsmuseum, Walenstadt 37301
Ortsmuseum, Weikertschlag 02799
Ortsmuseum, Zwentendorf 03057
Ortsmuseum Albisrieden, Zürich 37401
Ortsmuseum Altes Rathaus, Balgach 36491
Ortsmuseum Altstetten, Altstetten 36453
Ortsmuseum Beringen, Beringen 36537
Ortsmuseum Bern, Wangen an der Aare 37305
Ortsmuseum Brittnau, Brittnau 36589
Ortsmuseum Diessenhofen, Diessenhofen 36660
Ortsmuseum Dietikon, Dietikon 36661
Ortsmuseum Eglisau, Eglisau 36672
Ortsmuseum Erlenbach, Erlenbach (Zürich) 36686
Ortsmuseum Eschlikon, Eschlikon 36691
Ortsmuseum Flawil, Flawil 36701
Ortsmuseum Frenkendorf, Frenkendorf 36710
Ortsmuseum für Heimatkunde, Schlieren 37138
Ortsmuseum Gaiserwald, Sankt Josefen 37110
Ortsmuseum Hinwil, Hinwil 36804
Ortsmuseum Höngg, Zürich 37402
Ortsmuseum Kefiturm, Belp 36534
Ortsmuseum Kilchberg, Kilchberg, Zürich 36825
Ortsmuseum Küsnacht, Küsnacht 36840
Ortsmuseum Linthal, Linthal 36883
Ortsmuseum mit Karl-Jauslin-Sammlung, Muttenz 36977
Ortsmuseum Mollis, Mollis 36943
Ortsmuseum Mühle, Maur 36932
Ortsmuseum Neunkirch, Neunkirch 36988
Ortsmuseum Oberes Bad, Marbach (Sankt Gallen) 36921
Ortsmuseum Oberuzwil, Oberuzwil 37003
Ortsmuseum Oetwil, Oetwil am See 37005
Ortsmuseum Rüschlikon, Rüschlikon 37076
Ortsmuseum Sankt Veit, Sankt Veit im Mühlkreis 02617
Ortsmuseum Schleitheim, Schleitheim 37136
Ortsmuseum Schmitten, Schmitten (Albula) 37140
Ortsmuseum Spreitenbach, Spreitenbach 37197
Ortsmuseum Steinmaur, Sünikon 37221
Ortsmuseum Sust, Horgen 36809
Ortsmuseum Trotte, Arlesheim 36468
Ortsmuseum Urdorf, Urdorf 37269
Ortsmuseum Ursulastift, Gerstetten 17262
Ortsmuseum Vechigen, Boll 36576
Ortsmuseum Wallisellen, Wallisellen 37302
Ortsmuseum Weiach, Weiach 37309
Ortsmuseum Wetzikon, Wetzikon 37314
Ortsmuseum Wiesendangen, Wiesendangen 37318
Ortsmuseum Wila, Wila 37321
Ortsmuseum Wilchingen, Wilchingen 37322
Ortsmuseum Wilderswil, Wilderswil 37324
Ortsmuseum Wollishofen, Zürich 37403
Ortsmuseum Zollikon, Zollikon 37367
Ortsmuseum zur Farb, Stäfa 37200
Ortsmuseum zur Hohlen Eich, Wädenswil 37297
Ortssammlung Wettelsheim, Treuchtlingen 20200
Ortsstube, Bolligen 36577
Oružejnaja Palata, Moskva 33168
Orval Berry Museum, Frankford 05455
Orwell Corner Historic Village, Orwell 06058
Osage County Historical Society, Lyndon 45010
Osage County Historical Society Museum, Pawhuska 46314
Osage Village Historic Site, Lamar 44613
Osaka Castle Museum, Osaka 26660
Osaka City Museum of Modern Art, Osaka 26670
Osaka-furitsu Gendai Bijutsu Center, Osaka 26661
Osaka-furitsu Senboku Koko Shiryokan, Sakai 26697
Osaka Human Rights Museum, Osaka 26662
Osaka International Peace Center, Osaka 26663
Osaka-kenritsu Chikatsuasuka Hakubutsukan, Kanan 26304
Osaka-kenritsu Chu Hakabutsukan, Mino 26491
Osaka-kenritsu Sayamaike Hakubutsukan, Osaka-Sayama 26677
Osaka-kenritsu Waha Kamigata Bungeikan, Osaka 26664
Osaka Lottery Dream Museum, Osaka 26665
Osaka Maritime Museum, Osaka 26658
Osaka Municipal Museum of Art, Osaka 26669
Osaka Museum of History, Osaka 26666
Osaka Museum of Natural History, Osaka 26667
Osaka Nippon Mingeikan, Suita 26775
Osaka Prefectural Chikatsuasuka Museum, Kanan 26304
Osaka Prefectural Insect Museum, Mino 26491
Osaka Prefectural Museum of Kamigata Performing Arts, Osaka 26664
Osaka Prefectural Museum of Yayoi Culture, Izumi 26277
Osaka Prefectural Sayama Pond Museum, Osaka-Sayama 26677
Osaka Regional Contemporary Art Center, Osaka 26661
Osaka Science Museum, Osaka 26668
Osaka Senboku Area Archaeological Museum, Sakai 26697
Osaka-shiritsu Bijutsukan, Osaka 26669
Osaka-shiritsu Kindai Bijutsukan Kensetsu Jumbishitsu, Osaka 26670
Osaka-shiritsu Toyo Toji Bijutsukan, Osaka 26671
Osbane Museet, Fana 30486
Osborn-Jackson House, East Hampton 43049
Osborne House, East Cowes 38839
Oscar Anderson House Museum, Anchorage 41201
Oscar Getz Museum of Whiskey History, Bardstown 41504
Oscar Howe Art Center, Mitchell 45415
Oscarsborg Festningsmuseum, Oscarsborg 30723
Oscarshall Slott, Oslo 30757
Osen Bygdemuseum, Osen 30725
Osen Bygdetun, Steinsdalen 30895
Oseredok Ukrainian Art Gallery and Museum, Winnipeg 06836
Osgoode Township Museum, Vernon, Ontario 06709
Osh United Historical Cultural Museum-Preserve, Oš 27312
Oshawa Sydenham Museum, Oshawa 06060
Oshkosh Public Museum, Oshkosh 46206
Osinskij Kraevedčeskij Muzej, Osa 33273
Osipov-Woolf House-Museum, Puškinskie Gory 33343
Oskar Kokoschka Geburtshaus, Pöchlarn 02422
Oskar Luts Majamuuseum, Tartu 09381
Oskar Schlemmer Archiv, Stuttgart 20102
Oskar Schlemmer Theatre Estate and Collection, Oggebbio 24673
Oskara Kalpaka Muzejs Airīšu Piemiņas Vietā, Zirņi 27478
Oskars Kalpaks Museum in the Memorial Site Airītes, Zirņi 27478
Osler Historical Museum, Osler 06062
Oslo Bymuseum, Oslo 30758
Oslo City Museum, Oslo 30758
Osmalı Evi, Bursa 37647
Osmani Museum, Sylhet 03102
Osoyoos Art Gallery, Osoyoos 06063
Osoyoos Museum, Osoyoos 06064
Ośrodek Biograficzny Komisji Turystyki Górskiej, Kraków 31725
Ośrodek Budownictwa Ludowego w Szymbarku z filia w Bartnem, Sękowa 31968
Ośrodek Historii Dęblińskiego Węzła Kolejowego, Dęblin 31551
Ośrodek Muzealno-Dydaktyczny Wielkopolskiego Parku Narodowego, Mosina 31812
Ossining Historical Society Museum, Ossining 46212
Osškij Objedinennyj Istoriko-Kulturnyj Muzej-Zapovednik, Oš 27312
Ostarrichi-Kulturhof, Neuhofen an der Ybbs 02343
Ostasiatika-Sammlung Ehrich, Hattingen 17636
Østasiatiska Museet, Stockholm 36271
Ostdeutsche Heimatstube, Bad Zwischenahn 15784
Ostdeutsche Heimatstube, Fellbach 16991
Ostdeutsche Heimatstube, Schwäbisch Hall 19869
Ostdeutsche Kultur- und Heimatstuben mit Schönbacher Stube, Heppenheim 17713
Osterburgsammlung, Bischofsheim an der Rhön 16169
Ostereimuseum, Sonnenbühl 19998
Osterley Park House, Isleworth 39320
Osterøy Museum, Lonevåg 30653
Osterville Historical Museum, Osterville 46213
Osterzgebirgsmuseum, Lauenstein 18351
Das Ostfriesische Teemuseum und Norder Heimatmuseum, Norden 19113
Ostfriesisches Landesmuseum und Emder Rüstkammer, Emden 16850
Ostfriesisches Landwirtschaftsmuseum, Krummhörn 18255
Ostfriesisches Schulmuseum Folmhusen, Westoverledingen 20545
Osthofentor-Museum, Soest 19979
Ostholstein-Museum, Eutin 16979
Ostholstein-Museum Neustadt, Neustadt in Holstein 19081
Ostindiefararen Götheborg, Göteborg 35917
Ostpreußisches Landesmuseum, Lüneburg 18561
Ostravské Muzeum, Ostrava 08527
Ostrobothnia Australis, Vaasa 10160
Ostrobothnian Museum, Vaasa 10161
Ostrogožskij Rajonnyj Istoriko-chudožestvennyj Muzej im. I.N. Kramskogo, Ostrogožsk 33276
Ostrovsky House Museum, Moskva 33041
Østsamisk Museum, Neiden 30706
Østsjællands Museum, Stevns Museum, Store Heddinge 09080
Osuuspankkimuseo, Helsinki 09517
Oswego Historical Museum, Oswego 46214
Oswestry Transport Museum, Oswestry 40137
Ōta Kinen Bijutsukan, Tokyo 26912
Ōta Memorial Museum of Art, Tokyo 26912
Otago Military Museum, Dunedin 30150
Otago Museum, Dunedin 30151
Otago Settlers Museum, Dunedin 30152
Otago Vintage Machinery Club Museum, Dunedin 30153
Otakou Marae Museum, Dunedin 30154
Otani Memorial Art Museum Nishinomiya City, Nishinomiya 26606
Otar Memlekettik Archeologicalik Korik Muzej, Čimkent 27079
Otaru Museum, Otaru 26679
Otaru Science Center, Otaru 26680
Otaru-shi Hakubutsukan, Otaru 26679
Otaru-shi Seishonen Kagakugijutsukan, Otaru 26680
Otautau and District Local History Museum, Otautau 30222
Otello Kalesi, Gazimağusa 08220
Othello's Tower, Gazimağusa 08220
Othmar Jaindl-Museum, Villach 02760
Otis Gallery, Los Angeles 44936
Otley Museum, Otley 40138
Otoe County Museum of Memories, Syracuse 47905
Oton Župančič Collection, Vinica 34163
Otrar State Archaeological Park Museum, Shymkent 27096
Otraženie - Muzej Voskovych Figur, Moskva 33169
Ottawa County Historical Museum, Port Clinton 46592
Ottawa Scouting Museum, Ottawa 46219
Ottenby Naturum, Degerhamn 35852
Otter Tail County Historical Museum, Fergus Falls 43313
Otterton Mill Centre and Working Museum, Budleigh Salterton 38391
Otterup Museum, Otterup 09021
Ottmar-Mergenthaler-Museum, Bad Mergentheim 15694
Otto-Dill Museum, Neustadt an der Weinstraße 19078
Otto-Dix-Haus, Gera 17247
Otto-Dix-Haus Hemmenhofen, Gaienhofen 17191

Otto-Flath-Kunsthalle, Bad Segeberg 15741
Otto-König von Griechenland-Museum, Ottobrunn 19329
Otto-Lilienthal-Museum, Anklam 15495
Otto Modersohn Museum, Ottersberg 19326
Otto Pankok Museum, Hünxe 17861
Otto-Schwabe-Museum, Hochheim am Main 17774
Otto-von-Guericke-Museum in der Lukasklause, Magdeburg 18586
Otto Wagner Hofpavillion Hietzing, Wien 02966
Otto Wagner Pavillion Karlsplatz, Wien 02967
Ottoman House, Bursa 37647
Otwock Agricultural Museum, Otwock 31871
Oud Amelisweerd Museum, Bunnik 29036
Ouddorps Raad- en Polderhuis, Ouddorp 29694
De Oude Aarde, Giethoorn 29282
Oude Ambachten en Speelgoedmuseum, Terschuur 29869
Oude Bakkerij, Medemblik 29584
De Oude Drostdy, Tulbagh 34390
Oude Kerk Volksmuseum, Tulbagh 34391
't Oude Raadhuis, Beek en Donk 28967
Het Oude Raadhuis, Leerdam 29507
Het Oude Raadhuis, Oud-Beijerland 29689
Het Oude Raadhuis, Urk 29892
Het Oude Slot Heemstede, Heemstede 29357
Het Oude Stadhuis, Hasselt 29350
Oudheidkamer, Bruinisse 29032
Oudheidkamer, Den Burg 29089
Oudheidkamer, Koudekerk 29492
Oudheidkamer, Steenwijk 29852
Oudheidkamer, Wijngaarden 30005
Oudheidkamer Beilen, Beilen 28971
Oudheidkamer Bleiswijk, Bleiswijk 28987
Oudheidkamer Boerderij Strunk, Raalte 29721
Oudheidkamer Brederwiede, Vollenhove 29960
Oudheidkamer Buisjan Enter, Enter 29244
Oudheidkamer Dantumadeel, Zwaagwesteinde 30078
Oudheidkamer de Oude Pastory, Heiloo 29378
Oudheidkamer Doorn, Doorn 29168
Oudheidkamer Eemnes, Eemnes 29199
Oudheidkamer Geervliet, Geervliet 29266
Oudheidkamer Heerde, Heerde 29359
Oudheidkamer Hellevoetsluis, Hellevoetsluis 29392
Oudheidkamer Hoolt'n, Holten 29434
Oudheidkamer Horst, Horst 29449
Oudheidkamer Ijsselstreek, Wijhe 30003
Oudheidkamer in het Stadhuis, Bolsward 28995
Oudheidkamer Leiderdorp, Leiderdorp 29528
Oudheidkamer Lemster Fiifgea, Lemmer 29536
Oudheidkamer Leshuis, Dedemsvaart 29073
Oudheidkamer Lunteren, Lunteren 29552
Oudheidkamer/ Museum Mr. Andreae, Kollum 29488
Oudheidkamer Nederlandse Kaap-Hoornvaarders, Hoorn 29444
Oudheidkamer Nunspeet, Nunspeet 29651
Oudheidkamer Renswoude, Renswoude 29727
Oudheidkamer Ridderkerk, Ridderkerk 29731
Oudheidkamer Rozenburg, Rozenburg 29782
Die Oudheidkamer tot Medenblick, Medemblik 29585
Oudheidkamer Vreeswijk, Nieuwegein 29620
Oudheidkamer Wassenaar, Wassenaar 29984
Oudheidkamer Weststellingwerf, Wolvega 30019
Oudheidkamer Wieringerwaard het Polderhuis, Wieringerwaard 30001
Oudheidkamer Willem Van Strijen, Zevenbergen 30058
Oudheidkundeige Verzameling, Schinveld 29806
Oudheidkundig Museum, Sint Michielsgestel 29821
Oudheidkundig Museum Arnemuiden, Arnemuiden 28933
Oudheidkundig Museum Sint-Janshospitaal, Damme 03369
Oudheidkundig Museum van het Begijnhof, Turnhout 03805
Oudheidkundige Verzameling, Sluis 29836
Oulaisten Kotiseutumuseo, Oulainen 09889
Oulu City Art Museum, Oulu 09892
Oulun Automuseo, Oulu 09891
Oulun Taidemuseo, Oulu 09892
Oulun Yliopiston Eläinmuseo, Oulu 09893
Oulun Yliopiston Geologinen Museo, Oulu 09894
Oulun Yliopiston Kasvimuseo, Oulu 09895
Oulunsalon Kotiseutumuseo, Oulunsalo 09899
Oundle Museum, Oundle 40139
Our Heritage Museum, Adelaide 34169
Our House State Memorial, Gallipolis 43605
Our India Project Museum, Narendrapur 21966
Our Lady of Mercy Museum, Port-au-Port 06152
L'Oustal des Abeilles, Faugères 11706
Outagamie Museum and Houdini Historical Center, Appleton 41240
Outeniqua Railway Museum, George 34245
Outjo Museum, Outjo 28768
Outlook and District Heritage Museum and Gallery, Outlook 06086
Outokummun Kaivosmuseo, Outokumpu 09900
Outreach Collection, West Malling 40826
Outward Bound Museum, Aberdovey 37945
Ouvrage de la Ligne Maginot, Leutenheim 12567
Ouvrage Maginot de Rohrbach, Rohrbach-les-Bitche 14010
Ouyen Local History Resource Centre, Ouyen 01349
Ovens Museum, Riverport 06275
Overfield Tavern Museum, Troy 48073
Overholser Mansion, Oklahoma City 46122
Overland Trail Museum, Sterling 47803
Owatonna Arts Center, Owatonna 46225
Owela Display Centre, Windhoek 28782
Owen Sound Marine and Rail Museum, Owen Sound 06089
Owens Art Gallery, Sackville 06298
Owens-Thomas House, Savannah 47482
Owensboro Area Museum of Science and History, Owensboro 46229
Owensboro Museum of Fine Art, Owensboro 46230
Owls Head Transportation Museum, Owls Head 46231
Owo Museum, Owo 30360
Owyhee County Historical Museum, Murphy 45570
Oxford Bus Museum Trust, Long Hanborough 39822
Oxford Library Museum, Oxford 46235
Oxford Museum, Oxford 30225
Oxford Museum, Oxford 46236
The Oxford Story, Oxford 40150
Oxford University Museum of Natural History, Oxford 40151
Oxford University Press Museum, Oxford 40152
The Oxfordshire Museum, Woodstock 40925
Oxon Cove Park Museum, Oxon Hill 46246
Oyamazumi-jinja Kokuhokan, Omishima 26638
Oyamazumi Jinja Treasure House, Omishima 26638
Øyfjell Bygdemuseum, Vinje 30996
The Oyster and Maritime Museum of Chincoteague, Chincoteague 42383
Ozark Folk Center, Mountain View 45548
Ozaukee Art Center, Cedarburg 42163
Ozaukee County Historical Society Pioneer Village, Saukville 47468
P. and Al. Canellopoulos Museum, Athinai 20898
P. Jacinto Zamora Historical Museum, Manila 31389
P. Ramlee Memorial, Kuala Lumpur 27649
P.A. Krasikov House-Museum, Krasnojarsk 32949
Paamiune Katersugausivik, Paamiut 21235
Paarl Museum, Paarl 34321
Paattinen District Museum, Paattinen 09901
Paattisten Kotiseutumuseo, Paattinen 09901
Paavolan Kotiseutumuseo, Paavola 09902
PAC - Padiglione d'Arte Contemporanea, Milano 24414
PAC - Poste d'Arte Contemporain, Fribourg 36719
Pacem in Terris, Warwick 48320
Pacific Arts Center, Seattle 47542
Pacific Asia Museum, Pasadena 46303
Pacific County Historical Museum, South Bend 47684
Pacific Great Eastern Station, North Vancouver 06026
Pacific Grove Art Center, Pacific Grove 46252
Pacific Grove Museum of Natural History, Pacific Grove 46253
Pacific Islands Museums Association, Suva 49154
Pacific Lumber Company Museum, Scotia 47505
Pacific Museum, Yongin 27303
Pacific Northwest Truck Museum, Brooks 41956
Pacific Science Center, Seattle 47543
Pacific University Museum, Forest Grove 43362
Packwood House, Lapworth 39424
Packwood House Museum, Lewisburg 44722
Paço dos Duques de Bragança, Guimarães 32279
Paço Imperial, Rio de Janeiro 04399
Padasjoen Kotiseutumuseo, Nyystölä 09878
Padasjoen Kotiseutumuseo, Padasjoki 09903
Padasjoen Kotiseutumuseo, Torittu 10112
Padre Burgos National Museum, Vigan 31465
Padstow Museum, Padstow 40157
Päämajamuseo, Mikkeli 09833
Paekakariki Railway Museum, Wellington 30306
Pängelanton-Eisenbahnmuseum, Münster 18944
Pärnu Muuseum, Pärnu 09344
Paeroa and District Historical Society Museum, Paeroa 30226
Pätärin Talomuseo, Ylijärvi 10215
PAF Museum, Karachi 31031
Pagode de Chanteloup, Amboise 10315
Pagodenburg Rastatt, Rastatt 19487
Pahiatua and District Museum, Pahiatua 30227
Pahl Museum, Mainhardt 18595
Paignton and Dartmouth Steam Railway, Paignton 40160
Paikkari Cottage, Sammatti 10020
Paikkarin Torppa, Sammatti 10020
Paimion Kotiseutumuseo, Paimio 09904
Paine Art Center, Oshkosh 46207
Painted Bride Art Center Gallery, Philadelphia 46438
Painters's Hall, London 39739
Paipoonge Historical Museum, Thunder Bay 06547
Paisley Museum and Art Gallery, Paisley 40161
Pajar Museo, Ojacastro 35166
Pajaro Valley Historical Museum, Watsonville 48456
Pajulan Koulumuseo, Somero 10046
Pakistan Air Force Museum Peshawar, Peshawar 31050
Pakistan Army Museum, Rawalpindi 31056
Pakistan Forest Museum, Abbottabad 31012
Pakistan Museum of Natural History, Islamabad 31026
Pákozdi Csata Emlékmüve, Pákozd 21496
Pakruojis Manor House, Pakruojis 27524
Palác Kinských, Praha 08608
Pałac Radziwiłłów w Nieborowie, Nieborów 31822
Pałac Sztuki w Krakowie, Kraków 31726
Pałac w Dobrzycy, Dobrzyca 31556
Pałac w Rogalinie, Świątniki 32012
Palace and Museum of Antiquities, Padmanabhapuram 21971
Palace - Architectural-Park Complex, Balčik 04609
Palace Armoury, Valletta 27704
Palace Collection, Roskilde 09041
Palace Huis Ten Bosch Museum, Sasebo 26724
The Palace Museum, Beijing 06983
Palace Museum, Ulaanbaatar 28686
Palace Museum, Zanzibar 37469
Palace Museum of Peter the III at the Museum-Preserve, Lomonosov 32987
Palace Museum of Wilanów, The Royal Residence, Warszawa 32117
Palace of Holyroodhouse, Edinburgh 38903
Palace of Peter the Great, Strelna 33567
Palace of Physics, Kazanlăk 04703
Palace of Royal Jewelleries, Zizinia 09311
Palace of the Governors, Santa Fe 47429
Palace of the Grand Masters, Rhodos 21144
Palace of Vouni, Lefke 08233
Palace of Westminster, London 39740
Palacerigg House, Palacerigg 40162
Palacete del Embarcadero, Santander 35434
Palacio Arzobispal, Cusco 31161
Palácio Conde dos Arcos, Goiás 04117
Palácio das Laranjeiras, Rio de Janeiro 04400
Palacio de la Granja, Orihuela 35189
Palacio de Lebrija, Sevilla 35491
Palacio de Montemuzo, Zaragoza 35730
Palacio de Pedralbes, Barcelona 34589
Palacio de Viana, Córdoba 34743
Palacio del Mar, Donostia-San Sebastián 34779
Palacio del Mate, Posadas 00486
Palácio Guanabara, Rio de Janeiro 04401
Palácio Gustavo Capanema, Rio de Janeiro 04402
Palácio Nacional da Pena, Sintra 32351
Palácio Nacional de Mafra, Mafra 32319
Palacio Nacional de Queluz, Queluz 32340
Palacio Real, Madrid 35058
Palacio Real de Aranjuez, Aranjuez 34472
Palacio Real de El Pardo, El Pardo 35253
Palacio Real de Madrid, Madrid 35059
Palacio Real de Riofrío, Riofrío 35322
Palacio Real la Almudaina, Palma de Mallorca 35235
Palacio Real y Museos de Tapices, San Ildefonso 35376
Palacio Taranco, Montevideo 41031
Palaeobotanisch Museum, Utrecht 29908
Paläontologisches Museum, Offenhausen 02384
Paläontologisches Museum der Universität Zürich, Zürich 37404
Paläontologisches Museum München, München 18893
Paläontologisches Museum Nierstein, Nierstein 19103
Palaepaphos Museum, Kouklia 08187
Palæsamlingerne, Roskilde 09041
Palais Bénédictine, Fécamp 11713
Palais de Glace, Buenos Aires 00251
Palais de la Découverte, Paris 13651
Palais de la Miniature, Lyon 12752
Palais de la Miniature, Saint-Pourçain-sur-Sioule 14428
Le Palais de l'Art Traditionnel, Constantine 00059
Palais de l'Ile, Annecy 10363
Palais de Tokyo, Paris 13652
Palais des Beaux-Arts, Bruxelles 03339
Palais des Beaux-Arts, Charleroi 03355
Palais des Expositions Chinagora, Alfortville 10289
Palais des Papes et Musée du Vieil Avignon, Avignon 10535
Le Palais du Chocolat, La Côte-Saint-André 12162
Palais du Roure, Avignon 10536
Palais du Tau, Reims 13934
Palais für aktuelle Kunst, Glückstadt 17305
Palais Grand Ducal, Luxembourg 27569
Palais Jacques Coeur, Bourges 10867
Palais Liechtenstein, Feldkirch 01830
Palais Minéral, Granville 11915
Palais Palffy, Wien 02968
Palais Papius, Wetzlar 20557
Palais Princier, Monaco 28672
Palais Rihour, Lille 12605
Palais Surreal, Wien 02969
Palamas Museum, Athinai 20899
Palamuse O. Lutsu Kihelkonnakoolimuuseum, Palamuse 09346
Palata na Fizikata, Kazanlăk 04703
Palau Ducal dels Borja, Gandía 34837
Palawan Museum, Puerto Princesa 31424
Palawan National Museum, Quezon 31426
Palawan State University Museum, Puerto Princesa 31425
Palazzina Marfisa, Ferrara 23799
Palazzo Apostolico ed Archivio Storico della Santa Casa, Loreto 24216
Palazzo Armeria, Zurrieq 27719
Palazzo Attems-Petzenstein, Gorizia 24036
Palazzo Barolo, Torino 25763
Palazzo Belgiojoso, Lecco 24172
Palazzo Borromeo, Stresa 25643
Palazzo Bricherasio, Torino 25764
Palazzo Castelmur, Stampa 37203
Palazzo Castiglioni, Cingoli 23567
Palazzo del Principe, Genova 24010
Palazzo del Senato, Pinerolo 24933
Palazzo della Ragione, Padova 24750
Palazzo della Triennale, Milano 24415
Palazzo delle Esposizioni, Roma 25263
Palazzo Ducale, Genova 24011
Palazzo Ducale, Venezia 25946
Palazzo Grassi, Venezia 25947
Palazzo Medici Riccardi, Firenze 23883
Palazzo Orlandi, Busseto 23236
Palazzo Pfanner e Giardino, Lucca 24232
Palazzo Pubblico, San Marino 33768
Palazzo Reale, Torino 25765
Palazzo Reale-Reggia di Caserta, Caserta 23375
Palazzo Taffini, Savigliano 25501
Palazzo Tozzoni, Imola 24091
Palazzo Vertemate Franchi, Piuro 24966
Palazzo Vescovile, Reggio Emilia 25100
Paleis Het Loo - Nationaal Museum, Apeldoorn 28928
Paleontologic Collection, Roma 25168
Paleontological and Geological Museum of the University of Athens, Athinai 20900
Paleontological Museum, Asenovgrad 04605
Paleontological Museum, Tuxtla Gutiérrez 28572
Paleontological Park, Rudabánya 21520
Paleontologičen Muzej, Asenovgrad 04605
Paleontologičeskij Muzej im. Ju.A. Orlova, Moskva 33170
Paleontologo-stratigrafičeskij Muzej pri Kafedre Istorii Geologii, Sankt-Peterburg 33474
Paleontology Museum, Moskva 33170
Paleorama - Museo Itinerante, Don Torcuato 00333
Palestinian Archaeological Museum, Birzeit 31066
The Palette and Chisel, Chicago 42356
Pallant House Gallery, Chichester 38564
Palm Beach Institute of Contemporary Art, Lake Worth 44600
Palm Springs Desert Museum, Palm Springs 46267
Palma Rosa Museum, Hamilton, Brisbane 01086
Palmer/Gullickson Octagon Home, West Salem 48546
Palmer House, Northfield 46024
Palmer Museum, Jewell 44342
Palmer Museum of Art, University Park 48154
Palo Alto Art Center, Palo Alto 46273
Palo Alto Junior Museum, Palo Alto 46274
Palóc Múzeum, Balassagyarmat 21310
Palomuseo, Helsinki 09518
Palomuseo, Kuusankoski 09731
Palomuseo, Lahti 09745
Palos Verdes Art Center, Rancho Palos Verdes 46787
Palotavárosi Skanzen, Székesfehérvár 21559
Pålsjö Kvarn, Helsingborg 35954
Paltamon Kotiseutumuseo, Paltamo 09906
Palucka Izba Muzealna, Kcynia 31652
Památník, Dolní Domaslavice 08331
Památník Adolfa Kaspara, Loštice 08463
Památník Antonína Dvořáka, Nelahozeves 08495
Památník Antonína Dvořáka, Vysoká u Příbrami 08732
Památník Antonína Dvořáka, Zlonice 08753
Památník Bedřicha Smetany, Jabkenice 08377
Památník Bedřicha Václavka, Čáslavice 08289
Památník Bible Kralické, Kralice nad Oslavou 08427
Památník Bitvy 1813, Chlumec u Ústi nad Labem 08311
Památník Bitvy 1866 na Chlumu, Všestary 08729
Památník Bohuslava Martinů, Polička 08556
Památník Boženy Němcové, Červený Kostelec 08293
Památník Bratří Křičků, Kelč 08408
Památník Bratří Mrštíků, Diváky 08327
Památník Dr. Emila Axmana, Chropyně 08319
Památník Dr. Emila Holuba, Holice v Čechách 08357
Památník Dr. Františka Křižíka, Plánice 08541
Památník Františka Palackého, Hodslavice 08355
Památník Jana Ámoše Komenského, Bílá Třemešná 08248
Památník Jana Ámoše Komenského, Fulnek 08342
Památník Jana Ámoše Komenského, Horní Branná 08360
Památník Jiráskova Pokladu, Potštejn 08559
Památník Jiřího Melantricha z Aventýna, Roždalovice 08640
Památník Josefa Hybeše, Dašice 08325
Památník Josefa Ladislava Piče, Mšeno u Mělníka 08490
Památník Josefa Mánesa, Čechy pod Košířem 08290
Památník Josefa Suka, Křečovice 08432
Památník Karla Čapka, Stará Huť u Dobříše 08661
Památník Karla Havlíčka Borovského, Havlíčkův Brod 08348
Památník Karla Hynka Máchy, Doksy 08330
Památník Karla Jaromíra Erbena, Miletín 08477
Památník Karla Václava Raise, Lázně Bělohrad 08444
Památník Krále Jiřího z Poděbrad a Lapidarium, Poděbrady 08550
Památník Leoše Janáčka, Brno 08275
Památník Leoše Janáčka, Hukvaldy 08373
Památník Lidice, Lidice 08453
Památník Města, Police nad Metují 08552
Památník Mikoláše Alše, Mirotice 08479
Památník Mistra Jana Husa, Husinec 08375
Památník Mohyla míru, Prace u Brna 08560
Památník Národní Svobody, Hrabyně 08366
Památník Národního Písemnictví (Muzeum České Literatury), Praha 08609
Památník Otakara Štáfla, Havlíčkův Brod 08349
Památník Petra Bezruče, Kostelec na Hané 08422
Památník Petra Bezruče, Opava 08520
Památník Prokopa Diviše, Znojmo 08757
Památník Romániu Aloise Jiráska Skály, Teplice nad Metují 08678
Památník Selského Povstání, Rtyně v Podkrkonoší 08644
Památník Svatopluka Čecha, Obříství 08513
Památník Svatopluka Čecha, Ostředek 08529
Památník Terezín, Terezín 08680
Památník Terezy Novákové, Proseč u Skutče 08628
Památník Václava Beneše Třebízského, Třebíz 08689
Památník Václava Beneše Třebízského a Svatopluka Čecha, Liten 08454
Památník Venkovského Lidu, Žumberk 08759
Památník W.A. Mozarta a Manželů Duškových, Praha 08610

Památník Zdeňka Fibicha, Všeborice 08728
Památník Životické Tragedie, Havířov 08346
Pambasang Museo ng Pilipinas, Manila 31390
Pamětní Síň Jana Ámoše Komenského, Brandýs nad Orlicí 08257
Pametnik na Kulturata Zemenski Manastir, Zemen 04931
Pamplin Park Civil War Site, Petersburg 46374
PAN Kunstforum Niederrhein, Emmerich 16860
Panachrantos Monastery, Falika 20950
Panaddaman-Cagayan State University Museum, Tuguegarao 31461
Panaët Chitov Memorial House, Sliven 04821
Panamin Museum, Pasay 31416
Panarcadic Archeological Museum of Tripolis, Tripoli 21204
Panhandle-Plains Historical Museum, Canyon 42092
Pankhurst Centre, Manchester 39901
Pannonhalmi Főapátság Gyűjteménye, Pannonhalma 21497
Pannonisches Heimatmuseum, Neusiedl am See 02357
Panorama de la Bataille de Waterloo, Braine-l'Alleud 03237
Panorama Kreuzigung Christi, Einsiedeln 36675
Panorama Mesdag, Den Haag 29121
Panorama Museum, Bad Frankenhausen 15644
Panorama Plevenska Epopeja 1877, Pleven 04769
Panorama Racławicka, Wrocław 32192
Panos Aravantinos Theatrical Museum of Painting and Stage Design, Piraeus 21125
Pansarmuséet, Axvall 35827
Panssarimuseo, Parola 09913
Państwowe Muzeum Archeologiczne, Warszawa 32139
Państwowe Muzeum Etnograficzne, Warszawa 32140
Państwowe Muzeum Gross-Rosen w Rogoźnicy, Rogoźnica 31950
Państwowe Muzeum im. Przypkowskich, Jędrzejów 31628
Państwowe Muzeum na Majdanku, Lublin 31796
Państwowe Muzeum Stutthof, Sztutowo 32036
Państwowe Muzeum Stutthof w Sztutowie, Sopot 31989
Państwowe Muzeum w Białymstoku, Białystok 31489
Państwowe Muzeum w Oświęcimiu-Brzezince, Oświęcim 31868
Państwowe Zbiory Sztuki, Sułoszowa 32007
Panteão da Pátria Tancredo Neves, Brasília 04009
Panthéon, Paris 13653
Pao Galleries at Hong Kong Art Centre, Hong Kong 07108
Papadopoulos Picture Gallery, Tinos 21200
Papakura and District Historical Society Museum, Papakura 30232
Paper Museum, Espoo 09436
Paper Museum, Tokyo 26866
Paperimuseo, Espoo 09436
Paphos District Archaeological Museum, Paphos 08215
Papiergeschichtliche Sammlung, Bergisch Gladbach 15898
Papiermachermuseum, Steyrermühl 02695
Papiermolen de Schoolmeester, Westzaan 29999
Papiermuseum, Düren 16718
Papiliorama-Nocturama Foundation, Kerzers 36823
Papírna Museum, Velké Losiny 08712
Papplewick Pumping Station, Ravenshead 40291
Paprika Múzeum, Kalocsa 21436
Paprikamúzeum, Szeged 21552
Papua New Guinea Display Centre, Crafers 00951
Papua New Guinea National Museum and Art Gallery, Boroko 31090
Papyrusmuseum und Papyrussammlung, Wien 02970
Paqgoeta Park Information Center, Aia 34414
Para/Site Art Space, Hong Kong 07109
Parade of Presidents Wax Museum, Keystone 44477
Paradise Mill Silk Industry Museum, Macclesfield 39866
Parafia Ewangelicko - Augsburska Wang, Karpacz 31642
Parafialne Muzeum Regionalne, Krasnobród 31732
Parainen District Museum, Parainen 09907
Parainen Industrial Museum, Parainen 09908
Parasite Museum, Bangkok 37492
Parc Archéologique, Antoing 03134
Parc Archéologique de la Pointe-du-Buisson, Melocheville 05837
Parc Archéologique de Larina, Hières-sur-Amby 12025
Parc Archéologique Européen de Bliesbruck-Reinheim, Bliesbruck 10768
Parc Ardèche Miniature, Soyons 14800
Parc & Château de Valençay, Valençay 15048
Parc de la Préhistoire, Tarascon-sur-Ariège 14864
Parc de l'Artillerie, Québec 06210
Parc de Préhistoire de Bretagne, Malansac 12781
Parc de Reconstitution Archéologique, Villeneuve-d'Ascq 15222
Parc Howard Museum and Art Gallery, Llanelli 39546
Parc Miniature Alsace-Lorraine, Saint-Ame 14103
Parc National de la Culture des Ethnies, Vientiane 27322
Parc Préhistorique Animalier Dino-Zoo, Charbonnières-les-Sapins 11172
Parc Préhistorique des Grottes de Fontirou, Castella 11070
Parc Préhistorique Imaginaire, Chamoux 11149
Parc Zoologique Arche de Noé et Amazonia, Saint-Clément-des-Baleines 14160
Parco Monumentale di Pinocchio, Collodi 23617
Parco Museo Minerario, Abbadia San Salvatore 22793
Parco Nazionale delle Incisioni Rupestri, Capo di Ponte 23328
Parco Scherrer, Morcote 36949
Pardee Home Museum, Oakland 46068
Parfum-Flacon-Museum, München 18894
Parfummuseum, Hochfelden 36806
Parham Elizabethan House & Gardens, Pulborough 40273
Parikkalan Kotiseutumuseo, Parikkala 09910
Paris Gibson Square Museum of Art, Great Falls 43782
von Parish-Kostümbibliothek, München 18895
Parish Museum, Dobra 31554
Parish Museum, Grybów 31613
Parish Museum, Krynica 31741
Parish Museum, Paszyn 31876
Parish Museum, Rzepiennik Strzyżewski 31958
Parish Museum, Złota 32221
Parishville Museum, Parishville 46287
Park City Museum, Park City 46289
Park Farm Museum, Milton Abbas 39960
Park Gallery, Falkirk 38969
Park House Museum, Amherstburg 04989
The Park-McCullough House, North Bennington 45983
Park-Museum Skobelev, Pleven 04771
Park-muzej General V.Z. Lavrov, Gorni Dabnik 04677
Park-muzej im. A.K. Tolstogo, Brjansk 32711
Park-Muzej Vladislav Varnenčik, Varna 04905
Park-Villa Rieter, Zürich 37405
Parkanon Kotiseutumuseo, Parkano 09911
Parkanon Metsämuseo, Parkano 09912
Parkdale-Maplewood Community Museum, Barss Corner 05054
Parker-O'Malley Air Museum, Ghent 43666
Parker Tavern Museum, Reading 46804
Parkland College Art Gallery, Champaign 42188
Parks Canada Visitor Reception Centre, Churchill 05251
Parkside Cottage Museum, Narrandera 01305
Parkzicht, Ermelo 29252
Parlamentsausstellung des Deutschen Bundestages "Wege, Irrwege, Umwege", Berlin 16079
Parliament House Art Collection, Canberra 00889
Parliament In-Exile Museum, Kauhajoki 09636
Parliamentary Memorial Museum, Tokyo 26913
Parnell Museum, Rathdrum 22532
Parnham House, Beaminster 38135
Parochialkirche, Berlin 16080
Paroles d'Objets Africains du Togo, Blangy-sur-Bresle 10758
Parque Arqueológico Cueva Pintada, Galdar 34833
Parque Arqueológico El Caño, Natá 31075
Parque Etnográfico do Río Arnoia, Allariz 34450
Parque Museo el Catillo, Los Realejos 35310
Parque-Museo La Venta, Villahermosa 28613
Parque Regional de la Cuenca Alta del Manzanares, Manzanares El Real 35085
Parris Island Museum, Parris Island 46296
Parrish Art Museum, Southampton 47707
Parroquia de Santa María, Oliva 35170
Parry Mansion Museum, New Hope 45706
Pars Museum, Shiraz 22281
Parson Fisher House, Blue Hill 41756
Parsons Historical Society Museum, Parsons 46299
Parsonsfield-Porter History House, Porter 46619
The Parthenon, Nashville 45622
Partridge Island Museum, Saint John 06335
Parys Museum, Parys 34322
Pasadena City College Art Gallery, Pasadena 46304
Pasadena Historical Museum, Pasadena 46305
Pascack Historical Society Museum, Park Ridge 46293
Pashova Kăshta, Melnik 04735
Pasinger Fabrik, München 18896
Pasmans Huus, Ruinen 29784
Pass of Killiecrankie Visitor Centre, Killiecrankie 39358
Passages Centre d'Art Contemporain, Troyes 15009
Passaic County Community College Galleries, Paterson 46309
Passaic County Historical Society Museum, Paterson 46310
Passauer Glasmuseum, Passau 19359
Past Times, Blindley Heath 38260
Pásztói Múzeum, Pászto 21502
Pásztormúzeum, Bugac 21393
Pataka, Porirua 30240
Patan Museum, Kathmandu 28791
Pate Museum of Transportation, Cresson 42696
Patee House Museum, Saint Joseph 47107
Patek Philippe Museum, Genève 36753
Pateniemen Sahamuseo, Oulu 09896
Pateniemi Sawmill Museum, Oulu 09896
Patenschaftsmuseum Goldap in Ostpreußen, Stade 20025
Patent Model Museum, Fort Smith 43459
Pater Jon Sveinsson Memorial Museum, Akureyri 21622
Pater Peter Singer-Museum, Salzburg 02546
Paterson Court House, Adamstown 00701
Paterson Museum, Paterson 46311
Pathein Museum, Pathein 28741
Pathological Museum, London 39741
Pathologisch-anatomisches Bundesmuseum, Wien 02971
Pathology and Bacteriology Museum, Lucknow 21929
Pathology Museum, Kabul 00005
Pathology Museum, Mumbai 21953
Pathology Museum, Pretoria 34352
Patikamúzeum, Győr 21421
Patikamúzeum, Kőszeg 21465
Patna Museum, Patna 21978
The Patrick and Beatrice Haggerty Museum of Art, Milwaukee 45371
Patrick Collection Motor Museum, Birmingham 38226
Patrick Taylor Cottage Museum, Albany 00724
Patrijaršie Palaty, Moskva 33171
Patrimoine Historique et Études du Repassage, Sebourg 14686
Patriots Point Naval and Maritime Museum, Mount Pleasant 45540
Patten Lumberman's Museum, Patten 46312
Patterson Heritage Museum and Family History Centre, Birchington 38202
Patterson Homestead, Dayton 42804
Patterson's Spade Mill, Templepatrick 40682
Pattijoen Kotiseutumuseo Ojala, Pattijoki 09915
Patton Museum of Cavalry and Armor, Fort Knox 43406
Paul Anton Keller-Museum, Lockenhaus 02247
Paul Bunyan Logging Camp, Eau Claire 43076
Paul Dresser Memorial Birthplace, Terre Haute 47985
Paul Ernst-Gedenkstätte, Sankt Georgen an der Stiefing 02565
Paul Gugelmann-Museum, Schönenwerd 37142
Paul H. Karshner Memorial Museum, Puyallup 46752
Paul Jönska Gården, Viken 36408
Paul Laurence Dunbar State Memorial, Dayton 42805
Paul Revere House, Boston 41823
Paul-Röder-Museum, Marktoberdorf 18650
Paul Stradin Museum of the History of Medicine, Riga 27434
Paul W. Bryant Museum, Tuscaloosa 48116
Paul Whitney Larson Gallery, Saint Paul 47165
Paula Modersohn-Becker Museum. Museum im Roselius-Haus. Bernhard Hoetger Sammlung, Bremen 16331
Paula Modersohn-Becker-Stiftung, Bremen 16332
Paula Stradiņa Medicīnas Vēstures Muzejs, Rīga 27434
Pauline E. Glidden Toy Museum, Ashland 41293
Paulise de Bush Costume Collection, Broadclyst 38364
Pauselijk Zouavenmuseum, Roeselare 03704
Pavel Kuznetsov House-Museum, Saratov 33505
Paviljon Katalnoj Gorki, Lomonosov 32991
Pavillon Audrey Hepburn, Tolochenaz 37248
Pavillon Chinois et Tour Japonaise, Bruxelles 03340
Pavillon de l'Arsenal, Paris 13654
Pavillon de Vendôme, Aix-en-Provence 10257
Pavillon des Arts, Paris 13655
Pavillon des Princes, Plombières-les-Bains 13762
Pavillon Flaubert, Canteleu 11028
Pavillon Saint-Arnaud, Trois-Rivières 06647
Pavilon Anthropos, Brno 08276
Pāvilosta Museum of Local Studies, Pāvilosta 27392
Pāvilostas Novadpētniecības Muzejs, Pāvilosta 27392
Pavle Beljanski Memorial Collection, Novi Sad 33873
Pavlodar Historical and Regional Museum, Pavlodar 27089
Pavlodarskij Istoriko-Kraevedčeskij Muzej, Pavlodar 27089
Pavlos Vrellis Museum of Greek History, Ioannina 20971
Pavlovskij Istoričkij Muzej, Pavlovo 33284
Pawiak Prison Museum, Warszawa 32131
Pawilon Wystawowy, Gdynia 31589
Pawnee City Historical Society Museum, Pawnee City 46317
Pawnee Indian Village, Republic 46843
Paxson Gallery, Missoula 45407
Paxton House, Berwick-upon-Tweed 38177
Payne Gallery, Bethlehem 41669
Paynes Creek Historic State Park, Bowling Green 41848
Paznauner Bauernmuseum, Mathon 02279
P.D. Korin House-Museum, Palech 33281
Pea Ridge National Military Park, Garfield 43625
Peabody Essex Museum, Salem 47198
Peabody Museum of Archaeology and Ethnology, Cambridge 42049
Peabody Museum of Natural History, New Haven 45698
Peabody Place Museum, Memphis 45248
Peace Memorial Museum, Zanzibar 37470
Peace Museum, Bradford 38300
The Peace Museum, Chicago 42357
Peace Museum Project, Amsterdam 28880
Peace River Centennial Museum, Peace River 06102
Peachland Museum, Peachland 06103
Peacock, Aberdeen 37941
Peacock Heritage Centre, Chesterfield 38556
Peak District Mining Museum, Matlock 39923
Peak Rail Museum, Matlock 39924
Pearce Institute, Glasgow 39058
Pearl S. Buck Birthplace, Hillsboro 44023
Pearl S. Buck House, Perkasie 46352
Pearn's Steam World, Westbury 01594
Pearse Museum, Dublin 22451
Pearson Air Museum, Vancouver 48201
The Pearson Museum, Springfield 47741
The Peary-MacMillan Arctic Museum, Brunswick 41972
Peasant House, Święty Krzyż 32018
Peasant Museum, Kälviä 09608
Pebble Hill Plantation, Thomasville 48001
Pechermuseum, Hernstein 02024
Peckover House, Wisbech 40906
Pecos Park, Pecos 46324
Pedagogické Muzeum Jana Ámoše Komenského, Praha 08611
Pedagoški Muzej, Beograd 33815
Peekskill Museum, Peekskill 46327
Peel Castle, Peel 40168
Peel Heritage Complex, Brampton 05114
Peelmuseum, Ospel 29683
Peggy Guggenheim Collection, Venezia 25948
Peirce-Nichols House, Salem 47199
Pejepscot Historical Society Museum, Brunswick 41973
Peking Man in Zhoukoudian, Beijing 06984
Pékmúzeum, Sopron 21536
Pelastusarmeijan Museo, Helsinki 09519
Pelgrom Museum Poorterswoning, Antwerpen 03167
Pelham Art Center, Pelham 46328
Pelkosenniemen Kotiseutumuseo, Pelkosenniemi 09916
Pella Historical Village, Pella 46329
Pellisier House Museum, Bethulie 34180
Pellon Kotiseutumuseo, Pello 09917
Pellonpään Talonpoikaistalo, Pertteli 09921
Peltola Cotters Museum, Tammijärvi 10073
Peltolan Mäkitupalaismuseo, Tammijärvi 10073
Peltotyökalumuseo, Somero 10047
Pelzerhaus, Emden 16851
Pemba Museum, Chake Chake 37457
Pember Museum of Natural History, Granville 43770
Pemberton Museum, Pemberton 06105
Pembina Hills Regional Art Gallery, Morden 05940
Pembina Lobstick Historical Museum, Evansburg 05420
Pembina State Museum, Pembina 46332
Pembina Threshermen's Museum, Winkler 06816
Pembroke Historical Museum, Pembroke 46333
Pen and Brush Museum, New York 45862
Pena-Peck House, Saint Augustine 47070
Penang Forestry Museum, Pulau Pinang 27682
Pencarrow House, Bodmin 38267
Pence Gallery, Davis 42793
Pendarvis, Mineral Point 45379
Pendeen Lighthouse, Pendeen 40172
Pendennis Castle, Falmouth 38974
Pendle Heritage Centre, Barrowford 38097
Pendleton District Agricultural Museum, Pendleton 46337
Pendon Museum, Long Wittenham 39824
Penetanguishene Centennial Museum, Penetanguishene 06108
Pengsjö Nybyggarmuseum, Vännäs 36375
Peninsula and Saint Edmunds Township Museum, Tobermory 06553
Peninsula Fine Arts Center, Newport News 45939
Penkill Castle, Girvan 39035
Penlee House Gallery and Museum, Penzance 40181
Penneshaw Maritime and Folk Museum, Penneshaw 01361
Pennsbury Manor, Morrisville 45514
Pennsylvania Academy of the Fine Arts Gallery, Philadelphia 46439
Pennsylvania Anthracite Heritage Museum, Scranton 47520
Pennsylvania Dutch Folk Culture Society Museum, Lenhartsville 44715
Pennsylvania Federation of Museums and Historical Organizations, Harrisburg 49528
Pennsylvania German Cultural Heritage Center, Kutztown 44530
Pennsylvania Lumber Museum, Galeton 43601
Pennsylvania Military Museum and 28th Division Shrine, Boalsburg 41763
Pennsylvania Trolley Museum, Washington 48418
Pennypacker Mills, Schwenksville 47501
Pennyroyal Area Museum, Hopkinsville 44100
Penobscot Marine Museum, Searsport 47527
Penrhos Cottage, Llanycefn 39558
Penrhyn Castle, Bangor, Gwynedd 38083
Penrith Museum, Penrith 40176
Penrith Regional Gallery and The Lewers Bequest, Emu Plains 01019
Pensacola Historical Museum, Pensacola 46344
Pensacola Museum of Art, Pensacola 46345
Penselmuseet i Bankeryd, Bankeryd 35828
Penshurst Place and Toy Museum, Penshurst 40178
Penwith Galleries, Saint Ives, Cornwall 40407
Penyo Penev House-Museum, Dimitrovgrad 04649
Penzenskaja Kartinnaja Galerija im. K.A. Savickogo, Penza 33293
Penzenskij Gosudarstvennyj Obedinennyj Kraevedčeskij Muzej, Penza 33294
Penzenskij Muzej Odnoj Kartiny, Penza 33295
People's Gallery, El Paso 43123
People's History Museum, Manchester 39902
The People's Museum, Belfast 38157
People's Museum, Melaka 27672
People's Museum of Labin, Labin 07734
People's Palace Museum, Glasgow 39059
People's Story Museum, Edinburgh 38904
Peoria Historical Society, Peoria 46350
Peppers Art Gallery, Redlands 46823
Peppin Brown Art Gallery, Whittlesford 40865

Perachora Museum, Perachora 21117
Perak Royal Museum, Kuala Kangsar 27636
Perak State Museum, Taiping 27689
Perbadanan Muzium Melaka, Melaka 49287
Perc Tucker Regional Gallery, Townsville 01547
Percival David Foundation of Chinese Art, London 39742
Percy Pilcher Museum, Lutterworth 39847
Pères Blancs - Saint Anne, Jerusalem 22655
Pereslavl-Zalesskij Gosudarstvennyj Istoriko-architekturnyj i Chudožestvennyj Muzej-zapovednik, Pereslavl-Zalesskij 33299
Pereslavl-Zalessky Museum-Preserve of History, Art and Architecture, Pereslavl-Zalesskij 33299
Performance Space, Redfern 01410
Performing Arts Collection of South Australia, Adelaide 00712
Performing Arts Museum, Melbourne 01239
Perfume Museum, Niagara-on-the-Lake 06004
Perhon Kotiseutumuseo, Perho 09919
Perkins Bull Collection, Peterborough 06121
Perkins Center for the Arts, Moorestown 45486
Perkins County Historical Society Museum, Grant 43766
Perkinson Gallery, Decatur 42834
Perlis State Museum, Kangar 27625
Perlmuttdrechslerei, Riegersburg, Niederösterreich 02514
Perm State Art Gallery, Perm 33307
Permanent Exhibition of Votive Pictures Sanctuary of our Lady of Trsat, Rijeka 07762
Permanenten Vestlandske Kunstindustrimuseum, Bergen 30427
Permskaja Gosudarstvennaja Chudožestvennaja Galereja, Perm 33307
Permskij Oblastnoj Kraevedčeskij Muzej, Perm 33308
Perniön Museo, Perniö 09920
Perranzabuloe Folk Museum, Perranporth 40183
Perrault's Museum, Val Marie 06660
Perry County Lutheran Historical Society Museum, Altenburg 41156
Perry's Cider Mills, Ilminster 39288
Perry's Victory and International Peace Memorial, Put-in-Bay 46748
Perryville Battlefield Museum, Perryville 46358
Persepolis Museum, Marvdashd 22264
Persepolis Museum, Shiraz 22282
Persmuseum, Amsterdam 28892
Perspective Gallery, Blacksburg 41729
Perth Museum, Perth 06114
Perth Museum and Art Gallery, Perth 40185
Perth Regiment Museum, Stratford 06500
Perttelin Kotiseutumuseo, Pertteli 09922
Peshawar Museum, Peshawar 31051
Peshtigo Fire Museum, Peshtigo 46365
Peštera Rabiša Muzej, Belogradčik 04618
Pesterzsébeti Múzeum, Budapest 21377
Petalax Hembygdsmuseum, Petalax 09924
Petaluma Adobe State Historic Park, Petaluma 46366
Petaluma Wildlife and Natural Science Museum, Petaluma 46367
Pete and Susan Barrett Art Gallery, Santa Monica 47441
Peter and Paul Fortress, Sankt-Peterburg 33475
Peter Anich-Museum, Oberperfuss 02374
Peter Anson Gallery, Buckie 38385
Peter Benoitmuseum, Harelbeke 03476
Peter Conser House, Heavener 43980
Peter Handke-Ausstellung, Griffen 01943
Peter J. McGovern Little League Baseball Museum, South Williamsport 47706
Peter Rice Homestead, Marlboro 45168
Peter Rosegger-Museum, Krieglach 02165
Peter Roseggers Geburtshaus, Alpl 01658
Peter Scott Gallery, Lancaster 39416
Peter Stuyvesant Collection, Amsterdam 28893
Peter Stuyvesant Stichting, Zevenaar 30057
Peter the Great House Museum, Sankt-Peterburg 33391
Peter the Great Museum of Anthropology and Ethnography - Kunstkamera, Sankt-Peterburg 33427
Peter Van den Braken Centrum, Sterksel 29856
Peter Wentz Farmstead, Worcester 48759
Peter Whitmer Sr. Home and Visitors Center, Waterloo 48437
Peter-Wiepert-Museum, Burg auf Fehmarn 16410
Peter Yegen Jr. Yellowstone County Museum, Billings 41690
Pētera Barisona Muzejs, Staburags 27453
Pētera Upīša Piemiņas Muzejs, Dobele 27349
Peterborough Centennial Museum and Archives, Peterborough 06122
Peterborough Historical Society Museum, Peterborough 46368
Peterborough Museum and Art Gallery, Peterborough 40188
Peterhof State Museum Reserve, Sankt-Peterburg 33406
Petersburg Area Art League, Petersburg 46375
The Petersburg Museums, Petersburg 46376
Petersburg National Battlefield, Petersburg 46377
Petersfield Museum, Petersfield 40194
Petersham Historical Museum, Petersham 46381
Petes Museigård, Havdhem 35947
Petit Écomusée de Cinve, Pandrignes 13459
Petit Musée, Clair 05253
Petit Musée Ambulant de la Musique Mécanique, Villeneuve-la-Garenne 15227
Petit Musée d'Art Camerounais, Yaoundé 04963
Le Petit Musée de la Bicyclette, La Batie-Montgascon 12124
Petit Musée de la Chartreuse Saint-Hugon, Arvillard 10442
Petit Musée de la Poupée, Dijon 11532
Petit Musée de la Table, Paris 13656
Petit Musée de l'Argenterie, Paris 13657
Petit Musée des Silos de Jouques, Jouques 12095
Petit Musée du Feu, Schoeneck 14684
Petit Musée du Métier de Tonnelier, Saint-Yzans-de-Médoc 14513
Petit Musée Fantastique de Guignol, Lyon 12753
Le Petit Musée Maison de Mariette, Saint-Laurent-du-Pont 14314
Petit Musée Minéraux et Faune de l'Alpe, Bourg-Saint-Maurice 10857
Petit Musée Rural, Varaire 15087
Petit Palais, Genève 36754
Petit-Palais, Paris 13658
Petite Anglicane, Forestville 05433
Petite Maison de Le Corbusier, Corseaux 36650
La Petite Provence du Paradou, Paradou 13464
Petko and Pencho Slaveykov Memorial House, Sofia 04836
Petoëfi Irodalmi Múzeum, Budapest 21378
Petőfi Museum of Hungarian Literature, Budapest 21378
Petőfi Emlékmúzeum, Kiskoërös 21456
Petőfi Múzeum, Aszód 21307
Petone Settlers Museum, Hutt City 30183
Petone Settlers Museum, Wellington 30307
Petra Museum, Petra 27065
Petran Museum, Haltdalen 30527
Petrefaktensammlung, Bad Staffelstein, Oberfranken 15749
Petrie Museum of Egyptian Archaeology, London 39743
Petrified Creatures Museum of Natural History, Richfield Springs 46853
Petrified Forest of the Black Hills, Piedmont 46483
The Petroleum Museum, Midland 45329
Petrolia Discovery, Petrolia 06125
Petropavlovskaja Krepost - Istoriko-kulturnyj Zapovednik, Sankt-Peterburg 33475
Petrov-Vodkin Memorial Art Museum, Chvalynsk 32746
Pettaquamscutt Museum, Kingston 44497
Petter Dass-Museet på Alstahaug, Sandnessjøen 30827
Petter Dass-Museum at Alstahaug, Sandnessjøen 30827
Petterson Museum of Intercultural Art, Claremont 42418
Pettis County Historical Society Museum, Sedalia 47555
The Petworth Cottage Museum, Petworth 40197
Petworth House and Park, Petworth 40198
Peuran Museo, Rautalampi 09987
Pewabic Pottery Museum, Detroit 42934
Pewsey Heritage Centre, Pewsey 40200
Peyo Yavorov Memorial House, Sofia 04835
Pfahlbaumuseum Unteruhldingen, Uhldingen-Mühlhofen 20256
Pfahlbausammlung Dr. h.c. Carl Irlet, Twann 37257
Pfahlbautenmuseum, Pfyn 37023
Pfalzgalerie Kaiserslautern, Kaiserslautern 17970
Pfalzmuseum, Forchheim, Oberfranken 17020
Pfalzmuseum für Naturkunde (POLLICHIA-Museum), Bad Dürkheim 15630
Pfarrmuseum, Dießen am Ammersee 16601
Pfarrmuseum, Flintsbach 17014
Pfefferminzmuseum, Eichenau 16799
Pferde-Eisenbahn Museum, Rainbach im Mühlkreis 02478
Pferde- und Kutschenmuseum, Chieming 16473
Pferdekuranstalt, Bern 36548
Pfingstritt-Museum Kötzting, Kötzting 18192
Pfinzgaumuseum, Karlsruhe 18000
P.H. Sullivan Museum and Genealogy Library, Zionsville 48825
Pharaonic Museum, Cairo 09283
Phare-Musée de Penmarch, Penmarch 13686
Pharmaceutical and Medical Museum of Bohuslav Lavička, Ljubljana 34116
Pharmaceutical Museum, Moskva 33044
Pharmaceutical Society Late Victorian Pharmacy, Edinburgh 38905
Pharmacy Museum, Győr 21421
Pharmacy Museum, Kőszeg 21465
Pharmacy Museum, Kouvola 09702
Pharmazie-Historisches Museum der Universität Basel, Basel 36516
Phathai Cave, Lampang 37510
Phe, Rayong 37531
Phelps House, Burlington 41998
Phelps Store Museum, Palmyra 46271
Phi Kappa Psi Fraternity-Heritage Hall, Indianapolis 44233
Philadelphia Art Alliance, Philadelphia 46440
Philadelphia Mummers Museum, Philadelphia 46441
Philadelphia Museum of Art, Philadelphia 46442
Philadelphia Museum of Judaica-Congregation Rodeph Shalom, Philadelphia 46443
Philatelic Centre of French Polynesia, Papeete 15345
Philatelic Museum, Athinai 20904
Philatelic Museum, Tokyo 26869
Philatelistisches Museum der Vereinten Nationen, Genève 36755
Philbrook Museum of Art, Tulsa 48107
Philip and Muriel Berman Museum of Art, Collegeville 42528
Philip L. Wright Zoological Museum, Missoula 45408
Philipp-Matthäus-Hahn-Museum, Albstadt 15422
Philipp-Reis-Gedächtnisstätte, Friedrichsdorf, Taunus 17145
Philipp-Reis-Haus Friedrichsdorf, Friedrichsdorf, Taunus 17146
Philipp Schäfer II Museum, Riedstadt 19606
Philippine Air Force Aerospace Museum, Pasay 31417
Philippine Army Museum, Makati 31355
Philippine House Museum, Shepparton 01450
Philippine Museum of Ethnology, Pasay 31418
Philippine Navy Museum, Cavite 31305
Philippine Presidential Museum, Malacañang 31358
Philippine Radiation Science Museum, Manila 31391
Philippine Science Centrum, Manila 31392
Het Philips Gloeilampenfabriekje anno 1891, Eindhoven 29217
Philipse Manor Hall, Yonkers 48786
The Phillips Collection, Washington 48389
Phillips Countryside Museum, Brokerswood 38374
Phillips County Museum, Helena 43982
Phillips County Museum, Holyoke 44064
Phillips Historical Society Museum, Phillips 46467
The Philmont Museum, Seton Memorial Library and Kit Carson Museum, Cimarron 42396
Phipitapan Haeng Chart Phra Pathom Chedi, Nakhon Pathom 37516
Phipitapan Laeng Chart, Suphan Buri 37541
Phipitapan Laeng chart Chantharakasem, Ayutthaya 37472
Phipitapan Laeng chart Chao Sam Phraya, Ayutthaya 37473
Phipitapan Laeng Chart Ram Khamhaeng, Sukhothai 37539
Phipitapantasatan Haeng Chart Nakhon Si Thammarat, Nakhon Si Thammarat 37519
Phipittapan Tasatan Haengchart, Khon Kaen 37508
Phippen Museum, Prescott 46688
Phititapan Haeng Chart, Chiang Mai 37503
Phoebe Apperson Hearst Museum of Anthropology, Berkeley 41648
Phoenix Art Museum, Phoenix 46477
Phoenix Museum of History, Phoenix 46478
Phoros-Éco Parc, Bédarieux 10662
Photographers' Gallery, London 39744
Photographers Gallery, Saskatoon 06403
Photographic Investments Gallery, Atlanta 41355
Photographic Resource Center, Boston 41824
Photographisch-optisches Museum, Biedenkopf 16151
Photography Museum, Šiauliai 27528
Photomuseum, Zarautz 35732
Photomuseum des Landes Oberösterreich, Bad Ischl 01710
Phra Borommathat National Museum, Nakhon Si Thammarat 37520
Phra Chetuponwimonmangkhalaram National Museum, Bangkok 37493
Phra Pathom Chedi National Museum, Nakhon Pathom 37516
Phra Phuttachinnarat National Museum, Phitsanulok 37528
Phu Khanh Museum, Phu Khanh 48999
Phukradung, Loei 37513
Phulsanda Religious Arts Museum, Phulsanda 21980
Phupan, Sakon Nakhon 37532
Phuthadikobo Museum, Mochudi 03937
Phyletisches Museum, Jena 17947
Physics Museum, Brisbane 00840
P.I. Tchaikovsky Museum-Estate, Votkinsk 33737
P.I. Tchaikovsky State Memorial House, Klin 32933
Pi Yandong Xue Yi Zhi Display Center, Guilin 07076
Piano Museum Collection, Hereford 39229
Pianola Museum, Amsterdam 28894
Piatra-Neamţ Art Museum, Piatra-Neamţ 32565
Piatra-Neamţ Ethnography Museum, Piatra-Neamţ 32566
Piatt Castles, West Liberty 48533
Piatt County Museum, Monticello 45473
Pic du Midi, La Mongie 12208
Picasso-Museum, Luzern 36915
Piccolo Antiquarium, Fossato di Vico 23927
Piccolo Museo dei Popoli, Lodi 24205
Piccolo Museo della Moneta, Vicenza 25996
Piccolo Museo di San Paolo, Reggio Calabria 25093
Piccolo Museo Navale, Laives 24129
Piccolo Museo Parrocchiale, Torgnon 25728
Piccolo Museo Parrocchiale, Valsavarenche 25885
Pickens County Museum of Art History, Pickens 46481
Picker Art Gallery, Hamilton 43882
Pickering Museum Village, Pickering 06126
Pickford's House Museum, Derby 38718
Picton Community Museum, Picton 30236
Pictou County Historical Museum, New Glasgow 05979
Picture Gallery, Bhaktapur 28785
Picture Gallery of Minusinsk, Minusinsk 33015
Picture Gallery of Olonetsk, Olonec 33251
Picture Gallery of P.M. Gretchishkin, Stavropol 33561
Picture Gallery of Tchajkovsky, Čajkovskij 32715
Picture Gallery of the Adygean Republic, Majkop 33004
Picture Gallery of the Serbian Cultural Association, Novi Sad 33869
Piddig Museum, Piddig 31421
Piece Hall Art Gallery, Halifax 39154
Piedmont Arts Museum, Martinsville 45192
Piedra Lumbre Visitors Center, Abiquiu 41058
Pieksämäen Museo, Pieksämäki 09925
Pielaveden Kotiseutumuseo, Pielavesi 09928
Pielavesi Local History Museum, Pielavesi 09928
Pielisen Museo, Lieksa 09781
Pienmäen Talomuseo, Niemisjärvi 09861
Pienmäki Farm Buildings Museum, Niemisjärvi 09861
Pier Arts Centre, Stromness 40637
Pier Pander Museum, Leeuwarden 29513
Pierce Manse, Concord 42606
Pierides Museum, Larnaka 08191
Pierides Museum of Ancient Cypriot Art, Athinai 20901
Pierides Sculpture Garden, Larnaka 08192
Pierpont Morgan Library, New York 45863
Pierre Gildesgame Maccabi Sports Museum, Ramat Gan 22734
Pierre Menard Home - State Historic Site, Ellis Grove 43160
Pierrepont Museum, Canton 42085
Pietarin Radan Museo, Lahti 09746
Pieter Claesen Wyckoff House Museum, Brooklyn 41949
Pieter Vermeulen Museum, Ijmuiden 29458
Pigeon Island, Castries 33755
Pigeon Valley Steam Museum, Wakefield 30283
Pighouse Collection, Cornafean 22406
Pihlajaveden Kotiseutumuseo, Pihlajavesi 09929
Pihtiputaan Kotiseutumuseo, Pihtipudas 09930
Pijpenkabinet & Smokiana, Amsterdam 28895
Pike County Museum, Milford 45343
Pila Museum, Pila 31422
Pilchard Works, Newlyn 40048
Pilgrim Hall Museum, Plymouth 46561
Pilgrim Monument and Provincetown Museum, Provincetown 46729
Pilgrim's Rest Museum, Pilgrim's Rest 34330
The Pillsbury Art Collection, Minneapolis 45393
Pilon Gallery, Ajdovščina 34083
Pilonova Galerija, Ajdovščina 34083
Pilot Mound Cenntenial Museum, Pilot Mound 06132
Pilot Station, Uusikaupunki 10153
Pilots Cottage Museum, Kiama 01144
Pilz-Lehrschau, Villach 02761
Pima Air and Space Museum, Tucson 48091
Pimeria Alta Historical Society Museum, Nogales 45960
Pin Art Gallery, Klaaswaal 29481
Pinacoteca, Castelfiorentino 23397
Pinacoteca, Córdoba 00313
Pinacoteca, Ploaghe 24971
Pinacoteca, Teramo 25688
Pinacoteca, Varallo Sesia 25892
Pinacoteca Ambrosiana, Milano 24416
Pinacoteca Andrea Alfano, Castrovillari 23443
Pinacoteca Barão de Santo Angelo, Porto Alegre 04288
Pinacoteca Benedicto Calixto, Santos 04455
Pinacoteca Cantonale Giovanni Züst, Rancate 37041
Pinacoteca Capitolina, Roma 25264
Pinacoteca Carmelita del Convento del Carmen, Trujillo 31265
Pinacoteca Chiesa di San Giovanni, Pieve Torina 24924
Pinacoteca Chiesa di San Tomaso Becket, Padova 24751
Pinacoteca Civica, Abano Terme 22791
Pinacoteca Civica, Ascoli Piceno 22955
Pinacoteca Civica, Asti 22975
Pinacoteca Civica, Baiardo 23009
Pinacoteca Civica, Cento 23474
Pinacoteca Civica, Cepagatti 23476
Pinacoteca Civica, Crotone 23692
Pinacoteca Civica, Fermo 23782
Pinacoteca Civica, Iesi 24080
Pinacoteca Civica, Imola 24092
Pinacoteca Civica, Imperia 24096
Pinacoteca Civica, Montelupone 24535
Pinacoteca Civica, Monza 24560
Pinacoteca Civica, Pieve di Cento 24921
Pinacoteca Civica, San Gimignano 25367
Pinacoteca Civica, Santarcangelo di Romagna 25459
Pinacoteca Civica, Savona 25513
Pinacoteca Civica, Spello 25616
Pinacoteca Civica, Vado Ligure 25866
Pinacoteca Civica A. Modigliani, Follonica 23902
Pinacoteca Civica A. Ricci, Monte San Martino 24500
Pinacoteca Civica Bruno Molajoli, Fabriano 23748
Pinacoteca Civica Carlo Servolini, Collesalvetti 23615
Pinacoteca Civica d'Arte Moderna, Latina 24160
Pinacoteca Civica e Gipsoteca U. Gera, Ripatransone 25128
Pinacoteca Civica F. Duranti, Montefortino 24526
Pinacoteca Civica Francesco Podesti e Galleria Comunale d'Arte Moderna, Ancona 22885
Pinacoteca Civica G. Cattabriga, Bondeno 23160
Pinacoteca Civica Melozzo degli Ambrogi, Forli 23917
Pinacoteca Civica Tosio Martinengo, Brescia 23209
Pinacoteca Comunale, Assisi 22969
Pinacoteca Comunale, Bosa 23182
Pinacoteca Comunale, Castiglion Fiorentino 23430
Pinacoteca Comunale, Cesena 23507
Pinacoteca Comunale, Città di Castello 23581
Pinacoteca Comunale, Deruta 23710
Pinacoteca Comunale, Locarno 36886
Pinacoteca Comunale, Manciano 24276
Pinacoteca Comunale, Massa Fermana 24316

Pinacoteca Comunale, Massa Marittima 24327
Pinacoteca Comunale, Matelica 24333
Pinacoteca Comunale, Mondavio 24472
Pinacoteca Comunale, Narni 24610
Pinacoteca Comunale, Ostra 24718
Pinacoteca Comunale, Quistello 25061
Pinacoteca Comunale, Ravenna 25084
Pinacoteca Comunale, Ripe San Ginesio 25129
Pinacoteca Comunale, San Benedetto del Tronto 25336
Pinacoteca Comunale, San Severino Marche 25414
Pinacoteca Comunale, Sarnano 25475
Pinacoteca Comunale, Spoleto 25626
Pinacoteca Comunale, Verucchio 25980
Pinacoteca Comunale A. Moroni, Porto Recanati 25014
Pinacoteca Comunale Alberto Martini, Oderzo 24666
Pinacoteca Comunale D. Stefanucci, Cingoli 23568
Pinacoteca Comunale d'Arte Antica e Moderna, Faenza 23757
Pinacoteca Comunale E. Giannelli, Parabita 24791
Pinacoteca Comunale e Museo A. De Felice, Terni 25696
Pinacoteca Comunale F. Galante Civera, Margherita di Savoia 24298
Pinacoteca Comunale Foresiana, Portoferraio 25022
Pinacoteca Comunale Francesco Cozza, Stilo 25636
Pinacoteca Comunale V. Bindi, Giulianova 24031
Pinacoteca D. Inzaghi, Budrio 23226
Pinacoteca Dantesca F. Bellonzi, Torre de Passeri 25770
Pinacoteca d'Arte Antica, Gemona del Friuli 23972
Pinacoteca d'Arte Contemporanea, Smerillo 25593
Pinacoteca d'Arte Francescana, Lecce 24168
Pinacoteca d'Arte Moderna, Avezzano 22994
Pinacoteca d'Arte Sacra, Alcamo 22845
Pinacoteca Davide Bergh', Calice al Cornovoglio 23267
Pinacoteca de la Escuela Provincial de Bellas Artes Dr. Figueroa Alcorta, Córdoba 00314
Pinacoteca de la Facultad de Bellas Artes, Manizales 07510
Pinacoteca de la Universidad de Concepción, Concepción 06894
Pinacoteca de Nuevo León, Monterrey 28241
Pinacoteca dei Cappuccini, Voltaggio 26050
Pinacoteca del Ateneo, Saltillo 28371
Pinacoteca del Centro de la Profesa, México 28211
Pinacoteca del Duomo, Cittadella 23584
Pinacoteca del Estado Juan Gamboa Guzmán, Mérida 28086
Pinacoteca del Pio Monte della Misericordia, Napoli 24604
Pinacoteca del Templo de La Compañía, Guanajuato 27978
Pinacoteca della Cassa di Risparmio, Cesena 23508
Pinacoteca della Certosa, Firenze 23884
Pinacoteca della Chiesa di San Francesco, Mercatello sul Metauro 24359
Pinacoteca della Rocca Ubaldinesca, Sassocorvaro 25492
Pinacoteca dell'Abbazia di Novacello, Varna 25901
Pinacoteca dell'Accademia Carrara, Bergamo 23066
Pinacoteca dell'Accademia dei Concordi e del Seminario, Rovigo 25298
Pinacoteca dell'Accademia di Belle Arti, Carrara 23359
Pinacoteca di Brera, Milano 24417
Pinacoteca di Corinaldo, Corinaldo 23654
Pinacoteca di San Silvestro, Montecompatri 24515
Pinacoteca Diego Rivera, Xalapa 28618
Pinacoteca Diocesana di Arte Sacra, Senigallia 25538
Pinacoteca do Estado de São Paulo, São Paulo 04545
Pinacoteca e Biblioteca Rambaldi, Sanremo 25426
Pinacoteca e Musei Civici, Jesi 24116
Pinacoteca e Musei Comunali, Macerata 24251
Pinacoteca e Museo Civici, Camerino 23291
Pinacoteca e Museo Civico, Bettona 23072
Pinacoteca e Museo Civico, Volterra 26053
Pinacoteca e Museo de Napoli, Terlizzi 25689
Pinacoteca Eduardo Ramírez Castro, Aranzazu 07369
Pinacoteca G. A. Levis, Racconigi 25063
Pinacoteca Giovanni e Marella Agnelli, Torino 25766
Pinacoteca Giovanni Morscio, Dolceacqua 23717
Pinacoteca Giuseppe Stuard, Parma 24812
Pinacoteca in Palazzo Volpi, Como 23631
Pinacoteca Internazionale dell'Età Evolutiva A. Cibaldi, Rezzato 25107
Pinacoteca M. Cascella, Ortona 24701
Pinacoteca Malaspina, Pavia 24829
Pinacoteca Manfrediana, Venezia 25949
Pinacoteca Municipal de Guadalupe, Guadalupe 27965
Pinacoteca Municipal de la Provincia de Corongo, Corongo 31150
Pinacoteca Municipal Ignacio Merino, Lima 31227
Pinacoteca Municipal Leoncio Lugo, Paucartambo 31235
Pinacoteca Municipal Miguel Ângelo Pucci, Franca 04105
Pinacoteca-Museo Beato Sante, Mombaroccio 24464
Pinacoteca, Museo delle Ceramiche, Pesaro 24861
Pinacoteca Nazionale, Bologna 23145
Pinacoteca Nazionale, Cagliari 23255
Pinacoteca Nazionale, Cosenza 23668
Pinacoteca Nazionale, Ferrara 23800
Pinacoteca Nazionale, Siena 25578
Pinacoteca Parrocchiale, Buonconvento 23230
Pinacoteca Parrocchiale, Castroreale 23440
Pinacoteca Parrocchiale, Corridonia 23658
Pinacoteca Provinciale Corrado Giaquinto, Bari 23029
Pinacoteca Repossi, Chiari 23528
Pinacoteca Rossetti Valentini, Santa Maria Maggiore 25439
Pinacoteca Universitaria, Colima 27840
Pinacoteca Vaticana, Città del Vaticano 48885
Pinacoteca Virreinal de San Diego, México 28212
Pinacoteca Zelantea, Acireale 22798
Pinakothek der Moderne, München 18897
Pinakothiki Kouvoutsaki, Kifissia 21016
Pincacoteca E. Notte, Ceglie Messapica 23468
Pinchbeck Marsh Engine and Land Drainage Museum, Spalding 40563
Pine County Historical Society Museum, Askov 41304
Pine Creek Museum, Pine Creek 01365
Pine Grove Historic Museum, Pontiac 46585
Pine Islet Lighthouse, Mackay 01193
Pine Ridge Car Museum, Main Ridge 01197
Pinecrest Historical Village, Manitowoc 45115
Pinewood Museum, Wasagaming 06746
Ping Jin Zhan Yi, Old Zhi Display Center, Yangliuqing 07314
Pingdu City Museum, Pingdu 07198
Pinggu Shangzhai Cultural Display Center, Beijing 06985
Pinnacles National Monument, Paicines 46261
Pinnaroo Heritage Museum, Pinnaroo 01368
Pinnaroo Printing Museum, Pinnaroo 01369
Pinson Mounds State Archaeological Area, Pinson 46497
Pinzgauer Heimatmuseum, Saalfelden am Steinernen Meer 02531
Pioneer Arizona Living History Museum, Phoenix 46479
Pioneer Auto Museum, Murdo 45563
Pioneer Corner Museum, New Holstein 45704
Pioneer Farm Museum and Ohop Indian Village, Eatonville 43073
Pioneer Florida Museum, Dade City 42738
Pioneer Heritage Center, Cavalier 42143
Pioneer Heritage Center, Shreveport 47614
Pioneer Historical Connors Museum, Connors 05272
Pioneer-Krier Museum, Ashland 41285
Pioneer-Krier Museum, Ashland 41286
Pioneer Log Cabin, Manhattan 45109
Pioneer Museum, Fabius 43256
Pioneer Museum, Fairmont 43272
Pioneer Museum, Silverton 34375
Pioneer Museum, Watford City 48450
Pioneer Museum, Wild Rose 48619
Pioneer Museum and Vereins Kirche, Fredericksburg 43532
Pioneer Museum of Alabama, Troy 48067
Pioneer Rum Museum, Beenleigh 00788
Pioneer Settlement Museum, Swan Hill 01486
Pioneer Town, Wimberley 48674
Pioneer Village, Farmington 43302
Pioneer Village, Silverdale 30254
Pioneer Village Museum, Beauséjour 05066
Pioneer Village Museum, Burnie 00864
Pioneer Woman Statue and Museum, Ponca City 46582
Pioneerimuseo, Koria 09690
Pioneers of Aviation Museum, Kimberley 34292
Pioneers, Trail and Texas Rangers Memorial Museum, San Antonio 47256
Piopio and District Museum, Piopio 30237
Piper Aviation Museum, Lock Haven 44839
Pipestone County Historical Museum, Pipestone 46498
Pipestone National Monument, Pipestone 46499
Piqua Historical Area State Memorial, Piqua 46500
Pirate Contemporary Art Oasis, Denver 42896
Pirot Ethnographical Museum, Pirot 33884
Piskarevskoe Memorialnoe Kladbišče - Muzej, Sankt-Peterburg 33476
Pitäjämuseo ja Nymann Talo ja Apteekkimuseo, Tohmajärvi 10109
Pitäjäntupa-Museo, Joutseno 09587
Piteå Museum, Piteå 36157
Pitkänpellon Talomuseo, Kangasniemi 09620
Pitlochry Festival Theatre Art Gallery, Pitlochry 40205
Pitot House Museum, New Orleans 45738
Pitstone Green Farm Museum, Pitstone 40206
Pitt Meadows Museum, Pitt Meadows 06134
Pitt Rivers Museum, Oxford 40153
Pittencrieff House Museum, Dunfermline 38810
Pittock Mansion, Portland 46640
Pittsburg State University Natural History Museum, Pittsburg 46504
Pittsburgh Center for the Arts, Pittsburgh 46523
Pittsburgh Children's Museum, Pittsburgh 46524
Pittsford Historical Society Museum, Pittsford 46536
Pittsworth and District Historical Museum, Pittsworth 01370
Pitzhanger Manor-House and Gallery, London 39745
Piulimatsivik - Nain Museum, Nain 05955
Pivovarské Muzeum, Plzeň 08544
Pivovarski Muzej, Ljubljana 34117
Pixian Museum, Pixian 07199
Pjatigorsk Regional Museum, Pjatigorsk 33322
Pjatigorskij Kraevedčeskij Muzej, Pjatigorsk 33322
P^BDjóðmenningarhúsið, Reykjavík 21661
P^BDjóðminjasafn Islands, Reykjaník 21647
P.K. Koslov Memorial Apartment Museum, Sankt-Peterburg 33419
PLA Naval Museum, Qingdao 07202
Placentia Area Museum, Placentia 06136
Plaine des Dinosaures, Mèze 12972
Plains Art Museum, Fargo 43293
Plains Indians and Pioneers Museum, Woodward 48748
Plains Vintage Railway and Historical Museum, Ashburton 30100
Plainsman Museum, Aurora 41401
Plamondon and District Museum, Plamondon 06137
Plan-Weseritzer Heimatstuben mit Archiv, Tirschenreuth 20179
Planet Earth Museum, Newhaven 40047
Planetron - Aards Paradijs, Dwingeloo 29186
Planšarski Muzej, Bohinjsko Jezero 34087
Plantahaus - Chesa Planta, Samedan 37095
Plantation Agriculture Museum, Scott 47509
Plantation Historical Museum, Plantation 46543
Plantation of Ulster Visitor Centre, Draperstown 38775
Plas Mawr, Conwy 38627
Plas Newydd, Llanfairpwll 39549
Plas Newydd, Llangollen 39555
Plassenburg, Kulmbach 18270
Plaster Rock Museum, Plaster Rock 06138
Plastic Club, Philadelphia 46444
Plastov Museum of Modern Art, Uljanovsk 33667
Plastov Picture Gallery, Uljanovsk 33658
Platenhäuschen, Erlangen 16922
Platform 1 Heritage Farm Railway, Littlehampton 01181
Platt R. Spencer Special Collections and Archival Room, Geneva 43644
Plattner Bienenhof Museum, Soprabolzano 25605
Plattsburgh Art Museum, Plattsburgh 46549
Plauener Spitzenmuseum, Plauen 19412
Plaza de La Raza, Los Angeles 44937
Pleasant Point Railway and Historical Society Museum, Pleasant Point 30238
Please Touch Museum, Philadelphia 46445
Plesskij Gosudarstvennyj Istoriko-Architekturnyj i Chudožestvennyj Muzej-Zapovednik, Ples 33325
Pleven Art Gallery - Donation Svetlin Russev Collection, Pleven 04763
Plimsoll Gallery, Hobart 01103
Pluimvee Museum, Barneveld 28964
Plum Coulee and District Museum, Plum Coulee 06140
Plum Grove Historic Home, Iowa City 44246
Plumas County Museum, Quincy 46756
Plumb Farm Museum, Greeley 43786
Plumershuuske, Diepenheim 29151
Plunket Museum of Irish Education, Dublin 22452
Plymouth Plantation Museum, Plymouth 46562
Plymouth Antiquarian Society Museum, Plymouth 46563
Plymouth Arts Centre, Plymouth 40211
Plymouth Historical Museum, Plymouth 46565
Poble Espanyol, Palma de Mallorca 35236
Pocahontas County Iowa Historical Society Museum, Laurens 44680
Pocahontas County Museum, Marlinton 45172
Podhorácké Muzeum, Tišnov 08682
Podium Kunst, Schramberg 19847
Podjavorinské Múzeum, Nové Mesto nad Váhom 34038
Podještědské Muzeum Karoliny Světlé, Český Dub 08301
Podlipanské Museum, Český Brod 08300
Podpolianske Múzeum Detva, Detva 33987
Podpolnaja Tipografija CK RSDRP, Moskva 33172
Podravka Museum, Koprivnica 07719
Podřipské Museum, Roudnice nad Labem 08639
Podtatranské Múzeum, Poprad 34045
Pöljä Local History Museum, Pöljä 09934
Pöljän Kotiseutumuseo, Pöljä 09934
Pörtom Hembygdsmuseum, Pörtom 09935
Poet Jovaras House, Šiauliai 27529
Pöytyän Kotiseutumuseo, Pöytyä 09936
Pohjanmaan Museo, Vaasa 10161
Pohjois-Karjalan Museo, Joensuu 09581
Pohjois-Pohjanmaan Museo, Oulu 09897
Pohronské Múzeum v Novej Bani, Nová Baňa 34037
Point Amour Lighthouse, Saint John's 06347
Point Ellice House, Victoria 06728
Point of Honor, Lynchburg 45007
Point Pelee Natural History Museum, Leamington 05740
Pointe-à-Callière - Musée d'Archéologie et d'Histoire de Montréal, Montréal 05927
Pointe Coupee Museum, New Roads 45745
Pointe-Noire - Parc Marin du Saguenay, Baie-Sainte-Catherine 05036
Pojani Museum, Pojani 00030
Pokrajinski Muzej, Kočevje 34095
Pokrajinski Muzej, Maribor 34127
Pokrajinski Muzej, Murska Sobota 34134
Pokrajinski Muzej, Strumica 27596
Pokrajinski Muzej Celje, Celje 34090
Pokrajinski Muzej Koper, Koper 34097
Pokrajinski Muzej Ptuj, Ptuj 34141
Pokrov Church Museum, Moskva 33031
Pokrovskij Sobor-chram Vasilija Blažennogo, Moskva 33173
Polabské Muzeum, Poděbrady 08551
Polabské Národnopisné Muzeum, Přerov 08623
Polarmuseet, Andenes 30387
Polarmuseet i Tromsø, Tromsø 30933
Polarmuseum in Tromsø, Tromsø 30933
Poldark Mine and Heritage Complex, Helston 39216
Poldermuseum, Antwerpen 03168
Poldermuseum, Puttershoek 29719
Poldermuseum de Hooge Boezem Achter Haastrecht, Haastrecht 29335
Poldermuseum Den Huijgen Dijck, Heerhugowaard 29365
Poldermuseum Het Grootslag - Nationaal Saet en Cruytmuseum, Andijk 28920
Poldowrian Museum of Prehistory, Coverack 38647
Polemiko Mouseio, Athinai 20902
Polenmuseum Rapperswil, Rapperswil, Sankt Gallen 37044
Polenz-Museum, Cunewalde 16518
Polesden Lacey, Dorking 38756
Polesden Lacey, Great Bookham 39121
Poli Museo della Grappa, Bassano del Grappa 23041
Polibinskij Memoralnyj Muzej-usadba S.V. Kovalevskoj, Polibino 33327
Police and Pioneer Museum, Shoal Lake 06446
The Police Museum, Belfast 38158
Police Museum, Hong Kong 07110
Police Museum, Imphal 21856
Police Station and Courthouse, Auburn 00755
Police Station Museum, Mount Barker 01280
Polish American Museum, Port Washington 46609
Polish Army Museum, Kołobrzeg 31670
Polish Association of Members of the Museum Professions, Kraków 49335
Polish Aviation Museum, Kraków 31713
Polish Cultural Institution Gallery, London 39746
Polish Estate Museum, Plochocin 31885
Polish Maritime Museum, Gdańsk 31563
Polish Military Museum, Warszawa 32133
Polish Museum of America, Chicago 42358
Polish Museums Association, Kraków 49337
Polishistoriska Museet, Stockholm 36272
Polistekniska Museet, Solna 36220
Politechničskij Muzej, Moskva 33174
Political Life Museum, Amman 27059
Politie-Petten Museum, Slochteren 29834
Politiemuseum, Wommelgem 03846
Politiemuseum Oudaan, Antwerpen 03169
Politimuseet i Oslo, Oslo 30759
Polizeihistorische Sammlung Berlin, Berlin 16081
Polizeimuseum, Aarau 36428
Polk County Heritage Gallery, Des Moines 42907
Polk County Historical Museum, Cedartown 42164
Polk County Historical Museum, Crookston 42706
Polk County Historical Museum, Osceola 46202
Polk County Historical Society, Des Moines 42908
Polk County Memorial Museum, Livingston 44835
Polk County Museum, Balsam Lake 41446
Polk Museum of Art, Lakeland 44604
Pollismolen, Bos-en Pijpenmuseum, Bree 03244
Pollock's Toy Museum, London 39747
Pollok House, Glasgow 39060
Polly Woodside Melbourne Maritime Museum, Southbank 01465
Polokwane Art Museum, Polokwane 34331
Polson Park and Museum, Hoquiam 44102
Poltava Art Museum, Poltava 37897
Poltava State Museum, Poltava 37898
Põltsamaa Muuseum, Põltsamaa 09347
Põlva Talurahvamuuseum, Karilatsi 09329
Polygnotos Vagis Museum, Thassos 21174
Polynesian Cultural Center, Laie 44577
Polytechnical Museum, Moskva 33174
Polyteekkarimuseo, Espoo 09437
Pomarkun Kotiseutumuseo, Pomarkku 09942
Pomázer Heimatstube, Sinsheim 19971
Pommeranian Military Museum, Bydgoszcz 31516
Pommersches Bettenmuseum, Peenemünde 19363
Pommersches Landesmuseum, Greifswald 17390
Pomona College Museum of Art, Claremont 42419
Pomorski i Povijesni Muzej Hrvatskog Primorja, Rijeka 07763
Pomorski Muzej, Dubrovnik 07700
Pomorski Muzej, Zadar 07807
Pomorski Muzej Crne Gore, Kotor 33848
Pomorski Muzej Sergej Mašera, Piran 34138
Pomorskie Muzeum Wojskowe, Bydgoszcz 31516
Pompallier House, Russell 30252
Pompejanum, Aschaffenburg 15527
Pompey Museum of Slavery and Emancipation, Nassau 03077
Pomskizillious Museum of Toys, Xaghra 27715
Ponce de León's Fort, Santo Domingo 09116
Ponce DeLeon Inlet Lighthouse, Ponce Inlet 46583
Ponce History Museum, Ponce 32381
Ponce Museum of Art, Ponce 32380
Pondicherry Museum, Pondicherry 21983
Pongauer Heimatmuseum im Schloß Goldegg, Goldegg 01903
Ponitrianske Múzeum, Nitra 34035
Ponshu-kan-Echigo Sake Museum, Yuzawa 27036
De Pont, Tilburg 29881
Pontefract Castle Museum, Pontefract 40217
Pontefract Museum, Pontefract 40218
Pontifical Biblical Institute Museum, Jerusalem 22656
Pontypool and Blaenavon Railway, Blaenavon 38251
Pontypool Museums, Pontypool 40221
Pontypridd Museum, Pontypridd 40223
Pony Express Museum, Saint Joseph 47108
Pope County Historical Museum, Glenwood 43699
Pope's Tavern Museum, Florence 43344
Poplar Grove Historic Plantation, Wilmington 48662
Popol Vuh Archaeological Museum, Guatemala 21275
Poppen en Poppenhuis Museum 't Duvelke, Breda 29024
Poppen- en Speelgoedmuseum, Tilburg 29882

Poppenhuis Carmen, Utrecht 29909
Poppenhuismuseum, Heesch 29371
Poppenmuseum, Ter Apel 28923
Poppenmuseum, Maastricht 29570
Poppenmuseum Christus Koning, Wetteren 03838
Poppenspe(e)lmuseum, Vorchten 29964
Popppenhuismuseum Alida's Kleine Wereldje, Veendam 29925
Poptaslot Heringa-State, Marssum 29581
Popular Art Centre, Al-Bireh 31062
Popular Arts Museum, San Juan 32407
Popular Traditions Museum Qasrelazem, Damascus 37437
Porcelain Museum, Herend 21426
Porcelainmuseum, Hollóháza 21429
Porcelánmúzeum, Hollóháza 21429
Porcupine Plain and District Museum, Porcupine Plain 06147
Porfyrmuseet, Älvdalen 35785
Pori Art Museum, Pori 09944
Porin Taidemuseo, Pori 09944
Porirua Hospital Museum, Porirua 30241
Porlammi Local History Museum, Porlammi 09948
Porlammin Kotiseutumuseo, Porlammi 09948
Porsanger Museum, Lakselv 30625
Porsche Automuseum Helmut Pfeifhofer, Gmünd, Kärnten 01890
Porsche Museum, Stuttgart 20103
Porsche Traktorenmuseum, Altreiteregg 01668
Porselein Dierenpark, Wildervank 30006
Porsgrunn Bymuseum, Porsgrunn 30780
Port Albert Maritime Museum, Port Albert 01377
Port Angeles Fine Arts Center, Port Angeles 46589
Port Arthur Historic Site, Port Arthur 01378
Port-au-Choix Site, Port-au-Choix 06151
Port-aux-Basques Railway Heritage Centre, Port-aux-Basques 06154
Port Carling Pioneer Museum, Port Carling 06156
Port Chalmers Museum, Port Chalmers 30242
Port Clements Museum, Port Clements 06157
Port Colborne Historical and Marine Museum, Port Colborne 06158
Port Columbus National Civil War Naval Center, Columbus 42576
Port Community Art Centre, Port Adelaide 01374
Port Discovery - Children's Museum in Baltimore, Baltimore 41485
Port Dover Harbour Museum, Port Dover 06160
Port Elizabeth Museum, Port Elizabeth 34333
Port Fairy Historic Lifeboat Station, Port Fairy 01381
Port Fairy History Centre, Port Fairy 01382
Port Gamble Historic Museum, Port Gamble 46593
Port Hardy Museum, Port Hardy 06162
Port Hastings Museum, Port Hastings 06163
Port Huron Museum, Port Huron 46597
Port-la-Joye-Fort Amherst, Charlottetown 05229
Port MacDonnell and District Maritime Museum, Port MacDonnell 01385
Port Macquarie Historic Museum, Port Macquarie 01386
Port Moody Station Museum, Port Moody 06167
Le Port-Musée, Douarnenez 11562
Port Natal Maritime Museum, Durban 34231
Port of Morgan Historic Museum, Morgan 01275
Port Phillip City Collection, Saint Kilda, Victoria 01436
Port Pirie National Trust Museum, Port Pirie 01387
Port Royal National Historic Site, Annapolis Royal 04998
Port-Said Museum, Port Said 09303
Port Stephens Shell Museum, Corlette 00946
Port Sunlight Heritage Centre, Port Sunlight 40236
Port Townsend Marine Science Center, Port Townsend 46606
Port Union Museum, Port Union 06170
Port Victor Gallery, Victor Harbor 01566
Port Victoria National Trust Museum, Port Victoria 01389
Portage and District Arts Council, Portage-la-Prairie 06173
Portage County Historical Society Museum, Ravenna 46800
Portage County Museum, Stevens Point 47808
Portanje's Vespa Scooter en Nostalgie Collectie, Bunnik 29037
Portchester Castle, Portchester 40239
La Porte County Historical Society Museum, La Porte 44555
Porte de Hal, Bruxelles 03341
Porter County Old Jail Museum, Valparaiso 48193
Porter-Phelps-Huntington Foundation, Hadley 43863
Porter Thermometer Museum, Onset 46162
Porterville Historical Museum, Porterville 46620
Portfolio Gallery, Edinburgh 38906
Porthcawl Museum, Porthcawl 40240
Porthcurno Telegraph Museum, Porthcurno 40241
Porthmadog Maritime Museum, Porthmadog 40242
Portholes Into the Past, Medina 45226
Portico Gallery, Helensburgh 39209
Portico Library and Gallery, Manchester 39903
Portikus, Frankfurt am Main 17070
Portland Art Museum, Portland 46641
Portland Basin Museum, Ashton-under-Lyne 38034
Portland Castle, Portland 40244
Portland CEMA Arts Centre, Portland 01391
Portland Children's Museum Second Generation, Portland 46642
Portland Maritime Discovery Centre, Portland 01392
Portland Museum, Louisville 44974
Portland Museum, Portland 40245
Portland Museum of Art, Portland 46626
Portland State University Galleries, Portland 46643
Portobello Gallery, Saint James 03105
Portsmouth Athenaeum, Portsmouth 46652
Portsmouth Museum, Portsmouth 46658
Portsmouth Museum of Military History, Portsmouth 46664
Portsmouth Naval Shipyard Museum, Portsmouth 46665
Porvoon Museo, Porvoo 09954
Porzellanmuseum, Rödental 19629
Porzellanmuseum Reichmannsdorf, Reichmannsdorf 19548
Porzellansammlung, Dresden 16704
Posavje Museum, Brežice 34088
Posavski Muzej Brežice, Brežice 34088
Poshalostin Memorial House-Museum, Solotča 33545
Posion Kotiseutumuseo, Posio 09958
POSK Gallery, London 39748
Post and Telecommunication Museum, Wrocław 32183
Post Museum, Helsinki 09520
Post Museum, Vyšší Brod 08735
Post Office Museum, Hollókő 21431
Post Office Museum, Nagyvázsony 21490
Post Rock Museum, La Crosse 44535
Post & Tele Museum, København 08947
Postal and Philatelic Museum, Tel Aviv 22772
Postal Museum, Amman 27060
Postal Museum, Budapest 21379
Postal Museum, Cairo 09284
Postal Museum, Praha 08612
Postal Museum, Seoul 27266
Postal Museum, Stockholm 36273
Postal Museum, Storby 10057
Postal Museum, Taipei 07354
Postal Museum and Philatelic Library, Manila 31393
Postal Museum Botswana, Gaborone 03935
Postamúzeum, Balatonszemes 21313
Postamúzeum, Budapest 21379
Postamúzeum, Hollókő 21431
Postamúzeum, Nagyvázsony 21490
Postcard Museum, Holmfirth 39254
Poste de Traite Chauvin, Tadoussac 06533
Poster Museum, Hoorn 29441
Postimuseo, Helsinki 09520
Postmaster Museum, Vyra 33743
Póstminjasafn Íslands, Hafnarfjörður 21636
Postmuseet, Oslo 30760
Postmuseum, Balatonszemes 21313
Postmuseum des Fürstentums Liechtenstein, Vaduz 27517
Postmuseum Mettingen, Mettingen 18722
Postmuseum Rheinhausen, Oberhausen-Rheinhausen 19176
Postojannaja Požarno-techničeskaja Vystavka, Sankt-Peterburg 33477
Poštovní Muzeum, Praha 08612
Poštovní Muzeum, Vyšší Brod 08735
Postrotemuseet, Storby 10057
Postville Courthouse Museum, Lincoln 44774
Potchefstroom Museum, Potchefstroom 34335
Potland Museum, Basildon 38100
Potsdam-Museum, Potsdam 19436
Potsdam Public Museum, Potsdam 46669
Pottekarie, Dranouter 03394
Pottenbakkerij De Brinksteen, Dwingeloo 29187
Pottenbakkerij Het Ovenhuis, Ruinerwold 29787
Pottenbakkerij Museum, Kattendijke 29476
Potter County Historical Society Museum, Coudersport 42671
The Potteries Museum and Art Gallery, Stoke-on-Trent 40609
Potters Bar Museum, Potters Bar 40262
Potter's Museum, Somero 10048
Potter's Museum of Curiosity and Smugglers's Museum, Bolventor 38273
Potts Inn Museum, Pottsville 46672
Pottsgrove Manor, Pottstown 46671
Pouce Coupe Museum, Pouce Coupe 06174
Pouch Cove Museum, Pouch Cove 06175
Pound Ridge Museum, Pound Ridge 46679
Považské Múzeum, Žilina 34079
Povčenno-agronomičeskij Muzej im. V.R. Viljamsa, Moskva 33175
Powder Magazine, Beechworth 00785
Powder Magazine, Charleston 42226
Powderham Castle, Kenton 39340
Powell-Cotton Museum, Quex House and Gardens, Birchington 38203
Powell County Museum, Deer Lodge 42848
Powell River Historical Museum, Powell River 06176
Power Plant Contemporary Art Gallery, Toronto 06601
Power Station- and Engineering Museum, Mynämäki 09849
Power Station Museum of Helsinki City Museum, Helsinki 09548
Powerhouse House and Car Museum, Portland 01393
Powerhouse Museum, Ultimo 01558
Powerhouse Museum Yanco, Yanco 01624
Powers Museum, Carthage 42126
Powis Castle, Welshpool 40816
Pownalborough Court House, Dresden 42987
Powysland Museum and Montgomery Canal Centre, Welshpool 40817
P.P. Chistyakov House-Museum, Puškin 33335
Pra Site Museum, Bogor 22091
Prabhas Patan Museum, Prabhas Patan 21984
Prachatické Muzeum, Prachatice 08562
Prácheňské Muzeum, Písek 08540
Pracownia - Muzeum Józefa Ignacego Kraszewskiego, Poznań 31914
Praedicantenbibliothek der Nikolaikirche, Isny 17931
Prähistorische Privatsammlung, Mühlen 02326
Prähistorische Siedlung Pestenacker, Weil am Lech 20433
Prähistorisches Heimatmuseum, Veringenstadt 20303
Prämonstratenser-Chorherrenstift mit Stiftssammlungen, Geras 01874
Prague Castle Gallery, Praha 08607
Prahova District Museum of History and Archaeology, Ploieşti 32572
Prairie County Museum, Des Arc 42904
Prairie Gallery, Grande Prairie 05520
Prairie Homestead, Philip 46465
The Prairie Museum of Art and History, Colby 42517
Prairie Panorama Museum, Czar 05300
Prairie Pioneer Museum, Craik 05285
Prairie River Museum, Prairie River 06177
Prairie Trails Museum of Wayne County, Corydon 42661
Prairie Village, Madison 45064
Prairie West Historical Centre, Eston 05416
Sri Pratap Singh Museum, Srinagar 22028
Pratermuseum, Wien 02972
Praters Mill, Varnell 48204
Pratt County Historical Society Museum, Pratt 46686
Pratt Manhattan Gallery, New York 45864
Pratt Museum, Homer 44068
The Pratt Museum of Natural History, Amherst 41181
Pre-Industrial Museum, Halifax 39155
Precious Stones Museum, Polanica Zdrój 31892
Predjama Castle, Postojna 34140
Predjamski Grad, Postojna 34140
Prefectural Assambly Memorial Hall, Niigata 26597
Prefectural Sakitama Archaeological Hall, Gyoda 26160
Prefectural Science Museum Joetsu, Joetsu 26283
Prefectural Torii Memorial Museum, Naruto 26590
Préhisto-Parc, Tursac 15021
Préhisto-Parc et Grottes, Réclère 37047
Le Préhistorama, Rousson 14065
Prehistory Museum, Tripoli 27509
Preiļi History and Applied Art Museum, Preiļi 27397
Preilu Vēstures un Lietišķās Mākslas Muzejs, Preiļi 27397
Prempeh II Jubilee Museum, Kumasi 20797
Prentenkabinet Universiteit Leiden, Leiden 29523
Presbyterian Historical Society Museum, Montreat 45481
Presbyterian Historical Society Museum, Philadelphia 46446
Prescot Museum, Prescot 40264
Prescott House Museum, Port Williams 06171
Presentatieruimte de Overslag, Eindhoven 29218
Presentation House Gallery, North Vancouver 06027
Presentazione Scenografica Gioacchino Murat, Pizzo 24970
Prešernov Spominski Muzej, Kranj 34101
Présház, Tokaji 21598
President Andrew Johnson Museum, Greeneville 43803
President Benjamin Harrison Home, Indianapolis 44234
President Chester A. Arthur Historic Site, Fairfield 43270
President Pretorius Museum, Potchefstroom 34336
The Presidential Museum, Odessa 46094
President's Cottage Museum, White Sulphur Springs 48592
Presidio La Bahia, Goliad 43723
Presnja Istoriko-memorialnyj Muzej, Moskva 33176
Presque Isle County Historical Museum, Rogers City 46987
Presqu'ile Provincial Park Museum, Brighton 05133
Press Museum, Amsterdam 28892
Press Museum, İstanbul 37695
Preston Hall Museum, Stockton-on-Tees 40600
Preston Manor, Brighton 38342
Preston Mill and Phantassie Doocot, East Linton 38846
Prestongrange Museum, Prestongrange 40270
Prestwould Foundation, Clarksville 42438
Pretoria Art Museum, Pretoria 34353
Preußen-Museum Nordrhein-Westfalen, Wesel 20536
Preveli Monastery, Myrthios 21081
Prežihov Spominski Muzej, Ravne na Koroškem 34145
Price Tower Arts Center, Bartlesville 41515
Pricketts Fort, Fairmont 43273
Prickwillow Drainage Engine Museum, Prickwillow 40271
Priental-Museum, Aschau im Chiemgau 15534
Prieré d'Airaines, Airaines 10245
Priest House, West Hoathly 40824
Priesterhäuser, Zwickau 20777
Priest's House, Easton-on-the-Hill 38863
Priest's House Museum, Wimborne Minster 40879
Prieuré du Vieux Logis, Nice 13327
Prignitz-Museum Havelberg, Havelberg 17650
Prilukin National Museum of the Karelian Livviki people, Olonec 33252
Primer Museo de las Abejas en México, Colonia Condesa 27842
Primer Museo Permanente del Boxeo Argentino, Buenos Aires 00252
Primorskaja Kraevaja Kartinnaja Galereja, Vladivostok 33708
Primorskij Gosudarstvennyj Muzej im. V.K. Arseneva, Vladivostok 33709
Prince Albert Historical Museum, Prince Albert 06184
Prince Albert National Park Nature Centre, Waskesiu Lake 06748
Prince Chichibu Memorial Sports Museum, Tokyo 26835
Prince Edward Island Museum, Charlottetown 05230
Prince Edward Island Potato Museum, O'Leary 06050
The Prince Edward Island Regiment Museum, Charlottetown 05231
Prince of Wales Fort, Churchill 05252
Prince of Wales Martello Tower, Halifax 05561
Prince of Wales Museum of Western India, Mumbai 21954
Prince of Wales Northern Heritage Centre, Yellowknife 06870
Prince Rupert Fire Museum, Prince Rupert 06190
Princess of Wales's Royal Regiment and Queen's Regiment Museum, Dover 38769
Princess Patricia's Canadian Light Infantry Museum, Calgary 05178
Princessehof Leeuwarden, Leeuwarden 29514
Princeton and District Museum, Princeton 06192
Princeton Museum, Princeton 46702
Princeton University Art Museum, Princeton 46703
Princeton University Museum of Natural History, Princeton 46704
Pringle Cottage Museum, Warwick 01584
Prins Eugens Waldemarsudde, Stockholm 36274
Prins Hendrik de Zeevaarder Museum, Egmond aan Zee 29205
Print and Picture Collection, Philadelphia 46447
The Print Center, Philadelphia 46448
Print Collection of the National and University Library, Zagreb 07818
Print Consortium, Kansas City 44405
Print Room of the Polish Academy of Arts and Sciences, Kraków 31686
Print Room of the Warsaw University Library, Warszawa 32084
Printing House Museum, Cockermouth 38604
The Printing Museum, Carson 42115
Printing Museum, Esbjerg 08805
Printing Museum, Kungsgården 36024
Prirodnjački Muzej, Beograd 33816
Prirodnjački Muzej Crne Gore, Podgorica 33890
Prirodonaučen Muzej, Belogradčik 04619
Prirodonaučen Muzej, Burgas 04636
Prirodonaučen Muzej, Černi Osăm 04638
Prirodonaučen Muzej, Kotel 04720
Prirodonaučen Muzej, Plovdiv 04782
Prirodonaučen Muzej, Varna 04906
Prirodonaučen Muzej na Makedonija, Skopje 27592
Prirodoslovni Muzej, Rijeka 07764
Prirodoslovni Muzej, Split 07785
Prirodoslovni Muzej Slovenije, Ljubljana 34118
Prirodovedčeskij Muzej, Smolensk 33533
Přírodovědecké Muzeum, Praha 08613
Přírodovědecké Oddělení, Opava 08521
Prírodovedné Múzeum, Bratislava 33977
Prison Model Museum, Nueva Gerona 08062
Prison Museum, Hämeenlinna 09456
Prittlewell Priory Museum, Southend-on-Sea 40553
Private Ethnographic Museum, Góra Kalwaria 31604
Private Lebzelt- und Buttermodelabdrucksammlung, Pressbaum 02454
Private Museum of Grammophones an Phonographs, Sankt-Peterburg 33382
Private Sammlung Mechanischer Musikinstrumente, Wohlhausen 20645
Privatmuseum Hans Klein, Prichsenstadt 19448
Privatmuseum Im Blauen Haus, Appenzell 36464
Privatmuseum Sammlung Holzinger, München 18898
Privatsammlung A.F. Fleischer, Wien 02973
Privatsammlung Burg Runkel, Runkel 19719
Privatsammlung Franz Pinteritsch, Pichling 02414
Privatsammlung Hermine Brandstetter, Ostermiething 02389
Privatsammlung Leo Gesell, Triefenstein 20206
Privatsammlung Piaty, Waidhofen an der Ybbs 02787
Privatsammlung Silvester Berner, Lengenfeld bei Krems 02206
Pro Arts Gallery, Oakland 46069
Pro Rodeo Hall of Fame and Museum of the American Cowboy, Colorado Springs 42541
Pro Urba, Orbe 37014
Probstei-Museum, Schönberg, Holstein 19824
Prochorovo Field - Museum-preserve of Military History, Prochorovka 33328
Proclamation of Independence Memorial, Melaka 27666
Proctor House Museum, Brighton 05134
Produktionsmuseum Klostermühle, Boitzenburg 16223
Produzentengalerie - OHa Kunst im Wasserturm, Eutin 16980
Proed, Santiago de Chile 06920
Prof. Aleksandra Biezina Muzejs, Madona 27385
Prof. Eidenberger-Museum, Niederwaldkirchen 02363
Prof.-Fritz-Behn-Museum, Bad Dürrheim 15633
Prof. Gerstmayr-Museum, Mauthausen 02290
Profanierte Marienkapelle, Ludwigsstadt 18529
Programa de Museo y Parques, San Juan 32408
Programme for Museum Development in Africa, Mombasa 49266
Project Art-University of Iowa and Clinics, Iowa City 44247
Project Arts Center, Dublin 22453

Prokofyev-Museum, Moskva 33148
Prome Museum, Prome 28742
Promont House Museum, Milford 45342
Pronkkamer Uden-Museum Hedendaagse Kunst, Uden 29885
Propst House and Marple Grove, Hickory 44008
Prora-Museum, Ostseebad Binz 19313
Prorokov House-Museum, Ivanovo 32825
Proserpine Historical Museum, Proserpine 01395
Prospect Hill Museum, Meadows 01220
Prouty-Chew Museum, Geneva 43642
Provan Hall House, Glasgow 39061
Provand's Lordship, Glasgow 39062
Provan's Mechanical Museum, Colac 00936
La Provence Miniature, Saint-Galmier 14225
Proviant-Eisen Museum, Gresten 01940
Providence Athenaeum, Providence 46723
Providence Children's Museum, Providence 46724
Province House, Charlottetown 05232
Provincetown Art Museum, Provincetown 46730
Provincetown Heritage Museum, Provincetown 46731
Provinciaal Archeologisch Museum, Velzeke-Ruddershove 03807
Provinciaal Archeologisch Museum-Ename, Oudenaarde 03677
Provinciaal Archeologisch Museum van Zuid-Oost-Vlaanderen, Zottegem 03858
Provinciaal Domein Rivierenhof Galerij, Deurne 03383
Provinciaal Museum Bulskampveld, Beernem 03205
Provinciaal Museum Stijn Streuvels, Ingooigem 03519
Provinciaal Openluchtmuseum Bokrijk, Genk 03432
Provinciaal Veiligheidsinstituut, Antwerpen 03170
Provincial Museum, Kočevje 34095
Provincial Museum, Strumica 27596
Provincial Museum of Alberta, Edmonton 05384
Provincial Museum of History of Pinal del Río, Pinar del Río 08077
Provincial Museum of Kymenlaakso, Kotka 09700
Provincial Museum of Lapland, Rovaniemi 10001
Provincial Museum of Newfoundland and Labrador, Saint John's 06348
Provincial Natuurhistorisch Museum Natura Docet, Denekamp 29140
Provincial Open-Air Museum, Genk 03432
Provinzialrömische Sammlung und Antikenkabinett, Graz 01929
Provinzmuseum der Franziskaner, Wien 02974
Provost Skene's House, Aberdeen 37942
Prøysenhuset, Rudshøgda 30811
Prudence Crandall Museum, Canterbury 42082
Prunkräume in der Residenz, Kempten 18064
První České Muzeum Velocipédu, Chotěboř 08316
Prywatne Muzeum Etnograficzne, Góra Kalwaria 31604
Prywatne Muzeum Etnograficzno-Historyczne, Bielsk Podlaski 31493
Przhevalsk Regional Museum, Prževalsk 27314
P.S. 1 Contemporary Art Center, Long Island City 44870
P.S. Industry Museum, Renmark 01413
Pskov Memorial Museum of V.I. Lenin, Pskov 33333
Pskov Museum-Preserve of History, Architecture and Art, Pskov 33332
Pskovskij Gosudarstvennyj Istoričesko-architekturnyj i Chudožestnennyj Muzej-zapovednik, Pskov 33332
Pskovskij Memorialnyj Muzej V.I. Lenina, Pskov 33333
Psychiatrie-Museum, Bern 36549
Psychiatrie-Museum, Emmendingen 16856
Psychiatrie Museum im Philippshospital, Riedstadt 19607
Psychiatriemuseum Haina, Haina, Kloster 17494
Psykiatrihistoriska Museet, Uppsala 36359
Psykiatrihistoriska Museet, Växjö 36389
P.T. Boat Museum, Germantown 43659
P.T. Boat Museum, Germantown 43660
Ptolemais Museum, Tolmeitha 27503
PTT Museum of Denmark, København 08947
PTT Muzej Zajednice Jugoslovenskih Pošta, Telegrafa i Telefona, Beograd 33817
Pu Le Temple, Chengde 07019
Public Library and Museum, Herne Bay 39233
Public Library Gallery, Llanelli 39547
Public Museum, Mali Lošinj 07738
Public Museum of Grand Rapids, Grand Rapids 43759
Public Service Memorial, Kuala Lumpur 27650
Public Transportmuseum Brussel, Bruxelles 03329
Publiekscentrum voor Beeldende Kunst, Enschede 29239
PUC Minas Museum of Natural Sciences, Belo Horizonte 03985
Pucuk Rebung Royal Gallery Museum, Kuala Lumpur 27651
Pudasjärven Kotiseutumuseo, Pudasjarvi 09959
Pueblo County Historical Society Museum, Pueblo 46739
El Pueblo de Los Angeles Historical Monument, Los Angeles 44938
Pueblo Grande Museum, Phoenix 46480
La Puente Valley Historical Society Museum, La Puente 44558
Puerta de Isabel II Gallery, Manila 31394
Puerto Galera National Museum, Puerto Galera 31423
Puffing Billy Steam Museum, Menzies Creek 01246
Puget Sound Coast Artillery Museum at Fort Worden, Port Townsend 46607
Puhoi Historical Society Museum, Puhoi 30243
Puke Ariki, New Plymouth 30215
Pukkila Manor, Piikkiö 09931
Pukkilan Kartanomuseo, Piikkiö 09931
Pukkilan Kotiseutumuseo, Pukkila 09960
Pulandian City Museum, Dalian 07040
Pulkauer Gewerbemuseum, Pulkau 02462
Pulkautaler Weinbaumuseum, Hadres 01986
Pulkkilan Kotiseutumuseo, Pulkkila 09961
Pullman Museum, Chicago 42359
La Pulperie de Chicoutimi, Chicoutimi 05247
Pulszky Society - Hungarian Museums Association, Budapest 49230
Pump House Center for the Arts, Chillicothe 42380
Pump House Gallery, London 39749
Pump House of Regional Arts, La Crosse 44537
Pump House Steam Museum, Kingston 05686
Pumphouse Educational Museum, London 39750
Punct Muzeal, Moroeni 32552
Punct Muzeal Gospodăria Tărănească, Enisala 32517
Punjab Archives Museum, Lahore 31042
Punkaharjun Kotiseutumuseo, Punkaharju 09963
Punkt Etnograficzny w Rogierówku, Rogierówko 31948
Punkt Muzealny w Supraśli, Supraśl 32008
Puolakan Talomuseo, Kouvola 09704
Puppen-, Bären- und Spielzeugmuseum, Bad Wimpfen 15772
Puppen- und Spielzeugmuseum, Holzminden 17831
Puppen- und Spielzeugmuseum, Lichtenstein, Sachsen 18458
Puppen und Spielzeugmuseum, Mödling 02313
Puppen- und Spielzeugmuseum, Solothurn 37187
Puppen- und Spielzeugmuseum, Wien 02975
Puppen- und Spielzeugmuseum Sammlung Katharina Engels, Rothenburg ob der Tauber 19680
Puppenausstellung des Steinauer Marionetten-Theaters, Steinau an der Straße 20043
Puppenhausmuseum, Basel 36517
Puppenmuseum, Einöde 01800
Puppenmuseum, Oberlienz 02370
Puppenmuseum Falkenstein, Hamburg 17563
Puppenmuseum im Kunsthof, Herten 17741
Puppenmuseum in Villach, Villach 02762
Puppenmuseum Jeannine, Kreuzlingen 36837
Puppenmuseum Kärntner Eisenwurzen, Hüttenberg 02052
Puppenmuseum Sasha Morgenthaler, Zürich 37406
Puppentheatermuseum, Kaufbeuren 18043
Puppentheatermuseum, Mistelbach an der Zaya 02302
Puppentheatermuseum mit Abteilung Schaustellerei, München 18899
Puppentheatersammlung, Radebeul 19470
Puppet Centre, Toronto 06602
Puppet Museum, Tallinn 09369
Puratatva Sangrahalaya, Gorakhpur 21813
Purdue University Calumet Library Gallery, Hammond 43887
Purdue University Galleries, West Lafayette 48532
Puri Gamelan Suar Agung, Denpasar 22098
La Purisima Mission, Lompoc 44852
Purmerends Museum, Purmerend 29717
Purton Museum, Swindon 40663
Purvattatva Sangrahalaya Madhya Pradesh Shasan, Damoh 21753
Pusat Latihan Kesenian & Pertukangan Tangan Brunei, Bandar Seri Begawan 04600
Pushkin Museum, Toržok 33619
Pushkin Museum in Bernov, Bernov 32686
Pushkin Museum of Fine Arts, Moskva 33113
Pustozerskij Kompleksnyj Istoriko-prirodnyj Muzej, Narjan-Mar 33199
Pusulan Museo, Pusula 09965
Putkinotko, Savonlinna 10025
Putkiradiomuseo, Kouvola 09705
Putnam Cottage, Greenwich 43833
Putnam County Historical Society and Foundry School Museum, Cold Spring 42518
Putnam County Historical Society Museum, Kalida 44382
Putnam Museum of History and Natural Science, Davenport 42786
Putney Historical Society Museum, Putney 46749
Puuhkalan Talomuseo, Ylivieska 10218
Puukohola Heiau National Historic Site, Kawaihae 44419
P.V. Alabin History and Regional Museum, Samara 33378
P.W. Vorster Museum, Middelburg Cape 34308
Pyhäjärven Kotiseutumuseo, Pyhäjärvi 09967
Pyhäjoen Kotiseutumuseo, Pyhäjoki 09968
Pyhäjoki Local History Museum, Pyhäjoki 09968
Pyhämaan Kotiseutumuseo, Pyhämaa 09969
Pyhännän Kotiseutumuseo, Pyhäntä 09970
Pyhtään Kotiseutumuseo, Pyhtää 09971
Pykäri Nuutajärven Lasimuseo, Nuutajärvi 09876
Pyramid Hill and District Historical Museum, Pyramid Hill 01397
Pyramid Hill Sculpture Park and Museum, Hamilton 43884
Pyynikinlinna, Tampere 10083
Qalipakkanik Katersugaasivik, Ilulissat 21230
QANTAS Founders Outback Museum, Longreach 01186
Qaqortup Katersugaasivia, Qaqortoq 21237
Qasigiannguit Katersugaasiviat, Qasigiannguit 21238
Qasr Al-Gawharah, Cairo 09285
Qasr Al-Ibrahim, Cairo 09286
Qasr Ali Ibrahim, Zamalek 09309
Qatar National Museum, Doha 32417
QCA Gallery, Brisbane 00841
QCC Art Gallery, Bayside 41549
Qedem Museum, Kedumim 22673
Qeqertarsuaq Museum, Qeqertasuaq 21239
Qi Guo Gucheng Yi Zhi Museum, Zibo 07338
Qianling Museum, Qian Xian 07200
Qijiang Stone Engraving Museum, Gunan 07078
Qin Dai Zhan Guan, Xian 07295
Qin Shi Huan Bingmayong Museum, Xian 07296
Qingdao City Folklorish Museum, Qingdao 07203
Qingdao Municipal Museum, Qingdao 07204
Qingdao Painting Gallery, Qingdao 07205
Qingpu Museum, Shanghai 07218
Qom Museum, Qom 22274
Qozhaya Museum, Qozhaya 27492
Quaco Museum and Archives, Saint Martins 06366
Quadrat Bottrop, Bottrop 16265
Quadreria Cesarini, Fossombrone 23929
Quadreria Comunale, Offida 24672
Quadreria Comunale, Prato 25049
Quadreria Comunale, San Constanzo 25352
Quadreria dei Girolamini, Napoli 24605
Quadreria della Cassa Depositi e Prestiti, Roma 25265
Quadreria della Società Economica, Chiavari 23534
Quadreria e Pinacoteca Civica, San Giovanni in Persiceto 25374
Quaid-i-Azam Birthplace and Museum, Karachi 31032
Quaker Museum, Ballytore 22373
Quaker Yearly Meeting House, Mount Pleasant 45539
Quanzhou Maritime Museum, Quanzhou 07206
Quanzhou Painting Gallery, Quanzhou 07207
Quarry Bank Mill, Styal 40640
Quartel de Santa Cruz, Rio de Janeiro 04403
Quarzsandbergwerk-Museum, Buchs, Zürich 36597
Quaternary Period Qlacier Traces Exhibition Hall, Beijing 06986
Queanbeyan and District Historical Museum, Queanbeyan 01399
Quebec House, Westerham 40832
Queen Charlotte's Cottage, Richmond, Surrey 40321
Queen Elizabeth II Army Memorial Museum, Waiouru 30275
Queen Elizabeth National Park Museum, Lake Katwe 37830
Queen Elizabeth's Hunting Lodge, London 39751
Queen Emma Gallery, Honolulu 44086
Queen Emma Summer Palace, Honolulu 44087
Queen Mary Museum, Long Beach 44862
Queen Street Mill Textile Museum, Burnley 38400
Queen Victoria Museum, Harare 49033
Queen Victoria Museum and Art Gallery, Launceston 01170
Queen Victoria Rifles Museum - Hill 60, Zillebeke 03852
Queens County Farm Museum, Floral Park 43342
Queens County Museum, Liverpool 05759
Queens County Museum, Tilley House and Court House, Gagetown 05472
The Queen's Gallery, Edinburgh 38907
The Queen's Gallery, London 39752
Queens Historical Museum, Flushing 43356
Queen's Lancashire Regiment Museum, Preston 40269
Queens Library Gallery, Jamaica 44306
Queens Museum of Art, Flushing 43357
Queen's Own Cameron Highlanders of Canada Regimental Museum, Winnipeg 06837
Queen's Own Hussars Museum, Warwick 40791
Queen's Own Rifles of Canada Regimental Museum, Toronto 06603
Queen's Own Royal West Kent Regimental Museum, Maidstone 39878
Queen's Royal Irish Hussars Museum, Eastbourne 38855
The Queen's Royal Lancers Regimental Museum, Grantham 39112
Queen's Royal Surrey Regiment Museum, Guildford 39141
Queen's Royal Surrey Regiment Museum, West Clandon 40823
Queen's York Rangers Regimental Museum, Toronto 06604
Queenscliffe Historical Museum, Queenscliff 01401
Queenscliffe Maritime Museum, Queenscliff 01402
Queensferry Museum, South Queensferry 40536
Queensland Air Museum, Caloundra 00875
Queensland Art Gallery, South Brisbane 01459
Queensland Maritime Museum, South Brisbane 01460
Queensland Military Memorial Museum, Fortitude Valley 01032
Queensland Museum, South Bank 01458
Queensland Pioneer Steam Railway, Blackstone 00809
Queensland Police Museum, Brisbane 00842
Queensland University of Technology Art Collection, Kelvin Grove 01140
Queenstown and Frontier Museum, Queenstown 34365
The Queenstown Story, Cobh 22400
Quesnel and District Museum, Quesnel 06216
Quest - Center for Earth Science And Discovery, Makati 31356
Questacon The National Science and Technology Centre, Canberra 00890
Quetico Provincial Park Heritage Pavilion, Atikokan 05018
Quezonia Museum, Manila 31395
Quidi Vidi Battery, Saint John's 06349
Quiet Valley Living Historical Farm, Stroudsburg 47855
Quilpie Museum, Quilpie 01404
Quilters Hall of Fame, Marion 45159
Quincy and Adams County Museum, Quincy 46759
Quincy Art Center, Quincy 46760
Quincy Historical Museum, Quincy 46765
The Quincy Museum, Quincy 46761
La Quinta, Madrid 35060
Quinta das Cruzadas, Sintra 32352
Quinte Educational Museum, Ameliasburgh 04985
Quirindi and District Historical Cottage and Museum, Quirindi 01405
Quorn Mill Museum, Quorn 01406
Qurm Museum, Qurm 31011
Qutb Shahi Museum, Hyderabad 21845
Qwensel House and Pharmacy Museum, Turku 10118
Råå Museum för Fiske och Sjöfart, Råå 36158
Raabe-Haus, Braunschweig 16303
Raahe Museum, Raahe 09972
Raahen Museo, Raahe 09972
Raasay Heritage Museum, Kyle 39407
Rábaközi Múzeum, Kapuvár 21443
Rabekk Museum, Moss 30693
Rabindra Bharati Museum, Kolkata 21910
Rabindra Bhavan Art Gallery, Delhi 21782
Rabindra Bhavana, Santiniketan 22011
Rabiša Cave Museum, Belogradčik 04618
Raby Castle, Darlington 38698
Raccolata Comunale G.C. Corsi, Cantiano 23318
Raccolta Alberto della Ragione e Collezioni del Novecento, Firenze 23885
Raccolta Archeologica, Narni 24611
Raccolta Archeologica, Scheggia 25523
Raccolta Archeologica, Terni 25697
Raccolta Archeologica, Tolentino 25723
Raccolta Archeologica Alberto Pisani Dossi, Corbetta 23645
Raccolta Archeologica e Paleontologica, Corciano 23648
Raccolta Archeological, Bevagna 23075
Raccolta Civica, Città di Castello 23582
Raccolta Civica d'Arte Contemporanea, Molfetta 24460
Raccolta Civiche di Storia, Albino 22838
Raccolta Comunale, Acquasparta 22801
Raccolta Comunale, Celenza Valfortore 23471
Raccolta Comunale, Sigillo 25580
Raccolta Comunale d'Arte, Frontone 23938
Raccolta d'Arte, Città della Pieve 23575
Raccolta d'Arte, Roccalbegna 25140
Raccolta d'Arte C. Lamberti, Codogno 23605
Raccolta d'Arte Contemporanea R. Pastori, Calice Ligure 23268
Raccolta d'Arte della Provincia, Modena 24450
Raccolta d'Arte e Archeologia, Piazza Armerina 24901
Raccolta d'Arte Pagliara, Napoli 24606
Raccolta d'Arte Sacra, Figline Valdarno 23811
Raccolta d'Arte Sacra, Scarperia 25522
Raccolta d'Arte Ubaldiana, Piandimeleto 24897
Raccolta dei Padri Passionisti, Paliano 24781
Raccolta della Chiesa di Santa Maria Maggiore, Alatri 22828
Raccolta dell'Avifauna delle Marche, Montefortino 24527
Raccolta dell'Avifauna Lombarda, Arosio 22938
Raccolta delle Piastrelle di Ceramica, Sassuolo 25498
Raccolta dell'Opera del Duomo, Oristano 24693
Raccolta di Cose Montesine, Montese 24548
Raccolta di Fisarmoniche d'Epoca, Camerano 23281
Raccolta di Fossili Francesco Angellotti, Ostra 24719
Raccolta di Ingegneria Navale, Genova 24012
Raccolta di Opere d'Arte, Solarolo 25594
Raccolta di Sant'Urbano, Apiro 22905
Raccolta di Scienze Naturali, Vicenza 25997
Raccolta di Vasi da Farmacia, Roccavaldina 25143
Raccolta E Guatelli, Collecchio 23612
Raccolta Etnografica, Cerreto di Spoleto 23483
Raccolta Etnografica, Roseto Capo Spulico 25281
Raccolta Etnografica, Vallo di Nera 25883
Raccolta Etnografica del Centro Studi Pugliesi, Manfredonia 24281
Raccolta Etnografica della Civiltà Contadina, San Giorgio Piacentino 25369
Raccolta Guatelli, Ozzano Taro 24726
Raccolta Judica, Palazzolo Acreide 24760
Raccolta Kalefati, Oria 24689
Raccolta Lapidaria Capitolina, Roma 25266
Raccolta Memoria e Tradizioni Religiose, Serramanna 25547
Raccolta Naturalistica, Tagliolo Monferrato 25667
Raccolta Ornitologica F. Stazza, Tempio Pausania 25684
Raccolta Osservatorio di Apicoltura Giacomo Angeleri, Pragelato 25033
Raccolta Paleontologica e Preistorica, Narni 24612
Raccolta Parocchiale, Valpelline 25884
Raccolta Permanente sulla Lavorazione della Canapa, Buonconvento 23231
Raccolta Privata Toraldo di Francia, Tropea 25841
Raccolta Russo-Ortodossa, Merano 24355
Raccolta Storica della Vita Materiale dell'Antico, Altopascio 22866
Raccolta Temporanea, Cosenza 23669
Raccolte d'Arte dell'Ospedale Maggiore di Milano, Milano 24418
Raccolte del Dipartimento di Scienze Radiologiche, Roma 25267
Raccolte dell'Istituto di Clinica delle Malattie Tropicali e Subtropicali, Roma 25268

Raccolte dell'Istituto di Clinica Otorinolaringoiatrica, Roma 25269
Raccolte dell'Istituto di Clinica Urologica, Roma 25270
Raccolte di Palazzo Tursi, Genova 24013
Raccolte Frugone Villa Grimaldi-Fassio, Genova 24014
Racemotormuseum Lexmond, Lexmond 29537
Rachana Open Air Museum, Rachana 27493
Rachel Carson Homestead, Springdale 47734
Rachel Kay Shuttleworth Textile Collections, Padiham 40156
Racine Heritage Museum, Racine 46768
Rackstadmuseet, Arvika 35817
Rada Galerii České Republiky, Praha 49134
Ráday Museum of the Danubian District of the Hungarian Reformed Church, Kecskemét 21445
Radbrook Culinary Museum, Shrewsbury 40509
Råde Bygdetun, Råde 30783
Rademacher Forges, Eskilstuna 35871
Rademachersmedjorna, Eskilstuna 35871
Radetski-Ship National Museum, Kozloduj 04722
Radetzky-Gedenkstätte Heldenberg, Kleinwetzdorf 02136
Radford University Art Museum, Radford 46769
Radio Amateur Museum, Reusel 29728
Radio and Television Museum, Šiauliai 27530
Radio and TV Museum, Lahti 09747
Radio- en Speelgoed Museum, Onstwedde 29664
Rádió és Televízió Múzeum, Diósd 21402
Radio- ja TV-Museo, Lahti 09747
Radio Matterhorn Museum, Zermatt 37358
Radio- og Motorcykel Museet, Stubbekøbing 09082
Radio-Television Museum, Bowie 41847
Radiomuseet i Göteborg, Göteborg 35918
Radiomuseet i Jönköping, Jönköping 35978
Radiomuseum, Bad Bentheim 15600
Radiomuseum, Berneck 36556
Radiomuseum, Borculo 29002
Radiomuseum, Grödig 17409
Radiomuseum, Rottenburg an der Laaber 19693
Radiomuseum, Waldbronn 20354
Radishchev Art Museum, Saratov 33504
Radmuseum anno dazumal, Altmünster 01667
Radnorshire Museum, Llandrindod Wells 39539
Radstädter Museumsverein, Radstadt 02476
Rääkkylän Kotiseutumuseo, Rääkkylä 09973
Rælingen Bygdetun, Fjerdingby 30492
Ränkimäen Ulkomuseo, Lapua 09768
Rätisches Museum, Chur 36636
Rättviks Konstmuseum och Naturmuseum, Rättvik 36159
Raevangla Fotomuuseum, Tallinn 09371
Rafail Popov Museum, Madara 04732
Ragailong Museum, Imphal 21857
Ragged School Museum, London 39753
Raglan and District Museum, Raglan 30245
Ragley Hall, Alcester 37961
Raha- ja Mitalikokoelma, Helsinki 09521
Rahr West Art Museum, Manitowoc 45116
Rail Transport Museum, Bassendean 00772
Railco Museum, Ravenshoe 01407
Railroad and Heritage Museum, Temple 47976
Railroad House Historical Museum, Sanford 47396
Railroad Museum of Long Island, Riverhead 46915
Railroad Museum of Pennsylvania, Strasburg 47847
Railroader's Memorial Museum, Altoona 41158
Rail's End Gallery, Haliburton 05544
Railway Age, Crewe 38666
Railway and Forestry Museum, Prince George 06187
Railway and Industry Museum, Hagfors 35938
The Railway Exposition, Covington 42681
Railway Heritage Network, Linden 44803
Railway Museum, Athinai 20879
Railway Museum, Beograd 33821
Railway Museum, Livingstone 49018
Railway Museum, Nynäshamn 36130
Railway Museum, Pieksämäki 09926
Railway Museum, Ravenglass 40287
Railway Preservation Society of Ireland, Whitehead 40858
Railway Station Museum, Castlegar 05215
Railway Station Museum, Uitenhage 34394
Railway Station Museum, Wonthaggi 01613
Railway Village Museum, Swindon 40664
Railways to Yesterday, Rockhill Furnace 46965
Railworld, Peterborough 40189
Raimund-Gedenkstätte, Gutenstein 01978
Raiņa Literatūras un Mākslas Vēstures Muzejs, Rīga 27435
Raiņa Memoriālais Muzejs Jasmuiža, Aizkalne 27327
Raiņa Muzejs Tadenava, Tadaine 27454
Raiņa un Aspazijas Memoriālā Vasarnīca, Jūrmala 27372
Rainbow - Culture Centre and Exhibition Hall, Uljanovsk 33659
Rainermuseum Salzburg, Salzburg 02547
Rainham Hall, Rainham 40278
Rainis and Aspazija Cottage, Majori Jūrmala 27386
Rainis and Aspazija House, Rīga 27436
Rainis and Aspazija Memorial Summer Cottage, Jūrmala 27372
Rainis Memorial Museum Jasmuiža, Aizkalne 27327
Rainis Museum, Preiļi 27398
Rainis Museum of the History of Literature and Art, Rīga 27435
Rainis Museum Tadenava, Jēkabpils 27363
Rainy Hills Historical Society Pioneer Exhibits, Iddesleigh 05611
Rainy River District Women's Institute Museum, Emo 05407
Rais-ali-delvary Museum, Bushehr 22235
Raitioliikennemuseo, Helsinki 09522
Raja Dinkar Kelkar Museum, Pune 21994
Rajalahden Talomuseo, Virrat 10205
Rajalahti House Museum, Virrat 10205
Rajamäen Tehtaiden Museo, Nurmijärvi 09874
Rajamuseo, Imatra 09566
Rajkiya Sangrahalaya, Udaipur 22045
Rajoloteca Salvador Miquel, Vallromanes 35637
Rajputana Museum, Ajmer 21685
Rakennuskulttuuritalo Toivo ja Korsmanin talo, Pori 09945
Rakhine State Museum, Sittwe 28743
Rakhtshuy-Khaneh Museum, Zanjan 22338
Rakiura Museum, Stewart Island 30255
Rakkestad Bygdetun, Rakkestad 30784
Rákóczi Múzeum, Sárospatak 21524
Raku Museum, Kyoto 26446
Rakushikan, Kyoto 26447
Rakvere Linnakodaniku Muuseum, Rakvere 09348
Rakvere Linnus-Muuseum, Rakvere 09349
Rakvere Näitustemaja-Muuseum, Rakvere 09350
Raleigh City Museum, Raleigh 46779
Sri Rallabandi Subbarao Government Museum, Rajahmundry 22001
Rallarmuseet, Moskosel 36104
Ralli Museum, Caesarea 22583
Ralls Historical Museum, Ralls 46781
Ralph Allen Memorial Museum, Oxbow 06091
Ralph Foster Museum, Point Lookout 46573
Ralph Milliken Museum, Los Banos 44953
Ralph Waldo Emerson House, Concord 42602
Ram Mala Museum, Comilla 03081
Raman Science Centre, Nagpur 21964
Ramitscheder-Mühle, Edlbach 01787
Ramkhamhaeng National Museum, Sukhothai 37539
Ramla Museum, Ramla 22738
Ramlingappa Lamture Museum, Osmanabad 21970
Rammerscales, Lockerbie 39562
Ramón Magsaysay Memorabilia Museum, Manila 31396
Ramsauer Getreidemühle, Ramsau am Dachstein 02483
Ramsay House, Alexandria 41133
Ramsay Museum, Honolulu 44088
Ramsey Center for Arts, Shoreview 47610
Ramsey House Museum Plantation, Knoxville 44523
Ramsey Rural Museum, Ramsey, Cambridgeshire 40279
Ramsgate Museum, Ramsgate 40283
Ran-In-Ting Museum, Taipei 07355
Rana Museum, Mo i Rana 30674
Rana Museum, Mo i Rana 30675
Rancho Los Alamitos, Long Beach 44863
Rancho Los Cerritos, Long Beach 44864
Randaberg Bygdemuseum, Randaberg 30786
Randall House Museum, Wolfville 06858
Randall Library Museum, Stow 47841
Randall Museum, San Francisco 47333
Randers Kunstmuseum, Randers 09026
Randolph County Historical Museum, Winchester 48676
Randolph County Museum, Beverly 41674
Randolph Historical Society Museum, Randolph 46791
Rangau-Handwerkermuseum, Markt Erlbach 18643
Rangau-Heimathaus, Cadolzburg 16440
Rangiora Museum, Rangiora 30246
Rangpur Archaeological Museum, Rangpur 03100
Rani Laxmi Bai Palace Sculpture Collection, Jhansi 21873
Rankin House Museum, Miramichi 05862
Rankin House State Memorial, Ripley 46904
Rankin Museum, Ellerbe 43154
Rankin Museum, Rankin 46792
Rannarootsi Muuseum, Haapsalu 09319
Rannikkotykistömuseo, Helsinki 09523
Ransom County Historical Society Museum, Fort Ransom 43446
Rantasalmen Museo, Rantasalmi 09976
Rantsilan Kotiseutumuseo, Rantsila 09977
Ranuan Pappila- ja Pitäjämuseo, Ranua 09978
Rapid City Museum, Rapid City 06217
Raritätensammlung Bruno Gebhardt, Zwönitz 20785
Rariteiten- en Ambachtenmuseum 't Krekelhof, Koksijde 03536
Ras-al-Tin Palace Museum, Ras-al-Tin 09304
Rasht Museum, Rasht 22275
Rasmussen Art Gallery, Angwin 41212
Rassan Arabzadeh Carpet Museum, Teheran 22322
Rassegna Attrezzi e Oggetti del Passato, Belluno 23049
Ráth György Museum, Budapest 21380
Rathaus-Galerie, Berlin 16082
Rathausgalerie, Bad Harzburg 15657
Rathausgalerie, Castrop-Rauxel 16451
Rathausgalerie, Sankt Veit an der Glan 02613
Rathausgalerie, Waidhofen an der Ybbs 02788
Rathausgalerie der Stadt Brühl, Brühl, Rheinland 16378
Rathausgalerie Grimma, Grimma 17402
Rathausgalerie München, München 18900
Rathausgalerie Munster, Munster 18960
Rathausgalerie Vellmar, Vellmar 20299
Rathausmuseum, Sempach Stadt 37161
Rathausmuseum Nieder-Ohmen, Mücke 18798
Rathaussammlung, Stein am Rhein 37216
Rathgen-Forschungslabor, Berlin 49213
Rathgory Transport Museum, Dunleer 22465
Ratnapura National Museum, Ratnapura 35760
Raton Museum, Raton 46799
Ratsuväkimuseo, Lappeenranta 09763
Rattlesnake Museum, Albuquerque 41108
Ratvolden, Røros 30805
Rauchfangkehrermuseum, Wien 02976
Rauchstubenhaus, Gündorf 01967
Rauchstubenhaus, Sankt Johann im Saggautal 02575
Rauhaniemen Kotiseutumuseo, Sulkava 10058
Rauma Art Museum, Rauma 09984
Rauman Museo, Rauma 09983
Rauman Taidemuseo, Rauma 09984
Rauriser Talmuseum, Rauris 02492
Rautalammin Museo, Rautalampi 09988
Rautalampi Museum, Rautalampi 09988
Rautatieläiskotimuseo, Kouvola 09706
Rautenstrauch-Joest-Museum, Köln 18164
Raution Kotiseutumuseo, Rautio 09989
Ravalli County Museum, Hamilton 43877
Raverty's Motor Museum, Echuca 01004
Ravintolamuseo, Lahti 09748
Ravmuseet, Oksbøl 09017
Rawhide Old West Museum, Scottsdale 47513
Rawls Museum Arts, Courtland 42678
Ray E. Powell Museum, Grandview 43764
Raymond Chow Art Gallery, Vancouver 06686
Raymond M. Alf Museum of Paleontology, Claremont 42420
Raymore Pioneer Museum, Raymore 06218
Raynham Hall Museum, Oyster Bay 46249
Razstavni Salon Rotovž, Maribor 34128
R.B. Ferguson Museum of Mineralogy, Winnipeg 06838
RCMP Centennial Celebration Museum, Fairview 05421
R.E. Olds Transportation Museum, Lansing 44645
R.E. Stevenson Museum, Colenso 34217
Rea Museum, Murfreesboro 45566
Reaction and Lesson Palace and National Palace, Teheran 22308
Reader's Digest Art Gallery, Pleasantville 46556
Reading Abbay Gateway, Reading 40297
Reading Historical Society Museum, Reading 46805
Reading Historical Society Museum, Reading 46810
Reading Public Museum and Art Gallery, Reading 46809
Readsboro Historical Society Museum, Readsboro 46812
Real Cartuja, Valldemosa 35633
Real Cartuja de Miraflores, Burgos 34636
Real Casa del Labrador, Aranjuez 34473
Real Fábrica de Tapices, Madrid 35061
Real Monasterio de San Jerónimo, Granada 34881
Real Monasterio de San Juan de la Peña, San Juan de la Peña 35378
Real Monasterio de Santa María de El Puig, El Puig de Santa Maria 35302
Real Museo Mineralogico, Napoli 24607
Real Patronato de Sargadelos, Cervo 34710
Real Pinacoteca, Tres Casas 35575
Real World Computer Museum, Boothwyn 41792
Rebbaumuseum am Bielersee, Ligerz 36881
Rebecca Nurse Homestead, Danvers 42775
Reblandmuseum, Baden-Baden 15789
Rechnermuseum der Gesellschaft für wissenschaftliche Datenverarbeitung, Göttingen 17339
Rechtshistorisches Museum, Karlsruhe 18001
Recinto Casa Benito Juárez, Saltillo 28372
Reckturm, Wiener Neustadt 03020
Record Office for Leicestershire, Leicester and Rutland, Leicester 39469
Red Barn Museum, Morristown 45511
Red Bay Historic Site, Red Bay 06219
Red Brick Arts Centre and Museum, Edson 05398
Red Clay State Historical Park, Cleveland 42486
Red Deer and District Museum, Red Deer 06222
Red Dot Design Museum im Design Zentrum Nordrhein-Westfalen, Essen 16961
Red Hill-Patrick Henry National Memorial, Brookneal 41955
Red House Glass Cone Museum, Stourbridge 40616
Red House Museum, Gomersal 39092
Red House Museum and Art Gallery, Christchurch 38578
Red Lake Museum, Red Lake 06223
Red Lodge, Bristol 38359
Red Mill Museum Village, Clinton 42498
Red Monastery, Červený Kláštor 33986
Red Pepper Museum, Szeged 21552
Red River and Northern Plains Regional Museum, West Fargo 48522
Red River Historical Society Museum, Clay City 42440
Red River Valley Museum, Vernon 48218
Red Rock Museum, Church Rock 42394
Red Sea Maritime Museum, Eilat 22588
Redcliff Museum, Redcliff 06224
Redcliffe Historical Museum, Redcliffe 01409
Redding Museum of Art and History, Redding 46819
Reddingshuisje, Vliehors-Vlieland 29953
Reddingsmuseum Abraham Fock, Hollum 29432
Redhill Museum, Redhill 01411
Redington Museum, Waterville 48448
Redland Museum, Cleveland 00927
Redningsselskapets Museum, Horten 30567
Redoña Residence Museum, Tacloban 31453
Redpath Museum, Montréal 05928
Redpath Sugar Museum, Toronto 06605
Reðsafn Íslands, Reykjavík 21662
Redwater and District Museum, Redwater 06225
Redwood County Museum, Redwood Falls 46827
Redwood Library and Athenaeum, Newport 45932
Reed Gold Mine, Midland 45323
Reed Gold Mine State Historic Site, Stanfield 47771
Reedville Fishermen's Museum, Reedville 46828
Reese Bullen Gallery, Arcata 41247
The Reeves Center, Lexington 44761
Refectory of the Hosios Loukas Monastery, Boeotia 20911
Referat Volkskunde, Graz 01930
Reflex Miniatuur Museum voor Hedendaagse Kunst, Amsterdam 28896
Református Kollégiumi és Egyházművészeti Múzeum, Debrecen 21400
Le Refuge de Grasla, Les Brouzils 12530
Refuge Fortifié Muséalisé, Dossenheim-sur-Zinsel 11556
Refugio County Museum, Refugio 46829
Reghthuys, Giessenburg 29278
Regimental Museum of 1st The Queen's Dragoon Guards, Cardiff 38482
Regimental Museum of the 13th/18th Royal Hussars and Kent Dragoons, Cawthorne 38515
Regimental Museum of the 9th/12th Royal Lancers, Derby 38719
Regimental Museum of the Black Watch, Perth 40186
Regimental Museum of the Oxfordshire and Buckinghamshire Light Infantry, Oxford 40154
Regimental Museum of the Royal Dragoon Guards and the Prince of Wales's Own Regiment of Yorkshire, York 40967
Regimental Museum of the Royal Scots Dragoon Guards, Edinburgh 38908
Regimental Museum of the Sherwood Foresters, Nottingham 40114
Regimental Museum The Highlanders, Inverness 39301
Regina Firefighters Museum, Regina 06239
Regina Plains Museum, Regina 06240
Reginalds Tower, Waterford 22554
Regionaal Museum 1940-1945 Schagen en Omstreken, Schagen 29796
Regionaal Natuurmuseum Westflinge, Sint Pancras 29826
Regional Art Gallery, Burgas 04635
Regional Art Gallery, Kaluga 32882
Regional Art Gallery, Liberec 08450
Regional Art Gallery, Pleven 04768
Regional Art Gallery, Razgrad 04796
Regional Art Gallery, Sliven 04825
Regional Art Gallery, Stara Zagora 04867
Regional Art Gallery, Vidin 04927
Regional Art Gallery, Vraca 04930
Regional Art Gallery Georgi Papazov, Jambol 04682
Regional Art Museum, Uljanovsk 33668
Regional Children's Picture Gallery, Vladivostok 33698
Regional Ethnographic Museum, Smižany 34059
Regional Gallery of Fine Arts in Zlín, Zlín 08750
Regional Gallery of Modern Art, Hradec Králové 08367
Regional Historical Museum, Chaskovo 04641
Regional Historical Museum, Pazardžik 04757
Regional Historical Museum, Pernik 04759
Regional Historical Museum, Ruse 04807
Regional Historical Museum, Sliven 04824
Regional Historical Museum, Smoljan 04826
Regional Historical Museum, Vidin 04926
Regional Historical Museum, Vraca 04929
Regional Historical Museum of Varna, Varna 04907
Regional History Museum, Pleven 04770
Regional History Museum, Targovište 04883
Regional History Museum, Veliko Tărnovo 04920
Regional Museum, Balachna 32669
Regional Museum, Berane 33822
Regional Museum, Biecz 31490
Regional Museum, Biłgoraj 31497
Regional Museum, Borisoglebsk 32698
Regional Museum, Bučovice 08283
Regional Museum, Cedynia 31521
Regional Museum, Čeljabinsk 32725
Regional Museum, Chomutov 08314
Regional Museum, Chrudim 08321
Regional Museum, Djakovica 33836
Regional Museum, Dobczyce 31553
Regional Museum, Elec 32792
Regional Museum, Enisejsk 32796
Regional Museum, Glazov 32805
Regional Museum, Głogówek 31596
Regional Museum, Hajdúböszörmény 21425
Regional Museum, Herceg-Novi 33841
Regional Museum, Irkutsk 32814
Regional Museum, Iskitim 32822
Regional Museum, Ivanovo 32828
Regional Museum, Jurjevec 32865
Regional Museum, Kaliningrad 32871
Regional Museum, Kościan 31674
Regional Museum, Kozienice 31680
Regional Museum, Kraśnik 31731
Regional Museum, Krasnokamsk 32959
Regional Museum, Krasnystaw 31733
Regional Museum, Kutno 31745
Regional Museum, Lubań 31784
Regional Museum, Łuków 31798
Regional Museum, Magadan 32999
Regional Museum, Maribor 34127
Regional Museum, Miechów 31801

Regional Museum, Mielec 31806
Regional Museum, Murska Sobota 34134
Regional Museum, Narovčat 33201
Regional Museum, Novokuzneck 33237
Regional Museum, Orël 33267
Regional Museum, Penza 33294
Regional Museum, Perm 33308
Regional Museum, Ptuj 34141
Regional Museum, Puškin 33337
Regional Museum, Puškino 33341
Regional Museum, Sergač 33518
Regional Museum, Škrip 07777
Regional Museum, Sokolov 08660
Regional Museum, Środa Śląska 31993
Regional Museum, Staraja Russa 33555
Regional Museum, Stary Sącz 31999
Regional Museum, Staryj Oskol 33559
Regional Museum, Szczecinek 32030
Regional Museum, Tambov 33591
Regional Museum, Tarnów 32043
Regional Museum, Tomsk 33617
Regional Museum, Valdaj 33673
Regional Museum, Velikie Luki 33676
Regional Museum, Vetluga 33685
Regional Museum, Volgograd 33719
Regional Museum, Voronež 33736
Regional Museum, Vyborg 33742
Regional Museum, Wągrowiec 32070
Regional Museum, Wronki 32194
Regional Museum, Xinhui 07310
Regional Museum, Zaječar 33930
Regional Museum, Żytomyr 37914
Regional Museum and Gallery, Česká Lípa 08294
Regional Museum Center, Sankt-Peterburg 33473
Regional Museum Fergana, Fergana 48836
Regional Museum in Teplice, Teplice 08677
Regional Museum Iron Gates, Drobeta-Turnu Severin 32516
Regional Museum Jagodina, Jagodina 33842
Regional Museum Kristianstad, Kristianstad 36018
Regional Museum Niš, Niš 33865
Regional Museum of Andrzeja Kaube, Wolin 32169
Regional Museum of Boskovice, Boskovice 08253
Regional Museum of Dr. Bohuslav Horák, Rokycany 08636
Regional Museum of Eternal Frost - Permafrostmuseum, Igarka 32811
Regional Museum of Hadsund, Hadsund 08853
Regional Museum of History, Kardžali 04688
Regional Museum of History, Kjustendil 04710
Regional Museum of History, Loveč 04728
Regional Museum of History, Montana 04741
Regional Museum of History, Plovdiv 04780
Regional Museum of History, Stara Zagora 04868
Regional Museum of Kamtchatka Region, Petropavlovsk-Kamčatskij 33310
Regional Museum of Lgov, Lgov 32981
Regional Museum of Lomonosov, Lomonosov 32990
Regional Museum of Miass, Miass 33010
Regional Museum of Mineralnye Vody, Mineral'nye Vody 33012
Regional Museum of Natural History, Bhopal 21723
Regional Museum of Pinczov, Pińczów 31882
Regional Museum of South-Eastern Moravia, Napajedla 08493
Regional Museum of Spartanburg County, Spartanburg 47716
Regional Museum of Świebodzin, Świebodzin 32015
Regional Museum of Tarnowskie Góry, Tarnowskie Góry 32045
Regional Museum of the Bulgarian National Revival period and Liberation Movement, Plovdiv 04781
Regional Museum of the Jewish Autonomous Region, Birobidžan 32689
Regional Museum of the Kemerovo region, Kemerovo 32912
Regional Museum of the Khabarovsk Region, Chabarovsk 32737
Regional Museum of the North Ladoga Lake Region, Sortavala 33547
Regional Museum of the Republic Khakassiya, Abakan 32627
Regional Museum of the Republic Mordoviya, Saransk 33497
Regional Museum of the Tchukotsky Autonomous Region, Anadyr' 32638
Regional Museum of the Zbąszyń Region, Zbąszyń 32215
Regional Museum Specialized in Gold, Jílové u Prahy 08393
Regional MuseumCelje, Celje 34090
Regional Muzeum of the Požeška Valley, Požega 07756
Regional Parish Museum, Krasnobród 31732
Regional Picture Gallery, Vladivostok 33708
Regional Room of the PTTK, Sulejów 32005
Regional Science and Discovery Center, Horseheads 44106
Regional Science Centre, Bhopal 21724
Regional Science Centre, Guwahati, Assam 21827
Regional Science Centre, Lucknow 21930
Regional Science Centre, Tirupati 22039
Regional Science Centre and Planetarium, Kozhikode 21916
Regional Science Centre Bhubaneswar, Bhubaneshwar 21727
Regional- und Telegrafenmuseum, Stegersbach 02676
Regionale Heemmusea Bachten de Kupe, Izenberge 03525
Regionalen Istoričeski Muzej, Kardžali 04688
Regionalen Istoričeski Muzej, Kjustendil 04710
Regionalen Istoričeski Muzej, Pazardžik 04757
Regionalen Istoričeski Muzej, Pleven 04770
Regionalen Istoričeski Muzej, Ruse 04807
Regionalen Istoričeski Muzej, Stara Zagora 04868
Regionalen Istoričeski Muzej, Šumen 04876
Regionalen Istoričeski Muzej Varna, Varna 04907
Regionales Eisenbahnmuseum der Museumseisenbahn Hamm im Maximilianpark, Hamm, Westfalen 17578
Regionales Heimatmuseum für das Renchtal, Oppenau 19260
Regionalgeschichtliches Museum, Lutherstadt Eisleben 18573
RegionalHistorical Museum, Šumen 04876
Regionali Muzej, Djakovica 33836
Regionalmuseum, Sremska Mitrovica 33914
Regionalmuseum, Stockstadt am Rhein 20064
Regionalmuseum Alsfeld, Alsfeld 15437
Regionalmuseum Alte Schule, Kaufungen, Hessen 18045
Regionalmuseum Binn, Binn 36567
Regionalmuseum der Stadt Lobenstein, Lobenstein 18487
Regionalmuseum Fritzlar, Fritzlar 17154
Regionalmuseum Neubrandenburg, Neubrandenburg 19013
Regionalmuseum Reichelsheim Odenwald, Reichelsheim, Odenwald 19540
Regionalmuseum Schwarzwasser, Schwarzenburg 37148
Regionalmuseum Wolfhagen, Wolfhagen 20655
Regionalmuseum Xanten, Xanten 20729
Regionalna Izba Muzealna, Poddębice 31888
Regionalne Muzeum Młodej Polski - Rydlówka, Kraków 31727
Regionalne Muzeum Prasy i Drukarstwa Śląskiego, Pszczyna 31928
Regionalni Muzej, Bihać 03912
Regionální Muzeum, Mikulov na Moravě 08476
Regionální Muzeum, Náchod 08492
Regionální Muzeum, Žďár nad Sázavou 08744
Regionální Muzeum K.A. Polánka, Žatec 08738
Regionální Muzeum v Chrudimi, Chrudim 08321
Regionální Muzeum v Jílovém u Prahy, Jílové u Prahy 08393
Regionální Muzeum v Kolíně, Kolín 08417
Regionální Muzeum v Teplicích, Teplice 08677
Regionální Muzeum ve Vysokém Mýtě, Vysoké Mýto 08733
Regionalnyj Muzej Severnogo Priladožja, Sortavala 33547
Regionmuseet Kristianstad, Kristianstad 36018
Regionmuseum Västra Götaland, Vänersborg 36373
Het Regthuijs, Abbekerk 28799
Regthuis Oudkarspel, Oudkarspel 29703
Regthuis t'Schou, Schipluiden 29810
Rehoboth Art League, Rehoboth Beach 46831
Rehoboth Museum, Rehoboth 28769
Reial Academia Catalana Belles Arts Sant Jordi, Barcelona 34590
Reiat-Museum, Thayngen 37238
Reichenberger Heimatstube und Archiv, Augsburg 15565
Reichsdorf-Museum Gochsheim, Gochsheim 17310
Reichskammergerichtsmuseum, Wetzlar 20558
Reichspräsident-Friedrich-Ebert-Gedenkstätte, Heidelberg 17672
Reichsstadtmuseum, Rothenburg ob der Tauber 19681
Reichsstadtmuseum im Ochsenhof, Bad Windsheim 15777
Reichsstadtmuseum Weißenburg, Weißenburg in Bayern 20492
Reichsstädtisches Archiv, Rathaushalle und Ratsstube, Mühlhausen, Thüringen 18809
Reichsstädtisches Museum, Bad Wimpfen 15773
Reichstagsmuseum, Regensburg 19529
Reigate Priory Museum, Reigate 40308
Reinberger Galleries, Cleveland 42478
Reinessanceschloss Rosenburg, Rosenburg am Kamp 02526
Reipin Museo, Pirkkala 09933
Reisjärven Kotiseutumuseo, Reisjärvi 09990
Reiss-Engelhorn-Museen, Mannheim 18615
Reitz Home Museum, Evansville 43246
Reitzin Säätiön Kokoelmat, Helsinki 09524
Relais de la Muse du Van les Bayles, Saint-Symphorien-sous-Chomerac 14484
Religieus Museum Kijk-je Kerk-Kunst, Gennep 29276
Religionskundliche Sammlung der Philipps-Universität, Marburg 18632
REME Museum of Technology, Arborfield 38009
Remick Country Doctor Museum and Farm, Tamworth 47948
Remington Carriage Museum, Cardston 05206
Remington Firearms Museum and Country Store, Ilion 44195
Renaissance des Automates Éma, Lyon 12754
Renaissance-Lapidarium, Pécs 21514
Renaissance Schloss Greillenstein, Röhrenbach 02518
The Renaissance Society at the University of Chicago, Chicago 42360
Renaissance- und Barock-Schloß Weilburg, Weilburg 20446
Reneszánsz Kőtár, Pécs 21514
Renfrew Museum, Waynesboro 48482
Rengebu-ji Temple, Ogi 26618
Renishaw Hall Museum and Art Gallery, Renishaw 40309
Renmin Kang Ri Zhan Zhen Memorial Hall, Beijing 06987
Rennebu Bygdemuseum, Rennebu 30789
Rennesøy Bygdemuseum, Rennesøy 30790
Reno County Museum, Hutchinson 44184
Rensselaer County Historical Society Museum, Troy 48071
Rensselaer Russell House Museum, Waterloo 48432
Renton Museum, Renton 46841
Renville County Historical Society Museum, Mohall 45429
Renwick Gallery of the Smithsonian American Art Museum, Washington 48390
Renwick Museum, Renwick 30247
Replikate der Welt-Kunst im Schloss, Miltach 18738
Replot Hembygdsmuseum, Replot 09992
Reppuniemen Ulkomuseo, Pöytyä 09937
Repslagarmuseet, Älvängen 35783
Republic County Historical Society Museum, Belleville 41591
Republican Museum of Nature, Taškent 48859
Rescue House, Vliehors-Vlieland 29953
Resenhof, Bernau, Baden 16122
Réserve Géologique de Haute-Provence, Digne-les-Bains 11515
Reserve Officer School Museum, Hamina 09460
Réserves Nationales des Arts et Traditions Populaires Picardie, Saint-Riquier 14458
Reserviupseerikoulun Museo, Hamina 09460
Reshaw Exhibit, Evansville 43247
Residency Museum, York 01633
Residenz Ansbach, Ansbach 15504
Residenz Ellingen, Ellingen, Bayern 16831
Residenz und Hofgarten Würzburg, Würzburg 20701
Residenzgalerie Salzburg, Salzburg 02548
Residenzmuseum, München 18901
Residenzschloß Oettingen, Oettingen 19237
Resim ve Heykel Müzesi, İstanbul 37705
Resistance Museum, Akko 22568
Resistance Museum, Nueva Gerona 08057
Resistance Museum, Santiago de Cuba 08139
Resistance Museum Friesland, Leeuwarden 29516
Respublikanskij Istoriko-Kraevedčeskij i Chudožestvennyj Muzej, Dušanbe 37446
Respublikanskij Istoriko-Kraevedčeskij Muzej im. Rudaki Abuabdullo, Pendžikent 37450
Respublikanskij Literaturnyij Memorialnyj Muzej Abaja, Semey 27092
Respublikanskij Prirodovedčeskij Muzej, Taškent 48859
Respublikanskij Vystavočnyj Zal, Joškar-Ola 32862
Restaurant Museum, Lahti 09748
Restigouche Gallery, Campbellton 05190
Restigouche Regional Museum, Dalhousie 05301
Reston and District Historical Museum, Reston 06252
Restoration House, Mantorville 45129
Rétközi Múzeum, Kisvárda 21462
Returned Services League War Museum, Stawell 01475
Retzer Erlebniskeller, Retz 02508
Reubacher Heimatmuseum, Rot 19669
Reuben and Edith Hecht Museum, Haifa 22611
Reuben H. Fleet Science Center, San Diego 47285
Reuel B. Pritchett Museum, Bridgewater 41895
Réunion des Musées Nationaux, Paris 49192
Reuterhaus mit Richard-Wagner-Sammlung, Eisenach 16817
Rev. Krzysztof Kluk Museum of Agriculture, Ciechanowiec 31538
Revelstoke Court House, Revelstoke 06253
Revelstoke Museum, Revelstoke 06254
Revelstoke Railway Museum, Revelstoke 06255
Reventlow-Museet Pederstrup, Horslunde 08901
Revillon Frères Museum, Moosonee 05938
Revolution House, Chesterfield 38557
Revolutionary History Museum, Guangzhou 07072
Revolutionary Museum, Altanbulag 28673
Revolutionary Museum Ho Chi Minh City, Ho Chi Minh City 48989
Revolutionary Museum of the Jinggang Mountains, Jinggang Mountains 07139
Revolving Museum, Boston 41825
Rewa's Village, Kerikeri 30194
Reykjanes Museum, Reykjanesbaer 21646
Reykjavik Art Museum - Harbour House, Reykjavík 21650
Reykjavik Art Museum - Kjarvalsstaðir, Reykjavík 21651
Reykjavík Electricity Museum, Reykjavík 21664
Reykjavík Museum of Photography, Reykjavík 21656
Reynold Rapp Museum, Spalding 06479
Reynolda House, Winston-Salem 48703
Reynolds Homestead, Critz 42703
Reynolds Museum, Wetaskiwin 06779
Reza Abbasi Museum, Teheran 22323
Reza Shah Museum, Johannesburg 34282
Rezerwat Archeologiczny-Gród Piastowski w Gieczu, Oddział Muzeum Pierwszych Piastów na Lednicy, Dominowo 31557
Rezerwat Archeologiczny i Muzeum w Krzemionkach k. Ostrowca, Krzemionki koło Ostrowca 31742
Rezerwat Archeologiczny na Zawodziu, Kalisz 31636
Rezydencja Księży Młyn, Łódź 31779
Rhayader and District Museum, Rhayader 40311
Rhein-Museum Koblenz, Koblenz 18123
Rheingauer Weinmuseum Brömserburg, Rüdesheim am Rhein 19707
Rheinisches Bildarchiv, Köln 18165
Rheinisches Eisenkunstguss Museum, Bendorf, Rhein 15875
Rheinisches Freilichtmuseum und Landesmuseum für Volkskunde Kommern, Mechernich 18669
Rheinisches Industriemuseum, Engelskirchen 16873
Rheinisches Industriemuseum, Oberhausen, Rheinland 19178
Rheinisches Industriemuseum, Ratingen 19496
Rheinisches Industriemuseum, Solingen 19986
Rheinisches Industriemuseum Bergisch Gladbach, Bergisch Gladbach 15899
Rheinisches Industriemuseum Euskirchen, Euskirchen 16977
Rheinisches Landes Museum Bonn, Bonn 16246
Rheinisches Landesmuseum Trier, Trier 20212
Rheinland-Pfälzisches Freilichtmuseum Bad Sobernheim, Bad Sobernheim 15742
Rheinmuseum, Emmerich 16861
Rhinebeck Aerodrome Museum, Rhinebeck 46848
Rhinelander Logging Museum, Rhinelander 46849
Rhinopolis, Gannat 11837
Rhode Island Black Heritage Society Museum, Providence 46725
Rhode Island Historical Society Exhibition, Providence 46726
Rhode Island Museum Network, Pawtucket 49529
Rhodes Cottage Museum, Muizenberg 34313
Rhodes Memorial Museum and Commonwealth Centre, Bishop's Stortford 38240
Rhodes Museum of Classical Antiquities, Grahamstown 34253
Rhön-Museum, Fladungen 17010
Rhöner Naturmuseum, Tann, Rhön 20142
Rhondda Heritage Park, Trehafod 40725
Rhondda Museum, Llwynypia 39560
Rhuddlan Castle, Rhuddlan 40312
Rhyl Library, Museum and Arts Centre, Rhyl 40313
Rialto Museum, Rialto 46850
Ribarsko-Biološka Zbirka, Novi Dojran 33866
Ribchester Roman Museum, Ribchester 40314
Ribe Kunstmuseum, Ribe 09029
Ribe Raadhussamling, Ribe 09030
Ribniški Muzej, Ribnica na Dolenjskem 34146
Rice County Museum of History, Faribault 43294
The Rice Museum, Crowley 42714
The Rice Museum, Georgetown 43655
Rice University Art Gallery, Houston 44133
Ricewolrd Museum, Los Baños 31346
Richard Billinger-Gedenkraum, Sankt Marienkirchen bei Schärding 02584
Richard-Brandt-Heimatmuseum Bissendorf, Wedemark 20416
Richard F. Brush Art Gallery and Permanent Collection, Canton 42086
Richard Gallery and Almond Tea Gallery, Cuyahoga Falls 42736
Richard H. Schmidt Museum of Natural History, Emporia 43185
Richard-Haizmann-Museum, Niebüll 19094
Richard Jefferies Museum, Swindon 40665
Richard L. Nelson Gallery and the Fine Arts Collection, Davis 42794
Richard Salter Storrs House, Longmeadow 44876
Richard-Simoncic-Museum, Rabensburg 02471
Richard Sparrow House, Plymouth 46564
Richard Teschner-Gedenkraum, Wien 02977
Richard-Wagner-Museum, Bayreuth 15858
Richard Wagner-Museum, Luzern 36916
Richard-Wagner-Museum Graupa, Pirna 19406
Richards-Dar House, Mobile 45424
Richardson-Bates House Museum, Oswego 46216
Richborough Castle - Roman Fort, Sandwich 40447
Richey Historical Museum, Richey 46851
Richey Historical Society, Richey 46852
Richibucto River Museum, Richibucto 06258
Richland County Historical Museum, Wahpeton 48274
Richland County Museum, Lexington 44755
Richmond Art Center, Richmond 46859
Richmond Art Gallery, Richmond 06263
Richmond Art Museum, Richmond 46862
Richmond County Historical Society Museum, Melbourne 05832
Richmond Gaol Museum, Richmond, Tasmania 01414
Richmond Main Mining Museum, Pelaw Main 01359
Richmond Museum, Richmond 06264
Richmond Museum, Richmond 34367
Richmond Museum of History, Richmond 46860
Richmond National Battlefield Park, Richmond 46885
Richmond River Historical Museum, Lismore 01179
Richmond Vale Railway Museum, Pelaw Main 01360
Richmondshire Museum, Richmond, North Yorkshire 40317
Ric's Art Boat, Bruxelles 03342
Riddarholmen Church, Stockholm 36275
Riddarholmskyrkan, Stockholm 36275
Riddarhuset, Stockholm 36276
Ridderhof Martin Gallery, Fredericksburg 43540
Ridderhofstad Gunterstein, Breukelen 29027
Riddoch Art Gallery, Mount Gambier 01281
Rideau District Museum, Westport 06776
Rider University Art Gallery, Lawrenceville 44692
Ridge House Museum, Ridgetown 06267
Ridgeway Battlefield Museum, Ridgeway 06269
Riding School Exhibition Hall, Praha 08582

Rieck-Haus / Vierländer Freilichtmuseum, Hamburg 17564
Riedenburger Bauernhofmuseum, Riedenburg 19599
Riedmuseum, Rastatt 19488
Riel House, Winnipeg 06839
Riemland Museum, Heilbron 34261
Rien Poortvlietmuseum, Middelharnis 29596
Riesengebirgsmuseum, Marktoberdorf 18651
Riesengebirgsstube, Würzburg 20702
Riesenrundgemälde Schlacht am Bergisel, Innsbruck 02077
Rieser Bauernmuseum, Maihingen 18592
Rieskrater-Museum, Nördlingen 19108
Rietgaverstede, Nevele 03656
De Rietgors, Papendrecht 29711
Rietveld Schröderhuis, Utrecht 29910
't Rieuw, Nuis 29649
Rievaulx Abbay, Rievaulx 40324
Rıfat Ilgaz Culture Center, Kastamonu 37730
Rıfat Ilgaz Kültür Merkezi, Kastamonu 37730
Rifle Creek Museum, Rifle 46900
Riga Dome Church, Rīga 27437
Riga Film Museum, Rīga 27438
Rīga Motor Museum, Rīga 27439
Riga Technical University Museum, Rīga 27440
Rīgas Doma Baznīca, Rīga 27437
Rīgas Kino Muzejs, Rīga 27438
Rīgas Motormuzejs, Rīga 27439
Rīgas Tehniskās Universitātes Muzejs, Rīga 27440
Rīgas Ūdensapgādes Muzejs, Ādaži 27325
Rīgas Vēstures un Kugniecības muzejs, Rīga 27441
Riihimäen Kaupunginmuseo, Riihimäki 09993
Riihimäen Taidemuseo, Riihimäki 09994
Riihimäki Art Museum, Riihimäki 09994
Riihimäki City Museum, Riihimäki 09993
Riihimuseo, Peräseinäjoki 09918
Riihipiha Museo, Vuolijoki 10211
Rijdend Electrisch Tram Museum, Amsterdam 28897
Rijksarchief, Brugge 03265
Rijksmuseum, Amsterdam 28898
Rijksmuseum Hendrik Willem Mesdag, Den Haag 29122
Rijksmuseum Twenthe, Enschede 29240
Rijksmuseum van Oudheden, Leiden 29524
Rijksmuseum voor Volkenkunde, Leiden 29525
Rijksprentenkabinet, Amsterdam 28899
Rijssens Museum, Rijssen 29734
Rijtuigenmuseum, Bree 03245
Rijwiel- en Bromfietsmuseum, Zoutkamp 30067
Rikosmuseo, Vantaa 10181
Riksantikvaren, Oslo 30761
Riksutstallningar, Stockholm 36277
Rila Monastery National Museum, Rilski Manastir 04800
Riley County Historical Museum, Manhattan 45110
Riley House Museum of African American History and Culture, Tallahassee 47937
Rimrocker Historical Museum of West Montrose County, Naturita 45637
Rimska Grobnitsa Silistra, Silistra 04816
Rimsky-Korsakov Memorial House, Tichvin 33599
Rimsky-Korsakov Memorial Museum-Reserve Loubensk-Vechasha, Pljussa 33326
Rimu Street Gallery, Wellington 30308
Rincón de Historia, Salto 00546
Rindal Bygdemuseum, Rindal 30791
Ringe Museum, Ringe 09031
Ringelnatz-Museum, Wurzen 20721
Ringerikes Museum, Hønefoss 30561
Ringkøbing Museum, Ringkøbing 09032
Ringsaker Vekter- og Brannhistoriske Museum, Moelv 30678
Ringsted Museum, Ringsted 09033
Ringve Museum, Trondheim 30941
Ringwood Miners Cottage, Ringwood 01416
Rinno-ji Jokodo Treasure House, Nikko 26604
Rio Grande Valley Museum, Harlingen 43914
Rio Hondo College Art Gallery, Whittier 48597
Riordan Mansion, Flagstaff 43331
Ripley Castle, Ripley, North Yorkshire 40326
Ripley County Historical Society Museum, Versailles 48224
Ripley's Believe it or not!, Key West 44471
Ripley's Believe It or Not Museum, Niagara Falls 05998
Ripon College Art Gallery, Ripon 46906
Ripon Historical Society Museum, Ripon 46907
Ripon Prison and Police Museum, Ripon 40328
Ripon Workhouse Museum, Ripon 40329
Rippl-Rónai Emlékház, Kaposvár 21441
Rippon Lea Estate, Melbourne 01240
Rippon Lea House Museum, Elsternwick 01014
Riserva Naturale Speciale del Sacro Monte di Varallo, Varallo Sesia 25893
Rishon Le-Zion Museum, Rishon Le-Zion 22741
Rising Sun Tavern, Fredericksburg 43541
Risør Museum, Risør 30792
Rissa Bygdemuseum, Rissa 30794
Risten-Lakviks Järnväg, Åtvidaberg 35825
Rittergut Haus Laer, Bochum 16199
Ritterhaus Bubikon, Bubikon 36594
Rittersaalmuseum, Kirchbichl 02112
Rittman Historical Society Museum, Rittman 46908
Riuttalan Talonpoikaismuseo, Karttula 09631
River and Rowing Museum, Henley-on-Thames 39220
River Arts Center, Clinton 42491
River Brink, Queenston 06215
River Hills Park Museum, Chesterfield 42289
River Legacy Living Science Center, Arlington 41262
River Museum, Wellsville 48502
River Museum of the Southern Sea, Salango 09225
River Valley School Museum, Virden 06735
River View Ethnographic Museum, Bear River 05064
Riverdale Mansion, Riverdale Park 46913
Riverside Art Museum, Riverside 46921
Riverside Municipal Museum, Riverside 46922
Riverside Museum, La Crosse 44538
Riverside Museum at Blake's Lock, Reading 40298
Riverton Museum, Riverton 46925
Riverview at Hobson Grove, Bowling Green 41851
Rivnenski Museum of Regional Studies, Rivne 37899
Rizal Technological and Polytechnic Institute Museum, Morong 31402
Rize Devlet Güzel Sanatlar Galerisi, Rize 37773
Rize State Gallery, Rize 37773
Riznica Franjevačkog Samostana Split, Split 07786
Riznica Katedrala, Dubrovnik 07701
Riznica Katedrala, Split 07787
Riznica Katedrala, Trogir 07795
Riznica Manastira Studenica, Raška 33900
Riznica Samostana Svetog Frane, Zadar 07808
Riznica Srpske Pravoslavne Crkve u Kotoru, Kotor 33849
Riznica Zagrebačke Katedrala, Zagreb 07836
Riznica Župne Crkve, Nin 07744
Rjazanskij Gosudarstvennyj Istoriko-architekturnyj Muzej-zapovednik, Rjazan 33351
Rjazanskij Oblastnoj Chudožestvennyj Muzej im. I.P. Požalostina, Rjazan 33352
RLB-Kunstbrücke, Innsbruck 02078
R.L.S. Silverado Museum, Saint Helena 47092
R.M. Bohart Museum of Entomology, Davis 42795
RMIT Gallery, Melbourne 01241
R.N. Atkinson Museum, Penticton 06110
Road Museum, Helsinki 09542
Road Museum, Tarnów 32044
Roald Amundsens Hjem Uranienborg, Svartskog 30909
Roald Amundsens Minne, Borge Sarpsborg 30443
Roan Bygdetun, Roan 30797
Roanoke Island Festival Park, Manteo 45127
Roaring Twenties Antique Car Museum, Hood 44094
Rob Roy and Trossachs Victor Centre, Callander 38439
Robben Island Museum, Robben Island 34369
Robbins Hunter Museum, Granville 43774
Robbins Museum of Archaeology, Middleborough 45305
Roberson Museum and Science Center, Binghamton 41700
Robert A. Bogan Fire Museum, Baton Rouge 41533
Robert A. Peck Gallery, Riverton 46926
Robert A. Vines Environmental Science Center, Houston 44134
Robert and Mary Montgomery Armory Art Center, West Palm Beach 48539
Robert Brady Museum, Cuernavaca 27878
Robert Burns Centre, Dumfries 38791
Robert Burns House, Dumfries 38792
Robert C. Williams American Museum of Papermaking, Atlanta 41356
Robert E. Lee Memorial Association, Stratford 47851
Robert Edward Hart Memorial Museum, Souillac 27741
Robert Fulton Birthplace, Quarryville 46754
Robert Gordon University Museum, Aberdeen 37943
Robert Hamerling - Museum, Kirchberg am Walde 02110
Robert Hull Fleming Museum, Burlington 42009
Robert Hytha-Museum, Oberwölbling 02379
Robert-Koch-Museum, Berlin 16083
Robert Langen Gallery, Waterloo 06756
Robert Louis Stevenson Memorial Cottage, Saranac Lake 47450
Robert Louis Stevenson Museum, Vailima 33758
Robert McLaughlin Gallery, Oshawa 06061
Robert Mills Historic House and Park, Columbia 42565
Robert Musil-Literatur-Museum, Klagenfurt 02132
Robert Newell House, Saint Paul 47168
Robert Owen Memorial Museum, Newtown, Powys 40071
Robert R. McCormick Museum at Cantigny, Wheaton 48584
Robert S. Kerr Museum, Poteau 46668
Robert S. Peabody Museum of Archaeology, Andover 41209
Robert-Schumann-Haus Zwickau, Zwickau 20778
Robert Sheane's Agricultural Museum, Glenealy 22478
Robert-Sterl-Haus, Struppen 20080
Robert Stolz Museum Graz, Graz 01931
Robert Tait McKenzie Memorial Museum and Mill of Kintail, Almonte 04981
Robert Toombs House, Washington 48411
Robert V. Fullerton Art Museum, San Bernardino 47268
Robert W. Ryerss Museum, Philadelphia 46449
Robertinum, Halle, Saale 17519
Roberts County Museum, Miami 45296
Robertson Museum and Aquarium, Millport 39957
Robin Hood's Bay and Fylingdale Museum, Robin Hood's Bay 40331
Robinson Visitors Center, Hartsville 43950
Robson Gallery, Selkirk 40470
Rocanville and District Museum, Rocanville 06280
Rocca Borromeo, Angera 22890
Rocca Sanvitale, Fontanellato 23905
Roccolta d'Arte Sacra, San Piero a Sieve 25406
Rochdale Art and Heritage Centre, Rochdale 40332
Rochdale Pioneers Museum, Rochdale 40333
Rocher Saint-Léon, Dabo 11480
Rochester Art Center, Rochester 46936
Rochester Hills Museum at Van Hoosen Farm, Rochester Hills 46949
Rochester Historical and Pioneer Museum, Rochester 01419
Rochester Historical Society Museum, Rochester 46943
Rochester Museum, Rochester 46944
The Rock and Roll Hall of Fame and Museum, Cleveland 42479
Rock Art Centre, Tanumshede 36322
Rock County Historical Society Museum, Janesville 44319
Rock Creek Station State Historic Park, Fairbury 43259
Rock House Museum, Wytheville 48770
Rock Island Arsenal Museum, Rock Island 46956
Rock Island County Historical Museum, Moline 45431
Rock 'n Roll Museum Arum, Arum 28945
Rock Springs Historical Museum, Rock Springs 46958
Rockbourne Roman Villa, Fordingbridge 39002
Rockbridge Historical Society Museum, Lexington 44762
Rockcavern, Beechworth 00786
Rockefeller Archeological Museum, Jerusalem 22657
Rockefeller Museum, Jerusalem 22658
Rockford Art Museum, Rockford 46962
Rockford College Art Gallery/Clark Arts Center, Rockford 46963
Rockhampton and District Historical Museum, Rockhampton 01420
Rockhampton Art Gallery, Rockhampton 01421
Rockhill Trolley Museum, Rockhill Furnace 46966
Rockingham, Princeton 46705
Rockingham Castle, Market Harborough 39916
Rockingham Free Museum, Bellows Falls 41606
Rockland County Museum, New City 45687
Rockoxhuis, Antwerpen 03171
Rockport Art Association Museum, Rockport 46969
Rockwell Museum of Western Art, Corning 42638
Rockwood Museum, Wilmington 48655
Rocky Ford Historical Museum, Rocky Ford 46979
Rocky Lane School Museum, Fort Vermilion 05454
Rocky Mount Arts Center, Rocky Mount 46981
Rocky Mount Children's Museum, Rocky Mount 46982
Rocky Mount Museum, Piney Flats 46495
Rocky Mountain College of Art and Design Galleries, Denver 42897
Rocky Mountain Conservation Center, Denver 42898
Rocky Mountain National Park Museum, Estes Park 43217
Rocky Mountain Quilt Museum, Golden 43715
Rocky Mountain Rangers Museum, Kamloops 05640
Rocky Reach Dam, Wenatchee 48506
Rød Bygdetunet, Uskedalen 30961
Rodgers Tavern, Perryville 46359
Rodin Museum, Philadelphia 46450
Rodman Hall Arts Centre, Saint Catharines 06310
Rodný Domek Adalberta Stiftera, Horní Planá 08361
Rodný Domek Aloise Jiráska, Hronov 08372
Rodný Domek Otokara Březiny, Počátky 08549
Roebourne Old Goal Museum, Roebourne 01423
Roedde House Museum, Vancouver 06687
Röhsska Museet, Göteborg 35919
Röhsska Museum of Design and Applied Art, Göteborg 35919
Römer und Bajuwaren Museum Burg Kipfenberg, Kipfenberg 18085
Roemer- und Pelizaeus-Museum, Hildesheim 17760
Römerbad, Schwangau 19876
Römerbadmuseum, Hüfingen 17852
Römerhalle, Bad Kreuznach 15681
Römerhaus Walheim, Walheim 20375
Römerkastell Saalburg, Bad Homburg v.d.Höhe 15666
Römermuseum, Mainhardt 18596
Römermuseum, Mautern, Niederösterreich 02285
Römermuseum, Obernburg 19183
Römermuseum, Osterburken 19291
Römermuseum Augst, Augst 36479
Römermuseum Bedaium, Seebruck 19914
Römermuseum in der Grundschule Rißtissen, Ehingen, Donau 16793
Römermuseum Kastell Boiotro, Passau 19360
Römermuseum Multerer, Grabenstätt 17365
Römermuseum Stettfeld, Ubstadt-Weiher 20242
Römermuseum Teurnia, Lendorf 02205
Römermuseum Wallsee-Sindelburg, Wallsee 02792
Römermuseum Weißenburg, Weißenburg in Bayern 20493
Römerzeitliches Museum, Ratschendorf 02488
Römisch-Germanisches Museum, Köln 18166
Römisch-Germanisches Zentralmuseum, Mainz 18606
Römische Baureste Am Hof, Wien 02978
Römische Ruinen unter dem Hohen Markt, Wien 02979
Römische Thermenanlage, Weißenburg in Bayern 20494
Römische Villa Rustica Möckenlohe, Adelschlag 15393
Römischer Weinkeller Oberriexingen, Oberriexingen 19196
Römisches Freilichtmuseum, Hechingen 17657
Römisches Haus - Goethe-Nationalmuseum, Weimar, Thüringen 20469
Römisches Museum, Augsburg 15566
Römisches Museum für Kur- und Badewesen, Neustadt an der Donau 19072
Römisches Museum Remagen, Remagen 19561
Römisches Museum und Naturkunde-Museum, Kempten 18065
Römisches Parkmuseum, Aalen 15385
Röntgen-Gedächtnisstätte, Würzburg 20703
Rörbäcksnäs Hembygdsgård, Lima 36037
Roerstreekmuseum, Sint Odiliënberg 29822
Rogaland Bilmuseum, Vigrestad 30991
Rogaland Fiskerimuseum, Åkrehamn 30370
Rogaland Krigshistorisk Museum, Sola 30862
Rogaland Kunstmuseum, Stavanger 30887
Rogaland Museum of Fine Arts, Stavanger 30887
Rogendorfer-Ausstellung, Pöggstall 02428
Roger Guffey Gallery, Kansas City 44406
Roger Raveelmuseum, Machelen 03604
Roger Tory Peterson Institute of Natural History Museum, Jamestown 44313
Roger Williams National Memorial, Providence 46727
Rogers Daisy Airgun Museum, Rogers 46984
Rogers Historical Museum, Rogers 46985
Rogers House Museum and Gallery, Ellsworth 43163
Rogue Gallery and Art Center, Medford 45220
Rohnstädter Heimatstube, Weilmünster 20451
Roja Museum of Maritime Fishing, Roja 27445
Rojas Jūras un Zvejniecības Muzejs, Roja 27445
Rojstna Hiša Pesnika Otona Župančiča, Vinica 34163
Rojstna Hiša Simona Gregorčiča, Vrsno 34165
Rokeby Museum, Ferrisburgh 43316
Rokokomuseum Schloß Belvedere, Weimar, Thüringen 20470
Rokuharamitsu-ji Treasure House, Kyoto 26448
Rokuonji, Kyoto 26449
Rokuzan Art Museum, Hotaka 26232
Rokuzan Bijutsukan, Hotaka 26232
Roland Gibson Gallery, Potsdam 46670
Røldal Bygdemuseum, Røldal 30800
Rolf Bergendorffs Radio Museum, Lessebo 36031
Rolla Minerals Museum, Rolla 46992
Rollag Bygdetun, Rollag 30801
Rollettmuseum, Baden bei Wien 01729
Rollin Art Centre, Port Alberni 06150
Rollo Jamison Museum, Platteville 46546
Rolls-Royce Museum, Dornbirn 01771
Római Katolikus Egyházi Gyűjtemény, Sárospatak 21525
Római Katonai Fürdő, Budapest 21381
Római Kötár, Szentendre 21574
Roman Army Museum, Greenhead 39130
Roman Bath House, Lancaster 39417
Roman Baths Museum, Bath 38121
Roman grave, Silistra 04816
Roman-Katholic Church Museum, Sárospatak 21525
Román Kori Kőtár, Pécs 21515
Roman Legionary Museum, Caerleon 38431
Roman Painted House, Dover 38770
Roman Soldier Museum, Pordim 04786
Roman Theatre of Verulamium, Saint Albans 40376
Roman Villa, Brading 38306
Roman Villa Museum at Bignor, Pulborough 40274
Romanian Ethnic Art Museum, Cleveland 42480
Romanian Naval Museum, Constanța 32502
Romanian Peasants Museum, București 32470
Romanov's Chambers in Zaryadye, Moskva 33177
Romanovskie Palaty v Zarjade, Moskva 33177
Romantikerhaus, Jena 17948
Romany Folklore Museum and Workshop, Selborne 40466
Rome Art and Community Center, Rome 46997
Rome Historical Society Museum, Rome 46998
Romney Toy and Model Museum, New Romney 40016
Romsdalsmuseet, Molde 30687
Ron Morel Memorial Museum, Kapuskasing 05644
Ronald Reagan Boyhood Home, Dixon 42953
Rondeau Provincial Park Visitor Centre, Morpeth 05942
Rongyu Guan, Jiangyin 07125
Roniger Memorial Museum, Cottonwood Falls 42667
Roodepoort Museum, Florida Park 34240
Rooseum, Malmö 36079
Roosevelt Campobello, Lubec 44993
Roosevelt Campobello International Park, Welshpool 06768
Roosevelt County Museum, Portales 46618
Root House Museum, Marietta 45146
Roots of Norfolk at Gressenhall, Gressenhall 39132
Roparshaugsamlinga, Isdalstø 30580
Rørosmuseet, Røros 30806
Rosalie House, Eureka Springs 43235
Rosalie House Museum, Natchez 45633
Rosalie Shire Historical Museum, Goombungee 01064
Rosalie Whyel Museum of Doll Art, Bellevue 41599
Roscoe Village Foundation, Coshocton 42663
Roscommon County Museum, Roscommon 22534
Roscrea Heritage Centre, Roscrea 22535
Rose Art Museum, Waltham 48298
Rose Center Museum, Morristown 45513
Rose Hill Mansion, Geneva 43643
Rose Hill Museum, Bay Village 41548
Rose Hill Plantation State Historic Site, Union 48146
Rose House Museum, Picton 06128
Rose Lawn Museum, Cartersville 42123
Rose Museum at Carnegie Hall, New York 45865
Rose Seidler House, Wahroonga 01572

Rose Valley and District Heritage Museum, Rose Valley 06282
Roseau County Historical Museum, Roseau 47002
Rosebud Centennial Museum, Rosebud 06283
Rosebud County Pioneer Museum, Forsyth 43364
Rosemont Plantation, Woodville 48744
Rosemount Art Gallery, Regina 06241
Rosemount Museum, Pueblo 46740
Rosenbach Museum, Philadelphia 46451
Rosenberg Gallery, Baltimore 41486
Rosenborg Castle, København 08948
Rosenborg Slot, København 08948
Den Rosendahlske Bibelsamling, Esbjerg 08809
Rosendal Palace, Stockholm 36278
Rosendals Slott, Stockholm 36278
Rosenholm Slot, Hornslet 08893
Rosenlew-museo, Pori 09946
Rosenlew Museum, Pori 09946
Rosenlöfs Tryckerimuseum, Kungsgården 36024
Rosenmuseum Steinfurth, Bad Nauheim 15699
Rosenthal Gallery of Art, Caldwell 42028
Rosenwald-Wolf Gallery, Philadelphia 46452
Rosersbergs Slott, Rosersberg 36163
Rosetown Museum and Art Center, Rosetown 06285
Rosewall Memorial Shell Museum, Port Lincoln 01384
Rosewood Scrub Historical Museum, Marburg 01209
Roseworthy Agricultural Museum, Roseworthy 01425
Rosgartenmuseum, Konstanz 18206
Roshdestveno Museum-Estate, Roždestveno 33359
Rosicrucian Egyptian Museum, San Jose 47354
Roskilde Domkirkemuseum, Roskilde 09042
Roskilde Museum, Roskilde 09043
Roskilde Museums Købmandsgård, Roskilde 09044
Roslagens Sjöfartsmuseum, Väddö 36371
Roslagsmuseet, Norrtälje 36124
Roslavl Historical and Art Museum, Roslavl 33353
Roslavlskij Istoriko-chudožstvennyj Muzej, Roslavl 33353
The Ross C. Purdy Museum of Ceramics, Westerville 48556
Ross Castle, Killarney 22493
Ross County Historical Society Museum, Chillicothe 42381
Ross Farm Museum, New Ross 05981
Ross House Museum, Winnipeg 06840
Ross Memorial Museum, Saint Andrews 06303
Ross Thomson House Museum, Shelburne 06435
Ross Thomson Museum, Halifax 05562
Rossburn Museum, Rossburn 06286
Rossendale Footware Heritage Museum, Rawtenstall 40292
Rossendale Museum, Rawtenstall 40293
Rossijskij Ėtnografičeskij muzej, Sankt-Peterburg 33478
Rossijskij Komitet Meždunarodnogo Soveta Muzeev (IKOM Rossii), Moskva 49347
Rossland Historical Museum, Rossland 06287
Rosslyn Chapel, Roslin 40342
Rosso Bianco-Auto Museum, Aschaffenburg 15528
Rostejn Castle, Telč 08675
Rostov Kremlin - State Museum Reserve, Rostov (Jaroslavskaja obl.) 33355
Rostovskij Kreml - Gosudarstvennyj Muzej-zapovednik, Rostov (Jaroslavskaja obl.) 33355
Rostovskij Oblastnoj Muzej Kraevedenija, Rostov-na-Donu 33358
Roswell Museum and Art Center, Roswell 47016
Rot-Kreuz-Museum, Regenstauf 19534
Rotary Museum of Police and Corrections, Prince Albert 06185
Rotch-Jones-Duff House and Garden Museum, New Bedford 45663
Roter Haubarg, Witzwort 20639
Rothe House Museum, Kilkenny 22488
Rotherham Art Gallery, Rotherham 40345
Rothko Chapel, Houston 44135
Rothmühler Heimatmuseum und Archiv, Oestrich-Winkel 19232
Rothschild House, Port Townsend 46608
Rotkreuz-Museum, Nürnberg 19157
Rotkreuz-Museum Berlin, Berlin 16084
Rotkreuzmuseum, Hofheim, Unterfranken 17801
Rotorua Museum of Art and History, Rotorua 30249
Rotovž Art Gallery, Maribor 34128
Rottauer Museum für Fahrzeuge, Wehrtechnik und Zeitgeschichte bis 1948, Pocking 19424
Rotterdams Radio Museum, Rotterdam 29773
Rottingdean Grange Art Gallery and National Toy Museum, Brighton 38343
Rottneros Park, Rottneros 36164
Rottnest Island Museum, Rottnest Island 01427
The Rotunda, Charlottesville 42250
Rotunda Gallery, Brooklyn 41950
Rotunda Museum of Archaeology and Local History, Scarborough 40455
Roudaki Abuabdullo Republican Historical and Regional Museum, Pendžikent 37450
Rough and Tumble Engineers Museum, Kinzers 44501
Rouleau and District Museum, Rouleau 06290
Roulston Museum, Carstairs 05212
Round Top Center for the Arts - Arts Gallery, Damariscotta 42768
Rouse Hill Estate, Rouse Hill 01428
Roussi Chorbadzhi House-Museum, Žeravna 04934
Rovaniemen Kotiseutumuseo, Rovaniemi 10003
Rovaniemen Taidemuseo, Rovaniemi 10004
Rovaniemi Art Museum, Rovaniemi 10004
Rovaniemi Museum, Rovaniemi 10003
Rowan Museum, Salisbury 47220
Rowley Historical Museum, Rowley 47021
Roxbury Historical Museum, Roxbury 47023
Roy Boyd Gallery, Chicago 42361
The Roy Rogers-Dale Evans Museum, Victorville 48235
Roy Whalen Regional Heritage Centre, Deer Lake 05317
Royal Academy of Arts Gallery, London 39754
Royal Air Force Air Defence Radar Museum, Norwich 40098
Royal Air Force Museum, London 39755
Royal Air Force Museum, Shifnal 40499
Royal Air Force Museum 201 Squadron, Saint Peter Port 40426
Royal Air Force Museum Reserve Collection, Stafford 40570
Royal Albert Memorial Museum and Art Gallery, Exeter 38957
Royal Anglian Regiment Museum, Duxford 38830
Royal Armouries, London 39756
Royal Armouries at Fort Nelson, Fareham 38975
Royal Armouries Museum, Leeds 39450
Royal Armoury, Stockholm 36256
Royal Army Dental Corps Historical Museum, Aldershot 37969
Royal Army Educational Corps Museum, Beaconsfield 38133
Royal Army Veterinary Corps Museum, Aldershot 37970
Royal Armymuseum, Delft 29079
Royal Art Museum, Berlin 16085
Royal Arts Foundation, Newport 45933
Royal Atlantic Wax Museum, Hunter River 05609
Royal Australian Air Force Museum, Point Cook 01371
Royal Australian Corps of Transport Museum, Puckapunyal 01396
Royal Australian Infantry Corps Museum, Singleton 01453
Royal Bank of Scotland Art Collection, London 39757
Royal Barges National Museum, Bangkok 37494
Royal Berkshire Yeomanry Cavalry Museum, Windsor 40902
Royal Borough Collection, Maidenhead 39874
Royal Borough Museum Collection, Windsor 40903
Royal Brierley Crystal Museum, Dudley 38783
Royal British Columbia Museum, Victoria 06729
Royal British Society of Sculptors, London 39758
Royal Brunei Armed Forces Museum, Bandar Seri Begawan 04601
Royal Cabinet of Paintings, Den Haag 29105
Royal Cambrian Academy of Art, Conwy 38628
Royal Canadian Air Force Memorial Museum, Astra 05016
Royal Canadian Artillery Museum, Shilo 06445
Royal Canadian Military Institute Museum, Toronto 06606
Royal Canadian Mint, Winnipeg 06841
Royal Canadian Mounted Police Museum, Regina 06242
Royal Canadian Ordnance Corps Museum, Montréal 05929
The Royal Canadian Regiment Museum, London 05773
Royal Carriage Museum, Bulaq-el-Dakrur 09251
Royal Castle in Warsaw, Warszawa 32143
Royal Ceremonial Dress Collection, London 39759
Royal Coin Cabinet, Leiden 29519
The Royal Coin Cabinet, Stockholm 36251
Royal Collection of Coins and Medals, København 08934
Royal College of Art, London 39760
Royal College of Obstetricians and Gynaecologists Collection, London 39761
Royal College of Surgeons in Ireland Museum, Dublin 22454
Royal Cornwall Museum, Truro 40730
Royal Crown Derby Museum, Derby 38720
Royal Danish Arsenal Museum, København 08953
Royal Danish Naval Museum, København 08946
Royal Engineers Museum, Chatham 38532
Royal Engineers Museum, Gillingham, Kent 39033
Royal Flying Doctor Service Visitors Centre, Edge Hill 01007
Royal Fusiliers Regimental Museum, London 39762
Royal Glasgow Institute of the Fine Arts, Glasgow 39063
Royal Gloucestershire, Berkshire and Wiltshire Regiment Museum, Salisbury 40436
The Royal Governor's Mansion, Perth Amboy 46361
Royal Green Jackets Museum, Winchester 40891
Royal Gunpowder Mills, Waltham Abbey 40778
Royal Hamilton Light Infantry Heritage Museum, Hamilton 05575
Royal Hampshire Regiment Museum, Winchester 40892
Royal Highland Fusiliers Regimental Museum, Glasgow 39064
Royal Holloway College Picture Gallery, Egham 38923
Royal Hospital Chelsea Museum, London 39763
Royal Incorporation of Architects in Scotland Gallery, Edinburgh 38909
Royal Inniskilling Fusiliers Regimental Museum, Enniskillen 38941
Royal Irish Fusiliers Museum, Armagh 38020
Royal Irish Regiment Museum, Ballymena 38070
Royal Jewelry Museum, Alexandria 09246
Royal Lazienki Museum, Warszawa 32109
Royal Lincolnshire Regiment Museum, Lincoln 39502
Royal Logistic Corps Museum, Deepcut 38712
Royal London Hospital Archives and Museum, London 39764
Royal London Wax Museum, Victoria 06730
Royal Malaysian Air Force Museum, Kuala Lumpur 27652
Royal Malaysian Navy Museum, Lumut 27659
Royal Malaysian Navy Museum, Melaka 27674
Royal Marines Museum, Portsmouth 40257
The Royal Mews, London 39765
Royal Military Academy Sandhurst Collection, Camberley 38444
Royal Military College of Canada Museum, Kingston 05687
Royal Military Police Museum, Chichester 38565
Royal Mint Sovereign Gallery, London 39766
Royal Museum, Edinburgh 38910
Royal Museum, Kota Bharu 27629
Royal Museum, Seoul 27267
Royal Museum and Art Gallery, Canterbury 38474
Royal Museum Sri Menanti, Seremban 27685
Royal Museums of Art and History, Bruxelles 03337
Royal National Lifeboat Institution Headquarters Museum, Poole 40228
Royal Naval Museum Portsmouth, Portsmouth 40258
Royal Naval Patrol Service Association Museum, Lowestoft 39840
Royal Navy Submarine Museum, Gosport 39102
Royal New Zealand Army Medical Corps Museum, Christchurch 30131
Royal New Zealand Navy Museum, Devonport 30142
Royal Newfoundland Constabulary Museum, Saint John's 06350
Royal Norfolk Regimental Museum, Norwich 40099
Royal Norwegian Navy Museum, Horten 30565
Royal Observatory Greenwich, London 39767
Royal Observer Corps Museum, Eastleigh 38861
Royal Ontario Museum, Toronto 06607
Royal Palace Amsterdam, Amsterdam 28869
Royal Pavilion, Brighton 38344
The Royal Photographic Society Octagon Galleries, Bath 38122
Royal Pump Room Museum, Harrogate 39171
Royal Regalia Gallery, Bandar Seri Begawan 04595
Royal Regiment of Fusiliers Museum, Warwick 40792
Royal Research Ship Discovery, Dundee 38804
Royal Saint John's Regatta Museum, Saint John's 06351
Royal Saskatchewan Museum, Regina 06243
Royal Scots Regimental Museum, Edinburgh 38911
Royal Scottish Academy Collections, Edinburgh 38912
Royal Shakespeare Company Collection, Stratford-upon-Avon 40629
Royal Signals Museum, Blandford Forum 38257
Royal Summer Palace, Praha 08586
Royal Sussex Regiment Museum, Eastbourne 38856
Royal Thai Navy Museum, Samut Prakan 37534
Royal Tyrrell Museum of Palaeontology, Drumheller 05342
Royal Ulster Rifles Regimental Museum, Belfast 38159
Royal Welch Fusiliers Regimental Museum, Caernarfon 38434
Royal Western Australian Historical Museum, Nedlands 01312
Royal Wiltshire Yeomanry Museum, Swindon 40666
Royal Winnipeg Rifles Museum, Winnipeg 06842
Royall House, Medford 45216
Royalton Historical Society Museum, Royalton 47026
Røyrvik Bygdatun, Limingen 30645
Royston and District Museum, Royston 40348
Rozelle House Galleries, Ayr 38052
Rozmberk's House - Hussite Museum, Soběslav 08658
Rožmberský Dům, Soběslav 08658
R.P. Strathearn Historical Park, Simi 47636
R.S. Barnwell Memorial Garden and Art Center, Shreveport 47615
RSA Library, London 39768
Rubelle and Norman Schafler Gallery, Brooklyn 41951
Rubenianum, Antwerpen 03172
Rubens Maskinhistoriska Samlingar, Götene 35924
Rubenshuis, Antwerpen 03173
Rubin Museum, Tel Aviv 22773
Ruby Green Contemporary Arts Foundations, Nashville 45623
Rudd House Museum, Kimberley 34293
Ruddell Gallery, Spearfish 47721
Ruddick's Folly, Suffolk 47867
Ruddington Framework Knitters' Museum, Ruddington 40351
Ruddington Village Museum, Ruddington 40352
Rudolf Steiner Archiv, Dornach 36665
Rudolf Weinwurm-Museum, Göpfritz 01899
Rūdolfa Blaumaņa Memoriālais Muzejs Braki, Ērgļi 27355
Rudolph E. Lee Gallery, Clemson 42458
Rudolph Tegners Museum, Dronningmølle 08800
Rübeländer Tropfsteinhöhlenmuseum, Rübeland 19702
Rübesams Da Capo Oldtimermuseum, Leipzig 18412
Rügen-Museum, Ostseebad Binz 19314
Rüstkammer, Dresden 16705
Rufford Old Hall, Rufford 40353
Rugby Art Gallery and Museum, Rugby 40356
Rugby Museum, Newlands 34314
Rugby School Museum, Rugby 40357
Ruggles House, Columbia Falls 42572
Ruhlaer Tabakpfeifenmuseum und Museum für Stadtgeschichte, Ruhla 19710
Ruhlaer Uhrenmuseum, Ruhla 19711
Ruhmeshalle und Bavaria, München 18902
Ruhnu Muuseum, Ruhnu 09351
Ruhrlandmuseum Essen, Essen 16962
Ruhrtalmuseum, Schwerte 19903
Ruïne van Brederode, Santpoort 29790
Ruins of Gour and Pandua, Malda 21936
Ruiskumestarin Talo, Helsinki 09525
Rūjiena Exhibition Hall, Rūjiena 27447
Rūjienas Izstāžu Zāle, Rūjiena 27447
Rumford Historical Museum, North Woburn 46012
Rundāle Palace Museum, Pilsrundāle 27394
Rundāles Pils Muzejs, Pilsrundāle 27394
Rundetaarn, København 08949
Rundfunkmuseum der Stadt Fürth, Fürth, Bayern 17166
Rundfunkmuseum Schloß Brunn, Emskirchen 16870
Rundgang Urchigs Terbil, Törbel 37247
Rundlet-May House, Portsmouth 46653
Rundlingmuseum Wendlandhof-Lübeln, Küsten 18263
Runeberg's Cottage, Jakobstad 09575
Runebergs stugan, Jakobstad 09575
Runestone Museum, Alexandria 41119
Rungehaus, Wolgast 20668
Ruokolahden Kotiseutumuseo, Ruokolahti 10005
Ruokolahti Local History Museum, Ruokolahti 10005
Ruoveden Kotiseutumuseo, Ruovesi 10008
Ruovesi Local History Museum, Ruovesi 10008
Rupert Museum, Stellenbosch 34382
Rupertinum, Salzburg 02549
Rural Life Centre, Farnham 38983
Rural Life Museum, Steenwerck 14802
Rural Life Museum and Windrush Gardens, Baton Rouge 41534
Rural Museum on Folk Art and Archaeology, Bagnan 21699
Rural Residence Museum, Takamatsu 26792
Rush County Historical Society Museum, Rushville 47031
Rushen Abbey, Ballasalla 38063
Rushworth Museum, Rushworth 01429
Rusk County Historical Society Museum, Ladysmith 44565
Ruskin Library, Lancaster 39418
Ruskin Museum, Coniston 38625
Ruskon Kotiseutumuseo ja Rindellin Mäkitupalaismuseo, Rusko 10009
Russell Cave Museum, Bridgeport 41887
Russell Collection of Early Keyboard Instruments, Edinburgh 38913
Russell-Cotes Art Gallery and Museum, Bournemouth 38286
Russell Gallery of Fine Art, Peterborough 06123
Russell Hill Rogers Galleries, San Antonio 47257
Russell Museum, Russell 30253
Russian Historical and Ethnographic Museum, Toržok 33620
Russian Museum of Ethnography, Sankt-Peterburg 33478
Russian Museum of Photography, Nižnij Novgorod 33225
Russian Museums Association, Tula 49345
Russian State Museum of the Arctic and Antarctic, Sankt-Peterburg 33479
Russkij Gosudarstvennyj Muzej Arktiki i Antarktiki, Sankt-Peterburg 33479
Russkij Muzej Fotografii, Nižnij Novgorod 33225
Rust en Vreugd Museum, Cape Town 34209
Rustington Heritage Exhibition Centre, Rustington 40360
Rusty Relics Museum, Carlyle 05209
Ruth Eckerd Hall, Clearwater 42453
Ruth Hall Museum of Paleontology, Abiquiu 41059
Ruth Youth Wing, Jerusalem 22659
Rutherford B. Hayes Presidential Center, Fremont 43556
Rutherford House, Edmonton 05385
Ruthin Craft Centre, Ruthin 40361
Ruthmere House Museum, Elkhart 43142
Rutland County Museum, Oakham 40122
Rutland Railway Museum, Cottesmore 38638
Ruununmylly, Hämeenlinna 09453
Ruurd Wiersma Hûs, Burdaard 29040
RV/MH Heritage Foundation, Elkhart 43143
The R.W. Norton Art Gallery, Shreveport 47616
Ryan Fine Arts Center, Abilene 41054
Ryazan Historical-Architectural Museum Reservation, Rjazan 33351
Ryazan Regional Art Museum, Rjazan 33352
Rybinsk historical, Architectural and Art Museum-Preserve, Rybinsk 33362
Rybinskij Gosudarstvennyj Istoriko-architekturnyj i Chudožestvennyj Muzej-zapovednik, Rybinsk 33362
Rydal Mount, Ambleside 37997
Rydals Museum, Rydal 36166
Rye Art Gallery, Rye 40363
Rye Castle Museum, Rye 40364
Rye Heritage Centre Town Model, Rye 40365
Rye Historical Society Museum, Rye 47043
Ryedale Folk Museum, Hutton-le-Hole 39281
Ryfylkemuseet, Sand 30819
Rygge Museum, Larkollen 30628
Rygnestadtunet, Rysstad 30813
Ryhope Engines Museum, Sunderland 40648
Rymättylä Local History Museum, Rymättylä 10010
Rymättylän Kotiseutumuseo, Rymättylä 10010
Ryosan Museum of History, Kyoto 26450
Ryotsu Folk Museum, Ryotsu 26687
Ryuga-Do Cave Museum, Tosayamada 26962

Ryushi Memorial Hall, Tokyo 26914
S. Ray Miller Auto Museum, Elkhart 43144
SA Breweries World of Beer, Johannesburg 34283
S.A. Otkrytka, Moskva 33178
Saad Zaghlul Museum, Munira 09302
SAAF Museum Swartkop, Pretoria 34354
SAAF Museum Ysterplaat, Ysterplaat 34406
Saalburgmuseum, Bad Homburg 15663
Saalfelder Feengrotten, Saalfeld, Saale 19720
Saamelaismuseo Siida, Inari 09569
Saanich Historical Artifacts Society, Saanichton 06295
Saanich Pioneer Log Cabin Museum, Saanichton 06296
Saaremaa Muuseum, Kuressaare 09336
Saarijärven Museo, Saarijärvi 10012
Saarländisches Bergbaumuseum, Bexbach 16137
Saarländisches Künstlerhaus e.V., Saarbrücken 19726
Saarland Museum, Saarbrücken 19727
Saaser Museum, Saas Fee 37079
Saatchi Gallery, London 39769
Sabac National Museum, Sabac 33902
Sabae CCI Art Museum, Sabae 26689
Sabah Art Gallery, Kota Kinabalu 27632
Sabah State Museum, Kota Kinabalu 27631
Sabā's House, Teheran 22324
Saçaklı Ev - Kültür ve Sanat Merkezi, Lefkoşa 08239
Sacavém Municpal Pottery Museum, Loures 32317
Sachem Historical Society Museum, Holbrook 44049
Sachs Harbour Museum, Sachs Harbour 06297
Sackets Harbor Battlefield State Historic Site, Sackets Harbor 47045
Saco Museum, Saco 47046
Sacramento Mountains Historical Museum, Cloudcroft 42504
Sacred Circle Gallery of American Indian Art, Seattle 47544
Sacrewell Farm and Country Centre, Thornhaugh 40701
Sacro Convento Castillo de Calatrava la Nueva, Aldea del Rey 34442
Sa'dabad Museums, Teheran 22325
Sadbek Hanım Museum, İstanbul 37706
Sadberk Hanım Müzesi, İstanbul 37706
Saddleworth Museum and Art Gallery, Uppermill 40752
Sądecki Park Etnograficzny, Nowy Sącz 31836
Sadelmakare Öbergs Hus, Solna 36221
Sado Archaeology Museum, Ogi 26619
Sado Hakabutsukan, Sawata 26727
Sado Kokokan, Ogi 26619
Sado-koku Ogi Folk Museum, Ogi 26620
Sado Museum-Art and Natural History of Sado, Sawata 26727
Sado Nohgaku-no-sato, Ryotsu 26688
Sadriddin Aini Memorial Museum, Samarkand 48851
Sääksmäen Kotiseutumuseo, Sääksmäki 10013
Sääksmäki Museum, Sääksmäki 10013
Säätyläiskotiseutumuseo, Kolkanlahti 09686
Sæby Museum and Sæbygaard Manor Museum, Sæby 09051
Sächsischer Lehr- & Besucherbergwerk-Himmelfahrt-Fundgrube, Freiberg, Sachsen 17103
Sächsischer Museumsbund e.V., Dresden 49214
Sächsisches Apothekenmuseum Leipzig, Leipzig 18413
Sächsisches Eisenbahnmuseum, Chemnitz 16471
Sächsisches Psychiatriemuseum, Leipzig 18414
Sächsisches Schmalspurbahn-Museum Rittersgrün, Rittersgrün 19618
Sächsisches Strafvollzugsmuseum, Waldheim 20365
Säffle Marinmotor Museum, Säffle 36167
Säfsnäs Arbetarmuseum och Hembygdsgård, Fredriksberg 35894
Sägereimuseum, Richterswil 37057
Sägmühlmuseum Marhördt, Oberrot 19197
Säimenen Mylly, Rökönvaara 09999
Säkylän Kotiseutumuseo, Säkylä 10015
Sängermuseum, Feuchtwangen 16999
Säräisniemen Kotiseutumuseo, Vaala 10156
Särestad Lantbruksmuseum, Grästorp 35928
Särestöniemi-Museo, Kaukonen 09641
Säters Hembygdsmuseum, Säter 36170
Sætersgårds Samlinger Dølmotunet, Tolga 30924
Säyneisten Kotiseutumuseo, Säyneinen 10016
Safe Haven, Oswego 46217
Safety Harbor Museum of Regional History, Safety Harbor 47058
Saffron Walden Museum, Saffron Walden 40368
Safier Heimatmuseum, Safien 37082
Safn Ásgrims Jónssonar, Reykjavík 21663
Safn Rafmagnsveitu Reykjavíkur, Reykjavík 21664
Safnahusid Húsavík, Húsavík 21640
Sag Harbor Whaling and Historical Museum, Sag Harbor 47061
Saga-kenritsu Bijutsukan, Saga 26690
Saga-kenritsu Hakubutsukan, Saga 26691
Saga-kenritsu Kyushu Toji Bunkakan, Arita 26103
Saga Prefectural Art Museum, Saga 26690
Saga Prefectural Museum, Saga 26691
Sagalund Museum, Kimito 09669
Sagalunds Museum, Kimito 09669
Sagamore Hill National Historic Site, Oyster Bay 46250
Sagasco Historical Group Museum, Brompton 00848
Saginaw Art Museum, Saginaw 47063
Sagstua Skolemuseum, Sagstua 30815
Saguache County Museum, Saguache 47064
Såguddens Museum, Arvika 35818
Sahan Museo, Puumala 09966
Sahitya Parishad Museum, Midnapore 21943
Saijo Municipal Local Museum, Saijo 26692
Saikyo-ji Treasure Hall, Hirado 26201
Sailor's House, Uusikaupunki 10154
Sailor's Memorial Museum, Islesboro 44268
Saimaa Canal Museum, Lappeenranta 09764
Saimaan Kanavan Museo, Lappeenranta 09764
Sainsbury Centre for Visual Arts, Norwich 40100
Saint Albans Historical Museum, Saint Albans 47065
Saint Albans Organ Museum, Saint Albans 40377
Saint Andrews Cathedral Museum, Saint Andrews 40383
Saint Andrews College Museum, Christchurch 30132
Saint Andrews Museum, Saint Andrews 40384
Saint Andrews Preservation Museum, Saint Andrews 40385
Saint Andrews University Museum Collections, Saint Andrews 40386
Saint Angela's Museum, Prelate 06178
Saint Anne's Chapel and Old Grammar School Museum, Barnstaple 38094
Saint Asaph Cathedral Treasury, Saint Asaph 40388
Saint Augustine Historical Society Museum, Saint Augustine 47071
Saint Augustine Lighthouse and Museum, Saint Augustine 47072
Saint Augustine's Abbey, Canterbury 38475
Saint Barbe Museum and Art Gallery, Lymington 39854
Saint Barnabas Icon and Archaeological Museum, Gazimağusa 08221
Saint Bartholomew's Hospital Museum, London 39770
Saint Basil Cathedral, Moskva 33173
Saint Basile Chapel Museum, Saint-Basile 06306
Saint Bernard's Hospital Museum and Chapel, Southall 40541
Saint Bride's Crypt Museum, London 39771
Saint Catharines Museum, Saint Catharines 06311
Saint Catherine's National School Museum, Aughrim 22363
Saint Charles County Museum, Saint Charles 47081
Saint Charles Heritage Center, Saint Charles 47077
Saint Clair County Historical Museum, Belleville 41590
Saint Claude Museum, Saint Claude 06312
Saint Clements Island-Potomac River Museum, Colton Point 42546
Saint David's Hall, Cardiff 38483
Saint Dominic Church Museum, Macau 07169
Saint Elie Pioneer Church Museum, Inglis 05618
Saint Francis Art Collections, Zadar 07808
Saint Gaudens National Historic Site, Cornish 42639
Saint George Epanosifis Monastery, Iráklion 20978
Saint George's Historical Society Museum, Saint George's 03888
Saint Georges Regional Museum, Hurstville 01115
Saint George's United Methodist Church Museum, Philadelphia 46453
Saint Helens History Room, Saint Helens 01431
Saint Helens Transport Museum, Saint Helens 40397
Saint Ives Museum, Saint Ives, Cornwall 40408
Saint Ives Society of Artists Members Gallery (Norway Gallery) and Mariners Gallery, Saint Ives, Cornwall 40409
Saint James Cavalier, Valletta 27705
Saint James' House, Fredericksburg 43542
Saint James Museum and Library, Jerusalem 22660
Saint John and Coningsby Medieval Museum, Hereford 39230
Saint John Jewish Historical Museum, Saint John 06336
Saint John Sports Hall of Fame, Saint John 06337
Saint John's Church and Parish Museum, Hampton 43897
Saint John's Co-Cathedral and Museum, Valletta 27706
Saint John's House, Warwick 40793
Saint John's Museum of Art, Wilmington 48663
Saint John's Northwestern Military Academy Museum, Delafield 42860
Saint John's Schoolhouse Museum, Reid 01412
Saint John's Theatre and Arts Centre, Listowel 22509
Saint Johnsbury Athenaeum, Saint Johnsbury 47099
Saint Joseph College Art Gallery, West Hartford 48528
Saint Joseph Island Museum Village, Richards Landing 06257
Saint Joseph Museum, Saint Joseph 47109
Saint Joseph's College Museum, Tiruchirappalli 22037
Saint Joseph's University Gallery, Philadelphia 46454
Saint-Laurent Art Museum, Montréal 05930
Saint Lawrence College Art Gallery, Kingston 05688
Saint Lawrence Memorial Miner's Museum, Saint Lawrence 06362
Saint Louis Art Museum, Saint Louis 47134
Saint Louis Artists' Guild Museum, Saint Louis 47135
Saint Louis County Historical Museum, Duluth 43002
Saint Louis Science Center Museum, Saint Louis 47136
Saint Louis University Museum of Arts and Culture, Baguio 31284
Saint Lucie County Historical Museum, Fort Pierce 43441
Saint Luke's Gallery, Paxton 46320
Saint Mamas Manastırı İkon Müzesi, Güzelyurt 08229
Saint Mamas Monastery Icon Museum, Güzelyurt 08229
Saint Margaret's Museum, Saint Margaret's Bay 40413
Saint Mary Magdalene Treasury, Newark-on-Trent 40024
Saint Marys and Benzinger Township Museum, Saint Marys 47145
Saint Mary's Galeria, Orchard Lake 46177
Saint Marys Museum, Saint Marys 06367
Saint Mary's Museum of Maxstone, Assiniboia 05015
Saint Mary's River Marine Centre, Sault Sainte Marie 06412
Saint Mary's University Art Gallery, Halifax 05563
Saint Mawes Castle, Truro 40731
Saint Mel's Diocesan Museum, Longford 22511
Saint Michael's Historical Museum, Chatham, New Brunswick 05236
Saint Michael's Loft Museum, Christchurch 38579
Saint Mullins Heritage Centre, Saint Mullins 22538
Saint Mungo Museum of Religious Life and Art, Glasgow 39065
Saint Neots Museum, Saint Neots 40416
Saint Nicholas Priory, Exeter 38958
Saint Nicolas' Church Museum, Tallinn 09368
Saint Norbert Provincial Heritage Park, Winnipeg 06843
Saint Patrick's Museum, Sydney 06528
Saint Patrick's Trian, Armagh 38021
Saint Paul Museum, Randleman 46788
Saint Peter Hungate Church Museum, Norwich 40101
Saint Peter's Bunker, Saint Peter 40421
Saint Peter's Church, Sunderland 40649
Saint Peter's Church Museum, Kanturk 22483
Saint Peter's College Art Gallery, Jersey City 44341
Saint Petersburg Museum of History, Saint Petersburg 47175
Saint Petersburg State Museum of Theatre and Music, Sankt-Peterburg 33481
Saint Philip's Fortress, Santo Domingo 09117
Saint Photios Greek Orthodox National Shrine, Saint Augustine 47073
Saint Robert's Cave, Knaresborough 39401
Saint Sharbel Museum, Annaya 27479
Saint Simons Island Lighthouse Museum, Saint Simons Island 47182
Saint Sophia of Kiev, Kyïv 37876
Saint Tammany Art Gallery, Covington 42682
Saint Theresa's College Folklife Museum, Cebu 31314
Saint Thomas-Elgin Public Art Centre, Saint Thomas 06376
Saint Thomas More Art Gallery, Saskatoon 06404
Saint Thomas' Old Garrison Church Museum, Saint John's 06352
Saint Vigeans Museum, Arbroath 38013
Saint Vincent Church Museum, Isandlwana 34265
Saint Volodymyr Museum, Winnipeg 06844
Saint Walburg and District Historical Museum, Saint Walburg 06380
Sainte Genevieve Museum, Sainte Genevieve 47185
Sainte Maison de la Flocellière, La Flocellière 12182
Sainte Marie among the Iroquois, Liverpool 44830
Sairaalamuseo, Lahti 09749
De Saisset Museum, Santa Clara 47407
Sait Faik Müzesi, Burgaz Adası 37642
Sait Faik Museum, Burgaz Adası 37642
Saitama-kenritsu Hakubutsukan, Omiya 26639
Saitama-kenritsu Kindai Bijutsukan, Saitama 26693
Saitama-kenritsu Rekishi Shiryokan, Ranzan 26685
Saitama-kenritsu Sakitama Shiryokan, Gyoda 26160
Saitama-kenritsu Shizenshi Hakubutsukan, Nagatoro 26562
Saitama Museum of Natural History, Nagatoro 26562
Saitama Prefectural Historical Museum, Ranzan 26685
Saitama Prefectural Museum, Omiya 26639
Saito Ho-on Kai Museum of Natural History, Sendai 26734
Saito Ho-on Kai Shizenshi Hakubutsukan, Sendai 26734
Sajanskaja Kartinnaja Galereja, Sajansk 33363
Sakai City Museum, Sakai 26699
Sakai Cutting Tools Museum, Sakai 26700
Sakai Greenery Museum Harvest Hill, Sakai 26698
Sakai House, Osaka 26672
Sakai-shiritsu Hakubutsukan, Sakai 26699
Sakai-shiritsu Hamono Hakubutsukan, Sakai 26700
Sakaide Civic Art Museum, Sakaide 26702
Sakrale Kunst in der Sankt-Anna-Kapelle, Cham 16459
Sakraler Austellungsraum, Groß Siegharts 01950
Sakralna Baština Muzej, Senj 07769
Saksische en Museumboerderij Erve Brooks Niehof, Gelselaar 29270
Sakura Bank Exhibition Room, Kyoto 26451
Sakura City Museum of Art, Sakura 26707
Sala A. De Carolis, Montefiore dell'Aso 24524
Sala Cadafe, Caracas 48928
Sala d'Arqueologia i Gabinet Numismàtic, Lleida 34972
Sala de Arqueología del Municipio de Mújica, Múgica 28256
Sala de Arte Carlos F. Sáez, Montevideo 41032
Sala de Arte Prehispánico, Santo Domingo 09128
Sala de Exhibitiones Temporales del Banco Central, San José 07663
Sala de Exposiciones Edificio Historico, Oviedo 35206
Sala de Exposiciones El Pasaje, Alcázar de San Juan 34433
Sala de Exposiciones Rekalde, Bilbao 34616
Sala de los Bomberos, La Habana 08002
Sala de Memorias Culturales, Mogotes 07526
Sala de Memórias de Chapada dos Guimarães, Chapada dos Guimarães 04049
Sala de Recuerdos de la Escuela Militar de Montaña, Jaca 34921
Sala de Trofeos del Duque de Arión, Plasencia 35275
Sala del Costume e delle Tradizioni Popolari, Corinaldo 23655
Sala d'Exposicions de la Fundació la Caixa, Madrid 35062
Sala Girona de la Fundació la Caixa, Girona 34859
Sala Histórica de la Facultad de Medicina, Mitras 28222
Sala Histórica del Regimiento de Infantería Mecanizado 24, Río Gallegos 00518
Sala Historica General Savio, Buenos Aires 00253
Sala Homenaje a Juárez, Guelatao de Juárez 27980
Sala Ipostel, Caracas 48929
Sala Josefa Rodriguez del Fresno, Santa Fé 00610
Sala Melchor Ocampo, Morelia 28254
Sala Mendoza, Caracas 48930
Sala Montcada de la Fundació la Caixa, Barcelona 34591
Sala Muncunill, Terrassa 35528
Sala Museo Literario, Bogotá 07434
Sala Museo Pablo Sarasate, Pamplona 35250
Sala Piano Museum, Cebu 31315
Sala Reus, Reus 35315
Sala Sergio Larrain, Santiago de Chile 06921
Sala Traktormuseum, Sala 36173
Salamanca Arts Centre, Hobart 01104
Salamanca Rail Museum, Salamanca 47187
Salangen Bygdetun, Sjøvegan 30839
Salar Jung Museum, Hyderabad 21846
Salas Municipales de Arte Sanz-Enea, Zarautz 35733
Salcombe Maritime Museum, Salcombe 40428
Saldus History and Art Museum, Saldus 27450
Saldus Vēstures un Mākslas Muzejs, Saldus 27450
Sale Historical Museum, Sale 01438
Salem 1630 Pioneer Village, Salem 47200
Salem County Historical Society Museum, Salem 47204
Salem Historical Society Museum, Salem 47205
Salem Maritime National Historic Site, Salem 47201
Salem Museum, Salem 47211
Salem Witch Museum, Salem 47202
Salford Museum and Art Gallery, Salford 40432
Salgo Trust for Education, Port Washington 46610
Salich Sajdashev Museum, Kazan 32904
Salida Museum, Salida 47212
Salina Art Center, Salina 47213
Salinas Pueblo Missions National Monument, Mountainair 45549
Saline County Historical Society Museum, Dorchester 42959
Saline- und Heimatmuseum, Bad Sulza 15753
Salinenmuseum Unteres Bohrhaus, Rottweil 19697
Salisbury and South Wiltshire Museum, Salisbury 40437
Salisbury Folk Museum, Salisbury 01439
Salisbury Historical Society Museum, Salisbury 47222
Salisbury House, Des Moines 42909
Salisbury Mansion, Worcester 48755
Salisbury State University Galleries, Salisbury 47217
Sallan Kotiseutumuseo, Salla 10017
Sallands Landbouwmuseum de Laarman, Luttenberg 29554
Salle Alfred Pellan, Laval 05736
Salle de Traditions de la Garde Républicaine, Paris 13659
La Salle des Étiquettes, Épernay 11631
Salle des Illustres, Auch 10472
Salle des Souvenirs, Lisieux 12623
Salle d'Exposition du Centre Archéologique des Hauts Cantons, Villemagne-l'Argentière 15213
Salle d'Exposition Haras du Pin, Le Pin-au-Haras 12463
Salle d'Honneur du 44e, Mutzig 13230
Salle d'Honneur du 516e Régiment du Train, Toul 14925
Salle Dorée du Palais Episcopal, Lisieux 12624
Salle Gallo-Romaine, Florange 11750
Salle-Musée du Spitfire, Saulty 14640
Salle Panoramique de Notre-Dame-de-Monts, Notre-Dame-de-Monts 13366
Sally Lunn's Refreshment House and Kitchen Museum, Bath 38123
Salmagundi Museum of American Art, New York 45866
Salmo Museum, Salmo 06386
Salmon Arm Museum, Salmon Arm 06387
Salmon Brook Historical Society Museum, Granby 43739
Saloinen Local History Museum, Arkkukari 09417
Saloisten Kotiseutumuseo, Arkkukari 09417
Salomons Memento Rooms, Southborough 40550
Salón de Artes Plásticas Antonia F. Rizzuto, Villa Carlos Paz 00662
Salón de la Fama del Beisbol Profesional de México, Monterrey 28242
Salon de l'Automobile Miniature, Ally 10295
Salon de Peinture Permanent, Montbard 13056
Salón Electo Brizuela, Concepción del Uruguay 00286
Salon Muzyczny im. Fryderyka Chopina, Antonin 31472
Salone Villa Romana, Firenze 23886
Salonik Chopinów, Warszawa 32141
Salons voor Schone Kunsten, Sint-Niklaas 03743

Salpalinja-Museo, Miehikkälä 09826
Salpalinjan Bukkerialue, Ala-Philaja 09412
Salt Archaeological Museum, Salt 27066
Salt Folklore Museum, Salt 27067
Salt Lake Art Center, Salt Lake City 47232
Salt Museum, Liverpool 44831
Salt Museum, Northwich 40088
Salt Road Museum, Itoigawa 26267
Salt Spring Island Museum, Ganges 05475
Saltash Heritage Centre, Saltash 40438
Saltdal Museum, Rognan 30799
Salter Museum, Argonia 41254
Saltram House, Plymouth 40212
Saltstraumen Museum, Saltstraumen 30818
Saltykv-Shchedrin House-Museum, Kirov 32918
Saltykv-Shchedrin Museum, Tver 33636
Salvador Dali Museum, Saint Petersburg 47176
Salvage Fisherman's Museum, Salvage 06388
Salvation Army George Scott Railton Museum, Toronto 06608
Salvation Army International Heritage Centre, London 39772
Salvation Army Southern Historical Museum, Atlanta 41357
The Salvation Army Territorial Archives and Museum, Wellington 30309
Salvatorianerkloster, Gurk 01974
Salzbergwerk Berchtesgaden, Berchtesgaden 15887
Salzburger Barockmuseum, Salzburg 02550
Salzburger Freilichtmuseum, Großgmain 01953
Salzburger Landes-Skimuseum, Werfenweng 02823
Salzburger Museum Carolino Augusteum, Salzburg 02551
Salzkammer, Pratteln 37033
Salzkammergut-Lokalbahn-Museum, Mondsee 02322
Salzmagazin, Stans 37206
Salzmuseum, Bad Nauheim 15700
Salzmuseum, Bad Sooden-Allendorf 15747
Salzmuseum, Bad Sülze 15751
Salzwelten Altaussee, Altaussee 01660
Salzwelten Salzburg-Bad Dürrnberg, Hallein 01998
Sam Bell Maxey House, Paris 46286
Sam Brown Memorial Park, Browns Valley 41963
Sam Houston Historical Schoolhouse, Maryville 45198
Sam Houston Memorial Museum, Huntsville 44176
Sam Noble Oklahoma Museum of Natural History, Norman 45976
The Sam Rayburn Museum, Bonham 41780
Sam Roi Yod, Phachuab Khiri Khan 37525
Sam Tung Uk Museum, Hong Kong 07111
Sam Waller Museum, The Pas 06098
Samara Art Gallery Maria, Samara 33375
Samara Art Museum, Samara 33377
Samara Zoological Museum, Samara 33379
Samarra Museum, Samarra 22356
Samarskaja Chudožestvennaja Galereja Marija, Samara 33375
Samarskij Eparchialnyj Cerkovno-istoričeskij Muzej, Samara 33376
Samarskij Oblastnoj Chudožestvennyj Muzej, Samara 33377
Samarskij Oblastnoj Istoriko-kraevedčeskij Muzej im. P.V. Alabina, Samara 33378
Samarskij Zoologičeskij Muzej, Samara 33379
Samegården med Museum, Tärnaby 36320
Samford and District Historical Museum, Samford 01441
Sámi Museum and Northern Lapland Nature Centre, Inari 09569
De Samiske Samlinger, Karasjok 30590
Sammenslutningen af Grønlandske Lokalmuseer, Sisimiut 49224
Sammlung Antiker Kleinkunst, Jena 17949
Sammlung Berger, Amorbach 15486
Sammlung Berggruen - Picasso und seine Zeit, Berlin 16086
Sammlung Bodingbauer, Steyr 02689
Sammlung Buchheim - Museum der Phantasie, Bernried, Starnberger See 16129
Sammlung der Städtischen Galerie, Lüdenscheid 18549
Sammlung der Universität für angewandte Kunst Wien mit Oskar Kokoschka Zentrum, Wien 02980
Sammlung des Ägyptologischen Instituts, Heidelberg 17673
Sammlung Domnick, Nürtingen 19165
Sammlung Dr. Berkowitz, Hannover 17610
Sammlung Dr. Irmgard von Lemmers-Danforth, Wetzlar 20559
Sammlung Ernst Schneider, Düsseldorf 16741
Sammlung Essl - Kunst der Gegenwart, Klosterneuburg 02142
Sammlung Flörl, Hall in Tirol 01994
Sammlung Fossilien des Jura, Lichtenfels, Bayern 18456
Sammlung Friedhof Hörnli, Riehen 37062
Sammlung Friedrichshof, Zurndorf 03056
Sammlung für Papier- und Druckgeschichte, Frankenberg, Sachsen 17028
Sammlung Gauselmann, Espelkamp 16942
Sammlung Geyer-zu-Lauf, Emmendingen 16857
Sammlung Goetz, München 18903
Sammlung handgeschriebener Choralbücher, Kiedrich 18069
Sammlung Hauser und Wirth, Sankt Gallen 37107
Sammlung Heinrich Brechbühl, Steffisburg 37212
Sammlung Herzoglicher Kunstbesitz, Coburg 16485
Sammlung historischer Maschinen und Geräte, Calau 16442
Sammlung historischer Mikroskope von Ernst Leitz, Wetzlar 20560
Sammlung historischer Prägestempel, Wien 02981
Sammlung historischer Tasteninstrumente Neumeyer-Junghanns-Tracey, Bad Krozingen 15684
Sammlung Hoffmann, Berlin 16087
Sammlung im Obersteg, Oberhofen am Thunersee 36999
Sammlung industrielle Gestaltung, Berlin 16088
Sammlung Irmgard Friedl, Bad Griesbach im Rottal 15653
Sammlung Jagdkunde, Graz 01932
Sammlung landwirtschaftlicher Geräte, Unterpleichfeld 20270
Sammlung Ludwig in Bamberg, Bamberg 15815
Sammlung Meinrad Burch-Korrodi, Sarnen 37124
Sammlung Mittelalterliche Kunst in Thüringen, Eisenach 16818
Sammlung Oskar Reinhart 'Am Römerholz', Winterthur 37339
Sammlung Patt, Willisau 37326
Sammlung Prinzhorn, Heidelberg 17674
Sammlung Religiöser Volkskunst, Wien 02982
Sammlung Rosengart Luzern, Luzern 36917
Sammlung Schloß Aichberg, Rohrbach an der Lafnitz 02522
Sammlung Warburg im Planetarium, Hamburg 17565
Sammlungen Burg Bernstein, Bernstein, Burgenland 01735
Sammlungen der Benediktiner-Abtei Braunau, Rohr, Niederbayern 19641
Sammlungen der Burg Hochosterwitz, Launsdorf 02193
Sammlungen der Schule für Gestaltung Basel, Basel 36518
Sammlungen der Stadt Amstetten auf Schloß Ulmerfeld, Ulmerfeld-Hausmening 02750
Sammlungen der Technischen Universität Dresden, Dresden 16706
Sammlungen des Archäologischen Instituts der Universität, Göttingen 17340
Sammlungen des Augustiner Chorherrenstiftes, Sankt Florian 02563
Sammlungen des Instituts für Hochschulkunde der Deutschen Gesellschaft für Hochschulkunde, Würzburg 20704
Sammlungen des Kunstvereins, Ibbenbüren 17875
Sammlungen des Marktamtes, Wien 02983
Sammlungen des Stiftes Sankt Lambrecht, Sankt Lambrecht 02579
Sammlungen des Zisterzienserstiftes Rein, Rein 02503
Sammlungen im Adelmannschloß, Landshut 18311
Sammlungen Schloß Moosham, Mauterndorf 02287
Sammy Marks Museum, Pretoria 34355
Sammy Miller Motorcycle Museum, New Milton 40014
Samobor Museum, Samobor 07767
Samocvety, Moskva 33179
Samoilov Memorial Apartment Museum, Sankt-Peterburg 33418
Samoy Art Museum, Bacoor 31280
Samson-Haus, Leer 18367
Samson V Maritime Museum, New Westminster 05986
Samsun Devlet Güzel Sanatlar Galerisi, Samsun 37777
Samsun State Gallery, Samsun 37777
Samsung Children's Museum, Seoul 27268
Samsung Museum of Publishing, Seoul 27269
Samuel Cupples House, Saint Louis 47137
Samuel Dorsky Museum of Art, New Paltz 45741
Samuel F.B. Morse Historic Site, Poughkeepsie 46677
Samuel Johnson Birthplace Museum, Lichfield 39492
Samuel K. Fox Museum, Dillingham 42948
Samuel P. Harn Museum of Art, Gainesville 43584
Samuel S. Fleisher Art Memorial, Philadelphia 46455
Samvirkemuseet, Gjettum 30512
San Agustin Museum Intramuros, Manila 31397
San Angelo Museum of Fine Arts, San Angelo 47242
San Antonio Abad, Madrid 35063
San Antonio Children's Museum, San Antonio 47258
San Antonio Missions Museum, Jolon 44357
San Antonio Missions Visitor Center, San Antonio 47259
San Antonio Museum of Art, San Antonio 47260
San Bernardino County Museum, Redlands 46824
San Buenaventura Mission Museum, Ventura 48209
San Carlos Cathedral Museum, Monterey 45459
San Diego Aerospace Museum, San Diego 47286
San Diego Automotive Museum, San Diego 47287
San Diego Hall of Champions Sports Museum, San Diego 47288
San Diego Historical Society Museum, San Diego 47289
San Diego Maritime Museum, San Diego 47290
San Diego Mesa College Art Gallery and African Art Collection, San Diego 47291
San Diego Model Railroad Museum, San Diego 47292
San Diego Museum of Art, San Diego 47293
San Diego Museum of Man, San Diego 47294
San Diego Natural History Museum, San Diego 47295
San Diego Viceregal Art Gallery, México 28212
San Dieguito Heritage Museum, Encinitas 43187
San el-Haggar Museum, Sharqiya 09305
San Fernando Historical Museum, Mission Hills 45400
San Francisco African American Historical and Cultural Society Museum, San Francisco 47334
San Francisco Camerawork, San Francisco 47335
San Francisco Fire Department Museum, San Francisco 47336
San Francisco Maritime National Historical Park, San Francisco 47337
San Francisco Museum of Contemporary Hispanic Art, San Francisco 47338
San Francisco Museum of Modern Art, San Francisco 47339
San Gabriel Mission Museum, San Gabriel 47347
San Jacinto Museum, San Jacinto 47348
San Jacinto Museum of History, La Porte 44557
San Joaquin County Historical Museum, Lodi 44843
San Jose Institute of Contemporary Art, San Jose 47355
San Jose Museum of Art, San Jose 47356
San Jose Museum of Quilts and Textiles, San Jose 47357
San Juan Bautista State Historic Park, San Juan Bautista 47359
San Juan County Historical Museum, Silverton 47635
San Juan County Museum, Bloomfield 41735
San Juan Historical Society Museum, Friday Harbor 43561
San Juan Island National Historical Park, Friday Harbor 43562
San Juan National Historic Site, San Juan 32409
San Luis Obispo Art Center, San Luis Obispo 47362
San Luis Obispo County Historical Museum, San Luis Obispo 47363
San Marco Gallery, San Rafael 47376
San Marcos de Apalache Historic State Park, Saint Marks 47141
The San Mateo County Arts Council, Belmont 41608
San Mateo County Historical Museum, Redwood City 46826
San Miguel Mission Church, Santa Fe 47430
San Pedro Museo de Arte, Puebla 28344
Sanandaj Museum, Sanandaj 22277
Sanati Museum, Kerman 22253
Sanchez Adobe Historic Site, Pacifica 46255
Sancta Birgitta Klostermuseum, Vadstena 36368
Sanctuary Wood Museum - Hill 62, Zillebeke 03853
Sand Bakkens Medisinske Museum, Flekkefjord 30496
Sand Springs Cultural and Historical Museum, Sand Springs 47378
Sandal Castle, Sandal 40440
Sandauer Heimatstube, Arzberg, Oberfranken 15516
Sande Historielags Bygdesamlinger, Sande 30821
Sandefjord Bymuseum, Sandefjord 30823
Sandefjord Maritime Museum, Sandefjord 30824
Sandefjord Sjøfartsmuseum, Sandefjord 30824
Sandefjord Town Museum, Sandefjord 30823
Sandefjordmuseene, Sandefjord 30825
Sandellmuseet, Ramkvilla 36160
Sandelsches Museum, Kirchberg an der Jagst 18087
Sandgate and District Historical Museum, Sandgate 01443
Sandnesmuseet, Sandnes 30826
Sandon Museum, New Denver 05975
The Sandor Teszler Gallery, Spartanburg 47717
Sandown Historical Museum, Sandown 47381
Sandpoint Lighthouse, Escanaba 43206
Sandringham House Museum, Sandringham 40445
Sands-Willets House, Port Washington 46611
Sandsteinmuseum Kloster Cornberg, Cornberg 16496
Sandtoft Transport Centre, Doncaster 38744
Sandtorg Bygdetun, Sørvik 30871
Sanduo Tang Museum, Taigu 07256
Sandvikens Konsthall, Sandviken 36180
Sandwich Glass Museum, Sandwich 47388
Sandwich Historical Society Museum, Center Sandwich 42168
Sandwich Historical Society Museum, Sandwich 47385
Sandy Bay Historical Museums, Rockport 46970
Sandy Spring Museum, Sandy Spring 47392
Sanford Museum, Cherokee 42274
Sanford Museum, Sanford 47394
Sangerberger Heimatstube, Regenstauf 19535
Sangji Vocational College Museum, Andong 27130
Sangli State Museum, Sangli 22009
Sangre de Cristo Arts Center and Buell Children's Museum, Pueblo 46741
Sanilac County Historical Museum, Port Sanilac 46603
Sanin Historical Collection, Yonago 27029
Sanitärmuseum, Wien 02984
Sanitätsmuseum, Großpösna 17436
Sanjay Sharma Museum, Jaipur, Rajasthan 21864
Sanjusangendo, Kyoto 26452
Sankei-en Garden, Yokohama 27017
Sankt-Annen-Museum und Kunsthalle, Lübeck 18542
Sankt Marien, Müntzergedenkstätte, Mühlhausen, Thüringen 18810
Sankt Matthäus-Kirche im Kulturforum, Berlin 16089
Sankt Patrokli-Dom-Museum Soest, Soest 19980
Sankt-Peterburgskij Muzej Chleba, Sankt-Peterburg 33480
Sankt-Peterburgskij Muzej Teatralnogo i Musykalnogo Iskusstva, Sankt-Peterburg 33481
Sankt-Peterburgskij Muzej V.V. Nabokova, Sankt-Peterburg 33482
Sankta Karins Kyrkoruin, Visby 36417
Şanlıurfa Devlet Güzel Sanatlar Galerisi, Şanlıurfa 37778
Şanlıurfa State Gallery, Şanlıurfa 37778
Sannidal Bygdetun, Sannidal 30828
Sannomiya Local Museum, Isehara 26256
Sano Art Museum, Mishima 26497
Sanquhar Tolbooth Museum, Sanquhar 40449
Santa Ana College Art Gallery, Santa Ana 47401
Santa Barbara Contemporary Arts Forum, Santa Barbara 47402
Santa Barbara Historical Museum, Santa Barbara 47403
Santa Barbara Museum of Art, Santa Barbara 47404
Santa Barbara Museum of Natural History, Santa Barbara 47405
Santa Cruz Art League Museum, Santa Cruz 47413
Santa Cruz Museum of Natural History, Santa Cruz 47414
Santa Fe Children's Museum, Santa Fe 47431
Santa Fe Community Museum, Santa Fe 31443
Santa Fe Gallery, Gainesville 43585
Santa Fe Trail Museum, Larned 44656
Santa Fe Trail Museum, Trinidad 48065
Santa Fe Trail Museums of Gray County, Ingalls 44236
Santa Giulia - Museo della Città, Brescia 23210
Santa Maria Museum of Flight, Santa Maria 47436
Santa Maria Valley Historical Society Museum, Santa Maria 47437
Santa Monica Museum of Art, Santa Monica 47442
Santa Rosa Junior College Art Gallery, Santa Rosa 47447
Santarella Museum and Gardens, Tyringham 48133
Santiago do Cacém Museu Municipal, Santiago do Cacém 32342
Santiaoshi History Museum, Tianjin 07262
Santo Niño Shrine and Heritage Museum, Tacloban 31454
Santuario Casa Santa Caterina, Siena 25579
Santuario de Nuestra Senora de Guadalupe, Santa Fe 47432
Santuario della Beata Vergine della Salute, Solarolo 25595
Santuario Eucaristico, Bolsena 23149
Sanuki Folk Art Museum, Takamatsu 26790
Sanying Pagoda and Museum of Dinosaur, Shaoguan 07230
Sapper Museum, Koria 09690
Sapporo Art Park Museum, Sapporo 26717
Sapporo Geijutsu no Mori Bijutsukan, Sapporo 26717
Sapporo Science Center, Sapporo 26718
Sapporo Sculpture Museum, Sapporo 26719
Sapporo Waterworks Memorial Museum, Sapporo 26720
Sapporo Winter Sports Museum, Sapporo 26721
Sapulpa Historical Museum, Sapulpa 47449
Sapumal Foundation Gallery, Colombo 35752
Sara Hildén Art Museum, Tampere 10084
Sara Hildénin Taidemuseo, Tampere 10084
Sarafkina Kašta Gradski Bit, Veliko Tărnovo 04921
Sarah Campbell Blaffer Foundation, Houston 44136
Sarah Campbell Blaffer Gallery, Houston 44137
Sarah Moody Gallery of Art, Tuscaloosa 48117
Sarah Orne Jewett House, South Berwick 47686
Sarah Spurgeon Gallery, Ellensburg 43152
Sarah Vaughan Museum, Sioux Lookout 06458
Sarakatsani Folklore Museum, Serres 21152
Sarasota Classic Car Museum, Sarasota 47454
Sarat Smriti Granthagar, Panitras 21974
Saratoga Museum, Saratoga 47458
Saratoga National Historical Park, Stillwater 47812
Saratoga Springs Museum, Saratoga Springs 47462
Saratov Museum of Ethnography, Saratov 33509
Saratov Museum of Local History, Nature and Culture, Saratov 33511
Saratov Museum of the Glory of the Fighters, Saratov 33510
Saratovskij Ėtnografičeskij Muzej, Saratov 33509
Saratovskij Gosudarstvennyj Muzej Boevoj Slavy, Saratov 33510
Saratovskij Kraevedčeskij Muzej, Saratov 33511
Sarawak Police Museum, Kuching 27657
Sarawak State Museum, Kuching 27658
Sarcee People's Museum, Calgary 05179
Sardar Patel University Museum, Vallabhvidyanagar 22053
Sardar Vallabhbhai Patel Museum, Surat 22030
Sarehole Mill, Birmingham 38227
Sargent House Museum, Gloucester 43705
Sarguinetti Century House Museum, Yuma 48818
Saris Museum, Bardejov 33952
Šarišská Galéria, Prešov 34048
Šarišské Múzeum, Bardejov 33952
Sarjeant Gallery - Te Whare o Rehua, Wanganui 30285
Sárközi Népművészeti Tájház, Decs 21401
Sarnia Public Library and Art Gallery, Sarnia 06392
Sárospataki Református Kollégium Tudományos Gyűjteményei Múzeum, Sárospatak 21526
Sarpy County Historical Museum, Bellevue 41594
Sarrat Museum, Sarrat 31446
Sasebo Culture and Science Museum, Sasebo 26725
Sasebo-shi Bunka Kagakukan, Sasebo 26725
Saskatchewan Arts Board Collection, Regina 06244
Saskatchewan Baseball Hall of Fame and Museum, Battleford 05062
Saskatchewan Craft Gallery, Saskatoon 06405
Saskatchewan Military Museum, Regina 06245
Saskatchewan Pharmacy Museum, Regina 06246
Saskatchewan River Valley Museum, Hague 05540
Saskatchewan Science Centre, Regina 06247
Saskatchewan Sports Hall of Fame and Museum, Regina 06248
Saskatchewan Western Development Museum, Yorkton 06873

Saskatchewan Wildlife Federation Museum, North Battleford 06015
Satakunnan Museo, Pori 09947
Satakunta Museum, Building Heritage House Toivo and The Home of the Korsman Family, Pori 09945
The Satirical World Art Museum, Waco 48267
Satiricum, Greiz 17393
Sato Art Museum Toyama, Toyama 26967
Satrosphere, Aberdeen 37944
Satterlee Clark House, Horicon 44103
Satu Mare District Museum, Satu Mare 32587
Sauda Museum, Sauda 30832
Sauerland-Museum, Arnsberg 15512
Saugus Iron Works, Saugus 47466
Sauk County Historical Museum, Baraboo 41502
Sauk Prairie Area Historical Society Museum, Prairie du Sac 46685
Saukkojärven Kotiseutu- ja Koulumuseo, Ranua 09979
Saukkojärvi Local and School Museum, Ranua 09979
Sault de Sainte Marie Historical Sites, Sault Sainte Marie 47469
Sault Sainte Marie Museum, Sault Sainte Marie 06413
Saunders County Historical Museum, Wahoo 48273
Saunders Memorial Museum, Berryville 41656
Saurier-Museum, Frick 36721
Sauriermuseum Aathal, Aathal-Seegräben 36431
Saurierpark, Traismauer 02734
Sautee-Nacoochee Museum, Sautee 47475
Sauvon Kotiseutumuseo, Sauvo 10023
Sauwald-Heimathaus, Sankt Roman 02606
Sava Filaretov House-Museum, Žeravna 04935
Savannah College of Art and Design Galleries, Savannah 47483
Savaria Múzeum, Szombathely 21587
Savenvalajamuseo, Somero 10048
Savez Muzejskih Društva Hrvatske, Zagreb 49126
Savings Banks Museum, Ruthwell 40362
Savio-museet, Kirkenes 30594
Savitsky Picture Gallery of Penza, Penza 33293
Savon Radan Museo, Pieksämäki 09926
Savonlinna Art Gallery, Savonlinna 10027
Savonlinna Provincial Museum, Savonlinna 10026
Savonlinnan Maakuntamuseo, Savonlinna 10026
Savonlinnan Taidemuseo, Savonlinna 10027
Savremena Galerija Umetničke Kolonije Ečka, Zrenjanin 33933
Savupirttimuseo, Kuopio 09723
SAW Gallery, Ottawa 06085
Sawanworanayok National Museum, Sukhothai 37540
Sawhill Gallery, Duke Hall, Harrisonburg 43931
Sawin Memorial Building, Dover 42971
Sawyer's Sandhills Museum, Valentine 48184
Saxtead Green Post Mill, Saxtead 40452
Sayansk Picture Gallery, Sajansk 33363
Sayner Gießhalle, Bendorf, Rhein 15876
Sayville Historical Society Museum, Sayville 47490
Sayward-Wheeler House, York Harbor 48797
Scadding Cabin, Toronto 06609
Scalamandre Archives, Long Island City 44871
Scalloway Museum, Scalloway 40453
Scanderbeg Museum, Kruja 00028
Scandinavia House, New York 45867
Scandinavian Museum Association, Icelandic Section, Reykjavik 49234
Scantic Academy Museum, East Windsor 43064
Scapa Flow Museum, Hoy 39271
Scaplen's Court Museum, Poole 40229
Scarborough Art Gallery, Scarborough 40456
Scarborough Historical Museum, Scarborough 06414
Scarborough Historical Museum, Scarborough 47491
Scarfone and Hartley Galleries, Tampa 47944
Scarsdale Historical Society Museum, Scarsdale 47492
Scavi Archeologici di Velia, Ascea 22945
Scavi di Ercolano, Ercolano 23737
Scavi di Oplontis, Torre Annunziata 25769
Scavi di Ostia, Ostia Antica 24716
Scavi di Pompei, Pompei 24987
Scavi di Stabiae, Castellammare di Stabia 23402
Scavi e Museo Archeologico di S. Restituta, Napoli 24608
The Scein-Joseph International Museum of Ceramic Art, Alfred 41137
Schaár Erzsébet Gyüjtemény, Székesfehérvár 21560
Schack-Galerie, München 18904
Schäfertanz-Kabinett, Rothenburg ob der Tauber 19682
Schaeffer House Museum, Grafton 01072
Schaffhauser Weinbaumuseum, Hallau 36791
Schamser Talmuseum, Zillis 37362
Schatkamer Sint Lambertuskerk, Horst 29450
Schatkamer Sint Walburgis Basiliek, Arnhem 28944
Schatkamer van de Basiliek van Onze Lieve Vrouwe, Maastricht 29571
Schatkamer van de Kathedrale Basiliek Sint-Bavo, Haarlem 29329
Schatkamer van de Sint-Salvatorskathedraal, Brugge 03266
Schatkamer van de Sint-Servaasbasiliek, Maastricht 29572
De Schatkamer van de Ouze-Lieve-Vrouwekerk, Sint-Truiden 03752
Schattenburg Feldkirch, Feldkirch 01831
Schattleitenmühle, Garsten 01870
Schatz von Sankt Johann, Osnabrück 19284
Schatzhaus in der Lausitz, Göda 17311
Schatzkammer, Altötting 15465
Schatzkammer, Frauenkirchen 01847
Schatzkammer der Basilika Sankt Ludgerus, Essen 16963
Schatzkammer der Evangelisch-Lutherischen Sankt Andreaskirche, Weißenburg in Bayern 20495
Schatzkammer der Kath. Pfarrkirche Sankt Servatius, Siegburg 19944
Schatzkammer der Residenz München, München 18905
Schatzkammer der Wallfahrtskirche, Hohenpeißenberg 17810
Schatzkammer der Wallfahrtskirche Maria Dreieichen, Stockern 02700
Schatzkammer der Wallfahrtskirche Maria Schutz, Maria Schutz am Semmering 02271
Schatzkammer des Münsters, Reichenau, Baden 19543
Schatzkammer Grafenrheinfeld, Grafenrheinfeld 17373
Schatzkammer Kloster Sankt Marienstern, Panschwitz-Kuckau 19343
Schatzkammer - Turmmuseum der Pfarrkirche, Sankt Wolfgang im Salzkammergut 02621
Schatzturm zu Schwyz, Schwyz 37152
Schaubergwerk Barbarastollen, Leogang 02213
Schaubergwerk Büchenberg, Elbingerode, Harz 16829
Schaubergwerk Grillenberg, Payerbach 02394
Schaubergwerk Hochfeld, Neukirchen am Großvenediger 02344
Schaubergwerk Kupferplatte, Jochberg 02090
Schaubergwerk Seegrotte, Hinterbrühl 02029
Schaubergwerk Teufelsgrund, Münstertal 18954
Schaubergwerk und Heimatmuseum der Gemeinde Arzberg, Passail 02392
Schaubergwerk Zum Tiefen Molchner Stolln, Pobershau 19422
Schaudenkmal Gaszentrale, Unterwellenborn 20271
Schauglashütte, Uetendorf 37259
Schaulager, Münchenstein 36966
Schaumuseum Alte Huf-und Wagenschmiede, Gmünd, Niederösterreich 01892
Schauräume im Glockenturm, Graz 01933
Schauraum, Eggenfelden 16788
Schauraum über Geschichte und Brauchtum, Weitensfeld im Gurktal 02806
Schauwerkstatt Historische Handweberei, Oederan 19224
Scheepswerf De Delft, Rotterdam 29774
Scheepvaartmuseum, Baasrode 03194
Scheepvaartmuseum, Bornem 03230
Scheepvaartmuseum, Gasselternijveen 29264
Schefflenztal-Sammlungen, Schefflenz 19769
Scheldemuseum de Notelaer, Bornem 03231
Schelmenturm, Monheim am Rhein 18786
Schelpen Museum, Zaamslag 30031
Schenectady County Historical Society Museum, Schenectady 47497
Schenectady Museum, Schenectady 47498
Schepenzaal Stadhuis, Zwolle 30085
Scherjon's Klompenmakerij en Museum, Noardburgum 29639
Schick Art Gallery, Saratoga Springs 47463
Schiefer- und Ziegelmuseum Dörfles-Esbach, Dörfles-Esbach 16630
Schiefermuseum, Ludwigsstadt 18530
Schiele Museum of Natural History, Gastonia 43632
Schiffahrts- und Schiffbaumuseum, Wörth am Main 20643
Schiffahrtsmuseum, Spitz 02671
Schiffahrtsmuseum auf dem Traditionsschiff, Rostock 19667
Schiffahrtsmuseum der Oldenburgischen Weserhäfen, Brake, Unterweser 16271
Schiffahrtsmuseum mit Nordseeaquarium Nordseeheilbad Langeoog, Langeoog 18339
Schiffahrtsmuseum Nordfriesland, Husum, Nordsee 17871
Schifferstadt Architectural Museum, Frederick 43530
Schifffahrt Museum, Düsseldorf 16742
Schifffahrtsmuseum Haren (Ems), Haren 17619
Schifffahrtsmuseum Rostock, Rostock 19668
Schiffleutmuseum, Stadl-Paura 02672
Schiffmühle Höfgen, Grimma 17403
Schiffs- und Marinemuseum, Senden, Westfalen 19937
Schiffsmuseum Seitenradschleppdampfer "Württemberg", Magdeburg 18587
Schilder- en Bakkerijmuseum 't Steenhuis, Niebert 29612
Schilderijenzaal Prins Willem V, Den Haag 29123
Schiller-Museum, Bauerbach 15830
Schiller-Nationalmuseum und Deutsches Literaturarchiv, Marbach am Neckar 18619
Schillerhäuschen, Dresden 16707
Schillerhaus, Leipzig 18415
Schillerhaus, Ludwigshafen am Rhein 18520
Schillerhaus, Goethe-Nationalmuseum, Weimar, Thüringen 20471
Schillers Gartenhaus der Friedrich-Schiller-Universität, Jena 17950
Schillers Geburtshaus, Marbach am Neckar 18620
Schingoethe Center for Native American Cultures, Aurora 41398
Schirn Kunsthalle Frankfurt, Frankfurt am Main 17071
Schleifmühle Schwerin, Schwerin 19898
Schleimuseum, Kappeln 17984
Schlepper-, Auto- und Gerätemuseum Hesse, Aidhausen 15411
Schlesisch-Oberlausitzer Dorfmuseum, Markersdorf bei Görlitz 18636
Schlesisches Museum zu Görlitz, Görlitz 17325
Schleswig-Holsteinisches Freilichtmuseum, Molfsee 18783
Schleswig-Holsteinisches Landwirtschaftsmuseum und Dithmarscher Bauernhaus, Meldorf 18696
Schliekau-Museum, Bad Bevensen 15614
Schlösschen Borghees, Emmerich 16862
Schlößchen Vorder Bleichenberg Biberist, Biberist 36562
Schloß, Jegenstorf 36819
Schloss Achberg, Achberg 15390
Schloss Agathenburg, Agathenburg 15400
Schloß Ambras, Innsbruck 02079
Schloß Arolsen, Bad Arolsen 15592
Schloß Augustusburg, Brühl, Rheinland 16379
Schloß Baldern, Bopfingen 16254
Schloß Berleburg, Bad Berleburg 15610
Schloß Brake - Das Weserrenaissance-Museum, Lemgo 18431
Schloss Braunfels, Braunfels 16288
Schloß Bruchsal, Bruchsal 16369
Schloß Bürgeln, Schliengen 19800
Schloß Burgau, Burgau 01756
Schloss Cappenberg, Selm 19935
Schloss Dottenwil, Wittenbach 37347
Schloss Drachenburg, Königswinter 18184
Schloß Egg, Bernried, Niederbayern 16128
Schloß Eggenberg, Graz 01934
Schloss Ehrenburg, Coburg 16486
Schloß Ettersburg, Ettersburg 16973
Schloß Faber-Castell, Stein, Mittelfranken 20040
Schloß Falkenlust, Brühl, Rheinland 16380
Schloß Farrach, Zeltweg 03053
Schloß Favorite, Rastatt 19489
Schloß Friedberg, Volders 02771
Schloss Glienicke, Berlin 16090
Schloß Groß Leuthen, Groß Leuthen 17417
Schloss Großkühnau - Verwaltung, Dessau 16582
Schloss Güstrow, Güstrow 17458
Schloß Hämelschenburg, Emmerthal 16864
Schloß Hallwyl, Seengen 37157
Schloss Harburg, Harburg 17615
Schloss Hegi, Winterthur 37340
Schloß Heidelberg, Heidelberg 17675
Schloß Heiligenberg, Heiligenberg, Baden 17693
Schloß Heubach, Heubach, Württemberg 17749
Schloß Höchstädt, Höchstädt an der Donau 17780
Schloss Hof und Schloss Niederweiden, Engelhartstetten 01815
Schloß Hohenschwangau, Schwangau 19877
Schloss Hundisburg-Sammlung Apel, Hundisburg 17864
Schloss Johannisburg mit Schlossgarten, Aschaffenburg 15529
Schloß Kochberg mit Liebhabertheater, Großkochberg 17432
Schloß Leitzkau, Leitzkau 18427
Schloß Lichtenstein, Lichtenstein, Württemberg 18459
Schloß Linderhof, Ettal 16972
Schloß Loosdorf mit Prunkräumen und Zinnfigurensammlung, Loosdorf, Bez. Mistelbach 02253
Schloss Ludwigsburg, Ludwigsburg, Württemberg 18513
Schloss Ludwigslust, Ludwigslust 18527
Schloß Lustheim, Oberschleißheim 19205
Schloß Mannheim, Mannheim 18616
Schloß Marienburg, Pattensen 19361
Schloß Miltach, Miltach 18739
Schloß Mörsburg, Stadel (Winterthur) 37199
Schloß Moosham, Tamsweg 02712
Schloss Mosigkau, Dessau 16583
Schloß Naudersberg, Nauders 02338
Schloss Neuburg, Neuburg an der Donau 19018
Schloss Neuhardenberg, Neuhardenberg 19031
Schloß Neunhof, Nürnberg 19158
Schloß Neuschwanstein, Schwangau 19878
Schloss Oranienbaum, Oranienbaum 19263
Schloß Peigarten, Dobersberg 01766
Schloß Pfaueninsel, Berlin 16091
Schloss Pöllau, Pöllau 02431
Schloß Reinbek, Reinbek 19551
Schloß Rheinsberg, Rheinsberg 19592
Schloß Rosenau, Rödental 19630
Schloss Salem, Salem, Baden 19733
Schloß Sargans, Sargans 37120
Schloß Schallaburg, Loosdorf, Bez. Melk 02251
Schloß Schönbrunn, Wien 02985
Schloß Schwetzingen, Schwetzingen 19905
Schloß Seehof, Memmelsdorf 18703
Schloß Solitude, Stuttgart 20104
Schloß Spiez, Spiez 37193
Schloß Strünkede, Herne 17729
Schloß Tarasp, Tarasp 37229
Schloß Thunstetten, Thunstetten 37245
Schloß Trachselwald, Trachselwald 37250
Schloß Tratzberg mit Sammlungen, Jenbach 02087
Schloss Trebsen, Trebsen 20196
Schloß- und Goldbergbaumuseum, Großkirchheim 01954
Schloß und Gurschner Museum, Pram 02446
Schloss und Hofgarten Dachau, Dachau 16526
Schloss- und Kirche Sankt Bartholomä, Berchtesgaden 15888
Schloß und Park Schönbusch, Aschaffenburg 15530
Schloß und Schloßpark Bad Homburg, Bad Homburg v.d.Höhe 15667
Schloss und Schlosspark Charlottenburg mit Schinkelpavillon, Belvedere und Mausoleum, Berlin 16092
Schloß und Schloßpark Wilhelmsthal, Calden 16445
Schloß- und Spielkartenmuseum, Altenburg, Thüringen 15452
Schloß Unteraufseß, Aufseß 15548
Schloß Urbach, Urbach 20272
Schloß Veitshöchheim, Veitshöchheim 20292
Schloß Vianden, Vianden 27580
Schloß Villa Ludwigshöhe mit Max-Slevogt-Galerie, Edenkoben 16780
Schloß vor Husum, Husum, Nordsee 17872
Schloß Weikersheim, Weikersheim 20431
Schloß Weissenstein, Pommersfelden 19427
Schloß Werdenberg, Werdenberg 37311
Schloß Wernigerode, Wernigerode 20529
Schloß Wetzdorf-Fichtl, Kleinwetzdorf 02137
Schloß Weyer, Gmunden 01897
Schloss Wiederau, Pegau 19365
Schloß Wildegg, Wildegg 37323
Schloß Wilflingen, Langenenslingen 18333
Schloss Wörlitz und Englisches Landhaus, Wörlitz 20642
Schloß Wolfstein mit Jagd- und Fischereimuseum und Galerie Wolfstein, Freyung 17134
Schloss Wolkenburg, Wolkenburg-Kaufungen 20669
Schloßausstellung, Dresden 16708
Schloßbergmuseum, Chemnitz 16472
Schloßgalerie Kastenscheuer, Eberdingen 16761
Schloßgalerie Mondseeland, Mondsee 02323
Schloßmuseum, Arnstadt 15514
Schloßmuseum, Bad Bentheim 15601
Schlossmuseum, Bad Iburg 15670
Schlossmuseum, Burgdorf 36608
Schloßmuseum, Ellwangen 16836
Schloßmuseum, Erbach, Donau 16886
Schloßmuseum, Gotha 17363
Schloßmuseum, Haitzendorf 01989
Schloßmuseum, Herberstein 02022
Schloßmuseum, Höchstädt, Oberfranken 17781
Schloßmuseum, Kirchberg an der Jagst 18088
Schlossmuseum, Kirchentellinsfurt 18091
Schloßmuseum, Kronburg 18248
Schloßmuseum, Krummennaab 18252
Schlossmuseum, Langenburg 18332
Schlossmuseum, Linz 02241
Schloßmuseum, Oberhofen am Thunersee 37000
Schloßmuseum, Ortenburg 19271
Schloßmuseum, Quedlinburg 19464
Schloßmuseum, Schrozberg 19855
Schlossmuseum, Schwerin 19899
Schloßmuseum, Sigharting 02662
Schloßmuseum, Texing 02725
Schloßmuseum, Weimar, Thüringen 20472
Schloßmuseum Amerang, Amerang 15483
Schloßmuseum Aulendorf-Kunst des Klassizismus-Altes Spielzeug, Aulendorf 15575
Schlossmuseum Darmstadt, Darmstadt 16548
Schloßmuseum der Stadt Aschaffenburg, Aschaffenburg 15531
Schloßmuseum Heidegg, Gelfingen 36723
Schloßmuseum Hohenlohe-Schillingsfürst, Schillingsfürst 19780
Schloßmuseum Hubertusburg, Wermsdorf 20523
Schloßmuseum Ismaning, Ismaning 17928
Schloßmuseum Jagsthausen, Jagsthausen 17936
Schlossmuseum Jever, Jever 17957
Schloßmuseum Landeck, Landeck 02180
Schloßmuseum Mespelbrunn, Mespelbrunn 18717
Schlossmuseum mit Bauernkriegsmuseum, Oberösterreichischer Landeskrippe und Georg-von-Peuerbach-Ausstellung, Peuerbach 02411
Schloßmuseum mit Brüder-Grimm-Gedenkstätte, Steinau an der Straße 20044
Schloßmuseum Murnau, Murnau 18962
Schloßmuseum Niederleis, Niederleis 02360
Schlossmuseum Oranienburg, Oranienburg 19266
Schlossmuseum Reckahn, Reckahn 19511
Schloßmuseum Rimpar, Rimpar 19615
Schlossmuseum Sondershausen, Sondershausen 19996
Schloßmuseum Thun, Thun 37241
Schlossmuseum und Königliches Schloss, Berchtesgaden 15889
Schloßmuseum Warthausen, Warthausen 20405
Schlossmuseum Weitra, Weitra 02808
Schloßpark Tiefurt, Weimar, Thüringen 20473
Schloßparkmuseum, Bad Kreuznach 15682
Schlüsselburg Fortress Oreshek, Šlisselburg 33526
Schlumberger Wein- und Sektkellerei, Wien 02986
Schmalspurbahn-Museum, Frojach 01857
Schmelenhaus Museum, Windhoek 28783
Schmidt House Museum, Grants Pass 43768
Schmiede Burg Schlitz, Burg Schlitz 16412
Schmiede im Hammergraben, Helfenberg 02018
Schmiedemuseum, Fulpmes 01860
Schmiedemuseum, Hatten, Oldenburg 17632
Schmiedemuseum, Hohen Demzin 17804
Schmiedemuseum, Lölling 02249
Schmiedemuseum Arfeld, Bad Berleburg 15611
Schmiedemuseum Bremecker Hammer, Lüdenscheid 18550
Schmiedemuseum Kirchlauter, Kirchlauter 18099
Schminck Memorial Museum, Lakeview 44607
Schmuckmuseum Gablonzer Industrie, Enns 01819

Schmuckmuseum Pforzheim im Reuchlinhaus, Pforzheim 19389
Schnapsmuseum, Kötzting 18193
Schnarch-Museum Alfeld, Alfeld, Leine 15429
Schnauferlstall, Ruhpolding 19718
Schneider Museum of Art, Ashland 41296
Schnopfhagen-Stüberl, Oberneukirchen 02373
Schnupftabakmuseum, Grafenau, Niederbayern 17368
Schocken Institute of Jewish Research, Jerusalem 22661
Schöffer Museum, Kalocsa 21437
Schoellkopf Geological Museum, Niagara Falls 45951
Schoemansdal Museum, Louis Trichardt 34302
Schönberg-Haus in Mödling, Mödling 02314
Schoenbrunn Village State Memorial, New Philadelphia 45742
Schönbuch Museum, Dettenhausen 16593
Schoharie Colonial Heritage Association Museum, Schoharie 47500
Schoharie Crossing, Fort Hunter 43400
Schokoland Alprose, Caslano 36615
SchokoMuseum in SchokoLand, Peine 19367
Scholte House Museum, Pella 46330
Scholz Park Museum, Riverton 01417
Schomburg Center for Research in Black Culture, New York 45868
School Books Museum, Salt 27068
School Marine Museum, Bolesławiec 31508
School Museum, Littoinen 09790
School Museum, Munsala 09841
School Museum, Nukari 09870
School Museum, Somero 10046
School Museum, Trjavna 04889
School Museum, Yttilä 10220
School Museum of Helsinki City Museum, Helsinki 09504
School Museum of the Visually Handicapped, Jyväskylä 09596
School of Art and Art History Gallery, Denver 42899
School of Art Gallery, Baton Rouge 41535
School of Art - Gallery, Bozeman 41859
School of Art Gallery and Museum, Aberystwyth 37956
School of Earth Sciences Museum, Townsville 01548
School of Fine Arts Gallery, Bloomington 41748
School of Nations Museum, Elsah 43172
School of Political and Social Inquiry Museum, Clayton 00924
School of the Art Institute of Chicago Gallery, Chicago 42362
Schoolhouse Museum, Ridgewood 46899
Schoolmuseum Michel Thiery, Gent 03449
Schooltijd Schoolmuseum, Terneuzen 29866
Schoonewelle, Zwartsluis 30080
Schoonhovens Edelambachtshuys, Schoonhoven 29814
De Schotse Huizen, Veere 29932
Schott GlasMuseum, Jena 17951
Schraube Museum, Halberstadt 17503
Schreibmaschinen-Museum, Pfäffikon (Zürich) 37022
Schreibmaschinenmuseum Baggenstos, Wallisellen 37303
Schreinereimuseum, Ibach 36812
Schreinermuseum, Altishofen 36451
Schreinermuseum, Ettiswil 36697
Schrift- und Heimatmuseum Bartlhaus, Pettenbach 02410
Schriftmuseum J.A. Dortmond, Amsterdam 28900
Schubert Geburtshaus und Adalbert Stifter-Gedenkräume, Wien 02987
Schubert Sterbewohnung, Wien 02988
Schüttesägemuseum, Schiltach 19783
Schützenhaus Glaucha, Halle, Saale 17520
Schützenmuseum der Königlich privilegierten Feuerschützengesellschaft Weilheim, Weilheim, Oberbayern 20449
Schützenscheibenmuseum, Scheibbs 02630
Schützenscheibensammlung, Mainbernheim 18593
Schulgeschichtliche Sammlung, Magdeburg 18588
Schulgeschichtliche Sammlung Bremen, Bremen 16333
Schulgeschichtliche Sammlung im Main-Taunus-Kreis, Kriftel 18240
Schulheimatmuseum, Asbach-Bäumenheim 15518
Schulhistorische Sammlung Cruismannschule, Bochum 16200
Schullandheim Sassen, Sassen, Vorpommern 19760
Schulmuseum, Bad Kissingen 15675
Schulmuseum, Hundisburg 17865
Schulmuseum, Neumark 19044
Schulmuseum Bergisch Gladbach, Bergisch Gladbach 15900
Schulmuseum des Bezirkes Urfahr-Umgebung, Bad Leonfelden 01714
Schulmuseum des Bezirks Unterfranken, Bad Bocklet 15616
Schulmuseum Friedrichshafen am Bodensee, Friedrichshafen 17148
Schulmuseum Fronau, Roding 19626
Schulmuseum Lilienthal, Lilienthal 18467
Schulmuseum Mozartschule Rheingönheim, Ludwigshafen am Rhein 18521
Schulmuseum Nordwürttemberg in Kornwestheim, Kornwestheim 18212
Schulmuseum Nürnberg im Museum Industriekultur, Nürnberg 19159
Schulmuseum Steinhorst, Steinhorst, Niedersachsen 20052
Schulmuseum und Hallenhaus, Middelhagen, Rügen 18734
Schulmuseum Vechelde, Vechelde 20289
Schulmuseum - Werkstatt für Schulgeschichte Leipzig, Leipzig 18416
Schulmuseum Wildenhain, Wildenhain bei Großenhain, Sachsen 20587
Schulstub'n-Glockenhäusl, Sankt Peter am Wimberg 02598
Schultehuis, Diever 29155
Schulze-Delitzsch-Haus, Delitzsch 16565
Schumacher Gallery, Columbus 42592
Schumann-Haus, Leipzig 18417
Schunkelhaus, Obercunnersdorf 19171
Schutterskamer, Sneek 29840
Schuyler County Historical Society Museum, Montour Falls 45475
Schuyler-Hamilton House, Morristown 45510
Schuyler Jail Museum, Rushville 47030
Schuyler Mansion, Albany 41086
Schwäbisches Bauern- und Technikmuseum, Eschach 16930
Schwäbisches Bauernhofmuseum Illerbeuren, Kronburg 18249
Schwäbisches Handwerkermuseum, Augsburg 15567
Schwäbisches Krippenmuseum im Jesuitenkolleg, Mindelheim 18743
Schwäbisches Schnapsmuseum, Bönnigheim 16218
Schwäbisches Schützenmuseum, Kronburg 18250
Schwäbisches Turmuhrenmuseum, Mindelheim 18744
Schwäbisches Volkskundemuseum und Bauernhofmuseum Staudenhaus, Gessertshausen 17270
Schwälmer Dorfmuseum, Schrecksbach 19849
Schwartz Collection of Skiing Heritage, Tiburon 48004
Schwartz Heritage House, Altona 04983
Schwartzsche Villa, Berlin 16093
Schwarz-Afrika-Museum, Vilshofen 20326
Schwarzachtaler Heimatmuseum, Neunburg vorm Wald 19049
Schwarzenberger Skulpturenpark, Schwarzenberg am Böhmerwald 02644
Schwarzwälder Freilichtmuseum Vogtsbauernhof, Gutach, Schwarzwaldbahn 17467
Schwarzwälder Mineralienmuseum, Neubulach 19016
Schwarzwälder Mühlenmuseum, Grafenhausen 17372
Schwarzwälder Trachtenmuseum, Haslach 17627
Schwarzwald-Museum, Triberg 20203
Schwazer Silberbergwerk, Schwaz 02650
Schwedenspeicher-Museum, Stade 20026
Schweine-Museum, Bad Wimpfen 15774
Schweinfurth Memorial Art Center, Auburn 41374
Schweizer Filmmuseum, Basel 36519
Schweizer Jazzmuseum, Uster 37271
Schweizer Kamm-Museum, Mümliswil 36962
Schweizer Kindermuseum, Baden 36489
Schweizer Museum für Wild und Jagd, Utzenstorf 37273
Schweizerische Landesbibliothek, Bern 36550
Schweizerische Theatersammlung, Bern 36551
Schweizerisches Alpines Museum, Bern 36552
Schweizerisches Dampfmaschinenmuseum Vaporama, Thun 37242
Schweizerisches Feuerwehrmuseum, Basel 36520
Schweizerisches Freilichtmuseum für ländliche Kultur, Brienz, Bern 36587
Schweizerisches Gastronomie-Museum, Thun 37243
Schweizerisches Meteoriten-und Mineralienmuseum, Schönenwerd 37143
Schweizerisches Museum für Landwirtschaft und Agrartechnik Burgrain, Alberswil 36444
Schweizerisches Schützenmuseum, Bern 36553
Schweizerisches Sportmuseum, Basel 36521
Schweizerisches Zentrum für Volkskultur, Burgdorf 36609
Schwemmgut-Museum, Finsing 17003
Schwenkfelder Library and Heritage Center, Pennsburg 46341
Schwerkolt Cottage Museum, Mitcham 01260
Schwules Museum, Berlin 16094
Schwurgerichtssaal 600, Nürnberg 19160
Sci-Port Discovery Center, Shreveport 47617
Sci-Tech Center of Northern New York, Watertown 48443
Science Activity Centre, Sirsa 22027
Science Activity Corner, Gwalior 21831
Science and Industry Collections Group, London 49441
Science and Technology Museum of Atlanta, Atlanta 41358
Science Center, Trollhättan 36335
Science Center of Connecticut, West Hartford 48529
Science Center of Iowa, Des Moines 42910
Science Center of Pinellas County, Saint Petersburg 47177
Science Center of Thessaloniki and Technology Museum, Thessaloniki 21192
Science Center of West Virginia, Bluefield 41759
Science Centre for Education, Bangkok 37495
Science City Museum, Kolkata 21911
Science Discovery Center of Oneonta, Oneonta 46160
The Science Factory, Eugene 43227
Science Imaginarium, Waterloo 48433
Science Museum, Alexandria 09247
The Science Museum, Cebu 31316
Science Museum, Dhaka 03093
Science Museum, Giza 09296
Science Museum, Kabul 00006
Science Museum, London 39773
Science Museum, Tokyo 26864
Science Museum, Upton 48162
Science Museum la Caixa, Barcelona 34560
Science Museum of Long Island, Manhasset 45104
Science Museum of Minnesota, Saint Paul 47166
Science Museum of Virginia, Richmond 46886
Science Museum of Western Virginia, Roanoke 46930
Science Museum Wroughton, Wroughton 40945
Science North, Sudbury 06512
Science Spectrum, Lubbock 44992
Science Station Museum, Cedar Rapids 42162
Science Works!, Marikina 31401
Sciencenter, Ithaca 44274
Scienceworks, Spotswood 01468
Scienceworks Museum, Melbourne 01242
Scientific Collections, Forssa 09443
Scientific Oceanographic Museum, Kaliningrad 32874
Scientific Researches Museum, Cairo 09287
Scitech, Aurora 41399
Scituate Historical Museum, Scituate 47502
Scituate Maritime and Irish Mossing Museum, Scituate 47503
Sciworks, Winston-Salem 48704
Scolton Manor Museum, Haverfordwest 39191
Scone and Upper Hunter Historical Museum, Scone 01445
Scone Palace, Perth 40187
Scotch Whisky Heritage Centre, Edinburgh 38914
Scotchtown, Beaverdam 41575
Scotia-Glenville Children's Museum, Scotia 47507
Scotland Heritage Chapel and Museum, Scotland 47508
Scotland Street School Museum, Glasgow 39066
Scotland's Secret Bunker, Saint Andrews 40387
The Scott Gallery, Hawick 39196
Scott Monument, Edinburgh 38915
Scott Polar Research Institute Museum, Cambridge 38461
Scottish Fisheries Museum, Anstruther 38004
Scottish Football Museum, Glasgow 39067
Scottish Industrial Railway Centre, Dalmellington 38694
Scottish Infantry Divisional Museum, Penicuik 40174
Scottish Jewish Museum, Glasgow 39068
Scottish Maritime Museum, Irvine 39312
Scottish Mining Museum, Newtongrange 40066
Scottish Museum of Woollen Textiles, Walkerburn 40766
Scottish Museums Council, Edinburgh 49442
Scottish Museums Federation, Hamilton 49443
Scottish National Gallery of Modern Art Gallery, Edinburgh 38916
Scottish National Portrait Gallery, Edinburgh 38917
Scottish Rugby Union Museum, Edinburgh 38918
Scotts Bluff National Monument, Gering 43658
Scottsdale Museum of Contemporary Art, Scottsdale 47514
Scout Museum of Finland, Turku 10130
Scouting Museum de Ducdalf, Rotterdam 29775
Scouting Museum Haagse Randstad, Den Haag 29124
Scriver Museum of Montana Wildlife and Hall of Bronze, Browning 41961
Scryption, Tilburg 29883
Scugog Shores Historical Museum, Port Perry 06168
Sculpture Center, Long Island City 44872
Scuola Dalmata dei Santi Giorgio e Trifone, Venezia 25950
Scuola Grande Arciconfraternita di San Rocco, Venezia 25951
Scuola Grande di San Giovanni Evangelista, Venezia 25952
Scurry County Museum, Snyder 47662
Ščusev Museum, Chişinău 28662
Sea Museum, Petrozavodsk 33317
Sea Museum, Toba 26823
Sea World, Durban 34232
Seabrook Village, Midway 45333
Seafood Museum, Qingdao 07201
Seaford Historical Museum, Seaford 47524
Seaford Museum of Local History, Seaford 40461
Seaforth Highlanders of Canada Regimental Museum, Vancouver 06688
Seal Island Light Museum, Barrington 05053
Sealife Scheveningen, Den Haag 29125
SEARCH-Centre, Gosport 39103
Searcy County Museum, Marshall 45175
Seashore Trolley Museum, Kennebunkport 44436
Seaton Delaval Hall, Seaton 40462
Seattle Art Museum, Seattle 47545
Seattle Asian Art Museum, Seattle 47546
Sebastian-Kneipp-Museum, Bad Wörishofen 15778
Sebežskij Muzej Prirody, Sebež 33514
Sebnitzer Kunstblumen- und Heimatmuseum Prof. Alfred Meiche, Sebnitz 19908
Second Street Gallery, Charlottesville 42251
Second World War Experience Centre, Leeds 39451
Secwepemc Museum and Heritage Park, Kamloops 05641
Sed Gallery, Athens 41321
Sederholm House of Helsinki City Museum, Helsinki 09526
Sederholmin Talo, Helsinki 09526
Sedgewick Museum and Gallery, Sedgewick 06417
Sedgwick-Brooklin Historical Museum, Sedgwick 47557
Sedgwick Museum of Geology, Cambridge 38462
Sedona Arts Center, Sedona 47558
Seedamm Kulturzentrum, Pfäffikon (Schwyz) 37020
Seelackenmuseum, Sankt Veit im Pongau 02618
Seemuseum in der Kornschütte, Kreuzlingen 36838
Seevogel-Museum Neusiedlersee, Rust, Burgenland 02528
Sefel Collection, Volos 21214
Segantini-Museum, Sankt Moritz 37115
Segedunum Roman Fort, Baths and Museum, Wallsend 40769
Segontium Roman Museum, Caernarfon 38435
Seguine House, Staten Island 47786
Segwun Heritage Centre, Gravenhurst 05526
Şehir Müzesi, Beşiktaş 37634
Seigfred Gallery, Athens 41325
Seiji Togo Memorial Sompo Japan Museum of Art, Tokyo 26915
Seikado Library and Art Museum, Tokyo 26916
Seinäjoen Luonto-Museo, Seinäjoki 10029
Seinäjoki Natural History Museum, Seinäjoki 10029
Seisonkaku, Kanazawa 26311
Seiyun in Wadi Hadhramaut Museum, Seiyun 49012
Sejarah Mesjid Banten Museum, Banten 22080
Sejong College Museum, Seoul 27270
Sekiguchi Ko Museum Yuzawa, Yuzawa 27037
Sekitan Kinenkan, Ube 26982
Sekkeh Museum, Kerman 22254
Sekkeh Museum, Teheran 22326
Sekken Museum, Sekken 30833
Selbu Bygdemuseum, Selbu 30834
Selbu Strikkemuseum, Selbu 30835
Selby Gallery, Sarasota 47455
Selçuk Müzesi, Konya 37745
Self Help Graphics Gallery, Los Angeles 44939
Seljuk Museum, Konya 37745
Selkirk College Mansbridge Kootenay Collection, Castlegar 05216
Sellner Glashütte, Lohberg 18494
Selly Manor Museum, Birmingham 38228
Selsey Lifeboat Museum, Selsey 40472
Selsor Gallery of Art, Chanute 42195
Šeltozerskij Vepsskij Ėtnografičeskij Muzej, Šeltozero 33515
Semenovskij Gosudarstvennyj Kraevedčeskij Istoriko-chudožestvennyj Muzej, Semenov 33516
Seminole Canyon State Historical Park, Comstock 42596
Seminole Nation Museum, Wewoka 48577
Semipalatinsk Historical and Regional Museum, Semey 27093
Semipalatinskij Istoriko-Kraevedčeskij Muzej, Semey 27093
Semmelweis Museum for the History of Medicine, Budapest 21382
Semmelweis Orvostörténeti Múzeum, Budapest 21382
Semsey Andor Múzeum, Balmazújváros 21315
Senate House, Kingston 44494
Senator George Norris State Historic Site, McCook 45022
Senator John Heinz Pittsburgh Regional History Center, Pittsburgh 46525
Senćanski Muzej, Senta 33903
Senckenberg-Forschungsinstitut und Naturmuseum, Frankfurt am Main 17072
Sendai City Museum, Sendai 26736
Sendai Music Box Museum, Sendai 26735
Sendai-shi Hakubutsukan, Sendai 26736
Sendergalerie Dobl, Dobl 01767
Seneca County Museum, Tiffin 48006
Seneca Falls Historical Society Museum, Seneca Falls 47567
Seneca-Iroquois National Museum, Salamanca 47188
Senhouse Roman Museum, Maryport 39919
Senj Municipal Museum, Senj 07770
Senjehesten Kystforsvarsmuseum, Moen 30682
Senko-ji Treasure House, Ono 26640
Sennerei-Museum und Heimatmuseum, Unterwasser 37268
Sen'oku Hakukokan Museum, Kyoto 26453
Sensen-Schmiede-Museum/ Klangwelten, Micheldorf 02294
Sensen- und Heimatmuseum, Achern 15391
Sensler Museum, Tafers 37228
Senta Museum, Senta 33903
Seoul Art Museum, Seoul 27271
Seoul Design Museum, Seoul 27272
Seoul Education Museum, Seoul 27273
Seoul Metropolitan Museum of Art, Seoul 27274
Seoul National Science Museum, Seoul 27275
Seoul National University Museum, Seoul 27276
Seoul Olympic Museum, Seoul 27277
Seoul Station Hall, Seoul 27278
Sepänmäen Käsityömuseo, Mäntsälä 09809
Sepänmäki Handicraft Museum, Mäntsälä 09809
Septem Maria Museum, Adria 22809
Sequoyah Cabin, Sallisaw 47223
Serbian Church Museum, Szentendre 21577
Serbian Heritage Museum of Windsor, Windsor, Ontario 06811
Serbski muzej - Sorbisches Museum, Bautzen 15835
Serbski muzej/ Wendisches Museum, Cottbus 16505
Šeremetevskij Dvorec - Fontannyj Dom, Sankt-Peterburg 33483
Serengeti Museum, Arusha 37455
Sergačskij Kraevedčeskij Muzej, Sergač 33518
Sergei Parajanov Museum, Erevan 00688
Sergej Borodin Muzej, Taškent 48860
Sergej Esenin Museum-Preserve, Konstantinovo 32937

Sergiev-Posad State History and Art Museum-Reserve, Sergiev Posad 33521
Sergievo-Posadskij Gosudarstvennyj Istoriko-chudožestvennyj Muzej Zapovednik, Sergiev Posad 33521
Seriemuseet Comicland, Ullared 36344
Serpent Mound Museum, Peebles 46326
Serpentine Gallery, London 39774
Serpentine Vintage Tractors and Machinery Museum, Serpentine 01447
Serpentinsteinmuseum Zöblitz, Zöblitz 20765
Serpuchovskij Istoriko-chudožestvennyj Muzej, Serpuchov 33522
Serra Museum, San Diego 47296
Serrallés Castle Museum, Ponce 32379
Service historique de la Police, Bruxelles 03343
Serviceton Historic Railway Station, Serviceton 01448
Sesquicentennial Museum, Toronto 06610
Session Cottage Museum, Turriff 40735
Setagaya Art Museum, Tokyo 26917
Setagaya-kuritsu Bijutsukan, Tokyo 26917
Setesdalsbanen Stiftelsen, Vennesla 30985
Setesdalsmuseet, Rysstad 30814
Seto Ceramics Center, Seto 26741
Seto City Folk Historical Material Museum, Seto 26740
Seto Inland Sea Folk History Museum, Takamatsu 26791
Seto-shi Rekishi Minzoku Shiryokan, Seto 26740
Seto Tojiki, Seto 26741
Seton Centre, Carberry 05201
Seton Hall University Museum, South Orange 47700
Setor de Malacologia, Juiz de Fora 04160
Setsuryosha Art Museum, Niigata 26598
Setsuryosha Bijitsukan, Niigata 26598
Settlers Museum, Brewarrina 00831
Settlers Museum, Himeville 34263
Settlers' Museum, Mahone Bay 05799
Seurasaaren Ulkomuseo, Helsinki 09527
Seurasaari Open Air Museum, Helsinki 09527
Seven Oaks House Museum, Winnipeg 06845
Sevenoaks Museum and Gallery, Sevenoaks 40475
Severn Valley Railway, Bewdley 38185
Severo-osetinskij Gosudarstvennyj Obedinennyj Muzej Istorii, Architektury i Literatury, Vladikavkaz 33690
Severo-osetinskij Literaturnyj Muzej im. K.L. Četagurova, Vladikavkaz 33691
Severočeská Galerie Výtvarného Umění v Litoměřice, Litoměřice 08457
Severočeské Muzeum v Liberci, Liberec 08451
Seville Great House and Heritage Park, Ocho Rios 26080
Sewall-Belmont House, Washington 48391
Seward County Historical Society Museum, Goehner 43708
Seward House, Auburn 41375
Seward Museum, Seward 47572
Sewerby Hall Art Gallery and Museum, Bridlington 38329
Sexmuseum Amsterdam Venustempel, Amsterdam 28901
Sexton's Cottage Museum, Crows Nest 00956
Seymour and District Historical Museum, Seymour 01449
Seymour Art Gallery, North Vancouver 06028
Seymour Community Museum, Seymour 47575
Sezon Museum of Modern Art, Karuizawa 26313
S.F. Klonowic Museum of the Sulmierzyce Region, Sulmierzyce 32006
SFA Galleries, Nacogdoches 45589
De Sfeer van Weleer, Rekken 29725
S.H. Ervin Gallery, Sydney 01507
Shaanxi Chinese Painting Gallery, Xian 07297
Shaanxi History Museum, Xian 07298
Shackerstone Railway Museum, Shackerstone 40476
Shades of the Past, Carbonear 05203
Shadi Abdel Salam Museum, Alexandria 09248
The Shadows-on-the-Teche, New Iberia 45708
Shaftesbury Abbey and Museum, Shaftesbury 40477
Shaftesbury Town Museum, Shaftesbury 40478
Shaftsbury Historical Society Museum, Shaftsbury 47577
Shah Alam Art Gallery, Shah Alam 27688
Shaheed-e-Azam Bhagat Singh Museum, Khatkar Kalan 21888
Shahrood Museum, Semnan 22279
Shahryar Museum, Tabriz 22286
Shaker Heritage Society Museum, Albany 41087
Shaker Historical Society Museum, Shaker Heights 47578
Shaker Museum, New Gloucester 45690
Shaker Museum, Old Chatham 46131
Shaker Museum, South Union 47705
Shaker Village of Pleasant Hill, Harrodsburg 43935
Shakespeare Birthplace Trust, Stratford-upon-Avon 40630
Shakespeare's Globe Exhibition and Tour, London 39775
Shakir Ali Museum, Lahore 31043
Shakowi Cultural Center, Oneida 46158
Shalom Aleichem Museum, Tel Aviv 22774
Shalyapin Hall in the Bogoyavlenskij Clock Tower, Kazan 32889
Shalyapin House Museum, Moskva 33042
Shalyapin House Museum, Sankt-Peterburg 33454
Shambles Museum, Newent 40044
Shambyu Museum, Shambyu 28770
Shamrock and Cotehele Quay Museum, Saint Dominick 40394
Shamrock Museum, Shamrock 06426
Shan Rong Cultural Display Center, Beijing 06988
Shan State Museum, Taunggyi 28745
Shand House Museum, Windsor, Nova Scotia 06809
Shandong Painting Gallery, Jinan 07133
Shandong Provincial Museum, Jinan 07134
Shandong Stone Engraving Art Museum, Jinan 07135
Shandy Hall, Coxwold 38652
Shandy Hall, Geneva 43645
Shanghai History Museum, Shanghai 07219
Shanghai Luxun House, Shanghai 07220
Shanghai Museum, Shanghai 07221
Shanghai Natural History Museum, Shanghai 07222
Shanghai Science & Technology Museum, Shanghai 07223
Shankar's International Dolls Museum, Delhi 21783
Shantou Archaeology Museum, Shantou 07228
Shantytown, Greymouth 30170
Shanxi Painting Gallery, Taiyuan 07258
Sharadin Art Gallery, Kutztown 44531
Sharia Museum, Cairo 09288
Sharif Kamala Museum, Kazan 32905
Sharjah Archaeology Museum, Sharjah 37921
Sharjah Art Museum, Sharjah 37922
Sharjah Heritage Museum, Sharjah 37923
Sharjah Islamic Museum, Sharjah 37924
Sharjah Natural History Museum, Sharjah 37925
Sharjah Science Museum, Sharjah 37926
Sharlot Hall Museum, Prescott 46689
Sharon Arts Center, Sharon 47580
Sharon Museum, Emek Hefer 22591
Sharon Museum Emek Hefer, Midreshet Ruppin 22714
Sharon Temple Historic Site, Sharon 06427
Sharpsteen Museum, Calistoga 42034
Shasta College Museum, Redding 46820
Shaw Island Historical Society Museum, Shaw Island 47584
Shawano County Museum, Shawanao 47585
Shawneetown Historic Site, Old Shawneetown 46134
Shawnigan Lake Historical Museum, Shawnigan Lake 06431
Shawqi Museum, Cairo 09289
Shaw's Corner, Ayot-Saint-Lawrence 38048
Shchelykovo - Memorial Museum-Estate of Aleksander Ostrovsky, Ščelykovo 33513
Shchusev State Museum of Architecture, Moskva 33068
Shearwater Aviation Museum, Shearwater 06432
Sheboygan County Historical Museum, Sheboygan 47590
Shed im Eisenwerk, Frauenfeld 36708
Shedhalle-Rote Fabrik, Zürich 37407
Shedhalle Sankt Pölten, Sankt Pölten 02604
Shee Alms House, Kilkenny 22489
Sheehan Gallery at Whitman College, Walla Walla 48286
Sheffield Bus Museum, Sheffield 40488
Sheffield City Museum and Mappin Art Gallery, Sheffield 40489
Shefton Museum of Greek Art and Archaeology, Newcastle-upon-Tyne 40041
Sheikan Museum, El-Obeid 35762
Sheikh Saeed's House, Dubai 37917
Shelburne County Museum, Shelburne 06436
Shelburne Museum, Shelburne 47593
Sheldon Jackson Museum, Sitka 47650
Sheldon Memorial Art Gallery and Sculpture Garden, Lincoln 44791
Sheldon Museum, Haines 43870
Sheldon Peck Museum, Lombard 44849
Shell Lake Museum, Shell Lake 06437
Shellin Antiques and Irish Lace Museum, Enniskillen 38942
Shelter House, Emmaus 43180
Shelter Island Historical Society Museum, Shelter Island 47599
Shenandoah Valley Folk Art and Heritage Center, Dayton 42808
Shenshu-Bunko Museum, Tokyo 26918
Shenyang Palace Museum, Shenyang 07236
Shenzhen Art Gallery, Shenzhen 07241
Shenzhen Museum, Shenzhen 07242
Shenzhen Painting Gallery, Shenzhen 07243
Shephela Museum, Kibbutz Kfar Menahem 22692
Shepherd Wheel, Sheffield 40490
Shepherd's Museum, Bugac 21393
Shepherd's Museum, Hortobágy 21433
Sheppard Fine Arts Gallery, Reno 46836
Shepparton Art Gallery, Shepparton 01451
Sheppy's Farm and Cider Museum, Bradford-on-Tone 38302
Shepton Mallet Museum, Shepton Mallet 40493
Sherborne Castle, Sherborne 40494
Sherborne Museum, Sherborne 40495
Sherbrooke Village, Sherbrooke, Nova Scotia 06438
Sherburne County Historical Museum, Becker 41576
Sheremetyev Palace - Fountain House, Sankt-Peterburg 33483
Sheringham Museum, Sheringham 40498
Sherlock Holmes Museum, London 39776
Sherlock Holmes-Museum, Meiringen 36935
Sherman House, Lancaster 44622
Sherrier Resources Centre, Lutterworth 39848
Sherwood-Davidson House, Newark 45897
Sherwood Forest Plantation, Charles City 42202
Shetland Croft House Museum, Dunrossnes 38817
Shetland Museum, Lerwick 39479
Sheung Yiu Folk Museum, Hong Kong 07112
Shevchenko Apartment-Museum at Museum of the Russian Academy of Art, Sankt-Peterburg 33455
Shfela Museum, Kibbutz Kfar Menahem 22693
Shi Liao Display Center, Nanjing 07187
Shibayama Haniwa Hakubutsukan, Shibayama 26743
Shibayama Haniwa Museum, Shibayama 26743
Shibden Hall Museum, Halifax 39156
Shibunkaku Museum of Art, Kyoto 26454
Shicheng County Museum, Ganzhou 07059
Shido-dera Treasure House, Shido 26745
Shido-ji Homotsukan, Shido 26746
Shido-ji Treasure House, Shido 26746
Shiga-kenritsu Kindai Bijutsukan, Otsu 26683
Shiga-kenritsu Omi Fudoki-No-Oka Shiryokan, Azuchi 26116
Shiga Prefectural Fudoki-No-Oka Exhibition, Azuchi 26116
Shigaraki-yaki Pottery Museum, Koga 26361
Shihezi Junken Museum, Shihezi 07245
Shijiazhuang City Museum, Shijiazhuang 07247
Shiko Munakata Memorial Museum of Art, Aomori 26100
Shikoku Minka Hakubutsukan, Takamatsu 26792
Shillong Tribal Research Institute, Shillong 22018
Shiloh Museum of Ozark History, Springdale 47733
Shiloh National Military Park and Cemetery, Shiloh 47606
Shima Marineland, Ago 26086
Shimane Daigaku Hobungakubu Kokogaku Kenkyushitsu-nai, Matsue 26471
Shimane-kenritsu Hakubutsukan, Matsue 26472
Shimane Prefectural Museum, Matsue 26472
Shimane Prefectural Yakumodatsu Fudoki No Oka History Hall, Matsue 26473
Shimane University Archaeological Collection, Matsue 26471
Shimazu Foundation Memorial Hall, Kyoto 26455
Shimoda Marine Biological Station, Kamo, Izu 26301
Shimonoseki City Art Museum, Shimonoseki 26753
Shimosuwa Museum, Shimosuwa 26755
Shin-Yokohama Ramen Hakubutsukan, Yokohama 27018
Shinagawa Historical Museum, Tokyo 26919
Shinano Drawing Museum, Ueda 26983
Shinchon Museum, Shinchon 27124
Shingen-Ko Treasure House, Enzan 26136
Shinshu-shinmachi Art Museum, Shinshiyuushin 26756
Shinuiju Historical Museum, Shinuiju 27125
Shinyanga Mazingira Museum, Shinyanga 37465
Shinyoung Cinema Museum, Namwon 27215
Shio-no-michi Hakabutsukan, Itoigawa 26267
Shiogama Shrine Museum, Shiogami 26757
Shiozawa Tsumugi Commemorative Museum, Shiozawa 26760
Ship Museum, Eskifjörður 21630
Shipley Art Gallery, Gateshead 39028
Shippensburg Historical Society Museum, Shippensburg 47609
Ships of the Sea Maritime Museum, Savannah 47484
Shipwreck Heritage Centre, Hastings 39186
Shipwreck Museum, Bredasdorp 34195
Shipwreck Museum, Cairns 00874
Shipwreck Museum, Girne 08223
Shirahata Shiro World Mountains Photograph Collection, Yuzawa 27038
Shirane Memorial Museum, Tokyo 26920
Shire Hall Gallery, Stafford 40571
Shire of Landsborough Historical Society, Landsborough 01163
Shire of Wondai Museum, Wondai 01611
Shirehall Museum, Little Walsingham 39513
Shiretoko Museum, Shari 26742
Shirley-Eustis House, Boston 41826
Shirley Plantation, Charles City 42203
Shiseido Art House, Kakegawa 26291
Shishi Kaikan, Takayama 26810
Shitamachi Museum, Tokyo 26921
Shizuoka City Toro Museum, Shizuoka 26766
Shizuoka-kenritsu Bijutsukan, Shizuoka 26767
Shizuoka Prefectural Museum of Art, Shizuoka 26767
Shkodër Museum, Shkodër 00032
Shoal Creek Living History Museum, Kansas City 44407
Shodo Hakubutsukan, Tokyo 26922
Shoe Museum, Street 40635
Shoe Museum, Zlín 08752
Shohada Museum, Ghazvin 22237
Shoji Ueda Museum of Photography, Kishimoto 26338
Shoko Shuseikan Historical Museum, Kagoshima 26290
Shokokan Museum, Mito 26505
Shokokuji Jotenkaku Museum, Kyoto 26456
Sholem Asch House, Bat Yam 22578
Shore Line Trolley Museum, East Haven 43050
Shore Road Pumping Station, Birkenhead 38206
Shore Village Museum, Rockland 46967
Shoreham Aircraft Museum, Shoreham 40502
Shoreham Airport Historical Exhibition, Shoreham-by-Sea 40504
Shoreline Historical Museum, Seattle 47547
Shoren-in Treasure House, Kyoto 26457
Shorter Mansion Museum, Eufaula 43219
Shoshone Tribal Cultural Center, Fort Washakie 43468
Shosoin Treasure Repository, Nara 26583
The Shoto Museum of Art, Tokyo 26923
Shotts Heritage Centre, Shotts 40505
Show Gallery, Toronto 06611
Shpakovsky Regional Museum of Essentuki, Essentuki 32798
Shreemanthi Bai Memorial Government Museum, Mangalore 21939
Shrewsbury Castle, Shrewsbury 40510
Shrewsbury Museum and Art Gallery, Shrewsbury 40511
Shrewsbury Windle House, Madison 45059
Shri Chhatrapati Shivaji Maharaj Museum, Satara 22013
Shri Girdharbhai Sangrahalaya, Amreli 21696
Shrikrishna Science Centre, Patna 21979
Shrine of the Book, Jerusalem 22662
Shropshire Regimental Museum, Shrewsbury 40512
Shtekelis Prehistory Museum, Haifa 22612
Shugborough Estate Museum, Milford, Staffordshire 39954
Shukshin Memorial Preserve, Srostki 33551
Shushenskoye State Museum-Preserve of History and Etnography, Šušenskoe 33569
Shuttleworth Collection, Old Warden 40127
Si Salon, Wellington 30310
S.I. Taneev Museum in Dyutkovo, Zvenigorod 33750
Siatista Botanical Museum, Siatista 21154
Šiauliai Aušros Museum, Šiauliai 27531
Sibbesgården, Sipoo 10038
Sibbo Jordbruksmuseum, Sipoo 10039
Sibeliuksen Syntymäkoti, Hämeenlinna 09454
Sibelius Museum, Turku 10127
Sibiu Natural History Museum, Sibiu 32592
Sibley County Historical Museum, Henderson 43989
Sibley Historic Site, Mendota 45252
Siboney Farm Museum, Santiago de Cuba 08136
Sibsagar College Museum, Sibsagar 22023
Sicamous and District Museum, Sicamous 06447
Sichuan Museum, Chengdu 07024
Sichuan University Museum, Chengdu 07025
Sid Richardson Collection of Western Art, Fort Worth 43492
Side Müzesi, Side 37781
Side Museum, Side 37781
Side Street Projects, Los Angeles 44940
Sidenväveri Museum, Stockholm 36279
Sidmouth Museum, Sidmouth 40515
Sidney and Gertrude Zack Gallery, Vancouver 06689
Sidney Historical Association Museum, Sidney 47626
Sidney Historical Museum, Sidney 06449
Sidney Lanier Cottage, Macon 45047
Sidney Marine Museum, Sidney 06450
Sidney Mishkin Gallery of Baruch College, New York 45869
Sieben-Keltern-Museum, Metzingen 18726
Sieben-Schwaben-Museum, Türkheim 20234
Siebenberg House, Jerusalem 22663
Siebenbürgisches Museum Gundelsheim, Gundelsheim, Württemberg 17462
Siebengebirgsmuseum, Königswinter 18185
Sieblos-Museum Poppenhausen, Poppenhausen, Wasserkuppe 19428
Siebold Memorial Museum, Nagasaki 26560
Siebold-Museum, Würzburg 20705
Siege Museum, Petersburg 46378
Siegelmuseum Schloß Waldenburg, Waldenburg, Württemberg 20362
Siegerlandmuseum mit Ausstellungsforum Haus Oranienstraße, Siegen 19950
Siegfried Charoux-Museum, Langenzersdorf 02188
Siegfried H. Horn Archaeological Museum, Berrien Springs 41655
Sielmuseum der Hamburger Stadtentwässerung, Hamburg 17566
Siemens-Forum in Berlin, Berlin 16095
SiemensForum, München 18906
Sierra Arts Foundation, Reno 46837
Sierra Leone National Museum, Freetown 33935
Sievin Kotiseutumuseo, Sievi 10033
Sigdal og Eggedal Museum, Prestfoss 30782
Siggebohyttans Bergmansgård, Nora 36112
Siglhaus, Sankt Georgen bei Salzburg 02567
Sigmund Freud Museum, Sankt-Peterburg 33466
Sigmund Freud-Museum, Wien 02989
Signal Hill Gallery, Weyburn 06782
Signal Hill National Historic Site, Saint John's 06353
Signal Museum, Riihimäki 09998
Sigtuna Museer, Sigtuna 36183
Sigtuna Rådhus, Sigtuna 36184
Sigurhaedir - Hús Skáldsins Museum, Akureyri 21623
Sigurjón Ólafsson Museum, Reykjavík 21654
Siikaisten Kotiseutumuseo, Siikainen 10034
Sikar Museum, Sikar 22024
Sikinos Archeological Collection, Sikinos 21157
Sikkens Schildersmuseum, Sassenheim 29793
Siksika Nation Museum, Siksika 06452
Silas Wright Jr. Historic House, Canton 42087
Silberbergwerk, Ramingstein 02480
Silbereisenbergwerk Gleißinger Fels, Fichtelberg 17000
Silberstollen Geising, Geising 17217
Silberwaren- und Bijouteriemuseum, Schwäbisch Gmünd 19863
Silcher-Museum Schnait, Weinstadt 20486
Sildarminjasafnid a Siglufirdi, Siglufjörður 21669
Silesian Museum, Opava 08520
Silesian Museum, Opava 08522
Silesian Technical University Cz. Poborski Mineral Deposits Museum, Gliwice 31592
Silifke Mosaic Museum, Narlıkuyu 37765
Silifke Mozaik Müzesi, Narlıkuyu 37765
Silifke Müzesi, Silifke, Içel 37782

Silifke Museum, Silifke, Içel 37782
Siliman University Anthropology Museum, Dumaguete 31326
Siljansfors Skogsmuseum, Mora 36101
Siljustøl Museum, Paradis 30778
Silk Hakubutsukan, Yokohama 27019
Silk Museum, Gangnae 27165
Silk Museum, Soufli 21162
Silk Museum, Yokohama 27019
Silkeborg Kulturhistoriske Museum, Silkeborg 09052
Silkeborg Kunstmuseum, Silkeborg 09053
Silkeborg Museum of Art, Silkeborg 09053
Silkmuseum, Meliskerke 29588
Silla University Museum, Busan 27144
Siloam Springs Museum, Siloam Springs 47627
Silomuseum, Waidhofen an der Thaya 02785
Silpakorn University Art Centre, Bangkok 37496
Silvanum Forestmuseum, Ockelbo 36131
Silvanum Skogsmuseet, Ockelbo 36131
Silver City Museum, Silver City 47629
Silver Cliff Museum, Silver Cliff 47631
Silver Eye Center for Photography, Pittsburgh 46526
Silver Ledge Hotel Museum, Ainsworth Hot Springs 04968
Silver Mines Museum, L'Argentière-la-Bessée 12344
Silver River Museum, Ocala 46082
Silver Stream Railway Museum, Hutt City 30182
Silvercreek Museum, Freeport 43550
Silverman Heritage Museum, Toronto 06612
Silvermine Guild Arts Center, New Canaan 45682
Silvermuseet, Arjeplog 35810
Silverton Gaol Museum, Silverton 01452
Silvery Slocan Museum, New Denver 05976
Símaminjasafnið, Reykjavík 21665
Simcoe County Museum, Minesing 05857
Simeon Perkins House, Liverpool 05760
Simferopol Art Museum, Simferopol 37905
Simferopolskij Chudožestvennyj Muzej, Simferopol 37905
Simingshan Revolutionary Martyr Memory, Yuyao 07322
Simón Bolívar's Birthplace, Caracas 48897
Simon Fraser Gallery, Burnaby 05151
Simon Gfeller-Gedenkstube, Heimisbach 36800
Simon Gregorčič Collection, Vrsno 34165
Simon Kotiseutumuseo, Simo 10037
Simon Paneak Memorial Museum, Anaktuvuk Pass 41195
Simon van Gijn Museum aan Huis, Dordrecht 29178
Simon Wiesenthal Center, Los Angeles 44941
Simon Wiesenthal Center - Museum of Tolerance, Los Angeles 44942
Simon's Town Museum, Simon's Town 34376
Simsbury Historical Society Museum, Simsbury 47637
Le Simserhof, 2004 L, Siersthal 14749
Sincheonji Art Museum, Aeweol 27127
Sinclair-Haus, Bad Homburg v.d.Höhe 15668
Sinclair Lewis Museum, Sauk Centre 47467
Sind Provincial Museum, Hyderabad 31021
Sindringer Heimatmuseum - Stadtmühle, Forchtenberg 17022
Sinebrychoff Art Museum - Finnish National Gallery, Helsinki 09528
Sinebrychoffin Taidemuseo, Helsinki 09528
Singapore Art Museum, Singapore 33941
Singapore History Museum, Singapore 33942
Singapore History Museum at Riverside Point, Singapore 33943
Singapore Science Centre, Singapore 33944
Singer Museum, Laren, Noord-Holland 29499
Singida Museum, Singida 37466
Singleton Historical Museum, Singleton 01454
Singsås Museum, Singsås 30837
Sining Makiling Gallery, Los Baños 31347
Sinop Culture Center, Sinop 37784
Sinop Devlet Güzel Sanatlar Galerisi, Sinop 37783
Sinop Kültür Merkezi, Sinop 37784
Sinop Müzesi, Sinop 37785
Sinop Museum, Sinop 37785
Sinop State Gallery, Sinop 37783
Sint-Baafskathedraal Gent, Gent 03450
Sint-Dimpna en Gasthuismuseum, Geel 03427
Sint-Godelievemuseum, Gistel 03461
Sint-Janshuismolen en Koeleweimolen, Brugge 03267
Sint Jansmuseum De Bouwloods, 's-Hertogenbosch 29410
Sint-Pieters Museum op de Lichtenberg, Maastricht 29573
Sint-Plechelmusbasiliek met Schatkamer, Oldenzaal 29659
Sion Hill Hall, Thirsk 40697
Sioux City Art Center, Sioux City 47638
Sioux City Public Museum, Sioux City 47639
Sioux Empire Medical Museum, Sioux Falls 47645
Sioux Indian Museum, Rapid City 46798
Sioux Lookout Museum, Sioux Lookout 06459
Siouxland Heritage Museums, Sioux Falls 47646
Sipahi Ay. Trias Bazilikası ve Kantara Kalesi, Kantara 08231
Sipalaseequtt Museum, Pangnirtung 06093
Siping City Museum, Siping 07249
Sipiweske Museum, Wawanesa 06759
Sippola Museum, Sippola 10040
Sippolan Kotiseutumuseo, Sippola 10040
Sir Alexander Galt Museum, Lethbridge 05747
Sir Alfred Munnings Art Museum, Dedham 38711
Sir Choturam Memorial Museum, Sangaria 22008
Sir Edgeworth David Memorial Museum, Kurri Kurri 01154
Sir Francis Cook Gallery, Augrès 38040
Sir Frank Hutson Sugar Museum, Saint James 03106
Sir Henry Doulton Gallery, Stoke-on-Trent 40610
Sir Henry Jones Museum, Llangernyw 39551
Sir Henry Royce Memorial Foundation, Paulerspury 40164
Sir Isaac and Lady Edith Wolfson Museum, Jerusalem 22664
Sir John Soane's Museum, London 39777
Sir Max Aitken Museum, Cowes 38650
Sir Seewoosagar Ramgoolam Memorial Centre, Plaine Verte 27737
Sir Walter Scott's Courtroom, Selkirk 40471
Sir Wilfred Grenfell College Art Gallery, Corner Brook 05274
Sırçalı Medrese Müzesi, Konya 37746
Sırçalı Medrese Museum, Konya 37746
Sisi Museum zum Andenken an Kaiserin Elisabeth, München 18907
Sisimiut Katersugaasiviat, Sisimiut 21240
Sisimiut Museum, Sisimiut 21240
Siskin Museum of Religious and Ceremonial Art, Chattanooga 42265
Siskiyou County Museum, Yreka 48813
Site Archéologique, Alba-la-Romaine 10269
Site Archéologique de Saint-Blaise, Saint-Mitre-les-Remparts 14378
Site Archéologique La Cave Peinte, Brain-sur-Allonnes 10887
Site-Chantier de Fouilles Archéologiques, Charavines 11171
Site Fortifié des Bois de Cattenom, Cattenom 11086
Site Fortifié Hillmann, Colleville-Montgomery 11347
Site Gallery, Winnipeg 06846
Site Gallo-Romain de Grand, Grand 11901
Site-Historique du Banc-de-Paspébiac, Paspébiac 06099
Site Préhistorique de Castel Merle, Sergeac 14717
Site Santa Fe, Santa Fe 47433
Sitio Arqueológico de Cumbemayo, Cumbemayo 31151
Sítio Roberto Burle Marx, Rio de Janeiro 04404
Sitka National Historical Park, Sitka 47651
Sitorai Mochi-Khosa, Buchara 48833
Sittingbourne and Kemsley Light Railway, Sittingbourne 40522
Sittingbourne Heritage Museum, Sittingbourne 40523
Situation Kunst, Bochum 16201
Siuntion Kotiseutumuseo, Siuntio 10041
Sivas Atatürk Culture Center, Sivas 37789
Sivas Atatürk Kültür Merkezi, Sivas 37789
Sivas Devlet Güzel Sanatlar Galerisi, Sivas 37790
Sivas State Gallery, Sivas 37790
Six Nations Indian Museum, Onchiota 46155
Sixth Floor Museum at Dealey Plaza, Dallas 42757
Sizdah Aban Museum, Teheran 22327
Sizergh Castle, Kendal 39339
Sjöfartmuseet, Oskarshamn 36154
Sjöfartsmuseet, Göteborg 35920
Sjöfartsmuseet, Kristiinankaupunki 09710
Sjöhistoriska Institutet vid Åbo Akademi, Turku 10128
Sjöhistoriska Museet, Stockholm 36280
Sjøfartsmuseet i Porsgrunn, Porsgrunn 30781
Sjølingstad Uldvarefabrik, Mandal 30666
Sjóminja- og Vélsmiðjusafn, Reykjavík 21666
Sjóminjasafn Austurlands, Eskifjörður 21630
Sjóminjasafn Islands, Hafnarfjörður 21637
Sjóminjasafnid á Eyrarbakka, Eyrarbakki 21632
Sjukehusmuseet i Molde, Molde 30688
Sjukehusmuseet i Skien, Skien 30846
Ska-Nah-Doht Iroquoian Village and Museum, Mount Brydges 05947
Skaalurensamlinga - Skipsbyggingsmuseet i Rosendal, Rosendal 30810
Skärgårdens Sågverksmuseum, Holmsund 35962
Skärgårdsmuseet, Lappoby-Åland 09767
Skärgårdsmuseet, Stavsnäs 36227
Skagafjördur Folk Museum, Varmahlid 21672
Skagen By- og Egnsmuseum, Skagen 09057
Skagens Museum, Skagen 09058
Skagit County Historical Museum, La Conner 44533
Skagway City Museum, Skagway 47652
Skanderborg Museum, Skanderborg 09059
Skandinavisk Museumförbund - Skandinaavinen Museoliitto, Finnish Section, Helsinki 49159
Skandinavisk Museumsforbund, Danske Afdeling, København 49145
Skandinavisk Museumsforbund, Norwegian Section, Tønsberg 49324
Skandinavisk Museumsforbund, Swedish Section, Stockholm 49382
Skånland Museum, Evenskjer 30481
Skansen Archeologiczny w Mrówkach, Mrówki 31814
Skansen Górniczy Królowa Luiza, Zabrze 32201
Skansen i Muzeum Pszczelarstwa im prof. Ryszarda Kosteckiego, Swarzędz 32011
Skansen Kultury Ludowej Pogórza Sudeckiego, Kudowa Zdrój 31744
Skansen Kurpiowski im. Adama Chętnika, Nowogród 31832
Skansen Open Air Museum, Stockholm 36242
Skansenowska Zagroda Sitarska, Biłgoraj 31499
Skånska Lasses Hus, Mjölby 36095
Skara Järnvägsmuseum, Skara 36193
Skara Railway Museum, Skara 36193
Skattkammaren, Stockholm 36281
Skattkammaren - Uppsala Domkyrkas Museum, Uppsala 36360
Skaun Bygdamuseum, Børsa 30445
Skellefteå Museum, Skellefteå 36197
Skeppsvarvet sjöfartsutställning, Västanfjärd 10169
Skerryvore Museum, Hynish 39282
Ski Museum, Lahti 09740
Ski Museum, Vimpeli 10200
Ski- und Heimatmuseum, Kurort Oberwiesenthal 18273
Ski- und Heimatmuseum, Sankt Anton am Arlberg 02558
Ski- und Heimatmuseum Upfingen, Sankt Johann, Württemberg 19752
Skidans Hus, Boden 35836
Skidby Windmill and Museum of East Riding Rural Life, Skidby 40525
Skimuseet, Oslo 30762
Skimuseum, Oberreute 19194
Skimuseum, Vaduz 27518
Skinner Museum of Mount Holyoke College, South Hadley 47694
Skiptvet Bygdemuseum, Skiptvet 30849
Skirball Cultural Center, Los Angeles 44943
Skirball Museum of Biblical Archaeology, Jerusalem 22665
Skironio Centrum Kifissa, Néa Kifissia 21098
Skironio Museum Polychronopoulos, Mégara 21063
Skissernas Museum, Lund 36064
Skive Kunstmuseum, Skive 09060
Skive Museum, Skive 09061
Skjern-Egvad Museum, Skjern 09065
Skjern Vindmølle, Skjern 09066
Skjoldborgs Barndomshjem, Vesløs 09106
Sklářské Muzeum, Kamenický Šenov 08399
Sklářské Muzeum Moser, Karlovy Vary 08402
Sklářské Muzeum Nový Bor, Nový Bor 08507
Sklenka Muzeum v Železném Brodě, Železný Brod 08748
Skobelev Park-muzej, Pleven 04771
Škoda Auto Museum, Mladá Boleslav 08481
Skövde Konsthall och Konstmuseum, Skövde 36198
Skövde Stadsmuseum, Skövde 36199
Skogs- och Motorsågsmuseum, Sunne 36311
Skogsmuseet i Lycksele, Lycksele 36066
Skogsmuséet på Römmen, Mörsil 36099
Skogsmuseum, Åsele 35820
Skoindustrimuseet, Kumla 36022
Skokloster Castle, Skokloster 36201
Skokloster Motormuseum, Skokloster 36200
Skoklosters Slott, Skokloster 36201
Skolmuseet, Östra Ljungby 36150
Skolmuseum Bunge, Farösund 35885
Školoto Muzej, Trjavna 04889
Školska Zbirka Odžaci, Odžaci 33878
Skopje Museum of Contemporary Art, Skopje 27591
Skottvångs Gruva, Mariefred 36087
Skovbrugsmagasinet på Corselitze, Nykøbing Falster 08997
Skovgaard Museet i Viborg, Viborg 09111
Skowhegan History House, Skowhegan 47653
Skrolsvik Fiskebruksmuseum, Moen 30683
Skulpturen-Museum, Heilbronn 17691
Skulpturenhain vor Marleben, Trebel 20195
Skulpturenmuseum Glaskasten Marl, Marl, Westfalen 18655
Skulpturenmuseum im Hofberg, Landshut 18312
Skulpturenpark, Bad Nauheim 15701
Skulpturenpark Kramsach, Kramsach 02154
Skulpturens Hus, Stockholm 36282
Skulpturensammlung, Dresden 16709
Skulpturensammlung und Museum für Byzantinische Kunst, Berlin 16096
Skulpturenweg, Emmendingen 16858
Skulpturhalle Basel, Basel 36522
Skupnost Muzejev Slovenije, Ljubljana 49362
Skye and Lochalsh Area Museums, Portree 40246
Skyscraper Museum, New York 45870
Skyttalan Museo, Parainen 09909
Slaait'n Hoes, Onstwedde 29665
Slabsides, West Park 48541
Sládečkovo Vlastivědné Muzeum v Kladně, Kladno 08410
The Sladmore Gallery of Sculpture, London 39778
Slag van de Somme Museum, Schagen 29797
Slagelse Museum for Handel, Håndværk og Industri, Slagelse 09071
Slagterbutikken anno 1920, Roskilde 09045
Slate Run Living Historical Farm, Ashville 41303
Slate Valley Museum, Granville 43771
Slater Memorial Museum, Norwich 46037
Slater Mill Historic Site, Pawtucket 46318
Slaughter Ranch Museum, Douglas 42962
Slaveikovi House Museum, Trjavna 04887
Slavonic Benevolent Order of the State of Texas Museum, Temple 47977
Slawenburg Raddusch, Raddusch 19467
Sledmere House, Sledmere 40529
Sleire Skulemuseum, Hosteland 30568
Slesvigske Vognsamling, Haderslev 08850
Slevogthof Neukastel, Leinsweiler 18379
Slezské Zemské Muzeum, Opava 08522
Slidell Art Center, Slidell 47654
Sliedrechts Museum, Sliedrecht 29830
Slifer House, Lewisburg 44723
Šlisselburgskaja Krepost Orešek, Šlisselburg 33526
Sloan Museum, Flint 43340
Sloane-Stanley Museum and Kent Furnace, Kent 44444
Slöinge Lanthandelsmuseum, Slöinge 36205
Slöjdmuseet, Ånge 35804
Sloss Furnaces National Historic Landmark, Birmingham 41708
Slot Loevestein, Poederoijen 29714
Slot Zeist, Zeist 30051
Slot Zuylen, Oud-Zuilen 29692
Slough Museum, Slough 40530
Slovácké Muzeum, Uherské Hradiště 08698
Slovácko Museum, Uherské Hradiště 08698
Slovak Museum of Nature Protection and Speleology, Liptovský Mikuláš 34017
Slovak Museums Association, Liptovský Mikuláš 49359
Slovak National Gallery, Bratislava 33978
Slovak National Gallery - Schaubmar Mill - Gallery of Native Art, Pezinok 34042
Slovak National Literary Museum of the Slovak National Library, Martin 34026
Slovak National Museum, Bratislava 33979
Slovak Technical Museum, Košice 34005
Slovakian Museum of Local History, Békéscsaba 21320
Slovakian National Gallery, Dunajská Streda 33991
Slovakian National Museum, Holíč 33998
Slovene Ethnographic Museum, Ljubljana 34119
Slovenian Agricultural Museum, Nitra 34036
Slovenian Museum of Firefighting, Metlika 34131
Slovenian Museum of Natural History, Ljubljana 34118
Slovenian School Museum, Ljubljana 34121
Slovenská Národná Galéria, Bratislava 33978
Slovenská Národná Galéria, Dunajská Streda 33991
Slovenská Národná Galéria - Galéria Insitného Umenia - Schaubmar Mill, Pezinok 34042
Slovenská Národná Galéria - Kaštieľ Strážky, Spišská Béla 34063
Slovenská Národná Galéria - L'udovit Fulla Galéria, Ružomberok 34054
Slovenská Národná Galéria - Zvolenský Zámok, Zvolen 34082
Slovenské Banské Múzeum, Banská Štiavnica 33951
Slovenské Múzeum A.S. Puškina, Brodzany 33983
Slovenské Múzeum Ochrany Prírody a Jaskyniarstva, Liptovský Mikuláš 34017
Slovenské Národné Literárne Múzeum, Martin 34026
Slovenské Národné Múzeum, Bratislava 33979
Slovenské Národné Múzeum, Holíč 33998
Slovenské Národné Múzeum - Múzeum Betliar, Betliar 33954
Slovenské Národné Múzeum - Múzeum Bojnice, Bojnice 33956
Slovenské Polnohospodárske Múzeum, Nitra 34036
Slovenské Technické Múzeum, Košice 34005
Slovenski Etnografski Muzej, Ljubljana 34119
Slovenski Gasilski Muzej, Metlika 34131
Slovenski Gledališki Muzej, Ljubljana 34120
Slovenski Šolski Muzej, Ljubljana 34121
Slovensko Konservatorsko Društvo, Ljubljana 49363
Slovensko Muzejsko Društvo, Ljubljana 49364
Slovintzian Homestead, Kluki 31666
S.M. Kirov Memorial Appartment Museum, Vladikavkaz 33688
S.M. Kirov Museum, Sankt-Peterburg 33436
Smålands Bil, Musik och Leksaksmuseum, Rydaholm 36165
Smalands Cars, Toys and Musicmuseum, Rydaholm 36165
Smålands Konstarkiv, Värnamo 36377
Smålands Militärhistoriska Museum, Eksjö 35864
Smålands Museum, Växjö 36390
Small Mansions Arts Centre, London 39779
Small Museums Association, Clinton 49530
Smallwood's Retreat, Marbury 45138
Smeaton's Tower, Plymouth 40213
Smedemuseet, Øster-Assels 09020
Smederij Museum Wijlen dhr Verkley, Nieuwkoop 29623
Smetanamuseet, Göteborg 35921
Smidt Múzeum, Szombathely 21588
Smiske Museum, Rijmenam 03698
Smiterlöwsche Sammlung, Franzburg 17086
Smith Art Gallery, Brighouse 38335
Smith College Museum of Art, Northampton 46015
Smith County Historical Society Museum, Tyler 48131
Smith-McDowell House Museum, Asheville 41282
Smith Robertson Museum, Jackson 44286
Smith-Zimmermann Museum, Madison 45065
Smithers Public Art Gallery, Smithers 06463
Smithills Hall Museum, Bolton 38272
Smith's Cove Historical Museum, Smith's Cove 06464
Smiths Falls Railway Museum of Eastern Ontario, Smiths Falls 06467
Smith's Fort Plantation, Surry 47896
Smithsoniam American Art Museum, Washington 48392
Smithsonian Institution, Washington 48393
Smithtown Historical Society Museum, Smithtown 47657
Smoke Cabin Museum, Kuopio 09723
Smoki Museum, Prescott 46690
Smoky Hill Museum, Salina 47214
Smøla Museum, Smøla 30856
Smolensk Art Gallery, Smolensk 33534
Smolensk Cathedral, Smolensk 33537
Smolensk Historical Museum, Smolensk 33535
Smolensk State Museum-Preserve, Smolensk 33536
Smolenskaja Chudožestvennaja Galerja, Smolensk 33534

Smolenskij Istoričeskij Muzej, Smolensk 33535
Smolenskij Muzej-Zapovednik, Smolensk 33536
Smolenskij Sobor, Smolensk 33537
Smrcka's House - Hussite Museum, Soběslav 08659
Smrčkův Dům, Soběslav 08659
Smyth County Museum, Marion 45165
Snake River Heritage Center, Weiser 48492
Snake River Heritage Center, Weiser 48493
Snappertunan Talomuseo, Snappertuna 10042
Snåsa Bygdamuseum, Snåsa 30857
Snibston Discovery Park, Coalville 38599
The Snite Museum of Art, Notre Dame 46044
Snoqualmie Valley Historical Museum, North Bend 45982
Snow Country Tree Museum, Shiozawa 26761
Snowden House, Waterloo 48434
Snowshill Manor, Broadway 38369
Snug Harbor Cultural Center, Staten Island 47787
The Snyder County Historical Society Museum, Middleburg 45306
Snyder Museum and Creative Arts Center, Bastrop 41519
Søby Brunkulslejer og Brunkulsmuseet, Herning 08870
Søbygård, Søby Ærø 09073
Social History Collections, Cape Town 34210
Social History Curators Group, Newcastle-upon-Tyne 49444
Socialmuseet Det Gamle Syge-Plejehjem, Hinnerup 08875
Società per le Belle Arti ed Esposizione Permanente, Milano 24419
Societas Museologia, Český Těšín 49135
Société des Musées Québécois, Montréal 49105
Society for Contemporary Craft Museum, Pittsburgh 46527
Society for Contemporary Photography, Kansas City 44408
Society of Arts and Crafts Exhibition Gallery, Boston 41827
Society of County Museum Officers, Taunton 49445
Society of Decorative Art Curators, Liverpool 49446
Society of Illustrators Museum of American Illustration, New York 45871
Society of Museum Archaeologists, London 49447
Society of the Cincinnati Museum, Washington 48394
The Society of the Four Arts Gallery, Palm Beach 46265
Sočinskij Chudožestvennyj Muzej, Soči 33542
Socrates Sculpture Park, Long Island City 44873
Sod House Museum, Aline 41139
Sod House Museum, Arctic Bay 05005
Sod House Museum, Gothenburg 43734
Sodankylän Kotiseutumuseo, Sodankylä 10043
Sodbuster Archives Museum, Strome 06504
Sodus Bay Historical Society Museum, Sodus Point 47664
Söderbärke Hembygdsgård, Söderbärke 36208
Söderhamns Stadsmuseum, Söderhamn 36209
Söderlångvik Museum, Dragsfjärd 09423
Söderlångvikin Museo, Dragsfjärd 09423
Södertälje Art Gallery, Södertälje 36211
Södertälje Konsthall, Södertälje 36211
Sölje Bygdegård, Glava 35903
Sölvesborgs Museum, Sölvesborg 36215
Sörmlands Museum, Nyköping 36128
Sörmlandsgården, Eskilstuna 35872
Søfarts og Fiskerimuseet, Læsø 08969
Søfartssamlingerne i Troense, Svendborg 09086
Sofia Art Gallery, Sofia 04859
Sofiero Slott, Helsingborg 35955
Sofijska Gradska Chudožestvena Galerija, Sofia 04859
Sofijski Istoričeski Muzej, Sofia 04860
Software Museum, Hünfeld 17857
Sogetsu Art Museum, Tokyo 26924
Sogetsu Bijutsukan, Tokyo 26924
Søgne Bygdemuseum, Søgne 30859
Sogo Museum of Art, Yokohama 27020
Soho House, Birmingham 38229
Soil and Agronomy Museum W.R. Williams, Moskva 33175
Soinin Museo, Soini 10045
Sojun Art Museum, Siheung 27292
Sokang University Museum, Seoul 27279
Soklič Museum, Slovenj Gradec 34151
Sokličev Muzej, Slovenj Gradec 34151
Soknedal Bygdemuseum, Soknedal 30860
Solar Boats Museum, Giza 09297
Solar de Dom João VI, Rio de Janeiro 04405
Solar Grandjean de Montigny, Rio de Janeiro 04406
Le Soldat Artiste, Nouvron-Vingre 13367
Soldattorpet i Ytterjeppo, Uusikaarlepyy 10152
Soldiers' Memorial Military Museum, Saint Louis 47138
Soldiers National Museum, Gettysburg 43665
Soldiers of Gloucestershire Museum, Gloucester 39085
Soleleitungsmuseum Brunnhaus Klaushäusl, Grassau, Chiemgau 17379
Soli Archaeological Site, Lefke 08232
Solikamsk Municipal Museum, Solikamsk 33543
Solikamskij Gorodskoj Kraevedčeskij Muzej, Solikamsk 33543
Solinger Fotoforum, Solingen 19987
Sollefteå Museum, Sollefteå 36216
Søllerød Museum, Holte 08892
Solna Hembygdsmuseum, Solna 36222
Soloman Island National Museum and Cultural Centre, Honiara 34167
Solomon R. Guggenheim Museum, New York 45872
Solomos Museum, Corfu 20934
Soloveckij Gosudarstvennyj Istoriko-Architekturnyj i Prirodnyj Muzej-Zapovednik, Soloveckij 33546
Solovetsky State Historical, Architectural and Natural Museum-Reserve, Soloveckij 33546
Solway Aviation Museum, Crosby-on-Eden 38676
Soma Gyofu Kinenkan, Itoigawa 26268
Soma Gyofu Memorial Museum, Itoigawa 26268
Somali National Museum, Mogadishu 34168
Sombor Municipal Museum, Sombor 33910
Sombra Township Museum, Sombra 06469
Somdet Phra Narai National Museum, Lopburi 37514
Somero Museum, Somero 10049
Someron Museo, Somero 10049
Someron Torppamuseo, Somero 10050
Somers Historical Society Museum, Somers 47667
Somers Mansion, Somers Point 47669
Somerset and Dorset Railway Trust Museum, Washford 40798
Somerset Brick and Tile Museum, Bridgwater 38325
Somerset County Museum, Taunton 40677
Somerset Cricket Museum, Taunton 40678
Somerset East Museum, Somerset East 34379
Somerset Historical Center, Somerset 47670
Somerset Military Museum, Taunton 40679
Somerset Place, Creswell 42701
Somerset Rural Life Museum, Glastonbury 39072
Somervell County Museum, Glen Rose 43685
Somerville Museum, Somerville 47671
Somesville Museum, Mount Desert 45527
Somme Heritage Centre, Newtownards 40075
Sommerhuber-Kachelofenmuseum, Steyr 02690
Sømna Bygdetun, Sømna 30863
Somogyi Megyei Múzeumok Igazgatósága, Kaposvár 21442
Sonargaon Folk Art and Craft Museum, Sonargaon 03101
Sønderjyllands Kunstmuseum, Tønder 09093
Søndhordland Motormuseum, Valevåg 30969
Sondre Nordheimstova, Morgedal 30691
Song Qingling Former Residence, Shanghai 07224
Song Qingling Tongzhi Former Residence, Beijing 06989
Songam Art Museum, Incheon 27192
Songjiang County Museum, Shanghai 07225
Songsin Teachers College Museum, Seoul 27280
Sonkajärven Kotiseutumuseo, Sonkajärvi 10053
Sonoma County Museum, Santa Rosa 47448
Sonoma State Historic Park, Sonoma 47676
Sons of the American Revolution, Roselle 47006
Sons of the American Revolution Museum, Louisville 44975
Sontg Hippolytus, Veulden 37284
Sony Wonder Technology Lab, New York 45873
Soo Line Historical Museum, Weyburn 06783
Sood Sangvichien Prehistoric Museum, Bangkok 37497
Sooke Region Museum, Art Gallery and Historic Moss Cottage, Sooke 06470
Sookmyung Women's University Museum, Seoul 27281
Sooner Ga Museum, Dhaka 03094
Sophienburg Museum, New Braunfels 45670
Sopwell Nunnery, Saint Albans 40378
Sør-Senja Museum, Stonglandseidet 30899
Sorbische Bauernstube, Heinersbrück 17696
Sorbische Heimatstube Rohne, Schleife-Rohne 19789
Sordoni Art Gallery, Wilkes-Barre 48622
Sørlandets Kunstmuseum, Kristiansand 30615
Sørli Museum, Sørli 30867
Sorø Amts Museum, Sorø 09076
Sørsamiske Samlinger, Snåsa 30858
Sosnovoborskij Chudožestvennyj Muzei Sovremennogo Iskusstva, Sosnovyj Bor 33549
Sóstói Múzeumfalu, Sóstógyógyfürdő 21540
Sotamuseo, Helsinki 09529
Sotavallan Tuulimylly, Lempäälä 09775
Sotilaslääketieteen Museo, Lahti 09750
Sotkamon Kotiseutumuseo, Sotkamo 10054
Sotterley Plantation Museum, Hollywood 44061
Soun Museum, Ashikaga 26109
Sound School House Museum, Mount Desert 45528
Sound Visitor Centre, Port Saint Mary 40234
Sounds of Yesteryear, Winnipeg 06847
Souter Johnnie's House, Kirkoswald 39396
Souterroscope des Ardoisières, Caumont-l'Eventé 11093
South African Jewish Museum, Cape Town 34211
South African Maritime Museum, Cape Town 34212
South African Mint Museum-Coin World, Centurion 34216
South African Museum, Cape Town 34213
South African National Gallery, Cape Town 34214
South African National Museum of Military History, Saxonwold 34374
South African National Railway Museum, Auckland Park 34173
South African Police Service Museum, Pretoria 34356
South Arkansas Arts Center, El Dorado 43106
South Australian Aviation Museum, Port Adelaide 01375
South Australian Maritime Museum, Port Adelaide 01376
South Australian Museum, Adelaide 00713
South Australian Police Museum, Thebarton 01531
South Bannock County Historical Center, Lava Hot Springs 44683
South Bend Regional Museum of Art, South Bend 47681
South-Bohemian Museum in České Budějovice, České Budějovice 08299
South Boston-Halifax County Museum of Fine Arts and History, South Boston 47687
South Canterbury Museum, Timaru 30265
South Cariboo Historical Museum, Clinton 05258
South Carolina Artisans Center, Walterboro 48295
South Carolina Confederate Relic Room and Museum, Columbia 42566
South Carolina Cotton Museum, Bishopville 41718
South Carolina Federation of Museums, Columbia 49531
South Carolina Historical Society Museum, Charleston 42227
South Carolina Law Enforcement Officers Hall of Fame, Columbia 42567
South Carolina Military Museum, Columbia 42568
South Carolina National Guard Museum, Sumter 47878
South Carolina State Museum, Columbia 42569
South Carolina Tennis Hall of Fame, Belton 41617
South Charleston Museum, South Charleston 47688
South Coast Railroad Museum at Goleta Depot, Goleta 43720
South County Museum, Narragansett 45605
South Dakota Amateur Baseball Hall of Fame, Lake Norden 44591
South Dakota Art Museum, Brookings 41932
South Dakota Discovery Center, Pierre 46485
South Dakota Hall of Fame, Chamberlain 42183
South Devon Railway, Buckfastleigh 38381
South-East Armed Force Museum, Ho Chi Minh City 48990
South Eastern Federation of Museums and Art Galleries, Bromley 49448
South Florida Museum, Bradenton 41863
South Florida Museum of Natural History, Dania Beach 42773
South Florida Science Museum, West Palm Beach 48540
South Grey Museum and Historical Library, Flesherton 05427
South Hero Bicentennial Museum, South Hero 47696
South Hill Park Arts Centre, Bracknell 38293
South Holland Historical Museum, South Holland 47697
South Karelia Artmuseum, Lappeenranta 09761
South London Gallery, London 39780
South Midlands Museums Federation, Saffron Walden 49449
South Milwaukee Historical Society Museum, South Milwaukee 47698
South Molton and District Museum, South Molton 40533
South Moravian Museum, Znojmo 08756
South Nottinghamshire Hussars Museum, Bulwell 38392
South Otago Historical Museum, Balclutha 30116
South Park City Museum, Fairplay 43274
South Pass City State Historic Site, South Pass City 47701
South Peace Centennial Museum, Beaverlodge 05068
South Perth Heritage House, South Perth 01462
South Rawdon Museum, South Rawdon 06475
South Ribble Museum and Exhibition Centre, Leyland 39488
South River Meeting House, Lynchburg 45008
South Shields Museum and Art Gallery, South Shields 40538
South Simcoe Pioneer Museum, Alliston 04978
South Similkameen Museum, Keremeos 05663
South Street Seaport Museum, New York 45874
South Sutton Old Store Museum, South Sutton 47704
South Taranaki District Museum, Patea 30235
South Texas Museum, Alice 41138
South Tipperary County Museum, Clonmel 22398
South Tynedale Railway Preservation Society, Alston 37988
South Wales Borderers and Monmouthshire Regimental Museum of the Royal Regiment of Wales, Brecon 38318
South Wales Miner's Museum, Port Talbot 40238
South Wales Police Museum, Bridgend 38320
South West Museums Council, Bathpool 49450
South Western Federation of Museums and Art Galleries, Bournemouth 49451
South Wood County Historical Museum, Wisconsin Rapids 48719
Southampton Art Gallery, Southampton 06477
Southampton City Art Gallery, Southampton 40546
Southampton Hall of Aviation, Southampton 40547
Southampton Historical Museum, Southampton 47708
Southampton Maritime Museum, Southampton 40548
Southchurch Hall Museum, Southend-on-Sea 40554
Southeast Arts Center, Atlanta 41359
Southeast Missouri State University Museum, Cape Girardeau 42096
Southeast Museum, Brewster 41884
Southeast Museum of Photography, Daytona Beach 42812
Southeastern Center for Contemporary Art, Winston-Salem 48705
Southeastern Museums Conference, Baton Rouge 49532
Southeastern Railway Museum, Duluth 42996
Southend Central Museum, Southend-on-Sea 40555
Southend Pier Museum, Southend-on-Sea 40556
Southern African Development Community Association of Museums and Monuments, Harare 49551
Southern African Museums Association, Grahamstown 49366
Southern Alberta Art Gallery, Lethbridge 05748
Southern Alleghenies Museum of Art, Loretto 44884
Southern Alleghenies Museum of Art at Johnstown, Johnstown 44354
Southern California Chapter Railway and Locomotive Museum, Los Angeles 44944
Southern Exposure Gallery, San Francisco 47340
Southern Forest World Museum, Waycross 48473
Southern Highland Craft Guild at the Folk Art Center, Asheville 41283
Southern Museum of Flight, Birmingham 41709
Southern Newfoundland Seamen's Museum, Grand Bank 05508
Southern Ohio Museum and Cultural Center, Portsmouth 46657
Southern Oregon Historical Society Museum, Medford 45221
Southern Oregon University Museum of Vertebrate Natural History, Ashland 41297
Southern Ostrobothnia Museum, Seinäjoki 10028
Southern Plains Indian Museum, Anadarko 41193
Southern Ute Indian Cultural Center, Ignacio 44194
Southern Vermont Art Center, Manchester 45102
Southern Vermont College Art Gallery, Bennington 41630
Southern Vermont Natural History Museum, Marlboro 45171
Southey and District Museum, Southey 06478
The Southland Art Collection, Dallas 42758
Southland Fire Service Museum, Invercargill 30185
Southland Museum and Art Gallery, Invercargill 30186
Southold Historical Society Museum, Southold 47710
Southold Indian Museum, Southold 47711
Southsea Castle, Portsmouth 40259
Southside House, London 39781
Southward Museum, Paraparaumu 30234
Southwest Museum, Los Angeles 44945
Southwest Museum of Science and Technology, Dallas 42759
Southwest Virginia Museum, Big Stone Gap 41684
Southwestern College Art Gallery, Chula Vista 42393
Southwestern Häme Museum, Forssa 09442
Southwestern Michigan College Museum, Dowagiac 42978
Southwestern Ontario Heritage Village, Kingsville 05690
Southwestern Saskatchewan Oldtimer's Museum, Maple Creek 05811
Southwestern University Museum, Cebu 31317
Southwestern Utah Art Gallery, Saint George 47091
Southwick Hall, Peterborough 40190
Southwold Museum, Southwold 40561
Souvenirs de Temps Passé, Sarralbe 14618
Sovereign Hill, Ballarat 00765
S.P. Engelbrecht Museum of the Nederduitsch Hervormde Kerk van Afrika, Pretoria 34357
S.P. Korolev House Museum, Moskva 33074
Spaarnestad Fotoarchief, Haarlem 29330
Space 101 Gallery, Pittsburgh 46528
Space Center Houston, Houston 44138
Space Expo, Noordwijk, Zuid-Holland 29646
Space Farms Zoological Park and Museum, Sussex 47897
Space One Eleven, Birmingham 41710
Spaces, Cleveland 42481
Spadina Museum, Toronto 06613
Spakenburgs Museum 't Vurhuus, Bunschoten Spakenburg 29039
Spalding Gentlemen's Society Museum, Spalding 40564
The Spam Museum, Austin 41403
Spanish Governor's Palace, San Antonio 47261
Spanish Institute, New York 45875
The Spanish Quarter Museum, Saint Augustine 47074
Sparebankmuseet, Oslo 30763
Sparekassemuseet, Korsør 08965
Spargelmuseum, Schlunkendorf 19807
Spark Gallery, Denver 42900
Sparkassen-Museum, Greding 17382
Sparkassen-Museum der Erste Bank, Wien 02990
Sparresholm Vognsamling, Holme-Olstrup 08886
Spartanburg County Museum of Art, Spartanburg 47718
Spartanburg Science Center, Spartanburg 47719
Spårvägsmuseet, Stockholm 36283
Spasskoe Lutovinovo - I.S. Turgenev Museum-Estate, Spasskoe-Lutovinovo 33550
Spathareion Museum of the Shadow Theatre, Maroussi 21058
SPC Pioneer Museum, San Francisco 47341
Speed Art Museum, Louisville 44976
Speelgoedmuseum De Brug, Eerbeek 29201
Speelgoedmuseum De Kijkdoos, Hoorn 29445
Speelgoedmuseum Deventer, Deventer 29146
Speelgoedmuseum Mechelen, Mechelen 03617
Speelgoedmuseum Op Stelten, Oosterhout 29671
Speicherstadtmuseum, Hamburg 17567
Speke Hall, Liverpool 39527
Speldjesmuseum, Klaaswaal 29481
Spellman Museum of Stamps and Postal History, Weston 48570

Spelman College Museum of Fine Art, Atlanta 41360
Spelthorne Museum, Staines 40573
Spencer and Gillen Gallery, Alice Springs 00738
Spencer Entomological Museum, Vancouver 06690
Spencer House, London 39782
Spencer Museum of Art, Lawrence 44686
Spencer-Peirce-Little Farm, Newbury 45907
Spendiarians Museum, Erevan 00689
Spengler-Museum, Sangerhausen 19743
Sperrgebiet Museum, Oranjemund 28767
Sperrin Heritage Centre, Plumridge 40208
Spertus Museum, Chicago 42363
Spessartmuseum, Lohr am Main 18499
Spetses Museum, Spetses 21168
Spice's Gewürzmuseum, Hamburg 17568
spiegel, München 18908
Spiel Kultur, München 18909
Spielkartensammlung Piatnik, Wien 02991
Spielzeug anno dazumal - Museum Beilngries, Beilngries 15871
Spielzeug-Museum Bad Herrenalb, Bad Herrenalb 15658
Spielzeugeisenbahn- und Zweiradmuseum, Affoltern am Albis 36435
Spielzeugmuseum, Bad Lauterberg 15690
Spielzeugmuseum, Davos Platz 36655
Spielzeugmuseum, Görlitz 17326
Spielzeugmuseum, Hemau 17707
Spielzeugmuseum, Ingolstadt 17910
Spielzeugmuseum, Loosdorf, Bez. Melk 02252
Spielzeugmuseum, Michelstadt 18733
Spielzeugmuseum, Nürnberg 19161
Spielzeugmuseum, Salzburg 02552
Spielzeugmuseum, Schkeuditz 19787
Spielzeugmuseum, Trier 20213
Spielzeugmuseum, Zwiesel 20780
Spielzeugmuseum Alsfeld, Alsfeld 15438
Spielzeugmuseum Bebra, Bebra 15863
Spielzeugmuseum, Dorf- und Rebbaumuseum, Riehen 37063
Spielzeugmuseum im Alten Rathausturm, München 18910
Spielzeugmuseum im Alten Schloß, Sugenheim 20120
Spielzeugmuseum/Kellerkunstmuseum im Auktionshaus Boltz, Bayreuth 15859
Spielzeugmuseum - Sammlung Depuoz, Zürich 37408
Spiers Gallery, Brevard 41881
Spillemands-Jagt og Skovbrugsmuseet i Rebild, Skørping 09067
Spindletop and Gladys City Boomtown Museum, Beaumont 41571
Het Spinozahuis, Rijnsburg 29733
Spirit of '76 Museum, Elyria 43178
Spirit of '76 Museum, Wellington 48500
Spiro Mounds Archaeological Center, Spiro 47725
Spišské Múzeum, Levoča 34012
Spital Hengersberg, Hengersberg 17709
Spitalmuseum, Aub 15541
Spitfire and Hurricane Memorial Museum, Ramsgate 40284
SPLIA Gallery, Cold Spring Harbor 42519
Split Archaeological Museum, Split 07779
Split Ethnographical Museum, Split 07780
Split Rock Lighthouse Historic Site, Two Harbors 48128
Spode Museum, Stoke-on-Trent 40611
Spoke Wheel Car Museum, Charlottetown 05233
Społeczne Muzeum Konstantego Laszczki, Dobre 31555
Spomen Galerija Ivana Meštrovića, Vrpolje 07803
Spomen Kuća Bitke na Sutjesci, Tjentište 33920
Spomen-Kuća Vladimira Gortana, Beran 07679
Spomen-Muzej Prosvetitelja i Pisca Kirila Pejčinovića, Lesak kod Tetova 33858
Spomen Muzej Prvog Zasjedania ZAVNOBiH-a, Mrkonjić Grad 33861
Spomen Muzej Prvog Zasjedanja ZAVNOBiH-a, Mrkonjić Grad 03919
Spomen Muzej Stojana Araliče, Otočac 07751
Spomen-Park Kragujevački Oktobar, Kragujevac 33854
Spomen Park-Kumrovec, Kumrovec 07731
Spomen-Zbirka Pavla Beljanskog, Novi Sad 33873
Spominska Zbirka Pisatelja Ivana Cankarja, Vrhnika 34164
Spoor- en Tramweg Verzameling, Loppersum 29548
Spoorwegmuseum van Miniatuurmodellen, Heist-op-den-Berg 03490
Sport Museum at Luzhniki, Moskva 33150
Sportmuseum Berlin, Berlin 16097
Sportmuseum Leipzig, Leipzig 18418
Sportmuseum Vlaanderen, Hofstade 03500
Sports Car Museum of Japan, Gotemba 26159
Sports Hall of Memories, Trail 06629
Sports Museum Borås, Borås 35839
Sports Museum of Finland, Helsinki 09534
The Sports Museum of New England, Boston 41828
Sports Museum Pierre de Coubertin, La Falda 00380
Sporveismuseet Vognhall 5, Oslo 30764
Sporvejsmuseet Skjoldenæsholm, Jystrup Midtsj 08910
Spotsylvania Historical Museum, Spotsylvania 47729
Spreewald-Museum Lübbenau/Lehde, Lübbenau 18532
Sprengel Museum Hannover, Hannover 17611
Spring Mill State Park Pioneer Village and Grissom Memorial, Mitchell 45411
Spring Street Historical Museum, Shreveport 47618
Springbank Visual Arts Centre, Mississauga 05873
Springfield Armory Museum, Springfield 47749
Springfield Art Gallery, Springfield 47742
Springfield Art Museum, Springfield 47754
Springfield Historical Society Museum, Springfield 47755
Springfield Museum, Springfield 47758
Springfield Museum of Art, Springfield 47757
Springfield Museum of Old Domestic Life, High Point 44016
Springfield Science Museum, Springfield 47750
Springhill Costume Museum, Moneymore 39974
Springhill House, Magherafelt 39872
Springhill Miner's Museum, Springhill 06482
Springs Museum, Springs 47761
Springvale and District Historical Museum, Springvale 01472
Springville Museum of Art, Springville 47763
Spruce Row Museum, Waterford 06749
Spruill Gallery, Atlanta 41361
Spurlock Museum, Urbana 48164
Spurn Lightship, Kingston-upon-Hull 39382
Spy Museum, Tampere 10097
Spydeberg Bygdetun, Spydeberg 30873
Squam Lakes Natural Science Center, Holderness 44050
Squamish Valley Museum, Garibaldi Heights 05476
Squerryes Court, Westerham 40833
Średzki Ośrodek Kultury Galeria, Środa Śląska 31994
Srinakharinwirot Art Exhibition Hall, Bangkok 37498
SS Great Britain Museum, Bristol 38360
S.S. Meteor Maritime Museum, Barkers Island 41505
S.S. Moyie National Historic Site, Kaslo 05647
St Janhuis Mill & Koelewei Mill, Brugge 03267
Staatliche Antikensammlungen und Glyptothek, München 18911
Staatliche Bücher- und Kupferstichsammlung Greiz, Greiz 17394
Staatliche Graphische Sammlung München, München 18912
Staatliche Kunsthalle Baden-Baden, Baden-Baden 15790
Staatliche Kunsthalle Karlsruhe, Karlsruhe 18002
Staatliche Kunstsammlungen Dresden, Dresden 16710
Staatliche Münzsammlung, München 18913
Staatliche Museen Kassel, Kassel 18029
Staatliche Museen zu Berlin - Preußischer Kulturbesitz, Berlin 16098
Staatliche Museumsberatung für Nordhessen, Kassel 18030
Staatliche Sammlungen in der Residenz, München 18914
Staatlicher Schloßbetrieb Schloß Nossen / Kloster Altzella, Nossen 19128
Staatliches Museum Ägyptischer Kunst, München 18915
Staatliches Museum für Ägyptische Kunst, Seefeld, Oberbayern 19915
Staatliches Museum für Naturkunde, Karlsruhe 18003
Staatliches Museum für Naturkunde Görlitz, Görlitz 17327
Staatliches Museum für Naturkunde Stuttgart, Stuttgart 20105
Staatliches Museum für Völkerkunde Dresden, Dresden 16711
Staatliches Museum für Völkerkunde München, München 18916
Staatliches Naturhistorisches Museum, Braunschweig 16304
Staats- und Stadtbibliothek, Augsburg 15568
Staats- und Universitätsbibliothek Hamburg Carl von Ossietzky, Hamburg 17569
Staatsarchiv Bamberg, Bamberg 15816
Staatsbibliothek Bamberg, Bamberg 15817
Staatsbibliothek zu Berlin, Berlin 16099
Staatsbibliothek zu Berlin, Berlin 16100
Staatsburgh State Historic Museum, Staatsburg 47765
Staatsgalerie am Schaezler-Palais, Augsburg 15569
Staatsgalerie im Hohen Schloß, Füssen 17169
Staatsgalerie im Leeren Beutel, Regensburg 19530
Staatsgalerie im Neuen Schloß, Oberschleißheim 19206
Staatsgalerie in der Benediktiner-Abtei, Ottobeuren 19328
Staatsgalerie in der Burg, Burghausen, Salzach 16423
Staatsgalerie in der Kunsthalle, Augsburg 15570
Staatsgalerie in der Neuen Residenz, Bamberg 15818
Staatsgalerie in der Residenz, Ansbach 15505
Staatsgalerie in der Residenz Würzburg, Würzburg 20706
Staatsgalerie moderner Kunst in der Pinakothek der Moderne, München 18917
Staatsgalerie Stuttgart, Stuttgart 20106
Stabbursnes Naturhus og Museum, Indre Billefjord 30578
Stabler-Leadbeater Apothecary Museum, Alexandria 41134
Stables Art Gallery of Taos Art Association, Taos 47952
Stacy's Tavern Museum and Glen Ellyn Historical Society, Glen Ellyn 43682
Stadhuis, Gent 03451
Stadhuis van Antwerpen, Antwerpen 03174
Stadhuismuseum, Zierikzee 30062
Stadsboerderij Het Wevershuisje, Almelo 28810
Stadsgalerie Engels Tuin, Ootmarsum 29679
Stadsgalerie Gouda, Gouda 29298
Stadsgalerij Heerlen, Heerlen 29368
Stadsmuseet i Gråbrödraklostret, Ystad 36422
Stadsmuseet och Ahlbergshallen, Östersund 36148
Stadsmuseum Doetinchem, Doetinchem 29162
Stadsmuseum Groenlo, Groenlo 29303
Stadsmuseum IJsselstein, IJsselstein 29462
Stadsmuseum Woerden, Woerden 30016
Stadsmuseum Zoetermeer, Zoetermeer 30064
Stadt-, Glas- und Steinmuseum, Gmünd, Niederösterreich 01893
Stadt-Museum, Weil der Stadt 20440
Stadt- und Bädermuseum, Bad Salzuflen 15730
Stadt- und Bädermuseum Bad Doberan, Bad Doberan 15625
Stadt- und Bergbaumuseum Freiberg, Freiberg, Sachsen 17104
Stadt- und Brauereimuseum, Pritzwalk 19452
Stadt- und Burgmuseum, Eppstein 16884
Stadt- und Dampfmaschinenmuseum, Werdau, Sachsen 20517
Stadt- und Fachwerkmuseum Alte Universität, Eppingen 16882
Stadt- und Festungsmuseum im Ludwigstor, Germersheim 17254
Stadt- und Heimatmuseum, Heidenreichstein 02013
Stadt- und Heimatmuseum, Kusel 18277
Stadt- und Heimatmuseum, Marienberg 18634
Stadt- und Heimatmuseum der Stadt Marl, Marl, Westfalen 18656
Stadt- und Heimatmuseum mit Galerie, Waischenfeld 20351
Stadt- und Hochstiftmuseum, Dillingen an der Donau 16612
Stadt- und Industriemuseum-Lottehaus, Wetzlar 20561
Stadt- und Kreisgeschichtliches Museum, Hünfeld 17858
Stadt- und Kulturgeschichtliches Museum, Torgau 20186
Stadt- und Landesbibliothek Dortmund, Artothek, Dortmund 16664
Stadt- und Manfred-Kyber-Museum, Löwenstein 18493
Stadt- und Parkmuseum, Bad Muskau 15698
Stadt- und Regionalmuseum Landshut, Landshut 18313
Stadt- und Steirisches Eisenmuseum, Eisenerz 01802
Stadt- und Turmmuseum, Bad Camberg 15623
Stadt- und Universitätsbibliothek, Frankfurt am Main 17073
Stadt-und Wagenmuseum Oschatz, Oschatz 19273
Stadt- und Wallfahrtsmuseum, Walldürn 20379
Stadtarchiv mit städtischen Sammlungen, Lauf an der Pegnitz 18353
Stadtarchiv und Stadtbibliothek, Lindau, Bodensee 18475
Stadtbibliothek Reutlingen, Reutlingen 19579
Stadtbibliothek Trier - Schatzkammer und Ausstellung, Trier 20214
Stadtgalerie, Osnabrück 19285
Stadtgalerie Altena, Altena 15444
Stadtgalerie Altötting, Altötting 15466
Stadtgalerie am Minoritenplatz, Wolfsberg, Kärnten 03043
Stadtgalerie Bamberg - Villa Dessauer, Bamberg 15819
Stadtgalerie Bern, Bern 36554
Stadtgalerie im alten Herrenhaus, Ternitz 02723
Stadtgalerie im Elbeforum, Brunsbüttel 16384
Stadtgalerie in Bruneck, Brunico 23220
Stadtgalerie Kiel, Kiel 18079
Stadtgalerie Klagenfurt, Klagenfurt 02133
Stadtgalerie Lünen, Lünen 18563
Stadtgalerie Saarbrücken, Saarbrücken 19728
Stadtgeschichtliche Sammlung, Velbert 20295
Stadtgeschichtliches Museum, Pfullingen 19394
Stadtgeschichtliches Museum, Tangermünde 20140
Stadtgeschichtliches Museum im Landrichterhaus, Karlstadt 18009
Stadtgeschichtliches Museum Jülich, Jülich 17966
Stadtgeschichtliches Museum Leipzig, Leipzig 18419
Stadtgeschichtliches Museum Schabbellhaus, Wismar 20618
Stadtgeschichtliches Museum Spandau, Berlin 16101
Stadtgeschichtliches Museum Weißensee, Berlin 16102
Stadtgeschichtliches Zentrum, Lutherstadt Wittenberg 18578
Stadtgeschichts- und Schradenmuseum, Ortrand 19272
Stadtgeschichtsmuseum Schwerin, Schwerin 19900
Stadthaus am Dom, Wetzlar 20562
Stadthaus-Galerie, Münster 18945
Stadthaus Olten, Olten 37011
Stadthaus Ulm, Ulm 20260
Stadthistorisches Museum, Bad Salzdetfurth 15728
Stadtmauermuseum Nördlingen, Nördlingen 19109
Stadtmuseum, Apolda 15509
Stadtmuseum, Baunatal 15833
Stadtmuseum, Freilassing 17120
Stadtmuseum, Melk 02291
Stadtmuseum, Penzberg 19373
Stadtmuseum, Rothenburg, Oberlausitz 19686
Stadtmuseum, Wusterhausen 20723
Stadtmuseum Aarau, Aarau 36429
Stadtmuseum "Alte Burg" Wittenberge, Wittenberge 20625
Stadtmuseum Alte Post, Ebersbach an der Fils 16767
Stadtmuseum Amberg, Amberg, Oberpfalz 15478
Stadtmuseum Amtsturm, Lübz 18546
Stadtmuseum Andernach, Andernach 15488
Stadtmuseum Arelape-Bechelaren, Pöchlarn 02423
Stadtmuseum Bad Bergzabern, Bad Bergzabern 15603
Stadtmuseum Bad Berneck, Bad Berneck 15612
Stadtmuseum Bad Cannstatt, Stuttgart 20107
Stadtmuseum Bad Soden, Bad Soden am Taunus 15745
Stadtmuseum Bad Wildungen, Bad Wildungen 15766
Stadtmuseum Baden-Baden, Baden-Baden 15791
Stadtmuseum Baden-Baden, Baden-Baden 15792
Stadtmuseum Bautzen, Bautzen 15836
Stadtmuseum Beckum, Beckum 15865
Stadtmuseum Bergkamen, Bergkamen 15902
Stadtmuseum Bocholt, Bocholt 16190
Stadtmuseum Bonn, Bonn 16247
Stadtmuseum Borken, Westfalen, Borken, Westfalen 16258
Stadtmuseum Brakel, Brakel 16272
Stadtmuseum Breuberg-Neustadt, Breuberg 16359
Stadtmuseum Bruck an der Leitha, Bruck an der Leitha 01752
Stadtmuseum Burgdorf, Burgdorf, Kreis Hannover 16416
Stadtmuseum Burgstädt, Burgstädt 16431
Stadtmuseum Coesfeld und Städtische Turmgalerie, Coesfeld 16491
Stadtmuseum Colditz, Colditz 16494
Stadtmuseum Cottbus, Cottbus 16506
Stadtmuseum Cuxhaven, Cuxhaven 16519
Stadtmuseum Damme, Damme, Dümmer 16534
Stadtmuseum Deggendorf, Deggendorf 16560
Stadtmuseum Delmenhorst, Delmenhorst 16569
Stadtmuseum der Landeshauptstadt Düsseldorf, Düsseldorf 16743
Stadtmuseum Ditzingen, Ditzingen 16626
Stadtmuseum Döbeln/Kleine Galerie, Döbeln 16628
Stadtmuseum Dornbirn, Dornbirn 01772
Stadtmuseum Dresden, Dresden 16712
Stadtmuseum Eilenburg, Eilenburg 16810
Stadtmuseum Eisenberg, Eisenberg, Thüringen 16822
Stadtmuseum Erlangen, Erlangen 16923
Stadtmuseum Esslingen, Esslingen 16970
Stadtmuseum Eupen, Eupen 03413
Stadtmuseum Euskirchen, Euskirchen 16978
Stadtmuseum Fellbach, Fellbach 16992
Stadtmuseum Fembohaus mit Noricama, Nürnberg 19162
Stadtmuseum Friesach, Friesach 01855
Stadtmuseum Fürstenfeldbruck, Fürstenfeldbruck 17161
Stadtmuseum Fürth, Fürth, Bayern 17167
Stadtmuseum Gardelegen, Gardelegen 17199
Stadtmuseum Gehrden, Gehrden, Hannover 17210
Stadtmuseum Geithain, Geithain 17220
Stadtmuseum Gera, Gera 17248
Stadtmuseum Gerlingen - Gerlinger Heimatmuseum - Museum der Deutschen aus Ungarn, Gerlingen 17252
Stadtmuseum Giengen, Giengen an der Brenz 17275
Stadtmuseum Göhre, Jena 17952
Stadtmuseum Grafenau, Grafenau, Niederbayern 17369
Stadtmuseum Groß-Gerau, Groß-Gerau 17416
Stadtmuseum Gütersloh, Gütersloh 17460
Stadtmuseum Gunzenhausen, Gunzenhausen 17465
Stadtmuseum Hadamar, Hadamar 17474
Stadtmuseum Hagen, Hagen, Westfalen 17483
Stadtmuseum Hall in Tirol, Hall in Tirol 01995
Stadtmuseum Hartberg, Hartberg 02003
Stadtmuseum Hattingen, Hattingen 17637
Stadtmuseum Haus Kupferhammer, Warstein 20404
Stadtmuseum Herrenmühle, Hammelburg 17579
Stadtmuseum Herzogenaurach, Herzogenaurach 17744
Stadtmuseum Hildburghausen, Hildburghausen 17753
Stadtmuseum Hofgeismar, Hofgeismar 17798
Stadtmuseum Hofheim am Taunus, Hofheim am Taunus 17799
Stadtmuseum Holzminden, Holzminden 17832
Stadtmuseum Horb, Horb 17841
Stadtmuseum Hornmoldhaus, Bietigheim-Bissingen 16160
Stadtmuseum Hüfingen, Hüfingen 17853
Stadtmuseum im Alten Forstamt, Stockach 20062
Stadtmuseum im Augustinerkloster, Bad Langensalza 15687
Stadtmuseum im Knochenhauer-Amtshaus, Hildesheim 17761
Stadtmuseum im Prinz-Max-Palais, Karlsruhe 18004
Stadtmuseum im Spital, Crailsheim 16507
Stadtmuseum im Weveldhaus, Neuburg an der Donau 19019
Stadtmuseum Ingolstadt im Kavalier Hepp, Ingolstadt 17911
Stadtmuseum Iserlohn, Iserlohn 17922
Stadtmuseum Judenburg, Judenburg 02092
Stadtmuseum Kassel, Kassel 18031
Stadtmuseum Kaufbeuren, Kaufbeuren 18044
Stadtmuseum Killingerhaus, Idstein 17882
Stadtmuseum Klostermühle, Bad Urach 15757
Stadtmuseum Klosterneuburg, Klosterneuburg 02143
Stadtmuseum Leimen - Sankt Ilgen, Leimen, Baden 18374
Stadtmuseum Leonberg, Leonberg, Württemberg 18443
Stadtmuseum Leun, Leun 18445
Stadtmuseum Lichtenfels, Lichtenfels, Bayern 18457

Stadtmuseum Lindau, Lindau, Bodensee 18476
Stadtmuseum Ludwigshafen, Ludwigshafen am Rhein 18522
Stadtmuseum Lüdenscheid, Lüdenscheid 18551
Stadtmuseum Meersburg, Meersburg 18678
Stadtmuseum Meißen, Meißen 18692
Stadtmuseum Meppen, Meppen 18709
Stadtmuseum mit Weinmuseum, Bad Vöslau 01721
Stadtmuseum Mosbach, Mosbach, Baden 18796
Stadtmuseum Mühlberg, Elbe, Mühlberg, Elbe 18802
Stadtmuseum Mühlheim, Mühlheim am Main 18811
Stadtmuseum Münster, Münster 18946
Stadtmuseum Mutzschen, Mutzschen 18965
Stadtmuseum Naumburg, Naumburg, Saale 18981
Stadtmuseum Neumarkt, Neumarkt, Oberpfalz 19047
Stadtmuseum Neuötting, Neuötting 19056
Stadtmuseum Neustadt an der Waldnaab, Neustadt an der Waldnaab 19073
Stadtmuseum Nittenau, Nittenau 19106
Stadtmuseum Nördlingen, Nördlingen 19110
Stadtmuseum Norderstedt, Norderstedt 19118
Stadtmuseum Nürtingen, Nürtingen 19166
Stadtmuseum Obermühle, Braunfels 16289
Stadtmuseum Oberwölz und Österreichisches Blasmusikmuseum, Oberwölz 02380
Stadtmuseum Oldenburg, Oldenburg, Oldenburg 19259
Stadtmuseum Pforzheim, Pforzheim 19390
Stadtmuseum Pinkafeld, Pinkafeld 02416
Stadtmuseum Pinneberg, Pinneberg 19400
Stadtmuseum Pirna, Pirna 19407
Stadtmuseum Povelturm, Nordhorn 19124
Stadtmuseum Pulsnitz, Pulsnitz 19454
Stadtmuseum Quakenbrück, Quakenbrück 19456
Stadtmuseum Radolfzell, Radolfzell 19473
Stadtmuseum Rastatt, Rastatt 19490
Stadtmuseum Rottweil, Rottweil 19698
Stadtmuseum Saalfeld im Franziskanerkloster, Saalfeld, Saale 19721
Stadtmuseum Sachsenheim, Sachsenheim 19730
Stadtmuseum Sankt Pölten, Sankt Pölten 02605
Stadtmuseum Sankt Veit, Sankt Veit an der Glan 02614
Stadtmuseum Schelklingen, Schelklingen 19772
Stadtmuseum Schladming, Schladming 02632
Stadtmuseum Schleswig, Schleswig 19796
Stadtmuseum Schloß Hoyerswerda, Hoyerswerda 17848
Stadtmuseum Schloss Wolfsburg, Wolfsburg 20663
Stadtmuseum Schlüsselfeld, Schlüsselfeld 19806
Stadtmuseum Schongau, Schongau 19841
Stadtmuseum Schorndorf, Schorndorf, Württemberg 19844
Stadtmuseum Schramberg, Schramberg 19848
Stadtmuseum Schwabach, Schwabach 19857
Stadtmuseum Schwandorf mit Falkenauer Heimatstube, Schwandorf 19874
Stadtmuseum Schwedt, Schwedt 19887
Stadtmuseum Siegburg, Siegburg 19945
Stadtmuseum Sindelfingen, Sindelfingen 19965
Stadtmuseum Stadtoldendorf, Stadtoldendorf 20033
Stadtmuseum Steinfurt, Steinfurt 20047
Stadtmuseum Stolpen, Stolpen 20070
Stadtmuseum Stubenhaus, Staufen 20038
Stadtmuseum Sulzbach-Rosenberg, Sulzbach-Rosenberg 20126
Stadtmuseum Teterow, Teterow 20161
Stadtmuseum Teterow, Teterow 20162
Stadtmuseum Tharandt, Tharandt 20171
Stadtmuseum Traiskirchen, Möllersdorf 02316
Stadtmuseum Traiskirchen, Traiskirchen 02731
Stadtmuseum Trostberg, Trostberg 20219
Stadtmuseum Tübingen, Tübingen 20229
Stadtmuseum und Fürstlich Starhembergisches Familienmuseum, Eferding 01788
Stadtmuseum Waldkraiburg, Waldkraiburg 20369
Stadtmuseum Weilheim, Weilheim, Oberbayern 20450
Stadtmuseum Weimar, Weimar, Thüringen 20474
Stadtmuseum Wels, Wels 02815
Stadtmuseum Wels-Burg - Agrargeschichtliche Sammlung, Wels 02816
Stadtmuseum Wiener Neustadt, Wiener Neustadt 03021
Stadtmuseum Wienertor Hainburg, Hainburg an der Donau 01988
Stadtmuseum Wil, Wil 37320
Stadtmuseum Zistersdorf, Zistersdorf 03055
Stadtmuseum Zweibrücken, Zweibrücken 20773
Stadtmuseum Zwettl, Zwettl, Niederösterreich 03061
Stadtraum Vilshofen, Vilshofen 20327
Stadtresidenz Landshut, Landshut 18314
Stadttormuseum, Wehrheim 20422
Das Städel, Frankfurt am Main 17074
Städtische Ausstellungshalle, Münster 18947
Städtische Dauerausstellung zur Geschichte der Aschaffenburger Juden, Aschaffenburg 15532
Städtische Galerie, Bietigheim-Bissingen 16161
Städtische Galerie, Dreieich 16674
Städtische Galerie, Eisenhüttenstadt 16824
Städtische Galerie, Ettlingen 16976
Städtische Galerie, Lienz 02221
Städtische Galerie, Paderborn 19340
Städtische Galerie, Ravensburg 19507
Städtische Galerie, Schieder-Schwalenberg 19776
Städtische Galerie, Traunstein 20191
Städtische Galerie ada Meiningen, Meiningen 18687
Städtische Galerie am Markt Wurzen, Wurzen 20722
Städtische Galerie Böblingen, Böblingen 16214
Städtische Galerie Brückenturm, Mainz 18607
Städtische Galerie Delmenhorst, Delmenhorst 16570
Städtische Galerie Die Fähre, Bad Saulgau 15732
Städtische Galerie Eichenmüllerhaus, Lemgo 18432
Städtische Galerie Erlangen, Erlangen 16924
Städtische Galerie Fauler Pelz, Überlingen 20244
Städtische Galerie Filderhalle, Leinfelden-Echterdingen 18377
Städtische Galerie Filderstadt, Filderstadt 17002
Städtische Galerie Fruchthalle Rastatt, Rastatt 19491
Städtische Galerie Haus Seel, Siegen 19951
Städtische Galerie im Alten Rathaus, Fürstenwalde, Spree 17162
Städtische Galerie im Buntentor, Bremen 16334
Städtische Galerie im Cordonhaus, Cham 16460
Städtische Galerie im Königin-Christinen-Haus, Zeven 20754
Städtische Galerie im Kornhaus, Kirchheim unter Teck 18097
Städtische Galerie im Kulturforum, Offenburg 19243
Städtische Galerie im Lenbachhaus und Kunstbau, München 18918
Städtische Galerie im Park, Viersen 20314
Städtische Galerie im Rathaus, Balingen 15800
Städtische Galerie im Rathauspark, Gladbeck 17292
Städtische Galerie im Schloßpark Strünkede, Herne 17730
Städtische Galerie im Theater Ingolstadt, Ingolstadt 17912
Städtische Galerie in der Alten Schule, Sigmaringen 19958
Städtische Galerie In der Badstube, Wangen im Allgäu 20394
Städtische Galerie in der Reithalle, Paderborn 19341
Städtische Galerie Iserlohn, Iserlohn 17923
Städtische Galerie Kaarst, Kaarst 17969
Städtische Galerie Karlsruhe, Karlsruhe 18005
Städtische Galerie Leerer Beutel, Regensburg 19531
Städtische Galerie Lehrte, Lehrte 18371
Städtische Galerie Liebieghaus, Frankfurt am Main 17075
Städtische Galerie Lovis-Kabinett, Villingen-Schwenningen 20320
Städtische Galerie Mennonitenkirche, Neuwied 19087
Städtische Galerie Nordhorn - Kunstwegen, Nordhorn 19125
Städtische Galerie Ostfildern, Ostfildern 19298
Städtische Galerie Peschkenhaus, Moers 18778
Städtische Galerie Peter Breuer, Zwickau 20779
Städtische Galerie Reutlingen, Reutlingen 19580
Städtische Galerie Rosenheim, Rosenheim 19653
Städtische Galerie Schwarzes Kloster, Freiburg im Breisgau 17116
Städtische Galerie sohle 1, Bergkamen 15903
Städtische Galerie Stapflehus, Weil am Rhein 20437
Städtische Galerie Villa Streccius, Landau in der Pfalz 18301
Städtische Galerie Villa Zanders, Bergisch Gladbach 15901
Städtische Galerie Waldkraiburg, Waldkraiburg 20370
Städtische Galerie Wesseling, Wesseling 20540
Städtische Galerie Wolfsburg, Wolfsburg 20664
Städtische Gemäldegalerie, Füssen 17170
Städtische Kunstgalerie im Deutschordenshaus, Donauwörth 16641
Städtische Kunstgalerie Torhaus Rombergpark, Dortmund 16665
Städtische Kunsthalle, Recklinghausen 19513
Städtische Kunstsammlung, Eschweiler 16937
Städtische Kunstsammlung, Murrhardt 18964
Städtische Kunstsammlung Schloß Salder, Salzgitter 19735
Städtische Kunstsammlungen, Ausstellungsgebäude, Darmstadt 16549
Städtische Münzsammlung im Archiv der Hansestadt Lübeck, Lübeck 18543
Städtische Museen Heilbronn, Heilbronn 17692
Städtische Museen Junge Kunst und Viadrina, Frankfurt/Oder 17085
Städtische Museen Wangen im Allgäu, Wangen im Allgäu 20395
Städtische Sammlungen, Adelsheim 15397
Städtische Sammlungen, Amstetten 01670
Städtische Sammlungen Freital, Freital 17125
Städtische Wessenberg-Galerie, Konstanz 18207
Städtisches Feuerwehr-Museum, Eisenhüttenstadt 16825
Städtisches Heimatmuseum, Ballenstedt 15802
Städtisches Heimatmuseum, Höchstadt an der Aisch 17778
Städtisches Heimatmuseum, Landau in der Pfalz 18302
Städtisches Heimatmuseum, Lippstadt 18485
Städtisches Heimatmuseum, Mengen 18707
Städtisches Heimatmuseum, Meßkirch 18719
Städtisches Heimatmuseum, Naila 18972
Städtisches Heimatmuseum, Reinfeld, Holstein 19552
Städtisches Heimatmuseum, Taucha bei Leipzig 20146
Städtisches Heimatmuseum Erding, Erding 16891
Städtisches Heimatmuseum im Waldemarturm, Dannenberg, Elbe 16536
Städtisches Hellweg-Museum, Geseke 17269
Städtisches Hutmuseum, Lindenberg im Allgäu 18479
Städtisches Kießling-Museum, Drosendorf an der Thaya 01775
Städtisches Kramer-Museum, Kempen 18058
Städtisches Kunstmuseum Singen, Singen, Hohentwiel 19967
Städtisches Kunstmuseum Spendhaus Reutlingen, Reutlingen 19581
Städtisches Lapidarium, Stuttgart 20108
Städtisches Museum, Aschersleben 15536
Städtisches Museum, Bad Reichenhall 15718
Städtisches Museum, Bruchsal 16370
Städtisches Museum, Eisenhüttenstadt 16826
Städtisches Museum, Halberstadt 17504
Städtisches Museum, Iserlohn 17924
Städtisches Museum, Kalkar 17975
Städtisches Museum, Kitzingen 18105
Städtisches Museum, Korbach 18210
Städtisches Museum, Menden 18706
Städtisches Museum, Mülheim an der Ruhr 18818
Städtisches Museum, Pfungstadt 19396
Städtisches Museum, Schärding 02623
Städtisches Museum, Überlingen 20245
Städtisches Museum, Welzheim 20507
Städtisches Museum, Werl 20522
Städtisches Museum, Wiesloch 20582
Städtisches Museum, Zeulenroda 20750
Städtisches Museum Abteiberg, Mönchengladbach 18772
Städtisches Museum Abtshof, Jüterbog 17967
Städtisches Museum Braunschweig, Braunschweig 16305
Städtisches Museum/ Daniel-Pöppelmann-Haus, Herford 17720
Städtisches Museum Einbeck, Einbeck 16813
Städtisches Museum Engen galerie, Engen 16874
Städtisches Museum Fürstenwalde, Fürstenwalde, Spree 17163
Städtisches Museum Gelsenkirchen, Gelsenkirchen 17230
Städtisches Museum Göppingen im Storchen, Göppingen 17321
Städtisches Museum Göttingen, Göttingen 17341
Städtisches Museum Hann. Münden, Hann Münden 17591
Städtisches Museum im ehemaligen Heiliggeistspital, Munderkingen 18957
Städtisches Museum im Hospital, Nidderau 19091
Städtisches Museum im Kornhaus Bad Waldsee, Bad Waldsee 15759
Städtisches Museum Kamen, Kamen 17977
Städtisches Museum Ludwigsburg, Ludwigsburg, Württemberg 18514
Städtisches Museum Peterskirche, Vaihingen 20282
Städtisches Museum Rosenheim, Rosenheim 19654
Städtisches Museum Schloß Rheydt, Mönchengladbach 18773
Städtisches Museum Seesen, Seesen 19923
Städtisches Museum Simeonstift, Trier 20215
Städtisches Museum Sprucker Mühle, Guben 17451
Städtisches Museum Tuttlinger Haus, Tuttlingen 20239
Städtisches Museum Vogthaus, Ravensburg 19508
Städtisches Museum Wesel, Wesel 20537
Städtisches Museum Wesel, Wesel 20538
Städtisches Museum Zirndorf, Zirndorf 20759
Städtisches Naturkundliches Museum, Göppingen 17322
Städtisches Ortsmuseum Schwamendingen, Zürich 37409
Städtisches Propsteimuseum mit Römerthermen, Zülpich 20770
Städtisches Schulmuseum, Lohr am Main 18500
Städtisches Zentrum für Geschichte und Kunst, Riesa 19609
Ständerhaus, Buus 36611
Staff College Museum, Camberley 38445
Staffanstorps Konsthall, Staffanstorp 36225
Staffin Museum, Isle-of-Skye 39318
Staffin Museum, Staffin 40568
Stafford Castle and Visitor Centre, Stafford 40572
Staffordshire Regiment Museum, Lichfield 39493
Stafsjö Bruksmuseum, Falkenberg 35878
Stagecoach Inn Museum Complex, Newbury Park 45908
Stained Glass Museum, Ely 38935
Stała Ekspozycja Muzealna Ziemi Sierakowickiej, Sierakowice 31974
Stalheim Folkemuseum, Stalheim 30875
Stalna Izložba Stilskog Namještaja 18.-19. St., Čelarevo 33830
Stamford Brewery Museum, Stamford 40576
Stamford Historical Society Museum, Stamford 47767
Stamford Museum, Stamford 40577
Stamford Museum and Nature Center, Stamford 47768
Stamp Museum, Budapest 21330
Stampwise Info Square, Pretoria 34358
Stan Hywet Hall and Gardens, Akron 41074
Standard Bank Gallery, Johannesburg 34284
Standing Conference on Archives and Museums, York 49452
Stanford Hall Motorcycle Museum, Lutterworth 39849
Stanislav Dospevski Memorial House, Pazardžik 04756
Stanislav Dospevsky Art Gallery, Pazardžik 04753
Stanisław Noakowski Museum, Nieszawa 31825
Stanley Museum, Kingfield 44485
The Stanley Picker Gallery, Kingston-upon-Thames 39386
Stanley Spencer Gallery, Cookham 38629
Stanley-Whitman House, Farmington 43297
Stanly County Historic Museum, Albemarle 41093
Stanmer Rural Museum, Brighton 38345
Stansbury Museum, Stansbury 01473
Stansted Mountfitchet Windmill, Stansted Mountfitchet 40580
Stanthorpe Regional Art Gallery, Stanthorpe 01474
Stanton County Museum, Pilger 46486
Star City Heritage Museum, Star City 06487
Star Mound School Museum, Snowflake 06468
Star of the Republic Museum, Washington 48421
Star-Spangled Banner Flag House and 1812 Museum, Baltimore 41487
Stará Huť v Josefovském Údolí, Adamov 08241
Stará Škola, Police nad Metuji 08553
Stark Museum of Art, Orange 46172
Staro Selo Kumrovec, Kumrovec 07732
Staročerkasskij Istoriko-architekturnyj Muzej-zapovednik, Staročerkassk 33556
Staroladožskij Istoriko-Architekturnyj i Archeologičeskij Muzej-Zapovednik, Staraja Ladoga 33553
Starooskolskij Kraevedčeskij Muzej, Staryj Oskol 33559
Starorusskij Kraevedčeskij Muzej, Staraja Russa 33555
Starved Rock State Park, Utica 48168
Starý Královský Palác, Praha 08614
Starý Zámek, Jevišovice 08387
Statarmuseum Mejeriet, Örebro 36140
State Academic Bolshoi Theatre Museum, Moskva 33099
State Academic Mariinsky Theatre Museum, Sankt-Peterburg 33434
State Agricultural Heritage Museum, Brookings 41933
State Apartments of the Royal Palace, Stockholm 36284
State Archaeological Museum, Kolkata 21912
State Archaeological Museum, Warszawa 32139
State Archives of West Bengal, Kolkata 21913
State Art Collection, Sułoszowa 32007
State Art Gallery, Kaliningrad 32869
State Art Museum of Karakalpakstan, Nukus 48846
State Art Museum of the Kalmyk Republik, Elista 32793
State Art Museum R. Mustafaev, Baku 03069
State A.S. Pushkin Museum, Moskva 33063
State Authority of Museums, Rīga 49277
State Ayurvedic College Museum, Hardwar 21836
State Capital Publishing Museum, Guthrie 43856
State Central Museum, Ulaanbaatar 28688
State Central Museum of Contemporary History of Russia, Moskva 33050
State Central Theatre Museum A.A. Bakhrushin, Moskva 33051
State Ceramics Museum and 18th Century Kuskovo Estate, Moskva 33114
State Circus Museum, Sankt-Peterburg 33430
State Coal Mine Museum, Wonthaggi 01614
State Ethnographic Museum, Warszawa 32140
State Exhibition Hall Small Manege, Moskva 33088
State Exhibition Hall Zamoskvorechie, Moskva 33069
State Folk Art Museum of Armenia, Erevan 00690
State Fretwork Museum, Erevan 00691
State Gallery, Banská Bystrica 33949
State Gallery of Contemporary Cypriot Art, Lefkosia 08206
State Gallery of Fine Arts, Cheb 08309
State Health Institute Museum, Lucknow 21931
State Hermitage Museum, Sankt-Peterburg 33397
State Historical and Architectural Museum-reserve Shirvan Shahs' Palace, Baku 03070
State Historical Museum, Kamenec-Podolskij 37857
State Historical Museum, Moskva 33054
State Historical Museum of Kyrgyzstan, Biškek 27309
State Historical Society of Iowa Museum, Des Moines 42911
State Historical Society of Missouri Museum, Columbia 42554
State Historical Society of North Dakota Museum, Bismarck 41722
State History and Art Museum, Bolšoe Muraškino 32697
State History, Art and Architecture Museum-Preserve, Lomonosov 32988
State History Museum of Armenia, Erevan 00692
The State House-Museum of I.V. Stalin, Gori 15355
State Kala Akademi Museum, Imphal 21858
State Library and Museum, Kyaukpyu 28732
State Library and Museum, Mawlamyine 28737
State Literature and Memorial Anna Akhmatova Museum at Fountain House, Sankt-Peterburg 33399
State Literature Museum, Moskva 33057
State Literature Museum of Georgia, Tbilisi 15365
State Memorial A.V. Suvorov Museum, Sankt-Peterburg 33400
State Museum, Bhopal 21725
State Museum, Hyderabad 21847
State Museum, Kohima 21894
State Museum, Mandalay 28734
State Museum, Trichur 22042
State Museum at Majdanek, Lublin 31796
State Museum Gatchina Palace and Park, Gatčina 32802
State Museum of Abkhasia, Suchumi 15357
State Museum of Adjar, Batumi 15353
State Museum of Applied Art and Design, München 18890
State Museum of Art, Rīga 27444
State Museum of Art, Taškent 48853
State Museum of Azerbaijan Carpets and Applied Art Letif Kerimov, Baku 03071

State Museum of Ethnography, Arts and Crafts, Lviv 37888
State Museum of Fine Arts, Ašgabat 37811
State Museum of Folk Art of Karelia, Archangelsk 32646
State Museum of Georgia, Tbilisi 15366
State Museum of History, Architecture, Art and Nature Tsaritsyno, Moskva 33055
State Museum of Natural History of NAS of Ukraine, Lviv 37889
State Museum of Pennsylvania, Harrisburg 43925
State Museum of South Sumatra Province Balaputra Dewa, Palembang 22169
State Museum of the East Nusa Tenggara Province, Kupang 22149
State Museum of the History of Aviation, Sankt-Peterburg 33402
State Museum of the History of Cosmonautics K.E. Tsiolkovsky, Kaluga 32877
State Museum of the History of Religion, Sankt-Peterburg 33403
State Museum of the History of Saint Petersburg - Peter and Paul Cathedral, Sankt-Peterburg 33404
State Museum of the South-Ossetian Autonomous District, Chinvali 15354
State Museum of the Writers of the Ural, Ekaterinburg 32773
State Museum-Panorama Battle of Stalingrad, Volgograd 33715
State Museum Pavlovsk Palace and Park, Pavlovsk 33285
State Museum-Preserve of History, Gorki Leninskie 32807
State Museum-Preserve of History and Literature Alexander Pushkin with Estates Vjasemy and Zakharovo, Bolšie Vjazemy 32696
State Museum-Reserve Kolomenskoye, Moskva 33052
State Museum Reserve of History, Architecture, Nature and landscape - Izborsk, Izborsk 32834
State Museum Tsarsky village - Alexander Palace, Puškin 33334
State Museum Tsarsky Village - Palace of Cathrine II. the Great, Puškin 33336
State Open Air Museum Kizhi of Architecture, History and Ethnography, Kiži 32931
State Open Air Museum Kizhi of Architecture, History and Ethnography, Petrozavodsk 33315
State Park Museum on the Monuments of Ancient Taraz, Džambul 27082
State Russian Museum - Benois Wing, Sankt-Peterburg 33408
State Russian Museum - Marble Palace, Sankt-Peterburg 33423
State Russian Museum - Mikhailovsky Palace, Sankt-Peterburg 33407
State Russian Museum - Saint Michael's or Engineer's Palace, Sankt-Peterburg 33409
State Russian Museum - Stroganov Palace, Sankt-Peterburg 33484
State Studio Museum of the Sculptor A.S. Golubkina, Moskva 33061
State Stutthof Museum, Sopot 31989
State Stutthof Museum, Sztutowo 32036
State Theatrical Museum, Tbilisi 15367
State Tribal Museum, Chhindwada 21748
Statek-Muzeum Dar Pomorza, Gdańsk 31581
Statek-Muzeum Dar Pomorza, Gdynia 31590
Statek-Muzeum Sołdek, Gdańsk 31582
Staten Island Children's Museum, Staten Island 47788
Staten Island Ferry Collection, Staten Island 47789
Staten Island Historical Society Museum, Staten Island 47790
Staten Island Institute of Arts and Sciences, Staten Island 47791
Statens Historiska Museum, Stockholm 36285
Statens Museum for Kunst, København 08950
Statens Världskulturmuseet, Göteborg 35922
The Station Gallery, Whitby 06786
Station House, Culcairn 00960
Stationhouse Gallery, Williams Lake 06803
Štátna Galéria, Banská Bystrica 33949
Státní Galerie Výtvarného Umění, Cheb 08309
Státní Hrad a Zámek, Frýdlant v Čechách 08341
Státní hrad Bouzov, Bouzov 08254
Statthaus Böcklerpark, Berlin 16103
Statue Museum Balai Arca, Nganjuk 22163
Statue of Liberty National Monument and Ellis Island Immigration Museum, New York 45876
Statue Park, Budapest 21384
Staufergedächtnisstätte und Museum Wäscherschloß, Wäschenbeuren 20339
Stauffenberg-Schloß und Stauffenberggedächtniszimmer, Albstadt 15423
Staufferhaus - Sammlung Alt Unterentfelden, Unterentfelden 37262
Staunton Augusta Art Center, Staunton 47798
Staurothek, Domschatz und Diözesanmuseum Limburg, Limburg an der Lahn 18473
Stauth Memorial Museum, Montezuma 45464
Stavanger Brannmuseum, Stavanger 30888
Stavanger Maritime Museum, Stavanger 30889
Stavanger Museum, Stavanger 30890
Stavropol Museum of Fine Arts, Stavropol 33564
Stavropolskij Kraevedčeskij Muzej im. G.N. Prozriteleva i G.K. Prave, Stavropol 33563
Stavropolskij Muzej Izobrazitelnych Iskusstv, Stavropol 33564
Stawell Historical Museum, Stawell 01476
Steam Engine Museum, Mabel 45016
Steam Mill, Halfweg 29337
Steam Museum, Penrith 40177
The Steam Museum, Straffan 22543
STEAM Museum of the Great Western Railway, Swindon 40667
Steamboat Arabia Museum, Kansas City 44409
Steamboat Bertrand Museum, Missouri Valley 45409
Steamboat Dock Museum, Keyport 44472
Steamboat Museum, Bowness-on-Windermere 38291
Steamship Collection, Baltimore 41488
Steamship Keewatin, Douglas 42963
Steamship William G. Mather Museum, Cleveland 42482
Steamtown National Historic Site, Scranton 47521
Steamtown Railway Museum, Carnforth 38495
Stearns Collection of Musical Instruments, Ann Arbor 41221
Stearns History Museum, Saint Cloud 47086
Stedelijk Archeologisch Museum, Oudenburg 03680
Stedelijk Brouwerijmuseum, Leuven 03564
Stedelijk Museum, Alkmaar 28806
Stedelijk Museum, Damme 03370
Stedelijk Museum, Oudenaarde 03678
Stedelijk Museum Aalst, Aalst 03125
Stedelijk Museum Alfons Blomme, Roeselare 03705
Stedelijk Museum Amsterdam, Amsterdam 28902
Stedelijk Museum Brusselpoort, Mechelen 03618
Stedelijk Museum Bureau Amsterdam, Amsterdam 28903
Stedelijk Museum De Lakenhal, Leiden 29526
Stedelijk Museum Diest, Diest 03386
Stedelijk Museum Diksmuide, Diksmuide 03389
Stedelijk Museum Het Domein, Sittard 29827
Stedelijk Museum Het Toreke, Tienen 03778
Stedelijk Museum-Hoevemuseum, Sint-Truiden 03753
Stedelijk Museum Hof van Busleyden, Mechelen 03619
Stedelijk Museum Hoogstraten, Hoogstraten 03502
Stedelijk Museum Huize Ernest Claes, Scherpenheuvel 03728
Stedelijk Museum Ieper, Ieper 03517
Stedelijk Museum Kampen, Kampen 29474
Stedelijk Museum Lokeren, Lokeren 03594
Stedelijk Museum Roermond, Roermond 29743
Stedelijk Museum Schepenhuis, Mechelen 03620
Stedelijk Museum Schiedam, Schiedam 29804
Stedelijk Museum Van der Kelen-Mertens, Leuven 03565
Stedelijk Museum Vianen, Vianen 29943
Stedelijk Museum voor Actuele Kunst, Gent 03452
Stedelijk Museum voor Folklore en Regionale Geschiedenis, Ronse 03712
Stedelijk Museum voor Heemkunde en Folklore, Aarschot 03126
Stedelijk Museum voor Pijp en Tabak, Harelbeke 03477
Stedelijk Museum Zutphen, Zutphen 30077
Stedelijk Museum Zwolle, Zwolle 30086
Stedelijk Onderwijsmuseum Ieper, Ieper 03518
Stedelijk Prentenkabinet, Antwerpen 03175
Stedelijk Textielmuseum, Ronse 03713
Stedelijk Waagmuseum, Enkhuizen 29233
Stedelijke Academie voor Schone Kunsten, Roeselare 03706
Stedelijke Musea, Sint-Niklaas 03744
Stedelijke Musea, Torhout 03787
Stedelijke Musea Kortrijk, Kortrijk 03543
Stedelijke Oudheidkamer, Genemuiden 29272
Stedelijke Oudheidkamer De Roos, Geertruidenberg 29265
Stedman Art Gallery, Camden 42060
Steele County Museum, Hope 44096
Steenbakkerijmuseum Rupelklei te Terhagen, Terhagen 03771
Steenbakkerijmuseum 't Gelleg te Rumst, Rumst 03716
Steenkolenmijn Daalhemergroeve, Valkenburg, Limburg 29919
Steenmuseum, Gent 03453
Steensland Art Museum, Northfield 46023
Steep and Brew Gallery, Madison 45071
Stefan Cel Mare District Museum, Vaslui 32624
Stefan Fadinger-Museum, Sankt Agatha 02557
Stefan-George-Museum im Stefan-George-Haus, Bingen am Rhein 16165
Stefan Procopiu Science and Technics Museum, Iași 32539
Stefan Żeromski Museum, Nałęczów 31821
Steiglitz Court House, Steiglitz 01477
Steilacoom Historical Museum, Steilacoom 47801
Stein- und Bauernmuseum Großdöllnerhof, Rechberg 02493
Stein- und Beinmuseum, Weiterstadt 20504
Stein- und Fossiliensammlung Albert, Sulzdorf 20129
Steinhauermuseum, Randersacker 19482
Steinhauermuseum Mühlbach, Eppingen 16883
Steinhausen-Museum, Frankfurt am Main 17076
Steinhuder Spielzeugmuseum, Steinhude 20054
Steinkohlen-Besucherbergwerk Rabensteiner Stollen, Ilfeld 17884
Steinmuseum, Solothurn 37188
Steinsburg-Museum, Römhild 19635
Steinscher Hof Kirberg, Hünfelden 17860
Steinsland Klyngetun, Harstad 30534
Steinzeitmuseum, Korb 18209
Steinzeitmuseum, Thunstetten 37246
Steirisches Feuerwehrmuseum, Groß Sankt Florian 01947
Steirisches Glaskunstzentrum und Glasmuseum Bärnbach, Bärnbach 01731
Steirisches Holzmuseum, Sankt Ruprecht 02607
Steirisches Obstbaumuseum, Puch bei Weiz 02458
Steirisches Uhren-, Musikalien- und Volkskundemuseum, Arnfels 01679
Stellenbosch Museum, Stellenbosch 34383
Stenenexpositie de Molen - Museum Batjuchin, Borculo 29003
Stenersenmuseet, Oslo 30765
Stengel-True Museum, Marion 45164
Stenneset Bygdetun, Mo i Rana 30676
Stenneset Open Air Museum, Mo i Rana 30676
Steno Museet, Århus 08773
Steno Museum, Århus 08773
Stephanie Ann Roger Gallery, Frostburg 43569
Stephansson House, Edmonton 05386
Stephen A. Douglas Tomb, Chicago 42364
Stephen C. Foster State Park, Fargo 43289
Stephen Foster Folk Culture Center, White Springs 48590
Stephen G. Beaumont Museum, Wakefield 40763
The Stephen Girard Collection, Philadelphia 46456
Stephen Leacock Museum, Orillia 06055
The Stephen Phillips Memorial House, Salem 47203
Stephens African-American Museum, Shreveport 47619
Stephens Collection, London 39783
Stephens County Historical Society Museum, Duncan 43008
Stephens Museum, Fayette 43307
Stephenson County Historical Society Museum, Freeport 43551
Stephenson Railway Museum, North Shields 40080
Stephenville Museum, Stephenville 47802
Steppingstone Museum, Havre de Grace 43966
Sterbehaus Ferdinand Raimunds, Pottenstein 02437
Sterkstroom Museum, Sterkstroom 34388
Sterling and Francine Clark Art Institute, Williamstown 48634
Sterling Hill Mining Museum, Ogdensburg 46102
Sterling Historical Society Museum, Sterling 47805
Sterling-Rock Falls Historical Society Museum, Sterling 47804
Sternberg Museum of Natural History, Hays 43971
Šternberský Palác, Praha 08615
Sterne-Hoya Museum, Nacogdoches 45590
Stettler Town and Country Museum, Stettler 06490
Steuben House Museum, River Edge 46910
Stevedoring Museum, Kotka 09699
Stevenage Museum, Stevenage 40583
Stevens-Coolidge Place, North Andover 45980
Stevens County Gas and Historical Museum, Hugoton 44148
Stevens County Historical Society Museum, Morris 45503
Stevens Museum, Salem 47189
Stevenson-Hamilton Memorial Information Centre, Skukuza 34377
Steves Homestead Museum, San Antonio 47262
Steveston Museum, Richmond 06265
Stevington Windmill, Stevington 40584
Stewart Collection, Pocklington 40214
Stewart Historical Museum, Stewart 06491
Stewart Indian Cultural Center, Carson City 42120
Stewart M. Lord Memorial Museum, Burlington 42002
Stewart Museum at the Fort Ile Sainte-Hélène, Montréal 05926
Stewarton and District Museum, Stewarton 40585
The Stewartry Museum, Kirkcudbright 39393
Steyning Museum, Steyning 40586
Stichting Atlas Van Stolk, Rotterdam 29776
Stichting de Appel, Amsterdam 28904
Stichting De Brakke Grond, Amsterdam 28905
Stichting Huis Bergh, 's-Heerenberg 29361
Stichting Joden Savanna, Paramaribo 35777
Stichting Oosterkerk, Amsterdam 28906
Stichting Santjes en Kantjes, Maastricht 29574
Stichting Veranneman, Kruishoutem 03545
Stichting Zeeland 1939-1945, 's-Heer Abtskerke 29358
Stichting Zeeuwse Schaapkudde, Heinkenszand 29381
Stickereimuseum Eibenstock, Eibenstock 16798
Stickmaskinsmuseum, Glemminebro 35904
Sticks and Stones House, Corner Brook 05275
Stiefelmachermuseum, Rechnitz 02495
Stierhübelteichhaus, Karlstift 02100
't Stift, Susteren 29861
Stift Dürnstein, Dürnstein, Niederösterreich 01776
Stift Fischbeck, Hessisch Oldendorf 17746
Stift Melk, Melk 02292
Stift Obernkirchen, Obernkirchen 19189
Stiftelsen Musikkulturens Främjande, Stockholm 36286
Stiftlandmuseum, Waldsassen 20372
Stiftsbibliothek, Einsiedeln 36676
Stiftsgården, Trondheim 30942
Stiftskirchenmuseum, Himmelkron 17765
Stiftsmuseum, Bad Buchau 15622
Stiftsmuseum, Garsten 01871
Stiftsmuseum, Mattsee 02283
Stiftsmuseum, Millstatt 02299
Stiftsmuseum, Vomp 02772
Stiftsmuseum, Zwettl, Niederösterreich 03062
Stiftsmuseum der Stadt Aschaffenburg, Aschaffenburg 15533
Stiftsmuseum Praemonstratenser-Chorherren Stift Schlägl, Aigen-Schlägl 01652
Stiftsmuseum Schatzhaus Kärntens, Sankt Paul 02597
Stiftsmuseum Steyr-Gleink, Steyr-Gleink 02692
Stiftsmuseum und Domschatzkammer, Xanten 20730
Stiftssammlungen des Zisterzienserstiftes Rein, Gratwein 01908
Stiftssammlungen Lambach, Lambach 02178
Stiftssammlungen Wilten, Innsbruck 02080
Stiftung Aratym, Gutenstein 01979
Stiftung Aschenbrenner, Garmisch-Partenkirchen 17203
Stiftung AutoMuseum Volkswagen, Wolfsburg 20665
Stiftung Bauhaus Dessau, Dessau 16584
Stiftung B.C. Koekkoek-Haus, Kleve 18108
Stiftung Bundeskanzler-Adenauer-Haus, Bad Honnef 15669
Stiftung DKM, Duisburg 16756
Stiftung Dr. Edmund Müller, Beromünster 36559
Stiftung Fritz und Hermine Overbeck, Bremen 16335
Stiftung für Eisenplastik, Zollikon 37368
Stiftung für Konkrete Kunst, Reutlingen 19582
Stiftung für Konkrete Kunst Roland Phleps, Freiburg im Breisgau 17117
Stiftung Hans Arp und Sophie Taeuber-Arp, Remagen 19562
Stiftung Haus der Geschichte der Bundesrepublik Deutschland, Bonn 16248
Stiftung Haus der Geschichte der Bundesrepublik Deutschland, Leipzig 18420
Stiftung Käthe-Kollwitz-Gedenkstätte, Moritzburg 18792
Stiftung Keramion, Frechen 17094
Stiftung Kloster Michaelstein/Museum, Blankenburg, Harz 16178
Stiftung Kohl'sche Einhorn-Apotheke, Weißenburg in Bayern 20496
Stiftung Künstlerhaus Boswil, Boswil 36579
Stiftung Mecklenburg, Ratzeburg 19501
Stiftung Moritzburg, Halle, Saale 17521
Stiftung Preußische Schlösser und Gärten Berlin-Brandenburg, Potsdam 19437
Stiftung Rebhaus Wingreis, Twann 37258
Stiftung Römermuseum Homburg-Schwarzenacker, Homburg 17837
Stiftung Sammlung E.G. Bührle, Zürich 37410
Stiftung Scheibler-Museum Rotes Haus, Monschau 18787
Stiftung Schloß Ahrensburg, Ahrensburg 15407
Stiftung Schloß Eutin, Eutin 16981
Stiftung Schloß Glücksburg, Glücksburg, Ostsee 17303
Stiftung Stadtmuseum Berlin, Landesmuseum für Kultur und Geschichte Berlins, Berlin 16104
Stiftung Stadtmuseum Sursee, Sursee 37227
Stiftung Starke, Berlin 16105
Stiftung Stift Neuzelle, Neuzelle 19088
Stiftung Weimarer Klassik und Kunstsammlungen, Weimar, Thüringen 20475
Stiftung Wilhelm Lehmann, Niederhelfenschwil 36990
Stiftung Wilhelm Lehmbruck Museum, Duisburg 16757
Stiklestad Nasjonal Kultursenter, Verdal 30987
Stiklestad National Cultural Center, Verdal 30987
Still National Osteopathic Museum, Kirksville 44503
Stille Nacht-Museum, Hallein 01999
Stille-Nacht- und Heimatmuseum Bruckmannhaus, Oberndorf bei Salzburg 02372
Stills Gallery, Edinburgh 38919
Stinzenmuseum, Beers 28968
Stirk Cottage, Kalamunda 01131
Stirling Old Town Jail, Stirling 40594
Stirling Smith Art Gallery and Museum, Stirling 40595
Stjepan Gruber Museum, Županja 07844
Stjernsunds Slott, Askersund 35822
Stjørdal Museum KF, Stjørdal 30896
Stoani Haus der Musik, Gasen 01873
Stockbridge Library Historical Room, Stockbridge 47821
Stockholm City Museum, Stockholm 36290
Stockholm Historical Society Museum, Stockholm 47822
Stockholm School Museum, Stockholm 36289
Stockholm University Art Collections, Stockholm 36291
Stockholms Länsmuseum, Stockholm 36287
Stockholms Medeltidsmuseum, Stockholm 36288
Stockholms Skolmuseum, Stockholm 36289
Stockholms Stadsmuseum, Stockholm 36290
Stockholms Universitet Konstsamlingar, Stockholm 36291
Stockport Art Gallery, Stockport 40597
Stockport Museum, Stockport 40598
Stockton-on-Tees Museums and Heritage Service, Stockton-on-Tees 40601
Stockwood Craft Museum and Mossman Gallery, Luton 39846
Stofnun Arna Magnússonar, Reykjavík 21667
Stojan Aralič Memorial Museum, Otočac 07751
Stokke Bygdetun og Galleri Bokeskogen, Stokke 30897
Stoltze-Turm und Stoltze-Museum der Frankfurter Sparkasse, Frankfurt am Main 17077
Stondon Museum, Lower Stondon 39837
Stone Engraving Art Museum, Beijing 06990
Stone Engraving Museum, Fu 07051
Stone Fort Museum, Nacogdoches 45591
Stone House Gallery, Fredonia 43543

The Stone House Museum, Belchertown 41585
Stone Museum, Monroe Township 45446
Stone Sacristy, Mikkeli 09831
Stone Shop Museum, Grimsby 05533
Stone-Tolan House, Rochester 46945
Stonefield Historic Site, Cassville 42133
Stonehouse Museum, Vale 48182
Stones River National Battlefield, Murfreesboro 45569
Stone's Tavern Museum, Ligonier 44769
Stonington Stables Museum of Art, Malvern 01202
Stonnington Local History Collection - Malvern, Malvern 01203
Stonnington Local History Collection - Prahran, Prahran 01394
Stonor Park, Henley-on-Thames 39221
Stony Plain and District Pioneer Museum, Stony Plain 06495
Stony Point Battlefield State Historic Site, Stony Point 47833
Stoomgemaal Halfweg, Halfweg 29337
Stoomgemaal Hertog Reijnout en Bezoekerscentrum Arkemheen, Nijkerk 29628
Stoomgemaal Mastenbroek, Genemuiden 29273
Stoomhoutzagerij, Groenlo 29304
Stoomtrein Goes-Borsele, Goes 29287
Stoottroepen Museum, Assen 28952
Stor-Elvdal Museum, Koppang 30607
Stora Nyckelvikens Gård, Nacka 36109
Storchenturm-Museum, Zell am Harmersbach 20741
Storm King Art Center, Mountainville 45551
Storm P.-Museet, Frederiksberg 08827
Stormarnsches Dorfmuseum, Altes Bauernhaus am Thie, Hoisdorf 17821
Storno Collection, Sopron 21537
Storoževoj Korabl' 'Krasnyj Vympel' 1911 g., Vladivostok 33710
Storrowton Village Museum, West Springfield 48548
Storstrøms Kunstmuseum, Maribo 08982
Story House Historical Museum, Yamba 01622
Story of Castle Cornet, Saint Peter Port 40427
Story of People, Yorkton 06874
Stott Park Bobbin Mill, Ulverston 40749
Stoughton and District Museum, Stoughton 06496
Stoughton Historical Museum, Stoughton 47839
Stourhead House, Stourton 40617
Stow House, Goleta 43721
Stow West 1825 School Museum, Stow 47842
Stowarzyszenie Muzeów na Wolnym Powietrzu, Toruń 49336
Stowarzyszenie Zwiazek Muzeów Polskich, Kraków 49337
The Stoy Museum of the Lebanon County Historical Society, Lebanon 44705
Strabally Steam Museum, Stradbally 22542
Strachur Smiddy Museum, Strachur 40620
Strafvollzugsmuseum, Ludwigsburg, Württemberg 18515
Strahov Gallery, Praha 08616
Strahovská Obrazárna, Praha 08616
Stranahan House, Fort Lauderdale 43414
Stranda Hembygdsförening, Mönsterås 36098
Strandgaarden Museum, Ulfborg 09095
Strandhalle Ahrenshoop, Ostseebad Ahrenshoop 19303
Strandingsmuseum St. George, Ulfborg 09096
Strang Print Room, London 39784
Strangers Hall Museum of Domestic Life, Norwich 40102
Stranraer Museum, Stranraer 40622
Strasbourg and District Museum, Strasbourg 06497
Strasburg Museum, Strasburg 47849
Straßenbau - einst und jetzt, Waldbüttelbrunn 20356
Strategic Air & Space Museum, Ashland 41291
Strater Hotel, Durango 43015
Stratfield Saye House and Wellington Exhibition, Basingstoke 38103
Stratfield Saye House and Wellington Exhibition, Stratfield Saye 40623
Stratford and District Museum, Stratford 01478
The Stratford Historical Society and Catherine B. Mitchell Museum, Stratford 47850
Strathalbyn National Trust Museum, Strathalbyn 01479
Strathclair Museum, Strathclair 06501
Strathcona Archaeological Centre, Edmonton 05387
Strathcona County Heritage Foundation Museum, Sherwood Park 06444
Strathnaver Museum, Thurso 40708
Strathpeffer Spa Pumping Room Exhibition, Strathpeffer 40634
Strathroy Middlesex Museum, Strathroy 06503
Strathspey Railway, Aviemore 38043
Strauhof Zürich, Zürich 37411
Straumsnes Bygdemuseum, Kanestraum 30588
Strauß Gedenkstätte, Wien 02992
Straw and Grass Handicraft Museum, Seoul 27282
Strawbery Banke, Portsmouth 46654
Mr. Straw's House, Worksop 40935
Stražky Chateau of the Slovak National Gallery, Spišská Béla 34063
Strecker Museum Complex, Waco 48268
Středočeské Muzeum, Roztoky u Prahy 08643
Stredoslovenské Múzeum, Banská Bystrica 33950
Streekheemmuseum den Aanwas, Ossendrecht 29685
Streekhistorisch Centrum, Stadskanaal 29849
Streeklandbouwmuseum Agrimuda, Sluis 29837
Streeklandbowmuseum Agrimunda, Sint Anna ter Muiden 29818
Streekmuseum, Oudenaarde 03679
Streekmuseum Alphen, Alphen, Noord-Brabant 28814
Streekmuseum De Groote Sociëteit, Tiel 29875
Streekmuseum de Meesthof, Sint Annaland 29819
Streekmuseum de Moennik, Helden 29383
Streekmuseum De Oude Wolden, Bellingwolde 28974
Streekmuseum de Tolbrug, Bakel 28961
Streekmuseum De Vier Ambachten, Hulst 29457
Streekmuseum Goeree en Overflakkee, Sommelsdijk 29845
Streekmuseum Het Admiraliteitshuis, Dokkum 29164
Streekmuseum Het Dorp van Bartje, Rolde 29744
Streekmuseum Het Land van Axel, Axel 28956
Streekmuseum Het Rondeel, Rhenen 29729
Streekmuseum Hoeksche Waard, Heinenoord 29379
Streekmuseum Jan Anderson, Vlaardingen 29947
Streekmuseum Land van Valkenburg, Valkenburg, Limburg 29920
Streekmuseum Leudal, Haelen 29336
Streekmuseum Ommen, Ommen 29662
Streekmuseum Opsterland, Gorredijk 29292
Streekmuseum Oudheidkamer Reeuwijk, Reeuwijk 29724
Streekmuseum Schippersbeurs, Elsloo 29227
Streekmuseum Stevensweert/ Ohé en Laak, Stevensweert 29857
Streekmuseum van Klein-Brabant De Zilverreiger, Weert 03832
Streekmuseum Volkssterrenwacht, Burgum 29047
Streekmuseum voor de Krimpenerwaard Crimpenerhof, Krimpen aan den Ijssel 29494
Streekmuseum West Zeeuws-Vlaanderen, Ijzendijke 29463
Street Museum of Heslinki City Museum, Helsinki 09499
Streetcar and Electric Railway Museum, Milton 05855
Streetlife Museum, Kingston-upon-Hull 39383
Streichinstrumentensammlung, Einsiedeln 36677
Stretham Old Engine, Stretham 40636
Stretton Water Mill, Farndon 38979
Strigel-Museum und Antoniter-Museum, Memmingen 18705
Strindberg-Museum Saxen, Saxen 02622
Strindbergsmuseet Blå Tornet, Stockholm 36292
Striped House - Museum of Art, Tokyo 26925
Strømstads Museum, Strømstad 36304
Strömforsin Teollisuusmuseo, Ruotsinpyhtää 10006
Strömforsin Works Museum, Ruotsinpyhtää 10006
Strömsholms Slott, Kolbäck 36013
Strötzbacher Mühle, Mömbris 18767
Stroganov Church, Nižnij Novgorod 33226
Stroganovskaja Roždestvenskaja Cerkov, Nižnij Novgorod 33226
Stroganovskij Dvorec, Sankt-Peterburg 33484
Strohhaus, Muhen 36971
Strohhaus und Dorfmuseum, Kölliken 36830
Stromness Museum, Stromness 40638
Strong Museum, Rochester 46946
Strood Library Gallery, Rochester 40337
Stroom - Haags Centrum voor Visueel Kunst, Den Haag 29126
Strossmayer Gallery of Old Masters, Zagreb 07837
Strossmayerova Galerija Starih Majstora, Zagreb 07837
Stroud Mansion, Stroudsburg 47856
Strübhaus-Haus der Malkunst, Veringenstadt 20304
Struer Museum og Johs. Buchholtz Hus, Struer 09081
Struts Gallery, Sackville 06299
Struwwelpeter-Museum, Frankfurt am Main 17078
Stuart Collection, La Jolla 44549
Stuart House City Museum, Mackinac Island 45031
Stuart Town Gaol Museum, Alice Springs 00739
Stubnitz Gallery, Adrian 41067
Studebaker National Museum, South Bend 47682
Student Center Gallery, Wilmore 48665
Studiecentrum Perk, Eindhoven 29219
Studiensammlung der Lübecker Bodenfunde, Lübeck 18544
Studiensammlung der Universität Leipzig, Leipzig 18421
Studiensammlung historischer Ziegel, Irdning 02084
Studio A Otterndorf, Otterndorf 19323
Studio Capricornus, Eckernförde 16777
Studio Gallery, Washington 48395
Studio Glass Gallery, London 39785
Studio im Hochhaus, Berlin 16106
Studio im Zumikon, Nürnberg 19163
Studio-Museo di Giuseppe Pellizza, Volpedo 26049
Studio Museum in Harlem, New York 45877
Studio San Giuseppe Art Gallery, Cincinnati 42409
Studiogalerie Kaditzsch, Grimma 17404
Stuhlbau- und Heimatmuseum, Rabenau, Sachsen 19466
Stuhlmuseum Burg Beverungen, Beverungen 16136
Stuhr Museum of the Prairie Pioneer, Grand Island 43746
Sturdivant Hall, Selma 47563
Sturgeon River House, Sturgeon Falls 06505
Sturges Fine Arts Center, San Bernardino 47269
Sturgis Station House Museum, Sturgis 06506
Sturman Institute Museum of Regional Science, Afula 22565
Sturt House, Grange 01073
Stutsman County Memorial Museum, Jamestown 44308
Stuttgart Agricultural Museum, Stuttgart 47865
Stuttgarter Feuerwehrmuseum, Stuttgart 20109
Stuttgarter Gesellschaft für Kunst und Denkmalpflege, Stuttgart 20110
Stuttgarter Kunstverein, Stuttgart 20111
Stutzhäuser Brauereimuseum, Luisenthal 18567
Suan Pakkad Palace, Bangkok 37499
Subak Museum, Banjar Senggulan 22078
Subiaco Museum, Subiaco 01482
Submarine Force Museum and Historic Ship Nautilus, Groton 43845
Submarine Vesikko, Helsinki 09530
Subway Museum, Tokyo 26837
Sucharduv Dům, Nová Paka 08501
Sudan National Museum, Khartoum 35769
Sudan Natural History Museum, Khartoum 35770
Sudeley Castle, Winchcombe 40881
Sudetendeutsches Archiv, München 18919
Sudhaus Sorgendorf, Bleiburg 01738
Sudley House, Liverpool 39528
Sue Ryder Museum, Cavendish 38513
Südharzer Eisenhüttenmuseum, Bad Lauterberg 15691
Südhessisches Handwerksmuseum, Roßdorf bei Darmstadt 19655
Südmährer Heimatmuseum, Laa an der Thaya 02175
Südmährisches Landschaftsmuseum, Geislingen an der Steige 17219
Südostbayerisches Naturkunde- und Mammut-Museum, Siegsdorf 19953
Südsauerlandmuseum, Attendorn 15540
Südschwäbisches Archäologiemuseum im Jesuitenkolleg, Mindelheim 18745
Südtiroler Landesmuseum für Volkskunde, Brunico 23221
Sülchgau-Museum, Rottenburg am Neckar 19691
Suermondt-Ludwig-Museum, Aachen 15378
Suffolk City Council Libraries and Heritage, Ipswich 39307
Suffolk County Historical Society Museum, Riverhead 46916
Suffolk County Vanderbilt Museum, Centerport 42169
Suffolk Museum, Suffolk 47868
Suffolk Punch Heavy Horse Museum, Woodbridge 40919
Suffolk Regiment Museum, Bury Saint Edmunds 38418
Suffolk Resolves House, Milton 45354
Sugar Museum, Klaten 22147
Sugimoto Art Museum, Mihama 26488
Sugimoto Bijutsukan, Mihama 26488
Sugino Costume Museum, Tokyo 26926
Sugino Gakuen Isho Hakubutsukan, Tokyo 26926
Sui Tangyao Zhi Display Center, Chengdu 07026
Suider-Afrikaanse Museum-Assosiasie, Grahamstown 49366
Suifu Meitokukai Foundation Tokugawa Museum, Mito 26506
Suk Joo-sun Memorial Museum of Korean Folk Arts, Seoul 27283
Sukagawa Municipal Museum, Sukagawa 26777
Sukagawa-shiritsu Hakubutsukan, Sukagawa 26777
Sukanen Ship Pioneer Village and Museum of Saskatchewan, Moose Jaw 05935
Sukellusvene Vesikko, Helsinki 09530
Sukiennice. Galeria Związku Polskich Artystów Plastyków, Kraków 31728
Suksimuseo, Vimpeli 10200
Sukuma Museum - Bujora, Mwanza 37464
Sulabh International Museum of Toilets, Delhi 21789
Sulgrave Manor, Sulgrave 40643
Sulitjelma Gruvemuseum, Sulitjelma 30905
Sullivan County Historical Society Museum, Hurleyville 44179
Sulphide Street Station Railway and Historical Museum, Broken Hill 00847
Sulphur Creek Nature Center, Hayward 43974
Sultan Abdul Aziz Royal Gallery, Kelang 27626
Sultan Abu Bakar Museum Pahang, Pekan 27679
Sultan Alam Shah Museum, Shah Alam 27687
Sultan Ali Dianr Museum, El-Fasher 35761
Sultan Mahmud Badaruddin II Museum, Palembang 22170
Sultan's Armed Forces Museum, Muscat 31008
Sulu National Museum, Jolo 31332
Suma Aqualife Museum, Kobe 26352
Sumelocenna - Römisches Stadtmuseum, Rottenburg am Neckar 19692
Sumitomo Collection, Kyoto 26453
Sumiyoshi-jinja Treasure House, Shimonoseki 26754
Summerland Museum, Summerland 06513
Summerlee Heritage Park, Coatbridge 38600
Summit County Historical Society Museum, Akron 41075
Sumner/Redcliffs Historical Museum, Christchurch 30133
Sumo Hakubutsukan, Tokyo 26927
Sumo Museum of the Japan Sumo Association, Tokyo 26927
Sumpu Museum, Shizuoka 26768
The Sumter County Museum, Sumter 47879
Sumter Gallery of Art, Sumter 47880
Sumy State Art Museum, Sumy 37906
Sun Gallery, Hayward 43975
Sun Prairie Historical Museum, Sun Prairie 47881
SunAmerica Collection, Los Angeles 44946
Sunbury Great House, Saint Phillip 03109
Sunbury Shores Arts and Nature Centre, Saint Andrews 06304
Sund Bygdemuseum, Skogsvåg 30851
Sund Fiskerimuseum, Ramberg 30785
Sundby Samling Bryggergården, Nørresundby 08993
Sundby Samling Raschgården, Nørresundby 08994
Sundbybergs Museum, Sundbyberg 36306
Sunderland Museum, Sunderland 40650
Sundomin Kotiseutumuseo, Sundom 10062
Sundsbergs Gård Museum och Konsthall, Sunne 36312
Sundsvalls Museum, Sundsvall 36309
Sung-Am Archives of Classical Literature, Seoul 27284
Sung Kyun Kwan University Museum, Seoul 27285
Sungjon University Museum, Seoul 27286
Sungkok Art Museum, Seoul 27287
Sunnansjö Herrgård Galleri, Sunnansjö 36310
Sunndal Bygdemuseum, Sunndalsøra 30907
Sunnfjord Museum, Førde 30502
Sunnhordland Folkemuseum og Sogelag, Stord 30900
Sunnmøre Museum, Ålesund 30375
Sunnyhurst Wood Visitor Centre, Darwen 38704
Sunnyside Historical Museum, Sunnyside 47884
Sunnyside Museum, Hillside 39244
Sunnyvale Historical Museum, Sunnyvale 47886
Sunrise Museum, Charleston 42231
Sunrise Trail Museum, Tatamagouche 06535
Sunshine Coast Museum, Gibsons 05485
Suntory Bijutsukan, Tokyo 26928
Suntory Museum, Osaka 26673
Suntory Museum of Art, Tokyo 26928
Sunwatch Indian Village - Archaeological Park, Dayton 42806
Suojeluskuntamuseo, Seinäjoki 10030
Suolahden Museo, Suolahti 10065
Suomen Finnish Honeybee Museum, Juva 09592
Suomen Ilmailumuseo, Vantaa 10182
Suomen Jääkiekko-Museo, Tampere 10085
Suomen Järvikalastusmuseo ja Kerimäen Ulkomuseoalue, Kerimäki 09658
Suomen Jalkapallomuseo, Valkeakoski 10173
Suomen Joutsen, Turku 10129
Suomen Käsityön Museo, Jyväskylä 09604
Suomen Kansallismuseo, Helsinki 09531
Suomen Kansansoitinmuseo, Kaustinen 09643
Suomen Kellomuseo, Espoo 09438
Suomen Koulumuseo, Tampere 10086
Suomen Lasimuseo, Riihimäki 09995
Suomen Matkailumuseo, Imatra 09567
Suomen Merimuseo, Helsinki 09532
Suomen Metsästysmuseo, Riihimäki 09996
Suomen Museoliitto, Helsinki 49160
Suomen Nyrkkeilymuseo, Tampere 10087
Suomen Partiomuseo, Turku 10130
Suomen Rakennustaiteen Museo, Helsinki 09533
Suomen Rautatiemuseo, Hyvinkää 09556
Suomen Tietojenkäsittelymuseo, Jyväskylä 09605
Suomen Urheilumuseo, Helsinki 09534
Suomen Värimuseo, Kemi 09652
Suomen Valimomuseo ja Högforsin Masuuni, Karkkila 09628
Suomen Valokuvataiteen Museo, Helsinki 09535
Suomenlinna Island Fortress, Helsinki 09537
Suomenlinna-Museo, Helsinki 09536
Suomenlinna Museum, Helsinki 09536
Suomenlinna-Sveaborg, Helsinki 09537
Suomenlinna Toy Museum, Helsinki 09538
Suomenlinnan Lelumuseo, Helsinki 09538
Suomusjärven Kotiseutumuseo, Suomusjärvi 10066
Suonenjoen Kotiseutumuseo, Suonenjoki 10067
Supa-Ngwao Museum Centre, Francistown 03933
The Supreme Court of the United States Museum, Washington 48396
Suquamish Museum, Poulsbo 46678
Suquamish Museum, Suquamish 47892
Surahammars Bruksmuseum, Surahammar 36315
Surchondarë Vilojati Archeologija Muzeji, Termiz 48864
Surinaams Museum, Paramaribo 35778
Surnadal Bygdemuseum, Surnadal 30908
Surratt House Museum, Clinton 42493
Surrey Art Gallery, Surrey 06519
Surrey Heath Museum, Camberley 38446
Surrey Museum, Surrey 06520
Survey Museum, Roorkee 22006
Susan B. Anthony House, Rochester 46947
Susannah Place Museum, The Rocks 01422
Sushi Performance and Visual Art Museum, San Diego 47297
Susquehanna Art Museum, Harrisburg 43926
Susquehanna County Historical Society, Montrose 45484
Susquehanna Museum of Havre de Grace, Havre de Grace 43967
Sussex Combined Services Museum, Eastbourne 38857
Sussex County Historical Society Museum, Newton 45946
Sussex Farm Museum, Heathfield 39203
Sutcliffe Gallery, Whitby 40852
The Suter, Te Aratoi o Whakatu, Nelson 30211
Sutherland Steam Mill, Denmark 05326
Sutter's Fort, Sacramento 47054
Sutton-Ditz House Museum, Clarion 42426
Sutton Park, Sutton-on-the-Forest 40652
Sutton Windmill and Broads Museum, Sutton, Norwich 40651
Suur-Miehikkälän Kylämuseo, Miehikkälä 09827
Suur-Savon Museo, Mikkeli 09834
Suwa City Art Museum, Suwa 26779
Suwa-shi Bijutsukan, Suwa 26779
Suwałki Province Museum, Suwałki 32010
Suworow-Museum, Glarus 36765
Suzhou Art Gallery, Suzhou 07250

Suzhou Engraved Stone Museum, Suzhou 07251
Suzhou Museum, Suzhou 07252
Suzhou National Treasure Numismatics Museum, Suzhou 07253
Suzhou Silk Museum, Suzhou 07254
Suzuki Bokushi Kinenkan, Shiozawa 26762
Suzuki Bokushi Memorial Museum, Shiozawa 26762
S.V. Rachmaninov House-Museum, Ivanovka 32824
Svalbard-Museum, Longyearbyen 30655
Svaneholms Slott, Skurup 36203
Svedino's Automobile and Aviation Museum, Slöinge 36206
Svedinos Bil- och Flygmuseum, Slöinge 36206
Sveindal Museum, Kollungtveit 30600
Svelvik Museum, Svelvik 30910
Svendborg og Omegns Museum, Svendborg 09087
Svenska Museiföreningen, Stockholm 49383
Svenska Statens Porträttsamling, Mariefred 36088
Svenska Transportmuseet, Huskvarna 35970
Sverev Center of Modern Art, Moskva 33187
Sveriges Järnvägsmuseum, Gävle 35901
Sveriges Museimannaförbund, Nacka 49384
Sveriges Riksidrottsmuseum, Farsta 35886
Sveriges Rundradiomuseum, Motala 36107
Sveriges Sjömanshusmuseum, Uddevalla 36343
Sveriges Teatermuseum, Nacka 36110
Sveriges VVS-Museum, Katrineholm 36005
Švihov Hrad, Švihov 08670
Svijashsk Architectural and Artistic Museum-Preserve, Svijažsk 33570
Svijažskij Architekturno-chudožestvennyj Muzej, Svijažsk 33570
Svindersvik, Nacka 36111
Svjato-Troickij Sobor, Sankt-Peterburg 33485
Svjatogorskij Monastyr, Puškinskie Gory 33345
Svojanov Hrad, Polička 08557
Svyatogorsk Monastery, Puškinskie Gory 33345
Swaffham Museum, Swaffham 40653
Swakopmund Military Museum, Swakopmund 28772
Swakopmund Museum, Swakopmund 28773
Swalcliffe Barn, Swalcliffe 40654
Swaledale Folk Museum, Reeth 40305
Swan Hill Regional Art Gallery, Swan Hill 01487
Swan Valley Historical Museum, Swan River 06523
Swanage Railway, Swanage 40655
Swansea Museum, Swansea 40661
Swanton Mill, Ashford 38029
Swarovski Kristallwelten, Wattens 02797
Swarthout Memorial Museum, La Crosse 44539
Swayambunath Museum, Swayambunath 28792
Swaziland National Museum, Lobamba 35780
Sweden's Shipping Office Museum, Uddevalla 36343
Swedish Amber Museum, Höllviken 35957
Swedish American Museum Association of Chicago Museum, Chicago 42365
Swedish Association of Museum Curators, Nacka 49384
Swedish Federation of Friends of Museums, Stockholm 49385
Swedish House of Photography, Sundsvall 36307
Swedish Museum of Architecture, Stockholm 36231
Swedish Museum of Natural History, Stockholm 36267
Swedish Museums Association, Stockholm 49383
Swedish National Portrait Gallery, Mariefred 36088
Swedish Railway Museum, Gävle 35901
Swedish Sportsmuseum, Farsta 35886
Swedish Travelling Exhibitions, Stockholm 36277
Sweeney Art Gallery, Riverside 46923
Sweet Briar College Art Gallery, Sweet Briar 47901
Sweet Briar Museum, Sweet Briar 47902
Sweetwater County Historical Museum, Green River 43794
Swensbylijda, Svensbyn 36317
Swenson Memorial Museum of Stephens County, Breckenridge 41877
Swift County Historical Museum, Benson 41631
Swigart Museum, Huntingdon 44155
Swindler's Ridge Museum, Benton 41632
Swindon Museum and Art Gallery, Swindon 40668
Swinford Museum, Filkins 38991
Swisher County Museum, Tulia 48102
Swiss Historical Village, New Glarus 45689
Swiss Institute - Contemporary Art, New York 45878
Swiss Sports Museum, Basel 36521
Swiss-Type Automatic Lathe and History Museum of Moutier, Moutier 36959
Swissminiatur, Melide 36936
Switzerland County Historical Society Museum, Vevay 48226
Swope Art Museum, Terre Haute 47986
Swords and Ploughshares Museum, Manotick 05807
Swords Into Plowshares Peace Center and Gallery, Detroit 42935
Sydhimmerlands Museum, Nørager 08990
Sydney and Louisburg Railway Museum, Louisbourg 05783
Sydney Children's Museum, Merrylands 01251
Sydney Heritage Fleet, Pyrmont 01398
Sydney Jewish Museum, Darlinghurst 00969
Sydney Observatory, Sydney 01508
Sydney Tramway Museum, Loftus 01182
Sydsjællands Museum, Vordingborg 09115
Sygun Copper Mine, Beddgelert 38143
Sykepleiemuseum, Oslo 30768
Sykkylven Naturhistorisk Museum, Sykkylven 30913
Sylter Heimatmuseum, Sylt-Ost 20133
Sylvia Plotkin Judaica Museum, Scottsdale 47515
Synagoge, Bourtange 29010
Synagoge und Jüdisches Museum Ermreuth, Neunkirchen am Brand 19052
Synagogen-Museum, Urspringen 20275
Syndicat Mixte de Brouage, Hiers-Brouage 12026
Syon House, London 39786
Syracuse University Art Collection, Syracuse 47913
Sysmäen Kotiseutumuseo, Sysmä 10068
Syzranskij Gorodskoj Kraevedčeskij Muzej, Syzran 33581
Szabadtéri Néprajzi Gyűjtemény, Szenna 21566
Szabadtéri Néprajzi Múzeum, Szalafő 21543
Szabadtéri Néprajzi Múzeum, Szentendre 21575
Szabadtéri Vizügyi Múzeum, Szolnok 21586
Szadadtéri Erdei Múzeum, Szilvásvárad 21584
Szalay Collection of the Miskolc Gallery of Fine Arts - Petró House, Miskolc 21480
Szalay-Gyűjtemény - Petróház, Miskolc 21480
Szántó Kovács Múzeum, Orosháza 21494
Szatmári Múzeum, Mátészalka 21470
Széchenyi Emlékmúzeum, Nagycenk 21485
Széchenyi Memorial Museum, Nagycenk 21485
Szekler National Museum, Sfântu Gheorghe 32590
Szélmalom, Szeged 21553
Szent István Király Múzeum, Székesfehérvár 21561
Szentendrei Képtár, Szentendre 21576
Szépművészeti Múzeum, Budapest 21383
Szerb Egyházy Múzeum, Szentendre 21577
Szigetszentmiklós-Honismereti Gyűjtemény, Szigetszentmiklós 21581
Színháztörténeti és Színészmúzeum, Miskolc 21481
Szkolne Muzeum Morskie, Bolesławiec 31508
Szlovák Tájház, Békéscsaba 21320
Szoborpark, Budapest 21384
Szönyi István Emlék Múzeum, Zebegény 21616
Szövöház, Hollókö 21432
Szołayski House, Kraków 31691
Szombathelyi Képtár, Szombathely 21589
Szórakaténusz Játékmúzeum, Kecskemét 21452
Szórakaténusz Toy Museum, Kecskemét 21452
Szpitalki, Puck 31930
Sztuka Dalekiego Wschodu, Toruń 32055
T. Evseev National Museum of the Republic Marij El, Joškar-Ola 32861
Ta' Hagrat Copper Age Temples, Mgarr 27699
Ta' Kola Windmill, Xaghra 27716
Taalintehtaan Ruukinmuseo, Dalsbruk 09422
Tabak-Museum der Stadt Hockenheim, Hockenheim 17776
Tabak- und Zigarrenmuseum, Reinach (Aargau) 37051
Tabakhistorische Sammlung Reemtsma, Hamburg 17570
Tabakmuseum, Lorsch 18506
Tabakmuseum, Oberzeiring 02382
Tabako to Shio no Hakubutsukan, Tokyo 26929
Tabakspeicher, Nordhausen 19122
Taber and District Museum, Taber 06530
Table Rock Historical Society Museum, Table Rock 47914
Tabley House Collection, Knutsford 39405
Tabor Opera House Museum, Leadville 44701
Tabusintac Centennial Museum, Tabusintac 06531
Tacauz Museum, Tačauz 37819
Tačauz Muzej, Tačauz 37819
Tacoma Art Museum, Tacoma 47922
Tactual Museum, Athinai 20903
Tactual Museum, Kallithea 20990
Tadre Mølle, Hvalsø 08905
Tändsticksmuseet, Jönköping 35979
Taft Museum of Art, Cincinnati 42410
Taganrog Municipal Museum, Taganrog 33587
Taganrog Picture Gallery, Taganrog 33585
Taganrogskaja Kartinnaja Galereja, Taganrog 33585
Taganrogskij Gosudarstvennyj Literaturnyj i Istoriko-architekturnyj Muzej-zapovednik, Taganrog 33586
Taganrogskij Kraevedčeskij Muzej, Taganrog 33587
Taganrogskij Muzej im. A.P. Čechova, Taganrog 33588
Tagawa Bijutsukan, Tagawa 26783
Tagawa Museum of Art, Tagawa 26783
Tagore Memorial Museum, Santiniketan 22011
Taha Hussien Museum, Haram 09298
Tahydromiko Moyseio, Athinai 20904
Tai Hao Ling Museum, Zhoukou 07333
Taichang City Museum, Taichang 07255
Taidekeskus Mältinranta, Tampere 10088
Taidekoti Kirpilä, Helsinki 09539
Taidemuseo, Kokkola 09685
Taieri Historical Museum, Outram 30223
Taihape and District Museum, Taihape 30256
Tain and District Museum, Tain 40670
The Taipa Houses Museum, Macau 07170
Taipei Fine Arts Museum, Taipei 07356
Taiping Museum, Nanjing 07188
Tairawhiti Museum, Gisborne 30164
Taish-Machi Kominkan Fuzoku Taisha Kokokan, Taishiya 26786
Taisha Archaeological Collection, Taishiya 26786
Taivalkosken Kotiseutumuseo, Taivalkoski 10070
Taivassalon Museo, Taivassalo 10071
Taiwan Craft Center, Taipei 07357
Taiwan Folk Arts Museum, Taipei 07358
Taiwan Museum, Taipei 07359
Taiwan Museum of Art, Taichung 07342
Taiyuan Painting Gallery, Taiyuan 07259
Taizz Museum, Taizz 49013
Tájház, Buzsák 21394
Tájház, Mezőkövesd 21472
Tajmyr Regional Museum, Dudinka 32762
Tajmyrskij Okružnoj Kraevedčeskij Muzej, Dudinka 32762
Takamatsu City Museum of Art, Takamatsu 26793
Takamatsuzuka Wall Painting Museum, Asuka 26113
Takamura Art Museum, Minami-tsuru 26489
Takaoka Art Museum, Takaoka 26795
Takaoka Bijutsukan, Takaoka 26795
Takaoka Municipal Museum, Takaoka 26796
Takaoka Shiritsu Hakubutsukan, Takaoka 26796
Takasaki Museum of Art, Takasaki 26800
Takasaki-shi Bijutsukan, Takasaki 26800
Takasawa Folk Craft Museum, Niigata 26599
Takayama Jinya, Takayama 26811
Takayama Museum of Local History, Takayama 26812
Takayama-shiritsu Hakubutsukan, Takayama 26812
Takehisa Yumeji Ikaho Memorial Hall, Ikaho 26238
Takenouchi Kaido Rekishi Hakubutsukan, Taishi 26785
Takenouchi Road Historical Museum, Taishi 26785
Takht-e-Jamshid, Marvdashd 22264
Takht-e-Jamshid, Shiraz 22282
Tako no Hakubutsukan, Tokyo 26930
Tal-Museum, Engelberg 36682
Talana Museum and Heritage Park, Dundee 34222
Talbot Arts and Historical Museum, Talbot 01513
Talbot House, Poperinge 03688
Talbot Rice Gallery, Edinburgh 38920
Tales of the Old Gaol House, King's Lynn 39371
Talkeetna Historical Society Museum, Talkeetna 47930
Tallahassee Museum of History and Natural Science, Tallahassee 47938
Tallbo, Järbo 35974
Taller Puertorriqueno, Philadelphia 46457
Tallinn City Museum, Tallinn 09372
Tallinna Linnamuuseum, Tallinn 09372
Talmuseum, San Nicolò Ultimo 25402
Talmuseum Chasa Jaura, Valchava 37276
Talmuseum Kaunertal, Feichten 01824
Talmuseum Lachitzhof, Klein Sankt Paul 02135
Talmuseum Samnaun, Samnaun Compatsch 37096
Talmuseum Ursern, Andermatt 36458
Talomuseo, Kuortane 09725
Talonpoikaismuseo Yli-Kirra, Punkalaidum 09964
Talonpojanmuseo, Kälviä 09608
Talsi Museum of Local Studies and Art, Talsi 27456
Talsu Novadpētniecības un Mākslas Muzejs, Talsi 27456
Talvinen Cottage, Humppila 09554
Talvisen Työläismökki, Humppila 09554
Talvisotanäyttely, Kuhmo 09713
Tam O'Shanter Experience, Alloway 37981
Tama County Historical Museum, Toledo 48017
Tama Seiseki Kinenkan, Tama 26816
Tamagawa Modern Art Museum, Tamagawa 26817
Taman Warisan Merimbun, Tutong 04603
Tamborine Mountain Heritage Centre, Eagle Heights 00997
Tambov Picture Gallery, Tambov 33590
Tambovskaja Oblastnaja Kartinnaja Galereja, Tambov 33590
Tambovskij Oblastnoj Kraevedčeskij Muzej, Tambov 33591
Tammiharjun Sairaalamuseo, Ekenäs 09427
Tammio Museo, Tammio 10074
Tampa Bay History Center, Tampa 47945
Tampa Museum of Art, Tampa 47946
Tampere Art Museum - Regional Art Museum of Pirkanmaa, Tampere 10092
Tampere Mineral Museum, Tampere 10078
Tampere Museum of Contemporary Art, Tampere 10091
Tampere Natural History Museum, Tampere 10090
Tampereen Kaupunginmuseo, Tampere 10089
Tampereen Luonnontieteellinen Museo, Tampere 10090
Tampereen Nykytaiteen Museo, Tampere 10091
Tampereen Taidemuseo - Pirkanmaan Aluetaidemuseo, Tampere 10092
Tampereen Taidemuseon Muumilaakso, Tampere 10093
Tampereen Teknillinen Museo, Tampere 10094
Tamralipta Museum and Research Center, Tamluk 22031
Tamworth Castle Museum, Tamworth 40671
Tamworth City Gallery, Tamworth 01515
Tamyang Bamboo Museum, Tamyang 27294
Tan Oe Pang Art Studio, Singapore 33945
Tana Museum, Tana 30915
Tanabe Museum of Art, Matsue 26474
Tanah Art Museum, San Antonio 03869
Tanakami Mineral Museum, Otsu 26684
Tandanya, Adelaide 00714
Tandläkarmuseum, Sunne 36313
Tang Dai Art Museum, Xian 07299
Tang Teaching Museum and Art Gallery, Saratoga Springs 47464
Tanimura Art Museum, Itoigawa 26269
Tanimura Bijutsukan, Itoigawa 26269
Tank Museum, Axvall 35827
Tank Museum, Bovington 38289
Tank Museum, Parola 09913
Tank Museum, Poznań 31901
The Tanks of Aden, Aden 49008
Tanta Museum, Tanta 09307
Tantaquidgeon Indian Museum, Uncasville 48138
Tante Blanche Museum, Madawaska 45051
Tanum Museum of Rock Carvings, Tanumshede 36321
Tanums Hällristningsmuseum, Tanumshede 36321
Tanzimat Müzesi, İstanbul 37707
Taos Historic Museums, Taos 47953
Het Tapijtmuseum, Genemuiden 29274
Tapisseries Jean-Lurçat, Rocamadour 13989
Tappantown Historical Society Museum, Tappan 47954
Tapulimuseo, Lempäälä 09776
Tar Boat Canal, Kajaani 09612
Tar Tunnel, Coalport 38598
Tara and District Pioneer Memorial Museum, Tara 01518
Taralga Historical Museum, Taralga 01519
Tarble Arts Center, Charleston 42205
The Tareq Rajab Museum, Hawelli 27304
Tarpon Springs Cultural Center, Tarpon Springs 47956
Tarrytowns Museum, Tarrytown 47959
Tarskij Istoriko-kraevedčeskij Muzej, Tara 33592
Tarsus Müzesi, Tarsus 37791
Tarsus Museum, Tarsus 37791
Tartous Museum, Tartous 37443
Tartu Art House, Tartu 09382
Tartu Art Museum, Tartu 09383
Tartu Kunstimaja, Tartu 09382
Tartu Kunstimuuseum, Tartu 09383
Tartu Linnamuuseum, Tartu 09384
Tartu Mänguasjamuuseum, Tartu 09385
Tartu Toy Museum, Tartu 09385
Tartu Ülikooli Ajaloomuuseum, Tartu 09386
Tartu Ülikooli Geoloogiamuuseum, Tartu 09387
Tartu Ülikooli Kunstimuuseum, Tartu 09388
Tartu Ülikooli Zooloogiamuuseum, Tartu 09389
Tartu University History Museum, Tartu 09386
Tartu University Museum of Geology, Tartu 09387
Tartu University Museum of Zoology, Tartu 09389
Tartumaa Muuseum, Elva 09316
Tarusa Picture Gallery, Tarusa 33593
Tarusskaja Kartinnaja Galereja, Tarusa 33593
Tarusskij Kraevedčeskij Muzej, Tarusa 33594
Tarusskij Muzej Semji Cvetaevych, Tarusa 33595
Tarvasjoen Kotiseutumuseo, Tarvasjoki 10100
Tarvastu Kihelkonnamuuseum, Tarvastu 09390
Taş Eserler Müzesi - Lapidari, Lefkoşa 08240
Tashkent Historical Museum of the People of Uzbekistan, Taškent 48861
Tasiilaq Katersugaasivia, Tasiilaq 21241
Tåsinge Skipperhjem og Folkemindesamling, Svendborg 09088
Tasmania Distillery Museum, Hobart 01105
Tasmanian Museum and Art Gallery, Hobart 01106
Tasmanian Wool Centre, Ross 01426
Tasneem Arts Gallery, Peshawar 31052
Tassenmuseum Hendrikje, Amstelveen 28833
Tatabánya Múzeum, Tatabánya 21595
Tatar State Museum of Fine Arts, Kazan 32908
Tatarian Town - Archaeological Museum-Preserve, Stavropol 33565
Tatarskij Gosudarstvennyj Muzej Izobrazitelnych Iskusstv, Kazan 32908
Tatarskoe Gorodišče - Archeologičeskij i prirodnyj Muzej-zapovednik, Stavropol 33565
Tate Britain, London 39787
Tate Geological Museum, Casper 42131
Tate House, Portland 46627
Tate Liverpool, Liverpool 39529
Tate Modern, London 39788
Tate Saint Ives, Saint Ives, Cornwall 40410
Tatham Art Gallery, Pietermaritzburg 34328
Tatra Technical Museum, Kopřivnice 08421
Tatranská Galéria, Poprad 34046
Tatsuno Bijutsukan, Tatsuno 26820
Tatsuno Museum of Art, Tatsuno 26820
Tatsuuma Archaeological Museum, Nishinomiya 26607
Tatton Park, Knutsford 39406
Tattoo Art Museum, San Francisco 47342
Tattoo Museum, Amsterdam 28907
Tatura Irrigation and Wartime Camps Museum, Tatura 01521
Tauberfränkisches Landschaftsmuseum, Tauberbischofsheim 20145
Tauberländer Dorfmuseum, Weikersheim 20432
Tauernstraßen-Museum, Eben im Pongau 01777
Tauranga Museum, Tauranga 30259
Tauriska-Galerie, Neukirchen am Großvenediger 02345
Tavastilan Kotiseutumuseo, Mietoinen 09828
Tawhiti Museum, Hawera 30177
Tawi-Tawi Ethnological Museum, Bongao 31290
Taxameter-Museum, Hamburg 17571
Taxandriamuseum, Turnhout 03806
Taxinge Slott, Nykvarn 36129
Taylor Brown and Sarah Dorsey House, Midland 45330
Taylor-Grady House, Athens 41322
Taymori Hall, Isfahan 22247
T.B. Ferguson Home, Watonga 48453
TBA Exhibition Space, Chicago 42366
Tbilisi State Museum of Anthropology and Ethnography, Tbilisi 15368
T.C. Steele State Historic Site, Nashville 45611
T.Ch. Malsagov Regional Museum of Ingushetiya, Nazran 33203
Tcherkech Museum of Political Banishment in Yakutia, Čerkech 32735
Tchitinsk Art Museum, Čita 32750
Te Amorangi Trust Museum, Rotorua 30250
Te Awamutu Museum, Te Awamutu 30260
Te Kauri Lodge Museum, Hamilton 30173

Te Kuiti and District Historical Society Museum, Te Kuiti 30261
Te Manawa Art, Palmerston North 30230
Te Manawa Life Mind, Palmerston North 30231
Te Papa, Wellington 30311
Te Whare Taonga O Akaroa, Akaroa 30092
Te Whare Whakaaro o Pito-one, Hutt City 30183
Tea Museum, Bois-Cheri 27732
Tea Museum of Iran, Lahijan 22261
Teackle Mansion, Princess Anne 46694
Teatermuseet i Hofteatret, København 08951
Teatermuseet i Oslo, Oslo 30767
Teatralnyj Muzej, Kazan 32909
Teatre-Museu Dalí, Figueres 34819
Teatterimuseo, Helsinki 09540
Tecck an Phiarsaigh, Rosmuck 22536
Techni-Macedonian Artistic Association Kilkis, Kilkis 21018
Technical Museum, Zagreb 07838
Technical Museum of Slovenia, Ljubljana 34122
Technické Muzeum, Petřvald u Karviné 08538
Technické Muzeum Tatra, Kopřivnice 08421
Technické Muzeum v Brně, Brno 08277
Techniek Museum Delft, Delft 29087
Techniekmuseum Heim, Hengelo, Overijssel 29399
Technik anno dazumal - Museum Kratzmühle, Kinding 18083
Technik Museum Speyer, Speyer 20013
Technik- und Verkehrsmuseum, Stade 20027
Technikmuseum Magdeburg, Magdeburg 18589
Technikmuseum U-Boot "Wilhelm Bauer", Bremerhaven 16344
Technikon Natal Gallery, Durban 34233
Techniquest, Cardiff 38484
Technische Sammlungen der Stadt Dresden, Dresden 16713
Technisches Denkmal Kupferhammer, Thießen bei Dessau 20173
Technisches Denkmal Museumkalkwerk Lengefeld, Lengefeld, Erzgebirge 18433
Technisches Denkmal Neue Hütte, Schmalkalden 19809
Technisches Denkmal Neumannmühle, Ottendorf bei Sebnitz 19320
Technisches Denkmal Tobiashammer, Ohrdruf 19247
Technisches Denkmal Ziegelei Hundisburg, Hundisburg 17866
Technisches Halloren- und Salinenmuseum, Halle, Saale 17522
Technisches Landesmuseum, Schwerin 19901
Technisches Museum, Großröhrsdorf, Oberlausitz 17438
Technisches Museum Alte Wasserkunst, Bautzen 15837
Technisches Museum der Pforzheimer Schmuck- und Uhrenindustrie, Pforzheim 19391
Technisches Museum Frohnauer Hammer, Annaberg-Buchholz 15499
Technisches Museum Holzschleiferei Weigel, Rittersgrün 19619
Technisches Museum Ölmühle, Pockau 19423
Technisches Museum Papiermühle, Zwönitz 20786
Technisches Museum Silberwäsche Antonsthal, Breitenbrunn, Erzgebirge 16315
Technisches Museum Wien, Wien 02993
Technisches Schaudenkmal Gießerei Heinrichshütte, Wurzbach 20719
Technology Museum, Petřvald u Karviné 08538
Technopolis, Mechelen 03621
Technorama, Winterthur 37341
Teddy Bear Museum, Hof, Saale 17794
Teddy Bear Museum, Seogwipo 27221
The Teddy Bear Museum, Stratford-upon-Avon 40631
Teddy Bear Museum of Naples, Naples 45603
Teddy Bear Shop and Museum, Ironbridge 39310
Teddy Museum Berlin in Hof/Bayern, Hof, Saale 17794
Teddymuseum, Klingenberg am Main 18109
Tees Archaeology, Hartlepool 39178
Teeterville Pioneer Museum, Delhi 05320
Teeterville Pioneer Museum, Teeterville 06536
Tehkummah Township Museum, Tehkummah 06537
Tehnički Muzej, Zagreb 07838
Tehniški Muzej Slovenije, Ljubljana 34122
Teichmühle, Steinwiesen 20056
Teifi Valley Railway, Llandysul 39544
Teignmouth and Shaldon Museum, Teignmouth 40681
Teine Memorial Museum, Sapporo 26722
Teishin Sogo Hakubutsukan, Tokyo 26931
Teisko Museum, Tampere 10095
Teiskon Kotiseutumuseo, Tampere 10095
Tekakwitha Fine Arts Center, Sisseton 47648
Tekiho Memorial Museum of Art, Ogose 26621
Tekirdağ Devlet Güzel Sanatlar Galerisi, Tekirdağ 37792
Tekirdağ Müzesi, Tekirdağ 37793
Tekirdag Museum, Tekirdağ 37793
Tekirdağ State Gallery, Tekirdağ 37792
Tekisui Art Museum, Ashiya 26111
Tekniikan Museo, Helsinki 09541
Teknikens Hus, Luleå 36055
Teknikens och Sjöfartens Hus, Malmö 36080
Tekniska Kvarnen, Örebro 36141
Tekniska Museet, Stockholm 36293
Tekovské Muzeum v Leviciach, Levice 34010
Tel Aviv Museum of Art, Tel Aviv 22775
Tel Hai Museum, Tel-Hai 22779
Teleborgs Slott, Växjö 36391
Telecommunication Museum, Reykjavík 21665
Telecommunications Museum, Madrid 35028
Telefonmuseet, Hellerup 08859
Telefonmuseum Hittfelder Bahnhof, Seevetal 19925
Telefonmuseum im Greuterhof, Islikon 36817
Telefoonmuseum, Drouwen 29184
Telegalleria, Sonera 10051
Telemark og Grenland Museum, Skien 30847
Telemuseum, Stockholm 36294
Teleorman District Museum of History, Alexandria 32429
Telephone Historical Collection, Halifax 05564
Telephone Pioneer Museum, Saint John 06338
Telephone Pioneer Museum of New Mexico, Albuquerque 41109
Telfair Museum of Art, Savannah 47485
Telkwa Museum, Telkwa 06538
Tell-Museum, Bürglen 36600
Tell Qasile Archaeological Site, Tel Aviv 22776
Tellogleion Foundation, Thessaloniki 21193
Telorama, Regina 06249
Telstra Museum Brisbane, Clayfield 00922
Temecula Valley Museum, Temecula 47968
Temel Sanat Kolleksiyon, İstanbul 37708
Temiskaming Art Gallery, Haileybury 05542
Temlett House, Grahamstown 34254
Temmeksen Kotiseutumuseo, Temmes 10102
Tempe Arts Center, Tempe 47974
Tempe Historical Museum, Tempe 47975
Tempelmuseum Frauenberg, Leibnitz 02202
Temperance Tavern, Newcomerstown 45913
Tempietto Rossiniano della Fondazione Rossini, Pesaro 24862
Tempio Voltiano, Como 23632
Templar and Medieval Museum, Cogolin 11344
Temple des Mille Bouddhas, La Boulaye 12127
Temple Gallery, Philadelphia 46458
Temple Museum of Religious Art, Beachwood 41550
Temple Museum of Religious Art, Cleveland 42483
Temple Newsam House, Leeds 39452
Temple of Aphrodite, Kouklia 08188
Temple Réformé Mulhouse, Mulhouse 13216
Templerhaus, Amorbach 15487
Templin Historical Village, Boonah 00813
Templo Románico de San Martín, Fromista 34825
Temporäre Galerie Schloß Neersen, Willich 20597
Téms Swíya Museum, Sechelt 06416
Temuka Courthouse Museum, Temuka 30262
Ten Broeck Mansion, Albany 41088
Ten Duinen 1138, Koksijde 03537
Tenbury and District Museum, Tenbury Wells 40683
Tenby Museum and Art Gallery, Tenby 40684
Tenement House, Glasgow 39069
Tenholan Kotiseutumuseo, Tenala 10103
Tenino Depot Museum, Tenino 47980
Tenmon Museum of Art, Hirakata 26206
Tennent Art Foundation Gallery, Honolulu 44089
Tennessee Association of Museums, Piney Flats 49533
Tennessee Central Railway Museum, Nashville 45624
Tennessee Historical Society Museum, Nashville 45625
Tennessee State Museum, Nashville 45626
Tennessee Valley Art Association, Tuscumbia 48121
Tennessee Valley Railroad Museum, Chattanooga 42266
Tennismuseum Gasber, Oberhausen, Rheinland 19179
Tenri Gallery, Tokyo 26932
Tenri University Sankokan Museum, Tenri 26822
Tenterden and District Museum, Tenterden 40688
Tenterfield Centenary Cottage, Tenterfield 01523
Tentoonstellingsruimte 't Oute Hus, Burgh-Haamstede 29046
Tentoonstellingzaal Hessenhuis, Antwerpen 03176
Teo Otto-Gedenkraum, Wien 02994
Teodoro P. Resurreccion Memorial Museum, Luna 31348
Teollisuustyöväen Asuntomuseo, Imatra 09568
Tepco Denryokukan, Tokyo 26933
Tepco Electric Energy Museum, Tokyo 26933
Tepia, Kikai Sangyo Kinenkan, Tokyo 26934
Teplitz-Schönauer Heimatmuseum, Frankfurt am Main 17079
Teppich und Heimatmuseum, Oelsnitz, Erzgebirge 19228
Terengganu State Museum, Kuala Terengganu 27656
Teresia ja Rafael Lönnströmin kotimuseo, Rauma 09985
Terezín Memorial, Terezín 08680
Teriade Museum, Mytilini 21088
Terjärvs Hembygdsgård, Teerijärvi 10101
Természettudományi Múzeum, Aggetelek 21306
Ternopil Local Museum, Ternopil 37907
Terra Museum of American Art, Chicago 42367
Terra Mystica, Bad Bleiberg 01693
Terra Sancta Museum, Nazareth 22721
Terra-Vinea, Portel-des-Corbières 13848
Terrace Gallery, Orlando 46190
Terrace Hill Historic Site and Governor's Mansion, Des Moines 42912
Terracotta Warriors Museum, Dorchester 38752
Terrain Gallery, New York 45879
Terrebonne Museum, Houma 44114
Territoires du Jazz, Marciac 12809
Territorial Capital-Lane Museum, Lecompton 44707
Territorial Statehouse State Museum, Fillmore 43321
Territory Town USA, Old West Museum, Okemah 46109
Tersløsegaard, Dianalund 08794
Tervajärven Talomuseo, Sotkamo 10055
Tervakanava, Kajaani 09612
Terwilliger Museum, Waterloo 48438
Tesoro del Duomo, Messina 24366
Tesoro del Duomo, Milano 24420
Tesoro del Duomo, Monreale 24480
Tesoro del Duomo, Vigevano 26008
Tesoro della Cattedrale, Palermo 24779
Tesoro della Cattedrale, Rimini 25119
Tesoro della Chiesa di San Pietro, Calascibetta 23258
Tesoro della Santa Maria della Scala, Chieri 23541
Tesoro di Santa Maria La Stella, Militello in Val di Catania 24426
Tesouro-Museu da Sé de Braga, Braga 32244
Tessai Museum, Takaraduka 26797
Tessedik Sámuel Múzeum, Szarvas 21544
Testnevelési és Sportmúzeum, Budapest 21385
Tetbury Police Museum, Tetbury 40689
Tetley's Brewery Wharf, Leeds 39453
Tetovo Regional Museum, Tetovo 27598
Teulon and District Museum, Teulon 06541
Teutopolis Monastery Museum, Teutopolis 47989
Teuvan Museo, Teuva 10104
Teviot District Museum, Roxburgh 30251
Tewkesbury Museum, Tewkesbury 40692
Texana Museum, Edna 43095
Texarkana Museums System, Texarkana 47991
Texas Air Museum, Rio Hondo 46903
Texas Association of Museums, Austin 49534
Texas Baptist Historical Center Museum, Brenham 41880
Texas City Museum, Texas City 47992
Texas Energy Museum, Beaumont 41572
Texas Forestry Museum, Lufkin 44998
Texas Governor's Mansion, Austin 41420
Texas Heritage Museum, Hillsboro 44028
Texas Historical Museum, Texas 01527
Texas Maritime Museum, Rockport 46973
Texas Memorial Museum of Science and History, Austin 41421
Texas Military Forces Museum, Austin 41422
Texas Music Museum, Austin 41423
Texas Pharmacy Museum, Amarillo 41167
Texas Ranger Hall of Fame and Museum, Waco 48269
Texas Seaport Museum, Galveston 43614
Texas Sports Hall of Fame, Waco 48270
Texas Woman's University Art Galleries, Denton 42876
Textil- und Heimatmuseum, Sennwald 37162
Textil- und Rennsportmuseum, Hohenstein-Ernstthal 17815
Textilarkivet Västernorrland, Sollefteå 36217
Textildruckmuseum Mittelweiherburg, Hard, Vorarlberg 02001
Textile Conservation Centre, Winchester 40893
Textile Museum, Blönduós 21624
Textile Museum, Kuala Lumpur 27653
Textile Museum, Prato 25045
The Textile Museum, Washington 48397
Textile Museum of TIBA, Česká Skalice 08296
Textile Printing Museum of Premià de Mar, Premià de Mar 35295
Textilforum, Herning 08871
Textilmaschinenmuseum Neuthal, Bäretswil 36490
Textilmuseet, Borås 35843
Textilmuseet Högbo, Sandviken 36181
Textilmuseum, Hauptwil 36794
Textilmuseum, Neumünster 19048
Textilmuseum, Sankt Gallen 37108
Textilmuseum Die Scheune, Nettetal 19001
Textilmuseum Firma Franz Pischl, Telfs 02721
Textilmuseum im Jesuitenkolleg, Mindelheim 18746
Textilmuseum Max Berk im Kurpfälzischen Museum der Stadt Heidelberg, Heidelberg 17676
Textilmúzeum, Budapest 21386
Textilní Muzeum TIBA, Česká Skalice 08296
Teylers Museum, Haarlem 29331
Teysen's Woodland Indian Museum, Mackinaw City 45035
T.F. Chen Cultural Center, New York 45880
Thackray Museum, Leeds 39454
Thalassa - Aghia Napa Municipal Museum, Aghia Napa 08184
Thaler Keramikmuseum und Maria-Felchin-Sammlung, Matzendorf 36930
Thames Art Gallery, Chatham, Ontario 05241
Thames Museum, Newport 45934
Thames Police Museum, London 39789
Thames School of Mines and Mineralogical Museum, Thames 30263
Thames Valley Museum School, Burgessville 05143
Thameside Aviation Museum, East Tilbury 38850
Thamshavnbanen, Løkken Verk 30649
Thanjavur Art Gallery, Thanjavur 22032
The 7th Regiment Ulans Museum, Mińsk Mazowiecki 31808
The A.M. Gorki Appartment-Museum, Nižnij Novgorod 33215
The Anthropos Pavilion of the Moravian Museum, Brno 08276
The Argeş County Museum, Piteşti 32569
The Armory, Moskva 33168
The Art Museum, Iaşi 32532
The Arthur's Court - Dept of the Historical Museum, Gdańsk 31566
The A.S. Popov Central Museum of Communications, Sankt-Peterburg 33386
The Asia and Pacific Museum, Warszawa 32090
The Association of the State Literary Museums of the Republic of Belarus, Minsk 49066
The Badge of Honour State Museum of A.M. Gorky, Nižnij Novgorod 33207
The Belgrade City Museum, Beograd 33804
The Bishop's Courtyard - Moravian Museum, Brno 08262
The Bleschunov Municipal Museum of Personal Collections, Odessa 37896
The Brush Art Gallery and Studios, Lowell 44987
The Cathedral of the Archangel Michael, Moskva 33020
The City of Prague Museum, Praha 08596
The Coastal Heritage Museum, Stadsbygd 30874
The Coin Collection, University Museum of Cultural Heritage, Oslo 30745
The Danish Railway Museum, Odense 09007
The David Collection, København 08928
The District Museum, Náchod 08492
The Dutch Railway Museum, Utrecht 29906
The East Iceland Heritage Museum, Egilsstadir 21629
The Emperor Nicholas II Autograph Museum, Novosibirsk 33240
The Espoo Car Museum, Espoo 09430
The Far Eastern Art Museum, Chabarovsk 32739
The Faroese Museum of Natural History, Tórshavn 09408
The Feliks Nowowiejski Museum, Barczewo 31476
The Finnish Museum of Photography, Helsinki 09535
The Fire Technical Exhibition, Sankt-Peterburg 33477
The Fisherman's Cabin, Kauhava 09639
The Flamish Heritage, Groede 29302
The Fortress Museum Karlsborg, Karlsborg 35991
The Gem Museum, Ylämaa 10212
The Goncharov Museum, Uljanovsk 33657
The Gray Gallery, Quincy 46762
The Great Palace Mosaic Museum, İstanbul 37697
The Habourmuseum, Rotterdam 29750
The Historical Museum of the City of Cracow, Kraków 31707
The Historical Museum, University Museum of Cultural Heritage, Oslo 30736
The I.J. Padarowski and Polish Americans Museum, Warszawa 32103
The International Puppet Theatre Museum, Stockholm 36258
The Isaak Brodsky Apartment Museum, Sankt-Peterburg 33449
The Jan Matejko House, Kraków 31682
The Korean Museum Association, Seoul 49271
The Linnanmäki Toy and Game Museum, Helsinki 09510
The Little Cowboy Bar and Museum, Fromberg 43567
The Local Museum of Helsingør, Helsingør 08862
The Lönnström Art Museum, Rauma 09982
The Lomakov Museum of Oldtimers, Cars and Bikes, Moskva 33073
The Mayrau Mine Open Air Museum of Mining, Vinařice u Kladna 08719
The Memorial Museum of Yuldash Ahunbabayev, Margelan 48843
The Memorial of the Kralice Bible - Moravian Museum Brno, Kralice nad Oslavou 08427
The Monastic Museum of Denmark, Ry 09050
The Moravian Museum, Brno 08272
The Municipal Museum Anna Akhmatova - Silver Century, Sankt-Peterburg 33424
The Museum of Automobile Transport, Sankt-Peterburg 33412
The Museum of Children's Creation, Sankt-Peterburg 33432
The Museum of Civil Defence in Helsinki, Helsinki 09490
The Museum of History of Peterburg Conservatory, Sankt-Peterburg 33440
The Museum of History of Russian Military Schools (Cadet Corps), branch of the Military-Historical Museum of Artillery, Engineer and Signal Corps, Sankt-Peterburg 33472
The Museum of History Saint Petersburg University, Sankt-Peterburg 33444
The Museum of Modern Art, Kamakura and Hayama, Hayama 26185
The Museum of the Beskydy, Frýdek-Místek 08340
The Museum of Unique Dolls, Moskva 33155
The Museumship Pommern, Mariehamn 09817
The Nahum Goldmann Museum of the Jewish Diaspora, Tel Aviv 22748
The National Gallery of the Komi Republic, Syktyvkar 33578
The National Maritime Museum, Stockholm 36280
The National Pushkin Museum, Sankt-Peterburg 33489
The Nature and Forest Museum, Białowieża 31485
The Obretenov Family Museum, Ruse 04805
The Old Mine, Løkken Verk 30648
The Patriarch's Palace, Moskva 33171
The Polish Bar Museum, Warszawa 32086
The Poster Museum at Wilanów, Warszawa 32118
The Princes Czartoryski Museum, Kraków 31712
The Prokop Diviš Memorial, Znojmo 08757
The Pushkin Apartment Museum, Sankt-Peterburg 33453
The Pushkin Country House Museum, Puškin 33338
The Radziwill Palace in Nieborów, Nieborów 31822
The Road & Traffic Museum of Central Finland, Kintaus 09671
The Roy Rogers-Dale Evans Museum, Branson 41871
The Royal Academy of Fine Arts, Stockholm 36252
The Royal Mint Museum, Kongsberg 30601

The Saint Petersburg Vladimir Nabokov Museum, Sankt-Peterburg 33482
The Salvation Army Museum, Helsinki 09519
The Sholokhov Museum-Reserve, Vešenskaja 33683
The Slovak Mining Museum, Banská Štiavnica 33951
The Small Galery, Ljubljana 34108
The Soldiers' Uprising in 1918, Radomir 04795
The Sports Museum of Latvia, Rīga 27421
The State Art Museum of Altay Region, Barnaul 32672
The State Historical andMemorial Museum Smolny, Sankt-Peterburg 33398
The State Museum of Oriental Art, Moskva 33107
The State Museum of Political History of Russia, Sankt-Peterburg 33405
The State Museum of the Defense and Siege of Leningrad, Sankt-Peterburg 33401
The State Tretjakov Gallery, Moskva 33046
The Swedish Museum of Textile History, Borås 35843
The Tarusa Museum of the Tsvetaeva Family, Tarusa 33595
The Teresia and Rafael Lönnström Home Museum, Rauma 09985
The Theatre Museum in the Court Theatre, København 08951
The Tokugawa Art Museum, Nagoya, Aichi 26571
The Town Museum of Ústí nad Labem, Ústí nad Labem 08703
The Town Museum of Vrsac, Vršac 33928
The Treasury, Stockholm 36281
The Union Brewery Museum, Ljubljana 34117
The Upper Silesian Museum, Bytom 31519
The Village of Living History, Turku 10122
The Wielkopolskie Military Museum, Poznań 31915
The Yaroslavski Yakut State Museum of History and Culture of Northern Peoples, Jakutsk 32843
Thea G. Korver Visual Art Center, Orange City 46175
Theater Museum, Amsterdam 28908
Theatergeschichtliche Sammlung und Hebbel-Sammlung, Kiel 18080
Theatermuseum der Landeshauptstadt, Düsseldorf 16744
Theatermuseum Hannover, Hannover 17612
Theatermuseum in der Reithalle, Meiningen 18688
Theaterwissenschaftliche Sammlung, Köln 18167
Theatre Museum, Helsinki 09540
Theatre Museum, London 39790
Theatre Museum, Warszawa 32128
Theatre Museum of the Kasan Academic Bolshoy Theatre of Drama V.I. Kachalov, Kazan 32909
De Theefabriek, Houwerzijl 29451
Thelma Miles Museum, Matheson 05823
Themapark Openluchtmuseum De Spitkeet, Harkema 29344
Theo-Steinbrenner-Turm-Museum, Sommerach 19995
Theo Swagemakers Museum, Haarlem 29332
Theo Thijssen Museum, Amsterdam 28909
Theodor-Mommsen-Gedächtnisstätte, Garding 17200
Theodor-Storm-Haus, Husum, Nordsee 17873
Theodor-Zink-Museum und Wadgasserhof, Kaiserslautern 17971
Theodore Roosevelt Birthplace, New York 45881
Theodore Roosevelt Inaugural National Historic Site, Buffalo 41989
Theomin Gallery, Dunedin 30155
Theophilos Kairis Museum, Andros 20825
Theresienthaler Glasmuseum, Zwiesel 20781
Therisso Museum of Eleftherios Venizelos, Chania 20920
Thermae Maiores, Budapest 21381
Thermen-Museum Juliomagus, Schleitheim 37137
Thermenmuseum, Heerlen 29369
Thessaloniki Museum for the Macedonian Struggle, Thessaloniki 21194
Theta-Museet, Bergen 30428
Thetford Historical Society Museum, Thetford 47997
Thielska Galleriet, Stockholm 36295
Thingbaek Kalkminer Bundgaards Museum, Skørping 09068
Thinktank, Birmingham 38230
Third Cavalry Museum, Fort Carson 43377
Thirlestane Castle, Lauder 39428
Thirsk Museum, Thirsk 40698
This Century Art Gallery, Williamsburg 48631
This Is The Place Heritage Park, Salt Lake City 47233
Thomas Bewick's Birthplace, Mickley 39943
Thomas Carlyle's Birthplace, Ecclefechan 38866
Thomas Center Galleries, Gainesville 43586
Thomas Clarke House-Princeton Battlefield, Princeton 46706
Thomas E. McMillan Museum, Brewton 41885
Thomas Edison Birthplace Museum, Milan 45335
Thomas Edison House, Louisville 44977
Thomas-Foreman Home, Muskogee 45583
Thomas Foster Memorial Temple, Uxbridge 06656
Thomas Handforth Gallery, Tacoma 47923
Thomas Haney House, Maple Ridge 05814
Thomas Hart Benton Home and Studio, Kansas City 44410
Thomas J. Boyd Museum, Wytheville 48771
Thomas J. Walsh Art Gallery and Regina A. Quick Center for the Arts, Fairfield 43265
Thomas Jefferson House Monticello, Charlottesville 42252
Thomas K. Lang Gallery, Wien 02995
Thomas L. Kane Memorial Chapel, Kane 44387
Thomas-Mann-Archiv, Zürich 37412
Thomas McCulloch Museum, Halifax 05565
Thomas-Müntzer-Gedenkstätte, Heldrungen 17700
Thomas Muir Museum, Bishopbriggs 38237
Thomas Newcomen Museum, Exton 43255
Thomas P. Kennard House, Lincoln 44792
Thomas Price House, Woodruff 48734
Thomas Sappington House Museum, Crestwood 42700
Thomas T. Taber Museum, Williamsport 48632
Thomas Warne Historical Museum, Old Bridge Township 46130
Thomas Wolfe Memorial, Asheville 41284
Thomaston Historical Museum, Thomaston 47999
Thomasville Cultural Center, Thomasville 48002
Thonet-Museum, Friedberg 01853
Thong Nhat Palace, Ho Chi Minh City 48991
The Thoreau Institute at Walden Woods, Lincoln 44780
Thorma János Múzeum, Kiskunhalas 21460
Thornbury and District Museum, Thornbury, Gloucestershire 40699
Thorne-Sagendorph Art Gallery, Keene 44427
Thorney Heritage Centre, Thorney 40700
Thornhill Gallery, Kansas City 44411
Thornhill Historic Site and 19th Century Village, Chesterfield 42290
Thornton W. Burgess Museum, Sandwich 47389
Thorpe Water Mill, Bothwell 00818
Thorvaldsens Museum, København 08952
Thorvaldsens Samlingen på Nysø, Præstø 09024
Thousand Islands Museum of Clayton, Clayton 42445
Thracian Tomb, Kazanlăk 04704
Thrai Kao, Battani 37500
Thrasher Carriage Museum, Frostburg 43570
Three Rivers Museum, Muskogee 45584
Three Rivers Museum and Local History, Rickmansworth 40323
Three Village Historical Society Museum, Setauket 47570
Threlkeld Quarry and Mining Museum, Threlkeld 40705
Threshing Museum, Mellilä 09822
Threshing Museum, Mullinahone 22523
Threshing Museum, Peräseinäjoki 09918
Thronateeska Heritage Foundation, Albany 41082
Thua Thien Hue Museum, Thua Thien Hue 49003
Thünen-Museum-Tellow, Warnkenhagen 20403
Thüringer Freilichtmuseum Hohenfelden, Hohenfelden 17806
Thüringer Landesmuseum Heidecksburg, Rudolstadt 19700
Thüringer Museum Eisenach, Eisenach 16819
Thüringer Universitäts- und Landesbibliothek Jena, Jena 17953
Thürmer Pianoforte-Museum, Meißen 18693
Thunder Bay Art Gallery, Thunder Bay 06548
Thunder Bay Historical Museum Society, Thunder Bay 06549
Thunder Bay Military Museum, Thunder Bay 06550
Thunderbird Museum, Merrillan 45268
Thurles Famine Museum, Thurles 22546
Thurn und Taxis Museum, Regensburg 19532
Thurrock Museum, Grays 39117
Thursford Collection, Fakenham 38967
Thurso Heritage Museum, Thurso 40709
Thury György Múzeum, Nagykanizsa 21486
Thwaite Mills Watermill, Leeds 39455
Tiagarra Aboriginal Culture Centre and Museum, Devonport 00980
Tianjin Art Museum, Tianjin 07263
Tianjin Drama Museum, Tianjin 07264
Tianjin History Museum, Tianjin 07265
Tianjin Museum of Natural History, Tianjin 07266
Tianjin Painting Gallery, Tianjin 07267
Tianjin People's Science Hall, Tianjin 07268
Tianyi Ge Museum, Ningbo 07197
Tibet House Museum, Delhi 21785
Tibet Songtsen House, Zürich 37413
Tibetan Collection at the Kotoku-ji, Hanamaki 26182
Tibooburra Local Aboriginal Land Council Keeping Place, Tibooburra 01535
Tibro Museum, Tibro 36323
Ticho House, Jerusalem 22666
Tidaholms Konsthall, Tidaholm 36324
Tidaholms Museum, Tidaholm 36325
Tieling City Museum, Tieling 07271
Tiemuseo, Helsinki 09542
Tier- und Jagdmuseum, Bad Dürrheim 15634
Tiermuseum, Burgau, Schwaben 16415
Tiermuseum, Lenggries 18439
Tierwelt-Panorama, Ebikon 36668
Tieteelliset Kokoelmat, Forssa 09443
Tiflološki Muzej, Zagreb 07839
Tignish Cultural Centre Museum, Tighish 06551
Tikanoja Art Museum, Vaasa 10162
Tikanojan Taidekoti, Vaasa 10162
Tikotin Museum of Japanese Art, Haifa 22613
Tilbury Fort, Tilbury 40710
Till-Eulenspiegel-Museum, Schöppenstedt 19840
Tillamook County Pioneer Museum, Tillamook 48008
Tillamook Naval Air Station Museum, Tillamook 48009
Timber Creek Police Station Museum, Timber Creek 01536
Timber Museum of New Zealand, Putaruru 30244
Timber-rafting Museum, El Pont de Claverol 35280
Timber Village Museum, Blind River 05085
Timbertown Museum, Wauchope 01586
Time Bygdemuseum, Undheim 30960
Time Machine, Weston-super-Mare 40836
The Time Museum, Newark-on-Trent 40025
Time Museum, Teheran 22328
Timeball Tower, Deal 38710
Timespan Museum and Art Gallery, Helmsdale 39210
Timios Stavros Monastery, Mavradzei 21060
Timken Museum of Art, San Diego 47298
Timmermans-Opsomerhuis, Lier 03587
Timmins Museum, South Porcupine 06474
Timothy Hackworth Victorian Railway Museum, Shildon 40500
Tin Museum - Gedung Raja Abdullah, Kelang 27627
Tinelmuseum, Sinaai-Waas 03733
Tineriba Tribal Gallery and Museum, Hahndorf 01084
Tingvoll Museum, Tingvoll 30921
Tingwall Agricultural Museum, Gott 39104
Tinker Swiss Cottage Museum, Rockford 46964
Tinley Park Historical Society Museum, Tinley Park 48010
Tinn Museum, Rjukan 30796
Tintern Abbey, Chepstow 38547
Tintic Mining Museum, Eureka 43234
Tioga County Historical Society Museum, Owego 46226
Tioga Point Museum, Athens 41326
Tippecanoe Battlefield, Battle Ground 41540
Tippecanoe County Historical Museum, Lafayette 44569
Tipton County Museum, Covington 42683
Tipton-Haynes Museum, Johnson City 44348
Tiptree Museum, Tiptree 40711
Tipu Sahib Museum, Srirangapatna 22029
Tire Müzesi, Tire 37794
Tire Museum, Tire 37794
Tiroler Bauernhausmuseum, Kitzbühel 02119
Tiroler Bergbau- und Hüttenmuseum, Brixlegg 01750
Tiroler Kaiserjägermuseum Obergricht, Serfaus 02659
Tiroler Kunstpavillon Kleiner Hofgarten, Innsbruck 02081
Tiroler Landesmuseum Ferdinandeum, Innsbruck 02082
Tiroler Volkskunstmuseum, Innsbruck 02083
Tirpitz-Stillingen, Blåvand 08786
Titan Missile Museum, Green Valley 43795
Titanicmuseum, Bad Wildungen 15767
Tithe Barn Museum and Art Centre, Swanage 40656
Titus Brandsma Museum, Bolsward 28996
Tiverton Museum of Mid Devon Life, Tiverton 40712
Tjolöholms Slott, Fjärås 35891
Tjumen Picture Gallery, Tjumen 33609
Tjumen Region Museum named after I.Ya. Slovtsov, Tjumen 33610
Tjumen Regional Museum of Fine Art, Tjumen 33611
Tjumenskaja Kartinnaja Galereja, Tjumen 33609
Tjumenskij Oblastnoj Kraevedčeskij Muzej im. I.Ja. Slovcova, Tjumen 33610
Tjumenskij Oblastnoj Muzej Izobrazitelnych Iskusstv, Tjumen 33611
TM Gallery, Crestview 42699
T.N. Chrenikov House-Museum, Elec 32789
T.N. Granovsky House-Museum, Orël 33260
To-ji Homotsukan, Kyoto 26458
To-ji Temple Treasure House, Kyoto 26458
Toad Hole Cottage Museum, Ludham 39841
Tobacco and Match Museum, Stockholm 36296
Tobacco and Salt Museum, Tokyo 26929
Tobacco Farm Life Museum, Kenly 44433
Tobacco Museum, Ljubljana 34123
Tobacco Museum, Texas 01528
Tobačni Muzej, Ljubljana 34123
Tobaks- och Tändstickmuseum, Stockholm 36296
Tobias Community Historical Society Museum, Tobias 48015
Tobias-Mayer-Museum, Marbach am Neckar 18621
Tobias Smollett Museum, Alexandria 37971
Tobolsk Picture Gallery, Tobolsk 33612
Tobolsk State Historical and Architecture Museum-Estate, Tobolsk 33613
Tobolskaja Kartinnaja Galereja, Tobolsk 33612
Tobolskij Gosudarstvennyj Istoriko-architekturnyj Muzej-zapovednik, Tobolsk 33613
Tochigi-kenritsu Bijutsukan, Utsunomiya 26993
Tochigi-kenritsu Hakubutsukan, Utsunomiya 26994
Tochigi Prefectural Museum, Utsunomiya 26994
Tochigi Prefectural Museum of Fine Arts, Utsunomiya 26993
Todai-ji Treasure Hall, Nara 26584
Todd Madigan Gallery, Bakersfield 41441
Todmorden Mills Heritage Museum and Arts Centre, Toronto 06614
Todor Kableshkov Memorial House, Koprivštica 04715
Töllinmäen Museo, Hämeenkyrö 09446
Töllinmäki Museum, Hämeenkyrö 09446
Töllstorps Industrimuseum, Gnosjö 35908
Töpferei und Museum im Kannenofen, Höhr-Grenzhausen 17786
Töpfereimuseum, Langerwehe 18340
Töpfereimuseum Raeren, Raeren 03691
Töpfermuseum, Duingen 16745
Töpfermuseum, Kohren-Sahlis 18198
Töpfermuseum, Rödermark 19631
Töpfermuseum, Stoob 02702
Töpfermuseum Im alten Kannenofen, Ransbach-Baumbach 19484
Töpfermuseum Thurnau, Thurnau 20174
Töpferstube mit Keramikmuseum, Bad Wiessee 15760
Törngrens Krukmakeri, Falkenberg 35879
Töysän Museo, Töysä 10107
Tofield Historical Museum, Tofield 06554
Toggenburger Museum, Lichtensteig 36874
Toggenburger Schmiede- und Handwerksmuseum, Bazenheid 36524
Tohoku Daigaku, Kokoshiryoshitsu, Sendai 26737
Tohoku Historical Museum, Tagajou 26782
Tohoku Rekishi Shiryokan, Tagajou 26782
Tøjhusmuseet, København 08953
Tokai Daigaku Kaiyo Kagaku Hakubutsukan, Shizuoka 26769
Tokaji Múzeum, Tokaji 21599
Tokat Müzesi, Tokat 37795
Tokat Museum, Tokat 37795
Token Hakubutsukan, Tokyo 26935
Toki No Sato History Hall, Mano 26465
Tokmok Historical and Regional Museum, Tokmok 27316
Tokomairiro Historical Society Museum, Milton 30203
Tokomaru Steam Engine Museum, Tokomaru 30267
Tokoname Togei Kenkyujyo, Tokoname 26824
Tokugawa Bijutsukan, Nagoya, Aichi 26571
Tokushima-kenritsu Hakubutsukan, Tokushima 26825
Tokushima-kenritsu Kindai Bijutsukan, Tokushima 26826
Tokushima-kenritsu Torii Kinen Hakubutsukan, Naruto 26590
Tokushima Modern Art Museum, Tokushima 26826
Tokushima Prefectural Local Culture Hall, Tokushima 26827
Tokushima Prefecture Museum, Tokushima 26825
Tokyo Central Art Museum, Tokyo 26936
Tokyo Central Bijutsukan, Tokyo 26936
Tokyo Fuji Art Museum, Hachioji 26166
Tokyo Kokuritsu Hakubutsukan, Tokyo 26937
Tokyo Kokuritsu Kindai Bijutsukan, Tokyo 26938
Tokyo Kokuritsu Kindai Bijutsukan, Film Center, Tokyo 26939
Tokyo Kokuritsu Kindai Bijutsukan Kogeikan, Crafts Gallery, Tokyo 26940
Tokyo Kokusai Bijutsukyoukai, Tokyo 26941
Tokyo Metropolitan Art Museum, Tokyo 26944
Tokyo Metropolitan Geijutsu High School Museum, Tokyo 26942
Tokyo Metropolitan Museum of Photography, Tokyo 26946
Tokyo Metropolitan Teien Art Museum, Tokyo 26947
Tokyo National Museum, Tokyo 26937
Tokyo Noko Daigaku Kogakubu Fuzoku Sen'i Hakubutsukan, Koganei 26364
Tokyo Station Gallery, Tokyo 26943
Tokyo-to Bijutsukan, Tokyo 26944
Tokyo-to Gendai Bijutsukan, Tokyo 26945
Tokyo-to Shashin Bijutsukan, Tokyo 26946
Tokyo-to Teien Bijutsukan, Tokyo 26947
Tokyo University Archaeological Collection, Tokyo 26948
Tolbooth Art Centre, Kirkcudbright 39394
Tolbooth Museum, Stonehaven 40613
Toledo Museum of Art, Toledo 48021
Tolgus Tin Mill and Streamworks, Redruth 40304
Tolhouse Museum and Brass Rubbing Centre, Great Yarmouth 39127
Tolland County Jail and Warden's Home Museum, Tolland 48023
The Tolman Collection, Tokyo 26949
Tolmin Museum, Tolmin 34155
Tolminski Muzej, Tolmin 34155
Tolpuddle Martyrs Museum, Tolpuddle 40715
Tolsey Museum, Burford 38395
Tolson Memorial Museum, Huddersfield 39274
Toltec Mounds Archeological State Park, Scott 47510
Tolvmansgården, Kruunupyy 09711
Tom Brown School Museum, Uffington 40746
Tom Collins House, Swanbourne 01488
Tom Mix Museum, Dewey 42941
Tom Thomson Memorial Art Gallery, Owen Sound 06090
Tom Tits Experiment, Södertälje 36212
Tomakomai-shi Seishonen, Tomakomai 26961
Tomakomai Youth Science Museum, Tomakomai 26961
Tomball Community Museum Center, Tomball 48024
Tombe Reali di Casa Savoia, Torino 25767
Tome Parish Museum, Tome 48025
Tomelilla Konsthall, Tomelilla 36326
Tomimoto Kenkichi Memorial Museum, Ando 26098
Tomintoul Museum, Tomintoul 40716
Tomioka Museum, Tokyo 26950
Tomsk Museum of Wooden Art, Tomsk 33615
Tomsk Regional Museum of Art, Tomsk 33616
Tomskij Muzej Derevjannogo Zodčestva, Tomsk 33615
Tomskij Oblastnoj Chudožestvennyj Muzej, Tomsk 33616
Tomskij Oblastnoj Kraevedčeskij Muzej, Tomsk 33617
Ton Duc Thang Museum, Ho Chi Minh City 48992
Ton Sak Yai, Uttaradit 37545
Ton Smits Huis, Eindhoven 29220
Ton Trai, Phuket 37530
Tonawandas Museum, Tonawanda 48028
Tønder Museum, Tønder 09094
Tong-Jin Irrigation Folk Museum, Kimje 27204
Tongan County Museum, Xiamen 07291
Tongarra Museum, Albion Park 00727
Tongass Historical Museum, Ketchikan 44459
Tongdosa Museum, Yangsan 27298
Tongxian Museum, Beijing 06991
Tongzhou District Museum, Beijing 06992
Toni-Merz-Museum, Sasbach bei Achern, Baden 19759
Tonto National Monument, Roosevelt 47000

Toos Museum, Mashad 22268
Toowoomba Historical Museum, Toowoomba 01541
Toowoomba Regional Art Gallery, Toowoomba 01542
Top of Oklahoma Historical Museum, Blackwell 41730
Topkapı Palace Museum, İstanbul 37709
Topkapı Sarayı Müzesi, İstanbul 37709
Topographie des Terrors, Berlin 16107
Topoisten Ulkomuseoalue, Nousiainen 09869
Toppenish Museum, Toppenish 48036
Toppler-Schlößchen, Rothenburg ob der Tauber 19683
Topsfield Historical Museum, Topsfield 48037
Topsham Museum, Topsham 40717
Torajiro Kojima Memorial Hall, Kurashiki 26385
Torbay Museum, Torbay 06557
Torbogenmuseum, Königsbronn 18171
Torekällbergets Museum, Södertälje 36213
Torekovs Sjöfartsmuseum, Torekov 36327
Torenmuseum, Goedereede 29285
Torenmuseum, Mol 03630
Torenverplaatsingsmuseum, Bocholt 03221
Torfaen Museum, Pontypool 40222
Torfmuseum, Neustadt am Rübenberge 19070
Torfschiffwerftmuseum, Worpswede 20686
Torhalle, Frauenchiemsee 17089
Torhalle Frauenchiemsee und Vikarhaus, Chiemsee 16474
Torhaus Dölitz, Leipzig 18422
Torhaus Markkleeberg, Markkleeberg 18638
Torhaus-Museum, Siegburg 19946
Torhaus Otterndorf, Otterndorf 19324
Tornaritis Pierides Municipal Museum of Paloentology, Larnaka 08193
Tornionlaakson Maakuntamuseo, Tornio 10115
Tornyai János Múzeum, Hódmezővásárhely 21428
Torogan House, Pasay 31419
Toronto Aeropspace Museum, Toronto 06615
Toronto Center for Contemporary Art, Toronto 06616
Toronto Dominion Gallery of Inuit Art, Toronto 06617
Toronto Outdoor Art Exhibition, Toronto 06618
Toronto Scottish Regimental Museum, Toronto 06619
Toronto Sculpture Garden, Toronto 06620
Toronto's First Post Office, Toronto 06621
Toronto's Waterfront Museum, Toronto 06622
Torpedo Factory Art Center, Alexandria 41135
Torquay Museum, Torquay 40718
Torre Abbey Historic House and Gallery, Torquay 40719
Torre del Conde, San Sebastián de La Gomera 35392
Torre dels Enagistes, Manacor 35079
I Torre Guaita, San Marino 33769
Torreón Fortea, Zaragoza 35731
Torres Strait Museum, Thursday Island 01534
Torrington Historical Society Museum, Torrington 48040
Torrington Museum, Torrington 40721
Torsby Finnkulturcentrum, Torsby 36328
Torsby Fordonsmuseum, Torsby 36329
Torum Maa Ethnographic Open Air Museum, Chanty-Mansijsk 32742
Tørvikbygd Bygdemuseum, Tørvikbygd 30927
Toshiba Kagakukan, Kawasaki 26330
Toshiba Science Institute, Kawasaki 26330
Toshodai-ji Treasure House, Nara 26585
Total Open-Air Museum, Yangju 27297
Toten Ecomuseum, Bøverbru 30447
Toten Ecomuseum, Kapp 30589
Toten Økomuseum, Bøverbru 30447
Toten Økomuseum, Kapp 30589
Totius House Museum, Potchefstroom 34337
Totnes Costume Museum, Totnes 40723
Totnes Elizabethan Museum, Totnes 40724
Tottori Folk Art Museum, Tottori 26963
Tottori-kenritsu Hakubutsukan, Tottori 26964
Tottori Prefectural Museum, Tottori 26964
Touchstone Center for Crafts, Farmington 43301
Tougaloo College Art Collection, Tougaloo 48041
Tour de Constance, Aigues-Mortes 10237
Tour de la Motte-Forte, Arnay-le-Duc 10422
Tour de Moricq, Angles 10352
Tour des Voleurs, Riquewihr 13979
Tour-Musée de Velaux, Velaux 15109
La Tour Royale, Toulon (Var) 14934
Touring Exhibitions Group, London 49453
Touristik-Museum, Unterseen 37264
Toussaint Forge, Givet 11874
Towada Natural History Museum, Towadako 26966
Towe Auto Museum, Sacramento 47055
Tower Bridge Exhibition, London 39791
Tower Fine Arts Gallery, Brockport 41908
Tower Museum, Londonderry 39818
Tower Museum of Prosphorion, Ouranoupoli 21103
Tower of David, Jerusalem 22667
Tower of the Livonian Order Castle, Tukums 27460
Town and Crown Exhibition, Windsor 40904
Town and Regional Museum of Skagen, Skagen 09057
Town Creek Indian Mound Historic Site, Mount Gilead 45530
Town Exhibition Hall, Petrozavodsk 33314
Town Hall, Brugge 03252
Town Hall Art Gallery, Kranj 34099
Town History Exhibition, Sopron 21538
Town History Museum and New Hungarian Gallery, Székesfehérvár 21563
Town House, Culross 38683
Town House Museum of Lynn Life, King's Lynn 39372
Town Museum, East Grinstead 38841
Town Museum, Gödöllő 21416
Town Museum, Ledeč nad Sázavou 08445
Town Museum, Moravská Třebová 08485
Town Museum, Nurmes 09873
Town Museum, Šibenik 07772
Town Museum, Skuteč 08653
Town Museum, Stříbro 08666
Town Museum, Valašské Klobouky 08705
Town Museum, Zbiroh 08740
Town Museum of Příbor, Příbor 08624
Town Museum of the Art of Omsk, Omsk 33253
Town Museum of Tokaji, Tokaji 21599
Town Museum Rijeka, Rijeka 07761
Town of Clarence Museum, Clarence 42424
Town of Manlius Museum, Manlius 45122
Town of North Hempstead Museum, Westbury 48551
Town of Ontario Historical and Landmark Preservation Society Museum Complex, Ontario 46165
Town of Warwick Museum, Warwick 48321
Town War Museum for Peace, Trieste 25814
Towneley Hall Art Gallery and Museums, Burnley 38401
Towner Art Gallery and Local Museum, Eastbourne 38858
Township Museum, Lwandle 34303
Townsville Museum, Townsville 01549
Toy and Miniature Museum, Stellenbosch 34384
Toy and Miniature Museum of Kansas City, Kansas City 44412
Toy and Teddy Bear Museum, Lytham Saint Anne's 39862
Toy Museum, Davos Platz 36655
Toy Museum, Moirans-en-Montagne 12999
The Toy Museum, Soultz-Haut-Rhin 14796
Toy Museum, Stockholm 36247
Toy Museum Prag & Barbie Museum, Praha 08591
Toy-Toy Museum, Rotterdam 29777
Toyama Kenminkaikan Bijutsukan, Toyama 26968
Toyama-kenritsu Kindai Bijutsukan, Toyama 26969
Toyama Kinenkan, Hiki 26191
Toyama Kinenkan Fuzoku Bijutsukan, Kawashima, Saitama 26332
Toyama Memorial Art Museum, Kawashima, Saitama 26332
Toyama Municipal Folkcraft Village, Toyama 26970
Toyama Museum, Toyama 26971
Toymuseum Deventer, Deventer 29146
Toyohashi City Art Museum, Toyohashi 26972
Toyohashi-shiritsu Bijutsukan, Toyohashi 26972
Toyota Automobile Museum, Nagakute 26526
Toyota Municipal Museum of Art, Toyota, Aichi 26974
Toys Museum, Hoorn 29445
Trabzon Culture Center, Trabzon 37798
Trabzon Devlet Güzel Sanatlar Galerisi, Trabzon 37797
Trabzon Kültür Merkezi, Trabzon 37798
Trabzon State Gallery, Trabzon 37797
Trachten- und Heimatmuseum, Weiltingen 20453
Trachten- und Volkskunstmuseum, Seebach, Baden 19911
Trachtenhaus Jatzwauk, Hoyerswerda 17849
Trachtenmuseum, Ochsenfurt 19219
Tracy Maund Historical Collection, Carlton South 00898
Trader Windmill, Sibsey 40514
Traditiekamer Regiment Stoottroepen, Assen 28953
Traditiekamer Typhoon, Volkel 29959
Traditiekamer Vliegbasis Twenthe, Enschede 29241
Tradition Room of the Air Force Signals School, Tikkakoski 10105
Traditional Heritage Museum, Sheffield 40491
Traditional Village, Virrat 10206
Træe, Bryne 30454
Tragor Ignác Múzeum, Vác 21602
Trail End State Historic Museum, Sheridan 47602
Trail Museum, Trail 06630
Traill County Historical Society Museum, Hillsboro 44025
Trailside Nature and Science Center, Mountainside 45550
Trailside Nature Center and Museum, Cincinnati 42411
Trailside Nature Museum, Cross River 42711
Train Historique du Lac de Rillé, Rillé 13970
Train Museum, Ambarawa 22065
Train Station of Bejucal, Bejucal 07864
Trainland U.S.A., Colfax 42521
Les Trains de Saint-Eutrope, Evry 11682
Trakai Historical Museum, Trakai 27534
Trakijska Grobnica, Kazanlăk 04704
Traktoren-Museum Kempen, Horn-Bad Meinberg 17842
Traktorenmuseum, Vordernberg 02779
Traktorenmuseum, Westerkappeln 20542
Traktorveteranensammlung Dorf an der Pram, Wendling 02818
Tram Museum, Rio de Janeiro 04366
Tram Museum of Helsinki City Musuem, Helsinki 09522
Tram Museum Rotterdam, Rotterdam 29778
Tram Museum Zürich, Zürich 37414
Trambahn-Museum, München 18920
Trammell and Margaret Crow Collection of Asian Art, Dallas 42760
Trammuseum, Schepdaal 03727
Tramway Museum, Bendigo 00796
Tramway-Museum Graz, Graz 01935
Tramway Museum Tramshed 5, Oslo 30764
Tranby House, Maylands 01219
Tranquilino Sandalio de Noda Museo de Ciencias Naturales, Pinar del Río 08078
Tranquilino Sandalio de Noda Museum of Natural Science, Pinar del Río 08078
Transcona Historical Museum, Winnipeg 06848
Transgariep Museum, Philippolis 34324
TransNamib Museum, Windhoek 28784
Transnet Heritage Foundation Library, Johannesburg 34285
Transport Museum, Budapest 21352
Transport Museum, Stockholm 36283
Transportation Exhibits, Nevada City 45656
Transportation Museum, Cairo 09290
Transportation Museum, Tokyo 26875
Transvaal Museum, Pretoria 34359
Transylvania Museum, Lexington 44745
Trapezium House, Petersburg 46379
Trapholt, Kolding 08960
Traquair House, Innerleithen 39291
Trastad Samlinger, Borkenes 30444
Travel Town Museum, Los Angeles 44947
Traveler's Rest State Historic Site, Toccoa 48016
Travellers Rest Historic House Museum, Nashville 45627
Traverse County Historical Society Museum, Wheaton 48586
Traversothèque, Mulhouse 13217
Treadgolds Museum, Portsmouth 40260
Treasure Hall of the Kamakuragu Shrine, Kamakura 26294
Treasure Hall of the Yōgen-In Temple, Kyoto 26461
Treasure House of Serbian-Orthodox Church, Kotor 33849
Treasure House of the Eiheiji Temple, Eiheiji 26135
Treasure House of the Hotoku Ninomiya Shrine, Odawara 26612
Treasure House of the Kikuchi Shrine, Kikuchi 26333
Treasure House of the Myōhōin Temple, Kyoto 26437
Treasure Trove Shipwreck Museum, Port Douglas 01380
Treasurer's House, York 40968
Treasures of the Earth, Corpach 38635
Treasures of the Rokuonji Temple, Kyoto 26449
Treasures of the Sea Exhibit, Georgetown 43650
Treasury of the Cathedral Saint Vlaho, Dubrovnik 07701
Treasury of the Parish Church, Nin 07744
Treasury of Zagreb Cathedral, Zagreb 07836
Treasury - Uppsala Cathedral Museum, Uppsala 36360
Treaty House, Waitangi 30280
Treaty Museum, Pattijoki 09914
Treaty Site History Center, Saint Peter 47170
Třebechovické Muzeum Betlémů, Třebechovice pod Orebem 08684
Tredegar House and Park, Newport, Gwent 40052
Treherne Museum, Treherne 06631
Het Trekkermuseum, Nisse 29638
Trelleborgs Museum, Trelleborg 36333
Trembowla Cross of Freedom Museum, Dauphin 05310
Tremont Gallery, Boston 41829
Trenčianske Múzeum, Trenčín 34074
Trentham Agricultural and Railway Museum, Trentham 01551
Trenton City Museum, Trenton 48059
Trenton Historical Museum, Trenton 48051
Trepassey Area Museum, Trepassey 06632
Trerice, Newquay 40060
Tresfjord Museum, Tresfjord 30929
Tresoar, Frisian Historic and Literature Centre, Leeuwarden 29515
Tresoar, Frysk Histoarysk en Letterkundich Sintrum, Leeuwarden 29515
Trésor de la Basilique Saint-Materne, Walcourt 03825
Tresor de la Catedral, Girona 34860
Trésor de la Cathédrale de Troyes, Troyes 15010
Trésor de la Cathédrale Notre-Dame, Moulins (Allier) 13189
Trésor de la Cathedrale Notre-Dame, Tournai 03797
Trésor de la Cathédrale Notre-Dame-du-Glarier, Sion 37176
Trésor de la Cathédrale Saint-Nicolas, Fribourg 36720
Trésor de la Collégiale, Huy 03513
Trésor de la Collegiale Sainte-Waudru, Mons 03637
Trésor de l'Eglise Primaire Saint-Sebastien, Stavelot 03767
Trésor de Saint Foy, Conques 11397
Trésor d'Église, Marseille 12872
Trésor d'Église, Narbonne 13272
Trésor du Frère Hugo d'Oignies, Namur 03652
Trésor et Musée de la Collegiale Sainte-Begge, Andenne 03130
Trésor Saint-Gervais, Avranches 10543
Tresorama, La Ferté-Macé 12171
Tresure Room Gallery of the Interchurch Center, New York 45882
Trev Deeley Motorcycle Museum, Richmond 06266
Trevi Flash Art Museum, Trevi 25800
Trevithick Cottage, Camborne 38449
Tri-Cities Museum, Grand Haven 43745
Tri-County Historical Society and Museum, Herington 43999
Tri-State Mineral Museum, Joplin 44363
Trianon Museum and Art Gallery, Denver 42901
Trias-Museum, Ochsenfurt 19220
Tribal Museum, Ahmedabad 21682
Tridaya Eka Dharma Museum, Bukittinggi 22093
Triestingtaler Heimatmuseum, Weissenbach an der Triesting 02801
Trift- und Holzfällermuseum, Bad Großpertholz 01703
Triglavska Muzejska Zbirka, Mojstrana 34132
Trillarium, Cleebronn 16477
Trinity Church in Nikitniki, Moskva 33033
Trinity Heights - Saint Joseph Center-Museum, Sioux City 47640
Trinity House, Newcastle-upon-Tyne 40042
Trinity House National Lighthouse Centre, Penzance 40182
Trinity Interpretation Centre, Trinity 06635
Trinity Museum, Trinity 06636
Trinity Museum of the Parish of Trinity Church, New York 45883
Triton Museum of Art, Santa Clara 47408
Troadkasten, Freinberg 01849
Troadkasten, Sauerlach 19762
Troadkasten, Schardenberg 02625
Troadkasten Fornach, Fornach 01843
Trochu and District Museum, Trochu 06637
Trøgstad Bygdemuseum, Trøgstad 30930
Troickij Sobor, Serpuchov 33523
Trojanski monastery, Orešak 04748
Trollenäs Slott, Eslöv 35875
Trolley Museum of New York, Kingston 44495
Trollhättans Museum och Saab Museum, Trollhättan 36337
Trompetenmuseum, Bad Säckingen 15725
Het Tromp's Huys, Vlieland 29955
Troms Forsvarsmuseum, Bardu 30411
Tromsø Folkemuseum, Tromsø 30934
Tromsø Universitets Museum, Tromsø 30935
Trondarnes Distriktmuseum, Harstad 30535
Trøndelag Folkemuseum, Trondheim 30943
Trondheim Kunstmuseum, Trondheim 30944
Trondheim Politimuseum, Trondheim 30945
Trophäensaal, Altenfelden 01662
Trosterud Skolemuseum, Rømskog 30803
Trottenmuseum, Schliengen 19801
Trout Gallery, Carlisle 42105
Trova Foundation, Saint Louis 47139
Trowbridge Museum, Trowbridge 40729
Trowulan Archeological Museum, Mojokerto 22162
Troxell-Steckel House and Farm Museum, Egypt 43102
Troy Museum, Çanakkale 37651
Troy Museum and Historic Village, Troy 48068
Troyanski Manastir, Orešak 04748
Troyzky Cathedral, Serpuchov 33523
TRUCK Centre, Calgary 05180
True's Yard Fishing Heritage Centre, King's Lynn 39373
Trützschler's Milch- und Reklamemuseum, Hildburghausen 17754
Truppenmuseum, Straß in Steiermark 02704
Truva Müzesi, Çanakkale 37651
Try Museum, Dronninglund 08798
Tryart Gallery, Louisville 44978
Tryon Palace, New Bern 45667
Trysil Bygdemuseum, Trysil 30948
Tržiška Galerija, Tržič 34159
Tržiški Muzej, Tržič 34160
TS-Auto- & Viestintämuseo, Turku 10131
TS Car Museum, Turku 10131
Tsa Mo Ga Memorial Museum, Plains 46539
Tschechisches Zentrum-CzechPoint, Berlin 16108
Tsiolkovsky House-Museum, Kaluga 32875
Tsubouchi Memorial Theatre Museum, Waseda University, Tokyo 26954
Tsuchida Bakusen Art Museum, Sawata 26728
Tsuchida Bakusen Bijutsukan, Sawata 26728
Tsui Museum of Art, Hong Kong 07113
Tsukuba Bijutsukan, Tsukuba 26978
Tsukuba Museum of Art, Tsukuba 26978
Tsumeb Cultural Village, Tsumeb 28775
Tsumeb Museum, Tsumeb 28776
Tsurui Bijutsukan, Niigata 26600
Tsurui Museum of Art, Niigata 26600
Tsuwano Gendai Photo Gallery, Tsuwano 26981
Tsvetaeva House Museum, Moskva 33037
Tsvetaeva Museum-Appartement in Bolshevo, Korolev 32940
TTD Museum, Tirupati 22040
TU-Endie-Wei State Park, Point Pleasant 46576
Tuam Mill Museum, Tuam 22549
Tuapsinskij Kraevedčeskij Muzej im. N.G. Poletaeva, Tuapse 33622
Tuatapere Bushmans Museum, Tuatapere 30268
Tubac Center of the Arts, Tubac 48076
Tube Receiver Museum, Kouvola 09705
Tuberculosemuseum Beatrixoord, Appelscha 28930
Tubman African-American Museum, Macon 45048
Tubman Centre of African Culture, Cape Mount 27497
Tucherschloss mit Hirsvogelsaal, Nürnberg 19164
Tuchmacher-Museum Bramsche, Bramsche 16273
Tuchmuseum Lennep der Anna-Hardt-Stiftung, Remscheid 19567
Tuck Museum, Hampton 43892
Tucker House Museum, Saint George's 03889
Tucker Tower Nature Center Park Museum, Ardmore 41253
Tucson Children's Museum, Tucson 48092
Tucson Museum of Art and Historic Block, Tucson 48093
Tucumcari Historical Research Institute Museum, Tucumcari 48099
Tuddal Bygdetun, Tuddal 30949
Tudor House, Margate 39913
Tudor House, Weymouth 40844
Tudor House Museum, Southampton 40549
Tudor Place Museum, Washington 48398

Tüötten-Museum, Mettingen 18723
Türk Islam Eserleri Müzesi, İstanbul 37710
Türk Seramik Müzesi, Konya 37747
Türk Vakıf Hat Sanatları Müzesi, İstanbul 37711
Türk ve Islam Eserleri Müzesi, Edirne 37666
Türr István Múzeum, Baja 21309
Tüshaus-Mühle, Dorsten 16655
Tüzoltó Múzeum, Budapest 21387
Tufts University Art Gallery, Medford 45217
Tugnet Ice House, Spey Bay 40567
Tugu Nasional Museum, Jakarta 22139
Tukaj House-Museum, Košlauč 32941
Tukaj Memorial Museum Complex, Novyj Kyrlaj 33249
Tukuma Audēju Darbnīcas, Tukums 27461
Tukuma Muzejs, Tukums 27462
Tukums Museum, Tukums 27462
Tukums Weavers' Workshops, Tukums 27461
Tula Cremlin, Tula 33629
Tula Museum of Fine Arts, Tula 33632
Tula Museum of Regional Studies, Tula 33633
Tula Museum of Weapons, Tula 33631
Tula Samovar Museum, Tula 33628
Tulane University Art Collection, New Orleans 45739
Tulare County Museum, Visalia 48254
Tularosa Basin Historical Society Museum, Alamogordo 41078
Tullgarns Slott, Vagnhärad 36394
Tullie House - City Museum and Art Gallery, Carlisle 38490
Tullis-Toledano Manor, Biloxi 41697
Tullmuseum, Stockholm 36297
Tullner Museen im Minoritenkloster, Tulln 02747
Tullow Museum, Tullow 22550
Tulsi Sangrahalaya Ramvan, Satna 22014
Tul'skij Gosudarstvennyj Muzej Oružija, Tula 33631
Tulskij Muzej Izobrazitelnych Iskusstv, Tula 33632
Tulskij Oblastnoj Kraevedčeskij Muzej, Tula 33633
Tumanyans Museum, Erevan 00693
Tumbergs Skol- och Hembygdsmuseum, Vårgårda 36399
Tumut and District Historical Museum, Tumut 01555
Tun Abdul Razak Memorial, Kuala Lumpur 27654
Tunabygdens Gammelgård, Borlänge 35846
Tunbridge Wells Museum and Art Gallery, Tunbridge Wells 40732
Tune Bygdemuseum, Sarpsborg 30831
Tung Salaeng Luang, Phitsanulok 37529
Tunica-Biloxi Native American Museum, Marksville 45167
Tunku Abdul Rahman Memorial, Kuala Lumpur 27655
Tuomarinkylä Museum - Helsinki City Museum, Helsinki 09543
Tuomarinkylän Museo, Helsinki 09543
Tupelo Artist Guild Gallery, Tupelo 48110
Tupou College Museum, Nuku'alofa 37551
Tupperville School Museum, Bridgetown 05129
Turabo University Museum, Gurabo 32374
Turaida Museum Reserve, Sigulda 27451
Turaidas Muzejrezervāts, Sigulda 27451
Turčanska Galéria, Martin 34027
De Turfschuur, Kolhorn 29487
Turkansaaren Ulkomuseo, Oulu 09898
Turkansaari Open Air Museum, Oulu 09898
Turkeyenhof, Bredene 03241
Turkish Ceramics Museum, Konya 37747
Turkish Sports Museum, Şişli 37787
Turkmen Carpet Museum Gurbansoltan Eje, Aşgabat 37813
Turku Art Museum, Turku 10135
Turku Biological Museum, Turku 10132
Turku Cathedral Museum, Turku 10137
Turku Health Care Museum, Turku 10136
Turku Historical Museum, Turku Castle, Turku 10133
Turku Provincial Museum, Turku 10134
Turkuvaz Art Gallery, Ankara 37620
Turkuvaz Sanat Galerisi, Ankara 37620
Turlough Park House, Castlebar 22389
Turm 9 - Stadtmuseum Leonding, Leonding 02215
Turmmuseum, Breitenbrunn, Neusiedlersee 01749
Turmmuseum, Pillichsdorf 02415
Turmmuseum Sankt Magnus, Esens 16941
Turmmuseum Schloß Mengerskirchen, Mengerskirchen 18708
Turmmuseum Stadt Blankenberg, Hennef 17711
Turmuhren- und Heimatmuseum Bockenem, Bockenem 16204
Turmuhrenmuseum, Naunhof 18982
Turner Curling Museum, Weyburn 06784
Turner House Gallery, Penarth 40170
Turner House Museum, Hattiesburg 43958
The Turner Museum, Sarasota 47456
Turner Valley Gas Plant, Turner Valley 06650
Turnpike Gallery, Leigh, Lancashire 39471
Turquoise Museum, Albuquerque 41110
Turtle Mountain Chippewa Heritage Center, Belcourt 41586
Turtola Village Museum, Turtola 10139
Turtolan Kylämuseo, Turtola 10139
Turton Tower, Turton Bottoms 40736
Turun Biologinen Museo, Turku 10132
Turun Kaupungin Historiallinen Museo, Turun Linna, Turku 10133
Turun Maakuntamuseo, Turku 10134
Turun Taidemuseo, Turku 10135
Turun Terveydenhuoltomuseo, Turku 10136
Turun Tuomiokirkkomuseo, Turku 10137
Tuskegee Institute National Historic Site, Tuskegee Institute 48123
Tutankhamun Exhibition, Dorchester 38753
Tute-Natura, Bennekom 28977
Tuupalan Museo, Kuhmo 09714
Tuusniemen Kotiseutumuseo, Tuusniemi 10142
Tuvinskij Respublikanskij Kraevedčeskij Muzej im. Aldan Maadyr, Kyzyl 32979
TV Toys Dieren, Dieren 29152
Tvedestrand Museum, Tvedestrand 30953
Tveit Bygdemuseum, Tveit 30954
Tveitens Samlinger, Eggedal 30469
Tver Regional Art Gallery, Tver 33638
Tver State Museum, Tver 33639
Tverskaja Oblastnaja Kartinnaja Galereja, Tver 33638
Tverskoj Gosudarstvennyj Obedinennyj Muzej, Tver 33639
Tvorčeskij Centr i Vystavočnyj Zal Fëdor, Sankt-Peterburg 33486
T.W. Wood Gallery and Arts Center, Montpelier 45477
Tweed and Area Heritage Centre, Tweed 06651
Tweed Museum of Art, Duluth 43003
Tweed River Regional Art Gallery, Murwillumbah 01294
Tweeddale Museum, Peebles 40166
Tweewielermuseum Tankstop, Workum 30023
Twillingate Museum, Twillingate 06652
Twin Falls County Museum, Twin Falls 48125
Twin Falls Museum, Mullens 45553
Twinsburg Historical Society Museum, Twinsburg 48126
TWO 10 Gallery, London 39792
Two Hills and District Museum, Two Hills 06653
Two Turtle Iroquois Fine Art Gallery, Ohsweken 06044
Ty Gwyn and Ty Crwn, Barmouth 38086
Ty Mawr Wybrnant, Dolwyddelan 38739
Tybee Museum and Tybee Island Light Station, Tybee Island 48129
Tydal Museum, Tydal 30955
Tykarpsgrottan Kalkmuseum, Hässleholm 35936
Tyler Art Gallery, Oswego 46218
Tyler Museum of Art, Tyler 48132
Tylldalen Bygdetun, Tylldalen 30956
Tymperleys Clock Museum, Colchester 38614
Tyndalemuseum, Vilvoorde 03816
Tynset Bygdemuseum, Tynset 30957
Työväen Keskusmuseo, Tampere 10096
Työväenasuntomuseo, Helsinki 09544
Työväenasuntomuseo, Kuusankoski 09732
Typewritermuseum, Parcines 24792
Tyresö Slott, Tyresö 36340
Tyrnävän Kotiseutumuseo, Tyrnävä 10146
Tyrvää Regional Museum, Vammala 10176
Tyrvään Seudun Museo, Vammala 10176
Tyrwhitt-Drake Museum of Carriages, Maidstone 39879
Tytus Chałubiński Tatra Museum, Zakopane 32209
Tytyrin Kalkkikaivosmuseo, Lohja 09793
Tyutchev Museum-Estate Muranovo, Lugovskoe 32994
The U. Nahon Museum of Italian Jewish Art, Jerusalem 22668
U-Thong National Museum, Suphan Buri 37541
U Zlaté Koruny, Brno 08278
UBC Fish Museum, Vancouver 06691
Ube Municipal Coal Museum, Ube 26982
Učebno-chudožestvennyj Muzej im. I.V. Cvetaeva, Moskva 33180
Uckermärkische Heimatstuben, Fürstenwerder 17164
Uckermärkisches Volkskundemuseum Templin, Templin 20158
Udivitelnoe v Kamne - Muzej Mineralov, Rud, Samocvetov, Teberda 33598
Udmurtskij Respublikanskij Muzej Izobrazitelnych Iskusstv, Iževsk 32837
UDT-SEAL Museum, Fort Pierce 43442
Überseemuseum Bremen, Bremen 16336
Ueno Royal Museum, Tokyo 26951
Ürgüp Müzesi, Ürgüp 37799
Ürgüp Museum, Ürgüp 37799
Uesugi Shrine Treasure House, Yonezawa 27031
Ufa Picture Gallery, Ufa 33648
Uffenheimer Gollachgaumuseum, Uffenheim 20253
Ufimskaja Kartinnaja Galereja, Ufa 33648
Uganda Museum, Kampala 37829
Ugbrooke House, Chudleigh 38580
Uhrenindustriemuseum, Villingen-Schwenningen 20321
Uhrenmuseum, Bad Grund 15655
Uhrenmuseum, Bad Iburg 15671
Uhrenmuseum, Regensburg 19533
Uhrenmuseum, Wien 02996
Uhrenmuseum Beyer, Zürich 37415
Uhrenmuseum Glashütte, Glashütte, Sachsen 17295
Uhrenmuseum Matthäus, Obernzenn 19192
Uhrensammlung Kellenberger, Winterthur 37342
Uhrentechnische Lehrschau Hennig, Kurort Hartha 18271
Uilenspiegel Museum, Damme 03371
Uiryeong Museum, Uiryeong 27295
Uitamonkosken Myllymuseo, Multia 09840
Ukiyo-e and Pottery Museum, Osaka 26674
Ukraina Museum, Saskatoon 06406
Ukrainian-American Archives and Museum, Hamtramck 43899
Ukrainian-American Museum, Warren 48308
Ukrainian Canadian Archives and Museum of Alberta, Edmonton 05388
Ukrainian Catholic Women's League Museum, Edmonton 05389
Ukrainian Cultural Heritage Museum, Sandy Lake 06389
Ukrainian Cultural Heritage Village, Edmonton 05390
Ukrainian Museum, Cleveland 42484
Ukrainian Museum, New York 45884
Ukrainian Museum, Torrens Park 01544
Ukrainian Museum of Canada, Saskatoon 06407
Ukrainian Museum of Canada, Vancouver 06692
Ukrainian Museum of Canada - Alberta Branch, Edmonton 05391
Ukrainian Museum of Canada - Manitoba Branch, Winnipeg 06849
Ukrainian Museum of Canada - Ontario Branch, Toronto 06623
Ukrainian Museum of Folk and Decorative Art, Kyïv 37877
Ukrainian National Museum, Chicago 42368
Ukrainian Peoples Home of Ivan Franco, Angusville 04995
Ulaanbaatar City Museum, Ulaanbaatar 28687
Uleybury School Museum, One Tree Hill 01343
Uljanovskij Oblastnoj Chudožestvennyj Muzej, Uljanovsk 33668
Uljanovskij Oblastnoj Kraevedčeskij Muzej im. I.A. Gončarova, Uljanovsk 33669
Ullapool Museum, Ullapool 40747
Ullensaker Bygdemuseum, Jessheim 30582
Ullevål Sykehus Museum, Oslo 30768
Ulmer Museum, Ulm 20261
Ulricehamns Museum, Ulricehamn 36345
Ulrika museum, Ulrika 36346
Ulriksdal Palace, Solna 36223
Ulriksdals Slott, Solna 36223
Ulster-American Folk Park, Omagh 40131
Ulster County Historical Society Museum, Marbletown 45137
Ulster Folk and Transport Museum, Holywood 39258
Ulster History Park, Omagh 40132
Ulster Museum, Belfast 38160
Ulsyn Töw Muzei, Ulaanbaatar 28688
Ulug-Beg Memorial Museum, Samarkand 48852
Ulverstone Local History Museum, Ulverstone 01559
Umatilla County Historical Society Museum, Pendleton 46335
Umeå Energicentrum, Umeå 36348
Umekoji Steam Locomotive Museum, Kyoto 26459
Uměleckoprůmyslové Muzeum v Praze, Praha 08617
Umetnička Galerija Nadežda Petrović, Čačak 33828
Umetnička Zbirka Flögel, Beograd 33818
Umetnostna Galerija Maribor, Maribor 34129
Umezawa Memorial Gallery, Tokyo 26952
Umi-no Hakubutsukan, Toba 26823
U'Mista Cultural Centre, Alert Bay 04973
Umjetnička Galerija, Dubrovnik 07702
Umjetnička Galerija, Mostar 03918
Umjetnička Galerija, Skopje 27593
Umjetnička galerija Bosne i Hercegovine, Sarajevo 03924
Umjetnička Galerija Josip-Bepo Benkovic, Herceg-Novi 33840
Umjetnička Galerija Rizah Stetić, Brčko 03915
Umjetnička Galerija Velimir A. Leković, Bar 03911
Umjetnički Paviljon u Zagrebu, Zagreb 07840
Umlauf Sculpture Garden and Museum, Austin 41424
Umm Qais Archaeological Museum, Umm Qais 27069
Umoona Opal Mine and Museum, Coober Pedy 00941
Umstädter Museum Gruberhof, Groß-Umstadt 17422
Un Village se Raconte, Lourdios-Ichère 12699
Uncle Remus Museum, Eatonton 43072
Uncle Tom's Cabin Historic Site, Dresden 05339
Underground City Museum, Kaymaklı 37731
Underground Passages, Exeter 38959
Underground Prisoners Museum, Jerusalem 22669
Underhill Museum, Idaho Springs 44193
Ungarie Museum, Ungarie 01560
Ungarn-deutsche Heimatstuben, Langenau, Württemberg 18328
Ungarndeutsches Heimatmuseum Backnang, Backnang 15587
Unguri Manor, Raiskums 27399
Ungurmuiža, Raiskums 27399
Unhyang Art Museum, Bugil 27134
Uniacke Estate Museum, Mount Uniacke 05949
Unidad Museológica Municipal de La Banda, La Banda 00374
Union Art Gallery, Baton Rouge 41536
Union-Art Gallery, Milwaukee 45372
Union County Heritage Museum, New Albany 45660
Union County Historical Complex, Creston 42698
Union County Historical Foundation Museum, Union 48147
Union County Historical Society Museum, Blairsville 41731
Union County Historical Society Museum, Marysville 45195
Union County Museum, Lewisburg 44724
Union County Museum, Union 48145
Union County Public Library Union Room, Monroe 45444
Union Gallery, Adelaide 00715
Union Mills Homestead and Grist Mill, Westminster 48564
UNISA Art Gallery, Pretoria 34360
Unité Musée Numismatique, Port-au-Prince 21296
United Counties Museum, Cornwall 05278
United Empire Loyalist Museum, Bloomfield 05086
United States Air Force Academy Museum, El Paso 43110
United States Air Force Museum, Wright-Patterson Air Force Base 48766
United States Army Air Defense Artillery Museum, Fort Bliss 43370
United States Army Aviation Museum, Fort Rucker 43450
United States Army Center of Military History, Fort McNair 43424
United States Army Chaplain Museum, Fort Jackson 43402
United States Army Communications-Electronics Museum, Fort Monmouth 43430
United States Army Engineer Museum, Fort Leonard Wood 43420
United States Army Finance Corps Museum, Fort Jackson 43403
United States Army Heritage and Education Center, Carlisle 42106
United States Army Medical Department Museum, Fort Sam Houston 43452
United States Army Museum of Hawaii, Fort DeRussy 43386
United States Army Ordnance Museum, Aberdeen Proving Ground 41047
The United States Army Quartermaster Museum, Fort Lee 43418
United States Army Signal Corps and Fort Gordon Museum, Fort Gordon 43396
United States Army Transportation Museum, Fort Eustis 43393
United States Army Women's Museum, Fort Lee 43419
United States Brig Niagara, Homeport Erie Maritime Museum, Erie 43203
United States Capitol Visitor Center, Washington 48399
United States Cavalry Museum, Fort Riley 43449
United States Coast Guard Museum, New London 45712
United States Department of the Interior Museum, Washington 48400
United States Federation of Friends of Museums, Baltimore 49535
United States Grant Ancestral Homestead, Dungannon 38813
United States Grant's Home, Galena 43595
United States Hockey Hall of Fame, Eveleth 43248
United States Holocaust Memorial Museum, Washington 48401
United States-International Council on Monuments and Sites, Washington 49536
United States Marine Corps Air-Ground Museum, Quantico 46753
United States Marine Corps Museum, Washington 48402
United States Mint-Philadelphia, Philadelphia 46459
United States National Ski Hall of Fame and Museum, Ishpeming 44263
United States Naval Academy Museum, Annapolis 41230
United States Navy Art Gallery, Washington 48403
United States Navy Supply Corps Museum, Athens 41323
United States Senate Commission on Art Collection, Washington 48404
United States Space and Rocket Center, Huntsville 44175
Unites States National Committee of the ICOM, Washington 49537
Unity and District Heritage Museum, Unity 06655
Unity House, Detroit 42916
Univers Maurice Rocket Richard, Montréal 05931
Universeum, Göteborg 35923
Universität der Künste Berlin, Berlin 16109
Universitäts- und Landesbibliothek Bonn, Bonn 16249
Universitäts- und Landesbibliothek Münster, Münster 18948
Universitätsbibliothek, München 18921
Universitätsbibliothek der Humboldt-Universität zu Berlin, Berlin 16110
Universitätsbibliothek der Universität Leipzig, Leipzig 18423
Universitätsbibliothek Salzburg, Salzburg 02553
Universitätsbibliothek Wien, Wien 02997
Universitätssammlung antiker und nachantiker Münzen und Medaillen, Tübingen 20230
Universitätssammlungen Kunst Technik, Dresden 16714
Université du Vin, Suze-la-Rousse 14848
Universiteitsbibliotheek Gent, Gent 03454
Universiteitsmuseum, Groningen 29316
Universiteitsmuseum De Agnietenkapel, Amsterdam 28910
Universiteitsmuseum Utrecht, Utrecht 29911
Universitetets Oldsaksamling, Oslo 30769
University Archaeology Museum, Birmingham 38231
University Art Galleries, Murray 45572
University Art Galleries, Vermillion 48215
University Art Gallery, Bridgeport 41892
University Art Gallery, Carson 42116
University Art Gallery, Chico 42374
University Art Gallery, Irvine 44258
University Art Gallery, Jackson 44288
University Art Gallery, La Jolla 44550
University Art Gallery, Mount Pleasant 45537
University Art Gallery, North Dartmouth 45991
University Art Gallery, Pittsburgh 46529
University Art Gallery, Potchefstroom 34338
University Art Gallery, Rohnert Park 46989
University Art Gallery, San Diego 47299
University Art Gallery, Stony Brook 47832

University Art Gallery, Turlock 48111
University Art Museum, Albany 41089
University Art Museum, Albuquerque 41111
University Art Museum, Binghamton 41701
University Art Museum, Lafayette 44572
University Art Museum, Santa Barbara 47406
The University Art Museum, Tokyo National University of Fine Arts and Music, Tokyo 26853
University at Buffalo Art Galleries, Buffalo 41990
University College Dublin Classical Museum, Dublin 22455
University College of Cape Breton Art Gallery, Sydney 06529
University College Zoological Museum, Cork 22405
University Fine Art Collection, Hobart 01107
University Galleries, Akron 41076
University Galleries, Clarion 42427
University Galleries, Edinburg 43089
University Gallery, Alexandria 41118
University Gallery, Amherst 41182
University Gallery, Boca Raton 41769
University Gallery, Commerce 42595
University Gallery, Gainesville 43587
University Gallery, Hays 43972
University Gallery, Newark 45888
The University Gallery, Newcastle-upon-Tyne 40043
University Gallery, Oxford 46238
University Gallery Leeds, Leeds 39456
The University Gallery of the University of the South, Sewanee 47571
University Historical Museum, Musuan 31404
University Medical Museum, Charleston 42228
University Museum, Carbondale 42102
University Museum, Dundee 38805
The University Museum, Edwardsville 43098
The University Museum, Fayetteville 43308
The University Museum, Indiana 44213
University Museum, Martin 45189
University Museum, Port Harcourt 30362
The University Museum, Tokyo 26953
University Museum, Vallabhvidyanagar 22054
University Museum and Art Gallery, Hong Kong 07114
University Museum of Anthropology, Quezon City 31437
University Museum of Archaeology and Anthropology, Cambridge 38463
University Museum of Science and Culture, Aligarh 21687
University Museum of Zoology, Cambridge 38464
University Museum - Sasol Art Museum, Stellenbosch 34385
University Museums, Oxford 46239
University Museums Group, Liverpool 49454
University of Alaska Museum, Fairbanks 43258
University of Alberta Museums, Edmonton 05392
University of Arizona Mineral Museum, Tucson 48094
University of Arizona Museum of Art, Tucson 48095
University of Arizona Union Galleries, Tucson 48096
University of Arkansas at Little Rock Art Galleries, Little Rock 44826
University of Brighton Gallery, Brighton 38346
University of Bristol Theatre Collection, Bristol 38361
University of Calgary Museum of Zoology, Calgary 05181
University of California Berkeley Art Museum, Berkeley 41649
University of Colorado Museum, Boulder 41837
University of Dundee Exhibitions Department, Dundee 38806
University of Essex Exhibition Gallery, Colchester 38615
University of Fort Hare Museum, Alice 34170
University of Hawaii Art Gallery, Honolulu 44090
University of Hawaii at Manoa Art Gallery, Honolulu 44091
University of Helsinki Agricultural Museum, Helsinki 09494
University of Helsinki Museum of Medical History, Helsinki 09493
University of Helsinki, The K.E. Kivirikko Collection of Birds and Mammals, Helsinki 09500
University of Iowa Museum of Art, Iowa City 44248
University of Iowa Museum of Natural History, Iowa City 44249
University of Kansas Ryther Printing Museum, Lawrence 44687
University of Kentucky Art Museum, Lexington 44746
University of Lethbridge Art Gallery, Lethbridge 05749
University of Liverpool Art Gallery, Liverpool 39530
University of Mandalay Collections, Mandalay 28735
University of Michigan Museum of Art, Ann Arbor 41222
University of Nebraska Art Gallery at Omaha, Omaha 46153
University of Nebraska State Museum, Lincoln 44793
University of New Brunswick Art Centre, Fredericton 05467
University of North Dakota Zoology Museum, Grand Forks 43744
University of North Texas Art Gallery, Denton 42877
University of Northern Iowa Museum Museums & Collections, Cedar Falls 42151
University of Northern Philippines Museum, Vigan 31466
University of Nueva Caceres Museum, Naga 31407
University of Oregon Museum of Art, Eugene 43228
University of Oulu, Zoological Museum, Oulu 09893
University of Pennsylvania Museum of Archaeology and Anthropology, Philadelphia 46460
University of Pretoria Art Collection, Pretoria 34361
University of Queensland Art Museum, Brisbane 00843
University of Rhode Island Fine Arts Center Galleries, Kingston 44498
University of Richmond Museums, Richmond 46887
University of Rochester Memorial Art Gallery, Rochester 46948
University of San Carlos Anthropology Museum, Cebu 31318
University of San Carlos Biological Museum, Cebu 31319
University of Santo Tomas Museum of Arts and Sciences, Manila 31398
University of South Australia Art Museum, Adelaide 00716
University of South Carolina at Spartanburg Art Gallery, Spartanburg 47720
University of South Carolina Beaufort Art Gallery, Beaufort 41560
University of Southern Philippines Museum, Cebu 31320
University of Southern Queensland Art Collection, Toowoomba 01543
University of Stellenbosch Art Gallery, Stellenbosch 34386
University of Swaziland Library Museums Collection, Kwaluseni 35779
University of Sydney Art Collection, Sydney 01509
University of Toronto Art Centre, Toronto 06624
University of Virginia Art Museum, Charlottesville 42253
University of Waterloo Art Gallery, Waterloo 06757
University of West Florida Art Gallery, Pensacola 46346
University of Wisconsin Zoological Museum, Madison 45072
University of Wyoming Anthropology Museum, Laramie 44649
University of Wyoming Art Museum, Laramie 44650
University of Zambia Library Museums Collection, Lusaka 49022
University Place Art Center, Lincoln 44794
Universum, Museo de las Ciencias de la UNAM, México 28213
Universum Science Center Bremen, Bremen 16337
UNLV Barrick Museum, Las Vegas 44674
Uns lütt Schiffsmuseum, Cuxhaven 16520
Unser kleines Museum, Gries im Pinzgau 01941
UNSW Art Collection, Sydney 01510
Untamalan Kotiseutumuseo, Laitila 09756
Unterfränkisches Grenzmuseum, Bad Königshofen 15677
Unterfränkisches Verkehrsmuseum, Gemünden am Main 17233
Untersbergmuseum Fürstenbrunn, Grödig 01945
Unterwarter Heimathaus, Unterwart 02755
Untzi Museoa - Museo Naval, Donostia-San Sebastián 34780
Uodu Buried Forest Museum, Uodo 26990
Uodu History and Folklore Museum, Uodo 26991
Upernavik Museum, Upernavik 21242
Upham Mansion, Marshfield 45187
UPIDIV Galerija, Novi Sad 33874
Upminster Mill, Upminster 40750
Upminster Tithe Barn Museum, Upminster 40751
Uppark Exhibition, Petersfield 40195
Upper Canada Village, Morrisburg 05944
Upper East Region Museum, Bolgatanga 20790
Upper Musselshell Historical Society Museum, Harlowtown 43915
Upper Paxton Township Museum, Millersburg 45347
Upper Room Chapel Museum, Nashville 45628
Upper Snake River Valley Historical Museum, Rexburg 46847
Upper Waitaki Pioneer Museum and Art Gallery, Kurow 30195
Upper Wharfdale Folk Museum, Grassington 39115
Upper Yarra Valley Museum, Yarra Junction 01627
Upperclass Home Museum, Kolkanlahti 09686
Upperlands Eco-Museum, Derry 38723
Uppertown Firefighters Museum, Astoria 41312
Upplandsmuseet, Uppsala 36361
Uppsala Konstmuseum, Uppsala 36362
Uppsala Medicinhistoriska Museum, Uppsala 36363
Uppsala Universitet Myntkabinett, Uppsala 36364
Uppsala University Art Collection, Uppsala 36355
Uppsala University Museum, Uppsala 36358
Upstairs Gallery, Winnipeg 06850
Upton House, Banbury 38076
Ur-Donautal-Museum, Wellheim 20506
Ur- und Frühgeschichtliche Ausstellung, Sömmerda 19976
Ur- und frühgeschichtliche Eisenindustrie im Bezirk Oberpullendorf - Schauraum, Oberpullendorf 02375
Ur- und Frühgeschichtliche Sammlung, Erlangen 16925
Ur-und frühgeschichtliche Sammlungen, Graz 01936
Ur-Wolpertinger-Museum, Kreuth 18237
Ura-Tube Historical and Regional Museum, Ura-Tjube 37451
Urahoro-cho Kyodo Hakubutsukan, Urahoro 26992
Urahoro Municipal Museum, Urahoro 26992
Urajärven Kartanomuseo, Urajärvi 10147
Urajärvi Manor, Urajärvi 10147
Ural Geological Museum V.V. Vakhrushev, Ekaterinburg 32783
Uralsk Regional and Historical Museum, Uralsk 27098
Uralskij Geologičeskij Muzej V.V. Vachrušev, Ekaterinburg 32783
Uralskij Istoriko-Kraevedčeskij Muzej, Uralsk 27098
Urban Institute for Contemporary Arts, Grand Rapids 43760
Urban Public Transport Museum, Budapest 21389
Urbanarts, Boston 41830
Ure Museum of Greek Archaeology, Reading 40299
Urfa Müzesi, Urfa 37800
Urfa Museum, Urfa 37800
Urgeschichtliche Sammlung, Engerwitzdorf 01817
Urgeschichtliches Freilichtmuseum Keltendorf Mitterkirchen, Mitterkirchen 02304
Urgeschichtliches Museum und Galerie Vierzigtausend Jahre Kunst, Blaubeuren 16183
Urgeschichtssammlung und Heimtmuseum, Jedenspeigen 02085
Urho Kekkonen Museo Tamminiemi, Helsinki 09545
Uri and Rami Nechushtan, Kibbutz Ashdot Yaakov 22678
Urios College Museum, Butuan 31298
Urjala Museum, Urjala 10148
Urjalan Museo, Urjala 10148
Urmensch-Museum, Steinheim an der Murr 20051
Uroomieh Museum, Uroomieh 22333
Urquhart Castle, Drumnadrochit 38779
Urras Eachdraibh Sgire Bhearnaraidh, Bernera 38171
Urskog-Hølandsbanen, Sørumsand 30868
Ursula Blickle Stiftung, Kraichtal 18218
Ursuline Hallway Gallery, San Antonio 47263
Urumchi City Museum, Urumchi 07274
Urwelt-Museum Hauff, Holzmaden 17829
Urwelt-Museum Oberfranken, Bayreuth 15860
Urweltmuseum, Pirna 19408
Urweltmuseum Aalen, Aalen 15386
Urzeitmuseum Nußdorf ob der Traisen, Traismauer 02735
US Army Military Police Corps Museum, Fort Leonard Wood 43421
US Patent and Trademark Office - Museum, Arlington 41267
Usadba Izmajlovo, Moskva 33181
Uşak Archeological Museum, Uşakş 37801
Uşak Arkeoloji Müzesi, Uşakş 37801
Usher Gallery, Lincoln 39503
Usine-Musée de l'Espadrille, Saint-Laurent-de-Cerdans 14306
Usk Rural Life Museum, Usk 40753
USM Art Gallery, Gorham 43731
Usman Jusupov Memorial Museum, Jalta 37856
Usman Jusupov Memorial Museum, Jangi-Jul 48838
Uspenskij Sobor, Moskva 33182
USS Alabama Battleship Memorial Park, Mobile 45425
USS Arizona Memorial, Honolulu 44092
USS Bowfin Submarine Museum, Honolulu 44093
USS Constitution Museum, Boston 41831
USS Lexington Museum on the Bay, Corpus Christi 42647
USS Radford National Naval Museum, Newcomerstown 45914
Ussishkin House, Kibbutz Dan 22681
Ust-Ilimsk Picture Gallery, Ust'-Ilimsk 33671
Ust'-Ilimskaja Kartinnaja Galereja, Ust'-Ilimsk 33671
Ústecká Bus Historické Muzeum, Chlumec u Ústi nad Labem 08312
Utah Field House of Natural History State Park, Vernal 48217
Utah Museum of Fine Arts, Salt Lake City 47234
Utah Museum of Natural History, Salt Lake City 47235
Utah Museums Association, Salt Lake City 49538
Utah State Historical Society Museum, Salt Lake City 47236
Ute Indian Museum, Montrose 45483
Utica Museum, Hobson 44045
Utstein Kloster, Mosterøy 30694
Utsukushigahara Kogen Bijutsukan, Takeshi 26814
Utsukushigahara Open-Air Museum, Takeshi 26814
Uttar Pradesh State Museum, Lucknow 21932
Uttoxeter Heritage Centre, Uttoxeter 40754
Utvandrarnas Hus, Växjö 36392
Uudenkaupungin Kultuurihistoriallinen Museo, Uusikaupunki 10155
Uummannap Katersugaasivia, Uummannaq 21243
Uummannaq Museum, Uummannaq 21243
Uusikaupunki Cultural History Museum, Uusikaupunki 10155
Uus't Olde Maat, Giethoorn 29283
UVAN Historical Museum, Winnipeg 06851
Uwajima Date Museum, Uwajima 26995
Uwajima-shiritsu Date Hakubutsukan, Uwajima 26995
Uxbridge-Scott Museum, Uxbridge 06657
Uzbekistan Art Academy, Taškent 48862
Uzbekistan Art Academy, Taškent 48863
Uzbekistan Public Health Museum, Taškent 48858
V.A. Rusanov House-Museum of the Orël Regional Museum, Orël 33262
Vaajakosken Työläiskotimuseo, Jyväskylä 09606
Vaal Teknorama Cultural Museum, Vereeniging 34396
Vaasa Car- and Motormuseum, Vaasa 10163
Vaasan Auto- ja Moottorimuseo, Vaasa 10163
Vaasan Merimuseo, Vaasa 10164
Vacaville Museum, Vacaville 48173
Vachel Lindsay Home, Springfield 47743
Vadim Kozin Memorial Museum, Magadan 33000
Vadim Sidur State Museum, Moskva 33064
Vadsbo Museum, Mariestad 36091
Vadsø Museum - Ruija Kvenmuseum, Vadsø 30966
Vadstena Slott, Vadstena 36369
Vadstena Stadsmuseum, Vadstena 36370
Vääksyn Vesimylly- ja piensähkölaitosmuseo, Vääksy 10166
Vähänkyrön Museo, Vähäkyrö 10167
Väike-Männiku Talumuuseum, Kõpu 09334
Väinontalo - Järviseudun Museo, Vasikka-Aho 10189
Vämöparken, Karlskrona 36001
Vänermuseet, Lidköping 36035
Vänersborgs Museum, Vänersborg 36374
Værløse Museum, Værløse 09098
Värmlands Museum, Karlstad 36003
Värtsilän Myllymuseo, Värtsilä 10168
Väsby Kungsgård, Sala 36174
Västerås Flygande Museum, Västerås 36379
Västerås Flygmuseum, Västerås 36380
Västerås Konstmuseum, Västerås 36381
Västerås Skolmuseum, Västerås 36382
Västerbottens Museum, Umeå 36349
Västergötlands Museum, Skara 36194
Västernorrland Textile Archive, Sollefteå 36217
Västerviks Museum, Västervik 36387
Västmanlands Läns Museum, Västerås 36383
Västra Göinge Hembygdsmuseum, Hässleholm 35937
Vättehult - Pälle Nävers Diktarstuga, Vetlanda 36404
Vagnmuseet, Malmö 36081
Vagnshistoriska Museet, Fristad 35895
Vagonářské Muzeum, Studénka 08667
Vaijnorský L'udový Dom - Etnografická Expozícia, Bratislava 33980
Vaile Mansion - Dewitt Museum, Independence 44208
Vajda Lajos Emlékmúzeum, Szentendre 21578
Vakıf Halı Müzesi, İstanbul 37712
Vakıf İnşaat ve Sanat Eserleri Müzesi, İstanbul 37713
Vakıf Kilim ve Düz Dokuma Yaygılar Müzesi, İstanbul 37714
Vakoilumuseo, Tampere 10097
Val Gardena Heritage Museum, Ortisei 24698
Valaam Island Scientific Museum Preserve of Religion, Archeology and Nature, Sortavala 33548
Valaamskij Naučno-issledovatelskij Cerkovno-archeologičeskij i Prirodnyj Muzej-zapovednik, Sortavala 33548
Valašské Muzeum v Přírodě, Rožnov pod Radhoštěm 08642
Vâlcea District Museum, Râmnicu Vâlcea 32578
Valdajskij Kraevedčeskij Muzej, Valdaj 33673
Valdemārpils Forest Museum, Valdemārpils 27463
Valdemārpils Mežu Muzejs, Valdemārpils 27463
The Valdez Museum, Valdez 48179
Valdivia Museo, Valdivia 09230
Valdosta State University Fine Arts Gallery, Valdosta 48181
Valdres Folkemusum, Fagernes 30484
Vale and Downland Museum, Wantage 40782
Valemount and Area Museum, Valemount 06662
Valence House Museum and Art Gallery, Dagenham 38690
Valencian Toys Museum, Ibi 34911
Valens Log Cabin, Ancaster 04993
Valentia Island Heritage Centre, Knightstown 22501
Valentin-Karlstadt Musäum, München 18922
Valentin Serov Memorial Museum of Art in Domotkanovo, Krasnaja Nov' 32945
Valentine Richmond History Center, Richmond 46888
Valentown Museum, Victor 48232
Våler Torvdriftsmuseum, Våler i Solør 30968
Valga Muuseum, Valga 09392
Valhalla Museum, Tresco 40726
The Valiant Soldier, Buckfastleigh 38382
Valka Museum of Local Studies, Valka 27464
Valkas Novadpētniecības Muzejs, Valka 27464
Vallachian Open-Air Museum, Rožnov pod Radhoštěm 08642
Vallance Cottage, Alexandra 30094
Vallby Friluftsmuseum, Västerås 36384
Valle de los Caídos, Valle de Cuelgamuros 35634
Vallejo Naval and Historical Museum, Vallejo 48185
Valley Art Center, Clarkston 42434
Valley Community Historical Society Museum, Valley 48186
Valley County Pioneer Museum, Glasgow 43677
Valley Forge National Historical Park, Valley Forge 48189
Valley Museum, McBride 05793
Valmiera Museum of Local Studies, Valmiera 27466
Valmieras Novadpētniecības Muzejs, Valmiera 27466
Valsts Elektrotehniskās Fabrikas Vēstures Muzejs, Rīga 27442
Valsts Mākslas Muzejs Izstazu Zale Arsenāls, Rīga 27443
Valsts Mākslas Muzeju, Rīga 27444
Valtakunnallinen Työväentalomuseo, Riihimäki 09997
Vampulan Museo, Vampula 10177
Het Van Abbemuseum, Bonheiden 03224
Van Abbemuseum, Eindhoven 29221
Van Buren County Historical Society Museum, Keosauqua 44453
Van Cortlandt House Museum, Bronx 41926
Van Culture Center, Van 37803
Van de Poll-Stichting, Zeist 30052
Van-der-Werf's Wedgwoodmuseum, Zuidwolde, Groningen 30073
Van Devlet Güzel Sanatlar Galerisi, Van 37802
Van Gogh Documentatiecentrum, Nuenen 29648
Van Gogh Museum, Amsterdam 28911
Van Gybland-Oosterhoff Collection, Pretoria 34362
Van Kültür Merkezi, Van 37803
Van Meter State Park, Miami 45295

Van Müzesi, Van 37804
Van Museum, Van 37804
Van Nostrand-Starkins House, Roslyn 47010
Van Riper-Hopper House, Wayne 48479
Van State Gallery, Van 37802
Van 't Lindenhoutmuseum, Nijmegen 29637
Van Tilburg Collection, Pretoria 34363
Van Wyck Homestead Museum, Fishkill 43325
Vanaja Local History Museum, Hämeenlinna 09455
Vanajan Kotiseutumuseo, Hämeenlinna 09455
Vance Kirkland Museum, Denver 42902
Vancouver Art Gallery, Vancouver 06693
Vancouver Arts Centre, Albany 00725
Vancouver Holocaust Education Centre, Vancouver 06694
Vancouver Maritime Museum, Vancouver 06695
Vancouver Museum, Vancouver 06696
Vancouver Naval Museum, West Vancouver 06774
Vancouver Police Centennial Museum, Vancouver 06697
Vandalia State House, Vandalia 48203
Vanderbilt Mansion National Museum, Hyde Park 44189
Vanderbilt University Fine Arts Gallery, Nashville 45629
Vanderhoof Community Museum, Vanderhoof 06699
Vang Church, Karpacz 31642
Vanguard Centennial Museum, Vanguard 06700
Vanha-Rantalan Talomuseo, Pertunmaa 09923
Vanhalinna Museum, Vanhalinna 10178
Vankilamuseo, Hämeenlinna 09456
Vann House, Chatsworth 42257
Vantaa City Museum, Vantaa 10183
Vantaa City Museum - Visual Arts, Vantaa 10184
Vantaan Kaupunginmuseo, Vantaa 10183
Vantaan Kaupunginmuseo - Kuvataideasiat, Vantaa 10184
Vanuatu Cultural Centre and National Museum, Port Vila 48866
Vaos Collection, Athinai 20905
Vapentekniska Museet, Eskilstuna 35873
Varala Museum of Gymnastics, Tampere 10098
Varalan Liikuntamuseo, Tampere 10098
Varanger Museum Sør, Kirkenes 30595
Varaždin Municipal Museum, Varaždin 07797
Varaždinske Toplice Muzej, Varaždinske Toplice 07798
Varde Artillerimuseum, Varde 09102
Varde Museum, Varde 09101
Varden Redningsmuseum, Narbø 30703
Vardømuseene, Vardø 30974
Varendra Research Museum, Rajshahi 03099
Varga Imre Kiallitas, Budapest 21388
Vargas Museum and Art Gallery, Mandaluyong 31366
Varistaipaleen Kanavamuseo, Karvion Kanava 09633
Varjjat Sámi Musea, Varangerbotn 30973
Varkauden Museo, Varkaus 10186
Varkauden Taidemuseo, Varkaus 10187
Varkaus Art Museum, Varkaus 10187
Varkaus Museum, Varkaus 10186
Vármúzeum, Dunaföldvár 21403
Vármúzeum, Esztergom 21414
Vármúzeum, Kisvárda 21463
Vármúzeum, Siklós 21529
Vármúzeum, Simontornya 21530
Vármúzeum, Sümeg 21542
Vármúzeum, Veszprém 21609
Varner-Hogg Plantation, West Columbia 48520
Varnum Memorial Armory and Military Museum, East Greenwich 43042
Városi Képtár, Orosháza 21495
Városi Képtár, Székesfehérvár 21562
Városi Múzeum, Kőszeg 21466
Városi Tömegközlekedési Múzeum, Budapest 21389
Várostörténeti Kiállítás, Sopron 21538
Várostörténeti Múzeum, Pécs 21516
Várostörténeti Múzeum, Székesfehérvár 21563
Varpaisjärven Kotiseutumuseo, Varpaisjärvi 10188
Varpunen House Museum, Anjalankoski 09416
Várrom és Népi Müemlék, Kisnána 21461
Varteig Bygdemuseum, Varteig 30977
Varusschlacht im Osnabrücker Land, Bramsche 16274
Vasa Lutheran Church Museum, Vasa 48205
Vasa Museum, Stockholm 36298
Vasalopps Museet Mora, Mora 36102
Vasalopps Museet Sälen, Transtrand 36331
Vasamuseet, Stockholm 36298
Vasarely Múzeum, Budapest 21390
Vasarely Múzeum, Pécs 21517
Vaseaux Lake Galleries, Oliver 06052
Vashon Maury Island Heritage Museum, Vashon 48206
Vasi Múzeumfalu, Szombathely 21590
Vasil Kolarov Memorial House, Šumen 04874
Vasil Levski Memorial House, Loveč 04729
Vasil Levski Museum, Karlovo 04691
Vasily Eroshenko Memorial Museum of Literature, Staryj Oskol 33558
Vasnetsov Apartment Museum, Moskva 33080
Vassdragsmuseet Labro, Skollenborg 30852
Vassiliou Collection, Thessaloniki 21195
Vat Sisaket, Vientiane 27323
Vat Xiengkhouane, Vientiane 27324
Vaucluse House, Vaucluse 01565
Vaxholm Fortress Museum, Vaxholm 36401
Vaxholms Fästnings Museum, Vaxholm 36401
Vay Adám Múzeum, Vaja 21603
Veen Park, Barger Compascuum 28963
Het Veenkoloniaal Museum, Veendam 29926
Veenmuseum het Vriezenveense Veld, Vriezenveen 29968
Vefsn Museum, Mosjøen 30692
Vega Bygdemuseum, Vega 30981
Vegårshei Bygdetun, Vegårshei 30982
Vegmuseet - Rogaland, Stavanger 30891
Vegreville Regional Museum, Vegreville 06703
Vehmaan Kivityömuseo ja Huolilan Kotiseutumuseo, Vehmaa 10190
Vejen Kunstmuseum, Vejen 09103
Vejle Kunstmuseum, Vejle 09104
Vejle Museum, Vejle 09105
Vekkilän Kotiseutumuseo, Tammela 10072
Vektermuseet i Valbergtårnet, Stavanger 30892
Velenje Museum, Velenje 34162
Veletržní Palác, Praha 08618
Velfjord Bygdemuseum, Hommelstø 30558
Velikolukskij Kraevedčeskij Muzej, Velikie Luki 33676
Velikosoročinskij literaturno-memorialnyj muzej im N.V. Gogolja, Velikie Soročintsy 37910
Velikoustjugskij Gosudarstvennyj Istoriko-Architekturnyj i Chudožestvennyj Muzej-Zapovednik, Velikij Ustjug 33681
Velimir Chlebnikov House-Museum, Astrachan 32662
Veliš Lekovič Memorial Gallery, Bar 33789
Velká Synagoga, Plzeň 08545
Veluws Klederdrachtenmuseum, Epe 29247
Veluws Museum Nairac, Barneveld 28965
Veluws Museum van Oudheden - Stadsmuseum, Harderwijk 29342
Venango Museum of Art, Science and Industry, Oil City 46106
Venclauskiu House, Šiauliai 27532
Vendsyssel Historiske Museum, Hjørring 08877
Vendsyssel Kunstmuseum, Hjørring 08878
Venetsanos Museum of Modern Art, Piraeus 21126
Vennel Gallery, Irvine 39313
Vennesla Bygdemuseum, Vennesla 30986
Vent Haven Museum, Fort Mitchell 43429
Ventnor Heritage Museum, Ventnor 40756
Ventspils Jūras Zvejniecības Brīvdabas Muzejs, Ventspils 27471
Ventspils Museum, Ventspils 27472
Ventspils Muzejs, Ventspils 27472
Ventspils Open-Air Museum of Maritime Fishing, Ventspils 27471
Ventura College Art Galleries, Ventura 48210
Ventura County Maritime Museum, Oxnard 46245
Ventura County Museum of History and Art, Ventura 48211
Vepssk Ethnographic Museum of Sheltozero, Šeltozero 33515
Verband der Museen der Schweiz, Zürich 49388
Verband Österreichischer Privatmuseen, Bad Wimsbach-Neydharting 49060
Verband Rheinischer Museen, Solingen 49215
De Verbeelding Kunst Landschap Natuur, Zeewolde 30050
Das Verborgene Museum, Berlin 16111
Verdant Works, Dundee 38807
The Verdier House, Beaufort 41561
Verdmont Historic House Museum, Smith's Parish 03890
Verein Kunstsammlung Unterseen, Unterseen 37265
Vereinigung der Mund- und Fussmalenden Künstler in aller Welt e.V., Schaan 27511
Vereinigung Westfälischer Museen, Münster 49216
Vereniging van Rijksgesubsidieerde Musea, Amsterdam 49307
Vereschagin Museum, Čerepovec 32733
Verfmolen de Kat, Zaandam 30040
Vērgale Parish Museum, Vērgale 27473
Vērgales Pagasta Muzejs, Vērgale 27473
Verger's Museum, Loppi 09797
Veria Byzantine Museum, Veria 21209
Verkehrshaus der Schweiz, Luzern 36918
Verkehrsmuseum, Frankfurt am Main 17080
Verkehrsmuseum Dresden, Dresden 16715
Verkehrsmuseum Karlsruhe, Karlsruhe 18006
Verkehrsmuseum Sankt Veit an der Glan, Sankt Veit an der Glan 02615
Verla Mill Museum, Verla 10191
Verlagsmuseum der Unternehmensgruppe Ravensburger, Ravensburg 19509
Verlan Tehdasmuseo, Verla 10191
Vermessungskundliche Sammlung, Linz 02242
Vermilion County Museum, Danville 42777
Vermont Folklife Center, Middlebury 45309
Vermont Historical Society Museum, Montpelier 45478
Vermont Marble Museum, Proctor 46709
Vermont Museum and Gallery Alliance, Woodstock 49539
Vermont State Craft Center at Frog Hollow, Middlebury 45310
The Vermont State House, Montpelier 45479
Vernadsky State Geological Museum, Moskva 33053
Vernisaž Art Podvalčik, Chabarovsk 32740
Vernon County Museum, Viroqua 48253
Vernon Historical Museum and Pond Road Chapel, Vernon 48219
Vernon Public Art Gallery, Vernon, British Columbia 06708
Vernonia Historical Museum, Vernonia 48221
Verpleeghuis Cornelia, Zierikzee 30063
Verpleegkundig Historisch Bezit, Amersfoort 28827
Verran Museum, Malm 30661
Verrerie d'Art, Claret 11312
Verrerie de Coulonbrines, Ferrières-les-Verreries 11722
Vértes Múzeum, Csákvár 21396
Vértesszőllősi Bemutatóhely, Vértesszőllős 21606
Vértesszőllősi Open-air Exhibition, Vértesszőllős 21606
Verulamium Museum, Saint Albans 40379
Verwood Community Museum, Verwood 06711
Very Special Arts Gallery, Albuquerque 41112
Verzameling Steenbakker Ten Bokkel Huinink, Neede 29609
Verzamelmuseum, Veendam 29927
Verzetsmuseum Amsterdam, Amsterdam 28912
Verzetsmuseum Friesland, Leeuwarden 29516
Verzetz Museum Zuid-Holland, Gouda 29299
Vest-Agder Fylkesmuseum, Kristiansand 30616
Vest-Lindsey House, Frankfort 43515
Vest-Telemark Museum, Dalen i Telemark 30459
Vestal Museum, Vestal 48225
Vesterålsmuseet, Melbu 30671
Vesterheim Norwegian-American Museum, Decorah 42839
Vestfold Fylkesmuseum, Tønsberg 30926
Vestfyns Hjemstavnsgård, Glamsbjerg 08839
Vesthimmerlands Museum, Års 08774
Vesting Bourtange, Bourtange 29011
Vestingmuseum, Nieuweschans 29622
Vestingmuseum Oudeschans, Oudeschans 29700
Vestisches Museum, Recklinghausen 19514
Vestlandske Skolemuseum, Stavanger 30893
Vestry House Museum, London 39793
Vestsjællands Kunstmuseum, Sorø 09077
Vestvågøy Museum, Leknes 30635
Vetelin Museo, Veteli 10192
Veterans Federation of the Philippines Museum, Taguig 31456
Veterans'Memorial Military Museum, Kensington 05659
Veterinärhistoriska Museet, Skara 36195
Veterinärmedizinhistorisches Museum der Tierärztlichen Hochschule Hannover, Hannover 17613
Veterinary Medicine Museum of the Rev. K.Kluk Museum of Agriculture, Ciechanowiec 31539
Veterinary Museum, London 39794
Veterinary Pathology and Anatomy Museum, Ozzano dell'Emilia 24724
Vetlanda Museum, Vetlanda 36405
Vetlanda Skolmuseum, Vetlanda 36406
Vetlužskij Kraevedčeskij Muzej, Vetluga 33685
Větrný Mlýn, Rudice 08645
Veturimuseo, Toijala 10111
Vevelstad Bygdetun, Vevelstad 30990
V.G. Belinski State Memorial Museum-Estate, Belinskij 32679
V.G. Korolenko House-Museum, Gelendžik 32803
V.I. Chapaev Museum, Čeboksary 32722
V.I. Lenin House-Museum, Samara 33370
V.I. Nemirovich-Danchenko Apartment Museum, Moskva 33127
V.I. Surikov Art Museum, Krasnojarsk 32950
V.I. Surikov Museum-Estate, Krasnojarsk 32957
Via Artis, Bad Aussee 01692
Viborg Stiftsmuseum, Viborg 09112
Vicente Manansala Museum, Binangonan 31288
Vicksburg National Military Park-Cairo Museum, Vicksburg 48230
Victor and Apollinaris Vasnetsov Regional Art Museum, Kirov 32919
Victor and Appolinari Vasnetsov Memorial House-Museum, Rjabovo 33348
Victor-Schultze-Institut für christliche Archäologie und Geschichte der kirchlichen Kunst, Greifswald 17391
Victor Valley Museum and Art Gallery, Apple Valley 41237
Victoria and Albert Museum, London 39795
Victoria and Albert Museum, Mumbai 21955
Victoria Art Gallery, Bath 38124
Victoria County Historical Society Museum, Lindsay 05756
Victoria County Museum, Baddeck 05033
Victoria Falls Information Centre, Livingstone 49019
Victoria Hydro Station Museum, Carbonear 05204
Victoria Jubilee Museum, Cawthorne 38516
Victoria Jubilee Museum, Vijayawada 22060
Victoria Mansion, Portland 46628
Victoria Memorial Hall, Kolkata 21914
Victoria School Museum, Carleton Place 05208
Victoria School Museum and Archives, Edmonton 05393
Victoria Tower, Huddersfield 39275
Victoria West Regional Museum, Victoria West 34398
Victorian College of the Arts Gallery, Southbank 01466
Victoria's First Hardware Museum, Sorrento 01457
Victoria's Tramway Museum, Bylands 00869
Video Museum and Theater, Grass Valley 43777
Vieille Maison des Jésuites, Québec 06211
Vielstedter Bauernhaus, Vielstedt 20310
Vien Bao Tang Lich Sa Viet Nam, Ha Noi 48980
Vierschaar Museum, Veere 29933
Viestikeskus Lokki, Mikkeli 09835
Viestimuseo, Riihimäki 09998
Viet Nam History Museum Ho Chi Minh City, Ho Chi Minh City 48993
Viet Nam National Fine Arts Museum, Ha Noi 48981
Viet Nam Revolution Museum, Ha Noi 48982
Viet Nam Women's Museum, Ha Noi 48983
Vietnam Era Educational Center, Holmdel 44063
Vietnam Museum of Ethnology, Ha Noi 48972
Vietnam Veterans Museum, San Remo 01442
Vieux Grand Port Archaeological Site, Old Grand Port 27736
Le Vieux Logis, Mons 03638
Vieux Presbytère de Batiscan, Batiscan 05058
Vigado Galeria, Budapest 21391
Vigan House Museum, Vigan 31467
Vigatunet, Hjelmeland 30550
Vigeland, Sør-Audnedal 30865
Vigeland-Museet, Oslo 30770
The Vigeland Museum, Oslo 30770
Vigo County Historical Museum, Terre Haute 47987
Vihannin Kotiseutumuseo, Vihanti 10194
Vihanti Local History Museum, Vihanti 10194
Vihavuoden Myllymuseo, Sappee 10021
Vihdin Museo, Vihti 10195
Viirilän Kotiseutumuseo, Ruotsinpyhtää 10007
Viitainahon Kotiseutumuseo, Piippola 09932
Viitasaaren Metsätyömuseo, Viitasaari 10198
Vikedal Bygdemuseum, Vikedal 30994
Vikens Sjöfartsmuseum, Viken 36409
Viking Historical Museum, Viking 06732
The Viking Museum, Højbjerg 08881
Viking Ship Museum, Roskilde 09046
Viking Ship Museum, University Museum of Cultural Heritage, Oslo 30771
Viking Union Gallery, Bellingham 41602
Vikingemuseet Moesgård, Højbjerg 08881
Vikingeskibsmuseet, Roskilde 09046
Vikingmuseet på Borg, Bøstad 30446
Vikingsholm, Tahoma 47929
Vikingskiphuset, Oslo 30771
Vikram Kirti Mandir Museum, Ujjain 22047
Viktor Rydbergsmuseet, Jönköping 35980
Viļa Plūdoņa Memoriālā Māja Muzejs, Ceraukste 27341
Vila Tugendhat, Brno 08279
Viljamakasiinimuseo, Vihti 10196
Viljandi Muuseum, Viljandi 09395
Viljandimaa Gümnaasiumi Muuseum, Viljandi 09396
Villa Aichele, Lörrach 18491
Villa am Aabach, Uster 37272
Villa Arson, Nice 13328
Villa Bagatelle, Sillery 06454
Villa Bergzicht/Brouwerijmuseum Raaf, Heumen 29413
Villa Cicogna Mozzoni, Bisuschio 23090
Villa d'Este, Tivoli 25712
Villa et Jardins Ephrussi de Rothschild, Saint-Jean-Cap-Ferrat 14271
Villa Farnesina, Roma 25271
Villa Flora Winterthur, Winterthur 37343
Villa Foscari La Malcontenta, Mira 24430
Villa Gallo-Romaine de Saint-Ulrich, Haut-Clocher 11997
Villa Gallo-Romaine de Séviac, Montréal-du-Gers 13137
Villa Godi Malinverni, Lugo di Vicenza 24240
Villa Grècque Kérylos, Beaulieu-sur-Mer 10640
Villa Gyllenberg, Helsinki 09546
Villa Gyllenberg Art Collection, Helsinki 09546
Villa Imperiale, Pesaro 24863
Villa Kruger, Clarens 36638
Villa Lattes, Istrana 24109
Villa Louis Historic Site, Prairie du Chien 46683
Villa Majorelle, Nancy 13246
Villa Manin, Codroipo 23606
Villa Mansi, Capannori 23324
Villa Menafoglio Litta Panza, Varese 25898
Villa Merkel, Esslingen 16971
Villa Mirabello, Varese 25899
Villa Montezuma Museum, San Diego 47300
Villa Museo Puccini, Viareggio 25986
Villa Oppenheim, Berlin 16112
Villa Pelsser, Henri-Chapelle 03491
Villa Pisani, Strà 25639
Villa Romana, Piazza Armerina 24902
Villa Romana a Mosaici, Desenzano del Garda 23713
Villa San Michele, Anacapri 22878
Villa Strassburger, Deauville 11489
Villa 't Eksternest, Roeselare 03707
Villa Terrace Decorative Arts Museum, Milwaukee 45373
Villa Torrigiani, Camigliano 23293
Villa Vauban, Luxembourg 27570
Villa Verdi, Villanova sull'Arda 26019
Villa Wessel, Iserlohn 17925
Villacher Fahrzeugmuseum, Villach 02763
Le Village des Pêcheurs, Canet-en-Roussillon 11022
Village Historical Society Museum, Harrison 43929
Village Historique Acadien, Caraquet 05199
Village Miniature, Marchesieux 12805
Village Miniature avec Jardins et Plan d'Eau in Situ, Saint-Martin-de-Villenglose 14352
Village Minier de Bourlamaque, Val d'Or 06659
Village-Musée, Fos-sur-Mer 11789
Village Museum, Dar-es-Salaam 37459
Village Museum, Hollókő 21430
Village Museum, Kfar Tavor 22676
Village Museum, Kouřim 08425
Village Museum, Skjern 09062
Village Museum, Stellenbosch 34387
Village Museum of Göcsej, Zalaegerszeg 21613
Village Museum of Local History, Chihaya-Akasa 26126
Village of Elsah Museum, Elsah 43173
Village Québecois d'Antan, Drummondville 05345
Villanova University Art Gallery, Villanova 48236

Ville delle Rose, Bologna 23146
Vilniaus Paveikslu Galerija, Vilnius 27539
Vilnius Picture Gallery of the Lithuanian Art Museum, Vilnius 27539
Vilppulan Museo, Vilppula 10199
Vilstaler Bauernmuseum, Eichendorf 16801
Vin- och Sprithistoriska Museet, Stockholm 36299
Vina Cooke Museum of Dolls and Bygone Childhood, Newark-on-Trent 40026
The Vinalhaven Historical Society Museum, Vinalhaven 48237
Vinarium, Cleebronn 16478
Vincent Art Gallery, Townsville 01550
Vincent Price Gallery, Monterey Park 45462
Vindonissa-Museum, Brugg 36592
Vingelen Kirke- og Skolemuseum, Vingelen 30995
Vingerhoedmuseum, Veenendaal 29929
Vinjestoga, Vinje 30997
Vinnitsa Museum of Local Lore, Vinnica 37911
Vinorama - Musée du Vin, Bordeaux 10821
Vintage Aircraft Museum, Masterton 30200
Vintage Car and Carriage Museum, Inishowen 22481
Vintage Museum of Photography, London 39796
Vintage Toy and Train Museum, Sidmouth 40516
Vintage Wireless Museum, London 39797
Viranşehir Culture Center, Viranşehir 37805
Viranşehir Kültür Merkezi, Viranşehir 37805
Virden Pioneer Home Museum, Virden 06736
Virgil I. Grissom State Memorial, Mitchell 45412
Virgilkapelle, Wien 02998
Virginia Air and Space Center, Hampton 43898
Virginia Association of Museums, Richmond 49540
Virginia Aviation Museum, Richmond International Airport 46894
Virginia Baptist Historical Society Museum, Richmond 46889
Virginia Beach Maritime Museum, Virginia Beach 48249
Virginia City Madison County Historical Museum, Virginia City 48251
The Virginia Discovery Museum, Charlottesville 42254
Virginia Historical Society Museum, Richmond 46890
Virginia Institute of Marine Science, Fish Collection, Cloucester Point 42503
Virginia Living Museum, Newport News 45940
Virginia M. McCune Community Arts Center, Petoskey 46384
Virginia Marine Science Museum, Virginia Beach 48250
Virginia Military Institute Museum, Lexington 44763
Virginia Museum of Fine Arts, Richmond 46891
Virginia Museum of Natural History, Martinsville 45193
Virginia Museum of Transportation, Roanoke 46931
Virginia Sports Hall of Fame and Museum, Portsmouth 46666
The Virginia War Museum, Newport News 45941
Virgo Labour Museum, Oravais 09883
Virje Local History Museum and Fine Arts Gallery, Virje 07800
Virkki-käsityömuseo, Helsinki 09547
Virkki Museum of Handicrafts, Helsinki 09547
Viroconium Museum, Wroxeter 40946
Virolahden Kotiseutumuseo, Virolahti 10201
Virovitica Municipal Museum, Virovitica 07801
Virtain Perinnekylä, Virrat 10206
Virtasalmen Kotiseutumuseo, Virtasalmi 10207
Visafslag Elburg, Elburg 29225
Visceglia Art Gallery, Caldwell 42030
Vischpoort en Kazematten, Elburg 29226
Viski Károly Múzeum, Kalocsa 21438
Visserij- en Cultuurhistorisch Museum, Woudrichem 30026
Visserijmuseum, Breskens 29026
Visserijmuseum, Bruinisse 29033
Visserijmuseum, Vlaardingen 29948
Visserijmuseum Zoutkamp, Zoutkamp 30068
Vistula River Museum, Tczew 32046
Visual Arts and Galleries Association, Ely 49455
Visual Arts Annex Gallery, San Antonio 47264
Visual Arts Center, Portsmouth 46667
Visual Arts Center of Northwest Florida, Panama City 46278
Visual Arts Gallery, Birmingham 41711
Visual Arts Gallery, Pensacola 46347
Visual Arts Museum, New York 45885
Visvesvaraya Industrial and Technological Museum, Bangalore 21705
Vitenskapsmuseet, Trondheim 30946
Vitlycke Museum, Tanumshede 36322
Vitoslavlitsy - Museum of Folk Wood Carving, Velikij Novgorod 33678
Vitra Design Museum, Weil am Rhein 20438
Vitra Design Museum Berlin, Berlin 16113
Vitrine Présentée à la Médiathèque, Rougiers 14061
Vivarium, Lautenbach-Zell 12357
Vivarium, Quito 09220
Vizcaya Museum, Miami 45292
Vjatskaja Kunstkamera, Kirov 32924
V.K. Krishna Menon Museum and Art Gallery, Kozhikode 21917
Vlaams Mijnmuseum, Beringen 03212
Vlaams Tram- en Autobusmuseum, Berchem 03211
Vlaamse Museumvereniging, Antwerpen 49076
Vlachos Collection, Mytilini 21089
Vladimir Raevsky Museum, Bogoslovka 32695
Vladimir Serov Memorial House-Museum, Emmaus 32795
Vladimir-Suzdal Museum of Art, History and Architecture, Vladimir 33692
Vladimir-Volynski Local Museum, Vladimir-Volynski 37912
Vladislava Loča Latgaliešu Rakstniecības Muzejs, Pilcene 27393
Vladislavs Locis Letigallian Literature Museum, Pilcene 27393
Vladivostok Fortress - Military Historical Museum of Fortification, Vladivostok 33711
Vladivostokskaja Krepost' - Voenno istoričeskij Fortifikacionnyj Muzej, Vladivostok 33711
Het Vlaemsche Erfgoed, Groede 29302
Vlasbewerkingsmuseum It Braakhok, Ee 29195
Vlastivedné a Literárne Múzeum, Svätý Jur 34069
Vlastivědné Muzeum, Bělá pod Bezdězem 08244
Vlastivědné Muzeum, Broumov 08280
Vlastivědné Muzeum, Horšovský Týn 08363
Vlastivědné Muzeum, Kamenice nad Lipou 08398
Vlastivědné Muzeum, Kyjov 08441
Vlastivědné Muzeum, Litomyšl 08458
Vlastivedné Múzeum, Nové Zámky 34039
Vlastivědné Muzeum, Nymburk 08512
Vlastivedné Múzeum, Považská Bystrica 34047
Vlastivedné Múzeum, Prešov 34049
Vlastivědné Muzeum, Slany 08654
Vlastivědné Muzeum, Žirovnice 08749
Vlastivědné Muzeum Dr. Hostaše v Klatovech, Klatovy 08412
Vlastivědné Muzeum Jesenicka, Jeseník 08386
Vlastivědné Muzeum pro Vysoké nad Jizerou a Okolí, Vysoké nad Jizerou 08734
Vlastivedné Múzeum v Galante, Galanta 33995
Vlastivedné Múzeum v Hlohovci, Hlohovec 33997
Vlastivědné Muzeum v Olomouci, Olomouc 08516
Vleeshal, Middelburg 29594
Vleeshuis, Antwerpen 03177
Vleeshuismuseum, Dendermonde 03378
Vliegend Museum Lelystad, Lelystad 29534
Vliegend Museum Seppe, Bosschenhoofd 29008
V.M. Vasnetsov Memorial House Museum, Moskva 33077
Voas Museum, Minburn 45375
Vodné Kasárne, Bratislava 33981
Völkerkundemuseum der Archiv- und Museumsstiftung Wuppertal, Wuppertal 20716
Völkerkundemuseum der Universität Zürich, Zürich 37416
Völkerkundemuseum der von Portheim-Stiftung, Heidelberg 17677
Völkerkundemuseum Herrnhut, Herrnhut 17738
Völkerkundemuseum Sankt Gallen, Sankt Gallen 37109
Völkerkundesammlung, Lübeck 18545
Völkerkundliche Sammlung, Winterthur 37344
Völkerkundliche Sammlung der Philipps-Universität, Marburg 18633
Völkerkundliche Sammlung der Universität, Göttingen 17342
Völkerkundliches exotisches, zoologisches und heimatkundliches Missionsmuseum, Bad Driburg 15628
Völkerschlachtdenkmal und Forum 1813, Museum zur Geschichte der Völkerschlacht, Leipzig 18424
Voenno-istoričeski Muzej, Gorna Studena 04676
Voenno-istoričeski Muzej, Pleven 04772
Voenno-istoričeski Muzej Osvoboditelna Vojna 1877-1878, Bjala 04623
Voenno-istoričeskij Muzej Artillerii, Inženernych Vojsk i Vojsk Svjazi, Sankt-Peterburg 33487
Voenno-istoričeskij Muzej Tichookeanskogo Flota, Vladivostok 33712
Voenno-medicinskij Muzej, Sankt-Peterburg 33488
Voenno-morskoj Muzej Severnogo Flota, Murmansk 33191
Voergård Slot, Dronninglund 08799
Voerman Museum Hattem, Hattem 29353
Vörösmarty Mihály Emlékmúzeum, Kapolnásnyék 21439
Vötter's Oldtimermuseum, Kaprun 02099
Vöyri Museum, Vörå 10210
Vöyrin Kotiseutumuseo, Vörå 10210
Vogelmuseum, Waging 20344
Vogelmuseum-Die Vogelwelt des Böhmerwaldes, Aigen im Mühlkreis 01650
Vogelsberger Heimatmuseum, Schotten 19845
Vogteimuseum mit Blumenauer Heimatstube, Aurach 15577
Vogtländisches Dorfmuseum, Erlbach 16926
Vogtländisches Freilichtmuseum, Erlbach 16927
Vogtländisches Freilichtmuseum Landwüst, Landwüst 18315
Vogtlandmuseum Plauen, Plauen 19413
Voimalamuseo, Helsinki 09548
Voipaalas Taidekeskus, Sääksmäki 10014
Voithenberghammer, Furth im Wald 17182
Vojenské Technické Muzeum, Krhanice 08433
Vojni Muzej Beograd, Beograd 33819
Vojvodina Museum, Novi Sad 33875
Vojvodjanski Muzej, Novi Sad 33875
Volcano Art Center, Hawaii National Park 43968
Volda Bygdetun, Volda 30999
Voldemāra Jākobsona Memoriālā Māja Muzejs, Bebri 27337
Volendam Windmill Museum, Milford 45341
Volendams Museum, Volendam 29958
Volgograd Art Museum, Volgograd 33718
Volgograd History Museum of the State Museum-Panorama Battle of Stalingrad, Volgograd 33717
Volgogradskij Memorialno-istoričeskij Muzej, Volgograd 33717
Volgogradskij Muzej Izobrazitelnych Iskusstv, Volgograd 33718
Volgogradskij Oblastnoj Kraevedčeskij Muzej, Volgograd 33719
Volkening Heritage Farm at Spring Valley, Schaumburg 47496
Volkenkundig Museum Gerardus van der Leeuw, Groningen 29317
Volksbuurtmuseum, Den Haag 29127
Volksbuurtmuseum Wijk, Utrecht 29912
Volkskunde-Museum, Rudolstadt 19701
Volkskunde Museum Hesterberg, Schleswig 19797
Volkskunde Sammlung, Kassel 18032
Volkskunde- und Freilichtmuseum, Konz 18208
Volkskunde- und Mühlenmuseum, Waltersdorf bei Zittau 20385
Volkskundemuseum, Antwerpen 03178
Volkskundemuseum, Mödling 02315
Volkskundemuseum, Reitzengeschwenda 19555
Volkskundemuseum, Salzburg 02554
Volkskundemuseum, Schönberg, Mecklenburg 19826
Volkskundemuseum des Bezirks Unterfranken, Bad Bocklet 15617
Volkskundemuseum Deurne, Deurne 03384
Volkskundemuseum Spiralschmiede, Lasberg 02192
Volkskundemuseum Treuchtlingen, Treuchtlingen 20201
Volkskundemuseum Wyhra, Wyhratal 20725
Volkskundig Educatie Museum, Susteren 29862
Volkskundlich-Landwirtschaftliche Sammlung, Stainz 02674
Volkskundliche Sammlung, Hengsberg 02021
Volkskundliche Sammlung, Mömbris 18768
Volkskundliche Sammlung, Osnabrück 19286
Volkskundliche Sammlung alter bäuerlicher Geräte, Ludesch 02255
Volkskundliche Sammlung des Fichtelgebirgsvereins, Weidenberg 20428
Volkskundliche Sammlungen, Witzenhausen 20638
Volkskundliche und kirchliche Sammlungen, Straßburg 02705
Volkskundliches Berufe- und Handwerker-Museum, Aspang 01684
Volkskundliches Freilichtmuseum im Stadtpark Speckenbüttel, Bremerhaven 16345
Volkskundliches Gerätemuseum, Arzberg, Oberfranken 15517
Volkskundliches Museum, Deutschlandsberg 01763
Volkskundliches Museum Alois Alphons, Hirschwang 02032
Volksmuseum Deurne, Antwerpen 03179
Volksschulmuseum, Maria Taferl 02272
Volo Antique Auto Museum and Village, Volo 48257
Vologda Historical, Architectural and Artistic Museum Reserve, Vologda 33724
Vologda Regional Art Gallery, Vologda 33723
Vologodskaja Oblastnaja Kartinnaja Galereja, Vologda 33723
Vologodskij Gosudarstvennyj Istoriko-Architekturnyj i Chudožestvennyj Muzej-Zapovednik, Vologda 33724
Volta Regional Museum, Ho 20793
Volunteer Committees of Art Museum, New Orleans 49541
Volunteer Firemen's Mall and Museum of Kingston, Kingston 44496
Volynian Regional Museum, Luck 37880
Volynskyj Krajeznavčyj Muzej, Luck 37880
Vom Kloster zum Dorf, Creglingen 16510
Von der Heydt-Museum, Wuppertal 20717
The von Liiebig Art Center, Naples 45604
Vonderau Museum, Fulda 17178
Voorhistorisch Museum, Zonhoven 03855
Voormalig Stoombierbrouwerij De Keijzer N.A. Bosch, Maastricht 29575
Voortrekker Monument Heritage Site, Pretoria 34364
Voortrekker Museum, Pietermaritzburg 34329
Vor- und Frühgeschichtliche Sammlung, Kassel 18033
Vor- und Frühgeschichtliches Museum, Thalmässing 20168
Vorarlberger Landesmuseum, Bregenz 01746
Vorarlberger Militärmuseum, Bregenz 01747
Vorbasse Museum, Vorbasse 09114
Vorderasiatisches Museum, Berlin 16114
Vorgeschichtliche Sammlung, Nabburg 18970
Vorgeschichtsmuseum der Oberpfalz, Amberg, Oberpfalz 15479
Vorgeschichtsmuseum im Grabfeldgau, Bad Königshofen 15678
Vorkuta Regional Museum, Vorkuta 33728
Vorkutinskij Mežrajonnyj Kraevedčeskij Muzej, Vorkuta 33728
Voronezh Art Museum I.N Kramskoy, Voronež 33735
Voronežskij Chudožestvennyj Muzej im. I.N. Kramskogo, Voronež 33735
Voronežskij Oblastnoj Kraevedčeskij Muzej, Voronež 33736
Vorres Museum, Paiania 21104
Võrumaa Muuseum, Võru 09397
Voss Folkemuseum, Skulestadmo 30854
Vostočno Kazachstanskij Etnografičeskij Muzej, Ust-Kamenogorsk 27100
Votivsammlung der Wallfahrtskirche Maria Kirchental, Sankt Martin bei Lofer 02587
Votivschatz der Wallfahrtskirche, Sankt Jakob-Breitenau 02572
Vouros Eftaxias Museum, Athinai 20906
Vouvalis Mansion, Kalymnos 20993
Vox Populi Gallery, Philadelphia 46461
Voyageur Heritage Centre, Mattawa 05825
Voyageurs National Park Museum, International Falls 44241
V.P. Sukachev Regional Art Museum, Irkutsk 32813
Vredespaleis, Den Haag 29128
Vrindavan Research Institute Museum, Mathura 21941
Het Vrouwenhuis, Zwolle 30087
Vryburg Museum, Vryburg 34399
V.S. Meyerhold Museum, Moskva 33126
V.S. Vysotskiy Cultural Centre and Museum, Moskva 33071
VSE Elektro-Museum, Illingen 17889
Vserossijskij Istoriko-ėtnografičeskij Muzej, Toržok 33620
Vserossijskij Memorialnyj Muzej-zapovednik V.M. Šukšina, Srostki 33551
Vserossijskij Muzej Dekorativno-Prikladnogo i Narodnogo Iskusstva, Moskva 33183
Vserossijskij Muzej Puškina, Sankt-Peterburg 33489
Vsevoložskij Gosudarstvennyj Istoriko-kraevedčeskij Muzej, Vsevoložsk 33740
VU Centre de Diffusion et de Production de la Photographie, Québec 06212
Vughts Historisch Museum, Vught 29972
Vukov i Dositejev Muzej, Beograd 33820
Vuni Sarayi, Lefke 08233
Vuorela's Author Home, Keuruu 09660
V.V. Bianki Local Museum, Bijsk 32687
V.V. Mayakovsky State Museum, Moskva 33060
VW-Käfermuseum, Ingering 02057
Vyborgskij Kraevedčeskij Muzej, Vyborg 33742
Východočeská Galerie, Pardubice 08533
Východočeské Muzeum, Pardubice 08534
Východoslovenské Múzeum, Košice 34006
Vylym-Hütte, Userin 20277
The Vyne, Basingstoke 38104
Vysočna County Gallery, Jihlava 08391
Výstavní Síň Muzea, Ústí nad Orlicí 08704
Výstavní síň Muzea Těšínska, Český Těšín 08306
Výstavní Síň Muzea Těšínska, Orlová 08523
Výstavní síň Muzeum Těšínska, Jablunkov 08381
Vystavočnye Zaly v Dome Aksakovych, Moskva 33184
Vystavočnyj Zal, Čerepovec 32734
Vystavočnyj Zal, Ekaterinburg 32784
Vystavočnyj Zal, Kirov 32925
Vystavočnyj Zal, Kirov 32926
Vystavočnyj Zal, Krasnoturinsk 32962
Vystavočnyj Zal, Tula 33634
Vystavočnyj Zal, Volgograd 33720
Vystavočnyj Zal, Vologda 33725
Vystavočnyj Zal Biblioteki im. A.A. Bloka, Sankt-Peterburg 33490
Vystavočnyj Zal Doma Učenych, Novosibirsk 33245
Vystavočnyj Zal g. Smolenska, Smolensk 33538
Vystavočnyj Zal Karelskoj Gosudarstvennoj Filarmonii, Petrozavodsk 33320
Vystavočnyj Zal Moskovskogo Sojuza Chudožnikov, Moskva 33185
Vystavočnyj Zal Permskogo Oblastnogo Kraevedčeskogo Muzeja, Perm 33309
Vystavočnyj Zal Raduga, Čeboksary 32723
Vystavočnyj Zal - Russkie Chudožniki v Samarskoj Gubernii, Žigulevsk 33749
Vystavočnyj Zal Sojuza Chudožnikov Rossii, Sankt-Peterburg 33491
Vystavočnyj Zal Spasskaja Cerkov, Irkutsk 32821
Vystavočnyj Zal Tverskoj Oblastnoj Kartinnoj Galerei, Tver 33640
Vystavočnyj Zentr -Galereja, Iževsk 32838
Vystavočnyj Zentr Sankt-Peterburgskogo Otdelenija Sojuza Chudožnikov Rossii, Sankt-Peterburg 33492
Vytautas The Great War Museum, Kaunas 27523
Výtvarné Centrum Chagall, Ostrava 08528
W. and J. Kulczyckich Art Gallery, Zakopane 32204
W. Henry Duvall Tool Museum, Upper Marlboro 48158
W. Hourston Smithy Museum, Saint Margaret's Hope 40414
W.A. Scout Museum, West Perth 01592
Het Waaierkabinet, Amsterdam 28913
Het Waalres Museum, Waalre 29973
Waba Cottage Museum, White Lake 06788
Wabash Frisco and Pacific Association Museum, Glencoe 43686
Wabasha County Museum, Reads Landing 46811
Wabasso Historical Society Museum, Wabasso 48259
Wabaunsee County Historical Museum, Alma 41152
Wabowden Historical Museum, Wabowden 06737
Wachaumuseum, Weißenkirchen in der Wachau 02804
Wachiraprasat Museum, Phetchaburi 37526
Wachsstöcklkabinett - Wachzieher- und Lebzelter-Museum, Viechtach 20309
Waddesdon Manor, Waddesdon 40757
Wade House and Wesley Jung Carriage Museum, Greenbush 43797
Wadena and District Museum and Gallery, Wadena 06738
Wadsworth Atheneum, Hartford 43944
Wadsworth-Longfellow House, Portland 46629
Währungsreform von 1948 und Konklave in Rothwesten, Fuldatal 17179
Wäinö Aaltonen Museum of Art, Turku 10138
Wäinö Aaltosen Museo, Turku 10138
Wälderbähnle, Bezau 01737
Wäschepflegemuseum, Rainbach im Mühlkreis 02479
Wäscherei-Museum Omas Waschküche, Berlin 16115

Wafangdian City Museum, Wafangdian 07277
Waffenkammer im Munot-Turm, Schaffhausen 37133
Waffenmuseum, Oberndorf am Neckar 19186
Waffenmuseum Suhl, Suhl 20122
Waffensammlung Willibald Folger, Bruck an der Mur 01753
Wagenburg im Schloß Schönbrunn, Wien 02999
Wagenmakersmuseum, Leiden 29527
Wagga Wagga Art Gallery, Wagga Wagga 01570
Wagin Historical Village Museum, Wagin 01571
Wagnalls Memorial, Lithopolis 44816
Wagner Free Institute of Science, Philadelphia 46462
Wagner P.A. Museum, Rondebosch 34371
Wagon Wheel Regional Museum, Alix 04975
Wagstädter Heimatstube, Bad Neustadt an der Saale 15707
Wahkiakum County Historical Museum, Cathlamet 42140
Waiheke Island Historical Society Museum, Waiheke Island 30271
Waihi Arts Centre and Museum Association, Waihi 30272
Waikato Museum of Art and History, Hamilton 30174
Waikawa District Museum, Tokanui 30266
Waikouaiti Museum, Waikouaiti 30273
Waimate Historical Museum, Waimate 30274
Wainwright Museum, Wainwright 06739
Waipara County Historical Society Museum, Hawarden 30176
Waipu Heritage Centre, Waipu 30277
Waipukurau Museum, Waipukurau 30278
Wairoa Museum Kopututanga, Wairoa 30279
Waitomo Museum of Caves, Waitomo Caves 30281
Waiuku Museum, Waiuku 30282
Wakaw Heritage Museum, Wakaw 06741
Wakayama-kenritsu Hakubutsukan, Wakayama 26997
Wakayama-kenritsu Kindai Bijutsukan, Wakayama 26998
Wakayama Prefectural Museum, Wakayama 26997
Wake Forest University Fine Arts Gallery, Winston-Salem 48706
Wakefield Art Gallery, Wakefield 40764
Wakefield Historical Museum, Wakefield 48279
Wakefield House Museum, Blue Earth 41755
Wakefield Museum, Wakefield 40765
Wakefield Museum, Wakefield 48278
Wako Hakubutsukan, Yasugi 27010
Wald- und Lönsmuseum, Heinade 17695
Wald- und Moormuseum Berumerfehn, Großheide 17431
Waldbauernmuseum, Gutenstein 01980
Waldgeschichtliches Museum Sankt Oswald, Sankt Oswald, Niederbayern 19755
Waldhufen-Heimatmuseum Salmbach, Engelsbrand 16872
Waldmuseum, Burg, Dithmarschen 16411
Waldmuseum, Furth im Wald 17183
Waldmuseum, Mehlmeisel 18681
Waldmuseum, Münstertal 18955
Waldmuseum, Surwold 20130
Waldmuseum, Zwiesel 20782
Waldmuseum Dr. Kanngiesser, Braunfels 16290
Waldmuseum Göhrde, Göhrde 17312
Waldmuseum im Wildpark Neuhaus, Holzminden 17833
Waldmuseum Stendenitz, Stendenitz 20060
Waldmuseum Wassermühle, Wingst 20608
Waldmuseum Watterbacher Haus, Kirchzell 18100
Waldnaabtal-Museum in der Burg Neuhaus, Windischeschenbach 20607
Waldschmidt-Ausstellung, Eschlkam 16934
Waldschmidthaus Waldfrieden, Kötzting 18194
Waldviertler Bauernhaus-Museum, Weitra 02809
Waldviertler Bauernhof-Museum, Gföhl 01878
Waldviertler Eisenbahnmuseum, Sigmundsherberg 02663
Waldviertler Puppenmuseum, Waldkirchen 02791
Walhalla, Donaustauf 16635
Walkaway Station Museum, Walkaway 01573
The Walker, Liverpool 39531
Walker Art Center, Minneapolis 45394
Walker Art Collection of the Garnett Public Library, Garnett 43628
Walker Hill Art Center, Seoul 27288
Walker Street Gallery, Dandenong 00968
Walker Wildlife and Indian Artifacts Museum, Walker 48283
Walker's Point Center for the Arts, Milwaukee 45374
Wall-Museum, Oldenburg in Holstein 19252
Wall Roman Site and Museum - Letocetum, Lichfield 39494
Wallace Area Museum, Wallace Bridge 06742
The Wallace Collection, London 39798
Wallace District Mining Museum, Wallace 48287
Wallace Early Settlers Museum, Riverton 30248
Wallace House, Somerville 47673
The Wallace Museum Foundation, Montgomery 45468
Wallaroo Heritage and Nautical Museum, Wallaroo 01574
Wallenfels'sches Haus, Abteilung Vor- und Frühgeschichte, Archäologie und Völkerkunde, Gießen 17284
Wallfahrts- und Heimatmuseum, Altötting 15467
Wallfahrtsbasilika Mariazell, Mariazell 02276
Wallfahrtsmuseum, Bruckmühl 16372
Wallfahrtsmuseum, Legau 18368
Wallfahrtsmuseum, Maria Enzersdorf am Gebirge 02265
Wallfahrtsmuseum, Maria Taferl 02273
Wallfahrtsmuseum, Neukirchen beim Heiligen Blut 19040
Wallfahrtsmuseum, Steingaden 20048
Wallfahrtsmuseum Inchenhofen, Inchenhofen 17897
Wallingford Historical Society Museum, Wallingford 48288
Wallingford Museum, Wallingford 40767
Wallington Hall, Cambo 38447
Wallis Museum at Connors State College, Warner 48305
Walliser Reb- und Weinmuseum, Salgesch 37093
Wallraf-Richartz-Museum - Fondation Corboud, Köln 18168
Walmer Castle, Walmer 40770
Walmstedtska Gårdens Museivåning, Uppsala 36365
Walnut Canyon National Monument, Flagstaff 43332
Walnut Grove Plantation, Roebuck 46983
Walpurgishalle Thale, Thale 20167
Walsall Leather Museum, Walsall 40774
Walsall Local History Centre, Walsall 40775
Walsall Museum, Walsall 40776
The Walsenburg Mining Museum and Fort Francisco Museum of La Veta, Walsenburg 48293
Walser Heimatmuseum, Triesenberg 27513
Walserhaus Gurin, Bosco/Gurin 36578
Walsermuseum, Alagna Valsesia 22825
Walsermuseum, Riezlern 02517
Walsermuseum Lech-Tannberg, Lech 02200
Walt Whitman Birthplace State Historic Site, Huntington Station 44170
Walt Whitman House, Camden 42061
Walter and McBean Galleries, San Francisco 47343
Walter Anderson Museum of Art, Ocean Springs 46087
Walter Elwood Museum, Amsterdam 41187
Walter P. Chrysler Boyhood Home and Museum, Ellis 43159
Walter P. Chrysler Museum, Auburn Hills 41378
Walter Phillips Gallery, Banff 05044
Walter Rothschild Zoological Museum, Tring 40728
Walter Runeberg Sculpture Collection, Porvoo 09955
Walter Runebergin Veistoskokoelma, Porvoo 09955
Walter Wright Pioneer Village, Dawson Creek 05315
Walters Art Museum, Baltimore 41489
Waltham Historical Society Museum, Waltham 48299
The Waltham Museum, Waltham 48300
Walton Hall Heritage Centre, Warrington 40788
Walton Hall Museum, Linford 39504
Walton House Museum, Centerville 42171
Walton Maritime Museum, Walton-on-the-Naze 40779
Waltscher Heimatstube, Neckargemünd 18988
Waltzing Matilda Centre and Qantilda Museum, Winton 01606
Walvis Bay Museum, Walvis Bay 28777
Wan Zhou District Museum, Chongqing 07033
Wanapum Dam Heritage Center, Beverly 41673
Wandle Industrial Museum, Mitcham 39969
Wandsworth Museum, London 39799
Wangaratta Exhibitions Gallery, Wangaratta 01576
Wangaratta Museum, Wangaratta 01577
Wangmiao Display Center, Dujiangyan 07046
Wannenmacher-Museum, Emsdetten 16868
Wanuskewin Heritage Park, Saskatoon 06408
Wapello County Historical Museum, Ottumwa 46222
War and Hospital Museum, Ridderkerk 29730
War and Peace Exhibition, Oban 40124
War in the Pacific National Historical Park, Asan 21257
War in the Pacific National Historical Park, Piti 21259
War Memorial, Dublin 22456
War Memorial Carillon Tower and Military Museum, Loughborough 39832
War Memorial Gallery of Fine Arts, Sydney 01511
War Museum, Addis Ababa 09401
War Museum, Athinai 20902
War Museum, Yangon 28753
War Museum of the Boer Republics, Bloemfontein 34193
War Remnants Museum, Ho Chi Minh City 48994
War Room and Motor House Collection, Harrogate 39172
Ward County Historical Society Museum, Minot 45398
Ward Hall, Georgetown 43652
The Ward Museum of Wildfowl Art, Salisbury 47218
Ward O'Hara Agricultural Museum of Cayuga County, Auburn 41376
Warden's House Museum, Stillwater 47811
Ware Museum, Ware 40783
Wareham Town Museum, Wareham 40784
Warehouse Gallery, Lee 44708
Warhol Family Museum of Modern Art, Medzilaborce 34028
Warkums Erfskip, Workum 30024
Warkworth and District Museum, Warkworth 30290
Warmia and Mazuries Museum, Olsztyn 31852
Warmuseum The Consciousness, Borculo 29000
Warner Archive, Milton Keynes 39963
Warner Museum, Springville 47762
Warooka and District Museum, Warooka 01578
Warracknabeal Historical Centre, Warracknabeal 01580
Warragul and District Historical Museum, Warragul 01581
Warrandyte Historical Museum, Warrandyte 01582
Warren County Historical Society Museum, Lebanon 44704
Warren County Museum, Warren 48313
Warren Historical Museum, Warren 48307
Warren ICBM and Heritage Museum, Frances E. Warren Air Force Base 43503
Warren Rifles Confederate Museum, Front Royal 43568
Warrick County Museum, Boonville 41789
Warrington Museum and Art Gallery, Warrington 40789
Warrnambool Art Gallery, Warrnambool 01583
Warsaw Agriculture University Experimental Forest Station - Museum of Forestry and Wood, Rogów 31949
Warsaw Historical Museum, Warsaw 48318
Warta and River Warta Museum, Warta 32145
Wartburg, Eisenach 16820
Warther Museum, Dover 42974
Warwick Castle, Warwick 40794
Warwick Doll Museum, Warwick 40795
Warwick Museum of Art, Warwick 48323
Warwick Regional Art Gallery, Warwick 01585
Warwickshire Museum, Warwick 40796
Warwickshire Museum of Rural Life, Moreton Morrell 39986
Warwickshire Yeomanry Museum, Warwick 40797
Wasch-en Strijkmuseum, Boxtel 29016
De Wascht en Strekt, Gilze 29284
Wasco County Historical Museum, The Dalles 42763
Waseca County Historical Society Museum, Waseca 48325
Waseda Daigaku Tsubouchi Hakushi Kinen Engeki Hakubutsukan, Tokyo 26954
Washakie Museum, Worland 48760
Washburn County Historical Society Museum, Shell Lake 47598
Washburn Historical Museum, Washburn 48327
Washington Center for Photography, Washington 48405
Washington County Historical Association Museum, Fort Calhoun 43375
Washington County Historical Society Museum, Portland 46644
Washington County Historical Society Museum, Washington 48413
Washington County Historical Society Museum, Washington 48419
Washington County Historical Society Museum, West Bend 48512
Washington County Museum, Akron 41071
Washington County Museum, Sandersville 47380
Washington County Museum of Fine Arts, Hagerstown 43867
Washington Crossing Historic Park, Washington Crossing 48423
Washington Dolls House and Toy Museum, Washington 48406
Washington Historical Museum, Washington 48412
Washington Museum, Washington 48414
Washington Museum Association, Bellevue 49542
Washington National Cathedral, Washington 48407
Washington Old Hall, Washington, Tyne and Wear 40800
Washington Pavillion of Arts and Science, Sioux Falls 47647
Washington State Capital Museum, Olympia 46142
Washington State Historical Society Museum, Tacoma 47924
Washington University Gallery of Art, Saint Louis 47140
Washington's Headquarters, Newburgh 45905
Washington's Lands Museum and Sayre Log House, Ravenswood 46801
Waskada Museum, Waskada 06747
Wassenberg Art Center, Van Wert 48197
Wasserburg Haus Kemnade, Hattingen 17638
Wasserkraftmuseum, Ziegenrück 20755
Wasserkraftmuseum Leitzachwerk, Feldkirchen-Westerham 16989
Wasserkunst von 1535, Bad Arolsen 15593
Wasserleitungsmuseum, Reichenau an der Rax 02496
Wasserleitungsmuseum, Wildalpen 03027
Wassermühle Höfgen, Grimma 17405
Wassermühle Kuchelmiß, Kuchelmiß 18256
Wasserschloß Mitwitz, Mitwitz 18759
Wassertor-Museum, Isny 17932
Wasserwelt Erlebnismuseum, Ostseebad Binz 19315
Waste Products Museum, Zwolle 30082
Wastlbauernhof, Siegsdorf 19954
Wastlmühle, Lainbach 02177
Wasyl Negrych Pioneer Homestead, Gilbert Plains 05486
Wat Ko Museum, Phetchaburi 37527
Wat Phra Thart Lampang Luang Museum, Lampang 37511
Watari Museum of Contemporary Art, Tokyo 26955
Watari-Um, Tokyo 26955
Watchet Market House Museum, Watchet 40801
Water Barracks of the Slovak National Gallery, Bratislava 33981
Water Mill, Mikkeli 09829
Water Mill Museum, Water Mill 48426
Water Museum, Moskva 33158
Water Ski Hall of Fame, Polk City 46578
Water Supply Museum, Weymouth 40845
Water Supply Museum of Riga, Ādaži 27325
Water Tower Museum, Gunnedah 01081
Waterford Historical Museum, Waterford 48429
Waterford Treasures at the Granary, Waterford 22555
Waterfront Gallery, Westport 22556
Waterfront Museum, Poole 40230
Waterfront Museum and Showboat Barge, Brooklyn 41952
Waterland Neeltje Jans, Vrouwenpolder 29969
Waterloo Area Farm Museum, Grass Lake 43775
Waterloo Center of the Arts, Waterloo 48435
Watermen's Museum, Yorktown 48800
Watermill Museum, Vääksy 10166
Watertown Historical Society Museum, Watertown 48439
The Watervliet Arsenal Museum, Watervliet 48449
Waterways Museum, Goole 39095
Waterways Visitor Centre, Dublin 22457
Waterwheel Museum, Salisbury 01440
Waterworks Museum - Hereford, Hereford 39231
Waterworks Visual Arts Center, Salisbury 47221
Watford Museum, Watford 40803
Watkins Community Museum of History, Lawrence 44688
Watkins Gallery, Washington 48408
Watkins Institute Art Gallery, Nashville 45630
Watkins Museum, Taylorsville 47963
Watkins Woolen Mill, Lawson 44693
Watson Crossley Community Museum, Grandview 05522
Watson-Curtze Mansion, Erie 43204
Watson Farm, Jamestown 44315
Watson Gallery, Norton 46031
Watson Museum, Rajkot 22002
Watson's Mill, Manotick 05808
Watters Smith, Lost Creek 44956
Watts Gallery, Compton, Surrey 38621
Watts Towers Arts Center, Los Angeles 44948
Wauchope District Historical Museum, Wauchope 01587
Wauconda Township Museum, Wauconda 48458
Waukesha County Museum, Waukesha 48460
Waveland Museum, Lexington 44747
Wawel Royal Castle - State Art Collections, Kraków 31729
Wawota and District Museum, Wawota 06760
Wax Museum, Byblos 27490
Wax Museum, Dublin 22458
Wax Museum Český Krumlov, Český Krumlov 08304
Wax Museum Karlštejn, Karlštejn 08405
Wax Museum Prague, Praha 08598
Wax Museum Prague, Praha 08599
Waxworks Museum, Moskva 33169
Wayland Historical Museum, Wayland 48474
Wayne Art Center, Wayne 48481
Wayne Center for the Arts, Wooster 48750
Wayne County Historical Museum, Richmond 46863
Wayne County Historical Society Museum, Lyons 45014
Wayne County Historical Society Museum, Wooster 48751
Wayne County Museum, Honesdale 44071
Wayne State University Museum of Anthropology, Detroit 42936
Wayne State University Museum of Natural History, Detroit 42937
Wayside Folk Museum, Zennor 40975
Wayville Latvian Museum, Brooklyn Park 00849
W.C. Handy Home Museum, Florence 43345
Weald and Downland Open Air Museum, Singleton 40519
Weapons Museum, Eskilstuna 35873
Weardale Museum, Weardale 40805
Weather Dicovery Center, North Conway 45990
Weatherspoon Art Museum, Greensboro 43819
Weaver's Cottage, Kilbarchan 39355
Weavers' House, Hollókö 21432
Weavers' Triangle Visitor Centre, Burnley 38402
Weaverville Joss House, Weaverville 48487
Weaving and Silk Museum, Bussières 10960
The Webb-Deane-Stevens Museum, Wethersfield 48575
Webb House Museum, Newark 45898
Weber State University Art Gallery, Ogden 46101
Weberei- und Heimatmuseum, Laichingen 18293
Weberei- und Heimatmuseum Ruedertal, Schmiedrued 37139
Webereimuseum, Breitenberg, Niederbayern 16313
Webereimuseum, Haslach 02008
Weberhaus Marlesreuth, Naila 18973
Weberhausmuseum, Schauenstein 19767
Webermuseum, Heidenreichstein 02014
Weberstube Jonsdorf, Kurort Jonsdorf 18272
Webster County Historical Museum, Red Cloud 46815
Webster House Museum, Elkhorn 43145
Wedding and Custom Museum, Kuah 27635
Wedgwood Museum, Stoke-on-Trent 40612
Wednesbury Museum and Art Gallery, Wednesbury 40806
Weegmuseum de Oude Waag, Someren 29844
Weeks Air Museum, Miami 45293
Weems-Botts Museum, Dumfries 43006
Frankie G. Weems Gallery & Rotunda Gallery, Raleigh 46780
Weenen Museum, Weenen 34401
Weeping Water Valley Historical Society Museum, Weeping Water 48491
Weg des Friedens, Purgstall an der Erlauf 02465
Wegmachermuseum, Wasserburg am Inn 20409
Wehrgeschichtliches Museum Rastatt, Rastatt 19492
Weicheltmühle, Reichenau bei Dippoldiswalde 19544
Weidmann Cottage Heritage Centre, Muswellbrook 01296
Weil Art Gallery, Corpus Christi 42648
Wein- und Heimatmuseum, Durbach 16758

Weinbau-Museum, Chur 36637
Weinbau Museum, Neckermarkt 02339
Weinbau- und Heimatmuseum, Klingenberg am Main 18110
Weinbau- und Landwirtschaftsmuseum, Hadersdorf 01985
Weinbaumuseum, Flörsheim-Dalsheim 17016
Weinbaumuseum, Oetwil am See 37006
Weinbaumuseum, Reidling 02502
Weinbaumuseum Alte Kelter, Erlenbach, Kreis Heilbronn 16928
Weinbaumuseum am Zürichsee, Au, Zürich 36475
Weinbaumuseum der Winzergenossenschaft, Ortenberg, Baden 19268
Weinbaumuseum im Herrenhof, Neustadt an der Weinstraße 19079
Weinbaumuseum Jenins, Jenins 36820
Weinbaumuseum Meersburg, Meersburg 18679
Weinbaumuseum Stuttgart-Uhlbach, Stuttgart 20112
Weinberg Nature Center, Scarsdale 47493
Weingart Galleries, Los Angeles 44949
Weingreen Museum of Biblical Antiquities, Dublin 22459
Weingutmuseum Hoflößnitz, Radebeul 19471
Weinlandmuseum, Asparn an der Zaya 01687
Weinmuseum, Güssing 01970
Weinmuseum, Vaihingen 20283
Weinmuseum Kitzeck, Kitzeck im Sausal 02120
Weinmuseum Prellenkirchen, Prellenkirchen 02452
Weinmuseum Schlagkamp-Desoye Senheim, Senheim 19940
Weinstadtmuseum Krems, Krems 02160
Weinviertler Museumsdorf, Niedersulz 02362
Weinviertler Naturmuseum, Jetzelsdorf 02088
Weinviertler Oldtimermuseum Poysdorf, Poysdorf 02442
Weir Farm, Wilton 48671
Weißenhorner Heimatmuseum, Weißenhorn 20501
Weissenstein-Museum, Weissenstein bei Solothurn 37310
Weißgerbermuseum, Doberlug-Kirchhain 16627
Weisův Dům, Veselí nad Lužnicí 08716
Weizmann Archives and House, Rehovot 22739
The Welch Regiment Museum (41st/ 69th Foot) of the Rpyal Regiment of Wales, Cardiff 38485
Welcome-Church of Our Lady, Brugge 03251
Welholme Galleries, Grimsby 39134
Welkom Museum, Welkom 34402
Wella Museum, Darmstadt 16550
Welland Historical Museum, Welland 06762
Wellbrook Beetling Mill, Cookstown 38630
Wellcome Library for the History and Understanding of Medicine, London 39800
Wellcome Museum of Anatomy and Pathology, London 39801
Wellesbourne Wartime Museum, Wellesbourne 40809
Wellesley Historical Society, Wellesley Hills 48496
Wellfleet Historical Society Museum, Wellfleet 48498
Wellingborough Heritage Centre, Wellingborough 40811
Wellings Landsbymuseum, Lintrup 08974
Wellington Arch, London 39802
Wellington Aviation Museum, Moreton-in-Marsh 39985
Wellington B. Gray Gallery, Greenville 43826
Wellington Community Historical Museum, Wellington, Ontario 06763
Wellington County Museum, Fergus 05423
Wellington Courthouse Museum, Wellington 01589
Wells Auto Museum, Wells 48501
Wells County Historical Museum, Bluffton 41760
Wells County Museum, Fessenden 43318
Wells Fargo History Museum, Los Angeles 44950
Wells Fargo History Museum, Minneapolis 45395
Wells Fargo History Museum, Sacramento 47056
Wells Fargo History Museum, San Diego 47301
Wells Fargo History Museum, San Francisco 47344
Wells Fargo History Museum Old Sacramento, Sacramento 47057
Wells Museum, Wells 06766
Wells Museum, Wells 40812
Wells Walsingham Light Railway, Wells-next-the-Sea 40814
Welser Puppenweltmuseum, Wels 02817
Welsh Highland Railway Museum, Porthmadog 40243
Welsh Slate Museum, Llanberis 39536
Welshpool and Llanfair Light Railway, Llanfair Caereinion 39548
Weltkulturerbe Völklinger Hütte, Völklingen 20328
Welwyn Roman Baths Museum, Welwyn 40818
Wen Tianxiang Temple, Beijing 06993
Wenatchee Valley Museum, Wenatchee 48507
Wenceslao Vinzons Historical Landmark Museum, Vinzons 31468
Wendell Gilley Museum, Southwest Harbor 47712
Wenham Museum, Wenham 48508
Wenmiao Museum, Tianjin 07269
Wentworth-Coolidge Mansion, Portsmouth 46655
Wentworth Gardner and Tobias Lear Houses, Portsmouth 46656
Wenzel-Hablik-Museum, Itzehoe 17935
Weoley Castle, Birmingham 38232
Werberger Stuben, Motten 18797
Werdenfelser Museum, Garmisch-Partenkirchen 17204
Wereld Bodem Museum, Wageningen 29977
Wereldmuseum Rotterdam, Rotterdam 29779
Werkhof Bistrica, Sankt Michael 02588
Werksmuseum Achse, Rad und Wagen, Wiehl 20567
Werksmuseum der Amazonen-Werke, Gaste 17206
Werksmuseum der Firma Linke-Hofmann-Busch, Salzgitter 19736
Werksmuseum der MTU, München 18923
Werksmuseum der Waechtersbacher Keramik, Brachttal 16268
Werksmuseum Koenig & Bauer AG, Würzburg 20707
Werkspoor Museum, Amsterdam 28914
Werkzeugmuseum Zur Eisenbahn, Ermatingen 36687
Werner-Berg-Galerie der Stadt Bleiburg, Bleiburg 01739
Werner-Egk-Begegnungsstätte, Donauwörth 16642
Wernher Collection at Ranger's House, London 39803
Werra-Kalibergbau-Museum, Heringen, Werra 17723
Werribee and District Historical Museum, Werribee 01591
Wertpapier-Museum, Zürich 37417
Weslaco Bicultural Museum, Weslaco 48509
Wesley's House and Museum, London 39804
Wesselstuerne, København 08954
West Allis Historical Society Museum, West Allis 48510
West Baton Rouge Museum, Port Allen 46587
West Bend Art Museum, West Bend 48513
West Berkshire Museum, Newbury 40030
West Blatchington Windmill, Hove 39270
West Bohemian Gallery in Plzeň, Plzeň 08546
West Bohemian Museum, Plzeň 08547
West Chicago City Museum, West Chicago 48519
West Coast Historical Museum, Hokitika 30179
West Coast Maritime Museum, Tofino 06555
West Coast Museum of Flying, Sidney 06451
West Coast Pioneer's Memorial Museum, Zeehan 01635
West Cork Model Railway Village, Clonakilty 22395
West Cork Regional Museum, Clonakilty 22396
West End Gallery, Edmonton 05394
West Gate Towers, Canterbury 38476
West Highland Museum, Fort William 39011
West Java Museum, Bandung 22075
West Kalimantan Museum, Pontianak 22179
West Kilbride Museum, West Kilbride 40825
West Midlands Police Museum, Birmingham 38233
West-Moravian Museum in Třebíč, Třebíč 08687
West-Moravian Museum in Třebíč - Museum Jemnice, Jemnice 08384
West Norway Museum of Decorative Art, Bergen 30427
West of the Pecos Museum, Pecos 46325
West Overton Museums, Scottdale 47511
West Park Museum and Art Gallery, Macclesfield 39867
West Parry Sound District Museum, Parry Sound 06097
West Pasco Historical Society Museum, New Port Richey 45743
West Point Lighthouse Museum, O'Leary 06051
West Point Museum, West Point 48543
West River Museum, Philip 46466
West Somerset Railway, Minehead 39964
West Somerset Rural Life Museum, Allerford 37976
West Stow Anglo-Saxon Centre, Bury Saint Edmunds 38419
West Sumatrian Museum, Padang 22165
West Torrens Railway, Signal Telegraph and Aviation Museum, Brooklyn Park 00850
West Valley Art Museum, Surprise 47893
West Vancouver Museum, West Vancouver 06775
West Virginia Independence Hall, Wheeling 48588
West Virginia Northern Community College Alumni Association Museum, Wheeling 48589
West Virginia State Farm Museum, Point Pleasant 46577
West Virginia State Museum, Charleston 42232
West Virginia University Mesaros Galleries, Morgantown 45500
West Wales Arts Centre, Fishguard 38994
West Wycombe Motor Museum, West Wycombe 40829
West Wycombe Park House, West Wycombe 40830
Westallgäuer Heimatmuseum, Weiler-Simmerberg 20448
Westbury Manor Museum, Fareham 38976
Western Aerospace Museum, Oakland 46070
Western Approaches, Liverpool 39532
Western Archeological and Conservation Center, Tucson 48097
Western Art Gallery and Museum, Dillon 42950
Western Australian Maritime Museum, Fremantle 01038
Western Australian Medical Museum, Subiaco 01483
Western Australian Museum, Perth 01364
Western Australian Museum Geraldton, Geraldton 01049
Western Canada Aviation Museum, Winnipeg 06852
Western Colorado Center for the Arts, Grand Junction 43749
Western Development Museum, Saskatoon 06409
Western Gallery, Bellingham 41603
Western Hennepin County Pioneers Museum, Long Lake 44874
Western Heritage Center, Billings 41691
Western Hotel Museum, Lancaster 44617
Western Illinois University Art Gallery, Macomb 45042
Western Kentucky University Gallery, Bowling Green 41852
Western Museum, Abilene 41052
Western Museum of Mining and Industry, Colorado Springs 42542
Western Museums Association, Oakland 49543
Western New Mexico University Museum, Silver City 47630
The Western Railway Museum, Suisun City 47871
Western Reserve Historical Society Museum, Cleveland 42485
Western Rhode Island Civic Museum, Coventry 42679
Western Springs Museum, Western Springs 48553
Westerwolds Crashmuseum, Oude Pekela 29695
Westfälisch-Niederländisches Imkereimuseum, Gescher 17267
Westfälischer Kunstverein, Münster 18949
Westfälisches Feldbahnmuseum, Lengerich, Westfalen 18437
Westfälisches Freilichtmuseum Detmold, Detmold 16590
Westfälisches Freilichtmuseum Hagen, Hagen, Westfalen 17484
Westfälisches Glockenmuseum, Gescher 17268
Westfälisches Industriemuseum, Bochum 16202
Westfälisches Industriemuseum, Dortmund 16666
Westfälisches Industriemuseum, Hattingen 17639
Westfälisches Industriemuseum, Petershagen, Weser 19379
Westfälisches Industriemuseum, Waltrop 20388
Westfälisches Industriemuseum, Textilmuseum, Bocholt 16191
Westfälisches Landesmuseum für Kunst und Kulturgeschichte Münster, Münster 18950
Westfälisches Museum für Archäologie, Herne 17731
Westfälisches Museum für Naturkunde, Münster 18951
Westfälisches Schulmuseum, Dortmund 16667
Westfalia-Auto-Museum, Rheda-Wiedenbrück 19586
Westfield Heritage Village, Rockton 06281
Westfries Museum, Hoorn 29446
Westgate Museum, Winchester 40894
Westlands Museum voor Streek- en Tuinbouwhistorie, Honselersdijk 29435
Westman's Cottage, Jakobstad 09576
Westmansmors stugan, Jakobstad 09576
Westminster Abbey Museum, London 39805
Westminster College Art Gallery, New Wilmington 45749
Westminster Dragoons Museum, London 39806
Westminster Historical Society Museum, Westminster 48565
Westmoreland Museum of American Art, Greensburg 43821
Westmoreland Sanctuary, Bedford Corners 41584
Weston Park, Weston-under-Lizard 40837
Westonzoyland Pumping Station Museum, Bridgwater 38326
Westover House, Charles City 42204
Westpac Museum, Sydney 01512
Westphalsches Haus, Markkleeberg 18639
Westport Historical Museum, Westport 48573
Westport House, Westport 22557
Westport Maritime Museum, Westport 48574
Westpreussisches Landesmuseum, Münster 18952
Westsächsisches Textilmuseum Crimmitschau, Crimmitschau 16514
Westslovaki Museum in Trnava, Trnava 34075
Westville Gallery, Durban 34234
Westville Historic Handicrafts Museum, Lumpkin 45000
Westwallmuseum Gerstfeldhöhe, Pirmasens 19404
Westzaanse Bodemvondsten Kok-Voogt, Westzaan 30000
Wetaskiwin and District Museum, Wetaskiwin 06780
Wethersfield Museum, Wethersfield 48576
Wetsfälisches Industriemuseum Zeche Nachtigall, Witten 20623
Wetterau-Museum, Friedberg, Hessen 17139
Weverijmuseum, Geldrop 29269
Wexford Arts Centre, Wexford 22560
Wexford County Historical Museum, Cadillac 42024
Wexford County Museum, Enniscorthy 22469
Wexner Center for the Arts, Columbus 42593
Weyers-Sampson Art Gallery, Greenville 43828
Weygang-Museum, Öhringen 19226
Weymouth Museum, Weymouth 40846
Weymouth Woods-Sandhills Nature Preserve Museum, Southern Pines 47709
W.H. Over Museum, Vermillion 48216
W.H. Smith Museum, Newtown, Powys 40072
The W.H. Stark House, Orange 46173
Whakatane District Museum and Gallery, Whakatane 30313
Whale Museum, Friday Harbor 43563
Whaleworld Museum, Albany 00726
Whaley Thorns Heritage Centre and Museum, Whaley Thorns 40847
Whanganui Regional Museum, Wanganui 30286
Whanganui Riverboat Centre Museum, Wanganui 30287
Whangarei Art Museum, Whangarei 30315
Whangarei Museum, Whangarei 30316
Whangaroa County Museum, Kaeo 30187
Whanki Museum, Seoul 27289
Wharton County Historical Museum, Wharton 48579
Wharton Esherick Museum, Malvern 45087
Whatcom Museum of History and Art, Bellingham 41604
Wheal Martyn Cornwall's Museum of the Clay, Saint Austell 40390
Wheat Ridge Sod House Museum, Wheat Ridge 48580
Wheaton History Center, Wheaton 48585
Wheeler Gallery, Providence 46728
Wheeler Historic Farm, Salt Lake City 47237
Wheels O' Time Museum, Peoria 46351
Wheelwright Museum of the American Indian, Santa Fe 47434
Whetung Craft Centre and Art Gallery, Curve Lake 05298
Whipple House Museum, Ashland 41294
Whipple Museum of the History of Science, Cambridge 38465
Whistler House Museum of Art, Lowell 44988
Whitaker Center for Science and the Arts, Harrisburg 43927
Whitbourne Museum, Whitbourne 06785
Whitburn Community Museum, Whitburn 40849
Whitby Abbey Museum, Whitby 40853
Whitby Museum, Whitby 40854
Whitchurch Silk Mill, Whitchurch, Hampshire 40855
Whitchurch-Stouffville Museum, Gormley 05503
White County Historical Museums, Carmi 42111
White County Historical Society Museum, Cleveland 42461
White County Historical Society Museum, Monticello 45474
White Deer Land Museum, Pampa 46275
White Fox Museum, White Fox 06787
White Gallery, Portland 46645
White Hall Historic Site, Richmond 46865
The White House, Washington 48409
White House, Westbury 01595
White House Museum of Buildings and Country Life, Aston Munslow 38037
White Memorial Conservation Center, Litchfield 44814
White Mill Rural Heritage Centre, Sandwich 40448
White Pillars Museum, De Pere 42817
White Pine Public Museum, Ely 43176
White River Museum, Meeker 45227
White River Valley Museum, Auburn 41377
White Rock Museum, White Rock 06790
White Water Gallery, North Bay 06018
Whitechapel Art Gallery, London 39807
Whitefield House Museum, Nazareth 45640
Whitefriars, Coventry 38646
Whitehall, Cheam 38534
Whitehead Memorial Museum, Del Rio 42858
Whitehern Historic House and Garden, Hamilton 05576
Whitemouth Municipal Museum, Whitemouth 06795
Whiteshell Natural Historic Museum, Seven Sisters Falls 06424
Whitewater Canal Historic Site, Metamora 45276
Whitewater Historical Museum, Whitewater 48595
Whitewood Historical Museum, Whitewood 06797
Whithorn - Cradle of Christianity, Whithorn 40860
Whithorn Priory and Museum, Whithorn 40861
Whitingham Historical Museum, Whitingham 48596
Whitley County Historical Museum, Columbia City 42571
Whitney Museum of American Art, New York 45886
Whitney Museum of American Art at Champion, Stamford 47769
Whitstable Museum and Gallery, Whitstable 40862
Whitstable Oyser and Fishery Exhibition, Whitstable 40863
Whittier Fine Arts Gallery, Wichita 48609
Whittlesey Museum, Whittlesey 40864
The Whitworth Art Gallery, Manchester 39904
Whitworth Historical Society Museum, Whitworth 40866
Whowhatwherewhenwhy W5, Belfast 38161
Whyalla Maritime Museum, Whyalla 01597
Whyte Museum of the Canadian Rockies, Banff 05045
Wichita Art Museum, Wichita 48610
Wichita Center for the Arts, Wichita 48611
Wichita Falls Museum and Art Center, Wichita Falls 48614
Wichita-Sedgwick County Historical Museum, Wichita 48612
Wick Heritage Centre, Wick 40868
Wickaninnish Gallery, Vancouver 06698
Wickliffe Mounds, Wickliffe 48616
Wickman Maritime Collection, Zabbar 27717
Wide Bay and Burnett Historical Museum, Maryborough 01217
Wide Bay Hospital Museum, Maryborough 01218
Widener Gallery, Hartford 43945
Widener University Art Collection and Gallery, Chester 42285
Widukind-Museum, Enger 16875
Wiechers Woon Oase, Dwingeloo 29188
The Wiegand Gallery, Belmont 41609
Wieland-Archiv, Biberach an der Riß 16139
Wieland-Gartenhaus, Biberach an der Riß 16140
Wieland-Gedenkzimmer, Achstetten 15392
Wieland-Schauraum, Biberach an der Riß 16141
Wielandgut Ossmannstedt mit Wieland-Gedenkstätte, Ossmannstedt 19287
Wielkopolski Park Etnograficzny, Lednogóra 31753
Wielkopolskie Muzeum Pożarnictwa PTTK, Rakoniewice 31943
Wielkopolskie Muzeum Wojskowe, Poznań 31915
Wien Museum Hermesvilla mit Schauräumen der Modesammlung, Wien 03000
Wien Museum Karlsplatz, Wien 03001
Wiener Bestattungsmuseum, Wien 03002
Wiener Feuerwehrmuseum, Wien 03003
Wiener Glasmuseum, Wien 03004
Wiener Kriminalmuseum, Wien 03005
Wiener Porzellanmanufaktur Augarten, Wien 03006

Wiener Secession, Wien 03007
Wiener Stadt- und Landesbibliothek, Wien 03008
Wiener Straßenbahnmuseum, Wien 03009
Wiener Teddybärenmuseum, Wien 03010
Wiener Tramwaymuseum, Wien 03011
Wiener Ziegelmuseum, Wien 03012
't Wienkeltje van Wullempje, Hoedekenskerke 29426
Wieringer Boerderij, Den Oever 29137
Wieża Więzienna i Katownia, Gdańsk 31583
Wigan Pier, Wigan 40872
Wiggertaler Museum, Schötz 37145
Wightwick Manor, Wolverhampton 40917
Wignall Museum and Gallery, Rancho Cucamonga 46784
Wijnklder Soniën, Overijse 03683
Het Wijnkopersgildehuys, Amsterdam 28915
Wijnmuseum Maastricht, Cadier en Keer 29051
Wikinger Museum Haithabu, Busdorf bei Schleswig 16433
Wilber Czech Museum, Wilber 48617
Wilberforce House, Kingston-upon-Hull 39384
Wilbur D. May Museum, Reno 46838
Wilbur Wright Birthplace and Interpretive Center, Hagerstown 43864
Wilder Memorial Museum, Strawberry Point 47852
Wilderer-Museum Sankt Pankraz, Sankt Pankraz 02593
Wilderness Park Museum, El Paso 43124
Wilderness Road Regional Museum, Newbern 45903
Wildlife Education Centre, Entebbe 37824
Wildlife Gallery, Toronto 06625
Wildlife Interpretive Gallery, Royal Oak 47025
Wildlife Museum, Eksjö 35863
Wildlife Museum, Rio de Janeiro 04345
Wildlife Museum, Ulaanbaatar 28689
Wildlife Wonderlands Giant Worm Museum, Bass 00771
Wildwood Center, Nebraska City 45642
Wile Carding Mill Museum, Bridgewater 05131
Wilfrid Israel Museum of Oriental Art and Studies, Kibbutz Hazorea 22690
Wilhelm-Busch-Geburtshaus, Wiedensahl 20565
Wilhelm-Busch-Gedenkstätte, Seesen 19924
Wilhelm-Busch-Mühle, Ebergötzen 16763
Wilhelm-Busch-Museum Hannover, Hannover 17614
Wilhelm Fabry-Museum, Hilden 17756
Wilhelm-Hack-Museum Ludwigshafen am Rhein, Ludwigshafen am Rhein 18523
Wilhelm Kienzl-Museum, Waizenkirchen 02789
Wilhelm-Morgner-Haus, Soest 19981
Wilhelm-Ostwald-Gedenkstätte, Großbothen 17426
Wilhelmietenmuseum, Huijbergen 29452
Wilhelmsturm Dillenburg Museum, Dillenburg 16610
Wilkes Art Gallery, North Wilkesboro 46011
Wilkie and District Museum, Wilkie 06801
Wilkin County Historical Museum, Breckenridge 41876
Wilkinson County Museum, Woodville 48745
Will Rogers Memorial Museums, Claremore 42423
Will Rogers State Historic Park, Pacific Palisades 46254
Willa Cather State Historic Site, Red Cloud 46816
Willamette Science and Technology Center, Eugene 43229
The Willard House, Evanston 43243
Willard House and Clock Museum, Grafton 43736
Willem Prinsloo Museum, Rayton 34366
Willemoesgårdens Mindestuer, Assens 08779
Willenhall Lock Museum, Willenhall 40873
Willenhall Museum, Willenhall 40874
Willi Dickhut Museum, Gelsenkirchen 17231
William A. Farnsworth Art Museum and Wyeth Center, Rockland 46968
William A. Quayle Bible Collection, Baldwin City 41444
William B. Ide Adobe State Historic Park, Red Bluff 46814
The William Benton Museum of Art, Storrs 47837
William Blizard Gallery, Springfield 47751
William Bonifas Fine Arts Center, Escanaba 43207
William Booth Birthplace Museum, Nottingham 40115
William Breman Jewish Heritage Museum, Atlanta 41362
William Carey Museum, Leicester 39470
William Clark Market House Museum, Paducah 46257
William Cullen Bryant Homestead, Cummington 42728
William D. Lawrence House, Halifax 05566
William Fehr Collection, Cape Town 34215
William Grant Still Art Center, Los Angeles 44951
William H. Harrison Museum/ Grouseland, Vincennes 48242
William H. Van Every jr. and Edward M. Smith Galleries, Davidson 42789
William Hammond Mathers Museum, Bloomington 41749
William Henry Steeves House, Hillsborough 05597
The William Herschel Museum, Bath 38125
William Holmes McGuffey Museum, Oxford 46243
William Howard Taft National Historic Site, Cincinnati 42412
William Humphreys Art Gallery, Kimberley 34294
William King Regional Arts Center, Abingdon 41055
William Lamb Memorial Studio, Montrose 39984
William M. Colmer Visitor Center, Ocean Springs 46088
William Morris Gallery and Brangwyn Gift, London 39808
The William Morris Society, London 39809
William Pryor Letchworth Museum, Castile 42135
William Ray House, Dartmouth 05306
William S. Hart Museum, Newhall 45918
William S. Webb Museum of Anthropology, Lexington 44748
William Scarbrough House, Savannah 47486
William Trent House, Trenton 48060
William Whitley House, Stanford 47773
William Woods University Art Gallery, Fulton 43576
Williams College Museum of Art, Williamstown 48635
Williams County Historical Museum, Montpelier 45476
Williams Lake Museum, Williams Lake 06804
Williamson Art Gallery and Museum, Birkenhead 38207
Williamson County Historical Society Museum, Marion 45157
Williamstown Historical Museum, Williamstown 01601
Willibaldsburg, Eichstätt 16808
Willie Monks Museum, Lusk 22513
Willis Museum, Basingstoke 38105
Willistead Manor, Windsor, Ontario 06812
Willoughby-Baylor House, Norfolk 45972
Willoughby Historical Museum, Niagara Falls 05999
Willow Bunch Museum, Willow Bunch 06807
Willowbrook at Newfield, Newfield 45916
Wilmersdorf Archiv, Berlin 16116
Wilmette Historical Museum, Wilmette 48646
Wilmington Priory, Wilmington 40876
Wilmington Railroad Museum, Wilmington 48664
Wilson Castle, Proctor 46710
Wilson County Historical Society Museum, Fredonia 43544
Wilson Historical Museum, Wilson 48670
Wilson MacDonald Memorial School Museum, Selkirk 06421
Wilson Museum of Narberth, Narberth 40001
Wilson's Creek National Battlefield, Republic 46845
Wilton Historical Museums, Wilton 48672
Wilton House, Wilton, Salisbury 40878
Wilton House Museum, Richmond 46892
Wilton Windmill, Wilton, Marlborough 40877
Wiltondale Pioneer Village, Bonne Bay 05096
Wiltshire Fire Defence Collection, Potterne 40261
Wiltshire Heritage Museum and Gallery, Devizes 38726
Wiltshire Regiment Museum, Devizes 38727
Wimbledon Lawn Tennis Museum, London 39810
Wimbledon Society Museum of Local History, London 39811
Wimbledon Windmill Museum, London 39812
Wimmera Mallee Pioneers Museum, Jeparit 01124
Wimpole Hall and Home Farm, Royston 40349
Wincanton Museum, Wincanton 40880
Winchcombe Folk and Police Museum, Winchcombe 40882
Winchcombe Railway Museum, Winchcombe 40883
Winchelsea and District Historical Records Centre, Winchelsea 01604
Winchelsea Museum, Winchelsea 40884
Winchendon Historical Museum, Winchendon 48675
Winchester Cathedral Triforium Gallery, Winchester 40895
Winchester City Museum, Winchester 40896
Winchester College Treasury, Winchester 40897
Winchester-Frederick County Historical Society Museum, Winchester 48679
Winckelmann-Museum, Stendal 20059
Wind River Historical Center Dubois Museum, Dubois 42990
Windermere Steamboat Museum, Windermere 40898
Windermere Valley Museum, Invermere 05622
Windham Textile and History Museum, Willimantic 48637
Windmill and Milling Museum, Polegate 40216
Windmill Island Municipal Park Museum, Holland 44057
Windmill Museum, Korsnäs 09695
Windmill Museum, Szeged 21553
Windmühle, Podersdorf 02419
Windmühle, Retz 02509
Windmühle Vahrel, Varel 20288
Windsor Castle, Windsor 40905
Windsor's Community Museum, Windsor, Ontario 06813
Wine and Spirits Historical Museum, Stockholm 36299
The Wine Museum, Kelowna 05654
Wine Museum in Osaka, Osaka 26645
Wine Museum of Greyton H. Taylor, Hammondsport 43889
Wine Press, Tokaji 21598
Winedale Historical Center, Round Top 47018
Wing Luke Asian Museum, Seattle 47548
Wings of Freedom, Huntington 44158
Wings of History Air Museum, San Martin 47368
Wings of Love, Clinton 42494
Winkelriedhaus, Stans 37207
Winnebago Area Museum, Winnebago 48692
Winnetka Historical Museum, Winnetka 48693
Winnie Davis Museum of History, Gaffney 43580
Winnipeg Art Gallery, Winnipeg 06853
Winnipeg Police Museum, Winnipeg 06854
Winnipegosis Museum, Winnipegosis 06856
Winns Historic Bakehouse Museum, Coromandel Valley 00947
Winona County Historical Museum, Winona 48696
Winser Museumshof, Winsen, Aller 20612
Winslow Crocker House, Yarmouth Port 48780
Winston Churchill Memorial and Library in the United States, Fulton 43577
Winterset Art Center, Winterset 48711
Wintersport-Museum, Davos Platz 36656
Winterthur Museum, Winterthur 48712
Winthrop University Galleries, Rock Hill 46951
Winzer Museum, Eggenburg 01794
Winzerhaus, Poppendorfberg 02435
Winzermuseum Rauenberg, Rauenberg 19502
Wiregrass Museum of Art, Dothan 42961
Wireless Hill Telecommunications Museum, Applecross 00745
Wirrabara Forestry Museum, Wirrabara 01607
Wirral Museum, Birkenhead 38208
Wirtschaftsgeschichtliches Museum Villa Grün, Dillenburg 16611
Wirtz Gallery, Miami 45294
Wisbech and Fenland Museum, Wisbech 40907
Wisconsin Automotive Museum, Hartford 43946
Wisconsin Federation of Museums, Wausau 49544
Wisconsin Historical Museum, Madison 45073
Wisconsin Maritime Museum, Manitowoc 45117
Wisconsin National Guard Memorial Library and Museum, Camp Douglas 42069
The Wisconsin Union Galleries, Madison 45074
Wisconsin Veterans Museum King, King 44484
Wisconsin Veterans Museum Madison, Madison 45075
Wise County Heritage Museum, Decatur 42837
Wiseman and Fire House Galleries, Grants Pass 43769
Wishtower Puppet Museum, Eastbourne 38859
Wistariahurst Museum, Holyoke 44066
De Wit - Royal Manufacturers of Tapestries, Mechelen 03622
Withernsea Lighthouse Museum, Withernsea 40908
Witney and District Museum and Art Gallery, Witney 40911
Witte de With, Rotterdam 29780
Witte Museum, San Antonio 47265
Wittelsbachermuseum Aichach, Aichach 15409
Wittenberger Freilichtmuseum, Edewecht 16782
Witter Gallery, Storm Lake 47834
Witte's Museum, Axel 28957
Wittumsmuseum, Urbach 20273
Wittumspalais - Goethe-Nationalmuseum, Weimar, Thüringen 20476
Wixhäuser Dorfmuseum, Darmstadt 16551
W.K.P. Kennedy Gallery, North Bay 06019
Wladyslaw Orkan's House 'Orkanówka', Poręba Wielka 31894
Wladyslaw Orkan's Museum, Rabka 31936
W.M. Keck Museum, Reno 46839
Woburn Abbey, Woburn 40912
Wocher-Panorama der Stadt Thun um 1810, Thun 37244
Wocoal Art Center, Tokyo 26956
Wohl Archaeology Museum Herodian Mansions, Jerusalem 22670
Wohnmuseum Egga, Visperterminen 37293
Wohnmuseum Schellenberg, Schellenberg 27512
Wojewódzkie Muzeum Pożarnictwa, Włocławek 32164
Woksengs Samlinger, Rørvik 30808
Wolcott House Museum Complex, Maumee 45205
Wolf House Museum, Manhattan 45111
Wolf Point Area Historical Society Museum, Wolf Point 48721
Wolfson Museum, Jerusalem 22671
The Wolfsonian, Miami Beach 45300
Wolfsteiner Heimatmuseum im Schramlhaus, Freyung 17135
Woljeon Art Museum, Seoul 27290
Wolkoff House Museum, Lappeenranta 09765
Wolkoffin Talomuseo, Lappeenranta 09765
Wollaston Heritage Museum, Wollaston 40914
Wollondilly Heritage Centre, The Oaks 01342
Wollongong City Gallery, Wollongong East 01610
Wolseley Community Museum, Wolseley 06859
Wolverhampton Art Gallery, Wolverhampton 40918
Wolverine Hobby and Historical Society Museum, Spy Hill 06485
Womankraft, Tucson 48098
Women and Their Work, Austin 41425
Women's Art Registry of Minnesota Gallery, Saint Paul 47167
Women's Heritage Museum, San Francisco 47345
Women's History Museum, West Liberty 48534
Women's Museum, Dallas 42761
Women's Museum in Denmark, Århus 08771
Won Kwang College Museum, Iri 27193
Wonder in Stones - Museum of Minerals, Ores and Jewels, Teberda 33598
Wonder Works Children's Museum, The Dalles 42764
Wonders of the Sea, Jdeidet El-Metn 27491
Wongan Ballidu and District Museum, Wongan Hills 01612
Wonnerup House and Old School, Busselton 00867
Wonsan Historical Museum, Wonsan 27126
Woocoo Museum, Brooweena 00854
Wood County Historical Center, Bowling Green 41854
Wood End Museum, Scarborough 40457
Wood Library-Museum of Anesthesiology, Park Ridge 46292
Wood Mountain Post, Regina 06250
Wood Mountain Ranch and Rodeo Museum, Wood Mountain 06860
Woodbine International Fire Museum, Woodbine 48726
Woodbridge Museum, Woodbridge 40920
Woodburn Plantation, Pendleton 46338
Woodchester Villa, Bracebridge 05108
Woodchurch Village Life Museum, Woodchurch 40921
Wooden House Museum, De Rijp 29069
Wooden Nickel Historical Museum, San Antonio 47266
Wooden Shoe Museum Gebr. Wietzes, Eelde 29197
Wooden Shoes Museum, Soucht 14782
Woodend and District Local and Family History Resource Centre, Woodend 01615
Woodhall Spa Cottage Museum, Woodhall Spa 40922
Woodhorn Colliery Museum, Ashington 38030
Woodland Heritage Museum, Westbury 40831
Woodland Museum, Szilvásvárad 21584
Woodlands Art Gallery, London 39813
Woodlands Pioneer Museum, Woodlands 06862
Woodlawn Museum, Ellsworth 43164
Woodlawn Plantation, Alexandria 41136
Woodloes Homestead Folk Museum, Cannington 00891
Woodmere Art Museum, Philadelphia 46463
Woodrow Wilson Birthplace and Museum, Staunton 47799
Woodrow Wilson House, Washington 48410
Woodruff Museum of Indian Artifacts, Bridgeton 41894
Woods Hole Oceanographic Institution Exhibit Center, Woods Hole 48735
Woodside National Historic Site, Kitchener 05699
Woodside Store Historic Site, Woodside 48736
Woodson County Historical Museum, Yates Center 48781
Woodstock Art Gallery, Woodstock 06864
Woodstock Artists Gallery, Woodstock 48740
Woodstock Historical Society Museum, Bryant Pond 41975
Woodstock Historical Society Museum, Woodstock 48738
Woodstock Historical Society Museum, Woodstock 48743
Woodstock Museum, Woodstock 06865
Woodstock Museum of Shenandoah County, Woodstock 48741
Woodville Museum, Rogue River 46988
Woodville Pioneer Museum, Woodville 30318
Woodwork Museum, Bhaktapur 28786
Wookey Hole Cave Diving and Archaeological Museum, Wookey Hole 40926
Woolaroc Museum, Bartlesville 41516
Woolpit and District Museum, Woolpit 40927
Woolstaplers Hall Museum, Chipping Campden 38569
Woomera Heritage Centre, Woomera 01618
Woonbootmuseum, Amsterdam 28916
Worcester Art Museum, Worcester 48756
Worcester Center for Crafts, Worcester 48757
Worcester City Museum and Art Gallery, Worcester 40932
Worcester Historical Museum, Worcester 48758
Worcester Museum, Worcester 34405
Worcestershire County Museum, Kidderminster 39353
Worcestershire Yeomanry Cavalry Museum, Worcester 40933
Words and Pictures Museum, Northampton 46016
Wordsworth House, Cockermouth 38605
Worker Housing Museum of Helsinki City Museum, Helsinki 09544
Workers Arts and Heritage Centre, Hamilton 05577
Worker's Home Museum, South Bend 47683
Worker's Museum, Kemi 09651
Workers' Museum, København 08921
Workers' Museum, Kuusankoski 09732
Workhouse Museum, Londonderry 39819
Working-Class Home Museum in Vaajakoski, Jyväskylä 09606
Workman and Temple Family Homestead Museum, City of Industry 42415
The Works, Newark 45899
Works of Art Collection, Rosebank 34373
Workshop and Stores, Grangemouth 39109
Worksop Museum, Worksop 40936
World Federation of Friends of Museums, Paris 49178
World Figure Skating Museum and Hall of Fame, Colorado Springs 42543
World Forestry Center, Portland 46646
World Golf Hall of Fame, Saint Augustine 47075
World in Wax Museum, Echuca 01005
World Kite Museum and Hall of Fame, Long Beach 44865
World Methodist Museum, Lake Junaluska 44589
World Museum of Mining, Butte 42019
World Museum of Natural History, Riverside 46924
World O' Tools Museum, Waverly 48467
World of Country Life, Exmouth 38961
World of Energy, Fremantle 01039
World of Energy at Keowee-Toxaway, Seneca 47565
World of Glass, Saint Helens 40398
World of Wings Pigeon Center Museum, Oklahoma City 46123
The World Organization of China Painters, Oklahoma City 46124
Worldwide Butterflies and Lullingstone Silk Farm, Sherborne 40496
Wormsloe State Historic Site, Savannah 47487
Worsbrough Mill Museum, Barnsley, South Yorkshire 38092
Worthing Museum and Art Gallery, Worthing 40937

Worthington Historical Society Museum, Worthington 48764
Wortley Top Forge, Thurgoland 40707
Wosinsky Mór Megyei Múseum, Szekszárd 21565
Wotton Heritage Centre, Wotton-under-Edge 40938
Wowan and District Museum, Wowan 01619
Wrackmuseum, Cuxhaven 16521
Wrather West Kentucky Museum, Murray 45573
Wray Museum, Wray 48765
Wren's Nest House Museum, Atlanta 41363
Wrest Park, Silsoe 40518
Wrexham Arts Centre, Wrexham 40943
Wrexham County Borough Museum, Wrexham 40944
Wright Brothers National Memorial, Kill Devil Hills 44480
Wright County Historical Museum, Buffalo 41980
Wright Museum, Wolfeboro 48724
Wright Museum of Art, Beloit 41616
Wright State University Art Galleries, Dayton 42807
Wright's Ferry Mansion, Columbia 42556
Wriston Art Center Galleries, Appleton 41241
Writers Museum, Dublin 22460
The Writers' Museum, Edinburgh 38921
Wroclaw University Museum, Wrocław 32190
Württembergische Landesbibliothek, Stuttgart 20113
Württembergischer Kunstverein Stuttgart, Stuttgart 20114
Württembergisches Landesmuseum Stuttgart, Stuttgart 20115
Württembergisches Trachtenmuseum, Pfullingen 19395
Wuhan City Museum, Wuhan 07281
Wuhou Museum, Chengdu 07027
Wujiang Museum, Wujiang 07284
Wulastook Museums, Fredericton 05468
Wupatki National Monument, Flagstaff 43333
Wuppertaler Uhrenmuseum, Wuppertal 20718
Wurzel- und Heimatmuseum, Amel 03128
Wuxi City Museum, Wuxi 07286
Wuxi Engraved Stone Display Center, Wuxi 07287
Wuxi Revolutionary Display Center, Wuxi 07288
Wyalkatchem C.B.H. Agricultural Museum, Wyalkatchem 01620
Wyalong Park Private Museum, Maddington 01194
Wyandot County Historical Society Museum, Upper Sandusky 48161
Wyandotte County Museum, Bonner Springs 41782
Wyandotte Museum, Wyandotte 48767
Wyannie Malone Historical Museum, Hope Town 03072
Wyatt Earp Birthplace, Monmouth 45435
Wyck Museum, Philadelphia 46464
Wycombe Museum, High Wycombe 39241
Wylam Railway Museum, Wylam 40947
Wylie House Museum, Bloomington 41750
Wymondham Heritage Museum, Wymondham 40948
Wyndham Museum, Wyndham 30319
Wynn Collection, Las Vegas 44675
Wynyard and District Museum, Wynyard 06866
Wyoming Arts Council Gallery, Cheyenne 42299
Wyoming Dinosaur Center, Thermopolis 47995
Wyoming Pioneer Home, Thermopolis 47996
Wyoming Pioneer Memorial Museum, Douglas 42965
Wyoming State Museum, Cheyenne 42300
Wyoming Territorial Park, Laramie 44651
Wysing Arts, Bourn 38284
Wystan Hugh Auden-Dokumentationsräume, Kirchstetten 02116
Wythenshawe Hall, Manchester 39905
XA Ytem Museum, Mission 05866
Xantus János Múzeum, Győr 21422
Xavier University Art Gallery, Cincinnati 42413
Xavier University Museum (Museo de Oro), Cagayan de Oro City 31300
Xawery Dunikowski Museum of Sculpture-Królikarnia Palace, Warszawa 32124
Xi Bao Celadon Museum, Shenzhen 07244
Xiamen City Museum, Xiamen 07292
Xian Banpo Museum, Xian 07300
Xian Beilin Museum, Xian 07301
Xian Forest of Stone Tablets Museum, Xian 07302
Xian Highway Display Center, Xian 07303
Xiangtan City Museum, Xiangtan 07305
Xianyang City Museum, Xianyang 07306
Xiaoshan City Museum, Xiaoshan 07308
Xiaoyanta Bag Guan Museum, Xian 07304
Xin Hai Shouyi Mausoleum of Fallen Heroes, Wuhan 07282
Xincheng District Museum, Nanning 07192
Xingping Maoling Museum, Xianyang 07307
Xinjiang Museum, Urumchi 07275
Xinjiang Painting Gallery, Urumchi 07276
Xinle Yi Zhi Museum, Shenyang 07237
Xizhou Yandu Yi Zhi Museum, Beijing 06994
Xperiment Huset, Växjö 36393
Xu Bei-Hong Memorial Hall, Beijing 06995
Xuchang City Museum, Xuchang 07311
Xuzhou Museum, Xuzhou 07312
Xylon Museum, Schwetzingen 19906
Ya Pian Zhan Zhen Museum, Dongguan 07044
Yacimiento-Museo Arqueologico, Ambrona 34462
Yacimiento-Museo Arqueológico, Garray 34838
Yad Labanim Museum and Memorial Center, Petah Tikva 22727
Yad Lashiryon Museum, Latrun 22707
Yad-Lebanim Memorial Center, Rehovot 22740
Yad Vashem Art Museum, Jerusalem 22672
Yad Yaari Museum of Jewish Youth Movement, Givat Haviva 22593
Yaegaki-jinja Treasure Storehouse, Matsue 26475
Yaeyama Museum, Ishigaki 26258
Yagai Hakubutsukan, Gasshozukuri Minkaen, Shirakawa 26763
The Yager Museum, Oneonta 46161
Yahiko-jinja Treasure House, Yahiko 27000
Yakage Museum, Yakage 27001
Yakima Valley Museum, Yakima 48774
Yakushi-ji Treasure House, Nara 26586
Yakyu Taiiku Hakubutsukan, Tokyo 26957
Yaldhurst Museum of Transport and Science, Christchurch 30134
Yale Center for British Art, New Haven 45699
Yale University Art Gallery, New Haven 45700
Yale University Collection of Musical Instruments, New Haven 45701
Yalvaç Müzesi, İsparta 37690
Yalvaç Müzesi, Yalvaç 37806
Yalvaç Museum, İsparta 37690
Yamagata Bijutsukan, Yamagata 27002
Yamagata-kenritsu Hakubutsukan, Yamagata 27003
Yamagata Museum of Art, Yamagata 27002
Yamagata Prefectural Museum, Yamagata 27003
Yamaguchi Hoshun Memorial Hall, Hayama 26186
Yamaguchi-kenritsu Bijutsukan, Yamaguchi 27004
Yamaguchi-kenritsu Hakubutsukan, Yamaguchi 27005
Yamaguchi Museum, Yamaguchi 27005
Yamaguchi Prefectural Museum of Art, Yamaguchi 27004
Yamamoto Isoroku Kinenkan, Nagaoka 26539
Yamamoto Isoroku Memorial Museum, Nagaoka 26539
Yamamoto Kanae Memorial Museum, Ueda 26984
Yamanashi-kenritsu Bijutsukan, Kofu 26360
Yamanashi-kenritsu Koko Hakubutsukan, Higashi-Yatsushiro 26190
Yamanashi Prefectural Museum of Archaeology, Higashi-Yatsushiro 26190
Yamanashi Prefectural Museum of Art, Kofu 26360
Yamanouchi-jinja Treasure History Hall, Kochi 26357
Yamatane Bijutsukan, Tokyo 26958
Yamatane Museum of Art, Tokyo 26958
Yamauchi Library, Yokohama 27021
Yamazaki Museum of Art, Kawagoe 26322
Yanaga Hokkaido Museums, Sapporo 26723
Yanbian Autonomous Prefecture Museum, Yanji 07316
Yaneff International Art, Caledon East 05157
Yangliuqing Museum, Tianjin 07270
Yangzhou Museum, Yangzhou 07315
Yanhuang Art Center, Beijing 06996
Yanka Kupala Literary Museum, Minsk 03117
Yankalilla District Historical Museum, Yankalilla 01625
Yankee Air Museum, Belleville 41593
Yankee Air Museum, Willow Run Airport 48643
Yankee Candle Car Museum, South Deerfield 47691
Yannis Tsarouchis Museum, Maroussi 21059
Yao Xian Museum, Yao Xian 07317
Yard Gallery, Nottingham 40116
Yarmouth County Museum, Yarmouth 06869
Yarraman Heritage Centre, Yarraman 01628
Yass Railway Museum, Yass 01631
Yataro Noguchi Art Museum, Nagasaki 26561
Yatsuhashi-An & Shishu-Yakata, Kyoto 26460
Yayoi Museum, Tokyo 26959
Yazılı Kaya Müzesi, Çifteler 37654
Yazılıkaya Museum, Çifteler 37654
Yazoo Historical Museum, Yazoo City 48782
Ybor City State Museum, Tampa 47947
Ydessa Hendeles Art Foundation, Toronto 06626
Yeats Tower - Thoor Ballylee, Gort 22479
Yeiser Art Center, Paducah 46258
Yeleswasam Pavilion, Hyderabad 21848
Yellow Medicine County Historical Museum, Granite Falls 43765
Yellowstone Art Museum, Billings 41692
Yellowstone Gateway Museum of Park County, Livingston 44833
Yelverton Paperweight Centre, Yelverton 40954
Yeongil Folk Museum, Pohang 27218
Yeraltı Müzesi, Kaymaklı 37731
Yerba Buena Center for the Arts, San Francisco 47346
Yerebatan Cistern Museum, İstanbul 37715
Yerebatan Sarnıcı, İstanbul 37715
Yerevan Children's Picture Gallery, Erevan 00694
Yeshiva University Museum, New York 45887
Yester-Year Artifacts Museum, Rowley 06293
Yester-Years Community Museum, Dinsmore 05332
Yesteryear Costume Gallery, Orroroo 01348
Yesteryear House-Central Mine, Clarkston 42433
Yesteryear Museum, Captains Flat 00892
Yesteryear Museum, Pamplin 46276
Yesteryears Doll and Toy Museum, Sandwich 47390
Yeungnam University Museum, Kyongsan 27208
Yi Jun Peace Museum, Den Haag 29129
Yi Zhi Shi Liao Guan, Shanghai 07226
Yiannoulis Halepas Museum and Museum of Tinian Artists, Panormos Tinou 21107
Yichang City Museum, Yichang 07318
Yigal Allon Center, Ginnosar 22592
Yıldız Şale, İstanbul 37716
Yingkou City Museum, Yingkou 07320
Yivli Minare Sanat Galerisi, Antalya 37625
Yixing Porcelain Corporation Museum, Yixing 07321
Ylä-Savon Kotiseutumuseo, Iisalmi 09558
Ylämaan Jalokivimuseo, Ylämaa 10212
Yläne Local Histoy Museum, Yläne 10213
Yläneen Kotiseutumuseo, Yläne 10213
Yli-Kirra Museum, Punkalaidum 09964
Yli-Laurosela Farmhouse Museum, Ilmajoki 09562
Yli-Lauroselan Talomuseo, Ilmajoki 09562
Ylihärmän Kotiseutumuseo, Ylihärmä 10214
Ylikiimingin Kotiseututalo ja Museo, Ylikiiminki 10216
Ylistaron Kotiseutumuseo, Ylistaro 10217
Ymir Museum, Ymir 06871
Yogen-In Homotsukan, Kyoto 26461
Yogi Berra Museum, Little Falls 44819
Yokohama Archives of History, Yokohama 27024
Yokohama Bijutsukan, Yokohama 27022
Yokohama Doll Museum, Yokohama 27023
Yokohama Kaikou Shiryokan, Yokohama 27024
Yokohama Maritime Museum and Nippon-Maru Memorial Park, Yokohama 27025
Yokohama Museum of Art, Yokohama 27022
Yokosuka City Museum, Yokosuka 27027
Yokosuka-shi Hakubutsukan, Yokosuka 27027
Yokoyama Taikan Memorial Hall, Tokyo 26960
Yoldosh Oxunboboev Memorial Muzeyi, Margelan 48843
Yolo County Historical Museum, Woodland 48732
Yonago City Museum of Art, Yonago 27030
Yonago-shi Bijutsukan, Yonago 27030
Yongfeng County Museum, Enjiang 07047
Yonsei University Museum, Seoul 27291
Yorba-Slaughter Adobe Museum, Chino 42384
Yordan Yovkov Memorial House, Žeravna 04933
York and Lancaster Regimental Museum, Rotherham 40346
York City Art Gallery, York 40969
York County Museum, York 48796
York Minster Undercroft Treasury and Crypt, York 40970
York Quay Gallery at Harbourfront Centre, Toronto 06627
York Racing Museum, York 40971
York Story, York 40972
York Sunbury Historical Society Museum, Fredericton 05469
Yorkshire Air Museum, Elvington 38932
Yorkshire Air Museum, Canada Branch, Saint-Laurent 06361
Yorkshire and Humberside Federation of Museums and Art Galleries, Doncaster 49456
Yorkshire Museum, York 40973
Yorkshire Museum of Carriages and Horse Drawn Vehicles, Wensleydale 40819
Yorkshire Museum of Farming, York 40974
Yorkshire Museums Council, Leeds 49457
Yorkshire Sculpture Park, West Bretton 40820
Yorkton Arts Council, Yorkton 06875
Yorktown Historical Museum, Yorktown 48798
Yorktown Museum, Yorktown Heights 48803
Yorktown Visitor Center, Yorktown 48801
Yorktown Visitor Center Museum, Yorktown 48802
Yorozu Tetsugoro Memorial Museum of Art, Towa 26965
The Yosemite Museum, Yosemite National Park 48804
Yoshimizu-jinja Collection, Yoshino 27033
Yoshimizu-jinja Yoshinoyama, Yoshino 27033
Yoshimoto Bungeikan, Osaka 26675
Yoshinogawa Sake Museum Hisago-tei, Nagaoka 26540
Yoshizawa Kinenkan, Joetsu 26285
Yoshizawa Memorial Museum, Joetsu 26285
Yotvata Museum and Visitors Center, Yotvata 22785
Young at Art Children's Museum, Davie 42790
Young's Brewery Museum, London 39814
Youth Club Museum, Muhniemi 09837
Youth Museum of Southern West Virginia, Beckley 41577
Youth Science Institute, San Jose 47358
Yozgat Culture Center, Yozgat 37808
Yozgat Devlet Güzel Sanatlar Galerisi, Yozgat 37807
Yozgat Kültür Merkezi, Yozgat 37808
Yozgat State Gallery, Yozgat 37807
Ypäjän Kotiseutumuseo, Ypäjä 10219
Ypsilanti Historical Museum, Ypsilanti 48811
Yrjar Heimbygdslag, Opphaug 30718
Yrjö A. Jäntin Taidekokoelma, Porvoo 09956
Yrjö Liipola Art Collection, Koski 09698
Yrjö Liipolan Taidekokoelma, Koski 09698
Ystads Konstmuseum, Ystad 36423
Yttilän Museokoulu, Yttilä 10220
Yturri-Edmunds Historic Site, San Antonio 47267
Yu.A. Fedkovich Memorial Museum, Černivci 37840
Yucaipa Adobe, Yucaipa 48816
Yugtarvik Regional Museum, Bethel 41660
Yukara Ori Folkcraft Museum, Asahikawa 26107
Yuki Bijutsukan, Osaka 26676
Yuki Museum of Art, Osaka 26676
Yukon Beringia Interpretive Centre, Whitehorse 06793
Yukon Historical and Museums Association, Whitehorse 49106
Yukon Transportation Museum, Whitehorse 06794
Yuma Territorial Prison Museum, Yuma 48819
Yumeji Art Museum, Okayama 26629
Yunnan Museum Provincial, Kunming 07146
Yunus Emre Müzesi, Yunus Emre 37809
Yunus Emre Museum, Yunus Emre 37809
Yu.P. Spegalsky Museum-Apartement, Pskov 33331
Yurii Gagarin Memorial Museum, Gagarin 32799
Yurinkan Art Museum, Kyoto 26462
Yusupov's Palace, Sankt-Peterburg 33411
Yutoku Shrine Museum, Kashima, Saga 26319
Yuzawa History and Folk Museum, Yuzawa 27039
Yuzen Art Museum, Kyoto 26411
Yuzhang Bo Wu Yuan, Nanchang 07175
YYZ Artists' Outlet, Toronto 06628
Z33, Hasselt 03484
Zaanlandse Oudheidkamer Honig Breet Huis, Zaandijk 30043
Zaans Museum, Zaandam 30041
De Zaanse Schans, Zaandam 30042
Zabbar Sanctuary Museum, Zabbar 27718
Zabol Museum, Zabol 22336
Zabytkowa Cerkiew w Bartnem, Bartne 31479
Zabytkowa Huta Żelaza, Chlewiska 31525
Zabytkowa Kuźnia Wodna, Gdańsk 31584
Zabytkowa Kuźnia Wodna w Starej Kuźnicy, Stara Kuźnica 31995
Zabytkowa Zagroda Świętokrzyska, Bodzentyn 31502
Zacheta Gallery of Art, Warszawa 32142
Zacheta Państwowa Galeria Sztuki, Warszawa 32142
Zaduzbina Kralja Petra I Karađorđevića, Topola 33921
Zählermuseum, München 18924
Zahari Stoyanov House-Museum, Ruse 04803
Zahedan Museum, Zahedan 22337
Zahnärztliches Museum, Tübingen 20231
Zahnhistorische Sammlung, Coburg 16487
Zahnradbahnschuppen, Puchberg 02459
Záhorské Múzeum, Skalica 34058
Zakarpatsk Regional Museum, Užgorod 37909
Zakarpatskij Kraeznavčij Muzej, Užgorod 37909
Zakhari Stpyanov House-Museum, Medven 04733
Het Zakkendragershuisje, Rotterdam 29781
Zakład Narodowy im. Ossolińskich, Wrocław 32193
Zakynthos Byzantine Museum, Zakynthos 21222
Zakynthos Museum of the Natural Heritage, Zakynthos 21223
Zaldivar Museum, Albuera 31273
Žaliūkių Windmill, Šiauliai 27533
Zaltbommels Stoom- en Energiemuseum, Zaltbommel 30045
Zamboanga National Museum, Zamboanga 31470
Zámecké Muzeum, Kravaře 08431
Zámek, Hradec nad Moravicí 08369
Zámek, Jirkov 08395
Zámek, Nové Město nad Metují 08505
Zámek, Vrchotovy Janovice 08727
Zámek Brandýs, Brandýs nad Labem 08256
Zámek Budišov, Budišov u Třebíče 08284
Zámek-Kinski, Chlumec nad Cidlinou 08310
Zámek Kinských, Valašské Meziříčí 08706
Zamek Królewski na Wawelu - Państwowe Zbiory Sztuki, Kraków 31729
Zamek Królewski w Warszawie, Warszawa 32143
Zámek Lemberk, Jablonné v Podještědí 08380
Zámek Libochovice, Libochovice 08452
Zámek Ličkov - Galerie O. Brázda, Žatec 08739
Zámek Lysice, Lysice 08469
Zámek Manětín, Manětín 08471
Zámek Moravský Krumlov - Galerie Slovanská Epopej Alfonse Muchy, Moravský Krumlov 08488
Zámek Nelahozeves, Nelahozeves 08496
Zámek Sychrov, Sychrov 08672
Zámek Troja, Praha 08619
Zámek Velké Březno, Velké Březno 08710
Zámek Veltrusy, Veltrusy 08714
Zámek Vizovice, Vizovice 08720
Zamek w Czersku, Czersk 31543
Zamek w Gniewie, Gniew 31599
Zanabazar Museum of Fine Arts, Ulaanbaatar 28690
Zandenbos, Nunspeet 29652
Zandlopermuseum Glanerbrug, Enschede 29242
Zandvoorts Museum, Zandvoort 30046
Zane Grey Museum, Lackawaxen 44561
Zanesville Art Center, Zanesville 48821
Zanzibar National Archives and Museums Department, Zanzibar 37471
Západočeská Galerie v Plzni, Plzeň 08546
Západočeské Muzeum, Plzeň 08547
Západomoravské Muzeum v Třebíči, Třebíč 08687
Západomoravské Muzeum v Třebíči - Muzeum Jemnice, Jemnice 08384
Západoslovenské Múzeum v Trnave, Trnava 34075
Zaporožeskij Kraevedčeskij Muzej, Zaporože 37913
Zaporozhe Local Museum, Zaporože 37913
Zara Clark Folk Museum, Charters Towers 00906
Zarajsk Kremlin - History, Architecture, Archeological and Art Museum, Zarajsk 33746
Zavičajna Galerija, Novi Sad 33876
Zavičajni Muzej, Bar 33790
Zavičajni Muzej, Baška 07677
Zavičajni Muzej, Bileća 03913
Zavičajni Muzej, Bileća 33823
Zavičajni Muzej, Biograd na Moru 07680
Zavičajni Muzej, Buzet 07686
Zavičajni Muzej, Čazma 07690
Zavičajni Muzej, Danilovgrad 33835
Zavičajni Muzej, Doboj 33837
Zavičajni Muzej, Herceg-Novi 33841
Zavičajni Muzej, Jaša Tomić 33843
Zavičajni Muzej, Nikšić 33864
Zavičajni Muzej, Nova Gradiška 07745
Zavičajni Muzej, Ogulin 07747
Zavičajni Muzej, Otočac 07752
Zavičajni Muzej, Pljevlja 33885
Zavičajni Muzej, Prijedor 03920
Zavičajni Muzej, Ruma 33901
Zavičajni Muzej, Travnik 03926
Zavičajni Muzej, Trebinje 33922
Zavičajni Muzej, Ulcinj 33924
Zavičajni Muzej, Visoko 03931
Zavičajni Muzej Aleksinac, Aleksinac 33786
Zavičajni Muzej Grada Rovinja, Rovinj 07766
Zavičajni Muzej Našice, Našice 07741
Zavičajni Muzej Ozlja, Ozalj 07753

Zavičajni Muzej Poreštine, Poreč 07755
Zavičajni Muzej Trebinje, Trebinje 03927
Zavičajni Muzej u Jagodini, Jagodina 33842
Zavičajni Muzej Zemuna, Zemun 33931
Zavod za Zaštita na Spomenicite na Kulturata, Prirodnite Retkosti i Muzej, Strumica 27597
Zbiory Historyczne Ziemi Wadowickiej, Wadowice 32069
Zbiory Historyczno-Etnograficzne, Oświęcim 31869
Zbiory Metrologiczne Głównego Urzędu Miar, Warszawa 32144
Zbiory Sprzętu Ratownictwa Kolejowego, Poznań 31916
Zbiory Sztuki, Włocławek 32165
Zbiory Sztuki na Jasnej Górze, Częstochowa 31548
Zbirka Anke Gvozdanović, Zagreb 07841
Zbirka Bratovštine Gospe od Utjehe, Korčula 07724
Zbirka Bratovštine Sv. Nikole, Perast 07725
Zbirka Crkve Gospe od Skrpjela, Perast 33882
Zbirka Crkve Sv. Nikole, Perast 33883
Zbirka Crkvene Umjetnosti, Šibenik 07773
Zbirka Eparhije Banatski, Vršac 33929
Zbirka Franjevačkog Samostana, Sinj 07775
Zbirka Franjevačkog Samostana Visovac, Visovac 07802
Zbirka Ikona Bratovštine Svih Svetih, Korčula 07726
Zbirka Poduzeća Naftagas, Novi Sad 33877
Zbirka Rudnika Majdanpek, Majdanpek 33860
Zbirka Umjetnina Franjevačkog Samostana, Hvar 07708
Zbirka Umjetnina Juraj Plančić, Stari Grad 07790
Zbirka Umjetnina KAIROS, Trogir 07796
Zbirka Župne Crkve, Prčanj 33894
Zebulon B. Vance Birthplace, Weaverville 48488
Zee- en Havenmuseum de Visserijschool, Ijmuiden 29459
Zeemuseum, Den Haag 29130
Zeeuws Biologisch Museum, Oostkapelle 29673
Zeeuws Maritiem Muzeeum, Vlissingen 29956
Zeeuws Museum, Middelburg 29595
Zeeuws Poppen- en Klederdrachten Museum, Zoutelande 30066
Zehnthaus, Jockgrim 17958
Zeidel-Museum, Feucht 16995
Zeiler Foto- und Filmmuseum, Zeil am Main 20736
Zeilopleidingsschip Mercator, Oostende 03672
Žeimelis Žiemgalos Museum, Žeimelis 27540
Zeiselmairhaus, Schrobenhausen 19854
Zeitreise - Renner Vila Gloggnitz, Gloggnitz 01885
Zeitspurenmuseum Altheim, Altheim 01665
Zeittunnel Wülfrath, Wülfrath 20689
Železářské Muzeum, Komárov u Horovic 08418
Zeleznički Muzej, Beograd 33821
Zelienople Historical Museum, Zelienople 48822
Zemaljski Muzej, Sarajevo 03925
Zemědělská Sbírka na Zámku Kačina, Kutná Hora 08440
Zemědělské Muzeum Ohrada, Ohrada 08514
Zemljepišni Muzej Slovenije, Ljubljana 34124
Zempléni Muzeum, Szerencs 21580
Zempliňske Múzeum, Michalovice 34029
Zenetörténeti Múzeum, Budapest 21392
Zengcheng City Museum, Zengcheng 07324
Zenko-ji Tendai Sect Treasure House, Nagano 26530
Zentralarchiv, Berlin 16117
Zentrum für Außergewöhnliche Museen, Kreuth 18238
Zentrum für Außergewöhnliche Museen, München 18925
Zentrum für Internationale Lichtkunst, Unna 20266
Zeppelin-Museum, Neu-Isenburg 19005
Zeppelin Museum Friedrichshafen, Friedrichshafen 17149
Zeppelin-Museum Meersburg, Meersburg 18680
Zerain Cultural Park, Zerain 35735
Zetland Lifeboat Museum, Redcar 40301
Zetlin Museum, Ramat Gan 22735

Zettl Langer Collection, Sopron 21539
Zettl Langer gyüjtemény, Sopron 21539
Zgodovinski Arhiv i Muzej Univerze v Ljubljani, Ljubljana 34125
Zhabei Revolutionary Shi Liao Display Center, Shanghai 07227
Zhan Tianyou Former Residence, Wuhan 07283
Zhan Tianyou Memorial Hall, Beijing 06997
Zhangjiagang City Gallery, Zhangjiagang 07325
Zhangqiu Arts and Crafts Guan, Jinan 07136
Zhangqiu Museum, Jinan 07137
Zhaoling Museum, Liquan Xian 07153
Zhejiang Museum, Hangzhou 07087
Zhejiang Natural Museum, Hangzhou 07088
Zhengding County Display Center, Shijiazhuang 07248
Zhengzhou Museum, Zhengzhou 07329
Zhenjiang Museum, Zhenjiang 07330
Zhi Li Victory Museum, Baoding 06938
Zhonghua Nation Museum, Beijing 06998
Zhongshan Museum, Zhongshan 07332
Zhou Hejing County Museum, Hejing 07092
Zhuhai Museum, Zhuhai 07336
Zibo City Museum, Zibo 07339
Zichy Mihály Emlékmúzeum, Zala 21612
Židovské Muzeum v Praze, Praha 08620
Ziegel- und Kalkmuseum, Winzer 20615
Ziegelei-Museum, Cham 36622
Ziegeleimuseum, Jockgrim 17959
Ziegeleipark Mildenberg, Mildenberg 18737
Ziekenhuis- en Verpleegkundig Museum, Deventer 29147
Zielhaus am Klausenpass, Spiringen 37195
The Zigler Museum, Jennings 44334
Zijdemuseum, Meliskerke 29588
Zijper Museum, Schagerbrug 29798
Zilla Samgrahasala, Purulia 21997
Zille Museum, Berlin 16118
Zillertaler Goldschaubergwerk, Zell am Ziller 03051
Zilvermuseum Sterckshof Povincie Antwerpen, Antwerpen 03180
Zimmer Children's Museum, Los Angeles 44952
Zimmerei-Museum, Feldkirch 01832
Zimmermannshaus Lackinger, Windhaag bei Freistadt 03039
Zimmertoren, Lier 03588
Zinnfiguren-Klause im Schwabentor, Freiburg im Breisgau 17118
Zinnfiguren-Museum, Bad Bergzabern 15604
Zinnfigurenmuseum, Grüningen 36783
Zinnfigurenmuseum, Herzberg am Harz 17743
Zinnfigurenmuseum, Zürich 37418
Zinngießerhäusl, Mattighofen 02282
Zinngrube Ehrenfriedersdorf, Ehrenfriedersdorf 16795
Zinnkeller, Weidenberg 20429
Zinovyev House-Museum, Djagilevo 32757
Zion Historical Museum, Zion 48823
Zion National Park Museum, Springdale 47735
Zippo and Case Visitors Center Company Museum, Bradford 41864
Zirkelmuseum, Wilhelmsdorf, Mittelfranken 20590
Zirkus und Varieté Archivsammlung Reinhard Tetzlaff, Hamburg 17572
Ziska Gallery, Bracebridge 05109
Zisterzienserabtei Mehrerau, Bregenz 01748
Zisterzienserkloster Bebenhausen, Tübingen 20232
Zisterziensermuseum Riddagshausen, Braunschweig 16306
Zisterzienserstift, Lilienfeld 02224
Zisterzienserstift und Stiftssammlungen, Stams 02675
Žitnoostrovské Múzeum, Dunajská Streda 33992
Ziya Gökalp Müzesi, Diyarbakır 37663
Ziya Gökalp Museum, Diyarbakır 37663
ZKM Medienmuseum, Karlsruhe 18007
Zlatý Klíč Muzeum, Karlovy Vary 08403
Znojemský Hrad, Znojmo 08758

Zoar State Memorial, Zoar 48826
Zoll- und Finanzgeschichtliche Sammlung, Linz 02243
Zoll- und Heimatmuseum, Perwang 02407
Zollmuseum, Wegscheid 20420
Zollmuseum Friedrichs, Aachen 15379
Zollverein Ausstellungen, Essen 16964
Zoltán Kodály Memorial Museum, Budapest 21351
Zomerkoestal uut 't Wold, Ruinerwold 29788
Zompenmuseum, Enter 29245
Zonal Anthropological Museum, Shillong 22019
Zonal Museum, Dehradun 21761
Zone Gallery, Adelaide 00717
Zonengrenz-Museum Helmstedt, Helmstedt 17706
Zonguldak Devlet Güzel Sanatlar Galerisi, Zonguldak 37810
Zonguldak State Gallery, Zonguldak 37810
De Zonnehof, Centrum voor Moderne Kunst, Amersfoort 28828
Zoölogisch Museum Amsterdam, Amsterdam 28917
Zoological Museum, Addis Ababa 09402
Zoological Museum, Bukittinggi 22094
Zoological Museum, Dublin 22461
Zoological Museum, Faizabad 21803
Zoological Museum, Gorakhpur 21814
Zoological Museum, Hardwar 21837
Zoological Museum, Helsinki 09480
Zoological Museum, Jaunpur 21869
Zoological Museum, Lahore 31044
Zoological Museum, Meerut 21942
Zoological Museum, Oslo 30772
Zoological Museum, Pematangsiantar 22178
Zoological Museum, Teheran 22329
Zoological Museum, Tel Aviv 22777
Zoological Museum, Zografou 21227
Zoological Museum at Agricultural College, Karaj 22249
Zoological Museum of the Babeş-Bolyai University, Cluj-Napoca 32496
Zoological Museum of the Far East State University, Vladivostok 33713
Zoological Museum of the Institute of Zoology, Erevan 00695
Zoological Museum of the Jagiellonian University, Kraków 31723
Zoological Museum of the Kasan University, Kazan 32910
Zoological Museum of the M.V. Lomonosov Moscow State University, Moskva 33186
Zoological Museum of the Syktyvkar State University, Syktyvkar 33580
Zoological Museum of the Tomsk State University, Tomsk 33618
Zoologičeskij Muzej, Kazan 32910
Zoologičeskij Muzej, Syktyvkar 33580
Zoologičeskij Muzej, Vladivostok 33713
Zoologičeskij Muzej Kafedry Zoologii Pozvonočnych, Sankt-Peterburg 33493
Zoologičeskij Muzej Moskovskogo Gosudarstvennogo Universiteta M.V. Lomonosova, Moskva 33186
Zoologičeskij Muzej Rossijskogo Gosudarstvennogo Pedagogičeskogo Universiteta im. A.I. Gercena, Sankt-Peterburg 33494
Zoologičeskij Muzej Rossijskoj Akademii Nauk, Sankt-Peterburg 33495
Zoologičeskij Muzej Tomskogo Gosudarstvennogo Universiteta, Tomsk 33618
Zoologische Sammlungen des Institutes für Zoologie, Halle, Saale 17523
Zoologische Schausammlung, Tübingen 20233
Zoologische Staatssammlung, München 18926
Zoologisches Forschungsinstitut und Museum Alexander Koenig, Bonn 16250
Zoologisches Museum der Universität, Göttingen 17343
Zoologisches Museum der Universität Hamburg, Hamburg 17573

Zoologisches Museum der Universität Heidelberg, Heidelberg 17678
Zoologisches Museum der Universität Zürich, Zürich 37419
Zoologisches Museum zu Kiel, Kiel 18081
Zoologisches und Tiermedizinisches Museum der Universität Hohenheim, Stuttgart 20116
Zoologisk Museum, Grindsted 08845
Zoologisk Museum, København 08955
Zoologisk Museum, Oslo 30772
Zoologisk Museum Svendborg, Svendborg 09089
Zoologiska Museet, Lund 36065
Zoologiska Utställingar, Uppsala 36366
Zoology and Botany Museum, Ernakulam 21798
Zoology Museum, Annamalai Nagar 21698
Zoology Museum, Brisbane 00844
Zoology Museum, Ibadan 30341
Zoology Museum, Johannesburg 34286
Zoology Museum, Kanpur 21883
Zoology Museum, Kingston 26077
Zoology Museum, Legon 20801
Zoology Museum, Lucknow 21933
Zoology Museum, Muzaffarnagar 21958
Zoology Museum, Winnipeg 06855
Zoology Section, Museum of Evolution, Uppsala 36366
Zorn Collections, Mora 36103
Zornsamlingarna, Mora 36103
Zoshukan, Hanamaki 26182
Zoutmuseum Delden, Delden 29075
Zrinyi Miklos Castle Museum, Szigetvár 21582
Zrinyi Miklós Vármúzeum, Szigetvár 21582
Zsolnay Ceramic and Porcelain Exhibition of JPM, Pécs 21518
Zsolnay Kerámia Kiállitás, Pécs 21518
Zsolnay-Keramik-Porzellan-Museum, Potzneusiedl 02439
Zucker-Museum, Berlin 16119
Zuckmantler Heimatstube, Bietigheim-Bissingen 16162
Zürcher Abwassermuseum Kläranlage Werdhölzli, Zürich 37420
Zürcher Spielzeugmuseum, Zürich 37421
Zuid-Limburgse Stoomtreinmaatschappij, Simpelveld 29817
Zuiderkerk, Amsterdam 28918
Zuiderzeemuseum, Enkhuizen 29234
Zuidwestbrabants Museum, Halle 03470
Zuigan-ji Hakabutsukan, Matsushima 26482
Zuigan Museum, Matsushima 26482
Zululand Historical Museum, Eshowe 34238
Zunfthaus zur Meisen, Zürich 37422
Zunfthaus zur Meisen Keramiksammlung, Zürich 37423
Zungeninstrumenten-Sammlung Zwota, Zwota 20787
Zupski Muzej Lopud, Lopud 07735
Zupski Ured, Ston 07791
Zväz muzei na Slovensku, Liptovský Mikuláš 49359
Zvenigorodskij Istoriko-architekturnyj i Chudožestvennyj Muzej, Zvenigorod 33751
Zverevskij Centr Sovremennogo Iskusstva, Moskva 33187
Zwanenbroedershuis, 's-Hertogenbosch 29411
Zwangsarbeiter Gedenkstätte, Leipzig 18425
Zweigmuseum des Staatlichen Museum für Völkerkunde, Oettingen 19238
Zweiradmuseum Bühler, Wolfhausen 37350
Zweiradmuseum Havel-Auen-Werder, Werder, Havel 20519
Zwijvekemuseum, Dendermonde 03379
Zwingligeburtshaus, Wildhaus 37325
Zwischen den Deichen, Büsum 16408
Zwischen Venn und Schneeifel, Saint-Vith 03724

Index of Persons

Directors, curators, presidents and academic staff of museums

Aalund, Dorothy 45429
Aamodt, David 44207
Aaraas, Olav 30750, 30751
Aarhus, Aasne 30430
Aaronson, Diana 48103
Aarsen, John 43309
Aarsrud, Christian 36373
Aarstrand, Kjetil 30651
Aartomaa, Ulla 09744
Aarts, H.J. 30086
Aartsen, J. 29106
Aasberg, Dagny 30510
Aase, Jean 30609
Aaserud, Anne 30932
Aashagen, Kjersti Haugen 30793
Aasland, Odd 05286
Aasted, Elsebeth 08770
Aav, Marianne 09477
Abab, Khamib Hj. 27660
Abad, Dr. Andres 09160
Abad, María Jesús 35628
Abadesa, R.M. 34628
Abadese, M. 35102
Abadom, Monica 30346
Abadzic, Sabaheta 03925
Abadzieva, Sonia 27591
Abal de Russo, Prof. Clara 00435
Abaño, Isidro C. 31398
Abaraonye, Dr. Felicia Ihuoma 30334
Abbas, Muhammad 31042
Abbasi, Saeed 22292
Abbassi, Q. 22239
Abbate, Dr. Vincenzo 24764
Abbott, Dan 41896
Abbott, James 41454
Abbott, P. 39450
Abbott, Phyliss 41542
Abbott, Will 44050
Abcouwer, Dr. N.F. 29533
Abdo Mahgoub, Prof. Dr. Mohamed 09244
Abdol-Alipoor, M. 22313
Abdol-Alipour, Mohammad 22291
Abdolalipour, Mohammad 22288, 22295, 22297, 22298, 22301, 22305, 22310, 22325
Abdoolrahaman, S. 27733, 27736, 27737, 27740, 27741, 27742
Abdulla, Ayesha 37916
Abdulla, K. 37468
Abdullah, Mohamed Yusuf 27656
Abdullin, Rif Mudarisovič 33641
Abdullina, Svetlana Aleksandrovna 33742
Abdunov, Georgi 04750
Abdurazakov, A. 37856
Abe, Hiroshi 26259
Abegg, Dr. Angelika 19793
Abejide, Ola 30360
Abel, Marianne 16512
Abel, Dr. Susanne 20583
Abel, Tiina 09358
Abelanet, Jean 14872
Abele, S. 20113
Abele, Susan 45944
Abeler, Jürgen 20718
Abell, Carl T. 45224
Abella, Carmencita T. 31396
Abella, Jordi 34810
Abels, Peggy 44423
Abensour, Dominique 13893
Abildgaard, Hanne 08921
Abitz, Gerald 44460
Ablak, Mehmet 37727
Abner, Steve 42440
Abraham, Debbie 00814
Abraham, Julian 38123
Abraham-Roelants, Josiane 03275
Abrahams, Katy 34244
Abrahams-Willis, Gabeba 34210
Abrahamson, Dana 43648
Abram, Ruth J. 45827
Abramek, Bogusław 32154
Abramović-Miletić, Ljiljana 33810
Abrams, Catherine 47043
Abrams, Linda C. 44876
Abrão, Flávio Jorge 04026
Abravanel, Claude 22654
Abrell, Dr. Herbert 01745
Abreu, Jorge M. de 32355
Abreu, Juana Ines 28143
Abreu Nunes, Dr. Maria Luisa 32297
Abric, Christian 11245
Abril, Joana Mari 35671
Abring, Hans-Dieter 16949
Absi, Nuha 27058
Absolon, Eric 40813
Abu Hadba, Abdul Aziz H. 31061
Abubakar, Ali Mohamed 27109
Abueg, Dr. Nelle F. 31424
Abungu, Lorna 49264
Aburai, Masakazu 26796
Acalija, Sanja 07714
Accardi, Dr. Giuseppina 23429
Acda, G.M.W. 29314, 29315
Acevedo Basurto, Sara 31222
Aceves Romero, David 28113
Achaah Ndumbi, Patrick 04953
Achatz, Erika 01892
Achenbach, Dr. Nora von 17560
Achenbach, Dr. Sigrid-Ute 16033

Achi, Y. 22669
Achtelig, Dr. M. 15563
Achuri, Julio César 07499, 07500
Ackerman, Andrew S. 45781
Ackerman, Mary Anne 43505
Ackermann, Dr. Marion 20090
Ackermann, Paul R. 48543
Ackerson, Rex D. 48029
Ackley, Clifford S. 41817
Ackroyd, Paul 39729
Acorn, Eleanor 06182
Acosta Guerrero, Elena 35240
Acosta Mohalem, José de Jesús 07542
Acton, David 48756
Adachi, Hogara 26324
Adachi, Takanori 27009
Ådahl, Dr. Karin 36259
Adair, Mary J. 44684
Adam, Thomas 16370
Adamczyk-Pogorzelska, Bożena 31784
Adami, Valerio 24343
Adamik, John 43746
Adamo, Giuseppe 24985
Adams, Anne 44126
Adams, Dr. Beverly 46477
Adams, Bill J. 47288
Adams, Celeste M. 43756
Adams, Cheryl 42799
Adams, Cindy 44578
Adams, David 39037
Adams, E. Charles 48082
Adams, Elizabeth 42597
Adams, Eloise 45589
Adams, F. 05220
Adams, G. Rollie 46946
Adams, Henry 42466
Adams, J. Marshall 44280
Adams, Jay 41391
Adams, Jean 38836
Adams, J.M. 38338
Adams, John D. 06722
Adams, Kate 41408
Adams, Kathy 46581
Adams, Kenneth 06095
Adams, Larry 41786
Adams, Lorraine Margaret 49033
Adams, Mazie M. 44611
Adams, Mel 46579
Adams, N.C. 38329
Adams, Roxana 45090
Adams, Stephen 37992
Adams, Steve 46761
Adams, Vivian 41623
Adams Muranaka, Dr. Therese 47296
Adamsom, Noel 01381
Adamson, Alberta 48585
Adamson, J. 39000, 39283
Adamson, Tony 37984
Adamsson, Anneli 35941
Adamyan, M.S. 00695
Adar, Yossi 22567
Addenbrooke, Rosie 38643
Adderley, D.E. 06713
Addison, K.A. 20789
Addoms, Andrew 44036
Adedayo, Oluremi F. 30352
Adediran, Nath Mayo 30349
Adelantar, Jonas O. 31448
Adelsberger, Paul 16891
Aderman, Ella 47501
Adesina, Bode 30342
Adey, Dr. Elizabeth 39845
Adiletta, Dawn C. 43939
Adisumarto, Dr. Soenartono 22120
Adkin, Tammy 05770
Adkins, Dean 47742
Adkins, Todd 45264
Adlbauer, Dr. Karl 01922
Adleman, Debra 45484
Adler, Helmut 02753
Adler, Peter 01293
Adler, Rosa 02261
Adler, Tracy L. 45816
Adlı, Nadir 37665
Adlung, Dr. Philipp 17529
Adolfsson, Stig 35926
Adolphs, Dr. Volker 16242
Adorno, Prof. Francesco 23876
Adriaens Pannier, Anne 03300
Adriaensens, Annemie 03180
Adriaensens, Werner 03337
Adrian, Dolab Jorge 00165
Adriani, Prof. Dr. Götz 17998, 20227
Adriansen, Inge 09074
Adrimi-Sismani, Vassiliki 21211
Adsenius, Mikael 36262
Adsett, Virginia 38544
Adunka, Roland 01666
Adžemlerski, Svetoslav 04789
Aebersold, Marianne 37374
Aebi, Richard E. 37162
Aescht, Dr. Erna 02228
Afzal, Dr. Muhammad 31026
Agarwal, R.C. 21862
Agee, Sheila 47647
Ageeva, Marina Vladimirovna 33227
Agenjo, Xavier 35430
Ager, Kathleen 39036
Agliati Ruggia, Dr. Mariangela 37041

Agnelli, Marella 25766
Agnelli Caracciolo, Marella 25947
Agner, Raul Dumas 31452
Agnesi, Prof. V. 24775
Agostini, Giuseppe 24836
Agostini, Dr. Grazia 23800
Ágota, Kasper 21617
Ágotnes, Dr. Anne 30419, 30421
Agrawal, Rajesh 21779
Agrech, F. 14634
Ågren, Gertie 35996
Agrenius, Helen 35977
Agresti, Giannicola 22888
Agten, Beate 19119
Agthe, Dr. Johanna 17047
Aguayo, José 42893
Agudo Cadarso, Christina 35616
Ague, Jay 45698
Aguero Moras, Alfonso 31135
Aguiar Branco, Dr. Fernando 32337
Aguilar Piedra, Raúl 07648
Aguillera, Kristin 45840
Aguiló, Anna 34443
Aguiló Ribas, Catalina 35221
Aguinaldo, Rosalinda 31337
Aguirre, Joel O. 27810
Brandão Aguirre, Maria Beatriz 04498
Aguirre, Pierre 11304
Agúndez García, José Antonio 35077
Agusti, Jorge 35346
Ahern, Maureen 44427
Ahlberg, Leif 36023
Ahlbrecht, Helmut 19926
Ahlefeldt Laurvig Bille, Michael 08966
Ahlers, Silvia 04201
Ahlfort, Barbro 35912
Ahlqvist, Ingemar 36165
Ahlstrand, J.T. 36064
Ahmad, Awang Haji Adam bin Haji 04597
Ahmad, Mushtaq 31035
Ahmad, Dr. Razi 21977
Ahmady, B. 22323
Ahmaogak, George N. 41195
Ahmas, Kristina 09684
Ahmed, Amrani 28716
Ahmedzade, T.Z. 03066
Ahola, Tuija 10189
Ahonon, Léonard 03872
Ahrendt, Dorothee 20468
Ahrens, Claus 19259
Ahrens, Elke 16087
Ahrens, Regi 44399
Ahrndt, Dr. Wiebke 16336
Åhsberger, Douglas 35881
Ahtela, Eero 09792
Ahtola-Moorhouse, Leena 09474
Ahumada Valencia, Jacob 06928
Aichelburg, Dr. Wladimir Graf 01681
Aicher, Ernst 18803
Aichner, Dr. Ernst 17905
Aida, Susumu 26623
Aidara, Abdoul Hadir 33784
d'Aigneaux, Jean 14548
Aigner, Carl 02603
Aigner, Ottilie 02179
Aiken, Dr. Edward A. 47909
Aikens, C. Melvin 43224
Ailonen, Riitta 09476, 09527, 09536, 09545
Aimé About, Assamoa 07669
Ainhirn, Karola 01691
Ainsley, Anne 38130
Airey, Laura 41114
Aistars, John 42144
Aitken, Catherine 36479
Aitken, Terry 48766
Aizpurua, Inaki 34414
Ajmetov, Ramis Kijamovič 32905
Ajzenberg, Prof. Dr. Elza 04514
Akabiamu, Martin 03489
Akam, Prof. Michael 38464
Akamati-Lilimbaki, Dr. Maria 21116
Akanbiemu, Martin Ogunayo 30347
Akasheh, Anahid 45839
Akbar, Prof. Dr. Omar 16584
Akbulut, Nazim 37755
Åkerman, Charlotte 35948, 35949
Akers, Charlene 47662
Akers, John 47975
Akers, Lloyd 46577
Akersten, Dr. William A. 46571
Åkesson, Bernt-A. 36185, 36187
Akgül, Nebi 37631
Akgün, Ünal 37730
Akgulian, Mark 47268
Akimova, G. 27070
Akın, Gülşen 37676
Akin, Joseph 47085
Akinpelu, David Ano 30347
Akins, Ken 42783
Akins, Louise 44238
Akins, Rebecca 45269
Akioka, Yasuji 26254
Akira, Nagoya 26813
Akiyama, Yoshi 45100
Akkaya, Mustafa 37693, 37697
Akker, C. 29815
Akmamedova, Maja 37820
Aknazarov, N.A. 27084
Akomolafe, Tunde 30356

Akpan, Aniefiok Udo 30355
Akramov, N. 48852
Aksajskij, Ivan Grigorjevič 33600
Aksënova, Alisa Ivanovna 33692
Aksoy, Sule 37710
Al-Arifi, Dr. Nassir S. 33771
Al-Bubu, Sana' 27066
Al-Diban, Martina 18976
Al-Esawi, Talaat 09290
Al-Farsi, Said Ali Said 31006
Al-Hameed, Hazim A. 22351
Al-Khalifa, Nayla 03078
Al-Maamari, Moussa 27486
Al-Qaisy, Rabie 22346
Al-Robaae, Dr. Khalaf 22349
Al-Saud, Abdullah S. 33773
Al-Shibli, Alae 22344
Al-Sid, Siddig M. Gasm 35769
Al-Wohaibi, Dr. Fahed 27306
Alam, Dr. Shamsul 03090, 03096, 03098, 03100
Alam, Syamsir 22169
Alan, David 48358
Aland, Prof. Dr. Barbara 18933
Alaniz, Gilbert 46903
Alaoui, Brahim 13577
Alarcão, Adília 32264
Alarcon, Anne 47781
Alarcón, Enrique 34555
Alarcón Lotero, José Félix 07555
Alarcón Osorio, Gonzalo 28111
Alario, Prof. Leonardo 23381
Alasalmi, Jikka 10211
Alaurin, Alice A. 31323
Alausy, Abdalla 27115
Alba, Dominique 13654
Alba Alvarez, Dionisio 35713
Albacete, M.J. 42089
Alban, Marc 12387
Albaneso, Virginia 42357
Albani, Lino 23620
Albarian, Kimberly 44547
Albee, Suzanne 48498
Albendea Solis, Juan Manuel 35473
Alber, Merike 09362
Alberdi, Juan B. 00659
Alberg, Dr. Werner 16743
Alberigi, Merry 47375
Alberrán, Fernando 28647
Albers, Birgit 01745
Albers, Edward S. 44517
Albers, Hannes 15881
Albers, Dr. M. 29362, 29363, 29835
Albers, Mary 06215
Albert, Dr. J.S. 43581
Albert, Karen T. 43987
Albert, Peggy 14293
Albert, Shea 34211
Albertelli, Prof. Giancarlo 24000, 24009
Alberti, Dr. Walter 24392
Albertin, Anne-Marie 11753
Albertini, L. 36472
Albertis, Serge de 13332
Alberto, Dr. Giordano 23947
Albertsson, Kristinn J. 21621
Albertus, Dana 18419
Albertus, Jürgen 18351
Alberty, Beth 41940
Albiol Sampietro, Vicente F. 35140
Albisetti, Guiseppe 36436
Alborino, Dr. V. 16783
Albrecht, Constanze 15932
Albrecht, Marvin 48579
Albrecht, Wolfgang 48768
Albrecht-Weinberger, Dr. Karl 02903, 02948
Albrechtsen, Bo 21242
Albright, Dr. L. Barry 43329
Albright, Liz 46164
Albright, Shirley 48057
Albright, Terrence 45987
Albufera, E. d' 13090
Alcock, Rodney 40846
Alcolea Blanch, Santiago 34545
Alcouffe, Daniel 13603
Aldama, Dulce 47973
Aldeguer Gordiola, Daniel 34444
Aldema, Yehuda Levy 22664
Alder, Barbara 36880
Alder, M. 39146
Alder, Ruedi 37270
Alderdice, Dr. David 01505
Alderfer, Joel D. 43912
Alderfer, Kenny 47044
Alderton, Michéle 06223
Aldhizer, H.T. 43442
Aldini, Tobia 23918
Aldrich, William M. 46042
Aldridge, Carolyn 40641
Aldridge, G.E. 38392
Aldunate del Solar, Carlos 06908
Alebo, Lena 36189
Alegria, Dr. Ricardo E. 32396
Alegría Manegat, María 34549
Aleksandrova, Marija 04934
Aleksandrova, Nataša 04793
Aleksandrovič, Natalja Jurjevna 32949
Aleksandrovna, Marija 34933, 04935
Alekseev, Nikolaj Makarovič 33361
Alekseev, Vladimir Petrovič 32706
Alekseeva, Aida Nikolaevna 32844

Alekseeva, Galina Ivanovna 32680
Aleksiuk, Galina A. 33709
Aleksoska-Baceva, Zaharinka 27591
Alemany, Uiso 35678
Alemany, Véronique 12766
Alencar, Vera de 04314, 04321
Alessio, Pado 25764
Alex, Erdmute 16582
Alex, Dr. Reinhard 16582
Alexander, Andrew 41823
Alexander, Beatrix 18150
Alexander, Brian 41229
Alexander, Darsie 41454
Alexander, Eric 43759
Alexander, G. 40884
Alexander, H.E. 39633
Alexander, Irene O. 42550, 42551
Alexander, Jane 01164, 40506
Alexander, Jean 48024
Alexander, Julia 45699
Alexander, Karen 39584
Alexander, Kimberly 47198
Alexander, Kristi 42507
Alexander, Margareta 42365
Alexander, Nancy 46831
Alexander, Prof. Richard D. 41220
Alexander, Robert 00964
Alexander, Ron J. 45440
Alexandre, Claude 12520
Alexie, Eric 46931
Alexis, Gerald 21292
Alfageme Sánchez, Vitaliano 35712
Alfaro, Ana 35601
Alfaro Castillo, Andrés José 07410
Alfter, Dr. Dieter 15713
Algar, Maria Angela 36508
Algeri, Dr. Giuliana 24289
Alhaainen, Kari M. 09637
Alho, Anna-Liisa 09533
Ali, H.-A. 22345
Ali, Mazhar 31060
Ali, Mohamed 37457
Ali, Samirah Mohd 27654
Ali, Sanaa 09234
Alicante, Apolinario 31400
Aliev, Kazi Magomet Ibragimovich 32736
Alig, Joyce L. 42165
Alilović, Ivica 33839
Alimonti, Keith 05654
Alin, Margareta 36059, 36060
Alisch, Joachim 16172
Aliyasak, Munasor 27626
Alkema, J. 28941
Allaire, Kay 45788
Allan, David 40243
Allan, John 38957
Allan, Laurie 41336
Allan, Randy 41674
Allan, Shona 40161
Allansson, Jón 21618
Allard, Bob 38108
Allard, Jeanine 47095
Allard, Sarah 38716
Allas, Anu 09358
Allason-Jones, L. 40040, 40041
Allderidge, Patricia 38141
Allegrini, Prof. Piero 24332
Allemand, Eolo 23015
Allemand, Evelyne-Dorothée 14961
Allemand, Jacqueline 14587
Allemanlus, Elizabeth 44582
Allemann, Martin 36972
Allen, Anne 41259
Allen, Armin 45931
Allen, Babara 47821
Allen, Brian 48634
Allen, Bruce 47613
Allen, Catherine 42524
Allen, Dale 42851
Allen, David 38000, 38001
Allen, Dick 48186
Allen, Graham 38214
Allen, Jeff 46304
Allen, Jill 39484
Allen, Kay 44899
Allen, Kim 05865
Allen, Louise 39080
Allen, Lucy 44285
Allen, Marilyn 41771
Allen, Nancy L. 46009
Allen, Richard 42758, 44138
Allen, Roger 41558
Allen, Susan 47450
Allen, Suzanne 40007
Allen, Timothy S. 48070
Allen, Trudy J. 43704
Allen, Virginia S. 41789
Allen, William M. 46924
Allen Fleming, Kathy 47072
Allender, Chris 40966
Allie, Stephen J. 43416
Alilkvee, Anu 09358
Allington, Peter 40394
Allione, Patricia 12132
Allison, C. 40869
Allison, David 30114
Allison, Glenn 06751
Allison, Jim 42300
Allison, N. 30203

Allison, Tammy 44874
Allison Rogers, Traude 49038
Allman, Mary 44828
Allman, William G. 48409
Alloisi, Dr. Sivigliano 25163
Allsop, Julie 40432
Allwood, Rosamond 39481
Alm, Björn 35921
Alm, Göran 36233
Almagro Gorbea, M.J. 35036, 35047
Almarri, Ali 37924
Almeda, Ermelo 31406
Almeev, Robert V. 48832
Almeida, Joel 32296
Almeida Campos, Diogenes de 04357
Almeida Dias, Manuel Mateus de 00098
Almeras 12560
Almirante, Julián 35601
Almosara, Emelita V. 31388
Almquist, Katarina 36171
Almquist, Kathleen 48145
Alms, Barbara 16570
Alonso, Alejandro G. 07990
Alonso, Alicia 34996
Alonso, Jésus 35700
Alòs Trepat, Carme 34523
Alowan, Zoe 46339
Alper, Mara 45596
Alper, Richard 48366
Alphons, Alois 02032
Alpözen, T. Oõuz 37637
Alram, Dr. Michael 02918
Alsaker, Sigmund 30808
Alsobrook, Dr. David E. 42525
Alsteens, S. 13487
Alston, David 38670
Alston, Joseph 43740
Alsvik, Elling 30943
Alswanis, Hope 47593
Altamont, Earl of 22557
Altay, Denizay 37798
Alteen, Glenn 06678
Alter, Klaus 20714
Alterio, Italo 07624
Althaus, Marceline 36989
Althoff, Bruno 20605
Althoff, Ralf 16751
Altmann, Ferdinand 02301
Altmann, Katja 19468
Altmeder, Prof. Susanne 02939
Altner, Renate 16104
Altstatt, Rosanne 19253
Alvarado Gonzalo, Manuel de 34641
Alvarez, Helena 36258
Alvarez, José Carlos 32310
Alvarez, Josefina 00543
Alvarez, Juan 43054
Alvarez, Sergio Antonio 00138
Alvarez, Walter 41646
Alvárez Arévalo, Miguel 21273
Alvárez Masso, Montserrat 34565
Alvárez Polo, Giesela 08041
Alvarez Rojas, Antonio 34647
Alvarez Valverde, Dr. José J. de 09118
Alves, C. Douglass 47665
Alves, Hélio Osvaldo 32277
Alves, Dr. Sónia 32328
Alves Costa, Catarina 32308
Alves de Sousa, Dr. Pio G. 32244
Alves Gomes, José António 04188
Alves Pinto, José F. 32277
Alvina, Corazon S. 31382
Alvina, Corazón S. 31390
Alvud, Laura 42389
Alymer, John 38303
Amack, Rex 45641
Amadei, Daniel 06084
Amann, Bernd 02042
Amann, Henry 11139
Amarel Gourgel, Dr. Anicete do 00096
Amaro das Neves, António 32277
Amash, Carissa 41629
Amat Amer, José Maria 34795
Amato, Ann 46643
Amato, Prof. Domenico 24459
Amato, Pietro 48872, 48878, 48884
Ambroise, Guillaume 13668
Ambrose, David 48310
Ambrose, Pamela E. 47137
Ambrose, Richard 42231
Ambrosetti, Dr. Giancarlo 25094
Ambrosino, Guy 47416
Ambrosio, Prof. Augusto C. 25002
Ambrosio, Piero 23176
Ambrosio, Thomas J. 45449
Amdreoli, Prof. Annararie 23959
Amelin, Olov 36268
Amelingmeier, Dr. Eckard 20698
Amell, Alexander 43026
Amemiya, Tadashi 26835
Amend, Brad 43107
Amend, Debbie 43107
Amendolagine, Dr. Beatrice 24335
Ament, Sharon 39733
Amer, Prof. Mordechai 22730
Ames, Gerhard 19724
Ames Sheret, Mary 45221
Ametrano, Dr. Silvia 00392
Amic, S. 13132

Amidon, Catherine 46566
Amidon, Eleanor 43901
Amies, Sandra 38143
Aminova, Svetlana Gašimovna 32997
Amir, H. 27738
Amir, Mohammad 22088
Amiranišvili, S.J. 15359
Amlow, Lothar 16115
Ammann, Christopher 36821
Ammann, Prof. Dr. Gert 02082, 02118
Ammann, Hugo 37429, 37431
Ammann, Katharina 37185
Ammann, Sandra 36479
Amnehäll, Jan 35922
Amo, Dr. Toshino 26825
Amo y de la Era, Mariano del 35214
Amon, Prof. Dr. Karl 01691
Amonson, John 44287
Amor, Kebbour 00071
Amoretti, Guido 25760
Amoriñ, Prof. Dr. José L. 00206
Amoroso, Dr. Domenico 23273
Amoroso, Richard L. 46182
Amory, Dita 45794
Amprímoz, François Xavier 12473
Amprímoz, M.F.X. 14926
Ampuero, Gonzalo 06898
Amrein, Dr. Heidi 37393
Amsallem, Christiane 14790
Amselgruber, Prof. Dr. 20116
Amsler, Cory 42985
Amstad, Hans 37401
An, Tran Huy 48985
Anand, Dr. Y.P. 21775
Anati, Prof. Emmanuel 23326
Anawalt, Patricia 44900
Ancheotti, Dr. Angelo 23788, 23795
Ančiporov, A.I. 33328
Anda, Tone 30375
Andami, Parisa 22314
Ander, Dr. Angelika 02955
Ander, Heike 18867
Andergassen, Dr. Leo 23211
Anderjack, George M. 47403
Anderl, Dick 48759
Anderle, Charlotte 02165
Anderle, Peter 02006
Anderlik, Heidemarie 15939
Anders, Brian 48817
Anders, Ines 17323, 17324
Anders, Win 06842
Andersen, Britta 08781
Andersen, Håkon 30939
Andersen, H.C. 08849
Andersen, Jeffrey W. 46133
Andersen, Jens 08854
Andersen, John 08834
Andersen, Kjell 30506
Andersen, Kurt 08976
Andersen, Lise 08852, 08853
Andersén, Peter 09855
Andersen, Randi 30652, 30653
Andersen, Thyge 08997
Andersen, Verginia 04245
Anderson, Annette 42490
Anderson, Ary 42833
Anderson, Betsy 44854
Anderson, Bonnie 47424
Anderson, Bruce 41839
Anderson, Carol 40925
Anderson, Christine 47642
Anderson, Claude 47563
Anderson, Claudia 47974
Anderson, Craig 42350
Anderson, D. 43753
Anderson, Dale W. 43946
Anderson, David 39795, 46125
Anderson, Donald B. 47013
Anderson, Douglas 41906
Anderson, Duane 44096, 47425
Anderson, Dr. Duane 47427
Anderson, Ellen 06575
Anderson, Eve 47999
Anderson, Fred 46889
Anderson, Garry 05287
Anderson, George 43446
Anderson, Hilary 44750
Anderson, J. 29947
Anderson, Jill 44648
Anderson, Joe 44695
Anderson, Judy 45136
Anderson, Kathi 44780
Anderson, Kathy 48464, 48521, 48522
Anderson, Kris 44608
Anderson, Lynn 47924
Anderson, Margaret 40706
Anderson, Mark 42648
Anderson, Maxwell 45886
Anderson, Michael 44243, 44244
Anderson, Peter 47551
Anderson, Ray 48016
Anderson, Richard R. 47660
Anderson, Rolf 48428
Anderson, Steve 46841
Anderson, Susan K. 41505
Anderson, Susan M. 41751
Anderson, Tracy D. 44096
Anderson, W.M. 47599

Anderson-Densmore, Mari C. 44533
Andersson, Beritne 09440
Andersson, Göran 35916
Andersson, Henrik 36256
Andersson, Karin 36147
Andersson, Lars 35990, 36022
Andersson, Solveig 35928
Andersson, Ulla 36194
Andersson Flygare, Irene 36361
Andersson Møller, Vibeke 08961
Andjelković Dmitrijević, Branislava 33812
Ando, Barbara 41644
Andorfer, Gregory Paul 41479
Andrade, Rosemary 35780
Andral, Jean-Louis 10372, 10377
Andrási, Gábor 21369, 21370
André, Frédéric 03640
André, Dr. Georges 03367
André, Mervyn 01020
André-Schellner, Prof. Brigitte 02939
Andreadaki-Vlasaki, Maria 20915, 21137
Andreasen, Vagn 08979
Andreassen, Dag 30754
Andreassi, Dr. Giuseppe 23020, 25305, 25672
Andreasson, Sven-Glov 35829
Andreeva, Antonina Borisovna 33681
Andrefsky, William 46744
Andrell, Pauline 30236
Andren, Martin 36060
Andres, Louis M. 44994
Andres, Morrie 42686
Andresen, Thomas Bjorkan 30856
Andreu, Dr. Jaime Sancho 35600
Andrew, K.J. 39993
Andrew, Marcia 48253
Andrews, Bernice 05192
Andrews, Janine 05392
Andrews, Kathy 41274
Andrews, Dr. Peter 38255
Andrews, Richard 47535
Andrews, Schuyler Gott 47118
Andrews, Shelly L. 41079
Andrews, Susan 43812
Andrews, Thomas F. 44925
Andrews Trechsel, Gail 41706
Andriamanantena, Ranaivoarivelo 27604
Andrian-Werburg, Dr. Irmtraud Freifrau von 19139
Andrich, Dr. Uwe 17403, 17404
Andries, Pool 03144
Andrieu, Esther 00477
Andrishak, Steve 05402
Andrušaite, Dzintra 27419
Anelli, Dr. Giuseppe 25563
Anene, Francis 30330
Angarita Jiménez, Edgar 07535
Angel de Marco, Dr. Miguel 00143
Angelett, Prof. Luciana Rita 25219
Angelinetti de Elizalde, Sara 00331
Angelo, Therese 30121
Angeloni, Araldo 25383, 25384
Angelov, Anastas 04648
Angelov, Emil 04896
Angelova, Ilka 04883
Anger, Maksymilian 31760
Anger, Virginia 06158
Angerbauer, Dr. W. 19211
Angerer, Ferdl 02649
Angerer, Prof. Dr. Dr. Joachim 01874
Angerer, Dr. Martin 19524, 19526, 19529, 19531
Angert, Rina 22703
Anglin Burgard, Timothy 47311, 47325
Angst, H. 15623
Anguiano Lozano, Juan Manuel 28174
Angus, Barbara J. 43117
Angus, E. 40709
Anh, Tran Hong 48988
Anibas, Martin 03059
Anić, Hanja 07779
D'Aniello, Dr. Antonia 25398
Anılır, Burhanettin 37636
Aniol, Roland 19793
Anisi, Ali Reza 22318
Aniz Montes, Mercè 34805
Anken, Thomas 36694
Ankert, Kerstin 35882
Ankudinova, Elena Andreevna 32849
Anlagan, Çetin 37706
Anna, Dr. Susanne 16742, 16743
Annear, Judy 01490
Annemans, Jan 03194
Annett, John 39806
Annette, Dr. Jutta 42636
Annibaldi, Dr. Cesare 25131, 25947
Annicchiarico, Silvana 24381
Annison, F. 30194
Anosovskaja, Alla Vasiljevna 32851
Anraku, Yoshio 26764
Ansel, Dr. Valerie 14830
Ansell, Erynne 44140
Anselm, Gudrun 36128
Anselm, Paul S. 46085
Ansett, Tony 01045
Anthenaise, Claude d' 13551
Anthes, Hedi 18733
Anthes, Prof. Helmut 18733
Anthoine, Robert 45774
Anthony, Ginger 48137
Anthony, James S. 06579
Anthony, Jo 39050

Anthony, Lenard 05716
Anthony, Vincent 41337
Antihi, Adriana
Antillano Armas, Sergio 48916
Antinori, Alessandra 25238
Antipas 21112
Antipenkov, Boris N. 33125
Antl, Prof. Gerhard 02696
Antognini, Marco 36899
Antoime, Janeen 47304
Antoine, Elisabeth 13637
Antoli Candela, Fernando 35678
Antonelli, Dr. Angelo 25076
Antonen, Rusty 44591
Antoniadou, Sofia 20901
Antonić, Dr. Dragomir 33794
Antonietti, Thomas 36826, 37173
Antonino, Dr. Biancastella 23105, 23138
Antoniuk, Aleksander 31486
Antonoglou, Manolis 21143
Antonov, Anton 04658
Antonov, Teodosi 04737, 04740
Antonova, Irina A. 33113
Antonova, Ljubov Vladimirovna 33676
Antonsen, Lasse B. 45991
Antti-Poika, Jaakko 09537
Anttila, Eila 09968
Anttila, R. 05019
Anttila, Ritva 09588
Antweiler, Dr. Wolfgang 17756
Anyaegbuna, Felicia Chinwe 30336
Anyanwu, Dr. Starling E.N. 30333
Anzai, Ikuro 26427
Anzola, Sonia 48916
Anzuoni, Robert 43371
Aoki, Shigeru 26464
Aoki, Yoshiharu 26507
Apalkov, Jurij Aleksandrovič 32698
Apap Bologna, Daniela 27706
Aparin, Dr. Boris F. 33385
Apelbaum, Laura C. 48366
Apetrei, Maria 32567
Apfel, Prof. Kurt 02852
Apking, Barbara 44520
Aponte, Dr. Nilda E. 32376
Aponte Galvis, Alonso 07609
Apostolou, Eva 20897
Apostolov, Šanko 04905
Apostolova, Anna 04622
Apostolova, Lili 04676
Apothéloz, Gustave 36777
Appel, G. 29580
Appel, H.H. 08953
Appel, Dr. Michaela 18916
Appelboom, Prof. Thiérry 03305
Appelhof, Ruth 43046
Appenzeller, Hans 19970
Appignanesi, Paolo 23565
Appleby, Roger 39609
Applegate, Matthew 40125
Appleton, Maggie 40583
Aprill, Gregg 42099
Aprison, Dr. Barry 42349
Apschnikat, Kenneth 44046
Apsega, Alejo 00495
Apsemetov, Azhibay 27082
Aquilera Cerni, Vicente 35678
Aquiloni, Laura 24552
Aquilué, Dr. Xavier 34800
Aquino, Amelia M. 31361
Arab, Mona 00070
Arai, Toshizo 26274
Arakčeev, Boris Serafimovič 33404, 33475
Aralica, Miodrag 33928
Aramaki, Teiichi 26422
Aramova, Lidija Grigorjevna 33747, 33748, 33749
Aranburu, Xabier 34603
Aranda-Alvarado, Rocio 44340
Arango, Jaime 07530
Arango Trujillo, Ignacio 07452
Aranjo, Dr. Augusto C. de 00097
Aranne, Heikki 09611
Araño, Susana 34434
Arapoyanni, Xeni 20837
Araújo, Emmanoel 04545
Araujo, Marcelo 04540
Araujo, Samuel M. 04320
Aravantinos, Dr. Vassilis 21175
Arbart, Kazimierz 31560
Arbelo de Mazzaro, Prof. Aurora Catalina 00321
Arbeteta, Letizia 35039
Årbu, Grte 30727
Arbuckle, John B. 44726
Arbucó, Susana Maria 00235
Arbulla, Dr. Deborah 25823
Arbury, Steve 46769
Arcand, Jessica 46506
Arcangel, Norberto 31364
Arcangel, Norberto S. 31365
Arcangeli, Lino 22953
Arce Torres, Susana 31182
Arces, Prof. Antonio 24061
Arch, Nigel 39759
Archabal, Nina M. 47162
Archambault, Alan H. 43422
Archangelskij, Venjamin 33223
Archer, James Ronald 30632
Archer, Kent 06398
Archer, Prof. Michael 01492

Archibald, Allene 46920
Archibald, Dr. Joanna 38545
Archibald, Dr. Robert R. 47128
Archimanaritis, Alexios 21069
Archontidou-Argyri, Aglaia 20921, 21079, 21083
Archuleta, Margaret 46476
Arco-Zinneberg, Ulrich Graf 02520
Arcos, Hermana Ana Rosa 07551
Arcuri, Arthur 04158
Ardid, Jordi 34535
Ardila, Marsha T. 42567
Arduini, Dr. Franca 23822
Arefyeva, G.V. 37906
Arell, Berndt 09486
Arena, Albert A. 48300
Arena, Dr. Maria Stella 25198
Arenas Abello, Rosaema 07416
Arenas i Sampera, Josep A. 34559
Arenas Morales, Lía Esther 07498
Arends, Dr. T. 29508
Arens, A. 17269
Arenz, Deb 43746
Arenz, Deborah 44787
Arestizáhal, Irma 00185
Arfelli, Guido Arch 25698
Argente Oliver, José Luís 34461, 35506
Argun, A.A. 15357
Argungu, Emir of 30331
Arhaldo, Liboni 24616
Ariano, Terry 47667
Arickx-George, M. 03646
Arih, Prof. Aleš 34141
Ariizumi, Haruhiro 26323
Arima, Shin-Ich 26459
Aris, Evangelinos 21091
Arisholm, Torstein 30752
Aristizábal Giraldo, Tulio 07458
Arizzoli-Clémentel, Pierre 15143, 15145
Arkadjevna, A.A. 33665
Arkio-Laine, Leena 09482, 09488, 09499, 09504, 09508, 09522, 09525, 09526, 09543, 09544, 09548
Arkley, J. 40365
Arko-Pijevac, Milvana 07764
Arman, Kivanç 37704
Armater, Raymond J. 46675, 46677
Armella Maza, Virginia 28154
Armenta Camacho, Juan 28342
Armin, Karlen 37247
Arminio, Roberta Y. 46212
Armirail, Sandrine 12568
Armiros, Konstantinos 42332
Armitage, Dr. Philip L. 38362
Armour, David A. 45029, 45030
Armour, Erica 43286
Armstrong, Alison C. 39327
Armstrong, Charlotte 45836
Armstrong, Elizabeth 45935
Armstrong, Fredrick 42232
Armstrong, James A. 42043
Armstrong, Jane C. 45028
Armstrong, Joan T. 45165
Armstrong, Lauraine 05452
Armstrong, Richard 46510
Armstrong, Steve 46982
Armstrong-Gillis, Kathy 47257, 47263
Armstrong Touchine, Maxine 42394
Arna, Angela 20053
Arna, Dr. Angela 20054
Arnaudo de Schanton, Veldis 00505
Arnaudova, Bojanka 04843
Arnault, Jean-Charles 11277
Arnăutu, Nicoleta 32437
Arndt, Gerda 16279
Arnemann, Heinrich 15673
Arneodo, Sergio 25422
Arnesson, Ingemar 36250
Arnesson, Kerstin 35880
Arnhold, Dr. Hermann 18950
Arning, Bill 42047
Arnhold, Dr. Charles D. 06870
Arnold, Beate C. 20681
Arnold, Dr. Charles D. 06870
Arnold, Clara von 36203
Arnold, Dorothea 45833
Arnold, Erich 36600
Arnold, Francis 44448
Arnold, Gotthard 19968
Arnold, J. 40012
Arnold, Karl Heinz 17066
Arnold, Dr. Ken 39792
Arnold, Lothar 18813
Arnold, Mary Bea 43724
Arnold, Peter S. 43031
Arnold, Prof. Rainer 20725
Arnold, Sarah 44691
Arnold, Susan 38042
Arnold, Dr. Sven 15987
Arnold, Ute U. 20750
Arnold-Biucchi, Carmen F. 45760
Arnolli, G. 29508
Arnon, Carmella 22682
Arnot, Sally 43231
Arnott, Alastair 40548, 40549
Arnoult, Hubert 13783
Arnoux, Louis 13056
Arnst, Caris-Beatrice 15908
Arobba, Daniele 23818
Arocha Rovira, José A. 08151
Aron, Dr. Alfred 01922

Aron, Kathy 44408
Aronowitz-Mercer, Richard 39577
Arons, Dr. Kärlis-Ēriks 27434
Aronson, Julie 42400
Arpin, Odette 10935
Arpin, Pierre 06712
Arpin, Roland 06202, 06204
Arraras, Maria Teresa 32402
Arrasmith, Anne 41710
Arrate-Hernandez, Danilo M. 08103
Arriaga, Brenda 42255
Arrieta, Katrin 19665
Arriola, Juan Carlos Juárez 34956
Arroues, Heidi 43903
Arroyo, Marta 35599
Arroyo Martín, Dr. José Víctor 34615
Arsenault, Linda 06164
Arseneau, Steve 42978
Arslan, Dr. Ermanno A. 24373, 24375
Arteaga, Agustín 00169, 28160
Artëmov, Evgenij 33405
Arterburn, Lesa 41555
Artero-Pamplona, Rafael 35177
Arthur, Catherine 41470
Arthur, Lloyd 05530
Articus, Dr. Rüdiger 17545
Artime, José 15357
Artman jr, Paul C. 43824
Artmann, Dr. 02163
Arts-Vehmeyer, M. 29961
Artykov, B.R. 48839
Aru, Krista 09374
Arunga Sumba, Owen 27105
Aruz, Joan 45833
Arvola, Silja 30595
Arzadeh, Kamal 22322
Arzur, Anna-Vari 13780
Asakura, Tetsuo 26364
Ašanin, Snezana 33827
Asano, Toru 26565
Asánsi Catalán, Maria Dolores 35061
Asbury, Michael J. 40200
Ascarelli Blayer Corcos, Dr. Anna 25222
Ascencio, Michaelle 48914
Aščeulova, Tatjana Stanislavovna 33235
Asch, Georges 13788
Aschauer, Manfred 02214, 02215
Asche, Dr. Susanne 18000, 19242
Aschengreen Piacenti, Dr. Kirsten 23881
Aschim, Jan 46960
Aschkenes, Anna M. 46501
Aschwanden, Stefan 37150, 37393
Aselmeier, Marianne 18615
Asensio Llamas, Susana 34845
Ash, Carol 43417
Ash, Nancy 46442
Ash Ezersky, Lorinda 45796
Ashaye, Ibironke P. 30344
Ashcroft, Robert 41605
Ashdjian, Peter H. 08191
Ashe, James S. 44685
Ashe, Janet 42466
Asher, Dave 30248
Asher, Dorothy J. 43167
Ashley, Brian 40104, 40112
Ashley, Catherine 42988
Ashley, James 44299
Ashley, Raymond E. 47290
Ashman, Stuart A. 47428
Ashooh Lazos, Marylou 45098
Ashraf, Dr. Mohammad 31058
Ashton, Alan 39859
Ashton, Joanne G. 45665
Ashton, Kate 01226
Ashton, L. 40424
Ashton, Lynn 44968
Ashton, Dr. S. 38454
Ashton, Vicki 46592
Ashworth, A. Lawrence 40763
Ashworth, Ben 38053
Ashworth, Jim 01108
Ashworth, Meg 40432
Ashworth, S. 39414
Ashworth, Sue 39332
Ašimbaeva, N. 33414
Аširov, Jagšimurad 37815
Askali, Nurhusih 31331
Askew, J. 38924
Aslani, Q. 22261
Asmaramah, Rasanubari 27638
Asmundsson, Johann 21645
Asmus, Cathy 47803
Asmuss, Dr. Burkhard 15939
Aso, Keiko 26969
Asolati, Dr. Michele 24736
Asomaddin, Abdugayyumi 37447
Asparuchov, Milko 04769
Asparužov, Dr. Milko 04772
Aspe, Virginia Armella de 28212
Aspen, Peder 38874
Aspenwall, Jim 45538
Aspes, Dr. Alessandra 25971
Asprov, Ognian 04721, 04759
Assaàd, Khaled 37441
Assadulina, Maja 37818
Assaf, Amnon 22696
Assel, Dr. Marina von 15852
Assmann, Dr. Peter 02228, 02234, 02241
Assoghba, Romain-Philippe 03878

Assouline, Hadassah 22628
Assunção, Dr. Ana Paula 32317, 32318
Ast, Hiltraud 01980
Astaa, Mikko 01943
Astachova, Irina Valerjevna 33706
Aster, Robert 45666
Astier, Michel 11944
Astika, Tjokorda Bagus 22213
Astini, Piero 24241
Astley Cooper, Patricia 39799
Astro, C. 13324
Åström, Kjell 36216
Åströmad, Kenneth 35872
Astrua, Dr. Paola 25735
Astrup, Yngve 30478
Astrup Bull, Knut 30939
Astui, Aingeru 34604
Asunción Mateo, María 35300
Asztalos, István 21307
Atac, Robert 47869
Atanasova, Neli 04752
Atanga, Peter S. 04952
Atasever, Gülümser 37786
Atasever, Yaşar 37748
Ateş, Sevim 37648
Athanasiadis, Tasos 20899
Athanasiadis, Yanni 00941
Athani, Shankar S. 21749
Athayde, Sylvia 04427
Athens, Joe 42394
Atherly, Mary 41171
Atherton, Lois 46564
Atiyeh, Walid 39683
Atkins, Michael 48133
Atkinson, Elmer F. 46415
Atkinson, J. 01506
Atkinson, Jennifer 41909
Atkinson, Jo 39729
Atkinson, Karen 44940
Atkinson, Lesley 40224
Atkinson, N.K. 38011
Atkinson, Scott 47293
Attack, Paul H. 05852
Attali, Zohara 22572
Atter, Kerri 42892
Attewell, Alex 39636
Attila, Dimény 32615
Attum, Elaine 43079
Attuquayefio, Dr. Dan K. 20801
Attwood, Maryon 48757
Atvur, Orhan 37781
Atwater, William F. 41047
Atwell, Cheryl 42810
Atwell, Michael 48532
Atwood, Carol Ann 43314
Atwood, John R. 45027
Atwood, Leland 42521
Atwood, Valdine C. 45027
Aubagnac, Gilles 11575
Aubele, Jayne 41107
Aubert, Ben 43104
Aubert, Glenda 05096
Aubert, L. 36745
Aubrecht, Dr. Gerhard 02228, 02228
Aubrun, Max 11255
Aubry, Françoise 03330
Aucella, Frank J. 48410
Auchterlonie, Fiona 38866
Audinet, Gérard 13548
Audisio, Aldo 25759
Audley, Paul 41890
Auel, Lisa B. 43582
Auer, Dr. Alfred 02079, 02918
Auer, Dr. Anita 20316
Auer, Helmut 01645
Auer, Wilfried 19806
Auerbach, Dr. Konrad 18275, 18276
Auffant, Luisa 09120
Auffret, M.J. 12409
Aufgebauer, Peter 16266
Augé, Jean-Louis 11084
Auger, Michele 44988
Augier, Jean-Pierre 12569
Augusti, Dr. Adriana 25918
Augustin, Josef 01716
Aujard-Catot, Eliane 10533
Aulan, Comte d' 10482
Aulich, C. 20528
Ault, Lee 38367
Aumüller, Prof. 18631
Aunela, Jorma A. 09953
Aupetitallot, Yves 11938, 36860
Auping, Michael 43489
Aurandt, David 06310
Aurél, Szakál 21460
Aurell, Pirkko 10195
Auserve, Philippe 13222, 13223
Ausfeld, Margaret Lynne 45467
Ausiàs, Vera 11692
Auska, Adolf 01899
Austad, Dan 47860
Austigard, Bjørn 30687
Austin, George 44673
Austin, Kelly 43069
Austin, Pat 44521
Austin, Ramona 43896
Austin, Rowe 47898
Auth, Dr. Susan 45892

Autio, Tuula 36352, 36361
Auvergnat, Dr. Arielle 14943
Auwärter, Konrad 20085
Auwera, Joost Vande 03299
Auxerre, Alain 11572
Auzet, Didier 10535
Avalos Valenzuela, Ana 06927
Avant, Joanne 47247
Avdeeva, M.V. 33236
Avdeeva, Taisija Dmitrievna 33561
Avendaño, Clarissa L. 31398
Averjanova, Élvira Valentinovna 32931, 33315
Averoff-Ioannou, Tatiana 20851, 21070
Avery, Dr. D.M. 34213
Avery, Dr. G.A. 34213
Avery, Joseph T. 45805
Avery, Kim 05539
Avery, Laura 47455
Avery, Louise 05700
Avery-Gray, Adrienne 39464
Avesani, Ricciarda 24734
Avest, H.P. ter 29345
Avić, Mirsad 03925
Avila Bardají, José R. 35015
Avila de Monroy, María 07511
Avila Martínez, Jairo Hernando 07513
Avrandt, David 06061
Avril, Ellen 44272
Avsom, Richard 43756
Awald, John C. 41933
Awouters, Maria 03317
Awouters, Mia 03337
Awwal, Dr. Iftikhar ul 03082, 03085
Ax, Goeran 36174
Ax, Michael 09057
Ayalon, E. 22766
Ayalon, Dr. E. 22767
Aydin, M. Sezai 37638
Ayerbe, Santiago 07564
Ayers, Betty 05212
Ayers, Marilyn L. 41620
Ayerve, José M. 09147
Aykaş, Satı 37645
Aylesbury, Pat 01300
Ayling, Emma 40879
Aymon, Marie-F. 36923
Ayob, Dato Muslim 27652
Ayrault, Jacqueline 10320, 10321
Ayres, Dr. Anne 44936
Ayres, William 47830
Ayscue, Gene 48657
Aytar, Sefer 37805
Aytuğ, Şükriye 37621
Ayvaz, Melahat 37792
Azarcon, Romualdo A. 31409
Azarmehr, G. 22246
Azeim Mahmoud, Dr. Rifa'at Abdel 09274
Azevedo Abreu, Arienei 04285
Azevedo de Silva, Dr. Nearch 04352
Azimi, Esmail 22316
Aziz, Kapt Nazri 27652
Azizbekova, P.A. 03067
Aznar, Henry 00106
Aznar-Alfonso, Dr. Lydia 31317
Azuar, R. 34446
Azuma, Hisao 27012
Azzarelli, Vincent 44105
Baad Pedersen, Margit 08855
Baagøe, Jette 08899
Baakabe, Ali Salim 27105
Baalbergen, W. 29645
Baartman, H. 34246
Baartvedt, Randi 30958
Baas, F.K. 17893
Baatz, Henning 15439
Babajceva, Nadežda Borisovna 33591
Babanazarova, Marinika 48846
Babb, Ellen 44654
Babboni, Dr. Marina 23357
Babcock, Catherine 44642
Babcock, Sidney H. 45863
Babel, Jerzy 31742
Babelon, Jean-Pierre 11756
Baber, Charlotte 40546
Babić, Nikola 03914
Babic, Sherry 42263
Babin, Anikca 07714
Babini, Tino 25302
Babre, Dace 27409
Babu, Omari 27113
Bacallado Aránega, Juan José 35414
Bacalles, Lorraine 45771
Baccetti, Dr. Nicola 24725
Baccheschi, Dr. Edi 23994
Bacchetta, Véronique 36732
Baccini, Dr. Stefano 24489
Baccolo, Maria Grazia 23433
Baccrabere, G. 14939
Bačeva, Irina 04833
Bach, Beverly 46243
Bach, Dana 19273
Bach, Kim 43553
Bach-Nielsen, Hanne 09068
Bach Østergaard, Bjarne 08950
Bachčevanov, Ivan 04863
Bachelder, Laura 46964
Bacher, Fabian 15457
Bachler-Rix, Margit 02619
Bachman, Dona R. 42102

Bachmann, Alois 36835
Bachmann, Gaby 36475
Bachmann-Tonelli, Karen 06474
Bachmisov, Éduard Konstantinovič 32719, 32720
Bachniakon, Vaso 00034
Bachorz, Hanna 32195
Bachvarov, Ivan 04812, 04816
Bacigalupi, Dr. Don 47293
Bacin, Mark S. 46245
Bâciu, Dr. Florea 32503
Back, Lane 48082
Backer, Julie P. 42454
Backer, Kathleen L. 48324
Backhaus, Dr. 20444
Backhaus, Fritz 17057, 17069
Backhouse, Andrew 40640
Backhurst, Timothy D. 45526
Backlund, Connie 43335
Backström, Ragnar 09701
Bacon, Caroline 38147
Bacon, Weldon 05334
Bacourou, Emilia 21082
Bacquet, Emmanuel 13207
Bačvarov, Ivan 04675, 04815
Bączyk, Jarosław 31900
Badaró Nadal, Enrique 40988
Badas, Ubaldo 26020
Badder, Susan 48341
Badders, Hurley E. 46337
Bade, Mary 44484
Badel, Doris 18105
Badenhorst, S. 34359
Bader, Joerg 36731
Badgley, Carole 06028
Badham, Mark 05683
Badoúin, Gerhard 19504
Badovinac, Zdenka 34108, 34112
Badre, Dr. Leila 27481
Badura-Triska, Dr. Eva 02949
Bächle, Anke 20106
Bäcker, Erich 16636
Bähr, Gustav-Adolf 19079
Baehr, Dr. M. 18926
Baehrend, John 42293
Baeke, Jan 28852
Bækkelund, Björn 30478
Baele, A. 03857
Baena Alcántara, María Dolores 34737
Baensch, Joachim 17350
Baensch, Norbert 17333
Baepler, Dr. Donald H. 44674
Bär, Dr. Frank P. 19139
Baer, Jan Hodges 43996
Baer, Dr. Rudolf 36467
Bärnighausen, Hendrik 18800
Baerwaldt, Wayne 06601
Baeten, Herman 03685
Baets, A. de 03623
Báez Plaza, Anastasio 34594
Baggenstos, Thomas 37303
Bagheri-Zenouz, Dr. E. 22249
Bagle, Eyvind 30754
Bagnell, Warren 05783
Bagnoli, Dr. Alessandro 25578
Bahadar Khan, Mohammad 31018
Baharin Bin Buyong, Dr. Kamarul 27647, 27677, 27689
Bahe, Michelle 41393
Bahena García, Jaime Arturo 28142
Bahm, Linda 41111
Bahn, Erich 03024
Bahn, Dr. Peter 16357
Bahnmaier, Paul M. 44707
Bahrami, M. 22321
Baier, Berthold 17858
Baier, Patrick 16364
Baik, Jo Gang 27126
Bail, Anne le 15332
Bailey, Ann S. 45903
Bailey, Billie K. 48431, 48432, 48433, 48434
Bailey, Chris H. 41900
Bailey, Colin B. 45802
Bailey, Courtney 46771
Bailey, David 43748
Bailey, Elizabeth 42097
Bailey, Erin 41346
Bailey, Fiona 39489
Bailey, Jack C. 47773
Bailey, Jann L.M. 05638
Bailey, Margaret 45984
Bailey, Michael 38051, 43852
Bailey, Patricia 05122
Bailey, Patricia E. 43770
Bailey, Prof. Reeve M. 41220
Bailey, Robert 40045
Bailey, Stephen F. 46253
Bailey, Steve 38109
Bailleux-Delbecq, Martine 11677
Bailly-Maitre, Marie-Christine 12309
Bain, Heather 44977
Bainbridge, Carol 45954
Bainbridge, David S. 47679, 47680, 47683
Baird, James 46381
Bairlein, Prof. Dr. Franz 20593
Baitchiba-Afalna, Kloumtouin 06885
Baiza, Lee 47000
Baj, Janina 31665
Bajac, Quentin 13596
Bajada, John 27711

Bajanik, Dr. Stanislav 33968
Bajcurová, Dr. Katarína 33978
Bajević, Maja 03924
Bajic, Svetlana 03925
Bajko, Daria 45884
Bajpayee, Aparna 21719
Bajuk, Laura 44954, 44955
Bak, Aase 08763
Bak, Anna 31968
Bak, Jolán 21415
Bak, Dr. S.M. 29508
Bakajutova, Ljudmila M. 33386
Bakal, Jeniffer 45809
Bakalarz, Krystyna 31829
Bakalov, Michail 04862
Bakárdžieva, Cenka 04709
Bakárdžijev, Dimităr 04689
Bakarić, Lidija 07809
Bakay, Prof. Dr. Kornél 21466
Bakels, Dr. P. 29006
Baker, Alex 46439
Baker, Dr. Allan 06607
Baker, Alyson 44873
Baker, Amanda 01238
Baker, Barbara J. 41124
Baker, Billy P. 43684
Baker, Charlotte 41153
Baker, Chris 38700
Baker, Christopher 38898
Baker, Diane 01542
Baker, Gary E. 45963
Baker, James 46386, 47184, 47185, 48061
Baker, James W. 46562
Baker, Janet 40934
Baker, Dr. Janet 46477
Baker, Janet 47399
Baker, Jeanne 48490
Baker, John 40029, 40596, 40598
Baker, Joyce 46765
Baker, Kathryn 40381
Baker, Kendall 42030
Baker, Larry L. 41735
Baker, Peggy M. 46561
Baker, Rachel 42339
Baker, Dr. Robert 44991
Baker, Scott 48362
Baker, Sue 42696
Baker, Susan K. 48460
Baker, Warren L. 41124
Baker Driscoll, Dr. Jeanne 48333
Bakić, Ljiljana 33928
Bakker, C. 29446
Bakker, F. 29115
Bakker, G. 28844
Bakker, Henriette den 29120
Bakker, Dr. Lothar 15566
Bakker, W. 28971
Bakkevig, Sverre 30877
Bakouti, Moncef 37581
Bakr, Nemat 09232
Bakreeva, Ljubov Anatoljevna 33014
Bákula Budge, Cecilia 31201
Bal, Danielle 11942
Balabanov, Dimitar 04808
Balagtas, Alex 31362
Balagtas, Alex L. 31360
Balakina, Natalja Michajlovna 33449
Balan, Sandrine 13055
Balandraud, O. 12738
Balanza, Ferran 35094, 35095
Balao, Angel 35058
Balard, Prof. Michel 14840
Balas, Shawna 06836
Balaštiková, Eva 08643
Balatti, Ambrogio 23536
Balawejder, Edward 31796
Balázs, Dr. György 21367
Balbaugh, Joe 44382
Balciunas, Vytautas 27539
Bald, H. 18499
Baldaia, Peter J. 44174
Baldarrago Umpire, Prof. Miguel 31113
Baldellou, Vicente 34907
Baldemair, Vinzenz 02283
Balden, Friedesine 17413
Baldeón, Dr. Amelia 35698
Balderi, Felice 24228
Balderstone, Michael 01322
Baldeschi, Nino 25856
Baldewijns, Jeannine 03434
Baldini, Marino 07755
Baldit, Alain 13912
Baldoni, Lorenzo 24453
Baldwin, Deirdre 43648
Baldwin, Jane 41462
Baldwin, Susan 42331
Baldwin Rehbein, Valerie B. 46851
Balen, Dubravka 07809
Balen, Jacqueline 07809
Balestra, Nino 25274
Baley, Susan G. 45974
Balfet, Hélène 11725
Balic, Haris 02963
Balie, Dr. Isaac 34243
Baligand, Françoise 11560
Bálint, Magdolna 21386
Balist, Valerie 44143
Balistrieri, Bruce 46311
Balk, Dr. Claudia 18841

Balkanska, Veneta 04736
Ball, Baldev 47427
Ball, Dr. Daniela 36870, 37157
Ball, Elizabeth 05216
Ball, Glenys 01571
Ball, JoAnn 46538
Ball, Rex 47253
Ball, Sabine 17650
Balla, Wesley 41083
Ballak, Theo 19860
Ballantine, Dr. David 32376
Ballantine, Thomas 05543
Ballantyne, Dorothy 44042
Ballantyne, Weyman 30244
Ballard, Margot 46935
Ballard, Mark 45920
Ballbé, Xavier 34657
Ballerini, Rosangela 24228
Ballesta, J. 35655
Ballesta Gómiz, Pedro 35146
Ballesteros, Prof. Miguel 00530
Balletto, Prof. Emilio 25752
Ballinger, James K. 46477
Ballinger, J.C. 45164
Ballot, Prof. Dr. G.M. 34338
Ballweber, John 42119
Balmer, John 48772
Balogh, Mihály 21374
Balsama, Joseph 47899
Balsamo, Prof. Renato 23660
Balta, Zdravko 03932
Baltasar Coll Tomas, M.I.S.D. 35230
Baltensperger, Marianne 37205, 37206, 37207
Baltes, Peter 16521
Baltz, Gerald W. 47123
Balza, Raimundas 27524, 27525, 27527, 27531, 27532, 27540
Balzekas, R. 42307
Balzekas, Robert 42307
Balzekas, Stanley 42307
Bamala, Louis 07642
Bambara, Parfait Z. 04942
Bamberger, Gerald 16150
Bambery, Anneke 38716
Bamert, Markus 37152
Bamesa, Prof. Tshungu 07638
Bamforth, Janice 41612
Ban, Gheorghe 32592
Bana, Giovanni 22938
Banach, Wiesław 31967
Banach, Witold 31865
Banai, Merav 22609
Bańbura, Prof. Dr. Jerzy 31775
Banchieri, Daria 25895
Bancroft, William 42602
Bandaranaike, Sunethra 35746
Bandeira, Dr. Dione da Rocha 04150
Bandes, Dr. Susan J. 43053
Bandrowski, Margaret 47755
Bandt, J. 01268
Bandurraga, Peter L. 46834
Bandy, Mary Lea 44869
Bandyopadhyay, Dr. Banya 21699, 22055
Banfi, Enrico 24387
Banfield, Audray M. 00728
Bang, Mogens 08856
Bang Andersen, Sveinung 30877
Bang Larsen, Bent 09051
Bangcas, Salamon L. 31326
Bangcaya, Regino Z. 31436
Bange, Maja 30740
Banghard, Karl 19231
Banholzer, Dr. Max 37181
Banière, François 10304
Banker, Amy 42880
Banker, Maureen 46780
Bankert, John 42091
Bankes, Dr. G. 39894
Bánki, Esther 29562
Banks, Jaqueline 38720
Banks, R. 01097
Banks, Robert 48031
Bannicke, Elke 16044
Bannister, Jenny 01046
Bannister, R. 38260
Bannon, Anthony 46941
Banova, V. 04926
Banova, Vera 04925
Banović, Miroslav 33853
Bantivoglio, Barbar 45886
Bantle, Tom 43759
Banu Syed, Rehana 28788
Banz, Richard 48795, 48796
Banzato, Dr. Davide 22942, 24731, 24733, 24750
Baptista, Dr. Teresa 32265
Baptista Pereira, Fernando António 32346
Baquero, Dr. Angeles Ramos 31087
Baquero Velásquez, Ramón 07433
Bar-Gera, Dov 22573
Bar-Gera, Kenda 22573
Bar-Or, Galia 22589
Bar Semech, Vered 22584
Bar-Yosef, Dr. O. 22649
Barabaş, Dr. Neculai 32432
Barahona, Rolando 07655
Baral, Jody 44916
Barale, Joseph 11924
Baran, Iwona 32037
Barañano, Kosme de 35599

Barandun, Plasch 37284
Barangulova, Farida F. 33644
Baranova, M.N. 33496
Baranowska, Janina 39748
Baranowski, Dr. Jerzy 31823
Bárány, Anders 36268
Barattuci, Maurizio 47441
Barbagallo, Dr. Alfredo I. 00215
Barbalić, Željko 07763
Barbanera, Prof. Marcello 25199
Barbara, Sibille 13372, 13374
Barbeau, Bruce 06598
Barber, Dan 45554
Barber, Jacquey 41644
Barber, John 01628
Barber, R.G. 40448
Barberet-Girardin, E. 15048
Barberini, Maria Giulia 25233
Barbier, Jean 32422, 32423
Barbier, Jean-Paul 36742
Barbier, Nicole 11769
Barbier-Ludwig, Georges 11431
Barbier-Mueller, Monique 36742
Barbieri, Frances T. 47567
Barbieux, José 14959
Barbina, Prof. Alfredo 25151
Barbizet, Laure 13594
Barbosa, Artemio 31341
Barbosa Godefroid, Leonardo 04239
Barbour, Mark 42115
Barbour Strickland, C. 43825
Barbry jr, Earl J. 45167
Barbu, Cristian 32470
Barcel, Ellen 47711
Barcellos, Lauro 04408
Barcik, Jan 31691
Barclay, Craig 39379
Barclay, Don 42951
Barcus, Leisha 42906
Bardeau, Andreas Graf 01826
Bardelli, Alvaro 22923
Bardiaux, David 14781
Bardiová, Dr. Mariana 33947
Bareinz, Reinhard 16442
Barendsen, J.E. 29352
Barens, H. 46101
Barents, Els 28861
Barés, Athos 00537
Baretow, Steven G. 45253
Barger, Judith M. 44604
Barghini, Sandra 46264
Bargholz, Christina 17555
Bargiel, Réjane 13563
Barillas, Nuria E. de 31081, 31088
Barilleaux, Rene Paul 44280
Barina, Miloslav 08501
Barisch, G. 16153
Barisch, M. 16153
Barišić, Josip 07791
Barison, Mara 22997
Baritault du Carpia, M. de 12908, 12909
Barjou, François 12562
Barkefeld, Anna 19998
Barkemeyer, Dr. Werner 17013
Barker, Alex 42752
Barker, Amy 38087
Barker, Betty 46785
Barker, Deborah 46220
Barker, G. 01501
Barker, G. Carl 45467
Barker, Garry 45494
Barker, Lisa M. 45577
Barker, Marie 47563
Barker, Dr. Nicolas 38652
Barker, Ray 40959
Barker, Rod 43015
Barker, Stuart 38382
Barker, Wendy 43209
Barker, William 45941
Barketov, Vladimir Aleksandrović 33510
Barkhofen, Dr. Eva-Maria 15919
Barkley, Terry 41895
Barkoun, Gennady 03113
Barksdale, Daryl 45146
Barlek, Josip 07813
Barlow, Keith 40079
Barlow, Martin 39542
Barlow, Victoria 39647, 40803
Barmore, Jim 42118
Barndollar, Lue 42512
Barnea, Dr. Jackob 02305
Barnes, Althemese 47937
Barnes, James H. 43442
Barnes, Judy 45220
Barnes, Lolly 41694
Barnes, Lucinda 41649, 41771
Barnes, Marion 40956
Barnes, Ralp 47996
Barnes, Richard 44148
Barnes, William 40304
Barnet, Peter 45784, 45833
Barnett, Eric B. 43098
Barnett, George 39467
Barnett, James F. 45632
Barnett, James K. 41198
Barnett, Jim 48415
Barnett, June 47596
Barnett, Lawrence 48256
Barnett, Norman 47596

Barney, Edres 46488
Barnhart, Audrey 48639
Barnhill, Michael 41567
Barnhill, Pam 45585
Barnosky, Anthony 41646
Barnum, Lorie 46947
Barnwell, Andrea D. 41360
Barocelli, Prof. Francesco 24812
Baroff, Deborah 44695
Baroies-Fronty, Isabelle 12958
Baron, David 06243
Baron, Donna 48575
Baron, Dr. Jacques 13215
Baron, Richard 43112
Baron, Robert 42200
Baroni, Fabio 23376
Baroni, Laura 23723
Baronne, Geriool 45733
Barons, Richard I. 47708
Barr, Cheryl B. 41642
Barr, Edward 48034
Barr, Mike 38581
Barr, Norma 05324
Barr, Dr. Peter J. 41066
Barr, Tom 43425
Barr, Warren N. 46050
Barracane, Gaetano 23025
Barrachina, Jaime 35266
Barraclough, Bruc 45801
Barral Iglesias, Alejandro 35443
Barrand, Janine 01228, 01239
Barrera Bassols, Marco 28131
Barrett, Candace 44896
Barrett, Maurine 47728
Barrett, Michael 00733
Barrett, Wendy 47222
Barrett-Lennard, Amy 01435
Barrie, Brooke 43878
Barrientos, J. Oscar 21272
Barringer, George Martin 48358
Barrington, Robin 05832
Barro, Aminata 07671
Barron, G.D. 30155
Barron, Stephanie 44921
Barroso Panatieri, Angélica 04268
Barrow, Ira E. 06608
Barrowclough, Dr. George F. 45759
Barry, Alexis 47892
Barry Byrne, Brenda 05415
Barryte, Bernard 47772
Barsalou, Victoria 06102
Barsch, Dr. Barbara 16005
Barsch, Wolfgang 20757
Barson, Jerry 47416
Barsotti, Gianfranco 24194
Barstow, Norman 43862
Barsuglia, Dr. Bruno 24228
Barszcz, Janusz 32071
Barszczewska, Krystyna 32199
Bart, Barbara M. 44170
Barta, Andy 48639
Barta-Fliedl, Dr. Ilsebill 02904, 02906
Bartel, Janet 47280
Bartels, Dr. Christoph 16193
Bartels, Wolfgang 17594
Bartenev, Aleksandr Igorevič 33431
Barter, Judith A. 42304
Barth, Dr. Angelika 20164
Barth, Frank 17541
Bárth, Dr. János 21446, 21447, 21448, 21451
Barth, Linda J. 44947
Barth, Luiz Fernando 04273
Barth, Dr. Robert 37168
Barth, Dr. Robert L. 46650
Barthel, Günter 18196
Barthel, J. 18965
Barthelmess, Dr. Stephan N. 17790
Bartholow, Cheryl 41940
Bartik, Dr. Juraj 33958
Bartków-Domagala, Jadwiga 32183
Bartkowski, Gregor 16372
Bartl, Anna 36500
Bartl, Johanna 16577
Bartlett, Prof. Christopher 48047
Bartlett, Margaret 00922
Bartlett, R.W. 39163
Bartley, James A. 48691
Bartlinski, Jim 41481
Bartmuß, Prof. Dr. Hans-Joachim 17130
Bartolf, M. 06091
Bartolini Bussi, Prof. Maria Giuseppina 24433
Bartolomé Arraiza, Alberto 35044
Barton, Anita S. 45142
Barton, C. Michael 47973
Barton, Fayette Belle 45039
Barton, William R. 46277
Barton Billman, Hilary 44431
Barton Brown, Ann 48516
Barton Campbell, J.A. 46883
Barton Thurber, T. 43907
Bartoś, Magdalena 31811
Bartos, Paul I. 43714
Bartoš, Václav 08630
Bartosz, Adam 32043
Bartosz, Anna 32042
Bartram, Rita 43564
Bartsch, Monika 18880
Bartuš, Marta 31490
Bartz, Rolf-Peter 20403

Barufke, Regina 15698
Barwick, Kent 45837
Barzakova, Maria 04637
Barzen, Jeb 41501
Bas, Michael le 38255
Basamakov, Christo 04604
Basamakov, Ilko 04782
Basanieri, Giovanni 23664
Basante, Enar 07547
Basart 04516
Basbous, Alfred 27493
Bascom, Mansfield 45087
Başer, İsmail 37769, 37770
Basile, Kenneth A. 47217, 47218
Basir, Abdul 22223
Baškirova, Marija Michajlovna 32786
Bašnjak, Jurij Michajlovič 32686
Bass, Anneta Jakovlevna 33377
Bass, Carol 48710
Bass, Clayton 46087
Bass, Jacquelynn 41641
Basseches, Joshua 42041
Bassegoda Nonell, Juan 34551
Bassett, Christa 42104
Bassett, Fannie 42295
Bassett, Dr. M.G. 38481
Bassi, George 44679
Bassi, Dr. Roberto 25932
Bassi, Rosemarie 19559
Bassin, Aleksander 34110
Bassinger, Marilyn 46093
Basso, Dr. Laura 24389
Bassús, María M. 00166
Bast, Douglas G. 41788
Bastard, Laurent 14971, 14972
Basterretxea-Moreno, Dr. Amaia 34611
Bastia, France 03293
Bastidas, Hugo Xavier 44339
Basu Ray Chaudhuri, S. 21968
Bata, Philippe 13787
Bata, Sonja 06562
Bataillard, Marianne 36670
Batchelor, Elisabeth 44404
Batchelor, Trevor 06094
Bateman, Jill 41322
Bateman, Dr. Richard 39733
Bateman, Suellen 43741
Bater, John 43508
Bates, Charles 44772
Bates, Craig D. 48804
Bates, F. 40509
Bates, Geoffrey 44841
Bates, Michael L. 45760
Bates, Sandy 46352
Bates, Tom 45348
Bateva, Mimi 04726
Bath, Marquess of 40787
Bathe, I. 06059
Batista, Alvaro 32229
Batkin, Jonathan 47434
Batkin, Norton 41224
Batori, Dr. Armicla 25204
Batova, Anna Nikolaevna 33294
Battaglini, Dr. Giuseppe 25022
Battcher, Reinhard 41904
Battel, Angelo 25418
Batten, Andrew C. 45801, 46249
Batterson, Loren 44807
Battinou, Zanet 20861
Battins, Niccholas 45864
Battle, Dr. Thomas C. 48363
Batty, Tim 38747
Baty, Catherine 48563
Bauch, Herbert 18323
Bauch, Hermann 02634
Bauche, Dean 06012
Bauchhenß, Dr. Gerhard 16246
Baucum-Fields, Penny 46257
Baud, Arlette 36477
Baud, Georges 12036
Bauder, Charles C. W. 43642
Baudet, Jean-Charles 15057
Baudet, Jean-Michel 13749
Baudisson, C. 12260
Bauduin, Jean-Loup 12247, 12248, 12252
Bauer, Arthur 02879
Bauer, Christoph 19967
Bauer, Douglas F. 43352
Bauer, Franz 02523
Bauer, Fritz 20782
Bauer, Georg 02940
Bauer, Gudrun 17707
Bauer, Hans 16124
Bauer, Heidrun 20134, 20135
Bauer, Dr. Helmut 18880
Bauer, Herbert 15466
Bauer, Prof. Dr. Ingolf 18833, 19190
Bauer, Lloyd 47625
Bauer, Dr. Markus 17325
Bauer, Peter 18480
Bauer, Richard 47975
Bauer, Sigrud 16124
Bauer, Dr. Snejanka D. 17056
Bauer, Stéphane 16030
Bauer, Susan 05845
Bauermeister, Janneke 18946
Bauernfeind, Günther 19040
Baulard, Hervé 11173
Baule, John A. 48774

Baum, Bruce 41832
Baum, Prof. Dr. E. 20637
Baum, Jo Ann 41789
Baum, Kristina 20389
Baum, Prof. Peter 02235
Baum, Rainer 36500
Baum, Wolfgang 19944
Bauman, Victor-Henrich 32619
Bauman Taylor, Paula 43503
Baumane, Inta 27369
Baumann, Anton 02403
Baumann, Daniel 36544
Baumann, Evelies 16499
Baumann, Dr. Kirsten 16584
Baumann, Klaus 17386
Baumann, Leonie 16074
Baumann, Dr. Maria 19518, 19519
Baumann-Eisenack, Dr. Barbara 20125
Baumann-Huber, Margrit 37330
Baumbach, Susan M. 40212
Baumberger, Moritz 36998
Baume, Nicholas 43944
Baumeier, Prof. Dr. Stefan 16590
Baumeister, Dr. Annette 16743
Baumeister, Dr. Ralf 15621
Baumgärtel, Dr. Bettina 16738
Baumgärtner, I. 19488
Baumgärtner, Iris 19490
Baumgardner, George 42118
Baumgardt, Manfred 16094
Baumgarten, Detlef 16293
Baumgarten, Dr. K. 15711
Baumgarten, Ute 17846
Baumgartner, Josef 01796
Baumgartner, Dr. Jutta 01930
Baumgartner, Dr. Michael 36544
Baumgartner, Dr. Sieglinde 02512
Baumgartner, Walter 02945
Baumstark, Prof. Dr. Reinhold 18824, 18832, 18889, 18904, 18917
Baur, Andreas 16967, 16971
Baur, Karl 37121
Bausart, Lucie 03166
Bause, George S. 46292
Bausier, Karine 03187
Bauske, Clay R. 44202
Baussan, Magali 15077
Baußmann, Dr. Edda 18946
Bavnshøj, Peter 08780
Bavoni, Dr. Umberto 26051
Bawden, Dr. Garth L. 41104
Bawinkel, Betty 43550
Bawinkel, Russel 43550
Baxter, Alan 38419
Baxter, Clare 37985, 37986
Baxter, Connie 06262
Baxter, Ellen 46510
Bayard, Jean 04956
Bayard, Pierre 04957
Bayarri, Carlos 35370
Bayden, Ian 48286
Bayer-Niemeier, Dr. Eva 18260
Bayet 03795
Bayles, Jennifer 41981
Baylis, Lisa 46934
Baylis, Timothy 40881
Bayliss, Joan 38083
Bayliss, Keith 40660
Bayliss, Dr. Paul 34266
Baymuradov, N. 37450
Bayona, Wilhelm A. 31462
Bayou, Charlie 13919
Bayram, Metin 37688
Baysal, H. Hüseyin 37658
Bayuelo Castellar, Soraya 07472
Bazanov, Valerij Anatoljevič 32759
Bazely, Sue 05679
Bazin, J. 12993
Bazley, Shirley 01247
Bazzoni, Maurizio 25080
Bazzotti, Prof. Ugo 24284
Beach, James 44685
Beach, Jane 42171
Beach, Dr. Milo C. 48335
Beady, Charles H. 46496
Beal, Bradley L. 45689
Beal, Graham W.J. 42924
Beal, Isabel C. 43846
Beal, Robert J. 46467
Beale, Arthur C. 41817
Beale, Carolyn 42703
Beale, Denise 38734
Beall, Brent 46114
Beall, Charlotte 47532
Beall, William 44515
Beam, Michael J. 45544
Beam, Michael N. 42280
Beamis, Frances D. 41977
Bean, Dr. Susan 47198
Beans, Daniel J. 47499
Bearcroft, Don 37951
Beard, David 46419
Beard, Dr. James S. 45193
Beard, Rick 41333
Beard-Simpkins, Doreen 47917
Beardsley, Theodore S. 45815
Beardsmore, R.J. 30223
Bearis, Lynn 05908
Beasley, James M. 47754

Beasley, Lorraine 41396
Beasley, Pam 47655
Beaton, Stuart 05098
Beattie, Natalie 01363
Beattie, Stuart 40342
Beatty, Steven 44483
Beatty, Thomas P. 48244
Beatyy, John T. 46977
Beaucamp, Dr. Barbara 18615
Beaud, Marie-Claude 27562
Beaudin Saeedpour, Dr. Vera 41944
Beaudry Dion, Jacqueline 06358
Beauffet, Jacques 14199
Beaufort, Dr. Christian 02897
Beaufort-Spontin, Dr. Christian 02918
Beaugrand, Prof. Dr. Andreas 16158
Beaumont, Helen 22444
Beaumont, Robert N. 48288
Beauregrand, Becky 42688
Beausoleil, Jeanne 10836
Beavers, Randell A. 44134
Beavin, H.A. 39246
Beavis, Dr. Ian 40732
Beccari, Giuseppe 26045
Beccaria, Marcella 25131
Beccart, Christine 11904
Becchi, Casimiro 24871
Bećević, Azra 03925
Bech, Marianne 09040
Bechelet, Florence 40419
Becher, Inge 17242
Bechers, H.H 29882
Bechet, Georges 27568
Bechly, Dr. Günter 20105
Bechtel, Anna 42300
Bechtol, Nancy 42303
Bechtold, Dr. Ekkehard 01770
Bečić, Berina 03925
Beck, Alison 41408
Beck, Gerald 43291
Beck, Prof. Dr. Herbert 17074, 17075
Beck, Jane C. 45309
Beck, Jerry 41825
Beck, Mike 44165
Beck, Monica 47876
Beck, Noldi 27518
Beck, Rolf 20557, 20560
Beck, Stefan 37022
Beck, Tom 41447
Beck-Lipsi, Gabrielle 14037
Beck Silveria, Sheli 45923
Beckelman, Laurie 45872
Beckemeyer, Clemens 18722
Becken, Ellen 08789
Becker, Addie 47698
Becker, Dr. Annette 17035
Becker, Dr. Christoph 37386
Becker, Douglas L. 41485
Becker, Edwin 28911
Becker, Gail R. 44970
Becker, Dr. H. 17198, 17199
Becker, Horst R. 17050
Becker, Jürgen 16943
Becker, Lawrence 48756
Becker, Lisa 44989, 45015
Becker, Marjorie 44546
Becker, Dr. Michael 01953
Becker, Peter 17440
Becker, Dr. Peter-René 16336
Becker, Dr. Rayda 34277
Becker, Dr. Rolf 20084
Becker, Dr. Rudolf 19723
Becker, Sara 41134
Becker, Scott R. 48418
Becker, Ulrich 18485
Becker, Ulrike 02918
Becker, Ursula 19897
Beckers, Marion 16111
Beckett, D. 38927
Beckett, Michael D. 44693
Beckford, Chip 48512
Beckley, Frank J. 40339
Beckmann, Michael 01122, 01459
Beckmann, Dr. Ralf 16992
Beckmann, Werner J. 16747
Becks, Jürgen 20537, 20538
Becks, Dr. Leonie 18132
Beckström, Alf 30883
Becucci, Dr. Sandra 23418, 25614
Bedal, Albrecht 19867
Bedal, Prof. Dr. Konrad 15775, 15776
Bedaux, Dr. R. 29525
Bedell, Lisa 45836
Bedenham, M.D. 38537
Bedenig, Dr. K. 37412
Bedford, Emma 34214
Bedia García, Juana 34906
Bedouin, Regan 43020
Bedoya de Rendón, Martha Elena 07557
Bedula, Jane 45507
Bee, Dr. Andreas 17067
Beebe, John 43203
Beebe, Mary L. 44549
Beech, Mike 39012
Beeck, Sonja 16584
Beeden, Keith 40488
Beeker, Angela 44030
Beeks, Bonny 43716
Beele, F. 03146

Beer, Dieter 37374
Beer, Dr. Günther 17336
Beer, Dr. Manuela 18163
Beerli, Klaus 36963
Beerts, Harry 03728
Beesch, Ruth 45821
Beeson, George 42837
Beets-Anthonissen, M. 03150
Beevers, David 38342
Begg, Ken 00886
Beggin, Suzy 43551
Begić, Veselko 07793
Bégin, Carmelle 05484
Begley, John P. 44972
Begouin, Bernard 10986, 10987, 10990, 10991
Begue, Christelle 14903
Béguin, Gilles 13540
Béguin, Pierre Henri 36581
Behler, Mark 48507
Behm, Stefan 01970
Behne, Dr. Axel 19322
Behnke, Jean 46365
Behnke, Martin 17431
Behr, Lothar 20282
Behr Richards, Anita 41778
Behrends, Carey F. 46094
Behrendt, Klaus 02963
Behrendt, Martina 16097
Behrens, Friedrich 19768
Behrens, Sarah 46288
Behrens, Todd 44604
Behroozy, N. 22769
Behwke, Arlene 46365
Beier, Aasmund 30780, 30781
Beier, Dr. H.-J. 20517
Beier-de Haan, Prof. Dr. Rosmarie 15939
Beiersdörfer, Dr. Kurt 19334
Beiersdorf, Maciej 31705
Beil, Judith 47958
Beil, Leslie 47695
Beilharz, Horst F. 20665
Beilmann-Schöner, Dr. Mechthild 19590
Beimel, Alice 47145
Bein, Peter von 20534
Beiranvand, Asadollah 22255
Beirne, T. 39179
Beisel, P. 18986
Beisken, Angela 17634
Béistegui de Robles, Dolores 28105
Beitchman, Marsha 45755
Beitl, Dr. Klaus 02982
Beitl, Matthias 02117, 02960
Beitz, Dr. Uwe 16776
Bejenaru, Ionel 32514, 32588
Bekmuradov, I. 48842
Bekouan, Hortense Zagbayou 07666
Bela, Dr. Zbigniew 31702
Bélafi, Dr. B. 20171
Bélair, Guy 05906
Belaja, Z.A. 33564
Belan, Judy 45431
Belbin, J. 01311
Belčeski, Rubinčo 27588
Belčeva, Tonja 04659, 04660, 04661
Belda Navarro, Dr. Cristóbal 35150
Beldeanu, Katharina 18206
Belder, Marie de 03756
Beldon, Stanford T. 41143
Belenis 21032
Belfield, John 01306
Belgado Camblor, Victoria 34672
Belgin, Dr. Tayfun 02157
Belie, Liesbeth de 03299
Belin, Jacques 10979
Belinskis, Andrejs 27439
Belisario, Alessandro 23883
Beljaev, A.A. 33572
Beljaeva, Nadešda V. 33307
Beljaeva, Svetlana A. 33578
Belk, Brad 44361, 44363
Belkowitz, Shirley S. 46873
Bell, Brendan 34328
Bell, Chee Chee 44192, 44193
Bell, Christine 38074
Bell, Doug 45217
Bell, Elizabeth 42122
Bell, Eunice 46084
Bell, Dr. Graham A.C. 05928
Bell, Greg 47920
Bell, Gregory 44493
Bell, Harold 43702
Bell, Julia 39949
Bell, Lynn 41408
Bell, Margaret 30214
Bell, Michael 06078
Bell, P.J. 08964
Bell, Robert 00886
Bell, Steve 41677
Bell, Valerie 43256, 44830
Bella, Miguel Angel di 00527
Bellaigue, Dominique de 10789
Bellais, Leslie 45073
Bellamore, Stan 30234
Bellamy, James 43997
Bellamy, Dr. Martin 40439
Bellamy-Jawor, Deborah 42359
Bellando, Francesco 23015
Bellanger, Françoise 13469

Bellani, Giancarlo 24073
Bellanová, S. 34079
Bellar, Gail 43916
Bellas, Gerald M. 42409
Bellaton, Jean-Louis 14232
Bellavia, Kim 44509
Bellazzi, Dr. Pietro 26008
Bellec, Henri 06312
Bellehumeur, Alain 05076
Beller, Janet 44981
Bellerby, Greg 06672
Bellettini, Dr. Pierangelo 23100, 23108, 23111
Belli, Dr. Gabriella 25292, 25293, 25791
Bellier, C. 03800
Bellifemine, Graziano 23091
Bellin, Ines 15920
Bellinger, David 43404
Bellini, Lucette 11024
Bellini, R. 36470
Bellmore, Audra 47695
Bello Morales, Marinelly 48904
Belloni, Luigi Mario 24713
Bellucci, Alberto Guillermo 00226, 00228
Bellucci, Dr. Bruno 25399
Belluscio, Dr. Costantino 22864
Belluscio, Lynne J. 44697
Belluscio, Tara 45450
Bellwald, Tony 36826
Belmondo, Dr. Rosalba 25499
Belmonte, Patty 46141
Bělochová, Olga 08398
Belonović, Eleonora Nikolaevna 33507
Belonovich, Galina Ivanovna 32933
Belotti, Dr. Ione 23528
Beloubek-Hammer, Dr. Anita 16033
Belous, J.P. 37898
Belousova, Natalj Aleksandrovna 32914
Belov, Vladimir Ivanovič 33716
Belova, N.H. 33465
Belser, Eduard J. 36507
Belsey, Hugh 40642
Belsham, J. W. 40564
Belsley, Kathryn 46350
Belt, Virginia 41387
Belter, Rüdiger 18867
Beltrán, Carlos 27961
Beltran, Josel 31409
Beltrán Figueredo, Martín 07525
Beltrán Lloris, Miguel 35721, 35722, 35723, 35724
Beltrani, Francesco 24317, 24318
Belušić, Andreja 07822
Belvin, Robert 45677
Bem, Marek 32166
Beman, Lynn S. 41183
Bemis, William 41179
Bemmes, Robert 46805
Bemporad, Dr. Dora Liscia 23875
Ben, Dr. Arie 22763
Ben-Barak, I. 22689
Ben-Chaôbane, Abderrazzak 28700
Ben-Gal, Dr. Ely 22679
Ben-Nuftali, Aya 22780
Ben-Shimon, Eytana 22785
Benachetti, Sandra 15060
Benavides Becquis, Maria del Carmen 07401, 07575
Benayahu, Dr. Y. 22777
Benbow, Colin 03881
Benbow, Julie 47327
Benda, Susanne 48033
Bender, Brynn 48097
Bender, Claudia 19743
Bender, Joseph 47761
Bender, Patricia L. 43162
Bender, Phil 42896
Bender Hadley, Joy 45173
Bender-Wittmann, Uschi 18749
Bendixen, Maren 17838
Bendixen, Uwe 17838
Bendyukova, Natalia 37901
Benedetti, Prof. Laudomia 24326
Benedetti, Sergio 22446
Benedict, Hope 47224
Benedict, Kay 42127
Benedik, Dr. A. Christian 02830
Benedik, Kristie 43009
Beneš, Dr. Luděk 08480
Benesch, Dr. Evelyn 02840
Benetti, Attilio 25907
Benezra, Neal 47339
Benford, Joseph 46447
Bengston, Rod 41076
Bengtson, Keith 44026
Bengtson, Prof. S.A. 36065
Bengtsson, Bengt 36225
Benington, Jon 38124
Benítez, Antonio Maria 07595
Benitez, Moya 31370
Benito, Fernando 35601
Benito Goerlich, Dr. Daniel 35604
Benjamin, Bart 46912
Benjamin, Brent 47134
Benjamin, Jeremy 45789
Benjamin, Dr. Tritobia H. 48362
Benke, Dr. Harald 20073
Benke, Uwe 15923
Benn, Carl 06591
Benner, Sue 00838
Bennerhag, Carina 36054
Benneth, Dr. Solbritt 36260, 36288

Bennett, Dr. Betsy 46777
Bennett, Charles 47427, 47429
Bennett, Christobel 01482
Bennett, Dorthy E. 42053
Bennett, Fernanda 47009
Bennett, Graham 40756
Bennett, Harold D. 42053
Bennett, Isabel 22370
Bennett, James 43297, 43678
Bennett, James A. 40149
Bennett, Judson E. 43424
Bennett, Kurt Updegraff Mary 42013
Bennett, Michael 42466
Bennett, Michael W. 44843
Bennett, Dr. Nicholas 39496
Bennett, Dr. Peter 41863
Bennett, Ruby 06156
Bennett, Sally B. 45512
Bennett, Sandra 41361
Bennett, Sharon 42211
Bennett, Shelley 47366
Bennett, Susan 38925
Bennett, Swannee 44824
Bennett, Tony 03937
Bennett, Valerie 41419
Bennett, William P. 44010
Bennington, Jeanette 44075
Bennington, Seddon 46512
Bennyworth, J.P. 38081
Benova, Katarina 33978
Beňovský, Jozef 34026
Benscheidt, Dr. Anja 16340, 16342
Bensen, Pat 47458
Benson, Barbara E. 48650
Benson, Benjamin Foley 47445
Benson, Claire 41320
Benson, Dave 05237, 05240
Benson, Patricia 43128
Bentabet, Mohamed 00053
Bente, Jodi 44537
Bente, Klaus 17532
Bente, Prof. Dr. Klaus 18404
Bentheim, Oskar Prinz zu 15601
Bentinck, Baron B.W. 28869
Bentley, Alan 39199
Bentley, Donna 45920
Bentz, Sylviane 14004
Benvie, R. 39984
Benvie, Rachel 39983
Benyovsky, Lucija 07822
Benz, Edward 41794
Benz, Paul 19749
Benz, Robert G. 48742
Benzel, S. 18088
Beran, Antonia 17237
Beran, Helmut 15856
Beran, Pavel 08660
Beránek, Petr 08524
Beránková, Dr. Helena 08267
Beránková, Dr. Jana 08348, 08445
Bérard-Azzouz, Odile 10229
Béraud, Isabelle 11809
Berberkić, Alija 33920
Berchoux, Pierre 10960
Berchtold, Marianne 36541
Berding, Dr. Hans-Henning 17577
Berdjajeva, Tatjana Jurjevna 33547
Bereczky, Dr. Lóránd 21360
Beresford, P. 40889
Bereska, Norbert 18975
Berežanskij, Aleksandr Samuilovič 32985
Berg, Hans-Jürgen 20021
Berg, Kaare 30734
Berg, Karin 30762
Berg, Kristian 36246, 36285
Berg, Manfred 15880
Berg, Peter 15724
Berg, Dr. Richard B. 42018
Berg, Roger 44412
Berg, Dr. Stephan 17603
Berg Lofnes, Solveig 30842, 30844
Bergamaschi, Cirillo 24078
Bergamini, Dr. Giuseppe 25845, 25846, 25848
Bergdahl, Ewa 36121
Bergé, H. 29404
Bergé, Pierre 28700
Bergé Slager, S. 29404
Bergen, Terry 41240, 44418
Bergendahl, Mathias 47175
Bergenthal, Dr. T. 17925
Bergeon, Annick 10809
Berger, Aaron 41081, 45143
Berger, Prof. Albert 01917
Berger, Andrea 01735
Berger, Claudio 36941
Berger, Elfriede 02739
Berger, Erwin 15655
Berger, Dr. Eva 19276, 19280
Berger, Eva-Marie 15486
Berger, Ewald 01917
Berger, Dr. Frank 17055
Berger, Georg 16806
Berger, Ingrid 30820
Berger, Jerry A. 47754
Berger, Karin 15655
Berger, Marianne 19707
Berger, Michael 20213, 20573
Berger, Moshe Tzvi 22650
Berger, Paul 36568

Berger, Shelly 48603
Berger, Teresa J. 45306
Berger, Theodor 18521
Berger, Tobias 30102
Berger, Dr. Ursel 15975
Bergeret, Anne-Marie 12029, 12030, 12031
Bergeret, Jean 12621, 14236
Bergero, Susana 00314
Bergeron, André 05917, 05921
Bergeron, Arthur W. 46374
Bergeron, Myrna 45738
Bergès, Catherine 10229
Berggård, Ingeborg 30955
Berggten, Jan 36297
Bergheger, Brian F. 43166
Bergholm, Synnöve 09954
Berghout, Dr. P.-J. 29206
Bergin, Christer 35882
Bergler, Andrea 16514
Bergman, Bill 46761
Bergman, Ingela 35810
Bergman, Kaj 35902
Bergmann, Eva-Maria 19104
Bergmann, Jóhanna 21629
Bergmann, Prof. Marianne 17340
Bergmann, Sven 16729
Bergmann, Ulrike 16843
Bergra, Cliff 46692
Bergroth, Tom 10134
Bergs, Irene-Annette 17989
Bergs, Lilita 46976
Bergsten, Wayne 45377
Bergström, Anna-Lena 36128
Bergström, Anne 09907, 09908, 09909
Bergström, Carin 36201
Bergström, Eva-Lena 36265
Bergström, Lars 35893
Bergström, Matti 09556
Bergstrom, Prof. Stig M. 42591
Bergstrøm, Ture 08941
Bergundthal, Hermann 36797
Beringer, Emile 11727
Berinskat, Michael 17830
Berke, Debra 48400
Berkel, R.R. 29883
Berkemeier, Dr. Marie-Claire 36499, 36500
Berkes, Jill 43194
Berkes, Peter 36509
Berkey, Vernon 47670
Berkovitz, Sam 46526
Berkowitz, Dr. Roger M. 48021
Berktold, Dr. Werner 02036
Berkvens, Dirk 03144
Berlichingen, Hans Reinhard Freiherr von 17936
Berliet, Paul 12726
Berlin, K.W. 01461
Berliner, Nancy 47198
Bérliņš, Guntis 27371
Berman, Elizabeth Kessin 48338
Berman, Jerôme 41676
Berman, Tosh 48208
Berman-Miller, Cynthia 44060
Bernabo Brea, Dr. Luigi 25671
Bernabò Brea, Dr. Maria 24802
Bernard, A. 03313
Bernard, Charles 11741
Bernard, Christian 36739
Bernard, Fernand 03689
Bernard, Goetz 13059
Bernard, Loic 05751
Bernard, Marie-Thérèse 14537
Bernard, Mary Ann 44571
Bernard, Michel 03421
Bernard-Grit, Jeanne 14351
Bernardi, Dr. Vito 25689
Bernardini, Dr. Carla 23140
Bernardini, Paolo 25455
Bernardini, Toni 22961
Bernardinis, Domenico de 36774
Bernasconi, John G. 39381
Bernat, Chris 41781
Bernat, Clark 06003
Bernatzky, Eva 02664
Bernaudeau, Chloé 12620
Bernauer-Keller, Christine 16532
Bernay, Claude 13142
Berndes, Claske 48320
Berndt, Siegfried 20504
Berner, Dr. Hermann 18780
Bernesconi, César 41041
Berney, Adrienne 45731
Bernhard, Friedolin 17296
Bernhard-Walcher, Dr. Alfred 02918
Bernhardt, D. 17423
Bernhardt, Harold O. 42132
Bernhardt, Josef 01841
Bernier, Ronald R. 48622
Bernier, Suzie 05271, 05272
Bernini, C. 37412
Bernklau, Maria 02955
Berns, Christiane 27567
Berns, Marla C. 44900, 47406
Berns, Peter 29296, 29297
Bernsmeier, Dr. Uta 16321
Bernstein, Bruce 45852
Berntsen, Gunnar 30827
Bero, Meg 41398

Beron, Prof. Petar 04853
Beroza, Barbara L. 48804
Berraute, Luis Bernardo 00566
Berrend, Nico 27577
Berreth, David S. 43533
Berridge, Peter 38608
Berrin, Kathleen 47311, 47325
Berrones-Molina, Patricia 45960
Berry, A. Joyce 47100
Berry, Barbara 48465
Berry, Diane 43078
Berry, James M. 44313
Berry, Jim 43340
Berry, Dr. P.F. 01364
Berry, Susan 47629
Berry, Violet 46564
Berry, Warren 38725
Berry, William B. 41646
Berryman, Jill 46837
Berryman, Val 43054
Bers, Miriam 15968
Bersch, Alexandra 17056
Bersirov, A.M. 33004
Berswordt-Wallrabe, Prof. Dr. Kornelia von 18527, 19896, 19899
Bert, James 48220
Bert, Putter 41598
Bertalan, Karin 19226
Bertani, Licia 23824
Bertaud, Henri 10305
Bertazzolo, Prof. Luigi 25276
Berthaud, Gérard 12911
Bertheaud, Michael 48423
Berthelsen, David 01043
Berthod, Dr. Bernard 12730
Berthold-Hilpert, Monika 17165, 19816
Bertholi, Jean 14472
Berti, Dr. Fausto 24533
Bertie, Dr. David M. 38077, 39025, 39302, 39967, 40191, 40613
Bertini, Dr. Pierluigi 24263
Bertl, Richard 02473
Bertling, Dr. Markus 18937
Bertola, Carinne 36993
Bertolini, Madalen 47780
Bertone, Aureliano 23551
Bertout, Ernest 12812
Bertram, Dr. Marion 16059
Bertram-Neunzig, Evelyn 18165
Bertrand, Claire 39351
Bertrand-Sabiani, Julie 13431
Bertsch, Patricia 45550
Bertschi, Victor 36759
Bertuleit, Dr. Sigrid 19891
Bertus, Jean-Paul 12817
Beruete Calleja, Francisco 34807
Berup, Christina 35998
Berwick, Hildegarde 39958
Beryt, Andrzej 31797
Besio, Remo 37341
Beširov, Ilija 04930
Beskrovnaja, Nina Sergeevna 32929
Besom, Bob 47733
Bessa Luis Baldaque, Laura Mónica 32338
Bessant, Louise 39855
Bessborough, Madeleine 38851
Besse, Nadine 14198
Bessignano, Timothy 46362
Bessire, Mark 46623
Besson, Christine 10346
Besson, Elisabeth 11942
Bessone, Dr. Silvana 32312
Bessor, Joyce M. 48822
Bešťáková, Dr. Kamila 08512
Besten, G.J. den 29643
Besterman, Tristram 39894
Beštok, Chabas Korneevič 33194
Bestrom, Beth 46752
Betancourt, Julián 07406
Betancur, Víctor Raúl 07370
Betanio, Nemesio V. 31404
Bétemps, Alexis 25310
Bethell, Chris 39709
Bethell, Philip 40950
Bethge, Dr. Ulrich 18413
Bethmann-Hollweg, C. von 15453
Betrim 28756
Betschart, Madeleine 36566
Betscher, Hermann 18447, 18448
Betsky, Aaron 29767
Betsy, Dr. Bryan 41473
Bett, David 39016
Betta, Dr. Carlo 23460
Bettendorf, Josef 18750
Bettenhausen, Brad L. 48010
Bettens, Doug 01372
Bettison, Dr. Cynthia Ann 47630
Betton, Richard A. 43818
Betton, Thomas 26064
Betts, Jonathan 40706
Betts, Kathleen 48394
Betts, Shirley 06079
Betts, Wendy 05461
Betz, Eden 46101
Betz, Julia P. 46259
Betz, Martin 45081
Beu, Liliana Marinela 32578
Beuchel, Thomas 02540
Beuf, Jean-Claude 14413, 14414

Beugeling, Dr. Niels 28892
Beuker, J. 28950
Beukers, Prof. H. 29518
Beukes, Engela 34388
Beumer, A.C. 30058
Beumers, C.E.L. 29779
Beurskens, N. 29303
Beuster, Stephanie 19735
Beutelspacher, Prof. Dr. A. 17283
Beutelspacher, Martin 18749
Beuze, Lyne-Rose 27725
Bevan, Jennifer 00952
Beveridge, Albert J. 44759
Bevers, Dr. Holm 16033
Bevilacqua, Jean-Paul 11115
Bevilecqua, Emanuele 25263
Bex, Florent 03156
Beyeler, Ernst 37060
Beyer, Patrick 06042
Beyer, René 37415
Beyer, Dr. Roland 16656
Beynon, Jon 40684
Bezemek, Dr. Ernst 02045
Bezerra Rolim, Valéria Laena 04100
Bezin, C. 15044
Bezlaj Krevel, Ljudmila 34122
Bezold, Franz 19139
Bezzola, Dr. Tobia 37386
Bhagwati, Dr. Annette 15987
Bhan, Kuldeep K. 22501
Bhandari, Dr. J.S. 21764
Bhargava, P.C. 21730
Bhatt, Vikas 21721
Bhattacharya, Therese 36544
Bhaumik, P.K. 21780
Bhave, Dr. S.M. 21987
Bhering Cardoso, Marcio 04329
Bhikul, Tassanee 37503
Bhreathnach-Lynch, Dr. Sighle 22446
Bhullar, Akbar Ali 31042
Bhuyan, G.N. 21806
Biagini, Lorena 25390
Bianchi, Loredana 36531
Bianchi, Matteo 36529
Bianchi Gilangon, Sergio 23850
Bianchini, Dr. Gregorio 25802
Bianco, Prof. Vito Donato 25330
Biancolini, Daniela 22810, 25765
Bianconi, Teresa 25227
Biasini, Cathèrine 20011
Biasio, Elisabeth 37416
Biass-Fabiani, Sophie 12881
Biba, Prof. Dr. Otto 02888
Bibbins, M. Wyllis 42039
Bibby, Deirdre 43944
Biberin, Vladimír Nikolaevič 33638
Bibler, Helen Ann 43877
Bibra, G. von 01189
Bickel, John 38029
Bickell, Lara 46595
Bickford, Christpher P. 44497
Bickford, George P. 42466
Bickford-Berzock, Kathleen 42304
Bicklmeier, Lori 05308
Bicknell, Katharine 45250
Bicknell, Terry 30298
Bidar, A. 13326
Bidault, Alain 12954
Biddlecombe, Julie 39286
Biderman, Ellen 47431
Bidstrup, Wendy 45160
Bidwell, John 45863
Bidwell, Paul 40537
Bidwell, Richard 48461
Biedenharn, Murray 45439
Biedermann, Dr. Gottfried 01909
Biefel, H. 16885
Biefel, I. 16885
Bieg, Werner 15383
Biegel, Dr. Gerd 16293, 20509
Biegel, Gerd 20651
Biegel, Susanne 15575
Biehl, Martin 30741
Bielamowicz, Zbigniew 31920
Bielański, Janusz 31711
Bielby, Jane 38329, 40525
Bielejec, Stephanie 41374
Bielinski, Regula 37182
Bielkin, Kenneth 45758
Biemans, Johan 28980
Biemans, Dr. Jos A.A.M. 28900
Bienedell, Arturo Alberto 00560
Biener, Herbert 01898
Bieńkowski, Joachim 32078
Bier, Carol 48397
Bier, F. 11613
Bierens de Haan, J.C. 29497, 29914
Bieri, Susanne 36550
Bieri Thomson, Helen 36758
Bierinckx, Cis 45394
Biermann, Prof. Dr. Günther 02269
Biersack, Werner 17374
Bierwisch, Heidi 16899
Biesboer, Dr. P. 29324
Biesenbach, Klaus 16034
Bieske, Dr. Dorothee 17012
Bievenour, Ginger 44221
Biezaitis, M. 00849
Biffiger, Steffan 37211

Bigay, Victorino 31276
Bigda, Daisy R. 42227
Bigelow, May 48571
Biggart, Norman 42000
Biggs, Kate 40532
Biggs-Craft, Katherine 06336
Bignasca, Dr. Andrea 36495
Bihan, Olivier le 10812
Bihler, A. 16809
Bijelić, Dubravka 33810
Bijleveld, W. 28888
Bijleveld van Lexmond, Caspar 36823
Biktaševa, Natalija Nikolaevna 33360
Bilbey, Sue Ann 48217
Bilderback, Jeffrey 47483
Bilek, Alena 02837
Bilenduke, Florence 06105
Biles, Leanna S. 43461
Biles, LeAnna S. 43462
Bilgin, Mehmet 37774
Biličenko, Valentina Andreevna 33424
Bilich, Ivanka 07714
Billard, Marie Claude 10526
Billerbeck, Barb 45902
Billich, Dorie 05503
Billier, Philippe 14649
Billig, Pamela 41916
Billinge, Rachel 39729
Billings, Larry 41975
Billings, Loren 42348
Billings, Vernon N. 44638
Billingsley, Pam 47012
Billisics-Rosenits, G. 01806
Billops, Camille 45813
Billups, Di 40344, 40346
Biloparlović, Ivo 07764
Biloslav, Toni 34096, 34137
Bin Ismail, Halal 27646
Binaud, Daniel 10764
Binder, Caroline 40451
Binder, Christian 17134
Binder, Doug 39151
Binder, Gerhard 20736
Binder, Hanspeter 37017
Binder, Stefi 36487
Bindereif, Hugo 19261
Bindija, Mosar 33836
Bines, Dr. Joan P. 48568
Binette, Dennis 43282
Bing, Jens 08827
Bingham, David S. 43444
Binikowski 20413
Binkley, David 48374
Binnendijk, S. 29901
Bins, Coleen 43099
Bintz, Carol 48021
Biqijand, Colette 14992
Biran, Prof. Avraham 22665
Biraud, Guy 10343
Bircher, Prof. Dr. Martin 36641
Bircumshaw, John 46478
Bird, David M. 43141
Bird, P. 06176
Bird, Richard 42177
Bird, S. 38114
Birdick, Birdy 46158
Birdsall, Derrick 44176
Birdseye, William S. 48350
Birdsong, Sherri 41570
Bireley, Ellen K. 44227
Birk, Sherry C. 48387
Birk, Walter 19729
Birke, Katja 20106
Birkebæk, Frank A. 09041, 09043
Birker, Susanne 17576
Birklid, Richard 43446
Birks, Mary 45244
Birley, Robin 39237
Birman de Bessudo, Raquel 28148
Birmanova, M. 27075
Birnbaum, Dr. Daniel 17070
Birney, Elmer C. 45387
Birnie, Ian 44921
Birnie Danzker, Jo-Anne 18887
Biro, Miriam 47927
Birol, Çiğdem 37701
Birrer, Sibylle 36425
Birsak, Dr. Kurt 02551
Birthälmer, Dr. Antje 20717
Birtwhistle, Marjorie 48676
Bisanz-Prakken, Dr. Marian 02830
Bisbano, Beth 42555
Bischler, Gaston 18885
Bischof, Klaus 20103
Bischoff, Dr. Cäcilia 02918
Bischoff, Dieter 20000
Bischoff, Dr. Franz 16025
Bischoff, Dr. Harald 16897
Bischoff, Dr. Ulrich 16682
Bischoff, Walter 20740
Biscoito, M.J. 32276
Bishof, John 47557
Bishop, Adrian 38500
Bishop, Art 47287
Bishop, Barbara 43682
Bishop, Dr. C. 38082
Bishop, Eliza H. 42704
Bishop, Dr. Gale 47792
Bishop, Gale A. 46797

Bishop, Henry 05303
Bishop, Janet C. 47339
Bishop, Jean 45264
Bishop, Knox 42753
Bishop, Dr. Leslie 46861
Bishop, Dr. Michael 40054
Bishop, Michael 40055
Bishop, Dr. Mike 40056
Bishop, Ron 43435
Bishop, Russell J. 47604
Bishop, Tommy 48147
Bishopone, Iain R. 40728
Biskupić, Margareta 07799
Bisol, David 47403
Bissell, James 42467
Bisset, El 30138
Bissette, Carolyn B. 41432
Bissière, Caroline 12968
Bissonnette, Anne 44447
Bissonnette, Daniel 06702
Biström, Prof. Olof 09480
Biswas, Dr. T.K. 22056
Bither, Philip 45394
Bitner, Carol 47226
Bitomsky, Michael 15957
Bitsch, Dr. Helmut 19516
Bitschnau, Dr. Martin 02082
Bittel, Dr. Christoph 15693
Bitterli, Konrad 37102
Bittner, Regina 16584
Bivens, Peg 44511
Bivingou-Nzeingui 07646
Bixler, Ed 47494
Bizzarri, Laura 23015
Bjarnason, Páll V. 21648
Bjarnesen, Lynne 42780
Bjelić, Dobrila 33837
Bjerg, Ida 08818
Bjerkestrand, Steinar 30528, 30529
Bjerre, Henrik 08950
Bjerregaard, Jørgen O. 08782
Bjerregaard, Kirsten 08800
Bjerring Jensen, Knud 09052
Bjerrkjar, Anne 08898
Björk, Barbro 36309
Björklund, Anders 36240, 36280
Björkman, Sten 09431
Björn, Eva 36356
Björnemalm, Barbro 36361
Bjørgen, Asle B. 30648, 30649
Bjork, Alan 47020
Bjork, Tim 46485
Bjørklund, Prof. Kjell R. 30735
Blaas, Karl 37311
Blacharska, Wiktoria 31570
Black, Barbara 47670
Black, Bettye 44637
Black, Bill 01377
Black, Prof. C.M. 39723
Black, George B. 45603
Black, Jack 43305
Black, Jay 48270
Black, Joe 43746
Black, Kenneth N. 46967
Black, L. 01170
Black, William N. 43456
Black Petersen, S. 08859
Blackaby, Anita D. 43925
Blackburn, Dr. Bob 43016, 43192, 46121, 47223
Blackburn, M.A.S. 38454
Blackburn, Rachael 44401
Blackman, Barbara W. 47291
Blackman, Leona 43346
Blackmar, Charles B. 44327
Blackwelder, Martha 47260
Blackwood, Frank E. 05527
Bladen, Martha 48226
Blades, John M. 46264
Blades, Julian 40924
Blades, Kent 05197
Bladt, Inger K. 08762
Blæsild, Benno 08770
Blaettler, Roland 36740
Blagg, Margaret 41091
Blagg, Tim 43807
Blagov, Jurij Alekseevič 32909
Blair, Allan 05983
Blair, A.R. 44615
Blair, David 44900
Blair, Kay 48606
Blair, Robert 01326
Blair, William 38069
Blajan, Ion 32470
Blake, Dan 48164
Blake, Dr. Eugenia 44596
Blake, Janet 44575
Blake, Leo D. 42061
Blake, Paul 40951
Blake, Ruby 47035
Blake, Steven 38544
Blake Roberts, Gaye 40612
Blakey, Ellen Sue 47994
Blanc, Monique 13586
Blanchard, Cathérine 13449
Blanchard, Marian 30238
Blanchard, P.E. 06294
Blanchard, Raoul 36785
Blanchard-Gross, Diana 45939
Blanchebarbe, Prof. Dr. Ursula 19950

Blanchegorge, Eric 11375, 11376
Blanchette, Normand 05343
Blanchette, Odile 40425
Blanck, Denis 15312
Blanco, Bobby 31458
Blanco, Cristina 35024
Blanco, Hipólito S. del 00332
Blanco Sansa, Helena 34582
Bland, Bart 47791
Bland, Bruce F. 43035
Bland, Gaye K. 46985
Bland, Julia W. 45730
Blank, Maxine 44500
Blankenberg, Dr. H.M. 29904
Blankenship, Blanton 43852
Blankenship, Ken 42276
Blanquez, Juan 35390
Blas Pascual, Javier 35376
Blaschke, Shirley 46113
Blaser, Christophe 36863
Błaszczyk, Bożena 31941
Blatchford, Ian 39795
Blatter, Bernard 37289
Blauert, Elke 16025
Blaugrund, Dr. Annette 45849
Blavia, Francisco 48895
Blazevic, April 47646
Błażewicz, Sławomir 32105
Blazewiczea, Stanisław 31558
Blazwick, Iwona 39807
Blazy, Guy 12735, 12741, 14388
Blazy, Simone 12745
Bleakley, Bruce 47286
Bleathman, William 01106
Bled, Max 14779
Bleecker Blades, Margaret 43472
Bleiberg, Elizabeth W. 45038
Bleich, Gerhard 16416
Bleistein, Joachim 19151
Bleker, Klaus 16006
Bles, H. de 29134
Blessing, Jennifer 45872
Blethen, H. Tyler 42723
Bley, Karl 19106
Bley, Werner 19457
Bleymehl-Eiler, Dr. Martina 15737
Blicke, Linda 41978
Blickle, K.H. 17655
Blickle, Ursula 18218
Bliemeister, Jeffrey 48482
Blinov, Viktor Filippovič 32675
Bliss Coleman, Amy 43874
Blitz, Amy 45751
Bljudova, Ljudmila Grigorjevna 32762
Bloch, Dorete 09408
Bloch Ravn, Thomas 08770
Block, Deborah 45789
Block, Diana 42877
Block, Merle 43734
Block, Phillip 45817
Block, René 18021
Bloem, H. 29235
Bloem, M. 28902
Bloemen, H.A.C. 29237
Blohm Pultz, Janet 42839
Blok, R.S. 13487
Blok, Dr. W. 29974
Blom, J. 29007
Blomberg, M.G. 35884, 35885
Blomberg, Nancy 42885
Blome, Prof. Peter 36495
Blome, Ulrike 16112
Blomen, Bärbel 20597
Blommaert, Georges 03139
Blommel, Henry H. 42610
Blomquist, Fredrik 36128
Blomquist, Shirley 42034
Blomstedt, Severi 09533
Blomster, Pontus 10096
Blondel, Madeleine 11523, 11525
Blondin, Linda 06652
Bloom, Alan 38733
Bloomer, Harlan 45121
Bloomfield, Sara J. 48401
Blosser, Jack 46180
Blouin, Mike 42912
Blount, Rob 47857
Blue, John 06500
Blübaum, Doris 17191
Blühm, Andreas 28911
Bluhm, Hans-Georg 18052
Blum, Dilys 46442
Blum, Jürgen 17856
Blum-Spicker, Helene 16646
Blumberg, Linda 47313
Blume, Dr. Eugen 15981
Blume, Sharon 47768
Blume, Torsten 16584
Blumenthal, Arthur R. 48708
Blumenthal, Prof. Dr. W. Michael 16009
Blumentritt, R. 19772
Blundell, Kathi 47732
Blustain, Malinda S. 41209
Blyth, Mary 40498
Blyth-Hill, Victoria 44921
Boa, Valerie N.S. 39131
Boada, Eulalia 35048
Boal, Robert 46072
Boal Lee, Mathilde 41762

Boano, Giovanni 23348
Boarman, Don 43988
Boarowy, Innocenta 32067
Boas, Bob 39703
Boas, Lena 19683
Boas, Natasha 47448
Boase, Colin 01574
Boast, Mair 40238
Boatman, Linda 42356
Boatright, Neva 42904
Bob, Murray L. 44309
Bobar, Maja 03924
Bober, Anna 31507
Bober, Jonathan 41412
Boberg, Scott 44650
Bobinger, Wanda L. 44835
Bobkina, Tatjana Gennadjevna 33675
Bobkov, Konstantin Vasilevič 33009
Bobnjarić, Venija 07693
Bočanová, Vanda 08578
Bočarov, Lev Nikolaevič 33702
Bocca, Massimo 23518
Boccanera, Prof. Giacomo 23289
Boccardo, Dr. Piero 23983
Bocchieri, Prof. Franco 25821
Bocci, Giampiero 23483
Boccolari, Prof. Giorgio 24449
Bochenek, Marceli 32044
Bochenek, Dr. Władysław 31958
Bochenski, Leslie 46930
Bochmann, Deb 41149
Bochnakov, Nikola 04785
Bock, Britta 41980
Bock, Dr. Robert 17032
Bockelman, James 47573
Bockius, Dr. Ronald 18604, 18606
Bockwoldt, Michael 42821
Bocvarova-Plavevska, Marika 27591
Bod, Roy 42361
Bode-Hempton, Sharon 44657
Bodenstein, Anton 02803
Bodenstein, John Gilbert 19111
Bodilsen, Inge 08833
Bodine jr, William B. 46509
Bodine jr., William B. 46516
Bodine jr, William B. 46517
Bodingbauer, Prof. Adolf Karl 02689
Bodinger, John 43211
Bodini, Prof. Arturo 24384
Bodini, Prof. Floriano 23359
Bodini, Mauro 25601
Bodirsky, Peter 16487
Bodish, Glenn 42016
Bodnaryk, Randy 46407
Bodner, Connie 45554
Bodó, Dr. Sándor 21331
Bodoky, Dr. Tamás 21335
Bodorová, Olga 34051
Bodrova, Zoja Evgenjevna 33509
Bodsch, Dr. Ingrid 16235, 16247
Bøe, Kaare 30407
Böcher, Friederike 15680
Böcher, Hans-Georg 17665
Böck, Elfriede 17579
Boeck, Lorraine 47774
Boeckh, Dr. Hans 36753
Böckle, Karlheinz 19968
Bödewadt, Uwe 36250
Böge, Rainer 15434
Bögel, Christoph 18168
Bögels, C. 29897
Boeglin, Yves 14880
Böhle, Hans-Theo 16587
Böhle, Rainer 15722
Böhler, Dr. Bernhard 02880
Böhm 19599
Böhm, Helmut 02964
Boehme, Dr. Sarah E. 42510
Böhme, Prof. Dr. Wolfgang 16250
Böhmer, Otmar 16728
Böhmer, Sylvia 15378
Böhnert, Marlies 17034
Böhnke, Bärbel 16838
Böhnlein, E. 19107
Böker, Wolfgang 36549
Boelen, Jan 03484
Boelens, Christ 29823
Bölke, Dr. Wilfried 15493
Böller, Susanne 18918
Bömer, Jana 08587
Bönig, Dr. Jürgen 17555
Böning, Heinrich 19456
Bönnen, Dr. Gerold 20677
Bönnighausen, Helmut 16666
Bönninghausen, D.E.J. von 28879
Bönsch, Dr. Peter 02323
Boer, A. den 29194
Boer, Dr. A.M. 29106
Boer, Birgit de 16743
Boer, F.G. de 29668
Boer, P. den 29166
Börjesson, Klas 35987
Boers, T. 28875
Boers, Waling 15933
Boersma, W. 29666
Börste, Dr. Norbert 19332, 19335
Bösch, Dr. Gabriele 02142
Böse, Hans-Joachim 20624
Böser, Wolfgang 17287, 20052

Boesmans, Annick 03432
Boesner, Robert 02700
Böthig, Dr. Peter 19591
Boëthius, Lena 03478
Böttcher, Andreas 16303
Boettcher, Chris 47333
Böttcher, Dr. Ronald 20105
Boetzkes, Prof. Manfred 17761
Boffa, Prof. Giovanni 36436
Bogan, Alan 43433
Bogan, Dr. Michael A. 41105
Bogardus, Lorraine B. 45511
Bogatyrev, E. 33063, 33079
Bogdan, Gene 44355
Bogdanov, Pavel 33034
Bogdanova, Lidija Aleksandrovna 33636
Bogdanova, Marija 04623
Bogdanovič, Nikola 07778
Bogdanova, Vera Ivanovna 33554
Bogdanowicz, Prof. Wiesław 32102
Bøge Henriksen, Kirsten 09033
Bogetti, Dr. Anita 22972
Boggio, Stefano 25890
Boggs, Mac 47715
Boggs, Rex 43376
Bogman, Suzanne 28911
Bognanni, Filippo 24900
Bogner, Peter 02912
Bogoljubskaja, A.V. 33737
Bogomolova, M.T. 33127
Bogurat, W. 32048
Bogusky, Alfred M. 05698
Boguszewicz, Ireneusz 31516
Boguwolski, Ryszard 31610, 31611, 31612
Bogyirka, Enil 21377
Boheme, Prof. Dr. Enrico 25258
Bohl, Samuel D. 41747
Bohlen, Dr. H. David 47737
Bohlin-Davis, Stephen 47480
Bohlmann, Dieter-Theodor 17962
Bohman, Stefan 36264
Bohnenkamp-Renken, Anne 17046
Bohnert, G. 18289, 18290
Bohórquez, Jorge Alfonso 07504
Bohr, G. Ted 46144
Boice, Linda S. 41379
Bois, Dr. M. de 28950
Boiseneau, Gerard 43181
Boissard, Jerome de 11849
Boisselle, Lynn 06113
Boissevain, C.F.C.G. 29145, 29146
Boissière, Yves 11817
Boitani, Dr. F. 25237
Boits, Paul 03167
Bojani, Prof. Gian Carlo 23754, 24861
Bojar, Hans-Peter 01922
Bojarczuk, Helena 31615
Bojarskij, Dr. Viktor I. 33479
Bojko, Elena Michajlovna 33557
Bojko, Nina Vladimirovna 32959
Bojkova, Irina Petrovna 33729
Bojkova, Margarita Alekseevna 32771
Bojović, Nevenka 33827
Bojović, Radivoje 33827
Bok, Franciszek 32017
Bok, Klaus 17840
Bokbot, Dr. Youssef 28702
Bokchun, Youngja 27224
Bol, Marsha C. 47424
Bol, Prof. Dr. Peter C. 17075
Boland, Angela 00845
Boland, Raymond 42069, 45075
Bolas, Gerald D. 42196
Bolderman, J.C.L. 28940
Bolduan, Anka 16336
Bolenz, Dr. Eckhard 19496
Boley, Shawn 41703
Bolge, George S. 41765
Bolger, Doreen 41454
Bolger, Dr. Francis 05228
Bolick, Dr. Margaret R. 44793
Bolin, Jerry 45036
Boling, Ron 47244
Bolipata, Alfonso Corpus 31439
Bolívar, Julián Gil 07380
Bolla, Dr. Margherita 25969, 25974, 25975
Bolle, Pierre 03355
Bolleville, Jean 12467
Bolling, Richard G. 43818
Bologna, Alberto 24173
Bolognani, Betty 46812
Bolotov, Valentin A. 33108
Bolotova, G.P. 33391
Bolsinger, Daniel 36502
Bolster, Jane 45754
Bolster, Molly 46655
Bolt, Ed L. 46481
Bolten, Harald 18231
Bolten Rempt, Dr. H. 29526
Boltesilverman, Diane 43267
Bolton, Bruce D. 05893, 05926
Bolton, David 38957
Bolz, Dr. Peter 15945
Bombard, LuAnn 48519
Bomberger, Bruce 44629
Bomford, David 39729
Bommerlyn, Loren 42695
Bommert, Rainer 16322
Bonaccorsi, R. 12260

Bonačić Mandinić, Maja 07779
Bonagura, Pasquale 25947
Bonamini, Eros 27511
Bonansinga, Kate 43118
Bond, Anthony 01490
Bond, Debra 46346
Bond, Emma 39255, 40721
Bond, Hallie 41758
Bond, Karen 43633
Bond, Kaye 46356
Bond, Wanda L. 43839
Bond-Fahlberg, Margareta 36268
Bondar, Dr. Vitalij Vjačeslavovič 32947
Bondareva, Valentina Nikolaevna 32796
Bondaz, Gilles 14896
Bondil, Nathalie 13636
Bondjers, Rune 35882
Bone, Oliver 40694
Bonemaison, Michel 12727
Bonet Armengol, Jordi 34590
Bonet Correa, Antonio 35027
Bonet Planes, Juan Manuel 35041
Bonet Rosado, Helena 35603
Bonev, Ivan 04877
Boneva, Leonora 04846
Bongaarts, J. 29394
Bongaerts, Ursula 25150
Bongard, Rolf B. 16137
Bongers, H. 29759
Bonias, Zisis 21010
Bonifay, Suzanne 14174
Bonilla, Irene 35599
Bonilla, Mary Yamilet 48953
Bonin, Flavio 34138
Bonini, Julia 01196
Bonini, Laurie 01196
Bonn, Greg 44592
Bonnard, Jacques 13507
Bonnard Yersin, Pascale 37290
Bonnefille, J. Lovis 14147
Bonnefoi, Geneviève 11867
Bonnet, P. 29067
Bonnet Borel, Francoise 37275
Bonnett, Dr. Richard B. 44164
Bonnevialle, Gilles 14162
Bonnier, Bernadette 03651
Bonnin, Jean-Claude 12874
Bono, Sam 41106
Bonofiglio, Marta Maria 00521
Bonoli, Prof. Fabrizio 23117
Bonomi, Prof. Alfredo 24844
Bonomi, Dr. S. 22808
Bonsanti, Dr. Giorgio 23863
Bonvalet, Louis-Georges 12906
Bonzel, Helen 17177
Boo, Irene de 38217
Booknight, Alice 42563
Boomstra Van Raak, M.A.C. 29507
Boon, Loren 46905
Boone, Nathaniel A. 45101
Boonmark, Urith 37495
Boonstra, Dr. J.R. 28845
Booream, Rick 45949
Boorsch, Suzanne 45700
Boos, Dr. Andreas 19524
Boot, C. 29880
Boot, Kay 46208
Boot, M. 28902
Booth, Amanda 40059
Booth, Beverley 30130
Booth, C.M. 40338
Booth, Helen 05635
Booth, William H. 48019
Boothman, Colin 39813
Bootman, Karen 38901
Bora, Dr. D.K. 21860
Borbolla, Dr. Sol Rubin de la 28187
Borchardt, Dr. Albert 17664
Borchardt, Felicitas 15491
Borchardt, Susan A. 45201
Borchers, Karl-Hans 20287, 20288
Borchert, Till Holger 03246, 03253, 03254
Borčić, Goran 07783
Bordaz, Odile 15265
Bordeau, Annette 28669
Borden, Tamika 45744
Bordinskich, Gennadij Aleksandrovič 33543
Bore, Ove Magnus 30879, 30880, 30890
Boreham, Peter 40335
Borek, Henning 16306
Borel, François 36985
Borel, Dr. Gilles 36858
Borén, Ingjerd 35919
Borettaz, Omar 22902
Borg, Carles 27702
Borg, Prof. Dr. Vince 27697
Borgegård, Eva 36381
Borges, Prof. F. Sodré 32334
Borges, Grethe 30518
Borges, Richard 41629
Borges, Wolfgang 18319
Borges Rosales, Prof. J.C. 48951
Borgeson, Jaquelyn L. 42194
Borggrefe, Dr. Heiner 18431
Borghi, Gian Paolo 23790
Borić Brešković, Bojana 33820
Borisenko, Irina Gavrilovna 33164
Borisenko, Viktor Ivanovič 33627
Borisov, Boris 04791

Borisova, Diana 04653, 04654, 04655
Borisova, Tanja 04787
Borisova, Valentina Vladimirovna 32644
Borja-Santiago, Monina Katherina 31385
Borja-Villel, Manuel J. 34552
Bork, Prof. Dr. Hans Rudolf 19547
Borkopp-Restle, Dr. Birgitt 18833
Borman, Dennes 45463
Borman, R.Th.A. 28941
Borms, Gwen 03146
Born, J.G.M. 29369
Born, Dr. Klaus 18615
Born, Richard 42322
Bornacelli Guerrero, Humberto 07590
Bornecrantz, Mona 36309
Bornemann, Daniel 14806
Bornfriend, Carl 43565
Bornman, A.R. 34174
Borns, Harold 46195
Borodavkin, Andrej Viktorovič 33253
Borodina, Valentina Ivanovna 32746
Borošak Marjanović, Jelena 07822
Borovinskich, Nadežda Petrovna 33616
Borowski, Batya 22625
Borowsky, Gwen 46435
Borpuzari, D. 21825
Borremans, Dr. R. 03470
Borriello, Dr. Mariarosaria 24577
Borromeo, Dr. Georgina 46721
Borrowdale-Cox, Deborah 44746
Borrup, Tom 45386
Borsanyi, Jackie 45229
Borsboom, Leo 30015
Borsdorf, Prof. Dr. Ulrich 16960, 16962
Borselli, Lucilla 25520
Borsig, Josef 08242
Bortolan, Gino 25940
Bortolotti, Dr. Marco 23099, 23120
Borusiewicz, Mirosław 31777, 31779
Bory, Jean-René 36648
Borys, Stephen 46076
Borzan, Maria 32580
Bos, Agnès 11599
Bos, Saskia 28904
Bos, W. 29830
Bosano Ansaldo, Dr. Carlos de 00107
Bosch i Cornellà, Salvador 35402
Boscher, Jean-Yves 10809
Boschi, Prof. Enzo 23736
Boschiero, Dr. Gemma 22971, 22973, 22975
Boser, Dr. Elisabeth 16523, 16525
Boserup, Dr. Ivan 08925
Boshoff, Jaco 34210
Boshouwers, F. 29305
Bosi, Erio 24228
Bosinski, Prof. Dr. Gerhard 18606
Bosioković, Sava 33824
Bosiy, Pavel V. 37861
Boskamp, Ute 17809
Boškova, Tatjana 27592
Bošković, Dora 07822
Bosma, M. 29897
Bosman, K. 03303, 03303
Bosmans, A. 03146
Bošnakov, Nikola 04766
Bosnan Salihagić, Željka 07839
Bošniak, Jurij Michailovič 33639
Bošnjak, Karlo 07708
Boss, George 38830
Boss, Dr. M. 16915
Bossa Herazzo, Donaldo 07457
Bossaert 03592
Bossan, Marie-Josèphe 14016
Bossart, Hans Peter 37386
Bosse, David 42850
Bossé, Laurence 13548
Bosse, Maurice 42020
Bosshard, Daniel 37018
Bosshard, Reymond 36957
Bosshard-Frischknecht, Hulda 37268
Bosshard-Gorrite, Nuria 36950
Bossine, Lesley 39349
Bostanci, Gülten 08235
Bostander, Nellie 34398
Bostic, Connie 41277
Boston, A. 38430
Boston, David 40832
Boston, J. Audrey 38429
Boston, Katrina M. 45938
Bostrem, Lidija Andreevna 32653
Boswell, Mary Rose 44564
Bosworth, John 38241
Bot, Nadia 36735
Bot Riera, Issa 35672
Botero, Dr. Clara Isabel 07415
Botha, R. 34180
Bothe, Günter 15656
Bothe, Heinrich 16204
Bothe, Prof. Dr. Rolf 20455, 20466, 20470, 20472
Bothmer, Dietrich von 45833
Botineau, Pierre 10805
Botirov, I.T. 48864
Botsaris, Markos S. 20848
Botte, Prof. Virgilio 24596
Bottengård, Else 30935
Bottero, Giuliana 25761
Bottini, Dr. Angelo 23852
Bottlaender, Michael 17576
Bottrel Tostes, Vera Lúcia 04385

Botwinick, Michael 48785
Botzong, A. 10747, 10748
Bouaïche, Claire-Lise 37038, 37039
Bouchard, Guy 06278
Bouchard, Marie 13536
Bouchard, Yann 14647
Bouché, R. 20113
Boucher, George 43050
Boucher, Michel 10886, 10887
Boucher, Sid 01373
Bouchet, Denis 12539
Bouchet, J.-C. 01002
Bouchon, Chantal 13586
Bouchon, Juan Santiago 00459
Bouck, Jill 43082
Bouckaert, Odile-Marie 03258
Boudia, Soraya 13543
Boudier, Pierre 11493
Boudou, Dominique 13175
Boudreau, Luce Marie 05244
Boudrot, Donna 05006
Bouffault, Colette 13407
Boughton, Peter 38552
Bougia, Polyxeni 00897
Bouglé, Frédéric 14885
Boujamid, Azzouz 28693
Boukli, Aïcha 00044
Boulanger, Patrick 12856
Boulbes, M. 11653
Bould, Gillian 40479
Boulet, Jean 15062
Boulliard, Jean-Claude 13485
Boulton Elliott, Helen 06736
Boulton Stroud, Marion 46408
Bounous, Jewell P. 48178
Bouquet, B. 13480
Bourassa, Marie 06137
Bourbon, Prof. Giulio 23365
Bourbon Busset, Jean-Louis de 10571
Bourbonnais, Alain 05058
Bourbonnais, Caroline 11505
Bourcier, Paul 45073
Bourdin, Monika 14487
Bourdon, Don 05045
Bourdon, Kate 06264
Boureima, Konfé 04940
Bourel, Yves 14486
Bouret, Brigitte 13985
Bourgat, Robert 13707
Bourgeois, Jean 03827
Bourgeois, Valérie 06639
Bourgoin, Colette 05190
Bourgougnon, Eric 10733, 13104
Bourgoz, Michel 36476
Bourke, Marie 22446
Bourlet, Michel 11619
Bournazel, Comtesse de 13868
Bourne, Susan 38401
Bourque, Bruce 41390
Bourriaud, Nicolas 13652
Bouše, Petr 08472
Bouska, Marianne 42388
Bousmanne, Bernard 03275
Bousquet, Nicolas 10291
Boussard 13407
Bousska, Prof. Dr. Vladimira 02865
Boustany, Bernadette 12272
Bouteiller, Hubert 11476
Bouthat, Chantal 06198
Boutry, Pierre 33753
Bouttemy, Marie-Françoise 12599
Bouvier, Prof. Dr. Beatrix 20210
Bouvy, Michel 11013
Bouvy, P. 29561
Bouwman, J.W.M. 28795
Bouxin, Marc 13933
Bouzón Gallego, Avelino 35580
Bovewizer, Austin 22533
Bovey, Patricia E. 06853
Bowden, Cindy 41356
Bowden, Mitchell D. 46474
Bowdery, J. 38608
Bowdrey, Jeremy 38613
Bowen, Allyson 45795
Bowen, Duncan 39110
Bowen, Graham 38201
Bowen, John 46716
Bowen, Linnell R. 41225
Bower, Alan 40672
Bower, Barbara A. 43393
Bower, Corinna 08002
Bower, Finn 06436
Bower, Helen 39452
Bower, Mary 43246
Bowers, Prof. M. Deane 41837
Bowes, Murray 01583
Bowes, Peter 40805
Bowes-Crick, C.P. 39762
Bowie, Dr. Gavin 38404
Bowle, Jean 38403
Bowles, G. 38537, 38538
Bowman, Beth 47408
Bowman, Dr. S. 39586
Bowman, Travis 42460
Bowman, Trina 43944
Bownan, JoAnn 45810
Bownan, Leslie Green 48712
Bowron, Julian 01252
Box, David 01123

Boxall, Michael 38190
Boxer, David 26069
Boxer, Graham 39525
Boxhall, Patricia 00864
Boxley, Robert F. 48679
Boyce, David Y. 44712
Boychev, Petr 04891, 04892
Boyd, Beatrice 48224
Boyd, L. 05619
Boyd, Peter 40511
Boyd, Robert 41623
Boyd, Susan 48351
Boydell, Owen 38852
Boyden, Dr. P. 39728
Boyer, Cindy 46939, 46945
Boyer, Jean-Marc 14738
Boyer, John Vincent 43940
Boyer, Sylvain 10528
Boyette, Kathrin 42057
Boyette, Todd 41281
Boylan, Olive S. 45561
Boyle, Catherine 42107
Boyle, Chris 43655
Boyle, Dorothy 47214
Boyle, Gail 38351
Boyle, William J.S. 06627
Boym, Per Bj. 30744
Boyneburgh, Dorette von 20003
Boynton, Hugh 39190
Boysen, Jesper 08892
Boysen, Renate 18335
Boysson, Bernadette de 10811
Bozell, John R. 44787
Božič, Bojan 34098
Bozkurt, Batuhan 37750
Bozok, Erdoğan 35977
Bozzone, Christine 36931
Braack, Craig R. 41610
Braam, Dr. P. 29207
Braarud, Reni 30719
Braat-Voorhuis, T.M.A. 30059
Braaten, Alicia L. 42424
Braaten, Ivar Gunnar 30375
Braaten, Trond 30408
Brabant, Diane 06261
Brabec, Jiří 08631
Brace, Denise 38902, 40536
Brace, Jeffrey C. 05016
Bracegirdle, H. 40050
Bracegirdle, Robert 39828
Brachaczek, Zofia 32016
Bracher, Sylvia 37355
Brachner, Dr. Alto 18839
Brack, Dr. P. 37376
Brack, Peter 37390
Bracke, Norbert 03560
Brackenreg, Philip 00753
Brackenridge, Kirsty 40147
Bradbury, Christopher 40887
Bradbury, David 39654
Bradbury, J. Robert 05980
Bradbury, Karen 39518
Brademann, Margret 16391
Braden, Gerald 46824
Bradfield, Gerald 44587
Bradford, Anna 05571
Bradford, Dr. Bruce C. 42815
Bradford, Colleen 44587
Bradford, Jan 45725, 45726
Bradford, Mary 47794
Bradić, Mihajlo 07690
Bradley, Allen 45902
Bradley, Betsy 44280
Bradley, Bob 39917
Bradley, Dean 06246
Bradley, Douglas E. 46044
Bradley, Fiona 38882
Bradley, Graeme 30206
Bradley, J. 40131
Bradley, J.M. 38724
Bradley, Laurel 46019
Bradley, Loris 47346
Bradley, Richard 45581
Bradley, Ron 06726
Bradley, Dr. William Steven 42785
Bradman, Susan 38656
Bradshaw, Bill 44823
Bradshaw, John P. 46929
Bradshaw, Julia 30179
Bradshaw, Paul 48680
Bradt, Rachelle 45887
Bradtke, Jerzy 31580
Brady, Christine 38181, 39377
Braekeleer, Catherine de 03546
Brændholt Lundgaard, Ida 08902
Brändle, Christian 37397
Brändle, Hans 39978
Bräuer, Jörg 15499
Brafford, C.J. 45483
Bragagnolo, Dr. Pietro 23809
Bragg, Cheryl H. 41231
Bragg, Gary O. 46351
Bragotă, Gheorghe 32518
Braham, George O. 06637
Braham, Helen 39615
Brahim, Natalia Majluf 31205
Brahm-Lindberg, Lisa 48760
Brahma Chary, P. 21884

Braica, Silvio 07780
Braillard, Marie-Christine 14589
Brain, Danielle 43798
Bramah, Edward 39582
Bramberger, Alfred 01870
Bramlette, Teresa 41331
Branca, Luigi 24974
Brancaccio, Jim 44742
Brancaleoni, V. 03763
Brancati, Prof. Antonio 24857
Brancato, Prof. Francesco 24768
Brancel, Esther 48560
Brancelj, Andreja 34130
Brancucci, Dr. Michel 36514
Brand, Hermann 20709
Brand, Dr. Michael 46891
Brand, Dr. Ruth 36592
Brand, Ruth 37400
Brand-Claussen, Dr. Bettina 17674
Brânda, Nicolae 32438
Brandauer, Aline 47424
Brandão, J. 32303
Brandáo, Maria Luiza 04115
Brandauer, Aline 47427
Brandenburg, Dr. Hajo 17527
Brandenburg, Dr. Winfried 19751
Brandenburger-Eisele, Dr. Gerlinde 19243
Brandenstein, Ameli von 19805
Brander, Prof. A. 09441, 09443
Brander, Alli 09584
Brandl, Andrea 19889
Brandl, Franz 01738
Brandler, Gotthard 17393, 17394
Brandoli, Susan 06708
Brandon, Cath 00915
Brandon, G. 05264
Brandon, Reiko 44079
Brandson, Lorraine 05250
Brandt, Dr. Joachim 16025
Brandt, Dr. Klaus 19793
Brandt, Dr. Klaus J. 20099
Brandt, Dr. Michael 17757
Brandt, Monique 05351
Brandt, Dr. Reinhard 20495
Brandt, Thomas 19065
Brandt, Tova 42839
Brandt, Wayne 43259
Brannon, Jim 48075
Branscome, Curtis 47827
Branscome, Kimberly 46278
Bransom, Jennifer 42756
Brantley, R. Brit. 42259
Brascamp, M.H. 29482
Brasie, Jeff 42399
Brasil do Amaral, Paulo Cesar 04278
Braß, Dr. M. 20113
Brassel, Dirk 16272
Braswell, Alvin L. 46777
Bråthen, Magne 30602
Bratke, Dr. Elke 16242
Bratschi-Tschirren, Max 36685
Brattig, Dr. Patricia 18157
Bratton, Clara Ann 44641
Bratton, D. 40275
Bratton, Randall 48704
Bratuž, Ciril 34138
Brauen, Dr. Martin 37416
Brauer, Gerald J. 42855
Braufman, Sheila 41645
Braun, Dr. Andreas 02797
Braun, Annette 12112
Braun, Dr. Claudia 18615
Braun, Dr. Emanuel 16804
Braun, Hannes 02555
Braun, Dr. J.K. 45976
Braun, Joseph 12111
Braun, Karen 46768
Braun, Märta 36408
Braun, Mary E. 47152
Braun, Matthew 44270
Braun, Monika 18003
Braun, Peter 02542
Braun, Thomas 15757
Braun, Wilhelm 18788
Braunegger, Reinhold 02410
Braunlein, John 43621
Braunlein, John H. 45740
Braunová, Helena 08399
Brauns, Dmitri G. 47330
Braunstein, Susan L. 45821
Braunsteiner, Dr. Michael 01643
Braut, Else 30641
Bravo, John 47518
Braxton, Gail G. 43539, 43541, 43542
Bray, Alida 47351
Bray, Bill 43350
Bray, Rick 42769
Bray, Tamara 42936
Bray, Xavier 39729
Brayer, Hermione 12529
Brayner, Vânia 04302
Braz Teixeira, Dr. Madalena 32311
Brázdová, Marie 08739
Brearley, A. 39111
Brebeck, Wulff E. 16405
Brecciaroli, Dr. Luisa 25745
Brechbühl, Christof 37212
Brecht, Fatima 45838
Brechter, Steves 46228

Breckner, Thomas W. 44947
Bredenkamp, Dalene 34197
Bredereck, Wolfgang 00944
Bredow, Florentine C. 17794
Bredow, Sabine 15382
Bredsdorff, Eva B. 39556, 40069, 40817
Breede, Claus 05497
Breen, John D. 47478
Breese, Dr. Kathryn 44284
Breeze, Margaret 48614
Bregar, Marjeta 34136
Bregeaut, Pierre 11000
Bregovac Pisk, Marina 07822
Brehm, Georgia 44996
Brehm, Dr. Margrit 02549
Brehm, Dr. Thomas 19139
Brehme, Sylvia 15914
Breidbach, Prof. Dr. Dr. O. 17938
Breiler, Ronald 19682
Breinegaard, Jens 08860
Breiter, Michael 41084
Breitfuß, Dr. Anton 02553
Breithaupt, Brent H. 44647
Breithaupt, Julia 16728
Breitkreuz, Petra 17077
Breitmeier, Uwe 16538
Breitner, Suzy 45290
Breitwieser, Dr. Sabine 02887
Brejon, Barbara 12599
Brejon de Lavergnée, Arnauld 12599
Breker, Uwe H. 18159
Brekke, Borghild 30721
Brekke, Paul D. 47727
Brembeck, Josef 18755
Bremer, D. Neil 43165
Bremer, Stanley 29779
Bremner, R.W. 38778
Brendel-Pandich, Susanne 47958
Brendow, Dr. Volker 15763, 15766
Brendstrup, Dagmar 08803
Brengle, Anne B. 45662
Brennan, Anita 45510
Brennan, Anne G. 48663
Brennan, Edward 45866
Brennan, Kate 40526
Brennan, Nancy 46562
Brennan, Paul 41886
Brennan, Robert 22462
Brenneman, David 41348
Brenneman, Jan 43492
Brenner, Itzhak 22741
Brenner, Dr. Klaus-Peter 17338
Brenner, Theo E. 37382
Brennsteiner, Hans 02307
Brent, Brian 38658
Brent, Marty 06030
Bréon, Emmanuel 10837
Breščak, Mateja 34114
Breslauer, David 45507
Bresler, Zinaida Ivanovna 32641
Bresnahan, Bob 45265
Bresser, G.J. de 29411
Bressi, Dr. Nicola 25823
Bresticker, Stanley 46502
Breth, Renzo 47447
Breton, Audrée 06314
Breton, Gérard 12428
Bretón, Prof. Raúl 28110
Bretscher, Peter 36706
Bretscher, Renzo 36760
Bretschneider, Jürgen 19544
Brettner, Friedrich 01885
Breu, Zita 02993
Breuer, Brad 47243
Breuer, Dieter 20575
Breuker, P. 29260
Breunesse, Caroline 28911
Breuze, Marc 10612
Brevik, Bernt 30874
Breville, Tristan 27739
Brewer, Billy 41165
Brewer, Constance 42429
Brewer, Dr. Douglas J. 48163, 48164
Brewer, Esther Vivian 42931
Brewer, R. 38481
Brewster, Carrie 45491
Brewster, Christine 38200
Brewster, Linda 38828, 38829
Brewster, Pete 05042
Brewster, Rae 01480
Brewster, Suzanne G. 41055
Brewster, William F. 45075
Brey, F.J. 16985
Brey, Karen 42070, 42071, 46255
Brez, Wendy 43355
Breza, Bogusław 32149
Breza, Michael 46206
Brian, J. Andrew 45285
Brichet, Michel 03304
Brichtová, Dobromila 08476
Brick, Elizabeth M. 46008
Brickman, Penny 47492
Bridenstine, James A. 44379
Bridge, Louise 06621
Bridger, Tozzy 38980
Bridges, Edwin C. 45465
Bridges, Dr. E.M. 38966
Bridges, Mary 41155
Bridges, Roger D. 43556

Bridges, Tim 40933
Bridgford, Todd C. 43898
Bridgman, Norma 34248
Briedenhann, M.M. 34186, 34187
Briedis, Agris 27406
Briel, Gerhard 17796
Briend, J. 13550
Brier, Ida 44143
Briere, Florence 12401
Briese, Jodie G. 48726
Briest, Francis 15151
Brigandi, Phil 47348
Briggs, Kate Halle 47712
Briggs, Michael 38120
Briggs, Dr. Peter S. 48095
Briggs-Jude, Wendy 06776
Briggs Murray, James 45868
Brigham, David 48756
Bright, Bill 43510
Bright, Robert 48620
Brighton, T. 39112
Brillonet, Jean-Marc 14460
Brind, R.A. 38146
Brindeau, Irène 12412
Brindle, Nicole 06195
Brindley, Lynne 39585
Bringager, Frithjof 30746
Brink, Siegfried 20544
Brink, Dr. Sonja 16738
Brinkley, Mike 44282
Brinklow, R. 38800
Brinkman, L.D. 44456
Brinkmann, Dr. Bodo 17074
Brinkmann, Dr. Jens-Uwe 17341
Brinkmann, Petra 18749
Brinkmann, Dr. Vinzenz 18911
Brinkmann, Dr. W. 37404
Brisch, Brigitte 17085
Brisebois, Marcel 05914
Briški, Mika 34112
Brissard, Michel 15164
Brissette, Serge 11735
Brisson, Steven C. 45029, 45030, 45032, 45034
Brito Joao, Benedito 28729
Brito Moreira, Alvaro de 32343
Britschgi, Markus 36682
Britt, Nelson 42991
Britton, Marion 44847
Brivio, Dr. Ernesto 24394
Brix, Thorsten 11461
Břízová, Zuzana 08340
Brkić, Staniša 33854
Broach, Barbara K. 43343, 43345
Broad, Sandy 06469
Broadbert, D. 41725
Broaderick, Tom 41508
Broadfoot, Jan 48661
Broady, Duncan 39887
Brobst, William A. 46671
Brocas, Jon 30195
Brock, Mary 46489
Brocke, Dr. Edna 16944
Brockhaus, Prof. Dr. Christoph 16757
Brockhoff, Joan 06504
Brockmeier, Royna L. 43999
Brocksch, Dr. Dieter 19181
Brodanec, Vlado 07813
Broderick, Janice K. 47113
Brodeur, Bill 06107
Brodie, Ian J. 30284
Brodie, Suzanne M. 43338
Brodl, Michaela 02955
Brodneva, Adelja Vladimirovna 32954
Broege, Wallace W. 46916
Bröhan, Dr. Margrit 15930
Broeker, Dr. Holger 20662
Broekgaarden, A. 28866
Brönner, Dr. Melitta 16059
Brogiolo, Prof. G. Pietro 25323
Broglie, Charles Edouard Prince de 11143
Broidl, Erich 02703
Brok, Dr. Barbara den 36880
Brolsma, Allen 42706
Brom, Jodi 48696
Bromberg, Dr. Anne 42751
Brombierstäudl, Andreas 17916
Bromley, Fran 43920
Bromovsky, Fabia 40757
Broo, Dr. Hanno 16541
Broocks, Steven 47534
Brook, G.W.T. 01089
Brooke, Janet M. 05672
Brooke, Patrick 40712
Brooker, Melanie 37937
Brooking, Charles 38699
Brookman, Philip 48341, 48342
Brooks, Carol 48888
Brooks, Carolyn 44964
Brooks, Daniel F. 41704
Brooks, Dr. Earl 41211
Brooks, Eric 44736
Brooks, Leonard L. 45690
Brooks, Lindsay 40430
Brooks, Maggie 43773
Brooks, Peggy 43647
Brooks, Philip R.B. 40947
Brooks, Ruth 48549
Brooks jr., William F. 45310
Brooks Joyner, J. 46149

Brooks-Myers, Inez 46067
Brooksbank, Mike 39083
Brooslin, Michael 47748
Brophy, Dr. Gerald P. 41181
Broschinski, Dr. Annette 17607
Brose, Barbara H. 42742
Brose, David S. 43632
Brose, Lawrence F. 41987
Brosi, Dr. Sibylle 17995, 18002
Brosnahan, Seán 30152
Brosnan, Susan 45696
Brost, Leif 35957
Brothers, Michael M. 42811
Brotherton, Barbara 47545
Brouard, Michael 37090
Broucke, Remi 03360
Brougher, Kerry 48361
Broughton, H.E. 39915
Brouillet, Johanne 06440
Brouillette, Denis 06508
Brouillette, Penny 42128
Broun, Elizabeth 48390
Broun, Dr. Elizabeth 48392
Brousseau, Francine 05483, 05484
Brouwer, Dr. M. 29632
Brouwer, Norman 45874
Brouwer, T. de 29648
Brovčenkova, Valentina Ivanovna 32722
Brovinsky, Boris 34122
Brow, Charlotte 43554
Brower, Ken 48537
Brower, Paul 41603
Browes, Judi 38643
Brown, Alastair 30460
Brown, Alex 40703
Brown, Anne 46846
Brown, Anthony 01106
Brown, Ashley 41318
Brown-Bern Will 06010
Brown, Bruce 46971
Brown, Carol 34225, 39574
Brown, Charles B. 44439
Brown, Charles T. 45341
Brown, Dr. Charlotte V. 46778
Brown, Dr. Christopher 40141
Brown, Dr. Claudia 46477
Brown, Curtis E. 46427
Brown, Dan 47218
Brown, Daniel 46893
Brown, Dr. Daniel T. 47081
Brown, Dr. Dann 46617
Brown, Darlene 44362
Brown, David 26069, 42131
Brown, David Alan 48373
Brown, Don 43767, 44079
Brown, Dona 44815
Brown, Dorothy 06667
Brown, Elizabeth A. 47535
Brown, Ellsworth H. 46512
Brown, Eric 38235
Brown, Forrest 46020, 46022
Brown, Geoffrey I. 48682
Brown, Georgina 05335
Brown, Gordon 40288, 40289
Brown, Hannah 48115
Brown, Harold 06172, 44044
Brown, Harold L. 43921
Brown, Helen 38544
Brown, Ian 38616, 38819, 38820, 39024, 39334, 40468, 40470, 40471
Brown, James A. 43954
Brown, Jane 42222
Brown, Janene 44391
Brown, Jean 39431
Brown, Jocelyn 30232
Brown, Johanna 48701
Brown, Julia 45872
Brown, Karon 47983
Brown, Kate 40802
Brown, Kevan 39940
Brown, Kevin 39564
Brown, Leanne 48271
Brown, Lee N. 13342
Brown, M. 05030
Brown, Margaret 38196, 38197, 38198
Brown, Marjorie 43883
Brown, Marlene 48169
Brown, Marlin 05447
Brown, Mary Anne 42378
Brown, Michael K. 44129
Brown, Nancy 48559
Brown, Nancy F. 45396
Brown, Neil 06523
Brown, Nicolas 46719
Brown, Patricia 42462
Brown, Peter B. 40962
Brown, Rich 46508
Brown, Richard D. 43273
Brown, Rick 44536, 44538, 44539
Brown, R.J. 47093
Brown, Robert 38139
Brown, Robert M. 45405
Brown, Rondalyn 46281
Brown, Dr. S. 38220
Brown, Scott 40971
Brown, Stephen 47547
Brown, T. Robins 44041
Brown, Terrence 45871
Brown, Vinita 43359

Brown, Vivian A. 31426
Brown, W. 40084
Brown, William 43876
Brown, Dr. William 44077
Brown Hirst, Kaye 47220
Brownawell, Christopher J. 43066
Browne, Charles C. 47098
Browne, J. 22358
Browne, Mary-Louise 30109
Browne, Patrick 43029
Brownell, Carlton C. 44817
Browning, Dawn C. 45208
Browning, Mark 45336
Brownlee, Reuben 48274
Browns, Doug 43789
Brownson, Ron 30103
Broy, Erich 18381
Brubaker, Bob 48479
Bruce, Donald 45744
Bruce, Dorene 41586
Bruce, E. 05059
Bruce, Elspeth 40187
Bruce, Jeffrey 43896
Bruce, Michael 43855, 43856
Bruch, Claudia 16977
Bruchhäuser, A. 16136
Bruck, Anton 02974
Brück, Martin 16584
Brueck, Siegfried 19991
Brückner, Heike 16584
Brückner, Sigrid 20140
Brüderlin, Dr. Markus 37060
Brüggerhoff, Dr. Stefan 16193
Brühlmann, Fritz 36484
Brülisauer, Annemarie 37026
Brüning, Henning 16584
Brüninghaus-Knubel, Cornelia 16757
Bruer, Dr. Stephanie-Gerrit 20057, 20059
Brugeman, Tim 43323
Bruges Moreu, Gladys Marina 07576
Brugge, Dr. J.P. ter 29948
Bruggeman, Jean 15220
Bruggen, Bill 44224
Brugger, Dr. Ingried 02840
Brugnoli, Renzo 25294
Brugnoli Bailoni, Francisco 06910
Brugo, Carlo 25272
Bruguière, Philippe 13558
Bruhin, Felix 36709
Bruhn, Thomas P. 47837
Bruijn, Dr. J. de 28858
Bruijn, J.A. 29142
Bruin, Joan 44922
Bruin, Dr. R.E. de 29897
Bruinjes, Wilhelm 16762
Bruintjes, Jaap C.N. 29179
Brulomié, Agnes 10809
Brumbauch, Mary 45004
Brumbaugh, Lee 46834
Brumberg, Esther 45842
Brumder, Robert B. 48466
Brumelis, Andrew 06589
Brumen, Patrizia 01927
Brumgardt, Dr. John R. 42211
Brummer, Guntram 20245
Brummer, Hans Henrik 36274
Brun, Dominique 12726
Brun, Laura 47322
Brunacci, Prof. Dr. Aldo 22962, 22967
Brunacci, Maurizio 23483
Brunckhorst, Dr. Friedl 15667
Brundin, Martha 42792
Brune, Thomas 17680, 20115
Brunecker, Frank 16138
Brunel, Georges 13541
Brunelle, Danielle 05905
Brunet, P. 13166
Brunette, T. 06687
Brunetti, Armando 23538
Brungard, Charlene K. 41589
Bruni, Dr. Gaetano 25167
Bruni, Giovanni 23455
Bruni, Stephen T. 48649
Brunin, Ph. 03796
Bruning, Angela 16156
Brunius, Staffan 36240
Brunn-Lundgren, Maria 35909
Brunnemann, Eric 21259
Brunner, Dr. 12734
Brunner, Alois 19354
Brunner, Dieter 17691, 17692
Brunner, Dorla 41691
Brunner, Heinz 02959
Brunner, Dr. Michael 20244
Brunner, Paul 15694
Bruno, Prof. Gianfranco 23994
Brunovský, Ferdinand 34074
Bruns, James H. 48383
Brunscheen, Scott 42909
Brunschwyler, Greta 46046
Brunson, Jeana 47936
Brunson, Neal E. 44338
Brunson, Theodore 44338
Brunson Frisch, Marianne 46556
Bruschetti, Dr. Paolo 23663
Bruse, Ralf 19013
Brusila, Johannes 10127
Brussa, Carlos A. 41028
Brussat, Tracey K. 46715

Brussee, G.J. 29688
Brust, Alexander 36508
Bruton, Prof. David L. 30735
Brutvan, Cheryl 41817
Bruy Beyer, Mette 08933
Brüvere, Solvita 27398
Bruwier, Marie-Cécile 03640
Bruy, Pauline 03582
Bruyn, Dr. Jean-Pierre de 03440
Bruyn, M.A. de 29800
Bruyninx, Prof. Dr. E. 03437
Brvar, C. 29901
Bryan, Dr. Betsy 41449
Bryan, Dr. Charles F. 46890
Bryan, Tim 40664, 40667
Bryan, Tracey 46890
Bryan Hood, Mary 46230
Bryant, James 46922
Bryant, Jim 46615
Bryant, Julius 40738
Bryant, Steve 39584
Bryck, Jack 41442
Bryde, John A. 30806
Bryer, Stephen 40855
Bryman, Donna 05323
Bryson, Mary 48066
Bryzensky, Nicole 01474
Brzeziński, Prof. Tadeusz 32026
Brzeziński, Dr. Wojciech 32139
Brzon, Narveen 46843
Brzozowski, Jerzy 32010
Brzozowski, Leszek 31605
Bsteh, Prof. Dr. Andreas 02310
Bubb, Shirley 44630
Buberl, Dr. Brigitte 16662
Buccellato, Prof. Laura 00171
Buccheri, Prof. G. 24775
Bucci, Jonathan 48408
Bucciferro, Rose 44840
Buccino Grimaldi, Marchese Luigi 25611
Buccleuch, Duke of 40467, 40469
Buch, Carl E. 30538, 30539
Buchal, Dr. Sabine 19259
Buchan, Andrew 39487
Buchanan, David 44225
Buchanan, Dennis 38393
Buchanan, John 01081
Buchanan jr., John E. 46641
Buchanan, Karen 45007
Buchanan-Dunlop, R. 39644
Buchel, M. 28889
Bucher, Friedrich 02392
Bucher, Prof. Dr. H. 37404
Bucher, Hans 17136
Bucher, Regina 36944
Bucher-Häberli, E. 36786
Buchheim, Prof. Dr. Lothar-Günther 16129
Buchholtz, Annegret 18161
Buchholz, Sabine 18026
Buchholz-Todoroska, Małgorzata 31988
Buchi, Danielle 10880
Buchner, Dr. Gabriele 19413
Buchner, U. Ernest 05418
Buchs, Denis 36603
Buchtmann, Hans-Georg 20286
Bučinskaja, Valentina Stanislavovna 27072
Buck, Dennis 41394
Buck, Prof. Dr. Elmar 18167
Buck, Kathleen 48105
Buck, Kurt 19345
Buckaloo, Terence 47804
Buckellew, Shari Spaniol 41741
Buckie, Valerie 04989
Buckingham, John 40157
Buckley, Annette 38131
Buckley, Juanita 46479
Buckley, Kerry W. 46014
Buckley, Laurene 43357, 45674
Buckley, Oliver 40773
Bucknill, Greg 40190
Buckridge, Martin 40222
Buckson, Deborah 46092
Bucur, Corneliu-Ioan 32591
Buczkowski, Hans 02437
Buczynski, Bodo 16096
Budarov, Viktor Viktorovič 33730, 33732
Budde, Bernhard 16319
Budde, Dr. Rainer 18168
Buddle, Allan 44238
Buderer, Dr. Hans-Jürgen 18612, 18615
Budiastra, Putu 22096
Budiati, Dr. Tinia 22106
Budimir, Dr. Ante 07786
Budka, Mikołaj 31491
Budko, Prof. Dr. Anatolij A. 33488
Budney, Jen 06080
Budrovich, Tony 44894
Budrys, Milda 42338
Budrys, Romualdas 27536
Budzynski, Lillian 42621
Büche, Wolfgang 17521
Büchler, Dr. Hans 36874
Büchler-Mattmann, Dr. Helene 36559
Bücken, Véronique 03299
Buecker, Thomas R. 42689
Bückling, Dr. Maraike 17075
Bügel, Christian 18151
Buehler, J. Marshall 48719
Bühler, R.E. 37350

Bühlmann, Isolde 36679
Bühner, Dr. Jan-A. 20086
Buell, Pamela 06179
Buendía García, Mercedes 35629
Buenrostro Alba, Manuel 28156
Bürger, Werner 15503
Bürgin, Christoph 36919
Bürgin, Dr. Toni 37106
Bürke, Dr. Bernhard 36662
Bürki, Prof. Hermann 36540
Buerlein, Robert A. 46870
Buermeyer, Chris 43858
Büscher, Marietta 18951
Buesing, Kay 44865
Büsser, Roger E. 37314
Bütikofer, Prof. Alfred 37329, 37340
Bützer, Michael 16739
Büyükçapar, Ahmet 37722
Bufano, Ralph A. 47539
Buford, Elizabeth F. 46776
Bugaeva, Galina Alekseevna 33569
Bugalho Semedo, C.M. 32289
Bugalová, Dr. Edita 33966
Bugarski, Astrida 03925
Bugg, Mathias 37119
Buggeland, Tord 30641
Buggle, Claudia 20480
Bugnon, Prof. Pierre-André 37287
Buhler, Leslie L. 48398
Buhlmann, Dr. Britta E. 17970
Buić, Evgenije 33810
Buijs, H.W.J. 29930
Buijs, J. 13487
Buisson, René 05924
Bujakowska, Beata 31616
Bujić, Marija 33810
Bujold, Michel 06141
Bukač, Václav M. 08359
Bukačová, Dr. Irena 08429, 08471
Bukowska, Halina Lubomiła 31820
Bulaty, Dr. Milan 16110
Bulei, Gheoghe 32604
Bulei, Gheorghe 32601, 32602, 32603
Bulgarelli, Grazia Maria 25238
Bulger, Ralph 06051
Bulgin, Lloyd 05358
Buljević, Zrinka 07779
Bull, Hege Sofie 30635
Bullard, E. John 45735
Buller, Osmo 10070
Bullinger, Dr. Thomas 09111
Bullock, Christopher 40888
Bullock, Margaret 46641
Bulova, Gretchen M. 41127
Bulthuis, P. 30044
Bumgardner, Tim 44273
Bumiller, Manfred 15812
Bumpass, Terry 47419, 47424
Bunbury, Theresa 04996
Bunce, Mark 38356
Bunch, Lonnie G. 42318
Bunch, Nancy B. 42560
Bunch, Rosemary 48746
Bund, Dr. Konrad 17385
Bung, Maria-Hildegard 15788
Bungert, Petra 03278
Bunke, Jim 47550
Bunker-Lohrenz, Jackie 47040
Bunkichi, Ito 27011
Bunyan, Vicki 01211
Buonanno, Prof. Roberto 25178
Burak, Marek 32179
Buran, Dr. Dusan 33978
Buranelli, Dr. Francesco 48868, 48872
Burbank, Jane 46895
Burbano, Ignacio 07552
Burch, Danielle 43982
Burch, Ivan 05929
Burch, Prof. John B. 41220
Burch, Wanda 44350
Burchard, Helen 41579
Burchfield, Stanley G. 47195, 47200
Burckhardt, Dr. Daniel 36514
Burdak, Elisabeth 37424
Burdick, Funi 43251
Burdick, Richard L. 47001
Burdychová, Milena 08321
Burel, Bernard 13825
Burford, Beverley 39649
Burganov, Aleksandr 33116
Burge, Don 46693
Burge, Roisin 39229
Burge, Sarah 38297
Burger, Bernadette 36907
Burger, Dr. Hans 36444
Burger, Richard L. 45698
Burger, W. 17892
Burgère, André 11424
Burgess, Brian 01130
Burgess, Cynthia 48260
Burgess, Jerry G. 43419
Burgess, Jo 41750
Burgess, Ken 45329
Burgess, Norman 39783
Burgess, Robert 45748
Burgess, Susan M. 38929
Burghardt, Glenn 46058
Burghardt, Dr. Rainer 02312
Burgiss, Ken 30158

Burgos Cantor, Roberto 07396
Burgraff, Joseph 03455
Burik, Tatjana Borisovna 33559
Burkarth, Dr. Axel 20115
Burke, Adele 44943
Burke, Bonnie 05138
Burke, Bridget 42882
Burke, Daniel 46422
Burke, Gregory 30213
Burke, Jo 42856
Burke, Joan T. 42268
Burke, Marcus B. 45815
Burke, Maryellen 46649
Burke, Susan M. 05697
Burkel, Don 42268
Burkert, Richard A. 44352, 44353
Burkhalter, Françoise 36946
Burkhardt, Guido 15889
Burkhardt-Aebi, Rosmarie 36811
Burkhart, Linda 42274
Burki, Erika 36607
Burleson, D. 05560
Burleson, Rita 44651
Burlingham, Cynthia 44905
Burluaux-Blanchard, Odile 13548
Burman, Michael 40797
Burman, Peter 36185
Burman, Rickie 39677, 39678
Burmann, Peter 36187
Burmeister, Artur 18322
Burmeister, Prof. Dr. E.-G. 18926
Burmeister, Helmut 17798
Burmester, Dr. Andreas 18842
Burn, Dr. L. 38454
Burn-Murdoch, R.I. 40405
Burne, Colleen 42941
Burnett, Dr. A. 39586
Burnett, Kay Taylor 45631
Burnett, La Jean 44043
Burnett, Mark R. 41493
Burnett, Richard 39105
Burnett, Wayne 47094
Burnette, David 45540
Burnham, Laura 44333
Burns, Courtney 46181
Burns, Jane 43140
Burns, Kelly S. 44182
Burns, Laura 41486
Burns, Nancy 46339
Burns, Norman O.. 45612
Burns, Pamela 05942
Burns, Richard 38411
Burns, Rick 43137
Burns McAndrew, F. 47108
Burnside, Madeleine H. 44469
Burny, Jeannine 03332
Burojević, Zoran 07776
Buron, Gildas 10604
Buron, René 14399, 14402
Burpee, Jane 05350
Burr, Dr. Brooks M. 42102
Burrell, J.E. 38331
Burresi, Dr. Mariagiulia 24953
Burri, Mario 37363
Burris, Erna 42054
Burroughs, Judy 46832
Burroughs, Stuart 38117
Burscheidt, Margret 16970
Bursell, Barbro 36256
Bursey, M.L. 34236
Bursić, Herman 07758
Burt, Ann 46193
Burtch, Michael 06410
Burton, John 43330, 44602
Burton, Margaret 43689
Burton, Val 00852
Burtschi, Mary 48202
Busack, Dr. Stephen 46777
Busceme, Greg 41563
Busch, Anna 36268
Busch, Fritz B. 20648
Busch, Dr. Ina 16541
Busch, Ingo 17605
Busch, Jean 48037
Busch, Wolf-Rüdiger 17209
Buschhoff, Dr. Anne 16328
Busching, Dr. Wolf-Dieter 18191
Buser, Pierre 36890
Busetto, Dr. Giorgio 25934
Bush, Dianne 05823
Bush, Walter 46487
Bush Tomio, Kimberley 48132
Bushby, Debra L. 38092
Busine, Laurent 03503
Busjan, Béatrice 20618
Busk Laursen, Bodil 08927
Buskirk, Dr. William H. 46861
Buskov, Poul 09113
Buss, Leo W. 45698
Bussac, Monique 10356
Busse, Bettina M. 02929
Busse, Dr. Klaus 16250
Busse, Valerie 45184
Bussees, Dr. Helena 03297
Bussers, Helena 03299
Bussers, Dr. Helena 03298
Bussinger, André 10896
Bußmann, Prof. Dr. Klaus 18950
Bußmann, Maria 02929

Bustard, Wendy 45592
Bušueva, Margarita Viktorovna 33268
Busuladžić, Adnan 03925
Butala, Daniel 07713
Butler, Charles Thomas 42574
Butler, Connie 44930
Butler, David 39982, 48599
Butler, Gay 42255
Butler, Gerald 41523
Butler, John 38191
Butler, Joyce 46629
Butler, Maria V. 46345
Butler, Mary 41538
Butler, Maurice 06296
Butler, R. 34318
Butler, Samuel 45859
Butler, S.R. 39485
Butler, T. 39305
Butler, Tony 38649, 40055
Butnaru, Ioan 32559
Butt, Raymond 40237
Buttacavoli, Eva 41406
Buttar, Lyn 30309
Buttarazzi, Silvestro 23370
Buttel, Larry 43550
Butter, Jelena 16061
Butter, Mary 40454
Butterfield, DeAnne 41833
Butterfield, Tom 41729
Buttini, Eric 27568
Buttlar-Elberberg, Dr. Gertrud 03020
Button, Lawrence 43518
Butts, H. Daniel 45125
Butty, Dr. Pierre 37285
Butz, Dr. Herbert 16057
Buurma, Hilbrand 29834
Buurman, H. 29095
Buus, Henriette 08842
Buvelot, Q. 29105
Buyandelger, U. 28689
Buyko, Malgorzata 31682
Buys, C. 29525
Buyssens, Danielle 36728
Buzzi, Alessandro 25003
Buzzoni, Dr. Andrea 23786, 23796, 23799
Byambasüren, P. 28677
Byčkova, Marina Nikolaevna 33659
Bye, Joellen 45659
Byers, Bill 41881
Byers, James B. 48333
Byh, Per-Olov 36002
Bykov, Dr. Aleksandr 33722
Bykova, Jekaterina Vladimirovna 33213
Bykovceva, L.P. 33098, 33121
Bylicki, Tomasz 32083
Byman, Bertyl 09817
Bynum, Marci 44823
Byong, Ha Min 27285
Byrd, Cathy 41345
Byrd, Eugene 47776
Byrn, Brian 43140
Byrne, Debra J. 47534
Byrne, Douglas 40463
Byrne, Lisa 10826
Byrne, Paddy 22465
Byrne, Roger 41646
Byrne, Sue 39080
Byrtusová, Jana 08306
Byström, Lars 36262
Bytkovskij, Oleg 33272
Byvanck, Dr. F.V. 29595
Byzewski, Leah 43741
Caballero Barnard, Prof. José M. 28542
Cabanes, Francisco 35611
Cabano-Dempsey, Annali 34172
Cabaret, Michel 13940
Cabel, Oswalda A. 31332
Cabell, Kathleen 43725
Cabello Carro, Dr. Paz 35016
Cabezas, Hervé 12168, 14434
Cable, Christopher B. 41200
Cabot, Ian 40418
Cabot, Lee A. 43237
Cabot, Paul 06615
Cabral, Dr. Elisabeth 32291, 32297
Cabrera, Asun 35062
Cabrera, E. 43280
Cabrera, Geles 28166
Cabrera Cachón, Teresa 28569
Caccia, Antonietta 25518
Cachola Schmal, Peter 17035
Cad, Gabriel 31322
Cadavid López, Susana 07598
Cadenne, Ivan 11188
Cadier, Gérard 13864
Cagigós i Soró, Antonio 35470
Cagli, Prof. Bruno 24862
Çağman, Dr. Filiz 37709
Cahen, Daniel 28862
Cahen, Joël 1. 28862
Cahen-Delhaye, Anne 03337, 03337, 03340
Cahill, Ann 40117
Cahill, John 22535
Cahill, Kevin M. 45757
Caho, Ismet 33861
Caiado, José Pedro 32308
Caicedo, Iván 07469
Caicedo de Gómez, Hilda María 07445

Caicedo Lourido, María Isabel 07454
Caille, Georges 37248
Cain, Glena 46480
Cain, Prof. Dr. Hans-Ulrich 18384
Caines, M. 38823
Caivano, Felice 43945
Caji, Jaroslav 33788
Čajka, Vladimír Michailovič 33699, 33710, 33712
Čajkovskij, Bogdan N. 37886
Çakmak, Hacı 37626
Calame, Caroline 36888
Calandra, Eliana 24774
Calasan, Kovilįka 33789
Calatayud Cases, José Vte 35317
Calbiac, Christoph de 12646
Calboutin, A. 34403
Caldeira, Ernesto 48745
Caldeira, Prof. Dr. Helena 32258
Caldeira, Vasco 04515
Calder, Jacqueline 45478
Calderan, Gianni 25252
Calderer Serra, Joaquín 35502
Caldwell, Brenda B. 48122, 48123
Caldwell, Carey 46067
Caldwell, Desiree 42598
Caldwell, Frank 40671
Caldwell, Joan G. 45739
Caldwell, Dr. J.P. 45976
Caldwell, Judy 45233
Caldwell, K. 38688
Caldwell, Roy 41646
Calhoun, Angela 43521
Calhoun, Ralph 45439
Calisi, Dr. Marinella 25178
Caliz, Dr. Luis E. 32373
Calkins, Christopher 46377
Calkins, Jack 05393
Call, Linda 48781
Callaghan, Madelein 06414
Callaghan, Richard 38855, 38856, 38857
Callahan, Christine 45930
Callahan, Colin J. 42604
Callahan, Colleen 46888
Callahan, Elizabeth 43057
Callahan, Martin L. 43451
Callahan, William 42569
Callan, Josi Irene 47921
Callanan, Mary 22479
Calland, Gary 40617
Callatÿ, François de 03275, 03277
Callaway, Judson 47237
Callebert, Fernand 03707
Calleen, Dr. Justinus Maria 20628
Callegher, Dr. Bruno 24736
Callen, Bonnie 05423
Callewaert, Ferdy 03703
Callies, Prof. Dr. H. 20019
Callis, Charles 30305
Callison, Brian 38802
Callison, Chris 48165
Calloway, Bertha 46148
Calomiris, Ellen 44864
Calonne, Sylvain 15221
Caltik, Heidi 02929
Calvarin, Margaret 10952, 11429
Calvert, Peter S. 46868
Calvesi, Prof. Maurizio 23577
Calvi di Bergolo, Ippolito 25462
Calvin, Prudence K. 48445
Calvo, B. 35038
Calvo, Ernesto 07655
Calvo, Luis María 00603
Calvocoressi, Richard 38876, 38916
Calzada, S. 34548
Camacho, Dr. João Carlos 32250
Camacho Cadaval, Fernando 35488
Camara, Dr. Abdoulaye 33783
Camara, Calvin 41237
Camara, Prof. Edeltrudes 03985
Camasse, Dr. Michele M. 24155
Camber, Diane W. 45298
Cameron, Dan 45855
Cameron, E. 30104
Cameron, Elizabeth 38795
Cameron, Fran 06084
Cameron, Gary L. 45185
Cameron, John 38252
Cameron, Joyce M. 47728
Cameron, Rosanna 01107
Cameron of Lochiel, Sir Donald 40566
Camfield, Paul 43532
Camin, Philippe 13027, 14594
Camm, Simon 40303
Cammarata, Paolo 25316
Cammarota, Dr. Giampiero 23128
Camnitzer, Luis 45794
Camós Alvarez, Pilar 35718
Camoys, Lord 39221
Camp, Janet G. 47886
Camp, Kimberly 45266
Campagna, Dr. Francesca 24364
Campagnolo, Matteo 36743
Campanalli, Dr. Adele 23548
Campbell, Bruce 40051
Campbell, C.A. 40589
Campbell, Catherine A. 43613
Campbell, Clayton 47440
Campbell, Colin 48627
Campbell, Connie 06001

Campbell, D. 39202
Campbell, Daniel T. 47669
Campbell, Deborah 41213
Campbell, Ellen F. 43458
Campbell, Francis D. 45760
Campbell, George 05657
Campbell, Ina 41734
Campbell, Jacklyn 41357
Campbell, Prof. J.D. 30148
Campbell, John 45702
Campbell, Kathleen 46829
Campbell, Kathryn 47527
Campbell, Kay 01464
Campbell, Lesa 42996
Campbell, Levin 41814
Campbell, Loraine 48068
Campbell, Lorne 39729
Campbell, Mabel 06104
Campbell, Mei 44991
Campbell, Mungo 39050
Campbell, Nancy 44481
Campbell, Neil 05791
Campbell, Richard 45391
Campbell, Roy G. 46777
Campbell, Sara 46302
Campbell, Shearon 42391
Campbell, Tacie N. 42993
Campbell, Tracey 45467
Campbell, Wallace 46321
Campbell-Ferguson, Gail 41879
Campbell McMurray, H. 40258
Campbell-Shoaf, Heidi 43527
Camphausen, Ute 18398
Campo, Marta 34542
Campodonico, Dr. Piero 24006
Campofiorito, Italo 04226
Campos, Alexander 44304
Campos, Prof. Antonio Celso de Arruda 04208
Campos, Maria Lucia Rocha 04522
Campredon, Elisabeth 11486
Campuzano Ruiz, Enrique 35452
Camus, Marie-France 12323
Canal, Dr. Guillermo C. de la 00173
Canales, Rocio Gonzalez de 28232
Cañamás, Marita 35599
Canbey, Maşuk 37802
Cândea, Ionel 32444
Candeloro, Ilaria 25296
Cândido, Maria João 32346
Candlin, Dierdre 39733
Candon, Anthony 40132
Candy, Ron 06706
Caneer, Ann 46583
Canini, Alberto 25201
Canizales Montoya, Luis Fernando 07558
Cankova, Tatjana 34457
Cannata, Dr. Roberto 25166
Cannatella, David C. 41421
Cannegieter, Dr. D.A.S. 29240
Canning-Lacroix, Johane 05930, 06360
Cannon, Annetta 46036
Cannon, Janet 05531
Cannon, P. 40030
Cannon-Brookes, Peter 39405
Cano, Luis Martín 28211
Cano, Rose Marie 44937
Cano de Martín, Marta 00294
Cano Rivero, Ignacio 35485
Cano Salas, Gilda 28149
Canogar, Rafael 35678
Canonne, Xavier 03350
Canovai, Dr. Roberto 24228
Canright, Steve 47337
Cantinho, Dr. Manuela 32302
Cantley, John 47904
Cantor, Helen 43518
Canulli, Richard G. 48236
Capa, José 35232
Capa Eiriz, Dr. José 34763
Capanna, Prof. Ernesto 25206
Capano, Dr. Antonio 25953
Capazza, Gérard 13234
Capdevila, Dr. Ricardo 00180, 00187
Capella Molas, Anna 34817
Capin, Djordje 33840, 33841
Capin, Jean 14923
Capion, Ole 08769
Capistrano Barker, Dr. Florina H. 31352
Capitani, Dr. François de 37031, 37393
Capitanio, Fabrizio 23064
Čapková, Dr. Jana 08362
Capomolla, Soccorso 24543
Capon, Barry 38374
Capon, Edmund 01490, 01491
Capon, S.H. 40831
Capot, Stéphane 12611
Capovilla, Prof. Sergio Carlos 00554
Cappelletti, Prof. Vincenzo 24945
Capper, Rosi 39324
Capponi, Dr. Carlo 24411
Capps, Jennifer 44234
Capps, Larry 44175
Capralos, Souli 20804, 20855
Caproni di Taliedo Guasti, Firmina 25175
Carabo, Lucille 41627, 41628
Caradec, Marie-Anne 11477
Caramazza, O.G. 24328
Caramelle, Dr. Franz 02063
Caramelli, Fernando 24923

Carazzetti, Prof. Riccardo 36885, 36886, 36891
Carbajal, Londi 47431
Carbajal, Sergio 28162
Carballo, José Rodriguez 35445
Carbert, R.W. 05854
Carbery, David 22469
Carbonell, Sílvia 35525
Carbonell i Esteller, Eduard 34585
Card, Nan 43556
Cardarelli, Andrea 24438, 24439
Cardelli, Patrice 12753
Carden, Martha 42812
Carden, Willie F. 42411
Cárdenas Marcaida, María Caridad 07892
Cárdenas Tovar, Jairo Simón 07619
Cardenas Troncoso, Gloria 06890
Carder, Julia 39517
Cardim Ribeiro, José 32350
Cardin, Deborah 41472
Cardinaels, Marie-Jeanne 03242
Cardinale, Vincenzo 16255
Cardini, Giuliano 25643
Cardon, Dorothy 46751
Cardon, Véronique 03300
Cardona, Hermana Martha 07593
Cardone, Veronique 12384
Cardoner, F. 34532
Cardoso, Prof. Dr. António 32235
Cardoso Botelho, Americo G. 32240
Cardot, A. 37278
Carduner, Michel 14326
Cardwell, E. 40131
Carevic Rivera, Alvaro 06896
Carey, Betsy 47952
Carey, Edith 37289
Carey, Hon Hug L. 45757
Carfano, M. Susan 48807
Cargeeg, G. 01592
Cariello, Dr. Rubina 25611
Carignani, Dr. Mario 24581
Cariou, André 13901
Carl, Christine S. 43609
Carl, Christy 43606
Carlano, Annie 47426
Carle, Michele 43383
Carlén, Staffan 36032
Carles, Gilbert 14967
Carlestam, Håkan 35933
Carleton, Dr. Don 41408, 48172
Carli, Dr. Laura 25654
Carlier, Sylvie 15211
Carlier, Yves 11769
Carlile, Janet 05009
Carlin, Scott 01565
Carlosama Mora, Rosa Cecilia 07501
Carlquist, Thomas 36494
Carlsen, Dr. Charles 46223
Carlsen, Margaret 46705
Carlson, Elizabeth 48693
Carlson, Jeffrey 46345
Carlson, Jim 47629
Carlson, Joseph 43139
Carlson, Linda 43381
Carlson, Norman P. 44311
Carlson, Robert 41781
Carlson, Dr. Shawn 48421
Carlsson, Ann-Britt 36342
Carlsson, Eva 35882
Carlström, Dr. Ann-Kristin 36115
Carlstrom, Terry 43918, 47582, 48355, 48368, 48388
Carmack, Brent 44787
Carman, Michael D. 46471, 46474
Carmen Lema Pensado, María del 41021
Carmer, Craig 44885
Carmichael, Dr. Ian 41644
Carmichael, J. 39671
Carmichael, Kristina 42238
Carmona Lancheros, Carlos Alberto 07442
Carmount, Laurie 05544
Carnahan, John W. 45445
Carnap-Bornheim, Prof. Dr. C. von 16433
Carnap-Bornheim, Prof. Dr. Claus von 19793
Carnazzi, Umberto 23081
Carner, Gil 44572
Carnerini, Carla 24812
Carnes, Griffiths 44455
Carnes, John 44772
Carnes, William H. 43403
Carney, Barbara 47987
Carney, Dr. Margaret 41137
Carney, Terry J. 39117
Carniello, Peter 05443
Caroeva, Ludmila R. 37911
Carolan, Janet 38738
Carollo, Albert H. 48258
Carollo, Eugene R. 48258
Caron, Euclid 46205
Caron, Jacqueline 05634
Carpenter, Dean 42178, 43073
Carpenter, Ele 40647
Carpenter, Frank 38743
Carpenter, Dr. M.A. 38462
Carpenter, Matthew 41240
Carpenter, Dr. Richard 42827
Carpenter, T.F. 33333
Carpenter Correa, Laura 41926
Carpenter Troccoli, Joan 42885
Carpentier, Régine 03274

Carpio, Agustín 00469
Carr, Carolyn 48382
Carr, Eve 48659
Carr, Josh 45751
Carr, Layton 47568
Carr, Lucia C. 45047
Carr, N.J. 38306
Carr, Shelvie 42808
Carr-Griffin, Paul 39549
Carr-Whitworth, Caroline 38740
Carradice, Prof. Ian A. 40386
Carrara, Dr. Giancarlo 23543
Cararo, Dr. Francine 44290
Carré, Dr. Enrique González 31221
Carreau, Raphaële 11249, 11250
Carreck, Marjorie W. 39218
Carregha, Luz 28407
Carreira, Dr. Isabel 32265
Carrel, Michel 14441
Carreño, Irving 48901
Carreño Díaz, Prof. Esboardo 27894
Carrera Hontana, Enrique de 35029
Carretero Rebes, Salvador 35431
Carrier, Alan 46197
Carrier, Nicole M. 44273
Carrlee, Ellen 44370
Carrol, Brian 41964
Carroll, Daine L. 48055
Carroll, M. Lyda 43837
Carroll, Richard E. 48544
Carroll, Rowan 30242
Carroll, Scott 44368
Carroll, Sue 46728
Carroll, William B. 39257
Carron, Christian G. 43759
Carruthers, Karen 38258
Carruthers, Ray 06535
Carruzzo, S. 37286
Cars, Laurence des 13596
Carson, Heather 39720, 39804
Carson, John 46800
Carson, Michael 42364
Carstensen, Dr. Jan 16590
Carswell, A.L. 38900
Cart, Doran L. 44403
Cartacci, Marcello 25259
Carter, Bennett 43782
Carter, Curtis L. 45363
Carter, Dr. Curtis L. 45371
Carter, Hazel 45159
Carter, John S. 46419
Carter, Julia 44058, 44058
Carter, Kathy 44545
Carter, Martha C. 47729
Carter, Michael 45784
Carter, Mike 41863
Carter, Penelope 38898
Carter, R. 00847
Carter, Susan 47942
Carter, W.J. 38632
Cartwright, Colin M. 38180
Cartwright, Derrick R. 43907
Cartwright, Thomas 43522
Carty, Paul 22429
Caruana, Sebastian 27718
Carucci, Arturo 25321
Carus, Benno 16000
Carusi, Corina 42331
Caruso, Dr. Ida 23596
Caruso, Romy 48489
Carustrom, Terry 41265
Carvalho, Joseph 47746, 47747
Carvallo, Henri 15172
Carver, Dan 46258
Carver, Kate 39262
Carvey-Stewart, Elizabeth 46953
Cary, Farrin 43046
Cary, PeeWee 43008
Carzou, Jean-Marie 12795
Čas, Alenka 34089
Casadei, Dr. Sauro 23757
Casado Soto, José Luis 35432
Casagrande, Louis B. 41804
Casagrande, Rodrigo Fernando 04571
Casagrande, Tiziana 23771, 23772
Casal, Gabriel 31368
Casaldi, Silvano 24617
Casale, Tommaso 25666
Casalini, Dr. Antonio 24801
Casanelles, Eusebi 35527
Casanovas, María Antonia 34556
Casaro, Massimo 24410
Casarola, Albino 24553
Casartelli, Marisa Helena Cestari 04454
Casas, Imma 34591
Cascales Ayala, Manuel 34468
Caselli Wijsbek, H.E.J. 29919
Casetti, Christoph 36635
Casey, Dawn 00828, 00887
Casey, Laura 47587
Casey, Lynn R. 43618
Casey, Prof. Michael T. 22518
Cash, Reva 42906
Cash, Sarah 48341, 48342
Cashatt, Dr. Everett D. 47737
Cashbaugh, Todd M. 41217
Cashman, William 41574
Casini, Dr. Stefania 23061
Casjens, Laurel 47235

Câşlaru, Constantin 32436
Casler, Jennifer R. 43487
Caso, Kristin 41081
Caspers, Martha 17055
Caspersen, Kim 38875
Cass, Michael 39795
Cass-Hassol, Nicholas 45854
Cassan, Dagmar de 02217
Cassan, Ferdinand de 02217
Cassanelli, Dr. Roberto 24558, 24560
Cassell, Valerie 44118
Cassels, Patrick 38109
Casseminho Meira, Mariana 04285
Cassiano, Dr. Antonio 24167
Cassidy, Terry P. 48427
Castagnoli, Prof. Pier Giovanni 25734
Cãstãian, Mihai 32563
Castaño Cruz, Hermana Cecilia 07447
Castañón Albo, Luis 35015
Castanyer Bachs, Narcis 35645
Castel, Marie-Chantal 13732
Castel-Branco Pereira, Dr. João 32292
Castele, Theodore J. 42474
Castellà Reial, Josep 35294
Castellana, Dr. Gruiseppe 22816
Castelletti, Dr. Lalfredo 23632
Castelletti, Dr. Lanfredo 23627, 23630, 23631
Castelnuovo, Sheri 45069
Casteret, Norbert 11760
Castex, Jessica 13548
Castier, Annie 12599
Castilla, Francisca 35601
Castillo Tovar, Carlos Arturo 07484
Castle, Charles E. 44548
Castle, Lynn P. 41562
Castle, Myra 43836
Castleberry, May 45886
Castor, A. 13709
Castor González, Jesús 28138, 28158
Castrillón Urrera, Carlos Alberto 07379
Castro, Milagros 32389
Castro Benítez, Daniel 07382, 07384
Castro Mejía, María Eugenia 07378
Castro Meza, Raúl 28431
Castronovo, Simona 25736
Català Gorgues, Angel 35596
Cataldi, Dr. Maria 25674
Cataldi Gallo, Dr. Maria 23984
Catchpole, Julie 30230, 30231
Catchpole, Nancy 38110
Catchpole, Ron 39304
Cate, Phillip Dennis 45678
Cates, David L. 03074
Cates, Michael 40281
Catford, B.L. 01348
Cathcart, Rosemary 38942
Cathrin, Marcel 14370
Catleugh, Jon 39620
Catlin, Erica 41945
Catlin-Legutko, Cinnamon 46364
Cato, John S. 47878
Catolin, Eufemia B. 31470
Catron, Joanna D. 43533
Catroppa, Frank 41351
Catrysse, Bernard 26643
Catta, Javier 09187
Cattaneo, Claudia 37328
Cattaneo, Pascal 36940
Cattelain, P. 03800
Catton, Jonathan 39117
Cau, Ettore 26048, 26049
Caubet, Annie 13603
Caudoux, Michel 15096
Cauk, Françoise 10558
Cauldwell, Amanda 46858
Caulkins, Bethel I. 46856
Caumon, Annette 12712
Caurie, Philippa 40935
Čauševa, Dora 04691
Cauvin, Sylvette 15069
Cauwe, Nicolas 03337
Cavaglion Bassani, Laura 22718
Cavagnis Sotgiu, Dr. Maria Carla 25185
Cavaillès, Maria 13662
de Paiva Cavalanti, Lauro Augusto 04399
Cavalcante, Raquel 04008
Cavalchini, Pieranna 41811
Cavalho-Roos, Dr. T. Rosa de 28928
Cavalier, Odile 10528
Cavalier, Sebastien 12748
Cavalli, Attilio 24397
Cavalli, Germano 26018
Cavalli-Björkman, Åsa 36236
Cavalli-Björkman, Görel 36265
Cavanagh, Gwendolyn 42670
Cavanaugh, Joe 43531
Cavatrunci, Claudio 25238
Cavazzi Palladini, Dr. Lucia 25156
Cavelti, Dr. Urs J. 36770
Cavendish, Kim L. 43412
Cavenee, Dee 41979
Cavić, Aldo 07790
Cavnor, Julie Ann 41476
Cay Henry, Mary 42665
Cayer, Richard 41148
Çaylak, İsmail 37653
Cayphas, Jean-Paul 03521
Cazacu, Silvia 32470
Cazakoff, Ingrid 06428

Cazarez-Rueda, Luis 43722
Cazé, Sophie 12062
Cazes, Daniel 14952
Ceballos, Orlando Toro 07581
Ceballos Carrero, Rosa Maria 27985
Cebrián, Enriqueta 35601
Cebucoprea, Dr. Alexandru 32452
Ceccarelli, Giampiero 25625
Cecchetto, Dr. Giacinto 23400
Cecchi, Dr. Alessandro 23840
Ceccini de Dallo, Ana María 00610
Cecil, William A.V. 41276
Čecov, Prof. Dr. V.P. 33162
Cederlund, Dr. Johan 36355
Cedersand, Kerstin 36240
Cederstrøm, Elisabeth 08950
Cedro, Dr. Bernard 32025
Ceesay, B.A. 15352
Ceesay, Hassoum 15352
Cega, Fani Celio 07794
Celant, Germano 45872
Celayir, İsmail Hakkı 37699, 37716
Celenko, Theodore 44248
Celestina, Susan 46472
Céleyran, Tapié de 13274
Celi, Maria 45789
Siqueira Celidonio, Helio Fernando 04001
Celio-Scheurer, Marie-Eve 36955
Celis, Augustin de 35678
Celli, Jeanann 47783
Celma, Cécile 27721
Celuzza, Dr. Mariagrazia 24056
Celuzza, Dr. M.G. 24059
Cembrano, Rita 31293, 31296
Cembrola, Robert 45929
Cendo, Nicolas 12852
Ceni, Giuseppe Riccardo 25973
Ceniceros Herreros, Javier 35154
Cenni, Mario 24228
Censky, Ellen J. 47835
Centenay, Florence 13516
Centore, Prof. Giuseppe 23339
Čepič, Taja 34123
Cepon, Miloska 34122
Čeran, Branko 07830
Cerar, Estera 34122
Čerba, Larisa Valerjanovna 33634
Čerče, Peter 34138
Ceriotti, Guido 23238
Cerişer, Nicolae 32530
Čerkalin, Sergej Dmitrievič 33362
Čerkasova, Olga Anatoljevna 32839
Černá, Margit 08481
Cernat, Ivona Elena 32532
Černavin, Lev Davidovyč 33447
Černín, Dr. Svatomír 08667
Černjak, Éduard Isaakevič 33617
Černobai, Prof. Dr. Juri 37889
Cerny, Dr. P. 06838
Cerny, Zbynek 08308
Ceron, Clodualdo N. 31407
Cerón, Pablo 28136
Cerón Mireles, Prof. José Luis 28134
Ceroni, Nadia 25084
Cerovac, Branko 07760
Cerović, Dr. Ljubivoje 33875
Cerretelli, Claudio 25047, 25048
Certo, Michael 41111
Ceruti, Mary 44872
Cerutti, Dr. Antonio 25066
Cerutti, Lilia P. de 00674
Cervellino, Miguel 06895
Cervetti, Dr. Valerio 24794, 24800
Cervini, Dr. Fulvio 25730
Cesari, Gene 48685
Cesbron, Pierre 14303
Češková, Stanislava 08628
Česnova, Ljudmila Alekseevna 32779
Cession Louppe, Jacqueline 03640
Cetinić, Ljiljana 33805
Ceulemans, Louisa 03492
Ceunynck, Christoph de 11459, 11460
Ceut 11864
Ceynowa-Barth, Tatjana 17304
Chabard, Dominique 10500
Chabert, Noëlle 13649
Chacala Nuñulo, Pedro 00093
Chačatrian, Šahen 00687
Chačikjan, Svetlana Melkonovna 33357
Chadbourne, Janice 41801
Chadima, John 42630
Chadli, Mohammed 28694
Chadwick, Adam 39706
Chadwick, Phyllis 46203
Chadwick, P.J. 34371
Chadwick-Case, Wendy 44311
Chadžiev, N. 04844
Chafe, Dr. K.S. 30348
Chaguaceda Toledano, Ana 35357
Chai, Paris K. 44082
Chaik, Pak In 27124
Chaimerez, M. G. 22707
Chainé, Françoise 06645
Chait, Karen 45751
Chakraborti, R.M. 21952
Chakravarti, Rasmohan 03081
Chakravarti, Dr. S.K. 21905

Chald, Elisabeth 40390
Chalfant, Rhonda 47555
Chalker, Mary 01519
Challen, John 38594, 38595, 38596, 39308
Challener, Elisbeth 47457
Challis, Liz 00975
Challis, Paul 00975
Chalmers, Kim 41852
Chalmers, Sir Neil 39733
Chalmers, Dr. Neil R. 40728
Chalmers, Peggy 39730
Chalupa, Josef 08502
Chamay, Jaques 36645
Chambareau, René 10476
Chamberlain, Brewster 48401
Chamberlain, Lori 06376
Chamberlin, Edward M. 43616
Chambers, Coleen B. 44210
Chambers, Cullen 48129
Chambers, Elizabeth 46641
Chambers, Emma 05999
Chambers, Keith 00935
Chambers, Kristin 42465
Chambers, Michael A. 06073
Chambers, T.B. 01259
Chambon, Cati 12406
Chambon, Fabrice 13151
Chambon, Marion S. 45719
Chamil, Iskhakov 08261
Chamonikola, Dr. Kaliopi 08270, 08271
Champanil, Vira 37480
Chan, Elise 48442
Chan, Peng Sam 07166
Chanazarov, Kalbay 48455
Chance, Delores 42158
Chance, Dr. John 47973
Chancel-Bardelot, Béatrice de 10862, 10864, 10866
Chandès, Hervé 13501
Chandler, Charles 42858
Chandler, Christine 42786
Chandler, Kenneth 44225
Chandler, Pam 44225
Chandon, Melissa 42794
Chandran, P.R. 22035
Chandžieva, Evelina 04652
Chandžieva, Radka 04634
Chanel, Pierre 12712
Chankers, Natalie 38075
Chanler, James 45909
Channels, Noreen 43945
Channer, L.J. 39666
Channing, Susan R 42481
Channon, Ann 38533
Chanson, Robert 37125
Chansou, Dr. Michel 37085
Chapalain, Jean-Philippe 12645
Chapin, Angela 06275
Chapin, Jean 48329
Chapin, Mona 42400
Chaplin, Sylvia 39864
Chapman, Alan 38024
Chapman, Allison 45080
Chapman, A.T. 05119
Chapman, Gordon 01575
Chapman, H. 40044
Chapman, Dr. Jefferson 44519
Chapman, J.R. 40316
Chapman, Dr. S.T. 40176
Chapman, Prof. Stanley 40351
Chapman Banks, Barbara 44784
Chapnick, Harold 43355
Chapoose, Betsy 43391
Chapp, Belena S. 45888
Chappey, Frédéric 12626
Chapron, Philippe 10618
Chapuis, Julien 45784
Charbonneau, Reine 05881
Charette, Joanne 06084
Chariot, C. 03817
Charitatos, Katerina 21076
Charitonov, Christo 04917
Charles, Dorothée 13586
Charles, Steve 47544
Charlier, P. 03655
Charlot, Colette 13123
Charlton, Dr. Christopher 38674, 38675
Charlton, K. 30275
Charlton-Jones, D. 30216
Charmayne Young, J. 47088
Charmelo, Julie 42354
Charpentier, Corinne 11491
Charrière, Edmond 36627
Chartier, Catherine 14316
Chartrain, Michèle 11912
Charzynska, Jadwiga 31564
Chase, Ed 41289, 41290
Chase, Jim 44749
Chaserant, Françoise 12437, 12438, 12439
Chassaing, Jean-François 12079
Chassé, Sonia 05767
Chasseval, Geneviève de 12131
Château, Georges 14323
Chatelain, Prof. E. 12815
Chatenet, Georges 14947
Chatfield, Linda 42968
Chatland, Gordon 43321
Chatman, Patrina 42918
Chatterjee, Dr. H.J. 39648

Chatterjee, Dr. Sankar 44991
Chatterjee, Sunil Kumar 21839
Chaturvedi, Naresh 21951
Chaudet, M.-H. 37286
Chauffeteau, Claude 10810
Chaumet, Danièle 13751
Chauvel, Marie Claire 12137
Chauvin, Dr. Robert S. 42815
Chauvirviere, Comte de la 14856
Chavanne, Blandine 13241
Chavannes, Virgile Alexandre 00568
Chavarria, Antonio 47425
Chaves, Dr. Julio César 31108
Chaves, Manuel Wenceslao 31103
Chavez, Melinda N. 47947
Chavez, Thomas 47429
Chavez, Walter J. 32409
Chayes, William 41645
Chazal, Gilles 13658
Cheatham, Jim 42939
Chebanova, N. 48860
Chebitwey, Jane 27104
Checefsky, Bruce 42478
Chedal, Jean-Claude 13328
Cheetham, Elizabeth 40354
Cheevers, James W. 41230
Chefdebien, Anne de 13630
Cheikh, Aboubakar 07630
Chelbi, Fethi 37557
Chelius, Margot 19005
Chellah, Mwimanji Ndota 49015
Chemera, Lyn 43036
Chen, Jian Ming 07010
Chen, Julie 45880
Chen, Lucia 45880
Chen, Shih-Bey 07353
Chen, S.S.H. 29101
Chen, Zu-E 07253
Chen-Lee, Margaret 07347
Chenault, Amanda 42505
Cheney, Dotty 43600
Cheney, Dr. John T. 41181
Cheney, Rebecca 38532
Cheng, Hon Seng 47315
Cheng-Sheng, Tu 07351
Chenoufi, Brahim 00077
Chenoweth, Bob 47713
Chenoweth, Richard 47437
Chepp, Mark 47757
Cheptum, Andrew 27103
Cherchi Usai, Paolo 46941
Cherek, Dr. Janina 31528, 31529
Cherif, Housine Med 00076
Cherix, Dr. Daniel 36859
Chermak, Glenda L. 44567
Cherry, Stella 22402
Chesbrough, Herbert A. 47460
Chesebrough, David 41985
Chesi, Prof. Gert 02648
Chesneau-Dupin, Laurence 11342, 11745
Chester, Timothy J. 43759
Chesters, Dr. Robin 39533
Cheval, François 11126
Chevalier, Alain 15280
Chevalier, Ann 03571, 03572
Chevalies, Ségolène le 11537
Chevallier, Bernard 12045, 14075
Chevallier, Denis 12863
Chew, Nigel 40443
Chew, Ron 47548
Chew Matsuda, Fay 45841
Chez Checor, José 09127
Chia, Khoo Boo 27681
Chiacchierini, Prof. Ernesto 25214
Chiappini, Dr. Marco 22939
Chiappini, Dr. Rudy 36583, 36617, 36900, 36901
Chiara Bettini, Dr. Maria 23349
Chiaramonte, Dr. Giuseppe 24774
Chiarchiaro, Charles 46231
Chiarini, Dr. Marco 23821, 23844
Chiarucci, Dr. Giuseppe 22830, 24139
Chiba, Mizuo 26965
Chicharro Chamorro, José Luis 34924
Chicoineau, Pierre 11966
Chidavaenzi, R.P. 49028
Chidsey, Dr. Jennifer L. 41532
Chiego, William J. 47255
Chiesa, Franco 36614
Chiesi, Dr. Giuseppe 36526, 36530
Chikhaoui-Trachene, Prof. Henia 28695
Chikkamare Gowda, B.M. 21703
Chilcote, Doug 47106, 47107
Chilcote, Gary 47106, 47107
Child, M. 40561
Childress, Ann 42732
Childress, P.L. 46251
Childrey, Brooke 44266
Chilton, D.G. 40436
Chilton, Meredith 06580
Chimello, Sylvain 14888
Chimier, Brigitte 15035
Chiminelli, Baldassare 23401
Chin, Song-gi 27196
Chin Foo, Brenda 15347
Chinea Brito, Carmen D. 34937
Chinen, Satoru 26217
Chinery, Derek 40306
Chiocchetti, Dr. Fabio 25032
Chiong, Dr. Chew Tuan 33944

Chiriac, Aurel 32560, 32561, 32562
Chirită, Lenuta 32539
Chitaley, Dr. Shya 42467
Chitoshi, Matsuo 26290
Chivers, Jim 30096
Chlebarova, Marija 04628
Chlebecek, Friedrich 02107
Chmara, Gitta von 17839
Chmelinova, Dr. Katarina 33978
Chmelnickaja, Ljudmila 03123
Chmielak, Jadwiga 31790
Chmielewska, Wiesława 31956
Chmielewski-Hagius, Dr. Anita 17934
Chmurzyński, Wojciech 32104
Cho, Byoung Soon 27284
Choate, J.R. 43971, 43971
Chocholáč, Ivo 08500
Chodasiewicz, Jerzy 32018
Choe, Sung Eun 27231
Choetf, Betsy 44209
Choi, Prof. Duck-Keun 27276
Choi, Eric 07161
Choi, Il Sung 27153
Choi, Kim Sang 27119
Choi, Man-Li 27180
Choiselat, Roland 06007
Choisne, Franck 14644
Cholette, Yvon 06532
Cholewa, Anita 45387
Chołodowska, Małgorzata 32222
Chomič, Svetlana Viktorovna 32935
Chong, Alan 41811
Chongkol, Chira 37491
Chopping, George C. 06796
Choremi, Dr. Alkestis 20871
Choremis, Alketis 20898
Choriev, Kiem 48828
Chorunženko, V.A. 32798
Chou, Ju-Hsi 42466
Choudhury, B. 21805
Choudhury, Dr. R.D. 21807
Chow, Kai-Wing 48164
Chow, Kim-Fung 07101
Chowdhuri, Dr. M.K. 21902
Chowdhury, Prof. Dr. Saifuddin 03099
Chrest, Gwen 42491
Chrisanov, Petr Aleksandrovič 33542
Chrisholm, Donna 39361
Chrisman, D. Kent 46929
Christ, Nelda M. 41745
Christaffersen, Erna 08872
Christen, Benoît 10708
Christen, François 36989
Christen, Thomas 36600
Christensen, Henry 30198
Christensen, J.O. 08953
Christensen, Lisbeth 08849
Christensen, Margaret 05622
Christensen, Peter M. M. 08892
Christensen, Ruth 27511
Christensen, Svend 08892
Christenson, Goran 36076
Christian, J.A. 47039
Christian, Jay 43296
Christian, John 47454
Christian, Joshua W. 41474
Christiansen, Calvin 48437
Christiansen, Jette 08944
Christiansen, Prof. Dr. Jörn 16321, 16329
Christiansen, Sherie 47584
Christie, David 46339
Christie, Gordon A. 38998
Christie, Nancy 46339
Christman, David C. 43987
Christodoulakos, Yannis 20915
Christoffel, Udo 16017, 16116
Christoffer, Ed 05448
Christoph, Susi 02721
Christopher, Terry 47625
Christophersen, Axel 30946
Christou, Dr. Demos 08216
Christov, Christo 04662
Christov-Bakargiev, Carolyn 25131
Christova, Emilia 04694
Chrzan, Stanisław 31500
Chrzanowski, Jerzy 32216
Chu, Dr. Christina 07094
Chu, Doris 41829
Chubbuck Weinstein, Elizabeth 41527
Chudjakova, Lidija Aleksandrovna 32773
Chughtai, Arif Rahman 31033
Chuma-Ibe, Gloria Chianu 30350
Chun, Sung Woo 27233
Chunchu, Ai 06952
Chung, Prof. Jing-Won 27138
Chung, Yang-Ho 27264
Chuoc, Cu Van 48979
Chupin, Olivier 10999
Church, B. A. 43243
Church, Dorian 40487
Church, Rena J. 41395
Church, Susan 44199
Churchill, Viscount 38935
Churchill, Edwin 41390
Churchill, Robin 41454
Chushupal, E.N. 27316
Chusnutdinova, Rušanija Salichovna 32899
Chwałek, Roman 31962

Chwaliński, Andrzej 31838
Chwalisz, Zofia 32171
Chylak, Ana 38014
Chytilo, Prof. Lynne 41096
Ciamos, Christian 10296
Ciancio, Dr. Angela 24027
Cianciulli, John 43519
Ciapponi Landi, Bruno 24258
Ciaran, Dr. Fiona 30264
Ciardi, Dr. Roberto Paolo 25400
Ciarla, Dr. Roberto 25231
Ciavolino, Prof. Giuseppe 25771
Cibulová, Dr. Vlasta 08610
Cicala, Francesco 24785, 24787
Cicala Campagna, Dr. Francesca 25585
Cicali, Francesco 24786
Çiçeksız, İbrahim 37691
Ciceri, Angela 23735
Cichecka, Barbara 32145
Cichocki, Max 15917
Cicierski, Ernest 06836
Cicimov, Aleksandar 27597
Cicimurri, David 42455
Cicognani, Giorgio 23216
Cidenova, Rita Badmaeva 33651
Ciecholewski, Dr. Roman 31877
Ciecior, Gabriele 17600
Ciepiela, Elżbieta 32202
Cierna, Katarína 33978
Cierpka, Heinz 17414
Cieślak, Bogdan 32172
Cifelli, Dr. R.L. 45976
Cifuentes, Joaquín 28173
Ciganok, Nina 37845
Cigarroa, Melissa 44652
Cigliano, Flavia 41820
Cihan Özsayıner, Zübeyde 37711
Čikin, Vladimir Iljič 37900
Čilašvili, L.A. 15366
Cilona, Filippo Ferdinando 23770
Cimdiņa, Ruta 27408
Činč-Juhant, Dr. Breda 34118
Cinc-Mars, François 06542
Cingolani, Lauro 25088
Cingolani, Lilias 44492
Cini, Amato 25859
Cini, Stephen 27707
Činovec, Igor 08652
Cinquepalmi, Angela 23768
Cintulova, Erika 34001, 34002
Cioce, Dr. Pasquale 23092
Cioci, Antonio 23850
Ciôfalo, Manfred 25692
Cioffari, Gerardo 23021
Cioppi, Dr. Elisabeth 23866
Cipolletti, Dr. Maria S. 16226
Cipollone, Dr. Rosa 24691
Ciprian, Dr. Pavel 08269, 08273, 08279, 08755, 08756, 08757, 08758
Cipriani, Curzio 23871
Cirani, Simona 25337
Cirill, T. 21497
Cirillo, Gail 45975
Cirjakovic, Ivana 33827
Čirkova, Larisa I. 33421
Ciro Galotta, Brás 04539
Cirule, Astrīda 27386
Ciseri, Dr. Ilaria 24488
Cisle, Carrie 46794
Cisneros, Jose 44332
Cisneros, Mario Toledo 28381
Cist, O. 02224
Ciubotă, Dr. Viorel 32587
Ciugudean, Horia Ion 32428
Civai, Mauro 25572
Číž, Marian 34068
Claassen, Garth 42028
Claassen, Uwe 18360
Clabby, Paul 45695
Claes, Gabrielle 03321
Claessens Peré, Nanette 03180
Claesson, Anna Maria 35977
Clair, Cynthia 45802
Clam-Martinic, Dr. M.C.D. 02134
Clancey, Erin 44943
Clancy, John L. 48231
Clap, Sylvestre 10530
Clapham, Peter 40723
Clapperton, Raymond 30157
Clarck, Trinkett 41178
Clare, Roy 39731, 39767
Clarés, María Jesús 35601
Claret, Sawador 35495
Claret de Gouvêia, Antônio M. 04240
Clarin jr., Oligario L. 31344
Clark, Andrew 01459
Clark, Becky 46073
Clark, Charles T. 42449
Clark, Christa 46747
Clark, Donald 43738
Clark, Elaine R. 43801
Clark, Gayle 46898
Clark, Helen 38904
Clark, James 46400
Clark, Joann 45332
Clark, Kathy M. 46179
Clark, L.R. 01170
Clark, Mary K. 46777
Clark, Michael J. 48176, 48177

Clark, Neva 42010
Clark, Dr. Niki R. 46605, 46607
Clark, Patrick S. 47488
Clark, Peter 43545
Clark, Peter P. 42620
Clark, Phillip 44876
Clark, Richard H. 48543
Clark, Robert A. 38195
Clark, Roger 38301, 38351
Clark, Ronilee 47284
Clark, Scott 47105
Clark, Tom 48201
Clark, Vicky A. 46523
Clark, William 44435
Clark jr., William 45820
Clark, William H. 41582
Clark-Bedard, Sharon 06016
Clark-Langager, Sarah 41603
Clarke, A.H. 00857
Clarke, Alicia 47394
Clarke, B. 38454
Clarke, Cliff 05403
Clarke, David 30095
Clarke, Ignatius 22512
Clarke, Jane 40704
Clarke, Jay 42304
Clarke, Jeremy 40335
Clarke, Jerrie 48179
Clarke, Jo 40432
Clarke, Judith 40176
Clarke, Michael 38898
Clarke, Patrick 47799
Clarke, Robert 37958
Clarke, Ron 38643
Clarke, T. Henry 48472
Clarke Di Vico, Carol 41509
Clary, Owen 41068
Clason, Anders 35913
Clatworthy, J.C. 38223
Claude, Étienne 03271
Clausen, Charles 45343
Clausen, H. Erhardt 08779
Clausen, Jochen 18316
Clausen, Kim 08864, 09062, 09064, 09065, 09066
Clausen, Kirstin 05135
Clausen, Willy 36690
Clausnitzer, Regina 17424
Clauß, Dr. Gisela 18606
Clauß, Horst 18596
Claussen, Louise Keith 41386
Clavel, Sylvie 13552
Clavier, Michel 03628
Clavijo, Martha Isabel 07602
Clavijo Colom, Moraima 07987
Clawson, Rita 41555
Clay Chace, Helen 45802
Clayden, K. 39603
Clayden, Stephen 06334
Cleal, Rosamund 38041
Clear, Celia 39787, 39788
Clearwater, Bonnie 45997
Cleary, Chris 01360
Cleasby, I.W.J. 38009
Cleere, Sonny 47242
Clegg, R.E. 05578
Clegg, Dr. W.H. 40713
Clemens, George 41631
Clemens, Dr. Lukas 20212
Clemens, M. 12828
Clemens, William 42775
Clemens, William A. 41646
Clemenson, Gaye 44400
Clement, Christine 39772
Clement, Constance 45699
Clement, M. 13108
Clement, Rika 41772
Clement, T.A. 40917
Clement von Rehekampff, Uta 18331
Clemente, Milagros 31287
Clements, D.E. 39713
Clements, Gayle 48104
Clements, Louis 46847
Clements, Lynn B. 48250
Clemons, Veda 45175
Clendaniel, Dianne 41499
Clerc, Jacques 36582
Clergue, Yolande 10414
Clette, Michele 03316
Cleveland, David 40092
Cleveland, James C. 46846
Cleveland, Richard L. 47534
Cleven, E. 39017
Clevenger, A. Colin 43526
Clevenger, Martha 47128
Clevenger, Martha R. 44877
Clews, Stephen 38121
Cleyet-Merle, J.J. 12538
Cliffe, L. 40557
Clifford, B. 39756
Clifford, Timothy 38898, 38916
Clifton, Dan 43038
Clifton, James 44129
Clifton, Dr. James 44136
Clifton, Julia 47425
Clin, Marie-Véronique 13595
Cline, Garry 41189
Cline, Ann 43559
Cline, Raymond 46047
Clinger, Melinda 46932

Clinkingbeard, Brion 44967
Clinton, Tom 43760
Clitheroe, G. 40201
Clodfelter, Lee 41925
Clos Llombart, Jordi 34575
Close, Elisabeth 00972
Close, Freddy 03398
Close, Oliver 00856
Cloudman, Ruth 44976
Clouter, Carl 05474
Clow, John R. 48510
Clow, Jon 44336
Clow, Wayne 47865
Cluff, Raydene 47060
Cluver, Dr. M.A. 34219
Clyve, Lynda 41494
Coates, G. 05526
Coates, Ross 46745
Cobarg, Dr. Merete 19012
Cobb, Myrna 05215
Cobban, Janet 05587, 06813
Cobbe, Toy L. 45192
Cobble, Kelly 46763
Cobbold, A.G.B. 38418
Cobert, William 45757
Cobo, Maria 41945
Cobos Colmenares, Carlos Eduardo 07570
Cobos Wilkins, Juan 35115
Cobridges, Robert 45500
Coburn, Dr. Carol 44411
Coburn, Oakley H. 47717
Cocartă, Adrian 32519
Cocea, Sergio Eduardo 00677
Cochat, L. 14894
Cochener, Margaret M. 46928
Cochran, Barbara 42125
Cochran, Dorothy 45882
Cochrane, G. 38774
Cochrane, Tim 43752
Cockrill, Pauline 00732, 00736
Cocks, Dr. R. 39733
Cocordas, Eleni 45820
Cocuz, Prof. Ioan 32600
Coday, Jean C. 45124
Codding, Mitchell A. 45815
Codega, Antonio 25052
Codicé Pinelli, Dr. Ferruccio 23224
Codreanu, Elena 32552
Cody, George 45680
Coe, John G. 42299
Coekelbergs, Prof. R. 03840
Coelewij, L. 28902
Coelho, Conceição 32340
Coelho Bartholo, Dr. Maria de Lourdes 32245
Coellen, Claudia 37370
Coenen, Luc 03586, 03587
Coënen, Michel 15318
Coers, Frits 29898
Coetzee, F.P. 34348
Coffelt, Jon 41703
Coffen, Charles 06432
Coffey, Jeanne 44035
Coffey, John W. 46775
Coffrini, Ermes 23199
Cogan, Stanley 43354, 43356
Cogar, William 45588
Cogeval, Guy 05918, 13636
Cogswell, Arnold 44007
Cohalan, Mary Lou 43051
Cohen, A. 22735
Cohen, Evelyne 13557, 13557
Cohen, Françoise 13333, 13338
Cohen, Jack 46441
Cohen, Janie 42009
Cohen, Judith 22742
Cohen, Marvin K. 45317
Cohen, Nancy 47877
Cohen, Patricia 00230
Cohen, Richard S. 46305
Cohen, Sandor 41416
Cohen, Sylvia 43115
Cohen-Straytner, Barbara 45859
Cohn, Arthur B. 48212
Cohn, Marjorie B. 42042, 42042
Cohon, Dr. Robert 44404
Cohrs, Karin 17871
Cohrs, Peter 17871
Coibanu, Doina 32477
Coish, Theresa 45661
Coker, Gylbert 48002
Čolakov, Dimităr 04882
Colardelle, Michel 13635
Colardelle, Renée 11940
Colassi, David 45809
Colato, Juan 44950
Colazo, Susana 00510
Colbert, Brigitte de 13128
Colburn, Bolton 44575
Colby, James 44310, 44312
Coldren, James 43156
Cole, Burna 41160
Cole, Everett 42150
Cole, Felicity 40063
Cole, Garrett 41493
Cole, Geoffrey 38056
Cole, Ina 40406, 40410
Cole, Jane 05960
Cole, K. 34236
Cole, Paul B 06768

Cole, Richard 39726
Cole, Vicki 47364
Cole, William H. 41455
Cole-Will, Becky 41496, 41497
Colegial Gupierrez, Juan Diego 07439
Coleman, C. Allen 46481
Coleman, Don 43351
Coleman, Dorothy J 45718
Coleman, Evelyn 22498
Coleman, Jane 41851
Coleman, Mary Ruth 41123
Coleman, Rhonda 47249
Coleman, Roddy 39643
Coleman, Winifred E. 48528
Coles, Alec 40035, 40038, 40537, 40650
Coles, David 40438
Coley, Dwaine C. 44012
Colin, N. 03422
Colina, Gay 48426
Colitti, Raffaele 23303
Coll, Tom 48799
Coll Conesa, Dr. Jaume 35608
Coll Gormley, Jean 43978
Colla, Francis 03417
Collado, Elisa 35203
Collas, Josiane 11548
Colle, Jean-Pierre 11867
Colle, Marcella 03495
Collens, David R. 45551
Collett, Keith L. 00850
Collett, Morine 44253
Collett, V. 40148
Collette, Dr. Alfred T. 47909, 47913
Collette, Louis Jeffery 45283
Collier, Caroline 38347
Collier, Ric 47232
Collier, Shirley 39584
Collin, Dr. Gérard 10719
Collin, Ludo 03450
Colling, Guy 27568
Collings, Donna 05883
Collins, Anne 40815
Collins, Belva 41727
Collins, Craig 41792
Collins, D. 45105
Collins, D. Cheryl 45106, 45109, 45110, 45111
Collins, David 45686
Collins, Dr. Des 06607
Collins, George 43803
Collins, James H. 42952, 45430
Collins, John 41758
Collins, Lin 40027
Collins, Louanne 39867
Collins, Lynn 01565
Collins, Mary 46744
Collins, Michael 44997
Collins, Paul W. 47405
Collins, Philip 39939
Collins, Thom 42403
Collins, Thomas F. 42050
Collins, Toni I. 43195
Collins, Vickie 46434
Collins Blackmon, Mary 41409
Collins Coleman, Clara 47126
Collinson, Howard 44248
Collu, Cristiana 24661
Colman, Devin A. 47159
Colombi Ferretti, Dr. Anna 23755
Colombié, Ervé 14384
Colombino, Carlos 31094, 31101
Colombo, Dr. Tarcisio 23436
Colombo Gougoud, R. 36745
Colomer, Laia 34437
Colon, Anibal 47087
Colon, Constance B. 47828
Colonna, Cécile 14048
Colonna, Vittoria 23293
Colonna Ceccaldi, Michel 15142
Colossi, David 45809
Colović, Milosav 33906
Colpaert, Hilde 03522, 03523
Colt, Elizabeth R. 48508
Colton, Elizabeth 47345
Colton, Fiona 39194, 39195, 39196, 39325
Columbano, Dr. Juan Carlos 00431
Columbo, Colleen 05498
Colvia, Dr. Anna 25225
Colvin, Richard D. 45079
Colwell, Bruce 46021
Comanducci, Dr. Francesco 25427
Comas Estatella, Dr. Antonio 35658
Comba, Steve 42419
Combe, Anette 37013, 37014
Combe, Jean 37279
Comber, Robert James 05602
Combs, Dr. Dave 44894
Combs, Robert K. 43420
Comeau, Cy 05057
Comeault, Maurice 06365
Comer, Karen 41339
Comer, Michael 45715
Comingore, B.J. 47560
Comish, James R. 46055
Comlan Godonou, Alain 03877
Commandeur, Beatrix 15899
Commock, Tracy 26069, 26076
Communeau, Matthieu 11490
Compagno, Dr. L.J.V. 34213
Compagno-Roeleveld, M.A. 34213

Compaore, Benilde 04942
Comparin, Guy 11932
Complo, Jennifer 44217
Compton, Richard 40327
Comte, Philippe 13666
Comtois, George S. 44749
Cona, Dr. Cherubino 25454
Conable, Mary 48318
Conceição Correia, Maria da 32268
Condeescu, Dan Alexandru 32462
Conder, Marjorie D. 47231
Condette, Jean-François 15003
Condos, Lena 00966, 00967
Condurache, Val 32541
Cone, Ellen 46247
Coneva, Tanja 04828
Confessore, Lisa-Marie 47451
Conforti, Michael 48634
Cong, Pham Van 48989
Conger, Ivan A. 46232
Conihout, Isabelle de 13474
Conijn, G.H. 29191
Conijn, N.W. 28928
Conisbee, Philip 48373
Conkle Davis, Gloria 41316
Conklin, David 42916
Conklin, Jo-Ann 46717
Conkright, Lance 48518
Conley, Alston 42294
Conley, Angela 39904
Conley, Carolyn 48612
Conley, Maria 41062
Conlon, Beth 42444
Conlon, Tim 42991
Connaughton, Vincent 22511
Conneau, Jean-Claude 11386
Connell, Dr. D.P. 39376
Connell, John 05236
Connell, Louise 40106
Connelly, Nancy 42555
Connelly, Stephen 38445
Connemann, Elfi 16453
Connemann, Hans-Joachim 16453
Conner, Dorisanna 46256
Conner, Jill 43687
Connolly, Thomas 43224
Connolly, Tracy 30144
Connor, Brian 30150
Connor, Kathy 46941
Connor, Lorraine 45060
Connors, Dennis 47912
Conocido, Domicilio 27894
Conopask, Karen 46318
Conover, Margaret 47570
Conrad, Dr. Christofer 20106
Conrad, Geoffrey 41749
Conrad, Dr. J. 17285
Conrads, Margaret 44404
Consagre, Franesca 47134
Consey, Kevin 41649
Considine, Brian 44913
Conso, Prof. Giovanni 25271
Console, Dr. Ester Maria 48872
Constable, S. 40084
Constant Noanti, Mahoun 03874
Constantino De La Penna, Carol 35501
Constantopoulos, Dr. Jim 46616
Consuelo Dominguez Cuanalo, Delia del 28344
Contarino, Dr. Giuseppe 22798
Contassot, Cécile 11933
Conte, Cynthia 42248
Conte, Dr. Robert S. 48592
Conte, Roxana Diaz 00504
Contessa, Gregorio 24277
Conti, Prof. Dr. Luigi Francesco 23968
Conti, Richard C. 45969
Conti, Roberto 24559
Conticello, Prof. Dr. Baldassare 23186, 25617
Conticello, Dr. Baldo 24429
Contiguglia, Georgianna 42882, 48062, 48063, 48065
Contini, Dr. Roberto 15974
Contreras, Mamerto 31423
Contreras, Pilar 28140
Contreras Martínez, José Eduardo 28562
Contro, Antonia 42340
Conway, Allen C. 45658
Conway, Cari 45910
Conway, James 42923
Conway, Steven 03886
Conwell, Idella M. 45128
Conyers, Wayne 45049
Conzen, Dr. Fritz 16719
Conzen, Dr. Ina 20106
Coode, Linda 39080
Coogan, Steve 46962
Cook, Emma 40806, 40822
Cook, Janel 45013
Cook, Jenny 46741
Cook, Joyce A. 43356
Cook, Mary Jo 45559
Cook, Patrick 40875
Cook, Robert 46286
Cook, Silas B. 46634
Cook, Steven 05339
Cook, Thomas 42556
Cook, Wendy 40931

Cooke, Bill 44740
Cooke, Glenn 01459
Cooke, Krista 06098
Cooke, Lynne 41552, 45793
Cooke, Michael 26066, 26070, 26072, 26082
Cooke, Pat 22440, 22451
Cooke, Patrick 38746
Cooke, Pattie 44958
Cooke, Susan 39829
Cooke, Victoria 45735
Cooke, Vina 40026
Cookendorfer, Betty 43929
Coolidge, Jennifer 42813
Coolidge, John 44630
Coombe, JoAnne 43002
Coombs, Charles R. 43027
Coombs, Gary B. 43720
Coombs, Dr. Margery C. 41181
Coombs, Robert 48596
Coombs, Dr. Walter A. 41181
Coomer, Robert 43160, 48203
Cooney Frelinghuysen, Alice 45833
Coopen, Barry 41429
Cooper, Andrea 42528
Cooper, Avis 30156
Cooper, Bernard F. 47640
Cooper, Grant 30134
Cooper, Harry 42042
Cooper, Helen 45700
Cooper, Jo-Ann 01229
Cooper, John 39524
Cooper, Linda G. 48803
Cooper, Linda L. 48487
Cooper, Norman 05797
Cooper, Rhonda 47832
Cooper, Robert L.D. 38885
Cooper, Ronna 46390
Cooper, Rosemary 40053
Cooper, S. 39274
Cooper, Todd 45230
Cooper, Virginia 06569
Cooper Case, Carolyn 46866
Coopmans, H. 28936
Coote, Sylvia 40631
Cop, Eddy 03174
Cope, Michael W. 39330
Copeland, Jackie 41489
Copeland-Burns, Carla 44753
Copeley, William N. 42605
Copp, V.E. 38285
Coppens, Marguerite 03337
Coppernoll, Lee 45371
Coppieters, Pierre 03636
Coppola, Gianfranco 25346
Coppola, Regina 41182
Coppus, G.M. 29853
Coquemelle, Lucie 12637
Corazza, Dr. Carla 23787
Corbat, Marc 37025
Corbet, Glenn 46899
Corbett, Agnes 42063
Corbett, Gary 01294
Corbett, Patricia 12787
Corbett-Cyr, Susan 06106
Corbier, René 11023
Corbin, Dr. James E. 45591
Corbin, Kendall W. 45387
Corbould, Lola 01028
Corbu, Emilia 32599
Corcoran, M. 22448
Corcos, Sidney 22648
Corcuera, Catalina 28092
Cordaro, Dr. Michele 25157
Cordell, Prof. Linda S. 41837
Corder, Russ 46554
Cordero, Dr. Mario 23696
Cordero Miranda, Prof. Gregorio 03902
Cordes, D. 30117
Cordes, David 42912
Cordonnier, Aude 11585
Cordova-Gonzalez, Julia 06889
Coreth, Peter 02790
Corey, Mark 43801
Coria, Rodolfo 00479
Corio, Amedeo 25959
Corkern, Wilton C. 41060
Corkill, Nick 40167, 40168
Corkum, Kate 45663
Cormack, Anna E. 40734, 40735
Cormack, Malcolm 46891
Cormier, Angèle 05877
Cormier, George Ann 46600
Cormier, Lisette 05243
Cornejo Gutiérrez, Miguel Angel 31159
Cornelis, J.P. 03674
Cornelissen, Leo M. 28905
Cornelissen, S. 29756
Cornelius, Betty L. 46294
Cornelius, Patsy 48469
Cornelius, Dr. St. 34315, 34316
Cornelius, Steffi 16133
Corner, Rita 06552
Cornet, Josep 34554
Cornett, James 46267
Cornez, G. 03708
Corniani, Maurizio 24285
Cornick, N. 03688
Cornini, Dr. Guido 48872
Cornu, Bernard 12785

Cornwall, Bev 44508
Cornwell, John 01144
Coroiu, Dr. Ioan 32496
Corominas de Basso, Raquel 00399
Coronel, Maria Delia 31314
Corrado, Fabrizio 25736
Correa Sutil, Dr. Sofía 06915
Correia, Dr. Alberto 32360, 32361
Correia, Dr. Virgilio H. 32266
Corrigan, David J. 43942
Corrin, Lisa 47545
Corry, Corrine 06263
Corry, L. 40131
Corser, Elizabeth 05265
Corsini, Principessa 23838
Cort, Cynthia 43773
Cort, Louise 48335, 48357
Cortenova, Prof. Giorgio 25967
Cortes, Prof. Erlinda S. 31461
Cortés Gomez, Carlos 28097
Cortés, Prof. Gemma 25217
Corteville, Julie 13097
Cortina, Leonor 28114
Cory, David H. 47061
Cory, Jeff 42311
Corzo, Miguel-Angel 46452
Corzo Sánchez, Jorge Ramón 35479
Cosandier, Juliane 36855
Coşereanu, Valentin 32542
Cosgrove, Patricia 41377
Coski, Dr. John M. 46883
Cosmetatos, Helen 20835
Cossa, Egidio 25238
Cossart, Graham 00862
Cossignani, Dr. Tiziano 23700
Cosson, Maurice 11203
Costa, Diane 47390
Costa, Elisabeth 32297
Costa, Dr. Gian Paolo 23751
Costa, Prof. Giovanni 23449
Costa, John 46848
Costa jr., Luís da 28726
Costamagna, Dr. Alba 25225
Costamagna, Liliana 25623
Costantini, Dr. Lorenzo 25231
Costar, John 30259
Costard, Matthew P. 40391
Costas Loyola, José E. 32379
Coste, Pierre 10587
Costello, Noel 01133
Costelloe, Jean 22531, 22532
Costely, Nigel 40715
Coster, Annie de 03844
Costersian, John 43682
Costescu, Cornelia 32584
Costie, Gord 04993
Costopoulos Weeks, Jeanne 42332
Costoulas, Costas 20968
Coté, Michel 12750
Cote, Richard 48346
Cotie, Donna 06371
Cott, Peter 39119
Cotter, Patrick 22404
Cotter, Suzanne 40147
Cotter, William 48447
Cotterill, F.D.P. 49028
Cottino, Prof. Alberto 25748
Cottino, Peter 22878
Cotton, Areca 48827
Cotton, Carol 43677
Cotton, Gordon A. 48229
Cottrell, Robert 47948
Cotty, Céline 12298
Couaille, C. le 13125
Couch, Charles Walter 41285
Coudrot, Jean-Louis 11243
Coudurier, Yvonne 13235
Coughlan, M. 01311
Coughlin, Richard J. 44502
Coulombe, Marie-Christine 06658
Coulombier, Jean-Luc 14286
Coulon, François 13943
Coulon, Gérard 12226, 14082
Coumans, Paul 28819
Coumans, P.M.W. 28828
Counot, Bernard 12586
Cour Dragsbo, Peter la 09074
Courson, Bruce A. 47388
Courtelarre, Henry 11009
Courter, Sally 41784
Courtial, M.C. 12706
Courtiour, Jon 40720
Courtney, Janice 47083
Courtney, Kathryn 43545
Courtney, Vernon 48618
Courtois, Jean-Pierre 03456
Couser, Carol 44823
Cousillas, Ana María 00193
Cousin, M. 10670
Cousino, Beate 10623
Cousinou, Olivier 12852
Coutagne, Denis 10255
Coutheillas, Didier 11666
Coutts, Herbert 38921
Coutts, Howard 38087
Couturas, Francis 13692
Couture, André 06209
Couture, Llyr E. 42972
Couture, Raoul F. 42972

Couty, Paul-Henry 10736
Coventry, Susan 39680
Covey, Dustin 05379
Cowan, Joan 05408
Cowart, Jack 48341
Cowburn, Ian 12344
Cowden, Chris 41425
Cowden, Dorothy C. 47944
Cowell, Lorraine 48278
Cowell, R. 39520
Cowell, Tom 06795
Cowley, Liz 38184
Cowley, Paul 38792
Cowling, A. 40084
Cowling, Dr. Mary 38923
Cowling, Sue 46171
Cox, Arrington 42561, 42564
Cox, Charlotte 45489
Cox, Dan 45144
Cox, Dr. Douglas C. 46735
Cox, Eileen 38814
Cox, Janet 42461
Cox, Janson L. 41718
Cox, Katherine 44165
Cox, Marilyn 45482
Cox, N.R. 39081
Cox, Richard 41942
Cox, Rosemary 41564
Cox, Steven 41390
Cox-Paul, Lori 44205
Coxe, Trudy 45931
Coxson, Michael 40953
Coyle, D.C. 06192
Coyne, Richard F. 42473
Cozza, Prof. Lucas 25171
Crabtree, Andrew 38282
Crabtree, John 48142
Cracket, Alan 40599
Craft, John J. 46399
Crago, Jody 48582
Craig, Gerry 47025
Craig, Joanna 42065
Craig, Len 01403
Craig, Martin 48532
Craig, Neil 40594
Craighead, Linda 46273
Crailsheim, Freiherr Ortholf von 15483
Crain, Sandra 44230
Cramer, Carole 46713
Cramer, Jeffrey S. 44780
Cramer, John 48425
Cramer, Patricia T. 48557
Cramer, Sue 01502
Cramer, Wendy 45704
Cramer-Petersen, Lars 08791
Crampton, Lewis S.W. 46959
Crampton, S. 34192
Crampton, Sharon 34189
Crandall, Daniel T. 46640
Crane, Karen R. 44368, 47650
Crane, Prof. Peter 39350
Crane, Susan 47514
Cranson, Diane 00727
Craughwell-Varda, Kathy 47492
Craven, Jane 44296
Craven, K. 40432
Craven, Tim 40546
Crawford, C. 06257
Crawford, Dr. Clifford 43583
Crawford, Henry B. 44991
Crawford, James 42074
Crawford, Louise J. 45427
Crawford, Nina 05307
Crawford, Dr. Richard 43744
Crawford, Robert 39890
Crawford, R.W.K. 39671
Crawford, Shirley 41115
Crawford, Vivian 26069
Crawford-Gore, Betsy 44656
Crawley, Tracey 40577
Creal, Carolyn 47716
Creamer, Winifred 42854
Crean, Kristen 46627
Creary, Marilou 46034
Creasey, Michael 46727
Creddes, Jean 05606
Credland, Arthur G. 39375, 39380, 39382
Creech, C.L. 44513
Creecy, Kerry 01076
Creedon, Denise 45486
Creemers, Guido 03781, 03782
Creemers, Harry 42243
Crégut, Dr. Evelyne 10534
Creighton, Martha 48294
Crelot, Stefan 03627
Cremer, Kurt 15379
Cremers, Filip 03803
Crenshaw, Louise 42533
Crenzien, Helle 08902
Crépin-Leblond, Thierry 10769, 10771, 10774
Crésis, Eric 03551
Crespo, Michael 41535
Crespo-Burgos, Dr. Antonio 09215
Crespo Guliérrez, Victoria 35052
Cressey, Dr. Pamela J. 41120
Creste, Chantal 13119
Creutzburg, Gerlinde 19302
Creutzburg, Ralf 18029
Creuz, Serge 03289

Crevecœur, Claude F. 03834
Crew, Keith 46465
Crews, Gerald 05508
Crick, Monique 36736
Crider, Gwendolyn 41404
Cripe, Roy 44812
Crippa, Flavio 23962
Crippen, Donna 43109
Crişan, Eva 32491
Crise jr., Robert 42922
Crispini, Prof. Giuseppe 25368
Cristofoli, Raoul 25741
Cristofoli, Vincent 12197, 13357, 13359
Cristofolini, Prof. Renato 23445
Critchlow, William H. 05836
Crites, Dr. Gary 44519
Crittin, Jean-François 36623
Crnković, Prof. Vladimir 07819
Crociata, Mariano 24306
Crocker, P.A. 38434
Crocker, Piers 30884
Croft, Brenda L. 00886
Croft, Evelyn 47064
Croke, Fionnuala 22446
Croker, R.C. 30115
Crokett, James 41465
Croll, Prof. Dr. Gerhard 02541
Croll, Helen 00883
Crombe, Polly 46165
Cromer, Lorelei 43349
Crompton, John 38274
Cronin, J.J. 39278
Cronin, Michael 45857
Cronin, Thomas E. 48286
Cronlund, Carl-Johan 36272
Crook, Rosemary 39149
Crook, Rosie 39154
Cropera, Dr. Carla 23802
Cropp, Aubrey 30120
Cros, Caroline 13548
Crosby, Bill 39129
Crosby Tasker, Sheila 46971
Crosman, Christopher B. 46968
Cross, Christine 41573
Cross, Dave 06866
Cross, Sharon 38446
Cross, Tony 37990, 37991
Crossland, Leonard B. 20800
Crossland, Maynard 44717
Crothers, George M. 44748
Croton, G. 30171
Crotti, Pierre 36857
Crouch, Ned 42435
Crouch, Philip 40934
Crous, Dr. D. 34212
Crouy-Chanel, Bernard de 12196
Crowdy, Hannah 39486
Crowe, Dr. D. 41319
Crowe, K.L. 40555
Crowell, Darryl 05171
Crowell, Stephen 46752
Crowell, Stewart A. 45740
Crowl, Bill 45918
Crowley, Noel 22467
Crowley, Terry 01061
Crowter, Philip 38312
Croy, David E. 42667
Crozemarie, Gilles 11297
Crozzolin, Umberto 25807
Crué, Emmanuel 11313
Cruège, Robert 14890
Crüzer, Cristina 37203
Cruise, Sandra 40293
Crum, Katherine 47707
Crum, Dr. Katherine B. 46065
Crum, Patricia 46739
Crum, Rebecca 48419
Crump, Caroline 34286
Crusan, Ronald L. 43501
Crusoe, Lewis S. 45031
Crutchfield, Sharon 41363
Cruvinel, Márcio Borges 04574
Cruz, Amparo Magdaleno de la 35617
Cruz, Fe M. de la 31383
Cruz, Martin 35639
Cruz, Prudenciana C. 31372, 31395
Cruz, Sumra I. de la 31335
Csaplar, Dr. Ferenc 21348
Csar, Mary 41764
Cséfalvay, Pál 21412
Cserei, Dr. Ladislav 34053
Cseri, Dr. Miklós 21575
Cserményi, Vajk 21561
Cservenyák, László 21470
Csillag, Péter 21364
Csobádi, Jozef 34052
Csütörtöky, Jozef 34003
Čtvrtník, Dr. Pavel 08612, 08735
Cuadrado, Emeterio 35143
Čubareva, Roza Petrovna 33269
Cubrić, Ljiljana 33820
Cucchi, Franco 25565
Cuccuini, Dr. Piero 23865
Čučković, Lazo 07713
Cuda, Dr. Maria Teresa 23514
Cudahy, Michael J. 45361
Cudbill, Carolyn 38324
Čudnova, Lidija Aleksandrovna 33551
Cudworth, Keith R. 44814

Cuello, Juan Pablo 41029
Cuervo de Jaramillo, Elvira 07429
Cuevas, Elena 31393
Cuevas y Lara, Mónica 28193
Čuhelová, Blanka 08671
Ćuk, Prof. Dragan 33933
Cukić, Milica 33810
Ćuković, Petar 33833
Cukrov, Tončika 07835
Culbertson, Gary 48781
Čulig, Igor 07713
Cullen, Deborah 45838
Cullen, Maggie 38716
Cullen, M.L. 40751
Culligan, Jenine 44165
Cullinan, Deborah 47320
Cullingford, N.A. 38861
Cullman, Lewis B. 47707
Cullmann, Dorothy 47707
Culot, Maurice 03284, 03298
Culpepper, Marilyn 45423
Culver, Michael 46104
Cumbey, Susan G. 41125
Cumming, Glen 06810
Cummings, Dorothy A. 33935
Cummings, Ernst E. 43281
Cummings, Fern P. 42002
Cummings, Mary Lou 45696
Cummings, Ruth S. 45214
Cummins, Alissandra 03107
Cummins, Dr. D. Duane 41659
Cummins, Heather 40524
Cummins, Karen 48057
Cummins McNitt, R. 41158
Cunard, Gail C. 43733
Cunia, Claudia 03016
Cunliffe-Lister, E.S. 38407
Cunning, Lois 43095
Cunningham, Beth 44875
Cunningham, Clark 48164
Cunningham, Deirdre 46941
Cunningham, Denyse M. 43408, 43409
Cunningham, Eleanor W. 43810
Cunningham, Jewel 06341, 06353
Cunningham, Jo 40650
Cunningham, Kim 44302
Cunningham, Michael R. 42466
Cunningham, Noreen 40061, 40062
Cunningham, Patrick 06841
Cunningham, Patrick J. 41984
Cunningham, Scott 44302
Cuno, Prof. James 39615
Cunz, Dr. Rainer 17607
Cunz, Dr. Reiner 17608
Cupitt, John 39729
Cupp, Franzas 47903
Curbastro, Riccardo Ricci 23337
Curda, Dr. Andreas 02882
Curdy, Philippe 37171
Curiger, Bice 37386
Curling, Marianne J. 43940
Curran, Donald 44010
Curran, Emily 41821
Currat, Joseph 37279
Currell, M. 00770
Currey, David 45627
Currie, Gloria 06386
Currier, Janice 44980
Currin, Robert 43601
Curry, Collette 40598
Curry, Larrie Spier 43935
Curry, Michael 44852
Curry, Michael P. 43895
Curtet, Jean-Christophe 36727
Curtin, Donna D. 46563
Curtis, Brian 45271
Curtis, Dr. J. 39586
Curtis, John 41140
Curtis, Linda 04972
Curtis, Neil 37940
Curtis, Nellie K. 46083
Curtis, Penelope 39445
Curtis, Ron 00824
Curtis, S. 04978
Curtis, Sue 38690
Curtis, Vaughn 40315
Curtiss, Courtney P. 41765
Curto, Argeo 07766
Curto, Domenico 23347
Curto i Homedes, Albert 35569
Ćus Rukonić, Jasminka 07691, 07742
Čušenkov, Valerij Gennadjević 33191
Cushing, Dr. Paula E. 42887
Cushing, Raymond L. 42472
Cushing, Stanley 41798
Cushman, Brad 44826
Cusiac, Dragoş 32576
Cusick, Bonnie A. 42998
Cusming, J.R. 38967
Čusova, Elena 33048
Cussner, Alice 48775
Cutler, Scott 43113
Cutler, Walter L. 48369
Cutright, Marjorie E. 44155
Cuyper, Chris de 03841
Cuyper, Meve jo de 03126
Cuzin, Jean Pierre 13603
Čvančara, Alois 08451
Cvetaw, Dragica 07711

Cvetkova, Natalija 04664
Cvetković, Branislav 33842
Cvetković, Marija 33798
Cvitanović, Ivan 07787
Čvorović, Božena 03925
Cybulski, Antoni 32168
Cygański, Janusz 31852
Cyman, Patricia 41104
Cyncar, Nadia 05389
Cypress, Billy L. 41679
Cyr, Jean-Claude 05092
Cytacki, Joe 43412
Cywin, Allison 46726
Czajka, Jacek 31993
Czajkowski, Józef 32099
Czankus, Ruth 41611
Czapiewska, Aleksandra 39746
Czaplewski, Dr. N.J. 45976
Czapska, Zofia 31970
Czarny, Eugenunsz 31621
Czchodzińska-Przybysławska, Anna 31952
Czech, Tony 42431
Czerannowski, Dr. Barbara 16580
Czére, Dr. Andrea 21383
Czerniak, Robert Michał 31935
Czernin, Dr. Martin 02946
Czerw, Ewa 32157
Czerwinski, Bogdan 32001
Czichos, Raymond L. 48674
Czoma, László 21454
Czopek, Sylwester 31960
Czub, Zofia 31965
Czubaczyński, Ryszard 31770
Czuma, Stanisław 42466
Czymmek, Dr. Götz 18168
Czyżyk, Władysław 32196
Da Pra Galanti, Dr. Lorenzo 25132
Daalder, Dr. R. 28888
D'Abate, Richard 46624, 46629
Dabell, Simon 38245
Dabić, Ljubica 33819
Dabižić, Miodrag 33931
Dabney, Mary K. 46413
Dąbrowska, Anna 31532
Daby, Rebecca 01629
Daccó, Dr. Gian Luigi 24170, 24171, 24172
Dacey, Tim 41488
Dackerman, Susan 41454
Dadabaev, K. 48844
Dae, Sung Kwon 27259
Daele, Durandy van den 12336
Daelemans, Danny 03408
Daelemans, Frank 03275
Daellenbach, Dennis 43755
Daems, Gérard 14749
Daenens, L. 03435
Daenzer, Denise 37400
D'Afflitto, Dr. Chiara 24957
Dagan, Zvi 22639
Dagdar, L. 22296
Dage, Carol J. 44201
Dagon, Yoav 22771
Dagorne, Richard 13043, 13045
Daguerre de Hureaux, Alain 14946
Dahan, Arie 22715, 22724, 22778
Dahesh, Dr. A.S.M. 27480, 27483
Dahl, Erling 30776
Dahl, Torveig 30589
Dahlberg, Anne Marie 36256
Dahlbring, Magnus 35922
Dahle, Bernhard 17355
Dahle, Sigrio 06817
Dahlgren, Dorothy 42511
Dahlie, Paul N. 44836
Dahlitz, Ray 00768
Dahlstrom, Harry 44051
Dahm, Klaus 18831
Dahmani, Dr. Saïd 00048
Dahmke, Prof. Dr. A. 18072
Dai, Linyan 07284
Daijoji, Yoshifumi 27031
Dailey, John R. 48371
Daily, Charles 47421
Daily, Greg 47912
Daily, Steven L. 45367
Daim, Prof. Dr. Falko 02312, 18606
Dajani, Virginia 45754
Daker, Emma 40916
Dakin Hastings, Lynne 48046
Dalborg, Björn 36283
Dalby, Åge 30642
Dale, A.P. 37949
Dale, Charles 47074
Dale Zemlansky, Denise 43881
Dalen, Mary G. 05701
D'Alessandro, Laura 42355
Daley, Jean 43131
Dalhousie, Earl of 38799
Dalichow, Dr. Bärbel 19434
Dalla Vecchia, Fabio M. 24475
Dallago, Antonio 25995
Dallaj, Dr. Arnalda 24375
Dallam, Fred 43067
Dallas, John 38057
Dalleo, Bruce 45683
Dalli, Alberto 25451, 25453
Dallman, Armin 48259
Dallman, Dr. John E. 45072
Dallmeier, Dr. Martin 19521, 19522, 19523

Dalous, Pierre 14953
Daloze, M. 03235
Dalsgaard Larsen, Keld 09052
Dalton, Bryan 42003
Dalton, Carolyn 38741
Dalton, Jake 43183
Dalton, Ron 45305
Dalton, Shirley B. 46612
Daly, Beth 48052
Daly, Dr. Eleanor 44281
Daly, James 45835
Daly, Tess 30262
Daly, Thomas 48188
Dalyell, Kathleen 39506
Dám, Dr. László 21491
Dam-den-Gnam, Pithaya 37539
Dama, Prof. Salvatore Cirillo 06905
Damamme, Jeanne 13784, 13785
Daman, F.J. 03147
Damaskinos 21024
D'Amato, Dr. Alfonso 23129
D'Amato, Aurelia 25304
Dambaev, Munko Žartam 32630
Dambergs, Guntis 27472
D'Ambrosio, Anna T. 48170
D'Ambrosio, Dr. Antonio 24987
D'Ambrosio, Paul 42618
D'Ambrosio, Paul 42619
Damdinsuren, Tsedmaa 28679
Damdoumi, Vasiliki 21206
Dame, Susan 42954, 47214
Damgaard, Ellen 08971, 08972
Damgaard Sørensen, Tinna 09046
Damian, Paul 32467
Damianov, Nikola 04826
D'Amico, Prof. Claudio 23127
Damito, Dr. Ronaldo 04386
Damjanova, Katerina 04629
Damm, Dr. Inciser 18166
D'Amore, Dr. Paola 25231
Dampman, Allan 44179
Damsgaard, Nina 09104
Damy, Ken 23207
Dana, Rae 48505
Dana, Richard 42035
Danailov, Boris 04832
Dance, Pat 06848
Dancey, Jenny 39933
Danchev, Dancho 04702
Dăncuș, Mihai 32594
Dandaura, M. 30347
Dander, Dr. Marilena 24118
Dandison, Basil 48779
Dandwate, P.P. 21986
Danelzik-Brüggemann, Dr. Christoph 16738
Danesi, Claudio 23708
Dangel, Gerhard 17107
D'Angelo, Starlyn 46131
Danh, Prof. Dr. Trinh 48977
Daniel, Alain 10478
Daniel, Andy 43729
Daniel, Françoise 10910
Daniel, Mary 42859
Daniel, Rochette 03296
Daniel McElroy, Susan 40406, 40410
Daniels, Christopher 43825
Daniels, John P. 46342
Daniels, Marsha 42188
Daniels, R. 39178
Danielsson, Ing-Mari 36309
Danielsson, Ralf 35841
Danielsson, Rolf 35843
Danielsson, Dr. Roy 36065
Danini, Gianluca 24097
Daniylopoulou, Olga 20942
Danjo, Prof. Tatsuo 26117
Dankbar, Johannes 20201
Dankl, Dr. Günther 02082
Danly, Dr. Laura 42887
Dann, Alan O. 45170
Dann, Gaston 12584
Danna, Tracy 41563
Danne, Rainer 17923
Danneel, M. 03303
Dannhus, H. 18428
Dano, Dr. Ján 34010
Dansako, Tetsuya 27001
Dansberger, Dorthory 42813
Danson, Stuart 01593
Danšova, Olga Nikolajevna 33252
Dante Coronel, Hugo 00114
Dantinne, Claude 12492
Danzer, Dr. Gudrun 01927
Danzl, Barbara 02647
Dapkyunas, Jeanne 23117
Dapsens, J.-C. 03611
Darakčieva, Uljana 04741
Darakčiova, Uljana 04739
Darby, Daniel 06868
Darde, Dominique 13337
Darga, Dr. Robert 19953
Darke, Don F. 44385
Darling, Denise L. 42804
Darling, L.A. 06631
Darling, Sharon 47495
Darling-Finan, N. 40495
Darmstädter, Dr. Beatrix 02918

Darr, Alan P. 42924
Darst, Lise 43610
Dart, John 38485
Dary 14573
Dary, Anne 10392, 11541, 12662
Das, Chandranath 21756
Das, Dilip A. 45681
Das, Dr. Jithendra 21891
Dasbach, Th. P. 28945
Dashiell, David A. 46462
Dassas, Frédéric 13558, 13636
Date, Tatumi 26889
Daubendiek, James 44322
Daubert, Debra 46206
Dauda, J.Y. 30351
Daudelin, Robert 05901
Dauge, Alexandra 12165
Daugelis, Osvaldas 27521
Daughdrill, Kay 42781
Daughhetee, Mark 44368
Daughterman-Maguire, Dr. Eunice 41473
Dauphin, Jean 03555
Daure, Regine 11065
Dauskardt, Dr. Michael 17484
Dautermann, Dr. Christoph 18228
Dautermann Ricciardi, Dana 43502
Dauth, Louise 00889
Dautović, Andrea 03925
Dauwe, Marc 03558
Dávalos de Camacho, Maya 28184
Davaras, Dr. C. 20810
Davatz, Dr. Jürg 36978
Davenport, Kimberly 44133
Davey, Arnold 40262
David, Dr. 42467
David, Dr. A.R. 39894
David, Catherine 29780
David, Johan 03462
David, Josiane 12962
David, Karen 43136
David, Mihai 32443
David, Norma Jean 43822
David, Paul 40872
David, Romeo G. 31299
David, Walfried 17185
David, Wendy 13285
David-Weill, Hélène 13556, 13563, 13586, 13642
Davidov, Dr. Dinko 33798
Davidović, Jasna 33913
Davidović, Jelena 33854
Davidow, Joan 42748
Davidse, I. 29681
Davidson, Anne 46275
Davidson, Prof. C.W. 38277
Davidson, Dan 42687
Davidson, Denny 46503
Davidson, Heather A. 06858
Davidson, John H. 40071
Davidson, Kate 01494
Davidson, Scott 05525
Davies, Alan 38764
Davies, Andrew 39409
Davies, Brian 40223
Davies, Deborah 38262
Davies, Eluned 39534
Davies, Erica 39639
Davies, Hugh M. 44548, 47281
Davies, Jane 05435, 06268
Davies, Jean S. 46536
Davies, Jenny 39852
Davies, Kate 42980
Davies, Kirsty 01570
Davies, Lucy 39563
Davies, M.P. 38796
Davies, Pascal 10479
Davies, Peggy 39078
Davies, R.H. 38242
Davies, Rick 45318
Davies, Rita 06574
Davies, S. 01501
Davies, Simon 40121, 40122
Davies, Steve 39852
Davies, Su 39346, 39348
Davies, Suzanne 10241
Davies, Dr. W.V. 39586
Davignon, Étienne 03339
Dávila, Alejandro 00307
Davila, Julio V. 31219
Davis, Alice M. 43236
Davis, Dr. Ann 05176
Davis, Ann 41327
Davis, Audrey P. 41121
Davis, Beryl 06529
Davis, Beth 42543
Davis, Betty J. 46147
Davis, Carol A. 43274
Davis, Catherine 43299
Davis, Darwin R. 47102
Davis, David L. 46184
Davis, Dustin P. 43569
Davis, Ellen 45654
Davis, Elliot 41817
Davis, Gainor B. 45478
Davis, Gordon 41393, 41393
Davis, Helen 45157
Davis, Jacqueline B. 43451
Davis, Janet 06770
Davis, Jaqueline Z. 45859
Davis, Joanne 48474

Davis, John 43465
Davis, Karen Lee 45387
Davis, Kate 06238
Davis, Katherine 45864
Davis, Kay 42508
Davis, Kieth 30182
Davis, Dr. Leroy 46176
Davis, Lesia 05187
Davis, Dr. Leslie B. 41858
Davis, Lloyd 46071
Davis, M. 22612
Davis, Michael 47828, 47829
Davis, Nancy 41483
Davis, P.A.C. 30247
Davis, Phillip V. 47741
Davis, Priscilla 05353
Davis, Robert O. 47231
Davis, Ron 05704
Davis, Ruth 41114
Davis, Sarah 45758
Davis, Susan S. 44485
Davis, Tod 48051
Davis, Todd A. 06727
Davis, Walter R. 42092
Davis, William B. 41870
Davis, William J. 45964
Davis, Zina 48525, 48526
Davis Anderson, Brooke 45756, 45798
Davis Gardner, Katie 42536
Davison, Fiona 39657
Davison, Hazel 39344
Davison, Liane 06519
Davison, Dr. Patricia 34210
Davisson, Scott 47658
Davletov, B. 48834
Davson, Victor 45889
Davy, Geukens 03544
Davydova, Linaida Aleksandrovna 33384
Davydova, Natalja Alekseevna 33337
Dawans, Francine 03576
Dawe, Phillip 39026
Dawey, Dr. Chris 45402
Daws, Russell S. 47938
Dawson, Amy 47333
Dawson, Barbara 22432
Dawson, Chris 42470
Dawson, David 38325, 40677
Dawson, E.A. 38520
Dawson, J. 38454, 38625
Dawson, Dr. Mary R. 46511
Dawson, P. 22491
Dawson Penniman, H. 46423
Day, Brenda 41443
Day, Edward 46913
Day, Ginette 12027
Day, Jackie 47830
Day, John A. 48215
Day, Michael 39097, 39662, 40399, 40400, 40401, 40404
Day, Patricia 43818
Day, Richard 38542, 48240
Day, Sally 37966
Day, Theodorsa 46284
Dayan, Prof. T. 22777
Dayrit, Marina 31375
Dayson, Diane H. 45876
De Angelis, Prof. Giuseppe 25124
De Filippis, Dr. Elena 25893
De Floren, R. 41063
De Franceschi, Antonio Fernando 04328
De Herdt, René 03404
De Kelver, Jan 03395
De Lorentiis, Decio 24261
De Luca, Dr. Bianca 23545
De Luca, Maurizio 48872
De Lucia Brolli, Maria Anna 23592
De Marchi, Dr. Andrea G. 25161
De Marco, Dr. Marco 23806
De Martin, Prof. Gian Candido 24918
De Martin, Prof. Giancandido 24914, 24915, 24917
De Mier Riaño, Elisa 07420
De Paepe, Pantxika 10222
De Palma, Prof. Luigi Michele 24459
De Palma, Dr. Maria Camilla 23977
De Paolis, Rosario 24165
De Pasquale, Vicenzo 24338
De Polo Saibanti, Claudio 23870
De Pompeis, Claudio 24868
De Reymaeker, Michel 03633, 03635
De Rochambeau, M. 14898
De Santi, Claudio 24470, 24471, 24472
De Siena, Antonio 24647
De Simone, Dr. Emilio 22870
De Smet, Urbain 03832
De Strobel, Dr. Anna Maria 48872
De Vincentiis, Prof. Italo 25269
De Vito, Natalie 06593
De Waal, Dr. Lydia M. 34385, 34386
De Witte, Hubert 03247, 03248, 03249, 03250, 03252
Deagan, Dr. K.A. 43581
Deakin, G.T. 01185
Deal, Cliff 44571
Dealy, Anne F. 43642
Dean, Deborah 40103
Dean, Don 42125
Dean, Jeanne 48125
Dean, Jim 45498
Dean, Kevin 47455

Dean, M. 38730
Dean, Sharon 42467
Dean Krute, Carol 43944
Dean Stock, Michele 47188
Deaner, Beth J. 45707
Deans, Arthur 37930
Dear, Elizabeth 43780
Dearing, Vicki 41970
Dearinger, Dr. David 45849
Deaton, Linda 47938
Debain, Yvette 05028
Debal-Morche, Anne 10311, 10314
Debarge, René 11991
Deblanc Magnée, Marie-Paule 03808, 03810
Debo, Thomas A. 46573
Debočički, Valentin 04705, 04706, 04707, 04708, 04710
Dębowska, Alina 31492
Debrabandère, Béatrice 13317
Debrah, Dr. Issac N. 20788
Debray, Cécile 13548
Debrincat, Saviour 27708
DeBruyn, David L. 43759
Debruyn, Raphaël 03561
Debry, Jaques 11228
Debryn, Johan 03746
Debus-Steinberg, Astrid 20110
DeBuse Potter, Gail 42180, 44384
Deca, Eugen 32578
Decames, Jean-Claude 12889
DeCamp, Alta J. 45646
Decán Gambús, Ivanova 48933
Decatur, Raylene 42887
Decavele, Dr. Johan 03443
Dechaux, Carine 03701
Decker, Carla 45904
Decker, E. 14623, 14624
Decker, Dr. K.P. 16397
Decker, Raymond 15141
Decker, Scott E. 44210
Deckers, Yolande 03146
Decoodt, Wim 15860
Decraene, A. 03146
Decroix, Philippe 14107
Decron, Benoît 12555
Decter, Avi Y. 41472
Dectot, Xavier 13637
Dedenroth-Schou, Poul 08959
Dedic, Bernard 07788
Dedíková, Soňa 08288
Deecke, Prof. Dr. Thomas 16330
Deedes, C.M.J. 38742
Deegan, Dr. Ann 42384, 46783, 46824, 48815, 48816
Deegan, Denise 42231
Deer, Naomi 44254
Deering, Stan 05203
Deernose, Kitty 42712
Deerpalsingh, Salni 27734
Deeva, Valentina Kirillovna 32831
Defauwes, Georges 03368
Defeo, Prof. Rúben D.F. 31431
Degel, Hermann 20106
Degel, Kirsten 08902
Degen, Dr. Ch. 37271
Degen, Jenna 46448
Degen, Kurt 19759
Deggelsegger, M. 02593
Degon, Pierre 14055
Degreif, Dr. Uwe 16138
DeGroft, Aaron 47453
Degueurce, C. 12776
Deguglielmo, M. 10574
Deguillaume, Marie-Pierre 14845
DeGuzman, Rene 47346
Deharde, Ewald 16434
Dehejia, Dr. Vidya 48335, 48357
Dehrkoop, Prestene 43121
Deiber-Kumm, Michele 42274
Deigendesch, Roland 18928
Deigendesch, Dr. Roland 18929, 18930
Deiker, Dr. Tom 42273
Deimel, Dr. Claus 18407
Deiser, Leopoldine 01812
Deisler-Seno, Jane 42645
Deitsch, Elka 45814
Deitz, Judith 47624
Deitz, M. Ph. 03580
Dejardin, Dr. Fiona M. 46161
Dekiert, Dr. Markus 18832
Dekker, H. 29350
Dekker, M. 28919
Deknop, A. 03276, 03288
Del Bagno, Rober 45858
Del Falco, Vittorio 25255
Del Frate, Dr. Gabriella 24783
Del-Prete, Sandro 36818
Del Testa, Luise 20753, 20754
Del Vivo, Tommaso 23731
Dela, Feliks 31818
Delacoste, Raymond 36945
Delacote, Goery 47316
Delaender, Georges 03822
Delage, Dominique 14774
Delahant, John M. 47450
Delahaye, Marie-Claude 10505
Delaine, Joël 13209, 13214
Delaney, Chris 38493
Delaney, C.J. 38493

Delangle, J.F. 10734
Delannoy, Agnès 14241
Delannoy, Jean 12605
Delany, Max 01025
Delaousie, Renée 13401
Delaquis, Christian 06820
Delarge, Alexandre 11815
Delattre, Jean-Luc 03661
DeLay, Matthew 41170
Delay, Matthew 41171
Delbaere, Stefaan 28939
Delbos, Andrée 14140
Delcourt-Vlaeminck, Dr. Marianne 03790
Delehanty, Suzanne 45289
Delépine, Francine 03294
Delgado, Alvaro 34989
Delgado, Avella 34923, 34925
Delgado, Eric 10475
Delgado, James P. 06695
Delgado, Jane 45751
Delgado, Lino Torres 27753
Delgado, Sally 41324
Delgado Restrepo, Gloria 07446
Delhaise, Christophe 03236, 03237
Delialioğlu, Salih 37652
Delisle, André J. 05920
DeLisle, Godfray 05262
Delivorrias, Prof. Dr. Angelos 20878
Delker, Martin 16863
Dell, Roger 43326
Dell, Sharon 30286
Della Casa, Bettina 36898
Della Fina, Giuseppe M. 24706
Della Toffola, Leomberto 25935
Dellacroce, Raymond 43274
Dellamore, Hilona 10761
Dell'Antonia, Dario 15232
Dellantonio, Elio 25051
Dellbeck, Johan 36361
Dellin, Edward J. 44646
Dellinger, Mary H. 43535
Dell'Oca Fiordi, Dr. Angela 25603
Delmas, Jean 14006
Delmas, Luc 15188
DelMonico, Mary 45886
Delmont, Patrick 15287
Delobel, Jean 10569
Deloffre, Véronique 10611
Deloing, Evelyne 10421
Deloncle, Jacques-Gaspard 13704
DeLong, Dr. Marilyn 47154
DeLorme, Harry 47485
Delorme, Yves 13984
Delperdange, Roland 03197
Delporte, Luc 03802
Delroy, A. 01364
Deltedesco, Franco 24189
Deltour-Levie, Claudine 03337
Delye, Emmanuel 03573
Demaerschalk, Sylvain 03272
DeMaio, Bonnie 47019
Demard, Jean-Christophe 11159
Demaret, Nicole 03789
Demarez, Leonce 03190, 03191, 03219
DeMars, Louise L. 41901
Demarteau, J. 29050
Demazure, Michel 13651
Dembiniok, Marian 31540
Dembski, Prof. Dr. G. 01818
Dembski, Prof. Dr. Günther 02918, 02981
Dembski, Dr. Ulrike 02963
Demčenko, Ljubov Grigorjevna 32748
Demeester, Veerle 03146
Demel, Dr. Bernhard 02950
DeMenocal, Linda 41580
Demere, Dr. Thomas 47295
Demerling, Rod 06457
Demetis, Ioannis 21221
Demetriou, Maro 08193
Demetriou, Myra 01256
Demetz, Dr. Stefan 23153
Demeurie, Dirk 03388
Demidenko, Olga Moiseeva 33189
Demidovich, Peter 44162
Deminey, E. 34245, 34285
Deming, Diane 46835
Demirci, Süheyla 37788
Demke, Siegfried G. 44925
Demo, Dr. Željko 07809
Dempsey, Rey 22450
Dempsey, Terrence E. 47130
Demski, Tadeusz 31978
Demuth, Renate 19588
DeMuzio, David 46442
Denaro, Dolores 36563
Denelli, Gjergj 00031
Denenberg, Thomas 43944
Denford, Geoffrey 40887
Denford, Dr. G.T. 40894
Dengate, James 48164
Denis, Paul 06607
Denise, Danièle 11769
Denison, Ruth 38597
Denissen, Sabine 03140
Deniz, Sebahattin 37758
Denizli, Hikmet 37612
Denk, Dr. Roswitha 02918
Denker, Eric 48342
Denman, Ron 05248

Dennerly, Peter 30142
Denney, Alan 38451
Denning, Elizabeth 43282
Dennis, Mary 44526
Dennis, Sue M. 45882
Dennison, Foster K. 06774
Dennison, Lisa 45872
Dennler, William V.A. 48020
Denny, Tyra 44390
Dennys, Vincent 10347
Densapa, Tashi 21804
Densen, Paul M. 47381
Dent, G.J.H. 40199
Denton, Amy 43258
Denton, Joanna 40558
Dentraygues, D.J. 10395
Denys, Lama 10442
Denzel, H. 01667
Deon, Luca 36906
DeOrsay, Paul B. 42520, 46419
Deparpe, Patrice 12486
Depauw, Carl 03173
Depierre, Marie-Colette 12361
DePietro, Anne 44161
Depoid, Henry 11380
DeQueiroz, Prof. Alan 41837
Dequidt, Luk 03687
Deranian, Janet 42605
Derbic, Rupert 01759
Derbier, Josselin 13992
Derby, Newton 47846
Derbyshire, Janine 38716, 38718
D'Ercole, Dr. Vincenzo 23548
Dercon, Chris 18855
Dercon, C.P.E. 29759
Dercourt, J. 12009
Derda, Dr. Hans-Jürgen 16293
Derefaka, Dr. Abi Alabo 30362
Derenthal, Dr. Ludger 16025
Deriks, M. 29854
Dering, Dr. Florian 18880, 18899
Dering, Dr. Peter 15866
Derion, Brigitte 10809
Derjabin, Vladimir Ignatevič 33382
Derksen, J. 29169
Derksen, J.J.V.M. 29896
Dermitzakis, Prof. Dr. M.D. 20900
Dernmerle, Rita 02945
DeRosa, Donald 47825
Derosier, Paul 46017
Deroux, Kenneth 44368
Derriks, Claire 03640
Dertazzo, Ludovico M. 24735
Desai, Vishakha N. 45768
Desaix, Ingmari 35912
DeSantis, Diana Ortega 47427
Desaulniers, Guy 03044
Desbarax, Dr. P.M. 03158
Desbenoit, Martine 10854
Desborough, Jeff 48614
Descamps, Patrick 12007
Desel, Jochen 15672
DeSeyter, Craig 44054
Desfossés Le Page, Carmen 06641
DeShon, Richard N. 47108
Deshpande, Dr. P.N. 21795
Désirat, Georges 14586
DesJardins, Edward 47021
Desjardins, Robert Y. 06429
Desjardins-Ménégalli, Marie-Hélène 11711, 11712
Desmarais, Charles 42403
Desmedt, An 03146
Desmet, Don 44379
Desmet, Viviane 03314
Desmules, Olivier 12816
Despotidis, Emmanouil 20819
DesRoches, C. 05824
Dessens, H.J.A. 28888
Desserud, Thore 30474
Dessornes, Maria E. 48003
Destefani, Joseph 28667
DeStefano, Giacomo R. 46311
Desvigne, M. 14612
Desy, Dr. Elizabeth A. 45180
Desy, Margherita 41831
Detch, Rosalie S. 44725
Dethlefs, Dr. Gerd 18950, 49216
Detrani, Geoffrey 45885
Detrée, Jean-François 14494
Detrich, Kalman 45846
Detten, Jayne 46582
Dettmer, Dr. Frauke 19569
Dettmer, Hans-Georg 17355
Deuber-Ziegler, E. 36745
Deuchar, Stephen 39787
Deuchert, Dr. Norbert 16429
Deutmann, Karl Heinrich 16662
Deutsch, Fred 23044
Deutsch, Prof. Dr. H. 36533
Deutsch, Dr. J. 36533
Deutschbauer, Franz 02644
Dev, Anand 21782
Devaney, Richard 38685
Devanik, Dave 05936
Devaux, Bernard 13570
Devé, Jean 11866
Deveau, Bertha 47381
Deveau, Carole 05874
Devendorf, Meredith 45333

Devereux, Dr. B.J. 38452
Devereux, David 38502, 39393, 39394
DeVille, Sue 46168
Devin, Pierre 11565
Devine Nordstrom, Alison 42812
Devine-Reed, Pat 42309
Devlin, Dr. Felicity 22442
Devlin, Joseph T. 46456
Devonshire, Amana 40913
DeVonyar-Zansky, Jill 46556
Devos, Danny 03165
Devos, E. 03711, 03712, 03713
Devries, Fred 45303
DeVries, Karl 47486
Devroye-Stilz, Anne 13313
Devynck, Danièle 10276
Dewald, Ann 46262
DeWalt, Billie R. 46511
Dewan, L. Georg 06050
Deweerdt, Jean 11586
Dewey, Alice 38916
Dewey, S. 40767
Dewhurst, Dr. C. Kurt 43054
Dewhurst, Stephen 41552, 45793
Dewilde, Annick 03542
Dewilde, Jan 03514, 03515, 03516, 03517, 03518
Dewing, David 39641
DeWitt, Martin 43003
Dewitz, Dr. Bodo von 18128
DeWys-VanHecke, Amy 42923
Dexter, James 00896
Dexter, Susan 43325
Deyle, Betty 41626
DeYoung, Jeri 43333
Deyoung, Mildred 44558
Deysenroth, Paul 48566
Dezellus, Eric 14066
Dezutter, Willy P. 03264, 03267
Dhaene, Sylvie 03439, 03788
Dhaliwal, Theresa 39691
Dhaulakhandi, V.N. 21981
Dholakia, P.V. 21876
Dhombres, M. Jean 13520
Di Belgiojoso, Dr. Giuseppe B. 25452
Di Fabio, Clario 23982, 23992, 23998
Di Felice, Dr. Paola 25688
Di Flumeri, Dr. Gabriella 25231
Di Geronimo, I. 23448
Di Girolami, Dr. Paola 23437, 23635, 24062, 24493, 24537, 25126, 25289, 25332
Di Grazia Costa, Ivani 04515
Di Ianni, Angelo 24881
Di Lorenzo, Maria Teresa 25407
Di Malfetta, Dr. Felice 24459
Di Mario, Dr. Mario 25699
Di Martino, Maria 24931
Di Niro, Dr. Angela 23304
Di Paolo, Luciana 24923
Di Pascale, Paolo 23015
Di Pietrantonio, Dr. Giacinto 23060
Di Pietro, Gaetano 24869
Di Stefano, Dr. Carmela Angela 24765
Di Tommaso, Francis 45885
Diaconescu, Nicolae 32472
Diaconescu, Petru 32601
Diakite, Sinkoun 21284
Diamantakis, Stavros 02396
Diamond, Dr. Judy 44793
Dianto, Herkus 22128
Dianzinga, Dias-Théodore 07646
Diaper, Hilary 39456
Diaper, Dr. Hilary 39456
Dias, Dr. Maduro 32237
Dias, Robério 04404
Dias Duarte, Luiz Fernando 04388
Diaw, Amadou Tahirou 33777
Díaz, Dr. Jimena Perera Diaz 41024
Díaz, Joaquín 35588
Díaz, Luis H. 07466
Díaz, Miguel 35048
Díaz de Mazzoldi, Olga 07546
Díaz García, Dr. José Luis 35048
Díaz García, José Luís 35157
Díaz Padróns, Dr. Matías 35048
Díaz Pardo, Isaac 35352
Díaz-Tusham, Rafael 45754
Díaz Ungría, Dr. Adelaida de 48953
Dibbets, W.A.G. 28955
Dičeva, Vera 04849
Dick, Hans-Gerd 20770
Dick, James 47017
Dicke, James F. 45671
Dickens, Denise 46772
Dickenson, Joanne 46614
Dickenson, Victoria 05910
Dickerman, Dr. Robert W. 41105
Dickermann, Dr. Fred 02126
Dickerson, Amy 43586
Dickerson, Patricia 46124
Dickerson, Robin 43566
Dickerson Lind, Anne 47473
Dickey, Michael 41271
Dickhaut, Monique F.A. 29567
Dickinson, Cindy 41177
Dickinson, Gavé 45747
Dickinson, Pat 06612
Dickinson, Robert 40665, 40668
Dickinson, Roger 45685

Dickson, Carl A. 43923
DiCosimo, Joanne 06072
Didier, Alain 13892
Didier, Prof. Arturo 25681
Didier, Hebert 12607
Didrichsen, Maria 09478
Didrichsen, Peter 09478
Diebel, C. 30104
Dieck Jackson, Anke Tom 47707
Dieckhoff, Dr. Reiner 18150
Diederen, Roger 45789
Diederichs, Dr. Urs 19565
Diedrich, Dr. Stephan 18161
Diehes, Dr. Gerhard M. 01914
Diehl, Reinhard 18506
Diehl, Dr. Richard 48112, 48114
Diehl, Dr. Ruth 16242
Diekmann, Klemens 15598, 15599
Diekmann, Rolf 20118
Dieleman, Peter A. 29638
Diem, Peter 36830
Diemer, Dr. Kurt 15736
Diene, Baidy 33779
Dienes, Dr. Gerhard M. 01916, 01931
Dienst, Robert 02197
Dierking, Gary R. 43448
Dierks-Staiger, Regine 20106
Dießner, Dr. Petra 18417
Dietel, Volker 19028
Dieter, Raymond 42335
Diethorn, Karie 46418
Dietl, Dr. Gerhard 20105
Dietrich, Bev 05536, 05537
Dietrich, Dorothea 45678
Dietrich, Eva 37382
Dietrich, Dr. Gerhard 18157
Dietrich, Dr. Helmut 17388
Dietrich, Suzanne 43097
Dietrich, Tanja 36880
Dietschi, Cornelia 36912
Dietschi, Jean-Pierre 37365
Dietz, Günter 20406
Dietz, Karl-Heinz 16755
Dietz, Paddy 48654
Dietz, Stefanie 20425
Dietz, Steffen 15399
Dietz, Thomas A. 44380
Dietz, Ulysses G. 45892
Diez Valdez, Oscar 31133
DiFerdinando, Charles A. 43014
Diffily, James P. 43485
Difuccia, Mike A. 45434
Digby, Linda 05361
Digel, Brigitte 20664
Digger, Jo 40773
Dignef, Leo 03206
Dijkstra, J.G. 29627
Dijkstra, Rob 29309
Dijols, Pierre 13135
Diklev, Torben 21236
Dikun, Z.M. 32937
Dilas, Milica 07760
Dilcher, Dr. D.L. 43581
Dill, Chris 43785, 43786
Dill, Cynthia 45741
Dillard Mitchell, Shannon 44826
Dillard Rech, Lori 46395
Diller, Douglas 47403
Diller, Dr. J. 18926
Dilley, Cherry 34376
Dilley, Mary Lou 45172
Dillon, Alice 47877
Dillon, Idelle 46340
Dillon, John 47333
Dillon, Mike 40188
Dilly, Georges 10686
Dilo, Lefter 00023
Dilts, Bonnie 45475
Dimaandal, Carmelita 31377
Dimaki, Sofia 20843
DiMaria, Tom 46063
DiMeo Carlozzi, Annette 41412
Dimitrić, Dragan 33902
Dimitrijević, Bora N. 33930
Dimitrov, Ass.Prof. Dr. Bojidar 04846
Dimitrov, Ivan 04792
Dimitrova, Stanka 04900
Dimmick, Walter 44685
Dimova, Ljubov Ivanovna 33726
Dimpelfeld, William 47497
Dimt, Dr. Heidelinde 02241
Dimuchametova, Svetlana Aleksandrovna 33308
Dina, Diana le 36864
Dinard, N. Jean 12109
Diner, Mónica 28177
Dinger, Brigitte 16887
Dingertz, Stig 36254
Dinges, Christiane 18129
Dings, Mindie M. 42235
Dingwall, Fiona 39007
Dinkelspiel, Florence 44866
Dinkhauser, Lienhard 02811
Dinkins, Dr. Leon 46504
Dinsmoie, Elizabeth 05406
Diogo, Joanne 42059
Diogo Ribeiro, José 32266
Dion, Jean-Noël 06322
DiPaolo, Michael 44720
Dippel, Robert 48267

Dippold, Günter 15855
Dippold Vilar, Dalmo 04533
Dirican, Alan 41454
Dirnbacher, Karl 01884
Dirnbacher, Kurt 01683
Dirnbacher, Sonja 01682, 01684
Dirschel, Angelika 17668
Dirun, Moh Lativ 27653
Dishman, Jay 45276
Disney, Betty 42737
Disney, Jenny 47214
Distel, Anne 13596
Distel, Dr. Barbara 16524
Dîte, Dr. Tibor 34075
Ditmanson, Dennis 48454
Dittberner, Stephen 46685
Dittertová, Dr. Eva 08307, 08308
Dittler, Ingeborg 16673
Dittmann, Britta 18534
Dittmar, Monika 20300
Dittmar, Volker 18652
Dittrich, Dr. Erika 17144, 17145, 17146
Divall, Colin 40966
Divelbiss, Maggie 46741
Dixey, Judy 39572
Dixon, Annette 41222
Dixon, Bonnie 43619
Dixon, Carol 45113
Dixon, David J. 41698
Dixon, Debbie 47452
Dixon, Elaine 46749
Dixon, Gerald 43728
Dixon, Hugh 39943
Dixon, Jill P. 42978
Dixon, Kate 45239
Dixon, Rick 40663
Dixon, Wendy M.C. 01163
Dixon, William 48014
Diz Ardid, Emilio 35184
Djabbar, Abd. 22211
Djačenko, N.D. 37905
Djadaibaev, Amir Jalinovich 27072
Djalal, Dr. Zaidir 22119
Djamba K. Shungu, Joseph 07638
Djanguenane, Nayondjoua 37549
Djepbarov, Redjep 37817
Djevori, Bozidar 33899
Djordjević, Nenad 33854
Djordjević, Zivadin 33907
Djurdjekanović, Sladjana 33824
Djurdjević, Ivo 07795
Djuve, Kjetil 30836
Dlin, Elliott 42750
Dlugač, Vladimir Vladimirovič 32654
Długoszewska-Nadratowska, Hanna 31537
Dłużwska-Sobczak, Anna 31751
Dmitriev, Prof. I.S. 33429
Dmitrovic, Katarina 33827
Dmytrykiw, Danylo 43899
Doak, Elaine M. 44502
Doane, Erin 47462
Dobbelstein, H. 29227
Dobbie, Allison 30146
Dobbie, Dave 05944
Dobbratz, Alferna 44103
Dobke, Dr. Dirk 17533
Dobkowski, Mieczysław 31519
Dobney, Jayson 48214
Dobosi, Dr. Viola 21606
Dobras, Dr. Wolfgang 18603
Dobrea, George 42480
Dobrev, Marin 04867
Dobrik, Dr. Istváan 21481
Dobrik, Dr. István 21479, 21480
Dobrileit, Margitta 16735, 16736
Dobritzsch, Elisabeth 17357
Dobson, Stewart 38230
Dočev, Spas 04727
Dočeva, Penka 04711
Dočeva-Peeva, Elka 04846
Docog, Angelica 45271
Dodd, Dr. Donald B. 41709
Dodd, Jennifer 44014
Dodd, Nicholas 40915, 40918
Dodd, Nick 40489
Dodd, Philip 39673
Dodd, Roger 38617
Dodds, E. 39305
Dodds, Richard 47665
Dodge, Alan 01363
Dodge, Carol A. 47676
Dodge, Laura 43183
Dodier, Virginia 42109
Dodina, Tatjana Alekseevna 33718, 33720
Dodson, Gin 48462
Dodson, Howard 45868
Dodsworth, Roger C. 38782
Dodwell, A. 39693
Dodwell, P. 39693
Döllinger, Theodor 19350
Dörfer, Dr. Anja 19123
Dörhöfer, Friedrich 16393
Döring, Dr. Jürgen 17560
Döring, Martel 19167
Döring, Dr. Thomas 16297
Dörnenburg, Manuela 16167
Doerr, Marjorie A. 43173
Doersch, Lee 43095
Doetsch, Dr. Rainer 18123

Doezema, Marianne 47693
Doffey, Marie-Christine 36550
Dogan, Salih 37715
Dogariu, Octavian 32614
Doggatt, Henry 47896
Doherty, Ann 45817
Doherty, Laura 43028
Doherty, Peggy M. 42856, 42857
Doherty, Roisin 22521
Dohertyld, Erin 30118
Dohnal, Karel 08373
Dohrman, Stewart. 47477
Doht, Sabine 16815
Doiron, Sue 06318
Dojčev, Nejčo 04753
Dolan, Douglas C. 42982, 42985
Dolan, Joseph J. 43039
Dolata, Jan 32057
Dolby, Joe 34214
Dolby, Malcolm J. 40310, 40936
Dolce, Dr. Sergio 25811, 25823
Dolczewski, Zygmunt 31911
Dolenz, Dr. Heimo 02417
Doletsky-Rackham, Nina 42943
Doleva, John 47748
Dolgopolova, Zinaida Stepanovna 33549
Doll, Mary H. 44480
Doll, Nancy 43819
Dollinger, Hannes 37156
Dolor, Danny 31342
Doltenkov, V.V. 32679
Dolženko, Fëdor Nikolaevič 32761
Domagała, Roman 32049
Domaine, Elmo 23774
Domański, Edward 32119
Dombrowski, Dieter 20311
Domènech, Glòria 34538
Domenech de Celles, Yann 11945
Domenighim, Attilio 23850
Domingos, Tadeu 00089
Dominguez, Antonio Franco 34519
Domínguez, German 06914
Domínguez Cabrera, Gonzalo 08042
Domínguez Cadeño, Nelson 07930
Domínguez Salazar, José Antonio 35027
Dominjak, Aleksandr Vladimirovič 33302
Domitruk, Daryl 05939
Dommer, Olge 16666
Dompierre, Louise 05567
Dompnier, Pierre 14282
Domröse, Ulrich 15919
Don Angelo, Maria 24064
Donadio, Emmie 45308
Donadoni Roveri, Dr. Anna Maria 25753
Donahue, Gail 41136, 45545
Donahue, John J. 42532
Donahue, Susan F. 43245
Donaldson, E. 00779
Donaldson, John 38459
Donaldson, Susan 47730
Donat, Olivier 15249
Donath, David A. 48742
Donath, Wolfram 16083
Donati, Prof. Bruno 36619, 36762
Donbaz, Veysel 37702
Donchez Mowers, Charlene 41664, 41665, 41666, 41668
Donders van den Aardweg, M.G. 28943
Dondo-Tardiff, Michelle 06068
Donegá, Dr. Giuseppe 25947
Donelli, Ivo 07779
Donelly, P. 39414
Donetzkoff, Alexis 12599
Donevski, Peti 04878, 04879, 04880, 04881
Donlon, Dr. D. 01498
Donnell, Courtney G. 42304
Donnellon, Maureen 00804
Donnelly, George J. 44557
Donnelly, John 48201
Donnelly, Peter 39360, 39413
Donner, Drs. E.M. 28868
Donner, Josef 02496, 03027
Donnermeyer, Reinhold 18723
Donoghue, Gail 48162
Donoghue, Michael 45698
Donohue, Deidre 45817
Donohue, Lorena 44828
Donoso Guerrero, Rosa 35053
Donzé, Frédéric 37086
Donzé, Roger 37036
Donzelli, Rodolfo 25271
Dooley, Bill 48117
Doove, Edith 03382
Dopffer, Anne 10766
Doppelfeld, Dr. Basilius 19880
Doppelstein, Jürgen 20414
Doppermann, Cäcilia 02625
Doppler, Prof. Dr. Alfred 02539
Doppler, Elke 03001
Doppler, Margarete 01744
Dor, Ehud 22690
Doračić, Damir 07809
Dorado Ortega, Oscar Javier 07450
Doran, J. 40531
Doran, Patricia A. 44533
Dordevic, Radisav 33901
Dore, Dr. Anna 23109
Dore, Giovanni 25664
Dorée, Yves 14596

Doren, Jo-an' Van 42498
Dorgans 10581
Dorgerloh, Prof. Dr. Hartmut 19437
Dorhs, Michael 17798
Doring Van Buren, Denise 41553
Doriot, Sylvie 36869
Dorling, M. 38462
Dorman, Craig 48101
Dornan, Duncan 38845
Dornan, Vorin 46198
Dorner, Ernst 02167
Dornert, Nadine 10742
Dornieden, Horst 20154
Dornisch, Richard 47145
Doroshenko, Peter 03452, 45364
Dorosiev, J. 04716
Dorsaz, Pierre 37283
Dorsch, Dr. Klaus J. 19498, 19500
Dorsch, Roberta 02830
Dorsett, A.G. 38493, 39546
Dorst, A. 29799
Dortch, Steve 43192
Dose, Dr. Hanna 15708, 15709
Doseva, Iva 04846
Dosi, Ferdinando 25253
Dosik, Jeffrey 45876
Dosoudil, Dr. Ilse 02997
Dossi, Dr. Barbara 02830
Dost, Dr. Wolfgang 20632
Doth, Diane 06831
Doubek, Franz 01818
Doublard du Vigneau, Simone 11968
Doucet, C. 15048
Doucet, Donna 05518
Doucet, Jean 10753
Doucet, M. 15047
Doudiet, Norman 42136
Dougherty, Erin 45508
Dougherty, Marijo 41089
Dougherty, Molly 46414
Dougherty, Thomas A. 45821
Doughty, P.S. 38160
Doughty, Richard 39134
Douglas, Dr. B. 01275
Douglas, Marietta 36042
Douglass, Amy A. 47975
Douglass, Ardith 45227
Douglass, Larry 41897
Douglass, Michael 46683
Douroux, Xavier 11518, 11520
Douvette, Herny d'Otreppe de 03813
Dow, George F. 45958
Doway, Stella 33934
Dowell, Michael B. 46742
Dowell, Wanda S. 41125
Dowie, Peggy 40556
Dowlan, Neil 39447
Dowling, J.R. 40755
Dowling, Valerie 22442
Down, Geoffrey 01357
Downend, A.V 40364
Downer, Dr. 22377
Downes, Elizabeth 01176
Downes, Marcia W. 45899
Downey, Dharmena 45135
Downey, Martha J. 41716
Downey, Dr. Robert H. 41867
Downie Banks, Dr. Margaret 48214
Downing, Clayta 48316
Downs, Alex 41059
Downs, Gerald 46191
Downs, John 43513
Downs, Stuart 43931
Doyle, John 46167
Doyle, Louise 00873
Doyle, Paul 22388
Doyon, Jean-Pierre 05892
Drabow, Kerstin 19445
Drachman, Lorraine 48084
Dräger, Ulf 17521
Draganić, Danica 07801
Draganov, Dr. Dimitar 04680, 04681
Dragićević, Mate 03916
Drăgoi, Dr. Livia 32494
Dragoni, Prof. G. 23126
Dragsbo, Peter 08790
Dragt, G.I.W. 29164, 29600
Draheim, Heidi 16722
Drahoňovský, Jan 08461
Drahošová, Viera 34058
Drake, Chip 45513
Drake, Ellen Mary 05721
Drake, Lisa 43290
Drake, Pia 17599
Drake, Tommi 43769
Dran, Jean-Luc 11880
Draper, Amanda 40266
Draper, Jill 37957
Draper, Jo 39853
Draper, Steven C. 43398
Drapkin, Adrienne 44245
Draps, M. Willem 03329
Drašković, Dragan 33855
Draughn, Raymond 46981
Drayman-Weisser, Terry 41489
Draževa, Conja G. 04632
Dražić, Jovanka 33913
Dražin Trbuljak, Lada 07835
Drda, Dr. Miloš 08658, 08659, 08673, 08716

Drechsler, Dr. Wolfgang 02949
Dreckow, T. 00926
Drees, Dr. Jan 19794
Dreezen, J. 03494
Dreher, Derick 46451
Dreher, Nancy 45515
Dreier, Bruno 18035
Dreier, Prof. Martin 36551
Dreier, Max 36486
Dreishpoon, Douglas 41981
Drejholt, Nils 36256
Drempetić-Hrcic, Nikola 07703
Drenker-Nagels, Dr. Klara 16230
Drenkhahn, Prof. Dr. Rosemarie 17599
Dresch, Dr. Jutta 17991
Drescher, Georg 19888
Dresco, Jean-Pierre 37015
Dressel, Barry 41378
Dressel, Ina-Maria 15513
Dressel, Jan 46054
Dreuzy, Jehan de 14216
Drew, Alejandrina 43123
Drew, Stephen E. 47049
Drewes, C. 34335
Drewnowski, Benedykt 37184
Drews, Ute 19793
Drexel, Hermann 02490
Drexler, Ray 44432
Drexler, Toni 19832
Dreycus, Dominique 12657
Dreydoppel, Susan M. 45640
Dreyer, Dr. Andreas 30530
Dreyer, Chris 46049
Dreyer, Dr. Elfriede 34360
Dreyer, K. 17206
Dreyer, Prof. L. 34352
Dreyer, Dr. Wolfgang 18081
Dreyfus, Renee 47311, 47325
Dreyfuss, James 43893
Drezgić, Olivera 33913
Drias, Lakhdar 00045
Driesbach, Janice 44791
Drieselmann, Jörg 15948
Driesens, F.J.J. 29728
Driessen, Hendrik 29881
Driessens, Mevrouw Colette 03412
Driewer, Ginny L. 48793
Drinjaković, Milica 33827
Drinkard, Joel F. 44966
Drioli, Anton 02538
Driscoll, David 45073
Driskell, Julia 41753
Driver, Rod 00981, 00982
Drlić, Predrag 07745
Drobney, Dr. Jeffrey A. 44437
Drocklehurst, E. 39739
Dröscher, Elke 17563
Drössler, Stefan 18848
Dröbler, Stefan 18880
Droguet, Vincent 11769
Dromgoole, P.S.B.F. 39035
Dronkers, Ben 28856
Dronkers, S.L. 28809
Dror, Mira 22651
Drosinou, Paraskevi 20915
Droste-Vischering-Galen, Hubertus 01903
Drozd, Henryk 31969
Dru Burns, Mary 41138
Druček, A.A. 33128
Drucha-Graber, Barbara 02659
Druesedow, Jean 44447
Druick, Douglas 42304
Drummer, Karen A. 45070
Drummond, H. Maury 41528
Drutt, Matthew 44126
Družak, Antonija 07713
Dryfhout, John 42639
Dsuve, Kjetil 30899
du Fayet de la Tour, Alain 11751
Duarte, Carlos F. 48911
Duarte Ferreira, Selma 04564
Duarte Rodriguez, Rafael Enrique 07422
Dubarry, Dominique 49162
Dubb, Prof. Asher 34267
Dubé, Lisa 41143
Dubedat, Paul 14475
Dubick, David 43080
Dubler, Linda 41348
Dubois, Alan B. 44822
Dubois, Arlette 14052
Dubois, Danielle 05925
Dubois, Oliver 13915
Dubrisay, Pascal 12640
Dubrović, Ervin 07761
Dubrovin, Sergej Michajlovič 33242
Dubrovin, V.M. 32642
Dubuc, André 12574
Ducastelle, Jean-Pierre 03187, 03188, 03605
Ducey, Dr. Peter K. 42653
Duchamp, Luc 12836
Duchemin, Michael 44891
Duchesne, Prof. Jean-Patrick 03568
Duchesne, Jean-Patrick 03583
Duckers, Peter 40512
Duckworth, Elisabeth 05639
Duclos, Jean-Claude 11941, 11943
Duco, D.H. 28895
Ducor, J. 36745
Ducourau, Vincent 10620, 10622

Ducreux, Anne-Claire 12798
Duda, Eugeniusz 31699
Dudant, Didier 03132, 03133
Dudar, Dr. Wiesław 31879
Dudavt, Didier 03134
Dudeck, Dr. Volker 20761, 20762, 20763
Dudenhöffer, Franz 20012
Dudley, Andrew 01459
Dudley, Caroline 40730
Dudley, Clarissa 44094
Dudnik, I.E. 37869
Dudź, Jerzy 32030
Dudzik, Przemysław 31626
Dueck, Lois 05068
Dücker, Dr. Elisabeth von 17555
Düger, Şaban 37784
Dühr, Dr. Elisabeth 20215
Duell, Charles H.P. 42224
Duell, Marshall 47400
Dümas, Dieter 18615
Dümmel, Karlheinz 19016
Duenkel, Bob 43410
Dünnebier, Dr. Michael 16715
Duensing, Darrell 46684
Duerr, Mark 45071
Dürrenmatt, Dieter 36519
Dürüce, Servet 37807
Düspohl, Martin 16018
Düsterwald, Dr. Brigitte 18391
Dütschler, H.R. 37242
Dufek, Mike 43637
Dufet-Bourdelle, Rhodia 13538
Duff, Ana 41926
Duff, Doris 48491
Duff, James H. 42175
Duffels, Dr. J.P. 28917
Duffy, Prof. A. 34363
Duffy, Henry J. 42639
Dufilho, Diane 47613
Dufour, Albertine 47822
Dufour, Christophe 36986
Dufour, Gary 01363
Dufour, Pierre 06659
Dufrasne, F. 03763
Dufrenne, Michèle 28671
Dugall, Berndt 17073
Dugan, Walter 38183
Duggan, Ervin S. 46265
Duggen Below, Ina 19400
Dugmore, I.M. 34241
Dugot, Joël 13558
Dugué, Prof. J. 13628
Duguid, Meg 42362
Dugulin, Dr. Adriano 25810, 25812, 25813, 25814,
    25815, 25816, 25818, 25819, 25824
Duhm, Burghard 16584
Duits, Th. te 29506, 29759
Duivesteijn, John 29127
Dujardin, Paul 03339
Dujmović-Kosovac, Ljubica 07760
Dukat, Zdenka 07809
Duke, Jacqueline 47426
Duke, Judy 42615
Dulaban, Alta 42495
Dulaney, H.G. 41408, 41780
Dulaney, W. Marvin 42208
Dulda, Mustafa 37597
Dulgheru, Lia Maria 32570, 32572, 32622, 32623
Dulibić, Ljerka 07837
Dulière, Cecile 03640
Dulin, Étienne 15193
Dumalag, Filemon R. 31277
Dumančić, Ljubica 07803
Dumanoir, Thierry 12211, 13934
Dumaret, Isabelle 36613
Dumas, Cyril 12525, 12526, 12528, 12529
Dumitrescu, Horia 32520, 32521
Dumitrescu, Ilinca 32469
Dumitroaia, Gheorghe 32439, 32568, 32612
Dumitru, Țeicu 32581
Dummer, S. 39305
Dumon, Noël 03255
DuMont, Bruce 42343
Dumont, Fabienne 03280
Dumont, Françoise 03576
Dumortier, Christian 14260
Dumortier, Claire 03337
Dumortier, Philippe 14260
Dumoulin, J. 03797
Dumville, John P. 43270, 44141, 47026, 47759,
    47844
Dunand, Michele 12242
Dunbar, Elizabeth 48599
Dunbar, Lisa 46342
Duncan, Jenepher 00923
Dundass, Kay 30208
Dundon, Margo 44299
Dundore, Mary Margaret 46632
Dunfjeld, Sigbjørn 30858
Dunford, Fred 41882
Dungan, Erica Howe 41857
Dunham, Anne 47358
Dunham, Elizabeth L. 47945
Dunina, Elena Michajlovna 32968
Dunkel, Dr. Peter 17971
Dunkelman, Arthur 45301
Dunkerton, Jill 39729
Dunkley, Diane L. 48344
Dunkley, Tina 41340

Dunlap, Melissa L. 44842
Dunlap, Susan 46983
Dunlop, J.M. 38941
Dunn, Alberta 43639
Dunn, Carol 47362
Dunn, Cathey 44877
Dunn, David W. 47847
Dunn, Deborah F. 44080, 44084
Dunn, Delores 45717
Dunn, Forrest 47612
Dunn, Hedy 44888
Dunn, Lawren 43300, 46574
Dunn, Lindsley A. 42426
Dunn, Madeline 42969
Dunn, Nancy 41272
Dunn, Richard 38532
Dunne, John 22515
Dunne, Maxine 05425
Dunning, Fred 39168
Dunning, Louise 38716
Dunton, Anna Mary 42073
Duparc, F.J. 29105, 29123
Duperray, Eve 10799, 11759, 11761
Dupeux, Cécile 14827
Duplančić, Arsen 07779
DuPont, Diana 47404
DuPont, George 44599
Dupont, Jean-Pierre 15125
Dupont, Joel 14469
Dupont, Paule 03505
Dupont, Roland 15261
Dupont-Bauverie, Caroline 10738
Dupont-Logié, Cécile 14678
Duppré, Hans Jörg 16533
Duprat, Andrés 00125, 00128
Duprat, Jean-Marie 14774
Dupraz, Cathérine 11221
Dupree, Sherry 42928
DuPree Richardson, Jane 47882
Dupret, Sandra 42920
Dupriez, Françoise 03830
Dupuis, Burno 12922
Dupuis-Sabron, Geneviève 10809
Dura, Ulrike 18419
Duraj, Paweł 31888
Durán Gómez, Eduardo 07436
Durán Nájera, Juan José 28081
Durán Solís, Leonel 28192
Durand, Agnes 12853, 12864
Durand, Alain 11655
Durand, André 11707
Durand, Micheline 10509, 10511
Durand, Régis 13483
Duranthon, Francis 14953
Durben, Silvan 46225
Durden, Chris J. 41421
Durdyeva, Tuvakbibi Kurbanovna 37813
Duret, Evelyne 14451
Duret, Michel 11707
Durham, A. Scott 45553
Durhône, Marise 10639
Durić, Vladimir 33793
Durkin, Birgid 42770
Durko, Prof. Janusz 32101
Durman, Prof. Mick 38213
Durmaz, Ş. Nihal 37772
Durnford, Louise 06237
Durnoff, M. 11794
Durr, Andy 38339
Durracq, Roger-Pierre 11873
Durrani, Prof. Farzaud 31047
Durrleman, Sophie 13556, 13563, 13586, 13642
Durschlag, Richard 48471
Dursi, Jen 46274
Durst, Duane R. 43905
Durst, John 47876
Dursum, Brian A. 42628
Durye, Joseph 15234
Dusar, Mark 03753
Duscher, Michael 02143
Dusheshe, Tanny 21259
Dussex, Armand 36460
Dutescu, Mihai 32507
Dutoit, Albert 36951
Dutra, James 48456
Dutschke, G.K. 01388, 01389
Duty, Michael W. 44457
Duval, Dennis 42422
Duval Reese, Becky 43116
Duvall, Tracy 48082
Duvernois, Bruno 11989
Duvivier, Christophe 13832, 13833
Duvoisin, Olivier 36958
Duvosquel, Jean-Marie 03827
Duyckaerts, E. 03600
Duysters, K. 28941
Duzenberry, Jeanelle 46573
Dvir, Orah 22692
Dvořáková, Dr. Hana 08267
Dwyer, Christine M. 41093
Dwyer, Tessa 01024
Dybbro, Inge 08912
Dybing, Leif 30466, 30467
Dyck, Angela 06762
Dyckmans, Heinrich 18964
Dye, Dr. Joseph M. 46891
Dyer, David 45408
Dyer, Deborah 41498
Dyer, John 01073

Dyer, John T. 48402
Dyer, Michael P. 47579
Dyer, Thomas 44673
Dyes, Brian 39306
Dykhuis, Peter 05545
Dyl, Stanley J. 44113
Dynak, Sharon 42451
Dysart, William 47290
Dzalilov, A. 48840
Džanaeva, Alla Akimovna 33686
Dzeko, Lebiba 03925
Dzeranov, Timur Efimovič 33690
Dzhalilov, T. 37448
Dziechciaruk-Maj, Bogna 31692
Dzięciołowski, Edwin 31591
Dziedzic, Bogusław 31481
Dziembowski, Bettina von 19027
Dziewior, Yilmaz 17551
Dziurzyński, Tadeusz 31689
Eade, Coila 43900
Eager, Barry W. 41651
Eakin, Eric 41548
Eames, Fred 01619
Earenfight, Philip 44154
Earenfight, Dr. Phillip 42105
Earl, L.M. 01201
Earl, Phillip I. 46834
Earle, Edward 45817
Earle, Susan 44686
Earls-Solari, Bonnie 47309
Early, Dr. Ann M. 41255
Early, J. W. 30104
Early, Judy 41269
Earnest, Ola May 46553
Earnst, Arlene E. 42965
Eastleigh, Lord 28664
Eastman, James 46213
Easton, Elizabeth 41941
Easton, Lois 44450
Easton-Moore, Barbara 42678
Eastty, Gary 42754
Eastwood, S.A. 38487
Eatman-Jackson, Rebecca 43311
Eaton, Alex 40747
Eaton, Jennifer 45801
Eaton, Kenneth M. 44069
Eaton, Mary Candace 46383
Eaton, Nellie 06092
Eaton, Virginia M. 46784
Eatts, M. 01146
Eayrs, Walter F. 41934
Ebbers, Klaus 18219
Ēbedžāns, Svetlana Georgievna 33229
Eberhardt, Dr. Hans-Joachim 18912
Eberl, Dr. Wolfgang 18124
Eberle, Josef 27513
Eberle, Lidia 32092
Eberle, Dr. Martin 16292, 16305
Eberle, Urs 36673, 36674
Eberli, Ulrich 37427
Ebert, Glenn 05060
Eberwein, Dr. Roland 02127
Ebie, Teresa H. 43116
Ēbinger, Margarita Astemirovna 32754
Ebner, Dr. Lois 02220, 02369
Ebnet, David F. 47086
Ebtehaj, V. 22287
Echeverría Llanos, Clemente 07583
Ecjanov, A. 27079
Eckardt, Hans J. 37137
Eckenrode-Lewis, Emma 44172
Ecker, Dr. Berthold 02936
Ecker, Reingard 02817
Eckerbom, Jonas 35998
Eckerle, Dr. Klaus 17991
Eckerson, Rosemary 46752
Eckert, Lisa 47775
Eckert, Dr. Rainer 18420
Eckert-Schweizer, Angela 16738
Eckertn, Bob 45093
Eckhardt, Prof. Dr. Andreas 16231
Eckhardt, Cyndy 45985
Eckhardt, Mária 32507
Eckhardt, Susan 44379
Eckhel, Nerina 07813
Eckhoff, Audun 30412, 30413, 30414
Eckhout, Debbra 41634
Eckloff, Dr. Wolfram 18539
Eckmann, Sabine 47140
Eckstein, Beate 16239
Eckstrom, Carolyn 43183
Edblommery, Mats 36252
Eddie, I. 30227
Ēdeleva, Inessa Aleksandrovna 32889
Edelmann, Asher B. 37037
Edelmann, Dr. Martina 20291
Eden, Dave 45444
Edenfield, W. Vernon 43536
Eder, Dr. Johanna 20105
Ederer, Walter 19088
Ederndorfer, Gerhard 02880
Edgar jr., Arthur C. 45331
Edge, Yvonne 39901
Edgert, Elizabeth 45599
Edgren, Bengt 35935
Edhofer, Elisabeth M. 02955
Edidin, Stephen R. 45789
Edina, Mèri 21501
Edinborough, Lisa 38588

Edinger, Dorothy 30317
Edison, Carol 47227
Edison, Robert D. 48081
Edland, Svein 44877
Edler, Dr. Doris 17230
Edler, Hans 02607
Edlinger, Matth. 02353
Edlund, D. 38579
Edmondson, J. 39520
Edmonson, Dr. James M. 42471
Edmunds, Allan L. 46397
Edo, Austin 31092
Edson, Gary 44991
Edson Way, Dr. J. 47419
Eduard, Ebner 01778
Edvardsen, Erik Henning 30737
Edward, Barbara 40882
Edwards, Ashley 47459
Edwards, Darwin 48306
Edwards, David 47924
Edwards, Denise 38555
Edwards, Geoffrey 01044
Edwards jr., Harford 43450
Edwards, Janet 00820
Edwards, Jim 44845
Edwards, John 37931
Edwards, Karen 06031
Edwards, Kathy 44248
Edwards, N. 37981
Edwards, Nancy E. 43487
Edwards, Nat 37980
Edwards, Pamela 45717
Edwards, Paul C. 45779
Edwards, Paula 43998
Edwards, Rita 43592
Edwards, Dr. Scott 47529
Edwards, Dr. S.R. 39894
Edwards, Susan H. 44416
Edwards, Wanda 44299
Edwards, William 39645
Eekhof, H.R. 29898
Eekhout, L.L.M. 29502
Eenhuis, Drs. M.C. 29101
Effenberger, Dr. Arne 16096
Efimovskij, A.F. 32950
Efrati, Y. 22789
Eftekhari, M. 22317
Egami, Namio 26870
Egan, Caroline 38309
Egan, Dominic 22372
Egawa, Tokusuke 26605
Egbaylar, Enis 37779
Egbert jr, Francis 44337
Egelseder, Berthold 02293
Egermann, Gerhard 02438, 02439
Egg, Prof. Dr. Markus 18606, 18606
Egge, Dr. Reimer 20248
Eggen, S. 03131
Egger, Dr. Franz 36500
Egger, Norbert 02125
Eggers, Bernardo 06900
Eggers, Dr. José Carlos 04475
Eggerstorfer, Alfred 02008
Eggl, Christine 02668
Eggleston Jamieson, Grace 42201
Egholm, Aage 08895
Egilsson, Kristjan 21674
Egipciaco, Wanda 45751
Egli, Markus 36930
Egloff, Prof. Dr. Michel 36796
Egloffstein, Dr. Albrecht Graf von und zu 19347
Egorova, Ljudmila Semenovna 33672
Egoryčev, Viktor Vasiljevič 33055
Egounlety, Micheline 03875
Egret, Daniel 13476
Eguía, Dr. José 35696, 35697, 35702
Ehls, Heiner 17798
Ehm, Rainer 19520
Ehn, Prof. Friedrich 01793
Ehrenberg, Johanna 36776
Ehrenberg, Rolf 18785
Ehrenfellner, Dr. Karl 02551
Ehrenheim, Jacob von 35867
Ehrenhuber, Franz 01704
Ehrenkranz, Joel S. 45886
Ehrentraud, Adolf 01964
Ehres, Maria 36381
Ehrhart, Bernhard 18357
Ehrle, Dr. Peter Michael 17989
Ehrlich, Dr. Richard 41524
Ehrlich, Richard L. 42485
Ehrmann-Schindlbeck, Anna-Maria 17939
Ehry, Carl A. 43143
Ehser, Claudia 19120
Eibl, Simon 18354
Eiblmayr, Dr. Silvia 02065
Eichelberger, Allison 44630
Eichenauer, Jürgen 19240
Eichenberger, Peter 36542
Eichhorn jun., Georg 02829
Eichhorn, Dr. Helmut 16851
Eichhorn, Herbert 16161
Eichler, Heidrun 18640
Eichmann, Erland 37323
Eichorn, Cornelia 41073
Eichhorst, Dr. William S. 44405
Eickmann, Margaret 46642
Eickmann, Theodore 43050
Eidam, Hardy 16903

Eidemüller, Gisela 16165
Eidlin, Nathan 22744
Eidsaune, Thor Helge 30674
Eielson, Kerry 41196
Eifrig, Jennifer S. 48575
Eigler, Gerd 17622
Eigner, Gerda 02956
Eikelmann, Dr. 17876
Eikelmann, Dr. Renate 18061, 18062, 18833,
 19198, 19199, 19203, 19532
Eiken, Dr. Douglas 44563
Eikenoord, R.G. 29775
Eikermann, Silke 16384
Eiland, William U. 41318
Eilat, Galit 22618
Eilertsen, John 46914
Eilertson, Orie 46685
Eillott, John 01473
Eilschou Holm, Niels 08948
Eimbeck 28754
Eimer, Prof. Gerhard 17860
Eimert, Dr. Dorothea 16717, 16718
Einarsdóttir, Björg 21675
Einecke, Claudia 46149
Einhorn, Peggi 41940
Einreinhofer, Nancy 48477
Eins, Annaleen 28780
Einstein, Laura 45680
Eipper, Paul-Bernhard 37429
Eiraku, Toru 26683
Eirola, Martti 28766
Eis, Ruth 41645
Eiselt, Gerhard 18554
Eisenberg, Joseph 00752
Eisenburger, Dr. C.M.S. 28978
Eisenhofer, Dr. Stefan 18916
Eisenmann, Mark 45688
Eisl, Sigmund 02707
Eisler, Dr. János 21383
Eisley, Patricia 48281
Eisley, Susan 46531
Eisner, Michael 44579
Eissenhauer, Dr. Michael 15765, 18011, 18014,
 18017, 18018, 18022, 18024, 18026, 18028,
 18029, 18032, 18033
Eitam, David 22606
Eiynck, Dr. A. 18482
Eizenberg, Arie 22581
Ek-Nilsson, Katarina 36292
Ekberg, Anna 36128
Ekblom, Bengt 36359
Ekelhart-Reinwetter, Dr. Christine 02830
Ekinci, H. Ali 37641
Eklund, Dr. Sigrid 36269
Ekpo, Violeta I. 30364
Ekström, Börje 36054
Ekström, Kjell 09815, 09818
Ekström Söderlund, Birgitta 09463
El-Amrani, Dr. Ahmed 28717
El-Bahtimi, M. 09259
El-Bedawi, Mohammed Ahmed 09257
El-Hajj, Amal Abu 22629
El-Hajraoui, Mohamed Abdelwahed 28704
El-Husseini, Dr. Mehrez 09245
El-Kasri, Houceine 28706
El-Moussli, Majed 37440
El-Nur, Prof. Osama A. 35765, 35768
El-Ouafi, Prof. Boubker 28696
El-Younsi, Dr. Amin 28714
Elas-Necel, Karol 31526
Elayyan, Khaled 31062
Elba La Gioiosa, Rosa 00355
Eldamaty, Dr. Mamdouh 09261
Elder, E.J. 06801
Elder, Kym 48356
Elderfield, John 44869
Eldredge, Bruce B. 44795, 47728
Eldridge, Harold 38381
Eldridge, Karen 44712
Eldridge, Ruth 38567
Elen, A. 29759
Elena-Torralva, Maria 47251
Elerd, Udo 19259
Elfström, Gunnar 36040
Elgen, Fran 41685
Elger, Dr. Dietmar 17611
Elgstrand, Greg 05161
Elias, Prof. Giacomo 25789
Elias, Ramon Jan 44323
Elias Ortiz, Alejandrina 28453
Eliasen, Kirstin 08995
Eliason, Sara 36415
Eliasson, Ulla 36231
Eliëns, Prof. Dr. T.M. 29095
Eliezer-Brunner, Henrietta 22755
Eliot, D. 40679
Elis, Dr. Karlpeter 01913
Elk, Sara Jane 46403
Elkhadem, Hossam 03275
Elkin, Geoff 39954
Elkin, G.U. 33033
Elkington, Marian 37997
Elkington, Peter 37997
Elkjær, Trine 08770
Ellen, David M. 39996
Ellenbroek, Dr. F.J.M. 29879
Ellender, Dan 44580
Ellensint Kremer, M. 20274
Eller, E. 19865

Ellerman, Deborah L. 41274
Ellermann-Minda, Petra 01911
Ellermeier, Dr. Friedrich 17616
Ellermeyer, Dr. Jürgen 17555
Ellersdorfer, Heinz 02611, 02612, 02614
Ellin, Simone 41472
Ellingsen, Harry 30439, 30440
Ellington, Howard W. 48611
Elliott, Dana R. 43307
Elliott, Fiona 39454
Elliott, George 06852
Elliott, J.H. 41335
Elliott, Lucy 42995
Elliott, Mary Gene 41335
Elliott, Patrick 38916
Elliott, Rachael 01083
Ellis, Amy 43944
Ellis, Anita 42400
Ellis, Caroline 39584, 39721, 40732
Ellis, David W. 41818
Ellis, Evelyn M. 44804
Ellis, George R. 44079
Ellis, Gillian 38228
Ellis, J. 22392
Ellis, J.C. 44669
Ellis, Joe 42130
Ellis, Lori 05045
Ellis, Pam 42145
Ellis, Robert E. 44378
Ellis, Steven 42123
Ellis-Peckham, Courtney 43213
Ellison, Dr. Curtis W. 46243
Ellison, Rosemary 41193
Elliston Weiner, Sarah 45834
Ellmers, Prof. Dr. Detlev 16339
Ellmeyer, Stephan 02503
Ellsworth, Lynn 45534
Ellwood, Tony 01237
Elmén Berg, Anna 36157
Elmore, Fletcher L. 44975
Elmore, George 44655
Elmqvist, Inga 36270
Elo, Maija 10051
Elorduy, Julieta Gil 27747
Elorza Guinea, Juan Carlos 34630
Eloy, Paul 03601
Eloy, Vicente 34501
Elsasser, Kilian 36918
Elsbree, Carl J. 41737
Elsbury, Kathy 42011
Elsen, Dr. Thomas 15552, 15564
Elšin, Sergej Veniaminovič 32920
Elsner, Dr. Tobias von 18581
Elsom, Sarah 39493
Elsposch, Friedrich 16750
Elston, Tim 46339
Elsworth, Jo 38361
Elustondo, André 14279
Eluyemi, Dr. Omotoso 30326, 30329
Elvira Barba, Miguel Angel 35013
Ely, Bruno 10252, 10257
Elyasiv, Isaac 22740
Elzenga, Dr. E. 28928
Elzinga, Dr. C. 29508
Éma, Robert 12754
Emack Cambra, Jane 47960
Emanuel, Ludovit 08611
Emanuel, Nina 18379
Emanuelli, Dr. Giuseppe 24893
Ember, Dr. Ildikó 21383
Embertsén, Lena 36055
Emenegger, Ashley 44902
Emerick, Emily W. 45433
Emerson, David 41375
Emerson, Francis 48770, 48771
Emerson, Julie 47545
Emerson, Lucius J. 22537
Emerson, Myra 44619
Emerson, Pam 48043
Emerson, Philip G. 48629
Emerson, Robert L. 48805
Emery, Dominique 11814
Emery, Dr. K.F. 43581
Emigholz, Dr. Björn 20302
Emiliani, Prof. Andrea 23145
Eminger, Dr. Jürgen 20190
Emmanuel, Victoria 38225
Emmendörffer, Dr. Christoph 15561
Emonson, Janet 06427
Emont Scott, Deborah 44404
Encinas, Isabel 35024
Enciso Núñez, José Antonio 27839
End, Reinhard 17236
Ende, Arlyn 47571
Endenburg, Constanze 29771
Enders, Don 47090
Enders, Donald L. 37231
Endersbe, Susan U. 47511
Endert, D. van 15479
Endicott, John 38530
Endo, Koichi 26795
Endraß, Max 15506
Endzweig, Pamela 43224
Enei, Flavio 25440
Enei, Vicente 00471
Enevoldsen, V. 08953
Engberg, Siri 45394
Engdahl, Sarah 42446, 42447
Engel, Beate 36554

Engel, Birgit 15920
Engel, Donald J. 43050
Engel, Edmée 27568
Engel, Melissa 32223
Engel, Michael 44685
Engel, Robert 41913
Engel, Volker 16233
Engel, Dr. Walter 16724
Engelbach, Dr. Barbara 19949
Engelbosch, Christa 03751
Engelbrecht, Dr. C.M. 34183, 34184, 34189
Engelbrecht, Dean Mark 41172
Engelkemier, Catherine 41163
Engelmann, Christine 19070
Engelmann, Judith 17785
Engels, C.L.M. 29247
Engels, D. 30088
Engels, Kim 20572
Engels, Maria 15374
Engelsman, Dr. S.B. 29525
Engeman, Richard 46637
Engen, Jorunn 30472
Engen, Luc 03511
Engeseter, Aage 30591
Engesser, Dr. Burkart 36514
Engfors, Christina 36231
Enghoff, Dr. Henrik 08955
England, Ann 41345
Englebright, Steven E. 47831
Englert, Emil 20481
Englick, Gerd 15734
English, Catherine 06254
English, Charles L. 48684
English, Donise 46673
English, Louella F. 48684
English, Marie 46237
English, Patrick 45803
Engström, Johan 36232
Engström, Urban 36083
Enguita, Nuria 34538
Enkhtsetseg, Dashdavaa 28678
Enne, Eva 02297
Ennen, Dr. J. 20113
Enriqueta del Castillo y Mejía, María 28169
Enriquez, Felonilla D. 31320
Enseki, Carol 41940
Ensign, Garald 44146
Enslow, Ellen 48517
Ensslen, D. 05391
Enticott, Delyth 40031
Entin, Daniel 45861
Entwistle, R. 39305
Enz, Peter 37372
Enzler, Jerome A. 42992, 42993
Epp, Bear 05357
Eppensteiner, Heinz 02223
Eppich, Linda 46708, 46726
Epping, Nancy J. 43129
Eppinger, Virginia 41899
Epple, Sabine 18398
Eppler, Dr. Peter 03001
Eppler-Jehle, Ursula 15420, 15423
Epprecht, Dr. Katharina 37398
Epps, Renee 45827
Erancis, Dr. R.W. 40814
Erasmus, Prof. Theuns 34342
Erašova, Galina 33232
Erb, Christian 17048
Erbach-Erbach, Franz Graf zu 16888
Erbentraut, Dr. Regina 17458
Erbguth, Dr. Horst 19517, 19520
Erbschwendtner, Josef 02566
Ercolani, Fausto 25906
Erdem, Emin 37734
Erdem, Mehmet 37687
Erdenebat, P. 28685
Erdmann, Walter Johannes 17356
Erdoğan, Mustafa 37808
Eregina, Galina Nikolaevna 33413
Eremina, Natalija Aleksandrovna 33270
Eren, Metin 37736
Erf, Lisa K. 42327
Erffa, Dr. Axel von 18009
Erftemeijer, A.F.W. 29324
Ergert, Bernd E. 18838
Ergin, Muhlis 37698
Ergino, Nathalie 12854
Erhart, Heinrich 02636
Erhart, Ingeborg 02081
Erhatic Širnik, Romana 34122
Erias Martinez, Alfredo 34607
Ericani, Dr. Giuliana 23037, 23040
Erice Lacabe, Romana 35720, 35725
Erich, Frasl 02504
Erichsen, Dr. Johannes 18269, 18270
Erichsen, John 08901
Erichson, Ulf 19593
Ericini, Carlo 23179
Erickson, Bruce R. 47166
Erickson, Florence 05820
Erickson, Marsha 44417
Erickson, Ruth 46365
Erickson, Willis D. 41446
Eriksson, Håkan 36361
Eriksson, Maud 36046
Eriksson, Nadja 35991
Eriksson, Susan C. 41728
Eringen, P. 46782
Eritsyan, Elena Sergeevna 33114

Erk, Werner 17297
Erkelens, Dr. A.M.L.E. 28928
Erkinova, Rimma Michajlovna 32808
Erlande-Brandenburg, Alain 11599
Erlandsen, Roger 30902
Erlindo, Vittorio 24431
Erlinger, Fritz 02557
Ermacora, Dr. Beate 18227
Ermeling, Andreas 18945
Ermert, Axel 16006
Ermischer, Dr. G. 15533
Ermolaeva, Ljudmila Nikolaevna 33016
Ernet, Dr. Detlef 01922
Ernst, Alfred 18794
Ernst, Gay 41437
Ernst, Hannelore 19994
Ernst, Joey 34196
Ernst, Jürgen 18403
Ernst, Mathias 19994
Ernst, Dr. Rainer 17005
Ernst-Adolf, Kloth 17702
Ernstell, Eva-Sofi 36256
Erochin, Viktor Ivanovič 33649
Erol, Dr. Erdogan 37739, 37742, 37744, 37745, 37746, 37747
Erramah, Mourad 37565
Erskine, David 38046
Eršova, Valentina Petrovna 33329
Ertel, Dr. Christine 02285
Ertjukova, Nadežda Semenovna 32841
Ertman, Willis 44037
Erts, Keith 41997
Erwin, Douglas H. 48379
Erwin, Renee 43485
Erwin, Sarah 48104
Eržen, Miro 34132
Erzsébet, Dr. Kovácsné Bircher 21534
Escalas, Román 34562
Escallon, Ana Maria 48334
Escandor, Beatriz 44900
Escat, Monique 14315, 14787
Esche, Charles 36079
Eschebach, Dr. Erika 16305
Eschenburg, Dr. Barbara 18918
Escobar, Ticio 31094
Escobar, Washington 41042
Escoffier, André 14637
Escriche, Carmen 35530
Escriche Jaime, Carmen 35480
Escrivà, J. Ramon 35599
Escudero, Juan Miguel 31441
Esera, T. 33757
Esguerra, Liwliwa 31294
Eshenroder, Glenda 44109
Eskildsen, Prof. Ute 16959
Eskritt, Jodi Ann 05016
Esman, J. 29880
Esparza, Richard R. 46922
Espeland, Else 30728
Espinagosa Marsà, Jaume 35518
Espinola, Vera 47172
Espinós, Adela 35601
Espinosa, Deborah 46738
Espinosa, Gina Agnes 31329
Espinosa Jiménez, Eleazar 08092
Espinosa Rodriguez, Antonio 27703, 27713
Espinosa Ruiz, Antonio 35656
Espinosa Yglesias, Angeles 28317
Espinoza, Carlos A. 06912
Espinoza, Felipe 28119
Espinoza Arrubarrena, Luis 28129
Espinoza Mella, Adelaida 07411
Espinoza Pérez, Egdar 30322
Espírito Santo Bustorff Silva, Dr. Maria João 32287
Espiritu Gaston, Lynell 31447
Espointour, Elizabeth 41304
Espuiagosa Marsa, Jaume 35517
Eßbach, Elke 20787
Esseiva, Renato 37199
Essen, Dr. Manfred von 19118
Esser, Dr. Werner 19165
Essers, Dr. Volkmar 16728
Essig, Timothy 44629
Estall i Poles, Vicent 35178, 35179
Esteban Darder, Vicente 35570
Estep, Connie 46855
Esterhuizen, Valerie 34362
Estes, Dr. James R. 44793
Estes, Judith 44159, 44160, 44162
Esteve, Y. 12022
Estévez González, Fernando 34936
Estham, Inger 36356
Estrada, Cesar P. 31305
Estrada Sánchez, Ramiro 27777
Estrela, Tiago 06876
Etches, Richard A. 43591
Etgar, Raphie 22653
Ethelberg, Per 08849
Etling, Russell 45291
Ettema, Michael J. 48615
Etter, Dr. Walter 36514
Ettrich, Berthold 16501
Eubanks, Ray 47718
Eugster, Willi 37117
Euler, Dr. Andrea 02241
Euler-Schmidt, Dr. Michael 18150
Eure, Linda Jordan 43081
Eutsler, Therese 44803
Eva, Jan 00851

Evan, Paul 39450
Evangelist, Andrea 45014
Evanich, Joan 48693
Evans, Bob 05962
Evans, Catherine 42587
Evans, Cathy 42220
Evans, D.W. 40195
Evans, Ed 05100
Evans, Elaine L. 41578
Evans, Edward 40144
Evans, Elaine A. 44519
Evans, G.H. 38493
Evans, Helen H. 43515
Evans, Jonathan 39764
Evans, Linda 47883
Evans, Margaret 42585, 43886
Evans, Megan E. 43875
Evans, Michael 41538
Evans, N. 30250
Evans, Paul 39756
Evans, Steven 41552, 45793
Evans, Sylvia B. 46892
Evans, Viola 05421
Evares, J. 40753
Evascovich, Mildred 41078
Evdokimov, Vladimir Aleksandrovič 33026
Evdokimov, Vladimir Nikolaevič 32791, 32792
Eveleigh, David J. 38350, 38351
Eveler, Kimberly 47680
Evelyn, Douglas E. 45852
Evensen, Anne Bjørg 30645
Everard, R.H.A.J. 29329
Everbrand, Lars-Åke 35826
Everett, Julienne 05069
Everett, Martin 38318
Everly, Nancy 42697
Evers, Prof. Dr. Bernd 16025
Evers, Bisse 35919
Evers, Cécile 03337
Evers, Richard 44010
Evers, Dr. Ulrika 19366
Eversberg, Dr. Gerd 17873
Eversmann, Pauline K. 48712
Evetts, Deborah 45863
Evgenidou, Despina 20897
Evgeniev, Todor 04635
Evstigneeva, Irina V. 33481, 33483
Evtimov, Dejan 04870
Ewald, Jill 46023
Ewell, Matson 43275
Ewell G. Sturgis jr 42568
Ewen, Les 45496
Ewers, William 42356
Ewert, George H. 45418, 45422
Ewertowski, Zbigniew 31830
Ewigleben, Dr. Cornelia 20011
Ewing, Phyllis 43917
Ewing, Steve 45540
Ewing, William A. 36863
Ewington, Julie 01459
Ex, Dr. K.M.T. 29897, 29910
Exnarová, Alena 08320
Eyb, Alexander Freiherr von 20644
Eyb, Silvia Freifrau von 20644
Eychner, George 44237
Eyland, Cliff 06826
Eyler, Carolyn 43731
Ezell-Gilson, Carol 42213
Ezquerra, Beatriz 35530
Ezsöl, Adolf 02651
Fabbri, Fabio 24845
Fabbri, Dr. Francesco 23056
Fabbri, Dr. Franco 23908, 23909, 23910, 23911, 23914, 23917
Fabbri, Jennifer S. 34332
Fabela, Pamela K. 48035
Fabényi, Dr. Júlia 21365
Faber, Alain 27568
Faber, Dr. Elfriede 02859
Faber, Dr. Michael 18669
Faber, Dr. Monika 02830
Faber, O. 28968
Faber, Ole 08784, 08785, 08786, 08991, 09016, 09017, 09100, 09101, 09102
Faber, P. 28866
Faberman, Hilarie 47772
Fabian, Dr. Claudia 18831
Fabian, Rick 42168
Fabiani, Rossella 25831
Fabiankowitsch, Gabriele 02929
Fabich, Uwe 18355
Fabing, Suzannah 46015
Fabiny, Dr. Tibor 21337
Fabisiak, Wojciech 31984
Fabre, Eric 11919, 13559, 13560
Fabregues, M. de 12894
Fabrezi, Dr. Marissa 00539
Fabricius, Karen M. 08764, 08765, 08766, 09073
Fabris, Dr. Corrado 22959
Fabris, Jean 14603
Fabritius, Dr. Ruth 19589
Fabrizio, Fernando di 24838
Fabyan, Dr. E. Joseph 48242
Facchinetti, Claudio 23336
Facchini, Prof. Fiorenzo 23124
Faccinto, Victor 48698, 48706
Facciolongo, Sabino 23317
Fachrudin, H. 22125
Fadani, Dr. Andrea 20258

Fadden, John 46155
Fadeev, Igor 33034
Fae Kamm, Marie 42754
Fährig, Ute 17508
Faelmar-Abad, Mary 31307
Faenzi, Giovanna 23843
Færøy, Frode 30748
Fässler, Klaus 36464
Fagaly, William A. 45735
Fagbohunmi, Johnson 30341
Fage, André 13505
Fagerli, Karl A. 30711
Fagerstedt, Elisabeth 36338
Fagnant, Susan 44683
Faherty, William B. 43977
Fahey, John M. 48352
Fahey, Peggy 05584
Fahl, Dr. Andreas 17597
Fahl-Dreger, Axel 20290
Fahlund, Michael 45789
Fahrenbruch, Melanie 42658
Fahrer, Uwe 16312
Fahy, Everett 45833
Faietti, Dr. Marzia 23103
Failla, Dr. Donatella 23989
Faille d'Huysse, B. Baron della 03856
Faine, Susan 01434
Fair, Eileen 47390
Fair Sleeper, Sara 41113
Fairbank, Lynn 42841
Fairbanks, Theresa 45699
Fairclough, Oliver 38481
Fairfax, Anne 45832
Fairfax, James A. 48402
Fairfull, Thomas M. 43386
Fairman, Elisabeth 45699
Fairweather, Valerie A. 40590
Faißner, Waltraud 02234
Faivre, Bernard 12204
Fakundiny, Robert H. 41085
Falabrino, Ugo 25834
Falaschi, Prof. Pierluigi 23283, 23291
Falcão, Prof. José Antonio 32233
Falco, João 04031
Falco, Joseph 15179
Falconbridge, Liz 39369
Fales, Allen 44265
Falgayrettes, Christiane 13545
Falk, Dr. Birgitta 16948
Falk, Dr. Fritz 19389
Falk, Martin 01869
Falk, Rita 02081
Falke, Ulla 12098
Falkenberg, Edward 06568
Falkenberg, Dr. Regine 15939
Falkenberg, Dr. Uwe 16686
Falkenstien-Doyle, Cheri 47434
Falkner, Dr. Gerd 19410
Falletti, Dr. Franca 23842
Fallon, Steve 48270
Falomir Faus, Dr. Miguel 35048
Faltings, Dr. Dina 17673
Falvy, Dr. Zoltán 21392
Falz, A. 19905
Falz, Andreas 17675, 18616
Falz, Bernd 17726
Famà, Dr. Maria Luisa 25785
Famuyiwa, M.B. 30340
Fanciotto, Cristiana 24882
Fanelli, Doris 46405
Fang, Madeleine 41648
Fangarezzi, Dr. Riccardo 24635
Fankhauser, Heinz 36608
Fanni, Dr. Ignazio 26016
Fanning, Dale A. 46731
Fanony Fulgence 27609
Fansa, Prof. Dr. Mamoun 19257
Fanti, Mario 23131
Fanzun, Jon 37229
Farabee, Ann 41731
Farah, Ahmed 34168
Farahmanesh, Nazi 22255
Farar, Bill 42715
Farbaky, Dr. Péter 21350
Farber, Janet 46149
Faria, Dr. João Carlos Lázaro 32230
Farina, Dr. Ermes 25951
Fariña Busto, Francisco 35182, 35198, 35318
Faringdon, Lord 38977
Faris, Douglas D. 47583
Faris, M.P. 32044
Faris, Peter 41393
Farkas, Jesse 43207
Farley, G. 43971
Farley, Gayle 46111
Farley, Henry G. 48042
Farley, Dr. Linda E. 42881
Farley-Harger, Sara 43512
Farmer, Dennis 42291
Farmer, Dorothy 05340
Farmer, Sid 40284
Farnden, Bob 01149
Farnell, C. 33179
Farnham, Priscilla 43278
Farnhill, Elizabeth 38539
Farnós y Bel, Alex 34464
Farnyk, Patricia Barnett Diane 45802
Farooqi, Dr. Anish 21774
Farr, Amanda 40070

Farr, Fonda 46075
Farr, Raye 48401
Farrajota Ataíde Garcia, Dr. Maria Madalena 32297
Farrand, Dr. William R. 41219
Farrar, Ellyn M. 48005
Farrar, H.D. 46105
Farrar, Robert A. 44022
Farre, Pascal 36880
Farrell, Harold 38271, 38272
Farrell, Kathleen 46942
Farrell, Laurie 44868
Farrell, Lesley 40552
Farrell, Thomas L. 46682
Farrenkopf, Dr. Michael 16193
Farrington, Charles W. 45992
Farrington, Jane 38214
Farsan, Dr. N.M. 17670
Farver, Bonnie 41753
Farver, Jane 42047
Farwell, Richard S. 45292
Farwell-Gavin, Robin 47426, 47427
Fasching, Josef 01766
Fasciati, Luciano 36704
Fasel, André 36716
Fasold, Dr. Peter 17031
Fasold, Dr. Regina 17685
Fassati, Tomáš 08246
Fassbinder, Dr. S. 17390
Fasse, Dr. Norbert 16258
Fasser, Ernst 37112
Fast, Dr. Kirsten 16969, 16970
Fastlicht, Dr. Samuel 28146
Fateh, Suzanne 48329
Fatehi, F. 22245
Fatimah, T. 22081
Fatka, Jaroslav 08565, 08571, 08572, 08576, 08577, 08619
Faton, Louis 13482
Fauchille, Bernard 13060
Faude, Wilson H. 43943
Faul, Beverly 46620
Faulds, W. Rod 41769
Faulkner, D. Lindsay 30268
Faulkner, John 42440
Faulkner, Peter 01533
Faulkner, Rebecca 45796
Faulkner, Tim 39340
Faull, Dr. Margaret 40761
Faure-Comte, Karen 15178
Fauria, Dr. Carmen 34577
Faust, Alexis 48087
Faust, Pierre-Paul 14057
Faust, Dr. Sabine 20212
Fautin, Daphne 44685
Fauver, Lynn N. 45536
Fava, Lourdes 28637
Favata, Alexa 47940
Favell, Gene H. 44508
Favell, Georg 44132
Favre, Lee M. 44844
Favre, Dr. Pascal 36880
Favre, Séverine 37291
Favro, Diane 42312
Fawaz, Salma 27490
Fawell, Anne 44548
Fawzi, Ibrahim 22658
Faxe, Birgitta 35987
Faxon, Susan 41207
Fay, David 43288
Fay, Joyce 42001
Fay, Martin 43952
Fayard, Armand 11947
Faydali, Erol 37771
Fayet, Dr. Roger 37132
Fayet, Roger 37395
Fazekas, Patricia L. 45679
Fazel, Asghar M. 22320
Fazia, Gloria 23892
Fazzi, Kim 46900
Fazzini, Richard 41941
Fazzone, Mary Ann 45686
Fearn, Peter 01168
Feaster, Richard 45789
Feather, Philip H. 44705
Fechter, E. 17491, 17492
Fedele, Prof. F.G. 24588
Federico, Jean 41126
Federle Orr, Dr. Lynn 47311, 47325
Fediw, Mary 46434
Fedorenko, Tamara Grigorjevna 33442
Fëdorova, Ljubov Nikolaevna 33248
Fëdorova, Ljudmila Ivanovna 32881
Fëdorova, Natalja Viktorovna 32826
Fedorowicz, Władysław 31733
Fedyna, Holger 18994
Fedynsky, Andrew 42484
Feeley, Betsey 45754
Feely, Dr. Martin 22473
Feeney, Lawrence 42581
Feeney, Warren 30125
Feffee, Claudette 46670
Fefjuca, T.A. 37835
Fehér, Béla 21475
Fehér, Dr. György 21359
Fehérvári, Béla 21462
Fehle, Dr. Isabella 18602
Fehlemann, Dr. Sabine 20715, 20717
Fehlhammer, Prof. Dr. Dr. Wolf Peter 18839
Fehlhammer, Prof. Dr. Wolf Peter 18840

Fehlhammer, Prof. Dr. Dr. Wolf Peter 19200
Fehr, Horst 18495
Fehr, Dr. Michael 17480, 17481
Feichtlbauer, Brunhilde 01671
Feickert, Rudolf 20443
Feigel, Martine 13208
Feihler, Tim 41777
Feil, Fr. Carl 48025
Feinberg, Larry 42304
Feitknecht, Dr. Thomas 36550
Fejös, Dr. Zoltán 21367
Fekeza, Lidija 03925
Felbauer, Josef 02194
Felbauer, Maria 02194
Felber, Christine 37393
Felber, Michael 45758
Felborg, Jan 30571
Felbermayer, Dietrich 02453
Feldbauer, Sara 43955
Feldberg, Michael 45758
Feldborg, Jan 30571
Feldkamp, Dr. Jörg 16465
Feldkamp, Ursula 16339
Feldman, Kaywin 45242
Feldman, M.M 22638
Feldmane, Milda 27390
Feldmann, Dorothee 19427
Feldmer, Peter 17628
Felgenhauer-Schmiedt, Prof. Dr. Sabine 02727
Felhösné-Csiszár, Dr. Sarolta 21605
Felice, Silvio 27696
Felisati, Vittorio 23789
Fellay, André 36621
Felley, Jean-Paul 36725
Fellmeth, Dr. Ulrich 20101
Fellner, Fritz 01851
Fellner, Manuela 02993
Fellner, Marianne 07509
Felsher, Lynn 45839
Felshin, Nina 45314
Felz, Joseph 43572
Fenger, Lars 08902
Fennema, A.T. 29071
Fenner, Gloria J. 48097
Fenoglio, Norma 00498
Fenoglio, Norma C. 00499
Fensterstock, Lauren 47046
Fenton, David 48199
Fenton, Dr. Frank M. 48636
Fenton, John 00871
Fentress, Steven 46944
Ferarresi, Roberto 23816
Ferasin, Luigi 12577
Ferber, Linda 41941
Ferchland, Andrea 15920
Ferdi, Sabah 00079
Ferebee, Peggy V. 43818
Ferenczy, Dr. Mária 21344
Ferez Kuri, Maria del Carmen 28196
Fergola, Dr. Lorenzo 25769
Ferguson, Ian 30290
Ferguson, Moira 39367
Ferguson, Patricia 06580
Ferguson, Randy 46699
Ferguson, Ray 46974
Ferguson, Robert S. 39060
Fergusson, Ian L.C. 39761
Feria, Dr. Rafael 35024
Ferigo, Dr. Giorgio 25725
Ferino-Pagden, Dr. Sylvia 02918
Ferleger Brades, Susan 39661
Fermont, W.J.J. 29525
Fernan, Marissa N. 31316
Fernandes, Albano 32234
Fernandes, Isabel Maria 32278
Fernandes Gomes, João José 32232
Fernández, Dr. Antonio 06891
Fernández, Jorge H. 34785, 34787
Fernandez, Jorge Osvaldo 00191
Fernández, José Antonio 35574
Fernández, Kathleen M. 41776
Fernández, Luis Alfonso 03903
Fernandez, Luisito F. 31427
Fernández, Maria Angélica 00501
Fernandez, Nohema 44258
Fernández Bal, María Luisa 35318
Fernández Camargo, Gustavo 07604
Fernández Castañón Carrasco, José Antonio 35204
Fernández Cid, Miguel 35436
Fernández de Calderón, Cándida 28170
Fernández de Córdova Marquesa de Mirabel, Dr. Hilda 35275
Fernández de Henestrosa, Carlos 35057
Fernández de Ulibarri, Rocío 07654
Fernández Gómez, Fernando 35478
Fernández Lóp, Olga 35628
Fernández Ugalde, Antonio 34783
Fernández Villaverde, Duque Alvaro 35058, 35380
Fernholm, Ragnhild 36042
Fernier, Jean-Jaques 13438
Ferolla Frizzi, Dr. Vanda 23375
Ferrandi, Dr. Giuseppe 25796
Ferrara, Giovanni 24605
Ferraresi, Roberto 23815
Ferrari, Alessio 24533
Ferrari, Amedeo 23679
Ferrari, Ciro 23434, 24290
Ferraris, Francesco 25960
Ferraris, Pietro 22825

Ferrazzini, Petra 36615
Ferré, Rosario 32380
Ferreau, Christine 19178
Ferreira, Bernardo 42771
Ferreira, Claudia Marcia 04359
Ferreira, Ivette Senise 04505
Ferreira, João Carlos A. 04365
Ferreira, José 00101
Ferreira Brandão, Dr. Carlos Roberto 04526
Ferreira Calado, Dr. Luis 32288
Ferreira da Costa, Paulo 32308
Ferreira da Cunha, Sergio Henrique 04262
Ferrell, John 42369
Ferren, Dick 48307
Ferrer jr., Dominador 31394
Ferrer Ciari, Agustín 34460
Ferrer Dalgà, María Rosa 34857
Ferrer-Joly, Fabien 10471
Ferrer Soria, José Luis 34837
Ferrero, Marcelo 00145
Ferres, Katleen 43756
Ferreyra, Prof. Carlos Alfredo 00382
Ferries, D. 40065
Ferrill, Winifred 44608
Ferriol 14862
Ferris, Alison 41971
Ferriso, Brian 45366
Fersen, Vera von 09514
Fertig-Möller, Heidelore 20524
Festa, Mario 22795
Festanti, Dr. Maurizio 25096
Festini, Prof. Zvonko 07815
Fett, T. 30420
Fetter, Rosemary 41463
Feuß, Prof. Dr. Axel 17527
Fewkes, Nancy 42320, 42345
Fewster, Dr. Kevin 01508, 01558
Feyertag, Gertrude 02272
Feyler, Gabrielle 14661, 14662, 14664
Fiala, Claudia 17890
Fiala Erlich, Chris 43667
Fiallo Hernández, Eduardo 09126
Fiaschetti, Maria Egizia 25227
Fibicher, Dr. Bernhard 36543
Fibiger, Susanne 08876
Fichner-Rathus, Prof. Dr. Lois 48053
Fick, Dr. Astrid 17869, 17870, 17872, 20497, 20499
Fickert, Hildegard 16420
Fideucci, Elaine 43951
Fidler, Stephen David 40309
Fiechter, Hermann 37258
Fiedler, Dr. Elisabeth 01927
Fiedler, Marek 31934
Fiedler, Uwe 16472
Fiedler Streng, Evelyn 47559
Field, Caroline 01202
Field, Hannah 38035
Field, Monica 05291, 05292, 06650
Field, Peter 40081, 40082, 40084
Field, Dr. Richard 44212
Fielden, Dr. Kate 38441
Fielding, Andrew 40087
Fielding, James 06845
Fields, Edward D. 41773
Fields, Hoyt 47377
Fields, Laura 41552
Fields, Vilma S. 42258
Fierro Gossman, Julieta N. 28213
Fierz, Gaby 36508
Fietsam, Robert 41590
Fietz, Dr. Rudolf 19255
Fifield, Donald 47997
Fifiiță, Mariana 32527
Figari, G.B. Roberto 23294
Figlarowicz, Stefan 31567
Figueiredo, Alexandrine 11427
Figueres, Roger 12895
Figueroa, Elisa 06926
Figuerolar, Prof. I. 34561
Figuti, Midory Kimura 04497
Fike, Nancy J. 48140
Filieri, Dr. Maria Teresa 24230, 24231
Filina, Larissa 33074
Filipčić-Maligec, Vlatka 07703
Filipetti, Dr. Giuseppe 24158
Filipova, F. 04923
Filipová, Maria 08549
Filipović, Marica 03925
Filipow, Dr. Krzysztof 31488
Filipowicz, Zygmunt 32009
Filippi, Dr. Giorgio 48872
Filippo, Giuseppe 22980
Filippone, Christine 46448
Filippova, Éleonora Anatoljevna 32802
Fillman, Joseph B. 41144
Filtvedt, Per Kr. 30784
Fimpeler-Philippen, Annette 16742, 16743
Finaldi, Dr. Gabriele 35048, 39729
Finamore, Dr. Daniel 47198
Finamore, Prof. Nino 25480
Finat, Joelle 12452
Finch, Jon 39500, 39502
Finch, Patricia 40653
Finch, Rick 48166
Finch, Sarah 38438
Finch-Crisp, Sarah 40662
Finckh, Dr. Gerhard 18452
Finding, Gerhard 02122
Findley, Alvin 06468

Findley, David 46775
Fine, Ruth 48373
Fink, David G. 41073
Fink, Martin 19393, 19394, 19395
Fink, Dr. Verena 17560
Fink, Prof. William L. 41220
Finke, Karl 16868
Finkele, Diana 19730
Finkelstein, Christine 43878
Finkelstein, Jacqueline A. 04387
Finkelstein, Lori Beth 45063
Finks, Harvey 42962
Finlay, James 40965
Finlay, John 48538
Finlay, Nancy 43938
Finlayson, Prof. J.C. 20802
Finlayson, Jim 01059
Finley, James P. 43399
Finley, Janet 43715
Finley, Valerie 05790
Finneiser, Klaus 15908
Finnemore, Donnice 48448
Finnemore, Harry 48448
Finnerty, Sinéad 44902
Finney, Libby 38741, 39468
Finnigan, Stephen 43845
Finotti, Franco 25291
Finweg, Sabine 20759
Finžgar, Maja 34112
Finzi, Dr. Ranny 22748
Fionik, Doroteusz 31493
Fioning, Dr. Hubertuns 16947
Fiorentino, Alessandro 25610
Fiorenza, Joseph 43607
Fiori, Dennis A. 41483
Fiori, Dr. Pietro 24407
Fiorillo, Anthony 42752
Fiorio, Dr. Maria Teresa 24375, 24376, 24378, 24389
Fiouri, E. 08198
Firl, Wolfgang 17301
Firmenich, Andrea 15668
Firnges, Jörg 17769
Firstenberg, Jean 44890
Firszt, Stanisław 31630
Firth, Neil 40637
Fischbacher, Marianne 36813
Fischer, Dr. Alfred 18161
Fischer, Andrea 19751
Fischer, Angelika 17496
Fischer, Barbara 05869
Fischer, Christian 09052
Fischer, Dr. Eberhard 37398
Fischer, Dr. Eckhard 20659
Fischer, Felice 46442
Fischer, Dr. Fritz 15575, 20115
Fischer, Dr. Gert 19945
Fischer, Gertrud 02963
Fischer, Gottlieb 18651
Fischer, Hannelore 18147
Fischer, Dr. Hartwig 36505
Fischer, Helmut 16477, 16478
Fischer, Hermann von 36819
Fischer, Ilse 17543
Fischer, Ingrid 18473
Fischer, Karl-Günther 16291
Fischer, Klaus 16573
Fischer, Manfred W.K. 02372
Fischer, Dr. Manuela 15945
Fischer, Mark 43977
Fischer, Prof. Dr. Martin S. 17947
Fischer, Martina 18692
Fischer, Peter 02576, 36912
Fischer, Reinhold 19167
Fischer, Ron 42210
Fischer, Steffen 17309
Fischer, Susanne 17020
Fischer, Thomas 15878
Fischer, Prof. Dr. Volker 17062
Fischer, Dr. Werner 18719
Fischer-Elfert, Prof. Dr. Hans-W. 18382
Fischer-Huelin, Danièle 36743
Fischer Jonge, Ingrid 08939, 08942
Fischetti, Amy 43342
Fischhaber, Martin 18735
Fischlin, Jean-Mario 36478
Fisecker, August 02043
Fish, Paul 48082
Fish, Suzy 48082
Fishback, Pat 46886
Fisher, Alice 42683
Fisher, Claire 40704
Fisher, Clive 40229, 40230
Fisher, Debra 41908
Fisher, D.L. 30194
Fisher, Forest K. 44734
Fisher, Frederick J. 48360
Fisher, F.S. 42204
Fisher, Jay 41454
Fisher, John R. 47966
Fisher, Kathleen 45485
Fisher, Kathryn 06413
Fisher, Kevin M. 44765
Fisher, Larry 41500
Fisher, Lilian 48232
Fisher, M. 43035
Fisher, Susan 45845
Fisher, Ted 46917
Fisher, Dr. Wesley 46436

Fisher Sterling, Dr. Susan 48381
Fishman, Bernard P. 41145
Fisk, Jan 44434
Fiske, David A. 47800
Fiske, Nancy E. 47779
Fiske, Patricia 48374
Fisken, Judith A. 38970
Fiskesjö, Dr. Magnus 36271
Fisseha, Girma 18916
Fitch, James A. 43655
Fite, Susan 42524
Fitschen, Dr. Jürgen 16323
Fitts, Catherine 48396
Fitz, Erwin 01747
Fitz, Prof. Jenoë 21557
Fitz, Péter 21338
Fitzgerald, Annamary 46139
Fitzgerald, E. 46765
Fitzgerald, Elizabeth 47127
Fitzgerald, Jane 45356
Fitzgerald, Mary Ann 45068
Fitzgerald, Maryann 47462
Fitzhugh, Robin 43271
Fitzpatrick, Gareth 39347
Fitzpatrick, M. 49028
Fitzpatrick, Mike 22507
Fitzpatrick, Pat 06860
Fitzpatrick, Robert 42344
Fitzpatrick, Tom 22656
Fitzsimmons, Rita 44983
Fitzsimons, Gray 44983
Fitzsimons, Dr. J. Michael 41532
Fiumi, Prof. Enrico 26052
Fix, Dr. Andrea 18514
Fjellhøi 30372
Fjermedal, Torkell 30979
Flacke, Dr. Monika 15939
Flacke, Robert 44587
Flagge, Prof. Dr. Ingeborg 17035
Flaherty, Mary A. 41201
Flaherty, Tom 46512
Flaksman, Sandy 44968
Flanagam, Michael 48594
Flanagan, Anne 01490
Flanagan, Brendan 39406
Flanagan, I.D. 38835
Flanagan, Shelia M. 45422
Flannery, Kent V. 41219
Flannery, Prof. Tim 00713
Flashar, Dr. M. 17106
Flask, David 45050
Flasza, Jan 31501
Flatau, Astrid 18843, 18844, 18845, 18907, 18925
Flaud, Jackie 15022
Flavin, Samantha 39440
Flechas Corredor, Jorge Arturo 07617
Fleck, Robert 13249
Fleck, Dr. Robert 17530
Fleckenstein, Jutta 17165, 19816
Fleet, Dr. A. 39733
Fleet, Judy 43636
Flegel, Andreas 16810
Flegel-Wantier, Klaus 19926
Fleisch, Prof. Henri 27482
Fleischer, Alexander Franz 02973
Fleischer, Donna H. 47512
Fleischer, Dr. Martina 02886
Fleischman, Stephen 45069
Fleischmann-Heck, Dr. Isa 18223
Fleishman, Eve 44121
Fleissner, Alfred 02275
Fleming, Anne 39584
Fleming, Dr. David 40235
Fleming, Elizabeth A. 42216
Fleming, Elvis 47015
Fleming, Jeff 42905
Fleming, Jennifer 43561
Fleming, Leslie 46064
Fleming, Marty 48411
Fleming, Sam 38068
Flensburg, Brigitta 36120
Flensburg, Britta 35912
Flentje, Rachel 41751
Fletcher, Ann 30165
Fletcher, Carrol 45182
Fletcher, Charles 45582
Fletcher, Corinne 48666
Fletcher-Williams, Ann 39028
Fletling, Walter 17095
Flett, Dr. Alistair M. 37944
Flett, Harry 39166
Fleurov, Ellen 43208, 43210
Fleury, Nathalie 36657
Fliegel, Brigitte 18419
Flinn, Karen 48057
Flinsch, Stefanie 02551
Flinspach, Joan L. 43478
Flintoff, Paul 38242, 38244, 38246
Flodin, Göran 36230
Flögel, Dr. Evelyn 20366
Flögel-Kostić, Lela 33818
Flörl, Johann 01994
Flößer, Dr. Reinhard 15630
Flon, André 14301
Flon, Dominique 13239, 13243
Flood, Ellen 45268
Flood, Richard 45394
Flood, Rick 48783
Flood, Robert 45268

Flood, Timothy 42360
Florance, Robyn 01337
Florentino, M. Raquel 32294
Florenzano, Clorinda 24564
Florer, Michael R. 43662
Flores, Ana 32340
Flores, Antonio 31308
Flores, Crystal 44776
Flores, Juan C. 48952
Flores, Ricardo E. 31173
Flórez, Alberto 07606
Flórez, Helmer de Jesús 07599
Flórez de Grajales, Aura 07607
Florian, Carmen 32465
Floridi, Dr. Massimiliano 24010
Floris, Prof. Giovanni 23253
Floris, Lene 08884
Florizoone, Jan 03665
Flory, Maurice 12701
Floryan, Dr. Margrethe 08952
Flotow, Julia von 06602
Flour, Joke 03804
Flourentzos, Dr. Pavlos 08198
Flowers, Betty Sue 41416
Floyd, Alex 45945
Floyd, David 41534
Floyd, Roger 47556
Flucker, Turry 44286
Flude, Kevin 39737
Flückiger, Dr. Peter F. 37010
Flügge, Matthias 15909
Flühler, Dr. Dione 37393
Flug, Josef 02337
Fluke, Pam 40501
Fluke, Phil 40501
Fluksi, Josip 07809
Fluri, Annette 36518
Flury, Dorothea 36518
Flutsch, Laurent 36867
Flynn Johnson, Robert 47311, 47325
Flynt, Suzanne 42850
Foa, Piers 00786
Foa, Robyn 00786
Foanaota, Lawrence 34167
Foard, Douglas 44710
Fobbs, Archie 48378
Focht, Brenda 46922
Focht, John 41554
Foe, Peter 47940
Föller, R. 16968
Foelsche, Gudrun 02312, 02315
Fölster, Dieter 20264
Först, Dr. Elke 17545
Foerster, Dr. Cornelia 16155
Förster, Karin 20115
Förster, Roswitha 19481
Föttinger, Franz 02680
Fogarasi, Zsuzsa 21445
Fogarty, Lori 47473
Fogliazza, Virginio 24204
Foissner, Elisabeth 02953, 02954
Foister, Dr. Susan 39729
Fojtik, Miroslav 08525, 08719
Fok, Oliver 17955
Folch, María Jesús 35599
Folch, Stella 34540
Foldøy, Oddveig 30877
Foley, Doris 45656
Foley, J.A. 30274
Foley, Jim 42290
Foley, Mim 46589
Foley, Suzanne 42253
Foley, W.M. 38329
Folga-Januszewska, Dorota 32115
Folger, Peter 44436
Folger, Willibald 01753
Folgić-Korjak, Angelina 33810
Folie, Dr. Sabine 02914
Folk, Luther 41868
Folkins, Alice 05336
Follbert, Léon 10427
Follett, Joanna 40530
Follin, Ann 36277
Follmann-Schulz, Dr. Anna-Barbara 16246
Folsach, Dr. Kjeld von 08928
Folwell Krueger, Hilary 43473
Fong, Lawrence 43228
Fonio, Prof. Ezio 25750
Fonseca Ferreira, Aurora da 00094
Fonsmark, Anne-Birgitte 08793
Font, Walter 43474
Font-Réaulx, Dominique de 13596
Font Sentias, Josep 34884
Fontaine, Axel 11267
Fontaine, Christian 14930
Fontaine, Patrick 13764
Fontaine, Dr. Thomas 20212
Fontana, Armon 36704
Fontana, Dr. Eszter 18410
Fontana, Lilia 45287
Fontaneda, Cristina 34465
Fontenioue, Henri du 11771
Fontenot, Michelle 45731
Fontenote-Jamerson, Belinda 44928
Fontenoy, Paul 41558
Fonts-Reaulx, Dominique de 13636
Foote, W.T. 01460
Fopp, Dr. Michael A. 39755
Foppa, Christian 36634

Forand, Ed 48529
Forand, Peggy 47704
Foray, J.-M. 10740
Foray, Jean-Michel 13322, 15061
Forbes, A.A. 37968
Forbes, Duncan 38917
Forbes, Jamie 06630
Forbes, Dr. John M. 41444
Ford, Chris 42845
Ford, Cynthia 42885
Ford, Dabney 45592
Ford, David 05505
Ford, H. 06392
Ford, Peggy A. 43785
Ford, Richard I. 41219
Ford, Dr. S.D. 46504
Ford jr., Thomas 31327
Fordham, Gerald J. 47187
Fordham, Michael 39148
Fordyce, Dr. R. Ewan 30148
Forellad, Dolors 35345
Foreman, Martin 39379
Forero, Dr. Enrique 07405
Foresman, Dr. Kerry 45408
Forest, Dominique 13586
Forest, Gilles 12015
Forest, Marie-Cécile 13618
Forgan, Dr. Sophie 40850
Forgang, David M. 48804
Forgeng, Jeffrey L. 48753
Forget, Patrice 15273, 15274, 15275
Forhaug, Helén 36034
Forkl, Dr. Hermann 20099
Forman, Bob 46382
Forman, Weldon 42617
Formanek, Verena 37060
Formanová, Markéta 08544
Forment, Francina 03337
Formery, Valerie 03547
Formicone, Luigi 24639
Fornals Villalonga, Francisco 34689
Fornara, Livio 36733, 36738
Fornari Schianchi, Dr. Lucia 24799
Fornasari, Giuseppe 24553
Forner Caballero, Ester 35691
Forney, Jack D. 42888
Forni, Prof. Gaetano 25452
Forrer, Dr. M. 29525
Forrest, Richard 05792
Forrester, Gillian 45699
Forrester, Hugh 38158
Forrester, Jim 39890
Forsberg, Anders 30877
Forsberg, Helena 36349
Forsberg, Dr. Peter K. 43955
Forsberg, Virpi 09457
Forschler, Dr. Anne 41706
Forssblad, Marianne 47541
Forster, Helen 05011
Forster, Michael 15461
Forster, Werner 18833
Forsythe, Dee 44683
Fort, Thomas A. 43088
Fortenberry, Kay 45634
Forti, Fabio 23171
Forti, Dr. Micol 48872
Fortin, James 06511
Fortin, Verna 45051
Fortino, Sally 15684
Fortunat Černilogar, Damjana 34155
Fortune, C.F. 34287, 34290, 34291, 34292
Fortune, Linda 34205
Foschi, Dr. Pier Luigi 25115, 25117
Fosdick, Pamela A. 45451
Fosen-Schlichtinger, Petra 01654
Fosmine, Francis G. 41607
Foss, Birgit 30789
Foss, Marybeth 47934
Fossati, Alessandro 36899
Fosse, Martine 11003
Fossum, Finn 30411
Foster, Alasdair 01351
Foster, Dr. Allan 06861
Foster, Carter 42466
Foster, Clarence 05233
Foster, David R. 46380
Foster, Dr. E.J. 39449
Foster, Kathleen 46442
Foster, Keith 45271
Foster, Laura 46103
Foster, Linda 48102
Foster, Marusia 06849
Forget, Preston 42617
Foster, R.A. 39520
Foster, Stephen 40545, 47223
Foster, Velma 06101
Foster Owen, J. 47221
Fotchi Chian, Mansoor 22282
Fotoghi, M. 22274
Fotter, Ludwig 01663
Foucart, Bruno 10834
Foucher, Jean-Pascal 14691
Fouhse, Sally 43559
Foulds, Kris 04964
Foulon, Pierre-Jean 03640
Fouray, Monique 14050
Fourie, Dr. H. 34359

Fournet, Claude 13320
Fournier, Johanne 05822
Fournier, Lydia 36460
Fournier, Dr. M. 29521
Fourny-Dargere, Sophie 12462, 15239
Foust, Dorothy 45052
Fouts, Chris 05039
Fouts, David 44443
Fowkes, Dudley 40325
Fowler, James 47376
Fowler, Jon 48084
Fowler, Martin 38517
Fowler, Sophie 38552
Fowler, Stephen 00872
Fowler, Victoria 48561
Fowler, William M. 41814
Fowler Shearer, Christine 44610
Fox, Andrew 38004
Fox, Catherine 38587
Fox, Charles 47670
Fox, Christopher D. 48005
Fox, Emily 47752
Fox, Eugene 43833
Fox, Dr. Georgia 42373
Fox, Howard 44921
Fox, Jill 40569
Fox, Julie 40723
Fox, Maureen 30184
Fox, Michael 44891
Fox, Mike 42300
Fox, Patric 42538
Fox, Richard 46269
Fox, Dr. Ronald 45998
Foyer, Marle 12404
Fraas, Susanne 17805
Fraaye, Dr. R.H.B. 29015
Fraccaro, Prof. Marco 24828
Frady, Jackie L. 46833
Fraipont, J. de 03646
Fraisset, M.M. 10249
Frakes, Rita 45212
Framke, Dr. Gisela 16658, 16662
Framnes, Svein 30670
Franc, Karl 02724
França, Prof. Alexandre 04579
France, Glenda 42686
Francell, Larry 44501
Francès, Henry 11349
Franceschini, Luca 24314
Franceschini, Maria Anna 23847
Francesconi, Gino 45865
Francia, Ennio 48883
Franciolli, Marco 36898
Franciosi, Dr. Ario 23507
Francis, Dr. Carl A. 42046
Francis, Dermot 39819
Francis, Elaine 38409
Francis, Jerry 46534
Francis, Jesse 42290
Francis, John 40499
Francis, Kathy 41811
Francis, Dr. R. 39006
Francis, Tim 47764
Francis, Wayne 45174
Francisco, Emmanuel J. 45322
Francisco, Irving 48027
Francisco, Lisa 45231
Francisco, Silvestre António 00095
Franck, Dr. Frederick 48320
Franck, Marketta 10082
Franco, Alfredo 45678
Franco, Barbara 48359
Franco, Leoncio Verdera 34754
Franco, Patà 37189
François, Lionel 11667
Francou, Dr. Carlo 23407
Francová, Zuzana 33965
Frâncu, Simona 32441
Frandsen, Lene B. 08785, 08786, 08991, 09016, 09017, 09100, 09101, 09102
Frangos, Ioannis 21218
Frank, Claude 11358
Frank, Donald 43500
Frank, Dr. Günter 16356
Frank, Heinrich 04282
Frank, Larry 44700
Frank, Peggy 45600
Frank, Richard J. 41765
Frank, Richard W. 43416
Frank, Stuart M. 47579
Frank, Thomas 17903
Frank, Thomas H. 18261
Franke, Anselm 16034
Franke, Dr. Judith A. 44731, 47737
Frankel, Joan 46404
Frankel, Robert H. 47404
Frankel Nathanson, Marjorie 42497
Frankenberger, Anette 16129
Frankezo, Marianne 18916
Frankignoul, Daniel J. 03295
Frankl, Beatrice 18894
Franklin, Ailesia 43012
Franklin, Dr. David 06084, 06084
Franklin, Joyce 41194
Franklin, Karen S. 41921
Franko, Blanche 06479
Franková, Božena 08654, 08688
Franković, Dr. Bernard 07685

Franks, Carolyn J. 41252
Franks, Clara 45181
Franks, Curtis J. 42208
Franks, R.J. 05948
Fransen, Dr. H. 34207
Fransen, Linda 48681
Fransen, Martin 06255
Fransson, Elisabeth 36045
Frantz, James H. 45833
Frantz, Lewis 44501
Frantzen, Ole L. 08953
Frantzen-Heger, Gaby 27580
Franulic, Markita 07835
Franz, Dr. Erich 18950, 18950
Franz, Prof. Dr. G. 20214
Franz jr., L.R. 43581
Franze, Dr. Manfred 16764
Franzel, Frank E. 45209
Franzén, Ann 36266
Franzén, Darlyne S. 48742
Franzén, Eva-Lotta 35979
Franzke, Dr. Irmela 17991
Franzke, Dr. Jürgen 19135
Franzolin Trevisan, Amélia 04539
Frapporti, Giovanni 22630
Fraser, David 38716
Fraser, Dr. Nicholas C. 45193
Fraser, Nonie 05224, 05405, 06514
Fratelli, Dr. Maria 24371, 24406
Fratzke, Dieter 17978
Frauendorfer, Dr. Bernd 17528
Fraueneder, Dr. Hildegard 02535
Frawley, Sylvia 22444
Frayler, John 47201
Frayling, Prof. Christopher 39760
Frazer, John 05067
Frazer, Kay J. 44526
Frazer, Robert 45594
Frazier, Ronald F. 42840
Freaney, Linda 48740
Frèches, Claire 13596
Frechuret, Maurice 10803
Freddi, Dr. Loris 23463
Frederici, Joan 41883
Frederick, Frances 46508
Frederick, Karen 47492
Fredj, Jacques 13605
Free, Abigail 46007
Free, Adam 00704
Freece, David W. 44430
Freed, Douglass 47554
Freed, Howard 43302
Freed, Peter 43302
Freed, R. Mitchell 43180
Freed, Rita E. 41817
Freedman, Myron 47128
Freedman, Robert A. 42453
Freegman, David 40179
Freeland, Clara 42057
Freeland, George W. 44576
Freeling, Dr. Doris 42747
Freeman, A. 40335
Freeman, B.J. 41319
Freeman, Craig C. 44685
Freeman, D. Carl 42937
Freeman, Dottie 48561
Freeman, George 44589
Freeman, Lenette 45557
Freeman, Marina 44858
Freeman, Michael 37955
Freeman, Dr. Patricia W. 44793
Freeman, Rusty 45613
Freeman, Sue 44301
Freemantle, Andrew 40228
Freer, Elene J. 05107, 05108
Frehner, Dr. Matthias 36544
Frei, Beat 36574
Frei, Prof. Dr. Hans 19020
Frei, Hans-Peter 36594
Frei, Thomas 37157
Frei, Urs-Beat 37080, 37081
Freidberg, Dr. A. 22777
Freises, M. 14731
Freitag, Dr. Anne 36859
Freitag, Matthias 19526
Freitag, Winfried 16769
Freitag-Mair, Claudia 19851, 19852, 19853, 19854
Freitas, Dr. Henrique de 04111
Freixinet, Mercè 34964
Freland, Colin 30111
Frémaux, Thierry 12749
Frembgen, Dr. Jürgen 18916
Fremd, T. 44481
French, Ann 39904
French, B.G. 41052
French, Brenda 38706
French, David 39614
French, Dr. Frank 47792
French, Mary 42552
Frenkley, Helen 22708
Frennet, Raymond 03130
Frenssen, Dr. B. 17390
Frenz, Achim 17055
Frenz, Dr. Hans Gerhard 18606
Frenza, James P. 41214
Frenzel, Hans-Holger 15528
Frerichs, Dr. Klaus 16439
Frésard, Claude 36973
Freschi Conti, Dr. Graziella 23178

Frese, Dr. Annette 17668
Fresk, Klas 36212
Fresneda Padilla, Eduardo 34880
Freudenberg, Dr. Mechtild 19793
Freudenheim, Tom L. 39642
Freuenschlag, Jörg 02124
Freund, Franzika 02804
Freus, Dan 43324
Frey, Barbara 42595
Frey, Dietrich 20507
Frey, Dr. Eberhard 18003
Frey, Dr. Georg 20240
Frey, Dr. Jennifer K. 46617
Freyberg, Wolfgang 16830
Freyburger, J.-Claude 13248
Freyer, Bryna 48374
Freymann, Dr. Klaus 18839
Friary, Donald R. 42849
Frías Acosta, Alvaro Francisco 07628
Friberg, Gösta 35852
Friborg, Flemming 08944
Frick, C. Kevin 46884
Frick, William R. 45367
Fricke, Inge 18306, 18307
Fricke, Dr. Ronald 20105
Frickman, Linda 43382
Fridfinnsson, Jóhann 21673
Frieb, M.T. 15809
Friebel, V. 18356
Fried, Grace 43070
Fried, S. 36241
Friedel, Prof. Dr. Helmut 18918
Friederich, Dr. Christoph 16923
Friederich, M. 36851
Friedhofen, Barbara 15875
Friedl, Gerlinde 15653
Friedlander, Michal 41645
Friedman, Dr. Alan J. 43355
Friedman, Maxine 47790
Friedman, Robert 42550, 42551
Friedrich, Hanns 15677
Friedrich, Heinz-Jürgen 20746
Friedrich, Holger 19969
Friedrich, Dr. Sven 15845, 15848, 15858
Friedrich, Till 16674
Friedrich-Sander, Harald 17795
Friel, Dr. I. 38559, 38562
Frieling, Robert 44055
Frielinghaus, Volker 16199
Friemark, Dan 41652
Friemerding, Wolfgang 16534
Friend, Charlotte 46072
Friend, Glenda 48328
Frierson, Amy H. 42262
Fries, Dee 41626
Friese, Dr. Elisabeth 18057, 18058
Friesen, Steve 43712, 43712
Friesenbichler, Gerhard 02489
Friesenecker, Josef 02592
Friesinger, Prof. Dr. Herwig 01868, 01869
Friis, Birte 08879, 08990
Friis-Hansen, Dana 41406
Friis Møller, Søren 09516
Frimodig, Heidemarie 19826
Frinchillucci, Dr. Gianluca 23779, 23781
Frinsko, Linda M. 43730
Fripp, Gayle H. 43813
Frisbee, John L. 42605
Frisch, Patricia L. 47663
Frisk Coffman, Mary 46044
Frith, Caroline 39248
Fritsch, Julia 13637
Fritsch, Martin 16013
Fritts, Teresa 43008
Fritz, Anita 44544
Fritz, Beatrice 17669
Fritz, Dr. Ingomar 01922
Fritz, Dr. U. 16702
Frizzi, Dr. Vanda 23374
Frlan, Damodar 07813, 07813
Frodl, Dr. Gerbert 01990, 02838, 02953, 02954
Froehlich, Conrad G. 42192, 42193, 42194, 42195
Fröhlich, Günter 03001
Frohriep, Monika 19743
Froitzheim, Dr. Eva-Marina 16214
Frolcova, Dr. Milada 08698
Frolec, Dr. Ivo 08698
Frolova, Aleksandra Anatoljevna 32758
Frolova, T.V. 33736
From-Brown, Kristy 44171
Frommhage-Davat, Gudrun-Sophie 20565
Fromont, Chantal 10638
Froning, Prof. Dr. H. 18622
Froning, Dr. Hubertus 16959
Frontalini, Costantino 23566
Frorud, Harald 30848, 30849
Frosdick, Fiona 38175
Frost, Cheryl A. 44194
Frost, Katarina 36010
Frost, Natalie 40038
Frost, R. 38927
Frost-Pennington, Peter 40285
Frotscher, Matthias 18346
Froud, Alan 00886
Fry, Judith 01260
Fry, Stephen 05565
Fryberger, Betsy 47772
Frýda, Dr. František 08543, 08547
Fryda, Hildegard 18841

Fryer, Jonathan 40480
Fryer, Molly 43268
Fu, Dr. Tse Tak 07105
Fuchs, Dr. Carl Ludwig 17668, 17676
Fuchs, Dr. Detlef 19592
Fuchs, E. 31767
Fuchs, Elisabeth 02329
Fuchs, Dr. Emanuel 02878
Fuchs, Ernfried 02919
Fuchs, Dr. Friedrich 19518, 19519
Fuchs, Dr. Gerald 02171
Fuchs, Matthias 02606
Fuchs, Max 36675
Fuchs, Monique 14835
Fuchs, Dr. Rainer 02949
Fuchs, Ronald 02329
Fuchs, Sandra 48521, 48522
Fuchssteiner, Ingrid 02037
Füköh, Dr. Levente 21417
Füllner, Dr. Karin 16726
Fülöp, Dr. Eva Maria 21592
Fülöp, Dr. Éva Maria 21593
Fülöp, Dr. Gyula 21496, 21561
Fünfgeld, F. 17699
Fünfgelder, Konrad 19368
Fünfschilling, Sylvia 36479
Fürészné-Molnár, Anikó 21595
Fürle, Gisela 20301
Fürnkranz, Sonja 02945
Füvessy, Anikó 21596
Fugami, Tracey 45794
Fugaro, Anthony F. 48213
Fugate, Charlotte 46166
Fugate, Dody 47425
Fugazza, Prof. Stefano 24888
Fugazzola Delpino, Maria Antonietta 25238
Fuge, Rex 00912
Fugger-Babenhausen, Markus Graf 15582
Fuglie, Gordon L. 44918
Fuglsang, Harald 08834
Fuhrman, Loretta 46575
Fuji, Hishizu 26492
Fujii, Miyako 26397
Fujii, Yoshitugu 26397
Fujii, Zenzaburou 26397
Fujisaki, Aya 26217
Fujita, Chikako 26644
Fujita, Kyoko 26368
Fujita, Yukio 26142
Fukagawa, Masafumi 26328
Fukuda, Hiroko 26217
Fukuda, Mamoru 26275
Fukuhara, Yoshiharu 26946
Fukuji, Eiji 26186
Fukushima, Hiroyuki 26968
Fulconis, Marie-Madeleine 14204, 14205
Fulda, Anna-Barbara 36636
Fulfer, Glenn 45549
Fulford, Prof. M.G. 40517
Fulga, Ligia 32448
Fulghum, Joyce 43543
Fuller, Alfred W. 41962
Fuller, Candy 43406
Fuller, C.D. 29248
Fuller, Craig 47236
Fuller, Don Michael 47940
Fuller, Elaine L. 42722
Fuller, Elizabeth E. 46451
Fuller, Ellen 41998
Fuller, Janae 44751
Fullerton, Jane 06334
Fullhart, W.C. 46122
Fulop, Lajos 32508
Fulton, Jeff 47484
Fulton, William 40646
Fulton, William Duncan 42986
Funck, Ludwig 16358
Funk, Dr. Frank E. 48664
Funk, Michael 16666, 19379
Funk, Tamara 45379
Funk, Uli 15961
Funsho Adedayo, Oluremi 30358
Furber, Rich 46737
Furey, Linda 46027
Furey, Patrick W. 47110
Furger, Dr. Alex 36479
Furger, Dr. Andres 36722, 37393, 37394, 37406
Furgol, Dr. Edward 48386
Furiesi, Dr. Alessandro 26053
Furingsten, Agne 36016
Furlan, Giuseppe 22958
Furlong, James 45826
Furlow, Elizabeth 47540
Furman, Evelyn E. 44701
Furnival, Gloria 45995
Furrer, Dr. H. 37404
Furry, Nancy 47907
Fursdon, E.D. 38428
Furshong, Peg 43292
Fursova, Irina Alekseevna 33247
Furtner, Alois 15465, 15467
Furtwengler, Marusia 15658
Furtwengler, U. 15787
Furu, Helen 30752
Furuta, Ryo 26938
Fusi, Pietro 23430
Fustig, Manuela 17274
Futter, Christina 44404
Futter, Ellen V. 45759

Futzel, Charles 48336
Fux, Franz 01878
Fyfe, R. 30124
Fyke, James 45618
Fylypčuk, Dr. D. 37840
Gaaff, G. 29067
Gaál, Dr. Attila 21564, 21565
Gaasch, Cynnie 43546
Gabarra, Josep Feliu 34482
Gabat, Waltraud 02812
Gabay, Oshra 22716
Gabbard, Dennis 43485
Gabbitas, Victoria 38705
Gabet, Francis 36866
Gabici, Dr. Franco 25082
Gable, Edward 41736
Gaborit, Jean-René 13603
Gabra, Dr. Gwadat 00977
Gabriel, Prof. Reinhold 02139
Gabriel, Rosemary 45756
Gabriel, Siegfried 17079
Gabrielson, Bengt 35992
Gabršek Prosenc, Meta 34128, 34129
Gabyševa, Asja Lvovna 32845
Gachet, Luis-Jean 11142
Gačková, Dr. Lýdia 34029
Gadd, Richard W. 45456
Gaddis, Eugene R. 43944
Gaddy, Kenneth 48116
Gadebusch, Raffael D. 16053
Gądor, Józef 31932
Gädeke, Dr. Thomas 19794
Gaedtke-Eckardt, Dr. Dagmar 17607
Gähler, Walter 36765
Gänsheimer, Dr. Susanne 18918
Gänsicke, Christian 16757
Gärtner, Monika 02059
Gäßler, Prof. Dr. Ewald 19254, 19259
Gafert, Alfred 17713
Gaffino Rossi, Rodolfo 25743
Gaffney, T.J. 46597
Gafurov, G.G. 48829
Gagarina, Dr. Elena 33056, 33168
Gage, Mike 43788
Gagge, Carl-Magnus 36383
Gagnaison, Jean-Claude 14666
Gagneur, Didier 10391
Gagneux, Dominique 13548
Gagneux, Yves 13521
Gagnon, Rhéal 05706
Gagosian, Robert 48735
Gagro, Ivan 07809
Gaida, Dr. Maria 15918
Gaier, Dr. Claude 03574
Gaigalat, Michael 19178
Gaillard, Dr. Karin 29514
Gain, Prof. D.B. 34253
Gaines, Robert 43171
Gair, Michael 05041
Gais Muller, Deborah del 46721
Gaisbauer, Ernst 01691
Gaisberger, Karl 01691
Gaissert Jackson, Mary 41122
Gaitán de Santamaria, Magdalena 07471
Gaither, Edmund B. 41819
Gajdukova, Nadežda Michajlovna 32893
Gajewski, Dr. Pawel 24330
Gajski, Zora 07822
Galan, Brenda de 03458
Galanti Papola, Mary 46425
Galard, Jean 13603
Galassi, Peter 44869
Galassi, Susan Grace 45802
Galasso, Prof. Elio 23053
Galasso, Dr. Giovanna 23048
Galati, Dr. Roberto 23065
Galatis, Bill 41828
Galbraith, Marie 48427
Galbreath, Desiree 45627
Galčenko, J.A. 37873
Gale, Marilyn 48555
Galea, Victoria 27716
Galeazzi, Dr. Claudio 25001
Gałecki, Zdzisław 32108
Galendo, Dr. Pedro G. 31397
Galeotti, Prof. Piero 23557
Gałęza, Jarosław 31860
Galicer, Jorgelina 00427
Galicki, Piotr 31485
Galiègue, Josette 10655
Galili, Avner 22706
Galimberti, Dr. Paolo 24418
Galindo, Luis 48916
Galindo Rosales, Hortensia 28108
Galindo Steffens, Margarita 07377
Galkina, Inna Konstantinovna 32672
Galkina, Tatjana Ivanovna 33338
Gallacher, Daniel T. 05484
Gallagher, Marlys 41631
Gallagher, Marsha V. 46149
Gallagher, Patrick 22497
Gallagher, Susan 43746
Gallagher, Dr. Thomas H. 43146
Galland, Madelon 45816
Gallant, Aprile 46015
Gallant, Cécile 05231
Gallant, Greg 05231
Gallardo, Luis 28207
Gallasch, Harold E. 01084

Gallatin, Morgan Dean 48314
Galleano, Dr. Franco 23960
Gallego Londoño, María Elena 07573
Gallegos Franco, Francisco 28485, 28486
Galler, Peter 37062
Gallert, Andrea 20689
Galli, Dr. Cinzia 23681
Galli, Fiorenzo 24408
Gallico, Prof. Claudio 24287
Gallifant, David W. 40827
Galliffet, P. de 12522
Galliker-Tönz, Robert 36559
Gallimore, Janet 48457
Galliot, Gérard 10702
Gallivan, Dr. P.A. 01098
Galljamova, Dolaris G. 32785, 32787
Gallo, Denis 47347
Gallo, Prof. Pietro 25207
Gallois, J.L. 10310
Galloway, Dr. Ian 01458
Galluzzi, Prof. Paolo 23848
Galočkina, Svetlana Jurjevna 33682
Galonska, Ann 47836
Galonska, Julie 43456
Galopim de Carvalho, Prof. A.M. 32309
Galscott, Joseph 01065
Galtier, Jacques 13336
Galvani, Bill 44473
Galvin, Frank 40598
Galvin, John E. 45056
Galvin, Maureen 41980
Galvis, Hermana Martha Lucía 07518
Gálviz Muñoz, Rosalba 07541
Gama Mota, Prof. Dr. Paulo 32255
Gamache 11379
Gamasin, Gleb 16584
Gamazo Barrveco, Mercedes 35029
Gambin, Kenneth 27712
Gamboa, Lyn 31447
Gamboa, Marilyn B. 31279
Gamet, Prosper 15015
Gamillscheg, Prof. Dr. Ernst 02955
Gammersvik, Aagot 30501
Gammersvik, Ågot 30641, 30963
Gamolin, Vladimir Danilovič 33278
Gamperer, Franz 02282
Gamsjäger, Rudolf 02000
Gamsjäger, Siegfried 02377
Gamwell, Lynn 41701
Gamzatova, Patimat Saidovna 32995, 32996
Gancarski, Jan 31736
Gančev, Rumjan 04805
Gandee, Cynthia 47942
Gandhi, K.M. 22015
Gandhi, M. 21946, 22059
Gandino, Guido 23986
Gandioso, Carmen Roman 04561
Gandolfi, Dr. Lia 24369
Gandon, Gérard 10285
Ganebnaja, Nina Evgenjevna 32766
Gangi, Sabine 15149
Gangkofner, M. 20781
Gangloff, Deborah 42819
Gangloff, Roland 43258
Gangwere, Stanley K. 42937
Ganiev, A. 48851
Ganijon, Alijonov 48843
Ganino, Luigi 22901
Gannett, Michael R. 42640
Gannon, Thomas 43001
Ganozova, Radoslava 04838
Ganpat, Ganesh 42162
Gansohr-Meinel, Dr. Heidi 16246
Gansz, Kevin 47646
Gantenberg, Anette 19178
Gantner, Bernard 12150
Gantner, Ellen 48598
Gantner, Dr. Hildegard 36880
Gantt, Judy M. 41347
Gantzert-Castrillo, Erich 18842, 18842
Ganz, James A. 48634
Ganzelewski, Dr. Michael 16193
Ganzer, Dr. Gilberto 25007
Ganzkow, Martin 17822
Ganzoni, Ursina 37154
Gappmayer, Helga 02286
Gappmayer, Sam 41331
Garami, Erika 21328
Garanne Modise, Rogoff 03939
Garaudy, Roger 34735
Garavaglia, Gianluigi 23693
Garavaglia, Dr. Giuseppe 24369
Garay, Nora Cecilia 07371
Garbarini Islas, Dr. Guillermo 00244
Garbe, Dr. Detlef 17553
Garbes, Pam 30190
Garbutt, Kirstie 38201
Garcia, Denis 15080
Garcia, Elizabeth F. 45043
Garcia, Françoise 10804
García, Joaquín Emilio 07582
Garcia, José 45289
Garcia, Julian 34639
García, Lola 35601
Garcia, Magdalena A. 46150
Garcia, Rene R. 31456
Garcia, Susana 35725
García Arévalo, Manuel Antonio 09128
García de Del Valle, Prof. Delia 48953

García de la Rosa, Ignacio 34938
García-Frias Checa, Carmen 35634
García Limón, Fernando 28337
García López, Dr. J.R. 34984
Garcia-Lorca de los Ríos, Laura 34870
García Martinez, Carlos 35448
García Menárguez, Antonio 34889
García Moreno, Beatriz 07395
García Mota, Francisco 35070
García Muriano, Felipe O. 34600
Garcia-Nakata, Lorraine 47324
Garcia Paz, Dr. Carlota 35442
García Pérez, Fernando 35434
García Rozas, Rosario 35714
García Ruíz, María Esther 27818
García Serrano, Rafael 35534, 35538, 35541, 35542
García Soto, Rubén 31236
García-Tuñon, Guillermo 34847
García Vanegas, Rubén Darío 07522
García Velasco, Francisco 34803
Garcías y Truyols, Joan 34489
Gard, Jean-Michel 36925
Gard, Jean-Noël 10913, 13323, 13631, 13843, 13996, 14000, 14493, 14933, 14934
Gardent, Bruno 12195
Gardi, Dr. Bernhard 36508
Gardi Dupré, Maria Grazia 23807
Gardiner, Mary N. 41296
Gardner, David 01371
Gardner, John 44285
Gardner, Nicki 40916
Gardner jr., William F. 45054
Gardner Begell, Ruth 48173
Gardner Broske, Janet 45888
Gardner-Stilwell, Jill 43380
Garduño Pulido, Blanca 28116, 28167
Garey, Rose 47905
Garfield, Leonard 47540
Garía, Susana 35720
Garibaldi, Dr. Patrizia 23986, 23999
Garibaldi, Dr. Vittoria 24848
Gariboldi, Leopoldo 24559
Garifdžanova, Roza G. 32749
Garimorth, Julia 13548
Garín Llombart, Felipe Vicente 35601
Garín Ortiz de Tarancón, Felipe 35601
Garland, Jeff 43842
Garland, Joan 45073
Garland, Kathleen 44404
Garland, Steve 38269
Garland, Wilma 41294
Garlinski, M. 36745
Garlits, Donald G. 46081
Garmer, Lars 36195
Garncarzová, Hana 08282
Garner, Les 45543
Garner, Sheila 01555
Garnham, Peter 06449, 06450
Garniche, Marie José 12152
Garnier, J.F. 15236
Garnier, Laurent 11301
Garnier, Maurice 13534
Garnier, Nicole 11164
Garrels, Gary 44869
Garret, Patty 42032
Garretson, Stacey 45517
Garrett, Anne 06472
Garrett, Franklin M. 41333
Garrett, Jim 45008
Garrett, Jural J. 44934
Garrido, Emilio M. 31380
Garriga, Francesc 35399
Garrigue, Philippe 14570
Garrison, Elizabeth 46641
Garrity, Lois 06547
Garrity jr, Marilyn 44633
Garrity, Marilyn 44634
Garrott, Martha 46898
Garrut, Dr. J.M. 34532
Garry, William 44369
Garside, Sioux 01509, 01511
Garstenauer, Karl 02499
Garton, Diane 06102
Garua, Marina Prieto 34427
Garuti, Alfonso 23353
Garweg, Udo 20717
Garwood, Pat 44184
Gary, Grace 41306
Garza, Michael A. 43423
Garza Camino, Dr. Mercedes de la 28183
Gasc, Michel 12985
Gasco, Yves 10631
Gascon, France 05633
Gąsior, Stanisław 31883
Gąska, Wiesław 31961
Gaskell, Ivan 42042
Gaskin, Vivienne 39040
Gaspar, Burghard 01792
Gaspar, Filorena 32229
Gaspari, Prof. Gianmarco 24405
Gaspari, Kristin H. 48537
Gašparović, Miroslav 07834
Gasperment, Dr. Philippe 14540
Gasquet, Comtesse de 14857
Gass, Monika 17784
Gassen, Dr. Richard W. 18523
Gasser, Dr. Christoph 23552
Gasser, Ferdinand 23553

Gasset y Salafranca, Josep M. 34965
Gaßner, Prof. Hubertus 16959
Gast, Dr. Otto 19139
Gastal, Ney 04279
Gastaut, Amélie 13563
Gaston, Elizabeth 45370
Gastou, François-Régis 14942
Gateau, Fabienne 12576
Gateau, Laurence 13328
Gatellier, Michel 11774
Gately, Barbara 42538
Gatenbröcker, Dr. Silke 16297
Gates, Andrea 46367
Gates, Charles 41397
Gates, Daphnea 30187
Gates, Jay 48389
Gates, Jim 42620
Gates, Merryn 00699
Gates, Michael 40798
Gates, Pat 40478
Gates, Sue 41045
Gates, William 42590
Gatewood, Bill 44825
Gatti, Dr. Sandra 24780
Gattineau-Sterr, Dr. Susanne 18895
Gatzweiler, Wilfried 16241
Gau, Sönke 37407
Gaubert, Philippe 12232
Gaudencio de Germani, Marta 00217
Gaudet-Blavignac, Richard 36642
Gaudichon, Bruno 14044
Gaudio, Jennifer 45011
Gaudio, Linda 41568
Gaudlitz, Winfried 19787
Gaudnek, Prof. Dr. Walter 15469
Gaudzinski, Dr. Sabine 18606
Gaudzinski, Prof. Dr. Sabine 19086
Gauffin, Sten 36146
Gaugele, Roland 17319
Gaughran, Gerard 47710
Gauhar, Hasan 31054
Gaul, Roland 27549
Gauley, Sherrie 46149
Gaulke, Dr. Karsten 18024
Gault, Sam 38497
Gaulupeau, Yves 14056
Gaumé, Jean-Charles 13185
Gaurilius, K.K. 27538
Gausling, Helga 15401
Gauss, Dr. Ulrike 20106
Gaustad, Randi 30741
Gauthier, Jacques A. 45698
Gautier, Irène 13089
Gautier, Jean 03755
Gautier, Sandra K. 34227
Gautschi, Karl 36971
Gautschin, Hanspeter 36609
Gavagan, Mary 39416
gavin, Glenda 48011
Gavin, John 42297
Gavín Moya, Julio 35351
Gaviria, Alba 07443
Gavish, Galia 22640
Gavran, Dr. Ignacije 03930
Gavranic, Cynthia 37373
Gavranic, Cynthia 37397
Gavrilaki, Eirini 20915
Gavrilova, Marija Jurjevna 33216
Gavrilović, Miladin 33921
Gay, Hebe Dina 00297
Gay, Millicent 46977
Gay, Pierre-Raymond 11344
Gayler, Billie Sue 48102
Gazda, Elaine K. 41218, 41218
Gazzaway, Ofiera 48747
Gealt, Adelheid M. 41746
Gear, Emily T. 47781
Gear, Dr. Gilian 39575
Gearan, Donald 43623
Gearinger, Robert E. 43529
Geary, Adam 39362
Gebhardt, Hans 15843
Gebhardt, Matt 46909, 46910
Gebhardt, Dr. Rainer 15496
Gebhardt, Dr. Ute 18003
Gebühr, Dr. Michael 19793
Geddes, Jim 30166
Geden, Dennis 06019
Gedeon, Lucinda H. 46747
Gee, Christina M. 39679
Gee, Rosalyn 40659
Gee, Rosalyn P. 40661
Geeraerts, Liene 03734
Geerdinck, J.J.M. 29540
Geeroms, Luc 03125
Geerts, Dr. T. 29240
Geeslin, Phyllis 44234
Gefahun, Dr. Abebe 09402
Geft, Liebe 44942
Gehlfuß, Gundula 16725
Gehör, Dr. Seppo 09894
Gehri, Emil 36782, 36783
Gehrig, Bruno 36569
Gehrig, Elisabeth 15532
Gehrmann, Lucas 02914
Gehrmann, Rudi 16189
Gehrt, Gertrude 41152
Geibig, Dr. Alfred 16483
Geidner, Oskar 20656

Geier, Bob 46099, 46100
Geiger 19196
Geiger, H. 18242, 18243, 18244
Geiger, Hans 20382
Geiger, Maurice 13743
Geiger, Michael 02154
Geiger, R. 17193
Geiges, Michael 37391
Geigle, R. 15755
Geil, Bernd 18287
Geir, Reinhard 02903
Geiser, Alain 36643, 36644
Geiser, Anne 36865
Geisler, David A. 45563
Geisler, John 45563
Geißel, Helmut 20601
Geisser, Hans 36465
Geissl, Gerhard 03017
Geißler, G. 19502
Geissler, Josef 02362
Geißler, Ramona 19609
Geist, Dr. Joseph E. 43306
Gelao, Clara 23029
Gelburd, Dr. Gail 44708
Geldenhuys, M. 34188
Geldin, Sherri 42593
Gelfer-Jørgensen, Mirjam 08927
Gélinas, Cécile 06441
Gelius, Dr. William 08952
Gelszinnis, Hans Joachim 19634
Gelzer, Bev 45961
Gemmell, Michael 06493
Gemmingen, Freiherr von 17630
Gencer, Necdet 37735
Gencsi, Zoltán 21433
Gendre, Cathérine 15144
Gendron, Christian 13343, 13345, 13346
Generali, Genevieve 42489
Genev, Hristo 04697
Genger, Angela 16734
Genod, Jean-Claude 36864
Genorio, Rado 34124
Gens, María L. Alonso 35142
Genschow, Cäcilia 19443
Gentele, Glen P. 47126
Gentet, M.A. 37088
Gentile, Dr. Gerardo 24866
Gentile, Mannie 43759
Gentili, Lamberto 25622, 25626
Gentilini, Dr. Anna Rosa 23753
Gentis, Thierry 41906
Gentle, Bill 42298, 42964, 43373
Gentry, Dr. Johnnie L. 43308
Gentry, Marsha 45188
Gentry, Vicki 45018
Geoffroy, Pierre 14900, 14901
Geominy, Dr. Wilfred 16225
Geoppa, Judith 42782
Georg, Rolf 19989
George, Dave 47246
George, Hardy 46118
George, Kerrianne 01512
George, M.R. 01170
George, Prof. Ron 40760
George, Sarah B. 47235
George, Tamsen E. 41826
Georgel, Chantal 13596
Georgel, Pierre 13632
Georges, Joseph 36793
Georges, Sonia 37074
Georgescu, Valeriu 32547
Georget, Luc 12862
Georghiades, A. 08198
Georghiou, G. 08198
Georgia, Karamitrou 21035
Georgia, Olivia 47787
Georgieva, Elene 04651
Georgieva, Tanička 04806
Georgieva, Teodora 04924
Georgsson, Agust 21637
Geppert, K. 19691, 19692
Gerace, Gloria 44906
Geraci, Ester 23628
Gérard, Peter 20479
Gérard, Raphaël 10949
Gerasimčuk, Olga 33464
Gerasimidi, Elena Ivanovna 32666
Gerbauckas, Maryanne 48536
Gerber, Bruno 36654
Gerber, Daniel 36756
Gerber, Jan 42687
Gerber, Olive 47591
Gerber, Dr. Peter R. 37416
Gerber, Theodore 41799
Gercke, Hans 17666
Gerdur-Gunnardóttir, Gudny 21648
Gereau, Rebecca 43692
Gerena, Victor M. 32406
Gergely, Dr. Katalin 21342
Gergen, Rich 46498
Gerhards, Dr. Eva 17105
Gerhardt, Barbara 36587
Gerhardt, E. Alvin 43802
Gerhardt, Dr. Gunther 20383
Gerharz, Michael 19484
Gerhold-Knittel, Dr. Elke 20115
Gerichhausen, Heinz 20419
Gerini, Fiorenzo 22833
Gerke, Lucien 03829

Gerlach, Murney 46726
Gerlach, Walter 16554
Germain, P. 11573
Germann, Joachim 17531
Germann, Philip 46759
Germann-Bauer, Dr. Peter 19524, 19526, 19529
Germano, Anna 25905
Germiny, Comte Gabriel de 13827
Gerner, Dr. Cornelia 15994
Gerner, Dr. Joachim 20260
Gerold, Alfons 37170
Gerrard, Jane 40361
Gerrietts, Frank 41565
Gershon, Stacey 45780
Gertjejansen, Doyle 45723
Gertsch, Fritz 36868
Gertsch, Liliane 37090
Gervais, Alex 04974
Gervais, Louise 42731
Gesemann, Dr. Björn 18606
Gęsicki, Waldemar 31510
Gesing, Dr. Martin 15865
Gesquière, Dominique 12445, 12923
Gessener, Andrew 45791
Gesser, Susanne 17055, 17058
Gessie, Dwight 06544
Gessl, Paul 02156
Gestin, Jean-Pierre 14470
Gestsson, Magnús 21627
Gestwicki, Theone 42635
Getchell, Katherine 41817
Gether, Christian 08906
Getman, Z.D. 33454
Getson, Ralph 05788
Gettinger, Maria 02155
Gettler, Peter 19249
Geurts, Joe 05484, 06076
Geus, Prof. Dr. Armin 19017
Geuze, M.A. 29819
Gevas, Sophia 43262
Gewald, A. 29095
Geyer, Prof. Dr. A. 17937, 17949
Geyer, Jeannette 34259
Geyer, Dr. Roderich 02744, 02747
Gfeller, Claude 36889
Gfeller, Irma E. 44802
Ghaeni, Farzaneh 22287
Ghandgar, J. 22283
Gharrity, Mary Lou 45340
Gherardi, Dr. Pierluigi 24911
Ghesquières, L.-E. 12602
Ghez, Prof. Claude 36754
Ghez, Susanne 42360
Ghiara, Prof. Maria Rosaria 24607
Ghidini, Elena 24655, 24656
Ghini, Dr. Giuseppina 24613
Ghiorsi-Hart, Carol 47657
Ghiron, Yves 12785
Ghisalberti, Annie 00890
Ghiță, Ioana 32478
Ghoniem, Atef 09269
Ghorbani, M. 22333
Ghoshroy, Kajal 44658
Giacomini, Dr. Giovanni 23412
Giacomini, Dr. Pietro 23562
Giaimo, Catherine L. 46426
Giaj, Ezio 24930
Giamarchi, Paulette 12256
Giambuti, Lia 26018
Giampaolo, Francesca 24191
Gianadda, Léonard 36924, 36927, 36928
Gianaroli, Onofrio 23141
Gianelli, Ida 25131
Gianelli, Sarah 45789
Gianfranco, Armando 23190
Giannasi, Dr. D. 41319
Giannetti, Prof. Antonio 25122, 25123, 25128
Giannetti, Elio 24701
Gianni, Dr. Ginsberti 23124
Gianora, Giulietta 37160
Giarmoleo, Giuseppe 25235
Gibavic, Annette 44719
Gibb Roff, Samantha 43207
Gibbon, Richard 40966
Gibbon, Wilda V. 06490
Gibbons, Cindy 06219
Gibbons, Michael L. 41451
Gibbs, Gail 05703
Gibbs, Ivor 40347
Gibbs, Judith 41454
Gibbs, Margaret 43134
Gibbs, Marie 22536
Gibbs, Roger 44564
Gibbs, Vivienne W. 06597
Gibert-Balboni, Françoise 15009
Gibson, Charlotte 48067
Gibson, Hilda 40849
Gibson, John 40064
Gibson, Keith E. 44763, 45716
Gibson, Ken 45074
Gibson, Ralph 48613
Gibson Garvey, Susan 05550
Gică, Secție-Băeștean 32586
Giebelhaus, L. 06703
Gieben, Servus 25224
Gielen, J.K. 29369
Gier, Dr. Helmut 15551, 15568
Gier, Dr. Klaus 17527

Gieschen, Margarete 17307
Giese, Dr. Dale F. 47630
Giesen, Sebastian 17536
Giesenschlag, Bill 42031
Giesler, Dr. Jochen 16246
Giesler, Dr. Ulrike 18166
Giezendanner, Heini 36455
Giffault, Michèle 10467
Gifford, P. 40603
Gigandet, Eric 37047
Giglierano, Geoff 45856
Giglio, Alessia 36900
Giglio, Alessio 36617
Gigou, Laure 12545, 13724
Giguet, Aurore 44674
Gil, Dr. Euzebiusz 31744
Gil de los Reyes, Soledad 34680
Gil de Prado, Eva 34941
Gil Imaz, Maria Cristina 35727
Gilardi Polar, Hernando 07388
Gilbert, Abby 46412
Gilbert, André 06212
Gilbert, Barbara 44943
Gilbert, Chris 42905
Gilbert, David 40345
Gilbert, Glen L. 46646
Gilbert, Rendal B. 48131
Gilbert, Sylvie 05909
Gilbertson, Elsa 41064
Gilbertson, Laurann 42839
Gilchrist, Angela 48391
Gilchrist, Dr. Ellen 46080
Gilchrist, Rod 47314
Gilder, T.J. 39014
Giles, Laura 46703
Giles, Mel 05401
Giles, Nicole 38916
Giles, Sue 38351
Gilfillan, Richard M. 48499
Gilg, Karen 41389
Gilhaus, Dr. Ulrike 16666
Gili, Dr. Antonio 36903
Gill, B. 30104
Gill, Cecil 45296
Gill, John 39605
Gill, Peter 01295
Gill, Stephen J. 27496
Gill, T. D. 38089
Gillatt, V. 01382
Gillcrest, Christopher H. 45257
Gille, Martha 28769
Gille, Prof. Dr. P. 18884
Gillerist, Christopher 48213
Gilles, Dr. Karl-Josef 20212
Gilles, Matthieu 11633
Gillespie, Gordon 46707
Gillespie, Margaret 42408
Gillespie, Maria 38276
Gillespie, Marilyn 44670
Gillespie, Rosemarie G. 41642
Gillespie, Sarah 22398
Gillespie, Shane 22477
Gillett, Marnie 47335
Gillette, Dr. David D. 43329
Gilliam, Georgen 45598
Gilliam-Beckett, Elizabeth 44420, 44767
Gilliand, Michel 36480
Gillies, A. 40870
Gillies, Rachel 30282
Gillioz, Jean-Maximin 36815
Gillis, Jean 47386
Gillis, Nancy S. 41490
Gillis, Stuart 39132
Gillman, Derek 46439
Gillow, Norah 39808
Gilman, Robert G. 43985
Gilmore, Jerry 41834
Gilmore-House, Gloria 44885
Gilmour, J.A. 40131
Gilmour, K. 39399
Gilmour, Rosemary 38559, 38562
Gilpin, Deborah J. 41062
Gilpin, Melinda 45162
Giltaij, J. 29759
Gimborn, C.H. von 16859
Gimenez, Carmen 45872
Giménez Carrazana, Dr. Manuel 03905, 03906, 03907
Ginalski, Jerzy 31966
Ginette, Eric 42023
Ginger, Greg 41597
Gingerich, Jim 47865
Gini, John 44357
Ginlund, Hans 09422
Ginnever, J. 38329
Ginter, Donald W. 45994
Ginton, Ellen 22775
Gioacchini, Delfo 24697
Giobbi, Maria Paola 22954
Giombini, Dr. L. 23581
Gion, Alois 46830
Gionio, Maria Teresa 24417
Giordano, Prof. Christian 36712
Giordano, Claudio 23334
Giorgetti, Pia 36899
Giorgi, Dr. Angelo 23197
Giorgi, Dr. Marisa 25231
Giorolano, Fabris 25808
Giovanna 25159

Giovanni, Ferrini 37189
Giovetti, Dr. Paola 23109
Giovine, Dr. Francesco Paolo 25903
Gips, Terry 42522
Giradeau, Ted 05178
Girard, Alain 10565, 10566, 13817, 13818, 15229
Girard, Benoît 37027
Girard, Hélène 05024
Girard, Robert 06207
Girardin, Daniel 36863
Giraud, Milou 13689
Giraudy, Daniele 12846
Girgenti, Cecilia 00136
Girić, Milorad 33845
Giroir Luckett, Jeannie 46587
Gironde, Herberto 00265
Girouard, Terry 42542
Girousse, Laurent 10653
Giroux, Patrice 06143
Girsberger, Jürg 36672
Girst, Roswitha 17054
Girvan-Brown, Chris 01035
Gisbert Santonja, Josep Antoni 34771
Gisep, Claudio 37030
Gish, William 48167
Gisler, H. 37175
Gisler-Jauch, Dr. Rolf 36447
Gittelman, Steve 42169
Giubilei, Dr. Maria Flora 23978, 24005, 24014
Giudice, Rosa Maria 24763
Giuliani, Prof. Dr. Luca 18882
Giuliano, Prof. Carlo 25733
Giuliano, Dr. Laura 25231
Giuntini, Trey 45245
Giurescu, Dinu C. 32470
Giuricco, Judith 45876
Giusti, Dr. Annamaria 23863
Givnish, Gerry 46438
Gizatulin, Marat R. 33298
Gjedsted, Kirsten 08967, 08968, 08969
Gjerdi, Trond 30758
Gjipali, Ilir 00037
Gjmacan 35522
Gjurašin, Hrvoje 07777
Gjurinovic Canevaro, Pedro 31204
Gladiß, Dr. Almut von 16054
Gladstone, Prof. M. 21746
Gladwin, Jim 42852
Gläser, Dr. Manfred 18544
Gläßel, Adolf 20372
Glaister, Jane 39327
Glaizot, Dr. Olivier 36859
Glanzer, Harvey W. 46856
Glanzer, Michelle 41933
Glaser, Prof. Dr. Franz 01882, 02127, 02205
Glaser-Schnabel, Dr. Silvia 19139
Glasgow, Istiharoh 44892
Glass, Brent D. 43214, 48014
Glass, Dorothy F. 45784
Glass, Frank 06285
Glass, Jennifer 43473
Glass, Patrice 42259
Glassel, Jim 43360
Glasser, Susan 46878
Glasser, W. 01527, 01528
Glassman, Elizabeth 42367
Glassman, Susan 46462
Glassner, Prof. Dr. Gottfried 02292
Glasson, Michael 40774
Glaubinger, Jane 42466
Glauser, Daniel 37091
Glauser, Lori 06875
Glavočić, Daina 07760
Glaw, Dr. F. 18926
Glaz, Kazimir 06616
Glaze, George 41730
Gleason, Catherine 43210
Gleaton, Henry 45645
Gleaton, Sonja 45645
Gleeson, Elizabeth 00977, 01276
Gleffe, Waltraud 15494
Gleichenstein, Elisabeth von 18206
Gleirscher, Dr. Paul 02127
Gleissner, Stephen 48610
Gleixner, Johann 20336
Gleizer, Raquel 04542
Glenholme, Ian 39453
Glenn, Constance W. 44858
Glenn, Sherrian 44607
Glevenko, Elena Jurjevna 33417
Glick, Dr. Shmuel 22661
Glimme, Dr. Hans Peter 16850
Gliozheni, Lorenc 00027
Glistak, John 01417
Gliszczyńska, Elżbieta 31476
Glock, Walter 19606
Glocker, Dr. Jürgen 16251, 17371, 19747
Glöckner, Prof. Harry 02857
Gloor, Dr. Lukas 37410
Gloria, Dr. Heidi K. 31325
Gloria, Rogelia 31354
Gloßner, F.X. 19045
Glósz, Dr. József 21565
Glot, Claudine 11383
Gloudemans, M. 29654
Glover, Jack 47887
Glover, Lynn 46627
Glover, Mike 40269
Glover, Sarah Elizabeth 05064

Glover, Thomas 43880
Gluchova, Tatjana Vladimirovna 32837
Gluck, Daniel 45844
Gluck Steinberg, Judith 45756
Glüber, Dr. Wolfgang 16541
Glückert, Ewald 18453
Glueckert, Stephen 45403
Glüsing, Dr. Jutta 17011
Glušenkova, Ljudmila Nikolaevna 32707
Gluskova, Marina 32921
Glusstein, Bruno 36714
Glutting, Keith 45784
Glynn, Kathleen D. 46862
Gmelch, Christa 19579
Gnecco, Prof. María Julia 00573
Gnidovec, Dale 42591
Gnilšak, Ida 34142
Go, Sugil 27149
Gobbi, Elmar 24350, 24352
Gobel, Mary 44376
Goble, Rebecca 42835
Gockel-Böhner, Christoph 19337
Gockerell, Dr. Nina 18833, 20076
Gockov, Ilija 34450
Gócsáné-Móró, Csilla 21591
Gocz, Teodor 32062
Godart, Freddy 03366
Godbout, Dominique 05709
Goddard, Stephen 44686
Godefroy, Hubert 14327
Godelet, Andre 03512
Godfrey, Gerard 40780
Godfrey, Honor 39810
Godfrey, Judith 41053
Godfrey, Stephen J. 47665
Godkin, David 39729
Godlewska, Mirosława 31989
Godoli, Antonio 23840
Godoy, Arnaldo Augusto 03987
Godoy, José 36743
Godoy Muñoz, Maria Antonieta 21262
Godwin, Mary 40241
Godwin, Sharon 06548
Goebel, Susanne 15418, 15419, 15422
Göbel, Prof. Dr. Dr. Ulf 16083
Goebl, Dr. Renate 02993
Göçmen, Ali Bülent 37810
Goedicke, Dr. Christian 49213
Gökten, Serdar 37614
Göldner, Andrea 20488
Göller, Luitgar 15804
Görcke, Bärbel 19069
Göres, Dr. Burkhardt 16007, 16090, 16091, 16092, 19266, 19437
Görgner, Ernst 16579
Goerke-Shrode, Sabine 48173
Görlich, Manfred 03003
Görner, Dr. Irina 18033
Görner, Klaus 17067
Goertzen, Peggy 44024
Goertzen, Peter 05519
Goes, B.R. 28895
Goes, Dr. Georg 15828
Goess-Enzenberg, Ulrich Graf 02087
Goessen, J. 29574
Gößwald, Udo 16064
Göthberg, Elisabeth 36091
Goethert, Dr. Klaus-Peter 20211
Goethert-Polascheck, Dr. Karin 20212
Götte, Dr. Gisela 16332, 19063
Götz, Matthias 36510
Götz, Dr. Norbert 18880
Götz, Rudolf 37298
Goetz, Scott 47701
Götz, Dr. Ulrike 17122
Götze, Barbara 16117
Götze, Dr. Bettina 19493
Götze, Dr. Jürgen 01644
Goetze, Lisel 43216
Götze, Robby Joachim 17299
Goetzman, Richard 44263
Goff, Alex P. 43063
Goff, Nick 40835
Goffe, Gwendolyn H. 44129
Goffman Cutler, Judy 45928
Goheen, Marion 46854
Golay, Laurent 36864
Golay, Muriel 37163
Golbin, Pamela 13556
Gold, Dr. Helmut 17065
Gold, Ruth C. 47848
Gold Levi, Vicki 41365
Goldbacher, Alexandra 02839
Goldberg, Beth 47374
Goldberg, Beverly 48151
Goldberg, Elizabeth 47569
Goldberg, Marsea 44935
Goldberg, Shalom 41768
Golden, Jacqueline 40197
Golden, Julia 44927
Golden, Rorey 45777
Golden, Thelma 45877
Goldenkova, Vera Anatoljevna 33502
Goldfinger, I. 22595
Goldfinger, Yaffa 22775
Goldfuhs, Ingeborg 01788
Goldin, Rafael 30739
Golding, Norman 30243
Goldman, Debra 45887

Goldman, Martin 48401
Goldman, Stephen M. 47171
Goldman, Steven 46189
Goldnagl, Friedrich 01765
Goldner, Cheri 45896
Goldner, George R. 45833
Goldovski, Dr. Boris 33101
Goldsmith, A. 40579
Goldsmith, Cynthia A. 45985
Goldsmith, Jeremy 40578
Goldsmith, John 39277
Goldsmith, Robert B. 45802
Goldstein, Ann 44930
Goldstein, Carolyn 44983
Goldstein, G. 45887
Goldstein, Gabriel M. 45887
Goldstein, Lisa 43183
Goldstein, Sid 47134
Goldwasser, Edwin 48377
Goley, Mary Anne 48353
Golf, Anamani 44318, 44319
Golinelli, Jean 15110
Golinski, Dr. Hans Günter 16198, 17633, 17635, 17636, 17638
Goll, Jürg 36622, 36970
Goll, Dr. Jürg 37276
Gollberg, Maralee 41281
Golloway, Zoe C. 46757
Gollwitzer, Horst 19139
Golofast, Larisa 37902
Gologranc Zakonjšek, Bronislava 34089
Golonka, Jan 31548
Golovčenko, Ljudmila 37902
Golshan, J. 22304
Goltz, R. von der 16035
Gołubiew, Zofiasz 31715
Golz, Dr. Jochen 20459
Gomá Lanzón, Javier 35007
Gombert, Florence 12599
Gomel, Luc 13340
Gomendio Kindelán, Montserrat 35045
de Menezes Gomes, Geraldo 04523
Gomes, José Antonio Alves 04189
Gomes, Maryann 39900
Gomes de Pinho, António 32335
Gomes Leite, Gisélia Antonia 04433, 04434
Gómez, Arley 07507
Gomez, Carla 47417
Gómez, Carlo Humberto 07409
Gomez, Nadine 11514
Gómez, Roque Manuel 00447, 00541, 00542
Gomez, Victor 43111
Gómez Arnanz, Miguel 34509
Gómez Ayvilera, Fernando 35519
Gómez Hildawa, Isidro 31384
Gómez Hildawa, Sid 31411
Gómez Macías, Juan Antonio 35390
Gomig, Dr. Leo 01768
Gomozkova, Marina 33057
Mendes Gonçalves, Maria Arlete 04364
Gončarova, Elena Alekseevna 32825
Goncerut Estèbe, Véronique 36726
Goncharov, Kathleen 42047
Gong, Stephen 41649
Gonos, Arthur 43484
Gonschior, Dr. Hannelore 18831
Gonseth, Marc-Olivier 36985
Gonyea, Ray 44217
Gonzaga Bastidas Ortíz, Rodrigo 07479
Gonzalas, Fabian 48334
Gonzales, Ben 31408
Gonzales, Gil 43556
Gonzales, Michael E. 46110
Gonzales Baldoui, Mariano 35704
Gonzales-Belleza, Erlinda 31340
Gonzalez, Arturo Gonzalez 28368
González, Aurelio 34944
Gonzalez, Christine 11789
González, Jaime 07601
González, Jorge 07381, 07389
Gonzalez, Dr. Juan G. 32376
Gonzalez, Julieta 44914
Gonzalez, Manuel 45780
González, Milagros 48914
Gonzalez, Sylvie 14180
González Antón, Rafael 35413
Gonzalez Azcoaga, Miguel Fernando 00322
González Cevallos, María A. 00166
González Cristóbal, Margarita 35058
González de Amezúa, Mercedes 35027
Gonzalez de Durana, Javier 35694
González de León, Antonio 28115
González de Santiago, Ignacio María 34631
González Entidad, María Inocencia 07580
González González, Ignacio 28509
González Gozalo, Dr. Elvira 34801
González-Hontoria y Allendesalazar, Guadalupe 35017
González Lorente, Margarita 07923
González Padrón, Antonio María 35521
González Parra, Samuel 07374
González Penagos, Claudio 07363
González Pons, Esteban 34911
González Rodríguez, Rosalía 34928
Gonzalo Andrade, Luis 07612
Good, Les 38351

Good, Liz 45736
Good, Patricia 44773
Goodale, Thomas 43240
Goodband, Lara 40969
Goodchild, Anne 40484
Goode, Barb 04970
Goode, Dr. David 06503
Goode, Mack 45817
Goode, Rita 39082
Goodell, Steve 48401
Goodend, Olivia 40903
Goodger, Margaret 38417
Goodin, Kitty 44367
Gooding, Brian 39509
Gooding, Janda 01363
Goodlett, Chris 44968
Goodman, A. 05113
Goodman, Barbara 44294
Goodman, Carl 41307
Goodman, Norman 40863
Goodman, Susan 45821
Goodman, Wallace 48001
Goodrich, Dr. James W. 42554
Goodridge, Janet 39236
Goodridge, W. 40657
Goodsell, Leo J. 41654
Goodwin, John 43188, 43190
Goodwin, Marsi 46367
Goodwin, Murray 30163
Goodwin, Robert 45706
Goodwin, Sue 47662
Goodwinl, Patricia 45586
Goody, Dick 46933
Goodyear jr., Frank H. 46476
Goodyear, Hal E. 48486
Goolsby, Elwin L. 47601
Goos, D. 16382
Goossens, Dr. E.J.H.P. 28869
Goossens, Gerda 03842
Gor-Arie, D. 22727
Gorbenko, Anatolij Aleksandrovič 32668
Gorbey, Ken 30311
Gorbunova, Eleonora Grigorjevna 32828
Gorczyca, Krzyštof 31814
Gorczynski, Bohdan 42358
Gordenker, Emilie 38898
Gordon, Alec 38780
Gordon, Alexander 38078
Gordon, B. 34218
Gordon, David 45366
Gordon, Dr. Dillian 39729
Gordon, Don 06420
Gordon, Donnarae 46840
Gordon, Lindsay 37941
Gordon, Nick 39464
Gordon, Stanley 48292
Gordon-Smith, Peter 38740
Gorduza, Victor 32434
Gordy, Christopher M. 42833
Gordy Edwards, Esther 42933
Goren, Dr. M. 22777
Goren, Nili 22775
Goreta, Aleksandra 07713
Goretti, Ndayarinze M. 04944
Gorewitz, Shalom 45077
Gorham, Linda 41445
Gorham, Marilyn R. 44785
Gori, Beatrice 23464, 23465
Gorini, Prof. Giovanni 24736
Gorini Esmeraldo, Eugênia 04515
Gorjão, Sérgio 32322, 32323, 32324
Gorka, Steffi 16900
Gorman, Jill 41599
Gorman, Dr. Martyn 37932
Gorman, N. 01356
Gormley, John 48077
Gormley, Nina Z. 47712
Gormsen, Gudrun 09061
Gorny, Dagmar 19337
Goroch, Tansija Vladimirovna 33619
Gorochov, Vladimir Aleksandrovič 32966
Gorodnij, Aleksandr Ivanovič 33696
Gorove, Margaret 46238
Gorroño de Crespo, Maria del Carmen 00384
Gorschlüter, Peter 16731
Gorski, Michelle D. 48439
Górski, Mirosław 31667
Gorski, Stefan 31822
Gorsline, Marie 10962
Gosden, Dr. Chris 40153
Goshen, R. 22690
Goshow, Nancy 45835
Gosse, Rita 47575
Gosselin, Claude 05899
Gossy, Reinhard 02581
Gostick, Misha 05887
Gostisha, Don 41151
Gostwick, Martin 38671
Goswami, Raj Ratna 21984
Goswamy, Samares 21901
Gotcher, Jack 41369
Gotgelf, Lev K. 32635
Goto, Hidehiko 26992
Gottfried, Claudia 19496
Gottfried, Heinz 02324
Gottfried, Dr. Michael 43054
Gotthardt, Ruth 02955
Gottlieb, Jaromir 08388
Gottlieb, Paul 45774

Gottschalk, Dr. Jack W. 41433
Gottskálksdóttir, Júliana 21653
Gou Vernet, Assumpta 35667
Gouble, Philippe 11456
Goudry, Gail 05111
Goudy, David 46041
Gough, David 42928
Gough, Joan 00876
Gouinguenet, Hélène 10389
Goujat, Bérangère 10393
Goulaine, Marquis de 11998
Goulandris, Niki Angelos 21015
Gould, Alac 48802
Gould, Alec 44316
Gould, Claudia 46420
Gould, Jonathan H. 48501
Gould, Marilyn 48672
Gould, Richard 46843
Gould, William 43713
Goulden, M.R.R. 39203
Goulding, Kathleen 46724
Goumand, Bruno 12895
Gounarie, Dr. Emmanuela 21189
Gourcuff, Isabelle de 11147
Gourdin, Michel 03233
Gouriotis, G. 21044
Gouriotis, Lena 21042
Gourley, Hugh J. 48447
Gout, Jacques 11226
Goutayer, Virginie 11336
Goutorche, Christian 11482
Gouveia, Tiago Patricio 32247
Gouy-Gilbert, Cécile 12315
Govan, Michael 41552, 45793
Gove, Domingos Zefanias 28727
Gover, Isabel H. 41432
Gowdy, Marjorie E. 41696
Gowing, Laura 43251
Goycea, Ana Maria 00394
Gozani, Tal 44943
Gozdowski, Krzysztof 32011
Gozzi, Dr. Fausto 23472, 23474
Graaf, D.Th. de 29569
Graaf, F.M. de 30016
Graas, Lucette 03182
Grabar, Olga 37902
Grąbczewski, Wiktoryn 32121
Grabensberger, Dr. Peter 01933
Graber, Claudia 36546
Graber, Cleon 43548
Grabert, Walter 17455
Grabher, Gerhard 01746
Grabka, Dr. Marion 16540
Grabner, Adolf 01962
Grabner, Dr. Sabine 02953
Grabow, Astrid 16588
Grabowska, Genowefa 31955
Grabowska-Chałka, Janina 32036
Grabowski, Dr. Jörn 16117
Graça, Filipe 32345
Grachos, Louis 47433
Gradin, Eva 36054
Gradova, Dina Aleksandrovna 33389
Gradwohl, Hans 01718
Graefe, Frank 20106
Graells, Eulàlia 34532
Grämiger, Hans 37097
Graen, Dr. Monika 19332, 19337, 19340
Graepler, Dr. Daniel 17340
Gräser, Dr. 20508
Grässlin, Karola 16298
Graeve-Ingelmann, Dr. Inka 18832
Graf, Andre 36918
Graf, Dr. Angela 17560
Graf, Prof. Dr. Bernhard 16006
Graf, Bernhard 37063
Graf, Brigitte 16106
Graf, Felix 37394
Graf, Dr. Rudolf 36446
Graf, Ulrich 17672
Graf, Werner 36611
Grafenauer, Michael 01693
Graff, Allison 42654, 42655
Graff, Elizabeth 43866
Graff, Nicholas 47073
Graff, Terry 06400
Graffagnino, J. Kevin 43509
Graffam, Olive 48344
Grafton, Duke of 40696
Graham, Lady 40003
Graham, Angela 40606
Graham, Barry 39630
Graham, Douglass J.M. 47456
Graham, Fiona 39468
Graham, J. 38927
Graham, Sir James 40003
Graham, John 01429
Graham, John R. 45042
Graham, Kenneth 22542
Graham, Michael S. 45690
Graham, Sir Peter 37937
Graham, Dr. Rusell W. 42887
Graham, Shelby 47410
Graham, Tom 42206
Graham LeBlanc 05198
Graham Lee, Jean 45694
Graham Wade, Karen 42415
Grahammer, Veronika 18916
Grahn, Göran 36286

Grahn, Martin 38643
Grai, K. 40891
Gralter, Margaret 39694
Gram, Dr. Magdelena 36269
Gramatikov, Georgi 04641
Gramatikov, Jančo 04783
Gramer, Kevin 42879, 42890
Gramm, Jean-Jacques 37066
Grammenos, Dr. D. 21179
Grams, Greg 48257
Grančarov, Michail 04767, 04770, 04771
Grančarova, Kamelia 04626
Grand, Stanley I. 42096
Grandchamp, Gilbert 36948
Grande, Prof. Nuno 32344
Grande, Prof. Dr. Nuno 32344
Grander, Johann 02090
Grandidier, Daniel 14187
Grandjean, Gilles 13496
Grandmont, Jean-François 05710
Grandrud, Dr. Reba 42962
Grange, Bill 38716
Grangé, Claire 10272
Grange, Sylvie 11095, 11097
Granger, Brenda 43091
Granier, Jean-Marie 13627
Granitto, Andrew 48774
Granitz, Gerhard 02319
Grannan, Jill 42923
Grannis, Sue Ellen 45208
Granomont, Josée 06643
Granqvist, Eirik 09952, 14065
Grant, A.E. 38007
Grant, Anne 01390
Grant, Bronwyn 30239
Grant, Elinah 03937
Grant, Elizabeth 38120
Grant, Frank F. 05754
Grant, Gillian 30093, 30094
Grant, Hugh 42902
Grant, J. 38064
Grant, Laurence 05536, 05537, 38043
Grant, Rachel 39074
Grant, Richard 42572
Grant Morrisey, Marena 46188
Grantčarov, Michail 04677
Granville, Lee Z. 47653
Granville, Sharon 40080
Grape-Albers, Dr. Heide 17607, 17607
Grapin, Claude 10290
Grasberger-Lorenz, H. 20409
Graskoski, Debra 46035
Grasmann, Lambert 20322
Grasmug, Dr. Rudolf 01827
Grass, Yasmin 00708
Grasse, Carola 16854
Grasse, Marie-Christine 11917, 11922, 11923
Grassegger, Karl 02681
Grasselli, Margaret Morgan 48373
Grassetti, Jessica 42669
Grassi, Dr. Renzo 25573
Graßmann, Dr. A. 18543
Grassmayr, Johannes 02066
Grasso, Giacomo 23997
Graswinkel, J. 29078
Gratacós Teixidor, Georgina 34528
Grate, Steve 44945
Grattan, Patricia 06340
Gratte, Stan 01573
Gratvol, Eran 22716
Gratz, Dr. Reinhard 02533
Gratzer, Heinz 02945
Grau, Prof. Dr. Jürke 18836
Grau, Salvador 35671
Grau Lobo, Luís A. 34948, 34949
Graudina, Anna 46976
Grauer, Michael R. 42092
Graumlich, Anne 48211
Grauwiller-Straub, Kathrin 36877
Grave, Marion 40748
Gravel, Mabel 05048
Graves, Tolley 44735
Graves-Brown, Carolyn 40657
Gray, Alan 30241
Gray, Dr. Anna 00886
Gray, Bonnie 05808
Gray, Campbell B. 46734
Gray, Ian 05173
Gray, John 30287
Gray, John L. 44891
Gray, Les 01148
Gray, Michael 39408
Gray, Muriel 01148
Gray, Peter 01439, 40078, 40270
Gray, Richard 38622
Gray, Sam 46132
Gray, Sarah 38046
Gray, Dr. Sharon R. 47763
Gray, Susan Inskeep 43260
Gray, Xanthi 46047
Graybill, Maribeth 41222
Grayburn, Patricia 39139
Graze, Sue 41413
Grąziewicz-Chludzińska, Barbara 32148
Graziola, Claudio 24899
Grazzini, Patricia J. 45391
Grbic, M. 29818
Greaves, Debbie 40688
Greaves, Kerry 48222

Grébert, Eliane 14525
Grečenko, Ljudmila Pavlovna 32957
Grech, Frances 27710
Gredler, Martin 02538
Grédy, Jean 36889
Greeff, I.B. 34203
Green, Cheryl 45850
Green, Chris 38173, 40371, 40375, 40379
Green, Dr. D. 39894
Green, E. 39493
Green, Erica 00716
Green, Eveleth 43150
Green, James 40266
Green, John F. 47719
Green, Jonathan 46917
Green, Linda 47753
Green, Lisa 00797
Green, Louise 47599
Green, Nancy 44272
Green, Richard 40969
Green, R.M. 01321
Green, Dr. William 41615
Green, William Davis 47038
Green, Dr. William E. 42092
Greenbaum, Elizabeth R. 41751
Greenberg, Joel 47476
Greenberg, Judy A. 48365
Greene, A. Wilson 46374
Greene, Joseph A. 42043
Greene, Lynda 46552
Greene, Marilyn 39659
Greene, Rose Mary 46841
Greene, Virginia 46460
Greener, Peter 38036
Greenfield, Mark S. 44948
Greenfield, Prof. Susan 39708
Greenhill, John 40683
Greenhow, Dr. Desna 38391
Greenlee, Hal 42661
Greenlee, Nina 45161
Greenlee, Sandy 42577
Greeno, Judy 06744
Greenough, Sarah 48373
Greensted, Mary 38484
Greenwald, LouAnne 48531
Greenway, Lord 40045
Greenwood, E.F. 39520
Greenwood, Gail 00707
Greenwood, Mike 40488
Greenwood, Tom 44449
Greer, Alberta 46940
Greer, Connie 45284
Greer, Judy 46792
Greer, Kim E. 47216
Greer, Rina 06620
Greer, William 46591
Greff, Ken 47530
Greff, Pierre 14813
Greffrath, Dr. Bettina 20658, 20660, 20663
Grefstad, Ola 30943, 30943
Gregersen, Bo 09050
Gregersen, Thomas 42864
Gregg, David 41906
Gregg, David W. 48570
Gregg, Rosalie 42837
Gregl, Dr. Zoran 07809
Gregoire, Jean 10385
Gregoor, Yves 28909
Gregori i Berenguer, Joan 35613
Gregors, Tommy 41082
Gregory, Gail 06610
Gregory, Joseph 41646
Gregory, Linda 32410
Gregory, Susan 41644
Gregory, Tabitha 48179
Gregson, Brian 01081
Greguski, Eva 47830
Greif, B. 16509
Greiff, Dr. Susanne 18606
Greig, John 38678
Greimel, Susanne 02549
Grein, Gerd J. 19330
Greinwald, Dr. Elisabeth 01698
Greisenegger, Dr. Vana 02963
Grelier, Joseph 14307
Grella, Consalvo 22989
Grellier, Gérard 12416
Gremillet, E. 14854
Grenda, Edward 05677
Grenis, Dr. Michael 41699
Grenon, Prof. Ernesto A. 00621
Grenter, Steve 40944
Grenville, John H. 05673
Grépier, Gabriel 11496
Greppi, Graciela B. 00524
Grepstad, Ottar 30570
Greschny, Nicolaï 12838
Greuter, Prof. W. 15925
Greve, Jürgen 17576
Grever, T.F. 28879
Grewenig, Dr. Meinrad Maria 20328
Grexa, Dr. Susanne 16025
Grezinger, August 18472
Gribble, Michael 30204
Gribbon, Deborah 44913
Grice, Jean 38308
Gricenko, Vladimir Petrovič 33624
Grider, George 42779
Griebel, Dr. Rolf 18831

Griebl, Monika 02933
Griebler, Reinhold 02508
Grieder, Susanne 36552
Griepink, Dr. B. 29702
Grieshofer, Prof. Dr. Franz 02117, 02960, 02982
Grießmair, Dr. Hans 23221, 23262
Griff, Hanna 45796
Griffeuille, Marie F. 14254
Griffeuille, Marie-Françoise 14252
Griffin, Dale 41369
Griffin, Dave 42884
Griffin, David J. 22433
Griffin, Elizabeth P. 44131
Griffin, Jennifer 42968
Griffin, Jonathan 38973
Griffin, Kjerstin 30877
Griffin, O.T. 39498
Griffis, Larry L. 44806
Griffith, Lee Ellen 43547
Griffith, William 46239
Griffiths, A. 39586
Griffiths, Bill 39962
Griffiths, Caitlin 40879
Griffiths, David 08312
Griffiths, D.F. 39547
Griffiths, Dr. G. 38353
Griffiths, Jayne 38322
Griffiths, Jean 38620
Griffiths, Mary 39904
Griffiths, Pauline 40001
Griffiths, Peter 40089
Griffiths, R. John 40264
Griffo, Dr. Alessandra 22922
Griffo, Dr. Pietro 24429
Griggs, David W. 42112
Griggs, K. 01220
Grignon, Prof. Georges 15078
Grigo, Dr. M. 18139
Grigorian, Anelka 00692
Grigorian, Prof. Dr. Gurgen G. 33174
Grigorova, Emiliya 04672
Grigsby, Roger 42635
Gril, Cajetán 02522
Grimaldi, Dr. David 45759
Grimaldi, Floriano 24215, 24216
Grimaldi, Gloria 21303
Grimaud, Patricia 13317
Grimes, John 47198
Grimm, Albert 37302
Grimm, Dr. Alfred 18915
Grimm, Dr. Eric 47737
Grimm, Prof. Dr. Günter 20211
Grimm, Monika 18769
Grimm, Tess C. 43246
Grimmer, Dietgard 02537
Grimod, Dr. Ivana 25311
Grimpe, Rusty 48105
Grimsrud, Halvard 30795
Grinage, Jeanine 41085
Grinbaum, Blanche 11278
Grinell, Sheila 46473
Grinenko, Lucy 37902
Griner, Robert F. 46901
Grinëv, Nikolaj N. 33680
Gringmuth-Dallmer, Prof. Dr. Eike 16059
Grinnell, Debbie 45600
Gripenberg, M. 09439
Grisebach, Dr. Lucius 19156
Grišina, Ekaterina Vasiljevna 33335
Grissom, Don 45024
Grissom, Joi 47588
Griswold, Sarah 48729
Gritt, Stephen 06084
Grjaznova, Ann 33338, 33453
Groat, John 45714
Grob, Dr. B.W.J. 29521
Grobler, I. 34377
Groce, Prof. Aldo A. 00607
Groce, Dr. W. Todd 47479
Grodskova, Tamara 33504
Grodwohl, Marc 15026
Grodzicki, Prof. Andrzej 32177
Gröbl, Dr. Lydia 02918
Gröger, Walter 02174
Groen, Ir.B. 28928
Groen, M.F. 29757
Grönbold, Dr. Günter 18831
Groenendijk, Drs. G.H. 29079
Groenendyk, Ed 46208
Groeneveld, A. 29779
Groeneveld, A.C. 29807
Groenewald, A. 34188
Groenewald, M. 34298
Groenewold, Rod 48255
Groenewoud, G.J.M.M. 29113
Grönholm, Kirsti 09496
Gróf, József 21456
Groff, John M. 46464
Groft, Tammis K. 41083
Groh, Dr. Klaus 16781
Groiß, Dr. Albert 01661
Groleau, Michel 06321
Gromer, Kim 47975
Gromova, Ljudmila Ivanovna 33420
Grondman, Dr. A.C.M. 29144, 29382, 30084
Gronenborn, Dr. Detlev 18606
Gronert, Dr. Stefan 16242
Grøngaard Jeppesen, Torben 08775, 09005, 09006, 09009, 09010, 09011

Groninga, Janet 41051
Grønn Iversen, Trine 30720
Gronne, Claus 08944
Grønnegaard, Torben 09012
Gronning, Norman 47577
Grønvold, Ulf 30726
Groom, Gloria 42304
Groom, Simon 39529
Groos, Dr. Ulrike 16731
Grooss, Dr. K.S. 29521
Groot, E. de 29759
Groot, J.P. de 29318
Groot, Rolf de 19188
Grooth, Dr. M. de 29564
Grootveld, Cor 28906
Grootveld, Robert W. 46813
Grootveld-Parrée, C. 29748
Gros, C. 36745
Gros, Dr. Patrick 02545
Grosboll, Sue 42151
Groschner, Dr. Gabriele 02548
Grosfeld, Dr. J.F. 29020
Groß, Hans Kurt 02188
Gross, Jennifer 45700
Groß, Klaus M. 19610
Gross, Miriam 45778
Gross, Renee 45778
Groß, Thea 18672
Grosshans, Dr. Rainald 15974
Grossi, George 46367
Großkinsky, Dr. Manfred 17049
Grossman, Cissy 45787
Grossman, David J. 42529
Grossman, Grace Cohen 44943
Grossman, Richard 41824
Grossmann, Elisabeth 37378
Großmann, Prof. Dr. G. Ulrich 19139, 19140, 19158
Grossmann, Robert 14807
Grosspietsch, J. 20128
Grøtan, Geir A. 30700
Grote, Dr. Dietmar 19282
Grote, Dr. Hans-Henning 20654
Grote, Dr. Udo 18934, 18935, 20730
Grothe, Hans 16753
Grotkamp-Schepers, Dr. Barbara 19984
Grotz, Helmut 20308
Grove, David 47125
Grover, Ruth 42261
Groves, Bonnie Sue 42958
Grower, Steve 00879
Grozdanić, Nadežda 33904
Grozin, Vladimir 33058
Gruat, Philippe 12306, 13150
Grub, Adolf 16166
Grubb, Tom 43311
Grubbauer, Alfred 01670
Grube, Walter 18958
Gruben, Eva-Maria 16735, 16736
Gruber, Erich 02073
Gruber, F. 02173
Gruber, Franz 01938, 01961
Gruber, Dr. Gabriele 16541
Gruber, Dr. Gerlinde 02918
Gruber, Herbert 01742
Gruber, Dr. Herbert 16758
Gruber, Petra 19358
Gruber, Rosina 01960
Gruber, Sabine 20090
Gruber, Thilo 18392
Gruber, Wolfgang 01752
Grubessi, Prof. Dr. Odino 25215
Grubler, Mitchell 43354
Grubola, Prof. James 44960
Grubola, James 44973
Grudzinska, M. 16723
Grüger, Dr. Andreas 20074
Grün, Hans 18842, 18842
Gründel, Dr. Winfried 16452
Gründig, Rita 17521
Grünwald, Karin 18581
Grünwald, Manfred 02457
Grünwald, Prof. Michael 01861
Grünzweil, K. 40084
Grütter, Daniel 37132
Gruetzmacher, Mark 47945
Gruetzner, Sara Jane 05166
Gruffydd, Alun 38138, 39550
Gruhs, Ernie 05605
Grujić, Dragana 33824
Grunaugh, Darlene 47591
Grunberg, Evelina 04295
Grund, Dr. Rainer 16698
Grundnig, Christine 02131
Grundschober, Dr. Franz 02941
Grunenberg, Christoph 39529
Grunewald, Curtis 47468
Grunz, Karin 15959, 15963
Grupe, Prof. Dr. Gisela 18826
Grusman, V.M. 33478
Gruzdeva, Tatjana Aleksandrovna 33568
Grygiel, Prof. Ryszard 31768
Grynszpan, Anna 31625
Grynsztejn, Madeleine 47339
Grys, Dr. Iwona 32126
Gryspeert, Hans 03461
Grzechca-Mohr, Dr. Ursula 17074
Grzegorczyk, Dr. Detlef 18951
Grzesiak, Marion 44340
Grześkowiak, Andrzej 31607

Grzymkowski, Andrzej 31810
Gschwantler, Dr. Kurt 02877, 02918
Gschwendtner, Stefan 02241
Gstrein, Josef 02055
Guadarrama Guevara, Jorge 28132
Gualdoni, Flaminio 25895
Guardiola, Juan 34552
Guarino, Dr. Ariberto 25240
Guarnieri, M. Chiara 23750
Guati Rojo, Prof. Alfredo 28189
Guay, Serge 06142
Guayasamín, Pablo 09208
Gubb, A.A. 34237
Gubčevskaja, Ljudmila Aleksandrovna 33553
Gubel, Eric 03337
Gubin, V.V. 33051
Gudde, Irene 45649
Gudmundsdottir, Anna Lísa 21648
Gudmundson, Per 35882
Gudnadóttir, Kristin 21652
Gudnason, Thorarinn 21635
Gue, Robin 47625
Gügel, Dominik 37092
Gül, Sebahat 37710
Guelbert de Rosenthal, Eva 00451
Güler, Ali 37613
Güler, M. Güven 37717
Güllüoğlu, F. Nevin 37778
Guenat, François 37029
Günaydin, Celal 37657
Gündogdu, Veysel 37654
Gündüz, Yaşar 37752
Guenette, Irene 06505
Guennec, Aude Le 11300
Günter, Werner 19216
Güntert, Prof. Dr. Marcel 36547
Günther, Albert J. 16807
Guenther, Bruce 46641
Günther, Clas 36240
Günther, Michael 18204
Günther, Rolf 17125
Günther, Dr. Sigrid 01802
Guenther, Todd 44632
Günzler, Lilo 17052
Guerbabi, Ali 00078
Guerber, Steve 41774
Guerci, Prof. Antonio 23995
Guerdy Lissade, Joseph 21296
Guerin, Charles A. 48095
Guerin, Kerry 01346
Guermont, Mauricette 14455
Guerra, Yolanda 07621
Guerra Pizòn, Olga 09177
Guerrero, Doris 07451
Guerrero, Javier 47294
Guerrero Alvarez, Guillermo 07553
Guerreschi, Prof. Antonio 25531
Guerri, Dr. Roberto 24396, 24399, 24401
Gürtler, Dr. Eleonore 02082
Gürtler, Dr. W. 01806
Guest, Fiona 38012, 39341
Guest, P. 38431
Guest, Raechel 48427
Gueury, Marie-Claire 03572, 03582
Guevara Hernández, Jorge 28518
Güzel, Selahattin 37679
Guffee, Eddie 46540
Guffee, Patti 46540
Gugelberger, Rachel 45885
Guggeis, Karin 18916
Guggenberger, Hans 02153
Gugger, Beat 37150
Gugole, Jean 13137
Guhl, Klaus 36661
Guibal, Jean 10382
Guichard, Christiane 14359
Guichard, Marie-Claire 12059
Guichard, Vincent 13064
Guichaumon, Jean-Louis 12809
Guichon, Françoise 10259, 10260
Guidon, Suzanne 11414
Guidotti, Prof. Francesco 24349
Guidotti, Nives 23235
Guidry, Keith 46169
Guiducci, Dr. Anna Maria 25578
Guiffre, Florence 43361
Guigo, Elsa 13548
Guihaumé, Antoine 14362
Guilardian, D. 03308
Guilbaud, Laurence 15117
Guilbert, Manon 05484
Guilbride, Kurt 05714
Guild, John 47782, 47790
Guilhot, Jean-Olivier 11644
Guillard, Alain 12638
Guillaut, Laurent 10996
Guillemin, Daniel 10411, 11977
Guillemin, Jean-Claude 10691
Guillemot, Hélène 12380
Guillén Jiménez, Marilú 28576
Guillerme, Lucienne 13199
Guillermo, Joseph 31274
Guilliem Arroyo, Salvador 28150
Guillot-Chene, G. 11681
Guimarães, Prof. Dr. Edi Mendes 03999
Guinid, Rosario 31338
Guinn, Kevin 44062
Guinness, Alison 43211
Guinness, Robert 22543

Guion, Jacques 14171
Guiotto, Prof. Dr. Mario 25639
Guisolan, Dr. M. 37216
Guiver, Pam 38319
Gulbina, Anna Alekseevna 33707
Gulbrandson, Alvhild 30644
Guldemond, J. 29759
Guljaev, Vladimir Andreevič 33183
Gullickson, Nancy 42995
Gullsvåg, Per Morten 30981
Gulyes, Andreas 02959
Gumă, Nicoleta 32488
Gumerman, George J. 48082
Gumpert, Lynn 45809
Gunarsa, Dr. Nyoman 22148
Gunby, Stephen G. 42575
Gundel, Dr. Marc 17691, 17692
Gunder, Jacques 12509, 12510
Gunderson, Catherine F. 06401
Gunderson, Dan 42814
Gunderson, Robert A. 44200
Gundlach, Prof. F.C. 17546
Gundler, Dr. Bettina 18840
Gundry, Beverly F. 43897
Gunér, Tullan 35997, 35998, 36001
Gunjić, Ranko 07699
Gunn, Lorna 05650, 05654
Gunn, Robert 46252
Gunnarsson, Ann-Marie 35882
Gunnarsson, Torsten 36265
Gunning, Judy 01459
Gunnlaugsdóttir, Elin 21621
Gunter, Kristen C. 44604
Gunther, Minette 42518
Gunther, Paul 45858
Gunther, Uwe 34361
Guo, Xingjian 07029
Guohua, Gu 07186
Gupta, Chitta Ranjandas 21731
Gupta, Preeti 43355
Gupta, Dr. Vibha 22061
Gupta, V.N. 21887
Guralnik, Nehama 22775
Guratzsch, Prof. Dr. Herwig 16396, 17410, 19794, 19797
Gurba, Norma 44616, 44617
Gurevič, Dr. E. 33140
Gurgel, Felizardo Jesus 00091
Gurkina, Tatjana Aleksandrovna 33005
Gurley, Diana 05038
Gurney, Helen 39234
Gurney, Marilyn 05555
Gurney-Pringle, Chantal 00750
Guse, Ann 45211
Gusel, Erich 02186, 02188
Gusenleitner, Fritz 02228
Gusev, Vladimir 33407, 33408
Gushulak, Ruth 05429
Gust, Donald F. 41596
Gustafson, Donna 42497
Gustafson, Elaine D. 47946
Gustafson, James 44794
Gustafson, Sharon 44783
Gustafsson, Harry 05112
Gustafsson, Malin 35912
Gustafsson Ekberg, Kent 35815
Gustavson, Carrie 41714
Gustavson, Todd 46941
Gustavsson, Karin 35949
Gustavsson, Lars-Åke 35949
Gut, Andreas 16834
Gut, Ursula 37141
Gut, Werner 37253
Gutbrod, Dr. Helga 19008
Gutek, Dr. František 33952
Guth-Dreyfus, Dr. Katia 36501
Guthier, Mark 45074
Guthman, Howard 43278
Guthrie, Alyce N. 43659, 43660
Guthrie, C. Gay 06054
Guthrie, Giles 39877
Guthrie, Jeanne 42032
Guțică-Florescu, Laurențiu 32597, 32598
Gutiérrez, Marisa 47053
Gutiérrez, Guillermo Giraldo 07512
Gutiérrez, José A. 00189
Gutiérrez Alba, D. Julio 35488
Gutiérrez Campos, Yolanda Milagros 08176
Gutiérrez Carcia, Inés 07994
Gutiérrez Coto, Fernando 07650
Gutiérrez García, María Angeles 35147
Gutiérrez Jodar, Ricard 34541
Gutiérrez Salamanca, Carlos Julio 07526
Gutierrez-Solana, Carlos 41948
Gutiérrez Velásquez, Amado 07440
Gutker de Geus, Sven E. 29692
Gutman, Kevel Jane 42981
Gutmann, Gabriela 02844
Gutmann, Dr. Veronika 36499, 36500, 36500, 36513
Guttormsen, Sissel 30941
Guy, Dr. A. 39728
Guy, Frances 38564
Guy, Grant 06817
Guy, Troger 02947
Guye, Francis 37089
Guyonneau, Olivier 12208
Guzman, Antonio 15053
Guzmán, Manuel Gil 28130
Guzzi, B. Anthony 44003

Guzzo, Enrico Maria 25970
Guzzo, Prof. Pietro Giovanni 23402, 23737, 24987, 25769
Gvišiani, G.M. 15360
Gwan, Pak Yong 27125
Gwara, Czesław 31986
Gwarda, Zofia 32005
Gwiazda, Bronisław 31886
Gwilim, Ian 37927
Gwyn, Brenda 45165
Gye, Peggy 39917
Gyger, Patrick 37353
Gyger, R. 37280
Gyllenberg Pernevi, Bodil 35919
Gyllenhaal, C. Edward 41976
Gyllkrans, Monika 36325
Györe, Pál 21305
Gysin, Jacques 36975, 36977
Gyula, Dr. Ernyey 21357
Haag, Olinde S. 45745
Haag, Dr. Sabine 02918
Haagen Pictet, Loa 36748
Haak, Dr. Bill 43700
Haakanson, Sven 44524
Haakestad, Jorunn 30427
Haaland, Anders 30426
Haamer, Kaia 09368
Haan, David de 39309
Haan, Maartje de 29112
Haan, Drs. Peter de 29911
Haapala, Anu 10201
Haar, Frauke von der 18776
Haas, Gordon 43258
Haas, Prof. Dr. Helmuth 02870
Haas, James R. 42846, 42847, 42848
Haas, Josef 08333
Haas, Dr. Richard 15945
Haas, Ruth 48659
Haas, Sabine 18301
Haas, Dr. U. 18208
Haase, Prof. Dr. Claus-Peter 16054
Haase, Dr. Evelin 16305
Haase, Werner 20702
Haavaldsen, Per 30877
Habartova, Dr. Romana 08698
Habditch, Max 39853
Habecker, Dr. Eugene B. 45803
Habegger, Dr. Ueli 36916
Haberhauer, Günther 15769, 15770, 15773
Haberman, Patty 45270, 47974
Habermann, Dr. Sylvia 15846
Habermann, Yvonne 19720
Habersatter, Dr. Thomas 02548
Haberstroh, Sarah 45360, 45373
Habes, Scott 42523
Habibi, Mohammed 28705, 28712
Habrich, Prof. Dr. Dr. Christa 17906
Hachet, Michel 14924
Hachmer, Hendrik 29926
Hack, Angelica 16452
Hack, Dr. C. 29422
Hack, Janice 44586
Hack, Shery N. 42083
Hackenburg, Randy 42106
Hacker, Deannaopher 41400
Hackett, Brian 42803
Hackett, I. O. M. 40114
Hackett, Phoebe 47427
Hackford, Clive 38725
Hackhofer, Wilhelm 02559
Hackl, Prof. Dr. A. 02807
Hackler, Cornelia 19894
Hackman, John 10125
Hacksley, Malcolm 34221
Hacksley, M.M. 34251
Hackstein, Hermann 17479
Haddad, Regina Clélia 04577
Hadders, Rieks 28852
Haddington, Earl of 39096
Haddock, Brent 46692
Haddow, Carol 38600, 39988
Hadjicosti, Dr. M. 08198
Hadjisavvas, Dr. Sophocles 08190, 08201, 08208, 08210
Hadjistephanou, Prof. Costas E. 08194
Hadjusarnas, S. 08189
Hadland, Brian 06190
Hadley, Diana 48082
Hadley, V.J. 38647
Haduch, Henryka 31474
Haeck, Jules 03419
Häcki, Iren 37375
Haedo, Dr. José Antonio 00584
Häffner, Martin 20218
Häfliger, Pius 36444
Häfliger, Toni 36906
Hägele, U. 16593
Häggman, Gunvor 09882
Häggström, Stig 09462, 09625
Haenel, Johanna 01705
Haenel, Dr. Matthias 18831
Hänggi, Dr. Ambros 36514
Hänggi, Dr. Christoph 37158
Hänggi, René 36592
Haenlein, Dr. Carl 17598
Hänsel, Dr. Alix 16059
Hänsel, Dr. Volker 02738
Häring, Dr. Friedhelm 17278, 17279, 17281, 17284
Haese, Jürgen 17300

Häßler, Dr. Hans-Jürgen 17607
Häuser, Dr. Christoph 20105
Häußler, Theodor 15583
Hafenecker, Ingo 16765
Haffenden, Peter 01212
Haffner, Dr. Marianne 37402
Haffner, Z. 21421
Hafner, Dr. Mark S. 41532
Hafok, Barbara 02993
Hagan, Annemarie 05868, 05870
Hagan, Marylee 47985, 47987
Hagberg, Magnus 35806
Hagdorn, Dr. Hans 17898
Hagedorn Olsen, Claus 08897
Hagedorn-Saupe, Monika 16006
Hagemeier, Anna Mae 47803
Hagen, Dr. Bettina 02886
Hagen, Dr. Harold H. 47521
Hagen, Inga 16586
Hagen, John 43869
Hagen, Rien 28852
Hagen, Werner 02195
Hagendorfer, Dr. Johann 02035
Hager, Franz 02278
Hager, H. 34258
Hager, Joan DiChristina 42389
Hager, Joyce 45558
Hager, Dr. Michael W. 47295
Hagerup, Asbjørn 30701
Haggart, M.W. 05827
Hagler, James 43434
Hagloch, Jenny 47207
Hagnau, Dr. Carola 18163
Hagström, Lars 36038
Hagström, Torkel 35916
Hahling, Albert 36440
Hahn, Dr. Andreas 16227
Hahn, Prof. Dr. Dietbert 20703
Hahn, Gabriele 01818
Hahn, Dr. Klaus-Dieter 16979
Hahn, Dr. Sylvia 17121
Hahn Pedersen, Morten 08808
Hahnenberg, Tom 45536
Hahnl, Prof. Dr. Adolf 02283
Haider, Adolf 03063, 03064
Haider, Prof. Gertrude 02736
Haider, Johann 03035
Haigh, Brian 38127, 38728
Haigh, Louise 01281
Haight, Pete 48692
Haiko, Pertti 09773
Haile, Priscilla F. 47880
Hailey, Dabney 48495
Hain, Dr. Beatrix 02993
Hainard, Jacques 36985
Haindl, Dominik 01679
Haine, Heiko 16827
Haine, Prof. Dr. Malou 03317
Haine, Malou 03337
Haines, Jeniffer 41375
Hainfellner, Gerhard 02723
Haininger, Robert 01721
Hair, Denny G. 44125
Hair, Julia 43923
Haja, Simion 32625
Hajdamach, Charles 39245, 40616
Hajdamach, Charles R. 38782
Hajduk, Stjepan 07798
Hájek, A. 08604
Hájíček, Dr. Jaroslav 33985
Hakamata, Akihiro 26179
Hakasalo, Kalevi 09839, 09840
Hake, Helga 19396
Hakenjos, Dr. Bernd 16727, 16741
Hakes, Jay E. 41353
Hakobyan, Lilit 00679
Halamish, Uzi 22694
Halbgebauer, Peter 02886
Halbreich, Kathy 45394
Haldemann, Dr. Anita 36505
Haldemann, Dr. Matthias 37426
Halder, Dr. U. 36427
Haldimann, Marc-André 36743
Haldner, Bruno 36510
Haldo, Soeren 30650
Haldy, Lanny 41163
Hale, Donald G. 46475
Hale, J.K. 39212
Hale, Pat 43008
Hale, Dr. Stephen 47792
Halén, Widar 30741
Halevy, Maya 22626
Haley, Helen 06475
Haley, Jeanette 42191
Halfpenny, Geoff 48651
Halilagić, Rasim 33838
Hall, Alan 01577
Hall, Alma 48721
Hall, Anne M. 47344
Hall, Brian 38402
Hall, Charles W. 44136
Hall, D. 40914
Hall, Dale 46384
Hall, Doug 01459
Hall, Eli 30940
Hall, Gail 44754
Hall, Herbert 46658
Hall, Jenny 38128
Hall, Jim 43417

Hall, Mark 40185, 45197
Hall, Marlene 42058
Hall, Melissa 40020
Hall, Michael D. 42691
Hall, Mike 45564
Hall, M.J. 40022
Hall, Nancy 48678
Hall, Peter J. 34278
Hall, Philip 40164
Hall, Robert 39272
Hall, Robin 39923
Hall, Russell J. 42106
Hall, Tim 48683
Hall-Dodd, Jean 44293
Hall-Patton, Mark P. 43991
Hallam, Doug 06418
Hallan, Knut Christian 30749
Hallas-Murula, Karin 09357
Hallatt, Kim 46476
Hallberg, Sara 46076
Halldorsson, Gudni 21639, 21640
Hallé, Antoinette 14739
Hallen, Phillip 43250
Haller, Prof. Dr. Heinrich 37359
Haller, Dr. Kerstin 16337
Haller, Dr. Klaus 18831
Haller, P. 15409
Hallett, Bob 06074
Hallett, Vic 40699
Hallgrimsdóttir, Margrét 21647
Halliday, Tom 41166
Halliwell, Richard 40782
Hallin, Jens 08892
Halling, Finn 30868
Hallman, Charles V. 48154
Hallman, Christina 36267
Hallmanns, Dieter 17895
Hallmark, Dr. Donald P. 47736
Hallock, Robert 42685
Hallonová, K. 34079
Hallová, Dr. Markéta 08432, 08495, 08595
Halls, E.J. 38167
Hally, Dr. D.J. 41319
Halma, Sidney 45945
Halmágyi, Dr. Pál 21467, 21468
Halmová, Dr. Mária 34022, 34024
Halonen, Maija-Liisa 10069
Halota, Marianna 31721
Halouzková, Marcela 08733
Halsey Gardiner, Margaret 45832
Halstead, Graham 38222
Halter, Marc 12037
Halusa, Gerhard 02959
Ham, Jenny 45816
Ham, Mrs. Robert 43205
Hama, Atsushi 26127
Hamacher, Werner 16946
Hamada, Naotsugu 26736
Hamada, Dr. Takashi 26360
Hamann, Dr. Klaus 17588
Hamann, Dr. Matthias 19139
Hamano, Tokuei 26743
Hamans, Dr. P. 29872
Hamberger, Heike 18118
Hamblin, Edward L. 41678
Hambolu, Dr. M.O. 30354
Hambrecht, Dr. Rainer 15816
Hamed, Dr. Dawi Musa 35770
Hamed, Mohammed 35766
Hamel, W.A. 29128
Hamelin, Joël 12100
Hamelmann, Cordula 16619
Hamer, Diana 00517
Hamer, Fritz 42569
Hamer, Linnea 48387
Hamilton, Duke of 39143
Hamilton, Barbara 40185
Hamilton, Betsy 45660
Hamilton, Dan 42753
Hamilton, David 42215
Hamilton, Elaine 30255
Hamilton, Gaye 01242
Hamilton, James 38212
Hamilton, Dr. James 38220
Hamilton, James 38231
Hamilton, Jimmy V. 45236
Hamilton, John 00855
Hamilton, Laura 39042
Hamilton, Lynn 48007
Hamilton, Mary 42100
Hamilton, Mary Ellin 41504
Hamilton, Mort 42207
Hamilton, Olivia 40226
Hamilton, Roy 44900
Hamilton, R.V. 01170
Hamilton, S. 40424
Hamilton, W. 30168
Hamilton-Smith, Katherine 48457
Hamlin, Frank 45919
Hammar, Britta 36060
Hammell, Brian 47654
Hammell, Peter 47461
Hammer, Anders 36073
Hammer, Bettina 16540
Hammer, C. 38537
Hammer, Dr. Karen Elisabeth 19294, 19295, 20680, 20685
Hammer, William R. 46955
Hammerman, Toby 00969

Hammern, Dr. Karen-Elisabeth 20683
Hammerschmidt, Elmar 17921
Hammerschmied, Gerhard 02746
Hammersla, Keith E. 45191
Hammond, Barbara M. 42401
Hammond, Eleanor A. 41841
Hammond, Gary R. 41442
Hammond, Georgina 39116
Hammond, Karen L. 43591
Hammond, Niall 38236
Hammond, Theresa N. 43814
Hammond-Tooke, Prof. W.D. 34275
Hammontree, Nina 45614
Hamoniaux, Jacky 11535
Hamooya, C. 49021
Hamp, Steven K. 42825
Hampshire, Camilla 38957
Hampson, Leslie 39845
Hampson, Louise 40970
Hampton, Jan 30132
Hamraeva, G. 48856
Hamran, Ulf 30390, 30392
Hamre, Harald 30889
Hamrin, Örjan 35882
Hamshere, John 40481, 40486
Hamzabegović, Amra 03925
Hamzaev, A. 48837
Han, Yong 06951
Han Keuk 27155
Hanak, Werner 02903
Hanau, E. 34349
Hanauer, Christine 43739
Hance, Ben 46070
Hanchant, Deanne 01530
Hancock, Robert 46883
Hand, John 48373
Handerson, Dr. Harold 41264
Handler, Jeremy 42483
Handley, Jerry 42578
Handley, Neil 39587
Handley, Pamela 06017
Handlon, Jerry 47496
Handlos, Donald 46851
Handlos, Helga 18477
Hando, Justin 37455
Handy, Ilke 19808
Hanebutt-Benz, Dr. Eva-Maria 18600
Hanejko, Eugeniusz 32047
Hanemann, Dr. Regina 15808, 15815, 15819
Hanemza, Jarett 47037
Hanes, Alice C. 46661, 46665
Hanfstengel, E. 16808
Hangl 20407
Hanhardt, John 45872
Hanhart, Karin 06491
Hanisak, Dr. Dennis 43440
Hank, Jack 42089
Hankel, Lillian 00918
Hankewych, Jaroslaw J. 42368
Hankins, Roger 42792, 48754
Hanley, James 48649
Hanley, Joanne 43300
Hanley, Robin 39370, 39372
Hanley, Theresa 46163
Hanlin, Dr. R. 41319
Hann-Ruff, Stacey 41854
Hanna, Annette Adrian 42903
Hanna, Dan 43172
Hanna, Martha 06071, 06084
Hanna, Rebecca 42390
Hanna, Richard 45854
Hannah, Dr. Michael 30291
Hannay, Rosemary 40166
Hanner, Frank 43366
Hannesen, Dr. Hans Gerhard 15909
Hannibal, Dr. Joseph 42467
Hannick, P. 03182, 03183, 03185
Hanniffy, Constance 22365
Hanniffy, Kieran 22365
Hannula, Betsy 43327
Hannus, L. Adrien 47643
Hanor, Stephanie 44548
Hanreich, Georg 02444, 02446
Hanreich, Liselotte 02444
Hansch, Dr. Wolfgang 17689, 17692
Hansel, Anna-Elisabeth 17426
Hanselman, David S. 43393
Hansen, Arlette 42820
Hansen, Arne 05492
Hansen, Barbara 46696
Hansen, D. 01106
Hansen, David J. 42731
Hansen, David K. 48200
Hansen, Don 46365
Hansen, Dr. Dorothee 16328
Hansen, Emma 42510
Hansen, E.P.H. 03751
Hansen, Eva Maria 46468
Hansen, Frederikke 37407
Hansen, Dr. Harriet M. 08985
Hansen, Jean 46365
Hansen, Jeff 41259
Hansen, Jesper Vang 08949
Hansen, Klaus Georg 21240
Hansen, Larry 43708
Hansen, Maiken 09032, 09095
Hansen, Mogens 08774, 08843, 08844, 08844, 09114
Hansen, Moya 42882

Hansen, Nicola 40450
Hansen, Palle Birk 08987
Hansen, Prof. Pearl 48476
Hansen, Shannon 46590
Hansen, Sidsel 30824
Hansen, Dr. Stephen D. 47639
Hansen, Thor Gunnar 30666
Hansen, Prof. Dr. Dr. Volkmar 16725
Hansen, Wayne 42297
Hansford, Michele 42126
Hansky, Sabine 18839
Hanslok, Andreas 16627
Hanson, Brent 47091
Hanson, Chris 45414
Hanson, Christopher 44459
Hanson, Collen W. 47569
Hanson, Dr. John 44053
Hanson, Justin 47504
Hanson, Lisa 45487
Hanson, Luther D. 43418
Hanson, Stephen 42219
Hanson, Sue 46867
Hanson, William R. 42180, 44384
Hanssen, L.H. 29779
Hanssen-Bauer, Françoise 30746
Hanssens, Marjolaine 03729
Hansson, Hans-Erik 35876
Hanta, Dr. Rajoharison 27607
Hantschmann, Dr. Katharina 18833, 19203
Hanus-Möller, Christl 19767
Hanz, Dr. Günter Martin 19761
Hanzal, Andrea 03001
Hapkemeyer, Andreas 23151
Happe, Michael 17806
Haque, Dr. Enamul 03102
Hara, Toshio 26744, 26855
Harada, Heisaku 26483
Harada, Minoru 26207
Harbert, Dave 41202
Harbige, Sarah 38044
Harbin, Melanie M. 42503
Harboe, Jytte 08961
Harck, Lorraine A. 44566
Hard, John 41085
Hardacre, John 40895
Hardberger, Linda 47255
Harden, Bob 48020
Harden, R. 38118
Harden, Victoria A. 41662
Hardenbrook, Ruth 47774
Harder, H. 29469
Harder, Katie 05329
Harder, Dr. Matthias 17305
Harder, Dr. Ruth E. 37137
Hardiati, Dr. Endang Sri 22124
Hardiman, Thomás 22472
Hardiman, Tom 46652
Hardin, Jennifer 47174
Hardin, Pam 41123
Harding, J.C. 40698
Harding, Keith 40086
Harding, Maureen 48515
Harding, Shelley 06148
Harding-Davis, Elise 04988
Hardingham, Dennis 38826
Hardjonagoro, K.R.T. 22205
Hardman, Dean 48572
Hardman, Genee 47014
Hardman, Robert 42148
Hardmeier, Prof. Dr. Christof 17389
Hardt, Nis 16537
Hardwick, Tommy 05289
Hardy, Anne 40916
Hardy, Channing C. 43133
Hardy, Dr. Florent 41529
Hardy, G.A. 40785
Hardy-Marais, Laurence 12890
Hare, Sandra J.. 44454
Harel, Joram 02916
Harent, Sophie 13241
Hargaden, Mary 45345
Harger, Sara 43514
Harima, Michihiro 26942
Harinen, Dot 06167
Harju, Jouni 09710
Harker, Robert 47590
Harkins, Michael J. 41512
Harleman, Kathleen 41597
Harlen, Willie 47189
Harling, Nick 38242, 38244
Harltow, Harvey 06473
Harman, Elizabeth 44061
Harman, Fred C. 46260
Harman, Robert L.B. 43286
Harmon, Darla 43612
Harmon, Elaine 43384
Harmon, Horace E. 44756
Harmon, Leonard 46012
Harmon, Mark S. 42979
Harmsworth, Lord 39625
Harn, Alan D. 44731
Harnesk, Helena 36361
Harnett, Margaret 41714
Harnly, Marc 44913
Harnoncourt, Anne d' 46442, 46450
Harold, Steve 45112, 48049
Harp, Ann 05170
Harper, Avis 41517
Harper, Mary Kay 46977

Harper, Robert W. 47068
Harper Lee, Laura 41849
Harrauer, Prof. Dr. Hermann 02955, 02970
Harre Hérin, A. 03624
Harreld Love, Josephine 42929
Harrell, Deloris 45127
Harrer, Anton 02291
Harrer, Nicole 02959
Harrewijn, H. 29278
Harriett, Rebecca 43911
Harrington, Beverly 41239
Harrington, Bill 01262
Harrington, Caren Anne 41585
Harrington, Gary 44255
Harrington, Judith A. 48436
Harrington, Katie 43981
Harrington, Lisa 46236
Harrington, Sian 39589
Harris, Adam Duncan 44290
Harris, Amy 41216
Harris, Dr. C. 40153
Harris, Deborah 06560
Harris, Dee 47214
Harris, Dr. E.C. 03885
Harris, Florence E. 47774
Harris, Gene E. 42175
Harris, Harper 44437
Harris, Ivan 06570
Harris, James T. 41501
Harris, Jane 45762
Harris, Jennifer 39904
Harris, Joanna Ruth 45667
Harris, Joe 44022
Harris, Prof. Judith A. 41837
Harris, Kaye 01085
Harris, Mac R. 44659
Harris, Miriam B. 43378
Harris, Nathanial C. 45450
Harris, Neville 30295
Harris, Ottawa 42878
Harris, René 43117
Harris, Rhian 39638
Harris, Richard 40519
Harris, Rosemary 39757
Harris, Sandra L. 44671
Harris, Scott H. 45716
Harris, Sharon 37993
Harris, Tina B. 44321
Harris-Fernandez, Al 47638
Harrison, Betsy 45554
Harrison, Camilla 40966
Harrison, Christina 39991
Harrison, Eunice 40272
Harrison, Harrie 46387
Harrison, Dr. J. 34359
Harrison, Jefferson 45963
Harrison, John 38203, 40725
Harrison, Kathy 43532
Harrison, M. 39520
Harrison, Marie 30273
Harrison, Michael 38457
Harrison, Monica 45073
Harrison, Myra 41935, 41936
Harrison, Stephen 38760, 41348
Harriss, Joan 06527
Harrow, Edward D. 48091
Harsch, René 36471
Harstad, Peter T. 44222
Hart, Brooks 06021
Hart, Karen 44114
Hart, Katherine 43907
Hart, Macy B. 44283
Hart, Myrna 48416
Hart, Nancy 43506
Hart, Peter R. 38833
Hart, Robert L. 44659
Hart, Ron 48199
Hart, Susan E. 48658
Hart, William 47114
Hart Hennessey, Maureen 47820
Harte, Jeremy 38954
Harte, Miriam 38136
Hartenhoff, Nancy 41931
Hartfield, Libby 44281
Harth, Marjorie L. 42419
Harthorn, Sandy 41771
Hartigan, Lynda R. 48392
Hartkopf, Herbert 16779
Hartl, Christa 19357
Hartl, Georg L. 16128
Hartlage, Ken 43837
Hartland, Ian 40705
Hartleb, Silvia Waltraud 03053
Hartleben, Ralph Erik 18906
Hartleib, Dr. Rudolf 17068
Hartley, C. 38454
Hartley, David B. 46484
Hartley, Keith 38916
Hartley, Kristin 47055
Hartman, Bruce 46223
Hartman, C. 34302
Hartman, Janice 41158
Hartman Becker, Heather 44625
Hartmann, Andy 37118
Hartmann, Bonnie 47863
Hartmann, Felix 37118
Hartmann, Joseph 15584, 17000
Hartmann, K. 19647
Hartnigk-Kümmel, Dr. Christa 17992

Harto, Edward S. 45349
Hartshorn, Willis 45817
Hartung, Lee 43696
Hartweger, Hans 02959
Hartwell, Carroll T. 45391
Hartwell, Jane 39711
Hartwich, Bernd 19377
Hartwick, Sue 43365
Hartwig, Laurie 46493
Hartwigsen, Peter Lorenz 19093
Hartz, Jill 42253
Hartz, Susanne 08902
Hartzell, Matthew D. 42869
Hartzold, Susan 41744
Harvey, A.M. 34313
Harvey, Conrad 46557
Harvey, Deborah 47792
Harvey, G.J. 38329
Harvey, Iris 39911
Harvey, Liz 44858
Harvey, M. 40424
Harvey, Paul 42617
Harvey, Phyllis 45871
Harville, Vickie 44999
Harwon, Ipn 00837
Haryu, Tsutomu 26391
Haschke, Walter 02993
Haşdeu, N. Titus 32447
Hasegawa, Koichi 26297
Hasegawa, Mariko 26856
Hasegawa, Sakae 26909
Hasegawa, Takashi 26486
Hasegawa, Tei 26693
Hasegawa, Tokushichi 26315
Hashagen, Joanna 38087
Hashimoto, Akinobu 26095
Hashimoto, Isao 26189
Hashimoto, Masao 26391
Hashimoto, Takeshi 26368
Hashimoto, Tsutomu 26518
Hashimov, Bahodir Djuraevič 48836
Hashitomi, Hiroki 26388
Hashtroodi, A. 22283
Hasitschka, Dr. Peter 02941
Haskell, Barbara 44594
Haskell, Dr. Eric T. 42417
Haskell, Heather 47746, 47747
Haskins, James 43483
Håskoll Haugen, Liv 30601, 30603, 30605
Haslauer, Dr. Elfriede 02918
Haslehner, Hubert 02411
Hasler, Norbert W. 27512, 27516
Hasprunar, Jill 43517
Haß, Heike 17664
Hassan, Mohamed Omar 27107
Hassan, Syed Jamal 21765, 21771
Hassbecker, Egon 17671
Hassdenteufel, Dr. Erwin 18599
Hasse, Dr. Claus-Peter 18581
Hasselbalch, Kurt 42048
Hassen, Carol 48773
Hassinen, Esa 09742
Hassler, Donna 48071
Hassler, Hermann 27517
Hassmann, Dr. Elisabeth 02918
Hassol, Milton D. 45854
Hasson, Janet S. 45612
Hasson, Rachel 22646
Hastaba, Dr. Ellen 02082
Hasted, Rachel 38677
Hastedt, Catherine A. 42526
Hastie, J. Drayton 42223
Hastings, Lord 40462
Hastings, Bill 44828
Hasvold, Carol 42839
Haszprunar, Prof. Dr. Gerhard 18926
Hata, Nobuyuki 26196
Hataguchi, Minoru 26216
Hatchell, Steven J. 42541
Hatcher, Alexandra 06300
Hatcher, Alison 41743
Hatcher, Stephen 38665
Hatcher, V. 40110
Hatfield, P. 38951
Hathaway, Merle 01110
Hathaway, Michael 44568
Hathaway, Nadine 47435
Hathaway, Wesley 43485
Hatibv, H. 37465
Hatoum, Hassan 37442
Hatschek, Christoph 02895
Hatswell, D.A. 38841
Hattam, Edward 01174
Hattingh, J. 34193
Hattori, Gene 42118
Hattrick, Elspeth 39729
Hatzitaki-Kapsomenou, Prof. Ch. 21182
Hau, Hal 44499
Haubold, Prof. Dr. H. 17512
Hauck, Richard 46102
Haudiquet, Annette 12427
Haudot, Charles 12218, 12219
Hauer, Armin 17085
Hauer, Karl 02861
Hauer, Ulrich 17506
Hauff, Rolf Bernhard 17829
Haufschild, Kurt 19929
Haug, Prof. Dr. Andreas 16921
Haug, Dr. Tilman 18883

Hauge, Tore 30679, 30816, 30866
Haugen, Charleen 47002
Hauger, Therese 30485
Haugg, Hans 16438
Hauglid, Anders Ole 30501, 30641
Hauk, Roman 31854
Haumesser, Giselher 17982
Haun, Elizabeth 42719
Haupenthal, Dr. Uwe 19094
Haupt, Eva 18040
Haupt, Dr. Herbert 02918
Hauptmann, Dr. Andreas 16193
Hauptner, Brigitte 02953
Hauregard, Léon J. 03129
Haurie, Michel 13442
Haus, Anny-Claire 14805
Haus, Mary 45886
Hausammann, Hans Peter 37209
Hauschild, Dr. Jan-Christoph 16726
Hausding, Michaela 16688
Hauser, Emil 36810
Hauser, Erin 48273
Hauser, Hans-Jörg 17989
Hauser, Larry 43994
Hauser, Monika 19653
Hauser, Peter 37383
Hauser, Reine 41990
Hauser, Robert 45662
Hauser, Urban 36585
Hauser-Schäublin, Prof. Dr. Brigitta 17342
Hausmann, Dr. A. 18926
Hausmann, Doris 46300
Hauss, M. 12074
Haußmann, Dr. Eberhard 16767
Haussonville, Comte d' 36647
Haussteiner, Franz 01742
Haustein-Bartsch, Dr. Eva 19512
Hauswald, Dr. Kenneth 41287
Haut, Sheryl 42785
Hautekeete, Stefaan 03299
Hauthaway, Elisabeth L. 46560
Havard, Carine 03675
Havas, Sandra H. 46097
Havassy, Péter 21423
Havel, Joseph 44129
Havelund, Jørgen 09031
Havens, Patricia 47636
Havens, Ron 43804
Haveri-Nieminen, Marja-Liisa 10028
Haverkamp, Frode 30746
Haverkamp-Begemann, Egbert 45863
Havlíček, Jaroslav 08656
Havlíčková, Dr. Miloslava 08473
Havron, Rina 22579
Haw, Jane 46309
Hawadi, T. 49030
Hawelka, Dr. Walter 17251
Hawell, Dr. Steve 47529
Hawes, Denise 46333
Hawes, Irene 48142
Hawfield, Michael C. 44068
Hawhsford, Catherine 44145
Hawk, Alan 48378
Hawk, Bob 44244
Hawke, Jenny 34238
Hawke-Smith, Cameron 38450
Hawkes, Juliet 38357
Hawkey, Diane 47973
Hawkins, Del 43228
Hawkins, Lynda 42679
Hawkins, Marilyn 45021
Hawkins, Renee 44879
Hawkins, Dr. Ruth 44359
Hawkins, Dr. Seth C. 47158
Hawkins, Trystan 38284
Hawley, Anne 41811
Hawley, Greg 44409
Hawley, Henry 42466
Hawley, Ken 40707
Hawley, Pam 05437, 05438
Haworth, Brenda 44016
Hawvermale, Hettie G. 41650
Haxhiu, Prof. Dr. Idriz 00035
Haxton, Jason 44503
Hay, Irma 39573
Hay, Malcolm 39740
Hay, Mary 39316
Hay, Susan 46721
Hayashi, Hirotumi 26876
Hayashi, Kiichiro 26263
Hayashi, Masayoshi 27027
Hayashi, Misa 26995
Hayashibara, Ken 26624
Haycock, Dr. Lorna 38726
Hayes, C. Daniel 43255
Hayes, Chuck 46228
Hayes, David 38496
Hayes, Fiona 39059
Hayes, Neila C. 47626
Hayes, Randall 46145
Hayes, Virginia B. 47774
Hayhow, Simon 38995
Haylings, Peter 40926
Hayman, Judy 42984
Hayman, Louise 43085
Haynes, Bruce 05501
Haynes, Carol 44064
Haynes, Jackie 41210
Haynes, John H. 40565

Haynes, Peter 00884, 01529
Haynes, Tom 38960
Haynie, Ron 48408
Hayoz, Roger 36959
Hays, Bonnie 46270
Hays, George W.S. 47205
Haysom, David 40656
Hayter, Stephen 05120
Hayton, Brian 39377
Hayward, Alexander 39307
Hayward, Gardner 44749
Hayward, Merle 44185
Hayward, M.R. 39305
Hayward, Ron 30100
Hayward, Susan P. 40639
Haywood, Dr. C. 22455
Hayworth, P. 40920
Hazelrigg, Scott 41291
Hazelwood, Bevyn L. 42886
Head, Sandra 05121
Headland, R.K. 38461
Headley, Dr. David 46594
Headrick, Dennis 44851
Heady, Karen 46209
Healy, James 44931
Heaman, Ken 05576
Hearn, Brian 46118
Hearn, Redell 44893
Heath, Amie 46826
Heath, Betty 47802
Heath, Hether 06477
Heath, Pat 39404
Heathcote, Richard 01240
Heaton, Alice 41503
Heaume, R.L. 39004
Heaver, Stephen G. 45001
Heazlewood, Brenton 01594
Hebden, M.J. 39122
Heberling, Judith A. 44153
Hebestreit, Dr. Franz 18906
Hebler, Ingo 16379, 16380
Hebron, Victoria 40897
Hebsacker, Friedrich 20243
Hecher, Markus 20198
Hecht, Dr. Winfried 19695, 19696, 19697, 19698
Heck, Brigitte 17991
Heck, Suzanne 44017
Heckenbenner, Dominique 14622
Heckenberg, Dr. Norman 00840
Heckendorf, Kitty 43990
Heckert, Virginia 48538
Heckes, Jürgen 16193
Heckscher, Morrison H. 45833
Hectors, Jan 03409, 03410
Heddon, Gordon 39554
Hedegaard, Esben 09083, 09085, 09086, 09087
Hedel-Samson, Brigitte 10740
Hedelin, Jean-Louis 10483
Heder, Terence 45265
Hedger, Michael 00880
Hedges, Kenneth 47294
Hedin, Marika 36268
Hedin, Svante 36162
Hedinger, Dr. Bärbel 17527, 17547
Hedrick, Nancy 44733
Hee, Lee Hyun 27280
Heege, Dr. Elke 16813
Heen, E. de 29961
Heer, Ed de 28876
Heerebout, G.R. 29475
Heerink, B. 29320
Heermann, Dr. Ingrid 20099
Heey, H.F. 40021
Hefele, Bernhard 18831
Hefele, Dr. Gabriel 18473
Hefermehl, Norbert 16148
Hefferhan, Tom 01254
Heffern, Marion 06388
Heffley, Scott 44404
Heflin, Kirk 43433
Heflin, Tori 47294
Hefner, L. 19183
Hegan, M. 38070
Hege, Betsy 42764
Hegel, Andrea von 15939
Hegeman, Carol A. 43662
Heger, Gabriele 02685
Heggade, Dr. D. Veerendra 21791
Heggen, Bert 29918
Hegnar von Ubisch, Frederikke 30574, 30575
Hegseth Garberg, Ann Siri 30943
Heguerte de Soria, María del Carmen 41006
Heibein, Debbie 47392
Heide, Dr. Birgit 18602
Heide, Diana 07813
Heidecke, Dr. D. 17523
Heidemann, Dr. Stefan 17946
Heiden, Karl-Josef zu 19980
Heidenkreis, Walfart 37208
Heidenreich, Barbara 31533
Heidenreich, Walter 02199
Heidrich, Dr. Hermann 18783
Heigl, J. 15393
Heij, Dr. J.J. 28950
Heijmans, Dr. H.G. 29077, 29087
Heil, Gerd 19661
Heil, Jean-François 10492
Heilbrun, Françoise 13596
Heilbrunn, Margaret 45858

Heiliger, Don 44484
Heiligmann, Dr. Jörg 18201
Heilman, Anna Bea 45023
Heilman, Patrick 41552
Heilmann, Dr. Angela 18476
Heilmeyer, Prof. Dr. Wolf-Dieter 15914
Heiman, Mary-Ellen 05126
Heimann, Sybille 20392, 20393
Heimann-Jelinek, Dr. Felicitas 02903
Heimberg, Dr. Ursula 16246
Heimrath, Dr. Ralf 18969
Heimühle, Bernd 15688
Hein, Carolyn 05820
Hein, Ivar-Kristjan 09358
Hein, Jørgen 08920
Hein, Lisbet 08900
Hein, Louise 43633
Heinämies, Kati 09491
Heinänen, Seija 09600, 09604
Heindl, Alex 44674
Heindrichs, Horst 16873
Heine, Sabine 16250
Heinemann, Dr. Christiane 18585
Heinemann, Ingo F. 17850
Heinerud, Jans 36349
Heines, Carolyn 43760
Heinicke, Dr. Janet 44235
Heinisch, Dr. Severin 02156
Heinlein, Roland 15620
Heinmiller, Lee D. 43869
Heinonen, Jouko 09740, 09741, 09742, 09743, 09744, 09745, 09747, 09749
Heinrich, Dr. Chirstoph 17541
Heinritz, Dr. Reinhard 15805
Heins, Dr. 30127
Heintzelman, Scott A. 47882
Heintzman, John 46348
Heinz, Dr. Marianne 18028
Heinz, Ulrich von 16003
Heinzelmann, P. 17681
Heinzer, Dr. F. 20113
Heinzerling, Werner 18839
Heinzl, Richard 02990
Heischmann, Dr. Günter 18921
Heise, Bernd 16694
Heise, Dr. Brigitte 18542
Heise, Dr. Karin 18713
Heiser, Jerry 41558
Heising, Cornelia 16728
Heiss, Herbert 36688
Heiß, Ulrich 18041
Heißig, Prof. Dr. Kurt 18893
Heitele, Thomas 18251
Heitmann, Dr. Bernhard 17560
Heitz, Henri 14662
Heizer, Lois 47625
Heizmann, Dr. Elmar 20105
Hejdová, Dagmar 08335
Heks, Silke 19001
Helavuori, Hanna-Leena 09540
Helbig, Gabriele 16984
Helbig, Heike 19709, 19710
Helbling, R. 37206, 37207
Helbling, Regine 37205
Held, Peter 43983
Helfenstein, Dr. Josef 42187
Helfenstein, Marie-Therese 37161
Helfrich, Kurt 47406
Helg, Lukas 36677
Helgesson, Michael 35998
Helke, Dr. Gabriele 02918
Hellberg, Kerstin 15605
Helleland, Allis 08950
Hellenkemper, Prof. Dr. Hansgerd 18166
Heller, Barbara 42924
Heller, Dr. Erna 45803
Heller, Kurt 02961
Heller, Laura 46749
Heller, Margot 39780
Heller-Karneth, Dr. Eva 15477
Heller-Winter, Dr. Elisabeth 18880, 18895
Hellfaier, Detlev 16588
Helliesen, Dr. Sidsee 30746
Hellmann, Birgitt 17952
Hellmund, Dr. M. 17512
Hellrung, Reinhard 17229, 17230
Hellstern, Dr. John R. 41116
Helm, Charles 42593
Helm, Cherie 47885
Helm, Erika 03046
Helm, Lorna 42424
Helm, Dr. Reinhardt 20450
Helm, Richard S. 43748
Helmberger, Dr. 15527, 15529, 15530
Helmberger, Dr. Werner 15814, 18528
Helme, Andrew 39978
Helme, Mekis 09361
Helmecke, Gisela 16054
Helmerding, Willy 15710
Helmerson, Klas 36280, 36298
Helmig, Loeda 44855
Helminen, Hilkka 09571
Helminen, Liisa 09507
Helminen, Ritva 10049
Helms, Cheryl V. 45932
Helmus, L.M. 29897
Helmy, Kwathar 09238
Helsby, Kenneth M. 46501
Helsell, Charles P. 43388

Helstrom, Linnea 45746
Helton, Debra M. 47618
Helviö, Helena 09750
Helzel, Florence 41645
Helzer, Richard 41859
Héman, S. 28902
Hemby, Lisa 42749
Hemdal, Jay F. 48020
Hemdorff, Olle 30877
Hemetsberger, Matthias 02657
Hemm, Marsha 46709
Hemm, Michael 01742
Hemmendorff, Ove 36146
Hemmer, J. 29018
Hemmes, H.H. 29898
Hempel, Dr. Gudrun 02960
Hemsley, Jacqueline 00846
Henar, A.F. 29565
Henchley, Gillian 39795
Hendel, Dr. Margarete 19021
Hendeles, Ydessa 06626
Hender, Diane 41208
Henderby, D. 38789
Henderson, Cherel 44517
Henderson, Diana 38025
Henderson, Donald C. 43813
Henderson, D.T. 38691
Henderson, E. Ray 42412
Henderson, G. 01364
Henderson, Graeme 01038
Henderson, Jai 44893
Henderson, Kevin 30233
Henderson, M. 01179
Henderson, Marie 06251
Henderson, Robbin L. 41640
Henderson, Sam R. 43332
Henderson, Stan 06448
Henderson Fahnestock, Andrea 45847
Hendler, Karla 16077
Hendricks, Albert J. 48039
Hendricks, Dr. Alfred 18951
Hendricksh, M. 34310
Hendrickson, Dean A. 41421
Hendrickson, Riley 45381
Hendricx, Hilde 03748
Hendrikx, R. 30076, 30077
Hendrix, Lee 44913
Hendrix, Mittie B. 47179
Hendryx, Michael 48813
Heneberry, June L. 45740
Hengelhaupt, Regine 18463
Hengstenberg, Thomas 19935
Hengster, Sabine 17584, 17586
Hengstman, G. 29131
Henke, James 42479
Henke, Jerry D. 43496
Henkel, Dr. Katharina 20090
Henkens-Lewis, Helen 38534
Henley, Michael 46640
Henmi, Yoshiharu 26601
Henn, Catherine E. C. 41821
Henn, Char 46817
Hennaut, Eric 03298
Henneman, Inge 03144
Hennessey, Dr. William 45963, 45968, 45972, 48243
Hennessy, Thomas F. 47988
Hennig, Eckhard 17438
Hennig, Lutz 18800
Henning, Darrell D. 42839
Henning, Dirk 19721
Henning, Ulrich 19564
Henning, William T. 46740
Hennuy, Claude 03776
Hennze, Dr. Joachim 17690, 17692
Henriksen, Kenneth Roy 08861
Henrikson, Steve 44368
Henrikssen, Tracey 06548
Henrion, Pierre 03583
Henriot, André 13138
Henriot, Elisabeth 11417
Henry, Barbara 45874, 46067
Henry, Cassandra L. 44992
Henry, Chris 39101
Henry, Christopher 38975
Henry, John B. 43339
Henry, Karen A. 05148
Henry, Lawrence 45574
Henry, Patricia 42725
Henry-Barnaudière, Elise 15328
Henrykowska, Anna 31933
Henrysson, Harald 35845
Henschke, Dr. Ekkehard 18423
Hensel, Diethardt 19068
Hensel, Dr. Karen 43043, 43044, 43045, 43048, 43049
Henseler, Petra 19047
Henseler, Rainer 19716
Henshall, Barbara E. 42194
Henshall, W.A. 40967
Henshaw Jones, Susan 48372
Hensley, Dr. Dannie 32376
Hensley, Trevor 40923
Henson, Harvey 42102
Henson, Leonora 41989
Henson, Trevis 41468
Hente, Joke 28880
Henton, Marty 44742
Hentschel, Barbara 18405

Hentschel, Dr. Martin 18225, 18227, 18229
Henwood, Peter C. 30188
Hepburn, Lorna 39069
Hepp, Dr. Frieder 17668, 17676
Héran, Emmanuelle 13596
Herb, Reinhard 20456
Herbage, M.-B. 14191
Herbata, Peter P. 03019
Herbaugh, Karen 44982
Herber, Bob 48149
Herberg, Mayde 47401
Herberger, Mark 47735
Herberstein, Andrea Gräfin 02022
Herbert, Jacky 14704
Herbert, Lynn M. 44118
Herbert, Sharon C. 41218
Herbert, Susan 00886
Herbst, Detlev 20279
Herbst, Dr. Helmut 20348, 20350
Herbst, John H. 43324
Herbuveaux, Arlette 14870
Herce, Ana I. 35530
Herda, Isabel 17113
Herdits, H. 01806
Heredia Cortés, Gabriel 28624
Herger, Madeleine 36910
Herger, Dr. Peter 36914
Herger-Kaufmann, Josef 37194, 37263
Hergovich, Marianne 02918
Herholdt, Nancy 42232
Herkenhoff, Paulo 04389
Herlinger, Andreas 02959
Herlinger, Grete 02959
Hermalyn, Dr. Gary D. 41914, 41918, 41923
Herman, Eileen 42738
Herman, Judy 43960
Herman, Monica 43492
Herman, Richard 43440
Hermand, Michel 13418
Hermand, Nathalie 03556
Hermann, Prof. A. 20439
Hermann, Adolf 20203
Hermann, Claudia 36910
Hermann, Dr. Oliver 20625
Hermann, Reyh 19779
Hermann, Dr. Siegfried W. 02429
Hermann-Szabó, Sara 09121
Hermans, Georges 03481
Hermansdorfer, Mariusz 32182, 32186, 32189
Hermellin, G. 14707
Hernandez, Annie 14523
Hernández, Carlos Arturo 07393
Hernández, Jo Farb 47353
Hernandez, John 44695
Hernández, Rodolfo 28200
Hernandez, Sofia 45761
Hernández Carrión, Emiliano 34932
Hernández Gutiérrez, Jorge 07438
Hernández Hervás, Emilia 35354
Hernández Nieves, Román 34518
Herne, Shawn 41450
Herold, G. 19157
Herold, Dr. Inge 18612
Herold, Joyce L. 42887
Herold, Prof. Roland 02851
Herold, Prof. Roland-Peter 02103
Herr, Beth 42711
Herrán, Alfonso Carcero 07497
Herranen, Merja 09954
Herrbach-Schmidt, Dr. Brigitte 17991
Herreman, Frank 44868
Herren, Hans 36576
Herren, Robert 37233
Herren, Walter 36800
Herrera Acosta, Elvira 28201
Herrera de la Muela, Ignacio 35341
Herrera Salazar, Germán 07478
Herrero, Prof. Eutimio 34896
Herreshoff, Halsey C. 41907
Herrick, Phyllis M. 44252
Herrick O'Hara, Virginia 42175
Herring, Madeline 41519
Herring, Sarah 39729
Herrman, Diana 41387
Herrmann, Ger-Ulrich 19919
Herrmann, John 41817
Herrmann, Jürgen 20376
Herrmann, Karen 47258
Herrmann, Dr. Klaus 20088
Herrmann, Matthias 03007
Herrmann, Samuel 36846
Herrmann, Uwe 17983
Herrmann, Dr. Volker 17762
Herrmann Fiore, Dr. Kristina 25225
Herron, James 46297
Herron, Mary 44190
Herselman, D.E. 34382
Hershfield, Shauna 45454, 45455
Herskowitz, Sylvia A. 45887
Herta, Ana 32426
Hertel, Prof. Dr. Hannes 18836
Hertford, Marquess of 37961
Hertiš, Iris 34089
Hertner, Max 37142
Hertzlieb, Gregg 48192
Hervey Bathurst, James Sarah 39439
Herzer, Wolfgang 20426
Herzog, Dr. Georges 36819
Herzog, G.H. 17078

Herzog, John E. 45840
Herzog, Melinda 45090, 48268
Herzog, Rainer 16778
Herzogenrath, Prof. Dr. Wulf 16328
Hesketh-Campbell, Lorraine 39941
Heslewood, Emma 40266
Hess, Carsten 08908
Hess, Dr. Daniel 19139
Hess, Roman 37411
Hessaby, Mohandes Iraj 22302
Hesse, Gisela 17927
Hesse, Dr. Sabine 20115
Hesse-Mohr, Dr. Petra 18615
Heston, Charlton 43261
Heston, Dana 44566
Heth, Charlotte 45852
Hett, Ulrike 15972
Hettingg, Mary Jane 48464
Heuberger, Georg 17057, 17069
Heuberger, Vera 37000
Heublein, Dr. Brigitte 17355
Heuckeroth, Erwin 18684
Heuer, Christoph 19926
Heufelder, Jochen 18154
Heufelder, Michael 18863
Heukemes, Dr. Berndmark 18284
Heulot, Laurent 10341
Heunemann 20030
Heusden, G. van 29336
Heuser 16697
Heuser, Prof. Dr. August 17038
Heuser, Frederick J. 46446
Heuser, Dr. Mechthild 36550
Heusinger, Prof. Dr. Lutz 18624
Heußner, Karen 20291
Heuwinkel, Christiane 16156
Heuwinkel, Dr. Hubert 16737
Hevers, Dr. J. 16304
Hevia, Agustin 35205
Hew Wing, Micheal 45841
Hewitt, H.D. 40129
Hewitt, Karen 42187
Hewitt, Susan 01567
Hewitt, Timothy M. 46094
Hewitt-Dower, Bill 00932
Hewson, Alan 37952
Hewson, Karen E. 06037
Hewson, Paul 00715
Hewson, Rose 30224
Hewson, Shirley O. 01612
Heyburn, Tim 39303, 39305
Heyd, Paul 19225
Heyden, Dr. Thomas 19156
Heyen, Lora 41435
Heyes, John 38892
Heyl, Cornelius A. von 20679
Heyler, Joanne 44946
Heym, Dr. Sabine 18901, 18902, 18905
Heymans, Dr. Hubert 03602
Heyneman, C. 03261
Heynen, Arnold 37316
Heynen, Dr. Julian 16729
Hibbitt, Karen 48344
Hickey, Leo J. 45698
Hickey, Michael 05180
Hicklin, Karen 42376
Hickman, Carole S. 41646
Hickman, Gerry 41368
Hickman, Warren 48310
Hickman, Manfred 19407
Hickock, Paul 44110
Hicks, Anna Lee 45670
Hicks, Christine 13861
Hicks, Hilarie M. 45667
Hicks, Hugh Francis 41482
Hicks, Louis 41121
Hidasi, Prof. José 04110
Hidber, Alfred 37430
Hideo, Kurita 26108
Hideshima, Tatsumi 26103
Hidook, Tatjana 37853
Hiebel, Kaye 45173
Hiebler, Prof. Dr. Herbert 02778
Hieblinger, Faith 05696
Hiekisch-Picard, Sepp 16198, 17638
Hiéret, Jean-Pierre 10809
Hiesinger, Kathryn B. 46442
Hiesmayr, Herbert 02608
Higginbotham, Evangeline 47051
Higgs, Jane 38867
High, Laura 41254
High, Steven S. 46835
Hightower, John B. 45937
Higman, David 39538
Hignette, Michel 13634
Higuchi, Dr. Keiji 26570
Higuchi, Dr. Takayasu 26453
Higueras Rodríguez, Dolores 35049
Hiis Søftestad, Hanne 30381
Hijiwara, Takshi 26638
Hilaire, Michel 13126, 13132
Hilberg, Thomas D. 45225
Hilberg, Dr. Volker 19793
Hilbrand, Ingrid 01691
Hilbun, Dorinda 41531
Hildawa, Isidro 31414
Hildebran, Julia 42505
Hildebrand, Carla 48616
Hildebrand, Dr. Josephine 16028

Hildebrand, Walter 01866
Hildebrandt, Bernd 15996
Hildebrandt, Dr. Rainer 16042
Hildebrandt, Sandra 45908
Hildenbrand, Manfred 17626
Hiles, Wayne 48455
Hilger, Charles 47411
Hilger, H. 20113
Hilger, Dr. Wolfgang 02936
Hilgers, Patrick 03201
Hilkenbach, Rainer 18069
Hilkhuijsen, J. 29079
Hill, Andrew 45698
Hill, Andrew F. 38079
Hill, Barbara A. 45604
Hill, Brian O. 48059
Hill, Carla 41520
Hillis, Carolyn 46118
Hill, Charlie 06084
Hill, Christine C. 43930
Hill, Dr. Christopher L. 41858
Hill, Donald C. 44551
Hill, John 46121
Hill, June 39149
Hill, Katherine 42816
Hill, Lindsay 06155
Hill, Mary 47211
Hill, Michelle 41747
Hill, Pamela K. 43819
Hill, Peter 39270
Hill, Ray 46835
Hill, Robert D. 43924
Hill, Robin 39353
Hill, Sergej Ivanovič 32632
Hill, Shannen 42899
Hill, Steve 41284, 44225
Hill Carter, Charles 42203
Hill-Festa, Lisa 47541
Hill Perrell, Franklin 47009
Hillam, Penelope 00746
Hillard, Elbert R. 44278
Hillebrand, Dr. Melanie 34332
Hiller, Dr. Hilde 17115
Hiller, Dr. Hubertus 19837
Hiller, N. 30124
Hiller von Gaertringen, Dr. Julia 16588
Hiller von Gaertringen, Dr. Rudolf 18387, 18395, 18421
Hillerman, Barbara 02995
Hillesheim, Dr. Jürgen 15551
Hillhouse, David 38208
Hillhouse, Susan 47408
Hilliard, Elbert R. 44279
Hillier, Kenneth 38027
Hillis, Florence E. 44514
Hillsman, Matthew 46614
Hillstrom, Richard L. 45389
Hilpert Stuber, Susanne 36946
Hiltermann, Elisabeth 15715, 15887
Hilti, Joseph 36771
Hiltula, Leena 10183
Hilz, Dr. Helmut 18839
Hilzhood, Nancy 44416
Himanen, Hilke Liisa 09781
Himawan, Joice 41056
Himber, René 11086
Himmelbauer, Robert 02030
Himmelein, Prof. Dr. Volker 20115
Himmelstrand, Erik 36401
Hincapié, Alberto 07489
Hincapié Santa Maria, Jaime 07545
Hinchliffe, Robin 47372
Hind, Charles 39626, 39688
Hindelang, Eduard 18325
Hinderer, S. 17192
Hindman, James 44890
Hinds, Roger 41663
Hine, Marjorie 06648
Hine, N.A. 38550
Hinerman, Lenore 43677
Hines, Tommy 47705
Hingst, Eckhard 17782
Hinkley, Marilyn J. 48778
Hinman, Marilyn 43920
Hinnant, Vandorn 43817
Hinrichsen, Dr. Torkild 17527, 17544
Hinsch, Werner 18350
Hinson, Tom E. 42466
Hintermaier, Dr. Ernst 02541
Hinton, Dr. Brian 39017
Hinton, Verdell 44181
Hinton, William 44959
Hinz, Günther 16151
Hinz, Dr. Hans-Martin 15939
Hiott, William D. 42456, 42457
Hippe, Margarethe 02517
Hipps, Will 41478
Hipschman, Dorrie 47823
Hipwell, John 06734
Hír, Dr. János 21502
Hirabayashi, Kunio 26633
Hirako, Akihiko 26157
Hiramatsu, Hideki 26129
Hirano, Irene 44914
Hirano, Itaru 26693
Hirano, Naoki 26875
Hirata, Shozo 26808
Hirayama, Miyako 26693

Hirci, Andrej 34114
Hird, Maureen 39837
Hirner, Dr. René 17679
Hiroshi, Doi 26208
Hiroshi, Ito 26954
Hiroya, Yukiatu 26679
Hirsch, Jan 47615
Hirsch, John 41414
Hirsch, Marjorie 48198
Hirschbiegel, Dieter 18221
Hirschel, Anthony G. 44228
Hirschler, Christa 19996
Hirst, M. 34295
Hirst, Marlys 41541
Hirth, Dr. Antoine 10729
Hirthe, Dr. Thomas 17607
Hirtle, Wade 05718
Hirvonen, Anna-Riikka 09661, 09662
Hiscock, Rosella 06170
Hislop, Kare 46814
Hiss, Elfi 36964
Hitchings, Sinclair 41801
Hitchmough, Dr. Wendy 38992
Hite, Andy 46500
Hite, Jessie Otto 41412
Hittaller, Hans Martin 01731
Hitzing, Jörg 19572
Hiukka, Toini 09888
Hjermind, Jesper 09112
Hjorth, Carl-Gustav 36315
Hladky, Sylvia 18840
Hlaváčková, Dr. Miroslava 08638
Hlôška, L. 34079
Hnateyko, Olha 45884
Ho, Keimei 26386
Ho, Lynn 41338
Ho Ho, Ying 33937
Hoag, Everett H. 45663
Hoard, Constance G. 41968
Hoare, Adrian D. 40948
Hoare, Nell 40893
Hobaugh, J.H. 47469
Hobbs, Patricia A. 44760
Hobein, Beate 17482, 17483
Hoberg, Dr. Annegret 18918
Hobin, Ellen 05570
Hobolth, Nina 08763
Hobson, Marlena 47796
Hobson, Richard 38087
Hoch, Manfred 19769
Hochberg, Dr. F.G. 47405
Hochberger, Ernst 17994
Hochdörfer, Achim 02949
Hoche, Frank 17650, 19290
Hochleitner, Dr. Martin 02234
Hochstrasser, M. 37188
Hochuli, Dr. P. 37404
Hochuli-Gysel, Dr. Anne 36481
Hocking, Sheldon 48210
Hockman, Winnie 06274
Hodel, Daniel E. 36904
Hodel, R. 29508
Hodge, Anne 22446
Hodge, Dr. G. Jeannette 45720
Hodges, Rhoda 45114
Hodgins-Wollan, Sonya 05628
Hodgson, Beverly 45814
Hodgson, Clarence 05431
Hodgson, Kenneth O. 45957
Hodgson, Tom 38608, 38611
Hodkinson, Wendy 39894
Hodslavská, Lenka 08420, 08421
Hodson, Janice 42044
Höbler, Dr. Hans-Joachim 18404
Höck, Anton 02082
Höck, Dr. Christoph 17989
Höck, Georg 02169
Höfchen, Dr. Heinz 17970
Höfer, Dr. Hubert 18003
Höfer, Dr. Klaus 20242
Hoeffel, Joan 47512
Höfler, Franz 02467
Höfler, Werner Oskar 17699
Höfliger, Yvonne 37272
Höfling, Eckart Hermann 04353
Høeg, Asger 08857
Högberg, Lena 36289
Hoegen, Friedrich 18709
Hoegh Brand, Anne 30770
Högl, Dr. Günther 16660
Höglander, Agneta 36128
Höhl, Dr. Claudia 17757
Höhne, Annett 17400
Höibo, Roy 30819
Hoeker, Kristen 45578
Hoeksema, B.W. 29522
Hoekstra, Drs. Ridsert 29743
Hoekstra-van Vuurde, C.J. 29102
Hoel, Arild 30716
Hoel, Randall 45780
Höller, Silvia 02078
Hoelscher, Dr. Monika 15437
Hölscher, Dr. Petra 18890
Hölscher, Prof. Tonio 17662
Höltge, Dr. Kathrin 16297
Höltl, Georg 15649, 19359, 20181
Hoeltzel, Susan 41922
Hölz, Marjatta 20236
Hölzel, Josef 01719

Hoelzeman, Buddy 45502
Hölzer, Dr. Adam 18003
Hölzinger, Nora 16540
Hölzl, Dr. Christian 02918
Hölzl, Dr. Regina 02918
Höneisen, Markus 37132
Hoenig, Thomas M. 44406
Hönigmann, Alexandra 03001
Hönigmann, Andrea 03001
Höper, Dr. Corinna 20106
Hoepner, Leon 41673
Höppl, Birgit 18649
Hörker, Alois 02044
Hörmann, Barbara 17739
Hörmann, Fritz 02822
Hörner García, Gabriel 28353
Hoerschelmann, Dr. Antonia 02830
Hösch, Jürgen 17068
Höser, Dr. Norbert 15451
Hoesgen, Jennifer 05608
Hoesli, Hans Rudolf 36586
Hösli, Marc 37091
Hoeve, S. ten 29838
Höylä, Risto 09671
Hofbauer, Erwin 01844
Hofbauer, John D. 41676
Hofer, Manfred 02084
Hofer, Rudolf 02181, 02182
Hoff, Dr. Marlise 16020
Hoff, Svein Olav 30640
Hoff Jørgensen, Jan 30477
Hoffberger, Rebecca 41448
Hoffer, Andreas 02142
Hofferer, Robert 02258
Hoffert, Tonia 48006
Hoffman, Dan 05973
Hoffman, Hollace 45550
Hoffman, Dr. Kerstin 16752
Hoffman, Marilyn 47584
Hoffman, Max 43054
Hoffman, Michael E. 45774
Hoffman, Dr. Richard S. 45193
Hoffman, Thomas 47391
Hoffmann, Almut 16050
Hoffmann, Audrey 01585
Hoffmann, Christian 10135
Hoffmann, Dr. H. 16626
Hoffmann, Helmut W. 19077
Hoffmann, Jörn 16338
Hoffmann, John 42348
Hoffmann, Justin 18867
Hoffmann, Karen 16039
Hoffmann, Kim 46765
Hoffmann, Paul 02062
Hoffmann, Dr. Per 16339
Hoffmann, Dr. R.J. 18919
Hoffmann, Susanne 19351
Hoffmann, Tobias 17909
Hoffmann, Walter 19646
Hoffmann, Will 27575
Hoffpauer, Diane 42714
Hofinger, Franz 02069
Hofmacher, Anna 02464
Hofman, Andreas 17222
Hofman, Jack 44684
Hofman, O. 22727
Hofmann 19430
Hofmann, Dr. B. 36547
Hofmann, C. 28776
Hofmann, Christa 02955
Hofmann, Dr. Ernst 19997
Hofmann, Gertrud 18042
Hofmann, Helmut 02273
Hofmann, Irene 41738, 45935
Hofmann, Jürgen 17887
Hofmann, Lois 02072
Hofmann, Martina 18802
Hofmann, Rainer 19438
Hofmeister, Walter 17810
Hofschen, Dr. Heinz-Gerd 16321
Hofstad, Turid 30987
Hofstätter, Dr. Ulrike 01922
Hofstetter, Adolf 19358
Hofstetter, Willy 37357
Hofwolt, Gerald 44093
Hogan, Jacqueline 41701
Hogan, Tim 41837
Hogben, Barbara 01056
Hogben, Ian 01056
Hoge, Joan R. 43067
Hoge, Philip 48653
Hogestøl, Mari 30877
Hogg, C.G.O. 38174
Hogg, Gavin 40940
Hogsved, Åse 36229
Hogue, Kate 44499
Hoguet, Jean 13573
Hohbaum, R. 17249
Hoheisel, Tim 48444
Hoheisel-Huxmann, Reinhard 16339
Hohenberg, Anita Fürstin von 01681
Hohenlohe, Prinz Constantin von 19780
Hohenlohe-Bartenstein, Ferdinand Fürst zu 19855
Hohenlohe-Langenburg, Fürst zu 18329, 18332
Hohenlohe-Oehringen, Katharina Fürstin zu 19029
Hohenlohe-Waldenburg, F.K. Fürst zu 20362
Hohensee, Falko 16643
Hohensinner, Harald 01819
Hohenzollern, Dr. Johann Georg Prinz von 18865

Hohl, Erhard 01731
Hohl, J. 15780
Hohmann, H.-J. 17723
Hohri, Sasha 45769
Hohut, Khrystyna 05388
Høibo, Roy 30550
Høie, Bjørn K. 30696
Højer Petersen, Anne 08982
Højgaard, Johnny 08822
Hokanson, Randi 45503
Hol Haugen, Bjørn Sverre 30475
Holben Ellis, Margaret 45863
Holbrook, Maureen 01253
Holc, Elwira 31859
Holcomb, Gary 43226
Holcomb, Grant 46948
Holcombe, David C. 42468
Holcombe, Holly 42482
Holden, Charles 39120
Holden, Florence 42606
Holden, Sally 38467
Holden, Steve 43597
Holden, Thomas 43000
Holder, Heidi 44868
Holderegger, Katharina 37331
Holderness, Christine 41872
Holdren, Greg 41672
Holdsworth, Jane A. 45934
Hole, Frank 45698
Holeman, Claude A. 42798
Holen, Dr. Stephen 42887
Holeva, Daniel 45328
Holländer, Tove 10135
Holland, J. 01501
Holland, Kim 46020
Holland, M. 34264
Holland, Rudolf 20771
Holland-Beickert, Dana 45242
Hollander, Stacy 45756, 45798
Hollander, Volker 16563
Hollein, Max 17071
Hollender, G. 37412
Holler, Christiane 01922
Holler, Dr. Wolfgang 16692
Holler-Schuster, Günther 01927
Hollerbach, Dr. R. 18139
Holleufer, Lars 08768
Holliday, Dr. John 39319
Holliger, C. 36591
Hollinetz, Alfred 02774
Hollinger, Gail 41199
Hollingworth, John 39590
Hollingworth, Mar 44893
Hollis, Phil 39432
Hollister, Jack 41544
Holloman, Jim 42291
Hollosy, Gyuri 45262
Holloway, Douglas 47310
Holloway, James 38917
Holloway, Leonard B. 45955
Hollstein, Dr. Wilhelm 16698
Hólm, Geir 21630
Holm, Torben 09081
Holm-Johnsen, Hanne 30566
Holm Sørensen, Bodil 08916
Holman, Clyde 48450
Holman, Graham 05979
Holman, Kurt 46358
Holman, Paul 42370
Holman, William M. 42960
Holmes, Carolyn C. 42246
Holmes, Erskine J. 38164
Holmes, Saira 38222
Holmes, Selean 42324
Holmes, Willard 45886
Holmes, Dr. William 45271
Holmes, William C. 42536
Holmes Helgren, Heidi 42080
Holmesland, Liv 30855
Holmgrain, Ardith 45754
Holmgren, Bengt 36155
Holmlund, Bertil 09882
Holmquist, Dr. Jeffrey G. 32376
Holmstrand-Krueger, Lena 36198
Holmström, Lars 10088
Holo, Dr. Selma 44899
Holodňáková, Dr. Radmila 08738
Holowacz, Eric V. 41560
Holozet, Andrée 15345
Holpainen, Anja 09648
Holsbeke, Mireille 03141
Holst, Prof. Dr. Christian von 20106
Holst, Gerd 20687
Holst, Lars 08863
Holstein, Lars 36349
Holsten, Christina 35939
Holsten, Dr. Siegmar 18002
Holt, Daniel D. 41049
Holt, Frank 46186, 46190
Holt, Joyce 45103
Holt, Phillip 00874
Holtby, J.M. 39112
Holte, Bettye 42437
Holten, Arnfinn J. 30400
Holten, Lars 08970
Holthof, Marc 03143
Holthuis, Dr. Gabriele 19861, 19862, 19863
Holtman, Marjorie 47687
Holton, Linda 43727

Holtz, Jerzy 36281
Holtz, Wolfgang 15998
Holtzapple, John C. 42570
Holtzhausen, A. 34319
Holubizky, Ihor 05652
Holverson, John H. 47549
Holz, Uwe 16175, 20650
Holzer, Dr. Elmar 20447
Holzer-Weber, Ruth 37421
Holzinger, Hans 18898
Homa-Rożek, Ewa 31549
Homann, Dr. Klaus 20269
Homberger, Lorenz 37398
Homburg, Cornelia 47134
Homen, Prof. Zoran 07730
Homering, Liselotte 18615
Hommell, Michel 12649
Homolova, Dr. Alexandra 33978
Homs-Chabbert, Arlette 13084
Honadel, Elroy 46051
Honcoopova, Dr. Helena 08574
Honda, Masami 26305
Honda, Masuo 26701
Honda, Shizuo 26488
Honermann, Josefine 16722
Honerød, Anne Grete 30809
Honeyman, Robert E. 43232
Hong, Kathleen 44073
Hong, Trinh Van 48985
Honkanen, Pekka 09534
Hood, Betty 42117
Hood, Michael 44213
Hood, Sadie Ann 48664
Hoogenboom, W. 28976
Hoogendonk, M.H. 29324
Hook, I.D. 38537, 38540
Hook, John 01459
Hook, Sam 45614
Hooker, Saralinda 42076
Hooks, Terri 42613
Hooper, C.L. 39163
Hooper, Dr. John 01458
Hoopes, John 44684
Hoopfer, Ann 48049
Hoops, Erik 16339
Hoorn Bakker, A. 29786
Hoover, Bessie 46811
Hoover, Charles 47062
Hoover, Rhonda J. 48313
Hooymayers, Dr. J.M.M. 29521
Hoozee, Dr. Robert 03448
Hope, Eve 05591
Hopfengart, Dr. Christine 36544
Hopfinger, Rebecca 42443
Hopfner, Dr. Rudolf 02918
Hopgood, Dr. James F. 44018
Hopkin, Dieter 40966
hopkin, Dr. Steve 40294
Hopkins, Anthea 38512
Hopkins, Dave 06295
Hopkins, Debra 47514
Hopkins, Linda 43091
Hopkins, S.K. 40442
Hopkins, Terri M. 45194
Hopkins Coughlin, Joan 48498
Hopkinson, Susan 40458, 40459, 40460
Hopmann, Gerd 16865
Hopp, Doris 17046
Hoppe, Barbara G. 44529
Hoppe, Günther 18189
Hoppe, Martin 17583
Hoppe, Michael 16665
Hoppe, Dr. Werner 15785
Hoppe-Oehl, Dr. Ulrike 18491
Hoppenworth, Bodo 17538
Hopper, Barbara 48301
Hopping, Robert 01383
Hoptman, Laura 46510
Horacio Aranguren, Juan José 00565
Horat, H. 36905
Horat, Dr. Heinz 36910
Horber, Dr. R. 14101
Hordyński, Piotr 31724
Horgen, Randi 30574
Hori, Robert 44903
Hori, Tomosaburo 26363
Horkheimer, Jack 45291
Horký, Milan 08295
Horman, Trevor 00718
Horn, Damian 40418
Horn, David 39652
Horn, Elizabeth 46704
Horn, Dr. Gabriele 19437
Horn, Henning 20087
Horn, Ken 44910
Horn, Dr. Luise 18867
Horn, Dr. Reinhard 18831
Horn, Robert 42350
Horn, Sigrun 19662
Hornback, Kristina 43559
Hornbostel, Prof. Dr. Wilhelm 17560
Hornburg, Rainer 17761
Hornby, D. Mary 38590
Horndasch, Mickey 41268
Horne, Daphne 01082
Horne, Gene 30317
Horne, Graham 01039
Horne, Meade B. 47955
Horner, John R. 41858

Hornig, Dieter 20686
Hornik, Dr. Heidi 48264
Hornstrup, Nils 08857
Hornung, Herb 47296
Hornung, Prof. Dr. Maria 02962
Hornyak, Deanna 41273
Horowitz, Lawrence P. 47543
Horpeniak, Dr. Vladimír 08407, 08669
Horray, Henrietta 43732
Horrigan, William 42593
Horsley, Juliet 40644, 40650
Horsnall, P. 38962
Horst, Bill 46620
Horst, Dr. Katarina 17991
Horst, Prof. Dr. Kurt 18560
Horst, Randy 42950
Horsten, Frans 03502
Horsting, Archana 41643
Horstmann, Dr. G.G. 28950
Horton, Lon 42163
Hortz, Laura 47646
Horváth, Dr. Béla 21414
Horvath, Eugen 02247
Horváth, György 21360
Horváth, Dr. István 21410
Horváth, Dr. László 21486
Horvath, Dr. Michael J. 46601
Horvath, Ursula 02330
Horvatić, Franjo 07718
Horwath, Alexander 02957
Horwitz, Leon 41700
Horwood, Michelle 30286
Horžen, Vesna 34146
Hosack, George 42289
Hosaka, Kenjiro 26938
Hosar, Kåre 30641
Hose, Henry 48054
Hoskin, Rebecca 00806
Hoskins, Jeff 44027
Hoskins, Rebecca 45505
Hoskins, William J. 47646
Hoskinson, Susan 46544
Hoskisson, Don 45436
Hoško, Dr. Franjo Emanuel 07762
Hošková, Jitka 08558, 08676, 08690
Hosley, William 43937
Hosoe, Eikoh 26794
Hosokawa, Morisada 26843
Hosokawa, Toshiro 26883
Hossain, Shamsul 03079
Hossaka, Luiz 04515
Hosseloot, Eric 10914
Hosta Rebés, Assumpció 34851
Hostetter, David 44571
Hostyn, Norbert 03668, 03670, 03671
Hotalling, Don 46794
Hotard, Patrick 41693
Hotchner, Holly 45755
Hoti, Prof. Afrim 00015
Hotvedt, Heidi 42012
Hotz, Benedict 36914
Hotz, Claus-Dieter 17378
Hotz, Dr. Gerhard 36514
Houby-Nielsen, Dr. Sanne 36259
Houdamer, Chloé 10861
Hough, Douglas R. 46279
Hough, Katherine 46267
Hough, Melissa E. 46398
Houghtling, Kim 06524
Houghton, J. 45579
Hougue, Veronique de la 13586
Houkjaer, Ulla 08927
Houlden, Penny 06348
Houliston, Laura 39680
Hoult, R. 30131
Hourant, Francis 03764, 03766
House, George M. 41077
House, Kirk 43888
Houseago, Avril 40096
Housego, Bill 00979
Housen, Jean 03583
Houssinot, Jean-Claude 14117
Houston, David 42458
Houston, Joe 46962
Houston, John 46903
Houston, L.S. 45282
Houston, Dr. Margaret 44682
Houston, Sandra J. 42293
Houts, Mary D. 44004
Hovagimian, Vahan 02938
Hoveng, Dot 41270
Hovens, P. 29525
Hovi, Jouko 09418
Hovington, Raphael 05034
Hovish, Joseph J. 44218
Høvsgaard, Thomas 09078
Howard, Donna J. 44605
Howard, J. 34171, 39834
Howard, James 45570
Howard, Jan 46721
Howard, Jerome 06048
Howard, Jerry 45271
Howard, John 43528
Howard, John H. 44314
Howard, Louise 45600
Howard, Nora 41428
Howard, Paul 40973
Howard, Stephen R. 42293
Howard, Val 43874

Howe, Eileen 46796
Howe, Katherine S. 44129
Howe, Kathleen 41111
Howe, Philip 30265
Howe, Sherman M. 48743
Howell, A.C. 40424
Howell, Beverly 44656
Howell, Busser 48073
Howell, George L. 43170
Howell, Karen 39737
Howell, Kathy 48254
Howell, N. 40048
Howells, David 40629
Howese, Stephen 42727
Howett Smith, Catherine 41352
Howland, Robert 47690
Howoldt, Dr. Jenns E. 17541
Hoyd, Ed 42642
Hoyer, Dr. Eva Maria 18398
Hoyer, Klaus 15523
Hoyer, Lindy 46152
Hoyle, Gary 41390
Hoyle, Prof. R.W. 40295
Hoyle, Wayne 46339
Hoyos, Hans 02526
Hoyos Galarza, Melvin 09177
Hoyt, Marilyn 43355
Hoyt, Richard P. 48474
Hoyt, Robert 41141
Hoyum, Wanda 41621
Hrabánková, Dr. Světlana 08438, 08439
Hrastović, Ivica 07731
Hrebíčková, Marta 34048
Hrisenková, Nataša 34028
Hristov, Dr. Ivan 04846
Hristov, Dr. Martin 04848
Hristova, Mariana 04848
Hristova-Radoeva, Vessela 04859
Hroch, David 08651
Hron, Vincent 41754
Hrtánková, Valéria 33978
Hruška, Václav 08422, 08629
Hsieh, Kun-Shan 27511
Huang, Kuang-Nan 07350
Huang, Yaohua 07204
Huard, Micheline 06422
Huart, Nicole d' 03319
Hubacher, Dr. Hans 37258
Hubbard, Bob 43760
Hubbard, Dr. Charles M. 43936
Hubbard, Dr. Jane 40907
Hubbard, Wendy L. 45136
Hubbs, Heather 42366
Hubbs, Jenice 04984
Huber, Alfred 36871
Huber, Arthur 36588
Huber, Dr. Bernhard 16250
Huber, Christoph Anselm 03286
Huber, Franz 02766
Huber, Dr. Hannelore 02993
Huber, Markus 37131
Huber, Mary 42150
Huber, Dr. Waldemar 01871
Huber, Wolfgang 02141
Huber-Bitzer, Anne 20106
Hubert, François 13939, 13941
Hubinger, Horst 01686
Huchard, Viviane 13637
Huck, Thomas 17362
Huckaby, Barbara 44108
Hudák, Julianna 21418
Huddleston, David 06434, 06435
Hudeczek, Dr. E. 02202
Hudeczek, Dr. Erich 01929
Hudson, Fred 41592
Hudson, Giles 40149
Hudson, Dr. Julian D. 42438
Hudson, Louise 46788
Hudson, Mark S. 43527
Hudson, Dr. Neville 30108
Hue, Michel 11390, 11593, 12503, 12627, 12987, 12990, 15052
Hueber, Prof. Dr. Friedmund 01691
Hueber, Régis 11357
Hübl, Prof. Dr. Richard 02747
Hübner, Dr. A. 19390
Hübner, Heinz 01641
Hübner, Dr. John 01937
Hübner, Simone 16850
Hübner, Dr. Ute 17190
Hübsch, Norbert 15840
Hückel, Angela 18880
Hückstädt, Antje 19316
Hüls, Johannes 16188
Hülsewig-Johnen, Dr. Jutta 16156
Hülsmann, Gaby 19590
Huemer, Dr. Peter 02082
Huenefeld, Wesley C. 41401
Hünninghaus-Böckmann, Ute 02692
Hürkey, Dr. Edgar J. 17029
Huerta, Benito 41260
Huerta, Enrike 34781
Hüsam, Gernot 16495
Huescar, Duque de 35009
Hüsers-Doehmen, Dr. Katharina 17383
Hüsken, Wim 03618, 03619, 03620
Hüßner, Reinhard 17914
Huet, Dr. 12734
Hueter, Diana 42759

Hütt, Dr. Michael 20316
Hüttel, Dr. Richard 18405
Hüttner, Michaela 02918
Hüttner, Rudolf 02776
Huff, Richard E. 44259, 44260
Huffman, Bill 06507
Huffman, Joan 43934
Huffman, John 47840
Huffman, Vincent 05828
Hufnagl, Prof. Dr. Florian 18890
Hufschmid, Thomas 36479
Hufschmidt, Dr. Anke 16743
Hufschmied, Richard 02895
Hug, Guy 12570
Hug, Hannes 36515
Hug, Shamsul 03101
Hugel, André 12113, 13978, 13979
Hugentobler, Hanspeter 36817
Huges, Bryn 39176
Huggert, Anders 36349
Hughbanks, Bette 46850
Hughes, Anne-Marie 38087
Hughes, Dr. David 48603
Hughes, Debra 48652
Hughes, Elaine M. 43034
Hughes, Eugene M. 43329
Hughes, Gareth 40366, 40518
Hughes, Gary 06334
Hughes, Ginny 47595
Hughes, Helga 39092
Hughes, James T. 48438
Hughes, Janet 00886
Hughes, John 39551
Hughes, Kathleen 48113
Hughes, K.C. 40901
Hughes, Marianne 45684
Hughes, Mark 40061
Hughes, P. 01106
Hughes, Philip 40361
Hughes, Richard Ll. 39541
Hughes, Susan 06614
Hughes, Thomas A. 45905
Hugo 34199
Hugonich, J. Yves 14555, 14556, 14557, 14559
Huguet, Jean-Pierre 36983
Huhtamäki, Tuula 10214
Huhtamäki, Ulla 09528
Hui, Hwang Sun 27122
Huijs Janssen, Dr. Paul 29407
Huijts, Stijn 29827
Huiskes, Bert 29955
Huizi, María Elena 48914
Hulbert, Dr. Richard C. 47792
Hull, Prof. Andrea 01466
Hull, Dale 46382
Hull, Howard 38624
Hull, Karen 40296, 40298
Hull, Priscilla 38390
Hullah, S. 39038
Hulló, István 33918
Hulse, E. 38313
Hulse, Sir Edward 38312
Hulse, Robert 39591
Hulser, Kathleen 45858
Hulshof, G. 28949
Hulston, Nancy 44392
Hultgren, Mary Lou 43896
Humbert, Jean-Baptiste 31071
Humbert, Vincent 12295
Hume, J. Wilbert 05209
Hume, Ted 05485
Humer, Diethard 02129
Humer, Franz 01694, 02408, 02409
Humes, Alex B. 46413
Hummel, Alfred 18663
Hummer, Hermann 02960
Humphrey, J. Steven 43069
Humphrey, L. 38449
Humphrey, M. 01501
Humphrey, Rosanne 41837
Humphrey, Sylvia 40036
Humphreys, Mary 38319
Humphreys, Richard 39787
Humphries, Alan 39454
Humphries, Martin 39608
Humphries, Michael E. 42546
Humpl, Christine 02142
Hundt, Graf W.-D. von 15554
Hundt-Esswein, Hans U. 16376
Hùng, Nguyễn Quôê 48994
Hunger, Mattli 37082
Hunnewell, Elizabeth 48496
Hunold, Andrew 47075
Hunold, Dr. Angelika 18606
Hunt, Adrian P. 41107
Hunt, Alice 46827
Hunt, C. 40555
Hunt, Christopher J. 39891
Hunt, Clare 40551
Hunt, Dr. D.A. 39488
Hunt, David 46172
Hunt, Dr. Donald W. 41326
Hunt, Eugene A. 44422
Hunt, Michael 43064
Hunt, Phillip 41800
Hunt, Rhonda 01295
Hunt, Dr. Robert M. 44793
Hunt, Tony 30162
Hunt, Wilma 42663

Hunt Chamberlain, Carola 47482
Hunt Miller, Lee 47311, 47325
Hunter, Charles 48821
Hunter, Elizabeth 04984, 06127, 38015
Hunter, Fredericka 45140
Hunter, Jamie 05846
Hunter, Jessica 43782
Hunter, Jim 38578, 39002
Hunter, John 44331
Hunter, Judith 40904
Hunter, Julia 41390
Hunter, Ken 40570
Hunter, Lance 46227
Hunter, Liz 39198
Hunter, Paul 45797
Hunter, Richard 46172
Hunter, Terry 43956
Hunter, Thomas 47912
Hunter, Tom 43607
Hunter, Valerie 38898
Hunter-Stiebel, Penelope 46641
Huntington, Jeffrey L. 47113
Huntoon, Katherine 45971
Huntzinger, John 45339
Hunziker, Armando T. 00291
Hunziker, John 46935
Huo, Prof. Wei 07025
Huopainen, Raili 10001
Hupponen, Elina 10005
Huret, J. 14884
Hurezan Pascu, Geoghe 32543
Hurezan Pascu, George 32430
Hurkmans, Riek 29271
Hurley, Arthur L. 42233
Hurley, Richard 38629
Hurry, S.P. 38729
Hursey, Dick 44769
Hurtado Londoño, Gloria 07402
Hurum, Prof. Jørn H. 30735
Hurvitz, Uri 22779
Hurwitz, Avi 22709
Hušáková, Ivana 08654
Husband, John 30184
Husband, Timothy 45784
Husedžinović, Amela 03924
Huskisson, Christine 43651
Husmann, Karin C.E. 29646
Huss, John 45094
Hussaini, Syed Mohammad 22265
Hussein, Dató Ibrahim 27680
Husseini, Frederic 27484
Husseini, Frédéric 27489
Hussey, Noelene 30193
Hussey-Arntson, Kathy 48646
Husslein, Dr. Agnes 02549
Husso, Tuula 09925
Husted, Christine 43633
Huston, Louise 47793
Husty, Peter 02551
Huszár, Zoltán 21503, 21504, 21505, 21506, 21507, 21508, 21510, 21511, 21513, 21514, 21516, 21517, 21518
Hutchcrot, Sally 44511
Hutchings, Lamar 44713
Hutchins, Patricia 42136
Hutchins Bobyrk, Dawn 47637
Hutchinson, J. Dwight 45316
Hutchinson, John 22419
Hutchinson, Lawrence 41740
Hutchinson, Lydia C. 45316
Hutchinson, Susan 01455
Hutchison, John 42765
Huth, Nancy 45555
Huthwohl, Joël 13475
Hutin, Albert 42197
Hutt, Marilyn 47803
Hutter, Dr. Ernestine 02551, 02554
Hutterer, Dr. Karl 47405
Hutterer, Dr. Rainer 16250
Hutto, Dr. Richard 45408
Hutton, Susan 47631
Hutula, Betsy 42331
Hutz, Dr. Ferdinand 01751
Huuskola, Arto 10073
Huuskonen, Kari 09579
Huvenne, Dr. Paul 03146
Huwer, Elisabeth 17664
Huwyler, Dr. Edwin 36587
Hux, P. Meinrado 00412
Huxley, Geralyn H. 46506
Huyge, Dirk 03337
Huygens, Ch.E.C. 29779
Huysza, Hans 03031
Huzel, Karl 18376
Hwang, Pae Gang 27227
Hyams, Prof. Dr. Helge-Ulrike 18628
HyangAn, Kim 27289
Hyatt, John 40847
Hýbl, Dr. František 08622
Hyde, H. 40072
Hyde, J.R. 45246
Hyde, Lex 22488
Hyer, Warren W. 48763
Hygate, Nadine 38659
Hyland, Douglas 45674
Hylmarsová, Eva 08470
Hyman, Dr. P. 39845
Hyman, Ryan 45507
Hynes, Patricia 45755

Hynes, William Q. 47608
Hyross, Dr. Peter 33957, 33960, 33961, 33962, 33964, 33965, 33969, 33970, 33975, 33980
Hyšková, Veřa 08360
Hyson, Dr. John M. 41463
Hyss, Dr. Lothar 18952
Hytha, Prof. Dr. Robert K. 02379
Iaconoy, Nello 43688
Iacopi, Dr. Irene 25148, 25244
Iaing, Bonnie 05356
Iancu, Emilia 32573
Ianeva, Olga 04846
Iannelli, Dr. Maria Teresa 25987
Iannucci, Anna Maria 25081
Ibarra, Jorge A. 21268
Ibbertson, Prof. H.K. 30106
Ibbotson, Michael P.S. 30191
Ibing-Harth, Krista 15861
Ibragimov, T.S. 27092
Ibragimov, Ulykbek Šarachynovič 27077
Ibrahim, Abbas 27690
Ice, Dr. Joyce 47426, 47427
Icershaw, Mary J. 39169
Ichijo, Akiko 26938
Ickowicz, Pierre 11507, 13053
Ide, Evan 41937
Ide, Richard 19841
Idemitsu, Shosuke 26859
Idiens, Dale 40011
Idleman, Paul 42186
Idris, Hassan Hussein 35769
Idrisov, G. 27095
Idshinnorov, S. 28683
Iemura, Katsuyuki 26992
Iercoşan, Neţa 32489
Ieronymidou, M. 08198
Ievleva, Nina Vasiljevna 33368
Ifland, Dorothee 15921
Ifsits, Marguerite 33001
Igel, Dr. Walter 17105
Iglesias Grande, Manuel 34704
Igna, Ion 32497
Igna, Mary Ann 41305
Ignatev, Viktor Jakovlevič 32943
Igrakova, Natalja Ivanovna 33320
Ihrenberger, Elisabeth 02549
Ikeda, Sakae 26815
Ikeda, Yushi 26206
Ikefuji, Kiyoshi 26914
Ikejima, Kazuo 26994
Ikitian, H. 00694
Iles, Chissie 45886
Ilg, Werner 36834
Ilg, Dr. Wolfgang 01830
Ilias, Sakalis 20840
Ilić, Dragica 33810
Ilich-Klančnik, Breda 34112
Iliescu, Prof. Constantin 32528
Iliev, Christo 04638
Iliev, Petăr 04749
Ilieva, Marija 04646
Ilisch, Dr. Peter 18950
Iljin, Vadim Jurjevič 32711
Iljina, Ljudmila Ivanovna 32658
Ilkjær, Marianne 08878
Ilkosz, Jerzy 32175
Illa i Vilà, Montserrat 35666
Ille-Kopp, Regina 16160
Illich, Dr. Inge 02545
Illuzzi, Dr. Michael C. 47517
Ilmonen, Anneli 10092, 10093
Ilon, Gabor 21500
Ilse-Neuman, Ursula 45755
Ilshöfer, B. 20283
Imai, Yoko 26938
Imami-Paydar, Niloo 44228
Imamura, Prof. Keiji 26948
Imanse, G. 28902
Imbeault, Nisk 05877
Imber, Sofia 48912
Imbernor, Laurence 13943
Imbert, Christiane 11055, 11057, 11058, 11059
Imhoff, Bert C. 06379
Imiela, Edward 31996
Immel, Dr. Wolfgang 16561
Immelman, Dr. Paul 34267
Immenkamp, Dr. Andreas 16666
Immerzeel, A.A.G. 29435
Immisch, T.O. 17521
Immonen, Kari 10138
Immonen, Olli 09760, 09761, 09762, 09763, 09765
Imori, Tsugio 26628
Imponente, Anna 24147
Impraim, Mary 20788
Imychelova, E.C. 33655
Inaba, Hisao 26603
Inaba, Yoshinori 26693
Inai, Keijirõ 26851
Inama, Dr. Johannes 02041
Inauen, Roland 36462
Inazuka, Hiroko 26969
Inbar, Yehudit 22636, 22672
Inboden, Prof. Dr. Gudrun 20106, 20106
Incardona, Dr. Angela 22820
İnce, R. Sefa 37790
Ince, Sterling 06375
Inch, John 30140
Incze, Dr. Kálmán 21345
Indahl, Trond M. 30427

Indáns, Juris 27415
Indeck, Dr. Jeff 42092
Indra, Dr. W.I. Pandji 22114
Ineba, Pilar 35601
Infante, Victor Manuel 00293
Ingber, Abie 42407
Ingebrigtsen, Dr. Kristian 30756
Ingelheim, gen. Echter von Mespelbrunn, Graf zu 18717
Ingilby, Sir Thomas C.W. 40326
Ingle, R. 38531
Inglis, Elspeth 44380
Inglis, Marion L. 05129
Inglis, R. 40716
Inglis, Robin 06025, 06026
Inglis, Stephen 05484
Ingmarsson, Niklas 36060
Ingram, Bill 43284
Ingram, Cathy 48356
Ingram, Daniel 44352, 44353
Ingram, Doris 42287
Ingram, J. 38104
Ingram, Jack 30258
Ingram, Jack E. 43427
Ingram, Lynn 41646
Ingvordsen, Jens 08770
Iniesta González, Montserrat 35659
Inkova, Mariela 04846
Inman, Edward 38456
Innes, J.F. 06059
Innes, Kathryn V. 46825
Innes, Moira 39448
Innocenti, Pierluigi 22889
Ino, Hironobu 26213
Ino, Koushin 26694
Inojatov, K.Ch. 48854
Inostroza Saavedra, Jorge E. 06925
Inoue, Kouki 26146
Inoue, Tadashi 26237
Inselmann, Andrea 44272
Inserra, Margaret 47981
Internoscia, David 45153
Intihar Ferjan, Jana 34112
Inui, Kazuo 26261
Io, Lau Si 01770
Ioanid, Radu 48401
Ion, Prof. Dr. I. 32534
Ionesco, G. 13500
Ionescu, Ruxandra 32481, 32571
Ionesov, Anatoly 48849
Ioniţă, Ionel 32451, 32453, 32454
Ioniţă, Ionel 32455
Ioniţă, Ionel 32459, 32461
Iotta, Ivana 23680
Iovinelli, Maria Teresa 25261
Iozzo, Mario 23555
Iprajian, Avedis 22660
Ireland, Lynne 45022
Ireland, Terese 42934
Irén, Kállai 21321
Iriarte, Prof. Elba Esther 00550
Iribarren Avilés, Rodrigo 06929
Irie, Yoshiro 26938
Irie, Yoshiyuki 26291
Irinina, Elena 04613, 04614, 04615
Ironside, A. 40550
Irša, Dr. Rudolf 34020
Irvin, Mary A. 41672
Irvin, Stan 41410
Irving, Gillian 38643
Irving, James 39771
Irving, Mary L. 47976
Irwin, Charles W. 41783, 46096
Irwin, Ruth E. 44536
Irwin Meyer, Elaine 45977
Irwinnson, Charles W. 41785
Isaac, Preston 38672
Isajiw, Sophia 48111
Isaković, Aziz 03915
Isaksen, Knud Fink 08850
Isawumi, Prof. Dr. M.A. 30343
Isbell, Linda 46781
Iseki, Masaaki 26947
Iser, Wunibald 18974
Isert, Ingo Rüdiger 20096
Ishag, Ali 31053
Ishibashi, Kentaro 26217
Ishiga, Harue 26205
Ishihama, Beniko 26658
Ishii, I. 26169
Ishii, Mitsuru 26336
Ishii, Susumu 26706
Ishikawa, Chiyo 47545
Ishikawa, Koichi 26367
Ishikawa, M. 26172
Ishikawa, MitsuoSakari 26993
Ishikawa, Tetsuko 26217
Ishizuka, Kaname 26178
Ishtiaq Khan, Muhammad 31027
Isifidis, Kaplanis 21011
Iske, Gary 41594
Iskender, Prof. Kemal 37705
Islamova, Tatjana Michajlovna 33610
Isler, Andreas 37418
Isler, Prof. Dr.H.P. 37369
Isler, Jacques 37348
Isler, Norman J. 48037
Ismai, Reza 22324
Isman, Eileen 06859

Isohauta, Teija 09593
Isomäki, Irmeli 09474
Ison, Susan P. 44980
Isoz, Nicolas 36438, 36439
Israel, Sue 45158
Israfilovglu, I.R. 03068
Issanjour, Guy 11956
Isshi, Kaihei 26232
Istas, Dr. Yvonne 20062
István, Dr. Berta 21352
Itai, Josef 22686
Itami, Kaneo 27029
Iten, André 36734
Ito, Masakazu 26623
Ito, Tomoyuki 26635
Itoa, Yukio 26329
Itoh, Hiroji 26593
Itoh, Ikutaro 26671
Itter, Wolfgang 18179
Ittmann, John 46442
Ivančević, Nataša 07760
Ivanenko, Pjotr Ivanovič 37860
Ivannikova, Ljudmila 33097
Ivanov, Aleksandr Aleksandrovič 33002
Ivanov, Ivan 04790, 04797, 04893
Ivanov, Stefan 04717
Ivanov, Vladimir Alexandrovič 33352
Ivanova, Galina Olegovna 32915, 33642
Ivanova, Katja 04850
Ivanova, Maja I. 33353
Ivanova, Natalja Vasiljevna 32726
Ivanova, Silvia 41701
Ivanova, Tatjana Nikolaevna 33744
Ivanovski, Nikola 27584
Ivanuš, Rhea 07822
Ivask, Krista 09358
Ivaškina, Ljudmila 33660
Ivčević, Sanja 07779
Ivelic, Milan 06916
Ivens, R. 29551
Iversen, Mette 09112
Iverson, Dr. John B. 46861
Iverson, Stephen C. 44864
Ives, Alicia 41115
Iveson, Jon 38766
Ivetić, Marija 07754
Ivey, Donald J. 44654
Ivić, Prof. Vinko 07830
Ivkanec, Ivanka 07813
Ivory, Ken 30283
Ivory, Margaret 30225
Iwamoto, Mitsuo 26252
Iwasaki, Yohachiro 26235
Iwata, Tadao 26250
Iyoku, Hideaki 26886
Izaqirre, Manu 34415
Izdebska, Barbara 32085, 32131
Izsatovska, Dora 04620
Izui, Hidekazu 26693
Jaacks, Prof. Dr. Gisela 17558
Jaakkola, Markku 09459
Jaatinen, Aija 09721
Jaatinen, Carina 09431
Jaatinen, Toimi 10075, 10076, 10081, 10090
Jaber Al-Jaber, Ibrahim 32417
Jablonská, Dr. Beáta 33978
Jablonska, Teresa 31527
Jabłońska, Teresa 32209
Jabłońska, Tereza 32205
Jablovska, Gaida 27436
Jabtonska, Teresa 32208
Jackley, Michael 43428
Jacklitch, Prof. Paul 41637
Jackowska, Anna 32051
Jackson, Bee 05485, 06416
Jackson, Bev 41094
Jackson, Bryan 05441
Jackson, G.B. 38516
Jackson, Henry 38983
Jackson, Jerry 46981
Jackson, Kenneth T. 45858
Jackson, Margaret 42628
Jackson, Paul 33755
Jackson, Robert L. 41061
Jackson, Sailor 41529
Jackson, Steven B. 41858
Jackson, Susan 39594
Jackson, Toby 39788
Jackson, Tony 38291, 40898
Jackson-Forsberg, Eric 45952
Jackson Quillen, Debra 44542
Jacob, Dr. Christina 17686, 17692
Jacob, Eric 12040
Jacob, François 36737
Jacob, John 39803
Jacob, Milner 30098
Jacob, Dr. Wenzel 16241
Jacob-Friesen, Dr. Holger 18002
Jacobacci, Emilia 25227
Jacobeit, Dr. Sigrid 17158
Jacobi, Dr. Fritz 16075
Jacobi, H.W. 29519
Jacobs, Charles 45205
Jacobs, Edwin 29684
Jacobs, F.J. 34193
Jacobs, Flora Gill 48406
Jacobs, John 43792
Jacobs, Joseph 45892
Jacobs, Karen 47393

Jacobs, Marty 45847
Jacobs, Ted Seth 12532
Jacobsen, Anne Marie 08849
Jacobsen, Bent Sonne 08988
Jacobsen, Gaute 30641
Jacobsen, Harald 30877
Jacobsen, Robert 45391
Jacobsen, Signe 09104
Jacobson, Alice 43187
Jacobson, Andrew 45985
Jacobson, Harold 44433
Jacobson, L. 34290
Jacobson, LouAnn 42957
Jacobson, Sally 43193
Jacobson, Thomas N. 46353
Jacobson, Thora E. 46455
Jacobson Zuckerman, Heidi 41649
Jacobsson, Ingela 36333
Jacobsson, Nils E. 36154
Jacobsson, Yvonne 36249
Jacoupy, Charles 14752
Jacquat, Jeannine 37028
Jacquat, Marcel S. 36629
Jacqué, B. 13983
Jacquemin, Hervé 14196
Jacquemyn, Erik 03621
Jacques, Annie 13494
Jacques, Gary E. 42005
Jacques, R.A. 14841
Jacquesson, Alain 36728
Jacquet, Alain 14969
Jacquot, Dominique 14832
Jadid Hashim Bin, Mohamed 04595, 04596
Jadoda, Rachel 44924
Jaeger, Anders 08787
Jäger, Dr. Hagen 16816
Jäger, Hans 02383
Jäger, Dr. Joachim 15981
Jäger, Leo 17310
Jäger, Dr. M. 16670
Jaeger, Dr. Monika 01920
Jaeger, Steven D. 45372
Jäger, Veronika 17798
Jaegere, Isabelle De 03540, 03541, 03543
Jaeggi, Dr. Annemarie 15916
Jäggi, Hans 36792
Jaehner, Inge 19278, 19280
Jämbäck, Juha 09954
Jäppinen, Jere 09488
Järliden, Barbro 36003
Järvinen, Marja-Liisa 10014
Järvinen, Vesa 09465
Jaffe, Steven 45858, 45874
Jagdfeld, Monika 17674
Jagenteufel, Hermann 03052
Jager, Dr. G.W.M. 29812
Jaggi, Konrad 37393
Jahan-Giry, Dr. Ali 22260
Jahn, Dr. Peter 16045
Jahn, Thomas 18038
Jahn, Dr. Wolfgang 16850
Jahnigen, Rick 42401
Jahnke-Lowis, Ilse 19001
Jaillet, G. 37277
Jain, Dr. Jyotindra 21768
Jaindl, Franz 02760
Jajčević, Zdenko 07825
Jakeman, Estelle 40812
Jakeuchi, Yoichi 26354
Jakeway, Robert 46964
Jaki, Barbara 34114
Jaklin, Dr. Ingeborg 02859
Jakober, Yannick 34439
Jakobi, Jan 18747
Jakobsen, Björn M. 35958
Jakobsen, Egil Olav 30486
Jakobsen, S.E. 08870
Jakobson, Hans-Peter 17244
Jakobsons, Imants 27325
Jakomin, Dušan 25828
Jakoubĕová, Dr. Vladimíra 08694
Jakovleva, G.A. 33138
Jakovleva, Marina Dmitrievna 33480
Jakovleva, Nadežda Petrovna 33673
Jakovljević, Goran 07681
Jakubowski, Dr. Krzysztof 32137
Jakuševa, Valentina Maksimovna 33743
Jalal, Masoody 22335
Jalandoni, Carlos L. 31329
Jalava, Mari 09615, 10153, 10154, 10155
Jaletzke, Christian 16274
Jalilian, S.J. 22307
Jalon, Rita 03137, 03161
Jamal, Syed 27639
Jambon, Marcel 12123, 12124
James Jr., Alton 45850
James, Beth 43106
James, Betty 05416
James, Debbie 38125
James, Jon G. 48720
James, Louise 48748
James, Marion E. 43026
James, Sigrid 05432
James-Sarazin, Ariane 13574
Jamieson, Louise 01586
Jamieson, P.M. 05937
Jaminon, Martine 03570
Jamison, Wayne 42870
Jamkhedkar, Dr. A.P. 22009

Jammot, Dr. Dominique 13433
Jampen, Ulrich 37351
Jamro, Ron D. 45601
Jamščikova, Natalja Borisovna 33684
Jan, Darja 34089
Janas, Stanisław 31876
Jančár, Dr. Ivan 33963
Jančenko, Natalja Andreevna 33708
Janda, Martin 02647
Jandl, Ferdinand 01678
Janecek, James 46714
Janek, Eva 21368
Janes, Todd 05378
Janev, Georgi 04866
Jangoux, Prof. M. 03314
Janics, Dr. Hunert 01969
Janik, Michael 02127
Janjić, Gordan 33862
Jankavs, Peter 36194
Janke, Volker 19897
Jankov, Dr. Peter 20259
Jankova, Julia 04678
Jankova Kazakova, Rumjana 04647
Janković, Ljubica 33905
Jankovskij, Anatolij A. 37841
Jankowski, Andrzej 31659
Janků, Miloslav 08315
Jankulovski, Plamen 04764
Janneau, O. 10963
Jannek, Norbert 17967, 18116
Jannet, Monique 13318
Jannke, William 48446
Janović, Ognjana 07746
Janovy, Karen 44791
Jans, Mares 36718
Janscó, Istvan 34487
Janse, K.P.J. 28894
Jansen, Edward 47989
Jansen, F.W. 39430
Jansen, G. 29759
Jansen jr, John D. 42557
Jansen, Kristian 30497
Jansén, Maija 10123
Jansen, Siri 30415, 30423
Jansen, Dr. Steve 44688
Jansen Bramer, T. 29967
Janser, Andres 37397
Janssen, David 42156
Janssen, Dr. J.A.M.M. 29843
Janssen, Laura 48549
Janssen, Peter G. 18254
Janssen, S. 03146
Janssens, Dominique-Charles 10503
Janssens, Jan 03616
Jansson, Björn 36220
Jansson, Kyle R. 47209
Jansson, Tarja 09771
Jantjes, Gavin 30571
Jantsch, Karl 01980
Janu, Jan A. 02706
Janus, Jerzy 31530
Januszkiewicz, Bolesław 31910
Janzen, Thomas 18225, 18227, 18229
Janzweert, Jan 17490
Jaouen, Jean-Pierre 10695
Jaques, S.A. 39883
Jara, Dr. Holguer 09194
Jaramillo Agudelo, Darío 07404
Jaramillo Salazar, Juan Andrés 07563, 07567
Jardim, Frank 43406
Jarh, Dr. Orest 34122
Jarocka-Bieniek, Jolanta 32022
Jaros, John R. 41394
Jaros, Susan 42466
Jaros, Urszula Maria 31873
Jarosch, Jessica 01699
Jaroševskaja, Valentina Michajlovna 32952
Jaroszewicz, Mieczysław 31980
Jarquín Pacheco, Ana María 28069
Jarratt, Ardell 46697
Jarrell, Gordon 43258
Jarrige, Jean-François 13633
Jarron, Matthew 38805
Jarvie, Robert 40185
Jarvis, Anthea 39886, 39892
Jarvis, Antony 38737
Jarvis, P.D. 39428
Jarzembowski, Prof. Dr. E. 39877
Jasbar, Dr. Gerald 20261
Jasim, Dr. Sabah 37921
Jasiuk, Jerzy 31971, 32129
Jaskanis, Paweł Olaf 32117
Jaskowiak, Jennifer 44899
Jaskulski, Janusz 31905
Jastram-Porsche, Sabine 19301
Jastrebova, Raisa 33234
Jastrzębski, Jerzy 31780
Jatti Bredekamp, Prof. Henry C. 34200, 34201, 34206
Jaukkuri, Maaretta 09501
Jaupaj, Arben 00011
Jauslin, Dr. J.-F. 36550
Jávor, Anna 21360
Jaworowicz, Hanna 31634
Jay, Hilary 46402
Jaynell, Chambers 44488
Jaysane, A. Patricia 44689
Jean, Louis 37964
Jeanbrau, Héléne 12527

Jeandron, Angela 44472
Jeanes, K.I. 34245
Jeanmart, Jacques 03649
Jeanneney, Jean-Noël 13478
Jeannot, Bernard 13569, 13653
Jeanselme, Brigitte 14974
Jeansson Kock, Brgitta 36281
Jebreil Zadeh, A. 22273
Jecha, James 44535
Jeck, Siegrun 17848
Jeckel, J. 29898
Jedda McNab, Barbara 47131
Jędrzejewski, Antoni 32031
Jefferies, Dr. Chris 43007
Jefferies, Richard 38621
Jefferies, Susan 06580
Jeffery, Gordon 06649
Jeffet, William 47176
Jeffrey, Susan 39395
Jeffries, Bill 06027
Jegorov, Boris Michajlovič 32647
Jehl, Dr. Rainer 17917
Jehle, Michael 45662
Jehle-Schulte Strathaus, Dr. Ulrike 36496
Jeitler, Johannes 02785
Jekov, Vasko 04847
Jelavić, Zeljka 07813
Jeletich, Dr. F. 29222
Jelfs, Ann 30246
Jeličić, Janko 07822
Jelinek, Dr. Zdeněk 08563
Jelinková, Jaroslava 08747, 08748
Jeliseeva, Tatjana 33177
Jelvakova, Irena A. 33075
Jemison, Gerald Peter 48231
Jenal, Christian 37096
Jenal, Ludwig 37096
Jenderko-Sichelschmidt, Dr. Ingrid 15522, 15526, 15531, 15533
Jenisch, R. Dietlinde 17318
Jenkins, Adrian 38087
Jenkins, Carol 46370
Jenkins, Charles 38262
Jenkins, Donald 46641
Jenkins, Frances Susong 43652
Jenkins, Sabra 47649
Jenkins, Sue 38095
Jenkner, Ingrid 05557
Jenko, Helena 34117
Jenko, Mojca 34114
Jenks, Tracey 41238
Jenne, Hans-Jörg 16855
Jenneman, Eugene A. 48050
Jenni, Rudi 00917
Jennings, Lucille 46074
Jennings, Peter 40390
Jennings, Sibley 41229
Jensch, Dr. Rainer 20395
Jensen, B. 30256
Jensen, Carol Ann 43187
Jensen, Ellen Elisabeth 09098
Jensen, Erik 08947
Jensen, Harold 41435
Jensen, Herbert 17881
Jensen, Dr. Inken 18615
Jensen, Dr. Jacob B. 08896
Jensen, James 44073, 44074
Jensen, Johan M. 08933
Jensen, Dr. Jürgen 18074
Jensen, Kathleen A. 47758
Jensen, Ken 45176
Jensen, Loring 47871
Jensen, M. Wayne 48008
Jensen, Mona 48016
Jensen, Niels Erik 08962
Jensen, Ole G. 21241
Jensen, Otto 06471
Jensen, Pam 42852
Jensen, Sterling 05974
Jensen, Tom 05973
Jensen, Vivi 08959
Jensner, Magnus 35948
Jenssen, Ragnar 30450
Jentsch, Dr. F. 17100
Jenvold, Birgit 08959
Jeppesen, Hans 08861
Jepson, D. 40115
Jerg, Alfred 18359
Jerković, Dragan 33819
Jerlich, Walter 01695
Jerner, Ingbritt 36153
Jerome, Jeff 41464
Jerris, Rand 43288
Jervois, W. 34250
Jésman, Prof. Czesław 31774
Jesretić, Miroslav 33913
Jessat, Mike 15451
Jesse, Bernd 42304
Jessewitsch, Dr. Rolf 19985
Jessop, L. 40036
Jessup, Scott 01328
Jeszenszky, Dr. Sándor 21355
Jette, Carol 41188
Jette, David 45883
Jetzer, Gianni 37101
Jeufroy, Pierre 11859
Jeutter, Dr. Ewald 16485
Jevdjević, Ivana 03924
Jevtović, Jevta 33796

Jevtović, Mila 33810
Jewell, Brian 39172
Jeziorowski, Tadeusz 31915
Jezler, Peter 36541, 36691, 37000
Jezman, Meike 20161, 20162
Ježowitzová, Jiřina 08381
Ji, Gon Gil 27183
Ji, Qian 07184
Jian, Li 42801
Jibah, Matassim Bin Haji 04598
Jillis, Nellie 34259
Jiménez, Angel 35400
Jiménez Chávez, Alma Rosa 28209
Jiménez Espejo, Francisco J. 35137
Jiménez Vásquez, Gustavo 07548
Jimeno Santoyo, Myriam 07428
Jiminez, Jill A. 45421
Jimison, Tom 45567
Jimmie, Charles 43869
Jin, Jon Moon 27120
Jing, Guo 07146
Jing Weng, Liao 06995
Jirmusová, Hana 08302
Joachim, Karin 15704
Joannette, Michelle 05624
Joans, Dr. Barbara 46064
Jobin, Pamela A. 48663
Jobke, Ryszard 31817
Jobst-Rieder, Marianne 02955
Joch, Peter 16545
Jochem, Marlene 17971
Jochims, Richard 17212, 17697
Jochum, Franz 02367
Jockel, Nils 17560
Jodice, Dorothy 45094
Jodłowski, Prof. Antoni 32153
Joel, Judy 40409
Joenniemi, Sirpa 10091
Jönsson, Bertil 35874
Jönsson, Tomas 36003, 36116
Jörg, Christiaan 29309
Jöris, Dr. Olaf 18606, 19086
Joffre, Roland 12472
Joger, Prof. Dr. Ulrich 16304
Johannessen, Arild 30495
Johannessen, Jeanette 48293
Johannessen, Kåre 09070
Johannessen, Preben L. 30561
Johannesson, Birgitte 08931
Johannewes, Alice 47930
Johannsen, Hermann 18334
Johannsen, Ilona 20613
Johannsen, Karin 17314
Johannsen, Ruby 44180
Johannson, Sigfus 05787
Johansen, Annette 09058
Johansen, Jens 08892
Johansen, Rikke 09112
Johansson, Börje 35783
Johansson, Conny 36060
Johansson, Hjördis 36309
Johansson, Jan 36048
Johansson, Karin 36122
Johansson, Kennet 36072, 36077, 36078, 36080, 36081
Johansson, Ketty 08993, 08994
Johansson, Kjell 36016, 36257
Johansson, Lars G. 36035
Johansson, Marie 36326, 36342
Johansson, Sonny 36336
Johansson, Tina 36309
Johansson, Ulf 09883
Johansson, Ulrica 36349
John, J. 08535
John-Willeke, Bettina 16539, 16548
Johncock, M. 01135
Johnes, John 41334
Johns, Dana 41461
Johns, Daniel 44156
Johns, Sharleen 43008
Johns, Valerie 43747
Johnsen, Aksel 30905
Johnsen, Berit Åse 30590
Johnsen, Duane 43550
Johnson, Alfred E. 44684
Johnson, Allen 43995
Johnson, Amy Jo 46572
Johnson, Andrew 38872
Johnson, Anne J. 46283
Johnson, Arden 43959
Johnson, Audrey 47714
Johnson, Barbara B. 44291
Johnson, Brooks 45963
Johnson, Byron 45570
Johnson, Byron A. 48269
Johnson, C. 39894
Johnson, C. Clayton 46657
Johnson, Carl 06272
Johnson, Christine 30306
Johnson, Colin 38484
Johnson, Craig 47151, 47157
Johnson, D. Thomas 41539
Johnson, Dale 38075
Johnson, David 46515
Johnson, David A. 48119
Johnson, David T. 42410
Johnson, Diana 45614
Johnson, Diane 42726
Johnson, Dorothy E. 41734

Johnson, Drew 46067
Johnson, Dwayne 43611
Johnson, Edward 47791
Johnson, Dr. Eileen 44991
Johnson, Elsie 05583
Johnson, Frank 34283
Johnson, Gerardo 21300
Johnson, Gina 47812
Johnson, Grace 47294
Johnson, Harold 47488
Johnson, Dr. Heide-Marie 45271
Johnson, James 42279
Johnson, James L. 43340
Johnson, Jean 42241
Johnson, Jeanne 47389
Johnson, Jennifer L. 42586
Johnson, Jeremy 00763, 00765
Johnson, Jerome Martin 44573
Johnson, Joan 40733
Johnson, Dr. John R. 47405
Johnson, Kathleen E. 47957
Johnson, Kaytie 43799
Johnson, Kenneth R. 43599
Johnson, Kevin 38205
Johnson, Dr. Kirk R. 42887, 42887
Johnson, Kurt 43034
Johnson, Laurel 00762
Johnson, LaVern M. 45012
Johnson, Lewis 48577
Johnson, Libba 42582
Johnson, Louis 45751
Johnson, Lydia 42146
Johnson, Mark M. 45467
Johnson, Marlo L. 44421
Johnson, Mary 48582
Johnson, Mary A. 47230
Johnson, Maurianna 44695
Johnson, Maxine 48216
Johnson, Melinda 45578
Johnson, Melissa 44950
Johnson, Nancy T. 45442
Johnson, Ned K. 41647
Johnson, Nichola 40100
Johnson, Nina 43785
Johnson, Patricia 01086
Johnson, Penny 39646
Johnson, Polly 44506
Johnson, Richard 41828
Johnson, Dr. Richard E. 46743
Johnson, Robert E. 48219
Johnson, Robert S. 43426
Johnson, Robin 38643
Johnson, Dr. Ron 06753
Johnson, Sandra L. 46344
Johnson, Sarah 43655
Johnson, Sharon 42739, 47965
Johnson, Sheila A. 06865
Johnson, Steven 42839
Johnson, Stuart 45569
Johnson, Suni 41475
Johnson, Terry 45278
Johnson, Thomas B. 48792
Johnson, Tom 48790
Johnson, Twig 45450
Johnson, Vanessa 47912
Johnson, William C. 43636
Johnson, William M. 42911
Johnson Bowles, Kay 43304
Johnsson, Anders 35860
Johnston, Alan 38860
Johnston, Catherine 06084
Johnston, Phillip 46721
Johnston, Renée 05577
Johnston, Richard 47172
Johnston, Sally 41487
Johnston, Sona 41454
Johnston, Stephen 40149
Johnston, Virginia 42947
Johnston, William R. 41489
Join-Diéterle, Catherine 13615
Jojo, Eva 45399
Jolie, Renee 47426
Jolivel, D. 11061
Jolliff, Dawna 43990
Jolly, Dr. Anna 37064
Jolly, Guy 12063
Jomppanen, Tarmo 09569
Jonaitis, Aldona 43258
Jones, Alan 40547
Jones, Amanda C. 45137
Jones, Andy B. 48606
Jones, Anita 41454
Jones, Ann 38887
Jones, Anne 38982
Jones, Prof. B. 05381
Jones, Barbara L. 43821
Jones, Brenda 48601
Jones, Dr. Cheri A. 42887
Jones, Claire 38087
Jones, Clive 38563
Jones, C.R. 42618, 42619
Jones, Cynthia L. 43870
Jones, D. Keith 38648
Jones, D.L. 39305
Jones, Donna 06403
Jones, Donna P. 47664
Jones, Dr. Douglas S. 43581, 43581
Jones, Duffie 44346
Jones, E. Michael 03888

Jones, E.B. 30278
Jones, Edward 43571
Jones, Prof. E.L. 38219
Jones, Elisabeth 42402
Jones, Eric 38577
Jones, Erin 43829
Jones, Glenn 43776, 45655
Jones, Gwyneth 38628
Jones, Harvey 46067
Jones, Hugh R. 45002
Jones, Huw 38643
Jones, Jeanne 39827
Jones, Jeff 46229
Jones, Jill 47538
Jones, J.M. 38825
Jones, Joan 40608, 40610
Jones, Joanna 40557
Jones, Joy 05794
Jones, Julie 45833
Jones, Kathy 05191, 43077
Jones, Keith 00986, 39091
Jones, Larry A. 44956
Jones, Lester 38563
Jones, Lial A. 47050
Jones, Linda 42173, 42709, 47815
Jones, Lisa 00842
Jones, Lowell N. 42382
Jones, Margaret Ann 46174
Jones, Marilyn 44278, 46678, 47892
Jones, Mark 39795, 40011
Jones, Mike 47938
Jones, Nia 39972
Jones, R. 05935
Jones, Rhian 41102
Jones, Richard 38480
Jones, Dr. Robert 44281
Jones, Ronald D. 42024
Jones, Sian 40549
Jones, Stephen 46576
Jones, Sue 39001
Jones, Suzi 41197
Jones, Thomas 45328
Jones, Prof. Tom 38218
Jones, Trevor 38768
Jones, W.J. 30275
Jones Cox, Beverly 48382
Jones Harper, Suzanne 45044
Jong, C.C. de 29446
Jong, Dr. H. de 28917
Jong, Dr. Jutta de 20688
Jong, L. de 03146
Jong, Dr. M.A. de 29121
Jong, S. de 29759
Jonge, Eddy de 29309
Jonge, J.M. de 29358
Jonge, P. de 29686
Jongh, Marja de 29729
Jongh-Vermeulen, Dr. A. de 28823
Jonghe, Mieke de 03369
Jongs, Carel 05440
Jongstra, Jaap 29514
Jonin, Marie-Thérèse 11234
Jonker, Dr. A. 29136
Jonsson, Ingrid 36215
Jónsson, Petur 21626
Joo-Sik, Kim 27201
Joohee, Kim 27243
Joos, Cristian 37362
Joppien, Dr. Rüdiger 17560
Joppig, Dr. Gunther 18880, 18888
Jordaens, Lode 03409, 03410
Jordan, Brenda 44536, 44538, 44539
Jordan, Daniel P. 42252
Jordán, Dr. František 08731
Jordan, Kurt 17470
Jordan, Prof. Dr. Lothar 17083
Jordan, Manuel 43995
Jordan, Mary Alice 47379, 47380
Jordan, Peter 37188
Jordan, Robert 05302
Jordan, Thomas E. 43668
Jordan Wass, Catherine H. 45963, 48243
Jordanov, Ivan 04784
Jordanova, Zojca 04609
Jordanović, Branislava 33815
Jordon, G. 00869
Jordon, J. Greg 43183
Jørgensen, Anja 08962
Jørgensen, Erik 08849
Jørgensen, Mogens 08944
Jorgensen, Roy 43325
Jorikson, Håkan 35927
Joris, J.L. 03513
Joris, Yvònne G.J.M. 29405
Jorquera Caro, Sonia Alexandra 28280
Jorrand, C. 12339
Jorrín García, J.A. 35151
Josanu, Vitalie 32612
Joselu, Sergio 23167
Joseph, Carolyn 43963
Joseph, Jean-Louis 10385
Joseph, Laurel 38534
Joseph, Sarah 43758
Joseph-Debaque, Sandrine 11287
Josephson, Magnus 36128
Josephsson, Eva 36120
Joshi, Prof. B.D. 21837
Joshi, Mallickarjun 22057
Joshi, Vishwanath N. 21972

Josias, Anthea 34178
Josić, Zoran 33787
Josifovich, Jorge A. 00474
Joslin, Stewart 48023
Joss, Laura 41467
Jossifova, Maria 04846
Jost, Gerda 17226
Jost, Loren 46925
Jost, Stephan 46065
Jost-Przesłakowska, Maria 32038
Josvai, Jason 44318, 44319
Jósvai, Dr. Katalin Dankó 21524
Jotov, Petko 04855
Jotterand, Suzanne 36437
Joubeaux, Hervé 11194
Joubert, Alain 12199, 12200, 12876, 13365
Jouen, Jean-Pierre 12156
Jourdan, Aleth 10286, 10287
Jourdan, Patrick 13163
Jouzeau, Marie-Hélène 13251
Jovanov, Dr. Jasna 33873
Jovanović, Igor 33824
Jovel Castro, Walter E. 07661
Jovelić, Marijana 33819
Jović, Vukašin 33824
Joy, Catdlind 35279
Joyaux, Alain 45555
Joyce, Dan 44441
Joyce, Martin J. 22363
Joyce, Rosemary 41648
Joyeux, Y. 03235
Joyner, Elizabeth 48227, 48230
Joyner, Roger D. 43818
Ju, Calvin 07348
Juárez, Marcelo O. 00209
Juárez Nieto, M. Magdalena Sofía 28336
Juchli, Cornelia M. 37193
Juchniewich, Daniel 45116
Judd, Martha 44058
Judge, Joseph M. 45965
Judge, Vancy 48693
Judson, E. 34350
Judson, Etta 34366
Judson, Dr. Horace 46549
Judson, Jack 47254
Judson, William D. 46510
Juelich, Clarence 48586
Jülich, Dr. Theo 16541
Jüllig, Carola 15939
Jürries, Wolfgang 18263
Jufa, Marija 33314
Juffinger, Dr. Roswitha 02548
Juhl, Kirsten 30877
Jul, Ole 09093
Jules Kouloufoua, Jean Gilbert 07645
Julia, I. 13639
Julia y Macias, Manuel 35119
Juliusburger, Thomas 41892
Julkunen, Pirjo 09831, 09832, 09833, 09834
Jullian, Nathalie 13489
Jullien, Pierre 14936
Jumala, Francis C. 31469
Jumalla, Joesilo C. 31295
Jumalon, Julian N. 31290
Jumalon, Prof. Julian N. 31313
Jumelet, J. 29032
Jumping Bull, Calvin 46492
Juncà Bonal, Mariona 34528
Juncosa, Enrique 22436
Juneau, Madeleine 05923
Junek, David 08554, 08555, 08556
Jung, H. 29650
Jung, Heinrich 17384
Jung, Ilse 02918
Jung, Ludwig 19604
Jung, Mark 45369
Jung, Dr. Michael 25231
Jungbluth, Carmen 41785
Junge, Brigitte 15578
Junge, Claudia 18387
Junge, Dr. Michael 17818
Junge, Dr. Peter 15945
Junghans, Dr. Günther 18629
Junginger, Ernst 18326, 18327
Junhem, Inga 36296
Junier, Caroline 36984
Junker, Almut 17055
Junker, Patricia 43480
Junkins, Tom 43480
Junno, Johanna 10202, 10205, 10206
Junno-Pennanen, Johanna 09900
Juntikka, Ilse 09897
Juntunen, Judy 46469
Juranek, Christian 20529
Jurchuk, Dmitri 16008
Jurdana, Ela 07822
Jurdyga, Judy 06406
Jurecka, Małgorzata 31940
Jurevičius, J. 27523
Jurgemeyer, Marne 43432
Jurić, Radomir 07743, 07804
Jurica, Varina 07703
Jurkāne, Anna 27451
Jurkiewicz, Jan Gustaw 32201
Jurovics, Toby 46703
Jurriaans-Helle, Dr. G. 28835
Jusić, Enisa 03912
Jussila, Neil 41689
Just, Arthur 02959

Just, Helmut 02853
Just, Dr. Johannes 16701, 19470
Just, Rüdiger 17522
Justus, Dr. Antje 18606, 19086
Justus, Dirk 17534
Justus, Mary Beth 41317
Jutkeit, A. 18940
Juton, Alain 12986
Jutras, Michel 06638
Juul, Steffen 09056
Juul Holm, Michael 08902
Juva, Antti 09936, 09937
Juvonen-Eskola, Annamari 09431
Juzwenko, Dr. Adolf 32193
Kaack, Dr. Joachim 18832
Kaak, L. Joachim 18124
Kaarto, Sari 09983
Kaasen, Gunnar 30680, 30682
Kaasen, Svanhild Alver 30508
Kaba, Sory 21279
Kabat, Nora 47433
Kabayama, Koichi 26873
Kabić, Dušan 33824
Kábrtova, Jiřina 08527
Kabrud, Jack 45384
Kabus, Dr. Ronny 18561
Kačalova, Alisa D. 32701
Kačírek, Ľuboš 33969
Kaczarová, Iveta 34019
Kaczmarczyk, Witold 32002
Kaczynski, Prof. Dr. R. 18868
Kadake, Henrich 44375
Kaden, Antje 16406
Kadlec, Dr. František 08569, 08582, 08583, 08586, 08590, 08607, 08614
Kadota, Keizo 26487
Kadovitz, Sherri 44952
Kadowaki, Akira 26962
Kadurina, Elena 04798
Kadurina, Emilija 04799
Kadyrov, A.S. 37445
Käär, Pekka 10132
Käch, Robert 37049
Kaehr, Roland 36985
Kaelcke, Wolfgang 19348, 19349
Kämpf, Michael 18280
Kämpfner, Gabriele 16263
Kaenel, Gilbert 36857
Känsälä, Risto 09643
Kärgling, Dr. Karlheinz 18581, 18584
Kärki, Sirpa 36114
Kärnefelt, Prof. Ingvar 36056
Käs, Rudolf 19145, 19162
Kaeser, Dr. Bert 18911
Kaeser, Dr. Marc-Autoine 37393
Kaeser, Olivier 36725
Kaesler, Roger L. 44685
Kästner, Dr. Klaus Peter 16711
Kästner, Dr. Klaus-Peter 17738
Kästner, Ursula 15914
Kästner, Dr. Volker 15914
Käyhkö, Unto 09650
Kafetsi, Anna 20894
Kager, Stephen J. 48728
Kagioka, Masanori 26355
Kahan, Mitchell 41072
Kahari, Prof. George P. 49032
Kahin, Dr. Sharon 42990
Kahle, Patricia 45708
Kahle, Sharon M. 42926
Kahler, Caroline 44808
Kahn, David M. 43938
Kahn, Leo 47432
Kahn, Tammie 44117
Kahng, Eik 41489
Kaijt, W.P.A.M. 28915
Kailashnathan 21678
Kaindl, Heimo 01912
Kaiqu, Liu 06956
Kaire, Inese 27401
Kaiser, Dr. Barbara 01934
Kaiser, Friederike 18823
Kaiser, F.W. 29095
Kaiser, H. 17866
Kaiser, Dr. Hermann 16479
Kaiser, Michael 19138
Kaiser, Miriam 28199
Kaiser, Peter 37008
Kaiser, Philipp 36505
Kaiser, Dr. Stephan 18183
Kaiser-Reka, Berol 16278
Kaißer, Paul 20339
Kaizuka, Tsuyoshi 26832
Kaján, Imre 21413
Kajanus, Pirkko 09557
Kajdarov, A. 48859
Kajikawa, Yoshitomo 26407
Kajitani, Nobuko 45833
Kakko, Leena 10080
Kakourou-Chrossi, Dr. Georgia 21166
Kakuda, Arata 26217
Kakui, Hiroshi 26923
Kakusei, Miki 26292
Kal, W.H. 28866
Kalajainen, Jason 44055
Kalanj, Marko 33832
Kalantzes, Isabelle 47234
Kalašnik, Tatjana Nikolajevna 32834
Kalašnikov, Nikolaj Ivanovič 33556

Kalčev, Kamen 04670
Kalčev, Petar 04868
Kalchthaler, Peter 17107, 17114
Kaldewei, Dr. Gerhard 16567, 16569
Kaldor, Cynthia 45210
Kaldy, Robert 02956
Kale, Matt 44628
Kalela-Brundin, Maarit 36066
Kalenberg, Angel 41017
Kalenitchenko, Liliane 14074
Kalicki, Jerzy 31678
Kalina-Vidić, Ivana 33810
Kalinová, Dr. Alena 08267
Kalinsky, Nicola 38917
Kalista, Dagmar 02969
Kalkhoff, Gabriele 19258
Kalkmann, Hans-Werner 15727
Kallas, Nick 48139
Kallberg, Ulla 10120
Kallicas, Antonia 08183, 08184
Kalligas, P. 20844
Kallinich, Prof. Dr. Joachim 16055
Kallio, Maija-Riitta 09744
Kallista, Dr. Antonín 08314
Kalmite, Lelde Alida 45302
Kalmring, Sven 19793
Kalnins, Indulis 47056
Kalokerinos, Alexis 20975
Kalpakova, Akgul 37821
Kalpickaja, Elena Jakovlevna 33409
Kalsan, Prof. Vladimir 07687
Kaltenberger, Johann 02583
Kaltenbrunner, Regina 02550
Kalter, Prof. Dr. Johannes 20099
Kaltsas, Dr. Nikolaos 20873
Kaltved, Kenneth 43218
Kalus, Dr. Jaromír 08518, 08520, 08522
Kamada, Masataka 26701
Kamakura, Gizo 26182
Kamal, Hassan 37437
Kamansky, David 46303
Kamarun, Prof. Ham Rabeah 27686
Kamber, Ljubomir 33854
Kamber, Robert 36848
Kamber, Urs 36434
Kamburg, Petra 17637
Kamenov, Dr. Petar 04846
Kamer, S.J. 29613
Kamerling, Leonard 43258
Kamii, Monsho 26989
Kamijo, Kazuo 26758
Kamilia, Gharbi 37568
Kamino, Yoshiharu 26359
Kaminski, Jane 15918
Kamiya, Yukio 26183
Kamm, David 42838
Kamm, James J. 45235
Kammel, Dr. Frank Matthias 19139
Kamp 19711
Kamp, Dr. Diane D. 47961
Kampe, Allen 45746
Kamper, Gerard de 34341
Kamphausen, Dr. Donat 19438
Kamps, F. 29369
Kamps, Toby 44548
Kamuhangire, Dr. E 37829
Kamyšova, Antonina Abramovna 32715
Kan, G. 30023
Kan, Zhung 07319
Kana Anderson, Gail 45974
Kanabe, Albert 05404
Kanaga, Marian 44801
Kanaseki, Hiroshi 26607
Kanavrov, Darin 04611
Kanazawa, Tadao 26502
Kandeler-Fritsch, Martina 02929
Kandl, Veronica 43759
Kane, Debbie 43251
Kane, Debra 30260
Kane, Katherine 43939
Kane, Linda 05297
Kane, Patricia 45700
Kane, Randy 48639
Kane, Richard 45827
Kane, Robert E. 48632
Kaneichi, Ninomiya 26243
Kaneko, Kenji 26938
Kaneko, Yuriko 26693
Kanev, Ivajlo 04846
Kang, Prof. Joeng-Won 27276
Kania, Rolf 19178
Kania-Schütz, Monika 17443
Kankaala, Katri 09838
Kannan, Dr. R. 21744
Kanner, Debbie 43251
Kannu, T. 33939
Kano, Betty 46069
Kano, Kenji 26345
Kano, Takumi 26959
Kanowski, Dr. Claudia 19794
Kant Monteith, Joanita 45415
Kanter, Laurence B. 45833
Kantvilas, G. 01106
Kao, Deborah 42042
Kapches, Dr. Mima 06607
Kapelkova, Kristina 04846
Kapeller, Anne 37393
Kapfer, Otto 02363
Kapfer, Rudolf 02752

Kapinan, Catherine 48343
Kapinčeva, Dr. Iskra 04902
Kaplan, Dave 44819
Kaplan, David 44525
Kaplan, Ilee 44858
Kaplan, Luděk 08357
Kaplan, Nitzah 22592
Kaplan, Dr. Susan A. 41972
Kaplan, Wendy 44921
Kapler, Joseph 44907
Kapp de Thouzellier, Annemarie 17421
Kappeler, Richard 46248
Kappelmark, Ragnhild 36316
Kapronczay, Dr. Károly 21325, 21382
Kaptain, H.J. 08799
Kaptein, Helen 01487
Kapusta, Jan 08491
Kapustina, Nadežda Ivanovna 37846, 37848, 37849, 37850
Karabaic, Milena 19178
Karačevcev, Vladimir F. 32803
Karadi, Gabriella 06591
Karadontis, Fleurette 20824
Karajotov, Dr. Ivan 04631
Karakas, Steve 46630
Karakuzov, Kumekbay 27087
Karamaliki, Nota 20915
Karaman, Antun 07688, 07702
Karamanou, Aglaia 20928
Karamanou, Dr. Aglaia 20932
Karamitrou-Mentesidi, Georgia 20813
Karamzin, Alex 47330
Karanitsch, Peter 02312
Karantzali, Efthymia 21039
Kararadeva, Svetozara 04822
Karas, Lourdes 46523
Karasawa, Masahiro 26938
Karaseva, Alevtina Pavlovna 32660
Karaska, Dušan 33990
Karastamati, Dr. Helen 20872
Karbacher, Ursula 37108
Kardon, Nina 43470
Kardong, Don 47726
Kardosh, Judy 06681
Karegar, M. 22311
Karge, Dr. Wolf 19901
Karhoff, Brent 43087
Karhu, Jari 09520
Karhunen, Pentti 09433
Karibo, Lou 43511, 43515
Karijord Snørvik, Kjersti 30794
Karimov, S. 48853
Karinen, Helge 36224
Karingi, Lina 27111
Karinja, Snježana 34138
Karis, Sirje 09384
Karjalainen, Tuula 19501
Kärkliņa, Rūta 27410
Karlinger, Friedrich 02756
Karlsdottir, Anna Stella 30813, 30814
Karlsson, Anders 36349
Karlsson, Eva-Lena 36088
Karlsson, Henrik 09816
Karlsson, Lars Olov 35786
Karlsson, Stig 35823
Karlsson, Willy 36156
Karlstedt, Harry 09882
Karman Ohlberger, Christina 36124
Karmazin, N.I. 32987, 32989, 32991
Karnath, Sonja 20001
Karnauchova, Galina Georgievna 32661
Karner, Dr. Regina 03001
Karnes, Andrea 43489
Karneth, Dr. Rainer 15477
Károly, Simon 21346
Karon, Stephen A. 47910
Karosas, Gintaras 27535
Karov, Zdravko 04779
Karpf, Kurt 02527
Karpińska, Zofia 32050
Karpova, M.I. 33516
Karpowicz, Ewa 32008
Karppinen, Eira 09699, 09700
Karppinen, Hannu 09415, 09416
Karr, Ed F. 46319
Karrenbrock-Berger, Anneli 18122
Karsalainen, Tuula 09487
Karsch, Sylvia 18568
Karsmizki, Kenneth W. 41858
Karstadt, Bruce N. 45380
Karstens, E. 34368
Kartio, Kai 09471
Karttunen, Matti 09656
Karvonen-Kannas, Kerttu 09432
Karwatzki, Dr. Barbara 19578
Karwowski, Lech 32023, 32027, 32028, 32029
Kasal, Václav 08352, 08514
Kaschkat, Dr. Hannes 19201
Kasfir, Dr. Sidney 41352
Kashima, Noriyuki 26504
Kashima, Teishin 27032
Kasilag, Emma Y. 31427
Kašírin, Oleg Semënovič 33623, 33629, 33633
Kasl, Ronda J. 44228
Kasperovič, K.K. 37834
Kasperska, Helena 31738
Kass, Emily S. 47946

Kassal-Mikula, Dr. Renate 03001
Kaštelan, Jure 07831
Kastell, Christina 42160
Kastler, Daniel 10576
Kastler, Dr. Raimund 02551
Kastner, Carolyn 47329
Kastner, Erich 02956
Kasumov, Nazym Kasumovič 32756
Kasym, Sofija Vesiljevna 33425
Kaszak, Carole 40348
Kąsiołka, Stanisław 32221
Kaszubkiewicz, Andrzej 31752
Katagishi, Shoji 26969
Katakami, Syusaku 26692
Kataoka, Chogoro 26681
Katayama, Takashi 26791
Katerinkino, Lidija P. 32984
Kates, Sam W. 42961
Katevenidou, Tassoula 20915
Kathane, M. Y. 21963
Katili, Dr. Ekki Husein 22108
Katiskoski, Kaarina 10138
Katkevich, Walter 41905
Katkova, Maria 33178
Kato, Bruce 44368, 47650
Kato, Jatsuo 26792
Kato, Sadao 26500, 26885
Katoh, Yuji 26328
Katona, Dr. András 21352, 21363, 21389
Katsalaki, Georgia 20975
Katsiff, Bruce 42984
Katsimpalis, Tom 44980
Katsura, Nobuo 26714
Kattanek, Prof. Dr. Siegfried 18586
Katz, Alain 11298, 11299, 11300
Katz, Jane 41466
Katz, Paul 41167
Katzensteiner, Peter 02827
Katzinger, Dr. Willibald 02236, 02238
Kauder, Hans-Peter 02140
Kauder-Steiniger, Dr. Rita 18946
Kauders, Audrey S. 44424
Kauffmann, André 10387
Kaufmann, Bert Antonius 16738
Kaufmann, Carol 34214
Kaufmann, Dr. Christian 36508
Kaufmann, Christine 02945
Kaufmann, Christoph 18419
Kaufmann, Don 42607
Kaufmann, Heinz 36974
Kaufmann, Jürg 36656
Kaufmann, Manfred 02945
Kaufmann, Sabine 20011
Kaukiainen, Hannu 09460
Kaukiainen, Heli 09702, 09703, 09706
Kaulbach, Dr. Hans-Martin 20106
Kaumanns, Kurt 15874
Kaumeyer, Kenneth 47665
Kaupang, Brit 30741
Kaus, Dr. K. 01806, 02660
Kaus, Peter 15528
Kauschat, Gerda 16871
Kauth, K.O. 44180
Kauth, Robert R. 43408
Kava, Ritva 09464
Kavanagh, Dr. R. 05463
Kavanagh, Thomas 41749
Kavanash, Donald 47010
Kavanaugh, Martha 05193
Kavasch, E. Barrie 48424
Kavrečić, Ivan 07676
Kawabata, Hiroshi 26886
Kawaguchi, Kei 26566
Kawaguchi, Kimio 26873
Kawaguchi, Masako 26873
Kawai, Masaki 26972
Kawai, Suyako 26408
Kawaiaea, Daniel 44419, 44419
Kawakami, Kunihiko 26317
Kawanabe, Kusumi 26999
Kawasaki, Matsuju 26224
Kawasaki, Shoichiro 26838
Kawashima, Etsuko 26649
Kawiorski, Wacław 31740, 31835, 31836, 31889
Kay, Hannah 38240
Kay, Jeremy 47438
Kaya, Settar 37726
Kaye, Carole 44895
Kaye, Jennifer 06595
Kayombo, Dr. Norbert Andrew 37458
Kaysel, Dr. Roger 36489
Kayser, Christine 12703
Kayser, David 47201
Kayser, Gisela 15965
Kayser, Horst 19074
Kayser, Thomas A. 44009
Kaźmierczyk, Adam 31613
Kazus, Igor A. 33068
Kazutoschi, Kato 26134
Kazychanova, Marisa Grigorjevna 33713
Kazyhanov, E.B. 27078
Keall, Dr. Edward 06607
Kean, John 48144
Kean, Roger 46695
Keane, Terry 46145
Kearney, Brian 41746

Kearney, John 42321
Kearney, Lynn 42321
Keasal, Debra L. 39956
Keasler, Suzy 45141
Keates, Eve 04975
Keating, Neal B. 44140
Keatinge, H.D.H. 40892
Keaveney, Raymond 22446
Keck, Gabriele 36541
Keck, John 43850, 47838
Keckeisen, Robert J. 48033
Kedde, M.C. 29136
Kędzierski, Sławomir 32132
Kędziora, Prof. Dr. Andrzej 31913
Keeble, Phyllis 38639
Keech, Brenda 44359
Keefe, John 45735
Keefer, Dr. Erwin 20115
Keegan, Daniel T. 47356
Keegan, Dr. W.F. 43581
Keenan, Edward 48351
Keene, John 34374
Keene Fields, Catherine 44813
Keene Muhlert, Jan 48154
Keery, John 40635
Keesecker, Martin 45191
Kehrer, Helma 15474
Keil, Dirk 19442
Keil, Franka 18213
Keil, Matthias 02208
Keim, Cheryl 42690
Keim, Dr. Helmut 15481
Keimel, Reinhard 02993
Keinänen, Timo 09533
Keinan, Ofra 22565
Keiper, Elke 20369, 20370
Keiper, Dr. Joe 42467
Keisch, Dr. Christiane 16028
Keisuke, Iwamoto 26112
Keith, Barbara W. 43414
Keith, Dorothy 45086
Keith, Jack 41366
Keith, Larry 39729
Kejariwal, Dr. O. P. 21781
Kejzar, Josef 02615
Kekäle, Leena 09981
Kekeke, Daniel O. 30338
Kelch, Prof. Dr. Jan 15974
Kéler, Yves 14727
Kell, Dr. Klaus 17837
Kellams, Marty 43129
Kellar Mahaney, Edie 48824, 48825
Kellein, Dr. Thomas 16156
Keller, Dr. Christine 37393
Keller, Esther 36500
Keller, Dr. Eva 37374
Keller, Janet 48164
Keller, Jaroslav 08305
Keller, Linn 43913, 43914
Keller, Dr. Peter 02533
Keller, Peter C. 47399
Keller, Pierre 36854
Keller, Dr. Rolf 37428
Keller, Sylvia M. 46511
Keller, Tim 47804
Keller, Urs Oskar 36538
Kellerer, Anna 01978
Kellerhoff, Reinhard 20521
Kellett, Deborah 41777
Kellett, John 41453
Kelley, Barbara 41706
Kelley, Joyce J. 46802
Kelley, Timothy 46235
Kellgren, Ola 36349
Kelling, Paisley 46328
Kellner, Heike 02331
Kelly, Agnes R. 45137
Kelly, Amanda 47834
Kelly, Barbara 41837
Kelly, Bonny 47101
Kelly, Dr. Christopher 38458
Kelly, Cindy 41466, 41470
Kelly, D. 05317
Kelly, Eamonn 22442
Kelly, Elaine 41699
Kelly, Franklin 48373
Kelly, Gemey 06298
Kelly, Gillian 38815
Kelly, Jack 45506
Kelly, Jim 47536
Kelly, Karen 45793
Kelly, Linda 06433
Kelly, Michelle 37996
Kelly, Nancy 46153
Kelly, Rose 46858
Kelly, Sheila 06248
Kelly, Vonda 41752
Kelly, Wendy 41890
Kelm, Bonnie G. 47406, 48630
Kelm, Rüdiger 15416
Kelnberger, Raimund 19632
Kelner, Sara 44120
Kelsey Foley, Kathy 48463
Kelso, J. 39925
Kelthoum Kitouni, Daho 00058
Keltti, Pia 09421
Kemdal, Anne Louise 36293
Kemkes, Martin 15381
Kemkes, Dr. Martin 19196, 19695

Kemm, B. 36560
Kemmer, Kim 43293
Kemmerer, Allison 41207
Kemp, Alan 40350
Kemp, Blanch 45025
Kemp, Jane 42838
Kemp, Jo 40107
Kemp, N.R. 01106
Kemp, Dr. T.S. 40151
Kemp, W. Bradley M. 44685
Kemper, Heinrich 16752
Kemper, Julie 44759
Kemper Fields, Laura 44396
Kempf, Jürgen 10185
Kempf, Klaus 18831
Kempf, Peter 19956
Kempling, Steven 05341
Kempton, Peggy 43952
Kenagy, Dr. James 47529
Kendall, Andrew 41301
Kendall, Andy 42728
Kendall, Clifford P. 41158, 43303
Kendall, Harvey 38389
Kendrick, Marcia 42257
Kendrigan, Ernie 01160
Kenen, Susan 45676
Kenkel, Jens 19689
Kennedy, Arlene 05771
Kennedy, Dr. Brian 00886
Kennedy, Caroline 46587
Kennedy, Cheryl 45076
Kennedy, Chris 38716
Kennedy, Clay W. 41967
Kennedy, Elaine 38788
Kennedy, Elizabeth 42367
Kennedy, Dr. George L. 47275
Kennedy, Ian 44404
Kennedy, Mary C. 41398
Kennedy, R.H. 06604
Kennedy, Sally E. 46853
Kennedy, S.B. 38160
Kennedy, Tim 05160
Kennedy, William 42799
Kennedy, Prof. W.J. 40151
Kenney, Chris 42090
Kenney, Kimberley 42090
Kennis 28979
Kenny, Jessica 38615
Kenny, Kevin 43361
Kenny, Michael 22444
Kensler, Terry 32387
Kent, Dr. Jacquelyn S. 43436
Kent, Jerry 47127
Kent, Joan 46611
Kent, Liz 44194
Kent, Rachel 01502
Kenworthy, M. 38148, 38375
Kenwright, Carole 38527
Kenwright, Peter 40680
Kenyon, Colleen 48739
Kenyon, Sir George 38675
Kenyon, Kathleen 48739
Kenyon, Sarah 40368
Keo, Pich 04950
Keogh, Anthony J. 34332
Keough, Tracey 46722
Kepford, Kris S. 46401
Kephart, Betsy 46285
Keppert, Jozef 33995
Keracher, Susan 40385
Kerber Walrond, Frances 47120
Kerefov, Betal Muradinovič 33197
Kerekesh, Michael 46663
Kerelezova, Vera 04846
Keren, S. 22614
Kerimova, L.L. 48831
Kerkhoven, Dr. R. 29106
Kermode, Deborah 38222
Kern, Dr. Georg von 17905
Kern, James E. 48185
Kern, Robert 15718
Kern, Steven 47293
Kern, Ursula 17055
Kernaghan, Nan 06654
Kernan, Thomas J. 44820
Kerndler, Werner 01691
Kerner, Johann 18328
Kernhan, John 05993
Kerr, Andrea J. 40161
Kerr, Fred 00998
Kerr, John 38862
Kerr, Paul K. 41614
Kerr, Peter 01340
Kerr-Wilson, Ian 05572
Kerrin, Nancy 44311
Kerschbaum, Rupert 03001
Kershaw, Mary J. 39171
Kersing-Blok, Drs. I. 29075
Kersten, Michiel C.C. 29324
Kerstges, Andrea 16079
Kersting, Dr. Hannelore 18772
Kersting, Rita 16733
Kert, Christian 10250
Kervern, Jeannine 10737
Kervezee, Ruth 28911
Kerwood, Adrian 38549
Kesaeva, E.A. 33691
Kesler, Jonathan G. 46758
Kesselman, Steve 47201, 47466

Kessler, Adolf 36997
Kessler, Earl 21784
Keßler, Matthias 19793
Kessler, Dr. Michael 36516
Kessler, Monika 16546
Kessler, Nava 22668
Kessler, Werner 36790
Kestel, Michael 20056
Kesteman, Emile 03293
Kestenbaum, Stuart J. 42844
Kester, Marilyn 42052
Ketchum, Clark 43805
Ketelsen, Dr. Thomas 16692
Ketner, Joseph D. 48298
Ketteler, Georg 16190
Kettemann, Dr. Otto 18249, 18250
Kettula, Suvi 09431
Keulen, W.J. 28893
Keunecke, Dr. Hans-Otto 16918
Keuning, R.H. 29686
Keurs, P. ter 29525
Keuter, J.H.G. 28963
Keutgens, Eric 03211
Kevenhörster, Markus 01831
Keweloh, Hans-Walter 16339
Key, Eric 48604
Keyaerts, Geneniève 14376
Keyaerts, Magali 14376
Keyes, George S. 42924
Keyser, Ignace de 03317, 03337
Keyser, Ralph 42140
Keyworth, John 39571
Kezich, Giovanni 25396
Khabibullaev, Nozim 48857
Khachatrian, Shahen 00685
Khalid, Syed Ali 27644
Khan, Aurangzeb 31051
Khan, Gulzar Muhammad 31059
Khan, M. Ikramullah 31044
Khan, Muhammad Afzal 31037
Khan, Nazir Ahmad 31057
Khan Jatoi, Saeed 31046
Khasanov, S.R. 48855
Khasawneh, Alia 27062
Khazam, Sandra 01434
Kheel-Cox, Claudia 45731
Khevenhüller-Metsch, Maximilian 02193
Khewhok, Carol D. 44079
Khewhok, Sanit 44078
Khodair Kassim, Kassim 27305
Khotko, P.S. 03116
Khulani-Mkhize, Leo 34263
Kibritova, Vanja 04754
Kıcıman, Kerim 37759
Kida, Takuya 26938
Kidd, Benton 42553
Kidd, Jane 40161
Kidd, Pat 40355
Kidner, Laura 40937
Kidston, Jamie 06707
Kieberl, Wolff 01833
Kiebert, Susan 47382
Kiedel, Klaus-Peter 16339
Kiefer, Theresia 18523
Kieffer-Olsen, Jakob 09027, 09030
Kiehl, David 45886
Kiel, Dennis 42400
Kielak, Bernard 31864
Kielholz, Walter B. 37386
Kielland, Morten 30988
Kielwein, Dr. Matthias 16681
Kiely, Ann 40819
Kiely, David 40819
Kiemele, E. 16930
Kiendl, Anthony 05044
Kienholz, Kathleen 45754
Kienitz, Gerlinde 19808
Kientz, J.J. 10946
Kienzle, Karen 47407
Kiereś, Małgorzata 32156
Kiermeier-Debre, Prof. Dr. Joseph 18705
Kiers, J. 28875
Kietlińska-Michalik, Dr. Barbara 31703
Kiewel, Ann 44052, 44056
Kift, Dr. Dagmar 16202, 16666
Kiger, Robert W. 46518
Kigozi, F. 34295
Kihiyo, Jackson M. 37459
Kihlberg, Eva 36343
Kiiski-Finel, Päivi 10138
Kilaghbian, Elia 25933
Kilani, Huda 27053, 27054
Kilby, Virginia 44349
Kilger, Dr. Gerhard 16657
Kilham, D.D. 43919
Kilian, Ewa 31801
Kilian, Dr. H. 20113
Kilian, Dr. Ruth 18592
Kilian Dirlmeier, Dr. Imma 18606
Kiliti, Zsuzsanna 21459
Killacky, John 47346
Killoran, Elizabeth 46320
Kilpatrick, Susie 41445
Kilroy, Frank 39860
Kilsdonk, Betty 43216
Kilvington, Ken 39164
Kim, Chi-Eun 27275
Kim, Christine Y. 45877
Kim, Hongnam 27232

Kim, Jong Chull 27156
Kim, Dr. Ke Chung 48152
Kim, Kumja Paik 47308
Kim, Nam Kyun 27293
Kim, Sun-Jung 27184, 27223
Kim, Sung-Rae 27206
Kim, Sunggu 27202
Kim, Wook-Han 27184
Kim, Yun Soon 27300
Kimball, Cathy 47355
Kimball, Kathryn A. 45628
Kimfoko-Madoungou, Joseph 07647
Kimihiko, Hori 26131
Kimmig, Ingeborg 20098
Kimsey, Dr. Lynn S. 42795
Kimura, Hidenori 26822
Kimura, Shigenobu 26347
Kin, Wook-Han 27223
Kincaid, Jean E. 05025
Kincses, Károly 21450
Kindgren, Hans 36342
Kindler, Dr. Gabriele 17991
Kindrachuk, William 06740
Kindred, Peter 39013
Kindschy, Errol 48545, 48546
Kindt, Diane 45426
Kindt, Jean 03460
King, Alan 46040
King, Andy 38351, 38352
King, B.R. 40681
King, Brad 39665
King, Brian 05163
King, Carolyn 22382, 42302
King, Charles 42067
King, Dexter Scott 41350
King, D.F. 45916
King, Douglas R. 47136
King, Dr. Duane H. 44945
King, Edward 38290, 39336, 39338
King, Elspeth 40595
King, Dr. F.W. 43581
King, George G. 47418
King, G.G. 01170
King, Graham 38634
King, Gwen G. 46262
King, Harry 44522
King, Hugh R. 43047
King, John 30153
King, Karma S. 44522
King, Lyndel 45383
King, Margaret H. 39005
King, Margery 46506
King, Michael D. 38773
King, Prof. Phillip 39754
King, Tamara 45405
King, William C. 45253
King Torrey, Ella 47343
Kingan, Beryl A. 40938
Kingdon, Charles 05859
Kingery, James 43690, 45895
Kingsbury, Bernard 30139
Kingsbury, Paul 45614
Kingsford Hale, James 39213
Kingsley, April 43053
Kingston, Jean T. 48667
Kinnear, J. 40184
Kinno, Seiichi 26515
Kinoshita, Kyuichiro 26854
Kinoshita, Masafumi 26477
Kinoshita, Yumi 43558
Kinsell, Tracey 45249
Kinsey, Danna 42544
Kinsman, Jane 00886
Kinsolving, Lucie 45849
Kinson, Alan 00756
Kintisch, Christine 02844
Kinzinger, Nancy 47868
Kioseva, Ass.Prof. Dr. Tsvetana 04846
Kipiani, M.A. 15361
Kipkorir, Daniel 27101
Kipnis, Jeffrey 42593
Kippes, Dr. Wolfgang 02904, 02985
Kiprop, Nancy 27102
Király, Elvira 21366
Kirby, Chris 40692
Kirby, Jo 39729
Kirby, John 05523
Kirby, Michael 48631
Kirch, Patrick V. 41648
Kirchhauser, Hannes 18003
Kirchhoff, Hans 20345
Kirchmayer, Christian 02159
Kirchmeier Andersen, J.C. 08953
Kirchner, Dr. Ferdinand 02547
Kirchner, Gertrud 02037
Kirchweger, Dr. Franz 02918
Kiričenko, E.I. 32925
Kiričenko, Galina Vladimirovna 32951
Kirigin, Branko 07779
Kirilova, Lena 04653, 04654
Kirk, Natalie 48304
Kirk, Ruth 42571
Kirk, Wendy 39622
Kirkbride, Cinoy 05409
Kirkby, Patrick 40890
Kirkeby Andersen, Dorte 09053
Kirker, Anne 01459
Kirkham, Thomas G. 38157
Kirklin, Deborah 47444

Kirkman, John 01019
Kirkpatrick, Andrea 06334
Kirkpatrick, David 38676
Kirkpatrick, Dr. Gail B. 18947
Kirkpatrick, May 38068
Kirkwood, Michael 43120
Kirmeß, Max 19204, 19205
Kirov, Stefan 04901
Kirrane, Siobhan 39845
Kirsch, Eva 47268
Kirsch, Dr. Jeffrey W. 47285
Kirsch, Dr. John A.W. 45072
Kirsch, Dr. Steven 44630
Kirschberg-Grossman, Reva G. 45787
Kirschensteiner, Brian 43054
Kirwan King, Martin 47894
Kirwin, Timothy B. 44123
Kischkewitz, Dr. Hannelore 15908
Kisdemaker, Drs. R.E. 28868
Kisëv, Ërdan 04813
Kishida, Tamiya 27010
Kishioka, Yukio 26104
Kisić, Anica 07700
Kisielowicz, Marcin 32114
Kisjova, Vera 04778
Kisler, Mary 30103
Kisler, Shuli 22775
Kisman, A.K. 29161, 29162
Kiss, K. 39618
Kisser, Gerhard 01875
Kissi, Flavio 24709
Kissiov, Kostadin 04775
Kissling, Bertrand 37019
Kißro, Reinhard 19272
Kistner, Hans-Jürgen 17977
Kitagawa, Kazuo 26444
Kitagawa, Seika 26602
Kitagawa, Shigeto 26850
Kitamura, Hitomi 26938
Kitamura, Sadao 26388
Kitauo, Tsuguto 26528
Kitazawa, Toshio 26778
Kitchen, Dr. M. 38824
Kitchin, Cameron 48246
Kitchin, Simon 38559, 38562
Kitching, Matthew 34273
Kite Powell, Rodney 47945
Kittelmann, Udo 17067
Kittleson, Darrell 41446
Kittner, Ed 44105
Kittredge, Cindy 43781
Kityo, Robert Martin 37825
Kitz, Hilary 48104
Kitzler, Gottfried 02359
Kitzmann, Andrew 47907
Kiuchi, Kazuhiro 26107
Kiupčupov, Georgi 04823
Kivi, Mirja 10092
Kivimäe, Juta 09358
Kivimäki, Kati 09982, 09985
Kiziltan, Sabri 37702
Kiziltan, Zeynep 37702
Kjær, Birgitte 08770
Kjeldbæk, Esben 08929
Kjeldgaard, Inge Merete 08806
Kjeldsberg, K. 30564
Kjeldsberg, Peter Andreas 30941
Kjeldsen, Kjeld 08902
Kjellberg, Anne 30741
Kjems, Folke 08889, 08891
Kjerström Sjölin, Eva 36060
Kjupčupov, Georgi 04821, 04824
Kjuptčupov, Georgi 04819
Klaasen, Lizet 03146
Kładna, Dr. Aleksandra 32026
Klages, Dr. Claudia 16246
Klameth, Wolfgang 17045
Klammt, Annerose 17323, 17324
Klang Eriksson, Eva 36060
Klanicová, Dr. Evženie 08258, 08259
Klapczyński, Stanisław 31524
Klapthor, Frances 41454
Klar, Annika 35997, 35998, 36001
Klar, Herma 18971
Klarić, Josip 07836
Klassen, John 45202
Klasson, Gunnar 36342
Klatt, David 05933, 06014, 06393, 06409, 06873,
  06874
Klatt, Dr. Ingaburgh 18537
Klauda, Manfred 18233, 18234, 18235, 18236,
  18237, 18238
Klaus, Franz Josef 02223
Klaus, Judy 30205
Klaus, Dr. Sabine 48214
Klauser, K.D. 03724
Klaußecker, Fritz 20253
Klebe, Kurt E. 46628
Kleeberg, John M. 45760
Kleeblatt, Norman 45821
Kleefisch, Stephen J. 46545, 46546
Kleemann, Kurt 19561
Kleespies, Gavin 45541
Klei, Mary 44704
Klein, A. 29501
Klein, Adaire 44942
Klein, Dr. Angela 16293
Klein, Anton 02928
Klein, Beatrixe 20572

Klein, Carolyn 43157
Klein, Christhilde 29324
Klein, Christophe 13023
Klein, Dr. Emanuel 45609
Klein, Janice B. 43239, 43242
Klein, Jean-Claude 14138
Klein, Matthias 15514
Klein, Dr. Michael 18602
Klein, Peter 47881
Klein, Regine 19393, 19394, 19395
Klein, Thomas 16620, 16621
Klein, Dr. Ulrich 20115
Klein, Valérie 12995
Klein-Langner, Wolfgang 20705
Kleindorfer-Marx, Dr. Bärbel 20363
Kleine, Dr. Joachim 20751
Kleiner, Gerald 45446
Kleiner, Michael 20297
Kleiner-Frick, Beat 37399
Kleiner-Frick, Dorothee 37399
Kleinert, Dr. Annette 17875
Kleinertz, Dr. Everhard 18143
Kleinhans, M. 34392, 34393, 34394
Kleinhofer, Erna 03000
Kleinschmidt, Torsten 17937
Kleinschmidt-Altpeter, Dr. Irene 16242
Kleipaß, Dr. Herbert 16861
Kleisner, Ted J. 48592
Kleist, Monika von 15613
Klejman, N.I. 33115
Klemenz, Wolfgang 18265
Klemińska, Izabella 32120
Klemm, Dr. Christian 37386
Klemm, Federico 00151
Klemm, Randy 43789
Klemm, Susanne 16997
Klemp, Dr. Klaus 17059
Klencke, Lippold von 16864
Klenner, Hans-Christian 19437
Klenow, Rosemary E. 43061
Klepač, Koraljka 07764
Klerk, Frank de 29286
Klesman, Kees 28870
Klettner, Emmi 01903
Kletz, Ursula 18918
Kley, Dr. Stefan 19152
Klicka, Dr. John 44674
Kliege, Dr. Melitta 19156
Klietmann, Wolfgang 02701
Klim, T.B. 33051
Klimaszewski, Cathy 44272
Klimek, Larry 45409
Klimenova, Tamara Aleksandrovna 32742
Klimesch, Dr. Gertraud 01804
Klimmer, Hans 02422
Klimov, Vladislav Petrovič 32727
Klimova, Anna Danilovna 32755, 33745, 33746
Klimova, Elena Michajlovna 33595
Kline, John 42617
Kline, Dr. John 42915
Kline, Katy 41971
Kling, Burkhard 20042
Kling, Gudrun 36546
Klingelhöfer, Claudia 19943
Klinger, Dr. H.C. 34213
Klinghardt, G. 34213
Klinghardt, Gerald 34210
Klingler, Michael 02082
Klingman, Catherine 42923
Klink, Alfonso Caballero 34721
Klink, R. 20221
Klinkow, Michaela 19255
Klis, Dr. Rita 18113
Kljajić, Damijan 34162
Kljueva, Valentina Ivanovna 32764
Klobe, Tom 44090, 44091
Kloch, Ove 09110
Klochko, Deborah 47317
Klöpfer, Anette 18313
Kloosterboer, A.E. 29735
Klootwijk, L.P. 29738
Kloppenborg, David N. 42954
Klose, Dr. Dietrich 18913
Klose, Simon 00793
Kloster, Johan 30752
Klostermeier, David 47078
Kloub, Ola 27067
Klucas, Kevin 42772
Kluchko, Halya 06623
Klučina, Petr 08588
Klüver, Heinrich 18466
Klug, Dr. C. 37404
Kluge, Dr. Arnd 17793
Kluge, Prof. Arnold G. 41220
Kluge, Prof. Dr. Bernd 16044
Kluge, Martin 36498
Kluge, W. 18641
Kluger, Reinhard 01754
Klukina, Anna I. 33034
Klumpe, Josef 16866
Klumpp, Sibylle 13216
Klupp, Krzysztof 31914
Kluska, Adam 32003
Kluss, Dr. Maciej 31927
Kluza, Radosław 31800
Klykova, Galina Ivanova 33273
Klytcheva, Bibi 37814
Kmieck, Anne T. 42468
Kmínek, Petr 08247, 08745

Knabe, Hans-Jürgen 19618
Knape, Gunilla 35910
Knapen, I.A.M. 29711
Knapp, D.R. 39552
Knapp, S. 39552
Knapp, Steve 46233
Knapp, Trevor 40778
Knappertsbusch, Dr. Michael 36514
Knauer, Wilfried 20652
Knauss, Carol 41214
Knauss, Dr. Florian 18911
Knauss, Jürgen 16513
Kneale, John Brian 40389
Knebelsberger, Caroline 41602
Knee, Arthur 01521
Knee, Lurline 01521
Kneubühl, Dr. Urs 36552
Kneuss, Martine 37191
Knibb, Dennis 06333
Knibiely, Philippe 14329, 14330
Knick, Dr. Stanley 46334
Kniefeld, Lothar 20159
Knieriem, Dr. Michael 20710, 20713
Knierriem, Peter 18426, 19620
Knigge, Horst 17593
Knigge, Prof. Dr. Volkhard 20458
Knight, Bob 48605
Knight, David J. 44019
Knight, Frank 48541
Knight, Gregory 42317
Knight, Irene 06040
Knight, Jean 38498, 39599
Knight, Jeremy 39265
Knight, Jim 42569
Knight, Katie 43983
Knight, Michael 47308
Knight, Robert 41692
Knight, V.M. 39654
Knight, Yvonne 44330
Knill, Phyllis 43158
Knipe, Peter 44040
Knipp, Otto 17862
Knippenberg, Dr. W.H.Th. 29654
Knipping, Mark 43797
Knipprath, Ute 16246
Knittel, Pierre 15316
Knittel, W. 19035
Knížák, Dr. Milan 08608
Knízák, Milan 08618
Knobloch, Stephan 17074
Knoch, Francis 27558
Knoch, Susan 43284
Knoche, Norma 42959
Knocke, Erich 16956
Knode, Marilu 45364
Knöchlein, Dr. Bernhard 19960
Knödel, Dr. Susanne 17561
Knödler-Kagoshima, Brigitte 17989
Knöpfel, Sylvia 17205
Knofler, Dr. Monika 02921
Knogler, Helmut 02479
Knoke, Christine 46302
Knol, Egge 29309
Knoll, Andrew H. 42038
Knoll, Annegret 18211
Knolle, Dr. P. 29240
Knoop, Ulrich 17741
Knop Kallenberger, Christine 48107
Knopp, Dr. Hans-Georg 15987
Knoppers, K. 29017
Knorowski, Mariusz 31862
Knorre, Dr. Alexander von 17728, 17729, 17730
Knott de Arechaga, Deborah 46869
Knowles, A.M. 38554, 38557
Knowles, Elizabeth 40549
Knowles, John 45614
Knowles, Prof. Lacey 41220
Knowles, P. 22386
Knowles, Peter 47656, 48245
Knox, J. 38159
Knox, Judy 41869
Knox, Lu 46013
Knox, R. 39586
Knuab, Donald E. 42871
Knubben, Dr. Thomas 19507
Knudsen, Ann Vibeke 08847, 09037, 09038
Knudsen, Henning 08923
Knudsen, Herluf 09021
Knudsen, Jesper 08873
Knudsen, Karsten 09063
Knudsen, Svend Aage 08792
Knudsen, Trine-Lise 30735
Knuth, Dr. Michael 15976, 16096
Knutsen, Jim 47721
Kob, Karin 36479
Kobald, Peter 02096
Kobayashi, Akira 26764
Kobayashi, Fumio 26957
Kobayashi, Kiroku 26711
Kobayashi, Koichi 26820
Kobayashi, Moriaki 26998
Kobayashi, Naoji 26138
Kobayashi, Saburo 26887
Kobayashi, Shigeko 26918
Kobayashi, Tadashi 26120
Kobayashi, Dr. Tatsuo 26537
Kobayashi, Toshinobu 26312
Kobosil, Karel 08263
Kobusiewicz, Zofia 31809

Koç, Sema 37617
Koca, Osman 37760
Kočankov, Dr. Nikolaj 04846
Koççoban, Cahit 37719
Kocebenkova, Vera Ivanovna 32869
Kočevar, Sanda 07713
Koch, Dr. Alexander 37393
Koch, Christian 48540
Koch, Claudia 02886
Koch, Cynthia M. 44187
Koch, Friederike 17979
Koch, Heidemarie 20716
Koch, Ira 17457
Koch, Johannes Hugo 19081
Koch, Dr. Lars-Christian 15945
Koch, Dr. Michael 18833
Koch, Prof. Dr. Rainer 17055
Koch, Sven 17048
Koch, Werner 16209
Koch, Wilhelm 18711
Kochanova, Ljudmila Petrovna 33674
Kochendörfer, Reinhard 18358
Kočik, Zdeněk 08304, 08405, 08598, 08599
Kociolek, J. Patrick 47312
Kock, G.M. de 29873, 29875
Kock, Prof. Hans 18073
Kock, R.D. de 34255
Kocsis, Dr. Gyula 21395
Koczur, Anton 01949
Koda, Harold 45833
Kodama, Ikuo 26512
Kodani, Susan 44081
Köb, Edelbert 02949
Köberl, Rudolf 02416
Koechlin, Bernard 36748
Köck, Dr. Michaela 02852
Köcke, Dr. Ulrike 16959
Koefoed, Lizette 08965
Köger-Kaufmann, Dr. Annette 18375
Kögl, Reinhard 19814
Kögler, Johannes 17139
Köhl, Gudrun 18922
Köhler, Birte 17560
Köhler, Eva 19703
Köhler, Georg 02810
Köhler, Dr. Juliana 17471
Köhler, N. 29324
Köhler, Otto 17807
Köhler, R. 17610
Köhler, Thomas 20662
Köhlmeier, Ernst 20001
Köhn, Regine 16571
Koehnline, Lyn 42196
Kölbl, S. 16183
Kölbl-Ebert, Dr. M. 18853
Kölbl-Ebert, Dr. Martina 16805
Köll, Helmut 02621
Köllhofer, Dr. Thomas 18612
Kölmel, Dr. Reinhard 15801
Könenkamp, Dr. Wolf 18695, 18696
König, G. 16174
König, Dr. Gabriele 17177
König, H. 15749
König, Heinz 17701
König, Helmut 17798
König, Josef 02862
König, Prof. Kasper 18161
König, Lotte 02956
König, Dr. Margarethe 20212
König, Reginald 20090
Koenig, Robert J. 47979
König, Prof. Dr. Viola 15945, 16012
Koenigsmarková, Dr. Helena 08617, 08693
Koeninger, Kay 42802
Könke, Dr. Jörn 15407
Köntös, László 21498
Köpf, Prof. Ernst Ulrich 17399
Köpke, Ingeborg 17150
Köpke, Prof. Dr. Wulf 17561
Köppen, Thomas 20567
Koerber, Susannah 46927
Koerhuis, E. 30072
Környei, Dr. Attila 21485, 21532, 21533, 21535,
  21537, 21538
Koesoemowarni, Endang 22181
Köster, Hein 16088
Köster, Dr. Reinhard 18606
Koevend, Mary Helen de 45637
Kofler, Claudia 02929
Kofler, Gertraud 02048
Kofuku, Akira 26873
Koga, Kim 44932
Kogan, Lee 45756, 45798
Kogler, Leopold 02805
Kogure, Susumu 26238
Kohan, Carol E. 48514
Kohlbauer-Fritz, Dr. Gabriele 02903
Kohlberg, Ilona 17130
Kohler, Ruth 47589
Kohlschmidt, Ulrich 19034
Kohn, Klaus G. 19032
Kohn Loncarica, Prof. Dr. Alfredo G. 00179, 00220
Kohnke, Dr. Hans-Georg 16284, 16285
Kohout, K. 01818
Kohút, Dr. Teodor 34000
Koike, Tomio 26571
Koja, Dr. Stephan 02953
Kojaev, M. 27096
Kok, Harry de 03806

Kokki, Kari-Paavo 09469, 09470
Kokkotidis, Dr. Klaus Georg 20115
Kokošinek, Nataša 34092
Kokoska, Monika 16942
Kokot, Juliusz 31495
Kokroko, Grace Juliet 20793
Kolaric, Dr. Juraj 07812
Kolb, Ingrid 18161
Kolb, Jennifer 45073
Kolb, Nancy D. 46445
Kolb, Rainer 15523
Kolbach, B. 29379
Kolbasina, Larisa Aleksandrovna 33238
Kolbe, Joachim 18324
Kolber, Peggy 48459
Kolberg, Dr. Gerhard 18161
Kold, Anders 08902
Kolde, H. 17968
Kolenberg, Hendrik 01490
Koles, L.A. 01358
Kolesnikova, Ljudmila Arsenjevna 32859
Kolesnikova, Ljudmila Petrovna 33052
Kolesov, S.N. 33570
Koletsky, Susan 41550
Kolev, Cvetan 04885, 04888
Koll, Kersti 09354, 09358
Kolland, Dr. Dorothea 16021
Kollar, Mary 44804
Kollbaum, Marc 47122, 47124
Kollbaum-Weber, Jutta 20726
Koller, Dr. Johann 18842
Koller, Karl 02868, 03012
Koller, Margaret H. 42860
Koller-Jones, Kimberly B. 45686
Kolling, Dr. Alfons 19375
Kollmann, Dr. Karl 16936
Kollmann-Caillet, Virginie 10408
Kolltveit, Bård 30752
Kolm, Herbert 02426
Kolmos, Dr. Alfred S. 48595
Kolner, Brian A. 41867
Kolodziejak, Adeline 05839
Kołodziejski, Dr. Adam 32013
Kolomceva, Raisa Michajlovna 33094
Kolonas, L. 21113
Kolonas, Lazaros 20811, 20833
Kolonia, Rozina 20936
Kolonoas, Lazaros 20925
Koloski, Laura 43472
Koloskova, T.G. 33130
Kolosov, V. 48835
Kolosova, Ekaterina Matveevna 33443
Kolsio, Hannele 09944
Kolsteren, Steven 29309
Kolt, Ingrid 06519
Kolt, Sheryl 06848
Kolter, Horst 17631
Koltz, Jean-Luc 27567
Koludrović, Ivana 07799
Kolveši, Željka 07830
Kolyesnik, Ljudmila Michajlovna 32814
Komanecky, Michael 42801, 46477
Komarek, Beverly 43779
Komarl, Debra 41104
Komarov, Ilja Iljič 33072, 33089
Komatu, Nario 26703
Kombu, Anatolij Stepanovič 32978, 32979
Komick, J. 06703
Komissarov, Eha 09358
Kommer, Dr. Björn R. 15552, 15556, 15561
Komnenović, Ilija 33870
Komor, Valerie 45858
Komzyuk, Vera 37862
Koncevaja, Tatjana Leonidovna 33539, 33541
Kondakova, Nina Viktorovna 33626
Kondratenko, Tatjana Michailovna 32946
Kondziela, Mariusz 31992
Konečná, Katarína 34037
Konecny, Dr. Andreas 01694
Konevskaja, Tatjana Ivanovna 33358
Konieczny, Marian 31849
Konieczny, Władysław 32040, 32198
Konkle, Scott 04992
Konnikov, Boris Aleksandrovič 33257
Kono, Osamu 26374
Konomi, Thomas 00018
Kononov, Alexander 34299
Kononova, Natalia 34299
Konova, Ljubava 04846
Konrád, György 15909
Konst, Thomas 42114
Konstantinus, Lahurakis 21202
Konstantios, Dr. Dimitris 20853
Konsten, Marie-Thérèse 29299
Konukiewitz, Insa 16362
Konvalinka, Danilo 48717
Konz, Klaus 18443
Kooiman, R. 29920
Kooiskra, L. 29292
Kooistra-Manning, Kevin 41691
Koolkin, Kenneth 22581
Koolmees, Dr. P. 29902
Koontz, Darlene 42845
Koop, Kathy 45749
Koopmans, G. 29508, 29516
Koopmans, J.J.G. 29778
Koopmans, Y. 28941
Koopmans-Witt, C.E. 28990
Koos, Greg 41744

Kooten, C.V. 29686
Kopálová, Dr. Danka 34041
Kopbosinova, R.T. 27072
Kopco, Mary A. 42819, 42820
Kopczak, Dr. Chuck 44894
Kopec, Diane 41496, 41497
Kopecky, Carle J. 47499
Kopeinig, Josef 02710
Koperkiewicz, Adam 31571, 31576
Koperski, Kate 45952
Kopf, Sibylle 15863
Kopf, Vicki C. 48705
Koponen, Sanna 09988
Kopówka, Edward 31677
Kopp, Klaus 20570
Kopp, Dr. Marianne 15702
Kopp, Siegfried 02492
Kopp, Werner 16082
Koppel, Greta 09358
Koppel, John 08778
Koppel, Merike 09358, 09368
Koppel de Ramírez, Elsa 07426
Koppenhöfer, Dr. Johanna 17145
Koppensteiner, Dr. Erhard 02551
Koppensteiner, Norbert 03021
Kopplin, Dr. Monika 18943
Koppy, Ann 45981
Kopydłowski, Janusz 31520
Koralova, Ilina 18394
Korb, Uwe 18584
Korčagin, E.N. 33388
Korčevnikova, I.L. 33135
Kordina, Julia 02157
Kordiš, Ivan 34095
Kordowska, Barbara 32167
Koref, Barbara 15588
Koren, Elisabeth 30397
Koren, Johannes 01924
Korff, David 46596
Korhonen, Paavo 10078
Korhoven, Teppo 09494
Korkmasova, Maimusat Arslan-Alievna 32998
Korkmaz, Abdurrahman 37743
Korman, Sandy 05214
Korn, Brigitte 15388
Korn, Dagmar 18581
Korn, Dr. Werner 16484
Kornacki, Krzysztof 31638
Kornatek, Anna 32075
Kornetchuk, Elena 47574
Korobar, Klime 27589
Korotaeva, Ljudmila Dmitrievna 33724, 33725
Korotkij, Aleksandr Nikolaevič 32992
Korovina, Vera Vasiljevna 33325
Korppi, Svea 09948
Korres, Manolis 20866
Korschan, Werner 20783
Koršikov, Anatolij Semёnovič 33274
Korsmeier-Humbert, Helga 18939
Kort, Drs. Toon 28820
Korte-Böger, Dr. Andrea 19946
Korten, Noel 44923
Korteweg, Drs. A. J. 29101
Kortländer, Dr. Bernd 16726
Kortlander, Christopher 43631
Kortschak, Dr. Werner 02826
Kortunova, M. 33435
Korzeniewska, Iwona 31700
Kos, Dr. Peter 34115
Kos, Stanisław 31963
Kos, Dr. Dr. Wolfgang 02845, 02848, 02894, 02931,
02932, 02952, 02966, 02967, 02972, 02978,
02979, 02987, 02988, 02992, 02996, 02998,
03000, 03001
Košacký, Petr 08386
Košambekova, Rayan K. 27071
Kosanji, Kozo 26975
Kosasih, Dikdik 22072
Koschatko, Alois 02773
Koschnik, Dr. Leonore 15939
Kościńska, Halina 31513
Kościołko, Eugeniusz 31787
Koshalek, Richard 44930
Kosiba, Leokadia Ewa 31637
Kosicka, Anna 32054, 32055
Kosinski, Dr. Dorothy 42751
Kosinski, Joan 42358
Koski, Ann 45073
Koski, Elizabeth 41302
Koski, Janne 09984
Koskijoki, Maria 09435
Koskimies-Envall, Marianne 10161
Koskinen, Maija 10135
Koskinen, Pekka 10176
Kośko, Maria 31902
Kosler, Barbara 18860
Kosmadaki, Polina 20824
Kosok, Dr. Lisa 17555
Kosonen, Elina 09963
Kosonen, Juhani 09789
Kosorić, Despa 33885
Kosova, Parim 33897
Koss, Sarah 44430
Kossatz, Dr. Tilman 20697
Kosta, Bernard 43941
Kostadinova, Snežana 04795
Kostede, Ulrich 17976
Kostelny, Elizabeth 46880, 47656, 47894, 48245,
48248

Koster, Dr. A. 29632
Koster, F. 29256
Koster, Dr. J. 29464
Koster, John 48214
Koster, Koos 29558
Koster, Richard de 48542
Kostet, Juhani 09901, 10118, 10122, 10132, 10133,
10134
Kostina, N.V. 33574
Kostková, Magda 34067
Kostołowski, Andrzej 32217
Kostov, Georgi 04913
Kostova, Penka 04610
Kostrowicki, Andrzej 31891
Kostyál, Dr. László 21614
Kostynowicz, Roman 32024
Kosunen, Mirja 09877, 10025, 10026, 10027
Kosvincev, Boris Jurjevič 32690
Kosvinceva, Tatjana Dmitrievna 32689
Koszkul, Jan 31999
Kosznik, Danuta 31652
Koszutski, Oskar 31890
Kot, Malgorzata 42358
Kotai-Ewers, Trisha 01488
Kotasiak, Wojciech 31866
Kothe, O. 18374
Kothe, Robert J. 43670
Kotik, Charlotta 41941
Kotilainen, Eija-Maija 09505
Kotilainen, Kari 10012
Kotkin, Lauren 41062
Kotljakova, N.V. 33007
Kotooka, Mitsushige 26372
Kotouč, Friederike 19889
Kotrba, Dr. M. 18926
Kotrošan, Dražen 03925
Kotsch, Natalie 44169
Kotschwar, Sandra 02234
Kotsiubynsky, Igor 37837
Kottcamp, Edward 43255
Kottenbrink, Magdalene 19475
Kotterer, Michael 19527
Kottmann, Ingeborg 20317, 20321
Kotula, Krystyna 32165
Kotzan, Peter 18462
Kotzur, Dr. H.J. 18598
Kouakou Thierry, Konan 07672
Kouchi, Osami 26970
Koukal, Petr 08519
Koukal, Dr. Vitezlaw 08642
Koumantakis, Prof. I. 21226
Kourinou, Eleni 20873
Kourouma, Moussa 21283
Koutsomallis, Kyriakos 20824
Kouvaras, Fotini 21169
Kouvoutsakis, Panagiotis 21016
Kouzin, E. 32877
Kouzmin, Alexander 33400
Kovačev, Dimitar 04605
Kovačević, Dr. Bojan3a 33804
Kovačević, Goranka 07703, 07728
Kovačić, Marcelo 07764
Kovačić, Vladimir 07755
Kovács, Irén 21379
Kovács, Péter 21554, 21555, 21556, 21560
Kovács, Dr. Tibor 21361
Kovácsné Ládi, Katalin 21473
Kovacsovics, Dr. Wilfried 02532, 02551
Kovalenko, Donna 47534
Kovalskij, Sergej Viktorovič 33380
Kovalenko, Marja-Leena 09715
Kovarik, Jiri 08409
Kovrakis, Stavros 21099
Kovtun, Vladimir Vasiljevič 33751
Kowalczyk, Longin 31798
Kowalczyk, Wiktor 31650
Kowald, Dr. Margaret 01458
Kowalewska, Dr. Agnieszka 32163
Kowalewski, S. 41319
Kowalski, Beth 45073
Kowalski, Dr. James A. 45776
Kowalski, Michael 17906
Kowalski, Zygfryd 31812
Kowarik, Prof. Wilfried 02292
Kowark, Dr. Hannsjörg 20113
Kowski, Robert 43816
Kox, Jo 27559
Koyama, Dr. Hiroshi 26840
Koyama, Miturn 26139
Kozáková, M. 34079
Kozel, Jennifer 45781
Kozen, Hiroshi 26424
Kozerski, Paweł 31511
Kozhachev, M. 27081
Kozijn, W.I. 29034
Kožišková, Lenka 08477
Kozlova, T.D. 33524
Kozlova, Vera Danilovna 32703
Kozlovskaja, Nadežda Borisovna 32708
Kozlowski, Kazimiera 42082
Kozma, LuAnne 43054
Kozubek, Gwalbert 31553
Kožucharov, Dimitar 04742
Kozyra, Peter H. 05066
Kozyreff, Chantal 03337
Kraber, Rosa 47806
Kraciak, Aniela 31926
Kracke, Toni 45131
Kräftner, Dr. Johann 02926

Krähenbühl, Dr. Hans 36998
Krämer, Dirk 16756
Krämer, Gerd 15897
Kraemer, Jörg 16256
Kränzle, Beate 18916
Kraev, Vladimir Alekseevič 37843
Krafczyk, Alois 17627
Kraft, Gro 21659
Kraft, Joe C. 45652
Kraft, Karl Ludwig 15676
Kraft, Dr. Perdita von 16500
Kraft, Dr. R. 18926
Kragelund, Patrick 08935
Kragh, Birgitte 08760
Kragh, Mogens 09099
Kraglund, Ivar 30748
Kragness, Kurt K. 41576
Krahn, Susan 05486
Krahn, Dr. Volker 16096
Krajasich, Dr. P. 02676
Krajewski, Sara 45069
Krajneva, Anna Anatoljevna 33011
Krajniak, Paul J. 45361
Krakauer, Dr. Thomas H. 43024
Krakow, Peter 18401
Kralev, Krali 04864
Kralevska, Julijana 27591
Kraljević, Marija 07722
Kramarczyk, Andrea 16472
Kramatschek, Christopher 18829
Kramer, Dr. Dieter 02418, 17047, 17061
Kramer, Prof. Dr. Diether 01936
Kramer, Dr. E. 29508
Kramer, Finn Erik 08874
Kramer, Hermann 02743
Kramer, M. 19388
Kramer, Drs. M. 29101
Kramer, Dr. Mario 17067
Kramer, Trudy C. 47707
Kramme, Dr. Mike 45535
Kramp, Dr. Mario 18122
Krane, Susan 41834
Kranjc, Igor 34112
Kranjc, Katja 34112
Krankenhagen, Prof. Gernot 17555
Kranl, Christine 01727
Kranner, Romana 02013
Kranz, Betsy 44214
Kranz, Prof. Dr. P. 16915
Kranzelbinder, Norbert 01779
Krapež, Mateja 34114
Krapf, Eva 02846
Krapf, Dr. Michael 02953, 02954
Krapish, Anne 43704
Krasilnikov, Grigorij Vladimirovič 32628
Kraske, Bernd M. 19550, 19551
Kraskin, Sandra 45869
Krasnokutskaja, Lidiya Ivanovna 33322
Krasovskaja, Nonna 37902
Krasowska, Dorothy 45791
Kraspycki, Dr. Sylvia 17061
Krasteva, Dimitijka 04846
Krâsteva, Natasha 04693
Krátká, Drahomíra 08650
Kratochvil, Jiří 08517
Kratochvilová, Alena 08632
Kratochvilová, Irena 08358
Kratochwil, Franz 02862
Kratsas, James R. 43755
Kratzert, Martin 17930, 17932
Kraupe, Thomas W. 17565
Kraus, E. 24481
Kraus, Gerhard 15428
Kraus, Jeannie W. 41558
Kraus, Dr. Jürgen 17905
Kraus, Dr. Michael 02525
Kraus, Peter 20262
Kraus, Dr. Stefan 18135
Kraus, Werner 19651
Krause, Bernd 16318
Krause, Ines 18516
Krause, Dr. Jürgen 18950
Krause, Manfred 19986
Krause, Dr. Markus 16873
Krause, Martin F. 44228
Krause, Ortrud 17355
Krause, Dr. Siegfried 19139
Krause, Walt 46849
Krause-Willenberg, Horst 17468
Krauß, M. 17960
Krauss, Dr. Rolf 16059
Kravcov, Igor Nikolaevič 33562
Kravcova, Ljudmila Petrovna 32912
Krazmien, Mindy 44306
Kreamer, Todd A. 45422
Krebernik, Prof. Dr. Manfred 17943
Krech, Shepard 41906
Krečič, Peter 34104
Kreem, Tiina-Mall 09358
Kregar, Tone 34089
Krehe, Lynette 42369
Kreibich, Matthias 16795
Kreim, Dr. Isabella 17908
Krein, Sandra 45011
Kreindl, Richard 02192
Kreiner, Dr. Michael 02922
Kreisel, Dr. Gerd 20099
Krejči, Irena 08708
Krejci, Jim 48793

Krekel, Dr. Michael 15669
Kremer, Elisabeth 16584
Kremer, Dr. Roberta 06694
Krempel, Prof. Dr. Ulrich 17611
Kremsreiter, Hans 19387
Kren, Thomas 44913
Krenn, Prof. Dr. Peter 01923
Krens, Thomas 45810, 45872
Krenzlin, Kathleen 15971
Kreps, Dr. Christina 42894
Kress, Brady 42056
Kreß, Hannelore 17433
Kress, Dr. Theo 18667
Krestin, Steffen 16505, 16506
Kret, Robert A. 42263, 46242
Kretschmer, Karl 18795
Kretzschmar, Dr. R. 20094
Kretzschmar, Ulrike 15939
Kreuger, S.C.P. 29606
Kreul, Dr. Andreas 16328
Kreutz, Ellen 16720
Kreutzer, Teresa 43956
Kreuzberger, Robert 47336
Kreuzer, Dr. Barbara K. 47695
Kreuzer, Hermine 02923
Krichman, Michael 47277
Krick, Robert K. 43534
Krieg, M. 10593
Krieger, Edino 04348
Krieger, Friedrich 01967
Kriegsman, L. 29522
Kriemler, Andrea 36508
Krier, Jean 27567
Krier, Patricia 43224
Krikken, J. 29522
Kriller, Beatrix 02918
Krings, Dr. Michael 18893
Krippner, Regina 19817
Krischel, Dr. Roland 18168
Krischka, Karl 02201
Krishnappa, Dr. M.V. 21703
Krishtalka, Dr. Leonard 44685
Kristament, Werner 02285
Kristan, Dr. Markus 02830
Kristensen, Hans H. 09074
Kristensen, Tenna 08849
Kristfinnsson, Örlygur 21669
Kristiansen, Peter 08920
Kristic, Dr. Danilo 21577
Kristinsdottir, Gudrun 21620
Kristinsson, Axel 21625
Kristjansdottir, Gudbjorg 21642
Krištof, Andreas 02929
Kristoffersen, Åge 30500
Kristy, Ben 43479
Kritsotakis, Dr. Konstantin 18606
Kritzas, Charalambos 20859
Kritzman, George 44945
Kriuacrk, Kathi 46759
Krivitz, James 45368
Krivokapič, Momčilo 33849
Krivoshejev, Vladimir 33926
Krivova, N.N. 33222
Križ, Borut 34136
Križ, Ivica 34136
Krizanac, Milica 33810
Krizner, L.J. 45858
Krjakunova, Nadežda PProkofjevna 32769
Krjukov, Anatolij Charlampievič 32804
Kroča, K. 08403
Kroča, Květoslav 08401, 08754
Krock, Andreas 18615
Kroczak, Czesław 31521
Kroczyński, Hieronim 31670
Kroeber-Wolf, Dr. Gerda 17047, 17061
Kröger, Dr. Jens 16054
Kröhnert, Gesine 19897
Kröhnert, Dr. Gesine 19900
Krönke, Rudolf 18181
Krönsjö, Marianne 36164
Kroeper, Dr. Karla 15908
Kröplin, Detlef 20734
Krog, Paul 37418
Krogedal, David 42721
Krogh, Leila 08832
Krogh-Nielsen, Anna 08769
Krogstad, Bjørn R. 30673
Krohm, Prof. Dr. Hartmut 16096
Krohn, Robin 41695
Król, Adam 31874
Królik, Janusz 31855
Kroll, Sigrun 17576
Kromann, Erik 08983
Kronbichler, Dr. Johann 02600
Kronenbers, Johannes 16963
Kronenfeld, Daniel 45751
Kronenwett, Heike 15791
Kronig, Karl 36546
Kronjäger, Dr. Jochen 18612
Kronquist, Bo 10150
Kroon, Rita 09358
Kropf, Dr. Christian 36547
Kropf, Joan 47176
Krogh, Finn E. 30885
Krotky, Gene 44810
Krouse, Dr. Susan 43054
Krouthen, Mats 30941
Kroy, Eadwierd 46151
Krpan, Sonja 07809

Krpata, Dr. Margit 02945
Krucký, Marian 08700
Kruczyński, Dr. Andrzej 32128
Krueger, Alice F. 45267
Krüger, Frank 17700
Krüger, Dr. Gundolf 17342
Krüger, Hans 15521
Krueger, Hilary 48423
Krüger, Dr. Ingeborg 16246
Krüger, Prof. Dr. Kersten 19660
Krüger, Dr. M. 34359
Krüger, Martin 18547
Krueger, Thomas 17159
Krüger, U. 18513
Krüger, Ulrich 18095
Krüper, Jochen 16964
Krug, Martina 17591
Krug, Wolfgang 02603
Kruger, Gert 28777
Kruk, Karol 32169
Krukowski, Wojciech 32080
Krull, Regine 16875
Krumova, Božura 04840
Krumpöck, Dr. Ilse 02895
Krupa, Alain-Gérard 03578
Krupa, Dr. Vladimír 34043
Krupp, Dr. Ingrid 20477
Kruppa, Gail 48040
Kruschen, Franziska 06857
Kruse, Anette 09042
Kruse, Hans 08918
Kruse, Dr. Hans-Joachim 19419
Kruse, James 43258
Kruse, Prof. Dr. Joseph A. 16726
Kruseman, Pauline W. 28836, 28882
Kruska, Peter 18079
Kruszynski, Dr. Anette 16728
Krutina, Dr. Ivan 08255
Krutisch, Dr. Petra 19139
Krutova, Marina Anatoljevna 32636
Kruus, Ülle 09354, 09358
Kruytz, Rick 43557
Krużel, Krzysztof 31686
Krylov, V.M. 33472, 33487
Krylova, Raisa Nikolaevna 33552
Kryza-Gersch, Dr. Claudia 02918
Krzemiński, Jerzy 31964
Krzemiński, Prof. Wiesław 31718
Krzesinska, Caroline 40487
Krzeszowiak, Aleksander 32004
Krzmarzick, Pam 45748
Krznarić, Stjepan 07678
Krzykowska, Zofia 32045
Krzyżaniak, Prof. Lech 31898
Kseniak, Dr. Mieczysław 31795
Kubadinow, Irina 02955
Kubassek, Dr. János 21409
Kube, Dr. Alfred 16340, 16342
Kube, Jan K. 15777, 20120
Kubiak, Anna 31483
Kubizek, Mathilde 01704
Kublanovskaja, Natalija Alekseevna 33231
Kubli, Dr. Renate 18352
Kuboschek, Andreas 17354
Kuboshima, Seiichiro 26983
Kubota, Gaylord 46750
Kubota, Dr. Tadashi 26769
Kubrak, Zygmunt 31783
Kucharski, Karen 43169
Kuchorenko, Konstantin Gavrilovič 32874
Kuchyňka, Zdeněk 08410
Kučinskij, Stanislav A. 33403
Kuck, Barbara 46716
Kuckertz, Josefine 15908
Kucra, Scott 41558
Kučuk, Julija Valerjevna 32990
Kuczek, Irena 31816
Kuczyńska, Urszula 31832
Kudo, Masahide 26209
Kudrjavcev, Aleksandr Abakarovič 33565
Kudrjavceva, Olga 33390
Kübler, Christof 37393
Kübler, Dr. Gabriele 19582
Kübler, Sabine 15699
Küchler, Dr. Thomas 16159
Kuefstein, Elisabeth Gräfin 02518
Kühbacher, Andrea 02082
Kühebacher, Dr. Egon 25342
Kühhas, Margareta 02781
Kuehhas, Thomas A. 46248
Kuehl, Tracey K. 41670
Kühle, Sandra 19164
Kühling, Karin 18419
Kühn, Christine 16025
Kühnel, Dr. Anita 16025
Kuehnert, Leonard A. 41156
Kümmel, Dr. Birgit 15591
Künnapuu, Kalver 09391
Künnecke, Otto 16203
Kuenzel, Kurt 43626
Künzl, Dr. Ernst 18606
Künzl, Dr. Susanna 18606
Künzle, Fredy 36873
Künzler, Walter 37186
Kürten, Hans Peter 19560
Küster, Babette 18398
Küster, Dr. Bernd 19256
Küster-Heise, Katharina 18615
Küttner, Sybille 17545

Kufel, Tadeusz 31853
Kufeld, Klaus 18517
Kugel, Natalija Arkadjevna 33292
Kugina, Marija Borisovna 32677
Kugler, Andrea 19110
Kugler, Georg 02927
Kugler, Hans 16799
Kugler, Dr. Lieselotte 15940
Kugler, Dr. Walter 36665
Kuhfeld, Ellen 45381
Kuhl, Jane R. 45053
Kuhl, Dr. Uta 19794
Kuhlmann-Hodick, Dr. Petra 16692
Kuhn, Anja 16666, 17639
Kuhn, Prof. Dr. Axel 18442
Kuhn, Dieter 37348
Kuhn, Reinhilde 17989
Kuhn, Thomas G. 42381
Kuhn, Werner 18995
Kuhnke, Manfred 16987
Kuijers, Arie 34185
Kuiper, A. 29445
Kuiper, Dr. J. 29067
Kuiper, J. 29089
Kuitunen, Antero 09586
Kujukina, Tatjana Savvateevna 33638
Kujundžić, Zilka 03925
Kukk, Inge 09388
Kukko, Timo 09962
Kukla, Gabriele 15955
Kukla, Dr. Jon 41955
Kuklik, Mirosław 31929
Kuklová, Zdenka 08753
Kukovalska, Nelya M. 37876
Kukuruzova, Nina V. 33411
Kulakov, Viktor Evgenevič 32745
Kulczycka, Wanda 31508
Kuldna, Kersti 09358
Kulęgowski, Mieczysław 31884
Kulemeyer, Jorge Alberto 00597
Kulesa, Chester 41298, 43080, 47520
Kulichikchin, Vladimir 37847
Kulik, Gary 48712
Kulik, Zbigniew 31640
Kulikowski, Jenny 46779
Kulinčenko, Galina Aleksandrovna 32993
Kuljachtina, Ljubov Fëdorovna 32801
Kulkarni, B.S. 21793
Kulke, Willi 16666, 18285
Kullenberg, Ulrika 36166
Kulling, Catherine 36864
Kullnigg, Johann 02777
Kulmala, Matti 10144
Kulnyté, Biruté 27537
Kulygina, Svetlana Sergeevna 33254
Kumada, Tsukasa 26670
Kumar, Jitendra 21932
Kumar, Samarendra 21918
Kumar, Dr. Sarvash 21759
Kumasaka, Yoshihiro 26339
Kumazawa, Hiroshi 26853
Kume, Atsuko 26878
Kumela, Marjut 09472
Kumirai, Albert 49025, 49028
Kumler, Delorise M. 42439
Kumler, Phyllis 41600
Kummer, Edelbert 37059
Kummer, Prof. Dr. Stefan 20697
Kumpfmüller, Peter 02523
Kunac, Ana 07736
Kunar, Dr. Arun 21758
Kundar, Cynthia A. 45672
Kunde, Harald 15375
Kung-Haga, Vivian 45235
Kuniholm, Thor H. 28710
Kunow, Prof. Dr. Jürgen 20690
Kunst, Beate 15918
Kuntz, Edward 42617, 46222
Kunz, Hartmut 02510
Kunz, John 48443
Kunz, Jürgen 18831
Kunz, Mary Ellyn 45514
Kunz, Richard 30228
Kunz, Veronika 02510
Kunze, Prof. Dr. Max 20059
Kunze, Prof. Dr. Walter 02320, 02321
Kunzemann, Dr. Thomas 19446
Kuo, Shi Yu 07306
Kuononoka, Américo António 00099
Kuosmanen, Hannes 09558
Kupec, Dr. Tomas 08603
Kuper, A. 28922
Kupiec, Janina 32155
Kupka, Andreas 17964
Kuprijanov, Aleksandr Alekseevič 33134
Kuragina, Ljudmila Anatoljevna 32924
Kuraishi, Dr. Mahmud 03084
Kurant, Dr. Bogdan 32107
Kuraya, Mika 26938
Kurban, Michael J. 42342
Kurdiovsky, Horst W. 01848
Kurella, Dr. Doris 20099
Kuri, Prof. Vilson 00036
Kuring, Alfons 19342
Kuring, Gertrud 19342
Kurosawa, Hiroshi 26887
Kuroyanagi, Tetsuko 26836
Kurpik, Maria 32118
Kurre 17746

Kurth, Joanna 10138
Kurtz, Dr. John K. 41978
Kurtz Schaefer, Guillermo S. 34516
Kuručev, Dragana 33928
Kurz, A. 19699
Kurz, Birgit 20090
Kurz, Elmar 02279
Kurz, Friedhelm 18804
Kurz, Helma 16999
Kurz, Dr. Herbert 16642
Kurz, Dr. Hugo 36494
Kurz, Jürgen 16877
Kurz, Manfred 20582
Kurze, Gisela 18422
Kurzel-Runtscheiner, Dr. Monica 02918, 02999
Kurzenberger, Jim 47672, 47673
Kusche, Dagmar 18849
Kushwaha, M.R.S. 21929
Kusnecova, Anna Grigorevna 32629
Kussé, Kristel 03401
Kussi, Kurt 20741
Kussmann-Hochhalter, Andreas 19185, 19186
Kuster, Emma Maria 15647
Kuster, Dr. P. 29764
Kusuma, Agung 22216
Kusumajaya, Dr. Made 22100
Kutluay, Sevgi 37710
Kutsioğlu, F. Suzan 37628
Kutter, Fritz 01698
Kutz, Artur 15811
Kuuioka, Yasuo 26964
Kuusk, Sven 01142
Kuuskemaa, Jüri 09358
Kuutsa, Tommi 09627
Kuvšinskaja, Ljudmila Anatoljevna 32860
Kuwahara, Keiichi 26747
Kuysters, Janneke 29538
Kuzeev, Rail Gumerovič 33645
Kuzel, Prof. Hans-Jürgen 16919
Kuzina, Marina Nikolaevna 33632
Kužma, Pavel 33984
Kužma, Teresa 31616
Kuzmanić Pierotić, Ivo 06888
Kuzmić, Zdenko 07830
Kuzmin, Aleksej 33486
Kuzmin, Kirill Stanislavovič 33415
Kuzmits, Dr. Wolfgang 01808
Kuznecov, Nikolaj 33234
Kuznecova, Ljudmila Valentinovna 33378
Kuznecova, Natalija 33430
Kvaran, Gunnar B. 30727
Kvaran, Dr. Olafur 21655, 21663
Kvisle, Colleen 06799
Kvist, Kari 09457
Kwack, Dong Suk 27177
Kwakernaak, A.D. 29735
Kwang-ho, Dr. Hahn 27241
Kwasigroh, David 46218
Kwaśniewicz, Dr. Włodzimierz 31758
Kwasnik, Elizabeth I. 38051, 38052
Kwiadas-Wierzbicka, Ludwika 31639
Kwiatkowski, Prof. Marek 32109
Kwiatkowski, Phillip C. 44643
Kwiatkowski, Zygmunt 31602
Kwiecinski, William 43111
Kwok, Dr. Kenson 33936
Kwok, Kian Chow 33941
Kyas, Dr. Vojtěch 08255
Kyazim, K.M. 03069
Kyek, Martin 02545
Kyle, Peter 39775
Kyler, Duane 42422
Kyllönen, Elva 09431
Kyø Hermansen, Cathrine 08823
Kyparissi-Apostolika, Dr. Aikaterini 20843, 21039
Kyriazi, Nelli 20880
Kyriazopoulos, Prof. Basil 21078
Kyriazopoulou, Katerina 20915
Kytr, Hobe 44196
Kyupchupov, Georgi 04820
La Bianca, Domenico 23732
La Fayette, Aubert 15285
La Gamba, Prof. Filippo 22812
La Katos, Donald R. 44706
La Malfa, Francesca 24337
La Morgia, Dr. Jasmine 24228
La Porte, John Thomas 44620
La Regina, Prof. Adriano 25239
La Roche, A.J. 30228
La Rosa, Jean-Louis 11362
Laabs, Dr. Annegret 18582
Laajo, Eero 09564
Laaksonen, Tapio 09718, 09719
Laballe, Gérard 11207
Labanič, Eugen 34005
LaBar, Laurie 41390
Labarque, Ineke 03146
Labarre, Angélique de 11077
Labarthe, Olivier 36747
Labastar, Henri 05193
Labaste, Jacqueline 13474
Labat, Béatrice 15167
Labaune, Patrick 15050
L'Abbate, Vito 23641
Labbé 12359
Labbe, Armand 47399
Labbe, Daniel 14974
Laber, Philip 45196
Laberee, E.F. 05364

LaBier, Brenda 48246
Labonne, Michel 10641
Laborderie, Gérard 14853
LaBorwit, Melanie 44662
Labourdette, Anne 15140
Labovvić Marinković, Liljana 03909
Labrador, Ana Maria Theresa P. 31434
Labrails, Marie-Dominique 14953
Labuda, Dr. Jozef 33951
Labuschagne, L. 34311
Lacabanne, Marie 05278
Lacabe, Jean-Marc 14937
Lacasse, Johanne 06439
Lacchi, G. 24066
Lâce, Mara 27444
Lace, Simon 39879, 40320
Lacena, Daniel L. 31321
Lacerna, Daniel L. 31333
Lacey, Eileen A. 41647
Lacey, Michael 01007
Lacey, Susan J. 41514
LaChance, Michelle 06709
Lachatenere, Diana 45868
Lacher, Gerhard 02986
Lachinger, Dr. Johann 02225
Lachish, Z. 22756
Lachmuth, Uwe 16784
Łaciuk, Adam 31509
Lackey, Doris 44631
Lackner, Franz 02974
Lackner, Dr. Helmut 02993
Lackner, Thomas 02265
LaComb, Gerald 46043
Lacovara, Dr. Peter 41352
Lăcrămioara, Marin 32433
Lacy, Kyleen 44236
Laczko, Valerie 43276
Ladd, Audrey 45909
Ladenburger, Dr. Michael 16231
Ladi, Adrian 42930
Ladier, E. 13047
Ladišić, Jure 07735
Ladleif, Dr. Christiane 15525
Ladlow, Nick 39461, 39468
LaDouceur, Philip Alan 48821
Laduceur, H. 06326
Laenen, Marc 03749
Läufer, Egbert 17562
Laevskaja, Galina Leonidovna 33245
Lafargue, Guy 10802
Lafer, Celso 04491
Laffon, GÈrard de 11877
Laffon, Juliette 13548, 13548
LaFollette, Diane 44823
LaFollette, Mary 43558
Lafon, Alain 12668
Lafond, Frédéric 12214
Lafont-Couturier, Hélène 10809
LaFontaine, Charles 47344
LaFontaine, Mary 48023
Lafontant Vallotton, Chantal 36984
Laforet, Andrea 05484
Lafragette, Florence 14512
LaFrance, Liselle 41084
Lagabrielle, Sophie 13637
Lagardere, Geneviève 14767
Lagaso, N. Trisha 47340
Lagercrantz, Jacob 36163
Lagercrantz, Kristian 36240
Lagerkrans, Jacob 35853, 35854, 36394
Lagerwaard, Drs. Cornelieke 19758
Łagiewski, Dr. Maciej 32178
Lagiglia, Dr. Humberto A. 00594
Lagnel, Cosette 36865
Lagoria, Georgiana 44073, 44074
Lagos, Marta 42916
Lagree, Dr. Kevin 44235
Laguiche, Comte R. de 10413
Lagumdžija, Ermana 03925
Lagvik, Elisabeth 35870, 35871, 35873
Lahcéne, Zghidi Mohamed 00062
Laher, Herman 01662
Lahikainen, Dean 47190, 47198
Lahn, Tore 30477
Lahr, Jason 47681
Lahti, Markku 09593
Lahtinen, Maija 10036
Lahulla, F. 35035
Lai, Piero 23897
Laier, Dr. Heinrich 16386
Lainesse, M. Sylvain 06661
Laing, D.W. 38424
Laing, Greg 43962
Laing, Henry 03887
Laing-Malcolmson, Bonnie 43782
Lainhoff, Thomas A. 45201
Lais, Bruno 19821
Laitinen, Suvi 09478
Laitman, Nanette 45755
Lajoie, Léon 05636
Lajos, Asperjan 21437
Lajos, Dargay 21437
Lajoux, Jacques 11865
Lake, Susan 48361
Laken, L. 29369
Lakin, W.G. 40171
Lal Gaur, Banwari 21767
Lalaounis, Ioanna 20867
Lalev, Ivan 04684, 04728, 04729

Lalevic, Olga 03925
Lallemant, Marie-Françoise 11081
Lally, Michael H. 44988
Lalošević, Aleksander 33881
LaLouche, Judith 46818
Laloue, Christine 13558
Lam, Andrew 07106, 07107
Lam, Anita 45078
Lam, Prof. Peter Y.K. 07093
Lam, Tiffany 07098
Lama, Luís 31197
Lamaestre, Laurence de 11860
Lamard, Maria 18470
Lamasters, Raymond 43859
Lamb, Donna 41374
Lamb, Jennifer 01069
Lamb, Joseph 41221
Lamb, Nancy 47507
Lamb, Rebecca B. 41282
Lamb, Susan 40406, 40410
Lambacher, Lothar 16028
Lambaša, Gojko 07772
Lambel, T. de 11748
Lambers, Drs. P. 29911
Lambert, Al 45097
Lambert, Alice 46320
Lambert, Anne 45067
Lambert, Don 47655
Lambert, Françoise 37288
Lambert, Dr. Frederick A. 48587
Lambert, Helen 43336
Lambert, John 38822
Lambert, Kirby 43984
Lambert, Marie-Jeanne 11153, 12660
Lambert, Ruth 39869
Lambert, Susan 39795
Lambert, Thierry 03606, 03607
Lambert, William E. 42646
Lambert, Yves 10525
Lambertson, John Mark 44207
Lambeth, Linda 05269
Lambley, Alex 40410
Lambon, Corinne 14591
Lambousy, Greg 45731
Lambraki-Plaka, Prof. Dr. Marina 20860
Lambrecht, Miriam 03337
Lambrechts, Lilian 41807
Lambrigger, Josef 36968
Lambropoulos, Iraklis 21131
Lamesch, Chantal 11321
Laminou, Souley 30325
Lammassaari, Taina 09451
Lammertse, F. 29759
Lamonaca, Marianne 45300
Lamontagne, Nicole 06317
Lamouret, Prof. Alfredo Daniel 00148
Lamp, Frederick 41454
Lampard, D. 39305
Lampe, Dr. Angela 16156
Lampe, Dr. Karl-Heinz 16250
Lampens, Dieter 03146
Lampinen, Pekka 09455
Lampl, Johann 02778
Lampl, Dr. Sixtus 20284
Lamprecht, Anett 18398
Lamprecht, M.S. 34334, 34335
Lamschus, Dr. Christian 18556
Lamy, Laurence 15013
Lancaster, Robert 39480
Lancelot, Antoine 14106
Lancmanis, Imants 27366, 27394
Land, Mary 38593
Land, Winfried 01832
Landau, Dr. Sandra 18962
Landauer, Susan 47356
Lande Moe, Tore 30900
Landen, A. Wayne 06088
Landeraasen, Paul 47504
Landert, Markus 37307
Landes, Carolyn 45272
Landes, Christian 12353
Landis, Prof. Dr. Anna Maria 24082
Landis, Ellen 41099
Landis, Jamye 47378
Landis, Judy 46384
Landis, Mary Ann 41168
Landman, Dr. Neil H. 45759
Landmann, Jörg 15547
Landmann, Jürgen 19032
Landová, Blanka 34032
Landress, Helen T. 41519
Landrum-Bittle, Jenita 41325
Landry, Edmond 05507
Landry, Frédéric 05589, 05613
Landsbergen, Michael 01558
Landsmann, Hannah 02948
Lane, Dr. Andrew 39373
Lane, Dr. John R. 42751
Lane, Joshua W. 42849
Lane, Kathleen 48224
Lane, Kerstin 42365
Lane, Margaret Anne 41559
Lane, Maria 48677
Lane, Martin 06081
Lane, Nick 38937
Lane, Oliver 38076
Lane, Richard B. 47084
Lane, Steve 38643
Lane, William 48597

Lang, Alfred 16129
Lang, Anton 02854
Lang, Prof. Berthold 02956
Lang, Brian 43249
Lang, Brian J. 46522
Lang, Elisabeth 14838
Lang, Ewald 17435
Lang, Frank 20115
Lang, Gabriele 15999, 19403
Lang, Dr. Helmut 02955
Lang, Irma 33909
Lang, Manfred M. 02525
Lang, Merike 09365
Lang, Dr. Odo 36676
Lang, Paul 36743
Lang, Sabine 18931
Lang, Tom 47398
Lang, Ulrich 17067
Lang Walker, Barbra 05158
Langan, Lorie 46962
Langbein, Wolfram 19697
Langberg, Dr. Harald 08954
Lange, Dr. Albert de 19235
Lange, Allynne 44493
Lange, Andrzej 31976
Lange, Christian 18707
Lange, Cortina 36242
Lange, Dieter G. 19562
Lange, Dietmar 20404
Lange, Prof. Frederick W. 41837
Lange, Gerhard 19951
Lange, Jane 47374
Lange, Dr. John 40148
Lange, Karl Wilhelm 17154
Lange, Monika 18615
Lange, Rich 48082
Lange Malinverni, Jonas R. 04162
Langel, Carmen 42161
Langelan, Mary 48391
Langelier, Jacques 14651
Langer, Dr. 18314, 19595
Langer, Agnes von 21539
Langer, Brian 01515
Langer, Dr. Brigitte 16418, 18050, 18308, 19018
Langer, Dr. Heiderose 20294
Langford, E. 40636
Langham, B. 01190
Langhammer, Peter 02151
Langhammerová, Dr. Jiřina 08605
Langhof, Jörgen 35888
Langhorne, Richard 38163, 40615
Langkafel, Sonja 17720
Langland, Leo 45271
Langley-Ware, Lyntia 42612
Langlois, Daniel 06370
Langman, David 30301
Langner, Inge 17353
Langner, Kerstin 18400
Langos, Barbara 15444
Langrell, Opal 06862
Langsbury, Hoani 30154
Langston, Linda 42160
Langton, B.R. 38327
Langton jr., Sara 47352
Långvik-Huomo, Marianne 09431
Lanham, Tracy 45342
Lanier, Lance 48194
Lanigan Wood, Helen 38939
Lankford, Éamon 22539
Lannerbro Norell, Maria 35882
Lanning, Bruce 47517
Lannon, John 41798
Lannoye, Henri 03227
Lansdown, Robert R. 41516
Lanser, Dr. Klaus Peter 18951
Lansky, Aaron 41180
Lanszweert, Willem 03666
Lanth, Lynn 42853
Lantos, Titus 02171, 02418
Lantz, Jerry A. 43602
Lantz, Marcel 14328
Lantz, William 43139
Lanyon, Scott M. 45387
Lanz, Dr. Hanspeter 37393, 37423
Lanzarini, Viviana 23119, 23125, 23137, 23142
Lanzinger, Dr. Michele 24461, 25797
Lapa, Dr. Pedro 32300
Lapalus, Marie 12757, 12758
Lapetra, Damaso 34467
Lapeyre, Jean-François 14953
Lapi Ballerini, Dr. Isabella 23878
Łapiak, Dorota 31538, 31539
Laplana, Josep de C. 35125
Lapor, Ardin 47881
Laporte, Gerald 41264
Lapp, Holger 18835
Lappalainen, Ari 09996
LaPrelle, Robert 42744
Lapsley, Peter 03883
Laqua, Prof. Dr. Wolfgang 17282
Laquatra, Carolyn 42250
Laqueste, Marc 11478
Laquindanum, Felicidad 31422
Laranjeira de Schroeder, Prof. Viviana Nuñes 00363
Laray, Carolyn J. 44061
Larcher, Pedro Bruno 04159
Larco de Alvarez Calderon, Isabel 31200
Lareida, Andrea 36666
Larey, Frank 38775

Large, Carol 46136
Large, Christine 38259
Large, Joan T. 46431
Large, Stephen 01378
Larguem, Salima 00073
Lark, Thomas C. 41099
Larkins, Catherine 48472
Larl, Rupert 02064
Larner, Bronwyn 01178
Laroche, Walter Ernesto 41003
Larocque, Peter 06334
LaRosa, Gail 41499
LaRose, Helen 05731
LaRowe, Annette 43822
Larque, Beverley 44702
Larquin, Olivier 13626
Larrañaga, Juan Ramón 34944
Larrañaga, Maria Isabel de 00172
Lars, Roger 12317
Larsch, Georg 17008
Larsen, Carsten U. 08922, 08943
Larsen, Karen 48565
Larson, Dr. Andre P. 48214
Larson, Ara 47927
Larson, Barbara 48307
Larson, Bradley 46206
Larson, Donald 47731
Larson, Francine 42855
Larson, Harry 47605
Larson, John 44102
Larson, Dr. Judy L. 46927
Larson, Julie 47207
Larson, Neal L. 44022
Larson, Sidney 42554
Larson, Silvia 06780
Larson, Steve 47702
Larsson, Åke 35809
Larsson, Hans-Ove 36242
Larsson, Hugo 36242
Larsson, Lars-Erik 36235
Larsson, Peter 36042
Larsson, Thorbjörn 36239
Larsson, Ulf 36268
Larsson Modin, Anita 36322
LaRue, Dr. Hélèna 40142
LaRue, Dr. Hélène 40153
Lárusdóttir, Unnur 21648
Larvová, Hana 08577
Lary, Christian de 12898
Lasansky, Jeannette 44724
Lasansky, Leonardo 47155
Lasfargues, Jacques 12731, 14461
Lash, Michael 42351
Lasheras Corruchaga, José Antonio 35453
Lasić, Višnja 07713
Lasius, Dr. Angelika 18689
Laskey, Jane 39919
Lasley, Tom 46960
Lasmane, Daina 27449
Lasowa, Teresa 32147
Lassen, Thomas W. 08980, 08981
Lassere, Odile 13291
Lassnig, Johann 36816
Lasson, Dr. E. 19237
Lassotta, Dr. Arnold 16191, 16666
Laštovková, Dr. Věra 08450
Lastra, Cristina 00181
Lastu, Didier 14977
László, Dr. Gabor 21558
László, Dr. Péter 21499
Laszlo, Želimir 07835
Latady, Bill 41838
Latanza, Dr. Antonio 25232
Lategan, L. 34188
Laterza Parodi, José 31105
Latham, Charles 47997
Latham, Stanley A. 48263
Latimer, Dr. Bruce 42467
Latondress, Paul 05263
Latour, Patrick 13474
Latourelle, Philippe 14446
Latsay, Brenda 05849
Latschar, Dr. John A. 43662, 43663
Lattanzi, Dr. Elena 23688, 23689, 25987
Lattanzi, Vito 25238
Latu, Jacques 13046
Latuconsina, Dr. Achmad 22133
Laturner, Sybille 19793
Latvala, Anja 10008
Lauand, Débora 04515
Laub, Dr. Peter 02551
Laub, Dr. Richard S. 41985
Laubach, Simone 17935
Laube, Kurt 18918
Laube, Robert 16666, 17639
Laubenberger, Dr. Manuela 02918
Laubie, M. 15088
Laubier, Lucien 13481
Laudat, František 08606
Laudenbacher, Konrad 18842
Lauder, Leonard A. 45886
Lauder, William T. 41185
Lauderdale, David 44422
Laue, Christoph 17720
Lauenborg, Michael 08805
Lauens, Joël 12325
Lauer, Dr. Bernhard 18012
Lauer, Keith G. 41332
Lauermann, Dr. Ernst 01685, 02733

Lauermann, Frank 45154
Laughlin, Patricia J. 47801
Laughlin, Phyllis 43105
Laughton, Barbara 42269
Laughton, Rodney 47491
Laugier, Pierre-Henri 10368
Laukkanen, Rauni 10171, 10172
Launchbury, Michael 39718
Laurencin, André 11127
Laurent, Dominique 05482
Laurent, Elizabeth M. 46456
Laurent, Isabelle 03353
Laurenza, Joseph 43735
Lauridsen, Henning Ringgaard 09109
Lauridsen, Inger 08883, 09094
Lauridsen, Laurie 45713
Laurière, Claudine 13179, 13181
Lauring, Kåre 08861
Lauritzen, Ruth 43794
Lauro, Dr. Maria Giuseppina 25197
Laus, Harry 04091
Lausson, Mirja 36299
Lautanen-Raleigh, Marcia 43166
Lautenberg, W. 34216
Lauter, Prof. Dr. H. 18622
Lauter, Dr. Marlene 20700
Lauter, Dr. Rolf 18612
Lautz, Thomas 18138
Lauwers, J. 03164
Lauxerois, Roger 15163
Lauxmann, Dr. U. 20105
Lauzière, Yves 06442
LaValle, Nancy 43221
Lavalle Argudín, Mario 28176
Lavanchy, Jean-Claude 36546
Lavanchy, John 42962
Lavandera López, José 35241
Lavandeyra-Schöffer, Eléonore de 13470
Lavarnway, Carrie 41933
Laveck, Jocelyn 06794
Lavédrine, Marc 11118
Lavelle, Phyllis 41865
Lavergne, Laurence 11956
LaVerne, Thomas 47625
Laverty, Bruce 46392
Lavery, Sally Ann 41175
Lavie, Pierre 12573
Lavigne, Emma 13558
Lavin, Lucienne 48424
Lavino, Jane 44290
Laviolette, Suzanna 47142, 47143
Lavis, Tom 05485
Lavoie, Suzanne 06330
Lavoy, Carl L. 05241
Lavoyer, Martin 10942
Lavrenyuk, Benedikt Antonovich 37907
Law, Erica 40305
Lawes, Glen 38598, 39308
Lawitschka, Valérie 20224
Lawley, I. 40609
Lawrance, Sarah 38631
Lawrason, Helena 05300
Lawrence, Brad 06235
Lawrence, D.R. 01400
Lawrence, John 44542, 45037
Lawrence, John H. 45727
Lawrence, T.G.B. 40311
Lawrence, Wade 42214
Lawrimore, Katrina P. 43654
Lawson, Amanda 00774
Lawson, H. William 48806
Lawson, Julie 38917
Lawson, Karol 45006
Lawson, Pam 01114
Lawson, Paul 39287
Lawson, Paul W.G. 38295
Lawson, Scott J. 46756
Lawton, Ann L. 42508
Lawton, Peter 40260
Lawton, Rebecca 43480
Lawton, Simon R. 40690, 40691
Laxton, Ailisa 38119
Lay, Chan Kim 27661
Lay, Diana 38408
Layher, Hermann 19968, 20013
Layne, Janice 43605
Layton, Dwight 41680
Lazareva, Lilija Georgievna 32743
Lázaro López, Agustin 34629, 34632
Lazárová, Eva 33954
Lazarus, Fred 41478
Lazenby, William C. 46374
Lažetić, Predrag 33819
Lazov, Gavrail 04846
Lazzarini, Dr. Antonio 24950
Le, Ma Luong 48973
Le, Trung 48993
Le Bail, Jean-Marc 13757
Le Bailly de Tilleghem, Serge Baron 03794
Le Bihan, Olivier 13317
Le Blanc, Lisette 30004
Le Cieux, Laurence 32420
Le Foll, Typhaine 13158
Le Gall, Régine 13252
Le Gendre, Bernard 12362
Le Grange, Judy 34260
Le Grelle, Daniël Graaf 03168
Le Harivel, Adrian 22446
Le Leyzour, Philippe 10549, 14970

Le Maître, Claude 10835
Le Minor, J.-M. 14819
Le Nouëne, Patrick 10344, 10346, 10349, 10350
Le Rouzic-Giovanneli, Gisèle 12642
Le Saux, Marie-Françoise 15082, 15083
Le Stum, Philippe 13900
Le Tissier, P. 40424
Le Van Ho, Mireille 13474
Le Vay, Jonathan 39973
Leach, John 40712
Leach, Mark 42244
Leach, Patricia 44003
Leader, Prof. Mary 22454
Leafdale, Norris 43921
League, Alice 42945
Leah, Mervyn 39474
Leahy, K.A. 40460
Leahy, Mary 45479
Leal, José H. 47397
Leal Spengler, Eusebio 07961
Leaman, David L. 48031
Leandry, Mario 05260
Lear, Paul 46215
Leatherman, Lawrence 47910
Leavesley, Dr. James 01483
Leavey, Jane 41362
Leavitt, Christie 43990
Leavitt, Tracey 05851
Lebas, Frédéric 17560
Lebeau, Monique 13220
Lebedeev, P.I. 33046
Lebedeva, Alla Markovna 33215
Lebegern, Robert 20184
Leberknight, Alan 41485
LeBlanc, Bernard 05880
LeBlanc, Denise 41062
LeBlanc, Guy R. 47703
Leblanc, Jacqueline 14454
LeBlanc, Karen M. 48296
Leblanc, Pascal 15007, 15008
LeBlanc, Suzanne 44672
LeBlond, Dan 46565
Lebouteiller, Claire 15289
LeBouthillier, Louis 05199
Lebrasseur, Marie-Josée 06099
Lebrero Stals, José 35474
Lebrun, Jacques 15138
Lebsack, Ren 06220
LeCato, J.M. 42209
Lečev, Dečko 04731, 04732, 04773, 04774, 04869, 04871, 04872, 04873, 04874, 04876
Lecher, Belvadine 42178
Lechien Durant, Françoise 03301
Lechner, Dr. Gregor Martin 01861
Lechner, Martin 02729
Lechowski, Andrzej 31489
Lechuga, Dr. Ruth 28117
Leclair, Alain 12311
Leclair, Tom 06058
Leclef, Louis 03155
LeCleire Taylor, Gay 45350
Leclerc, Claudette 06833
Leclerc, Marie-Andrée 05882
Leclerc, Patrick 10891
Leclerc, Paul 45859
Leclerc, Paul-André 05707
Leclercq, Jean-Paul 13556
Leclert, Hélène 14021
LeCompte, Sarah 41437
Leconte, Philippe 03590
Lecoq-Ramond, Sylvie 11361, 11361
L'Ecotais, Emmanuelle de 13548
LeCount, Charles 46776
Lecouturier, Yves 10980
Lecuillier, Michel 10613
Lecuyer, Françoise 13351
Leder, Carolyn R. 39738
Lederer, Carrie 48290
Lederer, Irene 17744
Lederer, Nan 41837
Ledermair, Martin 02650
Ledet, Claudette 06201
Ledford, Thomas G. 45005
Ledoux, François 05805
Leduc, Dawn 04980
Lee, Bok Hyung 27205
Lee, Chris 40161
Lee, Christopher 41762
Lee, Colin 39490
Lee, Cynthia 45841
Lee, David L. 47234
Lee, David S. 46777
Lee, Ellen W. 44228
Lee, Eric M. 45974
Lee, Hee-Jae 27281
Lee, Hyun-Sook 27253
Lee, Jackie 48317
Lee, Janie C. 45886
Lee, Jean 45692
Lee, Prof. Jong-Sang 27276
Lee, Karen 06009
Lee, Lawrence 42540, 46145
Lee, Lila J. 48135
Lee, Linda 39490
Lee, Molly 43258
Lee, Ra Hee Hong 27301
Lee, Robert 45769
Lee, Roslyn 39240
Lee, Seung-Koo 27163

Lee, Steven 41459, 41469
Lee, William B. 47373
Lee, William D. 41933
Lee, Wuh-Kuen 07342
Lee Lindsey, Treva 42191
Lee Moss, Barbara 48191
Lee Pederson, Laura 45870
Lee Reid, Katharine 42466
Leebrick, Gilbert 43826
Leech, William J. 41763
Leeder, P.G. 40693
Leedy, Harriet 43634
Leedy, Sherry 44402
Leen, Frederik 03300
Leen, Mary 42048
Leenes, Tony 29535
Lees, Diane 39712
Leestma, Jeffrey K. 42822
Leeuw, G. de 29186
Leeuw, Prof. R. de 28898
Lefarth, Ute 20662
Lefébure, Amaury 11769
Lefebvre, Pascal 03569
Lefebvre-Canter, Michelle 42423
Lefever, Joel 44056
Lefevre, Gérard 13143
LeFevre, John 42543
Lefèvre, Prof. Patrick 03336
LeFevre-Stratton, Leslie 45740
Leff, Kathy 45300
Lefftz, M. 03600
Lefki, Michaelidou 08203, 08204
Lefort, Jacques 13118
Lefour, Pierre 14915
Lefrançois, Michèle 10837, 10838
Lefrançois, Thierry 12241, 12243, 12245
Lefrancq, Janette 03337
Legac, Mirjana 07764
Legarda, Eduardo 31356
Legarda, Rosalita R. 31356
LeGath, Judith B. 47956
Legault, Jocelyne 06572
Legendre, Françoise 14046
Legêne, Dr. S. 28866
Legg, Dr. G. 38338
Legget, J.A. 39465
Legleiter, Kim 45464
Legout, Gérard 10432
Legrand, Edith 12140
Legrand, Sybille 03233
Legros, Charles 03812
Leh, Dennis E. 41855
Lehan, Kathy 38311
Lehberger, Prof. Dr. Reiner 17542
Lehmann, Christine 19738, 19739
Lehmann, Gérard 12567
Lehmann, Dr. Hans-Ulrich 16692
Lehmann, Kai 19808
Lehmann, Dr. Karin 19913
Lehmann, Klaus 17770
Lehmann, Randall 43641
Lehmann, Dr. Ulrike 18523
Lehmann, Ursula 20523
Lehmann-Enders, Christel 18369, 18532
Lehnemann, Dr. Wingolf 18562
Lehner, Adam 45794
Lehnert, Marie Josée 27571
Lehnherr, Dr. Yvonne 36711, 36715
Lehodey, Colette 13935
Lehr, Dr. André 28954
Lehr, William 43926
Lehtinen, Dr. Martti 09502
Leiber, Christian 17446, 17447
Leibnitz, Dr. Thomas 02955
Leibrand, Sue 47504
Leich, Jeffrey R. 43504
Leicht, Walter 19650, 19654
Leichty, Erle 46460
Leidner, Udo 19080
Leidy, Susan 45096
Leif, Elizabeth 47839
Leighton, John 28911, 29112, 29122
Leijen, A.J.M. 28981
Leijerzapf, Dr. I.Th. 29523
Leijon, Anna-Greta 36242
Leijten, C.J.M. 29254
Leikauf, Barbara 01922
Leilund, Helle 08961
Leimu, Tuula 10178
Lein, Sharon 42868
Leinfelder, Prof. Dr. R. 18893
Leinicke, Kris Q. 46956
Leinonen, Paula 10075
Leinweber, Dr. Ulf 18032
Leinz, Dr. Gottlieb 16757
Leipold-Schneider, Gerda 01746
Leiseth, Sylvia 48450
Leismann, Burkhard 15403
Leistner, Dr. Gerhard 19527
Leite, Ana Cristina 32290, 32294, 32315
Leite, Prof. Michael 42179
Leitgeb, Dr. Franz 01827, 01916
Leitgeb, Otto 02135
Leitmeyer, Wolfgang 20011
Leitnaker, Connie 44622
Leitner, Andreas 02742
Leitner, Dr. Friedrich W. 02127
Leitner, Norbert 02623
Leitner, Stefan 01658

Leitner-Böchzelt, Susanne 02209
Leitner-BÖchzelt, Susanne 02210
LeJambre, L.A. 41793
Lejeune, Louis 03185
Lejnieks, Dr. Janis 27413
Lekholm, Kerstin 35919
Lekson, Steve 41837
LeLacheur, Melinda 41176
Lelieur 13477
Leloup, Michel 11701
Lemaire, Michèle 10863
Lemaire, Philippe 14736
Lemal Mengeot, Chantal 03351
Lemańska, Stefania 31586
Lemaster, Leroy 45213
Lemasters, Howard 41506
Lemback, Jack 45229
Lembert, Dan 41443
Lembke, S. 16035
Lemcke, J. Peter 16461
Lemelle, François 13472
Lemercier, Christian 10826
Lemeunier, Albert 03577
LeMieux, Linda D. 42542
Leming, C.F. 40551
Lemire, Marie 05919
Lemky, Barbara 05294
Lemle, Robert 43619
Lemmon, Dr. Alfred 45727
LeMoine, Dr. Geneviève 41972
Lemoine, Serge 13596
Lemons, C.R. 43406
Lemos, Nikolas S. 21102
Lemothe, Peter Thomas 45697
Lempka, Wayne 45741
Lenaers, J.H. 29202
Lenaghan, Patrick 45815
Lenarczyk, Leszek 31594
Lenarduzzi, Nelson 00371, 00372
Lenarz, Michael 17057
Lencquesaing, May-Eliane de 13671
Lengerken, Prof. Dr. von 17516
Lenglet, Marie-Cornélie 12596
Lengyel-Kiss, Katalin 21371
Lenk, Elfriede 02440
Lenk, Dr. Sabine 16722
Lenkiewicz, Jolanta 31712, 31714
Lenković, Mario 07068
Lennard, John Barret 00953
Lennig, Dr. Petra 15918
Lenoir, Yves 03275
Lensen, Jean-Pierre 03819
Lenski, Jean-Pierre 14686
Lenssen, Dr. Jürgen 20333, 20691
Lent, Eric 42069
Lentini, Dr. Maria Constanza 23970
Lentino, Miguel 48901
Lentz, Lamar 47017
Lentz, Dr. Thomas 48335, 48357
Lenz, Berta 17294
Lenz, Gerhard 16257
Lenz, Helmut 17042
Lenz, Iris 20097
Lenz, Mary Jane 45852
Lenz-Weber, Dr. Diana 17576
Leo, Dana 46226
León, Imelda de 27839
Leon, Lamgen 45841
León Rivera, Jorge de 28109
León Rivera, Melba Rocío 07418
Leonard, Amy 41062
Leonard, Claude 13107
Leonard, Douglas 05045
Léonard, Georges 13251
Leonard, Glen M. 47231
Leonard, Jessie 45358
Leonard, Jim 06122
Leonard, Mark 44913
Leonard, R.A. 38750
Leonard, Robert 45087
Leonardo-Finger, Jascin 45597
Leoncini, Dr. Luca 23996
Leone, Carol 48304
Leonhardt, Günter 18279
Leonhardt, Rainer 18754
Leonori, Dr. Maria Chiara 23777, 23782
Leontiev, Andrej 33355
Leontjeva, Sofija Jakovlevna 33250
Leopardi, Anna 25085
Leopold, Prof. Dr. Rudolf 02924
Lepage, Jean 13267, 13271
Lepdor, Catherine 36860
Lepe, Marcella 28350
Lepičić, Janko 33834
Lepine, André 03348
Lepine, Brigitte 10490
Lépine, Luc A. 06302
Lepley, John G. 43367, 43368
Leppala, Vesa 09466, 10021
Lepper, Beate 20454
Lepper, Dr. Katharina B. 16757
Leppiniemi-Järvinen, Anita 09634
Leproust, Evelyne 13902
Lepší, Miroslav 08400
Leray, Victor 12700
Lerch, Michaela 13533
Lerebours, Lionel 21293
Leresche, Anne 36864
Léri, Jean-Marc 13498, 13539

Leritt, Sarah 39459
Lernbaß, H. 18262
Lerner, Adam 41461
Lerner, Peter 41924
Lernout, Françoise 10324
Leron-Lesur, Pierre 14448
Lerouge-Benard, Jean-Pierre 11921
Leroux, Doug 06108
Leroux, Jean-François 15186
Lerov, Trifon 04682
Leroy, Gilbert 12656
Leroy, Jacques 10504
Leroy, Vincent 01894
Lerrick, Dr. Yacob 22149
Lervy, Annick 12982
Lesaffre, Jean-Marie 12600
Lesák, Dr. Barbara 02963
Leschhorn, Prof. Dr. Wolfgang 16297
Lescombes, Germain 10998
Lescroat-Cazenave, Elizabeth 13414
Leser, Rupert 15759
Lesher, Ronald E. 47149
Leshikar, Howard B. 47977
Leskien, Dr. Hermann 18831
Lesko, Diane B. 47482, 47485
Leskova, Marina 27591
Leskovar, Peter 34151
Leskovec, Ivana 34091
Leslie, James 38072
Leslie, Mike 46116
Lesniewicz, Paul 17663
Leśniewska, Józefa Ewa 31750
Lesser, Ann 48312
Lesser van Waveren, Hans-Georg 15842
Lessmann, Dr. Johanna 17560
Lessmann, Dr. Sabina 16242
Lester, Colleen C. 48076
Lester, Ellen 44525
Lester, Mary P. 48769
Lestraden, M.P. 28982
Leszczyński, Wojciech 32191
Letenayova, Dr. Zdenka 33974
Letendre, Julie 42841
Letertre, J.B. 14849
Leth, Gwen I. 46855
Letourneur, Céline 11700
Letroye, Marcelle 03610
Letsatsi, Reginald 34170
Letschert, Edmund 20445
Lettany, Lieve 03618
Lettner, Christoph 02622
Letts, A. 34240
Letz, Andrea 18116
Leu-Barthel, Angelika 17530
Leuba, Marion 10648, 10649, 10651
Leumann, Alexander 36706
Leuschner, Dr. Jörg 19735
Leušin, Viktor Vladimirovič 32688
Leutenegger, Dr. Marco 36473, 37183
Leutenegger-Kröni, Tanja 36778
Leuzinger, Dr. Urs 36707
Lev-Ari, Y. 22681
Levá, Kimmo 09617
Levander, Karin 36381
Levčenko, Vitalij Vasiljevič 32974
Levens, Dwight R. 42919
Leventon, Melissa 47311, 47325
Leverton, Raymond 44263
Lévesque, André 06384
Levey, Georges 14662
Levi, A. 22684
Levi, Preston 43410
Levièvre, Francine 05927
Levin, Annika 13517
Levin, Dalia 22616
Levin, Mai 09358
Levin, Nikolaj Iljič 33550
Levin, Pamela 47515
Levine, Beverly 43470
Levine, Janet 45876
Levine, Kenneth 45870
Levine, Dr. Louis 45842
Levine, Phyllis 45817
Levinho, José Carlos 04369
Levinthal, Beth E. 44161
Levitt, S. 39462, 39465
Levkin, Jaroslav Borisovič 33319
Levy, David C. 48341, 48342
Levy, Harry A. 45996
Levy, Sue M. 46398
Lew, Dr. Irena 31842
Lewallen, Constance 41649
Lewandowski, Marian 31899
Lewandowski, Ryszard 31825
Lewars, James 48725
Lewenhaupt, Dr. Inga 36110
Lewerken, Dr. Heinz-Werner 16705
Lewicki, Ireneusz 31804
Lewin, Jackie 47109
Lewin, S.J. 38524
Lewis, Anne V. 46524
Lewis, Forrest 48662
Lewis, Frank C. 41241
Lewis, George 47777
Lewis, Greg 48158
Lewis, Larry 48739
Lewis, Lesley 06600
Lewis, Louise 46028
Lewis, Maisie 00781

Lewis, Merri 41106
Lewis, Michael 41104
Lewis, Oli 44667
Lewis, Richard 46374
Lewis, Robert 41390
Lewis, Robert K. 44736
Lewis, Steve 43253
Lewis, T. 38317
Lewis, Vel A. 37552
Lewis, William 48621
Lewis, William R. 46469
Lewis-Crosby, Meg 38032
Lewis Schaal, Cynthia 42236
Ley, Dr. Andreas 18876, 18880
Leyoudec, Maud 14685
Leys, K. 03273
Leys, Kathleen 03287
Leysen, Veerle 03596
Leyten, C.J.M. 29891
Leyva, Maria 48334
Lezarrdiere, A. de 12149
Lhagvasüren, I. 28681
L'Hostis, Denez 11562
Li, Lifu 07005
Li, Linna 07070
Li, Qianbin 07077
Liabeuf, Brigitte 14886
Liagouras, Angelos 20925
Liaño, Marta 48914
Liao, Kui-Yin 07344
Liapis, Kostas 20808
Liavas, L. 20877
Libbus Boon, Edna 05346
Libby, Reis 47071
Liberatore, Laurie 43169
Libert, Laura L. 46426
Libin, Laurence 45833
Liby, Håkan 36352, 36361, 36361, 36365
Lică, Paul 32486, 32487
Lichenecker, Christian 02704
Lichte, Dr. Claudia 20696
Lichtlé, Francis 12113
Lichty, Robert C. 42088
Lickleder, Dr. Hermann 18051
Lickteig, Dorothy L. 43627
Licky, Maurice 06878
Liczkov, Sergej Nikolajevič 32629
Liddell, Lynne 39359
Liddle, Peter 38745
Liddle, Dr. Peter 39451
Lideń, Magnus 36357
Lidequist, Dr. Christina 36207
Lidman, Roger 46480
Lidtke, Thomas D. 48513
Liďuma, Ilze 27389
Lieb, Hartmut 17473
Liebelt, Glenn T. 01181
Liebenberg, O.J. 34188
Lieber, Vincent 36994
Lieberman, Chrissy 48096
Lieberman, Richard K. 44867
Lieberman, William S. 45833
Liebgott, Dorion 06563
Liebgott, Niels-Knud 08920
Liebhart, Prof. Dr. Wilhelm 15470, 15471
Liebich, Haimo 18861
Liebscher, Sabine 18581
Liechtenstein, Friedrich 02515
Liechti, W. G. 37200
Liedekerke Beaufort, Comte Hadelin de 03347
Liekonen, Marita 09653
Lien, Mary 46570
Lienau, Jennifer 47414
Lienerth, J. 16966
Lienhard, Kurt 36520
Lienhard, Ulrich 37366
Liensdorf, Klaus 20173
Liepold-Moser, Bernd 01943
Lierville, Sylviane 11607
Liesbrock, Dr. Heinz 16265
Liesch, F. 18736
Liesens, Liliane 03298
Lieth, Elke-Luise von der 16116
Lif, Malka 22749
Lifshitz, S. 22699
Liggett, G. 43971
Light, Brad 48689
Light, Dr. Helen 01434
Light, Lyn 39031
Light, Natalie de 19132
Lightbourn, Brian 03880
Lightfoot, Ricky 42651
Lighthall, Penny L. 06648
Ligne, Michel Prince de 03209
Lignori, Prof. Laura 25742
Ligon, Doris H. 42548
Ligon, Dr. J. David 41105
Ligon, Samantha M. 41884
Ligthart, Elisabeth 02959
Ligúde, Ginsa 27367
Liikkanen, Hilkka 10004
Liknes, Fern 05420
Lilienthal, Dr. Georg 17472
Lillehammer, Grete 30877
Lilley, Clare 40820
Lilly, Bruce 47163
Lilly, Stephanie 42232
Lilly, Tina 45055
Lim-Yuson, Dr. Nina 31386

Lima, Alida de la 31079
Lima, Dr. Francisco 32237
Lima Greene, Alison de 44129
Limbach, Dr. Adelheid 20314
Limbacher, Dr. Gabor 21310, 21522, 21546
Limburg-Stirum, Comtesse F. de 14902
Limme, Luc 03337
Limón Delgado, Antonio 35484
Limpo Pérez, Luis Alfonso 35171
Lin, Lee Chor 33942, 33943
Linaeque, Dr. P.M. 28763
Liñán Guijarro, Eladio 35729
Linasi, Marjan 34150
Linciano, Dr. Antonio 23948
Lincoln, Lee 42858
Lincoln, Louise 42323
Lind, Axel 09055
Lind, Dr. Christoph 18615
Lind, Ed 46734
Lind, Evgenij Alekseevič 33426
Lind-Sinanian, Gary 48440
Lind-Sinanian, Susan 48440
Lindahl, Per 35949
Lindauer, H. 30253
Lindberg, Annika 36349
Lindberg, David R. 41646, 41646
Lindberg, Janelle 46145
Lindberg, Kathy M. 43313
Lindbom, tina 36052
Lindemann, Prof. Dr. 20231
Lindemann, Prof. Dr. Bernd 36505
Linden, Grace 47639
Linden, Jaap ter 29765
Lindén, Lena M. 35968
Linden, Peppy G. 42254
Lindenhofer, Harald 02959
Linder, Brad 45221
Linder, Prof. H. P. 37372
Linder, Karin 45932
Linder, Maria 36003
Linder, Marja-Liisa 10092
Linderer, Steve 44655
Linderman, Mike 43244
Lindert, Reinhard 17335
Lindgren, Göran 35096
Lindh, Anders 36115
Lindh, Marianne 36398
Lindhartseni, Ole 30974
Lindhorst, André 19281
Lindley, Ralph 40329
Lindloff, Dr. Axel 20655
Lindmayr, Burgi 02541
Lindner, Gerd 15644
Lindner, Dr. Helmut 16713
Lindner, Mathias 16470
Lindner, Walter 17231
Lindquist, Carl 44247
Lindquist, Everett 48205
Lindquist, Sven-Olof 36413
Lindquist, Catharina 36268
Lindqvist, Per-Inge 35999
Lindqvist, Svante 36268
Lindsay, Frances 01237
Lindsay, Judy 38748
Lindsay, Mike 41313
Lindsay, S.J. 40186
Lindsay, Tom 47350
Lindsay Baker, Dr. T. 44028
Lindsberger, Josef F. 01954
Lindseth, Knuth 30663
Lindsey, David 39321
Lindsey, Jack 46428, 46442
Lindsey, Jimmy 41082
Lindsey, Rob 44568
Lindström, Anneli 09539
Lindstrom, Janet 45680
Lindvall, Martin 36128
Lineberry, Heather S. 47970
Lineros, Ricardo 34681
Lines, S. 38712
Ling, Steven 41298, 47520
Lingier, Rafael 03381
Lingstadt, Kirsty 38844, 39160
Linhares, Philip 46067
Linhart, Dr. Eva 17062
Linke, Irmgard 02425
Linkov, Krasimir 04777
Linkowski, Zdzisław 31606
Linley, Jim 39295
Linn, Joe Dale 46698
Linna, Markku 10106
Linnehan, Sharon 42946
Linnel, Eric 41756
Linnemann, Dr. Ulf 16700
Linnerr, Pip 01317
Linnertz, Rudolf 16289
Linnichenko, Antonina 37878
Linnie, Martyn J. 22461
Linnikova, Nina Jakovlevna 33460
Linou, Marie-Josée 13972, 13973
Lins, P. Andrew 46442
Linschinger, Josef 01895
Linsenmaier, Dr. Walter 36668
Linsky, Carol 46969
Linsmann, Dr. Maria 20216
Linthorne, Marguerite 05093
Linton, Dr. M. 01033
Linton, Meg 47402
Lintott, B. 30128

Linus, Frederick 44351
Linville, Tony 47814
Liot, David 13928
Liotta, Jorge 05779
Lipchinsky, Zelek L. 41635
Lipfert, Nathan 41522
Lipinski, Henry 39219
Lipka, Dieter 15657
Lipkens, Myriam 03482
Lipo, Frank 46054
Lipońska-Sajdak, Jadwiga 31646
Lipovanski, Georgi 04857
Lippe, Edward J. von der 43818
Lippens, Kathleen 03316
Lippert, Dr. Wolfgang 18836
Lippi, Angelo 24226
Lippi, Dr. Emilio 25804
Lippincott, Louise 46510
Lippman, Irvin M. 42587
Lippman, Judith 41480
Lipps, Jere 41646
Lisai, Virginia 48565
Lisberg Jensen, Ole 08946
Liščáková, Daniela 08498
Lisicyn, Viktor Borisovič 33721
Lisk, Susan J. 43863
Lisk-Hurst, Corrie 43812
Liška, Dr. Pavel 19527
Liška, Peteras 34073
L'Isle, Viscount de 40178
Lisowski, Silvia 20525
Liss, David 06034
Lissague, Bernard 10885
Lissens, Paul 03302
Listen, Simon 38837
Lister, Alison 39675
Listoe, Philip 06399
Listopad, John 47772
Lithén, Hans-Olof 10160
Litochleb, Dr. Jiří 08613
Little, Faye 38544
Little, John 41934
Little, L. 43171
Little, Tom 46959
Little, Tricia 44006
Littlefield, Jennifer 46484
Littleton, Kim 48007
Littlewood, Barry 38645
Litvak, Silvia 00316
Litwin, Dr. Jerzy 31563, 31579, 31581, 31582,
31590, 31614, 32046
Litz, Dr. Christine 18161
Litzenburg, Thomas V. 44761
Liu, Cary Y. 44703
Liu, Guang Rui 07030
Liu, Guang Tang 07037
Liu, Yuchuan 07031
Lium, Randi N. 30944
Lively, Carter C. 41228
Livengood, Donald L. 48605
Livengood, R. Mark 44714
Liverani, Dr. Paolo 48872, 48873, 48876, 48879
Livesay, Thomas A. 41604
Livezey, Dr. Bradley C. 46511
Livingston, Glenda A. 48272
Livingston, Jan 46863
Livingston, Judith 44813
Livingston, Dr. Valerie 47561
Livingstone, Judy A. 05319, 05320
Livland, Haakon 30604, 30926
Livneh, M. 22681
Livsey, Karen E. 44311
Liwei, Cheng 06965
Lixfeld, Gisela 19848
Lizarazo, Plata 07375
Lizzadro, John S. 43167
Ljiljak, Aleksandar 03922
Ljøkjell, J. 30588
Ljubaščenko, Anna Ivanovna 33592
Ljubić, Josip 07800
Ljubimov, Vladimir Alekseevič 32648
Ljubović, Prof. Blaženka 07770
Ljungberg, Louise 36180
Llabrés, Pere-Joan 35234
Llagostera Martínez, Dr. Agustín 06906
Llanas, Joan 35671
Llanes, Manuel 35535
Llanes-Myers, Susan 44122
Llazari, Vasil 00032
Llewellyn, David 39228
Llewellyn, Mike 39197
Llinas, Chr. 13127
Llobet, Guy 11349
Llongarriu, Marissa 35173
Llorens, Tomás 35057
Llorente, Sofía 35024
Llorente, Tina 44129
Lloveras, Fernando 32377
Lloyd, Alan 01490
LLoyd, Alison 40181
Lloyd, Deanna S. 45132
Lloyd, Kenita 44868
Lloyd, Kristin B. 41132
Lloyd, Stephen 38917
Lloyd Harvey, Peter 40219
Lmas, Jean de 11648
Lo Schiavo, Dr. Fulvia 25488
Loaring, A. 40030

Lobanova, Galina Pavlovna 32767, 32775
Lobaõ, Dr. Paulo 32237
Lobas, Aleksandr 27083
Lobb, Muriel 44799
Lobb, Sylvia 44311
Lobbig, Lois 41157
Lobjakas, Kai 09362
Lobkareva, Antonina Vasilevna 33657
Lobo, Dr. Wibke 15945
Lobos Lápera, Victor 06893
Lochman, Dr. Tomas 36495, 36522
Lochmann, Reinhart 15396
Lochrane, Dr. Charles G. 47281
Lock, Alan 38839
Lock, Victoria A. 44554
Lock-Weir, Tracey 00704
Locke, Dr. H. 05978
Locke, Michelle 42643
Lockett, Daniel 39842
Locklair, Paula 48701
Lockwood, Dave 42976
Lockwood, David 38788, 38790, 38791, 38792
Lockwood, D.C. 30272
Lockwood, Dr. Yvonne 43054
Loderer, Klaus J. 15587
Lodewijk, W. 29342
Lodge, Penny 46524
Lodowski, Dr. Jerzy 32173
Loeb, Gwen 47369
Löb, Heidrun 37400
Löbach, Prof. Bernd 16511
Löber, Eva 18574
Löbert, Dr. Horst W. 20117
Löbke, Dr. Matthia 17688
Löcken, Monika 15540
Loeffler, Robert J. 45488
Löffler, Ruth 16751
Löfquist, Barbro 35912
Löfström, Lena. A 36306
Löher, Jochen 16662, 16667
Löhr, Dr. Alfred 16321
Löhr, H. 17519
Löhr, Dr. Hartwig 20212
Loehr, Scott W. 41380
Löliger-Henggeler, Elisabeth 37032
Lönnebo, Lovisa 36262
Lönnström, Yvonne 10169
Loera Chávez y Peniche, Dr. Margarita 28188
Loers, Dr. Veit 18772
Lösch, Bernhard 25342
Lösche, Wolfgang 18852
Loest, Mark A. 47116
Lötsch, Prof. Dr. Bernhard 02951
Lövgren, Amanda 36208
Löwenkopf, A.Z. 22585
Lofgren, Donald 42420
Lofgren, John Z. 48222
Loft, Elaine P. 44101
Lofthus, Brian 43743
Loftin, Jack 41249
Loftin, Jim 43579
Loftus, John 19903
Loftus, Sydney L. 46156
Logan, Brad 44684
Logan, Burt 41831
Logan, Joyce 06147
Logan, Judy 43827
Loge, Øystein 30462, 30463
Logger, R. 28897
Logghe, Marc 03784, 03786, 03787
Lohe, Michael 18867
Lohiniva, Leena 10004
Lohmann, Dr. Frank 36920
Lohmann, J.H.A. 29360
Lohmann, Uwe 20478
Lohmeier, Prof. Dr. Dieter 18076
Lohrenz, Mary 44279
Lohse, Dr. E.S. 46571
Loichemol, Hervé 11719
Loidl, Josef 01709
Loikkanen, Kirsi 09881
Loiko, Patricia 41817
Loisel, Dr. Ulrike 02433
Loitfellner, Tamara 02953
Loizeau, Sigolène 10809
Loizou Hadjigavriel, Loukia 08202
Lojdová, Ivona 08666, 08674
Løken, Trond 30877
Lokensgard, Dr. Lynne 41566
Lokin, Dr. D.H.A.C. 29082, 29083, 29084
Lokki, Juhani 09511
Lomaheftewa-Slock, Tatiana 47421
Lomakov, Dmitrij Aleksandrovič 33073
Loman, D.E. 29308
Lomatter, Odilor 37079
Lomax, James 39452
Lomax, Jenni 39596
Lombardi, Gloria R. 45940
Lombardi, Michele 12592
Lombardo, Dr. Giovanna 25231
Lombardo, Marta Alicia 00353
Lombardo, Romualda 31077
Lombino, Mary-Kay 44858
Łonak, Wojciech 31847
Londoño, Jaime Manzur 07408
Londos, Eva 35977
Londt, Dr. Jason 34327
Lonergan, Gillian 40333
Long, Avis 41995

Long, Betty 43717
Long, Charles 47256
Long, Greg 48751
Long, J. Grahame 42211
Long jr., Paul V. 46690
Long, Philip 38916
Long, Phillip C. 42410
Long, Sachia 42980
Long, Steve 45827
Longbourne, Dr. D. 39935
Longcore, Robert R. 45946
Longenecker, Martha W. 47279
Longenecker, Vickie 43419
Longevialle, Ghislain de 11878
Longhauser, Elsa 47442
Longhi, Alberto 25301
Longhi, Janice 38368
Longhi, L.A. 38365
Longley, Dione 45315
Longo, Prof. Giuseppe 25692
Longtin, Barbara C. 45575
Longuein, Paul 14498
Longwell, Alicia 47707
Lonnberg, Thomas R. 43245
Look, Johannes 15866
Looper, Gail S. 47658
Loose, Annegret 17501
Loose, Helmut 15589
Loosli, Jean-Pierre 36947
Lopas, Julie 43791
Lopata, Robert 41647
Łopatkiewicz, Zdzisław 31627
Lopatkin, Michail Vasiljevič 33546
Lopes, Manuel Teixeira 32358
López, Al Ignatius G. 31430
López, Ana María 35545
Lopez, Donald 48371
López, Edgar 07460
López, Jorge 28182
Lopez, Julie Anna 47417
López, Magdalena 35024
López, Manuel R. 09313
López, María Jose Muñoz 34739
López, Mónica Alejandra 00138
López Alvárez, Joaquín 34846
López de Arriba Reyes Durán, Mercedes 35024
López Fernández, Francisco Javier 34723
López Franco, Amparo 07505
López Hervás, Maria Victoria 35029
López Ortiz, Amparo 35433
López Pimentel, María del Carmen 07924
López Portillo Romano, Carmen 28147
López-Vidriero, Luisa 35058
López Wehrli, Silvia 35693
Loppa, Linda 03149
Lopreato, Paola 23588
Loquenz, Norbert 02507
Lorbeer, Marie 16039
Lorblanchet, Hélène 13121
Lorck, Bjorn 28773
Lord, Allyn 46985
Lord, Anne 01550
Lord, Gary T. 46025
Lord, Victoria 44459
Lord, Victoria A. 44458
Lorek, Amy E. 44015
Loren, Diane 42049
Lorenčak, Marja 34114
Lorenz, Dr. Angelika 18950
Lorenz, Barbara 01725
Lorenz, Dr. Harald 17346
Lorenz, Margaret 39374
Lorenz, Dr. Ulrike 17246, 17247
Lorenzen, Dr. Heidrun 19663
Lorenzi, Franco 24379
Lorenzi, Georges 14754
Lorenzo, Liliana Ema 00231
Lorenzo Rosales, Elaine 08026
Lorenzoni, Dr. Mario 25575
Loret, John 45104
Lorian, F. 15559
Loring Brace, C. 41219
Łos, Ewa 31792
Los, Dr. W. 28917
Losavio, Sam 41527
Losch, Michael 48562
Loshi, Ygal 22725
Loskott, Herbert 01649
Lossnitzer, Carin 16840
Lossnitzer, Dr. Thomas 16480
Lotfullin, Galim F. 33249
Loth, Jan 44654
Lott-Büttiker, Dr. Elisabeth 36825
Lottermann, W. 15623
Lotz, Theo 48708
Lotze, Manfred 18460
Lotze, Ulrich 15893
Lotzwig, Hartmut 19938, 19939
Lou, Xia 07257
Louati, Ali 37591
Loud, Patricia C. 43487
Louderback, Paul 48105
Lõugas, Anne 09358
Loughton, Gregory 09645
Louis, Hubert 10845, 10846
Louma, Mark 45560
Lounsbury, Kathryn 41050
Lourdes Barreto, Maria de 04086
Loureiro Saavedra Machado, João de 32321

Louring, Aage 08838
Loustau, Alain 12561
Louvencourt, Amaury de 11106
Louvi, Dr. Aspasia 20938, 21162, 21167, 21190
Louw, Prof. D.J. 34381
Louw, Dr. D.J. 34381
Louw, J.P. 34320
Louw, P. 34297
Louwagie-Neyens, Linda 06374
Louwman, E.V.N. 29722
Lovdžieva, Marija 04836
Love, Jackie 45986
Love, Mindi 43083
Loveland, Linda 47753
Lovell, Carol 44771, 47850
Lovell, Charles M. 47950
Lovell, Russell A. 47389
Lovell, Shirley 05617
Lovén, Lucie 30767
Lovenz, Marianne 44668
Loverin, Jan 42118
Lovett, Margaret 44771
Lovick, Emily 43456
Lovie, Robert 39020
Loving, Charles R. 46044
Lovis, Dr. William 43054
Lovrinović, Nikola 03926
Low, Dr. James 05685
Low, William 44728
Lowe, Carole 46578
Lowe, Dr. D. 39741
Lowe, Janet 05258
Lowe, John 42988
Lowe, Joseph 42589
Lowe, Susan 27715
Lowell, Kathleen 44060
Lowell, Molly W. 42985
Lowenfeld, David 42476
Lowly, Tim 42310
Lowrey, Annie 48609
Lowrey, Carol 45850
Lowrey, Timothy K. 41105
Lowry, Dale 05205
Lowry, Glenn D. 44869, 44870, 45843
Loxa, Juan de 34831
Loyau, Anne 10628, 10629
Loynes, G. 40921
Loyrette, Henri 13603
Lozada Arias, José 07365
Lozado de Solla, Noemi 00111
Lozano, Prof. Luis-Martín 28126
Lozano Forero, Martha Janet 07622
Lozano Peña, Carlos 07626
Lozanova, Dr. Ralitsa 04846
Lu, Wensheng 07134
Lu Allen, Dr. Marti 46736
Lubac, Marcel 11816
Lubbe, T.A. 34190, 34191, 34194, 34323, 34378, 34402, 34404
Lubic, James E. 43928
Lubimova, L.M. 33065, 33066
Lubina, Michail 31953
Lubitz, Dr. Telse 17660
Lubomir, Martiner 08310
Lubowsky Talbott, Susan 42905
Luboznski, Joe 43530
Luca, Claudia 32621
Lucas, Annemarie 18936
Lucas, Cynthia L. 43802, 43803
Lucas, Daniel 12958
Lucas, Enriqueta T. 31459
Lucas, Judith S. 42406
Lucas, Martyn 39471
Lucas, Mike 38388
Lucas, Palma B. 46441
Lucas, Ritchie 42626
Lucas, Robert 44030
Lucchese, Dr. Angiolo del 25956
Lucchesi Ragni, Dr. Elena 23201, 23209, 23210
Lucchini, Mario 36761
Luce, Donald T. 45387
Luce, H. Christopher 45783
Lučevnjak, Silvija 07741
Lucey, Denis 22492
Luchetti, Dr. Glauco 23813
Luchs, Alison 48373
Luchter-Krupińska, Lidia 31552
Lucidi, Augusto 23483
Luck, Barbara R. 48624
Lucke, Dr. Arne 17771
Luckeneder, Walter 02627
Luckhardt, Prof. Dr. Jochen 16297
Luckhardt, Dr. Ulrich 17541
Luckhurst, Ailene 42430
Luckow, Dr. Dirk 18075
Łuczkowski, Jan 31856
Luderowski, Barbara 46521
Ludewig, Dr. Thomas 19063
Ludington, Link 45058
Ludvigsen, Lucia 21243
Ludvigsen, Peter 08921
Ludwig, Andreas 16823
Ludwig, Dr. Jochen 17113
Ludwig, Jürgen 16615
Ludwig, Dr. Renate 17668
Ludwig, Rudolf 02112
Ludwig, Ursula 15741
Luebbers, Dr. Leslie 45231
Lübbers-Ukena, A. 16585
Lübeck, Elisabet 35994

Lübeck, Karla-Kristine 19897
Lüchinger, Paul 37269
Lüder-Zschiesche, Adelheid von 16678
Lüders, Dr. Klaus 19501
Lüderwaldt, Dr. Andreas 16336
Lüdi, Heidi 36881
Lüdke, Dr. Dietmar 18002
Lüdtke, Dr. Hartwig 16245
Lueg, Dr. Gabriele 18157
Lührs, Günter 17126
Lüll, M. 20113
Lüpkes, Dr. Vera 18431
Lüps, Dr. P. 36547
Lüps, Dr. Peter 37273
Lüscher, Hans 37420
Lüscher, Regula 37108
Lütgens, Dr. Annelie 20662
Lüth, Dr. Friedrich 17419, 19761
Lueth, Virgil W. 47663
Lüthi, Werner 36608
Lüthy, Dr. Hans A. 36616
Lütkemeyer, Ursula 19590
Lütken, Ilona 20102, 20106
Lüttichau, Dr. Mario-Andreas von 16959
Lufkin, John C. 42911
Luft Dávalos, Rafaela 28307
Lugaski, Dr. Thomas P. 46839
Lugger, Leopold 02267
Luginbill, Troy 45009
Luginbühl-Wirz, Regulae 36541
Lugosi, Dr. József 21341
Lugtenburg, Anneke 34345
Luh, Willi 16398
Luhs Agrilar, José María 35086
Luhta, Caroline 42475
Luijten, G. 28899
Luisi, Vincent 43011
Luisi-Potts, Billy 47566
Lukáč, Ján 33999
Lukacs, Maria 32525
Lukas, Clemens 15841
Lukasch, Dr. Bernd 15495
Lukasiewicz, Nancy 41320
Łukaszewski, Andrzej 31979
Lukaszuk-Ritter, Joanna 02934
Lukatis, Dr. Christiane 18018
Luke, Gregorio 44861
Luke, Suzanne 06756
Lukeš, Dr. Michal 08602
Lukesch, I. 02896
Lukeschitsch, H. 02757
Lukić, Ivan 33828
Lukičeva, Alla Stepanovna 33062
Lukina, Inna Nikolaevna 33333
Lukowczyk, Evelyn 17521
Lukšić, Hilar 07765
Lulav, S. 22585
Lum, Shawn 48173
Luma, Ramon E.S. 31429
Lumley, SimonWhite 39573
Lummel, Heinz 18008
Lummel, Dr. Peter 15950
Lumpkin, Libby 45788
Luna, Dr. Juan J. 35048
Luna Moreno, Luís 35626
Lunardi, Prof. Ernesto 23985
Lund, Arnstein 30943
Lund, Elaine H. 45177
Lund, Mikael 08910
Lund, Tora Jervell 30477
Lundberg, Åsa 36349
Lundberg, Carl-Anders 09709
Lundbergh, Hans 36370
Lunde, Oeivind 30937
Lundgreen, James 45119
Lundgren, Britta 36349
Lundgren Nielsen, Hanne 08866
Lundh, Göran 36199
Lundin, Sally 46719
Lundkvist, Anders 35884, 35885
Lundrigan, Dr. Barbara 43054
Lundström, Dr. Agneta 36218, 36223, 36244, 36263, 36275, 36278, 36281
Lundström, Agneta 36284
Lundström, Sven 35940, 35941
Lungarotti, Dr. Maria Grazia 25726
Lunger, Brian 05626
Lunger-Valentini, Eva 02180
Lunghi, Enrico 27559
Lungu, Alexandru 32592, 32593
Lunn, Will 46159
Lunning, Elizabeth 44126
Lunsford, P. Celina 17041
Lunsingh Scheurleer, Dr. R.A. 28835
Lunt, Amanda 44908
Lunt, Sara 39126, 39494, 40946
Luojus, Susanna 10135
Lupal, Kimberly A. 05147
Luperini, Prof. Ilario 24942
Luptáková, Eva 33989, 34033
Lupton, Ellen 45788
Lurie, Doron J. 22775
Lusa Monforte, Guillermo 34547
Lusardi, Richard A. 46845
Lusardy, Martine 13515
Lusby, D.A. 30251
Luse, Vel 44453
Lushear, Jen 45736
Lussi, Kurt 36696, 36910

Lussky, Richard 42811
Luštinec, Jan 08392
Lutaenko, Konstantin Anatoljevič 33704
Luten Schuitema, E.A. 29927
Luterbach-Renggli, Hansjörg 37145
Luterbacher, Hannes 36779
Luther, Charles 42631
Luti, Claudio 24658
Lutnes, Kjell 30441
Lutnesky, Dr. Marvin 46617
Lutsic, Jennifer 47300
Luttinger, Ingrid 02081
Lutyens-Humfrey, A. 38537
Lutz, Dr. Albert 37379, 37398, 37405
Lutz, Gottlob 36794
Lutz, Marian 44129
Lutz, Nancy 48083
Lutz, Peter 20580
Lutz, Robert 41966
Lutz, Tina 48110
Lutz, Dr. Volker 02686
Lutz, William 43473
Lux, D. Ruth 46202
Lux, Simonetta 25227
Lux, Ulla 16732
Luxán, Elena 35034
Luxford, Bob 30229
Luyken, Dr. Gunda 15919
Luymes, H. 29514
Luz, David W. 46341
Luz, Henrique 04515
Luz Paula Marques, Maria da 32332
Luz Ramirez Estrada, Maria de la 07951
Luzin, Sergej Stepanovič 32928
Lyall, Clare 40729
Lyall, Dr. D.C. 20113
Lybeck, Shirley 42283
Lydakis, Prof. Dr. Stelios 20890
Lydamore, Chris 39165
Lydon, Andrea 22446
Lydon, Kate 46527
Lyell, D.I. 39925
Lyke, Linda 44949
Lyle, Charles T. 43630
Lyle, Janice 46267
Lyles, Pelham 48694
Lynam, Seamus 22444
Lynch, Cindy 42579
Lynch, Geraldino 22516
Lynch, Harry P. 41074
Lynch, Kevin 39494
Lynch, Thomas F. 41974
Lynch, Thomas J. 41856
Lyndaker, Vernon 42705
Lynesmith, P. 39977
Lyngby, Thomas 09074
Lynn, Bob 30099
Lynn, Judy G. 42676
Lynn, Ralph 05846
Lynx, David 48774
Lyon, David Peter 01342
Lyon, Katharine 44821
Lyons, Don 42977
Lyons, Jana 48395
Lyons, Joan 42977
Lyons, Dr. John D. 45072
Lyons, Michael 40861
Lyons, Michele 41662
Lyons, Rex 43507
Lyra, Fernando Soares 04302
Lysogórski, Krzysztof 31592
Lyssaris, Agelos 21159
Lytjen, Lokey 44289
Lytle Lipton, Susan 45821
Lytton Cobbold, Martha 39402
Lytwyn, Stephen 06856
Ma, Wei-du 06966
Maanit, G. 22690
Maarek, Lucien 14761
Maas, Klaus 16756
Maas, Wilhelm 19042
Maaß, Prof. Dr. Michael 17991
Maass, R. Andrew 43411
Maat, Erik 29279
Maaz, Dr. Bernhard 15912, 17432, 20457, 20460,
20461, 20464, 20469, 20471, 20473, 20476
Mabon, Richard 38925
Mabungule Chissano, Alberto 28728
Mac Phee, S.D. 05410
MacAdam, Barbara J. 43907
McAfee, Michael J. 48543
McAffee, Dionne 06628
MacAffer, John 41088
McAlister, Judith 41841, 43287
McAllister, Lowell 46103
McAlpine, Clark 43563
McAlpine, Dr. Donald 06334
McAnliffe, Dr. Chris 01233
McArthur, Meher 46303
MCarty, Kenneth W. 46426
MacAulay, Donald 05033
MacAulay, Margot 05033
McAuley, Joyce 41434
McAuley, Kathleen E.A. 41914, 41918, 41923
McAuley, Paul 38915
McBay, Ann 40204
Macbeth, James A. 47068
MacBratney-Stapleton, Deborah 41202
MacBride, Frank 00836

McBride, Heather 41055
McBride, Joe 41192
McBride, Michael A. 43851
McBride, Peggy 46766
McCabe, C. Kevin 48139
McCafferty, Estelle 47758
McCaffrey, John 39795
McCall, Janet L. 46527
McCalla, Mary Bea 43604
McCallum, Cheryl 44117
MacCallum, Jack 05109
McCallum, Sue 46369
McCalman, Dr. Janet 01236
McCamphill, Debbie 38021
McCandless, Barbara 43480
McCann, Mac 42027
McCarroll, Stacey 41802
McCarte jr., John W. 42325
McCarter, John W. 42326
McCarthy, Christine 46730
McCarthy, Frances 42225
McCarthy, J. 01609
McCarthy, John J. 47427
McCarthy, Judith 22503
McCarthy, K. 30124
McCarthy, Robert 41791
McCarthy, Wayne 48299
McCartney, Dr. Nancy G. 43308
McCarty, Cara 47134
McCarty, Gayle 46803
McCarty, Kimberly 45514
McCarty, Laura 43501
McCarty, R. Paul 43392
McCaskey, Jane 45476
McCauley, John F. 41796
McCay, Bill 44325
Macchi, M. 14760
Macciotta, Prof. Giampaolo 23250, 23254
McClain, Ronald 43906
McCleave, John 06258
McClellan, Nancy 45973
McClelland, Jesse 42340
McClenny, Bart 41160
McCloskey, Anne M. 44838
McClung, Elizabeth 45319
McClure, Donna 45472
McClure, Kent 45472
McClure, Nancy 47602
McClure, Richard 48305
McCluskey, Holly H. 48587
McClusky, Pamela 47545
McCollough, Pam 45452
McCollum, Jay 42533
McComb, Joseph 45501
MacComb, Prof. Leonard 39754
McConachie, Jackie 41107
McCone, John 41174
MacConnel, Cal 43364
McConnell, Bridget 39039, 39054, 39062, 39065,
39066
McConnell, Glenn 46126
MacConnell, Raymond 41638
McCooey, Patrick 05510
McCord, Dr. Robert 45271
McCord-Rogers, Suzette 44017
McCormick, Donald 45859
McCormick, Edgar L. 44445
McCormick, Todd 41588
McCorquodale, Ross 01474
McCosh, John 30160
McCourt, Frank A. 46211
McCourt, Steve 00778
McCowan, Kurt 47001
McCoy, James P. 46388
McCoy, Jeff 47034, 47036
McCoy, Kathy 45447
McCoy, Nancy 44882
McCracken, Patrick 41164
McCracken, Ursula E. 48397
McCrary, Joel 42487
McCrary, Patrick C. 44983
McCray, Phil 47912
McCreary, Kathleen 44065
McCree, Timothy 41092
McCudden, Bruce 38307
McCue, Debbie 41678
McCue, Denise 48233
McCue, Donald 46822
McCuistion, Mary Ann 48218
McCullagh, Suzanne 42304
McCullick, Nancy 45206
MacCulloch, Alexandra 38046
McCulloch, Bruce 30218
McCulloch, Judith 43702
McCullough, Catherine 38017
McCullough, Hollis K. 47485
McCully, Robert 43387
McCurtis, Barbara S. 47274
McCusker, Alisa 44868
McCusker, Carol 47283
McDaid, Cecilia 39395
McDaniel, George W. 42214
McDaniel, Phyllis 43520
McDaniel, Robert 43014
McDaniels, Warren E. 45734
McDermott, Robin 40961
McDiannid, Gordon 05116
MacDonald, Catherine 39438
MacDonald, Colin 40217

MacDonald, Colinn 38503, 40765
MacDonald, Craig 06438
McDonald, Donald M. 01278
McDonald, Doris 06064
McDonald, Douglass W. 42402
MacDonald, Elizabeth H. 46444
McDonald, Garry 45339
MacDonald, Dr. George 47529
MacDonald, Gerald J. 45815
Macdonald, I.H. 40585
MacDonald, Jessie 06371
McDonald, Jim 44282
McDonald, John 39292
McDonald, J.P. 44997
MacDonald, Dr. L. 01420
McDonald, Marty 41199
MacDonald, Mary V. 42823
McDonald, Michael 42988
McDonald, Michele A. 45292
MacDonald, Ned 05623
McDonald, Paul 41375
MacDonald, Peter 39398
McDonald, Rebecca A. 44124
Macdonald, Robert R. 45847
MacDonald, Ruby 05275
MacDonald, S. 39743
McDonald, Susan 41954
McDonald, Sussanne 05434
McDonald, Tessa 44097
MacDonald-MacLeod, Beryl 06163
McDonnell, Jeanne 47345
McDonnell, Dr. Patricia 47922
McDonough, Stephen 41175
MacDougal, Bruce 47245, 47262, 47267
McDougall, Jamie 05099
McDougall, Kim 05484
McDowell, Anna 40477
MacDowell, Dr. Marsha 43054
McDowell, Susanne 16456
McDowell, Suzanne 42723
McEachern, Mark 48040
Macedonio, Prof. Giovanni 23736
Macek, Stanislav 08338
McElhone, William K. 41713
McElroy, L.J. 45605
McElroy, Prof. Michael B. 42046
McElroy, Sara 41412
McElwee, J.A.C. 39121
McEneaney, Eamonn 22555
McEnroe, Natasha 39625
McEntee, Holly 45072
MacEnulty, Bill 42534
Maceroni, Prof. Giovanni 25111
McEwen, Amy 45768
McEwen, Bob 44265
McEwen, Gloria 44265
MacFadden, Dr. B.J. 43581
McFadden, David 45755
MacFadden, Lila 05268
McFadden, P. 34222
McFalls, W.J. 05581
McFarland, Seth 42396
MacFarlane, Aynsley 05031
MacFarlane, Nathalie 06460
MacFarlane, Sheena 40128
McFeely, Marie 22446
McFerrin, Jean 47240
McGahen, DeAnn 41139
McGarry, John H. 45577, 45578
McGary, Nancy 45821
McGaugh, Houston 48421
McGee, Maureen 44905
McGee, Prof. Mike 43573
McGee, Patrick 22427
McGehee, Thomas C. 47993
McGill, Forrest 47308
McGill, Shirley 42971
McGillivray, Allan 06657
McGillivray, Don 05966
McGillivray, Dr. W. Bruce 05384
McGinley, Edward 48323
McGinley, Dr. Jack 22435
McGinnis, Melissa S. 47917
McGirr, Margo 47798
McGivern, Andrew J. 48463
McGlumphy, D. 48106
McGlynn, Robert 45859
McGovern, Robert M. 42138
McGovern, Thomas 44937
McGowan, Jeanie L. 42103
McGrady, Dr. Patrick J. 48154
McGranahan, Denis 46118
McGrath, Joe 00902
McGrath, Steph 48582
McGraw, Linda 42614
McGraw, Steve 47532
McGreevy, Candace 47853, 47854, 47856
MacGregor, Neil 39586, 39729
McGrew, Rebecca 42419
McGuffie, Ian 06676
McGuinne, Niamh 22446
McGuinness, Ben 00976
McGuinness, Jim 48780
McGuire, Donna 06045
McGuire, Janice 43497
McGuire, Dr. Jim A. 41532
McGuire, Raymond J. 45877
MacGunnigle, Bruce C. 43040, 43042
Mach, Jiří 08329

Machan, Dallas 38832
McHenry, Kathryn 48698
Macheret, Elisabeth 36641
Machhammer, Helmut 01799
Machinek, Hubert 19948
Machkovski, Petko 04743, 04916
Machneva, Margarita A. 32917
Macho, Erwin 02937
Machon, Abdurremane 28719
McHugh, Eileen 41373
McHugh, Dr. J. 41319
McHugh, Joseph 06693
McHughs, David 43499
MChuny, V.B. 34245, 34285
Maciejewski, Andrzej 32103
Maciejunes, Nannette V. 42587
McIlhargey-Wigert, Dawn 43760
MacIlreith, Rob 05070
McInerney, Gay 41543
McInnes, Marilyn 38679
McIntosh, Jean 06148
McIntosh, Mildred 45207
McIntosh, Muriel 39075
McIntyre, Art 06279
McIntyre, Barbara 06366
McIntyre, Chris 39187, 40374
MacIntyre, Ronald 40124
Macintyre, Roy 39022
McIntyre, Stella 38257
Macintyre, Trish 39881
MacIsaac, Kim 46322
McIver, Duncan 43898
McIver, J.H. 41873
Mack, Angela 42216
Mack, J. 39586
Mack, Jeanne P. 43685
Mack, Joanne 46044
Mack, Joseph 44213
Mack, Vanessa 01501
McKague, Margot 05646
McKale, William 43449
MacKay, Allan 05698
Mackay, Andrew 40527
Mackay, Angus 39463
Mackay, Jim 41132
Mackay, John L. 42239, 42245
McKay, Kelly 05469
MacKay, Kevin 05097
MacKay, Dr. Lachlin 44504
McKay, Maria 47597
McKay, Mary Alice 45854
McKay, Patrick 46949
MacKay, Robert B. 42519
Mackay, Thomas 40708
Mackay, W.A.F. 06242
Mackechnie, John 39047
McKee, Barry 05575
McKee, Julia 45578
McKee, Kathleen 43268
McKee, Marshall 39258
McKee, Pamela 41228
McKee, Paul 38544
MacKellar, Dr. John 01271
McKellar, Stacey 05125
McKenna, George L. 44404
McKenna, James 46129
McKenna, Sharon L. 46322
McKenrick, Fremont 43077
Mackensen, Dr. Götz 16336
Mackenzie, Althea 39223
McKenzie, Cameron 38779
McKenzie, Colin 45768
McKenzie, Graham 39040
Mckenzie, Micahel 34198
McKenzie, Molly 42025
Mackenzie, Philippa 39153
MacKenzie, Stuart C. 42385
McKenzie, Wendy 05640
McKenzie Smith, An 38883
McKeown, Jack J. 43707
McKernan, Robert 42384, 46783, 48816
McKernan, Robert L. 46824
Mackey, Brian 39510
Mackey, David M. 44098
Mackey, Estel 48228
Mackey, Marjorie R. 41313
Mackey, Ted 48228
Mackie, Louise 42466
Mackie, Thomas 42663
McKillop, Joan 40130
Mackin, Richard E. 43431
Mackinlay, Betty 43471
McKinlay, Dawn 05834
McKinlay, Iain A. 38506
McKinley, Iain 38508, 38509
McKinley, Nancy R. 45327
McKinley, Robert 44157
McKinney, D. Frank 45387
McKinney, David 45833
McKinney, Frank B. 42200
McKinney, Jack 48262
McKinney, Janice 48608
McKinney-Tandy, Ruth 43199
McKinsey, Kristan H. 46349
McKitterick, Michael 47558
McKnight, Peg 41584
Mackowiak, Reinhild 18552
Maclagan, Dr. Helen 40793

Maclagan, Helen 40795, 40796
McLain, Charles 44474
McLain, Guy 47745
McLallen, Helen M. 44482
McLaren, Hazel 41507
McLaren, M. 01166
McLary, Kathleen 44224
McLaughlin, Barbara 48085
McLaughlin, Belinda J. 42278
McLaughlin, Pat 45836
McLaughlin, Robert 47760
McLaughlin, Stacey B. 47003
McLaughlin, William F. 42932
McLaughlir, Dr. John 05458
McLaurin, Genette 45868
McLea 47226
McLean, Al 40499
McLean, Genetta 44728
McLean, Dr. Janice V. 41154
McLean, Kathleen 06029
McLean, Libby 38813
McLean, Linda E. 44143
Maclean, Marge 05528
MacLean, Roderick 05546
MacLean, Rusty 40357
McLean, Steve 40036
McLean Ward, Dr. Barbara 46651
McLellan, Darlene 43092
MacLellan, Heather 06135
MacLellan, Iain 45095
McLellan, Richard A. 42176
Maclennan, F. 39407
MacLeod, Cynthia 46885
MacLeod, Dr. Ian 01364
MacLeod, Kathleen 05331
MacLeod, Patricia 47202
McLeod, Roddy 39056
McLeod, Susan M. 43074
McLerran, Jennifer 41324
McLorys, Jan 42358
McLoughlin, Kevin 38337
MacLoy, David 00812
McMahon, Cynthia 42359
McMahon, James 44004
McMahon, James E. 43666
MacMahon, Rose 39555
McMahon, Stephen 47819
McMahon, Steve 47818
McManus, Carol 47387
McManus, Greg W. 30249
McManus, Marcia 43402
McManus Zurko, Kathleen 48749
McMaster, Shannon 43760
McMasters, Thomas O. 43452
McMeekin, Rebeeca B. 46790
McMenamin, Brendan 39817
McMichael, Sindy 42866
MacMillan, Bruce 42923
MacMillan, C.J. 39420
Macmillan, Prof. Duncan 38920
McMillan, Edward 42496
McMillan, Dr. R. Bruce 47737
McMorris, Sharon 42773
McMullen, Darlene 06049
McMurtie, I. 38870
McMurtrie, I. 38893
McNabb, Debra 06489
MacNabb, Vicky 47167
McNaboe, Tracey 38926
McNally, Ginger 48805
McNally, Margaret 01541
McNamara, C. J. 43341
McNamara, Carole 41222
McNamara, Mary E. 45882
McNaught, William 38106
McNeal, Joanne 42703
McNealy, Terry 45706
McNear, Sara 42345
McNeely, Don 47771
MacNeil, Malcolm 39314
McNeill, Anne E. 40963
McNeill, C. 01556
McNelly, Kath 00927
McNelly, Dennis 46454
McNichol, Susan 06114, 06465
McNicol, Jean 06771
McNicol, Morag 39956
McNulty, E.C. 43234
McNulty, F.M. 43513
McNulty, J.L. 43234
McNutt, Jim 47265
Macon, Robert 46343
McOuat, Gordon 05855
McOwan, Daniel 01088
MacPhee, Dr. Ross D.E. 45759
McPherson, Beth Ann 46298
McPherson, Dan 42734
MacPherson, Kate 38731
McPherson, Loretta 01022
McPherson, Mark 43843
McPherson, Tommy 46298
McQuaid, Matilda 45788
Macquart, Bruno 13629
Macquart-Moulin, X. 13303
McQueen, Jack 47365, 47367
McQuillis Iscrupe, Shirley 44770
McReynolds, Anne 38155
McScowan, James 40411
McVay, Darice 48195

McWayne, Barry 43258
McWhorter, Nancy 44878
McWilliams, Edward R. 42969
McWilliams, Mary 42042
Macyszyn, Dr. Jacek 32133
Maczulis, Norbert 31643
Madanian, M. 22271
Madden, Jennifer 47386
Madden Leitner, Cynthia 43191
Maddox, Iva Jean 43441
Maddox, Margaret 44516
Mader, Annita 02917, 02918
Mader, Dr. Gerald 02673
Maderek, Dorota 31951
Madersbacher, Dr. Ernst 02374
Madin, John 38957
Madjarov, Mitko 04642
Madkour, Christopher 45102
Madonia, Ann C. 48630
Madrid, Candy L. 46982
Madrid Rojas, Juan José 07579
Madsen, Inge 08848
Madsen, Jan Skamby 08880
Madsen, John 48082
Madsen, Lennart S. 08849
Madsen, Orla 08849
Madsen, Per Kristian 09105
Madshus, Eva 30726
Madurini, Dr. Giulio 24384
Madžarac, Nada 34112
Madzik, Józef 31479
Maeder, Edward F. 42849
Mädl, Else 15849
Mädl, Wilhelm 15849
Maeght, Adrien 13180
Mähl, Andrea 20650
Maek-Gérard, Dr. Michael 17074
Mäkelä, Asko 09535
Mäkelä, Sirkku 09808, 09809
Mäkeläinen, Reijo 09830
Mäki, Riitta 09759
Mäkinen, Antti 09610
Mäkinen, Marketta 09597
Mael, Stephen 39475
Mänd, Anu 09610
Maeng, Injae 27203
Männchen, Dr. Julia 17389
Mänttäri, Roy 09533
Märker, Dr. Peter 16541
Maerz, Jürgen 17082
März, Dr. Roland 16075
Maes de Wit, Yvan 03622
Maesen, Mathieu 03694
Mäuser, Dr. Matthias 15813
Maeyama, Mikio 26967
Maeyama, Yuji 26693
Maffia, Prof. Cesare 24516
Maffioli, Dr. Monica 23870
Mafre, Christian 10277
Magacz, Joanna 16687
Magajne, Miljojka 34091
Magalhães, Carlos 04540
Ribeiro de Magalhães, Thales 04362
Magaña Cota, Gloria E. 27970
Magdich, Bob 48020
Magdolna, Simon 21449
Magee, Eileen M. 46392
Magee, Eugene 05783
Magee, Henry J. 46409
Magendans, J.R. 29524
Mager, Gerald Paul 19696, 19698
Mager, Dr. Karl 02060
Magersuppe, Karl 20043
Maggi, Ersilio 25058
Maggi, Gianfranco 22829
Maggi, Roberto 23530
Maggioli, Andrea 23130
Magglo-Serra, Dr. Rosanna 25731, 25758
Magidson, Phyllis 45847
Magielsen, A.F. 29480
Magill, Ronald E. 47204
Magill, Scott 45706
Magill, Tina M. 46586
Magilton, Jack 05682
Magiru, Maria 32500
Maglica, Nadja 07813
Magnago, José Carlos 00576
Magnaguagno, Guido 36511
Magnan, Oscar 44341
Magnetti, Daniela 25764
Magnin 10560
Magnin, B. 10559
Magnini, Prof. Marsilio 23710
Magnussen Svare, M. 08941
Magnusson, Inga-Lill 36020
Mago, Norma A. 31468
Magolfi, Dr. Miria 23899
Magomedova, Seir Seitovna 33597
Magras, M. 21250
Magré, Piet 29458
Magro, Antonio 22917
Magro, Pasquale 22968
Magsaysay, Dr. Eulogio Amang 31377
Maguin-Gonze, J. 36861
Maguindanao, Macmod 31399
Maguire, Cathy 47461
Maguire, Dr. Eunice 41449
Maguire, Nancy 42060
Magurany, J.D. 47122, 47124

Mahaffay, Suzanne 48291
Mahamadou, Kelessé 30324
Mahé, Lucien 11965
Mahecha Useche, Ernesto 07492, 07493
Mahéo, Noël 10324
Maher, Kathleen 41889
Maher, Kristie 46485
Maher, Michael 22381
Maher, Tina 37975
Maher-Kamprath, Audrey 46551
Mahida, Bhamini A. 22030
Mahilom, Mila M. 31319
Mahlknecht, Dr. Eduard 02123
Mahmoud, Assad 37438
Mahmoud, Ibrahim 27106
Mahmudor, N. 48848
Mahon, Rose 40313
Mahran, Younes 09255
Mai, Prof. Dr. Ekkehard 18168
Mai Hung, Prof. Dr. Pham 48982
Maia e Castro, Catarina 32338
Maiben, Dean 41512
Maier, Daniela 16974, 16975, 16976
Maier, Erhard 02584
Maier, Jakob 15482
Maier, Josef 02388
Maier, Marco 37217
Maier, Stefan 20077
Maier, Thomas 22655
Maier-Schöler, Barbara 20346
Maierhofer, Fritz 02145
Maikweki, James 27112
Mailer, Allison 06670
Mailhot, Philippe R. 06307
Maillard, Anne 12912
Maillé, Jacqueline 14179
Maillot, Suzanne 32418
Main, Sally 45737
Mainds, Paul E. 39220
Maine, Ian 37966
Mainella, Fran P. 41236
Mainieri Piedade, Leticia 04346
Mainland, Katrina 38234
Mainzer, Prof. Dr. Udo 18787
Mair, Walter 01893
Maire, Marcel 13416
Mairesse, François 03640
Mairinger, Jutta 02825
Mairot, Philippe 14574
Mairs, Kirsty 40752
Mais, Dr. Karl 02907
Maisak, Dr. Petra 17046
Maisel, Oscar 15853
Maislinger, Gerlinde 01816
Maison, Jack 45783
Maissen, Prof. Alfons 36813
Maistrello, Roberto 24271
Maitilasso, Mario 25838
Maitland, Richard 47898
Maitre-Allain, Olivier 13352
Maiwald, Dr. Christine 17560
Maiwald, Gabriele 18315
Majahad, Carol 45979
Majburova, Irina Borisovna 32777
Majcen, Jože 41655
Majewska, Grażyna 31861
Majka, Mary 06276
Major, Jürgen 20069
Majorov, Aleksandr Gennadjevič 32810
Majstorovic, Prof. Božo 07781
Majstorović, Ljuba 13819
Majstorski, Georgi 04908
Majumdar, Prof. Swapan 22011
Makabe, Tadahiko 26381
Makarewicz, Anna 32065
Makarov, Nikolaj Michajlovič 32714
Makarova, N.B. 33051
Makeeva, I.F. 33666
Maketz-Anderle, Sabine 02165
Makholm, Kristin 45366
Maki, Linda 42435
Makkonen, Esko 09255
Maklansky, Steven 45735
Makoev, Feliks H. 33521
Makoni, P. 49028
Makovičková, Marie 08488
Makowiecki, Wojciech 31895
Makowska, Bożena 31559
Maksić, Nemanja 33913
Maksić, Slobodan 33913
Maksimova, L.D. 33631
Makwana, R.K. 22048
Mal, Olivia 06555
Malá, Olga 08577
Malagón Castro, Dimas 07391
Malak, Gregory 42423
Malakar, Diana 43640
Malao, N. 34350
Malaspina, Bartolomeo 25754
Malatare, Marilyn 48035
Malatesta, Giuseppe 22949
Malausssena, Paul-Louis 13311
Malawski, Wiesław 31649
Malceva, Ljudmila Dmitrievna 33356
Malcolm, Megan 30249
Malcom, Corey 44469
Maldent, Dominique 10831
Maldon Fitch, M. Derek 39880

Maldonado, Eduard M. 42319
Maldonado, Laural R. 46987
Maldonado, Nivia 41974
Malec, Dr. Franz 18027
Maleev, Dr. Michail 04851
Malek, Peter 02698
Maleković, Vladimir 07841
Malenfant, Robert 06271
Malenke, Patti 42662
Malet Ybern, Rosa María 34539
Malewicz, J. 29500
Malewicz, P.A. 29500
Malgeri, Dina G. 45082
Malgin, Andrej 37903, 37904
Malgorzewicz, Anna 00973, 01232
Malherbe, C. 34359, 34359
Malicky, Michael 02228
Maliet, Vincent 10709
Malik, Sajid Anwar 31040
Malikova, D. 34079
Malin, Regula 37374
Malinar, Branka 43065
Malinick, Cynthia B. 48345
Malinová, Miluše 08538
Malinverni, Pierluigi 24240
Mališeva, Valentina Pavlovna 32936
Maljković, Rada 33798
Malkočev, Angel 04617, 04618
Małkowski, Dr. Krzysztof 32094
Mallalieu, William P. 03104
Mallamo, J. Lance 42169
Mallery, W. David 43314
Mallinson, Justin 38330
Mallo Area, Alberto 35092
Malloy, Dean 06576
Malmberg, Brita 38649
Malme, Arnfinn 30631
Malme, Heikki 09474
Malmlöf, Maria 35988
Malmquist, Hilmar 21643
Malnati, Dr. Luigi 24309
Malniča, Andrej 34135
Malocha, Mary 47063
Malone, Gail 06351
Malone, Mary 22373
Malone, Pam 44651
Malone, Peter 41943
Malone, Terry 44451
Malonly, Rachelle 48127
Malov, Nikolaj Michajlovič 33511
Malsch, Dr. Friedemann 27514
Maltais, Marie E. 05467
Maltby, Janet 06525, 06526, 06527, 06528
Maltezou, Prof. Chryssa 25936
Malushi, Petrit 00021
Małuszyńska, Krystyna 31546
Maluțan, Cornelia 32510
Malý, Dr. František 08275
Malý, Karel 08390, 08675
Malyševa, Tatjana Vasiljevna 32916
Mamaev, Aleksandr A. 32662
Mambetova, D. 27311
Mamer, Helen 06781
Mampaso Boj, Loreto 35053
Mamuro, Yoshitake 26944
Man, Grigore 32435
Manabe, Masahiko 26466
Manakidou, Dr. Eleni 21189
Manakou, Paraskevi 21187
Manau, Ferran 35394
Mančal, Dr. Josef 15562
Mancaş, Ioan 32624
Manceau, Sophie 12459
Manchak, Barry 05990
Manchester, Dr. S.R. 43581
Mancinelli, Dr. Fabrizio 48868
Mancini, Prof. Franco 25714
Manconi, Dr. Dorica 24850
Manconi, Francesca 25015
Mancuso, Francesco 24776
Mandanas Esquito, Joven 31381
Mandel, David 41107
Mander, Gabriela 17975
Mandeville, Jeffrey 44755
Mandeville, Joyce 45477
Mandis, Alexander 20832, 20839, 21090
Mandiwana, T. 34359
Mandracchia, James 46315
Manera, Brigida 13622
Manera, Settimo 25027
Manes, John 43433
Maness, David C. 45940
Manfredini, Prof. Alessandra 25203
Manfrina, Mario 36814
Manfull, William 46656
Mangan, Dianne 01576
Mangan, Richard 39704
Mangani, Elisabetta 25238
Mangani, Dr. Elisabetta 25569
Mangels, W. Gilbert 46579
Mangia, Dr. Paola 25225
Mangiagalli, B. 34389
Mangiagalli, Tizzie 34389
Mangion, Eric 12848
Mangis, Julie 41263
Mangnus, G. 29635
Mango, Dr. E. 37369
Mangold, Dr. Meret 36539
Mangus, John 48313

Manguso, John M. 43451
Manhart, Marcia Y. 48107
Manhart, Patty 43555
Manheim, Drs. Ron 15866
Manhès, Bruno 12282
Manibusan, Rose 21259
Manicastri, Dr. Claudio 25183
Maniez, Erica S. 44269
Maniguet, Thierry 13558
Maninger, Peter 17203
Manini, Paula 48062, 48063, 48065
Maniurka, Dr. Piotr 31858
Manka, Riitta 09905
Manke, Elke 18274
Mankin Kornhauser, Elizabeth 43944
Mańkowska, Ewa 31737
Mankus, Edward 42307
Mann, Esther 39695
Mann, Harald J. 19476
Mann, Dr. James 44668
Mann, Judith 47134
Mann, LaDonna 48470
Mann, Dr. Stephan 17309
Mann, Theresa 47718
Mann, Vivian 45821
Mannberg Wretin, Karin 36361
Manne, Robert 47505
Manneby, Hans 36194
Manneby, Dr. Hans 36342
Mannering, Ken 38088
Manni, Dr. Riccardo 25216
Manning, Anne 41412
Manning, Carolyn 43835, 44875
Manning, Gladys E. 41569
Mannini, Maria Pia 25044, 25049
Manns, John 01613
Mano, Livio 23696
Manojlović, Miroljub 33893
Manrho, Jet 29754
Manring, Yvonne 48556
Mansell, Jefferson 41559, 41561
Manser, Jurg 36905
Mansfield, Dr. Bernard M. 43603
Mansfield, Lisa 45789
Mansfield, Nicholas 39899, 39902
Manske, Dr. Hans-Joachim 16334
Manson, Wayne 44507
Mansour Naguib, Sylvia 41353
Mansperger, Linda W. 46210
Manssen, W.J. 28965
Mantel, Ken 39727
Mantovani, Prof. Giuseppe 25774
Mantzke, Irmgard 18155
Manuel, R.S. 06110
Manuhutu, W. 29900
Manus, Dieter 17901
Manyon, Ellen 48584
Manzanares, Rick 43394
Manzanilla, Dr. Linda 28157
Manzato, Prof. Eugenio 25803, 25805
Manzini Gazzani, Giorgio Mario 07554
Mapfarakora, Jacques 04945
Maphet, L. Ernestine 43633
Maple, William T. 45596, 45597
Maples, Philip G. 46938
Maquet, Nadine 03578
Maquiso, Dr. Teresita R. 31403
Mara, Kanfela 21286
Marafioti, Dr. Sergio 24785, 24786, 24787, 24788
Marais, Caroline 39750
Marandel, J. Patrice 44921
Marangon, Maria 21139
Marapana, P.B. 35758, 35759
Maraval, P. 10661
Maravelaki, Noni 20915
Marazzi, Laura 25896
Marbach, Wilhelm 16476
Marble, Lori L. 45650
Marc, Denis 15041
Marcantel, Gregory 44334
Marcantonio, Donna 42040
Marcato, Paolo Stefano 24724
Marcel, Louis 12002, 12340
Marcet, Roger 34583
March, Dr. Eugene 44962
March and Kinrara, Earl of 38561
Marchado, Philippe 12294
Marchant, Dr. D.J. 38329
Marchant, Dr. R. 36858
Marchant Smith, Dick 40877
Marchante, Carlos M. 07970
Marchart, Bruno 02514
Marchenko, Leonid V. 37902
Marchés, Dominique 10644
Marchesi, Dr. Marinella 23109
Marchetti, Prof. P.G. 23102
Marchetti, Roberto 22970
Marchington, Andrea 38266
Marchini, Gian Paolo 25976
Marchione, Kenneth 47768
Marchois, Bernard 13611
Marcia, Graff 47114
Marció, Pietro 24550
Marco, Sixio 34791
Marcode Flores, Giancarlo 31214
Marcon, Gaby 13087
Marcos, Ludovic 13555
Marcos, Mariano 14865
Marcos V., Emilio 35204

Marcu, Aurora 32522
Marcum, Donald 43042
Marcum-Estes, Leah 46057
Marcus, Evelyn 43907
Marcus, Jed 45870
Marcus, Joyce 41219
Mård, Hans 36101
Mardles, Tracey 39385
Maréchal, Dominique 03300
Marechal, Ph. 03772
Marek, Danuta 31603
Marek, Stanisław 31837
Marenco, Jean-Jacques 14042
Mareneo, Simeone 25767
Mareno, Luisa López 35482
Marepo Eoe, Soroi 31090
Mares, Dr. Michael A. 45976
Marešić, Jagoda 07779
Maret, J.F. 29583
Marfà i Riera, C. 35098, 35100
Marghieri, Roland 13325
Margita, George 06467
Margkudilaga, Sufwandi 22134
Margles, Judy 46638
Margolis, Bernard 41801
Margrey, Peter 42100
Margulies, Stephen N. 42253
Mariani, Prof. Franco 23746
Mariani, Gabriel 13680
Mariani, Giuseppe Antonio 23547
Máriássy, Eva-Maria von 17394
Marić, Dušan 33790
Marichal, Rémy 13701
Maričić, Dušanka 33819
Maricki-Ostojić, Vesna 33913
Maries, John 37977
Marijan, Jassmina 34114
Marin, Dr. Emilio 07739
Marin, Prof. Emilio 07779
Marín, Fabio 07441
Marin, Jean-Yves 10981
Marin, Jeanne 14077
Marín Vázquez, Gilberto 28107
Marinac, Bogdana 34138
Marinazzo, Dr. Angela 23212
Marincig, Harald 03009
Marincola, Michele 45784
Marinelli, Dr. Giampiero Gabrio 23974
Marines, Sheila R. 45063
Maringer, Christine 03001
Marini, Gabriele 24143
Marini, Dr. Giorgio 25974
Marini, Mariagrazia 25505
Marini, Marinella 25505
Marini, Dr. Paola 25972, 25974
Marinis, Dr. Giuliano de 22881
Marinković, Ive 07682
Marino, Mari 04518
Marinoiu, Vasile 32605, 32606
Marinoiu, Prof. Vasile 32607
Marinov, Evstati 04927
Marinska, Dr. Rouja 04839, 04856
Marioni, Tom 47328
Mariono, Christy 41571
Marits, Ülle 09325
Mark, Guido 02770, 02795, 02796
Mark, Lory 46200
Markel, Stephen A. 44921
Markelova, Nina Konstantinovna 33190
Marken, Kevin 48171
Marker, Peggy 45399
Markert, Günther 17164
Markert, Leo 17442
Markgraf, Monika 16584
Markham, Philip 30300
Markiewicz, Katarzyna 31924
Markina, Natalja Petrovna 33593
Markishtum, Merlee 47544
Markko, Helvi 09570
Markland, Eleanor 39845
Marko, Dr. Eva 01920
Markoe, Glenn 42400
Markon, Genya 48401
Markonish, Denise 41909
Markoulaki, Stavroula 20915
Markov, Dr. Nikolaj 04846
Markovčič, Albin 34140
Marković, Mirjana 33908
Marković, Prof. Slavica 07826
Marković, Srdjan 33859
Markowicz, Kazimierz 31741
Markowitz, John 46346
Marks, Dede 40971
Marks, Edward 47807
Marks, Jacqueline 20551
Marks, Jacqueline S. 46787
Marks, John C. 43642, 44015
Marks, Katherine Duer 44809
Marks, Michael 20551
Marks, Michael J. 44033
Marks, Sherry 44674
Markus, Russell P. 42809
Marler, Brooke 43238
Marley, Rita 26065
Marlow, Martha 42994
Marlowe, Dean 47698
Marloyannis, Georgi 21121
Marmolejo, Martha Lucía 07475
Marnetté-Kühl, Dr. Beatrice 16305

Maroević, Prof. Igor 07799
Maroević, Igor 07810
Marović, Metodija 07809
Marøy Hansen, Arild 30417
Marquardt, Claudia 19156
Marquardt, Regine 19895
Marquardt, Dr. W.H. 43581
Marquart, Dr. M. 15533
Marques, Luiz 04515
Marques, Willy 37053
Marquet, Helmut 03128
Marquet, Jean-Claude 12418, 12882
Marquet, Sybil 14195
Marquete, Ronaldo 04335
Márquez Martínez, Teresa 28194
Márquez Rojas, Margoth 07510
Marquis, Jean M. 36613
Marren, James 48190
Marri, Dr. Franca 24040
Marriott, Wayne P. 30210
Marsac, Michel 14251
Marsan, Geneviève 12698
Marsch, Peter 30312
Marschall, Jolanta 31946
Marsden, Dale 45026
Marsden, Melinda 43866
Marsden, Peter 39186
Marsden, Susan 06188, 06189
Marseille, Barbara 46605
Marseille, Jeremias 22781
Marsh, Geoff 39790
Marsh, Joanna 43944
Marsh, John S. 46363
Marsh, Tracy 05267
Marsh, Warwick 00732
Marsh-Matthews, Dr. F. 45976
Marshall, Alan 12733
Marshall, Dr. Cora 45673
Marshall, Danny 47096
Marshall, Francis 40266
Marshall, Jerry 45583
Marshall, Karen 44533
Marshall, Dr. Larry 45271
Marshall, Robert A. 43860
Marshall, Steven 39854
Mársico de Larribité, Viviana 00129
Marsland, Joanna Ruth 47526
Marson, Luigi 26040
Marstein, Nils 30761
Marszalec, Roman 31732
Marszałek, Zygmunt 32097
Marszewski, Tadeusz 31948
Marte, Philomena 06178
Marteljanova, Elisaveta Vladimirovna 33284
Martens, Caspar 29309
Martens, H.E.D. 28941
Martens, Jean 03220
Martens, Prof. Dr. K.R.I.M. 28917
Martens, Melissa 41472
Martens, Warburg 19302
Martensen, Robert L. 44392
Marth, Dr. Regine 16297
Martí Aixalà, Joseph 35511
Martí Armengol, Teresa 34539
Martí Bonet, José María 34574
Martí i Llambrich, Miquel 35211
Martig, Dr. Peter 36819
Martin, Alvia D. 46130
Martin, Amanda 40415
Martín, Andrés Peláez 34451
Martin, Anthea 34223
Martín, Aurora 34854, 35586
Martin, Bob 45731
Martin, Carol 06564
Martin, Collen 44463
Martin, Corlene 42390
Martin, Danny 40016
Martin, Erin L. 45687
Martin, François 11201, 11202, 11416, 12206, 14096, 15092
Martin, Frank 46176
Martin, Jacques 05395
Martin, James E. 46797
Martin, Jay C. 45117
Martin, Jean-Claude 10284
Martin, Jean-Hubert 16738
Martin, Jennifer 45508
Martin, Jerry 48730
Martin, J.G. 39464
Martin, JoAnne 05004
Martin, Dr. Joanne M. 41468
Martin, John 43219
Martin, L.A. 38580
Martin, Larry 44685
Martin, Loretta 48064
Martin, Loris 05313
Martin, Dr. Lutz 16114
Martin, M. 39050
Martín, Macarena Alés 34955
Martin, Marietta 41506
Martín, Marilyn 34214
Martin, Mary C. 43004
Martin, Dr. Michael 18302
Martin, Michael 46156
Martin, Pascal 13155
Martin, Paul 43377
Martin, Dr. Paula 38518
Martin, Dr. Peter-Hugo 17991
Martin, Pierre de 14803

Martin, Rebecca J. 48033
Martin, Richard 42867
Martin, Rick 43186
Martin, Robert 00449
Martin, Roger 05080
Martin, Sandra 39892
Martin, Dr. Shéonagh 38884
Martin, Terry 43576
Martin, Ètienne 14831
Martin, Tracy N. 41962
Martin, William 48569
Martin, William J. 46888
Martin, Wilson 47236
Martín Flores, Alfonso 35029
Martin-Vignes, Nicole 10254
Martindale, Bruce 06539
Martindale, Wendy 06222
Martínek, Jaroslav 08384, 08486, 08687
Martinelli, Massimo 24119
Martinelli, Patricia A. 43890
Martinelli, Dr. Roberta 25020, 25021
Martinet, Jean-Louis 12296
Martínez, Dr. Armando Luis 28151
Martinez, Connie 47350
Martinez, Daniel 44092
Martinez, Edward 46836
Martínez, Gonzalo 07485
Martínez, José Luis 28161
Martínez, Maite 35599
Martínez, Margarita 48901
Martínez, Ramiro 28203
Martinez, Ray 41058
Martínez, Ricardo Ariel 07560
Martínez Alvárez, Dr. José María 35110
Martínez Arvizu, Jesus 28277
Martínez Cortés, Ariel 07588
Martínez Fuentes, Dr. Antonio J.F. 07935
Martínez Mestre, Miguel 28168
Martínez Rodríguez, Andrés 34982
Martinez Saravia, Carlos A. 00203
Martínez Sarria, Victoria 07566
Martínez Vargas, Enrique 28069
Martini, Prof. Dr. Erlend 19428
Martini, Dr. Luciana 25081
Martiniani-Reber, Marielle 36743
Martinizi-Lemke, Tania 44919
Martínková, Jana 08485
Martino, Giuseppe 23716
Martino, Mike 46980
Martino, Dr. Ronald L. 44164
Martinović, Jovan 33848
Martinović, Niko 33864
Martins, Josephine 44424
Martins, Michael 43282
Martins Carneiro, José Manuel 32351
Martins Catharino, Henriqueta 04437
Martins e Silva, José 32298
Martins Fernandes, Francisco R. 32277
Martinson, Gordon 41876
Martis, Ela Helgi 09386
Martis, Val 42307
Martoana, Alan 45216
Martonová, T. 08354
Martorell, Jaume 35227
Marty, Michel 14249
Martykánová, Marie 08698
Martynova, Nina Petrovna 32919
Martynova, Raisa Fёdorovna 32836
Marugg, Richard 37153
Maruschke, Thomas 16276
Marusic, Irena 34122
Maruszeczka, Dave 05601
Maruyama, Mariko 26153
Maruyama, Masatake 26936
Maruyama, Tamiko 26969
Marvin, Anne 47586
Marvin, Anne M. 48033
Marwell, Dr. David G. 45842
Marwick, Fiona C. 39011
Marwick, Guy 46082
Marx, Dr. Erich 02532, 02534, 02551, 02552, 02554
Marx, Prof. Dr. Harald 16684
Marx, Mary 46066
Marx, Prof. R. 34297
Maryon, Mike 38408
Marzahn, Dr. Joachim 16114
Marzatico, Dr. Franco 23071, 25790
Marzio, Frances 44129
Marzio, Peter C. 44129
Marzolf, John G. 41392
Marzoli, Dr. Dirce 20115
Más Vilaplana, Antonio 34958
Masahide, Maekawa 26707
Masana, Megan 45467
Masanori, Ichikawa 26563
Mašanović, Pavle 33923
Masaracı, Yasemin 37634
Mašátová, Ivana 08250
Masau Dan, Dr. Maria 25817
Masayuki, Ogata 26508
Mascarenhas, Dr. Aubrey A. 21949
Mascherbauer, Michael 01676
Mascheroni, Achille 25450
Mascia, Sara 47959
Maseberg, G. 17504
Maselli Scotti, Dr. Franca 22907, 22908
Masemore, Dr. Ira 44839
Masen, Larz 45390
Masing, Maia 09368

Masino, H. 20354
Masjoan, Prof. Estela 00243
Maske, Andrew 47198
Maslarova, Iljana 04922
Maslov, V.I. 33163
Mason, Barbara 47741
Mason, Bonnie N. 46242
Mason, Carl 41237
Mason, Charles 46076
Mason, D.A. 06432
Mason, Darielle 46442
Mason, Erik 44877
Mason, G. 40036
Mason, Julia 38320
Mason, Dr. Kevin 38262
Mason, Laurie 05932
Mason, Michael E. 43098
Mason, Ngahirika 30103
Mason, Rainer Michael 36729
Mason, Richard 40828
Mason, R.P. 38911
Mason, Wally 46196
Mason, William J. 43861
Mason-Chaney, Lisa 43155
Maspoli, Guido 36899
Masriera, Alicia 34558
Massada, Satê 27061
Massalsky, Joachim 16344
Massari, Dr. Stefania 25234
Massaro, Marilyn 46715, 46722
Massart, Claire 03337
Massenbach, Elisabeth von 18879
Massengill, Myers 46495
Massey, Lewis 41358
Massey, S.L. 06240
Massey, William P. 42238
Massicotte, Jean 05803
Massie Lane, Rebecca 47901
Massimbe, Julieta 28725
Massobrio, Dr. Giulio 22849
Masson, Colette 05713
Masson Rusinowski, Fabienne 03495
Massy, Jean-Baptiste 37294
Mastemaker, Lorie 43891
Master-Karnik, Paul 44777
Mastorgio, Carlo 22943
Mastoris, Steph N. 38599
Mastorito, Susana 00338
Mastrogiuseppe, Joy 46744
Mastrovic, Mikica 07818
Masuda, Hideaki 26187
Masuda, Rei 26938
Mašulovic, Branimir 33910
Masuo, Tano 26356
Masuyer, François 11487
Mata, Rene Luis S. 31374, 31394
Mata González, Juan C. de la 35058
Matajis, Andrijana 33810
Matakieva, Ass.Prof. Dr. Teofana 04846
Matamoros, Joséphine 11110, 11351
Matasci, Mario 37231
Matat, L.N. 37874
Matauschek, Katja 20106
Mataušić, Nataša 07822
Mátéffy, Dr. Balázs 21332
Matei, Rodica 32466
Matejić, Slavoljub 33786
Matenga, Edward 49037
Maternati-Baldouy, Danielle 12869
Materón Salcedo, Edgar 07453
Maters, Drs. Petra 29926
Mateu y Miró, Josep 34690
Mateva, Borjana 04679
Matharan, Paul 10809
Matheis, Adam 18595
Matheny, Paul 42569
Mathes, Wayne 46061
Matheson, Susan 45700
Matheson, Trueman 05774
Mathew, Helen 46815
Mathewes, Charles P. 45667
Mathews, George K. 45940
Mathews, Mary 42800
Mathews, Nancy 44441
Mathews, Susan 38935
Mathez, Dr. Edmond A. 45759
Mathias, Gérard 11713
Mathiassen, Tove E. 08770
Mathieson, Julia 06339
Mathieu, Caroline 13596
Mathieu, Dr. Kai R. 16445, 17225, 19932, 20446
Mathis, Bernhard 36681
Mathis, Walti 36910
Mathison, Judy 48253
Mathusa, Parker D. 47562
Matias, Bienvenida 45382
Matijaca, Ivo 07723
Matijevič, Jožef 34136
Matile, Michael 37377
Matilsky, Barbara 42196
Matino, Dr. Lucia 24414
Matiskainen, Dr. Heikki 09993, 09995
Matkin, Dan 44262
Matland, Susan 30639
Mato, Nancy 46265
Matochik, Dr. John A. 43392
Matos, Dr. Lúcia de 32338
Matos Moctezuma, María Fernanda 27946
Matos Reis, Dr. António 32356

Matoušek, Dr. Branislav 33979
Matoušková, Martina 08621
Matschiner, Dieter 02609
Matskási, Dr. István 21362
Matson, Dr. Timothy 42467
Matsubayashi, Hosai 26988
Matsuda, Hiroshi 26217
Matsuda, Motoi 26629
Matsuhashi, Hiroto 26163
Matsumoto, Takeshi 26527
Matsumoto, Tohru 26938
Matsuo, Yasumasa 26490
Matsuoka, Masao 26557
Matsuoka, Mieko 26882
Matsura, Akira 26200
Matsushita, Kensuke 26089
Matsuura, Kunio 26764
Matsuzaki, Yukiko 26853
Matsuzawa, Shigefumi 27019
Matt, Edvin 44694
Matt, Dr. Gerald 02914, 02915
Mattausch-Schirmbeck, Dr. Roswitha 15665
Matteotti, Mario 25130
Matter, Kuno 37139
Matter, Victor 36872
Mattern, Dr. T. 18622
Mattes, Glenda 42971
Matteson, Judith M. 43401
Mattet, Laurence 36742
Matthäi, Bernhard 18135
Matthaes, Goffried 24393
Matthes, Lilian 08849
Matthes, Olaf 17557
Matthew, A.T. 34241
Matthew, Malcom 47261
Matthewman, Su 40966
Matthews, Anita 22522
Matthews, B. 45615
Matthews, Dr. B. 45976
Matthews, Dr. B.E. 38881
Matthews, Christy 42918
Matthews, Daniel Paul 45883
Matthews, John 00771
Matthews, Julia 06607
Matthews, Keith 40960
Matthews, Marsha 46637
Matthews, Martin 39214
Matthews, Nancy 48369
Matthews, Zara 38933
Matthews Hoffmann, Catherine 44752
Matthey, Prof. François 36954
Matthias, Diana 46044
Matthias, Kevin 38714
Matthiesen, Kjell Marius 30641
Matthiessen, Joy A. 42913
Matti, Arnold 37432
Matticks, Rebecca 43107
Mattila, Karen 05947
Mattioni, Fernando 24923
Mattl-Wurm, Dr. Sylvia 03001
Mattlin, Håkan 09426
Matton, A. 03476, 03477
Matton, Ann 03475
Mattox, Boyd 47966
Mattson, James 43138
Mattsson, Christina 36269
Matuella, Barbara 02945
Matukova, Marija Bajramovna 32861
Matuschka, Dagmar Gräfin von 19762
Matuska, Mike von 36247
Matuss, Dr. Márta 21405
Matuszczyk, Andrzej 31725
Matveeva, Tatjana Sergeevna 32651
Matvenov, Evgenij Rostitovič 32794
Matyniak, Margaret 48319
Matz, Darrell 47923
Matzke, Klaus 19786
Matzon, Ea 09076
Maubano, M. 12424
Maubant, Jean-Louis 15249
Maudet, Serge 27511
Maué, Dr. Hermann 19139
Mauerhan, Joëlle 10703
Mauersberger, Dr. Klaus 16706
Maugain, Gregory 13173
Mauldin, Barbara 47426, 47427
Mauler, Norbert 01940
Maulhardt, Dr. Heinrich 20316
Maulsby, Richard 41267
Maumont, A. 14953
Maung, U Min Khin 28736
Mauoloux, Herman 03765
Maur, Dr. Karin von 20102
Maurer, C.F. William 45169
Maurer, Eberhard 20112
Maurer, Eleonore 02029
Maurer, Ellen 45334
Maurer, Prof. Dr. Friedemann 17645
Maurer, Dr. Rudolf 01729
Maurer, Sherry C. 46952
Maurer, Simon 37381
Maurer-Zilioli, Dr. Ellen 18890
Maurice-Chabard, Brigitte 10499
Maurin, Ange 13884
Maurin, Bernard 14602
Maurin, Ray 44255
Maurirere, Naomi 30164
Maurizio, Dr. R. 37201
Maurizio, Dr. Remo 37202

Mauron, Christophe 36603
Mausel, Olivia 44066
Mautner-Markhof, Dr. Marietta 02830
Mauws, Eveline 06173
Mavric, Kaye 00938
Mavrodiev, Zdravko 04858
Mavrotas, Takis 29963
Mavuso, Makana R. 35779
Maw, Dr. Martin 40152
Mawdsley, Simon 31063
Mawe, Theodore 31091
Mawleke, M. 34285
Maxey, Michael 47211
Maxfield, Dorothy 48670
Maxfield, Mike 39896
Maxham, Marjorie P. 41867
Maxham, R.S. 43450
Maxheimer, Greta 42852
Maxholmes, Thomas 01634
Maxim, Dr. Elena 32456
Maximilien, Diana 37252
Maxwell, Gregory 48815
Maxwell, Jennifer 40633
Maxwell, Lowell 46362
Maxwell, Robert N. 44191
Maxwell, Robyn 00886
Maxwell, Dr. Thomas 45908
Maxwell Stuart, Catherine 39291
May, Eve 38268
May, Guy 27576
May, J. Alan 43632
May, James 41165, 44224
May, Jane 39468
May, John M. 42539
May, Pauline 40541
May, Philip 46086
May, Thérèse 27576
Mayberg, Magnus 36245
Mayberry, Matthew 42536
Mayer, August 02637
Mayer, Gregory C. 45072
Mayer, Günter 02811
Mayer, Günther 02836
Mayer, H. 20109
Mayer, Hedwig 01775
Mayer, Herbert 02901, 02955
Mayer, Jannie 13598
Mayer, John 46654
Mayer, M. 18704
Mayer, Olafa 18661
Mayer, Ronald 47690
Mayer, Walter 41983
Mayer-Thurman, Christa C. 42304
Mayers, Lise 46679
Mayes, Catherine 43028
Mayes, James 46973
Mayfield, Signe 46273
Mayhew, Kim 45901
Mayle, A.H. 39640
Maynard, Helen B. 43653
Maynard, Marie-Noëlle 11043
Maynard, Rex 41617
Mayo, Dr. Margaret Ellen 46891
Mayo, Martha 44985
Mayo, Marti 44118
Mayor, N. 10858
Mayorga Sanchón, D. Juan 35543
Mayou, Roger 36748
Mayr, Dr. Helmut 18893
Mayr, Herbert 18610
Mayr, Josef 01843
Mayr, Jürgen 17461
Mayr, Karin 17263
Mayr, Manfred 16601
Mayr, Peter 02822
Mayr, Walter 02478
Mayr-Oehring, Dr. Erika 02548
Mayrhofer, Martin 02658
Mayrhofer, Meinrad 02445
Mayrhofer, Monika E. 03049
Mayrhuber, Petra Gerti 02789
Mays, N. 00754
Maysonnaue, J. 15330
Maytk, Paul 48484
Maywald-Pitellos, Dr. Claus 18600
Maza, Roberto Ramos 28575
Mazeika, Dr. Rasa 05872
Maziarka, Włodzimierz 31619
Mazitova, Svetlana Vladimirovna 32945
Mazlish, Anne 47674
Mazlumoğlu, Hasan 37672
Maznev, Kostadin 04703
Mazonowicz, Douglas 45804
Mazor, Robin 44413
Mazourek, Paul 01597
Mazow, Dr. Leo 48154
Mazur, Leonid Viktorovič 33739
Mazurkiewicz, Janina 32053
Mazza, Germana 23364
Mazza, Thomas C. 45785
Mazzari, Roberto 23094
Mazzei, Dr. Lapo 23861
Mazzei, Marina 24280
Mazzeo, Dr. Donatella 25231
Mazzeroli, Paolo 24852
Mazziotti Gillan, Maria 46309
Mazzocchi, G. 25300
Mazzolti, Prof. Mario 25079
Mazzoni, Anne-Hélène 14024

Mazzoni, Prof. Francesco 23486
Mazzoni de Bravo, Helga 00256
Mazzotta, Gabriele 24383
Mazzotti, Dr. Stefano 23787
Mazzullo, Thomas 42499
Mbe, John C. Jacques 40476
Mbodji, Abdoulaye 33785
Mbokashanga, Nyimi Kuete 07643
McGarry, James R. 44471
Mead, Barry 38030
Meade, C. Wade 47039
Meade, Diane 43036
Meade, John 44699
Meador-Woodruff, Robin 41218
Meadors, William 44853
Meadows, Larry G. 42440
Meagher, George E. 42207
Meagher, Kathy 05465
Meagher, Tom 05782
Mealey, Brian 45291
Mealing, David 30183, 30302
Mearwah, Reena 21830
Mecham, Denny H. 47221
Mechan, Dallas 38403
Mechell, Barbara 48266
Mechler, Sabine 17674
Meck, Gerhard 19436
Mecklin, Kai 10106
Mecredy, Stephen D. 05675
Medaković, Anica 33928
Medeiros, Francisco 32281
Medek, Prof. Robert 02867
Medernach, Marcel 27564
Mederski, Mark 46482
Medica, Dr. Massimo 23112
Medicus, Christine 02545
Medina, Dennis H.J. 41049
Medina i Montes, Susana 35528
Medley, Mark 45614
Medlin, Tina 44121
Medlock, Leon 46584
Medlycott, Sir Mervyn 40441
Medri, Prof. Gianluca 23756
Medri, Dr. Litta 23846, 24976
Medurić, Jovan 33791
Medvedev, Nikolaj Jurjevič 33380
Medvedow, Jill 41810
Medzihradská, Dr. Elena 34015
Meehan, Brian 05763, 05772
Meehan, Joseph M. 43328
Meek, Kenneth 41516
Meek, Noel 30159
Meeke, Dr. Noel 39231
Meeker, David 39584
Meekers, Christa 03484
Meena, K.L. 21871
Mees, Dr. Allard 18604, 18606
Meester de Heyndonck, B. de 03189
Meeusen, M. 03783
Meewis, Menno 03166
Meffre, Pierre 15043
Meglio, Luciano di 24100
Mehaska, Dr. Walter 43925
Mehl, Dr. Heinrich 19794
Mehler, Sarah 37407
Mehring, Albert G. 43925
Mehring, Karen 43358
Mehta, A.P. 21695
Meiborg, E. 29597
Meidell, Bjarne A. 30425
Meidenbauer, Roy 45664
Meidinger, Ronald J. 41300
Meier, Andreas 37020
Meier, Anton C. 37352
Meier, Helmut 36768
Meier, Prof. Dr. Jens 16777
Meier, Jürgen 17355
Meier, Michelle 45885
Meier, Rupert 36524
Meier, Stefan 36498
Meier, Dr. Werner 37222
Meier, Wolfgang 17019
Meighörner, Dr. Wolfgang 17149
Meijer, M. 28941
Meillat, Eric 10298
Meillat, Joël 13088
Meillon, Anne 11956
Meinderts, Drs. A.J.M. 29096
Meinderts, Drs. A.J.M 29109
Meindre, Colette 12671, 14078
Meinelschmidt, C. 17801
Meiners, Dr. Jochen 16452
Meiners, Prof. Dr. Uwe 16479
Meinig, U. 15572, 15573
Meinrad-Meier, Dr. Anton 36780
Meir, Cecilia 22764
Bastos Gambogi Meireles, Alexa 04028
Meiring, Barbara 43447
Meiringer, Susanne 01773
Meirose, Jan-Dirk 16782
Meirovics, Prof. Imauts 27418
Meisch, Jim 27568
Meisser, Dr. N. 36858
Meissimilly-Rosin, Martine 15150
Meissner, Roman 31897
Meißner, Uwe 17522
Meissonnier, J. 11617
Meister, Arthur 36595
Meister, Mark 42799, 42806

Meister, Nicolette 41615
Meiszies, Dr. Winrich 16744
Meixner, J. Alfred 15748
Mejdahl, Ulla 08807
Mejer, Robert Lee 46762
Mejia, Javier 07587, 07591
Mejía Maya, Rafael 07620
Méla, Prof. Dr. Charles 36641
Melamed, Nuril 22765
Melander, Dr. Torben 08952
Melcher, Horst 18787
Melcher, Dr. Ralph 19727
Melchionne, Kevin 46458
Meldgård, Bjarne 08867
Melencio, Jet 31353
Melgarejo Cabrera, Elizabet 08111
Meli, Pietro 24184
Melichar, Dr. Herbert 02312, 02312
Melisi, Prof. Francesco 24582
Melke, Gunta 27348
Melki, Dr. Loutfalla 27485
Melkonyan, Hasmik 00682
Mella, Joseph S. 45629
Mellander, Barbo 35788
Mellander, Barbro 36018
Mellbye, Maren-Otte 30930
Mellemsether, Hanna 30943
Meller, Dr. Harald 17515
Mellinger, A. Clair 43930
Mello, Luiz Carlos 04360
Mellon, Lori A. 42898
Mellor, Stephen 48374
Mellott, Tina 41902
Mellow, Ralph 05268
Melničuk, Andrej Fёdorovič 33305
Melnik, Alison G. 45629
Melnikova, I.F. 27091
Melnikova, Natalija Ivanovna 32820
Melnikova, Tamara Michajlovna 32980
Melnyk, Anatolij Ivanovič 37875
Melo, B. de 32238
Melo, Jorge Orlando 07386, 07387
Melo Miranda, Selma 04416
Melody, Paul 30196
Melomina, Olga Alekseevna 32663
Melone, Dr. Francesco 24657
Meloni, Alberto C. 47109, 48424
Melrose, A. 01106
Melson, Claudia 42969
Melton, Babs 47848
Meltzer, J.L. 34215
Meltzer, Lalou 34210
Melville, Terry 30269
Melzer, Ellen 17392
Melzer, Gustav 02423
Melzer, Dr. Miloš 08484
Melzer, Miloš 08668
Melzer, Dr. Miloš 08702
Melzer, Miloš 08736
Melzer, Dr. R. 18926
Memoire, Natalie 10820
Mena Marqués, Dr. Manuela 35048
Mena Segarra, Prof. Enrique 40986
Menaker Rothschild, Deborah 48635
Ménard, Jean 14353
Menard, Jean-Daniel 14910, 14911
Menard, Joan 41135
Menardi, Dr. Herlinde 02083
Menato, Prof. Giuliano 25870
Menconeri, Kate 48739
Mencucci, Angelo 25537
Mendel, Shlomoh 22736
Mendell, Seth F. 45204
Mendelssohn, Dr. Gabriele 17900
Mendelssohn, Prof. H. 22777
Mendenhall, Winnifred 42508
Mendes, Albano 21289
Mendes Bürgi, Dr. Bernhard 36505, 36509
Mendes Marques, Dr. Maria da Concerção 32279
Méndez, Dr. Marion 17408
Méndez Lecanda, Dr. Elia Josefina 28204
Méndez López, Nohra Isabel 07470
Mendoza Garriga, Cristina 34553
Mendoza Ramírez, Patricia 28118
Menefee, Antonio 47023
Menegazzi, Dr. Alessandra 24742
Meneguzzo, Giobatta 24270
Meneses, Adriana 48925
Meng, Jim 41179
Meng, Qingjin 07035
Meng, Ung Vai 07163
Menga, Prof. Angelo 24477
Mengden, Dr. Lida von 18523
Menge, Heide 16336
Mengele, Mark 47875
Menghin, Prof. Dr. Wilfried 16059
Mengis, Tim 45016
Menhes, Prof. Dr. S.B.J. 28917
Menig, Irene 15779
Menis, Gian Carlo 25849
Menk, S. 19370
Menke, Dr. Annette 20335
Menke, Hubertus 17963
Menke, Wilhelm 17618
Menke, William V. 48239, 48241
Menn, Richard J. 42110
Menna, Edith 47230
Menne, Gilbert 03429
Mennel, Suzanne 36541

Mennicke, Christiane 16691
Mennicken, R. 03691
Mennucci, Dr. Antonello 25362, 25367
Mens, Drs. I.J.A. 30055
Mensch, Bernhard 19177
Mensink, O. 29095
Mentzelopoulos, Constantine 21196
Menu, Daniel 15218
Menu, Louis 03626
Menz, Dr. Cäsar 36733, 36738, 36740, 36743,
   36744, 36751
Menz, Martin 19926
Menzel, Joachim 20018
Menzies, Donald 48727
Menzies, G.M. 37946
Menzies, Jackie 01490
Meoard-Blondel, Anne 12871
Merabet, Née 00044
Meral, A. Seda 37615
Merali, Shaheen 15987
Mercadal i Fernández, Oriol 35303
Mercado Lopez, Eugenio 28253
Mercandino Jucker, Gabriella 24380
Mercede, Nevin 48784
Mercer, Anna 40416
Mercer, Bill 46641, 46895
Mercer, L.H.S. 38627
Mercer, Régis 15254
Mercier, Poppi 41766
Mercuri, Joan B. 42328, 46052
Mercuri, Mariano 24885
Merdjanov, Plamen 04683, 04718, 04719
Merdžanov, Plamen 04733
Meredith, Jill 41178, 41178
Meredith, Mary Ellen 47925
Merene-Wiesbauer, Dr. Elisabeth 02908
Merhiou, Olivier de 12933
Merino Acosta, Dr. Luz 07987
Merino Santisteban, José 35078
Mèriot, Christian 10815
Merk, Dr. Anton 17584
Merk, Jan 18819
Merk, Zsuzsa 21309
Merkel, Dr. Michael 17545
Merkert, Prof. Jörn 15919
Merlin, Georges 10547
Merlin-Anglade, Véronique 13692
Merling, David 41655
Merling, Mitchell 47453
Mermet, Christian 13199
Merrell, Ed 43132
Merrell Domingo, Merle 31343
Merriam, Robert W. 43041
Merrill, Kimberly 41077
Merrill, Dr. Linda 48357
Merrill, Michael 47632
Merrill, Robert 40004
Merrill, Ross 48373
Merrill-Mirsky, Dr. Carol 44907
Merrill Roenke, H. 43643
Merriman, Larry 43947
Merrin, Keith 39323
Merrit, Carrie 43698
Merritt, Jody A. 41364
Merritt, Roxanne M. 43372
Mersseman, Denise 03811
Merta, Klaus-Peter 15939
Merten, Jürgen 20212
Merten, Dr. Klaus 20431
Mertens, Carlos Frederico 00426
Mertens, Dr. Sabine 18602
Mertens, Dr. Veronika 15417
Mertes, Lorie 45289
Merveldt, Catherine Gräfin von 16654
Mery, Estelle 15299
Merzenich, Hildegard 18846
Mes, Dr. U. H. M. 29940
Mesa, José de 03893, 03895, 03896, 03897
Mesbahi, Sh. 22296
Meščerina, Nadežda Alekseevna 33277
Meschede, Dr. Friedrich 15935
Mesejo Maestre, Eduardo 07926
Mešerjakov, Vladimir 33433
Meserve, Edward N. 47839
Meshke, R. 05285
Meskin, Maria 44763
Meslin-Perrier, Chantal 12617
Mesnil du Buisson, Laurent du 15189
Mesquida García, Dr. Mercedes 35257
Mesquita, Ivo 04517
Messel, Nils 30746
Messenger, Jane 00704
Messenger, Janet M. 46283
Messenger, Margaret 05197
Messer, David J. 43857
Messer, Jennifer 46957
Messer, Renate 19212
Messerli, Jakob 36546
Messerli, N. 36879
Messerli, Ursula 37148
Messiaen, Marcel 03525
Messika, Natalie 22738
Messimer, Susan 44629
Messinger, Carla 41147
Messmer, Alois 20163
Messmer, Dorothee 37307
Messner, John 40398
Messner, Kathrin 02947
Messner, Reinhold 23392, 23559

Meštan, Prof. Pavol 33976
Mészáros, Dr. Ferenc 21362
Métais, Michel 13044
Metcalf, Charles D. 48766
Metcalf, Craig 06055
Metcalf, Elizabeth 45794
Metcalf, Mike 47628
Metcalf, Susan E 42746
Metcalf, William E. 45760
Metcalfe, Duncan 47235
Metcalfe, Edward C. 45171
Meteku Zekeke, Endalew 09404
Metham, Penny 01316
Methven, John 01442
Metropolis, William C. 42046
Mets, Esta 09392
Mettala, Teri 46107
Metternich, Wolfgang 17063
Mettjes, Dr. Gerd 20022, 20023, 20024, 20026
Metz, Edward 41282
Metz, Lance 43069
Metz, Thomas 16780, 18120
Metz, Wolfgang 18418
Metzger, Amy 43867
Metzger, Frederick W. 06665
Metzger, Dr. Wolfram 17991
Metzler, Jeannot 27567
Metzler, Dr. Sally 42339
Metzner, Dietrich 19537, 19538
Meulemeester, Jean Luc 03680
Meulenbeld, B.C. 28866
Meurant, Anne 03317, 03337
Meurer, Dr. Heribert 19695
Meûter, Ingrid de 03337
Mevludin, Ekmečić 03928
Mewborn, Frankie 48303
Mewes, Claus 17549
Mewton-Hynds, Sally 40770
Meybohm, Amy E. 41383
Meyer, Alain 13167
Meyer, Alberto 36546
Meyer, Bob 28864
Meyer, Charles G. 41439
Meyer, Dr. Christian 02314, 02835
Meyer, Dr. Christian A. 36514
Meyer, Ellen L. 41330
Meyer, Fifi 34217
Meyer, Franz 15730
Meyer, G. 19877
Meyer, Helen 44698
Meyer, Hubert 14698
Meyer, Irin von 17560
Meyer, J.B. 29361
Meyer, Jochanan 22577
Meyer, Dr. Jochen 18619
Meyer, Karl 18999
Meyer, Kurt 19305, 19309, 19310, 19312
Meyer, Lioba 19259
Meyer, M. 28935
Meyer, Marc 27568
Meyer, Marie-Emmanuelle 15130
Meyer, Niels 08770
Meyer, Peter S. 08960
Meyer, Rachel 46274
Meyer, Stefan 19467
Meyer, Steve 44139
Meyer, Dr. Susanne 16273
Meyer, Thomas 37371
Meyer, Werner 17317
Meyer-Büser, Dr. Susanne 18867
Meyer-Friese, Dr. Boye 17527
Meyer-Kröger, Hagen 18864
Meyer Utne, Janneke 30640
Meyer zu Schwabedissen, Doris 18987
Meyerdierks, Judith 42133
Meyere, J.A.L de 29907
Meyers, Amy 45699, 47366
Meyers, Joel 44708
Meyerson, Barbara 45269
Meyerson, Randy 48020
Meyrick, Robert 37956
Meysner 20142
Meza, Ruben 44234
Mezan Barrera, Jesús Manuel 28090
Mezhlumyan, G.B. 00681
Mežinski, Jelena 33978
Mezvinski-Smithgall, Elsa 48389
Mezzatesta, Dr. Michael P. 43019
Mhute, Josiah Rungano 49035
Miano, Ederick C. 31312
Michael, Dean 01157
Michael, Dr. Eckhard 18559
Michael, Dr. Elisabeth 18831
Michael, Helene 37362
Michael, Janet 38439
Michael, Linda 00923
Michael, William H. 44197
Michaelidon, Maria 21142
Michaelis, Bonni-Dara 45887
Michaelis, Dr. Rainer 15974
Michaelsen, Miah 46026
Michailov, Christo 04621
Michailov, Igor 33438
Michajlov, A.B. 33620
Michajlova, Ljudmila Vasiljevna 33441
Michajlova, Zdravka 04725, 04875
Michajlovna, Jelena 33057
Michalka, Matthias 02949
Michalka, Prof. Dr. Wolfgang 19486

Michaud, Bruce P. 47202
Michaud, François 13548
Michaud, Jean-Marc 12413, 14002, 14628
Michaud, Raynald 05922
Michavila, Joaquín 35678
Michel, D. 13131
Michel, Ernest W. 45797
Michel, Gundega 27420
Michel, Helmut 20422
Michel, Jean-François 11240, 11241, 11242
Michel, Samuel 36781
Michel, Prof. Dr. Thomas 20099
Michelet, Annick 13878
Michelotti, Dr. Francesca 33759, 33761, 33765,
   33769
Michels, Dr. Anette 20223
Michels, Dr. Hubertus 16590
Michels, Dr. Norbert 16576
Michélsen, Pia 36063
Michie, Thomas 46721
Michieli, Catalina Teresa 00109
Michoutouchkine, N. 48865
Mickelson-Lukach, Joan 43502
Mickenberg, David 43241, 48495
Micklich, Judy 47212
Micklich, Dr. Norbert 16541
Micklim, Lynne 42913
Micko, Ingeborg 02815
Mickschat, Klaus-Dieter 19308
Miclescu, Constanţa 32623
Micol, P.M. 11757
Mičurová, M. 34079
Middag, B.M. 29499
Middelbasch, Max 29720
Middlemost, Thomas A. 01568
Middleton, J. 01106
Middleton, J.W. 38466
Middleton, S.I. 38466
Midleton, Viscount 38416
Miedema, B. 28994
Mielke, Dr. Heinz-Peter 17383
Mielsch, Prof. Dr. Harald 16225
Mierkiewicz, Edward 32122
Mierzwiński, Mariusz 31799
Miesbeck, Peter 19649
Miesenberger, Martin 02351
Miessgang, Dr. Thomas 02914
Mießl, Peter 02126
Mieth, Katja Margarethe 20080
Miethe, Susann 19302
Mietke, Dr. Gabriele 16096
Miggitsch, Jörg 02309
Miglbauer, Dr. Renate 02813, 02814, 02815, 02816
Miglinas, Skirmante 42338
Migliori, Gabriele 24533
Mignot, D. 28902
Migritone Gondwe, Michael 27613
Miguet, Danièle 11181, 11182
Mihai, Raul 32445
Mihail, Benoît 03343
Mihailović, Milica 33800
Mihalić, Jana 07713
Mihelić, Sanjin 07809
Mihevc, Bibijana 34124
Miho, Terao 26290
Mihovilić, Kristina 07757
Mihut, Elena 32473
Mijić, Suzanalav 33824
Mijin, Vesna 33916
Mijnlieff, E.M. 29296, 29297
Mikaelsen, Laila 21238
Mikelson, Mary 06789
Mikes, Johannes H. 01874
Mikeskova, Irina 04846
Mikeson, Mary 47774
Mikhalevsky, A.V. 27099
Mikkelsen, Dr. Egil 30731, 30736, 30745, 30769,
   30771
Mikkelsen, Falk 08837
Mikkola, Ari 09844
Mikkola Huk, Eira 09792
Miklas, Lois 44004
Mikołajska, Ewa 32007
Mikonranta, Kaarina 09593
Mikoszewski, Jerzy 32144
Mikulaštík, Dr. Tomáš 08730
Mikus, Joan 43413
Mikuž, Marjeta 34113
Milani, Arch 46024
Milani, Dr. Domenico 24805, 24810
Milanich, Dr. J.T. 43581
Milano, Dean 43168
Milano, Prof. Ernesto 24435
Milbank, Bill 30285
Milbrath, Dr. S. 43581
Milchram, Gerhard 02903, 02948
Milchner, Dr. Paul 02127
Mildner, Dr. U. 19494
Miles, Bernice 44178
Miles, Blanche 47231
Miles, Bradley R. 42112
Miles, Carolyn P. 47111
Miles, Carolyn W. 41068
Miles, Christine M. 41083
Miles, David A. 48742
Miles, Ed 41697
Miles, Ellen 48382
Miles, Gwyn 39795
Miletić, Jelena 33824

Mileusnić, Slobodan 33813
Mileusnić, Snježana Radovanlija 07835
Milev, Svetoslav 04825
Milhazes, Dr. Maria Cláudia C. 32241
Miliadzidou-Ioannou, Dr. E. 21181
Milian, Mihai 32618
Milius, James 43695
Milivojević, Radmila 33851
Milkofsky, Brenda 48576
Mill, Dennis J. 46178
Millan, William I. 38126
Millar, Jim 06167
Millar, Joyce 06144
Millard, Ellen 06535
Millard, Jamie 44739
Millard, Rhoda 05325
Millas, Dr. Rolando 45291
Millaud, Hiriata 15348
Millberg, Per-Olof 35976, 35977
Mille, Dr. Diana Dimodica 43265
Millen, A.J. 05010
Miller, Alan 00848
Miller, Dr. Albrecht 16831, 19148
Miller, Alison 38093
Miller, Andree 41145, 42138, 43102
Miller, Angus 39113
Miller, Archie W. 05984
Miller, Bob 46919
Miller, Charles 46198
Miller, C.J. 43853
Miller, Corinne 39442
Miller, David 47463
Miller, David M. 45261
Miller, Denise 42320
Miller, Don 43454
Miller, Douglas 45514
Miller, E.M.J. 38097, 39858
Miller, Prof. George 43973
Miller, George 46550
Miller, Gerald J. 47360
Miller, Gordon 42346
Miller, Prof. Dr. H. 18853
Miller, Harriet 45900
Miller, Howard L. 43942
Miller, Jacky 38177
Miller, Dr. James 44745
Miller, Janelle 47052
Miller, John 40685, 43844
Miller, Dr. J.Y. 43581
Miller, Dr. Kathy Ann 47919
Miller, Kevin R. 42812
Miller, Kristin 41131
Miller, Dr. L.D. 43581
Miller, Lenore D. 48347
Miller, Linda L. 43144
Miller, Lisa 41143
Miller, Lois 44128
Miller, Margaret A. 47940
Miller, Marguerite 41141
Miller, Dr. Markus 16802
Miller, Mary 44967
Miller, Michael 46632, 47706
Miller, Nan L. 46874, 46874
Miller, Nancy Lee 41835
Miller, Pamela 46693
Miller, Paul F. 45931
Miller, R. Craig 42885
Miller, Randy 06334
Miller, Roger 48656
Miller, Rosemary 01104
Miller, Ruby 41063
Miller, Sammy 40014
Miller, Sandy 47845
Miller, Stephen 44588, 44629
Miller, Steve 45508
Miller, Steven 40359
Miller, Susan 47332
Miller, Tammy 43136
Miller, Terry J. 43595
Miller, Tom 05490
Miller, Tracy 41638
Miller, Walter 47911
Miller, William 38979, 39769
Miller, William K. 42999
Miller Batty, Nancy 48649
Miller-Betts, Christine 41384
Miller Zohn, Kristen 41081
Millet, Teresa 35599
Millett, Prof. Martin 38459
Milli, Konrad 17959
Milligan, Frank D. 45598
Milligan Ryan, Barbara 48779
Millin, Laura J. 45403
Milller, Marcus 06085
Millman, David 44673
Millroth, Thomas 36423
Mills, Brendon 44593
Mills, Cynthia K. 41712
Mills, Dan 44721
Mills, David 45699
Mills, Dinah 48233, 48234
Mills, Ellsworth 44020
Mills, Gina 44329
Mills, J. 40885
Mills, John 38922
Mills, John K. 46706
Milius, Nigel 40807
Mills, R.G. 40792
Mills, Susan 37979

Milne, Julie 40038
Milne, Lee 01087
Milne, V. 00721
Milne, William K. 39967
Milne, W.K. 39279
Milner, Renate 48180
Milnor, Nancy 43610
Milojković, Jelica 33891
Milonjić, Miroslav 07767
Milosavljević, Branka 33819
Milošević, Prof. Ante 07774, 07784
Milosevich, Joe B. 44356
Milosis, Themis 20956
Miloux, Yannick 12609
Milovanović, Dušan 33810
Milson, Andrew 38945
Milstren, Dr. Gerhard 36321
Milton-Elmore, Kara 46011
Milton-Tee, Ann 30164
Milyov, Simeon 04846
Min, Choi Hyong 27118
Mina, Dr. Gianna A. 36882
Minahan, Nancy M. 47889
Minar, Rena 47935
Minard, Barbara 44196
Minassian, Levon 22244
Minchinton, J. 40084
Mindell, Prof. David P. 41220, 41220
Minder, Nicole 37289
Mine, William K. 38079
Mineau, Marc 06471
Mineeva, Valentina Alekseevna 32721
Minegishi, Sumio 26799
Miner, Curt 43925
Miner, Donald J. 47065
Minerva, Michael 45842
Minetti, Dr. Alessandra 25481
Minish, Marveen 45252
Minke, Prof. Dr. Alfred 03413
Minkenberg, Dr. Georg 15372
Minkkinen, Aimo 10080
Minmeister, J.C. 11563
Minney, Michael J 44626
Minns, Dr. Jonathan E. 39268
Mino, Dr. Yutaka 26669
Minse, C. 29333
Minter, Sue 39604
Minto, Don 44315
Minto, Heather 44315
Minton, Dwayne 21259
Mints, Carolyn 42243
Mintz, Ann 46532
Mintz, Deborah Martin 43310
Minx, Jim 46119
Mion-Jones, Esta 40546
Miotkandal, Oddvar 30715
Mir, Dr. Ronen 41399
Mir-khalaf, A. 22245
Mira, Vegar 07680
Mira Bonomi, Angelo Vittorio 23953, 25555
Mirabdolbaghi, Zia 15113
Mirabella Roberti, Prof. Mario 25899
Miranda, Gaudenzio 24674
Mirelez, Cathy 43675
Mirmoghtadaie, S. 22246
Mirnik, Dr. Ivan 07809
Mirolo, Diana 36471
Miron, Dr. Andrei 19725
Miron, Dr. O. 22690
Mironneau, Paul 13670
Mironowicz-Panek, Maria 31821
Mirzejewska, Maria 32088
Misago, Dr. Kanimba 33752
Miscault, René de 12341
Mischke, Petra 17694
Mischkewitz, Franz 19013
Mišečkina, Marija V. 32811
Mishima, Tadao 26610
Mishima, Yashuhisa 26638
Mishima, Yoshinori 26638
Mishne, Merle H. 45226
Mishra, H. P 21724
Mišina, Ljudmila Aleksandrovna 33347
Miskovic, Svetlana 06811
Miskowski, Antoniny 48057
Mislej, Irene 34083
Misner, Mary 05185
Misočnik, Svetlana Michajlovna 33544
Misof, Dr. Bernhard 16250
Miss, Dr. Stig 08952
Mitanov, Petăr 04860
Mitchel, Gary 42709
Mitchell, Archie 48142
Mitchell, Barbara 44112
Mitchell, D.I. 40555
Mitchell, Freda 41877
Mitchell, Harold 00897
Mitchell, James 42232
Mitchell, Jena 47003
Mitchell, Joan 01003
Mitchell, Joanne 41133
Mitchell, Kay 45566
Mitchell, Leah 44308, 45893
Mitchell, Marjorie 46922
Mitchell, Paul 05284
Mitchell, Dr. Peter 40153
Mitchell, Renee 44486, 44487
Mitchell, Sandra 45084

Mitchell, Sue 01520
Mitev, P. 04800
Miteva, Kremena 04656
Mitheis, Christine 01689
Mitkevič, V.M. 32649, 32650
Mitne, Debra 44236
Mitre, Dr. Jorge Carlos 00224
Mitrev, Dimităr 04755, 04757, 04817
Mitrović, Miodrag 33927
Mitsuoka, Tadanari 26111
Mittas, Nicole 17111
Mittelberg, Antje 17527
Mitten, David 42042
Mittendorfer, Gabriele 02590
Mitterhöfer, Dr. Jakob 02310
Mitterwenger, Dr. Christine 02399, 02400, 02401, 02402
Mittmann, Dr. Hans-Walter 18003
Mittwoch, Wolfgang 16995
Mitzel, Horst 20505
Mitzel, June 05419
Mitzevich, Nick 01316
Mitzscherlich, Dr. Birgit 15834
Miwa, Kenjin 26938
Miyagawa, Ellen 46272
Miyaji, Nobuo 26626
Miyake, Akiko 26342
Miyake, Tetsuhisa 27020
Miyamoto, Akio 26286
Miyaoka, Kiyomi 26771
Miyatani, Masayuki 26789
Miyazaki, Katsumi 26832
Miyazaki, Takashi 26580
Miyazawa, Akimichi 26568
Miyazima, Hisao 26773
Mizerová, Hana 08561
Mizerski, Dr. Włodzimierz 32098
Mizina, Ljudmila V. 33575
Mizinga, Flexon Moono 49023
Mizukami, Iwao 26231
Mizukami, Takeo 26714
Mizukami, Takeshi 26268
Mizuno, Keizaburo 26536
Mizuno, Takashi 26693
Mizuno Elliott, Nancy 46859
Mizuta, Dr. Akira 26578
Mizutani, Takeshi 26938
Mjøs, Lise 30770
Mlecz, Stella C. 46853
Mleczko, Radoslaw 32124
Mlynarčík, Dr. Jozef 34025
Mlynarski, Ryszard 32190
Mo, Charles 42243
Moacir Maia, Prof. Pedro 04429
Moberg, Jack 45150
Mobley, Ree 47426
Moc, Joan S. 45212
Mochi Onori, Dr. Lorenza 25162, 25857
Mochola, Tatiana 31632
Mochoruk, Mike 06006
Mochova, Jelena Fillipovna 32629
Mock, Rayonna 41152
Moctezuma, Allessandra 47291
Modegi, Masaaki 26930
Modersohn, Christian 19326
Modest, Wayne 26069
Modi, Amrutbhai 21679
Modonesi, Dr. Denise 25975
Modotti, Luigi 23589
Modrzejewska, Dr. Irena 31482
Moe, Barbara 43780, 44473
Moe, Helene 30712, 30713
Moe, Richard 48385
Möbius, Ingrid 18791
Moed, G.J. 29634
Moeferdt, Dr. Horst 16623
Möhlenkamp, Dr. Klaus 18773
Möhlmeyer, Erich 19292
Möhring, Barbara 17590
Möhring, Dr. Helmut 19681
Moehring, Markus 18490
Möller, Axel 15976
Möller, Kristina 36211
Moeller, Prof. Magdalena 15931
Möller, Marie von 30412, 30413, 30414
Möller, Peter 36342
Möller, Dr. Reimer 19978, 19979, 19981
Möller, Dr. Werner 16584
Möller-Arnsberg, Birgit 18864
Moen, Eivind 30924
Moench, Esther 10531
Mönig, Dr. Roland 18107
Mönkkönen, Mikko 09893
Moens, Dominique 03667, 03745, 03847
Moens, Karel 03177
Mörgeli, Markus 36961
Mörike, Dr. Doris 20105
Moering, Dr. Renate 17046
Moerman, Dr. I.W.L. 29526
Moers, Rainer 17507
Mörtinger, Franz 01740
Mörzer Bruyns, W.F.J. 28888
Moes, K. 28921
Moeske, Ulrich 16664
Mössinger, Ingrid 16466
Mössner, Dr. Wolfgang 18267, 18268
Moetlo, Nancy 34358
Moffat, Jill 43560
Mofford, Juliet 41208

Moga, Jack 43789
Moga, John 43792
Mogensen, Ove 09093
Moget, Layla 14750
Mohamadi, Naghme 22277
Mohammadrezaie, P. 22254
Mohan, S. 35776
Mohl, Dr. Max 15821
Mohr, John 48057
Mohr, Julie 39897
Mohr, Peter 39897
Mohr, Vibeke 30847
Mohring, Marilyn 46974
Moigne, Roland de 10868
Moilanen, Arja 10088
Moisala, Prof. Pirkko 10127
Moisen Lechuga, Patricia 28180
Moises, Loly Keith 31339
Mojica, Brenda 31336
Mojseeva, T.M. 33456
Mojzer, Miklós 21383
Mojžíšová, Dr. Olga 08377, 08594
Mokarram Hossain, Mahmud 03095
Mokhtar Bin Abu Bakar, Dato Mohamed 27679
Mokre, Jan 02890, 02955
Mol 03793
Mol, I. 29067
Mol, W. 29022
Moland, Arnfinn 30748
Moldenhauer, Susan 44650
Molen, Dr. J.R. ter 28928
Molenda, Remigiusz 31704
Molesworth-Saint Aubyn, Lady Iona 38267
Molin, Dr. Paulette 43896
Molina, Prof. Mario 31073
Molina Cabal, Alvaro José 07474
Molina Pico, Horacio 00634
Molinare, Rod 39584
Molinari, Arno 03002
Molinari, Danielle 13524, 40425
Molinari, Giovanni 25532
Molinaro, Ettore 23193
Molinaro, Marcene J. 44434
Molins, Javier 35599
Molist, Miguel 34550
Molitor, Anne 03289
Mollano, Prof. Olga 00468
Mollay, Catherine 05816
Møller, Dan E. 09112
Møller, Lars Kærulf 08846
Møller, Stig B. 08762
Møller-Hansen, Keld 09115
Moller-Pedersen, Kurt 08773
Moller-Racke, Heidi 18601
Molles, Dr. Manuel C. 41105
Mollett, Fran 48057
Mollfulleda i Borrell, Joaquin 34481
Mollo, B. 38869
Molloy, Dr. Peter M. 46475
Molnar, August J. 45679
Molnár, Dr. Erzsébet 21457, 21458
Molnár, Sándor 21603
Mols, P. 29934
Molsbergen, B. 29106
Molteni, A. 12537
Moltesen, Mette 08944
Moltke-Hansen, David 46417
Molvær, Edvard 30553
Momas, Jacques 10895
Momčilov, Dimčo 04692
Monachon, Danuta 13502
Monaco, Dr. Giuseppe 25178
Monaghan, A. 40432
Monaghan, Bryan 05376
Monaghan, Ciaran 37929
Monaghan, Nigel 24423
Monahan, Gloria 05798
Moncrief, Dr. Nancy D. 45193
Moncur, Shannon 45090
Mond, Ulrike 16236
Mondini, Massimo 23194
Mondragón, Lourdes 28096
Mondragón, Martín Antonio 28477
Monds, Kathy 46588
Monedoñedo Espinoza, Juan 31224
Monery, Jean-Paul 14491
Mones, Prof. Alvaro 41018
Money, Eric 40363
Monfort, Catherine 03693
Mongan, Barbara 42602
Monge, Janet 46460
Monge, Maria de Jesus 32359
Mongellaz, Jacqueline 14645, 14648
Mongon, Alain 10425
Moniak, Eugeniusz 32225
Monigan, Michael F. 48402
Monin, Christophe 13603
Moniot, François 10809
Monk, Suny 47900
Monkhouse, Christopher 45391
Monmousseau, Patrice 14642
Monnani, Walter 01698
Monnet, C. 12598
Monney, Paul 37084
Monnier, Georges 37163
Monnier, Jean-Laurent 13685
Monod, Frédéric 13003
Monot, Michel 15256

Monrad, Kasper 08950
Monroe, Dan L. 47191, 47193, 47194, 47196, 47197, 47198
Monroe, Dr. Sam 46590
Monschaw, Elline von 22446
Montag, Dr. Ulrich 18831
Montagne, Dr. C. 29106
Montagne of Beaulieu, Lord 38370, 38371
Montaner, Jaume 34563
Montani, Miro 07817
Montanini, Deborah 46495
Montebello, Philippe de 45833
Montefiore, Don 01132
Monteil, Esclarmonde 10915
Montenegro, Dr. Raffaele 23033
Montenegro Carneiro, Maria Margarida V. 32319
Montero, Alberto E. 06886
Montero, Prof. Paula 04512
Montero Agüerz, Ildefonso 34741
Montesano, Frank 42647
Montesdeoca García-Sáenz, Antonio Daniel 35243
Montet-White, Anta 44684
Monteyne, Nathalie 03146
Montfort, Helen G. 43859
Montgomery, A. 39294
Montgomery, Alexander 06580
Montgomery, Alexandra 40347
Montgomery, Cathie 40620
Montgomery, D. Bruce 42168
Montgomery, Erick D. 41381
Montgomery, Florence 41803
Montgomery, Dr. John 46614
Montgomery, Küllike 36351
Montgomery, N. 34188
Montgomery, Dr. Sally 38161
Montgomery, S.E. 40794
Montgomery, Prof. W.I. 38154
Montgomery Tyler, Kay 42202
Monti, Canco Pietro 24608
Monticelli, Dr. Paolo 24648
Montileaux, Paulette 46798
Montin, Kim 10120, 10128
Montjalin, Olaf de 14659
Montmany, Marta 34564
Montñés García, Carmen 35718
Montoya Soto, Sonia 07464
Montserrat Martí, Dr. J.M. 34568
Monzó, Josep Vicent 35599
Moodie, Laura 05151
Moodie, Sandra 26073
Moody, Dr. Barry 04997
Moody, Eric N. 46834
Moody, Tammy 42954
Mooij, Dr. Charles de 29407
Moombolah-Goagoses, Esther U. 28781, 28782
Moombolah-Joagoses, Esther U. 28778
Moon, Diane 39702
Moon, John P.C. 46876
Moons, L.J.M. 29332
Moore, Anne 39987
Moore, Barbara 46234
Moore, Bennett 43892
Moore, Carleton B. 47971
Moore, Dr. Carlton 45271
Moore jr., Dan 41328
Moore, Dan 41328
Moore, David 38316
Moore, Dona 05652
Moore, Duane 48099
Moore, Dr. Dwight 43185
Moore, Dr. Elizabeth A. 45193
Moore, Fran 05316
Moore, Gary F. 48104
Moore, George 43416
Moore, Harold D. 47648
Moore, J. Roderick 43317
Moore, James C. 41099
Moore, Jennifer 43811
Moore, Juanita 44394
Moore, Kevin 40268
Moore, Linda 45584
Moore, Margaret 45595
Moore, Margaret Jane 41494
Moore, Michael R. 46867
Moore, Nick 38708, 38964, 39098, 40136, 40239, 40447
Moore, Richard 01169
Moore, Richard H. 43683
Moore, Rod 38603
Moore, S. 05364
Moore, Susan J. 44104
Moore, Terry 44005
Moore, Prof. Thomas E. 41220
Moore, Dr. Viola 46280
Moore, William J. 43813
Moore, William S. 42937
Moore Cole, Alisha 44407
Moore Stucker, Kathryn 46491
Moorefield, Amy G. 46871
Moorer, Bill 05484
Moores-Franklin, Lolisa 46541
Moos, Dr. David 41706
Moppett, Ronald 05169
Moqimi-zadeh, Hamid 22252
Mor, Judith 22786
Mora, Alejandra 28275
Mora, Dr. Rafael A. 00188
Mora García, Carlos 28602
Morabito, Dr. Leo 23991

Moraes Branco, Pércio de 04281
Moraes Sophia, Eunice 04515
Moragas, Cora Romy 06897
Moraitou-Apostolopoulou, Dr. Maria 21227
Moral, Mary del 46163
Morales, April 44547
Morales, Dr. Michael 43182
Morales-Coll, Eduardo 32386
Morales Gómez, Antonio 28262
Morales Gómez, David 28263
Morales Pérez, Eduardo 28572
Morales Ramón, José María 35086
Moran, Liz 40592
Moran, Maryann 47516
Moran, Paula G. 41075
Moran, Vivienne 01545
Moran-Zerda, Leticia 31392, 31401
Moraña, Prof. Oscar 48907
Morand, J. 05359
Morand, Lynn L. 45029, 45030, 45032, 45034
Morand, Marie-Claude 37087, 37111, 37172, 37173, 37174
Morandini, Dr. Carlo 25850
Morante López, Dr. Rubén Bernardo 28615
Morash, Terrence 41824
Morath-Vogel, Dr. Wolfram 16893, 16895
Moravčík, J. 34079
Moravec, Tomaš 08526
Morawietz, Doris 18058
Morawinska, Agnieszka 32142
Mórawski, Karol 32135
Morawski, Mike 44464
Morbach, Philippe 13625
Morbán Laucer, Dr. Fernando 09125
Morbis, Daniela 23036
Morcom, G. 34064
Morcos Gayyed, Mervat 09294
Mordasini, Andrea 36607
Mordi, Pietro 24126
More-Molyneux, Michael 39140
Moreau, Susie K. 05621
Morehouse, Dorothy V. 44801
Morel, Michel 05344
Morel, Pascal 14185
Morel, Sylvie 05484
Morel-Deledalle, Myriame 12865
Morelli, Gianni 25084
Morello, Dr. Giovanni 48881, 48882
Morelock, Dr. Jerry 43577
Moreno, Amanda 38020
Moreno, Anne Marie 31449
Moreno, Barry 45876
Moreno, Enrique 35024
Moreno, Maria Cristina 07506
Moreño de Medellín, Patricia 28587
Moreno Garrido, Maria Jesús 34737
Moreno Ulloa, Graciela 07653
Moret, J.-L. 36861
Moretti, Dr. A. Maria 25237
Moretti, Dr. Giovanni 23748
Moretti, Dr. Mario 23491
Moretti, Prof. Mario 25412, 25414
Moretti, Dr. Mario 26033
Morey, Mark 41164
Morgan, B.V. 05985
Morgan, Chris 38426, 40017, 43395
Morgan, Dahlia 45281
Morgan, Dave 45422
Morgan, David 44285
Morgan, Gary 01036
Morgan, Dr. Gary 01364
Morgan, Dr. J.D. 46578
Morgan, Jeremy 06244
Morgan, Jessica 41810
Morgan, K. 30103
Morgan, Kerry 42187
Morgan, Martin 41247
Morgan, Peter J. 40521
Morgan, Peter M. 45616
Morgan, Ron 38641
Morgan, Zane 43121
Morgan-Welch, Beverly 41816
Morgenegg, Hans 36656
Morgenroth, Heiner 18112
Morhun, Sue 05442
Mori, Masatoshi 26234
Moriarty, M.J. 38558
Moriarty, Steve 46044
Morier-Genoud, Gabriel 36625, 36626
Morigi Govi, Dr. Cristiana 23109
Morillo León, Anabel 35476
Morin, Cathy J. 45576
Morin, Robert G. 45576
Morinelli, Dom Leone 23458
Morishigue, Akifumi 26641
Morison, J. 39157
Moritsch, Dr. Otmar 02993
Moritz, Craig 41647
Moritz, Franz 18173
Moritz, Heidi 16775
Moritz, Dr. Marina 16905
Moritz, Per 36054
Moriyama, Mayumi 26902
Moriyama, Ryoichi 26134
Mork, Eileen 43959
Morkowski, J. 37044
Morl, Dr. Claudia 23899
Morletta, Martine 39561
Morley, Stephen H. 41976

Morlok, Dr. Wolfgang 19844
Morman, C. 29035
Morna, Dr. Teresa 32299
Morneburg, Otto 15838
Moro, Alberto E. 00380
Moro, Luigi 22804
Moroder, Robert 24698
Moroyama, Masanori 26938
Morozov, Ivan Ivanovič 32958
Morozov, Vladimir Vasilevič 33132
Morozova, Ludmila Ivanovna 33321
Morozova, T.V. 32878
Morral, Eulàlia 35525
Morrall, Dr. Andrew 45771
Morran, Gerald 05522
Morretta, Rosemary 46897
Morrill, Andreu 42096
Morrin, Peter 44976
Morris, Charles 42232
Morris, C.I. 39081
Morris, Clive 38482
Morris, D. 38570
Morris, David 39904, 46847
Morris, Derek 39758
Morris, Jack 05647
Morris, Jeffory 46729
Morris, Joan 39426
Morris, John 03865
Morris, Johnathan 01013
Morris, Lynda 40097
Morris, Mark 47170
Morris, Martha 48376
Morris, Nell 44584
Morris, Pamela 46641
Morris, Patricia A. 47182
Morris, Susan 41645
Morris Hambourg, Maria 45833
Morrison, Andrew 38172, 38651, 39256, 40324, 40675, 40853
Morrison, Angela 40381
Morrison, Charlotte K. 42866
Morrison, Cindi 44628
Morrison, D. 01452
Morrison, David A. 05484
Morrison, Garth 39142
Morrison, James F. 44351
Morrison, Kim 44038
Morrison, Lynn 40368
Morrison, Lynne 44623
Morrison, Mark T. 47169
Morrison, Philip R. 45966
Morrison, Renee 41231
Morrison, Sandra 46289
Morrisroe, Julia 45537
Morrissey, Dr. Kris 43054
Morrissey, Tom 44798
Morsch, Prof. Dr. Günter 19264
Morsch, Nathalie 15085
Morscheck, Charles 46430
Morscher, Lukas 02067
Morscher, Dr. Lukas 02068
Morse, Carla 06584
Morse, F.E. 42395
Morsiani, Paola 44118
Mort, Mark 44685
Mortensen, Ingrid 09107
Mortenson, Marianne 44888
Morteveille, Gérard 14553
Morteyrol, Amélie 14892
Mortimer, Kristen 43711
Morton, Craddock 00888
Morton, Doug 42440
Morton, E. 06651, 40036
Morton, Geneva 46282
Morton, Lisa 43021
Morton, Susan 40759
Morucci, Alberto 25324
Moś, Ignacy 31906
Mosby, Dewey F. 43882
Moschig, Günther 02118
Mosco, Dr. Marilena 23854, 23860
Mosconi, Prof. Andrea 23678, 23683
Moscoso Möller, M.A. Fernando 21271
Mosdal, Brita 08841
Mosel, Günter 17592
Moseley, Bruce M. 46157
Mosena, David R. 42349
Mosenfelder, Mrs. Robert 43206
Mosenstine, Ken 42068
Moser, Audrey 42988
Moser, Dr. Bernd 01922
Moser, Christopher L. 46922
Moser, Dr. Juliane 16981
Moser, Rene 42705
Moser-Gautrand, Claire 10939
Moses, H. Vincent 46922
Moses, Stephen A. 45725, 45726
Moses Nesmith, Cynthia 42565
Mosharraf Hossain, M. 03080
Moshenson, Edna 22775
Moshier, Wendy 47213
Mosica, Phillippe 14399
Moskovaja, Ljudmila Ivanovna 33275, 33276
Mosneagu, Marian 32502
Moss, Ed 41970
Moss, Gillian 45788
Moss, Kay K. 43632
Moss, Kenneth 45835
Moss, Michael E. 48543

Moss, Rick 46059
Moss, Dr. Roger W. 46392
Mossman, Kate 05469
Moster-Hoos, Dr. Jutta 19254
Mostert, Antoinette 28757
Mothe, Florence 13849
Mothe, Hubert 12364
Motlotle, Ntikwe Pene 03937
Motornaja, Larisa Ivanovna 33209
Motoyama, Yoshiao 26869
Mott, Joyce 44726
Mottart, Eugène 03675
Motte, Vic 03773
Motte Saint-Pierre, Marquise de la 13098
Mottram, Graham 39284, 40957
Motyka, Jerzy 31536
Motyka, Maria 31735
Moudry, Mary Lou 41866
Mouely-Koumba, Marie-Agnès 15350
Mougel, René 12116
Moughdad, S. 37434
Mougin, Denis 05123
Mouillaud, Jean 11825
Mould, Laurel 05590
Moulias, Christos 21115
Moulin, Hélène 15051
Moulin, Pierre 10486
Moult, Lynne 39477
Mounier, Bernard 14852
Mount, Steven 45945
Mountbatten of Burma, Countess 38028
Mountfort, Dick 41687
Moura, Fernando 32296
Moura Delphim, Angelo Alberto de 04170
Mouralová, Blanca 16108
Mourão, R. 04236
Mourlet, Gérard 14546
Mousley, Patricia K. 44107
Moussa Nene, Djamil 06883
Mousseigne, Alain 14940
Moussellard, Renaud Pascal 11054
Mousset, Jean-Luc 27567
Moutashar, Michèle 10417
Mouton, Romona 44570
Mouw, Christine 48515
Movan, Lisa 39949
Movillon, Mario M. 31346
Mowat, Dr. P. 40131
Mowll Mathews, Nancy 48635
Mowrey, Debbie 41278
Mowry, Robert 42042
Moxeme, Oscar O. 46625
Moxley, Richard W. 46869
Moy, Henry 44190
Moya Pons, Frank 09124
Moya-Valgañón, José Gabriel 35058
Moyce, Greg 47414
Moye, L.M. 45000
Moye, Matthew M. 45000
Moyes, Nick 38716
Moyle, N. 40210
Moyle, Nicola 40209
Moynes, Debbie 04985
Moynihan, George P. 47543
Moyroud, Raymond 10904
Mozales, José 34868
Mpouna Coline, Samuel 21285
Mrabet, Ridha 37577
Mrachacz, Maria 18144
Mravlincić, Ivan 07792
Mraz, Dr. Gottfried 02892
Mroczkowski, Dennis P. 43431
Mršić, Vjekoslav 07839
Mrugalska-Banaszak, Magdalena 31904
Mrva, Dr. Marián 34079
Mrvová, J. 34079
Msemwa, Dr. Paul J. 37458
Msimanga, A. 49028
Msonge, Andreas 37464
Mtshiza, Zola 34214
Muceus, Cheryl 41057, 41059
Muchametčina, Lejla Munirovna 32941
Muchanov, Gennadij Stepanovič 32907
Muchitsch, Dr. Wolfgang 01922
Mucnjak, Prof. Alois 02858
Mudd, Margaret 45406, 45407
Mudd, Michael 44168
Muddiman, Susi 01071
Mühlbacher, Anton 02420
Mühlbacher, Peter 19533
Mühlbauer, Heinrich 18368
Mühlberger, Dr. Kurt 02834
Mühldorfer-Vogt, Christian 19458, 19460, 19462, 19464
Mühlegger-Heuhapel, Dr. Christiane 02963
Mühlemann, Yves 36636
Mühlhäußer, Werner 17464, 17465
Muehlig, Linda 46015
Mühne, Dr. Christian 19406
Mülhaupt, Freya 15919
Müllauer, Gerhard 03061
Müllejans-Dickmann, Dr. Rita 17212, 17697
Müller, A. 19702
Müller, Dr. Adelheid 19139
Müller, Andreas 17118
Müller, Anette 20778
Müller, Berit 20684
Müller, Bruno 01777
Mueller, Carlyn 44868

Müller, Dr. Christian 36505, 36506
Müller, Dr. Claudius C. 18916
Müller, Conrad 17152
Müller, Erwin 18731
Müller, Eugen 02224
Müller, Prof. Dr. Felix 36541
Müller, Dr. Gino 36861
Müller, Gisela 17090
Mueller, Dr. Gordon H. 45732
Müller, H. 16259
Müller, Dr. H. P. 37099
Müller, Hans 02823
Müller, Dr. Hans-Peter 18384
Müller, Heike 19250, 19251, 19252
Müller, Heinz-Willi 15593
Müller, Hermann 36573
Müller, Dr. Ingeborg 15908
Müller, Prof. Dr. Irmgard 16197
Mueller, Jane 41979
Müller, Johann 37068
Müller, Johann Paul M. 02071
Mueller, John 45017
Mueller, Judith 45811
Müller, Dr. Jürg P. 36633
Müller, Dr. Karsten 20090
Müller, Klaus 16271
Müller, Dr. Klaus-Peter 19255
Müller, Dr. Maria 16728
Müller, Dr. Markus 18938
Müller, Markus 36498
Mueller, Prof. Marlene 48476
Müller, Dr. Martin 16860, 17243, 17248, 20727
Müller, Matthias 17803
Müller, Dr. Maya 36508
Müller, Michael 18203
Müller, Peter 20132, 20133
Müller, Dr. Peter 21375
Müller, Dr. R. 20095
Müller, Dr. Róbert 21453
Müller, Dr. Roland 20107, 20108
Müller, Roland 36683
Müller, Rolf 37258
Müller, Rudolf 37312
Müller, Sabine 17093
Mueller, Shirley 48798
Müller, Dr. Siegfried 16193, 19256
Müller, Stefan 18793, 18796
Müller, Prof. Telmo Lauro 04475
Müller, Thomas 18414
Müller, Dr. Thomas 20122
Müller, Thomas 37367
Müller, Urs 36479
Müller, Dr. Volker 20313
Müller, Walter 15392
Müller, Werner 16728
Müller, Prof. Dr. Werner 19660
Müller, Wolfgang 16653, 16655
Müller, Zsuzsanna 36240
Müller-Bahlke, Dr. Thomas 17509
Müller-Gaebele, Erich H. 17148
Müller-Karpe, Dr. Michael 18606
Müller-Krumbach, Dr. Renate 15830
Müller-Merz, Dr. Edith 37186
Müller-Serre, Helga 19566
Müller-Späth, Esther 17798
Müller-Tamm, Dr. Pia 16728
Müller-Westermann, Dr. Iris 36262
Müller-Wirth, Sabine 17991, 18002
Münch, Eugen 20235
Muench Navarro, Pablo 28569, 28572, 28576
Münch-Severin, Kornelia 15956
Muenkel, Harold 45026
Münzel, Prof. Dr. Mark 18633
Mürner, Rolf 36914
Muertegui, Charles 31308
Müsch, Dr. Imgard 20115
Mugavero, C.J. 41142
Muggeridge, Rosalind 45836
Muhlena, David 42161
Muir, Eleanor 40593
Muirhead, Frank H. 38673
Mujta, Dr. Józef Stanisław 31668
Mukai, Tetsuya 26805
Mukai, Tomoko 26853
Mukanova, N. 27074
Mukasa, Josephine 37828
Mukela, Manyando 49016
Mukulu 28765
Mulcahy, Fran 43411
Mulcahy, Michael 22499
Mulder, Dr. E.W.A. 29140
Mulder, Jenny 29069
Muldoon, Patrick L. 45927
Mulford, Hansen 46188
Mulholland, Hugh 38156
Mulk, Dr. Inga-Maria 35982
Mulka, Denise 39928
Mulkey, Terry 45519, 45520
Mull, Astrid 13976
Mullally, Matt 47027
Mullen, Beverly J. 42380
Mullen, Cindy 46074
Mullen, Kathy 46611
Muller, Dena 45752
Muller, Donald 41900
Muller, Jean-Paul 13213
Muller, Joe 44111
Muller, John 43417

Muller, Judith 45805
Muller, M. Gilles 49169
Muller, Norman 46703
Muller, Pam 47101
Mullers Bast, G.J. 29341
Mulligan, Dermot 22383
Mulligan, Therese 46941
Mullin, Amanda 46402
Mullin, D. 38168
Mullin, Marsha A. 44003
Mullins, Colleen 47153
Mullins, James 22484
Mullins, Margaret 22470
Mullins, Monica 37998
Mullins, Rose 38273
Mullins, Roy 46317
Mullins, Sam 39701
Mullio, Cara 48531
Mullis, Connie 45471
Mulqueen, Grace 22502
Mulvaney, Rebecca 41046
Mulvany, Dr. John 42320
Mummery, Brian 39289
Mun, Kyong Hyun 27157
Munakata, Pariji 26296
Munch, Jytte 09088
Munck, Jacqueline 13548
Munday, Graham K. 38305
Mundel, Ernst 15728
Munder, Heike 37389
Mundorff, Angelika 17161
Mundus, Doris 18419
Mundwiller, Mollye C. 44002
Mundy, James 46674
Muney Moore, Julia 44226
Munk, Dr. Jan 08680
Munk Pedersen, Hans 08828, 08829, 08831
Munksgaard, Jan Henrik 30616
Munktell, Ing-Marie 36358
Munnerlyn, Ron J. 41628
Munns, Judith 47652
Muno, Ed 46116
Muno Jordan, Iris 43091
Munoz, Carol 43119
Muñoz, Concha Carmona 35090
Munrde, Pamela E. 44559
Munro, Dr. David M. 39389
Munro, Gale 48403
Munro, J.A. 38454
Munro, Lewis 39271
Munroe, Alexandra 45820
Munroe, Dan L. 47192
Munroe, Pam 48293
Munroe Hjerstedt, E. 46205
Munshi, Prof. Supriya 21710
Munsick, Lee R. 46276
Munson, Julie 44105
Munson, Larry 47594
Munson, Robin 43609
Munstermann, Leonard 45698
Munt, Martin 40444
Munteanu, Simona 32492
Munteanu, Vasile 32535
Munthe, Adam 39781, 39992
Muntildeoz Rivera, Lorena 07419
Munyer-Branyan, Cheryl 45633
Munyikwa, D. 49028
Muolo, Vicenzo 24478
Mur, Pilar 34616
Mura-Smith, Collin 45885
Mura Sommella, Dr. Anna 25147, 25173, 25241, 25266
Muradjan, Rima Gevkorovna 33188
Muradov, Oraz 37819
Murakami, Isamu 26217
Murakami, Toshimasa 26793
Muramatsu, Masafumi 26897
Muramatsu, Teijiro 26249
Murariu, Dr. Dumitru 32468
Murase, Masao 26143
Murat, Francine 21291
Murata, Seiko 26578
Murati, Sulejman 33914
Muratore, P. Umberto 25642
Murauchi, Michimasa 26165
Murch, Cliff 05723
Murdin, Alexander 38288
Murdoch, Angus 46828
Murdoch, John 47366
Murdock, Gordon R. 45387
Murdock, Helen 01578
Murenina, G.P. 33508
Murerwa Kirigia, George 27108
Murgueítio de Montoya, Lucy 07459
Murillo Toro, Edificio 07432
Murken, Prof. Dr. Jan 19329
Murko, Matthias 19154
Murphey, F. Warren 44331
Murphy, Anne 46606, 47135
Murphy, Beth 45381
Murphy, D. 38911
Murphy, Dennis J. 45965
Murphy, J. 38750
Murphy, Dr. Jack A. 42887
Murphy, Joe 22509
Murphy, John 45355, 46437
Murphy, Kenny 41465
Murphy, Madge 44318
Murphy, Patricia 46077

Murphy, Patrick 42603
Murphy, Patrick T. 22413
Murphy, Paula 41159
Murphy, Randy 48809
Murphy, Rosalinde 22444
Murphy, Tricha J. 22405
Murphy, Valary 38144, 39690
Murra-Regner, Georg 16651
Murray, Alisdair 40843
Murray, Ann H. 46031
Murray, Holly 47751
Murray, Janice 40966
Murray, Jeffrey 43797
Murray, Johanne 05000
Murray, Karin G. 48181
Murray, Kay 22458
Murray, M. 05556
Murray, Mary 45456, 48170
Murray, Dr. Peter 00735, 00738
Murray, Peter 22403, 40820
Murray, Roddy 40614
Murrey, Grace 39355
Murzabekas, N. 27073
Musa, George 05140
Musango, Simon Peter 37829
Muscă, Luciana 32602
Muscat, Stefanie J. 44251
Muschwitz, Tanja 15903
Mușețeanu, Dr. Crișan 32467
Musgrave, Lee 43717
Musil-Jantjes, Angela 30741
Muširovski, Volodimir 37899
Muškalov, Sergej Michajlovič 32969
Musketa, Dr. Konstanze 17513
Musonda, Dr. Francis B. 49020
Musser, Bernice 42865
Musset, Daniele 12789
Mustaine, Beverly 44598
Musto, David F. 45698
Musty, Tony 38701, 38974, 38978, 39145, 40159, 40244
Muswasi, P. 35779
Musy-Ramseyer, Sylviane 36628
Muszała-Ciałowicz, Joanna 31937
Muto, Tetsu 26904
Muttenthaler, Dr. Roswitha 02993
Muya Wa Bitanko, Dr. Kamuanga 07641
Muzii, Dr. Rossana 24600
Mveng, Engelbert 04961
Mya, U San 28745
Mychajlunow, Lorraine 05368
Myerow, Cathy 48661
Myers, Dr. Arnold 38880
Myers, Bob 41108
Myers, Dr. Charles W. 45759
Myers, Jane 43480
Myers, Jeff 44224
Myers, Laura H. 48752
Myers, Maryann 43035
Myers, Mickey 47843
Myers, M.R. 39174
Myers, Pam 44612, 44613
Myers, Pamela L. 41275
Myers, Prof. Philip 41220
Myers, Dr. Thomas P. 44793
Myers Breeze, Camille 47810
Mygh, Liselotte 08996
Myhrén, Sture 35916
Myhrvold, Sissel 30741
Myland, Conny 38859
Myland, Mel 38859
Myllyharju, Taina 09892
Myllylä, Pälvi 10170
Myllymaa, Marju 09428
Myllymäki, Viljo 09726
Myltygaševa, Ljudmila Petrovna 32627
Mylyadi, Dr. Wulan Rujiati 22107
Myon, Kim Ik 27117
Mytton-Famié, Elisabeth 11569
Myzgina, V.V. 37842
Myzina, Larisa Ivanovna 32913
Naab, Michael 44458, 44459
Naar, Harry I. 44692
Nabačikov, Dr. V.A. 33107
Nabaura, Trudy 22631
Nabika, Hideyuki 26429
Nachtigäller, Roland 19125
Nacímento Brito, M.F. do 04354
Nacke, Josef 17276
Nad-Jerkovic, Erika 07687
Nadan, José 12414
Nadel, D. 22612
Nader, Georges S. 21295
Nadkarni, Dnyaneshwar 21950
Nadler, Dr. Rajaa 19052
Nadler Thomas, Genny 41533
Nadzeika, Bonnie-Lynn 45504
Naef, W. 44913
Naegel, Marie-Luise 37110
Nägele, Dr. R. 20113
Näse, Li 09669
Näslund, Erik 36238
Naess, Jenny-Rita 30877
Naeßl-Doms, Vinzenz 18673
Nätscher, Dr. Wolfgang 19351
Nævestad, Dag 30752
Nafziger, Helen 41254
Nagai, Akio 26217
Nagai, Dr. Akira 26749

Nagai, Taizan 26174
Nagai, V.G. 37877
Nagai, Yoshitaka 26195
Nagasaki, Motohiro 26623
Nagashima, Gyozen 26321
Nagashima, Kosuke 26289
Nagel, Prof. Dr. Günter 18871, 18886
Nager, Hans-Werner 36458
Naghawy, Aida 27052
Nagielło, Zbigniew 31763
Nagl, Michaela 02837
Nagorskij, Nikolaj Viktorovič 33410, 33462
Nagueira, Dr. Lenita W. Mendes 04021
Nagy, Dr. Aniko S. 21358
Nagy, Dr. Árpád 21383
Nagy, Imre 21427, 21428
Nagy, Dr. István 21383
Nagy, László 21493
Nagy, Rebecca 43584, 46775
Nagy-Molnár, Dr. Miklós 21444
Nahabedian, Mildred 48440
Nahon, Pierre 15114
Nahser, Dr. Siegmar 15945
Naidoo, Peter 34268
Nail, Nancy 42425
Nairne, Andrew 40147
Naish, Carolyn 39684
Naito, Makio 26779
Naivne, Sandy 39732
Najafi, M. 22281
Najera, Lionel 48334
Naji Sari, Ahmed 49011
Nakabayashi, Kazuo 26938
Nakagawa, Hajime 26742
Nakagawa, Misao 26969
Nakajima, Atsushi 26107
Nakajima, Prof. Jimi Naoki 04575
Nakajima, Tokuhiro 26347
Nakamura, Hiroshi 26660, 26696
Nakamura, Junsuke 26582
Nakamura, Makoto 26693
Nakamura, Minoru 26905
Nakamura, Nobuo 26342
Nakamura, Reiko 26938
Nakamura, Saihachi 26118
Nakamura, Satoru 26122
Nakano, Masaki 26152
Nakano, Seijiro 26821
Nakano, Yuzo 41643
Nakashima, Kunio 26099
Nakashima, Michiko 26567
Nakayama, Prof. Kimio 26798
Nakazawa, Ryuhei 27033
Nakrem, Prof. Hans Arne 30735
Nally, Flaget 41504
Namiki, Masashi 26571
Nance, Paul J. 44856
Nanfeldt, Mikael 35919
Nannen, Eske 16847
Nanni, Romano 26026
Nanu, Dan Basarab 32523
Nanzer, Angel Omar 00575
Naoki, Togawa 26854
Naomichi, Ishige 26774
Napier, John H. 45466
Náplavová, Dr. Marie 08698
Nápoli, Prof. Dr. José 00194
Naramore, Bruce E. 42460
Narbutaite, Gražina 27529
Nardelli, Lucia 23156
Nardi, Christopher J. 43281
Nardin, A. 13572
Narinskaja, Natalija Efimovna 33364
Narr, Claudia 19808
Narzt, Karl 02591
Nasalski, Zygmunt 31793
Nasarov, N. 37451
Nasby, Judith M. 05538
Nascimento, Leo 04136
Nash, Alyce 45602
Nash, Carol 44021, 44021
Nash, Lesley 44597
Nash, Dr. Steven A. 47311, 47325
Nasi, Stefano 24514
Nasir, Pervin T. 31029
Naski-Multanen, Marke 10143
Naski-Multanen, Marki 10145
Nasko, Siegfried 02601
Nasky, Cindy 43711
Nason, Dr. James 47529
Nason Davis, Robert 46967
Nasset, Yvette 43290
Nassi, Talma 22593
Nasu, Takayoshi 26667
Nasybullin, Émir Salimovič 32904
Natali, Dr. Antonio 23840
Nathan, Jaqueline S 41853
Nathans, David 42499
Natier, Michel 12704
Natter, Dr. Tobias G. 02953
Natterer, Sylvia 02764
Naturel, Michèle 11227
Natuschke, Peter 15472
Naudascher, Josef 18591
Nauderer, Ursula Katharina 16522
Nauert, Prof. Dr. Dr. Claudia 17391
Nauhaus, Dr. Gerd 20778
Naukkarinen, Tiina 09506
Nault, Gilles 06381

Naumann, Prof. Dr. Clas M. 16250
Naumann, Dr. Friedrich 18883
Naumann, Gerd 19413
Naumann, Heike 15989
Naumann, Peter 19132
Naumann, Rolf 17954
Naumann, Thomas 20378
Naumann-Steckner, Dr. Friederike 18166
Naumer, Sabine 18029
Naupp, Thomas 02772
Nause, Jean Pierre 11011
Nauta, Dr. J.F 29494
Nauta, Patience 42923
Nava, Dr. Cecilia 31278
Naval Mas, Antonio 34908
Navarro, Daisy A. 31383
Navarro, Elías Terés 34502
Navarro, Dr. Fausta 23856
Navarro, Mariana Varela 07400
Navarro Guitart, Jesús 34970
Navarro Linares, Antonio 34866
Navas Gutiérrez, Mariano 07571
Navascués, Pedro 35043
Navascués Benlloch, Pilar 34626
Navascués Benlloch, Pilar de 35014
Nave, Dr. Francine de 03152, 03175
Naveau, Jaques 12099
Naveaux, Ralph 45443
Navia, Olga Lucía 07448
Naville, Marc F. 37365
Nawafleh, Sami 27065
Nawka, Tomasz 15835
Nawrocki, Czesław 31471
Naylor, Dr. Bruce G. 05342
Naylor, Eleanor 47806
Nazieblo, Dr. Jerzy 32227
Nazionale, Nina 45858
Ndacyayisenga, Albert 33754
Ndege, Conchita F. 43817
Neaf, Oscar Angel 00387
Neagu, Marian 32479
Neal, George 43932
Neal, Dr. John R. 42377
Neale, Susan 06122, 06168
Nealis, Sharon 42724
Néar, Marie-José 14986
Neault, Caroline 42580
Neave, Ruth 38797
Nebel, Dr. Martin 20105
Nebes, Prof. Dr. Norbert 17946
Nebl, Rudolf 02632
Nebuloni, Dr. Gabriela 24175
Nečasová, Eva 08251
Necker, Hans 15685
Necker, L. 36646
Necker, Louis 14895
Nedelčeva, Cvetanka 04861
Nedelja, Anatoli Ivanovič 37838
Nedeljković, Dragana 33913
Nedelkovska-Dimitrovska, Liljana 27591
Nedeva, Galja 04932
Nedoma, Petr 08579
Neeb, Vanessa 48020
Needham, Dr. Claude 46339
Needham, Melanie 06792
Needle, John 38215
Neef, Almut 20011
Neel, David 43774
Neely, Alastair 05765
Neergaard, Mogens de 08958
Nees Holcomb, Sara 44741
Neff, Emily 44129
Neff, Jean W. 41183
Neff, John 48703
Nefzi, Tarak 37555
Negro Cobo, Marta 34630
Nehrer, Manfred 02912
Neich, R. 30104
Neichl, Brigitte 02933
Neidert, David 41203
Neidhart, Herbert 02428
Neighbours, Dr. K.F. 45911
Neil, Erik 45737
Neill, Teda W. 43385
Neilsen, Henry L. 48321
Neilsen, Kathrine 48623
Nejdl, Josef 08332
Neka, Suteja 22102
Nekrasov, Aleksandr Michailovič 33340
Nekrasov, Sergej Michailovič 33489
Nel, M. 34188
Nelgares Raye, José 34922
Nelišerová, Dr. Eva 33977
Nelje, Kerstin 36054
Nelley, Betty 30201
Nelly, Catherin 13806
Nelsen, Rick 47967
Nelson, Amanda 44251
Nelson, Arthur 48296
Nelson, Bob 46958
Nelson, Bryan 05529
Nelson, Carolyn 44648
Nelson, Cindy J. 44440
Nelson, Cortland 41838
Nelson, Daniel A. 44648
Nelson, Darrel 42820
Nelson, Doug 43096
Nelson, Ellie 05102
Nelson, Eric 48809

Nelson, Geoff 41062
Nelson, Gwen 42954
Nelson, Harold B. 44860
Nelson, Helen 47347
Nelson, Henry 38619
Nelson, Howard 44058
Nelson, James R. 42649
Nelson, John 39342, 43865, 43866
Nelson, Julie D. 46760
Nelson, Dr. Larry 46357
Nelson, Lee Ann 43804
Nelson, Lori 05656
Nelson, Mike 47443
Nelson, Mindy Honey 45898
Nelson, Morris 41717
Nelson, Nancy 42599
Nelson, Philip 39342
Nelson, Sarah E. 41145
Nelson, Stephen R. 47371
Nelson-Balcer, Mona 48642
Nelson-Mayson, Lin 47163
Nelsson, Cecilia 36061
Nelsson, Sigvard 36098
Němeček, Jaroslav 08327
Nemes, András 21536
Nemeth, Alice 06812
Nemeth, Elaine 06546
Németh, Pál 21334
Németh, Dr. Péter 21492
Nemeth Ehrlich, Dorica 07809
Nemetz, Johann 03015
Nemetz, Norbert 20673
Nemiroff, Diana 06084
Nenno, Dr. Rosita 19239
Nenonen, Yrjo 10130
Nenov, Dr. Nikolai 04803, 04804, 04807
Nenquin, Prof. Dr. J. 03433
Nentwig, Dr. Franziska 16814
Nenz, Cornelia 19574
Nenzioni, Gabriele 25377
Nepi, Dr. Chiara 23865
Nepočatych, Viktor Alekseevič 32747
Nepomuceno, Susan 41575
Nepputh, Fritz 16812
Néray, Katalin 21353
Nerchesseau, Daniel 13568
Nerdinger, Prof. Dr. W. 15549
Nerdinger, Prof. Dr. Winfried 18828
Neretniece, Anastasija 27376
Nerheim, Gunnar 30754
Neri, Joanne 40944
Nero, Don 48305
Nesbilt, Bill 05571
Nesbitt, Bill 05569
Nesbitt, Dr. Elizabeth 47529
Nesbitt, Melissa 47990
Neset, Karsten T. 30920
Nesheim, Jan 45279
Neshushtan, M. 22678
Nesin, Jeffrey D. 45243
Nesje Bjørlo, Aslaug 30820
Nesme, H. 12270
Nesmith, Michael 47422
Nespoli, T. 28917
Ness, Arlin E. 41097
Ness, Gary C. 42590, 45147, 45151
Ness, Dr. Gary C. 45742
Ness, Kim G. 05574
Nessell Colglazier, Gail 45098
Nesselrath, Dr. Arnold 48869, 48872, 48885
Nestler, Dr. Iris 18484
Nestler-Zapp, Dr. Angela 15681, 15682
Nestorova, Ani 04639
Neszmelyi, Adrienne 42984
Netel, Lies 29605
Stille Neto, Bernardo 04366
Neto, Luis 32346
Nette, Mary 45152
Netten, Dr. John 06352
Netter, Esther 44952
Netterlund, Karin 36217
Netuschil, C.K. 16544
Netzer, Dr. Nancy 42294
Neu, Noreen 06231
Neu, Dr. Stefan 18166
Neu-Kock, Dr. Roswitha 18165
Neubert, André 17813
Neubert, George W. 47260, 47260
Neubert, Hermann 18740
Neuburger, Dr. Susanne 02949
Neuer, D. 17667
Neufeld, Alice 06782
Neufeld, Carol E. 47918
Neuffer, Dr. Fr. O. 18605
Neugebauer, Rud. 15502
Neugebauer, Prof. Dr. Wolfgang 02874
Neugebauer-Maresch, Dr. J.-W. 02735
Neugent, Susan E. 41341
Neuhaus, A.F. 29489
Neuhaus, Dorothy E. 48216
Neuhaus, Johann Diederich 20620
Neuhoff, Stephan 18142
Neuhuber, Prof. Dr. W.L. 16914
Neuland-Kitzerow, Dr. Dagmar 16051
Neulinger, Adolf 01849
Neulinger, P. Maximilian 02178
Neumann, B. 01199
Neumann, Christoph 18763
Neumann, Dr. Dieter 02759

Neumann, Herbert 01848
Neumann, Timothy C. 42850
Neumann, Dr. U. 20228
Neumann-Eisele, Petra 18049
Neumayer, Dr. Heino 16059
Neumayer, W. 01667
Neumüllers, Marie 16584
Neuner, Ernst 03054
Neuner, Meinhard 02074, 02082
Neuner, Wolfgang 02082
Neunzert, Hartfrid 18303, 18305
Neuwirth, Karin 02963
Neuwirth, Karl 02695
Neuwirth, Waltraud 02929
Nevermann, Ulrike 17606
Neves, Julio 04515
Neves, Maria da Soledade S. 32277
Neveux, Yannick 13154
Nevill, Armanda 38299
Neville Blakey, W.H. 38333
Nevin, Michael E. 48252
Nevins, Christopher B. 43263
Nevitt, Elizabeth 41238
Nevraumont, Marcel 03457
Nevskaja, Galina N. 32701
Nevskij, Aleksej 33057
Newbery, C. 40257
Newbery, David 40254
Newbery, G. 40156
Newbery, Maria 40045
Newbury, Barbara 38283, 38405
Newcomb, Nancy 45858
Newhard-Farrar, Nancy 42490
Newhouse, Larry 48810
Newkirk, Sally 45657
Newland, Judy 41616
Newlands, David 05559
Newman, Ed 05575
Newman, Joanne K. 45587
Newman, Lilly 46864
Newnham, Kate 38351
Newsome, Mary 43012
Newsome, Steven C. 48332
Newton, Bette 42740, 44150
Newton, Christina 46872
Newton, Gael 00886
Newton, Paula H. 43147
Newton Gibson, Yasabel 46178
Neyer, Dr. Hans Joachim 17614
Neylon, Christina 22385
Neylon, Nicholas 46313
Neyses, Mechthild 20212
Neysters, Dr. Silvia 16738
Nezu, Kohichi 26900
N'Gele, Edward O. 27498
Nghien, Nguyen Thi 48983
Ngoubeli, Joseph 07645
Ngozi, Niobe 44117
Nguyên, T.P. 36724
Nhlane, Dr. Med 27611, 27614
Nias, Peter 38300
Niaufre, M. 13970
Niazi, Dr. Liaquat Ali Khan 31038
Nicandri, David L. 47924
Nicholas, Darcy 30240
Nicholas, Jeremy 40772
Nicholl, Boyd 41714
Nicholls, David 41197
Nicholls, Jane 45983
Nicholls, Stephen 38548
Nichols, Charlotte 47700
Nichols, John 47443
Nichols, Lawrence W. 48021
Nichols, Madeleine 45859
Nichols, Sarah 46510
Nichols, William O. 48230
Nicholsen, Charles 44045
Nicholson, Joseph 46463
Nicholson, Marilyn L. 43968
Nicholson, Robert 22439, 22460
Nicholson, Rosemary 39715
Nichterlein, Peter 20526
Nick, Lloyd 41500
Nickel, Douglas R. 47339
Nickell, Jeff 41440
Nickels, Sarah 45777
Nickens, Harry 46930
Nickerson, Cindy 42668
Nickerson, Dr. M.A. 43581
Nickl, Dr. B.E. 16119
Nicklaus, Jörg 15497
Nickles, Karen 43090
Nicod, Annelise 36738, 36743
Nicod, Bernard 37234
Nicod, Caroline 36860
Nicodemus, Dr. Victoria 28761
Nicola, A. 29949
Nicolai, Dr. B. 17502
Nicolai, David 46068
Nicolaisen, C. 09069
Nicolaisen, Dr. Jan 18405
Nicolas, Alain 12860
Nicolas, Jean 10364
Nicolau, Antoni 34573
Nicolau, Irina 32470
Nicolau, Sanda Gabriela 32622
Nicolaysen, Katja 30581
Nicolescu, Costion 32470
Nicoletta, Catherine 11361

Nicolini, Renato 25263
Nicoll, Jessica 46626
Nicolls, Andrea 48374
Nicolosi, Anthony S. 45929
Nicols, Marian 39845, 39846
Nicosia, Angelo 22910
Nicosia, Prof. Umberto 25216
Nicu, Mircea 32613
Niederalt, Michael 19885
Niederer, Robert 36801
Niederhöfer, Hans-Jörg 20105
Niederl, Dr. Reinhold 01922
Niedzielenko, Andrzej 31754, 31755
Niedźwiecki, Jan 31880
Niehaus, Dr. Andrea 16234
Niehoff, Dr. Franz 18309, 18310, 18313
Nield, M.J. 40749
Nield, Thenetta 47645
Niell-LLabrés, Francisca 35222
Nielsen, Anna Kathrine 08798
Nielsen, Christin 36028, 36029
Nielsen, Debbie 06304
Nielsen, Erik 09082
Nielsen, Ervin 09008
Nielsen, Hans 09054
Nielsen, Jan 46095
Nielsen, Jennifer 43491
Nielsen, Jens N. 08762
Nielsen, Johannes 09034
Nielsen, Jytte 08904, 09091
Nielsen, Keld 08783
Nielsen, Kim 48386
Nielsen, Kori L. 42673
Nielsen, Niels Jul 08933
Nielsen, Ole 08849
Nielsen, Poul Bryde 09071
Nielsen, Teresa 09103
Nielsen, Wendy 06266
Nielson, Jay 43390
Niemann, Dr. Carsten 17612
Niemann, Willi 18942
Niemeyer, Kirk 46112
Niemi, Marja 09983
Niemitz, Prof. Dr. Hans-Ulrich 18388
Nienur, Jennifer 43756
Nier, Eberhard 15802
Nieraad, Karla 20260
Niermann, Katrin 16264
Niero, Antonio 25949
Niesel, Bernd 17179
Niesner, Dr. Tomáš 08282, 08434
Nieszczerzewska, Elżbieta 31844
Nieuwdorp, Hans 03151
Nieuwstraten, Frits 29323
Nievera, Dr. Eduardo 31391
Nievergelt, Frank 37319
Nieves, Marysol 41915
Nieweg, J. 29443
Niewęgłowski, Stanisław 31995
Niewerth, Herbert 16666, 20388
Niggemann, Dr. Stefan 17921
Nigratschka, Kurt 17859
Nigro, Dr. Lorenzo 48872
Niinistö-Alanne, Arja 09920
Niizeki, Kimiko 26853
Nijsten, J. 29227
Nikbakhsh, M. 22273
Nikiforov, Valerij Ivanovič 33165
Nikita, Eleni S. 08206
Nikitine, Serge 12436
Nikitović, Lidija 33827
Niklasch, Wilfried 16553
Nikolaev, V.A.. 33381
Nikolaeva, Irina Alekseevna 33145
Nikolaeva, Lidija Dmitrievna 33202
Nikolajenko, Galina 37902
Nikolaou, Yorka 20897
Nikolasch, Dr. Franz 02299
Nikoleišvili, M.V. 15356
Nikolić, Dragan 33819
Nikolić, Dušica 33824
Nikolić, Jadranka 07695
Nikolov, Prof. Dr. Vasil 04827
Nikolova, Asja 04686
Nikolova, Ass.Prof. Dr. Diana 04846
Nikolova, Erika 04758
Nikolova, Petja 04846
Nikolova, Radka 04738
Nikoltsios, Vasilios 21194
Nikonov, Aleksandr K. 33028
Nikulin, Valerij S. 33497
Nill, Annegreth T. 42587
Nilsen, Laurel 48496
Nilsen, Rolf Erik 30519
Nilsen, Tore L. 30417
Nilson, Göran 35916
Nilson, Ylva 36194
Nilsson, Bo 36255
Nilsson, Christer 30478
Nilsson, Christin 35998
Nilsson, Håkan 36420, 36422
Nilsson, Harald 36364, 36364
Nilsson, Karin 35998, 36001
Nilsson, Marianne 36305
Nilsson, Rune 35956
Nilsson, Torsten 36115
Nimmich, Dr. Gunter 15970
Nimri, Mohamed 37595
Nimz, Tim 41781

Niniou-Kindeli, Vanna 20915
Nisbet, A. 40952
Nisbet, Peter 42042
Nishi, Yukitaka 26391
Nishida, Dr. Hiroko 26900
Nishidera, Masaya 26787
Nishikawa, Kyotaro 27015
Nishimura, Atsushi 27007
Nishitakaesuji, Nobuyoshi 26132
Nishitani, Noboru 26911
Nishizawa, Jun-ichi 26734
Nishizawa, Keiichi 26621
Niskz, Siiri 09989
Nissen, Dan 08926
Nissen, M.A.J.M. 29218
Nit, A. 29351
Niţă, Gabriela 32604
Nitsch, Hubert 02230
Nitsch, Dr. Ulla M. 16333
Nitta, Hideo 26484
Nitter, Marianne 30877
Nittmann, Karl 01821
Nittve, Lars 36262
Nitzschke, Katrin 16677
Niven, Catharine 39300
Nivière, Marie-Dominique 10231
Niwa, Masatoshi 26248
Nix, Dr. J.C. 29776
Nix, M. 39174
Nix, Nicole 19055
Nixon, Chris 42973
Nixon, Isabelle 05727
Nixon, James D. 42973
Nixon, Nigel 38581, 39993
Nixon, Roderick A. 48559
Nixon, Taryn 39718
Nixon, W.A. 01156
Niyama, Sadamasa 26857
Nizamiev, Muzip Tazievič 32896
Nižegorodova, Elena Vladimirovna 32685
Nko'o, Hulio 04962
Niemchuku Anyanwu, Dr. Starling E. 30359
N.N. 12736, 15556, 16099, 16100, 16661, 16707, 16712, 17165, 17607, 17607, 18075, 18157, 20115, 20115, 20220, 22020, 34335, 44869
Noack, Wita 16043
Noah, Randy 47509
Nobis, Dr. Norbert 17611
Noble, Alexandra 39632
Noble, Douglas R. 44224
Noble, Dr. Douglas R. 45244
Noble, Rhonda 01235
Nóbrega, Enrique 48914
Noda Gómez, Onaysi 07932
Nodine, Jane 47720
Nodzyńska, Marta 32204
Noe, Adrianne 48378
Noe, Per 08998, 08999, 09000, 09020
Noe, Pierre 03760
Noeding, Faye S. 47949
Nöhammer, Josef 01871
Noel, Albert 03362
Noël, Jacques 13253
Noël, Étienne 13938
Noel, William 41489
Noelmans, L. 03780
Nörenberg, Bernd 15427
Noever, Prof. Peter 02889
Noever, Peter 02929
Noguchi, Mitsunari 26166
Noguchi, Reiichi 26853
Nogueira, Abrelino 30105
Nogueira, Sandy 30105
Nogueira da Costa, Maria Inés 28724
Noh, Joon Eui 27297
Nohsoh, Toshio 26150
Noirot, André 10849
Noko, Oarabilke J. 03936
Nolan, Amy 47175
Nolan, Edward V. 47924
Nolan, Gail 39584
Nolan, Julia 38633
Nolan, Linda P. 46345
Nolan, Patrick B. 44176
Nolan, Peg 45139
Nolan Jones, Nancy 42463
Noland, Martin R. 47116
Nold, Carl R. 45029, 45030, 45032, 45034
Nolen, John 43829
Noli, Gino 28758
Noll, Linda M. 43966
Noll, Dr. Petra 16788
Nollar, Philip 48173
Nolle, Karl 16695
Nolley, Lance 44823
Nolte-Fischer, Dr. Hans-Georg 16540
Nombluez, Pieter 03490
Nomura, Harukata 26443
Nonesteid, Mark 43037
Nonestied, Mark 46501
Nonnenmacher, Eugen 16215, 16216
Noon, Patrick 45391
Noon, Rosemary 48567
Noordermeer, Aly 28911
Nooter Roberts, Mary 44900
Noppe, Catherine 03640
Nørager Pedersen, Erik 08769
Nørbach, Lars Chr. 08992
Nørbach, Lars Christian 08762

Nørballe, Inge 08826
Norbart, Rianne 28911
Norberg, Deborah 47356
Norbut Suits, Linda 47738
Norby, Lory 45065
Nordahl, Per 36392
Nordal, Bera 36192
Nordberg, Henri 10115
Nordbrock, Carol 41396
Norden, Linda 42042
Nordgren, Suneken 30746
Nordheim, Lutz von 20745
Nordin, Maxine 05594
Nordine, Dr. Malki 00068
Nordlinder, Gunnar 36273
Nordlund, Ivar 09425, 10042
Nordmo, Per E. 30531
Nordmo, Sverre 30517
Nordon, Deborah 45839
Nordqvist, Jørgen 08788
Nordström, Lena 36144
Nordstrom, Ralf 10159
Norell, Dr. Mark A. 45759
Norgren, Philip E. 47767
Norheim, Kari 30524
Norheim, Svein 30524
Noriega, Natividad 31437
Norland, Lissie 30513
Norlund, Yvonne 36219
Norman, Dr. D.B. 38462
Norman, Heather L. 43598
Norman, Jan 43847
Norman, Margaret Jane 48577
Norman, W.H. 40801
Normanby, Lady 40854
Normand, P. 40535
Normand, Rick 45738
Normann, Mark 40141
Normann, Øystein 30535
Noro, Masahiko 18145
Norovtseren, Oyuntegsh 28690
Norrington, S. 01501
Norris, Adrian 39443
Norris, Andrea S. 44686
Norris, B. 30124
Norris, Baden N. 30129
Norris, Johnny 41868
Norris, Dr. Patrick 44380
Northam, J. 06217
Northcote, P.S. 30270
Northrop Adamo, Amy 45836
Northwood, John 01257
Norting, Jack 43764
Nortmann, Dr. Hans 20212
Norton, Elaine 42062
Norton, Fran 47873
Norton, George 48570
Norton, I.S. 01170
Norton, Jessica A. 41183
Norton, Lyle 44616
Norton, Mary Lynn 46950
Norton jr., Richard W. 47616
Norton, Scott L. 43421
Norton, Susan E.S. 48352
Norton Moffatt, Laurie 47820
Norvell, Edward 47220
Norwood, Nancy 46948
Nory, Jean-Marc 14089
Noryńska, Barbara 31977
Nose, Dr. Martin 18893
Nosek, Elizabeth 44608
Noske, Dr. H. 16991
Noskova, Alla Anatoljevna 32919
Nosovic, Milorad 33823
Nota, Dr. Maria Teresa 25179
Nothnagl, Hannes 02328
Nothnagl, Reinhold 02671
Notin, Véronique 12610, 12616
Nottage, James H. 44217, 44891
Notteghem, Patrice 12407
Notter, Annick 13432, 13435
Nougarède, Martine 13341
Nougué, Cendrine 13076
Nouvel, Odile 13586
Nouyrit, H. 10969
Novák, Dr. László 21487
Novák, Dr. Pavel 08396, 08440
Novak, Stanislav 07696
Novak, Timothy 42527
Nováková, Dr. Lenka 08267
Novakovska, Nada 27587
Novellis, Mark de 40741
Novgorodova, Prof. M.I. 33084
Novoselova, Rimma Vjačeslavovna 33303
Novotná, Dr. Mária 34012
Novotná, Mariana 34007
Novotny, Deborah 41117
Nowack, Meg 48410
Nowacki, Dr. Henryk 31671
Nowacki, Marek 32015
Nowak, Holger 16497, 17944, 17952
Nowak, Joanna 31947, 32012
Nowak, Romuald 32192
Nowak, Włodzimierz 31925
Nowakyniak, Dr. Edmund 31857
Nowers, John 39033
Nowobilski, Dr. Józef Andrej 31695
Nowojski, Paweł 31644
Noyes, Julia 44790

Nozaka, Motoyoshi 26184
Nozet, Hervé 15024
Ntsema Khitsane, Julia 27495
Nuber, Dr. W. 18957
Nuculov, Georgi 04788
Nudds, Dr. J.R. 39894
Nudelman, Robert 44909
Nüesch, Ernst 36491
Nüesch, Rosmarie 37236
Nugent, Charles 39904
Nugent, M. 05454
Nugent, Randolph 45882
Nuki, Tatuto 26293
Nummelin, Esko 09944
Nummelin, Maria 09424
Nummelin, Rauni 10071
Numonova, Gulchehra Tojitinovna 37446
Nunes, Dave 46593
Nunes de Vasconcelos junior, Walter 04379
Núñez, César Marku 35659
Nuñez, Ramon 34746
Núñez Centella, Ramón 34748
Nunley, John 47134
Nunley, Larry 48105
Nunn, Chris 40651
Nunn, Dr. Tey Marianna 47426, 47427
Nunziati, Anna 23350
Nupen, Nikki 28767
Nurfeisova, Nurshamal Bekvossunovna 27072
Nurger, Heli 09332
Nuri, Kedir 09406
Nurkkala, Yrjö 10113
Nurmi, Virpi 09983
Nurmi-Nielsen, Anna 09983
Nusbaum, Pat 43179
Nussbaum, Patricia 36960, 37009
Nussbaum, Prof. R.A. 41220
Nussbaumer, Christiana 02726
Nussbaumer, Paul 36615
Nußbaummüller, Winfried 01745
Nusupova, D.N. 27308
Nutkins, Geoff 40502
Nuttall, Rick 34192
Nuyttens, M. 03265
Nyakas, Dr. Miklós 21425
Nyamabondo, Constantinus M. 37452
Nybak, Arne 47362
Nye, Steve 40335
Nye, Tom 41917
Nyegaard, Georg 21237
Nyein, U Kyaw 28735, 28739
Nyerges, Alexander Lee 42801
Nyffenegger, Kathrin 36544
Nygaard, Knut M. 30489
Nygren, Bitte 36231
Nygren, Kris 05451
Nykänen, Veijo 09957
Nykolyshyn, Z. 06828
Nykyforov, Viktor S. 37895
Nylander, Jane 41809, 44779
Nylen, Bob 42118
Nylén, Lars 36371
Nyman, Ola 36253
Nyman, Sven-Eric 36375
Nynoen, Paal 30752
Nys, Wim 03180
Nystad, Marianne 30921
Nyström, Hazze 08920
Nysveen, Aagot 44025
Nyujtó, Zsuzsa 21329
Nyunt, Kyaw 28752
Oaklander, Christine I. 41143
Oakley, Lisa 44517
Oakley, Stephen 47936
Oaks, Martha 43705
Oandasan, Crescencion 31334
Oanh, Phan 48990
Oates, Sarah 41306
Oatman, Michelle 45670
Obal, Franc 34133
O'Bannion, Tami 45324
O'Baoill, Eilis 40073
Obedat, Nassim 27040
O'Beirne, M.J. 39672
Ober, Jerry 41783
Oberchristl, Monika 02234
Oberfrank, Wilhelm 02257
Oberg, Paul Chancy 30367
Oberhänsli, Silvia 36691
Oberhänsli, Dr. This 36918
Oberhaus, Betty 42700
Oberländer, Rolf 15744
Oberlin Steel, Virginia 42060
Obermaier, Dr. Walter 03008
Obermeier, Christoph 19056
Obermeyer Simmons, Helen 43327
Obernosterer, Beatrix 02121, 02133
Obhof, Dr. Ute 17989
O'Bomsawin, Nicole 06041
Obradović, Slobodan 33822
Obrascova, Maja Aleksandrovna 33370
Obrecht, Elsa 37186
O'Brian, John 43376
O'Brien, David 22523
O'Brien, Eileen 45098
O'Brien, Freda 30318
O'Brien, Dr. G.G. 38913
O'Brien, Judith 44061
O'Brien, Kevin 44569

O'Brien, Kevin J. 44463, 44467
O'Brien, Maureen 46721
O'Brien, Michael J. 42552
O'Brien, Pam 45729
O'Brien, Patrick J. 48209
O'Brien, Ruairí 16676, 16680
O'Brien, Suzanne 43213
Obrist, Hans-Ulrich 13548
O'Bryen, Antoinette 22407
Obud, Renate 02758
Ocampo, Juan Carlos 00454
Ocaña, Maria Teresa 34586
O'Carroll, Helen 22547
O'Casaide, Peadar 22384
Ocello, Claudia 45891
Ochi, Catherine Megumi 26841
Ochi, Yujiro 26347
Ochoa, Cristina 44939
Ochoa, Maria 43975
Ochonko, Nikolaj Anatoljevič 33563
Ochsenmeier, Peter 17180
Ockershausen, Cindy Lou 48382
O'Connell, Bernard 46466
O'Connell, Daniel M. 46530
O'Connell, Michael 22396
O'Connor, Andrew 22446
Oconnor, Prof. Barry M. 41220
O'Connor, David 00704
O'Connor, Karen 43365
O'Connor, M. 30236
O'Connor, Thomas P. 22422
O'Connor, Tony 40777
O'Conor Nash, Marguerite 22390
Odawara, Kaname 26390
Odden, Tor 30796
Ode, Robert 11068
Odegaard, Nancy 48082
Odehnal, Petr 08705
O'Dell, Kathryn 45365
Odendaal, E.A. 34383
Odenhoven, Dr. S.L. 29864
Odenthal, Dr. Johannes 15987
Oder, Karla 34144, 34144, 34145
Odess, Daniel 43258
Odin, Samy 13562
Odoj, Romuald 32000
O'Donnell, Janice 46724
O'Donnell, Molly 44329
O'Donnell, P. 40131
O'Donovan, Hugh J. 45433
Odrowąż-Pieniążek, Janusz 32110
Odum, R. Andrew 48020
Oechslin, Dr. Ludwig 36630
Oegema, D. 34353
Öhlinger, Walter 03001
Öhlknecht, Rupert 02663
Öhman, Nina 36295
Öhman, Volga 36049
Oehme, Ursula 18419
Oehms, Günter 19001
Öjesjö, Mona Lisa 36041
Ökten, Haydar 37764
Ölçer, Dr. Nazan 37710
Oellers, Dr. Adam C. 15377, 15378
Oelschlägel, Dr. Petra 15901
Oelschlaeger-Garvey, Barbara 45076
Oerichbauer, Edgar S. 44240
Örsi, Dr. Julianna 21600
Oertlin, Jean-Paul 13388
Oeschger, Dr. Bernhard 17991
Östberg, Maths 36410
Östberg, Wilhelm 36240
Österholm-Granqvist, Sonja 10160
Oesterlein, Arnulf 15632
Österlund, Petter 36307
Oesterreicher, Claudia 03001
Oesterwind, Dr. Bernd C. 18668
Oetterli, Christoph 37310
Oettingen-Wallenstein, Fürst zu 16254
Oettingen-Wallerstein, Fürst zu 17615, 20380
Oettinger, Dr. Marion 47260
Öttl, Josef 15839, 15857, 18264
Oexle, Dr. Judith 16693
Özbey, Şahin 37673
Özcan, Hilmi 37733
Özçelik, Serpil 37712, 37714
Özdemir, Abdulhalik 37630
Özek, Halil 37702
Özerdem, Hürrem 37609
Özeren, Öcal 37762
Özgen, Emine 37635
Özgerey, Mehmet 37707
Özkütük, Zafer 37640
Özsağır, Ahmet 37737
Öztürk, Erdal 37713
Offers, Donald 36479
Offringa, D.C. 34353
Offroy, Martine 14938
Offutt, Cathy 44208
O'Floinn, Raghnall 22444
O'Foighil, Prof. Diarmaid 41220
Ogata, Hisanobu 26171
Ogawa, Toshiro 26826
Ogden, Dale 44224
Ogden, Sharon 30123
Oggenfuss, Daniel 18918
Ogilive, Peter 40432
Ogle, Brian 38362
Ogle, Nigel 30177

Ogle, Susan F. 48648
Ogliari, Prof. Francesco 25071
Ogny, Jean d' 12144
O'Gorman, Dr. Jodie 43054
O'Gorman, Therese 41352
O'Gorman, Tim 43418
O'Grady, John 38413
Ogrodniczak, Tomasz 31901
O'Halloran, Jim 30261
O'Hanlon, Dr. Michael 40153
O'Hara, Bruce 48041
O'Hara, Michael 40784
Ohba, Masatoshi 26938
Ohe, Dr. Werner von der 16455
O'Hear, John 45401
O'Hern, John D. 43169
Ohlsen, Dr. Nils 16847
Ohlsson, Birger 35832
Ohm, Ruth 41639
Ohmann, Agathe 09024
Ohmura, Etumasa 26517
Ohnemus, Dr. Sylvia 16336
Ohngemach, Dr. Ludwig 16792
Ohno, Akira 27016
Ohno, Masaji 26587
Ohrt, Hans Dieter 05655
Ohrt, Karsten 09014
Ohrt, Nils 08989
Ohsaki, Kuninori 26490
Ohta, Yoshinori 26156
Ohtsubo, Kenji 26969
Øien, Elisabeth Adelheide 30481
Oiler, Gary 47855
Oiler, Sue 47855
Oilliamson, Comtesse d' 11765
Oinas, Tapani 10002
Ojalvo Prieto, Roberto 07524
Ojeda Sato, Alonso 07528
Ojha, M.B. 21830
Okabe, Nobuyuki 27002
Okachi, Yukio 26564
Okada, Akiko 26239
Okada, Hidenori 26938
Okajima, Hasashi 26938
Okamoto, Takenobu 26382
Okániková, M. 34079
Okano, Kiheita 26765
Okawa, Eiji 26335
Okaya, Michiko 43068
Okazaki, Kyoichi 27002
Okazawa, Kunro 26608
O'Keefe, Barbara K. 42629
O'Keeffe, Cheryl W. 41383
O'Keeffe, Tony 37977
Oker-Blom, Teodora 09492
Okimoto, Hiroshi 26214
Okkenhaug, Eli 30412, 30413, 30414
Okoshi, Hisako 26693
Okubo, Tokiko 27009
Okumiya, Kaku 26391
Okumura, Yoshitsugu 26514
Okura, Haruhiko 26400
Olachea, Elena 28101
Olaczola, Juanjo 34514
Olano Trujillo, Manuel José 07565
Olason, Vésteinn 21667
Olausson, Magnus 36088, 36265
Olbrantz, John 47208
Olde Dubbelink, R.A. 29657
Oldeman, Dr. L.R. 29977
Olden, Sam 48782
Oldenburg, Rie 21233
Oldenburger, Julie 41223
Oldham, Terry 47104
O'Leary, Daniel E. 46626
Olejniczak, Józef 31881
Olerud, Becky 42938
Olfra, Michelle 45438
Olijnyk, Michael 46521
Oliva, Francisco Miguel González de la 34865
Olivarelli, Sebastiano 24785, 24786, 24787
Olivas, Art 47427
Olivas, Arthur 47429
Olive Garrard, Jacqueline 00640
Olivé Serret, Prof. Enric 35513, 35514
Nunes de Oliveira, Adilson 04083
Oliveira, Dr. José Carlos 32242
Oliveira, Nicolas de 39716
Oliveira Caetano, Dr. Joaquim 32269
Oliveira Mesquita Spränger, Paulo Roberto 04390
Oliveira Rodrigues, Adélia E. de 03978
Oliver, André 11152
Oliver, Dr. Graham 38481
Oliver, Graham 39830
Oliver, Katherine C. 45047
Oliver, Keith 06846
Oliver, Robyn 01116
Oliver Joliffe, Ruth 41798
Oliveri del Castillo, Patrizia 26030
Olivié, Jean-Luc 13586
Olivier, Prof. J. 34317
Olivier, Louis 14309
Olivo, Sandra 45308
Ollenburger, Jeff 44183
Ollikainen, Anja 10186
Ollingen, Elisabeth 02141
Ollman, Arthur 47283
Olmedo, Freddy 09168
Olmedo Patiño, Dolores 28164

Olmo Fernández, Jesús del 34634
Olmos Muñoz, Pedro 06899
Olmstead, Dr. Richard 47529
Oloffson, Jan 35851
Olsberg, Nicholas 05894
Olsen, Dr. Arnold 43984
Olsen, Betsy 43348
Olsen, Claus 09029
Olsen, Johanne 21239
Olsen, John 30637
Olsen, Dr. Knapp 45952
Olsen, Maude 48716
Olsen, Phyllis J. 43720
Olsen, Sandra H. 41990
Olsnes, Aanund 30572
Olson, Alice 42143
Olson, David 45944
Olson, Dona A. 46535, 47042
Olson, Dorothy 41344
Olson, Janis 41604
Olson, Joan 47625
Olson, Kathleen 44758
Olson, Kathryne 46224
Olson, Kathy 46229
Olson, Kristina 45499, 45500
Olson, Nicky L. 42741
Olson, Oliver 47774
Olson, Paula 42545
Olson, Roberta 47467
Olson, Ruth Ann 44683
Olson, Susanne 48297
Otero, Suzanne 46621
Olson, Thomas H. 47042
Olson, William 06139
Olson Peters, Ruth 44656
Olsson, Daniel Sven 35882
Olsson, Daniels Sven 35883
Olsson, Mari-Louise 36097
Olszak, Eliane 11819
Olszanowski, Zdzisław 32187
Oltean, Dr. Vasile 32450
Olthoff, Gabriele 20522
Oltjenbruns, Dr. Kevin 43381
Oltmans, Kay 41835
Olucha Montins, F. 34693
O'Malley, Dennis M. 46718
O'Malley, Jeanette 46305
O'Malley, Kathleen 42513, 42514, 42515
Oman, Dr. Hiltrud 02567
Oman, Richard G. 47090
Omar, Hadmar 37471
Omar, Hamad H. 37457, 37468, 37469, 37470
Omar, R.H. 34228, 34229, 34230, 34231
O'Mara, John F. 06342
O'Meara, John 41303
Omedes, Dr. Anna 34557
Omer, Prof. Mordechai 22757, 22775
Ometto, Giulio 25748
Omieczyński, Witold 31757
Ommen, Dr. Eilert 19102
Onaga, Stephen 46750
Ondevilla, Alex 31288
Ondish, Andrea 48150
Ondrejčeková, Zora 33978
Ondrušeková, Dr. Anna 34046
O'Neil, Paul 41452
O'Neill, Anthony 39181
O'Neill, Caroline 00725
O'Neill, Colleen 05274
O'Neill, Heidi 45794
O'Neill, John 45815
O'Neill, John J. 41457
O'Neill, Mark 39039, 39046
O'Neill, Peter 01610
O'Neill, Sheila C. 48573
O'Neill, Vicki 01344
Onodera, Hiroshi 26611
Onodera, Reiko 26853
Onorevoli, Dr. Giuseppe 25698
Onyejekwe, Dr. Umebe N. 30363
Oomen, Dr. Th. 03146
Oost, T. 03742, 03743, 03744
Oost, Tony 03740
Oostdijk, Dr. Alexandra E. 29962
Oosterbaan, A. 29067
Oosterhof, H. 29880
Oosthoek-Bogaard, A.W. 29546
Oostra, Dr. R.J. 28881
Ootukasa, Mitukuni 26638
Ooyama, Masaaki 26494
Op de Beeck, Bart 03275
Op de Beeck, Jozef 03616
Op de Beek, R. 29031
Opan, Ahmet 37789
Opdenberg, Laurence 03283
Operta, Mevlida 03925
Opie, Robert 40871
Opinel, Annick 14299
Opolá, Valentina 27402
Opp, Edmund 43233
Oppenheim, Roy 36849
Oppenhimer, Ann 46877
Opperman, G. 34364
Oppermann, Prof. M. 17519
Oppitz, Prof. Dr. Michael 37416
Opstad, Jan-L. 30939
Oquendo, Dante 31440
Orač-Stipperger, Dr. Roswitha 01930, 02674

Oratowska, Barbara 31794
O'Rawe, A.C. 40131
Oražem, Prof. Dr. Vito 16961
Orbons, Dr. A. 29430
Orchard, Dr. Karin 17611
Ordine, Mauriziano 25645
Ordoš, Dr. Ján 34049
Ore, Phyllis 06280
Orear, Tammy S. 45010
Orebäck-Krantz, Elisabeth 36194
Oredsson, Prof. Lars-Göran 36058
Orefici, Giuseppe 31231
Oreglia, Luciano 23052
Orehovec, Martina 34122
O'Reilly, Margaret 48057
O'Reilly-Lawrence, Priscilla 45727
Oremus, Frederick L. 45648
Oren, Dan 22576
Orfali, Dalila 00046
Orgeix, Charles-Louis d' 12672
Orgonikidze, I. 15365
Oriol, Calvo 34483
O'Riordan, E. 22514
O'Riordan, Ian 38873
Orlandi, Giuseppe 26044
Orlando, Fran 45947
Orlando González, Jorge 07390
Orlić, Alfons 07808
Orloski, Julie 47517
Orlov, Evgenij Michajlovič 33461
Orlov, Viktor 32687
Orłowski, Jarosław 31622
Orlson Agbo, Raymond 20791
Ormerod, Robin 05694
Ormhaug, Knut 30412, 30413, 30414
Ormiston, O. 40067
Ormond, Dr. Rupert 39957
Ormonde, Dr. Helena 32237
Ornauer, Elisabeth 02963
Ornsby, Philip 39183
Oroianu, Silvia 32611
Orona, Blanca 43119
Oropeza Segura, Manuel 28355
Orosz, Helma 20503
Orozco, Prof. Margarita V. de 27942
Orozco, Sylvia 41417
Orozco Móron, Edna Maria 28191
Orr, Brenda P. 05879
Orr, Charlene 45274
Orr, Dr. Patrick J. 22473
Orr-Cahall, Christina 48538
Orrick, Mary Norton 46331
Orro, Leena 09591
Orsi, Dr. Oriana 24092
Orsini, Ph. 14928
Orskou, Gitte 08769
Ortal, Dr. R. 22637
Ortega, Enric 35671
Ortega, Luis Angel 35390
Ortega DeSantis, Diana 47429
Ortega Rivera, Enric 35671
Ortel, Gustav-A. 16397
Ortenzi, Prof. Alfio 22955
Ortiz, Emilio I. 47432
Ortiz, Gustavo A. 07397
Ortiz, Rosa 34572
Ortiz Crespo, Alfonso 09201
Ortíz Lan, José E. 27800
Ortíz Muñoz, Idania 07481
Ortiz Volio, Melania 07662
Ortmeier, Dr. Martin 18664, 18666
Ortner, Josef 02947
Ortner, M. Christian 02895
Orton, Anna 40816
Orton, Donald 47762
Oruch, Sam 46119
Orzsi, Zoltán 21316
Osamu, Dr. Izumi 26733
Osborn, Rachel 41143
Osborne, Bernard 48684
Osborne, Duncan 37976
Osborne, Lois I. 42486
Osborne, Peter 46599
Osborne, S. 39527
Osborne, Victoria 40969
Oscarsson, Ulla 36146
Oselies, David 04971
Oset, Hans Petter 30565
O'Shaughnessy, Margaret 22471, 45801
O'Shea, Deborah H. 46997
O'Shea, John 41219
O'Shea, Patrick B. 22501
O'Shea, William A. 05782
O'Shea Schmieg, Shannon 41326
Oshel, Laurie 43617
Oshima, Seiji 26917
Oslen, John C. 05367
Oslund, Christopher 05541
Osman, Prof. Ali Mohamed 35763
Osmond, Lynn 42314
Ospina Cubillos, Carlos Enrique 07427
Ospina de Muñoz, Esperanza 07540
Ospina Navia, Francisco 07589
Ospino de la Rosa, José 07476
Osrin, Myra 34202
Osses, Dietmar 16202, 16666
Ostapova, Svetlana 37896
Østårgård, Niels Jøan 09067
Ostarhild, Dr. H. 18726

Ostaszewska, Stanisława 32032
Østein Ustvedt, C.M. 30746
Osten, Dr. Till 20105
Ostendorf, Dr. Thomas 20155, 20156
Ostenrieder, Dr. Petra 19236
Østerås, Bodil 30894
Osterhus, Cynthia B. 47219
Ostermann, Françoise 36626
Ostermiller, Jerry 41309
Østervig, Torsten 08974
Osticresi, Dr. Patrizio 23862
Ostlund, Ralph 45746
Ostojić, Milan 33928
Ostrenko, Wit 47943
Ostritz, Dr. S. 19635, 20465
Ostrosky, Amelia 48539
Ostrouchova, Marina Georgievna 32981
Ostrow, Mindy 46218
Ostrow, Victor 47513
Ostrowski, Prof. Jan 31729
Ostrum, Meg 45309
O'Suilleabhain, Sean 22366
O'Sullivan, Dr. A.M. 22558
O'Sullivan, Keith M.C. 38470
O'Sullivan, Mary 22496
Oswald, Dr. Niklaus 37393
Osyra, Tadeusz 31679
Ôta, Motoji 26912
Otani, Kazuhiko 26899
Otani, Shogo 26938
Otaola, Pablo 35599
Otavová, Marie 08737
Otero, álvaro 07461
Otke, Natalja Pavlovna 32638
Otkovyč, Dr. Vasyl 37887
Otomo, Akira 27025
Otomo, Tsutomu 26562
O'Toole, Judith H. 43821
Otsuka, Ronald 42885
Otsuka, Yoshio 26978
Ott, Irene 17098
Ott, John H. 44750
Ott, Lili R. 46131
Ott, Prof. Dr. Ulrich 18619
Ott, Wendell 47968
Ott, Wolfgang 20501
Otte, Prof. 03573
Otte, Andreas 16654
Otte, Stacey A. 41426
Otte, Wulf 16293
Ottenbacher, V. 16139, 16140, 16141
Otterspeer, Prof. Dr. W. 29517
Ottilinger, Dr. Eva 02906
Ottinger, Bénédicte 14709, 14710, 14711
Otto, John 42080
Otto, Kristin 20738
Otto, Martha 42590
Otto, Dr. Sigrid 15920
Otto, Veronika 19743
Otto-Hörbrand, Martin 20099
Ottomeyer, Prof. Dr. Hans 15939
Otton, Dr. William G. 42643
Ottosson, Jon Gunnar 21658
Ottou Onana, Irène 04954, 04958
Ottrubay, Dr. Stefan 01942
Otttaviani, Jean-Claude 10283
Otwell, Maureen 47162
Otzen, Dr. Peter 17303
Ouarzazi, Abdul Wahed 34647
Ouellet, Nicole 06197, 06210
Ouellet, Raynald 05885
Ouellette, Lenore 44986
Ourecky, Irma 48617
Ourmieres, Jean-Guy 14489
Outerbridge, Amanda 03889, 03890
Ovalle Neira, Pedro Ubert 07585
Ovečkinaova, Olga 33434
Overbeck, Prof. Dr. Bernhard 18913
Overbeck, Gertrud 16335
Overdiep, Dr. G. 29155
Overlie, Jill 44877
Overmyer, Lorraine 43013
Overstreet, Laura 41133
Overton, Jonathan 38123
Oviedo de Coria, Beatriz 00569
Ovsjankina, Ljudmila Vladimirovna 33611
Owczarski, Marian 46177
Owczuk, Tadeusz 31985
Oweis, Iman 27064
Owen, Ann 39553
Owen, Gwilym 39553
Owen, Paula 47257, 47263
Owen, Richard 39472
Owen, Thomas S. 48043
Owen Walker, Elizabeth 42892
Owens, Heather 45544
Owens, Joseph J. 48249
Owens, Marshall 44092
Owens, Sue Ellen 42830
Owens-Celli, Morgyn 44857
Owers, Lorna 38808
Owyoung, Steven D. 47134
Oxley, Nicola 39716
Oya, Mina 26873
Oyama, Prof. K. 26420
Oygur, Dr. Sule 45892
Oyuela, Raul M. 42627, 45288
Ozaki, Masaaki 26938
Ozanam, M. Yves 13597

Ozay, Alev 37710
Ožegova, Ljudmila Ivanovná 32926
Ozola, Agrita 27462
Ozola, Ārija 27358
Ozolina, Vita 27402
Paajanen, Kyllikki 09659
Paap, Hans-Uwe 18339
Paarlberg, Bill 47697
Paarlberg, S. 29173
Paas, Dr. 16780
Paas, Dr. Sigrun 18602
Paaverud, Merl 41720, 48638
Paaverud, Merlan E. 41721, 41722, 46332
Pabian, Roger K. 44793
Pabst, Fieke 28911
Pabst, Stewart J. 42613
Pacciarelli, Dr. Marco 24092
Paccioretti, Cecilia 48479
Pace, Dr. Lorenzo 48159
Pace, Richard 40554
Pace-DeBruin, Margaret 41827
Pacere, Tifinga Frédéric 04939
Pačev, Nikolaj 04722
Pache, Pierre 37354
Pacheco, Anelise 04351
Pacheco, Diane 41910
Pacheco, Gustavo 04299
Pachiyanni, Phani 21028
Pachner, Joan 45551
Pachnicke, Prof. Peter 19177
Pacholik, Kazmimierz 32151
Pachomova, Nadežda Petrovna 32776
Pachter, Marc 48376, 48382
Pacini, Marina 45234
Pacjukov, Vladimir V. 32994
Packard, Vance 42617
Packauskas, R. 43971
Packer, Dr. Claude 26071
Packer, Nancy 46402
Packheiser, Michael 18765, 18766
Paczkowski, Dr. Jörg 20532
Paczkowski, Dr. Renate 18076
Paczos, Andrzej 31631
Padalkina, Olga Viktorovna 32671
Paddock, D. 40809
Paddock, Eric 42882
Paddock, Dr. J.M 38584
Paddock, Dr. John 40085
Paderni, Loretta 25238
Padgett, Michael 46703, 46911
Padhy, Dr. K. P. 21915
Padhy, Dr. K.P. 21880, 21995
Padian, Kevin 41646
Padurariu, Nicolae 32470
Pärdi, Heiki 09383
Paesano, Dr. Ciro 23548
Pätzold, Winfried 17820
Pagac, Gerald J. 45412
Pagano, Dr. Denise Maria 24598
Pagano, Sergio 48867
Page, Casey 47146
Page, Chris 38663
Page, Eric 44393
Page, Gregory A. 47702
Page, John 38122
Page, Dr. Jutta Annette 42637
Page, Kathryn 45731
Pagé, Suzanne 13548
Pagella, Dr. Enrica 25736
Pagès, Solange 12457
Pagliardi, M. Nicoletta 25239
Pagnotta, Philippe 14598
Pagot, Serge 13266
Pagulayan, Teresita L. 31373, 31379
Pahlke, Dr. Rosemarie E. 16661
Pahlow, Martina 20193
Paige Linn, Nancy 46698
Paillard, Ph. 12737
Pailler, Henri 11663, 13062
Paillet, Antoine 14797
Paillet, Patrick 14344
Pain, Ron 40339
Paine, Susan W. 41817
Paine, Dr. Timothy D. 46918
Paine, Tony 30122
Paine, Wesley M. 45622
Painter, Bill 44378
Painter-De Monte, Y.Z. 48078
Païpetú, Andreas 21033
Pais de Brito, Joaquim 32308
Pais Pinto, Joaquim 00088
Paisley Cato, Dr. 47295
Paiva, Ricardo Luís 32347
Paizis-Paradelis, Constantin 21124
Pajović, Maja 33634
Pajskrová, Dr. Jana 08349
Pak, Valentin V. 27076
Pakesch, Peter 01921, 01922
Pakkala, Taru 09411
Pakoma, Katariina 09593
Pakuningrat, Maulana 22095
Pakzad, Dr. Amir 17609
Pal, Raj 40806, 40822
Pal, S.N. 21903
Pala, Valter 25360, 25363
Palacios i Manuel, Josep 34655, 34656, 34658
Palacpac, Remedios 31350
Palacz, Tomasz 31862
Palágyi, Dr. Sylvia 21608

Palamarz, Elisabeth 10060
Palavonov, D. 37444
Palella, Dr. Graciela Elizabeth 00310
Palermo, Jeanne 42800
Palisse, A. 14907
Páll, Dr. István 21540
Pall, Martina 01917
Palladino-Craig, Allys 47931
Pallan, Norbert 02456
Pallanca, Dr. Claude 28670
Pallavicini, Maria Camilla 25153
Pallestrang, Kathrin 02960
Pallmert, Sigrid 37393
Pallozola, Christina 42530
Pálmason, Ólafur 21657
Palmberg Eriksson, Stina 36128
Palmeiri, John 41907
Palmenaer, Els de 03141
Palmer, Lord 38818
Palmer, A.B. 41372
Palmer, Cheryl 42243
Palmer, Dr. C.J. 39189
Palmer, Mike 38046
Palmer, Oonagh 38976, 39099
Palmer, Peregrine 40899
Palmer, Ros 40718
Palmer, Sharon S. 44482
Palmgren, Kaj 09427
Palmgren, Ola 35998, 36001
Palmquist, Dr. Lena 36269
Palmquist, Linda 42607
Palo-oja, Ritva 10086
Paloheimo, George B. 47417
Palokangas, Markku 09513, 09523, 09529, 09530
Palombo, Aldo 46010
Palombo, Ionah 22629
Palomero, Santiago 35545
Palomo, Antonio 21255
Palop, José Alcántara 34487
Palou Sampol, Joana M. 35233
Palov, Dr. József 21544
Palsa, Raija 09786, 09787
Palsa, Raja 09788
Pálsson, Lýdur 21631, 21632
Paltenghi, Barbara 36901
Paluck, Jayne 06406
Palzerová, Hana 08344, 08346
Pamart, Jean-Luc 13367
Pambrun, Sam 46335
Pamlényi, Klara 21443
Pamperin, David L. 44554
Pamuk, Ömer 37777
Pan, Giuseppe 24692
Pan, Junxiang 07219
Pan, Zheng 07223
Pan, Zhenzhou 06980
Panabière, Louis 28100
Panafieu, Bruno de 14290
Panagiotopoulou, Anastasia 20873
Panajotov, Vladimir 04723
Panamaroff, Emilia 06406
Pañares, Tonette 31315
Panaskin, Vladimir Vasiljevič 32710
Panawatta, Senarath 35757
Panayotova, Dr. S. 38454
Panazza, Dr. Gaetano 24207
Pančeva, Petrana 04608
Pančeva, Radka 04914
Panczenko, Dr. Russell 45067
Panda, Prof. C. 21914
Pandey, A.K. 21965
Pandey, Dr. S.N. 21728, 21790
Pandolfi, Sylvia 28206
Pandžić, Ankica 07822
Panek, Kornelia 16873
Paner, Henryk 31568
Panese, Prof. Dr. Francesco 36862
Pang, Toni 44256
Pangburn, D.A. 46899
Panhorst, Michael W. 47816
Panić, Djordje 33912
Paniccia, Antonio 25965
Panizza, Marco 25663
Panjević, Nikola 03929
Panjuškin, A.D. 33049
Pankok, Eva 17861
Pannabecker, Rachel K. 45999
Panne, Dr. Kathrin 16452
Panneton, Jean 06645
Pannewitz, Otto 19963
Panni, Frédéric 11978
Panoski, Naum 27595
Pansi, Dr. Heinz 02023
Pant, Kurt 02984
Pant, Dr. Madhu 21773
Panteghini, Ivo 23206
Pantellini, Claudia 36880
Panter, Dr. Armin 19864
Panter, John 47289
Pantoja, Dianne 42064
Pantoja, Hernán Gil 07520
Panțuru, Prof. N. Ioan 32463
Panvini, Dr. Rosalba 23274
Pany, Franz Norbert 19011
Panzanaro, Mauro 24144
Paola de Picot, Mercedes di 00167
Paoletta, Dr. Donald 44781
Paoli, Arturo 23280
Paoli, Feliciano 25853

Paolillo, Dr. Antonio 23686
Paolillo, Giuseppe 23031
Paolozzi Strozzi, Dr. Beatrice 23879
Paolucci, Dr. Antonio 23837
Papa, Prof. Cristina 23483, 25883
Papachristodoulou, Dr. Joannis 21141
Papadakis, N. 20810
Papadakis, Dr. Nikos 21158
Papademetriou, Dr. Eleni 08195
Papadopoulos, A. 08198
Papadopoulos, Prof. N. 20882
Papadopoulou, Eleni 20915
Papadopoulou-Pangou, K. 21018
Papaefthymiou, Eleni 20897
Papageorgiou, Ioannis 21048
Papagno, Dr. Francesco Saverio 24855
Papait, Jean 11170
Papakonstantinou, Maria-Photini 21039
Papaldo, Dr. Serenita 25149
Papangeli, Kalliopi 20944
Papantoniou, Ioanna 21092
Papararo, Jenifer 06593
Paparella Treccia, Raffaelle 24870
Paparone, Guiseppe 25665
Papazian, Aline 46309
Papazoglou, Lena 20873
Papco, Ján 33956
Papendieck, Dr. Christine 20390
Papendorf, Dorothee C. 19840
Papet, Edouard 13596
Papies, Dr. Hans Jürgen 16075, 16086
Papike, Dr. James J. 41102
Papillard, Marie Laure 15093
Papin-Drastik, Y. 11443
Papone, Elisabetta 23993
Papounaud, Benoît-Henry 14218
Papović, Stanko 33826
Pappas, Elizabeth 43251
Pappi, Evangelia 21090
Papuc, Gheorghe 32424, 32501
Paradis, Michèle 06005, 06646
Paradowski, Dr. Stefan 37300
Páramo, Amanda Lucía 07366
Paramonov, Vladimir Aleksandrovič 33631
Paraskevas-Gizis, Evaggelos 21197, 21199, 21200
Parberg, Dee 46702
Pardee, Jean 43052
Pardilla, Helena 07610
Pardini, Prof. Edoardo 23864
Pardo, Alfredo 07394
Pardo, Rengifo 07385
Pardue, Diana 46476
Pardue, Diana R. 45876
Pare, Glenn 47386
Paredes Giraldo, Maria Camino 35249
Parent, Béatrice 13548
Parent, Geraldine 06109
Parent, Dr. Thomas 16666
Paret, John J. 41392
Pargner, Dr. Birgit 18841
Parham, Herbert S. 43904
Parikka, Anne 09448
Parillo, James D. 47462
Parisch, Manfred 02442
Parise, Dr. Roberta 24736
Pariset, Jean-Daniel 13598
Parish, Suzanne D. 44378
Parisi, Prof. Vittorio 24809
Park, Janette A. 39397
Park, You Chul 27146
Park Curry, Dr. David 46891
Parke, David L. 44004
Parke, Julie 44969
Parke, Susan 44532
Parker, Cheryl Ann 48513
Parker, David 43389
Parker, Donna 41849
Parker, Eris 30119
Parker, Harry S. 47311, 47325
Parker, Herschell 45621
Parker, John 00891
Parker, Prof. John S. 38455
Parker, Julia 39611
Parker, Madeline 41283
Parker, Margaret 46580
Parker, P. 39838
Parker, Robert 43629
Parker, Sandi 41577
Parker, Steve 44737
Parker, Teresa 43165
Parker, Tim 05998
Parkes, Susan 22452
Parkhurst, Jo 43344
Parkin, Peg 04981
Parkinson, C.D. 37969
Parkinson, Glenn 43504
Parks, Dennis 47539
Parks, Gary W. 44723
Parks, Dr. Raymond 38880
Parks, Robert E. 45863
Parks, Ron 42674
Parks, Shirley 48675
Parks McClain, Patti 44566
Parlic-Barisic, Slobodanka 27591
Parma, Dr. Rita 25149
Parmalee, Dr. Paul 44519
Parman, Susan 43575
Parmentier, Damien 13218
Parmentier, J.-P. 12597

Parnell, Dr. G. 39756
Parnes, Stuart 43211
Parola, Publio 00497
Parpagiola, Dr. Giuseppe 24664
Parr, Jesse 45207
Parr, Melissa 46142
Parra, Raúl 28205
Parra Casamun, Gerardo 28178
Parra Santos, Alirio 07468
Parratt, D.M. 40575
Parreiras Horta, Maria de Lourdes 04263
Parreño, Prof. Manuel 27511
Parrilla de Alvarez, Estela 27915
Parrinello, Prof. Nicolo 24772
Parris, David 48057
Parrish, M. 39335
Parrott, Robert W. 45195
Parrott, Shirley 47019
Parry, Linda 39809
Parry, Wendy 40356
Parshall, Peter 48373
Paršina, Lidija Semënovna 32699
Paršina, Ljudmila Vladimirovna 33678
Parson, Helen 38347
Parsons, Brian 00948
Parsons, Clare 39383
Parsons, Jeffrey K. 41219
Parsons, Julien 38544
Parsons, K. 01499
Parsons, Louise 46109
Parsons, Ralph 40573
Parsy, Paul-Hervé 13393
Partin, Marc 48767
Parton, Neville 01105
Partyka, Józef 31845
Parusel, Janina 32214
Parušev, Todor 04899, 04904
Pârvan, Lucia 32442
Pârvan, Lucica 32513, 32514
Pârvan, Lucicia 32588
Parviainen, Helena 09740
Paša, Natko 07813
Pascal, Huston 46775
Pascale, Mark 42304
Pasch, Anne 43034
Paschke, Ilona 18546
Pascual, José 34911
Pascucci, Marisa 45467
Pashley, Bill 38447, 40406, 40410
Pasiciel, Stanisław 31803
Paskova, Spaska 04674
Pasler, Hermann 18596
Pasquali, Prof. Flavia 25563
Pasquier, Alain 13603
Pasquini-Barisi, Isabella 25712
Passaglia, Elio 24444
Passarin, Dr. Mauro 25994
Passe, Eugene 46811
Passi, Leena 09413
Paßlick, Tonio 20437
Pasté de Rochefort, Aymeri 11385
Pastellas, Dominiue 13621
Paster, Carol 46584
Pasternak, Natalija Anisimovna 33297
Pastor, Paloma 35375
Pastor Vázquez, Prof. J.F. 35619
Pastore, Heather 43165
Pastore, Prof. Michele 25673
Pastorek, Ivan 33997
Pastoriza, Juan A. 32374
Pasture, B. 03634
Paszowski, Cindy 05383
Patané, Dr. Rosario 23475
Patchen, Dr. Jeffrey 44215
Paten, Richard 40189
Patenaude, Val 05813
Pater, Dr. Józef 32174
Patka, Erika 02980
Patka, Dr. Marcus G. 02903
Patnode, J. Scott 47727
Patocchi, Luca 36897
Paton, W.J. 30135, 30136
Patorska, Joanna 31803
Patrich, Pat 48061
Patrick, Brian 30151
Patrick, J.A. 38226
Patrick, R.E 45547
Patrick, Ruth 46386
Patrick, Stephen E. 41843, 41844, 41845, 41846, 41847
Patros, Charlotte 48637
Patry, J. Michael 44729
Patten, Dan W. 43749
Patterschal, Donald 47689
Patterson jr., Aubrey B. 48108
Patterson, James 39584
Patterson, Ken 05089
Patterson, Lillian 41121
Patterson, Dr. Mark A. 41992
Patterson, Richard 48058
Patterson, Robert B. 47173
Patterson, Ruth 00886

Patterson-O'Regan, J.J. 38202
Patteson, Rita 48260
Pattie, M. 30247
Pattinson, G. 40445
Pattison, Alison 39088
Patton, Jody 47533
Patton, LuAnn W. 41119
Patton, Robert 48073
Patton, Dr. Sharon F. 46076
Patton, S.M. 41279, 41280
Patwa, Elizabeth 10700
Patzak, Dr. B. 02971
Patzer, George 05581
Patzig, Eberhard 18398
Paugh, James J. 48758
Pauka, T.R. 28927
Paukšte, Regīna 27328
Paul, April 45778
Paul, C.D. 40111
Paul, Frédéric 10735
Paul, Gayle 46660
Paul, Renee 30249
Paul, Ryan 42147
Paul, Shimrath 30151
Paul-Zinserling, Dr. V. 17949
Paula, Alberto de 00219
Paulay, Dr. G. 43581
Păuleanu, Dr. Doina 32499
Păuleanu, Doina 32548, 32616
Pauletić, Mirjana 07686
Pauley, Ed 46295
Paulicka-Nowak, Dr. Lucja 31672
Paulo, Dália 32272
Paulocik, Linda 06786
Paulsen, Nils 30491
Paulson, Christopher 46768
Paulson, Dr. Dennis R. 47919
Paulson, Warren 05017
Paulsrud, Geir 30483
Paulus, Norma 46637
Pauly, Dorothy 42181
Pausch, Gottfried 01784
Pausch, Dr. Oskar 02977
Pause, Dr. Carl 19063
Paust, Dr. Bettina 15866
Pautet, C. 12903
Pautrizel, Françoise 10725
Pavaloi, Dr. Margareta 17677
Pavelčík, Dr. Jiří 08698
Pavelcikova, Monika 33986, 34065, 34066
Pavelec, Karen 43223
Pavelka, Dr. Karel 08706, 08730
Pavia, Prof. Giulio 25749
Pavic, Stjepan 03930
Pavić, Vladimira 07835
Pavičić, Snježana 07822
Pavlát, Dr. Leo 08620
Pavletić, Mira 07684
Pavlides, Paul 11141
Pavliňák, Dr. Petr 08528
Pavlov, Aleksandr Anatoljevič 32704
Pavlova, Irina Vasiljevna 33663
Pavlović, Ivo 07692
Pavlu, Viktor 02911
Pavlunina, Ljudmila Fëdorovna 33738
Pavoni, Rosanna 49250
Pavúková, Olga 34030
Pawchuak, Linda 46789
Pawłowska, Krystyna Iwona 32161
Pawłowski, Dr. Antoni J. 31746
Payet, Hugues 32419
Payling, Catherine 25169
Payne, Elizabeth 05282
Payne, James 48285
Payne, Mary 44704
Payne, R.G. 40555
Payne, Prof. Robert B. 41220
Payne, Susan 40185
Payrich, Wolfgang 02027
Payton, Charles 40255
Payton, Sidney 42895
Paz, Boaz 49213
Paz, Diego Alonso 07562
Paz, Olivier 12950
Paz Morales Osorio, Maria de la 28128
Pazmandy Horvath, Margaret 46601
Pazoutova, Katerina 08391
Pčelinceva, Nelli Sergeevna 32938
Peabody, Ann F. 44442
Peabody Turnbaugh, Sarah 46321
Peace, Barb 06738
Peach Lynch, Ann 46997
Peacock, Pat 47865
Peake, Jane 48575
Pealer, Dr. Casius 46079
Pearce, Alan 40500
Pearce, Andrew 40332
Pearce, Barry 01490
Pearce, John N. 43537
Pearce, Michael 38888
Pearce, Pelham G. 42172
Pearce, Robert J. 05769
Pearlstein, Elinor L. 42304
Pearsall, Barbara 45995
Pearson, A. Faye 05580
Pearson, Dave 41309
Pearson, Fiona 38916
Pearson, Marion 48114

Pearson, N. 01223
Pearson, Paul 41940
Pearsons, Don 06818
Peaucelle, Denis 10357
Peavy, John M. 44295
Peces Rata, Felipe Gil 35493, 35494
Pech, Edwin 31642
Pech, Dr. Jürgen 16377
Pecháček, Ivo 08428
Pechal, Dorothy 47977
Pecharromán, Ricardo 35255
Pechlamer, Helmut 01815
Pechová, Dr. Jarmila 08267
Pecht, Ulrike 17668
Peci, Innocenzo 25127
Peck, Donald J. 46361
Peck, Elsie 42924
Peck, James F. 48107
Peck, Scott 42746
Peck, William H. 42924
Peck Bracy, Tralice 45432
Peckham, Cynthia A. 46970
Pecoraro, Joseph P. 42301
Peczelt, Ursula 01834
Pedder, John 39856
Pede, Miriam 41633
Peden, Harold R. 48156
Pedersen, Birgit 08769
Pedersen, Hans 30692
Pedersen, Jørgen 08770, 08802
Pedersen, Kenno 08811, 08862, 09092
Pedersen, Knud 08932
Pedersen, K.S. 08953
Pedersen, Lisbeth 08911
Pedersen, Lykke 08961
Pedersen, Naja 08902
Pedersen, T. 08953
Pederson, Curt 45380
Pederson, Jennifer 42379
Pedevillano, Diane 46676
Pedlar, Arthur 45365
Pedneault, Richard 06731
Pedretti, Cornelia 37115
Pedretti, Robert 42070, 42071
Pedrini, Dr. Claudia 24083, 24087, 24090, 24091, 24092
Peebles, Cheryl 06765
Peebles, Virginia T. 42575
Peek, Andre 47617
Peek, Thomas 19438
Peel, Prof. John S. 36353, 36354, 36366
Peele, Anna M. 43467
Peeperkorn-van Donselaar, Dr. L.A. 29747
Peers, Dr. Laura 40153
Peers-Gloyer, Axel 19440
Peery, Richard 48057
Peeters, Herman 03163
Peeters, L. 03179
Peeters, Ludo 03384
Peeters Saenen, E. 03386
Pehlivaner, Metin 37623
Peić Čaldarović, Dubravka 07822
Peičinova, Chaterina 04616
Peiffer, Jacques 12016
Peik, Karl-Heinz 17555
Pein, Max Gerrit von 20092, 20100
Peine, Arnold 15810
Peiry, Lucienne 36852
Peitler, Karl 01925
Pejković, Božidar 07715
Pejnović, Nikola 07751
Peković, Mirko 33819
Pela, Premysl 45750
Peláez Arbeláez, Leopoldo 07425
Peláez Tremols, Dr. Lucía 34848, 34849
Pelagalli, Prof. G.V. 24587
Pelanne, Marja 09532
Pélatan, Martial 10235
Pełczyk, Antoni 31753
Péligry, Christian 13474
Pelikánová, Jaroslava 08503
Pelkey, Ann 46536
Pella, Nicholas W. 46143
Pellard, Sandra-Diana 11214
Pellegrinetti, Jerri 06557
Pellegrini, Dr. Beatrice 36746
Pellegrino, Ronald J. 43858
Pellen, Robin 38681, 38683
Pellengahr, Dr. Astrid 18044
Pellmann, Dr. Hans 18585
Pellow, Robin 39280
Pelon-Ribeiro, Laurence 11473
Pelosio, Prof. Giuseppe 24811
Pelrine, Diane 41746
Pelser, R. 34396
Pelsers, Dr. L. 29240
Peltier, Cynthia 44721
Pelz, H. 16368
Pelzl, Prof. Dr. Leopoldine 01670
Pemberton, David 01106
Peña, José María 00186
Peña Castillo, Agustín 28085
Peña Javier, Estrellita 31433
Peña Reigosa, Maria Cristina 07913
Peñalver Gómez, Henriqueta 48953
Penard, Michel 15260
Penati, Fabio 24563
Pence, Debra 43965
Pence, Noel 44147

Pencèv, Ass.Prof. Dr. Vladimir 04846
Pender, Branko 07779
Pendleton, Chris 43434, 43437
Penent, Jean 14950, 14951
Penicaud, Pierre 11325
Penick, George 43921
Penick, Steven 47086
Penka, Bradley 44534
Penkina, Elena Ivanovna 32870
Penkov, Petio 04909, 04910, 04911, 04912, 04919, 04920, 04921
Penkova, Elka 04846
Penn, Joyce 42638
Penn, Michael 40565
Penn, Simon 38376
Penna, Liisa 41311
Pennanen, Tapani 10092
Pennas, Dr. Vasso 20854
Penndorf, Jutta 15450
Penner, E. Paul 06750
Penner, Lisa 41308, 41312
Pennestri, Dr. Serafina 25737
Penney, David 42924
Penney, S.F.J. 05963
Penney, Stephen 40088
Penning, Dr. Mark 34232
Pennington, Claudia 45937
Pennington, Claudia L. 44463, 44468
Pennington, Tom C. 44233
Pennino, Gaetano 24759
Penno-Burmeister, Karin 18282
Penny, Cheryl 06288
Penny, Dr. Nicholas 39729
Pensabene, Dr. Giovanni 24228
Pensom, Carole 05681
Pentrella, Dr. Ruggero 25236
Penvose, Jane 48028
Penz, Marta 25871
Penzin, Viktor 33139
Pèon, Marie-Thérèse 12755
Peoples, Jo 00712
Peora, Prof. Oscar Carlos 00230
Pepić, Eva 27510
Pepich, Bruce W. 46767
Pepion, Loretta 41960
Peppler, Tina 05141
Perac, Jelena 33810
Perales Piqueres, Rosa 34641
Peralta, Juan 31197
Peralta, Prof. Tole 06894
Peralta Juárez, Juan 34420
Peralta Vidal, Gabriel 06901
Perchinske, Marlene 42553
Percival, Arthur 39984
Perco, Daniela 23512
Percy, Ann B. 46442
Percy, David O. 42227
Perego, Graziella 24046
Pereira, Maria Isabel de Sousa 32239
Gomes Pereira, Prof. Sonia 04377
Pereira Cabral, Augusto J. 28722
Pereira de Araujo, J. Hermes 04384
Pereira Herrera, David M. 03892
Pereira Neto, Prof. João 32302
Pereira Viana, Dr. Maria Teresa 32338
Perelló, Antonia M. 34552
Perepelkina, Aleksandra Fëdorovna 33545
Peretti, Pierre de 13124, 13130
Peretto, Prof. Raffaele 25297
Pereyra Salva de Impini, Prof. Nydia 00608
Perez, Anthony 49247
Perez, Fernando Alberto 07559
Perez, Gabriel 45761
Pérez, Juan Fernando 09216
Perez, Patricia 31310
Pérez, Rosa María 21274
Pérez Aviles, José Javier 35590
Pérez Avilés, José Javier 35592
Pérez Basurto, Alejandro 28133
Pérez Camps, Josep 35080
Pérez Casas, Angel 34454
Pérez Espinosa, Juan Fidel 28323
Pérez Gollan, Dr. José Antonio 00205
Pérez Gónzález, Melba 08105
Pérez Gutiérrez, Arturo 28152
Pérez Maldonado, Raúl 21264
Pérez Mesuro, Dolores 35557
Pérez Moreno, Rafael 35012
Pérez Navarro, Marcos 35029
Pérez Ornes, Nora 09119
Pérez Outeiriño, Bieito 35439
Pérez Quintana, José Andrés 07931, 07962
Pérez Recio, Manuel 34947
Pérez Ruán, Liliana 07623
Pérez Villarreal, Pedro 07596
Pergament, Allen 47668
Perger, Dr. Richard 02859
Pergola, Prof. Philippe 25955
Pería, Alejandra 28160
Pericoli, Prof. Cecilia 25174
Périer-d'Ieteren, C. 03281
Perillat, Shirley 05347
Perin, Giovanni 25554
Périn, Dr. Patrick 14242
Périnet, Francine 06038, 06039
Perini, Mino 25102
Perisho, Sally L. 42880
Perišin, Stane 07689
Périssère, Michèle 10818

Perkins, Allison 41454
Perkins, Bob 47530
Perkins, Bruce C. 48712
Perkins, Deborah 47564
Perkins, Larry David 43584
Perkins, Martin 43031
Perkins, Sophie 35559
Perkins, Stephen 43790
Perkins, Viola 43871
Perkko, Mariliina 09431, 09434
Perkone, Inga 27438
Perl, Alexander 16392
Perlee, A. 28675, 28680, 28688
Perlein, Gilbert 13312
Perlman, Patsy 41462
Perlon, Dr. Diane 44894
Perlstein, Barbara 46106
Perman, David 40783
Pernas Ojeda, Maria Emma 28127
Pernot, M.M. 48060
Pernu, Esko 10003
Peron, Claude 13745
Perot, Jacques 10766, 11377, 11378
Perraudin, Marguerite 36893
Perrault, Lise 06660
Perrefort, Dr. Maria 17576
Perren, Stephan 37358
Perrenoud, Raymond 36639
Perret, Gilles 36984
Perret, Pascale 36862
Perrier, Dr. Danièle 15637
Perron, Jean L. 06354
Perron, Michelle M. 42917
Perrons, Margot 40231
Perrot, Annick 13643
Perrot, C. 13187
Perrot, Mollie 46219
Perrottet, Marie-C. 36638
Perroud, Paul 12158
Perry, Andy 44963
Perry, Bob 41491
Perry, Ed 48223
Perry, Gregory P. 45678
Perry, Hadley 40604
Perry, John 48500
Perry, Michael L. 42763
Perry, Nancy 44395, 46660
Perry, Peter 00900
Perry, Rachel 45694
Perry, Shannon 45236
Perry, Sheila 45200
Persak, Erica 00886
Persan, Marquis de 11881
Perse, Marcell 17964, 17965, 17966
Persengieva, Marina 04745
Peršin, Vladimir 07713
Person, Tage 35898
Persson, Ann-Charlotte 36115
Persson, Bertil 36053
Persson, Curt 36054
Persson, Dr. Per-Edvin 10180
Persson, Thomas 35998
Pertin, B. 21860
Pertola, Esko 09679, 09680
Péru, Dr. Laurent 13245
Perucchi, Dr. Ursula 37343
Peruga, Iris 48914
Pesarini, Dr. Fausto 23787
Pescaru-Rusu, Adriana 32511
Pesch, Dr. Dieter 18669
Peschel, Tina 16051
Pescia, Sergio 37198
Pese, Dr. Claus 19139
Pešek, Dr. Ladislav 08452
Pesenecker, Marita 17401
Pesi, Dr. Rossana 24228
Pešková, K. 34079
Peso, Jean-Michel del 14332
Pesqueira de Esesarte, Prof. Alicia 28274
Pesqueur, Jean-Yves 11006, 11007
Pessa, Joanna 45835
Pessa, Loredana 24005
Pessemier 's Gravendries, Paul de 03548
Pessey-Lux, Aude 10281
Pessoa, Miguel 32266
Pestalozzi, Prof. Karl 37169
Pestalozzi, Dr. Martin 36429
Pestel, Michael 46514
Pestiaux, Pierre 03608
Petchey, Tim 40883
Peter, Carolyn 44905
Peter, Christopher 34372, 34373
Peter, Elmar 02110
Peter, Frank-Manuel 18131
Peter, Horst 16314
Peter, Jack 47075
Peter, Dr. Markus 36479
Petercsák, Dr. Tivadar 21406
Petermann, Jörg 16822
Petermann, Ralf 15543
Peterposten, Carlo 36442
Peters, Dr. Dirk J. 16339
Peters, Dr. Gustav 16250
Peters, Heinrich 16299
Peters, Dr. Hermann 16842
Peters, Irmtrude 16737
Peters, Karen 39614
Peters, Larry D. 48031
Peters, M. 29173, 43388

Peters, Michael 16666, 16666, 20623
Peters, Sandra 15567
Peters, Ted H. 46541
Peters, Dr. Ursula 19139
Peters, W. 05165
Peters-Barenbrock, Sabine 19300
Peters Bowron, Edgar 44129
Peterseim, Dr. Siegfried 18951
Petersen, Christopher 40722
Petersen, Flemming 08783
Petersen, Jan 43146
Petersen, Jerome 43989
Petersen, Jim 41652
Petersen, John 47298, 48558
Petersen, Viggo 08762
Peterson, Alan 48061
Peterson, Allan 46347
Peterson, Allan E. 47301
Peterson, Barbara 42472
Peterson, Brian 42984
Peterson, Dr. Cheryl D. 44326
Peterson, Dennis 47725
Peterson, Glenn 45839
Peterson, James L. 47166
Peterson, Karin 44444
Peterson, Karin E. 43937
Peterson, Mark F. 48695, 48696
Peterson, Merlin 43699
Peterson, Mildred 41613
Peterson, Paula 45993
Peterson, Rebecca 45113
Peterson, R.J. 42963
Peterson, Roger 47385
Peterson, Thomas 41736
Peterson, Tom 48080
Peterson, Townsend 44685
Peterson, William 45588
Peterson-Moussaid, Kathleen 41418
Petersson, Håkan 36262
Petey-Hache, Philippe 14897
Peti, Viktorija 27586
Petit, Jean-Paul 10768
Petit, René 11093
Petit, Prof. Th. 14829
Petke, Debra 43940
Petkov, Dimitär 04841
Petkov, Pavel 04687, 04688
Petkov, Vladimir 04809
Petout, Philippe 14341, 14342
Petr-Marcec, Prof. Smiljana 07687
Petranov, Borislav 02893
Petre, John L. 30237
Petre, Prof. Vasile 32476
Petrelli, Dr. Flavia 24599
Petrenko, Vladimir Grigorjevič 33001
Petresu, Nicolae 32467
Petri, Gerda 08920
Petri, Susanne 18405
Petrie, Hugh 39607
Petrinski, Ivan 04846
Petrioli, Annamaria 23840
Petrioli Tofani, Dr. Annamaria 23836, 23840
Petrone, P. Paolo 24588
Petrov, Angel 04624
Petrov, Evgenij 37836
Petrov, Najden 04811
Petrova, Lidija 04895
Petrova, Nadežda 32848
Petrova, Velička 04695
Petrovic, Dejan 33827
Petrović, Dragutin 33928
Petrović, Marijana 33810
Petrović-Raić, Marijana 33810
Petrovnina, Galina Michajlovna 33299
Petrovski, Zoran 27591
Petrovszky, Dr. Richard 20011
Petrucci, Stefano 24876
Petruchno, Alla Sergeevna 32633
Petrus, Jerzy T. 31729
Petrus, Magdolna 21612
Petrussen, Thomas 21231
Petryta, Bliderişanu 32583
Petry, Michael 39716
Petryshyn, M. 05637
Petschar, Dr. Hans 02955
Petschek-Sommer, Birgitta 16559, 16560
Pett, Joachim 15538
Pettengill, Shirley 47926
Pettersson, Jan 35985
Pettersson, Kerstin 36301
Pettersson, Lennart 35912
Pettibone, Jody 48333
Pettibone, John W. 43703
Petty-Johnson, Gayle 48794, 48796
Pétursdóttir, Brynhildur 21622
Pétursson, Björn 21633
Pétursson, Halldór 21621
Petz, Emmerich 01650
Petzal, Monica 39637
Petznek, Dr. Beatrix 01694
Petznek, Friedrich 01752
Petzold, A. 16628
Petzold, Lorraine 05756
Peuckert, Valérie 03183, 03184
Peukert, Jörg 17131
Peuzin, Jean 13911
Pevahouse, Jerry 42688
Pevereit, S. 40084
Peverelli, Maria de 36616

Pevernagie 03342
Pewitt, Dr. J. Dudley 41709
Peyer, Ricard de 39866
Peyer, Richard de 39865
Peylhard, Anne-Marie 10527
Peyre, P. 12925
Peyton-Jones, Julia 39774
Pezarro, D. 28817
Pfaff, Patricia 18615
Pfaffenberger, Dr. Gary 46617
Pfaffenbichler, Dr. Matthias 02918
Pfaffenhuemer, Dr. Johannes 02294
Pfanner, Dario 24232
Pfanner, Ute 01746
Pfanz, Donald C. 43534
Pfau, F.D. 19800
Pfau, Gisela 04177
Pfeifer, Anton 01789
Pfeifer, Magdalena 02918
Pfeifer, Nezka 47388
Pfeiffenberger, Deborah 45675
Pfeiffer, Dr. Andreas 17686, 17690
Pfeiffer, Brian 41826
Pfeiffer, Gordon A. 48650
Pfeiffer, Günter 03727
Pfeiffer, Dr. Ingrid 17071
Pfeiffer, Rainer 19925
Pfeiffer, Wolfgang 01675
Pfeifhofer, Elisabeth 01890
Pfeifhofer, Helmut 01890
Pfeil, Elke 15929
Pfennings, Edgar 06921
Pferdehirt, Dr. Barbara 18604, 18606
Pfister, Emil 36637
Pfleger, Dr. Susanne 20664
Pflüger, Helmut 20610
Pflumm, Manfred 20319
Pfnorr, Reinhard 19089
Pfnuer, Linda 15884
Pfosser, Dr. Martina 02228
Pfotenhauer, Louise 43792
Pfretzschmer, Prof. Dr. Hans-Ulrich 20225
Phagan, Patria 46674
Phaneuy, Jim 41585
Phares, Jane 45329
Pharo, R.G. 38776
Phelan, Beverly 41624
Phelan, Wynne 44129
Phéline, Jean-Michel 14592
Phelps, Kathleen D. 48901
Pheney, Kathleen 41525
Pheysey, Dawn 46734
Phil, D. 21914
Philbin, Ann 44906
Philbin, Gail 43760
Philbrick, Harry 46896
Philbrick, Nathaniel 45595
Philbrick, Ruth T. 48373
Philbrook, Wyman 48237
Philipon, Peter 06510
Philipp, Dr. Claudia Gabriele 17560
Philipp, Werner 15979
Philippe, Pierre 36657
Philippon, Annie 14008
Philippot 13049
Philipson, Jean 01298
Philipson, Peter 39702
Phillip, D.M. 30137
Phillips, Amanda 39442
Phillips, Ann 38735
Phillips, Christopher 45817
Phillips, Colin 01230
Phillips, Dale 48238
Phillips, Gene 42907
Phillips, George 06186
Phillips, G.R. 34304
Phillips, James 42096
Phillips, John 38261
Phillips, Joseph R. 41390
Phillips, Dr. Kenneth E. 44894
Phillips, Lisa 45855
Phillips, Melissa 45886
Phillips, Robert F. 48021
Phillips, Prof. Ruth B. 06683
Phillips, Dr. Sandra S. 47339
Phillips, Stephen 48389
Phillips, Steven 43519
Phillips, Wayne 45731
Phillips Olmedo, Carlos 28165, 28172
Phillipson, Prof. David W. 38463
Phillp, John 38270
Philo, P. 40300
Philo, Phil 39946
Philotheou, G. 08198
Philp, B.J. 38770
Philp, Brian 40134
Philp, S. 39399
Philpatt, Vandan 47303
Philpot, Chris 38199
Philpott, Vandean 47334
Philson, William C. 45261
Phinney, Chad 47975
Phinney Kelley, Sarah 44722
Phippin, Susan 47502
Phipps, Rebecca J. 41782
Phleps, Dr. Roland 17117
Phuong, Pham Xuân 49003
Phuong, Tran Thi Thuy 48992
Piacentini, Dr. Paola 25231

Pianca, Dr. Vittorino 26039
Pianea, Dr. Elena 25326
Piasecka, Grażyna 32060
Piaskowski, Tadeusz 31572
Piastrella, Dr. Carlo 23676
Piatek, Bruce J. 46266
Piątek, Jacek 31916
Piatrowski, Kenn 44060
Piatt, Margaret 48533
Piatti, Verena 02253
Piaty, Karl 02787
Picard, Dr. Bertold 16884
Picard, Dennis 48548
Picard, Michel 13742
Picard, Thomas 45866
Picazo Verdejo, Elisa 34827
Piccardi, Dr. Marco 23864
Picciano, Eric 42381
Piccioli, Prof. Rossana 24124
Piccirilli, Guido 25650
Piccirillo, M. 22652
Piccoli, Prof. Adalberto 23463
Piccottini, Prof. Dr. Gernot 02417
Picelj, Zdenko 34136
Picha, Krzysztof Vincenc 31550
Piché, Thomas 06733, 47908
Picher, Claude 05221
Pichler, Gerd 02422
Pichler, Dr. Isfried H. 01652
Pichler, Jutta M. 02156
Pichorner, Dr. Franz 02918
Pickard, Carey 45048
Pickard, Kelli L. 43488
Pickering, Jane 42045, 42048
Pickering, Mona 45130
Pickin, John 40621, 40622
Pickles, Verna 05217
Pico, Dr. Teresa 32362
Picollet, Auguste 10272
Picon, Carlos 45833
Picpican, Isikias T. 31284
Pidault, Monique 13730
Pidcock, James 39757
Pido, Asuncion Q. 31367, 31389
Piek, W. 30019
Pieke, Hannelore 15565
Pienaar, S. 34295
Pienimaa, Vilho 09577
Pieplow, Jane 43285
Pierard, Christiane 03638
Pierce, Dr. Charles E. 45863
Pierce, Donna 42885
Pierce, Dr. Donna 47417
Pierce, Gene 41186
Pierce, Sally 41798
Piergollini, Alberto 24669
Pierides, Demetrios Z. 08192
Pierini, Dr. Paolo 25086
Pierrangeli, Prof. Carlo 25160
Pierrot-Bults, Dr. A.C. 28917
Piersantini, Dr. Michele 25861
Piersol, Daniel 45735
Pierson, Charles 41075
Pierson, Stacey 39742
Pieschacón González, Gabriel 07614
Pieschel, Janet 05164
Piet 03706
Pieters, Dr. Georges 03442
Pietri de Caldera, Alicia 48921
Pietropaolo, Dr. Lisa 24233
Pietrzak, Stanisław 32056
Pietrzak, Ted 41986
Pietrzyk, Prof. Zdisław 31724
Pietsch, Dr. Ted 47529
Pietsch, Dr. Ulrich 16704
Pietscher, Charles 44452
Pietschmann, Wolfgang 17824, 17825
Piette, Jacques 13353
Pihema, Joseph 30164
Pihlak, Jaak 09395
Pihlgren, Kjell 35931
Piirainen, Sari 09431
Piiroinen, Päivikki 09708
Pijaudier-Cabot, Joëlle 15217
Pijbes, W. 29756
Pijeaux, Dr. Lawrence 41705
Pijl, B.H. 29497
Pika-Biolzi, Dr. M. 37376
Pikal, Dr. Jaroslav 08394
Pike, Alan 34176
Pike, J.P. 05687
Pike, Stephen J. 45193
Pil, E. 03146
Pilar, Jacquelin 43558
Pilar Muñoz Jiménez, María del 07413
Pilati von Thassul-Filo della Torre, Francesca Gräfin 02002, 02513
Pilato, Dominique 14536
Pilchowski, Władysław 31807
Pilides, Dr. D. 08198
Pilioko, A. 48865
Pilkilton, Sue 48120
Pilkinton, Hunter M. 48467
Pillaert, E. Elizabeth 45072
Pillay, Ruven 39729
Piller, Ferdinand 36553
Piller, Gudrun 36500
Piller, Josienne N. 46529
Pillet, Gaby 37128

Pillichshammer, Johann 02346
Pilotti, Bianca Maria 23593, 23658
Pils, Walter 02243
Pilven, Denis 10867
Pilz, Anette 20671
Pilz, Bernd 17451
Pilz, Winfried 15376
Pim, James 46914
Pimentel, Cristina 32336
Pimmins, Rose 46781
Pinat, Bruno Augusto 24039
Pincemin, Cecilia 05670
Pindinelli, Prof. Elio 23955
Pine, Lynda 39260
Piñeiro, Alberto Gabriel 00210
Pinelli, Prof. Antonio 24944, 24947
Pinette, Matthieu 14702
Pinette, Matthiew 10323, 10324
Pingel, Carol 43808
Pingeot, Anne 13596
Pinheiro, Maria Joao 32296
Pinheiro-Fankhauser, Marie-Anne 37228
Pini, Lucia 24386
Pinigina, Taisija Viktorovna 33514
Pinilla, José 07488
Pinnix, Cleve 46308, 48690
Pino Morán, Mónica 06931
Pinson, Dr. Patricia 46087
Pintarić, Adam 07792
Pintarić, Snježana 07833
Pintarić, Tanja 07799
Pintea, June 43202
Pintea, Rodica 32526
Pinto, Dr. Bianca Alessandra 25164
Pinto, Dr. Ettore 23446
Pinto de Matos, Maria Antonia 32284
Pinto Simon, Elena 45771
Pinzl, Christoph 20672
Pinzón, Carlos 07627
Pinzón, Rito 07603
Pioch, Klaus 15920
Pionk, Richard 45866
Piot, Marc-Etienne 36670
Piotrovski, Michail 33397
Piotrowski, Jerzy 31496
Pipek, K. 08343
Piper, Catharina 36378
Piper, William 47120
Pipino, Dr. Giuseppe 25582
Pipkin, Roy 47878
Piquera, F. 12435
Piquereddu, Dr. Paolo 24662, 24663
Piquero López, Blanca 35027
Pirenne, R. 03801
Pires Martins, Prof. Calebe 04592
Pirie, Victoria 38286
Pirker, Hans 02506
Pirker, Rudolf 02763
Pirkkalainen, Heli 10135
Pirkmajer, Darja 34090
Pirkonen, Pekka 09729
Pirlot, Anne-Marie 03298
Pirnat, Miha 34114
Pirnie, M. 40207
Pisa, Regina M. 47671
Pisani, Étienne du 34247
Pisano, Dr. Jane 45918
Pisano, Dr. Jane G. 44934
Pisarev, S.V. 32897
Pischl, Rupert 02721
Pişiren, Tuncay 37763
Piskal, Irina Leonidovna 33558
Piskur, Bojana 34112
Piso, Prof. Dr. Ioan 32495
Pistono Grand, Mario 25463
Pištora, Jiří 08297
Pistorius, Dr. Agnes 02963
Pitard, Wayne 48164
Piterskaja, Larisa Karlovna 33393
Piteša, Ante 07779
Pithie, Helen 00729
Pitkänen, Erkki 09460
Pitkänen, Maritta 09810
Pitman, Bonni 42751
Pitot 03792
Pitre, Marc 05712
Pitt, James 21244
Pitt Jones, Priscilla 42970
Pittaway, Louise D. 47829
Pittner, K. Heinz 20027
Pittock, Tina 37965
Pitts, Priscilla 30145, 30152
Pitts, Terence 42157
Pittz, Franeis 42534
Pitxot, Antoni 34819
Pitzen, Marianne 16236
Piuma, Dr. Fabio 25955
Pixley, Patricia 46147
Pixner, Albin 25381
Pizitz, Jackie 45908
Pizzigoni, Prof. Gianni 24782, 25958
Pizzinini, Dr. Meinrad 02074, 02082
Pizziolo, Marina 24403
Pizzo, Tony 47486
Pizzollo, Sissy 46429
Pjankova, Svetlana Anatoljevna 32728
Pla, Josefina 31097
Plaat, Jaanus 09376
Plaine, Jean 13942

Planas, Marta 00086
Planas, Ramón 34570
Planchard, Ch. 14098
Planchon, Jacques 11506
Planck, Prof. Dr. Dieter 18201
Planes Torregassa, Ramón 35503
Planisek, Dr. Sandra 45033
Plank, Benedikt 02579
Plánka, Dr. Ivan 08751
Plankensteiner, Dr. Barbara 02945
Plant, C.D. 39282
Plantalamor, Luis 35067
Plante, Stella 05777
Plasser, Dr. Gerhard 02551
Plaßmann, Dr. Otmar 19810
Plaßmeyer, Dr. Peter 16696
Plastow, N. 39812
Plata Vega, Edith 07616
Platen, Dr. Michael 17508, 17942, 17950
Platero, Ramon 35205
Plath, Dr. Carina 18949
Plath, Margie J. 48174
Platonova, T.V. 32795
Platt jr., Geoffrey 46882
Platt, Nicholas 45768
Platt, Ron 48705
Platt, Ronald 43819
Platteter, Janet 44565
Plattner, Fritz 02677
Platz, Daniela 20684
Platz, Dr. Gertrud 15914
Platzgummer, Hanno 01772
Plavan, Tamara 37902
Plavec-Butkovic, Lidija 07687
Player, Elizabeth 22446
Plaza, Ben 46166
Plazotta, Carol 39729
Plenković, Ivo 07683
Plenter, Dr. H.A. 29950, 29951
Plesher, Dan 42624
Pleská, Leona 08649
Plessis, H. 34353
Plessis, M. du 34365
Pletnjov, Valentinr 04907
Plevin, Leon M. 44610
Pleyn, Dieter 16336
Plitek, Dr. Karl-Heinz 20708
Plöchinger, Prof. Dr. Benno 02312
Plöckinger, Veronika 02117
Plötz, Dr. Robert 18068
Płotkowiak, Wiesław 31620
Plotoagă, Gabriela 32498
Plotzek, Dr. Joachim M. 18135
Ploug, Mariann 08785, 08786, 08991, 09016,
   09017, 09100, 09101, 09102
Plouin, Suzanne 10730
Plourde, Nelie 41424
Plowright, Georgina 38573, 38631, 39238, 39276
Pluciński, Dr. Józef 32019
Pluhařová, Jana 08720
Plukavec, Lina 07836
Plume, Thierry 11646
Plumier, J. 03645
Plumley, Nicholas 39263
Plummer, Bill 46117
Plummer, Marguerite R. 47614
Plummer, Mary Ann 43517
Plummer, Sue J. 41388
Plummer, Val 40916
Plunkett, Stephanie 47820
Pluntke, Margitta 15451
Pochman, Kathryn K. 45596, 45597
Pochwała, Stanisław 31709
Pocius, D. 01335
Pocius, Edward 42307
Počivalova, Elena Ivanovna 32833
Počivavšek, Prof. Marija 34089
Počivavšek, Marija 34089
Pocsainé Eperjesi, Eszter 21526
Podany, Evelyn D. 42432
Podany, Jerry 44913
Podedworny, Carol 06757
Podestá, Horacio 00245
Podlesnik, Mateja 34110
Podmaniczky, Christine B. 42175
Podnar, Franc 34148
Podos, Lisa Beth 45771
Podzorski, Patricia 45231
Pögelt, Erika 17508
Poel, Dr. Peter te 29564
Pölcher, Bertold 16821
Pöllmann, Rotraud 19601
Poelman, Shannon 06794
Pöppelbaum, H. 19586
Pöppelmann, Dr. Heike 18581
Pörnbacher, Prof. Dr. Hans 20048
Pöss, Ondrej 33971
Poessiger, Peter M. 43369
Pöstinger, Eberhard 02662
Poethe, Lothar 18390
Poethke, Prof. Dr. Günther 15908
Poette, Simonne 15097
Pöttler, E. 02708
Pöttler, Prof. DDr. V.H. 02708
Pötzsch, Herbert 18620
Pogačnik Grobelšek, Helena 34112
Poggendorf, Renate 18842
Poggi, Patrizia 25084
Poggi, Dr. Roberto 23987

Poggiani-Keller, Raffaella 23328
Pogliani, Dr. Marisa 25865, 25866
Pogorzelska, Renata 31541
Pogt, Dr. Herbert 20717
Pohanka, Dr. Reinhard 03001
Pohjakallio, Lauri 09442
Pohl, Burkhart 47995
Pohl, G. 16304
Pohl, Gerhard 18704
Pohl, Dr. Klaus-Dieter 16541
Pohl-Schneider, Nadine 18612
Pohlman, Lynette 41170, 41171
Pohlmann, Dr. Ulrich 18850, 18880
Pohowsky, Carolyn 45461
Pointal, Jean-Louis 10775
Poirel, Evelyne 14048
Poirier, Daphne 06411
Poirier, Diane 05244
Poirier, Ulric 06764
Poissant, Margaret 44115
Poitevin, B. 12651
Poivet, Clémence 14965
Poivet, Cllémence 14964
Pokorná, Blanka 08441
Pokorná, Libuše 08489
Pokorný, Jaroslav 08707
Pokorny, Klaus 02953
Pokorný, Zdeněk 08347
Pokorny-Nagel, Kathrin 02929
Pol, A. 29519
Poláčková, Dr. Dagmar 33978
Polacsek, John 42923
Polacsek, John F. 42927
Polak, Dr. Jerzy 31494
Polak, Dr. J.J.H. 29937
Polak, Sarah 41401
Polanco de Laverde, Cecilia 07495
Polanía Ramírez, Tiberio 07463
Polanich, Judith K. 41888, 47929, 48074
Polanská, Zuzana 08562
Polat, Cemal 37669
Pole, Len 38957
Pole, Merle 01349
Polenov, Juri A. 32783
Poleske, Lee E. 47572
Poletti, Catherine 11148
Poli, Cristina Tessari 23041
Polich, Debra 41215
Polichetti, Maria Luisa 25536
Polichetti, Dr. Massimilano A. 25231
Polifka, Marcus 44072
Polikarpova, Marina Alekseevna 32863
Polioudovarda, Anna M. 20909
Polis, Crystal A. 46389
Poliščuk, Natalja 37893
Poliščuk, Svetlana Alekseevna 32694
Politopoulos, Catherine 44954
Poljakova, Valentina Alekseevna 33717
Polk, Vickie 48709
Poll, Lothar C. 16031
Poll, Dr. Roswitha 18948
Poll, Walter 19014
Poll-Frommel, Veronika 18842
Pollák, Dr. Róbert 34006
Pollan, Carolyn 43459
Pollard, Brent 40155
Pollard, David 38637
Pollard, Ian 40494
Pollard, S. 30124
Polley, Amy E. 41261
Polli, Kadi 09358
Polli, Dr. Vittorio 26058
Pollini, Lucia 36899
Pollock, Mallory 42428
Polnick, Bill 06412
Polo, Laura W. 45214
Polonovski, Max 13592
Polott, E. Leslie 44144
Poloznev, Dmitrij F. 32883
Polozova, Natalja Ivanovna 33711
Pols, Dr. Ivor 34329
Polverari, Dr. Michele 22885
Polvi, Arvo 09557
Polyarnaya, Janna 33396
Polychronopoulos, Mari Ellenca 21098
Polymerou-Kamilakis, Dr. Aik. 20865
Polzine, Roxann L. 48762
Poma Swank, Anna-Maria 45784
Pomar, Maria Teresa 27839
Pomeroy, Dan E. 45626
Pomeroy, Marilyn 48738
Pomeroy Draper, Stacy 48071
Pommeranz, Dr. Johannes 19139
Pommies, Marie-Anne 10807
Pompa, Vince 41456
Pomponi, Luigi 25616
Ponce de León, Carolina 47318
Ponciş, Gheorghe 32564
Pond-Anderson, Marcia 46312
Ponder, Gary 46573
Pongracz, Dr. Patricia 45803
Ponomareva, Galina B. 33123
Ponomareva, Tatjana 33482
Pons, Marc 35671
Pons-Pons, Fermí 35411
Ponsonnard, Christian 12443
Ponsoy, Teresita 31465
Pont, Jeanne 36743

Ponte, Emily 44123
Ponte, Dr. Susanne de 18841
Ponton d'Amecourt, Jean de 12107
Pontual, Sylvia 04301
Pontvianne, Jean-Paul 12294
Poodt, J.G.M. 29405
Poolaw, Linda 41191
Poole, Helen 39147
Poole, Helen E. 40503
Poole, J.E. 38454
Poonsil, Banteng 37508
Poorter, Nora de 03172
Poot, J.A. 28902
Pop, Valer 32608, 32609, 32610, 32611
Popa, Gabriela 32596
Popal, Najibulla 00004
Pope, Clare 40910
Pope, Linda 47409, 48461
Popelier, Betty 06125
Popelka, Dr. Pavel 08699
Popescu, Dr. A. 38454
Popescu, Ioana 32470
Popivoda, Mileva 33854
Poplack, Robert 41609
Popolla, Don Gianluca 25656
Popov, Aleksandr Nikolaevič 33703
Popov, Gennadij Viktorovič 33024
Popova, L.B. 33271
Popova, Nina Ivanovna 33399
Popovčak, Borivoj 07837
Popović, Bojana 33810
Popovic, Miroslav 27591
Popović, Pavle 33913
Popovici, Dragomir 32467
Poppa, Dr. Rudolf 16612
Poppi, Dr. Cesare 25032
Popski, Dragoljub 33817
Por, Prof. F.D. 22634
Porada, Jerzy 31831
Poras, E. Linda 44987
Porenta, Tita 34160
Porfírio, José Luís 32307
Porignaux, Jonathan 03485
Pornin, Claudie 15007
Poroszlai, Dr. Ildikó 21545
Porra-Kuteni, Valérie 10669
Porras, César Augusto 07531
Porrelli, D.M. 40028
Porsmose, Erland 08914, 08915
Port, Jane L. 46561
Portanje, B.K. 29037
Portatius, Botho von 17112
Porte, Patrick 13638
Portele, Helmut 03011
Portell, Rosa 47768
Porteous, Ken 06843
Porter, Ann 42009
Porter, Barbara A. 46162
Porter, Barry 48006
Porter, Dr. C.M. 43581
Porter, Emily 41779
Porter, Frances J. 45173
Porter, Herman 06159
Porter, John R. 06208
Porter, Julian 38186
Porter, Marty 44391
Porter, Marye 39215
Porter, Paul 47207
Porter, Phil 45029, 45030, 45032, 45034
Porter, Phillip 05328
Porter, Richard T. 46162
Porter, Russ 01533
Porter, Suzanne 30215, 43022
Portet, Angel 35280
Portiabohn, Ivece 45862
Portiglia, Hélène 10429
Portigliatti Barbos, Prof. Mario 25746
Porttier, W. 03157
Portugal Ortiz, Max 03899
Porzenheim, Maria 16596
Posch, Eva 16474
Poser, Steffen 18419, 18424
Posinjak, Jurij Michajlovič 33619
Pospisilova, Dr. Alena 08423
Possehl, Gregory L. 46460
Posselt, Dr. Martin 18038
Possémé, Evelyne 13586
Possèmé, Gilles 14345
Possenti, Dr. Elisa 24665
Post, Alfred 16703
Post, Dr. K. 30010
Post, Dr. William 42211
Postek, Roman 31764
Postel, Mitchell P. 46255, 46826, 48736
Postema-George, Deborah 45578
Poster, Amy 41941
Postier, Wilfried 16023
Postl, Dr. Walter 01922
Postles, Suella 40104
Poston, Jonathan 42219
Poston, Roger D. 42565
Potapov, Roald Leonidovič 33495
Poteau, Gérard 11795
Poteete, Timothy 44695
Potempa, Dr. Harald 16038
Potet, Jean-Pierre 15245
Potgieter, M.J. 34391, 34391
Pothan, Scott 30315
Potirakis, Georges 40349

Potochick, Andrea 41771
Potocka, Maria Anna 31824
Pototschnig, Alfred 02588
Potsch 01734
Pott, Karin 15985
Pott, Dr. Ute 17501
Potter, Byrn 44945
Potter, Edmund 47799
Potter, J.E. 40743
Potter, Linda 43760
Potter, Ron 44208
Potter, Ted 46871
Pottier, Marie Hélène 11731, 11733
Potts, Albert 46857
Potts, Prof. Daniel T. 01506
Potts, Timothy 43487
Potucek, Delvin 48309
Potužáková, Dr. Jana 08546
Potvin, Ronald 45926
Poueymirou, Frank 45809
Pouget, Daniel 11729, 14302
Poulain, Ivan 11958
Poulis, Helen 05671
Poullain, Christine 11942
Poulliot, Elizabeth A. 45965
Poulos, Ann 47975
Poulsen, Hanne 08861
Poulter, Gill 38804, 38807
Pounis Guntavid, Joseph 27631
Pourtalès, Laure de 10299
Pourtalet, P. 11898
Pourtaud, François 12110
Povedano, Balbino 34735
Poviliúnas, Virgilijus 27534
Povšič, Sabina 34112
Powar, N.V. 22013
Powders, Dr. Vernon 41162
Powell, Bob 39388
Powell, Bobbie 46921
Powell, Bruce 41898
Powell, Earl A. 48373
Powell, Gwendolen 39447
Powell, JoAnne 41558
Powell, John T. 41885
Powell, Maurice F. 18023
Powell, Michael 39885
Powell, Nancy S. 46404
Powell, Shana 43590
Powell, William V. 44512
Powell-Cotton, C. 38203
Powell Harold, Fran 47480
Power, Cathy 39606
Power, Christopher 01314
Power, Deirdre 22388
Power, Dennis M. 46067
Power, Nicola 40432
Powers, Catherine 41288
Powers, Claire 06018
Powers, Heather 43523
Powers, James L. 44172
Powers, Leland 43970
Powers, Linda 44552
Powers, Dr. Ramon 46201
Poyner, Noelle 01153
Pozsonyi, József 21315
Pozzi, Dr. Raffaella 23762
Pozzuoli, Prof. Maria Cristina 00391
Ppili, Leleala E. 00082
Prace, David 45743
Prackwieser, Walter 23803
Prada Pérez, Isaac 07483
Pradat, Marc-Marie 11890
Prader, Angela 36655
Prado, César O. 31165
Präger, Dr. Christmut 18612
Prätzel, Maritta 19609
Prag, Dr. A.J.N.W. 39894
Prágay, Dr. István 21328
Prahase, Mircea 32440, 32505, 32554
Prakapcov, Vladimir I. 03121
Prall, Steve 41291
Pralong-Salamin, Rachel 37165
Pralormo, Marcella 25766
Prammer, Dr. Johannes 20077
Pranza, Denise M. 47057
Prasch, Dr. Hartmut 02506, 02670
Prasolova, Elena Ivanovna 33452
Prasser, Gabriele 19155
Prasser, Karen L. 42464
Praßl, Johann 01827, 01828
Praszelik-Kocjan, Grażyna 31848
Prat, Jean-Louis 14398
Prather, Marla 45886
Prati, Dr. Luciana 23908, 23909, 23910, 23911,
   23914, 23917
Pratt, Gordon 44594
Pratt, Dr. William 44674
Prause, W. 46530
Pray, Jim 43034
Prayitno, Dr. R. Joko 22156
Praz, Jean-Claude 37174
Praženilová, Dr. Viera 34047
Pražic, Rastko 07733
Préaux, Alain 14053
Prebushewsky Danylink, Janet 06407
Preece, Geoff 38741
Preininger, Kristina 34114
Preising, Dr. Dagmar 15378
Preiss, Prof. Heinz 02162

Preiss, Slawomir 31997
Preissler, Leonilda Maria 04127
Preiswerk-Lösel, Dr. Eva-Maria 36488
Prem, Prof. Dr. Hanns J. 16226
Premack, Ellen 42891
Premerl, Nada 07830
Premoli Silva, Adolfo 24898
Premoli Silva, Dr. Isabella 24400
Premović-Aleksić, Dragica 33868
Prendergast, Dr. D.V. 40319
Prendergast, Mary B. 22387
Přenosilová, Dr. Vera 08580
Prentice Burkett, Hazel 41656
Prentiss, Margo 46550
Prescott, Janice 47699
Presgrave, A.D. 01063
Presley, Priscilla 45238
Presnell-Weidner, Denise 46567
Pressl, Hannes 01691
Presson, Virginia 48475
Prest, Véronique 13548
Prestegard, Tom 47858
Preston, Carol 47333
Preston, Dr. Charles R. 42510
Preston, John 42375
Preston, Jules 40645
Preston, P. Anthony 30126
Preston, Dr. P.M. 38881
Preszler, Robert E. 46796
Pretola, John P. 47750
Pretorius, A.F. 34294
Pretsch, Dr. Peter 18004
Pretty, Carol Anne 05183
Preuß, Helmut 18201
Preuß, Jürgen 16825
Prévost, Jean-Marc 13993
Prévost-Bouré, Pascal 13330
Prevosti, Marta 35295
Prevratil, Joseph F. 44862
Prew, R. 38525
Prewer, Steven 38099
Prewett, Vickie 42392
Preyer, Josef 02441
Pría, Melba 28186
Přibáňová, Dr. Svatava 08275
Pribbernow, Marcus 18585
Přibil, Vladimír 08530
Přibyla, Radomír 08369
Prica, Stanko 33895
Price, Anita 05305, 05306
Price, Brenda 46359
Price, John 45100
Price, Dr. Marla J. 43489
Price, Marti 42309
Price, Renée 45853
Price, Robert 41231
Price, Sally Irwin 41546
Price, Stephen 38351
Price, Thomas E. 42570
Price Shanis, Carole 46440
Prickett, Marcus 28755
Prickett, N.J. 30104
Pricolota, Olga 37881
Priddle, Th. 40975
Priddy, Dr. Bennie 20337
Prie, Jean-Yves 13755
Priego Fernández del Campo, Carmen 35006, 35040
Prière, Marc 10544
Prieto, Gabriel 07430
Prieto Vicioso, Esteban 09122
Prieur, Abel 15251
Prieur, P. 36775
Prigge, Dr. Walter 16584
Přikrylová, Ludmila 08488
Priljeva, Srdjan 33932
Prillinger, Judith 02325
Prima, Dana D. 45781
Primack, Ilene 45290
Primozic, Melanija 34158, 34160
Prince, David 47909, 47913
Prince, J.R. 39882
Prince, Nigel 38222
Prince, Shannon 06020
Prince, Todd 42147
Pringle, Harry 46621
Pringle, Roger 40624, 40625, 40626, 40627, 40628, 40630
Prinz, Gerhard 20115
Prinz, Ina 16228
Prinz, Peter 41710
Prinz, Dr. Ursula 15919
Prinzler, Hans Helmut 15946
Prior, Annette 35919
Prior, Claudine 05144
Prior, Terrence M. 46216
Pripačkin, I.A. 32973
Prister, Boris 07822
Prister, Lada 07822
Pritchard, Frances 39904
Pritchard, Leonard 42573
Pritchard, Philip 06585
Pritikin, Renny 47346
Prittwitz und Gaffron, Dr. Hans-Hoyer von 16246
Privette, David 44810
Prix, Jörg 01782
Prjamikova, Vera Pavlovna 32944
Probst, Heinz 18993
Probst, Peter 37180
Probst, Dr. Volker 17456

Procacci, Ugo 23858
Procelli, Dr. Enrico 25070
Prochaska, James J. 42173
Prochazka, Denise 43105
Prochina, Irina Evgenjevna 33148
Procopé Ilmonen, Susanne 09814
Procopiou, E. 08198
Proctor, Karen E. 46333
Proctor, R. 38454
Proctor, Rebecca 38450
Proctor, Vicki 43125
Próder, István 21604
Prod'Hom, Chantal 36856
Proebst, Walter 15398
Prösch, Dr. Christoph 20733
Prohaska, Prof. Dr. Wolfgang 02918
Prokisch, Dr. Bernhard 02241, 02243
Prokop, J. 08508
Prol, Elbertus 46902
Pronti, Dr. Stefano 24890
Propri, Mary Ann 48311
Prøsch Danielsen, Lisbeth 30877
Proschwitz, Ted von 35916
Proskynitopoulou, Rosa 20873
Pross, Ann 42909
Proß, Christian 19015
Prosser, M. 30247
Prota, Prof. Romolo 25484
Prothero-Brooks, C.C. 06445
Proto Pisani, Dr. Rosanna Caterina 23829, 23831, 23834, 23857
Protz, Edward L. 43613
Proud, Hayden 34214
Proust, Georges 13554
Prouty, Elisha 43737
Provick, A.M. 05413
Providi, Dr. Ioanna 20892
Provoyeur, M. Pierre 10528
Prpa Stojanac, Ika 07779
Prudhomme, James 45635
Prudhomme, Mary Louise 41529
Prudhomme, Suzanne M. 45441
Prugh, Burton 41996
Pruitt, John E. 47729
Prum, Richard O. 44685
Prunet, Pierre 14287
Prusinovsky, Rupert 19327
Pruska, Mariola 31749
Pryor, Eric 47877
Prys-Jones, Dr. R. 40727
Przeczewski, P. Marek 23932
Przekazinski, Andrzej 32089
Przigoda, Dr. Stefan 16193
Przybilla, Carrie 41348
Przybył, Grazyna 31593
Przybylska, Grażyna 31954
Przybysz, Jane 47357
Przygoda, Udo 17043
Przypkowski, Piotr Maciej 31628
Psarapoulou, Betty 20854
Psenner, Dr. Barbara 02064
Psota, Dr. Thomas 36541
Puccinelli, Lydia 48374
Puccini, Simonetta 25772
Puchner, Manfred 02239
Puckett, Jakobus 17878
Puckett, James 15580
Puckett, Margaret 41492
Puckett, Robert A. 48612
Puckett, Tom 43176
Puddy, Audrey 38319
Pudelska, Aleksandra 31899
Pudney-Schmidt, Birgid 16728
Puech, Laurent 12497
Pühle, Dr. Matthias 18589
Puentes de Valderrama, Ana Rosa 07594
Pürro, Gertrud 36593
Puerta, Prof. J. 34994
Puertas Tricas, Rafael 35072, 35073
Puerto, Dr. F. Javier 35025
Pütz, Ursula 19333
Püüa, Endel 09333, 09335, 09336
Puga, Rosa D. 06909
Pugačevskaja, Alla Aleksandrovna 33150
Puget, Catherine 13803
Puggaard, Ole 08894
Pugh, Connie 06146
Pugi, Guido 25045
Puharich, Nick 30141
Puhle, Dr. Matthias 18581, 18584
Puhlmann, Dr. Helga 18833
Puig, Felipe 41004
Pujol, Albert 34579
Pujol, Gloria 00084
Puklowski, Tracy 30197
Pule, Tickey 03934
Pulinka, Steven M. 46092
Pulle, Thomas 02605
Pullen, Bernice 46194
Pullen, Reg 45981
Pullen, Sue 39285
Pullin, Robert 38868
Pulnar, Janusz 31938
Pultz, John 44686
Pulvenis de Séligny, Marie-Thérèse 13321
Pumbaya, Ismael 31399
Pumphrey, Jim 42111
Pungerčar, Majda 34136
Puntman, Paul 30014

Pupo de Mogallón, Yolanda 07456
Purba, Suruhen 22158
Purdy, Dorothea 42011
Pure Via, Luis 35658
Purin, Bernhard 18859, 19816
Purin, Sergio 03337
Purke, Terry 48073
Purkis, Harriet 39815, 39816, 39818
Purrington-Hild, Sally 42039
Purslow, Martin 39579
Purves, W.M. 38894
Puscher 18197
Puschnig, Dr. André 36514
Pusineri, Prof. Adelina 31102
Pusineri Scala, Prof. Carlos Alberto 31100
Puste, Jennifer 42156
Pusterla-Cambin, Patrizia 36892
Pusztai, László 21356
Putman, Christy 45886
Putnam, Erna 41270
Putnam, Michael 41501
Putsch, Dr. Jochem 19986
Putyńska, Elżbieta 31512
Putz, Karl 20124
Putze, Alfred 17889
Puype, J.P. 29079
Puyplat, Lisa 16924
Puzanova, N.A. 27072
Puzrina, Oksana Jurjevna 33018
Py, Cyille 14063
Py, Jacques 14855
Pyatt, John 30178
Pycke, J. 03797
Pyhrr, Stuart 45833
Pyka, Henryk 31645
Pykäläinen, Mari 10109
Pyle, Hilary 22446
Pylkkänen, Heikki 09658
Pym-Hember, Peter 06067
Pynn, Jo Ann 06582
Pyrrou-Drivalou, Ourania 20858
Pysher, Ray 45218
Qëndro, Gëzim 00033
Qin, Xinghan 06977
Qiu, Fang 06948
Quaas, Achim 17555
Quaas, Dr. Gerhard 15939
Quackenbush, Bill 06766
Quackenbush, Laura J. 44714
Quackenbush, Molly 41989
Quackenbush, W.G. 05046
Quaghebeur, Marc 03270
Quail, Sarah 40248, 40249, 40250, 40251, 40256, 40259
Quairiaux, Yves 03640
Qualizza, Dr. Marino 25847
Qualmann, Kenneth 40896
Quam, Jeffery 45185
Quann, Byron 43927
Quarcooporne, Nii 45892
Quarles Van Ufford, Dr. C.C.G. 28829, 29914
Quartero, Dr. Luigi 26009
Quaß, Alois 03033
Quast, Dr. Dieter 18606
Quasthoff, Michael 17611
Quatember, Dr. Wolfgang 01781
Quattrocchi, A. 06414
Quattrociocchi, Maria Pia 24879
Quayle, Frederick M. 47895
Quéau, Jean-François 11008
Quellenberg, Björn 37386
Queree, Jennifer 30124
Querejazu Calvo, Dr. Jorge 03904
Quero Castro, Salvador 35029
Quetard, Patrice 10497
Quevedo, Emilio 07537
Quevedo, Jacinto 35242
Quibell, Batty J. 47058
Quick, Estelle 40670
Quien, Prof. Guido 07782
Quijano, Marcela 20257
Quilitzsch, Uwe 16582
Quilter, Jeffrey 48351
Quinata, Tom 21258
Quinet, Władysław 03799
Quinlan, Karen 00794
Quinlan, M. 38165
Quinn, Betty 22412
Quinn, James F. 45424
Quinn, Thomas 22482
Quinn, Vivienne 38423
Quint, Eduard 29452
Quintanilla, Faustino 41549
Quintart, A. 03223
Quintelier, Johan 03458
Quintens, Patricia 03269
Quintens, Roger 03563
Quintern, Dr. Henry 01995
Quintero Durán, Miguel 07537
Quinto, Christine 39227
Quinton, Cathy 47233
Quirce, Sylvie 12047
Quirke, S. 39743
Quist, Kris N. 45457, 47359
Quoc Binh, Prof. Dr. Truong 48981
Quoc Quan, Phạm 48980
Raabe, Dr. Eva Ch. 17047, 17061
Raaber, Achim 02959

Raacke, Norbert 45735
Raade, Prof. Gunnar 30735
Raahauge, Kristine 21232
Raassen Kruimel, E.J.C. 29499
Raath, A. 34343
Rabal Merola, Victoria 34674
Rabano, Isabel 35037
Rabben, Anne Lise 30746
Rabbidge, Ted 30319
Rabeder, Dr. G. 01691
Rabeling, C.M. 29159
Raber, Christie 48161
Rabie, L.N. 34242
Rabino Massa, Prof. Emma 25747
Rabinovitch, Victor 05894
Rabinowitz, Rivka 22734
Rabner, Mario 28198
Rabner Cymerman, Mauricio 27949
Rabold, Dr. Joachim Martin 15860
Raboud, Isabelle 37285
Raby, Dr. Julian 48457
Race, Anne Katrin 15650
Racey, Nicholas 47849
Rachewitz, Dr. Siegfried de 25708, 25709
Rachinger, Dr. Johanna 02955
Rachman Zeth, H.R.A. 22170
Rachmankulov, Ilgiz Šamiljevič 32898
Racine, Bruno 13629
Racine, Ellen 46017
Racine, Yolande 05247
Rack, Theo 17260
Racker, Barbara 47076
Rackham, J.E. 39491
Rackow, Marcia 45879
Racky, Kurt 19270
Raczka, Laurel 46438
Raczka, Robert 45215
Rada, Judith K. 48015
Radam, B. 40559
Radawetz, Natalia 06844
Radčenko, Olga Ivanovna 33376
Raddatz, Dr. Corinna 17561
Radday, Helmut 16476
Radecki, Ronald 47682
Rademacher, Henning 17567
Radford, Ron 00704
Radić, Danka 07794
Radić, Ljubica 07716
Radić, Mladen 07750
Radić, Nikola 07842
Radicke, Rüdiger 19827
Radigois, Bertrand 12601, 12603
Radigonda, Ron 46117
Radins, A. 27428
Radivojević, Milan 33821
Radley, Seán 22519
Radloff, Rodney 48619
Radman-Livaja, Ivan 07809
Radojčić, Milica 03910
Radovanović, Dragan 33887
Radović, Andelija 33819
Radović, Slobodan 03923
Radschinski, Margitta 20761
Radtke, Christian 19793
Radtke, Edward 31761
Radulescu, Speranta 32470
Radulović, Ema 33857
Radulović, Ksenija 33809
Radwan, Krzysztof 31713
Radycki, Dr. Diane 41669
Radzak, Lee 48128
Radziewicz, Mary Ellen 41511
Radzilowicz, John 46512
Radzina, K. 27441
Raemdonck, André 03325
Rafey, Souhad 45754
Raffaelli, Prof. Mauro 23865
Raffel, Suhanya 01459
Raffelt, L. 18842
Rafferty, Pauline 06729
Raffi, Prof. S. 23136
Rafuse, Linda 05759, 05760
Ragan, Charlotte 42085
Ragionieri, Dr. Pina 23825
Ragni, Dr. Elena 23201
Rago, Kara 44823
Ragon, Jacques 14322
Ragsdale, Tammie 45036
Raguindin, Ethelinda A. 31281
Rahaman, F. 22025
Rahe, Dr. 18496
Rahe, Gebhard 19746
Rahlff, Reiner 16410, 20543
Rahman Chuchu, Abdul 04602
Rahman-Steinert, Uta 16057
Rahmani, Dr. A.R. 21951
Rahmatulaev, I. 48841
Rai, Archana 21719
Raidl, Dieter 01859
Raihle, Jan 35882
Raimond, Jean-Bernard 10671
Raimondi, Dr. Ludovico 24031
Rainbird, Stephen 01140
Rainbow, Prof. P. 39733
Rainer, Gerhard Florian 02945
Raineri, Maguerite 44540
Raines, James L. 47231
Raines, K. 05815
Rainsbury, Anne 38546

Raiola, Jonathan 45808
Rais, Dagmar 05950
Raisor, Jerry 46864
Raiss, Gerhard 16931
Rait, Eleanor 43987
Raith, Robert 16635
Raithel, Andreas 18966
Raja, Dr. Mohamad J. 21985
Rajaram, K. 21983
Rajčeva, Vasilka 04794
Rajchevska, Tsvetana 04846
Rajić, Delfina 33827
Rajkinski, Dr. Ivan 04928
Rajkinski, Ivan 04929
Rajkumar, Kimcha 06677
Rakke, Jim 43785
Rakonjac, Srdjan 33810
Rakotoarisoa, Jean-Aimé 27600
Raku XV, Kichizaemon 26446
Rakusanová, Marie 08577
Ralčev, Prof. Georgi 04854
Ralli, Efterpi 20897
Ralls, Nick 40353
Ralston, B. 30104
Ramachandran, V.S. 21916
Ramade, P. 15054
Ramaekers, M.T. 03761, 03762
Ramage, Alastair 39049
Raman, Anna 37701
Ramazanoğlu, Muzaffer 37723
Rambelli, Faustolo 24302
Rambo, Dr. Deborah 47568
Rambourg, Bernard 13923
Rambow, Charles 43428
Ramesh, J. 21680
Ramet, Nathan 03615
Ramezan-nia, T. 22268
Ramharter, Dr. Johannes 02747
Ramirez, Angel Antonio 07491
Ramirez, Jan 45858
Ramirez, Joe 42130
Ramírez, José Juan 35519
Ramirez, Marcela E. 28114
Ramirez, Mari Carmen 44129
Ramírez, Suny 27952
Ramírez Casali, María Eliana 06917
Ramírez de Lara, Ligia 07467
Ramírez Hernández, Jose Luis 28474
Rammer, Gottfried 02147
Ramón Vilarasau, Sandra 48907
Ramond, Serge 15139
Ramoneda, Josep 34534
Ramoneda, Prof. Luis Alberto 00364
Ramos, Margarida 32313
Ramos, Salome D. 31455
Ramos Fernández, Dr. Rafael 34790
Ramos Horta, Dr. José 09130
Ramos Pérez, Froilán 28069
Ramos Ruíz, Martha 07529
Rampazzi, Filippo 36899
Rampl, Dr. Franziska 01728
Ramsauer, Dr. Gabriele 02543, 02544
Ramsay, Gael 00761
Ramsay, Peter 01282
Ramsay, Susan 06492
Ramsden, Alan R. 05970
Ramsden, S. 38329
Ramsden, William 47853, 47856
Ramsden-Binks, T. 38669
Ramseuer, Dr. Gabriele 02570
Ramsey, Peter 46140
Ramsey, Ron 00886
Ramsey, Steve 45984
Ramseyer, Dr. Denis 36796
Ramskjaer, Liv 30754
Ramušćak, Prof. Ljubica 07687
Ramuschi, Maria Cristina 25786
Ramut, Eliza 31473
Rana, A.K. 21760
Ranade, Dr. Hari Govind 21994
Ranaldi, Prof. Franco 25028
Rand, Michael 48451
Rand, Patrick 42504
Rand, Richard 48634
Randall, R. Dennis 44142
Randall, Ross 41136
Randall, Ross G. 45545
Randazzo, Giuseppe 24773
Randić Barlek, Mirjana 07813
Randow, Renate von 20568
Raney, Floyd 44829
Raney, Nancy 41683
Ranftl, Helmut 02242
Range, Dorothy 48731
Rangström, Lena 36256
Raninen-Siiskonen, Tarja 09580, 09581
Ranjbaran, Sa'eid 22290
Rank, Karin 17099
Rank-Beauchamp, Elizabeth 47580
Ranker, Prof. Thomas A. 41837
Rankin, John L. 05579
Rankin jr, P.R. 43154
Rankin, Ray 39610
Rankin, Shan 43088
Ransom Lehman, Karen 46066
Ransome Wallis, Rosemary 39644
Ranšová, Eva 08507
Rantanen, Reijo 10199
Rao, D.V. 22000

Rapetti, Rodolphe 13641
Rapisarda, Alfredo Pablo 00668
Rapkin, Grace 45821
Rapmund, J. 29759
Raposo, Luís 32306
Rapp, Karen 46923
Rappe-Weber, Dr. Susanne 20634
Raptou, E. 08198
Raptou, Dr. Eustathios 08215
Rardin Johnson, Sara 46657
Rarhein, Ingar 30484
Rasajski, Javor 33928
Rasario, Dr. Giovanna 23869
Rasbury, Patricia 45626
Rasch, Elisabeth 36349
Rasch, Tone 30754
Rasche, Dr. Adelheid 16025
Rash, Roswitha M. 46371, 46372, 46373, 46376, 46379
Rašidov, G.R. 48861
Rasjid, A. 22153
Rask, Sven 08839
Rasmusen, Milo 42502
Rasmussen, Alan H. 08909
Rasmussen, Frank Allan 08938
Rasmussen, Keith 44541
Rasmussen, Dr. Pamela 43054
Rasmussen, Robert 46343
Rasmussen, William 46890
Rasmusson, Allan 36421
Raspail, Thierry 12729
Rassweiler, Janet 45891
Rastas, Perttu 09501
Rašticová, Dr. Blanka 08698
Rataiczyk, Matthias 17514
Ratcliffe, Dr. Brett C. 44793
Ratcliffe, Shirley 38607
Rath, H. 19781
Rath, Dr. Harald 03004
Rath, Herbert 01902
Rath, I. 19781
Rath, L. 17801
Rathbone, Eliza 48389
Rathbun, Merrilyn 43413
Rathburn, Robert R. 41708
Rathfelder, Johannes 02798
Rathgeber, Paul 16447, 16449
Rathke, Dr. Christian 19239
Rathman, Deane 48183
Ratier, Hugo 00461
Ratner, Phillip 22788
Ratnikova, Marina Semënovna 33740
Rattemeyer, Dr. Volker 20576
Rattenborg, Cena 46071
Rattenbury, Richard 46116
Ratti, Dr. Enrico 25926
Ratti, Dr. Marzia 24123
Ratti, Pietro 24119
Rattigan, John 22466
Ratzeburg, Wiebke 16302
Ratzenböck, Hans-Jörg 02229
Ratzky, Dr. Rita 21378
Ratzloff, Betty Lou 45547
Rau, Lorraine 43318, 43318
Rau, Dr. Patrick 18201
Rau, Prof. Dr. Peter 17569
Rauch, L. 37153
Rauch, Margot 02079, 02918
Rauch, Werner 13439
Rauchbauer, Judith von 15478
Rauchensteiner, Dr. Manfried 02895
Rauchenwald, Alexandra 01694
Raud, Anu 09322
Raudsepa, Ingrida 27402
Raudsepp, Renita 09358
Rauf, Barb 42699
Raunio, Erkki 09419
Rauø, Kåre William 30490
Raus, Edmund 45091
Rausch, Amalia 03056
Rausch, Guy 27563
Rausch, Jürgen 19367
Rauschenberg, Chris 46631
Rauscher, August 02448
Rauscher, Hannelore 20486
Raussmüller, Urs 37130
Raussmüller-Sauer, Christel 37130
Rauzi, Prof. Estebar 00464
Ravagnan, Dr. Giovanna Luisa 25923
Ravanelli Guidotti, Dr. Carmen 23754
Ravaonatoandro, Aldine 27603
Ravasi, Prof. Gianfranco 24416
Ravasi, Gianfranco 25897
Ravasio, Dr. Tiziana 23044
Ravaux, J.-P. 11130, 11132
Rave, Dr. August B. 20106
Raved, Noga 22580
Raveendran, K. 22042
Raveh, Kurt 22719
Ravel, Christian 12800
Ravelo Virgen, Margarita 28576
Ravenal, John 46891
Ravenscraft, Pauline 48183
Raverty, Norm 01004
Ravid, Zami 22712
Raviv, Efraim 22731
Ravnik Toman, Barbara 34086, 34087, 34099, 34100, 34101, 34154
Ravoire, Olivier 13429

Ravonatoandro, Aldine 27602
Rawdon, David D. 34306
Rawle, Caroline 40818
Rawluk-Raus, Bożena 31945
Rawstern, Sherri 41045
Rawsthorn, Alice 39623
Ray, Dulce Ivette 43488
Ray, Dr. Ella Maria 42887
Ray, Jeffrey 46393
Ray, Justice A.N. 21904
Ray, Randy W. 44130
Ray, Romita 41318
Ray, Shirley 44449
Rayburn, Ella S. 47521
Rayburn, Nicholas 47041
Rayment, John 39412
Raymond, David 44391
Raymond, Nancy 06704
Raymond, Richard 48802
Raymond, Yvette 05642
Rayne, Angela 43711
Raynolds, Robert 45126
Rayworth, Shelagh F. 06482
Razafindratsima, Clarisse 27606
Razzaq Moaz, Dr. Abdal 37436
Read, Albert J. 46160
Read, B. 37974
Read, Bob 44663
Read, Liz 22444
Read, Peter 30152
Read, Robert F. 42733
Read, Rolly 22444
Real, Nelson A. 00348
Reale, Giuseppe 24574
Reale, Dr. Isabella 25846
Reale, Sara W. 44311
Reap, Mary 47519
Reason, Robert 00704
Reber, Dr. Alfred 36895
Reber, Eugene 42510
Reber, Dr. Markus 37179
Reber, Paul 48702
Rebhandl, Reinhold 02684
Rebman, Dr. Jon 47295
Rebmann, Dr. Martina 17989
Réboli, Eliana Moro 04078
Rębosz, Ireneusz 31841
Rebuschat, Karlheinz 17227
Recalt, Gustavo 00260
Recanati, Harry 06919
Recanatini, Cesare 22883
Reček, Antonín 08560, 08682
Rečev, Vasil 04818
Rech, Prof. Dr. Manfred 16321
Rechberger, Erwin 02007
Recht, Roland 14821
Recio Crespo, Miguel Angel 35058, 35380
Recio Crespoz, Miguel Angel 35552
Reck, Pat 41101
Reckitt, Helena 41331
Recouvrot, M. 14452
Rector, P. 34511
Recupero, Jacopo 22895
Reczek, Krzysztof 31680
Reddeker, Lioba 02842, 02843
Reddell, James R. 41421
Redding, Mary Anne 42242
Redenbach, Marj 05838
Redlaczyk, Janelle 48614
Redlich, Daniela 17056
Redlin, Jane 16051
Redmann, Sheila K. 47063
Redmond, Dr. Brian 42467
Redmond-Cooper, Helen 38897
Redolfi, Silke 37095
Redpath, Donna 05450
Redvale, Jolene 48815
Reed, Andy 01021
Reed, C. 40555
Reed, Caroline M. 39724
Reed, Dorothy 45223
Reed, Gerard 00702
Reed, Ian 38932
Reed, J. 39839
Reed, Leon B. 42671
Reed, Mark 46646
Reed, Mary 45518, 45639
Reed, Michael 44118
Reed, Patrick H. 43438
Reed, Philip 39595, 39671
Reed, Robin Edward 46883
Reed, Sharon 48743
Reed, Ursula 46424
Reeder, Deborah 46688
Reeder, Warwick 01231
Reedie, K.G.H. 38471, 38472
Reedy, Joan M. 48806
Reekie, Clara 45581
Reel, David M. 48543
Reel, Paula 41205
Reel, Robert 44757
Reenberg, Holger 08868
Rees, Diane 44965
Rees, Elfan 40834
Rees, James C. 45546
Rees, Monica 38184
Rees-Jones, Elizabeth 39489
Reese, Dr. Beate 20700
Reese, David L. 45808

Reese, Frances S. 46677
Reese, Gary 47923
Reese, Julie 46335
Reeskamp, E. 29897
Reeve, Anthony 39729
Reeve, William F. 06162
Reevees, D.W. 40930
Reeves, Dr. Deborah 48214
Reeves, Dennis 39521
Reeves, Don 46116
Reeves, Kate A. 45573
Reeves, Lee 41190
Reeves, Dr. Nicholas 38952
Refsum, Siri 30770
Regan, Brian 45863
Regan, Mary 43617
Regan, Michael 39597
Regêncio Macedo, Carlos António 32262
Regenvanu, Ralph 48866
Reggiori, Albino 24164
Regibus, Raymond de 37128
Regier, Charles 45999
Regli, Kurt 36791
Regnauer, Dr. A. 19914
Regnier, Gérard 13644
Regoli, Dr. Edina 25284
Regull, Enrique 35658
Řeháková, Dr. Hana 08532, 08533
Rehberg, Dr. Rolf 19452
Rehberg, Vivian 13948
Rehberger, Prof. Dr. Dr. Karl 02563
Rehde, Anders 08814, 08816
Reher, Charles A. 44649
Reher, Dr. Uwe 18030
Rehm, Dr. Heinrich 19267
Rehor, Ophelia 15836
Rei, M. 34326
Reiblich, Luisa 18615
Reich, Dr. Annette 17970
Reich, Christopher J. 42786
Reich, Dindy 43089
Reich, Jacqueline 14499
Reichard, Tim 48020
Reichel, Antje 17650
Reichel, Maik 18564, 18565
Reichel, Reinhard 17295
Reichen, Quirinus 36541
Reichenbach, Dr. Maria Cecilia von 00390
Reichenbach, Svenja Gräfin von 15937
Reicher, Elisabeth 02945
Reichert, Klara 18660
Reichholf, Prof. Prof. Dr. J. 18926
Reichl, Leo 02101
Reichmann, Dr. Christoph 18228
Reichmann, Hans-Peter 17036
Reichmann, Kurt 19270
Reichmuth, Bernhard 36812
Reickart, Harry 42450
Reid, Alan 38692
Reid, Alison 38987
Reid, David 38787
Reid, Dennis 06561
Reid, Gare B. 47579
Reid, Grace 41706
Reid, Graeme 44568
Reid, Dr. John S. 37933
Reid, Kevin 38732
Reid, Kim 06122
Reid, Marie-Claude 06313
Reid, Megan 48818
Reid, Michelle 43781
Reid, Richard 05514
Reid, Scott 39937, 39938
Reid, Prof. Seona 39048
Reid-Bavis, Glenda 05282
Reid Hardman, Mimi 44597
Reid-Wallace, Dr. Carolyn 45617
Reid Williamson, J. 42056, 44231
Reidel, Dr. Hermann 19518, 19519
Reidy, Susan 48157
Reifenscheid-Ronnisch, Dr. Beate 18121
Reijmers, M. 28866
Reijnders, Dr. W. 28983
Reiles, Paul 27567
Reilly, Ann-Marie 45756
Reilly, Gerry 48588
Reilly, John W. 43031
Reilly, Margaret T. 39052
Reilly, Robin 05018
Reilly, Valerie A. 40161
Reimann, Rella 46307
Reimann, Urs 36509
Reimer, Wayne 06140
Reimoneng, H. 21253
Rein, Dr. Anette 17061
Rein, Elfriede 15693
Reinbacher, Adolf 01853
Reinbold, Dr. Michael 19256
Reincken, Sharon 48332
Reinders, Dr. Carin E.M. 28924
Reinders, C.E.M. 29880
Reinders, P.J. 29178
Reinecke, Klaus 17981
Reinert, Frank 27567
Reinert, Hans-Walter 19176
Reines Josephy, Marcia 44924
Reinhard, Adelheid 19605
Reinhard, Erika 18209
Reinhard, Rolf 18209

Reinhard-Felice, Dr. Mariantonia 37214, 37339
Reinhardt, Dr. Brigitte 20257, 20261
Reinhardt, Dr. Georg 18452
Reinhardt, Hannelore 20247
Reinholdt, Bruce 48329
Reinholdt, Helle 09059
Reinig, Margot 17548
Reininghaus, Ruth 45866
Reinisch, Christine 02565
Reinisch, Dr. Tobias 02968
Reinius, Doris 17025
Reinke, Doris M. 43145
Reinsch, Prof. Dietmar 16300
Reis, Heitor 04428
Reis, Jennifer 45493
Reis, Dr. José 32265
Reisacher, Anton 36587
Reisch, Prof. Dr. Ludwig 16925
Reisetbauer, Hans 02562
Reising, Dr. Gert 18002
Reisner, Peter 19642
Reiss, Johannes 01810
Reisse, Hans Peter 18020
Reissenweber, E. 16375
Reißer, Gudrun 16636, 16637, 16638, 16639,
   16640, 16642
Reisz, Frederick S. 44920
Reiter, Alois 02618
Reiter, Carmen 01741
Reiter, Günther 02197
Reiter, Klaus Giselher 18906
Reiterer, Bruno 02551
Reithinger, Gilles 13491
Reitner, Prof. Dr. J. 17337
Reitz, Dr. E. 41319
Reitz, Thomas A. 05695
Reitzler, Anne 43030
Rejimbal, Tamara 45529
Rejn, J. Surya Narayara 21817
Rejune Adams, Gloria 42863
Rekker, L. 29931
Rell, Zofia 31893
Rem, Dr. P.H. 28928
Remen, Geir 30671
Remillon, Michel 12839
Remington, Charlotte 44855
Rémon, Régine 03567
Remsen, Dr. J.V. 41532
Renaux, Jean-Pierre 14802
Renda, Dr. Gerhard 16155
Render, Lorne E. 45108
Rendić-Miočević, Prof. Ante 07809
Renfrew, Katherine A. 45964
Renfro, Francis 42966
Renfro, Gladys 44148
Renger, Dr. Konrad 18832, 18832
Rengnath, Rudi 16603
Renken, Dr. Lisa 44850
Renn, Wendelin 20320
Rennicke, Stefan 19178
Rennie, Heather 05038
Rennie, Ian 38790
Rennie, Jennifer A. 37959
Rennie, Mairi C. 48260
Renning, Kenneth 45714
Rennox, Munuma 28759
Renouf, Nicholas 45701
Renouf, Phil 01398
Rensberger, Dr. John M. 47529
Rent, Dr. Clyda S. 42583
Renting, Dr. A.D. 28928
Renton, Alan 40182
Renton, John 40090
Rentoul, A. 00996
Rentzhog, Sten 36146, 36147
Renvall, Dr. Pertti 09720
Renz, Joachim 19003
Renz, Ruth 47468
Renzl, Ludwig 02407
Renzo, Luigi 25288
Reo, Danielle 47277
Repetto, Arnaldo 24053
Rephann, Richard 45701
Reppe, C. 19454
Requejo, Angel 35680
Reris, L.S.D. 35752
Reser, Dr. Ladislaus 36914
Rességuier, Bernadette de 13195
Ressel, Dr. Stephen 41499
Ressiter, Jeremy 40802
Ressmeyer, Richard 42232
Restall, Robin 48901
Restif, Claire le 12067
Restle, Prof. Dr. Conny 16070
Resurreccion jr., Teodoro R. 31348
Retallick, Leslie 40719
Rethly, Akos 21384
Retière, Ch. 11536
Retière, Marie-Noëlle 13376
Retno, Dr. Sulistianingsih S. 22117
Rettenbeck, Georg 16614
Rettenmund, Jürg 36811
Rettig, Wolfram 17556
Retzlaff, Detlef 19013
Reublin, Patricia 43784
Reuland, G. 27554
Reumer, Dr. J.W.F. 29766
Reus, B. de 29666
Reuße, Dr. Felix 17107

Reustle, M. Charles 42647
Reustle, Dr. S. 20611
Reuter, Cecelia 43405
Reuter, Horst 18361
Reuter, Laurel J. 43743
Reuter, Pat 43125
Reuter, Scott 41308, 41311, 41312
Reuter, Simone 15745
Reuter, Dr. Wolfgang 17220
Reuther, Dr. Manfred 19039
Reutimann, Daniel 37267
Revelard, Michel 03217
Revilla Uceda, Mateo 34872, 34876
Rew, Christine 37942
Rex Svansson, Karin 36372, 36374
Rex Svensson, Karin 36373
Rexwinkel, Nancy 41932
Rey, Marie-Catherine 11599
Rey-Delqué, Monique 14948
Rey-Vodoz, Véronique 36995
Reyer, Manfred 15862
Reyer-Völlenklee, Silvia 02075
Reyes, Manuel 21263
Reyes, Patricia 45863
Reyes Flórez, Graciela 07462
Reyes Mota, Dr. Alicia 28112
Reymann, Patrick H. 42485
Reymond, Catherine 36950
Reynaldo, Pia 48174
Reynies, Béatrice de 13617
Reynolds, Craig 44163
Reynolds, David 44762
Reynolds, Earl 45535
Reynolds, Edmond 47092
Reynolds, Elsie 06267
Reynolds, Janelle 06839
Reynolds, Jerry 48669
Reynolds, Jock 45700
Reynolds, Nancy 45677
Reynolds, R.G. 38494
Reynolds, Stanley G. 06779
Reynolds, Dr. Terry 44661
Reynolds, Valrae 45892
Reynolds Brown, C. 48660, 48663
Reys, M. 29582
Rezai, N. 22333
Rezeanu, Prof. Paul 32506
Rezler, Aleš 08437
Rezník, Branislav 33949
Rhamie, Barb 42162
Rhees, David J. 45381
Rhein, Dr. Stefan 18570, 18571, 18572, 18575,
   18576
Rhi, Prof. Ju-Hyung 27276
Rhie, Dr. Jong-chul 27254
Rho, Jean 45789
Rhoades, John S. 44887
Rhoback, Kristine 41183
Rhode, Michael 48378
Rhodes, Carleen 47161
Rhodes, John 39033
Rhodes, Dr. Michael 40719
Rhodes, Ulysses S. 41957
Rhodes, William 45761
Rhomberg, Kathrin 18149
Rhymer, Clarence 05452
Rhys-Michael, Cellan 38348
Riaño Bernal, Wolfram Armando 07424
Riaño Lozano, Fernando 35049, 35693
Ribas San Emeterio, Neus 34480
Ribbert, Dr. Margret 36499, 36500
Ribbrock, Dr. Gerhard 18816
Ribé Monge, Genis 35348
Ribeiro, Agostinho 32282
Ribeiro, Francisca 32346
Ribeiro de Faria, Manuel José Marques 32305
Ribeiro Martins, António 32277
Ribero, Michel 15059
Ribes, Sonia 32421
Ribeton, Olivier 10621
Ribey, Barbara 06476
Riboreau, Brigitte 10869
Ricart, Dolors 34539
Ricci, Massimo 25425
Ricci, Pat 45721
Ricciardi, Prof. Mario 25757
Riccòmini, Prof. Eugenio 23110, 23112, 23140
Rice, Annette 43183
Rice, Calvin 42055
Rice, Christopher 38209
Rice, David 39080
Rice, Donald 41674
Rice, Jane 46842
Rice, Nancy N. 47129
Rice, Sean 45698
Rice Irwin, John 45977
Rich, Andrea L. 44921
Rich, Beverly 47634, 47635
Rich, Hans 17110
Rich, Margaret 00761
Rich, Mark S. 46882
Rich, Merle 41272
Rich, Nancy 46015
Rich, Pat 47115
Richard, Alison F. 45698
Richard, Christopher 46067
Richard, Jack 42736
Richard, Judy Morrissey 06551
Richard, Michel 12716

Richard, M.L. 06056
Richard, Nancy 41822
Richards, Beth 46406
Richards, Dolores 41775
Richards, Jane 41443
Richards, Janet 41218
Richards, John 39128
Richards, L. Jane 45405
Richards, Nancy 44093
Richards, Nancy E. 45667
Richards, Pat 47465
Richards, Paul 40489
Richards, Ron 44224
Richards, W.R. 38189
Richardson, Catherine 39305
Richardson, Darlene 46931
Richardson, Don H. 47805
Richardson, E. 39305
Richardson, Edgar 47504
Richardson, Gary 38778
Richardson, Dr. James B. 46511
Richardson, Jeanette 30280
Richardson, Katherine 47879
Richardson, Larry D. 41547
Richardson, Lindsey 45590
Richardson, Margaret 39777
Richardson, Mary 47504
Richardson, Meredith J. 46352
Richardson, Michael 43457
Richardson, Roy 30167
Richardson, R.T. 39450
Richardson, Sarah 40038
Richardson, Vivian 48315
Richardt, Ursula 17991
Richart, Brigitte 11534
Richart, Christian 41278
Richartz, Christoffer 15920
Richaud, Maurice 15215
Riche, Nicole 10718
Riche-Descamps, Jeannine 03693
Richelson, Paul W. 45421
Richerson, Jim 46349
Richey, Susan 42571
Richmond, Alan 41179
Richmond, Art 44710
Richmond, Patricia 41860
Richmond-Rex, Phyllis E. 30365
Richner, Trudi 37262
Richon, Marco 36565
Richoux, Sylvie 12857
Richter, Bob 05737
Richter, Dr. Burkhard 17576
Richter, Donald 42777
Richter, Dr. Erhard 17395
Richter, Gert 17513
Richter, Gunnar 17468
Richter, Dr. Helmut 17167
Richter, Helmut 20492, 20494
Richter, Hiltrud 19270
Richter, Jenett 06832
Richter, Jörg 17500
Richter, Paul 01795
Richter, Paula 47198
Richter, Dr. S. 17100
Richter, Susie 44555
Richter, Tanya 44004
Richter, Dr. Thomas Michael 36541
Richter, Ursula 19454
Richthofen, Dr. Jasper von 17323, 17324
Richtsfeld, Dr. Bruno 18916
Richwagen, Sue 41970
Rick, Jane 39782
Rickards, Dr. R.B. 38462
Rickart, Eric 47235
Ricke, Dr. Helmut 16738
Rickenbach, Bertha von 36615
Rickenbach, Judith 37398
Ricker, Maria 06864
Ricker, Stephen A. 41584
Ricketts, Paul W. 48272
Ríčko, Oka 07704
Rico Perrat, Gabriela 27804
Riddell, Dr. Richard 38754
Riddle, Janet 30317
Riddle, Lola 46932
Ridgely, Barbara S. 43650
Riding, Gillian 39248
Riding, Jacqueline 39660
Ridley, David J. 38585
Ridley, Jackie D. 38747, 38749
Ridley, Jacqeline 38752
Ridley, Dr. Michael 38753
Ridpath, Marjorie 42052
Rieche, Dr. Anita 16246
Rieche, Christiane 17513, 17517
Riechert, Claudia 19886, 19887
Riechert, Karl-Ludwig 17596, 19361
Rieck, Silvana 15624, 15625
Ried, Martha 18246
Riedel, Andrea 19227
Riedel, Angela 22444
Riedel, Gerd-Rainer 16907
Riedel, Heinz 03002
Riedel, Dr. Matthias 18166
Riedel, Uwe 18772
Riedel, Walter G. 46172, 46173
Rieder, Alfred 37281
Riederer, Prof. Dr. Josef 49213
Riedesel, Rikarde 15609

Riedl, Monika 15717
Riedlmiller, Thomas 17168, 17170
Rieger, Sigrun 18833
Rieger-Jähner, Prof. Dr. Brigitte 17085
Riegler, Frank 02883
Riegler, Wolfgang 01657
Riego González, Angel 34667
Riehl, Ken 05143
Riek, Peter 16882, 16883
Riek, Rolf 18293
Rieken, Duane 44250
Riemann, Angelika 16646
Riemersma, Tiny 29133
Riepe, Ulrike 17620
Riepl, Heiner 19873
Riepniece, Ineta 27356
Riepula, Anne 09716
Ries, Christian 27568
Rieser, Gabriele 02788
Riesgo, Juan M. 35015
Riess, Gerhard 02937
Riestra de Cuevas, Bertha 28179
Riether, Dr. Achim 18912
Riethmüller, Dr. Marianne 17175
Riethmuller, Bruce 01518
Rietschel, Dr. Gerhard 18615
Rietvelt, Carol 44285
Rietzke, I. 15879
Rifaux, Yves 12801
Rife, Sandra B. 48632
Riffel, Carola 16844
Rifkin, Ned 48361
Riganti, Riccardo 25801
Rigby, Carol 39188, 40818
Rigby, S. 38242, 38244
Rigdon, Lois 41996
Rigdon, Marge 43008
Rigeade, Pascal 10668
Rigert, Markus 37328
Rigg, Frank 41812
Riggall, R.A. 01426
Riggins-Ezzell, Lois S. 45626
Riggio, Leonard 45793
Riggs, Carol 44998
Riggs, Gerry 42537
Riggs, Richard 44727
Riggs, Timothy A. 42196
Righetti, Olimpia L. 00618
Righolt, Niels 35948
Rigoli, Adriano 25867
Rigon, Lidia 25295
Řihová, Dr. Ivana 08663
Riibak, Renate 09367
Riker, Janet 41950
Rikkoert, A. 29814
Rikkonen, Mikko 10173
Riley, Angelika 17560
Riley, Barbara 44440
Riley, Cathy 48275
Riley, Cygred 43052
Riley, Grace 39776
Riley, Joseph P. 42213
Riley, Michael J. 47016
Riley, Norman 41376
Riley, Pat 43491
Riley, Peter 40433, 40434
Riley, Terence 44869
Rimer, G.J. 39450
Rimmö, Christina 36381
Rimoldi, Luciano 24729
Rimon, Ofra 22611
Rinaldi, Paolo 25697
Rinaldini, Dr. Francesco 23456
Rinck, Aksel 19035
Rinder, Lawrence R. 45886
Rindfleisch, Jan 42730
Rindlisbacher, Rolf 36964
Rindom Madsen, Finn 08975
Rindsfüsser, Annemarie 15696
Rinetti, Dr. Luigi 25983
Ring, Prof. Francis 38125
Ring, Klaus 16179
Ringelheim, Joan 48401
Ringgaard Lauridsen, Henning 09112
Ringler, Sarah 48511
Ringstad, Jan Erik 30822, 30823
Rink, Christine 18393
Rinker, Dr. Dagmar 20257
Rintala, Liisa 10077
Rintoul, Dr. Gordon 38886, 38895, 38899, 38910,
   40482, 40484, 40487
Riolini-Unger, Dr. Adelheid 17137
Rionda, Patricia Elena 00625
Riopelle, Christopher 39729
Riordan, Mary Ann 44477
Riordon, Bernard 05457, 05547
Ríos de Molina, Martha 28139
Rios de Saluso, María Luisa Adriana 00465
Ríos Montero, Sylvia 06911
Rios Rigau, Adlin 32363
Rios-Samaniego, Milita 47051
Riottot El-Habib, Béatrice 13655
Rioux, Alfred 05735
Ripatti, Marja-Liisa 09449, 09454
Ripley, John W. 48367
Ripoll, Rafael Romá 36935
Ripperová, Dr. Marie 08713
Rippstein, Laurence 37289
Rippy, C. 48105

Rippy, Linda 46558
Risani Dossi, Dr. Carola 23645
Risch, Laurie 42680
Riseman, Henry 41939
Riser, Cherie 45178
Rish, Sarah 44772
Rishel, Joseph 46421
Rishel, Joseph J. 46442, 46450
Risskov Sørensen, Kurt 08913
Rister, Faye 05600
Risthein, Helena 09358
Ristola, Ruth 46167
Ritch, Irene 06373
Ritchey, Robert L. 46594
Ritchie, Christina 06674
Ritschard, Claude-Janine 36743
Ritter, Martin 19211
Ritter, Michael 19020
Ritter, Mildred 41186
Ritter, Dr. Nicole 16378
Ritter, Wolfgang 16938
Rittler, Elisabeth 18916
Rittmann, Josef 02519
Rittwage, Roy 05134
Ritzmann, Dietrich-Wilhelm 19818
Riva, Davide 23320
Riva, Maurizio 23320
Rivard, Céline 06291
Rivas, Francisco 35238
Rivas, Helen 46622
Rivas Octavio, José A. 35032
Rivatton, Bernard 14201
Rivé, Isabelle 12724
Riveil, Gilbert 15024
Rivera, Dianna 41874
Rivera, George 47408
Rivera, Gigi 31442
Rivera, Mario 44190
Rivera, Prof. Osmin 21297
Rivera, Paula 47951
Rivera Caliz, Ramon E. 32373
Rivero Borrell, Héctor 28171
Rivers, Gabrielle 40265
Rivers, Mildred B. 43893
Rivière, Danielle 12748
Rivière, Dr. Dominique 13729, 15132
Rivoira, Prof. Giuseppe 25485
Rivolta, Barbara 48026
Riwar, Monique 36947
Rix, Peggy 42153
Rixhon, Maryse 03417
Rizzo, Antonio A. 00502
Rizzuto, Timothy C. 41528
Rjabov, Gennadij Evgenjevič 33581
Rjazanov, Aleksandr Michajlovič 32696
Rjazanova, Lilija Aleksandrovna 32763
Rjuken, Kjetil 30478
Roach, Ed 05739
Roaldset, Prof. Dr. Elen 30735, 30747, 30772
Robb, Doug 40098
Robb, Douglas 43888
Robb, Lisa 46328
Robbins, Anna 00783
Robbins, Carol 42751
Robbins, Carolyn 47514
Robbins, Daniel 39685
Robbins, Neil 39251
Robe, Sofia 32577
Robel, Sigrid 16503
Robelen, William G. 42862
Roberson, Jeanette W. 44589
Roberson, W. Allen 42566
Robert, Henri 11450
Robert, K.L. 05847
Roberts, Bette 45204
Roberts, Brady 46477
Roberts, Carty 45568
Roberts, Catsou 38347
Roberts, Coles 45985
Roberts, Dr. Dafydd 39534, 39536
Roberts, David 40488
Roberts, Day 05314
Roberts, Elaine 44690
Roberts, Gary 42286
Roberts, Sir Hugh 39752
Roberts, Hugh 39765
Roberts, James D. 47749
Roberts, Jan 42387
Roberts, Jill 45554
Roberts, John 38387
Roberts, Martin 38643
Roberts, Mary A. 48155
Roberts, Paige W. 41671
Roberts, Peg 41632
Roberts, Perri L. 42628
Roberts, Randy 47498
Roberts, Sir Samuel 38606
Roberts, Teresa 42652
Roberts-Douglass, Kathy 46973
Roberts-Walker, Gayle 41593
Róbertsdóttir, Gerdur 21648
Robertson, A. 38315
Robertson, Alexander 39442
Robertson, Beatrice L. 46342
Robertson, Beverly 45246
Robertson, Bruce 44921
Robertson, Byron 43645
Robertson, Charles J. 48392
Robertson, David 42322

Robertson, Dongwol Kim 42644
Robertson, Dr. H.G. 34213
Robertson, I. 39728
Robertson, I.G. 40442
Robertson, Lynn 42563
Robertson, Pamela B. 39050
Robertson, Pat 44172
Robertson, Preston 05951
Robertson, Rosalyn 46961
Robertson, Susan 48297
Robidoux, R.R. 46459
Robie, Kathlyn 47592
Robins, Dr. Gay 41352
Robinson, Alicia 39567
Robinson, Beulah 42371
Robinson, Bonnell 41797
Robinson, Bruce 01074
Robinson, Charles 38694
Robinson, Christine 47812
Robinson, Cliff 00875
Robinson, Dan 38552
Robinson, David 48212
Robinson, Deborah 40773, 40773
Robinson, D.N. 39834
Robinson, Don 41196
Robinson, Duncan 38454
Robinson, Franklin W. 44272
Robinson, Dr. George W. 44113
Robinson, Graham 30254
Robinson, Herb 05631
Robinson, Dr. James J. 44228
Robinson, John 43215
Robinson, John A. 01246
Robinson, Dr. Joyce 48154
Robinson, Julie 00704
Robinson, Katharine S. 42219, 42226
Robinson, Laurie 42630
Robinson, Louise 43493
Robinson, Malcolm J. 48077
Robinson, Michael 05167
Robinson, Michelle 42785
Robinson, Dr. Paul 38726
Robinson, Prof. Peter 41837
Robinson, Dr. Roger W. 43736
Robinson, Ruth 48640
Robinson, Thomas A. 43127
Robinson, Travis 44738
Robinson, William 42042
Robinson, William H. 42466
Robinson-Dowling, Martin 40736
Robison, Andrew C. 48373
Robles, José Angel 28400
Roblin, Laurent 11392
Robson, Judy 41302
Robson, Keith 40731
Roca, Teresa 34973
Rocca, Robert 11689
Rocchi, Dr. Silvano 25397
Roch, Dr. Heidi 17349
Roch, Neal 41109
Roch-Stübler, Dr. Heidi 17348, 17351, 17352
Rocha, Dr. Olivio 32237
Rocha Moreno, Leonor 07431
Rocha Virmond, Eduardo da 04070
Rochard, Dr. Patricia 17899
Rochat, Pierre 36523
Roche, Fr.S. 22037
Roche, James 42084
Rochefort, Hervé de 11451
Rochette, Christelle 12233
Rochette, Edward C. 42540
Rochmad, Edi 22065
Rockefeller, David 45761
Rockhill, King 45517
Rockhold, Jean 47015
Roda, Dr. Burkard von 36499, 36500, 36507
Roda, Dr. Hortensia von 37132
Rodák, Dr. Jozef 34070
Rodazie, M. 12723
Rodd, H.C. 40880
Roddick, J.H. 06732
Roddis, William H. 44975
Rodee, Marian 41104
Rodekamp, Dr. Volker 18383, 18409, 18415, 18418, 18419, 18424
Rodenburg, Teun 30036
Roder, Dr. Hartmut 16336
Roderick, Myron 47814
Rodes, David 44905
Rodeschini Galati, Dr. Maria Cristina 23060
Rodger, David 40674
Rodger, Robin 40185
Rodgers, James 44555
Rodgers, Jeff 42094
Rodgers, Kenneth G. 43023
Rodgers, Maureen 05118
Rodgers, Michael W. 43396
Rodgers, Michele 42121
Rodgers, Rachel A. 42098
Rodgers, Tommie 44679
Rodgers, Warren D. 43746
Rodgers, Z. 22459
Rodiek, Dr. Thorsten 18533, 18536, 18538, 18541, 18542, 18545
Rodimceva, I.A. 33032
Rodina, Lucia-Letiţia 32425
Rodini, Elizabeth 42322
Rodman, Vickie 47237
Rodney, Clayton 21290

Rodolfi, Rosanna 23905
Rodon, Francesc 35673
Rodrigo, Carmen 35601
Rodrigues, Dr. Paulo 04357
Rodrigues Meyer, Fernando 04274
Rodriguez, Carlos Armando 07444
Rodriguez, Carmen 42626
Rodriguez, Geno 45753
Rodriguez, John 42663
Rodríguez, José Alfonso 07449
Rodriguez, Roberto M. 42234
Rodríguez, Rosa 35601
Rodriguez, Teresa 48159
Rodriguez, Tomás 48914
Rodríguez Angarita, María Esther 07383
Rodríguez-Boette, Taryn 47069
Rodríguez-Boette, Taryn 47071
Rodríguez Culebras, Dr. Ramón 35458
Rodríguez de Montes, María Luisa 07364
Rodríguez del Camino, Marco 48914
Rodriguez Delucchi, Jorge 41010
Rodríguez Martín, Aurora 34997
Rodríguez-Mendoza, Amalia 41405
Rodríguez Ruza, Concepción 34764
Rodriquez, Jennie 47326
Rodríquez Culebras, Ramón 35678
Rodway, Em 42578
Röber, Dr. Ralph 18201
Röber, Wolf-Dieter 17299
Röck, Erwin 02462
Rödel, Klaus 08830
Roeder, Corinna 19255
Röder, Heinz 20631
Roeder, Paul 42698
Röder, Dr. Sabine 18225, 18227, 18229
Rödger, Ralf 15643
Rödiger-Diruf, Prof. Dr. Erika 18005
Röding, Lutz 16184
Roegiers, Prof. Dr. Jan 03562
Röhl, Johannes 15610
Roehmer, Dr. Marion 19113
Röhr, Angelika 03001
Röhrer-Ertl, Dr. Dr. O. 18826
Röhrig, Prof. Dr. Dr. Floridus 02141
Röhring, Micha 17798
Roelfsema-Hummel, Chris 46498
Roelink, Géke 28852
Röllig, Robert 18892
Roeloffs, Abigail 41767
Roelofs, Dr. P. 29632
Römer, Kurt 01710
Römer, Neria 36899
Römer, Stefan 18867
Römhild, Michael 17753
Roensch, Fred 44888
Röper, Dr. Martin 19992
Rösch, Dr. Mathias 18837
Röscher, Angela 16902
Roese, Ronnie L 42746
Roesink, Macha 28813
Röske, Dr. Thomas 17674
Roesler, Henry E. 45448
Rösner, Dr. Corinna 18890
Rössl, Dr. Joachim 02500, 02804
Rößler, Dr. Hans 19024
Rössler, Heiner 18697
Rössler, Prof. Leopold 02891
Rössler, Dr. R. 16468
Roest-den Hartogh, G.C. 29415
Röver-Kann, Dr. Anne 16328
Roffia, Dr. Elisabetta 23713, 25588
Rogalski, Dr. Andrzej 36902
Rogdeberg, Guttorm A. 30697
Rogé, Monique 14987
Roger, Will 47310
Rogers, Dianne 48722
Rogers, Floretta 41286
Rogers, James 43134
Rogers, James A. 48557
Rogers, James R. 43369
Rogers, June 45738
Rogers, Malcolm 41817
Rogers, Patricia 42637
Rogers, Peggy 43136
Rogers, Philippa 01623
Rogers, Rachael 37948
Rogers, Richard 45754
Rogers, Robert 43163
Rogers, Roy 48235
Rogers jr, Roy Dusty 41871
Rogers, Ted 47723
Rogers, Dr. T.L. 05562
Rogers-Barnett, Cheryl 48235
Rogerson, J.-C. 38769
Rogerson, L. 40156
Rogge, Marc 03807, 03858
Rogger, Prof. Iginio 25794
Roggero, Prof. Mario Federico 23479
Roggero, Sue 39138
Roggmann, Bettina 15400
Roggow, B. 20667, 20668
Rogić, Milena 07769
Rogiest, Peter 03146
Rogin, Ned 43212
Rogina, Bojana 34112
Rogl, Rudolf 01855
Roglán-Kelly, Dr. Mark 42755
Rogne, Odd 30909
Rogozińska, Ewa 31478

Roh, Michael 42558
Roháček, Dr. Jindřich 08521
Rohan, Antoinette Duchesse de 12090
Rohde-Hehr, Patricia 17560
Rohdt, Erwin 15740
Rohlfs, Stefan 16912
Rohner, John R. 41837
Rohner, Rudolf 36798, 36799
Rohr, Dr. Gerlinde 18418, 18419
Rohrbach, John 43480
Rohrer, Norbert 37204
Rohrer, Susan 46142
Rohsmann, Dr. Arnulf 02131
Rohwer, Dr. Sievert 47529
Roig Toqués, Francisco 35665
Roige, Annabella 46457
Roiß, Dr. Hubert 03034, 03035, 03036, 03039
Roitman, Dr. Adolfo D. 22662
Rojanova, Galina Iljinična 32879
Rojas de Moreno, María Eugenia 07613
Rojas Iragorri, Ximena 07407
Rojas Toro, Elizabeth 03907
Rojas y Cruzat, Oscar M. de 07881
Rojo Dominguez, Ana Cristina 34641
Rola, Stefan 31863
Roland, Dr. Berthold 15602
Roland, Debbie U. 47148
Roland, Greg 43806
Roland, Heather 42582
Roley, Scott 44202
Roll, Jarrod 41973
Roll, Kempton 41278
Rolla, Maureen 46510
Rolland, C. 11087
Rollenitz, Maria 02116
Roller, Dr. Hans-Ulrich 20359
Roller, Scott 45073
Roller, Dr. Stefan 20261
Rolley, Jean-Pierre 10288
Rollings, James R. 48540
Rollins, Avon W. 44512
Rollins, Fred H. 48442
Rollins, Ken 44653
Rolo Fajardo jr., Gaudioso 31443
Roloff, Prof. Dr. A. 20170
Romagnoli, Dr. Emilio 24550
Romagnoli, Martha Beatriz 00666
Romagnolo, Dr. Antonio 25298
Roman, Cynthia 43944
Román, Enrique 00316
Román Berrelleza, Juan Alberto 28163
Roman de Zurek, Teresita 07455
Romanelli, Prof. Giandomenico 25912, 25913, 25914, 25916, 25922, 25927, 25929, 25930, 25938, 25946
Romanenko, Maja Petrovna 33195
Romanenko, Vera Vladimirovna 32676
Romaniuc, Elvira 32529
Romanko, Jennifer 06778
Romano, Simona 24658
Romano, Socorro 34780
Romanova, Margarita Nikolevna 33653
Romanova, Raisa Michajlovna 32716
Romanowska, Marta 31719
Romard, Judith 05782
Romdhane, Khaled Ben 37553
Romeo, Paolo 24366
Rømer Sandberg, Ole 30524
Romero, Dr. Edgardo J. 00158
Romero, Mark 46618
Romero Ardila, Dídimo Ernesto 07502
Romero de Tejada, Pilar 35042
Romero de Torres, Rafael 34740
Roming, Lorenz 19846
Romińska, Elina 31840
Romito, Dr. Matilde 24627, 24753, 25317, 25319, 26005
Rommé, Dr. Barbara 18946
Rommel, Dr. Ludwig 17747
Romney, George 44206
Romney, George G. 44204
Romportlová, Simona 08275
Romsics, Imre 21438
Romualdi, Antonella 23840
Rona, Zeynep 37685
Ronaghan, Allen 05629
Ronald, William 01353
Ronchi, Dr. Benedetto 25783
Roncière, Florence de la 10550, 12777
Rončkevičová, Antónia 34062
Róncoli, Mónica 00107
Rondeau, James 42304, 42304
Rondot, Bertrand 13586
Ronfort, J.N. 13482
Ronig, Prof. Dr. Dr. Franz 20208
Ronning, Peggy 45166
Ronowicz, Małgorzata 31781
Ronte, Prof. Dr. Dieter 16242
Roode, I. de 28902
Roodt, Frans 34331
Roohfar, Z. 22311
Rooke, Daru 39447
Rooney, Dr. Brendan 22446
Rooney, Jan 45753
Rooney, Mary 30179
Roos, Dr. Klaus-Dieter 18990
Roosa, Jan 48225
Roose, B. 03265
Roosen, Jean-Paul 10958

Roosevelt, Christopher 44993
Roosing, Jan Jaap 20753, 20754
Root, Deane L. 46513
Root, Margaret 41218
Roots, Gerrard 39607
Roper, Donna K. 46337
Roper, Mark 38523
Ropp, Ann 44345
Ropp, Harry 42988
Roppelt, Dr. Tanja 16435
Ropponen, Liisa 09431
Roque Gameiro, Maria Alzira 32320
Roques, Thierry 11066
Roquette-Gept, Marie-Christine 14590
Rorem, Ned 45754
Rorschach, Kimerly 42322
Rosa, Jocelyn R. de la 31303
Rosa, Joseph 46510, 47339
Conceição Duarte Rosa, Maria da 04234
Rosa, Mercedes 04422
Rosales, Felipe 31286
Rosales Huatuco, Dr. Odón 31110
Rosales Vergas, Manuel 28145
Rosanbo, Richard de 12337
Rosas de Silva Rebelo, Dr. Margarida 32338
Rosasco, Betsy 46703
Rosberg, Ingemar 35838
Rose, Ben 48428
Rose, Gilles 11262
Rose, Mary 45400
Rose, Dr. Murray 38134
Rose, Rebecca 46883
Rose, Sally 38864, 38865
Rose, Susan 06128
Rose, Wilhelm 15870
Roselli, Bart A. 47498
Roselli, David L. 43019
Roselló, Núria 35671
Rosemann, Günther 18493
Rosen, Steven W. 41530
Rosenbaum, Joan 45821
Rosenbeck, Dr. Hans 15883
Rosenberg, Dr. H.I. 05181
Rosenberger, Pat 42434
Rosenblattl, Christina 01766
Rosenbleeth, Herb 48377
Rosenblum, Amy 45289
Rosenblum, Robert 45872
Rosenbluth, Betsy 42007
Rosendahl, Paul 08809
Roseneck, Prof. Dr. Reinhard 17355
Rosenfeld, Alla 45678
Rosenfield, Jamie 45842
Rosenfield Lafo, Rachel 44777
Rosengren, Kerstin 35904
Rosenkranc, Milan 08326
Rosenkrantz, Baron Erik Christian 08893
Rosenmeier, Edith Marie 09079
Rosenquist, Perry E. 42708
Rosenstock, F. 15380
Rosensweig, Larry 42864
Rosenthal, Deborah 47863
Rosenthal, Dina R. 47788
Rosenthal, Ellen 42891
Rosenthal, Mark 45872
Rosentrater, Jil 43783
Rosero Solarte, Luciano 07549
Rosetti, Evelyn 45782
Rosewitz, Mindy 43430
Rosher, Fiona 39193
Rosiak, Andrzej 32150, 32224
Rosiek, Barbara 32228
Rosing, Emil 21234
Rosing, M. 08930
Rosini, Prof. Dr. Corrado 22921
Rosinski, Dr. Rosa 16152
Rosiny, Dr. Claudia 36542
Rosito, Massimiliano G. 23849
Rosjat, Dr. Erika 15837
Rośkiewicz, Wiesław 32014
Rosoff, Susan 46188
Ross, Dr. Cathy 39718
Ross, David A. 43370
Ross, Donald A. 01516
Ross, Dugald Alexander 39318, 40568
Ross, Ian D. 05145
Ross, Jan 06716
Ross, Jay 48105
Ross, Jerry 43225
Ross, Dr. J.P. 43581
Ross, Judy 44182
Ross, Mari B. 41456
Ross, Marian 48036
Ross, Martin J.E. 05453
Ross, Phill 44044
Ross, Richard 46293
Ross, Sandria B. 41226
Ross, Stewart 00949
Ross, Wendy 44415
Ross Noble, R. 40068
Rossacher, Walter 01927
Rossellini, Laurence 12870
Rosser, Merlin 06513
Rosset-Magnat, Chantal 14015
Rossetti, Evelyn 45847
Rossetti de Scander, Dr. Antonio 25827
Rossi, Dr. Francesco 23066
Rossi, Guido 23986
Rossi, John S. 43303

Rossi, Rochelle 42075
Rossiter, Shannon 44488
Rossolimo, Dr. Olga L. 33186
Rostami 22312
Rostek, Charlotte 39208
Rostek, L. 01544
Rostholm, Hans 08869
Rostworowska, Dr. Magdalena 32176
Rosu, Georgeta 32470
Roszko, Grzegorz 31601
Rota, Anna Francesca 23535
Rota, Dr. Laura 23322
Rotaru, Georgeta Monica 32545
Roten, Hortensia von 37393
Roth, André 11633
Roth, Dr. Anja-Maria 17668
Roth, Dan 41323
Roth, Eric 45740
Roth, Flemming 08840
Roth, Gary G. 46774
Roth, John 00969, 41939
Roth, Jules 13284
Roth, Linda H. 43944
Roth, Prof. Dr. Martin 16710
Roth, Dr. Michael 16033
Roth, Dr. Peter 34045
Roth, Ronald C. 46809
Roth, Dr. Ursula 16726
Roth-Oberth, Dr. Erna 16994
Rothe-Wörner, Heidrun 17252
Rothen, Heidi 36915
Rothenberger, Manfred 19147
Rotheneder, Martin 02292
Rothermel, Barbara 45003
Rothfuss, Joan 45394
Rothkopf, Katherine 41454
Rothove, Billi R.S. 43635
Roths, Jaylene 45527, 45528, 47674
Rothschild, Eric de 13605
Rothschild, Baroness Philippine de 13674
Rotkale, Rita 27405
Rotonda-McCord, Lisa 45735
Rotovnik, Mitja 34107
Rotsart, John A. 47292
Rott, Dr. Herbert W. 18832
Rottermund, Prof. Andrzej 32143
Røtting, Dorrit 08978
Rottmann, Lee 47132
Rouchaud, Alain 13930
Roughley, Dr. R.E. 06829
Rouijel, Souad 28709
Roullot, Cédric 14483
Roulston, Peggy 45085
Roumm, David L. 44470
Rountree, Robin K. 47867
Rouquereol, N. 10489
Rouquet, Chantal 15000, 15005, 15006, 15007
Roura Güibas, Gabriel 34860
Roure, Patrick 12614
Rourke, Ralph 41920
Rouse, Virginia 42577
Rousseau, Marshall 47176
Roussel, Dominique 14762, 15242
Roussel, Louis 12779, 14734
Rousselot, Dr. Jean-Loup 18916
Rousset-Rouard, Yves 12926
Roussia, Pierre 12151
Roussier, François 15284
Routhier, Nathalie 05101
Routledge, M.A. 40650
Roux, Bertrand 11368, 14459
Roux, Jean-Pierre 11694, 11920
Roux, Nathalie 11322
Rovati, Clementina 24826
Rovine, Victoria 44248
Rowan, Edward 45097
Rowe, Alan L. 30221
Rowe, Ann 05189
Rowe, Ann P. 48397
Rowe, Barbara 48659
Rowe, C. 34330
Rowe, Donald 46137
Rowe, Dorothy 47625
Rowe, M. Jessica 42905
Rowe, Matthew 38858
Rowe, Michael 40841
Rowe, Timothy 41421
Rowe-Shields, Michele 47457
Rowinski, Dr. Stanislaw 17560
Rowland, Rodney 46654
Rowland Jones, Mark 38201, 40600
Rowles, H.E. 40102
Rowley, Dean 41351
Rowley, Matthew 46445
Rowley, Roger H.D. 46745
Rowold, Kathleen L. 41745
Rowsell, Wayde 06362
Rox-Schulz, Heinz 19722
Roxas Lim, Prof. Aurora 31428
Roxburghe, Duke of 39333
Roy, Dr. Archana 21900
Roy, Dr. Ashok 39729
Roy, Carolyn 46654
Roy, David T. 38050
Roy, Jan-Bernard 13280
Roy, Kenneth J. 45634
Roy, Nathalie 14048
Roy, Noëlle 13648
Royce, Bill 44576

Royce, Ralph 43612
Royer, Claude 12172
Royle, Ted 38536
Rozanov, Aleksej Jurjevič 33170
Rozenberg, Dr. Silvia 22657
Rozendaal, Prof. A. 34380
Rozenfeld, Boris Matveevič 32930
Rozewicz, Beverly L. 43985
Rozko, Laurie 46824
Rozłowski, Tadeusz 31651
Roznoy, Cynthia 47769
Rózsa, Gyula 21380
Rozzo, Dr. Ugo 25779
Rúa, Rosa Edith 07569
Ruas dos Santos, Dr. Margarida 32293
Rub, Timothy 42400
Ruban, Nikolaj Ivanovič 32737
Rubel, William 47412
Ruben, Bärbel 15990
Ruben Cuñeo, Dr. Nestor 00639
Rubidge, Prof. Bruce 34271
Rubin, Jane 45821
Rubin, Jean-François 36993
Rubin, Robert S. 41941
Rubinstein, Adam 46786
Rubinstein, Ernest 45882
Rubio, J. David 07490
Rubio Pediata, Luis 35737
Rubio Sánchez, Pedro 27904
Rucellai, Oliva 25557
Ruch, Pam 46701
Rucka, Barbara 31815
Ruckel, Jay G. 45806
Rucker, Dr. Henrike 20498
Rucker, Ken 47633
Ruckstuhl, Dieter 36723
Ruczynski, F.C.K. 29021
Ruda, M. 03935
Rudaz, Patrick 36624
Rudd, Karen 40435
Rudd, Robert 43189
Rudd, Shirley J. 46330
Ruddlesden, C. 38702
Ruddock, Joanna 38519
Rudi, Dr. Thomas 18398
Rudigier, Dr. Andreas 01872, 02641
Rudin, Vladimir Vasiljevič 33548
Rudisill, Horace F. 43449
Rudisill, Dr. Richard 47427, 47429
Rudkin, David J. 38560
Rudman, Karen 28768
Rudnik, Galina Anatolevna 33523
Rudolp, Dr. Andrea 19374
Rudolph, Beth 41112
Rudolph, Jeffrey N. 44894
Rudolph, Johanna 19465
Rudolph, Ulrich 17187
Rudzińska, Wanda M. 32084
Rübesam, Manfred 18412
Rücker, Dr. Thomas 02545
Rückert, Dr. Birgit 19733
Rückert, Hans 15397
Rueda, Horacio 09217
Rüdel, Dr. Holger 19795, 19796
Rüdiger, Bernd J. 17320
Ruedin, Pascal 37172
Rüede, Erich 37223
Rüger, Axel 39729
Ruegg, Dr. François 36712
Rühl, Karin 17088
Rühlig, Cornelia 18774, 18775
Rühmer, Erich 17812
Rührl, Helmut 16313
Rührnschopf, Elfriede 02847
Ruell, David 41294
Rünger, Dr. Gabriele 16978
Rürup, Prof. Dr. Reinhard 16107
Ruesch, Carol 48823
Rüschoff-Thale, Dr. Barbara 17731
Ruess, Andreas 15731, 15732
Rueß, Dr. Karl-Heinz 17315, 17316, 17321, 17322
Rüth, Dr. Uwe 18655
Rütsche, Dr. Claudia 37384
Ruette, Monique de 03337
Rütti, Beat 36479
Ruf, A. 17993
Ruf, Beatrix 37385
Ruf, Peter 18518, 18522
Ruf, Susanne 20106
Rufe, Laurie J. 47016
Ruff, Eric J. 06869
Ruff, Joshua 47830
Ruff, T.J. 40851
Ruffo, Joseph M. 44782
Ruggeri, Prof. Alessandro 23118
Ruggeri Augusti, Dr. Adriana 25928
Ruggiero, Dr. Laurence J. 48707
Rugoff, Ralph 46062, 47305
Rugsveen, Magne 30478
Rugunanau, S. 34257
Rugus, Dot 46882
Ruhe, Rikke 08962
Ruhl, Erwin 17719
Ruhl, Hans-Eberhard 16551
Ruhl, Horst 20427
Ruhlig-Lühnen, Dagmar 17893
Ruhnke, Steven 43449
Ruhstaller, Tod 47824
Ruivo, José 32266

Ruiz, Aureli 35315
Ruiz, Dimas Fernández-Galiano 34885
Ruiz, Jauier Luna 28381
Ruiz de Azua Murua, Asun 35711
Ruiz-Martinez, José D. 21228
Ruiz Sastre, Elena 34788
Ruiz-Torres, Maricarmen 46163
Rukavina, Vjeročka 07830
Ruley, Dennis 47003
Rulíšek, Dr. Hynek 08351
Rulle, Amy 48083
Rum, Piera 25074
Rumbach, Erseline 48572
Rumbaugh, Catherine 47097
Rumbaugh, Darlene 46468
Rumi, Satoh 26854
Rumjanceva, Valentina Pavlovna 33327
Rumly, Katrina 01316
Rummel, Dr. Ralf 16294
Rump, Elisabeth 42174
Rump, Elizabeth 46711
Rump, Dr. Oliver 17559
Rumpca, Ronette 46484
Rumrill, Alan F. 44425
Rumsby, J.H. 39274
Runde, Dr. Sabine 17062
Rundhovde, Eric 30418
Rundle, Stella 03933
Rundqvist, Dmitry V. 33053
Runey, Dennis I. 48724
Runte, Markus 19337
Runton, Bourke A. 48088
Runyon, Carol 44676
Ruossr, Dr. Mylène 37393
Rupert, Dr. Manfred 02118
Rupert Enriquez, Carola 41440
Rupf, Hans-Jürgen 19882
Rupley, Kathleen 46860
Rupp, Jane E. 45163
Ruppe, Dr. Harry O. 16994
Rupprecht, Dr. Klaus 15816
Rupprechter, Hanns-Michael 20111
Ruprechtsberger, Prof. Dr. Erwin M. 02238
Ruseckaitė, Aldona 27520
Rusev, Rusi 04612, 04830
Rush, Martin 39663
Rush, Dr. Michael 44600
Rushton, Ray 39699
Rusibaev, D.S. 48853
Rusina, Prof. Ivan 33978
Rusinová, Dr. Zora 33978
Ruske, Wolfgang 15520
Ruskule, Skaidrite 27414
Rusnell, Wesley A. 47016
Russe, Christel 17245
Russel, Jack 00795
Russell, Barry 05056
Russell, Brenda 05428
Russell, Brian J. 39100
Russell, Prof. Bruce 39386
Russell, Douglas 42657
Russell, J. Fiona 46016
Russell, John I. 41928
Russell, Kentdur 48753
Russell, Laurence J. 45335
Russell, Marilyn M. 46510
Russell, Nancy J. 44551
Russell, Pamela 43326
Russell, Paul 42371
Russell, Willie 47537
Russell Howe, Dr. Stanley 41661
Russi, Graciela 00343
Russo, Prof. Antonio 24436, 24445
Russo, Dr. Carmelo 23447
Russo, Dick 48737
Russo, Pam 48737
Russo, Ralph 45074
Russo de Fontela, Adriana 00555
Rust, Sandra 02918
Rust, Wilfried W. H. 43420
Rustichelli, Arlette 36476
Rustige, Rona 05072
Ruszczyc, Ferdynand B. 32115
Ruszel, Dr. Krzysztof 31959
Ruta Serafini, Dr. Angela 23743
Rutberg, Carl 47779
Ruthensteiner, Dr. B. 18926
Rutherford, Jessica 38340, 38344
Rutherford Conrad, Marth 05103
Rutherford Conrad, Martha 06057
Rutishauser, Werner 37132
Rutkowski, Czesław 31973
Rutledge, Ann 42507
Rutsch, Franz 19381
Rutte, Helgard 19808
Rutter, A. 39180
Rutter, Michael 05648
Rutter, Mike 38553
Ruttinger, Jacquelyn 44377
Ruttner, Nancy 46519
Ruus, Tina 42391
Ruuska, Aulis 10148
Ruy Van Beest Holle, C.J. du 29781
Ruyssinck, Micheline 03337
Ružić, Ivan 07830
Ruzo, Victor 37232
Rvijn, Benoît 03266
Ryan, Dana 44301
Ryan, Dr. E. 43389

Ryan, Graham 01334
Ryan, Hilary 40266
Ryan, Jack Dingo 45620
Ryan, Kay 47852
Ryan, Lynne 41580
Ryan, Michael 22417
Ryan, Paul 47796
Ryan, Robert 41790
Ryan, Steven P. 46816
Ryan, Thomas 44912
Ryan, Thomas R. 44627
Ryazonova, T.P. 27314
Ryba, Kurt 24792
Rybakov, Ivan Alekseevič 32629
Rybakova, Tamara Viktorovna 33082
Rybka, Walter P. 43203
Rybnikova, Larisa 33069
Rychener, Dr. Jürg 36479
Rychlik, Dr. Otmar 02365
Rychlíková, Marie 08696
Rychtarik, John 41932
Ryckman, Heather 06035
Rycquart, Walter 03246, 03247, 03248, 03249, 03250, 03251, 03252, 03253, 03254, 03257, 03260, 03264, 03267
Rydel, Maria 31727
Ryder, Michael J. 39726
Rydergård, Evy 36128
Rydzewski, Dr. Jacek 31693, 31694
Rylance, Mark 39775
Ryland, James 45443
Rylands, Philip 25948
Rynd, Chase 45619
Rynierse, H. 29229
Ryol, Thae Pyong 27123
Ryšánková, Dr. Milada 08692
Ryska, Norbert 19334
Rystedt, Prof. Eva 36062
Ryusawa, Aya 26571
Ryzdynski, Mark 43990
Ryžov, Stanislav 37902
Ryžova, Tamara Alaksandrovna 33215
Ryžova, Tamara Aleksandrovna 33207
Rzepecka, Mirosława 31867
Rzepiela, Urzula 31917
Rzeszotarski, Jan 31975
Sá Marques, Ana Rita 32308
Saabye, Marianne 08931
Saadé, William 10361, 10363
Saage, Wallace 44121
Saager-Bourret, Stephanie 46545, 46546
Saal, Agnès 13478
Saal, Dr. Wolfgang 18602
Saalmann, Ute 16754
Saar, A. 09363
Saaret, Tarmo 09358, 09368
Saarimaa, Hanna-Maija 09845
Saarinen, Jarmo 10120
Saarist, Tiiu 19345
Saarnio, Robert 47199
Saathoff, Joachim 19363
Saatsi, Niko 09873
Šabalin, Rostislav Viktorovič 33301
Sabapathy, Colin 34234
Sabaté, Antonio 35658
Sabaté i Piqué, Gemma 35644
Sabatini, L. 03579
Sabin, Carleen 45320
Sabin, Owen 45320
Sabina, Choclán 34954
Sabloff, Dr. Jeremy 46460
Sabogal, Bernardo 07477
Sabolic, Prof. Dubravka 07801
Sabotinova, Donka 04814
Sabran-Ponteves, E. Comte de 13867
Sabroe, Charlotte 09077
Šabunts, Natalja 37811
Sacarés Mas, Antoni 35501
Saccà, Daniela 16051
Sacco, Louise R. 42842
Saccocci, Prof. Andrea 24736
Šachalova, Natalja Vladimirovna 33057
Sachanbiński, Prof. Michał 32180
Sachs, Charles L. 41948
Sachs, Samuel 45802
Sachs, Sid 46452
Sachse, Jutta 18433
Sack, Dr. Birgit 16683
Sackett, Margot Magee 06303
Sackl, Dr. Peter 01922
Sackstetter, Susanna 16507
Sada, Ricardo J. 34927
Sadinsky, Rachael 44746
Sadion, Martine 11632
Sadjukov, Nikolaj I. 32718
Sadler, Bill 47368
Sadler, Dr. Donna 42829
Sadler, Patsy 46329
Sádlo, Dr. Václav 08492
Sadok, Nedjah 00063
Sadowski, Władysław 31698
Saeed, Tahir 31032
Säkkinen, Senja 09906
Sæland, Frode 30603
Sälejoki-Hiekkanen, Leena 09542
Sänger, Dr. Reinhard 17991
Sæther, Per 30375
Sæthre, Ellen 30887
Sættem, Nils 08907

Saeverud, Dag H. 30854
Safarnia, P. 22261
Saffiotti Dale, Maria 45067
Safford, Pete 42817
Safin, Françoise 03576
Safina, Zulfira Midechatovna 33192
Safonyuk, Vladimir 37912
Šafr, Pavel 08299
Safronova, V.V. 33263
Safsafi, Nourddine 28709
Saft, Marcia 45821
Saganic, Livio 45061
Sagar, Scott 42555, 48632
Sagdalen, Betty Jo 44475
Sagebiel, Chris 46824
Sagel, Dietmar 19001
Sager, Judy 43481
Saghaar-Bessiére, Francoise 14391
Saghi, Mohamed 28708
Sagmeister, Dr. Rudolf 01745
Sagov, Magomet Zakrievič 33203
Sagrera, Enric 34859
Sagristà, Ferran 35671
Saheki, Ryoken 26240
Şahin, Hüseyin 37639
Sahlstrand, James 43152
Sahm, Helena 00859
Said, Sanib 27658
Sailard, Olivier 13556
Sailer, Andreas 02620
Saines, Chris 30103
Sainio, Tuulu 10118
Sainsbury, Derek 38950
Saint-Affrique, Olga de 12251
Saint-Bris, Jean 10313
Saint Hippolyte, Mary 47661
Saint-Maur, P. de 13610
Saint-Pierre, Adrienne 43264
Saint-Pierre, François 12501
Saint-Pol, Pierre P. 11575
Saint Romain, P.W. 46539
Sainte-Fare-Garnot, Nicolas 13621
Sáinz González, Elena 28111
Saire, Marcel 11796
Saisí, Enrique 00462
Saissac, Prof. Rosa A. 00513
Saito, Osamu 26595
Saji, Nobutada 26928
Sakaeva, Guzel Rinatovna 32902
Sakai, Tadayasu 26185
Sakai, Tetsuo 26149, 26976
Sakai, Dr. Toshihiro 26689
Sakai, Yasuo 26715
Sakamoto, Bishop 26797
Sakari, Marja 09501
Sakata, Toshitaka 26551
Sakazume, Hideichi 26919
Sakli, Dr. Mourad 37582
Sakmirda, Marta 19823
Šakova, Marjana Kušbievna 33196
Sakrausky, Oskar 01852
Sakwerda, Jan 32203
Sala, Susan M. 31315
Salabert, Patricia 16336
Salachova, P.Ch. 33662
Salacki, Kim 37897
Sälåjean, Ioan 32475
Salajić, Prof. Silvija 07801
Salameh, Khader 22641
Salamon, Nándor 21589
Salas, Jaime de 35576
Salas Vázquez, Eduardo 35029
Salatino, Kevin 44921
Salaverria, Ana 34774
Salazar, Ernesto 09212
Salazar, Evangeline 48172
Salazar, Lucila A. 31410
Salazar Soto, José Aníbal 07368, 07369
Salcedo Zambrano, Alonso 07550
Salcher, Hubert 03030
Salcher, Johann 02267
Salchli, Jacqueline 37066
Saldan, Kathryn 46409
Salden, Hubert 01992
Saldo, Josip Ante 07775
Šale, Majda 07677
Salé, Marie-Pierre 13596
Saleh, Ali Ibrahim 09262
Salehi, M. 22321
Salerno, Osvaldo 31094
Sales Marques, José Luís de 07161
Saletić, Momčilo 33835
Saletti, Prof. Cesare 24823
Salgo, Nicolos 46610
Salib, Dr. Mahar 09258
Saliga, Pauline 42312
Saliger, Dr. Arthur 02953, 02954
Saliklis, Ruta 41143, 43070
Salin, Anne-Maj 10158, 10162
Salina, Xavier 36952
Salisbury, Joyce 45536
Salisbury, R.D.N. 40516
Salisbury, Ruth 40430
Salje, Prof. Dr. Beate 16114
Salkin, Asen 04696
Salkoranta, Marja 09853, 10134
Sall, Joan C. 46443

Salleh, Dr. Badriyah B.H. 27665, 27670, 27671, 27672, 27674, 27675
Salleh, Dr. Badriyat B.H. 27673
Sallen, Sheila 43425
Sallinen, Kari 10175
Salmen, Brigitte 18962
Salmen, Nora 42573
Salmi, Lyle 42832
Salmon, Béatrice 13556, 13563, 13586, 13642
Salmon, Irit 22666
Salmon, Patricia 47791
Salmona, Paul 13603
Salmona, Riccardo 45756, 45798
Salmons-Perez, Carl 47466
Salo, B.M. 33044
Salo, Prof. J. 10121
Salomatin, A.V. 33157
Salome, Elizabeth 44211
Salomé, Laurent 14047, 14049, 14054
Salomeia, Paul 32531
Salomon, Joel 46965
Salomón Zuebi, Alex Faruk 31227
Salomone, Mario R. 00149
Salonen, Jouni 09933
Saloniemi, Marjo-Riita 10076
Salsi, Dr. Claudio 24372, 24374, 24377
Saltamanikas, P. 21107
Salter, Ann C. 46943
Saltiel, Solita 21184
Salton, Jenny 39274
Saltonstall, Patrick 44524
Salu, Luc 03144
Salus, Ernst R. 22680
Salvador, Fred 05223
Salvador, Josep 35599
Salvador, Mari Lyn 41104
Salvador Zazurca, Alejandro 35716, 35717, 35730, 35731
Salvatierra, Julio 35678
Salvator, Markus 01706
Salvatore, Ferraro 22806
Salvatori, Prof. Franco 25196
Salven, Irmeli 09475
Salvesen, Ole Bjørn 30788
Salveson, Doug 43322
Salvi, Donato 37098
Salvig, Jakob 09089
Salvioni, Mario Casanova 36528
Salwiński, Jacek 31708
Salzgeber, Christoph 37045
Salzman, Alexej 08482
Salzmann, Prof. Dr. Dieter 18932
Samac, Dr. Šime 07802
Samaniego, Lydia 31413, 31418
Samarati, Dr. Luigi 24201
Samardžić, Nadežda 33819
Samek, Tomasz 18946
Sameli-Erne, Doris 36805
Sameshima, Satoru 26352
Sami-Azar, Dr. A.R. 22303
Samietz, Rainer 17360
Saminger, Herbert 02802
Sammallahti, Leena 09947
Sammer, Dr. Alfred 02950
Samochvalova, Ljudmila Nikolaevna 32918
Samodurov, Jurij Vadimovič 33104
Samon, Josep 35671
Samoy, Antenor R. 31280
Sampaio, Heli de Almeida 04436
Sampaolo, Prof. Valeria 24577
Sampil, Mamadou 21282
Sampson, Michael 43169
Samson, Dr. Bill 38801
Samson, Ditas R. 31352
Samson, Fr. Antonio S. 31300
Samson, James 30279
Samson, Louise 43407
Samson, Rémy 11235
Samsonova, Élvira Aleksandrovna 32972
Samuels, Clifford 47139
Samuels, Philip 47139
Samuelson, Laura 45961
Samyn, John 03835
San Agustin, Leonora P. 31282
San Carlos, Duque de 35059
San Diego, Rodolfo 31406
San Martín, Luis Marín de 35653
San Quirce, Sylvie 12046
Sana, Costantino 22860
Sanborn, Colin J. 42421
Sanborn, Michael 48647
Sanchez, Artero 04520
Sanchez, Basilio 04519
Sanchez, Maria José 35428
Sánchez, Osvaldo 28124
Sanchez, Roger 46799
Sánchez, Tomás 35024
Sánchez Aguilera, Marco 06892
Sánchez de Velandia, Myriam 07360
Sánchez Fuertes, Caayetano 34479
Sanchez Garcia, Javier 28239
Sánchez Hernández, Américo 28181
Sánchez Mastranzo, Nazario A. 28431
Sánchez Murguía, Socorro 27839
Sánchez Peña, Prof. José Miguel 34647
Sánchez Pérez, Luz María 28152
Sánchez Ramírez, Angeles 35734
Sánchez Recio, Miguel Angel 35010, 35011

Sánchez Rodríguez, Marciano 35364
Sánchez Ruiz, José Fernando 34432
Sánchez Trujillano, Teresa 34981
Sanchidrián, Rafael Ruiz 35033
Sanchis, Frank Emile 45837
Sanclemente Girón, Américo Alfonso 07486, 07487
Sand, Christiane 12153
Sand, Gabriele 17611
Sand, Karl 02435
Sand, Viki 46393
Sandahl, Jette 35922
Sandberg, Anja 10136
Sandberg, Fredrik 35882
Sandbichler, Veronika 02079
Sandbichler, Dr. Veronika 02918
Sandell, Stephen 45385
Sanden, Jarle 30685, 30687
Sander, Dr. Antje 17956, 17957
Sander, Dr. Birgit 17049
Sander, Dr. Dietulf 18405
Sander, E. 17258
Sander, Helmut 17560
Sander, Dr. Jochen 17074
Sanders, Dr. Albert E. 42211
Sanders, Boyd 48130
Sanders, G. 28928
Sanders, James 44201
Sanders, Jennifer 01558
Sanders, Mildred 48453
Sanders, William A. 43174
Sanderson, Cecil 43373
Sanderson, Dr. Dewey D. 44164
Sanderson, Eleonore P. 46652
Sanderson, R. 06445
Sanderson, Sue 48785
Sandheinrich, Bernard 47133
Sandkühler, Prof. Dr. St. 19043
Sandlofer, Michael 41925
Sandmann, Oskar 17736
Sandmeyer, Marilyn 45518
Sandmo, Sigurd S. 30424
Šandová, Dr. Miroslava 08328, 08636
Sandoval, Josefina de 48897
Sandoval, Raquel 07376
Sandoval, Sonia 09209
Sandrini, Dr. Francesca 24798
Sandrock, Dr. Oliver 16541
Sandström, Birgitta 36103
Sandström, Paul 09882
Sandstrom, Ake 35961
Sandu, Ion 32424
Sandvoß, Hans-Rainer 15972
Sandweiss, Eric 47128
Saner, Gerhard 37220
Sanfelice di Bagnoli, Fabio 25158
Sanford, Dr. Beverly S. 48704
Sanftner, Phyllis 45510
Sangalang, Debbie 31401
Sangl, Dr. Sigrid 18833
Sangmanee, Kitti Cha 13607
Sangster, Gary 41461
Sanguinetti, María Isabel 00489
Sangvichien, Dr. Sanjai 37481
Sangvichien, Prof. Sood M.D. 37497
Sangwill, Richard 35869
Sani, Michele 24552
Sanita, Dennis 44195
Sankowski, Janusz 32106
Sanna, Maria Antonia 25683
Sannibale, Dr. Maurizio 48872, 48875
Sano, Dr. Emily J. 47308
Sans, Bartolomé 34478
Sans, Jérôme 13652
Sansano Costa, Lina 35418
Sansom, Andrew 43121, 43722, 44275, 46691, 48520
Santa Ana Alvárez Ossorio, Florencio de 35055
Santa Elena, Barrio 07496
Santaca, Dr. Susanna 09489
Santamaria, Prof. Ulderico 48872
Santamarina, Guillermo 28104
Santana Quintana, Luis Carlos 28106
Santandreu, Edmundo 00199
Santaniello, Giovanni 24630
Santiago, Isabel 32296
Santiago, Mark 41077
Santiago, Mildred 43436
Santiago, Rubio 35591
Santinacci-Boitelle, Françoise 12262
Santis, Jorge 43411
Santomauro, Angelica M. 43872
Santoni, Dr. Vincenzo 23252
Santonja, Josep A. Gisbert 34772
Santonja, Dr. Manuel 35351
Santoro, Geraldine 45876
Santoro, Dr. Paola 24260
Santos, Prof. Eliane Aparecida 04576
Teles Dos Santos, Prof. Dr. Jocelio 04421
Santos, María Soares dos 14795, 14796
Santos, Osmar 41036, 41037
Santos, Turibio 04397
Santos Correia Victor, Ana Paula dos 00100
Santos González, José María 35460
Santos Ramírez, Marco Antonio 28623
Santos Sátz Gomes, Ilmo 34762
Santos Simões, Joaquim A. 32277
Santrot, Jacques 13258
Santzevlariz, David 35172
Santzevlàriz, David 35173

Sanucci, Dennis 44490
Sanz, Eduardo 35678
Sanz, Joaquim 35083
Sanz Gamo, Rubí 34419
Sanz Sánchez, Erundino 34527
Sanzi, Dr. Maria Rita 23544
Šapošnikova, Ljudmila Vasiljevna 33083
Sapouna-Sakellaraki, Dr. Efi 21055
Sarabhai, Gira 21677
Saragoza, Florence 13637
Saraiva da Costa Pecorelli, Carlos 32270
Saran, P.K. 21828
Saraver, Ida 05607
Sarda, Marie-Anne 10853
Sardella, Filomena 24593
Sardo, Delfin 32286
Sarelius, Seppo 10120
Sargeant, Erich 39584
Sargent, William 47198
Sargsyan, Zaven 00688
Sarholz, Dr. Hans-Jürgen 15638
Sari, Dr. Alireza 22329
Sarie, Pierre 12688
Sariego, Manuel Lucío Julio 07532
Sarioglu, M. Adnan 37633
Sariola, Helmiriitta 09474
Sarkisjan, David A. 33068
Sarl, P.M. 40422, 40423, 40424, 40426, 40427
Sarna, Micheal 42313
Sarosácz, György 21482
Saroyan, Ione 45858
Sarpong, Kwame 20792
Sarrail, Cécile 11052
Sarrazin, Dr. J. 16163
Sarrazin, Dr. Jenny 18552
Sarret, Françoise 12619
Sarsfield, Stanley 38693
Sarteanesi, Prof. Nemo 23577, 23578
Sartes, Minna 10117, 10119
Sarti, Fabiola 25553
Sarto, Pietro 36950
Sartori, Dean 42902
Sartori, Dr. Michel 36859
Sartorio, Matteo 24412
Sartorio Pisani, Dr. Giuseppina 25195
Sartorius, K. 16218
Sartorius, Tara 45467
Saruchanian, Saro 00690
Sarvis, Will 41189
Sas, Adrian 45765
Sasagawa, Takami 26467
Sasaki, Hideaki 26368
Sasaki, Hideya 26516
Sasaki, Masamine 26872
Sasaki, Yoneyuki 26404
Sasano, Takaaki 26716
Sasayama, Kazutoshi 26350
Saskiweicz, Sharon 47015
Şaşmaz, Abdülkadir 37602
Sassen, J.H. 28902
Sasso, Rosalie 42988
Sastri, C.L.N. 21694
Sastry, Dr. V.V. Krishna 21842, 22001
Sasymanov, Y.A. 27313
Sata, Gori 00020
Sather, Stanley 06743
Sato, Keichi 26377
Sato, Mitsuo 26311
Sato, Naoki 26873
Sato, Takeshi 26106
Sato, Toyozo 26571
Sato, Yoshio 26387
Sato, Yumika 26715
Satoko, Maemura 26290
Satsuma, Masato 26853
Sattelmair, Hartwig 16890
Satterfield, Foad 47376
Satterthwaitt, Dr. Leann 00835
Sattlecker, Dr. Franz 02904, 02985
Sattmann, Dietrich 03001
Satut, Jorge 41006
Satvé Oliván, Enrique 35350
Satyan, M.S. 21815
Satzer, Wolfgang 02174
Saubel, Katherine 41495
Sauceman, Jill 44360
Sauder, Carolyn 41248
Sauer, Dr. Albrecht 16339
Sauer, Daniel 04330
Sauer, Marc 10229
Sauer, Dr. Marina 15417
Sauer, Wilfrid 17847
Sauerborn, Ulrich 15381, 15386
Sauermann, Bernhard 18266
Sauers, Dr. Richard A. 47890
Sauerwein, Herbert 02200
Sauge, Birgitte 30726
Sauge, Brigitte 30726
Saul, Dainiel 05641
Saulnier, Lydwine 14715
Saulsbery, Jeff 41742
Saumade, Jeanine 12038
Saunders, Dr. David 39729
Saunders, Dr. Gail 03074, 03077
Saunders, Kristin 40724
Saunders, P.R. 40437
Saunders, Dr. Rebecca A. 41532
Saunders, Richard 45189
Saunders, Richard H. 45308

Saunders, Stuart 00802
Saunders, Dr. Timothy 19115
Saunier, Bernard 15187
Saurage, Hank 41533
Saury-Serres, Claudine 12575
Sauter, Pierre 36438
Sauter, Wolfgang 18044
Sautov, Ivan Petrovič 33334, 33336
Sautter, Dr. Heribert 16990
Sauvebeuf, B. de 11600
Savage, Harland 48673
Savage, Pamela 48673
Savage, Paula 30292
Savage, Ronald 41114
Savage, Terry 41800
Savard, Denise 06814
Savary, Lee 41111
Savčenko, Andrej Grigorjevič 32725
Savčenko, Nikolaj Jakovlevič 33596
Savcheva, Dr. Elizabeth 04846
Savel, Irena 34134
Savelja, Oleg 37902
Savelsberg, Dr. Wolfgang 16582
Savery, Suzanne T. 46371, 46372, 46373, 46376, 46378, 46379
Savi, Dr. Dario 25871
Savi, Dario 25872
Savickaja, Ljudmila Aleksandrovna 32971
Savidge, Amanda 40931
Savidis, Prof. G. 21078
Savigny, Marie-Anne 11599
Savill, Rosalind J. 39798
Saville, Ansley 46993
Saville, Jennifer 44079
Saville, R.J. 39422
Saville, Sue 38756
Saving, Barbara 44595
Savini, Thomas M. 45779
Savinič, Irina Borisovna 33493
Savko, Iraida Lvovna 33625
Savolainen, Kari 09741
Sawa, Ryuken 26393
Sawadogo, Alimata 04943
Sawauchi, Takashi 26888
Sawchuk, Barry 05618
Sawchuk, Sherry 45538
Sawdey, Michael P. 41398
Sawicka-Oleksy, Daniela 31534
Sawkins, Annemarie 45371
Sawyer, Carol 46891
Sawyer, Doug 46472
Sawyer, Ed 47059
Sawyer, Kenneth C. 00959
Sawyer, Laura 41760
Sawyer, Sean 41949
Sawyer, Tom 43298
Saxinger, Karl 20367
Saxsburg, Sheila 48092
Sayle, Kristina 38227
Sayler, John G. 44687
Sayunain, Selamat 27646
Sazdova, Katerina 27599
Sazonov, Valerij Petrovič 33293, 33295
Sazonova, T.V. 33012
Sbardellati, Max 03028
Sbarge, Robert 41370
Scafetta, Stefano 48392
Scaggs, Tom 48420
Scaglia, Orlando 00428
Scalera, Michelle 47453
Scalera Liaci, Prof. Lidia 23023
Scalia, Dr. Fiorenza 23845
Scalini, Mario 23484
Scalora, Salvatore 47837
Scandola, Dr. Pietro 36564
Scanlon, Scott B. 46217
Scannapieco, Carlos A. 00413, 00415, 00416
Scaramella, Julie 48535
Scaramellini, Guido 23536
Scărlătescu, Fl. 32509
Scarpetti, Ivo 24317
Scarpi, Prof. Paolo 24742
Scarratt, David 38891
Scarso Japaze, Eduardo 00239
Scenna, Prof. Desiderato 23549
Ščerbakova, I.T. 32887
Ščerban, Aleksandr Nikolaevič 32692
Schaack, Judy 47695
Schaaf, Ania 03716
Schaaf, Petra 18626
Schaaff, Dr. Holger 18606
Schaafsma, Curtis F. 47427
Schaal, Agnes 41755
Schaar, Dana 42129
Schaar, Elke 18419
Schaatsenberg, W.J.M. 29181
Schachtner, Dr. Sabine 15899
Schachtschneider, Perdita 15452
Schachtsiek, Richard 44774, 45542
Schack von Wittenau, Dr. Clementine Gräfin 19628, 16483
Schächter, Willid 17641
Schädel, Gisela 17537
Schädle, Bernarda 15778
Schädler, Ulrich 37249
Schäfer, Andreas 37186
Schäfer, Bernd 17363
Schaefer, Dr. Claudia 16746
Schaefer, D.E. 34289

Schäfer, Dr. Dorit 18002
Schäfer, Dr. Dorothee 18916
Schaefer, Elizabeth Meg 42556
Schäfer, Gerd 17920, 17922, 17924
Schäfer, Prof. Dr. H.-P. 17233
Schaefer, Dr. Hartmut 18831
Schäfer, Prof. Dr. Hermann 16248
Schäfer, Julia 18394
Schäfer, Dr. Klaus 15488
Schäfer, Klaus 18811
Schäfer, Leane 17230
Schaefer, Scott 44913
Schaefer, Dr. Stacy 42373
Schäfer, Dr. Wolfgang 20280
Schäffel, Brigitte 02501
Schäffel, Karl 02501
Schaeffer, Astrida 43025
Schäffer, Prof. Dr. Dr. Johann 17613
Schäffer, Rudolf 17581
Schäfke, Dr. Werner 18150
Schael, Alfredo 48924
Schaeps, J. 29523
Schärer, Dr. Martin R. 37285
Schärli, Beatrice 36500
Schaetzel, Désiré 10780
Schafer, Colin 39363
Schaffer, Dale 42735
Schaffer, Dr. Herbert 02384
Schaffer, Dr. Nikolaus 02551
Schaffer-Hartmann, Richard 17584, 17585
Schaffers Bodenhausen, Dr. K. 29098
Schaffgotsch, Marie-Elise Gräfin 02360
Schaffner, Arndt R. 20184
Schaffner, Ingrid 46420
Schafhausen, Nicolaus 17044
Schafmeister, Prof. Dr. Maria-Theresia 17388
Schafroth, Colleen 43717
Schagen, C. 29433
Schaible, Larry 48009
Schaible, Silvia 18812
Schaiek, Zvi 22782
Schakel, F. 28807
Schalhorn, Dr. Andreas 16033
Schalke, Prof. Dr. Thomas 15918
Schall, Jan 44404
Schall Agnew, Ellen 45006
Schallenkamp, Kay 43184
Schaller, Anne K. 47699
Schaller, Hydee 41227
Schaller, Irene 37218
Schallert, Dr. Elmar 01741
Schalles, Dr. Hans-Joachim 20729
Schallmayer, Prof. Dr. Egon 15666
Schaltenbrand, Therese 36880
Schaluschke, Anja 18029
Schamberger, Rolf 17172
Schampers, K.J.J. 29324, 29325
Schanche, Kjersti 30973
Schantl, Alexandra 02603
Schantz, Michael W. 46463
Schanz, K.H. 19167
Schaper, Henning 20662
Schapp, Rebecca M. 47407
Schardin, Anne 01294
Scharf, Tamara 38511
Scharfenberg, Bernd 17143
Scharff, Prof. Wolfram 19548
Scharioth, Dr. Babara 18857
Scharioth, Dr. Barbara 18858, 18875
Scharloo, Dr. M. 29331
Scharnowski, Joachim 16000
Scharnweber, Karl 16629
Schaschl, Sabine 36708
Schaschl-Cooper, Sabine 36976
Schatorje, Dr. Jos 29939
Schatteman, Alice 45451
Schatten, Gereon 15768
Schatz, Duane 43130
Schatz, Günther 02304
Schatz, Dr. W. 37404
Schatzmann, Prof. Urs 36548
Schauber, Dr. Gregor 02498
Schauer, Karl 02276
Schauerte, Alfred 18650
Schauerte, Dr. Günter 16098
Schaufel, Shirley 46045
Schaufelberger-Breguet, Simone 37105
Schaukal, Dr. Barbara 01911
Schaumann, Prof. Walther 02149, 02150
Schaumburg-Lippe, Wolfgang Prinz zu 02227
Schaunaman, Lora 41045
Schaus, Dick 44378
Schawaller, Dr. W. 20105
Schawe, Dr. Martin 18832
Schebesta, Dr. Kurt 02841
Scheck, Klaus Peter 19878
Scheckle, Marian 28758
Scheda, Nicole 19178
Schedin, Pernilla 36003
Schedler, Christian 18741, 18742, 18743, 18744, 18745, 18746
Scheef, Vera 16589
Scheele, Edward 41050
Scheele, Dr. F. 16850
Scheele-Schmidt, Gisela 28760
Scheelen, J. 03487
Scheen, Rolf 30733
Schefcik, Jerry A. 44664
Schefers, Dr. Hermann 18505

Scheffers, Albert A.J. 29905
Scheffler, Ina 16425
Scheffler, Jürgen 18429, 18430
Scheffner, Charles A. 46591
Schegg, Jakob 36555
Scheibert, Johann 02169
Scheiblechner, Margit 36479
Scheicher, Harald 02769
Scheid, Dr. Eva 17799
Scheider, Dr. Ulrich 19794
Scheifer, Joanne 48384
Scheifinger, Otto 02086
Schein, Valentin 34139
Schelde-Jensen, Bodil 08825
Schelfhaut, Andrée 03471
Schellack, Dr. Fritz 19961
Schellenberger, Simona 18195
Schelshorn, E. 20592
Schemm, Jürgen von 18612
Schemmel, Prof. Dr. Bernhard 15817
Schenck, Jean-Luc 14124
Schenck, Marvin 48134
Schenk, Joseph B. 45421
Schenk, L.J.B. 28866
Schenk, P. 29429
Schenk, Ueli 36546
Schenk Freiherr von Stauffenberg, Franz 18333
Schenker, Prof. Christoph 37387
Schepers, Heiner 18483
Schepers, Dr. Wolfgang 17599
Scheppink, Baukje 30021
Scher, Anne 45821
Scherbel, Dr. G. 19149
Scherer, Ernst 37146
Scherer, Jim 46568
Scherer, Dr. Kristine 17676
Scherer, Kurt 36483
Scherer, Manfred 37146
Scherer, Rodney 01279
Scherf, Angeline 13548
Scherf, Avner 22676
Scherney, Dr. Ingrid 01869
Scherrer, August 37215
Scherrer, M. 10897
Scherting, Bruce A. 44249
Scherzer, Beatrice 17852
Scheu, David R. 48656
Scheuerecker, Franz X. 19355
Scheuermann, Gernot 19422
Scheuers, Vera 19001
Scheuren, Elmar 18185
Scheurer, Bruno 36660
Schiborra, Ute 19000
Schick, Dr. Karin 20090
Schick, Martin 15585
Schick, Dr. Ulrike 19323
Schicklberger, August 02559
Schicklgruber, Dr. Christian 02945
Schidlowsky, V. 11131
Schieber, Matthias 19019
Schieber, Dr. Michael 19108
Schiebout, Dr. Judith A. 41532
Schieck, Dr. Martin 17085
Schiefelbein, Don 44029
Schiemann, Larry 41295
Schierle, Dr. Sonja 20099
Schiers, Jörge 15721
Schierz, Dr. Kai Uwe 16904
Schiess, Robert 36497
Schießl, Werner 16786
Schiestl, Dr. Michael 02092
Schietere de Lophem, A. de 03263
Schietinger, James 42832
Schietz, Ottar 30870
Schiff, Michael 42750
Schiffer, Tim 48211
Schiffino, Prospero 23295
Schiffmann, Dr. René 36706, 37306
Schilbach, Michael 19229
Schild, Hans 37224
Schild, Margit 16722
Schilder, A.M.Th. 28910
Schildkrout, Dr. Enid 45759
Schill, Jörg 19918
Schillemans, R. 28875
Schiller, J. 01190
Schilli, K. 17234
Schilling, Christiane 17607
Schilling, Wolfgang 19930
Schiltz, Kelly 43788
Schimek, Dr. Michael 17313
Schimmel, Dan 46407
Schimmel, Paul 44930
Schimmelpenninck Van der Oije, C.O.A. 29758
Schimpf-Reinhardt, Dr. Hans 15797, 15799
Schindlbeck, Dr. Ingrid 15945
Schindlbeck, Dr. Markus 15945
Schindler, Dr. Helmut 18916
Schindler, Dr. Margot 02960
Schindler-Kaudelka, Dr. Eleny 02417
Schinkel, Dr. Eckhard 16666, 20388
Schinnerl, Heimo 02128
Schinnerl, Dr. Heimo 02268, 02269
Schinnerling, Mechthild 20749
Schinović, Nataša 03931
Schiøtz, Ottar 30869
Schipper, P. 30044
Schipper, Drs. Peter W. 29063, 29873, 29875
Schirmbeck, Dr. Peter 19708

Schirmböck, Thomas 18611
Schisler jr, Lee C. 41903
Schitinger, Jim 42834
Schiwek, Thomas 20678
Schladebach, Tilman 15867
Schlag, Dr. Gerald 02203, 02375, 02660, 02676
Schlagkamp, Dieter 19940
Schlass, Gerhard 02946
Schlatter, Alexander 36512
Schlatter, Dr. Rudolf 18411
Schlegel, Adolf 20428
Schlegel, Dr. Konrad 02918
Schleher, Linda 42445
Schleich, Prof. Dr. H. Hermann 20711
Schleicher, John 44787
Schleicher, Dr. Lennart 17414
Schleider, Holger 16326
Schlemmer, C. Raman 24673
Schlenk, Christoph 02077
Schleper, Dr. Thomas 19178
Schleushner, Evelyn 44680
Schleyerbach-Breu, Christiane 18739
Schlicher, Fred J. 45216
Schlicht, Udo 16155
Schlichting, Art 46603
Schlichting, Heike 15507, 15509
Schlicting, Eunice 42786
Schlieben, Katharina 37407
Schliebs, Des 01190
Schliefsteiner, Herbert 02341
Schliekau, Jürgen 15614
Schliemann, Ulrich 16346, 16348, 16353
Schlieper, Hans 19993
Schlimmgen-Ehmke, Katharina 16590
Schlögl, Franz 02316, 02731
Schlombs, Dr. Adele 18158
Schloßbauer, Kurt 19485
Schlosser, Christa 18968
Schlosser, Christoph 36703
Schlosser, Prof. Katesa 18078
Schloßer, Rosemarie 16553
Schloter, John E. 47174
Schluchter, Dr. André 36699
Schluep, Charlotte 36808
Schlüter, Dr. Andreas 20105
Schlüter, D. 29140
Schlüter, Dr. J. 17554
Schlueter, Sue 45357
Schlüter, Dr. Wolfgang 19280
Schlup, Michel 36982
Schmälzle, Reinhard 19909
Schmalbrock, R.F. 17945
Schmalfuß, Dr. Helmut 20105
Schmaltz, Prof. Bernhard 18071
Schmalz, Lydia H. 45729
Schmandt, Dr. Matthias 16164
Schmauder, Dr. Michael 16246
Schmeh, Thomas J. 44510
Schmeja, Michael 01730
Schmelz, Dr. Bernd 17561
Schmid, A. 15735
Schmid, Dr. Anna 17607
Schmid, Debora 36479
Schmid, Elisabeth 37403
Schmid, Dr. Elmar D. 18891
Schmid, G. 19675
Schmid, Gerhard 37241
Schmid, Dr. Hanns 02477
Schmid, Hanspeter 37108
Schmid, Jakob 37281
Schmid, Dr. Margit 01769
Schmid, Dr. Peter 37396
Schmid, Reinhard 20306
Schmid, S. 19506
Schmid, U. 20105
Schmid, Dr. Ulla K. 19842
Schmid, Ute 45803
Schmid-Birri, Ingrid 36689
Schmid-Nafz, Gerlinde 18675
Schmidberger, Dr. Ekkehard 15765
Schmidberger, Prof. Dr. Ekkehard 18022
Schmidl, Dr. H. 01818
Schmidl, Karin 15920
Schmidl, Matthias 02015
Schmidt, Aiko 16850
Schmidt, Dr. Alfons 19437
Schmidt, Andreas 20755
Schmidt, B. 20277
Schmidt, Dwight 43709
Schmidt, Erwin 18286
Schmidt, Dr. Eva 16324
Schmidt, Franz Xaver 20105
Schmidt, Franziska 17604
Schmidt, Gavin 41695
Schmidt, Georg 17292
Schmidt, Gudrun 15910
Schmidt, Dr. Hans-Günter 20694
Schmidt, Dr. Hans-Werner 18405
Schmidt, Harro 17601
Schmidt, Hartmut 20555, 20558, 20559, 20561
Schmidt, Jan 18842
Schmidt, Karl 16498
Schmidt, Kirsten 08892
Schmidt, Klaus 20707
Schmidt, Lawrence R. 46090
Schmidt, Martin 17607
Schmidt, Dr. Peter 19061
Schmidt, Philipp 01722
Schmidt, Rolf 16121, 16122

Schmidt, Roman 18509
Schmidt, Dr. Rüdiger 17989
Schmidt, Dr. S. 18926
Schmidt, Dr. Sabine Maria 16757
Schmidt, Sebastian 17778
Schmidt, Siegfried 20564
Schmidt, Teresa 48193
Schmidt, Dr. Theun-M. 16096
Schmidt, Thomas 16610, 16611
Schmidt, Volker 16325
Schmidt, Wayne W. 48306
Schmidt, Willi 19803
Schmidt-Bergmann, Prof. Dr. Hansgeorg 17997
Schmidt-Dengler, Prof. Dr. Wendelin 02955
Schmidt-Esters, Gudrun 17094
Schmidt-Glintzer, Prof. Dr. Helwig 20653
Schmidt-Herwig, Dr. Angelika 17031
Schmidt-Lawrenz, Dr. Stefan 17656
Schmidt-Rutsch, Dr. Olaf 16666, 20623
Schmidt-Surdez, Maryse 36982
Schmied, Peter 37258
Schmiegel, Karol A. 42967
Schmieglitz-Otten, Juliane 16452
Schmigalle, Dr. Günther 17989
Schmink, Donna 44225
Schmith, Andreas 15536
Schmitt, Horst 20209
Schmitt, Prof. Dr. Michael 16250
Schmitt, Peter 17991
Schmitt, Robert 14700
Schmitt-Riegraf, Dr. Cornelia 18941
Schmitz, Dr. Bettina 17760
Schmitz, Brigitte 15912
Schmitz, Dr. Britta 15981
Schmitz, Doris 42148
Schmitz, Hans-Hermann 15894
Schmitz, Dr. Michael 17607
Schmitz, Silvia 17606
Schmitz, Uwe 16582
Schmitz von Ledebur, Dr. Katja 02918
Schmocker, Susan 01490
Schmöhl, Thomas 15873
Schmölzer, Othmar 02473
Schmolka, Gerhard 03001
Schmollgruber, Friedrich 02682
Schmook, Dr. R. 15645
Schmucker, Kristine 43709
Schmuttermeier, Elisabeth 02929
Schmutz, Daniel 36541
Schmutz, Dr. Hans Konrad 37338, 37344
Schmutzler, Ruth 17074
Schnackenburg, Dr. M.-L. 19275
Schnall, Dr. Uwe 16339
Schneede, Prof. Dr. Uwe M. 17541
Schneeweis, Dr. Felix 02117
Schneider, Dr. Alfred 15484
Schneider, Prof. Dr. Angela 15912, 15981, 16075
Schneider, Dr. Carola 16952
Schneider, Claire 41981
Schneider, Dr. Cornelia 18600
Schneider, Don 46234
Schneider, E. Lina 16029
Schneider, Eckhard 01745
Schneider, Dr. Erich 19889, 19890, 19892, 19893
Schneider, Ester 18724
Schneider, Dr. G.C. 28779
Schneider, H. 18006
Schneider, Dr. Hans 36876
Schneider, Hansjörg 18201
Schneider, Hélène 13799
Schneider, Dr. Herbert 19524
Schneider, Joanne 45307
Schneider, John 48516
Schneider, Josef 16421
Schneider, Dr. K. 17523
Schneider, Karl-Heinz 19679
Schneider, Dr. Katja 17521
Schneider, Kerry 46515
Schneider, Klaus 16766
Schneider, Dr. Klaus 18164
Schneider, M. 19159
Schneider, Malou 14817
Schneider, Dr. Manfred 02082
Schneider, Michael 16542, 36508
Schneider, Nadja 36764
Schneider, Paul 44897
Schneider, Reisa Sniley 06689
Schneider, René 10959
Schneider, Dr. Thomas 19277
Schneider, Prof. Dr. Ulrich 15379, 17062
Schneider, Ursula 17555
Schneider, Dr. Wolfgang 16541, 17291
Schneider-Kempf, Barbara 16099, 16100
Schneider-Mohamed, Rosemarie 16722
Schneidler, Dr. Herbert 19531
Schneidmiller, Kenneth A. 43818
Schnell, Frank 42574
Schnell, Gertrude H. 43524
Schnell, M. 10747
Schnell, Ronald 48041
Schnellhammer-Ocist, Norbert 02675
Schnepp, Patrick 12250
Schnepper, Mary S. 43245
Schneyer, Rosemary 47821
Schniek, Dr. Rüdiger 19793
Schnitzer, Dr. Claudia 16692
Schnitzler, Bernadette 14818
Schnitzler, Dr. Ludwig 15723
Schnurr, Marie 43036

Schober, Manfred 19908
Schober, Otto 01897
Schoberwalter, Anton 02138
Schobinger, Dr. Juan 00434
Schoch, Lois H. 41402
Schoch, Dr. R. 20105
Schoch, Dr. Rainer 19139
Schöb, Kathrin 37054
Schöbe, Lutz 16584
Schöbel, Dr. G. 20256
Schöbl, Ernst 02424
Schöck, Dr. Gustav 20115
Schoeller, Danielle 15227
Schöllmann, Dr. Lothar 18951
Schömann, Rainer 18842
Schoen, Kenneth 48273
Schön, Matthias D. 15595, 17477
Schönberger, Dr. Angela 16028, 16049
Schöne, Dr. Anja 20155, 20156
Schoene, Lynn 19850
Schoeneck, Edith 19191
Schönefeld, Dr. Bärbel 16081
Schönewald, Dr. Beatrix 17904, 17910, 17911
Schönfelder, Kathleen 18383
Schönfellner, Dr. Franz 02158, 02160
Schönhagen, Dr. Benigna 15558
Schönitzer, Prof. Dr. N. 18926
Schoenke, Marilyn 44085
Schönweger, Astrid 24353
Schoepf, D. 36745
Schoewe, Sherry 44601
Schofield, Roger 30314
Schokkenbroek, J. 28888
Scholl, Dr. Andreas 15914
Scholl, Ben 48024
Scholl, Dr. Lars U. 16339
Schollenberger, Werner 19167
Scholler, Dr. Markus 18003
Schollian, Gerd 17657
Schollmeier, Dr. Axel 18946
Scholtemeijer, G. 34353
Scholten, Lisa 41932
Scholz, Dr. Antony 01935
Scholz, C. 20113
Scholz, Carl 47862
Scholz, Dr. G. 16210, 16211, 16212
Scholz, Dr. Günter 16213
Scholz, Margitta 16283
Scholz-Bauer, U. 19598
Scholz-Strasser, Inge 02989
Scholze, Frank 15920
Schomers, Dr. Florian 02080
Schommers, Dr. Annette 18833, 19203
Schonewille, Dr. P. 28950
Schonlau, Ree 46144
Schoofs, M. 03531
Schooler, Jim 48817
Schoon, P.J. 29173
Schoonhoven Okken, W. 29059
Schoonover, Karen 06241
Schoonover, Larry 47728
Schoonover, Mary Ellen 41393
Schoppe, Karla 20775
Schopping, H. 29897
Schorta, Dr. Regula 37064
Schoske, Dr. Sylvia 18915, 19915
Schotsman, Liesbeth 03146
Schott, Vibehe 08820
Schott-Smith, Christine 21256
Schotte, Petra 18534
Schotten, Christoph 20295
Schou-Christensen, Jørgen 08927
Schoulepnikoff, Chantal de 37031, 37393
Schoutens, P. 28875
Schrade, Ewald 16791
Schrader, Kathleen 46891
Schrader, Wolfgang 19413
Schram, Prof. Dr. F.R. 28917
Schramer-Lorang, Fernande 27556
Schramm, Dr. Ágnes 43978
Schramm, Jeanne 48534
Schramm, Robert W. 48534
Schrank, Gustav 17776
Schratter, Rudolf 02049, 02050, 02051, 02052
Schreck, Anne-Katrin 19139
Schreiber, Dr. K. 20113
Schreiber, Mildred 42155
Schreier, Dr. Christoph 16242
Schreilechner, Waltraud 02070
Schrein, Catherine 41518
Schreiner, A. 19819
Schreiner, Josy 27545
Schreiner, Manuela 18201
Schrem, Wilfried 19010
Schrenk, Prof. Dr. Klaus 18002
Schrenk, Dr. Sabine 37064
Schrettl, Reinhold 02765
Schrick, Annette 15899
Schrijvers, N. 03146
Schriver, Stephanie 47413
Schroder, Dr. Anne 43019
Schröder, Lise Lotte 08875
Schrøder Vesterkjær, Siri 30896
Schroeder, Allen 42133, 45379
Schroeder, Bob 43476
Schröder, Christoph 15447, 15448
Schroeder, Chuck 46116
Schroeder, Dorothy 42304
Schröder, Dr. Heike 15756, 20115

Schröder, Dr. Klaus Albrecht 02830
Schroeder, N.H. 38023
Schroeder, P. 41319
Schroeder, Patricia 43319
Schroeder, Sharon 46817
Schröder, Till 17555
Schröder, Dr. U. 17390
Schrödl, Dr. M. 18926
Schröter, Jürgen 20177
Schröter, Dr. P. 18826
Schröter, Wolfgang 19930
Schroll, Ludwig 16870
Schroth, Dr. Adella 46824
Schroth, Dr. Sarah W. 43019
Schrub, Antoine 13727
Schten, Abigail 42836
Schubert, Armin 16281
Schubert, Jason 42396
Schubert, Dr. Kristina 15918
Schubert, Susan 16728
Schubert, Werner 02854
Schubert, Wolfgang 18402
Schuch, Herbert 17985
Schuchardt, Günter 16820
Schuchmann, Dr. Karl-Ludwig 16250
Schüle, Bernard A. 37393
Schuelke, Chris 43313
Schüllenbach, Konrad 28784
Schüly, Dr. Maria 17107
Schünemann, Dr. Gustav 15827
Schünemann, Karl 15425
Schünemann, Ulla 17232
Schüpbach, Beat 36544
Schüpbach, Ulrich 36568
Schürer 16798
Schürer, Ralf 19139
Schuerholz, Peter 47954
Schürmann, Dr. Kay U. 18630
Schütt, Charlotte 37392
Schütt, Dr. Jutta 17074
Schütt-Hohenstein, Dr. A. 20113
Schuette, Bobbie 43787
Schütte, Dr. Margret 19794
Schütz, Dr. Christian 20326
Schütz, Ilse 34408
Schütz, Jan 08317
Schütz, Dr. Karl 02918, 02918
Schütz, Volker 16170
Schütz, Wolfgang 20440
Schuh, Kurt 02942
Schuh, Walter 02355
Schuhmacher, Walter 17253
Schuhwerk, Dr. Franz 18836
Schulenburg, Gräfin Sonnhild von der 16983
Schulenburg, Stephan Graf von der 17062
Schuler, Romana 02924
Schuler, Shirley 46543
Schuler, Dr. Thomas 16472
Schulkin, Jerrold L. 44768
Schuller, Kurt 01827
Schuller, Tom 44460
Schuller tot Peursum-Meyer, Drs. J. 29911
Schullerus, M. 15455
Schulman, Daniel 42304
Schulman Jesse, Daniel 42304
Schulson, Henry H. 42260
Schulte, Dr. Birgit 17480, 17481
Schulte, Wolfgang 03491
Schulte-Hobein, Dr. Jürgen 15512
Schulte-Kemper, Hubert 18656
Schulte-Wülwer, Prof. Dr. Ulrich 17012
Schulten, Ton 29676
Schulters, Johannes 15806
Schultes, Alfred 02085
Schultes, Dr. Lothar 02234
Schultes, Peter 15470, 15471
Schultz, Brian 43951
Schultz, Douglas G. 41981
Schultz, Dr. Franz Joachim 15851
Schultz, Prof. Dr. Hartwig 17046
Schultz, J. Bernard 45500
Schultz, Jeffrey 43797
Schultz, Peter 36262
Schultze, Prof. Dr. H.-P. 16056
Schultze, Joachim 19793
Schulz, Dr. Ch. 37062
Schulz, Günther 15437
Schulz, Dr. Isabel 17611
Schulz, Marion 19546
Schulz, Max 44899
Schulz, Ralph J. 45615
Schulz, Rebekah 01115
Schulz, Regine 41489
Schulz, Volker 20539
Schulz-Hoffmann, Prof. Dr. Carla 18832
Schulz-Weddigen, Dr. Ingo 18202
Schulze, Dietmar 18415
Schulze, Nina 18107
Schulze, Dr. Sabine 17074
Schulze Altcappenberg, Prof. Dr. Hein-Th. 16033
Schulze-Dörrlamm, Dr. Mechthild 18606
Schulze-Neuhoff, Eckart 16738
Schumacher, Caroline 19177
Schumacher, Dr. Doris 17501
Schumacher, Hans-Joachim 18104
Schumacher, Rainald 18903
Schumacher, Dr. Renate 16244
Schumacher-Gebler, Eckehart 18406
Schumann, Maurice 12056

Schumann, Peter 43706
Schumann, Romzin 27560
Schumard, Ann 48382
Schummel, Helle 09080
Schupbach, Marianne 36546
Schuppli, Madeleine 37240, 37244
Schur, Chantel 06308
Schure, Edeltraut 20640
Schurig, Dr. Roland 15382, 15383
Schurkamp, Trish 41782
Schusser, Dr. Adalbert 03001
Schuster, Anna 01835
Schuster, Dr. Erika 01888
Schuster, Erwin 02686
Schuster, Eva 20572
Schuster, Franz 01950
Schuster, Prof. Dr. Gerhard 17891, 20467
Schuster, Kenneth L. 41680
Schuster, Prof. Dr. Peter-Klaus 15912, 15981, 16071, 16075, 16086, 16098
Schuster, Robin 45023
Schuth, Anton 18777
Schutte, Maria Christina 00112
Schutz, Carine 13726
Schutz, David 45479
Schutz, John 47363
Schutz, Kenneth J. 46930
Schutzbier, Heribert 02262
Schwab, K. 15789
Schwab, Maria 17207
Schwab, Rosl 01688
Schwab, S. 37949
Schwab, Sibylle 18615
Schwab, Sigrid 16550
Schwab-Dorfman, Debbie 45821
Schwabach, Dr. Thomas 20482, 20483, 20484, 20485
Schwabe, Uwe 18385
Schwager, Michael 46989
Schwaiger, Dr. Axel 17239
Schwaiger, Wilhelm 01873
Schwalenberg, Gregory 41451
Schwaller, M. 13348
Schwalm, Dr. Bodo 17398
Schwalm, Dr. Hans-Jürgen 19514
Schwalm, Helmut 19871
Schwank, Prof. Dr. Benedikt 16134
Schwar, Scott 46053
Schwark, Dr. Thomas 17597
Schwarm, Larry W. 43184
Schwarts, Eleanore 47885
Schwartz, Constance 47009
Schwartz, David 41307
Schwartz, Elizabeth 44391
Schwartz, Gary 48004
Schwartz, Janet 06590
Schwartz, Judith 06581, 06587
Schwartz, Michael 42469
Schwartz, Stephen H. 43549
Schwartzbaum, Paul 45872
Schwarz 19750
Schwarz, Dr. Dieter 37331
Schwarz, Ernst 02040
Schwarz, Dr. Helmut 19161
Schwarz, Prof. Dr. Karl 02881
Schwarz, Klaus 17948
Schwarz, Peter 19306, 19307
Schwarz, Walter A. 02895
Schwarzenberg, Karl Johann von 02920
Schwarzjirg, Dr. Helmuth 02186
Schwarzkopf, C.G. 47842
Schwarzkopf, Craig 41576
Schweiger, Andrea 36518
Schweigert, Dr. Günter 20105
Schweiggl, Wolfgang 23659
Schwein, Florence 43113
Schweiss, Christoph 36840
Schweizer, Dr. Hans Ulrich 37378
Schweizer, Nicole 36544
Schweizer, Dr. Paul D. 48170
Schweizer, Dr. Rolf 18963
Schwelle, Dr. Franz 02300
Schwemer, Florian 18842
Schwenker, Polly 41065
Schwering, Dr. Burkhard 18068
Schwertner, Dr. Johann 02127, 02268, 02269
Schwind, Stefan 16690
Schwind, Wilhelm 02237
Schwinden, Lothar 20212, 20212
Schwinn, Wolfgang 19540
Schwintek, Monika 19809
Schwinzer, Dr. Ellen 17576
Schwitter, Josef 36763
Schwoeffermann, Catherine 41700
Schwolger, David 44640
Schymalla, Joachim 19344
Sci, LaVerne 42805
Sciallano, Martine 12065
Scichilone, Dr. Giovanni 23548
Scirè Nepi, Dr. Giovanna 25920
Scoates, Christopher 47406
Scobey, Pati 41096
Scoccimarro, Fabio 25820
Scofield, P. 30124
Sconci, Maria Selene 25233
Scoon, Fergus 39851
Scotes, Helen 30138
Scott, Adrienne 42373
Scott, Andrew 40966

Scott, B. 01479
Scott, Barbara 45913
Scott, Bob 39898
Scott, Carol E. 46301
Scott, Dan 06362
Scott, Donna A. 45852
Scott, E. 34359
Scott, Elva 43032
Scott, Eric 46824
Scott, F.E. 39392
Scott, Dr. Gerry 47260
Scott, Jane 01596
Scott, John 01598, 43625
Scott, Julie 47354
Scott, Kitty 06084
Scott, Michael 40655, 44528
Scott, Preston 05085
Scott, Ron 06098
Scott, Rose 43768
Scott, Terri 43108
Scott, Vane S. 45914
Scott, Vanya 48607
Scott, Virginia 41837
Scott, William W. 47962
Scott Bouth, Karen 05698
Scott-Childress, Katie 43796
Scott Garrity, Noreen 42060
Scottez-de Wambrechies, Annie 12599
Scotti, Dr. Roland 36654
Scrase, D.E. 38454
Scribner, John C.L. 41422
Scriven, Brian 42135
Scriver, Lorraine 41961
Scriver, Dr. Robert M. 41961
Scrobotă, Paul 32427
Scudder, G.G.E. 06690
Scuderi, Helena 46609
Scudero, Domenico 25227
Scudieri, Dr. Magnolia 23869
Sculley, John 40597
Scully, Cammie V. 48435
Scully, Robert J. 48620
Seabold, Thomas 44451
Seage Person, Robin 43835
Seager, Pamela 44863
Seal, Ray 39707
Seald-Chudzinski, Romi 46670
Seale, Sir David 03108
Searl, Majorie 46948
Searle, Ross 00843
Sears, Ann 43287
Sears, Dennis 43578
Seaver, Tom 22513
Sebastián, Dr. Amparo 35046
Sebastian, Padmini 01234
Sebastiani, Prof. Antonio 25268
Sebayang, Nas 22157
Šebek, Dr. F. 08534
Šebesta, Dr. Pavel 08308
Sebire, H. 40424
Sebolt George, Alberta 47859
Secher Jensen, Dr. Thomas 08772
Seck, Dr. Amadou Abdoulaye 33782
Sedberry, Rosemary 41526
Seddon, Jane 38559, 38562
Seddon, Jeffrey 39751
Seddon, Joan 05738
Sedge, Jane 40474
Sedikova, Larisa 37902
Sedilek, F. 34079
Sedinko, Svetlana Alekseevna 33233
Sedioli, Giovanni 23114
Sedláček, Zbyněk 08300, 08425
Sedler, Irmgard 18212
Sedlmeier, Martin 19383
Sedlmeir, Wolfgang 16337
Sedman, Ken 39948
Sedova, Galina Michajlovna 33453
Sedova, Irina V. 33068
Seear, Lynne 01459
Seebeck, Eibe 16668
Seeber, Dr. Ekkehard 20285
Seeberg, Peter 01980
Seefried, Dr. Monique 41352
Seel, Dr. Peter C. 15987
Seele, Ralf-Michael 18687
Seeley, Daniel 45031
Seelig, Dr. Lorenz 18833, 19532
Seeliger, G. 20038
Seeliger, Dr. Matthias 17832
Seelinger, Evelyn 47236
Seemann, Esther 19568
Seemann, Hellmut 20462
Seemann, Hellmut Th. 20475
Seemann, R. 20399
Seewaldt, Dr. Peter 20212
Seewöster, H. 19030
Şefănescu, Radu 32446
Šefčík, Dr. Erich 08431
Sefcik, James F. 45731
Sefu, Mary 27110
Segal, Dror 22723
Segal, Merav 22739
Segalstad, Prof. Tom V. 30735
Segarra, Guido Barletta 32385
Segarra, Ninfa 45857
Seger, Joe 45401
Segerer, Dr. A. 18926
Segessenmann, Vreni 37013, 37014

Segger, Martin 06724
Seghatoleslami, Parvine Sadre 22300
Seghers, George D. 41129
Segieth, Dr. Clelia 16129
Seglie, Prof. Dario 24926, 24928, 24933
Segni Pulvirenti, Francesca 23255
Segovia Barrientos, Francisco 34584
Séguin, Louise 06359
Segura, Angela 35649
Segura, Avelino 42752
Segura Martí, J.M. 34435
Seib, Dr. Gerhard 18805, 18806, 18807, 18808, 18810
Seibel, Prof. Dr. Wilfried 16762
Seibert, Dr. Elke 20435, 20436
Seibert, Georg 20195
Seibert, Peter S. 44624
Seidel, Doris 18859
Seidel, W.A. 18283
Seidenberg, Ulrich 18728
Seider, Diana L. 44832
Seidl, Alfred 01986
Seidl, Dr. Katharina 02918
Seidl, Manfred 01805
Seif, Denise 42188
Seifermann, Ellen 19150
Seifert, Jörg 15498
Seiffert, Claudia 17991
Seifried, Doriann 05427
Seifriedsberger, Anna 02447
Seifriedsberger, Georg 02447
Seigo, Jinbo 26796
Seiji, Kamei 26739
Seilacher, Adolf 45698
Seiler, Prof. Dr. Michael 19437
Seiler, R. 36824
Seiler, Dr. Sven 18166
Sein, Joni L. 43093
Seip, Ivar 30558
Seipel, Prof. Dr. Wilfried 02917, 02918
Seisbøll, Lise 08984
Seitter, John R. 42059
Seitz, Anna 02716, 02718
Seitz, Becca 41454
Seitz, Erich 20410
Seitz, Oliver 15550
Seitz, Walter 17836
Seitz-Weinzierl, Beate 20579
Sejček, Zdeněk 08637
Šejleva, Gergana 04671
Sekera, Dr. Jan 08567
Sekerák, Jiří 08268
Sekete, A. 34193
Sekulian, Augustin 02938
Selbach, Josee 29309
Selbe, Nance 47032
Seleli, Prof. Y. 34224
Selenitza, Enin 00025
Self, Dana 44401
Selfridge, Anna B. 44772
Selfridge, Nancy 45458
Selig, Gary D. 05130, 05131
Seligman, Thomas K. 47772
Seligmann, Susan M. 48348
Seline, Janice 46118
Selirand, Urmas 09328
Selke, Gordon 46204
Sell, Manfred 20629
Sella, Lodovico 23078
Sellers, Kate M. 43944
Sellers, Mary B. 42910
Sellers, P. 01330
Sellers, P.E. 28826
Selles, Didier 13603
Sellés, José Pascual 34436
Selliere-Charon 03202
Sellinger, Dr. Günter 02699
Sellink, Manfred 03246, 03247, 03248, 03249, 03250, 03251, 03252, 03253, 03254, 03257, 03260, 03264, 03267
Sello, Thomas 17541
Selmayr, Prof. Dr. Gerhard 18613, 18614
Selmeczi, Dr. László 21398
Selmer, Jørgen 08933
Selmer Olsen, Knud 30388
Selmić, Leposava 33869
Selph, Judy 42875
Selsing, Lotte 30877
Selvorious, Clement 23975
Selway, Robert 47400
Selwyn, Sve 38968
Selzer, Erika 01691
Selzer, Helmut 03001
Semakova, Tatjana Gennadjevna 32920
Semënov, Ivan Grigorjevič 33228
Semenova, Galina 33144
Semënova, Tatjana Andreevna 32830
Semff, Dr. Michael 18830, 18912
Semočkin, Aleksandr Aleksandrovič 33359
Sen Gupta, Pradip Kumar 03088
Senadheera, S. 35754
Senanster, Hvon de 13766
Sender, Becky 46703
Sendl, Thomas 19373
Sendra, Gemma 34552
Senén López Gómez, Felipe 34753
Senf, Erika 19287
Senften, Penny 45107
Seng, Dr. Joachim 17046

Senge, Takatoshi 26784
Sengele, J.-M. 13205
Senior, Caroline 22553
Senior, David 39922
Seniuk, Jake 46589
Senn, Carol J. 42779
Senn, Dr. Matthias 36722, 37393
Sennequier, Geneviève 14048
Sens, Dr. Angelie 28892
Sensabaugh, David 45700
Sensen, Stephan 15442, 15443
Seo, Chiaki 26795
Seoighe, Mainchín 22379
Seokgi, Kim 27162
Sepioł, Afred 31623
Seppänen, Anne 35882
Sequeira, Dora 07657, 07663
Sequeira, Dora María 07658
Serafini, Flavio 24095
Serafińska-Domańska, Maria 31839
Serageldin, Dr. Ismail 09248
Seraja, Marina Leonidovna 33750
Serani Elliott, Daniela 06902
Šeravić, Ivana 07796
Şerban, Violeta 32565
Şerbănescu, Done 32558
Šerbec, Jože 34094
Šerbelj, Dr. Ferdinand 34114
Serdar, Elizabeta 07824
Serena, Dominique 10418
Serge, Pascal 15002
Sergeenko, Valentin Ivanovič 33312
Sergeeva, Elena Nikolaevna 33667
Sergeeva, I.N. 32789
Sergent Nemeth, Dana 41307
Serghini, Mohamed 28715
Seright, Susan 40341
Séris, Anne-Jean 12244
Serkownek, Edith 45256
Sermeno, Rhodora J. 31435
Serna, Marco A. 07516
Serna Muñoz, Martha Judith 07473
Serota, Sir Nicholas 39787, 39788
Serpe, Louis 14616, 14617
Serra, Florenci 35671
Serra, Sophie 12326
Serra de Manresa, Valentí 34576
Serra Ferreira, Dr. Ana Margarida 32251
Serra Rexach, Eduardo 35048
Serradj-Remili, Nedjma 00043
Serrano, Delmy 45796
Serré-Van Wijk, Brenda 28870
Sersha, Tom 43248
Serson, Christine 03233
Sérullaz, Arlette 13640
Servais Lebrun, Françoise 03627
Service, Pam 43230
Servis, Nancy M. 42793
Servitje de Lerdo de Tejada, Marinela 28159
Sesić, Maria 33808
Šestakova, Tamara Nikolaevna 33590
Sestan, Ivan 07813
Sethuraman, K. 21777
Setinský, Jiří 08283
Šetrakova, Svetlana N. 33087
Settle Cooney, Mary 48121
Settler, Faye 06850
Seuffert, Dr. Ottmar 16641
Seugwoo, Nam 27243
Sevastjanova, Lidija Ivanovna 32884
Sevda, Dadasheva 30370
Ševeček, Dr. Ludvík 08750
Sevellec, Jacques 10909
Sever, Nancy 00698, 00700
Severance, Christopher C. 05230
Severens, Martha R. 43830
Ševereva, Tamara Anatoljevna 33230
Severini, Pavel 33850
Sévery, Sébastien 13936, 13937
Sevi, Uriel J. 00221
Sevier, James 42861
Sevigney, Nichola 48322
Sevilla, Guillermo A. 00253
Sevinç, Nurten 37649
Ševkomud, Igor Dmitrievič 32738
Ševyrin, Sergej Andreevič 33306
Seward Hannam, Kim 05699
Sewell, Cynthia 41771
Sewell, Dennita 46477
Sewell, Jack 00954
Sewell, Jane S. 48564
Sexton, Nick 38660
Sexton, Robert 42780
Seybold, Russell G. 45988
Seybold, Silke 16336
Seyfried, Dr. Friederike 18382
Seyfried, Tina 02945
Seyl, Susan 46637
Seymour, C. 01432
Seymour, Dr. Claire 39753
Seyrl, Harald 02626, 02628, 03005
Seytkazieva, N.M. 27309
Sezen, Nuri 37622
Sezer, Tahsin 37702
Sezgin, Mustafa 37797
Seznec, A. 13899
Sforzi, Dr. Andrea 24058
Sfrappini, Dr. Alessandra 24247, 24249, 24251
Sgromo, V. Joseph 47047

Sgubin, Dr. Raffaella 24034, 24035, 24036
Sgubini Moretti, Dr. Anna Maria 23313
Shaak, Dr. Graig D. 43581
Shaath, Shawqi M. 37433
Shacham, Tzvi 22745
Shackelford, George T. M. 41817
Shady Solís, Dr. Ruth 31203
Shaffer, Marcy 41086
Shaffer, Randy 41235
Shaffer, Dr. Susan 45271
Shaffer, Terry 43054
Shaffer, Vivienne 47734
Shafi El-Sheikh, Hassan Abdel 09246
Shagonaby, Joyce 43909
Shah, Hiralal P. 21695, 21696
Shahi, M. 22239
Shahzad, Tasneem 31052
Shaiboub, Dr. Abdullah 27501, 27502, 27503, 27504, 27505, 27506, 27507, 27508, 27509
Shaiman, Jason 42563
Shaker, H. 22235
Shalev, Avner 22636, 22672
Shalgosky, Sarah 38644
Shamis, Bob 45847
Shamsbod, Mahmoud 22299
Shanahan, Carl 43638
Shanahan, J.P. 01032
Shane, Dr. Orrin 47166
Shank, Nicholas 45388
Shankle, Kent 48435
Shanley, Ellen 45839
Shanmugam, Dr. P. 21741
Shannon, Dr. Helen 48057
Shannon, Steve 38826
Shapiro, Denise 44665
Shapiro, Lynda 42622
Shapiro, Michael 41348
Shapiro, Dr. Michael E. 41343
Shapiro, Selma 46056
Sharan, Michael 22603
Sharer, Robert 46460
Sharma, Dr. O. P. 21707
Sharma, R.D. 21685
Sharman, Glen 39700
Sharon, Dr. Douglas 47294
Sharp, Corwin 48743
Sharp, Ellen 42924
Sharp, James 44957
Sharp, Jane 45678
Sharp, Kevin 48538
Sharp, Lewis I. 42885
Sharp, Lindsay 40945
Sharp, Paige 44568
Sharp, Randall 43148
Sharp, R.W.D. 40750
Sharpe, D. 40282
Sharpe, Dr. Lindsay 39773
Sharpe, Yvonne 06725
Sharrock, D.J. 39343
Sharygin, G.V. 33173
Shastri, Nandan 22053
Shastri, N.H. 22054
Shattuck, Jennifer B. 45433
Shattuck, John 41812
Shaudys, Vincent 47684
Shaughnessy, Beth 05689
Shaul, Nissim 22728
Shaver, Steve 47590
Shaw, Cindy 40431
Shaw, D. 01418
Shaw, David 38643
Shaw, Deirdre 48524
Shaw, Elizabeth 40819
Shaw, Harry 39435
Shaw, J. 38269
Shaw, Karen 43051
Shaw, Lana 06066
Shaw, Lytle 45794
Shaw, Margaret 00886
Shaw, R. Douglas 48547
Shaw, R.W. 39512
Shaw, W. 39064
Shawe-Taylor, Desmond 39627
Shawhan, Jeff 45258
Shawn, Gene 46385
Shawn Barber, Barbara 46385
Shaylor, Ellen 41282
Shea, Carol 42767
Shea, John C. 44429
Sheads, Scott 41467
Sheaffer, Ed 47609
Shearer, I.M. 38854
Shearer, Linda 48635
Shearer, Thelma 01012
Shedd, Linda 41553
Shedd, Nancy S. 44153
Sheedy, Gilles 05065
Sheedy, Tom 22380
Sheehan, Ron 44343
Sheets, Arian 48214
Sheets, H.L. 45172
Sheets, Jeff 41048
Sheets, John W. 48315
Sheffer, Ann E. 48573
Sheffield, Sir Reginald 40652
Shefsik, Kenneth 45740
Sheku, Nail 00038
Sheldon, Dr. Andrew 45408
Sheldon, Dr. Frederick H. 41532

Sheldon, Sara 41836
Sheley, David 43958
Shelhouse, Marvin 45338
Shellabarger, Harold L. 47801
Shelley, Majorie 45833
Shelley, Roger 38715
Shelley, Dr. Rowland 46777
Shelly, Roger 38716
Shelswell White, E.R.G. 22375
Shelton, L.T. 44329
Shelton, Ronald G. 42569
Shen, Dr. Lindsay 47154
Shendar, Yehudit 22672
Sheng, Yi Jia 07176
Shepard, Betty J. 44911
Shepard, Bruce 06396
Shepard, Charles A. 45710
Shepard, Joel 47346
Shephard, Diane 45011
Shepherd, Dr. Brian 00919
Shepp, James G. 45079
Sheppard, Jude 42385
Sheppard, Veronica 39747
Sheppy, Richard 38302
Sherck, Robin 41051
Sherer, Aaron 46207
Sherhofer, Ronald F. 48417
Sheridan, Barry 38335, 39156
Sheridan, Joan 48299
Sheridan, Tom 48082
Sheriff, Alice 45711
Sherin, Pamela V. 46700
Sherman, Alan 22722
Sherman, Cathy R. 42632
Sherman, Jacob 05988
Sherman, Mimi 45832
Sherman, Nancy 46815
Sherman, Seán 39656
Sherman, Sean 39734
Sherman, William 41229
Sherrer, John 42562
Sherrill, Sarah B. 45771
Sherry, Thomas 48558
Sherwood, Frederick 43050
Sherwood, Penelope 48234
Shestack, Alan 48373
Shetler, John 48048
Shetty, Prof. N.R. 21772
Shexnayder, Charlotte 43004
Shick, Andrew F. 46310
Shickles, Tim 43340
Shieh, Suewhei 48045
Shields, Ann 48153
Shields, Charlotte. 44020
Shields, Dorothy 44800
Shields, R. Michael 06688
Shields, Scott 47050
Shiels, Margaret M. 42987, 48714
Shiffman, Carol 46604
Shifman, Barry L. 44228
Shigaki, Betty 46936
Shih, Chia-Chun 43487
Shih, Minfa 07359
Shikada, Norimitsu 26609
Shikata, Miho 26988
Shilliday, Charles 06823
Shilo-Cohen, Nurit 22659
Shimada, Kazutaka 26887
Shimada, Kunio 26768
Shimazu, Misato 26853
Shimizu, Minoru 26764
Shimp, Dr. Robert E. 42510
Shin, Prof. Kwang Cho 27198
Shin, Tak Keun 27132
Shin, Young Koog 27278, 27296
Shin-tsu Tai, Susan 47404
Shinn, Deborah 45788
Shinoda, Aishin 26331
Shipley, Sandra 42402
Shipp, Kim 05764
Shippee Lambert, Lisa 42092
Shirahra, Yukiko 47546
Shirbacheh, Tahereh 22291
Shireman, Joyce A. 45638
Shirley, Pippa 40757
Shirley, Rosie 40546
Shirley, Shirley 48113
Shives, Jenny 44981
Shivvers, Mel 42907
Shlomo, Eli Ben 22714
Shlomo, Eliyahu-Ben 22591
Sho, Masaki 26654
Shoaff, Jeanne 43383
Shock, Helen 44157
Shockley, Richard 05745
Shoemaker, Innis H. 46442
Shoemaker, John 44583
Shoemaker, Rene D. 41321
Shokoofi, M.R. 22328
Sholl, Rachel 39539
Shonk, Scott L. 43195
Shôno, Prof. Susumu 26781
Shook, Rays 42804
Shopland, A. 05281
Shoreman, Mark 06745
Shorey, Prof. C.D. 01499
Short, John D. 44232
Short, William 47370
Shorter, Daniel A. 41161

Shoshani, Jesheskel 42937
Shostak, Anthony 44728
Shozo, Tamura 26290
Shrago, Esther 42790
Shrago, Mindy 42790
Shrake, Peter 41502
Shrestha, Dr. Keshab 28789
Shrigley, Ruth 39888, 39892
Shriver, James M. 48564
Shriver, Karen K. 44099
Shriver, Thomas L. 41233
Shrum, L. Vance 44293
Shubert, Gabrielle 41948
Shugart, Dr. Gary 47919
Shugart, Dr. Sanford 46185
Shulman, Steven E. 48331
Shultz, Cathee 44931
Shuman, Greg 41166, 48262
Shuman, Lynne 45148
Shupeck, Fern 45359
Shust, Maria 45884
Shuttleworth, Alec 37979
Shuttleworth, John 44158
Shydlovskyy, Ihor 37883
Siachoono, Stanford Mudenda 49024
Siano, Mary Ann 41922
Siber, Hans Jakob 36431
Sibeth, Achim 17047
Sibeth, Dr. Achim 17061
Sibille, Marie-Hélène 10415
Sibiril, Marceline 12919
Sibley, S.F. 40901
Sibley, Shelia M. 45944
Siboroski, Paul 43412
Sibson, Tracy 30260
Sibutha, Addelis 49027
Sicard, D. 14380
Sicilia, Fiorella 25103
Sidebottom, D.J. 39107
Siders, Phyllis 42928
Sidibé, Samuel 27691
Sidiropoulos, Kleanthis 20975
Sidner, Rob 47279
Sidorov, Konstantin Nikolaevič 32724
Sidorova, Elena Iljinična 32840
Siebenmorgen, Prof. Dr. Harald 16365, 16448, 17991, 17996, 17999, 19291, 20037
Sieber, W. 15571
Sieber Kirk, Ellen 41749
Sieberer, Dr. Wido 02118
Siebert, Andreas 15687
Siebert, Dr. Anne Viola 17599
Sieblist, Kerstin 18419
Siebol, Michael 48774
Siebrecht, Silke 19511
Siede, Dr. Irmgard 18615
Siedell, Daniel 44791
Siefert, Chris 46524
Siefert, Dr. Helge 11832, 19328
Siegal, Robert L. 32412
Siegel, Bernard 47607
Siegel, Bob 45259
Siegel, Eric 43355
Siegel, Gerlinde 17439
Siegel, Nancy 44154
Siegenthaler, Gustavo Bernardo 00613
Siegfried, Clifford A. 41085
Siegman, Joe 22722
Siegmann, William 41941
Siegrist, Urs 37366
Sielewonowski, Zenon 31972
Siembor, Natalie 46216
Siemen, Palle 08807
Siemen, Wilhelm 15517, 17805, 19930
Siener, William 41983
Sienkiewicz, Joanna 31944
Sierpowski, Prof. Dr. Stanisław 31673
Sierra Bello, Prof. Luz 28125
Sierra de la Calle, Blas 35627
Sierra Jones, Alvaro 07521
Siersma, Betsy 41182
Sietz, Phillip 46401
Sievernich, Gereon 16041
Sievers-Flägel, Dr. Gudrun 19131
Sievert, Annette 17530
Sifkovits, Dr. Adam 01707, 01708
Sigal, Bronia 28175
Sigal, Laurence 13546
Sigaud, Anne 12705
Sigg, Thierry 12067
Siggins, Michael 41763
Sigl, Bärbel 15885
Sigmond, Prof. P. 28898
Signore, Joseph A. 42871
Signorell, Victor 37126
Signorini, Prof. Rodolfo 24288
Sigo, Charles 47892
Sigurdardottir, Aldis 21671
Sigurdardóttir, Elin S. 21624
Sigurdardóttir, Maria Karen 21656
Sigurdardóttir, Sigridur 21672
Sigurdarson, Erlingur 21623
Sigurdson, Annchristine 36009
Sigurdsson, Helgi 21648
Sigurjonsdottir, Iris Ólöf 21628
Sigurjónsson Jonsdottir, Sigrun Asta 21646
Sigurpálsson, Jŏn 21641
Sigwing, Marty 48600
Sihm, Marcel Agang-Ang 31292

Sijarić, Mirsad 03925
Šikić, Vojko 07698
Sikorska, Janina 31617
Sikorski, Marek 31518
Sila, Dr. Ante 07832
Silas, Anna 47553
Silber, Dr. Evelyn 39443
Silber, H. 20226
Silber, Karl-Heinz 17578
Silcox, David 06624
Silek, Suzanne 43568
Siler, Charles 45731
Šilina, Ljudmila Semënovna 33534
Silla, Dr. Chiara 23835
Silla, Dr. Chiaretta 23853, 23868, 23874, 23882, 23885
Sillaks, A. 38372
Sillanpää, Pirkko 09431
Silliman, Thomas 45462
Sillner, Helmut 01720
Šilnikova, Inna Evgenjevna 33640
Šilov, Lev Alekseevič 33296
Šilov, Viktor Valentinovič 33522
Šilova, Tatjana Éduardovna 32637
Silva, Cyro Advincula da 04350
Silva, Dr. Heliodoro 32237
Silva, Isabel 32243
Silva, Ivan Mariano 04211
Silva, John 31304
Silva, Dr. Leonardo D. 04303
Silva, Mark 46729
Silva, Dr. P.H.D.H. de 35756, 35760
Silva de Oliveira, António Manuel 32327
Silva Maroto, Dr. Pilar 35048
Silva Montauntildea, Margarita 07597
Silva Silva, Párroco Isaac 07527
Silveira, Prof. Maria Auxiliadora 04225
Silveira Godinho, Isabel 32314
Silver, Jessica 45883
Silver, Joshua M. 46426
Silverio, Prof. Franco di 24904
Silverio, Dr. Loca di 24904
Silverman, David 46460
Silverman, Judd 45751
Silverman, Lanny 42317
Silvester, Suzanne 46115
Silvestre, Ines K. 31415
Silze, Peter 17534
Sim, Angela 33940
Sim, Lee 27250
Sim, Robin 46108
Simak, Ellen 42263
Simanjuntak, Pareli 22067
Simard, Guylaine 45705
Simard, Julie 06382
Simavi, Çigdem 37701
Simcock, Dr. J.P. 30106
Simeonova, Maria 04846
Simerly, E. 45198
Simić, Prof. Jasna 33913
Simina, Nicolae-Marcel 32589
Simister, Kirsten 39377
Simkins, Barbara 05719
Simková, Dr. Anežka 08662
Simmons, Amy 44945
Simmons, Arlene 44707
Simmons, Denise P. 48295
Simmons, Ian 40094
Simmons, Jamie 47990
Simmons, Julie M. 06515
Simmons, Mark 40185
Simmons, Susan 43051
Simo, Colleen M. 44708
Simon, C.M. 46492
Simon, Gerlinde 15560
Simon, Hal 42756
Simon, Helen 43272
Simon, Dr. László 21567, 21568, 21569, 21570, 21571, 21572, 21573, 21574, 21576, 21578
Simon, Nancy 48662
Simon, Robert 42908
Simon, Rolf 15618
Simon, Ronald 45845
Simon, Susanne 16763
Simona, Dr. Rafanelli 25982
Simončič, Alenka 34114
Simone, Suzanne 28665
Simonelli, Lynn 42799
Simonett, Dr. Jürg 36636
Simonetti, Dr. Farida 23984
Simoni, Kate 07809
Simoni, Rino 23964
Simonnet, Philippe 13926
Simons, Ulrich 19297
Simonson, George 44732
Simpel, Francis de 03827
Simpson, Ann 38916
Simpson, Colin M. 38207
Simpson, Helen J. 38834
Simpson, J.L. 40669
Simpson, John W. 05778
Simpson, Ken 38053
Simpson, Laurence 45801
Simpson, M.A. 05060
Simpson, Paula 40266
Simpson, Shannon 38469
Simpson, Shona 30220
Simpson, Prof. S.J. 40151

Simpson, Tracy 40943
Simpson, Wendell 48109
Sims, Judith 41406
Sims, Patterson 45450
Sims, Richard 46689
Sims-Burch, Wylene 42549
Simui, Muyoyeta 49022
Simundson, Peter 06603
Simunec, Josip 07843
Šimunić, Ljerka 07797
Sin, Jang Jong 27121
Sinaga, T. Moesa 22177
Sinanovitch, Laura 36517
Sinčić, Branko 07844
Sinclair, Dr. Bradley 16250
Sinclair, H.M. 40650
Sinclair, James J. 42773
Sinclair, Mark E. 44006
Sindermann, Sabine 19670
Sinding Steinsvik, Tone 30382
Singer, Ilana 22613
Singer, June 41044
Singer, Karl 18434
Singer, Dr. Marijane 46170
Singh, Dr. Bhanu Pratap 21885
Singh, Himmat 21863
Singh, Prof. I.B. 21926
Singh, S. 21732
Singh, S. Amolak 21697
Singh, Spoony 44908
Singh, Vidya Nand 21738
Singhvi, Dr. L.M. 21772
Singleton, Ed 42534
Singleton, G. David 48107
Sinha, Prof. Anshu Kumar 21922
Sinick, Chris 47258
Sinisalo, Soili 09474
Šinjaev, Nikolaj Ulanovič 32793
Sinn, Margaret 48325
Sinn, Prof. Dr. Ulrich 20697
Sinnig-Haas, Christiane 11210
Sinnott, George 06133
Sinopoli, C. 41219
Sinopoli, P.A. 00529
Sinsheimer, Karen 47404
Sintes, Claude 10416
Sinyard, Elizabeth 05987
Siokalo, Zoriana 42984
Sipes, Robert L. 47109
Šipková, Želmíra 34081
Sirech, Alexander 07966
Siri, Marta 24812
Širin, Jurij 33234
Širkanova, Maja Konstantinovna 33258
Sirot Smith, Martin 40643
Siry, Renaud 13355
Sisdal, Odelbjørn 30907
Sisi, Dr. Carlo 23839
Sisi, Carlo 23840
Sisi, Dr. Carlo 23841, 23877
Šišigin, Egor Spiridonovič 32843
Siska, József 21580
Šiškin, Anatolij Aleksandrovič 33401
Šiškova, Živka 04649
Sisley, Alan 01347
Sitar, Dr. Gerfried 02597
Sitarski, Steve 46405
Sithole, R. 49028
Sitjar, Corazon 31359
Sitkowska, Maryla 32087
Sitt, Dr. Martina 17541
Siudziński, Kazimierz 31587
Siváček, Dr. Vladimír 34031
Šivačev, Stefan 04780, 04781
Sivan, Pnina 22599
Sivcova, Natalja Viktorovna 33201
Sivertson, Al 04969
Sivkov, Dr. Janaki 04906
Sivkova, Svetlana G. 32873
Sivonen, Esa 09768
Sivrić, Marijan 33922
Sivrikaya, İsmet 37773
Sivula, Leena 09862
Sivusaari, Tiina 09849
Sivyer, M.J. 01198
Siwecki, Barbara 42807
Siwek, Alberyk 32066
Siwek, Jan 31472
Sixbey, Peter 42911
Siximons, Les 01040
Sizemore, Bernice 41583
Sjöberg, Ursula 36281
Sjöberg-Pietarinen, Solveig 10124
Sjöblom, Seth 36397
Sjöö, Robert 35901
Sjöskog, Per 09785
Sjöström, Mats 10134
Sjösvärd, Lars 35900
Skaarup, Bi 08933
Skaarup, J.C. 09039
Skaarup, Jørgen 09048
Skamby Madsen, Jan 08881
Skandera, Franz 19869
Skanis, M. 27335
Skar, Anne Kari 30877
Škarić, Mila 07809
Skarpia-Heupel, Prof. Dr. Xanthippi 21186
Skarsbø, Einar 30777
Skarstein, Sigrid 30966

Skarstøl, Gunnar 30464
Skartsounis Schwab, Diane 36631
Skatov, Nikolaj Nikolaevič 33416
Skavhaug, Kjersti 30562
Skeide, Cecilie 30640
Skelly, David 45698
Skenbuch, Urban 36269
Škiljan, Maja 07822
Skinner, J.F. 40553, 40555
Skip, R. 42883
Skipper, Eva 06433
Skippings, Lin 39598
Skirtz Althea Warren, Stefan A. 42397
Skjølberg, Erik 30487
Sklar, E. 05491
Sklenářová, Vilma 08715
Skobeleva, T.P. 33516
Škoberne, Želimir 07830
Skoda, Joan 47101
Skodak, Maria 01989
Skog, Fredik 36268
Skoghäll, Lars 36139
Skoglund, Eric Y.W. 35969
Skoglund, Ivar 30410
Skoglund, Urban 36197
Skonecki, Leonard 43495
Skopec, Dr. Manfred 02930
Skorikova, Svetlana Nikolaevna 32741
Skory, Gary F. 45322
Skotheim, Hege 30598
Skott, Inga 10157
Skov, Torben 08887, 08890
Skov Kristensen, Henrik 09023
Skowranet, Heide 20090
Skriebeleit, Jörg 17017
Škrinjarić, Srećko 07809
Skrobov, Sergej 32781
Skudal, Tina M. 30444
Skuja, Andrejs 27425
Škulj, Božica 07838
Škurko, Dr. A.I. 33054, 33177
Skutecki, Andreas 20500
Škvařilová, Božena 08581
Skvarla, Diane K. 48404
Škvarnová, M. 34079
Skwarlová, Alena 08743
Skwirowski, Krzysztof 31982
Skye, Stephen. 42718
Slabá, Jaroslava 08378
Slabakova, Ganka 04644, 04645
Slade, Norman 44685
Sladen, S. 40562
Slader, John 43374
Sladky, Vaclav 02975
Slamenová, Dr. Zuzanah 33973
Slaney, Deb 41099
Slanina, Súsanne 20029
Slapinski, Tim 42026
Slastunin, A.A. 32908
Slater, Elizabeth A. 39523
Slattery, Fiona 40185
Slavick, Allison D. 42022
Slavik, Jan 35922
Sławski, Marek 31949
Slear, Gary 44724
Śledź, Edward 31566
Sledzik, Paul 48378
Slehofer, Vera 36495
Slej, Dr. Karen 36259
Slenczka, Dr. Eberhard 19139
Slettjord, Lars 30705
Sleurs, Jean-Pierre 03473
Slichter, Jennifer 44980
Slim, Soumaya 28202
Slimon, Gary 06077
Slinger, Frederico 41030
Slivac, Barbara 44673
Śliwiński, Eugeniusz 31674
Sliwinski, Jennifer 42982
Sloan, Brent 47228
Sloan, Catherine 39835
Sloan, Mark 42217
Sloan, Sarah 27878
Slobodzian, John 05310
Slocum, Kay 42113
Sloof Vermeij, P. 29130
Sloss, Tencha 41965
Slotta, Prof. Dr. Rainer 16193
Slover, Louise 43993
Slovin, Rochelle 41307
Slowe, V.A.J. 38625
Složenikina, Valentina Ivanovna 33326
Sluis, R. ter 29316
Slyngborg, Mette 08807
Smadar, Harpazi 22776
Smailes, Helen 38898
Smal, M. 34356
Small, Jim 43801
Small, Lawrence M. 48393
Smudal, Lisa 45789
Small, Luke 06819
Small, Nicole G. 42752
Smalley, Patricia 45838
Smallman, Anne 42524
Smart, Pansy 44253
Šmatov, Victor 03120
Smedt, Raphaël de 03275, 03326
Smeets, H. 29900
Smerdel, Inja 34119

Smidt, D.A.M. 29525
Smidt, Erzsébet 21588
Smidt-Jensen, Jörgen 09025
Smietana, Evelyn 44652
Smiley, Kristine 45279, 45280
Smiljković, Koviljka 33919
Smilova, Dimitrina 04636
Smirnova, Natalja Petrovna 33519
Smirnova, N.V. 32753
Smit, K. 29200
Smit, Sandra 34177
Smit, Toril 30770
Smith, A. 39074
Smith, Adam. 46204
Smith, Agnes L. 43375
Smith, Alan 01002, 01469
Smith, Alistair 39904
Smith, Allan 30103
Smith, Amanda 47984
Smith, Dr. Amy C. 40299
Smith, Ann 38586, 40494, 48427
Smith, Anne 46897
Smith, Antony 40824
Smith, Art 06252
Smith, Becky 43641
Smith, Bertyne 41511
Smith, Betsy 42985
Smith, Bill 41313
Smith, Dr. B.J. 01170
Smith, Bradley 47847
Smith, Brian 44695
Smith, Bruce 42576
Smith, Byron C. 44456
Smith, Calvin B. 48265, 48268
Smith, Carol 43031
Smith, Carole 45312
Smith, Caron 47293
Smith, Chris 38838
Smith, Chuck 46505
Smith, Clive 30189
Smith, Colin 40859
Smith, D. Ryan 41572
Smith, Daniel J. 48512
Smith, David 05804, 45092
Smith, Dr. David A.S. 38950
Smith, Deborah A. 41973
Smith, Diane 47675
Smith, Dr. Donald 38890
Smith, Donna 05411, 05412
Smith, Donna M. 05054
Smith, Dottie 06820
Smith, Doug 41179
Smith, Duane 44152
Smith, Earl 48473
Smith, Elizabeth 42344, 47722
Smith, Elizabeth A. 45484
Smith, Francis 05088
Smith, Francis X. 41504
Smith, Fred T. 44446
Smith, Frederick G. 42268
Smith, Gary 43847
Smith, Gary D. 43924
Smith, Gary N. 42756
Smith, Gary T. 47215
Smith, Gloria A. 42127
Smith, Guy 47395
Smith, Dr. H. Duane 46735
Smith, Heather 05934
Smith, Howard 39892
Smith, Ian 40291
Smith, J. 30124, 40739
Smith, Dr. James N.M. 06675
Smith, Jan 45116, 45643
Smith, Jane 41966
Smith, JaNeen M. 43529
Smith, Janet 05755
Smith, Janice 05568
Smith, Jay 44184
Smith, J.B. 46314
Smith, Jean 05965
Smith, Jerry 48405
Smith, Joel 46674
Smith, John T. 44330
Smith, Judy 47427
Smith, Kelleen 44674
Smith, Kent 42334, 47737
Smith, Kevin 41985, 44645
Smith, Kevin P. 41906
Smith, Kory 44938
Smith, Kristine 43879
Smith, Kym 00796
Smith, Lisa Deanne 06628
Smith, M. 06367
Smith, Mariann 41981
Smith, Marilyn 05748, 06096, 42643
Smith, Mark 39964
Smith, Mary 06087, 06089
Smith, Maureen M. 46702
Smith, Maurice 05686
Smith, Michael 45558
Smith, Michael J. 44982
Smith, Michael O. 42911
Smith, Michele L. 48197
Smith, Dr. M.P. 38223
Smith, Nancy 22544
Smith, Norman 45352
Smith, Owen 41392
Smith, Pamela 47429
Smith, Pat A. 42500

Smith, Patricia F. 44772, 48723
Smith, Pauline M. 41332
Smith, Peggy 44621
Smith, R. 05168
Smith, R.D. 39450
Smith, Rebecca 43641
Smith, Rebecca A. 45285
Smith, R.E.G. 06184
Smith, Richard 47792
Smith, Dr. R.M.H. 34213
Smith, Robert A. 47998
Smith, Robert H. 48373
Smith, Robert J. 44684
Smith, Ron 06181
Smith, Ronald 44862
Smith, Sam 42692
Smith, Scott 47481
Smith, Shana 46593
Smith, Sharon 40746
Smith, Shauna 47753
Smith, Sheila 38276
Smith, Shirley 43567
Smith, Stan 42949
Smith, Stephanie 42322
Smith, Steve 47691
Smith, Sue 01421
Smith, Susan 47600
Smith, Terri 45613
Smith, Thomas 46532
Smith, Tim 44150
Smith, Tobi 47439
Smith, Todd 43293
Smith, Trevor 01363
Smith, Vivian DuRant 45893
Smith, Warwick 30217
Smith, Wayne C. 44614
Smith, W.D. 38495
Smith-Christmas, Kenneth L. 46753
Smith de Tarnowsky, Andrea 45611
Smith-Ferri, Sherrie 48134
Smith-Speelman, Dr. Khristina 42494
Smith Woods, Karen 41513
Smitherman, Joy 47522
Smithline, Howard 22702
Smits, F.A.Th. 29079
Smitten, Al 05526
Smoak, Janet 47236
Smogór, Anna 31480
Smola, Dr. Franz 02838, 02953
Smolders, R. 29141
Smole Gavrilovic, Margita 03925
Smolek, Michael A. 47110
Smolík, Luboš 08412
Smolkin, Robert 41675
Smorenburg, D. 29920
Smrcka, Mariann 45219
Smrekar, Dr. Andrej 34114
Smucker, Linda 48820
Smurthwaite, D. 39728
Smutná, Silva 08709
Smylski, Brian 05995
Smyth, Deirdre 39298
Smyth, R. 05773
Smyth, Victor 45868
Snars, Frank 01209
Sneddon, Russell C. 43101
Šneiter, G.G. 33043
Snell, Dr. Gesa 17575
Snell, Dr. Howard L. 41105
Snetselaar, Rebecca 48641
Snibbe, Robert M. 42452
Snichelotto, Paolo 25421
Snider, Gary 06488
Snider, James B. 43556
Snider, Katherine 45827
Snider, Phyllis 41262
Śniegocki, Michał 32123
Snoddy, Stephen 39961
Snoddy, Suzie 47870
Snodgrass, Dianna H. 43860
Snoeys, Johan 03167
Snørteland, Dr. Målfrid 30698
Snørteland, Målfrid 30699
Snørtzland, Dr. Målfrid 30703
Snow, David H. 47429
Snowden, Gilda 42925
Snowden, Karen 40455, 40457
Snowdon, Sam T. 43312
Snydacker, Daniel 45926
Snydal, Dave 05123
Snyder, Barbara C. 45218
Snyder, Craig 41128
Snyder, Howard 05206
Snyder, James 22643, 46793
Snyder, James S. 22657
Snyder, Jill 42465
Snyder, Jim 48804
Snyder, Marion 48461
Snyder, Michael B. 44300
Snyder, Rob 46745
So, Gretchen 45841
So, Dr. Jenny 48335, 48357
So, Nguyen 48987
Soane, Sir John 39745
Soans, Hanno 09358
Soares, Dr. Marie-Christine 37393
Soares de Souza, Prof. Jonas 04140
Sobczyk, Pawel 32162
Sobel, Dean 41305

Sobezyk, Stéphanie 11579
Sobieraj, Edward 31885
Sobieraj, Janusz Szczepan 31609
Sobieszek, Robert 44921
Sobiesznak-Marcimak, Margaret 32113
Sobita Devi, Dr. K. 21854
Soboleva, L.L. 32942
Sobolik, Bonnie 43743
Søborg, Hans Christian 30378
Sobótek, Czesław 32213
Socarrás, Carlos 07586
Soccoro R. Samson, Marlene 31318
Sochovolsky, Z. 22770
Socias, Luís G. 35221
Socorro Mallorca, Maria 31330
Sodagar, L. 22323
Sodatova, T.M. 37871
Soden, Jack 45238
Soden, Joanna 38912
Soechting, Dr. Dirk 19983
Söderlind, Lars 36142
Söderlind, Prof. Solfrid 36265
Söderlund, Göran 36274
Söderström, Marita 10134
Soeharto, Ki 22219
Soejanto, B.U.W. 22077
Soekiman, Dr. Djoko 22227
Sölder, Wolfgang 02082
Söllner, Jürgen 19857
Soemaatmadja, Atang 22122
Sömmer, Hermann 15626
Sönmez, Dr. Necmi 16958, 16959
Söptei, István 21527
Sörensen, Steinar 30477
Sörries, Prof. Dr. Reiner 18025
Soesilo Hadi, Dr. Hidayat 22218
Soetjipto, Dr. 22200
Soffiantino, Paola 25736
Softić, Dr. Aiša 03925
Softic, Ajsa 03925
Soganci, Dr. Marion 18972
Soggin, Gian Piero 24683
Sogoba, Djaié 27693
Sohal, Neena 40540
Sohinki, Arnie 46975
Sohl, Katrin 18419
Sohnle, Dr. W. 20113
Søholt, Petter 30672, 30943, 30943
Soika, Dr. Aya 38460
Soileau, Malbae 48414
Soja, Henryk 31666
Sojková, Dr. Jana 08725
Šoka, Milan 33950
Sokač-Štimac, Prof. Dubravka 07756
Soklove, Deborah 48343
Sokol, Vladimir 07771
Sokól-Augustyńska, Maria 31936
Sokolov, Dr. Aleksej 33383
Sokolov, Dr. Nikolaj N. 33042
Sokołowska, Beata 32197
Sokołowska, Renata 32034
Sokolowski, Thomas 46506
Sol i Bachs, Josep M. 34582
Solà Turell, Ramón 35278
Solander, Terry J. 43628
Solańska, Krystyna 31720
Solberg, Chet 47504
Solberg, Per 30419
Šolc, Dr. Josef 08475
Soldaini, Julio E. 00166
Soldatova, Nina Ivanovna 33518
Soldini, Dr. Simone 36938
Sole, Allen 28764
Sole, Laura M. 39323
Solé, Maties 35129, 35130
Soler García, José María 35685
Soles, Mary Ellen 46775
Solheim Pedersen, Einar 30877
Solias i Aris, Josep 34904
Šolić, Dr. Marija-Edita 07737
Solimon, Ron 41101
Solis, Claudia 44115
Solis, Isabel 06930
Solivar, Sonia 31297
Solms, Fürst zu 16288
Šolochov, Aleksandr Michajlovič 33683
Solomatenko, Marg 06180
Solomko, Juri 33078
Solomon, Elizabeth 46464
Solomon Kiefer, Carol 41178
Solórzano Pérez, Diana 27954
Solovev, Aleksandr Borisovič 33402
Solovëva, E.A. 03111
Solovjeva, Ljubov Pavlovna 32832
Soloyeni, Joanna 21086
Soltek, Dr. Stefan 19241
Soltis, Dr. P.S. 43581
Solymosi, Rosalia 21330
Some, Porosper 04937
Somers, David 05112, 05114
Somers, Stephen G. 42641
Somerville, Ann 30249
Somerville, Robert 05188
Somma, Dr. Thomas P. 43538, 43540
Sommani, Dr. Donatella 25775
Sommer, Dr. Achim 16847
Sommer, B.A. 06518
Sommer, Lawrence J. 44787
Sommer, Mogens 08810

Sommer, Dr. Roswitha 16394
Sommer, Susan 45859
Sommer, Dr. Susanne 16751
Sommer Ribeiro, José A. 32285
Sommerfeld, Renate 19824
Sommerfeldt Gikas, Carol 41527
Sommerhuber, Christian 02690
Sommers, Joyce A. 44226
Sommers, Larry 44792
Somoza, Maria E. 32393
Sonder, Lucien 45796
Søndergaard, Sidsel 08944
Sonderman, Jacque 46307
Song, Prof. Ki-Ho 27276
Sonke, Denton 41715
Sonnabend, Dr. Martin 17074
Sonnabend, Regina 16584
Sonnberger, Gerwald 45853
Sonnenberger, Dr. Franz 19133, 19134, 19144,
    19145, 19154, 19160, 19161, 19162, 19164
Sonnenburg, Hubert von 45833
Sonno, Dr. Viviana 22963, 22969
Sonntag, Dr. Dina 20115
Sonntag, Gabrielle 12714
Sonntag, Dr. Hans 18691
Sonntag, Johannes 16849
Sonntag, Dr. Johannes-Hendrik 17265, 17266,
    17267, 17268
Sonoyama, Hiroshi 26864
Soohey, Shirron 48193
Soosloff, Philip 46963
Sopóliga, Dr. Miróslav 34071
Sorber, Frieda 03149
Soregaroli, Dr. Art 05135
Sorell, M.E. 45255
Soren, Joshua 47524
Sørensen, Anne Birgitte 08849
Sørensen, Anny 08819
Sørensen, Einar 30463
Sørensen, Jens 09018, 09019
Sørensen, Jens Erik 08769
Sørensen, Marianne 09104
Sørensen, Ove 09004
Sørheim, Helge 30877
Soriano, Alain 10335
Soriano, Dr. Corazon 31402
Soriano, Dolores 34577
Sormsen, Ellen C. 46905
Sorokin, Igor Vladimirovič 33505
Sorokina, N.I. 33100
Sorsak, Maks 34112
Sosič, Sarival 34110
Sošin, Aleksandr Pavlovič 32857
Šošmin, Aleksandr Aleksandrovič 33476
Sosnovskaja, Marina Jurjevna 32770
Sossenheimer, Doris 20569
Sotheran, Cheryll 30311
Soto, Jules M.R. 04129
Soto Bastida, Nicolás 28155
Součková, Dr. Jana 08449, 08600
Souichi, Takahata 26676
Souka Séko, Cisse Nèe 03876
Soule, Robert M. 42266
Soult 15954
Souplet, Michel 12310
Sourakli, Judy 47535
Sourdeau 03792
Sousa, Maria José Rego 32249
Souster, L. 39915
Souter, Jill 47262
Souter, Teri 05610
South, Allison 47232
Southall, A. 40170
Southall, Tom 41348
Southard, Edna Carter 46242
Southern, John 38736
Southern, Kathy Dwyer 48340
Southwell, Carey 43712
Southworth, Edmund 38400, 39211, 39411, 39412,
    39413, 39414, 39415, 39417, 39520, 40267
Soutif, Prof. Daniel 25042
Souza, Amandio 32274
Sovaudjieva, Natalia 04657
Sovluk, Viktor Ivanovič 32955
Sowada, Dr. Karin 01506
Sowder, Marvin 42766
Sowers, Russ 44088
Sowinski, Larry 45696
Soyhan, Cihat 37710
Soylu, Nilüfer 37740
Sozio, Janet L. 45531
Space, Fred 47897
Space, Parker 47897
Špaček, Jaroslav 08292
Spackman, A.J. 39705
Spadavecchia, Fiorella 25928
Spadea, Dr. Roberto 23688, 23689
Späth, Annette 15615, 15617, 15675
Spagnola, Gina 43614
Spahr, Elisabeth 36702
Spahr, P. Andrew 45096
Spahr-Van der Hoek, Nynke 29514
Spaid, Sue 42403
Spalding, Jeffrey 05749
Spalding, Jeffrey J. 46078
Spalek, Dr. Ladislav 34021, 34064
Spancer, Donald B. 45042
Spang, Mathias 16144
Spang, Veronika 20106

Spangenberg, Kristin 42400
Spangenberg, L. 34297
Spanke, Dr. Daniel 20595
Spanos Nordan, Antoinette 41711
Spargo, Janet 38448
Sparks, Brian 44833
Sparks, Kevin S. 48665
Sparrow, John 40192
Sparrow, Judy 40192
Spassibenko, A.V. 27097
Spathari, Elizabeth 20821, 20831, 20979
Špatný, Jan 08657
Spaulding, Daniel 41231
Spautz, Andrea 17607
Spear, June 05436
Spear, Robert N. 44163
Speare, Jed 41815
Spearman, Grant 41195
Spears, Carolyn 45591
Spears, Dolores 44334
Spears, Kimberly 41204
Spears, Susan 45183
Specht, Barbara von 18916
Specht Corsi, Martha 25633
Speciale, Giovanni 23276
Speciale, Michael P. 48687
Speckels, Gabriele 19331
Specter, David 45854
Spector, Nancy 45872
Spedding, J.H.F. 39345
Spedding, Michael 30164
Spedini, Prof. Gabriella 25209
Speierl, Dr. Charles 42498
Spelak, Lucyna 31828
Spellazza, William Salvador 43244
Speller, Margaret 38771
Spen, Cathryn 38113
Spence, Millie 06151
Spence, Talbert B. 41740
Spencer, Elizabeth 38716, 38718
Spencer, Georgia 44281
Spencer, Jeff 46339
Spencer, Jim 42440
Spencer, Leonard H. 42023
Spencer, Ted 42620
Spencer, Wendy 47141, 47933
Spencer-Davies, Jenni 40658
Spencer-Longhurst, Dr. P. 38211
Spendel, Dr. Cölestin 02596, 03042
Spender, Michael 38847
Sperath, Albert 45572
Sperber, Dr. G. 05372
Sperber, Dr. Lothar 20011
Sperebet, Yilmaz 08238
Sperl, Karl Eberhard 18670
Sperling, F.A.H. 41642
Sperling, Marion 43097
Speth, John D. 41219
Spicer, Joaneath 41489
Spicer, Margaret E. 43907
Spichtig, Klara 37123
Špička, Dr. Dušan 08436, 08677
Spiegel, Elisabeth 18166
Spiegel, Lisa J. 41837
Spiegel, Marty 47542
Spiegelberg, Dr. U. 17767
Spiegelman, Deborah 45290
Spieler, Dr. Reinhard 36606
Spielmann, Prof. Heinz 17529
Spies, Heike 16725
Spies, Uta 19356
Spieß, Dieter 20556
Spiessens, Frans 03228
Spigo, Dr. Umberto 24187
Spilka, Abby R. 45842
Spilker, Rolf 19283
Spillemaecker, Chantal 12161
Spiller, Harriet 41982
Spiller, Mortimer 41982
Spiller, Steven T. 46821
Spillman, Jane S. 42637
Spillman, W.B. 44615
Spindle, Carol 46668
Spindler, Barbara 19437
Spindler, Gabriele 02234
Spindler, Jean-Charles 10781
Spinelli-Flesch, Marie 10698
Spinner, Helmut 17643
Spinola, Dr. Giandomenico 48872, 48880
Spires, Ruth 40533
Spiridonov, Jurij Ivanovič 32965
Spiro, Stephen B. 46044
Spitler, Bing G. 47581
Spitzack, Maynard A. 43294
Spitzbart, Ingrid 01896
Spivak, Lisa 42897
Spivey, Towana 43455
Splaine, Shirley 41293
Šplíchalová, Vladimíra 08732
Spliethoff, Dr. M. 28928
Splitt, Jerzy Aleksander 31635
Splitter, Dr. Rüdiger 18011
Spooner, Dr. S. 45397
Sporea, Radoje 33792
Sporer-Heis, Dr. Claudia 02074, 02082
Sportiello, Anne 12868
Spotts, George 43793
Spowart, Cliff 01397
Spoz, Andrzej 32076

Sprain, Donald 48560
Sprankling, Miriam 45908
Spratt, Andrew 40372
Sprayue, John 46916
Sprecher, Dr. Eva 36514
Sprecher, Dr. Dr. Thomas 37412
Spree, Tommy 15913
Spreer, Elmar 16939
Sprem Lovrić, Branka 07732
Spriggs, Lynne 41348
Spring, Marika 39729
Springer, Bill 41887
Springer, Donald C. 48287
Springer, Ernst 02039
Springer, Fred 47976
Springer, Jonathan 46810
Springer, Kathleen 46824
Springer, Dr. Tobias 19139
Springhorn, Prof. Dr. Rainer 16589
Sprink, Claus-Dieter 15991
Sproat, Dr. John G. 42561, 42564
Spruill, Sarah C. 42272
Spruill Redford, Dorothy 42701
Spruit, R.J. 29446
Sprung, Sigrid 02953
Sprung, Y. 22585
Spuler, Dr. Christof 15373
Spur, Birgitta 21654
Spurgeon, Lucy 48750
Spurney, Dr. Robert 47578
Spychała, Jerzy 31769
Spyropoulos, Prof. Dr. Theodoros 20841, 20966,
    21061, 21164, 21172, 21204
Squier, P.H.M. 38565
Squiers, Carol 45817
Squire, Richard J. 41581
Squires, Ann 44335
Sretenovic, Vesela 46717
Srimal, Swdip 21908
Srinivasan, Shanta 21783
Srivastava, Dr. G.P. 21922
Sroka, Steven 48217
Sroka, Teresa 31608
Srp, Karel 08577
St. Onge, Dave 05674
Staarman, A. 29079
Staat, D.W. 28940
Staber, Deborah 44034
Stableton, Mike 47504
Stachel, G. 18330
Stachel, M. 18330
Stack, Joan 42553
Stack, Lotus 45391
Stack, R. 01501
Stackpole, Matthew 43082
Stackpole, Renny A. 47527
Stacy, Kaye 01454
Stade, Anette 36671
Stadelmann, Kurt 36546
Stader, Anette 36965
Stadler, Eva Maria 01915
Stadler, Herbert 19144
Stadler, Hilar 36839
Stadler, Dr. Peter 02312
Stadler, Wilhelm 02529
Stadtman, Kenneth L. 46733
Staebell, Sandra 41849
Städtler, Leopold 00912
Stäheli, Charles E. 36816
Stähli, Alois 37111
Stämpfli, Markus 36577
Stäuble, Dr. Nicole 37285
Staffen, Dr. Zdeněk 08313
Stager, Prof. Lawrence 42043
Stagg, Barbara 47028
Stagleder, Linda 43295
Stagno, Dr. Laura 24010
Stahel, Urs 37327
Stahl, Alan M. 45760
Ståhl, Elizabet 35882
Stahl, Dr. Johannes 16229
Stahl, Judith R. 41536
Stahl, Kathleen P. 42066
Stahl, Konrad 18789
Stahl, Mongerité 12582
Stahl, Patricia 17055, 17060
Stahl, Prof. Paul H. 32464
Ståhlberg, Ninaka 10006
Stahlecker, Robert C.G.A. 29114
Stahn, Frank 16950
Staikova, Evdokia 04846
Stainback, Charles 47464
Stajčić, Milorad 33856
Staker, Mark L. 47231
Staker, Ron 43082
Stalder, Dieter 36878
Stalf, Oscar 20377
Stalling, Dr. Gesine 19139
Stallings, Diane G. 44316
Stallings, Tyler 44575
Stallwitz, Kurt 43005
Stalskaja, Lidija Mirzejusofovna 32657
Stalvey, Dorrance 44921
Stalvey, Rip 47941
Stambach, Dr. Rudi 37072
Stambaugh, James B. 48581
Stambran, Doris I. 17061
Štambuk, Slobodan 07706
Stamhuis, I.M. 29888

Stamm, Hannelore 15881
Stamm, Jörg 37238
Stamm, Dr. Karl 18153
Stamm, Dr. Rainer 16331
Stamm, Wolfgang 19921
Stammers, Michael 39522
Stammers, Mike 39525
Stancati, Antonella 25225
Stanciu, Ştefan 32524
Stancu, Dr. Radu 32569
Standen, J. 40437
Standen, Roger 39151
Standenat, Peter 02311
Standley, Janet 40908
Standring, Timothy 42885
Stanek, Barbara 31850
Stanek, Dr. Christian 02943
Stângă, Ion 32515, 32516
Stange, Lorraine 47183
Stangel, John 45115
Stangier, Thomas 18313
Stangl, Bernhard 02146
Stangl, Denise 41667
Stangl, Reinhard 18510
Stangler, Prof. Dr. Ferdinand 02312
Staniczek, Dr. Arnold 20105
Stanimitović, Angelina 33925
Stanislav, Dr. Ján 33948
Stanislavska, L.P. 37857
Stankiritz, Gina 41373
Stankov, Vesna 33928
Stanland, Richard C. 42562
Stanley, Allein 43632
Stanley, B. 48349
Stanley, Diane 43178
Stanley, Eric 47448
Stanley, Michael 38222
Stanley, Tom 46951
Stansberry, Lucy 43135
Stanshev, Stansho 04669
Stanton, Dr. J.E. 01310
Stanton, Meridith Z. 41960
Stanulis, Roxanne M. 42967
Stapel, R. 20646
Stapf, Arnulf 19103
Stappaerts, Greet 03166
Starbuck, robin 41607
Starcky, Emmanuel 11527, 11531
Starham, J.T. 39924
Stark, Dr. Barbara 18206, 18207
Stark, Dr. Frank 42377
Stark, Julie 48814
Stark, Linda 06404
Stark, Ole 20414
Stark, Peter 46091
Stark, William 43971
Stark, William G. 44644
Starke, Jörg 16105
Starkey, Marsha B. 43918
Starkey, Patsy 45420
Starlin, Mildred 41071
Starling, Kate 39718
Starling, P.H. 37967
Starnes, Wayne 46777
Starodubcev, Gennadij Jurjevič 32975
Starr Hart, Leslie 44349
Stasch, Dr. Gregor 17174, 17178
Stasinopoulou, Elisavet 20873
Stasiuk, Savelia 06692
Staski, Edward 44661
Stastna, Dr. Eva 33978
Staton, James D. 47872
Stattler, Rick 46726
Staub, Bettina 37227
Staub, Edith 36482
Štauber, Dr. Bedřich 08464, 08466
Stauber, Reinhard 17783
Stauber, Richard 36961
Staubermann, Dr. K. 29911
Staubli, Gallus 36546
Stauder, Heiner 18475
Staudinger, Wilhelm 17033
Stauffacher, Ueli 36842
Stauffer, Nancy 47030
Staunton, Bob 39821
Stauß, Christian 18831
Stave, Pari 45770
Stavem Arrowsmith, Valorie 42051
Stavitsky, Gail 45450
Stavropoulos, Savvas 21097
Stavrou, Dr. Patroclos 20976
Stawarczyk, Prof. Tadeusz 32184
Stawarz, Dr. Andrzej 32116
Stawowy, Grzegorz 32006
Stayton, Kevin 41941, 41941
Stažić, Andjelko 07827
Steacy, Archie M. 06669
Stead, Miriam 40618
Steadman, Dr. D.W. 43581
Stearns, Emily 48508
Stebbins, Theodore 42042
Steblecki, Edith 41823
Stecher, Anton 02056
Stecher, Dr. Hans Peter 02231
Stecker, Heidi 18394
Stecker, Prof. Dr. Raimund 19558
Steckley, John 43637
Stedall, Tony 40678
Steed, Martha J. 41699

Steehler, Dr. Kirk W. 43200
Steel, David H. 46775
Steel, Martin 45818
Steel, Philip 30175
Steele, Curtis 44358
Steele, Jeffrey 44000
Steele, Joe 06008
Steele, Robert 46274
Steele, Steven 42897
Steele, Dr. Valerie 45839
Steen, Johan 29258
Steen, Dr. Jürgen 17055
Steen, Laura 42528
Steen Jacobsen, Jan 08882
Steen Jensen, Jørgen 08934
Steen-Zuniga, Britt 42170
Steenbeek, Dr. T.G.D. 29963
Steenbruggen, Han 29309
Steensma, Jennifer 43760
Ştefan-Nicolin, Mihail 32460
Štefančíková, Dr. Alica 08465
Stefanelli, Claudio 24875, 24877
Stefanescu, Dan 32470
Ştefănescu, Radu 32449
Stefani, Claude 11194
Stefani, L. 21208
Stefanidou-Tiveriou, Prof. Dr. Th. 21189
Stefanov, Georgi 04663
Stefanova, Morena 04846
Stefánsdóttir, Ragnheidur 21619
Steffan, Anton 01762
Steffan, Ferdinand 20408
Steffan, Günther 01762
Steffan, Roland 37109
Steffan, Dr. Wallace A. 46959
Steffan, Wallen A. 47893
Steffen, Carlos 04277
Steffen, Geneviève 43035
Steffen, Paul 37139
Steffian, Amy 44524
Steffl, John 42997
Stege, Frank 18737
Stege, Dr. Heike 18842
Stegeman, E. 29017
Steger, Adrian 37326
Stegmann, Dr. Markus 37132
Steguweit, Dr. Wolfgang 16044
Stehlin, Vera 36512
Stehphan, H. J. 16675
Steidl, Erwin 02119
Steidl, Dr. Thomas 02282
Steiger, Ivan 08591, 18910
Steiger, Ricabeth 37393
Steigert, Roger 47756
Steigerwald, Steve 44326
Steigman, Kenneth 45038
Stein, Christin L. 44311
Stein, Hanspeter 02393
Stein, Jutta 16584
Stein, Longest F. 15966
Stein, Peter 47323
Stein, Simcha 22709
Stein, Susan R. 42249
Stein, Dr. Wolfgang 18916
Steinau, Marlies 19884
Steinau, Norbert 16452
Steinberg, Dr. David 41959
Steinborn, Vera 16666
Steinbrenner, Theophil 19995
Steinbring, Wally 05048
Steinbrügge, Bettina 18557
Steinegger, Karl 01993
Steiner, Barbara 18394
Steiner, Charles 27500
Steiner, Charles K. 48610
Steiner, Chris 41099
Steiner, Dietmar 02833
Steiner, Dr. Erich 02603, 02603
Steiner, Myrtha 37397
Steiner, Dr. Peter B. 17121
Steiner, Ralph 40370
Steinhauer, Dr. George 20803, 21120
Steinhauer, H. J 19916
Steinhauser, Prof. Dr. Monika 16196, 16201
Steinhauser, Norbert 17148
Steinhof, Dr. Monika 16336
Steininger, Prof. Erich 02602
Steininger, Florian 02840
Steininger, Prof. Dr. Fritz F. 17072
Steinkeller, Prof. Piotr 42043
Steinlage, Forrest F. 44330
Steinle, Dr. Christa 01927
Steinle, E. 19870
Steinle, Karl-Heinz 16094
Steinmann, Dr. Axel 02945
Steinmetz, Robert 10710
Steinmetz, Dr. Walter 02503
Steinmetz, Wolf-Dieter 16293
Steinmetz, Wolf Dieter 20651
Steinwendtner, Hans 01982, 01983
Stejskal, Václav 08697
Stejskalová, Eliška 08531
Štekar-Vidic, Verena 34084, 34102, 34142, 34143
Stelfox, Evearad 43222
Stella, Dr. Clara 23210
Steller, Tom 46067
Stellmacher, Bernhard 19955
Stellwes, Carla 47248
Stelzhamer, Ernst 02818

Štem, Galina Michajlovna 32702
Stemmer, Dr. Klaus 15907
Stemmrich, Dr. Daniel 19178
Stenberg, Gunilla 35965
Stender, D. 16977
Steneberg, Suzanne 36349
Steneker, J. 29005
Stengel, Karin 18015
Stengel, Tom 45416
Stengert, Monika 48732
Stenhouse, Roderick 39976
Stenkamp, Dr. Hermann-Josef 16191, 16666
Stenkula, Anna 36268
Stenman, Paul 09683, 09685
Stenning, Howard 37995
Stensholt, Morten Chr. 30910
Stenstrop, Georg 08835
Stepančič, Lilijana 34109
Stepanova, Anna Alekseevna 33599
Stepanova, Ljudmila Vasiljevna 32744
Stepanova, Maria 32799
Stephan 18580
Stephan, Eric 17952
Stephan, Peter 19467
Stephan, Ralph 19966
Stephen, Charla 41767
Stephen, Virginia 05373
Stephen Weppner, Mary Dessoie 41686
Stephens, Dawn 41933
Stephens, John R. 43736
Stephens, Matt 39379, 39383
Stephens, Retha 44438
Stephens, Ruby A. 47185
Stephens, Spencer 47619
Stephens, Xavier 45093
Stephens Kruize, Pricilla G. 45282
Stephenson, Holly 44377
Stephenson, Tim 38662
Stepic, Barbara 41953
Stepken, Angelika 17990
Šter, Janez 34160
Stergar, Branka 07753
Šterk, Slavko 07830
Sterly, Marita 17704, 17706
Stermer, Jenifer 44740
Stern, Barry 41959
Stern, Gail F. 46702
Stern, Günter 02976
Stern, Hans 04380
Stern, Jean 44257
Stern, V. 29390
Sternath-Schuppanz, Dr. Marie-Luise 02830
Sternback, Mike 42672
Sternberg, Dr. Carsten 18773
Sternecker, Dieter 15620
Sternschulte, Agnes 16590
Sternweiler, Dr. A. 16094
Stertz, Dr. Stephen 41914
Stets, Mary Anne 45588
Stetson, Daniel E. 44604
Steuer, Matthias 16836
Steuert, Patricia 44986
Steurbaut, W.W.G. 28926
Stevan Bathoorn, H. 29987
Steven, H. 01384
Steven, Jackie 42791
Stevens, Andrew 45067
Stevens, Dr. Crosby 38740
Stevens, F. Scott 48792
Stevens, George 41882
Stevens, H. 29079
Stevens, Jane 42334
Stevens, Jean 44380
Stevens, Jon 41593, 48643
Stevens, Lawrence 40216
Stevens, N. Lee 43925
Stevens, Norman S. 44388
Stevens, Scott 48787, 48788, 48789, 48790, 48791
Stevens, Timothy 39664
Stevens Hardeman, Dr. H.J.M. 28914
Stevensen, Sara 38917
Stevenson, Candace 05949
Stevenson, Colin 30267
Stevenson, Esma 30267
Stevenson, Fenners W. 41784
Stevenson, Judy 39223
Stevenson, Moira 39892
Stevenson, Victor 06664
Števko, Anton 34035
Steward, James 41222
Steward, Maureen 05542
Steward, Travis 45858
Stewardson, Joanne 39454
Stewart, Ann 22446
Stewart, Barbara 39310
Stewart, Beth A. 46565
Stewart, Brian 38972
Stewart, Doug 06082
Stewart, Fiona 00832
Stewart, Heather 39584
Stewart, Dr. I. 37934
Stewart, Lorelei 42330
Stewart, Mary 43241
Stewart, Pamela 47831
Stewart, Rick 43480
Stewart, Sarah 40702
Stewart, W. Lyn 05027
Stewart, Wilma 05799
Stewart-Leach, Sheila 45045, 45229

Stewart-Young, J. 38800
Steyer, Dr. 20293
Steyer, Rosemarie 20717
Steyn, Andrew 34370
Steyskal, Josef 02861
Stiassny, Dr. Melanie L.J. 45759
Stiawa, Wolfgang 02801
Štíbr, Dr. Jan 08455, 08457
Štíbrová, Eva 08456
Stichel, Dr. Rudolf 16540
Stidolph, Diana 30199
Stieb, Ernst 06001
Stief, Gerhard 16617
Stiefelmayer, Ulrike 17036
Stiefmiller, Helen 43855, 43856
Stiegel, Dr. Achim 16028
Stiegemann, Prof. Dr. Christoph 19333
Stieglitz, Leo von 20115
Stiehler, Ursula 15665
Stieneker, Uwe 18437
Stiepani, Ute 15972
Stieper, Jürgen 16411
Stier, Dr. Christine 20105
Stier, David 47750
Stierhof, Dr. Horst 17780
Stieve, Mary Farrell 41502
Stiewe, Dr. Heinrich 16590
Stiffler, David L. 41061
Stiggens, D.C. 29331
Stijns, H.J.M.R. 29714
Štika, Dr. Jaroslav 08642
Stilijanov-Nedo, Dr. Ingrid 19527
Stilje, Emma Kristina 36419
Stilling, Niels Peter 08892
Stillström, Gunilla 36309
Stimson, Judy 40169
Stinchcomb, Donna 46741
Stipperger, Prof. Walter 02009
Stippich, Wolfram 18066
Stirratt, Betsy 41748
Stiso Mullins, Kathleen 45480
Stitely, David 45222
Stiver, Louise 47427
Stiverson, Gregory 43085
Stiwich, Undine 16536
Stob, Susan E. 48582
Stobbs, Neil T. 38150
Stochr, Bernard 11359
Stock, S. 01267
Stockar, Rudolf 36899
Stockebrand, Marianne 45140
Stocker, Gerfried 02226
Stockhammer, Prof. Dr. Helmut 02130
Stockhaus, Heike 20414
Stockhoff, Val 48145
Stockinger, Dr. Ursula 01922
Stockman, Edgard 03222
Stockman, Dr. René 03444
Stockmann, Robert 17874
Stockwell, Denis 38142
Stoddard, Leah 42251
Stoddard, Sheena 38351
Stoddart, Simeon 42510
Stöckl, Gottfried 01739
Stöckl, Dr. Hannelore 02993
Stöckler, Elisabeth 02034
Stöckli, Edi 36514
Stöckli, Werner 36957
Stöckmann, Birgit 15981
Stöger, Gabriele 02918
Stögner, Stefan 01660
Stöllner, Dr. Thoms 16193
Stölting, Dr. Siegfried 16339
Stölzel, Eckhard 20785, 20786
Stössel, Dr. Iwan 37132
Stoessinger, Caroline 45751
Stößl, Dr. Marianne 19198, 19199
Stofferan, Jan 47622
Stoga, Alan 45761
Stoga, Dr. Andrzej 32086, 32109
Stohler, Peter 37395
Stoianov, Georgi 04801
Stoica, Georgeta 32464
Stojanov, Georgi 04734, 04735
Stojanov, Stojan 04653, 04654, 04747
Stojanovic, Jelena 44271
Stojič, Jelena 33928
Stojneva, Nadežda 04650
Stokes, Mike 40511
Stokes Sims, Lowery 45877
Stokesbury, Bria 05661
Stolberg-Wernigerode, Alexander Graf zu 19269
Stolk, Ton 29946
Stoll, Dr. Wilhelm 16540
Stolle, Dr. Walter 16541
Stoller, Blanche 45473
Stollman, S. 30124
Stolwerk, Rick 30277
Stolwijk, Chris 28911
Stolyarov, Gwen 45809
Stolzenburg, Dr. Andreas 17541
Stomberg, John R. 41802
Stone, Donna K. 44100
Stone, Gaynell 42594
Stone, Karen 41297
Stone, Linda 41516
Stone, Margaret 38336
Stone, Mike 38568
Stone, Nancy E. 43616

Stone, Nathan 46770
Stone, Pat 43838
Stone, Paul 06037
Stone, Robert E. 46006
Stone, Thelma 43486
Stone, Walker S. 43018
Stone, Walter 46725
Stone-Gordon, Tammy 43054
Stone-Miller, Dr. Rebecca 41352
Stoner, Sheila 47865
Stooss, Toni 36461, 36463
Stoppelaar, Dr. J.D. de 29911
Stoppioni, Maria Luisa 23457
Stopps, R.A. 38345
Storch, Nancy 45342
Storch, Dr. Ursula 03001
Storch, Prof. Dr. Volker 17678
Storck, Dr. Ekkehard 20152
Storer, Prof. Robert W. 41220
Storer, Russell 01502
Stork, Dr. Simone 16760
Storm, Alex 05781
Storms, Dale C. 46038
Storto, Fred 16607
Storvik, Jehans 30967
Storz, Dr. Dieter 17905
Stoscheck, Dr. Jeannette 18405
Stoter, Dr. M. 29508
Stothoff, Richard H. 43337
Stottrop, Ulrike 16957, 16962
Stoughton, Kathleen 44550
Stoullig, Claire 10701
Stoumann, Ingrid 08807
Stout, Patricia 38014
Stovall, Linda Joy 48579
Støvern, Håvard 30782
Stowell, Elwood A. 43849
Stoyas, Yannis 20897
Stoye, Wilfried 20776
Stoyell, Sue 45492
Strachova, Alevtina Gennadjevna 33281, 33282
Strackerjan, Wilfried 20310
Straczek, Dr. Tomasz 32130
Stradeski, Leigh-Anne 39152
Stradiotti, Dr. Renata 23201, 23203, 23209, 23210
Straehly, Christiane 10297
Straka, Barbara 15986
Stramm, Günter 19754
Strandberg, Hindrik 09493
Strandberg Aieta, Janelle 42435
Strandberg Olofsson, Prof. Margareta 35909
Strander, Esa 09983
Strandgaard, Kirsten 09002, 21229
Strang, Craig 41644
Strang, T.H. 48530
Strang, Tim 47621
Strange, Georgia 41748
Strange, Shirley 42492
Stránsky, Jiří 08319
Strassen, Hermann zur 18247
Straßer, Dr. Josef 18890
Straßer, Wilfried 19021
Strassner, Andrea 47686
Strate, Kenneth 41619
Strate, Ursula 17560
Stratfold, Graham 40966
Strathy, Mark 45673
Stratmann, Dr. Wilhelm 18773
Stratton, Ceilia M. 43397
Stratton, David C. 47205
Stratton, Frances R. 44264
Straukamp, Werner 19124
Straus, Gail 46873
Strauss, Dr. Frank B. 47507
Strauß, Josef 02003
Strauss, Dr. Karl W. 16475
Strauss, Linda 44891
Strauß, Michael 16402, 16403, 16404
Strazar, Dr. Marie D. 44032
Streatfield, George C. 39085
Street, Dr. Martin 18606, 19086
Street Settleman, Henry 45751
Streetman, John W. 43245
Streets, Kim 40489
Strehl, Dieter 02991
Streicher, Dr. Gebhard 15464
Streiff, Elsie 37042
Streiff, Dr. Hans Jakob 36659
Streihammer, Dr. Rudolf 03055
Streisselberger, Josef 02343
Streit, Ruth 48218
Streitberger, Christine 02255
Strekalova, Valentina Michajlovna 33579
Strelnitski, Vladimir 45596, 45597
Stremel, Ted 05403
Strémoouhoff, Catherine 14869
Strempfl, Dr. Heimo 02132
Stremsterfer, Joanne 47135
Strenge, Bernhard von 19041
Strick, Jeremy 44930
Strickland, Alice 43718
Strickland, Dan 06798
Strickland, D.H. 41880
Strickland, Katherine F. 46931
Strickland jr., William 46520
Strickler, Susan E. 45096
Strid, Prof. Dr. Karl-Gustav 35918
Strieder, Dr. Barbara 15866
Strigl, Alfred 02635

Striker, Don 41310
Strinati, Dr. Claudio 25233
Strine, Linda T. 46808
Stringer, Clare 40256
Strittmatter, Gabi 36850
Stritzler-Levine, Nina 45771
Strižnikova, Svetlana S. 33060
Strnadová, Z. 08596
Strobbe, Johan 03704
Strobel, Barbara 15902
Strobel, Margaret 42336
Strobel, Sigruth 19299
Strobl, Dr. Andreas 18912
Strocka, Prof. Dr. V.M. 17106
Strode, Molly 44328
Strode, Wendell 41850
Stroebel, G. 34188
Ströbele, Dr. Werner 19576, 19577
Ströle-Jegge, Dr. Ingeborg 19491
Strömbäck, Stig 35986
Strömberg, Karin 36308
Strömberg, Ulla 08951
Strömfors, Göran 09813
Strömsdörfer, Thomas 19883
Strohfeldt, Guido 17163
Strohhammer, Andreas 02238
Strohmaier, Franz 02251, 02252
Strom, George 43177
Strom, Peter 43205, 43206
Stromberger, Franz 02806
Strombo, Cathryn J. 47888
Strondl, Ruth 02918
Strong, Charles 41609
Strong, Dan 43840
Strong, Michael 00870
Stroobants, Dr. A. 03376, 03377, 03378, 03379
Stroobants, Bart 03618, 03619, 03620
Stroppel, Alice 47552
Stroud, Michael 27704
Strubel, Howell 46838
Struhs, David B. 42154
Štrumej, Lara 34112
Strumia, Prof. Franco 23260
Stryker, Richard R. 42645
Stryker Lewis, Evelyn 45651
Stuani, Guido 23433
Stuart, Ann 42874
Stuart, Bruce F. 44846
Stuart, Jacqueline 05021
Stuart, Jan 48335, 48357
Stuart Elliott, David 26893
Stubbe, Els 28905
Stubbe Østergaard, Jan 08944
Stubbendieck, James 44783
Stubbs, Fred 42923
Stubbs, Ruth 06216
Stubing, Paul 42843
Štubova, Elena Valentinovna 32774
Stuchlík, Ladislav 08443, 08444
Stuckenbruck, Corky 42876
Stucker, Noah Lon 46491
Stucker, Richard 46041
Stuckey, Robert 48195
Stuckless, Allyson 06344
Stucky, Anton 37120
Studencka, Jolanta 31663
Studencki, Zbigniew 31991
Studenroth, Zachary 46032
Studer, Dr. Daniel 37100, 37104
Studer, Winfried 19022
Studinka, Felix 37397
Studley, David 47238
Stüben, Jürgen 17560
Stüber, Dr. E. 02307
Stüber, Prof. DDr. Eberhard 02545
Stüning, Dr. Dieter 16250
Stütz, Michael 18170, 18171
Stüwe, Hartmut 18047
Stuhlman, Theresa 46449
Stuhr, Joanne 48093
Stulić, Anselmo 07759
Stults, Jeannine 45943
Stumbaum, Regina 18916
Stumpe, L. 39520
Stumpf, Dr. Gerd 18913
Stumpf, Magdalena 03056
Stuppner, Dr. Alois 02900
Šturc, Libor 08616
Sturdy, Tom C. 05820
Sturgell, Ron 43777, 45655
Sturgeon, Ava 05516
Sturgeon, Keni 45437
Sturm, Kirk 47377
Sturm, Ulli 02126
Sturtevant, Naomi 42288
Sturtz, Rodney 47511
Stussi, Edmond 15299
Stutzer, Dr. Beat 36632, 37115
Stutzinger, Dr. Dagmar 17031
Stuvøy, Ingunn 30844
Štvánová, Jana 08497
Štýbrová, Miroslava 08752
Styles, Bertha 47999
Stylianou, Petros 08196
Styron, Thomas W. 43830
Suanda, Wayan 22184
Suárez, José 07574
Suárez, Margarita 07956
Suárez Baldrís, Jordi 35314

Suárez Zuloaga, María Rosa 35739
Subler, Craig A. 44398
Šubová, Dana 34017
Suchan, Laura 46060
Suchanov, M.K. 33167
Suchinina, Svetlana Jurjevna 33501, 33503
Suchocki, Wojciech 31909
Suchy, Ladislao 24503
Suchy, Theodore D. 44811
Šuckaja, Galina Konstantinovna 33177
Sudarmadji, Dr. 22132
Suddaby, R.W.A. 39671
Sudduth, William M. 41342
Sudnischnikowa, Jaqueline 02969
Sudwidja, Ketut 22192
Südekum, Dr. Karl 20694
Süel, Mustafa 37619
Sünkel, Werner 19637
Sünwoldt, Sabine 19858
Sütterlin, Hans 36479
Sützl, Werner 01640
Suezo, Uwano 26162
Suffolk, Randall 43693
Sugawara, Eikai 26604
Sugden, K. 39894
Suggett, Martin 39520
Suggitt, Mark 38294, 38296
Suggs, Patricia 41557
Sugimoto, Lisa Ann 44411
Sugimoto, Yukio 26495
Sugino, Hideki 26969
Suhr, Dr. Norbert 18602
Suhrbier, Dr. Birgit 17047, 17061
Suhre, Terry 47121
Sui, Dr. Claude 18615
Suk, Joo-sun 27283
Sukpramool, Patcharin 37506
Sukumaran, Dr. C. 21727
Sulaiman, Dr. Nasruddin 22068
Sulayman, Dr. Tawfiq 37443
Šulce, Baiba 27334
Suldina, Elena Nikolaevna 33658
Şulea, Ioan 32609
Sulebust, Jarle 30375
Šuleř, Dr. Petr 08264, 08272
Suliga, Dr. Jan Witold 32140
Sullivan, B. 01170
Sullivan, Carole 41263
Sullivan, Christine M. 45353
Sullivan, Cyndi 46958
Sullivan, Irene 41925
Sullivan, Joanne 43961
Sullivan, John 44832
Sullivan, Kathryn D. 42588
Sullivan, Dr. Lynne 44519
Sullivan, Martin E. 47147
Sullivan, Michael 45417, 45419
Sullivan, P.O. 22483
Sullivan, Dr. Robert M. 43925
Sullivan, Tracy L. 41130
Sullivan Sturgeon, Catherine 42372
Sullivanons, Mary Louise 46388
Sultan, Samir M. 09253
Sultan, Terrie 44137, 48341, 48342
Sumalde, Dr. Augusto 31345
Sumalvico, Ulrike 20512
Sumawilaga, H. Djamhir 22196
Sumberg, Dr. Barbara 47426
Sumbulova, Nadežda Georgievna 33200
Sumers, Anne R. 46281
Summerfield, Jan 38475, 40710, 40770
Summers, Carl 44837
Summers, Jacquie 38759
Summers, John 06591, 42443
Summers, Marcia J. 45593, 47422
Summers, Ruth 41283
Summersgill, Robert H. 41822
Šumnaja, Dr. T.G. 33050, 33149
Sumner, Kent 42660
Sumoza, Rosa María 07465
Sumrall, Robert F. 41230
Šumskaja, Ljubov Vladimirovna 33015
Sun, Dr. Dennis 07108
Sun, Jixin 07018
Sunday Oyegbile, Olayinka 30327
Sundblad, Stefan 36210, 36213
Sundborg, Peter 36309
Sundelin, Åsa 36268
Sundell, Eva 35899
Sundell, Karin 36309
Sundin, Sven-Olov 36152
Sundström, Susanne 36349
Sundvoll, Bjorn 30735
Suné, Prof. J.M. 34561
Sunier, Sandra 36146
Suominen, Tapio 10092
Supamena, M.S. 09129
Supanz, Ewald 01855
Superchi, Toni 43632
Superior, P. 34305
Supriyatno, Y. 22221
Surace, Dr. Angela 23426
Šurdić, Borislav 33807
Sureau, Jean-Louis 11291, 14733
Surma, Henryk 31843
Surmann, Dr. Ulrike 18135
Surrett, Janet 47576
Surroca i Sens, Joan 34855, 34858
Surup, Axel 20635, 20636, 20638

Suryana, Otong 22073
Surzyńska-Błaszak, A. 31906
Suščenko, Evgenija Michajlovna 33237
Sušić, Željka 07839
Šušková, Helena 33951
Susoj, Elena Grigorjevna 33365
Šuštar, Branko 34121
Susumu, Shimasaki 26306
Sutakovič, Nataša 33896
Šutalo, Kata 07820
Suter, Daniel 36479, 36918
Suter, Dick 00819
Suter, Josef Ignaz 36558
Suter, Mary 43308
Sutherland, Cara 41266
Sutherland, Gordon 05762
Sutherland, Maire-Claire 03715
Sutherland, Maureen 05739
Sutherland, Norma 40968
Sutherland, Rene 00992
Sutherland, Dr. Stuart 06684
Suthers, Terence 39161
Sutloff, Catherine 41743
Sutoyo, R. 22201
Sutphin, Derik 48060
Sutschek, Felix 16253
Sutton, Cynthia 44386
Sutton, J.M. 37988
Suvitie, Osmo 09964
Suvorova, Tatjana 33872
Suwanasai, Avudh 37541
Suwentra, I. Ketut 22098
Suzuki, Katsuo 26938
Suzuki, Keizo 26298
Suzuki, Koji 26113
Suzuki, Makoto 26705
Suzuki, Naomitsu 26862
Suzuki, Prof. Norihiko 26498
Suzuki, Takatoshi 26314, 26951
Suzuki, Yoshikazu 26253
Suzuki, Yusai 26634
Švachová, Jarmila 08415
Svae, Karin 36128
Svanascini, Prof. Osvaldo 00227
Svartgrund, Anita 09695
Svedberg, Berit 36290
Svedfeldt, Bjorn 36206
Svedlow, Andrew Jay 45099
Svedova, Inga 37902
Svendsen, Sverre J. 30618
Svens, John-Erik 10208
Svenshon, Dr. Helga 16540
Svensson, Else Marie 35818
Sverrir Árnason, Gisli 21638
Svetina, Ivo 34120
Sviblova, Olga 33086
Svirčević, Rosa 33880
Svitkova, Ani 04831
Svoboda, Dr. Christa 02551
Svoboda, Kurt 01988
Swaan, Trudy 06187
Swadley, Ben H. 47509
Swagemakers, Walter 28852
Swager, Karen 42563
Swaile, B.D. 05104
Swain, Adrian 45494
Swain, Hedley 39718
Swain, Kristin 42638
Swainston, M. 00722, 00723, 00724
Swallow, Debby 39795
Swan, Daniel C. 48104
Swan, Delores 43766
Swanagan, Don Jo 42688
Swanee, Lois 44059
Swaner, Ivan 43868
Swank, Scott T. 42083
Swanson, Alan 48761, 48762
Swanson, Ann 46998
Swanson, Brook 48460
Swanson, Erik 42702
Swanson, Robert 05142, 45207
Swanson, Dr. Vern G. 47763
Swantek, John E. 48449
Swart, Donna 42738
Swartout, Dennis W. 43745
Swartzlander, Martha 46999
Swasey, Gilvano 03865
Swatosch-Dore, Michael 02956
Swatschina, Wilhelm 02039
Sweasy, Lisa 43429
Sweeney, Alan 47516, 48433
Sweeney, Bill 44225
Sweeney, Colin 40837
Sweeney, Dennis F. 45802
Sweeney, John 41937
Sweeney, Karen 46844
Sweeney, Margie 46999
Sweeney Price, Mary Sue 45892
Sweets, Henry 43904
Sweets, Judy 44688
Sweha, Dr. Fawzi 09273
Sweitzer, Rick 43744
Swensson, Lisa C. 45939
Swettenham, Christine 40839
Świda, Piotr 32111
Swiderski, Christine 06599
Swift, Carolyn 42101
Swift, John 46816
Swift, Juli 45668

Swift, M. 39305
Swift, R.G. 40740
Swigart, Arthur L. Stewart 48189
Swigart, Patricia B. 44155
Swigart, Stacey A. 48188
Swim, Ann 42081
Swinford, Mervyn 38991
Swingle, Mark 48250
Swinkels, Dr. L.J.F. 29632
Śwircz, Kazimierz 31734
Świst, Lucyna 31664
Switlik, Matthew C. 45443
Swozilek, Dr. Helmut 01746
Sy, Joaquin 31369
Syahali, Teuku Sahir 22135
Sydow-Blumberg, Karen von 19253
Sykes, Diana A. 40382
Sylvester, Judith 41749
Sylvester, Morten 09096
Sylyuk, Anatoli 37880
Syme, John 30113
Symes, Dr. Robert F. 40515
Symmes, Edwin C. 41355
Symmes, Marilyn 45788
Symons, Gwendolyn 44683
Symons, Prof. T.H.B. 06121
Synder, Judith 42059
Syndram, Prof. Dr. Dirk 16685
Syre, Dr. Cornelia 18832
Syré, Dr. Ludger 17989
Syring, Marie Luise 16738
Syrjänen, Anneli 09898
Syrjänen, Inkeri 10099
Systad, Gunnhild 30502
Sytek, Wioletta 31896
Syverson, Duane 43197
Syvertsen, Per Ole 30674, 30675
Szabo, Dr. Agneza 07830
Szabo, Andras 32550
Szabó, Dr. Botond Gáborjáni 21400
Szabó, Ernst 02755
Szabó, Dr. J. József 21579
Szabó, Lajos 21385
Szabó, Lilla 21390
Szabolcs-Király, Dr. István 21441, 21442
Szakacs, Dennis 45855
Szakmary, Joanna 45606
Szalay, Prof. Dr. Miklos 37416
Szameit, Prof. Dr. Erik 01868, 01869
Szaniawska, Wanda 32093
Szaraniec, Dr. Lech 31648
Szathmáry, László 21426
Szatmári, Dr. Imre 21318, 21319
Szczebak, Dr. Władysław 32041
Szczech, Bernard 32200
Szczepański, Marek 32020
Szczesiak, Rainer 19013
Szczygieł, Andrzej 31707
Szczypiorski, Krzysztof 31808
Szeemann, Dr. H. 36472
Szekely, Linda 47820
Szekeres, Viv 00709
Szentkuti, Károly 21484
Szewczuk, Mieczysław 31939
Szewczyk, Kazimierz 32072
Szewczyk-Smith, Diane 45578
Szinai, Stephan 02946
Szinvavölgyi, Oszkár 21477
Szkop, Henryk 31561
Szmolicza, József 21434
Szöke, Dr. Mátyás 21611
Szoényi, Dr. Eszter 21422
Szpakiewicz, Alina 31569
Szpakowska, Ewa 31931
Szram, Dr. Antoni 31771, 31776
Szuber, Robert 31629
Szücs, Dr. Judit 21397
Szücs-Irén, B. 21317
Szura, Andrzej 31660
Szuromi, Béla 21519
Szvircsek, Dr. Ferenc 21523
Szygenda, Lynn 38847
Szymańska, Dobrochna 32074
Szymańska, Ewa 31565
Szymczyk, Adam 36504
Szymusiak, Dominique 12396
Szyndzielorz, Albert 31596
Taaffe, Renee 45403
Taawo, Kjell 36128
Tabacu, Jenica 32480
Tabah, Béatrice 15007
Tabaka, M. 05992
Tabakoff, Sheil 45854
Tabakoff, Sheila 46037
Tabakov, Michail Ivanovič 33714
Tabaraud, Georges 11400
Tabata, Chihiro 26998
Tabb, Kathy 44743
Tabbernor, Christine 06835
Tabbert, Mark 44750
Tabeaud, Marcel 11688
Tabel-Gerster, Margit 17560
Taber, David 45025
Tac An, Dr. Nguyen 48998
Tackett, William 44327
Tadahisa, Sakai 26979
Tadaya, Imamura 26866
Tadiello, Dr. Roberto 25915
Taeckens, Michel 12600

Täube, Dr. Dagmar 18163
Täubrich, Hans-Christian 19134, 19160
Taft Andrews, Nathalie 44974
Taga, Yoshiya 26316
Tagaev, Muchtar 27312
Tagage, L.M. 29572
Tagesen, Fran 42448
Taggart, Travis 43971
Taghiyeva, Roya 03071
Taglang, Barbara-Ulrike 18558
Tagliasacchi, Dr. Paolo 23649
Taguchi, Yasuo 26271
Taha, Dr. Haji Adi bin Haji 27677
Taher, Salah E. 09275
Tahon, Eva 03257, 03260
Tait, Dr. Edward 39945
Tait, Leslie Bussis 45851
Tait, L.P. 34319
Tait, Ronald 38176
Tajedin-Noureldaim, Yousif 09315
Takács, Dr. Imre 21383
Takács, Mária 21530
Takahara, Mayako 26128
Takahashi, Akiya 26873
Takahashi, Prof. Susumu 26953
Takahide, Hidenobu 27017
Takakusa, Shigeru 26541
Takanashi, Mitsumasa 26873
Takano, Masahiro 26128
Takano Yoshizawa, Hirohisa 26128
Takase, Tamotsu 26971
Takashi, Prof. Sutoh 26737
Takashina, Shuji 26384, 26385
Takata, Yoshikazu 26341
Takebe, Toshio 26583
Takeda, Sharon 44921
Takehana, Rintaro 26094
Takemoto, Hiroshi 27030
Takenaka, Yasuhiko 26997
Takeuchi, Jun-ichi 26853
Takeuchi, Makoto 26362, 26842
Takeuchi, Tadashi 26569
Taki, Shigeko 26622
Takita, Minoru 26361
Taksami, Prof. Čuner 33427
Taktak, Fehmi 37689
Tal, Felix 28913
Tal, Ilan 12677
Tal, Dr. Nissim 22596, 22605, 22609
Talaga, Sally 44071
Talajić, Mirko 07694, 07701
Talalay, Lauren 41218
Talamo, Prof. Giuseppe 25182
Talamo-Kemiläinen, Maarit 10134
Tálas, Dr. László 21585
Talazov, Veselin 04720
Talbert, Candy 48133
Talbot, Dennis 39895
Talbot-Stanaway, Susan 45579, 46256
Talerman, Margaretha 46389
Talero Pinzón, Claudia 07629
Tall, J.J. 39102
Talla, Primitiva C. 31460
Talland, Valentine 41811
Talley, Dan R. 44531
Talley, Roy 41545
Talsky de Ronchi, Prof. Alicia 00605
Talvio, Tuukka 09521
Talzrow, Michael 43792
Tamari, Dr. Dov 22753
Tamba, Dumitru Gheorghe 32626
Tambini, Michael 38287
Tamblin, J. 40209
Tamburini, Pietro 23148
Tamindarova, Miljauša Amirovna 32892
Tamir, Peleg 22762
Tamis, Catherine M. 47010
Tamla, Toomas 09356
Tammen, Mike 45064
Tammenoka, Paavo 09770
Tammiksaar, Erki 09379
Tamminen, Jukka A. 09790
Tamminen, Marketta 09950, 09951, 09954, 09955
Tamminen, Osmo 09417
Tamplin, Illi-Maria 06116
Tanabe, Emi 26610
Tanabe, Mikinosuke 26873
Tanaka, Iwao 26478
Tanaka, Masayuki 26873
Tanaka, Takeyoshi 26102
Tanaka, Toshiya 26173
Tanaka, Yoshiaki 26471
Tänäsescu, Gabriela 32574
Tanata, Charles 44307
Tandefelt, Petra 09538
Tandy, Virginia 39888, 39892, 39905
Taneva, Radosveta 04846
Taneva, Valentina 04810
Tangco, Manny 31357
Tange, Ellen 08957
Tangen, Eigil 30783
Tangen, Kirsten 30451
Tani, Gohei 26343
Taniguchi, Dennis 47321
Taniguchi, Harumichi 26783
Tanino, Dr. Akira 27012
Tanke, Dr. Walter 16663
Tanko, Ivana 34136
Tankoano, Ounteni Ernest 04937

Tannehill, Suzette 41531
Tannen, Jason 42374
Tannenbaum, Barbara 41072
Tannenbaum, Judith 46721
Tannenbaum, Myles 46436
Tanner, Julia 39182
Tanner, Matthew 38360
Tanner, Paul 37377
Tannert, Christoph 16019
Tanninen-Mattila, Maija 09489
Tannous, Youssef 27492
Tantaquidgeon, Gladys 48138
Ţânţăreanu, Ecaterina 32429
Tantoco, José P. 31361
Tapias Moreno, Rito Antonio 07615
Tapié, Alain 10983
Tàpies, Miquel 34538
Tapken, Dr. Kai Uwe 18927, 19492
Tapliss, Sue 38105
Tappan, Amanda 43025
Tappe-Pollmann, Dr. Imke 16589
Tapsell, P. 30104
Taracchini, Alfredo 24085
Taragin, Davira 48021
Tarasek, Władysław 31554
Tarasenko, Tatjana Ivanovna 33670
Tarasova, Nadežda Petrovna 32772
Tarawneh, Khaled 27041
Tarbell, Mike 44140
Tarcalova, Dr. Ludmila 08698
Tardiem, Robert 12721
Targan, Alfons 16352
Taricco, Dr. Bruno 23520
Tarjeson, Jane 45119
Tarmann, Dr. Gerhard 02082
Tarnawesky, Prof. M. 06851
Tarnovskaja, Tatjana Nikolaevna 33241
Tarnow, Rosmarie 19117
Tarnowski, A. 38719
Taron, Dr. Douglas 42313
Tarplee, Peter 39437
Tarr, Blair D. 48033
Tarr, Dr. Edward H. 15725
Tarrant, Josh 00931
Tarrats Bou, Francesc 35167, 35515, 35516
Tarrús Galter, Josep 34527
Tarshish, Noa 22608
Tartaglio, Michael 41893
Tartarini, Jorge D. 00202
Tarus, Käpy 10024
Taruvinska, Pascall 49031
Tarver, Paul 45735
Tasaka, Sharon 44090
Tasanen, Terni 10111
Taschenmacher, Peter 15671
Tasić, Nikola 33814
Tasick, Julian 45122
Tasker, Diana 43148
Taşlialan, Dr. Mehmet 37690, 37718, 37806
Tasma, G.L. 29262
Tassell, C.B. 01170
Tassi, Prof. Franco 23089, 23597, 26023
Tassianari, Duilio 22959
Tassignon, Jean-Marie 03346
Tassini, Francesco 23575
Tatangelo, Mireille 15119
Tataru, Marius J. 17462
Tate, Barbara L. 45829
Tate, Belinda 48699
Tate, Pat G. 47563
Tatewaki, M. 26084
Tatlı, Salih 37803
Tatlıcan, Zerefşan 37783
Tátrai, Dr. Vilmos 21383
Tatro, Ron 43104
Tatsch, Madeleine 16496
Tatter, Paul 41100
Tatum, Dana Lee 44173
Taub, Liba 38465
Taube, Dr. Angelika 18182
Tauerová, Dr. Jarmila 08593
Taufi 28775
Taupe, Christina 34912
Taupe, Georg Ingrid 02762
Taut, Dr. Konrad 18397, 18579
Tautorat, Ina 16012
Tavares Garcia, Sonia Maria 04255
Tavassoli 22327
Tavčar, Dr. Lidija 34114
Tavel, Dr. Hans Christoph von 36545
Taveneaux, Benoît 14385
Tavernier, Bertrand 12749
Tavernier, Marc 14019
Taviani, Prof. Emilio Paolo 25254
Tavlakis, Ioannis 20806
Tawalba, Dia 27062
Tayler, Jayne 39384
Taylor, Alison 39845
Taylor, Barbara 38415
Taylor, Barbara E. 44015
Taylor, Chris 39151, 41315
Taylor, Darrell 42149
Taylor, David 37935
Taylor, David G. 06391
Taylor, Deborah 44174
Taylor, Denise M. 44590
Taylor, Donald B. 43498
Taylor, Edith 44685
Taylor, Gloria 05857

Taylor, Howard 47239, 47242
Taylor, J. Lawrence 44287
Taylor, J. William 42272
Taylor, Jeanette 05186
Taylor, Jeff 43340
Taylor, Jennifer 38791
Taylor, Jenny Lou 42375
Taylor, Jill E. 40745
Taylor, June 43126
Taylor, Kathryn T. 48552
Taylor, Kathy 39735
Taylor, Lillian 43889
Taylor, Linda 41190
Taylor, Lloyd 39328
Taylor, Dr. Louise 39616
Taylor, M. 40025
Taylor, M.A. 40185
Taylor, Marilyn S. 47109
Taylor, Mary Rose 41349
Taylor, Michael 40184
Taylor, Mike 30236
Taylor, Dr. Peter 34226
Taylor, Richard 41484
Taylor, Robertine 45859
Taylor, Ron 06554
Taylor, Saddler 42563
Taylor, Simon 43046
Taylor, S.K. 01217
Taylor, Sue Ellen 42517
Taylor, Susan H. 45705
Taylor, Susan M. 46703
Taylor, Thomas C. 47851
Taylor, Tom 44685
Taylor, Tracey 39947
Taylor, Dr. Trevor 39845
Taylor Bennett, Cheryl 47680
Tazlari, Marianne 20531
Tazzoli, Vittorio 24824, 24825
Tchen, Dr. John K. W. 45841
Tckcli, Gonul 37710
Teachout, Gerald E. 46483
Teagle, Rachel 44548
Teague, John 01092
Teague, Lynn 48082
Tear, Paul 39798
Teatero, Barbara E. 05147
Tebani, Shahzor Ali 31021
Tebbutt, J. Bernard 39167
Tebbutt, Michael L. 39927
Tecce, Dr. Angela 24571, 24584
Teckman, Jon 39584
Tederick, Lydia 48409
Tedeschi, Dr. Carlo 25658, 25660
Tedeschi, Martha 42304
Tedesco, Paul H. 42970, 42971
Tedesko, Frank W. 43346
Tedford, Catherine L. 42086
Tedrow, Allen 46571
Teehan, Virginia 22505
Teerimäki, Matti 09411
Teeson, Douglas H. 45588
Teeter, Stephen 45731
Teeter, Wendy 44900
Teets, James W. 47982
Teets, Robert G. 47982
Teets, Ruth E. 47982
Teeuwisse, Dr. J.B.J. 29107
Tegin, Taylan 37620
Tegou, Eva 20915
Teig, Catherine 46106
Teinilä, Soile 10213
Teinonen, Markku 09552
Teisen, Michael 08956
Teitelbaum, Jesse 48621
Teitelbaum, Matthew 06561
Teixeira, Joaquina B. 46725
Tejada, Susana 41981, 44904
Tejada Jiménez, Natalia 07515
Tekampe, Dr. Ludger 20011
Tekatlian, Dominique 10960
Tektaş, Mehmet 37610
Telford, D.B. 30116
Telford, Helen 30211
Tellechea, Helena C. 00209
Tellenbach, Dr. Michael 18615
Telleria de Gallardo, Prof. María E. 00373
Tellier, Arnaud 36753
Tellier, Dr. Cassandra 42592
Tellini, Dr. Alberto 25894
Tello Figueroa, Jimmer Jesús 07435
Teltingsrude, Rebecca 43784
Telsemeyer, Ingrid 16666, 20623
Telsnig, Dr. Lore 02551
Tělupilová, Marielav 08453
Temkin, Ann 46442
Temmer, James D. 45360, 45373
Temming, Dr. S.N. 29707
Tempal, Denison 44462
Tempel, B. 29756
Tempel, Norbert 16666
Tempelaars, P.A. 29254
Temperli, R. 37414
Tempesti, Giorgio 22993
Tempestini, Luciano 24958, 24960
Temple, Ann 22411
Temple, Prof. J. 38896
Temple, Patty 40023
Templeman, Jack 06854
Templer, Peggy 45251

Templin, Brigitte 18545
Tempone, Mario C. 41011
Tena, Asunción 35601
Tenabe, Gabriel S. 41471
Tenbergen, Dr. Bernd 18951
Tenenbaum, Ann 45793
Teneva, Dr. Nadežda 04845
Tengblad, Stefan 30316
Tengku, Abdul Hamid 27651
Tennent, Elaine 44089
Tennent, Mike 47180
Tennyson, Daniel 38002
Tenorio Vera, Ricardo 34875
Tent, J. 29197
Tentoni, Dr. Damiana 24968
Teofilov, Teofil 04918
Tëplyj, Nikolaj Ivanovič 33394
Ter Assatouroff, C. 03323
Tera, Mitsuhiko 26974
Teramoto, John 44228
Teran, Reba Jo 43468
Terasima, Yoko 26873
Terblanche, E. 34188
Tercan, Şenel 37682
Terčon, Nadja 34138
Terechov, Anatolij Vladimirovič 33311
Terechov, Vladimir Michajlovič 33206
Terentev, I.S. 33609
Terezhchuk, Volodymyr 37908
Tergun, Dr. Alimuddin 22118
Terlouw, Dr. Willem 29514
Terlutter, Dr. Heiner 18951
Terman Frederiksen, Finn 09026
Teropšić, Tomaž 34088
Terpening, Virginia L. 44223
Terra, Prof. Pedro 04196
Terrail, Claude 13656
Terrell, Walter D. 47493
Terrettaz, Roger 36926
Terrier, Claude-Cathérine 11062
Terrier, France 37354
Terry, A. 38927
Terry, Blanche S. 48229
Terry, Christopher J. 06069, 06070
Terry, Joe 45468
Terry, Ray 47001
Tersew, Sylvie 21248
Teruzzi, Dr. Giorgio 23070
Tervahauta-Kauppala, Liisa 09641
Terziev, Penjo 04698
Terzo, Dr. Fatima 25992
Tesch, Ilse 20045
Tesch, Sten 36182, 36183
Teschner, Adelheid 18801
Tesfatsion, Costentinos 09400
Teshigara, Akane 26924
Teske, Christe 16308
Teske, Robert T. 45367, 48466
Tesseraux, Hartmut 17775
Tessman, Norm 46689
Testoni, Marcus 00901
Testoni, Theresa 00901
Tétaz, Marie Noëlle 11326
Tête, Michel 11510
Tetlow, David 39887
Tetterode Ravestein, Elke 29246
Tetzlaf, Reinhild 16714
Teunissen, J. 29897
Tew, Julie 39029
Tewes, Max 18313
Texel, Mark 45505
Teysen, Kenneth 45035
Thacker, Murray 30219
Thackeray, Dr. F. 34359
Thakkar, V.M. 22048
Thal, Denise 42825
Thaler, Dr. Herfried 02238
Thaler, Janice M. 43604
Thalheimer, Patricia 42811
Thaller, Toni 37361
Thalmann, Jacqueline 40145
Thalmann, Rolf 36518
Thames, Charles 47150
Thaxton, Kate 40099
Thaxton Soule, Debora 46957
Thaxton-Ward, Vanessa 43896
Thayer, Candace 45460
Thayer, Dorothy 45304
Thayer, Patricia 47077
Théberge, Pierre 06084
Thein, U Soe 28734
Thein, Udo 17710
Theis, Heinz-Joachim 16014
Theis, Wolfgang 16094
Theissen, A. 16101
Theißen, Dr. Peter 16619
Thellung, Caterina 25736
Theodorescu, Roxana 32452, 32457, 32458, 32466, 32474
Theol, Christopher R.M. 38394
Thériault, Serge 06084
Theriot, Edward C. 41421
Therre, Marie-Line 15160
Therrien, Richard 05396
Thestrup, Poul 09007
Thestrup Truelsen, Susanne 08813
Theune-Großkopf, Dr. Barbara 18201
Theunis, Karin 03337
Thévenin, M. Claude 14160

Thevenon, Luc F. 13311, 13327
Theyhsen, Annette 15866
Theys, Guido 03538
Thi, Nguyen Toan 48986
Thi Nu, Ha 49000
Thiagarajan, Dr. Deborah 21956
Thibault, Barbara 41808
Thibault, Pascale 13879
Thibodeau, Tony 47425
Thiébaut, Philippe 13596
Thiel, Dr. Ulrich 17102, 17104
Thiels-Mertens, Lydia 03385
Thieme, Thomas 35920, 36395
Thieme, Wulf 17545
Thiemler, Dagmar 19986
Thier, Dr. Bernd 18946
Thier, Wolfgang 02031
Thierbach, Melanie 15553
Thierer, Prof. Dr. Manfred 18451
Thierry, Olivier 11067
Thiery, Robert 13111
Thiesen, Barbara A. 46000
Thiesen, Bill 45117
Thiesen, John D. 46000
Thiessen-Schneider, Gudrun 19026
Thijsse, L. 29085
Thilges, Malou 02929
Thill, Edmond 27567
Thimme, Danae 41746
Thingvold, Terje 30685
Thipodeau, Richard G. 42930
Thir, Karl 01648
Thir, Dr. Mike 20105
Thiroy, Richard 03739
Thistle, Paul C. 05311
Thoben, Peter 29215
Thobois, Elisabeth 02830
Thöner, Wolfgang 16584
Thöny, Christof 01757
Thörn, Eva 36323
Thörnberg, Magnus 36047
Thörne, Michael 36221
Thøgersen, Mogens 08877
Thogersen, T. 30504
Thole, Dr. Bernward 18626
Thoma, Ludwig 02338
Thoman-Oberhofer, Elisabeth 02072
Thomanek, Kurt 01998
Thomann, Marcel 12829
Thomas, Abigail 39269
Thomas, Angela 38269
Thomas, Anne 06084
Thomas, Dr. Beth 40395
Thomas, Beth A. 43854
Thomas, Brad 42789
Thomas, Celestine 26069
Thomas, Charles 41737
Thomas, Charles C. 44456
Thomas, David 39729
Thomas, Dean V. 38623
Thomas, Don 48711
Thomas, Eleanor 39848
Thomas, Dr. Floyd R. 48618
Thomas, Harold Pratt 42226
Thomas, Heidi 48284
Thomas, Joe 42427
Thomas, Kathryn 47125
Thomas, Linda L. 41181
Thomas, M. Simon 29759
Thomas, Marcel 20712
Thomas, Marge 46051
Thomas, Mark 39191
Thomas, Maureen 47210
Thomas, Nancy K. 44921
Thomas, Nicholas 40572
Thomas, Raymond 10440
Thomas, Prof. Dr. Renate 18166
Thomas, Robert G. 39847, 39849
Thomas, Rosalyn 40668
Thomas, S. 03778
Thomas, Sarah 00704
Thomas, Steve 46917
Thomas, Susan 43782
Thomas, Thelma 41218
Thomas, Valerie 13240
Thomas, Valérie 13246
Thomas, William G. 47337
Thomas, William T. 42531
Thomas, Y. 12155
Thomas-Ziegler, Sabine 18669
Thomason, Henry 47510
Thomasson, J.R. 43971
Thome, Teresa L. 43757
Thomenius, Kristina 09722
Thommen, Lynn 45821
Thommesen, Nils H. 30389
Thompson, Anna 36268
Thompson, Anna M. 47103
Thompson, Barb 04986
Thompson, Barbara 43907
Thompson, Bernard J. 06872
Thompson, Bernell 47525
Thompson, Brian 40581
Thompson, Brian C. 45840
Thompson, Carol 41348
Thompson, Claudia 44778
Thompson, Deborah 36362, 47472
Thompson, Dixie 42182
Thompson, Dr. F.G. 43581

Thompson, Ida 44127
Thompson, Isobel 40668
Thompson, J. 42100
Thompson, Jim 41266
Thompson, Jo 48653
Thompson, Joe H. 47487
Thompson, John 42017, 47472
Thompson, Joseph 45978
Thompson, Karen 44079
Thompson, Kathy 42716
Thompson, Kelly 44527
Thompson, Livia 45823
Thompson, Marc 43124
Thompson, Margaret 39224
Thompson, Mervyn 38733
Thompson, Murray 01386
Thompson, Dr. P. 39244
Thompson, P. 39414
Thompson, Paul 30299, 38643
Thompson, Pauline 06696
Thompson, Peter 40701
Thompson, Ronda 48503
Thompson, Roy 05693
Thompson, S. 40460
Thompson, Scott 42989
Thompson, Susan 45701
Thompson, Wilma 42724
Thomsen, Douglas 43038
Thomsen, Sanciea 43038
Thomson, Beth 40283
Thomson, Bruce 05472
Thomson, C. 38250
Thomson, David 39312
Thomson, Frances 01547
Thomson, Frank E. 41275
Thomson, Prof. K.S. 40151
Thomson, Dr. Philip 01101
Thømt, Torill 30707
Thonet, Anke 17026
Thongthew, Suvaporn 37533
Thorarinsson, Einar 21644
Thorbjornsdottir, Sonny 21660
Thorburn, Ken 38373
Thorkildsen, Åsmund 30463
Thorlacius, Ethel 48309
Thorláksson, Eiríkur 21649
Thorláksson, Eiríkur 21650, 21651
Thormann, Dr. Olaf 18398
Thorn, Brett 38046
Thorndahl, Jytte 08783
Thorndike, Ellen 47843
Thorne, Lynne 03885
Thorne, Martha 42304
Thornton, Leigh 39995
Thornton, Pam 46240, 46241
Thorp, Barbara 44274
Thorpe, Christine 38505
Thorpe, Linda 38626
Thorpe, Timothy 39370
Thorsager, Carl F. 30986
Thorsell, William 06607
Thorsen, Sue 47651
Thorsteinsson, Arne 09407
Thoulouze, Daniel 13587
Thouret, Nicole 10456, 10457
Thowsen, Atle 30417
Thrailkill, Helen 47776
Thrane, Finn 09015
Thresher, Leon 43910
Throckmorton, C. 37960
Throl, Dr. Hans-Joachim 20661
Thron, Rudolf 02519
Thümmler, Dr. Sabine 18014
Thuesen, Søren T. 21235
Thum, Marvin 47508
Thurley, Dr. Simon 39718
Thurlow, Irja 45467
Thurmann, Dr. Peter 18075
Thurmer, Robert 42469
Thurner, Ludwig 02336
Thúroczy, Dr. Csaba 21465, 21587
Thurow, Dr. Beate 19580, 19581
Thurow, Chuck 42333
Thuy, X. de 13141
Thwaites, Dr. Peter 38444
Thygesen, Anker 08849
Thykier, Claus 09090
Thyrring, Ulla 08865, 08869, 08871
Thys, Joseph 03315, 03836
Tiacci, Giovanni Battista 24851
Tibbits, Michaela 45093
Tiberi, Prof. Romolo 24705
Tiberio, Dr. Artioli 24921
Tichenor, Daryl L. 48251
Tichonov, Dr. Igor L. 33444
Tichonov, Vladimir Viktorovič 32812
Tiderman, Conny 35897
Tidow, Klaus 19048
Tiedemann, Klaus 19499
Tiedemann, Nicole 17527
Tiefenbach, Dr. J. 01806
Tiefenbach, Oskar 01827
Tielman, Prof. R.A.P. 29943
Tiendrebeogo, Prosper 04936, 04941
Tierney, J. 38329, 39094
Tierney, Janet 40525
Tiescen, Doug 43186
Tiesing, F. 29017
Tietjen, Hinrich 18465

Tietken, Antje 19254
Tietmeyer, Dr. Elisabeth 16051
Tietz, Annette 15928
Tietz, R.M. 34237
Tietzel, Prof. Dr. Brigitte 18223
Tiffany, Harold 43976
Tiffany, Sharon 47809
Tigchelaar, I. 29838
Tigert, Jennifer 05218
Tiitsar, Ketli 09362
Tijdink, W. 28998
Til, Barbara 16738
Tilarinos, George 46375
Tilbrook, Val 00916
Tildesley, J.M. 38785, 39041, 39312
Tiley, Sian L. 34346
Till, Dr. Wolfgang 18880
Tillequin, Prof. François 13580
Tiller, Helmut 02935
Tilley, Nicola 40409
Tilley, Peter 39628
Tilliabaev, R.A. 48830
Tillmann, Michael 16824, 16826
Tillmann, Walter 19001
Tilmant, France 03609
Timbrook, Mark 45398
Timlin, Aaron 42921
Timm, Kristal 43347
Timm, Robert 44685
Timmelmayer, Andreas 02959
Timmerman, B.W. 29903
Timmermann, Dietrich 08940
Timmermans, L. 29563
Timmins, John 30152
Timmons, P.J. 40791
Timms, Peter 43326
Timofeeva, Nina Vasiljevna 33555
Timothy, John 45580
Timotijevic, Milos 33827
Timpano, Anne 42404
Tinčev, Valentin 04665
Tindale, Bruce 01273
Tindel, Raymond D. 42355
Tindell, Daniel F. 43594
Ting, Dr. Joseph 07104
Ting, Dr. Joseph S. P. 07103
Ting, Joseph S.P. 07097
Tingley, Charles A. 47071
Tinguy de la Giroulière, Dominique de 12324
Tinius, Joanna 47475
Tinjum, Larry 46681
Tinnell, Jack L. 46127
Tinney, Donal 22541
Tinney, Harle H. 45924, 45933
Tinte, Francisco 00637
Tintori, Dr. Andrea 24097
Tio, Dr. Teresa 32363
Tip, J.C. 29678
Tippmann, Rainer 16472
Tira, Masa Morioka 44086
Tirado, Vincent 45293
Tirelli, Dr. Margherita 25059
Tirion Beijerinck, I.H. 29759
Tironi, Ivan 07747
Tischer, Achim 16327
Tisdale, Brenda 43122
Tisdale, Shelby J. 47951
Tisken, Jörg 20217
Tisserand, Gérard 11323
Tissier, Gève 11365
Tissier de Mallerais, Martine 11252, 12803
Titova, Larisa Michajlovna 32934
Titova, Valentina Vasiljevna 33267
Tittoni, Dr. Maria Elisa 25217, 25218
Tittoni Monti, Dr. Elisa 25230, 25264
Tivadar, Petercsák 21408
Tixier, Guy 12810
Tixier, J.M. 13800
Tjäder, Jan-Börge 30752
Tjan, R. 29036, 29897
Tjardes, Tamara 47426
Tjentland, L. 48681
Tjomlid, Steinar 30922
Tjupina, Lidija Afanasjevna 32695
Tjutčeva, Valentina Sergeevna 33398
Tkačeva, Irina Vladimirovna 33506
Tkach, Steven 48416
Tkačuk, J. 37863
Tkešelašvili, A.V. 15368
T'Kint de Roodenbeke, Juan Graaf 03374
Toase, Charles 39811
Tobe, Carol B. 44961
Tober, Barbara 45755
Tobias, Todd 47288
Tobin, Shelley 38364
Tobler, Beatrice 36546
Tobler, Dr. M. 37428
Tobón Arbeláez, Elvira 07578
Tocev, Petăr 04668
Tocheva, Natalia 04756
Tochigi, Akira 26938
Toczewski, Dr. Andrzej 32220
Tod, Chris 40586
Toda, Masayasu 26638
Todd, Carol 45453
Todd de Iramain, Margarita Tula 00586
Todolí, Vicent 35599
Todorov, Todor 04796
Todorova, Ani 04643

Todorova, Pepa 04690
Todorova-Stojanova, Kresa 04760
Todts, Herwig 03146
Toedtemeier, Terry 46641
Toejner, Poul Erik 08902
Toelle, Wolfgang 17380
Toepfer, Lutz 15679
Törmälä, Satu 09431
Törnblom, Görel 35997, 35998
Törnig-Struck, Jutta 18706
Tövsayhan, G. 28682
Toftegaard, Kirsten 08927
Toftgaard Poulsen, Søren 08869
Tohjoh, Kohkoh 26389
Toit, Elizabeth du 34262
Toivanen, Pekka 09573
Toivanen, Yrjö 10182
Toka, Arnita 27421
Tokarczyk, William 43644
Tokarski, Longin 31523
Tokuda, Toshiaki 26309
Tokugawa, Narimasa 26506
Tokugawa, Yoshinobu 26571
Toledo, Eva 31358
Tolentino, Onofre R.. 31417
Tolhurst, Robert 38366
Tollefson, Roy 05946
Tollet, André 11157
Tolmačeva, Valentina Michajlovna 32857, 32858
Tolmoff, Mati 09377
Tolnay, Dr. Alexander 16076
Tolnick, Judith E. 44498
Tolonen, Tatiana 10138
Tolson, Peter 48020
Tolstoj, Vladimir I. 32856
Tolstrup, Dr. Inger 08962
Tolton, Ray 05023
Tolu, Giuseppe 23051
Toluse, Joe 41774
Toma, Shiichi 26572
Tomaka, Janice 41989
Tomamichel, Leonhard 36578
Tomana, Makoto 26715
Tomar, Y.P.S. 21989
Tomaschett, Dr. Pius 37256
Tomasi, Marie-Cécile 10502
Tomašik, Gennadij Aleksandrovič 32691
Tomasović, Nives 07705, 07707
Tomassetti, Larissa 01887
Tomassini, Gabriella 25696
Tomasson, Thordur 21670
Tomaszewski, Robert 31819
Tomaz do Couto, Dr. Matilde 32246
Tombs, Sebastian 38909
Tomczak, Bogdan 32194
Tomea Gavazzoli, Dr. Maria Laura 24644, 24645, 24646, 24649
Tomey, J.K. 38592
Tomiyama, Hideo 26832
Tomiyasu, Reiko 26128
Tomkins, John 46547
Tomkins, Rachel 40147
Tomlin, Julian 39904
Tomlinson, Dr. Janis A. 48337
Tomlinson, Lori 46746
Tomljenović, Zvjezdana 07809
Tommassen, W. 29597
Tomobe, Naoshi 26332
Tomot, Dr. Michael 44884
Tomov, Lazar 04846
Tomova, Krasimira 04903
Tompkins, Jack D. 46822
Tomplak, Darinka 34157
Toms, Art 43762
Toms, Donald D. 44699
Toms, Dr. R. 34359
Tondre, Mary L. 46555
Toner, Dominga N. 41658
Toner, Eden R. 46825
Toney, Brian E. 40689
Tonezzer, Lucia 36622
Tonge, V. 39877
Toniolo, Elia 25968
Tonković, Snježana 07709
Tonneau-Ryckelynck, Dominique 11929
Tønneberg, Ingrid 30875
Tonon, Dr. Marco 23205, 25008
Tooby, Michael 38481
Tooker, Chad 47076
Toom, Maire 09358
Toomet, Tiia 09385
Toomey, Dr. Richard 47737
Toone, Keith 05159
Tooze, M. 38264
Toplovich, Ann 45625
Topoleanu, Florian 32620
Topoleanu, Florin 32517, 32617, 32618, 32619
Topolinsky, Verna 04994
Toraason, Mary C. 48167
Torataro, Yoneyama 26828
Torchia, Richard 43694
Torchia, Robert W. 45235
Torchio, Maurizio 25729
Torfs, Freya 03166
Torgersen, Ulf E. 30704
Torki, Nasser 22241
Torm, Helge 08963
Tornbörg, Kay 44909
Torno, Janet E. 41712

Torp, Lisbet 08941
Torra, Eduardo 35715, 35719
Torra, Emilio 24111
Torralba, Casiana C. 31298
Torrance, Joshua C. 43164
Torre, Antonio 25249
Torre, Prof. Danilo 23866
Torre, Fuensanta García de la 34738
Torre, Graciela de la 28185
Torre, José Ramón de la 32392
Torre, Dr. Paola 25231
Torre Bonachera, José Luis la 35583
Torre González, Norberto de la 28406
Torre Prados, Francisco de la 35074
Torremocha Silva, Antonio 34445
Torrence, Gaylord 44404
Torrent i Bagudà, Enric 35566
Torrente, Virginia 35628
Torrents, Carme 34820
Torrenzieri, Claudio 25698
Torres, Prof. Emmanuel 31429
Torres, John 47425
Torres, Julio 35024
Torres, Pedro Pablo Alberto 07556
Torres Correa de Migliorini, Beatriz 00587
Torres Orell, Francisca 35079
Torres Valderrama, Hernando 07421
Torres Varela, Hilda 00505
Torruella Leval, Susanna 45838
Tortolero, Carlos 42341
Torunsky, Dr. Vera 16246
Tosatto, Guy 11942, 13256
Tosdevin, M. 40209
Tošev, Miroslav 04746
Toševa, Svetla 04829
Tosi, Dr. Maria Teresa 24961
Tosini Pizzetti, Simona 24273
Tosswill, Richard 06710
Tostado, Dr. Conrado 28137
Tostevin, Patrick 40314
Toteva, Teodora 04627
Totevski, Totjo 04890
Toth, Elizabeth 42799
Tóth, Hajnalka 21599
Tóth, János 21435, 21615
Toti, Dr. Odoardo 22859
Tottis, Jim 42924
Touche, Hugues de la 12935, 12936, 12937, 12938, 12939
Touhey, Paula 44441
Toulmond, Dr. André 14034
Toumazis, Yannis A. 08191
Toumit, François 10984
Touret, Lydie 13581
Tourneux, Alain 11179
Tourta, A. 21188
Tourtillotte, William 47681
Tous, Rafael 34546
Toussaint, Christophe 14606
Toussaint, Jacques 03648
Toussaint, Mauricio 48085
Toussaint, Yolaine 05888
Towe, Andrew C. 42846, 42847, 42848
Towe, Ruth 41688
Towell, Debbie 06717
Towell, Gerry 39998
Tower, Joan B. 41069
Towl, Betsy 42197
Town, Geri 48781
Townley, Kim 30293
Townsend, Clifford 43084
Townsend, Richard F. 42304
Townsend, Richard P. 41515
Townsend, Simon 38075
Townsend, Wayne 06284
Townsend, Wilma T. 42077
Toyama, Tohru 26888
Toyoda, Takao 26378
Trabert, Ilona 15914
Trabitsch, Dr. Thomas 02963
Tracey, D. 38170
Tracy, Duane 45607
Tracy, Susan 06564
Träger, Anne 16499
Träger, Béatrice 19813
Trafford, Lynne 30207
Tragent, Henry 45312
Trager, Neil C. 45741
Tragner, Manfred 02993
Trahan, Eric 42074
Traikasem, Saengchan 37512
Trainor, Eugene N. 47503
Trakospoulou, Helen 21017
Traljić, Seid 07807
Trâmbaciu, Şefan 32483
Trâmbaciu, Stefan 32482
Tramer, Nancy 42956
Tramonte, Pietro 25057
Tramp, Lana 47803
Tramposch, Dr. Bill 30311
Transier, Dr. Werner 20011
Tranter, Rachel 40741
Trapani, Prof. Salvatore 24778
Trapnell, Simon H. 39084
Trapness, Thor 30573
Trapp, Gaudenz Graf 02771
Trapp, Graf Johannes 25589
Trapp, Dr. Oswald Graf 02771
Trappeniers, Maureen 29407

Trask, David 48709
Trask, Richard B. 42775
Tratebas, Ed 45610
Trauffer, Walter 36587
Traugott, Joseph 47424, 47427
Trautmann, Charles H. 44274
Trautwein, Dr. Wolfgang 15909, 15910
Trauzettel, Ludwig 16582
Travella, Eugenio A. 00528
Travelyan, Vanessa 40091
Travers, John 39956
Travis, Betsy L. 46669
Travis, David 42304
Travis, P. 30276
Traxler, Dr. Herbert 02616
Trazegnies, Marquis de 03361
Trček Pečak, Tamara 34114
Trebbi, Marco 30427
Trebilcock, Evelyn 44143
Trebilcock, Joanie 42947
Trebilcozk, Samantha 38351
Trebitsch, Dr. Thomas 02885
Tréboit, Marcel 12892
Treen, Robin 47531
Treff, Dr. Hans-Albert 18883
Trefný, Martin 08639
Tregaskis, Kate 38919
Tréguier, Frank 11513
Trehin, E. 13504
Tremain, Robert 05509
Trembath, Lynne 39696
Tremblay, Diane 06292
Tremblay, Ermenegildo 25010
Tremblay, M. Joland 05916
Tremble, Steve 47531
Treml, Robert 20372
Tremp, Prof. Ernst 37103
Tremper Hanover, Lisa 42528
Trendler, Meg 43227, 43229
Trenkmann, Heidemarie 16894
Trentin-Meyer, Maike 15693
Trepesch, Dr. Christof 19727
Treskow, Dr. Sieglinde von 16280
Tresnak, Lenka 23220
Tresseras, Miquel 35652
Trethewey, Graham 01361
Tretjakov, Nicolaj S. 33285
Tretjakova, Vera Dmitrievna 32760
Trett, Robert 40051
Treude, Dr. Elke 16589
Treuherz, Julian 39528, 39531
Trevelyan, Vanessa 38672, 40102
Treves, Dr. Samuel B. 44793
Trevisani, Dr. Enrico 23787
Trevisani, Dr. Filippo 24434, 24448
Trezzi, Daniela 25741
Triandaphyllos, Diamandis 21023
Triantafyllidis, Jutta 16920
Triantis, Alice 20925
Triapitsyn, Serguei V. 46918
Tribouillois, Serge 14438
Trice, Robbert 46339
Trickett, Jessica D. 48806
Trickett, Peter 40513
Tridente, Tommaso 24457
Triebel, Dr. Dagmar 18836
Trier, Dr. Markus 18166
Triesch, Dr. Carl 17561
Triet, Dr. Max 36521
Triffaux, J.M. 03182, 03185
Trifonova, Mariana 04931
Trifut, Viorica 32431
Trillos Lozano, Ariel 07482
Trimbacher, Hans-Peter 02725
Trimpe, Pam 44248
Tringali, Mario 25885
Trinidad, Miguel Angel 28243
Tripanier, Romain 06306
Trischler, Prof. Dr. Helmuth 18839
Trivelli, Mari Frances 47373
Trividic, Claude 13805
Trnek, Dr. Helmut 02918
Trnek, Dr. Renate 02886
Troché, Bruno 12154
Tröster, Dr. G. 17343
Trofast, Jan 36234
Trofimova, Nadežda Nikolaevna 33525
Troha, Nevenka 34156
Troiani, Dr. Stefano 25493, 25494, 25495, 25497
Troll, Tim 42948
Trollerudoy, Elin 30893
Trollope, John 44489
Troman, Louise 40771, 40776, 40874
Trommer, Markus 18920
Tromp, C.P. 29793
Tromp, Dr. G.H.M. 29723
Tron, Prof. Federico 24530
Tronchetti, Dr. Carlo 23245
Trone, Peter 46558
Tronem, Donatella 24419
Troniou, Marie-France 12765
Tronrud, Thorold 06549
Trop, Sandra 47908
Tropeano, Placido 24360
Trosper, Robert 41243
Trost, Maxine 41805
Trost, Dr. V. 20113
Trotnow, Dr. Helmut 15911

Trotter, Mark A. 43269
Trotter, Ruth 40038
Trotti-Bertoni, Prof. Anna 23756
Trottmann, Dr. Kajo 16743
Troubat, Catherine 11743
Troughton, Betty 48279
Trouplin, Vladimir 13579
Trout, Amy L. 45697
Trouw, Bernward 17759
Trowles, Peter 39048
Trox, Dr. Eckhard 18551
Troy, Gloria 45837
Troyer, Herbert 02664
Trtheway, Linda 43071
Trubicyna, Tatjana 33218
Truc, Sylvie 11939, 11946
Truchina, Galina Vasiljevna 33728
Trucksis, Jane 48764
Trudel, Marianne 04990
Trudgeon, Roger 00763
Trudzinski, Dr. Meinolf 17607
True, Marion 44913
Trueb, Linda 44685
Trücher, Karl 01763
Trueman, Debbie 05958, 05961
Trümper, H.-J. 16084
Trümpler, Dr. Charlotte 16945
Trümpler, Rico 36490
Trümpler, Dr. Stefan 37069
Trufanov, E.I. 33741
Trufini, Antonio 24502
Trullén i Thomàs, Josep María 35668
Trulock, Sue 46490
Trulock, Trent 42087
Trulssen, Torbjörn 30933
Truman, Nell 41569
Trumble, Edward P. 41836
Trumbower, Sarah P. 41657, 45351
Trummer, Manfred 02929
Trummer, Thomas 02838, 02953
Trumpie, Dr. Ank 29514
Trumps, Patricia 42593
Trumpy, Sigrid 41230
Trupp, Adam 40032
Truque, Angeles Penas 34750
Trusch, Dr. Robert 18003
Truškin, Michail Danilovič 32963
Tsafrir, Prof. Yoram 22624
Tsai, Eugenie 45886
Tsakos, Konstantinos 21134
Tsaneva, Svetla 04846
Tsang, Gerard C.C. 07096
Tsang, Kathleen 06790
Tsaoussis, Vassilis 21152
Tsatsos, Irene 44920
Tschach, Dr. M. 01806
Tschachotin, Peter 20106
Tschamber, Théo 13405
Tscherter, Erwin 15068
Tschirner, Manfred 16075
Tschoeke, Dr. Jutta 19133, 19141
Tscholl, Erich 36970, 37276
Tschopp, Walter 36984
Tschorsnig, Dr. Hans-Peter 20105
Tschudi, Gabriele 17674
Tse Bartholomew, Terese 47308
Tselekas, Panayotis 20897
Tselos, George 45876
Tsenoglou, Dr. Eleni 20975
Tsenor, Carey 05565
Tsipopoulou, Dr. M. 20810
Tsomondo, Tarisai 49029
Tsoukalas, P. 21192
Tsourti, Eos 20897
Tsoutas, Nicholas 01617
Tsugaru, Yoshisaburo 26732
Tsuji, Shigebumi 26606
Tsujii, Dr. Tadashi 26086
Tsujimoto, Isamu 26098
Tsujimoto, Karen 46067
Tsujimura, Tetsuo 26938, 26940
Tsukada, Masahiko 26873
Tsukitani, Atsufumi 26472
Tsuneishi, Fumiko 26938
Tsutsumi, Seiji 26313
Tsuzuki, Chieko 26938
Tua, Jean 36750
Tubaja, Roman 32052
Tucci, Franco 24050
Tuček, Helga 18508
Tuch, Gabriele 15987
Tuchel, Dr. Johannes 15972, 15973
Tucher, Bernhard Freiherr von 17973
Tucker, Andrew 38726
Tucker, Anne W. 44129
Tucker, Bob 44217
Tucker, Kevin W. 42558
Tucker, Mark S. 46442
Tucker, Michael S. 47048, 47054
Tucker, Paul L.C. 44280
Tucker, Prof. Priscilla K. 41220
Tucker, Sara 45793
Tucker, Suasan A. 45470
Tucker, Sue 43323
Tucker, Susan A. 45469
Tuckett, Noreen 00825
Tuckhorn, Nancy 48344
Tucoo-Chala, Jean 13194
Tudeer, E. 10057

Tudor, Kim 40571
Tuffs, Peter 40526
Tufrow, Kate 47341
Tugarina, Polina Innokentjevna 32819
Ţuglui, Traian 32546
Tuhumwire, Joshua 37823
Tuitjer, Regine 17607
Tulaeva, Marina Aleksandrovna 33628
Tulekova, Margarita Vasiljevna 32705
Tuleškov, Vencislav 04724
Tulku, Doboom 21785
Tulku, Mynak R. 03891
Tull, Earl B. 47523
Tullos, Mark A. 48261
Tumanova, Anna Andreevna 33499
Tumanyan, Tamar 00693
Tumidei, Stefano 23110
Tuminaro, Craig 41136
Tung, Wu 41817
Tungarova, Saran-Térél Sultimovna 33654
Tunheim, Arne 30514
Tunis, Dr. Angelika 15945
Tunnell, Bill 45425
Tunnicliff, Iris 40848
Tunsch, Dr. Thomas 16054
Tuomi, Marja-Liisa 09510
Tuomi, Timo 09533
Tuomi, Tuulia 09438
Tuominen, Laura 09431
Tuomola, Satu-Miia 09983
Tupper, Christine 05853
Tupper, J. 40274
Tupper, J.A. 05788
Tupper, Jon 05225
Tura, Jordi 34475
Turán, Róbert B. 21376
Turbanisch, Gérard 13192
Turcanu, Dr. Senica 32533
Turci, Dr. Mario 25457
Turdo, Mark A. 45640
Turek, Stanisław 31525
Turekanov, E.T. 27310
Turekian, Karl K. 45698
Turgeon, Christine 06206
Turicyna, T.K. 33664
Turk, James F. 47204
Turkov, Shura 22578
Turkova, Helga 08743
Turley, G. Pasha 42393
Turley, James 41540
Turnbow, Chris 47425
Turnbull, A. 00925
Turner, A.K. 30185
Turner, Annette 01183
Turner, David 42535
Turner, Edward E. 48543
Turner, Dr. Elaine 18606, 19086
Turner, Elizabeth 01106
Turner, Elizabeth Hutton 48389
Turner, Grady T. 45844
Turner, J. Rigbie 45863
Turner, Kathy 44242
Turner, Dr. Kenneth R. 43728
Turner, Laura 39377
Turner, Linda 47992
Turner, Nathan 43855, 43856
Turner, N.S. 40111
Turner, Sheridan 48645
Turner, Dr. Thomas F. 41105
Turnham, Stephanie 41618
Turnquist, Jan 42601
Turnquist, Dr. Jean E. 32387
Turovski, Jevgenij 37902
Turpin, Susan 46983, 47716, 48734
Turton, Alan 38101
Turunen, Eija 09972
Tusa, Prof. Vincenzo 25430
Tuschell, Peter 02983
Tustin, S. 34400
Tut, Dr. Ye 28751
Tutorov, Jasmina 33933
Tuttle, Barbara 43399
Tuttle, Lyle 47342
Tuttle Miller, Elisabeth 42398
Tutty, Lauren 05758
Tuve, Richard L. 45136
Tuyttens, Deborah 06775
Tuzar, Dr. Johannes M. 01791
Tvrtković, Dr. Nikola 07821, 07823, 07828
Twalba, Dia'a 27069
Tweneboa-Kodua, Maxwell Ohene 20795
Twist, William 05720
Twitchell, Linda 05852
Twohill, Nicholas 30263
Tworek, Dr. Elisabeth 18877
Twyford, Mark 43056, 45539
Txabarri, Myriam Gonzalez de 35733
Ty, Agustin 31306
Tyack, Gerry V. 39985
Tyagi, Prof. K.N. 21942
Tyamzarne, G.W.T. 49039
Tybring, Tina 36106
Tych, Felix 32138
Tydesley, Carole 40872
Tyler, Dr. Alan 40135
Tyler, Fielding L. 48249
Tyler, Frances P.B. 42202
Tyler, Grant 06827, 06837
Tyler, Jayne 39378

Tyler, Jean 43735
Tyler, John C.P. 48683
Tyler, Kim 00772
Tyrefelt, Ronny 35891
Tyrell, Dr. Albrecht 19495
Tysdal, Bobbie Jo 45912
Tyson, Rose 47294
Tytgat, Christiane 03337
Tzekova, Katia 04846
Tziafalias, Athanasios 20951, 21041
Úbeda de los Cobos, Dr. Andrés 35048
Ubl, Prof. Dr. Hansjörg 02744
Uburğe, Baiba 27402
Uccello, Vincenza 48528
Uchida, Akihiko 26884
Uchida, Toshio 26470
Uchiyama, Takeo 26425
Uchtmann, Daniel 02918
Ucik, Dr. Friedrich 02127
Uda, Makoto 26212
Uddin, Belen Y. 31332
Udø, Ovin G. 30611
Uduwara, J.S.A. 35743
Ueda, Ichiro 26708
Ueda, Shinya 26814
Uehira, Mitsugi 26430
Uehling, Russel 43555
Ueland, Hanne Beate 30727
Uelsberg, Dr. Gabriele 18814, 18815, 18816
Ueltschi, Hans-Peter 37210
Ueno, Katami 26929
Ueno, Takaaki 27004
Ueno, Tetsukazu 26110
Ürgová, Dana 07611
Uerscheln, Gabriele 16735, 16736
Uetz, Kitty 42413
Uffmann, Rüdiger 16155
Ufimcev, Valeri K. 32782
Ugarte-Peña, Alfredo 06907
Ugat, Pedro R. 31277
Ugawa, Masahiro 26702
Ugent, Dr. Donald 42102
Ugo, Prof. Gianni 00419
Ugren, Dragomir 33872
Uhernik, Boris 07727
Uhlemann, Dr. Silvia 16540
Uhlig, Dietmar 20121
Uhlig, Rainer 16563
Uhlmann, Klaus 15958
Uhrmacher, Erwin 15467
Ujiie, Seiichiro 26945
Ujváry, Dr. Péter 21383
Ukdah, Radi 37439
Ukena, H. 16585
Ul-Haq, Saleem 31037
Ulak, Dr. James 48335, 48357
Ulbrich, Marorie 41098
Ulbrich, Thomas 27241
Ulbricht, Dr. Ingrid 19793
Ulčar, Mirko 34085
Ulenberg, Dr. S.A. 28917
Ulianćić-Vekić, Prof. Dr. Elena 07755
Ulinskyte, Vilija 27528
Ulitin, Valerij G. 33488
Ullmann, Silke 18634
Ulloa, Gina 28236
Ulloa Rojos, Sergio 06922
Ullock, Jack 05862
Ullrich, Prof. Dr. Ferdinand 19512, 19513, 19514
Ullrich, Tyrena 19715
Ulm zu Erbach, Franz Freiherr von 16886, 20405
Ulmann, Dr. Arnulf von 19139
Ulmer, Dr. Renate 16547, 16549
Ulmer, Sean 41222
Ulmis, Janis 27381
Ulrich, Alan 46804
Ulrich-Hicks, Barbara 44184
Ultan, Prof. Lloyd 41914
Umari, Suna 44135
Umberger, Eugene 43792
Umberger, Leslie 47589
Umemoto, Michio 26223
Umeñaca, Juan 35247
Umezu, Gen 26693
Uminowicz, Glenn 42774
Umney, Nick 39795
Umorbeckov, Baytursun Esjanovič 27072
Unbehaun, Dr. Lutz 19700, 19701, 19881
Underwood, Katie 45296
Undesser, Gottfried 02905
Unge-Sörling, Suzanne 36259
Unger, Dr. Achim 49213
Unger, P. Karl 02587
Ungerfeld, M. 22750
Uno, Tomohisa 26915
Unraw, Peter 05943
Unruh, Dr. Frank 20212
Unsain, José María 34780
Untch, Katharine 46891
Unterdörfer, Dr. Michaela 37107
Unterreiner, Katrin 02904
Unterschultz, Judy 06494
Untersteiner, Eva 03060
Unverfehrt, Dr. Gerd 17334
Unzueta Reyes, Prof. Ana Geraldina 28121
Uoti, Maunu 09913
Uotila, Dr. Pertti 09498
Upeniece, Daiga 27402
Upp, Janeanne A. 47922

Upshaw, Lisa 47214
Upton, Alastair 38992
Upton, Graham 38853
Upton, Jan 38853
Uracz, Andrzej 31846
Urakova, Ljudmila Evgenjevna 32835
Uranić, Igor 07809
Uranija, Valentin 07806
Urban, Dr. Andreas 17597
Urban, Bettina 02953, 02954
Urban, Elke 18416
Urban, Erin 47784, 47785
Urban, Heinz 18680
Urban, Robin 41690, 42019
Urban, Wolfgang 19690
Urbaneck, Rotraud 20527
Urbanek, Erich 01904
Urbanek, Dr. Wilhelm 02850
Urbanelli, Lora 46721
Urbani, Vittorio 25945
Urbanová, V. 34079
Urbański, Andrzej 32211, 32212
Urbanski, Prof. Dr. Krysztof 31658
Urbas, Herbert 01836
Urbons, Klaus 18817
Urey-Weeks, Burdie 27499
Urgesi, Prof. Domenico 24362
Uribe, Gloria Zea de 07398, 07399
Uribe Ramón, Jorge 07605
Urio, Leonarda 36613
Urioste Avana, Jaime 03907
Urmas, Olli 09698
Urquina Llanos, Henry 07480
Urquiola, Beatriz S.A. 31378
Urrea, Ana Isabel 07625
Urrutia, Larry 47293
Urrutibehety, Clément 14395
Ursachi, Vasile 25822
Urschel, Joe 41266
Urschitz, Charlotte 01919
d'Ursel, Robert 03400
Ursić, Desanka 06904
Ursu, Mihai 28659
Urumov, Vanko 04894
Urumova, Rumjana 04633
Usaquén Ramos, Martha Lucía 07372
Usberghi, Dr. Gianni 25822
Uschner, Ralf 15692
Ušakov, Prof. S.A. 33160
Ušakova, Tamara Ivanovna 37865
Usanov, Evgenij Nikolaevič 32634
Uslaner, Diane 06588
Usler, Dr. Alexander 17275
Usquhart, Donald R. 38008
Ussenko, Valentina 27086
Ussing Olsen, Peter 08977
Ustaeva, Anna 37816
Ustinov, Vladimir Jurjevič 33735
Ustvedt, Østein 30765
Utech, Dr. Frederick H. 46511
Uthardt, Lorenz 09812
Uthemann, Ernst W. 19728
Utili, Dr. Mariella 24589
Utriainen, Onerva 10083
Utry, Dr. Attila 21478
Utsunomiya, Akiko 26217
Utter, Dr. Brad L. 48429
Utz, Karen 41708
Utz, Laura Lee 46005
Uure, Sarah 45935
Uvarova, Elena Anatolevna 33638
Uyttenhove, Prof. Dr. J. 03445
Uzubalieva, K.N. 27307
Uzunov, Nikolai 04666
Vaccaro, Dr. Luis Fernandez 00152
Vaccaro, Prof. Mario 23272
Vache, Bernd 17446, 17447
Vačiullin, Gali Fajzrachmanovič 33647
Väisänen, Raija 09596
Väkeväinen, Lea 09541
Välicki, Antti 09582
Vaelske, Urd 02551
Värtinen, Lea 09414, 09420, 09561, 09562, 09733, 09803, 09872, 09931, 10020, 10147
Vaessen, J.A.M.F 28942
Väterlein, Dr. Christian 15575
Vahey, John 41799
Vahl, Heidemarie 16726
Vaida, Lucian 32553
Vaillancourt, Sandra 47415
Vaillant, L. le 30104
Vaimbois, Laurent 13242
Vainorius, Julius 27533
Vaireaux, Bernard 14003
Vairo, Carlos Pedro 00650
Vaitkute, Karile 42307
Vajnerman, Viktor Solomonovič 33256
Vajšnorajte, I.A. 33635
Valadés Sierra, Juan M. 34641
Valaison, Marie-Claude 13708
Valat, Georges 11406
Válčev, Aleksandär 04852
Valcke, Ludo 03205
Valdeny da Rocha, Manoel 04552
Valderas, Elena Ruiz 34684
Valderrama de Díaz, Maritza 07533

Valdes, Nieves 31291
Valdes Gonzalez Salas, Ana Luisa 28093
Valdez, Ana Luisa 28135
Valdez, E.A. 44562
Valdez, Juan Carlos 28293
Vale, Jessica 38324
Vale, Prof. Dr. Maria da Graça Pratas do 32259, 32265
Valemtová, Dr. Jarmila 08424
Valencia, Alvaro Pío 07568
Valencia, Maria L. 32362
Valencia, Dr. Niels 31210
Valencia de Redondo, María Eugenia 07561
Valencia Ospina, José Aníbal 07361, 07362
Valenteijn, R. 29741
Valentin, J.C.P. 29253
Valentin, Jocelyne 14794
Valentin, Noel 45838
Valentine, Eunice E. 48291
Valentine, James W. 41646
Valentine, Kathryn 39956
Valentine, P. 34195
Valentiner, Gitte 08776
Valentini, Paolo 25721
Valentová, Dr. Jarmila 08417
Valenzuela, Hermana Carmen 07584
Valerio, Michele 23026
Valette, Jean 11823
Valeza, Luisa S. 31301
Valk, Marika 09354, 09358, 09367, 09368
Vall Petitpierre, Carmina 34555
Vallat, Pierre 10898
Valle, Dr. Marco 23062
Valle, Martha 46740
Valle Pérez, Dr. José Carlos 35284
Vallee, Dianne 05595
Vallejo Laso, Manuel 35305
Vallejo Triano, Antonio 34736
Vallery, Tullio 25950
Valles, Dave Anthony 31319
Valles-Bled, M. 12647
Vallette, Philippe 10841
Valley, Derek R. 46142
Valley, Mohawk 41187
Vallianos, Dr. Christopher 21215
Valliant, John R. 47149
Vallvieille, Michel de 14542
Valor, E. 00630
Valowitz, Rhoda 48004
Valter, Dr. Claudia 19891
Valtere, Mära 27363
Valtere, Mara 27454
Valuska, Dr. David 44530
Valz, Jean-Paul 10258
Vametova, Farida H. 32788
Vámos, Dr. Éva 21373
Van Adrichem, J. 28902
Van Allen, Victor 05257
Van Alphen, Jan 03141
Van Amerongen, R.A.M. 29077
Van Arsdel, Sara 46187
Van Autzen, Henning 20106
Van Baren, J.H.V. 29977
Van Beek, Dr. R. 28835
Van Beekhofff, D. 28818
Van Beers, H. 28902
Van Beheemen, P. 29146
Van Berge-Gerbaud, M. 13487
Van Berge Henegouwen, Dr. A.L. 29106
Van Bergen, W.J. 29405
Van Blyenburgh, Dr. Ninian Hubert 36745
Van Boheemen, P. 29145
Van Boorne, Geert 03453
Van Bossche, André 03472
Van Boven, Dr. M.W. 29117
Van Boxtel, E. 29759
Van Brakel, J.H. 28866
Van Brakel, J.W. 29976
Van Broeckhoven, Greet 03146
Van Broekhoven, L. 29525
Van Bussel, Gerard W. 02945
Van Campen, Dr. Jan 29614
Van Campenhout, Nico 03594
Van Cauteren, J. 29988, 29989
Van Clardt, V. 34405
Van Cleve, David 41795
Van Daele, Dr. Rik 03594
Van Damme 03536
Van Damme, I. 03303
Van de Beuque, Guy 04338
Van de Guchte, Dr. Maarten 44293
Van de Kerkhof, Véronique 03173
Van de Maele, Maurice 06903
Van de Perre, M. 03124
Van de Schoor, Dr. F.C.M. 29632
Van de Velde, Hildegard 03171
Van de Voorde, Veronique 03641
Van de Voort, Dr. J.P. 29948
Van de Wiele, Johan 03441
Van Delen, Wieke 34210
Van den Abeele, Jean-Pol 03756
Van den Akker, Ad 44057
Van den Berg, R. 29228
Van den Berg, S. 29717
Van den Bosch, Paula 29564
Van den Branden, Walter 03823
Van den Brink, Dr. Peter 29564
Van den Broeke, J. 29932
Van den Bussche, Willy 03526, 03669

Van den Donk, Drs. H.P.S.M. 29595
Van den Driessche, B. 03600
Van den Eijnde, Jerden 29971
Van den Elzen, Dr. Renate 16250
Van den Hout, A.H.P.J. 29901
Van den Meiracker, C. 29779
Van den Steen de Jehay, Comte Guy 03528
Van den Valentyn, Heike 16738
Van den Veen, J. 29649
Van der Auwera, M. 03488
Van der Beele, P. 29448
Van der Burgh, Dr. J. 29908
Van der Donckt, Marie-Claire 03677
Van der Elst, Els 03337
Van der Goes, Drs. André W.A. 16689
Van der Haegen, Erik 03837
Van der Heever, Chast 34367
Van Der Heijden, Merijn 43772
Van der Holst, A.P.J. 29808
Van der Kemp, Gerald 11871
Van der Laan, Anke 29324
Van der Laar, P. 29752
Van der Lelie, H. 29520
Van der Lugt, Dr. P. 29368
Van der Meiden, Kees 29313
Van der Meijden, Dr. Hellebora 36495
Van der Merwe, Jake 05046
Van der Merwe, T. 34219
Van der Merwe, Thijs 34210
Van der Meulen, G.P. 29251
Van der Ploeg, J. 30064
Van der Ploeg, P. 29105
Van der Spek, Dr. T.M. 29521
Van der Veer, Hugh G. 47851
Van Der Vin, J.P.A. 29519
Van der Wall, Dr. Frauke 20696
Van der Werdt, E.F.L.M. 29474
Van der Westhuizen, V. 34335
Van der Zalm, Leo 29282
Van der Zee, Jelga 29514
Van der Zijpp, Sue-An 29309
Van der Zwaag, M. 28869
Van Deun, Charles 03737
Van Deurs, Lone 08794
Van Deventer, Anriët 34331
Van Dijck, Leen 03135
Van Dijk, E.A. 30086
Van Dijk, J. 28866
Van Dongen, A.G.A. 29759
Van Dongen, P.L.F. 29525
Van Dooren, Rita 03151
Van Doorne, Geert 03451
Van Doorne, Veerle 03375
Van Dorst, Drs. M.H.J. 29941
Van Duuren, D.A.P. 28866
Van Dyck, Ann 03144
Van Dyk, Pieter 01375
Van Dyk, Stephen H. 45788
Van Dyke, Dore 41368
Van Dyke, Jonathon 43926
Van Egmond, C. 29391
Van Endert, Dr. Dorothea 18745
Van Faasen, Drs. S.A.J. 29101
Van Frank, M. 44027
Van Geluwe, Johan 03826
Van Gennip, J. 29330
Van Genuchten, S. 29978
Van Gerwen, Dr. Ch. 29923
Van Gijseghem, A.M. 03449
Van Ginneken, Lily 29126
Van Gompel, F. 03629
Van Grevenstein, Alexander 29564
Van Grootheest, J. 29106
Van Haaften, Joel 44848, 44849
Van Haaren, Joke 29324
Van Haaren, S. 29901
Van Haarlem, Dr. W.M. 28835
Van Hablem, M. 29605
Van Haecke, Bert 03371
Van Harinxma, Barones K.L. 29931
Van Harten Boers, H. 29832
Van Hattem, M. 29079
Van Heerden, H. 34297
Van Heerden, Martie 28777
Van Hees, Eva 45289
Van Heesch, Dr. A. 29632
van Helmond, Mary 38468
Van Hengstum, R. 29522
Van Heugten, Sjraar 28911
Van Heuven-Van Nes, Dr. E. 28928
Van Hoof, Werner 03178
Van Hoofstat, Jan 03726
Van Hoonacker, Albin 03557
Van Hoonacker, Marie-Henriette 03557
Van Hoorn, Dr. M.A.M. 29331
Van Horn, Walter 41197
Van Hout, I.C. 28866
Van Hout, N. 03146
Van Huis, Edwin 29420
Van Huy, Prof. Dr. Hguyen 48972
Van Kampen, Dr. Iefke Johanna 23919
Van Kerkhouen, Laurence 03246
Van Kerkhoven, Geertrin 03678
Van Klinken, M.F. 28931
Van Koughnett, W.J. 05086
Van Krimpen, M. 29095
Van Krugten, Dr. D. 17933
Van Kruistum, G. 29477
Van Laar, Barb 47644

Van Laarhoven, H. 28984
Van Laarhoven, Dr. Jan 29375, 29407
Van Laer, M. 03418
Van Leeuwen, P.C. 28965
Van Leeuwen, P.P.H. 30035
Van Lennep, Jacques 03300
Van Leverink, J. 29585
Van Liebergen, Dr. L.C.B.M. 29884
Van Lier, F.J. 29044
Van Lingen, C. 29756
Van Loo, R. 03488
Van Loon, V. 28916
Van Looy, Walter 03698
Van Marion, A.J.H. 29906
Van Meerbeeck, Patrick 03545
Van Meerten, M.M. 30060, 30062
Van Melsen, Frances 34233
Van Mensch, Dr. 29419
Van Mol, Bruno 03632
Van Mullekom, Elisabeth 01111
Van Ness, Sally D. 43505
Van Nieuwenhuijzen, M. 28902
Van Noort, Dr. S. 34213
Van Noten, Francis 03285, 03322, 03341
Van Nüss, Berndt 20596
Van Oijen, M.J.P. 29522
Van Olst, C. 29438
Van Orman, John 45548
Van Pelt, Peter 43033
Van Peteghem, Dr. Sylvia 03454
Van Pottelberghe, Michel 03827
Van Praët, Michel 13512
Van Proyen, Mark 47310
Van Putten, J.H.J. 35778
Van Raalte, Christopher 47319
Van Raalte, Ronald C. 47005
Van Raay, Stefan 38564
Van Raemdonck, Marie 03337
Van Ravensteyn, Fr. 03427
Van Regteren, R. 29637
Van Remoortel, P. 03235
Van Rensburg, F.S. 34357
Van Rijnswall, M. 29562
Van Rijswick, Dr. A. 29863
Van Rosmeilen 28770
Van Schalkwyk, Frieda 34351
Van Schalkwyk, Thea 34351
Van Schie, A. 29898
Van Seters, A.G.J. 28912
Van Shields 45020
Van Shields, W. 46950
Van Soest, Dr. R.W.M. 28917
Van Sprang, Sabine 03299
Van Straaten, Dr. E.J. 29686
Van Stuivenberg, F. 29238
Van Suchtelen, A. 29105
Van 't Veen, Cees 29514
Van Tilborgh, Louis 28911
Van Tilburg, B. 29701
Van Tilburg, C. 29367
Van Tol, J. 29522
Van Tooren, M.M. 29081
Van Tuyl, Prof. Gijs 20662
Van Tuyll Van Serooskerken, Dr. C. Baron 29331
Van Twist, Kees 29309
Van Veen, J.W. 29314
Van Vierzen, Barb 06122
Van Vilsteren, Dr. V.T. 28950
Van Vleet, Sue 47072
Van Vlijmen, Dr. P.M.L. 29906
Van Vollenharen, A.C. 34375
Van Volsem, Cindy 06148
Van Voorhis, Joan 41551
Van Voorst Van Beest, R. 29331
Van Wagner, Alison G. 41210
Van Waterschoot, J. 28874
Van Weelden, J.F. 29175
Van Wegen, Dr. Rik 29564
Van Wesemael, Willy 03774
Van Westerop, W.C.J. 29808
Van Wetten, Katja 20106
Van Wezel, H. 29531
Van Zante, Gary 42048
Van Zijl, J.J.R. 34186
Van Zijl, M.I.E. 29897, 29897
Van Zyl, S. 34333
Van Zÿverden, J. 29757
Váňa, R. 08254
Vanadzinjs, A. 27344
Vanater, Holli M. 42815
Vanausdall, John 44217
Vanautgaerden, Alexandre 03273, 03287
Vance, Alex D. 45643
Vance, Ann 48553
Vance, Tom 44717, 44718
Vanco, John L. 43200
Vančugov, V.P. 37892
Vandamme, Dr. E. 03146
Vandamme, Heidi 28911
Vandecan, Suzanne 03652
Vandekerchove, Veronique 03565
Vandelannoote, Jean-André 14269
Vanden Berghe, E. 03259
Vandenbroek, Dr. Paul 03146
Vandenbulcke, Anne 03276, 03288, 03323
Vandenheuvel, William 46029
Vandenven, Marc 03172
Vandepitte, Dr. Francisca 03297, 03300
Vandeput, Ann 03483

Vander, Joan 43807
Vanderbeck, LeeAnne 46785
Vanderhenst, Clara 03154
Vanderhust, Guido 03292
VanderLeest, Merlyn 46329
Vanderlip, Dianne 42885
Vandermaesen, M. 03265
Vanderpijpen, Willy 03275
Vanderpool, Guy C. 47990, 47991
Vanderschooten, Alain 14550
Vandervellen, Pascale 03317, 03337
Vanderwerff, Laverne 41270
Vandever, William 43465
Vandevivere, I. 03600
Vándor, Dr. László 21613, 21614
Vandormael, Dr. H. 03424
Vandulek, Márta 21351
Vandura, Djuro 07837
Vane-Wright, R. 39733
Vanegas López, Walberto 07494
Vanek, Helga 03001
Vanerck, Patricia 03354
Vanhaelen, M. 03318
Vanhalewijn, Rudy 03535
Vanheusden, Margot 03165
Vanja, Dr. Christina 17494
Vanja, Prof. Dr. Konrad 16051
Vanlatum, Anne 14625
Vannini, Prof. Marco 23872
Vannoni, Filippo 03489
Vanns, Michael 38379, 39322
Vannson, Françoise 10302
Váňová, Kristina 08661
Vanreuerm-Rossetto, Roxane 11587
Vanrie, André 03647
Van't Veen, Dr. Cees 29508, 29513
Vantrimpont, Jean-Denis 03549
Varadinis, Mirjam 37386
Varaksina, Tamara Ivanovna 32673
Varaldo, Prof. Carlo 22831, 22832, 22834, 23164
Vardanjan, Irina Valerjevna 33262
Vare, Talis 09318
Varela, Katia 07986
Varela, Matias 41608
Varenius, Linnéa 35977
Varga, Vincent J. 05702
Vargas, Heriberto 07503
Vargas, Maria Cristina 07392
Vargas, Mercedes L. 31420
Vargas Cuervo, Roberto 07534
Vargas de Martínez, Evelia 07538
Vargas Guadarrama, Dr. Luis Alberto 28208
Vargoz, Sylvine 13561
Vargyas, Herbert 02528
Varignana, Dr. Franca 23101
Varjonen, Risto 09475
Varnado, R. Brien 42211
Várnav, Prof. Remus 32555, 32556
Varno, Edward 42077
Varrak, Maruta 09372
Vartiainen, Ulla 09836
Váry, Dr. László 21387
Vasconcelos, Maria João 32330, 32332
Vaseva Dimeska, Viktorija 27593
Vasher-Dean, April 45693
Vasić, Dr. Vojislav 33816
Vasicek, Werner 01791
Vasileva, Dineta 04884
Vasileva, Rumjana 04842
Vasilevič, Georgij N. 33344
Vasiliu, Lucian 32536
Vasilui, Lucian 32537, 32538, 32540, 32551
Vassallo, Dr. Adriana 25214
Vassallo de Cettour, Crsitina 00287
Vasseur, Bernard 14116
Vasseur, Dominique 47757
Vasseur, Marie-Madeleine 12319
Vassiliadis, Dimitrios 21024
Vassilika, Dr. Eleni 17760
Vassilyeva, Valentina 27085
Vasudeva Bhatta, K. 21705
Vašut, Karel 08711
Vatksy, Sharon 43357
Vatutin, Konstantin Ivanovič 33244
Vaucher, Laurence 36956
Vaughan, Ellen 42247
Vaughan, Dr. Gerard 01237
Vaughan, Dr. Jefferson 43744
Vaughan, Roger 38054, 38643
Vauth, Henry 16728
Vavilova, Anna Pavlovna 33323
Vavilova, N.I. 33318
Vavra, Jan 48606
Vázquez Agraz, Joaquín 27839
Vázquez Ramírez, Nelson 27777
Vazquez Zuleta, Sixto 00365
Vazzana, Dr. Angelo 25092
Vdovin, Dr. Gennadij Viktorovič 33090
Vecarić, Nenad 07689
Vecchio, Marji 42305
Večerková, Dr. Eva 08267
Vedeznikova, Galina I. 33109
Vedjaeva, Natalja Anatoljevna 33291
Védrine, Laurent 14219
Védrine, Mireille 11140
Vedsted, Jakob 08801
Veeneman, Dr. G.A.C. 29521
Veenvliet, J. 29140
Veerabhadra Rao, K. 21816

Veerman, Hein 29958
Vees, L. 17655
Vega, Carmen L. 32400
Vegelin Van Claerbergen, Ernst 39615
Vegesack, Alexander von 20438
Vegesack, Baron Henrik von 36276
Vehma-Çiftçi, M. 19265
Vehniä, Harri 09724, 09725
Vehns, Johannes 17580
Veil, Dr. Stephan 17607
Veisz, Ottó 21469
Veit, Johann 01651
Veit, Prof. Dr. Willibald 16057
Veitch Alexander, Mary 45273
Vejle, Jan 08795, 08796, 08797
Vejlstrup, Tove 08902
Vela de la Torre, Antonio 35412
Velado Craña, Bernardo 34497
Velani, Dr. Livia 22915
Velaochaga Rey, Irene 31207
Velasquez, Dr. Geraldine 44609
Vélasquez, Dr. M. Manuel 32237
Velázquez, Agustín 35110
Velázquez, Efrain 41655
Velázquez Martínez del Campo, Roxana 28195
Velde-Conyers, Ellayne 45179
Velder, Linda 45915
Velers, J.B.A. 29659
Vélez, Jesús Hernán 07508
Velez, Pedro 42366
Vélez, Pilar 34566, 34578
Velfi, Dr. Josef 08625
Velghe, Brita 03290, 03300
Velikanova, Olga Alekseevna 33459
Velikova, Elena 04802
Velikova-Kesheleva, Violeta 04846
Velilla Moreno, Pilar 07514
Vella, Antonino 40764
Vella, John J. 27698
Vellacott, Robert B. 00978
Vellekoop, Marije 28911
Veller, Prof. M. 34274
Velluto, Giovanna 25837
Veloccia Rinaldi, Dr. Maria Luisa 23920, 25710, 25711
Veloso, Abraã9 32357
Veltheim, M. von 17703
Veltzke, Dr. Veit 20536
Venborg Pedersen, Dr. Mikkel 08962
Vences, Dr. M. 28917
Vendeuvre, Elyane de 15116, 15115
Veneman, Katherine 48280
Venizelos, Eleftherios 20891
Venkataraman, R. 21934
Vento, Minna 09431
Venkatesh Jois, Dr. K.G. 21886
Ventre, Dr. Riccardo 23339
Ventrudo, Meg 45840
Ventschen, Warren 48187
Venturo Rubino, Donata 22861
Vera, Gina C. de 31289
Vera, Teresa N. de 31347
Verardo, Bonnie 41111
Verbanck Piérard, Annie 03640
Verbeeck, Luc 03225
Verberová-Stifter, Jana 08245
Verbrugghen, Johanna M. 46291
Vercler, Dr. 42611
Verderame, Dr. Lori 41146
Verdi, Prof. Richard 38211
Verdugo Santos, Javier 35454
Veremeeva, Irina L. 37870
Veres, Dr. László 21476
Vereščagina, Tatjana Fëdorovna 33668
Verey, A.P. 40902
Vergara Rodríguez, Ancízar 07367
Vergara Torres, David 06918
Verge, Laurie 42493
Verger, Sylvestre 13604
Vergho, Dr. Helge 15871, 18083
Vergne, Philippe 45394
Vergnetta, Angela 25493
Verhaagh, Manfred 18003
Verhaard, A.J.G. 29660
Verhaeghe, Y.-C. 03799
Verhoeff, R.N.S. 29334
Verhoeven, Carolina 28929
Verkest, Idesbalo 03127
Vermeesch, Gerald 41702
Vermeulen, S. 34188
Verna, Gaëtane 05742
Verner Hamilton, Elizabeth 42215
Verney, Antoine 10615
Vernon, C.J. 34236
Vernon, G.N. 34236, 34237
Verone, Amy 46250
Verrando, Joyce 43953
Verrill, John H. 46154
Verroen, Dr. Th.L.J. 29167
Verschelden, G. 03771
Verschoor, M. Lynn 41932
Verschuur, P. 29204
Versluis, John 43656
Versluis, P. 28941
Verster, J.L. 29745
Vertenten, A. 03402
Verthamon, Henri de 10329
Verwey, Drs. A.D.M. 28855
Verwiebe, Dr. Birgit 15912

Verwimp, Gunter 03146
Verževikina, Marina 33589
Verzosa, Fe Angela 31376
Verzuh, Valerie 47425
Vesio-Steinkamp, Susan 42398
Veskovic, Esad 03925
Vest, Ladonna 42199
Vest, Windsor 47659
Vestergaard, Ole Schou 08844
Vestermanis, Margers 27404
Vettel, Greg 43743
Vetter, J.W.M. 29218
Vetter, Manfred 19078
Vetter, Maureen 44789
Vetter, Remo 37235
Veyradier, Henri 12461
Vezzosi, Alessandro 26025
Via, Marie 46948
Vial, Marie-Paule 12862
Vialla, Andre 12089
Vialla, Gérard 13891
Vianin, Georges 37364
Viar, Javier 34609
Viatgé, Karine 10371
Viatte, Françoise 13603
Vibe, Ellen S. de 30729
Vice, Lola 41966
Vice, Mary L. 47178
Vice, Michael L. 43663
Vicente, Jaime D. 35530
Vicini, Dr. Donata 24822, 24827, 24829
Vicini, Maria Lucrezia 25166
Vicino, Giuseppe 23818
Vickers, Irene 39517
Vickery, Michael 44708
Vicq Carvalho, Beatriz de 04381
Vida, Štefan 34039
Vidal, Nélida 28123
Vidal, Pierre 13578
Vidal, Silvia M. 48949
Vidal de Alba, Beatriz 28190
Vidal Huguet, Carme 34972
Vidal Inglès, Anton 34812
Vidali, Dr. Gloria 25939
Vidarte, Juan Ignacio 34612
Vidovic, Prof. Josip 07687
Vidulich, Tullio 25795
Viehmeier, Klaus 20588
Vienet, Bernard 11934
Vienonen, Inga 09883
Viens, Katheryn P. 47960
Viera, Ricardo 41667
Vierhauser, Emil 01851
Vierk, Viola 17568
Vierny, Dina 13626
Vierock, Ronald 16052
Vietti, Paola 25109
Vietze, Arwed 20761, 20763
Vieux, Jacky 11875
Vigarani, Guido 24447
Vigié-Chevalier, Béatrice 12865
Vigna Taglianti, Prof. Augusto 55220
Vignau-Wilberg, Dr. Thea 18912
Vigorelli, Prof. Giancarlo 24405
Vigreux, Jean 14135
Viguier, Florence 13048
Vihovde, Anne Brit 30419
Viinikainen, Kari 09779
Viita, Jorma 09690
Vikan, Dr. Gary 41489
Vikström, Lena 36096
Viktorova, Jelena 27402
Vikulova, V.P. 33039
Vila, Dominique 11232, 11233
Vila, Emma R. 00127
Vilà Noguera, Francesc 35082
Vilà Planas, Xavier 35671
Vilademunt, Josep 35671
Vilain, André 03559
Vilain, Jacques 12960, 13532
Vilaplana, Susana 35601
Vilas, Felipe Arias 34698
Vílchez Vílchez, Carlos 34873
Viler, Darko 34091
Viletová, Dagmar 08740, 08741
Vilhu, Raimo 09447
Viljoen, H. 34347
Viljoen, L. 34188
Vilks, Dr. Ilgonis 27407
Vilkuna, Janne 09598, 09599
Villa, Azucena 31444, 31445, 31457
Villadier, Francis 12959
Villagran Valdespino, Manuel Angel 28296
Villamayor Coto, José 28153
Villamizar Duarte, Eduardo Adolfo 07543
Villamizar Lamus, Eduardo 07544
Villanueva, Gustavo M. 30320
Villarroya i Font, Joan 34520
Ville, Roy de 41117
Ville, Roy V. de 41118
Villegas de Aneiva, Teresa 03900
Villela, Milu 04517
Villeneove, Daniel 06196
Villeneuve, Pat 44686
Villeon, H. de la 12541
Villiers, Jaline de 34321
Villiger, Dr. Verena 36715
Villoutreix, Pascal 12547
Vilman, Vladimir 34122

Vilsmeier, Cäcilie 19084
Vilus, Ljiljana 07813
Vimpari, Maritta 09843
Vimpère, Jean 12139
Viñayo, Antonio 34951
Vincent, Ariel 14526
Vincent, François 05779
Vincent, Dr. Gilbert T. 42618, 42619
Vincent, Glenda 47874
Vincent, Hélène 11942
Vincent, Jean-Claude 13688
Vincent, Victor 45291
Vincentelli, Moira 37954
Vincenti, Dr. Patrick 43965
Vincenzi, Marco 23728
Vine, Pat 47291
Viner, David 38582
Vingtain, Dominique 10535
Vinje, Tor 30693
Vinke, Albert 19587
Vinogradov, Z. 22585
Vinogradova, V.I. 37867
Vinsen, Bob 30212
Vinyet Estebanell, Josep 34976
Vinzens, Brigitte 37342
Vio, Ettore 25931, 25942
Virasoro, Carlos Alberto 00609
Virgin, Louise 48756
Virieu, A. de 11756
Virole, Agnès 14240
Virtanen, Prof. Ismo 09493
Virtanen, Risto 09895
Vis-Best, A. 29599
Visbach, Alida 06191
Vischer, Dr. Theodora 36966
Visentin, Prof. Dr. Mario 23618
Visini, Patrick 15032
Viskari, Leena 09782
Višnevskaja, Julija 33155
Vispi, Maria 24075
Visser, Dr. Anna Maria 23783
Visser, H. 28902
Visser, Johann 19116
Visser, Mattijs 16738
Visser, Dr. S. H. 28959
Visser, Susan R. 47681
Visser, Tina 05407
Viswanadham, M. 22023
Vitáček, Zdeněk 08294, 08330
Vitagliano, Carol Edith 00214
Vital, Christophe 12533, 14793
Vital, M. 11772, 13037
Vitali, Christoph 37060
Vitali, Tiziana 24552
Viti, Paolo 25947
Vitie, Heikki 09517
Vitković Zikić, Milena 33810
Vitmayer, Janet 39668
Vitous, Frantisek 08490
Vitt, Dr. L.J. 45976
Vivanco Vega, Manuel 07423
Viver, F. Xavier 35554
Vivies, Bertrand de 11833, 11835
Vizi, Dr. József Kriston 21452
Vizi, Ondrej 33890
Vizirito, Jackie 42145
Vjalikov, P.F. 33023
Vjalych, Ljudmila Makarovna 32976
Vješnic, Borko 07779
Vlachou, Elia 20897
Vlack, Donald J. 45859
Vladimirova, Galina A. 33469
Vlaemynck, Joris 03389
Vlasáková, Beata 34069
Vlašić, Andrija 07748
Vlatković, Radmila 33884
Vlcek, Dr. Tomas 08570
Vliegenthart, Dr. A.W. 28926
Vlieghe, Prof. Dr. Hans 03138
Vlk, Antonin 08402
Vlnas, Dr. Vit 08584, 08585
Vlnas, Dr. Vít 08615
Vlok, Rochelle 34398
Voce, Yolanda 47269
Vodret, Dr. Rossella 25162
Vögele, Dr. Christoph 37185
Völcker-Janssen, Dr. Wilhelm 18210
Voélin-Dubey, Monique 36994
Voelkel, David B. 43537
Völker, Angela 02929
Voelker, Gary 44674
Völker, Heike 15920
Völker, Reinhard 20254
Völkl, Rosemarie 19517
Voelkle, William M. 45863
Vörös, Dr. Gabriella 21547, 21551
Voet, Albert 03170
Vötter-Dankl, Susanna 02345
Vogeding, Dr. Ralf 20131
Vogel, Christian 19139
Vogel, Klaus 16679
Vogel, Dr. Michael 15886
Vogel, Robert 47811
Vogel, Wilhelm Dieter 17076
Vogelaar, Dr. C.J.J. 29526
Vogelbacher, Martin 20180
Vogeler, Dr. Hildegard 18542
Vogels, J.J. 29296, 29297
Vogelsang, Harald 16195

Vogelsang, W.J. 29525
Vogelsanger, Dr. Cornelia 37416
Vogelstein, John L. 45821
Vogl, Elisabeth 20126
Vogler, Franz 02852
Vogler-Zimmerli, Brigitta 36544
Vogt, George L. 48652
Vogt, Dr. Renate 16249
Vogt, Sharon L. 45490
Vogt, Wolfgang 18744
Vogtenhuber, Peter 02228
Vogue, Louis de 11371
Vogüé, Comte B. de 13396
Vogüé, Patrice de 12773
Vogüé, T. Comtesse de 14979
Voicu, Mariana 32570
Voigt, Dr. Kirsten 18002
Voigt, Sigrun 17808
Voigt, Dr. Wolfgang 17035
Voigt Andersen, Mogens 21230
Voisin, Bernard 11272
Voisin-Thiberge, Claire 13260
Voithofer, Waltraud 01743
Volkert, James 45852
Volkmann, Jürgen 17416
Volkov, Sergej Pavlinovič 33220
Volkova, Valentina Borisovna 32882
Volkwein, Peter 17912
Vollert, Adalbert 17051
Vollgraaff, Helene 34210
Vollmer, David 47986
Vollmer, Erich 44414
Vollmer, Janis 43636
Vollmer, Jennifer 43071
Volmar, Michael 43952
Voločkova, Olga Kuzminična 33332
Volosenkova, Nadežda 33536
Volosova, Galina Pavlovna 33490
Volovenskaja, Ljudmila Vladimirovna 32829
Volpe, Jorge 00155
Volskij, Svjatoslav O. 33240
Volz, Günther 15603
Volz, Jochen 17070
Volz, Robert L. 48633
Vomm, Dr. Wolfgang 15896, 15901
Vomsattel, Gerold 37293
Von der Mieden, O.J.E. 29964
Vondras, Barbara 44754
Vonhof, M.J. 29686
Vonier, Franz 01771
Vonk-Hennig, Davien 28800
Voogt, Leo 29111
Vookles, Laura L. 48785
Voordendaf, A.G. 29858
Voorhies, Dr. Michael 44793
Vorachek, Pamela 47206
Vorano, Tullio 07734
Vorel, Otakar 08393
Vorländer, Dr. Hermann 19023
Voropanov, Vladimir Valentinovič 33723
Vorre, Birgit 08961
Vorres, George 21104
Vorres, Ian 21104
Vorsteher, Dr. Dieter 15939
Vort-Ronald, Michael P. 01128
Vorwig, Dr. Carsten 18669
Vos, H.N. 34383
Vos, K. 29525
Voss, Dr. J. 03566
Voss, Kurt 43614
Voß, Dr. Rolf 19013
Voss, William J. 43485
Vostrikov, Vladimir Ivanovič 33348
Votaw, John F. 48583
Votroubková, Dr. Iva 08308
Voûte, Alexander 37393
Voute, Dr. A.M. 29911
Vovk Čepič, Taja 34111
Voyadzis, G. 20890
Voyame, Christian 36546
Voyles, Robert 43390
Voza, Dr. Giuseppe 25429, 25586
Voznicky, Boris G. 37885
Vrabec, Vesna 07830
Vraesos, Alexis 10640
Vrat, Prof. Prem 22006
Vrba, Elisabeth 45698
Vrčic, Vjeko 07710
Vrebos, M. 03276, 03288
Vrellis, Paul P. 20971
Vriarte, Miriam de 47329
Vriend, Anita 28911
Vries, D.P. de 29515
Vries, J. de 29163
Vries, Dr. M.E.A. de 28806
Vrieze, John 28830
Vroede, Erik de 03500
Vrousos, Alexis 14271
Vrtiska, Floyd 47914
Vuadens, G. 37279
Vuigner, J.L. 36936
Vuille, Roger 37083
Vuilloud, R. 36945
Vujčić, Davorin 07715
Vujičić, Jasminka 07813
Vujnović, Andrej 33799

Vuk, Vili 34127
Vukadin, Hela 07830
Vukašinović, Dragomir 33867
Vukotić, Biljana 33851
Vuković, Prof. Radovan 07840
Vukovich, Franz 02277
Vulf, Galina Gerasimovna 32960, 32961, 32962
Vuorikoski, Timo 10084
Vuorinen, Pirjo 09594
Vusoniwailala, Kate 09409, 30174
Vuyk, Dr. K. 28908
Vydrina, Ljudmila Sergeevna 33448
Vykoukal, Dr. Jiří 08309
Vykydal, Vlastimil 08277
Vyskocil, Hubert 02983
Vysockij, Nikita Vladimirovič 33071
Vyvyan-Robinson, Richard 38265
Waage, Einy 30714
Waal, M. de 34188
Wachna, Pamela 06592
Wachs, Diane C. 44738
Wachsmund, Ulrike 16867
Wachten, Dr. Johannes 17057
Wachter, Dr. Markus 02408, 02409
Wacker, Ursel 20748
Wackerfuß, Winfried 17007
Wacs, Darin 46274
Wada, Kunibo 26790
Wade, Blake 43980, 44070
Wade, Dennis 00899
Wade, Don 47884
Wade, Dr. Edwin L. 43329
Wade, Hilary 38489, 38490
Wade, J. Blake 41514
Wade Thomas, Randall 43552
Wadensten, Hillevi 36349
Wadsley, Amanda 39079
Wadsworth, David H. 42513, 42514, 42515
Wächter, Gabriele 18048
Waechter, James 46863
Wäldchen, Günter 19988
Wälder, Manfred 18459
Wærdahl, Tove 30577
Wäre, Dr. Ritva 09531
Waern, Karl Erik 35793
Wäspe, Roland 37102
Wagemakers, C. 28850
Wageman, Patty 29309
Wagener, Danièle 27561, 27565, 27570
Wagensberg, Jorge 34560
Wagesreiter, Viktoria 03001
Waggener, Lynda 45544
Waghorne, N. 40335
Wagini, Dr. Susanne 18912
Wagner, Connie 47033
Wagner, Dieter 16716
Wagner, Eckard 19974
Wagner, Florence 45023
Wagner, Gerhard A. 16287
Wagner, Günther 19404
Wagner, Herbert 01850
Wagner, Hermann 01833
Wagner, Dr. Jens-Christian 19121
Wagner, Kay 47273
Wagner, Lynn 44433
Wagner, Maria 01713
Wagner, Patrice 41640
Wagner, René 19469
Wagner, Rita 18150
Wagner, Ruth 47591
Wagner, Dr. Siegfried 18980, 18981
Wagner, Thomas K. 43075
Wagner, Dr. Velten 16874
Wagner, Vivian 42411
Wagner-Gnan, Angela 19166
Wagoner, Ian 41104
Wagrodzki, Jerzy 32136
Wagstaff, Sheena 39787, 39788
Wahdan, Tracey 38765, 40447
Wahl, Hans-Rudolf 37360
Wahl, Johann 02792
Wahl, Sonja 42444
Wahle, Michael 16144
Wahlöö, Claes 36060
Wahlquist, Håkan 36240
Wahnsiedler, Angel 45694
Wain, Lisa 00957, 00958
Waintraub, Aron 22587
Waisbrot, Ann 45186
Waite, Dawn D. 42142
Wajima, Kunio 26262
Wakamatsu, Motoi 26969
Wake, David B. 41647
Wake, William 38821
Wakeling, Melissa 05063
Waker, William 47200
Wakitani, Masami 26804
Wakiyama, Yoshitaka 26175
Wal, Eva 16240
Walaszczyk, Anna 32218
Walaszczyk, Antoni 31618
Walberczyk, Jerzy 31551
Walburg, Dr. Reinhold 17048
Walch, Heribert 01813
Walch, Nicole 03275
Walch, Peter 41111
Walch, Timoth 48515
Wald, Albrecht 17010
Walde, Prof. Dr. Elisabeth 01768, 02075, 02219

Walden, Ian N. 38781
Waldherr, Johann 02405
Waldherr, Kaspar 18439
Waldkirch, Bernhard von 37386
Waldman, Glenys A. 46426
Waldmann, Fritz 37246
Waldmann-Glaser, Dr. Erich 02709
Waldmeier, Kurt 36666
Waldon, Arnold 46466
Waldren, Dr. William 34768
Waldron, Richard 46389
Walentowicz, T. 38537
Walgamott, Libby 46825
Walgenbach, H. 29752
Walgrave, René 03563
Waligurski, Carolyn M. 44177
Waligurski, Stephen S. 44177
Walk, Deborah 47453
Walk, Stephen G.W. 45932
Walkensteiner, Wolfgang 02126
Walker, Alexandra 40266
Walker, Anita 42911
Walker, Anne Noel 47964
Walker, Barry 44129
Walker, Bill 40377
Walker, Carol 40075
Walker, Catherine 39261
Walker, Celia 45613
Walker, Christopher 38395
Walker, Daniel 45833
Walker, David A. 39072
Walker, Dean 46442
Walker, Edwin G. 42831
Walker, Eleanor 06047
Walker, Gavin 40352
Walker, Gerald 47028
Walker, I. 40914
Walker, John 40964
Walker, June 44489
Walker, Kate 01561
Walker, Dr. K.J. 43581
Walker, Lauren 06755
Walker, Lulen 48358
Walker, Neil 40105
Walker, Nicola 39904
Walker, Pam 48719
Walker, Peter 38250
Walker, Rob 05040
Walker, Roslyn A. 48374
Walker, Sam 39580
Walker, Scott 45894, 45897
Walker, Sonia 41434
Walker, Stephen 40528, 48105
Walker, Tim 30180
Walker, William 45094
Walker Mecky, Debra 43832
Wall, Dora 05800
Wall, Gordon 43076
Wall, Kathleen 05536, 05537
Wallace, A. 06783
Wallace, Amanda 39892
Wallace, Anaret 34187
Wallace, Dr. C. 01546
Wallace, George 46027
Wallace, Hilt 06747
Wallace, I. 39520
Wallace, J. Don 45326
Wallace, James A. 45247
Wallace, James E. 43509
Wallace, Joseph 43858
Wallace, Judy 45247
Wallace, Lynda 30092
Wallace, Meghan 41184
Wallace, Mike 45375, 46355
Wallace, Pat 38636
Wallace, Dr. Patrick F. 22388, 22442, 22444, 22445
Wallace, Stephen R. 47045
Wallace, Teresa 42599
Wallace, Dr. Terry 48094
Wallace, William D. 48755, 48758
Wallach, Nancy 44416
Wallbrecht, Dr. Andreas 16361
Wallcraft, Wilma K. 05708
Waller, Bret 44216
Waller, Richard 46887
Waller, Susan R. 47219
Wallers-Bulot, Danielle 11309
Wallet, Marie 11025, 11026
Walley, G.P. 40111
Walling, Mary 45821
Wallis, Brian 45817
Wallis, Deborah L. 44788
Wallis, Jonathan 38716
Wallis, W.-C.K.H. 38997
Wallmann, Dr. Margarete 02117
Wallner, Sabine 02860
Wallner, Dr. Thomas 37184
Wallner-Bărbulescu, Luminiţa 32544
Walloschek, Arnold 19756
Wallwork, John 43522
Wallwork-Wright, Jan 38948
Walmsley, Frances 05957
Walser, Stefan 37270
Walseth, J. 08953
Walsh, Alice 46720
Walsh, Brian 22463
Walsh, David 46185
Walsh, Debbie 22400
Walsh, H. Ben 43719

Walsh, John 01484
Walsh, Larry 22508
Walsh, Mary 45516
Walsh, Nigel 39442
Walsh, Noa Martin 22394
Walsh, Pat 46838
Walsh, Paul 45393
Walsh-Piper, Kathleen 44746
Walsted, Anne-Lise 08921
Walt, Barbara 37125
Waltenberg, Horst 16763
Waltenspül, Walter 36450
Walter, A. 19173
Walter, Alfred 16622
Walter, Andreas 16178
Walter, Bernadette 37377
Walter, H. 20033
Walter, Katharina 02082
Walter, Max 02475
Walter, Michael 19968
Walter, Patricia 41591
Walter, Philippe 13152
Walter, Susanne 19076
Waltereit, Manfred 16846
Waltermire, Joan 46041
Walters, Cheryl 48000
Walters, Cliff 38257
Walters, John A. 47797
Walters, Margaret 48619
Walters, N. 34355
Walther, Alois 16698
Walther, Gerd 17166
Walther, Hubert 15321
Walther, Jim 41106
Walther Cuevas, Georgina 28091
Walton, Ann 43466
Walton, John 01005
Walton, Karin 38351, 38355, 38359
Walton, Les 40271
Waltoś, Prof. Dr. Stanisław 31722
Walty, J. 36766
Waltz, James 42098
Walujo, Dr. Ekoparoto 22087
Walz, Dr. Alfred 16297
Walz, Carol 45532
Walz, Glenn 06485
Walz, Jack 45532
Walzer, Herwig 02326
Wam, H. ten 29149
Wamers, Dr. Egon 17031
Wamser, G. 20145
Wamser, Prof. Dr. Ludwig 17449, 18827, 19007, 19360, 20493
Wamulungwe, Patrick Lisina 49018
Wan, Jamaluddin 27644
Wan, Norhiyati Ibrahim 27645
Wan, Robert 15346
Wan, Yusoff 27644
Wan Ahmad, Wan Ali Bin 27630
Wanachiwanawin, Prof. Darawan 37492
Wand-Seyer, Dr. Gabriele 17728, 17729
Wander, Evelyne 14169
Wandrei, Ellen A. 41583
Wandrooij, O.D. 29239
Wandschneider, Dr. Andrea 19332, 19337, 19340, 19341
Wang, Prof. Lianmao 07206
Wang, Mian Hou 07235
Wang, Ragnhild 30767
Wang, Xi Rong 07220
Wånge, Cecilia 35949
Waning, Alexander 29534
Wankel, James 05399
Wanner, Prof. Dr. E. 18261
Wanostrocht, C.A. 40446
Wappenschmidt, Dr. Kathrin 19643
Wappis, Erich 02127
Warburton, Stuart 39458, 39459
Warchałowski, Walerian 31782
Ward, Alberta 41359
Ward, Andrew 38661
Ward, Barry J. 44556
Ward, Barry K. 43006
Ward, David D. 38733
Ward, Esmé 39904
Ward, Joan 40744
Ward, Kathy 41539
Ward, Kimberley D. 43006
Ward, Dr. Lauck W. 45193
Ward, Mark 41448
Ward, Michael 39870
Ward, Mike 37973
Ward, Nancy 44354
Ward, Prof. Paul 37419
Ward, Ralph E. 43935
Ward, Robert W. 48490
Ward, Roger B. 48538
Ward, Scott 46787
Ward Grubb, Barbara 46394
Ward Povse, Sandra 47519
Ward Shannon, Dr. George 41558
Ward Shannon jr., George 46595
Warda, Rebecca M. 42285
Warden, Donald 47627
Warden, Greg 42755
Warden, P. 37454
Wardius, Janine 30412, 30413, 30414
Wardlaw, Alivia 44129
Wardle, Michelle 44445

Wardropper, Ian 42304, 45833
Ware, Katherine 46442
Ware, Mark 47670
Ware, Robert 41103
Warfel, Stephen G. 43925
Warger, Julia M. 47833
Wargo, Richard 41778
Warigai, Tsutomu 26224
Waring, Brian 39971
Waring, H.B.H. 39878
Waring, Jeff 46416
Warinsie Kankpeyeng, Benjamin 20790
Warkiewicz Laine, Christian K. 42315
Warming, Dagmar 08973
Warne, Pam 34214
Warner, Henry 39147
Warner, Jan 44818
Warner, Joanne 45788
Warner, John D. 47543
Warner, Judith 47500
Warner, Malcolm 43487, 45699
Warner, R. 38160
Warnes, Dr. Carl E. 45556
Warp, Harold G. 45376
Warren, David B. 44116, 44129
Warren, Eleanor 42429
Warren, Elizabeth 45756, 45798
Warren, Emma 39387
Warren, Harry 48593
Warren, Katherine V. 46923
Warren, Maggie 40188
Warren, Rebecca 42270
Warren, Sally 06122
Warrilow, Walt 38479
Warstler, Pasqua 43207
Wartenberg, Ute 45760
Warth, Werner 37320
Warther, David R. 42974
Wartke, Dr. Ralf-Bernhard 16114
Warton, Sue 40509
Warwick Thompson, Paul 45788
Warzecha, Newton M. 43723
Warzecha, Zygmunt 32021
Washbrook, Harry 05365
Washington jr, W. Curtis 42228
Washington Goyaud, Rolando 00369
Washizuka, Hiromitsu 26581
Waskowic, Lorraine 06177
Wass, Ann 46913
Wass, Janice 47737
Wasser, Larry 47171
Wasserman, Nadine 45741
Wassermann, Fred 45821
Wassing, A. 29779
Wassmann, Harry 41624
Wassmer, Edouard 36717
Wassnig, Gerhard 02221
Wat, Kathryn 41072
Watanabe, Hisashi 26533
Watanabe, Junko 26212
Watanabe, Kiriko 26969
Watanabe, Kousho 26704
Watanabe, Makoto 26190
Watanabe, Osamu 26817
Watanabe, Seiichiro 26096
Watanabe, Shinsuke 26873
Watanabe, Taeko 26497
Watanabe, Takao 26445
Watanabe, Yasuhiro 26894
Watanate, Akiyoshi 26880
Watari, Shizuko 26955
Watelet, Pierre 13257
Waterlow Oam, Nick 01352
Waterman, Amy E. 45796
Waters, Davis 43017
Waters, Deborah D. 45847
Waters, F. 40066
Waters, Martha 42518
Watkin, Alan 40939
Watkin, Jeffrey 39436
Watkin, Mel 47117
Watkins, Dr. David K. 44793
Watkins, Jonathan 38222
Watkins, Kathleen 40407
Watkins, Rod 45362
Watkinson, Patricia 43476
Watne, Eva 30976
Watson, Andy 42500
Watson, Bob 39095
Watson, Claudia 42803
Watson, Daryl 43593
Watson, Sir David 38346
Watson, Doreen 38149
Watson, Edwin W. 43535
Watson, Helen 40456
Watson, Iain 40036
Watson, Dr. Ian 40145
Watson, John 01486
Watson, Julian 39650
Watson, Julie 40038
Watson, Lisa 40266
Watson, Mark 38690
Watson, Maureen 40864
Watson, Maxine 45694
Watson, Philip 38214
Watson, Ronald 43490
Watson, Dr. Rubie 42049
Watson, Sara C. 43834
Watson, Scott 06682

Watson, Sheena 40283
Watson, Dr. Sheila 39123, 39124, 39125, 39127
Watson, Wendy 47694
Watson, Wendy M. 47693
Watson, William S. 38918
Watson-Armstrong, Francis 38073
Watt, David 38877
Watt, James C.Y. 45833
Watt, Michael 47978
Watt, Robert 04987
Watt, T. 38817, 39478, 39479
Watteck, Arno 02307
Wattenberg García, Eloisa 35621
Wattenmaker, Dr. Richard J. 48333
Watters, Jane 01507
Watterson, Norma 43072
Watteyne, Damien 03719, 03720, 03722, 03723
Watton, Graham C. 30226
Watton, Janet 46790
Watts, Kelly 44063
Watts, L. 01395
Watts, Martin 39281
Watts, Michael 42205
Watts, Pete 48781
Watts, Peter 01011, 01336, 01422, 01424, 01428, 01495, 01497, 01504, 01565, 01572
Watts, Steve 39483
Watts McKinney, Sylvia 41938, 46440
Waugh, Carmen 06913
Waurick, Dr. Götz 18606
Wawrzyk, Henryk 31833
Wawrzyniak, Andrzej 32090
Wawzonek, Donna 06299
Way, Angela 41683
Way, Catherine A. 44309
Way, Paul 38863
Way-Jones, M.F. 34250
Wayne, Cynthia 41447
Wayne, Kenneth 41981
Wcześny, Marek 31834
Weadick, Nathalie 22487
Weaner, Arthur 43661
Wear, Lisa 47219
Wearne, Richard B. 45642
Weatherby, Ken 05861
Weathers, Allen 45263
Weaver, Henry 05604
Weaver, John 41232
Weaver, Luella 45232
Weaver, Nigel 40367
Weaver, Pat 47181
Weaver, R. 39305
Weaver, Randall 41273
Weaver, Sarah 44478
Weaver, Susan 43992
Weaver, Suzanne 42751
Weaver, Vey O. 41050
Webb, Alan 38321
Webb, Belinda 01510
Webb, Eddie 46666
Webb, Heather 06117
Webb, Hugh 46636
Webb, Judy 46978
Webb, Keith 40788
Webb, Dr. S.D. 43581
Webb, Vaughan 43317
Webber, Barry 45962
Webber, Chris 39824
Webber, Eddie 00817
Webber, Maurie 40126
Webel, Sophie 13503, 13691
Weber 20044
Weber, Dr. Annette 17057
Weber, Brigitta 20766
Weber, C. Sylvia 18259, 19868
Weber, Cornelia 36544
Weber, C.S. 18258
Weber, Dr. Erich 20233
Weber, Francis J. 45400
Weber, Dr. Gerhard 18063
Weber, Dr. Gregor 18017
Weber, Dr. Hans Ruedi 37386
Weber, Heidi 37380
Weber, Heiko 18758
Weber, Jean 27583
Weber, Johanne 20119
Weber, John S. 47339
Weber, Karl 15667
Weber, Dr. Klaus 15916
Weber, K.R. 47436
Weber, Dr. Marion 07523
Weber, Michael 28773
Weber, Olaf 17005
Weber, Otto 19167
Weber, Dr. Peter 32549
Weber, Robin 06189
Weber, Stephan W. 01652
Weber, Ute 19221
Weber, Vera 41195
Weber, Warren 47367
Weber, Drs. W.I.M. 29956
Weber, Dr. Winfried 20207
Weber, Yvette 12802
Weber-Brosamer, Dr. Bernhard 16749
Weber-Lehmann, Dr. Cornelia 16196
Weber Soros, Dr. Susan 45771
Weberg, William 46707
Webersberger, Josef 02282
Webley, Dr. L. 34249

Webley, Dr. W. 34250
Webster, Barbara 42015
Webster, Harvey 42467
Webster, Robert 48020
Webster, Roger J. 38263
Webster, Susan 43813
Webster, Prof. William 01498
Wechner, Wilma 02082
Wechs, Thomas 15661
Wechsler, Jeffrey 45678
Weckbacher, Vernon 45017
Weckerle, Prof. Hans 17570
Weckström, Gunnar 10179
Weddegjerde, Per 30375
Weddle, Sam 44881
Weeda, K.A. 29234
Weedmark, Lillian 06462
Weekley, Carolyn 48624, 48625, 48626
Weekly, Nancy 41986
Weeks, Ross 47964
Weems, Marcia 48119
Weenink, G.J. 29541
Weerdt, G.A. de 29868
Wefers, Dr. Sabine 17953
Wegener-Welte, Kathrin 15597
Wegge, Aslak 30985
Wegmann, Dr. Peter 37333, 37337
Wegner, Gene 31302
Wegner, Hartmut 16177
Wegner, Karl-Hermann 18031
Wehgartner, Dr. Irma 20697
Wehling, Arno 04370
Wehmeyer, Egon 15596
Wehmeyer, Pete 41411
Wehrberger, Gerhard 02286
Wehrberger, Kurt 20261
Wehrle, Karl 19542
Weibel, Prof. Peter 01927, 18007
Weibezahn, Dr. Ingrid 16320
Weibull, Nina 36291
Weichselbaum, Dr. Hans 02539
Weichselbaum, Karl 02373
Weichselberger, Ingrid 02669
Weick, Wolfgang E. 16658, 16662
Weick-Krohn, Dr. Helga 17057
Weidel, Geraldine 44143
Weidemann, Dr. Friedegund 15981
Weidinger, Alfred 02830
Weidisch, Peter 15674
Weidl, Beverly 44098
Weidner, Marietta 18916
Weidner, Dr. Thomas 18880
Weidner, Timothy 43692
Weidner, William 46567
Weiermair, Prof. Peter 23104
Weigel, Jay 45722
Weigelt, Jürgen 16125
Weight, A. 39671
Weigl, Stephan 02228
Weigle, Petra 19151
Weiglin, Peter 41608
Weigt, Karin 16580
Weil, Benjamin E. 47339
Weil, Gilbert 10881
Weil, Dr. Mark S. 47140
Weil-Seigeot, Claude 11310
Weiland, Linde 17176
Weilepp, Bruce 47684
Weiler, Gerhard 20692, 20701
Weiler-Streichsbier, Dr. Doris 19256
Weilter, Theresia 02376
Weimert, Dr. Helmut 17682
Weinberg, Adam D. 41207
Weinberg, H. Barbara 45833
Weinberger, Prof. Gabriel 03032
Weinelt, Hannes 01947
Weinelt, Wendeline 17171
Weinert, Renate 15642
Weingärtner, Rudi 02195
Weingartner, Heinrich 02944
Weinhart, Dr. Martina 17071
Weinheber-Janota, Brigitte 02115
Weinheimer, Corinna 30941
Weinig, Prof. Dr. 20089
Weinke, Jane 48463
Weinland, Dr. Martina 16062
Weinmayr, Stefanje 18312
Weinmeister, Konstanze 17413
Weinshrott, William J. 43360
Weinstein, Michael 45796
Weintraub, Aviva 45821
Weinzapfel, Connie 45692
Weir, Margaret 39956
Weir, Margaret S. 47861
Weirauch, Annette 19406
Weisbach, Rainer 16584
Weisberg, Frank F. 44972
Weise, Sigrid 15920
Weiserová, Dr. Jana 08371, 08592
Weiskircher, Arrand 14782
Weisman, Billie Milam 44901
Weisman, Bruce 44476
Weiss, Alfred 02312
Weiß, Bernd 19384
Weiß, Berthold 01863
Weiss, Brigitte 16460
Weiss, Christian 18085
Weiß, E. 19790
Weiß, Ferdinand 01822

Weiß, Frank 19413
Weiss, Dr. Gabriele 02945
Weiss, Ján 33982
Weiss, Jeffrey 48373
Weiß, Johannes 01746
Weiss, Lois 47493
Weiss, Martin 43355
Weiss, Olga 42363
Weiss, Prof. Dr. Rainer-Maria 17545
Weiss, Sabine 20415
Weiss, Dr. Thomas 16581, 16582, 16583, 19263, 20641, 20642
Weiß, Dr. Ulrike 17597
Weissenbach, Peter 36475
Weißenböck, Jarmila 02963
Weissend, Patrick 41521
Weisser, Amy S. 41552
Weisser, Dr. Bernhard 16044
Weisser, Dr. Jürgen 17467
Weistengruber, Dr. Thekla 02241
Weit, Janina 16246
Weitzendorfer, Dr. Alfred 02207
Weitzer, Julia 02918
Weium, Frode 30754
Welander-Berggren, Elsebeth 35919
Welborn, Ann 48075
Welborn, Patricia 48765
Welch, Richard 43299
Welch, Robert M. 43578
Weldon, Eleanor 05878
Wellens, Luc 03180
Weller, Dennis P. 46775
Weller, Susan J. 45387
Wellicome, Lavinia 40912
Wellington, John P. 47469
Wellington, Judith 42229
Wellman, Lesley 43907
Wells, Edna 42914
Wells, Elizabeth 39717
Wells, Gerald 39797
Wells, Keith 46745
Wells, Kenneth D. 41855
Wells, Licia A. 47331
Wells, Nicole 45858
Wells, Penny 05511, 05512
Wells, Peter 43863
Wells, Stephen D. 43420
Wells, Trevor C. 27511
Wells-Cole, Anthony 39452
Wells Zaia, Kay 46039
Wellspeak, Charles 42767
Wellwood, Bridget 30235
Welsh, Caroline 41758
Welsh, Jane 42524
Welsh, Melissa 45578
Welsh, Susan 38544
Welter, Barbara 36485
Welter, Matt 43792
Welty, Claude 13212
Welu, James A. 48756, 48756
Welzig, Ingrid 19128
Wemhoff, Prof. Dr. Matthias 19338
Wemmlinger, Raymond 45812
Wemyss, Dallas 39391
Wendel, Candice 44236
Wendel, Michael G. 41717
Wendel, Siegfried 19704
Wendel, Vickie 41232
Wendl, Dr. Tobias 15847
Wendling, Britt 36149
Wendling, Pia 11985, 11986
Wendling, Urs 36881
Wendorf, Richard 41798
Wendt, Birgitta 36239
Wenger, Rhona 05532
Wenham, Julia 40879
Weniger, Prof. Dr. Gerd-C. 18725
Weninger, Gehard 02405
Wenn, Diane 06763
Wenn, Norbert 16383
Wennerholm jr., Roy 47090
Wentworth, Peggy 41494
Wenzel, Gundula 20491
Weon-Kettenhofen, Hae-Yon 16250
Wepfer, Dr. Hans-Ulrich 36838
Wepler, Bill 44224
Werd, Drs. Guido de 18107, 18108
Werf, Hans van der 14839
Werkmäster, Daniel 36123
Werkmäster, Lisskulla 35882
Wern, Christine 17057
Werneburg, Dr. Ralf 19799
Wernecke, Dr. Ingrid 19463
Werner, Dr. Anne-Marie 19727
Werner, Bernd 17518, 17520
Werner, Constanze 19168
Werner, Dietrich 47007
Werner, Dr. Edwin 17513, 17517
Werner, Harald 01677
Werner, Heinz 17740
Werner, Jane 46524
Werner, Dr. Sigrid 19912
Werner, Dr. Winfried 18893
Wernevik, Lena 36128
Werneyer, Rita 19156
Wernicke, Prof. Dr. Joachim 19311, 19313, 19315
Wernz-Kaiser, Heike 15703
Werring, Ole A. 30732
Wert, Nancy L. 45347

Werth, Linda 48446
Wertkin, Gerard C. 45756, 45798
Wertz, Dinyelle 46398
Wéry, Benoît 03814
Weschenfelder, Dr. Klaus 16483, 19628
Wescoat, Dr. Bonna D. 41352
Wesenberg, Dr. Angelika 15912
Wesler, Kit W. 48616
Wesney, Russell 30222
Wessel, Marilyn F. 41858
Wessel, Dr. Ruth 16735, 16736
Wesseler, Jürgen 16341
Wessels, E.M. 34193
Wessels, Reinhard 17619
West, Andrew 30181
West, Barbara 44241
West, Chris 38352
West, Gerald C. 42383
West, J. Martin 44770
West, J. Thomas 05177
West, Janis 45086
West, Jeff 42757
West, Jenny 30173
West, Pat 38081
West, Dr. Patricia 44483
West, Penelope A. 44770
West, Richard 47045
West, Richard V. 47534
West, Thomas 43862
West, W. Richard 45852
Westbrook, Nicholas 48005
Westbrook, T.G. 38783, 40931
Westby, Alan 46204
Westenhuber, Karl-Heinz 19524
Wester la Torre, Carlos 31195
Westerbeck, Colin 42304
Westerkamp, P.W. 29084
Westerlund, Jens 09072
Westermann-Angerhausen, Prof. Dr. Hiltrud 18163
Westers, Drs. Abraham 29618
Westfall, Deborah 41733
Westfehling, Dr. Uwe 18168
Westheider, Dr. Rolf 17460
Westhoff, Julia 16317
Westholm, Gun 36413
Westling, Stefan 36019
Westlund, Frances 05835
Westmacott, Jean 43588
Westman, Anne 35820
Westmoreland, Debra 45504
Westmorland, Lamont 44898
Westoby, Carolyn 05355
Weston, Catherine 38046
Weston, D.W.V. 38488
Weston, E. 39906
Weston, Gill 39930
Weston-Lewis, Aidan 38898
Westphal, Jean 12217
Westphal, Dr. Martin 19570
Westphal, Ursula 16575
Westra, J.F. 28838
Westrop, Dr. S. 45976
Westwood, Ros. 38427
Wetenhall, Dr. John 45613
Wetenhall, John 47453
Wetherell, Virginia 43315
Wetherington, Mark V. 44965
Wetmore, Shirley 48094
Wettengl, Dr. Kurt 17055
Wetter, Ellen de 06174
Wetterau, G. 43443
Wetton, Allan 00747
Wettre, Håkan 35912
Wetzel, Brigitte 17410
Wetzel, Dietrich 19412
Wetzel, Elaine 41777
Wetzel, James K. 42865
Wetzel, Walter 36597
Wetzstein, Jim 45562
Weydemann, Ingrid 02350
Weyerhaeuser, Charles A. 43028
Weyers, E. 34335
Weygandt, Virginia 47756
Whaley, Martha 44347
Whallon, Robert 41219
Whang, Prof. Won-Koo 27291
Whatmoor, D.J. 40140
Wheary, Dale C. 46882
Wheatcroft, F.B. 38501
Wheaton, R. 01411
Wheeldon, Jenny 41966
Wheeler, Karla 41615
Wheeler, Lawrence J. 46775
Wheeler, Mary 44412
Wheeler, Matthew 38169
Wheeler, Robert K.L. 45335
Wheelock, Arthur 48373
Whelan, Mary C. 46089
Wheldon, G.H. 39331
Wheltle, Bruce 41258
Whetstone, Lucy 40037
Whisman, Evelyn 46756
Whissell, Raymond 06301
Whistance, John 40873
White, A.C. 40742
White, Adam 37947, 39452
White, Babs 42782
White, Barbara 47615
White, Betsy K. 41055

White, Blair H. 44344
White, Courtney 45873
White, C.S. 40258
White, David 06636, 39791, 44803
White, Diane 43379
White, Donald 46460
White, Donna 05520
White, Donny 05831
White, Elisa 45753
White, Gail W. 48022
White, Sir George 39612, 39687
White, James J. 46518
White, Joe L. 44479
White, Julia 44079, 48675
White, Kathryn 38127
White, Kristy 42634
White, Marcelle 42766
White, Mark 47813
White, Mary 40511
White, Matthew 45989, 45990
White, Maylon 48250
White, Matthew 41570
White, Richard S. 48090
White, Dr. Sally 40937
White, Tim 41646
White, Timothy J. 42298
White, Turner 44400
White, Warren O. 43103
Whitehead, F. 38432
Whitehead, J.K. 40328
Whitehouse, Adrienne 39206
Whitehouse, C.M. 38216
Whitehouse, David B. 42636, 42637
Whiteley, Jim 44695
Whiteman, Rowland 43697
Whiter, Robert 01006
Whitey, Matthew 39442
Whitfield, Carol 05782
Whiting, Dr. Cliff 30311
Whitley, Ann Marshall 47902
Whitlock, Pamela 01055
Whitlow, Paula 06043
Whitmal, Angela M. 41080
Whitman-Grice, Lisa 46857
Whitmore, Damien 39795
Whitmore, Dennis 41475
Whitney, Richard 42942
Whitt, Teresa C. 47688
Whittaker, Dr. J. 38515
Whittall, Dafydd 39559
Whitten, Norman 48164
Whittington, Michael 42243
Whitworth, Kent 44517
Whitworth, Peggy 42156
Whorlow, David 39173
Whyel, Rosalie 41599
Whyte, Alan 06749
Whyte, Robert A. 47327
Wiatr, Al 42190
Wiberg, Ewa 36294
Wible, Carole 44061
Wiblé, François 36928
Wible, Dr. John R. 46511
Wichert-Meissner, Dr. Susanne 16241
Wichrowski, Zbigniew 31730, 31731
Wick, Peter 36908
Wick, Susan B. 48136
Wick Reaves, Wendy 48382
Wickenden, N.P. 38537
Wickers, Tine 08950
Wickham, Ann 39136
Wickham, W.C. 43908
Wicklund, Doug 43261
Wickman, Viktor 27717
Wickramasinghe, Dr. Nanda 35747, 35751
Wicks, Alice 47855
Wicks, Dr. Fred 06607
Wicks, Phyllis 48716
Wicks, Stephen C. 44520
Widbom, Mats 36277
Widdowson, Prof. J.D.A. 40491
Widemann, Norbert 17105
Widén, Britt-Marie 35912
Widener, George D. 46450
Widenheim, Cecilia 36262
Widjeskog, Susanna 09954
Widmann, Dr. Marion 16246
Widschwendter, Martin 01755
Widulin, Navena 15918
Wiebe, Charles M. 47574
Wiebe, Dave 44024
Wiebel, Dr. Christiane 16483
Wiechert, Ralph D. 47138
Wiechmann, Dr. A.H.C.A. 29521
Wieczorek, Prof. Dr. Alfried 18615
Wieczorek, Jan 31912
Wied, Fürst zu 19719
Wied, Dr. Alexander 02918
Wied, M. Prinz zu 19719
Wiedemann, Dr. Konrad 18019
Wiedemann, Wilfried 18496
Wiedenhofer, Dr. Josef 02281
Wieg, Cornelia 17521
Wiegand, Dawn Michelle 43142
Wiegand, Gesine 17355
Wiegand, Otto 18702
Wiegand, Tanya 05127
Wiegand, Winfried 18685, 18686, 18688
Wiegmann, Dr. Karlheinz 18130

Wiehager, Dr. Renate 15936
Wiehart, Michael 02946
Wiehl, Wolfgang 18361
Wieklander, Dan 48326
Wielek, Jan 31762
Wiell, Stine 08849
Wiemann, Dr. Elsbeth 20106
Wiemer, Regine 18488
Wienand, Paul 20442
Wiene, Inger 08933
Wienecke, Joachim 17715
Wieninger, Johannes 02929
Wiens, Dr. John J. 46511
Wier, Nan 46169
Wier, Tom 47160
Wierecky, Norbert 17566
Wiermann, Susanne 15621
Wierzbicka, Alina 31813
Wierzbowska, Ilona 31515
Wiese, Dr. André 36495
Wiese, Joyce 48017
Wiese, Kerstin 18389
Wiese, Larry 45272
Wiese, Prof. Dr. Rolf 18782, 19648
Wiese, Dr. Rüdiger 20463
Wiese, Sharon A. 41270
Wiese, Dr. Stephan von 16738
Wiese, Dr. W. 19489
Wieseman, Betsy 42400
Wiesen, Richard A. 41983
Wiesenhofer, Franz 02463, 02465
Wiesenmüller, H. 20113
Wieser, Gertrud 03001
Wiesmann-Emmerling, Adelheid 16541
Wiesner, Tomáš 08703
Wietholt, Charlotte 29324
Wiethorn, Hans 20014
Wieting, Margaret 44246
Wiewelhove, Dr. Hildegard 16157
Wiget, Dr. Josef 37149, 37151
Wiggins, Denise 45073
Wigh, Leif 36262
Wight, Anthony 42329
Wight, David 44176
Wigmore, John R. 06715
Wijesooriya, Bandusena 35742
Wijn, Drs. J.J.A. 29829
Wikström, Anne-Maj 10103
Wikström-Haugen, Inger 35915
Wilcox, Bill 48514
Wilcox, Dr. David R. 43329
Wilcox, John 42617
Wilcox, Mike 43093
Wilcox, Richard 45168
Wilcox, Scott 45699
Wilcox, Susan 43328
Wilcox, Thomas R. 41522
Wilcox, Tim 39892
Wilczak, Susan 47102
Wilczek jun., Alexander Graf 02712
Wild, Jane 06122
Wild, Maxine F. 01015
Wild, Norbert 37397
Wildberger, Anne-Käthi 36495
Wilde, Cathleen 46579
Wilde, Dr. Eliane de 03300
Wilde, Kevan A. 30281
Wilde, Dr. Manfred 16564, 16565
Wildeman, G.J.D. 28888
Wilder, Cecile 46789
Wilder, Jacalin W. 41929, 41930
Wilder, Sofie 03165
Wildes, Deborah 45357
Wildgans, Ilse 02308
Wildgust, D. 40221
Wildgust, Patrick 38652
Wildhagen, Harald 17650
Wildman, Janet 39103
Wildman, S.G. 39418
Wildung, Prof. Dr. Dietrich 15908
Wilekans, Martine 29846
Wiles, Stephanie 45313
Wiley, E.O. 44685
Wiley, Florence 42958
Wiley, John 05854, 40927
Wilezek, Alexander 02287
Wilfong, Terry 41218
Wilhelm, Ada 42573
Wilhelm, Angelika 20720, 20722
Wilhelm, Elliot 42924
Wilhelm, Franz 16793
Wilhelm, Martin 01846
Wilhelm, Robert 43969
Wilhelmer, Erika 15774
Wilhelmer, Hans-Sieghart 01674
Wilhelmson, Pia 09799
Wilhelmy, Dr. W. 18598
Wilhite, Janet 42745
Wilk, Zbigniew 31584
Wilke, Erich 20600
Wilkens, Dr. Barbara 24228
Wilkens, Prof. Dr. Horst 17573
Wilker, Klaus-J. 20194
Wilkes, Regi 46657
Wilkes, Woody 43412
Wilkie, Jo-Anne 45524
Wilkins, Prof. David G. 46529
Wilkins, Margaret 38990
Wilkinson, D.J. 39566

Wilkinson, MaryAnn 42924
Wilkinson, Patty 41759
Wilks, John 38697
Will, Heinz 17474
Willander, Dr. Alfred 02521
Willard, David 43635
Willburger, Dr. Nina 20115
Willeboordse, A. 29836
Willeboordse, A.C.J. 28797
Willeboordse, Arco 29837
Willems, Alfons 03838
Willems, Carmen 03781
Willems, Jean 03614
Willemsen, M. 29079
Willenbrink, Brunhilde 16645
Willer, Thérèse 14808
Willers, Prof. Dietrich 36539
Willers, Dr. Johannes 19139
Willesme, Jean-Pierre 13479
Williams, Alice 43654, 44762
Williams, Barb 46825
Williams, Bill 44971
Williams, Bob 44007
Williams, Clay 44285
Williams, Dr. D. 39586
Williams, David 39526
Williams, Debby 47588
Williams, Don 45751
Williams, Dorothy 43459
Williams, Ed 41450, 43155
Williams, Edna 45111
Williams, Eric K. 45956
Williams, Fred 42623
Williams, Gareth H. 38433
Williams, Dr. George 48551
Williams, Gloria 46302
Williams, Greg 47278, 47289, 47300
Williams, Henry G. 41087
Williams, Hilary 39965, 40939
Williams, I.B. 38061, 40949
Williams, Janice C. 46776
Williams, Jay 42563
Williams, Jenny 39225
Williams, Jimmy 46666
Williams, Judy 30303
Williams, Karen 35356, 30257
Williams, Kathy 43457
Williams, Kay P. 45667
Williams, Dr. Keith 48507
Williams, Kevin 45387
Williams, Laura 39657
Williams, Linda 40362
Williams, Lisa 45014
Williams, Dr. Lorraine 48057
Williams, Lyle 47255
Williams, M. 41319
Williams, Mary-Louise 01493
Williams, Michael 40104, 40108, 40112
Williams, Dr. Michael 42467
Williams, Morag 38786
Williams, Dr. N.H. 43581
Williams, Pamela 41846
Williams, Paul 47233
Williams, Peter J. 01600
Williams, Richard 39216
Williams, Robert J. 47577
Williams, Stacy 47229
Williams, Stephen 39681
Williams, Stephen R. 46597
Williams, Teri 41329, 41356
Williams, Thomas 45133
Williams, Tommy 44868
Williams, Victoria 39184, 39185
Williams-Davies, John 40395
Williamson, Armand J. 41947
Williamson, Eleanor 47765
Williamson, J. Reid 44220
Williamson, Jan 47440
Williamson, Jane 43316
Williamson, Mary 42137
Williamson, Paul 39795
Williamson, Roberta 43334
Willis, Carol 45870
Willis, James 41574
Willis, Dr. Jeff 48734
Willis, Kelly B. 44736
Willis, Leanne 01451
Willis, Michael 46585
Willis, Pamela 39722
Willis, Patricia 39581
Willis, Robert 42744
Willis, William 46687
Willisch, Susanne 18842
Willits, Mary Lou 43771
Willmann, Prof. Dr. R. 17343
Willmer, Prof. P.G. 40380
Willmitch, Thomas R. 41759
Willmont, Joanne 44730
Willms, Dr. Christoph 17031
Willms, Karl 16345
Willomitzer, Gerry 06793
Willoughby, Alan 45486
Willoughby, Brenda 42778
Willoughby, Sue 46688
Willour, Clint 43608
Willow, Hai Chang 45783
Wills, Carol 47109
Willscheid, Bernd 19085
Wilmes, Dr. Ulrich 18161

Wilmot, Patricia J. 43948
Wilmot, Robert 38888
Wilms, Kurt 15604
Wilner Stack, Trudy 48083
Wilpert, Dr. Clara B. 36508
Wilsdon, D.E. 01467
Wilsey, Bart 43299
Wilson, A. 40032
Wilson, Dr. A. 40574
Wilson, Alan 01459
Wilson, Dr. Alan 38033, 38034
Wilson, Amy 43170
Wilson, Arnold 38111
Wilson, Audrey 05794
Wilson, B. 40638
Wilson, Beth 42021
Wilson, Carol 44061
Wilson, Chris 22393, 37928, 39537, 48668
Wilson, Christine 38681, 38683
Wilson, Clifford 41288
Wilson, Courtney B. 41450
Wilson, Dale 43107
Wilson, Dan 43770
Wilson, Diane 41592
Wilson, Dorothy 38224
Wilson, Eric 40488
Wilson, Floyd S. 42237
Wilson, Gill 40808
Wilson, Gillian 40302, 44913
Wilson, Gordon 47067
Wilson, Gordon J. 47066
Wilson, H. 38285
Wilson, I.A. 38080
Wilson, Inge 05603
Wilson, J. Keith 44921
Wilson, Jane 46230
Wilson, Jay 48798
Wilson, Jerry 42797
Wilson, Jim 43894
Wilson, John 38160, 44606
Wilson, Karen L. 42355
Wilson, Kay 43841
Wilson, Keri 39073
Wilson, Kevin 01526
Wilson, Dr. L. 46161
Wilson, Lamar 47595
Wilson, Lesley 38551
Wilson, Marc F. 44397, 44404
Wilson, Mark 29309
Wilson, Michael 39729
Wilson, Nancy 44997
Wilson, Peter 39787, 39788
Wilson, Prof. R.J.A. 40113
Wilson, Rob 46819
Wilson, Robert C. 47838
Wilson, Robin 40196
Wilson, Dr. Rodney 30104
Wilson, Roger N. 45943
Wilson, Roy 40205
Wilson, Sophia 38544
Wilson, Steven 43936
Wilson, Tom 48704
Wilson, Wayne 05650, 05653
Wilson, William 39857
Wilson Davine, Blossom 46710
Wilson Jenkins, Kay 43840
Wilson-McKee, Marie 42300
Wilsony, Thomas A. 47427
Wilsterman, James 43104
Wiltfang, Helga 19112
Wiltzius, Ruth 46365
Wiluś, Bogusława 31872
Wilusz, Mike 47826
Wilz, Mick 41958
Wimberger, Dr. Peter 47919
Wimmer, Franz 02423
Wimpress, Kate 38005
Wimsett, Brian 38763
Win, U Kyaw 28751
Winans, Cathie 47578
Winbladh, Marie-Louise 36259
Winch, Barbara 47696
Winchell, Jane 47198
Winchester, Dr. Judi A. 42510
Wincke, Claus-Jürgen 15576
Wind, D.A. 29804
Winders, Dr. Bruce 47243
Windham, Michael 47235
Winding, Dr. Norbert 02545
Windl, Dr. Helmut 01685, 02733
Windle, Ann S. 45059
Windrum, Robert 06499
Windsor, Deirdre 44982
Windsor, Noel 00799
Wine, Dr. Humphrey 39729
Winegrad, Dr. Dilys V. 46391
Wines, Claudia 43146
Winey, Michael J. 42106
Wingate, Lloyd R. 34295, 34296
Wingfield, Carolyn 40368
Wingo, Calvin 43219
Winkelmeyer, Iris 18918
Winklbauer, Andrea 02948
Winkler, Anke 17299
Winkler, Dr. G. 01806
Winkler, Gerhard 01697
Winkler, Dr. Gerhard 01809
Winkler, Howard 41257
Winkler, J. 45328

Winkler, Dr. Kurt 15982, 16040, 16050, 16060, 16063, 16065, 16066, 16068, 16069, 16072, 16104
Winkler, Paul 44119
Winkler, Dr. Raffael 36514
Winkler, Reinhard 20379
Winkler, Steffen 17299
Winkler, Susanne 03001
Winkler, Ursula 18059
Winkler-Hermaden, Burkhardt 02097
Winkler Prins, Dr. C.F. 29522
Winkworth, David R. 38604
Winn, Allan 40840
Winnekes, Dr. Katharina 18135
Winnicki, Tomasz 32063
Winnicott, Caroline 40147
Winning, Fiona 01410
Winnink, Dr. G.J.G. 29058
Winrerborham, Nick 39455
Winslow, Bruce B. 45321
Wint, Dennis M. 46411
Winteler, Florence 36439
Winter, Amy 43353
Winter, Dr. B. 05150
Winter, C. 30147
Winter, Emil 17750
Winter, Gerhard 17641
Winter, Dr. Heike 17048
Winter, Dr. Heinz 02918
Winter, Hilda 39833
Winter, Joan G. 00860
Winter, Kevin 43258
Winter, Małgorzata 31514
Winter, Petra 16117
Winter-Berger, Robert 45812
Winterbotham, N. 39440
Winterbotham, Nick 37947, 39442, 39447, 39452
Winterhalter, Greg 41630
Winterick, Douglas E. 42004
Winters, Laurie 45366
Wintersteen Parmenter, Marian 47307
Wintgens, Dr. D. 29526
Wintz, Klaudius 02161
Winzeler, Marius 17323, 17324
Winzen, Dr. Matthias 15790
Winzingerode, Margit Freifrau von 19439
Wiotte-Franz, Claudia 19729
Wippermann, Hartmut 18698
Wippert, Bernd 18239
Wipplinger, Hans-Peter 19356
Wirenfeldt Asmussen, Marianne 09049
Wirnsberger, Karlheinz 01932
Wirsperger, Dr. Peter 02286
Wirtanen, Lyle 42665
Wirth, Dr. Klaus 18615
Wirth, Peter 47431
Wirth, Prof. Dr. Volkmar 18003
Wirthgen, G. 18399
Wirz, Arno 15820
Wirz, Charles 36749
Wise, Ann 40937
Wise, Carol 44382
Wise, Philip 38608
Wise, Raymond 39729
Wise, Dr. Stephen R. 46296
Wise, Tess 45078
Wise, Theodore F. 43396
Wiséhn, Ian 36251
Wiseman, Christopher 44361, 44363
Wiseman, William 48568
Wishart, E. 01106
Wismar, Franz Werner von 19567
Wismeijer, P.J. 29174
Wismer, Beat 36424
Wisowaty, Elaine 44831
Wißkirchen, Dr. Hans 18534, 18535
Wissler, Richard 42586
Wissler-Thomas, Carrie 43922
Wistar, Caroline 46422
Wistoft, Birgitte 08947
Wisuri, Marlene 42502
Wit, B.H. de 28999
Wit, Prof. Dr. G.W. de 29768
Witcherly, Zak 48589
Witcox, David E. 45959
Witenstein, Michael 44859
Withnell, J.H. 05366
Withycombe, C. 38454
Witkofsky, Adrien 43831
Witmer, Linda F. 42104
Witschey, Walter R.T. 46886, 46894
Witschi, Heinz 36819
Witschi, Dr. Peter 36802
Witt, David 47950
Witt-Dörring, Dr. Christian 02889
Witt-Dörring, Christian 02929
Witte, Amy 41974
Witte, David 47641
Witte, Hubert De 03251
Witte de Haelen, Didier de 03466
Wittenbauer, Christine 18457
Wittendorfer, Dr. Frank 18906
Witter, Thomas 18115
Wittig, Peer 15495
Wittington, Dr. Stephen 48700
Wittke, Norbert 17693
Wittkopp, Gregory M. 41738
Wittmann, Dr. Helmut 02545
Wittmer, Heike 19401

Wittmer, Marcilene 42628
Wittstock, Dr. Jürgen 18629
Witty, Anne 41522
Witty, Robert M. 47278, 47289, 47296, 47300
Witzbauer, Dr. Harald 02549
Witzleben, Alexander von 17939
Witzmann, Nora 02960
Witzmann, Dr. Reingard 03001
Wlattnig, Robert 01783, 02127, 02769
Włodarczyk, Tadeusz 32185
Wodiunig, Tina 37400
Woehl, Betty 47508
Wöhrer, Hannes 01696
Wöhrer, Josef 02277
Woelfl-Graff, Elisabeth 03001
Woelk, Dr. Moritz 16709
Wörlen, Hanns Egon 19356
Woertman, Rick 28841
Wörtz, Walter 18053, 18997, 19640
Wörz, Dr. Arno 20105
Wöß, Gerhard 02751
Woestenburg, K. 29712
Wognum, Nick 43002
Wojciechowski, Jerzy 31654
Wojciechowski, Zbigniew 31585
Wójcik, Adam 32039
Wojewoda, Maciej 31987
Wojtowicz, Wit Karol 31748
Wojtusiak, Prof. Janusz 31723
Wojtysiak, Władysława 31786, 31789
Wolanin, Dr. Barbara A. 48399
Wolbert, Dr. Klaus 16547, 16549
Wolde, H.B. ten 29466
Wolden, Arnold 47470
Wolenitz, Dorit 22732
Wolf, Alexandra 02736
Wolf, Dr. Barbara 15549
Wolf, Dr. Beate 20106
Wolf, Connie 47323
Wolf, Dieter 16437
Wolf, Dr. Helmut 15544, 18257
Wolf, Prof. Dr. Jörn Henning 18077
Wolf, Martha Leigh 46701
Wolf, Maurice de 03673
Wolf, Patricia B. 41197
Wolf, Reinmar 02312
Wolf, René 28852
Wolf, Sabine de 03146
Wolf, Sara 42243
Wolf, Sarah 46960
Wolf, Sylvia 42304, 45886
Wolf, Vicki 47297
Wolf, Werner 01926
Wolfe, Adam 01049
Wolfe, Dr. Cheri L. 43483
Wolfe, Douglas 45271
Wolfe, L. 05981
Wolfe, Sara 45774
Wolfe, Susan 43691
Wolfe, Townsend 44822
Wolfensberger, Dr. Rolf 36546
Wolfer, Johannes 01766
Wolfer, Dr. Martin 01766
Wolff, Martha 42304
Wolff, Dr. Tobias 16337
Wolff, W. 18367
Wolford, Craig 42441
Wolfová, Dr. Eva 08609
Wolfs, R. 29759
Wolfschlag, Robert 45057
Wolfson, R.D. 29594
Woliung, Dorothy 41600
Wolkow, Gary 42818
Woll, Gunda 20237, 20238, 20239
Wollan, Alexa 05628
Wollert, Christian 15915
Wolleswinkel, E.J. 29727
Wollkopf, Peter 18206
Wollmann, Dr. Klaus 19339
Wollner, Dr. Bernd 18727
Wołodko, Wiesław 31574
Wolpers, Emily G. 46586
Wolsdorff, Dr. Christian 15916
Wolsk, Nancy 44744
Wolter, Bernd 19539
Wolters, Dr. Christof 16006
Wolters, R. 29029
Wolters, Prof. Dr. Reinhard 20230
Wolters, Susan 46954
Wolterstorff, Robert 46628
Wolthoorn, Dr. R. 29526
Woltman, Bob 41099
Wolz, Robert J. 44466
Wolzogen, Wolf von 17055
Womack, Gayle 47368
Wombell, Paul 39744
Wong, Allison 44073, 44074
Wong, Carly 39904
Wong, Michele 45809
Wong, S.J. 05847
Wong-Uparaj, Acharn Damrong 37479
Wonisch-Langenfelder, Dr. Renate 02551, 02552
Wood, Brian 05124
Wood, Bryen 38421
Wood, Carolyn 42196
Wood, Charles A. 46753
Wood, David 42598
Wood, Dr. Donald A. 41706
Wood, Edward 43669

Wood, Elaine 42240
Wood, H. 40607
Wood, James N. 42304
Wood, Jeff 45324
Wood, Jeremy 39716
Wood, Katherine 38610
Wood, Kaye 00807
Wood, Lydia 42546
Wood, Mara-Helen 40043
Wood, Margaret 46365
Wood, Margaret K. 43732
Wood, Marion 38687
Wood, Nancy 01387
Wood, P. 38522
Wood, Ronald M. 44995
Wood, Vicki 39241
Wood, Virginia 48225
Wood, Willis 48485
Wood, Wilma 05747
Woodage, Claire 38711
Woodcock, Vivi 46382
Woodings, David J. 30186
Woodrey, Mark 44281
Woodrow, James 38140
Woods, Christine 39904
Woods, Claude N. 43979
Woods, Dana V. 46970
Woods, James C. 48124
Woods, Jean 43867
Woods, John S. 45967
Woods, Margaret M. 41858
Woods, Mark H. 45311
Woods, Pearley 43345
Woods, Trudy 44880
Woods, William 43240
Woodson, Shirley 42931
Woodson, Yoko 47308
Woodward, Charles J. 38686
Woodward, Christopher 38115
Woodward, Geoff 40769
Woodward, Hiram 41489
Woodward, John 38289
Woodward, Mac 44176
Woodward, Martin 38162
Woodward, Peter 38748
Woodward, Richard 46891
Woodward, Robert F. 46889
Woodward, Roland H. 48517
Woody Cywink, Linda 47421
Woof, Dr. Robert 39114
Woog, Dr. Friederike 20105
Woolcott, Isabelle S. 42664
Woolf, Derrick 40010
Woolfall, Steve 38552
Woolliscroft, Pam 40611
Woolmore, J.D. 38566
Woolrich, Gill 40489
Woolsey, Sam 42762
Woosley, Anne 47969
Woosley, Dr. Anne I. 42986
Wooten, Jerry 47705
Wootton, James E. 42246
Worcester, Mike 42516
Word, Levi 41851
Worden, Gretchen 46432
Worden, John 46920
Worden, Pamela 41830
Workington, Dawn 40266
Workman, David A. 48279
Workman, Robert 43480
Workmann, Tom 44381
Worm, Dr. Heinz-Lothar 18478
Wormald, M. 01190
Worn, Ethel 42729
Worschech, Kathrin 15451
Worschech, Thomas 17036
Worsdale, Godfrey 39948
Worswick, Clark 47198
Worth, Claudia R. 48580
Worth, Cyril 44058
Worth, Tim 06822, 06840
Worthen, Amy N. 42905
Worthen jr., William B. 44824
Worthington, Gary 46548
Worton, Graham 38782
Worton, James 47132
Worts, Martin 30537
Wotovic, Audrey 11717
Woycicki, Dr. Kazimierz 18396
Woyda, Stefan 31918
Woytowicz, Barbara 45817
Wpadhyays, Dr. Chandrakant B. 21682
Wradzidlo, Dr. Isolde 16159
Wragg, Gary 38102
Wray, JaLayne 48607
Wrębiak, Celestyn 31484
Wretemark, Mia 36194
Wrey, Dr. James D. 46339
Wright, Amina 38115
Wright, Anthony 30124
Wright, Belinda 00863
Wright, David M. 48724
Wright, Ethan 44225
Wright, George 38999
Wright, Henry T. 41219
Wright, Joanne 40105
Wright, John 44025
Wright, Kevin 46910
Wright, Lesley 43840

Wright, Lynne 04964
Wright, M. 40437
Wright, Margot 37940
Wright, Mavis 48523
Wright, Michael 44285
Wright, Nigel 38574
Wright, Raymond 48478
Wright, Rita 30097
Wright, Dr. Robin K. 47529
Wright, Dr. S. 40111
Wright, Simon 00841
Wright, Steven J. 46399
Wright, Vicki C. 43025
Wright Millard, Elizabeth 47117
Wright-Parsons, Ann 42854
Wrigley, John 00878
Wrobel, Horst 17286
Wróbel, Leszek 31907
Wróblewska-Straus, Hanna 32096, 32141
Wróblewski, Jerzy 31868
Wroczyńska, Ewa Maria 32061
Wroz, Winfried 18045
Wu, Cheng-Shang 07349
Wu, Chu Pang 07165
Wu, Dang Wei 07231
Wu, Hongzhou 07217
Wu, Hung Yuen 07043
Wu, Ke Shun 07244
Wu, Prof. Shi-Kuei 41837
Wu, Dr. Shun-Chi 15945
Wudel, Tom 45413
Wünsche, Prof. Dr. Raimund 18911
Würgler, Andreas 36934
Würmli, Dr. M. 20240
Würsch, Paul 37144
Würthner, Robert 02088
Würzelberger, Jörg 02745
Wüst, Léonard 37225
Wüthrich, Dr. Lucas 37048
Wulf, Karin 16224
Wulf, Rüdiger 16662
Wulkan, Reba 45887, 45887
Wunderer, Dr. Hansjörg 19528
Wunderlin, Dominik 36508
Wunsch, G. 17018
Wurda, Andreas 18577, 18578
Wurfel, Max 01367, 01368, 01369
Wurmfeld, Sanford 45816
Wurster, F. 19391
Wurzer, Günther 02127
Wurzinger, Erika 01980
Wustrack, Dr. Michael K. 17030
Wuthenau von Pietsch, Carlota von 28457
Wyatt, Frederica 44366
Wyatt, Mary Pat 44370
Wyatt, Shannon 46882
Wyatt, Steve 45921
Wyckoff, Dr. D. 45976
Wyczółkowski, Mariusz 31655
Wydler, Henry 36918
Wye, Deborah 44869
Wykerslooth, Baron E. de 03238
Wyld, Lesley 39920
Wyldster, Martin 39729
Wylie, Charles 42751
Wyman, Devik 41606
Wyman, James 41324, 43587
Wymbs, Norm 42953
Wijnandts, Dr. H. 29509
Wynn, Rachel 46612
Wynne, M.V 38571
Wynnemer, Donald 48325
Wyrsch, Dr. Jürg 37296
Wyse Jackson, Dr. Patrick N. 22428
Wysk, Susan C. 47841
Wyss, Matthias von 37251
Xamena, Miguel A. 00255
Xanke, Uwe 16609
Xavier, Andrew 39624
Xerri, Alda 27714
Xiae, Guo Cui 07188
Xiao, Runjun 07331
Xiejun, Chen 07221
Xin, Xue Jian 41939
Xinmiao, Zheng 06983
Xiong, Qiu Shi 07232
Xu, Jay 42304, 47546
Xun, Gao You 07147
Xylander, Prof. Dr. Willi 17327
Y, Dr. Rainer 20115
Yaacobi, Effi 22722
Yabacıoğlu, Ömer 37655
Yabe, Yoshiaki 26371
Yager, Bob 45114
Yaghobi 22326
Yagid, Meira 22775
Yahn Kramer, Bettie 47623
Yajima, Loretta 44076
Yakar, Saffet 37738
Yalakki, C.S. 22033
Yaldız, Fethiye 37686
Yaldiz, Prof. Dr. Marianne 16053
Yamada, Rikuzou 26691
Yamada, Yasuhisa 27005
Yamaga, Motoko 26199
Yamagishi, Youichi 26637
Yamaguchi, Kakutaro 26111
Yamaguchi, Matsuzo 26969
Yamakawa, Kazutoshi 26740

Yamamoto, Akira 26097, 26932
Yamamoto, Atsuo 26526
Yamamoto, Chikyo 26373
Yamamoto, Kazumaro 26511
Yamamoto, Dr. Masao 26529
Yamamoto, Shuji 26997
Yamamoto, Yasukazu 26571
Yamamoto, Yoshiko 47302
Yamanaka, Osamu 26345
Yamanaka, Sadanori 26935
Yamazaki, Midori 26368
Yamazaki, Tomiji 26958
Yambo, Francisco Xavier 00092
Yanagi, Munemichi 26775
Yanagi, Sori 26906
Yanagihara, Masaki 26969
Yanamoto, Akira 26827
Yanari, Sachi 43476
Yancey, Shirley S. 48468
Yande, R. 03182, 03185
Yandle, Ashley 42227
Yaneff, Greg 05157
Yanega, Doug A. 46918
Yáñez Anllo, Lucila 34987
Yang, Xiaoneng 44404
Yanik, Kadir 37791
Yaniv, Shosh 22667
Yank, Paul 42163
Yanko, Dick 41850
Yankov, Dr. Angel 04776
Yano Bretón, Dr. Sabino 28534
Yantorno, Suzanne 45789
Yap, Priscilla M. 31424
Yap, Virgilio 31309
Yapelli, Tina 47299
Yard, Dr. Sally 47276
Yarlow, Loretta 41951, 45864
Yaroshchuk, Mariya 37864
Yarsinske, Amy Waters 45970
Yasin, Dr. Walid 37915
Yassin, Robert A. 48093
Yasuda, Haruki 26900
Yasui, Teruo 26383
Yasuo, Hasimoto 26627
Yates, Jane M. 42212
Yates, R. 34213
Yates, Royden 34210
Yates, Sam 44518
Yates, Dr. Steve 47427
Yates, Dr. Steven A. 47424
Yates, Dr. Terry L. 41105
Yatim, Prof. Dr. Othman 27648
Yatras-Dehove, Elena 20850
Yazbeck, Janine 27491
Yeager, Shelley 46001
Yeager, William 06456
Yeatts, David L. 48742
Yébenes, M. Sierra 34735
Yee, Lydia 41915
Yeffeth, Laura 45885
Yelavich, Susan 45788
Yeler, Nihat 37611
Yellis, Ken 45925
Yellow Horn, Jo-Ann 05137
Yener, Emin 37627
Yerdon, Lawrence J. 46533
Yerhot, Judith 41751
Yerkovich, Dr. Sally 45891
Yeroulanos, Marinos 20878
Yersin, Jean-Marc 37290
Yetkin, Mehmet 37600
Yeudall, Robert 05375
Yeung, C.T. 07114
Yi, Shu 06981
Yi, Zhu 06963
Yıldız, Adem 37662
Yıldız, Hacı Ahmet 37599
Yılmaz, Ayla 37703
Yip, Chee-Kuen 07100
Ylioja, Merja 10012
Ylvisåker, Anne Britt 30427
Yochim, Jordan 44685
Yoder, Harold E. 46807
Yoder, Robert Lee 44543
Yoder, Sandy 48166
Yoki, Aharon 47939
Yokomizo, Hiroko 26853
Yoneya, Tetsuo 26719
Yoneyama, Torataro 26916
Yoon, Prof. Se-Young 27252
York, Beverly 48637
York, Brian 41291
Yorty, Faith A. 47754
Yosef, A. 22766
Yoshida, Kazuo 26712
Yoshida, Mitsuo 26503
Yoshida, Shoji 26963
Yoshihisa, Suto 26109
Yoshikata, Ishihara 26823
Yoshikawa, Miho 26571
Yoshinaka, Yasumaro 26218
Yoshioka, Akemi 26900
Yoshioka, Kenjiro 26767
Yoshioka, Yoji 26115, 26176
Yotsutsuji, Hideki 26571
You, Mee Chung 27259
Youck, Ingrid 06497
Young, Amber M. 43825
Young, Bobbie 42650

Young, Brian 44822
Young, C. 38800
Young, Charles 43754
Young, Cynthia 42923
Young, Dan 05553
Young, Dede 46747
Young, Dr. D.J. 38944
Young, Ernest 44419
Young, Frank 48550
Young, Gary 06397
Young, Holly 46480
Young, Jocelyn 41197
Young, John J. 06550
Young, Joyce 46148
Young, Judi 06568
Young, Karen S. 47953
Young, Kyle 45614
Young, Dr. Marcia 41742
Young, Marvin R. 47614
Young, Mary Jane 41625
Young, Michael 01437
Young, Sir Nicholas 39588
Young, Patrice 47772
Young, Richard L. 42129
Young, Steve 43264
Young Lee, Nan 27185
Young-Sanchez, Margaret 42885
Young-Vignola, Eilee 46410
Youngken, M. Joan 45926
Youngs, Christopher 46806
Younker, Randall W. 41655
Younkin, Elva 46895
Yount, Frank 44764
Yount, Sylvia 41348
Youssoufian, Jerry 06004
Yozak, Roman 37884
Ysel, H.J.D. 34339
Ysenburg und Bündingen, Casimir Erbprinz zu 19644
Yu, Louis 07108
Yu, Sun 06974
Yu, Teng Kuei 07354
Yüksek, Mustafa 37729
Yuergniaux, Danièle 13851
Yuichi, Tatsuno 26217
Yuki, Ryogo 26542
Yuko, Isazawa 26854
Yun, Jang Sub 27240
Yunus bin Zakaria, Dr. Mohd 27682
Yut, Joyce 42090
Yzereef, Dr. Gerard 28822, 28824
Zabarovskij, Vladimir Ivanovič 33027
Zabehlicky-Scheffenegger, Dr. Susanne 02417
Zabel, Barbara 31669
Zabel, Igor 34112
Zabel, Jürgen 20784
Zabusch, Prof. Stephanie 02856
Zaccaguini, Dr. Marisa 25162
Zaccome, Dr. Gian Maria 25742
Zacepina, Olga Vasiljevna 33512
Zachariou, E. 08198
Zacharkiw, Irene 48308
Zacharuk, Dr. Richard 17056
Zache, D. 19362
Zacher, J. 00759
Zachorowska, Maria 31701
Zachos, Dr. K. 20967
Zachou, Eleni 20843, 21039
Zack, Wendy 05266
Zadgorska, Valentina 04846
Zadka, Ruth 22623
Zäch, Benedikt 37332
Zaffarano, Antonio 25998
Zaffino, Antonio 25544
Zafran, Eric 43944
Žagar, Zora 34138
Zagnoli, Roberto 48872, 48877
Zagrina, Natalja Aleksandrovna 33350
Zahaniciuc, Marcel 32484
Žahirović, Prof. Šaban 03917
Zahler, Robert 01701
Zahn, Donald 42414
Zahn-Biemüller, Dr. Eva 20696
Zahner, Anton 36981
Zahrádka, Jiří 08275
Zahradník, Dr. Zdeněk 08368, 08729
Zaitsev, Nikolai Alekseevič 27100
Zaitsu, Nagatsugi 26753
Zając, Zdzisława 32206
Zajączkowski, Wiesław 31562, 31597
Zajceva, Natalija Leonidovna 32922
Zajic, Václav 08411
Zak, Thomas 42467
Zakatova, Anastasija Vasiljevna 32709
Zakian, Michael 45083
Zakrevskaja, G.P. 33387
Zakrzewski, R.J. 43971
Zakythinos, Prof. D. 21078
Zalba, Pat E. 42181
Zaldivar, Brenda Projas 28461
Zaleski, Pierre 13528, 13535
Zamanillo, Jorge 45285
Zamarchi Grassi, Dr. P. 22920
Zambrano de Gentile, Flor 48908
Zamora Canellada, Alonso 35465, 35468
Zanche, Prof. Vittorio de 24740
Zander, Charlotte 16217
Zander, Dr. Gisela 18583
Zander-Seidel, Dr. Jutta 19139
Zandler, Richard 44677

Zanella, Prof. S. 23950
Zanella Manara, Dr. Emma 23951
Zanelli, Dr. Gianluca 23984
Zanetta, Michèle 36645
Zang, Dr. Joachim 17879
Zangenfeind, Hermann 02561
Zangs, Dr. Christiane 19063, 19064
Zankman, Pat 43751
Zannas, D.K. 21194
Zanni, Dr. Annalisa 24409
Zannieri, Nina 41823
Zanola, Oscar Pablo 00649
Zansitis, Peter Paul 42338
Zant, Herbert 02184
Zantfrisco, Liana 03491
Žantudieva, Elizaveta Magamedovna 33193
Zapałowa, Jadwiga 31894
Zapałowa, Kazimiera 31657
Zapata, Marian 21298
Zapolis, Frank 42307
Zaporožskaja, Valentina Aleksandrovna 32739
Zappa, Armanda 37098
Zappa, Giancarlo 36651
Zaracki, Kathleen 45451, 45451
Zaragüeta, Vicente 34779
Zarb, Michael 06728
Zaremba, Ewa 31923
Zaremba, Tadeusz 31887
Zarev, Dr. Kosio 04700, 04701, 04704
Zarimi, Dominique 14667
Zarina, Elena Gennadjevna 33316
Zarling, Ronald 45703
Zarri, Dr. Enrico 24228
Zarrilli, Dr. Carla 25574
Zarubin, V.I. 33099
Zarzuelo Villaverde, Manuel 35254
Zarzycka, Joanna 32077
Zarzycka, Dr. Zyta 31756
Zasur, Dahas 04344
Zatloukal, Dr. Pavel 08515
Zau, Daw Nu Mya 28743
Zausch, Bärbel 17521
Zavada, Jeanne L. 46318
Závala, Ignacio M. 34512
Zavattaro, Dr. M. 23864
Zavjalova, Irina Vasiljevna 32895
Zavodnick, George A. 48800
Zawisza, Norbert 31765
Zawol, Zofia 32070
Zawrel, Dr. Peter 02871
Zayani, Abdelhak 28701
Zbarnea, Tudor 28658
Žbikowska, Janina 31919
Žbikowski, Dr. Dörte 18075
Zborowski, Janusz 31805, 31806
Zdesenko, Vjačeslav Iosifovič 32807
Zdravkovski, Dr. Dragiša 27590
Zea, Philip 42849, 44315, 45906, 45907, 46653, 47817, 48780
Zealand, A. 38800
Zeberg, Rolf 35989
Zecca, Walter 25851
Zecha, Horst 19965
Zeder, O. 13132
Zegadłowicz-Rudel, Atessa 32068
Zegher, Catherine de 45794
Zeh, Manfred 02010
Zehavi, Zvi 22699
Zehentmeier, Dr. Sabine 19930
Zehnder, Angela 34214
Zehnder, Prof. Dr. Frank Günter 16246
Zehnder, W. 37278
Zehnter, Dr. Annette 16584
Zeidler, Ingrid 19471
Zeigerer, Wolfgang 18079
Zeik, Travis 48587
Zeileis, Georg 01865
Zeillinger, Josef 02448
Zeiner, Ulrich 17511
Zeipel, Agneta von 36342
Zeitler, Dr. Kurt 18912
Zeitlin, Marilyn 47970
Zekaria, Ahmed 09398
Zekorn, Beate 17053
Zeković, Marina 33819
Zeldenrust, I. 29106
Zelenović, Radoslav 33806
Želev, Ivan 04744
Železnik, Adela 34112
Zelfel, Prof. Dr. Hans Peter 01807
Zelfel, Dr. Hans Peter 02312
Zelie, M. 34390
Zella, Robbin 41891
Zelleke, G. 42304
Zeller, Anselm 02772
Zeller, Kurt W. 01997, 01999
Zeller, Regine 16725
Zemanová, Jana 08653
Zemanova, Zita 08684
Zembala, Dr. Dennis 42923
Zembik, Andrzej 31545
Zemer, Avshalom 22609
Zemovičs, Elmārs 27432
Zemp, Dr. Heinrich 36918
Zemter, Dr. Wolfgang 20622
Zenegas-Millan, Dorenda 46325
Zenks, Ralph 20360
Zenz, Gerhard 02459
Zepecaner, Eugen 32557

Zeppenfeld, Dr. Burkhard 19178
Zerdina, V. 27422
Zerrudo, Eric 31412
Žertogova, Izabella Jakovlevna 32735
Zeschick, Dr. Johannes 19641
Zeskinskay, Nelly 37894
Zettel, Ernest 01900
Zetterström, Margareta 36250
Zettl, Charleen 41878
Zettler, Richard 46460
Zeuli, Prof. Errico 25211
Zeuli, Maria Francesca 25227
Zevallos Quinones, Dr. Jorge 31260
Zevi, Dr. Anna Gallina 24714, 24715, 24716
Zevi, Anna Gallina 25242
Ževrnja, Prof. Nediljko 07785
Zgaga, Višnja 07835
Zhang, Cheng Zhi 07216
Zhang, Jing 07066
Zhang, John 41636
Zhang, Lizhi 07300
Zhang, Wei 07005
Zhang, Wen Long 07273
Zhang, Xiao Jun 07194
Zhi, Yunting 07236
Zhitao, Huang 07189
Zhou, Zhao 07021
Zhu, Jiping 07222
Zhuber-Okrog, Karoline 02918
Ziąbka, Leszek 31636
Ziauddin, Muhammad 03086
Zibelius-Chen, Prof. Dr. K. 20220
Zibelo, Fisseha 09403
Zibler, Barbara 15997
Zichner, Prof. Dr. L. 17037
Zidić, Igor 07829
Zidlick, Pauline 41510
Zieglar, Ken 46467
Ziéglé, Anne 10809
Ziegler, Christiane 13603
Ziegler, Dr. Reinhard 20105
Ziegler, Dr. Susanne 15945
Ziehe, Dr. Irene 16051
Zielinski, Melissa L. 41246
Zielke, Bridgett 45075
Zielonka, Mariusz 31981
Ziemann-Heitkämper, Sonja 17720
Zierden, Martha 42211
Zierke, Franciszek 32215
Zieselman, Ellen 47424
Ziessow, Dr. Karl-Heinz 16479
Zięzio, Ryszard 31661
Ziffer, Dr. Irit 22752
Zifferero, Dr. Andrea 25724
Žigalov, Valerij Alekseevič 33527
Žiganova, Nina Iljinična 32901
Zigler Becker, Janis 41562
Zigmunde, Alida 27440
Zijp, R.P. 29234
Zika, Paul 01103
Zilianti, Dr. Romualdo 23132
Žiljanina, Tatjana Vladimirovna 32865
Zillenbiller, Prof. Dr. Erwin 20303, 20304
Zimina, I.D. 33637
Zimmer, Jim L. 44841
Zimmer, Patricia 05026
Zimmerer, Kathy 42116
Zimmerman, Anne 42155
Zimmerman, Daniel W. 43387
Zimmerman, Diane 46979
Zimmerman, Ryan 42960
Zimmerman, Sara C. 45903
Zimmerman, Vickie 43008
Zimmermann, Grety 36562
Zimmermann, Dr. Karl 36541
Zimmermann, Prof. Dr. Konrad 19666
Zimmermann, Dr. Margret 17107
Zimmermann, Oliver L. 18119
Zimmermann, Paul 17802
Zimmermann, Pedro 36579
Zimmermann, Peter 15910
Zimmermann, Pius 36937
Zimmern, Emily F. 42241
Zindler, Debra 45254
Zingarelli, Thomas V. 43265
Zingg, Ernst 37011
Zink, Bob 45387
Zinke, Dr. Detlef 17107
Zinn, Nancy 41489
Zinnkann, Dr. Heidrun 17062
Zintel, Diana 45694
Zintz, Daniel 14749
Ziolkowski, Anne 42694
Zippelius, Dr. K. 18001
Zipursky, Gerry 06689
Zirnitis, P. 27435
Zischka, Dr. Ulrike 18880
Ziswiler, Prof. V. 37396
Žitko, Duška 34138
Zitko, Salvator 34097
Žižić, Olivera 33886
Zjablicki, A.J. 27093
Zjumčenko, Ljudmila Petrovna 33540
Zlatar, Milena 34149
Zlattinger, Klaus 02669
Zlobina, Nina Nikolaevna 32923
Žmuda, Anna 31785
Žmuda, Maurycy 31745
Znamenov, V.V. 33406

Žnidarič, Dr. Marjan 34126
Znojek, Jerzy 31882
Zoe, Vivian F. 48527
Zöhrer, Georg 01956
Zöller, Achim 19933, 19934
Zöller, Dr. Helge 20696
Zöller-Stock, Dr. Bettina 18542
Zoer, J.A. 29172
Zoete, Johan de 29327
Žogina, Viktorija Stepanovna 33432
Zoli, Renato Giancarlo 25698
Zolli, Barbara T. 46557
Zolotareva, Tatjana Nikolaevna 33324
Zolotina, I.A. 33418
Zolotinkina, Dr. Larissa Igorevna 33422
Zoltán, Kató 32590
Zombork, Márta 21601
Zomborka Szűcsné, Márta 21602
Zomlefer, W. 41319
Zommer, Raya 22590
Zona, Louis A. 48807
Zonneveld-Kouters, M.C. 29698
Zopes, Elaine 43252, 45709, 46648, 47471, 47685
Zopf, August 01857, 02322
Zopf, Johann 02678
Zorbo, Lorrie 41537
Zorić, Ivanka 33810
Zoridis, Pandeli 21062
Zorn, Dr. Bettina 02945
Zorn, Dr. Olivia 15908
Zorzi, Dr. Marino 25921
Zoubek, Ernst 02748
Zrebiec, Alice 42885
Zrelov, Vladimir Andreevič 33367
Zsidi, Dr. Paula 21324
Zsusza, Dr. Fodor 21608
Zuback, Lynne 44372
Zubčie, Pavao 07744
Zuber, Michaela 17023
Zuberer, Peter 20434
Zubiaurre, Pablo 00123
Zubov, Aleksandr Nikolaevič 33656
Zubrij, Elena Stanislavovna 32813
Zuccali, Jean-Pierre 12659
Zuckerman, B. Michael 42097
Zuckriegl, Dr. Margit 02549
Züchner, Dr. Christian 16925
Zünd, Peter 37002
Züst, Ernst 37349
Zueva, Ljubov Vasiljevna 33585
Zufferey, Anne-D. 37093, 37167
Žugan, Vitalij Ivanovič 33598
Zugay, Gabriele 02918
Zugaza Miranda, Miguel 35048
Zugni Tauro, Anna Paola 23773
Zuidervaart, Dr. Huib J. 29673
Žuk, Stanisław 31503
Žukauskienė, Genovaite 27526, 27530
Zukauskienė, Genovaite 27532
Zukiwski, Wilson 06806
Zukowsky, John 42304
Zukulis, Ivars 27429
Zuleta, Pilar 07412
Zumaeta Zúñiga, Hector 06923
Zumbini, Vincenzo 23665
Zumpfe, Dr. Dieter 02312
Zuna-Kratky, Dr. Gabriele 02993
Zunk, Bodo 19552
Zupančič, Mirina 34093
Žuravlev, M.N. 03110
Žuravleva, Tatjana Jurjevna 33198
Zurawski, Jarosław 32219
Zurbuchen, Max 36871
Zurcher, Sarah 36713
Zurfluh, Dr. Anselm 37034
Zurfluh, M. 11237
Zuris, Donald P. 42645
Zuris, Kay A. 43759
Zuskinová, Dr. Iveta 34013
Zutautas, Sofia 42317
Žutikov, Aleksandr Ivanovič 33264
Zutter, Dr. Jorg 00886
Zuver, W. Marc 48354
Zvelebil, Miloš 08641
Zviguilsky, Dr. Alexandre 10832
Zvirin, Prof. Yoram 22610
Zwaenepoel, Dr. J. 03498
Zwaka, Petra 16011
Zwanger, Meryl 45794
Zwart, A. 29459
Zweifel, Gwen 05470
Zweifel, Regula 37393
Zweite, Prof. Dr. Armin 16728, 16729
Zwez, Annelise 37257
Zwez, John 48302
Zwicker, Jörg 01908, 02503
Zwickl, Alfred 37345, 37346
Zwicky, P. 36561
Zwiener, Walter 16162
Zwierzyna, John 43925
Zwink, Dr. E. 20113
Zwolak, Adam 31475
Zydlik, Stanisław 32073
Zygmun, Kathy 47278
Zykaner, Michaela 02930
Zykov, Andrej Viktorovič 32911
Zyman, Daniela 44926

Personality Index

Aakjær, Jeppe 09047
Aalto, Alvar 09559
Aaltonen, Wäinö 09810
Aas, Nils 30577
Aasen, Ivar 30570
Abbe, Ernst 17945
Abélard, Pierre 12459
Abramov, Fëdor 32647, 33682
Abt, Franz 16810
Abu Sina, Abu Ali 48828
Achmatova, Anna Andreevna 33399, 33424
Adam, Robert 39096, 39320, 39786, 39927
Adami, Valerio 03633
Adams, Robert 45774
Addams, Chas 36502
Adenauer, Konrad 15669
Adimoolam, K.M. 22059
Adler, Friedrich 18359
Ady, Endre 21322
Adzak, Roy 13529
Affandi 22216
Agoncillo, Marcela M. 31450
Agricola, Georgius 16472, 17299
Aguéli, Ivan 36171
Aicard, Jean 14766
Ajvazovskij, I.K. 37853
Akersloot-Berg, Betzy R. 29955
Aksakov, S.T. 32632
Alain-Fournier, Henri 11634
Albert, Eduard 08737
Albert Prince of Saxe-Coburg-Gotha 38839
Alberti, Friedrich August von 19697
Alberti, Rafael 35300
Aldridge, John 40367
Aldrovandi, Ulisse 23105
Alechinsky, Pierre 03546
Alecsandri, Vasile 32551
Aleichem, Shalom 22774
Aleš, Mikoláš 08371, 08372, 08479, 08592
Alesio, Perez de 31218
Alfaro Siqueiros, David 28160
Alfelt, Else 08866
Alfieri, Vittorio 22972
Allen, William Herbert 37990
Allilueva, Nadežda 33448
Allmayer, Josefine 02107
Allmers, Hermann 19742
Altamirano, Ignacio Manuel 28516
Altdorfer, Albrecht 19518
Alves, Castro 04424
Aman, Teodor 32473
Amaral, Tarsila do 04514
Ambrosi, Gustinus 02838
Amiet, Cuno 36424, 37185
Ammannati, Bartolomeo 24742
Amorsolo, Fernando 31352
Ámos, Imre 21567
Ampère, André-Marie 13788
Amundsen, Roald 30443, 30734, 30909, 30933
Andersen, Hans Christian 09011
Andersen, Magnus 30632
Andersson, Dan 36051
András, Jósa 21492
Andrea, Pat 03546
Andrée, Salomon 35927
Andreev, L.N. 33259, 33266
Andreotti, Libero 24877
Anhalt-Dessau, Leopold Friedrich Franz Fürst von 19511
Anheuser, P. Clemens 15599
Anich, Peter 02374
Anker Aurdal, Synnøve 30939
Anna Amalia, Herzogin von Sachsen-Weimar-Eisenach 20476
Anna, Margit 21567, 21578
Anselmi, Mickelangelo 24799
Anslinger, Harry 15983
Anson, Peter 38385
Antes, Horst 07514
Antonelle, Patrick 41142
Antonioni, Michelangelo 23788
Apacible, Galiciano 31449
Apacible, Leon 31449
Apel, Heinrich 17864
Apollinaire, Guillaume 03766
Appel, Karel 29804
Appia, Adolphe 36551
Appiani, Guiseppe 18677
Aquitaine, Aliénor d' 14417
Aragay, Josep 34623
Araki, Nobuyoshi 26855
Aralič, Stojan 07751
Arany, János 21487
Aratym, Hubert 01979
Aravantinos, Panos 21125
Arbaud, Paul 10256
Arbuzov, Aleksandr E. 32688, 32893, 32900
Arbuzov, Boris A. 32893, 32900
Archer, Colin 30632
Archipenko, Alexander 19727
Arden, Mary 40627
Ariosto, Ludovico 23783
Arkwright, Sir Richard 38675
Armand, Inessa 33341
Armando 29804
Armbruster, Ludwig 15950
Arndt, Ernst Moritz 16235, 17205, 20074
Arndt, H. 30211
Arnim, Achim von 20569

Arnim, Bettina von 20569
Arntz, Gerd 19565
Arp, Hans 08902, 12833, 14199, 18259, 19562, 19868, 36886
Arramidis, M. 21185
Arrieta, Agustín 28319
Artschwager, Richard 01927
Asakura, Fumio 26829
Asbjørnsen, Peter Christen 30561
Asch, Sholem 22578
Asger, Jorn 16692
Astrup, Nikolai 30978
Atatürk 37605, 37643, 37659, 37675, 37717, 37739, 37776, 37786, 37796
Atenbourg, Gerhard 16692
Auberjonois, R. 36424
Aubry, Emile 00051
Auden, W.H. 02116
Audrain, Wayne 40404
Auerbach, Berthold 17840
Augundson, Thorgeir Øygarden 30787
August der Jüngere 20653
Augustinčić, Antun 07715
Austen, Jane 38533
Auwera, J.W. von der 20697
Avakian, Hrandt 32457
Aventinus, Johannes 15389
Avercamp, Barent 29474
Averkin, A.P. 33512
Axman, Emil 08319
Azorín 35127
Babits, Mihály 21564
Bach, Johann Sebastian 15513, 16814, 18189, 18389, 19246
Bach, Wilhelm Friedemann 17513
Bacher, Karl 03052
Bachmann, August 16346, 16348, 16353
Bachmann, Ingeborg 02132
Backer, Harriet 30413
Bacon, Francis 08902, 13629, 19949, 30727, 39272, 40100
Baden-Powell, Robert Stephenson Smyth 39570
Baelz, Erwin von 16160
Bärtschi, Arnold 36667
Bahr, Hermann 02225
Bain, George 40341
Baird, John 38686
Bajcsy-Zsilinszky, Endre 21607
Bajén, Francisco 13011
Baker, Sir Herbert 34313
Bakunin, Michail 36472
Bakusen, Tsuchida 26727, 26728
Balaguer y Cirera, Víctor 35668
Balakirev 33194
Bald, J.W. 05846
Bálint, Endre 21578
Balkenhol, Stephan 18107
Balmes, Jaime 35650
Balzac, Honoré de 14082, 13521, 14738
Bandaranaike, Sirimawo W.R.D. 35746
Baracca, Francesco 24238, 24239
Barbey d'Aurevilly, Jules-Amédée 14469
Barbosa, Rui 04337
Barceló, Miquel 07514
Barcsay, Jenoë 21568
Bardini, Stefano 23853
Barlach, Ernst 17456, 17536, 19499, 20414
Barnard, Christian 34177
Barnes, William 38748
Barocci, F. 20697
Barrau y Buñol, Laureano 35417
Barrie, James M. 39399
Barry, Robert 20466
Bartholdi, Auguste 11357
Bartók, Béla 21329, 21392
Basedow, Johann Bernhard 19511
Baselitz, Georg 08902, 18161, 19868, 37060, 37386
Bauchant, André 16217
Bauer, Wilhelm 16612
Bauernfeld, Eduard von 02852
Baumbach, Rudolf 18685
Baumeister, Willi 20090
Baumgarten, Lothar 18107
Bawden, Edward 40367
Bažov, P.P. 32772, 32773, 32779
Beauchesne, G. de 14342
Beauharnais, Hortense de 37092
Bebel, August 16815
Becher, Bernd u. Hilla 19949
Bechstein, Ludwig 18685
Bechteler, Eduard 16390
Beck, Richard 17099
Beckmann, Max 16661, 17970, 18161, 19868, 20106
Becquerel, Henry 17960
Bede, the Venerable 39323
Beecher Stowe, Harriet 43939
Beer, Johann 02225
Beethoven, Ludwig van 01726, 02155, 02845, 02846, 02847, 02848, 16231, 21469
Behn, Fritz 15633
Belanger, François-Joseph 12777
Belgrano, Manuel 00386
Belinskij, Vissarion Grigorevič 32678, 32679
Bell, Alexander Graham 05031, 05124
Bellamy, John 39045
Bellany, John 38789
Bellay, Joachim du 12620

Belli, Valerio 25993
Bellini 25951
Bellini, Giovanni 23066, 25043, 25927, 25951, 38211
Bellini, Vincenzo 23446
Bellman, C.M. 36237
Bellotto, Bernardo 24799
Ben-Gurion, David 22749
Benczúr, Gyula 21492
Benda, Franz 08245
Benda, Georg 08245
Benedito Vives, Manuel 34995
Benlliure, José 35596
Benlliure, Mariano 34759
Benlliure, Peppino 35596
Benoit, Peter 03476
Benz, Carl 18283, 18613
Berg, Werner 01739
Berija, L. 17960
Bering, Vitus 33311
Berlioz, Hector 12161
Bernadotte, Jean-Baptiste 13666
Bernadozzi, A. 28662
Bernard, Claude 14299
Bernard, Emile 28911
Bernhard, Thomas 02225
Bernhardi, Dr. Anton 16810
Berni, Antonio 00307
Bernier, J.E. 05757
Bernini, Gian Lorenzo 24434
Beron, Petăr 04719
Bertrand, Henri Gratien 11227
Berzelius, Jacob 36234
Best, Fritz 18247
Bethune, Norman 05525
Beuys, Joseph 04514, 13629, 15866, 15981, 16242, 16661, 16728, 18028, 18107, 18135, 18161, 20106, 37386, 45792
Bewick, Thomas 39943
Bezruč, Petr 08340, 08422, 08520
Bialik, Nachman 22750
Bickel, Karl sen. 37300
Biegas, Boleslaw 13535
Bieruma Oosting, Jeanne 29562
Bilderdijk, Willem 28846
Bílek, František 08323, 08565
Bilger, Margret 02635
Bilibin, I.Ja. 33395
Bill, Max 04514, 16042
Bismarck, Otto von 17150
Bjåland, Olav 30690
Bjarnadóttir, Halldóra 21624
Bjørnson, Bjørnstjerne 30501, 30622
Blackadder, Elizabeth 38789
Blackburne, Joseph 03890
Blagoev, Dimităr 04612, 04830
Blake, Robert 38324
Blake, William 40198
Blanche, Jacques-Emile 13387
Bláthy 21355
Blechen, Carl 16501
Bleken, Håkon 30537
Bleyl, Fritz 20776
Blicher, Steen Steensen 08865, 08918, 09109
Bligh, William 00855
Blixen, Karen 09049
Bloch, M.E. 16056
Blok, Aleksandr A. 33544
Blücher von Wahlstatt, Gebhard Leberecht 18035
Blüthgen, Victor 20766
Boccaccio, Giovanni 23486
Boccioni, Umberto 04514
Bodenstedt, Friedrich von 19366
Boeck, Félix de 03395
Boeckel, Lodewijk van 03587
Boeckhorst, Johann 18946
Böckler, Hans 20192
Böcklin, Arnold 37386
Boehle, Fritz 16855
Böhme, Jacob 17323
Boix-Vives, Anselme 17671
Bol, Peter 29259
Bolano, Italo 25018
Boldini, Giovanni 23795
Bolívar, Simón 07384, 07429, 07587, 07591, 48908, 48909, 48919
Boltanski, Christian 20662
Bombardier, J. Armand 06661
Bonaiuto, Andrea di 23874
Bonevardi, Marcelo 00307
Bonme, Rodrigo 00505
Bonzanigo, Guiseppe Maria 25736
Boon, Louis Paul 03125
Booth, E.T. 38338
Boratynskij, Evgenij 32994
Bordes, Antoine 14342
Bores, Francisco 03633, 35040
Borlach, Johann Gottfried 15679
Borodin, Sergej 48860
Bosch, Hieronymus 02886
Bose, Nataji Subhas 21909
Bose, Sarat Chandra 21909
Botero, Fernando 07429, 07514
Botev, Christo 04686
Bottema, Tjeerd 29477
Botticelli, Alessandro F. 23066, 38898
Botticelli, Sandro 13621, 23840, 23843
Botticini, Francesco 23730
Bouchard, Henri 13536

Boucher, Alfred 13353
Boucher, François 13621, 14832
Bouillon, Godefroy de 03233
Bourdelle, Antoine 13048
Bourdelle, Emile-Antoine 03600, 13048, 13538
Bourdon, Sébastien 40198
Bourgeoys, Marguerite 05925
Bouts, Albrecht 03565
Bovet, Claude 36643
Bowler, J.B. 38117
Boyle, Harry, Munro, Alice 06815
Boznanska, Olga 13535
Bozveli, Neofit 04719
Braak, Ivo 18657
Brahe, Tycho 08245
Brahms, Johannes 01896, 02329, 15785, 17659
Braille, Louis 11429
Braith, Anton 16138
Brâncuşi, Constantin 32506
Brands, Eugène 29804
Brangwyn, Frank 03246
Branly, Edouard 13612
Brant, Joseph 05147
Braque, Georges 11507, 13629, 15217, 25164, 37185
Brayer, Yves 11407
Brecht, Bertolt 15551, 15929, 16391
Brehm, Alfred Edmund 15451, 19572
Brehm, Christian Ludwig 19572
Breidvik, Mons 30713
Breithaupt, Friedrich August 17099
Bremer, Frederick 39793
Brenders, Carl 38736
Brennand, Francisco 04301
Breuer, Marcel 16136
Breughel, Pieter 25161
Breunig, Johann Michael 16407
Březina, Otokar 08549
Brigaud, Florentin 11860
Bristowe, Ethel S.G. 38502
Broch, Hermann 02718
Brodie, P.B. 40796
Brodski, Isaak Izrailevič 33449
Brontë, Anne 39199
Brontë, Branwell 39199
Brontë, Charlotte 39199
Brontë, Emily Jane 39199
Brontë, Patrick 39199
Broodthaers, Marcel 16729
Brookes, William Penny 39993
Brosch, Klemens 02234
Brown, Jenny 36488
Brown, Sidney 36488
Brozzi, Renato 25786
Bruce, Michael 39389
Bruckner, Anton 01676, 02166
Brüggemann, Hans 20383
Brueghel, Jan l 10853
Brueghel, Pieter 02918, 03151
Brunel, Isambard Kingdom 39591, 40667
Brunel, Sir Marc Isambard 39591
Brunelleschi, Filippo 23843, 23862
Brunovski, Albin 04652
Brus, Günter 01927
Brusau, René 00505
Bu, Amund K. 30962
Buchan, John 40737
Buchholz, Martin 16781
Budd, David 03633
Büchner, Georg 19601
Bücker, Carl Clemens 18120
Bürger, Gottfried August 18784, 20416
Bürkel, Heinrich 19401, 19402
Buisseret, Louis 03633
Bukovac, Vlaho 07829
Bull, Jacob Breda 30788
Bunin, Ivan Alekseevič 32791, 32792, 33265, 33266, 33732
Bunyan, John 38148, 38149
Burchfield, Charles E. 41986
Burgos, José 31465
Burnand, Eugène 36958
Burne-Jones, Sir Edward 38624, 40141
Burnot, C. Philippe 10639
Burns, Robert 37980, 38791, 38792, 38921, 38928, 39313, 39392, 39925, 40674
Burri, Alberto 23577
Busch, Wilhelm 16763, 17614, 19924, 20565
Busoni, F. 23728
Bustos, Hermengildo 27977
Buyx, Peter Michael 18068
Byron, George Gordon Noel Lord 21065, 25169, 40290
Caballero, José 35694
Caballero, Luis 07514
Cage, John 18135
Caillebotte, Gustave 13832
Čajkovskij, Pëtr Iljič 32933, 33136, 33440, 33737, 37858
Calder, Alexander 08902
Calderara, Antonio 22877
Callan, Nicholas 22518
Calloch, Jean-Pierre 12046
Calvin, Jean 13372, 36728
Calvo, Luis Antonio 07483
Camassei, Andrea 23074
Cameron, Julia Margaret 39017
Camos, Honoré 10591
Campbell, Donald 38625

Campbell, Sir Malcolm 38625
Campigli, Massimo 04514
Canaletto 14832, 39798
Cankar, Ivan 34164
Cano, Francisco Antonio 07514
Canova, Antonio 25027
Čapaev, V.I. 32722
Čapek, Josef 08470, 08661, 08701
Čapek, Karel 08470, 08661, 08701
Capella, Anna 34856
Capralos, Christos 20804, 20812, 20855
Caraffa, Emilio 00307
Caravaggio, Michelangelo Merisi da 13241, 25043, 25161, 25163
Carballo, Aida 00484
Carducci, Giosuè 23108, 24911
Carigiet, Alois 37256
Carlyle, Jane Welsh 39142, 39598
Carlyle, Thomas 38866, 39598
Carnacini, Ceferino 00659
Carnegie, Andrew 38808
Carneiro, Antônio 32332
Carneiro, Carlos 32332
Carneo, Antonio 25845
Carnielo, Rinaldo 23845
Carpaccio, Vittore 24273, 25845, 25927
Carr, Emily 06693, 06719
Carracci, Annibale 11560, 24799, 25161, 25163
Carriego, Evaristo 00248
Carroll, Lewis 39138
Carte, Anto 03633
Cartier, Jacques 14341
Casals, Pablo 13861, 35645
Castagno, Andrea del 23829
Castellani, Enrico 08868
Castro, Rosalía de 35208
Čavčavadze, Ilya 15363
Cavour, Camillo Benso Conte di 25462
Cazin, Jean-Charles 14596
Cazneau, Harold 01065
Čech, Svatopluk 08454, 08513, 08529
Čechov, Anton Pavlovič 33009, 33036, 33057, 33588
Cedercreutz, Emil 09464
Čelákovsky, František L. 08663
Celaleddin, Mevlana 37744
Čepeláková, Zdenka 08530
Černyševskij, Nikolaj Gavrilovič 32666, 33508
Cervantes Saavedra, Miguel de 34427, 35617
Céspedes, Carlos Manuel de 07858
Cézanne, Paul 10249, 13626, 13632, 18002, 24273, 37060, 37386, 39729, 43693
Chabot, Hendrik 29748
Chadži, Dimitǎr 04818
Chagall, Marc 02549, 03123, 13322, 13629, 22600, 26598, 37386, 45872
Chaillioux, Julien 11816
Chaissac, Gaston 03633
Champaigne, Philippe de 14832
Champlain, Samuel de 06106
Champneys, Basil 39891
Champollion, J.-F. 11731
Chandra, Prakash 22059
Chaplin, Charles Spencer 17033
Chappell, Reuben 39094
Chapu, Henri 12445, 12923
Charcot, Jean-Baptiste 14341
Charlemagne 17900
Charoux, Siegfried 02188
Chateaubriand, François-René de 11366, 14341
Chatterjee, Sarat Chandra 21974
Checa, Ulpiano 34729
Chéniers, André de 11043
Chéron, Emile 11215
Chiattone, Mario 24947
Chillida, Eduardo 03546, 18135, 34763, 34900
Chinnaraj, T. 22059
Chippendale, Thomas (the Younger) 40617
Chitov, Panaët 04821
Chittussi, Antonín 08637
Chlebnikov, Velimir Vladimirovič 32662
Chlebnikova Vera Vladimirovna 32662
Chochrjakov, Nikolaj N. 32916
Chodowiecki, Daniel 15672, 18219
Chopin, Frédéric 31472, 31905, 31985, 32076, 32096, 32141
Chrenikov, Tichon Nikolaevič 32789
Christie, Agatha 40718
Christo 18107, 18259
Christov, Ivan 04913
Chughtai, Muhammed Abdur Rahman 31033
Čintulov, Dobri 04819
Ciolkovskij, Konstantin Éduardovič 32760, 32875, 32877, 32921
Čišinski, Jakub-Bart 19342
Čistjakov, P.P. 33335
Čiurlionis, Mikalojus Konstantinas 27521
Claes, Ernest 03728
Claesz, Pieter 29505
Clark, Jim 38820
Claudius, Hermann 17821
Claudius, Matthias 19552
Claus, Carlfriedrich 15498
Claver, Pedro 35646
Clayton, John 38573
Cleillida, Eduardo 35694
Clémenceau, Georges 13616, 14507
Clemens August, Herzog von Bayern 15693, 19974
Cobbett, William 38982

Cockburn, Sir John 01123
Cocteau, Jean 12939, 12981
Coecke van Aelst, Pieter 03565
Coello, Alonso 31603
Coleridge, Samuel Taylor 40010
Colladon, J.D. 36746
Collingwood, W.G. 38625
Colón, Cristóbal 35240, 35245, 40997
Comenius, Jan Amos 08248, 08257, 08342, 08360, 08427, 08611, 08622, 08699, 17715, 29605
Comte, Auguste 13520
Comyn, Christine 29259
Conca, Sebastiano 24887
Constable, John 38898, 39729, 40773
Constant, Benjamin 04336
Cook, Francis 38040
Cook, James 00855, 30253, 39118, 39946
Cooper, T.S. 38474
Coper, Hans 40100
Copernicus, Nicolaus 31561, 32053
Copley, John Singleton 38917
Čorbadžijski, Dimitǎr Christov 04698
Corbin Lukis, Frederick 40424
Corelli, Arcangelo 23498
Corinth, Lovis 17970, 18028
Corneille, Pierre 12462, 14046, 29804
Coronel, Pedro 28637
Coronel, Rafael 28637
Corot, Camille 26360
Correggio, Antonio 24434, 24799, 25161
Coşbuc, George 32505
Cosimo, Piero di 23843
Cossit, Ranna 06526
Cotta, Bernhard von 17099
Cotta, Johann Friedrich 18619
Coubertin, Pierre de 36866
Courbet, Gustave 13438, 25164, 26360
Cousin, Jean 14902
Cowper, William 40130
Coxie, Michel 03565
Craig, Edward Gordon 40686
Cranach, Lucas (the Elder) 02886, 15529, 16692, 18243, 20472
Creangǎ, Ion 32537
Crişan, Eva 32491
Crome, John 40091
Cromwell, Oliver 39277
Cross, Henri Edmond 11560
Cruz, Oswaldo 04324
Cruz, San Juan de la 35584
Csallány, Gábor 21579
Čudomir 04698
Čukovskij, Kornej Ivanovič 33057, 33296
Curie, Marie 17960, 32113
Curros Enríquez, Manuel 34703
Curry, John S. 41316
Cuypers, Pierre 29743
Cvetaeva, Marina I. 32635, 32940, 33037, 33231, 33595, 33670
Czechowicz, Józef 31792
Czóbel, Béla 21569
Da Messina, Antonello 25736
Daan van Golden 29804
Dadd, Richard 38141
Dahl, J.C. 30412
Dal', Vladimir Ivanovič 33094
Dalén, Gustaf 36228
Dalí, Salvador 02969, 05457, 13500, 34553, 35232, 35694, 38916
Dalla Bella, Giovanni Antonio 32258
Danicourt, Alfred 13699
Danielson-Kalmari, Johan-Richard 10165
D'Annunzio, Gabriele 23959, 24866
Danov, Christo G. 04778
Dantan, J.P. 08551
Dante Alighieri 23824, 25080
Darder i Llimona, Francesc 34528
Dargent, Yan 14472
Darwin, Charles 00493, 38455, 38464, 38771
Dass, Petter 30827
Dastrac, Raoul 10240
Daubigny, Charles-François 13832
Daudet, Alphonse 11783
Daumier, Honoré 14180, 26261
Daura, Pierre 10996, 13708, 45003
Davey, Alan 38789
David, Gerard 28195
Davidis, Henriette 16658
Davie, Alan 39045
Davies, John 40100
Davitt, Michael 22544
Dawley, Joseph 41142
De Chirico, Giorgio 25164, 04514
De Maria, Walter 45792
Debeljanov, Dimcho 04712
Debussy, Claude 14240
Déchelette, Joseph 13985
Decurtins, Caspar 37256
Degas, Edgar 12736, 13618, 13626, 38211
Degottex, Jean 10853
Del Piombo, Sebastiano 24010
Del Vaga, Perino 24010
Delacroix, Eugène 12736, 13241, 13640
Della Ragione, Alberto 23885
Della Robbia, Luca 23862
Delvaux, Paul 03600, 03737, 26195
Demard, Albert 11159
Demidov, A. 32671

Denejka, A.A. 32973
Denis, Maurice 14241
Depero, Fortunato 25292, 25791
Depiau, Charles 12241
Derain, André 12881
Déri 21355
Derkovits, Gyula 21340
Deržavin, Gavrila R. 33416
Desiderio, Vincent 07514
Desmet, Jean 28852
Desmoulin, Fernand 10890
Despiau, Charles 13027
Desportes, Alexandre-François 11860
Destinnová, Ema 08394
Deubler, Konrad 01700
Deusser, August 37429
Dewantara, Ki Hadjar 22219
Dewey, Harold Nelson 40785
Di Bicci, Neri 23805
Di Cambio, Arnolfo 23862
Dias, Cícero 04301
Dickens, Charles 29030, 38365, 38367, 39624, 40248, 40334
Dickinson, Frank R. 39690
Diehn-Bitt, Kate 19665
Diesel, Rudolf 15560
Dietrich, Adolf 36538
Dietz, Günter 20406
Dill, Otto 19078
Dima, Gheorghe 32446
Dimitrov, Georgi 04721, 04849
Dimitrov-Majstora, Vladimir 04709
Dimov, Dimitǎr 04831, 04847
Dinglinger, Johann Melchior 16138
Dion, Mark 16971
Dios Mena, Juan de 00484, 00505
Disraeli, Benjamin 39240
Disteli, Martin 37009
Diviš, Prokop 08737, 08757
Dix, Otto 02549, 16692, 17191, 17247, 17970, 20090
Dobrovský, Josef 08322
Dobroljubov, N.A. 33206
Doderer, Heimito von 02850
Doerfler, Ludwig 19779
Doisneau 11850
Dollmann, Georg 17201, 17735
Domínguez, Lorenzo 00505
Domoto, Insho 26406
Donatello 23862, 24742
Doni, Adone 23074
Donizetti, Gaetano 23064
Doré, Gustave 10853
Doren, Emile van 03430
Dornier, Claude 18677
Dospevski, Stanislav 04756
Dostoevskij, Fëdor Michajlovič 27091, 32755, 33057, 33123, 33235, 33414, 33416, 33554
Douglas, C. 22059
Douwes-Dekker, E. 28874
Doyle, Arthur Conan 36935
Drachmann, Holger 09054
Drais, Karl von 18613
Drake, Sir Francis 40953
Droese, Felix 18135
Droste-Hülshoff, Annette von 17651, 18673, 18675, 18936
Drummonds, James 01537
Drużbacka, Elżbieta 32196
Duarte, Juan Pablo 09126
Dubois, Paul 13353
Dubuffet, Jean 13691, 14199
Ducros, Louis 36860
Duchamp, Marcel 01927, 13626, 14199, 25164
Dufy, Raoul 12881, 13626, 13708
Duguay-Trouin, René 14341
Dumas, Alexandre 15242
Dumont, Louise 16744
Dunant, Henry 36748, 36797
Duncker, Johann Heinrich August 19493
Dunikowski, Xawery 32124
Dunn, Harvey 41932
Dupain, Max 01065
Dupré, Amalia 23807
Dupré, Giovanni 23807
Dupré, Jules 12626
Durand, Marie 13864
Durand, Pierre 13864
Durova, Nadežda A. 32788
Dürer, Albrecht 02178, 02830, 02918, 11929, 13932, 16692, 18002, 19133, 21539, 23983, 24273, 24875
Dvořák, Antonín 08495, 08593, 08732, 08753
Dyck, Anton van 02926, 03171, 13621, 14832, 23844, 23983, 24213, 24799, 25993, 29836, 38898, 38917, 39798, 40198
Džalil, Musa 32902
Dzierzon, Jan 31665

Eardley, Joan 38789
Ebert, Friedrich 17672
Eckenfelder, Friedrich 15797
Eckermann, Johann Peter 20613
Eckl, Vilma 01918
Edelfelt, Albert 09810, 10005
Edelmann, Albert 36669
Edison, Thomas 40477, 45335
Eertvet, Andries van 29836
Egger, Albin 02220
Egk, Werner 16642

Eichendorff, Joseph Freiherr von 20392, 20395
Eichler, Ernst 20517
Einstein, Albert 36540
Eldh, Carl 36236
Elgar, Edward 39835
Eliot, George 40118
Elisabeth of Thuringia 17131
Elizabeth, Countess of Shrewsbury 38555
Elizalde, Fernando de 00331
Ellis, Richard 00726
Eluard, Paul 14180
Eminescu, Mihai 32538, 32542
Emma, Kunz 37352
Emre, Yunus 37809
Enckell, Magnus 09810
Endre, Ady 32560
Endre, Béla 21427
Enescu, George 32469, 32514
Engels, Friedrich 20710
Engström, Albert 35860, 35931, 35967
Enku 26640
Enríquez, Carlos 07968
Ensor, James 03668, 03670, 26195, 26261
Éovkov, Éordan 04933
Epstein, Sir Jacob 40773
Erasmus, Desiderius 03287, 36500
Erben, Jaromír 08477
Erichsen, Thorvald 30556
Erixson, Sven X. 36219, 36338
Erkel, Ferenc 21423
Erler, Erich 18305
Ermolova, M.N. 33038
Erni, Hans 36909
Ernst August Herzog von Sachsen-Weimar 16648
Ernst, Max 13629, 14199, 16377, 18161, 18259, 30414, 38640
Ernst, Paul 02565
Erošenko, Vasilij J. 33558
Erxleben, Dorothea C. 19462
Erzia, Stefan 00505
Eschenbach, Wolfram von 20656
Escher, Rolf 04652
Esenin, Sergej Aleksandrovič 32937, 33087
Eulenspiegel, Till 03371, 19840
Evans, Eva 17273
Evenepoel, Henri 03743
Exter, Julius 20246
Fader, Fernando 00367, 00419
Fałat, Julian 31494
Falger, Josef Anton 01813
Falk-Breitenbach, Eugen 17642
Falk, Johannes Daniel 20462
Falkberget, Johan 30805
Falken, Herbert 18135
Falla, Manuel de 00112, 34866
Fallada, Hans 16987
Falter, John 41316
Faraday, Michael 39708
Farey, Hélène 13371
Fath, Richard 11860
Fauconnier, Edouard 16486
Faust, Georg 18118
Faust, Heinrich 18118
Faust, Johann 18118
Federer, Heinrich 17080
Fedkovič, Jurij 37840
Fehling, Heinz 19768
Feininger, Lyonel 15916, 16584, 19463, 30414
Feluérez, Manuel 28637
Fenneker, Josef 16190
Fernández de Latorre, Néstor Martín 35243
Ferrari, Defendente 25736
Ferry, Jules 14187
Feuchtwanger, Josef Anton 18103
Fibich, Zdeněk 08728
Fičeto, Kolju 04660, 04661
Fichte, Johann Gottlieb 17948, 19481
Figl, Leopold 02296
Filla, Emil 08319, 08465
Firpo, Roberto 00544
Firth, Josiah 30202
Fischer, Camillo 18194
Fischer, Johann Georg 18103
Fischer, Johann Michael 16427
Fischer, J.T. 08755
Fizelle, Rah 01568
Fjell, Kai 30765
Flacius Illyricus, Matthias 07734
Flagstad, Kirsten 30529
Flaig, Waldemar 18677
Flath, Otto 15741
Flaubert, Gustave 11028, 11462, 14052
Flavin, Dan 41552, 45792, 45793
Fleming, Alexander 39564
Fleming, Paul 17622
Fleury, Sylvie 16971
Flinders, Matthew 01598
Flüe, Nikolaus von der 37081
Foch 14865
Fojita, Tsuguji 13626
Folles, Pierres 14287
Fonck, René 14187
Fontaine, Jean de la 11210
Fontana, Lucio 00505
Fontane, Theodor 19061, 20751
Forckenbeck, Oscar von 15373
Forel, Alexis 36950
Forster, Karl-August 17886
Forte, Vicente 00505

Fortunato Bartolomeo de, Félice 37354
Fortuny y Carbó, Mariano 34553
Foster, Norman 40100
Fouqué, Friedrich de la Motte 17083
Fowler, James 39834
Fra Angelico 23840, 23869, 25163
Fra Bartolomeo 23869
Fragonard, Jean-Honoré 02830, 11923, 12776
Francis, Sam 07514
Francke, August Hermann 17509
François I 11769
Frank, Anne 28838
Franke, Hanny 16931
Frankenthaler, Helen 07514
Franklin, John 38461
Franko, Ivan 06828, 37884
Franz Joseph I 01706, 02562
Franz, Robert 17513
Franz, Schmidt 02399
Fraser, Simon 06546
Fraunhofer, Joseph von 15877
Frenguelli, Joaquín 00621
Freud, Anna 39639
Freud, Lucian 19949, 39336
Freud, Sigmund 02989, 08624, 33466, 39639
Freundlich, Otto 13833
Frey, Günther 02473
Freytag, Gustav 17359, 20393, 20395
Fried, Erich 02850
Friedrich, Caspar David 20472
Friedrich I Barbarossa 17225
Fries, Adrian de 02926
Fröbel, Friedrich 17048, 19214
Fröding, Gustaf 36002
Fröhlich, Fritz 03032
Fronius, Hans 02401
Frunze, M.V. 27308
Fuchs, Ernst 02878
Fürstenberg, Heinrich Graf von 36664
Füssli, Johann Heinrich 37386
Fugger, Jakob 15554
Fujiwara, Kei 26119
Fumbuka, David Clement 37464
Furneaux, Tobias 00855
Furphy, Joseph 01488
Gabat, Rudolf 02812
Gabin, Jean 12943
Gabo, Naum 40637
Gaddi, Taddeo 23805
Gadegård, Paul 08868
Gagarin, Jurij 32799, 33536
Gainsborough, Thomas 38115, 38211, 38917, 39627, 39680, 40642
Gaitán, Jorge Eliécer 07383
Gaj, Ljudevit 07727
Gajdar, Arkadij P. 32655, 32982, 33545
Galaup, Jean-François de 10275
Galilei, Galileo 24945
Gallatin Hoit, Albert 42168
Gallen-Kallela, Akseli 09432, 09810
Gallois, Genevieve 15099
Gallop, H. 01568
Gambetta, Léon 10996, 14738
Gameiro, Roque 32320
Gandersheim, Roswitha von 15650
Gandhi, Mahatma 21679, 21710, 21718, 21775, 21924, 21977, 22015, 34397
Ganesh, Selva 22059
Ganghofer, Ludwig 18044
Gárate, Hermano Francisco 34512
Garborg, Arne 30575, 30959
García, Carlos P. 31372
García Lorca, Federico 34831, 34870
Gárdonyi, Géza 21406, 21408
Gargallo, Pablo 34553, 35694
Garibaldi, Giuseppe 23065, 24118, 24349
Garret, Georges 15149
Gasteiger, Anna Sophie 20281
Gasteiger, Mathias 20281
Gaudí, Antoni 34532, 34553
Gauguin, Paul 13626, 13804, 15347, 18002, 28911, 38211
Gaul, August 17585
Gay-Lussac, Louis-Joseph 14323
Gaya, Ramón 35149
Gayarre, Julián 35336
Gazdov, Ivan 04888
Gebauer, Walter 16406
Gebler, F. 32671
Gegenbaur, Joseph Anton von 20395
Geiger, Rupprecht 19949
Gellée, Claude 11134
Gellert, Christian Fürchtegott 17496
Gentz, Wilhelm 19061
Georganti, Loukia 20889
George IV, King of England 38344
George, Stefan 16165
Gercen, Aleksandr 33057, 33075
Géricault, Théodore 12736
Gerstein, Noemí 00505
Gertsch, Franz 18107, 36606
Gerung, Mathis 18357
Gesellius, Herman 09673
Gevork, Grigorian 00683
Geyer-zu-Lauf, Hans von 16857
Gezelle, Guido 03254
Gfeller, Simon 36800
Ghiberti, Lorenzo 23862
Ghirlandaio, Domenico 23828, 23843, 23869

Giacometti, Alberto 08902, 25164, 37386, 40100
Giacometti, G. 36424
Giallina, Angeliki 20927
Giallina, Angelos 20927
Giaquinto, Corrado 23029, 23074
Gibbons, Grinling 40198
Gibran, Khalil 27488
Gil de Palacio, Léon 35040
Gill, Henry 16061
Gillray, James 26261
Giordano, Luca 23883, 24887, 25163, 35040
Giorgione 24733, 25951
Giotto di Bondone 23840, 24731, 24733, 25991
Giovanoli, Samuele 37168
Giraudoux, Jean 10671
Gleim, Johann Wilhelm Ludwig 17501
Gleyre, Charles 36860
Glichenstein, Hanoch 22787
Glicznęr, Erazm 32224
Glinka, Michail I. 33246, 33536
Glöckner, Hermann 16692
Gluck, Christoph Willibald Ritter von 15883
Gökalp, Ziya 37663
Göschen, Georg Joachim 17400
Goethe, Johann Wolfgang von 15434, 16648, 14727, 15606, 15688, 16725, 16855, 17046, 17432, 17890, 17891, 17942, 20081, 20167, 20459, 20460, 20461, 20561, 25150
Goetz, Ferdinand 18408
Götz, K.O. 18107
Göz, Godefried Bernhard 17973
Goga, Octavian 32490
Gogh, Vincent van 03365, 10414, 10503, 14446, 25164, 28911, 29648, 29686, 30074, 37386, 38898, 39729, 40773, 43693
Gogol, Nikolaj Vasilevič 33039, 37910
Goitia, Francisco 28637
Goldblatt, S. 34317
Goldenvejzer, A.B. 33124
Goldie, C.F. 30264
Goldsworthy, Andy 39336
Goll, Claire 14187
Goll, Ivan 14187
Golovanov, N.S. 33122
Goltzius, H. 18068
Golubkina, A.S. 33061, 33745
Gómez, Martin 00501
Gončarov, Ivan Aleksandrovič 33416, 33657
Gončarova, Natalja 33522
González, Joaquín V. 00274
González, Julio 34553
Gordon, Charles George 38532
Gorkij, Maksim 19913, 32892, 33098, 33121, 33207, 33209, 33215, 33372
Gorsline, Douglas 10962
Gortan, Vladimir 07679
Gortani, Michele 25725
Gosselin, Joshua 40424
Goßmann, Gerhard 17163
Gotthelf, Jeremias 36608, 36895
Goudge, Edward 39110
Gounaropoulos, Giorgios 21224
Goya, Francisco de 10231, 11084, 14832, 24273, 28195, 34827, 35006, 35027, 35040, 35718, 35739
Goyen, Jan van 29526
Graber, Alfons 02677
Granovskij, T.N. 33260, 33266
Grass, Günter 18535
Grassi, Nicola 25845
Grebenščikov, G.D. 32673
El Greco 24434, 24799, 35535, 35739, 38898
Green, George 40107
Green, John 03890
Green, Thomas 39168
Grekov, M.B. 33232
Grela, Juan 00505
Grescny, Marie-Thérèse 12838
Gressly, A. 36664
Grétry, André Ernest Modeste 03584
Griboedov, Aleksandr Sergeevič 32745
Grieg, Edvard 30776
Grigorescu, Nicolae 32481
Grimm, Jacob 17506, 18012, 20042, 20044
Grimm, Ludwig Emil 18012, 20042
Grimm, Wilhelm 17506, 18012, 20042, 20044
Grimmelshausen, Johann Jakob Christoffel von 17226, 19180
Grin, Aleksandr S. 32917
Grinberg, Aleksandr 33086
Gris, Juan 36262
Grochtmann, Hermann 16553
Grock 19440
Gröbli, Isaak 37003
Grohmann, Will 20106
Gropius, Walter 15916, 16136, 16584
Groth, Klaus 17660
Groth, Lars 30887
Gruber, Franz Xaver 01640, 01999, 02179
Gründgens, Gustaf 16744
Grünenwald, Jakob 16766
Grünewald, Matthias 18002
Grundtvig, N.F.S. 08978
Guardi, Francesco 02886, 38115
Güiraldes, Ricardo 00550
Günther, Ignaz 15460
Guercino 23983
Guericke, Otto von 18586
Guérin, Maurice de 10335

Guillaumin, Émile 15328
Gulácsy, Lajos 21349, 21550
Gulbransson, Olaf 20152
Gulia, Dmitri 15357
Gully, John 30211
Gunarsa, Nyoman 22148
Gurschner, Gustav 02446
Gursky, Andreas 18107, 18161
Gustav II Adolf 18564, 20497
Gutenberg, Johannes 16842, 18600
Gutman, Nahum 22771
GutsMuths, Johann C. 19462, 19819
Gyokudo, Kawai 26634
Hablik, Wenzel 17935
Hacker, Dieter 07514
Hadjikyriakos-Ghikas, N. 20892
Hadjimichail, T. 21119
Haeckel, Ernst 17938
Händel, Georg Friedrich 17513
Hahn, Philipp Matthäus 15422, 15799
Haidar, Ali 22029
Haizmann, Richard 19094
Hall, John 40625
Halonen, Eemil 09759
Hals, Frans 28195, 29324, 38211
Hamada, Shoji 26468
Hamerling, Robert 02110
Hamil, Jan 41316
Hammerich, Gunnar 08766
Hanak, Anton 02186
Handke, Peter 01943
Hanrieder, Norbert 02467
Hansen, Helmer 30793
Hansjakob, Heinrich 17626
Harbutt, W. 38117
Hardy, Adolphe 03393
Hardy, Oliver 40748
Hardy, Thomas 38748, 39242
Haring, Keith 16042
Harrer, Heinrich 02051
Harris, Howell 38317
Harris, John 05763
Hart Benton, Thomas 41316
Hart, Robert Edward 27741
Harth, Philipp 15861
Hartmann, Oluf 08982
Hartung, Hans 19949
Hasdeu, Bogdan Petriceicu 32480
Hasdeu, Julia 32480
Hasenclever, Johann Peter 19565
Hathaway, Anne 40624
Hatry, Julius 18613
Hauptmann, Gerhart 16724, 16912, 18113, 31629
Hauser, Kaspar 15503
Hausner, Rudolf 18259
Haviland, Théodore 10299
Havlíček, Borovský Karel 08348
Haydn, Johann Michael 02541
Haydn, Joseph 01808, 01809, 02521, 02894, 21415
Haydn, Michael 02521
Hayet, Louis 13832
Hearn, Lafcadio 26470
Hebbel, Friedrich 02859, 18080, 20539
Hebel, Johann Peter 15597, 17644, 19842
Hébert, Ernest 12270, 13639
Hebroni, Josef 19569
Heckel, Erich 15931, 16893
Hecker, Friedrich 19486
Hedberg, Erik 35974
Heeg-Erasmus, Fritz 19842
Heel, Jan Van 29562
Heesters, Jan 29805
Hegel, Georg Wilhelm Friedrich 20095
Hein, Piet 08966
Heine, Ferdinand 17502
Heine, Heinrich 16726
Heine, Salomon 17544
Heinke, Curt 20762
Helm, Walter 15524
Helmcken, J.S. 06722
Helmschmid, Desiderius 35059
Helmschmid, Kolman 35059
Helye, Helyas 36557
Hem, Louise de 03517
Hemingway, Ernest 08103, 44464, 46053
Henner, Jean-Jacques 13641
Henry VIII 39756
Hepburn, Audrey 37248
Hepworth, Barbara 29686, 40406, 40637
Heras, Henry 21949
Herbin, Auguste 12396
Herder, Johann Gottfried 20462
Heredia, José-Maria de 13963
Herites, František 08722
Herkomer, Hubert von 18305, 18303
Hernandez, Don Jaime 31407
Hernández, José 00660
Hernández, Miguel 35183
Herold, Georg 16971
Herrliberger, David 36931
Herschel, Caroline 38125
Herschel, William 38125
Hertervig, Lars 30887
Herwegh, Georg 03859
Herzen, Alexander 33057, 33075
Herzer, Klaus 18781
Hesse, Hermann 16447, 16836, 17190, 26211, 36472, 36944
Heuber, Blasius 02374

Heydt, Eduard Baron v.d. 36472
Heyerdahl, Thor 30632, 30740
Hidalgo y Castulo, Miguel 27891
Hideyoshi, Toyotomi 26437, 26567
Hieronymus von Prag 18203
Higueras, Jacinto 35455
Hilberseimer, Ludwig 15916
Hildebrandt, Hugo 15451
Hill, Derek 22393
Hincz, Gyula 21601
Hinder, Frank 01568
Hippokrates 21032
Hirst, Damien 30727
His, Wilhelm 36494
Hjorth, Bror 36219, 36351
Hobhouse, Emily 34323
Hobrecht, James 16061
Hockaday, Hugh 44384
Hodgkins, Frances 30264
Hodler, Ferdinand 36424, 37185, 37386
Höbarth, Josef 02048
Höch, Hannah 16042
Hoel, Sigurd 30815
Hölderlin, Friedrich 18619, 20224
Hoelscher, Richard 15437
Höß, Crescentia 18036
Hoetger, Bernhard 16331
Hofer, Andreas 02062, 25381
Hoffman, Ernst Theodor Amadeus 15805
Hoffmann, Heinrich 17053, 17078
Hoffmann von Fallersleben, August Heinrich 20660
Hofmann, Hans 01818
Hofmann, Julius 17735, 19878
Hofner, Johann Baptist 19852
Hogarth, William 39666, 39729, 39777
Hogg, James 40469
Hohmann, Walter 17617
Hokusai, Katsushika 26980
Holbein, Hans (the Younger) 37185
Holberg, Ludvig 08794
Hollaender, Friedrich 16781
Holm-Møller, Olivia 08891
Holman Hunt, William 38624, 40141
Holst, Gustav 38545
Holub, Emil 08357
Holz, Paul 19353
Hopper, Edward 46048
Horch, August 18120
Horn, Rebecca 18135
Horn, Roni 18135
Hornel, E.A. 39392
Horstmann, G. 38117
Horta, Victor 03330
Horváth, Ödön von 18962
Houdin, Robert 10770
Houssay, Bernardo A. 00160
Howe, Oscar 41932, 45415
Howson, Peter 39045
Hrdlička, Aleš 08374
Hrdlicka, Alfred 02235, 19868
Hrozný, Bedřich 08468
Huber, Konrad 20274
Huber, Mida 02182
Hudetz, Karl Anton 20580
Hübsch, Heinrich 20480
Huet, Jan 03502
Hugo, Victor 10731, 13524, 15239, 27579, 40425
Huisman, Jopie 30021
Hulsdonck, Jacob van 12923
Humboldt, Alexander von 16003, 16056, 32671
Humboldt, Wilhelm von 16003
Hummel, Berta 18663
Hummel, Johann Nepomuk 33965
Hummel, M.I. 18663
Hundertwasser, Friedensreich 02916
Hunt, Robert 40303
Hunter, Adelaide 46318
Hunter, William 39051
Hus, Jan 08375, 18203
Hussein, Ibrahim 27680
Huys, Modest 03859
Hviezdoslav, Pavel O. 33990
Hybeš, Josef 08325
Iancu, Avram 32431
Ibsen, Henrik 30519, 30737, 30845
Ingres, Jean Auguste Dominique 13048, 13626
Iorga, Nicolae 32623
Iqbal, Allama Sheikh Muhammad 31036
Iramain, Juan Carlos 00586
Irving, Henry 40686
Isac, Emil 32493
Isepp, Sebastian 02365
Ishikawa, Takuboku 26818
Islandsmoen, Sigurd 30408
Istrati, Panait 32444
Itten, Johannes 16584, 20455
Ittenbach, Franz 18135, 18185
Ivens, Joris 28852
Izquierdo, María 28126
Jabotinsky, Zeev 22762
Jacobs, Ted 12532
Jacobsen, Jens Peter 09091
Jacobsen, Robert 18259
Jahn, Friedrich Ludwig 16064, 17130
Jaindl, Othmar 02760
Jakšić, Džuro 33916
James, John 41379
James, Joyce 22438, 22475
Jamsz-Teles jr. 04301

Janáček, Leoš 08265, 08272, 08275, 08340, 08373
Janco, Marcel 22590
Janicki, Klemens 32224
Janků, Miloslav 08315
Jans, Theo 29484
Jansson, Tove 10093
Jarošenko, Nikola 32929
Jauslin, Karl 36977
Javornickij, D.I. 37850
Javorov, Pejo K. 04646, 04835, 04847
Jawlensky, Alexej von 16661, 20576, 36470, 36884
Jean, Émile 15258
Jeanne-Claude 18259
Jedlik 21355
Jefferies, Richard 40665
Jenner, Edward 38168
Jensens, Johannes Vilhelm 08821
Jerome, Jerome K. 40772
Jesenský, Janko 33969
Jilemnický, Peter 34069
Jiménez, Juan Ramón 35115
Jindřich, Jindřich 08333
Jinnah, Mohammed Ali 31032
Jirásek, Alois 08371, 08372, 08592, 08678
Jochumsson, Matthías 21623
Jodrell, Sir Alfred 39038
Johann, Erzherzog von Österreich 02674
John, Augustus 40684
John, Gwen 40684
Johns, Jasper 18161, 26313
Johnson, Eyvind 35834
Johnson, Samuel 39492, 39625
Johnston, Franz 05846
Jókai, Mór 21311
Jomini, A.-H. 37018
Jones, Inigo 39573
Jones, Paul 01065
Jong, A.M. de 29615
Jonquieres, Eduardo 00505
Jónsson, Ásgrímur 21655, 21663
Jonsson, Einar 21653
Jónsson, Finnur 21655
Jordaens, Jacob 03171
Jorn, Asger 09053
Josephsohn, Hans 36760
Jourdain, Francis 14180
Jovellanos, Gaspar Melchor de 34848
Jovkov, Jordan 04656
Joyant, Jules-Romain 12626
Joyce, James 22439
József, Attila 21312, 21467
Juárez, Benito 28182, 28278
Judd, Donald 01927
Jüngst, Antonie 20524
Jularbo, Carl 35826
Juntoku, Emperor 26465
Jusupov, F. 33411
Jusupov, Usman 37856
Juvarra, Filippo 25736
Kableškov, Todor 04715
Kaempfer, Engelbert 18429
Kästner, Erich 16680, 16781
Kahlo, Frida 28126, 28172
Kahn, Albert 10836
Kaim, Lorenz 18244
Kairis, Theophilos 20825
Kaiser, Berta 18105
Kaiser, Georg 18583
Kalamaras, Dimitri 20958
Kalantiaw, Datu Benhadara 31286
Kallmann, Hans Jürgen 17927
Kaltenbrunner, Carl Adam 01818
Kalvoda, Alois 08655
Kamala, Šarif 32905
Kanakakis, Lefteris 21139
Kandinsky, Wassily 13626, 13629, 15916, 16584,
    16728, 18002, 18918, 18961, 26313, 36262,
    39615
Kandó 21355
Karalijčev, Angel 04828
Karavelov, Lyuben 04714
Karl V. 18195, 34760
Karlstadt, Liesl 18922
Karsten, Ludvig 30765
Kašpar, Adolf 08463
Kaspar, Johann 19175
Kasprowicz, Jan 31617, 32206
Kass, János 21549
Kassák, Lajos 21348
Kassner, Rudolf 37166
Kastriotis, George 21122
Kat, Otto de 29562
Katona, József 21446
Katz, Añex 07514
Kauffmann, Angelika 02645
Kaulbach, Wilhelm von 15591
Kausopson, Kausop 34194
Kawabata, Ryushi 26914
Kawaguchi, Kigai 26998
Kawai, Kanjiro 26408
Kawanabe, Kyosai 26999
Kazakov, Dimitar 04888
Kazantzakis, Nikos 20975, 20976
Keats, John 25169, 39679
Kekkonen, Urho Kaleva 09545
Kekulé, August 03445
Keller, Friedrich Gottlob 15734, 17497
Keller, Helen 48120
Keller, Paul Anton 02247

Kelley, Mike 16729
Kendall, Henry 01067
Kenkichi, Tomimoto 26098
Kenneth, King 22441
Kepler, Johannes 19526, 20439
Kerényi, Jenő 21571
Kerg, Theo 19850
Kern, Leonhard 19864
Kerner, Justinus 20481
Kernstock, Ottokar 01751
Khare, G.H. 21987
Khnopff, Fernand 26195
Kiefer, Anselm 15981, 20662, 26313, 30727
Kierkegaard, Søren 08933
Kießling, Franz 01775
Kim, N. 33394
King, Jessie M. 38789, 39393
Kipling, Rudyard 34313, 38409
Kirchner, Ernst Ludwig 16138, 18161, 36654, 38916
Kirov, Sergej Mironovič 33436
Kirste, Ernst 15451
Kisfaludi Strobl, Zsigmond 21614
Kisfaludy, Károly 21541
Kisfaludy, Sándor 21541
Kitchener, Horatio Herbert 38532
Kittelsen, Theodor 30610
Kivi, Aleksis 09905
Klaproth, Martin Heinrich 17960
Klassen, Peter 03633
Klee, Paul 15916, 16086, 16584, 16728, 26313,
    30414, 36470, 36917
Klein, Yves 18107, 18161
Kleist, Ewald Christian von 17083
Kleist, Franz Alexander von 17083
Kleist, Heinrich von 17083
Klenze, Leo von 19788
Klimt, Gustav 02235, 02549, 37185
Klinger, Max 18979
Ključevskij, V.O. 33289
Kløcker, Johannes Nicolai 30389
Klöpfer, Hans 01798
Klopstock, Friedrich Gottlieb 19462
Klotz, Matthias 18754
Klucis, Gustavs 27444
Kluk, Krzysztof 31538
Kmet, A. 34025
Kmetty, János 21572
Kneipp, Sebastian 15778
Knoll, Franz Xaver 20584
Knopp, Naum 00505
Knox, John 38890
Kobell, Ferdinand 15529
Kobro, Katarzyna 31777
Koch, Robert 16083
Kochanowski, Jan 31541
Kodály, Zoltán 21351
Köhler, Johann David 16492
Köleri, Johann 09393
König, Albert 20269
Körner, Theodor 18195, 20640
Kohán, György 21424
Kohlhaas, Michael 15629
Kohlhase, Hans 15629
Kojima, Torajiro 26385
Kokoschka, Oskar 02235, 02422, 02549, 37386,
    38917
Kolarov, Vasil 04874
Kolbe, Georg 15909
Kolbenheyer, Erwin Guido 17251
Kolcov, Aleksej Vasiljevič 33732
Kolig, Anton 02365
Kollwitz, Käthe 16013, 18147, 18792, 26261
Kolstø, Fredrik 30537
Kommerell, Max 18929
Konenkov, S.T. 33081, 33529, 33536
Konopnicka, Maria 31627, 32009
Konstantinov, Aleko 04879
Koons, Jeff 20662
Korin, P.D. 33076
Korniss, Dezső 21578
Korolenko, V.G. 32803
Korolev, S.P. 33074
Koschat, Thomas 02125
Kosciuszko, Tadeusz 37184
Kossuth, Lajos 21395, 21483
Kostka, Fertiš 34067
Kostov, Dončo 04725
Kosuth, Joseph 16971
Koszta, József 21579
Kounellis, Jannis 18135
Kovács, Attila 18135
Kovács, Margit 21420, 21573
Kovalevskaja, Sofja Vassilievna 33327
Kozin, Vadim Alekseevič 33000
Kozlov, P.K. 33419
Kraljević, Miroslav 07756, 07829
Kramskoj, Ivan Nikolaevič 33275, 33276
Kranewetter, Franz Josef 02336
Krasilnikov, G.D. 32835
Krasiński, Zygmunt 31855
Kraszewski, Józef Ignacy 16687, 31952
Kraus, Joseph Martin 16386
Kreibig, Erwin von 18846
Kreutzer, Conradin 18719
Křička, Jaroslav 08408
Křička, Petr 08408
Kristiansen, Herleik 30444
Křižík, František 08541
Krohg, Christian 30413

Kromer, Marcin 31490
Krúdy, Gyula 21492
Kruger, Paul 34345, 36638
Krumbacher, Karl 20584
Krupp, Alfred 16951
Krupp, Friedrich 16951
Krupp, Friedrich Alfred 16951
Krupp von Bohlen und Halbach, Alfried 16951
Krupp von Bohlen und Halbach, Gustav 16951
Kruse, Käthe 15679, 16639
Ku, Chieh Kuang 07359
Kuba, Ludvík 08260
Kubin, Alfred 02225, 02234, 02235, 02825, 36470
Kügelgen, Gerhard von 16688
Kuen, Martin 20274
Kuindži, Archip Ivanovič 33452
Kulisiewicz, Tadeusz 31635
Kullrich, F.W. 16531
Kumičić, Eugen 07685
Kunanbaev, Ibrahim Abaj 27092
Kupala, Janka 03117
Kuprin, Aleksandr Ivanovič 32801, 33200
Kurelek, William 06407
Kuri Breña, José 28637
Kuroda, Seiki 26880
Kurts, R. 28662
Kurz, Alfred 02218
Kurz, Hermann 19576
Kusama, Yayoi 26855
Kustodiev, Boris Michajlovič 33277
Kvapil, Jaroslav 08322
Kyber, Manfred 18493
La Villéon, Emmanuel de 11794
Laban, Rudolf 36472
Lachner, Franz 19476
Lachner, Ignaz 19476
Lachner, Vinzenz 19476
Laemmle, Carl 18359
Lafage, Raimond 12631
Lafran, Paul 14143
Lagerlöf, Selma 35882, 36149
Laib, Wolfgang 20090
Lam, Wifredo 08001, 08117
Lamartine, Alphonse de 12758, 04779, 10260
Lamb, William 39984
Lamennais, Felicité 14341
Lampi, Vilho 09787
Land, Peter 16971
Langenberg, Ferdinand 17309
Langenhoven, C.J. 34317
Lansyer, Emmanuel 12640
Laperouse 10275
Lara, Agustín 27793
Larbaud, Valéry 15159
Larese, Dino 36457
Largillière 14832
Larionov, M. 33522
Larn, Richard 40389
Larsen, Johannes 08914
Larsen, Thoger 08972
Larsson, Carl 36305
Lassnig, Maria 19949
Laurel, José P. 31444
Laurel, Stan 40748
Laurencin, Marie 03766, 26128
Laurens, Henri 15217
Laurier, Wilfrid 06731, 06733
Lauritzen, Jørgen 30991
Lavant, Christine 02132
Lawrence, David Herbert 38864
Lawrence, W.D. 05566
Lawson, Henry 01077
Lazaris, Theodoros 21053
Lázaro, Franco 27819
Le Corbusier 13504, 13717, 14187, 37380
Le Maire, Jacob 14342
Leacock, Stephen 06055
Léandre, Charles 11544
Leber, Hermann 18739
Leck, Bart van der 29686
Lecoq, Henri 11325
Ledoux, Claude Nicolas 10394
Lee, Ufan 26855
Leger, Alexis 21248
Léger, Fernand 04514, 10740, 11929, 12067,
    13629, 14199, 15217, 36262
Lehár, Franz 01707, 02923
Lehmann, Lotte 19749
Lehmbruck, Wilhelm 16757
Leibniz, Gottfried Wilhelm 20653
Leighton, A.C. 05170
Leighton, Frederic Lord 39685
Leistikow, Walter 31514
Leitz, Ernst 20560
Leković, Veliš 33789
Lemonnier, Camille 03293
Lenau, Nikolaus 02699
Lenbach, Franz von 18918, 19852
Lenin, Vladimir Iljič 10080, 32807, 32886, 33130,
    33370, 33656, 33662, 33665, 33666
León y Castillo, Fernando de 35521
León y Castillo, Juan 35521
Leonardo da Vinci 02830, 03783, 10313, 23840,
    24408, 24799, 26025, 26026, 31712, 39729,
    43693
Leonhardi, Eduard 16694
Leopardi, Giacomo 25085
Leopoldo, Camille 31514
Lepe, Manuel 28350

Leppänen, Lauri 09552
Lermontov, Michail Jurjevič 32980, 33040, 33057,
    33194, 33321, 33416
Leskov, Nikolaj S. 33261, 33266
Lessing, Gotthold Ephraim 17978, 20653
Lesueur, Charles Alexandre 12428
Levitan, Isaak Iljič 33323
Levski, Vasil 04684, 04691, 04729
LeWitt, Sol 01927, 03546, 20466
Leyde, Lucas de 14832
Leyden, Lucas van 29526
Leyster, Judith 29324
Liapis, Kostas 20808
Lichtenstein, H. 16056
Lichtenstein, Roy 14199, 18161
Liebermann, Max 17970, 19569, 29955
Liebig, Justus von 17282
Liebknecht, Karl 18508
Ligne, Ch.-J. de 03209
Liipola, Yrjö 09698
Lilienthal, Otto 15495
Lindemann, Gustav 16744
Lindgren, Armas 09673
Liner, Carl August 36461, 36463
Liner, Carl Walter 36461, 36463
Liniers, Virrey 00111
Linley, Sambourne 35689
Linnankoski, Johannes 09421
Linné, Carl von 35782, 36356, 36357
Linnqvist, Hilding 36219
Lippi, Filippo 23730, 23840, 24273, 25043, 25161
Lippmann, J. 17007
Lipsi, Morice 14037
List, Friedrich 19576
Liszt, Franz 02477, 15845, 20464, 21354
Livadićca, Ferde 07767
Livingstone, David 38258, 49017
Llonye, Antoni 25736
Lo-Johansson, Ivar 36248
Locmanov, A. 32779
Lönnrot, Elias 10020
Löns, Hermann 20383
Loewe, Carl 17513
Löwen, Axel Graf von 20074
Logan, Andrew 40815
Loganathan, K. 22059
Loisel, Wilhelm 02433
Lomonosov, Michail Vasilevič 32992, 33456
Long, Richard 15981, 18107
Loo, Jacob van 29836
Lope de Vega, Félix 34990
López de Legazpi, Miguel 35740
López Velarde, Ramón 28029
López y Planes, Vicente 00195
Lord, Ted 05846
Lorean, John de 22492
Lorrain, Claude 02830, 13241, 25161, 40198
Loseleur, Hector 12806
Lossen, Carl-Maximilian 15875
Loti, Pierre 14001, 14417
Lotter, Hieronymus 17273
Lotto, Lorenzo 23066, 25086, 25927
Lowry, Andrew 22537
Lowry, L.S. 40430, 40650
Loyola, San Ignacio de 34511
Lu Xun 06974, 07066, 07220, 07232
Lubbock, Sir John 40135
Ludwig II 16972, 17733, 19878
Ludwig, Otto 16827
Lünenschloß, C.A. 20697
Luna, Juan 31281
Lunačarskij, A.V. 33125
Lurçat, Jean 14187
Luro de Sansinenz, Agustina 00331
Luro, Pedro 00331
Luther, Katharina 20185
Luther, Martin 16816, 16820, 18570, 18571, 18572,
    18575, 18576
Lutz, Joseph Maria 19381
Luyten, Hendrik 29743
Lyon, Danny 45774
Mabini, Apolinario 31367
McCahon, C. 30211
McCarthy, Paul 16729
McCrae, Georgiana 01191
McCrae, John 05537
McCulloch, Thomas 06129
MacDiarmid, Hugh 38194
Macdonald, Sir John A. 05673, 05963
Maceo, Antonio 08131
McGillivray, William 06546
Mácha, Karel Hynek 08330
Machado y Ruiz, Antonio 35462
McIndoe, Ken 41142
Mack, Alexander 15607
Macke, August 16230, 16242, 16661, 18002
MacKenzie, Sir Alexander 05963
Mackenzie King, William Lyon 05699, 06590
Mackintosh, Charles Rennie 39050, 39208
Mackintosh, Margaret MacDonald 39208
McMillan, Angus 01262
McNaughton, Daniel 38141
Macpherson, Allan 05963
Madách, Imre 33988
Mader, Ernst 02048
Madigan, Elvira 09088
Märkli, Peter 36760
Maeterlinck, Maurice 03443
Maeztu, Gustavo de 34807

Magalhães, João Jacinto de 32258
Magellan, Fernão de 14342
Magnelli, Alberto 14199, 15060
Magritte, René 03600, 13629, 26195, 38916
Magsaysay, Ramón 31396
Mahé de la Bourdonnais, Bertrand 14341
Mahen, Jiří 08288
Mahler, Gustav 02680, 08389
Mahringer, Anton 02365
Maillol, Aristide 13626, 13708
Maironis, Jonas 27520
Maistorov, Nikolai 04888
Majakovskij, Vladimir Vladimirovič 33060
Majorelle, Louis 13246
Makarenko, A.S. 33132
Makariopolski, Ilarion 04663
Makarova, N.V. 32863
Makowski, Tadeusz 13535
Makuszyński, Kornel 32208
Malewitsch, Kasimir 18161
Malfatti, Anita 04514
Malhoa, José 32246, 32284
Mali, Christian 16138
Mallarmé, Stéphane 15298
Malraux, André 12427
Malyškin, A.G. 33018
Mamin-Sibirjak, D.N. 32769, 32773, 32779
Manansala, Vicente 31288
Mané-Katz 22608
Mánes, Josef 08290
Manet, Edouard 13241, 40773
Manigk, Otto 19665
Manjarris, Michael 44259
Manley, Victor 40785
Mann, Golo 36825
Mann, Heinrich 08628
Mann, Thomas 08628, 36825, 37412
Mannerheim, Carl Gustaf Emil 09420, 09514
Manrique, César 35519
Mansart, François 12777
Mansfield of Iveagh, Lord 39680
Mantegna, Andrea 13621, 23066
Manthe, Albert 15492
Manzoni, Alessandro 24170, 24405
Manzoni, Piero 08868
Manzu, Giacomo 25164
Mao Zedong 07231, 07313
Marc, Franz 18002, 18124, 36470
Marchese, Victor 00505
Marchionni, C 20697
Marcks, Gerhard 16323
Marconi, Guglielmo 24125
Marey, Etienne-Jules 10651
Marini, Marino 23877, 24961
Marks, Sammy 34355
Marot, Clément 10996
Márquez Figueroa, José 28322
Marsili, Luigi Ferdinando 23138
Marti, Hugo 36876
Martí, José 07951
Martin, Alexandre-Louis 03346
Martin-Bates, Pat 06724
Martin, Henri 10996
Martin, John 40038
Martin, Jonathan 38141
Martin, Sarah 39127
Martine 13011
Martínez, Efrain 07566
Martínez Murguía, Manuel 35208
Martini, Arturo 25804
Martinů, Bohuslav 08556
Marx, Jenny 19738
Marx, Karl 20210
Masaccio 23840
Maside, Carlos 35352
Masla, Antun 07697
Mason, Raymond 07514
Massier, Clément 12186
Mataré, Ewald 18107
Matisse, Henri 12396, 13321, 13626, 13629,
    13632, 13833, 14199, 16086, 36262, 37060,
    37185, 40773
Matsutani, Takesada 03546
Matta, Roberto 07514
Mauersberger, Erhard 17439
Mauersberger, Rudolf 17439
Maulbertsch, Franz Anton 18325
Mauracher, Hans 01918
Mauthner, Fritz 18678
Maximilian, Erzherzog 02063
Maximilian Franz von Österreich 15693
Maximilian II Emanuel 19204, 19205
Maximilian, Kaiser von Mexiko 02002
May, Karl 17813, 19469
Maydell, Baron Ernst von 17375
Mayer-Franken, Georg 17020
Mayer, Tobias 18621
Mayeurm le 22184
Mayrhuber, Sepp 02420
Mazies, Victor 12631
Mazoyer, Georges 10369
Mazzini, Giuseppe 24946, 36780
Meckenem, Israhel van 16190
Medrea, Cornel 32453
Medvedcka, Mária 34076
Meerwein, Carl-Friedrich 16855
Méheut, Mathurin 12311
Mehoffer, Józef 31683

Meiche, Alfred 19908
Meister von Osnabrück 19275
Meistermann, Prof. Georg 20628
Mejerchold, Vsevolod E. 33051, 33126, 33292
Melanchthon, Philipp 16356, 18576
Melantrich z Aventýna, Jiří 08640
Melba, Dame Nellie 01176, 01239
Meletta, Carlo 36891
Memling, Hans 03257, 25993
Mendel, Johann Gregor 08268, 08272
Mendeleev, Dmitri Ivanovič 32693, 33429
Mendelssohn-Bartholdy, Felix 18403
Menéndez y Pelayo, Marcelino 35430
Mengs, Raphael 20274
Menon, Vengalil Krishnan Krishna 21917
Mercator, Gerhard 03742, 16751
Mergenthaler, Ottmar 15694
Mernoz, Jean 10459
Merrick, Thom 16971
Merveldt, Hanns-Hubertus von 16654
Merz, Mario 15981
Merz, Toni 19759
Mesdag, Hendrik Willem 29112, 29121, 29955
Mesmer, Franz Anton 18678
Mesonero Romanos, Ramón 34992
Messina, Antonello da 24887
Meštrović, Ivan 07782, 07803, 07810
Metsys, Quentin 03565
Meyer-Amden, O. 36424
Meyer, Conrad Ferdinand 36825
Meyer, Joseph 17753
Meyer, Traugott 36434
Michelangelo 02830, 13494, 23822, 23825, 23842,
    23862, 40141
Michelangelo il Giovane 23825
Michelena, Arturo 48906
Michelsen, Christian 30777
Michoutouchkine, Nikolai 48865
Mickiewicz, Adam 13528, 32110, 32217
Miegel, Agnes 15702
Mieghem, Eugeen van 03142
Mies van der Rohe, Ludwig 08279, 15916, 16136
Migishi, Kotaro 26715
Mihelič, France 34083
Mikelson, Arnold 06789
Milcendeau, Charles 14793
Milev, Geo 04866
Miller, Hugh 38671
Milles, Carl 36032
Millet, Jean-François 10585, 26360
Milton, John 38520
Milyj 33194
Minkowski, Maurice 00222
Mirabeau, Honoré Gabriel Riqueti Comte de 10407
Miranda, Carmen 04334
Miró, Joan 14199, 15217, 25164, 35232, 35694,
    38916
Mirtschin, Alfred 19609
Mistral, Frédéric 12769
Mistral, Gabriela 06929
Mitre, Bartolomé 00224
Mitterhofer, Peter 24792
Modersohn-Becker, Paula 16331, 20683
Modersohn, Otto 19326
Modigliani, Amedeo 04514, 13241, 13632, 15217,
    25164, 40773
Modok, Mária 21569
Moe, Jørgen 30561
Möbius, Karl 16056, 18081
Mörike, Eduard 15693, 16174, 18619
Moholy-Nagy, László 16584
Mohr, Joseph 01999
Mohs, Carl Friedrich 17099
Moldagulova, Alia 27070
Molière, Jean-Baptiste 13724
Molina Campos, Florencio 00454
Moll, Karl 16878
Moltke, Helmuth Graf von 19348
Molwitz, Herbert 18756
Mommsen, Theodor 17200
Monaco, Lorenzo 23730, 23805
Mondrian, Piet 29095
Monet, Claude 11871, 11872, 13241, 13627,
    14199, 15140, 18002, 24273, 25164, 37386,
    38898
Moniuszko, Stanisław 32076
Montag, Karl 20416
Montaldo, Anna Maria 23244
Montecuccoli, Raimund von 01987
Monteiro, Vincente do Rego 04301
Montgomery, Lucy Maud 06657
Monticelli, Adolphe 28911
Montilla, Carmen 07941
Moore, Henry 08902, 09478, 26174, 29686, 40100
Móra, Ferenc 21457, 21458
Morales, Tomás 35142
Morandi, Giorgio 19949
Moreau de Maupertuis, Pierre Louis 14341, 36664
Moreau, Gustave 13618
Morelos y Pavón, José María Teclo 27870
Moretus, Balthasar 03152
Moretus, Jan 03152
Morgan, William 38739
Morgner, Wilhelm 19981
Morie, Ogihara 26232
Moroles, Jesus Bautista 44259
Morris, William 39808
Mossman, James 38890

Motzfeld, Benny 30939
Moulin, Jean 13527
Mozart, Leopold 02543, 15562
Mozart, Nannerl 02543
Mozart, Wolfgang Amadeus 02543, 02544, 02570,
    02932, 08610, 15562
Mucha, Alfons 08488
Muche, Georg 15916, 16584
Muchin, N.S. 33250
Mühsam, Erich 36472
Müllenhoff, Carl Victor 18657
Müller, Carl Otto 16803
Müller-Scheeßel, Ernst 19768
Müller, Walter 20684
Münchhausen, Hieronymus Karl Friedrich Freiherr von
    16209
Münster, Mia 19758
Münster, Sebastian 17900
Münter, Gabriele 18961, 18962
Müntzer, Thomas 15434, 17700, 18810, 20066
Münzer, Adolf 18305
Münzner, Rolf 04652
Muir, Thomas 38237
Mukanov, Sabit 27074
Mukhtar, Mahmoud 09271
Multscher, Hans 26028
Munakata, Shiko 26100
Munch, Edvard 30398, 30413, 30414, 30640,
    30743, 30746, 30765, 37386
Munirathinam, B. 22059
Munkácsy, Mihály 21319
Munnings, Sir Alfred 38711
Muñoz Rivera, Luis 32362
Munthe, Axel 22878
Murat, Joachim 12282
Muratori, Ludovico A. 24449
Murillo, Bartolomé Esteban 11084, 25163, 35479
Musäus, Johann Karl August 20462
Musil, Alois 08731
Musil, Robert 02132
Musorgskij, Modest Petrovič 33202
Musrepov, Gabit 27074
Myers, W.J. 38952
Mylonas, Alex 20845
Nabokov, Vladimir V. 33359, 33482
Näf, Matthias 37003
Näver, Pälle 36404
Nagaoka, Kounito 04652
Nagel, Gustav 15510
Nandino, Elías 27835
Nansen, Fridtjof 30734, 30933
Napoléon I 01759, 03590, 10262, 10267, 10375,
    10513, 10789, 11769, 12045, 25230, 37092
Napoléon III 11769, 37092
Nash, John 38344
Nash, Thomas 40628
Nasyri, Kajuma 32899
Natsagdorj, Dashdorjiyn 28684
Naumann, J.F. 18191
Necker, Jacques 36647
Negroli, Filippo 35059
Nehru, Jawaharlal 21781
Neidhardt von Gneisenau, August Wilhelm Anton Graf
    17308
Nekrasov, Nikolaj Alekseevič 32628, 32753, 32883,
    33417
Nelimarkka, Eero 09413
Nelson, Lord Horatio 39978, 40258
Němcová, Božena 08293, 08295, 08508
Němejc, Augustin 08497
Nemirovič-Dančenko, Vladimir I. 33127, 33135
Nerdrum, Odd 30640
Nervo, Amado 28494
Nesch, Rolf 30372, 30765
Netti, Francesco 23029
Neuber, Friederike Caroline 19546
Neubrand, Philipp 16879
Neukams, Gottfried 18244
Neumann, Balthasar 18677, 20696, 20701
Neuss, Wolfgang 15983
Neve, Hanneke de 41142
Newman, Chris 18135
Newton, Isaac 39111
Newton, John 40130
Niazy, Hamza Hakim-Zadé 48837, 48841
Nicholson, Ben 39336, 40637
Niebuhr, Carsten 18695
Niekerk, Chris Van 34194
Nielsen, Carl 08775, 09006
Nielsen Hauge, Hans 30802
Nielsen, Jens 08891
Niemeyer-Holstein, Otto 18213, 19665
Niemeyer, Oscar 04327
Nietzsche, Friedrich 18980, 20467, 37169
Nightingale, Florence 38047, 39636
Nilsen, Torstein 30444
Nivelt, Roger 13371
Noakowski, Stanisław 31825
Nobel, Alfred 35996, 36268
Noble, Roberto 00240
Noguchi, Hideyo 26247
Nøis, Hilmar 30793
Nolde, Emil 19039
Nonagase, Banka 26998
Nonell y Monturiol, Isidro 34553
Nordenskiöld, Adolf Erik 09872
Nordheim, Sondre 30691
Nordlander, Anna 36196

Nosilov, K. 32779
Nouveau, Henri 13833
Novák, Vítězslav 08398
Nováková, Tereza 08628
Novalis 17948, 20499, 20566
Nowak,Arthur 02048
Nowowiejski, Feliks 31476
Nüesch, Jacob 36491
Núñez, Rafael 07455
Oates, Frank 40465
Oates, Lawrence 40465
Oberkampf, Christophe-Philippe 12096
Oberlin, Jean-Frédéric 15299
Oberth, Hermann 16994
Obregón, Alvaro 37982
O'Connor, James 22557
O'Hara, Jack 41316
Ohmann, Friedrich 02408
Ohmeyer, Maria 02440
Oille, Lucille 05846
Okakura, Tenshin 26340
Okudžava, Bulat 33298
Ólafsson, Sigurjón 21654
Olbracht, Ivan 08652
Oldenburg, Claes 18161
Oldenburg, Ernst 20265
Ollier, Léopold 12560
Olsson Hagalund, Olle 36219
O'Neill Verner, Elizabeth 42215
Onley, Toni 06724
Opitz, Theodor 36876
Oppenheim, Meret 37185
Opsomer, I. Baron 03587
Oranien-Nassau, Wilhelm I von 16610
Orensanz, Angel 45763
Orff, Carl 16599
Orkan, Władisław 31894, 31936
Orley, Bernard van 10853
Orozco, José Clemente 27942, 28126, 28160
Orthman, Thomas 07514
Ortiz Echagüe, Antonio 00266
Osborn Cunningham, Marion 41439
Ossietzky, Karl von 16781
Ost, Alfred 03502, 03860, 29745
Ostrovskij, Aleksandr Nikolaevič 33041, 33051,
    33513
Ostrovskij, Nikolaj Alekseevič 33106, 33540, 37900
Ostwald, Wilhelm 17426
O'Sullivan, Timothy 45774
Oteiza, Jorge 35694
Otero Pedrayo, Ramón 35572
Othón, Manuel Jóse 28406
Owen, Robert 40012, 40071
Pacheco, Francisco 11084
Paderewski, Ignace J. 36952
Pahl, Manfred 18595
Paik, Nam June 16729
Palacios, Alfredo L. 00149
Palacios, Pedro 00385
Palacký, František 08355
Palamas, Kostis 20899
Palauzov, Dimităr Trifonov 04669
Palissy, Bernard 15672
Palitzsch, Johann Georg 16686
Pallas, P.S. 16056
Palma, Jacopo 24733
Panaitescu-Perpessicius, Dumitru 32444
Pancera, Ella 01705
Pander, Pier 29513
Pankok, Bernhard 18946
Pankok, Otto 17861
Pannini, Giovanni Paolo 24887
Paolo Veronese 23983, 24733, 25921, 25993
Papanastassiou, Alexandros 21046
Pappenheim, Gottfried Heinrich Graf zu 19347
Paracelsus, Theophrastus 36482
Paradise, Phil 41439
Parajanian, Sargis 00688
Parapunov, Nikola 04799
Pardo Bazán, Emilia 34747
Parmigianino 23905, 24799
Parnell, Charles Stewart 22531, 22532
Parry, Joseph 39938
Parthenis, K. 21200
Pascoli, G. 23017
Pass, Alfred A. de 34219
Pasternak, Boris L. 32748, 33057, 33297
Pasteur, Louis 10389, 11542, 13643
Pasteur, Vincent 12082
Patton, George S. 27557
Pátzay, Pál 21443
Paul, Jean 15848, 15849
Paustovskij, Konstantin G. 33072, 33545
Pavelic, Myfanwy 06724
Pavlov, A.P. 33053
Pavlov, Ivan Petrovič 33350, 33420
Pavlović-Barilli, Milena 33589
Pavlovskij, Evgenij Nikanorovič 32699
Pearse, Patrick 22451
Pecharromán, Ricardo 35255
Pechstein, Max 20776
Peck, Sheldon 44849
Pedersen, Carl-Henning 08866
Pelin, Elin 04608, 04847
Pellicer Cámara, Carlos 28604
Peltonen, Vihtori 09041
Penev, Penjo 04649
Pengelly, William 40718
Perantinos, Nikolaos 20896

Pérez Galdós, Benito 35244
Pérez, Genaro 00307
Perkins, Simeon 05760
Permeke, Constant 03526
Peroutka, Ferdinand 08661
Perraudin, Jean-Pierre 36893
Perugino 12736, 13241
Peské, Jean 11351
Pestalozzi, Johann Heinrich 36608, 37354
Peter I, the Great 30032, 33391, 33567, 33721
Petersson Döderhultarn, Axel 36153
Petőfi, Sándor 21307, 21456, 21457
Petrarca, Francesco 11759, 22942
Petrov-Vodkin, Kuzma Sergeevič 32746
Pettoruti, Emilio 00505
Petzval, Johann 34062
Peukert, August 17585
Peyrissac, Jean 10996
Peyton, Elizabeth 20662
Pezzani, Costante 17671
Pflug, Johann Baptist 16138
Pfohl, Alexander 17473
Piaf, Edith 13611
Pič, Ladislav 08490
Picabia, Francis 12881, 18161
Picard, Max 19842
Picasso, Pablo 03600, 08902, 10377, 10417,
    11003, 11929, 12736, 12939, 13241, 13626,
    13629, 13632, 13644, 13708, 14199, 15060,
    15061, 15217, 16086, 16728, 18161, 18938,
    20106, 26174, 26998, 30414, 34586, 34626,
    35232, 35694, 36262, 36915, 36917, 37060,
    37386, 38916, 43693, 45872
Piechowski, W. 31810
Pieck, Anton 29351
Piero della Francesca 25427
Piette, Ludovic 13832
Piffetti, Pietro 25736
Pijnenburg, R. 29580
Pilioko, Aloi 48865
Pilon, Veno 34083
Piłsudski, Józef 31697
Piotrowski, Maksymilian Antoni 31514
Pirandello, Luigi 22815, 25151
Piranese, Canaletto 12640
Pisanello 23066
Pisano, Giovanni 24731
Pisis, Filippo de 23788
Pissaro, Camille 13832, 18002, 40141, 40773
Pissarro, Lucien 13832
Pitman, I. 38117
Pius X 25109
Plantin, Christopher 03152
Plateau, J. 03445
Platter, Felix 36494
Plechanov, Georgi Valentinovič 32984, 32985
Plessis, Jean de 13963
Poey, Felipe 07960
Pol, Rein 29259
Pol, Wincenty 31789
Polenov, V.D. 33566
Polenz, Wilhelm von 16518
Poliakoff, Serge 13626
Polke, Sigmar 08902, 14199, 18161
Pollock, Jackson 26313
Polychronopoulos, Costas 21063
Ponce de León, Juan 09116
Popov, Aleksandr Stepanovič 32780, 32960, 32961,
    32965, 33422
Porras, Belisario 31078
Porsche, Ferdinand 01890, 20103
Porumbescu, Ciprian 32600
Post, Frans 04301
Potter, Beatrix 39198, 40451
Pound, Ezra 25709
Poussin, Nicolas 02830, 12516, 25163, 38898,
    39627
Povarova, V. 33394
Powell-Cotton, P.H.G. 38203
Požalostin, I.P. 33545
Prassinos, Mario 14450
Preriati, Gaetano 23788
Pretorius, M.W. 34336
Prieto, Gregorio 35591
Princip, Gavrilo 03914
Prišvin, Michail M. 32763, 33057
Prokofjev, Sergej Sergeevič 33148
Proust, Marcel 12056
Prus, B. 31820
Przybyszewski, Stanisław 31617
Puccini, Giacomo 24227, 25772, 25986
Pückler-Muskau, Hermann Fürst von 15698, 16501
Pueyrredón, Juan Martín de 00565
Pufendorf, Samuel Freiherr von 20784
Pugačëv, Emeljan 33273
Puig, Joseph 13709
Pułaski, Kazimir 32075
Pulitzer, Joseph 21468
Purrmann, Hans 17970, 18325, 19727
Puškin, Aleksandr Sergeevič 32686, 32696, 33063,
    33079, 33194, 33338, 33339, 33344, 33416,
    33453, 33489, 33619, 33743, 37858
Putz, Leo 18305
Puvis de Chavannes 28195
Queuille, Henri 13293
Quezon, Manuel L. 31435
Quinós, Bernardo Cesáreo de 00484
Raabe, Wilhelm 16303, 16933
Rabelais, François 14733

Rachmaninov, Sergej Vasilevič 32824
Račić, Josip 07829
Radetzky, Joseph Wenzel Graf 02136
Radiščev, Aleksandr Nikolaevič 33346
Radziwill, Franz 19256, 20285
Raevskij, Vladimir Fedoseevič 32695
Raffaello 02830, 02926, 13494, 14832, 23840,
    23844, 25161, 25856, 38898, 40141, 43693
Raimu 11345
Raimund, Ferdinand 01978, 02437
Rainer, Arnulf 02234
Rais, Karel Václav 08444, 08535
Rakovski, Georgi S. 04719
Raman, C.V. 21952
Ramoneda, Francisco 00364
Ran-In-Ting 07355
Ransome, Arthur 38625
Rapin, Aimée 37018
Rasmussen, Knud 08903
Rasputin, Grigorij 33411
Rathgeber, Valentin 19174
Rathinavelu, P.K. 22059
Rauch, Christian Daniel 15591
Rauf, H. Abdul 22108
Rauschenberg, Robert 07514, 15981
Ravel, Maurice 13086
Ravilious, Eric 40367
Raynaud, Jean-Pierre 26855
Razin, Stepan Timofeevič 33233, 33556
Rebreanu, Liviu 32554
Redon, Odile 13626
Redouté, H.-J. 03723
Redouté, P.-J. 03723
Rees, Lloyd 00774
Reger, Max 16277
Rehmann, Erwin 36849
Reich, Ferdinand 17099
Reichardt, Johann Friedrich 17513
Reid, George A. 06815
Reiffenstuel, Hans 19387
Reinhardt, Ad 01927
Reis, Philipp 17145, 17226
Rembrandt 02178, 02830, 02886, 02918, 02926,
    09025, 13621, 16692, 18002, 21539, 28855,
    28876, 28898, 29108, 29526, 38211, 38898,
    39627, 39680, 39729, 39798, 43693
Renan, Ernest 14989
Rendl, Georg 02566
Reni, Guido 23983, 24434, 25153, 25163
Renner, Karl 01885
Renoir, Auguste 13632, 24273, 43693
Renoudot, Théophraste 12675
Renz, Ernst Jakob 19440
Repin, Ilja Efimovič 33347, 33566
Rerich, Elena Ivanovna 33083, 33437
Rerich, Ju.N. 33083
Rerich, Jurij Nikolaevič 33437
Rerich, Nikolaj Konstantinovič 27444, 32673, 32839,
    33083, 33242, 33437, 45861
Rerich, Svjatoslav Nikolaevič 33083, 33437
Rešetnikov, F.M. 32770, 32773, 32779
Restle, Wilhelm 18678
Reuter, Fritz 16629, 16817
Reventlow, C.D.F. 08901
Reynolds, Joshua 38211, 39680, 39798, 40198
Rhodes, Cecil John 34313, 38240
Ribera, Jusepe de 25163
Ricci, Sebastiano 24799
Riccio, Andrea 24733
Rice, Edmund Ignatius 22552
Richards, Ceri 40658
Richelieu, Armand 13963
Richmond, James. C. 30211
Richter, Gerhard 14199, 18107, 18161, 30727
Richter, Johann Paul Friedrich 15848
Rie, Lucie 40100
Riehl, Elli 01800
Riemenschneider, Tilman 18243, 20696
Ries, Adam 15496
Riesener, Johann Heinrich 17291
Rietti, Ciro 00153
Rigaud, Hyacinthe 13708, 23983
Riley, Bridget 39336
Rilke, Rainer Maria 37166
Rilski, Neofit 04613, 04614
Rimski-Korsakov, Nikolaj Andreevič 33326, 33421,
    33599
Rinckart, Martin 16810
Ringelnatz, Joachim 16781, 20720
Rio Branco, Baron of 04384
Rippl-Rónai, József 21441, 21442
Rist, Pipilotti 20466
Ritter, Johann Wilhelm 17948
Rivel, Charly 16490
Rivera, Diego 27968, 28116, 28126, 28160, 28172
Rizal, José 31301, 31322, 31379
Rizzarda, Carlo 23771
Robbi, Andrea 37168
Robbia, Luca della 23843
Robert, Hubert 15051
Robertson, David 39957
Robinson, Joy 40795
Roca, Julio A. 00241
Rocha, Dardo 00394
Roché, Déodat 10426
Rochow, Friedrich Eberhard von 19511
Rodčenko, Aleksandr 33086
Rodin, Auguste 10260, 11003, 11131, 12960,
    13532, 14199, 38917

Rodríguez, Mariano 07932
Rodt, Christoph 20274
Röder, Paul 18650
Röntgen, Wilhelm Conrad 19564, 20703
Roerich, Nicholas 27444, 32673, 32839, 33083,
    33242, 33437, 45861
Roesch, Carl 36660
Rojas, Ricardo 00161
Romanino, Girolamo 24733
Rømer, Ole 09090
Romero de Torres, Julio 34740
Romney, George 39336
Roosevelt, Franklin D. 06768, 44186, 44187, 44188
Rops, Felicien 03651
Rosa, Salvator 24434
Rosegger, Peter 01657, 01658, 02164, 02165
Rossetti, Dante Gabriel 39787, 40141
Rossi, Gino 25804
Rossini, Gioacchino 24858, 24862
Roth, Dieter 17533, 20090
Rothenstein, Michael 40367
Rother, Richard 18105
Rothko, Mark 26313, 26998
Rousseau, Henri 16217
Rousseau, Jean-Jacques 11140, 11756, 13111,
    36728, 36749, 36954, 36982
Rousseau, Théodore 26360
Rożek, Marcin 32171
Rubcov, Nikolaj 32647
Rubens, Pieter Paul 02830, 02886, 02918, 02926,
    03152, 03171, 03173, 13241, 14832, 15529,
    18002, 22883, 23844, 24273, 28195, 29836,
    38211, 38898, 39573, 39627, 39798, 43693
Rubin, Reuven 22773
Rubinstejn, N.G. 33136, 33140, 33440
Rude, Olaf 08982
Rückert, Friedrich 16481
Rückriem, Ulrich 19643
Ruelas, Julio 28637
Ruhlmann, Jacques-Emile 11892
Ruisdael, Salomon Van 29108
Runeberg, Johan Ludvig 09951
Runeberg, Walter 09955
Runge, Friedlieb Ferdinand 19265
Runge, Philipp Otto 20074, 20667, 20668
Rupchan, Peter 06407
Ruppe, Hugo 18641
Rusiñol, Santiago 35497
Ruskin, John 38447, 38624, 38625, 39336, 39418
Russell, George 38017
Russell, John 39137
Rutherford, A.C. 05385
Ryba, Jakub Jan 08641
Ryggen, Hannah 30939
Rylands, John 39891
Ryti, Risto 09552
Saar, Ferdinand von 02852
Saarinen, Eliel 09673
Sabā, Aboul Hassan 22324
Sacharov, Andrej D. 33104, 33216
Saedeleer, Valerius de 03125
Saeki, Yuzo 26998
Sáenz, Manuelita 07384
Saint-Phalle, Niki de 36711
Saint-Saëns, Camille 11507
Sajdašev, Salich 32904
Sakatsoume, Atsouo 04652
Šaljapin, Fëdor 32801, 32889, 32892, 32927,
    33042, 33454
Saltykov-Ščedrin, Michail E. 32918, 33636
Salzillo, Francisco 35150
Salzmann, Christian Gotthilf 19819
Sami Durai, K. 22059
San Martín, José de 00214
Sanati 22253
Sand, George 11842, 12153, 13354
Sandby, Paul 01088
Sandell, Lina 36160
Sander, August 19949
Sándor, Petőfi 32497
Sansinenz de Elizalde, Elena 00331
Santa María, Andrés de 07514, 07429
Sante, Beato 24464
Sarian, M. 00685
Sarmiento, Domingo Faustino 00144, 00217, 00569
Sarpaneva, Timo 09559
Satie, Erik 13647
Saul, Peter 03633
Saura, Antonio 03633, 18135, 35694
Saussure, H.B. de 36746
Savio, John Andreas 30594
Savio, Manuel Nicolás Aristóbulo 00253
Ščekotichina-Potockaja, A.V. 33395
Ščerbov, P.E. 32801
Scharff, Edwin 19008
Schedoni, Bartolomeo 24799
Scheele, Carl-Wilhelm 20074
Scheffer, Ary 13568
Scheidt, Samuel 17513
Scheinpflugová, Olga 08661
Schelling, Friedrich 17948
Scherer, Alois 16618
Scherer, Joseph 16618
Scherer, Leo 16618
Scheving, Gunnlaugur 21655
Schiavo, Paolo 23829
Schiele, Egon 02235, 02348, 02743, 08302
Schiering, Kurt 18641

Schiestl, Rudolf 17167
Schikaneder, Emanuel 02923
Schill, Ferdinand von 20074
Schiller, Friedrich 15830, 16707, 17950, 18415,
    18520, 18619, 18620, 20459, 20471
Schindler, Oskar 08671
Schinkel, Karl Friedrich 19061
Schjerfbeck, Helene 09478, 09810
Schlegel, August Wilhelm 17948
Schlegel, Caroline 17948
Schlegel, Friedrich 17948
Schlegel, Hermann 15451
Schlemmer, Oskar 16584, 20102, 20106
Schleyer, Johann Martin 18348
Schliemann, Heinrich 15493, 19014
Schlosser, Cornelia 16855
Schlosser, Johann Georg 16855
Schmidt, Gustav 19366
Schmidt, Maximilian 16934, 18194
Schmidt-Rottluff, Karl 15931, 16466
Schmidtova, Natallie 17671
Schnabel, Julian 07514
Schneider, Friedrich 20385
Schnitzler, Arthur 16787
Schnopfhagen, Hans 02616
Schöffer, Nicolas 13470, 21437
Schoemaker, Ruud 29259
Schönberg, Arnold 02314, 02835
Schönburg, Grafen von 17299
Schönfeld, Johann Heinrich 16138
Scholl, Hans 17021
Scholl, Sophie 17021
Scholte, Dominie 46330
Schongauer, Martin 16692
Schoonhoven, Jan 29804
Schott, Otto 17945
Schouten, Cornelisz 14342
Schraemli, Harry 37243
Schreiber, Peter Conrad 17167
Schröter, Klaus 18305
Schubart, Christian Friedrich Daniel 15382
Schubert, Franz 01688, 02925, 02987, 02988
Schütte, Thomas 16729, 18107
Schütz, Christian Georg 15529
Schütz, Heinrich 15680, 20498, 20499
Schütz, Willi 16765
Schulenburg, Friedrich Werner Graf von der 16983
Schulten, Ton 29676
Schulze-Delitzsch, Hermann 16565
Schumacher, Emil 16661, 19949
Schumann, Clara 18417, 20778
Schumann, Robert 14685, 18417, 20778
Schumann, Viktor 18641
Schwarz, Joseph 16390
Schweitzer, Albert 11981, 12111, 17034, 20454
Schwind, Moritz von 18198, 19877
Schwitters, Kurt 13629, 14199, 39336, 40037
Scott, Robert Falcon 38461
Scott, Sir Walter 38921, 39931, 40471
Ščurovskij, G.E. 33053
Ščusev, A. 28662
Searle, Ronald 36502
Seckinger, Karl 17993
Sedlacek, Franz 02234
Seewald, Richard 36470
Segal, George 26998
Segantini, Giovanni 36920, 37115
Segovia, Andrés 34953
Segui, Antonio 03546
Seiko, Sawada 26269
Sell Cotman, John 40091
Sella, Vittorio 23078
Sellaio, Jacopo del 23805
Semmelweis, Ignác 21382
Semsey, Andor 21315
Sen, Sun Yat 07160
Šeremetev, V.P. 32863
Sergi, Sergio 00505
Serov, Valentin Aleksandrovič 32945
Serov, Vladimir Aleksandrovič 32795
Serra, Richard 18107
Seume, Johann Gottfried 17400
Ševčenko, Taras Grigorevič 33455, 37859, 37873
Shackleton, Ernest Henry 38461
Shakespeare, William 40624, 40625, 40627, 40628,
    40629, 40630
Shakir, Ali 31043
Shaw, George Bernard 38048
Shawqi, Ahmed 09289
Shelley, Percy Bysshe 25169
Shen Zong 07008
Shiro, Shitahata 27038
Shomu, Emperor 26583
Shortridge, G.C. 34295
Sibelius, Jean 09454, 09571, 10127
Siebner, Herbert 06724
Siebold, Philipp Franz von 20705
Siemens, Werner von 18906
Sienkiewicz, Henryk 31841, 32168
Signac, Paul 12881, 13832
Signer, Roman 37185
Silbermann, Gottfried 17090
Silcher, Friedrich 20488
Silva, Mário Augusto da 32258
Silva Paranhos, José Maria da 04384
Simberg, Hugo 09810
Singer, William H. 29499
Singh, S. Bhagat 21888
Siqueiros, David Alfaro 28126

Šiškin, Ivan Ivanovič 32786
Sison, Dolores 31407
Siswa, Taman 22219
Sivle, Per 30404
Skinner, J. Scott 38077
Skjoldborg, Johan 09106
Skovgaard, Joakim 09111
Skovgaard, Niels 09111
Skovgaard, P.C. 09111
Skrjabin, Aleksandr N. 33082
Sládek, Josef Václav 08741
Slavejkov, Pencho 04836, 04847
Slavejkov, Petko Racho 04836, 04847
Slevogt, Max 16780, 17970, 18379, 19727
Smet, Gustaaf de 03380
Smet, Léon de 03381
Smetana, Bedřich 08245, 08377, 08394, 08594, 35921
Smidovič, Vikentij Vikent'evič 33623
Smidt, Lajos 21588
Smirnenski, Christo 04829, 04847
Smith, Kiki 17970
Smits, Jakob 03629
Snellman, J.V. 09718
Śniadecki, Jan 32224
Śniadecki, Jędrzej 32224
Soane, Sir John 39627, 39777
Šogencukov, A.A. 33196
Sohos, A. 21197
Sokolow, Andrej 18569
Soldi, Raúl 00505
Šolochov, Michail Aleksandrovič 33683
Solomos, Dionysios 20934, 21221, 21222
Søndergaard, Jens 08971
Sørensen, Henrik 30556
Sorolla y Bastida, Joaquín 35055
Soto, Jesús 48933
Soudia, Fevronia 17671
Soulages, Pierre 14199
Soun, Tazaki 26109
Soundrajajan, N. 22059
Southey, Robert 39344
Soutter, Louis 36424, 36860
Sova, Antonín 08531
Spacca, Ascensidonio 23074
Španiel, Otakar 08383
Spanzotti, Giovanni Martino 25736
Spencer, Stanley 38629
Spicer, P. 40796
Spilimbergo, Lino 00307
Spilliaert, Leon 03670
Spinoza, Baruch de 29733
Spiridonov, Moisej S. 32721
Spitteler, Carl 36535, 36876
Spohr, Louis 18023
Spooner, Paul 39594
Spreitz, Karl 06724
Spyri, Johanna 36805
Spyropoulos, Jannis 20942
Stäbli, Adolf 36424
Staël, Madame de 36647
Šťáfl, Otakar 08349
Stalin, Jossif V. 33448
Stambolijski, Aleksandär 04817, 04837
Stanev, Emilijan 04847, 04914
Stanislavskij, Konstantin S. 33043, 33051, 33135
Stankowski, Anton 17230
Stašek, Antal 08652
Staszic, Stanisław 31615, 31881
Stażewski, Henryk 31777
Šteberl, Ondrej 17671
Steele, Theodore Clement 45611
Steen, Jan 29108, 29526
Stefansson, David 21619
Steichen, Edward 45774
Steiff, Margarete 17274
Steiger, Johann Ulrich 37431
Stein, Charlotte von 17432
Steinberg, Saul 36502
Steiner, Kilian von 18359
Steiner, Rudolf 01754
Steinway, William 19923
Stella, Frank 07514, 26998
Sten, John 35965
Stendhal 11946
Stephan, Heinrich von 16055
Stephenson, George 38697, 39026
Stern, Irma 34372
Sterne, Laurence 38652
Sterzel, Johann Traugott 16468
Stevenson, Robert Louis 38921
Stifter, Adalbert 02225, 02752, 02987, 08361
Stirner, Karl 16836
Stoddart, Margaret 30211
Stöhr, Gertrude 02774
Stojanov, Zachari 04733, 04803
Stoltze, Friedrich 17077
Stolz, Robert 01931
Stombuco, Andre 01086
Storck. Frederic 32451

Storm, P. 08827
Storm, Theodor 17685, 17873
Storno, Ferenc (jun) 21537
Storno, Ferenc (sen) 21537
Strand, Paul 45774
Straßner, Ernst 18739
Straub, Harriet 18678
Strauß, Johann 02992
Stravinskij, Igor 37908
Strigel, Bernhard 18705
Strindberg, August 02622, 36292
Stroux, Karl-Heinz 16744
Strozzi, Bernardo 23983
Strug, Andrzej 32088
Struth, Thomas 18107
Struve, Gustav 19486
Strzemiński, Władysław 31777
Stubbs, George 38115
Stuck, Franz von 18887, 20163
Stuckenberg, Fritz 16570
Štúr, Ludovit 34030
Sturt, Charles 01073
Sturtevant, Erich 17967
Stuyvaert, Victor 03443
Sucharda, Vojtěch 08501
Sudlow, Robert 41316
Suk, Josef 08432
Šukšin, Vasilij M. 32673, 33551
Sunyer, Joaquin 34553
Surcouf, Robert 14341
Susanin, Ivan 33568
Suter, August 36684
Sutter, Johann August 36608
Suvorov, Aleksandr Vasilevič 03112, 32936, 33400, 33679, 36765
Sveinsson, Jón 21622
Sverdrup, Otto 30734
Šverma, Jan 08483
Světlá, Karolina 08301
Svinhufvud, Pehr Evind 09803
Svoboda, Josef 08288
Svor, Anders 30563
Swagemakers, Theo 29332
Swann, Harry Percival 22537
Świętochowski, Aleksander 31601
Sypesteyn, C.H.C.A. van 29546
Szadurska, Kasia von 18677
Szántó, Piroska 21578
Széchenyi, István 21485
Szoényi, István 21616
Szukalski, Stanisław 32145
Taeuber-Arp, Sophie 19562
Tagore, Rabindranath 21899, 21910, 22011
Taiga, Ike 26404, 26428
Talbot, William Henry Fox 39408
Talkov, Igor 33105
Talvio, Maila 09465
Tamayo, Rufino 28126, 28160, 28274
Tamil Pandian, M.K. 22059
Tanaka, Kyokichi 26998
Taneev, Sergej Ivanovič 33194, 33750
Tanguy, Yves 14199
Tàpies, Antoni 07514, 34763, 35232
Tàpis, Antoni 19949
Taranci, Cahit Sitki 37660
Tarkovskij, Andrej 32865, 32866
Tasso, Torquato 25190
Tattarascu, Gheorghe M. 32459
Tavčar, Ivan 34148
Tavel, Rudolf von 36819
Tell, Wilhelm 36600
Tellgmann, Oscar 16936
Teniers, David 03171
Tennyson, Alfred Lord 39503
Tĕplyj, N.I. 33394
Terborch, Gerard 29145, 29505
Terbrugghen, Hendrik 29145
Terry, Ellen 40686
Terry, José Antonio 00637
Tersteegen, Gerhard 18815
Tesla, Nikola 33808
Tétar Van Elven, Paul 29085
Thaer, Albrecht Daniel 15950, 19547
Thatcher, Margaret 39111
Thek, Paul 18135
Theophilos 21206
Thoma, Hans 16121
Thoma, Ludwig 20149
Thomopoulos, Epaminondas 21114
Thonet, Michael 18120
Thorma, János 21460
Thorvaldsen, Bertel 09024, 38917
Ticho, Anna 22666
Ticiano 33898
Tidemand, Adolph 30663
Tieck, Ludwig 17948
Tiepolo, Giovanni Battista 14832, 20696, 20697, 20701, 20706, 25845, 25951, 25993
Tiepolo, Giovanni Domenico 20706
Tietz. Ferdinand 18703. 20696

Tiguely, Jean 37185
Tiljak, Djuro 07717
Timirjazev, Kliment Arkadevič 33128
Timlin, William 34294
Timmermans, Felix 03587
Tinel, Edgar 03733
Tinguely, Jean 36511, 36711
Tintoretto 12736, 13241, 23844, 24733, 25921, 25951
Tintoretto, Jacopo 24434
Tipu, Sultan 22029
Tischbein, Johann Friedrich 17494
Tischbein, Johann Heinrich 17494, 18028
Tischbein, Johann Heinrich Wilhelm 15592, 16979, 17494, 19256
Tito, Josip Broz 07731, 33805
Titov, German 32671
Tiziano 02886, 23840, 23844, 24273, 24733, 24914, 25161, 25921, 25951, 29798, 40141
Tjutčev, Fёdor Ivanovič 32994, 33278
Tkačev, Aleksej Petrovič 32709
Tkačev, Sergej Petrovič 32709
Tobón Mejía, Marco 07514
Todorov, Petko J. 04663
Toe Boelop, Mechteld 29474
Togo, Seiji 26915
Tokugawa, Ieyasu 26764
Toledo, Francisco 28126
Tollens, Peter 18135
Tolstoj, Aleksej Konstantinovič 32963
Tolstoj, Aleksej Nikolaevič 33057, 33129, 33374, 33416
Tolstoj, Lev Nikolaevič 32856, 33065, 33066, 33157, 33204, 33416, 33552
Topelius, Z. 10150
Topor, Roland 03546
Torner, Gustavo 34763
Tornyai, János 21427, 21428
Torrealba, Alberto Arvelo 48894
Torres Martínez, Manuel 35092
Torricelli, Evangelista 23756
Toscanini, Arturo 24794
Tóth, Menyhért 21427, 21449
Toulouse-Lautrec, Henri de 10276, 13274, 16692, 28911
Tour, Maurice-Quentin de la 14434
Tourguéniev, Ivan 10832
Townsend, Steven 38736
Trakl, Georg 02539
Traunfellner, Franz 02425
Třebízský, V.B. 08454, 08689
Trevithick, Richard 39349
Trockel, Rosemarie 16729
Troelstra, Pieter Jelles 29515
Tropinin, Vassilij A. 33154
Troyon, Constant 26360
Truman, Harry S. 43763, 44201, 44202, 44203, 44466, 44612
Tsangaris, Manos 18135
Tsarouchis, Yannis 21059
Tsouderos, E. 20975
Tucholsky, Kurt 16781, 19591
Tucović, Dimitrij 33829
Tübke, Werner 15644
Türk, Daniel Gottlob 17513
Tukaj, Gabdulla 32896, 32941, 33249
Tulloch, Bobby 40952
Tumanyan, Ovanes 00693
Tunnicliffe, C.F. 39867
Turgenev, Ivan Sergeevič 33263, 33266, 33416, 33550
Turner, Joseph M. William 38898, 39336, 39729, 39777, 39787, 40141, 40198, 47456
Tuttle, Richard 18135
Tvardovskij, A.T. 33528, 33744
Twombly, Cy 15981, 18107, 19949, 37386
Ubac 10245
Uccello, Paolo 13621, 23874
Uecker, Günther 18107
Ugalde, Miguel Angel 00501
Ulug-Beg 48852
Unamuno y Jugo, Miguel de 35357
Ungerer, Tomi 14808, 14831
Uniacke, Richard John 05949
Uriburu, José Evaristo 00542
Urteaga, Mario 31125
Uspenskij, Gleb Ivanovič 33524
Uthmann, Barbara 15496
Utrillo, Maurice 14603, 36470
Václavek, Bedřich 08289
Vagis, Polygnotos 21012, 21174
Vajda, Lajos 21578
Valadon, Suzanne 13626
Valand, Norvald 30537
Valdés, Manolo 07514
Valentin, Karl 16781, 18922
Valera, Eamonn de 22379
Valéry, Paul 14731
Valle, Evaristo 34847
Vallotton. Félix 36860

Vanderpoel, John H. 42337
Vaneev, A.A. 32797
Vanoni, Giovanni A. 36762
Vanorny, Otmar 08733
Vanvitelli, Luigi 23374
Vanzo, Julio 00505
Vapcarov, Nikola Ёnkov 04613, 04615, 04834, 04847
Vari, Sophia 07514
Varlin 36424
Varo, Remedios 28126
Vasarély, Victor 21517
Vasari, Giorgio 23868
Vasnecov, Apolinarij M. 33077, 33080, 33348
Vasnecov, Viktor M. 33077, 33080, 33348
Vaylet, Joseph 11649
Vazov, Ivan 04622, 04833, 04847
Vega 13011
Veit, Dorothea 17948
Vela, Lorenzo 36882
Vela, Spartaco 36882
Vela, Vincenzo 36882
Velarde, Pedro 35151
Velazquez, Diego 11084
Velázquez, Diego 23844
Velazquez, Diego 24434
Velázquez, Diego 25161, 23588, 38898, 39798
Velde, Henry van de 16406, 16464, 20455, 30939
Vélez, Eladio 07514
Veličkov, Konstantin 04754
Venevitinov, Dmitrij Vasiljevič 33248
Venizelos, Eleftherios 20858, 20878, 20891
Verdaguer, Jacinty 35639
Verdi, Giuseppe 23234
Veremans, Renaat 03587
Veres, Péter 21315
Veresaev, Vikentij Vikent'evič 33623
Vereščagin, Vasilij V. 32733
Verhaeren, Emile 03708, 03734
Verlaine, Paul 12105
Vermeer, Jan 29105, 23588, 39680
Vernadskij, V.T. 33053
Verne, Jules 10323
Veronese, Paolo 11560, 12736, 21539, 24434, 38211
Vesalius, Andreas 36494
Viani, Domenico 24887
Victoria Queen of England 38839
Vigeland, Emanuel 30730
Vigeland, Gustav 30746, 30770
Vignali, Pellegrino 17671
Vijayvelu, T. 22059
Vila Gorgoll, Emilio 19460
Villa-Lobos, Heitor 04397
Villebois-Marenil 34194
Villon, Jacques 13626
Vinje, Å.O. 30997
Vinzons, Wenceslao Q. 31468
Viola, Bill 16729
Vischer, Georg Matthäus 01649
Visdal, Jo 30967
Vitol, Jazep 27356
Vittoria, Alessandro 24742
Vivarini, Antonio 23029
Vivarini, Bartolomeo 23029
Vlaminck, Maurice de 11194, 12626
Vörösmarty, Mihály 21439
Vogel, Alfred 36434
Vogeler, Heinrich 20681, 20684
Voivenel, Paul 11036
Volanakis, K. 21200
Volta, Alessandro 23632
Voltaire 36737
Voß, Johann Heinrich 16979
Vostell, Wolf 16042
Vovčok, Marko 33195
Vuillard, Edouard 38916
Vulcan, Iosif 32561
Vysockij, Vladimir S. 33071
Wagenbauer, Max Joseph 17375
Waggerl, Karl Heinrich 02781
Wagner, J.M. von 20697
Wágner, Josef 08383
Wagner, Otto 02878
Wagner, Peter 20696
Wagner, Richard 15858, 16817, 17733, 19406, 36916
Waibl, Ignaz 16438
Wain, Louis 38141
Waldeck, Heinrich Suso 02616
Wall, Jeff 16729, 18161
Wallenstein, Albrecht Wenzel Eusebius von 08308
Waller, Sam 06098
Wallis, Alfred 40637
Wallis, Thomas Wilkinson 39834
Walpole, Hugh 39344
Walser, Karl 36551, 36564
Walser, Robert 36564
Walton, Izaak 40479
Wankel. Felix 18613

Waplington, Nick 45774
Warhol, Andy 14199, 15981, 18161, 20662, 26855, 34028, 37060, 45792
Washington, George 40643, 41129, 42532, 45546
Waterhouse, E.G. 01065
Waterton, Charles 40765
Watson, Budd 05846
Watt, Alison 39045
Watt, James 39131, 39349
Watts, G.F. 38621
Weber, A. Paul 19498
Weber, Carl Maria von 16678, 16979
Weber, Friedrich Wilhelm 15626
Weber-Lipsi, Hildegard 14037
Weber, Mili 37114
Wegener, Alfred 20734
Weidemann, Jakob 30765
Weidemeyer, Carl 36470
Weigel, Helene 15929, 16391
Weinert, Erich 18583
Weinheber, Josef 02115
Weininger, Andor 18135
Weisbach, Albin 17099
Weisgerber, Albert 17970, 19727, 19751
Weiß, Karl 16386
Weißkopf, Gustav 18447
Weizmann, Chaim 22739
Welk, Ehm 15491, 15624
Wellesley, Arthur 1st Duke of Wellington 03830, 39153, 39567
Welliver, Neil 07514
Wentworth, William C. 01565
Werefkin, Marianne von 36470
Werenskiold, Erik 30640
Werner, Abraham Gottlob 17099
Werner, Rolf 19912
Werth, Johann von 08245
Wesley, John 39720, 39804

Wessel, Johan Herman 08954
Wesselmann, Tom 14199
West, Franz 01927
Wet, C.R. de 34378
Wettstein, Johann Rudolf 37063
Weyden, Rogier van der 03565
Weygang, August 19226
Weysser, Karl 18000
Whistler, James McNeill 39050, 43693
Whistler, Rex 40201
White, Elizabeth 47880
White, Gilbert 40465
Whiteley, Brett 01485
Whitman, Walt 42061, 44170
Whittle, Sir Frank 38055
Whyte, Catharine 05045
Whyte, Peter 05045
Wicksteed, Thomas 39349
Widmann, Josef Viktor 36876
Widukind 16875
Wiegele, Franz 02365
Wiegersma, Hendrik 29141
Wieland, Christoph Martin 15392, 16139, 16140, 18619, 19287
Wiertz, Antoine 03290
Wilberforce, William 39384
Wildgans, Anton 02308
Wilhelm, Bröker 15679
Williams, Alfred 40665
Willumsen, J.F. 08832
Wimmer, Hans 19358
Winckelmann, Johann Joachim 20059, 25262
Winkler, Clemens A. 17100
Winter, Fritz 15401, 19949, 20090
Wirkkala, Tapio 09559
Wirth, Josef Alfons 18812
Wirth, Philipp 18740
Wislicenus, Hermann 17352

Wittelsbach, Clemens August von 16379
Witten, Hans 16472
Wittgenstein, Ludwig 02111
Wlérick, Robert 13027
Wocher, Marquard 37244
Wolf, Alexander 36537
Wolf, August 20480
Wolf, C. 36424
Wolf, Elise 36537
Wolf, Georg 20248
Wolf, Gustav 19233
Wolf, Hugo 02400
Wolfmüller, Alois 18305
Wolker, Jiří 08629
Wolseley, Frederick 22492
Wood Perry, E. 42168
Wood, W.J. 05846
Woollaston, Mountford Tosswill 30211
Wordsworth, William 37997, 38605, 39114, 39344
Worthington, Alfred 37955
Wouw, Anton van 34196
Wright, Frank Lloyd 45344, 45545, 46052
Wright, Joseph 38716
Wüsten, Johannes 17323
Wunderlich, Paul 04652
Wurm, Erwin 01927
Wybicki, Józef 31833
Wycliff, John 18203
Wyczółkowski, Leon 31514
Wynn, Steve 44675
Wyspiański, Stanisław 31719
Yaichi, Aizu 26594
Yamaga, Sokō 26199
Yeats, William Butler 22479
Yokoyama, Taikan 26340, 26960
Yole, Jean 14793
Yrurtia, Rogelio 00162
Zabaleta, Rafael 35305

Zadkine, Ossip 13649
Zambaccian, Krikor 32458
Zamora, José María 07514
Zaumseil, Andrea 17970
Zdarsky, Mathias 02223
Zedlitz-Leipe, Karl Abraham von 19511
Zegadłowicz, Emil 32068
Zeh, Franz 02010
Zeisig, Max 19376
Zeiss, Carl 17945
Zenetti, Leopold 01818
Zeppelin, Ferdinand Graf von 18680, 19005
Żeromski, Stefan 31657, 31821
Zetkin, Clara 16167, 18178
Zeune, Johann August 15923
Zeyer, Július 08722
Zichy, Mihály 21612
Zick, Januarius 18122
Ziegler, Jakob 17020
Ziem, F. 10648
Zille, Heinrich 16118
Zimmermann, Dominikus 18305
Zipernowsky 21355
Zlatarov, Asen 04640
Zobel, Fernando 31352, 34763
Zorbernig, Heimo 16971
Zorn, Anders 36103
Zoščenko, Michail Michajlovič 33415
Zubkov, G. 33394
Zuckmayer, Carl 37079
Žukov N.N. 32790
Žukovskij, Nikolaj Egorovič 33163, 33258, 33416
Zuloaga, Daniel 35468
Zuloaga, Ignacio 35259, 35468, 35739
Župančič, Oton 34163
Zurbar, Francisco de 31218
Zurbarán, Francisco de 28195, 35089, 35739
Zweig, Stefan 02859

Subject Index

List of Subjects

Agricultural Implements and Machinery
Agriculture
Amber
Anthropology → Ethnology
Apiculture → Bees
Archaeology
Archaeology, Christian and Medieval
Archaeology, Far Eastern
Archaeology, Greek and Roman
Archaeology, Ibero-American
Archaeology, Near and Middle Eastern
Architecture
Arms and Armour
Art
Art, African
Art, American
Art, Asian
Art, Australian
Art, European
Art, Greek and Roman
Art, Latin American
Art, Medieval
Art, Modern and Contemporary
Art, Oriental
Art, Russian
Astronomy
Automobiles → Vehicles
Aviation
Baking and Cookery
Balneology
Banks and Banking
Baskets
Bees
Bells
Biology
Birds
Boats and Shipping
Bones
Books, Book Art and Manuscripts
Botany
Brewing
Bronzes
Bullfights
Buttons
Cabaret → Performing Arts
Calligraphy
Cameras → Optics
Carpets
Carriages and Carts
Cartography
Carts → Carriages and Carts
Carving, Wood → Wood Carving
Castles and Fortresses
Ceramics → Porcelain and Ceramics
Chemistry
China (Porcelain) → Porcelain and Ceramics
Cigarettes → Tobacco
Cinematography
Circus → Performing Arts

Clocks and Watches → Horology
Clothing and Dress
Coaches → Carriages and Carts
Coffee → Tea and Coffee
Coins → Numismatics
Cookery → Baking and Cookery
Copper
Cosmetics
Costume → Clothing and Dress
Crafts → Handicraft
Criminology
Dairy Products
Dance → Performing Arts
Decorative and Applied Arts
Distilling → Wines and Spirits
Dolls and Puppets
Drawing
Ecology
Economics
Education
Egyptology
Electricity
Embroidery → Needlework
Enamel Works
Energy
Engraving → Graphic Arts
Entomology → Insects
Epitaphs → Inscriptions and Epitaphs
Ethnology
Expeditions → Scientific Expeditions
Explosives
Eyeglasses → Optics
Faience → Porcelain and Ceramics
Fashion → Clothing and Dress
Festivals
Fire Fighting and Rescue Work
Firearms → Arms and Armour
Fishing and Fisheries
Folk Art
Folklore
Food
Forest Products
Fortresses → Castles and Fortresses
Fossils
Fresco Painting → Mural Painting and Decoration
Fur → Hides and Skins
Furniture and Interior
Games → Toys and Games
Gas → Petroleum Industry and Trade
Gems → Precious Stones
Genealogy
Geography
Geology
Glass and Glassware
Globes → Cartography
Gold and Silver
Graphic Arts
Gravestones → Tombs
Handicapped

Handicraft
Heraldry → Genealogy
Hides and Skins
History
History, Early → Prehistory and Early History
History, Local and Regional
History, Maritime → Boats and Shipping
History, Medieval
History, Modern
History, Social → Social Conditions
Horology
Horses
Horticulture
Household Articles
Hunting
Hygiene → Medicine and Hygiene
Icons
Incunabula → Books, Book Art and Manuscripts
Indian Artifacts
Industry
Inscriptions and Epitaphs
Insects
Instruments of Torture
Ironwork → Metalwork
Ivory
Jewellery → Precious Stones
Judaica
Keys → Locks and Keys
Lace → Needlework
Lacquerwork
Lamps and Lighting
Language and Literature
Law
Lead and Tin Figures
Leather
Literature → Language and Literature
Locks and Keys
Lumber → Forest Products
Machines and Machinery
Majolica → Porcelain and Ceramics
Mammals
Man, Prehistoric
Manuscripts → Books, Book Art and Manuscripts
Maps → Cartography
Marine Archaeology
Marine Biology → Oceanography
Masks
Mass Media
Medals → Numismatics
Medicine and Hygiene
Metals and Metallurgy
Metalwork
Meteorites
Military History
Mills
Mineralogy
Miniature Painting
Mining Engineering
Mollusks
Monasteries
Money → Numismatics
Mosaics
Mummies

Mural Painting and Decoration
Museology
Music and Musical Instruments
Naive Art → Folk Art
Natural History
Needlework
Numismatics
Oceanography
Oenology → Wines and Spirits
Office Equipment
Oil → Petroleum Industry and Trade
Opera → Performing Arts
Optics
Ornithology → Birds
Painted and Stained Glass
Painting
Painting, 17th C.
Painting, 18th C.
Painting, 19th C.
Painting, 20th C.
Painting, English
Painting, European
Painting, French
Painting, German
Painting, Italian
Painting, Latin American
Painting, Medieval
Painting, Netherlandish
Painting, Renaissance
Painting, Spanish
Paleontology → Fossils
Paper
Peasant Life and Traditions
Performing Arts
Petroleum Industry and Trade
Pets
Pewter
Pharmacy
Philately → Postage Stamps
Philosophy
Photography
Physics
Pipes, Tobacco → Tobacco
Plaster Casts
Playing Cards
Police → Criminology
Politics and Government
Porcelain and Ceramics
Portraits
Postage Stamps
Postal Services
Posters
Pottery, Earthenware → Porcelain and Ceramics
Precious Stones
Prehistory and Early History
Press → Mass Media
Printing
Prints → Graphic Arts
Prisons → Criminology
Puppets → Dolls and Puppets
Radio → Mass Media
Railroads
Rare Books → Books, Book Art and Manuscripts

Religious Art and Symbolism
Religious History and Traditions
Reptiles
Rescue Equipment → Fire Fighting and Rescue Work
Rocks → Mineralogy
Salt
Sarcophagi → Tombs
Scientific Apparatus and Instruments
Scientific Expeditions
Sculpture
Shells
Shipping → Boats and Shipping
Shoes
Silk
Silver → Gold and Silver
Skeletons → Bones
Social Conditions
Speleology
Spirits → Wines and Spirits
Sports and Recreation
Stained Glass → Painted and Stained Glass
Stelae → Tombs
Stoves
Stucco
Sugar
Tapestries
Tea and Coffee
Technology
Telecommunications → Postal Services
Television → Mass Media

Terracotta
Textiles
Theatre → Performing Arts
Tin Figures → Lead and Tin Figures
Tobacco
Tombs
Tools
Tourism
Toys and Games
Trades and Guilds
Transport
Travel → Tourism
Treasuries
Typography → Books, Book Art and Manuscripts
Uniforms, Military
Vehicles
Veterinary Medicine
Viticulture → Wines and Spirits
Voyages of Discovery → Scientific Expeditions
Wallpaper
Water
Wax, Molded
Weapons → Arms and Armour
Weaving
Weights and Measures
Whaling → Fishing and Fisheries
Wines and Spirits
Wood → Forest Products
Wood Carving
Zoology

Agricultural Implements and Machinery

Australia
Ardrossan Historical Museum, Ardrossan 00749
Cleve National Trust Museum, Cleve 00925
Donald Agricultural Museum, Donald 00984
Doug Kerr Vintage Museum, Oaklands 01340
Farming Through the Ages, Whyte Yarcowie 01599
Mingenew Museum, Mingenew 01258
Pearn's Steam World, Westbury 01594

Austria
Bäuerliche Gerätesammlung, Buch bei Jenbach 01755
Bäuerliches Gerätemuseum und Venezianer-Gatter, Innervillgraten 02058
Bauern- und Heimatmuseum Haigermoos, Sankt Pantaleon 02594
Freilichtmuseum Stehrerhof - Dreschmaschinenmuseum, Neukirchen an der Vöckla 02346
Landtechnikmuseum, Leiben 02201
Landwirtschaftliches Museum und Pfarrer Franz Engel-Museum, Prinzendorf 02456
Museum für landwirtschaftliche Geräte, Grafenwörth 01907
Schloßmuseum, Sigharting 02662
Troadkasten, Freinberg 01849
Troadkasten Fornach, Fornach 01843

Belgium
Heemmuseum De Kaeck, Wommelgem 03845

Canada
Backus Heritage Village, Port Rowan 06169
British Columbia Farm Machinery and Agricultural Museum, Fort Langley 05440
Crossroads Museum, Oyen 06092
Frobisher Thresherman's Museum, Frobisher 05471
Heritage Farm Village, North Battleford 06014
Keystone Pioneer Museum, Roblin 06279
Missisquoi Museum, Stanbridge East 06486
Musée Saint-Joseph, Saint-Joseph 06354
Saanich Historical Artifacts Society, Saanichton 06295
Southwestern Saskatchewan Oldtimer's Museum, Maple Creek 05811
Swords and Ploughshares Museum, Manotick 05807
Teeterville Pioneer Museum, Teeterville 06536
Whitemouth Municipal Museum, Whitemouth 06795

Denmark
Blaavandshuk Egnsmuseum, Oksbøl 09016

Finland
Helsingin Yliopiston Maatalousmuseo, Helsinki 09494

France
Musée Agricole Vivant, Bissey-la-Pierre 10746
Musée Conservatoire de l'Agriculture, Chartres 11192
Musée de la Faux, Pont-Salomon 13819
Musée de la Machine Agricole, Vroncourt 15297
Musée de la Machine Agricole et à Vapeur, Ambert 10302
Musée de la Vie Rurale, Steenwerck 14802
Musée des Champs, Saint-Ségal 14470
Musée du Machinisme Agricole, Tullins-Fures 15015
Musée du Matériel Agricole, La Villeneuve-les-Convers 12274
Musée Régional du Machinisme Agricole, La Ferté-Milon 12173

Germany
Altdenzlinger Heimethüs mit Otto-Raupp-Stube, Denzlingen 16574
Bachgau-Museum, Großostheim 17435
Bäuerliches Heimatmuseum der Landtechnik, Geiselhöring 17214
Bauern- und Waldmuseum, Haidmühle 17486
Bauerngerätemuseum des Stadtmuseums, Ingolstadt 17904
Bauernhaus-Museum, Ruhmannsfelden 19713
Bauernhausmuseum des Landkreises Erding, Erding 16890
Bauernhofmuseum Hof, Kirchanschöring 18086
Bauernmuseum Liebenau, Liebenau bei Dippoldiswalde 18460
Bauernmuseum Mühlhausen, Villingen-Schwenningen 20315
Bauernmuseum Ostdorf, Balingen 15796
Bauernmuseum Pfarrscheuer, Bösingen 16220
Dorfmuseum Weckbach, Weilbach 20441
Freilichtmuseum Ostenfelder Bauernhaus, Husum, Nordsee 17869
Freilichtmuseum Scherzenmühle Weidenberg, Weidenberg 20427
Gerätesammlung Georg Bauer, Stadtlauringen 20032
Gerätesammlung Koch, Königsberg in Bayern 18169
Gottlieb-Häußler-Heimatmuseum, Filderstadt 17001
Heimat- und Bergbaumuseum, Nentershausen, Hessen 18993
Heimat- und Hafnermuseum, Heidenheim, Mittelfranken 17683
Heimatmuseum, Dietenhofen 16602
Heimatmuseum, Weissach im Tal 20489
Heimatmuseum Beutelsbach, Weinstadt 20483
Heimatmuseum Grafenau Schloß Dätzingen, Grafenau, Württemberg 17370
Heimatmuseum Grimmen "Im Mühlentor", Grimmen 17406
Heimatmuseum Holzgerlingen, Holzgerlingen 17827
Heimatmuseum Niederaichbach, Niederaichbach 19095
Heimatmuseum Stadtsteinach, Stadtsteinach 20035
Heimatmuseum Waldaschaff, Waldaschaff 20352
Heimatmuseum Weiler, Schorndorf, Württemberg 19843
Heimatmuseum Wertach, Wertach 20530
Heimatstuben im Oberen Tor, Scheinfeld 19771
Historische Ochsentretanlage im Brunnenhausmuseum, Schillingsfürst 19778
Kreisagrarmuseum, Dorf Mecklenburg 16643
Landmaschinenmuseum - Sammlung Speer, Rimbach bei Eggenfelden 19612
Landtechnik-Museum Gut Steinhof, Braunschweig 16299
Mittelschwäbisches Heimatmuseum Krumbach, Krumbach, Schwaben 18251
Museum Bad Füssing, Bad Füssing 15649
Museum für bäuerliche Arbeitsgeräte des Bezirks Oberfranken, Bayreuth 15855
Museum Wildberg, Wildberg, Württemberg 20586
Museumshof Lerchennest - Friedrich-der-Große-Museum, Sinsheim 19970
Museumsscheune, Bremervörde 16353
Museumsstadl, Bernried, Niederbayern 16127
Privatmuseum Hans Klein, Prichsenstadt 19448
Privatsammlung Leo Gesell, Triefenstein 20206
Riedenburger Bauernhofmuseum, Riedenburg 19599
Schlepper-, Auto- und Gerätemuseum Hesse, Aidhausen 15411
Schulheimatmuseum, Asbach-Bäumenheim 15518
Sensen- und Heimatmuseum, Achern 15391
Stadtmuseum Schloss Wolfsburg, Wolfsburg 20663
Städtische Sammlungen, Adelsheim 15397
Traktoren-Museum Kempen, Horn-Bad Meinberg 17842
Werksmuseum der Amazonen-Werke, Gaste 17206

Ireland
An Dun Transport and Heritage Museum, Ballinahown 22365
Threshing Museum, Mullinahone 22523

Israel
Museum of Pioneer Settlement, Kibbutz Yifat 22706

Italy
Museo della Tecnologia Contadina, Santu Lussurgiu 25467

Mexico
Museo Aperos de Labranza, Lerdo 28057

Namibia
Helmeringhausen Museum, Helmeringhausen 28756

Netherlands
Automuseum Histo-Mobil, Giethoorn 29279
Boerderij Klein Hulze, Almen 28811
Boerenwagenmuseum, Buren, Gelderland 29042
Fries Landbouw Museum, Exmorra 29257
Nationaal Museum Historisch Landbouwtechniek, Wageningen 29976
Plumershuuske, Diepenheim 29151
Streekmuseum Hoeksche Waard, Heinenoord 29379
Het Trekkermuseum, Nisse 29638

New Zealand
Pigeon Valley Steam Museum, Wakefield 30283

Norway
Auli Mølle, Årnes 30393
Egge Museum, Steinkjer 30894
Jærmuseet, Nærbø 30699

South Africa
Settlers Museum, Himeville 34263

Sweden
Sala Traktormuseum, Sala 36173

Switzerland
Heimatmuseum, Aesch, Basel-Land 36434
Heimatmuseum, Attiswil 36474
Musée Agricole, Coffrane 36639
Musée Romand de la Machine Agricole, Gingins 36759
Ortsmuseum Albisrieden, Zürich 37401
Ortsmuseum Wiesendangen, Wiesendangen 37318
Schweizerisches Museum für Landwirtschaft und Agrartechnik Burgrain, Alberswil 36444

United Kingdom
Combe Mill Beam Engine and Working Museum, Long Hanborough 39821
Fife Folk Museum, Ceres 38518
Greenfield Valley Museum, Greenfield 39128
Hezlett House, Coleraine 38618
Lackham Museum of Agriculture and Rural Life, Lacock 39409
Laidhay Croft Museum, Dunbeath 38795
March and District Museum, March 39908
Museum of Lincolnshire Life, Lincoln 39500
Northfield Farm Museum, New Pitsligo 40015
Sheppy's Farm and Cider Museum, Bradford-on-Tone 38302
Sussex Farm Museum, Heathfield 39203
Walton Hall Museum, Linford 39504
Wilmington Priory, Wilmington 40876

U.S.A.
Deere Museum, Moline 45430
Forest Park Museum, Perry 46355
Midwest Old Settlers and Threshers Association Museum, Mount Pleasant 45535
The National Agricultural Center and Hall of Fame, Bonner Springs 41781

Agriculture

Argentina
Museo de la Máquina Agrícola, Esperanza 00344
Museo Pampeano del Pergamino, Pergamino 00474

Australia
Avondale Discovery Farm, Beverley 00800
Churchill Island Agricultural Museum, Newhaven 01319
Court House Museum, Stroud 01481
Cunderdin Municipal Museum, Cunderdin 00961
Geralka Rural Farm, Spalding 01467
Gledswood Farm Museum and Homestead, Catherine Fields 00901
Gulf Station Historic Farm, Yarra Glen 01626
Maffra Sugarbeet Museum, Maffra 01195
Maitland Museum, Maitland, South Australia 01199
National Trust Museum, Streaky Bay 01480
North Western Agricultural Museum, Warracknabeal 01579
Old Council Chambers Museum, Cleve 00926
Roseworthy Agricultural Museum, Roseworthy 01425
Rouse Hill Estate, Rouse Hill 01428
Trentham Agricultural and Railway Museum, Trentham 01551
Waterwheel Museum, Salisbury 01440
Wyalkatchem C.B.H. Agricultural Museum, Wyalkatchem 01620

Austria
Alpsennereimuseum, Hittisau 02033
Bauernmuseum im Grottenhof, Kaindorf an der Sulm 02094
Bauernmuseum Sollinger-Bauer, Maria Schmolln 02270
Bergbauernmuseum, Alpbach 01656
Denkmalhof Gererhof, Annaberg 01673
Denkmalhof Maurerbauernhof, Zederhaus 03048
Freilichtmuseum, Bad Tatzmannsdorf 01719
Freilichtmuseum Mondseer Rauchhaus, Mondsee 02320
Haus des Moores, Heidenreichstein 02011
Heimatmuseum im alten Bruderhaus und in der Dechanatshofscheune, Altenmarkt im Pongau 01664
Kärntner Freilichtmuseum, Maria Saal 02269
Kapuzinerturm, Radstadt 02475
Kurmuseum des Österreichischen Moorforschungsinstituts, Bad Wimsbach-Neydharting 01723
Landwirtschaftsmuseum Schloss Ehrental, Klagenfurt 02128
Lavanttaler Obstbaumuseum, Sankt Paul 02596
Mentlhof-Bergbauernmuseum, Heiligenblut 02016
Mostviertler Bauernmuseum, Amstetten 01669
Nationalparkmuseum, Mittersill 02307
Obermühlviertler Denkmalhof Unterkagerer, Auberg 01689
Ötztaler Freilichtmuseum, Längenfeld 02176
Rauchstubenhaus, Gündorf 01967
Rauchstubenhaus, Sankt Johann im Saggautal 02575
Stadtmuseum Wels-Burg - Agrargeschichtliche Sammlung, Wels 02816
Urgeschichtliches Freilichtmuseum Keltendorf Mitterkirchen, Mitterkirchen 02304

Belgium
Bardelaere Museum, Lembeke 03558
Ecomusée du Pays des Collines, Lahamaide 03549
Havesdonckhoeve, Bornem 03228
Hopmuseum De Stadsschaal, Poperinge 03687
Karrenmuseum, Essen 03410
Landbouwmuseum Leiedal, Bissegem 03218
Musée de Hottemme, Durbuy 03397
Musée de la Vie Rurale Li Vîle Grègne, Erezée 03407
Musée du Cheval, de la Vie Rurale et du Tabac, Thuillies 03776
Museum Kempenland, Lommel 03596
Museum Rufferdinge, Landen 03551

Brazil
Fundação Museu do Zebu Edilson Lamartine Mendes, Uberaba 04574
Museu do Tropeiro, Castro 04045
Museu Fazenda, Nanuque 04216
Museu Municipal Visconde de Guarapuava, Guarapuava 04121

Brunei
Muzium Teknologi Melayu, Bandar Seri Begawan 04599

Bulgaria
Muzej na Bivolarstvoto i Konevădstvoto, Šumen 04875
Nacionalen Selskostopanski Muzej, Sofia 04854

Canada
1910 Boomtown, Saskatoon 06393
Agricultural Museum of New Brunswick, Sussex 06521
Beckoning Hills Museum, Boissevain 05089
Blair House Museum, Kentville 05660
Blockhouse Museum, Merrickville 05841
Bradley Museum, Mississauga 05870
Brownvale North Peace Agricultural Museum, Brownvale 05140
Canada Agriculture Museum, Ottawa 06068
Central Butte District Museum, Central Butte 05219
Cole Harbour Heritage Farm Museum, Cole Harbour 05265
Comber and District Historical Society Museum, Comber 05268
Compton County Historical Museum, Eaton Corner 05364
Gaspesian British Heritage Village, New Richmond 05980
Greater Sudbury Heritage Museum, Sudbury 06511
Hanna Pioneer Museum, Hanna 05581
Historic Hat Creek Ranch, Cache Creek 05155
Historic O'Keefe Ranch, Vernon, British Columbia 06707
Historic Stewart Farmhouse, Surrey 06518
International Fox Museum, Summerside 06515
Keillor House Museum, Dorchester 05336
Kelowna Museum, Kelowna 05653
Kilby Historic Store and Farm, Harrison Mills 05586
Kings Landing Historical Settlement, Prince William 06191
Lac Sainte-Anne and District Pioneer Museum, Sangudo 06390
The Log Farm, Nepean 05972
MacPherson's Mill and Farm Homestead, New Glasgow 05978
Manitoba Agricultural Hall of Fame, Brandon 05122
Manitoba Agricultural Museum, Austin 05023
Mayne Island Museum, Mayne Island 05827
Museum of the Cariboo Chilcotin, Williams Lake 06802
Ontario Agricultural Museum, Milton 05854
Orwell Corner Historic Village, Orwell 06058
Peace River Centennial Museum, Peace River 06102
Pouce Coupe Museum, Pouce Coupe 06174
River View Ethnographic Museum, Bear River 05064
Ross Farm Museum, New Ross 05981
Salt Spring Island Museum, Ganges 05475
South Peace Centennial Museum, Beaverlodge 05068
Story of People, Yorkton 06874
Victoria County Museum, Baddeck 05033

Chile
Museo de Arte y Artesanía de Linares, Linares 06899

Cuba
Museo La Isabelica, Santiago de Cuba 08148

Czech Republic
Kotulova Dřevěnka, Havířov 08344
Národní Zemědělské Muzeum Praha, Kačina 08396
Zemědělská Sbírka na Zámku Kačina, Kutná Hora 08440
Zemědělské Muzeum Ohrada, Ohrada 08514

Denmark
Bov Museum, Padborg 09022
Dansk Landbrugsmuseum, Auning 08780
Det Danske Hedeselskabs Museum, Viborg 09108
Fjordmuseet, Jyllinge 08909
Frilandsmuseet i Maribo, Maribo 08980
Den Fynske Landsby, Odense 09010
Glud Museum, Horsens 08896
Herning Museum, Herning 08869
Klosterlund Museum og Naturcenter, Engesvang 08804
Landbrugs- og Interiørmuseet, Farsø 08822
Landbrugsmuseet Melstedgård, Gudhjem 08847
Landbrugsmuseet Skarregaard, Nykøbing Mors 08998
Sydhimmerlands Museum, Nøtager 08990
Vestfyns Hjemstavnsgård, Glamsbjerg 08839

Egypt
Cotton Museum, Cairo 09259

Estonia
Eesti Põllumajandusmuuseum, Tõrvandi 09391
Väike-Männiku Talumuuseum, Kõpu 09334

Finland
Bragegården, Vaasa 10157
Etelä-Pohjanmaan Maakuntamuseo, Seinäjoki 10028
Isonkyrön Kotiseutumuseo, Isokyrö 09570
Jan Karlsgarden, Sund 10060
Jokioisten Pappilamuseo, Jokioinen 09584
Kalannin Kotiseutumuseo, Kalanti 09615
Karjalainen Kotitalo, Imatra 09565
Kauhajoen Museo, Kauhajoki 09637
Kaunislehdon Talomuseo, Hyrynsalmi 09555
Kemin Museo, Kemi 09649
Keuruun Kotiseutumuseo, Keuruu 09661
Kokemäen Maatalousmuseo, Kokemäki 09679
Laurinmäen Torpparimuseo, Janakkala 09578
Luopioisten Museo, Luopioinen 09801
Murtovaaran Talomuseo, Valtimo 10175
Mustialan Maataloushistoriallinen Museo, Mustiala 09844
Pielisen Museo, Lieksa 09781
Pienmäen Talomuseo, Niemisjärvi 09861
Pöljän Kotiseutumuseo, Pöljä 09934

Subject Index: Agriculture

Pyhäjoen Kotiseutumuseo, Pyhäjoki 09968
Reipin Museo, Pirkkala 09933
Reppuniemen Ulkomuseo, Pöytyä 09937
Ruoveden Kotiseutumuseo, Ruovesi 10008
Rymättylän Kotiseutumuseo, Rymättylä 10010
Someron Museo, Somero 10049
Talonpoikaismuseo Yli-Kirra, Punkalaidum 09964
Urjalan Museo, Urjala 10148
Vöyrin Kotiseutumuseo, Vörå 10210
Yläneen Kotiseutumuseo, Yläne 10213

France
L'Agriculture au Fil du Temps, Maniquerville 12790
Ecomusée Agricole du Pays de Fayence, Fayence 11709
Ecomusée de la Bresse Bourguignonne, Pierre-de-Bresse 13729
Écomusée de la Courneuve, La Courneuve 12163
Écomusée de la Forêt d'Orient, Brienne-la-Vieille 10927
Ecomusée de la Grande Lande Marquèze, Sabres 14081
Ecomusée de la Vallee d'Aspe, Accous 10226
Ecomusée de l'Ile-de-Groix, Ile-de-Groix 12046
Ecomusée de Marais Breton Vendéen, La Barre-de-Monts 12121
Écomusée du Liège, Gonfaron 11884
Ecomusée du Pays de Rennes, Rennes (Ille-et-Vilaine) 13939
Ecomusée du Vernon, Savigny-en-Vernon 14667
Ecomusée Picarvie, Saint-Valéry-sur-Somme 14498
Ferme-Musée de Bray, Sommery 14769
Ferme-Musée du Contentin, Sainte-Mère-Eglise 14547
Maison des Abeilles, Brignoles 10930
Musée Accous-Fermiers Basco-Béarnais, Accous 10227
Musée Agricole du Château de Didonne, Semussac 14704
Musée Briard et de la Crypte Mérovingienne, Jouarre 12091
Musée Conservatoire de la Vie Agricole et Rurale d'Autrefois, Gimont 11866
Musée d'Art et d'Histoire de Toul, Toul 14924
Musée d'Arts et de Traditions Populaires, Mussidan 13227
Musée de la Chapellerie, Espéraza 11653
Musée de la Coiffe et du Costume Oléronnais, Le Grand-Village-Plage 12419
Musée de la Dentelle, Mirecourt 12994
Musée de la Ferme et des Vieux Métiers, Bosquentin 10825
Musée de la Vie Rurale, Desaignes 11501
Musée de la Vie Rurale et Forestière, Saint-Michel-en-Thiérache 14372
Musée de l'Estérel, Les Adrets-de-l'Estérel 12515
Musée de l'Habitat Rural Passé et des Traditions, La Garnache 12189
Musée de l'Outillage Artisanal Rural et Bourguignon, Cruzille-en-Mâconnais 11466
Musée des Anciens Outils Agricoles, Saint-Mathurin 14361
Musée des Arts et Traditions Populaires, Marignane 12823
Musée des Arts et Traditions Populaires, Valbonne 15045
Musée des Traditions Agricoles du Ségala, Pradinas 13862
Musée des Vallées Cévenoles, Saint-Jean-du-Gard 14289
Musée Domaine de Samara, La Chaussée-Tirancourt 12154
Musée du Fromage de la Chèvrerie, Noirmoutier-en-l'Ile 13360
Musée du Mouton et de la Bergerie Nationale, Rambouillet 13911
Musée du Patrimoine Montagnard, Nages 13232
Musée du Revermont, Treffort-Cuisiat 14985
Musée Maison Déodat Roché, Arques (Aude) 10426
Musée Olivier-de-Serres, Mirabel (Ardèche) 12986
Musée Troglodytique, Louresse 12700
Un Village se Raconte, Lourdios-Ichère 12699

Germany
Ackerbürgermuseum, Reichenbach, Oberlausitz 19545
Agrar- und Freilichtmuseum, Crimmitschau 16513
Agrarhistorisches Museum, Schlepzig 19792
Agrarmuseum, Greußen 17396
Albrecht-Daniel-Thaer-Gedenkstätte-Landesausstellung, Reichenow 19547
Baudenkmal Hopfenhaus - Landwirtschaftliche Gerätesammlung - Alt-Seilerei - Ostdeutsche Heimatstube, Aidlingen 15412
Bauernhaus-Museum, Lindberg 18477
Bauernhausmuseum Amerang des Bezirks Oberbayern, Amerang 15481
Bauernhausmuseum Hattingen, Hattingen 17633
Bauernhofmuseum, Buchhofen 16388
Bauernhofmuseum Jexhof, Schöngeising 19832
Bauernmuseum Landkreis Bamberg, Frensdorf 17127
Bergisches Freilichtmuseum für Ökologie und bäuerlich-handwerkliche Kultur, Lindlar 18481
Bodanrück-Bauernmuseum, Allensbach 15432
Denkmalhof Rauchhaus Mölln, Mölln 18764
Deutsches Hirtenmuseum, Hersbruck 17739
Deutsches Landwirtschaftsmuseum, Stuttgart 20088
Erlichthof, Rietschen 19611
Europäisches Spargelmuseum, Schrobenhausen 19851
Fränkisches Freilandmuseum, Bad Windsheim 15776
Freilandmuseum Ammerländer Bauernhaus, Bad Zwischenahn 15782
Freilandmuseum Grassemann Naturpark-Infostelle, Warmensteinach 20401
Freilichtmuseum, Diesdorf, Altmark 16598
Freilichtmuseum, Stade 20022
Freilichtmuseum Alt Schwerin, Alt Schwerin 15439
Freilichtmuseum Domäne Dahlem, Berlin 15950
Freilichtmuseum Hessenpark, Neu-Anspach 19003
Freilichtmuseum Klausenhof, Herrischried 17736
Freilichtmuseum Lehde, Lehde bei Lübbenau 18369
Freilichtmuseum Massing, Massing 18664
Hanf-Museum, Berlin 15983
Haselünner Heimathäuser, Haselünne 17625
Heimatmuseum Buchenberg, Buchenberg bei Kempten 16387
Heimatmuseum der Marktgemeinde Wiggensbach, Wiggensbach 20584
Heimatmuseum im Hartmannhaus, Marktoberdorf 18648
Heimatmuseum im Wolfschneider-Hof, Taufkirchen, Kreis München 20148
Hopfen Erlebnis Hof, Altmannstein 15461
Isinger Dorfmuseum - Alte Kelter, Tübingen 20226
Jura-Bauernhof-Museum, Hitzhofen 17772
Kulturzentrum Sinsteden des Kreises Neuss, Rommerskirchen 19643
Landwirtschaftliches Museum Wetzlar, Wetzlar 20556
Landwirtschafts- und Heimatmuseum, Karben 17985
Landwirtschaftsmuseum, Rhede, Ems 19587
Landwirtschaftsmuseum, Weil am Rhein 20435
Landwirtschaftsmuseum Hof Espe, Bad Berleburg 15608
Lebendiges Museum, Bad Wildungen 15764
Mühlen- und Landwirtschaftsmuseum, Jever 17956
Mühlen- und Landwirtschaftsmuseum, Westfehmarn 20543
Museum der Elbinsel Wilhelmsburg, Hamburg 17556
Museum Dermbach, Dermbach 16575
Museum für ländliches Kulturgut, Landwirtschaft, Forsten und Jagd, Ulrichstein 20262
Museum für Landtechnik und Landarbeit, Emmerthal 16863
Museum Grossauheim, Hanau 17585
Museum Hüsli- Sammlung Schwarzwälder Volkskunst, Grafenhausen 17371
Museum im Schlößle, Freiberg am Neckar 17098
Museum Reichenau, Reichenau, Baden 19542
Museums-Gutshof Sonnekalb, Kleinheringen 18106
Museumsdorf Volksdorf mit Spiekerhus, Hamburg 17562
Museumsscheune Fränkische Schweiz, Hollfeld 17825
Niederbayerisches Landwirtschaftsmuseum, Regen 19516
Oberfränkisches Bauernhofmuseum, Zell, Oberfranken 20743
Oberpfälzer Freilandmuseum Neusath-Perschen, Nabburg 18969
Oberschwäbisches Museumsdorf Kreisfreilichtmuseum Kürnbach, Bad Schussenried 15736
Obstbaumuseum, Werder, Havel 20518
Ostfriesisches Landwirtschaftsmuseum, Krummhörn 18255
Riedmuseum, Rastatt 19488
Schäfertanz-Kabinett, Rothenburg ob der Tauber 19682
Schlesisch-Oberlausitzer Dorfmuseum, Markersdorf bei Görlitz 18636
Schleswig-Holsteinisches Freilichtmuseum, Molfsee 18783
Schleswig-Holsteinisches Landwirtschaftsmuseum und Dithmarscher Bauernhaus, Meldorf 18696
Schlossmuseum Reckahn, Reckahn 19511
Schwäbisches Bauernhofmuseum Illerbeuren, Kronburg 18249
Schwarzwälder Freilichtmuseum Vogtsbauernhof, Gutach, Schwarzwaldbahn 17467
Stadtmuseum Herrenmühle, Hammelburg 17579
Tauberländer Dorfmuseum, Weikersheim 20432
Technisches Museum Ölmühle, Pockau 19423
Vogtländisches Freilichtmuseum, Erlbach 16927
Volkskundliches Gerätemuseum, Arzberg, Oberfranken 15517
Westfälisches Freilichtmuseum Detmold, Detmold 16590

Hungary
Georgikon Majormúzeum, Keszthely 21455
Magyar Mezőgazdasági Múzeum, Budapest 21359
Paprika Múzeum, Kalocsa 21436
Paprikamúzeum, Szeged 21552

India
Agriculture Museum, Imphal 21849
Meghalaya State Museum, Shillong 22017
Museum of the Agricultural College and Research Institute, Coimbatore 21751
Regional Science Centre, Guwahati, Assam 21827
Victoria and Albert Museum, Mumbai 21955

Indonesia
Museum Subak Bali, Kediri 22145
Subak Museum, Banjar Senggulan 22078

Ireland
Ballinamore Local Museum, Ballinamore 22366
Crover Folk Museum, Mount Nugent 22522
Irish Agricultural Museum, Wexford 22558
Roscrea Heritage Centre, Roscrea 22535

Israel
Dagon Grain Museum, Haifa 22603
Farmer's House, Metulla 22713
Landscapes of the Holy Land Park, Tel Aviv 22766
Neot Kedumim, Lod 22708

Italy
Museo Agrario Tropicale, Firenze 23851
Museo Agricolo, Ronco Briantino 25277
Museo Agricolo della Civiltà Contadina L. Carminati, San Giuliano Milanese 25376
Museo Agricolo e del Vino Ricci Curbastro, Capriolo 23337
Museo Agricolo e Museo dell'Arte Conciaria, Castelfranco Veneto 23401
Museo Agro-Forestale San Matteo, Erice 23738
Museo Contadino della Bassa Pavese, San Cristina e Bissone 25353
Museo del Lavoro e della Civiltà Rurale, Palaia 24756
Museo del Po, Monticelli d'Ongina 24553
Museo del Trattore Agricolo, Senago 25533
Museo della Civiltà Contadina, Bentivoglio 23056
Museo della Civiltà Contadina ed Artigiana, Monterosso Calabro 24543
Museo della Civiltà Contadina Valle dell'Aniene, Roviano 25296
Museo della Civiltà Rurale, Altamura 22862
Museo della Frutticoltura Adofo Bonvicini, Massa Lombarda 24318
Museo della Val Venosta, Sluderno 25590
Museo della Vita e del Lavoro della Maremma Settentrionale, Cecina e Marina 23465
Museo dell'Agricoltura Meridionale, San Tammaro 25417
Museo delle Tradizioni Agroalimentari della Sardegna, Siddi 25566
Museo di Cultura Contadina, Oriolo 24690
Museo di Storia dell'Agricoltura, Cesena 23506
Museo di Storia dell'Agricoltura, Urbania 25854
Museo Enologico Grasso, Milazzo 24422
Museo Etnico della Civiltà Salentina Agrilandi Museum, Brindisi 23213
Museo Lombardo di Storia dell'Agricoltura, Sant'Angelo Lodigiano 25452
Museo Nazionale dell'Alta Val d'Agri, Grumento Nova 24065
Raccolta Permanente sulla Lavorazione della Canapa, Buonconvento 23231

Japan
Hida Minzoku-mura, Takayama 26804
Hokkaido Daigaku Nogakubu Hakubutsukan, Sapporo 26711
Jingu Nogyokan, Ise 26254
Nara-kenritsu Minzoku Hakubutsukan, Yamatokoriyama 27008
Nihon Minka Shuraku Hakubutsukan, Toyonaka 26973
Sakai Greenery Museum Harvest Hill, Sakai 26698

Korea, Republic
Agricultural Museum of Jeollanam-do, Samho 27219
Jeonju National Museum, Jeonju 27200
Korean Agricultural Museum, Seoul 27248

Latvia
Latvijas Lauksaimniecības Universitātes Muzejs, Jelgava 27367

Malaysia
Agricultural Museum, Jasin 27623

Mexico
Ecomuseo Los Torres, Lerdo 28056
Museo Agrarista de Tzurúmutaro, Pátzcuaro 28306
Museo Comunitario el Asalto a las Tierras, Mexicali 28088
Museo El Remate, Comala 27845
Museo Nacional de Agricultura, Texcoco de Mora 28508

Netherlands
Agrarisch Museum Westerhem, Middenbeemster 29598
Boerderij Museum Duurswold, Slochteren 29831
Boerderijmuseum De Bovenstreek, Oldebroek 29656
Boerderijmuseum De Lebbenbrugge, Borculo 28997
Boerderijmuseum Zelhem, Zelhem 30053
Boerenbondsmuseum, Gemert 29271
Cultuurhistorisch Streekmuseum De Acht Zaligheden, Eersel 29202
De Locht - Streekmuseum, Nationaal Asperge- en Champignonmuseum, Horst 29447
Fruitteeltmuseum, Kapelle 29475
De Garstkamp, Overasselt 29706
Goemanszorg - Streek- en Landbouwmuseum, Dreischor 29180
Hagedoorns Plaatse, Epe 29246
Heemkundemuseum Paulus Van Daesdonck, Ulvenhout 29891
Historisch Museum Ede, Ede 29192
Land- en Tuinbouwmuseum, Etten-Leur 29255
Landbouw- en Juttersmuseum Swartwoude, Buren, Friesland 29041
Landbouwmuseum Erve Niehof, Diepenheim 29150
Meierische Museumboerderij, Heeswijk-Dinther 29373
Museum Bebinghehoes, Exloo 29256
Museum Broeker Veiling, Broek op Langedijk 29029
Museum in de Veenen, Vinkeveen 29945
Museum Saet en Cruyt, Andijk 28919
Museum Veeteelt en K.I., Beers bij Cuyk 28969
Museumboerderij de Karstenhoeve, Ruinerwold 29786
Museumboerderij de Tip, Herveld 29412
Museumboerderij de Zwemkolk, Markelo 29578
Museumboerderij Erve Hofman, Hellendoorn 29387
Museumboerderij Scholten, Den Ham 29132
Museumboerderij Wendezoele, Ambt-Delden 28815
Museumsboerderij Oud Noordwijk, Noordwijk, Zuid-Holland 29645
Openlucht Laagveenderij Museum Damshûs, Nij Beets 29627
Openluchtmuseum Ellert en Brammert, Schoonoord 29815
Oudheidkamer Horst, Horst 29449
Peelmuseum, Ospel 29683
Pluimvee Museum, Barneveld 28964
Sallands Landbouwmuseum de Laarman, Luttenberg 29554
Stichting Zeeuwse Schaapkudde, Heinkenszand 29381
Streeklandbouwmuseum Agrimuda, Sluis 29837
Streeklandbowmuseum Agrimunda, Sint Anna ter Muiden 29818
Streekmuseum de Meesthof, Sint Annaland 29819
Streekmuseum Het Land van Axel, Axel 28956
Streekmuseum voor de Krimpenerwaard Crimpenerhof, Krimpen aan den Ijssel 29494
Veen Park, Barger Compascuum 28963
Vlasbewerkingsmuseum It Braakhok, Ee 29195
Wereld Bodem Museum, Wageningen 29977
Westlands Museum voor Streek- en Tuinbouwhistorie, Honselersdijk 29435
Wieringer Boerderij, Den Oever 29137

New Zealand
East Coast Museum of Technology, Gisborne 30163
Norsewood Pioneer Cottage Museum, Norsewood 30216
Waiuku Museum, Waiuku 30282

Norway
Åfjord Bygdetun, Åfjord 30369
Ål Bygdemuseum, Ål 30371
Andøymuseet, Risøyhamn 30793
Askim Museum, Askim 30402
Aurskog-Høland Bygdetun, Hemnes i Høland 30542
Bagn Bygdesamling, Bagn 30408
Bardu Bygdetun, Salangsdalen 30816
Brudavollen Bygdetun, Ørsta 30721
Bygdetunet Jutulheimen, Vågåmo 30967
Bygland Museum, Bygland 30455
Dokken, Hol i Hallingdal 30552
Eidsvoll Bygdemuseet, Eidsvoll Verk 30475
Enebakk Museet, Enebakk 30479
Fløtermuseet, Osen 30724
Foldalbruket, Kjøllefjord 30596
Folkenborg Museum, Mysen 30696
Forsand Bygdemuseum, Forsand 30503
Fossmotunet - Målselv Bygdemuseum, Moen 30679
Fyresdal Bygdemuseet, Fyresdal 30507
Gamle Hvam Museum, Årnes 30395
Gamle Kvernes Bygdemuseum, Averøy 30407
Glomdalsmuseet, Elverum 30477
Gol Bygdemuseet, Gol 30515
Granvin Bygdamuseum, Granvin 30516
Grødaland Bygdetun, Nærbø 30698
Grytøy Bygdetun, Lundenes 30658
Haltdalen Bygdetun, Haltdalen 30526
Havråtunet, Lonevåg 30652
Hedmarksmuseet og Domkirkeodden, Hamar 30528
Hemsedal Bygdatun, Hemsedal 30543
Hol Bygdemuseum, Hol i Hallingdal 30553
Hordamuseet, Fana 30485
Huldreheimen, Bykle 30457
Jærmuseet, Nærbø 30699
Kvæfjord Museum, Harstad 30533
Kviteseid Bygdetun, Kviteseid 30623
Kystmuseet i Øygarden, Rong 30804
Kystmuseet i Sør-Trøndelag, Hitra 30549
Landbruksmuseet for Møre og Romsdal, Vikebukt 30993
Lands Museum, Dokka 30460
Lårdal Bygdemuseum, Høydalsmo 30572
Lørenskog Bygdemuseum, Skårer 30840
Målselv Bygdemuseum, Moen 30680
Mandal og Opplands Folkemuseum, Mandal 30664
Måsøy Museum, Havøysund 30545
Meløy Bygdemuseum, Ørnes 30720
Meråker Bygdemuseum, Meråker 30673
Mosvik Museum, Mosvik 30695
Namsdalsmuseet, Namsos 30700
Ner Hole Museum, Åndalsnes 30383
Nesna Bygdemuseum, Nesna 30708
Nordre Husan, Alvdal 30380
Norsk Hagebruks Museum, Grimstad 30520
Norsk Landbruksmuseum, Ås 30397
Odalstunet Gårdsmuseum, Skarnes 30841
Orkdal Bygdetun, Fannrem 30487
Osterøy Museum, Lonevåg 30653
Rakkestad Bygdetun, Rakkestad 30784
Rennebu Bygdemuseum, Rennebu 30789
Rissa Bygdemuseum, Rissa 30794
Roan Bygdetun, Roan 30797
Sætersgårds Samlinger Dølmotunet, Tolga 30924
Sande Historielags Bygdesamlinger, Sande 30821
Sigdal og Eggedal Museum, Prestfoss 30782
Skiptvet Bygdemuseum, Skiptvet 30849

Sørli Museum, Sørli 30867
Spydeberg Bygdetun, Spydeberg 30873
Stenneset Bygdetun, Mo i Rana 30676
Sunndal Bygdemuseum, Sunndalsøra 30907
Sunnfjord Museum, Førde 30502
Toten Økomuseum, Bøverbru 30447
Toten Økomuseum, Kapp 30589
Trøgstad Bygdemuseum, Trøgstad 30930
Trysil Bygdemuseum, Trysil 30948
Tylldalen Bygdetun, Tylldalen 30956
Velfjord Bygdemuseum, Hommelstø 30558
Vestfold Fylkesmuseum, Tønsberg 30926
Volda Bygdetun, Volda 30999

Pakistan
Agricultural Museum, Faisalabad 31017

Poland
Muzeum Dworu Polskiego, Plochocin 31885
Muzeum Narodowe Rolnictwa i Przemysłu Rolno-Spożywczego w Szreniawie, Komorniki 31671
Muzeum Rolnictwa im. Ks. Krzysztofa Kluka, Ciechanowiec 31538
Muzeum Wiedzy o Środowisku, Poznań 31913
Muzeum Ziemi Krzeszowickiej, Krzeszowice 31743
Muzeum Ziemi Otwockiej, Otwock 31871
Zbiory Historyczne Ziemi Wadowickiej, Wadowice 32069

Portugal
Agricultural Museum of Entre Douro e Mino, Vila do Conde 32357
Jardim-Museu Agrícola Tropical, Lisboa 32289

Qatar
Al Khor Museum, Al Khor 32413

Réunion
Muséum Agricole et Industriel de Stella Matutina, Piton-Saint-Leu 32419

Romania
Muzeul Național al Satului, București 32464

Russia
Gosudarstvennyj Muzej Životnovodstva im Akademika E.F. Liskuna, Moskva 33067
Muzej-usadba A.T. Bolotova, Dvorjaninovo 32764
Povčenno-agronomičeskij Muzej im. V.R. Viljamsa, Moskva 33175

Slovakia
Slovenské Polnohospodárske Múzeum, Nitra 34036

Slovenia
Muzej Tomaža Godca, Bohinjska Bistrica 34086
Planšarski Muzej, Bohinjsko Jezero 34087

South Africa
Bathurst Agricultural Museum, Bathurst 34176
Cuyler Manor Museum, Uitenhage 34392
Howick Museum, Howick 34264
Willem Prinsloo Museum, Rayton 34366

Spain
Museu d'Eines del Camp Masia de Can Deu, Sabadell 35347
Museu del Pagès, Linyola 34958

Sweden
Åttingen Hantverk och Lantbruksmuseum, Aneby 35799
Gårdsmuséet, Åre 35807
Grans Lantbruksmuseum, Öjebyn 36132
Hägnan Friluftsmuseet i Gammelstad, Gammelstad 35902
Halmens Hus, Bengtsfors 35830
Julita Sveriges Lantbruksmuseums, Julita 35985
Kronobergs Lantbruksmuseum, Alvesta 35792
Kulturhistoriska Museet i Bunge, Farösund 35884
Lantbruksmuseum, Ingatorp 35972
Särestad Lantbruksmuseum, Grästorp 35928

Switzerland
Alpmuseum Riederalp, Riederalp 37059
Dorfmuseum, Bottmingen 36580
Heimatmuseum Nutli-Hüschi, Klosters 36827
Mazot-Musée de Plan-Cerisier, Martigny 36926
Ortsgeschichtliche Sammlung, Oberrieden 37001
Ortsmuseum Altes Rathaus, Balgach 36491
Sennerei-Museum und Heimatmuseum, Unterwasser 37268
Ständerhaus, Buus 36611
Strohhaus, Muhen 36971

United Kingdom
Aberdeenshire Farming Museum, Mintlaw 39967
Acton Scott Historic Working Farm, Church Stretton 38581
Agricultural Museum Brook, Dover 38763
Almond Valley Heritage Centre, Livingston 39533
Ardress House and Farmyard Museum, Annaghmore 38002
Barleylands Farm Museum, Billericay 38199
Battle and Farm Museum, Naseby 40002
Brattle Farm Museum, Staplehurst 40581
Bwlch Farm Stable Museum, Llanelli 39545
Bygones at Holkham, Wells-next-the-Sea 40813
Bygones Museum, Claydon 38587
Church Farm Museum, Skegness 40524
Cogges Manor Farm Museum, Witney 40910
Corfe Castle Museum, Corfe Castle 38632
Countryside Museum, East Budleigh 38837
Cousland Smiddy, Cousland 38640
Craigavon Museum, Craigavon 38655
Easton Farm Park, Easton 38862
Ellisland Farm, Ellisland 38928
Farmland Museum and Denny Abbey, Waterbeach 40802
Farmlife Centre, Thornhill, Central 40702
Gower Heritage Centre, Gower 39106
Hampshire Farm Museum, Botley, Hampshire 38283
Hamptonne Country Life Museum, Saint Lawrence 40412
Heaven Farm Museum, Uckfield 40744
Hirsel Homestead Museum, Coldstream 38617
Kingsbury Watermill Museum, Saint Albans 40372
Leslie Hill Open Farm, Ballymoney 38072
Llanyrafon Farm, Cwmbran 38689
Maldon and District Agricultural and Domestic Museum, Goldhanger 39090
Manor Farm, Bursledon 38405
Museum of English Rural Life, Reading 40295
Museum of Farming Life, Ellon 38929
Museum of Rural Industry, Sticklepath 40588
Museum of Scottish Country Life, East Kilbride 38845
Newham Grange Leisure Farm Museum, Middlesbrough 39950
Normanby Park Farming Museum, Scunthorpe 40459
Orkney Farm and Folk Museum, Birsay 38234
Park Farm Museum, Milton Abbas 39960
Pitstone Green Farm Museum, Pitstone 40206
Plantation of Ulster Visitor Centre, Draperstown 38775
Roots of Norfolk at Gressenhall, Gressenhall 39132
Rural Life Centre, Farnham 38983
Sacrewell Farm and Country Centre, Thornhaugh 40701
Shetland Croft House Museum, Dunrossnes 38817
Somerset Rural Life Museum, Glastonbury 39072
South Molton and District Museum, South Molton 40533
Tingwall Agricultural Museum, Gott 39104
Upminster Tithe Barn Museum, Upminster 40751
Upper Wharfdale Folk Museum, Grassington 39115
Warwickshire Museum of Rural Life, Moreton Morrell 39986
Whaley Thorns Heritage Centre and Museum, Whaley Thorns 40847
Wimpole Hall and Home Farm, Royston 40349
Yorkshire Museum of Farming, York 40974

U.S.A.
The 100th Meridian Museum, Cozad 42686
The Accokeek Foundation, Accokeek 41060
Adams County Museum, Brighton 41899
Agricultural Museum at Stone Mills, La Fargeville 44540
Alexander and Baldwin Sugar Museum, Puunene 46750
American Maple Museum, Croghan 42705
American West Heritage Center, Wellsville 48503
The Apple Trees Museum, Burlington 41995
Arches Museum of Pioneer Life, Winona 48695
Baldwin County Heritage Museum, Elberta 43126
Banner County Historical Museum, Harrisburg 43921
Barrington Living History Farm, Washington 48420
Belair Stable Museum, Bowie 41844
Billings Farm and Museum, Woodstock 48742
Blackberry Farm-Pioneer Village, Aurora 41396
Browntown Museum, Lake City 44584
Calumet County Historical Society Museum, New Holstein 45703
Carroll County Farm Museum, Westminster 48561
Center for Agricultural Science and Heritage, Indianapolis 44214
Central Washington Agricultural Museum, Union Gap 48149
Chippokes Farm and Forestry Museum, Surry 47895
Chisholm Trail Heritage Center Museum, Duncan 43007
Coley Homestead and Barn Museum, Weston 48566
Collin County Farm Museum, McKinney 45037
Craftsman Farms Foundation, Parsippany 46298
Delaware Agricultural Museum, Dover 42968
Drumlin Farm, Lincoln 44778
Erie Canal Village, Rome 46995
The Farm, Sturgeon Bay 47862
Farm House Museum, Ames 41171
Farmamerica, Waseca 48324
Farmamerica, Janesville 44317
The Farmers' Museum, Cooperstown 42618
Florence Ranch Homestead, Mesquite 45274
Florida Agricultural Museum, Palm Coast 46266
Fort Walla Walla Museum, Walla Walla 48285
Fosterfields Living Historical Farm, Morristown 45505
The Fryeburg Fair Farm Museum, Fryeburg 43571
Garfield Farm Museum, Lafox 44573
Georgia Agrirama, Tifton 48007
Gibbs Farm Museum, Falcon Heights 43278
Gibbs Museum of Pioneer and Dakotah Life, Falcon Heights 43279
Grant-Kohrs Ranch National Historic Site, Deer Lodge 42845
Hadley Farm Museum, Hadley 43862
Hale Farm and Village, Bath 41524
Hallockville Museum Farm, Riverhead 46914
Hamilton Grange, New York 45811
Harry's Truman Farm Home, Grandview 43763
Hathaway Ranch Museum, Santa Fe Springs 47435
Highland Maple Museum, Monterey 45461
Hillsboro Museum, Hillsboro 44024
Historic Schaefferstown, Schaefferstown 47494
Historic Stagville, Bahama 41431
Hofwyl-Broadfield Plantation, Brunswick 41969
Homestead National Monument of America, Beatrice 41556
Howard-Dickinson House Museum, Henderson 43993
Howell Living History Farm, Titusville 48012
Huddleston Farmhouse Inn Museum, Cambridge City 42056
Jackson's Mill Historic Area, Weston 48572
Jarrell Plantation Georgia, Juliette 44365
Jerome County Historical Society, Jerome 44337
Jewell County Historical Museum, Mankato 45118
John Brown Farm, Lake Placid 44593
Jourdan-Bachman Pioneer Farm, Austin 41414
Kittson County History Center Museum, Lake Bronson 44578
Kiwanis Van Slyke Museum Foundation, Caldwell 42027
Kline Creek Farm, Winfield 48688
Landis Valley Museum, Lancaster 44629
Landmark Park, Dothan 42960
Leaming's Run Garden and Colonial Farm, Cape May Court House 42099
Living History Farms Museum, Urbandale 48166
Longstreet Farm, Holmdel 44062
Malabar Farm State Park, Lucas 44994
Marjorie Kinnan Rawlings Historic State Park, Cross Creek 42710
Midwest Old Settlers and Threshers Association Museum, Mount Pleasant 45535
Miles B. Carpenter Museum, Waverly 48468
Mississippi Agriculture and Forestry/National Agricultural Aviation Museum, Jackson 44282
Mitchell County Historical Museum, Osage 46200
Moriarty Historical Museum, Moriarty 45501
Mountain Farm Museum, Cherokee 42275
Mulford House and Farm, East Hampton 43048
The National Agricultural Center and Hall of Fame, Bonner Springs 41781
National Apple Museum, Biglerville 41687
Neeses Farm Museum, Neeses 45645
Nelson Pioneer Farm and Museum, Oskaloosa 46208
New Hampshire Farm Museum, Milton 45355
New Jersey Museum of Agriculture, North Brunswick 45985
New Mexico Farm and Ranch Heritage Museum, Las Cruces 44659
New Sweden Farmstead Museum, Bridgeton 41893
Northeastern Montana Threshers and Antique Association Museum, Culbertson 42721
Old Trail Museum, Choteau 42390
Oliver Kelley Farm, Elk River 43138
Olmstead Place State Park, Ellensburg 43151
Oxon Cove Park Museum, Oxon Hill 46246
Pawnee City Historical Society Museum, Pawnee City 46317
Pendleton District Agricultural Museum, Pendleton 46337
Petaluma Adobe State Historic Park, Petaluma 46366
Pioneer Farm Museum and Ohop Indian Village, Eatonville 43073
Pioneer Florida Museum, Dade City 42738
Pioneer Museum of Alabama, Troy 48067
Piqua Historical Area State Memorial, Piqua 46500
Plantation Agriculture Museum, Scott 47509
Plumb Farm Museum, Greeley 43786
Queens County Farm Museum, Floral Park 43342
Quiet Valley Living Historical Farm, Stroudsburg 47855
Rice County Museum of History, Faribault 43294
Rough and Tumble Engineers Museum, Kinzers 44501
Seward County Historical Society Museum, Goehner 43708
Shaker Village of Pleasant Hill, Harrodsburg 43935
Silvercreek Museum, Freeport 43550
Slate Run Living Historical Farm, Ashville 41303
Sotterley Plantation Museum, Hollywood 44061
State Agricultural Heritage Museum, Brookings 41933
Steppingstone Museum, Havre de Grace 43966
Stonefield Historic Site, Cassville 42133
Stuttgart Agricultural Museum, Stuttgart 47865
Thetford Historical Society Museum, Thetford 47997
Tipton-Haynes Museum, Johnson City 44348
Tobacco Farm Life Museum, Kenly 44433
Troy Museum and Historic Village, Troy 48068
Volkening Heritage Farm at Spring Valley, Schaumburg 47496
Ward O'Hara Agricultural Museum of Cayuga County, Auburn 41376
Waterloo Area Farm Museum, Grass Lake 43775
Watters Smith, Lost Creek 44956
West Virginia State Farm Museum, Point Pleasant 46577
Wheeler Historic Farm, Salt Lake City 47237
Wolf Point Area Historical Society Museum, Wolf Point 48721

Amber

Denmark
Ravmuseet, Oksbøl 09017

Germany
Bernstein Museum, Bad Füssing 15647
Deutsches Bernsteinmuseum, Ribnitz-Damgarten 19593

Mexico
Museo del Ámbar de Chiapas, San Cristóbal de las Casas 28380

Russia
Muzej Jantarja, Kaliningrad 32872

Sweden
Bärnstensmuseet, Höllviken 35957

Anthropology → Ethnology

Apiculture → Bees

Archaeology

Albania
Archeological Museum of Durrës, Durrës 00015
Fier Archaeological Museum, Fier 00020
National Museum of Archaeology, Tiranë 00037

Algeria
Musée d'Archéologie, Béjaïa 00049
Musée de Cherchell, Cherchell 00055
Musée de Circonscription Archéologique, Sétif 00071
Musee de Plein de Cherchell, Cherchell 00056
Musee de Tipaza, Tipaza 00080
Musée d'Hippone, Annaba 00048
Musée du Temple de Minerve, Tebessa 00076
Musée National d'Archéologie de Sétif, Sétif 00073
Musée National des Antiquités, Alger 00045

Angola
Museu Nacional de Arqueologia, Benguela 00088

Argentina
Instituto de Investigaciones Arqueológicas y Museo Prof. Mariano Gambier, Albardón 00109
Museo Arqueológico, Aguilares 00108
Museo Arqueológico, Tafí del Valle 00626
Museo Arqueológico Adán Quiroga, San Fernando del Valle de Catamarca 00555
Museo Arqueológico del Instituto de Arqueología y Etnología, Mendoza 00434
Museo Arqueológico Provincial Andalgalá, Andalgalá 00114
Museo Arqueológico Provincial Condor Huasi (interim), Belén 00138
Museo Etnográfico Juán B. Ambrosetti, Buenos Aires 00205
Museo Etnográfico y Colonial Juan de Garay, Santa Fé 00603
Museo Histórico de La Rioja, La Rioja 00400
Museo Privado de Arqueología Regional Julio Gironde, Carmen de Patagonés 00265
Museo Rocsen, Nono 00459

Armenia
State History Museum of Armenia, Erevan 00692

Australia
Abbey Museum of Art and Archaeology, Caboolture 00870
John Elliott Classics Museum, Hobart 01098
Museum of Classical Archaeology, Adelaide 00710
Nicholson Museum, Sydney 01506

Austria
Archäologische Gedenkstätte, Klosterneuburg 02139
Archäologisches Museum Lavant, Lienz 02219
Ausgrabungen Wüstung Hard, Thaya 02727
Freilichtmuseum Römervilla in Brederis, Rankweil 02484
Keltenmuseum Gracarca, Sankt Kanzian 02577
Museen im Wehrturm, Perchtoldsdorf 02402
Museum von Abgüssen und Originalsammlung, Innsbruck 02075
Provinzialrömische Sammlung und Antikenkabinett, Graz 01929
Römermuseum Teurnia, Lendorf 02205
Römermuseum Wallsee-Sindelburg, Wallsee 02792
Römische Baureste Am Hof, Wien 02978
Rollettmuseum, Baden bei Wien 01729
Salzburger Museum Carolino Augusteum, Salzburg 02551
Stadtmuseum Sankt Pölten, Sankt Pölten 02605
Stadtmuseum Wels, Wels 02815
Städtisches Kießling-Museum, Drosendorf an der Thaya 01775
Turmmuseum, Pillichsdorf 02415
Ur-und frühgeschichtliche Sammlungen, Graz 01936
Urgeschichtliches Freilichtmuseum Keltendorf Mitterkirchen, Mitterkirchen 02304
Virgilkapelle, Wien 02998

Bahrain
Bahrain National Museum, Manama 03078

Bangladesh
Archaeological Museum, Mahastangarh 03096

Archaeological Museum, Paharpur 03098
Bangladesh National Museum, Dhaka 03085
Dhaka City Museum, Dhaka 03087
Dinajpur Museum, Dinajpur 03095
Rangpur Archaeological Museum, Rangpur 03100
Varendra Research Museum, Rajshahi 03099

Belarus
Muzej Starażytna Belaruskaj Kultury, Minsk 03120

Belgium
Archeologisch Museum Abdij, Affligem 03127
Archeologisch Museum Van Bogaert-Wauters, Hamme 03472
Bruggemuseum - Archeologie, Brugge 03247
Espace Gallo-Romain, Ath 03187
Gallo-Romeins Museum, Tongeren 03781
Gemeentelijk Archaeologisch Museum, Grobbendonk 03464
Gemeentelijk Museum, Melle 03623
Gemeentemuseum, Temse 03768
Groeningeabdij, Kortrijk 03541
Musée Archéologique, Namur 03645
Musée Athois, Ath 03188
Musée Communal Georges Mulpas, Elouges 03403
Musée d'Archéologie et Folklore, Verviers 03808
Musée d'Archéologie Préhistorique de l'Université de Liège, Liège 03573
Musée de la Pierre et Site des Carrières, Maffle 03605
Musée des Fagnes, Roly 03709
Musée des Francs et de la Famenne, Marche-en-Famenne 03609
Musée d'Histoire et d'Archéologie, Warneton 03827
Musée du Malgré-Tout, Treignes 03800
Musée du Monde Souterrain, Han-sur-Lesse 03474
Musée du Vieux-Cimetière, Soignies 03756
Musée Gallo-Romain, Rumes 03715
Musée Royal de Mariemont, Morlanwelz-Mariemont 03640
Museum 't Nieuwhuys Hoegaarden, Hoegaarden 03497
Rietgaverstede, Nevele 03656
Stedelijk Museum Aalst, Aalst 03125
Stedelijk Museum Brusselpoort, Mechelen 03618
Vleeshuis, Antwerpen 03177
Vleeshuismuseum, Dendermonde 03378

Bosnia and Herzegovina
Humačka Arheološko Zbirka, Ljubuški 03916
Muzej Grada Zenice, Zenica 03932
Muzej Istične Bosně, Tuzla 03929
Muzej Republike Srpske, Banja Luka 03910
Zavičajni Muzej, Prijedor 03920
Zemaljski Muzej, Sarajevo 03925

Brazil
Centro de Arqueologia Annete Laminge Emperaire, Lagoa Santa 04163
Centro Regional de Arqueologia Ambiental, Piraju 04265
Centro Regional de Pesquisas Archeológicas Mário Neme, Piraju 04266
Museu Arqueológico, Lagoa Santa 04164
Museu Arqueológico de Sambaqui Joinville, Joinville 04150
Museu de Arqueologia e Etnologia, Salvador 04426
Museu de Arqueologia e Etnologia da Universidade de São Paulo, São Paulo 04512
Museu Municipal de Arqueologia, Monte Alto 04209
Museu Paranaense, Curitiba 04078

Bulgaria
Archeological Preserve Nicopolis ad Istrum, Veliko Tărnovo 04909
Archeologičeska Ekspozicija Kreposta, Silistra 04812
Archeologičeska Ekspozicija v Džamia Achmed Bej, Kjustendil 04705
Archeologičeski Muzej, Burgas 04631
Archeologičeski Muzej, Plovdiv 04775
Archeologičeski Muzej, Radnevo 04791
Archeologičeski Muzej, Septemvri 04810
Archeologičeski Muzej, Sozopol 04862
Archeologičeski Muzej, Varna 04893
Archeologičeski Muzej, Veliko Tărnovo 04910
Archeologičeski Rezervat Starijat Grad Šumen i Šumenska Krepost, Šumen 04869
Gradski Archeologičeski Muzej, Nesebăr 04742
Gradski Istoričeski Muzej, Asenovgrad 04604
Gradski Istoričeski Muzej, Botevgrad 04627
Gradski Istoričeski Muzej, Karnobat 04692
Istoričeski Muzej, Blagoevgrad 04626
Istoričeski Muzej, Goce Delčev 04674
Istoričeski Muzej, Petrič 04761
Istoričeski Muzej, Pomorie 04783
Istoričeski Muzej, Provadia 04789
Istoričeski Muzej, Razgrad 04797
Istoričeski Muzej, Velingrad 04922
Istoričeski Muzej Targovište, Targovište 04883
Istoričeskij Muzej, Tutrakan 04892
Madara Nacionalen Istoriko-archeologičeski Rezervat, Madara 04731
Muzej Rafail Popov, Madara 04732
Nacionalen Istoriko-archeologičeski Rezervat i Muzej Veliki Preslav, Veliki Preslav 04908
Nacionalen Istoriko-archeologičeski Rezervat Pliska, Pliska 04774
Nikopolis ad Istrum-Antičen grad, Nikjup 04743
Okražen Istoričeski Muzej, Chaskovo 04641
Okražen Istoričeski Muzej, Sliven 04824
Peštera Rabiša Muzej, Belogradčik 04618
Regionalen Istoričeski Muzej, Stara Zagora 04868

Cameroon
Musée du Palais, Foumban 04957

Canada
Fort George and Buckingham House, Saint Paul 06368
Kingston Archaeological Centre, Kingston 05679
Murray's Museum of History, Neepawa 05968
Musée Canadien des Civilisations, Gatineau 05484
Musée Marguerite Bourgeoys, Montréal 05925
Museum of Archaeology and Ethnology, Burnaby 05150
Parc Archéologique de la Pointe-du-Buisson, Melocheville 05837
Pointe-à-Callière - Musée d'Archéologie et d'Histoire de Montréal, Montréal 05927
Prince of Wales Northern Heritage Centre, Yellowknife 06870
Red Bay Historic Site, Red Bay 06219
Royal British Columbia Museum, Victoria 06729
Ska-Nah-Doht Iroquoian Village and Museum, Mount Brydges 05947
Strathcona Archaeological Centre, Edmonton 05387
Surrey Museum, Surrey 06520
XA Ytem Museum, Mission 05866
Yukon Beringia Interpretive Centre, Whitehorse 06793

Central African Republic
Musée Labasso, Bangassou 06877

Chile
Museo Arqueológico R.P. Gustavo Le Paige S.J., San Pedro de Atacama 06906
Museo Arqueológico San Miguel de Azapa, Arica 06889
Museo de Hualpén, Concepción 06893
Museo Regional de Atacama, Copiapó 06895
Museo Regional de Iquique, Iquique 06897

China, People's Republic
Hong Kong Museum of History, Hong Kong 07097
Inner Mongolia Museum, Huhehot 07119
Municipal Museum, Baoji 06939

Colombia
Casa del Escribano Real Don Juan de Vargas, Tunja 07609
Colección Arqueológica, Génova 07484
Colección Arqueológica, Pijao 07559
Colección de Minerales y Arqueología, Villanueva 07625
Monumento a Cristo Rey, Belalcázar 07379
Muestra Arqueológica, Armenia 07370
Muestra Arqueológica, Montenegro 07529
Muestra Arqueológica, Quimbaya 07573
Muestra Arqueológica Colección Rosmary, Colosó 07465
Museo Antrológico, Cereté 07461
Museo Antropológico Tairona, Santa Marta 07585
Museo Arqueológica de Mongua, Mongua 07527
Museo Arqueológico, Aranzazu 07368
Museo Arqueológico, Cartago 07459
Museo Arqueológico, Curumaní 07470
Museo Arqueológico, Inzá 07499
Museo Arqueológico, La Tebaida 07503
Museo Arqueológico, Manizales 07506
Museo Arqueológico, Oiba 07538
Museo Arqueológico, Paéz 07539
Museo Arqueológico, Puerto Berrío 07569
Museo Arqueológico, Salamina 07581
Museo Arqueológico, Sogamoso 07597
Museo Arqueológico Casa de Madame Augustín, Santa Marta 07586
Museo Arqueológico Chimica, El Copey 07476
Museo Arqueológico de Guacarí, Guacarí 07486
Museo Arqueológico del Cesar, Valledupar 07616
Museo Arqueológico del Huila, Neiva 07533
Museo Arqueológico del Sinú, Tierralta 07605
Museo Arqueológico Julio César Cubillos, San Agustín 07582
Museo Arqueológico La Bagatela, Villa del Rosario 07623
Museo Arqueológico La Merced, Cali 07445
Museo Arqueológico Marco Fidel Micolta, Guamo 07491
Museo Arqueológico Regional Guane, Floridablanca 07481
Museo Arqueológico y Paleontológico de Guane, Barichara 07374
Museo Casa de Bolívar, Bucaramanga 07436
Museo Chairama, Santa Marta 07588
Museo de la Casa de la Cultura Martín Gamarra, Gamarra 07482
Museo del Canasto Cafetero y Muestra Arqueológica de la Cultura Quimbaya, Filandia 07478
Museo del Cobre, Bogotá 07414
Museo del Oro, Ipiales 07501
Museo del Oro Calima, Cali 07450
Museo del Oro Nariño, Pasto 07546
Museo del Oro Quimbaya, Armenia 07372
Museo del Oro Quimbaya, Manizales 07509
Museo Escolar María Goretti, Pasto 07547
Museo Ethnográfico, Florencia 07479
Museo Fotográfico, Calarcá 07443
Museo Histórico de la Casa de la Cultura, Ambalema 07366
Museo Histórico y Arqueológico, Belén de Umbría 07380
Museo Histórico y Arqueológico, Charalá 07462
Museo Indígena de Guatavita, Guatavita 07492
Museo Medardo Burbano, Pasto 07552
Museo Mineralógico y Antropológico, Ibagué 07498
Museo Nacional de Colombia, Bogotá 07429
Museo Universitario, Pasto 07554
Museo y Parque Arqueológico de Obando, Obando 07536

Congo, Democratic Republic
Musée de Mbandaka, Mbandaka 07642

Côte d'Ivoire
Musée des Civilisations de Côte d'Ivoire, Abidjan 07666

Croatia
Archeological and Natural History Museum, Brijuni 07684
Arheološka Zbirka, Metković 07739
Arheološka Zbirka Osor, Nerezine 07742
Brački Muzej, Škrip 07777
Collection of the Dominican Priory, Stari Grad 07788
Creski Muzej, Cres 07691
Glyptothèque, Zagreb 07817
Gradski Muzej Makarska, Makarska 07736
Gradski Muzej Siska, Sisak 07776
Gradski Muzej Virovitica, Virovitica 07801
Muzej Cetinjske Krajine, Sinj 07774
Muzej Franjevačkog Samostana Košljun, Punat 07759
Muzej Grada, Šibenik 07772
Muzej Grada Koprivnice, Koprivnica 07718
Muzej Hvarske Baštine, Hvar 07707
Muzej Korčula, Korčula 07722
Muzej Medjimurja, Čakovec 07687
Muzej Moslavine, Kutina 07733
Narodni Muzej Labin, Labin 07734
Senj Municipal Museum, Senj 07770
Zavičajni Muzej, Biograd na Moru 07680
Zavičajni Muzej, Otočac 07752
Zbirka Umjetnina KAIROS, Trogir 07796
Zupski Ured, Ston 07791

Cuba
Museo Arqueológico Guamuhaya, Trinidad 08159
Museo Chorro de Maita, Yaguajay 08178
Museo de la Provincia de Granma, Bayamo 07859
Museo Histórico Municipal de Regla, Regla 08089
Museo Memorial El Morrillo, Matanzas 08041
Museo Municipal de Rodas, Rodas 08092
Museo Provincial de Holguín La Periquera, Holguín 08009
Museo Provincial de Villa Clara y Museo Municipal, Santa Clara 08125

Cyprus
Kourion Museum, Episkopi 08186
Larnaca District Archaeological Museum, Larnaka 08189
Larnaca District Museum, Larnaka 08190
Paphos District Archaeological Museum, Paphos 08215
Pierides Museum, Larnaka 08191
Temple of Aphrodite, Kouklia 08188

Cyprus, Turkish Republic
Güzelyurt Müzesi, Güzelyurt 08228
Saint Barnabas Icon and Archaeological Museum, Gazimağusa 08221

Czech Republic
Archeological Open Air Museum in Březno u Loun, Louny 08464
Archeologické Muzeum, Břeclav 08258
Archeologické Pracoviště, Opava 08518
Archeologické Sbirky, Plzeň 08542
Chebský Hrad, Cheb 08307
Dietrichsteinský Palác, Brno 08264
Jihomoravské Muzeum ve Znojmě, Znojmo 08756
Kamenný Dům, Kutná Hora 08438
Měnínská Brána, Brno 08269
Městské Muzeum, Čelákovice 08292
Městské Muzeum, Dačice 08324
Městské Muzeum, Jesenice u Rakovnika 08385
Městské Muzeum, Mnichovo Hradiště 08483
Městské Muzeum, Nové Strašecí 08506
Městské Muzeum, Počátky 08548
Městské Muzeum, Valašské Klobouky 08705
Městské Muzeum, Veselí nad Moravou 08717
Městské Muzeum a Galerie, Břeclav 08259
Městské Muzeum a Galerie J. Karse, Velvary 08715
Městské Vrbasovo Muzeum, Ždánice 08742
Moravské Zemské Muzeum, Brno 08272
Muzeum Kouřimska, Kouřim 08424
Muzeum Mohelnice, Mohelnice 08484
Muzeum Prostějovska, Prostějov 08629
Muzeum Východních Čech v Hradci Králové, Hradec Králové 08368
Národní Kulturní Památník - Valy, Mikulčice 08475
Okresní Muzeum, Blovice 08252
Okresní Muzeum, Pelhřimov 08537
Okresní Muzeum a Galerie, Jičín 08388
Ostravské Muzeum, Ostrava 08527
Regionální Muzeum v Kolíně, Kolín 08417
Regionální Muzeum ve Vysokém Mýtě, Vysoké Mýto 08733
Sládečkovo Vlastivědné Muzeum v Kladně, Kladno 08410
Východočeské Muzeum, Pardubice 08534

Denmark
Den Antikvariske Samling, Ribe 09027
Arkaeologisk Museum, Korsør 08963
Blaabjerg Egnsmuseum, Nørre Nebel 08991
Danmarks Kloster Museum, Ry 09050
Djurslands Museum - Dansk Fiskerimuseum, Grenå 08841
Hobro Museum, Hobro 08879
Klosterlund Museum og Naturcenter, Engesvang 08804
Kulturhistorisk Museum, Randers 09025
Langelands Museum, Rudkøbing 09048
Lindholm Høje Museet, Nørresundby 08992
Vendsyssel Historiske Museum, Hjørring 08877
Viborg Stiftsmuseum, Viborg 09112

Ecuador
Museo Arqueológico, Cuenca 09149
Museo Arqueológico Atahualpa, Ibarra 09179
Museo Arqueoloógico y Etnográfico, Ibarra 09180
Museo Augustín Landívar, Cuenca 09150
Museo Benigno Malo, Cuenca 09152
Museo de las Culturas Aborígenes, Cuenca 09158
Museo Francisco Campos, Guayaquil 09173
Museo Los Amantes de Sumpa, Guayaquil 09176
Museo Mariano Acosta, Ibarra 09183
Museo Municipal de Guayaquil, Guayaquil 09177
Museo Vásquez Fuller, Otavalo 09190
Museos Arqueológico, Portoviejo 09191
Valdivia Museo, Valdivia 09230

Egypt
Museum of Islamic Art, Cairo 09274

Eritrea
Eritrean Archaeological Museum, Asmara 09315

Ethiopia
Aksum Archaeology Museum, Aksum 09403
National Museum of Ethiopia, Addis Ababa 09400

Faroe Islands
Føroya Fornminnissavn, Tórshavn 09407

Fiji
Fiji Museum, Suva 09409

Finland
Aboa Vetus - Arkeologis-historiallinen Museo, Turku 10117
Liedon Vanhalinna, Vanhalinna 10178

France
Aître Saint-Saturnin, Blois 10769
L'Archéodrome de Bourgogne, Meursault 12962
Archéosite Gallo-Romain des Flaviers, Mouzon 13200
Collections Archéologiques, Parmain 13661
Dépôt de Fouilles Gallo-Romaines et Préhistoriques de Montmaurin, Montmaurin 13106
Expositions du Château, Pierrefonds 13735
Maison du Patrimoine, Blanquefort 10761
Mise en Valeur du Site Archéologique, Barzan 10597
Musée Alfred Bonnot, Chelles 11266
Musée Antoine Vivenel, Compiègne 11375
Musée Archéologique, Bray-sur-Seine 10897
Musée Archéologique, Brumath 10946
Musée Archéologique, Champagnole 11153
Musée Archéologique, Corseul 11414
Musée Archéologique, Dijon 11522
Musée Archéologique, Escolives-Sainte-Camille 11644
Musée Archéologique, Lectoure 12503
Musée Archéologique, Nîmes 13337
Musée Archéologique, Pons 13797
Musée Archéologique, Saint-Gilles-du-Gard 14252
Musée Archéologique, Soyons 14799
Musée Archéologique, Strasbourg 14818
Musée Archéologique, Vachères 15037
Musée Archéologique, Eauze 11593
Musée Archéologique, Saintes 14555
Musée Archéologique d'Argentomagus, Saint-Marcel (Indre) 14344
Musée Archéologique de la Porte du Croux, Nevers 13303
Musée Archéologique de la Région de Breteuil, Breteuil 10915
Musée Archéologique de l'Institut Catholique, Toulouse 14939
Musée Archéologique Départemental, Saint-Bertrand-de-Comminges 14124
Musée Archéologique Départemental du Val-d'Oise, Guiry-en-Vexin 11976
Musée Archéologique du Gâtinais, Montargis 13043
Musée Archéologique - Eglise Saint-Laurent, Grenoble 11940
Musée Archéologique et de Paléontologie, Minerve 12984
Musée Archéologique et d'Histoire Locale, Saint-Emilion 14192
Musée Archéologique et Lapidaire, Blois 10771
Musée Archéologique Henri-Prades, Lattes 12353
Musée Archéologique Géologique et Ethnologique des Vans, Les Vans 12559
Musée Baroncelli, Saintes-Maries-de-la-Mer 14562
Musée Biochet-Brechot, Caudebec-en-Caux 11087
Musée Calvet, Avignon 10528
Musée Campanaire, L'Isle-Jourdain 12627
Musée Cappon, Marans 12799
Musée Champollion, Figeac 11731
Musée Charbonneau-Lassay, Loudun 12674
Musée Charles-Portal, Cordes 11406
Musée Crozatier, Le Puy-en-Velay 12473
Musée d'Archéologie, Izernore 12068
Musée d'Archéologie, Le Pègue 12461

Musée d'Archéologie du Jura, Lons-le-Saunier 12660
Musée d'Archéologie Méditerranéenne, Marseille 12853
Musée d'Archéologique, Saint-Raphaël 14442
Musée d'Archéologique Municipal, Martres-Tolosane 12883
Musée d'Art et d'Archéologie, Aurillac 10490
Musée d'Art et d'Archéologie, Laon 12339
Musée d'Art et d'Archéologie, Senlis 14709
Musée d'Art et d'Histoire, Chaumont (Haute-Marne) 11249
Musée d'Art et d'Histoire de Toul, Toul 14924
Musée d'Art et d'Histoire du Vieux Pérouges, Pérouges 13700
Musée de la Castre, Cannes 11025
Musée de la Société Archéologique et Historique de la Charente, Angoulême 10355
Musée de la Société d'Histoire et d'Archéologie, Briord 10933
Musée de la Tour aux Puces, Thionville 14888
Musée de la Vallée de l'Ubaye, Barcelonnette 10587
Musée de l'Ancienne Abbaye de Landévennec, Landévennec 12317
Musée de l'Ardenne, Charleville-Mézières 11179
Musée de Lodève, Lodève 12647
Musée de Melun, Melun 12923
Musée de Moulages, Strasbourg 14829
Musée de Provins et du Provinois, Provins 13878
Musée de Tauroentum, Saint-Cyr-les-Lecques 14171
Musée de Tautavel-Centre Européen de la Préhistoire, Tautavel 14872
Musée de Traditions Populaires et d'Archéologie, Chauvigny 11255
Musée Départemental de l'Oise, Beauvais 10655
Musée Départemental del'Ariège, Foix 11753
Musée Départemental des Antiquités de la Seine-Maritime, Rouen 14048
Musée Départemental des Hautes-Alpes, Gap 11838
Musée Départemental Jérôme-Carcopino, Aléria 10283
Musée des Antiquités Nationales, Saint-Germain-en-Laye 14242
Musée des Arts Décoratifs, Saumur 14645
Musée des Beaux-Arts, Blois 10774
Musée des Beaux-Arts, Dole 11541
Musée des Beaux-Arts et d'Archéologie, Rennes (Ille-et-Vilaine) 13943
Musée des Beaux-Arts et d'Archéologie, Vienne (Isère) 15163
Musée des Beaux-Arts et d'Archeologie Joseph Déchelette, Roanne 13985
Musée des Fontaines Salées, Saint-Père-sous-Vezelay 14409
Musée des Moulages, Montpellier 13127
Musée d'Evreux, Evreux 11681
Musée d'Histoire et d'Archéologie, Vannes (Morbihan) 15083
Musée d'Histoire et d'Archéologie René Bauberot, Châteauponsac 11223
Musée d'Histoire Naturelle, Rouen 14050
Musée Dobrée, Nantes 13258
Musée Domaine de Gourjade, Castres 11083
Musée du Berry, Bourges 10864
Musée du Biterrois, Béziers 10719
Musée du Châtillonnais, Châtillon-sur-Seine 11243
Musée du Cloître, Tulle 15014
Musée du Colombier, Alès 10287
Musée du Louvre, Paris 13603
Musée du Nord de la Vendée, Montaigu (Vendée) 13037
Musée du Noyonnais, Noyon 13374
Musée du Patrimoine, Néris-les-Bains 13282
Musée du Pays de Sarrebourg, Sarrebourg 14622
Musée du Perigord, Périgueux 13692
Musée du Trophée des Alpes, La Turbie 12271
Musée E. Chenon, Château-Meillant 11205
Musée Gallo-Romain de Tauroentum, Saint-Cyr-sur-Mer 14174
Musée Historique, Haguenau 11986
Musée Historique et Archéologique, Montségur 13152
Musée Historique et Archéologique de l'Orléanais, Orléans 13435
Musée Intercommunal d'Histoire et d'Archéologie, Louvres 12705
Musée Jeanne d'Aboville, La Fère 12168
Musée La Diana, Montbrison 13064
Musée Labenche d'Art et d'Histoire, Brive-la-Gaillarde 10939
Musée Languédocien, Montpellier 13134
Musée Le Minerve, Yzeures-sur-Creuse 15337
Musée Municipal, Châlons-en-Champagne 11131
Musée Municipal, Digne-les-Bains 11514
Musée Municipal, Nuits-Saint-Georges 13376
Musée Municipal, Saint-Amand-les-Eaux 14097
Musée Municipal, Saint-Dizier 14191
Musée Municipal A. Danicourt, Péronne 13699
Musée Municipal Ancienne Abbaye Saint-Léger, Soissons 14762
Musée Municipal Auguste Jacquet, Beaucaire 10631
Musée Municipal de Cambrai, Cambrai 11013
Musée Municipal de Millau, Millau 12980
Musée Municipal de Vendôme, Vendôme 15117
Musée Municipal d'Ernée, Ernée 11639
Musée Municipal des Beaux-Arts, Valence (Drôme) 15051
Musée Municipal d'Étampes, Etampes 11665
Musée Municipal Méditerranéen de Cassis, Cassis 11068
Musée Pierre Borrione, Aime-en-Tarentaise 10243
Musée Pierre Tauziac, Montcaret 13065
Musée Pincé, Angers 10350
Musée Rolin, Autun 10499
Musée Saint-Loup, Troyes 15007
Musée Saint-Raymond, Toulouse 14952
Musée Saint-Remi, Reims 13933
Musée Savoisien, Chambéry 11142
Musée Site Départemental d'Archéologie de Bavay, Bavay 10611
Musée Ziem, Martigues 12881
Musées de la Cour d'Or, Metz 12958
Parc Archéologique Européen de Bliesbruck-Reinheim, Bliesbruck 10768

Gambia
Gambia National Museum, Banjul 15352

Georgia
Tbilisi State Museum of Anthropology and Ethnography, Tbilisi 15368

Germany
Alamannenmuseum, Weingarten, Württemberg 20478
Alamannenmuseum Ellwangen, Ellwangen 16834
Antikenmuseum der Universität Leipzig, Leipzig 18384
Antikensammlung der Friedrich-Alexander-Universität Erlangen-Nürnberg, Erlangen 16915
Archäologiemuseum im Fränkischen Freilandmuseum, Bad Windsheim 15775
Archäologisch-Ethnographische Lehr- und Studiensammlung des Instituts für Altamerikanistik und Ethnologie der Universität Bonn, Bonn 16226
Archäologisch-Ökologisches Museum, Albersdorf 15416
Archäologische Sammlung, Essen 16945
Archäologische Sammlung Keltenhaus, Taufkirchen, Kreis München 20147
Archäologische Sammlung mit Heimatvertriebenen-stube und Kruk-Sammlung, Königsbrunn 18172
Archäologisches Freilichtmuseum Oerlinghausen, Oerlinghausen 19231
Archäologisches Landesmuseum, Schleswig 19793
Archäologisches Landesmuseum Baden-Württemberg, Konstanz 18201
Archäologisches Landesmuseum Mecklenburg-Vorpommern, Groß Raden 17419
Archäologisches Museum, Donauwörth 16636
Archäologisches Museum, Rimpar 19613
Archäologisches Museum der Stadt Kelheim, Kelheim 18049
Archäologisches Museum der Stadt Weißenhorn, Weißenhorn 20500
Archäologisches Museum Essenbach, Essenbach 16965
Archäologisches Museum Gablingen, Gablingen 17186
Archäologisches Museum im Rathaus, Weichering 20423
Archäologisches Museum in der Feldmühle, Rennertshofen 19571
Archäologisches Zentrum Hitzacker, Hitzacker 17771
Badisches Landesmuseum Karlsruhe, Karlsruhe 17991
Burg Neuhaus, Wolfsburg 20658
Clemens-Sels-Museum, Neuss 19063
Die Eulenburg, Rinteln 19617
Federseemuseum Bad Buchau, Bad Buchau 15621
Glauberg-Museum, Glauburg 17297
Haus zum Stockfisch - Stadtmuseum, Erfurt 16903
Hegau-Museum, Singen, Hohentwiel 19966
Heimatmuseum Adlhoch-Haus, Altdorf, Niederbayern 15441
Heimatmuseum Schlitz, Schlitz 19803
Heimatmuseum Zusmarshausen, Zusmarshausen 20772
Heinrich-Schliemann-Museum, Ankershagen 15493
Heuneburgmuseum, Herbertingen 17714
Historisches Museum im Marstall, Paderborn 19335
Hochburg-Museum, Emmendingen 16853
Keltenmuseum Hochdorf/Enz, Eberdingen 16760
Keltisch-Römisches Museum, Manching 18610
Landesmuseum Koblenz, Koblenz 18120
Landesmuseum Mainz, Mainz 18602
Münzkabinett und Archäologische Lehrsammlung der Universität Rostock, Rostock 19666
Museum Abodiacum, Denklingen 16573
Museum Bürgstadt, Bürgstadt 16407
Museum Burg Bederkesa, Bad Bederkesa 15595
Museum der Stadt Ettlingen, Ettlingen 16975
Museum der Stadt Worms, Worms 20678
Museum der Westlausitz Kamenz, Kamenz 17979
Museum für Archäologie und Volkskunde, Kösching 18188
Museum für Kloster- und Heimatgeschichte, Harsefeld 17620
Museum für Kunst und Kulturgeschichte der Stadt Dortmund, Dortmund 16662
Museum in der Kaiserpfalz, Paderborn 19338
Museum Quintana - Archäologie in Künzing, Künzing 18260
Museum Roemervilla, Bad Neuenahr-Ahrweiler 15704
Museum Römervilla, Grenzach-Wyhlen 17395
Museum Schloss Oberschwappach, Knetzgau 18117
Reiss-Engelhorn-Museen, Mannheim 18615
Rhön-Museum, Fladungen 17010
Robertinum, Halle, Saale 17519
Römer und Bajuwaren Museum Burg Kipfenberg, Kipfenberg 18085
Römerhalle, Bad Kreuznach 15681
Römerkastell Saalburg, Bad Homburg v.d.Höhe 15666
Römermuseum Multerer, Grabenstätt 17365
Römermuseum Stettfeld, Ubstadt-Weiher 20242
Römisches Museum und Naturkunde-Museum, Kempten 18065
Sammlung Antiker Kleinkunst, Jena 17949
Schlossmuseum, Bad Iburg 15670
Slawenburg Raddusch, Raddusch 19467
Torfmuseum, Neustadt am Rübenberge 19070
Ur- und Frühgeschichtliche Sammlung, Erlangen 16925
Varusschlacht im Osnabrücker Land, Bramsche 16274
Victor-Schultze-Institut für christliche Archäologie und Geschichte der kirchlichen Kunst, Greifswald 17391
Wall-Museum, Oldenburg in Holstein 19252
Westfälisches Museum für Archäologie, Herne 17731
Wikinger Museum Haithabu, Busdorf bei Schleswig 16433
Wittelsbachermuseum Aichach, Aichach 15409

Ghana
Ghana National Museum, Accra 20788
Museum of Archaeology, Legon 20800

Gibraltar
Gibraltar Museum, Gibraltar 20802

Greece
Archeological Museum, Chaironeia 20912
Archeological Museum, Delos 20935
Archeological Museum, Mykonos 21077
Vaos Collection, Athinai 20905

Greenland
Avanersuup Katersugaasivia, Qaanaaq 21236

Grenada
Grenada National Museum, Saint George's 21244

Guatemala
Museo Popol Vuh, Guatemala 21275

Hungary
Arany János Múzeum, Nagykőrös 21487
Balassa Bálint Múzeum, Esztergom 21410
Balatoni Múzeum, Keszthely 21453
Csongrádi Múzeum, Csongrád 21397
Déri Múzeum, Debrecen 21398
Dobó István Vármuzeum, Eger 21406
Dráva Múzeum, Barcs 21316
Erkel Ferenc Múzeum, Gyula 21423
Ferenczy Károly Múzeum, Szentendre 21570
Göcseji Múzeum, Zalaegerszeg 21614
Hajdusági Múzeum, Hajdúböszörmény 21425
Hansági Múzeum, Mosonmagyaróvár 21484
Herman Ottó Múzeum, Miskolc 21476
Intercisa Múzeum, Dunaújváros 21405
Jász Múzeum, Jászberény 21435
Jósa András Múzeum, Nyíregyháza 21492
Kubinyi Ferenc Múzeum, Szécsény 21546
Kuny Domokos Múzeum, Tata 21593
Laczkó Dezsoë Múzeum, Veszprém 21608
Magyar Nemzeti Múzeum, Budapest 21361
Mátyás Király Múzeum, Visegrád 21611
Móra Ferenc Múzeum, Szeged 21551
Rákóczi Múzeum, Sárospatak 21524
Reneszánsz Kőtár, Pécs 21514
Smidt Múzeum, Szombathely 21588
Szent István Király Múzeum, Székesfehérvár 21561
Tatabánya Múzeum, Tatabánya 21595
Tornyai János Múzeum, Hódmezővásárhely 21428
Tragor Ignác Múzeum, Vác 21602
Vármúzeum, Esztergom 21414
Wosinsky Mór Megyei Múseum, Szekszárd 21565
Xantus János Múzeum, Győr 21422

Iceland
Minjasafn Austurlands, Egilsstadir 21629
P^BDjóðminjasafn Islands, Reykjaník 21647

India
Akshaya Kumar Maitreya Museum, Siliguri 22025
Anthropological Museum, Guwahati, Assam 21826
Archaeological Museum, Amaravati 21694
Archaeological Museum, Bijapur 21729
Archaeological Museum, Bodhghaya 21732
Archaeological Museum, Delhi 21765
Archaeological Museum, Guntur 21816
Archaeological Museum, Gwalior 21828
Archaeological Museum, Halebidu 21832
Archaeological Museum, Hardwar 21835
Archaeological Museum, Jaunpur 21867
Archaeological Museum, Kamalapur 21880
Archaeological Museum, Khajuraho 21887
Archaeological Museum, Nalanda 21965
Archaeological Museum, Pune 21986
Archaeological Museum, Sanchi 22007
Archaeological Museum, Sarnath 22012
Archaeological Museum Konarak, Puri 21995
Archaeological Museum of Patiala, Patiala 21975
Archaeological Museum Red Fort Delhi, Delhi 21766
Archaeological Site Museum, Alampur 21686
Archaeology Museum, Chennai 21741
Archeological Museum, Trichur 22041
Assam State Museum, Guwahati 21819
Central Museum, Indore 21859
Central Museum, Nagpur 21963
Commercial Museum, Guwahati 21820
District Archaeological Museum, Dhar 21788
District Museum, Gulbarga 21815
District Museum, Pillalamari 21982
District Museum, Shimoga 22021
Gandhi Centenary Museum, Karimnagar 21884
Ganga Government Museum, Bikaner 21730
Government Museum, Ajmer 21684
Government Museum, Chennai 21744
Government Museum, Hassan 21838
Government Museum, Pudukottai 21985
Government Museum Jhalawar, Jhalawar 21871
Government Museum Vellore, Vellore 22059
Jeypore Branch Museum, Jaipur, Orissa 21861
Jhalawar Archaeology Museum, Jhalawar 21872
Junagadh Museum, Junagadh 21877
Kachchh Museum, Bhuj 21728
Keladi Museum, Keladi 21886
Kithur Rani Channamma Memorial Museum, Kittur 21890
Kolhapur Museum, Kolhapur 21895
Local Antiquities Museum, Chitradurga 21749
Local Museum, Bhanpura 21713
Mahant Ghasidas Memorial Museum, Raipur, Karnataka 21998
Museum of Antiquities, Jamnagar 21866
Museum of Archaeology, Vadodara 22051
Museum of Art and Archaeology, Mysore 21961
National Museum of India, Delhi 21776
Orissa State Museum, Bhubaneshwar 21726
Palace and Museum of Antiquities, Padmanabhapuram 21971
Patna Museum, Patna 21978
Sri Pratap Singh Museum, Srinagar 22028
Sri Rallabandi Subbarao Government Museum, Rajahmundry 22001
Ramlingappa Lamture Museum, Osmanabad 21970
State Archaeological Museum, Kolkata 21912
University Museum, Vallabhvidyanagar 22054
Victoria Jubilee Museum, Vijayawada 22060
Vikram Kirti Mandir Museum, Ujjain 22047
Yeleswasam Pavilion, Hyderabad 21848

Indonesia
Archaeological Museum Blitar, Blitar 22086
Archaeological Museum Kediri, Kediri 22144
Museum Daerah Blambangan, Banyuwangi 22081
Museum Gedung Arca, Gianyar 22100
Museum Nasional, Jakarta 22124
Statue Museum Balai Arca, Nganjuk 22163

Iran
Archaeological Museum, Neishaboor 22272
Hegmataneh Museum, Samedan 22276
Khalkhal Museum, Khalkhal 22256
Khoy Museum, Khoy 22259
Miandoab Museum, Urmieh 22331
Museum Falak-ol-Aflak, Khorram-Abaad 22257
National Museum, Teheran 22319
Qom Museum, Qom 22274
Shahrood Museum, Semnan 22279

Iraq
Mosul Museum, Mosul 22351

Ireland
Clare Museum, Ennis 22466
The Hunt Museum, Limerick 22505
Kerry County Museum, Tralee 22547
Meath Archaeological and Historical Museum, Trim 22548
Músaem Corca Dhuibhne, Ballyferriter 22370
Museum of Archaeology and History, Dublin 22442
Saint Catherine's National School Museum, Aughrim 22363

Israel
Antiquities Museum of Tel Aviv-Yafo, Tel Aviv 22745
Archaeological and Historical Museum, Ramat Hashofet 22736
Archaeological Collection, Yehi'am 22783
Archaeological Collection of Youth Village Nitzanim, Doar-Na Evtach 22587
The Archaeological Museum of Kfar-Saba, Kfar-Saba 22675
Archeological and Land Study Collection, Alumot 22570
Archeology Museum, Shamir 22743
Beit-Shean Museum, Beit Shean 22581
Center of Nautical and Regional Archaeology, Nahshonim 22719
Collection of Archaeology and Land Study, Nahshonim 22720
Ecce Homo, Jerusalem 22631
Genia Schreiber University Art Gallery, Ramat Aviv 22730
Greek Orthodox Museum, Jerusalem 22633
Israel Museum, Jerusalem, Jerusalem 22643
Qedem Museum, Kedumim 22673
Rockefeller Museum, Jerusalem 22658
Shephela Museum, Kibbutz Kfar Menahem 22692
Siebenberg House, Jerusalem 22663
Ussishkin House, Kibbutz Dan 22681

Italy
Antiquarium, Agropoli 22819
Antiquarium, Ariano Irpino 22928
Antiquarium, Avella 22988
Antiquarium, Borgia 23168
Antiquarium, Buccino 23223
Antiquarium, Caldarola 23263
Antiquarium, Castelseprio 23426
Antiquarium, Cesenatico 23509
Antiquarium, Cimitile 23564
Antiquarium, Filadelfia 23812

Antiquarium, Golasecca 24032
Antiquarium, Loreto Aprutino 24217
Antiquarium, Lugnano in Teverina 24237
Antiquarium, Massarosa 24329
Antiquarium, Mergozzo 24361
Antiquarium, Monasterace 24466
Antiquarium, Nonantola 24634
Antiquarium, Partinico 24813
Antiquarium, San Marzano sul Sarno 25392
Antiquarium, Serravalle Scrivia 25550
Antiquarium, Trieste 25809
Antiquarium, Boscoreale 23186
Antiquarium Cantianense, San Canzian d'Isonzo 25344
Antiquarium Civico, Bagnolo San Vito 23007
Antiquarium Civico, Vazzano 25904
Antiquarium Comunale, Colleferro 23613
Antiquarium Comunale, Contessa Entellina 23639
Antiquarium Comunale, Milena 24423
Antiquarium Comunale, Monte Romano 24498
Antiquarium Comunale, Sezze 25563
Antiquarium Comunale, Tiriolo 25707
Antiquarium Comunale N. Pansoni, Cossignano 23671
Antiquarium del Castello Eurialo, Siracusa 25584
Antiquarium del Parco della Forza, Ispica 24107
Antiquarium del Seminario Vescovile, Nola 24630
Antiquarium del Varignano, Portovenere 25025
Antiquarium di Canne, Barletta 23030
Antiquarium di Megara Hyblaea, Augusta 22985
Antiquarium di Monte Cronio, Sciacca 25527
Antiquarium di Nervia, Ventimiglia 25954
Antiquarium di Poggio Civitate, Murlo 24570
Antiquarium Di Sant'Appiano, Barberino Val d'Elsa 23013
Antiquarium di Tesis, Vivaro 26042
Antiquarium di Villa Romana, Patti 24817
Antiquarium e Archeologica Museo, Cuglieri 23694
Antiquarium Ipogeo dei Volumni, Perugia 24846
Antiquarium Jetino, San Cipirello 25348
Antiquarium Lucio Salvio Quintiano, Ossuccio 24713
Antiquarium Tellinum, Teglio 25682
Antiquarium Torre Cimalonga, Scalea 25514
Antiquarium - Villa Maritima, Minori 24428
Archeologica di Sovana, Sorano 25608
Castello di Giulio II, Ostia Antica 24714
Castello e Raccolta Archeologica, Montechiarugolo 24514
Castello Malaspina, Massa 24313
Centro Ambientale Archeologico, Legnano 24174
Centro di Documentazione Messapica, Oria 24685
Civica Raccolta e Ceramiche Rinascimentali, Camporgiano 23311
Civici Musei e Gallerie di Storia ed Arte, Udine 25845
Civico Museo Archeologico, Arsago Seprio 22943
Civico Museo Archeologico, Camogli 23294
Civico Museo Archeologico, Ozieri 24723
Civico Museo Archeologico L. Barni e Pinacoteca C. Ottone, Vigevano 26006
Civico Museo di Storia ed Arte e Orto Lapidario, Trieste 25815
Civico Museo Frignanese, Pavullo nel Frignano 24830
Civico Museo Ingauno, Albenga 22831
Civico Museo Storico Archeologico, Savona 25507
Collezione Martini Carissimo, Oria 24686
Collezione Meo-Evoli, Monopoli 24476
Collezioni dell'Istituto Universitario Orientale, Napoli 24573
Collezioni Egittologiche dell'Università di Pisa, Pisa 24943
Lapidario Civico, Gradisca d'Isonzo 24041
Lapidario Comunale, Osimo 24707
Mostra Archeologica G. Venturini, San Felice sul Panaro 25357
Musei Civici, Reggio Emilia 25096
Musei Civici, Pavia 24822
Musei Civici agli Eremitani, Padova 24733
Musei Civici e Pinacoteca L. Sturzo, Caltagirone 23272
Museo Alessi, Enna 23732
Museo Archeologica, Savignone 25503
Museo Archeologico, Acqualagna 22799
Museo Archeologico, Arborea 22911
Museo Archeologico, Artena 22944
Museo Archeologico, Bonorva 23161
Museo Archeologico, Caltanissetta 23274
Museo Archeologico, Camaiore 23279
Museo Archeologico, Carassai 23342
Museo Archeologico, Castello di Godego 23413
Museo Archeologico, Castiglione della Pescaia 23432
Museo Archeologico, Dorgali 23721
Museo Archeologico, Fermo 23777
Museo Archeologico, Follonica 23898
Museo Archeologico, Frosinone 23939
Museo Archeologico, Isola della Scala 24106
Museo Archeologico, Lentini 24177
Museo Archeologico, Molfetta 24457
Museo Archeologico, Monopoli 24477
Museo Archeologico, Ostiglia 24717
Museo Archeologico, Palazzuolo sul Senio 24761
Museo Archeologico, Povegliano Veronese 25031
Museo Archeologico, Priverno 25054
Museo Archeologico, Pula 25056
Museo Archeologico, Rocca di Mezzo 25135
Museo Archeologico, San Miniato 25398
Museo Archeologico, Santadi 25445
Museo Archeologico, Santorso 25466
Museo Archeologico, Scansano 25517
Museo Archeologico, Teramo 25687
Museo Archeologico, Varallo Pombia 25890
Museo Archeologico, Ventotene 25957
Museo Archeologico, Veroli 25964
Museo Archeologico, Villasimius 26022
Museo Archeologico, Cavriana 23463
Museo Archeologico Antiquarium Arborense, Oristano 24692
Museo Archeologico Antonio Santarelli, Forlì 23908
Museo Archeologico Aquaria, Soncino 25599
Museo Archeologico B. Antonucci, Pietrasanta 24912
Museo Archeologico Civico, Forlimpopoli 23918
Museo Archeologico Comprensoriale, Teti 25703
Museo Archeologico Comunale, Vicchio 25989
Museo Archeologico dei Campi Flegrei, Bacoli 22996
Museo Archeologico del Finale, Finale Ligure 23818
Museo Archeologico del Territorio, Cupra Marittima 23699
Museo Archeologico del Territorio - Antiquarium Suasanum, San Lorenzo in Campo 25383
Museo Archeologico del Territorio di Populonia, Piombino 24935
Museo Archeologico della Badia, Licata 24183
Museo Archeologico della Lucania Occidentale, Padula 24753
Museo Archeologico dell'Abruzzo, Crecchio 23675
Museo Archeologico dell'Alto Adige, Bolzano 23152
Museo Archeologico dell'Alto Canavese, Cuorgnè 23698
Museo Archeologico dell'Antica, Alife 22858
Museo Archeologico dell'Antica Calatia, Maddaloni 24256
Museo Archeologico dell'Antica Capua, Santa Maria Capua Vetere 25435
Museo Archeologico di Casteggio, Casteggio 23385
Museo Archeologico di Naxos, Giardini Naxos 24021
Museo Archeologico di Sepino, Sepino 25541
Museo Archeologico di Villa Sulcis, Carbonia 23344
Museo Archeologico e Antiquarium, Sala Consilina 25314
Museo Archeologico e d'Arte della Maremma, Grosseto 24056
Museo Archeologico e Paleontologico di Farneta, Cortona 23662
Museo Archeologico ed Etnografico, Ittireddu 24110
Museo Archeologico Etnografico, Paulilatino 24820
Museo Archeologico F. Milizia, Oria 24687
Museo Archeologico G. Allevi, Offida 24669
Museo Archeologico G. Rambotti, Desenzano del Garda 23711
Museo Archeologico Ibleo, Ragusa 25068
Museo Archeologico Isidoro Falchi, Vetulonia 25982
Museo Archeologico Iulium Carnicum, Zuglio 26061
Museo Archeologico Lametino, Lamezia Terme 24131
Museo Archeologico Liutprando, San Giovanni in Persiceto 25372
Museo Archeologico Lomellino, Garlasco 23961
Museo Archeologico Lucus Feroniae, Capena 23325
Museo Archeologico Luigi Donini, San Lazzaro di Savena 25377
Museo Archeologico Michele Janora, Irsina 24098
Museo Archeologico Nazionale, Cagliari 23245
Museo Archeologico Nazionale, Cassino 23382
Museo Archeologico Nazionale, Cividale del Friuli 23588
Museo Archeologico Nazionale, Crotone 23689
Museo Archeologico Nazionale, Eboli 23726
Museo Archeologico Nazionale, Firenze 23852
Museo Archeologico Nazionale, Manfredonia 24280
Museo Archeologico Nazionale, Mantova 24283
Museo Archeologico Nazionale, Spoleto 25623
Museo Archeologico Nazionale del Melfese, Melfi 24345
Museo Archeologico Nazionale della Sibaritide, Cassano allo Jonio 23380
Museo Archeologico Nazionale delle Marche, Ancona 22881
Museo Archeologico Nazionale dell'Umbria, Perugia 24850
Museo Archeologico Nazionale di Metaponto, Bernalda 23067
Museo Archeologico Nazionale Etrusco, Siena 25569
Museo Archeologico per la Preistoria e Protostoria del Tigullio, Chiavari 23530
Museo Archeologico Provinciale, Potenza 25028
Museo Archeologico Provinciale, Salerno 25317
Museo Archeologico Regionale, Aosta 22900
Museo Archeologico Regionale, Gela 23970
Museo Archeologico Regionale, Santa Croce Camerina 25429
Museo Archeologico Regionale Paolo Orsi, Siracusa 25586
Museo Archeologico Remo Fumagalli, Novara 24645
Museo Archeologico Sentinate, Sassoferrato 25494
Museo Archeologico Statale, Altamura 22861
Museo Archeologico Statale, Arcevia 22913
Museo Archeologico Statale, Teano 25678
Museo Archeologico Statale, Urbisaglia 25862
Museo Archeologico Statale V. Laviola, Amendolara 22876
Museo Archeologico Tifernum Mataurense, Sant'Angelo in Vado 25449
Museo Archeologico Villa Abbas, Sardara 25472
Museo Berenziano, Cremona 23679
Museo Bicknell, Bordighera 23164
Museo Canonicale, Verona 25970
Museo Capitolare delle Antichità Corfiniesi, Corfinio 23650
Museo Carlo Venturini, Massa Lombarda 24317
Museo Civico, Avola 22995
Museo Civico, Cosenza 23665
Museo Civico, Noto 24640
Museo Civico, Piedimonte 24906
Museo Civico, Pizzighettone 24968
Museo Civico, Ragogna 25066
Museo Civico, Riva del Garda 25130
Museo Civico, Susa 25654
Museo Civico, Viterbo 26033
Museo Civico, Sanremo 25425
Museo Civico, Nocera Umbra 24628
Museo Civico, Biella 23079
Museo Civico, Finale Emilia 23815
Museo Civico Albano, Albano Laziale 22830
Museo Civico Antiquarium, Nettuno 24616
Museo Civico Antiquarium Platina, Piadena 24895
Museo Civico Archeologica e Quadreria, Monterubbiano 24545
Museo Civico Archeologico, Angera 22889
Museo Civico Archeologico, Bologna 23109
Museo Civico Archeologico, Castrovillari 23441
Museo Civico Archeologico, Marciana 24295
Museo Civico Archeologico, Massa Marittima 24322
Museo Civico Archeologico, Nicotera 24620
Museo Civico Archeologico, Padria 24752
Museo Civico Archeologico, Ramacca 25070
Museo Civico Archeologico, Remedello 25102
Museo Civico Archeologico, Rutigliano 25304
Museo Civico Archeologico, Tolentino 25717
Museo Civico Archeologico, Treia 25788
Museo Civico Archeologico, Bene Vagienna 23052
Museo Civico Archeologico della Val Tenesi, Manerba del Garda 24278
Museo Civico Archeologico e Pinacoteca, Chiomonte 23551
Museo Civico Archeologico Eno Bellis, Oderzo 24665
Museo Civico Archeologico F Saverio Majellaro, Bisceglie 23086
Museo Civico Archeologico Genna Maria, Villanovaforru 26020
Museo Civico Archeologico Goffredo Bellini, Asola 22958
Museo Civico Archeologico P. Giovio, Como 23627
Museo Civico Archeologico Trebula Mutesca, Monteleone Sabino 24530
Museo Civico di Belriguardo, Voghiera 26046
Museo Civico di Scienze Naturali ed Archeologia della Valdinievole, Pescia 24876
Museo Civico Don Queirolo, Vado Ligure 25865
Museo Civico e Antiquarium, Latina 24158
Museo Civico e Pinacoteca A. Vernarecci, Fossombrone 23928
Museo Civico e Risorgimentale Don Giovanni Verità, Modigliana 24453
Museo Civico F. de Rocco, San Vito al Tagliamento 25418
Museo Civico G. Sutermeister, Legnano 24175
Museo Civico Pietro Lotti, Ischia di Castro 24099
Museo Civico-Pinacoteca, Vicenza 25993
Museo Civico Storico Archeologico, Leno 24176
Museo Civico U. Formentini, La Spezia 24123
Museo dei Grandi Fiumi, Rovigo 25297
Museo del Collezionista d'Arte, Milano 24393
Museo del Sannio, Benevento 23053
Museo del Santuario di Montevergine, Mercogliano 24360
Museo del Territorio, Riccione 25108
Museo della Città, Aquino 22910
Museo della Civiltà Locale, Trevi 25799
Museo della Regina, Cattolica 23457
Museo dell'Abazzia di San Colombano, Bobbio 23094
Museo dell'Abbazia di San Nilo, Grottaferrata 24060
Museo dell'Accademia Etrusca, Cortona 23663
Museo dell'Arte Classica, Sezione di Archeologia, Roma 25199
Museo delle Genti d'Abruzzo, Pescara 24868
Museo delle Navi Romane, Nemi 24613
Museo di Antichità Etrusche e Italiche, Roma 25208
Museo di Antropologia, Napoli 24588
Museo di Paletnologia, Polignano a Mare 24979
Museo di Scienze Archeologiche e d'Arte, Padova 24742
Museo e Pinacoteca Civica, Alessandria 22849
Museo e Pinacoteca Comunali, Gubbio 24075
Museo Etrusco Gasparri, Piombino 24938
Museo G. Whitaker, Marsala 24307
Museo Giovanni Antonio Sanna, Sassari 25488
Museo I. Mormino, Palermo 24776
Museo Irpino, Avellino 22989
Museo L. Ceselli, Subiaco 25646
Museo Lapidario del Duomo, Novara 24648
Museo Memorie Pollentine, Pollenza 24981
Museo Naturalistica-Archeologico, Vicenza 25995
Museo Nazionale, Reggio Calabria 25091
Museo Nazionale Archeologico, Chieti 23548
Museo Nazionale Archeologico di Egnazia, Fasano-Savelletri 23768
Museo Nazionale Atestino, Este 23743
Museo Nazionale Concordiese, Portogruaro 25023
Museo Nazionale d'Abruzzo, L'Aquila 24147
Museo Nazionale d'Arte Orientale, Roma 25231
Museo Nazionale dell'Agro Picentino, Pontecagnano 24995
Museo Nazionale di San Matteo, Pisa 24953
Museo Oraziano, Licenza 24185
Museo P. Vagliasindi, Randazzo 25073
Museo Palatino, Roma 25244
Museo Perrando, Sassello 25490
Museo Preistorico e Archeologico A.C. Blanc, Viareggio 25985
Museo Provinciale Campano, Capua 23339
Museo Provinciale Sigismondo Castromediano, Lecce 24167
Museo R. De Cesare, Spinazzola 25619
Museo Storico Archeologico G. Gabetti, Dogliani 23716
Museo Storico del Vetro e della Bottiglia J.F. Mariani, Montalcino 24492
Museo Territoriale del Lago di Bolsena, Bolsena 23148
Museo Tuscolano, Frascati 23933
Palazzo Belgiojoso, Lecco 24172
Raccolta Archeologica, Terni 25697
Raccolta Archeologica, Tolentino 25723
Raccolta Archeologica Alberto Pisani Dossi, Corbetta 23645
Raccolta Archeologica e Paleontologica, Corciano 23648
Raccolta Archeological, Bevagna 23075
Raccolta Lapidaria Capitolina, Roma 25266
Scavi Archeologici di Velia, Ascea 22945
Scavi di Ostia, Ostia Antica 24716
Scavi di Stabiae, Castellammare di Stabia 23402

Jamaica
Archaeological Museum, Spanish Town 26081
Museum of Historical Archaeology, Kingston 26074

Japan
Abashiri Kyodo Hakubutsukan, Abashiri 26084
Ainu Museum, Sapporo 26708
Chiba-kenritsu Boso Fudoki-No-Oka, Sakae 26694
Hiratsuka-shi Hakubutsukan, Hiratsuka 26208
Kyoto City Archaeological Museum, Kyoto 26419
Nagatoro Kyukokan, Chichibu 26125
Nakayama Archaeological Museum, Matsumoto 26478
Nara-kenritsu Kashihara Kokogaku Kenkyujo Fuzoku Hakubutsukan, Kashihara 26317
Oku Kokokan, Oku 26631
Osaka Prefectural Museum of Yayoi Culture, Izumi 26277
Shimane Daigaku Hobungakubu Kokogaku Kenkyushitsu-nai, Matsue 26471
Shiretoko Museum, Shari 26742
Taish-Machi Kominkan Fuzoku Taisha Kokokan, Taishiya 26786
Tatsuuma Archaeological Museum, Nishinomiya 26607
Tokushima-kenritsu Torii Kinen Hakubutsukan, Naruto 26590
Tokyo University Archaeological Collection, Tokyo 26948
The University Museum, Tokyo 26953

Jordan
Salt Archaeological Museum, Salt 27066

Kazakhstan
Otar Memlekettik Archeologicalik Korik Muzej, Čimkent 27079
Otrar State Archaeological Park Museum, Shymkent 27096

Kenya
Fort Jesus Museum, Mombasa 27109
Gede Museum and National Monument, Watamu 27115
Hyrax Hill Museum, Hyrax Hill 27102
Kariandusi Prehistoric Site Museum, Gilgil 27101

Kyrgyzstan
Muzej Architektury i Archeologii Vez Burana, Čujsk 27310

Latvia
Latvijas Vēstures Muzejs, Rīga 27428
Turaidas Muzejrezervāts, Sigulda 27451

Lithuania
Aušros Avenue Mansion, Šiauliai 27525
Ch. Frenkelis Mansion, Šiauliai 27527
Lietuvos Nacionalinis Muziejus, Vilnius 27537
Šiauliai Aušros Museum, Šiauliai 27531
Vytautas The Great War Museum, Kaunas 27523

Luxembourg
Musée Municipal, Diekirch 27548
Musée Municipal, Dudelange 27551
Musée National d'Histoire et d'Art, Luxembourg 27567

Macedonia
Makedonsko Archeološko Društvo - Zavod i Muzej Prilep, Prilep 27588
Muzej na Grad Skopje, Skopje 27589
Muzej na Makedonija - Arceološki, Etnološki i Istoriski, Skopje 27590
Muzej na Tetovskiot Kraj, Tetovo 27598
Naroden Muzej, Veles 27599
Naroden Muzej Dr. Nikola Nezlobinski, Struga 27595
Narodni Muzej, Štip 27594

Madagascar
Musée d'Art et d'Archéologie de l'Université d'Antananarivo, Antananarivo 27600

Malaysia
Archaeological Museum, Bedung 27619
Jabatan Muzium Sabah, Kota Kinabalu 27631
Muzium Arkeologi, Merbok 27677
Muzium Negara, Kuala Lumpur 27644
Muzium Sejarah National, Kuala Lumpur 27647

Malta
Archaeology Museum, Victoria 27707
National Museum of Archaeology, Valletta 27702

Mauritius
Historical Museum, Mahébourg 27733

Mexico
Museo de las Culturas de la Huasteca Potosina Tamuantzán, Valles 28587
Museo de las Culturas de Oaxaca, Oaxaca 28277
Museo Nacional de las Culturas, México 28192

Morocco
Musée Archéologique, Kassba 28696
Musée Archéologique, Larache 28697
Musée Archéologique, Tétouan 28714
Musée d'Archéologique, d'Arts et d'Folklorique Al-Kaçabah, Tanger 28712
Musée de la Kasbah, Rabat 28705
Musée des Antiquités de Volubilis, Moulay Driss 28702

Namibia
National Museum of Namibia, Windhoek 28781

Netherlands
Archeologisch Centrum C.W. Bruinvis, Alkmaar 28802
Archeologisch en Paleontologisch Museum Hertogsgemaal, 's-Hertogenbosch 29402
Archeologisch Museum Haarlem, Haarlem 29322
Breda's Museum, Breda 29020
Fluweelengrot Valkenburg, Valkenburg 29915
Gemeentelijk Archeologisch Museum, Aardenburg 28797
Gemeentelijke Oudheidkamer, Ermelo 29251
Gemeentelijke Oudheidkamer, Geldrop 29268
Geschied- en Oudheidkundig Museum 't Freulekeshuus, Venray 29941
Historisch Museum de Scheper, Eibergen 29207
Kasteelruïne Valkenburg, Valkenburg 29917
Museum De Roode Tooren, Doesburg 29159
Museum Dorestad, Wijk bij Duurstede 30004
Museum Het Valkhof, Nijmegen 29632
Museum Oud Westdorpe, Westdorpe 29994
Museum Schokland, Ens 29235
Museum Wierdenland, Ezinge 29258
Museumkelder Derlon, Maastricht 29568
Ruïne van Brederode, Santpoort 29790
Westlands Museum voor Streek- en Tuinbouwhistorie, Honselersdijk 29435

Nicaragua
Museo Arqueológico, Granada 30321
Museo Nacional de Nicaragua, Managua 30322

Niger
Musée National du Niger, Niamey 30324

Nigeria
Archaeology Museum, Nsukka 30353
Institute of Archaeology and Museum Studies, Jos 30346
National Museum Benin, Benin City 30334
National Museum Esie, Esie 30338
National Museum Ibadan, Ibadan 30340
National Museum Ile-Ife, Ife 30342
National Museum Kaduna, Kaduna 30348

Norfolk Island
Norfolk Island Museum, Kingston 30366

Norway
Hægebostad Bygdemuseum, Tingvatn 30920
Kon-Tiki Museum, Oslo 30740
Vitenskapsmuseet, Trondheim 30946

Oman
Muscat Gate Museum, Muscat 31004
Qurm Museum, Qurm 31011

Pakistan
Archaeological Museum, Karachi 31028
Archaeological Museum Harappa, Harappa 31018
Archaeological Museum Moen-Jo-Daro, Moen-Jo-Daro 31046
Archaeological Museum of Baluchistan Quetta, Quetta 31053
Archaeological Museum Peshawar, Peshawar 31047
Archaeological Museum Saidu Sharif, Saidu Sharif 31057
Bahawalpur Museum, Bhawalpur 31013
Chakdara Museum, Chakdara 31015
Museum of Archaeological Site Moenjodaro, Dokri 31016
National Museum of Pakistan, Karachi 31029
Peshawar Museum, Peshawar 31051

Palestine
Palestinian Archaeological Museum, Birzeit 31066

Peru
Monumento Arqueológico de Chavín, Huari 31176
Museo Amano, Lima 31198
Museo Arqueológical Rafael Larco Herrera, Lima 31200
Museo Arqueologico José María Morante de la Universidad Nacional de San Augustín de Arequipa, Arequipa 31113
Museo de Arqueología de la Universidad Nacional de Trujillo, Trujillo 31260
Museo de Sitio de Pachacamac, Lima 31214
Museo Regional de Ica María Reiche Gross Newman, Ica 31182

Philippines
Angono National Museum, Angono 31274
Daniel W. Tantoco jr. Collection, Manila 31376
Ethnological Museum, Zamboanga 31469
Pambasang Museo ng Pilipinas, Manila 31390
Siliman University Anthropology Museum, Dumaguete 31326
Southwestern University Museum, Cebu 31317
Zamboanga National Museum, Zamboanga 31470

Poland
Jacek Malczewski Muzeum, Radom 31938
Muzeum, Koszalin 31678
Muzeum Archeologiczne, Gdańsk 31568
Muzeum Archeologiczne, Gniew 31598
Muzeum Archeologiczne, Poznań 31898
Muzeum Archeologiczne, Wrocław 32173
Muzeum Archeologiczne i Etnograficzne, Łódź 31768
Muzeum Archeologiczne Środkowego Nadodrza, Świdnica 32013
Muzeum Archeologiczne w Biskupinie, Gąsawa 31562
Muzeum Archeologiczne w Krakowie, Kraków 31693
Muzeum Archeologiczne w Krakowie, Oddział w Nowej Hucie, Kraków 31694
Muzeum Archeologiczno-Historyczne, Głogów 31594
Muzeum Częstochowskie, Częstochowa 31545
Muzeum Historyczne w Sanoku, Sanok 31967
Muzeum im. Wojciecha Kętrzyńskiego, Kętrzyn 31655
Muzeum Lubelskie, Lublin 31793
Muzeum Miasta Pabianice, Pabianice 31873
Muzeum Miedzi, Legnica 31754
Muzeum Miejskie, Zabrze 32200
Muzeum Okręgowe, Konin 31672
Muzeum Okręgowe, Piotrków Trybunalski 31883
Muzeum Okręgowe, Rzeszów 31960
Muzeum Okręgowe, Sandomierz 31965
Muzeum Okręgowe, Suwałki 32010
Muzeum Okręgowe im. Leona Wyczółkowskiego, Bydgoszcz 31514
Muzeum Okręgowe Ziemi Kaliskiej, Kalisz 31635
Muzeum Początków Państwa Polskiego, Gniezno 31600
Muzeum Regionalne, Cedynia 31521
Muzeum Regionalne, Szczecinek 32030
Muzeum Regionalne, Szydłów 32037
Muzeum Regionalne, Wiślica 32157
Muzeum Regionalne im. Andrzeja Kaube, Wolin 32169
Muzeum Regionalne im. Janusza Petera, Tomaszów Lubelski 32047
Muzeum Regionalne im. Władysława Kowalskiego, Dobczyce 31553
Muzeum Regionalne PTTK, Golub-Dobrzyń 31602
Muzeum Śląska Opolskiego, Opole 31859
Muzeum Ślężańskie im. Stanisława Dunajewskiego, Sobótka 31984
Muzeum Starożytnego Hutnictwa Mazowieckiego, Pruszków 31918
Muzeum w Biskupinie, Głsawa 31597
Muzeum w Chrzanowie, Chrzanów 31536
Muzeum w Elblągu, Elbląg 31560
Muzeum w Kwidzynie, Kwidzyn 31746
Muzeum w Lęborku, Lębork 31749
Muzeum w Łowiczu, Łowicz 31782
Muzeum w Lubaczowie, Lubaczów 31783
Muzeum w Międzyrzeczu, Międzyrzecz 31803
Muzeum w Raciborzu, Racibórz 31937
Muzeum-Zamek Górków, Szamotuły 32020
Muzeum Ziemi Kępińskiej, Kępno 31654
Muzeum Ziemi Rawickiej, Rawicz 31945
Muzeum Ziemi Rawskiej, Rawa Mazowiecka 31944
Muzeum Ziemi Wieluńskiej, Wieluń 32154
Muzeum Ziemi Zawkrzańskiej, Mława 31810
Państwowe Muzeum Archeologiczne, Warszawa 32139
Rezerwat Archeologiczny i Muzeum w Krzemionkach k. Ostrowca, Krzemionki koło Ostrowca 31742
Rezerwat Archeologiczny na Zawodziu, Kalisz 31636
Skansen Archeologiczny w Mrówkach, Mrówki 31814

Portugal
Museo Arqueológico de Martins Sarmento, Guimarães 32277
Museu Arqueológico e Etnológico António Tomás Pires, Elvas 32267
Museu Arqueológico e Lapidar do Infante D. Henrique, Faro 32272
Museu Carlos Reis, Torres Novas 32355
Museu da Cidade, Lisboa 32294
Museu da Rainha Dona Leonor, Beja 32242
Museu Hipólito Cabaço, Alenquer 32232
Museu Municipal de Arqueologia, Silves 32348
Museu Municipal de Óbidos, Óbidos 32322
Museu Municipal do Seixal Núcleo Sede, Seixal 32345
Museu Municipal Quinta do Conventinho, Loures 32318

Puerto Rico
Turabo University Museum, Gurabo 32374

Romania
Muzeul Arheologic Adamclisi, Adamclisi 32424
Muzeul Arheologic Sarmizegetusa, Sarmizegetusa 32586
Muzeul Castelul Corvinestilor, Hunedoara 32530
Muzeul Civilizației Dacice și Române, Deva 32511
Muzeul Curtea Veche, București 32454
Muzeul de Arheologie, Săveni 32588
Muzeul de Arheologie Callatis Mangalia, Mangalia 32547
Muzeul de Arheologie Oltenița, Oltenița 32558
Muzeul de Arheologie și Etnografie, Corabia 32503
Muzeul de Istorie, Târgu Jiu 32606
Muzeul de Istorie al Moldovei, Iași 32533
Muzeul de Istorie Naționalá și Archeologie, Constanța 32501
Muzeul de Istorie și Arheologie, Tulcea 32619
Muzeul de Istorie și Artă Roman, Roman 32582
Muzeul Județean Argeș, Pitești 32569
Muzeul Județean de Istorie, Galați 32524
Muzeul Județean de Istorie, Piatra-Neamț 32568
Muzeul Județean de Istorie Brașov, Brașov 32449
Muzeul Județean Ialomița, Slobozia 32599
Muzeul Național al Unirii, Alba Iulia 32428
Muzeul Național de Istorie a României, București 32467
Muzeul Orășenesc de Istorie, Aiud 32427
Muzeul Taru Făgărasului, Făgăraș 32518

Russia
Anapskij Archeologičeskij Muzej-zapovednik, Anapa 32639
Archeologičeskij Muzej, Čerepovec 32729
Archeologičeskij Muzej, Azov 32667
Archeologičeskij Muzej Kazanskogo Universiteta, Kazan 32885
Astrachanskij Gosudarstvennyj Obedinennyj Istoriko-architekturnyj Muzej-zapovednik, Astrachan 32659
Azovskij Kraevedčeskij Muzej, Azov 32668
Biljarskij Gosudarstvennyj Istoriko-Architekturnyj i Prirodnyj Muzej-Zapovednik, Biljarsk 32688
Brjanskij Gosudarstvennyj Obedinennyj Kraevedčeskij Muzej, Brjansk 32706
Chabarovskij Kraevoj Kraevedčeskij Muzej im. N.I. Grodekova, Chabarovsk 32737
Chabarovskij Muzej Archeologii im. A.P. Okladnikova, Chabarovsk 32738
Chakasskij Respublikanskij Kraevedčeskij Muzej, Abakan 32627
Chvalynskij Kraevedčeskij Muzej, Chvalynsk 32747
Čuvašskij Nacionalnyj Muzej, Čeboksary 32719
Gosudarstvennyj Istoriko-architekturnyj i Prirodno-landšaftnyj Muzej Zapovednik Izborsk, Izborsk 32834
Gosudarstvennyj Nacionalnyj Muzej Ust-Ordynskogo Burjatskogo Avtonomnogo Okruga, Ust-Ordynsk 33672
Gosudarstvennyj Okružnoj Muzej Prirody i Čeloveka Goroda Chanty-Mansijsk, Chanty-Mansijsk 32744
Irkutskij Oblastnoj Kraevedčeskij Muzej, Irkutsk 32814
Istoriko-architekturnyj Muzej Kuzneckaja Krepost', Novokuzneck 33234
Istoriko-memorial'nyj Muzejnyj Kompleks Bobriki, Donskij 32760
Kaliningradskij Oblastnoj Istoriko-chudožestvennyj Muzej, Kaliningrad 32870
Kalmyckij Respublikanskij Kraevedčeskij Muzej im. Prof. N.N. Palmova, Ėlista 32794
Kamčatskij Oblastnoj Kraevedčeskij Muzej, Petropavlovsk-Kamčatskij 33310
Karelskij Gosudarstvennyj Kraevedčeskij Muzej, Petrozavodsk 33316
Kislovodskij Istoriko-kraevedčeskij Muzej Krepost', Kislovodsk 32928
Krasnodarskij Gosudarstvennyj Istoriko-archeologičeskij Muzej-zapovednik, Krasnodar 32947
Kurskij Gosudarstvennyj Oblastnoj Muzej Archeologii, Kursk 32975
Miasskij Kraevedčeskij Muzej, Miass 33010
Muzej 700 let - Landskrona, Nevskoe Ustje, Nienšanc, Sankt-Peterburg 33425
Muzej Archeologii, Syktyvkar 33575
Muzej Archeologii i Ėtnografii, Vladivostok 33703
Muzej Archeologii i Ėtnografii, Ufa 33645
Muzej Archeologii i Ėtnografii, Syktyvkar 33576
Muzej Archeologii Moskvy, Moskva 33091
Muzej Archeologii Prikamja, Perm 33305
Muzej 'Archeologija, Ėtnografija i Ėkologija Sibiri' Kemerovskogo Gosudarstvennogo Universiteta, Kemerovo 32914
Muzej Istorii i Kultury Srednego Prikamja, Sarapul 33503
Muzej Istorii Moskvy, Moskva 33109
Nacionalnyj Muzej Respubliki Baškortostan, Ufa 33647
Nacionalnyj Muzej Udmurtskoj Respubliki im. K. Gerda, Iževsk 32836
Narovčatskij Rajonnyj Kraevedčeskij Muzej, Narovčat 33201
Nižegorodskij Gosudarstvennyj Istoriko-architekturnyj Muzej-zapovednik, Nižnij Novgorod 33223
Novokuzneckij Kraevedeskij Muzej, Novokuzneck 33237
Roslavlskij Istoriko-chudožstvennyj Muzej, Roslavl 33353
Šeltozerskij Vepsskij Ėtnografičeskij Muzej, Šeltozero 33515
Severo-osetinskij Gosudarstvennyj Obedinennyj Muzej Istorii, Architektury i Literatury, Vladikavkaz 33690
Tatarskoe Gorodišče - Archeologičeskij i prirodnyj Muzej-zapovednik, Stavropol 33565
Tuapsinskij Kraevedčeskij Muzej im. N.G. Poletaeva, Tuapse 33622
Valaamskij Naučno-issledovatelskij Cerkovno-archeologičeskij i Prirodnyj Muzej-zapovednik, Sortavala 33548
Volgogradskij Oblastnoj Kraevedčeskij Muzej, Volgograd 33719

Saudi Arabia
King Saud University Museum, Riyadh 33772
National Museum, Riyadh 33773

Senegal
Musée d'Archéologie, Dakar 33776

Serbia-Montenegro
Arheološka Zbirka Crne Gore, Podgorica 33886
Arheološki Muzej, Prizren 33896
Gradski Muzej Sombor, Sombor 33910
Gradski Muzej Vršac, Vršac 33928
Kulturno Prosvetni Centar Bela Crkva-Muzejska Jedinica, Bela Crkva 33792
Muzej Grada Beograda, Beograd 33804
Muzej Grada Perasta, Perast 33881
Muzej Ras, Novi Pazar 33868
Muzej Srema, Sremska Mitrovica 33913
Muzejska Zbirka pri Narodnoj Biblioteki Dimitrije Tucović, Čajetina 33829
Narodni Muzej, Kragujevac 33853
Narodni Muzej, Požarevac 33893
Narodni Muzej, Smederevska Palanka 33908
Narodni Muzej, Užice 33925
Narodni Muzej, Vranje 33927
Narodni Muzej, Zrenjanin 33932
Narodni Muzej Čačak, Čačak 33827
Narodni Muzej Kikinda, Kikinda 33845
Narodni Muzej Kruševac, Kruševac 33857
Narodni Muzej Valjevo, Valjevo 33926
Zavičajni Muzej, Bar 33790
Zavičajni Muzej, Ruma 33901

Sierra Leone
Sierra Leone National Museum, Freetown 33935

Slovakia
Archeologické Múzeum, Bratislava 33958
Lesnícke a Drevárske Múzeum, Zvolen 34081
Slovenské Národné Múzeum, Bratislava 33979
Vlastivedné Múzeum, Nové Zámky 34039
Vlastivedné Múzeum, Prešov 34049
Západoslovenské Múzeum v Trnave, Trnava 34075

Slovenia
Dolenjski Muzej Novo Mesto, Novo Mesto 34136
Kamniški Muzej, Kamnik 34093
Pokrajinski Muzej, Kočevje 34095
Pokrajinski Muzej, Maribor 34127
Pokrajinski Muzej, Murska Sobota 34134
Pokrajinski Muzej Celje, Celje 34090
Pokrajinski Muzej Koper, Koper 34097
Pokrajinski Muzej Ptuj, Ptuj 34141
Posavski Muzej Brežice, Brežice 34088
Tolminski Muzej, Tolmin 34155

South Africa
Arend Dieperink Museum, Potgietersrus 34339
Mapungubwe Museum, Pretoria 34346
Museum of Anthropology and Archaeology, Pretoria 34348
National Museum Bloemfontein, Bloemfontein 34189
Schoemansdal Museum, Louis Trichardt 34302

Spain
Castell Cartoixa Vallparadis, Terrassa 35524
Clos Arqueologic Torre Llauder, Mataró 35098
Colección Arqueológica Municipal, Besalú 34605
Colección de Arqueología, Ciudad Real 34718
Colección de la Real Academia de la Historia, Madrid 35000
Collecions Municipals del Foment Arqueològic Excursionista Sallentí, Sallent 35369
Conjunt Monumental de la Esglésias de Sant Pere, Terrassa 35526
Conjunto Arqueológico de Madinat Al Zahra, Córdoba 34736
Deià Museo Arqueológico, Deià 34768
Euskal Arkeologia, Etnografia eta Kondaira Museoa, Bilbao 34611
Gabinete de Antigüedades, Madrid 35008
Museo Arqueològic Municipal Cal Guimerà, El Vendrell 35644
Museo Arqueológico, Nerja 35157
Museo Arqueológico, Osuna 35196
Museo Arqueológico, Sagunto 35354
Museo Arqueológico, Santa Cruz de Tenerife 35413
Museo Arqueológico Comarcal, Orihuela 35184
Museo Arqueológico de Asturias, Oviedo 35203
Museo Arqueológico de la Plana Baja, Burriana 34637
Museo Arqueológico Municipal, Cartagena 34684
Museo Arqueológico Municipal, Dénia 34771
Museo Arqueológico Municipal, Lorca 34982
Museo Arqueológico Municipal, Marchena 35088
Museo Arqueológico Municipal Cayetano Mergelina, Yecla 35708
Museo Arqueológico Municipal José María Soler, Villena 35685
Museo Arqueológico Nacional, Madrid 35013
Museo Arqueológico Provincial, Sevilla 35478
Museo Arqueológico Provincial de Orense, Orense 35182
Museo Arqueológico Provincial-MARQ, Alicante 34446
Museo Arqueológico y Termas Romanas, Caldes de Montbui 34655
Museo Comarcal Durán y Sanpere, Cervera 34706

Museo de Albacete, Albacete 34419
Museo de Almería, Almería 34454
Museo de América, Madrid 35016
Museo de Arqueología de Alava, Vitoria-Gasteiz 35698
Museo de Avila, Avila 34502
Museo de Burgos, Burgos 34630
Museo de Cáceres, Cáceres 34641
Museo de Ciudad Real, Ciudad Real 34721
Museo de Guadalajara, Guadalajara 34885
Museo de Huelva, Huelva 34906
Museo de los Concilios y de la Cultura Visigoda, Toledo 35541
Museo de Málaga, Málaga 35072
Museo de Manacor, Manacor 35078
Museo de Palencia, Palencia 35214
Museo de Pontevedra, Pontevedra 35284
Museo de Salamanca, Salamanca 35361
Museo de San Isidro, Madrid 35029
Museo de Santa Cruz, Toledo 35542
Museo de Segóbriga, Saelices 35353
Museo de Valladolid, Valladolid 35621
Museo del Foro Caesaraugusta, Zaragoza 35725
Museo Histórico Arqueológico, A Coruña 34753
Museo Histórico Municipal de Écija, Ecija 34783
Museo Municipal, Consuegra 34733
Museo Municipal, Valdepeñas 35592
Museo Municipal, Zuheros 35737
Museo Municipal Jerónimo Molina, Jumilla 34932
Museo Municipal Sala Dámaso Navarro, Petrer 35269
Museo Nacional de Arte Romano, Mérida 35110
Museo Numantino, Soria 35506
Museo Provincial, Teruel 35530
Museo Taller del Moro, Toledo 35547
Museu Arqueològic, Ponts 35285
Museu Arqueològic Comarcal, Banyoles 34527
Museu Arqueològic i Paleontològic, Baldomar 34524
Museu Arqueològic i Paleontològic, Moià 35117
Museu Arqueològic Municipal, Els Prats de Rei 35294
Museu-Arxiu Tomàs Balvey i Bas, Cardedeu 34678
Museu d'Arqueologia de Catalunya, Olèrdola 35167
Museu d'Arqueologia de Catalunya-Empúries, L'Escala 34800
Museu d'Arqueología de Catalunya Ullastret, Ullastret 35586
Museu de la Noguera, Balaguer 34523
Museu de la Vall de Lord, Sant Lorenç de Morunys 35405
Museu de Vilafranca-Museu del Vi, Vilafranca del Penedès 35659
Museu d'Eines Antigues, Torregrossa 35561
Museu d'Història de la Ciudad, Sant Feliu de Guíxols 35400
Museu Diocesa de Menorca, Ciudadela de Menorca 34726
Museu Egipci de Barcelona, Barcelona 34575
Museu Local Arqueològic, Artesa de Lleida 34490
Museu Monografic de Pol Lèntia, Alcúdia 34441
Museu Municipal Can Xifreda, Sant Feliu de Codines 35399
Museu Municipal Vicenç Ros, Martorell 35095
Museu-Poblat Ibèric, Tornabous 35555
Palacio de Lebrija, Sevilla 35491
Sala d'Arqueologia i Gabinet Numismàtic, Lleida 34972
Yacimiento-Museo Arqueológico, Garray 34838

Sri Lanka
Archaeological Museum, Colombo 35745
Archaeological Museum, Dedigama 35753
Colombo National Museum, Colombo 35747

Sudan
El-Ibied Regional Museum, Khartoum 35765
Sheikan Museum, El-Obeid 35762
Sudan National Museum, Khartoum 35769

Sweden
Arkeologiskt Museum Vuollerim 6000 år, Vuollerim 36419
Eketorps Borg, Degerhamn 35851
Forngården Hembygdsmuseum, Trollhättan 36334
Gällersta Forngård, Örebro 36134
Gene Fornby, Örnsköldsvik 36142
Göteborgs Stadsmuseum, Göteborg 35913
Hällristningsmuseet vid Brunnssalongen, Norrköping 36117
Härjedalens Fjällmuseum, Funäsdalen 35898
Helsingborgs Slott, Helsingborg 35952
Lappstaden, Arvidsjaur 35814
Museum Gustavianum, Uppsala 36358
Museum Tre Kronor, Stockholm 36263
Regionmuseet Kristianstad, Kristianstad 36018
Såguddens Museum, Arvika 35818
Tanums Hällristningsmuseum, Tanumshede 36321
Västmanlands Läns Museum, Västerås 36383

Switzerland
Archäologische Sammlung der Universität Zürich, Zürich 37369
Castello di Montebello, Bellinzona 36526
Didaktische Ausstellung Urgeschichte, Chur 36634
Fondation La Tène, Hauterive 36795
Klostermuseum, Müstair 36970
Laténium, Hauterive 36796
Münzkabinett und Antikensammlung der Stadt Winterthur, Winterthur 37332
Musée Cantonal d'Archéologie, Sion 37171
Musée d'Art et d'Histoire, Genève 36743
Musée Gyger, Vallorbe 37280
Musée Romain, Lausanne 36867
Musehum.BL, Liestal 36880
Museo Civico e Archeologico, Locarno 36885
Museum für Archäologie, Frauenfeld 36707
Museum Schwab, Biel, Kanton Bern 36566
Ortsmuseum Wetzikon, Wetzikon 37314
Pfahlbausammlung Dr. h.c. Carl Irlet, Twann 37257
Rätisches Museum, Chur 36636
Römermuseum Augst, Augst 36479
Steinzeitmuseum, Thunstetten 37246

Tanzania
Dar-es-Salaam National Museum, Dar-es-Salaam 37458

Thailand
Ban Kao Prehistoric Museum, Kanchanaburi 37507
Phipitapan Haeng Chart Phra Pathom Chedi, Nakhon Pathom 37516
Phipitapan Laeng Chart, Suphan Buri 37541
Phipitapan Laeng Chart Ram Khamhaeng, Sukhothai 37539
Phipittapan Tasatan Haengchart, Khon Kaen 37508
Phititapan Haeng Chart, Chiang Mai 37503
Somdet Phra Narai National Museum, Lopburi 37514
Sood Sangvichien Prehistoric Museum, Bangkok 37497

Tunisia
Musée Archéologique, Gafsa 37561
Musée Archéologique de Sfax, Sfax 37579
Musée Archeologique du Cap Bon, Nabeul 37576
Musée Lella Hadria, Midoun 37573
Musée les Thermes d'Antonin, Carthage 37556

Turkey
Adana Müzesi, Adana 37598
Afyon Arkeoloji Müzesi, Afyon 37601
Amasra Müzesi, Amasra 37608
Amasya Müzesi, Amasya 37610
Bergama Arkeoloji Müzesi, Bergama 37633
Burdur Müzesi, Burdur 37641
Bursa Arkeoloji Müzesi, Bursa 37644
Çorum Müzesi, Çorum 37656
Diyarbakır Arkeoloji ve Etnografi Müzesi, Diyarbakır 37661
Eregli Arkeoloji ve Etnografi Müzesi, Eregli 37668
Erzurum Arkeoloji ve Etnografi Müzesi, Erzurum 37671
Eskişehir Arkeoloji Müzesi, Eskişehir 37674
Fethiye Müzesi, Fethiye 37680
Gordion Müzesi, Ankara 37618
Haçıbektaş Müzesi, Nevşehir 37767
İzmir Arkeoloji Müzesi, İzmir 37718
Kahramanmaraş Müzesi, Kahramanmaraş 37724
Karaman Müzesi, Karaman 37725
Kars Müzesi, Kars 37728
Kayseri Arkeoloji Müzesi, Kayseri 37732
Kütahya Müzesi, Kütahya 37749
Malatya Müzesi, Malatya 37751
Manisa Arkeoloji Müzesi, Manisa 37754
Milas Müzesi, Milas 37761
Museum Seyitgazi, Seyitgazi 37780
Nevşehir Arkeoloji ve Etnografya Müzesi, Nevşehir 37768
Sinop Müzesi, Sinop 37785
Tarsus Müzesi, Tarsus 37791
Tokat Müzesi, Tokat 37795
Truva Müzesi, Çanakkale 37651
Ürgüp Müzesi, Ürgüp 37799
Urfa Müzesi, Urfa 37800
Uşak Arkeoloji Müzesi, Uşakş 37801
Van Müzesi, Van 37804
Yalvaç Müzesi, Yalvaç 37806

Ukraine
Kerčskij Gosudarstvennyj Istoriko-Kulturnyj Zapovednik, Kerč 37860
Krymski Respublikanskij Kraevedčeskij Muzej, Simferopol 37904
Odessa Archaeological Museum, Odessa 37892

United Arab Emirates
Sharjah Archaeology Museum, Sharjah 37921

United Kingdom
Abbot's House, Arbroath 38010
Anker's House Museum, Chester-le-Street 38553
Archaeology Centre, Bagshot 38056
Arnol Blackhouse Museum, Arnol 38022
Ashmolean Museum of Art and Archaeology, Oxford 40141
Axbridge Museum, Axbridge 38044
Basing House, Basing 38101
Beaumaris Castle, Beaumaris 38137
Beeston Castle, Tarporley 40675
Bessie Surtees House, Newcastle-upon-Tyne 40033
Binchester Roman Fort, Bishop Auckland 38236
Bredy Farm Old Farming Collection, Bridport 38330
The British Museum, London 39586
Bute Museum, Rothesay 40347
Camborne Museum, Camborne 38448
Canterbury Heritage Museum, Canterbury 38471
Canterbury Roman Museum, Canterbury 38472
Carnegie Museum, Inverurie 39302
Castle Museum, Norwich 40091
Castleford Museum Room, Castleford 38503
Cheddar Man and the Cannibals, Cheddar 38535
City Museum and Records Office, Portsmouth 40249
Clayton Collection Museum, Humshaugh 39276
Corinium Museum, Cirencester 38584
Creswell Crags Museum and Education Centre, Welbeck 40807
Criccieth Castle, Criccieth 38668
Crofton Roman Villa, Orpington 40134
Cuming Museum, London 39619
Deal Archaeological Collection, Deal 38707
Dewa Roman Experience, Chester 38551
Dover Museum, Dover 38766
Droitwich Spa Heritage Centre, Droitwich 38776
Egypt Centre, Swansea 40657
English Heritage South East Region, Guildford 39135
English Heritage South West Region, Bristol 38354
Five Council Museums East Headquarters, Cupar 38687
Forge Mill Needle Museum and Bordesley Abbey Visitor Centre, Redditch 40302
Groam House Museum, Rosemarkie 40341
Guardhouse Museum, Tattershall 40676
Guildford Museum, Guildford 39138
Gunnersbury Park Museum, London 39656
Hull and East Riding Museum, Kingston-upon-Hull 39379
Hunterian Museum, Glasgow 39051
Ipswich Museum, Ipswich 39305
Jewry Wall Museum, Leicester 39462
Jorvik Museum, York 40964
Kildonan Museum, Kildonan 39356
King's Lynn Museum, King's Lynn 39370
Kings Weston Roman Villa, Bristol 38358
Kirriemuir Gateway to the Glens Museum, Kerriemuir 39341
Kyngston House Museum, Saint Albans 40373
La Hougue Bie Museum, Saint Helier 40403
Lancaster City Museum, Lancaster 39414
Lindisfarne Priory, Holy Island 39256
Littlehampton Museum, Littlehampton 39514
Liverpool Museum, Liverpool 39520
London Borough of Bromley Museum, Orpington 40135
Maidstone Museum and Bentlif Art Gallery, Maidstone 39877
Maison Dieu, Faversham 38985
Manor House Museum and Art Gallery, Ilkley 39287
Marischal Museum, Aberdeen 37940
Moat Park Heritage Centre, Biggar 38198
Museum Nan Eilean, Steornabhagh, Stornoway 40615
Museum of Antiquities, Alnwick 37985
Museum of Antiquities, Newcastle-upon-Tyne 40040
Museum of Archaeology, Durham 38828
Museum of Archaeology, Classics and Oriental Studies, Liverpool 39523
Museum of Classical Archaeology, Cambridge 38459
Museum of Harlow, Harlow 39165
Museum of Sussex Archaeology, Lewes 39486
Newark Museum, Newark-on-Trent 40022
Norris Museum, Saint Ives, Cambridgeshire 40405
North Lincolnshire Museum, Scunthorpe 40460
Nottingham University Museum, Nottingham 40113
Old Rectory Museum, Loughborough 39831
Orkney Museum, Kirkwall 39397
The Oxfordshire Museum, Woodstock 40925
Penlee House Gallery and Museum, Penzance 40181
Perth Museum and Art Gallery, Perth 40185
Peterborough Museum and Art Gallery, Peterborough 40188
Pitt Rivers Museum, Oxford 40153
Powysland Museum and Montgomery Canal Centre, Welshpool 40817
Red House Museum and Art Gallery, Christchurch 38578
Rhuddlan Castle, Rhuddlan 40312
Rockbourne Roman Villa, Fordingbridge 39002
Roman Bath House, Lancaster 39417
Roman Baths Museum, Bath 38121
Royal Albert Memorial Museum and Art Gallery, Exeter 38957
Royal Museum, Edinburgh 38910
Saint Bride's Crypt Museum, London 39771
Salisbury and South Wiltshire Museum, Salisbury 40437
Sheffield City Museum and Mappin Art Gallery, Sheffield 40489
Skye and Lochalsh Area Museums, Portree 40246
Staffin Museum, Staffin 40568
Swansea Museum, Swansea 40661
Tees Archaeology, Hartlepool 39178
Time Machine, Weston-super-Mare 40836
Torre Abbey Historic House and Gallery, Torquay 40719
Tredegar House and Park, Newport, Gwent 40052
Ulster History Park, Omagh 40132
University Archaeology Museum, Birmingham 38231
University Museum of Archaeology and Anthropology, Cambridge 38463
Verulamium Museum, Saint Albans 40379
Warwickshire Museum, Warwick 40796
Wells Museum, Wells 40812
Welwyn Roman Baths Museum, Welwyn 40818
West Stow Anglo-Saxon Centre, Bury Saint Edmunds 38419
Whitby Abbey Museum, Whitby 40853
Wiltshire Heritage Museum and Gallery, Devizes 38726
Winchester City Museum, Winchester 40896
Yorkshire Museum, York 40973

Uruguay
Museo Municipal de Historia y Arqueología, Rivera 41037

U.S.A.
AAF Museum, Washington 48330
Abbe Museum at Downtown, Bar Harbor 41496
Abbe Museum at Sieur de Monts Spring, Bar Harbor 41497
Alaska Museum of Natural History, Eagle River 43034
Alexandria Archaeology Museum, Alexandria 41120
Alutiiq Museum and Archaeological Repository, Kodiak 44524
America's Stonehenge, North Salem 46006
The Amerind Foundation, Dragoon 42986
Anasazi Heritage Center, Dolores 42957
Anasazi State Park, Boulder 41838
Angel Mounds Historic Site, Evansville 43244
Anthropology Museum, DeKalb 42854
Anza-Borrego Desert Museum, Borrego Springs 41795
Archaeological Collection, Baltimore 41449
Archaeological Museum, Louisville 44962
Arizona State Museum, Tucson 48082
Aztec Ruins, Aztec 41430
Bandelier Site, Los Alamos 44886
Boone's Lick Site, Boonesboro 41787
Boonshoft Museum of Discovery, Dayton 42799
Brazos Valley Museum of Natural History, Bryan 41974
Brazosport Museum of Natural Science, Clute 42506
Cahokia Mounds State Historic Site, Collinsville 42530
California Museum of Ancient Art, Beverly Hills 41676
Carlsbad Caverns National Park, Carlsbad 42108
Carlsbad Museum and Art Center, Carlsbad 42109
Casa Grande Ruins, Coolidge 42616
Catalina Island Museum, Avalon 41426
Center for American Archeology, Kampsville 44386
C.H. Nash Museum-Chucalissa Archaeological Museum, Memphis 45232
Cobb Institute of Archaeology Museum, Mississippi State 45401
Colonial Pemaquid Historical Site, New Harbor 45691
Cottonlandia Museum, Greenwood 43835
Crow Canyon Archaeological Center, Cortez 42651
Crystal River State Archaeological Site, Crystal River 42717
Dickson Mounds Museum, Lewistown 44731
Effigy Mounds Museum, Harpers Ferry 43917
Etowah Indian Mounds Historical Site, Cartersville 42122
Evelyn Payne Hatcher Museum of Anthropology, Saint Cloud 47084
Favell Museum of Western Art and Indian Artifacts, Klamath Falls 44508
First National Bank of Chicago Art Collection, Chicago 42327
Florence Hawley Ellis Museum of Anthropology, Abiquiu 41057
Flowerdew Hundred Foundation, Hopewell 44099
Folsom Museum, Folsom 43359
Fort Mountain, Chattsworth 42267
Frank H. McClung Museum, Knoxville 44519
Gila County Historical Museum, Globe 43700
Glacier National Park Museum, West Glacier 48524
Grand Village of the Natchez Indians, Natchez 45632
Grave Creek Mound Historic Site, Moundsville 45521
Great Lakes Lighthouse Museum, Mackinaw City 45033
Gustav Jeeninga Museum of Bible and Near Eastern Studies, Anderson 41203
H. Earl Clack Museum, Havre 43964
Hampson Museum, Wilson 48666
Harvard University Semitic Museum, Cambridge 42043
Historic London Town, Edgewater 43085
Historic Morven, Princeton 46701
Homolovi Ruins State Park, Winslow 48697
Howland House, Plymouth 46559
Indian Museum of the Carolinas, Laurinburg 44682
The Institute For American Indian Studies, Washington Green 48424
Iraan Museum, Iraan 44253
Jay I. Kislak Foundation, Miami Lakes 45301
John Deere House, Dixon 42952
The Johns Hopkins University Archaeological Collection, Baltimore 41473
The Joseph A. Callaway Archaeological Museum, Louisville 44966
Journey Museum, Rapid City 46795
Kelsey Museum of Ancient Archaeology, Ann Arbor 41218
Kolomoki Mounds State Park Museum, Blakely 41732
The Lake Champlain Maritime Museum, Vergennes 48212
Lake Jackson Mounds Archaeological Park, Tallahassee 47933
L.C. Bates Museum, Hinckley 44034
Logan Museum of Anthropology, Beloit 41615
Long Island Culture History Museum, Commack 42594
Louden-Henritze Archaeology Museum, Trinidad 48064
Marin Museum of the American Indian, Novato 46045
Maxwell Museum of Anthropology, Albuquerque 41104
Mesa Southwest Museum, Mesa 45271
Mesa Verde National Park Museum, Mesa Verde 45272
Minute Man National Historical Park, Concord 42599
Mission San Diego de Alcala, San Diego 47280

Mission San Juan Capistrano Museum, San Juan Capistrano 47360
Moanalua Gardens Foundation, Honolulu 44085
Museum of Anthropology, Highland Heights 44018
Museum of Anthropology, Ann Arbor 41219
Museum of Anthropology, Columbia 42552
Museum of Art and Archaeology, Columbia 42553
Museum of Florida History, Tallahassee 47936
Museum of Peoples and Cultures, Provo 46736
Museum of Primitive Art and Culture, Peace Dale 46321
Museum of the Red River, Idabel 44190
Native American Exhibit, Fonda 43361
Navajo National Monument, Tonalea 48027
New York State Museum, Albany 41085
Ocmulgee National Monument, Macon 45046
Ohio Historical Society Museum, Columbus 42590
Old Mackinac Pointlightstation, Mackinac Island 45030
Oriental Institute Museum, Chicago 42355
Osage Village Historic Site, Lamar 44613
Pawnee Indian Village, Republic 46843
Peabody Museum of Archaeology and Ethnology, Cambridge 42049
Pecos Park, Pecos 46324
Phoebe Apperson Hearst Museum of Anthropology, Berkeley 41648
Pinson Mounds State Archaeological Area, Pinson 46497
Pueblo Grande Museum, Phoenix 46480
Puukohola Heiau National Historic Site, Kawaihae 44419
Robbins Museum of Archaeology, Middleborough 45305
Robert S. Peabody Museum of Archaeology, Andover 41209
Runestone Museum, Alexandria 41119
Russell Cave Museum, Bridgeport 41887
Safety Harbor Museum of Regional History, Safety Harbor 47058
Saint Clements Island-Potomac River Museum, Colton Point 42546
San Diego Museum of Man, San Diego 47294
Saratoga Museum, Saratoga 47458
Scotts Bluff National Monument, Gering 43658
Seminole Canyon State Historical Park, Comstock 42596
Seton Hall University Museum, South Orange 47700
Siegfried H. Horn Archaeological Museum, Berrien Springs 41655
Silver River Museum, Ocala 46082
South Florida Museum of Natural History, Dania Beach 42773
Southold Indian Museum, Southold 47711
Southwest Museum, Los Angeles 44945
Spencer-Peirce-Little Farm, Newbury 45907
Spiro Mounds Archaeological Center, Spiro 47725
Sunwatch Indian Village - Archaeological Park, Dayton 42806
Thomas E. McMillan Museum, Brewton 41885
Toltec Mounds Archeological State Park, Scott 47510
Tonto National Monument, Roosevelt 47000
Treasures of the Sea Exhibit, Georgetown 43650
University of Pennsylvania Museum of Archaeology and Anthropology, Philadelphia 46460
Van Meter State Park, Miami 45295
Van Nostrand-Starkins House, Roslyn 47010
Van Riper-Hopper House, Wayne 48479
Walnut Canyon National Monument, Flagstaff 43332
Wayne State University Museum of Anthropology, Detroit 42936
Western Archeological and Conservation Center, Tucson 48097
Wickliffe Mounds, Wickliffe 48616
Wilderness Park Museum, El Paso 43124
Winnebago Area Museum, Winnebago 48692
Wormsloe State Historic Site, Savannah 47487
Wray Museum, Wray 48765
Wupatki National Monument, Flagstaff 43333
Yellowstone Gateway Museum of Park County, Livingston 44833

Uzbekistan
Surchondarë Vilojati Archeologija Muzeji, Termiz 48864

Vanuatu
Vanuatu Cultural Centre and National Museum, Port Vila 48866

Venezuela
Museo J.M. Cruxent, Los Teques 48949

Vietnam
Thua Thien Hue Museum, Thua Thien Hue 49003

Yemen
National Museum, Aden 49007
Seiyun in Wadi Hadhramaut Museum, Seiyun 49012

Zimbabwe
Great Zimbabwe Site Museum, Masvingo 49037
Khami Ruins Site Museum, Bulawayo 49025
Museum of Human Sciences, Harare 49031
Nyahokwe Ruins Site Museum, Inyanga 49034

Archaeology, Christian and Medieval

Austria
Bischöfliches Diözesanmuseum Klagenfurt, Klagenfurt 02123
Dekanatsmuseum, Haus 02009
Instituts- und Studiensammlung des Instituts für Ur- und Frühgeschichte, Wien 02900
Ortsmuseum, Zwentendorf 03057
Römermuseum Teurnia, Lendorf 02205
Sammlungen des Zisterzienserstiftes Rein, Rein 02503

Bulgaria
Archeologičeski Muzej, Varna 04893

Croatia
Arheološka Zbirka i Lapidarij Dr. Grga Novak, Hvar 07705
Muzej Hrvatskih Arheoloških Spomenika, Split 07784

Denmark
Vikingemuseet Moesgård, Højbjerg 08881

Egypt
Monastery of Saint Catherine, Gebel Katherîna 09293

Finland
Suomen Kansallismuseo, Helsinki 09531

France
Crypte archéologique du Parvis de Notre-Dame, Paris 13498
Musée Archéologique de Viuz-Faverges, Faverges 11707
Musée Briard et de la Crypte Mérovingienne, Jouarre 12091
Musée d'Art et d'Histoire de Langres, Langres 12326
Musée de Notre-Dame-de-Paris, Paris 13583
Musée des Amis de Castrum Vetus, Châteauneuf-les-Martigues 11220
Musée Municipal, La Charité-sur-Loire 12152

Germany
Ausgrabungsmuseum Esslinger Stadtkirche, Esslingen 16966
Bajuwarenmuseum Waging am See, Waging 20343
Bibelmuseum, Beuron 16134
Bischöfliches Dom- und Diözesanmuseum, Trier 20207
Burgmuseum Altnußberg, Geiersthal 17211
Grabungsmuseum, Langenburg 18330
Grabungsmuseum Kirchhof, Coburg 16482
Römisch-Germanisches Museum, Köln 18166
Torhalle Frauenchiemsee und Vikarhaus, Chiemsee 16474

Greece
Byzantine Collection, Chalkida 20914

Hungary
Budapesti Történeti Múzeum, Budapest 21331

Ireland
Athlone Castle Museum, Athlone 22362
Waterford Treasures at the Granary, Waterford 22555
Weingreen Museum of Biblical Antiquities, Dublin 22459

Israel
Archeological Site Avedat, Avedat 22575
Benedictine Monastery - Church of the Multiplication of Loaves and Fish Tabgha, Tiberias 22781

Italy
Cripta e Museo di Sant'Anastasio, Asti 22971
Museo Archeologico Etneo, Adrano 22807
Museo Civico Archeologico, Verucchio 25978
Museo Diocesano, Ancona 22883
Museo Lapidario Estense, Modena 24448
Museo Paleocristiano, Aquileia 22908

Netherlands
Museum Abdij van Egmond, Egmond Binnen 29206

Poland
Gród Piastowski w Gieczu, Giecz 31591
Izba Regionalna Polskiego Towarzystwa Turystyczno-Krajoznawczego, Sulejów 32005
Muzeum Północno-Mazowiecke, Łomża 31780

Spain
Museo Misional de Nuestra Señora de Regla, Chipiona 34715
Museu Monogràfic del Castell de Llinars, Llinars del Vallés 34973

Sweden
Lödöse Museum, Lödöse 36048
Sigtuna Museer, Sigtuna 36183

Tunisia
Musée d'Enfidaville, Enfidaville 37560

Turkey
Ayasofya Müzesi, İstanbul 37693
Yeraltı Müzesi, Kaymaklı 37731
Yerebatan Sarnıcı, İstanbul 37715

United Kingdom
Archaeology Unit and Transport Museum, Gloucester 39079
Farleigh Hungerford Castle, Farleigh Hungerford 38978
Halesworth and District Museum, Halesworth 39148
Meigle Museum of Sculptured Stones, Meigle 39929
River and Rowing Museum, Henley-on-Thames 39220
Shaftesbury Abbey and Museum, Shaftesbury 40477
Whithorn Priory and Museum, Whithorn 40861

U.S.A.
Badè Institute of Biblical Archaeology and Howell Bible Collection, Berkeley 41639

Archaeology, Far Eastern

Cambodia
Musée, Kampong Thom 04948
Musée d'Archéologie, Battambang 04946

China, People's Republic
Chongqing Museum, Chongqing 07031
County Museum, Fufeng 07052
Dingling Museum, Beijing 06964
Henan Provincial Museum, Zhengzhou 07327
Hunan Provincial Museum, Changsha 07010
Luoyang City Museum, Luoyang 07159
Museum near the Ming Tombs, Changping 07008
Museum of Ningxia Autonomous Region of the Hui Nationality, Yinchuan 07319
Museum of the Guangxi Province, Nanning 07190
Nanjing Museum, Nanjing 07184
National Museum of Chinese History, Beijing 06980
Qianling Museum, Qian Xian 07200
Qin Shi Huan Bingmayong Museum, Xian 07296
Shantou Archaeology Museum, Shantou 07228
Sichuan Museum, Chengdu 07024
Suzhou Museum, Suzhou 07252
Urumchi City Museum, Urumchi 07274
Xian Banpo Museum, Xian 07300
Xianyang City Museum, Xianyang 07306
Xincheng District Museum, Nanning 07192
Yao Xian Museum, Yao Xian 07317
Zhaoling Museum, Liquan Xian 07153

China, Republic
Museum of the Institute of History and Philology, Academia Sinica, Taipei 07349

France
Musée Archéologique, Monségur 13022
Musée et Villa Gallo-Romain, Plassac 13750
Musée National des Arts Asiatiques Guimet, Paris 13633

Germany
Museum für Ostasiatische Kunst, Berlin 16057

India
Archaeological Museum Cochin, Kochi 21891

Indonesia
Museum MPU Tantular, Surabaya 22200
Museum Purbakala Trowulan, Mojokerto 22162

Israel
Burnt House Museum, Jerusalem 22627

Japan
Aikawa Kokokan, Isesaki 26257
Aomori-kenritsu Kyodokan, Aomori 26099
Beppu Daigaku Fuzoku Hakubutsukan, Beppu 26117
Biwa-ko Bunkakan, Otsu 26681
Chido Museum, Tsuruoka 26979
Chino-shi Togariishi Jomon Kokokan, Chino 26127
Hida Minzoku Kokokan, Takayama 26803
Hiraide Archaeological Museum, Shiojiri 26758
Kinreizuka Archaeological Collection, Kisaradu 26336
Kokugakuin University Archaeological Collection, Tokyo 26871
Korekawa Archaeological Museum, Hachinohe 26163
Kurashiki Archaeological Museum, Kurashiki 26381
Kyoto Daigaku Bungakubu Hakubutsukan, Kyoto 26420
Kyoto Daigaku Sougou Hakubutsukan, Kyoto 26421
Machida-shiritsu Hakubutsukan Machida City Museum, Machida 26463
Osaka-furitsu Senboku Koko Shiryokan, Sakai 26697
Sado Kokokan, Ogi 26619
Sannomiya Local Museum, Isehara 26256
Shimane Prefectural Yakumodatsu Fudoki No Oka History Hall, Matsue 26473
Shizuoka City Toro Museum, Shizuoka 26766
Tenri University Sankokan Museum, Tenri 26822
Yamagata-kenritsu Hakubutsukan, Yamagata 27003
Yamaguchi-kenritsu Hakubutsukan, Yamaguchi 27005
Yamanashi-kenritsu Koko Hakubutsukan, Higashi-Yatsushiro 26190

Korea, Republic
Busan University Museum, Busan 27138
Buyeo National Museum, Buyeo 27145
Daegwallyeong Museum, Gangneung 27167
Dong-eui University Museum, Busan 27140
Gongju National Museum, Gongju 27177
Gwangju National Museum, Gwangju 27183
Gyeongju National Museum, Gyeongju 27185
Jinju National Museum, Jinju 27202
Koryo Taehakyo Pakmulgwan, Seoul 27252
National Museum of Korea, Seoul 27264
Seoul National University Museum, Seoul 27276
Silla University Museum, Busan 27144
Uiryeong Museum, Uiryeong 27295

Myanmar
Archaeological Museum, Myohaung 28738
Archaeological Museum, Pagan 28739
National Museum of Art and History, Yangon 28751

Nepal
Kapilavastu Museum, Taulihawa 28793

Pakistan
Archaeological Museum, Swat 31058
Archaeological Museum, Taxila 31059

Philippines
Balanghai Archeological Site Museum, Butuan 31293
Fort San Pedro National Museum, Cebu 31312
University of San Carlos Anthropology Museum, Cebu 31318
Xavier University Museum (Museo de Oro), Cagayan de Oro City 31300

Russia
Gosudarstevnnyj Istoriko-architekturnyj i Chudožestvennyj Muzej-zapovednik Drevnij Derbent, Derbent 32756

Sri Lanka
Archaeological Museum, Anuradhapura 35743

Sweden
Østasiatiska Museet, Stockholm 36271

Syria
Deir ez-Zor Museum, Deir ez-Zor 37438
Hama National Museum, Hama 37439
Musée de Palmyra, Palmyra 37441
Tartous Museum, Tartous 37443

Thailand
Ancient City, Samut Prakan 37533
Kamphaeng Phet National Museum, Kamphaeng Phet 37506
Phipitapan Laeng chart Chantharakasem, Ayutthaya 37472
Phipitapan Laeng chart Chao Sam Phraya, Ayutthaya 37473
Phipitapantasatan Haeng Chart Nakhon Si Thammarat, Nakhon Si Thammarat 37519

United Kingdom
Terracotta Warriors Museum, Dorchester 38752

Uzbekistan
Surchondarë Vilojati Archeologija Muzeji, Termiz 48864

Archaeology, Greek and Roman

Albania
Pojani Museum, Pojani 00030

Algeria
Musée de Tazoult, Tazoult 00075
Musée de Tipasa, Tipasa 00079

Australia
Hellenic Antiquities Museum, Melbourne 01232

Austria
Archäologischer Park Carnuntum, Petronell 02408
Archäologischer Park Magdalensberg, Pischeldorf, Kärnten 02417
Ephesos-Museum, Wien 02877
Freilichtmuseum Petronell, Petronell 02409
Museum Aguntum, Dölsach 01768
Römermuseum, Mautern, Niederösterreich 02285
Römische Ruinen unter dem Hohen Markt, Wien 02979
Tempelmuseum Frauenberg, Leibnitz 02202

Belgium
Musée Archéologique, Charleroi 03349
Musée Curtius, Liège 03571
Musée de la Basilique et des Thermes Romains, Arlon 03182
Musée de la Tour Romaine, Arlon 03183
Musée du Poitier Gallo-Romain, Blicquy 03219
Musée Gallo-Romain, Berneau 03215
Musée Luxembourgeois, Arlon 03185
Provinciaal Archeologisch Museum van Zuid-Oost-Vlaanderen, Zottegem 03858

Bulgaria
Archeologičeski Institut s Muzej, Sofia 04827
Archeologičeski Muzej, Varna 04893
Burgaski Muzej, Burgas 04632
Gradski Archeologičeski Muzej, Chisar 04642
Gradski Archeologičeski Muzej, Sandanski 04809
Gradski Istoričeski Muzej, Balčik 04611
Gradski Istoričeski Muzej, Čirpan 04645
Gradski Istoričeski Muzej, Sozopol 04864

Istoričeski Muzej, Svištov 04880
Muzej na Mozaikite, Devnja 04648
Rimska Grobnitsa Silistra, Silistra 04816
Trakijska Grobnica, Kazanlăk 04704

Croatia
Arheološka Zbirka, Nin 07743
Arheološki Muzej Istre, Pula 07757
Arheološki Muzej u Splitu, Split 07779
Zbirka Franjevačkog Samostana, Sinj 07775

Cyprus
Archaeological Museum, Lemesos 08207
Cyprus Museum, Lefkosia 08198
Limassol District Museum, Lemesos 08210
Museum of the George and Nefeli Giabra Pierides Collection, Lefkosia 08203

Cyprus, Turkish Republic
Sipahi Ay. Trias Bazilikası ve Kantara Kalesi, Kantara 08231
Soli Archaeological Site, Lefke 08232

Egypt
Greco-Roman Museum, Alexandria 09238
Ismailia Museum, Ismailia 09300

France
Ancienne Mairie-Musée Annexe, Lillebonne 12606
Glanum, Saint-Rémy-de-Provence 14447
Musée Alésia, Alise-Sainte-Reine 10290
Musée Amphoralis, Sallèles-d'Aude 14576
Musée Archéologique, Saint-Martin-de-Bromes 14348
Musée Archéologique, Saint-Paulien 14407
Musée Archéologique, Soulosse-sous-Saint-Élophe 14794
Musée Archéologique, Vaison-la-Romaine 15043
Musée Archéologique de Rom-Sainte-Soline, Rom 14011
Musée Archéologique de Viuz-Faverges, Faverges 11707
Musée Archéologique et Lapidaire, Aix-les-Bains 10259
Musée Archéologique Municipal de Fréjus, Fréjus 11809
Musée Bastion Saint-André, Antibes 10371
Musée Celte - Gallo Romain, Seltz 14700
Musée d'Art et d'Archéologie, Château-Gontier 11204
Musée de la Civilisation Gallo-Romaine, Lyon 12731
Musée des Docks Romains, Marseille 12864
Musée d'Eysses, Villeneuve-sur-Lot 15236
Musée d'Histoire et d'Archéologie de Die et du Diois, Die 11506
Musée du Mas de la Pyramide, Saint-Rémy-de-Provence 14453
Musée et Site Archéologiques de Nice-Cimiez, Nice 13318
Musée et Sites Archéologiques de Saint-Romain-en-Gal-Vienne, Saint-Romain-en-Gal 14461
Musée Gallo-Romain, Biesheim 10730
Musée Horreum Romain, Narbonne 13270
Musée Lapidaire, Narbonne 13271
Musée Lapidaire Municipal, Saint-Sever (Landes) 14475
Musée Villien, Avesnes-sur-Helpe 10524
Muséosite de l'Amphithéâtre Gallo-Romain, Lillebonne 12608
Nécropole de Louis Cauvin, Gareoult 11841

Germany
Antikenmuseum und Abgußsammlung des Archäologischen Instituts der Universität Heidelberg, Heidelberg 17662
Antikensammlung, Berlin 15914
Archäologische Ausstellung in der Schule, Nassenfels 18974
Archäologische Sammlung der Universität, Freiburg im Breisgau 17106
Archäologischer Park Cambodunum - APC, Kempten 18063
Archäologischer Park mit Museums-Turm, Kellmünz 18053
Archäologischer Park Xanten, Xanten 20727
Archäologisches Museum, Burgheim 16424
Archäologisches Museum, Frankfurt am Main 17031
Freilichtmuseum am Rätischen Limes, Rainau 19478
Heimatmuseum Kösching, Kösching 18187
Heinrich-Schliemann-Gedenkstätte, Neubukow 19014
Kunstsammlungen der Ruhr-Universität Bochum, Bochum 16196
Museum im Römerbad, Heidenheim an der Brenz 17681
Museum Römische Villa Nennig, Perl 19375
Museum Villa Rustica, Möckenlohe 18761
Museum Villa Sarabodis, Gerolstein 17258
Rheinisches Landesmuseum Trier, Trier 20212
Römerbadmuseum, Hüfingen 17852
Römerhaus Walheim, Walheim 20375
Römermuseum, Mainhardt 18596
Römermuseum, Obernburg 19183
Römermuseum, Osterburken 19291
Römermuseum Bedaium, Seebruck 19914
Römermuseum in der Grundschule Rißtissen, Ehingen, Donau 16793
Römermuseum Kastell Boiotro, Passau 19360
Römisch-Germanisches Museum, Köln 18166
Römische Thermenanlage, Weißenburg in Bayern 20494
Römischer Weinkeller Oberriexingen, Oberriexingen 19196
Römisches Freilichtmuseum, Hechingen 17657
Römisches Museum, Augsburg 15566
Römisches Museum für Kur- und Badewesen, Neustadt an der Donau 19072
Römisches Museum Remagen, Remagen 19561
Sammlungen des Archäologischen Instituts der Universität, Göttingen 17340
Stadtgeschichtliches Museum Jülich, Jülich 17966
Stiftung Römermuseum Homburg-Schwarzenacker, Homburg 17837
Sumelocenna - Römisches Stadtmuseum, Rottenburg am Neckar 19692
Winckelmann-Museum, Stendal 20059

Greece
Agora Museum, Athinai 20844
Archaeological Museum of Ancient Corinth, Ancient Corinth 20821
Archaeological Museum of Argos, Argos 20832
Archaeological Museum of Epidaurus, Asklepieion Lygourio 20839
Archaeological Museum of Isthmia, Isthmia 20979
Archaeological Museum of Nemea, Archaia Nemea 20831
Archaeological Museum of Piraeus, Piraeus 21120
Archaeological Museum of Siteia, Siteia 21158
Archaeological Museum of Thebes, Thebes 21175
Archaeological Museums of Chania and Rethymnon, Chania 20915
Archeological Collection, Apeirathos 20829
Archeological Collection, Astypalaia 20842
Archeological Collection, Dimitsana 20937
Archeological Collection, Ermoupolis 20947
Archeological Collection, Farsala 20951
Archeological Collection, Folegandros 20959
Archeological Collection, Galaxidi 20960
Archeological Collection, Geraki 20962
Archeological Collection, Grevena 20964
Archeological Collection, Grevena 20965
Archeological Collection, Gythion 20966
Archeological Collection, Ios 20972
Archeological Collection, Istiaia 20980
Archeological Collection, Kardamyli 20994
Archeological Collection, Kastro 21008
Archeological Collection, Kea 21013
Archeological Collection, Kimolos 21019
Archeological Collection, Kos 21029
Archeological Collection, Kozani 21034
Archeological Collection, Lindos 21049
Archeological Collection, Lixouri 21054
Archeological Collection, Loutra Aidipsou 21055
Archeological Collection, Maroneia 21057
Archeological Collection, Mégara 21062
Archeological Collection, Messinia 21066
Archeological Collection, Mithymna 21072
Archeological Collection, Molyvos 21073
Archeological Collection, Navpaktos 21094
Archeological Collection, Néa Anchialos 21096
Archeological Collection, Neos Skopos 21100
Archeological Collection, Paramythia 21108
Archeological Collection, Platanos 21128
Archeological Collection, Preveza 21133
Archeological Collection, Pythagoreion 21136
Archeological Collection, Sifnos 21156
Archeological Collection, Tsotili 21205
Archeological Museum, Andros 20822
Archeological Museum, Argostolion 20833
Archeological Museum, Arhaia Olympia 20837
Archeological Museum, Atalanti 20843
Archeological Museum, Chalkida 20913
Archeological Museum, Chios 20921
Archeological Museum, Chora 20925
Archeological Museum, Corfu 20928
Archeological Museum, Dion 20939
Archeological Museum, Elefsis 20944
Archeological Museum, Eresos 20945
Archeological Museum, Eretria 20946
Archeological Museum, Florina 20955
Archeological Museum, Iráklion 20974
Archeological Museum, Kabos 20981
Archeological Museum, Kalamata 20982
Archeological Museum, Kalamos 20986
Archeological Museum, Kalymnos 20992
Archeological Museum, Kastelli Kisamou 21005
Archeological Museum, Kavala 21010
Archeological Museum, Kiato 21014
Archeological Museum, Kilkis 21017
Archeological Museum, Kórinthos 21028
Archeological Museum, Kos 21030
Archeological Museum, Lamia 21039
Archeological Museum, Lárissa 21041
Archeological Museum, Myrina 21079
Archeological Museum, Mytilini 21083
Archeological Museum, Naxos 21095
Archeological Museum, Paros 21110
Archeological Museum, Patrai 21113
Archeological Museum, Plaka 21127
Archeological Museum, Polygyros 21130
Archeological Museum, Rethymnon 21137
Archeological Museum, Rhodos 21141
Archeological Museum, Salamina 21145
Archeological Museum, Samos 21146
Archeological Museum, Samothráki 21150
Archeological Museum, Sicyon 21155
Archeological Museum, Spárti 21164
Archeological Museum, Thassos 21173
Archeological Museum, Thera 21176
Archeological Museum, Thermo 21178
Archeological Museum, Tinos 21198
Archeological Museum, Vathy 21207
Archeological Museum, Vravrón 21216
Archeological Museum, Karystos 21003
Archeological Museum of Agrinion, Agrinion 20811
Archeological Museum of Aiani, Aiani 20813
Archeological Museum of Aigina, Aegina 20803
Archeological Museum of Delphi, Delphi 20936
Archeological Museum of Ioannina, Ioannina 20967
Archeological Museum of Komotini, Komotini 21023
Archeological Museum of Nafplion, Nafplion 21090
Archeological Museum of Pella, Pella 21116
Archeological Museum of Somothraki, Palaiochora 21105
Archeological Museum of Stavros, Stavros Ithakis 21169
Archeological Museum of Veroia, Veria 21208
Archeology Museum of Kozani, Kozani 21035
Arhaiologiko Mouseio Thassaloniki, Thessaloniki 21179
Artemis Collection, Athinai 20849
Athanassakeion Archeological Museum, Volos 21211
Byzantine and Christian Museum, Athinai 20853
Byzantine Museum of Antivouniotissa, Corfu 20929
Chania Byzantine and Postbyzantine Collection, Chania 20916
Chios Museum of Byzantine and Postbyzantine Art, Chios 20922
Collection of Byzantine and Postbyzantine Art, Kythira 21038
Corfu Byzantine Collection, Corfu 20930
Economopoulos Collection, Athinai 20857
Goulandris Collection, Athinai 20862
Hadjidimou Collection, Athinai 20863
Ionnina Byzantine Museum, Ioannina 20970
Kastoria Byzantine Museum, Kastoria 21007
Lambropoulos Collection, Polygyros 21131
Manos Faltaits Museum, Euboea 20948
Megisti Museum, Kastellorizo 21006
Monemvasia Archeological Collection, Monemvasia 21074
Mouseio Akropoleos, Athinai 20871
Mouseio Ethnikon Archaiologikon, Athinai 20873
Mouseio Kerameikos, Athinai 20876
Mouseio Mpenaki, Athinai 20878
Museum Agios Nikolaos, Agios Nikolaos 20810
Museum Astros, Astros 20841
Museum Mistra, Mystras 21082
Museum of Casts and Archeological Collection, Thessaloniki 21189
Museum Papageorgiou, Limenaria 21048
P. and Al. Canellopoulos Museum, Athinai 20898
Palace of the Grand Masters, Rhodos 21144
Panarcadic Archeological Museum of Tripolis, Tripoli 21204
Perachora Museum, Perachora 21117
Pierides Museum of Ancient Cypriot Art, Athinai 20901
Sefel Collection, Volos 21214
Sikinos Archeological Collection, Sikinos 21157
Spetses Museum, Spetses 21168
Tower Museum of Prosphorion, Ouranoupoli 21103
Vassiliou Collection, Thessaloniki 21195
Veria Byzantine Museum, Veria 21209
Vouvalis Mansion, Kalymnos 20993
Zakynthos Byzantine Museum, Zakynthos 21222

Hungary
Aquincumi Múzeum, Budapest 21324
Görög-Római Szobormásolatok Múzeuma, Tata 21592
Gorsium Szabadtéri Múzeum, Székesfehérvár 21557
Román Kori Kőtár, Pécs 21515

Ireland
University College Dublin Classical Museum, Dublin 22455

Israel
Local Museum, Ashkelon 22574
Museum of Regional and Mediterranean Archaeology, Nir-David 22723
Wohl Archaeology Museum Herodian Mansions, Jerusalem 22670

Italy
Antiquarium, Brescello 23199
Antiquarium, Manduria 24277
Antiquarium, Numana 24659
Antiquarium, Palazzolo Acreide 24758
Antiquarium, Patti 24816
Antiquarium, Porto Torres 25015
Antiquarium, Santa Flavia 25430
Antiquarium, Santa Maria Capua Vetere 25434
Antiquarium, Sant'Antioco 25455
Antiquarium Comunale, Roma 25147
Antiquarium Comunale, Sutri 25658
Antiquarium del Serapeo, Tivoli 25710
Antiquarium delle Grotte di Catullo, Sirmione 25588
Antiquarium di Himera, Termini Imerese 25691
Antiquarium e Zona Archeologica, Lugagnano Val d'Arda 24236
Civico Museo Archeologico, Acqui Terme 22804
Civico Museo Archeologico e di Scienze Naturali Federico Eusebio, Alba 22829
Cripta e Museo di Sant'Anastasio, Asti 22971
Musei Capitolini, Roma 25173
Museo Antiquarium Archeologico, Falerone 23760
Museo Antiquarium Etrusco, Colle di Val d'Elsa 23608
Museo Archeologico, Cecina e Marina 23464
Museo Archeologico, Cesena 23497
Museo Archeologico, Faenza 23750
Museo Archeologico, Gropello Cairoli 24053
Museo Archeologico, Milano 24385
Museo Archeologico al Teatro Romano, Verona 25969
Museo Archeologico Comunale di Artimino, Carmignano 23349
Museo Archeologico dell'Agro Nocerino, Nocera Inferiore 24627
Museo Archeologico di Vallecamonica, Cividate Camuno 23590
Museo Archeologico e Antiquarium Nazionale, Formia 23920
Museo Archeologico e Paleontologico, Asti 22973
Museo Archeologico e Pinacoteca Comunale, Foligno 23897
Museo Archeologico e Storico Aristico, Bra 23192
Museo Archeologico Girolamo Rossi, Ventimiglia 25955
Museo Archeologico Nazionale, Adria 22808
Museo Archeologico Nazionale, Aquileia 22907
Museo Archeologico Nazionale, Capaccio 23322
Museo Archeologico Nazionale, Chieti 23544
Museo Archeologico Nazionale, Chiusi Città 23555
Museo Archeologico Nazionale, Gioia del Colle 24027
Museo Archeologico Nazionale, Metaponto 24367
Museo Archeologico Nazionale, Napoli 24577
Museo Archeologico Nazionale, Parma 24802
Museo Archeologico Nazionale, Quarto d'Altino 25059
Museo Archeologico Nazionale, Taranto 25672
Museo Archeologico Nazionale, Venosa 25953
Museo Archeologico Nazionale di Cosa, Orbetello 24683
Museo Archeologico Nazionale di Palestrina, Palestrina 24780
Museo Archeologico Nazionale e Antiquarium Statale, Locri 24199
Museo Archeologico Nazionale Etrusco, Cerveteri 23491
Museo Archeologico Oliveriano, Pesaro 24857
Museo Archeologico Provinciale, Bari 23020
Museo Archeologico Provinciale F. Ribezzo, Brindisi 23212
Museo Archeologico Regionale, Agrigento 22816
Museo Archeologico Regionale A. Salinas, Palermo 24765
Museo Archeologico San Giovanni in Compito, Savignano sul Rubicone 25502
Museo Archeologico Statale, Cingoli 23565
Museo Archeologico Statale V. Capialbi, Vibo Valentia 25987
Museo Civico, Asolo 22959
Museo Civico, Baranello 23011
Museo Civico, Cabras 23240
Museo Civico, Centuripe 23475
Museo Civico, Feltre 23772
Museo Civico, Guardiagrele 24070
Museo Civico, Iesi 24079
Museo Civico, Magliano Sabina 24260
Museo Civico, Tolfa 25724
Museo Civico, Trevignano Romano 25802
Museo Civico, Sesto Calende 25555
Museo Civico Antonino Olmo e Gipsoteca, Savigliano 25499
Museo Civico Archeologico, Bergamo 23061
Museo Civico Archeologico, Canosa di Puglia 23317
Museo Civico Archeologico, Cologna Veneta 23618
Museo Civico Archeologico, Fiesole 23806
Museo Civico Archeologico Arsenio Crespellani, Bazzano 23044
Museo Civico Archeologico C. Cellini, Ripatransone 25122
Museo Civico Archeologico O. Nardini, Velletri 25905
Museo Civico Archeologico Paleoambientale, Budrio 23224
Museo Civico Arecheologico delle Acque, Chianciano Terme 23522
Museo Civico Aufidenate, Castel di Sangro 23388
Museo Civico C. G. Nicastro, Bovino 23191
Museo Civico Castello Ursino, Catania 23447
Museo Civico e Foro Romano, Assisi 22963
Museo Civico e Teatro e Serbatoio Romano, Falerone 23761
Museo Civico G.B. Adriani, Cherasco 23520
Museo Civico Mambrini, Galeata 23949
Museo Civico Rogadeo, Bitonto 23092
Museo Correale di Terranova, Sorrento 25611
Museo del Opera Omnia R. Musa e Pinacoteca Parmigiani, Bedonia 23045
Museo del Patrimonium, Sutri 25660
Museo dell'Abbazia, Casamari-Veroli 23370
Museo dell'Abbazia, Castiglione a Casauria 23431
Museo delle Grigne, Esino Lario 23742
Museo delle Mura, Roma 25202
Museo di Preistoria e del Mare, Trapani 25784
Museo Didattico Archeologico, Laterza 24154
Museo Diocesano di Arte Sacra, Sarsina 25479
Museo e Pinacoteca Civici, Vasto 25903
Museo Etrusco, Asciano 22948
Museo Etrusco, San Gimignano 25365
Museo Etrusco Gasparri, Populonia 25006
Museo Etrusco M. Guarnacci, Volterra 26052
Museo Fondazione C. Faina e Museo Civico Palazzo Faina, Orvieto 24706
Museo Lapidario, Ferrara 23796
Museo Nazionale Archeologico, Sarsina 25480
Museo Nazionale della Siritide, Policoro 24978
Museo Nazionale di Santa Maria delle Monanche e Paleolitico, Isernia 24103
Museo Nazionale di Villa Guinigi, Lucca 24231
Museo Nazionale Etrusco di Villa Giulia, Roma 25237

Museo Nazionale Etrusco Pompeo Aria, Marzabotto 24309
Museo Nazionale Jatta, Ruvo di Puglia 25305
Museo Nazionale Romano-Terme di Diocleziano, Roma 25239
Museo Nicola Antonio Manfroce, Palmi 24788
Museo Nuovo - Museo del Conservatori, Roma 25241
Museo Ostiense, Ostia Antica 24715
Museo Palatino, Roma 25245
Museo Paleoveneto, Pieve di Cadore 24917
Museo Provinciale, Catanzaro 23455
Museo Romano, Tortona 25779
Museo Torlonia, Roma 25262
Nuovo Museo Provinciale Sannitico, Campobasso 23304
Raccolta d'Arte e Archeologia, Piazza Armerina 24901
Scavi di Ercolano, Ercolano 23737
Scavi di Oplontis, Torre Annunziata 25769
Scavi di Pompei, Pompei 24987
Scavi e Museo Archeologico di S. Restituta, Napoli 24608
Villa Romana a Mosaici, Desenzano del Garda 23713

Malta
Museum of Roman Antiquities, Rabat 27700

Netherlands
Allard Pierson Museum Amsterdam, Amsterdam 28835
Archaeologische Verzameling der Rijksuniversiteit, Utrecht 29896
Museum onder de N.H. Kerk, Elst 29228
Ouddorps Raad- en Polderhuis, Ouddorp 29694
Oudheidkundig Museum, Sint Michielsgestel 29821
Thermenmuseum, Heerlen 29369

Peru
Museo Nacional de Antropología, Arqueología e Historia del Perú, Lima 31221

Portugal
Museu Monográfico de Conimbriga, Condeixa-a-Nova 32266
Museu Nacional de Arqueologia, Lisboa 32306

Serbia-Montenegro
Arheološka Zbirka, Budva 33825

Slovakia
Antická Gerulata v Rusovciach, Bratislava 33957

Spain
Alcázar de los Reyes Cristianos, Córdoba 34734
Conjunto Arqueológico de Carmona, Carmona 34680
Conjunto Arqueológico de Itálica, Santiponce 35454
Museo Arqueológico Monogrófico de Cástulo Linares, Linares 34954
Museo Arqueológico Municipal, Alcúdia 34440
Museo Arqueológico Municipal Alejandro Ramos Folqués, Elche 34790
Museo Arqueológico Municipal Camilo Visedo Molto, Alcoi 34435
Museo Arqueológico Provincial, Badajoz 34516
Museo Catedralicio, Murcia 35145
Museo de Cádiz, Cádiz 34647
Museo de la Comisión Provincial de Monumentos, León 34948
Museo Monográfico de Clunia, Peñalba de Castro 35262
Museo Monográfico y Necrópolis Púnica de Puig des Molins, Eivissa 34787
Museo Municipal, Antequera 34468
Museo Municipal, Jérica 34929
Museu Arqueològic de l'Esquerda, Roda de Ter 35330
Museu d'Arqueologia de Catalunya, Barcelona 34550
Museu de Badalona, Badalona 34520
Museu Municipal, Tossa de Mar 35570
Museu Nacional Arqueològic de Tarragona, Tarragona 35516

Sweden
Antikmuseet, Göteborg 35909
Lunds Universitets Antikmuseum, Lund 36062
Medelhavsmuseet, Stockholm 36259

Switzerland
Historisches Museum der Stadt Baden, Baden 36485
Musée de la Villa Romaine de Pully, Pully 37038
Musée Gallo-Romain d'Octodure, Martigny 36928
Musée Romain, Avenches 36481
Musée Romain, Nyon 36995
Museo di Castelgrande, Bellinzona 36530
Thermen-Museum Juliomagus, Schleitheim 37137
Vindonissa-Museum, Brugg 36592

Tunisia
Musée Archéologique de Makthar, Makthar 37570
Musée d'Institut National de Archéologique d'El-Jem, El-Jem 37559
Musée d'Utique, Utique 37596
Musée National de Carthage, Carthage 37557

Turkey
Afrodisiyas Müzesi, Geyre Köyü Karasu Aydın 37684
Aydın Müzesi, Aydın 37627
Bodrum Sualtı Arkeolojisi Müzesi, Bodrum 37637
Çanakkale Müzesi, Çanakkale 37649
Efes Müzesi, Selçuk 37779
Hatay Müzesi, Hatay 37687
Hierapolis Arkeoloji Müzesi, Denizli 37658
Iznik Müzesi, Iznik 37720
Konya Müzesi, Konya 37742
Nigde Müzesi, Nigde 37771
Side Müzesi, Side 37781
Silifke Müzesi, Silifke, Içel 37782
Tire Müzesi, Tire 37794

Ukraine
National Preserve of Tauric Chersonesos, Sevastopol 37902

United Kingdom
Aldborough Roman Town Museum, Boroughbridge 38280
Arbeia Roman Fort and Museum, South Shields 40537
Calleva Museum, Silchester 40517
Castle Museum, Colchester 38608
Chedworth Roman Villa, Yanworth 40950
Chedworth Roman Villa Museum, Cheltenham 38543
Clayton Collection Museum, Chollerford 38573
Corbridge Roman Site Museum, Corbridge 38631
Fishbourne Roman Palace and Museum, Chichester 38560
Hereford City Museum and Art Gallery, Hereford 39225
Housesteads Roman Fort and Museum, Hexham 39238
Lullingstone Roman Villa, Eynsford 38964
Malton Museum, Malton 39884
Newport Roman Villa, Newport, Isle of Wight 40056
Ribchester Roman Museum, Ribchester 40314
Richborough Castle - Roman Fort, Sandwich 40447
Roman Army Museum, Greenhead 39130
Roman Legionary Museum, Caerleon 38431
Roman Painted House, Dover 38770
Roman Villa, Brading 38306
Segedunum Roman Fort, Baths and Museum, Wallsend 40769
Segontium Roman Museum, Caernarfon 38435
Senhouse Roman Museum, Maryport 39919
Thurrock Museum, Grays 39117
Ure Museum of Greek Archaeology, Reading 40299
Viroconium Museum, Wroxeter 40946
Wall Roman Site and Museum - Letocetum, Lichfield 39494

Vatican City
Museo Gregoriano Egizio, Città del Vaticano 48874

Archaeology, Ibero-American

Argentina
Museo Arqueológico, Gualeguaychú 00360
Museo Arqueológico de Chasicó, Chasicó 00273
Museo Arqueológico de Puerto Esperanza, Puerto Esperanza 00490
Museo Arqueológico de Salta, Salta 00537
Museo Arqueológico de Tilcara, Tilcara 00635
Museo Arqueológico Pío P. Díaz, Cachi 00255
Museo Arqueológico Provincial, San Salvador de Jujuy 00595
Museo Arqueológico Regional Anibal Montes, Río Segundo 00521
Museo Arqueológico Regional Inca Huasi, La Rioja 00395
Museo Arqueológico y Colonial, Fuerte Quemado 00350
Museo de Antropología, Córdoba 00292
Museo de Antropología y Ciencias Naturales, Concordia 00287
Museo de Arqueología de la Universidad Nacional de Tucumán, San Miguel de Tucumán 00581
Museo del Area Fundacional, Mendoza 00436
Museo Florentino Ameghino, Bolívar 00141
Museo Histórico Arqueológico Guillermo Magrassi, Mar del Plata 00426
Museo Jesútico Nacional de Jesús María, Jesús María 00371
Museo Pampeano de Chascomús, Chascomús 00272
Museo Provincial Arqueológico Eric Boman, Santa María de Catamarca 00611
Museo Provincial de Arqueología Wagner, Santiago del Estero 00618
Museo Rauzi, Palmira 00464
Museo Regional Dr. Adolfo Alsina, Carhué 00263
Museo Universitario Florentino y Carlos Ameghino, Rosario 00533

Belize
Altun Ha Archaeological Site, Altun Ha 03861
Ambergris Museum and Cultural Centre, Ambergris Caye 03862
Caracol Archaeological Site, Caracol 03866
Lamanai Archaeological Site, Lamanai 03867
Museum of Belize, Belize City 03865
Tanah Art Museum, San Antonio 03869

Bolivia
Museo Charcas, Sucre 03907
Museo Nacional de Arqueología, La Paz 03899
Museo Universitario, Cochabamba 03892

Brazil
Museu Câmara Cascudo, Natal 04218
Museu Comercial e Arqueológico do Sindicato dos Empregados, Maceió 04178
Museu Lasar Segall, São Paulo 04540
Museu Sitio Arqueológico Casa dos Pilões, Rio de Janeiro 04394

Canada
London Museum of Archaeology, London 05769

Chile
Museo Arqueológico de La Serena, La Serena 06898
Museo Chileno de Arte Precolombino, Santiago de Chile 06908
Museo de Antofagasta, Antofagasta 06888
Museo del Limari, Ovalle 06902

Colombia
Museo Arqueológico, Pasca 07545
Museo Arqueologico Casa del Marqués de San Jorge, Bogotá 07392
Museo Arqueológico Julio César Cubillos, Cali 07444
Museo del Río Magdalena, Honda 07495
Museo Luciano Rosero, Pasto 07549
Museo Maridiaz, Pasto 07551

Costa Rica
Museo Nacional de Costa Rica, San José 07662
Museo Sito Arqueológico Guayabo de Turrialba, Turrialba 07664

Cuba
Indo-Cuban Bani Museum, Banes 07854
Museo Antropológico Montané, La Habana 07935
Museo de Arqueología, La Habana 07955

Dominican Republic
Fortaleza de San Felipe, Santo Domingo 09117
Museo Natural de Historia y Geografía, Santo Domingo 09127
Sala de Arte Prehispánico, Santo Domingo 09128

Ecuador
Museo Antropológico del Banco Central, Guayaquil 09168
Museo Arqueologico Carlos Aiiercado, Esmeraldas 09163
Museo Arqueologico del Banco Central de Bahia, Bahia de Carácluez 09139
Museo Banco del Pacifico, Guayaquil 09169
Museo Carlos Emilio Grijalva, Tulcán 09228
Museo de Sitio de Ingapirca, Azogues 09138
Museo de Sitio del Rumicucho, San Antonio 09226
Museo del Banco Central de Manta, Manta 09188
Museo del Colegio Nacional Pedro Vicente Maldonado, Riobamba 09223
Museo del Colegio Stella Maris, Atacames 09137
Museo Francisco Huerta Rendón en la Casona Universitaria, Guayaquil 09174
Museo Nacional de la Dirección Regional del Banco Central del Ecuador, Quito 09216
Museo Nahim Isaias, Guayaquil 09178
Museo Sala de Exposición Banco Central de Esmeraldas, Esmeraldas 09164
Museo Santuario Nuestra Señora Natividad del Guayco, La Magdalena 09187
Museo Weilbauer, Quito 09219

El Salvador
Museo Nacional David J. Guzmán, San Salvador 09313

France
Musée des Jacobins, Auch 10471

Guatemala
Museo Nacional de Arqueología y Etnología, Guatemala 21271

Honduras
Museo Arqueológico de Comayagua, Comayagua 21298
Museo Regional de Arqueología Maya, Ciudad de Copán 21297

Italy
Castello D'Albertis, Genova 23977
Museo Americanistico Federico Lunardi, Genova 23985

Mexico
Museo Arqueológico Chiametlán, Rosario 28360
Museo Arqueológico Cuicuilco, México 28107
Museo Arqueológico de Apaxco, Apaxco 27775
Museo Arqueológico de Campeche, Campeche 27795
Museo Arqueológico de Cancún, Cancún 27803
Museo Arqueológico de Ciudad Guzmán, Guzmán 27981
Museo Arqueológico de Comitán, Comitán de Domínguez 27848
Museo Arqueológico de la Ciudad, Emiliano Zapata 27908
Museo Arqueológico de la Costa Grande, Zihuatanejo 28654
Museo Arqueológico de Lagos de Moreno, Lagos de Moreno 28047
Museo Arqueológico de Mazatlán, Mazatlán 28076
Museo Arqueológico de Nextlalpan, Nextlalpan 28266
Museo Arqueológico de Tepeapulco, Tepeapulco 28487
Museo Arqueológico de Tizatlán, Tizatlán 28518
Museo Arqueológico de Tonalá, Tonalá, Chiapas 28552
Museo Arqueológico de Tula Jorge R. Acosta, Tula de Allende 28565
Museo Arqueológico de Venustiano Carranza, Venustiano Carranza 28592
Museo Arqueológico de Xochimilco, México 28108
Museo Arqueológico del Cerro de la Estrella, México 28109
Museo Arqueológico del Soconusco, Tapachula 28455
Museo Arqueológico Dr. Román Piña Chan, Tenango del Valle 28477
Museo Arqueológico Juan Sepúlveda y Museo Eduardo Ruiz, Uruapán 28578
Museo Arqueológico Luis G. Urbina, México 28110
Museo Arqueológico Mesoamericano, Tijuana 28510
Museo Casa del Dr. Mora, Comonfort 27851
Museo Comunitario Shan-Dany, Santa Ana del Valle 28426
Museo David Ramírez Lavoignet, Misantla 28221
Museo de Antropología de Xalapa, Xalapa 28615
Museo de Arqueología, Acapulco de Juárez 27748
Museo de Arqueología, Ixtepec 28017
Museo de Arqueología de Córdoba, Córdoba 27856
Museo de Arqueología de León, León 28053
Museo de Arqueología de Occidente de México, Guadalajara 27948
Museo de Arqueología El Chamizal, Juárez 28036
Museo de Arqueología Nabor Rosales Araiza, Tolimán 28540
Museo de Arte Prehispánico de México Rufino Tamayo, Oaxaca 28274
Museo de la Ciudad, Mérida 28083
Museo de la Cultura Huasteca, Tampico 28453
Museo de la Cultura Maya, Chetumal 27817
Museo de la Pintura Mural y Museo Manuel Gamio, Teotihuacán 28481
Museo de La Quemada, Guadalupe 27964
Museo de San Lorenzo Tenochtitlán, Texistepec 28509
Museo de Sitio Boca de Potrerillos, Mina 28219
Museo de Sitio de Cacaxtla, Nativitas 28262
Museo de Sitio de Cempoala, Cempoala 27811
Museo de Sitio de Chalcatzingo, Chalcatzingo 27813
Museo de Sitio de Chichen Itza, Timun 28515
Museo de Sitio de Coatetelco, Coatetelco 27833
Museo de Sitio de Comalcalco, Comalcalco 27847
Museo de Sitio de El Tajín, Papantla 28304
Museo de Sitio de El Zapotal, Ignacio de la Llave 28010
Museo de Sitio de Higueras, Vega de Alatorre 28590
Museo de Sitio de La Venta, Huimanguillo 28006
Museo de Sitio de la Zona Arqueológica de Tzintzunzan, Tzintzuntzan 28577
Museo de Sitio de Monte Albán, Oaxaca 28279
Museo de Sitio de Ocuilan, Ocuilan 28288
Museo de Sitio de Palenque Alberto Ruz Lhuillier, Palenque 28298
Museo de Sitio de Pomona, Tenosique de Pino Suárez 28479
Museo de Sitio de Querétaro, Querétaro 28354
Museo de Sitio de San Lorenzo Tenochtitlán, Tenochtitlán 28478
Museo de Sitio de San Miguel Ixtapan, San Miguel Ixtapan 28412
Museo de Sitio de Tenayuca, Tlalnepantla 28524
Museo de Sitio de Teotihuacán, Teotihuacán 28482
Museo de Sitio de Toniná, Ocosingo 28285
Museo de Sitio de Tres Zapotes, Santiago Tuxtla 28440
Museo de Sitio de Uxmal, Santa Elena 28432
Museo de Sitio de Xochicalco, Xochicalco 28623
Museo de Sitio de Xochitecatl, Nativitas 28263
Museo de Sitio Degollado Jalisco, Degollado 27888
Museo de Sitio El Torreoncito, Torreón 28555
Museo de Sitio Ocotelulco, Totolac 28562
Museo de Sitio San Agustín, Juárez 28038
Museo de Sitio Talavera, México 28149
Museo de Sitio Tecpan, México 28150
Museo del Carmen, México 28154
Museo del Pueblo Maya Dzibilchaltún, Chablekal 27812
Museo del Templo Mayor, México 28163
Museo Dr. Atl, Pihuamo 28311
Museo El Jonotal, Playa Vicente, Veracruz 28313
Museo El Polvorín, Monclova 28226
Museo Fray Bernardo Padilla, Acámbaro 27743
Museo Omar Huerta Escalante, Jonuta 28033
Museo Porfirio Corona Covarrubias, El Grullo, Jalisco 27904
Museo Regional de Arqueología de Tuxpan, Tuxpan de Rodríguez Cano 28568
Museo Regional de la Laguna, Torreón 28560
Museo Regional Huasteco, Valles 28588
Museo Sac-be, Yaxcabá 28630
Museo San José el Mogote, San José el Mogote 28388
Museo Universitario de Arqueología de Manzanillo, Manzanillo 28069
Museo Universitario Lariab de Historia Antigua de la Huaxteca, Tamuín 28454
Sala de Arqueología del Municipio de Mújica, Múgica 28256

Netherlands
Amerika Museum Nederland, Cuijk 29059

Panama
Parque Arqueológico El Caño, Natá 31075

Peru
Instituto Regional de Ucayali, Pucallpa 31240
Muestrario Arqueológico de Amazonas, Chachapoyas 31141
Museo Arqueológico Alejandro Pezzia Aseretto, La Angostura 31191

Museo Arqueológico de Ancash, Huaraz 31174
Museo Arqueológico de Cajamarca y Museo Médico, Cajamarca 31126
Museo Arqueológico de la Universidad Nacional del Altiplano, Pucara 31241
Museo Arqueológico del Centro de Estudios Histórico Sociales Julio Espejo Nuñez, Jauja 31189
Museo Arqueológico e Histórico de Andahuaylas, Andahuaylas 31111
Museo Arqueológico Frederico Galvez Durand, Huancayo 31168
Museo Arqueológico Horacio Urteaga, Cajamarca 31127
Museo Arqueológico José Casinelli, Santa Inés 31248
Museo Arqueológico Municipal y Museo Municipal Miguel Justino Ramírez, Piura 31238
Museo Arqueológico Nacional Brüning, Lambayeque 31195
Museo Arqueológico Regional de Ancash, Ancash 31110
Museo Cabrera, Ica 31180
Museo Católica de Santa María, Cercado 31139
Museo Contisuyo, Moquegua 31229
Museo de Arqueología Josefina Ramos de Cox del Instituto Riva-Agüero, Lima 31202
Museo de Arqueología Samuel Humberto Espinoza Lozano, Huaytará 31177
Museo de Arqueología y Antropología, Lima 31203
Museo de Arte de Lima, Lima 31205
Museo de la Provincia El Dorado, El Dorado 31164
Museo de Oro del Perú y Armas del Mundo, Lima 31213
Museo de Sitio Arqueológico Kuntur Wasi, San Pablo 31247
Museo de Sitio Complejo Arqueológico de Sillustani, Atuncolla 31119
Museo de Sitio de Chan Chan, Trujillo 31263
Museo de Sitio de Chinchero, Urubamba 31266
Museo de Sitio de Paracas Julio C. Tello, Pisco 31236
Museo de Sitio de Puruchuco, Lima 31215
Museo de Sitio de San Isidro, Tembladera 31259
Museo de Sitio de Sipán, Zaña 31272
Museo de Sitio de Túcume, Campo 31136
Museo de Sitio de Wari, Wari 31267
Museo de Sitio El Algarrobal, El Algarrobal 31163
Museo de Sitio Wari, Ayacucho 31121
Museo de Sitio Wari Willca, Huancayo 31169
Museo del Centro de Investigación Arqueológica de Ancón, Lima 31216
Museo del Instituto Nacional de Cultura, Arequipa 31114
Museo Inca de la Universidad Nacional San Antonio Abad, Cusco 31160
Museo Lítico de Pukara, Pukara 31243
Museo Martínez de Compañon, Tambogrande 31258
Museo Municipal de Chincha, Chincha Alta 31143
Museo Municipal Dreyer, Dreyer 31162
Museo Regional de Arqueología de Junín, Chupaca 31147
Sitio Arqueológico de Cumbemayo, Cumbemayo 31151

Puerto Rico
Museum of History, Anthropology and Art, San Juan 32405

Spain
Colección de Arqueología y Etnografía Americana, Madrid 34996
Museo Arqueológico Municipal Precolombino, Benalmádena 34600

Uruguay
Palacio Taranco, Montevideo 41031

U.S.A.
Blackwater Draw Museum, Portales 46614
Chaco Culture National Historical Park, Nageezi 45592
El Morro National Monument, Ramah 46782
Salinas Pueblo Missions National Monument, Mountainair 45549

Archaeology, Near and Middle Eastern

France
Musée Arménien de France, Paris 13530
Musée de Bible et Terre Sainte, Paris 13550

Germany
Hilprecht-Sammlung Vorderasiatischer Altertümer der Friedrich-Schiller-Universität Jena, Jena 17943

Iran
Azarbayezan Museum, Tabriz 22283
Gorgan Museum, Gorgan 22239
Hakhamaneshi Museum, Shiraz 22280
Reza Abbasi Museum, Teheran 22323
Takht-e-Jamshid, Shiraz 22282
Uroomieh Museum, Uroomieh 22333

Iraq
Al Mawsil Museum, Nineveh 22355
Archaeological Site Nimrud (Calah), Nimrud 22354
Babylon Museum, Babylon 22340
Basrah Museum, Basrah 22348
Nasiriya Museum, Nasiriya 22353
Nergal Gate Museum, Mosul 22352
Samarra Museum, Samarra 22356

Israel
Akko Municipal Museum, Akko 22567
Arad Museum, Arad 22571
Archaeological Museum, Kibbutz Ein Dor 22682
Be'eri Archaeological Collection, Be'eri 22579
Beit Miriam-Museum, Kibbutz Palmachim 22699
Bible Lands Museum Jerusalem, Jerusalem 22625
Caesarea Museum, Kibbutz Sedot Yam 22703
Ceramics Museum, Tel Aviv 22752
Golan Archaeological Museum, Qatzrin 22728
Hanita Museum, Kibbutz Hanita 22689
Hazor Museum, Ayelet-Hashahar 22577
Herbert E. Clark Collection of Near Eastern Antiquities, Jerusalem 22635
Local Museum, Kibbutz Maabarot 22695
Local Museum, Kibbutz Sasa 22702
Museum, Ancient Synagogue and Necropolis, Beit Shearim 22582
Museum of Nahariya, Nahariya 22718
Nahsholim Museum, Hof Dor 22617
Pères Blancs - Saint Anne, Jerusalem 22655
Reuben and Edith Hecht Museum, Haifa 22611
Rockefeller Archeological Museum, Jerusalem 22657
Saint James Museum and Library, Jerusalem 22660
Shrine of the Book, Jerusalem 22662
Shtekelis Prehistory Museum, Haifa 22612
Skirball Museum of Biblical Archaeology, Jerusalem 22665
Tell Qasile Archaeological Site, Tel Aviv 22776
Terra Sancta Museum, Nazareth 22721

Japan
Okayama-shiritsu Oriento Bijutsukan, Okayama 26628

Jordan
Irbid Archaeological Museum, Irbid 27062
Jarash Archaeological Museum, Jarash 27064
Jordan Archaeological Museum, Amman 27052
Madaba Archaeology Museum, Ajloun 27040
Museum of Aqaba Antiquities, Aqaba 27061
Umm Qais Archaeological Museum, Umm Qais 27069

Lebanon
Musée Archéologique de l'Université Americaine, Beirut 27481
Musée National, Beirut 27484

Mexico
Museo de Historia de Tabasco, Villahermosa 28609
Parque-Museo La Venta, Villahermosa 28613

Netherlands
Bijbels Openluchtmuseum, Heilig Landstichting 29375

Oman
Bait Muzna Gallery, Muscat 31002

Pakistan
Islamabad Museum, Islamabad 31023

Palestine
Musée de l'Ecole Biblique et Archéologique Française, Jerusalem 31071

Turkey
Alacahöyük Arkeoloji Müzesi, Alacahöyük 37607
Anadolu Medeniyetleri Müzesi, Ankara 37612
Elazığ Arkeoloji ve Etnografi Müzesi, Elazığ 37667
Karatepe Açıkhava Müzesi, Kadirli 37721
Türk Seramik Müzesi, Konya 37747
Yazılı Kaya Müzesi, Çifteler 37654

United Arab Emirates
Al-Ain Museum, Al-Ain 37915

United Kingdom
Department of Semitic Studies Collection, Leeds 39444
Oriental Museum, Durham 38829

U.S.A.
Elizabeth P. Korn Gallery, Madison 45061
Hellenic Museum and Cultural Center, Chicago 42332

Yemen
Baihan Al Qasab Museum, Wadi Baihan 49014
National Museum, Sanaa 49011

Architecture

Albania
Architecture Museum, Bérat 00010

Australia
Burnett House and Myilly Point Heritage Precinct, Darwin 00972
City of Melbourne Collection, Melbourne 01225
Earlystreet, Norman Park 01323
Elizabeth Farm, Rosehill 01424
Miniature English Village and Brass Rubbing Centre, Flaxton 01027
Palma Rosa Museum, Hamilton, Brisbane 01086
Powder Magazine, Beechworth 00785
Quilpie Museum, Quilpie 01404
Rose Seidler House, Wahroonga 01572

Austria
Architekturzentrum Wien, Wien 02833
Ausstellungszentrum Heft, Hüttenberg 02049
Ausstellungszentrum Heiligenkreuzer Hof, Wien 02839
Ernst Fuchs-Privatmuseum, Wien 02878
Freilichtmuseum Ensemble Gerersdorf, Gerersdorf 01875
Kunstsammlung des Benediktinerstifts Seitenstetten, Seitenstetten 02658
Lehár-Schlößl, Wien 02923
Minimundus, Klagenfurt 02129
Östereichisches Brückenbaumuseum, Edelsbach bei Feldbach 01786
Salvatorianerkloster, Gurk 01974
Studiensammlung historischer Ziegel, Irdning 02084

Bangladesh
Varendra Research Museum, Rajshahi 03099

Belgium
Fondation pour l'Architecture, Bruxelles 03284
Kasteel van Gaasbeek, Gaasbeek 03424
Miniatuurstad, Antwerpen 03148
Musée d'Architecture - La Loge, Bruxelles 03298

Brazil
Fundaçao Oscar Niemeyer, Rio de Janeiro 04327
Museu da Casa Brasileira, São Paulo 04502
Museu da Limpeza Urbana - Casa de Banhos de Dom João VI, Rio de Janeiro 04349

Brunei
Muzium Teknologi Melayu, Bandar Seri Begawan 04599

Bulgaria
Architekturno-muzeen Rezervat Arbanassi, Veliko Tărnovo 04911
Architekturno-muzeen Rezervat Carevec, Veliko Tărnovo 04912
Architekturno-parkov Kompleks Dvorceva, Balčik 04609
Muzej Kolju Fičeto, Drjanovo 04661
Nacionalen Muzej na Bălgarskata Architektura, Veliko Tărnovo 04918
Okrăžen Istoričeski Muzej, Veliko Tărnovo 04920

Canada
Bellevue House, Kingston 05673
Brubacher House Museum, Waterloo 06750
Canadian Centre for Architecture, Montréal 05894
Jost House Museum, Sydney 06527
Westfield Heritage Village, Rockton 06281

China, People's Republic
Ancient Architecture Museum, Beijing 06940
Sam Tung Uk Museum, Hong Kong 07111
Sheung Yiu Folk Museum, Hong Kong 07112

Colombia
Museo de Arquitectura Leopoldo Rother, Bogotá 07395

Croatia
Archaeological Museum, Zadar 07804

Cuba
Casa de los Arabes, La Habana 07921
Museo Romántico, Trinidad 08163

Czech Republic
Expozice Josef Hoffmann, Brtnice 08281
Krajská Galerie Výtvarného Umeni ve Zlíně, Zlín 08750
Muzeum Lidových Staveb, Kouřim 08425
Národopisné Muzeum Třebíz, Třebíz 08688
Obec Architektů, Brno 08274
Vila Tugendhat, Brno 08279

Denmark
Den Gamle By, Århus 08770

Egypt
Coptic Museum, Cairo 09258

Estonia
Eesti Arhitektuurimuuseum, Tallinn 09357

Finland
Alvar Aalto Museum, Jyväskylä 09593
Hvitträsk, Kirkkonummi 09673
Sederholmin Talo, Helsinki 09526
Suomen Rakennustaiteen Museo, Helsinki 09533

France
Château d'Azay-le-Ferron, Azay-le-Ferron 10549
Ecomusée des Monts d'Arrée, Saint-Rivoal 14459
Ecomusée du Pays de Rennes, Rennes (Ille-et-Vilaine) 13939
Fondation Le Corbusier, Paris 13504
Institut Français d'Architecture, Paris 13516
Musée Biochet-Brechot, Caudebec-en-Caux 11087
Musée des Années 30, Boulogne-Billancourt 10837
Musée Le Corbusier, Pessac 13717

Germany
Alt-Rothenburger Handwerkerhaus, Rothenburg ob der Tauber 19676
Architekturmuseum der Technischen Universität München, München 18828
Architekturmuseum Schwaben, Augsburg 15549
Bauhaus-Archiv, Berlin 15916
Befreiungshalle Kelheim, Kelheim 18050
Betonzeitschiene, Dresden 16676
Deutsches Architektur Museum, Frankfurt am Main 17035
Fachwerkbaumuseum im Ständerbau, Quedlinburg 19458
Fagus-Gropius-Ausstellung, Alfeld, Leine 15425
Felsengarten Sanspareil mit Morgenländischem Bau, Wonsees 20675
Forum für Angewandte Kunst im Bayerischen Kunstgewerbeverein e.V., Nürnberg 19136
Henry van de Velde Museum, Chemnitz 16464
Kathree Häusle, Dettenhausen 16592
KdF-Museum, Ostseebad Binz 19309
Kunstsammlung Lorenzkapelle Rottweil, Rottweil 19696
Miniaturpark Klein-Erzgebirge, Oederan 19223
Museum Altes Land, Jork 17962
Museum der Stadt Waiblingen, Waiblingen 20350
Museumsdorf Bayerischer Wald, Tittling 20181
Museumskirche Sankt Katharinen, Lübeck 18541
Pelzerhaus, Emden 16851
Prunkräume in der Residenz, Kempten 18064
Regionalmuseum Wolfhagen, Wolfhagen 20655
Schloß Brake - Das Weserrenaissance-Museum, Lemgo 18431
Städtisches Museum/ Daniel-Pöppelmann-Haus, Herford 17720
Stiftung Bauhaus Dessau, Dessau 16584
Vitra Design Museum, Weil am Rhein 20438
Walpurgishalle Thale, Thale 20167
Wenzel-Hablik-Museum, Itzehoe 17935

Greece
Ethnological Museum of Pyrsogianni Stonemasons, Konitsa 21027

Hungary
Ernst Múzeum, Budapest 21336
Magyar Építészeti Múzeum, Budapest 21356

Iceland
Minjasafn Austurlands, Egilsstadir 21629

Ireland
Castletown, Celbridge 22391

Israel
Islamic Museum, Jerusalem 22641

Italy
Museo Civico, Busseto 23235
Museo della Linea Gotica, Montefiore Conca 24521
Museo di Architettura, Ferrara 23792
Museo di Architettura Militare, Bologna 23125
Museo di Palazzo Strozzi, Firenze 23867
Museo In Situ, Sulmona 25650
Museo Storico di Architettura Militare, Roma 25260
Oskar Schlemmer Theatre Estate and Collection, Oggebbio 24673
Palazzo Reale-Reggia di Caserta, Caserta 23375

Japan
Edo-Tokyo Tatemono-En, Koganei 26362
Hakubutsukan Meiji-Mura, Inuyama 26249
Sankei-en Garden, Yokohama 27017
Yagai Hakubutsukan, Gashozukuri Minkaen, Shirakawa 26763

Kyrgyzstan
Muzej Architektury i Archeologii Vez Burana, Čujsk 27310

Mexico
Museo Municipal Los Guachimontones y Museo de Arquitectura Prehispánica, Teuchitlán 28506
Museo Nacional de Arquitectura, México 28184

Moldova
Ščusev Museum, Chişinău 28662

Netherlands
ABC Architectuurcentrum Haarlem, Haarlem 29321
ARCAM Galerie, Amsterdam 28839
Architektuur Centrum Amsterdam, Amsterdam 28840
Madurodam, Den Haag 29104
Miniatuur Walcheren, Middelburg 29592
Nederlands Architektuurinstituut, Rotterdam 29767
Nederlands Baksteen en Dakpanmuseum de Panoven, Zevenaar 30056
Rietveld Schröderhuis, Utrecht 29910
Zuiderkerk, Amsterdam 28918

New Zealand
City Gallery Wellington, Wellington 30292
Rewa's Village, Kerikeri 30194

Nigeria
Jos National Museum and Museum of Traditional Nigerian Architecture, Jos 30347

Norway
Andøymuseet, Risøyhamn 30793
Arkitekturmuseet, Oslo 30726
Emanuel Vigeland Museum, Oslo 30730
Kvam Bygdemuseum, Norheimsund 30712
Midttunet, Skei i Jølster 30844
Riksantikvaren, Oslo 30761
Stiftsgården, Trondheim 30942
Tuddal Bygdetun, Tuddal 30949
Vennesla Bygdemuseum, Vennesla 30986

Pakistan
Shakir Ali Museum, Lahore 31043

Peru
Museo de Miniaturas, Huaraz 31175
Museo de Suelos, Iquitos 31185

Poland
Muzeum Architektury, Wrocław 32175
Muzeum Budownictwa Ludowego - Park Etnograficzny w Olsztynku, Olsztynek 31853
Muzeum Wsi Lubelskiej, Lublin 31795
Muzeum Wsi Opolskiej, Opole 31860

Russia
Aleksandrovskaja Sloboda - Gosudarstvennyj Istoriko-architekturnyj i Chudožestvennyj Muzej-zapovednik, Aleksandrov 32633
Architekturno-chudožestvennyj Ansambl byvšego Spaso-Jakovleskogo Monastyrja, Rostov (Jaroslavskaja obl.) 33354
Architekturno-ėtnografičeskij Muzej Derevjannogo Zodčestva Chochlovka, Perm 33300
Astrachanskij Kreml, Astrachan 32661
Bolšoj Dvorec, Lomonosov 32986
Elabužskij Gosudarstvennyj Istoriko-architekturnyj i Chudožestvennnyj Muzej-zapovednik, Elabuga 32785
Gosudarstvennyj Chudožestvenno-architekturnyj Dvorcovo-parkovyj Muzej-zapovednik Oranienbaum, Lomonosov 32988
Gosudarstvennyj Chudožestvennyj Istoriko-architekturnyj i prirodno-landšaftnyj Muzej-zapovednik Kolomenskoe, Moskva 33052
Gosudarstvennyj Istoriko-architekturnyj i Etnografičeskij Muzej-zapovednik Kiži, Kiži 32931
Gosudarstvennyj Istoriko-architekturnyj i Etnografičeskij Muzej-zapovednik Kiži, Petrozavodsk 33315
Gosudarstvennyj Istoriko-architekturnyj i Prirodno-landšaftnyj Muzej Zapovednik Izborsk, Izborsk 32834
Gosudarstvennyj Istoriko-Architekturnyj i Prirodnyj Muzej-Zapovednik Monrepo, Vyborg 33741
Gosudarstvennyj Istoriko-chudožestvennyj Dvorcovo-parkovyj Muzej-zapovednik Gatčina, Gatčina 32802
Gosudarstvennyj Istoriko-ėtnografičeskij i Architekturnyj Muzej-zapovednik Staraja Sarepta, Volgograd 33714
Gosudarstvennyj Istoriko-kulturnyj Muzej-zapovednik "Moskovskij Kreml", Moskva 33056
Gosudarstvennyj Istoriko-memorialnyj Zapovednik Rodina V.I. Lenina, Uljanovsk 33656
Gosudarstvennyj Muzej Zapovednik Petergof, Sankt-Peterburg 33406
Gosudarstvennyj Naučno-issledovatelskij Muzej Architektury im. A.V. Ščuseva, Moskva 33068
Gosudarstvennyj Vladimiro-Suzdalskij Istoriko-architekturnyj i Chudožestvennyj Muzej-zapovednik, Vladimir 33692
Irkutskij Architekturno-ėtnografičeskij Muzej Talcy, Irkutsk 32812
Karačaevo-Čerkesskij Istoriko-kul'turnyj i Prirodnyj Muzej-Zapovednik, Čerkessk 32736
Kargopolskij Gosudarstvennyj Istoriko-Architekturnyj i Chudožestvennyj Muzej, Kargopol 32884
Kirillo-Belozerskij Istoriko-Architekturnyj i Chudožestvennyj Muzej-Zapovednik, Kirillov 32915
Kostromskoj Gosudarstvennyj Istoriko-architekturnyj Muzej-zapovednik, Kostroma 32942
Memorial'nyj Muzej N.I. Beloborodova, Tula 33625
Muzej Architektury Byta Narodov Nižegorodskogo Povolžja, Nižnij Novgorod 33208
Muzej Architektury i Stroitelstva, Samara 33373
Muzej Derevjannogo Zodčestva Malye Karely, Archangelsk 32653
Muzej Goroda Jurjevca, Jurjevec 32865
Muzej Gradostroitelstva i Byta Taganroga, Taganrog 33583
Muzej Istorii Architektury i Architekturnogo Obrazovanija Sibiri, Novosibirsk 33241
Muzej Istorii Doma XIX-XX vekov, Tjumen 33605
Muzej Narodnogo Derevjannogo Zodčestva Vitoslavlicy, Velikij Novgorod 33678
Muzej Remesla, Architektury i Byta, Kaluga 32881
Muzej Semji Benua, Sankt-Peterburg 33464
Muzej Tul'skij Kreml', Tula 33629
Muzej-usadba Ostafjevo "Russkij Parnas", Ostafjevo 33274
Muzej-zapovednik Dmitrovskij Kreml, Dmitrov 32758
Muzej-zapovednik Kazanskij Kreml, Kazan 32906
Muzejno-vystavočnyj Kompleks Volokolamskij Kreml, Volokolamsk 33726
Nižegorodskij Gosudarstvennyj Istoriko-architekturnyj Muzej-zapovednik, Nižnij Novgorod 33223
Novgorodskij Gosudarstvennyj Muzej-zapovednik, Velikij Novgorod 33680
Plesskij Gosudarstvennyj Istoriko-Architekturnyj i Chudožestvennyj Muzej-Zapovednik, Ples 33325
Rjazanskij Gosudarstvennyj Istoriko-architekturnyj Muzej-zapovednik, Rjazan 33351
Šlisselburgskaja Krepost Orešek, Šlisselburg 33526
Soloveckij Gosudarstvennyj Istoriko-Architekturnyj i Prirodnyj Muzej-Zapovednik, Soloveckij 33546
Staročerkasskij Istoriko-architekturnyj Muzej-zapovednik, Staročerkassk 33556
Staroladožskij Istoriko-Architekturnyj i Archeologičeskij Muzej-Zapovednik, Staraja Ladoga 33553
Svijažskij Architekturno-chudožestvennyj Muzej, Svijažsk 33570
Svjatogorskij Monastyr, Puškinskie Gory 33345
Taganrogskij Gosudarstvennyj Literaturnyj i Istoriko-architekturnyj Muzej-zapovednik, Taganrog 33586
Velikoustjugskij Gosudarstvennyj Istoriko-Architekturnyj i Chudožestvennyj Muzej-Zapovednik, Velikij Ustjug 33681
Vologodskij Gosudarstvennyj Istoriko-Architekturnyj i Chudožestvennyj Muzej-Zapovednik, Vologda 33724

Spain
Casa-Museu Gaudí, Barcelona 34532
Conjunt Monumental de la Esglésias de Sant Pere, Terrassa 35526
Monasterio de Santa Clara de Tordesillas, Tordesillas 35552
Museo de la Colegiata de Santa Juliana y Claustro, Santillana del Mar 35451
Museo Nacional de Arquitectura, Madrid 35043
Museu d'Arquitectura de la Real Càtedra Gaudí, Barcelona 34551
Real Cartuja de Miraflores, Burgos 34636
Real Monasterio de San Juan de la Peña, San Juan de la Peña 35378

Sweden
Arkitekturmuseet, Stockholm 36231
Friluftmuseet Hallandsgården, Halmstad 35940
Friluftmuseet Skansen, Stockholm 36242
Gunnebo Slott och Trädgårdar, Mölndal 36096
Hembygdsgården Rots Skans, Älvdalen 35784

Switzerland
Architektur Forum Zürich, Zürich 37370
Architekturgalerie Luzern, Ausstellungsraum Partikel, Luzern 36906
Architekturmuseum, Basel 36496
Baugeschichtliches Archiv der Stadt Zürich, Zürich 37371
Châlet de l'Etambeau, Château-d'Oex 36625
Grubenmann-Sammlung, Teufen 37236
Ortsmuseum Eglisau, Eglisau 36672

Thailand
Gallery of the Faculty of Architecture, Bangkok 37484
Kamthieng House, Bangkok 37487

Turkey
Ahlat Açık Hava Müzesi, Ahlat 37604

United Kingdom
Ancient High House, Stafford 40569
Blackwell - The Arts and Crafts House, Bowness-on-Windermere 38290
Bramall Hall, Bramhall 38309
Brooking Collection, Dartford 38699
Building of Bath Museum, Bath 38113
Carew Manor and Dovecote, Beddington 38144
Design Museum, London 39623
Farleigh Hungerford Castle, Farleigh Hungerford 38978
Glasgow School of Art - Mackintosh Collection, Glasgow 39048
Guildhall, Leicester 39461
Hill House, Helensburgh 39208
House of Dun, Montrose 39981
Hughenden Manor, High Wycombe 39240
Kufa Gallery, London 39683
Loseley House, Guildford 39140
Mellerstain House, Gordon 39096
Museum of Domestic Design and Architecture MODA, Barnet 38088
Newark Town Treasures and Art Gallery, Newark-on-Trent 40023
Old Merchant's House and Row 111 Houses, Great Yarmouth 39126
Osterley Park House, Isleworth 39320
Pitzhanger Manor-House and Gallery, London 39745
Royal Incorporation of Architects in Scotland Gallery, Edinburgh 38909
Sainsbury Centre for Visual Arts, Norwich 40100
Scotland Street School Museum, Glasgow 39066
Sir John Soane's Museum, London 39777

U.S.A.
A.D. German Warehouse, Richland Center 46856
Art and Architecture Exhibition Space, San Francisco 47305
Bellamy Mansion Museum of History and Design Arts, Wilmington 48657
Bronck Museum, Coxsackie 42685
Chicago Architecture Foundation, Chicago 42314
Colonel Ashley House, Ashley Falls 41301
The Dana-Thomas House, Springfield 47736
Department of the Treasury Museum, Washington 48346
Edison and Ford Winter Estates, Fort Myers 43434
Ewing Gallery of Art and Architecture, Knoxville 44518
Fairbanks House, Dedham 42841
Frank Lloyd Wright's Pope-Leighey House, Mount Vernon 45545
Frederick Law Olmsted Historic Site, Brookline 41935
The Gardner Museum of Architecture and Design, Quincy 46758
Glessner House Museum, Chicago 42331
Grant-Humphreys Mansion, Denver 42890
Gropius House, Lincoln 44779
Hermann-Grima House, New Orleans 45726
Historic Lyme Village, Bellevue 41595
The House of the Seven Gables, Salem 47195
Jean Paul Slusser Gallery, Ann Arbor 41217
Koreshan Historic Site, Estero 43215
Lace House Museum, Black Hawk 41723
MAK Center for Art and Architecture, Los Angeles 44926
MAK Center for Art and Architecture, West Hollywood 48531
Museum of American Architecture and Decorative Arts, Houston 44128
National Building Museum, Washington 48372
The Octagon, Washington 48387
Plymouth Antiquarian Society Museum, Plymouth 46563
Price Tower Arts Center, Bartlesville 41515
Pullman Museum, Chicago 42359
Reshaw Exhibit, Evansville 43247
Ruthmere House Museum, Elkhart 43142
Schifferstadt Architectural Museum, Frederick 43530
Sed Gallery, Athens 41321
Skyscraper Museum, New York 45870
Spencer-Peirce-Little Farm, Newbury 45907
Spring Mill State Park Pioneer Village and Grissom Memorial, Mitchell 45411
The Stone House Museum, Belchertown 41585
Strater Hotel, Durango 43015
Van Cortlandt House Museum, Bronx 41926
William Whitley House, Stanford 47773
Wilton House Museum, Richmond 46892
The Wolfsonian, Miami Beach 45300

Venezuela
Museo de Arquitectura, Caracas 48910

Vietnam
National Museum of Cham Sculpture, Da Nang 48969

Arms and Armour

Argentina
Museo de Armas de la Nación, Buenos Aires 00166
Museo de Instituto Magnasco, Gualeguaychú 00361
Museo de la Policía del Chaco, Resistencia 00507
Museo General Lavalle, General Pinto 00356
Museo Tradicionalista El Rancho, Chacabuco 00270

Australia
Firearms Technology Museum, Orange 01346

Austria
Büchsenmacher- und Jagdmuseum, Ferlach 01836
Hexenmuseum, Riegersburg, Steiermark 02515
Hofjagd- und Rüstkammer des Kunsthistorischen Museums, Wien 02897
Landeszeughaus, Graz 01923
Museum der Stadt Steyr, Steyr 02686
Schützenscheibenmuseum, Scheibbs 02630
Waffensammlung Willibald Folger, Bruck an der Mur 01753

Belgium
Moervarststede, Wachtebeke 03822
Musée d'Armes de Liège, Liège 03574
Musée d'Armes et d'Histoire Militaire, Tournai 03792
Musée de la Compagnie Royale des Anciens Arquebusiers de Visé, Visé 03818
Musée de la Porte de Hal, Bruxelles 03306
Musée du Fort de Huy, Huy 03512
Musée Français - 1e Armée Française Mai 1940, Cortil-Noirmont 03362
Museum van de Kruisbooggilde Sint-Joris, Brugge 03261

Brazil
Casa de Osório, Rio de Janeiro 04318
Museu Aeroespacial, Rio de Janeiro 04329
Museu de Armas Ferreira da Cunha, Petrópolis 04262
Museu do Instituto Histórico, Carpina 04042
Museu Histórico de Sergipe, São Cristóvão 04460
Museu Histórico do Exército e Forte de Copacabana, Rio de Janeiro 04383
Museu José Bonifácio, São Paulo 04539
Museu Navio Comandante Bauru, Rio de Janeiro 04391
Museu Particular de Armas de Arlindo Pedro Zatti, Porto Alegre 04287

Brunei
Royal Brunei Armed Forces Museum, Bandar Seri Begawan 04601

Canada
Army Museum, Halifax 05546
Evergreen Firearms Museum, Belmont 05074
Lieutenant General Ashton Armoury Museum, Victoria 06723
Murney Tower Museum, Kingston 05684
Royal Military College of Canada Museum, Kingston 05687
Royal Winnipeg Rifles Museum, Winnipeg 06842

China, People's Republic
Chinese Museum of Military Weaponary, Tongzhou 07273

Croatia
Etnografski Muzej Split, Split 07780

Cuba
Casa de los Arabes, La Habana 07921
Complejo Museos Históricos Militares, La Habana 07925
Museo Armería 9 de Abril, La Habana 07936
Museo de la Revolución, La Habana 07962

Czech Republic
Východočeské Muzeum, Pardubice 08534

Denmark
Dragon- og Frihedsmuseet, Holstebro 08887
Hjemmevaernsmuseet, Holstebro 08888
Krudttaarnsmuseet, Frederikshavn 08831

Dominican Republic
Museo de las Casas Reales, Santo Domingo 09124

Egypt
Military Museum, Cairo 09270

Ethiopia
War Museum, Addis Ababa 09401

Finland
Ilmatorjuntamuseo, Tuusula 10144

France
Maison de la Manufacture d'Armes Blanches, Klingenthal 12115
Musée d'Armes Anciennes, La Cluse-et-Mijoux 12157
Musée de la Guerre au Moyen Age, Castelnaud-la-Chapelle 11076
Musée du Valois et de l'Archerie, Crépy-en-Valois 11456
Musée International des Hussards, Tarbes 14868

Germany
Bartholomäus-Schmucker-Heimatmuseum, Ruhpolding 19714
Bayerisches Armeemuseum, Ingolstadt 17905
Burg Meersburg, Meersburg 18673
Burg Neuhaus, Wolfsburg 20658
Burg Stolpen, Stolpen 20069
Burgmuseum, Ortenberg, Hessen 19269
Fürstlich Hohenzollernsche Sammlungen, Sigmaringen 19956
Historisches Waffenmuseum im Zeughaus, Überlingen 20243
Museum im Zwinger, Goslar 17354
Rüstkammer, Dresden 16705
Schloßmuseum Mespelbrunn, Mespelbrunn 18717
Schützenmuseum der Königlich privilegierten Feuerschützengesellschaft Weilheim, Weilheim, Oberbayern 20449
Schützenscheibensammlung, Mainbernheim 18593
Trillarium, Cleebronn 16477
Waffenmuseum, Oberndorf am Neckar 19186
Waffenmuseum Suhl, Suhl 20122

India
Fort Saint George Museum, Chennai 21743
Maharaja Banaras Vidya Mandir Museum, Varanasi 22058
Victoria Memorial Hall, Kolkata 21914

Ireland
Heraldic Museum, Dublin 22430

Italy
Armeria Reale, Torino 25730
Civico Museo di Guerra per la Pace Diego de Henriquez, Trieste 25814
Collezioni d'Armi e Ceramiche della Rocca Sforzesca, Imola 24083
Museo Civico, Pizzighettone 24968
Museo Civico delle Armi L. Marzoli, Brescia 23201
Museo dei Trombini di Lessinia, San Bortolo 25341
Museo delle Armi Antiche, Martinsicuro 24308
Museo delle Armi Antiche, Offagna 24667
Museo di San Michele, Sagrado 25309
Museo Fioroni, Legnago 24173
Museo Nazionale del Palazzo di Venezia, Roma 25233
Museo Nazionale dell'Arma della Cavalleria, Pinerolo 24931
Museo Nazionale di Castel Sant'Angelo, Roma 25236
Museo Stibbert, Firenze 23881
Museo Storico dela Caccia e del Territorio, Cerreto Guidi 23484
Museo Storico Italiano della Guerra, Rovereto 25294
Palazzo Ducale, Venezia 25946

Japan
Hirado Castle Donjon, Hirado 26198
Museum of Antique Armour Helmets and Swords, Kyoto 26435
Nishimura Museum, Iwakuni 26273
Oyamazumi-jinja Kokuhokan, Omishima 26638
Token Hakubutsukan, Tokyo 26935

Malta
Palace Armoury, Valletta 27704

Mexico
Museo de Historia de Lampazos de Naranjo y las Armas Nacionales, Lampazos de Naranjo 28049

Morocco
Musée d'Armes du Bordj Nord, Fèz 28694

Nepal
National Museum of Nepal, Kathmandu 28788

Netherlands
Bussemakerhuis, Borne 29006

Nigeria
Kanta Museum Argungu, Argungu 30331

Norway
Galtebosamlingen, Spydeberg 30872
Kongsberg Våpenfabrikks Museum, Kongsberg 30603

Peru
Museo de Oro del Perú y Armas del Mundo, Lima 31213

Poland
Muzeum Militariów Arsenal Miejski, Wrocław 32179
Muzeum Okręgowe, Zamość 32212
Muzeum Pierwszych Piastów na Lednicy, Lednogóra 31752
Muzeum Regionalne, Pyzdry 31935
Muzeum Wojska Polskiego, Warszawa 32133
Muzeum Zbrojownia, Liw 31764

Portugal
Museu Militar de Lisboa, Lisboa 32305

Russia
Centralnyj Voenno-morskoj Muzej, Sankt-Peterburg 33388
Ingušskij Gosudarstvennyj Muzej Kraevedenija im. T.Ch. Malsagova, Nazran 33203
Memorialnyj Kompleks 'Vorošilovskaja Batareja', Vladivostok 33700
Muzej Archeologii i Etnografii, Vladivostok 33703
Novorossijskij Gosudarstvennyj Istoričeskij Muzej Zapovednik, Novorossijsk 33238
Tul'skij Gosudarstvennyj Muzej Oružija, Tula 33631
Vladivostokskaja Krepost' - Voenno istoričeskij Fortifikacionnyj Muzej, Vladivostok 33711
Voenno-istoričeskij Muzej Tichookeanskogo Flota, Vladivostok 33712

San Marino
Museo delle Armi Antiche, San Marino 33761
Museo delle Armi Moderne, San Marino 33762

Serbia-Montenegro
Muzej Stara Livnica, Kragujevac 33851
Vojni Muzej Beograd, Beograd 33819

Slovakia
Expozícia Zbraní a Stredovekého Mestského Opevnenia, Bratislava 33961

Slovenia
Muzej Novejše Zgodovine Slovenije, Ljubljana 34113

South Africa
Fort Beaufort Historical Museum, Fort Beaufort 34241
Messina Museum, Messina 34307
Museum of Coast and Anti-Aircraft Artillery, Green Point 34256
R.E. Stevenson Museum, Colenso 34217

Spain
Alcázar de Segovia, Segovia 35460
Museo de Almería, Almería 34454
Museo de Armería de Alava, Vitoria-Gasteiz 35697
Museo de la Academia de Infantería, Toledo 35539
Museo Específico de la Academia de Caballería, Valladolid 35625
Museo José Serra Farré, La Riba 35316
Museo Naval de Cartagena, Cartagena 34686
Museu Militar, Barcelona 34584

Sweden
Livrustkammaren, Stockholm 36256
Vapentekniska Museet, Eskilstuna 35873

Switzerland
Kantonales Museum Altes Zeughaus, Solothurn 37183
Musée d'Histoire, La Neuveville 36989
Musée Militaire Vaudois, Morges 36951
Ortsmuseum Sust, Horgen 36809
Schloßmuseum Thun, Thun 37241

United Kingdom
Border History Museum, Hexham 39236
Cobbaton Combat Collection, Chittlehampton 38572
Dean Castle, Kilmarnock 39361
Delgatie Castle, Turriff 40733
Eastnor Castle, Ledbury 39439
Fawley Court Historic House and Museum, Henley-on-Thames 39219
Fire Power, the Royal Artillery Museum, London 39635
Fleet Air Arm Museum - Concorde, Yeovilton 40957
Fort Brockhurst, Gosport 39098
Havant Museum, Havant 39189
Infantry and Small Arms School Corps Weapons Collection, Warminster 40786
Preston Hall Museum, Stockton-on-Tees 40600
Ripley Castle, Ripley, North Yorkshire 40326
Royal Armouries, London 39756
Royal Armouries at Fort Nelson, Fareham 38975
Royal Armouries Museum, Leeds 39450
Royal Gloucestershire, Berkshire and Wiltshire Regiment Museum, Salisbury 40436
Royal Marines Museum, Portsmouth 40257
Scottish Infantry Divisional Museum, Penicuik 40174
Warwickshire Yeomanry Museum, Warwick 40797
West Gate Towers, Canterbury 38476

U.S.A.
Dane G. Hansen Memorial Museum, Logan 44844
Dixie Gun Works' Old Car Museum, Union City 48148
General Douglas L. McBride Museum, Roswell 47014
Higgins Armory Museum, Worcester 48753
National Firearms Museum, Fairfax 43261
Remington Firearms Museum and Country Store, Ilion 44195
Rogers Daisy Airgun Museum, Rogers 46984
Saunders Memorial Museum, Berryville 41656
UDT-SEAL Museum, Fort Pierce 43442

Vatican City
Museo Storico Vaticano, Città del Vaticano 48884

Yemen
Military Museum, Aden 49006

Zimbabwe
Zimbabwe Military Museum, Gweru 49029

Art

Albania
Fine Arts Gallery, Korçë 00024
Fine Arts Gallery, Tiranë 00033

Algeria
Musée Archéologique de Djemila, Sétif 00070
Musée de Constantine, Constantine 00057
Musée de Skikda, Skikda 00074
Musée de Timgad, Timgad 00078
Musée National des Beaux-Arts d'Alger, Alger 00046

American Samoa
Jean P. Haydon Museum, Pago Pago 00082

Argentina
Museo de Arte Eduardo A. Minnicelli, Río Gallegos 00513
Museo de Arte Gauchesco La Recova, San Antonio de Areco 00547
Museo de Bellas Artes de la Boca, Buenos Aires 00173
Museo de Bellas Artes Domingo Faustino Sarmiento, Mercedes 00442
Museo de Bellas Artes Dr. Juan Ramón Vidal, Corrientes 00320
Museo de Calcos y Esculturas Compardas, Buenos Aires 00174
Museo de Historia Reginal San Lorenzo y Galería del Libertador General San Martín, San Lorenzo 00575
Museo Fundación Naum Komp, Buenos Aires 00207
Museo Histórico de Arte, Morón 00456
Museo Histórico Municipal Brigadier General Juan Martín de Pueyrredón, San Isidro 00565
Museo Judío de Buenos Aires Dr. Salvador Kibrick, Buenos Aires 00221
Museo Municipal de Bellas Artes, Bahía Blanca 00128
Museo Municipal de Bellas Artes, La Calera 00375
Museo Municipal de Bellas Artes, La Paz 00383
Museo Municipal de Bellas Artes, Tandil 00630
Museo Municipal de Bellas Artes Prof. Amelio Ronco Ceruti, Metán 00446
Museo Pio Collivadino, Banfield 00132
Museo Provincial de Bellas Artes, Salta 00543
Museo Provincial de Bellas Artes Emiliano Guiñazu - Casa de Fader, Luján de Cuyo 00419
Museo Provincial de Bellas Artes Ramón Gómez Cornet, Santiago del Estero 00619
Museo Provincial de Bellas Artes Timoteo Eduardo Navarro, San Miguel de Tucumán 00587
Museo Regional y de Arte Marino, Puerto San Julián 00492
Museo Universitario de Artes, Mendoza 00441
Museo y Archivo Dardo Rocha, La Plata 00394
Pinacoteca de la Escuela Provincial de Bellas Artes Dr. Figueroa Alcorta, Córdoba 00314

Armenia
Yerevan Children's Picture Gallery, Erevan 00694

Australia
Adelaide Central Gallery, Norwood 01334
Albury Regional Art Gallery, Albury 00728
Art and Local History Collections, Mackay 01192
Art Gallery of South Australia, Adelaide 00704
Art Gallery of Western Australia, Perth 01363
Atwell House Gallery, Alfred Cove 00731
Ballarat Fine Art Gallery, Ballarat 00761
Benalla Regional Art Gallery, Benalla 00793
Bundaberg Arts Centre, Bundaberg 00860
City Art Gallery, Wagga Wagga 01569
Creswick Historical Museum, Creswick 00954
Cunningham Dax Collection of Psychiatric Art, Parkville, Victoria 01356
Drill Hall Gallery, Acton 00700
Eryldene Heritage House, Gordon 01065
Flinders University Art Museum, Adelaide 00707
Fremantle Arts Centre, Fremantle 01035
The George Adams Gallery, Melbourne 01228
George Paton Gallery, Victoria 01567
Glen Eira City Gallery, Caulfield 00903
Goethe-Institut Sydney, Woollahra 01616
Hamilton Art Gallery, Hamilton, Victoria 01088
Kingaroy Art Gallery, Kingaroy 01147
La Trobe University Art Museum, Melbourne 01235
Mildura Arts Centre, Mildura 01252
Museum of Fine Arts, Hobart 01102
Naracoorte Art Gallery, Naracoorte 01300
Narrogin Gallery, Narrogin 01307
National Gallery of Australia, Canberra 00886
Newcastle Region Art Gallery, Newcastle 01316
Plimsoll Gallery, Hobart 01103
Port Community Art Centre, Port Adelaide 01374
Queen Victoria Museum and Art Gallery, Launceston 01170
RMIT Gallery, Melbourne 01241
Salamanca Arts Centre, Hobart 01104
Spencer and Gillen Gallery, Alice Springs 00738
Stonington Stables Museum of Art, Malvern 01202
Toowoomba Regional Art Gallery, Toowoomba 01542
Uleybury School Museum, One Tree Hill 01343
Union Gallery, Adelaide 00715
University of Queensland Art Museum, Brisbane 00843
University of Sydney Art Collection, Sydney 01509
Vancouver Arts Centre, Albany 00725
Victorian College of the Arts Gallery, Southbank 01466
Walker Street Gallery, Dandenong 00968
Wangaratta Exhibitions Gallery, Wangaratta 01576
War Memorial Gallery of Fine Arts, Sydney 01511
Zone Gallery, Adelaide 00717

Austria
ABC-Galerie, Ansfelden 01675
Alpen-Adria-Galerie im Stadthaus, Klagenfurt 02121
Alte Galerie, Graz 01909
Ausstellungszentrum Heiligenkreuzer Hof, Wien 02839
BA-CA Kunstforum, Wien 02840
Barockmuseum, Reidling 02500
Basis Wien, Wien 02842
Basis Wien, Wien 02843
Dengel-Galerie, Reutte 02510
Figurencabinett Madamme Lucrezia, Rosegg 02524
Galerie der Stadt Schwaz, Schwaz 02647
Galerie der Stadt Vöcklabruck, Vöcklabruck 02766
Galerie im 44er Haus, Leonding 02214
Galerie im Taxispalais, Innsbruck 02065
Galerie Kulturzentrum Lerchhaus, Eibiswald 01797
Galerie Sala Terrena, Mödling 02309
Galerie Stephanie Hollenstein, Lustenau 02257
Galerie und Weinmuseum Schloß Gamlitz, Gamlitz 01867
Gemeindegalerie, Wiener Neudorf 03013
Grazer Stadtmuseum, Graz 01916
Haenel-Pancera-Familienmuseum, Bad Ischl 01705
Hangar-7, Salzburg 02540
Heidegalerie, Wels 02812
Kaiservilla, Bad Ischl 01706
Kammerhofgalerie der Stadt Gmunden, Gmunden 01895
Kubin-Haus, Wernstein am Inn 02825
Künstlerhaus Wien, Wien 02912
Kunsthalle Krems, Krems 02157
Kunsthalle Leoben, Leoben 02209
Kunsthalle Steyr, Steyr 02684
Kunsthaus Graz, Graz 01921
Kunsthaus Mürzzuschlag, Mürzzuschlag 02330
Kunsthistorisches Museum Wien, Wien 02918
Kunstraum Sankt Virgil, Salzburg 02542
Kunstsammlungen des Stiftes Kremsmünster, Kremsmünster 02161
Moderne Galerie im Weinstadtmuseum Krems, Krems 02158
Museen im Rathaus, Perchtoldsdorf 02401
Museum der Marktgemeinde Sankt Johann in Tirol, Sankt Johann in Tirol 02576
Museum der Stadt Bad Ischl, Bad Ischl 01708
Museum des Nötscher Kreises, Nötsch im Gailtal 02365
Museum im Schottenstift, Wien 02946
Neidhart Fresken, Wien 02952
Niederösterreichisches Landesmuseum, Sankt Pölten 02603
Österreichische Galerie Belvedere, Halbturn 01990
Prof. Eidenberger-Museum, Niederwaldkirchen 02363
Rathausgalerie, Sankt Veit an der Glan 02613
RLB-Kunstbrücke, Innsbruck 02078
Rupertinum, Salzburg 02549
Salzburger Museum Carolino Augusteum, Salzburg 02551
Sammlung der Universität für angewandte Kunst Wien mit Oskar Kokoschka Zentrum, Wien 02980
Sammlung Friedrichshof, Zurndorf 03056
Sammlungen Schloß Moosham, Mauterndorf 02287
Schloß Burgau, Burgau 01756
Schloß Eggenberg, Graz 01934
Schloß Farrach, Zeltweg 03053
Schubert Geburtshaus und Adalbert Stifter-Gedenkräume, Wien 02987
Stadtgalerie am Minoritenplatz, Wolfsberg, Kärnten 03043
Stadtgalerie im alten Herrenhaus, Ternitz 02723
Stadtmuseum Klosterneuburg, Klosterneuburg 02143
Städtische Galerie, Lienz 02221
Stiftssammlungen Wilten, Innsbruck 02080
Via Artis, Bad Aussee 01692
Werkhof Bistrica, Sankt Michael 02588
Wien Museum Hermesvilla mit Schauräumen der Modesammlung, Wien 03000

Azerbaijan
State Art Museum R. Mustafaev, Baku 03069

Bahamas
Angelo Roker's Art Centre and Museum, Nassau 03073

Bangladesh
Dhaka City Museum, Dhaka 03087

Barbados
Portobello Gallery, Saint James 03105

Belarus
Nacionalnyj Chudožestvennyj Muzej Respubliki Belarus, Minsk 03121
National Art Gallery, Minsk 03122

Belgium
Andre Garitte Foundation, Berchem 03210
Bijlokemuseum, Gent 03434
Bruggemuseum - Stadhuis, Brugge 03252
Centre Culturel des Roches, Rochefort 03701
Collection du Château d'Attre, Attre 03189
Design museum Gent, Gent 03435
Groeningemuseum, Brugge 03253
Huis Hellemans, Edegem 03401
Internationaal Exlibriscentrum, Sint-Niklaas 03740
Musée d'Art Differencie, Liège 03575
Musée des Francs et de la Famenne, Marche-en-Famenne 03609
Musée d'Iconographie Historique, Onoz 03664
Musée du Bois de Maredret-Galerie A la Fontaine, Maredret 03612
Musée du Sabot, Porcheresse 03689
Musée Gaspar, Arlon 03184
Musée Ribauri, Lasne-Chapelle-Saint-Lambert 03554
The Museum of Museums, Waregem 03826
Museum voor Schone Kunsten Gent, Gent 03448
Ric's Art Boat, Bruxelles 03342
Roger Raveelmuseum, Machelen 03604
Salons voor Schone Kunsten, Sint-Niklaas 03743
Stedelijk Museum Aalst, Aalst 03125
Stedelijk Museum Ieper, Ieper 03517
Stedelijke Academie voor Schone Kunsten, Roeselare 03706
Stedelijke Musea Kortrijk, Kortrijk 03543
Tentoonstellingzaal Hessenhuis, Antwerpen 03176
Het Van Abbemuseum, Bonheiden 03224
Vleeshuis, Antwerpen 03177

Bermuda
Bermuda National Gallery, Hamilton 03882
The Masterworks Foundation Collection, Hamilton 03884

Bolivia
Fundación de Fomento a las Artes, La Paz 03894
Galería de Arte Moderna, Sucre 03905
Museo Nacional de Arte, La Paz 03900

Bosnia and Herzegovina
Galerija Likovnih Umjetnosti Republike Srpske Banja Luka, Banja Luka 03909
Galerija Portreta Tuzla, Tuzla 03928
Umjetnička Galerija, Mostar 03918
Umjetnička Galerija Rizah Stetić, Brčko 03915

Brazil
Acervo Artístico Cultural dos Palácios do Governo, São Paulo 04481
Casa di Xilogravura, Campos de Jordão 04034
Ciências Educação e Artes Luiz de Queiráz, Piracibaba 04264
Coleção de Artes Visuais, São Paulo 04487
Fundação Casa de Jorge Amado, Salvador 04420
Fundação Clóuis Salgado - Palácio das Artes, Belo Horizonte 03979
Fundação Eva Klabin Rappaport, Rio de Janeiro 04325
Fundaçao Oscar Niemeyer, Rio de Janeiro 04327
Galeria de Arte do Instituto de Artes da Universidade Federal do Rio Grande do Sul, Porto Alegre 04273
Galeria de Arte Prof. Sylvio Vasconcellos, Belo Horizonte 03980
Galeria de Arte UNICAMP, Campinas 04022
Galeria Virtual da Casa das Rosas, São Paulo 04494
Museu Arquidiocesano de Mariana, Mariana 04196
Museu Carmen Miranda, Rio de Janeiro 04334
Museu da Arte Brasileira, Maceió 04179
Museu da Arte Pierre Chalita, Maceió 04180
Museu da Gravura Brasileira, Bagé 03963
Museu da Porcelana Senhor Adelino dos Santos Gouveia, Pedreira 04253
Museu de Arte, Belém 03973
Museu de Arte, Goiânia 04109
Museu de Arte, Joinville 04152
Museu de Arte, Londrina 04174
Museu de Arte Assis Chateaubriand, Campina Grande 04020
Museu de Arte Brasileira, São Paulo 04513
Museu de Arte Contemporânea de Pernambuco, Olinda 04231
Museu de Arte Contemporônea, Curitiba 04069
Museu de Arte da Pampulha, Belo Horizonte 03983
Museu de Arte da Universidade Fedral do Ceará, Fortaleza 04099
Museu de Arte de Santa Catarina, Florianópolis 04091
Museu de Arte do Paranà, Curitiba 04070
Museu de Arte do Rio Grande do Sul Aldo Malagoli, Porto Alegre 04278
Museu de Arte e Cultura Canjira, Itaobim 04134
Museu de Arte e História, Natal 04219
Museu de Arte e Histórico, Jaboticabal 04141

Museu de Arte Moderna, Resende 04308
Museu de Arte Moderna do Rio de Janeiro, Rio de Janeiro 04354
Museu de Arte Sacra, São Cristóvão 04459
Museu de Arte Sacra, São João Del Rei 04468
Museu de Arte Sacra, São Luís 04476
Museu de Arte Sacra, São Sebastião 04547
Museu de Arte Sacra, Taubaté 04558
Museu de Arte sacra de Angra dos Reis, Angra dos Reis 03945
Museu de Arte Sacra de Boa Morte, Goiás 04116
Museu de Arte Sacra de Iguape, Iguape 04126
Museu de Arte Sacra do Carmo / Paróquia do Pilar, Ouro Preto 04238
Museu de Arte Sacra do Estado de Alagoas, Marechal Deodoro 04195
Museu de Arte Sacra do Pará, Belém 03974
Museu de Artes Plásticas Quirino da Silva, Mococa 04204
Museu de Artes Sacras Iria Josepha da Silva, Mococa 04205
Museu de Artes Visuais, São Luís 04477
Museu de Artes Visuais Ruth Schneider, Passo Fundo 04246
Museu de Belas-Artes, Cataguases 04046
Museu de Ex-votos do Senhor do Bonfim, Salvador 04432
Museu de Images do Inconsciente, Rio de Janeiro 04360
Museu di Arte Contemporânea, Americana 03943
Museu Histórico Farroupilha, Piratini 04268
Museu Internacional de Arte Naïf do Brasil, Rio de Janeiro 04387
Museu Lasar Segall, São Paulo 04540
Museu Nacional de Belas Artes, Rio de Janeiro 04389
Museu Paranaense, Curitiba 04078
Museu Pinacoteca, Igarassu 04125
Museu Universitário de Arte, Uberlândia 04579
Pinacoteca Barão de Santo Angelo, Porto Alegre 04288
Pinacoteca Benedicto Calixto, Santos 04455
Pinacoteca Municipal Miguel Ângelo Pucci, Franca 04105
Sítio Roberto Burle Marx, Rio de Janeiro 04404

Brunei
Bangunan Alat Kebesaran Diraja, Bandar Seri Begawan 04595

Bulgaria
Chudožestvena Galerija, Balčik 04610
Chudožestvena Galerija, Blagoevgrad 04625
Chudožestvena Galerija, Chaskovo 04639
Chudožestvena Galerija, Drjanovo 04658
Chudožestvena Galerija, Gabrovo 04666
Chudožestvena Galerija, Gălăbovo 04671
Chudožestvena Galerija, Karlovo 04689
Chudožestvena Galerija, Kavarna 04694
Chudožestvena Galerija, Kazanlăk 04697
Chudožestvena Galerija, Levski 04724
Chudožestvena Galerija, Loveč 04727
Chudožestvena Galerija, Mezdra 04736
Chudožestvena Galerija, Michajlovgrad 04737
Chudožestvena Galerija, Provadia 04788
Chudožestvena Galerija, Radnevo 04792
Chudožestvena Galerija, Silistra 04813
Chudožestvena Galerija, Sozopol 04863
Chudožestvena Galerija, Svištov 04877
Chudožestvena Galerija Darenie Kollekcia Svetlin Russev, Pleven 04763
Chudožestvena Galerija Dobrič, Dobrič 04652
Chudožestvena Galerija Ilija Beškov, Pleven 04764
Chudožestvena Galerija Kiril Petrov, Montana 04740
Chudožestvena Galerija Nikola Marinov, Targovište 04882
Chudožestvena Galerija "Petar Persengiev", Novi Pazar 04745
Chudožestvena Galerija Stanislav Dospevski, Pazardžik 04753
Gradska Chudožestvena Galerija, Berkovica 04621
Gradska Chudožestvena Galerija, Plovdiv 04777
Gradska Chudožestvena Galerija Petko Čurčuliev, Dimitrovgrad 04650
Kăšta-muzej Ivan Lazarov, Sofia 04832
Kăšta-muzej s Dom-pametnik Jordan Jovkov, Dobrič 04656
Muzej na Chudožestvenata Akademija, Sofia 04840
Nacionalna Chudožestvena Galerija, Sofia 04856
Nacionalna Galerija za Čuždestranno Izkustvo, Sofia 04857
Okrăžna Chudožestvena Galerija Dimităr Dobrovič, Sliven 04825
Regionalen Istoričeski Muzej Varna, Varna 04907

Cameroon
Musée des Arts et des Traditions Bamboun, Foumban 04956

Canada
A Space, Toronto 06558
Academy of Spherical Arts, Toronto 06559
Ace Art, Winnipeg 06817
Agnes Etherington Art Centre, Kingston 05672
Agnes Jamieson Gallery, Minden 05856
A.K.A. Gallery, Saskatoon 06394
Alcan Aluminium Corporate Art Collection, Montréal 05886
The Alfoldy Gallery, Canyon 05195
Allen Sapp Gallery, North Battleford 06012
Amelia Douglas Gallery, New Westminster 05982
Annex Art Centre Gallery, Toronto 06560
Armstrong-Spallumcheen Museum and Art Gallery, Armstrong 05008
Art Cannon Gallery, Montréal 05887
Art Gallery, Etobicoke 05417
Art Gallery of Algoma, Sault Sainte Marie 06410
Art Gallery of Greater Victoria, Victoria 06712
Art Gallery of Hamilton, Hamilton 05567
Art Gallery of Mississauga, Mississauga 05867
Art Gallery of Northumberland, Cobourg 05262
Art Gallery of Nova Scotia, Halifax 05547
Art Gallery of Peel, Brampton 05112
Art Gallery of Southwestern Manitoba, Brandon 05116
Art Gallery of Swift Current National Exhibition Centre, Swift Current 06524
Art Gallery of the South Okanagan, Penticton 06109
Art Gallery of Windsor, Windsor, Ontario 06810
Atelier d'Estampe Imago, Moncton 05874
Atelier Ladywood Museum, Ladywood 05716
Beaverbrook Art Gallery, Fredericton 05457
Bernadette's Galleries, North Vancouver 06023
Bonnington Arts Centre, Nakusp 05956
Burnaby Art Gallery, Burnaby 05148
Cambridge Galleries, Cambridge 05185
Canadian Wildlife and Wilderness Art Museum, Ottawa 06077
Carleton University Art Gallery, Ottawa 06078
Centre Culturel de Verdun, Verdun 06704
Centre Culturel Franco-Manitobain, Winnipeg 06820
Centre d'Art, Baie-Saint-Paul 05035
Centre d'Art de Lévis, Lévis 05750
Centre d'Art de Saint-Georges, Saint-Georges, Quebec 06320
Centre d'Art du Mont-Royal, Montréal 05896
Centre d'Artistes Vaste et Vague, Carleton 05207
Centre des Arts de Shawinigan, Shawinigan 06429
Centre d'Exposition Art-Image, Gatineau 05481
Centre d'Exposition de Rouyon-Noranda, Rouyn-Noranda 06291
Centre d'Exposition de Saint-Hyacinthe, Saint-Hyacinthe 06321
Centre d'Exposition de Val d'Or, Val d'Or 06658
Centre d'Exposition Mont-Laurier, Mont-Laurier 05881
Centre d'Exposition Plein Sud, Longueuil 05775
Centre Missionnaire Sainte-Therèse, Montréal 05900
Centre National d'Exposition, Jonquière 05634
Cercle d'Art, Laval 05732
Chapel Gallery, Bracebridge 05107
Charles H. Scott Gallery, Vancouver 06672
Circle Craft Gallery, Vancouver 06673
Colville Lake Museum, Norman Wells 06010
Confederation Centre Art Gallery and Museum, Charlottetown 05225
Creative Spirit Art Centre, Toronto 06575
Dalhousie Art Gallery, Halifax 05550
Dawson Creek Art Gallery, Dawson Creek 05313
Dorval Art Gallery and Cultural Centre, Dorval 05337
Dr. V.L. Watson Allied Arts Centre, Dauphin 05307
Dunlop Art Gallery, Regina 06231
Durham Art Gallery, Durham 05357
Eastern Edge Art Gallery, Saint John's 06344
Edmonton Art Gallery, Edmonton 05373
Espace Virtuel, Chicoutimi 05246
Estevan National Exhibition Centre, Art Gallery and Museum, Estevan 05415
Exposure Gallery, Vancouver 06676
Ferry Building Gallery, West Vancouver 06773
Floating Gallery, Winnipeg 06823
Front Gallery, Edmonton 05377
Galarie du Centre, Saint-Lambert 06358
Galerie Colline, Edmundston 05395
Galerie d'Art de Matane, Matane 05821
Galerie d'Art du Parc, Trois-Rivières 06640
Galerie d'Art l'Union-Vie, Drummondville 05343
Galerie d'Art Stewart Hall, Pointe-Claire 06144
Galerie Dominion, Montréal 05904
Galerie Elizabeth LeFort, Cheticamp 05243
Galerie Georges-Goguen, Moncton 05876
Galerie l'Industrielle-Alliance, Montréal 05905
Galerie Montcalm, Gatineau 05482
Galerie Municipale au Palais Montcalm, Québec 06199
Galerie Port-Maurice, Saint-Léonard 06363
Galerie Sans Nom, Moncton 05877
Gallery 101.Galerie 101, Ottawa 06080
Gallery 44, Toronto 06578
Gallery Arcturus, Toronto 06579
Gallery Connexion, Fredericton 05460
Gallery Lambton, Sarnia 06391
Gallery on the Roof, Regina 06234
Gallery One One One, Winnipeg 06826
Gallery Stratford, Stratford 06499
Gibson Gallery, London 05766
Glenbow Museum, Calgary 05167
Glendon Gallery, North York 06032
Gordon Snelgrove Art Gallery, Saskatoon 06397
Grace Campbell Gallery, Prince Albert 06182
Grand Forks Art Gallery, Grand Forks 05514
Grunt Gallery, Vancouver 06678
Harbour Gallery, Mississauga 05871
Hart House, Toronto 06581
Heffel Gallery, Vancouver 06679
Homer Watson House and Gallery, Kitchener 05696
Hudson Bay Museum, Hudson Bay 05606
Humboldt and District Museum and Gallery, Humboldt 05608
Hunter West Gallery, Peterborough 06119
Huronia Museum, Midland 05846
Island Mountain Arts Public Gallery, Wells 06765
Joseph D. Carrier Art Gallery, Toronto 06586
Justina M. Barnicke Gallery, Hart House, Toronto 06587
Kenderdine Art Gallery, Saskatoon 06398
Kitchener-Waterloo Art Gallery, Kitchener 05698
Koffler Gallery, Toronto 06588
Langham Cultural Centre Galleries, Kaslo 05646
Latitude 53, Edmonton 05378
Leaf Rapids National Exhibition Centre, Leaf Rapids 05738
Leonard Bina Ellen Art Gallery, Montréal 05908
Lindsay Gallery, Lindsay 05755
Little Gallery, Prince Albert 06183
Lunenburg Art Gallery, Lunenburg 05789
Lynnwood Arts Centre, Simcoe 06457
Macdonald Stewart Art Centre, Guelph 05538
McIntosh Gallery, London 05771
MacLaren Art Centre, Barrie 05049
McMichael Canadian Art Collection, Kleinburg 05702
Maison Hamel-Bruneau, Sainte-Foy 06383
Maltwood Art Museum and Gallery, Victoria 06724
Maple Sugar Museum, Art Gallery and Pioneer Home, Sundridge 06517
Mendel Art Gallery, Saskatoon 06400
Moncur Gallery, Boissevain 05090
Morris and Helen Belkin Art Gallery, Vancouver 06682
Mount Royal College Gallery, Calgary 05172
Mount Saint Vincent University Art Gallery, Halifax 05557
Mountain View Gallery, Port Moody 06166
Musée-Atelier Calixa-Lavellée, Calixa-Lavallée 05182
Musée Beaulne, Coaticook 05260
Musée d'Art de Joliette, Joliette 05633
Musée d'Art de Mont-Saint-Hilaire, Mont-Saint-Hilaire 05882
Musée d'Art de Saint-Laurent, Saint-Laurent 06360
Musée des Beaux-Arts de Montréal, Montréal 05918
Musée des Beaux-Arts de Sherbrooke, Sherbrooke, Québec 06441
Musée Louis-Hemon, Peribonka 06113
Musée National des Beaux-Arts du Québec, Québec 06208
Musée Régional de la Côte-Nord, Sept-Iles 06422
Museum London, London 05772
Museum of Antiquities, Saskatoon 06401
Nanaimo Art Gallery and Exhibition Centre, Nanaimo 05960
National Gallery of Canada, Ottawa 06084
Nelson Museum, Nelson 05970
Niagara Falls Art Gallery - Kurlek Collection, Niagara Falls 05995
Northwestern National Exhibition Centre, Hazelton 05591
OCAD Gallery, Toronto 06599
Old School House Arts Centre, Qualicum Beach 06193
Open Space Gallery, Victoria 06727
Orillia Museum of Art and History, Orillia 06054
Osoyoos Art Gallery, Osoyoos 06063
Outlook and District Heritage Museum and Gallery, Outlook 06086
Owens Art Gallery, Sackville 06298
Peel Heritage Complex, Brampton 05114
Portage and District Arts Council, Portage-la-Prairie 06173
Prairie Gallery, Grande Prairie 05520
Prairie Panorama Museum, Czar 05300
Prince Edward Island Museum, Charlottetown 05230
Prince of Wales Northern Heritage Centre, Yellowknife 06870
La Pulperie de Chicoutimi, Chicoutimi 05247
Rail's End Gallery, Haliburton 05544
Raymond Chow Art Gallery, Vancouver 06686
Red Brick Arts Centre and Museum, Edson 05398
Restigouche Gallery, Campbellton 05190
River Brink, Queenston 06215
Robert Langen Gallery, Waterloo 06756
Robert McLaughlin Gallery, Oshawa 06061
Rodman Hall Arts Centre, Saint Catharines 06310
Rollin Art Centre, Port Alberni 06150
Rosemount Art Gallery, Regina 06241
Russell Gallery of Fine Art, Peterborough 06123
Saint Mary's University Art Gallery, Halifax 05563
Saint Thomas-Elgin Public Art Centre, Saint Thomas 06376
Saint Thomas More Art Gallery, Saskatoon 06404
Salle Alfred Pellan, Laval 05736
Sarnia Public Library and Art Gallery, Sarnia 06392
SAW Gallery, Ottawa 06085
Seymour Art Gallery, North Vancouver 06028
Sidney and Gertrude Zack Gallery, Vancouver 06689
Signal Hill Gallery, Weyburn 06782
Sir Wilfred Grenfell College Art Gallery, Corner Brook 05274
Site Gallery, Winnipeg 06846
Smithers Public Art Gallery, Smithers 06463
Sooke Region Museum, Art Gallery and Historic Moss Cottage, Sooke 06470
Southampton Art Gallery, Southampton 06477
Springbank Visual Arts Centre, Mississauga 05873
Stationhouse Gallery, Williams Lake 06803
Sunbury Shores Arts and Nature Centre, Saint Andrews 06304
Surrey Art Gallery, Surrey 06519
Temiskaming Art Gallery, Haileybury 05542
Thames Art Gallery, Chatham, Ontario 05241
Toronto Dominion Gallery of Inuit Art, Toronto 06617
Toronto Outdoor Art Exhibition, Toronto 06618
Two Turtle Iroquois Fine Art Gallery, Ohsweken 06044
University of Lethbridge Art Gallery, Lethbridge 05749
University of New Brunswick Art Centre, Fredericton 05467
University of Toronto Art Centre, Toronto 06624
Upstairs Gallery, Winnipeg 06850
Vaseaux Lake Galleries, Oliver 06052
Vernon Public Art Gallery, Vernon, British Colombia 06708
Wadena and District Museum and Gallery, Wadena 06738
Walter Phillips Gallery, Banff 05044
West End Gallery, Edmonton 05394
Whetung Craft Centre and Art Gallery, Curve Lake 05298
Whyte Museum of the Canadian Rockies, Banff 05045
Wickaninnish Gallery, Vancouver 06698
W.K.P. Kennedy Gallery, North Bay 06019
Woodstock Art Gallery, Woodstock 06864
Ydessa Hendeles Art Foundation, Toronto 06626
York Quay Gallery at Harbourfront Centre, Toronto 06627
Yorkton Arts Council, Yorkton 06875
YYZ Artists' Outlet, Toronto 06628

Chile
Museo Municipal de Bellas Artes de Valparaíso, Valparaíso 06928
Museo O'Higginiano y de Bellas Artes de Talca, Talca 06922

China, People's Republic
Galeria de Exposiçõnes Temporárias da CMMP, Macau 07161
Guangdong Art Gallery, Guangzhou 07060
Guangzhou Art Gallery, Guangzhou 07063
Hong Kong Visual Arts Centre, Hong Kong 07102
Nanjing International Culture and Arts Exchange Center, Nanjing 07183
Nanjing Museum, Nanjing 07184
National Museum of Chinese History, Beijing 06980
Qin Dai Zhan Guan, Xian 07295
Suzhou Art Gallery, Suzhou 07250
Tianjin Art Museum, Tianjin 07263
Yanhuang Art Center, Beijing 06996

China, Republic
National Taiwan Art Gallery, Taipei 07352
Taiwan Museum of Art, Taichung 07342

Colombia
Colección de Arte y Museo Botero, Bogotá 07386
Collectión Banco de la República, Bogotá 07390
Museo Casa Mosquera, Popayán 07562
Museo Casa Negret, Popayán 07563
Museo de Arte de Pereira, Pereira 07557
Museo de Arte Universidad Nacional de Colombia, Bogotá 07400
Museo de Artes y Tradiciones Populares, Espinal 07477
Museo de la Cultura de Albán, Albán 07363
Museo de los Niños, Bogotá 07407
Museo de Marionetas, Bogotá 07408
Museo del Carajo, Cali 07449
Museo del Cobre, Bogotá 07414
Museo del Siglo XIX, Bogotá 07416
Museo del Virrey Ezpeleta, Guaduas 07489
Museo Etnográfico, Albán 07364
Museo Gabriel Mateus, Sabanagrande 07580
Museo Mercedes Sierra de Pérez El Chico, Bogotá 07426
Museo Rayo, Roldanillo 07579
Museo Taminango de Artes y Tradiciones Populares de Nariño, Pasto 07553
Museo Universitario, Medellín 07524
Museo Universitario, Pasto 07554
Pinacoteca de la Facultad de Bellas Artes, Manizales 07510
Pinacoteca Eduardo Ramírez Castro, Aranzazu 07369

Costa Rica
Galeria Facultad de Bellas Artes, San José 07651
Galería Nacional y Museo de los Niños, San José 07652
Museo de Arte Costarricense, San José 07654
Sala de Exhibitiones Temporales del Banco Central, San José 07663

Croatia
Branko Deškovič Art Gallery, Bol 07682
Bukovac Art Gallery, Cavtat 07688
Galerija Jerolim, Stari Grad 07789
Galerija Klovićevi Dvori, Zagreb 07815
Galerija Sebastian, Dubrovnik 07695
Gallery of Naive Art, Zlatar 07843
Gradski Muzej Karlovac, Karlovac 07713
Gradski Muzej Virovitica, Virovitica 07801
Kaštela Gradski Muzej, Kaštel Lukšić 07714
Memorijalna Zbirka Antuna Masle, Dubrovnik 07697
Memorijalna Zbirka Eugena Kumičića, Brseč 07685
Muzej za Umjetnost i Obrt, Zagreb 07834
Spomen Galerija Ivana Meštrovića, Vrpolje 07803
Strossmayerova Galerija Starih Majstora, Zagreb 07837
Umjetnički Paviljon u Zagrebu, Zagreb 07840
Zbirka Umjetnina Juraj Plančić, Stari Grad 07790

Cuba
Centro de Desarrollo de las Artes Visuales, La Habana 07923
La Galería de Arte, La Habana 07929
Galería de Arte Universal, Santiago de Cuba 08128

Museo Acacia, La Habana 07934
Museo de Arte Colonial de la Habana, La Habana 07956
Museo de Arte Colonial de Palacio Valle Iznaga, Sancti-Spíritus 08111
Museo des Orígenes, La Habana 07967
Museo Mariano, La Habana 07974
Museo Nacional de Bellas Artes, La Habana 07987
Museo Oscar María de Rojas, Cárdenas 07881
Museo Sol y Mar, Matanzas 08043
Museo Wifredo Lam, La Habana 08001

Cyprus, Turkish Republic

Saçaklı Ev - Kültür ve Sanat Merkezi, Lefkoşa 08239

Czech Republic

Dům Umění, České Budějovice 08298
Dům Umění, Znojmo 08755
Dům Umění Města Brna, Brno 08266
Galerie Hlavního Města Prahy, Praha 08576
Galerie Hlavního Města Prahy, Praha 08577
Galerie Jamborův Dům, Tišnov 08681
Galerie Malovaný Dům, Třebíč 08686
Galerie Města Blanska, Blansko 08250
Galerie Portyč, Písek 08539
Hasičské Muzeum, Přibyslav 08626
Horácka Galerie, Nové Město na Moravě 08502
Hrad Roštejn, Telč 08675
Jihomoravské Muzeum ve Znojmě, Znojmo 08756
Jízdárna Pražskeho Hradu, Praha 08582
Městská Galerie, Polička 08554
Městské Muzeum, Rýmařov 08649
Micovna, Praha 08590
Moravská Galerie Brno - Místodrzitelsky Palác, Brno 08270
Muzeum Telč, Telč 08676
Muzeum Umění Olomouc, Olomouc 08515
Severočeská Galerie Výtvarného Umění v Litoměřice, Litoměřice 08457
Velká Synagoga, Plzeň 08545
Vlastivědné Muzeum v Olomouci, Olomouc 08516
Východočeská Galerie, Pardubice 08533
Výstavní Síň Muzea, Ústí nad Orlicí 08704
Západočeská Galerie v Plzni, Plzeň 08546
Znojemský Hrad, Znojmo 08758

Denmark

Bornholms Kunstmuseum, Gudhjem 08846
Danmarks Keramikmuseum, Middelfart 08984
Drachmanns Hus, Skagen 09054
Frederikshavn Kunstmuseum- og Exlibrissamling, Frederikshavn 08830
Fyns Kunstmuseum, Odense 09009
Grenen Kunstmuseum, Skagen 09055
Holstebro Kunstmuseum, Holstebro 08889
Horsens Kunstmuseum, Horsens 08897
Jens Nielsens Olivia Holm-Møller Museet, Holstebro 08891
Johannes Larsen Museet, Kerteminde 08914
Kunsthallen, København 08936
Kunsthallen Brandts Klaedefabrik, Odense 09014
Museet Psykiatrisk Hospital i Århus, Risskov 09034
Odsherreds Kunstmuseum, Asnæs 08776
Rundetaarn, København 08949
Storstrøms Kunstmuseum, Maribo 08982
Vestsjællands Kunstmuseum, Sorø 09077

Dominican Republic

Museo de Arte Moderno, Santo Domingo 09121

Ecuador

Museo de Arte Colonial, Quito 09202
Museo de Arte Moderno, Cuenca 09153
Museo de la Casa de la Cultura Ecuatoriana, Quito 09206
Museo Frey Pedro Bedón, Ibarra 09182
Museo Municipal de Guayaquil, Guayaquil 09177

Egypt

Anderson Museum, Cairo 09255

Estonia

Adamson-Eric Museum, Tallinn 09354
Eesti Kunstimuuseum, Tallinn 09358
Kunstigalerii, Narva 09340
Niguliste Muuseum, Tallinn 09368
Rakvere Näitustemaja-Muuseum, Rakvere 09350
Tartu Kunstimaja, Tartu 09382
Tartu Ülikooli Kunstimuuseum, Tartu 09388

Ethiopia

Ethnographic Museum, Addis Ababa 09398

Finland

Aineen Taidemuseo, Tornio 10113
Ålands Konstmuseum, Mariehamn 09814
Ålands Museum, Mariehamn 09815
Ateneumin Taidemuseo, Helsinki 09474
Etelä-Karjalan Taidemuseo, Lappeenranta 09761
Helsingin Taidehalli, Helsinki 09489
Hvitträsk, Kirkkonummi 09673
Jyväskylän Taidemuseo, Jyväskylä 09597
Kemin Taidemuseo, Kemi 09650
Keravan Taidemuseo, Kerava 09657
Kuopion Taidemuseo, Kuopio 09721
Lampi-Museo, Liminka 09787
Lönnströmin Taidemuseo, Rauma 09982
Maria de Lisitzin Fine Art and Historical Museum, Porvoo 09953
Mikkelin Taidemuseo, Mikkeli 09832
Museo Villa Urpo, Siivikkala 10036
Önningebymuseet, Mariehamn 09818
Orimattilan Taidemuseo, Orimattila 09885
Pohjanmaan Museo, Vaasa 10161
Porin Taidemuseo, Pori 09944
Pyynikinlinna, Tampere 10083
Reitzin Säätiön Kokoelmat, Helsinki 09524
Riihimäen Taidemuseo, Riihimäki 09994
Rovaniemen Taidemuseo, Rovaniemi 10004
Savonlinnan Taidemuseo, Savonlinna 10027
Sinebrychoffin Taidemuseo, Helsinki 09528
Tampereen Taidemuseo - Pirkanmaan Aluetaidemuseo, Tampere 10092
Turun Taidemuseo, Turku 10135
Vantaan Kaupunginmuseo - Kuvataideasiat, Vantaa 10184
Villa Gyllenberg, Helsinki 09546
Voipaalas Taidekeskus, Sääksmäki 10014

France

Carré d'Art, Nîmes 13333
Le Carré-Scéne Nationale, Château-Gontier 11203
Centre d'Art Contemporain, Bignan 10735
Centre d'Art Contemporain, Dijon 11518
Centre d'Art Contemporain, Pau 13664
Centre d'Art Contemporain, Pougues-les-Eaux 13851
Centre d'Art Contemporain, Tanlay 14855
Centre d'Art Contemporain le Quartier, Quimper 13893
Centre d'Art du Crestet, Crestet 11457
Centre d'Art et d'Exposition Jacques-Henri Lartigue, L'Isle-Adam 12625
Château Beaufief, Mazeray 12906
Château de Maisons-Laffitte, Maisons-Laffitte 12777
Château de Rochefort-en-Terre, Rochefort-en-Terre 14002
Château des Pêcheurs, La Bussière 12131
Château-Musée des XVIe-XVIIe s, Tanlay 14856
Collection Frits Lugt, Paris 13487
Le Creux de l'Enfer, Centre d'Art Contemporain, Thiers 14885
Donation François Mitterrand, Jarnac 12072
Ecomusée de Saint-Dégan, Brech 10899
Espace Culturel Hippolite-Mars, Équeurdreville-Hainneville 11636
Espace Joseph Besset, Vanosc 15084
Exposition du Cloître des Cordeliers, Tarascon (Bouches-du-Rhône) 14860
Exposition Permanente d'Art, Brasparts 10891
Galerie d'Exposition d'Art et d'Histoire, Villaries 15179
Galerie du Vitrail, Amiens 10322
Galerie Fernand Léger - Le Crédac, Ivry-sur-Seine 12067
Institut d'Art Contemporain, Villeurbanne 15249
Maison de l'Amandier, Saint-Rémy-de-Provence 14448
Maison et Atelier de Jean-François Millet, Barbizon 10585
Maison Lansyer, Loches (Indre-et-Loire) 12640
Maison-Musée des Sciences, Lettres et Arts de Cholet et de sa Région, Cholet 11297
Musée Archéologique de Touraine, Tours 14969
Musée Artisanal et Rural d'Arts, Ars 10433
Musée Arts et Histoire, Bormes-les-Mimosas 10823
Musée Barrois, Bar-le-Duc 10583
Musée Bernard Buffet, Paris 13534
Musée Bernard d'Agesci, Niort 13343
Musée Bossuet, Meaux 12912
Musée Campredon, L'Isle-sur-la-Sorgue 12628
Musée Charles Milcendeau-Jean Yole, Soullans 14793
Musée-Château, Grignan 11956
Musée Château d'Annecy et Observatoire Régional des Lacs Alpins, Annecy 10361
Musée-Château de Saint-Ouen, Saint-Ouen 14389
Musée Chintreuil, Pont-de-Vaux 13806
Musée Communal Robert Tatin, Cossé-le-Vivien 11417
Musée d'Art et d'Archéologie, Laon 12339
Musée d'Art et d'Histoire des Côtes d'Armor, Saint-Brieuc 14132
Musée d'Art et d'Histoire Louis Senlecq, L'Isle-Adam 12626
Musée d'Art et d'Industrie, Saint-Étienne 14198
Musée d'Art et d'Industrie - La Piscine, Roubaix 14044
Musée d'Art Moderne Jean Peské, Collioure 11351
Musée d'Art Religieux, Marsal 12838
Musée d'Art Roger Quilliot, Clermont-Ferrand 11322
Musée d'Art Sacré de Loukine, Arsonval 10435
Musée de Borda, Dax 11486
Musée de Brou, Bourg-en-Bresse 10853
Musée de Cosne, Cosne-Cours-sur-Loire 11416
Musée de la Castre, Cannes 11025
Musée de la Princerie, Verdun (Meuse) 15130
Musée de la Tour des Echevins, Luxeuil-les-Bains 12715
Musée de l'Art Culinaire, Villeneuve-Loubet 15232
Musée de l'Holographie, Paris 13575
Musée de l'Hôtel-Dieu, Mantes-la-Jolie 12798
Musée de l'Ile de France, Sceaux 14678
Musée de Lodève, Lodève 12647
Musée de Montmartre, Paris 13582
Musée de Morlaix et Maison du 9 Grand Rue, Morlaix 13163
Musée de Moulages, Strasbourg 14829
Musée de Peinture Louis-Français, Plombières-les-Bains 13761
Musée de Picardie, Amiens 10324
Musée Départemental des Hautes-Alpes, Gap 11838
Musée Départemental Hébert, La Tronche 12270
Musée Départemental Stéphane Mallarmé, Vulaines-sur-Seine 15298
Musée des Arts Africains, Océaniens, Amérindiens, Marseille 12860
Musée des Arts et de l'Enfance, Fécamp 11711
Musée des Arts Populaires, Reillanne 13924
Musée des Beaux-Arts, Dijon 11527
Musée des Beaux-Arts, Montbard 13054
Musée des Beaux-Arts, Vannes (Morbihan) 15082
Musée des Beaux-Arts et Arts Décoratifs Raymond Ritter, Morlanne 13164
Musée des Beaux-Arts et d'Archeologie Joseph Déchelette, Roanne 13985
Musée des Beaux-Arts et de la Dentelle, Alençon 10281
Musée des Beaux-Arts et d'Histoire, Saint-Lô 14326
Musée des Hospices Civils de Lyon, Lyon 12737
Musée des Moulages, Lyon 12738
Musée des Peintres du Pays, Saint-Cyprien 14166
Musée des Tapisseries, Aix-en-Provence 10252
Musée d'Evreux, Evreux 11681
Musée du Bizarre, Lavilledieu 12373
Musée du Gemmail, Lourdes 12690
Musée du Perigord, Périgueux 13692
Musée du Prieuré, Charolles 11187
Musée du Touquet, Le Touquet-Paris-Plage 12486
Musée Edouard Barthe, Montblanc 13061
Musée-Fondation Louis-Jou, Les Baux-de-Provence 12527
Musée Galerie Honoré Camos, Bargemon 10591
Musée-Galerie Raoul-Dufy, Nice 13320
Musée Girodet, Montargis 13045
Musée Henri Boez, Maubeuge 12890
Musée Henri-Giron, Le Vigan (Lot) 12498
Musée Hofer-Bury, Lavérune 12372
Musée International d'Arts Modestes, Sète 14730
Musée J.-E.-Blanche, Offranville 13387
Musée Jean-Charles Cazin, Samer 14596
Musée Jean Lurçat, Saint-Laurent-les-Tours 14315
Musée Lombard, Doullens 11568
Musée Magnelli, Vallauris 15060
Musée Mainssieux, Voiron 15284
Musée-Maison des Arts des Hauts-Cantons, Bédarieux 10661
Musée M'Am Jeanne, Fontenoy-en-Puisaye 11777
Musée Mine, Cagnac-les-Mines 10985
Musée Municipal, Hazebrouck 12007
Musée Municipal, Semur-en-Auxois 14702
Musée Municipal Auguste Grasset, Varzy 15092
Musée Municipal de Cambrai, Cambrai 11013
Musée Municipal de Saint-Maur, La Varenne-Saint-Hilaire 12272
Musée Municipal Max Claudet, Salins-les-Bains 14573
Musée Municipal Méditerranéen de Cassis, Cassis 11068
Musée Municipal Saraleguinea, Guéthary 11971
Musée Napoléonien du Château de Grosbois, Boissy-Saint-Léger 10789
Musée Nicéphore Niépce, Chalon-sur-Saône 11126
Musée Raimu, Cogolin 11345
Musée Raymond Lafage, Lisle-sur-Tarn 12631
Musée Régional Dupuy-Méstreau, Saintes 14559
Musée René Davoine, Charolles 11188
Musée Rupert-de-Chièvres, Poitiers 13786
Musée Saint-Loup, Troyes 15007
Musée Tavet-Delacour, Pontoise 13833
Musée Toffoli, Charenton-le-Pont 11174
Musée Villa Tamaris Pacha, La Seyne-sur-Mer 12263
Palais des Papes et Musée du Vieil Avignon, Avignon 10535
Pavillon des Arts, Paris 13655
Petit-Palais, Paris 13658
Prieré d'Airaines, Airaines 10245

Georgia

Georgian State Art Museum, Tbilisi 15359
Museum of Fine Arts, Tbilisi 15364

Germany

Airport Gallery 1 2, Frankfurt am Main 17030
Akademie der Künste, Berlin 15910
Alpenländische Galerie, Kempten 18061
Arithmeum, Bonn 16228
Artothek der Stadt und Regionalbibliothek Erfurt, Erfurt 16894
Ausstellungszentrum im Schloss, Schlettau 19798
Ausstellungszentrum Kloster Cismar, Grömitz 17410
Ausstellungszentrum Kroch-Haus, Leipzig 18387
Ausstellungszentrum Lokschuppen, Rosenheim 19649
Badhaus Museum und Galerie, Kulmbach 18265
Badischer Kunstverein, Karlsruhe 17990
Bahnwärterhaus, Esslingen 16967
Bauernmuseum Rothenburg, Rothenburg, Oberlausitz 19684
Besenmuseum Galerie, Ehingen, Donau 16791
Brandenburgische Kunstsammlungen Cottbus, Cottbus 16500
Brasilianisches Kulturinstitut, Berlin 15927
Bröhan-Museum, Berlin 15930
Die Brücke, Braunschweig 16294
Brüder Grimm-Haus Steinau, Steinau an der Straße 20042
Bucerius Kunst Forum, Hamburg 17529
Caricatura Galerie, Kassel 18013
Clemens-Sels-Museum, Neuss 19063
Deutsche Guggenheim, Berlin 15937
Deutsches Märchen- und Wesersagenmuseum, Bad Oeynhausen 15708
Deutsches Museum für Schulkunst, Hagen, Westfalen 17479
Digital Art Museum, Berlin 15941
E-Werk Freiburg, Freiburg im Breisgau 17108
Erotic Art Museum Hamburg, Hamburg 17537
Erotik-Museum, Berlin 15944
Erzbischöfliches Diözesanmuseum Köln, Köln 18135
Europäisches Kulturzentrum Galerie Villa Rolandshof, Remagen 19559
Fälschermuseum, Ostseebad Binz 19306
Felix-Nussbaum-Haus Osnabrück mit Sammlung der Niedersächsischen Sparkassenstiftung, Osnabrück 19278
Forum Konkrete Kunst - Peterskirche, Erfurt 16899
Franz Radziwill Haus, Varel 20285
Franz von Stuck Geburtshaus Tettenweis, Tettenweis 20163
Frauen Museum, Bonn 16236
Freies Deutsches Hochstift/ Frankfurter Goethe-Museum mit Goethe-Haus, Frankfurt am Main 17046
Gadebuscher Galerie am Schlossberg, Gadebusch 17187
Galerie 37. Kunst im Museum der Weltkulturen, Frankfurt am Main 17047
Galerie Alte Reichsvogtei, Schweinfurt 19889
Galerie Altes Rathaus, Worpswede 20682
Galerie am Prater, Berlin 15953
Galerie Arcus, Berlin 15954
Galerie Contact, Böblingen 16212
Galerie der Stadt, Bad Wimpfen 15768
Galerie der Stadt Backnang, Backnang 15585
Galerie der Stadt Fellbach, Fellbach 16990
Galerie der Stadt Plochingen, Plochingen 19418
Galerie der Stadt Sindelfingen, Sindelfingen 19963
Galerie der Stadt Waiblingen Kameralamt, Waiblingen 20348
Galerie des Kultur- und Festspielhauses Wittenberge, Wittenberge 20624
Galerie des Marburger Kunstvereins, Marburg 18627
Galerie Goethe 53, München 18851
Galerie Grünstraße, Berlin 15956
Galerie Haus Dacheröden, Erfurt 16900
Galerie im Amtshaus, Bad Wurzach 15779
Galerie im Bürgerhaus, Haigerloch 17492
Galerie im Fontanehaus, Berlin 15957
Galerie im Franck-Haus, Marktheidenfeld 18645
Galerie im Hörsaalbau, Leipzig 18395
Galerie im Körnerpark, Berlin 15959
Galerie im Körnerpark, Berlin 15960
Galerie im Kreishaus, Wetzlar 20552
Galerie im Prediger, Schwäbisch Gmünd 19861
Galerie im Saalbau, Berlin 15963
Galerie im Stadtmuseum, Jena 17941
Galerie in der Brotfabrik, Berlin 15967
Galerie Inkatt, Bremen 16322
Galerie Kunstbrücke Osteuropa, Berlin 15969
Galerie Marktschlößchen, Halle, Saale 17511
Galerie Münsterland, Emsdetten 16867
Galerie Palais Walderdorff, Trier 20209
Galerie Palette Röderhaus, Wuppertal 20712
Günter Grass-Kulturstiftung Hansestadt Lübeck, Lübeck 18535
Gustav-Wolf-Kunstgalerie, Östringen 19233
Gutshaus Steglitz, Berlin 15980
Haus am Lützowplatz, Berlin 15985
Haus der Landbrandenburg Lottogesellschaft, Potsdam 19435
Haus Esters, Krefeld 18225
Haus Giersch - Museum Regionaler Kunst, Frankfurt am Main 17049
Haus Opherdicke, Holzwickede 17834
Heiliggeistkirche, Landshut 18309
Heinrich Vogeler Stiftung Haus im Schluh, Worpswede 20684
Heussenstamm Stiftung, Frankfurt am Main 17054
Hohenhof, Hagen, Westfalen 17480
Horst-Janssen-Museum, Oldenburg, Oldenburg 19254
Humbert Collection, Münster 18939
ifa-Galerie Berlin, Berlin 16005
Internationale Tage Boehringer Ingelheim, Ingelheim am Rhein 17899
Jazz Art Galerie, Gelsenkirchen 17228
Jerusalemhaus mit Verwaltung der Städtischen Sammlungen Wetzlar, Wetzlar 20555
Jüdisches Museum Berlin, Berlin 16009
Jugendkunstschule Pankow, Berlin 16010
Kaiser Wilhelm Museum, Krefeld 18227
Kelsterbacher Museum für Porzellan, Kelsterbach 18054
Kinder-Akademie Fulda Werkraummuseum, Fulda 17177
Kinder- und Jugendgalerie Sonnensegel, Brandenburg an der Havel 16281
Kindermuseum, Karlsruhe 17995
Kirche am Hohenzollernplatz, Berlin 16015
Kloster-Kunstsammlung, Preetz, Holstein 19441
Klostergalerie, Zehdenick 20735
Kölnischer Kunstverein, Köln 18149
Kommunale Galerie, Darmstadt 16543
Kommunale Galerie, Berlin 16017
Kommunale Galerie Gelsenkirchen, Gelsenkirchen 17229
Kommunale Galerie im Leinwandhaus, Frankfurt am Main 17059
Kügelgenhaus, Dresden 16688
Künstlerforum Bonn, Bonn 16240
Künstlerhaus Bethanien, Berlin 16019

Künstlerhaus Marktoberdorf, Marktoberdorf 18649
Künstlerhaus Schloß Balmoral, Bad Ems 15637
Kulturamt Mitte, Berlin 16020
Kulturforum Alte Post, Neuss 19065
Kulturinstitut in der Italienischen Botschaft, Berlin 16022
Kulturzentrum Schloß Bonndorf, Bonndorf im Schwarzwald 16251
Kunst Archiv Darmstadt, Darmstadt 16544
Kunstbank, Berlin 16024
Kunstforum in der Grundkreditbank, Berlin 16027
Kunstgußmuseum Lauchhammer, Lauchhammer 18346
Kunsthalle am Goetheplatz, Weimar, Thüringen 20463
Kunsthalle Barmen, Wuppertal 20715
Kunsthalle der Hypo-Kulturstiftung, München 18865
Kunsthalle Dominikanerkirche, Osnabrück 19281
Kunsthalle Erfurt im Haus zum Roten Ochsen, Erfurt 16904
Kunsthalle Fridericianum, Kassel 18021
Kunsthalle Gießen, Gießen 17280
Kunsthalle in Emden, Emden 16847
Kunsthalle Jesuitenkirche, Aschaffenburg 15525
Kunsthalle Sparkasse Leipzig, Leipzig 18401
Kunsthalle Wilhelmshaven, Wilhelmshaven 20595
Kunsthaus Hamburg, Hamburg 17549
Kunsthaus Hohenlockstedt, Hohenlockstedt 17809
Kunsthaus Kannen, Münster 18940
Kunsthaus Kaufbeuren, Kaufbeuren 18041
Kunstkeller Annaberg, Annaberg-Buchholz 15498
Kunstmuseum Bayreuth mit Tabakhistorischer Sammlung, Bayreuth 15852
Kunstmuseum Celle mit Sammlung Robert Simon, Celle 16456
Kunstmuseum Heidenheim, Heidenheim an der Brenz 17679
Kunstpavillon, München 18866
Kunstraum Alter Wiehrebahnhof, Freiburg im Breisgau 17111
Kunstraum Berlin, Berlin 16029
Kunstraum Düsseldorf, Düsseldorf 16732
Kunstraum Kreuzberg/Bethanien, Berlin 16030
Kunstsammlung im Schloß Rheinstein, Trechtingshausen 20198
Kunstsammlungen Chemnitz, Chemnitz 16466
Kunstsammlungen der Stadt Limburg, Limburg an der Lahn 18470
Kunststätte Bossard, Jesteburg 17955
Kunstverein Grafschaft Bentheim, Neuenhaus 19026
Kunstverein Hannover, Hannover 17603
Kunstverein Köln rechtsrheinisch e.V., Köln 18155
Kunstverein Passau- Sankt Anna-Kapelle, Passau 19355
Kunstverein Ruhr e.V., Essen 16955
Kunstverein Springhornhof e.V., Neuenkirchen, Lüneburger Heide 19027
Kunstverein Talstrasse, Halle, Saale 17514
Kunstverein zu Frechen e.V., Frechen 17093
Landesmuseum Mainz, Mainz 18602
Lettl-Atrium, Augsburg 15559
Liebermann-Villa, Berlin 16037
Lindenau-Museum, Altenburg, Thüringen 15450
Marburger Universitätsmuseum für Kunst und Kulturgeschichte, Marburg 18629
Margret-Knoop-Schellbach-Museum, Körle 18186
Markgräfler Museum Müllheim, Müllheim, Baden 18819
Max-Ernst-Kabinett, Brühl, Rheinland 16377
Meininger Museen, Meiningen 18686
Morat-Institut für Kunst und Kunstwissenschaft, Freiburg im Breisgau 17112
Die Mühle, Eberswalde 16770
Museum Alte Post, Pirmasens 19402
Museum Baden, Solingen 19985
Museum der bildenden Künste Leipzig, Leipzig 18405
Museum der Stadt Ratingen, Ratingen 19494
Museum für aktuelle Kunst, Groß-Umstadt 17421
Museum für bildende Kunst im Landkreis Neu-Ulm, Nersingen 18997
Museum für Europäische Gartenkunst, Düsseldorf 16736
Museum für Fotokopie, Mülheim an der Ruhr 18817
Museum für Islamische Kunst, Berlin 16054
Museum für Kunst und Gewerbe Hamburg, Hamburg 17560
Museum für Kunst und Kulturgeschichte der Stadt Dortmund, Dortmund 16662
Museum für Naive Kunst, Bönnigheim 16217
Museum für Neue Kunst, Karlsruhe 17998
Museum Georg Schäfer, Schweinfurt 19891
Museum Haus Cajeth, Heidelberg 17671
Museum Haus Lange, Krefeld 18229
Museum Heylshof, Worms 20679
Museum im Kreuzgang, Landshut 18310
Museum Insel Hombroich, Neuss 19066
Museum Kartause Astheim, Volkach 20333
Museum Katharinenhof mit Mühlenturm und Stadtscheune, Kranenburg, Niederrhein 18219
Museum Kloster Bentlage, Rheine 19590
Museum Künstlerkolonie, Darmstadt 16547
Museum Kulturgeschichte der Hand, Wolnzach 20673
Museum Kunst Palast mit Sammlung Kunstakademie und Glasmuseum Hentrich, Düsseldorf 16738
Museum Osterzgebirgsgalerie im Schloß, Dippoldiswalde 16621
Museum Sankt Ingbert, Sankt Ingbert 19751
Museum Sankt Wendel, Sankt Wendel 19758
Museum Schloß Hundshaupten, Egloffstein 16790
Museum Schloss Oberschwappach, Knetzgau 18117
Museum Synagoge Gröbzig, Gröbzig 17408
Museum Synthese, München 18885
Museum und Stiftung Anton Geiselhart, Münsingen 18931
Museum Villa Haiss, Zell am Harmersbach 20740
Museum Wurzen mit Ringelnatzsammlung, Wurzen 20720
Museumsgalerie, Altomünster 15471
Museumshof-Galerie, Oldenburg in Holstein 19251
Neue Galerie, Dachau 16525
Neue Gesellschaft für bildende Kunst e.V., Berlin 16074
Neuer Sächsischer Kunstverein, Dresden 16703
Neues Kunsthaus Ahrenshoop, Ostseebad Ahrenshoop 19302
Neues Kunstquartier Berlin, Berlin 16077
Neues Museum, Nürnberg 19156
Niedersächsisches Landesmuseum Hannover, Hannover 17607
Oberpfälzer Künstlerhaus-Kebbel-Villa, Schwandorf 19873
Oldenburg-Museum, Unna 20265
Orangerie im Englischen Garten, München 18892
Otto-Flath-Kunsthalle, Bad Segeberg 15741
Palais für aktuelle Kunst, Glückstadt 17305
PAN Kunstforum Niederrhein, Emmerich 16860
Paula Modersohn-Becker Museum. Museum im Roselius-Haus. Bernhard Hoetger Sammlung, Bremen 16331
Pfalzgalerie Kaiserslautern, Kaiserslautern 17970
Pommersches Landesmuseum, Greifswald 17390
Privatmuseum Sammlung Holzinger, München 18898
Quadrat Bottrop, Bottrop 16265
Rathaus-Galerie, Berlin 16082
Rathausgalerie, Castrop-Rauxel 16451
Rathausgalerie der Stadt Brühl, Brühl, Rheinland 16378
Rathausgalerie Grimma, Grimma 17402
Rathausgalerie Munster, Munster 18960
Rathausgalerie Vellmar, Vellmar 20299
Replikate der Welt-Kunst im Schloss, Miltach 18738
Sammlung Buchheim - Museum der Phantasie, Bernried, Starnberger See 16129
Sammlung der Städtischen Galerie, Lüdenscheid 18549
Sammlung Domnick, Nürtingen 19165
Sammlung Goetz, München 18903
Sammlung Herzoglicher Kunstbesitz, Coburg 16485
Sammlung Prinzhorn, Heidelberg 17674
Sammlungen des Instituts für Hochschulkunde der Deutschen Gesellschaft für Hochschulkunde, Würzburg 20704
Schauraum, Eggenfelden 16788
Schirn Kunsthalle Frankfurt, Frankfurt am Main 17071
Schloß Brake - Das Weserrenaissance-Museum, Lemgo 18431
Schloss Braunfels, Braunfels 16288
Schloss Cappenberg, Selm 19935
Schloss Güstrow, Güstrow 17458
Schloss Hundisburg-Sammlung Apel, Hundisburg 17864
Schloss Johannisburg mit Schlossgarten, Aschaffenburg 15529
Schloss Neuhardenberg, Neuhardenberg 19031
Schloß Weikersheim, Weikersheim 20431
Schloßmuseum, Schrozberg 19855
Schwules Museum, Berlin 16094
Sinclair-Haus, Bad Homburg v.d.Höhe 15668
Staatliche Kunsthalle Baden-Baden, Baden-Baden 15790
Staatsgalerie Stuttgart, Stuttgart 20106
Stadtgalerie Altena, Altena 15444
Stadtgalerie Bamberg - Villa Dessauer, Bamberg 15819
Stadtgalerie Kiel, Kiel 18079
Stadthaus-Galerie, Münster 18945
Stadtmuseum Göhre, Jena 17952
Stadtmuseum Hadamar, Hadamar 17474
Stadtmuseum Münster, Münster 18946
Städtische Galerie, Dreieich 16674
Städtische Galerie, Eisenhüttenstadt 16824
Städtische Galerie, Ravensburg 19507
Städtische Galerie, Paderborn 19340
Städtische Galerie ada Meiningen, Meiningen 18687
Städtische Galerie am Markt Wurzen, Wurzen 20722
Städtische Galerie Delmenhorst, Delmenhorst 16570
Städtische Galerie Fauler Pelz, Überlingen 20244
Städtische Galerie Filderhalle, Leinfelden-Echterdingen 18377
Städtische Galerie Haus Seel, Siegen 19951
Städtische Galerie im Buntentor, Bremen 16334
Städtische Galerie im Königin-Christinen-Haus, Zeven 20754
Städtische Galerie im Rathaus, Balingen 15800
Städtische Galerie im Schloßpark Strünkede, Herne 17730
Städtische Galerie im Theater Ingolstadt, Ingolstadt 17912
Städtische Galerie In der Badstube, Wangen im Allgäu 20394
Städtische Galerie Iserlohn, Iserlohn 17923
Städtische Galerie Kaarst, Kaarst 17969
Städtische Galerie Lehrte, Lehrte 18371
Städtische Galerie Lovis-Kabinett, Villingen-Schwenningen 20320
Städtische Galerie Mennonitenkirche, Neuwied 19087
Städtische Galerie Reutlingen, Reutlingen 19580
Städtische Galerie Rosenheim, Rosenheim 19653
Städtische Galerie Villa Streccius, Landau in der Pfalz 18301
Städtische Galerie Villa Zanders, Bergisch Gladbach 15901
Städtische Galerie Wesseling, Wesseling 20540
Städtische Kunstgalerie Torhaus Rombergpark, Dortmund 16665
Städtische Kunstsammlungen, Ausstellungsgebäude, Darmstadt 16549
Städtisches Museum, Kalkar 17975
Städtisches Museum Gelsenkirchen, Gelsenkirchen 17230
Städtisches Museum Zirndorf, Zirndorf 20759
Steinhausen-Museum, Frankfurt am Main 17076
Stiftung Fritz und Hermine Overbeck, Bremen 16335
Stiftung für Konkrete Kunst Roland Phleps, Freiburg im Breisgau 17117
Stiftung Starke, Berlin 16105
Studiensammlung der Universität Leipzig, Leipzig 18421
Temporäre Galerie Schloß Neersen, Willich 20597
Theo-Steinbrenner-Turm-Museum, Sommerach 19995
Tschechisches Zentrum-CzechPoint, Berlin 16108
Universitätssammlungen Kunst Technik, Dresden 16714
Urgeschichtliches Museum und Galerie Vierzigtausend Jahre Kunst, Blaubeuren 16183
Ursula Blickle Stiftung, Kraichtal 18218
Das Verborgene Museum, Berlin 16111
Villa Aichele, Lörrach 18491
Weißenhorner Heimatmuseum, Weißenhorn 20501
Wenzel-Hablik-Museum, Itzehoe 17935
Westfälisches Landesmuseum für Kunst und Kulturgeschichte Münster, Münster 18950
Winckelmann-Museum, Stendal 20059
Zehnthaus, Jockgrim 17958
Zille Museum, Berlin 16118
ZKM Medienmuseum, Karlsruhe 18007

Greece
Jannis Spyropoulos Museum, Ekali 20942
Municipal Art Gallery of Xanthi, Xanthi 21219
Municipal Gallery of Corfu, Corfu 20931
Municipal Museum of Kavala, Kavala 21012
Museum-Art Collection of the National Bank, Athinai 20881
Museum of Works by Theophilos, Varia Lesbos 21206
Pinakothiki Kouvoutsaki, Kifissia 21016
Polygnotos Vagis Museum, Thassos 21174
Tactual Museum, Athinai 20903
Teriade Museum, Mytilini 21088

Greenland
Qalipakkanik Katersugaasivik, Ilulissat 21230

Guyana
Guyana Museum, Georgetown 21290

Haiti
Musée du Panthéon National Haïtien, Port-au-Prince 21293

Honduras
Galería Nacional de Arte, Tegucigalpa 21302

Hungary
Alföldi Galéria, Hódmezővásárhely 21427
Amerigo Tot Múzeum, Pécs 21503
Endre Nemes Múzeum, Pécs 21505
Ferenczy Károly Múzeum, Szentendre 21570
Kassák Museum, Budapest 21348
Miskolci Galéria - Rákóczi-ház, Miskolc 21479
Műcsarnok, Budapest 21365
Schaár Erzsébet Gyűjtemény, Székesfehérvár 21560
Szépművészeti Múzeum, Budapest 21383

Iceland
Hafnarborg Art Gallery, Hafnarfjörður 21634
Hafnarhúsið, Reykjavík 21650
Kjarvalsstaðir, Reykjavík 21651
Listasafn Kópavogs - Gerðasafn, Kópavogur 21642
Norræna Húsid, Reykjavík 21659
Safn Ásgríms Jónssonar, Reykjavík 21663

India
Allahabad Museum, Allahabad 21689
Art Museum, Thiruvananthapuram 22033
Barton Museum, Bhavnagar 21716
Bharat Kala Bhavan, Varanasi 22056
Commercial Museum, Guwahati 21820
Damerla Rama Rao Memorial Art Gallery, Rajahmundry 22000
District Museum, Barpeta 21709
Framgi Dadabhoy Alpaiwalle Museum, Mumbai 21947
Gallery of Musical Instruments, Delhi 21769
Ganga Government Museum, Bikaner 21730
Government Museum, Alwar 21693
Government Museum, Chennai 21744
Government Museum, Jodhpur 21874
Haryana Prantiya Puratatva Sangrahalaya, Jhajjar 21870
Indira Gandhi National Centre for the Arts, Delhi 21772
Kannada Research Institute Museum, Dharwar 21793
Karnataka Government Museum and Venkatappa Art Gallery, Bangalore 21703
Mahakoshal Art Gallery, Raipur, Madhya Pradesh 21999
Manipur State Museum, Imphal 21854
Maratha History Museum, Pune 21992
Marble Palace Art Gallery and Zoo, Kolkata 21907
Mehrangarh Museum, Jodhpur 21875
Museum of Art and Archaeology, Dharwad 21792
Shreemanthi Bai Memorial Government Museum, Mangalore 21939
State Museum, Hyderabad 21847

Indonesia
Agung Rai Museum of Art, Ubud 22212
Museum Kraton Yogyakarta, Yogyakarta 22222
Museum Seni, Denpasar 22097
Museum Taruna Akbari Udarat, Magelang 22152

Iran
Babol Museum, Babol 22231
Fine Arts Museum, Teheran 22298
Museum of Contemporary Articrafts, Teheran 22315
Sizdah Aban Museum, Teheran 22327

Ireland
AV Gallery, Limerick 22504
The Chester Beatty Library, Dublin 22417
Douglas Hyde Gallery, Dublin 22419
Galway Arts Centre, Galway 22472
Garter Lane Arts Centre, Waterford 22553
The Hunt Museum, Limerick 22505
Saint John's Theatre and Arts Centre, Listowel 22509
Waterfront Gallery, Westport 22556
Wexford Arts Centre, Wexford 22560

Israel
Art Gallery, Haifa 22597
Beit-Hagefen Art Gallery, Haifa 22598
Beit Ha'Omanim, Jerusalem 22623
Colosseum Art Gallery, Haifa 22602
Corin Maman Ashdod Museum, Ashdod 22572
David Palombo Museum, Jerusalem 22629
Herzliya Museum of Contemporary Art, Herzliya 22616
Ilana Goor Museum, Tel Aviv 22758
Israel Museum, Jerusalem, Jerusalem 22643
Jerusalem Artists' House, Jerusalem 22644
Kibbutz Art Gallery, Tel Aviv 22765
Mané-Katz Museum, Haifa 22608
Negev Museum, Be'ersheva 22580
Open Museum, Migdal-Tefen 22715
Open Museum, Omer 22724
Reuben and Edith Hecht Museum, Haifa 22611
Ruth Youth Wing, Jerusalem 22659
Shephela Museum, Kibbutz Kfar Menahem 22692
Yad Labanim Museum and Memorial Center, Petah Tikva 22727
Yad-Lebanim Memorial Center, Rehovot 22740
Yad Vashem Art Museum, Jerusalem 22672

Italy
Affresco di Piero della Francesca, Monterchi 24540
Casa Museo del Cima, Conegliano 23637
Casa Museo F. Scaglione, Sciacca 25528
Casa Museo Ivan Bruschi, Arezzo 22918
Casa Romei, Ferrara 23784
Castel Taufers, Campo Tures 23301
Castello del Buonconsiglio, Trento 25790
Castello della Manta, Manta 24282
Castello di Donnafugata, Ragusa 25067
Castello Ducale, Agliè 22810
Castello Pallotta, Caldarola 23264
Castello Principesco, Merano 24350
Castello Reale, Moncalieri 24467
Castello Reale, Racconigi 25062
Centro d'Arte Verrocchio, Casole d'Elsa 23378
Centro di Scultura Contemporanea, Cagli 23241
Chiostro dello Scalzo, Firenze 23831
Civica Galleria d'Arte G. Sciortino, Monreale 24479
Civica Galleria di Palazzo Rocca, Chiavari 23529
Civica Pinacoteca V. Crivelli, Sant'Elpidio a Mare 25460
Civica Raccolta d'Arte, Medole 24342
Civica Raccolta d'Arte, Roseto degli Abruzzi 25282
Civica Raccolta d'Arte B. Biancolini, Potenza Picena 25029
Civiche Raccolte d'Arte, Busto Arsizio 23237
Civici Musei di Villa Paolina, Viareggio 25984
Civico Museo d'Arte Orientale, Trieste 25810
Civico Museo G.V. Parisi-Valle, Maccagno 24246
Collegio del Cambio - Museo d'Arte, Perugia 24847
Collezione Berenson, Firenze 23832
Collezione Contini-Bonacossi, Firenze 23833
Collezione d'Arte della Banca Carige, Genova 23980
Collezione d'Arte di Santa Maria di Piazza, Ostra Vetere 24720
Collezione d'Arte Sacra, Saludecio 25325
Collezione di Carrozze, Maser 24310
Collezione Straka-Coppa, Spello 25615
Collezione Wolfson, Genova 23981
Collezioni d'Arte della Cassa di Risparmio, Savona 25508
Collezioni d'Arte e di Storia della Cassa di Risparmio, Bologna 23101
Collezionoe Sarda L. Piloni, Cagliari 23243
Dogana d'Arte, Atripalda 22982
Donazione Sambo, Trieste 25820
Enoteca Regionale del Monferrato, Vignale Monferrato 26009
Fondazione Antonio Mazzotta, Milano 24383
Fondazione Bandera per l'Arte, Busto Arsizio 23238
Fondazione M. Minucci, Vittorio Veneto 26038
Fondazione Palazz Coronini Cronberg, Gorizia 24033
Fondazione Palazzo Albizzini Collezione Burri, Città di Castello 23577
Fondazione T. Balestra, Longiano 24209

Galleria Civica d'Arte Contemporanea, Caltagirone 23270
Galleria Comunale d'Arte, Lecco 24169
Galleria Comunale d'Arte Contemporanea, Arezzo 22919
Galleria Comunale S. Croce, Cattolica 23456
Galleria Corsini, Firenze 23838
Galleria d'Arte Contemporanea V. Stoppioni, Santa Sofia 25443
Galleria d'Arte Moderna A. Discovolo, Bonassola 23159
Galleria d'Arte Moderna Comunale, San Severino Marche 25411
Galleria d'Arte Moderna F. Montanari, Moncalvo 24468
Galleria d'Arte Moderna O. Marchesi, Copparo 23643
Galleria d'Arte Rocca Sforzesca, Imola 24086
Galleria dell'Accademia di Belle Arti, Napoli 24575
Galleria di Palazzo degli Alberti, Prato 25043
Galleria Ferrari, Maranello 24293
Galleria G. Pedriali, Forlì 23907
Galleria Nazionale d'Arte Antica, Trieste 25821
Galleria Palazzo Cini, Venezia 25919
Galleria Pallavicini, Roma 25165
Gallerie di Palazzo Leoni Montanari, Vicenza 25992
Giardino Storico e Villa Garzoni, Pescia 24874
Gipsoteca, Lucca 24225
Gipsoteca F. Jerace, Catanzaro 23451
Gipsoteca M. Guerrisi, Palmi 24784
Il Mauriziano, Reggio Emilia 25095
Mostra Nazionale di Pittura Contemporanea, Marsala 24304
Mostra Permanenta P. Mariani, Bordighera 23163
Musei Civici Veneziani, Venezia 25922
Musei, Gallerie, Gabinetto Stampe e Archivio Fotografico, Roma 25174
Museo Alternativo Remo Brindisi, Comacchio 23620
Museo Antoniano, Padova 24735
Museo Archeologico e Pinacoteca Comunale, Foligno 23897
Museo Artistico della Bambola, Suvereto 25661
Museo Aurelio Castelli, Siena 25570
Museo Bagatti Valsecchi, Milano 24386
Museo Capitolare, Atri 22980
Museo Capitolare, Cagliari 23246
Museo Cappuccini Emiliani, Reggio Emilia 25097
Museo Casa del Duca, Venezia 25925
Museo Casa Natale di Giotto, Vicchio 25991
Museo Civico, San Gimignano 25362
Museo Civico, Biella 23079
Museo Civico Archeologica e Quadreria, Monterubbiano 24545
Museo Civico Archeologico, Montalto Marche 24493
Museo Civico Archeologico e Pinacoteca, Chiomonte 23551
Museo Civico d'Arte, Modena 24439
Museo Civico del Sigillo, La Spezia 24122
Museo d'Arte d'Ammobigliamento, Stupinigi 25645
Museo d'Arte Nuoro, Nuoro 24661
Museo d'Arte Orientale, Venezia 25928
Museo d'Arte Pietro Cavoti, Galatina 23948
Museo dei Burattini e delle Figure, Cervia 23492
Museo del Bigallo, Firenze 23855
Museo del Collezionista d'Arte, Milano 24393
Museo del Lazio Meridionale, Anagni 22879
Museo del Paesaggio e Museo Storico Artistico, Verbania Pallanza 25958
Museo del Tesoro, Lodi 24202
Museo della Città, Ancona 22882
Museo della Congregazione Mechitarista dei Padri Armeni, Venezia 25933
Museo della Pieve di Staggia, Poggibonsi 24975
Museo della Val Gardena, Ortisei 24698
Museo dell'Abbazia, Casamari-Veroli 23370
Museo dell'Accademia di Belle Arti, Perugia 24852
Museo dell'Arte Serica e Laterizia, Malo 24272
Museo delle Tavolette di Biccherna, Siena 25574
Museo dell'Opera Metropolitana, Siena 25575
Museo di Arte Contemporanea, Stia 25634
Museo di Arte Contemporanea e del Novecento, Monsummano Terme 24487
Museo di Arte e Giacimenti Minerari, Latina 24159
Museo di Arte e Storia delle Miniere, Massa Marittima 24325
Museo di Arte Sacra del Castello, Genga 23975
Museo di Palazzo Altieri, Oriolo Romano 24691
Museo di Palazzo della Penna, Perugia 24854
Museo di Palazzo Fortuny, Venezia 25937
Museo di Palazzo Gamilli, Nocera Umbra 24629
Museo di Palazzo Mirto, Palermo 24771
Museo di Palazzo Pepoli Campogrande, Bologna 23128
Museo di Palazzo Pretorio, Certaldo 23487
Museo di Roma, Roma 25217
Museo di San Francesco, Aversa 22991
Museo di San Mercuriale, Forlì 23912
Museo di Scienze Archeologiche e d'Arte, Padova 24742
Museo di Villa Cagnola, Gazzada 23968
Museo Diffuso, Pennabilli 24835
Museo e Pinacoteca delle Arti Epizephiri, Locri 24200
Museo E. Treccani, Milano 24403
Museo elle Arti e Tradizioni Contadine, Roccasecca dei Volsci 25142
Museo Ideale Leonardo Da Vinci, Vinci 26025
Museo Il Giardino dell'Arte, Portoferraio 25018
Museo Laboratorio di Arte Contemporanea, Roma 25227
Museo Mediceo della Petraia e Giardino, Firenze 23878
Museo Miniscalchi Erizzo, Verona 25976
Museo Piersanti, Matelica 24332
Museo Pietro Canonica, Stresa 25641
Museo Pietro della Vedova, Rima San Giuseppe 25112
Museo Pinacoteca dell'Arte dei Bambini, Smerillo 25592
Museo Regionale A. Pepoli, Trapani 25785
Museo Storico dela Caccia e del Territorio, Cerreto Guidi 23484
Museum Graphia, Urbino 25861
Palazzo del Principe, Genova 24010
Palazzo delle Esposizioni, Roma 25263
Palazzo Ducale, Genova 24011
Pinacoteca Andrea Alfano, Castrovillari 23443
Pinacoteca Chiesa di San Giovanni, Pieve Torina 24924
Pinacoteca Civica, Abano Terme 22791
Pinacoteca Civica, Asti 22975
Pinacoteca Civica, Baiardo 23009
Pinacoteca Civica, Cepagatti 23476
Pinacoteca Civica, Crotone 23692
Pinacoteca Civica, Montelupone 24535
Pinacoteca Civica, Savona 25513
Pinacoteca Civica, Vado Ligure 25866
Pinacoteca Civica A. Modigliani, Follonica 23902
Pinacoteca Civica d'Arte Moderna, Latina 24160
Pinacoteca Civica e Gipsoteca U. Gera, Ripatransone 25128
Pinacoteca Civica G. Cattabriga, Bondeno 23160
Pinacoteca Comunale, Bosa 23182
Pinacoteca Comunale, Deruta 23710
Pinacoteca Comunale, Manciano 24276
Pinacoteca Comunale, Matelica 24333
Pinacoteca Comunale, Narni 24610
Pinacoteca Comunale, Ostra 24718
Pinacoteca Comunale, Quistello 25061
Pinacoteca Comunale, Ripe San Ginesio 25129
Pinacoteca Comunale, San Benedetto del Tronto 25336
Pinacoteca Comunale A. Moroni, Porto Recanati 25014
Pinacoteca Comunale D. Stefanucci, Cingoli 23568
Pinacoteca Comunale E. Giannelli, Parabita 24791
Pinacoteca Comunale e Museo A. De Felice, Terni 25696
Pinacoteca Comunale F. Galante Civera, Margherita di Savoia 24298
Pinacoteca Comunale Francesco Cozza, Stilo 25636
Pinacoteca D. Inzaghi, Budrio 23226
Pinacoteca Dantesca F. Bellonzi, Torre de Passeri 25770
Pinacoteca d'Arte Antica, Gemona del Friuli 23972
Pinacoteca d'Arte Contemporanea, Smerillo 25593
Pinacoteca d'Arte Francescana, Lecce 24168
Pinacoteca d'Arte Sacra, Alcamo 22845
Pinacoteca Davide Bergh', Calice al Cornovoglio 23267
Pinacoteca dei Cappuccini, Voltaggio 26050
Pinacoteca della Cassa di Risparmio, Cesena 23508
Pinacoteca della Certosa, Firenze 23884
Pinacoteca della Rocca Ubaldinesca, Sassocorvaro 25492
Pinacoteca di Corinaldo, Corinaldo 23654
Pinacoteca di San Silvestro, Montecompatri 24515
Pinacoteca e Biblioteca Rambaldi, Sanremo 25426
Pinacoteca in Palazzo Volpi, Como 23631
Pinacoteca Internazionale dell'Età Evolutiva A. Cibaldi, Rezzato 25107
Pinacoteca-Museo Beato Sante, Mombaroccio 24464
Pinacoteca Nazionale, Cosenza 23668
Pinacoteca Parrocchiale, Castroreale 23440
Pinacoteca Rossetti Valentini, Santa Maria Maggiore 25439
Pincacoteca E. Notte, Ceglie Messapica 23468
Quadreria Comunale, Offida 24672
Quadreria Comunale, San Constanzo 25352
Quadreria della Società Economica, Chiavari 23534
Quadreria e Pinacoteca Civica, San Giovanni in Persiceto 25374
Raccolta Civica d'Arte Contemporanea, Molfetta 24460
Raccolta Comunale d'Arte, Frontone 23938
Raccolta d'Arte C. Lamberti, Codogno 23605
Raccolta d'Arte Contemporanea R. Pastori, Calice Ligure 23268
Raccolta d'Arte della Provincia, Modena 24450
Raccolta di Opere d'Arte, Solarolo 25594
Raccolta E Guatelli, Collecchio 23612
Raccolta Privata Toraldo di Francia, Tropea 25841
Riserva Naturale Speciale del Sacro Monte di Varalio, Varallo Sesia 25893
Santa Giulia - Museo della Città, Brescia 23210
Stadtgalerie in Bruneck, Brunico 23220
Villa Godi Malinverni, Lugo di Vicenza 24240

Japan
Amagasaki Bunka Art Gallery, Amagasaki 26097
Arai Memorial Museum of Art, Iwanai 26274
Bunkamura Museum of Art, Tokyo 26834
Chiba-kenritsu Bijutsukan, Chiba 26121
Choraku Homotsukan, Kamo, Izu 26299
Former Hong Kong and Shanghai Bank Museum, Nagasaki 26545
Fuji Art Museum, Fujinomiya 26139
Fukui-kenritsu Bijutsukan, Fukui 26143
Fukushima-kenritsu Bijutsukan, Fukushima 26149
Fukuyama Museum of Art, Fukuyama 26152
Gyokusenji Homotsukan, Kamo, Izu 26300
Hikone Castle Collection, Hikone 26193
Hokkaidoritsu Hakodate Bijutsukan, Hakodate 26173
Hokkaidoritsu Obihiro Bijutsukan, Obihiro 26611
Hokodate Museum of Art, Hokodate 26229
Ibara Municipal Denchu Art Museum, Ibara 26234
Iga Art and Industry Institute, Ueno 26986
Imura Art Museum, Kyoto 26405
Isetan Bijutsukan, Tokyo 26861
Itabashi Kuritsu Bijutsukan, Tokyo 26862
Iwate Museum of Art, Morioka 26516
Japan Amateur Art Museum, Ogi 26616
Kagawa-ken Bunka Kaikan, Takamatsu 26789
Kawasaki-shi Shimin Hakubutsukan, Kawasaki 26328
Kazuaki Iwasaki Space Art Gallery, Ito 26264
Kitakyushu-shiritsu Bijutsukan, Kitakyushu 26343
Kodai Yuzenen, Kyoto 26411
Komagata Jukichi Bijutsu Kinenkan, Nagaoka 26531
Komatsu Hitoshi Art Museum, Kyoto 26412
Koryo Museum of Art, Kyoto 26414
Koyama Keizo Art Museum, Komoro 26370
Kozu Kobunka Museum, Kyoto 26416
Kushiro Art Museum, Kushiro 26390
Manno Art Museum, Osaka 26653
Mirasaka Peace Museum of Art, Mirasaka 26494
Miyagi-ken Bijutsukan, Sendai 26732
MOA Bijutsukan, Atami 26115
Momoyama Art Museum, Kyoto 26434
Morishita Bijutsukan, Hinase 26197
Musée Bernard Buffet, Shizuoka 26765
Musée Marie Laurencin, Chino 26128
Nagoya-Boston Museum of Fine Arts, Nagoya, Aichi 26565
Nagoya-shi Bijutsukan, Nagoya, Aichi 26568
Nakamoura Kenichi Museum of Art, Koganei 26363
Nichido Bijutsukan, Kasama 26315
No Kaiga Art Museum, Kyoto 26442
The Ohsha'joh Museum of Art, Hiroshima 26223
Okyo and Rosetsu Art Museum, Kushimoto 26389
Rokuzan Bijutsukan, Hotaka 26232
Saitama-kenritsu Kindai Bijutsukan, Saitama 26693
Sakaide Civic Art Museum, Sakaide 26702
Sapporo Geijutsu no Mori Bijutsukan, Sapporo 26717
Seiji Togo Memorial Sompo Japan Museum of Art, Tokyo 26915
Setsuryosha Bijitsukan, Niigata 26598
Shibunkaku Museum of Art, Kyoto 26454
Shiseido Art House, Kakegawa 26291
Sogo Museum of Art, Yokohama 27020
Striped House - Museum of Art, Tokyo 26925
Suwa-shi Bitjutsukan, Suwa 26779
Takamatsu City Museum of Art, Takamatsu 26793
Takamura Art Museum, Minami-tsuru 26489
Takaoka Bijutsukan, Takaoka 26795
Tochigi-kenritsu Bijutsukan, Utsunomiya 26993
Tokyo Central Bijutsukan, Tokyo 26936
Tokyo Fuji Art Museum, Hachioji 26166
Tokyo Station Gallery, Tokyo 26943
The Tolman Collection, Tokyo 26949
Toyama Kenminkaikan Bijutsukan, Toyama 26968
Toyama Kinenkan Fuzoku Bijutsukan, Kawashima, Saitama 26332
Toyohashi-shiritsu Bijutsukan, Toyohashi 26972
Wocoal Art Center, Tokyo 26956
Yamanashi-kenritsu Bijutsukan, Kofu 26360
Yamauchi Library, Yokohama 27021
Yayoi Museum, Tokyo 26959
Yokohama Bijutsukan, Yokohama 27022
Yuki Bijutsukan, Osaka 26676

Kazakhstan
Muzej Izobrazitelnych Iskusstv, Astana 27076

Kenya
The Museum Studio and Arts Centre, Nairobi 27111

Latvia
Arzemju Mākslas Muzejs, Rīga 27402
Bauskas Novadpētniecības un Mākslas Muzejs, Bauska 27334
Daugavpils Muzeja Izstāžu Zāles, Daugavpils 27346
Izstāžu Zāle, Madona 27383
Liepājas Muzeja Izstāžu Zāles, Liepāja 27379
Raiņa Literatūras un Mākslas Vēstures Muzejs, Rīga 27435
Valsts Mākslas Muzeju, Rīga 27444

Lebanon
Musée des Beaux Arts, Beirut 27483
Musée Nicholas Ibrahim Sursock, Beirut 27485

Liechtenstein
Vereinigung der Mund- und Fussmalenden Künstler in aller Welt e.V., Schaan 27511

Lithuania
Ch. Frenkelis Mansion, Šiauliai 27527
Lietuvos Dailes Muziejus, Vilnius 27536
Šiauliai Aušros Museum, Šiauliai 27531
Venclauskiu House, Šiauliai 27532
Vilniaus Paveikslu Galerija, Vilnius 27539

Luxembourg
Galerie d'Art d'Esch, Esch-sur-Alzette 27555
Galerie d'Art du Château, Bettembourg 27543
Galerie d'Art Municipale, Oberkorn 27573
Galerie d'Art Municipale, Rumelange 27574

Macedonia
Muzej na Makedonija - Arceološki, Etnološki i Istoriski, Skopje 27590

Madagascar
Musée d'Art et d'Archéologie de l'Université d'Antananarivo, Antananarivo 27600
Musée du Palais de la Reine, Antananarivo 27602

Malaysia
Balai Seni Lukis Negara, Kuala Lumpur 27639
Museum and Art Gallery, Shah Alam 27686
Pucuk Rebung Royal Gallery Museum, Kuala Lumpur 27651
Sabah Art Gallery, Kota Kinabalu 27632
Shah Alam Art Gallery, Shah Alam 27688

Malta
National Museum of Fine Arts, Valletta 27703
Ta' Hagrat Copper Age Temples, Mgarr 27699

Mexico
Casa Siglo XIX, Chihuahua 27820
Centro Cultural Isidro Fabela, México 28093
Galería José María Velasco, México 28101
Instituto Mexicano Norteamericano de Jalisco, Guadalajara 27947
Museo Amparo, Puebla 28317
Museo Casa del Alfeñique, Puebla 28320
Museo de Arte José Luis Bello y González, Puebla 28323
Museo de la Secretaria de Hacienda y Credito Publico Antiguo Palacio del Arzobispado, México 28143
Museo José Luis Cuevas, México 28179
Museo Nacional de Arte Fantástico, Córdoba 27858
Museo Soumaya, México 28202
Museo Taller Luis Nishizawa, Toluca 28551
Museo Universitario de Ciencias y Artes, Roma, México 28207
Pinacoteca de Nuevo León, Monterrey 28241
Pinacoteca del Centro de la Profesa, México 28211
Pinacoteca Diego Rivera, Xalapa 28618
Robert Brady Museum, Cuernavaca 27878
San Pedro Museo de Arte, Puebla 28344

Moldova
Muzeul National de Arte Plastice, Chişinău 28658

Mongolia
Zanabazar Museum of Fine Arts, Ulaanbaatar 28690

Morocco
Musée d'Art Islamique, Marrakech 28700
Musée de Dar-El-Jamaï, Meknès 28701
Musée des Arts Traditionnels, Tétouan 28716

Mozambique
Museu Nacional de Arte, Maputo 28725

Myanmar
State Museum, Mandalay 28734

Namibia
National Art Gallery of Namibia, Windhoek 28780

Netherlands
Achter de Zuilen, Overveen 29708
Armando Museum, Amersfoort 28819
Beeldentuin Belling Garde, Bellingwolde 28972
Beurs van Berlage Museum, Amsterdam 28844
De Beyerd, Breda 29017
Brink 7 Galerij, Yde 30029
Centrum Beeldende Kunst, Groningen 29307
Centrum Beeldende Kunst Emmen, Emmen 29229
Collectie D.H.G. Bolten, Den Haag 29091
Galerie Anna Paulownahuis, Soest 29841
Galerie de Lange, Emmen 29230
Gemeentelijk Expositiecentrum Aemstelle, Amstelveen 28831
ID Galerie, Helmond 29395
Inter Art - Sonsbeek Art and Design, Arnhem 28939
Jachthuis Sint-Hubertus, Hoenderloo 29429
De Kabinetten van de Vleeshal, Middelburg 29591
Kasteel Heeze - Collectie H.N.C. Baron Van Tuyll Van Serooskerken Van Heeze en Leende, Heeze 29374
Kasteel Het Hijenhuis, Heino 29382
Kasteel-Museum Sypesteyn, Loosdrecht 29546
Kinderkunsthal Villa Zebra, Rotterdam 29754
Kunstcentrum De Waagh, Oldenzaal 29658
Kunstcentrum Pand Paulus, Schiedam 29801
Kunsthal Rotterdam, Rotterdam 29756
Kunstpaviljoen, Nieuw Roden 29614
't Kunstuus, Heinkenszand 29380
Kunstvereniging Diepenheim, Diepenheim 29149
Meppeler Expositie Centrum, Meppel 29590
Museum Boijmans Van Beuningen, Rotterdam 29759
Museum De Paviljoens, Almere 28813
Museum Galerie Rob Mohlman, Venhuizen 29938
Museum het Catharina Gasthuis, Gouda 29297
Museum HSF, Zwolle 30084
Museum Jan Cunen, Oss 29684
Museum Katendrecht, Rotterdam 29760
Museum Kranenburgh, Bergen, Noord-Holland 28982
Museum Swaensteyn, Voorburg 29962
Museum Van Bommel Van Dam, Venlo 29940
Museum Veluwezoom, Doorwerth 29171
Museum voor Figuratieve Kunst de Buitenplaats, Eelde 29198
Nederlands Museum van Knipkunst, Schoonhoven 29813
Oerka Irene Verbeek Museum, Raard 29723
Orangerie, 's-Hertogenbosch 29409
Presentatieruimte de Overslag, Eindhoven 29218
Rijksmuseum Hendrik Willem Mesdag, Den Haag 29122
Stadsmuseum Woerden, Woerden 30016

Stroom - Haags Centrum voor Visueel Kunst, Den Haag 29126
Studiecentrum Perk, Eindhoven 29219
Tattoo Museum, Amsterdam 28907
Theo Swagemakers Museum, Haarlem 29332
De Verbeelding Kunst Landschap Natuur, Zeewolde 30050
Verpleeghuis Cornelia, Zierikzee 30063
Vleeshal, Middelburg 29594
Voerman Museum Hattem, Hattem 29353
De Zonnehof, Centrum voor Moderne Kunst, Amersfoort 28828

New Zealand
Eastern Southland Gallery, Gore 30166
George Fraser Gallery, Auckland 30109
Lake Taupo Museum and Art Gallery, Taupo 30257
Left Bank Art Gallery, Greymouth 30169
Lopdell House Gallery, Auckland 30112
Sarjeant Gallery - Te Whare o Rehua, Wanganui 30285
Southland Museum and Art Gallery, Invercargill 30186
Te Manawa Art, Palmerston North 30230
Waikato Museum of Art and History, Hamilton 30174
Whangarei Art Museum, Whangarei 30315

Nigeria
National Museum Uyo, Uyo 30364

Norway
Agatunet, Nå 30697
Astruptunet, Skei i Jølster 30842
Beiarn Bygdetun, Moldfjord 30689
Bergen Kunstmuseum, Bergen 30412
Bergen Kunstmuseum - Rasmus Meyers Samlinger, Bergen 30413
Christianssands Billedgalleri, Kristiansand 30612
Drammens Museum, Drammen 30462
Eikaasgalleriet, Skei i Jølster 30843
Fedrenes Minne, Hidrasund 30548
Galleri Espolin, Kabelvåg 30586
Galleri Svalbard, Longyearbyen 30654
Haugar Vestfold Kunstmuseum, Tønsberg 30925
Ingebrigt Vik's Museum, Øystese 30775
Internasjonale Barnekunstmuseet, Oslo 30738
International Museum of Children's Art, Oslo 30739
Lillehammer Kunstmuseum, Lillehammer 30640
Magnus Dagestad Museet, Voss 31000
Mandal Bymuseum, Mandal 30663
Nord-Trøndelag Fylkesgalleri, Namsos 30701
Nordnorsk Kunstmuseum, Tromsø 30932
Nøstetangen Museum, Hokksund 30551
Savio-museet, Kirkenes 30594
Sørlandets Kunstmuseum, Kristiansand 30615
Stenersenmuseet, Oslo 30765
Stokke Bygdetun og Galleri Bokeskogen, Stokke 30897
Trastad Samlinger, Borkenes 30444
Vigeland, Sør-Audnedal 30865

Pakistan
Aiwen e Rifat Museum and Art Gallery, Karachi 31027
Children Art Palace, Islamabad 31022
Hyderabad Museum, Hyderabad 31020

Paraguay
Centro de Artes Visuales, Asunción 31094
Museo Bernardino Caballero, Asunción 31096
Museo Nacional de Bellas Artes y Antigüedades, Asunción 31105

Peru
Museo de Arte Colonial Pedro de Osma, Lima 31204
Pinacoteca Municipal Ignacio Merino, Lima 31227

Philippines
Bulwagang Helena Benitez Gallery, Manila 31371
CAP Art Center and Don Sergio Osmeña Memorabilia, Cebu 31307
Children's Museum, Quezon City 31430
Corredor, Gallery of the College of Fine Arts, Quezon City 31431
Cultural Museum, Kabacan 31333
Jumalon Museum and Art Gallery, Cebu 31313
Pambasang Museo ng Pilipinas, Manila 31390
University of Santo Tomas Museum of Arts and Sciences, Manila 31398

Poland
Dom Eskenów, Toruń 32049
Dom Jana Matejki, Kraków 31682
Dworek Jana Matejki w Krzesławicach, Kraków 31684
Galeria Bałucka, Łódź 31766
Galeria Miejeska Arsenał, Poznań 31895
Galeria Sztuki Dawna Synagoga, Nowy Sącz 31834
Galeria Sztuki im. W. i J. Kulczyckich, Zakopane 32204
Galeria Sztuki Wozownia, Toruń 32051
Galeria Władysława Hasiora, Zakopane 32205
Galeria Zamek w Reszlu, Reszel 31946
Muzeum Akademii Sztuk Pięknych, Warszawa 32087
Muzeum Diecezjalne Sztuki Religijnej, Lublin 31788
Muzeum Emila Zegadłowicza, Wadowice 32068
Muzeum Górnośląskie, Bytom 31519
Muzeum im. Adama Mickiewicza w Śmiełowie, Żerków 32217
Muzeum im. Anny i Jarosława Iwaszkiewiczów w Stawisku, Podkowa Leśna 31890
Muzeum im. Jerzego Dunin-Borkowskiego, Krośniewice 31734
Muzeum im. Oskara Kolberga, Przysucha 31924
Muzeum im. Stanisława Noakowskiego, Nieszawa 31825
Muzeum Jana Cybisa, Głogówek 31595
Muzeum Łazienki Krolewskie, Warszawa 32109
Muzeum Marii Konopnickiej, Suwałki 32009
Muzeum Miedzi, Legnica 31754
Muzeum Narodowe, Szczecin 32029
Muzeum Narodowe w Krakowie, Kraków 31715
Muzeum Narodowe w Warszawie, Warszawa 32115
Muzeum Narodowe we Wrocławiu, Wrocław 32182
Muzeum Okręgowe w Toruniu, Toruń 32054
Muzeum Pałac w Wilanowie, Warszawa 32117
Muzeum Parafialne, Iwkowa 31619
Muzeum Rzeźby im. Xawerego Dunikowskiego Królikarnia, Warszawa 32124
Muzeum Stanisława Wyspiańskiego, Kraków 31719
Muzeum Sztuki Dziecka, Warszawa 32127
Muzeum Sztuki Mieszczańskiej, Wrocław 32188
Muzeum Walewskich w Tubądzinie, Wróblew 32172
Muzeum-Zamek w Gołuchowie, Gołuchów 31603
Muzeum Zamkowe, Pszczyna 31927
Muzeum Ziemi Zaborskiej i Galeria Sztuki Ludowej, Wiele 32152
Ośrodek Biograficzny Komisji Turystyki Górskiej, Kraków 31725
Pałac Sztuki w Krakowie, Kraków 31726
Panorama Racławicka, Wrocław 32192
Punkt Muzealny w Supraśli, Supraśl 32008
Rezydencja Księży Młyn, Łódź 31779
Zamek Królewski w Warszawie, Warszawa 32143
Zbiory Sztuki, Włocławek 32165

Portugal
Casa Museu Abel Salazar da Universidade do Porto, São Mamede de Infesta 32344
Casa-Museu Dr. Anastácio Gonçalves, Lisboa 32284
Museu da Santa Casa da Misericórdia, Coimbra 32256
Museu de Angra do Heroísmo, Angra do Heroísmo 32237
Museu de Aveiro, Aveiro 32239
Museu de José Malhoa, Caldas da Rainha 32246
Museu Romântico da Quinta da Macieirinha, Porto 32339

Puerto Rico
Museo de Arte de Puerto Rico, San Juan 32394
Museo de Arte Francisco Oller, Bayamón 32364
Museo de Las Américas, San Juan 32396

Réunion
Musée Léon Dierx, Saint-Denis 32420

Romania
Muzeul de Artă, Braşov 32447
Muzeul de Artă, Iaşi 32532
Muzeul de Artă Piatra-Neamţ, Piatra-Neamţ 32565
Muzeul Judeţean Argeş, Piteşti 32569
Muzeul Naţional de Artă al României, Bucureşti 32466
Muzeul Naţional de Artă Cluj-Napoca, Cluj-Napoca 32494
Muzeul Naţional Peleş, Sinaia 32596
Muzeul Taru Făgărasului, Făgăraş 32518
Muzeul Theodor Pallady, Bucureşti 32474

Russia
Aleksandrovskaja Sloboda - Gosudarstvennyj Istoriko-architekturnyj i Chudožestvennyj Muzej-zapovednik, Aleksandrov 32633
Aleksandrovskij Chudožestvennyj Muzej, Aleksandrov 32634
Altajskij Respublikanskij Kraevedčeskij Muzej im. A.V. Anochina, Gorno-Altajsk 32808
Archangelskij Oblastnoj Muzej Izobrazitelnych Iskusstv, Archangelsk 32649
Architekturno-chudožestvennyj Ansambl byvšego Spaso-Jakovleskogo Monastyrja, Rostov (Jaroslavskaja obl.) 33354
Art Centr Puškinskaja 10, Sankt-Peterburg 33380
Baškirskij Respublikanskij Chudožestvennyj Muzej im. M.V. Nesterova, Ufa 33641
Bolšoj Dvorec, Lomonosov 32986
Burjatskij Respublikanskij Chudožestvennyj Muzej im. C.S. Sampilova, Ulan-Udė 33651
Centralnyj Dom Chudožnikov, Moskva 33022
Čitinskij Oblastnoj Chudožestvennyj Muzej, Čita 32750
Čuvašskij Gosudarstvennyj Chudožestvennyj Muzej, Čeboksary 32718
Dagestanskij Gosudarstvennyj Objedinennyj Istoriko-architekturnyj Muzej, Machačkala 32995
Dagestanskij Muzej Izobrazitelnych Iskusstv, Machačkala 32996
Dalnevostočnyj Chudožestvennyj Muzej, Chabarovsk 32739
Ekaterininskij Dvorec - Gosudarstvennyj Muzej Carskoje Selo, Puškin 33336
Galereja Le Vall, Novosibirsk 33239
Galereja Zarubežnogo Iskusstva im. Professora M.F. Gabyševa, Jakutsk 32842
Gosudarstvennyj Chudožestvenno-architekturnyj Dvorcovo-parkovyj Muzej-zapovednik Oranienbaum, Lomonosov 32988
Gosudarstvennyj Chudožestvenno-architekturnyj Dvorcovo-parkovyj Muzej-zapovednik Pavlovsk, Pavlovsk 33285
Gosudarstvennyj Chudožestvennyj Istoriko-architekturnyj i prirodno-landšaftnyj Muzej-zapovednik Kolomenskoe, Moskva 33052
Gosudarstvennyj Istoriko-architekturnyj, Chudožestvennyj i Landšaftnyj Muzej-Zapovednik Caricyno, Moskva 33055
Gosudarstvennyj Istoriko-chudožestvennyj Dvorcovo-parkovyj Muzej-zapovednik Gatčina, Gatčina 32802
Gosudarstvennyj Istoriko-kulturnyj Muzej-zapovednik "Moskovskij Kreml", Moskva 33056
Gosudarstvennyj Istoriko-literaturnyj Muzej-Zapovednik A.S. Puškina s usadbami Vjazemy i Zacharovo, Bolšie Vjazemy 32696
Gosudarstvennyj Memorial'nyj Istoriko-chudožestvennyj i Prirodnyj Muzej-zapovednik V.D. Polenova, Strachovo 33566
Gosudarstvennyj Muzej Izobrazitelnych Iskusstv Respubliki Kalmykija, Ėlista 32793
Gosudarstvennyj Muzej-masterskaja Skulptora A.S. Golubkinoj, Moskva 33061
Gosudarstvennyj Muzej A.S. Puškina, Moskva 33063
Gosudarstvennyj Muzej Zapovednik Petergof, Sankt-Peterburg 33406
Gosudarstvennyj Russkij Muzej, Sankt-Peterburg 33407
Gosudarstvennyj Vladimiro-Suzdalskij Istoriko-architekturnyj i Chudožestvennyj Muzej-zapovednik, Vladimir 33692
Irkutskij Oblastnoj Chudožestvennyj Muzej im. V.P. Sukačeva, Irkutsk 32813
Istoriko-Architekturnyj, Chudožestvennyj i Archeologičeskij Muzej "Zarajskij Kreml", Zarajsk 33746
Istoriko-Architekturnyj i Chudožestvennyj Muzej Ivangorodskaja Krepost, Ivangorod 32823
Istoriko-chudožestvennyj Muzej, Uglič 33649
Istoriko-memorialnyj i Architurno-chudožestvennyj Muzej, Tichvin 33600
Ivanovskij Oblastnoj Chudožestvennyj Muzej, Ivanovo 32829
Jaroslavskij Chudožestvennyj Muzej - Gubernatorskij Dom, Jaroslavl 32848
Jaroslavskij Istoriko-architekturnyj i Chudožestvennyj Muzej-zapovednik, Jaroslavl 32849
Jurinskij Istoriko-chudožestvennyj Muzej, Jurino 32863
Kabardino-Balkarskij Gosudarstvennyj Muzej Izobrazitelnych Iskusstv, Nalčik 33193
Kaliningradskaja Oblastnaja Chudožestvennaja Galereja, Kaliningrad 32869
Kaliningradskij Oblastnoj Istoriko-chudožestvennyj Muzej, Kaliningrad 32870
Kalužskij Oblastnoj Chudožestvennyj Muzej, Kaluga 32878
Karačaevo-Čerkesskij Istoriko-kul'turnyj i Prirodnyj Muzej-Zapovednik, Čerkessk 32736
Kartinnaja Galereja K. Vasiljeva, Kazan 32890
Kirovskij Oblastnoj Chudožestvennyj Muzej im. Viktora i Apollinarija Vasnecovych, Kirov 32919
Kostromskoj Gosudarstvennyj Istoriko-architekturnyj Muzej-zapovednik, Kostroma 32942
Kostromskoj Gosudarstvennyj Obedinennyj Chudožestvennyj Muzej, Kostroma 32943
Krasnojarskij Chudožestvennyj Muzej im. V.I. Surikova, Krasnojarsk 32950
Kulturno-vystavočnyj Centr Raduga, Uljanovsk 33659
Malojaroslaveckaja Gorodskaja Kartinnaja Galereja, Malojaroslavec 33005
Memorialnyj Muzej-Masterskaja Skulptora S.T. Konenkova, Moskva 33081
Memorialnyj Muzej-usadba Chudožnika N.A. Jarošenko, Kislovodsk 32929
Meždunarodnyj Centr-Muzej im. N.K. Rericha, Moskva 33083
Mitropoličji Palaty - Muzej Drevnerusskogo Iskusstva, Jaroslavl 32852
Mordovskij Muzej Izobrazitelnych Isskustv im. S.D. Ėrzi, Saransk 33496
Moskovskij Gosudarstvennyj Vystavočnyj Zal Malyi Manež, Moskva 33088
Muzej A Muzy ne Molčali, Sankt-Peterburg 33426
Muzej-institut Semji Rerichov, Sankt-Peterburg 33437
Muzej Izobrazitelnych Iskusstv im. A.S. Puškina, Moskva 33113
Muzej Izobrazitelnyh Iskusstv Respubliki Marij Ėl, Joškar-Ola 32860
Muzej Klassičeskogo i Sovremennogo Iskusstva, Moskva 33116
Muzej Krylova, Tula 33626
Muzej Nonkonformistskogo Iskusstva, Sankt-Peterburg 33461
Muzej Parka Iskusstv na Krymskoj Naberežnoj, Moskva 33146
Muzej Rossijskoj Akademii Chudožestv, Sankt-Peterburg 33463
Muzej Semji Benua, Sankt-Peterburg 33464
Muzej Sovremennogo Izobrazitelnogo Iskusstva im. A.A. Plastova, Uljanovsk 33667
Muzej-usadba im. N.K. Rericha, Izvara 32839
Muzej-zapovednik Dmitrovskij Kreml, Dmitrov 32758
Muzej-zapovednik Kazanskij Kreml, Kazan 32906
Muzejno-vystavočnyj Centr, Ivanovo 32833
Muzejno-vystavočnyj Centr Ego, Sankt-Peterburg 33471
Nacionalnaja Galereja Respubliki Komi, Syktyvkar 33578
Nižegorodskij Chudožestvennyj Muzej, Nižnij Novgorod 33222
Nižnetagilskij Municipalnyj Muzej Izobrazitelnych Iskusstv, Nižnij Tagil 33227
Nižnetagilskij Muzej-Zapovednik Gornozavodskogo Dela Srednego Urala, Nižnij Tagil 33228
Novokuzneckij Chudožestvennyj Muzej, Novokuzneck 33236
Oblastnaja Kartinnaja Galereja Obraz, Kaluga 32882
Oloneckaja Kartinnaja Galereja, Olonec 33251
Omskij Oblastnoj Muzej Izobrazitelnych Iskusstv im. M.A. Vrubelja, Omsk 33257
Pereslavl-Zalesskij Gosudarstvennyj Istoriko-architekturnyj i Chudožestvennyj Muzej-zapovednik, Pereslavl-Zalesskij 33299
Respublikanskij Vystavočnyj Zal, Joškar-Ola 32862
S.A. Otkrytka, Moskva 33178
Sergačskij Kraevedčeskij Muzej, Sergač 33518
Sergievo-Posadskij Gosudarstvennyj Istoriko-chudožestvennyj Muzej Zapovednik, Sergiev Posad 33521
Severo-osetinskij Gosudarstvennyj Obedinennyj Muzej Istorii, Architektury i Literatury, Vladikavkaz 33690
Smolenskaja Chudožestvennaja Galerja, Smolensk 33534
Smolenskij Muzej-Zapovednik, Smolensk 33536
Sosnovoborskij Chudožestvennyj Muzei Sovremennogo Iskusstva, Sosnovyj Bor 33549
Tarusskaja Kartinnaja Galereja, Tarusa 33593
Tatarskij Gosudarstvennyj Muzej Izobrazitelnych Iskusstv, Kazan 32908
Tjumenskij Oblastnoj Kraevedčeskij Muzej im. I.Ja. Slovcova, Tjumen 33610
Tomskij Oblastnoj Chudožestvennyj Muzej, Tomsk 33616
Učebno-chudožestvennyj Muzej im. I.V. Cvetaeva, Moskva 33180
Udmurtskij Respublikanskij Muzej Izobrazitelnych Iskusstv, Iževsk 32837
Uljanovskij Oblastnoj Chudožestvennyj Muzej, Uljanovsk 33668
Voronežskij Chudožestvennyj Muzej im. I.N. Kramskogo, Voronež 33735
Vystavočnyj Zal, Tula 33634
Vystavočnyj Zal Moskovskogo Sojuza Chudožnikov, Moskva 33185
Vystavočnyj Zal Sojuza Chudožnikov Rossii, Sankt-Peterburg 33491
Vystavočnyj Zentr Sankt-Peterburgskogo Otdelenija Sojuza Chudožnikov Rossii, Sankt-Peterburg 33492
Zvenigorodskij Istoriko-architekturnyj i Chudožestvennyj Muzej, Zvenigorod 33751

San Marino
Museo - Pinacoteca San Francesco, San Marino 33766

Serbia-Montenegro
Centar Savremene Umjetnosti Crne Gore, Podgorica 33887
Galerija Lazar Vozarević, Sremska Mitrovica 33912
Galerija Milan Konjović, Sombor 33909
Galerija Milene Pavlović Barilli, Požarevac 33891
Galerija Reprodukcija i Umetničkih Dela, Beograd 33797
Galerija Samoukih Likovnih Umetnika Svetozarevo, Svetozarevo 33919
Galerija Slika Save Sumanovića, Sid 33904
Galerija Sopoćanska Vidjenja, Novi Pazar 33867
Memorijalni Muzej u Goši, Smederevska Palanka 33907
Narodni Muzej Valjevo, Valjevo 33926
Zaduzbina Kralja Petra I Karađorđevića, Topola 33921

Slovakia
Múzeum a Galéria Hont Šahy, Šahy 34056
Múzeum Ferdiša Kostku, Stupava 34067
Múzeum vo Svätý Antone, Svätý Anton 34068
Oblastná Galéria P.M. Bohúňa, Liptovský Mikuláš 34016
Šarišská Galéria, Prešov 34048
Slovenská Národná Galéria, Bratislava 33978
Slovenské Banské Múzeum, Banská Štiavnica 33951

Slovenia
Cankarjev Dom, Ljubljana 34107
Galerija Božidar Jakac, Kostanjevica na Krki 34098
Galerija Likovnih Samorastnikov, Trebnje 34157
Galerija Mestne Hiše, Kranj 34099
Galerije Sivčeva Hiša, Radovljica 34143
Koroška Galerija Likovnih Umetnosti, Slovenj Gradec 34149
Obalne Galerije - Galerija Loža, Koper 34096
Obalne Galerije - Mestna Galerija, Piran 34137
Pilonova Galerija, Ajdovščina 34083
Pokrajinski Muzej, Murska Sobota 34134
Razstavni Salon Rotovž, Maribor 34128

South Africa
Anton Van Wouw House, Brooklyn 34196
Caledon Museum, Caledon 34198
Gencor Art Gallery, Auckland Park 34172
Jack Heath Art Gallery, Pietermaritzburg 34325
Johannes Stegmann Art Gallery, Bloemfontein 34185
Johannesburg Art Gallery, Johannesburg 34279
Mayibuye Centre Collection, Bellville 34178
Nelson Mandela Metropolitan Art Museum, Port Elizabeth 34332
Old Arts Gallery, Pretoria 34351
Oliewenhuis Art Museum, Bloemfontein 34192
UNISA Art Gallery, Pretoria 34360
University Museum - Sasol Art Museum, Stellenbosch 34385
University of Pretoria Art Collection, Pretoria 34361
Van Gybland-Oosterhoff Collection, Pretoria 34362
Van Tilburg Collection, Pretoria 34363
Works of Art Collection, Rosebank 34373

Spain
Bilboko Arte Eder Museoa / Museo de Bellas Artes de Bilbao, Bilbao 34609
Cartuja de la Asunción, Granada 34863
Casa de los Morlanes, Zaragoza 35716
Casa Museo de Rafael Alberti, El Puerto de Santa María 35300
Casa Natal de Isabel la Católica, Madrigal de las Altas Torres 35064
Castell Cartoixa Vallparadis, Terrassa 35524
Centre de Cultura Sa Nostra, Palma de Mallorca 35222
Colección de la Real Academia de la Historia, Madrid 35000
Colección Municipal de Arte Contemporáneo, Madrid 35004
Collección de Arte y Ciencias Naturales, Ciudad Real 34719
Conjunt Monumental de la Esglésias de Sant Pere, Terrassa 35526
Fundació Antoni Tàpies, Barcelona 34538
Fundació Joan Miró, Barcelona 34539
Fundació Pilar i Joan Miró, Palma de Mallorca 35228
Fundación César Manrique, Teguise 35519
Fundación Yannick y Ben Jakober, Alcúdia 34439
Koldo Mitxelena Kulturunea Erakustaret, Donostia-San Sebastián 34774
Monasterio de Nuestra Señora de Guadelupe, Guadelupe 34887
Museo Arqueologico Provincial de Orense, Orense 35182
Museo Artístico de Roncesvalles, Roncesvalles 35337
Museo Cerralbo, Madrid 35014
Museo de Arte Contemporáneo José María Moreno Galván, Sevilla 35483
Museo de Avila, Avila 34502
Museo de Bellas Artes, Valencia 35601
Museo de Bellas Artes de Asturias, Oviedo 35204
Museo de Bellas Artes de Castellón, Castellón de la Plana 34693
Museo de Bellas Artes de Sevilla, Sevilla 35485
Museo de Burgos, Burgos 34630
Museo de Ciudad Real, Ciudad Real 34721
Museo de Cuenca, Cuenca 34764
Museo de Gomellano, Gumiel de Hizán 34896
Museo de Guadalajara, Guadalajara 34885
Museo de la Encarnación, Corella 34745
Museo de las Telecomunicaciones, Madrid 35028
Museo de Palencia, Palencia 35214
Museo de Santa Cruz, Toledo 35542
Museo de Valladolid, Valladolid 35621
Museo de Zaragoza, Zaragoza 35724
Museo Español de Arte Contemporaneo, Madrid 35036
Museo Gregorio Prieto, Valdepeñas 35591
Museo Histórico de Requena y su Comarca, Requena 35311
Museo Marceliano Santa María, Burgos 34634
Museo Municipal, Reus 35313
Museo Nacional de Reproducciones Artísticas, Madrid 35047
Museo Thyssen-Bornemisza, Madrid 35057
Museu d'Art, Cadaqués 34644
Museu d'Art Casa Turull, Sabadell 35345
Museu d'Art Frederic Marès, Montblanc 35130
Museu de Granollers, Granollers 34883
Museu de la Ciutat, Valls 35638
Museu de l'Empordà, Figueres 34817
Museu de Montserrat, Monistrol de Montserrat 35125
Museu de Rubí, Rubí 35342
Museu de Vilafranca-Museu del Vi, Vilafranca del Penedès 35659
Palacio de Viana, Córdoba 34743
Rajoloteca Salvador Miquel, Vallromanes 35637
Reial Academia Catalana Belles Arts Sant Jordi, Barcelona 34590
Salas Municipales de Arte Sanz-Enea, Zarautz 35733
Templo Románico de San Martín, Fromista 34825

Sudan
Art Gallery of the College of Fine and Applied Arts, Khartoum 35763

Sweden
Åmåls Konsthall, Åmål 35795
Axel Ebbes Konsthall, Trelleborg 36332
Båtsmanskasernen, Karlskrona 35997
Bergsjö Konsthall, Bergsjö 35831
Bollnäs Konsthallen, Bollnäs 35837
Borås Konstmuseum, Borås 35840
Botkyrka Konsthall och Xet-Museet, Tumba 36338
Bror Hjorths Hus, Uppsala 36351
Dunkers Kulturhus, Helsingborg 35948
Höganäs Museum och Konsthall, Höganäs 35956
Karby Gård Konstcentrum, Täby 36319
Karlskoga Konsthall, Karlskoga 35995
Konstmuseum, Lund 36058
Konstmuseum Gösta Werner och Havet, Simrishamn 36188
Konstmuseum Gösta Werner och Rådhusets Konsthall, Örnsköldsvik 36143
Konstsamlingarna, Uppsala 36355
Kulturhuset, Stockholm 36250
Länsmuseet Gävleborg, Gävle 35900
Landskrona Konsthall, Landskrona 36028
Lidköpings Konsthall, Lidköping 36034
Liljevalchs Konsthall, Stockholm 36255
Ljungbergmuseet, Ljungby 36043
Lunds Konsthall, Lund 36061
Malmö Konsthall, Malmö 36075
Malmö Konstmuseum, Malmö 36076
Mjellby Konstmuseum, Halmstad 35942
Museet Kvarnen, Filipstad 35889
Museum Anna Nordlander, Skellefteå 36196
Museum Leonardo da Vinci Ideale, Karlskrona 36000
Nationalmuseum, Stockholm 36265
Nolhaga Slotts Konsthall, Alingsås 35791
Örebro Konsthallen, Örebro 36138
Östergötlands Länsmuseum, Linköping 36042
Olle Olsson-Huset, Solna 36219
Rackstadmuseet, Arvika 35817
Rättviks Konstmuseum och Naturmuseum, Rättvik 36159
Regionmuseet Kristianstad, Kristianstad 36018
Riksutstallningar, Stockholm 36277
Skissernas Museum, Lund 36064
Skövde Konsthall och Konstmuseum, Skövde 36198
Smålands Konstarkiv, Värnamo 36377
Staffanstorps Konsthall, Staffanstorp 36225
State Apartments of the Royal Palace, Stockholm 36284
Stockholms Universitet Konstsamlingar, Stockholm 36291
Strindbergsmuseet Blå Tornet, Stockholm 36292
Sundsbergs Gård Museum och Konsthall, Sunne 36312
Tidaholms Konsthall, Tidaholm 36324
Tomelilla Konsthall, Tomelilla 36326
Uppsala Konstmuseum, Uppsala 36362
Västerås Konstmuseum, Västerås 36381
Vasamuseet, Stockholm 36298

Switzerland
Andrea Robbi-Stiftung, Sils in Engadin 37168
Castello di Sasso Corbaro, Bellinzona 36527
Civica Galleria d'Arte Villa dei Cedri, Bellinzona 36529
Coninx Museum, Zürich 37373
Espace Jean Tinguely - Niki de Saint-Phalle, Fribourg 36711
Fondation de l'Hermitage, Lausanne 36855
Fondation Louis Moret, Martigny 36923
Fondation Pierre Gianadda, Martigny 36924
Fondazione Galleria Gottardo, Lugano 36897
Galerie Gersag Emmen, Emmenbrücke 36679
Hans Trudel-Haus Stiftung, Baden 36484
Heidi Weber-Museum, Zürich 37380
Kunst im Alten Schützenhaus, Zofingen 37365
Kunstforum Bâloise, Basel 36503
Kunsthalle Palazzo, Liestal 36879
Kunsthalle Prisma, Arbon 36466
Kunsthalle Winterthur, Winterthur 37330
Kunsthaus, Grenchen 36779
Kunsthaus Zürich, Zürich 37386
Kunsthaus Zug, Zug 37426
Kunsthof Zürich, Zürich 37387
Kunstmuseum Bern, Bern 36544
Kunstraum Aarau, Aarau 36426
Kunstsammlung Villa Schüpbach, Steffisburg 37211
Manoir de la Ville de Martigny, Martigny 36925
Martin-Lauterburg-Stiftung, Schloss Jegenstorf, Bern 36545
Musée Barbier-Mueller, Genève 36742
Musée Cantonal des Beaux-Arts, Sion 37172
Musée d'Art et d'Histoire, Fribourg 36715
Musée d'Art et d'Histoire Neuchâtel, Neuchâtel 36984
Musée de la Science-Fiction, de l'Utopie et des Voyages Extraordinaires, Yverdon-les-Bains 37353
Musée Léon Perrin, Môtiers 36955
Musée Rath, Genève 36751
Museo Cantonale d'Arte, Lugano 36898
Museo d'Arte Mendrisio, Mendrisio 36938
Museo d'Arte Moderna, Lugano 36901
Museo in Erba, Bellinzona 36531
Museo Wilhelm Schmid, Brè sopra Lugano 36583
Museum Casa Anatta, Casa Selma und Klarwelt der Seligen, Ascona 36472
Museum im Bellpark, Kriens 36839
Museum im Lagerhaus, Sankt Gallen 37105
Museum Jean Tinguely, Basel 36511
Museum Rietberg Zürich, Zürich 37398
Museum zu Allerheiligen, Schaffhausen 37132
Ortsmuseum Zollikon, Zollikon 37367
PAC - Poste d'Art Contemporain, Fribourg 36719
Park-Villa Rieter, Zürich 37405
Polenmuseum Rapperswil, Rapperswil, Sankt Gallen 37044
Sammlung Hauser und Wirth, Sankt Gallen 37107
Schlößchen Vorder Bleichenberg Biberist, Biberist 36562
Stiftung Künstlerhaus Boswil, Boswil 36579
Stiftung Stadtmuseum Sursee, Sursee 37227
Verein Kunstsammlung Unterseen, Unterseen 37265

Syria
National Museum of Damascus, Damascus 37436

Trinidad and Tobago
National Museum and Art Gallery of Trinidad and Tobago, Port-of-Spain 37552

Tunisia
La Nationale Galerie d'Art Alyssa, Bardo 37554

Turkey
Antalya Devlet Güzel Sanatlar Galerisi, Antalya 37622
Basin Müzesi Sanat Galerisi, İstanbul 37695
Beyoglu Sanat Merkezi, İstanbul 37696
Manisa Devlet Güzel Sanatlar Galerisi, Manisa 37755
Sadberk Hanım Müzesi, İstanbul 37706
Temel Sanat Kolleksiyon, İstanbul 37708
Yivli Minare Sanat Galerisi, Antalya 37625

Ukraine
Charkovskij Chudožestvennyj Muzej, Charkiv 37842
Dnepropetrovsk State Art Museum, Dnepropetrovsk 37847
Kartynna Galereya, Luck 37878
Kiev Taras Shevchenko National Museum, Kyïv 37873
Lviv Art Gallery, Lviv 37885
Museum of Fine Art, Lugansk 37882
Nacionalnij Muzej u Lvovi, Lviv 37887
Odessa Fine Arts Museum, Odessa 37893
Poltava Art Museum, Poltava 37897
Rivnenski Museum of Regional Studies, Rivne 37899
Simferopolskij Chudožestvennyj Muzej, Simferopol 37905
State Historical Museum, Kamenec-Podolskij 37857

United Arab Emirates
Emirates Very Special Arts, Sharjah 37920
Sharjah Art Museum, Sharjah 37922

United Kingdom
Abbot Hall Art Gallery, Kendal 39336
Aberdeen Arts Centre, Aberdeen 37930
Aberdona Gallery, Alloa 37978
Angel Row Gallery, Nottingham 40103
Apsley House, London 39567
Architecture Foundation, London 39568
Ards Art Centre, Newtownards 40073
Arts Centre, Washington, Tyne and Wear 40799
Ashmolean Museum of Art and Archaeology, Oxford 40141
Astley-Cheetham Art Gallery, Stalybridge 40574
Axiom Centre for Arts, Cheltenham 38541
Bankside Gallery, London 39572
Barbican Art, London 39574
Barreau Le Maistre Art Gallery, Saint Helier 40399
Bassetlaw Museum and Percy Laws Memorial Gallery, Retford 40310
Bedford Central Library Gallery, Bedford 38145
Beecroft Art Gallery, Southend-on-Sea 40551
Berwick Borough Museum and Art Gallery, Berwick-upon-Tweed 38173
Beverley Art Gallery, Beverley 38181
Billingham Art Gallery, Billingham 38201
Bilston Craft Gallery, Wolverhampton 40916
Blackburn Museum and Art Gallery, Blackburn, Lancashire 38242
Blenheim Palace, Woodstock 40924
Bondgate Gallery, Alnwick 37983
Borough Museum and Art Gallery, Newcastle-under-Lyme 40031
Boxfield Gallery, Stevenage 40582
Brecknock Museum and Art Gallery, Brecon 38316
Bristol City Museum and Art Gallery, Bristol 38351
Bromham Mill and Art Gallery, Bromham 38375
Broughton House and Garden, Kirkcudbright 39392
BSAT Gallery, Newmarket 40049
Burghley House, Stamford 40575
Bury Saint Edmunds Art Gallery, Bury Saint Edmunds 38415
Bushey Museum and Art Gallery, Bushey 38421
Camborne School of Mines Geological Museum and Art Gallery, Pool 40224
Camden Arts Centre, London 39596
Canada House Gallery, London 39597
Cannon Hall Museum, Barnsley, South Yorkshire 38090
Castle Museum, Norwich 40091
Castle Park Arts Centre, Frodsham 39018
Cecil Higgins Art Gallery, Bedford 38147
Central Art Gallery, Ashton-under-Lyne 38032
Chapman Gallery, Salford 40429
Cheltenham Art Gallery and Museum, Cheltenham 38544
Cheshire Military Museum, Chester 38550
Chisenhale Gallery, London 39605
Christchurch Mansion, Ipswich 39303
City Art Centre, Edinburgh 38873
City Gallery, Leicester 39460
City Museum and Art Gallery, Plymouth 40209
City Museum and Records Office, Portsmouth 40249
Cliffe Castle Museum, Keighley 39327
College Art Collections, London 39613
Commonwealth Institute, London 39614
Corridor Gallery, Glenrothes 39077
Crawford Arts Centre, Saint Andrews 40382
Crescent Arts, Scarborough 40454
Dalkeith Arts Centre, Dalkeith 38692
The Danish Cultural Institute, Edinburgh 38875
The Dean Clough Galleries, Halifax 39151
Denbigh Museum and Gallery, Denbigh 38714
Dick Institute Museum and Art Gallery, Kilmarnock 39362
Doncaster Museum and Art Gallery, Doncaster 38741
Dudley Museum and Art Gallery, Dudley 38782
Duleep Singh Picture Collection, Thetford 40695
Durham Light Infantry Museum and Durham Art Gallery, Durham 38826
Ealing College Gallery, London 39629
Eastwood House, Glasgow 39043
Eden Court Art Gallery, Inverness 39299
Fabrica, Brighton 38341
Farnhem Maltings Gallery, Farnham 38980
Fergusson Gallery, Perth 40184
Fitzwilliam Museum, Cambridge 38454
Flaxman Gallery, Stoke-on-Trent 40605
Focal Point Gallery, Southend-on-Sea 40552
Foundation for Women's Art, London 39637
Foyer Gallery/James Hockey Gallery, Farnham 38981
Fry Public Art Gallery, Saffron Walden 40367
The Gallery, Gateshead 39027
The Gallery, Luton 39844
Gallery II, Bradford 38298
Gallery of the Royal Scottish Academy, Edinburgh 38883
Gardner Arts Centre, Falmer 38971
Gillingham Library Gallery, Gillingham, Kent 39032
Glasgow School of Art - Mackintosh Collection, Glasgow 39048
Gomshall Gallery, Gomshall 39093
Graves Art Gallery, Sheffield 40484
Grays School of Art Gallery and Museum, Aberdeen 37939
Great Yarmouth Museums, Great Yarmouth 39124
Guernsey Museum and Art Gallery, Saint Peter Port 40424
Guild Gallery, Bristol 38356
Guildhall Gallery, Winchester 40887
Hamilton's Gallery, London 39658
Hanbury Hall, Droitwich 38777
Harewood House, Harewood 39161
Harris Museum and Art Gallery, Preston 40266
Hayloft Gallery, Armagh 38018
Hayward Gallery, London 39661
Hereford City Museum and Art Gallery, Hereford 39225
Holden Gallery, Manchester 39889
Horsham Arts Centre, Horsham 39264
Howard Gardens Gallery, Cardiff 38479
Hull University Art Collection, Kingston-upon-Hull 39381
Hunterian Art Gallery, Glasgow 39050
Ikon Gallery, Birmingham 38222
John Gershom-Parkington Collection of Timekeeping Instruments, Bury Saint Edmunds 38416
John Hansard Gallery, Southampton 40545
Kelly Gallery, Glasgow 39053
Keswick Museum and Art Gallery, Keswick 39344
King's Lynn Arts Centre, King's Lynn 39369
Kirriemuir Gateway to the Glens Museum, Kerriemuir 39341
Lauderdale House, London 39684
Leeds Metropolitan University Gallery, Leeds 39448
Leek Art Gallery, Leek 39457
Leighton House Museum, London 39685
Lewis Collection, Cambridge 38458
Lewis Elton Gallery, Guildford 39139
Lighthouse Poole Centre for the Arts, Poole 40226
Llandudno Museum and Art Gallery, Llandudno 39541
London Institute Gallery, London 39696
Longleat House, Warminster 40787
Lyth Arts Centre, Lyth 39857
McManus Galleries, Dundee 38800
MacRobert Gallery, Stirling 40592
Maidstone Library Gallery, Maidstone 39876
Maidstone Museum and Bentlif Art Gallery, Maidstone 39877
Manchester Art Gallery, Manchester 39892
Manx Museum, Douglas, Isle of Man 38760
Margaret Harvey Gallery, Saint Albans 40374
Marischal Museum, Aberdeen 37940
Medway Towns Gallery, Rochester 40336
Melbourne Hall, Melbourne 39930
Metropole Gallery, Folkestone 39001
Midlands Art Centre, Birmingham 38224
Milton Keynes Gallery, Milton Keynes 39961
Morley Gallery, London 39711
Museum and Art Gallery, Forfar 39005
Museum and Art Gallery, Letchworth 39481
Museum and Art Gallery, Newport, Gwent 40051
Museum of Installation, London 39716
Museums and Study Collection, London 39725
Narwhal Inuit Art Gallery, London 39727
National Museum and Gallery, Cardiff 38481
Nature in Art, Gloucester 39084
New Hall Women's Art Collection, Cambridge 38460
Newark Town Treasures and Art Gallery, Newark-on-Trent 40023
Newry and Mourne Arts Centre and Museum, Newry 40061
Northampton Museum and Art Gallery, Northampton 40084
Norwich Gallery, Norwich 40097
Nottingham Castle, Nottingham 40112
Old Museum Arts Centre, Belfast 38155
Orchard Gallery, Londonderry 39817
Oriel Davies Gallery, Newtown, Powys 40070
Oriel Mostyn Gallery, Llandudno 39542
Orleans House Gallery, Twickenham 40741
Parc Howard Museum and Art Gallery, Llanelli 39546
Park Gallery, Falkirk 38969
Pearce Institute, Glasgow 39058
Penlee House Gallery and Museum, Penzance 40181
Penrhyn Castle, Bangor, Gwynedd 38083
Peppin Brown Art Gallery, Whittlesford 40865
Peter Scott Gallery, Lancaster 39416
Petworth House and Park, Petworth 40198
Piece Hall Art Gallery, Halifax 39154
Pitlochry Festival Theatre Art Gallery, Pitlochry 40205
Plymouth Arts Centre, Plymouth 40211
Polish Cultural Institution Gallery, London 39746
Portico Gallery, Helensburgh 39209
Portico Library and Gallery, Manchester 39903
Renishaw Hall Museum and Art Gallery, Renishaw 40309
Robson Gallery, Selkirk 40470

Royal Albert Memorial Museum and Art Gallery, Exeter 38957
Royal Bank of Scotland Art Collection, London 39757
Royal Borough Collection, Maidenhead 39874
Royal Glasgow Institute of the Fine Arts, Glasgow 39063
Rozelle House Galleries, Ayr 38052
Ruskin Library, Lancaster 39418
Ruskin Museum, Coniston 38625
Russell-Cotes Art Gallery and Museum, Bournemouth 38286
Saddleworth Museum and Art Gallery, Uppermill 40752
Saint Barbe Museum and Art Gallery, Lymington 39854
Saint David's Hall, Cardiff 38483
Saint Ives Society of Artists Members Gallery (Norway Gallery) and Mariners Gallery, Saint Ives, Cornwall 40409
Salford Museum and Art Gallery, Salford 40432
The Scott Gallery, Hawick 39196
Sheffield City Museum and Mappin Art Gallery, Sheffield 40489
Sir Francis Cook Gallery, Augrès 38040
Small Mansions Arts Centre, London 39779
South Hill Park Arts Centre, Bracknell 38293
The Stanley Picker Gallery, Kingston-upon-Thames 39386
Stirling Smith Art Gallery and Museum, Stirling 40595
Strood Library Gallery, Rochester 40337
Tenby Museum and Art Gallery, Tenby 40684
Timespan Museum and Art Gallery, Helmsdale 39210
Turner House Gallery, Penarth 40170
TWO 10 Gallery, London 39792
Ulster Museum, Belfast 38160
University Museum, Dundee 38805
University of Brighton Gallery, Brighton 38346
University of Dundee Exhibitions Department, Dundee 38806
University of Liverpool Art Gallery, Liverpool 39530
Vennel Gallery, Irvine 39313
Victoria and Albert Museum, London 39795
Victoria Art Gallery, Bath 38124
Warrington Museum and Art Gallery, Warrington 40789
Watford Museum, Watford 40803
Whitstable Museum and Gallery, Whitstable 40862
Winchester College Treasury, Winchester 40897
Worcester City Museum and Art Gallery, Worcester 40932
Worthing Museum and Art Gallery, Worthing 40937
Yard Gallery, Nottingham 40116

Uruguay

Centro de Artistas Plásticos, Montevideo 40987
Galería Pocitos, Montevideo 40990
Museo de Bellas Artes Agustin Araujo, Treinta y Tres 41043
Museo Juan Manuel Blanes, Montevideo 41006
Museo Municipal de Artes Plásticas, Rivera 41036
Museo Nacional de Artes Visuales, Montevideo 41016
Museo Romántico, Montevideo 41022
Museo San Gregorio de Polanco, San Gregorio de Polanco 41040
Museo Virtual de Artes el Pais, Montevideo 41025
Sala de Arte Carlos F. Sáez, Montevideo 41032

U.S.A.

1890 House-Museum and Center for Victorian Arts, Cortland 42652
3M Art Collection, Saint Paul 47150
Abby Aldrich Rockefeller Folk Art Museum, Williamsburg 48624
Abington Art Center, Jenkintown 44333
Academy Art Museum, Easton 43066
Ackland Art Museum, Chapel Hill 42196
ACME Art Gallery, Columbus 42585
Adam East Museum Art Center, Moses Lake 45519
Adirondack Museum, Blue Mountain Lake 41758
Agnes Gallery, Birmingham 41703
Air Gallery, New York 45752
Akron Art Museum, Akron 41072
A.L. Fetterman Educational Museum, Fort Valley 43466
Albany Institute of History and Art, Albany 41083
Albany Museum of Art, Albany 41081
Albrecht-Kemper Museum of Art, Saint Joseph 47104
Albright-Knox Art Gallery, Buffalo 41981
The Albuquerque Museum of Art and History, Albuquerque 41099
Alexander Brest Museum, Jacksonville 44292
Alexandria Museum of Art, Alexandria 41117
Alford House-Anderson Fine Arts Center, Anderson 41202
Alice C. Sabatini Gallery, Topeka 48031
Allen Memorial Art Museum, Oberlin 46076
Allen R. Hite Art Institute, Louisville 44960
Allentown Art Museum, Allentown 41143
Allied Arts Center and Gallery, Richland 46854
Alternative Museum, New York 45753
Alton Museum of History and Art, Alton 41157
Alva DeMars Megan Chapel Art Center, Manchester 45095
Amarillo Museum of Art, Amarillo 41164
American Academy of Arts and Letters Art Museum, New York 45754
American Advertising Museum, Portland 46630
American Craft Museum, New York 45755
American Museum of Asmat Art, Saint Paul 47152
American Sport Art Museum and Archives, Daphne 42781
American Visionary Art Museum, Baltimore 41448
The Amerind Foundation, Dragoon 42986
Amon Carter Museum, Fort Worth 43480
Anacostia Museum, Washington 48332
Anchorage Museum of History and Art, Anchorage 41197
Ancient Spanish Monastery of Saint Bernard de Clairvaux Cloisters, North Miami Beach 45998
Anderson County Arts Center, Anderson 41204
Anderson Gallery, Richmond 46871
The Andy Warhol Museum, Pittsburgh 46506
Ann Arbor Art Center, Ann Arbor 41213
Anna Eaton Stout Memorial Art Gallery, Owensboro 46227
Annmary Brown Memorial, Providence 46713
Aperture Photo Gallery and EMU Art Gallery, Eugene 43220
Apex Museum, Atlanta 41328
Appleton Art Center, Appleton 41238
Appleton Museum of Art, Ocala 46078
A.R.C. Gallery, Chicago 42302
Arcadia University Art Gallery, Glenside 43694
Archer Gallery, Vancouver 48198
Arizona Gallery, Tucson 48079
Arizona Museum For Youth, Mesa 45269
The Arkansas Arts Center, Little Rock 44822
Arkansas State University Art Gallery, Jonesboro 44358
Arlington Arts Center, Arlington 41263
Arlington Museum of Art, Arlington 41259
Armstrong Collection, Olivet 46137
Arnot Art Museum, Elmira 43169
Arrowmont School of Arts and Crafts Collection, Gatlinburg 43635
Art and Culture Center of Hollywood, Hollywood 44060
Art Association of Harrisburg, Harrisburg 43922
Art Center at Fuller Lodge, Los Alamos 44885
Art Center Gallery, Warrensburg 48314
Art Center In Hargate, Concord 42604
Art Center of Battle Creek, Battle Creek 41537
Art Center of South Florida, Miami Beach 45297
The Art Center of Waco, Waco 48261
Art Center Sarasota, Sarasota 47451
Art Complex Museum, Duxbury 43028
Art Department Gallery, Warwick 48322
Art Galleries, Northridge 46028
Art Galleries of Ramapo College, Mahwah 45077
Art Gallery, Atlanta 41329
Art Gallery, Jamestown 44309
The Art Gallery, Decatur 42827
The Art Gallery, College Park 42523
The Art Gallery, Durham 43025
Art Gallery, San Antonio 47244
Art Guild of Burlington Gallery, Burlington 41996
The Art Gym, Marylhurst 45194
The Art Institute of Boston Main Gallery, Boston 41797
The Art Institute of Chicago, Chicago 42304
Art League of Houston, Houston 44115
Art League of Manatee County, Bradenton 41860
The Art Museum at Florida International University, Miami 45281
Art Museum of Greater Lafayette, Lafayette 44568
The Art Museum of Los Gatos and the Nature Museum of Los Gatos, Los Gatos 44954
Art Museum of Missoula, Missoula 45403
Art Museum of South Texas, Corpus Christi 42643
Art Museum of Southeast Texas, Beaumont 41562
Art Museum of the University of Memphis, Memphis 45231
Art Museum of Western Virginia, Roanoke 46927
The Art Studio, Beaumont 41563
Artemisia Gallery, Chicago 42305
Artful Deposit Galleries, Allentown 41142
Arthur A. Houghton Jr. Gallery and the Great Hall Gallery, New York 45766
Arthur M. Sackler Gallery, Washington 48335
Arthur Ross Gallery, Philadelphia 46391
Artists Association of Nantucket Museum, Nantucket 45594
Artist's Space, New York 45767
Artmobile, Newtown 45947
Artrain, Ann Arbor 41215
Arts Council of Fayetteville, Fayetteville 43310
Arts Council of Wayne County, Goldsboro 43718
Arts in the Academy, Washington 48337
Artspace-Lima, Lima 44773
Artswatch, Louisville 44963
Artworks, Trenton 48052
Arvada Center for the Arts and Humanities, Arvada 41274
Asheville Art Museum, Asheville 41275
Ashtabula Arts Center, Ashtabula 41302
Aspen Art Museum, Aspen 41305
Associated Artists of Pittsburgh Gallery, Pittsburgh 46508
The Athenaeum, Alexandria 41122
Athenaeum of Philadelphia, Philadelphia 46392
Atlanta Contemporary Art Center and Nexus Press, Atlanta 41331
The Atlanta Cyclorama, Atlanta 41332
Atlanta International Museum of Art and Design, Atlanta 41334
Atrium Gallery, Saint Louis 47111
Attleboro Museum, Attleboro 41368
Atwater Kent Museum - The History Museum of Philadelphia, Philadelphia 46393
Atwood Memorial Center, Saint Cloud 47083
Augustana College Art Gallery, Rock Island 46952
Aurora Public Art Commission, Aurora 41395
Austin Museum of Art, Austin 41406
The AXA Gallery, New York 45770
Babe Ruth Birthplace Museum, Baltimore 41451
Bakersfield Museum of Art, Bakersfield 41439
Ball State University Museum of Art, Muncie 45555
The Baltimore Museum of Art, Baltimore 41454
Bank One Fort Worth Collection, Fort Worth 43482
Barnard's Mill Art Museum, Glen Rose 43683
Barnsdall Junior Arts Center, Los Angeles 44892
Barton Museum, Wilson 48668
Bass Museum of Art, Miami Beach 45298
Bates College Museum of Art, Lewiston 44728
Beaufort Museum, Beaufort 41559
Beaumont Art League, Beaumont 41565
The Belknap Mill Museum, Laconia 44564
Bellevue Art Museum, Bellevue 41597
Belmont, Gari Melchers Estate and Memorial Gallery, Fredericksburg 43533
The Benjamin Banneker Museum, Baltimore 41459
The Bennington Museum, Bennington 41629
Berea College Doris Ulmann Galleries, Berea 41636
Bergen Museum of Art and Science, Hackensack 43857
Bergstrom-Mahler Museum, Neenah 45643
Berkshire Artisans, Pittsfield 46530
Berlin Art and Historical Collections, Berlin 41651
Bertha V.B. Lederer Fine Arts Gallery, Geneseo 43638
Betty Brinn Children's Museum, Milwaukee 45359
Beyond Baroque Art Gallery, Venice 48208
Bicentennial Art Center and Museum, Paris 46283
Biggs Museum of American Art, Dover 42967
Birger Sandzén Memorial Gallery, Lindsborg 44806
Birmingham Bloomfield Art Center, Birmingham 41712
Birmingham Museum of Art, Birmingham 41706
Blanden Memorial Art Museum, Fort Dodge 43388
Bloomington Art Center, Bloomington 41751
Blount-Bridgers House/ Hobson Pittman Memorial Gallery, Tarboro 47955
B'nai B'rith Klutznick National Jewish Museum, Washington 48338
Boal Mansion Museum, Boalsburg 41762
Boca Raton Museum of Art, Boca Raton 41765
Boehm Gallery, San Marcos 47364
The Bohen Foundation, New York 45773
Boise Art Museum, Boise 41771
Bolinas Museum, Bolinas 41775
Boothbay Region Art Foundation, Boothbay Harbor 41791
Boston Athenaeum, Boston 41798
Boston Public Library Art Collections, Boston 41801
Boston University Art Gallery, Boston 41802
Boulevard Arts Center, Chicago 42309
Bowdoin College Museum of Art, Brunswick 41971
The Bowers Museum of Cultural Art, Santa Ana 47399
Bowling Green State University Fine Arts Center Galleries, Bowling Green 41853
Bradford Brinton Memorial, Big Horn 41680
Bradley Gallery of Art, Plymouth 46567
Braithwaite Fine Arts Gallery, Cedar City 42146
Brandywine River Museum, Chadds Ford 42175
Branigan Cultural Center, Las Cruces 44657
Brattleboro Museum and Art Center, Brattleboro 41872
Brauer Museum of Art, Valparaiso 48192
Brenau University Galleries, Gainesville 43588
Brevard Museum of Art and Science, Melbourne 45229
Brigham City Museum-Gallery, Brigham City 41897
Brigham Young University Museum of Art, Provo 46734
Bromfield Art Gallery, Boston 41803
Bronx Museum of the Arts, Bronx 41915
Brookings Arts Council, Brookings 41931
Brooklyn Museum of Art, Brooklyn 41941
Brown County Art Gallery and Museum, Nashville 45609
Brownsville Museum of Fine Art, Brownsville 41965
Brueckner Museum, Albion 41097
Brunnier Art Museum, Ames 41170
Bry Gallery, Monroe 45440
Buchanan Center for the Arts, Monmouth 45434
Buckley Center Gallery, Portland 46632
Buffalo Bill Historical Center, Cody 42510
Burchfield-Penney Art Center, Buffalo 41986
Bush House Museum and Bush Barn Art Center, Salem 47207
Butler Institute of American Art, Youngstown 48807
California Palace of the Legion of Honor, San Francisco 47311
California African-American Museum, Los Angeles 44893
California Art Gallery, San Marino 47365
California Museum of Ancient Art, Beverly Hills 41676
California State University-Long Beach Art Museum, Long Beach 44858
Callanwolde Fine Arts Center, Atlanta 41336
Camp Gallery, Sweet Briar 47900
Campus Art Gallery, Santa Rosa 47444
Camron-Stanford House, Oakland 46061
Canadian Embassy Art Gallery, Washington 48339
Canajoharie Library and Art Gallery, Canajoharie 42074
Canton Museum of Art, Canton 42089
Cape Ann Historical Museum, Gloucester 43702
Cape Museum of Fine Arts, Dennis 42871
Caramoor Center for Music and the Arts, Katonah 44414
Cardinal Gallery, Annapolis 41225
Carleton College Art Gallery, Northfield 46019
Carlsbad Museum and Art Center, Carlsbad 42109
Carnegie Art Center, Walla Walla 48284
Carnegie Center for Art History, New Albany 45657
Carnegie Museum of Art, Pittsburgh 46510
Carney Gallery, Weston 48567
Carroll Reece Museum, Johnson City 44344
Castellani Art Museum, Niagara University 45952
Cazenovia College Chapman Art Center Gallery, Cazenovia 42144
CCAC Institute, Oakland 46062
CCC Weeks Gallery, Jamestown 44310
Cecelia Coker Bell Gallery, Hartsville 43947
Cecille R. Hunt Gallery, Sankt Louis 47398
Cedar Rapids Museum of Art, Cedar Rapids 42157
Center Art Gallery, Grand Rapids 43754
Center for Arts Criticism, Minneapolis 45382
Center for Cultural Arts, Gadsden 43578
Center for Exploratory and Perceptual Art, Buffalo 41987
Center for the Arts, Vero Beach 48222
Center for the Visual Arts, Denver 42880
Center for the Visual Arts, Philadelphia 46397
Center Galleries, Detroit 42917
Central Iowa Art Museum, Marshalltown 45184
Chadron State College Main Gallery, Chadron 42177
Chaffee Center for Visual Arts, Rutland 47041
The Chaim Gross Studio Museum, New York 45778
Chandler Gallery, Randolph 46790
Chappell Art Gallery, Chappell 42198
Charles A. Wustum Museum of Fine Arts, Racine 46767
Charles Allis Art Museum, Milwaukee 45360
Charles B. Goddard Center for Visual and Performing Arts, Ardmore 41251
Charlotte and Philip Hanes Art Gallery, Winston-Salem 48698
Chattahoochee Valley Art Museum, La Grange 44541
Cheekwood Museum of Art, Nashville 45613
Chester Art Guild, Chester 42287
Chesterwood Museum, Stockbridge 47816
Cheyenne Frontier Days Old West Museum, Cheyenne 42297
The Chicago Athenaeum - Museum of Architecture and Design, Chicago 42315
Chicago Cultural Center, Chicago 42317
Chieftains Museum, Rome 46993
Children's Art Museum, San Angelo 47239
Children's Museum of the Arts, New York 45782
Chinati Foundation, Marfa 45140
The Chrysler Museum of Art, Norfolk 45963
Chung-Cheng Art Gallery, Jamaica 44303
Cigna Museum and Art Collection, Philadelphia 46398
Cincinnati Art Museum, Cincinnati 42400
City Hall Council Chamber Gallery, Charleston 42213
City of Brea Gallery, Brea 41874
Clark Humanities Museum, Claremont 42417
Cleveland Center for Contemporary Art, Cleveland 42465
Cleveland Museum of Art, Cleveland 42466
Cleveland State University Art Gallery, Cleveland 42469
Clymer Museum of Art, Ellensburg 43148
C.M. Russell Museum, Great Falls 43780
Coastal Center for the Arts, Saint Simons Island 47179
Cobb Museum of Art, Marietta 45143
Colby College Museum of Art, Waterville 48447
College of Eastern Utah Art Gallery, Price 46692
College of New Jersey Art Gallery, Trenton 48053
College of Visual Arts and Gallery, Saint Paul 47153
The College of Wooster Art Museum, Wooster 48749
Colorado Gallery of the Arts, Littleton 44827
Colorado Springs Fine Arts Center, Colorado Springs 42535
Colorado University Art Galleries, Boulder 41834
Columbia College Art Gallery, Chicago 42320
Columbia Museum of Art, Columbia 42558
The Columbian Museum and Art Center, Wamego 48301
Columbus Cultural Arts Center, Columbus 42586
The Columbus Museum, Columbus 42574
Columbus Museum of Art, Columbus 42587
Combat Air Museum, Topeka 48032
Commencement Art Gallery, Tacoma 47916
Communications and History Museum of Sutton, Washington 48341
Community Arts Gallery, Detroit 42920
Community Fine Arts Center, Rock Springs 46957
Concord Art Association Museum, Concord 42597
Concordia University-Wisconsin Art Gallery, Mequon 45258
Conejo Valley Art Museum, Thousand Oaks 48003
Connecticut Historical Society Museum, Hartford 43938
Contemporary Art Museum, Raleigh 46772
Contemporary Arts Center, Cincinnati 42403
Contemporary Museum, Baltimore 41461
Cookeville Art Gallery, Cookeville 42614
Coos Art Museum, Coos Bay 42622
Copper King Mansion, Butte 42017
Copper Village Museum and Arts Center, Anaconda 41188

Coppini Academy of Fine Arts Gallery and Museum, San Antonio 47249
The Corcoran Gallery of Art, Washington 48342
Cornell Museum, Delray Beach 42863
Corvallis Art Center, Corvallis 42656
Courthouse Gallery, Portsmouth 46660
Courtney and Lemmerman Galleries, Jersey City 44339
Coutts Memorial Museum of Art, El Dorado 43108
Craft Alliance Gallery, Saint Louis 47118
Cranbrook Art Museum, Bloomfield Hills 41738
Crary Art Gallery, Warren 48312
Creative Arts Center, Kansas City 44397
Creative Arts Guild, Dalton 42765
Creative Growth Art Center, Oakland 46063
Cress Gallery of Art, Chattanooga 42261
Crocker Art Museum, Sacramento 47050
Crook County Museum and Art Gallery, Sundance 47883
Crossman Art Gallery, Whitewater 48594
Crowder College-Longwell Museum and Camp Crowder Collection, Neosho 45650
Crowley Art Association and Gallery, Crowley 42713
Cuban Museum of Arts and Culture, Miami 45283
The Cultural Center of Fine Arts, Parkersburg 46295
Cummer Museum of Art, Jacksonville 44293
Cuneo Museum, Vernon Hills 48220
Curfman Gallery and Duhesa Lounge, Fort Collins 43378
Currier Gallery of Art, Manchester 45096
Cy Twombly Gallery, Houston 44119
DAAP Galleries, Cincinnati 42404
Dahl Arts Center, Rapid City 46794
The Dallas Center for Contemporary Art, Dallas 42748
Dallas Museum of Art, Dallas 42751
Dalton Gallery, Decatur 42829
Dane G. Hansen Memorial Museum, Logan 44844
Danforth Museum of Art, Framingham 43501
Danville Museum of Fine Arts and History, Danville 42780
Daura Gallery, Lynchburg 45003
Davenport Museum of Art, Davenport 42785
The David and Alfred Smart Museum of Art, Chicago 42322
David Strawn Art Gallery, Jacksonville 44301
David Winton Bell Gallery, Providence 46717
Davidson County Museum of Art, Lexington 44753
Davis Art Gallery, Columbia 42550
Davis Museum, Wellesley 48495
Davison Art Center, Middletown 45313
Dawson Springs Museum and Art Center, Dawson Springs 42798
Dayton Art Institute, Dayton 42801
Dayton Visual Arts Center, Dayton 42802
De Land Museum of Art, De Land 42813
DeCordova Museum and Sculpture Park, Lincoln 44777
Degrazia Gallery in the Sun, Tucson 48084
Deines Cultural Center, Russell 47032
Delaware Art Museum, Wilmington 48649
Denison University Art Gallery, Granville 43772
Dennos Museum Center of Northwestern Michigan College, Traverse City 48050
Denver Art Museum, Denver 42885
DePaul University Art Gallery, Chicago 42323
DePauw University Art Center, Greencastle 43799
DePree Art Center and Gallery, Holland 44053
Des Moines Art Center, Des Moines 42905
Desert Caballeros Western Museum, Wickenburg 48615
Detroit Artists Market, Detroit 42921
The Detroit Institute of Arts, Detroit 42924
Detroit Repertory Theatre Gallery, Detroit 42925
Dia Center for the Arts, Quemado 46755
Diggs Gallery at Winston-Salem State University, Winston-Salem 48699
Dimock Gallery, Washington 48347
Dinnerware Contemporary Art Gallery, Tucson 48085
The Discovery Museum, Bridgeport 41890
Dishman Art Gallery, Beaumont 41566
District of Columbia Arts Center, Washington 48349
The Dixon Gallery and Gardens, Memphis 45235
Douglas F. Cooley Memorial Art Gallery, Portland 46634
Dowd Fine Arts Gallery, Cortland 42655
Downey Museum of Art, Downey 42980
Dubuque Museum of Art, Dubuque 42991
Duke University Museum of Art, Durham 43019
Duke University Union Museum and Brown Art Gallery, Durham 43020
Duluth Art Institute, Duluth 42997
Dumbarton Oaks Collections, Washington 48351
The Duncan Gallery of Art, De Land 42814
Dwight Frederick Boyden Gallery, Saint Mary's City 47146
East Campus Galleries, Orlando 46185
East Jordan Portside Art and Historical Museum, East Jordan 43052
East-West Center, Honolulu 44075
Eaton-Buchan Gallery and Marvin Cone Gallery, Cedar Rapids 42158
Eccles Community Art Center, Ogden 46097
Edison Community College Gallery of Fine Art, Fort Myers 43435
Edmonds Arts Festival Museum, Edmonds 43092
Edward and Marthann Samek Art Gallery, Lewisburg 44721
Edward M. Bannister Gallery, Providence 46718
Edwin A. Ulrich Museum of Art, Wichita 48599
Eighteenth Street Arts Complex, Santa Monica 47440
Eiteljorg Museum of American Indians and Western Art, Indianapolis 44217
El Paso Museum of Art, El Paso 43116
Elder Art Gallery, Lincoln 44781
Elisabet Ney Museum, Austin 41409
Elizabeth Myers Mitchell Art Gallery, Annapolis 41227
Elizabeth O'Neill Verner Studio Museum, Charleston 42215
Elizabeth P. Korn Gallery, Madison 45061
Elizabeth Rozier Gallery, Jefferson City 44328
Elizabeth Slocumb Galleries, Johnson City 44345
Ella Sharp Museum, Jackson 44276
The Ellen Noel Art Museum of the Permian Basin, Odessa 46093
Elmhurst Art Museum, Elmhurst 43165
Eloise Pickard Smith Gallery, Santa Cruz 47409
Elvehjem Museum of Art, Madison 45067
Emerson Gallery, Clinton 42499
Epcot, Lake Buena Vista 44579
Erie Art Museum, Erie 43200
Esther M. Klein Art Gallery, Philadelphia 46407
Evansville Museum of Arts and Science, Evansville 43245
Evergreen Galleries, Olympia 46140
Everhart Museum of Natural History, Science and Art, Scranton 47517
Everson Museum of Art, Syracuse 47908
The Exploratorium, San Francisco 47316
Ezra and Cecile Zilkha Gallery, Middletown 45314
The Fabric Workshop and Museum, Philadelphia 46408
Fairbanks Gallery, Corvallis 42657
Falkirk Cultural Center, San Rafael 47374
Fallingwater - Western Pennsylvania Conservancy, Mill Run 45344
Farnham Galleries, Indianola 44235
Father Weyland Gallery, Epworth 43198
Faulconer Gallery at Grinnell College, Grinnell 43840
Fayette Art Museum, Fayette 43305
Fayetteville Museum of Art, Fayetteville 43311
F.Donald Kenney Museum and Art Study Wing, Saint Bonaventure 47076
Federal Reserve Board Art Gallery, Washington 48353
Festival-Institute Museum, Round Top 47017
Fielding L. Wright Art Center, Cleveland 42462
Fine Art Gallery at Centro Cultural Aztlan, San Antonio 47250
Fine Arts Center for New River Valley, Pulaski 46742
Fine Arts Center Gallery, Maryville 45197
Fine Arts Center of Kershaw County, Camden 42064
Fine Arts Collection, Decorah 42838
Fine Arts Exhibitions, Austin 41410
Fine Arts Gallery, Breckenridge 41875
Fine Arts Gallery, Los Angeles 44898
Fine Arts Gallery, New Orleans 45723
Fine Arts Gallery, Omaha 46146
The Fine Arts Gallery, Las Vegas 44663
Firehouse Art Center, Norman 45973
Firehouse Art Gallery, Garden City 43618
Firehouse Gallery, Oak Bluffs 46049
First National Bank of Chicago Art Collection, Chicago 42327
First Tennessee Heritage Collection, Memphis 45237
Fisher Gallery, Los Angeles 44899
Fisk University Galleries, Nashville 45617
Fitchburg Art Museum, Fitchburg 43326
Flamingo Gallery, Las Vegas 44665
Flanagan Valley Campus Art Gallery, Lincoln 44798
Fleet Boston Financial Gallery, Boston 41807
Fleischer Museum, Scottsdale 47512
Flint Institute of Arts, Flint 43339
Florence Griswold Museum, Old Lyme 46133
Florence Museum of Art, Science and History, Florence 43348
The Florida Museum of Hispanic and Latin American Art, Coral Gables 42627
Florida State University Museum of Fine Arts, Tallahassee 47931
Ford Gallery and Slide Collection, Ypsilanti 48810
Fort Frederick, Big Pool 41681
Fort Smith Art Center, Fort Smith 43457
Fort Wayne Museum of Art, Fort Wayne 43476
Forum Gallery, Jamestown 44312
Foster Gallery, Eau Claire 43075
Founders Gallery, San Diego 47276
Fowler Museum of Cultural History, Los Angeles 44900
Frances Lehman Loeb Art Center, Poughkeepsie 46674
Francis Colburn Gallery, Burlington 42008
Francis McCray Gallery, Silver City 47628
Franklin G. Burroughs-Simeon B. Chapin Art Museum, Myrtle Beach 45586
Fred Harman Art Museum, Pagosa Springs 46260
Fred Jones Jr. Museum of Art, Norman 45974
Fred Wolf Jr. Gallery, Philadelphia 46412
Frederic Remington Art Museum, Ogdensburg 46103
Frederick R. Weisman Art Museum, Minneapolis 45383
Freedman Gallery, Reading 46806
Freeport Arts Center, Freeport 43549
Freer Gallery of Art, Washington 48357
French Art Colony, Gallipolis 43604
Fresno Art Museum, Fresno 43558
Fresno Metropolitan Museum, Fresno 43559
The Frick Art Museum, Pittsburgh 46516
Frick Collection, New York 45802
Frist Center for the Visual Arts, Nashville 45619
Frye Art Museum, Seattle 47534
Fuller Museum of Art, Brockton 41909
Furlong Art Gallery, Menomonie 45255
Gadsden Arts Center, Quincy 46757
Gadsden Museum of Fine Arts, Gadsden 43579
Galesburg Civic Art Center, Galesburg 43598
The Gallery, Trenton 48054
Gallery 101, River Falls 46911
Gallery 181, Ames 41172
Gallery 2, Chicago 42329
Gallery 400, Chicago 42330
Gallery 57, Cambridge 42040
Gallery '76, Wenatchee 48505
Gallery 825, Los Angeles 44902
Gallery 9, Los Altos 44889
Gallery A and Gallery G, San Pedro 47372
Gallery at Bristol-Myers Squibb, Princeton 46700
Gallery Gazelle, Philomath 46470
Gallery North, Setauket 47569
Gallery of Art, Overland Park 46223
Gallery of the Department of Art, Portales 46615
Gallery of Visual Arts, Missoula 45404
Gallery West, Alexandria 41128
Galveston Arts Center, Galveston 43608
Gardiner Art Gallery, Stillwater 47813
Gardner Museum, Gardner 43623
Gaston County Museum of Art and History, Dallas 42742
Gatov Gallery, Long Beach 44859
Genesee Country Village and Museum, Mumford 45554
George A. Spiva Center for the Arts, Joplin 44362
The George D. and Harriet W. Cornell Fine Arts Museum, Winter Park 48708
George J. Doizaki Gallery, Los Angeles 44903
George Washington's Mount Vernon, Mount Vernon 45546
Georgetown University Art Collection, Washington 48358
Georgia Museum of Art, Athens 41318
Georgia State University Art Gallery, Atlanta 41345
Gertrude Herbert Institute of Art, Augusta 41383
Gibbes Museum of Art, Charleston 42216
Gibson Barham Gallery, Lake Charles 44581
Gilcrease Museum, Tulsa 48104
Giustina Gallery, Corvallis 42658
The Glynn Art Association, Saint Simons Island 47181
Godwin and Ternbach Museum, Flushing 43353
Goethe-Institut New York - Exhibitions, New York 45807
The Goldie Paley Gallery, Philadelphia 46414
Governor's Gallery, Santa Fe 47419
Grand Rapids Art Museum, Grand Rapids 43756
Grants Pass Museum of Art, Grants Pass 43767
Great Lakes Lighthouse Museum, Mackinaw City 45033
Great Plains Art Collection in the Christlieb Gallery, Lincoln 44783
The Greater Reston Arts Center, Reston 46846
Green Hill Center for North Carolina Art, Greensboro 43811
Greensboro Artists' League Gallery, Greensboro 43812
Greensward Gallery, Corvallis 42659
Greenville County Museum of Art, Greenville 43830
Greenville Museum of Art, Greenville 43825
Grey Art Gallery, New York 45809
Grinnell College Art Gallery, Grinnell 43841
Grover M. Hermann Fine Arts Center, Marietta 45149
Guadalupe Cultural Arts Center, San Antonio 47251
Guild Hall Museum, East Hampton 43046
Guilford College Art Gallery, Greensboro 43814
Gulf Beach Art Center, Indian Rocks Beach 44209
Haas Gallery of Art, Bloomsburg 41754
Haggerty Museum of Art, Milwaukee 45363
The Haggin Museum, Stockton 47824
Halsey Gallery, Charleston 42217
Hammer Museum, Los Angeles 44906
Hammond Museum, North Salem 46007
Hampton University Museum, Hampton 43896
Handwerker Gallery of Art, Ithaca 44271
Harlow Gallery, Hallowell 43874
Harris Art Gallery, James M. Lykes Maritime Gallery and Hutchings Gallery, Galveston 43610
Harris Exhibit Hall, Oxford 46241
Hartnell College Gallery, Salinas 47215
Hartsville Museum, Hartsville 43948
Harvard University Art Museums, Cambridge 42042
Harwood Museum of Art of the University of New Mexico, Taos 47950
Hatton Gallery, Fort Collins 43382
Hawaii Pacific University Gallery, Honolulu 44078
Heard Museum, Phoenix 46476
Hearst Art Gallery, Moraga 45491
Heckscher Museum of Art, Huntington 44161
Helen Day Art Center, Stowe 47843
Helen E. Copeland Gallery, Bozeman 41857
Helen King Kendall Memorial Art Gallery, San Angelo 47240
Henry Art Gallery, Seattle 47535
The Henry Sheldon Museum of Vermont Histoy, Middlebury 45307
Herbert F. Johnson Museum of Art, Ithaca 44272
The Heritage Center, Pine Ridge 46492
Heritage Center of Lancaster County, Lancaster 44624
Heritage Hjemkomst Interpretive Center, Moorhead 45489
Heritage Library and Museum, Anchorage 41199
Hershey Museum, Hershey 44004
Heuser Art Center, Peoria 46348
Hibel Museum of Art - Jupiter, Jupiter 44372
Hickory Museum of Art, Hickory 44007
Hiddenite Center, Hiddenite 44012
High Museum of Art, Atlanta 41348
High Wire Gallery, Philadelphia 46416
Highlands Museum of the Arts, Sebring 47552
Hill-Stead Museum, Farmington 43295
Hillwood Art Museum, Brookville 41959
Hiram Blauvelt Art Museum, Oradell 46170
Hirshhorn Museum and Sculpture Garden, Washington 48361
Hispanic Society of America, New York 45815
Hockaday Museum of Arts, Kalispell 44384
Hofstra Museum, Hempstead 43987
Holland Area Arts Council, Holland 44055
The Holtzman Art Gallery, Towson 48047
Honolulu Academy of Arts Museum, Honolulu 44079
Hood Museum of Art, Hanover 43907
Hoosier Salon Gallery, Indianapolis 44221
Housatonic Museum of Art, Bridgeport 41891
Houston Harte University Center, San Angelo 47241
Howard University Gallery of Art, Washington 48362
Hoyt Institute of Fine Arts, New Castle 45686
Hoyt Sherman Place, Des Moines 42906
Hudson River Museum of Westchester, Yonkers 48785
Hunt Gallery, Staunton 47796
Hunt Institute for Botanical Documentation, Pittsburgh 46518
Hunter College Art Galleries, New York 45816
Hunterdon Museum of Art, Clinton 42497
Huntington Art Collections, San Marino 47366
Huntington Beach Art Center, Huntington Beach 44168
Huntington Museum of Art, Huntington 44165
Huntsville Museum of Art, Huntsville 44174
Hyde Art Gallery, El Cajon 43104
Hyde Collection Art Museum, Glens Falls 43693
Hyde Park Art Center, Chicago 42333
Illinois Art Gallery, Chicago 42334
Illinois State Museum, Springfield 47737
Ilwaco Heritage Museum, Ilwaco 44196
Imperial Calcasieu Museum, Lake Charles 44582
Indiana University Art Museum, Bloomington 41746
Indianapolis Art Center, Indianapolis 44226
Indianapolis Museum of Art - Columbus Gallery, Columbus 42578
Institute of Visual Arts, Milwaukee 45364
International Images, Sewickley 47574
International Institute of Metropolitan Detroit, Detroit 42930
International Museum of Art, El Paso 43120
International Museum of Cartoon Art, Boca Raton 41767
International Museum of the Horse, Lexington 44740
Intersection for the Arts Gallery, San Francisco 47320
I.P. Stanback Museum, Orangeburg 46176
Iredell Museum of Arts Heritage, Statesville 47794
Iris and B. Gerald Cantor Art Gallery, Worcester 48754
Iris B. Gerald Cantor Center for Visual Arts at Stanford University, Stanford 47772
Irvine Museum, Irvine 44257
Irving Arts Center, Irving 44259
Irving Arts Center, Irving 44260
Isabella Stewart Gardner Museum, Boston 41811
ISE Art Foundation, New York 45819
Islip Art Museum, East Islip 43051
Iupui Cultural Arts Gallery, Indianapolis 44229
J. Paul Getty Museum, Los Angeles 44913
J. Wayne Stark University Center Galleries, College Station 42526
Jack S. Blanton Museum of Art, Austin 41412
Jacqueline Casey Hudgens Center for the Arts, Duluth 42995
Jacques Marchais Museum of Tibetan Art, Staten Island 47783
Jamaica Center for Arts, Jamaica 44304
James A. Michener Art Museum, Doylestown 42984
James and Meryl Hearst Center for the Arts, Cedar Falls 42150
James E. Lewis Museum of Art, Baltimore 41471
James Howe Gallery, Union 48143
Jane Voorhees Zimmerli Art Museum, New Brunswick 45678
Japantown Art and Media Collection, San Francisco 47321
Jasper Rand Art Museum, Westfield 48557
Jay I. Kislak Foundation, Miami Lakes 45301
Jean Paul Slusser Gallery, Ann Arbor 41217
Jersey City Museum, Jersey City 44340
Jesse Peter Museum, Santa Rosa 47445
Jesus Jones and Justice Museum of Art, Los Angeles 44915
Jewett Hall Gallery, Augusta 41389
Jewish Institute for the Arts, Boca Raton 41768
The Jewish Museum, New York 45821
Joe and Emily Lowe Art Gallery, Syracuse 47909
John A. Hermann jr. Memorial Art Museum, Bellevue 41596
The John A. Noble Collection, Staten Island 47784
The John and Mable Ringling Museum of Art, Sarasota 47453
John G. Blank Center for the Arts, Michigan City 45302
John J. McDonough Museum of Art, Youngstown 48808
John Mariani Art Gallery, Greeley 43784
John Michael Kohler Arts Center, Sheboygan 47589

John Slade Ely House, New Haven 45695
Joseloff Gallery, West Hartford 48525
Joslyn Art Museum, Omaha 46149
Julia C. Butridge Gallery, Austin 41415
Jundt Art Museum, Spokane 47727
Juniata College Museum of Art, Huntingdon 44154
Kalamazoo Institute of Arts, Kalamazoo 44379
Karl Drerup Fine Arts Gallery, Plymouth 46566
Katherine Nash Gallery, Minneapolis 45388
Katonah Museum of Art, Katonah 44416
Kauai Museum, Lihue 44771
Kendall Campus Art Gallery, Miami 45287
Kennedy-Douglass Center for the Arts, Florence 43343
Kennedy Museum of Art, Athens 41324
Kenosha Public Museum, Kenosha 44441
Kent Art Association, Kent 44443
Kent Campus Museum and Gallery, Jacksonville 44297
Kent State University Art Galleries, Kent 44446
Kentuck Museum and Art Center, Northport 46026
Keokuk Art Center, Keokuk 44451
Key West Museum of Art and History, Key West 44468
Kiehle Gallery, Saint Cloud 47085
Kimball Art Center, Park City 46288
Kimbell Art Museum, Fort Worth 43487
Kipp Gallery, Indiana 44212
Kirkland Fine Arts Center-Perkinson Gallery, Decatur 42832
Kittredge Art Gallery, Tacoma 47920
Krannert Art Museum, Champaign 42187
The Kreeger Museum, Washington 48365
Kresge Art Museum, East Lansing 43053
La Raza-Galeria Posada, Sacramento 47053
La Salle University Art Museum, Philadelphia 46422
The Lab, San Francisco 47322
Lafayette College Art Gallery, Easton 43068
Lake George Historical Association Museum, Lake George 44588
Lakeside Studio, Lakeside 44606
Lakeview Museum of Arts and Sciences, Peoria 46349
Lakewood's Heritage Culture and the Arts Galleries, Lakewood 44608
Lamar Dodd Art Center, La Grange 44542
The Lamont Gallery, Exeter 43253
Lancaster Museum/Art Gallery, Lancaster 44616
Lancaster Museum of Art, Lancaster 44628
Lane Community College Art Gallery, Eugene 43221
Lansing Art Gallery, Lansing 44642
Larson Gallery, Yakima 48773
Lauren Rogers Museum of Art, Laurel 44679
L.C. Bates Museum, Hinckley 44034
L.D. Brinkman Art Foundation, Kerrville 44456
Leanin' Tree Museum of Western Art, Boulder 41836
Lehigh University Art Galleries/Museum, Bethlehem 41667
Leigh Yawkey Woodson Art Museum, Wausau 48463
The Lentz Center for Asian Culture, Lincoln 44784
Leslie-Lohman Gay Art Foundation, New York 45824
Licking County Art Association Gallery, Newark 45893
Lighthouse Gallery, Tequesta 47981
The Lithuanian Museum, Chicago 42338
The Living Arts and Science Center, Lexington 44742
Lockport Gallery, Lockport 44841
Long Beach Museum of Art, Long Beach 44860
Long Island Museum of American Art, History and Cariages, Stony Brook 47830
Longboat Key Center for the Arts, Longboat Key 44875
Longview Museum of Fine Art, Longview 44879
Longwood Center for the Visual Arts, Farmville 43304
Lore Degenstein Gallery, Selinsgrove 47561
Los Angeles County Museum of Art, Los Angeles 44921
Los Angeles Museum of the Holocaust, Los Angeles 44924
Los Angeles Valley College Art Gallery, Valley Glen 48190
Louisburg College Art Gallery, Louisburg 44959
Louisiana Arts and Science Center, Baton Rouge 41527
Louisiana State University Museum of Art, Baton Rouge 41530
Loveland Museum and Gallery, Loveland 44980
Lowe Art Museum, Coral Gables 42628
Lower Columbia College Fine Arts Gallery, Longview 44880
Luce Gallery, Mount Vernon 45543
Lyndon House Art Center, Athens 41320
Mabee-Gerrer Museum of Art, Shawnee 47588
Macalester College Art Gallery, Saint Paul 47159
McAllen International Museum, McAllen 45017
McLean County Arts Center, Bloomington 41743
McMullen Museum of Art, Chestnut Hill 42294
Madison Art Center, Madison 45069
Magnolia Plantation, Charleston 42223
Maier Museum of Art, Lynchburg 45006
Main Art Gallery, Fullerton 43573
Main Line Art Center, Haverford 43960
Maine Art Gallery, Wiscasset 48716
Maitland Art Center, Maitland 45079
MAK Center for Art and Architecture, Los Angeles 44926
MAK Center for Art and Architecture, West Hollywood 48531
Malden Public Library Art Collection, Malden 45082
Mansfield Art Center, Mansfield 45125
Margaret Fort Trahern Gallery, Clarksville 42437
Margaret Harwell Art Museum, Poplar Bluff 46586
Margaret Hutchinson Compton Gallery, Cambridge 42045
Marias Museum of History and Art, Shelby 47594
Marine Corps Art Collection, Washington 48367
Marion Koogler McNay Art Museum, San Antonio 47255
Mariposa County Gallery, Los Angeles 44927
Martin Art Gallery, Allentown 41146
Marxhausen Art Gallery, Seward 47573
Mary and Leigh Block Museum of Art, Evanston 43241
Mary Brogan Museum of Art and Science, Tallahassee 47935
Mary Porter Sesnon Art Gallery, Santa Cruz 47410
Mary Washington College Galleries, Fredericksburg 43538
Maryhill Museum of Art, Goldendale 43717
Maryland Art Place, Baltimore 41476
Maryland Institute Museum, Baltimore 41478
Marywood University Art Galleries, Scranton 47519
Mason County Museum, Maysville 45208
Massillon Museum, Massillon 45202
Masur Museum of Art, Monroe 45441
The Mattatuck Museum of the Mattatuck Historical Society, Waterbury 48427
Maude I. Kerns Art Center, Eugene 43223
Meadow Brook Art Gallery, Rochester 46933
Meadows Museum, Dallas 42755
Meadows Museum of Art, Shreveport 47613
Mellon Financial Corporation's Collection, Pittsburgh 46522
Memorial Union Art Gallery, Corvallis 42660
Memorial Union Art Gallery, Davis 42792
Memorial Union Gallery, Fargo 43292
Memorial Union Gallery, Tempe 47972
Memphis Brooks Museum of Art, Memphis 45242
Memphis College of Art Gallery, Memphis 45243
Mendocino Art Center Gallery, Mendocino 45251
The Menil Collection, Houston 44126
Mercer Gallery, Rochester 46942
Meridian International Center - Cafritz Galleries, Washington 48369
Meridian Museum of Art, Meridian 45265
The Merrick Art Gallery, New Brighton 45672
Metropolitan Museum of Art, New York 45833
Mexic-Arte Museum, Austin 41417
Mexican Fine Arts Center Museum, Chicago 42341
The Mexican Museum, San Francisco 47324
M.H. de Young Memorial Museum, San Francisco 47325
Miami Art Museum, Miami 45289
Miami University Art Museum, Oxford 46242
Michael C. Rockefeller Arts Center Gallery, Fredonia 43546
Michelson Museum of Art, Marshall 45183
Mid-Atlantic Center for the Arts, Cape May 42097
The Middlebury College Museum of Art, Middlebury 45308
Midwest Museum of American Art, Elkhart 43140
Miller Art Museum, Sturgeon Bay 47863
Millicent Rogers Museum of Northern New Mexico, Taos 47951
Milliken Gallery, Spartanburg 47715
Mills College Art Museum, Oakland 46065
Milwaukee Art Museum, Milwaukee 45366
Mingenback Art Center Gallery, Lindsborg 44808
Minneapolis College of Art and Design Gallery, Minneapolis 45390
Minneapolis Institute of Arts, Minneapolis 45391
Minnesota Museum of American Art, Saint Paul 47163
Mint Museum of Art, Charlotte 42243
Miriam and Ira D. Wallach Art Gallery, New York 45834
Mission Cultural Center for Latino Arts, San Francisco 47326
Mississippi Museum of Art, Jackson 44280
MIT-List Visual Arts Center, Cambridge 42047
Mitchell Museum at Cedarhurst, Mount Vernon 45544
Mobile Museum of Art, Mobile 45421
Modern Art Museum of Fort Worth, Fort Worth 43489
Montalvo Center for the Arts, Saratoga 47457
Montclair Art Museum, Montclair 45450
Monterey Museum of Art, Monterey 45456
Montgomery Museum and Lewis Miller Regional Art Center, Christiansburg 42391
Montgomery Museum of Fine Arts, Montgomery 45467
Morris Belknap Gallery, Dario Covi Gallery and SAL Gallery, Louisville 44973
Morris Museum of Art, Augusta 41386
Moss-Thorns Gallery of Arts, Hays 43970
Moudy Exhibition Hall, Fort Worth 43490
Mount Holyoke College Art Museum, South Hadley 47693
MSC Forsyth Center Galleries, College Station 42527
The Muchnic Gallery, Atchison 41316
Muckenthaler Cultural Center Gallery, Fullerton 43574
Mulvane Art Museum, Topeka 48034
Munce Art Center, Zionsville 48824
Municipal Art Society, New York 45837
Munson-Williams-Proctor Arts Institute Museum of Art, Utica 48170
Muscarelle Museum of Art, Williamsburg 48630
Muscatine Art Center, Muscatine 45575
Muse Art Gallery, Philadelphia 46429
Museo de Las Americas, Denver 42893
El Museo del Barrio, New York 45838
El Museo Latino, Omaha 46150
Museum and Arts Center in the Sequim Dungeness Valley, Sequim 47568
The Museum at Drexel University, Philadelphia 46430
Museum California Center for the Arts Escondido, Escondido 43210
Museum in the Community, Hurricane 44182
Museum of Ancient and Modern Art, Penn Valley 46339
Museum of Art, Pullman 46745
Museum of Art, Providence 46721
Museum of Art, Orono 46196
Museum of Art and Archaeology, Columbia 42553
Museum of Art and History, Santa Cruz 47411
The Museum of Arts and Sciences, Daytona Beach 42811
Museum of Arts and Sciences, Macon 45045
Museum of Arts Downtown Los Angeles, Los Angeles 44929
Museum of Bad Art, Dedham 42842
Museum of Central Connecticut State University, New Britain 45673
Museum of Children's Art, Oakland 46066
Museum of Conceptual Art, San Francisco 47328
The Museum of East Texas, Lufkin 44997
Museum of Fine Arts, Boston 41817
The Museum of Fine Arts, Houston 44129
Museum of Fine Arts, Missoula 45406
Museum of Fine Arts, Santa Fe 47424
Museum of Fine Arts, Springfield 47747
Museum of Fine Arts Saint Petersburg, Florida, Saint Petersburg 47174
Museum of Indian Arts and Culture, Santa Fe 47425
Museum of International Children's Art, Santa Cruz 47412
Museum of Nebraska Art, Kearney 44424
The Museum of Outdoor Arts, Englewood 43191
Museum of Texas Tech University, Lubbock 44991
Museum of the Dog, Saint Louis 47131
Museum of the Southwest, Midland 45328
Museum Quality Finishes, New York 45848
Muskegon Museum of Art, Muskegon 45579
Mystic Art Association Museum, Mystic 45587
Napa Valley Museum, Yountville 48809
Naples Museum of Art, Naples 45602
Nassau County Museum of Art, Roslyn 47009
Natalie and James Thompson Gallery, San Jose 47353
National Academy of Design Museum, New York 45849
National Art Museum of Sport, Indianapolis 44232
National Arts Club, New York 45850
National Center for American Western Art, Kerrville 44457
National Exhibits by Blind Artists, Philadelphia 46434
National Gallery of Art, Washington 48373
National Institute of Art and Disabilities, Richmond 46858
National Museum of American Illustration, Newport 45928
National Museum of Wildlife Art, Jackson 44290
National Museum of Women in the Arts, Washington 48381
National Portrait Gallery, Washington 48382
Nave Museum, Victoria 48234
The Nelson-Atkins Museum of Art, Kansas City 44404
Nemours Mansion and Gardens, Wilmington 48654
Neuberger Museum of Art, Purchase 46747
Nevada Museum of Art, Reno 46835
New England College Gallery, Henniker 43996
New Hampshire Institute of Art, Manchester 45099
New Image Art, Los Angeles 44935
New Jersey Center for Visual Arts, Summit 47877
New Jersey State Museum, Trenton 48057
New Mexico State University Art Gallery, Las Cruces 44660
New Orleans Artworks Gallery, New Orleans 45733
New Orleans Museum of Art, New Orleans 45735
New Visions Gallery, Marshfield 45186
New York Studio School of Drawing, Painting and Sculpture Gallery, New York 45860
New Zone Virtual Gallery, Eugene 43225
The Newark Museum, Newark 45892
Newcomb Art Gallery, New Orleans 45737
Newport Art Museum, Newport 45930
Nicolaysen Art Museum, Casper 42130
Niu Art Museum, DeKalb 42856
Noble Maritime Collection, Staten Island 47785
Nobles County Art Center Gallery, Worthington 48761
Nora Eccles Harrison Museum of Art, Logan 44845
Nordic Heritage Museum, Seattle 47541
Norman R. Eppink Art Gallery, Emporia 43184
Norman Rockwell Museum at Stockbridge, Stockbridge 47820
North Carolina Central University Art Museum, Durham 43023
North Carolina Museum of Art, Raleigh 46775
North Carolina State University Gallery of Art and Design, Raleigh 46778
North Country Museum of Arts, Park Rapids 46291
North Dakota Museum of Art, Grand Forks 43743
North Florida Community College Art Gallery, Madison 45054
Northcutt Steele Gallery, Billings 41689
Northeastern Nevada Museum, Elko 43146
Northern Arizona University Art Museum and Galleries, Flagstaff 43330
Northern Galleries, Aberdeen 41046
Northern Illinois University Art Gallery in Chicago, Chicago 42354
Northern Indiana Arts Association, Munster 45562
Northern Kentucky University Art Galleries, Highland Heights 44019
Northwest Gallery and Sinclair Gallery, Powell 46680
Norton Simon Museum, Pasadena 46302
Noyes Art Gallery, Lincoln 44790
The Noyes Museum of Art, Oceanville 46090
Oak Ridge Art Center, Oak Ridge 46057
Oakland Museum of California, Oakland 46067
The Octagon Center for the Arts, Ames 41173
Oglethorpe University Museum of Art, Atlanta 41354
The Ohr-O'Keefe Museum of Art, Biloxi 41696
Ojai Art Center, Ojai 46107
Okefenokee Heritage Center, Waycross 48472
Oklahoma City Museum of Art, Oklahoma City 46118
Olana State Historic Site, Hudson 44143
Old Dominion University Gallery, Norfolk 45971
The Old Jail Art Center, Albany 41091
Old State House, Hartford 43943
Olin Fine Arts Center, Washington 48417
On the Hill Cultural Arts Center, Yorktown 48799
Opelousas Museum of Art, Opelousas 46169
Opus 40 and the Quarryman's Museum, Saugerties 47465
Orange County Museum of Art, Newport Beach 45935
Oriental Institute Museum, Chicago 42355
Orlando Museum of Art, Orlando 46188
Ormond Memorial Art Museum, Ormond Beach 46193
Oscar Howe Art Center, Mitchell 45415
Ossining Historical Society Museum, Ossining 46212
Otis Gallery, Los Angeles 44936
Ozaukee Art Center, Cedarburg 42163
Pacific Arts Center, Seattle 47542
Pacific Asia Museum, Pasadena 46303
Pacific Grove Art Center, Pacific Grove 46252
Paine Art Center, Oshkosh 46207
The Palette and Chisel, Chicago 42356
Palm Beach Institute of Contemporary Art, Lake Worth 44600
Palm Springs Desert Museum, Palm Springs 46267
Palmer Museum of Art, University Park 48154
Palo Alto Art Center, Palo Alto 46273
Palos Verdes Art Center, Rancho Palos Verdes 46787
Paris Gibson Square Museum of Art, Great Falls 43782
Parkland College Art Gallery, Champaign 42188
Parrish Art Museum, Southampton 47707
Passaic County Community College Galleries, Paterson 46309
The Patrick and Beatrice Haggerty Museum of Art, Milwaukee 45371
Payne Gallery, Bethlehem 41669
The Peace Museum, Chicago 42357
Pelham Art Center, Pelham 46328
Pen and Brush Museum, New York 45862
Pence Gallery, Davis 42793
Peninsula Fine Arts Center, Newport News 45939
Pennsylvania Academy of the Fine Arts Gallery, Philadelphia 46439
Pensacola Museum of Art, Pensacola 46345
Perkins Center for the Arts, Moorestown 45486
Perkinson Gallery, Decatur 42834
Petersburg Area Art League, Petersburg 46375
Petterson Museum of Intercultural Art, Claremont 42418
Philadelphia Art Alliance, Philadelphia 46440
Philadelphia Museum of Art, Philadelphia 46442
Philbrook Museum of Art, Tulsa 48107
Philip and Muriel Berman Museum of Art, Collegeville 42528
The Phillips Collection, Washington 48389
The Philmont Museum, Seton Memorial Library and Kit Carson Museum, Cimarron 42396
Phoenix Art Museum, Phoenix 46477
Pickens County Museum of Art History, Pickens 46481
Picker Art Gallery, Hamilton 43882
Piedmont Arts Museum, Martinsville 45192
Pierpont Morgan Library, New York 45863
Pittsburgh Center for the Arts, Pittsburgh 46523
Plains Art Museum, Fargo 43293
Plattsburgh Art Museum, Plattsburgh 46549
Polish American Museum, Port Washington 46609
Polk County Heritage Gallery, Des Moines 42907
Polk Museum of Art, Lakeland 44604
Pomona College Museum of Art, Claremont 42419
Port Angeles Fine Arts Center, Port Angeles 46589
Portholes Into the Past, Medina 45226
Portland Art Museum, Portland 46641
Portland Museum of Art, Portland 46626
Portland State University Galleries, Portland 46643
Pratt Manhattan Gallery, New York 45864
Princeton University Art Museum, Princeton 46703
Providence Athenaeum, Providence 46723
Provincetown Art Museum, Provincetown 46730
Provincetown Heritage Museum, Provincetown 46731
Purdue University Galleries, West Lafayette 48532
Pyramid Hill Sculpture Park and Museum, Hamilton 43884
QCC Art Gallery, Bayside 41549
Queens Library Gallery, Jamaica 44306
Queens Museum of Art, Flushing 43357
Quincy Art Center, Quincy 46760
Radford University Art Museum, Radford 46769
Rahr West Art Museum, Manitowoc 45116
Ramsay Museum, Honolulu 44088
Rawls Museum Arts, Courtland 42678

Reader's Digest Art Gallery, Pleasantville 46556
Reading Public Museum and Art Gallery, Reading 46809
Red River Valley Museum, Vernon 48218
Redding Museum of Art and History, Redding 46819
The Reeves Center, Lexington 44761
Rehoboth Art League, Rehoboth Beach 46831
The Renaissance Society at the University of Chicago, Chicago 42360
Renwick Gallery of the Smithsonian American Art Museum, Washington 48390
Revolving Museum, Boston 41825
Reynolda House, Winston-Salem 48703
Reynolds Homestead, Critz 42703
Rhode Island Black Heritage Society Museum, Providence 46725
Richard F. Brush Art Gallery and Permanent Collection, Canton 42086
Richard Gallery and Almond Tea Gallery, Cuyahoga Falls 42736
Richard L. Nelson Gallery and the Fine Arts Collection, Davis 42794
Richmond Art Center, Richmond 46859
Richmond Art Museum, Richmond 46862
Ridderhof Martin Gallery, Fredericksburg 43540
Ripon College Art Gallery, Ripon 46906
River Arts Center, Clinton 42491
Riverside Art Museum, Riverside 46921
R.L.S. Silverado Museum, Saint Helena 47092
Roberson Museum and Science Center, Binghamton 41700
Robert and Mary Montgomery Armory Art Center, West Palm Beach 48539
Robert Hull Fleming Museum, Burlington 42009
Robert V. Fullerton Art Museum, San Bernardino 47268
Rockford Art Museum, Rockford 46962
Rockford College Art Gallery/Clark Arts Center, Rockford 46963
Rockport Art Association Museum, Rockport 46969
Rockwell Museum of Western Art, Corning 42638
Rocky Mount Arts Center, Rocky Mount 46981
Rocky Mountain College of Art and Design Galleries, Denver 42897
Rocky Reach Dam, Wenatchee 48506
Rodin Museum, Philadelphia 46450
Roger Guffey Gallery, Kansas City 44406
Rogers House Museum and Gallery, Ellsworth 43163
Rogue Gallery and Art Center, Medford 45220
Roland Gibson Gallery, Potsdam 46670
Rome Art and Community Center, Rome 46997
Rose Art Museum, Waltham 48298
Rosenberg Gallery, Baltimore 41486
Rosenthal Gallery of Art, Caldwell 42028
Rosenwald-Wolf Gallery, Philadelphia 46452
Roswell Museum and Art Center, Roswell 47016
Rotunda Gallery, Brooklyn 41950
Round Top Center for the Arts - Arts Gallery, Damariscotta 42768
R.S. Barnwell Memorial Garden and Art Center, Shreveport 47615
Rubelle and Norman Schafler Gallery, Brooklyn 41951
Rudolph E. Lee Gallery, Clemson 42458
Ruth Eckerd Hall, Clearwater 42453
The R.W. Norton Art Gallery, Shreveport 47616
Saco Museum, Saco 47046
Saginaw Art Museum, Saginaw 47063
Saint Gaudens National Historic Site, Cornish 42639
Saint John's Museum of Art, Wilmington 48663
Saint Joseph College Art Gallery, West Hartford 48528
Saint Joseph's University Gallery, Philadelphia 46454
Saint Louis Art Museum, Saint Louis 47134
Saint Louis Artists' Guild Museum, Saint Louis 47135
Saint Luke's Gallery, Paxton 46320
Saint Mary's Galeria, Orchard Lake 46177
Saint Peter's College Art Gallery, Jersey City 44341
De Saisset Museum, Santa Clara 47407
Salina Art Center, Salina 47213
Salisbury State University Galleries, Salisbury 47217
Salt Lake Art Center, Salt Lake City 47232
Samuel Cupples House, Saint Louis 47137
Samuel Dorsky Museum of Art, New Paltz 45741
Samuel P. Harn Museum of Art, Gainesville 43584
San Angelo Museum of Fine Arts, San Angelo 47242
San Antonio Museum of Art, San Antonio 47260
San Diego Mesa College Art Gallery and African Art Collection, San Diego 47291
San Diego Museum of Art, San Diego 47293
San Francisco Camerawork, San Francisco 47335
San Jose Museum of Art, San Jose 47356
San Luis Obispo Art Center, San Luis Obispo 47362
The Sandor Teszler Gallery, Spartanburg 47717
Sangre de Cristo Arts Center and Buell Children's Museum, Pueblo 46741
Santa Ana College Art Gallery, Santa Ana 47401
Santa Barbara Museum of Art, Santa Barbara 47404
Santa Cruz Art League Museum, Santa Cruz 47413
Santa Fe Gallery, Gainesville 43585
Santa Rosa Junior College Art Gallery, Santa Rosa 47447
Santarella Museum and Gardens, Tyringham 48133
Sarah Campbell Blaffer Foundation, Houston 44136
Sarah Campbell Blaffer Gallery, Houston 44137
Sarah Moody Gallery of Art, Tuscaloosa 48117
Sarah Spurgeon Gallery, Ellensburg 43152
The Satirical World Art Museum, Waco 48267
Sawhill Gallery, Duke Hall, Harrisonburg 43931
Scarfone and Hartley Galleries, Tampa 47944
Schenectady Museum, Schenectady 47498
Schick Art Gallery, Saratoga Springs 47463
Schneider Museum of Art, Ashland 41296
School of Art and Art History Gallery, Denver 42899
School of Fine Arts Gallery, Bloomington 41748
Schumacher Gallery, Columbus 42592
Schuyler Mansion, Albany 41086
Schweinfurth Memorial Art Center, Auburn 41374
Seattle Art Museum, Seattle 47545
Sedona Arts Center, Sedona 47558
Seigfred Gallery, Athens 41325
Selby Gallery, Sarasota 47455
Senate House, Kingston 44494
SFA Galleries, Nacogdoches 45589
Sharadin Art Gallery, Kutztown 44531
Sharon Arts Center, Sharon 47580
Sheehan Gallery at Whitman College, Walla Walla 48286
Sheldon Memorial Art Gallery and Sculpture Garden, Lincoln 44791
Side Street Projects, Los Angeles 44940
Sidney Mishkin Gallery of Baruch College, New York 45869
Silvermine Guild Arts Center, New Canaan 45682
Sioux City Art Center, Sioux City 47638
Sioux Indian Museum, Rapid City 46798
Skirball Cultural Center, Los Angeles 44943
Slater Memorial Museum, Norwich 46037
Slidell Art Center, Slidell 47654
Smith College Museum of Art, Northampton 46015
The Snite Museum of Art, Notre Dame 46044
Snyder Museum and Creative Arts Center, Bastrop 41519
Society for Contemporary Craft Museum, Pittsburgh 46527
Society of the Cincinnati Museum, Washington 48394
The Society of the Four Arts Gallery, Palm Beach 46265
Solomon R. Guggenheim Museum, New York 45872
Sordoni Art Gallery, Wilkes-Barre 48622
South Arkansas Arts Center, El Dorado 43106
South Boston-Halifax County Museum of Fine Arts and History, South Boston 47687
South Dakota Art Museum, Brookings 41932
Southeastern Center for Contemporary Art, Winston-Salem 48705
Southern Alleghenies Museum of Art, Loretto 44884
Southern Ohio Museum and Cultural Center, Portsmouth 46657
Southern Plains Indian Museum, Anadarko 41193
Southern Vermont Art Center, Manchester 45102
Southern Vermont College Art Gallery, Bennington 41630
The Southland Art Collection, Dallas 42758
Southwest Museum, Los Angeles 44945
Space One Eleven, Birmingham 41710
Spartanburg County Museum of Art, Spartanburg 47718
Speed Art Museum, Louisville 44976
Spelman College Museum of Fine Art, Atlanta 41360
Spencer Museum of Art, Lawrence 44686
Spiers Gallery, Brevard 41881
Springfield Art Gallery, Springfield 47742
Springfield Art Museum, Springfield 47754
Springfield Museum of Art, Springfield 47757
Springville Museum of Art, Springville 47763
Spruill Gallery, Atlanta 41361
Stables Art Gallery of Taos Art Association, Taos 47952
Stamford Museum and Nature Center, Stamford 47768
Stark Museum of Art, Orange 46172
Staten Island Institute of Arts and Sciences, Staten Island 47791
Staunton Augusta Art Center, Staunton 47798
Steensland Art Museum, Northfield 46023
Stephens Museum, Fayette 43307
Sterling and Francine Clark Art Institute, Williamstown 48634
Stone House Gallery, Fredonia 43543
Storm King Art Center, Mountainville 45551
Stuart Collection, La Jolla 44549
Studio Gallery, Washington 48395
Studio Museum in Harlem, New York 45877
Studio San Giuseppe Art Gallery, Cincinnati 42409
Sturges Fine Arts Center, San Bernardino 47269
Suffolk Museum, Suffolk 47868
Sumter Gallery of Art, Sumter 47880
Sunrise Museum, Charleston 42231
Sweeney Art Gallery, Riverside 46923
Sweet Briar College Art Gallery, Sweet Briar 47901
Swope Art Museum, Terre Haute 47986
Syracuse University Art Collection, Syracuse 47913
Tacoma Art Museum, Tacoma 47922
Taft Museum of Art, Cincinnati 42410
Tang Teaching Museum and Art Gallery, Saratoga Springs 47464
Tarble Arts Center, Charleston 42205
Tattoo Art Museum, San Francisco 47342
T.C. Steele State Historic Site, Nashville 45611
Telfair Museum of Art, Savannah 47485
Tempe Arts Center, Tempe 47974
Temple Gallery, Philadelphia 46458
Tennent Art Foundation Gallery, Honolulu 44089
Tennessee Valley Art Association, Tuscumbia 48121
Texas Woman's University Art Galleries, Denton 42876
The Brush Art Gallery and Studios, Lowell 44987
The Gray Gallery, Quincy 46762
This Century Art Gallery, Williamsburg 48631
Thomas Center Galleries, Gainesville 43586
Thomas Handforth Gallery, Tacoma 47923
Thomas J. Walsh Art Gallery and Regina A. Quick Center for the Arts, Fairfield 43265
Thomasville Cultural Center, Thomasville 48002
Thorne-Sagendorph Art Gallery, Keene 44427
Thornhill Gallery, Kansas City 44411
Timken Museum of Art, San Diego 47298
TM Gallery, Crestview 42699
Toledo Museum of Art, Toledo 48021
Torpedo Factory Art Center, Alexandria 41135
Tougaloo College Art Collection, Tougaloo 48041
Tower Fine Arts Gallery, Brockport 41908
Trianon Museum and Art Gallery, Denver 42901
Triton Museum of Art, Santa Clara 47408
Tubac Center of the Arts, Tubac 48076
Tucson Museum of Art and Historic Block, Tucson 48093
Tufts University Art Gallery, Medford 45217
Tulane University Art Collection, New Orleans 45739
Tupelo Artist Guild Gallery, Tupelo 48110
Turner House Museum, Hattiesburg 43958
The Turner Museum, Sarasota 47456
Turtle Mountain Chippewa Heritage Center, Belcourt 41586
T.W. Wood Gallery and Arts Center, Montpelier 45477
Tweed Museum of Art, Duluth 43003
Tyler Art Gallery, Oswego 46218
Tyler Museum of Art, Tyler 48132
Ukrainian Museum, Cleveland 42484
Union Art Gallery, Baton Rouge 41536
Union-Art Gallery, Milwaukee 45372
United States Capitol Visitor Center, Washington 48399
United States Naval Academy Museum, Annapolis 41230
United States Navy Art Gallery, Washington 48403
United States Senate Commission on Art Collection, Washington 48404
University Art Galleries, Murray 45572
University Art Galleries, Vermillion 48215
University Art Gallery, Bridgeport 41892
University Art Gallery, Mount Pleasant 45537
University Art Gallery, North Dartmouth 45991
University Art Gallery, Pittsburgh 46529
University Art Gallery, Rohnert Park 46989
University Art Gallery, Stony Brook 47832
University Art Gallery, Irvine 44258
University Art Gallery, San Diego 47299
University Art Gallery, La Jolla 44550
University Art Museum, Albany 41089
University Art Museum, Binghamton 41701
University Art Museum, Santa Barbara 47406
University Art Museum, Lafayette 44572
University Art Museum, Albuquerque 41111
University at Buffalo Art Galleries, Buffalo 41990
University Galleries, Akron 41076
University Galleries, Clarion 42427
University Gallery, Alexandria 41118
University Gallery, Gainesville 43587
University Gallery, Commerce 42595
University Gallery, Newark 45888
University Gallery, Amherst 41182
The University Gallery of the University of the South, Sewanee 47571
The University Museum, Edwardsville 43098
The University Museum, Indiana 44213
University Museums, Oxford 46239
University of Alaska Museum, Fairbanks 43258
University of Arizona Museum of Art, Tucson 48095
University of Arizona Union Galleries, Tucson 48096
University of Arkansas at Little Rock Art Galleries, Little Rock 44826
University of California Berkeley Art Museum, Berkeley 41649
University of Hawaii Art Gallery, Honolulu 44090
University of Iowa Museum of Art, Iowa City 44248
University of Kentucky Art Museum, Lexington 44746
University of Michigan Museum of Art, Ann Arbor 41222
University of North Texas Art Gallery, Denton 42877
University of Oregon Museum of Art, Eugene 43228
University of Rhode Island Fine Arts Center Galleries, Kingston 44498
University of Richmond Museums, Richmond 46887
University of Rochester Memorial Art Gallery, Rochester 46948
University of South Carolina Beaufort Art Gallery, Beaufort 41560
University of Virginia Art Museum, Charlottesville 42253
University of West Florida Art Gallery, Pensacola 46346
University of Wyoming Art Museum, Laramie 44650
Upper Room Chapel Museum, Nashville 45628
Upper Snake River Valley Historical Museum, Rexburg 46847
Urban Institute for Contemporary Arts, Grand Rapids 43760
Urbanarts, Boston 41830
USM Art Gallery, Gorham 43731
Utah Museum of Fine Arts, Salt Lake City 47234
Valdosta State University Fine Arts Gallery, Valdosta 48181
Valley Art Center, Clarkston 42434
Vanderbilt University Fine Arts Gallery, Nashville 45629
Venango Museum of Art, Science and Industry, Oil City 46106
Ventura College Art Galleries, Ventura 48210
Very Special Arts Gallery, Albuquerque 41112
Viking Union Gallery, Bellingham 41602
Virginia M. McCune Community Arts Center, Petoskey 46384
Virginia Museum of Fine Arts, Richmond 46891
Visceglia Art Gallery, Caldwell 42030
Visual Arts Center of Northwest Florida, Panama City 46278
Visual Arts Gallery, Birmingham 41711
Visual Arts Gallery, Pensacola 46347
Volcano Art Center, Hawaii National Park 43968
The von Liiebig Art Center, Naples 45604
Wadsworth Atheneum, Hartford 43944
Walker Art Center, Minneapolis 45394
Walker Art Collection of the Garnett Public Library, Garnett 43628
Walter and McBean Galleries, San Francisco 47343
Walter Anderson Museum of Art, Ocean Springs 46087
Walters Art Museum, Baltimore 41489
The Ward Museum of Wildfowl Art, Salisbury 47218
Warehouse Gallery, Lee 44708
Warther Museum, Dover 42974
Warwick Museum of Art, Warwick 48323
Washington County Museum of Fine Arts, Hagerstown 43867
Washington Pavillion of Arts and Science, Sioux Falls 47647
Wassenberg Art Center, Van Wert 48197
Waterloo Center of the Arts, Waterloo 48435
Waterworks Visual Arts Center, Salisbury 47221
Watkins Gallery, Washington 48408
Watson Gallery, Norton 46031
Watts Towers Arts Center, Los Angeles 44948
Wayne Center for the Arts, Wooster 48750
Weatherspoon Art Museum, Greensboro 43819
Weber State University Art Gallery, Ogden 46101
Weir Farm, Wilton 48671
Wellington B. Gray Gallery, Greenville 43826
West Bend Art Museum, West Bend 48513
West Valley Art Museum, Surprise 47893
West Virginia University Mesaros Galleries, Morgantown 45500
Western Art Gallery and Museum, Dillon 42950
Western Colorado Center for the Arts, Grand Junction 43749
Western Gallery, Bellingham 41603
Western Illinois University Art Gallery, Macomb 45042
Western Kentucky University Gallery, Bowling Green 41852
Westmoreland Museum of American Art, Greensburg 43821
Wexner Center for the Arts, Columbus 42593
Whatcom Museum of History and Art, Bellingham 41604
Whistler House Museum of Art, Lowell 44988
Whitaker Center for Science and the Arts, Harrisburg 43927
Whitney Museum of American Art at Champion, Stamford 47769
Whittier Fine Arts Gallery, Wichita 48609
Wichita Art Museum, Wichita 48610
Wichita Center for the Arts, Wichita 48611
Wichita Falls Museum and Art Center, Wichita Falls 48614
Widener Gallery, Hartford 43945
Widener University Art Collection and Gallery, Chester 42285
The Wiegand Gallery, Belmont 41609
Wignall Museum and Gallery, Rancho Cucamonga 46784
Wildlife Interpretive Gallery, Royal Oak 47025
Wilkes Art Gallery, North Wilkesboro 46011
The William Benton Museum of Art, Storrs 47837
William Bonifas Fine Arts Center, Escanaba 43207
William King Regional Arts Center, Abingdon 41055
William Woods University Art Gallery, Fulton 43576
Williams College Museum of Art, Williamstown 48635
Wing Luke Asian Museum, Seattle 47548
Wings of Love, Clinton 42494
Winterset Art Center, Winterset 48711
Winthrop University Galleries, Rock Hill 46951
Wiregrass Museum of Art, Dothan 42961
Wirtz Gallery, Miami 45294
The Wisconsin Union Galleries, Madison 45074
Wiseman and Fire House Galleries, Grants Pass 43769
Witter Gallery, Storm Lake 47834
Women and Their Work, Austin 41425
Women's Art Registry of Minnesota Gallery, Saint Paul 47167
Woodmere Art Museum, Philadelphia 46463
Woodstock Artists Gallery, Woodstock 48740
Woolaroc Museum, Bartlesville 41516
Worcester Art Museum, Worcester 48756
Words and Pictures Museum, Northampton 46016
The Works, Newark 45899
The World Organization of China Painters, Oklahoma City 46124
Wright Museum of Art, Beloit 41616
Wright State University Art Galleries, Dayton 42807
Wriston Art Center Galleries, Appleton 41241
Wyoming Arts Council Gallery, Cheyenne 42299
Xavier University Art Gallery, Cincinnati 42413
The Yager Museum, Oneonta 46161
Yale Center for British Art, New Haven 45699
Yale University Art Gallery, New Haven 45700

Yeiser Art Center, Paducah 46258
Zanesville Art Center, Zanesville 48821

Uzbekistan
Bucharskij Gosudarstvennyj Muzej, Buchara 48832
Gosudarstvennyj Muzej Iskusstv, Taškent 48853
Gosudarstvennyj Muzej Iskusstv Respubliki Karakalpakstan, Nukus 48846

Venezuela
Ateneo de Valencia, Valencia 48965
Centro Cultural Corp Group, Caracas 48898
Centro de Arte La Estancia, Caracas 48900
Galería de Arte Nacional, Caracas 48903
Museo Arturo Michelena, Caracas 48906
Museo de Arte Colonial, Mérida 48955
Museo de Arte Moderno Jesús Soto, Ciudad Bolívar 48933
Museo de la Fundación John Boulton, Caracas 48919
Museo Pedagógico de Historia del Arte, Caracas 48926

Vietnam
Exhibition Hall, Ha Noi 48975
Viet Nam National Fine Arts Museum, Ha Noi 48981

Art, African

Argentina
Museo Nacional de Arte Oriental, Buenos Aires 00227

Belgium
Africa-Museum, Tervuren 03772

Botswana
Botswana National Museum and Art Gallery, Gaborone 03934

Burkina Faso
Centre National d'Artisanat d'Art, Ouagadougou 04941

Cameroon
Musée d'Art Nègre, Yaoundé 04961

Czech Republic
Náprstkovo Muzeum Asijských, Afrických a Amerických Kultur, Praha 08600

France
Musée Africain, Lyon 12727
Musée Charbonneau-Lassay, Loudun 12674
Musée Dapper, Paris 13545
Musée d'Art Moderne, Troyes 15004
Musée d'Arts Africains, Langonnet 12325
Musée National des Arts d'Afrique et d'Océanie, Paris 13634

Germany
Iwalewa Haus, Bayreuth 15847
Makonde Art Museum, Bammental 15821

Italy
Museo Africano, Roma 25176
Museo di Arte Cinese ed Etnografico, Parma 24805
Museo e Villaggio Africano, Basella di Urgnano 23036

Morocco
Musée Dar-Si-Said, Marrakech 28699
Museum of Maroccan Arts, Tanger 28713

Netherlands
Afrika Museum, Berg en Dal 28978

Nigeria
Centre for Black and African Art and Civilization, Lagos 30350
Isenbaye Art Gallery and Cultural Troupe, Oshogbo 30356

Poland
Muzeum Afrykanistyczne im. Dr. Bogdana Szczygła, Olkusz 31848

Puerto Rico
Museo de Las Américas, San Juan 32396

Sao Tome and Principe
Museu Nacional, São Tomé 33770

Senegal
Musée d'Art Africain, Dakar 33777

South Africa
African Art Centre, Durban 34223
Ann Bryant Art Gallery, East London 34235
Durban Art Gallery, Durban 34225
Gertrude Posel Gallery, Johannesburg 34277
Irma Stern Museum of the University of Cape Town, Rosebank 34372
Julius Gordon Africana Centre, Riversdale 34368
Lichtenburg Museums and Art Gallery, Lichtenburg 34301
Museum of Southern African Rock Art, Johannesburg 34281
Polokwane Art Museum, Polokwane 34331
Potchefstroom Museum, Potchefstroom 34335
Pretoria Art Museum, Pretoria 34353
Rust en Vreugd Museum, Cape Town 34209
South African National Gallery, Cape Town 34214
Standard Bank Gallery, Johannesburg 34284
Tatham Art Gallery, Pietermaritzburg 34328
Technikon Natal Gallery, Durban 34233
Township Museum, Lwandle 34303
University Art Gallery, Potchefstroom 34338
University of Fort Hare Museum, Alice 34170
Westville Gallery, Durban 34234

Spain
Museo Africano Mundo Negro, Madrid 35012

Switzerland
Asia-Africa Museum, Genève 36724

Uganda
Makerere Art Gallery, Kampala 37828

United Kingdom
Danford Collection of West African Art and Artefacts, Birmingham 38220

U.S.A.
African Art Museum of Maryland, Columbia 42548
Black Arts National Diaspora, New Orleans 45720
Jackson Hall Gallery, Frankfort 43508
Lois E. Woods Museum, Norfolk 45967
Marianna Kistler Beach Museum of Art, Manhattan 45108
Museum for African Art, Long Island City 44868
The Museum of African Tribal Art, Portland 46625
Museum of the National Center of Afro-American Artists, Boston 41819
Museum of the National Center of Afro-American Artists, Roxbury 47022
National Museum of African Art, Washington 48374
Selsor Gallery of Art, Chanute 42195
Trout Gallery, Carlisle 42105

Zimbabwe
National Gallery of Zimbabwe, Harare 49032

Art, American

Canada
Art Gallery of Bancroft, Bancroft 05038
Atlantic Salmon Museum on the Miramichi River, Doaktown 05333
Bonavista North Regional Museum, Wesleyville 06770
Centre d'Exposition d'Amos, Amos 04990
City of Saint John Gallery, Saint John 06332
Cornwall Regional Art Gallery, Cornwall 05276
Enook Galleries, Waterloo 06754
Kelowna Art Gallery, Kelowna 05652
Maple Ridge Art Gallery, Maple Ridge 05812
Marion Scott Gallery, Vancouver 06681
Market Gallery, Toronto 06592
Moose Jaw Museum and Art Gallery, Moose Jaw 05934
Red Deer and District Museum, Red Deer 06222
Simon Fraser Gallery, Burnaby 05151
Tom Thomson Memorial Art Gallery, Owen Sound 06090
Workers Arts and Heritage Centre, Hamilton 05577

France
Musée National de la Coopération Franco-Américaine, Blérancourt 10766

Ireland
National Gallery of Ireland, Dublin 22446

Netherlands
Museum voor Valse Kunst, Vledder 29951

Uruguay
Museo de Arte Americano de Maldonado, Maldonado 40980

U.S.A.
Academy Gallery, New Orleans 45718
Addison Gallery of American Art, Andover 41207
Alaska Centennial Center for the Arts, Fairbanks 43257
A.R. Mitchell Memorial Museum of Western Art, Trinidad 48061
ARC Gallery, Chicago 42303
Arizona State University Art Museum, Tempe 47970
Armory Art Gallery, Blacksburg 41726
The Art Center, Mount Clemens 45524
Art Gallery, Brooklyn Park 41954
Art Gallery Marist College, Poughkeepsie 46673
Artist Gallery, San Francisco 47307
Arts Alliance Center at Clear Lake, Nassau Bay 45631
Arts Club of Washington, Washington 48336
Arts Midland Galleries, Midland 45321
Ashby-Hodge Gallery of American Art, Fayette 43306
Bank of Mississippi Art Collection, Tupelo 48108
Barron Arts Center and Museum, Woodbridge 48728
Bedford Gallery at the Dean Lesher Regional Center for the Arts, Walnut Creek 48290
Bergen Museum of Art and Science, Ho-Ho-Kus 44040
Berkeley Art Museum, Berkeley 41641
B.F. Larsen Gallery, Provo 46732
Biola University Art Gallery, La Mirada 44553
Bjarne Ness Gallery, Fort Ransom 43445
Black Mountain College Museum and Arts Center, Asheville 41277
Blackwell Street Center for the Arts, Denville 42903
Boarman Arts Center, Martinsburg 45190
Bowman, Megahan and Penelec Galleries, Meadville 45215
Braithwaite Fine Arts Gallery, Cedar City 42146
Cahoon Museum of American Art, Cotuit 42668
Carnegie Art Center, Mankato 45120
Charles H. MacNider Museum, Mason City 45200
Charles H. Taylor Arts Center, Hampton 43895
The Charles Hosmer Morse Museum of American Art, Winter Park 48707
Charles M. Auampato Discovery Museum, Charleston 42229
Chatham College Art Gallery, Pittsburgh 46514
Chief Oshkosh Native American Arts, Egg Harbor 43099
Clark Atlanta University Art Galleries, Atlanta 41340
Clough-Hanson Gallery, Memphis 45234
The Coburn Gallery, Ashland 41295
College of Marin Art Gallery, Kentfield 44448
Colter Bay Indian Arts Museum, Colter Bay Village 42544
Community College Art Gallery, Baltimore 41460
Coral Springs Museum of Art, Coral Springs 42629
Custer County Art Center, Miles City 45336
The David and Alfred Smart Museum of Art, Chicago 42322
DeRicci Gallery, Madison 45066
Detroit Focus Gallery, Detroit 42922
Doll Gardner Art GAllery, Portland 46633
Donna Beam Fine Art Gallery, Las Vegas 44664
Doreen Young Art Gallery, Great Barrington 43778
Dupont Gallery, Lexington 44758
El Camino College Art Gallery, Torrance 48038
Fairfield Art Museum, Fairfield 43267
Fawick Art Gallery, Berea 41637
Fine Arts Center of Hot Springs, Hot Springs 44108
Fine Arts Gallery, Columbus 42581
Fine Arts Gallery, Cypress 42737
Frame Gallery, Pittsburgh 46515
Frankenberger Art Gallery, Charleston 42230
Gallery of Art, Dickinson 42946
Gallery of the Department of Art and Art History, Lincoln 44782
Gallery XII, Wichita 48601
Gavilan Community College Art Gallery, Gilroy 43674
George Walter Vincent Smith Art Museum, Springfield 47746
Glyndor Gallery and Wave Hill House Gallery, Bronx 41919
Grace Museum, Abilene 41053
Guggenheim Museum Soho, New York 45810
Hallie Ford Museum of Art, Salem 47208
Helson Hall, Mankato 45121
Hera Gallery, Wakefield 48280
Heritage Conservancy, Doylestown 42983
Hicks Art Center, Newtown 45948
Higgins Art Gallery, West Barnstable 48511
Hoxie Gallery, Westerly 48552
Hui No'eau Visual Arts Center, Makawao 45081
Hunter Museum of American Art, Chattanooga 42263
Indian Arts Research Center, Santa Fe 47420
Institute of American Indian Arts Museum, Santa Fe 47421
Irene Cullis Gallery, Greensboro 43816
Iroquois Indian Museum, Howes Cave 44140
Jack R. Hennesey Art Galleries, Port Huron 46596
John B. Davis Gallery of Fine Art, Pocatello 46572
John H. Vanderpoel Art Gallery, Chicago 42337
John P. Barclay Memorial Gallery, Pittsburgh 46519
Johnson Heritage Post, Grand Marais 43753
Jonson Gallery, Albuquerque 41103
Junior Museum, Newark 45890
Kansas African American Museum, Wichita 48604
Kauffman Gallery, Shippensburg 47608
KBCC Art Gallery, Brooklyn 41943
Kearny Cottage, Perth Amboy 46360
King County Arts Commission Gallery, Seattle 47536
Laure A. Sprague Art Gallery, Joliet 44356
Lewistown Art Center, Lewistown 44733
Lillian and Coleman Taube Museum of Art, Minot 45396
Long Island Museum of American Art, History and Cariages, Stony Brook 47830
Loop Museum and Art Center, Seagraves 47525
Louisburg College Art Gallery, Louisburg 44959
Louise Wells Cameron Art Museum, Wilmington 48660
Lowell Telecommunications Corporation Museum, Lowell 44984
Lyman Allyn Museum of Art, New London 45710
Lynchburg Fine Arts Center, Lynchburg 45004
M. Christina Geis Gallery, Lakewood 44609
McPherson College Gallery, McPherson 45049
Manhattan Arts Center, Manhattan 45107
Marie Hull Gallery, Raymond 46803
Marwen Foundation, Chicago 42340
Mead Art Museum, Amherst 41178
Michigan Chapter Gallery, Detroit 42931
Middletown Fine Arts Center, Middletown 45318
Midtown Art Center, Houston 44127
Mill Grove, The Audubon Wildlife Sanctuary, Audubon 41379
Minority Arts Resource Council Studio Art Museum, Philadelphia 46427
Morris Graves Museum of Art, Eureka 43231
Moses Lake Museum and Art Center, Moses Lake 45520
Mount Wachusett Community College Art Galleries, Gardner 43624
El Museo Francisco Oller y Diego Rivera, Buffalo 41988
Museum of African American Art, Los Angeles 44928
Museum of Fine Arts, Springfield 47747
Museum of History and Art, Morehead City 45496
Museum of Northwest Art, La Conner 44532
Museum of the National Center of Afro-American Artists, Roxbury 47022
National Museum of American Art, Washington 48375
New Britain Museum of American Art, New Britain 45674
Nordstrand Visual Arts Gallery, Wayne 48476
North Carolina State University Gallery of Art and Design, Raleigh 46778
Northeastern Illinois University Art Gallery, Chicago 42353
Noyes and Read Gallery and Herndon Gallery, Yellow Springs 48784
Ogunquit Museum of American Art, Ogunquit 46104
Oklahoma Museum of African American Art, Oklahoma City 46120
Olin Art Gallery, Gambier 43615
Olive Hyde Art Gallery, Fremont 43553
Owatonna Arts Center, Owatonna 46225
People's Gallery, El Paso 43123
Perspective Gallery, Blacksburg 41729
Phippen Museum, Prescott 46688
The Pillsbury Art Collection, Minneapolis 45393
Price Tower Arts Center, Bartlesville 41515
Project Art-University of Iowa and Clinics, Iowa City 44247
Pump House of Regional Arts, La Crosse 44537
Ramsey Center for Arts, Shoreview 47610
Rankin Museum, Ellerbe 43154
Rider University Art Gallery, Lawrenceville 44692
Robert A. Peck Gallery, Riverton 46926
Ryan Fine Arts Center, Abilene 41054
Sacred Circle Gallery of American Indian Art, Seattle 47544
Salmagundi Museum of American Art, New York 45866
Sargent House Museum, Gloucester 43705
Sheldon Peck Museum, Lombard 44849
Sheppard Fine Arts Gallery, Reno 46836
Sid Richardson Collection of Western Art, Fort Worth 43492
Smithsoniam American Art Museum, Washington 48392
South Bend Regional Museum of Art, South Bend 47681
Southeast Arts Center, Atlanta 41359
Southern Alleghenies Museum of Art at Johnstown, Johnstown 44354
Steep and Brew Gallery, Madison 45071
Stephens African-American Museum, Shreveport 47619
Tekakwitha Fine Arts Center, Sisseton 47648
Terra Museum of American Art, Chicago 42367
Thea G. Korver Visual Art Center, Orange City 46175
Tryon Palace, New Bern 45667
University Art Gallery, Carson 42116
University Art Gallery, Chico 42374
University Art Gallery, Turlock 48111
University Galleries, Edinburg 43089
University Gallery, Oxford 46238
University of South Carolina at Spartanburg Art Gallery, Spartanburg 47720
University Place Art Center, Lincoln 44794
Victor Valley Museum and Art Gallery, Apple Valley 41237
Villanova University Art Gallery, Villanova 48236
Vincent Price Gallery, Monterey Park 45462
Wake Forest University Fine Arts Gallery, Winston-Salem 48706
Watkins Institute Art Gallery, Nashville 45630
Frankie G. Weems Gallery Rotunda Gallery, Raleigh 46780
Westminster College Art Gallery, New Wilmington 45749
Whitney Museum of American Art, New York 45886
William A. Farnsworth Art Museum and Wyeth Center, Rockland 46968
William Blizard Gallery, Springfield 47751
Womankraft, Tucson 48098
The Zigler Museum, Jennings 44334

Art, Asian

Argentina
Museo Nacional de Arte Oriental, Buenos Aires 00227

Australia
Asian Galleries, Sydney 01491
Queensland Art Gallery, South Brisbane 01459

Austria
MAK - Österreichisches Museum für angewandte Kunst, Wien 02929

Azerbaijan
Azerbaijan State Museum of Fine Arts, Baku 03065

Bangladesh
Bangladesh National Museum, Dhaka 03085
Institute of Arts and Crafts, Dhaka 03089
National Art Gallery, Dhaka 03092

Bhutan
National Museum of Bhutan, Paro 03891

Cambodia
Musée National de Phnom Penh, Phnom Penh 04950

China, People's Republic
Art Museum of the Chinese Univertity of Hong Kong, Hong Kong 07093
Beijing Art Museum, Beijing 06945
Boer Tala Zhou Museum and Gallery, Bole 07000
China Art Gallery, Beijing 06956
Dalian Gallery, Dalian 07034
Doumen County Fine Art Calligraphy Society, Zhuhai 07334
Guangzhou Art Museum, Guangzhou 07064
Hong Kong Museum of Art, Hong Kong 07096
Jinze Xuan Art Center, Shenzhen 07239
Liaoning Art Gallery, Shenyang 07234
Liaoning Museum, Shenyang 07235
Macau Museum of Art, Macau 07163
Museum of Sacred Art, Macau 07168
Museum of Shanxi Province, Taiyuan 07257
Museum of Site, Most I, Hong Kong 07106
Museum of Site, Most II, Hong Kong 07107
The Palace Museum, Beijing 06983
Shaanxi Chinese Painting Gallery, Xian 07297
Shandong Provincial Museum, Jinan 07134
Shenzhen Art Gallery, Shenzhen 07241
Sichuan University Museum, Chengdu 07025
Tang Dai Art Museum, Xian 07299
Tsui Museum of Art, Hong Kong 07113
University Museum and Art Gallery, Hong Kong 07114
Xian Forest of Stone Tablets Museum, Xian 07302
Yunnan Museum Provincial, Kunming 07146
Zhangjiagang City Gallery, Zhangjiagang 07325
Zhangqiu Arts and Crafts Guan, Jinan 07136

China, Republic
Chuan Cheng Art Center, Taipei 07345
National Palace Museum, Taipei 07351

Czech Republic
Expozice Asijského Umĕni Národní Galerie v Praze, Praha 08574
Muzeum Bedřicha Hrozného, Lysá nad Labem 08468
Náprstek Museum of Asian, African and American Cultures, Libĕchov 08449
Náprstkovo Muzeum Asijských, Afrických a Amerických Kultur, Praha 08600

Finland
Joensuun Taidemuseo, Joensuu 09580

France
Galeries du Panthéon Bouddhique du Japon et de la Chine, Paris 13513
Musée Cernuschi, Paris 13540
Musée d'Art Oriental Asiatica, Biarritz 10724
Musée d'Ennery, Paris 13585
Musée Georges-Labit, Toulouse 14950
Musée Municipal d'Arts Asiatiques, Toulon (Var) 14932
Musée National des Arts Asiatiques Guimet, Paris 13633

Georgia
Georgian State Museum of Oriental Art, Tbilisi 15360

Germany
Gentilhaus, Aschaffenburg 15522
Japanisches Kulturinstitut, Köln 18145
Museum für Frühislamische Kunst, Bamberg 15812
Museum für Indische Kunst, Berlin 16053
Museum für Ostasiatische Kunst, Köln 18158
Museum Villa Rot - Kunstsammlung Hoenes-Stiftung, Burgrieden 16429
Siebold-Museum, Würzburg 20705

Greece
Museum of Asian Art, Corfu 20932
New Museum of European and Eastern Art, Athinai 20895

Hungary
Hopp Ferenc Kelet-Ázsiai Müvészeti Múzeum, Budapest 21344
Ráth György Museum, Budapest 21380

India
Ananda Niketan Kirtishala, Bagnan 21699
Asutosh Museum of Indian Art, Kolkata 21898
India Arts Museum, Chennai 21745
Jehangir Art Gallery, Mumbai 21950
Madhavan Nair Foundation, Edapally 21796
Sri Meenakshi Sundaresvara Temple Museum, Madurai 21935
Nandan Museum-Vichittra and Art Gallery, Santiniketan 22010
Prince of Wales Museum of Western India, Mumbai 21954

Indonesia
Museum Istana Mangkunegaran, Surakarta 22202
Museum Kraton Kasepuhan, Cirebon 22095

Israel
Tikotin Museum of Japanese Art, Haifa 22613
Wilfrid Israel Museum of Oriental Art and Studies, Kibbutz Hazorea 22690

Italy
Messner Mountain Museum Juval, Castelbello 23392
Museo d'Arte Orientale, Venezia 25928
Museo d'Arte Orientale Edoardo Chiossone, Genova 23989
Museo di Arte Cinese ed Etnografico, Parma 24805
Museo Nazionale d'Arte Orientale, Roma 25231
Museo Ossenvanza, Bologna 23141
Museo Popoli e Culture, Milano 24410

Japan
Adachi Museum of Art, Yasugi 27009
Art Gallery of Seikado Library, Tokyo 26828
Chikkyo Art Museum Kasaoka, Kasaoka 26316
Chishaku-in Temple Storehouse, Kyoto 26392
Daikakuji Temple Treasure House, Kyoto 26395
Dazaifu Tenman-gu Hômotsuden, Dazaifu 26132
Dewazakura Art Museum, Tendo 26821
Egawa Museum of Art, Nishinomiya 26605
Eisei Bunko Museum, Tokyo 26843
Fujii Saisei-kai Yurinkan, Kyoto 26397
Fujita Museum of Art, Osaka 26644
Fukui Fujita Bijutsukan, Fukui 26142
Fukuoka-kenritsu Bijutsukan, Fukuoka 26145
Fukushima-ken Bunka Center, Fukushima 26148
Gangidori Bijutsukan, Joetsu 26280
Geidai Bijutsukan, Tokyo 26853
Gifu-ken Bijutsukan, Gifu 26157
Gyokudo Art Museum, Ome 26634
Hakuba Bijutsukan, Hakuba 26178
Hakutsuru Fine Art Museum, Kobe 26345
Hasegawa Bijutsukan, Tokyo 26856
Hatakeyama Collection, Tokyo 26857
Hayashibara Bijutsukan, Okayama 26624
Hida Takayama Bijutsukan, Takayama 26805
Higashi-Hiroshima-shiritsu Bijutsukan, Higashi-Hiroshima 26187
Hiratsuka Bijutsukan, Hiratsuka 26207
Hiroshima-kenritsu Bijutsukan, Hiroshima 26217
Hofu Tenmangu History Hall, Hofu 26227
Hokkaidoritsu Migishi Kotaro Bijutsukan, Sapporo 26715
Hokuetsu Bijutsukan, Nakajo 26573
Homma Museum of Art, Sakata 26703
Ibaraki-ken Rekishikan, Mito 26501
Ii Art Museum, Hikone 26194
Iida-shi Bijutsu Hakubutsukan, Iida 26237
Insho-Domoto Museum of Fine Arts, Kyoto 26406
Ishii Chawan Bijutsukan, Hagi 26169
Ishikawa-kenritsu Bijutsukan, Kanazawa 26306
Itami-shiritsu Bijutsukan, Itami 26261
Itsuo Bijutsukan, Ikeda 26239
Iwasaki Museum, Yokohama 27013
Iwata Senshinkan, Inuyama 26250
Kamiya Bijutsukan, Handa 26183
Kanagawa-kenritsu Kanazawabunko Museum, Yokohama 27014
Kanazawa-shiritsu Nakamura Kinen Bijutsukan, Kanazawa 26310
Kanuma Municipal Art Museum of Kawakami Sumio, Kanuma 26312
Kanzeon-ji Treasure House, Dazaifu 26133
Kathmandu - Hot Spring in the Art Museum, Yuzawa 27034
Katsushika Hokusai Bijutsukan, Tsuwano 26980
Kawaguchi Tibetan Collection, Sendai 26731
Kawaguchiko Bijutsukan, Kawaguchiko 26324
Kawamura Memorial Museum of Art, Sakura 26705
Kawasaki Municipal Industrial and Cultural Museum, Kawasaki 26327
Kitano Bijutsukan, Nagano 26528
Kitazawa Bijutsukan, Suwa 26778
Kochi-kenritsu Bijutsukan, Kochi 26355
Kodai Orient Hakubutsukan, Tokyo 26870
Kongosho-ji Treasure House, Ise 26255
Kosetsu Bijutsukan, Kobe 26351
Kotohira-gu Museum, Kotohira 26372
Koyasan Reihokan, Koya 26373
Kuboso Memorial Museum of Arts, Izumi 26276
Kumamoto-kenritsu Bijutsukan, Kumamoto 26377
Kumaya Bijutsukan, Hagi 26170
Kume Bijutsukan, Tokyo 26878
Kunaicho Sannomaru Shozokan, Tokyo 26879
Kurashiki City Art Museum, Kurashiki 26382
Kure Bijutsukan, Kure 26387
Kyoto Kokuritsu Hakubutsukan, Kyoto 26424
Kyoto-shi Bijutsukan, Kyoto 26430
Kyusei Atami Art Museum, Atami 26114
Marugame Bijutsukan, Marugame 26466
Matsunaga Memorial Hall, Odawara 26613
Matsuoka Museum of Art, Tokyo 26882
Meguro Gajoen Bijutsukan, Tokyo 26883
Menard Art Museum, Komaki 26367
Mie-kenritsu Bijutsukan, Tsu 26976
Miho Museum, Shigaraki 26748
Mitsukuni and Nariaki Tokugawa Memorial Collection, Mito 26504
Miyazaki-kenritsu Bijutsukan, Miyazaki, Miyazaki-ken 26512
Mori Hokokai Hakubutsukan, Hofu 26228
Murauchi Art Museum, Hachioji 26165
Musashino Museum, Kodaira 26359
The Museum Yamato Bunkakan, Nara 26578
Nagano-ken Shinano Bijutsukan, Nagano 26529
Nagasaki-kenritsu Bijutsu Hakubutsukan, Nagasaki 26553
Nara-kenritsu Bijutsukan, Nara 26580
Nara Kokuritsu Hakubutsukan, Nara 26581
Neiraku Museum, Nara 26582
Nezu Bijutsukan, Tokyo 26900
Niigata-shiritsu Bijutsukan, Niigata 26595
Nomura Art Museum, Kyoto 26443
Northern Culture Museum, Yokogoshi 27011
O Art Museum, Tokyo 26909
Ohara Bijutsukan, Kurashiki 26384
Oita-kenritsu Geijutsu Kaikan, Oita 26622
Okawa Bijutsukan, Kiryu 26335
Okayama-Kenritsu Bijutsukan, Okayama 26626
Okayama-kenritsu Hakubutsukan, Okayama 26627
Okura Shukokan Museum, Tokyo 26911
Ome-shiritsu Bijutsukan, Ome 26635
Onomichi Shiritsu Bijutsukan, Onomichi 26641
Osaka-shiritsu Bijutsukan, Osaka 26669
Ōta Kinen Bijutsukan, Tokyo 26912
Saga-kenritsu Bijutsukan, Saga 26690
Sano Art Museum, Mishima 26497
Sato Art Museum Toyama, Toyama 26967
Seisonkaku, Kanazawa 26311
Sekiguchi Ko Museum Yuzawa, Yuzawa 27037
Sen'oku Hakukokan Museum, Kyoto 26453
Shimonoseki City Art Museum, Shimonoseki 26753
Shizuoka-kenritsu Bijutsukan, Shizuoka 26767
The Shoto Museum of Art, Tokyo 26923
Sogetsu Bijutsukan, Tokyo 26924
Soun Museum, Ashikaga 26109
Sugimoto Bijutsukan, Mihama 26488
Sumpu Museum, Shizuoka 26768
Suntory Bijutsukan, Tokyo 26928
Suntory Museum, Osaka 26673
Suwa-shi Bitjutsukan, Suwa 26779
Tagawa Bijutsukan, Tagawa 26783
Tanabe Museum of Art, Matsue 26474
Tanimura Bijutsukan, Itoigawa 26269
Tatsuno Bijutsukan, Tatsuno 26820
Tekiho Memorial Museum of Art, Ogose 26621
Tekisui Art Museum, Ashiya 26111
Tessai Museum, Takaraduka 26797
Tokugawa Bijutsukan, Nagoya, Aichi 26571
Tokyo Kokuritsu Hakubutsukan, Tokyo 26937
Tokyo-to Bijutsukan, Tokyo 26944
Toyama Kinenkan, Hiki 26191
Tsukuba Bijutsukan, Tsukuba 26978
Tsurui Bijutsukan, Niigata 26600
Umezawa Memorial Gallery, Tokyo 26952
Wakayama-kenritsu Hakubutsukan, Wakayama 26997
Yamaguchi-kenritsu Bijutsukan, Yamaguchi 27004
Yamamoto Kanae Memorial Museum, Ueda 26984
Yamazaki Museum of Art, Kawagoe 26322
Yataro Noguchi Art Museum, Nagasaki 26561
Yokoyama Taikan Memorial Hall, Tokyo 26960
Yonago-shi Bijutsukan, Yonago 27030
Yoshimizu-jinja Yoshinoyama, Yoshino 27033
Yumeji Art Museum, Okayama 26629
Yurinkan Art Museum, Kyoto 26462
Zoshukan, Hanamaki 26182

Korea, Democratic People's Republic
Korean Art Gallery, Pyongyang 27119

Korea, Republic
Cheongju National Museum, Cheongju 27149
Donga University Museum, Busan 27141
Equine Museum, Gwacheon 27179
Gan-Song Art Museum, Seoul 27233
Geumho Museum of Art, Seoul 27234
Han Kuk Art Museum, Yongin 27300
Hanwon Art Museum, Seoul 27237
Ho-Am Art Museum, Yongin 27301
Horim Museum, Seoul 27240
Hwajeong Museum, Seoul 27241
Munsin Museum, Masan 27210
Museum of NaJu Pears, Naju 27213
Seoul Metropolitan Museum of Art, Seoul 27274
Seoul National University Museum, Seoul 27276
Sincheonji Art Museum, Aeweol 27127
Songam Art Museum, Incheon 27192
Unhyang Art Museum, Bugil 27134
Walker Hill Art Center, Seoul 27288
Whanki Museum, Seoul 27289

Malaysia
The Art Gallery, Kuala Lumpur 27637
Muzium Seni Asia, Kuala Lumpur 27648

Nepal
Swayambunath Museum, Swayambunath 28792

Pakistan
Chughtai Museum Trust, Lahore 31033

Philippines
Artists Center and Foundation, Makati 31351
CAP Art Center and Price Mansion, Tacloban 31451
Heritage Art Center, Quezon City 31432
Metropolitan Museum of Manila, Manila 31382
Museo ng Makati, Makati 31354
Museum of Philippine Art, Manila 31387
Sining Makiling Gallery, Los Baños 31347
Torogan House, Pasay 31419

Poland
Muzeum Azji i Pacyfiku, Warszawa 32090

Russia
Chudožestvennyj Muzej, Valujki 33674
Dagestanskij Gosudarstvennyj Objedinennyj Istoriko-architekturnyj Muzej, Machačkala 32995
Dalnevostočnyj Chudožestvennyj Muzej, Chabarovsk 32739
Gosudarstvennyj Istoriko-architekturnyj i Chudožestvennyj Muzej-zapovednik Drevnij Derbent, Derbent 32756
Gosudarstvennyj Muzej Izobrazitelnych Iskusstv Respubliki Kalmykija, Élista 32793
Ingušskij Gosudarstvennyj Muzej Kraevedenija im. T.Ch. Malsagova, Nazran 33203
Irkutskij Oblastnoj Chudožestvennyj Muzej im. V.P. Sukačeva, Irkutsk 32813
Kitajskij Dvorec-muzej, Lomonosov 32989
Muzej Iskusstva Narodov Vostoka, Moskva 33107

Singapore
NUS Museum, Singapore 33940
Singapore Art Museum, Singapore 33941

South Africa
Reza Shah Museum, Johannesburg 34282

Spain
Museo de Arte Oriental, Avila 34501
Museo Oriental, Valladolid 35627

Switzerland
Asia-Africa Museum, Genève 36724
Collections Baur, Genève 36736
Museo delle Culture Extraeuropee, Castagnola 36617

Thailand
The Art Center, Bangkok 37475
Art Gallery of the Faculty of Painting, Sculpture and Graphic Art, Bangkok 37476
Bangkok University City Gallery, Bangkok 37477
Burapha Museum of Art, Chon Buri 37505
D.R. Visual Art Center, Nakorn-Chaisri 37521
James H.W. Thompson House, Bangkok 37486
Silpakorn University Art Centre, Bangkok 37496
Srinakharinwirot Art Exhibition Hall, Bangkok 37498

Turkey
Bursa Türk-İslâm Eserleri Müzesi, Bursa 37646
Mardin Müzesi, Mardin 37757
Mevlâna Müzesi, Konya 37744
Türk Islam Eserleri Müzesi, İstanbul 37710
Türk ve Islam Eserleri Müzesi, Edirne 37666

Ukraine
Bogdan and Varvara Khanenko Museum of Arts, Kyïv 37867
Odessa State Museum of European and Oriental Art, Odessa 37895

United Kingdom
Hartlepool Art Gallery, Hartlepool 39175
Kufa Gallery, London 39683
Museum of East Asian Art, Bath 38119
Oriental Museum, Durham 38829
Powis Castle, Welshpool 40816
Snowshill Manor, Broadway 38369

U.S.A.
Asian-American Arts Centre, New York 45769
Asian Art Museum of San Francisco, San Francisco 47308
Asian Arts and Culture Center, Towson 48045
Asian Resource Gallery, Oakland 46060
China Institute Gallery, New York 45783
Chinese Culture Center of San Francisco, San Francisco 47315
George Walter Vincent Smith Art Museum, Springfield 47746
Japan Society Gallery, New York 45820
Nicholas Roerich Museum, New York 45861
Peabody Place Museum, Memphis 45248
Robert W. Ryerss Museum, Philadelphia 46449
Seattle Asian Art Museum, Seattle 47546
Trammell and Margaret Crow Collection of Asian Art, Dallas 42760
Tremont Gallery, Boston 41829

Vietnam
Fine Art University Exhibition Hall, Ha Noi 48976
Ho Chi Minh City Fine Arts Museum, Ho Chi Minh City 48986

Art, Australian

Australia
Art Gallery of New South Wales, Sydney 01490
Artarmon Galleries, Artarmon 00753
Berrima District Art Gallery, Bowral 00821
Brett Whiteley Studio Museum, Surry Hills 01485
Bribie Island Community Arts Centre, Bribie Island 00832
Brisbane City Gallery, Brisbane 00836
Bunbury Regional Art Galleries, Bunbury 00859
Burnie Regional Art Gallery, Burnie 00863
Cairns Regional Gallery, Cairns 00873
Campbelltown City Bicentennial Art Gallery, Campbelltown 00880
Castlemaine Art Gallery and Historical Museum, Castlemaine 00900
Charles Surt University Art Collection, Wagga Wagga 01568
Cooktown School of Art Gallery, Cooktown 00942

Cooperative Store Museum, Albany 00722
Emerald Art Gallery, Emerald 01015
Geelong Gallery, Geelong 01044
Geraldton Regional Art Gallery, Geraldton 01048
Gladstone Regional Art Gallery and Museum, Gladstone, Queensland 01055
Global Arts Link, Ipswich 01122
Heide Museum of Modern Art, Bulleen 00858
Heide Museum of Modern Art, Melbourne 01231
Horsham Regional Art Gallery, Horsham 01110
The Ian Potter Art Museum, Melbourne 01233
Jane Neville-Rolfe Gallery, Alpha 00742
Lady Franklin Gallery, Lenah Valley 01173
Lawrence Wilson Art Gallery, Crawley 00953
Light Square Gallery, Adelaide 00708
Logan Art Gallery, Logan 01183
McClelland Gallery, Langwarrin 01164
Manly Art Gallery and Museum, Manly 01207
Metro Arts, Brisbane 00838
Mining Industry House, Braddon 00828
Moonah Arts Centre, Moonah 01266
Mornington Peninsula Arts Centre, Mornington 01276
Museum and Art Gallery of the Northern Territory, Darwin 00973
Muswellbrook Regional Arts Centre, Muswellbrook 01295
Noosa Regional Art Gallery, Tewantin 01526
Old Ware House Gallery, Maryborough 01216
Orange Regional Gallery, Orange 01347
Port Victor Gallery, Victor Harbor 01566
Portland CEMA Arts Centre, Portland 01391
QCA Gallery, Brisbane 00841
Queensland Art Gallery, South Brisbane 01459
Queensland University of Technology Art Collection, Kelvin Grove 01140
Quilpie Museum, Quilpie 01404
Riddoch Art Gallery, Mount Gambier 01281
S.H. Ervin Gallery, Sydney 01507
Talbot Arts and Historical Museum, Talbot 01513
Tandanya, Adelaide 00714
Tasmanian Museum and Art Gallery, Hobart 01106
Umoona Opal Mine and Museum, Coober Pedy 00941
UNSW Art Collection, Sydney 01510
Vincent Art Gallery, Townsville 01550
Warrnambool Art Gallery, Warrnambool 01583
Warwick Regional Art Gallery, Warwick 01585

Netherlands
Aboriginal Art Museum, Utrecht 29893

New Zealand
Arts Centre of Christchurch, Christchurch 30122

United Kingdom
Hastings Museum and Art Gallery, Hastings 39184

U.S.A.
Australian Exhibition Center, Chicago 42306

Art, European

Austria
Galerie im Traklhaus, Salzburg 02537
Grazer Kunstverein, Graz 01915
Hipp-Halle, Gmunden 01894
MAK - Österreichisches Museum für angewandte Kunst, Wien 02929
Museum im Ballhaus, Imst 02056
Museum Stift Admont, Admont 01643
Österreichische Galerie Belvedere, Wien 02954

Belgium
Centrum voor de Vlaamse Kunst van de 16de en de 17de Eeuw, Antwerpen 03138
Musée d'Art Ancien, Bruxelles 03299
Musée de Louvain-la-Neuve, Louvain-la-Neuve 03600
Provinciaal Domein Rivierenhof Galerij, Deurne 03383

Chile
Museo Ralli, Santiago de Chile 06919

Croatia
Moderna Galerija, Zagreb 07829

Czech Republic
Alšova Jihočeská Galerie, Hluboká nad Vltavou 08351
Bílkova Vila, Praha 08565
Bílkův Dům v Chýnově, Chýnov u Tábora 08323
České Muzeum Výtvarných Umění, Praha 08567
Císařská Konírna, Praha 08569
Obrazárna Pražského Hradu, Praha 08607
Šternberský Palác, Praha 08615
Zámek Troja, Praha 08619

Denmark
Den Hirschsprungske Samling, København 08931
Kunstakademiets Bibliotek, København 08935
Nivågårds Malerisamling, Nivå 08989
Trapholt, Kolding 08960

Finland
Ateneumin Taidemuseo, Helsinki 09474
Hämeenlinnan Taidemuseo, Hämeenlinna 09451
Joensuun Taidemuseo, Joensuu 09580
Taidekoti Kirpilä, Helsinki 09539
Teresia ja Rafael Lönnströmin kotimuseo, Rauma 09985
Villa Gyllenberg, Helsinki 09546

France
Musée Cognacq-Jay, Paris 13541
Musée d'Art, Toulon (Var) 14926
Musée d'Art et d'Histoire, Nice 13311
Musée d'Art et d'Histoire de Langres, Langres 12326
Musée de Cognac, Cognac 11342
Musée des Années 30, Boulogne-Billancourt 10837
Musée Granet, Aix-en-Provence 10255
Villa Arson, Nice 13328

Germany
Altes Schoß, Abteilung Gemäldegalerie und Kunsthandwerk, Gießen 17278
Angermuseum, Erfurt 16893
Atelierhaus Philipp Harth, Bayrischzell 15861
Barkenhoff Stiftung Worpswede, Worpswede 20681
Bayerisches Nationalmuseum, München 18833
Dieter Roth-Museum, Hamburg 17533
Galerie am Kamp, Teterow 20160
Hessisches Landesmuseum Darmstadt, Darmstadt 16541
Hirschwirtscheuer-Museum für die Künstlerfamilie Sommer, Künzelsau 18258
Historischer Kunstbunker, Nürnberg 19145
Kunsthaus in Stade, Stade 20024
Kunstmuseum Nörvenich, Nörvenich 19111
Kunstwerk, Köln 18156
Mittelrhein-Museum, Koblenz 18122
Museum Villa Rot - Kunstsammlung Hoenes-Stiftung, Burgrieden 16429
Neue Sächsische Galerie, Chemnitz 16470
Neue Städtische Galerie Lüdenscheid, Lüdenscheid 18548
Sammlung Berggruen - Picasso und seine Zeit, Berlin 16086
Sammlung Geyer-zu-Lauf, Emmendingen 16857
Schloßmuseum Aulendorf-Kunst des Klassizismus-Altes Spielzeug, Aulendorf 15575
Schwurgerichtssaal 600, Nürnberg 19160
Stadtmuseum Weilheim, Weilheim, Oberbayern 20450
Städtische Galerie im Kornhaus, Kirchheim unter Teck 18097
Städtische Galerie Karlsruhe, Karlsruhe 18005
Städtische Museen Junge Kunst und Viadrina, Frankfurt/Oder 17085

Greece
New Museum of European and Eastern Art, Athinai 20895

Hungary
Koszta József Múzeum, Szentes 21579
Magyar Nemzeti Galéria, Budapest 21360

Ireland
Butler Gallery, Kilkenny 22487
GAA Museum, Dublin 22426

Israel
Ralli Museum, Caesarea 22583

Italy
Galleria Giorgio Franchetti alla Ca' d'Oro, Venezia 25918
Museo di Storia e Arte, Gorizia 24035
Pinacoteca Civica Tosio Martinengo, Brescia 23209

Japan
Kokuritsu Seiyo Bijutsukan, Tokyo 26873
Miyazaki-kenritsu Bijutsukan, Miyazaki, Miyazaki-ken 26512

Lithuania
M.K. Čiurlionis National Museum of Art, Kaunas 27521

Malta
Cathedral Museum, Mdina 27697

Mexico
Museo Nacional de San Carlos, México 28195

Netherlands
Anton Pieck Museum, Hattem 29351
Bonnefantenmuseum, Maastricht 29564
Cultureel Centrum van Gogh, Zundert 30074
Historisch Museum Rotterdam Het Schielandshuis, Rotterdam 29752
Jacques van Mourik Ruim, Mook 29603
Marie Tak van Poortvliet Museum, Domburg 29165
Museum Het Oude Raadhuis, Megen 29587
Museum Ianchelevici, Goudriaan 29300
Museum Kruijsenhuis, Oirschot 29655
Museum van Lien, Fijnaart 29259
Museum voor Valse Kunst, Vledder 29951
Stedelijk Museum Bureau Amsterdam, Amsterdam 28903

Norway
Haugesund Billedgalleri, Haugesund 30537
Jølstramuseet, Vassenden 30978

Poland
Gabinet Rycin Biblioteki Uniwersyteckiej w Warszawie, Warszawa 32084
Muzeum Książąt Czartoryskich, Kraków 31712
Muzeum Narodowe, Gdańsk 31572
Muzeum Śląskie, Katowice 31648
Muzeum Sztuki w Łodzi, Łódź 31777
Muzeum w Nysie, Nysa 31840
Państwowe Zbiory Sztuki, Sułoszowa 32007

Portugal
Museu Calouste Gulbenkian, Lisboa 32292
Museu do Caramulo, Caramulo 32247
Museu Municipal de Óbidos, Óbidos 32322
Museu Municipal Polinucleado de Tomae, Tomar 32354

Romania
Muzeul Colecţiilor de Artă, Bucureşti 32452
Muzeul de Artă, Târgovişte 32603
Muzeul de Artă, Tulcea 32617
Muzeul de Artă Constanţa, Constanţa 32499
Muzeul de Artă Craiova, Craiova 32506
Muzeul de Artă Dinu şi Sevasta Vintilă, Topalu 32616
Muzeul de Artă şi Artă Populară, Calafat 32478
Muzeul Judeţean de Artă, Ploieşti 32571
Muzeul Judeţean de Istorie şi Artă, Slatina 32598
Muzeul Judeţean Mureş-Secţia de Artă, Târgu Mureş 32609
Muzeul K.H. Zambaccian, Bucureşti 32458
Muzeul Memorial Gheorghe M. Tattarascu, Bucureşti 32459
Muzeul Naţional Brukenthal, Sibiu 32593
Muzeul Naţional Cotroceni, Bucureşti 32465
Muzeul Orăşenesc, Lipova 32543
Muzeul Romanaţiului Secţia de Artă Plastică, Caracal 32487

Russia
Gosudarstvennyj Muzej-usadba Archangelskoe, Archangelskoe 32654
Istoriko-Architekturnyj, Chudožestvennyj i Archeologičeskij Muzej "Zarajskij Kreml'", Zarajsk 33746
Kirovskij Oblastnoj Chudožestvennyj Muzej im. Viktora i Apollinarija Vasnecovych, Kirov 32919
Samarskij Oblastnoj Chudožestvennyj Muzej, Samara 33377
Uljanovskij Oblastnoj Chudožestvennyj Muzej, Uljanovsk 33668

Slovakia
Galéria Mesta Bratislavy, Bratislava 33963
Slovenská Národná Galéria, Bratislava 33978

Spain
Monasterio de San Lorenzo de El Escorial, San Lorenzo de El Escorial 35380
Museo Camón Aznar, Zaragoza 35718
Museo de Belas Artes da Coruña, A Coruña 34750
Museo de Bellas Artes de Alava, Vitoria-Gasteiz 35699
Museo de Cádiz, Cádiz 34647
Museo Pablo Gargallo, Zaragoza 35727
Museo Ralli, Marbella 35087
Museu Municipal Josep Aragay, Breda 34623
Museu Municipal Vicenç Ros, Martorell 35095
Palacio Real, Madrid 35058

Sweden
Eskilstuna Konstmuseum, Eskilstuna 35869
Norrtälje Konsthall, Norrtälje 36123
Sörmlands Museum, Nyköping 36128
Tallbo, Järbo 35974
Ystads Konstmuseum, Ystad 36423

Switzerland
Art ab dä Gass, Steckborn 37208
Huberte Goote Gallery, Zug 37425
Kunstmuseum Luzern, Luzern 36912
Musée des Beaux-Arts, Le Locle 36889
Musée Jurassien des Arts, Moutier 36960

Turkmenistan
Muzej Izobrazitel'nych Iskusstv, Ašgabat 37811

Ukraine
Bogdan and Varvara Khanenko Museum of Arts, Kyïv 37867
Charkovskij Chudožestvennyj Muzej, Charkiv 37842
Chudožestvennyj Muzei, Sevastopol 37901
Odessa State Museum of European and Oriental Art, Odessa 37895

United Kingdom
Art Collection, Stirling 40590
The Art Gallery, Hillsborough 39243
Barber Institute of Fine Arts, Birmingham 38211
Boughton House, Kettering 39347
Bowhill Collection, Selkirk 40467
Bowood House and Gardens, Calne 38441
City Museum and Art Gallery, Gloucester 39080
Compton Verney Collections, Compton Verney 38622
Ferens Art Gallery, Kingston-upon-Hull 39377
Foundling Museum, London 39638
Government Art Collection, London 39646
Hove Museum and Art Gallery, Hove 39269
Kenwood, London 39680
Museum of the Royal College of Physicians, London 39723
Newlyn Art Gallery, Penzance 40180
Osborne House, East Cowes 38839
Palace of Holyroodhouse, Edinburgh 38903
Pallant House Gallery, Chichester 38564
The Queen's Gallery, Edinburgh 38907
Royal Scottish Academy Collections, Edinburgh 38912
Rugby Art Gallery and Museum, Rugby 40356
Shire Hall Gallery, Stafford 40571
Squerryes Court, Westerham 40833
Torre Abbey Historic House and Gallery, Torquay 40719
University Gallery Leeds, Leeds 39456

U.S.A.
Dahesh Museum of Art, New York 45789
Guggenheim Museum Soho, New York 45810
The Martin D'Arcy Museum of Art, Chicago 42339
Museum of Fine Arts, Springfield 47747
Salgo Trust for Education, Port Washington 46610
Spanish Institute, New York 45875
The Zigler Museum, Jennings 44334

Art, Greek and Roman

Austria
Archäologischer Park Carnuntum, Petronell 02408
Archäologisches Museum Carnuntinum und Amphitheater, Bad Deutsch-Altenburg 01694
Freilichtmuseum Petronell, Petronell 02409
Museum Lauriacum, Enns 01818

Cyprus
Leventis Municipal Museum of Nicosia, Lefkosia 08202

Czech Republic
Muzeum Antického Umění, Hostinné 08364

France
Musée des Beaux-Arts, Agen 10231
Musée Gallo-Romain d'Aoste, Aoste 10382
Villa Grècque Kérylos, Beaulieu-sur-Mer 10640

Germany
Antikensammlung, Kiel 18071
Antikensammlung, Kassel 18011
Archäologisches Museum der Universität Münster, Münster 18932
Dominikanermuseum Rottweil, Rottweil 19695
Humboldt-Museum Schloß Tegel, Berlin 16003
Limesmuseum Aalen, Aalen 15381
Martin-von-Wagner-Museum der Universität Würzburg, Würzburg 20697
Staatliche Antikensammlungen und Glyptothek, München 18911
Städtisches Lapidarium, Stuttgart 20108

Greece
Archeological Collection, Anafi 20820
Byzantine and Christian Museum, Athinai 20853
Coumantaros Art Gallery of Sparta, Spárti 21166
Gallery of Florina Artists, Florina 20958
Gallery of the Society for Epirot Studies, Ioannina 20968
Gallery of the Society for Macedonian Studies, Thessaloniki 21183
G.I. Katsigras Museum, Lárissa 21043
Historical Museum of Arta, Arta 20838
Mouseio Vorre, Paiania 21104
Municipal Art Gallery, Thessaloniki 21187
Municipal Gallery of Herakleion, Iráklion 20977
Municipal Gallery of Lamia, Lamia 21040
Municipal Gallery of Volos, Volos 21213
Museum of Cycladic and Ancient Greek Art, Athinai 20883

Iran
Sa'dabad Museums, Teheran 22325

Israel
Museum of the Franciscan Convent, Jerusalem 22652

Italy
Antiquarium, Tindari 25705
Museo Agricolo e Museo dell'Arte Conciaria, Castelfranco Veneto 23401
Museo Archeologico Nazionale, Sperlonga 25617
Museo Archeologico Nazionale, Venezia 25923
Museo Civico Pio Capponi, Terracina 25699
Museo Lapidario Maffeiano, Verona 25975

Russia
Ivanovskij Oblastnoj Chudožestvennyj Muzej, Ivanovo 32829

South Africa
Rhodes Museum of Classical Antiquities, Grahamstown 34253
Social History Collections, Cape Town 34210

Spain
Colección de la Casa de Alba, Madrid 34998

Syria
Musée de Soueida, Soueida 37442

United Kingdom
Old Speech Room Gallery, London 39738
Shefton Museum of Greek Art and Archaeology, Newcastle-upon-Tyne 40041

U.S.A.
Kelsey Museum of Ancient Archaeology, Ann Arbor 41218

Vatican City
Museo Chiaramonti e Braccio Nuovo, Città del Vaticano 48873
Museo Pio Clementino, Città del Vaticano 48879

Art, Latin American

Argentina
Casa Museo Fernando Fader, Ischilín 00367
Centro Cultural España Córdoba, Córdoba 00289
Escuela Museo de Bellas Artes General Urquiza, Buenos Aires 00148
Galerías Pacífico de Centro Cultural Borges, Buenos Aires 00154
Museo Chavin de Huantar, Martínez 00431
Museo de Arte e História de Los Toldos, Los Toldos 00411
Museo de Arte Hispanoamericano Isaac Fernández Blanco, Buenos Aires 00168
Museo de Arte Latinoamericano de Buenos Aires, Buenos Aires 00169
Museo de Artes Plásticas Eduardo Sívori, Buenos Aires 00172
Museo de Bellas Artes, Lincoln 00407
Museo de Bellas Artes, Luján 00414
Museo de Bellas Artes Bonaerense, La Plata 00389
Museo de Bellas Artes Ceferino Carnacini, Villa Ballester 00659
Museo de Bellas Artes Claudio León Sempere, Burzaco 00254
Museo de Bellas Artes de Coronel Pringles, Coronel Pringles 00317
Museo de Bellas Artes Franklin Rawson, San Juan 00570
Museo de Bellas Artes Juan Yapari, Posadas 00481
Museo de Bellas Artes Laureano Brizuela, San Fernando del Valle de Catamarca 00556
Museo de Centro Cultural Recoleta, Buenos Aires 00175
Museo Evocativo y de Bellas Artes Osvaldo Gasparini, San Antonio de Areco 00549
Museo Florencio Molina Campos, Moreno 00454
Museo Histórico, Zapala 00676
Museo Histórico Provincial Brig. Estanislao López, Santa Fé 00605
Museo Juan Carlos Iramaín, San Miguel de Tucumán 00586
Museo Municipal de Arte, Rauch 00502
Museo Municipal de Artes Plásticas, Avellaneda 00122
Museo Municipal de Artes Plásticas Pompeo Boggio, Chivilcoy 00277
Museo Municipal de Artes Visuales, Concordia 00288
Museo Municipal de Bellas Artes, Godoy Cruz 00357
Museo Municipal de Bellas Artes, Pergamino 00473
Museo Municipal de Bellas Artes, San Nicolás de los Arroyos 00591
Museo Municipal de Bellas Artes de Campana, Campana 00258
Museo Municipal de Bellas Artes Dr. Genaro Perez, Córdoba 00307
Museo Municipal de Bellas Artes Dr. Genaro Pérez, Río Cuarto 00512
Museo Municipal de Bellas Artes Dr. Urbano Poggi, Rafaela 00499
Museo Municipal de Bellas Artes Juan B. Castagnino, Rosario 00530
Museo Municipal Lino Enea Spilimbergo, Unquillo 00647
Museo Municipal Primeros Pobladores, San Martín de los Andes 00578
Museo Pedro Luro, Dolores 00331
Museo Provincial de Artes de La Pampa, Santa Rosa 00612
Museo Provincial de Bellas Artes Emilio A. Caraffa, Córdoba 00310
Museo Provincial de Bellas Artes Rosa Galisteo de Rodríguez, Santa Fé 00608
Museo Rómulo Raggio, Vicente López 00655
Museo San Roque, Buenos Aires 00242
Salón de Artes Plásticas Antonia F. Rizzuto, Villa Carlos Paz 00662
Salón Electo Brizuela, Concepción del Uruguay 00286

Belize
Tanah Art Museum, San Antonio 03869

Bolivia
Museo Nacional Tihuanacu, La Paz 03902

Brazil
Fundação Cultural Ema Gordon Klabin, São Paulo 04491
Instituto Moreira Sales, São Paulo 04495
Museu da Abolição, Recife 04295
Museu do Índio, Florianópolis 04093
Museu Malinverni Filho, Lages 04162

Chile
Museo Ralli, Santiago de Chile 06919

Colombia
Collecíon de Antigüedades, San Andrés de Sotavento 07583
Museo Bolivariano de Arte Contemporáneo, Santa Marta 07587
Museo Casa de la Cultura de Cuacutecuta, Cuacutecuta 07467
Museo de la Caña de Azúcar, El Cerrito 07474
Museo Maestro Alfonso Zambrano, Pasto 07550

Cuba
Casa Natal de Regino Boti, Guantánamo 07915
Museo Benito Hortiz, Sancti-Spíritus 08108
Museo de Arte de Matanzas, Matanzas 08037
Museo de Arte Habana, La Habana 07957
Museo La Vigía, Matanzas 08040
Museo Servando Cabrera Moreno, La Habana 07998
Museo Teodoro Ramos Blanco, La Habana 07999
Museo Víctor Manuel, La Habana 08000

Ecuador
Museo Casa de Benalcazar, Quito 09197
Museo Convento de San Diego, Quito 09199
Museo Cultural del Instituto Geografico Militar, Quito 09200
Museo de la Fundación Guayasamin, Quito 09208
Museo de las Artes Populares Cidap, Cuenca 09156
Museo del Banco Central, Riobamba 09222
Museo Guillermo Perez Chiriboga del Banco Central, Quito 09211
Museo Nahim Isaias, Guayaquil 09178

Haiti
Musée d'Art Haïtien, Port-au-Prince 21292

Israel
Ralli Museum, Caesarea 22583

Mexico
Casa Museo Gene Byron, Guanajuato 27967
Colección de Roberto Montenegro, Guadalajara 27945
Galería de Arte de Tabasco, Villahermosa 28605
Galería de Arte Iztapalapa, México 28094
Galería de Escuela Nacional de Artes Plásticas, México 28095
Galeria del Sur, México 28099
Galería Dr. Miguel Angel Gómez Ventura, Villahermosa 28607
Galería IFAL, México 28100
Galería Universitaria Artistos, México 28103
Museo Casa del Maestro José Márquez Figueroa, Puebla 28322
Museo de Academia de San Carlos, México 28122
Museo de Arte Colonial, Morelia 28245
Museo de Arte de Mazatlán, Mazatlán 28077
Museo de Arte de Orizaba y del Estado de Veracruz, Orizaba 28290
Museo de Arte de Querétaro, Querétaro 28352
Museo de Arte de Sinaloa, Culiacán 27882
Museo de Arte en Ciudad Juárez, Juárez 28037
Museo de Arte Guillermo Ceniceros, Durango 27896
Museo de Arte José Luis Bello y Zetina, Puebla 28324
Museo de Arte Moderno, México 28126
Museo de Arte Popular de la Universidad, Puebla 28325
Museo de Arte Prehispánico, Mascota 28071
Museo de Arte Prehispánico Carlos Pellicer, Tepoztlán 28502
Museo de Arte Prehispánico de México Rufino Tamayo, Oaxaca 28274
Museo de Arte Virreinal de Taxco, Taxco de Alarcón 28457
Museo de Artes Visuales Aramara, Tepic 28497
Museo de Artes y Tradiciones Populares de Tlaxcala, Tlaxcala 28532
Museo de Bellas Artes de Toluca, Toluca 28542
Museo de Laca, Chiapa de Corzo 27818
Museo de las Artes, Guadalajara 27952
Museo Emilia Ortiz, Tepic 28498
Museo Francisco Goitia, Zacatecas 28637
Museo Frissel de Arte Zapoteca, Santa Ana del Valle 28428
Museo Hermila Domínguez de Castellanos, Comitán de Domínguez 27850
Museo José María Velasco, Toluca 28550
Museo Nacional de Virreinato, Tepotzotlán 28500
Museo Regional de Arte e Historia, Jerez de García Salinas 28030
Museo Sala de Arte, Tijuana 28514
Museo Universitario del Chopo, México 28209
Pinacoteca del Ateneo, Saltillo 28371
Pinacoteca del Estado Juan Gamboa Guzmán, Mérida 28086
Pinacoteca del Templo de La Compañía, Guanajuato 27978
Pinacoteca Municipal de Guadalupe, Guadalupe 27965
Pinacoteca Universitaria, Colima 27840

Peru
Museo del Instituto Americano del Arte, Cusco 31158
Pinacoteca Municipal Leoncio Lugo, Paucartambo 31235

Puerto Rico
Ateneo Puertorriqueno Gallery, San Juan 32386
Galería Nacional, San Juan 32391

Spain
Museo de América, Madrid 35016
Museo Ralli, Marbella 35087

Uruguay
Centro Municipal de Exposiciones Subste, Montevideo 40988
Museo Municipal de Historia del Arte, Montevideo 41012
Museo Municipal Precolombino y Colonial, Montevideo 41014
Museo Ralli, Punta del Este 41035
Museo Torres García, Montevideo 41024

U.S.A.
Arte Maya Tz'utuhil, San Francisco 47306
Casa de Unidad, Detroit 42916
Galeria de la Raza, San Francisco 47318
Latin American Art Museum, Miami 45288
Museum of Latin American Art, Long Beach 44861
Museum of Spanish Colonial Art, Santa Fe 47428
San Francisco Museum of Contemporary Hispanic Art, San Francisco 47338

Venezuela
Centro de Arte La Cañuela, Caracas 48899
Galería de Arte de la Escuela Armando Reverón, Barcelona 48888
Galería de la Asamblea Legislativa, Barcelona 48889
Galería del Museo Anzoátegui, Barcelona 48890
Museo de Arte Coro y Museo Alberto Henríquez, Falcón 48940
Museo El Sol de las Botellas, Barcelona 48893

Art, Medieval

Albania
National Museum of Medieval Art, Korçë 00027

Austria
Kunstausstellung Stift Herzogenburg, Herzogenburg 02027

Belgium
Musée d'Art Religieux et d'Art Mosan, Liège 03577
Musée des Arts Anciens du Namurois, Namur 03648

Bulgaria
Nacionalen Istoriko-archeologičeski Rezervat i Muzej Veliki Preslav, Veliki Preslav 04908

Cyprus
Cyprus Medieval Museum, Lemesos 08208

Czech Republic
Klašter Sv. Jiří, Praha 08585
Sládečkovo Vlastivědné Muzeum v Kladně, Kladno 08410

France
Musée d'Art et d'Histoire, Saint-Denis (Seine-Saint-Denis) 14180
Musée de Normandie, Caen 10981
Musée du Petit-Palais, Avignon 10531
Musée Municipal, Chartres 11194
Musée National du Moyen Age, Paris 13637
Musée Zervos, Vézelay 15154
Palais Jacques Coeur, Bourges 10867

Germany
Augustinermuseum, Freiburg im Breisgau 17107
Barfüßerkirche, Erfurt 16895
Diözesanmuseum Rottenburg, Rottenburg am Neckar 19690
Dominikanermuseum Rottweil, Rottweil 19695
Focke-Museum, Bremen 16321
Mittelrhein-Museum, Koblenz 18122
Museum Kurhaus Kleve, Kleve 18107
Museum Schnütgen, Köln 18163
Museumskirche Sankt Katharinen, Lübeck 18541
Sankt-Annen-Museum und Kunsthalle, Lübeck 18542
Staatsgalerie am Schaezler-Palais, Augsburg 15569
Strigel-Museum und Antoniter-Museum, Memmingen 18705
Ulmer Museum, Ulm 20261
Zisterzienserkloster Bebenhausen, Tübingen 20232

Greece
Museum of Byzantine Culture, Thessaloniki 21188

Italy
Galleria Regionale della Sicilia, Palermo 24764
Museo Civico Medievale, Bologna 23112
Museo della Basilica di San Marco, Venezia 25931
Museo dell'Alto Medioevo, Roma 25198
Museo Diocesano San Pietro, Teggiano 25681
Pinacoteca Malaspina, Pavia 24829

Poland
Muzeum Narodowe w Poznaniu, Poznań 31909

Slovenia
Posavski Muzej Brežice, Brežice 34088

Spain
Collección Eugenio Fontaneda, Ampudia 34465
Instituto de Valencia de Don Juan, Madrid 35009
Museo Diocesano, Jaca 34920
Museo Parroquial de San Cosme y San Damián, Covarrubias 34757
Museu Diocesà de Girona, Girona 34857
Museu Episcopal de Vic, Vic 35652

Sweden
Gotlands Fornsal med Fenomenalen, Visby 36413

Switzerland
Kirchenschatz des Chorherrenstiftes, Beromünster 36558

Ukraine
Rivnenski Museum of Regional Studies, Rivne 37899

United Kingdom
Boston Guildhall Museum, Boston 38282
Chapter House, London 39602
Norton Priory Museum, Runcorn 40359

U.S.A.
The Cloisters, New York 45784
Early American Museum, Mahomet 45076
Harrison Gray Otis House, Boston 41809
Homewood House Museum, Baltimore 41470
Humboldt County Old Settler's Museum, Livermore 44829
The Johns Hopkins University Archaeological Collection, Baltimore 41473
The Lane Place, Crawfordsville 42691
McAllister House Museum, Colorado Springs 42538
Michael C. Carlos Museum, Atlanta 41352
Oakley Pioneer Museum, Oakley 46073
Patent Model Museum, Fort Smith 43459
Saunders Memorial Museum, Berryville 41656
Stan Hywet Hall and Gardens, Akron 41074
Strater Hotel, Durango 43015

Art, Modern and Contemporary

Argentina
Fundación Federico Jorge Klemm, Buenos Aires 00151
Itimuseum, Buenos Aires 00155
Museo de Arte Contemporáneo, Bahía Blanca 00125
Museo de Arte Contemporáneo Fra Angélico, La Plata 00388
Museo de Arte Moderno, Buenos Aires 00170
Museo de Arte Moderno de la Ciudad de Buenos Aires, Buenos Aires 00171
Museo de Artes y Artesanías Enrique Estrada Bello, Santo Tomé 00620
Museo de Bellas Artes Octavio de la Colina, La Rioja 00397
Museo Fernán Félix de Amador, Luján 00417
Museo Municipal de Arte Moderno de Mendoza, Mendoza 00440

Armenia
Contemporary Art Museum of Yerevan, Erevan 00680

Australia
Art Collection, Acton 00698
Artarmon Galleries, Artarmon 00753
Arts Project Australia, Northcote 01332
Artspace, Woolloomooloo 01617
Australian Centre for Contemporary Art, Southbank 01464
Bathurst Regional Art Gallery, Bathurst 00774
Bega Valley Regional Art Gallery, Bega 00789
Bribie Island Community Arts Centre, Bribie Island 00832
Broken Hill Regional Art Gallery, Broken Hill 00846
Bunbury Regional Art Galleries, Bunbury 00859
Canberra Contemporary Art Space, Braddon 00826
Canberra Museum and Gallery, Canberra 00884
Contemporary Art Centre of South Australia, Parkside 01355
Contemporary Art Gallery, South Yarra 01463
Dubbo Regional Gallery, Dubbo 00992
Geraldton Regional Art Gallery, Geraldton 01048
Gippsland Art Gallery Sale, Sale 01437
Gold Coast City Art Gallery, Surfers Paradise 01484
Goulburn Regional Art Gallery, Goulburn 01069
Grafton Regional Gallery, Grafton 01071
Greenaway Gallery, Camberwell, Victoria 00876
Griffith Artworks, Nathan 01309
Griffith Regional Art Gallery, Griffith 01076
Heide Museum of Modern Art, Bulleen 00858
Ivan Dougherty Gallery, Paddington, New South Wales 01352
Lake Macquarie City Art Gallery, Booragul 00814
Latrobe Regional Gallery, Morwell 01279
Linden - Saint Kilda Centre for Contemporary Arts, Saint Kilda, Victoria 01435
Lismore Regional Art Gallery, Lismore 01178
Maitland City Art Gallery, Maitland 01198
Manning Regional Art Gallery, Taree 01520
Metro Arts, Brisbane 00838
Monash University Museum of Art, Clayton 00923
Moree Plains Gallery, Moree 01273
Museum of Contemporary Art Sydney, Sydney 01502
New England Regional Art Museum, Armidale 00752
Nolan Gallery, Tharwa 01529
Parliament House Art Collection, Canberra 00889
Penrith Regional Gallery and The Lewers Bequest, Emu Plains 01019
Perc Tucker Regional Gallery, Townsville 01547
Performance Space, Redfern 01410
Port Phillip City Collection, Saint Kilda, Victoria 01436
QCA Gallery, Brisbane 00841

Queensland University of Technology Art Collection, Kelvin Grove 01140
Rockhampton Art Gallery, Rockhampton 01421
Stanthorpe Regional Art Gallery, Stanthorpe 01474
Swan Hill Regional Art Gallery, Swan Hill 01487
University Fine Art Collection, Hobart 01107
University of South Australia Art Museum, Adelaide 00716
University of Southern Queensland Art Collection, Toowoomba 01543

Austria
Alte Seifenfabrik, Lauterach 02195
Artbox, Mattersburg 02281
Artothek-Galerie, Wien 02837
Ausstellungszentrum Heiligenkreuzer Hof, Wien 02839
BAWAG Foundation, Wien 02844
Burgenländische Landesgalerie, Eisenstadt 01804
Burggalerie Laa, Laa an der Thaya 02173
Egon Schiele-Museum, Tulln 02743
Ernst Fuchs-Privatmuseum, Wien 02878
Erzherzog Franz-Ferdinand Museum, Artstetten 01681
Frauenbad - Zentrum für zeitgenössische Kunst, Baden bei Wien 01727
Galerie Alte Schule, Vils 02764
Galerie der Mitte, Linz 02231
Galerie der Stadt Traun, Traun 02736
Galerie der Stadt Wels, Wels 02811
Galerie Freihausgasse, Villach 02758
Galerie Hausruck, Altenhof am Hausruck 01663
Galerie im Adalbert Stifter-Haus, Linz 02232
Galerie im Schloß Porcia, Spittal an der Drau 02669
Galerie im Stadtturm, Gmünd, Kärnten 01888
Galerie im Theater am Saumarkt, Feldkirch 01829
Galerie im Troadkasten, Pram 02444
Galerie in der Hauptschule, Ulrichsberg 02751
Galerie Kunst der Gegenwart, Salzburg 02538
Galerie Stephanie Hollenstein, Lustenau 02257
Galerie Theodor von Hörmann, Imst 02054
Galerie Weberhaus, Weiz 02810
Generali Foundation, Wien 02887
Haus Wittgenstein, Wien 02893
Inn-Galerie, Kufstein 02169
Künstlerhaus Graz, Graz 01919
Kunstforum Ebendorf, Wien 02913
Kunsthalle Tirol, Hall in Tirol 01992
Kunsthalle Wien, Wien 02914
Kunsthaus Bregenz, Bregenz 01745
KunstHausWien, Wien 02916
Kunsthistorisches Museum im Palais Harrach, Wien 02917
Kunstsammlung Volpinum, Wien 02919
Kunststätte Kuenburg, Payerbach 02393
Landesgalerie Oberösterreich, Linz 02234
Lebende Galerie, Graz 01924
Lentos Kunstmuseum Linz, Linz 02235
Leopold Museum, Wien 02924
MAK - Österreichisches Museum für angewandte Kunst, Wien 02929
Museum Alte Schmiede, Wien 02934
Museum auf Abruf, Wien 02936
Museum Kuenburggewölbe, Werfen 02822
Museum Moderner Kunst Kärnten, Klagenfurt 02131
Museum Moderner Kunst Stiftung Ludwig Wien, Wien 02949
Neue Galerie, Graz 01927
Niederösterreichisches Dokumentationszentrum für Moderne Kunst, Sankt Pölten 02602
Österreichische Galerie Belvedere, Wien 02953
Oskar Kokoschka Geburtshaus, Pöchlarn 02422
Palais Palffy, Wien 02968
Rathausgalerie, Waidhofen an der Ybbs 02788
Schloß Farrach, Zeltweg 03053
Schloss Pöllau, Pöllau 02431
Schloßgalerie Mondseeland, Mondsee 02323
Stadtgalerie Klagenfurt, Klagenfurt 02133
Sudhaus Sorgendorf, Bleiburg 01738
Thomas K. Lang Gallery, Wien 02995
Tiroler Kunstpavillon Kleiner Hofgarten, Innsbruck 02081
Wiener Secession, Wien 03007

Belgium
CCNOA, Bruxelles 03278
Centre d'Art Contemporain, Bruxelles 03280
Musée d'Art Moderne, Bruxelles 03300
Musée d'Art Moderne et d'Art Contemporain, Liège 03576
Musée des Arts Contemporains de la Communauté Française, Hornu 03503
Museum Dhondt-Dhaenens, Deurle 03382
Museum van Hedendaagse Kunst Antwerpen, Antwerpen 03156
Museum voor Moderne Kunst Oostende (PMMK), Oostende 03669
Museum voor Schone Kunsten, Oostende 03670
Stedelijk Museum voor Actuele Kunst, Gent 03452
Z33, Hasselt 03484

Bosnia and Herzegovina
Umjetnička galerija Bosne i Hercegovine, Sarajevo 03924

Brazil
Açude Museum, Rio de Janeiro 04314
Chácara do Céu Museum, Rio de Janeiro 04321
Museu de Arte Contemporâea, Jataí 04145
Museu de Arte Contemporânea, Feira de Santana 04086
Museu de Arte Contemporânea de Niterói, Niterói 04226
Museu de Arte Moderna da Bahia, Salvador 04428
Museu de Arte Moderna de São Paulo, São Paulo 04517

Bulgaria
Chudožestvena Galerija Elena Karamichajlova, Šumen 04870
Chudožestvena Galerija Prof. Ilija Petrov, Razgrad 04796
Chudožestvena Galerija Varna, Varna 04894
Gradska Chudožestvena Galerija, Plovdiv 04777
Nacionalna Chudožestvena Galerija, Sofia 04856
Okrăžna Chudožestvena Galerija, Stara Zagora 04867
Okrăžna Chudožestvena Galerija, Vraca 04930
Okrăžna Chudožestvena Galerija Georgi Papazov, Jambol 04682

Canada
Allie Griffin Art Gallery, Weyburn 06781
Anna Leonowens Gallery, Halifax 05545
Art Gallery of Bishop's University, Lennoxville 05742
Art Gallery of Calgary, Calgary 05161
Art Gallery of Newfoundland and Labrador, Saint John's 06340
The Arts Centre, Leamington 05739
Artspace, Peterborough 06117
Assiniboia, Regina 06227
Axe Néo-7 Art Contemporain, Gatineau 05480
Blackwood Gallery, Mississauga 05869
Burlington Art Centre, Burlington 05145
Campbell River and District Public Art Gallery, Campbell River 05186
Centre d'Exposition Raymond-Lasnier, Trois-Rivières 06638
Centre for Art Tapes, Halifax 05549
Centre for Experimental Art and Communication, Toronto 06571
Centre International d'Art Contemporain de Montréal, Montréal 05899
Contemporary Art Gallery, Vancouver 06674
Galerie d'Art, Moncton 05875
Galerie d'Art du Centre Culturel, Sherbrooke, Québec 06440
Grimsby Public Art Gallery, Grimsby 05532
Illingworth Kerr Gallery, Calgary 05169
Kamloops Art Gallery, Kamloops 05638
Kelowna Art Gallery, Kelowna 05652
Liane and Danny Taran Gallery, Montréal 05909
McIntyre Street Gallery, Regina 06237
McMaster Museum of Art, Hamilton 05574
Mercer Union - Centre for Contemporary Visual Art, Toronto 06593
Musée d'Art Contemporain de Montréal, Montréal 05914
Musée d'Art de Saint-Laurent, Saint-Laurent 06360
Musée de Lachine, Lachine 05712
Musée du Bas Saint-Laurent, Rivière-du-Loup 06278
Musée et Centre de Transmission de la Culture Daniel Weetaluktuk, Inukjuak 05621
Museum of Contemporary Canadian Art, North York 06034
The Nickle Arts Museum, Calgary 05176
Oakville Galleries, Centennial, Oakville 06038
Oakville Galleries, Gairloch, Oakville 06039
Power Plant Contemporary Art Gallery, Toronto 06601
Presentation House Gallery, North Vancouver 06027
Richmond Art Gallery, Richmond 06263
Saskatchewan Arts Board Collection, Regina 06244
Simon Fraser Gallery, Burnaby 05151
Southern Alberta Art Gallery, Lethbridge 05748
Struts Gallery, Sackville 06299
Thunder Bay Art Gallery, Thunder Bay 06548
Toronto Center for Contemporary Art, Toronto 06616
TRUCK Centre, Calgary 05180
University College of Cape Breton Art Gallery, Sydney 06529
University of Waterloo Art Gallery, Waterloo 06757
White Water Gallery, North Bay 06018
Winnipeg Art Gallery, Winnipeg 06853

Chile
Museo de Arte Contemporáneo, Santiago de Chile 06910
Museo de Arte Contemporaneo, Valdivia 06924

China, People's Republic
Jin Contemporary Shi Museum, Shenyang 07233
Museum of Fine Arts, Nanchang 07171
Pao Galleries at Hong Kong Art Centre, Hong Kong 07108
Para/Site Art Space, Hong Kong 07109

Colombia
Museo Bolivariano de Arte Contemporáneo, Santa Marta 07587
Museo de Antioquia, Medellín 07514
Museo de Arte Contemporáneo Moderno de Ibagué, Ibagué 07497
Museo de Arte Moderno de Barranquilla, Barranquilla 07378
Museo de Arte Moderno de Bogotá, Bogotá 07398
Museo de Arte Moderno de Bogotá II, Bogotá 07399
Museo de Arte Moderno de Bucaramanga, Bucaramanga 07437
Museo de Arte Moderno de Cartagena, Cartagena 07456
Museo de Arte Moderno de Medellín, Medellín 07515
Museo de Arte Moderno La Tertulia, Cali 07446
Museo de Arte Moderno Ramírez Villamizar, Pamplona 07544
Museo Nacional de Colombia, Bogotá 07429

Costa Rica
Museo de Arte y Diseño Contemporáneo, San José 07655

Croatia
Hrvatski Muzej Naivne Umjetnosti, Zagreb 07819
Muzej Hvarske Baštine, Hvar 07707
Muzej Suvremene Umjetnosti, Zagreb 07833

Cuba
Museo Provincial de Villa Clara y Museo Municipal, Santa Clara 08125

Cyprus
Byzantine Museum and Art Galleries, Lefkosia 08194
Nicosia Municipal Arts Centre, Lefkosia 08205
State Gallery of Contemporary Cypriot Art, Lefkosia 08206

Czech Republic
Dům u Černé Matky Boží, Praha 08570
Dům u Jonáše, Pardubice 08532
Dům u Kamenného Zvonu, Praha 08571
Dům u Zlatého Prstenu, Praha 08572
Galerie Benedikta Rejta v Lounech, Louny 08465
Galerie Rudolfinum, Praha 08579
Galerie Umění Karlovy Vary, Karlovy Vary 08400
Galerie Výtvarného Umění, Hodonín 08353
Galerie Výtvarného Umění, Náchod 08491
Krajská Galerie, Hradec Králové 08367
Krajská Galerie Výtvarného Umeni ve Zlíně, Zlín 08750
Královsky Letohradek, Praha 08586
Leica Galerija Praha, Praha 08587
Moravská Galerie Brno - Pražákův Palác, Brno 08271
Muzeum Umění Olomouc, Olomouc 08515
Obecní Dům, Praha 08606
Oblastní Galerie Vysočiny v Jihlavě, Jihlava 08391
Okresní Muzeum a Galerie, Jičín 08388
Orlická Galerie, Rychnov nad Kněžnou 08648
Podještědské Muzeum Karoliny Světlé, Český Dub 08301
Šternberský Palác, Praha 08615
Uměleckoprůmyslové Muzeum v Praze, Praha 08617
Veletržní Palác, Praha 08618

Denmark
Arken Museum of Modern Art, Ishøj 08906
Aros Aarhus Kunstmuseum, Århus 08769
Esbjerg Kunstmuseum, Esbjerg 08806
Herning Kunstmuseum, Herning 08868
J.F. Willumsens Museum, Frederikssund 08832
København Museum for Moderne Kunst, København 08932
Museet for Samtidskunst, Roskilde 09040
Nordjyllands Kunstmuseum, Aalborg 08763
Ribe Kunstmuseum, Ribe 09029
Silkeborg Kunstmuseum, Silkeborg 09053
Skive Kunstmuseum, Skive 09060
Sønderjyllands Kunstmuseum, Tønder 09093
Vendsyssel Kunstmuseum, Hjørring 08878

Ecuador
Museo Camilo Egas del Banco Central, Quito 09196
Museo Municipal de Arte Moderno, Cuenca 09162

Egypt
Museum of Modern Art, Cairo 09275

Estonia
La Galerie Passage, Tallinn 09366

Finland
Amos Andersonin taidemuseo, Helsinki 09471
Ars Nova - Nykytaiteen Museo, Turku 10119
Galleria Pinacotheca, Jyväskylä 09594
Helsingin Kaupungin Taidemuseo, Mejlahti, Helsinki 09486
Helsingin Kaupungin Taidemuseo, Tennispalatsi, Helsinki 09487
Kajaanin Taidemuseo, Kajaani 09611
Kiasma Nykytaiteen Museo, Helsinki 09501
Kluuvin Galleria - Glogalleriet, Helsinki 09503
Kouvolan Taidemuseo, Kouvola 09703
Kuntsin Taidekokoelma, Vaasa 10158
NIFCA - Nordic Institute for Contemporary Art, Helsinki 09516
Oulun Taidemuseo, Oulu 09892
Taidekeskus Mältinranta, Tampere 10088
Tikanojan Taidekoti, Vaasa 10162
Vantaan Kaupunginmuseo - Kuvataideasiat, Vantaa 10184
Varkauden Taidemuseo, Varkaus 10187
Villa Gyllenberg, Helsinki 09546

France
CAPC Musée d'Art Contemporain, Bordeaux 10803
Centre Artistique et Médiéval, Richerenches 13964
Centre d'Art Contemporain, Ginals 11867
Centre d'Art Contemporain, Lacoux-Hauteville-Lompnes 12294
Centre d'Art Contemporain, Rueil-Malmaison 14073
Centre d'Art Contemporain, Noisiel 13361
Centre d'Art Contemporain de Brétigny, Brétigny-sur-Orge 10916
Centre d'Art Contemporain de Castres, Castres 11081
Centre d'Art Contemporain de Vassivière en Limousin, Beaumont-du-Lac 10644
Centre Régional d'Art Contemporain, Montbéliard 13058
Château de Villeneuve, Vence 15113
Château d'Oiron, Oiron 13393
Château-Musée de Dieppe, Dieppe 11507
Château Musée Grimaldi, Cagnes-sur-Mer 10986
Collection Lambert, Avignon 10525
Espace d'Art Contemporain, Marseille 12848
Espace Mira Phalaina, Montreuil 13140
Fondation Cartier pour l'Art Contemporain, Paris 13501
Fondation Maeght, Saint-Paul (Alpes-Maritimes) 14398
Galerie Beaubourg, Vence 15114
Galerie d'Art Contemporain, Menton 12935
Galerie d'Art Contemporain, Sarlat-la-Canéda 14614
La Galerie de Noisy, Noisy-le-Sec 13362
Galerie des Beaux-Arts, Bordeaux 10804
Galerie Le Carré, Bayonne 10620
Galerie Nationale du Jeu de Paume, Paris 13511
L.A.C. Lieu d'Art Contemporain, Sigean 14750
Le Lavoir de Mougins, Mougins 13178
Maeght Musée, Paris 13519
Maison Levanneur, Chatou 11244
Municipal d'Arts Plastiques, Choisy-le-Roi 11295
Musée Angladon, Avignon 10527
Musée Auguste Rodin, Paris 13532
Musée Cantini, Marseille 12852
Musée-Centre d'Arts Plastiques Chanot, Clamart 11309
Musée-Centre de Documentation Alfred Desmasures, Hirson 12027
Musée d'Art Contemporain de Lyon, Lyon 12729
Musée d'Art et d'Histoire, Livry-Gargan 12637
Musée d'Art Moderne, Saint-Étienne 14199
Musée d'Art Moderne, Troyes 15004
Musée d'Art Moderne de la Ville de Paris, Paris 13548
Musée d'Art Moderne et Contemporain, Strasbourg 14821
Musée d'Art Moderne et d'Art Contemporain, Nice 13312
Musée d'Art Moderne Lille Métropole, Villeneuve-d'Ascq 15217
Musée d'Art Moderne Méditerranéen, Cagnes-sur-Mer 10987
Musée de l'Abbaye Sainte-Croix, Les Sables-d'Olonne 12555
Musée de Saint-Paul, Saint-Paul (Alpes-Maritimes) 14399
Musée Départemental d'Art Ancien et Contemporain, Épinal 11633
Musée Départemental d'Art Contemporain de Rochechouart, Rochechouart 13993
Musée Départemental Maurice-Denis, Saint-Germain-en-Laye 14241
Musée d'Orsay, Paris 13596
Musée du Valois, Vez 15151
Musée Hofer-Bury, Lavérune 12372
Musée Jean-Aicard, La Garde 12186
Musée Municipal d'Art Moderne, Céret 11110
Musée National d'Art Moderne, Paris 13629
Musée National Fernand Léger, Biot 10740
Musée Paul Arbaud, Aix-en-Provence 10256
Musée Paul Raymond, Pont-Saint-Esprit 13818
Musée Picasso, Paris 13644
Palais de Tokyo, Paris 13652
Passages Centre d'Art Contemporain, Troyes 15009

Germany
Albert-König-Museum, Unterlüß 20269
Art Gluchowe, Glauchau 17298
Art Kite Museum für Kunst Flugobjekte, Detmold 16586
Artothek, Köln 18129
Artothek der Zentral- und Landesbibliothek Berlin, Berlin 15915
Asyl der Kunst, Häuslingen 17475
AusstellungsHalle, Frankfurt am Main 17032
Bauhaus-Museum, Weimar, Thüringen 20455
Berlinische Galerie, Berlin 15919
Büro Friedrich, Berlin 15933
Büro Otto Koch, Dessau 16577
contact:c4, Berlin 15934
Cubus Kunsthalle, Duisburg 16746
DaimlerChrysler Contemporary, Berlin 15936
Deichtorhallen Hamburg, Hamburg 17530
DLM - Deutsches Ledermuseum/ Schuhmuseum Offenbach, Offenbach am Main 19239
Edith-Ruß-Haus für Medienkunst, Oldenburg, Oldenburg 19253
Ehemaliges Postfuhramt, Berlin 15943
Ernst Barlach Museum Wedel, Wedel 20414
Flottmann-Hallen, Herne 17727
Forum Konkrete Kunst - Peterskirche, Erfurt 16899
Fritz-Winter-Haus, Ahlen 15401
Galerie 100, Berlin 15952
Galerie am Dom, Wetzlar 20551
Galerie am Domhof, Zwickau 20775
Galerie am Graben, Augsburg 15555
Galerie an der Bleiche, Ludwigslust 18524
Galerie Bezirksamt Mitte, Berlin 15955
Galerie Bodenseekreis im Landratsamt, Friedrichshafen 17147
Galerie Bodenseekreis im Roten Haus, Meersburg 18676
Galerie der Stadt Stuttgart, Stuttgart 20090
Galerie der Stadt Tuttlingen, Tuttlingen 20236
Galerie der Stadt Wendlingen am Neckar, Wendlingen am Neckar 20512

Galerie des Kunstvereins Neustadt an der Weinstraße, Neustadt an der Weinstraße 19075
Galerie des Landkreises Rügen, Putbus 19455
Galerie für Zeitgenössische Kunst Leipzig, Leipzig 18394
Galerie im Kehrwiederturm, Hildesheim 17758
Galerie im Kunsthaus Erfurt, Erfurt 16901
Galerie im Malzhaus, Plauen 19411
Galerie im Polnischen Institut, Leipzig 18396
Galerie im Tor, Emmendingen 16852
Galerie im Willy-Brandt-Haus, Berlin 15965
Galerie K S, Berlin 15968
Galerie M, Berlin 15970
Galeriehaus, Nürnberg 19137
Georg-Kolbe-Museum, Berlin 15975
Georg-Meistermann-Museum, Wittlich 20628
Gesellschaft für Aktuelle Kunst, Bremen 16324
Grafik Museum Stiftung Schreiner, Bad Steben 15750
Graphothek Berlin, Berlin 15978
Gustav-Lübcke Museum, Hamm, Westfalen 17576
Halle für Kunst e.V., Lüneburg 18557
Hamburger Bahnhof - Museum für Gegenwart Berlin, Berlin 15981
Haus am Waldsee, Berlin 15986
Haus der Kunst, München 18855
Hochheimer Kunstsammlung, Hochheim am Main 17773
Junge Kunst, Wolfsburg 20661
K20 Kunstsammlung am Grabbeplatz, Düsseldorf 16728
K21 Kunstsammlung im Ständehaus, Düsseldorf 16729
Käthe Kollwitz Museum Köln, Köln 18147
Kallmann-Museum, Ismaning 17927
Karl Ernst Osthaus-Museum der Stadt Hagen, Hagen, Westfalen 17481
Kreisgalerie, Mellrichstadt 18701
Künstlerhaus Hooksiel, Hooksiel 17839
Kunst aus Nordrhein-Westfalen, Aachen 15374
Kunst-Museum Ahlen, Ahlen 15403
Kunst und Museum, Hollfeld 17824
Kunstbunker Tumulka, München 18863
Kunsthalle Bremerhaven, Bremerhaven 16341
Kunsthalle Darmstadt, Darmstadt 16545
Kunsthalle Dresden im Art'otel Dresden, Dresden 16690
Kunsthalle Düsseldorf, Düsseldorf 16731
Kunsthalle Göppingen, Göppingen 17317
Kunsthalle Lingen, Lingen 18483
Kunsthalle Nürnberg, Nürnberg 19150
Kunsthalle Tübingen, Tübingen 20227
Kunsthaus Apolda Avantgarde, Apolda 15508
Kunsthaus Dresden, Dresden 16691
Kunsthaus Essen, Essen 16952
Kunsthaus Kloster Gravenhorst, Hörstel 17789
Kunstmuseum Bonn, Bonn 16242
Kunstmuseum Dr. Krupp, Weinbach 20477
Kunstmuseum Wolfsburg, Wolfsburg 20662
Kunstraum Fuhrwerkswaage, Köln 18154
Kunstraum München, München 18867
Kunstsammlung Neubrandenburg, Neubrandenburg 19012
Kunststiftung Baden-Württemberg, Stuttgart 20098
Kunststiftung Poll, Berlin 16031
Kunstverein Heilbronn, Heilbronn 17688
Kunstverein in Hamburg e.V, Hamburg 17551
Kunstverein Weiden, Weiden, Oberpfalz 20426
KW Institute for Contemporary Art, Berlin 16034
KX., Hamburg 17552
Lände, Kressbronn am Bodensee 18232
Landesmuseum für Kunst und Kulturgeschichte Oldenburg, Oldenburg, Oldenburg 19256
Leopold-Hoesch-Museum Düren, Düren 16717
Ludwig-Forum für Internationale Kunst, Aachen 15375
Ludwig Galerie Schloß Oberhausen, Oberhausen, Rheinland 19177
Ludwig Museum im Deutschherrenhaus, Koblenz 18121
Märkisches Museum, Witten 20622
Malura-Museum, Unterdießen 20267
Mies van der Rohe Haus, Berlin 16043
Mönchehaus-Museum für moderne Kunst Goslar, Goslar 17353
Münter-Haus, Murnau 18961
Museum Bochum, Bochum 16198
Museum Burg Abenberg, Abenberg 15388
Museum der Stadt Borna, Borna bei Leipzig 16263
Museum der Stadt Gladbeck, Gladbeck 17291
Museum der Stadt Waiblingen, Waiblingen 20350
Museum für Gegenwartskunst Siegen, Siegen 19949
Museum für konkrete Kunst, Ingolstadt 17909
Museum für moderne Kunst, Cremlingen 16511
Museum für Moderne Kunst Frankfurt am Main, Frankfurt am Main 17067
Museum für Neue Kunst, Freiburg im Breisgau 17113
Museum Ludwig, Köln 18161
Museum Modern Art, Hünfeld 17856
Museum Moderner Kunst - Stiftung Wörlen, Passau 19356
Museum Morsbroich, Leverkusen 18452
Museum Schloss Hardenberg, Velbert 20294
Museum Schloss Moyland, Bedburg-Hau 15866
Museum SPUR Cham, Cham 16458
Museum Waldhof, Bielefeld 16158
Neue Galerie im Höhmann-Haus, Augsburg 15564
Neue Galerie Oberschöneweide der Karl-Hofer-Gesellschaft, Berlin 16073
Neue Nationalgalerie, Berlin 16075
Neue Sammlung, Passau 19357
Neues Museum Weimar, Weimar, Thüringen 20466
Neues Museum Weserburg Bremen, Bremen 16330
Nordische Botschaften Gemeinschaftshaus, Berlin 16078
Oberschwäbische Galerie Kloster Heiligkreuztal, Altheim bei Riedlingen 15457
Orangerie, Gera 17246
Panorama Museum, Bad Frankenhausen 15644
Parochialkirche, Berlin 16080
Pinakothek der Moderne, München 18897
Richard-Haizmann-Museum, Niebüll 19094
Robert-Sterl-Haus, Struppen 20080
Sammlung Berger, Amorbach 15486
Sammlung Hoffmann, Berlin 16087
Sankt-Annen-Museum und Kunsthalle, Lübeck 18542
Schloß Wolfstein mit Jagd- und Fischereimuseum und Galerie Wolfstein, Freyung 17134
Schloßgalerie Kastenscheuer, Eberdingen 16761
Schwartzsche Villa, Berlin 16093
Situation Kunst, Bochum 16201
Spital Hengersberg, Hengersberg 17709
Sprengel Museum Hannover, Hannover 17611
Staatsgalerie Stuttgart, Stuttgart 20106
Stadtgalerie, Osnabrück 19285
Stadthaus Ulm, Ulm 20260
Städtische Galerie, Traunstein 20191
Städtische Galerie Böblingen, Böblingen 16214
Städtische Galerie Filderstadt, Filderstadt 17002
Städtische Galerie Fruchthalle Rastatt, Rastatt 19491
Städtische Galerie im Cordonhaus, Cham 16460
Städtische Galerie Leerer Beutel, Regensburg 19531
Städtische Galerie sohle 1, Bergkamen 15903
Städtische Galerie Waldkraiburg, Waldkraiburg 20370
Städtische Galerie Wolfsburg, Wolfsburg 20664
Städtische Kunsthalle, Recklinghausen 19513
Städtische Kunstsammlung, Eschweiler 16937
Städtische Sammlungen Freital, Freital 17125
Städtisches Kunstmuseum Singen, Singen, Hohentwiel 19967
Städtisches Kunstmuseum Spendhaus Reutlingen, Reutlingen 19581
Städtisches Museum Abteiberg, Mönchengladbach 18772
Städtisches Museum Engen galerie, Engen 16874
Stiftung für Konkrete Kunst, Reutlingen 19582
Stiftung Hans Arp und Sophie Taeuber-Arp, Remagen 19562
Stiftung Moritzburg, Halle, Saale 17521
Studio A Otterndorf, Otterndorf 19323
Studio Capricornus, Eckernförde 16777
Studio im Hochhaus, Berlin 16106
Studio im Zumikon, Nürnberg 19163
Studiogalerie Kaditzsch, Grimma 17404
Stuttgarter Kunstverein, Stuttgart 20111
Villa Merkel, Esslingen 16971
Villa Oppenheim, Berlin 16112

Ghana
College of Art Gallery, Kumasi 20794

Greece
Averoff Gallery, Athinai 20851
Averoff Gallery, Metsovon 21070
Dimitreion Oikima House, Agios Georgios Nilias 20808
Dimitris Pierides Museum of Contemporary Art, Glyfada 20963
Florina Museum of Modern Art, Florina 20956
Gallery of Modern Greek Art of Kalamata, Kalamata 20983
Gallery of the Municipality of Patras, Patrai 21114
Lefteris Kanakakis Gallery, Rethymnon 21139
Macedonian Museum of Contemporary Art, Thessaloniki 21186
Municipal Gallery of Athens, Athinai 20880
Municipal Gallery of Lamia, Lamia 21040
Municipal Gallery of Livadia, Livadia 21053
Municipal Gallery of Piraeus, Piraeus 21122
Municipal Gallery of Rhodes, Rhodos 21143
Museum of Contemporary Art, Andros 20824
National Gallery of Corfu, Skripero 21161
National Museum of Contemporary Art, Athinai 20894
Skironio Museum Polychronopoulos, Mégara 21063
Techni-Macedonian Artistic Association Kilkis, Kilkis 21018
Venetsanos Museum of Modern Art, Piraeus 21126
Yannis Tsarouchis Museum, Maroussi 21059

Guatemala
Museo Nacional de Arte Moderno, Guatemala 21272

Haiti
Musée Nader, Port-au-Prince 21295

Hungary
Ámos-Anna Gyűjtemény, Szentendre 21567
Barcsay Gyűjtemény, Szentendre 21568
Budenz-Ház, Székesfehérvár 21554
Ernst Múzeum, Budapest 21336
Kecskeméti Képtár és Tóth Menyhért Emlékmúzeum, Kecskemét 21449
Kerényi Jenő Emlékmúzeum, Szentendre 21571
Kmetty Múzeum, Szentendre 21572
Kortárs Művészeti Múzeum - Ludwig Múzeum Budapest, Budapest 21353
Martyn Ferenc Gyűjtemény, Pécs 21508
Miskolci Galéria - Rákóczi-ház, Miskolc 21479
Modern Magyar Képtár I, Pécs 21510
Modern Magyar Képtár II, Pécs 21511
Óbudai Pincegaléria, Budapest 21369
Óbudai Társaskör Galéria, Budapest 21370
Schöffer Museum, Kalocsa 21437
Szentendrei Képtár, Szentendre 21576
Szombathelyi Képtár, Szombathely 21589
Vajda Lajos Emlékmúzeum, Szentendre 21578

Iceland
Listasafn Así, Àsmundarsalur, Reykjavík 21652
Listasafn Íslands, Reykjavík 21655
Nýlistasafnið, Reykjavík 21660

India
Museum of Fine Arts, Chandigarh 21739
National Gallery of Modern Art, Delhi 21774

Indonesia
Museum Affandi - Museum Seni, Yogyakarta 22216
Museum Puri Lukisan, Ubud 22213

Iran
Honarhaye Moaser Tehran, Teheran 22303

Ireland
Ashford Gallery, Dublin 22413
Butler Gallery, Kilkenny 22487
The Hugh Lane Municipal Gallery of Modern Art, Dublin 22432
Irish Museum of Modern Art, Dublin 22436

Israel
Art Centre, Haifa 22596
Digital Art Lab, Holon 22618
Genia Schreiber University Art Gallery, Ramat Aviv 22730
Helena Rubinstein Pavillon for Contemporary Art, Tel Aviv 22757
Mishkan Le'Omanut, Ein Harod 22589
Museum für verfolgte Kunst-Israel, Ashdod 22573
Museum of Israeli Art, Ramat Gan 22733
Tel Aviv Museum of Art, Tel Aviv 22775

Italy
Ca'Pesaro Galleria Internazionale d'Arte Moderna, Venezia 25912
Castello di Rivoli Museo d'Arte Contemporanea, Rivoli 25131
Centro per l'Arte Contemporanea Luigi Pecci, Prato 25042
Civica Galleria d'Arte Contemporanea, Lissone 24188
Civica Galleria d'Arte Contemporanea F. Scroppo, Torre Pellice 25774
Civica Galleria d'Arte Moderna, Milano 24371
Civica Galleria d'Arte Moderna, Genova 23978
Civica Galleria d'Arte Moderna E. Restivo, Palermo 24763
Civici Musei e Gallerie di Storia ed Arte, Udine 25845
Civico Museo d'Arte Contemporanea, Milano 24376
Collezione Calderara, Ameno 22877
Galleria Civica, Valdagno 25870
Galleria Civica d'Arte Contemporanea, Suzzara 25663
Galleria Civica d'Arte Contemporanea, Termoli 25693
Galleria Civica d'Arte Moderna, Santhià 25463
Galleria Civica d'Arte Moderna e Contemporanea, Torino 25734
Galleria Civica d'Arte Moderna e Contemporanea, Verona 25967
Galleria Comunale d'Arte Moderna, Bologna 23104
Galleria Comunale d'Arte Moderna e Contemporanea, Roma 25159
Galleria Comunale d'Arte Risorgimento, Imola 24085
Galleria d'Arte Contemporanea, Ascoli Piceno 22949
Galleria d'Arte Contemporanea, Assisi 22961
Galleria d'Arte Contemporanea L. Spazzapan, Gradisca d'Isonzo 24040
Galleria d'Arte Moderna, Udine 25846
Galleria d'Arte Moderna Arnoldo Bonzagni, Cento 23472
Galleria d'Arte Moderna e Contemporanea, Bergamo 23060
Galleria d'Arte Moderna Giannoni, Novara 24644
Galleria d'Arte Moderna Moretti, Civitanova Marche 23593
Galleria dell'Accademia Nazionale di San Luca, Roma 25160
Galleria Nazionale d'Arte Moderna-Arte Contemporanea, Roma 25164
Museion - Museo d'Arte Moderna e Contemporanea, Bolzano 23151
Museo Civico di Belriguardo, Voghiera 26046
Museo d'Arte Contemporanea, Torino 25738
Museo d'Arte Moderna e Contemporanea, Ferrara 23788
Museo d'Arte Moderna e Contemporanea di Trento e Rovereto, Trento 25791
Museo d'Arte Moderna L. Répaci, Palmi 24786
Museo d'Arte Moderna M. Rimoldi, Cortina d'Ampezzo 23660
Museo d'Arte Moderna Pagani, Castellanza 23405
Museo Marino Marini, Firenze 23877
Museo Marino Marini, Pistoia 24961
Museo Marino Marini, Milano 24406
Museo Mascagnano, Livorno 24193
Nuova-Icona, Venezia 25945
PAC - Padiglione d'Arte Contemporanea, Milano 24414
Pinacoteca Comunale, Verucchio 25980
Pinacoteca d'Arte Moderna, Avezzano 22994
Raccolta Alberto della Ragione e Collezioni del Novecento, Firenze 23885
Raccolte Frugone Villa Grimaldi-Fassio, Genova 24014
Trevi Flash Art Museum, Trevi 25800
Villa Menafoglio Litta Panza, Varese 25898

Japan
Akita-kenritsu Kindai Bijutsukan, Yokote 27028
Center for Contemporary Art Kitakyushu, Kitakyushu 26342
Garden of Fine Art Kyoto, Kyoto 26399
Gunma-kenritsu Kindai Bijutsukan, Takasaki 26798
Hara Bijutsukan, Tokyo 26855
Hiroshima-shi Gendai Bijutsukan, Hiroshima 26218
Hokkaidoritsu Kindai Bijutsukan, Sapporo 26714
Hyogo-kenritsu Bijutsukan, Kobe 26347
Ibaraki-ken Kindai Bijutsukan, Mito 26500
Kahitsukan - Kyoto Museum of Contemporary Art, Kyoto 26407
Kanagawa Kenritsu Kindai Bijutsukan, Hayama 26185
Kokuritsu Kokusai Bijutsukan, Suita 26773
Kurashiki City Art Museum, Kurashiki 26382
Kyoto Kokuritsu Kindai Bijutsukan, Kyoto 26425
Meguro Museum of Art, Tokyo 26885
Mito Geijutsukan Gendai Bijutsu Center, Mito 26503
Mori Bijitsukan, Tokyo 26893
Museum of Contemporary Art Sapporo, Sapporo 26716
Ohara Bijutsukan, Kurashiki 26384
Osaka-furitsu Gendai Bijutsu Center, Osaka 26661
Osaka-shiritsu Kindai Bijutsukan Kensetsu Jumbishitsu, Osaka 26670
Otani Memorial Art Museum Nishinomiya City, Nishinomiya 26606
Sakura City Museum of Art, Sakura 26707
Setagaya-kuritsu Bijutsukan, Tokyo 26917
Sezon Museum of Modern Art, Karuizawa 26313
Shiga-kenritsu Kindai Bijutsukan, Otsu 26683
Sogetsu Bijutsukan, Tokyo 26924
Tamagawa Modern Art Museum, Tamagawa 26817
Tokushima-kenritsu Kindai Bijutsukan, Tokushima 26826
Tokyo Kokuritsu Kindai Bijutsukan, Tokyo 26938
Tokyo Kokusai Bijutsukyoukai, Tokyo 26941
Tokyo-to Gendai Bijutsukan, Tokyo 26945
Toyama-kenritsu Kindai Bijutsukan, Toyama 26969
Toyota Municipal Museum of Art, Toyota, Aichi 26974
Wakayama-kenritsu Kindai Bijutsukan, Wakayama 26998
Watari-Um, Tokyo 26955

Jordan
Jordan National Gallery of Fine Arts, Amman 27055

Korea, Republic
Artsonje Center, Seoul 27223
Artsonje Museum, Gyeongju 27184
Deosugung Art Museum, Seoul 27228
Han Kuk Art Museum, Yongin 27300
Hanlim Museum, Daejeon 27161
Kukje Gallery, Seoul 27253
National Museum of Contemporary Art, Gwacheon 27180
Seoul Art Museum, Seoul 27271
Sungkok Art Museum, Seoul 27287
Total Open-Air Museum, Yangju 27297
Whanki Museum, Seoul 27289

Kyrgyzstan
Kyrgyz State Museum of Fine Arts G. Aitiyev, Biškek 27307

Latvia
Latvian Centre for Contemporary Art, Rīga 27412
Valsts Mākslas Muzejs Izstazu Zale Arsenāls, Rīga 27443

Liechtenstein
Kunstmuseum Liechtenstein, Vaduz 27514

Lithuania
Europos Parkas, Vilnius 27535

Luxembourg
Casino Luxembourg - Forum d'Art Contemporain, Luxembourg 27559
Galerie d'Art Contemporain Am Tunnel, Luxembourg 27560
Musée d'Art Moderne Grand-Duc Jean, Luxembourg 27562
Villa Vauban, Luxembourg 27570

Macedonia
Muzej na Sovremenata Umetnost Skopje, Skopje 27591

Mexico
Instituto Cultural Cabañas, Guadalajara 27946
Museo Chihuahuense de Arte Contemporáneo, Chihuahua 27822
Museo de Arte Abstracto Manuel Felguérez, Zacatecas 28635
Museo de Arte Alvar y Carmen T. de Carrillo Gil, México 28124
Museo de Arte Contemporáneo Alfredo Zalce, Morelia 28246
Museo de Arte Contemporáneo Ángel Zárraga, Durango 27895
Museo de Arte Contemporáneo Ateneo de Yucatán, Mérida 28080
Museo de Arte Contemporáneo de Chihuahua, Chihuahua 27823
Museo de Arte Contemporáneo de Monterrey, Monterrey 28230

Museo de Arte Contemporáneo de Oaxaca, Oaxaca 28273
Museo de Arte Contemporáneo Número 8, Aguascalientes 27755
Museo de Arte Moderno de Durango, Gómez Palacio 27936
Museo de Arte Moderno del Estado de México, Toluca 28541
Museo de la Ciudad de Querétaro, Querétaro 28353
Museo de Sitio Polyforum Siqueiros, México 28148
Museo Sala de Arte Moderno, Juchitán de Zaragoza 28040
Museo Tamayo Arte Contemporáneo, México 28203
Museo Universitario Contemporáneo de Arte, México 28206
Ninart Centro de Cultura, México 28210

Monaco
Monaco Modern Art Museum, Monaco 28664

Mongolia
Mongolian National Modern Art Gallery, Ulaanbaatar 28678

Netherlands
Arti et Amicitiae, Amsterdam 28841
Bergkerk Deventer, Deventer 29143
Bergkerk Museum, Deventer 29144
Centrum Beeldende Kunst Utrecht, Amersfoort 28820
Centrum Kunstlicht in de Kunst, Eindhoven 29208
Cobra Museum voor Moderne Kunst, Amstelveen 28830
Electric Ladyland, Amsterdam 28849
Frisia Museum, Spanbroek 29846
Gemeentelijke Expositieruimte Kampen, Kampen 29470
Gemeentemuseum, Maassluis 29562
Gemeentemuseum Helmond, Helmond 29394
De Hallen, Haarlem 29325
Kröller-Müller Museum, Otterlo 29686
Kunstenaarscentrum De Fabriek, Eindhoven 29213
Kunsthal Rotterdam, Rotterdam 29756
Mondriaanhuis - Museum voor Constructieve en Concrete Kunst, Amersfoort 28823
Museum Hedendaagse Grafiek en Glaskunst, Vledder 29950
Museum Henriette Polak, Zutphen 30076
Museum Het Valkhof, Nijmegen 29632
Museum voor Moderne Kunst, Arnhem 28941
Nederlands Instituut voor Mediakunst - Montevideo, Amsterdam 28887
Odapark, Venray 29942
Peter Stuyvesant Collection, Amsterdam 28893
Peter Stuyvesant Stichting, Zevenaar 30057
De Pont, Tilburg 29881
Pronkkamer Uden-Museum Hedendaagse Kunst, Uden 29885
Publiekscentrum voor Beeldende Kunst, Enschede 29239
De Rietgors, Papendrecht 29711
Rietveld Schröderhuis, Utrecht 29910
Stadsgalerij Heerlen, Heerlen 29368
Stedelijk Museum Het Domein, Sittard 29827
Stedelijk Museum Schiedam, Schiedam 29804
Stichting De Brakke Grond, Amsterdam 28905
Van Abbemuseum, Eindhoven 29221
Witte de With, Rotterdam 29780

New Zealand
Anderson Park Art Gallery, Invercargill 30184
Aratoi Wairarapa Museum of Art and History, Masterton 30197
Artspace, Auckland 30102
Centre of Contemporary Art, Christchurch 30125
City Gallery Wellington, Wellington 30292
Forrester Gallery, Oamaru 30217
Govett-Brewster Art Gallery, New Plymouth 30213
Left Bank Art Gallery, Greymouth 30169
Lopdell House Gallery, Auckland 30112
New Zealand Academy of Fine Arts Gallery, Wellington 30300
Pataka, Porirua 30240

Norway
Astrup Fearnley Museet for Moderne Kunst, Oslo 30727
Bergen Kunstmuseum - Stenersens Samling, Bergen 30414
Hå Gamle Prestegard, Varhaug 30976
Munch-museet, Oslo 30743
Museet for Samtidskunst, Oslo 30744
Nasjonalgalleriet, Oslo 30746

Pakistan
National Art Gallery, Islamabad 31025

Panama
Museo de Arte Contemporáneo, Panamá City 31079

Papua New Guinea
Papua New Guinea National Museum and Art Gallery, Boroko 31090

Peru
Centro de Arte Visuales, Lima 31197
Museo de Arte Contemporáneo, Cusco 31152

Philippines
Anita Gallery, San Antonio 31439
Cultural Center of the Philippines Museo, Pasay 31411
Gallery III, Makati 31353
GSIS Gallery, Pasay 31412
Jorge B. Vargas Museum and Filipiana Research Center, Quezon City 31434
Museo ng Makati, Makati 31354

Poland
Centrum Rzeźby Polskiej, Oronsko 31862
Centrum Sztuki Współczesnej, Warszawa 32080
Centrum Sztuki Współczesnej Łaźnia, Gdańsk 31564
Galeria Sztuki Wozownia, Toruń 32051
Galeria Sztuki Współczesnej, Szczecin 32023
Muzeum, Koszalin 31678
Muzeum Narodowe w Poznaniu, Poznań 31909
Muzeum Sztuki Nowoczesnem, Niepołomice 31824
Muzeum Sztuki Współczesnej, Radom 31939
Muzeum Sztuki Współczesnej, Wrocław 32189
Oddział Sztuki Współczesnej, Gdańsk 31580
Zacheta Państwowa Galeria Sztuki, Warszawa 32142

Portugal
Centro de Arte Moderna da Fundação Calouste Gulbenkian, Lisboa 32285
Museu de Serralves, Porto 32335
Museu do Chiado, Lisboa 32300
Museu Regional Abade de Baçal, Bragança 32245

Puerto Rico
Museo de Arte Contemporáneo de Puerto Rico, San Juan 32393

Romania
Muzeul de Artă, Medgidia 32548
Muzeul de Artă, Târgu Jiu 32605
Muzeul de Artă Vizuală, Galaţi 32523
Muzeul Municipal Dej ş Galeria de Artă, Dej 32510

Russia
Art Centr Puškinskaja 10, Sankt-Peterburg 33380
Belgorodskij Gosudarstvennyj Chudožestvennyj Muzej, Belgorod 32675
Centralnyj Vystavočnyj Zal Manež g. Sankt-Peterburga, Sankt-Peterburg 33389
Chudožestvenno-memorialnyj Muzej K.S. Petrova-Vodkina, Chvalynsk 32746
Chudožestvennyj Muzej, Staryj Oskol 33557
Chudožestvennyj Muzej, Valujki 33674
Chudožestvennyj Muzej im. M.S. Tuganova, Vladikavkaz 33686
D137, Sankt-Peterburg 33390
Dalnevostočnyj Chudožestvennyj Muzej, Chabarovsk 32739
Galereja Forum, Sankt-Peterburg 33394
Galereja-masterskaja Chudožnika G.S. Rajševa, Chanty-Mansijsk 32743
Galereja Novyj Passaž, Sankt-Peterburg 33395
Galereja Sovremennogo Iskusstva Arka, Vladivostok 33695
Galereja Sovremennogo Iskusstva Artëtaž, Vladivostok 33696
Gosudarstvennyj Istoriko-architekturnyj, Chudožestvennyj i Landšaftnyj Muzej-Zapovednik Caricyno, Moskva 33055
Gosudarstvennyj Muzej Izobrazitelnogo Iskusstva Rossijskogo Severa, Archangelsk 32650
Gosudarstvennyj Muzej Izobrazitelnych Iskusstv Respubliki Kalmykija, Ėlista 32793
Jaroslavskij Chudožestvennyj Muzej - Gubernatorskij Dom, Jaroslavl 32848
Kaliningradskaja Oblastnaja Chudožestvennaja Galereja, Kaliningrad 32869
Kartinnaja Galereja A.A. Plastova, Uljanovsk 33658
Kartinnaja Galereja Respubliki Adygeja, Majkop 33004
Krasnodarskij Chudožestvennyj Muzej im. F.A. Kovalenko, Krasnodar 32946
Krasnojarskij Gorodskoj Vystavočnyj Zal, Krasnojarsk 32951
Memorialnyj Muzej-kvartira M.S. Spiridonova, Čeboksary 32721
Municipalnaja Chudožestvennaja Galereja g. Kostromy, Kostroma 32944
Muzej Carskoselskaja Kollekcija, Puškin 33340
Muzej-institut Semji Rerichov, Sankt-Peterburg 33437
Muzej Nonkonformistskogo Iskusstva, Sankt-Peterburg 33461
Muzej Sovremennogo Izobrazitelnogo Iskusstva im. A.A. Plastova, Uljanovsk 33667
Novokuzneckij Chudožestvennyj Muzej, Novokuzneck 33236
Oblastnoj Muzejnyj Centr, Sankt-Peterburg 33473
Orenburgskij Oblastnoj Muzej Izobrazitelnych Iskusstv, Orenburg 33271
Penzenskaja Kartinnaja Galerija im. K.A. Savickogo, Penza 33293
Sosnovoborskij Chudožestvennyj Muzei Sovremennogo Iskusstva, Sosnovyj Bor 33549
Tambovskaja Oblastnaja Kartinnaja Galereja, Tambov 33590
Tjumenskaja Kartinnaja Galereja, Tjumen 33609
Tulskij Muzej Izobrazitelnych Iskusstv, Tula 33632
Tverskaja Oblastnaja Kartinnaja Galereja, Tver 33638
Tvorčeskij Centr i Vystavočnyj Zal Fëdor, Sankt-Peterburg 33486
Ufimskaja Kartinnaja Galereja, Ufa 33648
Vernisaž Art Podvalčik, Chabarovsk 32740
Vologodskaja Oblastnaja Kartinnaja Galereja, Vologda 33723
Vystavočnyj Zal Tverskoj Oblastnoj Kartinnoj Galerei, Tver 33640
Zverevskij Centr Sovremennogo Iskusstva, Moskva 33187

San Marino
Galleria Nazionale di Arte Moderna e Contemporanea, San Marino 33759

Serbia-Montenegro
Artmedia Art Gallery, Beograd 33793
Moderna Galerija, Podgorica 33888
Muzej Savremene Likovne Umetnosti, Novi Sad 33872
Muzej Savremene Umetnosti, Beograd 33812
Spomen-Zbirka Pavla Beljanskog, Novi Sad 33873
Umetnička Galerija Nadežda Petrović, Čačak 33828
Zavičajna Galerija, Novi Sad 33876

Singapore
Singapore Art Museum, Singapore 33941

Slovakia
Galéria J. Jakobyha, Košice 34004
Štátna Galéria, Banská Bystrica 33949
Warhol Family Museum of Modern Art, Medzilaborce 34028

Slovenia
Galerija Murska Sobota, Murska Sobota 34133
Moderna Galerija, Ljubljana 34112

South Africa
A.C. White Gallery, Bloemfontein 34181
Centre for African Studies Collection, Rondebosch 34370
Hester Rupert Art Museum, Graaff-Reinet 34247
Irma Stern Museum of the University of Cape Town, Rosebank 34372
UNISA Art Gallery, Pretoria 34360
University of Stellenbosch Art Gallery, Stellenbosch 34386

Spain
Artium - Centro Museo Vasco de Arte Contemporáneo, Vitoria-Gasteiz 35694
Centre de Cultura Contemporània de Barcelona, Barcelona 34534
Centro Andaluz de Arte Contemporáneo, Sevilla 35474
Centro Atlántico de Arte Moderno, Las Palmas de Gran Canaria 35238
Centro de Arte Moderno y Contemporáneo Daniel Vázquez Díaz, Nerva 35158
IVAM Centre Julio González, Valencia 35599
Metrònom, Barcelona 34546
Museo Angel Orensanz y Artes de Serralbo, Sabiñánigo 35350
Museo de Arte Abstracto Español, Cuenca 34763
Museo de Arte Contemporáneo, Sevilla 35482
Museo de Arte Contemporáneo, Toledo 35538
Museo de Cáceres, Cáceres 34641
Museo del Grabado Español Contemporáneo, Marbella 35086
Museo Extremeño e Iberoamericano de Arte Contemporáneo, Badajoz 34519
Museo Internacional de Arte Contemporáneo, Arrecife 34487
Museo Municipal, Valdepeñas 35592
Museo Nacional Centro de Arte Reina Sofía, Madrid 35041
Museo Patio Herreriano, Valladolid 35628
Museo-Pinacoteca de Arte Contemporáneo, Zarzuela del Monte 35734
Museo Popular de Arte Contemporáneo, Villafamés 35678
Museo Vostell-Malpartida de Cáceres, Malpartida de Cáceres 35077
Museu Comarcal de la Garrotxa, Olot 35172
Museu d'Art, Girona 34855
Museu d'Art Contemporani de Barcelona, Barcelona 34552
Museu d'Art Contemporani d'Eivissa, Eivissa 34788
Museu d'Art Espanyol Contemporani, Palma de Mallorca 35232
Museu d'Art Modern, Tarragona 35512
Museu d'Art Modern del MNAC, Barcelona 34553
Museu de L'Hospitalet de Llobregat, L'Hospitalet de Llobregat 34904
Museu Picasso, Barcelona 34586
Teatre-Museu Dalí, Figueres 34819

Sweden
Eksjö Museum med Albert Engströms Samlingarna, Eksjö 35860
Immigrant-institutets Museum, Borås 35842
Kalmar Konstmuseum, Kalmar 35987
Kristinehamns Konstmuseum, Kristinehamn 36019
Moderna Museet, Stockholm 36262
Norrköpings Konstmuseum, Norrköping 36120
Rooseum, Malmö 36079
Södertälje Konsthall, Södertälje 36211
Thielska Galleriet, Stockholm 36295
Zornsamlingarna, Mora 36103

Switzerland
attitudes, Genève 36725
Ausstellungsraum Klingental, Basel 36497
Bündner Kunstmuseum, Chur 36632
Centre Culturel-Exposition d'Artistes et d'Artisans, Collombey 36640
Centre d'Art Contemporain, Genève 36730
Centre pour l'Image Contemporaine Saint-Gervais, Genève 36734
Centro d'Arte Contemporanea Ticino, Bellinzona 36528
Collection de l'Art Brut, Lausanne 36852
Daros Exhibitions, Zürich 37374
Emma Kunz-Museum, Würenlos 37352
Espace Lausannoise d'Art Contemporain, Lausanne 36854
Fondation Beyeler, Riehen 37060
Fondation Saner, Studen 37220
Fri-Art, Fribourg 36713
Galerie art one, Zürich 37375
Hallen für neue Kunst, Schaffhausen 37130
Haus für Relief und Halbfiguren von Hans Josephsohn, Giornico 36760
Helmhaus, Zürich 37381
Kunsthalle Sankt Gallen, Sankt Gallen 37101
Kunsthalle Ziegelhütte, Appenzell 36461
Kunsthaus Glarus, Glarus 36764
Kunstmuseum Thun, Thun 37240
Kunstpanorama im Bourbaki, Luzern 36913
Mamco, Genève 36739
Migros Museum für Gegenwartskunst, Zürich 37389
Mili Weber-Haus, Sankt Moritz 37114
Musée d'Art Contemporain - FAE, Pully 37037
Musée des Beaux-Arts, La Chaux-de-Fonds 36627
Musée Jenisch, Vevey 37289
Museo Comunale d'Arte Moderna di Ascona, Ascona 36470
Museum Bickel, Walenstadt 37300
Museum Franz Gertsch, Burgdorf 36606
Museum für Gegenwartskunst, Basel 36509
Museum Liner Appenzell, Appenzell 36463
Pinacoteca Comunale, Locarno 36886
Sammlung Rosengart Luzern, Luzern 36917
Schaulager, Münchenstein 36966
Seedamm Kulturzentrum, Pfäffikon (Schwyz) 37020
Shed im Eisenwerk, Frauenfeld 36708
Villa am Aabach, Uster 37272
Villa Flora Winterthur, Winterthur 37343

Thailand
Bhirasri Museum of Modern Art, Bangkok 37479
Chiang Mai Contemporary Art Museum, Chiang Mai 37501

Tunisia
Maison des Arts, Tunis 37591

Turkey
Erzurum Resim ve Heykel Müzesi, Erzurum 37673
İzmir Resim ve Heykel Müzesi, İzmir 37719
Turkuvaz Sanat Galerisi, Ankara 37620

Ukraine
Center for Contemporary Art, Kyïv 37868

United Kingdom
198 Gallery, London 39563
Aberdeen Art Gallery, Aberdeen 37929
Aberystwyth Arts Centre, Aberystwyth 37952
Arnolfini, Bristol 38347
Batley Art Gallery, Batley 38128
Ben Uri Gallery, London 39577
Citadel's Artspace, Saint Helens 40396
Collins Gallery, Glasgow 39042
Delfina, London 39621
Edinburgh Printmakers Workshop and Gallery, Edinburgh 38877
Estorick Collection of Modern Italian Art, London 39632
Ferens Art Gallery, Kingston-upon-Hull 39377
Firstsite at the Minories Art Gallery, Colchester 38610
Fruitmarket Gallery, Edinburgh 38882
Gallery of Modern Art, Glasgow 39045
Harley Gallery, Welbeck 40808
Himley Hall, Himley 39245
Institute of Contemporary Arts, London 39673
John Creasey Museum, Salisbury 40434
Kettle's Yard, Cambridge 38457
Kingsgate Gallery, London 39681
Maclaurin Art Gallery, Ayr 38051
Mall Galleries, London 39703
Mead Gallery, Coventry 38644
Mission Gallery, Swansea 40660
Modern Art Oxford, Oxford 40147
Museum and Art Gallery Leicester, Leicester 39464
The Museum of Modern Art, Machynlleth 39869
The New Art Gallery Walsall, Walsall 40773
Northern Gallery for Contemporary Art, Sunderland 40647
Old Steeple, Dundee 38803
Ormeau Baths Gallery, Belfast 38156
Pier Arts Centre, Stromness 40637
Pitzhanger Manor-House and Gallery, London 39745
Pump House Gallery, London 39749
Rammerscales, Lockerbie 39562
Rotherham Art Gallery, Rotherham 40345
Rye Art Gallery, Rye 40363
Saatchi Gallery, London 39769
Sainsbury Centre for Visual Arts, Norwich 40100
Serpentine Gallery, London 39774
South London Gallery, London 39780
Talbot Rice Gallery, Edinburgh 38920
Tate Britain, London 39787
Tate Liverpool, Liverpool 39529
Tate Modern, London 39788
Tate Saint Ives, Saint Ives, Cornwall 40410
Tolbooth Art Centre, Kirkcudbright 39394
Turnpike Gallery, Leigh, Lancashire 39471
The University Gallery, Newcastle-upon-Tyne 40043
University of Essex Exhibition Gallery, Colchester 38615
West Wales Arts Centre, Fishguard 38994

Whitechapel Art Gallery, London 39807
Wrexham Arts Centre, Wrexham 40943

Uruguay
Museo de Arte Contemporáneo, Montevideo 40995

U.S.A.
1078 Gallery, Chico 42369
Aldrich Museum of Contemporary Art, Ridgefield 46896
Aljira Center for Contemporary Art, Newark 45889
American Indian Contemporary Arts, San Francisco 47304
Anderson Museum of Contemporary Art, Roswell 47013
Armory Center for the Arts, Pasadena 46300
Art Gallery, College Park 42522
Art Gallery Marist College, Poughkeepsie 46673
Art Museum of the Americas, Washington 48334
Art-Tech, San Jose 47349
Artforms Gallery Manuyunk, Philadelphia 46390
Arts Center of the Ozarks, Springdale 47732
Artspace, Raleigh 46771
Balboa Park Gallery, San Diego 47270
Bank of America Galleries, San Francisco 47309
Baton Rouge Gallery, Baton Rouge 41525
Bemis Center for Contemporary Arts, Omaha 46144
Ben Shahn Galleries, Wayne 48477
Benedicta Arts Center, Saint Joseph 47103
Berkeley Art Center, Berkeley 41640
Beverly Art Center, Chicago 42308
Black Rock Arts Foundation, San Francisco 47310
Bobbitt Visual Arts Center, Albion 41096
Bowman, Megahan and Penelec Galleries, Meadville 45215
Bridge Center for Contemporary Art, El Paso 43112
Buckham Fine Arts Project Gallery, Flint 43338
Buddy Holly Center, Lubbock 44990
Bunnell Street Gallery, Homer 44067
Butte Silver Bow Arts Chateau, Butte 42016
Cabot's Old Indian Pueblo Museum, Desert Hot Springs 42914
California Center for the Arts, Escondido 43208
Campbell Hall Gallery, Monmouth 45436
Capp Street Project, San Francisco 47313
Carlson Tower Gallery, Chicago 42310
Carnegie Art Museum, Oxnard 46244
Center for Contemporary Arts of Santa Fe, Santa Fe 47416
Center for Curatorial Studies, Annandale-on-Hudson 41224
Center for Maine Contemporary Art, Rockport 46971
Center on Contemporary Art, Seattle 47531
Centro Cultural de la Raza, San Diego 47272
Century Gallery, Sylmar 47904
City Gallery at Chastain, Atlanta 41338
City Gallery East, Atlanta 41339
Cleveland Artists Foundation at Beck Center for the Arts, Lakewood 44610
The Coburn Gallery, Ashland 41295
Commerce Bancshares Fine Art Collection, Kansas City 44396
Communications and History Museum of Sutton, Washington 48341
Contemporary Art Center of Fort Worth, Fort Worth 43484
Contemporary Art Center of Virginia, Virginia Beach 48246
Contemporary Art for San Antonio Blue Star Art Space, San Antonio 47248
Contemporary Art Museum, Tampa 47940
Contemporary Art Museum of Saint Louis, Saint Louis 47117
Contemporary Art Workshop, Chicago 42321
Contemporary Arts Center, New Orleans 45722
Contemporary Arts Museum, Houston 44118
The Contemporary Museum, Honolulu 44073
The Contemporary Museum at First Hawaiian Center, Honolulu 44074
Coyote Gallery, Oroville 46197
Creative Growth Art Center, Oakland 46063
Crestar Bank Art Collection, Richmond 46875
Dan Flavin Art Foundation Temporary Gallery, New York 45790
Danforth Gallery, Portland 46622
Daum Museum of Contemporary Art, Sedalia 47554
Davis Art Center, Davis 42791
Dia Art Foundation, New York 45792
Dia:Beacon, Beacon 41552
Dia:Chelsea, New York 45793
Dudley and Mary Marks Lea Gallery, Findlay 43322
Duncan-McAshan Visual Arts Center, Ingram 44237
Euphrat Museum of Art, Cupertino 42730
Evanston Art Center, Evanston 43238
Ewing Gallery of Art and Architecture, Knoxville 44518
Federal Reserve Bank of Boston Collection, Boston 41806
Fondo Del Sol, Washington 48354
Frederick R. Weisman Art Foundation, Los Angeles 44901
Frederick R. Weisman Museum of Art, Malibu 45083
Fugitive Art Center, Nashville 45620
Galeria Mesa, Mesa 45270
Gallery 210, Saint Louis 47121
The Gallery at UTA, Arlington 41260
Gallery of Art, Cedar Falls 42149
Gallery of Contemporary Art, Colorado Springs 42537
Georgetown College Gallery, Georgetown 43651
Georgia O'Keeffe Museum, Santa Fe 47418
Guild of Creative Art, Shrewsbury 47620
Gulf Coast Museum of Art, Largo 44653
Hamline University Galleries, Saint Paul 47155
Holter Museum of Art, Helena 43983
HUB Robeson Galleries, University Park 48153
Indianapolis Museum of Art, Indianapolis 44228
Installation Gallery Insite, San Diego 47277
Institute of Contemporary Art, Boston 41810
Institute of Contemporary Art, Portland 46623
Institute of Contemporary Art, Philadelphia 46420
Intermedia Arts Minnesota, Minneapolis 45386
Irvine Fine Arts Center, Irvine 44256
Jackson Art Center, Washington 48364
Jacksonville Museum of Modern Art, Jacksonville 44296
Jeannette Powell Art Center, Stockton 47825
John A. Logan College Museum, Carterville 42124
John Maxine Belger Center, Kansas City 44398
Jones Center for Contemporary Art, Austin 41413
Kemper Museum of Contemporary Art, Kansas City 44401
Kendall Gallery, Grand Rapids 43758
Knoxville Museum of Art, Knoxville 44520
Laband Art Gallery, Los Angeles 44918
Las Vegas Art Museum, Las Vegas 44668
Leedy-Voulke's Art Center, Kansas City 44402
Lehman College Art Gallery, Bronx 41922
LeMoyne Art Foundation, Tallahassee 47934
Lewis, James and Nellie Stratton Gallery, Columbia 42551
Littman Gallery, Portland 46635
Los Angeles Contemporary Exhibitions, Los Angeles 44920
Los Angeles Municipal Art Gallery, Los Angeles 44923
Louisville Visual Art Museum, Louisville 44972
Main Gallery of Henry Street Settlement, New York 45829
Margaret Thatcher Projects, New York 45830
Marie Walsh Sharpe Art Foundation, New York 45831
Martin Museum of Art, Waco 48264
Mass Moca, North Adams 45978
Mattress Factory Museum, Pittsburgh 46521
Mhiripiri Gallery, Edina 43086
Mobius Gallery, Boston 41815
Montclair State University Art Galleries, Upper Montclair 48159
Museo Italoamericano, San Francisco 47327
Museum Necca and New England Center for Contemporary Art, Brooklyn 41939
Museum of Art, Fort Lauderdale 43411
Museum of Contemporary Art, Chicago 42344
Museum of Contemporary Art, Fort Collins 43383
Museum of Contemporary Art, North Miami 45997
Museum of Contemporary Art, Washington 48370
Museum of Contemporary Art Denver, Denver 42895
Museum of Contemporary Art Los Angeles, Los Angeles 44930
Museum of Contemporary Art San Diego - Downtown, San Diego 47281
Museum of Contemporary Art San Diego - La Jolla, La Jolla 44548
Museum of Contemporary Religious Art, Saint Louis 47130
Museum of Modern Art at the Gramercy Theatre, New York 45843
Museum of Modern Art in Queens, Long Island City 44869
Museum of Neon Art, Los Angeles 44932
NAB Gallery, Chicago 42350
National Vietnam Veterans Art Museum, Chicago 42352
Neue Galerie New York, New York 45853
New Harmony Gallery of Contemporary Art, New Harmony 45693
New Museum of Contemporary Art, New York 45855
Nexus Foundatoin for Today's Art, Philadelphia 46437
No Name Exhibitions @ Soap Factory, Minneapolis 45392
North View Gallery, Portland 46636
Northern Illinois University Art Museum, DeKalb 42857
Northern Lights Art Gallery, Mayville 45210
Northern Michigan University Art Museum, Marquette 45174
Norton Museum of Art, West Palm Beach 48538
Oberlin College Gallery, Cleveland 42477
Olive DeLuce Art Gallery, Maryville 45196
Omaha Center for Contemporary Art, Omaha 46151
Painted Bride Art Center Gallery, Philadelphia 46438
Pasadena City College Art Gallery, Pasadena 46304
Paul Whitney Larson Gallery, Saint Paul 47165
Paxson Gallery, Missoula 45407
Phoenix Art Museum, Phoenix 46477
Pittsburgh Center for the Arts, Pittsburgh 46523
Pro Arts Gallery, Oakland 46069
Project Art-University of Iowa and Clinics, Iowa City 44247
P.S. 1 Contemporary Art Center, Long Island City 44870
Reese Bullen Gallery, Arcata 41247
Rice University Art Gallery, Houston 44133
Rio Hondo College Art Gallery, Whittier 48597
Rochester Art Center, Rochester 46936
Ruby Green Contemporary Arts Foundations, Nashville 45623
Russell Hill Rogers Galleries, San Antonio 47257
Salvador Dali Museum, Saint Petersburg 47176
San Francisco Museum of Modern Art, San Francisco 47339
San Jose Institute of Contemporary Art, San Jose 47355
San Marco Gallery, San Rafael 47376
The San Mateo County Arts Council, Belmont 41608
Santa Barbara Contemporary Arts Forum, Santa Barbara 47402
Santa Monica Museum of Art, Santa Monica 47442
Savannah College of Art and Design Galleries, Savannah 47483
School of Art Gallery, Baton Rouge 41535
Scottsdale Museum of Contemporary Art, Scottsdale 47514
Second Street Gallery, Charlottesville 42251
Sierra Arts Foundation, Reno 46837
Site Santa Fe, Santa Fe 47433
Socrates Sculpture Park, Long Island City 44873
Solomon R. Guggenheim Museum, New York 45872
Southwestern College Art Gallery, Chula Vista 42393
Space 101 Gallery, Pittsburgh 46528
Spaces, Cleveland 42481
Stedman Art Gallery, Camden 42060
Student Center Gallery, Wilmore 48665
Sun Gallery, Hayward 43975
SunAmerica Collection, Los Angeles 44946
Sushi Performance and Visual Art Museum, San Diego 47297
Susquehanna Art Museum, Harrisburg 43926
Tampa Museum of Art, Tampa 47946
TBA Exhibition Space, Chicago 42366
Terrace Gallery, Orlando 46190
T.F. Chen Cultural Center, New York 45880
Trova Foundation, Saint Louis 47139
Tryart Gallery, Louisville 44978
University Art Gallery, Jackson 44288
Ursuline Hallway Gallery, San Antonio 47263
Ventura County Museum of History and Art, Ventura 48211
Visual Arts Annex Gallery, San Antonio 47264
Vox Populi Gallery, Philadelphia 46461
Walker's Point Center for the Arts, Milwaukee 45374
Washington University Gallery of Art, Saint Louis 47140
Wayne Art Center, Wayne 48481
Weil Art Gallery, Corpus Christi 42648
Weingart Galleries, Los Angeles 44949
Wheeler Gallery, Providence 46728
Yellowstone Art Museum, Billings 41692
Yerba Buena Center for the Arts, San Francisco 47346

Venezuela
Galería Municipal de Arte Moderno, Barcelona 48891
Museo Alejandro Otero, Caracas 48904
Museo de Arte Contemporáneo de Caracas Sofía Imber, Caracas 48912
Museo de Arte Contemporáneo Francisco Narváez, Porlamar 48962
Museo de Arte Moderno, Mérida 48956
Sala Ipostel, Caracas 48929

Zimbabwe
National Gallery Bulawayo, Bulawayo 49027

Art, Oriental

Brazil
Açude Museum, Rio de Janeiro 04314

Cuba
Galería Oriente, Santiago de Cuba 08129

France
Musée Salies, Bagnères-de-Bigorre 10560

Iran
Abkar Museum, Teheran 22288
Behzad Museum, Teheran 22291
Farshchian Museum, Teheran 22297
Muséyé Honarha-ye Melli, Teheran 22317
Reza Abbasi Museum, Teheran 22323
Sanati Museum, Kerman 22253

Switzerland
Antikenmuseum Basel und Sammlung Ludwig, Basel 36495

Turkey
Etnografya Müzesi, Ankara 37617

United Arab Emirates
Sharjah Islamic Museum, Sharjah 37924

United Kingdom
Hartlepool Art Gallery, Hartlepool 39175
Hastings Museum and Art Gallery, Hastings 39184

Art, Russian

Kazakhstan
The Kasteyev State Museum of Arts of the Republic of Kazakhstan, Almaty 27072

Poland
Muzeum Nikifora, Krynica 31740

Russia
Aleksandrovskaja Sloboda - Gosudarstvennyj Istoriko-architekturnyj i Chudožestvennyj Muzej-zapovednik, Aleksandrov 32633
Aleksandrovskij Chudožestvennyj Muzej, Aleksandrov 32634
Archangelskij Gosudarstvennyj Muzej Zodčestva i Narodnogo Ikusstva - Malye Karely, Archangelsk 32646
Archangelskij Oblastnoj Muzej Izobrazitelnych Iskusstv, Archangelsk 32649
Architekturno-chudožestvennyj Ansambl byvšego Spaso-Jakovleskogo Monastyrja, Rostov (Jaroslavskaja obl.) 33354
Astrachanskaja Gosudarstvennaja Kartinnaja Galereja im. B.M. Kustodieva, Astrachan 32658
Baškirskij Respublikanskij Chudožestvennyj Muzej im. M.V. Nesterova, Ufa 33641
Belgorodskij Gosudarstvennyj Chudožestvennyj Muzej, Belgorod 32675
Belozerskij Muzej Narodnogo Dekorativno-prikladnogo Iskusstva, Belozersk 32681
Bolšoj Dvorec, Lomonosov 32986
Bratskij Chudožestvennyj Vystavočnyj Zal, Bratsk 32703
Brjanskij Oblastnoj Chudožestvennyj Muzej, Brjansk 32708
Čajkovskaja Kartinnaja Galereja, Čajkovskij 32715
Čeljabinskaja Oblastnaja Kartinnaja Galerija, Čeljabinsk 32724
Chudožestvenno-memorialnyj Muzej K.S. Petrova-Vodkina, Chvalynsk 32746
Chudožestvenno-vystavočnyj Kompleks, Sarapul 33501
Chudožestvennyj Muzej, Staryj Oskol 33557
Chudožestvennyj Muzej, Valujki 33674
Chudožestvennyj Muzej im. A.N. Radiščeva, Saratov 33504
Chudožestvennyj Muzej im. M.S. Tuganova, Vladikavkaz 33686
Čitinskij Oblastnoj Chudožestvennyj Muzej, Čita 32750
Dalnevostočnyj Chudožestvennyj Muzej, Chabarovsk 32739
Dom-muzej N.N. Chochrjakova, Kirov 32916
Dom-Muzej I.N. Kramskogo, Ostrogožsk 33275
Dom-muzej B.I. Prorokova, Ivanovo 32825
Dom-Muzej I.E. Repina, Žigulevsk 33747
Dom-muzej Skulptora A.S. Golubkinoj, Zarajsk 33745
Dom-muzej Velimira Chlebnikova, Astrachan 32662
Ekaterininskij Dvorec - Gosudarstvennyj Muzej Carskoje Selo, Puškin 33336
Galereja Forum, Sankt-Peterburg 33394
Galereja Novyj Passaž, Sankt-Peterburg 33395
Gatčinskij Literaturno-memorialnyj Muzej-usadba P.E. Ščerbova, Gatčina 32801
Gorodskoj Muzej Iskusstvo Omska, Omsk 33253
Gosudarstvennaja Tretjakovskaja Galerja, Moskva 33046
Gosudarstvennaja Tretjakovskaja Galerja na Krymskom Valu, Moskva 33047
Gosudarstvennyj Chudožestvenno-architekturnyj Dvorcovo-parkovyj Muzej-zapovednik Oranienbaum, Lomonosov 32988
Gosudarstvennyj Chudožestvenno-architekturnyj Dvorcovo-parkovyj Muzej-zapovednik Pavlovsk, Pavlovsk 33285
Gosudarstvennyj Istoriko-architekturnyj, Chudožestvennyj i Landšaftnyj Muzej-Zapovednik Caricyno, Moskva 33055
Gosudarstvennyj Istoriko-architekturnyj i Etnografičeskij Muzej-zapovednik Kiži, Kiži 32931
Gosudarstvennyj Istoriko-architekturnyj i Etnografičeskij Muzej-zapovednik Kiži, Petrozavodsk 33315
Gosudarstvennyj Istoriko-architekturnyj i Prirodno-landšaftnyj Muzej Zapovednik Izborsk, Izborsk 32834
Gosudarstvennyj Istoriko-Architekturnyj i Prirodnyj Muzej-Zapovednik Monrepo, Vyborg 33741
Gosudarstvennyj Istoriko-chudožestvennyj Dvorcovo-parkovyj Muzej-zapovednik Gatčina, Gatčina 32802
Gosudarstvennyj Istoriko-kulturnyj Muzej-zapovednik "Moskovskij Kreml", Moskva 33056
Gosudarstvennyj Istoriko-literaturnyj Muzej-Zapovednik A.S. Puškina s usadbami Vjazemy i Zacharovo, Bolšie Vjazemy 32696
Gosudarstvennyj Memorial'nyj Istoriko-chudožestvennyj i Prirodnyj Muzej-zapovednik V.D. Polenova, Strachovo 33566
Gosudarstvennyj Muzej Izobrazitelnych Iskusstv Respubliki Kalmykija, Ėlista 32793
Gosudarstvennyj Muzej Zapovednik Petergof, Sankt-Peterburg 33406
Gosudarstvennyj Russkij Muzej, Sankt-Peterburg 33407
Gosudarstvennyj Russkij Muzej, Sankt-Peterburg 33408
Gosudarstvennyj Vladimiro-Suzdalskij Istoriko-architekturnyj i Chudožestvennyj Muzej-zapovednik, Vladimir 33692
Gosudarstvennyj Vystavočnyj Zal Zamoskvorec^Bie, Moskva 33069
Inženernyj (Michailovskij) Zamok, Sankt-Peterburg 33409

Irkutskij Oblastnoj Chudožestvennyj Muzej im. V.P. Sukačeva, Irkutsk 32813
Irkutskij Oblastnoj Kraevedčeskij Muzej, Irkutsk 32814
Istoriko-Architekturnyj, Chudožestvennyj i Archeologičeskij Muzej "Zarajskij Kreml", Zarajsk 33746
Istoriko-memorialnyj i Architurno-chudožestvennyj Muzej, Tichvin 33600
Ivanovskij Oblastnoj Chudožestvennyj Muzej, Ivanovo 32829
Jaroslavskij Chudožestvennyj Muzej - Gubernatorskij Dom, Jaroslavl 32848
Jaroslavskij Istoriko-architekturnyj i Chudožestvennyj Muzej-zapovednik, Jaroslavl 32849
Jurinskij Istoriko-chudožestvennyj Muzej, Jurino 32863
Jusupovskij Dvorec, Sankt-Peterburg 33411
Kabardino-Balkarskij Gosudarstvennyj Muzej Izobrazitelnych Iskusstv, Nalčik 33193
Kamčatskij Oblastnoj Kraevedčeskij Muzej, Petropavlovsk-Kamčatskij 33310
Kartinnaja Galereja A.A. Plastova, Uljanovsk 33658
Kartinnaja Galereja Respubliki Adygeja, Majkop 33004
Kemerovskij Oblastnoj Muzej Izobrazitelnych Iskusstv, Kemerovo 32913
Kirillo-Belozerskij Istoriko-Architekturnyj i Chudožestvennyj Muzej-Zapovednik, Kirillov 32915
Kirovskij Oblastnoj Chudožestvennyj Muzej im. Viktora i Apollinarija Vasnecovych, Kirov 32919
Kostromskoj Gosudarstvennyj Istoriko-architekturnyj Muzej-zapovednik, Kostroma 32942
Kostromskoj Gosudarstvennyj Obedinennyj Chudožestvennyj Muzej, Kostroma 32943
Krasnodarskij Chudožestvennyj Muzej im. F.A. Kovalenko, Krasnodar 32946
Krasnojarskij Chudožestvennyj Muzej im. V.I. Surikova, Krasnojarsk 32950
Krasnojarskij Gorodskoj Vystavočnyj Zal, Krasnojarsk 32951
Krasnokamskaja Kartinnaja Galereja, Krasnokamsk 32958
Kurganskij Oblastnoj Chudožestvennyj Muzej, Kurgan 32971
Kurskaja Kartinnaja Galerija im. A.A. Denejki, Kursk 32973
Magnitogorskaja Kartinnaja Galereja, Magnitogorsk 33001
Malojaroslaveckaja Gorodskaja Kartinnaja Galereja, Malojaroslavec 33005
Memorialno-chudožestvennyj Dom-muzej Vladimira Aleksandroviča Serova, Emmaus 32795
Memorialnyj Chudožestvennyj Muzej Valentina Aleksandroviča Serova v Domotkanovo, Krasnaja Nov' 32945
Memorialnyj Dom-muzej I.I. Levitana, Ples 33323
Memorialnyj Dom-muzej I.P. Požalostina, Solotča 33545
Memorialnyj Dom-muzej Viktora i Apolinarija Vasnecovych, Rjabovo 33348
Memorialnyj Dom-muzej V.M. Vaznecova, Moskva 33077
Memorialnyj Muzej-kvartira A.M. Vasnecova, Moskva 33080
Memorialnyj Muzej-usadba Chudožnika N.A. Jarošenko, Kislovodsk 32929
Minusinskaja Chudožestvennaja Kartinnaja Galereja, Minusinsk 33015
Mitropoličji Palaty - Muzej Drevnerusskogo Iskusstva, Jaroslavl 32852
Mramornyj Dvorec, Sankt-Peterburg 33423
Municipalnaja Chudožestvennaja Galereja g. Kostromy, Kostroma 32944
Murmanskij Oblastnoj Chudožestvennyj Muzej, Murmansk 33188
Muzej Bratjev Tkačevych, Brjansk 32709
Muzej im. B.M. Kustodieva, Ostrovskoe 33277
Muzej Izobrazitelnych Iskusstv, Komsomolsk-na-Amure 32935
Muzej Izobrazitelnych Iskusstv, Rostov-na-Donu 33356
Muzej Krylova, Tula 33626
Muzej Narodnogo Chudožnika Rossii A.I. Morozova, Ivanovo 32832
Muzej Narodnogo Derevjannogo Zodčestva Vitoslavlicy, Velikij Novgorod 33678
Muzej Pejzaža, Ples 33324
Muzej Sovremennogo Izobrazitelnogo Iskusstva im. A.A. Plastova, Uljanovsk 33667
Muzej Tropinina i Moskovskich Chudožnikov Ego Vremeni, Moskva 33154
Muzej Tverskogo Byta, Tver 33637
Muzej-usadba V.E. Borsova-Musatova, Saratov 33507
Muzej Vereščaginych, Čerepovec 32733
Muzej-zapovednik Abramcevo, Abramcevo 32629
Muzej-zapovednik Dmitrovskij Kreml, Dmitrov 32758
Nacionalnyj Chudožestvennyj Muzej Respubliki Sacha (Jakutija), Jakutsk 32845
Nižnetagilskij Municipalnyj Muzej Izobrazitelnych Iskusstv, Nižnij Tagil 33227
Novgorodskij Gosudarstvennyj Muzej-zapovednik, Velikij Novgorod 33680
Novokuzneckij Chudožestvennyj Muzej, Novokuzneck 33236
Oblastnoj Chudožestvennyj Muzej, Petropavlovsk-Kamčatskij 33312
Oblastnoj Muzejnyj Centr, Sankt-Peterburg 33473
Omskij Oblastnoj Muzej Izobrazitelnych Iskusstv im. M.A. Vrubelja, Omsk 33257
Orenburgskij Oblastnoj Muzej Izobrazitelnych Iskusstv, Orenburg 33271
Orlovskij Oblastnoj Muzej Izobrazitelnych Iskusstv, Orël 33268
Ostrogožskij Rajonnyj Istoriko-chudožestvennyj Muzej im. I.N. Kramskogo, Ostrogožsk 33276
Patrijaršie Palaty, Moskva 33171
Penzenskaja Kartinnaja Galerija im. K.A. Savickogo, Penza 33293
Pereslavl-Zalesskij Gosudarstvennyj Istoriko-architekturnyj i Chudožestvennyj Muzej-zapovednik, Pereslavl-Zalesskij 33299
Permskaja Gosudarstvennaja Chudožestvennaja Galereja, Perm 33307
Plesskij Gosudarstvennyj Istoriko-Architekturnyj i Chudožestvennyj Muzej-Zapovednik, Ples 33325
Primorskaja Kraevaja Kartinnaja Galereja, Vladivostok 33708
Pskovskij Gosudarstvennyj Istoričesko-architekturnyj i Chudožestnennyj Muzej-zapovednik, Pskov 33332
Rjazanskij Gosudarstvennyj Istoriko-architekturnyj Muzej-zapovednik, Rjazan 33351
Rjazanskij Oblastnoj Chudožestvennyj Muzej im. I.P. Požalostina, Rjazan 33352
Roslavlskij Istoriko-chudožstvennyj Muzej, Roslavl 33353
Rostovskij Kreml - Gosudarstvennyj Muzej-zapovednik, Rostov (Jaroslavskaja obl.) 33355
Rybinskij Gosudarstvennyj Istoriko-architekturnyj i Chudožestvennyj Muzej-zapovednik, Rybinsk 33362
Sajanskaja Kartinnaja Galereja, Sajansk 33363
Samarskij Oblastnoj Chudožestvennyj Muzej, Samara 33377
Semenovskij Gosudarstvennyj Kraevedčeskij Istoriko-chudožestvennyj Muzej, Semenov 33516
Sergievo-Posadskij Gosudarstvennyj Istoriko-chudožestvennyj Muzej Zapovednik, Sergiev Posad 33521
Serpuchovskij Istoriko-chudožestvennyj Muzej, Serpuchov 33522
Sočinskij Chudožestvennyj Muzej, Soči 33542
Soloveckij Gosudarstvennyj Istoriko-Architekturnyj i Prirodnyj Muzej-Zapovednik, Soloveckij 33546
Staroladožskij Istoriko-Architekturnyj i Archeologičeskij Muzej-Zapovednik, Staraja Ladoga 33553
Starorusskij Kraevedčeskij Muzej, Staraja Russa 33555
Stavropolskij Muzej Izobrazitelnych Iskusstv, Stavropol 33564
Stroganovskij Dvorec, Sankt-Peterburg 33484
Svijažskij Architekturno-chudožestvennyj Muzej, Svijažsk 33570
Taganrogskaja Kartinnaja Galereja, Taganrog 33585
Tambovskaja Oblastnaja Kartinnaja Galereja, Tambov 33590
Tarusskaja Kartinnaja Galereja, Tarusa 33593
Tjumenskij Oblastnoj Muzej Izobrazitelnych Iskusstv, Tjumen 33611
Tomskij Oblastnoj Chudožestvennyj Muzej, Tomsk 33616
Troickij Sobor, Serpuchov 33523
Tverskoj Gosudarstvennyj Obedinennyj Muzej, Tver 33639
Ufimskaja Kartinnaja Galereja, Ufa 33648
Uljanovskij Oblastnoj Chudožestvennyj Muzej, Uljanovsk 33668
Ust'-Ilimskaja Kartinnaja Galereja, Ust'-Ilimsk 33671
Valaamskij Naučno-issledovatelskij Cerkovno-archeologičeskij i Prirodnyj Muzej-zapovednik, Sortavala 33548
Velikoustjugskij Gosudarstvennyj Istoriko-Architekturnyj i Chudožestvennyj Muzej-Zapovednik, Velikij Ustjug 33681
Vjatskaja Kunstkamera, Kirov 32924
Volgogradskij Muzej Izobrazitelnych Iskusstv, Volgograd 33718
Vologodskaja Oblastnaja Kartinnaja Galereja, Vologda 33723
Vologodskij Gosudarstvennyj Istoriko-Architekturnyj i Chudožestvennyj Muzej-Zapovednik, Vologda 33724
Voronežskij Chudožestvennyj Muzej im. I.N. Kramskogo, Voronež 33735
Vystavočnyj Zal, Čerepovec 32734
Vystavočnyj Zal, Kirov 32925
Vystavočnyj Zal, Tula 33634
Vystavočnyj Zal, Volgograd 33720
Vystavočnyj Zal Biblioteki im. A.A. Bloka, Sankt-Peterburg 33490
Vystavocnyj Zal Doma Učenych, Novosibirsk 33245
Vystavočnyj Zal - Russkie Chudožniki v Samarskoj Gubernii, Žigulevsk 33749
Vystavočnyj Zal Tverskoj Oblastnoj Kartinnoj Galerei, Tver 33640
Zvenigorodskij Istoriko-architekturnyj i Chudožestvennyj Muzej, Zvenigorod 33751

South Africa
Marvol Museum, Kuilsriver 34299

Ukraine
Charkovskij Chudožestvennyj Muzej, Charkiv 37842
Kiev Museum of Russian Art, Kyïv 37871

Astronomy

Argentina
Museo Geográfico Einstein, San Juan 00572

Australia
Sydney Observatory, Sydney 01508

Belgium
Museum voor de Geschiedenis van de Wetenschappen, Gent 03445

Brazil
Museu de Astronomia e Ciências Afins, Rio de Janeiro 04356

Canada
Brydone Jack Observatory Museum, Fredericton 05458
H.R. MacMillan Space Centre, Vancouver 06680
Ontario Science Centre, Toronto 06600

Denmark
Ole Rømer Museet, Taastrup 09090

Ecuador
Museo Los Amantes de Sumpa, Guayaquil 09176

France
Bibliothèque-Musée de l'Observatoire, Paris 13476

Germany
Heimat- und Palitzsch-Museum Prohlis, Dresden 16686
Kepler-Gedächtnishaus, Regensburg 19526
Keplermuseum, Weil der Stadt 20439
Sammlung Warburg im Planetarium, Hamburg 17565
Universum Science Center Bremen, Bremen 16337

Greece
Cultural Center Hellenic Cosmos, Athinai 20856

Italy
Museo Astronomico Copernicano, Roma 25178
Museo Astronomico e Geofisico, Modena 24437
Museo della Specola, Bologna 23117
Museo dell'Osservatorio, Monte Porzio Catone 24497
Museo dell'Osservatorio Astronomico di Capodimonte, Napoli 24585

Japan
Akashi-shiritsu Tenmon Kagakukan, Akashi 26092
Hiratsuka-shi Hakubutsukan, Hiratsuka 26208
Okayama Tenmon Hakubutsukan, Kamogata 26302

Kuwait
Educational Science Museum, Kuwait 27305

Mexico
Museo Planetario, Garza García 27931

Netherlands
Explorion, Heerlen 29366
Nationaal Ruimtevaart Museum, Lelystad 29531

Poland
Muzeum Mikołaja Kopernika, Frombork 31561
Muzeum Mikołaja Kopernika, Toruń 32053

Russia
Istoriko-memorial'nyj Muzejnyj Kompleks Bobriki, Donskij 32760

South Africa
Observatory Museum, Grahamstown 34252

Spain
Museo de la Ciencia y el Cosmos, La Laguna 34938

United Kingdom
Foredown Tower, Portslade-by-Sea 40247
Mills Observatory Museum, Dundee 38801
National Maritime Museum, London 39731
Royal Observatory Greenwich, London 39767
The William Herschel Museum, Bath 38125

U.S.A.
McKinley Museum and McKinley National Memorial, Canton 42090
Mitchell House, Nantucket 45597
Museum of Ancient and Modern Art, Penn Valley 46339
Suffolk County Vanderbilt Museum, Centerport 42169

Uzbekistan
Ulug-Beg Memorial Museum, Samarkand 48852

Automobiles → Vehicles

Aviation

Argentina
Museo Aeronáutico, Baradero 00133
Museo de la Aviación Naval, Bahía Blanca 00126
Museo de Tecnología Aeronáutica y Espacial, Córdoba 00298
Museo Histórico Fuerte Barragan, Ensenada 00341
Museo Histórico Sanmartíniano, Mendoza 00438
Museo Nacional de Aeronáutica, Buenos Aires 00225
Museo Tecnológico Aeroespacial, Las Higueras 00404

Australia
Australian Flying Museum, Archerfield 00748
Aviation Heritage Museum of Western Australia, Bull Creek 00857
Central Australian Aviation Museum, Alice Springs 00734
Fighter World, Williamtown 01602
Flypast Museum of Australian Army Flying, Oakey 01339
Mona Vale Aero Nautical Museum, Mona Vale 01265
Moorabbin Air Museum, Cheltenham 00908
Moorabbin Air Museum, Moorabbin 01270
QANTAS Founders Outback Museum, Longreach 01186
Queensland Air Museum, Caloundra 00875
Royal Australian Air Force Museum, Point Cook 01371
Royal Flying Doctor Service Visitors Centre, Edge Hill 01007
South Australian Aviation Museum, Port Adelaide 01375
West Torrens Railway, Signal Telegraph and Aviation Museum, Brooklyn Park 00850

Austria
Flugmuseum Aviaticum, Wiener Neustadt 03016
Hangar-7, Salzburg 02540
Österreichisches Luftfahrtmuseum, Feldkirchen bei Graz 01833

Brazil
Museu Aeroespacial, Rio de Janeiro 04329

Bulgaria
Muzej na Aviacijata, Krumovo 04723

Canada
Aero Space Museum of Calgary, Calgary 05159
Air Force Heritage Museum and Air Park, Winnipeg 06818
Alberta Aviation Museum, Edmonton 05369
Atlantic Canada Aviation Museum, Bedfords 05070
Billy Bishop Heritage Museum, Owen Sound 06087
British Columbia Aviation Museum, Sidney 06448
Canada Aviation Museum, Ottawa 06069
Canada's Aviation Hall of Fame, Wetaskiwin 06778
Canadian Museum of Flight, Langley 05725
Canadian Warplane Heritage Museum, Mount Hope 05948
Commonwealth Air Training Plan Museum, Brandon 05120
Comox Air Force Museum, Lazo 05737
Great War Flying Museum, Cheltenham 05242
Greenwood Military Aviation Museum, Greenwood, Nova Scotia 05529
Nanton Lancaster Air Museum, Nanton 05962
North Atlantic Aviation Museum, Gander 05474
Royal Canadian Air Force Memorial Museum, Astra 05016
Sarah Vaughan Museum, Sioux Lookout 06458
Shearwater Aviation Museum, Shearwater 06432
Toronto Aeropspace Museum, Toronto 06615
West Coast Museum of Flying, Sidney 06451
Western Canada Aviation Museum, Winnipeg 06852
Yorkshire Air Museum, Canada Branch, Saint-Laurent 06361

China, People's Republic
Astronautics Museum, Beijing 06943
China Aviation Museum, Beijing 06957

Czech Republic
Letecké Muzeum, Praha 08588

Denmark
Dansk Veteranflysamling, Skjern 09063

Ecuador
Museo Aeronautico y del Espacio, Quito 09193

Egypt
Airport Museum, Cairo 09254

Finland
Keski-Suomen Ilmailumuseo, Tikkakoski 10106
Luotsitupa, Uusikaupunki 10153
Suomen Ilmailumuseo, Vantaa 10182

France
Musée Aérorétro, Albon 10277
Musée Airborne, Sainte-Mère-Eglise 14548
Musée de l'Air et de l'Espace, Le Bourget (Seine-Saint-Denis) 12387
Musée de l'Aviation Charles-Noetinger, Perpignan 13706
Musée de l'Aviation Légère de l'Armée de Terre, Dax 11487
Musée de l'Invasion Aéroportée, Bénouville 10684
Musée des Débuts de l'Aviation, Douzy 11573

Germany
Aeronauticum - Deutsches Luftschiff- und Marinefliegermuseum Nordholz, Nordholz 19123
Art Kite Museum für Kunst Flugobjekte, Detmold 16586
Ballonmuseum Gersthofen, Gersthofen 17263

Bavaria Airways-Museum, Kirchdorf an der Amper 18089
Deutsche Raumfahrtausstellung, Morgenröthe-Rautenkranz 18789
Deutsches Museum - Flugwerft Schleißheim, Oberschleißheim 19200
Deutsches Segelflugmuseum mit Modellflug, Gersfeld 17260
Dorniermuseum im Neuen Schloß, Meersburg 18674
Erfatal-Museum Hardheim, Hardheim 17617
Flughafen Modellschau, Hamburg 17538
Flugpionier-Gustav-Weißkopf-Museum, Leutershausen 18447
Hermann-Köhl-Museum, Pfaffenhofen an der Roth 19384
Hermann-Oberth-Raumfahrt-Museum, Feucht 16994
Hubschraubermuseum, Bückeburg 16393
Internationales Luftfahrtmuseum, Villingen-Schwenningen 20319
Luftfahrt-Museum Laatzen-Hannover, Laatzen 18279
Luftfahrt- und Technik-Museumspark, Merseburg 18714
Luftfahrtausstellung im Alten Straßenbahndepot, Brandenburg an der Havel 16283
Luftfahrttechnisches Museum, Rothenburg, Oberlausitz 19685
Museum für Luftfahrt und Technik, Wernigerode 20528
Otto-Lilienthal-Museum, Anklam 15495
Zeppelin-Museum, Neu-Isenburg 19005
Zeppelin Museum Friedrichshafen, Friedrichshafen 17149
Zeppelin-Museum Meersburg, Meersburg 18680

Ireland
Foynes Flying Boat Museum, Foynes 22471

Italy
Museo Aeronautico, Padova 24734
Museo Aeronautico Caproni di Taliedo, Roma 25175
Museo Aeronautico Caproni di Taliedo, Vizzola Ticino 26043
Museo dell'Aeronautica G. Caproni, Trento 25793
Museo dell'Aviazione, Rimini 25116
Museo Storico-Aeronautica Militare, Bracciano 23194

Malaysia
Royal Malaysian Air Force Museum, Kuala Lumpur 27652

Netherlands
Avog's Crash Museum, Lievelde 29540
Ballon- en Luctvaartmuseum Zep/Allon, Lelystad 29529
Dutch Dakota Association Exhibition, Schiphol 29807
Luchtvaart Museum Texel, De Cocksdorp 29066
Luchtvaart Museum Twenthe, Enschede 29236
Militaire Luchtvaart Museum, Soesterberg 29843
Museum Vliegbasis Deelen, Deelen 29074
Nationaal Luchtvaart Museum Aviodome, Schiphol 29808
Old Aircraft Museum, Arnemuiden 28932
Space Expo, Noordwijk, Zuid-Holland 29646
Traditiekamer Typhoon, Volkel 29959
Traditiekamer Vliegbasis Twenthe, Enschede 29241
Vliegend Museum Lelystad, Lelystad 29534
Vliegend Museum Seppe, Bosschenhoofd 29008
Westerwolds Crashmuseum, Oude Pekela 29695

New Zealand
Air Force Museum, Christchurch 30121
Ashburton Aviation Museum, Ashburton 30096
Gore Airforce Museum, Gore 30167
Museum of Aviation, Paraparaumu 30233
New Zealand Fighter Pilots Museum, Wanaka 30284
New Zealand Fleet Air Arm Museum, Auckland 30114
Vintage Aircraft Museum, Masterton 30200

Pakistan
PAF Museum, Karachi 31031
Pakistan Air Force Museum Peshawar, Peshawar 31050

Peru
Museo de la Fuerza de Aviación Naval, Callao 31131

Philippines
Philippine Air Force Aerospace Museum, Pasay 31417

Poland
Muzeum Lotnictwa Polskiego, Kraków 31713

Portugal
Museu do Ar, Alverca do Ribatejo 32234

Russia
Centr Istorii Aviacionnych Dvigatelej im. N.D. Kuznecova, Samara 33367
Centralnyj Muzej Aviacii i Kosmonavtiki, Moskva 33023
Dom-muzej K.È. Ciolkovskogo, Kaluga 32875
Gosudarstvennyj Muzej Istorii Aviacii, Sankt-Peterburg 33402
Gosudarstvennyj Muzej Istorii Kosmonavtiki im. K.È. Ciolkovskogo, Kaluga 32877
Memorialnyj Dom-muzej Akademika S.P. Koroleva, Moskva 33074
Memorialnyj Dom-muzej N.E. Žukovskogo, Orechovo 33258
Memorialnyj Muzej Jurija Gagarina, Gagarin 32799
Memorialnyj Muzej Kosmonavtiki, Moskva 33078
Muzej Aviacii Severa, Archangelsk 32652
Muzej K. È. Ciolkovskogo, Aviacii i Kosmonavtiki, Kirov 32921
Naučno-memorialnyj Muzej N.E. Žukovskogo, Moskva 33163

South Africa
Pioneers of Aviation Museum, Kimberley 34292
SAAF Museum Swartkop, Pretoria 34354
SAAF Museum Ysterplaat, Ysterplaat 34406

Spain
Museo Aeronáutico Torreón de Gando, Telde 35522
Museo de Aeronáutica y Astronáutica, Madrid 35015

Sweden
Jämtlands Flyg och Lottamuseum, Östersund 36145
Landskrona Museum, Landskrona 36029
Västerås Flygande Museum, Västerås 36379
Västerås Flygmuseum, Västerås 36380

Switzerland
Flieger-Flab-Museum, Dübendorf 36666
Musée de la Naissance de l'Aviation Suisse, Avenches 36480

United Arab Emirates
Al-Mahatah - Sharjah Aviation Museum, Sharjah 37919

United Kingdom
448th Bomb Group Memorial Museum, Seething 40464
Brenzett Aeronautical Museum, Romney Marsh 40339
Carpetbagger Aviation Museum, Harrington 39167
City of Norwich Aviation Museum, Horsham Saint Faith 39266
Cornwall Aero Park, Helston 39212
Dumfries and Galloway Aviation Museum, Dumfries 38787
Fenland and West Norfolk Aviation Museum, West Walton 40828
Flambards Victorian Village and Gardens, Helston 39213
De Havilland Aircraft Heritage Centre, Saint Albans 40370
The Helicopter Museum, Weston-super-Mare 40834
Imperial War Museum Duxford, Cambridge 38456
Lashenden Air Warfare Museum, Headcorn 39202
Midland Air Museum, Baginton 38055
Military Aviation Museum, Tangmere 40672
Montrose Air Station Museum, Montrose 39982
Museum of Army Flying, Middle Wallop 39945
Museum of Flight, North Berwick 40077
Newark Air Museum, Newark-on-Trent 40021
Norfolk and Suffolk Aviation Museum, Flixton 38997
North East Aircraft Museum, Sunderland 40646
Percy Pilcher Museum, Lutterworth 39847
Royal Air Force Air Defence Radar Museum, Norwich 40098
Royal Air Force Museum, London 39755
Royal Air Force Museum, Shifnal 40499
Royal Air Force Museum 201 Squadron, Saint Peter Port 40426
Royal Air Force Museum Reserve Collection, Stafford 40570
Shoreham Aircraft Museum, Shoreham 40502
Shuttleworth Collection, Old Warden 40127
Solway Aviation Museum, Crosby-on-Eden 38676
Southampton Hall of Aviation, Southampton 40547
Spitfire and Hurricane Memorial Museum, Ramsgate 40284
Thameside Aviation Museum, East Tilbury 38850
Wellington Aviation Museum, Moreton-in-Marsh 39985
Yorkshire Air Museum, Elvington 38932

Uruguay
Museo Aeronáutico, Montevideo 40991

U.S.A.
Air Classic Museum of Aviation, Sugar Grove 47869
Air Force Armament Museum, Eglin Air Force Base 43101
Air Force Flight Test Center Museum, Edwards Air Force Base 43096
Air Heritage Museum of Santa Barbara/Goleta, Goleta 43719
Air Power Park and Museum, Hampton 43894
Air Victory Museum, Medford 45218
Airborne and Special Operations Museum, Fayetteville 43309
Airmen Memorial Museum, Suitland 47872
Airpower Museum, Ottumwa 46221
Alaska Aviation Heritage Museum, Anchorage 41196
Allied Air Force Museum, Allentown 41144
Amelia Earhart Birthplace Museum, Atchison 41314
American Airlines C.R. Smith Museum, Fort Worth 43479
American Airpower Heritage Museum, Midland 45324
American Helicopter Museum Education Center, West Chester 48516
Aviation Museum of Kentucky, Lexington 44737
Bergen Museum of Art and Science, Ho-Ho-Kus 44040
Carolinas Aviation Museum, Charlotte 42237
Castle Air Museum, Atwater 41369
Clark County Museum, Henderson 43990
College Park Aviation Museum, College Park 42524
Combat Air Museum, Topeka 48032
Crawford Auto-Aviation Museum, Cleveland 42470
EAA AirVenture Museum, Oshkosh 46204
Edward H. White II Memorial Museum, Brooks Air Force Base 41957
Empire State Aerosciences Museum, Glenville 43697
Evergreen Aviation Museum, McMinnville 45041
Exploration Station, Bourbonnais 41840
Fargo Air Museum, Fargo 43291
Frontiers of Flight Museum, Dallas 42753
Glenn H. Curtiss Museum, Hammondsport 43888
Grissom Air Museum, Peru 46363
Grumman Memorial Park, Calverton 42036
Hill Aerospace Museum, Hill Air Force Base 44021
Howard W. Cannon Aviation Museum, Henderson 43991
International Sport Aviation Museum, Lakeland 44602
International Women's Air and Space Museum, Cleveland 42475
Intrepid Sea-Air-Space Museum, New York 45818
Iowa Aviation Museum, Greenfield 43804
Kalamazoo Aviation History Museum, Kalamazoo 44378
Kansas Aviation Museum, Wichita 48605
Kansas Cosmosphere and Space Center, Hutchinson 44183
Kirkpatrick Science and Air Space Museum at Omniplex, Oklahoma City 46114
Lone Star Flight Museum/Texas Aviation Hall of Fame, Galveston 43612
Louisiana State Museum, Patterson 46313
March Field Museum, Riverside 46919
May Natural History Museum and Museum of Space Exploration, Colorado Springs 42539
Memphis Belle B17 Flying Fortress, Memphis 45241
Mid-America Air Museum, Liberal 44764
Mid Atlantic Air Museum, Reading 46808
Minnesota Air National Guard Exhibition, Saint Paul 47160
Mitchell Gallery of Flight, Milwaukee 45369
Museum of Aviation at Robins Air Force Base, Warner Robins 48306
Museum of Flight, Seattle 47539
NASA Lewis Research Center's Visitor Center, Cleveland 42476
National Air and Space Museum, Washington 48371
National Model Aviation Museum, Muncie 45558
National Museum of Naval Aviation, Pensacola 46343
National Soaring Museum, Elmira 43171
National Warplane Museum, Horseheads 44105
Neil Armstrong Air and Space Museum, Wapakoneta 48302
New England Air Museum of the Connecticut Aeronautical Historical Association, Windsor Locks 48687
New Mexico Wing-Commemorative Air Force, Hobbs 44044
North Carolina Museum of Life and Science, Durham 43024
Octave Chanute Aerospace Museum, Rantoul 46793
Oregon Air and Space Museum, Eugene 43226
Parker-O'Malley Air Museum, Ghent 43666
Pearson Air Museum, Vancouver 48201
Pima Air and Space Museum, Tucson 48091
Piper Aviation Museum, Lock Haven 44839
Rhinebeck Aerodrome Museum, Rhinebeck 46848
San Diego Aerospace Museum, San Diego 47286
Santa Maria Museum of Flight, Santa Maria 47436
Science Museum of Virginia, Richmond 46886
Smithsonian Institution, Washington 48393
Southern Museum of Flight, Birmingham 41709
Space Center Houston, Houston 44138
Strategic Air Space Museum, Ashland 41291
Texas Air Museum, Rio Hondo 46903
Tillamook Naval Air Station Museum, Tillamook 48009
United States Air Force Museum, Wright-Patterson Air Force Base 48766
United States Space and Rocket Center, Huntsville 44175
Virgil I. Grissom State Memorial, Mitchell 45412
Virginia Air and Space Center, Hampton 43898
Virginia Aviation Museum, Richmond International Airport 46894
Weeks Air Museum, Miami 45293
Western Aerospace Museum, Oakland 46070
Wings of Freedom, Huntington 44158
Wings of History Air Museum, San Martin 47368
Wonder Works Children's Museum, The Dalles 42764
Wright Brothers National Memorial, Kill Devil Hills 44480
Yankee Air Museum, Belleville 41593
Yankee Air Museum, Willow Run Airport 48643

Venezuela
Museo Aeronáutico Colonel Luis Hernan Paredes, Maracay 48952

Vietnam
Air Force Museum, Ha Noi 48970

Baking and Cookery

Australia
Charles Ferguson Museum, Mentone 01244
Miller Bakehouse Museum, Palmyra 01354
Winns Historic Bakehouse Museum, Coromandel Valley 00947

Austria
Bäckermuseum, Wien 02841
Bezirksmuseum Josefstadt, Wien 02860
Brot- und Mühlen-Lehrmuseum, Gloggnitz 01884
Burgenländisches Brotmuseum, Bad Tatzmannsdorf 01718
Österreichisches Getreidemuseum, Wels 02814

Belgium
Bakkerijmuseum, Groot-Bijgaarden 03465
Bakkerijmuseum, Veurne 03811

Canada
Maison J.A. Vachon, Sainte-Marie 06385
Musée de la Cuisine, Drummondville 05344

France
Musée de la Boulangerie, Bonnieux 10799
Musée des Ustensiles de Cuisine Anciens, Saint-Denis-la-Chevasse 14178

Germany
Badisches Bäckereimuseum und Erstes Deutsches Zuckerbäckermuseum, Kraichtal 18216
Bäckerei- und Dorfgeschichtliches Museum, Bremervörde 16347
Bäckereimuseum, Krummhörn 18253
Europäisches Brotmuseum, Ebergötzen 16762
Lebzelterei- und Wachsziehereimuseum, Pfaffenhofen an der Ilm 19382
Museum Alte Pfefferküchlerei, Weißenberg 20491
Museum der Brotkultur, Ulm 20258
Passauer Glasmuseum, Passau 19359

Italy
Museo Agricolo Brunnenburg, Tirolo di Merano 25709

Netherlands
Bakkerijmuseum, Huizen 29454
Bakkerijmuseum De Grenswachter, Luijksgestel 29551
Bakkerijmuseum de Meelzolder, Almelo 28808
Caddy's Diner, Purmerend 29716
Gerrit Valk's Bakkerij- en Ijsmuseum, Hellendoorn 29384
Haardplatenmuseum Klarenbeek, Klarenbeek 29482
Museum Bakkerij Mendels, Middelstum 29597
Nederlands Bakkerijmuseum Het Warme Land, Hattem 29352
Oude Bakkerij, Medemblik 29584
Schilder- en Bakkerijmuseum 't Steenhuis, Niebert 29612

Russia
Muzej Tul'skie Samovary, Tula 33628

Switzerland
La Maison du Blé et du Pain, Echallens 36670
Schweizerisches Gastronomie-Museum, Thun 37243

United Kingdom
Bakelite Museum, Williton 40875
Past Times, Blindley Heath 38260
Sally Lunn's Refreshment House and Kitchen Museum, Bath 38123

Balneology

Austria
Kurmuseum, Bad Tatzmannsdorf 01720

Croatia
Varaždinske Toplice Muzej, Varaždinske Toplice 07798

Czech Republic
Městské Muzeum, Františkovy Lázně 08338
Muzeum Jáchymovského Hornictví a Lázeňství, Jáchymov 08382
Vlastivědné Muzeum Jesenicka, Jeseník 08386
Zlatý Klíč Muzeum, Karlovy Vary 08403

Germany
Bademuseum, Bad Elster 15636
Heimatmuseum, Bad Orb 15712
Historische Kuranlagen und Goethe-Theater Bad Lauchstädt, Bad Lauchstädt 15688
Kur-und Stadtmuseum, Bad Ems 15638
Kurmuseum Bad Wildungen, Bad Wildungen 15763
Museum im Alten Rathaus, Bad Brückenau 15620
Salzmuseum, Bad Sülze 15751
Sebastian-Kneipp-Museum, Bad Wörishofen 15778
Stadt- und Bädermuseum, Bad Salzuflen 15730
Stadt- und Bädermuseum Bad Doberan, Bad Doberan 15625

Slovakia
Balneologické Múzeum, Piešťany 34043

Switzerland
Museum Altes Bad Pfäfers, Bad Ragaz 36482

Banks and Banking

Argentina
Museo Históricos del Banco de la Provincia de Buenos
Aires, Buenos Aires   00219
Museo Numismático del Banco Naciónal, Buenos
Aires   00233

Australia
ANZ Banking Museum, Melbourne   01221
Bank of Victoria Museum, Yackandandah   01621
Banking and Currency Museum, Kadina   01128
Westpac Museum, Sydney   01512

Austria
Sparkassen-Museum der Erste Bank, Wien   02990

Canada
Bank of Montreal Museum, Montréal   05888
Farmers Bank of Rustico, Rustico   06294
Old Bank of New Brunswick Museum, Riverside-
Albert   06276

Denmark
Sparekassemuseet, Korsør   08965

Finland
Bank Museum of Kansallis-Osake-Pankki,
Helsinki   09475
Osuuspankkimuseo, Helsinki   09517

Germany
Sparkassen-Museum, Greding   17382

Haiti
Unité Musée Numismatique, Port-au-Prince   21296

Iran
Money Museum, Teheran   22314
Sekkeh Museum, Teheran   22326

Ireland
The House of Lords, Dublin   22431

Israel
Bank Leumi Museum, Tel Aviv   22747

Japan
Former Hong Kong and Shanghai Bank Museum,
Nagasaki   26545
Sakai House, Osaka   26672

Korea, Republic
Chohung Museum of Finance, Seoul   27225

Mexico
Museo Túenl Casa Parker, Angangueo   27772

Mozambique
Museu Nacional da Moeda, Maputo   28724

Peru
Museo Banco Central de Reserva del Perú,
Lima   31201

Philippines
Museo ng Bangko Sentral ng Pilipinas, Manila   31383

South Africa
ABSA Group Museum, Johannesburg   34266

Spain
Museo Histórico BBVA, Bilbao   34615

Sweden
Gamla Bankgården, Vrigstad   36418

United Kingdom
Savings Banks Museum, Ruthwell   40362

Uruguay
Museos del Gaucho y de la Moneda,
Montevideo   41030

U.S.A.
Farmers Bank, Petersburg   46373
Fleet Boston Financial Gallery, Boston   41807
Higgins Museum, Okoboji   46126
Museum of American Financial History, New
York   45840
Old State Bank, Vincennes   48241
Wells Fargo History Museum, San Diego   47301
Wells Fargo History Museum, San Francisco   47344

Venezuela
Museo de la Moneda, Caracas   48920

Baskets

Germany
Deutsches Korbmuseum, Michelau   18727
Korbmacher-Museum, Malsfeld   18609
Stadtmuseum Lichtenfels, Lichtenfels, Bayern   18457

Netherlands
Nationaal Vlechtmuseum, Noordwolde   29647

Poland
Muzeum Wikliny, Olkusz   31851

U.S.A.
Gatekeeper's Museum and Marion Steinbach Indian
Basket Museum, Tahoe City   47927

Bees

Austria
Bienen- und Wagnereimuseum, Grieskirchen   01942
Heimat- und Bienenzuchtmuseum, Orth an der
Donau   02386
Imkereiausstellung Einst-Jetzt, Reidling   02501
Imkereimuseum, Pöggstall   02426
Imkereimuseum, Pramet   02448

Belgium
Bijenteeltmuseum Kalmthout, Kalmthout   03531

Canada
Musée de l'Abeille, Château-Richer   05235
Musée de l'Abeille, Québec   06203

France
Écomusée de l'Abeille, Grateloup   11924
Écomusée de l'Abeille, Le Faou   12412
Ecomusée la Cité des Abeilles, Saint-Faust   14212
Mesnil aux Abeille, Beautheil   10652
Musée de Miellerie, Saint-Saturnin-les-
Avignon   14464
Musée des Arts et Tradition Apicoles, Fontan   11770
Musée du Miel et de l'Abeille, Gramont   11900
Musée Vivant de l'Abeille, Corbeny   11403
Musée Vivant de l'Apiculture Gâtinaise, Châteaurenard
(Loiret)   11226

Germany
Bienenkundemuseum, Münstertal   18953
Deutsches Bienenmuseum, Weimar, Thüringen   20456
Heimatmuseum und Karl-August-Forster-
Bienenmuseum, Illertissen   17886
Hohberger Bienenmuseum, Hohberg   17802
Imkereigeschichtliche und bienenkundliche
Sammlungen, Celle   16455
Westfälisch-Niederländisches Imkereimuseum,
Gescher   17267
Zeidel-Museum, Feucht   16995

Italy
Mostra Culturale di Apicoltura, Porto Marghera   25013
Museo Apistico Didattico, Bregnano   23196
Museo dell'Apicoltura, Renon   25104
Museo dell'Apicultura, Abbiategrasso   22794
Museo di Apicoltura Guido Fregonese, Piavon di
Oderze   24899
Plattner Bienenhof Museum, Soprabolzano   25605

Netherlands
Bijenteeltmuseum De Bankorf, Amen   28816
Imkerijmuseum Poppendamme, Grijpskerke   29301

Norway
Norges Birøkterlags Museet, Billingstad   30430

Poland
Muzeum im. Jana Dzierzona, Kluczbork   31665
Skansen i Muzeum Pszczelarstwa im prof. Ryszarda
Kosteckiego, Swarzędz   32011
Skansen Kurpiowski im. Adama Chętnika,
Nowogród   31832

Slovenia
Čebelarski Muzej, Radovljica   34142

Switzerland
Bienenmuseum, Alberswil   36443
Imkereimuseum Grüningen, Wetzikon   37312

United Kingdom
IBRA Collection, Cardiff   38480

Bells

Austria
Glockenmuseum der Glockengiesserei,
Innsbruck   02066

Belgium
Klokkenmuseum van de Sint-Martinusbasiliek,
Halle   03468

China, People's Republic
Big Bell Gu Zhon Museum, Beijing   06954

Croatia
Ethnographic Museum of Istria, Pazin   07754

France
Collection de Cloches, Morteau   13172
Musée Campanaire, L'Isle-Jourdain   12627

Germany
Deutsches Glockenmuseum, Greifenstein   17385
Glocken-Museum, Siegen   19948
Glockenmuseum, Apolda   15507
Glockenmuseum, Laucha, Unstrut   18345
Westfälisches Glockenmuseum, Gescher   17268

Netherlands
Klokkengieterijmuseum, Vries   29965
Nationaal Beiaardmuseum, Asten   28954

Russia
Valdajskij Kraevedčeskij Muzej, Valdaj   33673

United Kingdom
Bellfoundry Museum, Loughborough   39828

Biology

Argentina
Museo de Ciencias Naturales, Salta   00539

Austria
Naturkundemuseum Haus der Natur, Salzburg   02545
Weinviertler Naturmuseum, Jetzelsdorf   02088

Belgium
Museum voor de Geschiedenis van de
Wetenschappen, Gent   03445

Brazil
Centro de Biologia Marinha, São Sebastião   04546
Museu de Biodiversidade do Cerrado,
Uberlândia   04575
Museu de Biologia Prof. Mello Leitão, Santa
Teresa   04447

Canada
Earth Sciences Museum, Waterloo   06752
Ontario Science Centre, Toronto   06600
Thomas McCulloch Museum, Halifax   05565

Chile
Museo Nacional de Historia Natural, Santiago de
Chile   06917

China, People's Republic
Beijing Natural History Museum, Beijing   06952

Colombia
Museo del Mar Mundo Marino, Santa Marta   07590

Czech Republic
Lesnické, Myslivecké a Rybářské Muzeum, Hluboká
nad Vltavou   08352
Vlastivědné Muzeum, Nymburk   08512
Východočeské Muzeum, Pardubice   08534

Denmark
Naturhistorisk Museum, Århus   08772

Egypt
Hydrobiological Museum, Alexandria   09239

France
Musée de la la Faune des Pyrénées, Nébias   13277
Petit Musée Minéraux et Faune de l'Alpe, Bourg-
Saint-Maurice   10857

Germany
Anthropologische Staatssammlung, München   18826
Biohistoricum, Neuburg an der Donau   19017
Müritz-Museum, Waren   20399
Museum der Natur und Umwelt Cottbus,
Cottbus   16503
Museum der Westlausitz Kamenz, Kamenz   17979
Museum für Naturkunde, Dortmund   16663
Naturkunde-Museum, Bielefeld   16159
Waldmuseum, Surwold   20130

Iceland
Reðsafn Íslands, Reykjavík   21662

India
Biological Museum, Imphal   21850
Zoology and Botany Museum, Ernakulam   21798

Indonesia
Museum Biologi UGM, Yogyakarta   22218

Iran
Natural History Museum, Hamedan   22242

Iraq
Natural History Museum of the University of Basrah,
Basrah   22349

Israel
Bloomfield Science Museum Jerusalem,
Jerusalem   22626
Man and the Living World Museum, Ramat Gan   22732
Museum of Natural History, Jerusalem   22648

Italy
Casa di Lazzaro Spallanzani, Scandiano   25516
Centro Museo Universitario di Storia Naturale e della
Strumentazione Scientifica, Modena   24433
Gabinetto Geologico e Botanico Piccinini,
Pergola   24841
Museo del Castagno, Pescaglia   24865
Museo della Vita, Castelmagno   23415
Museo di Biologia Marina, Porto Cesareo   25012
Museo di Biologia Marina, Fano   23763

Japan
Hiratsuka-shi Hakubutsukan, Hiratsuka   26208
Human Science Museum, Tokai University,
Shimizu   26749

Jordan
Biology Museum, Amman   27046

Mexico
Museo de Anatomía, México   28123
Museo Estatal de Patología, Puebla   28339

Poland
Muzeum Przyrodnicze Uniwersytetu Łódzkiego,
Łódź   31775
Muzeum Przyrodniczo-Leśne, Białowieża   31485

Romania
Complex Muzeal de Ştiinţele Naturii, Galaţi   32522

Russia
Gosudarstvennyj Biologičeskij Muzej im. K.A.
Timirjazeva, Moskva   33048
Muzei Permskogo Gosudarstvennogo Universiteta,
Perm   33304
Muzej Instituta Biologii Morja, Vladivostok   33704
Muzej Priroda Morja i eë Ochrana, Vladivostok   33707
Novosibirskij Muzej Prirody, Novosibirsk   33243
Zoologičeskij Muzej, Vladivostok   33713

Serbia-Montenegro
Senčanski Muzej, Senta   33903

South Africa
Sea World, Durban   34232

Sweden
Biologiska Museet, Örebro   36133
Biologiska Museet, Södertälje   36210
Biologiska Museet, Uppsala   36350
Biologiska Museet, Stockholm   36235

Switzerland
Museum der Anthropologie, Zürich   37396

Turkey
Afyon Etnografya Müzesi, Afyon   37603

United Kingdom
Biological Sciences Collection, Birmingham   38212
Down House, Downe   38771
Hawthorns Urban Wildlife Centre, Southampton   40544

U.S.A.
Alaska Museum of Natural History, Eagle River   43034
The Benjamin Banneker Museum, Baltimore   41459
New York State Museum, Albany   41085
Regional Science and Discovery Center,
Horseheads   44106

Birds

Argentina
Museo Ornitológico Patagónico, El Bolsón   00334

Australia
Murtoa Water Tower - Concordia Collage Museum,
Murtoa   01293

Austria
Mühlviertler Vogelkundeweg, Gutau   01977
Naturmuseum, Neuberg an der Mürz   02341
Seevogel-Museum Neusiedlersee, Rust,
Burgenland   02528
Vogelmuseum-Die Vogelwelt des Böhmerwaldes,
Aigen im Mühlkreis   01650

Belgium
Musée d'Histoire Naturelle de Mons, Mons   03634
Natuurpunt Museum, Turnhout   03804

Brazil
Museu Anchieta Ciencias Naturais, Porto
Alegre   04274
Museu da Fauna, Rio de Janeiro   04345
Museu de Ornitologia, Goiânia   04110

Bulgaria
Prirodonaučen Muzej, Burgas   04636
Prirodonaučen Muzej, Černi Osăm   04638

Canada
Birdtail Country Museum, Birtle   05082
Musée du Séminaire de Saint-Hyacinthe, Saint-
Hyacinthe   06322

Colombia
Museo de Historia Natural, Popayán   07564

Cuba
Museo de Historia Natural Felipe Poey, La
Habana   07960

Czech Republic
Zámek Budišov, Budišov u Třebíče   08284

Denmark
Zoologisk Museum, Grindsted   08845

Egypt
Entomological Society Museum, Cairo 09263
Ornithology and Entomology Museum, Cairo 09282

Finland
K.E. Kivirikon Lintu- ja Nisäkäskokoelma, Helsinki 09500

France
Ecomusée de la Brenne, Le Blanc 12380
Musée d'Allard, Montbrison 13062
Musée d'Histoire Naturelle, Nantes 13257
Musée d'Histoire Naturelle de Toulon, Toulon (Var) 14928
Musée d'Histore Naturelle Victor-Brun, Montauban 13047
Musée Joseph Abeilhe, Marciac 12808
Muséum d'Histoire Naturelle, Le Havre 12428

Germany
Harzer Roller-Kanarien-Museum, Sankt Andreasberg 19744
Heimatstube Cumlosen, Cumlosen 16517
Institut für Vogelforschung -Vogelwarte Helgoland, Wilhelmshaven 20593
Museum für Jagdtier- und Vogelkunde des Erzgebirges, Augustusburg 15573
Museum Heineanum, Halberstadt 17502
Natureum Niederelbe, Balje 15801
Naturkundliches Museum in der Harmonie, Schweinfurt 19893
Naumann-Museum, Köthen, Anhalt 18191
Norddeutsches Vogelmuseum, Osterholz-Scharmbeck 19295
Schloßmuseum Hohenlohe-Schillingsfürst, Schillingsfürst 19780
Staatliches Naturhistorisches Museum, Braunschweig 16304
Vogelmuseum, Waging 20344
Waldmuseum Wassermühle, Wingst 20608

Italy
Museo Civico di Scienze Naturali E. Caffi, Bergamo 23062
Museo Civico Ornitologico, Lonato 24206
Museo Civico Ornitologico e di Scienze Naturali Luigi Scanagatta, Varenna 25894
Museo di Scienze Naturali, Brescia 23205
Museo Geopaleontologico Naturalistico Antropico e Ornitologico Brancaleoni, Piobbico 24934
Museo Ornitologico, Poppi 25005
Museo Ornitologico, San Gimignano 25366
Museo Ornitologico C. Beni, Stia 25635
Museo Ornitologico Naturalistico S. Bambini, Pietralunga 24910
Museo Ornitologico U. Foschi, Forlì 23915
Museo Provinciale di Storia Naturale, Foggia 23895
Museo Provinciale di Storia Naturale, Livorno 24194
Raccolta Ornitologica F. Stazza, Tempio Pausania 25684

Japan
Shiretoko Museum, Shari 26742

Mexico
Museo de las Aves de México, Saltillo 28366
Museo de Pericos, Culiacán 27883

Netherlands
Natuurdiorama Holterberg, Holten 29433
Natuurhistorisch en Volkenkundig Museum, Oudenbosch 29697
Natuurmuseum Dokkum, Dokkum 29163
Natuurmuseum Rotterdam, Rotterdam 29766

New Zealand
Whanganui Regional Museum, Wanganui 30286

Panama
Museo de Historia Natural, Panamá City 31084

Poland
Jacek Malczewski Muzeum, Radom 31938
Muzeum Lasu i Drewna przy Lesnym Zakładzie Doświadczalnym SGGW, Rogów 31949

Romania
Muzeul Național de Istorie Naturala Grigore Antipa, București 32468

Russia
Zoologičeskij Muzej, Vladivostok 33713

Slovenia
Prirodoslovni Muzej Slovenije, Ljubljana 34118

Sudan
Sudan Natural History Museum, Khartoum 35770

Sweden
Fågelmuseet, Jönköping 35975
Ottenby Naturum, Degerhamn 35852

Switzerland
Museum Stemmler, Schaffhausen 37131

United Kingdom
Aberdeen University Natural History Museum, Aberdeen 37932
Ayscoughfee Hall Museum, Spalding 40562
Booth Museum of Natural History, Brighton 38338
Dunrobin Castle Museum, Golspie 39091
Natural History Museum, Tring 40727
Woodland Heritage Museum, Westbury 40831

U.S.A.
Birds of Vermont Museum, Huntington 44163
Carrie Weedon Natural Science Museum, Galesville 43600
Connecticut Audubon Birdcraft Museum, Fairfield 43263
Historical and Natural History Museum of Natick, South Natick 47699
International Crane Foundation Museum, Baraboo 41501
John James Audubon Museum, Henderson 43988
World of Wings Pigeon Center Museum, Oklahoma City 46123

Venezuela
Colección Ornitológica W.H. Phelps, Caracas 48901
Museo Ornitológico, Aragua 48887

Boats and Shipping

Argentina
Buque-Museo Fragata Presidente Sarmiento, Buenos Aires 00144
Museo Histórico de la Prefectura Naval Argentina, Tigre 00633
Museo Marítimo de Ushuaia y Presidio, Ushuaia 00650
Museo Marítimo y Naval de la Patagonia Austral, Río Gallegos 00516
Museo Naval de la Nación, Tigre 00634

Australia
Australian National Maritime Museum, Sydney 01493
Axel Stenross Maritime Museum, Port Lincoln 01383
Customs House Nautical Museum, Robe 01418
Devonport Maritime Museum, Devonport 00978
Geelong Naval and Maritime Museum, North Geelong 01325
Gladstone Maritime Museum, Gladstone, Queensland 01054
Golden City Paddle Steamer Museum, Ballarat 00764
HMAS Castlemaine - Museum Ship, Williamstown 01600
HMS Buffalo, Glenelg 01059
Lady Denman Maritime Museum, Huskisson 01116
Maritime Museum, Low Head 01188
Maritime Museum, Port Victoria 01388
Maritime Museum of Tasmania, Hobart 01099
Maritime Museum of Townsville, Townsville 01545
Naval and Maritime Museum, Ballina 00766
Newcastle Region Maritime Museum, Newcastle 01317
Penneshaw Maritime and Folk Museum, Penneshaw 01361
Pine Islet Lighthouse, Mackay 01193
Polly Woodside Melbourne Maritime Museum, Southbank 01465
Port Albert Maritime Museum, Port Albert 01377
Port Fairy Historic Lifeboat Station, Port Fairy 01381
Port MacDonnell and District Maritime Museum, Port MacDonnell 01385
Port Victoria National Trust Museum, Port Victoria 01389
Portland Maritime Discovery Centre, Portland 01392
P.S. Industry Museum, Renmark 01413
Queenscliffe Maritime Museum, Queenscliff 01402
Queensland Maritime Museum, South Brisbane 01460
Shipwreck Museum, Cairns 00874
South Australian Maritime Museum, Port Adelaide 01376
Sydney Heritage Fleet, Pyrmont 01398
Treasure Trove Shipwreck Museum, Port Douglas 01380
Western Australian Maritime Museum, Fremantle 01038
Western Australian Museum Geraldton, Geraldton 01049
Whyalla Maritime Museum, Whyalla 01597
Williamstown Historical Museum, Williamstown 01601

Austria
Oberösterreichisches Schiffahrtsmuseum, Grein an der Donau 01938
Schiffahrtsmuseum, Spitz 02671
Schiffleutmuseum, Stadl-Paura 02672

Belgium
Les Ascenceurs du Calal Historique du Centre, Houdeng-Aimeries 03504
Museum Rijn- en Binnenvaart, Antwerpen 03153
Nationaal Scheepvaartmuseum, Antwerpen 03161
Scheepvaartmuseum, Bornem 03230

Belize
Belize Maritime Terminal and Museum, Belize City 03864

Bermuda
Bermuda Maritime Museum, Mangrove Bay 03885
Bermuda National Trust Museum, Saint George's 03886

Brazil
Espaço Cultural da Marinha, Rio de Janeiro 04323
Museu da Escola Naval, Rio de Janeiro 04343
Museu de Pesca, Santos 04454
Museu Naval e Oceanográfico, Rio de Janeiro 04390

Bulgaria
Archeologičeski Muzej, Burgas 04631
Muzej na Morskoto Stopanstvo, Varna 04899
Nacionalen Voenno-morski Muzej, Varna 04904

Canada
Archelaus Smith Museum, Cape Sable Island 05197
Atlantic Statiquarium Marine Museum, Louisbourg 05781
Britannia Heritage Shipyard, Richmond 06260
Campbell River Optical Maritime Museum, Campbell River 05188
CFB Esquimalt Naval Museum and Military Museum, Victoria 06717
Collingwood Museum, Collingwood 05267
Cowichan Bay Maritime Centre, Cowichan Bay 05284
Green Park Shipbuilding Museum and Yeo House, Port Hill 06164
Gulf Museum, Port-aux-Basques 06153
HMCS Sackville, Halifax 05554
LaHave Islands Marine Museum, LaHave 05718
Lawrence House Museum, Maitland 05802
Marine Museum of Manitoba, Selkirk 06420
Marine Museum of Upper Canada, Toronto 06591
Mariners' Park Museum, Milford 05850
Maritime Command Museum, Halifax 05555
Maritime Museum of British Columbia, Victoria 06725
Maritime Museum of the Atlantic, Halifax 05556
Musée de la Mer, Havre-Aubert 05589
Musée de la Mer, Iles-de-la-Madeleine 05613
Musée de la Mer de Rimouski, Pointe-au-Père 06142
Musée du Navigateur Flottant, Saint-Joseph-de-Sorel 06356
Musée du Vieux-Phare, Matane 05822
Musée Maritime du Québec, L'Islet 05757
Muskoka Lakes Museum, Port Carling 06155
Nancy Island Historic Site, Wasaga Beach 06745
Naval Museum of Alberta, Calgary 05175
The Ned Shed Museum, Meldrum Bay 05834
Owen Sound Marine and Rail Museum, Owen Sound 06089
Pointe-Noire - Parc Marin du Saguenay, Baie-Sainte-Catherine 05036
Port Colborne Historical and Marine Museum, Port Colborne 06158
Quaco Museum and Archives, Saint Martins 06366
Saint Mary's River Marine Centre, Sault Sainte Marie 06412
Samson V Maritime Museum, New Westminster 05986
Segwun Heritage Centre, Gravenhurst 05526
Site-Historique du Banc-de-Paspébiac, Paspébiac 06099
Southern Newfoundland Seamen's Museum, Grand Bank 05508
Trinity Museum, Trinity 06636
Vancouver Maritime Museum, Vancouver 06695
Vancouver Naval Museum, West Vancouver 06774
Voyageur Heritage Centre, Mattawa 05825
West Coast Maritime Museum, Tofino 06555
William D. Lawrence House, Halifax 05566
Yarmouth County Museum, Yarmouth 06869

Chile
Museo Naval de Viña del Mar, Viña del Mar 06932

China, People's Republic
Maritime Museum of Macau, Macau 07165
PLA Naval Museum, Qingdao 07202
Quanzhou Maritime Museum, Quanzhou 07206

Croatia
Orebić Maritime Museum, Orebić 07749
Pomorski i Povijesni Muzej Hrvatskog Primorja, Rijeka 07763
Pomorski Muzej, Zadar 07807
Pomorski Muzej, Dubrovnik 07700
Zavičajni Muzej, Baška 07677

Cuba
Museo Histórico Naval, Cienfuegos 07892

Denmark
Aabenraa Museum, Aabenraa 08760
Flaske-Peters-Samling, Ærøskøbing 08765
Fregatten Jylland, Ebeltoft 08802
Handels- og Søfartsmuseet paa Kronborg, Helsingør 08861
Ladbyskibsmuseet, Kerteminde 08916
Limfjordsmuseet, Løgstør 08975
Marstal Søfartsmuseum, Marstal 08983
Orlogsmuseet, København 08946
Skagen By- og Egnsmuseum, Skagen 09057
Søfarts og Fiskerimuseet, Læsø 08969
Søfartssamlingerne i Troense, Svendborg 09086
Strandingsmuseum St. George, Ulfborg 09096
Vikingeskibsmuseet, Roskilde 09046

Egypt
National Maritime Museum, Alexandria 09245
Solar Boats Museum, Giza 09297

Estonia
Eesti Meremuuseum, Tallinn 09360

Finland
Ålands Sjöfartsmuseum, Mariehamn 09816
Ehrensvärd-Museo, Helsinki 09479
Forum Marinum, Turku 10120
Jakobstads Museum, Jakobstad 09573
K.H. Renlundin Museo, Kokkola 09683
Kymenlaakson maakuntamuseo, Kotka 09700
Raahen Museo, Raahe 09972
Rauman Museo, Rauma 09983
Sjöfartsmuseet, Kristiinankaupunki 09710
Sjöhistoriska Institutet vid Åbo Akademi, Turku 10128
Suomen Joutsen, Turku 10129
Suomen Merimuseo, Helsinki 09532
Uudenkaupungin Kultuurihistoriallinen Museo, Uusikaupunki 10155

France
Aquarium-Musée de la Mer, Dinard 11536
Château-Musée de Dieppe, Dieppe 11507
Ecomusée de Saint-Nazaire, Saint-Nazaire (Loire-Atlantique) 14380
L'Écomusée la Maison de l'Islandais, Gravelines 11928
Espace Maritime et Portuaire des Docks Vauban, Le Havre 12423
Maison du Patrimoine Maritime, Camaret-sur-Mer 11006
Musée à Flot de l'Escorteur d'Escadre, Nantes 13250
Musée d'Aquitaine, Bordeaux 10809
Musée d'Art Populaire Régional, Nantes 13251
Musée de la Batellerie, Conflans-Sainte-Honorine 11392
Musée de la Batellerie de l'Ouest, Redon 13919
Musée de la Construction Navale, Noirmoutier-en-l'Ile 13357
Musée de la Marine, Saint-Brévin-les-Pins 14130
Musée de la Marine de la Seine, Caudebec-en-Caux 11088
Musée de la Marine de Loire, Châteauneuf-sur-Loire 11221
Musée de la Marine et de l'Économie de Marseille, Marseille 12856
Musée de la Mer, Paimpol 13452
Musée de la Mer OCEAM, Les Sables-d'Olonne 12554
Musée de la Vilaine Maritime, La Roche-Bernard 12227
Musée des Mariniers du Rhône, Serrières 14724
Musée des Terre-Neuvas et de la Pêche, Fécamp 11712
Musée d'Histoire de la Ville et d'Ethnographie du Pays Malouin, Saint-Malo (Ille-et-Vilaine) 14341
Musée du Bateau, Douarnenez 11561
Musée du Canal de Berry, Audes-Reugny 10476
Musée Ernest Cognacq, Saint-Martin-de-Ré 14351
Musée Flottant-Architecture Navale, Audierne 10478
Musée Français des Phares et Balises, Ile-d'Ouessant 12052
Musée International du Long Cours Cap Hornier, Saint-Malo (Ille-et-Vilaine) 14342
Musée la Maison du Pêcheur et "Le Hope", Saint-Gilles-Croix-de-Vie 14251
Musée Maritime, Camaret-sur-Mer 11007
Musée Maritime, Le Mont-Saint-Michel 12456
Musée Maritime l'Esvale et Ostréicole, La Tremblade 12269
Musée National de la Marine, Brest 10913
Musée National de la Marine, Paris 13631
Musée National de la Marine, Port-Louis 13843
Musée National de la Marine, Rochefort (Charente-Maritime) 14000
Musée National de la Marine, Saint-Tropez 14493
Musée National de la Marine, Toulon (Var) 14933
Musée Naval de Nice, Nice 13323
Musée Naval de Sarcelles, Sarcelles 14607
Musée Naval Fort Balaguier, La Seyne-sur-Mer 12262
Naviscope Alsace, Strasbourg 14839
Le Port-Musée, Douarnenez 11562

French Polynesia
Musée de Marine, Faranui 15343

Germany
Altes Hafenamt, Dortmund 16656
Altonaer Museum in Hamburg, Hamburg 17527
Atrium an der Schleuse, Brunsbüttel 16382
Binnenschifffahrts-Museum Oderberg, Oderberg, Mark 19221
Buddelschiff-Museum, Wedel 20413
Deutsches Schiffahrtsmuseum, Bremerhaven 16339
Deutsches Sielhafenmuseum in Carolinensiel, Wittmund 20629
Donau-Schiffahrts-Museum-Regensburg, Regensburg 19520
Elbschiffahrtsmuseum mit stadtgeschichtlicher Sammlung, Lauenburg 18350
Fehn- und Schiffahrtsmuseum, Rhauderfehn 19583
Flensburger Schiffahrtsmuseum und Rum-Museum, Flensburg 17011
Heimat- und Schiffahrtsmuseum, Heinsen 17698
Heimatmuseum Haus Morgensonne, Ostseebad Zingst 19319
Informationszentrum am Wasserstraßenkreuz Minden, Minden, Westfalen 18748
Inselmuseum im Alten Leuchtturm, Wangerooge 20397
Kapitän Tadsen Museum, Langeneß 18335
Kieler Stadt- und Schiffahrtsmuseum, Kiel 18074
Klepper Museum, Rosenheim 19652
Küstenmuseum, Juist 17968
Museum der Deutschen Binnenschifffahrt Duisburg-Ruhrort, Duisburg 16752
Museum der Seefahrt, Geiselhöring 17215
Museum für Antike Schiffahrt des Römisch-Germanischen Zentralmuseums, Mainz 18604

Museumsfeuerschiff Amrumbank/Deutsche Bucht, Emden 16848
Museumslogger AE7 Stadt Emden, Emden 16849
Museumsschiff Mannheim des Landesmuseums für Technik und Arbeit, Mannheim 18614
Museumsschiff STÖR, Holzminden 17830
Neckarschiffahrts-Museum und Weinbau, Stadt- und Industriegeschichte, Heilbronn 17690
Prignitz-Museum Havelberg, Havelberg 17650
Rhein-Museum Koblenz, Koblenz 18123
Rheinmuseum, Emmerich 16861
Schiffahrts- und Schiffbaumuseum, Wörth am Main 20643
Schiffahrtsmuseum auf dem Traditionsschiff, Rostock 19667
Schiffahrtsmuseum der Oldenburgischen Weserhäfen, Brake, Unterweser 16271
Schiffahrtsmuseum mit Nordseeaquarium Nordseeheilbad Langeoog, Langeoog 18339
Schiffahrtsmuseum Nordfriesland, Husum, Nordsee 17871
Schifffahrt Museum, Düsseldorf 16742
Schifffahrtsmuseum Haren (Ems), Haren 17619
Schiffsmuseum Seitenradschleppdampfer "Württemberg", Magdeburg 18587
Stadtgeschichtliches Museum, Tangermünde 20140
Technikmuseum U-Boot "Wilhelm Bauer", Bremerhaven 16344
Torfschiffwerftmuseum, Worpswede 20686
Westfälisches Industriemuseum, Waltrop 20388
Wrackmuseum, Cuxhaven 16521

Greece
Aegean Maritime Museum, Mykonos 21076
Maritime Museum of Andros, Andros 20823
Maritime Museum of Thera (Santorini), Oia 21101
Maritime Tradition Museum, Piraeus 21121
Museum of the Merchant Marine, Piraeus 21123
Nautical Museum of Crete, Chania 20919
Nautical Museum of Galaxidi, Galaxidi 20961
Nautikon Mouseiontis Ellados, Piraeus 21124
Oinoussian Maritime Museum, Oinoussai 21102

Iceland
Sjóminja- og Vélsmiðjusafn, Reykjavík 21666
Sjóminjasafn Austurlands, Eskifjörður 21630
Sjóminjasafn Islands, Hafnarfjörður 21637
Sjóminjasafnid á Eyrarbakka, Eyrarbakki 21632

Indonesia
Museum Tni A.L. Loka Jala Carana, Surabaya 22201

Ireland
1796 Bantry French Armada Exhibition Centre, Bantry 22374
Arklow Maritime Museum, Arklow 22361
Cape Clear Heritage Centre, Skibbereen 22539
Kilmore Quay Maritime Museum, Kilmore Quay 22495
Kilmore Quay Maritime Museum, Wexford 22559
National Maritime Museum of Ireland, Dun Laoghaire 22462
Waterways Visitor Centre, Dublin 22457

Italy
Civico Museo del Mare, Trieste 25811
Galleria Storica del Lloyd Triestino, Trieste 25822
Museo Civico Marinaro Gio-Bono Ferrari, Camogli 23295
Museo dei Navigli, Milano 24391
Museo della Barca Lariana, Pianello del Lario 24898
Museo della Marineria dell'Alto e Medio Adriatico, Cesenatico 23511
Museo delle Navi e Antiche Carte Geografiche, Bologna 23119
Museo delle Navi Romane, Fiumicino 23889
Museo delle Navi Romane, Nemi 24613
Museo dello Sbarco, Anzio 22899
Museo dello Sbarco Alleato, Nettuno 24617
Museo Navale, Genova 24006
Museo Navale, Napoli 24601
Museo Navale Didattico, Milano 24407
Museo Navale Internazionale del Ponente Ligure, Imperia 24095
Museo Navale O. Zibetti, Caravaggio 23343
Museo Storico della Brigata Sassari, Sassari 25489
Museo Storico Navale, Venezia 25944
Museo Tecnico Navale, La Spezia 24125
Piccolo Museo Navale, Laives 24129
Raccolta di Ingegneria Navale, Genova 24012

Jamaica
Fort Charles Maritime Museum, Kingston 26066

Japan
Fune no Kagakukan, Tokyo 26847
Kobe Maritime Museum, Kobe 26349
Marine Transportation Museum, Ogi 26617
Naniwa-no Umino Jikukan, Osaka 26658
Tokai Daigaku Kaiyo Kagaku Hakubutsukan, Shizuoka 26769
Yokohama Maritime Museum and Nippon-Maru Memorial Park, Yokohama 27025

Korea, Republic
National Maritime Museum, Mokpo 27212
Naval Academy Museum, Jinhae 27201

Malaysia
Maritime Archaeology Museum, Melaka 27664
Maritime Museum, Melaka 27665
Muzium Tentera Laut Diraja Malaysia, Melaka 27674

Malta
Maritime Museum, Vittoriosa 27713
Wickman Maritime Collection, Zabbar 27717

Mexico
Museo Histórico Naval Central, México 28176
Museo Marino de Tecolutla, Tecolutla 28468
Museo Pablo Bush Romero, Puerto Aventura 28347

Monaco
Musée Naval, Monaco 28670

Netherlands
Batavia-Werf, Lelystad 29530
Droogdok Jan Blanken, Hellevoetsluis 29389
Fries Scheepvaart Museum, Sneek 29838
Gemeentemuseum Het Hannemahuis, Harlingen 29345
Het Havenmuseum, Rotterdam 29750
Maas- en Scheepvaartmuseum, Maasbracht 29559
Marinemuseum, Den Helder 29134
Maritiem en Jutters Museum, Oudeschild 29701
Maritiem Museum Rotterdam, Rotterdam 29758
Maritime Museum Zierikzee, Zierikzee 30060
Minischeepvaartmuseum, Ouwerkerk 29704
Museum de Verzamelaar, Zuidhorn 30069
Museum Nanning Hendrik Bulthuis, Leeuwarden 29512
Museumhaven Zeeland, Zierikzee 30061
Museumwerf 't Kromhout, Amsterdam 28883
Nationaal Reddingmuseum Dorus Rijkers, Den Helder 29136
Nationaal Scheephistorisch Centrum, Leylstad 29538
Nationaal Sleepvaartmuseum, Maassluis 29563
Nederlands Scheepvaartmuseum, Amsterdam 28888
Noordelijk Scheepvaartmuseum, Groningen 29315
Open Haven Museum, Amsterdam 28891
Oudheidkamer Nederlandse Kaap-Hoornvaarders, Hoorn 29444
Prins Hendrik de Zeevaarder Museum, Egmond aan Zee 29205
Scheepswerf De Delft, Rotterdam 29774
Scheepvaartmuseum, Gasselternijveen 29264
Zeeuws Maritiem Muzeeum, Vlissingen 29956
Zompenmuseum, Enter 29245

New Zealand
Bluff Maritime Museum, Bluff 30118
Museum of Wellington, City and Sea, Wellington 30299
New Zealand National Maritime Museum, Auckland 30115
Whanganui Riverboat Centre Museum, Wanganui 30287
Whangaroa County Museum, Kaeo 30187

Norway
Ålesunds Museum, Ålesund 30374
Berg-Kragerø Museum, Kragerø 30609
Bergens Sjøfartsmuseum, Bergen 30417
Frammuseet, Oslo 30734
Hurtigrutemuseet, Stokmarknes 30898
Ishavsmuseet Aarvak, Brandal 30448
Kystmuseet Hvaler, Vesterøy 30988
Kystmuseet i Sogn og Fjordane, Florø 30497
Larvik Sjøfartsmuseum, Larvik 30632
Lillesand By-og Sjøfartsmuseum, Lillesand 30644
Marinemuseet, Horten 30565
Mellemværftet, Kristiansund 30617
Museet Kystens Arv, Stadsbygd 30874
Nordnorsk Fartøyvernsenter og Båtmuseum, Gratangen 30517
Norsk Sjøfartsmuseum, Oslo 30752
Sandefjord Sjøfartsmuseum, Sandefjord 30824
Sjøfartsmuseet i Porsgrunn, Porsgrunn 30781
Skaalurensamlinga - Skipsbyggingsmuseet i Rosendal, Rosendal 30810
Stavanger Maritime Museum, Stavanger 30889
Sunnmøre Museum, Ålesund 30375
Svelvik Museum, Svelvik 30910
Vikingskiphuset, Oslo 30771

Peru
Buque Museo Yaraví, Puerto de Puno 31242
Museo de la Fuerza de Submarinos, Callao 31132
Museo Naval de Ilo, Ilo 31183
Museo Naval del Perú, Callao 31135

Philippines
Philippine Navy Museum, Cavite 31305

Poland
Centralne Muzeum Morskie, Gdańsk 31563
Muzeum Marynarki Wojennej, Gdynia 31585
Muzeum Okręt Błyskawica, Gdynia 31588
Muzeum Żuraw, Gdańsk 31579

Portugal
Colecção Maritima do Comandante Ramalho Ortigão, Faro 32270
Museu de Marinha, Lisboa 32298
Museu Municipal, Alcochete 32231

Russia
Centralnyj Voenno-morskoj Muzej, Sankt-Peterburg 33388
Gosudarstvennyj Severnyj Morskoj Muzej, Archangelsk 32651
Istoričeskaja Usadba Botik Petra I, Veskovo 33684
Kamčatskij Voenno-istoričeskij Muzej, Petropavlovsk-Kamčatskij 33311
Memorialnaja Gvardejskaja Krasnoznamënnaja Podvodnaja Lodka S-56 1939 g., Vladivostok 33699
Morskoj Muzej, Petrozavodsk 33317
Muzej AO Petrozavod, Sankt-Peterburg 33428
Muzej Istorii Dal'nevostočnoj Morskoj Akademii im. G.I. Nevel'skogo, Vladivostok 33705
Muzej-ledokol Angara, Irkutsk 32819
Muzej-ledokol Bajkal, Angarsk 32643
Muzej Morskogo Flota, Moskva 33134
Muzej Morskogo Flota Dal'nevostočnogo Morskogo Parochodstva, Vladivostok 33706
Muzej Rečnogo Flota, Nižnij Novgorod 33220
Storoževoj Korabl' 'Krasnyj Vympel' 1911 g., Vladivostok 33710
Voenno-istoričeskij Muzej Tichookeanskogo Flota, Vladivostok 33712
Voenno-morskoj Muzej Severnogo Flota, Murmansk 33191

Serbia-Montenegro
Muzej Rečnog Brodarstva, Beograd 33811
Pomorski Muzej Crne Gore, Kotor 33848

Singapore
Maritime Museum, Singapore 33939

Slovenia
Pomorski Muzej Sergej Mašera, Piran 34138

South Africa
Bartolomeu Dias Museum Complex, Mossel Bay 34311
Old Harbour Museum, Hermanus 34262
Port Natal Maritime Museum, Durban 34231
Shipwreck Museum, Bredasdorp 34195
Simon's Town Museum, Simon's Town 34376
South African Maritime Museum, Cape Town 34212

Spain
Archivo-Museo Don Alvaro de Bazán, Viso del Marqués 35693
Museo del Mar, Santa Pola 35428
Museo Marítimo de Asturias, Luanco 34984
Museo Marítimo del Cantábrico, Santander 35432
Museo Marítimo Torre del Oro, Sevilla 35488
Museo Massó, Bueu 34625
Museo Naval, Madrid 35049
Museu de Curiositats Marineres, Vilanova i la Geltrú 35665
Museu Marítim de Barcelona, Barcelona 34583
Untzi Museoa - Museo Naval, Donostia-San Sebastián 34780

Sri Lanka
National Maritime Museum, Galle 35755

Sweden
Dalälvarnas Flottningsmuseum, Sandviken 36178
Dyvelstens Flottningsmuseum, Forshaga 35892
Eldnäset Flottningsmuseum, Ånge 35803
Fartygsmuseet, Göteborg 35911
Holmöns Båtmuseum, Holmön 35961
Kalmar Sjöfartsmuseum, Kalmar 35989
Kanalmuseet, Trollhättan 36336
Marinmuseum, Karlskrona 35999
Museum för Utombordsmotorer, Varberg 36396
Råå Museum för Fiske och Sjöfart, Råå 36158
Roslagens Sjöfartsmuseum, Väddö 36371
Sjöfartmuseet, Oskarshamn 36154
Sjöfartsmuseet, Göteborg 35920
Sjöhistoriska Museet, Stockholm 36280
Skärgårdsmuseet, Stavsnäs 36227
Sveriges Sjömanshusmuseum, Uddevalla 36343
Teknikens och Sjöfartens Hus, Malmö 36080
Torekovs Sjöfartsmuseum, Torekov 36327
Vänermuseet, Lidköping 36035
Vasamuseet, Stockholm 36298
Vikens Sjöfartsmuseum, Viken 36409

Switzerland
Musée des Traditions et des Barques du Léman, Saint-Gingolph 37085

Thailand
Royal Barges National Museum, Bangkok 37494

United Kingdom
Aberdeen Maritime Museum, Aberdeen 37931
Arctic Corsair, Kingston-upon-Hull 39375
Barmouth Sailors' Institute Collection, Barmouth 38084
Bembridge Maritime Museum and Shipwreck Centre, Bembridge 38162
Birchills Canal Museum, Walsall 40771
Boat Museum, Ellesmere Port 38926
Bridlington Harbour Museum, Bridlington 38328
Buckler's Hard Village Maritime Museum, Buckler's Hard 38388
Caernarfon Maritime Museum, Caernarfon 38432
Canal Museum, Linlithgow 39505
Canal Museum, Llangollen 39552
Canal Museum, Stoke Bruerne 40602
Castle Cornet Military and Maritime Museums, Saint Peter Port 40422
Charlestown Shipwreck and Heritage Centre, Saint Austell 40389
Clipper Ship Cutty Sark, London 39611
Clydebank Museum, Clydebank 38593
Clydebuilt, Glasgow 39041
Cowes Maritime Museum, Cowes 38649
Deal Maritime and Local History Museum, Deal 38709
Denny Ship Model Experiment Tank, Dumbarton 38785
Dock Museum, Barrow-in-Furness 38095
Dolphin Sailing Barge Museum, Sittingbourne 40521
Fort Grey and Shipwreck Museum, Saint Peter Port 40423
Foxton Canal Museum, Foxton 39012
Frigate Unicorn, Dundee 38799
Harbour Museum, Londonderry 39816
Hartland Quay Museum, Bideford 38192
Hartland Quay Museum, Hartland 39174
Harwich Maritime Museum and Harwich Lifeboat Museum, Harwich 39179
Historic Dockyard Chatham, Chatham 38529
HMS Belfast, London 39665
HMS Trincomalee, Hartlepool 39176
HMS Victory, Portsmouth 40253
HMS Warrior 1860, Portsmouth 40254
Holyhead Maritime Museum, Holyhead 39257
House of Manannan, Peel 40167
Hovercraft Museum, Gosport 39100
Hull Maritime Museum, Kingston-upon-Hull 39380
Inveraray Maritime Museum, Inveraray 39296
John Paul Jones Birthplace Museum, Arbigland 38008
Lancaster Maritime Museum, Lancaster 39415
Local and Maritime Museum, Newhaven 40045
London Canal Museum, London 39694
Lowestoft and East Suffolk Maritime Museum, Lowestoft 39838
McLean Museum and Art Gallery, Greenock 39131
Maritime and Industrial Museum, Swansea 40659
Maritime Heritage Exhibition, Yarmouth 40951
Maritime Museum, Ramsgate 40281
Mary Rose Museum, Portsmouth 40255
Maryport Maritime Museum, Maryport 39918
Merseyside Maritime Museum, Liverpool 39522
The Motorboat Museum, Basildon 38099
Museum of Hartlepool, Hartlepool 39177
National Coracle Centre, Cenarth 38517
National Maritime Museum, London 39731
National Maritime Museum Cornwell, Falmouth 38973
National Waterways Museum, Gloucester 39083
Nautical Museum, Castletown 38508
North Carr Lightship, Dundee 38802
North Devon Maritime Museum, Appledore, Devon 38007
Old Lifeboat Museum, Poole 40227
Porthmadog Maritime Museum, Porthmadog 40242
Royal National Lifeboat Institution Headquarters Museum, Poole 40228
Royal Naval Patrol Service Association Museum, Lowestoft 39840
Royal Research Ship Discovery, Dundee 38804
Salcombe Maritime Museum, Salcombe 40428
Scottish Maritime Museum, Irvine 39312
Shamrock and Cotehele Quay Museum, Saint Dominick 40394
Shipwreck Heritage Centre, Hastings 39186
Southampton Maritime Museum, Southampton 40548
Southend Pier Museum, Southend-on-Sea 40556
Spurn Lightship, Kingston-upon-Hull 39382
SS Great Britain Museum, Bristol 38360
Steamboat Museum, Bowness-on-Windermere 38291
Trinity House National Lighthouse Centre, Penzance 40182
Valhalla Museum, Tresco 40726
Walton Maritime Museum, Walton-on-the-Naze 40779
Watchet Market House Museum, Watchet 40801
Waterfront Museum, Poole 40230
Whitstable Museum and Gallery, Whitstable 40862
Windermere Steamboat Museum, Windermere 40898
Zetland Lifeboat Museum, Redcar 40301

Uruguay
Museo Naval, Montevideo 41019

U.S.A.
American Merchant Marine Museum, Kings Point 44490
Antique Boat Museum, Clayton 42443
Baltimore Maritime Museum, Baltimore 41453
Barnegat Bay Decoy and Baymen's Museum, Tuckerton 48077
Battleship Cove - Maritime Heritage Museums, Fall River 43281
Battleship North Carolina, Wilmington 48656
Bremerton Naval Museum, Bremerton 41878
Buffalo and Erie County Naval and Military Park, Buffalo 41984
Cape Ann Historical Museum, Gloucester 43702
Captain Charles H. Hurley Library Museum, Buzzards Bay 42020
Captain Salem Avery House Museum, Shady Side 47576
Carpenter Museum of Antique Outboard Motors, Gilmanton 43672
Center for Wooden Boats, Seattle 47530
Chittenango Landing Canal Boat Museum, Chittenango 42389
City Island Nautical Museum, Bronx 41917
The Coffin School Museum, Nantucket 45595
Columbia River Maritime Museum, Astoria 41309
Connecticut River Museum, Essex 43211
Door County Maritime Museum, Gills Rock 43671
Door County Maritime Museum, Sturgeon Bay 47860
Dossin Great Lakes Museum, Detroit 42927
East and Seaport Museum, Greenport 43809
Essex Shipbuilding Museum, Essex 43213

Fairport Marine Museum, Fairport Harbor 43276
Great Harbor Maritime Museum, Northeast Harbor 46018
Great Lakes Naval Memorial and Museum, Muskegon 45576
Greater Port Jefferson Museum, Port Jefferson 46598
Hampton Roads Naval Museum, Norfolk 45965
Hawaii Maritime Center, Honolulu 44077
Hereford Inlet Lighthouse, North Wildwood 46010
Herreshoff Marine Museum/America's Cup Hall of Fame, Bristol 41907
Howard Steamboat Museum, Jeffersonville 44330
Hudson River Maritime Museum, Kingston 44493
Independence Seaport Museum, Philadelphia 46419
Inland Seas Maritime Museum of The Great Lakes Historical Society, Vermilion 48213
Intrepid Sea-Air-Space Museum, New York 45818
The John A. Noble Collection, Staten Island 47784
Keokuk River Museum, Keokuk 44452
Keweenaw County Historical Society Museum, Eagle Harbor 43033
Kittery Historical and Naval Museum, Kittery 44507
Lake Superior Maritime Visitors Center, Duluth 43000
Lake Waccamaw Depot Museum, Lake Waccamaw 44596
Long Island Maritime Museum, West Sayville 48547
Los Angeles Maritime Museum, San Pedro 47373
Maine Maritime Museum, Bath 41522
Marine Museum at Fall River, Fall River 43283
The Mariners' Museum, Newport News 45937
Maritime and Seafood Industry Museum, Biloxi 41695
Maritime Museum of Monterey, Monterey 45454
Mel Fisher Maritime Heritage Museum, Key West 44469
Michigan Maritime Museum, South Haven 47695
Mississippi River Museum, Dubuque 42993
Museum of Yachting, Newport 45927
Mystic Seaport, Mystic 45588
Nauticus, Norfolk 45969
Naval Undersea Museum, Keyport 44473
The Navy Museum, Washington 48386
New Jersey Naval Museum, Hackensack 43858
North Carolina Maritime Museum, Beaufort 41558
Old Lighthouse Museum, Michigan City 45303
The Oldest House Museum, Key West 44470
Patriots Point Naval and Maritime Museum, Mount Pleasant 45540
Penobscot Marine Museum, Searsport 47527
Port Columbus National Civil War Naval Center, Columbus 42576
Portsmouth Athenaeum, Portsmouth 46652
Portsmouth Naval Shipyard Museum, Portsmouth 46665
P.T. Boat Museum, Germantown 43659
P.T. Boat Museum, Germantown 43660
Queen Mary Museum, Long Beach 44862
Sailor's Memorial Museum, Islesboro 44268
San Diego Maritime Museum, San Diego 47290
San Francisco Maritime National Historical Park, San Francisco 47337
Sault de Sainte Marie Historical Sites, Sault Sainte Marie 47469
Scituate Maritime and Irish Mossing Museum, Scituate 47503
Ships of the Sea Maritime Museum, Savannah 47484
South Street Seaport Museum, New York 45874
S.S. Meteor Maritime Museum, Barkers Island 41505
Steamboat Arabia Museum, Kansas City 44409
Steamboat Bertrand Museum, Missouri Valley 45409
Steamship Collection, Baltimore 41488
Steamship Keewatin, Douglas 42963
Steamship William G. Mather Museum, Cleveland 42482
Submarine Force Museum and Historic Ship Nautilus, Groton 43845
Texas Seaport Museum, Galveston 43614
United States Coast Guard Museum, New London 45712
United States Naval Academy Museum, Annapolis 41230
USS Bowfin Submarine Museum, Honolulu 44093
USS Constitution Museum, Boston 41831
USS Lexington Museum on the Bay, Corpus Christi 42647
USS Radford National Naval Museum, Newcomerstown 45914
Virginia Beach Maritime Museum, Virginia Beach 48249
Waterfront Museum and Showboat Barge, Brooklyn 41952
Watermen's Museum, Yorktown 48800
Westport Maritime Museum, Westport 48574
Wisconsin Maritime Museum, Manitowoc 45117

Venezuela
Museo Naval, Catia la Mar 48931

Bones

Canada
Dinosaur Provincial Park, Patricia 06100

Denmark
Æbelholt Museum, Hillerød 08872

Germany
Anatomisches Museum, Greifswald 17387
Museum für Haustierkunde Julius Kühn, Halle, Saale 17516
Staatliches Naturhistorisches Museum, Braunschweig 16304
Stein- und Beinmuseum, Weiterstadt 20504

Greece
Museum of Anatomy of the Department of Anatomy, Athinai 20882

Netherlands
Gemeentelijke Oudheidkamer, Ermelo 29251
Schelpen Museum, Zaamslag 30031

Puerto Rico
Caribbean Primate Research Center Museum, San Juan 32387

United Kingdom
Anatomy Museum, Aberdeen 37934

Books, Book Art and Manuscripts

Argentina
Museo Biblioteca Municipal Cesar Fernández Navarro, Santa Fé 00601
Museo del Libro, San Javier 00566
Museo Judío de Buenos Aires Dr. Salvador Kibrick, Buenos Aires 00221
Museo y Biblioteca de la Literature Porteña, Buenos Aires 00248

Armenia
Matenadaran, Erevan 00686

Australia
Local Studies Collection, Marrickville 01213

Austria
Österreichische Nationalbibliothek, Wien 02955
Schrift- und Heimatmuseum Bartlhaus, Pettenbach 02410
Universitätsbibliothek Salzburg, Salzburg 02553

Belgium
Bibliothèque d'Art ENSAV de la Cambre, Bruxelles 03274
Musée du Livre et Cabinets de Donations de la Bibliothèque Royale de Belgique, Bruxelles 03326
Musée P.-J. Redouté et de l'Illustration Botanique, Saint-Hubert 03723
Rubenianum, Antwerpen 03172

Brazil
Biblioteca e Museu Regional Dr. Alípio de Araújo Silva, Rio Preto 04411
Museu Casa de Rui Barbosa, Salvador 04423

Cape Verde
Museu de Documentos Especials, Praia 06876

China, People's Republic
Book Cultural Museum, Shaoguan 07229
China First History Archive Museum, Beijing 06958

Croatia
Zbirka Umjetnina Franjevačkog Samostana, Hvar 07708

Czech Republic
Muzeum Jana Ámoše Komenského, Uherský Brod 08699
Muzeum Knihy, Ždár nad Sázavou 08743

Denmark
Danmarks Bogmuseum, København 08925
Den Rosendahlske Bibelsamling, Esbjerg 08809

Egypt
Library of the Greek Orthodox Patriarchate of Alexandria and All Africa, Alexandria 09240
Monastery of Saint Catherine, Gebel Katherîna 09293

France
Centre de Recherches Historiques sur les Maîtres Ebénistes, Paris 13482
Centre du Livre d'Artiste Contemporain, Verderonne , 15127
Fondation Dosne-Thiers, Paris 13502
Musée Départemental Stéphane Mallarmé, Vulaines-sur-Seine 15298
Musée Mathurin Méheut, Lamballe 12311
Musée Michel Braibant, Montolieu 13117

Germany
Badische Landesbibliothek, Karlsruhe 17989
Bayerische Staatsbibliothek, München 18831
Bibelmuseum Stuttgart, Stuttgart 20086
Bibliothek Otto Schäfer, Schweinfurt 19888
Buchmuseum der Sächsischen Landesbibliothek - Staats- und Universitätsbibliothek Dresden, Dresden 16677
Deutsches Buch- und Schriftmuseum der Deutschen Bücherei Leipzig, Leipzig 18390
Deutsches Buchbindermuseum, Mainz 18599
documenta Archiv für die Kunst des 20. und 21 Jahrhunderts, Kassel 18015
Einbecker Schreibmaschinenmuseum, Einbeck 16812
Freiligrath Museum, Rüdesheim am Rhein 19705
Fürst Thurn und Taxis Zentralarchiv und Hofbibliothek, Regensburg 19523
Göschenhaus / Seume-Gedenkstätte, Grimma 17400
Goethe- und Schiller-Archiv, Weimar, Thüringen 20459
Gutenberg-Museum, Mainz 18600
Handschriftenabteilung der Landes-, Universitäts- und Murhardschen Bibliothek, Kassel 18019
Herzog August Bibliothek, Wolfenbüttel 20653
Hessische Landes- und Hochschulbibliothek, Darmstadt 16540
Hochschul-und Landesbibliothek, Fulda 17175
Klingspor-Museum, Offenbach am Main 19241
Kupferstichkabinett - Sammlung der Zeichnungen und Druckgraphik, Berlin 16033
Landesbibliothek Oldenburg, Oldenburg, Oldenburg 19255
Monacensia-Literaturarchiv und Bibliothek, München 18877
Museum an der Krukenburg, Bad Karlshafen 15673
Museum Schloß Burgk, Burgk 16425
Sammlung handgeschriebener Choralbücher, Kiedrich 18069
Staatliche Bücher- und Kupferstichsammlung Greiz, Greiz 17394
Staats- und Universitätsbibliothek Hamburg Carl von Ossietzky, Hamburg 17569
Staatsbibliothek zu Berlin, Berlin 16099
Staatsbibliothek zu Berlin, Berlin 16100
Stadt- und Universitätsbibliothek, Frankfurt am Main 17073
Stadtarchiv und Stadtbibliothek, Lindau, Bodensee 18475
Stadtmuseum Hildburghausen, Hildburghausen 17753
Universitätsbibliothek der Humboldt-Universität zu Berlin, Berlin 16110
Württembergische Landesbibliothek, Stuttgart 20113

Greece
Teriade Museum, Mytilini 21088

Guatemala
Museo del Libro Antiguo, Antigua 21263

India
Asiatic Society Museum, Kolkata 21897
G.N. Jha Kendriya Sanskrit Vidyapeetha, Allahabad 21691
Museum of Gujarat Vidyasabha, Ahmedabad 21681
Museum of the Sarvajanik Wachanalaya, Nasik 21967
Sibsagar College Museum, Sibsagar 22023
Vrindavan Research Institute Museum, Mathura 21941

Indonesia
Museum Gedong Kirtya, Singaraja 22192

Ireland
Bolton Library, Cashel 22386
The Chester Beatty Library, Dublin 22417
Irish Architectural Archive, Dublin 22433

Israel
Berman Hall, Jerusalem 22624
Bible Museum, Tel Aviv 22751
Nahum Gutman's Museum, Tel Aviv 22771

Italy
Biblioteca Medicea Laurenziana, Firenze 23822
Casa di Pirandello, Agrigento 22815
Centro di Informazione e Documentazione Arti Visive, Prato 25040
Museo Carducci - Biblioteca e Casa, Bologna 23108
Museo Civico Didattico Gian Andrea Irico, Trino 25834
Museo Dantesco, Ravenna 25080
Museo del Cattedrale, Ferrara 23789
Museo dell'Istituto di Patologia del Libro, Roma 25204
Museo Marchigiano del Risorgimento G. e D. Spadoni, Macerata 24249

Japan
Chihiro Art Museum Azumino, Nagano 26527

Jordan
School Books Museum, Salt 27068

Liechtenstein
Liechtensteinische Landesbibliothek, Vaduz 27515

Luxembourg
Musée de l'Abbaye, Echternach 27552

Mexico
Museo Biblioteca Palafoxiana, Puebla 28318
Museo Biblioteca Pape, Monclova 28224

Netherlands
Museum Meermanno-Westreenianum, Den Haag 29111
Museum Oude Boekdrukkunst, Almen 28812
Schriftmuseum J.A. Dortmond, Amsterdam 28900
Scryption, Tilburg 29883

Philippines
Cavite City Library Museum, Cavite 31303
Lopez Memorial Museum, Pasig 31420

Poland
Biblioteka Sejmowa, Warszawa 32078
Muzeum Biblioteki Publicznej Warszawa-Bielany, Warszawa 32091
Muzeum Sztuki Książki, Wrocław 32186
Zakład Narodowy im. Ossolińskich, Wrocław 32193

Puerto Rico
Museo La Casa del Libro, San Juan 32402

Russia
Muzej Knigi, Moskva 33117

Serbia-Montenegro
Muzej Orijentalnih Rukopisa, Prizren 33898

Slovenia
Prežihov Spominski Muzej, Ravne na Koroškem 34145

Spain
Fundació Pública Institut d'Estudis Ilerdencs, Lleida 34965
Museo del Libro, Madrid 35034
Museu d'Història de la Ciudad, Sant Feliu de Guíxols 35400

Swaziland
University of Swaziland Library Museums Collection, Kwaluseni 35779

Sweden
Bernadottebiblioteket, Stockholm 36233
Biblioteksmuseet, Borås 35838

Switzerland
Biblioteca Fundaziun Planta Samedan, Samedan 37094
Fondation Martin Bodmer, Cologny 36641
Fonds Ancien de la Bibliothèque Cantonale Jurassienne, Porrentruy 37027
Öffentliche Bibliothek der Universität Basel, Basel 36515
Schweizerische Landesbibliothek, Bern 36550

Tanzania
Zanzibar National Archives and Museums Department, Zanzibar 37471

Turkey
Türk Vakıf Hat Sanatları Müzesi, İstanbul 37711

United Kingdom
British Library, London 39585
Canterbury Cathedral Archives and Library, Canterbury 38470
John Rylands Library, Manchester 39891
Leadhills Miners' Library Museum, Leadhills 39435
Mappa Mundi and Chained Library, Hereford 39227

U.S.A.
Armstrong Browning Library, Waco 48260
The Atlanta College of Art, Atlanta 41330
Brand Library and Art Galleries, Glendale 43687
Canajoharie Library and Art Gallery, Canajoharie 42074
Center for Book Arts, New York 45777
Chancellor Robert R. Livingston Masonic Library and Museum, New York 45779
Chapin Library of Rare Books, Williamstown 48633
Dwight D. Eisenhower Library-Museum, Abilene 41049
Fort Worth Public Library Arts and Humanities, Fort Worth 43486
Gerald R. Ford Library Museum, Grand Rapids 43755
Hamilton Library and Two Mile House, Carlisle 42104
Haverhill Public Library Special Collections, Haverhill 43962
Herbert Hoover Presidential Library-Museum, West Branch 48515
Historical Museum of the D.R. Barker Library, Fredonia 43545
James Monroe Museum and Memorial Library, Fredericksburg 43537
John F. Kennedy Presidential Library-Museum, Boston 41812
Kala Art Institute, Berkeley 41643
Living Word National Bible Museum, Aledo 41116
Lyndon Baines Johnson Museum, Austin 41416
Melton Art Reference Library Museum, Oklahoma City 46115
Museum of the Jimmy Carter Library, Atlanta 41353
Pierpont Morgan Library, New York 45863
Rosenbach Museum, Philadelphia 46451
Rutherford B. Hayes Presidential Center, Fremont 43556
Society of Illustrators Museum of American Illustration, New York 45871
State Capital Publishing Museum, Guthrie 43856
The Thoreau Institute at Walden Woods, Lincoln 44780
Tresure Room Gallery of the Interchurch Center, New York 45882
Wagnalls Memorial, Lithopolis 44816

Vatican City
Archivio Segreto Vaticano, Città del Vaticano 48867

Zambia
University of Zambia Library Museums Collection, Lusaka 49022

Botany

Argentina
Museo Botanico, Buenos Aires 00159
Museo Botánico, Córdoba 00291
Museo de Ciencias Naturales Dr. Amado Bonpland, Corrientes 00321
Museo Farmacobotánica, Buenos Aires 00206

Australia
Tasmanian Museum and Art Gallery, Hobart 01106

Austria
Biologiezentrum des Oberösterreichischen Landesmuseums, Linz 02228
Kräutermuseum - Naturpark Jauerling Wachau, Maria Laach am Jauerling 02266
Landesmuseum Joanneum, Graz 01922

Belgium
Musée d'Histoire Naturelle et Vivarium, Tournai 03796
Schoolmuseum Michel Thiery, Gent 03449

Brazil
Museu Botânico Dr. João Barbosa Rodrigues, São Paulo 04499
Museu Carpológico do Jardim Botânico do Rio de Janeiro, Rio de Janeiro 04335
Museu de História Natural, Belo Horizonte 03986
Museu do Eucalipto, Rio Claro 04312
Museu do Jardim Botânico, Rio de Janeiro 04371
Museu Regional da Fauna e Flora do Itatiaia, Itatiaia 04136
Museu von Martius, Teresópolis 04567
Sítio Roberto Burle Marx, Rio de Janeiro 04404

Bulgaria
Prirodonaučen Muzej, Burgas 04636

Central African Republic
Musée Botanique de Wakombo, M'Baiki 06880

Colombia
Museo Etnobotánico, Tuluá 07608
Museo Mundocaña, Cali 07451
Museo Mundocaña, Palmira 07540

Czech Republic
Botanické Oddělení Národního Muzea, Průhonice 08631
Dietrichsteinský Palác, Brno 08264
Mendelianum - Památnik Gregora Mendela, Brno 08268
Muzeum Těšínska, Český Těšín 08305
Rožmberský Dům, Soběslav 08658
Východočeské Muzeum, Pardubice 08534
Západomoravské Muzeum v Třebíči, Třebíč 08687

Denmark
Botanisk Museum, København 08923

Egypt
Scientific Researches Museum, Cairo 09287

Finland
Kasvimuseo, Turku 10121
Kasvimuseo, Helsinki 09498
Oulun Yliopiston Kasvimuseo, Oulu 09895

France
Exposition Botanique, Villar-d'Arène 15173
Galerie de Paléobotanique, Paris 13508
Maison de la Baie du Mont Saint-Michel, Vains 15041
Musée de Cerdagne d'Eyne, Eyne 11692
Musée d'Histoire Naturelle, Nantes 13257
Muséum d'Histoire Naturelle, Nice 13326
Muséum National d'Histoire Naturelle, Paris 13650

Germany
Azaleen-Museum, Bremen 16317
Bonsai Museum Heidelberg, Heidelberg 17663
Botanische Staatssammlung München, München 18836
Botanisches Museum, Hamburg 17528
Botanisches Museum Berlin-Dahlem, Berlin 15925
Fehn- und Schiffahrtsmuseum, Rhauderfehn 19583
Forst- und Jagdmuseum, Hofgeismar 17796
Landschloss Pirna-Zuschendorf-Botanische Sammlungen, Pirna 19405
Mooreichensammlung Johann Weber, Göppingen 17320
Museum für Naturkunde der Stadt Gera, Gera 17245
Naturhistorisches Museum, Mainz 18605

Greece
Botanical Museum of the National Gardens, Athinai 20852
Siatista Botanical Museum, Siatista 21154

Guinea
Musée Botanique, Conakry 21280

India
Botanical Survey Museum of India, Pune 21988
Botanical Survey of India, Dehradun 21759
Botany Museum, Faizabad 21800
Botany Museum, Gorakhpur 21812
Botany Museum, Jaunpur 21868
Botany Museum, Kanpur 21881
Botany Museum, Lucknow 21923
Central National Herbarium, Haora 21834
Government Museum, Chennai 21744

Indonesia
Museum Herbarium Bogoriensis, Bogor 22087

Israel
Ussishkin House, Kibbutz Dan 22681

Italy
Museo Agrario Tropicale, Firenze 23851
Museo Alpino Duca degli Abruzzi, Courmayeur 23674
Museo Botanico Cesare Bicchi, Lucca 24226
Museo dei Fossili e Mostra dei Funghi, Pioraco 24939
Museo del Fiore, Acquapendente 22800
Museo del Fungo e di Scienze Naturali, Boves 23190
Museo delle Erbe, Teggiano 25680
Museo di Botanica, Firenze 23865
Museo di Storia Naturale, Genova 24000
Museo Erbario, Roma 25223
Museo Friulano di Storia Naturale, Udine 25850
Museo Naturalistico del Parco, San Romano di Garfagnana 25409
Orto Botanico Hanbury, Genova 24009

Japan
Gifu-ken Hakubutsukan, Seki 26729

Mali
Musée National du Mali, Bamako 27691

Mexico
Museo Botánico, Tuxtla Gutiérrez 28569
Museo Herbario de la Facultad de Ciencias, México 28173

Nepal
Natural History Museum, Kathmandu 28789

Netherlands
Breda's Begijnhof Museum, Breda 29019
Museum de Zwarte Tulp, Lisse 29543

New Zealand
Rewa's Village, Kerikeri 30194

Norway
Natural History Museum, Oslo 30747

Oman
Oman Natural History Museum, Muscat 31006

Pakistan
Botanical Museum, Rawalpindi 31055

Russia
Botaničeskij Muzej, Sankt-Peterburg 33381
Muzei Permskogo Gosudarstvennogo Universiteta, Perm 33304
Novosibirskij Muzej Prirody, Novosibirsk 33243

Slovakia
Múzeum Tatranského Národného Parku, Tatranská Lomnica 34073
Ponitrianske Múzeum, Nitra 34035

Slovenia
Prirodoslovni Muzej Slovenije, Ljubljana 34118

South Africa
African Herbalist Shops, Johannesburg 34268
Albany Museum, Grahamstown 34249
National Museum Bloemfontein, Bloemfontein 34189

Spain
Museo de Ciencias Naturales, Onda 35177
Museo de Historia Natural, Santiago de Compostela 35442
Museu de l'Instituto Botánico, Barcelona 34568

Sweden
Botaniska Museet, Lund 36056
Evolutionsmuseet, Uppsala 36353
Linnémuseet, Uppsala 36356
Linnés Hammarby, Uppsala 36357

Switzerland
Botanisches Museum der Universität Zürich, Zürich 37372
Musée de Botanique, Lausanne 36861

United Kingdom
Botanic Gardens Museum, Southport 40558
Chelsea Physic Garden, London 39604
Falconer Museum, Forres 39008
Herbarium, Cambridge 38455
Kew Palace Museum of the Royal Botanic Gardens, Kew 39350
Margam County Park, Port Talbot 40237
Museum No 1, Richmond, Surrey 40319
Museum of Garden History, London 39715

Uruguay
Museo Botánico, Montevideo 40993
Museo y Jardin Botánico Profesor Atilio Lombardo, Montevideo 41028

U.S.A.
Botanical Museum of Harvard University, Cambridge 42038
Cranbrook Institute of Science, Bloomfield Hills 41740
Edison and Ford Winter Estates, Fort Myers 43434
Great Basin National Park, Baker 41436
Museum of Ancient Artifacts, Chicago 42342
Museum of Vintage Fashion, Lafayette 44566
Thomas Jefferson House Monticello, Charlottesville 42252
Wilderness Park Museum, El Paso 43124

Brewing

Austria
Biermuseum, Laa an der Thaya 02172
Bindereimuseum Hofbräu Kaltenhausen, Hallein 01996
Bräustüberlmuseum, Raab 02468
Brauereimuseum im Stift Göß, Leoben 02207
Braumuseum, Wieselburg an der Erlauf 03024
Erstes Südburgenländisches Schnapsbrennereimuseum, Kukmirn 02170

Belgium
Bocholter Brouwerij Museum, Bocholt 03220
Brouwershuis, Antwerpen 03137
Musée Bruxellois de la Gueuze, Bruxelles 03291
Musée de la Brasserie, Bruxelles 03304
Musée de la Cervoise, du Gruyt et des Bières Mediévales, Anthisnes 03131

Czech Republic
Pivovarské Muzeum, Plzeň 08544

Denmark
Fjerritslev Bryggeri- og Egnsmuseum, Fjerritslev 08824

France
Musée de la Bière, Stenay 14803
Musée Français de la Brasserie, Saint-Nicolas-de-Port 14385

Germany
Bayerisches Brauereimuseum Kulmbach, Kulmbach 18266
Brauerei-Kontor, Bochum 16192
Brauerei-Museum, Haßfurt 17629
Brauerei-Museum, Nesselwang 18999
Brauerei Museum Bürger-Bräu Hof, Hof, Saale 17791
Brauereikulturmuseum Gut Riedelsbach, Neureichenau 19057
Brauereimuseum, Aldersbach 15424
Brauereimuseum, Altomünster 15468
Brauereimuseum Bräu im Moos, Tüßling 20235
Brauereimuseum im historischen Kronen-Brauhaus zu Lüneburg, Lüneburg 18555
Brauereimuseum in der Brauerei Franz Xaver Glossner, Neumarkt, Oberpfalz 19045
Brauereimuseum Schöneck, Schöneck, Vogtland 19828
Brauhausmuseum, Stadtlauringen 20031
Felsenkeller-Labyrinth im Hirschberg - Brauereimuseum, Beilngries 15870
Fränkisches Brauereimuseum, Bamberg 15806
Hallertauer Hopfen- und Heimatmuseum, Geisenfeld 17216
Heimat- und Brauereimuseum, Pleinfeld 19414
Klosterbräu Brauereimuseum, Irsee 17918
Küppers Historisches Biermuseum, Köln 18151
Maisel's Brauerei- und Büttnerei-Museum, Bayreuth 15853
Stutzhäuser Brauereimuseum, Luisenthal 18567

Ireland
Guinness Storehouse, Dublin 22429

Luxembourg
Musée National d'Art Brassicole et Musée de la Tannerie, Wiltz 27583

Netherlands
Heineken Experience, Amsterdam 28857
Museumbrouwerij de Hemel, Nijmegen 29633
Museumbrouwerij De Roos, Hilvarenbeek 29417
Nederlands Biermuseum de Boom, Alkmaar 28804
Villa Bergzicht/Brouwerijmuseum Raaf, Heumen 29413
Voormalig Stoombierbrouwerij De Keijzer N.A. Bosch, Maastricht 29575

Slovenia
Pivovarski Muzej, Ljubljana 34117

Sweden
Arboga Bryggerimuseum, Arboga 35805

Switzerland
Ortsmuseum, Nürensdorf 36992

United Kingdom
Bass Museum of Brewing, Burton-upon-Trent 38408
Stamford Brewery Museum, Stamford 40576
Tetley's Brewery Wharf, Leeds 39453

U.S.A.
Hayner Cultural Center, Troy 48072

Bronzes

France
Collection de Sculptures, Peillon 13680

Italy
Museo Archeologico G. Cilnio Mecenate, Arezzo 22920

Japan
Shimane-kenritsu Hakubutsukan, Matsue 26472

Netherlands
Museum Mesdag, Den Haag 29112

United Kingdom
The Sladmore Gallery of Sculpture, London 39778

Vatican City
Museo Gregoriano Etrusco, Città del Vaticano 48875

Bullfights

Colombia
Museo Taurino, Cali 07453
Museo Taurino de Bogotá, Bogotá 07433

Mexico
Museo Centro Taurino Potosino, San Luis Potosí 28398

Peru
Museo Taurino de la Plaza de Acho, Lima 31225

Spain
Museo Municipal Taurino, Córdoba 34741
Museo Taurino, Madrid 35056
Museo Taurino, Valencia 35611
Museo Taurino de la Real Maestranza de Caballería de Ronda, Ronda 35341
Museu Taurí de la Monumental, Barcelona 34587

Buttons

Canada
Wellington Community Historical Museum, Wellington, Ontario 06763

Germany
Deutsches Knopfmuseum, Bärnau 15794

Netherlands
Speldjesmuseum, Klaaswaal 29481

Cabaret → Performing Arts

Calligraphy

China, People's Republic
Art Museum of Dazu Rock Carvings in Chongqing, Chongqing 07029
China Calligraphy Art Museum, Xian 07293
Lin San Zhi Art Display Center, Zhujiang 07337

France
Musée du Scribe, Saint-Christol-lès-Alès 14147

Germany
Graphische Sammlung der Universität, Erlangen 16918
Siebold-Museum, Würzburg 20705

Iran
Mir-Emad Calligraphy Museum, Teheran 22313

Japan
Basho Memorial Museum, Ueno 26985
Imabari City Kono Shiniichi Memorial Culture Hall, Imabari 26244
Jingu Museum of Antiquities, Ise 26253
Masaki Art Museum, Osaka 26654
Nihon Shodo Bijutsukan, Tokyo 26907
Saga-kenritsu Hakubutsukan, Saga 26691
Shodo Hakubutsukan, Tokyo 26922
Ueno Royal Museum, Tokyo 26951

Korea, Republic
Namjin Art Museum, Imhoe 27189
Woljeon Art Museum, Seoul 27290

Mexico
Museo de la Pluma, México 28141

Syria
Musée de Calligraphie et Epigraphie Arabe, Damascus 37435

Turkey
İstanbul Divan Edebiyatı Müzesi, İstanbul 37704
Türk Vakıf Hat Sanatları Müzesi, İstanbul 37711

United Kingdom
Ditchling Museum, Ditchling 38735

Cameras → Optics

Carpets

Armenia
State Folk Art Museum of Armenia, Erevan 00690

Azerbaijan
State Museum of Azerbaijan Carpets and Applied Art Letif Kerimov, Baku 03071

Belgium
Musée de la Tapiserie et des Arts du Tissu, Tournai 03793

Brazil
Fundação Eva Klabin Rappaport, Rio de Janeiro 04325

Bulgaria
Izložba na Stari Kotlenski Kilimi, Kotel 04717

Canada
Museum for Textiles, Toronto 06595

Germany
Orientteppich-Museum, Hannover 17609

Iran
Astan-e-Qods-e Razavi Museums, Mashad 22265
Farsh Museum, Teheran 22296
Rassan Arabzadeh Carpet Museum, Teheran 22322

Netherlands
Het Tapijtmuseum, Genemuiden 29274

Turkey
Edirne Arkoloji ve Etnografi Müzesi, Edirne 37664
Vakıf Halı Müzesi, İstanbul 37712
Yıldız Şale, İstanbul 37716

Turkmenistan
Turkmen Carpet Museum Gurbansoltan Eje, Ašgabat 37813

Carriages and Carts

Argentina
Museo del Carruaje El Tacu, Villa General Belgrano 00668

Australia
Carriage and Harness Museum, Beechworth 00784

Austria
Fiakermuseum, Wien 02882
Kutschen- und Heimatmuseum, Sillian 02664
Kutschen- und Schlittenmuseum, Großraming 01961
Wagenburg im Schloß Schönbrunn, Wien 02999

Belgium
Karrenmuseum, Essen 03410

Bermuda
Carriage Museum, Saint George's 03887

Canada
Clegg's Museum of Horse-Drawn Vehicles, Hamiota 05578
Remington Carriage Museum, Cardston 05206

Czech Republic
Vagonářské Muzeum, Studénka 08667

Denmark
Slesvigske Vognsamling, Haderslev 08850
Sparresholm Vognsamling, Holme-Olstrup 08886

Egypt
Royal Carriage Museum, Bulaq-el-Dakrur 09251

France
Musée des Attelages, de la Carrosserie et du Charronnage, Vonnas 15291
Musée des Carrosses, Versailles 15143
Musée National de la Voiture et du Tourisme, Compiègne 11377

Germany
Fürst Thurn und Taxis Marstallmuseum, Regensburg 19521
Hessisches Kutschen- und Wagenmuseum, Lohfelden 18495
Kutschen-, Schlitten- und Wagenmuseum Rottach-Egern, Rottach-Egern 19688
Kutschenmuseum, Gaildorf 17193
Kutschenmuseum, Ludwigslust 18525
Kutschenmuseum Hessisches Landgestüt, Dillenburg 16609
Kutschensammlung, Eigeltingen 16809
Marstallmuseum, München 18873
Museum für Kutschen, Chaisen, Karren, Heidenheim an der Brenz 17680
Museum Kutschen-Wagen-Karren, Gescher 17265
Werksmuseum Achse, Rad und Wagen, Wiehl 20567

Ireland
Vintage Car and Carriage Museum, Inishowen 22481

Italy
Mostra di Palazzo Farnese, Piacenza 24889
Mostra Permanente Le Carrozze d'Epoca, Roma 25172
Museo del Biroccio Marchigiano e Museo Beltrami, Filottrano 23813
Museo delle Carrozze, Catanzaro 23453
Museo delle Carrozze, Firenze 23859
Museo delle Carrozze, Napoli 24584
Museo delle Carrozze dell'Ottocento, Verona 25973
Museo di Auto e Moto d'Epoca, Vigolzone 26011

Netherlands
Agrarisch en Wagenmuseum, De Waal 29072
Cultuurhistorisch Streek- en Handkarrenmuseum De Wemme, Zuidwolde, Drenthe 30071
Kinderwagens van toen, Dwingeloo 29185
Het Koetshuis, Den Haag 29100
Nationaal Rijtuigmuseum, Leek 29502
Zijper Museum, Schagerbrug 29798

Portugal
Museu Nacional dos Coches, Lisboa 32312

Spain
Museo de Carruajes, Madrid 35019
Museo de Carruajes de Sevilla, Sevilla 35486

Sweden
Eriksborg Vagnmuseum, Ystad 36421
Livrustkammaren, Stockholm 36256
Vagnmuseet, Malmö 36081

Switzerland
Kutschenmuseum, Basel 36507
Kutschensammlung Robert Sallmann, Amriswil 36456

United Kingdom
Arlington Court, Arlington 38014
Tyrwhitt-Drake Museum of Carriages, Maidstone 39879

U.S.A.
Car and Carriage Museum, Pittsburgh 46509
Cheyenne Frontier Days Old West Museum, Cheyenne 42297
Thrasher Carriage Museum, Frostburg 43570

Vatican City
Museo Padiglione delle Carozza, Città del Vaticano 48878

Cartography

Austria
Dokumentationraum Georg Matthäus Vischer, Aigen bei Raabs 01649
Globenmuseum der Österreichischen Nationalbibliothek, Wien 02890
Peter Anich-Museum, Oberperfuss 02374
Vermessungskundliche Sammlung, Linz 02242

Belgium
Mercator Museum, Sint-Niklaas 03742

Brazil
Museu do Colono, Santa Leopoldina 04442

India
Survey Museum, Roorkee 22006

Italy
Mostra Cartografica, Mendatica 24347

Netherlands
Van de Poll-Stichting, Zeist 30052
Witte's Museum, Axel 28957

Norway
Norsk Kartmuseum, Hønefoss 30560

Slovenia
Zemljepišni Muzej Slovenije, Ljubljana 34124

Switzerland
Alpineum, Luzern 36904
Gletschergarten, Luzern 36908

United Kingdom
American Museum in Britain, Bath 38106

Carts → Carriages and Carts

Carving, Wood → Wood Carving

Castles and Fortresses

Algeria
Musée du Palais du Dey, Casbah 00054

Australia
Fort Scratchley Museum, Newcastle 01315

Austria
Ausgrabungsstätte Schanzberg, Gars am Kamp 01869
Barockjagdschloß Eckartsau, Eckartsau 01784
Burg Greifenstein, Greifenstein 01937
Burgenkundliches Museum des Steirischen Burgenvereins, Bärnbach 01730
Burgmuseum, Güssing 01969
Burgmuseum, Seebenstein 02655
Burgmuseum Clam, Klam 02134
Emperor Maximilian of Mexico Museum, Hardegg 02002
Esterházy-Ausstellung, Eisenstadt 01808
Festung Kniepaß, Unken 02753
Festungsmuseum, Salzburg 02534
Franzensburg, Laxenburg 02197
Gschlößl Leithaprodersdorf-Freilichtanlage, Leithaprodersdorf 02203
Hengistburgmuseum, Hengsberg 02020
Museum Burg Heidenreichstein, Heidenreichstein 02012
Paul Anton Keller-Museum, Lockenhaus 02247
Reinessanceschloss Rosenburg, Rosenburg am Kamp 02526
Renaissance Schloss Greillenstein, Röhrenbach 02518
Rittersaalmuseum, Kirchbichl 02112
Sammlungen Burg Bernstein, Bernstein, Burgenland 01735
Sammlungen der Burg Hochosterwitz, Launsdorf 02193
Schloss Hof und Schloss Niederweiden, Engelhartstetten 01815
Schloß Naudersberg, Nauders 02338
Schloß Tratzberg mit Sammlungen, Jenbach 02087
Schloßmuseum, Herberstein 02022

Azerbaijan
State Historical and Architectural Museum-reserve Shirvan Shahs' Palace, Baku 03070

Bangladesh
Ahsan Manzil Museum, Dhaka 03082
Lalbagh Fort Museum, Dhaka 03090

Belgium
Château de Beloeil, Beloeil 03209
Château de Rixensart, Rixensart 03699
Collection du Château des Princes, Chimay 03358
Fort Napoleon, Oostende 03667
Kasteel Achtendries, Gent 03440
Kasteel Beauvoorde, Wulveringem 03847
Musée Baillet-Latour, Latour 03555
Musée de la Chasse, de la Vénerie et de la Protection de la Nature, Lavaux-Sainte-Anne 03556
Musée du Château-Fort, Ecaussinnes-Lalaing 03400
Musée et Parc Archéologiques de Montauban, Buzenol 03345
Stedelijk Archeologisch Museum, Oudenburg 03680

Canada
Bastion, Nanaimo 05958
Castle Hill National Historic Park, Placentia 06135
Château Logue, Maniwaki 05805
Craigdarroch Castle Historical Museum, Victoria 06718
Fort-Numéro-Un de la Pointe-de-Lévy, Québec 06196
Fort Point Museum, LaHave 05717
Fort Saint Joseph National Historic Park, Saint Joseph Island 06357
Fort Selkirk, Whitehorse 06791
Fortress of Louisbourg, Louisbourg 05782
Musée du Fort Saint-Jean, Saint-Jean 06326
Old Fort Erie, Niagara Falls 05997
Old Fort William Historical Park, Thunder Bay 06546
Prince of Wales Fort, Churchill 05252

China, People's Republic
Museum of the Imperial Palace of Manchu State, Changchun 07005
Nan Yue Wang Palace Museum, Guangzhou 07071
Pu Le Temple, Chengde 07019

Cuba
Fortaleza de Nuestra Señora de los Angeles de Jagua, Jagua 08011
Museo Fuerte de la Loma, Victoria de las Tunas 08170

Cyprus, Turkish Republic
Girne Kalesi, Girne 08225
Otello Kalesi, Gazimağusa 08220
Sipahi Ay. Trias Bazilikası ve Kantara Kalesi, Kantara 08231
Vuni Sarayi, Lefke 08233

Czech Republic
Chebský Hrad, Cheb 08307
Helfštýn Hrad, Týn nad Bečvou 08695
Muzeum Betlémů, Karlštejn 08404
Náprstek Museum of Asian, African and American Cultures, Liběchov 08449
Švihov Hrad, Švihov 08670
Svojanov Hrad, Polička 08557
Zámecké Muzeum, Kravaře 08431
Zámek, Hradec nad Moravicí 08369
Zámek, Nové Město nad Metují 08505
Zámek, Vrchotovy Janovice 08727
Zámek Brandýs, Brandýs nad Labem 08256
Zámek-Kinski, Chlumec nad Cidlinou 08310
Zámek Libochovice, Libochovice 08452
Zámek Líčkov - Galerie O. Brázda, Žatec 08739
Zámek Lysice, Lysice 08469
Zámek Nelahozeves, Nelahozeves 08496
Zámek Sychrov, Sychrov 08672
Zámek Velké Březno, Velké Březno 08710
Zámek Veltrusy, Veltrusy 08714
Zámek Vizovice, Vizovice 08720

Denmark
Borgmuseum, Spøttrup 09078
Jægerspris Slot, Jægerspris 08907
Kronborg Slot, Helsingør 08863
Liselund Gamle Slot, Borre 08788
Palæsamlingerne, Roskilde 09041
Rosenholm Slot, Hornslet 08893
Voergård Slot, Dronninglund 08799

Egypt
Abdeen Palace Museum, Cairo 09252
Manial Palace Museum, Cairo 09269

Finland
Hanko Museo, Hanko 09463
Kastleholm Castle, Sund 10061
Olavinlinna Castle, Olavinlinna 09881
Suomenlinna-Museo, Helsinki 09536
Suomenlinna-Sveaborg, Helsinki 09537
Turun Kaupungin Historiallinen Museo, Turun Linna, Turku 10133

France
Château, Arlay 10413
Château Beaufief, Mazeray 12906
Château de Messilhac, Raulhac 13915
Château de Montmuran, Les Iffs 12541
Château de Rochefort-en-Terre, Rochefort-en-Terre 14002
Château de Talcy, Marchenoir 12803
Château-Musée, Carrouges 11062
Château-Musée d'Art Populaire et Religieux, Clermont (Haute-Savoie) 11326
Château-Musée de Terre-Neuve, Fontenay-le-Comte 11771
Château-Musée de Vollore, Vollore-Ville 15285
Château-Musée des Ducs, Duras 11587
Château-Musée du Suscinio, Sarzeau 14628
Château-Musée et Ecuries de Chaumont-sur-Loire, Chaumont-sur-Loire 11252
Château-Musée Mansart, Sagonne 14084
Château-Musée Municipal, Nemours 13279
Collections du Château du Breil de Foin, Genneteil 11849
Exposition du Château Fort du Fleckenstein, Lembach 12509
Mini-Château, Amboise 10310
Musée Arthur-Le-Duc, Torigni-sur-Vire 14919
Musée-Château de Haute-Goulaine, Haute-Goulaine 11998
Musée-Château de La Verrerie, Oizon 13396
Musée d'Art et d'Histoire, Schirmeck 14683
Musée des Plans-Reliefs, Paris 13592
Musée du Château, Dinan 11534
Musée du Château, Noirmoutier-en-l'Ile 13359
Musée du Château de Vincennes, Vincennes 15265
Musée du Château et des Anciennes Écuries, Montbard 13055
Musée du Manoir d'Argentelles, Villebadin 15189
Musée du Tire-Bouchon, Ménerbes 12926
Musée Fort de Sucy, Sucy-en-Brie 14841
Musée Fort Lagarde, Prats-de-Mollo-la-Preste 13865
Musée National des Châteaux de Versailles et de Trianon, Versailles 15145
Musée National du Château de Fontainebleau, Fontainebleau 11769
Musée National du Château de Pau, Pau 13670
Palais Rihour, Lille 12605

Germany
Allgäuer Burgenmuseum, Kempten 18060
Bergisches Museum Schloß Burg, Solingen 19983
Bettina und Achim von Arnim Museum, Wiepersdorf bei Jüterbog 20569
Burg Gnandstein, Kohren-Sahlis 18195
Burg Lauenstein, Ludwigsstadt 18528
Burg Mildenstein, Leisnig 18426
Burg Pappenheim mit Naturmuseum und Historischem Museum, Pappenheim 19347
Burg Prunn, Riedenburg 19595
Burg Trausnitz, Landshut 18308
Burg Trifels, Annweiler 15500
Burg- und Klosteranlage Oybin, Kurort Oybin 18274
Burg Zwernitz, Wonsees 20674
Burgenmuseum Eisenberg, Eisenberg, Allgäu 16821
Burgmuseum, Höhr-Grenzhausen 17783
Burgmuseum, Kirschau 18101
Burgmuseum, Lisberg 18486
Burgmuseum, Ortenberg, Hessen 19269
Burgmuseum Burg Guttenberg, Haßmersheim 17630

Burgmuseum der Wasserburg Kapellendorf, Kapellendorf 17983
Burgmuseum Grünwald, Grünwald 17449
Burgmuseum Marksburg, Braubach 16287
Dornburger Schlösser, Dornburg, Saale 16648
Felsenburg Neurathen, Lohmen, Sachsen 18497
Festung Königstein, Königstein, Sächsische Schweiz 18182
Festung Marienberg mit Fürstenbaumuseum, Würzburg 20692
Die Festung Rosenberg - Deutsches Festungsmuseum, Kronach 18242
Festung Wilhelmstein im Steinhuder Meer, Wunstorf 20709
Fürst Thurn und Taxis Schloßmuseum - Museum Kreuzgang, Regensburg 19522
Herzogschloss, Celle 16454
Historische Wehranlage, Mühlhausen, Thüringen 18806
Historisches Kabinett Burgruine Eckartsburg, Eckartsberga 16775
Jagdschoss Letzlingen, Letzlingen 18444
Kaiserburg Nürnberg, Nürnberg 19148
Kaiserpfalzruine, Gelnhausen 17225
Königshaus am Schachen und Alpengarten, Garmisch-Partenkirchen 17201
Konradsburg Ermsleben, Ermsleben 16929
Kulturhistorisches Museum Schloss Köthen, Köthen, Anhalt 18190
Kutschenmuseum, Augustusburg 15571
Landesmuseum Koblenz, Koblenz 18120
Museum Burg Frankenberg, Aachen 15377
Museum Burg Freyenstein, Freyenstein 17132
Museum Burg Kriebstein, Kriebstein 18239
Museum Burg Querfurt, Querfurt 19465
Museum Burg Ramsdorf, Velen 20297
Museum Burg Stein, Hartenstein bei Zwickau 17622
Museum Burg Stickhausen, Detern 16585
Museum im Alten Schloß, Altensteig 15455
Museum Schloss Fasanerie, Eichenzell 16802
Museum Schloss Friedrichsfelde, Berlin 16068
Museum Schloss Hardenberg, Velbert 20294
Museum Schloss Herzberg, Herzberg am Harz 17742
Museum Schloß Molsdorf, Molsdorf 18785
Museum Zitadelle, Jülich 17965
Neues Schloß Herrenchiemsee, Herrenchiemsee 17735
Neues Schloß Schleißheim, Oberschleißheim 19204
Neues Schloß und Instrumentenmuseum, Kißlegg 18103
Oberburg Giebichenstein, Halle, Saale 17518
Privatsammlung Burg Runkel, Runkel 19719
Renaissance- und Barock-Schloß Weilburg, Weilburg 20446
Residenz Ansbach, Ansbach 15504
Schloß Arolsen, Bad Arolsen 15592
Schloß Augustusburg, Brühl, Rheinland 16379
Schloß Berleburg, Bad Berleburg 15610
Schloß Egg, Bernried, Niederbayern 16128
Schloß Ettersburg, Ettersburg 16973
Schloß Falkenlust, Brühl, Rheinland 16380
Schloß Favorite, Rastatt 19489
Schloss Glienicke, Berlin 16090
Schloß Hämelschenburg, Emmerthal 16864
Schloss Harburg, Harburg 17615
Schloß Heiligenberg, Heiligenberg, Baden 17693
Schloß Hohenschwangau, Schwangau 19877
Schloß Leitzkau, Leitzkau 18427
Schloß Linderhof, Ettal 16972
Schloss Ludwigsburg, Ludwigsburg, Württemberg 18513
Schloss Ludwigslust, Ludwigslust 18527
Schloß Neuschwanstein, Schwangau 19878
Schloß Pfaueninsel, Berlin 16091
Schloß Rheinsberg, Rheinsberg 19592
Schloß Rosenau, Rödental 19630
Schloß Schwetzingen, Schwetzingen 19905
Schloss und Hofgarten Dachau, Dachau 16526
Schloß und Park Schönbusch, Aschaffenburg 15530
Schloß und Schloßpark Bad Homburg, Bad Homburg v.d.Höhe 15667
Schloß und Schloßpark Wilhelmsthal, Calden 16445
Schloß Unteraufseß, Aufseß 15548
Schloß Veitshöchheim, Veitshöchheim 20292
Schloß vor Husum, Husum, Nordsee 17872
Schloßmuseum, Arnstadt 15514
Schloßmuseum, Bad Bentheim 15601
Schloßmuseum, Erbach, Donau 16886
Schloßmuseum, Gotha 17363
Schloßmuseum, Kirchberg an der Jagst 18088
Schloßmuseum, Kronburg 18248
Schloßmuseum, Krummennaab 18252
Schloßmuseum, Ortenburg 19271
Schlossmuseum, Schwerin 19899
Schloßmuseum Amerang, Amerang 15483
Schloßmuseum Hohenlohe-Schillingsfürst, Schillingsfürst 19780
Schloßmuseum Hubertusburg, Wermsdorf 20523
Schloßmuseum mit Brüder-Grimm-Gedenkstätte, Steinau an der Straße 20044
Schlossmuseum Sondershausen, Sondershausen 19996
Schloßmuseum Warthausen, Warthausen 20405
Schmiede Burg Schlitz, Burg Schlitz 16412
Spielzeugmuseum im Alten Schloß, Sugenheim 20120
Stadt- und Kulturgeschichtliches Museum, Torgau 20186
Städtisches Heimatmuseum, Landau in der Pfalz 18302
Städtisches Museum Wesel, Wesel 20538
Toppler-Schlößchen, Rothenburg ob der Tauber 19683
Wartburg, Eisenach 16820
Wasserschloß Mitwitz, Mitwitz 18759
Willibaldsburg, Eichstätt 16808

Ghana
Manhyia Museum, Kumasi 20796

Hungary
Beethoven Emlékmúzeum, Martonvásár 21469
Diósgyőri Vármúzeum, Miskolc 21473
Festetics-Kastély, Keszthely 21454
Kastélymúzeum, Fertőd 21415
Kinizsi Vármúzeum, Nagyvázsony 21488
Nádasdi Ferenc Múzeum, Sárvár 21527
Vármúzeum, Dunaföldvár 21403
Vármúzeum, Siklós 21529
Vármúzeum, Simontornya 21530
Vármúzeum, Sümeg 21542
Vármúzeum, Veszprém 21609
Várrom és Népi Müemlék, Kisnána 21461
Vay Adám Múzeum, Vaja 21603
Zempléni Muzeum, Szerencs 21580

Iran
Baghcheh-Jaq Palace, Urmieh 22330
Golestan Palace Museum, Teheran 22300
Green Palace Museum, Teheran 22301
Mianposhteh Palace Museum, Bandar-Anzali 22232
Museum Falak-ol-Aflak, Khorram-Abaad 22257
Niavaran Palace, Teheran 22321

Ireland
Driminagh Castle, Dublin 22420
King John's Castle, Limerick 22506
Malahide Castle, Malahide 22516
Ross Castle, Killarney 22493

Israel
Museum of Acre, Acre 22563

Italy
Borgo e Castello Medioevale, Torino 25731
Castel Beseno, Besenello 23071
Castel Sant'Elmo, Napoli 24571
Castello Fénis, Fénis 23774
Museo del Castello di Porciano, Stia 25633
Museo del Castello di Sarre, Sarre 25477
Museo di Palazzo d'Arco, Mantova 24288
Museo di Palazzo Piccolomini, Pienza 24907
Museo Morando Bolognini, Sant'Angelo Lodigiano 25453
Museo Nazionale di Canossa N. Campanini, Ciano d'Enza 23558
Museo Storico del Castello di Miramare, Trieste 25831
Palazzo della Ragione, Padova 24750

Japan
Fukuyama-Jo Castle Museum, Fukuyama 26151
Heijokyuseki Shiryokan, Nara 26575
Hiroshima Castle, Hiroshima 26213
Kumamoto Castle, Kumamoto 26375
Odawara Castle Museum, Odawara 26615
Osaka Castle Museum, Osaka 26660

Laos
Ho Phrakèo, Vientiane 27319
Vat Sisaket, Vientiane 27323
Vat Xiengkhouane, Vientiane 27324

Latvia
Bauskas Pils Muzejs, Bauska 27335
Rundāles Pils Muzejs, Pilsrundāle 27394

Luxembourg
Schloß Vianden, Vianden 27580

Mexico
Museo Baluarte de Santiago, Veracruz 28593
Museo de la No Intervención Fuerte de Loreto, Puebla 28330
Museo de Sitio Castillo de Teayo, Castillo de Teayo 27807
Museo del Fuerte de San Felipe, Bacalar 27788
Museo del Fuerte de San Juan de Ulúa, Veracruz 28595
Museo Histórico Fuerte de San José el Alto, Campeche 27799

Nepal
Patan Museum, Kathmandu 28791

Netherlands
Fort Rammekens, Ritthem 29736
Fraeylemaborg, Slochteren 29832
De Groene Schuur, Culemborg 29061
Kasteel Amerongen, Amerongen 28818
Kasteel Ammersoyen, Ammerzoden 28829
Kasteel Cannenburch, Vaassen 29914
Kasteel De Doornenburg, Doornenburg 29169
Kasteel Duivenvoorde, Voorschoten 29963
Kasteel Groeneveld, Baarn 28959
Kasteel Heeswijk, Heeswijk-Dinther 29372
Kasteel Hernen, Hernen 29401
Kasteel Hoensbroek, Hoensbroek 29430
Kasteel Middachten, De Steeg 29071
Kasteel Radboud, Medemblik 29582
Kasteeltoren IJsselstein, IJsselstein 29461
Muiderslot, Muiden 29604
Museum Fort Kijkduin, Den Helder 29135
Museum Kasteel Wijchen, Wijchen 30002
Museum Menkemaborg, Uithuizen 29888
Het Nederlands Vestingmuseum, Naarden 29606
Poptaslot Heringa-State, Marssum 29581
Slot Loevestein, Poederoijen 29714
Slot Zeist, Zeist 30051
Slot Zuylen, Oud-Zuilen 29692
Stichting Huis Bergh, 's-Heerenberg 29361
Vestingmuseum, Nieuweschans 29622

Norway
Austråt Slott, Opphaug 30717
Baroniet Rosendal, Rosendal 30809
Bogstad Gård, Oslo 30728
Håkonshallen og Rosenkrantztårnet, Bergen 30421
Norges Hjemmefrontmuseum, Oslo 30748

Oman
Nahkl Fort Museum, Nahkl 31009

Poland
Muzeum Dworek Zabytkowy, Stryszów 32002
Muzeum Twierdza Wisłoujście, Gdańsk 31576
Muzeum Zamkowe w Malborku, Malbork 31799
Zamek w Czersku, Czersk 31543
Zamek w Gniewie, Gniew 31599

Puerto Rico
Castillo de San Felipe del Morro, San Juan 32388

Russia
Gosudarstvennyj Istoriko-architekturnyj i Prirodno-landšaftnyj Muzej Zapovednik Izborsk, Izborsk 32834
Istoriko-architekturnyj Muzej Kuzneckaja Krepost', Novokuzneck 33234
Memorialnyj Kompleks 'Vorošilovskaja Batareja', Vladivostok 33700
Muzej Kronštadtskaja Krepost, Kronštadt 32966
Petropavlovskaja Krepost - Istoriko-kulturnyj Zapovednik, Sankt-Peterburg 33475
Šlisselburgskaja Krepost Orešek, Šlisselburg 33526
Vladivostokskaja Krepost' - Voenno istoričeskij Fortifikacionnyj Muzej, Vladivostok 33711

San Marino
Palazzo Pubblico, San Marino 33768

Slovakia
Expozícia Zbraní a Stredovekého Mestského Opevnenia, Bratislava 33961

Spain
Museo del Alcázar, Toledo 35543
Palacio de Pedralbes, Barcelona 34589
Palacio Real de Aranjuez, Aranjuez 34472
Sacro Convento Castillo de Calatrava la Nueva, Aldea del Rey 34442

Sweden
Drottningholm Slott, Drottningholm 35853
Engsö Slott, Västerås 36378
Ericsbergs Slott, Mellösa 36093
Finspångs Slott, Finspång 35890
Glimmingehus, Hammenhög 35943
Gripsholms Slott, Mariefred 36084
Grönsöö Slott, Enköping 35867
Hallwylska Museet, Stockholm 36245
Kalmar Slott, Kalmar 35990
Kina Slott, Drottningholm 35854
Löfstad Slott Museum, Norrköping 36119
Målsåkers Slott, Stallarholmen 36226
Nolhaga Slotts Konsthall, Alingsås 35791
Nynäs Slott, Västerljung 36385
Ölands Forngård, Borgholm 35844
Rosersbergs Slott, Rosersberg 36163
Sofiero Slott, Helsingborg 35955
Strömsholms Slott, Kolbäck 36013
Taxinge Slott, Nykvarn 36129
Teleborgs Slott, Växjö 36391
Tjolöholms Slott, Fjärås 35891
Trollenäs Slott, Eslöv 35875
Tullgarns Slott, Vagnhärad 36394
Tyresö Slott, Tyresö 36340
Vadstena Slott, Vadstena 36369
Vaxholms Fästnings Museum, Vaxholm 36401

Switzerland
Burgenkundliche Sammlung im Burgenmuseum, Gossau (Sankt Gallen) 36770
Château, Gruyères 36785
Château de Chillon, Territet-Veytaux 37233
Château de Coppet, Coppet 36647
Château d'Oron, Oron-le-Châtel 37015
Museum Schloss Kyburg, Kyburg 36842
Museum Schloss Waldegg, Feldbrunnen 36699
Ortsmuseum Dietikon, Dietikon 36661
Schloß, Jegenstorf 36819
Schloß Hallwyl, Seengen 37157
Schloß Spiez, Spiez 37193
Schloß Werdenberg, Werdenberg 37311
Schloßmuseum Heidegg, Gelfingen 36723
Stadtmuseum Aarau, Aarau 36429

Thailand
Suan Pakkad Palace, Bangkok 37499

Turkey
Istanbul Hisarlar Müzesi, Bebek 37632

United Kingdom
Bamburgh Castle, Bamburgh 38073
Berkeley Castle, Berkeley 38167
Bickleigh Castle, Bickleigh 38190
Blair Castle, Blair Atholl 38253
Bodiam Castle, Robertsbridge 40330
Braemar Castle, Braemar 38307
Broughty Castle Museum, Dundee 38797
Buckingham Palace, London 39593
Caerphilly Castle, Caerphilly 38436
Caldicot Castle, Caldicot 38438
Cardiff Castle, Cardiff 38478
Castle and Regimental Museum, Monmouth 39977
Castle Cary and District Museum, Castle Cary 38499
Castle Coole, Enniskillen 38938
Castle Fraser, Sauchen 40450
Castle Menzies, Aberfeldy 37946
Castle Museum, York 40960
Castle of Saint John, Stranraer 40621
Castle Rushen, Castletown 38506
Cawdor Castle, Cawdor 38514
Compton Castle, Paignton 40158
Culross Palace, Culross 38681
Culzean Castle and Country Park, Maybole 39927
Deal Castle, Deal 38708
Dean Castle, Kilmarnock 39361
Denbigh Castle Museum, Denbigh 38713
Dover Castle, Dover 38765
Downhill Castle, Castlerock 38504
Drum Castle, Drumoak 38780
Dunimarle Castle, Culross 38682
Dunster Castle, Dunster 38821
Dunvegan Castle, Dunvegan 38822
Elizabeth Castle, Saint Helier 40400
Floors Castle, Kelso 39333
Frogmore House, Windsor 40900
Fyvie Castle, Fyvie 39020
Giant's Castle, Marazion 39907
Gilstrap Heritage Centre, Newark-on-Trent 40019
Glamis Castle, Glamis 39037
Harlech Castle, Harlech 39162
Harwich Redoubt Fort, Harwich 39180
Hever Castle and Gardens, Edenbridge 38868
Knaresborough Castle and Old Courthouse Museum, Knaresborough 39400
Lauriston Castle, Edinburgh 38891
Linlithgow Palace, Linlithgow 39507
Lunt Roman Fort, Baginton 38054
Mont Orgueil Castle, Gorey 39097
Mountfitchet Castle and Norman Village, Stansted Mountfitchet 40579
Muncaster Castle, Ravenglass 40285
Museum of Fulham Palace, London 39714
Museum of Local History and Industry, Llandrindod Wells 39537
Nothe Fort Museum of Coastal Defence, Weymouth 40843
Oakham Castle, Oakham 40121
Peel Castle, Peel 40168
Pendennis Castle, Falmouth 38974
Penkill Castle, Girvan 39035
Pontefract Castle Museum, Pontefract 40217
Sandal Castle, Sandal 40440
Sizergh Castle, Kendal 39339
Southsea Castle, Portsmouth 40259
Stafford Castle and Visitor Centre, Stafford 40572
Story of Castle Cornet, Saint Peter Port 40427
Sudeley Castle, Winchcombe 40881
Thirlestane Castle, Lauder 39428
Urquhart Castle, Drumnadrochit 38779
Victoria Tower, Huddersfield 39275
Warwick Castle, Warwick 40794
Weoley Castle, Birmingham 38232
Windsor Castle, Windsor 40905

U.S.A.
Belcourt Castle, Newport 45924
Castle Clinton, New York 45775
Fort Casey Interpretive Center, Coupeville 42675
Fort Clinch, Fernandina Beach 43315
Fort Delaware, Narrowsburg 45606
Fort Leboeuf, Waterford 48430
Fort Loudoun, Chambersburg 42184
Fort Nashborough, Nashville 45618
Fort Okanogan, Pateros 46308
Fort Scott National Historic Site, Fort Scott 43453
Fort Sumner, Fort Sumner 43463
Hammond Castle Museum, Gloucester 43703
Iolani Palace, Honolulu 44080
Miramont Castle Museum, Manitou Springs 45114
Old Castle Museum, Baldwin City 41443
The Walsenburg Mining Museum and Fort Francisco Museum of La Veta, Walsenburg 48293
Wilson Castle, Proctor 46710

Venezuela
Castillos de Guayana la Vieja, Guayana 48945

Ceramics → Porcelain and Ceramics

Chemistry

Canada
Ontario Science Centre, Toronto 06600

France
Maison de Louis Pasteur, Arbois 10389

Germany
Deutsches Chemie Museum, Merseburg 18712
Deutsches Kunststoff Museum, Düsseldorf 16720
Liebig-Museum, Gießen 17282
Museum der Göttinger Chemie, Göttingen 17336

Hungary
Magyar Vegyészeti Múzeum, Várpalota 21604

Italy
Museo di Chimica, Roma 25211

Russia
Dom-muzej D.I. Mendeleeva, Boblovo 32693
Memorialnyj Muzej Akademikov A.E. i B.A. Arbuzovych, Kazan 32893
Muzej-Archiv D.I. Mendeleeva, Sankt-Peterburg 33429
Muzej Kazanskoj Chimičeskoj Školy, Kazan 32900

United Kingdom
Catalyst, Widnes 40869
Michael Faraday's Laboratory and Museum, London 39708

China (Porcelain) → Porcelain and Ceramics

Cigarettes → Tobacco

Cinematography

Argentina
Museo del Cine Pablo C. Ducrós Hicken, Buenos Aires 00200

Armenia
Sergei Parajanov Museum, Erevan 00688

Austria
Bild- und Tonarchiv, Graz 01911
Filmsammlungen Laxenburg, Laxenburg 02196
Moviemento-Art-Galerie, Linz 02237
Österreichisches Filmmuseum Wien, Wien 02957

Belgium
Filmmuseum, Antwerpen 03143
Musée du Cinéma, Bruxelles 03321

Canada
Cinémathèque Québécoise - Musée du Cinéma, Montréal 05901

Denmark
Det Danske Filminstitut, København 08926

France
Musée Vivant du Cinéma, Lyon 12749

Germany
Berliner Kinomuseum, Berlin 15917
Deutsche Mediathek im Filmhaus, Berlin 15938
Deutsches Filmmuseum, Frankfurt am Main 17036
Filmmuseum, München 18848
Filmmuseum Berlin, Berlin 15946
Filmmuseum Landeshauptstadt Düsseldorf, Düsseldorf 16722
Filmmuseum Potsdam, Potsdam 19434
Industrie- und Filmmuseum Wolfen, Wolfen 20650
Münchner Stadtmuseum, München 18880
Museum für visuelle Kommunikation, Köln 18159
Zeiler Foto- und Filmmuseum, Zeil am Main 20736

Hungary
Mozimúzeum, Kaposvár 21440

Iceland
Kvikmyndasafn Islands, Hafnarfjörður 21635

Italy
Museo del Cinema, Milano 24392
Museo dell'Immagine, Cesena 23504
Museo Nazionale del Cinema, Torino 25756
Museo Nazionale del Cinema, Torino 25757

Japan
Tokyo Kokuritsu Kindai Bijutsukan, Film Center, Tokyo 26939

Korea, Republic
Shinyoung Cinema Museum, Namwon 27215

Mauritius
Musée de la Photographie, Port Louis 27739

Mexico
Museo del Cine, Durango 27899

Netherlands
Filmmuseum Foundation Nederlands, Amsterdam 28852
Omroepmuseum en Smalfilmmuseum, Hilversum 29420

New Zealand
Museum of Audio Visual Technology, Wellington 30298

Norway
Filmmuseet, Oslo 30732

Poland
Muzeum Kinematografii, Łódź 31771

Russia
Muzej Goroda Jurjevca, Jurjevec 32865
Muzej Kino, Moskva 33115
Muzej Andreja Tarkovskogo, Jurjevec 32866

Serbia-Montenegro
Muzej Jugoslavenska Kinoteka, Beograd 33806

Sweden
Film- och Biografmuseet, Säter 36168
Filmmuseet, Kristianstad 36016

Switzerland
Pavillon Audrey Hepburn, Tolochenaz 37248
Schweizer Filmmuseum, Basel 36519

Ukraine
Museum of Theatrical, Musical and Cinematographic Art of Ukraine, Kyïv 37874

United Kingdom
British Film Institute Collections, London 39584
Cinema Museum, London 39608
Laurel and Hardy Museum, Ulverston 40748

Uruguay
Galería de Cinemateca, Montevideo 40989

U.S.A.
The Academy Gallery, Beverly Hills 41675
American Advertising Museum, Portland 46630
The American Film Institute, Los Angeles 44890
The Andy Warhol Museum, Pittsburgh 46506
Birthplace of John Wayne, Winterset 48709
Film Forum - Film Archives, Collingswood 42529
Hollywood Heritage Museum, Los Angeles 44909
The Jimmy Stewart Museum, Indiana 44211
Light Factory, Charlotte 42242
McLarty Treasure Museum, Vero Beach 48223
Martin and Osa Johnson Safari Museum, Chanute 42194
The Movie Museum, Owosso 46234
University of California Berkeley Art Museum, Berkeley 41649

Circus → Performing Arts

Clocks and Watches → Horology

Clothing and Dress

Argentina
Museo Criollo de los Corrales, Buenos Aires 00163
Museo Nacional de la Histórico del Traje, Buenos Aires 00229

Australia
Benalla Costume and Pioneer Museum, Benalla 00792
Don Bank Museum, North Sydney 01327
Frances Burke Textile Resource Centre, Melbourne 01226
W.A. Scout Museum, West Perth 01592
Yesteryear Costume Gallery, Orroroo 01348

Belgium
Fashion Museum, Hasselt 03479
Modemuseum Provincie Antwerpen, Antwerpen 03149
Musée du Costume et de la Dentelle, Bruxelles 03323
Poldermuseum, Antwerpen 03168

Brazil
Museo Municipal Barão de Santo Angelo, Rio Pardo 04409

Bulgaria
Etnografska Ekspozicija, Svištov 04878
Istoričeski Muzej, Goce Delčev 04674

Canada
Costume Museum of Canada, Dugald 05351
Ermatinger, Sault Sainte Marie 06411
Musée Marsil, Saint-Lambert 06359
Ukrainian Catholic Women's League Museum, Edmonton 05389
Ukrainian Museum of Canada, Vancouver 06692
Ukrainian Museum of Canada - Manitoba Branch, Winnipeg 06849
Ukrainian Museum of Canada - Ontario Branch, Toronto 06623

Côte d'Ivoire
Musée National du Costume, Grand Bassam 07671

Croatia
Etnografski Muzej, Zagreb 07813
Etnografski Muzej Split, Split 07780

Czech Republic
Expozice Historického Nábytku 16.-19. a Oděvů 19. Století, Turnov 08693
Kloboučnické Muzeum, Nový Jičín 08509
Muzeum Krajky, Prachatice 08561

Denmark
Brede Værk, Kongens Lyngby 08961
Fanø Skibsfarts- og Dragtsamling, Fanø 08819

Ethiopia
City Museum, Makale 09405

Finland
Helsinge Hembygdsmuseum, Vantaa 10179
Kansallispukukeskus, Jyväskylä 09600
Nukke- ja Pukumuseo - Hatanpää Mansion, Tampere 10082

France
Atelier-Musée du Chapeau, Chazelles-sur-Lyon 11262
Centre d'Exposition du Costume, Avallon 10519
Château Beaufief, Mazeray 12906
Ecomusée de Salazie, Salazie 14567
Ecomusée du Pays de Montfort, Montfort-sur-Meu 13087
Musée d'Allauch, Allauch 10291
Musée de la Bonneterie, Troyes 15005
Musée de la Chapellerie, Le Somail 12482
Musée de la Coiffe, Blesle 10767
Musée de la Mode, Marseille 12857
Musée de la Mode et du Textile, Paris 13556
Musée de la Mode Retrovée, Digoin 11517
Musée de l'Automobile La Belle Époque, Pont-l'Évêque 13815
Musée de Traditions Populaires et d'Archéologie, Chauvigny 11255
Musée Départemental Breton, Quimper 13900
Musée du Costume, Château-Chinon 11201
Musée du Costume Civils, La Chapelle-Caro 12142
Musée du Costume Comtadin, Pernes-les-Fontaines 13697
Musée du Costume Comtois, Montgesoye 13089
Musée du Costume Provençal, Solliès-Ville 14765
Musée du Costume Trégor-Goëlo, Paimpol 13453
Musée du Folklore, Moulins (Allier) 13188
Musée du Terroir Marseillais, Marseille 12867
Musée du Vieux Honfleur, Honfleur 12029
Musée Galliéra, Paris 13615
Musée Pyrénéen, Lourdes 12698
Musée Textile de Haute-Alsace, Husseren-Wesserling 12040

Germany
Deutsches Phonomuseum, Sankt Georgen im Schwarzwald 19749
Fächerkabinett, Bielefeld 16153
Geburtshaus Levi Strauss Museum Jeans und Kult, Buttenheim 16435
Heimat- und Miedermuseum Heubach, Heubach, Württemberg 17748
Heimatmuseum Stade, Stade 20023
Hüttenberger Heimatmuseum, Linden, Hessen 18478
Kostüm-Museum im neuen Schloß Schleißheim, Oberschleißheim 19202
Modemuseum, München 18876
Museum der Deutschen Spielzeugindustrie, Neustadt bei Coburg 19080
von Parish-Kostümbibliothek, München 18895
Regionales Heimatmuseum für das Renchtal, Oppenau 19260
Rheinisches Industriemuseum, Ratingen 19496
Schwarzwälder Trachtenmuseum, Haslach 17627
Trachten- und Heimatmuseum, Weiltingen 20453
Trachtenmuseum, Ochsenfurt 19219
Tuchmuseum Lennep der Anna-Hardt-Stiftung, Remscheid 19567
Württembergisches Trachtenmuseum, Pfullingen 19395

Greece
Ethnological and Folklore Museum, Chios 20923
Folklore and Ethnological Museum of Macedonia and Thrace, Thessaloniki 21181
Folklore Museum, Karditsa 20997
Folklore Museum, Xanthi 21218
Folklore Museum of Thrace, Komotini 21025
Monastery of the Archangel Michael Panormitis, Chora 20926
Nafplion Folklore Museum, Nafplion 21092

Guadeloupe
Musée Municipal de Saint-Barthélemy, Saint-Barthélemy 21251

Guatemala
Museo Ixchel del Traje Indigena, Guatemala 21270

Hungary
Szombathelyi Képtár, Szombathely 21589

Iceland
Heimilisidnardarsafnid Halldórustofa, Blönduós 21624

India
Bharatiya Adim Jati Sevak Sangh Museum, Delhi 21767

Iraq
Baghdad Museum, Baghdad 22344

Ireland
Pighouse Collection, Cornafean 22406

Italy
Casa di Carlo Goldoni, Venezia 25914
Galleria del Costume, Firenze 23841
Mostra Permanente del Costume Arbereshe, Vaccarizzo Albanese 25864
Museo Civico, Amalfi 22869
Museo dei Costumi della Partita a Scacchi, Marostica 24303
Museo dei Magli, Ponte Nossa 24992
Museo del Cappello, Alessandria 22847
Museo del Cappello, Montappone 24496
Museo del Costume Arbereshe, Frascineto 23934
Museo del Costume e della Tradizione Nostra Gente, Guardiagrele 24071
Museo del Costume Farnesiano, Gradoli 24045
Museo del Costume R. Piraino, Palermo 24766
Museo del Costume Tradizionale, Grosio 24054
Museo del Vino e della Donna, Ciliverghe 23562
Museo della Donna E. Ortner, Merano 24353
Museo della Sindone, Torino 25742
Museo della Valle Cannobina, Gurro 24078
Museo di Palazzo Mocenigo, Venezia 25938
Museo Salvatore Ferragamo, Firenze 23880
Museo Stibbert, Firenze 23881
Sala del Costume e delle Tradizioni Popolari, Corinaldo 23655

Japan
Fuzoku Hakubutsukan, Kyoto 26398
Hirano Image Library, Osaka 26648
Kobe Fashion Museum, Kobe 26348
Oriamu Museum, Izumiotsu 26278
Sugino Gakuen Isho Hakubutsukan, Tokyo 26926

Jordan
Jordan Folklore Museum, Amman 27053

Korea, Republic
Korean Museum of Contemporary Clothing, Seoul 27251

Malaysia
Museum of Traditional Custumes, Alor Gajah 27615

Mexico
Museo de Cultura Populares del Estado de México, Toluca 28544
Museo de la Indumentaria Mexicana Luis Márquez Romay, México 28139
Museo de Sitio del Claustro de Sor Juana, México 28147
Museo del Traje en Tabasco, Villahermosa 28611
Museo Serfín de Indumentaria Indígena, México 28201

Netherlands
Drenthe's Veste Stedelijk Museum, Coevorden 29057
Hidde Nijland Museum, Hindeloopen 29422
Huizer Klederdrachtmuseum, Huizen 29455
Kostuummuseum De Gouden Leeuw, Noordhorn 29644
Museum Scheveningen, Den Haag 29113
Museum voor Klederdracht en Oud Speelgoed, Warnsveld 29980
'T Museumke, Handel 29338
Mutsen en Poffermuseum Sint-Paulusgasthuis, Sint Oedenrode 29825
Politie-Petten Museum, Slochteren 29834
Streekmuseum Ommen, Ommen 29662
Veluws Klederdrachtenmuseum, Epe 29247
Wasch-en Strijkmuseum, Boxtel 29016
De Wascht en Strekt, Gilze 29284
Zeeuws Poppen- en Klederdrachten Museum, Zoutelande 30066

New Zealand
Gore Historical Museum and Hokonui Heritage Research Centre, Gore 30168

Norway
Konfeksjonsmuseet, Molde 30686
Norsk Trikotasjemuseum, Salhus 30817
Setesdalsmuseet, Rysstad 30814

Poland
Muzeum Kamienica Orsettich w Jarosławiu, Jarosław 31622

Portugal
Museu Nacional do Traje, Lisboa 32311

Qatar
Al Wakra Museum, AL Wakra 32414

Russia
Čukotskij Okružnoj Kraevedčeskij Muzej, Anadyr' 32638
Muzej Etnografičeskogo Kostjuma na Kuklach, Moskva 33097
Muzej Ivanovskogo Sitca, Ivanovo 32831
Muzej Tverskogo Byta, Tver 33637

South Africa
Bernberg Fashion Museum, Johannesburg 34272
Drostdy Museum, Uitenhage 34393
Weenen Museum, Weenen 34401

Spain
Colección de la Casa de Alba, Epila — 34799

Sweden
Livrustkammaren, Stockholm — 36256

Turkey
Etnografi Müzesi, Antalya — 37624
Konya Etnografi Müzesi, Konya — 37741

United Kingdom
Bexhill Museum of Costume and Social History, Bexhill-on-Sea — 38187
Burton Court, Eardisland — 38834
Cavalcade of Costume, Blandford Forum — 38256
Chertsey Museum, Chertsey — 38548
Churchill House Museum and Hatton Gallery, Hereford — 39223
Fairlynch Museum, Budleigh Salterton — 38390
Gallery of Costume, Manchester — 39886
Hollytrees Museum, Colchester — 38611
Horsham Museum, Horsham — 39265
Mansfield Costume Study Centre, Colchester — 38612
Museum of Costume, Bath — 38118
Museum of Costume, New Abbey — 40011
Museum of Costume and Textiles, Nottingham — 40109
Nidderdale Museum, Harrogate — 39170
Paulise de Bush Costume Collection, Broadclyst — 38364
Royal Ceremonial Dress Collection, London — 39759
Saint John's House, Warwick — 40793
Totnes Costume Museum, Totnes — 40723
Vina Cooke Museum of Dolls and Bygone Childhood, Newark-on-Trent — 40026

U.S.A.
Alling Coverlet Museum, Palmyra — 46268
Black Fashion Museum, New York — 45772
Dar Museum First Ladies of Texas Historic Costumes Collection, Denton — 42874
Glove Museum, New York — 45806
The Hermitage, Ho-Ho-Kus — 44041
John E. and Walter D. Webb Museum of Vintage Fashion, Island Falls — 44264
Kent State University Museum, Kent — 44447
Mount Mary College Costume Museum, Milwaukee — 45370
Museum at the Fashion Institute of Technology, New York — 45839
Museum of Vintage Fashion, Lafayette — 44566
Owatonna Arts Center, Owatonna — 46225
Philadelphia Mummers Museum, Philadelphia — 46441
Reynolda House, Winston-Salem — 48703

Coaches → Carriages and Carts

Coffee → Tea and Coffee

Coins → Numismatics

Cookery → Baking and Cookery

Copper

Australia
Geralka Rural Farm, Spalding — 01467

Germany
Kupferschmiede-Museum, Tangermünde — 20139

Mexico
Museo Nacional del Cobre, Salvador Escalante — 28373

Netherlands
Koperslagersmuseum Van der Beele, Horst — 29448

Spain
Calcografía Nacional, Madrid — 34989

Cosmetics

Bulgaria
Kazanlăshka Roza, Kazanlăk — 04701

Canada
Perfume Museum, Niagara-on-the-Lake — 06004

France
Château-Promenade des Parfums, Chilleurs-aux-Bois — 11287
Musée de la Lavande, Cabrières-d'Avignon — 10971
Musée de la Parfumerie, Bastia — 10602
Musée de la Parfumerie, Paris — 13559
Musée de la Parfumerie Fragonard, Grasse — 11919
Musée de la Parfumerie Fragonard, Paris — 13560
Musée de la Parfumerie Galimard, Grasse — 11920
Musée des Arômes et du Parfum, Graveson — 11932

Musée International de la Parfumerie, Grasse — 11922
Musée Traditions Verrieres, Eu — 11678

Germany
4711-Museum, Köln — 18127
Parfum-Flacon-Museum, München — 18894
Wella Museum, Darmstadt — 16550

Korea, Republic
Pacific Museum, Yongin — 27303

Mexico
Museo de Navajas y Curiosidades del Mundo, Puebla — 28335

Spain
Museu del Perfum, Barcelona — 34570

Switzerland
Parfummuseum, Hochfelden — 36806
Schweizer Kamm-Museum, Mümliswil — 36962

U.S.A.
Museum of Cosmetology, Chicago — 42346

Costume → Clothing and Dress

Crafts → Handicraft

Criminology

Argentina
División Museo e Investigaciones Históricas de la Policía Federal, Buenos Aires — 00147
Museo de Gendarmería Nacional, Buenos Aires — 00178
Museo de la Policía del Chaco, Resistencia — 00507
Museo Histórico de la Policía de la Provincia de Misiones, Posadas — 00483
Museo Histórico Policial de La Plata, La Plata — 00393
Museo Penitenciario Argentino, Buenos Aires — 00237

Australia
Adelaide Gaol, Thebarton — 01530
Bridgetown Old Gaol Museum, Bridgetown — 00833
Fremantle Prison Precinct, Fremantle — 01037
Gladstone Gaol, Gladstone, South Australia — 01056
Hay Gaol Museum, Hay — 01094
Justice and Police Museum, Sydney — 01500
Old Dubbo Gaol, Dubbo — 00993
Old Gaol and Courthouse, York — 01632
Old Gaol Museum, Albany — 00723
Old Jail House, Croydon — 00958
Old Melbourne Gaol and Penal Museum, Melbourne — 01238
Old Police Station Museum Brookton, Brookton — 00851
Police Station and Courthouse, Auburn — 00755
Police Station Museum, Mount Barker — 01280
Port Arthur Historic Site, Port Arthur — 01378
Queensland Police Museum, Brisbane — 00842
Richmond Gaol Museum, Richmond, Tasmania — 01414
Roebourne Old Goal Museum, Roebourne — 01423
South Australian Police Museum, Thebarton — 01531
Stuart Town Gaol Museum, Alice Springs — 00739

Austria
Museum des Instituts für gerichtliche Medizin, Wien — 02940
Museum für Rechtsgeschichte, Pöggstall — 02427
Museum Pfleggerichtshaus, Abfaltersbach — 01636
Österreichisches Kriminalmuseum, Scharnstein — 02628
Wiener Kriminalmuseum, Wien — 03005

Belgium
Politiemuseum Oudaan, Antwerpen — 03169
Service historique de la Police, Bruxelles — 03343

Brazil
Museu da Companhia Independente do Palácio Guanabara, Rio de Janeiro — 04340
Museu da Polícia Civil, Rio de Janeiro — 04350

Canada
Calgary Police Service Interpretive Centre, Calgary — 05164
Canada's Penitentiary Museum, Kingston — 05674
Fort Saskatchewan Museum, Fort Saskatchewan — 05451
Halifax Police Museum, Halifax — 05553
Metropolitan Toronto Police Museum and Discovery Centre, Toronto — 06594
Old Carleton County Court House, Woodstock — 06863
Ontario Police College Museum, Aylmer — 05030
Rotary Museum of Police and Corrections, Prince Albert — 06185
Royal Canadian Mounted Police Museum, Regina — 06242
Royal Newfoundland Constabulary Museum, Saint John's — 06350
Vancouver Police Centennial Museum, Vancouver — 06697
Winnipeg Police Museum, Winnipeg — 06854
Wood Mountain Ranch and Rodeo Museum, Wood Mountain — 06860

China, People's Republic
Police Museum, Hong Kong — 07110

Cuba
Antigua Cárcel de Jaruco, Jaruco — 08013
Antiguo Ayuntamiento y Cárcel de Bejucal, Bejucal — 07863

Denmark
Fængselshiststoriske Museum, Horsens — 08895
Ribe Raadhussamling, Ribe — 09030

Egypt
Criminology Museum, Abbasiya — 09231
National Police Museum and Ancient Police Museum, Cairo — 09281

France
Musée des Collections Historiques de la Préfecture de Police, Paris — 13588

Germany
Bayerisches Strafvollzugsmuseum, Kaisheim — 17972
Heimatmuseum, Bernau bei Berlin — 16123
Historiengewölbe, Rothenburg ob der Tauber — 19677
Historische Lochgefängnisse im Alten Rathaus, Nürnberg — 19144
Kriminal- und Foltermuseum Henke, Brandenburg an der Havel — 16282
Mittelalterliches Kriminalmuseum, Rothenburg ob der Tauber — 19679
Polizeihistorische Sammlung Berlin, Berlin — 16081
Sächsisches Strafvollzugsmuseum, Waldheim — 20365
Strafvollzugsmuseum, Ludwigsburg, Württemberg — 18515
Zollmuseum, Wegscheid — 20420
Zollmuseum Friedrichs, Aachen — 15379

India
Jail Training School Museum, Lucknow — 21927

Indonesia
Museum Kepolisian Negara Republik Indonesia, Jakarta — 22119
Museum Kriminal-Mabak, Jakarta — 22121

Ireland
Garda Museum, Dublin — 22427
Kilmainham Gaol and Museum, Dublin — 22440

Italy
Museo del Brigante, Sonnino — 25604
Museo di Antropologia Criminale, Torino — 25746
Museo di Criminologia Medievale, San Gimignano — 25364
Museo di Criminologico, Roma — 25212
Museo Malacologico, Erice — 23741
Museo Storico dell'Arma dei Carabinieri, Roma — 25256

Japan
Meiji-Daigaku Keiji Hakubutsukan, Tokyo — 26886

Madagascar
Musée de la Gendarmerie, Toamasina — 27608

Malaysia
Briged Pasukan Polis Hutan, Kuching — 27657
Muzium Polis Diraja Malaysia, Kuala Lumpur — 27646

Malta
The Old Prison, Victoria — 27711

Mexico
Museo Calabozo de Hidalgo, Chihuahua — 27821
Museo de la Policía Preventiva de la Ciudad de México, México — 28142
Museo del Policía, Monterrey — 28235

Netherlands
Gevangenismuseum Veenhuizen, Veenhuizen — 29930
Museum de Gevangenpoort, Den Haag — 29109
Museum Historische Verzameling Nederlandse Politie, Zaandam — 30034
Museum 't Gevang, Doetinchem — 29161
Museum van de Koninklijke Marechaussee, Buren, Gelderland — 29044
Nederlands Politie Museum, Apeldoorn — 28927

New Zealand
New Zealand Police Museum, Porirua — 30239

Norway
Aurland Bygdetun og Lensmannsstova, Aurland — 30404
Trondheim Politimuseum, Trondheim — 30945

Philippines
Manila Police Department Museum and Gallery, Manila — 31381

Poland
Muzeum Więzienia Pawiak, Warszawa — 32131
Wieża Więzienna i Katownia, Gdańsk — 31583

Russia
Muzej Istorii Milicii, Sankt-Peterburg — 33438
Muzej Kriminalistiki, Barnaul — 32674

South Africa
South African Police Service Museum, Pretoria — 34356

Spain
Museo de la Escuela General de Policía, Madrid — 35023
Museo del Bandolero, Ronda — 35339

Sweden
Långholmens Fängelsemuseum, Stockholm — 36253
Polishistoriska Museet, Stockholm — 36272
Polistekniska Museet, Solna — 36220

Switzerland
Kriminalmuseum der Kantonspolizei Zürich, Zürich — 37383
Polizeimuseum, Aarau — 36428

United Kingdom
Bath Police Museum, Bath — 38108
Beaumaris Gaol and Courthouse, Beaumaris — 38138
City of London Police Museum, London — 39609
Dover Old Town Goal, Dover — 38767
Essex Police Museum, Chelmsford — 38539
Fire Police Museum, Sheffield — 40483
Galleries of Justice, Nottingham — 40106
Gloucester Prison Museum, Gloucester — 39082
Greater Manchester Police Museum, Manchester — 39887
HM Prison Service Museum, Rugby — 40354
Inveraray Jail, Inveraray — 39295
Jedburgh Castle Jail Museum, Jedburgh — 39324
Kent Police Museum, Chatham — 38530
Metropolitan Police Historical Museum, London — 39707
Mounted Branch Museum, East Molesey — 38849
Ripon Prison and Police Museum, Ripon — 40328
Sherlock Holmes Museum, London — 39776
South Wales Police Museum, Bridgend — 38320
Stirling Old Town Jail, Stirling — 40594
Tales of the Old Gaol House, King's Lynn — 39371
Tetbury Police Museum, Tetbury — 40689
Thames Police Museum, London — 39789
Tolhouse Museum and Brass Rubbing Centre, Great Yarmouth — 39127
West Midlands Police Museum, Birmingham — 38233

U.S.A.
The 1811 Old Lincoln County Jail and 1839 Jailer's House Museum, Wiscasset — 48714
American Police Center and Museum, Chicago — 42301
Andersonville Prison, Andersonville — 41206
Cauthorn Memorial Depot and Sutton County Jail, Sonora — 47677
Cleveland Police Museum, Cleveland — 42468
Eastern State Penitentiary Historic Site, Philadelphia — 46403
Houston Police Museum, Houston — 44125
Jacinto Courthouse, Corinth — 42633
Law Enforcement Museum, Roselle — 47005
Montana Auto Museum, Deer Lodge — 42846
The Museum of Death, Los Angeles — 44931
New York City Police Museum, New York — 45857
Old Fire House and Police Museum, Superior — 47891
Old Gaol Museum, York — 48790
Old Gaol Museum, Albion — 41095
The Old Jail Museum, Crawfordsville — 42692
The Old Jail Museum, Warrenton — 48317
Old Monterey Jail, Monterey — 45458
Old Prison Museum, Deer Lodge — 42847
Porter County Old Jail Museum, Valparaiso — 48193
Yuma Territorial Prison Museum, Yuma — 48819

Dairy Products

Canada
Creamery Museum, Eriksdale — 05411
Historic Markerville Creamery, Markerville — 05815

Denmark
Hjedding Mejerimuseum, Ølgod — 09018

Estonia
Eesti Piimandusmuuseum, Imavere — 09326

Finland
Meijerimuseo, Saukkola — 10022

France
Moulin-Musée de la Brosserie, Saint-Félix — 14213
Musée de la Meunerie, Courtelevant — 11438
Musée des Tradition de l'île, Noirmoutier-en-l'Ile — 13358
Musée du Bocage Normand, Saint-Lô — 14327
Musée du Camembert, Vimoutiers — 15261
Musée du Lait, Belvedere — 10678

Germany
Carl-Hirnbein-Museum, Missen-Wilhams — 18750
Heimatmuseum Hüttenberg, Hüttenberg — 17862
Historische Käsküche, Wiggensbach — 20585
Molkerei-Museum, Bernbeuren — 16124
Trützschler's Milch- und Reklamemuseum, Hildburghausen — 17754

Italy
Museo del Profumo, Milano — 24395
Museo del Sale, Paceco — 24727

Netherlands
Kaasboerderijmuseum de Weistaar, Maarsbergen — 29555
Kaaswaag Gouda, Gouda — 29294

Russia
Muzej Tul'skie Samovary, Tula 33628

South Africa
Riemland Museum, Heilbron 34261

Switzerland
Fromagerie de Démonstration de Gruyères, Pringy 37035
Milchwirtschaftliches Museum, Kiesen 36824

United Kingdom
National Dairy Museum, Ashurst 38035

U.S.A.
America's Ice Cream and Dairy Museum, Medina 45224

Dance → Performing Arts

Decorative and Applied Arts

Algeria
Musée Folklorique de Ghardaïa, Ghardaïa 00064
Le Palais de l'Art Traditionnel, Constantine 00059

Argentina
Fundación Banco Francés, Buenos Aires 00150
Museo Almacén El Recreo, Chivilcoy 00276
Museo Folklórico Regional de Humahuaca, Humahuaca 00365
Museo Nacional de Arte Decorativo, Buenos Aires 00226
Museo Patria Chica de Mohamed Diaz, Realicó 00504
Museo Tornambe de la Universidad Nacional de San Juan, San Juan 00574
Palais de Glace, Buenos Aires 00251

Armenia
State History Museum of Armenia, Erevan 00692

Australia
Powerhouse Museum, Ultimo 01558

Austria
Bardeau'sches Kultur- und Ausstellungszentrum, Feldbach 01826
Heimatmuseum Egg, Egg 01789
Im Kinsky-Museum, Wien 02899
Kulturhistorische Sammlung, Graz 01920
Sammlung Bodingbauer, Steyr 02689
Sammlung der Universität für angewandte Kunst Wien mit Oskar Kokoschka Zentrum, Wien 02980
Schloß Loosdorf mit Prunkräumen und Zinnfigurensammlung, Loosdorf, Bez. Mistelbach 02253
Schloß Moosham, Tamsweg 02712

Azerbaijan
State Museum of Azerbaijan Carpets and Applied Art Letif Kerimov, Baku 03071

Belgium
Bruggemuseum - Gruuthuse, Brugge 03250
Espace des Saveurs, Herve 03496
Maison du Roi, Bruxelles 03288
Musée d'Ansembourg, Liège 03572
Musée de l'Orfevrerie de la Communaute Française, Seneffe 03729
Musée du Cinquantenaire, Bruxelles 03322
Musées Royaux d'Art et d'Histoire, Bruxelles 03337
Museum Maagdenhuis, Antwerpen 03150
Stedelijk Museum Ieper, Ieper 03517

Brazil
Açude Museum, Rio de Janeiro 04314
Chácara do Céu Museum, Rio de Janeiro 04321
Museu de Arte Popular da Fortaleza dos Reis Magos, Natal 04220
Museu Henriqueta Catharino, Salvador 04437

Bulgaria
Chudožestvena Galerija, Žeravna 04932
Nacionalna Galerija za Dekorativni Izkustva, Sofia 04858

Canada
Joseph Schneider Haus, Kitchener 05697
Musée des Beaux-Arts de Montréal, Montréal 05918
Museum of Cape Breton Heritage, North East Margaree 06022
Nels Berggran Museum, Imperial 05615
New Brunswick College of Craft and Design Gallery, Fredericton 05463
Nova Scotia Centre for Craft and Design, Halifax 05558
Oseredok Ukrainian Art Gallery and Museum, Winnipeg 06836
Pavillon Saint-Arnaud, Trois-Rivières 06647
Prescott House Museum, Port Williams 06171
Ross Memorial Museum, Saint Andrews 06303
Whetung Craft Centre and Art Gallery, Curve Lake 05298

China, People's Republic
GianFu Classic Art Museum, Beijing 06966

Colombia
Museo Patio del Moro, Guaduas 07490

Costa Rica
Museo de Arte y Diseño Contemporáneo, San José 07655

Croatia
Muzej za Umjetnost i Obrt, Zagreb 07834
Zbirka Anke Gvozdanović, Zagreb 07841

Cuba
Centro de Diseño Ambiental, La Habana 07924
Museo Artes Decorativo, Gibara 07910
Museo de Ambiente Histórico Cubano, Santiago de Cuba 08134
Museo de Artes Decorativas de Palacio Salcines, Guantánamo 07916
Museo Nacional de Artes Decorativas, La Habana 07986
Museo Nacional de Artes Decorativas de Santa Clara, Santa Clara 08124

Cyprus, Turkish Republic
Folk Art Institute, Lefkoşa 08236
Güzel Sanatlar Müzesi, Girne 08226

Czech Republic
Design Centrum České Republiky, Brno 08263
Městské Muzeum, Aš 08242
Městské Muzeum, Chotěboř 08315

Denmark
Det Danske Kunstindustrimuseum, København 08927
Davids Samling, København 08928
Michael og Anna Anchers Hus og Saxilds Gaard, Skagen 09056
Museet for Varde By og Omegn, Varde 09101
Museet på Koldinghus, Kolding 08959
Trapholt, Kolding 08960

Estonia
Eesti Tarbekunsti- ja Disainimuuseum, Tallinn 09362

Finland
Alvar Aalto Museum, Jyväskylä 09593
Designmuseo, Helsinki 09477
Edelfelt-Vallgren Museo, Porvoo 09950
Hiekan Taidemuseo, Tampere 10077

France
Château de Champchevrier, Cléré-les-Pins 11317
Musée Angladon, Avignon 10527
Musée Anne de Beaujeu, Moulins (Allier) 13185
Musée Arménien de France, Paris 13530
Musée Baccarat, Paris 13533
Musée Baron Gérard, Bayeux 10615
Musée Boucher-de-Perthes, Abbeville 10222
Musée Bouilhet-Christofle, Paris 13537
Musée Bourdelle, Paris 13538
Musée d'Art et d'Histoire, Belfort 10670
Musée de la Nacre et de la Tabletterie, Méru 12948
Musée de la Vie Romantique, Paris 13568
Musée de l'Eventail, Paris 13573
Musée des Années 30, Boulogne-Billancourt 10837
Musée des Arts décoratifs, Lyon 12735
Musée des Arts Décoratifs, Paris 13586
Musée des Arts Décoratifs et de la Modernité, Gourdon (Alpes-Maritimes) 11892
Musée des Beaux-Arts, Blois 10774
Musée des Beaux-Arts, Reims 13928
Musée du Château, Laas 12276
Musée du Château, Siorac-en-Périgord 14752
Musée-Ecole de la Perrine, Laval (Mayenne) 12362
Musée Leblanc-Duvernoy, Auxerre 10511
Musée Municipal de l'Évêché, Limoges 12616
Musée National des Arts Asiatiques Guimet, Paris 13633
Musée Paul Dupuy, Toulouse 14951
Prieuré du Vieux Logis, Nice 13327
Villa Majorelle, Nancy 13246

Germany
Auto- und Motorrad-Museum, Öhringen 19225
Bauhaus-Archiv, Berlin 15916
Bayerisches Nationalmuseum, München 18833
Das Berta-Hummel-Museum im Hummelhaus, Massing 18663
Bröhan-Museum, Berlin 15930
Design Center Stuttgart des Landesgewerbeamtes Baden-Württemberg, Stuttgart 20087
Deutsches Drachenmuseum und Stadtmuseum, Furth im Wald 17180
Deutsches Plakat Museum, Essen 16947
Dreikronenhaus, Osnabrück 19276
Ehemaliges Jagdschloß Bebenhausen, Tübingen 20222
Fürstliches Residenzschloß, Detmold 16587
Fugger-Museum, Babenhausen, Schwaben 15582
Gablonzer Archiv Museum, Kaufbeuren 18038
Galerie Handwerk, München 18852
Gewerbemuseum der LGA im Germanischen Nationalmuseum, Nürnberg 19140
Glasschmelzofenbau-Hütte mit Glasausstellung, Plößberg 19420
Gotisches Haus, Wörlitz 20641
Grassimuseum Leipzig, Leipzig 18398
Heimatmuseum Scheeßel, Scheeßel 19768
Historisches Museum Hanau, Hanau 17584
Jugendstilmuseum Reissenweber, Brühl, Baden 16375
Kestner-Museum, Hannover 17599
Krippenmuseum, Glattbach 17296
Krippenstube-Heimatstube, Plößberg 19421
Kunst und Museum, Hollfeld 17824
Kunstgewerbemuseum, Dresden 16689
Kunstgewerbemuseum, Berlin 16028
Kunsthandwerk und Plastik Sammlung, Kassel 18022
Kunstsammlungen der Veste Coburg, Coburg 16483
Maximilianmuseum, Augsburg 15561
Museum beim Markt - Angewandte Kunst seit 1900, Karlsruhe 17996
Museum Corps de Logis, Düsseldorf 16735
Museum der RaumKunst aus Renaissance, Barock und Rokoko, Berlin 16049
Museum der Stadt Miltenberg und Porzellansammlung Kreis Dux, Miltenberg 18740
Museum der Stadt Zerbst mit Sammlung Katharina II., Zerbst 20746
Museum für Angewandte Kunst, Frankfurt am Main 17062
Museum für Angewandte Kunst, Gera 17244
Museum für Angewandte Kunst, Köln 18157
Museum für Europäische Gartenkunst, Düsseldorf 16736
Museum für Frühislamische Kunst, Bamberg 15812
Museum für schlesische Landeskunde im Haus Schlesien, Königswinter 18183
Museum Huelsmann, Bielefeld 16157
Museumsberg Flensburg, Flensburg 17012
Die Neue Sammlung, München 18890
Palais Papius, Wetzlar 20557
Red Dot Design Museum im Design Zentrum Nordrhein-Westfalen, Essen 16961
Residenzmuseum, München 18901
Rokokomuseum Schloß Belvedere, Weimar, Thüringen 20470
Schloß Heidelberg, Heidelberg 17675
Schlossmuseum, Langenburg 18332
Schloßmuseum der Stadt Aschaffenburg, Aschaffenburg 15531
Schloßmuseum Mespelbrunn, Mespelbrunn 18717
Schlossmuseum und Königliches Schloss, Berchtesgaden 15889
Schwäbisches Krippenmuseum im Jesuitenkolleg, Mindelheim 18743
Sebnitzer Kunstblumen- und Heimatmuseum Prof. Alfred Meiche, Sebnitz 19908
Spessartmuseum, Lohr am Main 18499
Stadtmuseum Fembohaus mit Noricama, Nürnberg 19162
Stadtmuseum Lindau, Lindau, Bodensee 18476
Städtisches Museum, Überlingen 20245
Städtisches Museum, Zeulenroda 20750
Vitra Design Museum, Weil am Rhein 20438
Werdenfelser Museum, Garmisch-Partenkirchen 17204

Greece
Decorative Arts Museum of Rhodos, Rhodos 21142
Konstandoglou Collection, Athinai 20869
Likion Ton Ellinidon Collection, Rethymnon 21140
Museum of Decorative Arts, Athinai 20884
Tellogleion Foundation, Thessaloniki 21193

Hungary
Iparművészeti Múzeum, Budapest 21346

India
Crafts Museum, Delhi 21768
Dr. Bhau Daji Lad Museum, Mumbai 21946
Government Central Museum, Jaipur, Rajasthan 21862
Maharaja Sawai Man Singh II Museum, Jaipur, Rajasthan 21863
Raja Dinkar Kelkar Museum, Pune 21994

Indonesia
Museum Batik, Yogyakarta 22217
Museum Radya Pustaka, Surakarta 22205

Iran
Astan-e-Qods-e Razavi Museums, Mashad 22265
Chehel-Stoun Museum, Ghazvin 22236
Chinikhaneh Museum, Ardebil 22230
Honarhaye Tazini - Rakibkhaneh, Isfahan 22246
Kandeloos Museum, Kojoor 22260
Malek Museum, Teheran 22309
Mellat Museum, Teheran 22310
Pars Museum, Shiraz 22281

Iraq
Mustansiriya School Collections, Baghdad 22347

Ireland
Glebe House and Gallery, Church Hill 22393
The Hunt Museum, Limerick 22505
Museum of Decorative Arts and History, Dublin 22444

Israel
L.A. Mayer Museum for Islamic Art, Jerusalem 22646

Italy
Collezione Permanente del Design Italiano '45-'90, Milano 24381
Museo Civico d'Arte Antica, Torino 25736
Museo Civico Gaetano Filangieri, Napoli 24581
Museo del Corallo, Ravello 25077
Museo del Corallo, Torre del Greco 25771
Museo del Presepe, Modena 24442
Museo del Presepio, Dalmine 23708
Museo del Presepio Tipologico Internazionale, Roma 25188
Museo dell'Arte del Cappello, Ghiffa 24019
Museo di Arte Contadina, Montegallo 24529
Museo di Palazzo Reale Genova, Genova 23996
Museo Missionario Francescano, Fiesole 23809
Oskar Schlemmer Theatre Estate and Collection, Oggebbio 24673
Palazzo Tozzoni, Imola 24091
Raccolte di Palazzo Tursi, Genova 24013

Japan
Fukuoka-shi Bijutsukan, Fukuoka 26146
Hida Takayama Bijutsukan, Takayama 26805
Suntory Museum, Osaka 26673
Tako no Hakubutsukan, Tokyo 26930
Tokyo-to Teien Bijutsukan, Tokyo 26947
Toyota Municipal Museum of Art, Toyota, Aichi 26974

Korea, Republic
Ewha Yoja Taehakkyo Pakmulgwan, Seoul 27232
Seoul Design Museum, Seoul 27272

Latvia
Dekoratīvi Lietišķās Mākslas Muzejs, Rīga 27403

Lebanon
Moussa Castle Museum, Beiteddine 27486

Luxembourg
Villa Vauban, Luxembourg 27570

Malaysia
Museum and Art Gallery, Shah Alam 27686
Muzium Negeri Kedah, Alor Setar 27618

Mexico
Galeria Mexicana de Diseño, México 28102
Museo Casa Ruth Lechuga, México 28117
Museo de Arte Olga Costa, Guanajuato 27969
Museo de la Casa de las Artesanías del Estado de Chihuahua, Bocoyna 27794
Museo de La Quemada, Guadalupe 27964
Museo Estudio Diego Rivera, México 28167
Museo Franz Mayer, México 28171
Museo Mural Diego Rivera, México 28181
Museo Nacional de Arte Popular, Mérida 28084
Museo Nacional de Virreinato, Tepotzotlán 28500
Museo Palacio de la Canal, San Miguel de Allende 28411
Museo Universitario Antigua Casa de los Muñecos, Puebla 28343

Nepal
National Museum of Nepal, Kathmandu 28788

Netherlands
Amsterdams Historisch Museum, Amsterdam 28836
Centraal Museum, Utrecht 29897
Collectie A. Veltman, Bussum 29048
Expositieruimte De Weem, Westeremden 29997
Fogelsangh State, Veenklooster 29931
Frans Hals Museum, Haarlem 29324
Galerie Numero 16, Noordbroek 29641
Het Gouverneurshuis, Heusden 29414
Hans van Riessen Museum, Vledderveen 29952
Herdenkingsbordenmuseum, Lochem 29544
Historisch Museum Deventer, Deventer 29145
Het Kantenhuis, Amsterdam 28863
Kasteel de Haar, Haarzuilens 29333
Merklappenmuseum, Dieteren 29153
Museum Boijmans Van Beuningen, Rotterdam 29759
Museum het Catharina Gasthuis, Gouda 29297
Museum het Tramstation, Schipluiden 29809
Nederlands Tegelmuseum, Otterlo 29688
Oudheidkamer in het Stadhuis, Bolsward 28995
Simon van Gijn Museum aan Huis, Dordrecht 29178
Stedelijk Museum, Alkmaar 28806
Stedelijk Museum Roermond, Roermond 29743
Stedelijk Museum Vianen, Vianen 29943
Stedelijk Museum Zutphen, Zutphen 30077
Streekmuseum Het Rondeel, Rhenen 29729
Het Waaierkabinet, Amsterdam 28913

New Zealand
The Dowse, Hutt City 30180

Norway
Kunstindustrimuseet, Oslo 30741
Nordenfjeldske Kunstindustrimuseum, Trondheim 30939
Permanenten Vestlandske Kunstindustrimuseum, Bergen 30427

Peru
Museo de la Reincorporación, Tacna 31254
Museo de Sitio de Narihualá, Catacaos 31138

Philippines
Casa Gorordo Museum, Cebu 31308
Museo ng Kalinangang Pilipino, Manila 31384
Santo Niño Shrine and Heritage Museum, Tacloban 31454

Poland
Muzeum Kultury Szlacheckiej, Łopuszna 31781
Muzeum Okręgowe w Toruniu, Toruń 32054
Muzeum Plakatu w Wilanowie, Warszawa 32118
Muzeum Sprzętu Gospodarstwa Domowego, Ziębice 32219
Muzeum Sztuk Użytkowych, Poznań 31911
Muzeum Zamoyskich w Kozłówce, Kamionka 31638
Sztuka Dalekiego Wschodu, Toruń 32055

Portugal
Casa de Vitorino Ribeiro, Porto 32329
Casa Museu Guerra Junqueiro, Porto 32330

Exhibition Centre, Lisboa 32286
Fundação Ricardo do Espírito Santo Silva, Lisboa 32287
Museu-Biblioteca da Fundacão de Casa de Bragança, Vila Viçosa 32359
Museu Calouste Gulbenkian, Lisboa 32292
Museu Condes de Castro Guimarães, Cascais 32249
Museu da Quinta das Cruzes, Funchal 32274
Museu da Regiao Flåviense, Chaves 32252
Museu Municipal, Pinhel 32326
Museu Municipal de Viana do Castelo, Viana do Castelo 32356
Museu Nacional de Machado de Castro, Coimbra 32264
Museu Nacional de Soares dos Reis, Porto 32338
Palácio Nacional de Mafra, Mafra 32319

Romania
Muzeul de Artă, Iaşi 32532
Muzeul de Artă, Târgovişte 32603
Muzeul Hrandt Avakian, Bucureşti 32457
Muzeul Judeţean Argeş, Piteşti 32569
Muzeul Naţional Brukenthal, Sibiu 32593
Muzeul Naţional Cotroceni, Bucureşti 32465
Muzeul Orăşenesc, Lipova 32543

Russia
Belozerskij Muzej Narodnogo Dekorativno-prikladnogo Iskusstva, Belozersk 32681
Bogorodickij Dvorec-muzej i Park, Bogorodick 32694
Čukotskij Okružnoj Kraevedčeskij Muzej, Anadyr' 32638
Dagestanskij Muzej Izobrazitelnych Iskusstv, Machačkala 32996
Dom-muzej A.A. Dydykina, Palech 33279
Dom-muzej I.I. Golikova, Palech 33280
Dom-Muzej P.D. Korina, Palech 33281
Dom-muzej N.M. Zinovjeva, Djagilevo 32757
Elaginoostrovskij Dvorec-Muzej Russkogo Dekorativno-Prikladnogo Iskusstva i Interjera XVIII-XX vv., Sankt-Peterburg 33393
Gosudarstvennyj Chudožestvennyj Muzej Altajskogo Kraja, Barnaul 32672
Gosudarstvennyj Istoričeskij Zapovednik Gorki Leninskie, Gorki Leninskie 32807
Gosudarstvennyj Muzej Istorii Sankt-Peterburga - Petropavlovskij Sobor, Sankt-Peterburg 33404
Gosudarstvennyj Muzej Palechskogo Iskusstva, Palech 33282
Gosudarstvennyj Muzej Zapovednik Petergof, Sankt-Peterburg 33406
Istoriko-Architekturnyj, Chudožestvennyj i Archeologičeskij Muzej "Zarajskij Kreml", Zarajsk 33746
Jurinskij Istoriko-chudožestvennyj Muzej, Jurino 32863
Krasnojarskij Chudožestvennyj Muzej im. V.I. Surikova, Krasnojarsk 32950
Muzej Dekorativno-prikladnogo Iskusstva, Sankt-Peterburg 33431
Muzej Dekorativno-prikladnogo Iskusstva Urala, Čeljabinsk 32726
Muzej Istorii Kamnereznogo i Juvelirnogo Iskusstva, Ekaterinburg 32776
Nižegorodskij Gosudarstvennyj Istoriko-architekturnyj Muzej-zapovednik, Nižnij Novgorod 33223
Oblastnoj Muzejnyj Centr, Sankt-Peterburg 33473
Oružejnaja Palata, Moskva 33168
Paviljon Katalnoj Gorki, Lomonosov 32991
Pereslavl-Zalesskij Gosudarstvennyj Istoriko-architekturnyj i Chudožestvennyj Muzej-zapovednik, Pereslavl-Zalesskij 33299
Rjazanskij Oblastnoj Chudožestvennyj Muzej im. I.P. Požalostina, Rjazan 33352
Samarskij Oblastnoj Chudožestvennyj Muzej, Samara 33377
Šeremetevskij Dvorec - Fontannyj Dom, Sankt-Peterburg 33483
Sergievo-Posadskij Gosudarstvennyj Istoriko-chudožestvennyj Muzej Zapovednik, Sergiev Posad 33521
Severo-osetinskij Gosudarstvennyj Obedinennyj Muzej Istorii, Architektury i Literatury, Vladikavkaz 33690
Uljanovskij Oblastnoj Chudožestvennyj Muzej, Uljanovsk 33668
Valaamskij Naučno-issledovatelskij Cerkovno-archeologičeskij i Prirodnyj Muzej-zapovednik, Sortavala 33548
Vserossijskij Muzej Dekorativno-Prikladnogo i Narodnogo Iskusstva, Moskva 33183

Serbia-Montenegro
Muzej Primenjene Umetnosti, Beograd 33810

South Africa
The Design Museum, Cape Town 34204
Melrose House, Pretoria 34347
Roodepoort Museum, Florida Park 34240
Van Gybland-Oosterhoff Collection, Pretoria 34362

Spain
Alcázar, Sevilla 35471
Centro del Diseño, Bilbao 34610
Museo Art Nouveau y Art Deco, Salamanca 35359
Museo de la Alhambra, Granada 34876
Museu de les Arts Decoratives, Barcelona 34564
Museu Frederic Marès, Barcelona 34578
Museu Local d'Artesania Terrissaire, Verdú 35647
Museu Romàntic Can Llopis, Sitges 35499
Palacio Real de Madrid, Madrid 35059
Palacio Real y Museos de Tapices, San Ildefonso 35376

Sweden
Hälsinglands Museum, Hudiksvall 35965
Jämtlands Läns Museum, Östersund 36146
Länsmuseet Halmstad, Halmstad 35941
Örebro Läns Museum, Örebro 36139
Röhsska Museet, Göteborg 35919
Skoklosters Slott, Skokloster 36201
Surahammars Bruksmuseum, Surahammar 36315

Switzerland
Abegg-Stiftung, Riggisberg 37064
Collection de la Fondation in Memoriam Comtesse Tatiana Zoubov, Genève 36735
Froschmuseum, Münchenstein 36964
Haus zum Kirschgarten, Basel 36499
Heimatmuseum und Buchdruckerstube, Beromünster 36557
Historisches Museum Bern, Bern 36541
Historisches Museum Luzern, Luzern 36910
Mudac-Musée de Design et d'Arts Appliqués Contemporains, Lausanne 36856
Musée d'Histoire, La Chaux-de-Fonds 36628
Musée Eugène Burnand, Moudon 36958
Musée Suisse, Zürich 37393
Museum für Gestaltung Basel, Basel 36510
Museum für Gestaltung Zürich, Zürich 37397
Museum in der Burg Zug, Zug 37428
Museum Lindengut, Winterthur 37336
Rathaussammlung, Stein am Rhein 37216
Sammlungen der Schule für Gestaltung Basel, Basel 36518
Stadtmuseum Wil, Wil 37320
Stiftung Dr. Edmund Müller, Beromünster 36559

Turkey
Galeri Suav ve Küsav, İstanbul 37701
Yıldız Şale, İstanbul 37716

United Kingdom
American Museum in Britain, Bath 38106
Art and Design Gallery, Hatfield 39187
Bantock House, Wolverhampton 40915
Belton House, Grantham 39110
Birmingham Institute of Art and Design, Birmingham 38213
The Bowes Museum, Barnard Castle 38087
Brighton Museum and Art Gallery, Brighton 38340
Charleston Trust, Firle 38992
Cheltenham Art Gallery and Museum, Cheltenham 38544
Cleveland Crafts Centre, Middlesbrough 39947
Clocktower Museum, Elsham 38930
Clotworthy Arts Centre, Antrim 38005
Coughton Court, Alcester 37960
Courtauld Institute Gallery, London 39615
Cragside House, Rothbury 40343
Crown Liquor Saloon, Belfast 38151
Design Museum, London 39623
Dimbola Lodge, Freshwater 39017
Doddington Hall, Doddington 38737
Dunhill Museum, London 39628
Fitzwilliam Museum, Cambridge 38454
Gawsworth Hall, Macclesfield 39863
Gilbert Collection, London 39642
Helena Thompson Museum, Workington 40934
Herbert Art Gallery and Museum, Coventry 38643
Holburne Museum of Art, Bath 38115
Kellie Castle, Pittenweem 40207
Laing Art Gallery, Newcastle-upon-Tyne 40038
Little Holland House, London 39690
Lotherton Hall, Aberford 37947
Manchester Art Gallery, Manchester 39892
Manor House, Sandford Orcas 40441
Merchant Adventurers' Hall, York 40965
Millennium Galleries, Sheffield 40487
Mompesson House, Salisbury 40435
Museum of Domestic Design and Architecture MODA, Barnet 38088
Museum of Farnham, Farnham 38982
Museum of the Order of Saint John, London 39722
Museums and Study Collection, London 39725
Newby Hall, Ripon 40327
Norton Conyers, Near Ripon 40003
Palace of Westminster, London 39740
Peckover House, Wisbech 40906
Pickford's House Museum, Derby 38718
Polesden Lacey, Great Bookham 39121
Potter's Museum of Curiosity and Smugglers's Museum, Bolventor 38273
Powell-Cotton Museum, Quex House and Gardens, Birchington 38203
Ragley Hall, Alcester 37961
Royal Museum and Art Gallery, Canterbury 38474
Scolton Manor Museum, Haverfordwest 39191
Speke Hall, Liverpool 39527
Sutton Park, Sutton-on-the-Forest 40652
Tatton Park, Knutsford 39406
Usher Gallery, Lincoln 39503
Victoria and Albert Museum, London 39795
Waddesdon Manor, Waddesdon 40757
Warner Archive, Milton Keynes 39963
Wernher Collection at Ranger's House, London 39803
West Berkshire Museum, Newbury 40030
West Wycombe Park House, West Wycombe 40830
William Morris Gallery and Brangwyn Gift, London 39808

Uruguay
Museo de Arte Industrial, Montevideo 40996
Museo del Azulejo Francés, Madonado 40979
Palacio Taranco, Montevideo 41031

U.S.A.
The 100th Meridian Museum, Cozad 42686
1890 House-Museum and Center for Victorian Arts, Cortland 42652
AAF Museum, Washington 48330
Adam Thoroughgood House, Virginia Beach 48243
Alleghany Highlands Arts and Crafts Center, Clifton Forge 42490
American Museum of Straw Art, Long Beach 44857
Ash Lawn-Highland, Charlottesville 42246
Asia Society and Museum, New York 45768
Asian Cultures Museum, Corpus Christi 42644
Astor House Hotel Museum, Golden 43711
Atlantic Wildfowl Heritage Museum, Virginia Beach 48244
The Bard Graduate Center for Studies in the Decorative Arts, Design, and Culture, New York 45771
Barnes Foundation, Merion 45266
Batsto Village, Hammonton 43890
Bayou Bend Collection, Houston 44116
Bellamy Mansion Museum of History and Design Arts, Wilmington 48657
Bellingrath Home, Theodore 47993
The Bennington Museum, Bennington 41629
Bergstrom-Mahler Museum, Neenah 45643
Bidwell House, Monterey 45460
Birks Museum, Decatur 42831
Boscobel Restoration, Garrison 43630
Brunnier Art Museum, Ames 41170
Buccleuch Mansion, New Brunswick 45676
California Heritage Museum, Santa Monica 47439
Campbell House Museum, Saint Louis 47113
Campbell Whittlesey House, Rochester 46939
The Carole and Barry Kaye Museum of Miniatures, Los Angeles 44895
CFCC Webber Center, Ocala 46079
Cincinnati Art Museum, Cincinnati 42400
The Columbian Museum and Art Center, Wamego 48301
Concord Museum, Concord 42598
Cooper-Hewitt National Design Museum, New York 45788
Coral Gables Merrick House, Coral Gables 42625
Crescent Bend/Armstrong-Lockett House and William P. Toms Memorial Gardens, Knoxville 44515
The Dana-Thomas House, Springfield 47736
Daughters of the American Revolution Museum, Washington 48344
Decatur House Museum, Washington 48345
Decorative Arts Center of Ohio, Lancaster 44620
Dedham Historical Museum, Dedham 42840
Department of the Treasury Museum, Washington 48346
Detroit Repertory Theatre Gallery, Detroit 42925
DeWitt Wallace Decorative Arts Museum, Williamsburg 48628
Dezign House, Jefferson 44323
Edsel and Eleanor Ford House, Grosse Pointe Shores 43844
Edward Dean Museum, Cherry Valley 42278
Elbert Hubbard-Roycroft Museum, East Aurora 43035
Elizabeth D. Walters Library, Stroudsburg 47854
Fallingwater - Western Pennsylvania Conservancy, Mill Run 45344
Fenimore Art Museum, Cooperstown 42619
Festival-Institute Museum, Round Top 47017
Fonthill Museum of the Bucks County Historical Society, Doylestown 42982
Forbes Collection, New York 45800
Fort Hunter Mansion, Harrisburg 43923
Founders Gallery, San Diego 47276
Fred Wolf Jr. Gallery, Philadelphia 46412
Frederic Remington Art Museum, Ogdensburg 46103
Fulton Mansion, Rockport 46972
Gallier House, New Orleans 45725
George Washington's Mount Vernon, Mount Vernon 45546
The Goldstein Museum of Design, Saint Paul 47154
Gomez Foundation for Mill House, Marlboro 45169
Harrison Gray Otis House, Boston 41809
Headley-Whitney Museum, Lexington 44738
Henry B. Plant Museum, Tampa 47942
Herbert and Eileen Bernard Museum, New York 45814
Heritage Center of Lancaster County, Lancaster 44624
Hermann-Grima House, New Orleans 45726
Hermitage Foundation Museum, Norfolk 45966
Hibel Museum of Art - Jupiter, Jupiter 44372
Hillwood Museum, Washington 48360
Hinckley Foundation Museum, Ithaca 44273
Historic Cherry Hill, Albany 41084
Historic Hope Foundation, Windsor 48683
The Historic Indian Agency House, Portage 46613
Horatio Colony House Museum, Keene 44426
House of Memories Museum, Wilson 48667
Houston Museum of Decorative Arts, Chattanooga 42262
Illinois Artisans and Visitors Centers, Whittington 48598
Indianapolis Museum of Art, Indianapolis 44228
Jacob Kelley House Museum, Hartsville 43949
Jamestown Settlement, Williamsburg 48629
Jeremiah Lee Mansion, Marblehead 45134
John A. Logan College Museum, Carterville 42124
The John and Mable Ringling Museum of Art, Sarasota 47453
John Brown House, Providence 46708
Joseph Manigault House, Charleston 42221
Julian H. Sleeper House, Saint Paul 47158
Kansas Museum of History, Topeka 48033
Kearney Mansion Museum, Fresno 43560
Kelton House Museum, Columbus 42589
Kemerer Museum of Decorative Arts, Bethlehem 41666
Kent State University Museum, Kent 44447
Kimberly Crest House, Redlands 46821
Ladew Manor House, Monkton 45433
Leffingwell House Museum, Norwich 46036
Leigh Yawkey Woodson Art Museum, Wausau 48463
Lemon Hill Mansion, Philadelphia 46423
Liberty Hall, Frankfort 43512
Lightner Museum, Saint Augustine 47068
Locust Lawn and Terwilliger House, Gardiner 43621
Longue Vue House, New Orleans 45729
Loudoun Mansion, Philadelphia 46424
Lower Cape Fear Historical Society Museum, Wilmington 48661
Luna Mimbres Museum, Deming 42868
McMinn County Living Heritage Museum, Athens 41327
Manchester Historical Society Museum, Manchester 45094
Maria Martinez Museum, Santa Fe 47423
Mary Todd Lincoln House, Lexington 44743
The Mattatuck Museum of the Mattatuck Historical Society, Waterbury 48427
Maymont, Richmond 46882
Memorial Hall Museum, Deerfield 42850
Middleton Place Foundation, Charleston 42224
Mint Museum of Craft and Design, Charlotte 42244
Montpelier Cultur Arts Center, Laurel 44677
Moody Mansion Museum, Galveston 43613
Morlan Gallery, Lexington 44744
Morris-Butler House Museum, Indianapolis 44231
Morris-Jumel Mansion, New York 45835
Moses Myers House, Norfolk 45968
Mount Clare Museum House, Baltimore 41481
MSC Forsyth Center Galleries, College Station 42527
Muscatine Art Center, Muscatine 45575
The Museum at Drexel University, Philadelphia 46430
Museum of American Architecture and Decorative Arts, Houston 44128
Museum of Decorative Art, Chicago 42347
Museum of Early Southern Decorative Arts, Winston-Salem 48701
Museum of Glass, Tacoma 47921
Museum of New Hampshire History, Concord 42605
The Museums of Oglebay Institute, Wheeling 48587
New Orleans Artworks Gallery, New Orleans 45733
New Visions Gallery, Marshfield 45186
The Newark Museum, Newark 45892
Nichols House Museum, Boston 41820
Noyes Art Gallery, Lincoln 44790
The Old Stone Jail Museum, Palmyra 46272
Osborn-Jackson House, East Hampton 43049
Owensboro Museum of Fine Art, Owensboro 46230
Parry Mansion Museum, New Hope 45706
Patterson Homestead, Dayton 42804
Peppers Art Gallery, Redlands 46823
Pittock Mansion, Portland 46640
Polynesian Cultural Center, Laie 44577
Potsdam Public Museum, Potsdam 46669
The Prairie Museum of Art and History, Colby 42517
Pump House Center for the Arts, Chillicothe 42380
Purdue University Calumet Library Gallery, Hammond 43887
Queen Emma Gallery, Honolulu 44086
Raynham Hall Museum, Oyster Bay 46249
Renfrew Museum, Waynesboro 48482
Ripley's Believe it or not!, Key West 44471
Riverview at Hobson Grove, Bowling Green 41851
Rockwell Museum of Western Art, Corning 42638
Rockwood Museum, Wilmington 48655
Royal Arts Foundation, Newport 45933
Ruthmere House Museum, Elkhart 43142
Salgo Trust for Education, Port Washington 46610
Sam Bell Maxey House, Paris 46286
Sanford Museum, Sanford 47394
Saratoga Springs Museum, Saratoga Springs 47462
Sargent House Museum, Gloucester 43705
Schuyler-Hamilton House, Morristown 45510
Slater Memorial Museum, Norwich 46037
Society of Arts and Crafts Exhibition Gallery, Boston 41827
Stamford Historical Society Museum, Stamford 47767
Stan Hywet Hall and Gardens, Akron 41074
Stauth Memorial Museum, Montezuma 45464
The Stephen Girard Collection, Philadelphia 46456
Sterling and Francine Clark Art Institute, Williamstown 48634
Stevens-Coolidge Place, North Andover 45980
Stone-Tolan House, Rochester 46945
Ten Broeck Mansion, Albany 41088
University of Rochester Memorial Art Gallery, Rochester 46948
Valentine Richmond History Center, Richmond 46888
Vance Kirkland Museum, Denver 42902
Varner-Hogg Plantation, West Columbia 48520
The Vermont State House, Montpelier 45479
Villa Terrace Decorative Arts Museum, Milwaukee 45373
Visual Arts Gallery, Pensacola 46347

Vizcaya Museum, Miami 45292
Warther Museum, Dover 42974
Webster House Museum, Elkhorn 43145
Wichita Center for the Arts, Wichita 48611
Willoughby-Baylor House, Norfolk 45972
Wilson Castle, Proctor 46710
Wilton House Museum, Richmond 46892
Winterthur Museum, Winterthur 48712
The Wolfsonian, Miami Beach 45300

Uzbekistan
Bucharskij Gosudarstvennyj Muzej, Buchara 48832

Venezuela
Museo de la Estampa y del Diseño Carlos Cruz Diez, Caracas 48918
Museo de la Fundación John Boulton, Caracas 48919

Distilling → Wines and Spirits

Dolls and Puppets

Australia
Heirloom Doll Museum, Airlie Beach 00720
Jerilderie Doll World Museum, Jerilderie 01125

Austria
Badener Puppen- und Spielzeugmuseum, Baden bei Wien 01725
Elli Riehl-Puppenmuseum, Treffen bei Villach 02739
Internationale Puppenausstellung, Sankt Wolfgang im Salzkammergut 02619
Puppen- und Spielzeugmuseum, Wien 02975
Puppenmuseum, Einöde 01800
Puppenmuseum in Villach, Villach 02762
Puppenmuseum Kärntner Eisenwurzen, Hüttenberg 02052
Waldviertler Puppenmuseum, Waldkirchen 02791
Welser Puppenweltmuseum, Wels 02817

Belgium
Musée Marial de Beauraing, Beauraing 03203
Musée Tchantchès - Musée de la République Libre d'Outre-Meuse, Liège 03585
Poppenmuseum Christus Koning, Wetteren 03838

Canada
House of International Dolls, Fredericton 05462
Mildred M. Mahoney Silver Jubilee Dolls' House Gallery, Fort Erie 05436
Puppet Centre, Toronto 06602

Czech Republic
Muzeum Loutkářských Kultur, Chrudim 08320

Estonia
Nukumuuseum, Tallinn 09369

Finland
Nukke- ja Pukumuseo - Hatanpäa Mansion, Tampere 10082
Nukkemuseo Suruton, Savonlinna 10024
Suomenlinnan Lelumuseo, Helsinki 09538

France
Collection Historial Cognacq-Jay, Paris 13488
Musée-Atelier de Poupées Francépoque, Nances-Lac d'Aiguebelette 13235
Musée de Jouet et da la Poupée Ancienne, L'Isle-sur-la-Sorgue 12629
Musée de la Poupée, Aubeterre-sur-Dronne 10460
Musée de la Poupée, Le Beausset 12378
Musée de la Poupée Ancienne, Cerisiers 11112
Musée de l'Automobile Miniature et des Poupées Anciennes, Nointel (Oise) 13355
Musée des Poupées, Josselin 12090
Musée du Folklore, Moulins (Allier) 13188
Musée Gadagne, Lyon 12745
Musée Miniatures et Poupées, Gréoux-les-Bains 11951

Germany
Café-Museum Zum Puppenhaus, Immenstaad 17894
Coburger Puppen-Museum, Coburg 16480
Erstes Ethnisches Puppenmuseum der Welt, Kreuth 18233
Hessisches Puppenmuseum, Hanau 17583
Käthe-Kruse-Puppen-Museum, Donauwörth 16639
Katharinas Puppenhaus, Pleystein 19415
Kindergartenmuseum, Bruchsal 16368
Kindheitsmuseum, Marburg 18628
Münchner Puppenmuseum, München 18879
Museen der Stadt Bad Kösen, Bad Kösen 15679
Museum der Deutschen Spielzeugindustrie, Neustadt bei Coburg 19080
Museum Klingelbeutel, Gaukönigshofen 17207
Musikinstrumenten- und Puppenmuseum, Goslar 17356
Norddeutsches Spielzeugmuseum, Soltau 19994
Oberrheinische Narrenschau, Kenzingen 18066
Puppen- und Spielzeugmuseum, Holzminden 17831
Puppen- und Spielzeugmuseum, Lichtenstein, Sachsen 18458
Puppen- und Spielzeugmuseum Sammlung Katharina Engels, Rothenburg ob der Tauber 19680
Puppenausstellung des Steinauer Marionetten-Theaters, Steinau an der Straße 20043
Puppenmuseum Falkenstein, Hamburg 17563
Puppenmuseum im Kunsthof, Herten 17741
Puppentheatermuseum, Kaufbeuren 18043
Puppentheatermuseum mit Abteilung Schaustellerei, München 18899
Sammlung Berger, Amorbach 15486
Schloßmuseum, Ellwangen 16836
Spielzeugmuseum, Bad Lauterberg 15690
Stadtmuseum Borken, Westfalen, Borken, Westfalen 16258
Steinhuder Spielzeugnuseum, Steinhude 20054
Stiftung Aschenbrenner, Garmisch-Partenkirchen 17203
Teddy Museum Berlin in Hof/Bayern, Hof, Saale 17794
Teddymuseum, Klingenberg am Main 18109

India
Shankar's International Dolls Museum, Delhi 21783

Indonesia
Museum Wayang, Jakarta 22138

Italy
Collezione di Marionette Ferrari, Parma 24797
Museo dei Burattini, Mantova 24285
Museo della Marionetta, Torino 25741
Museo Internazionale delle Marionette A. Pasqualino, Palermo 24777
Museo Internazionale di Burattini e Marionette, L'Aquila 24145

Japan
Omoide Museum, Kyoto 26444
Yokohama Doll Museum, Yokohama 27023

Korea, Republic
Teddy Bear Museum, Seogwipo 27221

Luxembourg
Musée Dicks, Vianden 27578

Mexico
Museo Casa de Carranza, México 28113
Museo Nacional del Títere, Huamantla 27994

Monaco
Musée National de Monaco, Monaco 28669

Netherlands
Historische Expositie Klederdracht en Visserijmuseum, Bunschoten Spakenburg 29038
Museum de Verzamelaar, Zuidhorn 30069
Poppen- en Speelgoedmuseum, Tilburg 29882
Poppenhuis Carmen, Utrecht 29909
Poppenhuismuseum, Heesch 29371
Poppenmuseum, Ter Apel 28923
Poppenmuseum, Maastricht 29570
Poppenspe(e)lmuseum, Vorchten 29964
Popppenhuismuseum Alida's Kleine Wereldje, Veendam 29925
Speelgoedmuseum De Brug, Eerbeek 29201
Speelgoedmuseum Op Stelten, Oosterhout 29671
Zeeuws Poppen- en Klederdrachten Museum, Zoutelande 30066

Russia
Chudožestvennaja Galereja - Dom Kukly Tatjany Kalininoj, Petrozavodsk 33313
Muzej Gosudarstvennogo Centralnogo Teatra Kukol pod Rukovodstvom Narodnogo Artista S.V. Obrazcova, Moskva 33101
Muzej Kukol i Detskoj Knigi Strana Čudes, Ekaterinburg 32777
Muzej Miniaturnych Kukol Malenkij Mir, Semipalatinsk 33517
Muzej Teatralnoj Kukly A.A Veselova, Voronež 33734
Muzej Unikalnych Kukol, Moskva 33155

Slovakia
Múzeum Bábkarských Kultúr a Hračiek Hrad Modry Kameň, Modrý Kameň 34031

Spain
El Mundode Muñecas, Icod de los Vinos 34912

Sweden
Dock- och Textilmuseum, Katrineholm 36004
Dockmuseum, Gärsnäs 35899
Hobby- och Leksaksmuseum, Stockholm 36247

Switzerland
Musée Suisse de la Marionette, Fribourg 36718
Puppenmuseum Jeannine, Kreuzlingen 36837
Puppenmuseum Sasha Morgenthaler, Zürich 37406
Spielzeugmuseum, Davos Platz 36655

United Kingdom
Abbey House Museum, Leeds 39440
Bear Museum, Petersfield 40192
Childhood and Costume Museum, Bridgnorth 38322
Coventry Toy Museum, Coventry 38641
The Dolly Mixture, Langbank 39420
Dorset Teddy Bear Museum, Dorchester 38749
Ethnic Doll and Toy Museum, Canterbury 38473
Lilliput Antique Doll and Toy Museum, Brading 38305
Mechanical Music and Doll Collection, Chichester 38563
Mellerstain House, Gordon 39096
Museum of Childhood, Boscombe 38281
Museum of Childhood, Sudbury, Derbyshire 40641
Museum of Childhood at Bethnal Green, London 39712
The Teddy Bear Museum, Stratford-upon-Avon 40631
Teddy Bear Shop and Museum, Ironbridge 39310
Vina Cooke Museum of Dolls and Bygone Childhood, Newark-on-Trent 40026
Warwick Doll Museum, Warwick 40795
Wishtower Puppet Museum, Eastbourne 38859

U.S.A.
American Museum of the Miniature Arts, Dallas 42745
Bread Puppet Museum, Glover 43706
Creatabilitoys! - Museum of Advertising Icons, Coral Gables 42626
Denver Museum of Miniatures, Dolls and Toys, Denver 42886
Doll Museum, Tucson 48086
Eliza Cruce Hall Doll Museum, Ardmore 41252
Enchanted Mansion Doll Museum, Baton Rouge 41526
Enchanted World Doll Museum, Mitchell 45413
Franks Antique Doll Museum, Marshall 45181
The Heritage Museum of Fine Arts for Youth, Detroit 42929
House of a Thousand Dolls, Loma 44847
Milan Historical Museum, Milan 45334
Rosalie Whyel Museum of Doll Art, Bellevue 41599
Teddy Bear Museum of Naples, Naples 45603
Toy and Miniature Museum of Kansas City, Kansas City 44412
Washington Dolls House and Toy Museum, Washington 48406
Yesteryears Doll and Toy Museum, Sandwich 47390

Venezuela
Museo de las Muñecas, Píritu 48961

Drawing

Argentina
Fundacion Museo de la Caricatura Severo Vaccaro, Buenos Aires 00152

Austria
Albertina, Wien 02830
Kupferstichkabinett, Wien 02921
Nordico - Museum der Stadt Linz, Linz 02238

Belgium
Alfred Ost Museum, Zwijndrecht 03860
Musée Constantin Meunier, Bruxelles 03297
Musée de la Ville d'Eaux, Spa 03761
Musée de l'Imprimerie, Bruxelles 03312
Stedelijk Prentenkabinet, Antwerpen 03175
Le Vieux Logis, Mons 03638

Brazil
Museu de Arte Contemporânea da Universidade de São Paulo, São Paulo 04514

Canada
Acadia University Art Gallery, Wolfville 06857

Croatia
Ivan Meštrović Gallery, Split 07782

Czech Republic
Galerie Umění, Ostrov nad Ohří 08530
Muzeum Umění, Benešov 08246
Palác Kinských, Praha 08608

Denmark
Museet for Dansk Bladtegning, København 08939
Vejen Kunstmuseum, Vejen 09103
Vejle Kunstmuseum, Vejle 09104

Finland
Tampereen Taidemuseon Muumilaakso, Tampere 10093

France
Collections de l'Abbaye Bénédictine de Saint-Louis-du-Temple, Vauhallan 15099
Collections de l'Ecole Nationale Supérieure des Beaux-Arts, Paris 13494
Fondation Le Corbusier, Paris 13504
Institut Tessin, Paris 13517
Musée Atger, Montpellier 13121
Musée Calvet, Avignon 10528
Musée-Chapelle Saint-Blaise-des-Simples, Milly-la-Forêt 12981
Musée des Beaux-Arts de Bordeaux, Bordeaux 10812
Musée du Luxembourg, Paris 13604
Musée Jean Cocteau, Menton 12939
Musée Magnin, Dijon 11530
Musée Maison Robert-Doisneau, Gentilly 11850
Musée Municipal de l'Évêché, Limoges 12616
Musée National Ernest Hébert, Paris 13639

Germany
Alf Lechner Museum, Ingolstadt 17902
Edwin Scharff Museum am Petrusplatz, Neu-Ulm 19008
Ernst Barlach Stiftung Güstrow, Güstrow 17456
Graphische Sammlung, Augsburg 15556
Kunsthalle Bremen, Bremen 16328
Kupferstichkabinett - Sammlung der Zeichnungen und Druckgraphik, Berlin 16033
Museum Corps de Logis, Düsseldorf 16735
Olaf-Gulbransson-Museum, Tegernsee 20152
Wilhelm-Busch-Museum Hannover, Hannover 17614

Greece
Alex Mylonas Museum, Athinai 20845
N. Hadjikyriakos-Ghikas Gallery, Athinai 20892

Iraq
Al Shaheed Monument and Museum, Baghdad 22343

Italy
Casa Buonarroti, Firenze 23825
Civico Gabinetto dei Disgeni, Milano 24375
Fondazione Europea del Disegno, Meina 24343
Museo, Biblioteca e Archivio, Bassano del Grappa 23037
Museo dell'Accademia Ligustica di Belle Arti, Genova 23994
Museo Internazionale della Caricatura, Tolentino 25721
Raccolta d'Arte Pagliara, Napoli 24606
Raccolte d'Arte dell'Ospedale Maggiore di Milano, Milano 24418

Japan
Masaki Art Museum, Osaka 26654
Shinano Drawing Museum, Ueda 26983

Mexico
Museo de la Caricatura, México 28133
Museo Francisco Sarabia, Lerdo 28061

Netherlands
Abraham's Mosterdmakerij, Eenrum 29200
Teylers Museum, Haarlem 29331

Portugal
Museu Rafael Bordalo Pinheiro, Lisboa 32315

Serbia-Montenegro
Galerija Srpske Akademije Nauka i Umetnosti, Beograd 33798

Spain
Museo de Bellas Artes, Córdoba 34738
Museo de Dibujo Castillo de Larrés, Sabiñánigo 35351

Sweden
Albert Engström-Museerna, Grisslehamn 35931
Museum Kasper, Norrtälje 36122
Seriemuseet Comicland, Ullared 36344

Switzerland
Kunstmuseum, Solothurn 37185
Kunstmuseum Winterthur, Winterthur 37331
Museum Sursilvan, Trun 37256

Turkey
İstanbul Büyükşehir Belediyesi Karikatür ve Mizah Müzesi, Fatih 37677

United Kingdom
Beatrix Potter Gallery, Hawkshead 39198
Courtauld Institute Gallery, London 39615
Drawings Collection, London 39626
Guildford House Gallery, Guildford 39137
Library Drawings Collection, London 39688
Linley Sambourne House, London 39689
The Lowry Gallery, Salford 40430
National Fairground Museum, Northampton 40083

U.S.A.
American Museum of Cartoon Art, Santa Monica 47438
Americas Society Art Gallery, New York 45761
Cartoon Art Museum, San Francisco 47314
Drawing Center, New York 45794
Hughes Fine Arts Center, Grand Forks 43742
International Museum of Cartoon Art, Boca Raton 41767
Joseph A. Cain Memorial Art Gallery, Corpus Christi 42646
Mabel Larson Fine Arts Gallery, Clarksville 42436
Marshall M. Fredericks Sculpture Museum, University Center 48150
Pete and Susan Barrett Art Gallery, Santa Monica 47441

Ecology

Argentina
Ecomuseo Regional Maipú, Maipú 00422

Belgium
Maison de la Forêt, Bon-Secours 03223

Brazil
Espaço Museu da Vida, Rio de Janeiro 04324

Canada
Cave and Basin National Historic Site, Banff 05043
Écomusée des Deux-Rives, Valleyfield 06663
Kortright Centre Museum, Woodbridge 06861
Lynn Canyon Ecology Centre, North Vancouver 06024
Musée Écologique Vanier, Laval 05735

Denmark
Naturhistorisk Museum, Århus 08772
Strandgaarden Museum, Ulfborg 09095

France
Ecomusée de Saint-Joseph, Fargues-sur-Ourbise 11705

Germany
Archäologisch-Ökologisches Museum, Albersdorf 15416
Elbschloss Bleckede, Bleckede 16184
Haus des Waldes, Köln 18141
Naturmuseum Lüneburg, Lüneburg 18560
Naturschutzausstellung der Naturschutzstation, Neschwitz 18998
Niedersächsisches Deichmuseum, Dorum 16668
Stadtmuseum Schlüsselfeld, Schlüsselfeld 19806

Italy
Civico Museo Naturalistico Ferruccio Lombardi, Stradella 25640
Museo di Ecologia e Storia Naturale, Marano sul Panaro 24294

Mexico
Museo Na-Bolom, San Cristóbal de las Casas 28382

Netherlands
Afval-Museum, Zwolle 30082
Bezoekerscentrum Oortjespad, Kamerik 29468
Milieu Educatie Centrum, Eindhoven 29214
De Verbeelding Kunst Landschap Natuur, Zeewolde 30050

Peru
Museo Multidisciplinario del Colegio La Salle, Lima 31220

Philippines
Dinosaur Museum, Malabon 31357

Poland
Muzeum Wiedzy o Środowisku, Poznań 31913

Russia
Muzej 'Archeologija, Ėtnografija i Ėkologija Sibiri' Kemerovskogo Gosudarstvennogo Universiteta, Kemerovo 32914

South Africa
Sea World, Durban 34232

Spain
Ingurugiro Etxea, Azpeitia 34513

Sweden
Aquaria Vattenmuseum, Stockholm 36230

Tanzania
Shinyanga Mazingira Museum, Shinyanga 37465

Tunisia
Ecomusée d'Ichkeul, Bizerte 37555

United Kingdom
Harestanes Countryside Visitor Centre, Ancrum 37999
River and Rowing Museum, Henley-on-Thames 39220

Uruguay
Museo Marítimo-Ecológico Malvín, Montevideo 41008

U.S.A.
Asri Environmental Education Center, Bristol 41903
Austin Nature and Science Center, Austin 41407
Coyote Point Museum for Environmental Education, San Mateo 47369
EcoTarium, Worcester 48752
Koke'e Natural History Museum, Kauai 44417
Robert A. Vines Environmental Science Center, Houston 44134
Weymouth Woods-Sandhills Nature Preserve Museum, Southern Pines 47709

Zambia
Copperbelt Museum, Ndola 49024

Economics

Argentina
Museo Histórico de la Dirección General Impositiva, Buenos Aires 00211

Austria
Österreichisches Gesellschafts- und Wirtschaftsmuseum, Wien 02959
Zoll- und Finanzgeschichtliche Sammlung, Linz 02243
Zoll- und Heimatmuseum, Perwang 02407

Canada
Lester-Garland Premises, Trinity 06634

France
Musée de la Douane et des Frontières, Hestrud 12019
Musée des Commerces Anciens, Doué-la-Fontaine 11567
Musée National des Douanes, Bordeaux 10818

Germany
Deutsches Zollmuseum, Hamburg 17532
Erstes Deutsches Historic-Actien-Museum, Kürnbach 18261
Heimat- und Naturkunde-Museum Wanne-Eickel, Herne 17728
NRW-Forum Kultur und Wirtschaft, Düsseldorf 16739
Wirtschaftsgeschichtliches Museum Villa Grün, Dillenburg 16611

Hungary
Magyar Kereskedelmi és Vendéglátóipari Múzeum, Budapest 21358

India
Commercial and Industrial Museum, Kanpur 21882
Commercial Museum, Gauhati 21808
Government Industrial and Commercial Museum, Kolkata 21903

Japan
Economical Document Collection, Hikone 26192
Takayama Jinya, Takayama 26811

Mexico
Museo Histórico Ex Aduana de Ciudad Juárez, Juárez 28039

Netherlands
Belasting en Douane Museum, Rotterdam 29747
Grenslandmuseum, Dinxperlo 29156

Norway
Bankmuseet, Stavanger 30878
Bergen Skolemuseum, Bergen 30416
Norsk Tollmuseum, Oslo 30755

Pakistan
Industrial and Commercial Museum, Lahore 31035

Russia
Muzej Istorii Otečestvennogo Predprinimatelstva, Moskva 33110
Nižnetagilskij Muzej-Zapovednik Gornozavodskogo Dela Srednego Urala, Nižnij Tagil 33228

Spain
Museo Histórico BBVA, Bilbao 34615

Sweden
Tullmuseum, Stockholm 36297

Switzerland
Museo Doganale Svizzero, Gandria 36722

United Kingdom
Opie's Museum of Memories, Wigan 40871

U.S.A.
Discovery World - The James Lovell Museum of Science, Economics and Technology, Milwaukee 45361

Education

Albania
Museum of Education, Elbasan 00019
Museum of Education, Korçë 00026

Algeria
Musée du Mont Riant, Alger 00043

Argentina
Eureka - Parque de la Ciencia, Mendoza 00432
Museo de Escuela de Educación Técnica Número 1, Dolores 00329
Museo de la E.E.M. Número 3, Dolores 00330
Museo de los Niños Barrilete, Córdoba 00296
Museo y Centro Estudios Históricos de la Facultad de Odontología, Buenos Aires 00249

Australia
Alumny Creek School Museum, Grafton 01070
Andrew Ross Museum, Kangaroo Ground 01134
Frankston Primary Old School Museum, Frankston 01034
Hale School Museum, Wembley Downs 01590
The Museum of Nursing, Camperdown 00883
Old School Museum, Merimbula 01247
Saint John's Schoolhouse Museum, Reid 01412
Sir Edgeworth David Memorial Museum, Kurri Kurri 01154
Uleybury School Museum, One Tree Hill 01343

Austria
Archiv der Universität Wien, Schausammlung, Wien 02834
Burgenländisches Schulmuseum, Lockenhaus 02246
Kindermuseum Zoom, Wien 02908
Kinderweltmuseum, Vöcklamarkt 02768
Niederösterreichisches Schulmuseum, Asparn an der Zaya 01686
Volksschulmuseum, Maria Taferl 02272

Azerbaijan
Baku Museum of Education, Baku 03066

Belgium
Stedelijk Onderwijsmuseum Ieper, Ieper 03518

Brazil
Museu Histórico e Pedagógico, Mococa 04206
Museu Histórico e Pedagógico Conselheiro Rodrigues Alves, Guaratinguetá 04123
Museu Histórico e Pedagógico Dr. Washington Luís, Batatais 03968
Museu Histórico e Pedagógico Fernão Dias Paes, Penápolis 04257
Museu Histórico e Pedagógico Marechal Cândido Rondon, Araçatuba 03953
Museu Histórico e Pedagógico Monteiro Lobato, Taubaté 04560
Museu Histórico e Pedagógico Pe. Manoel da Nóbrega, São Manuel 04479
Museu Histórico e Pedagógico Prof. Lourenço Filho, Porto Ferreira 04290
Museu Histórico e Pedagógico Zequinha de Abreu, Santa Rita do Passa Quatro 04446
Museu Histórico Pedagógico Conselheiro Dr. João da Silva Carrão, Americana 03944
Museu Histórico Pedagógico Índia Vanuíre, Tupã 04572

Bulgaria
Nacionalen Muzej na Obrazovanieto, Gabrovo 04670
Školoto Muzej, Trjavna 04889

Canada
Alex Youck School Museum, Regina 06226
Algonquin College Museum, Nepean 05971
Athol Murray College of Notre Dame Museum, Wilcox 06799
Bleakhouse Museum, Fogo Island 05430
Brocksden County School Museum, Stratford 06498
Cape Breton Centre for Heritage and Science, Sydney 06525
Century Schoolhouse, Toronto 06572
Children's Own Museum, Toronto 06573
East Coulee School Museum, East Coulee 05360
Ecole du Rang II, Authier 05024
Edmonton Public Schools Museum, Edmonton 05374
Enoch Turner Schoolhouse, Toronto 06576
Frontenac County Schools Museum, Kingston 05676
The Hamilton Children's Museum, Hamilton 05570
King Seaman School Museum, River Herbert 06273
Little School Museum, Lockeport 05762
Little White Schoolhouse, Truro 06649
McCulloch House Museum and Hector Exhibit Centre, Pictou 06129
Manitoba Children's Museum, Winnipeg 06831
Metchosin School Museum, Victoria 06726
Morrison Museum of the Country School, Islay 05629
Musée Acadien du Québec, Bonaventure 05092
Musée du College de Lévis, Lévis 05751
Museum of the North American Indian Travelling College, Cornwall 05277
Old Crofton School Museum, Crofton 05290
Quinte Educational Museum, Ameliasburgh 04985
River Valley School Museum, Virden 06735
Rocky Lane School Museum, Fort Vermilion 05454
Sesquicentennial Museum, Toronto 06610
Star Mound School Museum, Snowflake 06468
Thames Valley Museum School, Burgessville 05143
Tupperville School Museum, Bridgetown 05129
University of Alberta Museums, Edmonton 05392
Victoria School Museum, Carleton Place 05208
Victoria School Museum and Archives, Edmonton 05393
Wilson MacDonald Memorial School Museum, Selkirk 06421

Chile
Museo Pedagógico Carlos Stuardo Ortiz, Santiago de Chile 06918

China, People's Republic
Central Nation University Museum, Beijing 06955
Children's Museum, Shanghai 07209

China, Republic
National Taiwan Science Education Center, Taipei 07353

Costa Rica
Galería Nacional y Museo de los Niños, San José 07652

Croatia
Hrvatski Školski Muzej, Zagreb 07824
Hrvatski Sportski Muzej, Zagreb 07825

Cuba
Museo Abel Santamaria, Santa Clara 08119
Museo Nacional de la Alfabetización, La Habana 07989

Czech Republic
Krkonošské Muzeum, Paseky nad Jizerou 08535
Muzeum Komenského v Přerově, Přerov 08622
Okresní Vlastivědné Muzeum Nový Jičín, Příbor 08624
Pedagogické Muzeum Jana Ámoše Komenského, Praha 08611
Stará Škola, Police nad Metuji 08553

Denmark
Børnenens Museum, København 08922
Flakkebjerg Skolemuseum, Slagelse 09069

Egypt
Education Museum, Cairo 09260

Estonia
Õisu Tehnikumi Muuseum, Halliste 09321
Tartu Ülikooli Ajaloomuuseum, Tartu 09386
Viljandimaa Gümnaasiumi Muuseum, Viljandi 09396

Finland
Elimäen Koulumuseo, Elimäki 09429
Helsingin Yliopistomuseo, Helsinki 09491
Himangan Kotiseutumuseo, Himanka 09550
Jyväskylän Lyseon Museo, Jyväskylä 09595
Jyväskylän Näkövammaisten Koulun Museo, Jyväskylä 09596
Jyväskylän Yliopiston Museo - Kultuurihistoriallinen Osasto, Jyväskylä 09599
Kaurilan Koulumuseo, Tohmajärvi 10108
Koulumuseo, Helsinki 09504
Lastenmuseo, Helsinki 09508
Lastentarhamuseo, Helsinki 09509
Näkövammaismuseo, Jiris 09579
Saukkojärven Kotiseutu- ja Koulumuseo, Ranua 09979
Suomen Koulumuseo, Tampere 10086

France
Musée de Jouet et da la Poupée Ancienne, L'Isle-sur-la-Sorgue 12629
Musée de La Vieille École, Pernes-les-Fontaines 13695
Musée de l'École, Carcassonne 11042
Musée de l'Ecole, Chartres 11193
Musée de l'Ecole 1900, Saint-Martin-des-Olmes 14354
Musée de l'École d'Autrefois, Pontis 13828
Musée de l'Ecole Rurale, Trégarvan 14987
Musée de l'École Rurale d'Auvergne, Messeix 12953
Musée Départemental de l'Éducation, Saint-Ouen-l'Aumône 14391
Musée du Jeu de l'Oie, Rambouillet 13910
Musée la Vie des Jouets, Mauleon 12893
Musée-Maison d'Ecole, Montceau-les-Mines 13067
Musée National de l'Éducation, Rouen 14056
Musée Valentin Haüy, Paris 13648

Germany
Altdorfer Universitäts-Museum, Altdorf bei Nürnberg 15440
Bayerisches Schulmuseum, Ichenhausen 17876
Deutsches Museum für Schulkunst, Hagen, Westfalen 17479
Dorfschulmuseum, Ködnitz 18125
Ebersdorfer Schulmuseum, Chemnitz 16462
Erstes Allgäu-Schwäbisches Dorfschulmuseum, Erkheim 16911
Erstes Bayerisches Schulmuseum, Sulzbach-Rosenberg 20124
Exploratorium - Kindermuseum Stuttgart und Region, Stuttgart 20089
Faszinosum, Borna bei Leipzig 16262
Die Franckeschen Stiftungen zu Halle, Halle, Saale 17509
Fröbelmuseum, Keilhau 18048
Gedenkstätte für C.G. Salzmann und J.C.F. GuthsMuths, Schnepfenthal 19819
Hamburger Schulmuseum, Hamburg 17542
Heimat-und Handwerkermuseum, Leutershausen 18448
Heimatmuseum Hallstadt, Hallstadt 17525
Heimatstube Wendhausen, Schellerten 19773
Johann-Baptist-Graser-Schulmuseum, Bayreuth 15850
Jugendmuseum Schöneberg, Berlin 16011
Kinder- und Jugendmuseum München, München 18861
Kindermuseum, Frankfurt am Main 17058
Kindermuseum, Wuppertal 20714
Kindermuseum, Karlsruhe 17995
Kindermuseum Hamburg, Hamburg 17548
Kleines Museum - Kinder der Welt, Frankfurt/Oder 17082
Labyrinth Kindermuseum Berlin, Berlin 16035
Landschulmuseum Göldenitz, Göldenitz bei Rostock 17314
MACHmit! Museum für Kinder, Berlin 16039
Memorialmuseum Friedrich Fröbel, Oberweißbach 19214
Mobiles Kindermuseum im Freizeitheim Vahrenwald, Hannover 17604
Museum im Koffer, Nürnberg 19153
Museum Kindheit und Jugend, Berlin 16062
Museum zum Anfassen, Ostseebad Binz 19311
Museum zur Geschichte Hohenheims, Stuttgart 20101
Ostfriesisches Schulmuseum Folmhusen, Westoverledingen 20545
Sammlungen des Instituts für Hochschulkunde der Deutschen Gesellschaft für Hochschulkunde, Würzburg 20704
Schlossmuseum Reckahn, Reckahn 19511
Schulgeschichtliche Sammlung, Magdeburg 18588
Schulgeschichtliche Sammlung Bremen, Bremen 16333
Schulgeschichtliche Sammlung im Main-Taunus-Kreis, Kriftel 18240
Schulheimatmuseum, Asbach-Bäumenheim 15518
Schulhistorische Sammlung Cruismannschule, Bochum 16200
Schulmuseum, Hundisburg 17865
Schulmuseum, Neumark 19044
Schulmuseum des Bezirks Unterfranken, Bad Bocklet 15616
Schulmuseum Friedrichshafen am Bodensee, Friedrichshafen 17148
Schulmuseum Fronau, Roding 19626

Schulmuseum Lilienthal, Lilienthal 18467
Schulmuseum Mozartschule Rheingönheim, Ludwigshafen am Rhein 18521
Schulmuseum Nordwürttemberg in Kornwestheim, Kornwestheim 18212
Schulmuseum Nürnberg im Museum Industriekultur, Nürnberg 19159
Schulmuseum Steinhorst, Steinhorst, Niedersachsen 20052
Schulmuseum und Hallenhaus, Middelhagen, Rügen 18734
Schulmuseum - Werkstatt für Schulgeschichte Leipzig, Leipzig 18416
Schulmuseum Wildenhain, Wildenhain bei Großenhain, Sachsen 20587
Stadtmuseum Teterow, Teterow 20161
Städtisches Schulmuseum, Lohr am Main 18500
Theodor-Mommsen-Gedächtnisstätte, Garding 17200
Wasserwelt Erlebnismuseum, Ostseebad Binz 19315
Westfälisches Schulmuseum, Dortmund 16667

Greece
Athens University Museum, Athinai 20850
Hellenic Children's Museum, Athinai 20864

Guatemala
Museo Universitario de San Carlos, Guatemala 21276

Hungary
Albertfalvai Helytörténeti Gyűjtemény és Iskolamúzeum, Budapest 21323
Katona József Múzeum, Kecskemét 21447
Országos Pedagógiai Könyvtár és Múzeum, Budapest 21374

India
Bal Sangrahalaya, Lucknow 21921
Children's Museum, Bhavnagar 21717
Government Educational Museum, Etawah 21799
National Children's Museum, Delhi 21773
Nehru Children's Museum, Kolkata 21908
Regional Science Centre, Bhopal 21724
Regional Science Centre and Planetarium, Kozhikode 21916
Regional Science Centre Bhubaneswar, Bhubaneshwar 21727
Shri Girdharbhai Sangrahalaya, Amreli 21696

Ireland
Old Schoolhouse Museum, Ballintubber 22367
Plunket Museum of Irish Education, Dublin 22452

Israel
Havayeda Museum, Holon 22620

Italy
Museo dei Bambini Explora, Roma 25186
Museo della Scuola, Bolzano 23154
Museo della Scuola, Pramollo 25036
Museo Didattico, Niscemi 24623
Museo Didattico della Scuola Medica Salernitana, Salerno 25320
Museo per la Storia dell'Università di Pavia, Pavia 24828
Museo Scuola Odin-Bertot, Angrogna 22894

Japan
Children's Museum Big Bang, Sakai 26695
Historical Museum of Private Schools at the Foreign Settlement, Nagasaki 26547
Iwata-shi Kyu Mitsukegakko, Iwata, Shizuoka 26275
Muroran-shi Seishonen Kagakukan, Muroran 26522

Jordan
Children's Heritage and Science Museum, Amman 27047
School Books Museum, Salt 27068

Korea, Republic
Chonbuk University Museum, Jeonju 27198
Chonnam University Museum, Gwangju 27181
Daegu National University of Education Museum, Daegu 27155
Dan Kook University Museum, Seoul 27227
Deokpojin Educational Museum, Gimpo 27175
Dongguk University Museum, Seoul 27230
Gyeongju University Museum, Gyeongju 27186
Hanbat Education Museum, Daejeon 27160
Hansong Womens College Museum, Seoul 27236
Jeju Education Museum, Jeju 27195
Joongang University Museum, Seoul 27242
Kookmin College Museum, Seoul 27245
Kwangdong College Museum, Gangneung 27169
Kyongju University Museum, Kyongju 27207
Kyongnam College Museum, Masan 27209
Myong Ji University Museum, Seoul 27262
Samsung Children's Museum, Seoul 27268
Sangji Vocational College Museum, Andong 27130
Sejong College Museum, Seoul 27270
Seoul Education Museum, Seoul 27273
Sokang University Museum, Seoul 27279
Songsin Teachers College Museum, Seoul 27280
Sung Kyun Kwan University Museum, Seoul 27285
Won Kwang College Museum, Iri 27193
Yeungnam University Museum, Kyongsan 27208

Latvia
Rīgas Tehniskās Universitātes Muzejs, Rīga 27440

Lithuania
Museum of Pedagogics, Kaunas 27522

Malaysia
Malaysian Youth Museum, Melaka 27663

Mexico
La Burbuja-Museo del Niño, Hermosillo 27984
Museo Antiguo Colegio de San Ildefonso, México 28105
Museo del Niño, Santa Ana del Valle 28427
Museo del Niño Globo mi Ciudad Pequeña, Guadalajara 27958
Museo del Niño Papalote, México 28159
Museo del Recuerdo de la Academia Mexicana de la Lengua, México 28161
Museo Escolar de Sitio de la Matamba, Jamapa 28027
Museo Escolar y Comunitario de Acamalín, Xico 28620
Museo Histórico de la Educación Tecnológica en México, Chilpancingo 27830
Museo Interactivo de Ciencia, Tecnología y Medio Ambiente Sol del Niño, Mexicali 28090
Museo Interactivo del Centro de Ciencias de Sinaloa, Culiacán 27885
Museo Interactivo del Medio Ambiente, México 28178
Museo Interactivo El Rehilete, Pachuca 28296
Museo Interactivo La Avispa, Chilpancingo 27831
Museo Universitario, Mexicali 28091

Netherlands
Academisch Historisch Museum van de Universiteit Leiden, Leiden 29517
Comenius Museum, Naarden 29605
Historisch Documentatiecentrum voor het Nederlands Protestantisme 1800-Heden, Amsterdam 28858
Joodse Schooltje, Leek 29501
KIT Kindermuseum, Amsterdam 28865
Museum de Burghse Schoole, Burgh-Haamstede 29045
Museum Katendrecht, Rotterdam 29760
Nationaal Schoolmuseum, Rotterdam 29765
Onderwijsmuseum Educatorium, Ootmarsum 29677
De Ontdekhoek Kindermuseum, Rotterdam 29770
Schooltijd Schoolmuseum, Terneuzen 29866
Scouting Museum de Ducdalf, Rotterdam 29775
Scouting Museum Haagse Randstad, Den Haag 29124
Universiteitsmuseum, Groningen 29316
Universiteitsmuseum De Agnietenkapel, Amsterdam 28910
Van 't Lindenhoutmuseum, Nijmegen 29637

New Zealand
Saint Andrews College Museum, Christchurch 30132

Norway
Averøy Skolemuseum, Averøy 30406
Faleide Skulemuseum, Stryn 30904
Flatanger Bygdemuseum, Flatanger 30494
Gulli Skoletun, Andebu 30385
Holt Skolemuseum, Tvedestrand 30951
Lindås Skulemuseum, Isdalstø 30579
Meløy Bygdemuseum, Ørnes 30720
Modalen Skulemuseum, Modalen 30677
Saltstraumen Museum, Saltstraumen 30818
Sleire Skulemuseum, Hosteland 30568
Trosterud Skolemuseum, Rømskog 30803
Vestlandske Skolemuseum, Stavanger 30893

Oman
Children's Museum, Muscat 31003

Pakistan
Education Museum, Hyderabad 31019

Peru
Museo de la Universidad Nacional Hermilio Valdizán, Huánuco 31172
Museo Didáctico Antonini, Nasca 31231

Philippines
Brillantes Ancestral House, Tayum 31459
Cebu City State College Museum, Cebu 31311
Central Luzon State University Museum, Muñoz 31403
Centro Escolar University Museum and Archives, Manila 31375
Colegio de Santa Isabel Museum, Naga 31405
Museo de la Salle, Dasmariñas 31324
Museo Pambata, Manila 31386
Science Works!, Marikina 31401
University Historical Museum, Musuan 31404
University of Southern Philippines Museum, Cebu 31320
Urios College Museum, Butuan 31298

Poland
Muzeum Oświatowe, Puławy 31931
Muzeum Oświaty w Bydgoszczy, Bydgoszcz 31515
Muzeum Pedagogiczne, Gdańsk 31573
Muzeum Uniwersytetu Warszawskiego, Warszawa 32130
Muzeum Uniwersytetu Wrocławskiego, Wrocław 32190

Portugal
Museu Académico de Coimbra, Coimbra 32254

Puerto Rico
Museo del Niño, San Juan 32400

Romania
Muzeul Primei Şcoli Româneşti din Scheii Braşovului, Braşov 32450

Russia
Muzej Istorii Prosveščenija Komi Kraja, Syktyvkar 33577
Muzej Istorii Rossijskogo Gosudarstvennogo Pedagogičeskogo Universiteta im A.I. Gercena, Sankt-Peterburg 33443
Muzej Istorii Sankt-Peterburgskogo Universiteta, Sankt-Peterburg 33444
Muzej A.S. Makarenko, Moskva 33132
Muzej Narodnogo Obrazovanija Oblasti, Penza 33290
Muzej Narodnoje Obrazovanie Simbirskoj Gubernii v 70-80 gody 19 veka, Uljanovsk 33664
Muzej Simbirskaja Čuvašskaja Škola - Kvartira I.Ja. Jakovleva, Uljanovsk 33665
Muzej Simbirskaja Klassičeskaja Gimnazija, Uljanovsk 33666
Muzj Istorii Rossijskich Voennych Učilišč, Sankt-Peterburg 33472
Ogni Moskvy - Muzej Istorii Gorodskogo Osveščenija, Moskva 33166
Učebno-chudožestvennyj Muzej im. I.V. Cvetaeva, Moskva 33180

Serbia-Montenegro
Pedagoški Muzej, Beograd 33815

Slovakia
Museum of Special Educational System, Levoča 34011

Slovenia
Slovenski Šolski Muzej, Ljubljana 34121

South Africa
Edoardo Villa Museum, Pretoria 34341

Spain
Museo de la Academia de Infantería, Toledo 35539
Museo del Niño, Albacete 34420
Museo del Real Seminario de Bergara, Bergara 34603
Museo Scout-Guía, Madrid 35054

Sweden
Årbols Skolmuseum, Åmål 35796
Friluftmuseet Hallandsgården, Halmstad 35940
Helsingborgs Skolmuseum, Helsingborg 35951
Leksbergs Skolmuseum, Mariestad 36089
Moheda Skolmuseum, Moheda 36100
Skolmuseet, Östra Ljungby 36150
Skolmuseum Bunge, Farösund 35885
Stockholms Skolmuseum, Stockholm 36289
Universeum, Göteborg 35923
Västerås Skolmuseum, Västerås 36382
Vetlanda Skolmuseum, Vetlanda 36406

Switzerland
Musée d'Yverdon-les-Bains et sa Région, Yverdon-les-Bains 37354
Schweizer Kindermuseum, Baden 36489

United Kingdom
Andrew Carnegie Birthplace Museum, Dunfermline 38808
Auld Sköll, Fair Isle 38965
Böd of Gremista Museum, Lerwick 39478
Captain Cook Schoolroom Museum, Great Ayton 39118
Causeway School Museum, Bushmills 38423
Christ's Hospital Museum, Horsham 39263
Hands on History, Kingston-upon-Hull 39378
Haslemere Educational Museum, Haslemere 39182
Heriot-Watt University Museum and Archive, Edinburgh 38887
Islington Education Artefacts Library, London 39674
Livesey Museum for Children, London 39691
Museum of Childhood, Edinburgh 38892
Museum of Eton Life, Eton 38951
Museum of the History of Education, Leeds 39449
Old Grammar School, Castletown 38509
Ragged School Museum, London 39753
Rugby School Museum, Rugby 40357
Scaplen's Court Museum, Poole 40229
Scotland Street School Museum, Glasgow 39066
Staff College Museum, Camberley 38445
Tom Brown School Museum, Uffington 40746

Uruguay
Museo Didáctico Artiguista, Maldonado 40981
Museo Pedagógico José Pedro Varela, Montevideo 41021

U.S.A.
4-H Schoolhouse Museum, Clarion 42425
A.C. Gilbert's Discovery Village, Salem 47206
A.D. Buck Museum of Natural History and Science, Tonkawa 48029
Adams State College Luther Bean Museum, Alamosa 41079
Allen R. Hite Art Institute, Louisville 44960
Arkansas State University Museum, Jonesboro 44359
Austin Children's Museum, Austin 41404
Bay Area Discovery Museum, Sausalito 47473
Black Mountain College Museum and Arts Center, Asheville 41277
Brooklyn Children's Museum, Brooklyn 41940
Buffalo and Erie County Naval and Military Park, Buffalo 41984
Capital Children's Museum, Washington 48340
Chicago Children's Museum, Chicago 42316
Chief John Ross House, Rossville 47011
Children's Art Museum, San Angelo 47239
Children's Discovery Museum of North San Diego, Carlsbad 42107
Children's Discovery Museum of San Jose, San Jose 47350
Children's Discovery Museum of the Desert, Rancho Mirage 46785
The Children's Discovery Museum of Vermont, Burlington 42007
Children's Hands-On Museum, Tuscaloosa 48113
The Children's Metamorphosis, Londonderry 44854
Children's Museum, Detroit 42919
Children's Museum, Holyoke 44065
The Children's Museum, Seattle 47532
Children's Museum, San Diego 47273
The Children's Museum, Boston 41804
Children's Museum at La Habra, La Habra 44547
The Children's Museum at Saratoga, Saratoga Springs 47459
Children's Museum at Yunker Farm, Fargo 43290
Children's Museum in Dartmouth, South Dartmouth 47690
The Children's Museum in Easton, North Easton 45993
Children's Museum in New Braunfels, New Braunfels 45668
Children's Museum of Boca Raton, Boca Raton 41766
The Children's Museum of Cleveland, Cleveland 42464
Children's Museum of Denver, Denver 42881
The Children's Museum of Green Bay, Green Bay 43787
Children's Museum of History, Natural History and Science at Utica, New York, Utica 48169
The Children's Museum of Houston, Houston 44117
The Children's Museum of Indianapolis, Indianapolis 44215
The Children's Museum of Kansas City, Kansas City 44391
Children's Museum of Lake Charles, Lake Charles 44580
Children's Museum of Los Angeles, Los Angeles 44896
Children's Museum of Maine, Portland 46621
Children's Museum of Manhattan, New York 45781
The Children's Museum of Memphis, Memphis 45233
Children's Museum of Oak Ridge, Oak Ridge 46056
Children's Museum of Portsmouth, Portsmouth 46647
Children's Museum of Richmond, Richmond 46874
The Children's Museum of Rose Hill Manor Park, Frederick 43526
Children's Museum of South Carolina, Myrtle Beach 45585
Children's Museum of Spokane, Spokane 47726
Children's Museum of Stockton, Stockton 47823
Children's Museum of Tampa - Kid City, Tampa 47939
The Children's Museum of Utah, Salt Lake City 47228
Children's Museum of Virginia, Portsmouth 46659
The Children's Science Center, Cape Coral 42094
Childventure Museum, Fort Washington 43470
Cincinnati Museum Center, Cincinnati 42402
Cobb County Youth Museum, Marietta 45142
Coyote Point Museum for Environmental Education, San Mateo 47369
Creative Discovery Museum, Chattanooga 42260
The Curious Kids' Museum, Saint Joseph 47101
Discovery Center Museum, Rockford 46960
Discovery Center of the Southern Tier, Binghamton 41699
Discovery Creek Children's Museum of Washington DC, Washington 48348
The Discovery Museums, Acton 41062
Doozoo Children's Museum, Grand Junction 43747
Duke University Union Museum and Brown Art Gallery, Durham 43020
Duluth Children's Museum, Duluth 42998
Edventure, Columbia 42559
Elder Art Gallery, Lincoln 44781
Experience Children's Museum, Erie 43202
Exploration Place, Wichita 48600
Exploration Station, Boubonnais 41832
Exploris, Raleigh 46773
Family Museum of Arts and Science, Bettendorf 41670
Goodnow Museum, Manhattan 45105
Grand Rapids Children's Museum, Grand Rapids 43757
Great Explorations, Saint Petersburg 47173
Grout Museum of History and Science, Waterloo 48431
Hands On! Regional Museum, Johnson City 44346
Handwerker Gallery of Art, Ithaca 44271
Hannah Lindahl Children's Museum, Mishawaka 45399
Hawaii Children's Discovery Center, Honolulu 44076
Henderson State University Museum, Arkadelphia 41255
Historic Jefferson College, Washington 48415
Hudson Valley Children's Museum, Nanuet 45599
Imaginarium Hands-On Museum, Fort Myers 43437
Iquest Children's Museum, Bellevue 41598
Junior Museum, Troy 48070
The Junior Museum of Bay County, Panama City 46277
Kaleidoscope, Kansas City 44399
Kansas Health Museum, Halstead 43875
The Kansas Teachers' Hall of Fame, Dodge City 42956
Kauai Children's Discovery Museum, Kapaa 44413
Kearney Area Children's Museum, Kearney 44423

Kent Campus Museum and Gallery, Jacksonville 44297
Kidspace Children's Museum, Pasadena 46301
Kohl Children's Museum, Wilmette 48645
Lanesfield School, Edgerton 43083
Laredo Children's Museum, Laredo 44652
Las Vegas International Scouting Museum, Las Vegas 44669
Lexington Children's Museum, Lexington 44741
Lied Discovery Children's Museum, Las Vegas 44672
Lincoln Children's Museum, Lincoln 44785
Little Red School House Museum, Weyauwega 48578
Little Red Schoolhouse-Living Library, Beloit 41613
The Living Arts and Science Center, Lexington 44742
Long Island Children's Museum, Garden City 43619
Long Island Museum of American Art, History and Cariages, Stony Brook 47830
Louisiana Children's Museum, New Orleans 45730
Lutz Children's Museum, Manchester 45093
Madison Children's Museum, Madison 45070
Magic House-Saint Louis Children's Museum, Saint Louis 47127
Maxwell Museum of Anthropology, Albuquerque 41104
Melvin B. Tolson Black Heritage Center, Langston 44637
Miami Children's Museum, Miami 45290
Mid-Hudson Children's Museum, Poughkeepsie 46676
Minneapolis College of Art and Design Gallery, Minneapolis 45390
Minnesota Children's Museum, Saint Paul 47161
Mississippi University for Women Museum, Columbus 42583
Muncie Children's Museum, Muncie 45557
Museum and Archives of Georgia Education, Milledgeville 45345
Museum in the Community, Hurricane 44182
Museum of Anthropology, Columbia 42552
Museum of Art and Archaeology, Columbia 42553
Museum of Sex, New York 45844
New Britain Youth Museum, New Britain 45675
New Britain Youth Museum at Hungerford Park, Kensington 44442
New Jersey Children's Museum, Paramus 46281
New Mexico State University Museum, Las Cruces 44661
Norman Rockwell Museum at Stockbridge, Stockbridge 47820
Northern Indiana Center for History, South Bend 47680
Northwestern Oklahoma State University Museum, Alva 41162
Oklahoma Museum of Higher Education, Stillwater 47815
Old School House, York 48791
Omaha Children's Museum, Omaha 46152
Ottawa Scouting Museum, Ottawa 46219
Pittsburgh Children's Museum, Pittsburgh 46524
Please Touch Museum, Philadelphia 46445
Port Discovery - Children's Museum in Baltimore, Baltimore 41485
Portland Children's Museum Second Generation, Portland 46642
President Andrew Johnson Museum, Greeneville 43803
Princeton University Museum of Natural History, Princeton 46704
Providence Children's Museum, Providence 46724
Randall Museum, San Francisco 47333
Rocky Mount Children's Museum, Rocky Mount 46982
San Antonio Children's Museum, San Antonio 47258
Sangre de Cristo Arts Center and Buell Children's Museum, Pueblo 46741
Santa Fe Children's Museum, Santa Fe 47431
Science Museum, Upton 48162
Scitech, Aurora 41399
Scotia-Glenville Children's Museum, Scotia 47507
Seminole Nation Museum, Wewoka 48577
Sound School House Museum, Mount Desert 45528
Southeast Missouri State University Museum, Cape Girardeau 42096
Spertus Museum, Chicago 42363
Staten Island Children's Museum, Staten Island 47788
Stephens Museum, Fayette 43307
Tougaloo College Art Collection, Tougaloo 48041
Tucson Children's Museum, Tucson 48092
The University Museum, Edwardsville 43098
University Museum, Carbondale 42102
University Museums, Oxford 46239
University of Northern Iowa Museum Museums Collections, Cedar Falls 42151
The Virginia Discovery Museum, Charlottesville 42254
Wonder Works Children's Museum, The Dalles 42764
Wylie House Museum, Bloomington 41750
Young at Art Children's Museum, Davie 42790
Youth Museum of Southern West Virginia, Beckley 41577
Youth Science Institute, San Jose 47358

Venezuela
Museo de Los Niños de Caracas, Caracas 48921

Egyptology

Austria
Papyrusmuseum und Papyrussammlung, Wien 02970

Egypt
Egyptian Museum, Cairo 09261
Elephantine Island's Museum, Aswan 09249
Pharaonic Museum, Cairo 09283

France
Musée d'Egyptologie, Villeneuve-d'Ascq 15219
Musée Municipal de l'Évêché, Limoges 12616

Germany
Ägyptische Sammlung der Universität/ Museum Schloß Hohentübingen, Tübingen 20220
Ägyptisches Museum der Universität Leipzig - Interim, Leipzig 18382
Ägyptisches Museum und Papyrussammlung, Berlin 15908
Gustav-Lübcke Museum, Hamm, Westfalen 17576
Kestner-Museum, Hannover 17599
Roemer- und Pelizaeus-Museum, Hildesheim 17760
Sammlung des Ägyptologischen Instituts, Heidelberg 17673
Staatliches Museum Ägyptischer Kunst, München 18915
Staatliches Museum für Ägyptische Kunst, Seefeld, Oberbayern 19915
Vorderasiatisches Museum, Berlin 16114

Israel
Pontifical Biblical Institute Museum, Jerusalem 22656

Italy
Museo Egizio, Torino 25753

Netherlands
Allard Pierson Museum Amsterdam, Amsterdam 28835
Rijksmuseum van Oudheden, Leiden 29524

Spain
Museu Egipci de Barcelona, Barcelona 34575

Sweden
Medelhavsmuseet, Stockholm 36259
Museum Gustavianum, Uppsala 36358

United Kingdom
Blackburn Museum and Art Gallery, Blackburn, Lancashire 38242
Bolton Museum and Art Gallery, Bolton 38269
Egypt Centre, Swansea 40657
Hancock Museum, Newcastle-upon-Tyne 40036
Manchester Museum, Manchester 39894
Myers Museum, Eton 38952
Old Speech Room Gallery, London 39738
Petrie Museum of Egyptian Archaeology, London 39743
Tutankhamun Exhibition, Dorchester 38753
West Park Museum and Art Gallery, Macclesfield 39867

Uruguay
Museo Egipcio, Montevideo 41002

U.S.A.
Rosicrucian Egyptian Museum, San Jose 47354

Vatican City
Museo Gregoriano Egizio, Città del Vaticano 48874

Electricity

Argentina
Museo de la Energía, Embalse 00339

Australia
Longreach Power House Museum, Longreach 01185
Powerhouse House and Car Museum, Portland 01393
Powerhouse Museum Yanco, Yanco 01624

Belgium
Energeia - Museum voor het Industrieel erfgoed Electrabel, Gent 03436

Brazil
Museu da Eletricidade, Rio de Janeiro 04341

Canada
Cité de l'Énergie, Shawinigan 06430
Electrical Engineering Museum, Fredericton 05459
Manitoba Electrical Museum, Winnipeg 06832
Victoria Hydro Station Museum, Carbonear 05204

Czech Republic
Památník Dr. Františka Křižíka, Plánice 08541

Finland
Voimalamuseo, Helsinki 09548

France
Musée André-Marie-Ampère, Poleymieux-au-Mont-d'Or 13788
Musée EDF Electropolis, Mulhouse 13212

Germany
Ausstellung Historischer Elektromaschinenbau, Leipzig 18386
EAM-live-Museum Wasserkraftwerk Wülmersen, Kassel 18016
Elektrizitätszähler-Kabinett, Braunschweig 16295
Elektro-Museum Schleswag, Rendsburg 19568
Energiemuseum, Fürstenfeldbruck 17160
ESWE Technicum, Wiesbaden 20571
Heinrich-Mayer-Haus Elektromuseum, Esslingen 16968
Infozentrum und Elektromuseum, Ansbach 15501
Museum der Stadtwerke, Pirmasens 19403
Museum für Energiegeschichte(n), Hannover 17606
Rheinisches Industriemuseum, Engelskirchen 16873
SiemensForum, München 18906
VSE Elektro-Museum, Illingen 17889

Greece
Open-Air Water-Power Museum, Dimitsana 20938

Hungary
Magyar Elektrotechnikai Múzeum, Budapest 21355

Iceland
Safn Rafmagnsveitu Reykjavíkur, Reykjavík 21664

Iran
The Electrical Industry Museum, Teheran 22293

Italy
Museo dell'Energia Elettrica, Brescia 23204
Museo dell'Energia Elettrica, Brescia 23204

Japan
Asahikawa Youth Science Museum, Asahikawa 26105
Okukiyotsu Electric Power Museum, Yuzawa 27035

Mexico
Museo Tecnológico de la Comisión Federal de Electricidad, México 28204

Netherlands
Bedrijfsmuseum NUON-ENW Amsterdam, Amsterdam 28843
Blikmuseum De Blikvanger, Renesse 29726
Elektriciteits- en Techniekmuseum, Hoenderloo 29428
EnergeticA, Museum voor Energietechniek, Amsterdam 28850
Museum of Historical Philips Products, Eindhoven 29216
Museum Stoomgemaal Winschoten, Winschoten 30008
Het Philips Gloeilampenfabriekje anno 1891, Eindhoven 29217
Zaltbommels Stoom- en Energiemuseum, Zaltbommel 30045

Norway
Theta-Museet, Bergen 30428
Vassdragsmuseet Labro, Skollenborg 30852

Peru
Museo de la Electricidad, Lima 31211

Poland
Muzeum Energetyki Jeleniogórskiej, Szklarska Poręba 32033

Serbia-Montenegro
Muzej Nikole Tesle, Beograd 33808

Switzerland
Ecomusée de la Haute-Areuse, Saint-Sulpice, Neuchâtel 37089
Electrobroc, Broc 36590
Elektrizitätsmuseum, Münchenstein 36963
Elektro Museum, Baden 36483

Tajikistan
Muzej po Istorii Stroitelstva Gidroelektričeskogo Zavoda v Nurke, Nurek 37449

United Kingdom
Museum of Bath at Work, Bath 38117
Museum of Electricity, Christchurch 38577

U.S.A.
American Museum of Radio, Bellingham 41601
A.W.A. Electronic-Communication Museum, Bloomfield 41736
Con Edison Energy Museum, New York 45786
Hearthstone Historic House Museum, Appleton 41239
Niagara Power Project Visitors' Center, Lewiston 44730
Real World Computer Museum, Boothwyn 41792
Robinson Visitors Center, Hartsville 43950
World of Energy at Keowee-Toxaway, Seneca 47565

Venezuela
Museo de la Electricidad, Caracas 48917

Embroidery → Needlework

Enamel Works

Austria
Emailmuseum Gertrude Stöhr, Vorchdorf 02774

Canada
Canadian Clay and Glass Gallery, Waterloo 06751

France
Musée d'Art et d'Histoire Alfred-Douët, Saint-Flour (Cantal) 14218

Netherlands
Kachelmuseum De Drie Kronen, Boekel 28992

Switzerland
Musée de l'Horlogerie et de l'Emaillerie, Genève 36744

United Kingdom
Bilston Craft Gallery, Wolverhampton 40916

Energy

Australia
Longreach Power House Museum, Longreach 01185
World of Energy, Fremantle 01039

Belgium
Steenbakkerijmuseum Rupelklei te Terhagen, Terhagen 03771

Canada
Hamilton Museum of Steam and Technology, Hamilton 05572
Pump House Steam Museum, Kingston 05686

Czech Republic
Technické Muzeum v Brně, Brno 08277

Finland
Korvensuun Voimalaitos- ja Konepajamuseo, Mynämäki 09849

Germany
Atom Museum, Haigerloch 17491
Technisches Landesmuseum, Schwerin 19901
Wasserkraftmuseum, Ziegenrück 20755

India
Bardhaman Science Centre, Bardhaman 21706

Italy
Museo Italgas, Torino 25755

Japan
Gas Museum, Kodaira 26358
Gasu no Kagakukan, Tokyo 26852
Tepco Denryokukan, Tokyo 26933

Madagascar
Musée de l'Université de Tuléar, Tuléar 27610

Netherlands
Stoomhoutzagerij, Groenlo 29304

New Zealand
Engine House, Dunedin 30147

Norway
Fotland Kraftverk, Bryne 30453
Industrimuseet, Kopperå 30608
Norsk Oljemuseum, Stavanger 30885

Russia
Muzej Istorii OAO Gaz, Nižnij Novgorod 33212
Muzej Istorii Razvitija Mosenergo, Moskva 33111

Sweden
Umeå Energicentrum, Umeå 36348

Switzerland
EKZ-Museum Stromhaus Burenwisen, Glattfelden 36766
Kraftwerkmuseum Löntsch, Netstal 36981

Tajikistan
Muzej po Istorii Stroitelstva Gidroelektričeskogo Zavoda v Nurke, Nurek 37449

United Kingdom
Electric Mountain - Museum of North Wales, Llanberis 39534
Ellenroad Engine House, Milnrow 39959
Fakenham Museum of Gas and Local History, Fakenham 38966
Markfield Beam Engine and Museum, London 39705

U.S.A.
Coolspring Power Museum, Coolspring 42617
National Atomic Museum, Albuquerque 41106
North Anna Nuclear Information Center, Mineral 45378
Texas Energy Museum, Beaumont 41572
World of Energy at Keowee-Toxaway, Seneca 47565

Engraving → Graphic Arts

Entomology → Insects

Epitaphs → Inscriptions and Epitaphs

Ethnology

Albania
District Ethnographic Museum, Elbasan 00017
Ethnographic Museum, Bérat 00012
Ethnographic Museum, Durrës 00016
Ethnographic Museum, Gjirokastër 00022

Algeria
Musée National de Préhistoire et d'Ethnographie du Bardo, Alger 00044

Angola
Museu de Etnografia do Lobito, Lobito 00093
Museu Municipal, Nova Lisboa 00104
Museu Nacional de Antropologia, Luanda 00099

Argentina
Centro Mundo Aborigen, Córdoba 00290
Museo Arqueológico de Salta, Salta 00537
Museo Cacique Balata, La Cumbre 00378
Museo de Ciencias Antropológicas y Naturales, Santiago del Estero 00616
Museo de Ciencias Naturales y Antropológicas Juan Cornelio Moyano, Mendoza 00435
Museo de Ciencias Naturales y Misional del Colegio San José, Esperanza 00342
Museo del Indio, Los Toldos 00412
Museo del Mundo, Buenos Aires 00201
Museo Ethnográfico de las Obras Misionales Pontificias, Buenos Aires 00204
Museo Etnográfico Juán B. Ambrosetti, Buenos Aires 00205
Museo Etnográfico Municipal Dámaso Arce, Olavarría 00461
Museo Etnográfico y Archivo Histórico Enrique Squirru, Azul 00124
Museo Histórico Municipal y Colección de Arte Precolombino Arminio Weiss, Rafaela 00498
Museo Independencia, Córdoba 00303
Museo Indigenista, Esquel 00346
Museo Municipal de Lomas de Zamora, Lomas de Zamora 00410
Museo Nacional del Hombre, Buenos Aires 00231
Museo Privado de Arqueología Regional Julio Gironde, Carmen de Patagonés 00265
Museo Regional de Antropología, Resistencia 00510
Museo Rocsen, Nono 00459
Museo Runa de Antropología, Tafí del Valle 00628
Museo Salesiano Ceferino Namuncura, Córdoba 00311

Armenia
State History Museum of Armenia, Erevan 00692

Australia
Adelaide Lithuanian Museum and Archives, Norwood 01335
Alpenrail Swiss Model Village and Railway, Claremont, Tasmania 00917
Anthropology Museum, Brisbane 00835
Berndt Museum of Anthropology, Nedlands 01310
Boandik Cultural Museum, Beachport 00778
Chinese Museum, Melbourne 01224
Golden Dragon Museum, Bendigo 00795
Italian Historical Museum, Carlton South 00895
J.L. Shellshear Museum of Comparative Anatomy and Physical Anthropology, Sydney 01498
J.T. Wilson Museum of Human Anatomy, Sydney 01499
Macleay Museum, Sydney 01501
Miegunyah Pioneer Women's Memorial House Museum, Bowen Hills 00820
Philippine House Museum, Shepparton 01450
Queensland Museum, South Bank 01458
School of Political and Social Inquiry Museum, Clayton 00924
South Australian Museum, Adelaide 00713
Tandanya, Adelaide 00714
Templin Historical Village, Boonah 00813
Tineriba Tribal Gallery and Museum, Hahndorf 01084
Western Australian Museum, Perth 01364

Austria
Ethnographisches Museum Schloss Kittsee, Kittsee 02117
Haus der Völker, Schwaz 02648
Heimathaus Mörbisch, Mörbisch 02318
Heimatmuseum im Amonhaus, Lunz 02256
Missions-Ethnographisches Museum St. Gabriel, Mödling 02310
Museum - Begegnung der Kulturen, Krenglbach 02163
Museum für Völkerkunde, Wien 02945
Referat Volkskunde, Graz 01930
Richard-Simoncic-Museum, Rabensburg 02471
Volkskundliche Sammlung alter bäuerlicher Geräte, Ludesch 02255

Bangladesh
Bangla Academy Folklore Museum, Dhaka 03084
Chittagong University Museum, Chittagong 03079
Ethnological Museum, Chittagong 03080
Varendra Research Museum, Rajshahi 03099

Belarus
Muzej Staražytna Belaruskaj Kultury, Minsk 03120

Belgium
Africa-Museum, Tervuren 03772
Etnografisch Museum, Antwerpen 03141
Etnografische Collecties van de Universiteit Gent, Gent 03437
Musée Africain de Namur, Namur 03644
Musée de Chine, Bruxelles 03302
Musée de la Vie Wallonne, Liège 03578
Museum voor Volkskunde, Brugge 03264
Volkskundemuseum, Antwerpen 03178

Benin
Musée de Cotonou, Cotonou 03873
Musée de Natitingou, Natitingou 03874
Musée d'Homme, Porto-Novo 03877
Musée Ethnographique, Porto-Novo 03878

Bolivia
Museo Antropológico, Sucre 03906
Museo Nacional de Etnografía y Folklore, La Paz 03901

Bosnia and Herzegovina
Zemaljski Muzej, Sarajevo 03925

Botswana
Kgosi Bathoen II (Segopotso) Museum, Kanye 03936
Nhabe Museum, Nhabe 03938
Supa-Ngwao Museum Centre, Francistown 03933

Brazil
Museu da Cidade, São Paulo 04503
Museu de Arqueologia e Etnologia da Universidade de São Paulo, São Paulo 04512
Museu de Folclore Édison Carneiro, Rio de Janeiro 04359
Museu do Homem, Curitiba 04073
Museu do Homem do Nordeste, Recife 04302
Museu do Índio, Manaus 04191
Museu do Indio, Rio de Janeiro 04369
Museu do Instituto de Antropologia Câmara Cascudo, Natal 04222
Museu-Escola Esacro do Estado da Paraiba, João Pessoa 04149
Museu Paranaense, Curitiba 04078
Museus de História Natural e Etnologia Indígena, Juiz de Fora 04159

Bulgaria
Etnografska Ekspozicija, Pazardžik 04755
Etnografska Ekspozicija, Svištov 04878
Etnografski Muzej, Berkovica 04620
Etnografski Muzej, Dobrič 04654
Etnografski Muzej, Elchovo 04662
Etnografski Muzej, Plovdiv 04776
Etnografski Muzej, Silistra 04814
Etnografski Muzej, Varna 04895
Etnografski muzej, Burgas 04633
Etnografski Muzej Dunavski Ribolov i Lodkostroenie, Tutrakan 04891
Istoričeski Muzej, Batak 04616
Istoričeski Muzej, Dimitrovgrad 04651
Istoričeski Muzej, Razgrad 04797
Istoričeski Muzej Targovište, Targovište 04883
Istoričeskij Muzej, Tutrakan 04892
Kërpeeva Kašta, Kotel 04718
Okražen Istoričeski Muzej, Veliko Tărnovo 04920

Burkina Faso
Musée National de Burkina Faso, Ouagadougou 04943
Musée Provincial du Houet, Bobo-Dioulasso 04936

Burundi
Musée Vivant de Bujumbura, Bujumbura 04944

Cameroon
Musée de Diamare, Maroua 04958
Musée International de Akum, Bamenda 04952
Musée Municipal de Mokolo, Mokolo 04960

Canada
Arkona Lion's Museum, Arkona 05007
Eskimo Museum, Churchill 05250
Glenbow Museum, Calgary 05167
Haida Gwaii Museum at Qay'llnagaay, Skidegate 06460
Ksan Historical Village and Museum, Hazelton 05590
McCord Museum, Montréal 05910
Manitoba Museum of Man and Nature, Winnipeg 06833
Musée Canadien des Civilisations, Gatineau 05484
Musée de Baie Comeau, Baie Comeau 05034
Musée de Charlevoix, Pointe-au-Pic 06143
Musée de la Civilisation, Québec 06202
Musée des Abénakis, Odanak 06041
Musée du Bas Saint-Laurent, Rivière-du-Loup 06278
Musée du Bûcheron, Grandes-Piles 05521
Musée du Château Ramezay, Montréal 05920
Musée et Centre de Transmission de la Culture Daniel Weetaluktuk, Inukjuak 05621
Musée François Pilote, La Pocatière 05707
Musée Kateri Tekakwitha, Kahnawake 05636
Musée Kio-Warini, Loretteville 05779
Museum of Anthropology, Vancouver 06683
Museum of Archaeology and Ethnology, Burnaby 05150
North American Black Historical Museum, Amherstburg 04988
Northern Life Museum and National Exhibition Centre, Fort Smith 05452
Prince of Wales Northern Heritage Centre, Yellowknife 06870
La Pulperie de Chicoutimi, Chicoutimi 05247
Rainy River District Women's Institute Museum, Emo 05407
Royal British Columbia Museum, Victoria 06729
Surrey Museum, Surrey 06520
Transcona Historical Museum, Winnipeg 06848
Ukraina Museum, Saskatoon 06406
Ukrainian Canadian Archives and Museum of Alberta, Edmonton 05388
Ukrainian Cultural Heritage Village, Edmonton 05390
Ukrainian Museum of Canada, Saskatoon 06407
Ukrainian Museum of Canada - Alberta Branch, Edmonton 05391

Central African Republic
Musée Ethnographique Regional, Bouar 06879
Musée National Barthélémy Boganda, Bangui 06878

Chile
Museo Antropológico de Antofagasta, Antofagasta 06887
Museo Antropológico de Iquique, Iquique 06896
Museo Arqueológico San Miguel de Azapa, Arica 06889
Museo Regional Salesiano Maggiorino Borgatello, Punta Arenas 06905

China, People's Republic
Anthropological Museum, Beijing 06942
Anthropological Museum of Xiamen University, Xiamen 07289
Museum of the Cultural Palace of National Minorities, Beijing 06978
Peking Man in Zhoukoudian, Beijing 06984

China, Republic
Museum of the Institute of History and Philology, Academia Sinica, Taipei 07349

Colombia
Exposición Permanente de Cerámica Indígena, Manizales 07505
Museo Chairama, Santa Marta 07588
Museo de Artesanías del Mundo, Silvia 07592
Museo de Historia Natural, Bogotá 07405
Museo de la Cultura de Albán, Albán 07363
Museo de la Diversidad Biológica y Cultural del Pacífico, Quibdó 07572
Museo de Trajes Regionales de Colombia, Bogotá 07413
Museo Etnográfico, Albán 07364
Museo Etnográfico, Inzá 07500
Museo Etnográfico Madre Laura, Medellín 07518
Museo Etnográfico Miguel Angel Builes, Medellín 07519
Museo Histórico de la Casa de la Cultura, Ambalema 07366
Museo Indígena Regional Enin, Mitú 07525
Museo Inter-étnico de la Amazonía, Florencia 07480
Museo Nacional de Antropología, Bogotá 07428
Museo Nacional de Colombia, Bogotá 07429
Museo Paisa, Caicedonia 07442

Congo, Democratic Republic
Musée du Roi de Cuba, Mushenge 07643
Musée National de Kananga, Kananga 07633
Musée National de Lubumbashi, Lumumbashi 07641
Musée Regional, Kisangani 07639

Congo, Republic
Musée Régional André Grenard Matsoua, Kinkala 07646
Musée Régional Ma-Loango Diosso, Pointe-Noire 07647

Côte d'Ivoire
Musée des Civilisations de Côte d'Ivoire, Abidjan 07666

Croatia
Creski Muzej, Cres 07691
Etnografska Zbirka, Koprivnički 07720
Etnografska Zbirka Franjevačkog Samostana, Zaostrog 07842
Gradski Muzej, Bjelovar 07681
Gradski Muzej Karlovac, Karlovac 07713
Gradski Muzej Makarska, Makarska 07736
Gradski Muzej Virovitica, Virovitica 07801
Knežev Dvor, Cavtat 07689
Memorijalna Zbirka Eugena Kumičića, Brseč 07685
Muzej Moslavine, Kutina 07733
Muzejska Zbirka Krapina i Okolica, Krapina 07729
Narodni Muzej Labin, Labin 07734
Staro Selo Kumrovec, Kumrovec 07732
Zavičajni Muzej, Čazma 07690

Cuba
Museo Antropológico Montané, La Habana 07935
Museo Casa de Africa, La Habana 07939
Museo Casa de Asia, La Habana 07940
Museo Ciudades del Mundo, La Habana 07953
Museo Etnográfico, Madruga 08023
Museo Etnográfico, Santa Lucía 08127

Cyprus
Ethnographic Museum, Avgorou 08185
Ethnographical Museum, Paphos 08214

Cyprus, Turkish Republic
Canbulat Türbe ve Müzesi, Gazimağusa 08217
Dervish Pasha Mansion Ethnographical Museum, Lefkoşa 08235
Mevlevi Tekke Müzesi, Lefkoşa 08238

Czech Republic
Dietrichsteinský Palác, Brno 08264
Etnografické muzeum, Tovačov 08683
Etnografický Ústav, Brno 08267
Hrdličkovo Muzeum Člověka, Praha 08581
Lesnické, Myslivecké a Rybářské Muzeum, Hluboká nad Vltavou 08352
Městské Muzeum, Úpice 08701
Městské Muzeum, Valašské Klobouky 08705
Moravské Zemské Muzeum, Brno 08272
Muzeum Dr. Aleše Hrdličky, Humpolec 08374
Muzeum Jindřicha Jindřicha, Domažlice 08333
Muzeum Vysočiny Jihlava, Jihlava 08390
Náprstek Museum of Asian, African and American Cultures, Liběchov 08449
Náprstkovo Muzeum Asijských, Afrických a Amerických Kultur, Praha 08600
Národopisné Muzeum Plzeňska, Plzeň 08543
Sládečkovo Vlastivědné Muzeum v Kladně, Kladno 08410
Slovácké Muzeum, Uherské Hradiště 08698

Denmark
Djurslands Museum - Dansk Fiskerimuseum, Grenå 08841
Grindsted Museum, Grindsted 08844
Kulturhistorisk Museum, Randers 09025
Nordsjaellandsk Folkemuseum, Hillerød 08874
Vendsyssel Historiske Museum, Hjørring 08877

Dominican Republic
Museo del Hombre Dominicano, Santo Domingo 09125

East Timor
Museum Siwa Lima, Ambon 09129

Ecuador
Museo Antropológico Shuar, Quito 09194
Museo Azuayo del Folklore, Cuenca 09151
Museo de Etnografía, Quito 09204
Museo Etnografico del Cologio Nacional Mejia, Quito 09210

Egypt
Ethnological Museum, Cairo 09264

El Salvador
Museo Nacional David J. Guzmán, San Salvador 09313

Estonia
Eesti Põllumajandusmuuseum, Tõrvandi 09391
Eesti Rahva Muuseum, Tartu 09376
Rannarootsi Muuseum, Haapsalu 09319

Ethiopia
City Museum, Makale 09405
City Museum, Yirgalem 09406
Ethnographic Museum, Addis Ababa 09398

Fiji
Fiji Museum, Suva 09409

Finland
Ethnographisches Museum Pöykkölä, Rovaniemi 10000
Helinä Rautavaaran museo, Espoo 09435
Kettumäen Ulkomuseo ja Kotiseututalo, Kuusankoski 09730
Kulttuurien Museo, Helsinki 09505
Lapin Maakuntamuseo, Rovaniemi 10001
Liedon Vanhalinna, Vanhalinna 10178
Mäntyharjun Museo, Mäntyharju 09811
Perniön Museo, Perniö 09920
Rautalammin Museo, Rautalampi 09988
Ruokolahden Kotiseutumuseo, Ruokolahti 10005
Suomen Kansallismuseo, Helsinki 09531
Tornionlaakson Maakuntamuseo, Tornio 10115
Vanajan Kotiseutumuseo, Hämeenlinna 09455

France
Ecomusée de la Brenne, Le Blanc 12380
Ecomusée de la Margeride, Loubaresse 12671
Ecomusée de la Margeride, Ruynes-en-Margeride 14078
Ecomusée de l'Ile-de-Groix, Ile-de-Groix 12046
Ecomusée de Plein Air du Quercy, Sauliac-sur-Célé 14634
Ecomusée du Pays de Rennes, Rennes (Ille-et-Vilaine) 13939
Musée Africain, Ile-d'Aix 12044
Musée Alsacien, Haguenau 11985
Musée Arménien de France, Paris 13530
Musée Béarnais, Pau 13665
Musée d'Art et d'Histoire de Lisieux, Lisieux 12621
Musée Dauphinois, Grenoble 11941
Musée de Cosne, Cosne-Cours-sur-Loire 11416
Musée de la Camargue, Arles 10415

Musée de la Haute-Auvergne, Saint-Flour (Cantal) 14219
Musée de la Poupée, Paris 13562
Musée de la Vallée du Lot, Villeneuve-sur-Lot 15235
Musée de Traditions Populaires et d'Archéologie, Chauvigny 11255
Musée Départemental des Hautes-Alpes, Gap 11838
Musée des Arts Africains, Océaniens, Amérindiens, Marseille 12860
Musée des Beaux-Arts, Angoulême 10356
Musée d'Ethnographie de l'Université de Bordeaux II, Bordeaux 10815
Musée d'Histoire Naturelle, Rouen 14050
Musée d'Histoire Naturelle et d'Ethnographie, Colmar 11359
Musée du Biterrois, Béziers 10719
Musée du Château Saint-Jean, Nogent-le-Rotrou 13351
Musée du Patrimoine Rural, Dompierre (Orne) 11549
Musée du Pays de Luchon, Bagnères-de-Luchon 10562
Musée du Pays de Retz, Bourgneuf-en-Retz 10868
Musée Entomologique, Saint-Quentin (Aisne) 14435
Musée Ethnographique de l'Olivier, Cagnes-sur-Mer 10990
Musée Ethnographique du Donjon, Niort 13346
Musée-Fondation Alexandra David-Néel, Digne-les-Bains 11513
Musée Joseph-Vaylet, Espalion 11649
Musée Napoléonien, Ile-d'Aix 12045
Musée National de la Marine, Paris 13631
Musée National des Arts et Traditions Populaires, Paris 13635
Musée Portuaire, Dunkerque 11586
Museon Arlaten, Arles 10418
Muséum d'Histoire Naturelle de Toulouse, Toulouse 14953

French Polynesia
Musée de Tahiti et des Iles-Te Fare Iamanaha, Punaauia 15348

Georgia
Kutaisskij Gosudarstvennyj Muzej Istorii i Etnografii, Kutaisi 15356

Germany
Abenteuermuseum Saarbrücken - Sammlung Heinz Rox-Schulz, Saarbrücken 19722
Adelhausermuseum, Natur- und Völkerkunde, Freiburg im Breisgau 17105
Afrika-Museum, Bergen, Kreis Celle 15893
Afrikahaus Museum und Nold-Namibia-Bibliothek, Sebnitz 19907
Agrar- und Freilichtmuseum, Crimmitschau 16513
Anthropologische Sammlung der Universität Göttingen, Göttingen 17332
Archäologisch-Ethnographische Lehr- und Studiensammlung des Instituts für Altamerikanistik und Ethnologie der Universität Bonn, Bonn 16226
Brasilienmuseum im Kloster Bardel, Bad Bentheim 15598
Darß-Museum, Ostseebad Prerow 19316
Deutsches Albert-Schweitzer-Zentrum, Frankfurt am Main 17034
Deutsches Märchen- und Wesersagenmuseum, Bad Oeynhausen 15708
Ethnologisches Museum, Berlin 15945
Hamaland-Museum und Westmünsterländische Hofanlage, Vreden 20335
Haus Völker und Kulturen - Ethnologisches Museum, Sankt Augustin 19746
Iwalewa Haus, Bayreuth 15847
JuniorMuseum im Ethnologischen Museum, Berlin 16012
Kindheitsmuseum, Schönberg, Holstein 19823
Landesschau Äthiopien, Neulingen, Enzkreis 19043
Linden-Museum Stuttgart, Stuttgart 20099
Lippisches Landesmuseum, Detmold 16589
Ludwig-Harms-Haus, Hermannsburg 17725
Missionsmuseum, Sankt Ottilien 19756
Missionsmuseum der Mariannhiller Missionare, Würzburg 20699
Missionsmuseum der Spiritaner Knechtsteden, Dormagen 16647
Museum der deutschen Sprachinselorte bei Brünn, Erbach, Donau 16885
Museum der Weltkulturen, Frankfurt am Main 17061
Museum Europäischer Kulturen, Berlin 16051
Museum Forum der Völker, Werl 20521
Museum für Naturkunde und Völkerkunde Julius Riemer, Lutherstadt Wittenberg 18577
Museum für Regionalgeschichte und Volkskunde, Gotha 17362
Museum für Stadtgeschichte und Volkskunde, Heppenheim 17712
Museum für Völkerkunde, Witzenhausen 20637
Museum für Völkerkunde der Universität Kiel, Kiel 18078
Museum für Völkerkunde Hamburg, Hamburg 17561
Museum für Völkerkunde zu Leipzig/ Grassimuseum, Leipzig 18407
Naturhistorisches Museum, Nürnberg 19155
Niedersächsisches Landesmuseum Hannover, Hannover 17607
Rautenstrauch-Joest-Museum, Köln 18164
Reiss-Engelhorn-Museen, Mannheim 18615
Ruhrlandmuseum Essen, Essen 16962
Sammlung Buchheim - Museum der Phantasie, Bernried, Starnberger See 16129
Schwarz-Afrika-Museum, Vilshofen 20326
Staatliches Museum für Völkerkunde Dresden, Dresden 16711
Staatliches Museum für Völkerkunde München, München 18916
Überseemuseum Bremen, Bremen 16336
Ungarndeutsches Heimatmuseum Backnang, Backnang 15587
Ur-Wolpertinger-Museum, Kreuth 18237
Völkerkundemuseum der von Portheim-Stiftung, Heidelberg 17677
Völkerkundemuseum Herrnhut, Herrnhut 17738
Völkerkundesammlung, Lübeck 18545
Völkerkundliche Sammlung der Philipps-Universität, Marburg 18633
Völkerkundliche Sammlung der Universität, Göttingen 17342
Volkskundliche Sammlungen, Witzenhausen 20638
Wallenfels'sches Haus, Abteilung Vor- und Frühgeschichte, Archäologie und Völkerkunde, Gießen 17284
Zweigmuseum des Staatlichen Museum für Völkerkunde, Oettingen 19238

Ghana
Institute of African Studies Teaching Museum, Legon 20799

Greece
Anthropological-Ethnological Museum, Athinai 20847
Ethnographical Historical Museum of Lárissa, Lárissa 21042
Folklore Museum, Pogoniani 21129
Folklore Museum, Vitsa 21210
Mouseio Mpenaki, Athinai 20878
Museum of Cretan Ethnology, Vori 21215

Guatemala
Museo Nacional de Arqueología y Etnología, Guatemala 21271
Museo Regional, Chichicastenango 21264

Guinea
Musée Annexe de Youkounkoun, Youkounkoun 21287
Musée National de Conakry, Conakry 21282
Musée Préfectoral de Koundara, Koundara 21285
Musée Regional de Beyla, Beyla 21278

Guinea-Bissau
Musée da Guine Portugesa, Bissau 21288
Museu Etnografico Nacional, Bissau 21289

Honduras
Museo Antropologia e Historia Valle de Sula, San Pedro Sula 21301

Hungary
Csongrádi Múzeum, Csongrád 21397
Déri Múzeum, Debrecen 21398
Dráva Múzeum, Barcs 21316
Ferenczy Károly Múzeum, Szentendre 21570
Gyoërffy István Nagykun Múzeum, Karcag 21444
Intercisa Múzeum, Dunaújváros 21405
Jfj. Lele J. Néprajzi Gyűjteménye, Szeged 21548
Kanizsai Dorottya Múzeum, Mohács 21482
Kiskun Múzeum, Kiskunfélegyháza 21457
Kiss Pál Múzeum, Tiszafüred 21596
Kossuth Múzeum, Cegléd 21395
Laczkó Dezsoë Múzeum, Veszprém 21608
Matyó Múzeum, Mezőkövesd 21471
Munkácsy Mihály Múzeum, Békéscsaba 21319
Nemzeti Történeti Emlékpark, Opusztaszer 21493
Néprajzi Gyűjtemény, Sopron 21535
Néprajzi Kiállítás, Pécs 21512
Néprajzi Múzeum, Budapest 21367
Rábaközi Múzeum, Kapuvár 21443
Rákóczi Múzeum, Sárospatak 21524
Szántó Kovács Múzeum, Orosháza 21494
Szatmári Múzeum, Mátészalka 21470
Thorma János Múzeum, Kiskunhalas 21460
Thury György Múzeum, Nagykanizsa 21486
Türr István Múzeum, Baja 21309
Vármúzeum, Kisvárda 21463
Viski Károly Múzeum, Kalocsa 21438

Iceland
P^BDjóðminjasafn Islands, Reykjanik 21647

India
Anthropological Museum, Gauhati 21805
Anthropology Museum, Delhi 21764
Anthropology Museum, Ranchi 22003
Anthropology Museum, Lucknow 21919
Bharat Itihas Samshodhak Mandal Museum, Pune 21987
Bihar Tribal Welfare Research Institute Museum, Ranchi 22004
Cultural Research Institute, Kolkata 21902
Ethnological Museum, Pune 21989
Government Museum, Pudukottai 21985
Jawaharlal Nehru State Museum, Itanagar 21860
Kurukshetra Panorama Science Centre, Kurukshetra 21918
Prabhas Patan Museum, Prabhas Patan 21984
Ragailong Museum, Imphal 21857
State Museum, Kohima 21894
Tibet House Museum, Delhi 21785
Tribal Museum, Ahmedabad 21682
Victoria and Albert Museum, Mumbai 21955
Zonal Anthropological Museum, Shillong 22019
Zonal Museum, Dehradun 21761

Indonesia
Museum Loka Budaya, Jayapura 22141
Museum Negeri Propinsi Nusa Tenggara Timur, Kupang 22149
Museum Negeri Sumatera Utara, Medan 22158
Museum Pemda Balige, Balige 22067
Museum Wanua Paksinanta, Manado 22155
Subak Museum, Banjar Senggulan 22078

Iran
Ethnological Museum, Teheran 22294
Ethnological Museum, Teheran 22295
Ghoochan Museum, Ghoochan 22238
Kandelous Museum, Kandelous 22248
Khoy Museum, Khoy 22259
Mardom-shenasi-ye Kavir, Nayin 22271
Moaven Al- Molk Museum, Kermanshah 22255
Muséyé Kerman, Kerman 22252
Muséyé Mardom Shenassi, Teheran 22318
Rasht Museum, Rasht 22275
Sa'dabad Museums, Teheran 22325
Zabol Museum, Zabol 22336

Israel
Albadia Museum, Osafia 22726
Babylonian Jewry Museum, Or Yehuda 22725
Museum for Beduin Culture, Kibbutz Lahav 22694

Italy
Castello D'Albertis, Genova 23977
Museo Africano, Verona 25968
Museo Archeologico Etnografico, Paulilatino 24820
Museo Calabrese di Etnografia e Folklore R. Corso, Palmi 24785
Museo Civico Archeologico Etnologico, Modena 24438
Museo Civico di Numismatica, Etnografia e Arti Orientali, Torino 25737
Museo Civico Etnografico C.G. Franchini, Oleggio 24674
Museo Civico Etnografico M.G. Fontana, Sappada 25469
Museo dei Ferri Taglienti, Scarperia 25520
Museo del Bosco, Sovicille 25614
Museo del Po, Monticelli d'Ongina 24553
Museo del Sud-Ovest Americano, Cuveglio 23707
Museo della Gente dell'Appennino Pistoiese, Cutigliano 23704
Museo della Vita Contadina in Romagnolo, Russi 25302
Museo delle Culture Extraeuropee Dinz Rialto, Rimini 25117
Museo delle Genti d'Abruzzo, Pescara 24868
Museo delle Terre Marchigiane, San Lorenzo in Campo 25384
Museo delle Valli Valdesi, Torre Pellice 25775
Museo di Antropologia, Bologna 23124
Museo di Antropologia, Napoli 24588
Museo di Antropologia ed Etnografia, Torino 25747
Museo di Antropologia ed Etnologia, Firenze 23864
Museo di Antropologia G. Sergi, Roma 25209
Museo di Arte Cinese ed Etnografico, Parma 24805
Museo di Etnopreistoria, Napoli 24590
Museo Etiopico G. Massaia, Frascati 23932
Museo Etnico Arbereshe, Civita 23591
Museo Etno-Antropologico, Calatafimi 23259
Museo Etno-Antropologico, San Cipirello 25349
Museo Etno-Antropologico, San Mauro Castelverde 25394
Museo Etno-Antropologico, Scaletta Zanclea 25515
Museo Etno-Antropologico della Terra di Zabut, Sambuca di Sicilia 25329
Museo Etno-Antropologico della Valle del Belice, Gibellina 24025
Museo Etno-Antropologico delle Madonie, Geraci Siculo 24017
Museo Etnografico, Aprica 22906
Museo Etnografico, Aritzo 22934
Museo Etnografico, Bomba 23158
Museo Etnografico, Collinas 23616
Museo Etnografico, Faeto 23758
Museo Etnografico, Fossalta di Portogruaro 23924
Museo Etnografico, Fratta Polesine 23936
Museo Etnografico, Lusevera 24244
Museo Etnografico, Malborghetto Valbruna 24266
Museo Etnografico, Montodine 24555
Museo Etnografico, Novara di Sicilia 24652
Museo Etnografico, Oneta 24679
Museo Etnografico, Ortonovo 24703
Museo Etnografico, Ossimo Superiore 24712
Museo Etnografico, Parma 24810
Museo Etnografico, Ponte in Valtellina 24990
Museo Etnografico, Roccalbegna 25139
Museo Etnografico, Schilpario 25525
Museo Etnografico Africo, Bari 23026
Museo Etnografico Antico Mulino ad Acqua Licheri, Fluminimaggiore 23890
Museo Etnografico Cerginolano, Cerignola 23482
Museo Etnografico Civiltà Contadina, Forlì 23913
Museo Etnografico dei Cimbri, Selva di Progno 25532
Museo Etnografico del Carretto Siciliano, Terrasini 25701
Museo Etnografico del Pinerolese e Museo del Legno, Pinerolo 24930
Museo Etnografico del Ponente Ligure, Cervo 23495
Museo Etnografico della Cultura Contadina, Morigerati 24564
Museo Etnografico della Lunigiana, Villafranca in Lunigiana 26018
Museo Etnografico della Trinità, Botticino 23187
Museo Etnografico della Valle, Ultimo 25852
Museo Etnografico e della Stregoneria, Triora 25835
Museo Etnografico e di Scienze Naturali, Torino 25754
Museo Etnografico Francesco Bande, Sassari 25487
Museo Etnografico G. Carpani, Lizzano in Belvedere 24197
Museo Etnografico I Zuf, Vione 26027
Museo Etnografico Il Cicle della Vita, Quartu Sant'Elena 25060
Museo Etnografico La Steiva, Piverone 24967
Museo Etnografico San Domu de is Ainas, Armungia 22935
Museo Etnografico sulla Lavorazione del Legno, San Vito di Leguzzano 25421
Museo Etnografico Tiranese, Madonna di Tirano 24258
Museo Etnografico Tiranese, Tirano 25706
Museo Etnografico U. Ferrandi, Novara 24647
Museo Etnografico Vallivo, Val Masino 25868
Museo Etnologico della Apuane, Massa 24315
Museo Geopaleontologico Naturalistico Antropico e Ornitologico Brancaleoni, Piobbico 24934
Museo Indiano, Bologna 23137
Museo Missionario delle Grazie, Rimini 25118
Museo Nazionale Preistorico ed Etnografico Luigi Pigorini, Roma 25238
Museo Polare Etnografico Silvio Zavatti, Fermo 23781
Museo Storico Etnografico, Sampeyre 25331
Museo Storico Etnografico della Bassa Valsesia, Romagnano Sesia 25272
Museo Storico Etnografico Naturalistico, Chiesa in Valmalenco 23543
Museum Zeitreise Mensch, Cortaccia 23659
Raccolta Etnografica, Vallo di Nera 25883
Südtiroler Landesmuseum für Volkskunde, Brunico 23221

Japan
Abashiri Kyodo Hakubutsukan, Abashiri 26084
Imaizumi Museum, Shiozawa 26759
Kokuritsu Minzokugaku Hakubutsukan, Minpaku, Suita 26774

Jordan
The Anthropological National Folklore Museum, Amman 27044

Kazakhstan
Muzej Prezidentskogo Centra Kultury Respubliki Kazachstan, Astana 27077
Vostočno Kazachstanskij Ėtnografičeskij Muzej, Ust-Kamenogorsk 27100

Kenya
Kitale Museum, Kitale 27106
Meru Museum, Meru 27108

Korea, Democratic People's Republic
Korean Central Ethnographic Museum, Pyongyang 27120

Korea, Republic
Africa Museum, Seoul 27222
Latin American Cultural Center Museum, Koyang 27205
Pacific Museum, Yongin 27303
Sookmyung Women's University Museum, Seoul 27281

Kyrgyzstan
Gumbez Manace Literary Ethnographic Museum, Taš-Aryk 27315

Laos
Parc National de la Culture des Ethnies, Vientiane 27322

Latvia
Turaidas Muzejrezervāts, Sigulda 27451

Lesotho
Lesotho National Museum, Maseru 27495
Morija Museum, Morija 27496

Liberia
Africana Museum, Monrovia 27498
National Museum, Monrovia 27499

Lithuania
Aušros Avenue Mansion, Šiauliai 27525
Lietuvos Nacionalinis Muziejus, Vilnius 27537
Šiauliai Aušros Museum, Šiauliai 27531
Žeimelis Žiemgalos Museum, Žeimelis 27540

Luxembourg
Musée d'Art Rustique, Vianden 27576

Macedonia
Muzej i Galerija Bitola, Bitola 27584
Muzej na Makedonija - Arceološki, Etnološki i Istoriski, Skopje 27590

Malawi
Museum of Malawi, Blantyre 27611

Malaysia
Jabatan Muzium Sabah, Kota Kinabalu 27631
Malay Ethnographic Museum, Kuala Lumpur 27642
Museum of Aboriginal Affairs, Gombak 27620
Muzium Kecantikan, Melaka 27670
Muzium Negara, Kuala Lumpur 27644
Muzium Negeri Sarawak, Kuching 27658

Muzium Negeri Sembilan, Seremban 27684
Muzium Rakyat, Melaka 27672

Mali
Musée National du Mali, Bamako 27691

Malta
Inquisitor's Palace, Vittoriosa 27712
Ta' Kola Windmill, Xaghra 27716

Mexico
Museo Antropología e Historia, Victoria 28601
Museo Centro de Cultura Mayo de El Júpare Blas Mazo, Huatabampo 27999
Museo Coahuila y Texas, Monclova 28225
Museo Comunitario Raramuri, Guachochi 27939
Museo de Antropología de Xalapa, Xalapa 28615
Museo de Artes Populares, Tepic 28496
Museo de Cocula es El Mariachi, Cocula 27834
Museo de Culturas Populares de San Luis Potosí, San Luis Potosí 28399
Museo de Culturas Populares e Indígenas de Sonora, Hermosillo 27985
Museo de la Cultura Maya, Chetumal 27817
Museo de La Huaxteca, Amatlán de los Reyes 27770
Museo de la Soledad, Oaxaca 28276
Museo de las Californias, Los Cabos 28064
Museo de las Californias, Tijuana 28512
Museo de las Culturas, Saltillo 28367
Museo de las Culturas Afromestizas, Cuajinicuilapa 27867
Museo de las Culturas de la Huasteca Potosina Tamuantzán, Valles 28587
Museo de las Culturas de Occidente, Colima 27836
Museo de las Culturas Prehispánicas, Puerto Vallarta 28348
Museo de las Culturas Prehispánicas de Durango, Durango 27898
Museo de las Miniaturas Poblanas, Palmar de Bravo 28299
Museo de Sitio de Cholula, San Pedro Cholula 28422
Museo del Centro Cultural Universitario Quinta Gameros, Chihuahua 27826
Museo del Instituto de Investigaciones Antropológicas, México 28157
Museo del Origen, Santiago Ixcuintla 28437
Museo Étnico de los Seris, Hermosillo 27986
Museo Étnico de los Yaquis, Obregón 28282
Museo Etnográfico, Tuxtla Gutiérrez 28573
Museo Etnográfico Huichol Wixarica, Zapopan 28648
Museo Nacional de Antropología, México 28183
Museo Nacional de las Culturas, México 28192
Museo Naucalpan de la Cultura Tlatilca, Naucalpan de Juárez 28264
Museo Nuestro Pueblo y Museo Etnográfico de Tecpatán, Tecpatán 28471
Museo Regional de Actopán, Actopán 27752
Museo Regional de Antropología Carlos Pellicer Cámara, Villahermosa 28612
Museo Regional de Antropología e Historia de Baja California Sur, La Paz 28045
Museo Regional de Guadalajara, Guadalajara 27961
Museo Regional de Guerrero, Chilpancingo 27832
Museo Regional de Nayarit, Tepic 28499
Museo Regional de Yucatán, Mérida 28085
Museo Renacimiento Indígena, Huamuxtitlán 27996
Museo Sala, San Juan Bautista Tuxtepec 28390
Museo Tradicional Ik Al Ojov, Zinacantán 28657

Moldova
Muzeul National de Etnografie si Istorie Naturala, Chişinău 28659

Mongolia
Museum of Mongolian Ethnography, Ulaanbaatar 28681

Morocco
Musée Ethnographique, Tétouan 28717

Myanmar
University of Mandalay Collections, Mandalay 28735

Namibia
National Museum of Namibia, Windhoek 28781

Netherlands
Afrika Centrum, Cadier en Keer 29050
Afrika Museum, Berg en Dal 28978
Educatieve Boerderij en Zijdemuseum de Schans, Oud-Gastel 29691
Expositie Versteend Leven, Drouwen 29183
Gemeentegrot Valkenburg, Valkenburg 29916
KIT Tropenmuseum, Amsterdam 28866
Moluks Historisch Museum, Utrecht 29900
Museum Kennemerland, Beverwijk 28986
Museum Nusantara, Delft 29084
Museum Stapelen, Boxtel 29014
Museum Suriname, Amsterdam 28878
Natuurhistorisch en Volkenkundig Museum, Oudenbosch 29697
Nederlands Openluchtmuseum, Arnhem 28942
Nijmeegs Volkenkundig Museum, Nijmegen 29636
Rijksmuseum voor Volkenkunde, Leiden 29525
Wereldmuseum Rotterdam, Rotterdam 29779

New Zealand
Okains Bay Maori and Colonial Museum, Okains Bay 30219
Otago Museum, Dunedin 30151
Te Awamutu Museum, Te Awamutu 30260
Waikato Museum of Art and History, Hamilton 30174
Whanganui Regional Museum, Wanganui 30286

Niger
Musée National du Niger, Niamey 30324

Nigeria
Gidan Makama Museum, Kano 30349
Kanta Museum Argungu, Argungu 30331
Museum of the Institute of African Studies, Ibadan 30339
Museum of the Institute of African Studies, Oshogbo 30357
National Museum, Oshogbo 30358

Norway
Etnografisk Museum, Oslo 30731
Finnetunet, Grue Finnskog 30523
Kon-Tiki Museum, Oslo 30740
Østsamisk Museum, Neiden 30706
Varjjat Sámi Musea, Varangerbotn 30973

Panama
Museo Antropológico Reina T. de Araúz, Panamá City 31077

Papua New Guinea
J.K. MacCarthy Museum, Goroka 31091
Papua New Guinea National Museum and Art Gallery, Boroko 31090

Paraguay
Museo Etnográfico Andrés Barbero, Asunción 31102

Peru
Museo de Chusis de Sechura, Sechura 31249
Museo de la Cultura José Arens Berg, Sullana 31251
Museo del Centro de Investigación Arqueológica de Ancón, Lima 31216
Museo del Colegio Nacional Amauta, Chupaca 31146
Museo Etnográfico Santa Rosa de Ocopa, Concepción 31149
Museo Etnohistórico de Ayabacara, Ayabacara 31120
Museo Etnológico, Sechura 31250
Museo Nacional de la Cultura Peruana, Lima 31222
Museo Schaferrer, Oxapampa 31234
Museo y Biblioteca Leoncio Prado, Huánuco 31173

Philippines
Aga Khan Museum of Islamic Arts, Marawi 31399
Ayala Museum of Philippine History, Makati 31352
Baguio-Mountain Provinces Museum, Baguio 31282
Bahay Tsinoy Museum, Manila 31369
Barangay Museum, Mandaluyong 31363
Cotabato National Museum, Cotabato 31321
Cultural Center of the Philippines Museo, Pasay 31411
Divine Word University Museum, Tacloban 31452
Ethnological Museum, Zamboanga 31469
Museo Pambata, Manila 31386
Nayong Pilipino Museum, Pasay 31415
Notre Dame of Jolo College Museum, Jolo 31331
Palawan State University Museum, Puerto Princesa 31425
Pambansang Museo ng Pilipinas, Manila 31390
Panaddaman-Cagayan State University Museum, Tuguegarao 31461
Philippine Museum of Ethnology, Pasay 31418
Saint Louis University Museum of Arts and Culture, Baguio 31284
Saint Theresa's College Folklife Museum, Cebu 31314
Siliman University Anthropology Museum, Dumaguete 31326
Sulu National Museum, Jolo 31332
Tawi-Tawi Ethnological Museum, Bongao 31290
University Museum of Anthropology, Quezon City 31437
University of San Carlos Anthropology Museum, Cebu 31318
University of Santo Tomas Museum of Arts and Sciences, Manila 31398
Zamboanga National Museum, Zamboanga 31470

Poland
Górnośląski Park Etnograficzny, Chorzów 31533
Harcerskie Muzeum Etnograficzne przy Szkole Podstawowej nr 11 w Katowicach, Katowice 31644
Mission and Folklore Museum, Polanica Zdrój 31891
Muzeum, Koszalin 31678
Muzeum Etnograficzne, Toruń 32052
Muzeum Etnograficzne, Wrocław 32176
Muzeum Etnograficzne im. Franciszka Kotuli, Rzeszów 31959
Muzeum Etnograficzne im. Seweryna Udzieli, Kraków 31701
Muzeum Etnograficzne w Oliwie, Gdańsk 31570
Muzeum Etnograficzne w Zielonej Górze z Siedzibą w Ochli, Ochla 31842
Muzeum Etnograficzny, Tarnów 32042
Muzeum Historyczno-Etnograficzne, Chojnice 31528
Muzeum im. Jana Nikodema Jaronia, Olesno 31847
Muzeum-Kaszubski Park Etnograficzny w Wdzydzach Kiszewskich, Wdzydze Kiszewskie 32147
Muzeum Kaszubskie, Kartuzy 31643
Muzeum Kultury Ludowej, Kolbuszowa 31667
Muzeum Kultury Ludowej, Węgorzewo 32148
Muzeum Mazurskie, Szczytno 32032
Muzeum Misyjno-Etnograficzne, Pieniężno 31879
Muzeum Nadwiślański Park Etnograficzny, Babice 31474
Muzeum Pojezierza Łęczyńsko-Włodawskiego, Włodawa 32166
Muzeum Regionalne, Jarocin 31621
Muzeum Regionalne Dom Grecki, Myślenice 31816
Muzeum Regionalne im. Marcina Rożka, Wolsztyn 32171
Muzeum Regionalne PTTK im. Hieronima Ławinczaka, Krotoszyn 31738
Muzeum Rzemiosła Tkackiego, Turek 32060
Muzeum Tatrzańskie im. Tytusa Chałubińskiego, Zakopane 32209
Muzeum w Tomaszowie Mazowieckim, Tomaszów Mazowiecki 32048
Muzeum Wisły, Tczew 32046
Muzeum Wsi Kieleckiej, Kielce 31660
Muzeum Wsi Mazowieckiej, Sierpc 31975
Muzeum Zachodnio-Kaszubskie, Bytów 31520
Muzeum Ziemi Puckiej, Puck 31929
Orawski Park Etnograficzny, Zubrzyca Górna 32225
Ośrodek Budownictwa Ludowego w Szymbarku z filia w Bartnem, Sękowa 31968
Palucka Izba Muzealna, Kcynia 31652
Państwowe Muzeum Etnograficzne, Warszawa 32140
Prywatne Muzeum Etnograficzne, Góra Kalwaria 31604
Punkt Etnograficzny w Rogierówku, Rogierówko 31948
Sądecki Park Etnograficzny, Nowy Sącz 31836

Portugal
Museu Antropológico, Coimbra 32255
Museu de Azambuja, Azambuja 32240
Museu de Etnografia e História, Porto 32333
Museu de Olaria, Barcelos 32241
Museu Etnográfico da Sociedade de Geografia de Lisboa, Lisboa 32302
Museu Etnográfico e Arqueológico do Dr. Joaquim Manso, Nazaré 32321
Museu Municipal Quinta do Conventinho, Loures 32318
Museu Nacional de Etnologia, Lisboa 32308

Puerto Rico
Museo del Indio de Puerto Rico, San Juan 32399
Turabo University Museum, Gurabo 32374

Qatar
Ethnographical Museum, Doha 32416
Qatar National Museum, Doha 32417

Romania
Colecţia Etnografică, Poiana Sibiului 32575
Colecţia Etnografică, Răşinari 32579
Complexul Muzeal Măldăreşti, Măldăreşti 32546
Complexul Naţional Muzeal Astra, Sibiu 32591
Muzeal Conacul Bellu, Urlaţi 32622
Muzeul de Arheologie şi Etnografie, Corabia 32503
Muzeul de Artă Populară şi Etnografie, Tulcea 32618
Muzeul de Etnografie Braşov, Braşov 32448
Muzeul de Etnografie Piatra-Neamţ, Piatra-Neamţ 32566
Muzeul de Etnografie şi a Regimentului de Graniţă, Caransebeş 32488
Muzeul de Etnografie şi Artă Populară, Reghin 32580
Muzeul de Etnografie şi Artă Populară Orăştie, Orăştie 32563
Muzeul Etnografic, Vatra Dornei 32625
Muzeul Etnografic al Moldovei, Iaşi 32535
Muzeul Etnografic al Transilvaniei, Cluj-Napoca 32492
Muzeul Etnografic Lupşa, Lupşa 32545
Muzeul Etnografic Tehnici Populare Bucovinene, Rădăuţi 32576
Muzeul Judeţean de Etnografie, Slatina 32597
Muzeul Judeţean Mureş-Secţia de Etnografie şi Artă Populară, Târgu Mureş 32610
Muzeul Municipal Câmpulung-Secţia de Etnografie şi, Câmpulung 32483
Muzeul Orăşenecs de Istorie şi Etnografie, Beiuş 32438
Muzeul Tării Oaşului, Negreşti-Oaş 32556
Muzeul Taru Făgăraşului, Făgăraş 32518
Muzeul Vrancei, Focşani 32521
Punct Muzeal, Moroeni 32552

Russia
Adygejskij Respublikanskij Kraevedčeskij Muzej, Majkop 33003
Altajskij Respublikanskij Kraevedčeskij Muzej im. A.V. Anochina, Gorno-Altajsk 32808
Amurskij Gorodskoj Kraevedčeskij Muzej, Amursk 32637
Architekturno-ėtnografičeskij Muzej Angarskaja Derevnja, Bratsk 32702
Astrachanskij Gosudarstvennyj Obedinennyj Istoriko-architekturnyj Muzej-zapovednik, Astrachan 32659
Astrachanskij Kraevedčeskij Muzej, Astrachan 32660
Bratskij Gorodskoj Objedinennyj Muzej Istorii Osvoenija Angary, Bratsk 32704
Chakasskij Respublikanskij Kraevedčeskij Muzej, Abakan 32627
Čuvasškij Nacionalnyj Muzej, Čeboksary 32719
Dagestanskij Gosudarstvennyj Objedinennyj Istoriko-architekturnyj Muzej, Machačkala 32995
Dom Poėta A.N. Širjaevca - Muzej Krestjanskogo Byta, Žigulevsk 33748
Enisejskij Kraevedčeskij Muzej, Enisejsk 32796
Ėtnografičeskij Muzej Kazanskogo Universiteta, Kazan 32887
Ėtnografičeskij Muzej Narodov Zabajkalja, Ulan-Udė 33652
Ėtnografičeskij Muzej pod Otkrytym Nebom Torum Maa, Chanty-Mansijsk 32742
Ėvenkijskij Okružnoj Kraevedčeskij Muzej, Tura 33635
Gosudarstvennyj Istoriko-ėtnografičeskij Muzej-zapovednik Šušenskoe, Šušenskoe 33569
Gosudarstvennyj Nacionalnyj Muzej Ust-Ordynskogo Burjatskogo Avtonomnogo Okruga, Ust-Ordynsk 33672
Gosudarstvennyj Okružnoj Muzej Prirody i Čeloveka Goroda Chanty-Mansijsk, Chanty-Mansijsk 32744
Ibresinskij Ėtnografičeskij Muzej pod Otkryrym Nebom, Ibresi 32810
Ingušskij Gosudarstvennyj Muzej Kraevedenija im. T.Ch. Malsagova, Nazran 33203
Irkutskij Architekturno-ėtnografičeskij Muzej Talcy, Irkutsk 32812
Irkutskij Oblastnoj Kraevedčeskij Muzej, Irkutsk 32814
Istoriko-ėtnografičeskij Muzej Usadba Galskich, Čerepovec 32731
Jakutskij Gosudarstvennyj Muzej Istorii i Kultury Narodov Severa im. Jaroslavskogo, Jakutsk 32843
Jamalo-Neneckij Okružnoj Kraevedčeskij Muzej im. I.S. Šemanovskogo, Salechard 33364
Kalmyckij Respublikanskij Kraevedčeskij Muzej im. Prof. N.N. Palmova, Ėlista 32794
Kamčatskij Oblastnoj Kraevedčeskij Muzej, Petropavlovsk-Kamčatskij 33310
Kislovodskij Istoriko-kraevedčeskij Muzej Krepost', Kislovodsk 32928
Komi Respublikanskij Istoriko-Kraevedčeskij Muzej, Syktyvkar 33573
Krasnodarskij Gosudarstvennyj Istoriko-archeologičeskij Muzej-zapovednik, Krasnodar 32947
Literaturno-memorialnyj Dom-muzej Sulejmana Stalskogo, Ašaga-Stalsk 32657
Muzej Antropologii i Ėtnografii im. Petra Velikogo (Kunstkamera), Sankt-Peterburg 33427
Muzej Archeologii i Ėtnografii, Vladivostok 33703
Muzej Archeologii i Ėtnografii, Ufa 33645
Muzej Archeologii i Ėtnografii, Syktyvkar 33576
Muzej 'Archeologija, Ėtnografija i Ėkologija Sibiri' Kemerovskogo Gosudarstvennogo Universiteta, Kemerovo 32914
Muzej Ėtnografii, Istorii i Kultury Narodov Baškortostana, Ufa 33646
Muzej Istorii Aksaja, Aksaj 32631
Muzej Istorii Burjatii im. M.N. Changalova, Ulan-Udė 33653
Muzej Istorii i Kultury Srednego Prikamja, Sarapul 33503
Muzej Istorii Kolskich Saamov, Lovozero 32993
Nacionalnyj Muzej Respubliki Baškortostan, Ufa 33647
Nacionalnyj Muzej Respubliki Komi, Syktyvkar 33579
Nacionalnyj Muzej Respubliki Marij Ėl im. T. Evseeva, Joškar-Ola 32861
Nacionalnyj Muzej Udmurtskoj Respubliki im. K. Gerda, Iževsk 32836
Naučno-issledovatelskij Institut i Muzej Antropologii im. D.N. Anučina, Moskva 33162
Neneckij Okružnoj Kraevedčeskij Muzej, Narjan-Mar 33198
Nižnetagilskij Muzej-Zapovednik Gornozavodskogo Dela Srednego Urala, Nižnij Tagil 33228
Novokuzneckij Kraevedčeskij Muzej, Novokuzneck 33237
Oloneckij Nacionalnyj Muzej Karelov-Livvikov im. N.T.Prilukin, Olonec 33252
Omskij Gosudarstvennyj Istoriko-kraevedčeskij Muzej, Omsk 33255
Primorskij Gosudarstvennyj Muzej im. V.K. Arseneva, Vladivostok 33709
Pskovskij Gosudarstvennyj Istoričesko-architekturnyj i Chudožestvennyj Muzej-zapovednik, Pskov 33332
Roslavlskij Istoriko-chudožstvennyj Muzej, Roslavl 33353
Rossijskij Ėtnografičeskij muzej, Sankt-Peterburg 33478
Saratovskij Ėtnografičeskij Muzej, Saratov 33509
Šeltozerskij Vepsskij Ėtnografičeskij Muzej, Šeltozero 33515
Severo-osetinskij Gosudarstvennyj Obedinennyj Muzej Istorii, Architektury i Literatury, Vladikavkaz 33690
Taganrogskij Kraevedčeskij Muzej, Taganrog 33587
Tajmyrskij Okružnoj Kraevedčeskij Muzej, Dudinka 32762
Tarskij Istoriko-kraevedčeskij Muzej, Tara 33592
Tjumenskij Oblastnoj Kraevedčeskij Muzej im. I.Ja. Slovcova, Tjumen 33610
Tuapsinskij Kraevedčeskij Muzej im. N.G. Poletaeva, Tuapse 33622
Tuvinskij Respublikanskij Kraevedčeskij Muzej im. Aldan Maadyr, Kyzyl 32979
Vserossijskij Istoriko-ėtnografičeskij Muzej, Toržok 33620

Rwanda
Musée de Kabgayi, Kabgayi 33753
Musée National du Rwanda, Butare 33752

Serbia-Montenegro
Etnografski Muzej Crne Gore, Cetinje 33831
Etnografski Muzej Srbije, Beograd 33794
Etnološka Muzejska Zbirka, Jasenovo 33844
Kompleksi Monumental i Lidhjes Shqiptare të Prizrenit, Prizren 33897
Muzej Afričke Umetnosti-Zbirka Vede i Dr. Zdravka Pečara, Beograd 33803

Muzej Ponišavlja Pirot, Pirot 33884
Muzeji i Galerije Podgorica, Podgorica 33889
Muzejska Zbirka pri Narodnoj Biblioteki Dimitrije Tucović, Čajetina 33829
Narodni Muzej, Bački Petrovac 33788
Narodni Muzej, Kragujevac 33853
Narodni Muzej Kraljevo, Kraljevo 33855
Narodni Muzej Kruševac, Kruševac 33857
Narodni Muzej Toplice, Prokuplje 33899
Narodni Muzej Valjevo, Valjevo 33926
Vojvodjanski Muzej, Novi Sad 33875
Zavičajni Muzej Aleksinac, Aleksinac 33786

Singapore
Asian Civilisations Museum, Singapore 33936

Slovakia
Etnografické Múzeum, Martin 34022
Horehronské Múzeum, Brezno 33982
Múzeum, Bardejovské Kúpele 33953
Múzeum Kultúry Karpatských Nemcov, Bratislava 33971
Múzeum Kultúry Maďarov na Slovensku, Bratislava 33972
Okresné Vlastivedné Múzeum, Humenné 33999
Vajinorský L'udový Dom - Etnografická Expozícia, Bratislava 33980
Vlastivedné Múzeum, Prešov 34049
Západoslovenské Múzeum v Trnave, Trnava 34075

Slovenia
Belokranjski Muzej, Metlika 34130
Kurnikova Hiša, Tržič 34158
Loški Muzej, Škofja Loka 34148
Mestni Muzej Idrija, Idrija 34091
Pokrajinski Muzej, Kočevje 34095
Pokrajinski Muzej, Maribor 34127
Pokrajinski Muzej, Murska Sobota 34134
Posavski Muzej Brežice, Brežice 34088
Slovenski Etnografski Muzej, Ljubljana 34119
Tolminski Muzej, Tolmin 34155
Tržiški Muzej, Tržič 34160

Somalia
Somali National Museum, Mogadishu 34168

South Africa
Africana Museum, Mariannhill 34305
Anthropology Museum and Resource Centre, Johannesburg 34269
Barberton Museum, Barberton 34174
Duggan-Cronin Gallery, Kimberley 34287
Museum of Anthropology and Archaeology, Pretoria 34348
National Cultural History Museum, Pretoria 34350
University Museum - Sasol Art Museum, Stellenbosch 34385

Spain
Ecomuseu de les Valls d'Aneu, Esterri d'Aneu 34810
Euskal Arkeologia, Etnografia eta Kondaira Museoa, Bilbao 34611
Museo Africano Mundo Negro, Madrid 35012
Museo Angel Orensanz y Artes de Serralbo, Sabiñánigo 35350
Museo Canario, Las Palmas de Gran Canaria 35239
Museo de América, Madrid 35016
Museo de Antropología de Tenerife - Casa de Carta, La Laguna 34936
Museo de Artes y Costumbres Populares, Combarro 34731
Museo de Artes y Costumbres Populares, Jaén 34923
Museo de Artes y Costumbres Populares, Ribadavia 35318
Museo de Artes y Costumbres Populares, Piedrafita de El Cebrero 35270
Museo de Avila, Avila 34502
Museo de Bellas Artes, Mahón 35066
Museo de Cáceres, Cáceres 34641
Museo de Guadalajara, Guadalajara 34885
Museo de Zaragoza, Zaragoza 35723
Museo del Blat y de la Pagesia, Cervera 34707
Museo del Carro y la Labranza, Tomelloso 35550
Museo do Pobo Galego, Santiago de Compostela 35448
Museo Etnográfico, Arteta 34492
Museo Etnográfico de Azuaga de la Sierra y la Campiña, Azuaga 34515
Museo Etnográfico de Cantabria, Muriedas 35151
Museo Etnográfico de los Valles de Campoo, Canduela 34669
Museo Etnográfico de Oyón-Oion, Oyón 35207
Museo Etnográfico del Pueblo de Asturias, Gijón 34846
Museo Etnográfico Textil Pérez Enciso, Plasencia 35273
Museo Etnológico de la Diputación, Castellón de la Plana 34694
Museo Etnológico de Morella y del Meastrazgo, Morella 35141
Museo Municipal de San Telmo, Donostia-San Sebastián 34778
Museo Municipal Etnológico de la Huerta, Alcantarilla 34429
Museo Nacional de Antropología, Madrid 35042
Museo Parroquial de Arte Sacro y Etnología, Anso 34467
Museo Provincial, Teruel 35530
Museo Taurino, Salamanca 35365
Museu de la Fusta, Areu 34482
Museu de la Pedra i de l'Estable, Guimerà 34893
Museu de l'Acordió, Arsèguel 34488
Museu de Prehistòria i de les Cultures de València, Valencia 35613
Museu de Vilafranca-Museu del Vi, Vilafranca del Penedès 35659
Museu del Pagès, Castelldans 34691
Museu d'Etnografia d'Eivissa, Santa Eulària des Riu 35418
Museu Diocesà i Comarcal, Solsona 35503
Museu Etnogràfic de Ripoll, Ripoll 35325
Museu Etnològic de Barcelona, Barcelona 34577
Museu Etnologic de Guadalest, Guadalest 34886
Museu Etnològic del Montseny La Gabella, Arbúcies 34475
Museu Etnològic i Arqueològic, Juneda 34933
Museu Marès de la Punta, Arenys de Mar 34480
Museu Parroquial, Vinaixa 35690

Sri Lanka
Colombo National Museum, Colombo 35747
Museum of Ethnology and Folk Art, Ratnapura 35758
Ratnapura National Museum, Ratnapura 35760

Sudan
Ethnographical Museum, Khartoum 35766
Halfa Museum, Wadi Halfa 35775

Swaziland
Swaziland National Museum, Lobamba 35780

Sweden
Ájtte - Svenskt Fjäll- och Samemuseum, Jokkmokk 35982
Arboga Museum, Arboga 35806
Disagården, Uppsala 36352
Etnografiska Museet, Stockholm 36240
Fotevikens Museum, Höllviken 35958
Grekiskt Kulturcentrum, Stockholm 36243
Hantverks- och Sjörfartsmuseét på Norra Berget, Sundsvall 36308
Jamtli Historieland, Östersund 36147
Jukkasjärvi Museet, Jukkasjärvi 35984
Statens Världskulturmuseet, Göteborg 35922
Trelleborgs Museum, Trelleborg 36333

Switzerland
Afrika-Museum, Zug 37424
Ethnographische Sammlung, Fribourg 36712
Kulturama, Zürich 37384
Musée Cantonal d'Histoire, Sion 37173
Musée d'Ethnographie, Conches 36646
Musée d'Ethnographie, Genève 36745
Musée d'Ethnographie, Neuchâtel 36985
Museum der Kulturen Basel, Basel 36508
Museum für Völkerkunde, Burgdorf 36607
Tibet Songtsen House, Zürich 37413
Völkerkundemuseum der Universität Zürich, Zürich 37416
Völkerkundemuseum Sankt Gallen, Sankt Gallen 37109
Völkerkundliche Sammlung, Winterthur 37344

Togo
Musée d'Histoire et d'Ethnographie, Aneho 37546
Musée National du Togo, Lomé 37549

Tunisia
Musée de Mahdia, Mahdia 37569
Musée des Arts et Traditions Populaires, Djerba 37558
Musée des Arts et Traditions Populaires Dar Ben Abdallah, Tunis 37593
Musée des Jallouli, Sfax 37581
Musée du Village, Moknine 37574
Musée Régional des Arts et Traditions Populaires, Kef 37566

Turkey
Etnografya Müzesi, Ankara 37617
İzmir Arkeoloji Müzesi, İzmir 37718
Koyunoglu Müzesi, Konya 37743
Tarsus Müzesi, Tarsus 37791

Turkmenistan
Historical and Ethnographical Museum, Turkmenabat 37820
Muzej Kizyl-Arvata, Kizyl-Arvat 37816
National Museum of Turkmenistan, Ašgabat 37812

Uganda
Folk Museum, Mbarara 37831
Folk Museum, Soroti 37833

Ukraine
Etnografičeskij Muzej Tavrika, Simferopol 37903
State Historical Museum, Kamenec-Podolskij 37857
State Museum of Ethnography, Arts and Crafts, Lviv 37888

United Kingdom
Brunei Gallery, London 39590
Dunrobin Castle Museum, Golspie 39091
The Eastern Museum, Derby 38717
Gurkha Museum, Winchester 40888
Hancock Museum, Newcastle-upon-Tyne 40036
Hastings Museum and Art Gallery, Hastings 39184
Horniman Museum, London 39668
Liverpool Museum, Liverpool 39520
Marischal Museum, Aberdeen 37940
Pitt Rivers Museum, Oxford 40153
Powell-Cotton Museum, Quex House and Gardens, Birchington 38203
Rhodes Memorial Museum and Commonwealth Centre, Bishop's Stortford 38240
Royal Albert Memorial Museum and Art Gallery, Exeter 38957
Royal Engineers Museum, Gillingham, Kent 39033
Russell-Cotes Art Gallery and Museum, Bournemouth 38286
Saffron Walden Museum, Saffron Walden 40368
Sainsbury Centre for Visual Arts, Norwich 40100
University Museum of Archaeology and Anthropology, Cambridge 38463

Uruguay
Museo del Gaucho y de la Moneda, Montevideo 41001

U.S.A.
Abbe Museum at Downtown, Bar Harbor 41496
Abbe Museum at Sieur de Monts Spring, Bar Harbor 41497
Adan E. Treganza Anthropology Museum, San Francisco 47302
African-American Historical and Cultural Society Collection, San Francisco 47303
African Art Museum of the S.M.A. Fathers, Tenafly 47979
Afro-American Cultural Center, Charlotte 42236
Alabama-Coushatta Indian Museum, Livingston 44834
Alabama Museum of Natural History, Tuscaloosa 48112
Alaska Indian Arts, Haines 43869
Alutiiq Museum and Archaeological Repository, Kodiak 44524
American Museum of Asmat Art, Saint Paul 47152
American Swedish Institute, Minneapolis 45380
The Amerind Foundation, Dragoon 42986
Anasazi Heritage Center, Dolores 42957
Andrew J. Blackbird Museum, Harbor Springs 43909
Anthropology Museum, DeKalb 42854
Appalachian Center for Crafts, Smithville 47658
The Appaloosa Museum and Heritage Center, Moscow 45517
Arizona State Museum, Tucson 48082
Armenian Museum of America, Watertown 48440
The Balch Institute for Ethnic Studies, Philadelphia 46394
Baltimore's Black American Museum, Baltimore 41458
Balzekas Museum of Lithuanian Culture, Chicago 42307
Bernice Pauahi Bishop Museum, Honolulu 44072
Buechel Memorial Lakota Museum, Saint Francis 47088
Burke Museum of Natural History and Culture, Seattle 47529
Cahokia Mounds State Historic Site, Collinsville 42530
California African-American Museum, Los Angeles 44893
California State Indian Museum, Sacramento 47048
Capitol Reef National Park Visitor Center, Torrey 48039
Carnegie Museum of Natural History, Pittsburgh 46511
Carrie M. McLain Memorial Museum, Nome 45961
Carter County Museum, Ekalaka 43103
Castine Scientific Society Museum, Castine 42136
C.E. Smith Museum of Anthropology, Hayward 43973
Center for Intuitive and Outsider Art, Chicago 42311
C.H. Nash Museum-Chucalissa Archaeological Museum, Memphis 45232
Cherokee Heritage Centre, Tahlequah 47925
College of Eastern Utah Prehistoric Museum, Price 46693
Colorado River Indian Tribes Museum, Parker 46294
Croatian Heritage Museum, Eastlake 43065
Cultural Heritage Center Museum, Toppenish 48035
Cultural Rights and Protection/Ute Indian Tribe, Fort Duchesne 43391
CWU Anthropology Department Collection, Ellensburg 43149
Danish Immigrant Museum, Elk Horn 43137
DePauw University Anthropology Museum, Greencastle 43798
Douglas County Museum of History and Natural History, Roseburg 47003
Durham Center Museum, East Durham 43038
Eastern Arizona Museum, Pima 46488
Eastern California Museum, Independence 44197
Edge of the Cedars State Park, Blanding 41733
Eiteljorg Museum of American Indians and Western Art, Indianapolis 44217
Elgin Public Museum, Elgin 43129
Esther Prangley Rice Gallery, Westminster 48562
Etowah Indian Mounds Historical Site, Cartersville 42122
Evelyn Payne Hatcher Museum of Anthropology, Saint Cloud 47084
Exhibition of the Norwegian-American Historical Association, Northfield 46020
Favell Museum of Western Art and Indian Artifacts, Klamath Falls 44508
Five Civilized Tribes Museum, Muskogee 45581
Florence Hawley Ellis Museum of Anthropology, Abiquiu 41057
Fort Ancient Museum, Oregonia 46180
Fort Fetterman State Museum, Douglas 42964
Fort Recovery Museum, Fort Recovery 43447
Frisco Native American Museum and Natural History Center, Frisco 43565
Grace Hudson Museum and The Sun House, Ukiah 48134
Grand Village of the Natchez Indians, Natchez 45632
Haffenreffer Museum of Anthropology, Bristol 41906
Hartzler-Towner Multicultural Museum, Nashville 45621
Hawaii's Plantation Village, Waipahu 48276
Heard Museum, Phoenix 46476
The Heritage Center, Pine Ridge 46492
Heritage Library and Museum, Anchorage 41199
Herrett Center for Arts and Science, Twin Falls 48124
Heym-Oliver House, Russell 47035
High Desert Museum, Bend 41623
Hopewell Culture National Historic Park, Chillicothe 42379
Horry County Museum, Conway 42613
Hudson Museum, Orono 46195
Imperato Collection of West African Artifacts, Chanute 42192
Indian Center Museum, Wichita 48603
Indian City U.S.A., Anadarko 41191
Indian Museum of Lake County-Ohio, Painesville 46262
Indian Museum of North America, Crazy Horse 42694
Indian Museum of the Carolinas, Laurinburg 44682
Indian Temple Mound Museum, Fort Walton Beach 43467
The Institute For American Indian Studies, Washington Green 48424
Institute of American Indian Arts Museum, Santa Fe 47421
Institute of Texan Cultures, San Antonio 47253
International Museum of Cultures, Dallas 42754
Iroquois Indian Museum, Howes Cave 44140
Jacques Marchais Museum of Tibetan Art, Staten Island 47783
Jean Lafitte National Historical Park and Preserve, New Orleans 45728
Jensen Arctic Museum, Monmouth 45437
Jesse Peter Museum, Santa Rosa 47445
Journey Museum, Rapid City 46795
Ka-Do-Ha Indian Village Museum, Murfreesboro 45565
Kaw Mission, Council Grove 42674
The Kendall College Mitchell Museum of the American Indian, Evanston 43239
Koshare Indian Museum, La Junta 44552
The Kurdish Museum, Brooklyn 41944
Latvian Museum, Rockville 46976
Lesbian Herstory Educational Foundation, Brooklyn 41946
Logan Museum of Anthropology, Beloit 41615
Lompoc Museum, Lompoc 44850
Lucy Craft Laney Museum of Black History, Augusta 41384
MacCallum More Museum, Chase City 42255
Malki Museum, Banning 41495
Maxwell Museum of Anthropology, Albuquerque 41104
Merritt Museum of Anthropology, Oakland 46064
Miami County Museum, Peru 46364
Michel Brouillet House and Museum, Vincennes 48240
Middle Border Museum of American Indian and Pioneer Life, Mitchell 45414
Millicent Rogers Museum of Northern New Mexico, Taos 47951
Milwaukee Public Museum, Milwaukee 45368
The Morikami Museum and Japanese Gardens, Delray Beach 42864
Moundbuilders State Memorial and Museum, Newark 45895
Museum for African Art, Long Island City 44868
Museum of Afro-American History, Boston 41816
Museum of Anthropology, Chico 42373
Museum of Anthropology, Denver 42894
Museum of Anthropology, Fullerton 43575
Museum of Anthropology, Lawrence 44684
Museum of Anthropology, Pullman 46744
Museum of Anthropology, Tempe 47973
Museum of Anthropology, Winston-Salem 48700
Museum of Anthropology, Highland Heights 44018
Museum of Anthropology, Ann Arbor 41219
Museum of Anthropology, Columbia 42552
Museum of Indian Arts and Culture, Santa Fe 47425
Museum of Indian Culture, Allentown 41147
Museum of Peoples and Cultures, Provo 46736
Museum of Primitive Art and Culture, Peace Dale 46321
Museum of Russian Culture, San Francisco 47330
Museum of the Cherokee Indian, Cherokee 42276
Museum of the Red River, Idabel 44190
Nance Museum, Lone Jack 44856
National Hall of Fame for Famous American Indians, Anadarko 41192
Native American Museum, Terre Haute 47984
Native American Resource Center, Pembroke 46334
New Mexico State University Museum, Las Cruces 44661
Nez Perce National Historical Park, Spalding 47713
Norwegian-American Historical Museum, Northfield 46022
Old World Wisconsin, Eagle 43031
Oneida Nation Museum, De Pere 42816
Pawnee Indian Village, Republic 46843
Peabody Museum of Archaeology and Ethnology, Cambridge 42049

The Peary-MacMillan Arctic Museum, Brunswick 41972
Pella Historical Village, Pella 46329
Pennsylvania German Cultural Heritage Center, Kutztown 44530
Phoebe Apperson Hearst Museum of Anthropology, Berkeley 41648
Pipestone National Monument, Pipestone 46499
Plains Indians and Pioneers Museum, Woodward 48748
Polynesian Cultural Center, Laie 44577
Red Rock Museum, Church Rock 42394
Reuel B. Pritchett Museum, Bridgewater 41895
Riley House Museum of African American History and Culture, Tallahassee 47937
Robert Hull Fleming Museum, Burlington 42009
Romanian Ethnic Art Museum, Cleveland 42480
Saint Joseph Museum, Saint Joseph 47109
Samuel K. Fox Museum, Dillingham 42948
San Diego Museum of Man, San Diego 47294
Schingoethe Center for Native American Cultures, Aurora 41398
Schomburg Center for Research in Black Culture, New York 45868
Seminole Nation Museum, Wewoka 48557
Serpent Mound Museum, Peebles 46326
Sheldon Jackson Museum, Sitka 47650
Simon Paneak Memorial Museum, Anaktuvuk Pass 41195
Smoki Museum, Prescott 46690
Southern Plains Indian Museum, Anadarko 41193
Southern Ute Indian Cultural Center, Ignacio 44194
Southwest Museum, Los Angeles 44945
Stewart Indian Cultural Center, Carson City 42120
Suquamish Museum, Poulsbo 46678
Suquamish Museum, Suquamish 47892
Texas Memorial Museum of Science and History, Austin 41421
Teysen's Woodland Indian Museum, Mackinaw City 45035
The Roy Rogers-Dale Evans Museum, Branson 41871
Town Creek Indian Mound Historic Site, Mount Gilead 45530
The University Museum, Fayetteville 43308
University of Northern Iowa Museum Museums Collections, Cedar Falls 42151
University of Pennsylvania Museum of Archaeology and Anthropology, Philadelphia 46460
University of Wyoming Anthropology Museum, Laramie 44649
Ute Indian Museum, Montrose 45483
Vesterheim Norwegian-American Museum, Decorah 42839
Vincent Price Gallery, Monterey Park 45462
Western Archeological and Conservation Center, Tucson 48097
Western New Mexico University Museum, Silver City 47630
Wheelwright Museum of the American Indian, Santa Fe 47434
William Hammond Mathers Museum, Bloomington 41749
Wing Luke Asian Museum, Seattle 47548
Winnebago Area Museum, Winnebago 48692
The Yosemite Museum, Yosemite National Park 48804

Uzbekistan
Museum of the History of Termurids, Taškent 48857

Vanuatu
Vanuatu Cultural Centre and National Museum, Port Vila 48866

Vatican City
Museo Missionario Etnologico, Città del Vaticano 48877

Venezuela
Museo de Antropología e Historia, Maracay 48953
Museo Etnológico de Amazonas, Puerto Ayacucho 48963
Museo J.M. Cruxent, Los Teques 48949
Museo Nueva Cádiz, La Asunción 48947

Vietnam
Bao Tàng Dân Tôc Hoc Viêt Nam, Ha Noi 48972
Bao Tàng Văn Hóa Các Dân Tôc Viêt Nam, Thai Nguyen 49000
Nan Bo's Southern Women Museum, Ho Chi Minh City 48988
Viet Nam Women's Museum, Ha Noi 48983

Yemen
Ethnographical Museum, Aden 49005

Zambia
Choma Museum and Crafts Centré, Choma 49015
Copperbelt Museum, Ndola 49024
Moto Moto Museum, Mbala 49023

Zimbabwe
Museum of Human Sciences, Harare 49031

Expeditions → Scientific Expeditions

Explosives

Brazil
Museu Sitio Arqueológico Casa dos Pilões, Rio de Janeiro 04394

Poland
Muzeum Filumenistyczne, Bystrzyca Kłodzka 31518

United Kingdom
Royal Gunpowder Mills, Waltham Abbey 40778

Eyeglasses → Optics

Faience → Porcelain and Ceramics

Fashion → Clothing and Dress

Festivals

Brazil
Museu do Carnaval, Rio de Janeiro 04367

Cuba
Museo del Carnaval, Santiago de Cuba 08142

Germany
Georg Papendicks Faschings- und Karnevalsordenmuseum, Bad Reichenhall 15716

Fire Fighting and Rescue Work

Australia
Fire Museum, Kurwongbah 01156
Fire Services Museum of Victoria, East Melbourne 00998

Austria
Burgenländisches Feuerwehrmuseum, Eisenstadt 01805
Erlauftaler Feuerwehrmuseum, Purgstall an der Erlauf 02463
Erstes Österreichisches Rettungsmuseum, Hohenems 02040
Erstes Tiroler Feuerwehrmuseum, Schwaz 02646
Feuerwehrmuseum, Perchtoldsdorf 02397
Feuerwehrmuseum, Sankt Florian 02559
Feuerwehrmuseum, Steyrermühl 02694
Feuerwehrmuseum, Türnitz 02741
Feuerwehrmuseum, Wienerbruck 03022
Feuerwehrsmuseum, Tumeltsham 02749
Museum der Freiwilligen Feuerwehr, Laxenburg 02198
Naturkunde- und Feuerwehrmuseum, Dobersberg 01765
Niederösterreichisches Feuerwehrmuseum, Tulln 02745
Steirisches Feuerwehrmuseum, Groß Sankt Florian 01947
Wiener Feuerwehrmuseum, Wien 03003

Belarus
Fire Museum, Minsk 03114

Brazil
Museu Histórico do Corpo de Bombeiros Militar do Estado do Rio de Janeiro, Rio de Janeiro 04382

Canada
Dory Shop Museum, Shelburne 06434
Fire Fighting Museum, Toronto 06577
Firefighters' Museum of Nova Scotia and National Exhibition Centre, Yarmouth 06868
Firefighting Museum, Chatham, Ontario 05239
Kingston Fire Department Museum, Kingston 05680
Niagara Fire Museum, Niagara-on-the-Lake 06002
Prince Rupert Fire Museum, Prince Rupert 06190
Regina Firefighters Museum, Regina 06239

Cuba
Museo de los Bomberos, Matanzas 08038
Sala de los Bomberos, La Habana 08002

Denmark
Blåvand Redningsbådsmuseum, Blåvand 08785
Dansk Brandvæernshistorisk Museum, Næstved 08986

Ecuador
Museo Coronel Félix Luque Plata, Guayaquil 09170
Museo de los Bomberos, Guayaquil 09171

Finland
Palomuseo, Helsinki 09518
Palomuseo, Lahti 09745

France
Musée de la Mine et de Meunerie-Moulin de Marcy, Le Molay-Littry 12449
Musée Départemantal de des Sapeurs-Pompiers de l'Orne, Bagnoles-de-l'Orne 10563
Musée Départemental des Sapeurs-Pompiers du Val-d'Oise, Osny 13443
Musée des Pompiers, Wasquehal 15304
Musée des Pompiers, Fontainebleau 11767
Musée des Sapeurs-Pompiers de France, Montville 13155
Musée des Sapeurs-Pompiers du Grand Lyon, Lyon 12739
Musée du Sapeur-Pompier, Bouzigues 10883
Musée du Sapeur-Pompier, Mulhouse 13211
Musée du Sapeur Pompier, Saint-Hippolyte-du-Fort 14266
Musée du Sapeurs-Pompiers, Ille-sur-Têt 12055

Germany
Deutsche Arbeitsschutzausstellung, Dortmund 16657
Deutsches Feuerwehr-Museum, Fulda 17172
Feuerwehr-Museum Schloß Waldmannshofen, Creglingen 16508
Feuerwehrmuseum, Dietzenbach 16605
Feuerwehrmuseum, Kaufbeuren 18037
Feuerwehrmuseum, Lengenfeld, Vogtland 18434
Feuerwehrmuseum, Niederwiesa 19101
Feuerwehrmuseum, Rehau 19536
Feuerwehrmuseum, Roding 19625
Feuerwehrmuseum, Salem, Baden 19732
Feuerwehrmuseum, Spalt 20006
Feuerwehrmuseum, Stadtprozelten 20034
Feuerwehrmuseum, Wasserburg am Inn 20407
Feuerwehrmuseum des Landkreises Harburg, Marxen 18659
Feuerwehrmuseum Grethen, Parthenstein 19352
Feuerwehrmuseum Hannover, Hannover 17593
Feuerwehrmuseum Kalmbach, Riedbach 19594
Feuerwehrmuseum Musberg, Leinfelden-Echterdingen 18376
Feuerwehrmuseum Ravensburg, Ravensburg 19506
Feuerwehrmuseum Salzbergen, Salzbergen 19734
Feuerwehrmuseum Schröttinghausen, Preußisch Oldendorf 19446
Feuerwehrmuseum Winnenden, Winnenden 20610
Feuerwehrmuseum Zeven, Zeven 20752
Haller Feuerwehrmuseum, Schwäbisch Hall 19865
Heimat- und Feuerwehrmuseum, Schauenstein 19766
Historische Lehrsammlung der Feuerwehr Köln, Köln 18142
Historisches Feuerwehrmuseum Lüchow-Dannenberg, Dannenberg, Elbe 16535
Münchner Feuerwehrmuseum, München 18878
Niederbayerisches Feuerwehrmuseum, Eggenfelden 16787
Stadtmuseum Dresden, Dresden 16712
Städtisches Feuerwehr-Museum, Eisenhüttenstadt 16825
Stuttgarter Feuerwehrmuseum, Stuttgart 20109

Hungary
Tüzoltó Múzeum, Budapest 21387

Netherlands
Brandweermuseum, Wouwse Plantage 30028
Brandweermuseum en Stormrampmuseum, Borculo 28998
Brandweermuseum Wassenaar, Wassenaar 29982
Nationaal Brandweermuseum, Hellevoetsluis 29391
Nationaal Reddingsmuseum Dorus Rijkers, Den Helder 29136
Reddingshuisje, Vliehors-Vlieland 29953
Reddingsmuseum Abraham Fock, Hollum 29432

New Zealand
Fire Brigadesmens Museum, Wellington 30294
Southland Fire Service Museum, Invercargill 30185

Norway
Ringsaker Vekter- og Brannhistoriske Museum, Moelv 30678
Stavanger Brannmuseum, Stavanger 30888

Poland
Muzeum Pożarnictwa, Alwernia 31471

Romania
Muzeul Naţional al Pompierilor, Bucureşti 32463

Russia
Postojannaja Požarno-techničeskaja Vystavka, Sankt-Peterburg 33477

Slovenia
Slovenski Gasilski Muzej, Metlika 34131

Spain
Museo de Bomberos, Madrid 35018

Switzerland
Feuerwehrmuseum, Adligenswil 36433
Feuerwehrmuseum, Kreuzlingen 36834
Feuerwehrmuseum Kradolf-Schönenberg, Kradolf 36832
Schweizerisches Feuerwehrmuseum, Basel 36520

Turkey
İtfaiye Müzesi, Fatih 37678

United Kingdom
Balfour Museum of Hampshire Red Cross History, Winchester 40886
Braidwood and Rushbrook Museum, Edinburgh 38870
Chartered Insurance Institute's Museum, London 39603
Fire Police Museum, Sheffield 40483
Fire Service Museum, Hethersett 39235
Henry Blogg Lifeboat Museum, Cromer 38673
Lifeboat House, Margate 39910
London Fire Brigade Museum, London 39695
Lytham Lifeboat Museum, Lytham Saint Anne's 39860
Museum of Fire, Edinburgh 38893
Museum of the Royal National Lifeboat Institution, Eastbourne 38854
Royal National Lifeboat Institution Headquarters Museum, Poole 40228
Selsey Lifeboat Museum, Selsey 40472
Uppark Exhibition, Petersfield 40195
Wiltshire Fire Defence Collection, Potterne 40261

U.S.A.
Alma Firehouse and Mining Museum, Alma 41151
American Heritage "Big Red" Fire Museum, Louisville 44979
American Museum of Fire Fighting, Hudson 44142
Atlantic 1 Museum, Swampscott 47898
Bare Cove Fire Museum, Hingham 44436
Boston Fire Museum, Boston 41799
Cincinnati Fire Museum, Cincinnati 42401
Columbia Fire Department Museum, Columbia 42557
Conway Fire Museum Aka Vintage Fire Engines, New Albany 45658
County of Los Angeles Fire Museum, Los Angeles 44897
Eureka Fire Museum, Milltown 45349
Fire Museum of Maryland, Lutherville 45001
Fire Museum of Memphis, Memphis 45236
Fire Museum of Texas, Beaumont 41568
Fire Museum of York County, York 48794
Firehouse Museum, Ellicott City 43157
Firehouse Museum, Nevada City 45653
Fireman's Hall Museum, Philadelphia 46409
Fort Wayne Firefighters Museum, Fort Wayne 43475
Friendship Firehouse, Alexandria 41126
Hall of Flame - Museum of Firefighting, Phoenix 46475
Hinckley Fire Museum, Hinckley 44035
Houston Fire Museum, Houston 44123
Hull Lifesaving Museum, Hull 44149
Jacksonville Fire Museum, Jacksonville 44295
John J. Harvey Fireboat Collection, New York 45822
Maple Valley Historical Museum, Maple Valley 45130
Nevada State Fire Museum and Comstock Firemen's Museum, Virginia City 48252
New Bern Firemen's Museum, New Bern 45666
New England Fire and History Museum, Brewster 41883
New Orleans Fire Department Museum, New Orleans 45734
New York City Fire Museum, New York 45856
North Plainfield Exempt Firemen's Museum, North Plainfield 46002
Oklahoma Firefighters Museum, Oklahoma City 46119
Old Fire House and Police Museum, Superior 47891
Old Firehouse Museum, Greenville 43824
Plantation Historical Museum, Plantation 46543
Robert A. Bogan Fire Museum, Baton Rouge 41533
San Francisco Fire Department Museum, San Francisco 47336
Uppertown Firefighters Museum, Astoria 41312
Volunteer Firemen's Mall and Museum of Kingston, Kingston 44496
Woodbine International Fire Museum, Woodbine 48726

Firearms → Arms and Armour

Fishing and Fisheries

Australia
Eden Killer Whale Museum, Eden 01006
Fisherman's Cottage, Tooradin 01538
Old Wool and Grain Store Museum, Beachport 00779
Whaleworld Museum, Albany 00726

Austria
Kunstsammlungen des Stiftes Kremsmünster, Kremsmünster 02161
Österreichisches Donau- und Fischereimuseum, Orth an der Donau 02387

Belgium
Heemkundig Museum Sincfala, Knokke 03535
Nationaal Visserijmuseum van Oostduinkerke, Oostduinkerke 03666

Brazil
Museu de Pesca, Santos 04454

Brunei
Muzium Teknologi Melayu, Bandar Seri Begawan 04599

Canada
Basin Head Fisheries Museum, Souris 06472

Durrell Museum, Durrell 05358
Ellerslie Shellfish Museum, Tyne Valley 06654
Fisheries Museum of the Atlantic, Lunenburg 05788
Fisherman's Life Museum, Halifax 05551
Fisherman's Museum, Musgrave Harbour 05952
Fishermen's Museum, Port-de-Grave 06159
Gulf of Georgia Cannery, Richmond 06262
Margaree Salmon Museum, North East Margaree 06021
Northumberland Fisheries Museum, Pictou 06130
Port Dover Harbour Museum, Port Dover 06160
Provincial Museum of Newfoundland and Labrador, Saint John's 06348
Salvage Fisherman's Museum, Salvage 06388
Tehkummah Township Museum, Tehkummah 06537
William Ray House, Dartmouth 05306

Czech Republic
Lesnické, Myslivecké a Rybářské Muzeum, Hluboká nad Vltavou 08352

Denmark
Blåvand Museum, Blåvand 08784
Fiskeri- og Søfartsmuseet, Esbjerg 08808
Fjordmuseet, Jyllinge 08909
Gilleleje Museum, Gilleleje 08836
Museumscenter Hanstholm, Hanstholm 08854
Nordsømuseet, Hirtshals 08876
Søfarts og Fiskerimuseet, Læsø 08969

Egypt
Aquatics Museum - Institute of Oceanography and Fisheries, Suez 09306

Estonia
Karepa Kalame Talumuuseum, Vihula 09394

Finland
Ålands Jakt och Fiskemuseum, Eckerö 09424
Langinkoski Imperial Fishing Lodge, Kotka 09701
Merikarvian Kalastusmuseo, Merikarvia 09825
Runebergs stugan, Jakobstad 09575
Skärgårdsmuseet, Lappoby-Åland 09767

France
Ecomusée de la Pêche, Thonon-les-Bains 14896
Ecomusée de Montjean, Montjean-sur-Loire 13099
Maison de la Rivière et du Pêcheur, Saint-Georges-de-Montaigu 14231
Maison de l'Eau et de la Pêche, Besse-en-Chandesse 10705
Maison de l'Eau et de la Pêche, Neuvic (Corrèze) 13292
Maison du Patrimoine Maritime, Camaret-sur-Mer 11006
Maison Nationale de la Pêche et de l'Eau, Ornans 13437
Musée de la Conserverie Le Gall, Loctudy 12645
Musée de la Mer, Paimpol 13452
Musée de la Mer OCEAM, Les Sables-d'Olonne 12554
Musée de la Mytiliculture, Esnandes 11645
Musée de la Pêche, Concarneau 11380
Musée de la Vilaine Maritime, La Roche-Bernard 12227
Musée la Maison du Pêcheur et "Le Hope", Saint-Gilles-Croix-de-Vie 14251
Musée-Maison du Saumon et de la Rivière, Brioude 10936

Germany
Deutsches Jagd- und Fischereimuseum, München 18838
Deutsches Meeresmuseum, Stralsund 20073
Fischer- und Webermuseum Steinhude, Steinhude 20053
Fischereimuseum, Wassertrüdingen 20411
Jagd- und Fischereimuseum, Adelsdorf 15395
Jagd- und Fischereimuseum Schloss Tambach, Weitramsdorf 20505
Museum für Wattenfischerei, Wremen 20687
Museum im Malhaus, Wasserburg, Bodensee 20410
Museumslogger AE7 Stadt Emden, Emden 16849
Nationalpark-Haus, Butjadingen 16434
Norderneyer Fischerhausmuseum, Norderney 19116
Oberpfälzer Fischereimuseum, Tirschenreuth 20178
Schloß Wolfstein mit Jagd- und Fischereimuseum und Galerie Wolfstein, Freyung 17134

Iceland
Síldarminjasafnid a Siglufirdi, Siglufjörður 21669
Sjóminjasafn Islands, Hafnarfjörður 21637

India
Meghalaya State Museum, Shillong 22017
Museum of the Central Marine Fisheries Research Station, Mandapam Camp 21937

Israel
Fishing Museum, Kibbutz Ein Gev 22683

Italy
Museo della Pesca, Magione 24259
Museo della Tonnara, Milazzo 24421
Museo della Tonnara, Stintino 25637
Museo Ittico, Pescara 24869

Japan
Chiba-kenritsu Awa Hakubutsukan, Tateyama 26819
Iyoboya Salmon Museum, Murakami 26520
Seto Inland Sea Folk History Museum, Takamatsu 26791
Tokai Daigaku Kaiyo Kagaku Hakubutsukan, Shizuoka 26769

Korea, Republic
Bukyoung University Museum, Busan 27136

Netherlands
It Earmhus en Oud Friese Greidboerderij, Warten 29981
Gemeentemuseum Elburg, Elburg 29222
Historische Expositie Klederdracht en Visserijmuseum, Bunschoten Spakenburg 29038
Jan Vissermuseum, Helmond 29396
Museum 't Fiskershúske, Moddergat 29600
Museum in 't Houtenhuis, De Rijp 29069
Museum Scheveningen, Den Haag 29113
Museum van Egmond, Egmond aan Zee 29204
Oudheidkundig Museum Arnemuiden, Arnemuiden 28933
Visafslag Elburg, Elburg 29225
Visserij- en Cultuurhistorisch Museum, Woudrichem 30026
Visserijmuseum, Breskens 29026
Visserijmuseum, Bruinisse 29033
Visserijmuseum, Vlaardingen 29948
Visserijmuseum Zoutkamp, Zoutkamp 30068
Zee- en Havenmuseum de Visserijschool, Ijmuiden 29459

New Zealand
New Zealand Marine Studies Centre, Dunedin 30149

Norway
Andøymuseet, Risøyhamn 30793
Berlevåg Havnemuseum, Berlevåg 30429
Fiskerimuseet og Kunstsmie i Sund, Sund i Lofoten 30906
Fiskerimuseet på Hjertøya, Molde 30685
Fiskerimuseum i Måløy, Måløy 30662
Fossmotunet - Målselv Bygdemuseum, Moen 30679
Gamvik Museum 71N, Gamvik 30508
Grytøy Bygdetun, Lundenes 30658
Ishavsmuseet Aarvak, Brandal 30448
Karmøy Fiskerimuseum, Vedavågen 30980
Kommandør Chr. Christensen's Hvalfangst Museum, Sandefjord 30822
Kråksundet notnaust Sjøbruksmuseum, Tustna 30950
Kystmuseet i Sogn og Fjordane, Florø 30497
Leka Bygdemuseum, Leka 30634
Lenvik Bygdemuseet, Finnsnes 30490
Lofotmuseet, Kabelvåg 30587
Meløy Bygdemuseum, Ørnes 30720
Nordkappmuseet, Honningsvåg 30562
Nordlandsmuseet, Bodø 30440
Norges Fiskerimuseet, Bergen 30426
Norsk Fiskeindustrimuseum, Melbu 30670
Norsk Fiskerværsmuseet, Sørvågen 30869
Norsk Hermetikkmuseum, Stavanger 30884
Norsk Klippfiskmuseum, Kristiansund 30619
Norsk Skogbruksmuseum, Elverum 30478
Rogaland Fiskerimuseum, Åkrehamn 30370
Skrolsvik Fiskebruksmuseum, Moen 30683
Sund Fiskerimuseum, Ramberg 30785
Sunnhordland Folkemuseum og Sogelag, Stord 30900
Vestvågøy Museum, Leknes 30635

Poland
Muzeum Rybackie, Jastarnia 31624
Muzeum Rybołówstwa, Hel 31614

Portugal
Museu dos Baleeiros, Lajes do Pico 32281
Museu Oceanográfico, Setúbal 32347

Russia
Morskoj Muzej-Akvarium, Vladivostok 33702
Muzej Istorii Rybnoj Promyšlennosti Dagestana, Machačkala 32997
Muzej Ochoty i Rybolovstva, Moskva 33144

Senegal
Musée de la Mer, Gorée 33782

Serbia-Montenegro
Ribarsko-Biološka Zbirka, Novi Dojran 33866

South Africa
Old Harbour Museum, Hermanus 34262
Sea World, Durban 34232

Spain
Arrantzaleen Museoa, Bermeo 34604
Museu de la Pesca, Palamós 35211
Museu Marítim de Barcelona, Barcelona 34583

Sri Lanka
National Maritime Museum, Galle 35755

Sweden
Hälleviks Fiskemuseum, Sölvesborg 36214
Kukkola Fiskemuseum, Haparanda 35944
Nordvärmlands Jakt och Fiskemuseum, Sysslebäck 36318
Råå Museum för Fiske och Sjöfart, Råå 36158

Switzerland
Musée du Léman, Nyon 36993
Museo della Pesca, Caslano 36614
Seemuseum in der Kornschütte, Kreuzlingen 36838

United Kingdom
Arbuthnot Museum, Peterhead 40191
Brighton Fishing Museum, Brighton 38339
Brixham Museum, Brixham 38362
Buckhaven Museum, Buckhaven 38383
Buckie Drifter Maritime Museum, Buckie 38384
Eyemouth Museum, Eyemouth 38963
Fishermen's Museum, Hastings 39183
Forge Mill Needle Museum and Bordesley Abbey Visitor Centre, Redditch 40302
Golden Hind Museum, Brixham 38363
Hull Maritime Museum, Kingston-upon-Hull 39380
Izaak Walton's Cottage, Shallowford 40479
Lossiemouth Fisheries and Community Museum, Lossiemouth 39826
Maritime Museum for East Anglia, Great Yarmouth 39125
National Fishing Heritage Centre, Grimsby 39133
Scottish Fisheries Museum, Anstruther 38004
True's Yard Fishing Heritage Centre, King's Lynn 39373
Tugnet Ice House, Spey Bay 40567
Whitstable Oyser and Fishery Exhibition, Whitstable 40863

U.S.A.
The American Museum of Fly Fishing, Manchester 45100
Catskill Fly Fishing Center and Museum, Livingston Manor 44836
Clausen Memorial Museum, Petersburg 46369
Cold Spring Harbor Whaling Museum, Cold Spring Harbor 42520
Fishermen's Museum, Pemaquid Point 46331
National Fresh Water Fishing Hall of Fame, Hayward 43976
Reedville Fishermen's Museum, Reedville 46828
Sag Harbor Whaling and Historical Museum, Sag Harbor 47061
Virginia Institute of Marine Science, Fish Collection, Cloucester Point 42503
Whale Museum, Friday Harbor 43563

Folk Art

Algeria
Musée des Arts Populaires et Traditions, Casbah 00053

Argentina
Museo Cooperativo Eldorado, Eldorado 00337
Museo de Artes y Artesanías Enrique Estrada Bello, Santo Tomé 00620
Museo de Motivos Argentinos José Hernández, Buenos Aires 00193
Museo Monseñor José Fagnano, Río Grande 00519

Australia
Bega Valley Regional Art Gallery, Bega 00789
Latvian Museum, Wayville 01588
Man From Snowy River Folk Museum, Corryong 00949
Tiagarra Aboriginal Culture Centre and Museum, Devonport 00980

Austria
Anton-Museum, Zwettl, Niederösterreich 03058
Haus der Völker, Schwaz 02648
Heimatmuseum, Telfs 02720
Museum für Volkskultur Spittal an der Drau, Spittal an der Drau 02670
Österreichisches Museum für Volkskunde, Wien 02960
Private Lebzelt- und Buttermodelabdrucksammlung, Pressbaum 02454
Salzburger Museum Carolino Augusteum, Salzburg 02551
Sammlungen Schloß Moosham, Mauterndorf 02287
Tiroler Volkskunstmuseum, Innsbruck 02083
Walsermuseum Lech-Tannberg, Lech 02200

Bangladesh
Sonargaon Folk Art and Craft Museum, Sonargaon 03101

Belarus
Gallery of Traditional Ornamental Art, Minsk 03115
Grodnenski Gosudarstvennyj Istoričeskij Muzej, Grodno 03111

Belgium
Museum voor Volkskunde, Brugge 03264
Rariteiten- en Ambachtenmuseum 't Krekelhof, Koksijde 03536

Brazil
Museu Casa do Pontal, Rio de Janeiro 04338
Museu da Cultura e Arte Popular, João Pessoa 04148
Museu da Inconfidência, Ouro Preto 04236
Museu de Arte e Cultura Popular Coordenação de Cultura, Cuiabá 04059

Bulgaria
Etnografska Ekspozicija Stojova KäsB3ta, Radomir 04793
Nacionalen Etnografski Muzej, Sofia 04845
Nacionalna Izložba na Narodnite Chudožestveni Zanajati i Priložni Izkustva, Orešak 04747

Cameroon
Musée Bamilike, Dschang 04955

Canada
Lower Fort Garry, Selkirk 06419
Musée de Charlevoix, Pointe-au-Pic 06143

Chile
Museo de Arte Popular Americano, Santiago de Chile 06911
Museo Regional de la Araucania, Temuco 06923

China, People's Republic
Guangdong Folk Arts and Crafts Museum, Guangzhou 07061
Zhangqiu Arts and Crafts Guan, Jinan 07136

Colombia
Museo de Arte y Tradiciones Populares, Bogotá 07401

Costa Rica
Museo Indigeno, San José 07661

Croatia
Galerija Hlebine-Muzejska Zbirka, Hlebine 07704
Galerija Zavjetnih Slika Brodova, Dubrovnik 07696
Narodni Muzej, Zadar 07806

Cuba
Museo del Danza, La Habana 07965

Cyprus
Cyprus Folk Art Museum, Lefkosia 08195
Ethnographic Museum, Avgorou 08185
Folk Art Museum, Lemesos 08209
Folk Art Museum, Yeroskipos 08216
Pierides Museum, Larnaka 08191

Cyprus, Turkish Republic
Halk Sanatları Müzesi, Girne 08227

Czech Republic
Městské Muzeum, Česká Třebová 08297
Muzeum Beskyd Frýdek-Místek, Frýdek-Místek 08340
Muzeum Krajky, Prachatice 08561
Muzeum Krajky, Vamberk 08708
Oddělení Oblastního Muzea Jihovychodní Moravy, Zlín, Luhačovice 08467

Denmark
Lolland-Falsters Stiftsmuseum, Maribo 08981

Ecuador
Museo de Artesanias Cefa, Quito 09203
Museo de la Inmaculada Concepción, Cuenca 09154
Museo de las Artes Populares Cidap, Cuenca 09156

Finland
Emil Cedercreutzin Museo, Harjavalta 09464
Ilmajoen Museo, Ilmajoki 09561
Muurlan Kotiseutumuseo, Muurla 09845

France
Maison d'Offwiller, Offwiller 13388
Musée Abbaye d'Airvault, Airvault 10247
Musée Alsacien, Strasbourg 14817
Musée Catalan des Arts et Traditions Populaires, Perpignan 13704
Musée Cévenol, Le Vigan (Gard) 12497
Musée d'Art et d'Histoire de Puisaye, Villiers-Saint-Benoît 15257
Musée d'Art et Traditions Populaires, Nancy 13239
Musée d'Arts et Traditions Populaires, La Guérinière 12197
Musée d'Arts et Traditions Populaires Paul Reclus, Domme 11546
Musée de Cerdagne, Sainte-Léocadie 14536
Musée de Dol, Dol-de-Bretagne 11540
Musée de la Crèche Provençale, Cavaillon 11096
Musée de la Fève et de la Crèche, Blain 10753
Musée de l'Amour et des ses Traditions, Oger 13389
Musée Départemental de l'Oise, Beauvais 10655
Musée Départemental des Arts et Traditions Populaires du Perche, Saint-Cyr-la-Rosière 14169
Musée des Arts et Traditions Populaires, Cherves-Mirebeau 11281
Musée des Arts et Traditions Populaires, La Petite-Pierre 12218
Musée des Arts et Traditions Populaires et des Arts Appliqués, Moissac 13001
Musée d'Histoire et d'Archéologie René Bauberot, Châteauponsac 11223
Musée du Charroi Rural, Salmiech 14586
Musée du Rouergue Arts Métiers, Salles-la-Source 14585
Musée du Vieux-Château, Laval (Mayenne) 12361
Musée Municipal de Pithiviers, Pithiviers-le-Vieil 13745
Musée National des Arts et Traditions Populaires, Paris 13635
Musée Régional d'Arts et de Traditions Popoulaires, Grimaud 11957
Musée Vivant de la Passementerie, Jonzieux 12089

Gabon
Musée National des Arts et Traditions, Libreville 15350

Germany
Altonaer Museum in Hamburg, Hamburg 17527
Bauernhaus-Museum, Bielefeld 16152
Buddelschiff-Museum, Neuharlingersiel 19032
Buddelschiff-Museum, Tangerhütte 20137
Erzgebirgische Volkskunststube, Bermsgrün 16120

Erzgebirgischer Spielzeugwinkel, Obereisenheim 19173
Heimatmuseum, Bad Neustadt an der Saale 15705
Heimatmuseum, Deutschneudorf 16595
Heimatmuseum im Unteren Turm, Leutershausen 18449
Heimatmuseum Schloß Adelsheim, Berchtesgaden 15885
Heimatstube Freest, Freest 17096
Heimatstube für Volkskunst, Podelwitz 19425
Heimatstube Podersam-Jechnitz, Kronach 18245
Missionsmuseum des päpstlichen Missionswerks der Kinder in Deutschland, Aachen 15376
Museum Erzgebirgische Volkskunst "Buntes Holz" im Postgut am Altmarkt, Hohenstein-Ernstthal 17814
Museum für bergmännische Volkskunst Schneeberg, Schneeberg, Erzgebirge 19817
Museum für Sächsische Volkskunst, Dresden 16701
Museum für Volkskunst, Meßstetten 18721
Museum Knochenstampfe, Zwönitz 20784
Museum Otzberg, Otzberg 19330
Museum Rade am Schloß Reinbek, Reinbek 19550
Museumsdorf Bayerischer Wald, Tittling 20181
Nussknackermuseum, Neuhausen, Sachsen 19037
Oderlandmuseum, Bad Freienwalde 15645
Schloßmuseum Murnau, Murnau 18962
Siegerlandmuseum mit Ausstellungsforum Haus Oranienstraße, Siegen 19950
Theodor-Zink-Museum und Wadgasserhof, Kaiserslautern 17971
Volkskundemuseum des Bezirks Unterfranken, Bad Bocklet 15617

Greece
Archipelagos Cultural Center, Athinai 20848
Eleftheriadis Collection, Petra 21119
Folk Art Museum of the Metropolis of Kos, Kos 21031
Folklore Museum, Thessaloniki 21182
Historical and Folk Art Museum of Gavalohori, Chania 20917
Kyriazopoulos Collection, Thessaloniki 21185
Mouseio Ellinikis Laïkis Technis, Athinai 20872
Mouseio Vorre, Paiania 21104
National Historical Museum, Athinai 20893

Hungary
Magyar Naiv Művészek Múzeuma, Kecskemét 21451
Népmüvészeti Tájház, Balatonszentgyörgy 21314
Palóc Múzeum, Balassagyarmat 21310
Szabadtéri Néprajzi Múzeum, Szentendre 21575

India
Acharya Jogesh Chandra Purakirti Bhavan, Bishnupur 21731
Ananda Niketan Kirtishala, Bagnan 21699
Gurusaday Museum, Kolkata 21904
Kachchh Museum, Bhuj 21728
Lady Wilson Museum, Dharampur 21790
Madhya Pradesh Tribal Research and Development Institute, Bhopal 21721
Museum and Art Gallery, Burdwan 21734
State Tribal Museum, Chhindwada 21748

Indonesia
Museum Negeri Sumatera Barat, Padang 22165

Iran
Sanandaj Museum, Sanandaj 22277

Italy
Casa Natale di Pascoli, San Mauro Pascoli 25395
Museo Arti e Tradizioni Popolari del Gargano Giovanni Tancredi, Monte Sant'Angelo 24502
Museo Carnico delle Arti Popolari Michele Gortani, Tolmezzo 25725
Museo Civico delle Arti e Tradizioni Popolari, Micigliano 24368
Museo della Cultura Popolare e Contadina, Carrega Ligure 23361
Museo della Vita e delle Tradizioni Popolari Sarde, Nuoro 24663
Museo delle Tradizioni ed Arti Contadine, Picciano 24904
Museo e Pinacoteca della Comunità di Fiemme, Cavalese 23460
Museo Etnografico Siciliano Giuseppe Pitrè, Palermo 24774
Museo Ibleo delle Arti e Tradizioni Popolari S.A. Guastella, Modica 24452
Museo Nazionale delle Arti e Tradizioni Popolari, Roma 25234
Museo Nazionale delle Arti Naïves C. Zavattini, Luzzara 24245

Japan
Fujii Bijutsu Mingeikan, Takayama 26801
Gotoh Bijutsukan, Tokyo 26854
Hachiro Yuasa Memorial Museum, Mitaka 26498
Kochi-ken Kaitokukan, Kochi 26354
Kumamoto International Folk Art Museum, Kumamoto 26376
Kurashiki Mingeikan, Kurashiki 26383
Kyoto Prefectural Museum, Kyoto 26429
Matsumoto Folk Arts Museum, Matsumoto 26476
Nihon Mingeikan, Tokyo 26906
Okinawa-kenritsu Hakubutsukan, Naha 26572
Osaka Nippon Mingeikan, Suita 26775
Takasawa Folk Craft Museum, Niigata 26599
Tottori Folk Art Museum, Tottori 26963
Tottori-kenritsu Hakubutsukan, Tottori 26964

Korea, Republic
Duksung Women's University Art Museum, Seoul 27231
Gwangju Municipal Folk Museum, Gwangju 27182
Jeju-do Folklore and Natural History Museum, Jeju 27194
Jeonju National Museum, Jeonju 27200
Kuknip Minsok Pakmulgwan, Seoul 27254
Museum of Korea Indigenous Straw and Plant, Seoul 27258
Suk Joo-sun Memorial Museum of Korean Folk Arts, Seoul 27283

Latvia
Latvijas Etnogrāfiskais Brīvdabas Muzejs, Rīga 27415

Mexico
Museo Casa Ruth Lechuga, México 28117
Museo de Arte Popular de San Bartolo de Coyotepec, San Baltazar Chichicapan 28375
Museo de Arte Popular Poblano y Museo de Artesanías, Puebla 28326
Museo de Arte Popular Tlajomulco, Tlajomulco de Zúñiga 28523
Museo de Artes e Industrias Populares, Pátzcuaro 28307
Museo de Artes Populares, Tepic 28496
Museo de Artes y Tradiciones Populares de Tlaxcala, Tlaxcala 28532
Museo de Culturas Populares, Durango 27897
Museo de la Casa de las Artesanías del Estado de Chihuahua, Bocoyna 27794
Museo de la Platería, Taxco de Alarcón 28460
Museo de las Artes Populares de Jalisco, Guadalajara 27953
Museo de las Culturas, Saltillo 28367
Museo Michoacano de las Artesanías, Morelia 28252
Museo Nacional de Artes e Industrias Populares, México 28186
Museo Regional de Arte Popular La Huatápera, Uruapán 28579
Museo Sala de Arte Público David Alfaro Siqueiros, México 28199
Museo Universitario de Artes Populares, Colima 27839

Morocco
Musée Bert Flint, Agadir 28691
Musée Bert Flint, Marrakech 28698
Musée d'Art Populaire Marocain, Tétouan 28715
Musée Ethnographique, Chefchaouen 28692
Musée Sidi Med Ben Abdellah, Essaouira 28693

Namibia
Shambyu Museum, Shambyu 28770

Netherlands
Creativiteitscentrum Gouden Handen, 's-Heerenberg 29360
Flessenscheepjesmuseum, Enkhuizen 29232
Huize Nijenstede, Hardenberg 29341
Katwijks Museum, Katwijk aan Zee 29477
Multi Colour Museum, Middelburg 29593
Museum De Vier Quartieren, Oirschot 29654

New Zealand
Rotorua Museum of Art and History, Rotorua 30249
Whakatane District Museum and Gallery, Whakatane 30313

Nigeria
Isenbaye Art Gallery and Cultural Troupe, Oshogbo 30356

Norway
Bu Museum, Utne 30962
Hufthamartunet, Storebø 30901
Lågdalsmuseet, Kongsberg 30604
Maihaugen, Lillehammer 30641
Nordfjord Folkemuseum, Sandane 30820
Norsk Husflidsmuseum, Moen 30681
Oscarsborg Festningsmuseum, Oscarsborg 30723
Telemark og Grenland Museum, Skien 30847
Tinn Museum, Rjukan 30796
Vikedal Bygdemuseum, Vikedal 30994

Pakistan
Lok Virsa Museum, Islamabad 31024

Palestine
Maha Al Saqqa Center - Palestinian Folk Museum, Bethlehem 31065

Peru
Museo de Arte Popular de la Universidad Nacional San Cristóbal de Huamanga, Humanga 31179
Museo de Arte Popular de Quinua, Quinua 31244
Museo de Arte Popular del Instituto Riva-Agüero, Lima 31208
Museo de Filigrana de Cobre, La Esperanza 31192
Museo Histórico Hipólito Unanue, Ayacucho 31123

Philippines
Bahay Laguna Museum, Liliw 31341
Balay Negrense Museum, Silay 31447
Bayanihan Folk Arts Museum, Manila 31370
Bontoc Museum, Bontoc, Mountain Province 31292
Museo It Akean, Kalibo 31335

Poland
Muzeum Beskidzkie im. A. Podżorskiego, Wisła 32156
Muzeum Budownictwa Ludowego, Sanok 31966
Muzeum Etnograficzne, Poznań 31902
Muzeum Etnograficzne, Włocławek 32161
Muzeum Kultury Ludowej, Osiek nad Notecią 31863
Muzeum Lachów Sądeckich im. Zofii i Stanisława Chrząstowskich, Podegrodzie 31889
Muzeum Pomorza Środkowego, Słupsk 31980
Muzeum Regionalne, Łuków 31798
Muzeum Regionalne, Radomsko 31941
Muzeum Regionalne im. Seweryna Udzieli, Stary Sącz 31999
Muzeum Regionalne Ziemi Zbąszyńskiej PTTK, Zbąszyń 32215
Muzeum Rzemiosła, Krosno 31737

Portugal
Museu de Arte Popular, Lisboa 32297

Puerto Rico
Museo de Las Américas, San Juan 32396

Romania
Complexul Naţional Muzeal Astra, Sibiu 32591
Muzeul Arhitecturii Populare din Gorj, Bumbeşti-Jiu 32476
Muzeul Arta lemnului, Câmpulung Moldovenesc 32484
Muzeul de Artă Populară, Constanţa 32500
Muzeul de Artă Populară Prof. Dr. Nicolae Minovici, Bucureşti 32455
Muzeul de Artă Populară şi Etnografie, Tulcea 32618
Muzeul de Artă şi Artă Populară, Calafat 32478
Muzeul de Etnografie şi Artă Populară, Reghin 32580
Muzeul de Etnografie şi Artă Populară Orăştie, Orăştie 32563
Muzeul Judeţean Mureş-Secţia de Etnografie şi Artă Populară, Târgu Mureş 32610
Muzeul Maramureşului, Sighetu Marmaţiei 32594
Muzeul Municipal Câmpulung-Secţia de Etnografie şi, Câmpulung 32483
Muzeul Naţional al Satului, Bucureşti 32464
Muzeul Obiceiurilor Populare din Bucovina, Gura Humorului 32529

Russia
Adygejskij Respublikanskij Kraevedčeskij Muzej, Majkop 33003
Amurskij Gorodskoj Kraevedčeskij Muzej, Amursk 32637
Archangelskij Gosudarstvennyj Muzej Zodčestva i Narodnogo Ikusstva - Malye Karely, Archangelsk 32646
Architekturno-ėtnografičeskij Muzej Derevjannogo Zodčestva Chochlovka, Perm 33300
Chabarovskij Kraevoj Kraevedčeskij Muzej im. N.I. Grodekova, Chabarovsk 32737
Chudožestvennyj Muzej im. M.S. Tuganova, Vladikavkaz 33686
Čukotskij Okružnoj Kraevedčeskij Muzej, Anadyr' 32638
Dalnevostočnyj Chudožestvennyj Muzej, Chabarovsk 32739
Dom-Muzej I.E. Repina, Žigulevsk 33747
Ėtnografičeskij Muzej Narodov Zabajkalja, Ulan-Udė 33652
Ėtnografičeskij Muzej pod Otkrytym Nebom Torum Maa, Chanty-Mansijsk 32742
Ėvenkijskij Okružnoj Kraevedčeskij Muzej, Tura 33635
Gosudarstvennyj Istoriko-architekturnyj i Chudožestvennyj Muzej-zapovednik Drevnij Derbent, Derbent 32756
Gosudarstvennyj Istoriko-ėtnografičeskij Muzej-zapovednik Šušenskoe, Šušenskoe 33569
Gosudarstvennyj Moskovskij Muzej Naivnogo Iskusstva, Moskva 33058
Gosudarstvennyj Nacionalnyj Muzej Ust-Ordynskogo Burjatskogo Avtonomnogo Okruga, Ust-Ordynsk 33672
Ingušskij Gosudarstvennyj Muzej Kraevedenija im. T.Ch. Malsagova, Nazran 33203
Jakutskij Gosudarstvennyj Muzej Istorii i Kultury Narodov Severa im. Jaroslavskogo, Jakutsk 32843
Kargopolskij Gosudarstvennyj Istoriko-Architekturnyj i Chudožestvennyj Muzej, Kargopol 32884
Kirillo-Belozerskij Istoriko-Architekturnyj i Chudožestvennyj Muzej-Zapovednik, Kirillov 32915
Moskovskij Muzej-usad'ba Ostankino, Moskva 33090
Muzej Istorii Narodnych Chudožestvennych Promyslov, Nižnij Novgorod 33211
Muzej Narodnogo Iskusstva, Moskva 33138
Muzej Narodnogo Tvorčestva, Penza 33291
Muzej Narodnogo Tvorčestva, Uljanovsk 33663
Muzej Remesla, Architektury i Byta, Kaluga 32881
Muzej Vjatskie Narodnye Chudožestvennye Promysly, Kirov 32922
Nacionalnyj Muzej Respubliki Baškortostan, Ufa 33647
Rybinskij Gosudarstvennyj Istoriko-architekturnyj i Chudožestvennyj Muzej-zapovednik, Rybinsk 33362
Saratovskij Ėtnografičeskij Muzej, Saratov 33509
Tjumenskij Oblastnoj Muzej Izobrazitelnych Iskusstv, Tjumen 33611
Tuvinskij Respublikanskij Kraevedčeskij Muzej im. Aldan Maadyr, Kyzyl 32979
Udmurtskij Respublikanskij Muzej Izobrazitelnych Iskusstv, Iževsk 32837
Vserossijskij Muzej Dekorativno-Prikladnogo i Narodnogo Iskusstva, Moskva 33183
Zvenigorodskij Istoriko-architekturnyj i Chudožestvennyj Muzej, Zvenigorod 33751

Serbia-Montenegro
Galerija Naivnih Slikara, Kovačica 33850
Gradski Muzej, Foča 33838
Muzej Naivne Umetnosti, Sid 33905

Slovakia
Historické Múzeum, Bratislava 33964
Múzeum Kultúry Karpatských Nemcov, Bratislava 33971
Múzeum Kultúry Maďarov na Slovensku, Bratislava 33972
Múzeum Ždiarsky dom Ždiar, Ždiar 34078

Spain
Museo Municipal de Prehistoria, Gandía 34836
Museo Municipal Taurino, Córdoba 34741
Museo Parroquial, Ecija 34784
Museu d'Art Popular, Horta de Sant Joan 34903
Museu de l'Empordà, Figueres 34817
Museu Municipal, Molins de Rei 35119

Sri Lanka
Folk Museum, Anuradhapura 35744

Sweden
Dalarnas Museum, Falun 35882

Switzerland
Historisches Museum Murten, Murten 36974
Musée du Vieux-Pays d'Enhaut, Château-d'Oex 36626
Museo di Vallemaggia, Giumaglio 36762
Museum im Lagerhaus, Sankt Gallen 37105

Syria
Museé d'Art Populaire du Hauran, Bosra 37434
Popular Traditions Museum Qasrelazem, Damascus 37437

Tunisia
Musée des Arts Populaires et Traditions, Sfax 37580

Uganda
Makerere Art Gallery, Kampala 37828

Ukraine
Kolomya State Museum of Folk Art, Kolomja 37863
Nacionalnij Muzej u Lvovi, Lviv 37887
Ukrainian Museum of Folk and Decorative Art, Kyïv 37877

United Kingdom
Buxton Museum and Art Gallery, Buxton 38427
Polish Cultural Institution Gallery, London 39746

Uruguay
Museo del Indio y del Gaucho, Tacuarembó 41042

U.S.A.
Abby Aldrich Rockefeller Folk Art Museum, Williamsburg 48624
Academy Art Museum, Easton 43066
American Folk Art Museum, New York 45756
American Museum of Straw Art, Long Beach 44857
Americana Museum, El Paso 43111
Art and Culture Center of Hollywood, Hollywood 44060
Art Center of Battle Creek, Battle Creek 41537
Beck Cultural Exchange Center, Knoxville 44512
Bedford Gallery at the Dean Lesher Regional Center for the Arts, Walnut Creek 48290
Belair Mansion, Bowie 41843
Birmingham Bloomfield Art Center, Birmingham 41712
Blue Ridge Institute and Museum, Ferrum 43317
B'nai B'rith Klutznick National Jewish Museum, Washington 48338
Boone County Historical Center, Boone 41783
Branigan Cultural Center, Las Cruces 44657
Brattleboro Museum and Art Center, Brattleboro 41872
Brookings Arts Council, Brookings 41931
Bulloch Hall, Roswell 47012
Center for Cultural Arts, Gadsden 43578
Center for Intuitive and Outsider Art, Chicago 42311
CFCC Webber Center, Ocala 46079
Chase Home Museum of Utah Folk Art, Salt Lake City 47227
Chattahoochee Valley Art Museum, La Grange 44541
Columbus Cultural Arts Center, Columbus 42586
Creative Arts Center, Pontiac 46584
Cuban Museum of Arts and Culture, Miami 45283
Cultural Heritage Center, Dallas 42747
Delta Cultural Center, Helena 43981
Denver Art Museum, Denver 42885
Eide-Dalrymple Gallery, Sioux Falls 47643
Eva and Morris Feld Gallery, New York 45798
Falkirk Cultural Center, San Rafael 47374
Fayette Art Museum, Fayette 43305
Folk Art and Photography Galleries, Atlanta 41343
Folk Art Society of America, Richmond 46877
Four Rivers Cultural Center, Ontario 46166
Fowler Museum of Cultural History, Los Angeles 44900
Goschenhoppen Folklife Museum, Green Lane 43793
Grants Pass Museum of Art, Grants Pass 43767
The Greater Reston Arts Center, Reston 46846
Hambidge Center for the Creative Arts and Sciences, Rabun Gap 46766
Havre de Grace Decoy Museum, Havre de Grace 43965
Hellenic Museum and Cultural Center, Chicago 42332
Henry County Museum and Cultural Arts Center, Clinton 42495

Hiwan Homestead Museum, Evergreen 43249
Hungarian Folk-Art Museum, Port Orange 46601
International Institute of Metropolitan Detroit, Detroit 42930
Jaffrey Civic Center, Jaffrey 44302
Jamaica Center for Arts, Jamaica 44304
James and Meryl Hearst Center for the Arts, Cedar Falls 42150
Jimmie Rodgers Museum, Meridian 45264
Kentucky Art and Craft Foundation, Louisville 44967
Kentucky Folk Art Center, Morehead 45494
Liberty Village Arts Center and Gallery, Chester 42284
Lladro Museum, New York 45825
Los Angeles Craft and Folk Art Museum, Los Angeles 44922
Lyndon House Art Center, Athens 41320
McKissick Museum, Columbia 42563
Marian and Religious Museum, Brooklyn 41947
Meadow Farm Museum, Glen Allen 43679
Mennello Museum of American Folk Art, Orlando 46186
Mercer Museum of the Bucks County Historical Society, Doylestown 42985
Miles B. Carpenter Museum, Waverly 48468
Mingei International Museum, San Diego 47279
Mission Cultural Center for Latino Arts, San Francisco 47326
Mount Dora Center for the Arts, Mount Dora 45529
Museo Italoamericano, San Francisco 47327
El Museo Latino, Omaha 46150
Museum in the Community, Hurricane 44182
Museum of Craft Folk Art, San Francisco 47329
Museum of International Folk Art, Santa Fe 47426
Museum of the American Hungarian Foundation, New Brunswick 45679
National Hall of Fame for Famous American Indians, Anadarko 41192
Native American Museum, Terre Haute 47984
New England Carousel Museum, Bristol 41901
The Octagon Center for the Arts, Ames 41173
Oscar Howe Art Center, Mitchell 45415
Ozark Folk Center, Mountain View 45548
Parson Fisher House, Blue Hill 41756
Pelham Art Center, Pelham 46328
Pennsylvania Dutch Folk Culture Society Museum, Lenhartsville 44715
Petterson Museum of Intercultural Art, Claremont 42418
Plaza de La Raza, Los Angeles 44937
Polish American Museum, Port Washington 46609
Polish Museum of America, Chicago 42358
Ralph Milliken Museum, Los Banos 44953
Rialto Museum, Rialto 46850
Richland County Museum, Lexington 44755
Romanian Ethnic Art Museum, Cleveland 42480
Rose Center Museum, Morristown 45513
San Francisco African American Historical and Cultural Society Museum, San Francisco 47334
Sautee-Nacoochee Museum, Sautee 47475
Schweinfurth Memorial Art Center, Auburn 41374
Scottsdale Museum of Contemporary Art, Scottsdale 47514
Sedona Arts Center, Sedona 47558
Shaker Museum, Old Chatham 46131
Shenandoah Valley Folk Art and Heritage Center, Dayton 42808
Shoshone Tribal Cultural Center, Fort Washakie 43468
Snug Harbor Cultural Center, Staten Island 47787
South Arkansas Arts Center, El Dorado 43106
South Carolina Artisans Center, Walterboro 48295
Southern Highland Craft Guild at the Folk Art Center, Asheville 41283
Southern Ohio Museum and Cultural Center, Portsmouth 46657
Southern Vermont Art Center, Manchester 45102
Stephanie Ann Roger Gallery, Frostburg 43569
Stewart Indian Cultural Center, Carson City 42120
Swedish American Museum Association of Chicago Museum, Chicago 42365
Tennessee Valley Art Association, Tuscumbia 48121
Torpedo Factory Art Center, Alexandria 41135
Tucumcari Historical Research Institute Museum, Tucumcari 48099
Ukrainian-American Archives and Museum, Hamtramck 43899
Ukrainian Museum, Cleveland 42484
Ukrainian Museum, New York 45884
Ukrainian National Museum, Chicago 42368
Vermont Folklife Center, Middlebury 45309
Virginia Museum of Fine Arts, Richmond 46891
Volcano Art Center, Hawaii National Park 43968
Washington Pavillion of Arts and Science, Sioux Falls 47647
Wendell Gilley Museum, Southwest Harbor 47712
Wheelwright Museum of the American Indian, Santa Fe 47434
White River Museum, Meeker 45227
William Bonifas Fine Arts Center, Escanaba 43207
Worcester Center for Crafts, Worcester 48757

Venezuela
Museo de Arte Popular Venezolano, Juangriego 48946

Vietnam
Viet Nam National Fine Arts Museum, Ha Noi 48981

Folklore

Albania
Muzeu i Filmit Shkodër, Shkodër 00031

American Samoa
Jean P. Haydon Museum, Pago Pago 00082

Argentina
Centro Mundo Aborigen, Córdoba 00290
Museo Centro Cultural Pachamama, Amaicha del Valle 00113
Museo de Artesanías Tradicionales Folklóricas, Corrientes 00319
Museo de Esculturas Luis Perlotti, Buenos Aires 00177
Museo de la Artesanía Tradicional Juan Alfonso Carrizo, La Plata 00391
Museo del Traje, La Rioja 00398
Museo Etnográfico y Colonial Juan de Garay, Santa Fé 00603
Museo Folklórico, La Rioja 00399
Museo Folklórico Provincial, San Miguel de Tucumán 00585
Museo Gauchesco Ricardo Güiraldes, San Antonio de Areco 00550
Museo Histórico y de la Tradiciones Populares de la Boca, Buenos Aires 00218
Museo La Cinacina, San Antonio de Areco 00551
Museo Molino Nant Fach, Trevelin 00644
Museo Rafael Escriña, Santa Clara de Saguier 00600
Museo Rauzi, Palmira 00464
El Museo Viajero, Buenos Aires 00246
Museo y Archivo Histórico de San Nicolás, San Nicolás de los Arroyos 00592

Australia
Albany Residency Museum, Albany 00721
Armidale and District Folk Museum, Armidale 00751
Australian Children's Folklore Collection, Melbourne 01222
Barossa Valley Historical Museum, Tanunda 01516
Bowraville Folk Museum, Bowraville 00822
Brambuk Living Cultural Centre, Halls Gap 01085
Carbethon Folk Museum and Pioneer Village, Crows Nest 00955
Channel Folk Museum, Lower Snug 01189
Clarendon House, Nile 01321
Dawson Folk Museum, Theodore 01532
Daylesford and District Historical Museum, Daylesford 00974
Dowerin District Museum, Dowerin 00987
Dreamtime Cultural Centre, North Rockhampton 01326
Folk Museum, Deloraine 00975
Franklin House, Launceston 01168
Gawler Museum, Gawler 01042
Gippsland Heritage Park, Moe 01262
Gloucester Lodge Museum, Yanchep 01623
Hahndorf Academy Public Art Gallery and Museum, Hahndorf 01083
History House, Armadale, Western Australia 00750
Kadina Heritage Museum, Kadina 01129
Kempsey Historical and Cultural Museum, Kempsey 01141
Latrobe Court House Museum, Latrobe 01166
Mahogany Inn, Mahogany Creek 01196
Mingenew Museum, Mingenew 01258
Mount Laura Homestead Museum, Whyalla Norrie 01598
National Trust Museum, Balaklava 00759
Nor West Bend Museum, Morgan 01274
Old Blythewood, Pinjarra 01366
Old Mornington Post Office Museum, Mornington 01277
Old Newcastle Gaol Museum, Toodyay 01537
Old Wool and Grain Store Museum, Beachport 00779
Penneshaw Maritime and Folk Museum, Penneshaw 01361
Pioneer Settlement Museum, Swan Hill 01486
Port Pirie National Trust Museum, Port Pirie 01387
Redcliffe Historical Museum, Redcliffe 01409
Rockcavern, Beechworth 00786
Settlers Museum, Brewarrina 00831
Tamborine Mountain Heritage Centre, Eagle Heights 00997
Tibooburra Local Aboriginal Land Council Keeping Place, Tibooburra 01535
Wellington Courthouse Museum, Wellington 01589
Wonnerup House and Old School, Busselton 00867
Woodloes Homestead Folk Museum, Cannington 00891
Zara Clark Folk Museum, Charters Towers 00906

Austria
Gailtaler Heimatmuseum-Sammlung Georg Essl, Hermagor 02023
Heimat- und Landlermuseum, Bad Goisern 01700
Heimathaus mit Photographiemuseum, Mariazell 02274
Heimatkundliche Sammlung Strick, Bad Mitterndorf 01715
Heimatmuseum, Gleisdorf 01880
Krahuletz-Museum, Eggenburg 01791
Mährisch-Schlesisches Heimatmuseum, Klosterneuburg 02140
Mühlviertler Schlossmuseum Freistadt, Freistadt, Oberösterreich 01851
Museum der Stadt Lienz, Lienz 02220
Museum Lauriacum, Enns 01818
Österreichisches Museum für Volkskunde, Wien 02960
Ortskundliches Museum Jois, Jois 02091
Peter Roseggers Geburtshaus, Alpl 01658
Privatsammlung Piaty, Waidhofen an der Ybbs 02787
Schaubergwerk und Heimatmuseum der Gemeinde Arzberg, Passail 02392
Schloßmuseum Landeck, Landeck 02180
Stadtmuseum Judenburg, Judenburg 02092
Urgeschichtssammlung und Heimtmuseum, Jedenspeigen 02085
Volkskundemuseum, Mödling 02315
Volkskundliches Museum, Deutschlandsberg 01763
Volkskundliches Museum Alois Alphons, Hirschwang 02032
Weinlandmuseum, Asparn an der Zaya 01687

Barbados
Heritage Park Folk Museum, Saint Phillip 03108

Belgium
De Botermolen, Keerbergen 03533
Domein De Locht, Duffel 03396
Gemeentelijk Museum, Melle 03623
Geschiedkundig Museum Mesen, Mesen 03626
Heemkundig Museum Tempelhof, Beerse 03206
Heemkundig Museum Wetteren, Wetteren 03837
Heemmuseum Die Swane, Heist-op-den-Berg 03488
Heemmuseum Eeklo, Eeklo 03402
Hopmuseum De Stadsschaal, Poperinge 03687
Het Huis van Alijn, Gent 03439
Maison Tournaisienne, Tournai 03789
Musée Communal de Folklore Léon Maes, Mouscron 03641
Musée Communal Herstalien d'Archéologie et de Folklore, Herstal 03495
Musée de Folklore, Nismes 03658
Musée de la Porte, Tubize 03802
Musée du Folklore et de la Vie Montoise, Mons 03635
Musée du Vieux Nimy, Mons 03636
Museum De Kijkuit, Merksem 03625
Museum voor Folklore, Zottegem 03857
Museum voor Heem- en Oudheidkunde, Kontich 03538
Museum voor Volkskunde, Dendermonde 03377
Provinciaal Openluchtmuseum Bokrijk, Genk 03432
Rietgaverstede, Nevele 03656
Stedelijk Museum Het Toreke, Tienen 03778
Stedelijk Museum voor Folklore en Regionale Geschiedenis, Ronse 03712
Stedelijk Museum voor Heemkunde en Folklore, Aarschot 03126
Volkskundemuseum, Antwerpen 03178

Bolivia
Museo Nacional de Etnografía y Folklore, La Paz 03901

Brazil
Museu da Cultura e Arte Popular, João Pessoa 04148
Museu Folclorico da Divisão de Discoteca e Biblioteca de Música de São Paulo, São Paulo 04534
Museu Histórico e de Artes, Santana do Ipanema 04449
Museu Municipal do Folclore, Penápolis 04258

Canada
Basilian Fathers Museum, Mundare 05950
Black Creek Pioneer Village, North York 06030
Black Cultural Centre for Nova Scotia, Dartmouth 05303
Calgary Chinese Cultural Centre, Calgary 05162
Centre Culturel et Patrimonial la Poudrière de Windsor, Windsor, Québec 06814
Centre Franco-Ontarien de Folklore, Sudbury 06508
Doon Heritage Crossroads, Kitchener 05695
Dr. Henry N. Payne Community Museum, Cow Head 05282
Heritage Park - Historical Village, Calgary 05168
Highland Village Living History Museum, Iona 05625
Kinistino District Pioneer Museum, Kinistino 05691
Kitimat Centennial Museum, Kitimat 05700
Langley Centennial Museum and National Exhibition Centre, Fort Langley 05442
Latvian History Museum, Toronto 06589
McCord and District Museum, McCord 05794
Le Musée Acadien, Caraquet 05198
Musée Acadien, Gloucester 05496
Musée Québécois de Culture Populaire, Trois-Rivières 06646
Saint Basile Chapel Museum, Saint-Basile 06306
Serbian Heritage Museum of Windsor, Windsor, Ontario 06811
Ukrainian Peoples Home of Ivan Franco, Angusville 04995
U'Mista Cultural Centre, Alert Bay 04973

Central African Republic
Musée Ethnographique Regional, Bouar 06879

Chile
Museo Folklórico Araucano de Cañete Juan A. Ríos M., Cañete 06890

China, People's Republic
Baimasi Han Wei Gucheng Display Center, Luoyang 07156
Beijing Changcheng Hua Ren Huai, Beijing 06946
Beijing Cultural Relic Protection Foundation, Beijing 06947
Beijing Folklorish Museum, Beijing 06949
Folklorish Museum, Wuxi 07285
Fuzhou City Hualin Si, Fuzhou 07057
Law Uk Folk Museum, Hong Kong 07103
Li Zong Ren Display Center, Guilin 07075
Liangzhu Cultural Museum, Hangzhou 07083
Longgang Ke Jia Folklorish Museum, Shenzhen 07240
Luoyang City Folklorish Museum, Luoyang 07158
Museum of Dr. Sun Yat-Sen, Zhongshan 07331
Nanjing Folklorish Museum, Nanjing 07182
Ping Jin Zhan Yi, Old Zhi Display Center, Yangliuqing 07314
Pinggu Shangzhai Cultural Display Center, Beijing 06985
Qingdao City Folklorish Museum, Qingdao 07203
Shan Rong Cultural Display Center, Beijing 06988
Sui Tangyao Zhi Display Center, Chengdu 07026
Tongxian Museum, Beijing 06991
Wangmiao Display Center, Dujiangyan 07046
Yanbian Autonomous Prefecture Museum, Yanji 07316
Yuzhang Bo Wu Yuan, Nanchang 07175

Colombia
Casa de los Abuelos, Sonsón 07598
Museo de Antropología, Barranquilla 07377
Museo de Trajes Regionales de Colombia, Bogotá 07413
Museo Etnográfico de Colombia, Bogotá 07417
Museo Histórico de Cartagena Casa de la Inquisición, Cartagena 07457

Costa Rica
Museo de Cultura Popular Costa Rica, Heredia 07649

Cuba
Galería Bienes Culturales, Victoria de las Tunas 08169
Museo de las Parrandas de Remedios, Remedios 08090
Museo de los Orishas, La Habana 07963
Museo Etnográfico, Madruga 08023
Museo Histórico Municipal de Regla, Regla 08089

Czech Republic
Kotulova Dřevěnka, Havířov 08344
Muzeum Mladaboleslavska, Mladá Boleslav 08480
Národopisné Odděleni, Praha 08605
Okresní Muzeum, Tachov 08674
Polabské Národnopisné Muzeum, Přerov 08623

Denmark
Haastrup Folkemindesamling, Faaborg 08815
Hjerl Hedes Frilandsmuseum, Vinderup 09113
Museet for Holbæk og Omegn, Holbæk 08884
Odsherreds Museum, Nykøbing Sjælland 09002

East Timor
East Timorese Cultural Centre Museum Collection, Dili 09130

Ecuador
Museo Azuayo del Folklore, Cuenca 09151
Museo de la Casa de la Cultura Ecuatoriana, Quito 09206

Egypt
Folklore Museum, Cairo 09265

Estonia
Eesti Kirjandusmuuseum, Tartu 09374

Finland
Tenholan Kotiseutumuseo, Tenala 10103

France
Écomusée d'Alzen, Alzen 10298
Ecomusée de la Ferme et des Vieux Métiers, Lizio 12638
Ecomusée de Savigny-le-Temple, Savigny-le-Temple 14668
Ecomusée des Pays de l'Oise, Beauvais 10653
Maison des Archers, Quimperlé 13902
Musée Agathois, Agde 10228
Musée Basque et de l'Histoire de Bayonne, Bayonne 10621
Musée Comtadin, Carpentras 11055
Musée de la Corse, Corte 11415
Musée de l'Image Populaire, Pfaffenhoffen 13726
Musée de Sologne, Romorantin-Lanthenay 14020
Musée Départemental de Flandre, Cassel 11067
Musée des Arts et Traditions Populaires, Gaillac 11833
Musée des Arts et Traditions Populaires, Le Sel-de-Bretagne 12481
Musée des Tradition de l'île, Noirmoutier-en-l'Ile 13358
Musée des Traditions et Arts Normands, Martainville-Epreville 12876
Musée d'Ethnographie et d'Histoire de Conflans, Albertville 10273
Musée du Berry, Bourges 10864
Musée du Chablais, Thonon-les-Bains 14897
Musée du Crest-Cherel, Ugine 15024
Musée du Rouergue, Espalion 11648
Musée du Santon et des Traditions de Provence, Fontaine-de-Vaucluse 11762
Musée du Vieil Aix, Aix-en-Provence 10254
Musée Émile-Guillaumin, Ygrande 15328
Musée Municipal Méditerranéen de Cassis, Cassis 11068
Musée Provençal et Folklorique, Taradeau 14857

Musée Provençal et Folklorique Taradeau, Les Arcs 12518
Musée Traditions et Vie, Châtillon-sur-Chalaronne 11239
Musées Départementaux Albert Demard, Champlitte 11159

French Guiana
Musée des Cultures Guyanaises, Cayenne 15341

Germany
Bauernhofmuseum Jexhof, Schöngeising 19832
Burgmuseum Schönfels, Schönfels 19831
Erstes Niederrheinisches Karneval-Museum, Duisburg 16747
Erzgebirgisches Freilichtmuseum, Kurort Seiffen 18275
Fastnachtsmuseum Fasenickl, Kipfenberg 18084
Heimatmuseum Duderstadt, Duderstadt 16716
Heimatmuseum Warnemünde, Rostock 19662
Josefine-Weihrauch-Heimatmuseum, Neudenau 19021
Landesmuseum für Kunst und Kulturgeschichte, Schleswig 19794
Landschaftsmuseum Angeln, Langballig 18316
Landschaftsmuseum Schönhengstgau, Göppingen 17318
Museum für Thüringer Volkskunde Erfurt, Erfurt 16905
Museum für Volkskultur in Württemberg, Waldenbuch 20359
Museum im Alten Schloß, Altensteig 15455
Museum im Bierlinghaus, Bad Bayersoien 15594
Museum im Pflegschloss, Schrobenhausen 19853
Museum Der Kunststall, Dahlem 16528
Niederrheinisches Museum für Volkskunde und Kulturgeschichte, Kevelaer 18068
Privatsammlung Burg Runkel, Runkel 19719
Riedmuseum, Rastatt 19488
Riesengebirgsmuseum, Marktoberdorf 18651
Schwäbisches Volkskundemuseum und Bauernhofmuseum Staudenhaus, Gessertshausen 17270
Schweine-Museum, Bad Wimpfen 15774
Stadtmuseum, Wusterhausen 20723
Trachtenhaus Jatzwauk, Hoyerswerda 17849
Tüötten-Museum, Mettingen 18723
Volkskunde Museum Hesterberg, Schleswig 19797
Volkskunde Sammlung, Kassel 18032
Volkskundemuseum Treuchtlingen, Treuchtlingen 20201
Volkskundemuseum Wyhra, Wyhratal 20725
Volkskundliches Freilichtmuseum im Stadtpark Speckenbüttel, Bremerhaven 16345

Greece
Folklore Museum of Florina, Florina 20957
Folklore Museum of Thrace, Komotini 21025
Hellenic Folklore Research Centre, Athinai 20865
Historical Museum of Crete, Iráklion 20975
Mouseio Isrorias tis Ellinikis Endymasias, Athinai 20874
Mykonos Folklore Museum, Mykonos 21078
Sarakatsani Folklore Museum, Serres 21152

Guam
Faninadahen Kosas Guahan, Adelup 21255

Guatemala
Centro de Estudios Folklóricos, Guatemala 21267

Iceland
Byggðasafn Húnvetninga og Strandarmanna, Brú 21626
P^BDjóðmenningarhúsið, Reykjavík 21661
Stofnun Arna Magnússonar, Reykjavík 21667

India
Heras Institute of Indian History and Culture, Mumbai 21949

Iran
Babol Museum, Babol 22231
Hazrati Museum, Semnan 22278
Kandelous Museum, Kandelous 22248
Shahrood Museum, Semnan 22279

Ireland
Knock Folk Museum, Knock 22502
Muckross House Gardens and Traditional Farms, Killarney 22491
Museum of Country Life, Castlebar 22388
Turlough Park House, Castlebar 22389

Israel
Beit Hameiri, Zefat 22786
Kibbutz Negba Museum, Kibbutz Negba 22698

Italy
Civico Museo del Merletto al Tombolo, Rapallo 25074
Museo Civico delle Arti e Tradizioni Popolari, Micigliano 24368
Museo degli Usi e Costumi della Gente di Romagna, Santarcangelo di Romagna 25457
Museo degli Usi e Costumi della Valle di Goima, Zoldo Alto 26059
Museo degli Usi e Costumi delle Genti dell'Etna, Giarre 24022
Museo del Folklore e delle Tradizioni Popolari, Caltanissetta 23275
Museo della Civiltà Contadina Valle dell'Aniene, Roviano 25296
Museo delle Arti e delle Tradizioni Popolari, Sassoferrato 25497
Museo delle Tradizioni Popolari, Città di Castello 23580
Museo di Roma in Trastevere, Roma 25218
Museo Etnografico e del Folklore Valsesiano, Borgosesia 23178
Museo Etnografico Siciliano Giuseppe Pitrè, Palermo 24774
Museo Fittile, Ripatransone 25127
Museo Internazionale del Folklore e Civiltà Contadina, Atina 22979
Museo Statale, Anghiari 22892
Talmuseum, San Nicolò Ultimo 25402

Japan
Chita-shi Rekishi Minzoku Hakubutsukan, Chita 26129
Edo-Tokyo Museum, Tokyo 26842
Folk Museum of Meguro-ku, Tokyo 26844
Folk Museum of Ota-ku, Tokyo 26845
Gifu-ken Hakubutsukan, Seki 26729
Hiratsuka-shi Hakubutsukan, Hiratsuka 26208
Imari-shi Rekishi Minzoku Shiryokan, Imari 26245
Itsukaichi Folk Museum, Itsukaichi 26270
Japan Folk Art Museum, Osaka 26649
Kawasaki-shiritsu Nihon Minkaen, Kawasaki 26329
Kunisaki-machi Rekishi Minzoku Shiryokan, Kunisaki 26379
Matsumoto-shiritsu Hakubutsukan, Matsumoto 26477
Murakami Folk Museum, Murakami 26521
Nagasaki City Museum of History and Folklore, Nagasaki 26552
Nagasaki Kite Museum, Nagasaki 26555
Ogarako Folk Museum, Misawa 26495
Takayama-shiritsu Hakubutsukan, Takayama 26812
Toyama Municipal Folkcraft Village, Toyama 26970
Uodu History and Folklore Museum, Uodo 26991
Yamagata-kenritsu Hakubutsukan, Yamagata 27003

Jordan
The Anthropological National Folklore Museum, Amman 27044
Jordan Museum of Popular Tradition, Amman 27054
Salt Folklore Museum, Salt 27067

Kenya
Lamu Museum, Lamu 27107
Narok Museum, Narok 27113

Korea, Republic
Andong Folk Museum, Andong 27128
Cheongju University Museum, Cheongju 27150
Gongju Folk Drama Museum, Gongju 27176
Hangguk Minsok-chon, Kihung 27203
Kang Weon Folk Museums, Chunchon 27151
Kuknip Minsok Pakmulgwan, Seoul 27254
Kyungsung Museum, Busan 27143
Lotte World Folk Museum, Seoul 27256
National Folk Museum, Seoul 27263
Onyang Minsok Pakmulgwan, Asan 27132
Yeongil Folk Museum, Pohang 27218

Laos
Parc National de la Culture des Ethnies, Vientiane 27322

Lebanon
Moussa Castle Museum, Beiteddine 27486
Qozhaya Museum, Qozhaya 27492

Madagascar
Museum du Parc Tsimbazaza, Antananarivo 27605

Malta
Folklore Museum, Victoria 27708

Mauritius
Maison Creole Eureka, Moka 27735

Mexico
Casa Museo Leonardo Valdez Esquer, Etchojoa 27922
Museo Casa de Cultura de Ixtlán, Ixtlán del Río 28019
Museo Costumbrista de Sonora, Alamos 27765
Museo Cultura y Tradición de Jalcomulco, Jalcomulco 28022
Museo de Artes y Tradiciones Populares de Tlaxcala, Tlaxcala 28532
Museo de Cultura Popular Angel Gil Hermidas, Villahermosa 28608
Museo de Culturas Populares de Chiapas, San Cristóbal de las Casas 28377
Museo de Culturas Populares e Indígenas, Obregón 28281
Museo de Culturas Populares e Indígenas de Sonora, Hermosillo 27985
Museo de la Casa de Cultura de Tepeapulco, Tepeapulco Hidalgo 28489
Museo de la Charrería, México 28136
Museo de la Cultura Potosina, San Luis Potosí 28401
Museo de las Culturas del Norte, Monte Verde 28227
Museo de las Tradiciones Potosinas, San Luis Potosí 28403
Museo del Centro Cultural Patio de los Ángeles, Guadalajara 27955
Museo del Centro Cultural Zacualpan, Comala 27844
Museo Diego Rivera Anahuacalli, México 28164
Museo Estatal de Culturas Populares, Monterrey 28237
Museo Fomento Cultural Banamex, México 28170
Museo Instituto Cultural México Israel, México 28177
Museo Juárez del Jardín Borda, Cuernavaca 27875

Morocco
Musée Bert Flint, Marrakech 28698
Musée de la Kasbah, Rabat 28705

Namibia
Tsumeb Cultural Village, Tsumeb 28775

Netherlands
Cultureel Maçonniek Centrum Prins Frederik, Den Haag 29093
Educatieve Boerderij en Zijdemuseum de Schans, Oud-Gastel 29691
Folkloristisch Museum, Swalmen 29863
Goemanszorg - Streek- en Landbouwmuseum, Dreischor 29180
Holland Experience, Amsterdam 28859
Limburgs Museum, Venlo 29939
Museum Kameleon Dorp en Museum Hans Brinker, Terherne 29865
Nederlands Openluchtmuseum, Arnhem 28942
Het Regthuijs, Abbekerk 28799
Streekmuseum Jan Anderson, Vlaardingen 29947
Volksbuurtmuseum, Den Haag 29127
Volksbuurtmuseum Wijk, Utrecht 29912

New Zealand
Waikawa District Museum, Tokanui 30266

Nigeria
Jos National Museum and Museum of Traditional Nigerian Architecture, Jos 30347

Norway
Drangedal Bygdetun, Drangedal 30464
Fauske Museum, Fauske 30488
Finnetunet, Grue Finnskog 30523
Follo Museum, Drøbak 30465
Fossesholm Herregård, Vestfossen 30989
Hallingdal Folkemuseum, Nesbyen 30707
Hedrum Bygdetun, Larvik 30630
Hordamuseet, Fana 30485
Jutulheimen Bygdemuseum, Vaagaa 30965
Karmsund Folkemuseum, Haugesund 30538
Kittilbu Utmarksmuseum, Østre Gausdal 30773
Kvæven Bygdetun, Tjørhom 30922
Mattisrud Småbruksmuseum, Løten 30657
Meldal Bygdemuseum, Meldal 30672
Norsk Folkemuseum, Oslo 30751
Norsk Utvandrermuseum, Ottestad 30774
Ringerikes Museum, Hønefoss 30561
Sjukehusmuseet i Molde, Molde 30688
Sørsamiske Samlinger, Snåsa 30858
Stalheim Folkemuseum, Stalheim 30875
Tromsø Folkemuseum, Tromsø 30934
Trøndelag Folkemuseum, Trondheim 30943
Voss Folkemuseum, Skulestadmo 30854

Palestine
Artas Folklore Museum, Bethlehem 31063
Museum of Palestinian Popular Heritage, Al-Bireh 31061

Panama
Casa Manuel F. Zárate, Guarraré 31074
Museo Afro Antillano, Panamá City 31076

Paraguay
Centro Cultural Paraguayo-Americano, Asunción 31093
Centro Cultural Paraguayo-Argentino, Concepción 31106

Philippines
Bayanihan Folk Arts Museum, Manila 31370
Museo de la Salle, Dasmariñas 31324
Museo ng Buhay Pilipino, Pasay 31413
Museo ng Kalinangang Pilipino, Pasay 31414
Xavier University Museum (Museo de Oro), Cagayan de Oro City 31300

Poland
Muzeum Ludowych Instrumentów Muzycznych, Szydłowiec 32038
Muzeum Regionalne PTTK, Muszyna 31815
Muzeum Wsi Słowińskiej w Klukach, Kluki 31666
Skansen Kultury Ludowej Pogórza Sudeckiego, Kudowa Zdrój 31744

Puerto Rico
Caguana Indian Ceremonial Park and Museum, Utuado 32410
Centro Ceremonial de Caguana, San Juan 32389

Romania
Muzeul Arta Iemnului, Câmpulung Moldovenesc 32484
Muzeul de Artă Populară, Ploieşti 32570

Russia
Adygejskij Respublikanskij Kraevedčeskij Muzej, Majkop 33003
Amurskij Gorodskoj Kraevedčeskij Muzej, Amursk 32637
Archangelskij Gosudarstvennyj Muzej Zodčestva i Narodnogo Ikusstva - Malye Karely, Archangelsk 32646
Architekturno-ètnografičeskij Muzej Angarskaja Derevnja, Bratsk 32702
Bogorodickij Dvorec-muzej i Park, Bogorodick 32694
Chabarovskij Kraevoj Kraevedčeskij Muzej im. N.I. Grodekova, Chabarovsk 32737
Čukotskij Okružnoj Kraevedčeskij Muzej, Anadyr' 32638
Dom-muzej Semji Cvetaevych, Novo-Talicy 33231
Enisejskij Kraevedčeskij Muzej, Enisejsk 32796
Ètnografičeskij Muzej Narodov Zabajkalja, Ulan-Udė 33652
Ètnografičeskij Muzej pod Otkrytym Nebom Torum Maa, Chanty-Mansijsk 32742
Èvenkijskij Okružnoj Kraevedčeskij Muzej, Tura 33635
Gosudarstvennyj Istoriko-ètnografičeskij Muzej-zapovednik Šušenskoe, Šušenskoe 33569
Gosudarstvennyj Nacionalnyj Muzej Ust-Ordynskogo Burjatskogo Avtonomnogo Okruga, Ust-Ordynsk 33672
Ibresinskij Ètnografičeskij Muzej pod Otkryrym Nebom, Ibresi 32810
Istoki, Belozersk 32682
Jakutskij Gosudarstvennyj Muzej Istorii i Kultury Narodov Severa im. Jaroslavskogo, Jakutsk 32843
Jamalo-Neneckij Okružnoj Kraevedčeskij Muzej im. I.S. Šemanovskogo, Salechard 33364
Krasnodarskij Gosudarstvennyj Istoriko-archeologičeskij Muzej-zapovednik, Krasnodar 32947
Muzej Archeologii i Ètnografii, Ufa 33645
Muzej Tul'skie Samovary, Tula 33628
Muzej V Mire Skazok, Smolensk 33532
Nacionalnyj Muzej Respubliki Baškortostan, Ufa 33647
Tuvinskij Respublikanskij Kraevedčeskij Muzej im. Aldan Maadyr, Kyzyl 32979

Slovakia
Múzeum Kultúry Karpatských Nemcov, Bratislava 33971
Múzeum Kultúry Maďarov na Slovensku, Bratislava 33972
Múzeum Ľudovíta Štúra, Modra 34030
Múzeum Ukrajinsko-Rusínskej Kultúry, Svidník 34071
Národopisné Múzeum Liptova, Liptovský Hrádok 34013

South Africa
Pioneer Museum, Silverton 34375

Spain
Centre Bonastruç ça Porta, Girona 34851
Museo de Artes y Costumbres Populares, Sevilla 35484
Museo de Artes y Tradiciones Populares, Madrid 35017

Sweden
Friluftsmuseet Gammelgården, Köping 36009
Holmöns Båtmuseum, Holmön 35961
Kulturen i Lund, Lund 36059
Mångkulturellt Centrum, Tumba 36339
Nordiska Museet, Stockholm 36269
Norrbottens Museum, Luleå 36054
Torsby Finnkulturcentrum, Torsby 36328
Tunabygdens Gammelgård, Borlänge 35846

Switzerland
Appenzeller Brauchtumsmuseum, Urnäsch 37270
Appenzeller Volkskunde-Museum, Stein, Appenzell-Ausserrhoden 37218
Museum Dorf, Wittenbach 37345
Museum Oedenhof, Wittenbach 37346
Museum Sursilvan, Trun 37256
Schweizerisches Zentrum für Volkskultur, Burgdorf 36609
Walserhaus Gurin, Bosco/Gurin 36578
Wiggertaler Museum, Schötz 37145

Tanzania
Sukuma Museum - Bujora, Mwanza 37464
Village Museum, Dar-es-Salaam 37459

Thailand
Hill Tribes Museum, Bangkok 37485

Tunisia
Musée d'Art et Traditions Populaires, Sidi Boulbaba 37585
Musée des Arts et Traditions, Tozeur 37590
Musée des Arts et Traditions Populaires, Djerba 37558
Musée des Arts et Traditions Populaires Dar Ben Abdallah, Tunis 37593
Musée Régional des Arts et Traditions Populaires, Kef 37566

United Kingdom
Breadalbane Folklore Centre, Killin 39359
Calverton Folk Museum, Calverton 38442
Carmarthenshire County Museum, Carmarthen 38493
Cregneash Folk Village, Cregneash 38663
Cregneash Village Folk Museum, Port Saint Mary 40233
Curtis Museum, Alton 37991
Dalgarven Mill, Kilwinning 39367
Folk Museum, Câtel 38511
Folk Museum, Mevagissey 39942
Folk Museum, Millom 39955
Highland Folk Museum, Kingussie 39388
Highland Folk Museum, Newtonmore 40068
Jorvik Museum, York 40964
Museum of Welsh Life, Saint Fagans 40395
Ordsall Hall Museum, Salford 40431
Swaledale Folk Museum, Reeth 40305
Tolson Memorial Museum, Huddersfield 39274
Ulster-American Folk Park, Omagh 40131
Ulster Folk and Transport Museum, Holywood 39258
World of Country Life, Exmouth 38961

Uruguay
Museo Parque de Esculturas, Montevideo 41020
Museo y Centro Cultural AGADU, Montevideo 41027

U.S.A.
African American Museum, Cleveland 42463
African American Museum, Dallas 42743
Afro-American Cultural Center, Charlotte 42236
Akta Lakota Museum, Chamberlain 42182
Alaska State Museum, Juneau 44368
Alexandria Black History Resource Center, Alexandria 41121
American Swedish Historical Museum, Philadelphia 46389
Amherst County Museum, Amherst 41184
Amon Carter Museum, Fort Worth 43480
Anderson County Historical Museum, Garnett 43627
Andrew-Safford House, Salem 47190
Arthur M. Sackler Gallery, Washington 48335
Atrium Gallery, Saint Louis 47111
Avery County Museum, Newland 45919
Balzekas Museum of Lithuanian Culture, Chicago 42307
Beau Fort Plantation Home, Bermuda 41653
Beck Cultural Exchange Center, Knoxville 44512
Black American West Museum and Heritage Center, Denver 42878
Brick Store Museum, Kennebunk 44434
Bridgton Historical Museum, Bridgton 41896
Buechel Memorial Lakota Museum, Saint Francis 47088
Burke Museum of Natural History and Culture, Seattle 47529
Carter County Museum, Ekalaka 43103
Centro Cultural de la Raza, San Diego 47272
Charles A. Grignon Mansion, Kaukauna 44418
Charles H. Wright Museum of African American History, Detroit 42918
Chisholm Trail Museum, Kingfisher 44486
Connecticut River Museum, Essex 43211
Croatian Heritage Museum, Eastlake 43065
Czech Center New York, New York 45750
Daniel Boone Homestead, Birdsboro 41702
Delta Cultural Center, Helena 43981
Dubuque Museum of Art, Dubuque 42991
East-West Center, Honolulu 44075
Eastern Oregon Museum on the Old Oregon Trail, Haines 43871
Edwards Memorial Museum, Chesterfield 42288
Eiteljorg Museum of American Indians and Western Art, Indianapolis 44217
El Rancho de Las Golondrinas Museum, Santa Fe 47417
Eldridge Street Project, New York 45796
Five Civilized Tribes Museum, Muskogee 45581
Four Rivers Cultural Center, Ontario 46166
Frankenmuth Historical Museum, Frankenmuth 43505
Frontier Culture Museum, Staunton 47795
General Adam Stephen House, Martinsburg 45191
George W. Brown jr. Ojibwe Museum, Lac du Flambeau 44560
Goliad State Historical Park, Goliad 43722
Grand Mound History Center, International Falls 44239
Hammond-Harwood House Museum, Annapolis 41228
Hampton County Historical Museum, Hampton 43893
Historic Crab Orchard Museum and Pioneer Park, Tazewell 47964
Historic Saint Mary's City, Saint Mary's City 47147
Hopi Cultural Museum, Second Mesa 47553
Horry County Museum, Conway 42613
Hoskins House, Burlington 42006
House of Memories Museum, Wilson 48667
Howard County Center of African American Culture, Columbia 42549
Hudson River Museum of Westchester, Yonkers 48785
Hulihee Palace, Kailua-Kona 44374
Indian Center Museum, Wichita 48603
Irish American Heritage Museum, East Durham 43039
Jensen Arctic Museum, Monmouth 45437
Jonathan Hager House and Museum, Hagerstown 43865
Kanabec History Center, Mora 45490
Korean Museum, Los Angeles 44917
The Kurdish Museum, Brooklyn 41944
The Lacrosse Museum and National Hall of Fame, Baltimore 41474
Lahaina Restoration Foundation, Lahaina 44576
Latvian Museum, Rockville 46976
Linn County Historical Museum and Moyer House, Brownsville 41964
Lyman House Memorial Museum, Hilo 44032
Malki Museum, Banning 41495
Maramec Museum, Saint James 47096
Marblehead Historical Museum and J.O.J. Frost Folk Art Gallery, Marblehead 45136
Maritime Museum, Cohasset 42515
Mattye Reed African Heritage Center, Greensboro 43817
Maxwell Museum of Anthropology, Albuquerque 41104
Melrose Plantation Home Complex, Melrose 45230
Meriden Historical Society Museum, Meriden 45263
Meridian International Center - Cafritz Galleries, Washington 48369
Mexic-Arte Museum, Austin 41417
Mexican Fine Arts Center Museum, Chicago 42341
The Mexican Museum, San Francisco 47324
Michigan State University Museum, East Lansing 43054
Museo Italoamericano, San Francisco 47327
The Museum at Warm Springs, Warm Springs 48304
Museum of Afro-American History, Boston 41816
Museum of Amana History, Amana 41163
Museum of Appalachia, Norris 45977
Museum of Chinese in the Americas, New York 45841
Museum of Indian Arts and Culture, Santa Fe 47425
Museum of Russian Culture, San Francisco 47330
Museum of the American Hungarian Foundation, New Brunswick 45679
Museum of the Korean Cultural Center, Los Angeles 44933
National Afro-American Museum and Cultural Center, Wilberforce 48618
National Museum of African Art, Washington 48374
National Museum of Women in the Arts, Washington 48381
Native American Exhibit, Fonda 43361
Native American Museum, Terre Haute 47984
Nevada State Fire Museum and Comstock Firemen's Museum, Virginia City 48252
Nordic Heritage Museum, Seattle 47541
Northeast Louisiana Delta African American Heritage Museum, Monroe 45442
Northwest Museum of Arts and Culture, Spokane 47728
The Oldest House Museum, Key West 44470
Orcas Island Historical Museum, Eastsound 43071
Pacific Asia Museum, Pasadena 46303
Pacific University Museum, Forest Grove 43362
Paynes Creek Historic State Park, Bowling Green 41848
Pendarvis, Mineral Point 45379
Pennsbury Manor, Morrisville 45514
Pennsylvania German Cultural Heritage Center, Kutztown 44530
P.H. Sullivan Museum and Genealogy Library, Zionsville 48825
Piatt Castles, West Liberty 48533
Point of Honor, Lynchburg 45007
Pro Rodeo Hall of Fame and Museum of the American Cowboy, Colorado Springs 42541
Putney Historical Society Museum, Putney 46749
Richland County Museum, Lexington 44755
S. Ray Miller Auto Museum, Elkhart 43144
Schingoethe Center for Native American Cultures, Aurora 41398
Schwenkfelder Library and Heritage Center, Pennsburg 46341
Seabrook Village, Midway 45333
Shakowi Cultural Center, Oneida 46158
Shoal Creek Living History Museum, Kansas City 44407
Shoshone Tribal Cultural Center, Fort Washakie 43468
Sioux Indian Museum, Rapid City 46798
Skagit County Historical Museum, La Conner 44533
Smithsonian Institution, Washington 48393
Southern Plains Indian Museum, Anadarko 41193
Stephen Foster Folk Culture Center, White Springs 48590
Stewart M. Lord Memorial Museum, Burlington 42002
Strasburg Museum, Strasburg 47849
Swedish American Museum Association of Chicago Museum, Chicago 42365
Terrebonne Museum, Houma 44114
Teysen's Woodland Indian Museum, Mackinaw City 45035
Thousand Islands Museum of Clayton, Clayton 42445
Tubman African-American Museum, Macon 45048
Ukrainian Museum, Cleveland 42484
Ukrainian Museum, New York 45884
Wanapum Dam Heritage Center, Beverly 41673
Whitingham Historical Museum, Whitingham 48596
Wilber Czech Museum, Wilber 48617
Willa Cather State Historic Site, Red Cloud 46816
Yeshiva University Museum, New York 45887
Zoar State Memorial, Zoar 48826

Uzbekistan
Gosudarstvennyj Muzej Istorii Kultury i Iskusstva Uzbekistana, Samarkand 48848

Venezuela
Museo de Arte Popular Petare, Caracas 48913
Museo de Arte Popular Venezolano, Juangriego 48946

Yemen
Al-Mukalla Museum, Al-Mukalla 49009

Food

Australia
City of Gosnells Museum, Gosnells 01068
Old Council Chambers Museum, Norton Summit 01333

Austria
Volkskundlich-Landwirtschaftliche Sammlung, Stainz 02674

Belgium
Frietkotmuseum, Antwerpen 03145

Canada
Alberta Wheat Pool Grain Museum, Calgary 05160
Ingersoll Cheese Factory Museum, Ingersoll 05617
Maple Syrup Museum, Saint Jacobs 06323
Prince Edward Island Potato Museum, O'Leary 06050

China, People's Republic
Nanji Guan, Qingdao 07201

Croatia
Podravka Museum, Koprivnica 07719

France
Cassissium, Nuits-Saint-Georges 13375
Hameau du Fromage, Cléron 11330
Maison de la Pomme et de la Poire, Barenton 10589
Maison de l'Abeille et du Miel, Riez 13965
Maison des Fromages d'Auvergne, Egliseneuve-d'Entraigues 11603
Musée Amora, Dijon 11521
Musée Art du Chocolat, Lisle-sur-Tarn 12630
Musée de la Casse, Orcières 13420
Musée de la Mytiliculture, Esnandes 11645
Musée de la Pomme, Bourg-Saint-Maurice 10855
Musée de la Pomme et du Cidre et des Métiers Traditionnels, Rosay 14031
Musée de l'Art Culinaire, Villeneuve-Loubet 15232
Musée des Techniques Fromagères, Saint-Pierre-sur-Dives 14419
Musée du Bonbon Haribo, Uzès 15034
Musée du Foie Gras, Frespech 11817
Musée du Jus de Fruit, Saint-Andiol 14104
Musée du Lait, Montebourg 13071
Musée du Terroir et de la Volaille, Romenay 14018
Musée Vivant de l'Abeille, Valensole 15055
Le Palais du Chocolat, La Côte-Saint-André 12162

Germany
Bananenmuseum, Sierksdorf 19955
Deutsches Kartoffelmuseum Fußgönheim, Fußgönheim 17185
Deutsches Kochbuchmuseum, Dortmund 16658
Europäisches Spargelmuseum, Schrobenhausen 19851
Historisches Käsereimuseum, Altusried 15474
Imhoff-Stollwerck-Museum, Köln 18144
Das Kartoffelmuseum, München 18860
Museum der Brotkultur, Ulm 20258
Museum im Bock, Leutkirch im Allgäu 18451
Spice's Gewürzmuseum, Hamburg 17568

Greece
Museum of the Olive and Greek Olive Oil, Spárti 21167

Ireland
Cork Butter Museum, Cork 22401

Israel
Israel Oil Industry Museum, Haifa 22606

Italy
Museo Agrumario, Reggio Calabria 25089
Museo del Cioccolato, Norma 24638
Museo del Pane, Sant'Angelo Lodigiano 25451
Museo dell'Arte e della Tecnologia Confetteria, Sulmona 25647
Museo dell'Olivo, Imperia 24094
Museo dell'Olivo e dell'Olio, Torgiano 25727
Museo Nazionale delle Paste Alimentari, Roma 25235
Museo Storico degli Spaghetti, Pontedassio 24998

Korea, Republic
Kimchi Field Museum, Seoul 27243

Netherlands
Bakkerij Museum, Oosterhout 29669
Culinair Historisch Museum De Vleer, Appelscha 28929
Culinair Museum, Amersfoort 28821
Flipje en Jam Museum Tiel, Tiel 29873
Het Hollands Kaasmuseum, Alkmaar 28803
Kaasmuseum Bodegraven, Bodegraven 28991
Museum in den Halven Maen, Rockanje 29737

Norway
Meierimuseet, Ås 30396

Philippines
Grains Industry Museum, Cabanatuan 31299
Ricewolrd Museum, Los Baños 31346

South Africa
Elgin Apple Museum, Grabouw 34248

Spain
Museo del Chocolate, Astorga 34496
Museo Vasco de Gastronomía, Laudio 34941

Switzerland
Alimentarium, Vevey 37285
Appenzeller Schaukäserei, Stein, Appenzell-Ausserrhoden 37217
Schokoland Alprose, Caslano 36615

United Kingdom
MoCHA, London 39710
Mustard Shop Museum, Norwich 40096
Radbrook Culinary Museum, Shrewsbury 40509

U.S.A.
Beverage Containers Museum, Millersville 45348
Culinary Archives and Museum, Providence 46716
George Washington Carver House, Diamond 42944
New England Maple Museum, Pittsford 46535
The Rice Museum, Crowley 42714
The Spam Museum, Austin 41403

Forest Products

Argentina
Museo Histórico La Gallareta Forestal, La Gallareta 00381

Australia
Forest and Heritage Centre, Geeveston 01047
Manjimup Timber Museum, Manjimup 01206
Timbertown Museum, Wauchope 01586
Wirrabara Forestry Museum, Wirrabara 01607

Austria
Erstes Tiroler Holzmuseum, Wildschönau 03030
Forstmuseum, Reichraming 02499
KiK - Kultur im Kloster, Klostermarienberg 02138
Montanmuseum, Hieflau 02028
Mühlviertler Waldhaus, Windhaag bei Freistadt 03038
Museum Alte Brettersäge, Rappottenstein 02487
Österreichisches Forstmuseum Silvanum, Großreifling 01962
Steirisches Holzmuseum, Sankt Ruprecht 02607
Stierhübelteichhaus, Karlstift 02100
Trift- und Holzfällermuseum, Bad Großpertholz 01703
Waldbauernmuseum, Gutenstein 01980

Belgium
Bosmuseum, Hechtel 03486
Bosmuseum Wildert, Essen 03408
Musée Provincial de la Forêt, Namur 03650

Brazil
Laboratório de Anatomia e Identificação de Madeiras, Manaus 04189
Museu da Secção de Tecnologia do Serviço Florestal, Rio de Janeiro 04352
Museu Florestal Octávio Vecchi, São Paulo 04533

Brunei
Brunei Forestry Museum, Sungai Liang 04602

Canada
Alberta Forestry Service Museum, Hinton 05599
British Columbia Forest Discovery Centre, Duncan 05352
British Columbia Forest Service Museum, Victoria 06713
Forest Sandilands Centre and Museum, Winnipeg 06824
Penetanguishene Centennial Museum, Penetanguishene 06108
Pinewood Museum, Wasagaming 06746
Railway and Forestry Museum, Prince George 06187
Sherbrooke Village, Sherbrooke, Nova Scotia 06438

Denmark
Dansk Jagt- og Skovbrugsmuseum, Hørsholm 08899
Vorbasse Museum, Vorbasse 09114

Finland
Lapin Metsämuseo, Rovaniemi 10002
Lusto-Suomen-metsämuseo ja metsätietokeskus, Punkaharju 09962
Pielisen Museo, Lieksa 09781

France
Musée de la Schlitte et des Métiers du Bois, Muhlbach-sur-Munster 13205
Musée de la Vie Rurale et Forestière, Saint-Michel-en-Thiérache 14372
Musée du Bois et de la Forêt, La Chaise-Dieu 12138
Musée-Maison des Amis de la Forêt, Mervent 12949

Germany
Brandenburgisches Forstmuseum Fürstenberg/Havel, Fürstenberg, Havel 17157
Forst- und Jagdmuseum, Hofgeismar 17796
Forst- und Köhlerhof, Rostock 19661
Forstbotanisches Museum, Tharandt 20170
Forstliche und Jagdkundliche Lehrschau Grillenburg, Grillenburg 17399
Forstmuseum Heringen, Heringen, Werra 17722
Forstmuseum im Hochwildpark Karlsberg, Weikersheim 20430
Gemeinde- und Forstmuseum, Oftersheim 19244
Holzknechtmuseum Ruhpolding, Ruhpolding 19716
Holztechnisches Museum, Rosenheim 19650
Köhlereimuseum, Hasselfelde 17628
Museum für ländliches Kulturgut, Landwirtschaft, Forsten und Jagd, Ulrichstein 20262
Museum Wald und Umwelt, Ebersberg 16769
Sägmühlmuseum Marhördt, Oberrot 19197
Schönbuch Museum, Dettenhausen 16593
Schüttesägemuseum, Schiltach 19783
Technisches Museum Holzschleiferei Weigel, Rittersgrün 19619
Wald- und Moormuseum Berumerfehn, Großheide 17431
Waldgeschichtliches Museum Sankt Oswald, Sankt Oswald, Niederbayern 19755
Waldmuseum, Münstertal 18955
Waldmuseum, Zwiesel 20782

Waldmuseum im Wildpark Neuhaus, Holzminden 17833
Waldmuseum Stendenitz, Stendenitz 20060
Waldmuseum Wassermühle, Wingst 20608
Waldmuseum Watterbacher Haus, Kirchzell 18100

Guatemala
Centro de Estudios Conservacionistas, Guatemala 21266

Hungary
Szadadtéri Erdei Múzeum, Szilvásvárad 21584

India
Assam Forest Museum, Gauhati 21806
F.R.I. Museums, Dehradun 21760
Gass Forest Museum, Coimbatore 21750

Indonesia
Museum Manggala Wanabakti, Jakarta 22122

Italy
Museo Agro-Forestale San Matteo, Erice 23738
Museo del Legno, Cantù 23320
Orto Botanico, Palermo 24778

Japan
Uodu Buried Forest Museum, Uodo 26990

Korea, Republic
Forest Museum, Soheul 27293
Tamyang Bamboo Museum, Tamyang 27294

Malaysia
Forestry Research Institute Malaysia Museum, Kepong 27628
Penang Forestry Museum, Pulau Pinang 27682

Myanmar
Forest Museum, Taungdwingyi 28744

Netherlands
Boomkwekerijmuseum, Boskoop 29007

New Zealand
Timber Museum of New Zealand, Putaruru 30244

Norway
Fetsund Lenser Fløtingsmuseum, Fetsund 30489
Norsk Skogbruksmuseum, Elverum 30478
Sunnhordland Folkemuseum og Sogelag, Stord 30900

Pakistan
Forest Museum, Peshawar 31048
Pakistan Forest Museum, Abbottabad 31012

Poland
Muzeum Lasu i Drewna przy Lesnym Zakładzie Doświadczalnym SGGW, Rogów 31949

Slovakia
Lesnicke a Drevárske Múzeum, Zvolen 34081

Slovenia
Tehniški Muzej Slovenije, Ljubljana 34122

Sweden
Finnskogsmuseet, Viksjöfors 36410
Siljansfors Skogsmuseum, Mora 36101
Skärgårdens Sågverksmuseum, Holmsund 35962
Skogsmuséet på Römmen, Mörsil 36099
Tändsticksmuseet, Jönköping 35979

Switzerland
Bielen-Säge Museum, Unterschächen 37263
Musée du Bois, Aubonne 36478

Uganda
Forest Department Utilisation Division Museum, Kampala 37826

United Kingdom
Dean Heritage Museum, Soudley 40532
New Forest Museum and Visitor Centre, Lyndhurst 39855
Queen Elizabeth's Hunting Lodge, London 39751

U.S.A.
Camp 6 Logging Museum, Tacoma 47915
Camp Five Museum, Laona 44646
Chippokes Farm and Forestry Museum, Surry 47895
Fisher Museum of Forestry, Petersham 46380
Forest Capital State Museum, Perry 46354
Forest History Center, Grand Rapids 43761
Hoo-Hoo International Forestry Museum, Gurdon 43854
Klamath National Forest Interpretive Museum, Yreka 48812
Mississippi Agriculture and Forestry/National Agricultural Aviation Museum, Jackson 44282
Naomi Wood Collection at Woodford Mansion, Philadelphia 46433
New England Maple Museum, Rutland 47042
North Carolina Museum of Forestry, Whiteville 48593
Oklahoma Forest Heritage Center Forestry Museum, Broken Bow 41912
Paul Bunyan Logging Camp, Eau Claire 43076
Pennsylvania Lumber Museum, Galeton 43601
Rhinelander Logging Museum, Rhinelander 46849
Southern Forest World Museum, Waycross 48473
Texas Forestry Museum, Lufkin 44998
World Forestry Center, Portland 46646

Fortresses → Castles and Fortresses

Fossils

Argentina
Museo de Ciencias Naturales Luma, Tanti 00631
Museo de Geología y Paleontología, Neuquén 00458
Museo de História y Ciencias Naturales, Lobería 00408
Museo Escolar de Ciencias Naturales Carlos A. Merti, San Antonio de Areco 00548
Museo Municipal Carmen Funes, Plaza Huincul 00479
Museo Municipal de Ciencias Naturales Lorenzo Scaglia, Mar del Plata 00428
Museo Paleontológico Egidio Feruglio, Trelew 00639
Museo Paleontológico y Petrolero Astra, Comodoro Rivadavia 00283
Museo Prof. Dr. Juan Augusto Olsacher, Zapala 00677
Museo Provincial de Historia Natural de La Pampa, Santa Rosa 00613
Museo Universitario Florentino y Carlos Ameghino, Rosario 00533
Paleorama - Museo Itinerante, Don Torcuato 00333

Australia
Boulia Stone House Museum, Boulia 00819
Museum of Tropical Queensland, Townsville 01546
National Dinosaur Museum, Gungahlin 01080
Queensland Museum, South Bank 01458

Austria
Paläontologisches Museum, Offenhausen 02384

Belgium
Mineralogisch Museum, Merksem 03624
Musée de la Préhistoire en Wallonie, Flémalle 03419
Musée de l'Iguanodon, Bernissart 03216
Museum des Sciences naturelles de Belgique, Bruxelles 03338
Schoolmuseum Michel Thiery, Gent 03449

Brazil
Museu de Ciências da Terra - DNPM, Rio de Janeiro 04357
Museu de Ciências Naturais PUC Minas, Belo Horizonte 03985
Museu de Paleontologia, Monte Alto 04208

Bulgaria
Paleontologičen Muzej, Asenovgrad 04605

Canada
Courtenay and District Museum and Paleontology Centre, Courtenay 05281
Devil's Coulee Dinosaur Heritage Museum, Warner 06744
Dinosaur Provincial Park, Patricia 06100
Drumheller Dinosaur and Fossil Museum, Drumheller 05340
Garden Park Farm Museum, Alberta Beach 04971
Grande Prairie Museum, Grande Prairie 05519
London Regional Children's Museum, London 05770
Morden and District Museum, Morden 05939
Museum of Natural Sciences, Saskatoon 06402
Princeton and District Museum, Princeton 06192
Royal Tyrrell Museum of Palaeontology, Drumheller 05342
Yukon Beringia Interpretive Centre, Whitehorse 06793

Chile
Museo de Historia Natural de Valparaíso, Valparaíso 06927
Museo Histórico de Osorno, Osorno 06901

China, People's Republic
Dalian Natural History Museum, Dalian 07035
Sanying Pagoda and Museum of Dinosaur, Shaoguan 07230

Colombia
Museo Geológico José Royo y Gómez, Bogotá 07422
Museo Paleontológico, Mariquita 07513

Croatia
Gradski Muzej, Požega 07756
Muzej Krapinskog Pračovjeka, Krapina 07728
Stjepan Gruber Museum, Županja 07844

Cuba
Museo Paleontológico, Pinar del Río 08076

Cyprus
Tornaritis Pierides Municipal Museum of Paloentology, Larnaka 08193

Czech Republic
Městské Muzeum, Lanškroun 08442
Muzeum Českého Krasu v Berouně, Beroun 08247
Vlastivědné Muzeum, Slany 08654
Vlastivědné Muzeum, Litomyšl 08458
Zámek Budišov, Budišov u Třebiče 08284

Denmark
Fur Museum, Fur 08835
Geologisk Museum, København 08930
Molermuseet, Nykøbing Mors 08999

Ecuador
Museo David Paltan, Tulcán 09229

Finland
Kivimuseo, Tampere 10078

France
Collection Archéologique, Villarzel-Cabardes 15183
Écomusée de la Cévenne, Saint-Laurent-de-Trèves 14309
Galeries de Paléontologie et d'Anatomie Comparée, Paris 13512
Musée de la Pierre, Trambly 14983
Musée de la Thiérache, Vervins 15147
Musée de Paléontologie, La Voulte-sur-Rhône 12275
Musée de Paléontologie, Villers-sur-Mer 15244
Musée de Paléontologie, Villeurbanne 15251
Musée de Paléontologie Christian Guth, Chilhac 11286
Musée de Préhistoire Amédée Lemozi, Cabrerets 10969
Musée des Fossiles, Montceau-les-Mines 13066
Musée des Minéraux et Fossiles des Ardennes, Bogny-sur-Meuse 10784
Musée d'Histoire Naturelle, Dijon 11528
Musée d'Histoire Naturelle Philadelphe Thomas, Gaillac 11835
Musée du Cloître, Tulle 15014
Musée Municipal d'Archéologique, Murviel-les-Montpellier 13226
Musée Municipal de Préhistoire, Fismes 11739
Musée Municipal des Fossiles, Tourtour 14978
Musée Théophile Jouglet, Anzin 10381
Muséum d'Histoire Naturelle, Le Havre 12428
Muséum National d'Histoire Naturelle, Paris 13650

Germany
Archäologische Ausstellung in der Schule, Nassenfels 18974
Bürgermeister-Müller-Museum, Solnhofen 19992
Dinosaurier-Freilichtmuseum Münchehagen, Rehburg-Loccum 19539
Dobergmuseum/Geologisches Museum Ostwestfalen-Lippe, Bünde 16403
Eifelmuseum Blankenheim, Blankenheim, Ahr 16179
Erdgeschichtliches Werksmuseum der ZEAG, Lauffen am Neckar 18355
Fossilien- und Heimatmuseum, Messel 18718
Fossilienmuseum im Werkforum Rohrbach Zement, Dotternhausen 16670
Geiseltalmuseum der Martin-Luther-Universität, Halle, Saale 17512
Geologisch-Paläontologisches Museum, Münster 18937
Geowissenschaftliche Sammlungen, Freiberg, Sachsen 17099
Heimatmuseum Günzburg, Günzburg 17455
Heimatmuseum Niederaichbach, Niederaichbach 19095
Hohenloher Urweltmuseum, Waldenburg, Württemberg 20361
Mineralien-Fossilien-Museum, Neckartenzlingen 18991
Muschelkalkmuseum Hagdorn, Ingelfingen 17898
Museum Alzey, Alzey 15477
Museum beim Solenhofer Aktien-Verein, Maxberg 18667
Museum Bergér, Eichstätt 16806
Museum für Naturkunde der Humboldt-Universität zu Berlin, Berlin 16056
Museum im Hollerhaus, Dietfurt 16604
Museum Natur und Mensch, Greding 17381
Naturhistorisches Museum, Mainz 18605
Naturkunde-Museum Bamberg, Bamberg 15813
Naturkundliche Sammlung, Königsbrunn 18174
Odenwald- Spielzeugmuseum, Michelstadt 18732
Paläontologisches Museum München, München 18893
Paläontologisches Museum Nierstein, Nierstein 19103
Petrefaktensammlung, Bad Staffelstein, Oberfranken 15749
Privatmuseum Hans Klein, Prichsenstadt 19448
Sammlung Fossilien des Jura, Lichtenfels, Bayern 18456
Sieblos-Museum Poppenhausen, Poppenhausen, Wasserkuppe 19428
Stadtmuseum Stadtoldendorf, Stadtoldendorf 20033
Stein- und Fossiliensammlung Albert, Sulzdorf 20129
Südostbayerisches Naturkunde- und Mammut-Museum, Siegsdorf 19953
Trias-Museum, Ochsenfurt 19220
Urwelt-Museum Hauff, Holzmaden 17829
Urwelt-Museum Oberfranken, Bayreuth 15860
Urweltmuseum Aalen, Aalen 15386
Zeittunnel Wülfrath, Wülfrath 20689

Greece
Natural History Museum of the Aegean, Samos 21149
Natural History Museum of Tilos, Tilos 21196
Paleontological and Geological Museum of the University of Athens, Athinai 20900

Hungary
Mátra Múzeum, Gyöngyös 21417
Ősléntani Telep, Rudabánya 21520

Ireland
James Mitchell Museum, Galway 22473

Israel
House of the Scribe, Almog 22569

Italy
Civico Museo Naturalistico Ferruccio Lombardi, Stradella 25640
Istituto Italiano di Paleontologia Umana, Roma 25168
Mostra Permanente di Paleontologia, Terni 25694
Museo Archeologico della Sabbia, Gavardo 23964
Museo Civico Antiquarium, Nettuno 24616
Museo Civico di Paleontologia, Empoli 23729
Museo Civico di Scienze Naturali, Faenza 23751
Museo Civico di Scienze Naturali, Voghera 26044
Museo Civico di Scienze Naturali ed Archeologia della Valdinievole, Pescia 24876
Museo Civico Fossili, Besano 23070
Museo Civico Paleontologico, Macerata Feltria 24252
Museo dei Fossili, Vestenanova 25981
Museo dei Fossili, Zogno 26056
Museo dei Fossili Don Giuseppe Mattiacci, Serra San Quirico 25545
Museo dei Fossili e dei Minerali, Smerillo 25591
Museo dei Fossili e Minerali del Monte Nerone, Apecchio 22903
Museo dei Fossili e Mostra dei Funghi, Pioraco 24939
Museo del Fossile del Monte Baldo, Brentonico 23198
Museo di Fossili, Ronca 25276
Museo di Geologia e Paleontologia, Torino 25749
Museo di Geologia e Paleontologia, Padova 24740
Museo di Minerali e Fossili, Montefiore Conca 24522
Museo di Mineralogia e Paleontologia, Saint Vincent 25312
Museo di Mineralogia e Petrologia, Padova 24741
Museo di Paleontologia, Milano 24400
Museo di Paleontologia, Modena 24445
Museo di Paleontologia, Napoli 24595
Museo di Paleontologia, Roma 25216
Museo di Paleontologia dell'Accademia Federiciana, Catania 23448
Museo di Paleontologia e Mineralogia, Campomorone 23310
Museo di Paleontologia e Speleologia E.A. Martel, Carbonia 23345
Museo di Paleontologia G. Buriani, San Benedetto del Tronto 25334
Museo di Scienze Naturali Don Bosco, Alassio 22826
Museo Friulano di Storia Naturale, Udine 25850
Museo Geo-Paleontologico, Ferrara 23794
Museo Geologico e Paleontologico G. Capellini, Bologna 23136
Museo Geologico G.G. Gemmellaro, Palermo 24775
Museo Geopaleontologico dei Fossili della Lessinia, Velo Veronese 25907
Museo Paleontologico, Amandola 22873
Museo Paleontologico, Bova 23188
Museo Paleontologico, Fluminimaggiore 23891
Museo Paleontologico, L'Aquila 24148
Museo Paleontologico, Mondaino 24469
Museo Paleontologico, Monfalcone 24475
Museo Paleontologico, Montevarchi 24552
Museo Paleontologico M. Gortani, Portogruaro 25024
Museo Paleontologico Parmense, Parma 24811
Museo Paleontologico S. Lai, Ceriale 23480
Raccolta Archeologica e Paleontologica, Corciano 23648
Raccolta di Fossili Francesco Angellotti, Ostra 24719

Japan
Fukui-kenritsu Hakubutsukan, Fukui 26144
Mizunami-shi Kaseki Hakubutsukan, Mizunami 26514
Osaka Museum of Natural History, Osaka 26667

Korea, Republic
Gyeongbo Museum of Paleontology, Namjeong 27214

Lebanon
Fossils Museum, Byblos 27489

Luxembourg
Collection Eugène Pesch, Oberkorn 27572

Mexico
Museo Casa de la Plomada, Vallecillo 28586
Museo de Paleontología, Delicias 27889
Museo de Paleontología de Guadalajara, Guadalajara 27954
Museo de Paleontología de la Preparatoria, Apaxtla de Castrejón 27776
Museo de Paleontología de Rincón Gallardo, General Cepeda 27932
Museo de Paleontología Eliseo Palacios Aguilera, Tuxtla Gutiérrez 28572
Museo José de Jesús Almaza, Xicoténcatl 28621
Museo Palenteológico de la Laguna, Torreón 28559
Museo Universitario de Paleontología, México 28208

Netherlands
Natuurhistorisch Museum Maastricht, Maastricht 29569
Palaeobotanisch Museum, Utrecht 29908
Provincial Natuurhistorisch Museum Natura Docet, Denekamp 29140
Verzameling Steenbakker Ten Bokkel Huinink, Neede 29609

New Zealand
Geology Museum, Auckland 30108

Panama
Museo de Ciencias Naturales, Panamá City 31081

Philippines
Dinosaur Museum, Malabon 31357

Portugal
Museu Nacional de História Natural, Lisboa 32309

Romania
Muzeul de Ştiinte Naturale, Piatra-Neamţ 32567
Muzeul Naţional de Istorie Naturala Grigore Antipa, Bucureşti 32468

Russia
Gosudarstvennyj Geologičeskij Muzej im V.I. Vernadskogo, Moskva 33053
Paleontologičeskij Muzej im. Ju.A. Orlova, Moskva 33170

South Africa
Bernard Price Institute Paleontology Museum, Johannesburg 34271
Molteno Museum, Molteno 34309
South African Museum, Cape Town 34213

Spain
Museo Geominero, Madrid 35037
Museo Paleontologico, Zaragoza 35729
Museo Paleontológico Municipal, Valencia 35610
Museu de l'Institut Paleontològic Miquel Crusafont, Sabadell 35346

Sweden
Evolutionsmuseet, Paleontologi, Uppsala 36354

Switzerland
Geologisch-Mineralogische Ausstellung der Eidgenössischen Technischen Hochschule Zürich, Zürich 37376
Musée de Sciences Naturelles, Vevey 37287
Museo dei Fossili, Meride 36940
Paläontologisches Museum der Universität Zürich, Zürich 37404
Saurier-Museum, Frick 36721
Sauriermuseum Aathal, Aathal-Seegräben 36431

United Kingdom
Bolton Museum and Art Gallery, Bolton 38269
Booth Museum of Natural History, Brighton 38338
Cockburn Museum, Edinburgh 38874
Creetown Gem Rock Museum, Creetown 38662
Dinosaur Isle, Sandown 40444
Dinosaur Museum, Dorchester 38747
Dinosaurland, Lyme Regis 39852
Dorking and District Museum, Dorking 38755
Elgin Museum, Elgin 38925
Planet Earth Museum, Newhaven 40047
Portland Museum, Portland 40245
Staffin Museum, Isle-of-Skye 39318
Tithe Barn Museum and Art Centre, Swanage 40656

U.S.A.
Bergen Museum of Art and Science, Ho-Ho-Kus 44040
Big Bone Lick State Park Museum, Union 48141
Brigham Young University Earth Science Museum, Provo 46733
Dakota Dinosaur Museum, Dickinson 42945
Dinosaur Valley State Park, Glen Rose 43684
Dunn-Seiler Museum, Mississippi State 45402
Fernbank Museum of Natural History, Atlanta 41341
Fick Fossil and History Museum, Oakley 46074
Great Basin National Park, Baker 41436
John Day Fossil Beds National Monument, Kimberly 44481
Mulberry Phospate Museum, Mulberry 45552
Museum of Paleontology, Berkeley 41646
Petrified Creatures Museum of Natural History, Richfield Springs 46853
Ruth Hall Museum of Paleontology, Abiquiu 41059
Stone Museum, Monroe Township 45446
Wyoming Dinosaur Center, Thermopolis 47995

Fresco Painting → Mural Painting and Decoration

Fur → Hides and Skins

Furniture and Interior

Andorra
Museu Casa d'Areny-Plandolit, Ordino 00085

Argentina
Fundación Alfredo L. Palacios, Buenos Aires 00149
Museo Casa Padilla, San Miguel de Tucumán 00580
Museo Municipal de Arte Decorativo Firma y Odilo Estévez, Rosario 00529

Australia
Carrick Hill Museum, Springfield 01469
Clarendon House, Nile 01321
Cooma Cottage, Yass 01629
Dowerin District Museum, Dowerin 00987
Eryldene Heritage House, Gordon 01065
Franklin House, Launceston 01168
Gledswood Farm Museum and Homestead, Catherine Fields 00901
Rippon Lea House Museum, Elsternwick 01014
Rouse Hill Estate, Rouse Hill 01428
White House, Westbury 01595

Austria
Barockschloß Riegersburg, Riegersburg, Niederösterreich 02513
Bauernmöbelmuseum Propstkeusche, Malta 02259
Burgmuseum Ruine Dürnstein, Wildbad-Einöd 03028
Europäisches Museum für Frieden, Stadtschlaining 02673
Geymüller Schlössel, Wien 02889
Hirschbacher Bauernmöbelmuseum, Hirschbach 02030
Kaiserappartements, Sisi Museum und Silberkammer, Wien 02904
Kaiserliche Hofburg zu Innsbruck, Innsbruck 02070
Kaiserliches Hofmobiliendepot, Wien 02906
Kunstsammlungen Palais Schwarzenberg, Wien 02920
Kunstsammlungen und Graphische Sammlung, Furth bei Göttweig 01861
Lehár-Schlößl, Wien 02923
Museum des Zisterzienserstifts mit Margret Bilger-Galerie, Schlierbach 02635
Museum für Sozialkunde und Geschichte des Möbels, Gleisdorf 01881
Oberösterreichisches Freilichtmuseum Sumerauerhof, Sankt Florian 02561
Peter Rosegger-Museum, Krieglach 02165
Sammlungen des Augustiner Chorherrenstiftes, Sankt Florian 02563
Schloß Ambras, Innsbruck 02079
Schloß Peigarten, Dobersberg 01766
Schloß Schönbrunn, Wien 02985
Schloß Tratzberg mit Sammlungen, Jenbach 02087
Thonet-Museum, Friedberg 01853
Volkskundliche und kirchliche Sammlungen, Straßburg 02705

Belgium
Bormshuis, Antwerpen 03136
Design museum Gent, Gent 03435
Hôpital Notre-Dame de la Rose, Lessines 03561
Hotel-Museum Arthur Merghelynck, Ieper 03514
Kantmuseum, Olsene 03663
Musée de Groesbeeck de Croix, Namur 03646
Musée de la Haute Sûre, Martelange 03613
Musée de la Vie Régional des Rièzes et des Sarts, Cul-des-Sarts 03367
Musée du Château des Comtes de Marchin, Modave 03628
Musée Horta, Bruxelles 03330
Museum Onze-Lieve-Vrouw ter Potterie, Brugge 03260
Museum Smidt van Gelder, Antwerpen 03154
Museumkerk Sint Pieter, Rekem 03694
Provinciaal Museum Stijn Streuvels, Ingooigem 03519
Rockoxhuis, Antwerpen 03171
Sint-Dimpna en Gasthuismuseum, Geel 03427
Taxandriamuseum, Turnhout 03806
Le Vieux Logis, Mons 03638

Bermuda
Saint George's Historical Society Museum, Saint George's 03888
Tucker House Museum, Saint George's 03889
Verdmont Historic House Museum, Smith's Parish 03890

Brazil
Casa dos Sete Candeeiros, Salvador 04419
Fundação Eva Klabin Rappaport, Rio de Janeiro 04325
Museu Capela Santa Luzia, Vitória 04590
Museu Carlos Costa Pinto, Salvador 04422
Museu Casa de Rui Barbosa, Rio de Janeiro 04337
Museu da República, Rio de Janeiro 04351
Museu de Arte da Bahia, Salvador 04427
Museu Dom José, Sobral 04552
Museu Mariano Procópio, Juiz de Fora 04158
Museu Municipal, São João Del Rei 04469
Museu Solar Monjardim, Vitória 04592

Canada
Alan Macpherson House, Napanee 05963
Annandale National Historic Site, Tillsonburg 06552
Barbour's General Store Museum, Saint John 06331
Barnum House Museum, Grafton 05506
Battlefield House Museum, Stoney Creek 06492
Billings Estate Museum, Ottawa 06065
Brubacher House Museum, Waterloo 06750
Casa Loma, Toronto 06569
Colborne Lodge, Toronto 06574
Dalnavert Museum, Winnipeg 06822
Daly House Museum, Brandon 05121
Eldon House, London 05763
Erland Lee Museum, Stoney Creek 06493
Ermatinger, Sault Sainte Marie 06411
Eva Brook Donly Museum, Simcoe 06456
Fort La Reine Museum and Pioneer Village, Portage-la-Prairie 06172
Green Gables House, Charlottetown 05226
Green Park Shipbuilding Museum and Yeo House, Port Hill 06164
Grosvenor Lodge, London 05767
Helmcken House Pioneer Doctor's Residence, Victoria 06722
Hillcrest Museum, Souris 06473
Hiscock House, Trinity 06633
Kennedy House, Selkirk 06418
Lieu Historique National du Manoir-Papineau, Montebello 05884
Lucy Maud Montgomery Birthplace, Charlottetown 05228
Maison André-Benjamin-Papineau, Laval 05734
Maison du Calvet, Montréal 05912
Maison Lamontagne, Rimouski 06271
Maison Louis-Hippolyte Lafontaine, Boucherville 05101
Maison Maillou, Québec 06200
Manoir Mauvide-Jenest, Saint-Jean 06325
Milner House, Chatham, Ontario 05240
Musée Place-Royale, Québec 06209
North Hills Museum, Granville Ferry 05523
Peterborough Centennial Museum and Archives, Peterborough 06122
Point Ellice House, Victoria 06728
Proctor House Museum, Brighton 05134
Randall House Museum, Wolfville 06858
Roedde House Museum, Vancouver 06687
Roosevelt Campobello International Park, Welshpool 06768
Saint Marys Museum, Saint Marys 06367
Seven Oaks House Museum, Winnipeg 06845
Twillingate Museum, Twillingate 06652
Valens Log Cabin, Ancaster 04993
Vieux Presbytère de Batiscan, Batiscan 05058
Virden Pioneer Home Museum, Virden 06736
Whitehern Historic House and Garden, Hamilton 05576
Willistead Manor, Windsor, Ontario 06812
Woodchester Villa, Bracebridge 05108
Woodside National Historic Site, Kitchener 05699

Chile
Casa-Museo La Sebastiana, Valparaíso 06926

China, People's Republic
Li Xian Jun Former Residence, Nanjing 07179
Mao Dun Former Residence, Beijing 06972
Song Qingling Former Residence, Shanghai 07224
Song Qingling Tongzhi Former Residence, Beijing 06989
The Taipa Houses Museum, Macau 07170
Zhan Tianyou Former Residence, Wuhan 07283

Colombia
Museo El Castillo Diego Echavarría, Medellín 07517

Croatia
Dvor Trakoščan, Trakoščan 07792
Ivan Meštrović Gallery, Split 07782

Cuba
Castillo de los Tres Reyes del Morro, La Habana 07922
Museo Ambiente Cubano, Gibara 07909
Museo del Ambiente Histórico Cubano, Santiago de Cuba 08141
Museo Doña Rosario, Santiago de Cuba 08146
Museo La Isabelica, Santiago de Cuba 08148
Museo Romántico, Trinidad 08163

Cyprus
House of Hadjigeorgakis Kornesios, Lefkosia 08201

Cyprus, Turkish Republic
Lüzinyan Evi, Lefkoşa 08237

Czech Republic
Expozice Historického Nábytku 16.-19. a Oděvů 19. Století, Turnov 08693
Městské Muzeum, Holešov 08356
Nábytek jako umění a řemeslo, Duchcov 08335
Starý Královsky Palác, Praha 08614
Státní hrad Bouzov, Bouzov 08254

Denmark
Egnsmuseet Ll. Kolstrupgaard, Aabenraa 08761
Gammel Estrup Jyllands Herregårdsmuseum, Auning 08781
Michael og Anna Anchers Hus og Saxilds Gaard, Skagen 09056
Reventlow-Museet Pederstrup, Horslunde 08901
Tønder Museum, Tønder 09094

Dominican Republic
Museo de la Familia Dominicana Siglo XIX, Santo Domingo 09122

Egypt
Luxor Museum of Ancient Art, Al-Uqsur 09234
Qasr Al-Gawharah, Cairo 09285

Estonia
Memme-Taadi Kamber, Karksi 09331

Finland
Alikartano, Numminen 09872
Anjalan Kartanomuseo, Anjalankoski 09414
Askon Museo, Lahti 09739
Hankasalmen Kotiseutumuseo, Hankasalmi 09461
Hvitträsk, Kirkkonummi 09673
Kotkaniemi - Presidentti P.E. Svinhufvudin koti, Luumäki 09803
Lebell Residence, Kristiinankaupunki 09709
Louhisaaren Kartanolinna, Askainen 09420
Museet Ett Hem, Turku 10125
Nivalan Museo Katvala, Nivala 09865
Nokian Kotiseutumuseo, Nokia 09866
Paikkarin Torppa, Sammatti 10020
Pukkilan Kartanomuseo, Piikkiö 09931
Ruiskumestarin Talo, Helsinki 09525
Söderlångvikin Museo, Dragsfjärd 09423
Taivassalon Museo, Taivassalo 10071
Turkansaaren Ulkomuseo, Oulu 09898
Urajärven Kartanomuseo, Urajärvi 10147
Yli-Laurosela Talomuseo, Ilmajoki 09562

France
Château de Bouges, Bouges-le-Château 10831
Château de Langeais, Langeais 12323
Château de Lourmarin, Lourmarin 12701
Château de Saint-Aubin-sur-Loire, Saint-Aubin-sur-Loire 14118
Château du XVIe s, Ancy-le-Franc 10332
Château-Musée de la Grange, Manom 12792
Château Musée Grimaldi, Cagnes-sur-Mer 10986
Château-Musée Renaissance, Azay-le-Rideau 10550
Domaine National de Chambord, Chambord 11146
Institut Tessin, Paris 13517
La Maison de la Dordogne Quercynoise, Souillac 14785
Musée-Château de Saint-Germain-de-Livet, Saint-Germain-de-Livet 14236
Musée Comtois, Besançon 10698
Musée d'Armes Anciennes, La Cluse-et-Mijoux 12157
Musée d'Art et d'Histoire, Dreux 11579
Musée d'Art et d'Histoire de Provence, Grasse 11917
Musée de Jules Gounon-Loubens, Loubens-Lauragais 12672
Musée de la Faucillonnaie, Vitré 15274
Musée de la Folie Marco, Barr 10593
Musée de l'Hôtel de Berny, Amiens 10323
Musée de l'Hôtel-Dieu, Beaune 10647
Musée de l'Hôtel Sandelin, Saint-Omer 14386
Musée Départemental de l'Oise, Beauvais 10655
Musée du Vieux Honfleur, Honfleur 12029
Musée Garinet, Châlons-en-Champagne 11130
Musée Jacquemart-André, Fontaine-Chaalis 11756
Musée Lamartine, Mâcon 12758
Musée Louis-Philippe, Eu 11677
Musée Magnin, Dijon 11530
Musée National des Arts Asiatiques Guimet, Paris 13633
Musée National du Château de Compiègne - Musée du Second Empire, Compiègne 11378
Musée Palais Lascaris, Nice 13324
Parc Château de Valencay, Valençay 15048
Pavillon de Vendôme, Aix-en-Provence 10257

Germany
50er Jahre Erlebniswelt, Zusmarshausen 20771
Alt-Rothenburger Handwerkerhaus, Rothenburg ob der Tauber 19676
Alt-Segeberger Bürgerhaus, Bad Segeberg 15740
Altes Residenztheater, München 18825
Altes und Neues Schloß Eremitage, Bayreuth 15839
Altfriesisches Haus, Sylt-Ost 18595
Antikes Wohnmuseum, Weinheim, Bergstraße 20479
Bauernhausmuseum, Grafenau, Niederbayern 17367
Benedikt-Nimser-Haus, Wilhelmsdorf, Württemberg 20591
Burg Falkenberg, Falkenberg, Oberpfalz 16983
Burg Kronberg, Kronberg 18246
Burg Lauenstein, Ludwigsstadt 18528
Burg Meersburg, Meersburg 18673
Burg zu Burghausen, Burghausen, Salzach 16418
Coburger Puppen-Museum, Coburg 16480
Couven Museum, Aachen 15371
Friesenstube Honkenswarf, Langeneß 18334
Fürstenzimmer im Schloß Kirchheim, Kirchheim unter Teck 18095
Fürstlich Ysenburg- und Büdingensches Schloßmuseum, Büdingen 16397
Gentilhaus, Aschaffenburg 15522
Heimat- und Uhrenmuseum, Villingen-Schwenningen 20317
Heimatmuseum, Grabow, Mecklenburg 17366
Heimatmuseum, Immenstaad 17895
Heimatmuseum Beutelsbach, Weinstadt 20483
Heimatmuseum der Stadt Herrnhut, Herrnhut 17737
Heimatmuseum Spangenberg, Spangenberg 20008
Heimatmuseum Strümpfelbach, Weinstadt 20484
Heimatmuseum Wertach, Wertach 20530
Herrenhaus Altenhof, Altenhof 15453
Herrenhausen-Museum, Hannover 17596
Historische Räume des Stadtschlosses, Fulda 17174
Jenisch Haus, Hamburg 17547
Kavalierhaus Gifhorn- Museum für bürgerliche Wohnkultur, Gifhorn 17287
Kleines Stuck-Museum, Freiburg im Breisgau 17110
König Ludwig II.-Museum, Herrenchiemsee 17733
Kreismuseum, Neuwied 19085
Kulturhistorisches Museum Prenzlau im Dominikanerkloster, Prenzlau 19443
Münchner Stadtmuseum, München 18880
Museum Altes Bürgerhaus, Stolberg, Harz 20067
Museum Burg Falkenstein, Pansfelde 19344
Museum der Stadt Boppard, Boppard 16255
Museum Hohenzollern in Franken, Kulmbach 18269
Museum im Frey-Haus, Brandenburg an der Havel 16284
Museum Knoblauchhaus, Berlin 16063
Museum Nostalgie der 50er Jahre, Burgpreppach 16428
Museum Schloß Burgk, Burgk 16425
Museum Schloß Hundshaupten, Egloffstein 16790
Museum Schloss Lembeck, Dorsten 16654
Museum Schloß Molsdorf, Molsdorf 18785
Museum Schloss Neuenburg, Freyburg 17131
Museum Schloß Rochsburg, Lunzenau 18568
Museum Schloß Weesenstein, Müglitztal 18800
Museum Thonet, Frankenberg, Eder 17026
Museum und Kunstsammlung Schloß Hinterglauchau, Glauchau 17299
Neue Residenz, Bamberg 15814
Neues Schloß Bayreuth, Bayreuth 15857

Neues Schloss Wallerstein, Wallerstein 20380
Plassenburg, Kulmbach 18270
Pompejanum, Aschaffenburg 15527
Renaissance- und Barock-Schloß Weilburg, Weilburg 20446
Residenz und Hofgarten Würzburg, Würzburg 20701
Residenzschloß Oettingen, Oettingen 19237
Römisches Haus - Goethe-Nationalmuseum, Weimar, Thüringen 20469
Sammlung Dr. Irmgard von Lemmers-Danforth, Wetzlar 20559
Schloß Lustheim, Oberschleißheim 19205
Schloß Wernigerode, Wernigerode 20529
Schloß Wilflingen, Langenenslingen 18333
Schlossmuseum, Kirchentellinsfurt 18091
Schlossmuseum Darmstadt, Darmstadt 16548
Schlossmuseum Jever, Jever 17957
Schloßpark Tiefurt, Weimar, Thüringen 20473
Stadtgeschichtliches Museum, Tangermünde 20140
Städtisches Kramer-Museum, Kempen 18058
Stiftung Preußische Schlösser und Gärten Berlin-Brandenburg, Potsdam 19437
Stiftung Schloß Ahrensburg, Ahrensburg 15407
Stiftung Schloß Glücksburg, Glücksburg, Ostsee 17303
Stuhlbau- und Heimatmuseum, Rabenau, Sachsen 19466
Stuhlmuseum Burg Beverungen, Beverungen 16136
Technisches Museum Frohnauer Hammer, Annaberg-Buchholz 15499
Thüringer Landesmuseum Heidecksburg, Rudolstadt 19700
Tucherschloss mit Hirsvogelsaal, Nürnberg 19164
Vogtlandmuseum Plauen, Plauen 19413
Weingutmuseum Hoflößnitz, Radebeul 19471
Wittumspalais - Goethe-Nationalmuseum, Weimar, Thüringen 20476

Greece
Museum of Epirot Folk Art, Metsovon 21071

Guatemala
Museo de Arte colonial, Antigua 21260

Hungary
Fabricius-Ház, Sopron 21532
Nagytétényi Kastélymúzeum, Budapest 21366

India
Darbarhall Museum, Junagadh 21876

Indonesia
Museum Asserajah El Hasyimiah Palace, Bengkalis 22082

Ireland
Bantry House, Bantry 22375
Bunratty Castle and Folkpark, Bunratty 22380
Castletown, Celbridge 22391
Clonalis House, Castlerea 22390
Derrynane House, Caherdaniel 22381
Rothe House Museum, Kilkenny 22488
Tecck an Phiarsaigh, Rosmuck 22536
Westport House, Westport 22557

Israel
Liebermann House, Nahariya 22717

Italy
Appartamenti Monumentali, Firenze 23821
Casa da Noal, Treviso 25803
Casa Natale di A. Rosmini, Rovereto 25290
Castello Malaspina, Bobbio 23093
Civiche Raccolte d'Arte Applicata, Milano 24374
Civico Museo Revoltella e Galleria d'Arte Moderna, Trieste 25817
Civico Museo Sartorio, Trieste 25818
Fondazione Magnani Rocca, Mamiano di Traversetolo 24273
Museo Bagatti Valsecchi, Milano 24386
Museo Civico Casa Cavassa, Saluzzo 25326
Museo d'Arte e Ammobiliamento, Nichelino 24619
Museo del Castello di San Giusto e Lapidario Tergestino, Trieste 25824
Museo della Fondazione Horne, Firenze 23858
Museo dell'Arredo Contemporaneo, Russi 25303
Museo di Palazzo Reale Genova, Genova 23996
Museo e Pinacoteca Nazionale di Palazzo Mansi, Lucca 24230
Palazzina Marfisa, Ferrara 23799
Palazzo Pfanner e Giardino, Lucca 24232
Palazzo Reale, Torino 25765
Rocca Sanvitale, Fontanellato 23905
Villa San Michele, Anacapri 22878
Walsermuseum, Alagna Valsesia 22825

Jamaica
Greenwood Great House Museum, Greenwood 26064

Japan
Kagu no Hakubutsukan, Tokyo 26865
Niitsu House, Niigata 26596

Korea, Republic
Korean Furniture Museum, Seoul 27249

Luxembourg
Palais Grand Ducal, Luxembourg 27569

Malta
Palazzo Armeria, Zurrieq 27719

Mexico
Casa Luis Barragán, México 28092
Museo Casa de León Trotsky, México 28115
Museo Casa del Alfeñique, Puebla 28320
Museo Casa del Marques de Aguayo y Museo Municipal, Mazapil Zacatecas 28075
Museo Colonial del Conde de Sierra Gorda, Santander Jiménez 28436
Museo de las Leyendas, Guanajuato 27971
Museo Ex Hacienda San Gabriel de Barrera, Guanajuato 27975
Museo Jarocho Salvador Ferrando, Tlacotalpan 28520
Museo José María Morelos y Pavón, Cuautla 27871
Museo Palacio de la Canal, San Miguel de Allende 28411
Museo Timoteo L. Hernández, Villaldama 28614

Moldova
Ščusev Museum, Chişinău 28662

Monaco
Palais Princier, Monaco 28672

Namibia
Duwisib Castle, Maltahohe 28761

Netherlands
Borg Verhildersum, Leens 29503
Geelvinck Hinlopen Huis, Amsterdam 28855
Heemkundemuseum Paulus Van Daesdonck, Ulvenhout 29891
Heemkundig Streekmuseum Jan Uten Houte, Etten Leur 29254
Hidde Nijland Museum, Hindeloopen 29422
Hilleshuis Museum, Rotterdam 29751
Huis Verwolde, Laren, Gelderland 29497
Huis Zypendaal, Arnhem 28938
Huize Betje Wolff, Middenbeemster 29599
Jachthuis Sint-Hubertus, Hoenderloo 29429
Kasteel Huis Doorn, Doorn 29167
Kasteel Middachten, De Steeg 29071
Kasteel Rosendael, Rozendaal 29783
Koninklijk Paleis te Amsterdam, Amsterdam 28869
Het Koptisch Museum, Ruinerwold 29785
Muiderslot, Muiden 29604
Museum Ald Slot, Wergea 29992
Museum Beeckestijn, Velsen Zuid 29937
Museum Het Paleis, Den Haag 29110
Museum It Kokelhûs van Jan en Sjut, Earnewald 29189
Museum Spaans Gouvernement, Maastricht 29567
Museum van de Stichting Bisdom van Vliet, Haastrecht 29334
Museum Van Loon, Amsterdam 28879
Museum Willet-Holthuysen, Amsterdam 28882
Museumboerderij Gilde Koat, Zeddam 30049
Museumwoning de Kiefhoek, Rotterdam 29764
Ons Museum, Wintelre 30012
Saksische en Museumboerderij Erve Brooks Niehof, Gelselaar 29270
Schepenzaal Stadhuis, Zwolle 30085
Schultehuis, Diever 29155
Schutterskamer, Sneek 29840
Sint-Pieters Museum op de Lichtenberg, Maastricht 29573
Slot Loevestein, Poederoijen 29714
Stedelijk Museum Zwolle, Zwolle 30086
Verzamelmuseum, Veendam 29927
Wiechers Woon Oase, Dwingeloo 29188
't Wienkeltje van Wullempje, Hoedekenskerke 29426

New Zealand
Alberton, Auckland 30101
Ewelme Cottage, Auckland 30107
Theomin Gallery, Dunedin 30155

Norway
Asker Museum, Hvalstad 30574
Flekkefjord Museum, Flekkefjord 30495
Gamle Bergen Museum, Bergen 30420
Grindheim Bygdemuseum, Kollungtveit 30599
Herregården Museum, Larvik 30631
Leirvika Bygdesamling, Foldereid 30498
Merdøgård, Arendal 30392
Olav Holmegaards Samlinger, Mandal 30665
Roparshaugsamlinga, Isdalstø 30580
Selbu Bygdemuseum, Selbu 30834

Oman
Bait Al Zubair, Muscat 31001

Paraguay
Museo Doctor Francia, Yaguarón 31108

Philippines
Bernandino Jalandoni Ancestral House, Silay 31448
CAP Art Center and Don Sergio Osmeña Memorabilia, Cebu 31307
Casa Manila Museum, Manila 31374

Poland
Muzeum Narodowe w Poznaniu, Oddział w Rogalinie, Rogalin 31947
Muzeum w Oporowie, Oporów 31861
Muzeum Wnętrz Dworskich, Ożarów 31872
Muzeum Wnętrz Pałacowych w Choroszczy, Choroszcz 31532
Muzeum Wsi Lubelskiej, Lublin 31795
Muzeum Zamku w Niedzicy, Niedzica 31823
Muzeum Ziemi Średzkiej Dwór w Koszutach, Koszuty 31679
Pałac Radziwiłłów w Nieborowie, Nieborów 31822
Salonik Chopinów, Warszawa 32141
Zamek Królewski na Wawelu - Państwowe Zbiory Sztuki, Kraków 31729
Zamek w Gniewie, Gniew 31599

Portugal
Casa Museu Bissaya Barreto, Coimbra 32253
Museu Palácio Nacional da Ajuda, Lisboa 32314
Paço dos Duques de Bragança, Guimarães 32279
Palácio Nacional da Pena, Sintra 32351
Palacio Nacional de Queluz, Queluz 32340

Puerto Rico
Dr. Jose Celso Barbose Museum, Bayamón 32363
Museo Casa Blanca, San Juan 32392
Museo Castillo Serrallés, Ponce 32379
Museo José Celso Barbosa, Bazamón 32365

Romania
Muzeul Nicolae Iorga, Vălenii de Munte 32623

Russia
Dom-muzej E.M. Jaroslavskogo, Jakutsk 32840
Dom-muzej Gannibalov v Petrovskom, Puškinskie Gory 33342
Dom-muzej Pavla Kuznecova, Saratov 33505
Dom-muzej Osipovych-Vul'f v Trigorskom, Puškinskie Gory 33343
Dvorec-Muzej Petra I, Sankt-Peterburg 33392
Dvorec-muzej Petra III, Lomonosov 32987
Gosudarstvennyj Istoričeskij Zapovednik Gorki Leninskie, Gorki Leninskie 32807
Gosudarstvennyj Istoriko-ėtnografičeskij Muzej-zapovednik Šušenskoe, Šušenskoe 33569
Jurinskij Istoriko-chudožestvennyj Muzej, Jurino 32863
Memorialnyj Dom-muzej V.M. Vaznecova, Moskva 33077

Serbia-Montenegro
Stalna Izložba Stilskog Namještaja 18.-19. St., Čelarevo 33830

Slovakia
Museum of Home Décor, Kežmarok 34001
Múzeum Červený Kameň, Častá 33985
Nábytkové Múzeum, Markušovce 34021
Slovenské Národné Múzeum - Múzeum Betliar, Betliar 33954

Slovenia
Mestni Muzej Ljubljana, Ljubljana 34111

South Africa
Bertram House Museum, Cape Town 34200
Caledon Museum, Caledon 34198
Campbell Collections, Durban 34224
Drostdy Museum, Swellendam 34389
Dunluce House Museum, Kimberley 34288
Gately House, East London 34237
Graaf-Reinet Museum, Graaff-Reinet 34246
Great Fish River Museum, Cradock 34220
Jansen Collection, Pretoria 34344
Koopmans-De Wet House Museum, Cape Town 34206
Macrorie House Museum, Pietermaritzburg 34326
Marie Rawdon Museum, Matjiesfontein 34306
Montagu Museum, Montagu 34310
Natale Labia Museum, Muizenberg 34312
Old House Museum, Durban 34230
De Oude Drostdy, Tulbagh 34390
Oude Kerk Volksmuseum, Tulbagh 34391
Our Heritage Museum, Adelaide 34169
Richmond Museum, Richmond 34367
Rudd House Museum, Kimberley 34293
Somerset East Museum, Somerset East 34379
Stellenbosch Museum, Stellenbosch 34383
Temlett House, Grahamstown 34254
Worcester Museum, Worcester 34405

Spain
Casa de Pilatos, Sevilla 35473
Colección Vivot, Palma de Mallorca 35224
L'Enrajolada Casa-Museu Santacana, Martorell 35094
Museu Romantic Can Papiol, Vilanova i la Geltrú 35667

Sweden
Charlotte Berlins Museum, Ystad 36420
Ebbas Hus, Malmö 36072
Ekenäs Slott, Linköping 36039
Friluftmuseet Skansen, Stockholm 36242
Gustav III.'s Paviljong, Solna 36218
Julita Sveriges Lantbruksmuseums, Julita 35985
Kattlunds Museigård, Havdhem 35946
Läckö Slott, Lidköping 36033
Lundströmska Gården, Sigtuna 36182
Möbelindustrimuseum i Virserum, Virserum 36412
Nobynäs Säteri, Aneby 35801
Petes Museigård, Havdhem 35947
Rosendals Slott, Stockholm 36278
Skidans Hus, Boden 35836
Stjernsunds Slott, Askersund 35822
Sunnansjö Herrgård Galleri, Sunnansjö 36310
Svaneholms Slott, Skurup 36203
Ulriksdals Slott, Solna 36223

Switzerland
Château de Grandson, Grandson 36776
Château et Musée de Valangin, Valangin 37275
Engadiner Museum, Sankt Moritz 37112
Heimatmuseum Allschwil, Allschwil 36446
Heimatmuseum Schanfigg, Arosa 36469
Heimatmuseum Unterengadin, Scuol 37153
Musée Régional du Vieux-Coppet, Coppet 36648
Museum Bärengasse, Zürich 37394
Museum für Wohnkultur des Historismus und des Jugendstils, Hilterfingen 36803
Museum Langmatt, Baden 36488
Palazzo Castelmur, Stampa 37203
Plantahaus - Chesa Planta, Samedan 37095
Schloß Tarasp, Tarasp 37229
Schloßmuseum, Oberhofen am Thunersee 37000

Turkey
Osmalı Evi, Bursa 37647

Ukraine
Alupka State Palace and Park Preserve, Alupka 37834
The Bleschunov Municipal Museum of Personal Collections, Odessa 37896

United Kingdom
Anne Hathaway's Cottage, Stratford-upon-Avon 40624
Ardress House and Farmyard Museum, Annaghmore 38002
The Argory, Dungannon 38811
Arreton Manor, Arreton 38023
Ascott House, Leighton Buzzard 39473
Astley Hall Museum and Art Gallery, Chorley 38574
Aston Hall, Birmingham 38209
Athelhampton House, Dorchester 38746
Attingham Park, Shrewsbury 40506
Audley End House, Saffron Walden 40366
Banqueting House, London 39573
Belgrave Hall and Gardens, Leicester 39459
Belton House, Grantham 39110
Bishops' House Museum, Sheffield 40482
Blackwell - The Arts and Crafts House, Bowness-on-Windermere 38290
Bolling Hall Museum, Bradford 38294
Brodsworth Hall Gardens, Doncaster 38740
Buckland Abbey, Yelverton 40953
Building of Bath Museum, Bath 38113
Burton Constable Hall, Kingston-upon-Hull 39376
Castle Ward, Downpatrick 38772
Chethams's Hospital and Library, Manchester 39885
Chiswick House, London 39606
Church Farmhouse Museum, London 39607
Clarke Hall, Wakefield 40759
Claydon House, Middle Claydon 39944
Clergy House, Alfriston 37975
Cotehele House, Saint Dominick 40392
Cottage Museum, Lancaster 39411
Crathes Castle, Banchory 38078
Croxteth Hall, Liverpool 39517
Dalemain Historic House, Penrith 40175
Dan Winters House - Ancestral Home, Loughgall 39833
Drumlanrig Castle, Thornhill, Dumfriesshire 40704
Dudmaston House, Quatt 40276
Dunham Massey Hall, Altrincham 37992
East Riddlesden Hall, Keighley 39328
Eltham Palace, London 39631
English Heritage South East Region, Guildford 39135
English Heritage South West Region, Bristol 38354
Epworth Old Rectory, Epworth 38945
Erddig Agricultural Museum, Wrexham 40940
Fairfax House Museum, York 40962
Felbrigg Hall, Norwich 40093
Fenton House, London 39634
Firle Place, Firle 38993
Florence Court House, Enniskillen 38940
Florence Nightingale Museum, Aylesbury 38047
Ford Green Hall, Stoke-on-Trent 40606
Gainsborough Old Hall, Gainsborough 39021
Geffrye Museum, London 39641
Georgian House, Bristol 38355
The Georgian House, Edinburgh 38884
Glamis Castle, Glamis 39037
Guildhall, Bath 38114
Haddo House, Methlick 39941
Haden Hall, Cradley Heath 38653
Haden Hill House, Cradley Heath 38654
Hall-I'Th'-Wood Museum, Bolton 38271
Hall's Croft, Stratford-upon-Avon 40625
Hampton Court Palace, East Molesey 38848
Hardwick Hall, Chesterfield 38555
Haremere Hall, Etchingham 38949
Harewood House, Harewood 39161
Hauteville House, Saint Peter Port 40425
Heaton Hall, Manchester 39888
Hellen's House, Much Marcle 39992
Hezlett House, Coleraine 38618
Hill House, Helensburgh 39208
Hill of Tarvit Mansion House, Cupar 38688
Hinchingbrooke House, Huntingdon 39278
Hopetoun House, South Queensferry 40535
Ickworth House, Horringer 39262
Inveraray Castle, Inveraray 39294
Judges' Lodgings, Lancaster 39412
Kelmscott Manor, Kelmscott 39332
Kirkham House, Paignton 40159
Knebworth House, Knebworth 39402
Knole, Sevenoaks 40474
Lennoxlove House, Haddington 39143
Lydiard House, Swindon 40662
Lytham Hall, Lytham Saint Anne's 39858
Manor House, Donington-le-Heath 38745
Mary Arden's House and the Countryside Museum, Stratford-upon-Avon 40627
Melford Hall, Long Melford 39823
Michelham Priory, Hailsham 39147

Mount Edgcumbe House, Cremyll 38664
Mount Stewart House, Newtownards 40074
Nash's House and New Place, Stratford-upon-Avon 40628
National Portrait Gallery, Montacute 39979
Normanby Hall, Scunthorpe 40458
Nostell Priory, Wakefield 40762
Number 1 Royal Crescent Museum, Bath 38120
Oak House Museum, West Bromwich 40822
Oakwell Hall Country Park, Birstall 38235
Old Bridge House Museum, Dumfries 38790
Old House, Hereford 39228
Osborne House, East Cowes 38839
Packwood House, Lapworth 39424
Plas Newydd, Llangollen 39555
Preston Manor, Brighton 38342
Provan Hall House, Glasgow 39061
Provost Skene's House, Aberdeen 37942
Queen Charlotte's Cottage, Richmond, Surrey 40321
Rainham Hall, Rainham 40278
Red Lodge, Bristol 38359
Revolution House, Chesterfield 38557
Royal Pavilion, Brighton 38344
Rufford Old Hall, Rufford 40353
Scone Palace, Perth 40187
Seaton Delaval Hall, Seaton 40462
Selly Manor Museum, Birmingham 38228
Shakespeare Birthplace Trust, Stratford-upon-Avon 40630
Shibden Hall Museum, Halifax 39156
Shrewsbury Castle, Shrewsbury 40510
Smithills Hall Museum, Bolton 38272
Southchurch Hall Museum, Southend-on-Sea 40554
Southside House, London 39781
Spencer House, London 39782
Springhill House, Magherafelt 39872
Stourhead House, Stourton 40617
Strangers Hall Museum of Domestic Life, Norwich 40102
Stratfield Saye House and Wellington Exhibition, Stratfield Saye 40623
Sulgrave Manor, Sulgrave 40643
Syon House, London 39786
Tenement House, Glasgow 39069
Town House Museum of Lynn Life, King's Lynn 39372
Treasurer's House, York 40968
Trevithick Cottage, Camborne 38449
Tudor House Museum, Southampton 40549
Turton Tower, Turton Bottoms 40736
Ugbrooke House, Chudleigh 38580
The Vyne, Basingstoke 38104
Wallington Hall, Cambo 38447
Walmer Castle, Walmer 40770
Wightwick Manor, Wolverhampton 40917
Wilton House, Wilton, Salisbury 40878
Woburn Abbey, Woburn 40912
Wythenshawe Hall, Manchester 39905

U.S.A.
Ace of Clubs House, Texarkana 47990
Adsmore Museum, Princeton 46697
Alexander Ramsey House, Saint Paul 47151
Amos Herr House, Landisville 44635
The Apple Trees Museum, Burlington 41995
Ashtabula Plantation, Pendleton 46336
Barbara Fritchie House, Frederick 43525
Baxter House Museum, Gorham 43730
Beauchamp Newman Museum, Elizabeth 43131
Beauport-Sleeper-McCann House, Gloucester 43701
Bloom Mansion, Trinidad 48063
Boscobel Restoration, Garrison 43630
Burnside Plantation, Bethlehem 41664
Byers-Evans House Museum, Denver 42879
Campbell Whittlesey House, Rochester 46939
Carlen House, Mobile 45418
Carpenter Home Museum, Cle Elum 42446
Casa Navarro, San Antonio 47247
Cedar Grove Mansion, Philadelphia 46396
Chief John Ross House, Rossville 47011
Chinqua-Penn Plantation, Reidsville 46832
Codman House - The Grange, Lincoln 44776
Collinsville Depot Museum, Collinsville 42531
Copper King Mansion, Butte 42017
Cranbrook House and Gardens Auxiliary, Bloomfield Hills 41739
Crowninshield-Bentley House, Salem 47192
Cuneo Museum, Vernon Hills 48220
Cupola House, Egg Harbor 43100
Darnall's Chance, Upper Marlboro 48157
David Conklin Farmhouse, Huntington 44159
Derby-Beebe Summer House, Salem 47193
Dinsmore Homestead History Museum, Burlington 41999
Donkey Milk House, Key West 44462
Dumbarton House, Washington 48350
Dyckman Farmhouse Museum, New York 45795
Edison and Ford Winter Estates, Fort Myers 43434
Elizabeth Perkins House, York 48787
Excelsior House, Jefferson 44324
Ezekiel Harris House, Augusta 41381
Fabyan Villa Museum and Dutch Windmill, Geneva 43640
Fairbanks House, Dedham 42841
Fairlawn Mansion and Museum, Superior 47890
Fall River County Historical Museum, Hot Springs 44110
Fort Columbia House Museum, Chinook 42386
Gardner-Pingree House, Salem 47194
General Adam Stephen House, Martinsburg 45191
General Wait House, Waitsfield 48277
Gertrude Smith House, Mount Airy 45522
Gilbert House, Atlanta 41346
Glenn House, Cape Girardeau 42095
Gracie Mansion, New York 45808
Granger House, Marion 45155
Groton Historical Museum, Groton 43846
Hamilton House, South Berwick 47685
Hanley House, Clayton 42442
Harvey House Museum, Florence 43347
Henry Clay Frick Estate, Pittsburgh 46517
Heyward-Washington House, Charleston 42218
Hill-Hold Museum, Montgomery 45470
The Hill House, Portsmouth 46661
Hillforest House Museum, Aurora 41400
Historic General Dodge House, Council Bluffs 42673
Historic Newton Home, Decatur 42836
Historic Rosedale, Charlotte 42240
Hixon House, La Crosse 44536
Howard-Dickinson House Museum, Henderson 43993
Jacob Kelley House Museum, Hartsville 43949
James Dunklin House, Laurens 44681
Jeremiah Lee Mansion, Marblehead 45134
John Jay Homestead, Katonah 44415
John Wornall House Museum, Independence 44205
Josiah Quincy House, Quincy 46764
Julian H. Sleeper House, Saint Paul 47158
Kelly-Griggs House Museum, Red Bluff 46813
Kentucky New State Capitol, Frankfort 43511
Kimball House Museum, Battle Creek 41538
Lexington County Museum, Lexington 44756
Locust Grove, Poughkeepsie 46675
Locust Lawn and Terwilliger House, Gardiner 43621
Longfellow-Evangeline State Historic Site, Saint Martinville 47142
Loudoun Mansion, Philadelphia 46424
Lyle-Tapley Shoe Shop and Vaughn Doll House, Salem 47197
Mallory-Neely House, Memphis 45240
Mary Todd Lincoln House, Lexington 44743
Merchant's House Museum, New York 45832
Merwin House Tranquility, Stockbridge 47817
Molly Brown House Museum, Denver 42892
Montpelier Cultur Arts Center, Laurel 44677
Montpellier Mansion, Laurel 44678
Moss Mansion Museum, Billings 41688
Mount Clare Museum House, Baltimore 41481
Mount Pleasant, Philadelphia 46428
National Trust for Historic Preservation, Washington 48385
Old Constitution House, Windsor 48686
Old Hoxie House, Sandwich 47387
Old Westbury Gardens, Old Westbury 46136
Orlando Brown House, Frankfort 43514
Parry Mansion Museum, New Hope 45706
Pearl S. Buck House, Perkasie 46352
Peirce-Nichols House, Salem 47199
Pena-Peck House, Saint Augustine 47070
Phelps House, Burlington 41998
Philipse Manor Hall, Yonkers 48786
Pierrepont Museum, Canton 42085
Pieter Claesen Wyckoff House Museum, Brooklyn 41949
Pointe Coupee Museum, New Roads 45745
Pownalborough Court House, Dresden 42987
Propst House and Marple Grove, Hickory 44008
Rebecca Nurse Homestead, Danvers 42775
Restoration House, Mantorville 45129
Richards-Dar House, Mobile 45424
Riordan Mansion, Flagstaff 43331
Rising Sun Tavern, Fredericksburg 43541
Robert Fulton Birthplace, Quarryville 46754
Rosemont Plantation, Woodville 48744
Rotch-Jones-Duff House and Garden Museum, New Bedford 45663
Rothschild House, Port Townsend 46608
Sagamore Hill National Historic Site, Oyster Bay 46250
Sam Brown Memorial Park, Browns Valley 41963
Sayward-Wheeler House, York Harbor 48797
Schmidt House Museum, Grants Pass 43768
Scotchtown, Beaverdam 41575
Seguine House, Staten Island 47786
The Shadows-on-the-Teche, New Iberia 45708
The Stephen Girard Collection, Philadelphia 46456
The Stephen Phillips Memorial House, Salem 47203
Stone-Tolan House, Rochester 46945
Stuart House City Museum, Mackinac Island 45031
Taft Museum of Art, Cincinnati 42410
Taylor Brown and Sarah Dorsey House, Midland 45330
Thomas Jefferson House Monticello, Charlottesville 42252
Tinker Swiss Cottage Museum, Rockford 46964
Tullis-Toledano Manor, Biloxi 41697
Turner House Museum, Hattiesburg 43958
United States Department of the Interior Museum, Washington 48400
Victoria Mansion, Portland 46628
Wakefield House Museum, Blue Earth 41755
Ward Hall, Georgetown 43652
Waveland Museum, Lexington 44747
Wentworth Gardner and Tobias Lear Houses, Portsmouth 46656
Westover House, Charles City 42204
Wharton Esherick Museum, Malvern 45087
White Hall Historic Site, Richmond 46865
Will Rogers State Historic Park, Pacific Palisades 46254
The Willard House, Evanston 43243
Winslow Crocker House, Yarmouth Port 48780
Woodburn Plantation, Pendleton 46338
Wyck Museum, Philadelphia 46464

Venezuela
Casa San Isidro, Ciudad Bolívar 48932
Museo Biblioteca Rosauro Rosa Acosta, Pampatar 48959
Museo Inés Mercedes Gómez Álvarez, Guanare 48944

Games → Toys and Games

Gas → Petroleum Industry and Trade

Gems → Precious Stones

Genealogy

Australia
Australian Institute of Genealogical Studies, Blackburn 00808
Hope Cottage, Kingscote 01149

Austria
Esterházy-Ausstellung, Eisenstadt 01808
Großer Wappensaal im Landhaus, Klagenfurt 02124
Kammerhofmuseum der Stadt Gmunden, Gmunden 01896

Canada
Alberton Museum, Alberton 04972
Beaconsfield Historic House, Charlottetown 05224

Korea, Republic
Royal Museum, Seoul 27267

Latvia
Kurzemes Hercogu Kapenes, Jelgava 27366

Mexico
Museo Norawa, Guachochi 27940

Netherlands
Huygens Museum Hofwijck, Voorburg 29961
Museum Buren en Oranje, Buren, Gelderland 29043

New Zealand
Albertland and Districts Museum, Wellsford 30312
Waipu Heritage Centre, Waipu 30277

Philippines
Balay Negrense Museum, Silay 31447
Clarin Ancestral House, Loay 31344
Teodoro P. Resurreccion Memorial Museum, Luna 31348

South Africa
Huguenot Memorial Museum, Franschhoek 34242

Spain
Museo de Heráldica Alavesa, Mendoza 35109

United Kingdom
Clare Ancient House Museum, Clare 38585
Greenwich Local History Centre, London 39650
Mountbatten Exhibition, Romsey 40340

U.S.A.
Anoka County Historical and Genealogical Museum, Anoka 41232
Bellflower Genealogical and Historical Society Museum, Bellflower 41600
Camden Archives and Museum, Camden 42063
Dyer Memorial Library, Abington 41056
Fryer Memorial Museum, Munnsville 45561
Mayville Area Museum of History and Genealogy, Mayville 45209
Northampton County Historical and Genealogical Society Museum, Easton 43070
Saint Marys and Benzinger Township Museum, Saint Marys 47145
Town of Clarence Museum, Clarence 42424
Union County Museum, Lewisburg 44724

Geography

Austria
Lungauer Landschaftsmuseum, Mauterndorf 02286

Brazil
Museu Histórico e Geográfico de Poços de Caldas, Poços de Caldas 04271

France
Maison des Sirènes et des Siréniens, Castellane 11071

Germany
Universum Science Center Bremen, Bremen 16337

Italy
Museo della Società Geografica Italiana, Roma 25196

Netherlands
Abel Tasman Kabinet, Lutjegast 29553

Poland
Muzeum-Dworek Wincentego Pola, Lublin 31789

Russia
Russkij Gosudarstvennyj Muzej Arktiki i Antarktiki, Sankt-Peterburg 33479

Switzerland
Museum Langenthal, Langenthal 36846

United Kingdom
National Maritime Museum Cornwell, Falmouth 38973
Tower Bridge Exhibition, London 39791

U.S.A.
Explorers Hall, Washington 48352

Geology

Angola
Museu de Geológia, Paleontológia e Mineralógia, Luanda 00097

Argentina
Museo Mineralógico Prof. Manuel Tellechea, Mendoza 00439

Armenia
Geological Museum of the Institute of Geology, Erevan 00681

Australia
Albert Kersten GeoCentre, Broken Hill 00845
E. de C. Clarke Geological Museum, Crawley 00952
Norseman Historical and Geological Collection, Norseman 01324
School of Earth Sciences Museum, Townsville 01548
Tasmanian Museum and Art Gallery, Hobart 01106

Austria
Burgenländisches Landesmuseum, Eisenstadt 01806
Burgenländisches Steinmuseum, Landsee 02181
Geologische Sammlung Schloß Kapfenstein, Kapfenstein 02097
Geologisches Freilichtmuseum, Gmünd, Niederösterreich 01891
Landesmuseum Joanneum, Graz 01922
Mineralien-Fossilien-Bergbau, Langenlois 02185
Mineralienschau, Afritz 01647
Naturkundemuseum Haus der Natur, Salzburg 02545
Städtisches Museum, Schärding 02623
Terra Mystica, Bad Bleiberg 01693
Turmmuseum, Pillichsdorf 02415

Bangladesh
Geological Survey Museum, Dhaka 03088

Belgium
Musée de Minéralogie et de Géologie, Bruxelles 03313
Musée du Monde Souterrain, Han-sur-Lesse 03474
Musée Hydrogéologique, Chaudfontaine 03356

Brazil
Museu de Geociências, São Paulo 04522
Museu de Geociências da Universidade de Brasília, Brasília 03999
Museu de Geologia, Maringá 04200
Museu Geológico da Bahia, Salvador 04436
Museu Geológico Valdemar Lefèvre, São Paulo 04535

Canada
Banff Park Museum, Banff 05041
Daredevil Hall of Fame, Niagara Falls 05988
Miller Museum of Geology, Kingston 05683
Musée de Geologie, Sainte-Foy 06384
Museum of Geology, Edmonton 05381
M.Y. Williams Planet Earth Museum, Vancouver 06684

China, People's Republic
The Geological Museum of China, Beijing 06965

Colombia
Museo Casa Colonial, Pamplona 07543
Museo de Geología y Suelos, Armenia 07371
Museo de Historia Natural, Alta Suiza 07365
Museo Geológico José Royo y Gómez, Bogotá 07422
Museo Geológico Marino Arce Herrera, Bucaramanga 07439

Congo, Democratic Republic
Musée Geologique Sengier-Cousin, Jadotville 07632

Croatia
Hrvatski Narodni Zoološki Muzej, Zagreb 07821

Cuba
Museo del Transporte Terrestre, Santiago de Cuba 08145

Czech Republic
Krkonošské Muzeum, Jilemnice 08392
Městské Muzeum, Čáslav 08288

Městské Muzeum a Galerie T.F. Simona, Železnice 08746
Muzeum Těšínska, Český Těšín 08305
Okresní Vlastivědné Muzeum a Galerie, Česká Lípa 08294
Podhorácké Muzeum, Tišnov 08682
Rožmberský Dům, Soběslav 08658
Sládečkovo Vlastivědné Muzeum v Kladně, Kladno 08410

Denmark
Midtsønderjyllands Museum, Gram 08840
Naturhistorisk Museum, Århus 08772

Egypt
Cairo Geological Museum, Cairo 09257

Estonia
Tartu Ülikooli Geoloogiamuuseum, Tartu 09387

Finland
Kivimuseo, Helsinki 09502
Kivimuseo, Tampere 10078

France
Les Fosses d'Enfer, Saint-Rémy-sur-Orne 14454
Musée de l'Institut de Géologie et de Géoscience de Rennes, Rennes (Ille-et-Vilaine) 13942
Musée d'Histoire Naturelle de Toulon, Toulon (Var) 14928
Musée d'Histoire Naturelle et de Géologie, Lille 12601
Musée Geologique, Vernet-les-Bains 15137
Musée Régional de Géologie Pierre Vetter, Decazeville 11490
Museum de Géologie Provençale, La Roque-d'Anthéron 12255
Muséum d'Histoire Naturelle, Nice 13326

Germany
Audorfer Museum im Burgtor, Oberaudorf 19169
Bachmann-Museum Bremervörde, Bremervörde 16346
Deutsches Erdölmuseum Wietze, Wietze 20583
Deutsches Schiefermuseum Steinach/Thür., Steinach, Thüringen 20041
Dobergmuseum/Geologisches Museum Ostwestfalen-Lippe, Bünde 16403
Dr.-Carl-Haeberlin-Friesen-Museum, Wyk auf Föhr 20726
Eifelmuseum, Mayen 18668
Fossilien- und Heimatmuseum, Messel 18718
Geiseltalmuseum der Martin-Luther-Universität, Halle, Saale 17512
Geologisch-Paläontologisches Museum, Münster 18937
Geologische Landessammlung von Vorpommern, Greifswald 17388
Geologisches Museum der DSK-Saar, Saarbrücken 19723
Geologisches Museum München, München 18853
Geologisches und Mineralogisches Museum der Christian-Albrechts-Universität, Kiel 18072
GeoMuseum der Universität, Köln 18139
Geosammlung der Technischen Universität Clausthal, Clausthal-Zellerfeld 16475
Geowissenschaftliche Sammlungen, Freiberg, Sachsen 17099
Haus des Gastes mit heimatkundlicher Sammlung, Gößweinstein 17331
Heimatecke am Seifenbach, Beierfeld 15868
Heimatmuseum, Camburg 16450
Heimatmuseum, Mügeln bei Oschatz 18799
Heimatmuseum Bad Laer, Bad Laer 15686
Heimatmuseum Betzenstein, Betzenstein 16132
Heimatmuseum der Marktgemeinde Wiggensbach, Wiggensbach 20584
Heimatmuseum Günzburg, Günzburg 17455
Heimatmuseum Spangenberg, Spangenberg 20008
Heimatstuben im Oberen Tor, Scheinfeld 19771
Höhlenkundemuseum Dechenhöhle, Iserlohn 17921
Höhlenmuseum Kubacher Kristallhöhle und Freilicht-Steinemuseum, Weilburg 20445
Informationsstelle des Naturparks Fichtelgebirge, Zell, Oberfranken 20742
Institut und Museum für Geologie und Paläontologie, Tübingen 20225
Jura-Museum, Eichstätt 16805
Kreisheimatmuseum Weißes Haus, Rotenburg an der Fulda 19670
Kreismuseum Bad Liebenwerda, Bad Liebenwerda 15692
Landschaftsinformationszentrum (LIZ) Hessisches Kegelspiel Rasdorf, Rasdorf 19485
Müritz-Museum, Waren 20399
Muschelkalkmuseum Hagdorn, Ingelfingen 17898
Museum am Lindenbühl, Mühlhausen, Thüringen 18807
Museum der Natur, Gotha 17360
Museum der Natur und Umwelt Cottbus, Cottbus 16503
Museum der Westlausitz Kamenz, Kamenz 17979
Museum Dermbach, Dermbach 16575
Museum für Archäologie und Volkskunde, Kösching 18188
Museum für Geologie und Paläontologie am Geowissenschaftlichen Zentrum der Universität Göttingen, Göttingen 17337
Museum für Mineralogie und Geologie, Dresden 16700
Museum für Natur und Umwelt, Lübeck 18539
Museum für Naturkunde, Dortmund 16663
Museum für Naturkunde der Stadt Gera, Gera 17245
Museum Geologie/Paläontologie, Heidelberg 17670
Museum im Stadtpark, Grevenbroich 17398
Museum Schloß Bernburg, Bernburg 16125
Naturhistorisches Museum, Mainz 18605
Naturkunde-Museum, Bielefeld 16159
Naturkundemuseum Erfurt, Erfurt 16907
Naturkundemuseum Ostbayern, Regensburg 19528
Naturkundliche Sammlung, Königsbrunn 18174
Paläontologisches Museum München, München 18893
Peter-Wiepert-Museum, Burg auf Fehmarn 16410
Regionalmuseum Wolfhagen, Wolfhagen 20655
Rieskrater-Museum, Nördlingen 19108
Sieblos-Museum Poppenhausen, Poppenhausen, Wasserkuppe 19428
Stadtmuseum Coesfeld und Städtische Turmgalerie, Coesfeld 16491
Stadtmuseum Schelklingen, Schelklingen 19772
Stadtmuseum Schlüsselfeld, Schlüsselfeld 19806
Stadtmuseum Stadtoldendorf, Stadtoldendorf 20033
Städtisches Museum, Aschersleben 15536
Südmährisches Landschaftsmuseum, Geislingen an der Steige 17219
Südostbayerisches Naturkunde- und Mammut-Museum, Siegsdorf 19953
Urwelt-Museum Oberfranken, Bayreuth 15860
Waldnaabtal-Museum in der Burg Neuhaus, Windischeschenbach 20607

Ghana
Geology Museum, Legon 20798

Greece
Museum of Mineralogy, Petrology and Geology, Zografou 21226
Natural History Museum of the Aegean, Samos 21149
Paleontological and Geological Museum of the University of Athens, Athinai 20900

Guinea
Musée Géologique, Conakry 21281

Hungary
Országos Geológia Múzeum, Budapest 21372

India
Geological Museum, Varanasi 22057
Geology and Geophysics Museum, Roorkee 22005
Geology Museum, Lucknow 21926
Government Museum, Chennai 21744

Indonesia
Museum Geologi, Bandung 22072

Iran
Geological Museum, Teheran 22299

Ireland
Earth Science Museum, Dublin 22424
Geological Museum, Dublin 22428

Israel
Yotvata Museum and Visitors Center, Yotvata 22785

Italy
Civico Museo Naturalistico Ferruccio Lombardi, Stradella 25640
Collezioni Naturalistiche del Museo Comunale, Imola 24084
Museo Astronomico e Geofisico, Modena 24437
Museo Civico Craveri di Storia Naturale, Bra 23193
Museo Civico della Val Fiorentina Vittorino Cazzetta, Selva di Cadore 25531
Museo Civico di Scienze Naturali ed Archeologia della Valdinievole, Pescia 24876
Museo Civico di Storia Naturale, Ferrara 23787
Museo Civico Geologia e Etnografia, Predazzo 25051
Museo di Geologia, Camerino 23286
Museo di Geologia, Napoli 24592
Museo di Geologia, Roma 25213
Museo di Geologia e Paleontologia, Firenze 23866
Museo di Geologia e Paleontologia, Padova 24740
Museo di Scienza dela Terra, San Gemini 25359
Museo di Scienze della Terra U. Baroli, Crodo 23687
Museo di Storia Naturale dell'Accademia dei Fisocritici, Siena 25576
Museo Geo-Paleontologico, Ferrara 23794
Museo Geologico, Castell'Arquato 23407
Museo Geopaleontologico Alto Aventino, Arielli 22933
Museo Geopaleontologico del Castello, Lerici 24179
Museo Geopaleontologico Naturalistico Antropico e Ornitologico Brancaleoni, Piobbico 24934
Museo Sardo di Geologia e Paleontologia D. Lovisato, Cagliari 23254
Museo Vesuviano G. B. Alfano, Pompei 24986

Jamaica
Geology Museum, Kingston 26067

Japan
Fossa Magna Museum, Itoigawa 26266
Hiratsuka-shi Hakubutsukan, Hiratsuka 26208
Omi Natural History Museum, Omi 26637
Saito Ho-on Kai Shizenshi Hakubutsukan, Sendai 26734

Jordan
Geology Museum, Amman 27049

Madagascar
Musée National de Géologie, Antananarivo 27604

Malaysia
Geological Survey Museum, Ipoh 27621

Mexico
Museo de Geología de la UNAM, México 28129
Museo de Geología del IPN, México 28130
Museo de Geología Dr. Jenaro González Reyna, Morelia 28247
Museo de Mineralogía y Geología Ing. Luis Silva Ruelas, Morelia 28250

Mozambique
Museu Nacional de Geologia, Maputo 28726

Namibia
Geological Survey Museum, Windhoek 28779

Netherlands
Artis Geologisch Museum, Amsterdam 28842
Gelders Geologisch Museum, Velp 29936
Geologisch Museum Hofland, Laren, Noord-Holland 29498
Geologisch Streek-Museum de Ijsselvallei, Olst 29660
Kristalmuseum 't Los Hoes, Borculo 28999
Museum Freriks, Winterswijk 30014
Natuurmuseum Groningen, Groningen 29313
Oudheidkamer Heerde, Heerde 29359
Stenenexpositie de Molen - Museum Batjuchin, Borculo 29003

New Zealand
Alexander McKay Geological Museum, Wellington 30291
Geology Museum of the University of Otago, Dunedin 30148
Institute of Geological and Nuclear Sciences, Hutt City 30181

Norway
Geologisk Museum, Oslo 30735
Natural History Museum, Oslo 30747
Norsk Bremuseum, Fjærland 30491

Pakistan
Museum of Historical Geology and Geological Survey of Pakistan, Quetta 31054

Peru
Museo Geológico de la Universidad Nacional de Ingeniería del Perú, Lima 31219

Poland
Muzeum Geologiczne, Kraków 31703
Muzeum Geologiczne, Wrocław 32177
Muzeum Geologiczne Państwowego Instytutu Geologicznego, Warszawa 32098
Muzeum Geologiczne Uniwersytetu Szczecińskiego, Szczecin 32025
Muzeum Geologii Złóż im. Czesława Poborskiego, Gliwice 31592
Muzeum Górnicze, Bogatynia 31503
Muzeum Okręgowe, Konin 31672
Muzeum Puszczy Kampinoskiej, Kampinos 31639
Muzeum w Sosnowcu, Sosnowiec 31991
Muzeum Zbiorów Geologicznych, Kielce 31663
Muzeum Ziemi Polskiej Akademii Nauk, Warszawa 32137

Portugal
Museu Nacional de História Natural, Lisboa 32309

Russia
Centralnyj Geologorazvedočnyj Muzej im. Akademika F.N. Černyševa, Sankt-Peterburg 33383
Geologičeskij Muzej, Vorkuta 33727
Geologičeskij Muzej im. A.A. Černova, Syktyvkar 33572
Geologo-mineralogičeskij Muzej, Kazan 32888
Geologo-mineralogičeskij Muzej im. A.I. Kozlova, Vladivostok 33697
Gornyj Muzej, Sankt-Peterburg 33396
Gosudarstvennyj Geologičeskij Muzej im V.I. Vernadskogo, Moskva 33053
Muzei Permskogo Gosudarstvennogo Universiteta, Perm 33304
Muzej Geologii, Čeljabinsk 32727
Muzej Geologii Centralnoj Sibirii, Krasnojarsk 32955
Muzej Geologii, Nefti i Gaza, Tjumen 33603
Narodnyj Geologičeskij Muzej Volgageologija, Nižnij Novgorod 33221
Ore-Petrographic Museum, Moskva 33167
Paleontologo-stratigrafičeskij Muzej pri Kafedre Istorii Geologii, Sankt-Peterburg 33474
Regionalnyj Muzej Severnogo Priladožja, Sortavala 33547
Udivitelnoe v Kamne - Muzej Mineralov, Rud, Samocvetov, Teberda 33598
Uralskij Geologičeskij Muzej V.V. Vachruševa, Ekaterinburg 32783

Rwanda
Musée Géologique du Rwanda, Kigali 33754

St. Lucia
Pigeon Island, Castries 33755

Saudi Arabia
Geological Museum, Riyadh 33771

Senegal
Musée Géologique, Dakar 33779

Serbia-Montenegro
Zbirka Poduzeća Naftagas, Novi Sad 33877

Slovakia
Liptovské Múzeum, Ružomberok 34053
Slovenské Národné Múzeum - Múzeum Bojnice, Bojnice 33956

Slovenia
Prirodoslovni Muzej Slovenije, Ljubljana 34118

South Africa
Barberton Museum, Barberton 34174
Bleloch Museum, Johannesburg 34273
Geological Museum, Johannesburg 34276
Geology Education Museum, Durban 34227
Geology Museum of the University of Stellenbosch, Stellenbosch 34380
Geoscience Museum, Pretoria 34343

Spain
Museo de Ciencias Naturales, Pamplona 35248
Museo de Historia Natural, Santiago de Compostela 35442
Museo Geológico del Seminario, Barcelona 34548
Museo Nacional de Ciencias Naturales, Madrid 35045
Museo Paleontologico, Zaragoza 35729
Museu de Ciències Naturals, Lleida 34971
Museu de Geologia, Barcelona 34558
Museu de Geologia Valenti Masachs, Manresa 35083

Sudan
Geological Museum, Khartoum 35767

Switzerland
Geologisch-Mineralogische Ausstellung der Eidgenössischen Technischen Hochschule Zürich, Zürich 37376
Gletschergarten, Luzern 36908
Musée Cantonal de Géologie, Lausanne 36858
Musée des Glaciers, Lourtier 36893
Naturmuseum Olten, Olten 37010

Tunisia
Musée Géologique, La Charguia 37568

Uganda
Geological Survey and Mines Museum, Entebbe 37823
Geology Museum, Kampala 37827

United Kingdom
Amberley Working Museum, Amberley 37995
Bolton Museum and Art Gallery, Bolton 38269
Castle Museum, Clitheroe 38590
Clatteringshaws Forest Wildlife Centre, Clatteringshaws 38586
Department of Geological Sciences Collection, London 39622
Dewey Museum, Warminster 40785
Dick Institute Museum and Art Gallery, Kilmarnock 39362
Dudley Museum and Art Gallery, Dudley 38782
Dunrobin Castle Museum, Golspie 39091
Geological Museum of North Wales, Wrexham 40941
Geology Department Museum, Aberdeen 37936
Gosport Museum, Gosport 39099
Halesworth and District Museum, Halesworth 39148
Hugh Miller's Cottage, Cromarty 38671
Hunterian Museum, Glasgow 39051
La Hougue Bie Museum, Saint Helier 40403
Lapworth Museum of Geology, Birmingham 38223
Ludlow Museum, Ludlow 39842
Margate Caves, Margate 39911
Much Wenlock Museum, Much Wenlock 39993
Natural History Museum, Belfast 38154
Natural History Society and Folk Museum, Bacup 38053
Oxford University Museum of Natural History, Oxford 40151
Peterborough Museum and Art Gallery, Peterborough 40188
Powell-Cotton Museum, Quex House and Gardens, Birchington 38203
Ruskin Museum, Coniston 38625
Sedgwick Museum of Geology, Cambridge 38462
Shepton Mallet Museum, Shepton Mallet 40493
Staffin Museum, Staffin 40568
Treasures of the Earth, Corpach 38635
Tweeddale Museum, Peebles 40166

Uruguay
Museo Geológico del Uruguay, Montevideo 41004

U.S.A.
Alaska Museum of Natural History, Eagle River 43034
Anza-Borrego Desert Museum, Borrego Springs 41795
Berea College Burroughs Geological Museum, Berea 41635
Bob Campbell Geology Museum, Clemson 42455
Burpee Museum of Natural History, Rockford 46959
Carter County Museum, Ekalaka 43103
Colburn Gem and Mineral Museum, Asheville 41278
Colorado School of Mines Geology Museum, Golden 43714
Dinosaur Gardens Museum, Ossineke 46211
Dunn-Seiler Museum, Mississippi State 45402
E.C. Allison Research Center, San Diego 47275
Ed Clark Museum of Missouri Geology, Rolla 46990
Eleanor Barbour Cook Museum of Geology, Chadron 42179
Emporia State University Geology Museum, Emporia 43182
Fiedler Memorial Museum, Seguin 47559

Fort Peck Museum, Fort Peck 43439
Franklin Mineral Museum, Franklin 43519
Fryxell Geology Museum, Rock Island 46955
The Geological Museum, Laramie 44647
Geology Museum, Huntington 44164
Gerald E. Eddy Discovery Center, Chelsea 42271
Grand Canyon National Park Museum Collection, Grand Canyon 43740
Greene Memorial Museum, Milwaukee 45362
Henry S. Reuss Ice Age Visitor Center, Campbellsport 42072
Lora Robins Gallery of Design from Nature, Richmond 46881
Luzerne County Historical Museum, Wilkes-Barre 48621
Mammoth Site of Hot Springs, Hot Springs 44111
Mesa Southwest Museum, Mesa 45271
Mississippi Petrified Forest Museum, Flora 43341
Museum of Ancient Artifacts, Chicago 42342
Museum of Geology, Rapid City 46797
Museum of the Geological Sciences, Blacksburg 41728
New York State Museum, Albany 41085
Orton Geological Museum, Columbus 42591
Petrified Forest of the Black Hills, Piedmont 46483
Rolla Minerals Museum, Rolla 46992
Ruth Hall Museum of Paleontology, Abiquiu 41059
Schoellkopf Geological Museum, Niagara Falls 45951
Silver River Museum, Ocala 46082
Springfield Science Museum, Springfield 47750
Tate Geological Museum, Casper 42131
Vermont Marble Museum, Proctor 46709
Voas Museum, Minburn 45375
W.M. Keck Museum, Reno 46839

Vietnam
Geology Museum, Ha Noi 48977

Glass and Glassware

Australia
City Art Gallery, Wagga Wagga 01569
Colac Otway Shire Hammerton Bottle Collection, Colac 00935
Devonport Gallery and Arts Centre, Devonport 00977
Fusions Gallery, Fortitude Valley 01031
House of Bottles, Kinglake 01148
House of Bottles and Bottle Museum, Tewantin 01525
Wagga Wagga Art Gallery, Wagga Wagga 01570

Austria
Gläsermuseum, Gerersdorf 01876
Glasmuseum Zalto, Nagelberg 02335
Heimathaus Ulrichsberg, Ulrichsberg 02752
Heimatstube Schwarzenberg am Böhmerwald, Schwarzenberg am Böhmerwald 02643
Hinterglasmuseum, Sandl 02555
Museum Freudenthaler Glassammlung, Weißenkirchen im Attergau 02802
Palais Surreal, Wien 02969
Stadt-, Glas- und Steinmuseum, Gmünd, Niederösterreich 01893
Steirisches Glaskunstzentrum und Glasmuseum Bärnbach, Bärnbach 01731
Wiener Glasmuseum, Wien 03004

Belgium
Musée d'Histoire et des Arts Décoratifs, Tournai 03795
Musée du Verre, Liège 03582
Musée du Verre et Art et Technique, Charleroi 03353
Musée du Verre chez Val-Saint-Lambert Château, Seraing 03731
Villa 't Eksternest, Roeselare 03707

Canada
Canadian Clay and Glass Gallery, Waterloo 06751
Les Maisons de Bouteilles, Cap-Egmont 05196

Czech Republic
Muzeum Skla, Harrachov v Krkonoších 08343
Muzeum Skla a Bižuterie, Jablonec nad Nisou 08378
Muzeum Šumavy, Kašperské Hory 08407
Severočeské Muzeum v Liberci, Liberec 08451
Sklářské Muzeum, Kamenický Šenov 08399
Sklářské Muzeum Moser, Karlovy Vary 08402
Sklářské Muzeum Nový Bor, Nový Bor 08507
Sklenka Muzeum v Železném Brodě, Železný Brod 08748
Uměleckoprůmyslové Muzeum v Praze, Praha 08617
Východočeské Muzeum, Pardubice 08534
Východočeské Muzeum, Pardubice 08534

Denmark
Anneberg-Samlingerne, Nykøbing Sjælland 09001
Den Gamle Gaard, Faaborg 08814
Glasmuseet Ebeltoft, Ebeltoft 08803

Finland
Iittalan Tehtaan Museo, Iittala 09559
Pykäri Nuutajärven Lasimuseo, Nuutajärvi 09876
Suomen Lasimuseo, Riihimäki 09995

France
Atelier Musée du Verre, Trélon 14994
Galerie d'Art Moderne, Passavant-la-Rochère 13663
Musée-Atelier de la Cristallerie des Papes, Fontaine-de-Vaucluse 11758
Musée Calvet, Avignon 10528
Musée d'Art Moderne, Troyes 15004
Musée de La Glacerie, La Glacerie 12191
Musée de la Poterie et de la Céramique, Sadirac 14083
Musée de la Verrerie, Blangy-sur-Bresle 10756
Musée de l'Ecole de Nancy, Nancy 13240
Musée de l'homme et de l'Industrie, Le Creusot 12408
Musée de Traditions Populaires et d'Archéologie, Chauvigny 11255
Musée Despiau Wlérick, Mont-de-Marsan 13027
Musée du Verre, Blaye-les-Mines 10765
Musée du Verre, Sars-Poteries 14625
Musée du Vitrail, Gordes 11887
Musée International de la Parfumerie, Grasse 11922
Musée-Maison du Verre, Meisenthal 12917
Musée National Adrien Dubouché, Limoges 12617

Germany
Erich Mäder-Glasmuseum, Grünenplan 17446
Glas- und Keramikmuseum, Großalmerode 17423
Glasmuseum, Frauenau 17088
Glasmuseum, Immenhausen 17893
Glasmuseum, Warmensteinach 20402
Glasmuseum Boffzen, Boffzen 16221
Glasmuseum Grünenplan, Grünenplan 17447
Glasmuseum Hadamar, Hadamar 17473
Glasmuseum Rheinbach, Rheinbach 19589
Glasmuseum Steina, Bad Sachsa 15721
Glasmuseum Weisswasser, Weisswasser 20503
Glasmuseum Wertheim, Wertheim 20531
Goethe-Museum Stützerbach mit Museum zur Geschichte des technischen Glases, Stützerbach 20081
Heimat- und Uhrenmuseum, Villingen-Schwenningen 20317
Heimatmuseum Uelzen mit Gläsersammlung Röver, Uelzen 20248
Historische Fraunhofer-Glashütte, Benediktbeuern 15877
Museum des Kreises Plön mit norddeutscher Glassammlung, Plön 19419
Museum für Glaskunst, Lauscha 18360
Museum für Modernes Glas, Rödental 19628
Museum Kunst Palast mit Sammlung Kunstakademie und Glasmuseum Hentrich, Düsseldorf 16738
Museumsdorf und Technisches Denkmal, Baruth, Mark 15828
Neues Schloss Wallerstein, Wallerstein 20380
Passauer Glasmuseum, Passau 19359
Schott GlasMuseum, Jena 17951
Stadtmuseum Neustadt an der Waldnaab, Neustadt an der Waldnaab 19073
Stadtmuseum Waldkraiburg, Waldkraiburg 20369
Teplitz-Schönauer Heimatmuseum, Frankfurt am Main 17079
Theresienthaler Glasmuseum, Zwiesel 20781
Waldmuseum, Zwiesel 20782

Iran
Abgineh Va Sofalineh, Teheran 22287

Israel
Glass Museum, Tel Aviv 22755

Italy
Museo del Vetro, Venezia 25930

Japan
Notojima Glass Art Museum, Notojima 26610

Mexico
Museo del Vidrio, Monterrey 28236

Netherlands
De Drentse Glasbloazer, Dalen 29064
Nationaal Glasmuseum, Leerdam 29506
Nederlands Museum voor Glas en Glastechniek, Hoogeveen 29438
Ontmoetingscentrum de Veldkei, Expositie, Havelte 29354

Norway
Hadeland Glassverks Museum, Jevnaker 30583

Philippines
MPG Town Gallery, Odiongan 31408

Poland
Muzeum Karkonoskie, Jelenia Góra 31630

Russia
Gosudarstvennyj Chudožestvenno-architekturnyj Dvorcovo-parkovyj Muzej-zapovednik Pavlovsk, Pavlovsk 33285

South Africa
Our Heritage Museum, Adelaide 34169

Spain
Museo del Castillo de Peralada, Peralada 35266
Museo del Vidrio, San Ildefonso 35375
Museu del Vidre, Algaida 34444

Sweden
Glasbruksmuseet i Surte, Surte 36316
Smålands Museum, Växjö 36390

Switzerland
Fondation Neumann, Gingins 36758
Gewerbemuseum, Winterthur 37328
Mudac-Musée de Design et d'Arts Appliqués Contemporains, Lausanne 36856
Musée Ariana, Genève 36740
Musée du Verrier, Saint-Prex 37088
Museum Bellerive, Zürich 37395

United Kingdom
Bennie Museum, Bathgate 38126
Brierley Hill Glass Museum, Brierley Hill 38334
Broadfield House Glass Museum, Kingswinford 39387
Clevedon Court, Clevedon 38589
Dartington Crystal Glass Museum, Torrington 40720
Guildford House Gallery, Guildford 39137
Haworth Art Gallery, Accrington 37959
Himley Hall, Himley 39245
Red House Glass Cone Museum, Stourbridge 40616
Royal Brierley Crystal Museum, Dudley 38783
Shipley Art Gallery, Gateshead 39028
South Shields Museum and Art Gallery, South Shields 40538
Stained Glass Museum, Ely 38935
Studio Glass Gallery, London 39785
World of Glass, Saint Helens 40398
Yelverton Paperweight Centre, Yelverton 40954

U.S.A.
Blenko Museum of Seattle, Seattle 47528
Cambridge Glass Museum, Cambridge 42053
Corning Glass Center, Corning 42636
Corning Museum of Glass, Corning 42637
Degenhart Paperweight and Glass Museum, Cambridge 42054
Fenton Glass Museum, Williamstown 48636
The Glass Museum, Dunkirk 43012
Greentown Glass Museum, Greentown 43822
The Jones Museum of Glass and Ceramics, Sebago 47549
Museum of American Glass at Wheaton Village, Millville 45350
Museum of Glass, Tacoma 47921
National Heisey Glass Museum, Newark 45896
National Museum of Ceramic Art and Glass, Baltimore 41484
Neustadt Museum of Tiffany Art, New York 45854
Sandwich Glass Museum, Sandwich 47388

Globes → Cartography

Gold and Silver

Australia
Gold Museum, Ballarat 00763
Gold Treasury Museum, Melbourne 01229

Austria
Gold- und Silberschmiedemuseum, Wien 02891
Rauriser Talmuseum, Rauris 02492
Schloß- und Goldbergbaumuseum, Großkirchheim 01954

Belgium
Kasteelmuseum Slot van Laarne, Laarne 03548
Stedelijk Museum, Oudenaarde 03678
Trésor de la Collégiale, Huy 03513
Trésor de la Collegiale Sainte-Waudru, Mons 03637
Trésor du Frère Hugo d'Oignies, Namur 03652
Zilvermuseum Sterckshof Povincie Antwerpen, Antwerpen 03180

Bermuda
Tucker House Museum, Saint George's 03889

Bolivia
Museo del Oro y Metales Preciosos, La Paz 03897

Bulgaria
Etnografiski Kompleks na Istoričeski Muzej, Vraca 04928

Canada
Klondike National Historic Sites, Dawson City 05312
Sherbrooke Village, Sherbrooke, Nova Scotia 06438
Silvery Slocan Museum, New Denver 05976
Soo Line Historical Museum, Weyburn 06783

Colombia
Museo del Oro, Bogotá 07415

Costa Rica
Museo de Oro Precolombino, San José 07658

Cuba
Museo Casa de la Orfebrería, La Habana 07943

Czech Republic
Regionální Muzeum v Jílovém u Prahy, Jílové u Prahy 08393

Denmark
Tønder Museum, Tønder 09094

France
Collection Charles de l'Escalopier, Amiens 10320
Petit Musée de l'Argenterie, Paris 13657

Germany
Bergbau- und Heimatmuseum, Goldkronach 17345
Deutsches Goldschmiedehaus, Hanau 17581
Glashüttenmuseum des Erzgebirges, Neuhausen, Sachsen 19036
Grünes Gewölbe, Dresden 16685
Historisches Rathaus, Krempe 18231
Historisches Silbererzbergwerk Grube Samson und Heimatmuseum, Sankt Andreasberg 19745
Ikonenmuseum Schloß Autenried, Ichenhausen 17878
Museum im Goldschmiedehaus, Ahlen 15404
Städtisches Museum Wesel, Wesel 20537
Technisches Museum Silberwäsche Antonsthal, Breitenbrunn, Erzgebirge 16315

Italy
Museo Alessi, Enna 23732
Museo Civico, Lucignano 24234
Museo d'Arte e Storia Antica Ebraica, Casale Monferrato 23365
Museo del Duomo, Città di Castello 23578
Museo della Propositura di San Pietro, Montecatini Val di Nievole 24510
Museo e Pinacoteca della Città, Todi 25714
Museo Ebraica di Roma, Roma 25222
Museo Sacro, Pompei 24985
Tesoro del Duomo, Milano 24420
Tesoro della Cattedrale, Palermo 24779

Korea, Republic
Ewha Yoja Taehakkyo Pakmulgwan, Seoul 27232
National Museum of Korea, Seoul 27264

Latvia
Rīgas Vēstures un Kuģniecības muzejs, Rīga 27441

Mexico
Museo Guillermo Spratling, Taxco de Alarcón 28461

Netherlands
Collectie in het Gemmeentehuis, Brummen 29034
Nederlands Goud-, Zilver- en Klokkenmuseum, Schoonhoven 29812
Oudheidkamer Beilen, Beilen 28971
Schoonhovens Edelambachtshuys, Schoonhoven 29814

New Zealand
Clyde Historical Museum, Clyde 30136
Maniototo Early Settlers Museum, Naseby 30208

Norway
Norsk Bergverksmuseum, Kongsberg 30605

Portugal
Museu de Alberto Sampaio, Guimarães 32278

Russia
Almaznyj Fond, Moskva 33019

Spain
Cámara Santa de la Catedral de Oviedo, Oviedo 35202
Museo de Arte Sacro Antiguo, Villanueva de Lorenzana 35681

Sweden
Gruvmuseet, Sala 36172
Silvermuseet, Arjeplog 35810
Skattkammaren - Uppsala Domkyrkas Museum, Uppsala 36360

United Kingdom
Brodick Castle, Brodick 38373
Goldsmiths' Hall, London 39644
Ickworth House, Horringer 39262
Painters's Hall, London 39739
Treadgolds Museum, Portsmouth 40260

U.S.A.
Argo Gold Mine and Mill Museum, Idaho Springs 44191
Big Thunder Gold Mine, Keystone 44474
Custer Museum, Clayton 42441
Reed Gold Mine, Midland 45323

Vatican City
Museo Storico Artistico, Città del Vaticano 48883

Graphic Arts

Argentina
Museo Municipal de Bellas Artes Lucas Braulio Areco, Posadas 00484
Museo Nacional del Grabado, Buenos Aires 00230

Armenia
M. Sarians Museum, Erevan 00685

Austria
Albertina, Wien 02830
Franz Traunfellner-Dokumentation, Pöggstall 02425
Galerie Loisel Grafik, Pörtschach am Wörther See 02433
Karikaturmuseum Krems, Krems 02156
Kunstsammlungen und Graphische Sammlung, Furth bei Göttweig 01861
Kupferstichkabinett, Wien 02921
Palais Surreal, Wien 02969
Salzburger Museum Carolino Augusteum, Salzburg 02551

Werner-Berg-Galerie der Stadt Bleiburg, Bleiburg 01739

Belgium
Cabinet des Estampes et des Dessins, Liège 03567
Centre de la Gravure et de l'Image Imprimée de la Communauté Française de Belgique, La Louvière 03546
Collections Artistiques de l'Université de Liège, Liège 03568
Stedelijk Prentenkabinet, Antwerpen 03175

Bulgaria
Chudožestvena Galerija, Žeravna 04932
Sofijska Gradska Chudožestvena Galerija, Sofia 04859

Canada
Galerie de l'UQAM, Québec 06198
Glenhyrst Art Gallery of Brant, Brantford 05126
McMaster Museum of Art, Hamilton 05574
The Station Gallery, Whitby 06786
Yaneff International Art, Caledon East 05157

China, People's Republic
Changshu Engraved Stone Museum, Changshu 07013
Hong Kong Space Museum, Hong Kong 07101
Qijiang Stone Engraving Museum, Gunan 07078
Shandong Stone Engraving Art Museum, Jinan 07135
Stone Engraving Art Museum, Beijing 06990
Stone Engraving Museum, Fu 07051
Suzhou Engraved Stone Museum, Suzhou 07251
Wuxi Engraved Stone Display Center, Wuxi 07287

Colombia
Museo de Museos Colsubsidio, Bogotá 07411

Croatia
Grafička Zbirka Nacionalne i Sveučilišne Knjižnice, Zagreb 07818
Kabinet Grafike HAZU, Zagreb 07826

Cuba
Antigua Casa de los Marqueses de Campo Florido, San Antonio de los Baños 08097

Czech Republic
Galerie Výtvarného Umění, Havlíčkův Brod 08347
Palác Kinských, Praha 08608

Denmark
Kastrupgaardsamlingen, Kastrup 08912
Kunsthallen Brandts Klaedefabrik, Odense 09014
Storm P.-Museet, Frederiksberg 08827
Vejle Kunstmuseum, Vejle 09104

Finland
Jyväskylän Taidemuseo, Jyväskylä 09597

France
Cabinet des Estampes et des Dessins, Strasbourg 14805
Château de Lourmarin, Lourmarin 12701
Espace Salvador Dalí, Paris 13500
Institut Tessin, Paris 13517
Musée Adzak, Paris 13529
Musée de Nogent, Nogent-sur-Marne 13352
Musée des Beaux-Arts, Marseille 12862
Musée des Beaux-Arts de Bordeaux, Bordeaux 10812
Musée du Dessin et de l'Estampe Originale, Gravelines 11929
Musée Toulouse-Lautrec, Naucelle 13274

Germany
A. Paul Weber-Museum, Ratzeburg 19498
Artothek Worpswede, Worpswede 20680
Ausstellungsräume der Staatlichen Graphischen Sammlung, München 18830
Bibliothek Otto Schäfer, Schweinfurt 19888
Deutsches Werbemuseum, Düsseldorf 16721
Ernst Barlach Stiftung Güstrow, Güstrow 17456
Erwin von Kreibig-Museum, München 18846
Galerie Albstadt, Albstadt 15417
Galerie Parterre, Berlin 15971
Grafik Museum Stiftung Schreiner, Bad Steben 15750
Grafische Sammlung, Nürnberg 19141
Graphikmuseum Pablo Picasso Münster, Münster 18938
Graphische Sammlung, Kassel 18018
Graphische Sammlung, Augsburg 15556
Graphische Sammlung der Universität, Erlangen 16918
Heimatmuseum Scheeßel, Scheeßel 19768
Holzschnitt-Museum Klaus Herzer, Mössingen 18781
Hudetz-Turm, Wiesent 20580
Käthe-Kollwitz-Museum Berlin, Berlin 16013
Kunstbibliothek, Berlin 16025
Kunstforum Ostdeutsche Galerie, Regensburg 19527
Kunsthalle Bremen, Bremen 16328
Kunsthaus Meyenburg, Nordhausen 19120
Kupferstich-Kabinett, Dresden 16692
Ludwig-Doerfler-Galerie, Schillingsfürst 19779
Lyonel-Feininger-Galerie, Quedlinburg 19463
Martin-von-Wagner-Museum der Universität Würzburg, Würzburg 20697
Molwitz-Stube, Mitterteich 18756
Museum beim Solenhofer Aktien-Verein, Maxberg 18667
Museum Corps de Logis, Düsseldorf 16735
Museum Folkwang Essen, Essen 16959
Museum Rolf Werner, Seebad Bansin 19912
Museum Schloß Moritzburg, Zeitz, Elster 20738
Otto-Dix-Haus Hemmenhofen, Gaienhofen 17191
Otto Pankok Museum, Hünxe 17861
Sammlungen des Kunstvereins, Ibbenbüren 17875
Siegerlandmuseum mit Ausstellungsforum Haus Oranienstraße, Siegen 19950
Staatliche Graphische Sammlung München, München 18912
Staatsgalerie Stuttgart, Stuttgart 20106
Stadtmuseum Bocholt, Bocholt 16190
Städtische Galerie, Bietigheim-Bissingen 16161
Städtische Galerie Erlangen, Erlangen 16924
Städtische Galerie im Park, Viersen 20314
Stiftung Käthe-Kollwitz-Gedenkstätte, Moritzburg 18792
Struwwelpeter-Museum, Frankfurt am Main 17078
Westfälisches Landesmuseum für Kunst und Kulturgeschichte Münster, Münster 18950
Zille Museum, Berlin 16118

Greece
Museum of Engravings and Graphic Arts, Athinai 20886

Guam
Isla Center for the Arts at the University of Guam, Mangilao 21258

Hungary
Kass Galéria, Szeged 21549

Italy
Calcografia, Roma 25149
Civica Raccolta delle Stampe Achille Bertarelli, Milano 24372
Gabinetto dei Disegni e delle Stampe, Bologna 23103
Gabinetto Disegni e Stampe degli Uffizi, Firenze 23836
Gabinetto Disegni e Stampe-Dipartimento di Storia delle Arti dell'Università di Pisa, Pisa 24947
Gabinetto Nazionale delle Stampe, Roma 25157
Museo Casabianca, Malo 24270
Museo di Milano, Milano 24399
Pinacoteca Ambrosiana, Milano 24416

Japan
Center for Contemporary Graphic Art and Tyler Graphics Archive Collection, Sukagawa 26776
Engraving Print Village Art Museum, Aikawa 26088
Katsushika Hokusai Bijutsukan, Tsuwano 26980
Machida-shiritsu Kokusai Hanga Bijutsukan, Machida 26464
Munakata Prints Museum, Kamakura 26296
Munakata Shiko Kinenkan, Aomori 26100
Nagasaki-shiritsu Ukiyo-e Bijutsukan, Nagasaki 26559
Nihon Ukiyo-e Hakubutsukan, Matsumoto 26479
Ukiyo-e and Pottery Museum, Osaka 26674

Mexico
Casa Museo Vladimir Cora, Acaponeta 27745
Instituto de Artes Gráficas de Oaxaca, Oaxaca 28272
Museo de Arte Gráficas Juan Pablos, México 28125
Museo de la Estampa, Cuitzeo 27880
Museo de la Estampa del Estado de México, Toluca 28547
Museo de la Gráfica de la Historia Social de Taxco Siglo XX, Taxco de Alarcón 28458
Museo del Periodismo y las Artes Gráficas, Guadalajara 27959
Museo Franco Lázaro, Chiapa de Corzo 27819
Museo Gráfico de la Mujer Guerrenese, Chilpancingo 27829
Museo José Guadalupe Posada, Aguascalientes 27758
Museo Nacional de la Estampa, México 28190

Netherlands
Affiche Museum Hoorn, Hoorn 29441
Apeldoorns Museum, Apeldoorn 28924
Atelier Kea Homan, Assen 28948
Bierreclamemuseum, Breda 29018
Grafisch Museum Groningen, Groningen 29308
Jelly van den Bosch Museum, Roden 29739
Museum Het Rembrandthuis, Amsterdam 28876
Museum Jan Heestershuis, Schijndel 29805
Prentenkabinet Universiteit Leiden, Leiden 29523
Rien Poortvlietmuseum, Middelharnis 29596
Rijksprentenkabinet, Amsterdam 28899
Zandvoorts Museum, Zandvoort 30046
Zijper Museum, Schagerbrug 29798

New Zealand
Dunedin Public Libraries Artprint Collection, Dunedin 30146

Norway
Levende Grafisk Museum, Skjeberg 30850
Nesch-Museet, Ål 30372

Pakistan
Tasneem Arts Gallery, Peshawar 31052

Peru
Buque Museo Ex BAP América, Iquitos 31184

Philippines
Samoy Art Museum, Bacoor 31280

Poland
Biblioteka Narodowa, Warszawa 32077
Centrum Rysunku i Grafiki im. Tadeuza Kulisiewicza, Kalisz 31634
Gabinet Rycin Polskiej Akademii Umiejętności w Krakowie, Kraków 31686
Miejska Galeria Sztuki, Łódź 31767
Muzeum Karykatury, Warszawa 32104
Oddział Zbiorów Graficznych i Kartograficznych, Kraków 31724

Puerto Rico
Popular Arts Museum, San Juan 32407

Russia
Dom-Muzej N.N. Žukova, Elec 32790
Gosudarstvennyj Memorial'nyj Istoriko-chudožestvennyj i Prirodnyj Muzej-zapovednik V.D. Polenova, Strachovo 33566
Gosudarstvennyj Muzej Vadima Sidura, Moskva 33064
Muzej Knigi, Moskva 33117
Muzej Narodnoj Grafiki, Moskva 33139
Novosibirskaja Kartinnaja Galereja, Novosibirsk 33242
Regionalnyj Muzej Severnogo Priladožja, Sortavala 33547
Rybinskij Gosudarstvennyj Istoriko-architekturnyj i Chudožestvennyj Muzej-zapovednik, Rybinsk 33362
Valaamskij Naučno-issledovatelskij Cerkovno-archeologičeskij i Prirodnyj Muzej-zapovednik, Sortavala 33548

Serbia-Montenegro
Galerija Matice Srpske, Novi Sad 33869
Galerija Srpske Akademije Nauka i Umetnosti, Beograd 33798

Slovakia
Novohradská Galéria, Lučenec 34018

Slovenia
Mednarodni Grafični Likovni Centar, Ljubljana 34109

Sweden
Grafikens Hus, Mariefred 36083
Grafikmuseum, Korsberga 36014

Switzerland
Cabinet des Estampes du Musée d'Art et d'Histoire, Genève 36729
Graphische Sammlung der Eidgenössischen Technischen Hochschule, Zürich 37377
Herrliberger-Sammlung, Maur 36931
Karikatur und Cartoon Museum Basel, Basel 36502
Kirchner Museum Davos, Davos Platz 36654
Kupferstichkabinett, Basel 36506
Musée Alexis Forel, Morges 36950
Musée de l'Hôtel-Dieu, Porrentruy 37028
Museum für Gestaltung Zürich, Zürich 37397

Turkey
Ayşe ve Ercümend Kalmık Vakfı-Müzesi, Gümüşsuyu 37685

Ukraine
National Aivazovsky Picture Gallery, Feodosija 37853

United Kingdom
Bank of England Museum, London 39571
Beatrix Potter Gallery, Hawkshead 39198
Buddle Arts Centre, Wallsend 40768
Glasgow Print Studio, Glasgow 39047
Hogarth's House, London 39666
The John Southern Gallery, Dobwalls 38736
School of Art Gallery and Museum, Aberystwyth 37956

U.S.A.
Art Galleries at UAH, Huntsville 44171
Audubon State Historic Site, Saint Francisville 47089
Brand Library and Art Galleries, Glendale 43687
Centrum Arts and Creative Education, Port Townsend 46604
Claypool-Young Art Gallery, Morehead 45493
Esther Prangley Rice Gallery, Westminster 48562
Gallery II, Kalamazoo 44377
Grier-Musser Museum, Los Angeles 44904
Grunwald Center for the Graphic Arts, Los Angeles 44905
Harry D. Hendren Gallery, Saint Charles 47079
Hughes Fine Arts Center, Grand Forks 43742
Janet Turner Print Museum, Chico 42372
Joel and Lila Harnett Print Study Center, Richmond 46879
King Hooper Mansion, Marblehead 45135
Lassen Museum Waikiki, Honolulu 44083
Martin Art Gallery, Allentown 41146
Myra Powell Art Gallery and Gallery at the Station, Ogden 46099
Piedra Lumbre Visitors Center, Abiquiu 41058
Print and Picture Collection, Philadelphia 46447
The Print Center, Philadelphia 46448
Print Consortium, Kansas City 44405
Self Help Graphics Gallery, Los Angeles 44939
SFA Galleries, Nacogdoches 45589
Trout Gallery, Carlisle 42105
University of Hawaii at Manoa Art Gallery, Honolulu 44091
University of Nebraska Art Gallery at Omaha, Omaha 46153
Weyers-Sampson Art Gallery, Greenville 43828
William H. Van Every jr. and Edward M. Smith Galleries, Davidson 42789

Vatican City
Museo Profano, Città del Vaticano 48881

Gravestones → Tombs

Handicapped

Austria
Museum des Blindenwesens, Wien 02939

Canada
Show Gallery, Toronto 06611

Croatia
Tiflološki Muzej, Zagreb 07839

Czech Republic
Technické Muzeum v Brně, Brno 08277

Denmark
Blindehistorisk Museum, Hellerup 08856

Finland
Jyväskylän Näkövammaisten Koulun Museo, Jyväskylä 09596
Näkövammaismuseo, Jiris 09579

Germany
Blinden-Museum, Berlin 15923
Blindenmuseum, Hannover 17592

Russia
Centralnyj Muzej Vserossijskogo Obščestva Slepych, Moskva 33029
Literaturno-memorialnyj Muzej Vasilija Erošenko, Staryj Oskol 33558

U.S.A.
Museum on the History of Blindness, Watertown 48441

Handicraft

Argentina
Casa de Manuel Mujica Láinez, La Cumbre 00377
Museo de Arqueologia Colonial Rodolfo I. Bravo, Cafayate 00256

Australia
Bathurst Regional Art Gallery, Bathurst 00774
Tweed River Regional Art Gallery, Murwillumbah 01294

Austria
Buchdruckmuseum, Rohrbach in Oberösterreich 02523
Hofinge's Rahmenmuseum, Innsbruck 02069
Kaiser Franz-Josef-Museum für Handwerk und Volkskunst, Baden bei Wien 01728
Kapuzinerturm, Radstadt 02475
Maurermuseum und Dachdeckermuseum, Langenlois 02184
Messerermuseum, Steinbach an der Steyr 02681
Museum Steinmetzhaus, Eggenburg 01792
Museum Stoffels Säge-Mühle, Hohenems 02042
Papiermachermuseum, Steyrermühl 02695
Pechermuseum, Hernstein 02024
Rauchfangkehrermuseum, Wien 02976
Schmiedemuseum, Fulpmes 01860
Sensen-Schmiede-Museum/ Klangwelten, Micheldorf 02294
Wäschepflegemuseum, Rainbach im Mühlkreis 02479
Wiener Ziegelmuseum, Wien 03012
Zimmerei-Museum, Feldkirch 01832

Belgium
Folkloremuseum Florishof, Oostduinkerke 03665
Heemkundig Museum Boekhoute, Boekhoute 03222
Kempisch Museum, Brecht 03240
Musée de la Vie Réginal des Rièzes et des Sarts, Cul-des-Sarts 03367
Museum 't Nieuwhuys Hoegaarden, Hoegaarden 03497
Nationaal Borstelmuseum, Izegem 03522
Regionale Heemmusea Bachten de Kupe, Izenberge 03525
Streekmuseum van Klein-Brabant De Zilverreiger, Weert 03832

Brazil
Museu Vivo da Memória Candanga, Brasília 04008

Brunei
Muzium Teknologi Melayu, Bandar Seri Begawan 04599
Pusat Latihan Kesenian Pertukangan Tangan Brunei, Bandar Seri Begawan 04600

Bulgaria
Architekturno-etnografski Muzej Etăr, Gabrovo 04665
Nacionalna Izložba na Narodnite Chudožestveni Zanajati i Priložni Izkustva, Orešak 04747

Canada
Alcan Aluminium Corporate Art Collection, Montréal 05886

Carman House Museum, Iroquois 05627
Central New Brunswick Woodmen's Museum, Boiestown 05088
Huron County Museum, Goderich 05497
Milton Blacksmith Shop Museum, Milton 05853
Musée Acadien, Cheticamp 05244
Musée des Anciens Canadiens, Saint-Jean-Port-Joli 06328
Musée Maritime du Québec, L'Islet 05757
Le Noir Forge, Arichat 05006
Nova Scotia Centre for Craft and Design, Halifax 05558
Saskatchewan Craft Gallery, Saskatoon 06405
Turner Curling Museum, Weyburn 06784

China, People's Republic
China Silk Museum, Hangzhou 07080

Congo, Democratic Republic
Musée d'Anthropologie, Kinshasa 07634

Cuba
Galería Los Oficios, La Habana 07930

Czech Republic
Muzeum Krajky, Prachatice 08561
Muzeum Krajky, Vamberk 08708
Muzeum Prostějovska, Prostějov 08629
Muzeum Šumavy, Sušice 08669
Památník, Dolní Domaslavice 08331
Technické Muzeum v Brně, Brno 08277
Vlastivědné Muzeum pro Vysoké nad Jizerou a Okolí, Vysoké nad Jizerou 08734

Denmark
Holstebro Museum, Holstebro 08890
Museet for Thy og Vester Hanherred, Thisted 09091
Næstved Museum, Næstved 08987
Slagelse Museum for Handel, Håndværk og Industri, Slagelse 09071
Søfartssamlingerne i Troense, Svendborg 09086
Viborg Stiftsmuseum, Viborg 09112

Finland
Fransu-tupa, Himanka 09549
Gallen-Kallela Museum, Espoo 09432
Halikkon Museo, Halikko 09458
Luostarinmäen Käsityöläismuseo, Turku 10124
Lusto-Suomen-metsämuseo ja metsätietokeskus, Punkaharju 09962
Naantalin Museo, Naantali 09853
Porvoon Museo, Porvoo 09954
Satakunnan Museo, Pori 09947
Sepänmäen Käsityömuseo, Mäntsälä 09809
Suomen Käsityön Museo, Jyväskylä 09604
Väinontalo - Järviseudun Museo, Vasikka-Aho 10189
Virkki-käsityömuseo, Helsinki 09547

France
Ecomusée de la Ferme et des Vieux Métiers, Lizio 12638
Musée de la Coutellerie, Thiers 14886
Musée de l'Orfevrerie Boilhet-Christofle, Saint-Denis (Seine-Saint-Denis) 14181
Musée du Compagnonnage, Tours 14972
Musée du Feutre, Mouzon 13202
Musée Paul Dupuy, Toulouse 14951

Germany
Alte Wache, Groitzsch bei Pegau 17411
Bauernhofmuseum, Buchhofen 16388
Bergisches Museum für Bergbau, Handwerk und Gewerbe, Bergisch Gladbach 15896
Breuberg-Museum, Breuberg 16358
Brunnenmuseum, Goslar 17347
Deutsches Maler- und Lackierer-Museum, Hamburg 17531
Deutsches Vogelbauer-Museum, Walsrode 20382
Dorfmuseum Dietersweiler, Freudenstadt 17128
Erstes Deutsches Türmermuseum, Vilseck 20324
Erzgebirgsmuseum mit Besucherbergwerk, Annaberg-Buchholz 15497
Europäisches Klempner- und Kupferschmiede-Museum, Karlstadt 18008
Flößermuseum Unterrodach, Marktrodach 18653
Freilicht- und Heimatmuseum Donaumoos, Karlshuld 17988
Freilichtmuseum Glentleiten, Großweil 17443
Gedenkstätte Ehemalige Synagoge, Adelsheim 15396
Gewerbe-Museum, Spaichingen 20005
Gilde-Museum, Oldenburg in Holstein 19250
Grönegau-Museum, Melle 18698
Hammer- und Waffenschmiede-Museum Hexenagger, Altmannstein 15459
Handwerkerstuben, Feuchtwangen 16998
Handwerksmuseum, Deggendorf 16559
Handwerksmuseum Ovelgönne, Ovelgönne 19331
Handwerksmuseum und Friseurmuseum, Berlin 15982
Haselünner Heimathäuser, Haselünne 17625
Heimat- und Feuerwehrmuseum, Schauenstein 19766
Heimat-und Handwerkermuseum, Leutershausen 18448
Heimat- und Handwerks Museum Stolberg, Stolberg, Rheinland 20068
Heimathaus-Handwerkermuseum, Scheidegg 19770
Heimathaus Wendelstein, Wendelstein, Mittelfranken 20511
Heimatmuseum, Müllrose 18820
Heimatmuseum, Oederan 19222
Heimatmuseum, Ruhla 19709
Heimatmuseum Brackenheim, Brackenheim 16269
Heimatmuseum Leingarten Altes Rathaus Schluchtern, Leingarten 18378
Heimatmuseum Maßbach, Maßbach 18662
Heimatmuseum Roßwein, Roßwein 19657
Heimatmuseum Stadtilm, Stadtilm 20030
Heimatmuseum und Naturalienkabinett, Waldenburg, Sachsen 20360
Heimatmuseum Vilsbiburg - Kröninger Hafnermuseum, Vilsbiburg 20322
Heimatmuseum Wertingen, Wertingen 20533
Heimatstuben der Stadt, Titisee-Neustadt 20180
Heimschneidermuseum, Großwallstadt 17442
Historische Handwerkerstuben, Gingst 17289
Historische Spinnerei Gartetal, Gleichen 17300
Historisches Stadtmuseum, Burghausen, Salzach 16421
Kloster zum Heiligen Kreuz, Rostock 19663
Kolpings- und Handwerksmuseum im Faltertor, Dettelbach 16591
Kreisheimatmuseum, Demmin 16571
Kreismuseum Gräfenhainichen, Oranienbaum 19262
Kreismuseum Oranienburg, Oranienburg 19265
Kulturhistorisches Museum der Hansestadt Stralsund, Stralsund 20074
Landesmuseum Mainz, Mainz 18602
Lohgerber-, Stadt- und Kreismuseum, Dippoldiswalde 16620
Ludwig-Gebhard-Museum, Tiefenbach, Oberpfalz 20175
Mainfränkisches Museum Würzburg, Würzburg 20696
Museum "Alte Münze", Stolberg, Harz 20066
Museum am Markt / Schubarts Museum, Aalen 15382
Museum Dermbach, Dermbach 16575
Museum des Kreises Plön mit norddeutscher Glassammlung, Plön 19419
Museum ehemalige Klöppelschule Tiefenbach, Tiefenbach, Oberpfalz 20176
Museum für bäuerliches Handwerk und Kultur, Wilhelmsdorf, Württemberg 20592
Museum für Holzhandwerke, Sinzig, Rhein 19972
Museum Göltzsch, Rodewisch 19624
Museum im Alten Schloß, Altensteig 15455
Museum Kloster Asbach, Rotthalmünster 19694
Museum Schloss Moritzburg, Moritzburg 18791
Museum Schloß Neu-Augustusburg, Weißenfels 20499
Museum Schloß Wilhelmsburg, Schmalkalden 19808
Museumsscheune Fränkische Schweiz, Hollfeld 17825
Natur-Museum mit Bauerngarten, Goldberg, Mecklenburg 17344
Oberpfälzer Handwerksmuseum, Rötz 19639
Regionalmuseum Alsfeld, Alsfeld 15437
Schefflenztal-Sammlungen, Schefflenz 19769
Schiefer- und Ziegelmuseum Dörfles-Esbach, Dörfles-Esbach 16630
Schloss Braunfels, Braunfels 16288
Schwäbisches Handwerkermuseum, Augsburg 15567
Stadt- und Bergbaumuseum Freiberg, Freiberg, Sachsen 17104
Stadtmuseum Gardelegen, Gardelegen 17199
Städtisches Hutmuseum, Lindenberg im Allgäu 18479
Städtisches Museum Braunschweig, Braunschweig 16305
Stiftung Moritzburg, Halle, Saale 17521
Straßenbau - einst und jetzt, Waldbüttelbrunn 20356
Südhessisches Handwerksmuseum, Roßdorf bei Darmstadt 19655
Tabakspeicher, Nordhausen 19122
Technik anno dazumal - Museum Kratzmühle, Kinding 18083
Thüringer Museum Eisenach, Eisenach 16819
Voithenberghammer, Furth im Wald 17182
Volkskundliche Sammlung des Fichtelgebirgsvereins, Weidenberg 20428
Wachsstöcklkabinett - Wachzieher- und Lebzelter-Museum, Viechtach 20309
Waldnaabtal-Museum in der Burg Neuhaus, Windischeschenbach 20607
Wannenmacher-Museum, Emsdetten 16868
Wegmachermuseum, Wasserburg am Inn 20409
Westfälisches Freilichtmuseum Hagen, Hagen, Westfalen 17484
Zeiselmairhaus, Schrobenhausen 19854

Greece
Ethnological Museum of Pyrsogianni Stonemasons, Konitsa 21027
Vouvalis Mansion, Kalymnos 20993

Hungary
Kékfestő Múzeum, Pápa 21501
Kis Géza Ormánság Múzeum, Sellye 21528
Néprajzi Gyűjtemény, Sopron 21535

Iceland
Heimilisidnardarsafnid Halldórustofa, Blönduós 21624
Minjasafnid Burstarfelli, Vopnafjörður 21675

India
Arts and Crafts Museum, Bhavnagar 21715
Government Museum, Thiruvananthapuram 22035
Magan Sangrahalaya Samiti, Wardha 22061
Mahatma Phule Vastu Sangrahalaya, Pune 21991
Sree Moolam Shastyabdapurti Memorial Institute, Thiruvananthapuram 22036
Museum of Arts and Crafts, Lucknow 21928

Italy
Museo del Falegname T. Sana-Onlus, Almenno San Bartolomeo 22860
Museo della Civiltà Contadina ed Artigiana, Monterosso Calabro 24543
Museo della Paglia e dell'Intreccio D. Michalacci, Signa 25581
Museo dello Spazzacamino, Santa Maria Maggiore 25438
Museo dell'Ombrello e del Parasole, Gignese 24026

Japan
Bekko Museum, Nagasaki 26543
European Folkcraft Museum, Kawakami 26325
Gotoh Bijutsukan, Tokyo 26854
Ishikawa-kenritsu Dento Sangyo Kogeikan, Kanazawa 26307
Kyoto Gion Oil Lamp Museum, Kyoto 26423
Kyoto Museum of Traditional Crafts - Fureaikan, Kyoto 26428
Meiji-Daigaku Shouhin Hakubutsukan, Tokyo 26888
Nagasaki-shiritsu Hakabutsukan, Nagasaki 26557
Ohara Bijutsukan, Kurashiki 26384
Sapporo Geijutsu no Mori Bijutsukan, Sapporo 26717
Token Hakubutsukan, Tokyo 26935
Tokyo Central Bijutsukan, Tokyo 26936
Tokyo Kokuritsu Kindai Bijutsukan Kogeikan, Crafts Gallery, Tokyo 26940

Jordan
Jordan Museum of Popular Tradition, Amman 27054

Korea, Republic
Straw and Grass Handicraft Museum, Seoul 27282

Kuwait
The Tareq Rajab Museum, Hawelli 27304

Malaysia
Heritage Museum, Kuah 27633
Kemajuan Kraftangan Malaysia, Rawang 27683
Kuala Lumpur Craft Museum, Kuala Lumpur 27641

Morocco
Musée de Dar-El-Jamaï, Meknès 28701

Netherlands
Afdeling Nuttige en Fraaie Handwerken, Uithuizermeeden 29889
Atelier Na-iem, Gees 29267
Craftselijke Zadelmakerij Museum, Bellingwolde 28973
De Dubbele Palmboom, Rotterdam 29749
Kantmuseum, Uithuizen 29887
Museum De Grutterswinkel, Leeuwarden 29511
Museum de Koperen Knop, Hardinxveld-Giessendam 29343
Museum de Timmerwerf, De Lier 29068
Museum de Valkhof, Hellendoorn 29386
Museum Valkenheide, Maarsbergen 29556
Museum van het Ambacht, Den Haag 29114
Museumboerderij, Paasloo 29709
Museummolen de Nieuwe Palmboom, Schiedam 29802
Nederlands Baksteen en Dakpanmuseum de Panoven, Zevenaar 30056
Nederlands Centrum voor Handwerken, Breda 29023
Oude Ambachten en Speelgoedmuseum, Terschuur 29869
Stadsboerderij Het Wevershuisje, Almelo 28810
Streekmuseum Opsterland, Gorredijk 29292

New Zealand
Hawke's Bay Museum, Napier 30207

Niue
Huanki Cultural Centre, Alofi 30365

Norway
Bygdetunet Jutulheimen, Vågåmo 30967
Hardanger Folkemuseum, Utne 30963
Stjørdal Museum KF, Stjørdal 30896
Trastad Samlinger, Borkenes 30444

Poland
Muzeum Dawnego Kupiectwa, Świdnica 32014
Muzeum Miedzi, Legnica 31754
Muzeum Regionalne, Chojnów 31530
Muzeum Regionalne, Krasnystaw 31733
Muzeum Rzemiosł Artystycznych i Precyzyjnych, Warszawa 32123
Państwowe Muzeum Etnograficzne, Warszawa 32140

Russia
Gorodeckij Kraevedčeskij Muzej, Gorodec 32809
Muzej Istorii Narodnych Chudožestvennych Promyslov, Nižnij Novgorod 33211
Muzej Remesla, Architektury i Byta, Kaluga 32881
Muzej Vjatskie Narodnye Chudožestvennye Promysly, Kirov 32922
Novgorodskij Gosudarstvennyj Muzej-zapovednik, Velikij Novgorod 33680

Serbia-Montenegro
Gradski Muzej Sombor, Sombor 33910

Slovakia
Múzeum Umeleckých Remesiel, Bratislava 33975
Múzeum v Kežmarku, Kežmarok 34002

Slovenia
Mestni Muzej Ljubljana, Ljubljana 34111

South Africa
Zululand Historical Museum, Eshowe 34238

Spain
Colección Municipal, Granada 34869
Museo Etnológico de Navarra Julio Caro Baroja, Ayegui 34508

Sweden
Åttingen Hantverk och Lantbruksmuseum, Aneby 35799
Falkenbergs Hembygdsmuseum, Falkenberg 35876
Friluftsmuseum Färgargården, Norrköping 36116
Hantverks- och Sjörfartsmuseét på Norra Berget, Sundsvall 36308
Hantverksloftet, Simrishamn 36187
Hantverksmuseet, Ängelholm 35787
Läckö Slott, Lidköping 36033
Länsmuseet Gävleborg, Gävle 35900
Länsmuseet Varberg, Varberg 36395
Nora Museum, Gyttorp 35933
Sadelmakare Öbergs Hus, Solna 36221
Skellefteå Museum, Skellefteå 36197
Slöjdmuseet, Ånge 35804

Switzerland
Heimatmuseum, Reinach (Basel-Land) 37052
Historisches Museum Arbon, Arbon 36465
Historisches Museum Blumenstein, Solothurn 37182
Malermuseum Wetzikon, Wetzikon 37313
Musée des Arts et des Sciences, Sainte-Croix 37091
Musée du Vieux-Moudon, Moudon 36957
Musée Paysan et Artisanal, La Chaux-de-Fonds 36631
Museum Wasseramt, Halten 36792
Ortsmuseum, Kaltbrunn 36822
Ziegelei-Museum, Cham 36622

United Kingdom
Abingdon Museum, Abingdon 37957
Bewdley Museum, Bewdley 38184
Castle Park Arts Centre, Frodsham 39018
Cousland Smiddy, Cousland 38640
Crafts Council Collection, London 39616
Cumberland Pencil Museum, Keswick 39343
Devon Guild of Craftsmen Gallery, Bovey Tracey 38288
Fordyce Joiner's Visitor Centre, Fordyce 39003
Friary Art Gallery, Lichfield 39489
Gordon Brown Collection, Ravenshead 40288
Hat Works, Museum of Hatting, Stockport 40596
Hop Farm, Paddock Wood 40155
Jersey Battle of Flowers Museum, Saint Ouen 40419
Museum of Local Crafts and Industries, Burnley 38399
The Petworth Cottage Museum, Petworth 40197
Ruthin Craft Centre, Ruthin 40361
Saint Ives Museum, Saint Ives, Cornwall 40408
Shepherd Wheel, Sheffield 40490
Shire Hall Gallery, Stafford 40571
Somerset Rural Life Museum, Glastonbury 39072
Stockwood Craft Museum and Mossman Gallery, Luton 39846
Strachur Smiddy Museum, Strachur 40620
W. Hourston Smithy Museum, Saint Margaret's Hope 40414

U.S.A.
Alleghany Highlands Arts and Crafts Center, Clifton Forge 42490
American Craft Museum, New York 45755
Arrowmont School of Arts and Crafts Collection, Gatlinburg 43635
Arts Center of the Ozarks, Springdale 47732
Brookfield Craft Center, Brookfield 41928
Bunker Hill Museum, Charlestown 42233
Center for Book Arts, New York 45777
Chimneyville Crafts Gallery, Jackson 44277
Craft Alliance Gallery, Saint Louis 47118
Crafts Museum, Mequon 45259
Craftsman Farms Foundation, Parsippany 46298
Crowley Art Association and Gallery, Crowley 42713
Cultural Heritage Center, Dallas 42747
Dawson Springs Museum and Art Center, Dawson Springs 42798
Fowler Museum of Cultural History, Los Angeles 44900
Georgetown College Gallery, Georgetown 43651
Hambidge Center for the Creative Arts and Sciences, Rabun Gap 46766
Hammond Museum, North Salem 46007
Hand Workshop Art Center, Richmond 46878
Hartzler-Towner Multicultural Museum, Nashville 45621
Haystack Mountain School of Crafts Gallery, Deer Isle 42844
Historic Sauder Village, Archbold 41248
Hull Lifesaving Museum, Hull 44149
Kentucky Art and Craft Foundation, Louisville 44967
The London Brass Rubbing Centre in Washington D.C., Gaithersburg 43591
Longboat Key Center for the Arts, Longboat Key 44875
Lyndon House Art Center, Athens 41320
Macalester College Art Gallery, Saint Paul 47159
Manchester Craftsmen's Guild, Pittsburgh 46520
Mattye Reed African Heritage Center, Greensboro 43817
Mint Museum of Craft and Design, Charlotte 42244
Mississippi Crafts Center, Ridgeland 46898

Museum and Arts Center in the Sequim Dungeness Valley, Sequim 47568
Museum of the American Quilter's Society, Paducah 46256
Old Depot Museum, Ottawa 46220
Pioneer Log Cabin, Manhattan 45109
Pope County Historical Museum, Glenwood 43699
Red Rock Museum, Church Rock 42394
Renwick Gallery of the Smithsonian American Art Museum, Washington 48390
Richard Sparrow House, Plymouth 46564
Schingoethe Center for Native American Cultures, Aurora 41398
School of Nations Museum, Elsah 43172
Snug Harbor Cultural Center, Staten Island 47787
Society for Contemporary Craft Museum, Pittsburgh 46527
South Carolina Artisans Center, Walterboro 48295
Southwest Museum, Los Angeles 44945
Steppingstone Museum, Havre de Grace 43966
Tama County Historical Museum, Toledo 48017
Thomas E. McMillan Museum, Brewton 41885
Vermont State Craft Center at Frog Hollow, Middlebury 45310
Western Colorado Center for the Arts, Grand Junction 43749
Westville Historic Handicrafts Museum, Lumpkin 45000
Wharton Esherick Museum, Malvern 45087
Worcester Center for Crafts, Worcester 48757
World Kite Museum and Hall of Fame, Long Beach 44865

Yemen
Al-Mukalla Museum, Al-Mukalla 49009
Seiyun in Wadi Hadhramaut Museum, Seiyun 49012

Heraldry → Genealogy

Hides and Skins

Canada
Ermatinger, Sault Sainte Marie 06411
Fort Carlton, Regina 06233
Lieu Historique National du Commerce de la Fourrure, Lachine 05711
Nor' Wester and Loyalist Museum, Williamstown 06805
Port Royal National Historic Site, Annapolis Royal 04998
Sturgeon River House, Sturgeon Falls 06505

U.S.A.
Fort Clark Trading Post, Center 42167
Gingras Trading Post, Walhalla 48282

History

Albania
District Historical Museum, Përmet 00029
Museum of the Struggle for National Liberation, Tiranë 00034
Muzeu Historik Fier, Fier 00021

Algeria
History and Natural History Museum, Alger 00040
Musée Emir Abdelkader, Miliana 00067

Andorra
Museu Casa Rull, Sispony 00087

Angola
Centro Nacional de Documentação e Investigação Histórica, Luanda 00094
Museu da Escravatura, Luanda 00096
Museu do Reino do Koongo, Mbanza Koongo 00103

Argentina
Casa Natal de Sarmiento, San Juan 00569
Fuerte de la Punta del Sauce, La Carlota 00376
Galería Monumento Histórico Nacional a la Bandera, Rosario 00524
Museo Americanista, Lomas de Zamora 00409
Museo de la Administración Federal de Ingresos Públicos, Buenos Aires 00183
Museo de la Casa Histórica de la Independencia Nacional, San Miguel de Tucumán 00583
Museo de la Escuela Normal Alejandro Carbo, Córdoba 00295
Museo de los Corrales Viejos de Parque de los Patricios, Buenos Aires 00191
Museo de los Pioneros, Río Gallegos 00514
Museo General Belgrano, Buenos Aires 00208
Museo Hermanos Nacif Weiss, Rivadavia 00522
Museo Histórico Conventual San Carlos, San Lorenzo 00576
Museo Histórico de la Honorable Cámara de Diputados de la Nación, Buenos Aires 00212
Museo Histórico de la Provincia de Catamarca, San Fernando del Valle de Catamarca 00557
Museo Histórico Municipal Brigadier General Juan Martín de Pueyrredón, San Isidro 00565
Museo Histórico Nacional, Buenos Aires 00215
Museo Histórico Provincial Colonel Manuel José Olascoaga, Chos Malal 00278
Museo La Cinacina, San Antonio de Areco 00551
Museo Malvinas Argentinas, Río Gallegos 00515
Museo Metropolitano, Buenos Aires 00223
Museo Nacional Justo José de Urquiza, Concepción del Uruguay 00285
Museo Provincial Mario Brozoski, Puerto Deseado 00489
Museo Ramón Pérez Fernández, Rivadavia 00523
Museo Regional Aníbal Cambas, Posadas 00485
Museo Regional Carlos Funes Derieul, Coronel Dorrego 00316
Museo Regional Dr. José Luro, Pedro Luro 00471
Museo Regional Histórico y de Ciencias Naturales, Coronel Pringles 00318
Museo Regional José G. Brochero, Santa Rosa de Río Primero 00614
Museo Rural de la Posta de Sinsacate, Jesús María 00372
Museo Senador Domingo Faustino Sarmiento, Buenos Aires 00243
Museos Integrales de Antofagasta de la Sierra y Laguna Blanca, San Fernando del Valle de Catamarca 00559
Sala Josefa Rodriguez del Fresno, Santa Fé 00610

Armenia
State History Museum of Armenia, Erevan 00692

Australia
Adelaide City Council Civic Collection, Adelaide 00702
Adelaide Lithuanian Museum and Archives, Norwood 01335
Adelaide Masonic Centre Museum, Adelaide 00703
Australian Stockman's Hall of Fame and Outback Heritage Centre, Longreach 01184
Commissariat Store Museum, Brisbane 00837
Conservation Resource Centre, Glebe 01057
Edith Cowan University Museum of Childhood, Claremont, Western Australia 00919
Edmund Wright House, Adelaide 00706
Garrison Gallery, Historical and Military Museum, Millers Point 01256
Griffith Pioneer Park Museum, Griffith 01075
Hyde Park Barracks Museum, Sydney 01497
Melbourne Museum, Carlton South 00896
Migration Museum, Adelaide 00709
Monarch Historical Museum, Williamtown 01603
Museum of Sydney, Sydney 01504
Museum Victoria, Carlton South 00897
National Museum of Australia, Canberra 00887
Queen Victoria Museum and Art Gallery, Launceston 01170
Royal Western Australian Historical Museum, Nedlands 01312
Tasmanian Museum and Art Gallery, Hobart 01106
Torres Strait Museum, Thursday Island 01534
Ukrainian Museum, Torrens Park 01544
Western Australian Museum, Perth 01364
Yarraman Heritage Centre, Yarraman 01628

Austria
Ausstellung Hittisauer Lebensbilder aus dem 19. Jahrhundert, Hittisau 02034
Berg-Isel-Museum der Tiroler Kaiserjäger mit Andreas Hofer-Galerie, Innsbruck 02062
Cowboy-Museum Fatsy, Linz 02229
Erzherzog Johann-Dokumentationsstätte, Thernberg 02729
Fürstlich Esterházy'sche Sammlungen Burg Forchtenstein, Forchtenstein 01842
Goldenes Dachl-Maximilianeum, Innsbruck 02067
Historisches Stadtmuseum Innsbruck, Innsbruck 02068
K K-Museum, Türnitz 02742
K.u.k. Hausmuseum, Weyregg am Attersee 02829
Mährisch-Schlesisches Heimatmuseum, Klosterneuburg 02140
Malteser-Museum Mailberg, Mailberg 02258
Museum der Mechitharisten-Congregation, Wien 02938
Museum Laxenburg, Laxenburg 02199
Napoleon- und Heimatmuseum, Deutsch Wagram 01759
Otto Wagner Hofpavillion Hietzing, Wien 02966
Otto Wagner Pavillion Karlsplatz, Wien 02967
Rogendorfer-Ausstellung, Pöggstall 02428
Salzburger Museum Carolino Augusteum, Salzburg 02551
Schlossmuseum, Linz 02241
Schlossmuseum mit Bauernkriegsmuseum, Oberösterreichischer Landeskrippe und Georg-von-Peuerbach-Ausstellung, Peuerbach 02411
Schulmuseum des Bezirkes Urfahr-Umgebung, Bad Leonfelden 01714
Sigmund Freud-Museum, Wien 02989

Azerbaijan
Museum of the History of Azerbaijan, Baku 03067

Bahamas
Bahamas Historical Society Museum, Nassau 03074
Pompey Museum of Slavery and Emancipation, Nassau 03077

Bahrain
Bahrain National Museum, Manama 03078

Bangladesh
Bangabandhu Shek Mujibur Rahman Museum, Dhaka 03083
Chittagong University Museum, Chittagong 03079
Mukti Juddha Museum, Dhaka 03091

Barbados
Barbados Museum, Saint Michael 03107

Belarus
Gosudarstvennyj Muzej Istorii i Kultury Belarusa, Minsk 03116
Grodnenski Gosudarstvennyj Istoričeskij Muzej, Grodno 03111

Belgium
Archeologisch Museum Van Bogaert-Wauters, Hamme 03472
Bijlokemuseum, Gent 03434
Gallo-Romeins Museum, Tongeren 03781
Groeningeabdij, Kortrijk 03541
IJzertoren-Museum Oorlog-Vrede-Vlaamse Ontvoogding, Diksmuide 03388
Mercator Museum, Sint-Niklaas 03742
Musée Communal d'Archéologie, d'Art et d'Histoire, Nivelles 03661
Musée de Waterloo, Waterloo 03829
Musée des Archives de l'Etat à Namur, Namur 03647
Musée d'Histoire et d'Archéologie, Warneton 03827
Musée Luxembourgeois, Arlon 03185
Musées Royaux d'Art et d'Histoire, Bruxelles 03337
Pauselijk Zouavenmuseum, Roeselare 03704
Rietgaverstede, Nevele 03656
Stadhuis, Gent 03451
Stedelijk Museum Aalst, Aalst 03125
Stedelijke Musea Kortrijk, Kortrijk 03543
Torenmuseum, Mol 03630

Belize
Museum of Belize, Belize City 03865

Benin
Musée d'Histoire, Ouidah 03875
Musée Historique, Abomey 03871
Musée Historique d'Abomey, Abomey 03872
Musée National, Porto-Novo 03879

Bermuda
Bermuda Maritime Museum, Mangrove Bay 03885

Bosnia and Herzegovina
Memorijalni Muzej Gavrila Principa u Obljaju, Bosansko Grahova 03914
Muzej Hercegovine, Mostar 03917

Botswana
Khama III Memorial Museum, Serowe 03939

Brazil
Biblioteca e Museu Regional Dr. Alípio de Araújo Silva, Rio Preto 04411
Divisão de Museus, Patrimônio e Arquivo Histórico, Taubaté 04556
Museu Afro Brasileiro de Sergipe, Laranjeiras 04169
Museu Arquivo Histórico da Santa Casa, Belém 03970
Museu Banespa, São Paulo 04498
Museu Bi Moreira, Lavras 04170
Museu Casa de Portinari, Brodowski 04011
Museu da Associação Nacional dos Veteranos, São João Del Rei 04467
Museu da Família Colonial, Blumenau 03991
Museu de Arte e Histórico, Jaboticabal 04141
Museu de Folclore Saul Martins, Vespasiano 04584
Museu de História Natural, Crato 04058
Museu de Instrumentos de Cálculo Numérico, São Carlos 04458
Museu de Pedras Ramis Bucair, Cuiabá 04060
Museu de Tradições do Nordeste, Brasília 04000
Museu do Ceará, Fortaleza 04100
Museu do Estado da Bahia, Salvador 04433
Museu do Instituto Arqueológico, Histórico e Geográfico Pernam Bucano, Recife 04303
Museu do Instituto Geografico e Historico da Bahia, Salvador 04434
Museu do Instituto Histórico e Geográfico Brasileiro, Rio de Janeiro 04370
Museu do Instituto Histórico e Geográfico de Alagoas, Maceió 04183
Museu do Instituto Histórico e Geográfico do Rio Grande do Norte, Natal 04223
Museu do Minstério do Trabalho, Brasília 04002
Museu do Primeiro Reinado, Rio de Janeiro 04374
Museu do STF, Brasília 04003
Museu Educativo Gama d'Eça, Santa Maria 04444
Museu Guido Straube, Curitiba 04074
Museu Gustavo Barroso, Fortaleza 04101
Museu Histórico, Cambé 04018
Museu Histórico, Divinópolis 04081
Museu Histórico, Londrina 04175
Museu Histórico, Nova Ponte 04228
Museu Histórico, Rio Pomba 04410
Museu Histórico, São Francisco do Sul 04462
Museu Histórico Aurélio Dolabella, Santa Luzia 04443
Museu Histórico Bárbara Heliodora, São Gonçalo do Sapucaí 04465
Museu Histórico Beato José de Anchieta, Pedreira 04254
Museu Histórico Casa do Imigrante, Bento Gonçalves 03989
Museu Histórico Corália Venites Maluf, Sacramento 04418
Museu Histórico Cultural, Rio do Sul 04407
Museu Histórico da Cidade, Brasília 04005
Museu Histórico da Universidade Federal, Viçoasa 04586
Museu Histórico de Araxá - Don Beja, Araxá 03957
Museu Histórico de Jataí Francisco Honório de Campos, Jataí 04146
Museu Histórico do Senado Federal, Brasília 04006
Museu Histórico Dona Mariana Joaquina da Costa, Vespasiano 04585
Museu Histórico e de Ordem Geral Plínio Travassos dos Santos, Rebeirão Preto 04294
Museu Histórico e Diplomático do Itamaraty, Rio de Janeiro 04384
Museu Histórico Municipal, Carangola 04039
Museu Histórico Municipal e da Imigração Italiana Oswaldo Samuel Massei, São Caetano do Sul 04457
Museu Histórico Municipal Tuany Toledo, Pouso Alegre 04292
Museu Histórico Nacional, Rio de Janeiro 04385
Museu Histórico Regional, Apucarana 03948
Museu Histórico Regional, Itambacuri 04132
Museu Histórico Tenente Coronel PM Augusto de Almeida Garrett, Curitiba 04075
Museu Histórico Visconde de São Leopoldo, São Leopoldo 04475
Museu Joaquim José Felizardo, Porto Alegre 04284
Museu Julio de Castilhos, Porto Alegre 04285
Museu Leprológico, Curitiba 04076
Museu Meridional, Porto Alegre 04286
Museu Metropolitano de Arte, Curitiba 04077
Museu Municipal, Conquista 04051
Museu Nacional do Mar - Embarações Brasileiras, São Francisco do Sul 04463
Museu Patríco Corrêa da Câmara, Bagé 03965
Museu Paulista da Universidade de São Paulo, São Paulo 04542
Museu Regional D. Bosco, Campo Grande 04031
Museu Regional de Olinda, Olinda 04233
Museu Republicano Convenção de Itu, Itu 04140
Museu Sargento Edésio de Carvalho, Sousa 04554
Museu Theodormiro Carneiro Santiago, Itajubá 04131
Sala de Memórias de Chapada dos Guimarães, Chapada dos Guimarães 04049

Brunei
Constitutional History Gallery, Bandar Seri Begawan 04596
Muzium Brunei, Bandar Seri Begawan 04598

Bulgaria
Gradski Istoričeski Muzej, Jeravna 04683
Istoričeski Muzej, Batak 04616
Istoričeski Muzej, Drjanovo 04660
Istoričeski Muzej, Pravec 04787
Istoričeski Muzej Krastata Kazarma, Vidin 04923
Istoričeski Muzej - Preminavane na Ruskite Vojski pri Svištov, Svištov 04881
Istoričeski Muzej Targovište, Targovište 04883
Istoričeskij Muzej, Tutrakan 04892
Kăšta-muzej Bojan Chonos, Vidin 04924
Kăšta-muzej Christo G. Danov, Plovdiv 04778
Kăšta-muzej Christo i Ivan Michailovi, Michajlovgrad 04738
Kăšta-muzej Dimităr Poljanov, Karnobat 04693
Kăšta-muzej Dobri Voinikov, Šumen 04871
Kăšta-muzej Georgi Benkovski, Koprivštica 04713
Kăšta-muzej na Slivenskija Bit ot 19 Vek, Sliven 04820
Kăšta-muzej Neofit Rilski, Bansko 04614
Kăšta-muzej Panaět Volov, Šumen 04872
Kăšta-muzej Pančo Vladigerov, Šumen 04873
Kăšta-muzej Svetoslav Obretenov, Provadia 04790
Kăšta-muzej Zachari Stojanov, Medven 04733
Kăšta-muzej Zachari Stojanov, Ruse 04803
Memorialen Kompleks Balova Shuma, Gavril Genovo 04672
Muzej Kăkrinsko Chanče, Kăkrina 04684
Muzej na Văzroždeneto i Nacionalno-osvoboditelnite Borbi, Elena 04663
Muzej Semejstvo Obretenovi, Ruse 04805
Muzej Slivenski Zatvor, Sliven 04823
Muzej Vojniško Văstanie 1918, Radomir 04795
Nacionalen Istoričeski Muzej, Sofia 04846
Nacionalen Muzej Parachod Radecki, Kozloduj 04722
Nacionalen Muzej Roženski Manastir, Rožen 04801
Nacionalen Park-muzej Samuilova krepost, Petrič 04762
Nova Istoria na Veliko Tărnovo, Veliko Tărnovo 04919
Okrăžen Istoričeski Muzej, Veliko Tărnovo 04920
Panorama Plevenska Epopeja 1877, Pleven 04769
Park-muzej General V.Z. Lavrov, Gorni Dabnik 04677
Park-Muzej Vladislav Varnenčik, Varna 04905
Pashova Kăshta, Melnik 04735
Regionalen Istoričeski Muzej, Pleven 04770
Sarafkina Kăšta Gradski Bit, Veliko Tărnovo 04921
Skobelev Park-muzej, Pleven 04771
Voenno-istoričeski Muzej, Pleven 04772
Voenno-istoričeski Muzej Osvoboditelna Vojna 1877-1878, Bjala 04623

Cambodia
Musée du Palais Royal, Phnom Penh 04949

Canada
Admiral Digby Museum, Digby 05330
Art Gallery of Bishop's University, Lennoxville 05742
Avon River Heritage Museum, Hants County 05582
Campbell River Museum, Campbell River 05187
Cape Spear National Historic Site, Saint John's 06341
Cavalier Block, Halifax 05548

Cave and Basin National Historic Site, Banff 05043
Centre National d'Exposition, Jonquière 05634
Chatham-Kent Museum, Chatham, Ontario 05237
Cossit House Museum, Sydney 06526
Diefenbaker Canada Centre, Saskatoon 06396
Fort Anne, Annapolis Royal 04996
Fort Langley National Historic Site, Fort Langley 05441
Fort Malden, Amherstburg 04987
Fort Ostell Museum, Ponoka 06146
Fort Saint John-North Peace Museum, Fort Saint John 05450
Fultz House Museum, Lower Sackville 05784
Gaspesian British Heritage Village, New Richmond 05980
Head-Smashed-In Buffalo Jump, Fort Macleod 05444
Hermitage Gatehouse Museum, Ancaster 04992
Ireland House Museum, Burlington 05146
Keir Memorial Museum, Kensington 05658
Labrador Heritage Museum, Happy Valley 05583
Lieu Historique National du Canada de la Bataille-de-la-Ristigouche, Pointe-à-la-Croix 06141
Lithuanian Museum-Archives of Canada, Mississauga 05872
Log Cabin Museum, Murray Harbour 05951
McFarland House, Niagara Falls 05993
Manoir Leboutillier, Anse-au-Griffon 05000
Montgomery's Inn, Etobicoke 05418
Monument Lefebvre, Memramcook 05840
Musée Canadien des Civilisations, Gatineau 05484
Musée de l'Amérique Française, Québec 06204
Musée de Saint-Boniface, Saint-Boniface 06307
Musée des Pioneers, Saint-André-Avelin 06301
Musée des Ursulines, Trois-Rivières 06643
Musée d'Histoire et de Traditions Populaires, Gaspé 05479
Musée du Château Ramezay, Montréal 05920
Musée Laurier, Victoriaville 06731
Musée Stewart au Fort de Ile Sainte-Hélène, Montréal 05926
Museum London, London 05772
Myrtleville House Museum, Brantford 05127
Nanton Lancaster Air Museum, Nanton 05962
New Iceland Heritage Museum, Gimli 05488
Pioneer Historical Connors Museum, Connors 05272
Port Royal National Historic Site, Annapolis Royal 04998
Prince Edward Island Museum, Charlottetown 05230
Province House, Charlottetown 05232
Scadding Cabin, Toronto 06609
Secwepemc Museum and Heritage Park, Kamloops 05641
Signal Hill National Historic Site, Saint John's 06353
Sod House Museum, Arctic Bay 05005
Sodbuster Archives Museum, Strome 06504
Spadina Museum, Toronto 06613
Sukanen Ship Pioneer Village and Museum of Saskatchewan, Moose Jaw 05935
Thomas Foster Memorial Temple, Uxbridge 06656
Uncle Tom's Cabin Historic Site, Dresden 05339
UVAN Historical Museum, Winnipeg 06851
Villa Bagatelle, Sillery 06454
Walter Wright Pioneer Village, Dawson Creek 05315
Whyte Museum of the Canadian Rockies, Banff 05045
Wiltondale Pioneer Village, Bonne Bay 05096
Wood Mountain Post, Regina 06250

Chile
Museo de la Solidaridad Salvador Allende, Santiago de Chile 06913
Museo del Carmen de Maipú, Santiago de Chile 06914
Museo Histórico Regional de Magallanes, Punta Arenas 06904
Museo Martín Gusinde, Puerto Williams 06903
Museo O'Higginiano y de Bellas Artes de Talca, Talca 06922

China, People's Republic
Anhui Sheng Bo Wu Guan, Hefei 07091
Beijing Dabaotai Western Han Tomb Museum, Beijing 06948
China Great Wall Museum, Beijing 06959
China National Museum, Beijing 06961
Dayi Liu's Manor-House Museum, Chengdu 07021
Guangdong Museum, Guangzhou 07062
Hainan Museum, Haikou 07079
Hebei Museum, Shijiazhuang 07246
Hebei Provincial Museum, Wuhan 07280
Heilongjiang Province Nation Museum, Harbin 07089
History Museum of the Taiping Heavenly Kingdom in Nanjing, Nanjing 07176
Hunan Provincial Museum, Changsha 07010
Jiangnan Gongyuan History Display Center, Nanjing 07177
Jilin Museum, Changchun 07002
Liao Jincheng Yuan, Beijing 06970
Liaoning Museum, Shenyang 07235
Longhua Mausoleum of Fallen Heroes, Shanghai 07215
Mountain Resort Museum, Chengde 07018
Museum of Macao, Macau 07167
Museum of the Liangshan Autonomous Prefecture of the Yi Nationality, Xichang 07309
Museum of the Mausoleum of King Nanyue, Guangzhou 07070
Nation Museum, Beijing 06979
National Museum of Chinese History, Beijing 06980
Quaternary Period Qlacier Traces Exhibition Hall, Beijing 06986
Santiaoshi History Museum, Tianjin 07262
Shaanxi History Museum, Xian 07298
Shandong Provincial Museum, Jinan 07134
Shanghai History Museum, Shanghai 07219
Shenyang Palace Museum, Shenyang 07236
Xinjiang Museum, Urumchi 07275
Zhejiang Museum, Hangzhou 07087
Zhonghua Nation Museum, Beijing 06998

China, Republic
Museum of the Institute of History and Philology, Academia Sinica, Taipei 07349
National Museum of History, Taipei 07350
National Palace Museum, Taipei 07351

Colombia
Casa Museo 20 de Julio de 1810, Bogotá 07382
Casa Museo Quinta de Bolívar, Bogotá 07384
Cuadros Vivos de la Sabana, Corozal 07466
Museo Antonio Ricaurte, Villa de Leyva 07619
Museo Casa de la Cultura de Pensilvania, Pensilvania 07555
Museo Casa de la Cultura "Luis Camacho Rueda", Socorro 07596
Museo Casa del Fundador Ponzalo Suárez Rendón, Tunja 07611
Museo Casa Natal General Santander, Villa del Rosario 07624
Museo de Artes y Tradiciones Populares de Ráquira, Ráquira 07575
Museo de la Ferrería de La Pradera, Subachoque 07601
Museo del Hombre en el Universo, Sopó 07600
Museo Fotográfico, Calarcá 07443
Museo Histórico Casa de la Convención de Rionegro, Rionegro 07578
Museo Histórico y Arqueológico, Charalá 07462
Museo Luis A. Calvo, Agua de Dios 07360
Museo Quinta de San Pedro Alejandrino, Santa Marta 07591
Museo Taminango de Artes y Tradiciones Populares de Nariño, Pasto 07553
Museo Univérsitas, El Cerrito 07475

Comoros
Musée National, Moroni 07630

Congo, Republic
Musée National du Congo, Brazzaville 07645

Costa Rica
Museo Histórico Cultural Juan Santamaría, Alajuela 07648

Côte d'Ivoire
Musée des Civilisations de Côte d'Ivoire, Abidjan 07666

Croatia
Creski Muzej, Cres 07691
Gradski Muzej Virovitica, Virovitica 07801
Hrvatski Povijesni Muzej, Zagreb 07822
Memorijalna Zbirka Eugena Kumičića, Brseč 07685
Muzej Slavonije Osijek, Osijek 07750
Pomorski i Povijesni Muzej Hrvatskog Primorja, Rijeka 07763
Spomen-Kuća Vladimira Gortana, Beran 07679

Cuba
Museo 13 de Marzo, Pinar del Río 08070
Museo Casa Natal de Calixto Garcia, Holguín 08003
Museo Casa Natal de Carlos Manuel de Céspedes, Bayamo 07858
Museo Comandancia La Plata, Santo Domingo 08152
Museo de Ambiente Histórico Cubano, Santiago de Cuba 08134
Museo de Baracoa, Baracoa 07855
Museo de la Guerra Hispano-Cubano-Norteamericana, Santiago de Cuba 08138
Museo Historico de Ciego de Avila, Ciego de Avila 07887
Museo Histórico de Palma Soriano, Palma Soriano 08064
Museo Histórico Municipal de Guanabacoa, Guanabacoa 07913
Museo Máximo Gómez, La Habana 07975
Museo Memorial 26 de Julio, Victoria de las Tunas 08171
Museo Memorial El Morrillo, Matanzas 08041
Museo Memorial José Martí, La Habana 07977
Museo Memorial La Demajagua, Manzanillo 08032
Museo Memorial Los Malagones, Moncada 08050
Museo Memorial Vicente García, Victoria de las Tunas 08173
Museo Municipal del III Frente, Santiago de Cuba 08149
Museo Nacional de Camilo Cienfuegos, Sancti-Spíritus 08114
Museo Provincial de la Historia de Pinar del Río, Pinar del Río 08077

Cyprus
Cyprus Historical Museum, Lefkosia 08196
Museum of the History of Cypriot Coinage, Lefkosia 08204

Cyprus, Turkish Republic
Barbarlık Müzesi, Lefkoşa 08234

Czech Republic
Historické Muzeum, Praha 08580
Jihomoravské Muzeum ve Znojmě, Znojmo 08756
Lobkovicky Palác, Praha 08589
Masarykovo Muzeum, Hodonín 08354
Městské Muzeum v Železném Brodě, Železný Brod 08747
Muzeum Středniho Pootavi, Strakonice 08663
Muzeum v Bruntále, Bruntál 08282
Muzeum Východních Čech v Hradci Králové, Hradec Králové 08368
Národní Muzeum, Praha 08602
Památník Bedřicha Václavka, Čáslavice 08289
Památník Josefa Ladislava Piče, Mšeno u Mělníka 08490
Památník Krále Jiřího z Poděbrad a Lapidarium, Poděbrady 08550
Památník Lidice, Lidice 08453
Vlastivědné Muzeum v Olomouci, Olomouc 08516

Denmark
Aalborg Historiske Museum, Aalborg 08762
Amalienborg, København 08920
Ballerup Egnsmuseet, Ballerup 08782
Blaabjerg Egnsmuseum, Nørre Nebel 08991
Danmarks Kloster Museum, Ry 09050
Ebeltoft Museum, Ebeltoft 08801
Farums Arkiver og Museer, Farum 08823
Frøslevlejrens Museum, Padborg 09023
Grundtvigs Mindestuer i Udby, Lundby 08978
Horsens Museum, Horsens 08898
Lejre Forsøgscenter, Lejre 08970
Museet på Sønderborg Slot, Sønderborg 09074
Museet ved Trelleborg, Slagelse 09070
Nationalmuseet, København 08943
Silkeborg Kulturhistoriske Museum, Silkeborg 09052

East Timor
East Timorese Cultural Centre Museum Collection, Dili 09130
Museum Sonyine Malige, Halmahera Tengah 09132

Ecuador
Museo Casa de Sucre, Quito 09198
Museo Cultural del Instituto Geografico Militar, Quito 09200
Museo Historico Casa de los Tratados, Cuenca 09161

Egypt
Museum of the Faculty of Arts, Alexandria 09244

Estonia
Eesti Ajaloomuuseum, Tallinn 09356
Eesti Põllumajandusmuuseum, Tõrvandi 09391
Rakvere Linnakodaniku Muuseum, Rakvere 09348

Ethiopia
National Museum of Ethiopia, Addis Ababa 09400

Finland
Aboa Vetus - Arkeologis-historiallinen Museo, Turku 10117
Hämeen Museo, Tampere 10076
Lahden Historiallinen Museo, Lahti 09742
Mannerheim Museo, Helsinki 09514
Maria de Lisitzin Fine Art and Historical Museum, Porvoo 09953
Museokeskus Vapriikki, Tampere 10081
Suomen Kansallismuseo, Helsinki 09531

France
Ateliers de l'Abeille, Chavignon 11259
Château de Gratot, Gratot 11925
Château et Musée de Filain-Fort, Filain 11734
Château-Musée d'Aulteribe, Sermentizon 14721
Collections de l'Abbaye Bénédictine de Saint-Louis-du-Temple, Vauhallan 15099
Fondation Dosne-Thiers, Paris 13502
Galerie d'Exposition d'Art et d'Histoire, Villaries 15179
Historium de Sedan, Sedan 14689
Maison dite de la Duchesse Anne, Morlaix 13162
Mémorial Caen-Normandie, Caen 10979
Mémorial des Soldats de La Nouvelle France, Le Château-d'Oléron 12399
Musée America-Gold Beach, Ver-sur-Mer 15125
Musée Archéologique et Historique, Clichy 11333
Musée Arthur Batut, Labruguière 12288
Musee Bajén-Vega, Monesties 13011
Musée Bourbonnais, Moulins (Allier) 13186
Musée Centre Culturel, Vichy 15161
Musée Charles-VII, Mehun-sur-Yèvre 12915
Musée de Bretagne, Rennes (Ille-et-Vilaine) 13941
Musée de la Bataille de Tilly sur Seulles 1944, Tilly-sur-Seulles 14914
Musée de La Bouteille, Saint-Emilion 14193
Musée de la Bresse, Saint-Cyr-sur-Menton 14172
Musée de la Citadelle, Bitche 10747
Musée de la Curiosité et de la Magie, Paris 13554
Musée de la Déportation et de la Résistance, Tarbes 14866
Musée de la Guerre 1939-45, Pourrain 13853
Musée de la Monnaie, Paris 13557
Musée de la Résistance et Déportation, Blois 10773
Musée de la Résistance Henri-Queuille, Neuvic (Corrèze) 13293
Musée de la Vie d'Autrefois, Vivoin 15279
Musée de la Vie Romantique, Paris 13568
Musée de l'Ancien Havre, Le Havre 12424
Musée de l'Histoire de France, Paris 13574
Musée de l'Histoire de la Médecine, Vandœuvre-les-Nancy 15078
Musée de l'Hôtel de Barral, Soissons 14761
Musée de l'Ile de France, Sceaux 14678
Musée de l'Œuvre, Avignon 10529
Musée de Notre-Dame-de-Paris, Paris 13583
Musée de Tourisme et d'Artisanat, Lys-Saint-Georges 12755
Musée Départemental Albert-Kahn, Boulogne-Billancourt 10836
Musée Départemental de la Résistance et de la Déportation, Lorris 12670
Musée Départemental de la Résistance et de la Déportation, Tulle 15012
Musée Départemental de la Résistance et de la Déportation Jean Philippe, Toulouse 14945
Musée des Amis du Vieux Corbie, Corbie 11404
Musée des Traditions Comtadines, Pernes-les-Fontaines 13696
Musée des Traditions Populaires Marius Audin, Beaujeu 10639
Musée d'Izieu Mémorial des Enfants Juifs Exterminés, Izieu 12069
Musée d'Orange, Orange 13412
Musée du Biterrois, Béziers 10719
Musée du Café Gondrée, Bénouville 10685
Musée du Capitellu, Ajaccio 10264
Musée du Palais des Evêques, Saint-Lizier 14325
Musée du Patrimoine Religieux et des Croyances Populaires, Moustey 13194
Musée du Pays Rabastinois, Monesties 13012
Musée du Prieuré, Perrecy-les-Forges 13711
Musée du Septennat de François Mitterrand, Château-Chinon 11202
Musée Historique, Mulhouse 13214
Musée Historique de Graffiti Anciens, Marsilly 12874
Musée Historique du Domaine National, Saint-Cloud 14162
Musée Hospitalier, Charlieu 11182
Musée Intercommunal d'Histoire et d'Archéologie, Louvres 12705
Musée Lacoune, Lacaune 12291
Musée Laperouse, Albi 10275
Musée Lapidaire, Cabasse 10966
Musée Lautrecois, Lautrec 12358
Musée Lorrain, Nancy 13243
Musée Maison Déodat Roché, Arques (Aude) 10426
Musée Marcel Cachin, Choisy-le-Roi 11296
Musée-Mémorial National du Débarquement en Provence (1944), Toulon (Var) 14931
Musée Napoléonien, Ile-d'Aix 12045
Musée National de la Légion d'Honneur et des Ordres de Chevalerie, Paris 13630
Musée National des Arts Asiatiques Guimet, Paris 13633
Musée National du Château de Fontainebleau, Fontainebleau 11769
Musée Raymond Poincaré, Sampigny 14598
Musée Remenber 39-45, Léhon 12508
Musée Une Halte sur le Chemin de Saint-Jacques, Borce 10801
Musée Vivant de la Laine et du Mouton, Saint-Pierreville 14420
Petit Musée des Silos de Jouques, Jouques 12095
Refuge Fortifié Muséalisé, Dossenheim-sur-Zinsel 11556

Gabon
Musée National du Gabon, Libreville 15351

Gambia
Gambia National Museum, Banjul 15352

Georgia
State Museum of Georgia, Tbilisi 15366

Germany
Alpinmuseum, Kempten 18062
Altes Schloß Schleißheim, Sammlung zur Landeskunde Ost- und Westpreußen, Oberschleißheim 19199
Antifaschistische Mahn- und Gedenkstätte, Lieberose 18462
Ausstellungszentrum Kroch-Haus, Leipzig 18387
Bismarck-Museum, Schönhausen, Elbe 19833
Burg Hohenzollern, Bisingen 16172
Deutsches Bauernkriegsmuseum, Böblingen 16210
Deutsches Historisches Museum, Berlin 15939
Dokumentationszentrum Alltagskultur der DDR, Eisenhüttenstadt 16823
Domschatzkammer, Essen 16948
Emslandmuseum Schloß Clemenswerth, Sögel 19974
Erinnerungsstätte Baltringer Haufen Bauernkrieg in Oberschwaben, Mietingen 18736
Familienmuseum Bad Homburg, Bad Homburg v.d.Höhe 15664
Foltermuseum, Burghausen, Salzach 16419
Frauen Museum, Bonn 16236
Friedlandstube Hünfeld, Hünfeld 17855
Gartenkunst-Museum Schloss Fantasie, Eckersdorf 16778
Gedenkstätte Großbeeren 1813, Großbeeren 17424
Gerhart-Hauptmann-Haus, Düsseldorf 16724
Germanisches Nationalmuseum, Nürnberg 19139
Goslarer Zinnfiguren-Museum, Goslar 17350
Graf-Luxburg-Museum, Bad Bocklet 15615
Gustav-Adolf-Museum, Geleithaus, Weißenfels 20497
Heimatmuseum, Müllrose 18820
Heimatmuseum der Deutschen aus Bessarabien, Stuttgart 20096
Herfurthsche Haus, Hainichen, Sachsen 17497
Historisches Museum im Marstall, Paderborn 19335
Historisches Museum Regensburg, Regensburg 19524
Historisches Museum Schloß Bad Urach, Bad Urach 15756

Hofgarten an der Residenz, München 18856
Idstedt-Gedächtnishalle, Idstedt 17881
John-Wagener-Haus Sievern, Langen bei Bremerhaven 18322
Judenbad, Friedberg, Hessen 17138
Jüdisches Museum Berlin, Berlin 16009
Kaiserpfalz mit Sankt Ulrichskapelle, Goslar 17352
Kreismuseum Wittenberg, Prettin 19445
Kügelgenhaus, Dresden 16688
Kulturhistorisches Museum Magdeburg, Magdeburg 18581
Kyffhäuser-Denkmal, Bad Frankenhausen 15643
Melanchthonhaus Wittenberg, Lutherstadt Wittenberg 18576
Mindener Museum für Geschichte, Landes- und Volkskunde, Minden, Westfalen 18749
Moltke-Gedächtnisstätte, Parchim 19348
Museum Burg Abenberg, Abenberg 15388
Museum für Kommunikation Nürnberg im Verkehrsmuseum, Nürnberg 19152
Museum für schlesische Landeskunde im Haus Schlesien, Königswinter 18183
Museum Hoffmann'sche Sammlung, Kohren-Sahlis 18197
Museum im ehemaligen Augustiner-Chorherrenstift, Herrenchiemsee 17734
Museum Stadt Königsberg, Duisburg 16754
Museum und Studienstätte Schloss Nöthnitz, Bannewitz 15822
Museum zur brandenburg-preußischen Geschichte/ Zinnfigurenmuseum, Gusow 17466
Nordwestdeutsches Schulmuseum Friesland, Zetel 20748
Ostdeutsche Heimatstube, Fellbach 16991
Ostdeutsche Heimatstube, Schwäbisch Hall 19869
Otto-König von Griechenland-Museum, Ottobrunn 19329
Philipp-Reis-Haus Friedrichsdorf, Friedrichsdorf, Taunus 17146
Pommersches Landesmuseum, Greifswald 17390
Preußen-Museum Nordrhein-Westfalen, Wesel 20536
Priesterhäuser, Zwickau 20777
Reichskammergerichtsmuseum, Wetzlar 20558
Saalburgmuseum, Bad Homburg 15663
Schatzhaus in der Lausitz, Göda 17311
Schloß Brake - Das Weserrenaissance-Museum, Lemgo 18431
Schloss Trebsen, Trebsen 20196
Schloss Wiederau, Pegau 19365
Schloss Wolkenburg, Wolkenburg-Kaufungen 20669
Schwedenspeicher-Museum, Stade 20026
Stadtmuseum Meißen, Meißen 18692
Staufergedächtnisstätte und Museum Wäscherschloß, Wäschenbeuren 20339
Westpreussisches Landesmuseum, Münster 18952
Widukind-Museum, Enger 16875
Württembergisches Landesmuseum Stuttgart, Stuttgart 20115

Ghana
Cape Coast Castle Museum, Cape Coast 20791

Greece
Cultural Center Hellenic Cosmos, Athinai 20856
Eleftherios K. Venizelos Museum, Athinai 20858
Historical and Ethnological Museum of Patras, Patrai 21115
Historical Museum of Crete, Iráklion 20975
Mouseio Mpenaki, Athinai 20878
Pavlos Vrellis Museum of Greek History, Ioannina 20971
Therisso Museum of Eleftherios Venizelos, Chania 20920
Vouros Eftaxias Museum, Athinai 20906

Guatemala
Museo de Santiago de los Caballeros, Antigua 21262
Museo Nacional de Historia, Guatemala 21273

Guinea
Musée National de Guinée, Conakry 21283

Haiti
Musée du Panthéon National Haïtien, Port-au-Prince 21293

Honduras
Museo Antropologia e Historia Valle de Sula, San Pedro Sula 21301
Museo Nacional de Historia Colonial, Omoa 21300

Hungary
Bihari Múzeum, Berettyóujfalu 21321
Blaskovich Múzeum, Tápiószele 21591
Budavári Mátyás Templom Egyházmüvészeti Gyüjteménye, Budapest 21332
Csók István Képtár, Székesfehérvár 21555
Ferenczy Károly Múzeum, Szentendre 21570
Jantyik Mátyás Múzeum, Békés 21317
Laczkó Dezsoë Múzeum, Veszprém 21608
Magyar Nemzeti Múzeum, Budapest 21361
Német Nemzetiségi Muzeum, Tata 21594
Rákóczi Múzeum, Sárospatak 21524
Rétközi Múzeum, Kisvárda 21462
Római Katonai Fürdö, Budapest 21381
Várostörténeti Múzeum, Pécs 21516
Zrinyi Miklós Vármúzeum, Szigetvár 21582

Iceland
Byggðasafn Dalamanna, Búdardalur 21627

India
Bhagavan Mahavir Government Museum, Cuddapah 21752
Carey Museum, Hooghly 21839
Childrens Museum, Imphal 21851
Gandhi National Memorial, Pune 21990
Government Museum Vellore, Vellore 22059
Heras Institute of Indian History and Culture, Mumbai 21949
H.H. Maharaja Jayaji Rao Scindia Museum, Gwalior 21829
Leimarel Museum and Research Centre, Imphal 21853
Police Museum, Imphal 21856
Shillong Tribal Research Institute, Shillong 22018
Shri Chhatrapati Shivaji Maharaj Museum, Satara 22013
Tipu Sahib Museum, Srirangapatna 22029

Indonesia
Jakarta History Museum, Jakarta 22106
Monumen Nasional, Jakarta 22108
Museum Asia Africa, Bandung 22071
Museum Dewantara Kirti Griya, Yogyakarta 22219
Museum Joang '45, Medan 22157
Museum Kebangkitan Nasional, Jakarta 22117
Museum Negeri Kalimantan Timur Mulawarman, Tenggarong 22211
Museum Negeri of Aceh, Banda Aceh 22068
Museum Negeri Propinsi Nusa Tenggara Timur, Kupang 22149
Museum Pancacsila Sakti, Jakarta 22125
Museum Pangeran Diponegoro, Yogyakarta 22223
Museum Pendidikan Islam, Yogyakarta 22224
Museum Pers, Surakarta 22203
Museum Pugung Ulago Sembah, Donggala 22099
Museum Sasmita Loka A. Yani, Jakarta 22128
Museum Sono Budoyo, Yogyakarta 22227
Museum Sudirman, Magelang 22151
Museum Sumpah Pemuda, Jakarta 22133
Museum Tugu Nasional, Jakarta 22137
Museum Wanua Paksinanta, Manado 22155
Sultan Mahmud Badaruddin II Museum, Palembang 22170

Iran
Golestan Palace Museum, Teheran 22300
Khorassan Natural History Museum, Mashad 22266
Melli Museum, Teheran 22311
Nader Mausoleum, Mashad 22267
National Museum, Teheran 22319
National Museum of Kashan, Kashan 22250
Rais-ali-delvary Museum, Bushehr 22235
Sa'dabad Museums, Teheran 22325
Toos Museum, Mashad 22268

Iraq
Iraqi Museum, Baghdad 22346
Kirkuk Museum, Kirkuk 22350

Ireland
DeValera Museum and Bruree Heritage Centre, Bruree 22379
Donegal Historical Society Museum, Rossnowlagh 22537
Famine Museum, Strokestown 22545
Kerry County Museum, Tralee 22547
Michael Davitt National Memorial Museum, Straide 22544
National 1798 Visitor Centre, Enniscorthy 22468
The Queenstown Story, Cobh 22400

Israel
Bet Hashomer Museum, Kibbutz Kfar Giladi 22691
Edward and Helen Mardigian Museum, Jerusalem 22632
Eretz-Israel Museum Tel Aviv, Tel Aviv 22753
Hamizgaga Museum, Kibbutz Nachsholim 22697
Man in the Galilee Museum, Kibbutz Ginosar 22688
Medicine and Pioneers Museum, Menahimiya 22711
Museum of Taxes, Jerusalem 22651
Museum of Yarmukian, Kibbutz Shaar Hagolan 22705
Resistance Museum, Akko 22568
Tower of David, Jerusalem 22667
Weizmann Archives and House, Rehovot 22739
Yad Labanim Museum and Memorial Center, Petah Tikva 22727
Yad Yaari Museum of Jewish Youth Movement, Givat Haviva 22593

Italy
Castello di Masnago, Varese 25895
Fondazione Museo Glauco Lombardi, Parma 24798
Landesmuseum Schloß Tirol, Tirolo di Merano 25708
Monumenti Antichi, Medioevali e Moderni, Roma 25171
Museo Archeologico, Venafro 25909
Museo Archivio Sacrario di Storia Patria, Bagheria 22999
Museo Casa Walser, Macugnaga 24253
Museo Centrale dell'Istituto Storico della Resistenza, Imperia 24093
Museo Civico, Barga 23018
Museo Civico Archeologico, Anzio 22898
Museo Civico Archeologico, Castelleone di Suasa 23411
Museo Civico Archeologico, Castro dei Volsci 23438
Museo Civico Archeologico, Cavaion Veronese 23459
Museo Civico Archeologico, Concordia Sagittaria 23636
Museo Civico Archeologico, Gazzo Veronese 23969
Museo Civico Archeologico, Gottolengo 24037
Museo Civico Archeologico, Grotte di Castro 24063
Museo Civico Archeologico, Latronico 24161
Museo Civico Archeologico, Mel 24344
Museo Civico Archeologico, Mondragone 24474
Museo Civico Archeologico, Nepi 24614
Museo Civico Archeologico, Norma 24637
Museo Civico Archeologico, Pitigliano 24963
Museo Civico Archeologico, Portoferraio 25017
Museo Civico Archeologico, Roccagloriosa 25137
Museo Civico Archeologico, Sarteano 25481
Museo Civico Archeologico di Fregellae, Ceprano 23477
Museo Civico Archeologico e Paleobotanico, Perfugas 24840
Museo Civico Archeologico L. Fantini, Monterenzio 24542
Museo Civico Archeologico M. Petrone, Vieste 26004
Museo Civico Archeologico Sa Domu Nosta, Senorbì 25540
Museo Civico dei Villaggi Scomparsi, Villa Estense 26013
Museo Civico del Marmo, Carrara 23357
Museo Civico della Val Fiorentina Vittorino Cazzetta, Selva di Cadore 25531
Museo Civico delle Centuriazioni Romane Padovana, Borgoricco 23175
Museo Civico Messapico, Alezio 22850
Museo Civico Storico-Etnografico, Ripatransone 25123
Museo Comunale, Montaione 24490
Museo Comunale, Roggiano Gravina 25144
Museo Comunale Archeologico, Viddalba 26003
Museo Comunale della Valle dei Nuraghi, Torralba 25768
Museo degli Scavi, Piuro 24965
Museo del Brigante, Sonnino 25604
Museo del Lazio Meridionale, Anagni 22879
Museo del Medioevo e del Rinascimento, Sorano 25609
Museo del Paesaggio, Castelnuovo Berardenga 23418
Museo del Piccolo Regio, Torino 25739
Museo del Risorgimento, Santa Maria Capua Vetere 25436
Museo del Vicino Oriente, Roma 25192
Museo della Battaglia di San Martino, Desenzano del Garda 23712
Museo della Civiltà Messapica, Poggiardo 24973
Museo della Guerra Bianca, Temù 25685
Museo della Via Ostiense, Roma 25197
Museo dello Studio, Bologna 23120
Museo di Muggia e del Territorio, Muggia 24569
Museo di Palazzo Reale, Napoli 24593
Museo di Storia, d'Arte e d'Antichità Don Florindo Piolo, Serravalle Sesia 25551
Museo Didattico d'Arte e Vita Preistorica, Capo di Ponte 23327
Museo Didattico della Riserva Regionale Incisioni Rupestri, Ceto 23513
Museo Documentario della Città, Gradisca d'Isonzo 24042
Museo Etnografico dei Cimbri, Selva di Progno 25532
Museo Etnografico della Valle Brembana, Zogno 26058
Museo Garibaldino della Campagna dell'Agro Romano per la Liberazione di Roma 1867, Mentana 24349
Museo Laboratorio di Archeologia, Monsampolo del Tronto 24483
Museo Marsiliano, Bologna 23138
Museo Muratoriano, Modena 24449
Museo Napoleonico, Rivoli Veronese 25132
Museo Nazionale Archeologico di Vulci, Canino 23313
Museo Paleontologico Archeologico V. Caccia, San Colombano al Lambro 25350
Museo Preistorico, Paceco 24728
Museo Preistorico dell'Isolino, Biandronno 23076
Museo Storico, Voghera 26045
Museo Storico Archeologico, Cicagna 23561
Museo Storico Archeologico dell'Antica Nola, Nola 24633
Museo Storico Badogliano, Bari 23028
Museo Storico del Risorgimento della Società Economica, Chiavari 23533
Museo Villa Medicea, Poggio a Caiano 24976
Villa Pisani, Strá 25639

Jamaica
Institute of Jamaica, Kingston 26069

Japan
Akama-jingu Treasure House, Shimonoseki 26750
Asuka Shiryokan, Asuka 26112
Dewa San-Zan History Museum, Haguro 26171
Dosho-machi Pharmaceutical and Historical Museum, Osaka 26642
Former Hong Kong and Shanghai Bank Museum, Nagasaki 26545
Gifu-ken Hakubutsukan, Seki 26729
Gunma Prefectural Museum of History, Takasaki 26799
Hirado Kanko Shiryôkan, Hirado 26199
Hokkaido Kaitaku Kinenkan, Sapporo 26712
Iga-Ryu Ninja Yashiki, Ueno 26987
Kanagawa-kenritsu Kanazawabunko Museum, Yokohama 27014
Kinenkan Mikasa, Yokosuka 27026
Kokuritsu Rekishi Minzoku Hakubutsukan, Sakura 26706
Kunozan Toshogu Museum, Shizuoka 26764
Kyushu Rekishi Shiryokan, Dazaifu 26134
Museum in Kochi Park, Kochi 26356
Nagasaki-kenritsu Hakubutsukan, Nagasaki 26554
Nagoya City Hideyoshi and Kiyomasa Memorial Museum, Nagoya, Aichi 26567
Nyozezo Private Museum, Nagaoka 26538
Osaka-kenritsu Chikatsuasuka Hakubutsukan, Kanan 26304
Ryosan Museum of History, Kyoto 26450
Saitama-kenritsu Rekishi Shiryokan, Ranzan 26685
Sanin Historical Collection, Yonago 27029
Sasebo-shi Bunka Kagakukan, Sasebo 26725
Takaoka Shiritsu Hakubutsukan, Takaoka 26796
Takehisa Yumeji Ikaho Memorial Hall, Ikaho 26238
Takenouchi Kaido Rekishi Hakubutsukan, Taishi 26785
Tohoku Rekishi Shiryokan, Tagajou 26782
Toki No Sato History Hall, Mano 26465
Tokushima-kenritsu Hakubutsukan, Tokushima 26825
Tokyo Kokuritsu Hakubutsukan, Tokyo 26937
Yokohama Kaikou Shiryokan, Yokohama 27024

Jordan
Archaeological Museum, Amman 27045

Kazakhstan
Centralnyj Gosudarstvennyj Muzej Kazachstana, Almaty 27071
Gosudarstvennyj Muzej-Reservat Pamjatniki Drevnego Taraza, Džambul 27082
Kuybyshev Republican Memorial Museum, Kzyl-Orda 27088

Kenya
Fort Jesus Museum, Mombasa 27109

Korea, Democratic People's Republic
Haeju Historical Museum, Haeju 27116
Hamhung Historical Museum, Hamhung 27117
Korean Central Historical Museum, Pyongyang 27121
Shinuiju Historical Museum, Shinuiju 27125
Wonsan Historical Museum, Wonsan 27126

Korea, Republic
Bokcheon Municipal Museum, Busan 27135
Hyeonchungsa Shrine, Asan 27131
Independence Hall of Korea, Cheonan 27146
King Sejong The Great Memorial Exhibition, Seoul 27244
National Museum of Korea, Seoul 27264
Naval Academy Museum, Jinhae 27201
Royal Museum, Seoul 27267

Kuwait
Kuwait National Museum, Kuwait 27306

Kyrgyzstan
State Historical Museum of Kyrgyzstan, Biškek 27309

Laos
Musée National Lao, Vientiane 27321
National Museum, Luang Prabang 27318

Latvia
Cēsu Vēstures muzejs, Cēsis 27344

Lesotho
Lesotho National Museum, Maseru 27495

Lithuania
Aušros Avenue Mansion, Šiauliai 27525
Dionizas Poška Hollowed Trunks, Bijotai 27519
Lietuvos Nacionalinis Muziejus, Vilnius 27537

Luxembourg
General Patton Memorial Museum, Ettelbruck 27557
Musée National d'Histoire Militaire, Diekirch 27549

Macedonia
Istoriski Muzej, Kruševo 27586
Muzej na Makedonija - Arceološki, Etnološki i Istoriski, Skopje 27590

Madagascar
Musée Historique, Antananarivo 27603

Malawi
Museum of Malawi, Blantyre 27611

Malaysia
History and Legendary Museum, Kuah 27634
Jabatan Muzium Sabah, Kota Kinabalu 27631
Kedah Royal Museum, Alor Setar 27616
Malacca Museums Corporation, Malacca 27660
Memorial Pengisytiharan Kemerdekaan, Melaka 27666
Muzium dan Galeri Seni, Minden 27678
Muzium Diraja Abu Bakar, Johor Bahru 27624
Muzium Negeri Kelantan, Kota Bharu 27630
Muzium Negeri Sembilan, Seremban 27684
Muzium Sejarah National, Kuala Lumpur 27647
Perak Royal Museum, Kuala Kangsar 27636
Sultan Abdul Aziz Royal Gallery, Kelang 27626
Tun Abdul Razak Memorial, Kuala Lumpur 27654

Mali
Centre de Documentation Arabe, Timbuktu 27694

Mauritania
Musée National de Nouakchott, Nouakchott 27731

Mauritius
B. Bissoondoyal Memorial Centre, Tyack 27742
Historical Museum, Mahébourg 27733
Sir Seewoosagar Ramgoolam Memorial Centre, Plaine Verte 27737

Mexico
Casa de la Constitución de 1814, Apatzingán 27773
Casa Museo Cadete Juan Escutia, Tepic 28495
Galería de Historia o Museo del Caracol, México 28096
Museo Antiguo Colegio de San Ildefonso, México 28105
Museo Antropología e Historia, Victoria 28601
Museo Casa de Hidalgo La Francia Chiquita, San Felipe 28383
Museo Casa del General Alvaro Obregón, Huatabampo 27998
Museo Casa Dr. Belisario Domínguez, Comitán de Domínguez 27849
Museo Casa Natal de Morelos, Morelia 28244
Museo Colonial de Acolman, Acolman 27751
Museo Comunitario el Asalto a las Tierras, Mexicali 28088
Museo Comunitario General Francisco Villa, Durango 27894
Museo Comunitario Unidad Indígena Emiliano Zapata, Hueyapan de Ocampo 28003
Museo Cristero Ing. Efrén Quezada, Encarnación de Díaz, Jalisco 27911
Museo de Historia de Tabasco, Villahermosa 28609
Museo de Historia Mexicana, Monterrey 28232
Museo de la Amistad México-Cuba, Tuxpan de Rodríguez Cano 28567
Museo de la Independencia, Dolores Hidalgo 27892
Museo de la Insurgencia, Rincón de Romos 28358
Museo de la Lealtad Republicana, Chihuahua 27825
Museo de la Memoria, Tlaxcala 28533
Museo de la Revolución, Puebla 28332
Museo de la Revolución de San Pedro, San Pedro 28421
Museo de las Californias, Tijuana 28512
Museo de las Estelas Mayas, Campeche 27798
Museo de las Revoluciones Mariano Jiménez, San Luis Potosí 28402
Museo del Camino Real de Hecelchakan, Hecelchakán 27983
Museo del Centro de Estudios de la Revolución Mexicana, Jiquilpan 28031
Museo del General Toribio Ortega, Coyame 27863
Museo División del Norte, Canutillo 27805
Museo División del Norte, Lerdo 28060
Museo General Francisco Villa, San Juan del Río 28394
Museo Hermanos López Rayón, Tlalpujahua 28525
Museo Hidalgo, Salamanca 28364
Museo Histórico de Acapulco, Acapulco 27747
Museo Histórico de la Revolución Mexicana, Chihuahua 27827
Museo Histórico de la Sierra Gorda, Jalpan 28025
Museo Histórico del Oriente de Morelos, Cuautla 27870
Museo Histórico Ex Aduana de Ciudad Juárez, Juárez 28039
Museo Histórico Mexicano de Cananea, Cananea 27802
Museo José Luis Cuevas, Colima 27837
Museo Nacional de Historia, México 28188
Museo Regional de Antropología e Historia de Baja California Sur, La Paz 28045
Museo Regional de Guadalajara, Guadalajara 27961
Museo Regional de Historia, Hermosillo 27987
Museo Regional de Historia de Aguascalientes, Aguascalientes 27759
Museo Regional de Historia de Tamaulipas, Victoria 28602
Museo-Sala de los Símbolos Patrios, Hermosillo 27989
Sala Homenaje a Juárez, Guelatao de Juárez 27980

Moldova
Muzeul National de Istorie a Moldovei, Chişinău 28660

Mongolia
National Museum of Mongolian History, Ulaanbaatar 28683

Myanmar
Bogyoke Aung San Museum, Yangon 28747
Prome Museum, Prome 28742

Namibia
Alte Feste, Windhoek 28778
National Museum of Namibia, Windhoek 28781
Owela Display Centre, Windhoek 28782

Nepal
National Museum of Nepal, Kathmandu 28788

Netherlands
Bezoekerscentrum Binnenhof, Den Haag 29090
De Brede, Maasbree 29560
Dief- en Duifhuisje, Capelle aan den IJssel 29053
Drents Museum, Assen 28950
Fries Museum, Leeuwarden 29508
Geschied- en Oudheidkundig Museum 't Freulekeshuus, Venray 29941
Haags Historisch Museum, Den Haag 29096
Herinneringscentrum Kamp Westerbork, Hooghalen 29439
Historisch Museum, Capelle aan den IJssel 29054
Historisch Museum de Scheper, Eibergen 29207
Historisch Museum Haarlemmermeer, Hoofddorp 29436
Historisch Museum Rotterdam Het Schielandshuis, Rotterdam 29752
Historisch Museum Warsenhoeck, Nieuwegein 29619
Historisch Museum Zuid-Kennemerland, Haarlem 29326
Koninklijk Oudheidkundig Genootschap, Amsterdam 28868
Koninklijk Paleis te Amsterdam, Amsterdam 28869
Kralingsmuseum, Rotterdam 29755
Madurodam, Den Haag 29104
Museon, Den Haag 29106
Museum Buren en Oranje, Buren, Gelderland 29043
Museum De Helpoort, Maastricht 29565
Nationaal Monument Kamp Vught, Vught 29971
Oud Amelisweerd Museum, Bunnik 29036
Oudheidkamer Vreeswijk, Nieuwegein 29620
Paleis Het Loo - Nationaal Museum, Apeldoorn 28928
Stichting Atlas Van Stolk, Rotterdam 29776
Titus Brandsma Museum, Bolsward 28996
Universiteitsmuseum, Groningen 29316
Van-der-Werf's Wedgwoodmuseum, Zuidwolde, Groningen 30073
Van 't Lindenhoutmuseum, Nijmegen 29637
Zeeuws Museum, Middelburg 29595

New Zealand
Canterbury Museum, Christchurch 30124
Colonial Cottage Museum, Wellington 30293
Lake Taupo Museum and Art Gallery, Taupo 30257
South Otago Historical Museum, Balclutha 30116
Treaty House, Waitangi 30280
Waipara County Historical Society Museum, Hawarden 30176

Nicaragua
Museo Nacional de Nicaragua, Managua 30322

Niger
Musée National du Niger, Niamey 30324

Nigeria
National Museum, Abuja, Abuja 30329
National Museum of Colonial History, Aba 30326

Norway
Akershus Fylkesmuseum, Strømmen 30902
Bergen Museum, Bergen 30415
Emanuel Vigeland Museum, Oslo 30730
Halden Historiske Samlinger, Halden 30524
Herøy Kystmuseum, Herøy 30546
Historisk Museum, Oslo 30736
Hovden Jernvinnemuseum, Bykle 30456
Kaperdalen Samemuseum, Senja 30836
Kongsvinger Festningsmuseum, Kongsvinger 30606
Lørenskog Bygdemuseum, Skårer 30840
Museet i Mælandsgården, Skudeneshavn 30853
Nord-Jarlsbergmuseene, Holmestrand 30555
Norsk Seminmuseum, Stange 30876
Norske Grenselosers Museum, Bjørkelangen 30435
Ny Ålesund By- og Gruvemuseum, Ny-Ålesund 30715
Osen Bygdemuseum, Osen 30725
Polarmuseet i Tromsø, Tromsø 30933
Risør Museum, Risør 30792
Rogaland Krigshistorisk Museum, Sola 30862
Tromsø Universitets Museum, Tromsø 30935
Vardømuseene, Vardø 30974
Vevelstad Bygdetun, Vevelstad 30990
Vikingmuseet på Borg, Bøstad 30446

Oman
National Museum at Ruwi, Muscat 31005
Omani-French Museum Bait Fransa, Muscat 31007

Pakistan
Archaeological Museum Umarkot, Umarkot 31060
Punjab Archives Museum, Lahore 31042

Panama
Museo de Herrera, Panamá City 31082
Museo de Historia de Panamá, Panamá City 31083
Museo de la Historia de la Cultura José de Obaldia, David 31073
Museo de la Historia y la Tradición, Panamá City 31085
Museo de la Nacionalidad, Panamá City 31086

Papua New Guinea
Papua New Guinea National Museum and Art Gallery, Boroko 31090

Peru
Casa Museo Almirante Miguel Grau, Piura 31237
Museo Casa de Zela, Tacna 31253
Museo de Arte e Historia, Lima 31206
Museo Histórico Andrés Avelino Cáceres, Huamanga 31165
Museo Histórico Regional - Casa Garcilaso Cusco, Cusco 31159
Museo Memoria Coronel Leoncio Prado, Callao 31134
Museo Universitario y Museo de Anatomía General, Yanacancha 31268
Museos de la Universidad Nacional de Cajamarca, Cajamarca 31130

Philippines
Ayala Museum of Philippine History, Makati 31352
Baldomero Aguinaldo House, Kawit 31336
Bibak Museum, Baguio 31283
Carlos P. Romulo Collection, Manila 31373
Casa Real Shrine, Malolos 31360
Emilio Aguinaldo Shrine Museum, Kawit 31337
Geronimo Berenguer de los Reyes jr. Museum, Cavite 31304
José Rizal Shrine Museum, Manila 31379
Leon Apacible Historical Landmark Museum, Taal 31449
Malacañan Palace Presidential Museum, Manila 31380
Marcela M. Agoncillo Historical Museum, Taal 31450
Marcelo H. del Pilar Museum, Malolos 31362
Munting Museo Ng Namayan, Mandaluyong 31365
Museo ng Rebolusyon, San Juan 31440
Museo Valenzuela, Valenzuela 31462
Museums of Filipinana and Rizaliana, Sampaloc 31438
P. Jacinto Zamora Historical Museum, Manila 31389
Pambasang Museo ng Pilipinas, Manila 31390
Sulu National Museum, Jolo 31332
University of Nueva Caceres Museum, Naga 31407
Veterans Federation of the Philippines Museum, Taguig 31456

Poland
Centralne Muzeum Pożarnictwa, Mysłowice 31818
Centrum Pamięci Gen. Józefa Hallera, Władysławowo 32158
Dom Rodzinny Ojca Świętego Jana Pawła II, Wadowice 32067
Dwór Artusa, Gdańsk 31566
Muzeum Dom Wincentego Witosa, Wierzchosławice 32155
Muzeum Dworu Polskiego, Plochocin 31885
Muzeum Gross-Rosen, Wałbrzych 32071
Muzeum Historii Miasta, Szczecin 32027
Muzeum Historii Polskiego Rucha Ludowego, Piaseczno koło Gniewa 31878
Muzeum Historii Polskiego Ruchu Ludowego w Warszawie, Oddział w Sandomierzu, Sandomierz 31963
Muzeum Historii Żdów Polskich, Warszawa 32100
Muzeum Historyczne, Białystok 31486
Muzeum Historyczne Miasta Krakowa, Kraków 31707
Muzeum Historyczno-Etnograficzne, Chojnice 31528
Muzeum Ignacego Jana Paderewskiego i Wychodźstwa Polskiego w Ameryce, Warszawa 32103
Muzeum im. Jana Kasprowicza, Inowrocław 31617
Muzeum Małego Miasta, Bieżuń 31496
Muzeum Martyrologii Pod Zegarem, Lublin 31794
Muzeum Miedzi, Legnica 31754
Muzeum Miejskie, Wyszków 32197
Muzeum Pamiątek po Janie Matejce "Koryznówka", Nowy Wiśnicz 31839
Muzeum Pojezierza Łęczyńsko-Włodawskiego, Włodawa 32166
Muzeum w Darłowie, Darłowo 31550
Państwowe Muzeum Gross-Rosen w Rogoźnicy, Rogoźnica 31950
Państwowe Muzeum w Białymstoku, Białystok 31489

Portugal
Museu de Etnografia e História, Porto 32333

Puerto Rico
Luis Muñoz Rivera Museum, Barranquitas 32362
Museo y Parque Historico de Caparra, San Juan 32404

Romania
Complexul Muzeal Goleşti, Goleşti 32528
Memorial Museum B.P. Hasdeu, Câmpina 32480
Muzeul de Istorie al Moldovei, Iaşi 32533
Muzeul de Istorie Naţională şi Archeologie, Constanţa 32501
Muzeul de Istorie şi Artă Roman, Roman 32582
Muzeul Judeţean de Istorie, Piatra-Neamţ 32568
Muzeul Judeţean de Istorie Braşov, Braşov 32449
Muzeul Judetean de Istorie şi Arheologie Prahova, Ploieşti 32572
Muzeul Naţional al Unirii, Alba Iulia 32428
Muzeul Naţional de Istorie a României, Bucureşti 32467
Muzeul Naţional de Istorie a Transilvaniei, Cluj-Napoca 32495
Muzeul Naţional Peleş, Sinaia 32596
Muzeul Taru Făgărasului, Făgăraş 32518
Muzeul Unirii, Iaşi 32541

Russia
Aleksandrovskij Dvorec - Gosudarstvennyj Muzej Carskoje Selo, Puškin 33334
Astrachanskij Gosudarstvennyj Obedinennyj Istoriko-architekturnyj Muzej-zapovednik, Astrachan 32659
Astrachanskij Kraevedčeskij Muzej, Astrachan 32660
Belgorodskij Gosudarstvennyj Istoriko- Kraevedčeskij Muzej, Belgorod 32676
Biljarskij Gosudarstvennyj Istoriko-Architekturnyj i Prirodnyj Muzej-Zapovednik, Biljarsk 32688
Bogorodickij Dvorec-muzej i Park, Bogorodick 32694
Bratskij Gorodskoj Objedinennyj Muzej Istorii Osvoenija Angary, Bratsk 32704
Brjanskij Gosudarstvennyj Obedinennyj Kraevedčeskij Muzej, Brjansk 32706
Bunker Stalina, Samara 33366
Chabarovskij Kraevoj Kraevedčeskij Muzej im. N.I. Grodekova, Chabarovsk 32737
Čukotskij Okružnoj Kraevedčeskij Muzej, Anadyr' 32638
Čuvašskij Nacionalnyj Muzej, Čeboksary 32719
Dagestanskij Gosudarstvennyj Objedinennyj Istoriko-architekturnyj Muzej, Machačkala 32995
Diorama Kurskaja Bitva - Belgorodskoe Napravlenie, Belgorod 32677
Dom-muzej Istorii Molodëžnogo Dviženija, Rjazan 33349
Dom-muzej Petra Pervogo (Petrovskij Domik), Vologda 33721
Elabužskij Gosudarstvennyj Istoriko-architekturnyj i Chudožestvennyj Muzej-zapovednik, Elabuga 32785
Fort N5 - Muzej Istorii Velikoj Otečestvennoj Vojny, Kaliningrad 32868
Gorodskoj Kraevedčeskij Muzej, Elec 32792
Gosudarstvennyj Borodinskij Voenno-istoričeskij Muzej-zapovednik, Borodino 32701
Gosudarstvennyj Chudožestvennyj Istoriko-architekturnyj i prirodno-landšaftnyj Muzej-zapovednik Kolomenskoe, Moskva 33052
Gosudarstvennyj Istoričeskij Muzej, Moskva 33054
Gosudarstvennyj Istoričeskij Zapovednik Gorki Leninskie, Gorki Leninskie 32807
Gosudarstvennyj Istoriko-ėtnografičeskij i Architekturnyj Muzej-zapovednik Staraja Sarepta, Volgograd 33714
Gosudarstvennyj Istoriko-memorialnyj Sankt-Peterburgskij Muzej Smolnyj, Sankt-Peterburg 33398
Gosudarstvennyj Istoriko-memorialnyj Zapovednik Rodina V.I. Lenina, Uljanovsk 33656
Gosudarstvennyj Muzej-usadba Archangelskoe, Archangelskoe 32654
Gosudarstvennyj Voenno-istoričeskij i Prirodnyj Muzej-zapovednik Kulikovo Pole, Tula 33624
Gosudarstvennyj Voenno-istoričeskij Muzej-zapovednik Prochorovskoe Pole, Prochorovka 33328
Ingušskij Gosudarstvennyj Muzej Kraevedenija im. T.Ch. Malsagova, Nazran 33203
Istoričeskaja Usadba Botik Petra I, Veskovo 33684
Istoriko-memorialnyj Kompleks Gerojam Stalingradskoj Bitvy na Mamaevom Kurgane, Volgograd 33716
Istoriko-memorialnyj Muzej M.V. Lomonosova, Lomonosovo 32992
Istoriko-memorial'nyj Muzejnyj Kompleks Bobriki, Donskij 32760
Jakutskij Gosudarstvennyj Muzej Istorii i Kultury Narodov Severa im. Jaroslavskogo, Jakutsk 32843
Jamalo-Neneckij Okružnoj Kraevedčeskij Muzej im. I.S. Šemanovskogo, Salechard 33364
Kaliningradskij Oblastnoj Istoriko-chudožestvennyj Muzej, Kaliningrad 32870
Kalmyckij Respublikanskij Kraevedčeskij Muzej im. Prof. N.N. Palmova, Ėlista 32794
Karačaevo-Čerkesskij Istoriko-kul'turnyj i Prirodnyj Muzej-Zapovednik, Čerkessk 32736
Kirillo-Belozerskij Istoriko-Architekturnyj i Chudožestvennyj Muzej-zapovednik, Kirillov 32915
Komi Respublikanskij Istoriko-Kraevedčeskij Muzej, Syktyvkar 33573
Kostromskoj Gosudarstvennyj Istoriko-architekturnyj Muzej-zapovednik, Kostroma 32942
Kraevedčeskij Muzej Evrejskoj Avtonomnoj Oblasti, Birobidžan 32689
Krasnojarskij Kraevoj Kraevedčeskij Muzej, Krasnojarsk 32952
Memorialnyj Dom-muzej Gercena, Moskva 33075
Memorialnyj Dom-muzej G.V. Plechanova, Lipeck 32985
Memorialnyj Dom-muzej Uljanovych, Astrachan 32663
Memorialnyj Muzej-Kvartira S.M. Kirova, Vladikavkaz 33688
Mordovskij Respublikanskij Kraevedčeskij Muzej, Saransk 33497
Muzej 700 let - Landskrona, Nevskoe Ustje, Nienšanc, Sankt-Peterburg 33425
Muzej Archeologii Prikamja, Perm 33305
Muzej Arsenal - Muzej Velikoj Otečestvennoj Vojny, Voronež 33731
Muzej Avtogravov imeni Imperatora Nikolaja Vtorogo, Novosibirsk 33240
Muzej Boevogo i Trudovogo Podviga 1941-1945, Saransk 33498
Muzej Boevoj Slavy, Astrachan 32664
Muzej Cerkov Dekabristov, Čita 32751
Muzej Dekabristov, Minusinsk 33017
Muzej Dekabristov, Moskva 33095
Muzej Dekabristov - Dom Trubeckogo, Irkutsk 32816
Muzej Dekabristov - Dom Volkonskich, Irkutsk 32817
Muzej Diplomatičeskogo Korpusa, Vologda 33722
Muzej Ėtnografii, Istorii i Kultury Narodov Baškortostana, Ufa 33646
Muzej Istorii Burjatii im. M.N. Changalova, Ulan-Udė 33653
Muzej Istorii Kolskich Saamov, Lovozero 32993
Muzej Istorii Političeskoj Polcii Rossii - Gorochovaja 2, Sankt-Peterburg 33441
Muzej Istorii Političeskoj Ssylki, Bratsk 32705
Muzej Istorii Revoljucionno-demokratičeskogo Dviženija 1880-1890 gg, Sankt-Peterburg 33442
Muzej Konspirativnaja Kvartira Simbirskoj Gruppy RSDRP 1904-1906, Uljanovsk 33661
Muzej-panorama Borodinskaja Bitva, Moskva 33145
Muzej Podviga Ivana Susanina, Susanino 33568
Muzej Smolenščina v Gody Velikoj Otečestvennoj Vojny 1941 -1945, Smolensk 33530
Muzej Štab-kvartira V.K. Bljuchera, Tjumen 33608
Muzej Vladimira Raevskogo, Bogoslovka 32695
Muzej-zapovednik Dmitrovskij Kreml, Dmitrov 32758
Muzejno-vystavočnyj Centr - Diorama, Kirov 32923
Muzejno-vystavočnyj Centr Tul'skie Drevnosti, Tula 33630
Muzejno-vystavočnyj Kompleks Volokolamskij Kreml, Volokolamsk 33726

Nacionalnyj Muzej Respubliki Baškortostan, Ufa 33647
Nacionalnyj Muzej Respubliki Komi, Syktyvkar 33579
Nacionalnyj Muzej Udmurtskoj Respubliki im. K. Gerda, Iževsk 32836
Nižnetagilskij Muzej-Zapovednik Gornozavodskogo Dela Srednego Urala, Nižnij Tagil 33228
Novgorodskij Gosudarstvennyj Muzej-zapovednik, Velikij Novgorod 33680
Novočerkasskij Muzej Istorii Donskich Kazakov, Novočerkassk 33233
Novorossijskij Gosudarstvennyj Istoričeskij Muzej Zapovednik, Novorossijsk 33238
Oloneckij Nacionalnyj Muzej Karelov-Livvikov im. N.T.Prilukin, Olonec 33252
Omskij Gosudarstvennyj Istoriko-kraevedčeskij Muzej, Omsk 33255
Osinskij Kraevedčeskij Muzej, Osa 33273
Pavlovskij Istoričskij Muzej, Pavlovo 33284
Penzenskij Gosudarstvennyj Obedinennyj Kraevedčeskij Muzej, Penza 33294
Permskij Oblastnoj Kraevedčeskij Muzej, Perm 33308
Piskarevskoe Memorialnoe Kladbišče - Muzej, Sankt-Peterburg 33476
Plesskij Gosudarstvennyj Istoriko-Architekturnyj i Chudožestvennyj Muzej-Zapovednik, Ples 33325
Podpolnaja Tipografija CK RSDRP, Moskva 33172
Presnja Istoriko-memorialnyj Muzej, Moskva 33176
Primorskij Gosudarstvennyj Muzej im. V.K. Arseneva, Vladivostok 33709
Pskovskij Gosudarstvennyj Istoričesko-architekturnyj i Chudožestnennyj Muzej-zapovednik, Pskov 33332
Pskovskij Memorialnyj Muzej V.I. Lenina, Pskov 33333
Rjazanskij Gosudarstvennyj Istoriko-architekturnyj Muzej-zapovednik, Rjazan 33351
Roslavlskij Istoriko-chudožstvennyj Muzej, Roslavl 33353
Rostovskij Oblastnoj Muzej Kraevedenija, Rostov-na-Donu 33358
Saratovskij Gosudarstvennyj Muzej Boevoj Slavy, Saratov 33510
Saratovskij Kraevedčeskij Muzej, Saratov 33511
Šlisselburgskaja Krepost Orešek, Šlisselburg 33526
Soloveckij Gosudarstvennyj Istoriko-Architekturnyj i Prirodnyj Muzej-Zapovednik, Soloveckij 33546
Staročerkasskij Istoriko-architekturnyj Muzej-zapovednik, Staročerkassk 33556
Staroladožskij Istoriko-Architekturnyj i Archeologičeskij Muzej-Zapovednik, Staraja Ladoga 33553
Stavropolskij Kraevedčeskij Muzej im. G.N. Prozriteleva i G.K. Prave, Stavropol 33563
Taganrogskij Gosudarstvennyj Literaturnyj i Istoriko-architekturnyj Muzej-zapovednik, Taganrog 33586
Tambovskij Oblastnoj Kraevedčeskij Muzej, Tambov 33591
Tobolskij Gosudarstvennyj Istoriko-architekturnyj Muzej-zapovednik, Tobolsk 33613
Tomskij Oblastnoj Kraevedčeskij Muzej, Tomsk 33617
Uljanovskij Oblastnoj Kraevedčskij Muzej im. I.A. Gončarova, Uljanovsk 33669
Velikoustjugskij Gosudarstvennyj Istoriko-Architekturnyj i Chudožestvennyj Muzej-Zapovednik, Velikij Ustjug 33681
Volgogradskij Oblastnoj Kraevedčeskij Muzej, Volgograd 33719
Vologodskij Gosudarstvennyj Istoriko-Architekturnyj i Chudožestvennyj Muzej-Zapovednik, Vologda 33724
Voronežskij Oblastnoj Kraevedčeskij Muzej, Voronež 33736
Vserossijskij Istoriko-étnografičeskij Muzej, Toržok 33620
Vyborgskij Kraevedčeskij Muzej, Vyborg 33742

Rwanda
Musée National du Rwanda, Butare 33752

St. Lucia
Pigeon Island, Castries 33755

Samoa
Museum of Samoa, Apia 33757

San Marino
Museo delle Cere - Strumenti di Tortura, San Marino 33763
I Torre Guaita, San Marino 33769

Senegal
Musée Historique de Gorée, Dakar 33780
Musée Historique de Gorée, Gorée 33783

Serbia-Montenegro
Jevrejski Istorijski Muzej, Beograd 33800
Kompleksi Monumental i Lidhjes Shqiptare të Prizrenit, Prizren 33897
Muzej Istorije Jugoslavije, Beograd 33805
Narodni Muzej, Beograd 33814
Narodni Muzej, Kragujevac 33853
Narodni Muzej, Leskovac 33859
Narodni Muzej Kruševac, Kruševac 33857
Narodni Muzej Niš, Niš 33865
Spomen Kuća Bitke na Sutjesci, Tjentište 33920
Spomen Muzej Prvog Zasjedania ZAVNOBiH-a, Mrkonjić Grad 33861

Sierra Leone
Sierra Leone National Museum, Freetown 33935

Singapore
Singapore History Museum, Singapore 33942

Slovakia
Múzeum Kultúry Karpatských Nemcov, Bratislava 33971
Múzeum Kultúry Maďarov na Slovensku, Bratislava 33972
Múzeum Slovenských Národných Rád, Myjava 34032
Východoslovenské Múzeum, Košice 34006
Západoslovenské Múzeum v Trnave, Trnava 34075

Slovenia
Kobariški Muzej, Kobarid 34094
Narodni Muzej Slovenije, Ljubljana 34115
Predjamski Grad, Postojna 34140

South Africa
Arbeidsgenot, Oudtshoorn 34317
Bo-Kaap Museum, Cape Town 34201
Great Fish River Museum, Cradock 34220
National Cultural History Museum, Pretoria 34350
National Cultural History Museum, Pretoria 34350
Port Elizabeth Museum, Port Elizabeth 34333
South African Jewish Museum, Cape Town 34211
Voortrekker Museum, Pietermaritzburg 34329

Spain
Casa del Cordón, Vitoria-Gasteiz 35695
Colegio del Rey The King's College, Alcalá de Henares 34425
Museo-Archivo de Falset y Comarca, Falset 34812
Museo de la Vida Rural, L'Espluga de Francolí 34804
Museo Histórico Municipal, Cádiz 34649
Museo Municipal, Ayllón 34509
Museo-Palacio de Fuensalida, Toledo 35544
Museo Sinagoga de Santa María la Blanca, Toledo 35546
Museo Thermalia, Caldes de Montbui 34656
Museu Comarcal Salvador Vilaseca, Reus 35314
Sala de Exposiciones Edificio Historico, Oviedo 35206

Sudan
Khalifa's House Museum, Omdurman 35773

Swaziland
Swaziland National Museum, Lobamba 35780

Sweden
Aschanska Gården, Eksjö 35858
Birka Vikingastaden, Adelsö 35781
Ekehagens Forntidsby, Åsarp 35819
Ekomuseum Bergslagen, Smedjebacken 36207
Fågelsjö Gammelgård Bortom åa, Los 36050
Kullängsstugan, Askersund 35821
Kulturhistoriska Museet, Lund 36060
Kungsstugan och Cajsa Wargs Hus, Örebro 36136
Museet Malmahed, Malmköping 36070
Nyströmska Gården, Köping 36011
Östergötlands Länsmuseum, Linköping 36042
Riddarholmskyrkan, Stockholm 36275
Riddarhuset, Stockholm 36276
Stora Nyckelvikens Gård, Nacka 36109
Utvandrarnas Hus, Växjö 36392
Vasamuseet, Stockholm 36298

Switzerland
Bundesbriefmuseum, Schwyz 37149
Forum der Schweizer Geschichte, Schwyz 37150
Historische Sammlung Schloß Hegi, Winterthur 37329
Historisches Museum Basel, Basel 36500
Maison du Vieux-Zinal, Zinal 37364
Mazzini-Gedenkstätte, Grenchen 36780
Moulagensammlung des Universitätsspitals und der Universität Zürich, Zürich 37391
Musée Cantonal d'Histoire, Sion 37173
Musée d'Art et d'Histoire, Fribourg 36715
Musée des Suisses dans le Monde, Pregny-Chambésy 37034
Musée International de la Croix-Rouge et du Croissant-Rouge, Genève 36748
Musée National Suisse, Prangins 37031
Polenmuseum Rapperswil, Rapperswil, Sankt Gallen 37044
Suworow-Museum, Glarus 36765
Swissminiatur, Melide 36936
Tell-Museum, Bürglen 36600

Syria
National Museum of Damascus, Damascus 37436

Tajikistan
Respublikanskij Istoriko-Kraevedčeskij i Chudožestvennyj Muzej, Dušanbe 37446

Tanzania
Azimio la Arusha Museum, Arusha 37453
Beit al-Ajaib Museum with House of Wonders Museum, Zanzibar 37468
Livingstone and Stanley Memorial, Tabora 37467
Palace Museum, Zanzibar 37469
Pemba Museum, Chake Chake 37457
Zanzibar National Archives and Museums Department, Zanzibar 37471

Tonga
Tupou College Museum, Nuku'alofa 37551

Trinidad and Tobago
National Museum and Art Gallery of Trinidad and Tobago, Port-of-Spain 37552

Tunisia
Musée Dar Bourguiba, Tunis 37592

Turkey
19 Mayıs Müzesi, Samsun 37775
Birinci Millet Meclisi Müzesi, Ankara 37616
Eksi Şarkeserleri Müzesi, İstanbul 37700
Kurtuluş Savaşı ve Cumhuriyet Müzeleri, Ankara 37619
Mudanya Mutareke Evi Müzesi, Mudanya 37762
Tanzimat Müzesi, İstanbul 37707

Turkmenistan
Ancien Merv Historical Site, Mary 37817
National Museum of Turkmenistan, Ašgabat 37812

Uganda
Uganda Museum, Kampala 37829

Ukraine
Diorama "Bitva za Dnepr", Dnepropetrovsk 37846
Dneprodzerzhinsk History Museum, Dneprodzeržinsk 37845
Historical Museum by V. Tarnovsky, Černigiv 37838
Istoričeskij Muzej, Kyïv 37869
Istoričeskij Muzej, Dnepropetrovsk 37848
Kortelisy Historical Museum, Kortelisy 37864
Krasnojarskij Istoričeskij Muzej Memorial Pobedy, Krasnojarsk 37865
Lviv Historical Museum, Lviv 37886
State Historical Museum, Kamenec-Podolskij 37857

United Arab Emirates
Sheikh Saeed's House, Dubai 37917

United Kingdom
Anne Hathaway's Cottage, Stratford-upon-Avon 40624
Bannockburn Heritage Centre, Stirling 40591
Black Cultural Archives, London 39580
Blackburn Museum and Art Gallery, Blackburn, Lancashire 38242
Blakesley Hall, Birmingham 38217
Boswell Museum and Mausoleum, Auchinleck 38038
British Empire and Commonwealth Museum, Bristol 38353
British Red Cross Museum and Archives, London 39588
Brontë Parsonage Museum, Haworth 39199
Burston Strike School, Burston, Diss 38406
Captain Cook Memorial Museum, Whitby 40850
Castle Museum, Colchester 38608
A Celebration of Immigration, London 39600
Chiddingstone Castle, Chiddingstone 38567
Childhood and Costume Museum, Bridgnorth 38322
City and County Museum, Lincoln 39496
Clan Armstrong Museum, Langholm 39421
Clan Cameron Museum, Spean Bridge 40566
Clan Macpherson House and Museum, Newtonmore 40067
Commandery Museum, Worcester 40928
Crom Estate, Newtownbutler 40076
Cromarty Courthouse Museum, Cromarty 38670
Culloden Visitor Centre, Inverness 39298
Darby Houses, Coalbrookdale 38594
Devon and Cornwall Constabulary Museum, Exeter 38955
East Ham Nature Reserve, London 39630
Edinburgh Scout Museum, Edinburgh 38878
Elliot Colliery Winding House, New Tredegar 40017
Golden Hinde Educational Museum, London 39643
Guide Heritage Centre, London 39653
Her Majesty Tower of London, London 39662
Heritage World Centre, Dungannon 38812
Historic Scotland, Edinburgh 38888
Holst Birthplace Museum, Cheltenham 38545
Humber Estuary Discovery Centre, Cleethorpes 38588
Jewish Museum, London 39677
John Muir's Birthplace, Dunbar 38794
Lewes Castle and Barbican House Museum, Lewes 39484
Magdalen Museum, Wainfleet 40758
Marischal Museum, Aberdeen 37940
Mary Queen of Scots' House, Jedburgh 39325
Milestones: Hampshire's Living History Museum, Basingstoke 38102
Museum of Scotland, Edinburgh 38895
Museum - Treasures from the National Archives, Kew 39351
National Football Museum, Preston 40268
National Wallace Monument, Stirling 40593
New Lanark World Heritage Village, New Lanark 40012
Newark Town Treasures and Art Gallery, Newark-on-Trent 40023
Outreach Collection, West Malling 40826
The Oxford Story, Oxford 40150
Pass of Killiecrankie Visitor Centre, Killiecrankie 39358
People's Palace Museum, Glasgow 39059
Piece Hall Art Gallery, Halifax 39154
Ripon Workhouse Museum, Ripon 40329
Rob Roy and Trossachs Victor Centre, Callander 38439
Royal Army Educational Corps Museum, Beaconsfield 38133
Royal Borough Museum Collection, Windsor 40903
Royal Museum, Edinburgh 38910
Royal Naval Museum Portsmouth, Portsmouth 40258
SEARCH-Centre, Gosport 39103
Shoreham Airport Historical Exhibition, Shoreham-by-Sea 40504
Sopwell Nunnery, Saint Albans 40378
Tolpuddle Martyrs Museum, Tolpuddle 40715
Tower Bridge Exhibition, London 39791
Tudor House, Weymouth 40844
Ulster History Park, Omagh 40132
Ulster Museum, Belfast 38160
United States Grant Ancestral Homestead, Dungannon 38813
Wellington Arch, London 39802
Western Approaches, Liverpool 39532
Wheal Martyn Cornwall's Museum of the Clay, Saint Austell 40390
Wilberforce House, Kingston-upon-Hull 39384
Workhouse Museum, Londonderry 39819

Uruguay
Casa de Lavalleja, Montevideo 40984
Casa del General José Garibaldi, Montevideo 40985
Casa Rivera, Montevideo 40986
Museo Histórico Nacional Luis A. de Herrera, Montevideo 41005
Museo Juan Zorrilla de San Martín, Montevideo 41007

U.S.A.
The 100th Meridian Museum, Cozad 42686
Abraham Lincoln Museum, Harrogate 43936
A.D. Buck Museum of Natural History and Science, Tonkawa 48029
Adams House, Deadwood 42819
Adams National Historical Park, Quincy 46763
African American Museum, Dallas 42743
African-American Museum at Oakland, Oakland 46059
Afro-American Historical Society Museum, Jersey City 44338
Akta Lakota Museum, Chamberlain 42182
Albany Institute of History and Art, Albany 41083
The Albuquerque Museum of Art and History, Albuquerque 41099
Alton Museum of History and Art, Alton 41157
American Airpower Heritage Museum, Midland 45324
American Catholic Historical Society Museum, Philadelphia 46388
The American Historical Foundation Museum, Richmond 46870
American Independence Museum, Exeter 43251
American Irish Historical Society Museum, New York 45757
American Merchant Marine Museum, Kings Point 44490
American Printing House for the Blind, Callahan Museum, Louisville 44961
American Saddlebred Horse Museum, Mexico 45279
Americana Museum, El Paso 43111
America's Black Holocaust Museum, Milwaukee 45358
Anacostia Museum, Washington 48332
Anchorage Museum of History and Art, Anchorage 41197
Andrew J. Blackbird Museum, Harbor Springs 43909
Anna Bemis Palmer Museum, York 48793
Antietam National Battlefield, Sharpsburg 47582
Antiquarian and Landmarks Society Museum, Hartford 43937
Antique Gas and Steam Engine Museum, Vista 48255
Apex Museum, Atlanta 41328
Aptucxet Trading Post Museum, Bourne 41841
Arizona Historical Society Museum, Tucson 48080
Arkansas Museum of Science and History - Museum of Discovery, Little Rock 44823
Armenian Museum of America, Watertown 48440
Arrow Rock State Historic Site, Arrow Rock 41271
Arvada Center for the Arts and Humanities, Arvada 41274
Ashland - Henry Clay Estate, Lexington 44736
The Atlanta Cyclorama, Atlanta 41332
Audubon House, Key West 44461
Autry Museum of Western Heritage, Los Angeles 44891
Avery Research Center for African American History and Culture, Charleston 42208
Baca House, Trinidad 48062
Barnacle Historic State Park, Coconut Grove 42509
Barrett House, Forest Hall, New Ipswich 45709
Bates-Scofield Homestead, Darien 42782
Battle of Lexington State Historic Site, Lexington 44751
Beauregard-Keyes House, New Orleans 45719
Beauvoir, Biloxi 41693
Beaverhead County Museum, Dillon 42949
Bellamy Mansion Museum of History and Design Arts, Wilmington 48657
Ben-Hur Museum, Crawfordsville 42690
Bennington Battle Monument, Old Bennington 46128
Bennington Battlefield Exhibition, Walloomsac 48289
Bent's Old Fort, La Junta 44551
Beth Ahabah Museum and Archives, Richmond 46873
Betsy Ross House, Philadelphia 46395
Black Hawk State Historic Site, Rock Island 46953
Black Heritage Museum, Miami 45282
Black Hills Mining Museum, Lead 44699
Bob Burns Museum, Van Buren 48194
Bodie State Historic Park, Bridgeport 41888
Bollinger Mill State Historic Site, Burfordville 41993
Boone County Historical Center, Boone 41783
Boonsborough Museum of History, Boonsboro 41788
Boot Hill Museum, Dodge City 42954
Boston National Historic Park, Boston 41800
Brazos Valley Museum of Natural History, Bryan 41974

Brown County Historical Society Museum, New Ulm 45748
Brown House Museum, Sandersville 47379
Brucemore, Cedar Rapids 42156
Buffalo Bill Historical Center, Cody 42510
Buffalo Bill Memorial Museum, Golden 43712
Buffalo Bill Museum of Le Claire, Iowa, Le Claire 44696
Buffalo Bill Ranch, North Platte 46003
Bunker Hill Museum, Charlestown 42233
Butterfield Trail Historical Museum, Russell Springs 47037
Cabrillo National Monument, San Diego 47271
Cairo Museum, Vicksburg 48227
Caleb Lothrop House, Cohasset 42513
California African-American Museum, Los Angeles 44893
California Heritage Museum, Santa Monica 47439
Cape Fear Museum, Wilmington 48659
Capitola Historical Museum, Capitola Village 42101
Cappon House Museum, Holland 44052
Captain Forbes House Museum, Milton 45353
Captain George Flavel House Museum, Astoria 41308
Captain Phillips' Rangers Memorial, Saxton 47489
Carillon Historical Park, Dayton 42800
Carpinteria Valley Museum of History, Carpinteria 42112
Carroll County Farm Museum, Westminster 48561
Carroll Reece Museum, Johnson City 44344
Carter's Grove Visitor Center, Williamsburg 48626
Carver County Historical Society Museum, Waconia 48271
Cary Cottage, Cincinnati 42399
Castillo de San Marcos Museum, Saint Augustine 47066
Castle Tucker, Wiscasset 48715
Cedar Grove Mansion Inn, Vicksburg 48228
Centennial Village Museum, Greeley 43783
Center for American History, Austin 41408
Century Village Museum, Burton 42013
C.H. Nash Museum-Chucalissa Archaeological Museum, Memphis 45232
Chancellor Robert R. Livingston Masonic Library and Museum, New York 45779
Charles H. Wright Museum of African American History, Detroit 42918
Charles Towne Landing 1670, Charleston 42210
Chattanooga African-American Museum, Chattanooga 42258
Cherokee Heritage Centre, Tahlequah 47925
Cherokee Strip Museum and Henry S. Johnston Library, Perry 46356
Cheyenne Frontier Days Old West Museum, Cheyenne 42297
Chicago Historical Society, Chicago 42318
Chickasaw Council House Museum, Tishomingo 48011
The Children's Museum in Easton, North Easton 45993
Chisholm Trail Museum, Wellington 48499
Cigna Museum and Art Collection, Philadelphia 46398
The Citadel Archives and Museum, Charleston 42212
City of Las Vegas and Rough Riders Memorial Museum, Las Vegas 44662
Civil War Museum, Philadelphia 46399
Civil War Museum, Carrollton 42114
Civilian Conservation Corps Museum, Sebring 47551
Clara Barton Birthplace, North Oxford 46001
Clark County Museum, Henderson 43990
Clinton Academy Museum, East Hampton 43043
Coastal Discovery Museum, Hilton Head Island 44033
Coffin House, Newbury 45906
Colesville and Windsor Museum at Saint Luke's Church, Harpursville 43920
Collier Memorial State Park and Logging Museum, Chiloquin 42382
Colonial Michilimackinac, Mackinaw City 45032
Colorado Historical Society Museum, Denver 42882
Columbia River Maritime Museum, Astoria 41309
Columbia State Historic Park, Columbia 42547
Columbus-Belmont Civil War Museum, Columbus 42579
The Columbus Museum, Columbus 42574
Commonwealth Museum, Boston 41805
Constitution Square, Danville 42778
Coppini Academy of Fine Arts Gallery and Museum, San Antonio 47249
Coronado National Memorial, Hereford 43997
Cottonwood County Historical Society Museum, Windom 48681
Creek Council House Museum, Okmulgee 46125
Cultural Heritage Center Museum, Toppenish 48035
Cultural Rights and Protection/Ute Indian Tribe, Fort Duchesne 43391
Cumberland Gap National Historical Park, Middlesboro 45311
Custer Museum, Clayton 42441
Dade Battlefield Historic State Park, Bushnell 42015
Dahlonega Courthouse Gold Museum, Dahlonega 42739
Dakota County Historical Society Museum, South Saint Paul 47702
Dalton Defenders Museum, Coffeyville 42512
Daughters of the American Revolution Museum, Washington 48344
Dawson Springs Museum and Art Center, Dawson Springs 42798
Delaware and Hudson Canal Museum, High Falls 44014
Department of the Treasury Museum, Washington 48346
Depot Museum of the Mammoth Spring State Park, Mammoth Spring 45089
Depreciation Lands Museum, Allison Park 41150
Desert Caballeros Western Museum, Wickenburg 48615
Desoto National Memorial, Bradenton 41861
Deutschheim State Historic Site, Hermann 44001
Dillard Mill State Historic Site, Davisville 42797
Discovery Museum History Center, Sacramento 47051
Doak House Museum, Greeneville 43802
Donner Memorial and Emigrant Trail Museum, Truckee 48074
Door County Maritime Museum, Sturgeon Bay 47860
Douglass Historical Museum, Douglass 42966
Dr Pepper Museum and Free Enterprise Institute, Waco 48262
Drum Barracks Civil War Museum, Wilmington 48648
Du Page County Historical Museum, Wheaton 48582
Duke Homestead State Historic Site, Durham 43018
Dusable Museum of African-American History, Chicago 42324
E. St. Julien Cox House, Saint Peter 47169
Early American Museum, Mahomet 45076
East-West Center, Honolulu 44075
Edison National Historic Site, West Orange 48536
Eisenhower National Historic Site, Gettysburg 43662
El Morro National Monument, Ramah 46782
El Paso Museum of History, El Paso 43117
Elijah Clark Memorial Museum, Lincolnton 44800
E.M. Violette Museum, Kirksville 44502
Ephrata Cloister, Ephrata 43195
The Esther Thomas Atkinson Museum, Hampden-Sydney 43891
Eugene O'Neill National Historic Site, Danville 42776
Eustis Historical Museum, Eustis 43236
Exchange Hotel Civil War Museum, Gordonsville 43729
Exhibition of the Norwegian-American Historical Association, Northfield 46020
Fairfax Museum and Visitor Center, Fairfax 43260
Farmington Historic Home, Louisville 44964
Favell Museum of Western Art and Indian Artifacts, Klamath Falls 44508
Federal Hall National Memorial, New York 45799
Fick Fossil and History Museum, Oakley 46074
First Missouri State Capitol, Saint Charles 47078
First White House of the Confederacy, Montgomery 45466
Five Civilized Tribes Museum, Muskogee 45581
Florence McLeod Hazard Museum, Columbus 42582
Florida History Museum, Jupiter 44371
Florissant Valley Historical Society Museum, Florissant 43349
Forest Lawn Museum, Glendale 43689
Fort Boonesborough Museum, Richmond 46864
Fort Bowie, Bowie 41842
Fort Caroline Memorial Museum, Jacksonville 44294
Fort Clatsop National Memorial, Astoria 41310
Fort de Chartres Museum, Prairie du Rocher 46684
Fort Fisher, Kure Beach 44529
Fort Frederica, Saint Simons Island 47180
Fort Huachuca Museum, Fort Huachuca 43399
Fort King George Historic Site, Darien 42783
Fort Ligonier Museum, Ligonier 44770
Fort McHenry, Baltimore 41467
Fort Macon, Atlantic Beach 41364
Fort Massac, Metropolis 45278
Fort Matanzas, Saint Augustine 47067
Fort Roosevelt Natural Science and History Museum, Hanford 43903
Fort Saint Jean Baptiste, Natchitoches 45635
Fort Smith, Fort Smith 43456
Fort Union Trading Post National Historic Site, Williston 48639
Fort Vasquez Museum, Platteville 46544
Fort Worth Museum of Science and History, Fort Worth 43485
Fort Yargo, Winder 48680
Frank Lloyd Wright Home and Studio, Oak Park 46052
Franklin Pierce Homestead, Hillsborough 44031
Frederick C. Robie House, Chicago 42328
Frederick Douglass National Historic Site, Washington 48356
The French Legation Museum, Austin 41411
Frontier Times Museum, Bandera 41491
Gadsden Museum, Mesilla 45273
Ganondagan State Historic Site, Victor 48231
Gay 90's Mansion Museum, Barnesville 41506
General Grant National Memorial, New York 45805
General Henry Knox Museum, Thomaston 47998
General John J. Pershing Boyhood Home, Laclede 44563
George Rogers Clark Park Museum, Vincennes 48238
George W. Somerville Historical Library, Chillicothe 42376
George Washington Carver Museum, Tuskegee Institute 48122
George Washington Masonic National Memorial, Alexandria 41129
George Washington's Headquarters, Cumberland 42726
George Washington's Mount Vernon, Mount Vernon 45546
Georgia Mountains History Museum, Gainesville 43589
Geronimo Springs Museum, Truth or Consequences 48075
Gettysburg National Military Park, Gettysburg 43663
Gilcrease Museum, Tulsa 48104
Glendower State Memorial, Lebanon 44703
Glensheen Historic Estate, Duluth 42999
Goodhue County Historical Society Museum, Red Wing 46817
Gore Place, Waltham 48297
Governor Bent Museum, Taos 47949
Grand River Historical Society Museum, Chillicothe 42377
Great Blacks in Wax Museum, Baltimore 41468
Great Plains Black Museum, Omaha 46148
Green River Museum, Woodbury 48730
Grout Museum of History and Science, Waterloo 48431
The Haggin Museum, Stockton 47824
The Hagley Museum, Wilmington 48652
Hampton National Historic Site Museum, Towson 48046
Hampton University Museum, Hampton 43896
Hancock House, Hancock's Bridge 43902
Harn Homestead and 1889er Museum, Oklahoma City 46111
Harriet Beecher Stowe Center, Hartford 43939
Harry S. Truman Birthplace State Historic Site, Lamar 44612
Harry S. Truman Home, Independence 44201
Harry S. Truman Library Museum, Independence 44202
Harvard Historical Society Collection, Harvard 43953
Hearthstone Historic House Museum, Appleton 41239
Hellenic Museum and Cultural Center, Chicago 42332
Hennepin History Museum, Minneapolis 45384
Henry Whitfield State Historical Museum, Guilford 43851
Herbert Hoover National Historic Site, West Branch 48514
Hereford Inlet Lighthouse, North Wildwood 46010
Heritage Museum, Baltimore 41469
Herreshoff Marine Museum/America's Cup Hall of Fame, Bristol 41907
Hershey Museum, Hershey 44004
Hickories Museum, Elyria 43177
High Desert Museum, Bend 41623
High Plains Museum, Goodland 43727
Hinckley Foundation Museum, Ithaca 44273
Historic Bethany, Bethany 41659
Historic Columbus Foundation, Columbus 42575
Historic Edenton State Historic Site, Edenton 43081
Historic Landmarks Foundation of Indiana, Indianapolis 44220
Historic Langhorne Museum, Langhorne 44636
Historic Latta Plantation, Huntersville 44152
Historic Lyme Village, Bellevue 41595
Historic Mann House, Concord 42603
Historic Museum of Arkansas, Little Rock 44824
Historic Renville Preservation Commission Museum, Renville 46842
Historic Spanish Point, Osprey 46210
Historic W.H.C. Folsom House, Taylors Falls 47962
Historical Center for Southeast New Mexico, Roswell 47015
Historical Museum of Southern Florida, Miami 45285
Historical Society of Old Yarmouth Museum, Yarmouth Port 48779
History Museum of Western Virginia, Roanoke 46929
History San José, San Jose 47351
Horry County Museum, Conway 42613
House of Roses, Deadwood 42821
The House of the Seven Gables, Salem 47195
Howard University Museum, Washington 48363
Hubbardton Battlefield Museum, Hubbardton 44141
Huddleston Farmhouse Inn Museum, Cambridge City 42056
Huguenot Historical Society Museum, New Paltz 45740
Humboldt County Old Settler's Museum, Livermore 44829
Idaho State Historical Museum, Boise 41774
Ilwaco Heritage Museum, Ilwaco 44196
Indian City U.S.A., Anadarko 41191
Indian Mill Museum State Memorial, Upper Sandusky 48160
Indian Temple Mound Museum, Fort Walton Beach 43467
Indiana Historical Society Museum, Indianapolis 44222
Indiana State Museum, Indianapolis 44224
Indiana Territory Capitol, Vincennes 48239
Iraan Museum, Iraan 44253
Iron Mission Museum, Cedar City 42147
James K. Polk Ancestral Home, Columbia 42570
James Whitcomb Riley Birthplace and Museum, Greenfield 43805
Jamestown Settlement, Williamsburg 48629
Japanese American National Museum, Los Angeles 44914
Japanese Cultural Center of Hawaii, Honolulu 44081
Jefferson County Historical Society Museum, Port Townsend 46605
Jefferson National Expansion Memorial, Saint Louis 47125
Jerome State Historic Park, Jerome 44336
The Jewish Museum, New York 45821
John G. Neihardt Center, Bancroft 41490
John Kane House, Pawling 46316
Joseph Priestley House, Northumberland 46029
Joseph Smith Historic Center, Nauvoo 45638
Kalaupapa Historical Park, Kalaupapa 44381
Kandiyohi County Historical Society Museum, Willmar 48642
Kansas Barbed Wire Museum, La Crosse 44534
Kansas Museum of History, Topeka 48033
Kauai Museum, Lihue 44771
The Kendall College Mitchell Museum of the American Indian, Evanston 43239
Kennesaw Civil War Museum, Kennesaw 44437
Kennesaw Mountain National Battlefield Park, Kennesaw 44438
Kentucky Historical Society Museum, Frankfort 43509
Keweenaw County Historical Society Museum, Eagle Harbor 43033
Knights of Columbus Museum, New Haven 45696
Knox County Historical Society Museum, Edina 43087
Lake County Historical Society Museum, Two Harbors 48127
Lake Superior Maritime Visitors Center, Duluth 43000
Lane County Historical Museum, Eugene 43222
Last Indian Raid Museum, Oberlin 46075
Laura Ingalls Wilder-Rose Wilder Lane Historic Home and Museum, Mansfield 45124
Lea County Cowboy Hall of Fame and Western Heritage Center, Hobbs 44043
Levere Memorial Temple, Evanston 43240
Levine Museum of the New South, Charlotte 42241
Liberty Hall Museum, Union 48144
Liberty Memorial Museum of World War One, Kansas City 44403
Lincoln Homestead, Springfield 47744
Lincoln Memorial Shrine, Redlands 46822
The Lincoln Museum, Fort Wayne 43478
Lincoln Tomb, Springfield 47739
The Lithuanian Museum, Chicago 42338
Little Norway, Blue Mounds 41757
Lockerbie Street Home of James Whitcomb Riley, Indianapolis 44230
Locust Grove, Louisville 44969
Long Island Culture History Museum, Commack 42594
Long Island Museum of American Art, History and Cariages, Stony Brook 47830
Longfellow National Historic Site, Cambridge 42044
Longhorn Museum, Pleasanton 46555
Longyear Museum, Chestnut Hill 42293
Lost City Museum, Overton 46224
Louis E. May Museum, Fremont 43555
Louisiana Old State Capitol, Center for Political and Governmental History, Baton Rouge 41529
Louisiana State Museum, New Orleans 45731
Lower East Side Tenement Museum, New York 45827
Luzerne County Historical Museum, Wilkes-Barre 48621
The Lyceum - Alexandria's History Museum, Alexandria 41132
Lyndon Baines Johnson Museum, Austin 41416
McCollum-Chidester House Museum, Camden 42057
McKinley Museum and McKinley National Memorial, Canton 42090
McLarty Treasure Museum, Vero Beach 48223
Mahaffie Stagecoach Stop and Farm, Olathe 46127
Major John Bradford House, Kingston 44492
Mansfield State Historc Site, Mansfield 45123
Manship House Museum, Jackson 44278
Marais Des Cygnes Memorial Historic Site, Pleasanton 46554
Maramec Museum, Saint James 47096
The Margaret Mitchell House and Museum, Atlanta 41349
Marin Museum of the American Indian, Novato 46045
The Mariners' Museum, Newport News 45937
Maritime Museum, Cohasset 42515
Marjorie Kinnan Rawlings Historic State Park, Cross Creek 42710
Mark Twain Birthplace Museum, Stoutsville 47840
Mark Twain Home and Museum, Hannibal 43904
Mark Twain House, Hartford 43940
Marland's Grand Home, Ponca City 46581
Marrett House, Standish 47770
Marshall County Historical Museum, Holly Springs 44059
Marshall County Historical Society Museum, Warren 48309
Martin Van Buren Historic Site, Kinderhook 44483
Massachusetts Historical Society Museum, Boston 41814
Massillon Museum, Massillon 45202
The Mattatuck Museum of the Mattatuck Historical Society, Waterbury 48427
Mattye Reed African Heritage Center, Greensboro 43817
Melrose Plantation Home Complex, Melrose 45230
Melvin B. Tolson Black Heritage Center, Langston 44637
Memphis Pink Palace Museum, Memphis 45244
Mennonite Heritage Museum, Goessel 43709
Mercer Museum of the Bucks County Historical Society, Doylestown 42985
Meriwether Lewis National Monument, Hohenwald 44048
Methodist Church Museum - a Laura Ingalls Wilder Site, Spring Valley 47731
Michigan State University Museum, East Lansing 43054
Mill Grove, The Audubon Wildlife Sanctuary, Audubon 41379
Milton House Museum, Milton 45357
Minnesota Historical Society Museum, Saint Paul 47162

Minnesota Pioneer Park Museum, Annandale 41223
Minute Man National Historical Park, Concord 42599
Miracle of America Museum, Polson 46579
Mission San Carlos Borromeo del Rio Carmelo, Carmel 42110
Mississippi County Historical Society Museum, Charleston 42206
Mississippi Governor's Mansion, Jackson 44279
Missouri Historical Society Museum, Saint Louis 47128
Missouri State Museum, Jefferson City 44329
Missouri Town 1855, Lees Summit 44709
Monocacy National Battlefield, Frederick 43528
Monterey State Historic Park, Monterey 45457
Monticello, Home of Thomas Jefferson, Charlottesville 42249
Moody Mansion Museum, Galveston 43613
Mordecai Historic Park, Raleigh 46774
Morningside Nature Center, Gainesville 43583
Mount Rushmore National Memorial, Keystone 44476
Mountain Heritage Center, Cullowhee 42723
Muscatine Art Center, Muscatine 45575
Museo de Las Americas, Denver 42893
El Museo Latino, Omaha 46150
Museum and Arts Center in the Sequim Dungeness Valley, Sequim 47568
Museum of Afro-American History, Brookline 41938
Museum of American Frontier Culture, Staunton 47797
Museum of American Historical Society of Germans from Russia, Lincoln 44786
Museum of Art and History, Santa Cruz 47411
Museum of Chinese in the Americas, New York 45841
Museum of Connecticut History, Hartford 43942
The Museum of East Texas, Lufkin 44997
Museum of Florida History, Tallahassee 47936
Museum of History and Industry, Seattle 47540
Museum of Man in the Sea, Panama City Beach 46279
Museum of Nebraska History, Lincoln 44787
Museum of New Mexico, Santa Fe 47427
Museum of Science and History of Jacksonville, Jacksonville 44299
Museum of Southern History, Jacksonville 44300
Museum of Texas, Waco 48266
Museum of the Albemarle, Elizabeth City 43132
Museum of the Cape Fear Historical Complex, Fayetteville 43312
Museum of the Cherokee Indian, Cherokee 42276
Museum of the Fur Trade, Chadron 42180
Museum of the Mountain Man, Pinedale 46493
Museum of the Northern Great Plains, Fort Benton 43368
Napoleonic Society of America, Clearwater 42452
National Afro-American Museum and Cultural Center, Wilberforce 48618
National Border Patrol Museum and Memorial Library, El Paso 43122
National Center for the American Revolution, Valley Forge 48188
National Cowboy and Western Heritage Museum, Oklahoma City 46116
National Cowgirl Museum and Hall of Fame, Fort Worth 43491
National Czech and Slovak Museum, Cedar Rapids 42161
National Frontier Trails Center, Independence 44207
National Hall of Fame for Famous American Indians, Anadarko 41192
National Heritage Museum, Lexington 44750
National Museum of American History, Washington 48376
National Museum of American Jewish History, Philadelphia 46436
National Museum of Funeral History, Houston 44132
National Museum of the American Indian, Washington 48380
National Museum of the American Indian, New York 45852
National Society of the Children of the American Revolution Museum, Washington 48384
National Trust for Historic Preservation, Washington 48385
National Yiddish Book Center, Amherst 41180
Native American Exhibit, Fonda 43361
Native American Heritage Museum at Highland Mission, Highland 44017
Native American Museum, Terre Haute 47984
Naumkeag House, Stockbridge 47819
Nevada Historical Society Museum, Reno 46834
Nevada State Fire Museum and Comstock Firemen's Museum, Virginia City 48252
Nevada State Museum, Carson City 42118
New Echota, Calhoun 42033
New Jersey State Museum, Trenton 48057
New Mexico Farm and Ranch Heritage Museum, Las Cruces 44659
The Newseum, Arlington 41266
Nickels-Sortwell House, Wiscasset 48718
Nobles County Historical Society Museum, Worthington 48762
North Carolina Museum of History, Raleigh 46776
Northeast Louisiana Delta African American Heritage Museum, Monroe 45442
Northeastern Nevada Museum, Elko 43146
Northern Indiana Center for History, South Bend 47680
Norwich University Museum, Northfield 46025
Oakland Museum of California, Oakland 46067
Oaks House Museum, Jackson 44284
O'Fallon Historical Museum, Baker 41435
Ohio Historical Society Museum, Columbus 42590
Oklahoma Museum of History, Oklahoma City 46121
Oklahoma Territorial Museum, Guthrie 43855
Oktibbeha County Heritage Museum, Starkville 47777
Old Capitol Museum of Mississippi History, Jackson 44285
Old Colony Historical Museum, Taunton 47960
Old Fort Garland, Fort Garland 43394
Old Fort Western, Augusta 41391
The Old Manse, Concord 42600
Old Ordinary Museum, Hingham 44037
Old Spanish Fort and Museum, Pascagoula 46306
Old State House, Boston 41822
Old State House, Hartford 43943
The Old State House Museum, Little Rock 44825
Old Washington Museum, Washington 48328
Old World Wisconsin, Eagle 43031
Olde Colonial Courthouse, Barnstable 41509
Oldest House Museum Complex, Saint Augustine 47069
Oliver House Museum, Saint Martinville 47143
Olmsted County Historical Society Museum, Rochester 46935
Olustee Battlefield, Olustee 46138
Oregon Coast History Center, Newport 45921
Oregon Trail Regional Museum, Baker City 41438
Our House State Memorial, Gallipolis 43605
Owens-Thomas House, Savannah 47482
Pacific University Museum, Forest Grove 43362
Palmer Museum, Jewell 44342
Pardee Home Museum, Oakland 46068
The Park-McCullough House, North Bennington 45983
Parker Tavern Museum, Reading 46804
Paul H. Karshner Memorial Museum, Puyallup 46752
Paul Revere House, Boston 41823
Paynes Creek Historic State Park, Bowling Green 41848
The Peace Museum, Chicago 42357
Pembina State Museum, Pembina 46332
Pennsylvania Anthracite Heritage Museum, Scranton 47520
Pennsylvania Lumber Museum, Galeton 43601
Peoria Historical Society, Peoria 46350
Perry's Victory and International Peace Memorial, Put-in-Bay 46748
The Petroleum Museum, Midland 45329
Pierce Manse, Concord 42606
Pioneer Arizona Living History Museum, Phoenix 46479
Pioneer Florida Museum, Dade City 42738
Pioneer Heritage Center, Shreveport 47614
Pioneer Museum, Watford City 48450
Pioneer Woman Statue and Museum, Ponca City 46582
Pioneers, Trail and Texas Rangers Memorial Museum, San Antonio 47256
Pipestone County Historical Museum, Pipestone 46498
Pipestone National Monument, Pipestone 46499
Plum Grove Historic Home, Iowa City 44246
Plymoth Plantation Museum, Plymouth 46562
Polish American Museum, Port Washington 46609
Polish Museum of America, Chicago 42358
Porter-Phelps-Huntington Foundation, Hadley 43863
Portholes Into the Past, Medina 45226
Postville Courthouse Museum, Lincoln 44774
President Andrew Johnson Museum, Greeneville 43803
President Benjamin Harrison Home, Indianapolis 44234
The Presidential Museum, Odessa 46094
El Pueblo de Los Angeles Historical Monument, Los Angeles 44938
Pullman Museum, Chicago 42359
Putnam Museum of History and Natural Science, Davenport 42786
Railroad and Heritage Museum, Temple 47976
Red River Valley Museum, Vernon 48218
Redding Museum of Art and History, Redding 46819
Redwood County Museum, Redwood Falls 46827
Rensselaer Russell House Museum, Waterloo 48432
The Rice Museum, Georgetown 43655
Roanoke Island Festival Park, Manteo 45127
Roberson Museum and Science Center, Binghamton 41700
Rochester Museum, Rochester 46944
Rockingham, Princeton 46705
Roniger Memorial Museum, Cottonwood Falls 42667
Rosalie House, Eureka Springs 43235
Rosalie House Museum, Natchez 45633
Roscoe Village Foundation, Coshocton 42663
Rose Hill Plantation State Historic Site, Union 48146
Roseau County Historical Museum, Roseau 47002
Rowan Museum, Salisbury 47220
Royall House, Medford 45216
Ruggles House, Columbia Falls 42572
Rumford Historical Museum, North Woburn 46012
Rutherford B. Hayes Presidential Center, Fremont 43556
Safe Haven, Oswego 46217
Sag Harbor Whaling and Historical Museum, Sag Harbor 47061
Sagamore Hill National Historic Site, Oyster Bay 46250
Saint Augustine Lighthouse and Museum, Saint Augustine 47072
Saint Clements Island-Potomac River Museum, Colton Point 42546
De Saisset Museum, Santa Clara 47407
Salem Maritime National Historic Site, Salem 47201
Salem Witch Museum, Salem 47202
Salter Museum, Argonia 41254
Sam Houston Memorial Museum, Huntsville 44176
San Francisco African American Historical and Cultural Society Museum, San Francisco 47334
San Jacinto Museum of History, La Porte 44557
San Joaquin County Historical Museum, Lodi 44843
San Marcos de Apalache Historic State Park, Saint Marks 47141
Santa Fe Trail Museum, Trinidad 48065
Sault de Sainte Marie Historical Sites, Sault Sainte Marie 47469
Schomburg Center for Research in Black Culture, New York 45868
Seminole Nation Museum, Wewoka 48577
Senate House, Kingston 44494
Shaker Museum, New Gloucester 45690
Shaker Museum, South Union 47705
Shawneetown Historic Site, Old Shawneetown 46134
Sheldon Museum, Haines 43870
Shiloh Museum of Ozark History, Springdale 47733
Shirley-Eustis House, Boston 41826
Sibley Historic Site, Mendota 45252
Sinclair Lewis Museum, Sauk Centre 47467
Skirball Cultural Center, Los Angeles 44943
Slavonic Benevolent Order of the State of Texas Museum, Temple 47977
Smith Robertson Museum, Jackson 44286
Smith-Zimmermann Museum, Madison 45065
Smoky Hill Museum, Salina 47214
Snowden House, Waterloo 48434
Society of the Cincinnati Museum, Washington 48394
Sons of the American Revolution Museum, Louisville 44975
Sotterley Plantation Museum, Hollywood 44061
South Carolina Confederate Relic Room and Museum, Columbia 42566
South Carolina Historical Society Museum, Charleston 42227
South Dakota Hall of Fame, Chamberlain 42183
Southern Ute Indian Cultural Center, Ignacio 44194
Southwest Virginia Museum, Big Stone Gap 41684
Southwestern Michigan College Museum, Dowagiac 42978
Spirit of '76 Museum, Wellington 48500
Spurlock Museum, Urbana 48164
Star of the Republic Museum, Washington 48421
Star-Spangled Banner Flag House and 1812 Museum, Baltimore 41487
State Museum of Pennsylvania, Harrisburg 43925
Statue of Liberty National Monument and Ellis Island Immigration Museum, New York 45876
Stearns History Museum, Saint Cloud 47086
Stephen A. Douglas Tomb, Chicago 42364
Stephens Museum, Fayette 43307
Stevens County Gas and Historical Museum, Hugoton 44148
Steves Homestead Museum, San Antonio 47262
Stewart M. Lord Memorial Museum, Burlington 42002
Stockbridge Library Historical Room, Stockbridge 47821
Storrowton Village Museum, West Springfield 48548
Strecker Museum Complex, Waco 48268
Strong Museum, Rochester 46946
Sunwatch Indian Village - Archaeological Park, Dayton 42806
Surratt House Museum, Clinton 42493
Swindler's Ridge Museum, Benton 41632
Tate House, Portland 46627
Tennessee Historical Society Museum, Nashville 45625
Tennessee State Museum, Nashville 45626
Texas City Museum, Texas City 47992
Texas Memorial Museum of Science and History, Austin 41421
Texas Ranger Hall of Fame and Museum, Waco 48269
Theodore Roosevelt Birthplace, New York 45881
Theodore Roosevelt Inaugural National Historic Site, Buffalo 41989
Thomas Edison Birthplace Museum, Milan 45335
Thomas P. Kennard House, Lincoln 44792
Thomas Wolfe Memorial, Asheville 41284
Thousand Islands Museum of Clayton, Clayton 42445
Tippecanoe Battlefield, Battle Ground 41540
Trail End State Historic Museum, Sheridan 47602
Traverse County Historical Society Museum, Wheaton 48586
Treaty Site History Center, Saint Peter 47170
Tryon Palace, New Bern 45667
Tubman African-American Museum, Macon 45048
Turtle Mountain Chippewa Heritage Center, Belcourt 41586
Tuskegee Institute National Historic Site, Tuskegee Institute 48123
Ukrainian-American Archives and Museum, Hamtramck 43899
Ukrainian Museum, Cleveland 42484
Uncle Remus Museum, Eatonton 43072
United States Army Museum of Hawaii, Fort DeRussy 43386
United States Marine Corps Museum, Washington 48402
Utah State Historical Society Museum, Salt Lake City 47236
Valley Forge National Historical Park, Valley Forge 48189
Vandalia State House, Vandalia 48203
Vikingsholm, Tahoma 47929
Virginia Historical Society Museum, Richmond 46890
Wabasha County Museum, Reads Landing 46811
Wabasso Historical Society Museum, Wabasso 48259
The Wallace Museum Foundation, Montgomery 45468
Warden's House Museum, Stillwater 47811
Waseca County Historical Society Museum, Waseca 48325
Washington Crossing Historic Park, Washington Crossing 48423
Weir Farm, Wilton 48671
Wells Fargo History Museum, Los Angeles 44950
Wentworth-Coolidge Mansion, Portsmouth 46655
Western Archeological and Conservation Center, Tucson 48097
Western Hotel Museum, Lancaster 44617
Wilber Czech Museum, Wilber 48617
Will Rogers Memorial Museums, Claremore 42423
William Hammond Mathers Museum, Bloomington 41749
William Howard Taft National Historic Site, Cincinnati 42412
William M. Colmer Visitor Center, Ocean Springs 46088
Willowbrook at Newfield, Newfield 45916
Windham Textile and History Museum, Willimantic 48637
Wing Luke Asian Museum, Seattle 47548
Winnebago Area Museum, Winnebago 48692
Winnie Davis Museum of History, Gaffney 43580
Winona County Historical Museum, Winona 48696
Winston Churchill Memorial and Library in the United States, Fulton 43577
Winterthur Museum, Winterthur 48712
Witte Museum, San Antonio 47265
Women's Heritage Museum, San Francisco 47345
Women's History Museum, West Liberty 48534
Woolaroc Museum, Bartlesville 41516
Workman and Temple Family Homestead Museum, City of Industry 42415
The Works, Newark 45899
Wright Museum, Wolfeboro 48724
Wyoming State Museum, Cheyenne 42300
Yazoo Historical Museum, Yazoo City 48782
Yorba-Slaughter Adobe Museum, Chino 42384
Yorktown Museum, Yorktown Heights 48803
Yorktown Visitor Center, Yorktown 48801
Yorktown Visitor Center Museum, Yorktown 48802

Uzbekistan
Gosudarstvennyj Muzej Istorii Kultury i Iskusstva Uzbekistana, Samarkand 48848
Historical Museum of Uzbekistan M.T. Oibek, Taškent 48854
Karakalpakskij Istoričeskij Muzej, Nukus 48847
Sergej Borodin Muzej, Taškent 48860
Tashkent Historical Museum of the People of Uzbekistan, Taškent 48861
Yoldosh Oxunboboev Memorial Muzeyi, Margelan 48843

Venezuela
Casa Natal de José María España, La Guaira 48948
Casa Natal del Libertador Simón Bolívar, Caracas 48897
Museo Bolívariano, Caracas 48908
Museo Cristóbal Mendoza, Trujillo 48964
Museo de Historia y Artesanía de la Colonial Tovar, Colonia Tovar 48935
Museo Gran Mariscal de Ayacucho, Cumaná 48938
Museo José Antonio Páez, Acarigua 48886

Vietnam
Vien Bao Tang Lich Sa Viet Nam, Ha Noi 48980
Viet Nam History Museum Ho Chi Minh City, Ho Chi Minh City 48993

Zambia
Lusaka National Museum, Lusaka 49020
Moto Moto Museum, Mbala 49023

Zimbabwe
Queen Victoria Museum, Harare 49033

History, Early → Prehistory and Early History

History, Local and Regional

Afghanistan
Bamian Museum, Bamian 00001
Ghazni Museum, Ghazni 00002
Herat Museum, Herat 00003
Kabul Museum, Kabul 00004
Kandahar Museum, Kandahar 00007
Maimana Museum, Maimana 00008
Mazar-i-Sharif Museum, Mazar-i-Sharif 00009

Albania
Butrinti Museum, Butrint 00014
District Historical Museum, Bérat 00011
District Historical Museum, Vlorë 00038

Elbasan Museum, Elbasan 00018
Gjirokastër Museum, Gjirokastër 00023
Korçë Museum, Korçë 00025
National Historical Museum, Tiranë 00036
Scanderbeg Museum, Kruja 00028
Shkodër Museum, Shkodër 00032

Algeria
Musée Archéologique du Théâtre de Guelma,
Guelma 00065
Musée de Béjaïa, Béjaïa 00050
Musée de Djemila, Djemila 00060
Musée de Temouchent, Ain Temouchent 00039
Musée de Tiemcen, Tiemcen 00077
Musée de Tiemcen, Tiemcen 00081
Musée d'El-Oued, El-Oued 00063
Musée Marsa El-Kharez, El-Kala 00061
Musée National Ahmed Zabana - Demaeght Museum,
Oran 00068
Musée National Cirta, Constantine 00058
Musée National de Préhistoire et d'Ethnographie du
Bardo, Alger 00044
Musée Saharien de Ouargla, Ouargla 00069

American Samoa
Jean P. Haydon Museum, Pago Pago 00082

Andorra
Museu Viladomat d'Escultura, Escaldes-
Engordany 00084

Angola
Museu do Congo, Carmona 00090
Museu do Dundu, Chitato 00091
Museu do Pioneiro, Malange 00102
Museu Regional da Huila, Lumbango 00101
Museu Regional do Planalto Central, Huambo 00092

Argentina
Cartref Taid, Trevelin 00643
Casa de la Cultura, Curuzú Cuatiá 00326
Centro de Exposiciones La Casona de los Olivera,
Buenos Aires 00146
Complejo Histórico Chivilcoy, Chivilcoy 00275
Complejo Museológico La Estación, Cruz Alta 00325
Exposición de Gregorio de Laferrere, Gregorio de
Laferrere 00358
Fundación Archivo Gráfico y Museo Histórico de la
Ciudad de San Francisco y la Región, San
Francisco 00560
Museo Activo del Pago de los Arroyos, Rosario 00525
Museo Capitán Juan de Zevallos, Valle
Hermoso 00653
Museo Clarisse Coulombie de Goyaud,
Ituzaingó 00369
Museo Colonial e Histórico, Luján 00413
Museo Comunal de Chañar Ladeado, Chañar
Ladeado 00271
Museo Comunal Pedro Bargero, Emilio Bunge 00340
Museo Comunal Regional de San Guillermo, San
Guillermo 00563
Museo Coyug-Curá, Pigüé 00476
Museo de Antropología e Historia Natural Los
Desmochados, Casilda 00267
Museo de Arte e História de Los Toldos, Los
Toldos 00411
Museo de Chilecito, Chilecito 00274
Museo de Ciencias Naturales e Historia,
Posadas 00482
Museo de Firmat, Firmat 00348
Museo de Historia Reginal San Lorenzo y Galería del
Libertador General San Martín, San Lorenzo 00575
Museo de Historia Regional de Tristán Suárez, Trisán
Suárez 00646
Museo de la Casa Histórica de la Independencia
Nacional, San Miguel de Tucumán 00583
Museo de la Ciudad, Buenos Aires 00186
Museo de la Ciudad, Paraná 00466
Museo de la Ciudad, Salta 00540
Museo de la Ciudad, Victoria 00656
Museo de la Ciudad de Colón, Colón 00280
Museo de la Ciudad de San Francisco, San
Francisco 00561
Museo de la Colonización, Esperanza 00343
Museo de la Patagonia Dr. Francisco P. Moreno,
Bariloche 00136
Museo de La Plata, La Plata 00392
Museo de los Asentamientos, Federación 00347
Museo de Mitos y Leyendas, Tafí del Valle 00627
Museo del Este, Monte Caseros 00452
Museo del Fin del Mundo, Ushuaia 00649
Museo del Hombre y su Entorno, Caleta Olivia 00257
Museo del Periodismo Bonaerense, Capilla del
Señor 00261
Museo del Pueblo, Pirané 00478
Museo del Puerto de Ingeniero White, Ingeniero
White 00366
Museo El Reencuentro, Darregueira 00327
Museo General de Arequito, Arequito 00117
Museo Germán Guglielmetti, Benito Juárez 00139
Museo Histórico, Arqueológico y de Arte Pedro
Balduín, San Pedro de Jujuy 00593
Museo Histórico, Colonial y de Bellas Artes y Museo
de Ciencias Naturales Regional Mesopotámico,
Mercedes 00443
Museo Histórico Comunal, Villa Trinidad 00674
Museo Histórico Comunal de San Genaro Norte, San
Genaro Norte 00562
Museo Histórico de Arenaza, Arenaza 00116
Museo Histórico de Arrecifes, Arrecifes 00120
Museo Histórico de Cañuelas, Cañuelas 00260

Museo Histórico de Entre Ríos Martiniano
Leguizamón, Paraná 00468
Museo Histórico de Guatraché, Guatraché 00363
Museo Histórico de la Colonia San Carlos, San Carlos
Centro 00553
Museo Histórico de la Provincia, Santiago del
Estero 00617
Museo Histórico de Laborde, Laborde 00401
Museo Histórico de Navarro, Navarro 00457
Museo Histórico de Ranchos, Ranchos 00501
Museo Histórico General Julio de Vedia, 9 de
Julio 00106
Museo Histórico La Gallareta Forestal, La
Gallareta 00381
Museo Histórico Manuel A. Moreira, Laboulaye 00402
Museo Histórico Municipal, Bahía Blanca 00127
Museo Histórico Municipal Alfredo E. Múlgura,
General Belgrano 00353
Museo Histórico Municipal Andrés A. Roverano, Santo
Tomé 00621
Museo Histórico Municipal de Armstrong,
Armstrong 00119
Museo Histórico Municipal de Cañada de Gómez,
Cañada de Gómez 00259
Museo Histórico Municipal de Luque, Luque 00420
Museo Histórico Municipal de Pergamino,
Pergamino 00472
Museo Histórico Municipal de Villa Gesell, Villa
Gesell 00669
Museo Histórico Municipal General Levalle, General
Levalle 00354
Museo Histórico Municipal Hércules J. Rabagliati,
Ramallo 00500
Museo Histórico Municipal Juan Lavalle,
Baradero 00134
Museo Histórico Municipal La Para, La Para 00382
Museo Histórico Municipal Monte Grande, Monte
Grande 00453
Museo Histórico Municipal Víctor E. Míguez,
Mercedes 00444
Museo Histórico Municipal Villa Clara, Villa
Clara 00663
Museo Histórico Municipal Villa del Rosario, Villa del
Rosario 00666
Museo Histórico Municipal y Colección de Arte
Precolombino Arminio Weiss, Rafaela 00498
Museo Histórico Provincial Agustín V. Gnecco, San
Juan 00573
Museo Histórico Provincial de Rosario Dr. Julio Marc,
Rosario 00528
Museo Histórico Provincial Marqués de Sobremonte,
Córdoba 00302
Museo Histórico Regional, Alpachiri 00110
Museo Histórico Regional, Gualeguay 00359
Museo Histórico Regional de Ayacucho,
Ayacucho 00123
Museo Histórico Regional de Gaiman, Gaiman 00351
Museo Histórico Regional de la Colonia San José, San
José 00567
Museo Histórico Regional De la Isla, Isla del
Cerrito 00368
Museo Histórico Regional de Río Cuarto, Río
Cuarto 00511
Museo Histórico Regional de Urdinarrain,
Urdinarrain 00648
Museo Histórico Regional de Villa La Angostura, Villa
La Angostura 00670
Museo Histórico Regional Gabriel Campomar Cervera,
Salliqueló 00536
Museo Histórico Regional Ichoalay, Resistencia 00509
Museo Histórico Regional Municipal de Magdalena,
Magdalena 00421
Museo Histórico Regional Pablo Argilaga, Santo
Tomé 00622
Museo Histórico Regional Padre Francisco Cremasco,
Villa Concepción del Tío 00664
Museo Histórico San Ignacio de Loyola, San
José 00568
Museo Histórico y Natural de Lavalle, Lavalle Villa
Tulumaya 00406
Museo Histórico y Regional Pico Truncado, Pico
Truncado 00475
Museo Histórico y Tradicional de Barracas al Sud,
Avellaneda 00121
Museo Irureta, Tilcara 00636
Museo José Manuel Estrada, Suipacha 00625
Museo López Claro, Santa Fé 00606
Museo Municipal Carmen Funes, Plaza Huincul 00479
Museo Municipal de El Trébol, El Trébol 00336
Museo Municipal de Eldorado, Eldorado 00338
Museo Municipal de la Ciudad de Carcarañá,
Carcarañá 00262
Museo Municipal de la Ciudad de Rosario,
Rosario 00531
Museo Municipal de Porteña, Porteña 00480
Museo Municipal Dr. Rodolfo Doval Fermi,
Sastre 00623
Museo Municipal Histórico Regional Santiago
Lischetti, Villa Constitución 00665
Museo Municipal Ignacio Balvidares, Puan 00487
Museo Municipal José A. Mulazzi, Tres Arroyos 00641
Museo Municipal José Manuel Maciel,
Coronda 00315
Museo Municipal Punta Hermengo, Miramar 00450
Museo Municpal Dr. Santos F. Tosticarelli,
Casilda 00268
Museo Oncativo, Oncativo 00463
Museo Orlando Binaghi, Moreno 00455

Museo Paleontológico, Arqueológico e Histórico de la
Ciudad de Deán Funes, Deán Funes 00328
Museo Particular Los Abuelos, Franck 00349
Museo Patria Chica de Mohamed Diaz, Realicó 00504
Museo Polifacético Regional Vottero, Laguna
Larga 00403
Museo Provincial Dora Ochoa de Masramón, San
Luis 00577
Museo Pueblo de Luis, Trelew 00640
Museo Regional Castelli, Castelli 00269
Museo Regional Cayetano Alberto Silva, Venado
Tuerto 00654
Museo Regional de Cinco Saltos, Cinco Saltos 00279
Museo Regional de Claromecó, Balneario
Claromecó 00131
Museo Regional de la Ciudad de La Paz, La
Paz 00384
Museo Regional de Pigüé, Pigüé 00477
Museo Regional de Sacanta, Sacanta 00535
Museo Regional Dr. Federico Escalada, Río
Mayo 00520
Museo Regional Las Varillas, Las Varillas 00405
Museo Regional Malargüe, Malargüe 00423
Museo Regional Maracó, General Pico 00355
Museo Regional Municipal de El Calafate, El
Calafate 00335
Museo Regional Particular Epifanio Saravia, Santa
Catalina 00599
Museo Regional Patagónico, Comodoro
Rivadavia 00284
Museo Regional Provincial Padre Manuel Jesús
Molina, Río Gallegos 00517
Museo Regional Rincón de Vida, Villa Mirasol 00672
Museo Regional Rumi Mayu (Río de Piedra),
Sanagasta 00598
Museo Regional Salesiano de Rawson,
Rawson 00503
Museo Regional Trevelin, Trevelin 00645
Museo Regional Valcheta, Valcheta 00652
Museo Regional y de Arte Marino, Puerto San
Julián 00492
Museo Rocsen, Nono 00459
Museo San Antonio de Padua, Córdoba 00312
Museo Ucraniano, Apóstoles 00115
Museo Usina Vieja, San Antonio de Areco 00552
Museo y Monumento Histórico Las Bóvedas,
Uspallata 00651
Museo y Parque Libres del Sur, Dolores 00332
Rincón de Historia, Salto 00546
Unidad Museológica Municipal de La Banda, La
Banda 00374

Australia
Addington - Ryde House of Heritage, Ryde 01430
Adelaide House Museum, Alice Springs 00732
Albury Regional Museum, Albury 00729
Allora Historical Museum, Allora 00740
Allwood House, Hurstbridge 01114
Art and Local History Collections, Mackay 01192
Augusta Historical Museum, Augusta 00756
Australian Freethought Heritage Library,
Balwyn 00768
Bairnsdale Museum, Bairnsdale 00758
Ballan Shire Historical Museum, Ballan 00760
Bank of Victoria Museum, Yackandandah 01621
Barcaldine and District Historical Museum,
Barcaldine 00769
Bathurst and District Historical Museum,
Bathurst 00773
Beaudesert Museum, Beaudesert 00781
Beenleigh and District Museum, Beenleigh 00787
Bellarine Historical Museum, Drysdale 00989
Benalla Costume and Pioneer Museum,
Benalla 00792
Benga Oral Historic Centre, Dandenong 00966
Berkshire Mill Museum, Moora 01269
Berrima District Museum, Berrima 00798
Berry Museum, Berry 00799
Berwick Pakenham Historical Museum,
Pakenham 01353
Bicentennial Historical Museum, Cunnamulla 00962
Biggenden Museum, Biggenden 00801
Bingara Museum, Bingara 00803
Birchip Local History Museum, Birchip 00804
Birdsville Working Museum, Birdsville 00805
Bland District Historical Museum, West
Wyalong 01593
Bluestone Cottage and Museum, Coburg 00933
Bond Store Port of Maryborough Heritage Museum,
Maryborough 01214
Boolarra Historical Museum, Boolarra 00811
Boulia Stone House Museum, Boulia 00819
Bowraville Folk Museum, Bowraville 00822
Boyne Valley Historical Cottage, Ubobo 01557
Braidwood Museum, Braidwood 00829
Brewarrina Aboriginal Cultural Museum,
Brewarrina 00830
Bridgetown Old Gaol Museum, Bridgetown 00833
Broome Historical Society Museum, Broome 00852
Broomehill Museum, Broomehill 00853
Brunswick Valley Museum, Mullumbimby 01288
Buderim Pioneer Cottage, Buderim 00856
Bundaberg Historical Museum, Bundaberg 00861
Burke Museum, Beechworth 00783
Burnett House and Myilly Point Heritage Precinct,
Darwin 00972
Byfield and District Museum, Byfield 00868
Cairns Museum, Cairns 00872
Calala Cottage, Tamworth 01514

Camden Haven Historical Museum, Laurieton 01171
Camden Historical Museum, Camden 00878
Camperdown and District Museum,
Camperdown 00881
Canberra Museum and Gallery, Canberra 00884
Captain's Cottage Museum, Murray Bridge 01290
Carbethon Folk Museum and Pioneer Village, Crows
Nest 00955
Carcoar Historic Village, Carcoar 00893
Cardwell Shire Museum, Tully 01552
Carss Cottage Museum, Blakehurst 00810
Charles Ferguson Museum, Mentone 01244
Charleville Historic House Museum,
Charlesville 00905
Chillago Historical Centre, Chillagoe 00911
Chiltern Athenaeum, Chiltern 00912
Chinchilla and District Historical Society Museum,
Chinchilla 00915
City of Belmont Museum, Belmont 00791
City of Richmond and Burnley Historical Museum,
Richmond, Victoria 01415
City of Unley Museum, Unley 01561
C.L. Alexander Museum, Tumby Bay 01553
Clare National Trust Museum, Clare 00916
Claremont Museum, Claremont, Western
Australia 00918
Clarencetown and District Historical Museum,
Clarencetown 00921
Cloncurry and District Museum, Cloncurry 00929
Clunes Museum, Clunes 00930
Coal Creek Heritage Village, Korumburra 01153
Coalfields Museum, Collie 00938
Cohuna Historical Museum, Cohuna 00934
Coleraine Local History Museum, Coleraine 00937
Concord Heritage Museum, Concord 00940
Corrigin Museum, Corrigin 00948
Court House Museum, Stroud 01481
Cowra Museums, Cowra 00950
Creswick Historical Museum, Creswick 00954
Crystal Brook Heritage Centre, Crystal Brook 00959
Dance Cottage Museum, Ravensthorpe 01408
Dartmoor District Coach House Museum,
Dartmoor 00970
Denmark Historical Museum, Denmark 00976
Dromana and District Museum, Dromana 00988
Dubbo Museum, Dubbo 00991
Dungog Historical Museum, Dungog 00994
Dunolly Museum, Dunolly 00995
Echuca Museum, Echuca 01003
Edithburgh Museum, Edithburgh 01008
Eidsvold Historical Complex, Eidsvold 01009
Eldorado Museum, Eldorado 01010
Elizabeth Bay House, Elizabeth Bay 01011
Elmore Progress Association Station Museum,
Elmore 01012
Emerald Museum, Emerald 01016
Emu Park Historical Museum, Emu Park 01018
Endeavour Museum, Cessnock 00904
Eskbank House, Lithgow 01180
Esperance Museum, Esperance 01020
Eumundi Museum, Eumundi 01021
Eureka Museum, Ballarat 00762
Fairfield City Museum and Gallery, Smithfield 01455
Farmer's Arms Hotel Museum, Euroa 01022
Forbes Museum, Forbes 01030
Foster and District Historical Society Museum,
Foster 01033
Fremantle History Museum, Fremantle 01036
Furneaux Museum, Flinders Island 01028
Gascoyne Junction Museum, Gascoyne
Junction 01041
Gayndah Museum, Gayndah 01043
Geelong Heritage Centre, Geelong 01045
Gerringong and District Museum, Gerringong 01051
Gilgandra Museum, Gilgandra 01052
Gladstone Regional Art Gallery and Museum,
Gladstone, Queensland 01055
Glenreagh Memorial Museum, Glenreagh 01060
Gloucester Folk Museum, Gloucester 01061
Gloucester Lodge Museum, Yanchep 01623
Goolwa National Trust Museum, Goolwa 01063
Great Cobar Heritage Centre, Cobar 00931
Great Lakes Historical Museum, Tuncurry 01556
Grenfell and District History Museum, Grenfell 01074
Gumeracha and District History Centre,
Gumeracha 01078
Gundagai Historical Museum, Gundagai 01079
Gympie and District Historical and Gold Mining
Museum, Gympie 01082
Hamilton Heritage Museum, Hamilton,
Tasmania 01087
Hamilton Hume Museum, Yass 01630
Hastings-Western Port Historical Museum,
Hastings 01091
Hawker Museum, Hawker, South Australia 01092
Headland Historical Museum, Nambucca
Heads 01298
Henry Kendall Cottage and Historical Museum,
Gosford 01067
Heritage Hill Museum, Dandenong 00967
Hervey Bay Historical Society Museum, Hervey
Bay 01096
Historical Society of Saint Kilda, Saint Kilda,
Victoria 01433
Hobart Heritage Museum, Hobart 01097
Homestead Park Pioneer Museum, Port
Augusta 01379
Hope Cottage, Kingscote 01149
Horsham Historical Museum, Horsham 01109

Hunters Hill Historical Museum, Sydney 01496
Huntly and Districts Historical Museum, Huntly 01112
Huon Valley Apple and Heritage Museum, Huonville 01113
Ilfracombe Museum, Ilfracombe 01117
Illawarra Museum, Wollongong 01609
Inglewood District Historical Museum, Inglewood 01119
Innisfail and District Historical Museum, Innisfail 01120
Isis District Historical Complex, Childers 00910
James Cook Historical Museum, Cooktown 00943
Jamestown Museum, Jamestown 01123
Junee Historical Museum, Junee 01127
Kandos Bicentennial Industrial Museum, Kandos 01133
Kapunda Museum, Kapunda 01135
Katamatite Museum, Katamatite 01136
Katanning Historical Museum, Katanning 01137
Katherine Museum, Katherine 01138
Keith National Trust Museum, Keith 01139
Kempsey Historical and Cultural Museum, Kempsey 01141
Kew Historical Museum, Kew 01143
Kilkivan Historical Museum, Kilkivan 01145
Kimba and Gawler Ranges Historical Society Museum, Kimba 01146
King Island Historical Museum, Currie 00963
Kingston Pioneer Museum, Kingston 01151
Koorda Museum, Koorda 01152
Kyneton Museum, Kyneton 01157
Laidley District Historical Village, Laidley 01158
Lake Tabourie Museum, Lake Tabourie 01160
Lambing Flat Museum, Young 01634
Lancefield Court House Museum, Lancefield 01162
Land of the Beardies History House Museum, Glen Innes 01058
Langi Morgala Museum, Ararat 00747
Learmonth Museum, Learmonth 01172
Lighthouse Keepers Cottage, Carnarvon 00899
Linton and District Museum, Linton 01177
Local History Collection, Aberfoyle Park 00696
Lord Howe Island Museum, Lord Howe Island 01187
Loxton District Historical Village, Loxton 01190
McCrossin's Mill Museum, Uralla 01563
Mahogany Inn, Mahogany Creek 01196
Maldon Museum, Maldon 01200
Mallala and Districts Historical Museum, Mallala 01201
Mandurah Community Museum, Mandurah 01204
Manilla Historical Royce Cottage Museum, Manilla 01205
Mareeba District Rodeo Museum, Mareeba 01210
Mareeba Heritage Museum, Mareeba 01211
Maritime Museum, Port Victoria 01388
Masonic Temple, Hobart 01100
Melbourne's Living Museum of the West, Maribyrnong 01212
Melville Discovery Centre, Applecross 00744
Merriwa Colonial Museum, Merriwa 01250
Mid-Richmond Historical Museum, Coraki 00945
Miles and District Historical Village Museum, Miles 01254
Millicent National Trust Museum, Millicent 01257
Minlaton National Trust Museum, Minlaton 01259
Moe Historical Museum, Moe 01263
Molong Historical Museum, Molong 01264
Mont De Lancey Historical Museum, Wandin 01575
Moonta Mines Museum, Moonta 01267
Moonta National Trust Museum, Moonta 01268
Mooroopna Hospital, Mooroopna 01271
Morawa Old Police Station Museum, Morawa 01272
Mordialloc Historical Society Museum, Mentone 01245
Morven Historical Museum, Morven 01278
Mount Morgan Historical Museum, Mount Morgan 01283
Mount Victoria and District Historical Museum, Mount Victoria 01284
Mudgee Colonial Inn Museum, Mudgee 01285
Mundubbera and District Historical Museum, Mundubbera 01289
Murrumburrah-Harden Historical Museum, Murrumburrah 01291
Murrurundi Museum, Murrurundi 01292
Murtoa Water Tower - Concordia Collage Museum, Murtoa 01293
Museum of Wonders, Imbil 01118
Nandewar Historical Museum, Barraba 00770
Narembeen Historical Museum, Narembeen 01302
Narrabri Old Gaol Heritage Centre, Narrabri 01304
Narrogin Old Courthouse Museum, Narrogin 01308
Narryna Heritage Museum, Battery Point 00777
National Trust Museum, Streaky Bay 01480
Nepean Historical Museum, Sorrento 01456
Newcastle Regional Museum, Newcastle 01318
Nimbin Museum, Nimbin 01322
Noosa Shire Museum, Pomona 01372
Nor West Bend Museum, Morgan 01274
North Stradbroke Island Historical Museum, Dunwich 00996
Northcliffe Pioneer Museum, Northcliffe 01331
Nowra Museum, Nowra 01337
Nundah and Districts Historical Museum, Nundah 01338
Oakleigh and District Museum, Oakleigh 01341
Old Cable Station Museum, Apollo Bay 00743
Old Highercombe Museum, Tea Tree Gully 01522
Old Police Station Museum Brookton, Brookton 00851
Old School Museum, Merimbula 01247
Old Timers Traeger Museum, Alice Springs 00737
Ongerup and Needilup District Museum, Ongerup 01344
Ouyen Local History Resource Centre, Ouyen 01349
Paterson Court House, Adamstown 00701
Patrick Taylor Cottage Museum, Albany 00724
Pilots Cottage Museum, Kiama 01144
Pine Creek Museum, Pine Creek 01365
Pinnaroo Heritage Museum, Pinnaroo 01368
Pioneer Village Museum, Burnie 00864
Pittsworth and District Historical Museum, Pittsworth 01370
Police Station Museum, Mount Barker 01280
Port Fairy History Centre, Port Fairy 01382
Port Macquarie Historic Museum, Port Macquarie 01386
Port of Morgan Historic Museum, Morgan 01275
Port Phillip City Collection, Saint Kilda, Victoria 01436
Port Victoria National Trust Museum, Port Victoria 01389
Pringle Cottage Museum, Warwick 01584
Proserpine Historical Museum, Proserpine 01395
Prospect Hill Museum, Meadows 01220
Pyramid Hill and District Historical Museum, Pyramid Hill 01397
Queanbeyan and District Historical Museum, Queanbeyan 01399
Queenscliffe Historical Museum, Queenscliff 01401
Quirindi and District Historical Cottage and Museum, Quirindi 01405
Railway Station Museum, Wonthaggi 01613
Redhill Museum, Redhill 01411
Redland Museum, Cleveland 00927
Residency Museum, York 01633
Richmond River Historical Museum, Lismore 01179
Ringwood Miners Cottage, Ringwood 01416
Rippon Lea Estate, Melbourne 01240
Rochester Historical and Pioneer Museum, Rochester 01419
Rockhampton and District Historical Museum, Rockhampton 01420
Roebourne Old Goal Museum, Roebourne 01423
Rosalie Shire Historical Museum, Goombungee 01064
Rosewood Scrub Historical Museum, Marburg 01209
Rottnest Island Museum, Rottnest Island 01427
Rushworth Museum, Rushworth 01429
Saint Georges Regional Museum, Hurstville 01115
Saint Helens History Room, Saint Helens 01431
Sale Historical Museum, Sale 01438
Salisbury Folk Museum, Salisbury 01439
Samford and District Historical Museum, Samford 01441
Sandgate and District Historical Museum, Sandgate 01443
Schaeffer House Museum, Grafton 01072
Schwerkolt Cottage Museum, Mitcham 01260
Scone and Upper Hunter Historical Museum, Scone 01445
Serviceton Historic Railway Station, Serviceton 01448
Settlers Museum, Brewarrina 00831
Sexton's Cottage Museum, Crows Nest 00956
Seymour and District Historical Museum, Seymour 01449
Shire of Landsborough Historical Society, Landsborough 01163
Shire of Wondai Museum, Wondai 01611
Silverton Gaol Museum, Silverton 01452
Singleton Historical Museum, Singleton 01454
Sir Edgeworth David Memorial Museum, Kurri Kurri 01154
South Perth Heritage House, South Perth 01462
Springvale and District Historical Museum, Springvale 01472
Stansbury Museum, Stansbury 01473
Stawell Historical Museum, Stawell 01476
Steiglitz Court House, Steiglitz 01477
Stirk Cottage, Kalamunda 01131
Stonnington Local History Collection - Malvern, Malvern 01203
Stonnington Local History Collection - Prahran, Prahran 01394
Story House Historical Museum, Yamba 01622
Stratford and District Museum, Stratford 01478
Strathalbyn National Trust Museum, Strathalbyn 01479
Subiaco Museum, Subiaco 01482
Susannah Place Museum, The Rocks 01422
Talbot Arts and Historical Museum, Talbot 01513
Tara and District Pioneer Memorial Museum, Tara 01518
Taralga Historical Museum, Taralga 01519
Tatura Irrigation and Wartime Camps Museum, Tatura 01521
Tenterfield Centenary Cottage, Tenterfield 01523
Texas Historical Museum, Texas 01527
Timber Creek Police Station Museum, Timber Creek 01536
Tongarra Museum, Albion Park 00727
Toowoomba Historical Museum, Toowoomba 01541
Townsville Museum, Townsville 01549
Tranby House, Maylands 01219
Tumut and District Historical Museum, Tumut 01555
Ulverstone Local History Museum, Ulverstone 01559
Ungarie Museum, Ungarie 01560
Upper Yarra Valley Museum, Yarra Junction 01627
Wagin Historical Village Museum, Wagin 01571
Walkaway Station Museum, Walkaway 01573
Wallaroo Heritage and Nautical Museum, Wallaroo 01574
Waltzing Matilda Centre and Qantilda Museum, Winton 01606
Wangaratta Museum, Wangaratta 01577
Warooka and District Museum, Warooka 01578
Warracknabeal Historical Centre, Warracknabeal 01580
Warragul and District Historical Museum, Warragul 01581
Warrandyte Historical Museum, Warrandyte 01582
Water Tower Museum, Gunnedah 01081
Wauchope District Historical Museum, Wauchope 01587
Wayville Latvian Museum, Brooklyn Park 00849
Weidmann Cottage Heritage Centre, Muswellbrook 01296
Werribee and District Historical Museum, Werribee 01591
Wide Bay and Burnett Historical Museum, Maryborough 01217
Wimmera Mallee Pioneers Museum, Jeparit 01124
Winchelsea and District Historical Records Centre, Winchelsea 01604
Winns Historic Bakehouse Museum, Coromandel Valley 00947
Wollondilly Heritage Centre, The Oaks 01342
Wongan Ballidu and District Museum, Wongan Hills 01612
Woocoo Museum, Brooweena 00854
Woodend and District Local and Family History Resource Centre, Woodend 01615
Woomera Heritage Centre, Woomera 01618
Wowan and District Museum, Wowan 01619
Wyalong Park Private Museum, Maddington 01194
Yankalilla District Historical Museum, Yankalilla 01625
Yesteryear Museum, Captains Flat 00892

Austria

Aberseer Heimathaus, Strobl 02707
Aktion Museum M, Mistelbach an der Zaya 02300
Alpin- und Heimatmuseum, Hohe Wand-Stollhof 02038
Alte Anton Bruckner-Schule, Windhaag bei Freistadt 03033
Ausgrabungen Schanzberg bei Gars Thunau, Gars am Kamp 01868
Aussiedlermuseum im Schüttkasten, Allentsteig 01655
Bacher-Museum, Zellerndorf 03052
Bad Gasteiner Museum, Bad Gastein 01698
Bauern-Technik-Museum, Steyr-Gleink 02691
Bauern- und Heimatmuseum Haigermoos, Sankt Pantaleon 02594
Bergbau- und Heimatmuseum, Jochberg 02089
Bezirksheimatmuseum, Völkermarkt 02769
Bezirksheimatmuseum mit Zdarsky-Skimuseum, Lilienfeld 02223
Bezirksmuseum Alsergrund, Wien 02850
Bezirksmuseum Brigittenau, Wien 02851
Bezirksmuseum Donaustadt, Wien 02853
Bezirksmuseum Favoriten, Wien 02854
Bezirksmuseum Floridsdorf, Wien 02855
Bezirksmuseum Hernals, Wien 02856
Bezirksmuseum Hietzing, Wien 02857
Bezirksmuseum Innere Stadt, Wien 02858
Bezirksmuseum Josefstadt, Wien 02859
Bezirksmuseum Landstraße, Wien 02861
Bezirksmuseum Leopoldstadt, Wien 02862
Bezirksmuseum Margareten, Wien 02863
Bezirksmuseum Mariahilf, Wien 02864
Bezirksmuseum Meidling mit Galerie, Wien 02865
Bezirksmuseum Neubau, Wien 02866
Bezirksmuseum Ottakring, Wien 02867
Bezirksmuseum Penzing, Wien 02868
Bezirksmuseum Simmering, Wien 02869
Bezirksmuseum Stockerau, Stockerau 02699
Bezirksmuseum Währing, Wien 02870
Bezirksmuseum Wieden, Wien 02871
Bruckbacher Hoarstubn, Weyregg am Attersee 02828
Brunner Heimathaus mit Rudolf-Steiner-Gedenkstätte, Brunn am Gebirge 01754
Burgmuseum Reichenstein, Pregarten 02450
Denkmalhof Kösslerhäusl, Großarl 01951
Denkmalhof Rauchhaus Mühlgrub, Hof bei Salzburg 02036
Dokumentationsarchiv des österreichischen Widerstandes, Wien 02874
Dorfmuseum, Herrnbaumgarten 02025
Dorfmuseum, Katzelsdorf, Leitha 02102
Dorfmuseum, Nikitsch 02364
Dorfmuseum, Pöttelsdorf 02434
Dorfmuseum Mönchhof, Mönchhof 02317
Dorfmuseum Roiten, Rappottenstein 02486
Dorfmuseum Weinburg, Weinburg 02800
Dorfmuseum Zwingendorf, Zwingendorf 03063
Ehrwalder Heimatmuseum, Ehrwald 01795
Ennsmuseum Kastenreith, Weyer 02826
Erstes Österreichisches Friedensmuseum und Heimatstube, Wolfsegg 03044
Falger-Museum, Elbigenalp 01813
Fastnachtmuseum, Nassereith 02336
Folterkammer mit Heimatmuseum, Pöggstall 02424
Forum Hall, Bad Hall 01704
Frankenburger Heimatstube, Frankenburg 01844
Franz Michael Felder-Stube, Schoppernau 02638
Franz Stelzhamer-Geburtshaus, Pramet 02447
Freilichtmuseum Anzenaumühle, Bad Goisern 01699
Freilichtmuseum Himmelreich, Volders 02770
Freilichtmuseum Oberlienz, Oberlienz 02369
Freilichtmuseum Pelmberg, Hellmonsödt 02019
Freilichtmuseum Venetianersäge, Windhaag bei Freistadt 03036
Freilichtmuseum Vorau, Vorau 02773
Galerie im Bürger- und Gemeindezentrum Hofstetten-Grünau, Hofstetten-Grünau 02037
Galerie zum alten Ötztal, Oetz 02383
Gedächtnisstätte Mida Huber, Landsee 02182
Gemeindemuseum, Schweiggers 02652
Gemeindemuseum Absam, Absam 01637
Geschichtliches Museum Enns-Donauwinkel, Sankt Valentin 02609
Goldmarkgedenkhaus Deutschkreutz, Deutschkreutz 01761
Grazer Stadtmuseum, Graz 01916
Grillparzer-Gedenkzimmer, Wien 02892
Großmitterberger Troadkasten, Laussa 02194
Haager Heimatstuben, Haag am Hausruck 01981
Heimat-Museum, Millstatt 02298
Heimat- und Krippenmuseum, Zirl 03054
Heimat- und Montanmuseum in Schloß Oberkindberg, Kindberg 02108
Heimat- und Pfarrmuseum, Wildalpen 03026
Heimathaus Beandhaus, Sankt Johann am Walde 02573
Heimathaus des Heimatvereins Haslach, Haslach 02004
Heimathaus Ebensee, Ebensee 01780
Heimathaus Gallneukirchen, Gallneukirchen 01864
Heimathaus im alten Zollhaus, Kobersdorf 02144
Heimathaus Julbach, Julbach 02093
Heimathaus Königswiesen, Königswiesen 02147
Heimathaus Neufelden, Neufelden 02342
Heimathaus Neukirchen, Neukirchen bei Altmünster 02347
Heimathaus Obernberg am Inn, Obernberg am Inn 02371
Heimathaus Pregarten, Pregarten 02451
Heimathaus Raab, Raab 02469
Heimathaus Sankt Peter im Sulmtal, Sankt Peter im Sulmtal 02599
Heimathaus Schalchen, Schalchen 02624
Heimathaus Schörfling, Schörfling am Attersee 02637
Heimathaus Schwanenstadt, Schwanenstadt 02642
Heimathaus Spitalskirche/Bürgerspital, Bad Leonfelden 01712
Heimathaus Steinbach am Attersee, Steinbach am Attersee 02679
Heimathaus Stinatz, Stinatz 02697
Heimathaus Ulrichsberg, Ulrichsberg 02752
Heimathaus und Stadtmuseum, Perg 02403
Heimathaus Vöcklabruck, Vöcklabruck 02767
Heimathaus Wartenberg an der Krems, Wartberg an der Krems 02793
Heimatkundehaus und Münzkabinett, Sankt Marien 02582
Heimatkundesammlung Inzersdorf, Herzogenburg 02026
Heimatkundliche Sammlung Strick, Bad Mitterndorf 01715
Heimatkundliches Museum Medaria, Matrei in Osttirol 02280
Heimatkundliches Museum Wetzlhäusl, Sankt Gilgen 02569
Heimatmuseum, Arnoldstein 01680
Heimatmuseum, Bad Großpertholz 01702
Heimatmuseum, Bad Radkersburg 01717
Heimatmuseum, Bernhardsthal 01733
Heimatmuseum, Bezau 01736
Heimatmuseum, Fügen 01858
Heimatmuseum, Gaaden 01862
Heimatmuseum, Gablitz 01863
Heimatmuseum, Gleisdorf 01880
Heimatmuseum, Gnas 01898
Heimatmuseum, Gressenberg 01939
Heimatmuseum, Groß-Enzersdorf 01946
Heimatmuseum, Hadersdorf 01984
Heimatmuseum, Holzgau 02046
Heimatmuseum, Kals am Großglockner 02095
Heimatmuseum, Kematen an der Ybbs 02106
Heimatmuseum, Kirchham 02113
Heimatmuseum, Kirchschlag 02114
Heimatmuseum, Krieglach 02164
Heimatmuseum, Kuchl 02168
Heimatmuseum, Langenlois 02183
Heimatmuseum, Langenzersdorf 02187
Heimatmuseum, Litschau 02244
Heimatmuseum, Mank 02260
Heimatmuseum, Marchegg 02263
Heimatmuseum, Mautern in Steiermark 02284
Heimatmuseum, Mureck 02334
Heimatmuseum, Niederleis 02359
Heimatmuseum, Niederndorf 02361
Heimatmuseum, Oberhofen 02368
Heimatmuseum, Obertrum am See 02378
Heimatmuseum, Pfaffstätten 02412
Heimatmuseum, Pfunds 02413
Heimatmuseum, Pressbaum 02453
Heimatmuseum, Purkersdorf 02466
Heimatmuseum, Radstadt 02474
Heimatmuseum, Rietz 02516
Heimatmuseum, Sankt Koloman 02578
Heimatmuseum, Scheibbs 02629
Heimatmuseum, Schrems 02640
Heimatmuseum, Schwarzenberg in Vorarlberg 02645
Heimatmuseum, Siget 02661
Heimatmuseum, Tarrenz 02714

Heimatmuseum, Taufkirchen an der Pram 02715
Heimatmuseum, Teesdorf 02717
Heimatmuseum, Thaya 02728
Heimatmuseum, Traismauer 02732
Heimatmuseum, Trofaiach 02740
Heimatmuseum, Wartberg im Mürztal 02794
Heimatmuseum, Wörgl 03041
Heimatmuseum Achental, Achenkirch 01642
Heimatmuseum Aflenz, Aflenz 01646
Heimatmuseum Alberschwende, Alberschwende 01653
Heimatmuseum Altenmarkt, Yspertal 03047
Heimatmuseum Altlichtenwarth, Absdorf 01638
Heimatmuseum am Kobernaußerwald, Lohnsburg am Kobernaußerwald 02250
Heimatmuseum der Gemeinde Weißenkirchen, Perschling 02405
Heimatmuseum der Stadt Murau, Murau 02333
Heimatmuseum der Stadt Neunkirchen, Neunkirchen, Niederösterreich 02354
Heimatmuseum des Heimatkreises Scheiflingertal, Scheifling 02631
Heimatmuseum Elsbethen, Elsbethen-Glasenstein 01814
Heimatmuseum Feuerwehrzeugstätte, Neumarkt am Wallersee 02349
Heimatmuseum Grahhof, Ramsau am Dachstein 02482
Heimatmuseum Gröbming, Gröbming 01944
Heimatmuseum Großengersdorf, Großengersdorf 01952
Heimatmuseum Großes Walsertal, Sonntag 02666
Heimatmuseum Großschönau, Großschönau 01963
Heimatmuseum Guntramsdorf, Guntramsdorf 01973
Heimatmuseum im alten Marktturm, Fischamend 01839
Heimatmuseum Kalchofengut, Unken 02754
Heimatmuseum Kaumberg, Kaumberg 02103
Heimatmuseum Kautzen, Kautzen 02105
Heimatmuseum Kohbauernhaus, Köstendorf 02148
Heimatmuseum Lembach, Lembach 02204
Heimatmuseum Lölling, Lölling 02248
Heimatmuseum Losenstein, Losenstein 02254
Heimatmuseum Markt Piesting, Markt Piesting 02277
Heimatmuseum Michelhausen, Michelhausen 02295
Heimatmuseum mit Raimund von Montecuccoli-Gedenkraum, Hafnerbach 01987
Heimatmuseum Obdach, Obdach 02366
Heimatmuseum Oberbichl, Prägarten 02443
Heimatmuseum Pabneukirchen, Pabneukirchen 02391
Heimatmuseum Persenbeug-Gottsdorf, Persenbeug 02406
Heimatmuseum Pulkau, Pulkau 02461
Heimatmuseum Rabenstein, Rabenstein an der Pielach 02472
Heimatmuseum Rauchstubenhaus Edelschachen, Anger 01672
Heimatmuseum Rechnitz, Rechnitz 02494
Heimatmuseum Reith, Reith im Alpbachtal 02505
Heimatmuseum Rother Hof, Pottendorf 02436
Heimatmuseum Sankt Martin am Wöllmißberg, Sankt Martin am Wollmißberg 02586
Heimatmuseum Schloß Fels, Fels 01835
Heimatmuseum Schloß Hochhaus, Vorchdorf 02775
Heimatmuseum Schloß Pragstein, Mauthausen 02288
Heimatmuseum Schönau, Günselsdorf 01968
Heimatmuseum Tannheimer Tal, Tannheim 02713
Heimatmuseum und Keltenhaus, Ligist 02222
Heimatmuseum und Klöpferhaus, Eibiswald 01798
Heimatmuseum und Pfeifenmuseum, Sankt Aegyd am Neuwalde 02556
Heimatmuseum und Schiele Museum, Neulengbach 02348
Heimatmuseum Vogtturm, Zell am See 03050
Heimatmuseum Waidhofen, Waidhofen an der Thaya 02784
Heimatmuseum Waidhofen an der Ybbs, Waidhofen an der Ybbs 02786
Heimatmuseum Weng im Innkreis, Weng im Innkreis 02819
Heimatmuseum Windischgarsten, Windischgarsten 03040
Heimatstube der Deutsch-Reichenauer, Haslach 02005
Heimatstube Großraming, Großraming 01959
Heimatvertriebenen-Stuben, Traun 02737
Heinrich Suso Waldeck und Hans Schnopfhagen-Gedenkraum, Sankt Veit im Mühlkreis 02616
Hufschmiedemuseum, Engelhartszell 01816
Hundsmarktmühle, Thalgau 02726
Husslik-Heimatmuseum, Pöls 02432
Irrseer Heimathaus, Zell am Moos 03049
Jenbacher Museum, Jenbach 02086
Joslowitzer Heimatstube, Zwingendorf 03064
Kammerhofmuseum Ausseerland, Bad Aussee 01691
Kammerhofmuseum der Stadt Gmunden, Gmunden 01896
Karden-und Heimatmuseum, Katsdorf 02101
Karl Heinrich Waggerl-Haus, Wagrain 02781
Katschtaler Heimatmuseum, Rennweg 02507
Kellermuseum Das Preßhaus, Großkrut 01958
Kellerviertel Heiligenbrunn, Heiligenbrunn 02017
Kierlinger Heimatmuseum, Kierling 02107
Klostertal-Museum, Dalaas 01757
Koschatmuseum, Klagenfurt 02125
Kreuzstadelmuseum, Mogersdorf 02319
Kultur-Gut-Museum, Aigen-Schlägl 01651
Kulturhistorische Sammlung, Frankenmarkt 01846
Kutschen- und Heimatmuseum, Sillian 02664
Landesmuseum Kärnten, Klagenfurt 02127
Landschaftsmuseum der Kulmregion, Pischelsdorf in Steiermark 02418
Landschaftsmuseum im Schloß Trautenfels, Trautenfels 02738
Lavanttaler Heimatmuseum, Eitweg 01812
Lavanttaler Heimatmuseum, Wolfsberg, Kärnten 03042
Leopold Figl-Museum, Michelhausen 02296
Lichtentaler Pfarrmuseum, Wien 02925
Liechtenstein Schloss Wilfersdorf, Wilfersdorf 03031
LinzGenesis, Linz 02236
Literatur- und Heimatmuseum Altaussee, Altaussee 01659
Lungauer Heimatmuseum Tamsweg, Tamsweg 02711
Marchfeldmuseum, Weikendorf 02798
Montafoner Heimatmuseum Schruns, Schruns 02641
Mostmuseum und Heimathaus, Sankt Marienkirchen an der Polsenz 02583
Mostviertelmuseum Haag, Haag, Niederösterreich 01982
Mühlviertler Kulturgütermuseum, Sankt Johann am Wimberg 02574
Mühlviertler Schlossmuseum Freistadt, Freistadt, Oberösterreich 01851
Museum 15, Wien 02933
Museum Burg Golling, Golling an der Salzach 01904
Museum der Heimatvertriebenen, Wels 02813
Museum der Marktgemeinde Sankt Johann in Tirol, Sankt Johann in Tirol 02576
Museum der Stadt Bludenz, Bludenz 01741
Museum der Stadt Fürstenfeld, Fürstenfeld 01859
Museum der Stadt Gmünd, Gmünd, Kärnten 01889
Museum der Stadt Kapfenberg, Kapfenberg 02096
Museum der Stadt Köflach, Köflach 02146
Museum der Stadt Korneuburg, Korneuburg 02151
Museum der Stadt Leoben, Leoben 02210
Museum der Stadt Poysdorf, Poysdorf 02441
Museum der Stadt Schwaz, Schwaz 02649
Museum der Stadt Villach, Villach 02759
Museum der Stadt Vils, Vils 02765
Museum Geyerhammer, Scharnstein 02627
Museum Herzogsburg, Braunau am Inn 01744
Museum Hohenau an der March, Hohenau an der March 02039
Museum Ilz, Ilz 02053
Museum im Fürstenstöckl, Ebenau 01778
Museum im Grünen Haus der Marktgemeinde Reutte, Reutte 02511
Museum im Ledererhaus, Purgstall an der Erlauf 02464
Museum im Troadkostn zu Giem, Feldbach 01828
Museum im Zeughaus, Innsbruck 02074
Museum in der Gaststätte Scherrerwirt, Markt Piesting 02278
Museum in der Wegscheid, Ternberg 02722
Museum Kaprun, Kaprun 02098
Museum Kitzbühel, Kitzbühel 02118
Museum Kremayr, Ybbsitz 03046
Museum Kuenburggewölbe, Werfen 02822
Museum Lauriacum, Enns 01818
Museum Mannersdorf, Mannersdorf 02262
Museum Mödling, Mödling 02312
Museum Schloß Erla, Sankt Valentin 02610
Museum Schloß Pöllau, Pöllau 02430
Museum Schöngrabern, Hollabrunn 02044
Museum Wattens, Wattens 02796
Museumsdorf Krumbach, Krumbach 02167
Museumsstube, Eisgarn 01811
Neubistritzer Heimatstube, Reingers 02504
Neues Museum, Hollabrunn 02045
Neues Museum Schwechat, Schwechat 02651
Niederösterreichisches Freilichtmuseum, Haag, Niederösterreich 01983
Niederösterreichisches Museum für Volkskultur, Groß Schweinbarth 01948
Nordico - Museum der Stadt Linz, Linz 02238
Oberkärntner Brauchtums- und Maskenmuseum, Oberdrauburg 02367
Österreichisches Freilichtmuseum Stübing, Stübing bei Graz 02708
Österreichisches Pfahlbaummuseum und Museum Mondseeland, Mondsee 02321
Ortskundliches Museum Jois, Jois 02091
Ortsmuseum, Weikertschlag 02799
Pannonisches Heimatmuseum, Neusiedl am See 02357
Pinzgauer Heimatmuseum, Saalfelden am Steinernen Meer 02531
Pongauer Heimatmuseum im Schloß Goldegg, Goldegg 01903
Pratermuseum, Wien 02972
Privatsammlung Franz Pinteritsch, Pichling 02414
Proviant-Eisen Museum, Gresten 01940
Rauchstubenhaus, Gündorf 01967
Rauchstubenhaus, Sankt Johann im Saggautal 02575
Rauriser Talmuseum, Rauris 02492
Reckturm, Wiener Neustadt 03020
Regional- und Telegrafenmuseum, Stegersbach 02676
Salzburger Freilichtmuseum, Großgmain 01953
Sammlungen der Stadt Amstetten auf Schloß Ulmerfeld, Ulmerfeld-Hausmening 02750
Sauwald-Heimathaus, Sankt Roman 02606
Schattenburg Feldkirch, Feldkirch 01831
Schaubergwerk und Heimatmuseum der Gemeinde Arzberg, Passail 02392
Schauräume im Glockenturm, Graz 01933
Schiffleutmuseum, Stadl-Paura 02672
Schloßmuseum, Sigharting 02662
Schloßmuseum, Texing 02725
Schulstub'n-Glockenhäusl, Sankt Peter am Wimberg 02598
Seelackenmuseum, Sankt Veit im Pongau 02618
Siglhaus, Sankt Georgen bei Salzburg 02567
Silomuseum, Waidhofen an der Thaya 02785
Stadt- und Heimatmuseum, Heidenreichstein 02013
Stadtmuseum, Melk 02291
Stadtmuseum Arelape-Bechelaren, Pöchlarn 02423
Stadtmuseum Bruck an der Leitha, Bruck an der Leitha 01752
Stadtmuseum Dornbirn, Dornbirn 01772
Stadtmuseum Friesach, Friesach 01855
Stadtmuseum Hall in Tirol, Hall in Tirol 01995
Stadtmuseum Hartberg, Hartberg 02003
Stadtmuseum Judenburg, Judenburg 02092
Stadtmuseum Klosterneuburg, Klosterneuburg 02143
Stadtmuseum mit Weinmuseum, Bad Vöslau 01721
Stadtmuseum Oberwölz und Österreichisches Blasmusikmuseum, Oberwölz 02380
Stadtmuseum Pinkafeld, Pinkafeld 02416
Stadtmuseum Sankt Veit, Sankt Veit an der Glan 02614
Stadtmuseum Schladming, Schladming 02632
Stadtmuseum Traiskirchen, Möllersdorf 02316
Stadtmuseum Traiskirchen, Traiskirchen 02731
Stadtmuseum und Fürstlich Starhembergisches Familienmuseum, Eferding 01788
Stadtmuseum Wienertor Hainburg, Hainburg an der Donau 01988
Stadtmuseum Zistersdorf, Zistersdorf 03055
Stadtmuseum Zwettl, Zwettl, Niederösterreich 03061
Städtische Sammlungen, Amstetten 01670
Städtisches Kießling-Museum, Drosendorf an der Thaya 01775
Städtisches Museum, Schärding 02623
Stefan Fadinger-Museum, Sankt Agatha 02557
Stein- und Bauernmuseum Großdöllnerhof, Rechberg 02493
Stiftsmuseum, Vomp 02772
Stille-Nacht- und Heimatmuseum Bruckmannhaus, Oberndorf bei Salzburg 02372
Südmährer Heimatmuseum, Laa an der Thaya 02175
Talmuseum Kaunertal, Feichten 01824
Talmuseum Lachitzhof, Klein Sankt Paul 02135
Tauriska-Galerie, Neukirchen am Großvenediger 02345
Tiroler Kaiserjägermuseum Obergricht, Serfaus 02659
Triestingtaler Heimatmuseum, Weissenbach an der Triesting 02801
Troadkasten, Schardenberg 02625
Tullner Museen im Minoritenkloster, Tulln 02747
Turm 9 - Stadtmuseum Leonding, Leonding 02215
Turmmuseum, Breitenbrunn, Neusiedlersee 01749
Unterwarter Heimathaus, Unterwart 02755
Urgeschichtssammlung und Heimtmuseum, Jedenspeigen 02085
Vorarlberger Landesmuseum, Bregenz 01746
Walsermuseum, Riezlern 02517
Weinstadtmuseum Krems, Krems 02160
Weinviertler Museumsdorf, Niedersulz 02362
Wien Museum Karlsplatz, Wien 03001
Zeitspurenmuseum Altheim, Altheim 01665
Zimmermannshaus Lackinger, Windhaag bei Freistadt 03039
Zoll- und Heimatmuseum, Perwang 02407

Bahamas

Bahamas Museum, Nassau 03075
Nassau Public Library and Museum, Nassau 03076
Wyannie Malone Historical Museum, Hope Town 03072

Bangladesh

Ahsan Manzil Museum, Dhaka 03082
Bangladesh Shamorik Jadughar, Dhaka 03086
Osmani Museum, Sylhet 03102
Ram Mala Museum, Comilla 03081
Sooner Ga Museum, Dhaka 03094

Belgium

Archeologisch Museum Abdij, Affligem 03127
Het Arendonks Heemmuseum, Arendonk 03181
Begijnhofmuseum, Dendermonde 03376
Bruggemuseum - Belfort, Brugge 03248
Druivenmuseum, Overijse 03682
Gemeentelijk Heemkundig Museum, Hoeilaart 03499
Gemeentemuseum, Temse 03854
Grevenbroek Museum, Hamont-Achel 03473
Heemkundig Museum, Asse 03186
Heemkundig Museum, Borgerhout 03226
Heemkundig Museum, Bree 03242
Heemkundig Museum, Tervuren 03773
Heemkundig Museum, Wilrijk 03843
Heemkundig Museum, Zolder 03854
Heemkundig Museum Gerard Meeusen, Essen 03409
Heemkundig Museum Wissekerke, Kruibeke 03544
Heemmuseum de Zuiderkempen, Westerlo 03836
Maison du Roi, Bruxelles 03288
Meerhemmuseum, Gent 03442
Musée Charlier, Bruxelles 03294
Musée Communal de Huy, Huy 03511
Musée Communal de la Ville de Braine-le-Comte, Braine-le-Comte 03239
Musée Communal de Woluwe-Saint-Lambert, Bruxelles 03295
Musée d'Archéologie, Tournai 03790
Musée d'Arenberg, Rebecq 03693
Musée de Folklore et d'Histoire Armand Pellegrin, Opheylissem 03673
Musée de la Principauté de Stavelot-Malmedy, Stavelot 03764
Musée de la Tour Salamandre, Beaumont 03202
Musée de la Vie Régionale, Cerfontaine 03348
Musée de l'Entité de Walcourt, Walcourt 03824
Musée de l'Histoire et de la Vie Salmiennes, Vielsalm 03812
Musée de Waterloo, Waterloo 03829
Musée des Archives, Saint-Hubert 03721
Musée du Bailles, Nismes 03659
Musée Ducal, Bouillon 03233
Musée Gaspar, Arlon 03184
Musée Marchiennois d'Histoire et d'Archéologie Industrielle, Marchienne-au-Pont 03610
Musée National de la Résistance, Bruxelles 03333
Museum De Bres, Ruisbroek, Antwerpen 03714
Museum Gevaert-Minne, Sint-Martens-Latem 03738
MUseum Huize Bareldonk, Berlare 03213
Museum Stellingwerff-Waerdenhof, Hasselt 03482
Museum van de Willebroekse Vaart, Willebroek 03842
Museum van Deinze en de Leiestreek, Deinze 03375
Museum Vleeshuis, Antwerpen 03157
Museum voor Heem- en Volkskunde, Wenduine 03833
Oostends Historisch Museum De Plate, Oostende 03671
Oudheidkundig Museum Sint-Janshospitaal, Damme 03369
Porte de Hal, Bruxelles 03341
Stedelijk Museum Diest, Diest 03386
Stedelijk Museum Diksmuide, Diksmuide 03389
Stedelijk Museum Hof van Busleyden, Mechelen 03619
Stedelijk Museum Ieper, Ieper 03517
Stedelijk Museum Lokeren, Lokeren 03594
Stedelijk Museum Schepenhuis, Mechelen 03620
Stedelijke Musea, Torhout 03787
Taxandriamuseum, Turnhout 03806
Ten Duinen 1138, Koksijde 03537
Torenmuseum, Mol 03630
Volkskundemuseum Deurne, Deurne 03384
Volksmuseum Deurne, Antwerpen 03179
Zuidwestbrabants Museum, Halle 03470
Zwijvekemuseum, Dendermonde 03379

Belize

Ambergris Museum and Cultural Centre, Ambergis Caye 03862

Benin

Musée de Natitingou, Natitingou 03874
Musée de Plein Air, Parakou 03876

Bermuda

Bermuda Historical Society Museum, Hamilton 03881
Tucker House Museum, Saint George's 03889
Verdmont Historic House Museum, Smith's Parish 03890

Bolivia

Casa de la Libertad, Sucre 03904
Museo Costumbristá, La Paz 03895

Bosnia and Herzegovina

Regionalni Muzej, Bihać 03912
Zavičajni Muzej, Visoko 03931

Botswana

Botswana National Museum and Art Gallery, Gaborone 03934
Kgosi Bathoen II (Segopotso) Museum, Kanye 03936
Phuthadikobo Museum, Mochudi 03937
Supa-Ngwao Museum Centre, Francistown 03933

Brazil

Arquivo Histórico e Museu de Canonas Dr. Sezefredo Azambuja Vieira, Canoas 04038
Casa de Cultura Afrónio Peixoto, Lençóis 04172
Casa de Deodoro, Rio de Janeiro 04316
Casa de José Bonifácio, Rio de Janeiro 04317
Casa de Oliveira Vianna, Niterói 04224
Casa do Escultor Ervin Curt Teichmann, Pomerode 04272
Casa Roche Pombo, Morretes 04214
Centro de Estudos Murilo Mendes, Juiz de Fora 04155
Espaço Lucio Costa, Brasília 03995
Fundação Clóuis Salgado - Palácio das Artes, Belo Horizonte 03979
Museu Alfredo Varela, Jaguarão 04143
Museu Aníbal Ribeiro Filho, Paranaguá 04244
Museu Antonio Granemann de Souza, Curitibanos 04079
Museu Arquivo Histórico Florense, Flores da Cunha 04087
Museu Barão de Mauá, Mauá 04201
Museu Casa Cel. Joaquim Lacerda, Lapa 04166
Museu Casa da Hera, Vassouras 04582
Museu Casa do Anhanguera, Santana de Parnaíba 04448
Museu Casa dos Contos, Ouro Preto 04234
Museu Casa Fritz Alt, Joinville 04151
Museu Casa Pedro Américo, Areia 03960
Museu Comendador Ananias Arruda, Baturit 03969
Museu Corina Novelino, Sacramento 04417
Museu D. João VI, Rio de Janeiro 04339
Museu da Borracha, Rio Branco 04311
Museu da Casa da Cultura de Teresina, Teresina 04563

Museu da Cidade, Campinas 04023
Museu da Cidade de Recife, Recife 04296
Museu da Companhia Paulista, Jundiá 04161
Museu da Estrada de Ferro Sorocabana, Sorocaba 04553
Museu da Imigração, Santa Bárbara d'Oeste 04440
Museu da Inconfidência, Ouro Preto 04236
Museu da Limpeza Urbana - Casa de Banhos de Dom João VI, Rio de Janeiro 04349
Museu das Bandeiras, Goiás 04115
Museu das Monções, Porto Feliz 04289
Museu de Corrente, Corrente 04056
Museu de Rua Alto Paraná Ontem e Hoje, Alto Paran 03942
Museu de Santo André, Santo André 04451
Museu de Sertão, Petrolina 04261
Museu de Venâncio Aires, Venâncio Aires 04583
Museu do Automóvel, Arte História, São Francisco de Paula 04461
Museu do Cangaço, Triunfo 04570
Museu do Colégio Mauá, Santa Cruz do Sul 04441
Museu do Estado de Pernambuco, Recife 04301
Museu do Mamulengo, Olinda 04232
Museu do Piauí, Teresina 04564
Museu do Pio XII, Novo Hamburgo 04230
Museu do Porto do Rio, Rio de Janeiro 04373
Museu do Seridó, Caicó 04017
Museu do Sol, Penápolis 04256
Museu do Vaqueiro, Morada Nova 04213
Museu do Vinho, Videira 04588
Museu Dom Avelar Brandão Vilela, Teresina 04565
Museu dos Inhamuns, Tauá 04555
Museu e Arquivo Histórico, Itu 04139
Museu e Arquivo Histórico Municipal, Guapor 04119
Museu e Arquivo Público Municipal de Campo Belo, Campo Belo 04028
Museu e Biblioteca Pública Pelotense, Pelotas 04255
Museu Estadual do Carvão, Arroio dos Ratos 03961
Museu Farroupilha, Triunfo 04571
Museu Ferroviário de Pires do Rio, Pires do Rio 04269
Museu Getúlio Vargas, São Borja 04456
Museu Goiano Zoroastro Artiaga, Goiânia 04111
Museu Histórico, Igarassu 04124
Museu Histórico, Lavras 04171
Museu Histórico, Sertanópolis 04550
Museu Histórico, Siqueira Campos 04551
Museu Histórico Abílio Barreto, Belo Horizonte 03987
Museu Histórico da Cidade do Rio de Janeiro, Rio de Janeiro 04381
Museu Histórico de Brejo Madre de Deus, Brejo Madre de Deus 04010
Museu Histórico de Witmarsum, Palmeira 04242
Museu Histórico Desembargador Edmundo Mercer Júnior, Tibagi 04568
Museu Histórico e Artístico, Quitandinha 04293
Museu Histórico e Geográfico de Monte Sião, Monte Sião 04211
Museu Histórico e Geral da Cidade de São Vicente, São Vicente 04549
Museu Histórico Kiyoshi Takano, Ura 04580
Museu Histórico Muncipal José Chiachiri, Franca 04104
Museu Histórico Municipal, Dois Irmãos 04082
Museu Histórico Municipal, Montenegro 04212
Museu Histórico Municipal, Telêmaco Borba 04562
Museu Histórico Professor Jos' Alexandre Vieira, Palmas 04241
Museu Integrado de Roraima, Boa Vista 03992
Museu Jaguaribano, Aracati 03952
Museu João Pedro Nunes, São Gabriel 04464
Museu Municipal, Barbacena 03967
Museu Municipal, Caxias do Sul 04048
Museu Municipal, Garibaldi 04107
Museu Municipal, Itambaracá 04133
Museu Municipal, Missal 04203
Museu Municipal, Paulínia 04251
Museu Municipal, Pedras Grandes 04252
Museu Municipal, Rolândia 04412
Museu Municipal, Rosário de Oeste 04413
Museu Municipal, Uberlândia 04578
Museu Municipal, Visconde do Rio Branco 04589
Museu Municipal Adolfo Eurich, Turvo 04573
Museu Municipal Atílio Rocco, São José dos Pinhais 04473
Museu Municipal Capitão Henrique Jos' Barbosa, Canguçu 04037
Museu Municipal David Canabarro, Sant'Anna do Livramento 04450
Museu Municipal de Antônio Prado, Antônio Prado 03946
Museu Municipal de São José dos Campos, São José dos Campos 04472
Museu Municipal Deolindo Mendes Pereira, Campo Mourão 04033
Museu Municipal Domingos Battistel, Nova Prata 04229
Museu Municipal Elisabeth Aytai, Monte Mor 04210
Museu Municipal Embaixador Hélio A. Scarabôtolo, Marília 04198
Museu Municipal Francisco Manoel Franco, Itaúna 04137
Museu Municipal Francisco Veloso, Cunha 04061
Museu Municipal Joaquim de Bastos Bandeira, Perdões 04260
Museu Municipal Karl Ramminger, Mondaí 04207
Museu Municipal Oswaldo Russomano, Bragança Paulista 03994
Museu Municipal Pedro Laragnoit, Miracatu 04202
Museu Municipal Prof. Hugo Daros, Gramado 04118
Museu Municipal Wenceslau Braz, Itajubá 04130
Museu Municipal Wülson Jehovah Lütz Farias, Frederico Westphalen 04106
Museu Nossa Senhora Aparecida, Aparecida 03947
Museu Oswaldo Aranha, Alegrete 03940
Museu Padre Júlio Maria, Russas 04415
Museu Paranaense, Curitiba 04078
Museu Paulo Firpo, Dom Pedrito 04083
Museu Regional, Vitória da Conquista 04593
Museu Regional de São João Del Rei, São João Del Rei 04470
Museu Regional do Alto Uruguai, Erechim 04084
Museu Regional Olívio Otto, Carazinho 04041
Museu Salles Cunha, Rio de Janeiro 04393
Museu São Norberto, Pirapora do Bom Jesus 04267
Museu Tempostal, Salvador 04438
Museu Teresa Bernardes Adami de Carvalho, Sant Antônio do Monte 04439
Museu Territorial do Amapá, Macapá 04176
Museu Tinguí-Cuera, Araucária 03955
Museu Victor Bersani, Santa Maria 04445
Museu Vivo da Memória Candanga, Brasília 04008
Museu Zé Didor, Campo Maior 04032
O Museu do Marajó, Cachoeira do Arari 04015
Paço Imperial, Rio de Janeiro 04399
Palácio das Laranjeiras, Rio de Janeiro 04400
Palácio Guanabara, Rio de Janeiro 04401
Palácio Gustavo Capanema, Rio de Janeiro 04402
Setor de Malacologia, Juiz de Fora 04160
Solar de Dom João VI, Rio de Janeiro 04405
Solar Grandjean de Montigny, Rio de Janeiro 04406

Brunei
Taman Warisan Merimbun, Tutong 04603

Bulgaria
Architekturno-istoričski Muzej-rezervat, Boženci 04628
Drjanovski Manastir Muzej, Drjanovo 04659
Etnografska Ekspozicija, Svištov 04878
Etnografski Kompleks Starijat Dobrič, Dobrič 04653
Etnografski-vàzroždenski Kompleks, Kavarna 04695
Gradski Istoričeski Muzej, Čirpan 04645
Gradski Istoričeski Muzej, Dalgopol 04647
Gradski Istoričeski Muzej, Kavarna 04696
Gradski Istoričeski Muzej, Klisura 04711
Gradski Istoričeski Muzej, Lom 04726
Gradski Istoričeski Muzej, Melnik 04734
Gradski Istoričeski Muzej, Orjachovo 04749
Gradski Istoričeski Muzej, Panagjurište 04750
Gradski Istoričeski Muzej, Samakov 04808
Gradski Istoričeski Muzej, Sevlievo 04811
Gradski Istoričeski Muzej, Teteven 04884
Gradski Istoričeski Muzej Aleko Konstantinov, Svištov 04879
Gradski Istoričeski Muzej Iskra, Kazanlăk 04700
Istoričeski Muzej, Bansko 04613
Istoričeski Muzej, Bracigovo 04629
Istoričeski Muzej, Burgas 04634
Istoričeski Muzej, Čiprovci 04643
Istoričeski Muzej, Dobrič 04655
Istoričeski Muzej, Gabrovo 04668
Istoričeski Muzej, Goce Delčev 04674
Istoričeski Muzej, Gorna Orjachovica 04675
Istoričeski Muzej, Ichtiman 04678
Istoričeski Muzej, Isperich 04679
Istoričeski Muzej, Karlovo 04690
Istoričeski Muzej, Lovеč 04728
Istoričeski Muzej, Omurtag 04746
Istoričeski Muzej, Pavlikeni 04752
Istoričeski Muzej, Petrič 04761
Istoričeski Muzej, Pomorie 04783
Istoričeski Muzej, Popovo 04784
Istoričeski Muzej, Provadia 04789
Istoričeski Muzej, Razlog 04798
Istoričeski Muzej Silistra, Silistra 04815
Kăšta-muzej Angel Kănčev, Trjavna 04886
Kăšta-muzej Asen Razcvetnikov, Draganovo 04657
Kăšta-muzej Canko Cerkovski, Bjala Čerkva 04624
Kăšta-muzej Dimitar Pešev, Kjustendil 04706
Kăšta-muzej Iljo Vojvoda, Kjustendil 04707
Kăšta-muzej Neofit Rilski, Bansko 04614
Kăšta-muzej Nikola P. Karadžchata, Bradvari 04630
Kăšta-muzej Pejo K. Javorov, Čirpan 04646
Kăšta-muzej Rusi Čorbadži, Žeravna 04934
Kăšta-muzej Sava Filaretov, Žeravna 04935
Muzej, Pliska 04773
Muzej Aleksandăr Stambolijski, Slavovica 04817
Muzej Emfiedžieva Kăšta, Kjustendil 04708
Muzej-krepost Baba Vida, Vidin 04925
Muzej na Gradskij Bit Oslekova Kăšta, Koprivština 04716
Muzej na Gradskija Bit, Ruse 04804
Muzej na Kotlenskite Vazroždenci i Panteon na Georgi S. Rakovski, Kotel 04719
Muzej Rumănski Voin, Pordim 04786
Muzej Văzraždane i Učreditelno Săbranie, Veliko Tărnovo 04917
Nacionalen Istoriko-archeologičeski Rezervat i Muzej Veliki Preslav, Veliki Preslav 04908
Nacionalen Park-muzej Šipka-Buzludža, Kazanlăk 04702
Oblasten Istoričeski Muzej, Jambol 04681
Obščinski Istoričeski Muzej, Etropole 04664
Okražen Istoričeski Muzej, Montana 04741
Okrăžen Istoričeski Muzej, Smoljan 04826
Okrăžen Istoričeski Muzej, Vidin 04926
Okrăžen Istoričeski Muzej, Vraca 04929
Regionalen Istoričeski Muzej, Kardžali 04688
Regionalen Istoričeski Muzej, Kjustendil 04710
Regionalen Istoričeski Muzej, Pazardžik 04757
Regionalen Istoričeski Muzej, Šumen 04876
Regionalen Istoričeski Muzej Varna, Varna 04907
Školoto Muzej, Trjavna 04889
Sofijski Istoričeski Muzej, Sofia 04860

Burkina Faso
Musée Pobe Mengao, Mengao 04940
Musée Provincial du Houet, Bobo-Dioulasso 04936
Musée Provincial du Poni, Gaoua 04937
Musée Provincial du Sanmatenga, Kaya 04938

Burundi
Musée National de Gitega, Gitega 04945
Musée Vivant de Bujumbura, Bujumbura 04944

Cameroon
Musée de Maroua, Maroua 04959
Musée National de Yaoundé, Yaoundé 04962
Musée Provincial de Douala, Douala 04954

Canada
1910 Boomtown, Saskatoon 06393
Agassiz-Harrison Historical Museum, Agassiz 04967
Alberta Beach and District Museum, Alberta Beach 04970
Algonquin Park Logging Museum, Whitney 06798
Alliance and District Museum, Alliance 04977
Ameliasburgh Historical Museum, Ameliasburgh 04984
Andrew and District Local History Museum, Andrew 04994
Annapolis Valley Macdonald Museum, Middelton 05844
Anola and District Museum, Anola 04999
Anthony Henday Museum, Delburne 05318
Antigonish Heritage Museum, Antigonish 05002
Antler River Historical Society Museum, Melita 05836
Archibald Historical Museum, La Rivière 05708
Arcola Museum, Arcola 05004
Arnprior and District Museum, Arnprior 05009
Ashcroft Museum, Ashcroft 05011
Ashern Pioneer Museum, Ashern 05012
Assiginack Historical Museum and Norisle Heritage Park, Manitowaning 05804
Assiniboia and District Historical Society Museum, Assiniboia 05014
Atikokan Centennial Museum, Atikokan 05017
Atlin Historical Museum, Atlin 05019
Aurora Museum, Aurora 05021
Avonlea and District Museum, Avonlea 05025
Aylmer and District Museum, Aylmer 05026
Ball's Falls Historical Park, Allanburg 04976
Barkerville Historic Town, Barkerville 05046
Barr Colony Heritage Cultural Centre, Lloydminster 05761
Barrhead and District Centennial Museum, Barrhead 05048
Bateman Historical Museum, Bateman 05055
Batoche National Historic Site, Batoche 05059
Batoche National Historic Site, Rosthern 06288
Battleford National Historic Site, Battleford 05060
Beachville District Museum, Beachville 05063
Beau Village Museum, Saint Victor 06377
Beautiful Plains Museum, Neepawa 05966
Beaver River Museum, Beaverton 05069
Beckoning Hills Museum, Boissevain 05089
Bella Coola Museum, Bella Coola 05071
Belmont and District Museum, Belmont 05073
Beothuck Village, Grand Falls-Windsor 05511
Bethune Memorial House, Gravenhurst 05525
Big Bear Trails Museum, Loon Lake 05778
Big River Memorial Museum, Big River 05078
Biggar Museum and Gallery, Biggar 05079
Binscarth and District Gordon Orr Memorial Museum, Binscarth 05081
Black Creek Pioneer Village, North York 06030
Blackville Historical Museum, Blackville 05083
Blaine Lake Museum, Blaine Lake 05084
Blockhouse Museum, Merrickville 05841
Bonavista Museum, Bonavista 05093
Bonavista North Regional Museum, Wesleyville 06770
Botwood Heritage Centre, Botwood 05100
Boundary Museum, Grand Forks 05513
Bowden Pioneer Museum, Bowden 05102
Bowmanville Museum, Bowmanville 05103
Bralorne Pioneer Museum, Bralorne 05111
Brant Museum Archives, Brantford 05125
Bresaylor Heritage Museum, Paynton 06101
Briercrest and District Museum, Briercrest 05132
Broadview Museum, Broadview 05136
Brockville Museum, Brockville 05138
Brome County Historical Society Museum, Knowlton 05703
Brooks and District Museum, Brooks 05139
Bruce County Museum, Southampton 06476
Bruce Mines Museum, Bruce Mines 05141
Buckland Heritage Museum, Spruce Home 06483
Buffalo Bean Museum, Tompkins 06556
Bulkley Valley Museum, Smithers 06462
Burin Heritage House, Burin 05144
Burnaby Village Museum, Burnaby 05149
Buxton Museum, North Buxton 06020
By the Bay Museum, Lewisporte 05752
Cabri and District Museum, Cabri 05154
Cadillac Museum, Cadillac 05156
Callander Bay Heritage Museum, Callander 05183
Campbell House, Toronto 06564
Campbellford-Seymour Heritage Centre, Campbellford 05189
Campobello Island Museum, Welshpool 06767
Cannington Centennial Museum, Cannington 05192
Cannington Manor, Regina 06228
Canso Museum, Canso 05193
Canwood Museum, Canwood 05194
Cape Breton Centre for Heritage and Science, Sydney 06525
Carberry Plains Museum, Carberry 05200
Carscadden's Museum, Plenty 06139
Castor and District Museum, Castor 05217
Centennial Museum of Canmore, Canmore 05191
Centennial Park 1910 Logging Museum, Thunder Bay 06544
Central Butte District Museum, Central Butte 05219
Centre d'Exposition d'Amos, Amos 04990
Centre d'Histoire de Montréal, Montréal 05898
Centre d'Interpretation de la Métabetchouane, Desbiens 05327
Centre d'Interpretation de l'Ardoise, Richmond 06261
Centre d'Interpretation de l'Histoire de Sherbrooke, Sherbrooke, Québec 06439
Cereal Prairie Pioneer Museum, Cereal 05220
Channel-Port-aux-Basques Museum, Channel-Port-aux-Basques 05222
Chapel Hill Museum, Shag Harbour 06425
Chapleau Centennial Museum, Chapleau 05223
Chapman Museum, Brandon 05119
Charlotte County Museum, Saint Stephen 06373
Chase and District Museum, Chase 05234
Chestico Museum, Port Hood 06165
Chilliwack Museum, Chilliwack 05248
Claresholm Museum, Claresholm 05255
Clarke Museum, Orono 06057
Claude Crayston Museum, Glenora 05493
Clayton McLain Memorial Museum, Cutknife 05299
Climax Community Museum, Climax 05257
Cloyne Pioneer Museum, Cloyne 05259
C.O. Card Home, Cardston 05205
Cochrane Railway and Pioneer Museum, Cochrane 05263
Colchester Historical Museum, Truro 06648
Coldwater Canadiana Heritage Museum, Coldwater 05264
Cole Harbour Heritage Farm Museum, Cole Harbour 05265
Colville Lake Museum, Norman Wells 06010
Comber Pioneer Village, Holland Centre 05602
Compton County Historical Museum, Eaton Corner 05364
Conception Bay Museum, Harbour Grace 05584
Connors Museum, Connors 05271
Cook's Creek Heritage Museum, Dugald 05350
Copper Cliff Museum, Sudbury 06509
Coronach District Museum, Coronach 05279
Cossit House Museum, Sydney 06526
Cowichan Valley Museum, Duncan 05353
Craig Heritage Park Museum, Parksville 06094
Creston and District Museum, Creston 05289
Crowsnest Museum, Coleman 05266
Crystal City Community Museum, Crystal City 05293
Cumberland County Museum, Amherst 04986
Cumberland Heritage Village Museum, Cumberland, Ontario 05295
Cumberland Museum, Cumberland, British Columbia 05294
Cupar and District Heritage Museum, Cupar 05296
Cupids Museum, Cupids 05297
Darlingford School Heritage Museum, Darlingford 05302
Darlington Province Park Pioneer Home, Bowmanville 05104
Dartmouth Heritage Museum, Dartmouth 05304
Dawson City Museum, Dawson City 05311
Dawson Creek Station Museum, Dawson Creek 05314
DeBolt and District Pioneer Museum, DeBolt 05316
Delhi Ontario Tobacco Museum Heritage Centre, Delhi 05319
Deloraine Museum, Deloraine 05321
Delta Museum, Delta 05323
Denman Island Museum, Denman Island 05325
Desbrisay Museum and Exhibition Centre, Bridgewater 05130
Devil's Coulee Dinosaur Heritage Museum, Warner 06744
Dewberry Valley Museum, Dewberry 05328
Didsbury and District Museum, Didsbury 05329
Diefenbaker Homestead House, Regina 06230
Dodsland Museum, Dodsland 05334
Donalda and District Museum, Donalda 05335
Drayton Valley Museum, Drayton Valley 05338
Dryden and District Museum, Dryden 05346
Duck Lake Regional Interpretive Centre, Duck Lake 05347
Duff Community Heritage Museum, Duff 05348
Dufferin County Museum, Rosemont 06284
Dufferin Historical Museum, Carman 05210
Dundas Historical Society Museum, Dundas 05355
Dundurn Castle, Hamilton 05569
Dunwell and Community Museum, Weekes 06761
Ear Falls District Museum, Ear Falls 05359
East Hants Historical Museum, Maitland 05801
Eastend Museum, Eastend 05362
Eastend School Museum, Eastend 05363
Écomusée de la Haute-Beauce, Saint-Evariste 06317
Edgerton and District Museum, Edgerton 05366
Edinburgh Square Heritage and Cultural Centre, Caledonia 05158

Eildon Hall Sibbald Memorial Museum, Sutton, Ontario 06522
Ekfrid Township Museum, Appin 05003
Elbow Museum, Elbow 05399
Elk Lake Heritage Museum, Elk Lake 05401
Elman W. Campbell Museum, Newmarket 05987
Elrose Heritage Museum, Elrose 05406
Enderby and District Museum, Enderby 05408
Englehart and Area Historical Museum, Englehart 05409
Eptek National Exhibition Centre, Summerside 06514
Eriksdale Museum, Eriksdale 05412
Erland Lee Museum, Stoney Creek 06493
Esterhazy Community Museum, Esterhazy 05413
Estevan National Exhibition Centre, Art Gallery and Museum, Estevan 05415
Evergreen Historic House, Dartmouth 05305
Fairfield Museum, Bothwell 05099
Fanshawe Pioneer Village, London 05764
Fenelon Falls Museum, Fenelon Falls 05422
Fernie and District Historical Museum, Fernie 05424
Fieldcote Museum, Ancaster 04991
Flat Rock Museum, Flat Rock 05426
Flin Flon Museum, Flin Flon 05428
Foam Lake Museum, Foam Lake 05429
Forest-Lambton Museum, Forest 05431
Forestburg and District Museum, Forestburg 05432
Fort Calgary, Calgary 05166
Fort Chipewyan Bicentennial Museum, Fort Chipewyan 05434
Fort Dauphin Museum, Dauphin 05308
Fort Edmonton Park, Edmonton 05376
Fort Erie Historical Museum, Ridgeway 06268
Fort Frances Museum, Fort Frances 05437
Fort George Museum, Elk Point 05402
Fort Lennox, Saint-Paul-de-Ile-aux-Noix 06370
Fort Museum, Fort Macleod 05443
Fort Nelson Heritage Museum, Fort Nelson 05447
Fort Pelley and Livingston Museum, Pelly 06104
Fort Qu'appelle Museum, Fort Qu'appelle 05448
Fort Rodd Hill Museum, Victoria 06720
Fort Saint James National Historic Site, Fort Saint James 05449
Fort Saint Pierre, Fort Frances 05438
Fort Saskatchewan Museum, Fort Saskatchewan 05451
Fort Steele Heritage Town, Fort Steele 05453
Fort Walsh, Maple Creek 05809
Fortifications-de-Québec, Québec 06197
Fortress of Louisbourg, Louisbourg 05782
Frank Slide Interpretive Centre, Crowsnest Pass 05291
Fraser Lake Museum, Fraser Lake 05456
Frazer's Museum, Beauval 05067
Fred Light Museum, Battleford 05061
Frenchman Butte Museum, Frenchman Butte 05470
Galloway Station Museum, Edson 05397
Gananoque Museum, Gananoque 05473
George Johnston Tlingit Indian Museum, Teslin 06540
Georgina Pioneer Museum, Keswick 05665
Gibson House, North York 06031
Gillam Community Museum, Gillam 05487
Gladstone and District Museum, Gladstone 05491
Glanmore National Historic Site of Canada, Belleville 05072
Glen Ewen Community Antique Centre, Glen Ewen 05492
Glengarry Pioneer Museum, Dunvegan, Ontario 05356
Glentworth Museum, Glentworth 05494
Gloucester Museum, Gloucester 05495
Golden and District Museum, Golden 05498
Goldstream Region Museum, Victoria 06721
Goodsoil Historical Museum, Goodsoil 05500
Gowganda and Area Museum, Gowganda 05505
Grand Falls Museum, Grand Falls 05510
Grand Manan Museum, Grand Manan 05516
Grand-Pré National Historic Site of Canada, Grand-Pré 05518
Gravelbourg and District Museum, Gravelbourg 05524
Great Sandhills Museum, Sceptre 06415
Greater Sudbury Heritage Museum, Sudbury 06511
Greater Vernon Museum, Vernon, British Colombia 06706
Greenspond Court House, Greenspond 05527
Greenwood Museum, Greenwood, British Columbia 05528
Grenfell Community Museum, Grenfell 05530
Grey County Museum, Owen Sound 06088
Grimsby Museum, Grimsby 05531
Groundbirch Museum, Groundbirch 05535
Guelph Civic Museum, Guelph 05536
Haileybury Heritage Museum, Haileybury 05541
Haldimand County Museum, Cayuga 05218
Haliburton Highlands Museum, Haliburton 05543
Halton Region Museum, Milton 05852
Hamiota Pioneer Club Museum, Hamiota 05579
Harris Heritage and Museum, Harris 05585
Harry S. Washbrook Museum, Edam 05365
Hart-Cam Museum, Hartney 05588
Harvey Grant Heritage Centre Community Museum, Springdale 06480
Hecla Island Heritage Home Museum, Riverton 06277
Heritage Hazenmore, Hazenmore 05592
Heritage House Museum, Smiths Falls 06465
Heritage Museum, Langruth 05726
Heritage Park, Fort McMurray 05445
Heritage Park Museum, Terrace 06539
High Prairie and District Museum, High Prairie 05594
Highland Pioneers Museum, Baddeck 05032
Historic Ferryland Museum, Ferryland 05425
Historic Fort York, Toronto 06582
Historic Yale Museum, Yale 06867
Historical Museum and Pioneer Village, Sundre 06516
Historical Village and Pioneer Museum, Willingdon 06806
History Museum of Saint Paul, Saint Paul 06369
Hodgeville Community Museum, Hodgeville 05600
Holden Historical Society Museum, Holden 05601
Homestead Antique Museum, Drumheller 05341
Homestead Museum, Biggar 05080
Hope Museum, Hope 05603
House of Memories, Latchford 05731
Howard House of Artifacts, Old Perlican 06048
Hudson Bay Museum, Hudson Bay 05606
Hudson's Hope Museum, Hudson's Hope 05607
Humber-Bay of Islands Museum, Corner Brook 05273
Humboldt and District Museum and Gallery, Humboldt 05608
Huronia Museum, Midland 05846
Hymers Museum, Kakabeka Falls 05637
Ignace Heritage Centre, Ignace 05612
Imperial and District Museum, Imperial 05614
Indian Head Museum, Indian Head 05616
Innisfail and District Historical Museum, Innisfail 05619
Innisville and District Museum, Innisville 05620
Inverness Miners Museum, Inverness 05623
Iron Creek Museum, Lougheed 05780
Iroquois Falls Pioneer Museum, Iroquois Falls 05628
Irving House Historic Centre and New Westminster Museum, New Westminster 05984
Ituna Cultural and Historical Museum, Ituna 05630
Jasper Cultural and Historical Centre, Maple Creek 05810
J.A.V. David Museum, Killarney 05666
Jordan Historical Museum of the Twenty, Jordan 05635
Jost House Museum, Sydney 06527
Kamloops Museum, Kamloops 05639
Kamsack and District Museum, Kamsack 05643
Kaposvar Historic Site, Esterhazy 05414
Kawartha Settlers' Village, Bobcaygeon 05087
Keillor House Museum, Dorchester 05336
Kelliher and District Heritage Museum, Kelliher 05649
Kellross Heritage Museum, Leross 05743
Kelowna Museum, Kelowna 05653
Keno City Mining Museum, Keno City 05655
Kerrobert and District Museum, Kerrobert 05664
Killarney Centennial Museum, Killarney 05667
Kimberley Heritage Museum, Kimberley 05668
Kincaid Museum, Kincaid 05669
Kindersley Plains Museum, Kindersley 05670
King Township Historical Museum, King City 05671
Kings County Museum, Hampton 05580
Kings County Museum, Kentville 05661
Kings Landing Historical Settlement, Prince William 06191
Kipling District Historical Society Museum, Kipling 05692
Kitwanga Fort, Queen Charlotte 06213
Klondike National Historic Sites, Dawson City 05312
Kneehill Historical Museum, Three Hills 06543
Kootenai Brown Pioneer Village, Pincher Creek 06133
Kootenay Gallery of Art, History and Science, Castlegar 05214
Kwagiulth Museum, Quathiaski Cove 06194
Labrador Straits Museum, L'Anse-au-Loup 05001
Lac Cardinal Regional Pioneer Village Museum, Grimshaw 05534
Lac La Hache Museum, Barkerville 05047
Lake Country Museum, Okanagan 06046
Lake of the Woods Museum, Kenora 05656
Lakes District Museum, Burns Lake 05152
Lakeside Museum, Bulyea 05142
Lambton Heritage Museum, Grand Bend 05509
Lancer Centennial Museum, Lancer 05723
Lang Pioneer Village, Keene 05648
Langham and District Heritage Village Museum, Langham 05724
Lanigan and District Heritage Centre, Lanigan 05727
Lashburn Centennial Museum, Lashburn 05730
Laurier House, Ottawa 06082
Lennox and Addington County Museum and Archives, Napanee 05964
Leroy and District Heritage Museum, Leroy 05744
Lieu Historique National de Côteau-du-Lac, Côteau-du-Lac 05280
Lieu Historique National de Sir Wilfrid Laurier, Ville des Laurentides 06733
Lillooet District Museum, Lillooet 05753
Little Current-Howland Centennial Museum, Sheguiandah 06433
Little Prairie Heritage Museum, Chetwynd 05245
London Regional Children's Museum, London 05770
Londonderry Mines Museum, Londonderry 05774
Lord Selkirk Settlement, Charlottetown 05227
Loyalist Cultural Centre, Bath 05056
Loyalist House Museum, Saint John 06333
Lumsden Heritage Museum, Lumsden 05786
Lundar Museum, Lundar 05787
Lundy's Lane Historical Museum, Niagara Falls 05992
Luseland and Districts Museum, Luseland 05790
Lutz Mountain Meeting House, Moncton 05878
Lynn Lake Mining Town Museum, Lynn Lake 05791
Lytton Museum, Lytton 05792
Macaulay Heritage Park, Picton 06127
MacBride Museum, Whitehorse 06792
McCrae House, Guelph 05537
McKays Museum, Bowsman 05105
Mackenzie and District Museum, Mackenzie 05795
Macklin and District Museum, Macklin 05796
Macrorie Museum, Macrorie 05797
Madonna House Pioneer Museum, Combermere 05269
Magnetawan Historical Museum, Magnetawan 05798
Main Centre Heritage Museum, Main Centre 05800
Manitou Pioneer Museum, Neilburg 05969
Manitoulin Historical Society Museum, Gore Bay 05502
Manor Museum, Manor 05806
Maple Ridge Museum, Maple Ridge 05813
Maple Sugar Museum, Art Gallery and Pioneer Home, Sundridge 06517
Marble Mountain Community Museum, West Bay 06771
Markham Museum and Historic Village, Markham 05816
Marringhurst Pioneer Park Museum, Pilot Mound 06131
Marten River Logging Museum, Marten River 05817
Mary March Regional Museum and Logging Exhibition, Grand Falls-Windsor 05512
Maryfield Museum, Maryfield 05818
Marystown Museum, Marystown 05819
Massey Area Museum, Massey 05820
Matsqui Sumas Abbotsford Museum, Abbotsford 04964
Mattawa and District Museum, Mattawa 05824
Meadow Lake Museum, Meadow Lake 05828
Meaford Museum, Meaford 05829
Meanskinisht Museum, Kitwanga 05701
Medicine Hat Museum and Art Gallery, Medicine Hat 05831
Melfort and District Museum, Melfort 05835
Melville Heritage Museum, Melville 05838
Mennonite Heritage Village, Steinbach 06488
Miami Museum, Miami 05843
Middle Lake Museum, Middle Lake 05845
Middleville Museum, Lanark 05722
Milden Community Museum, Milden 05849
Millet and District Museum, Millet 05851
Milton Blacksmith Shop Museum, Milton 05853
Miniota Municipal Museum, Miniota 05858
Minnedosa and District Museum, Minnedosa 05859
Minto Museum, Minto 05860
Mirror and District Museum, Mirror 05863
Mission Museum, Mission 05865
Mockbeggar Plantation, Bonavista 05095
Moncton Museum, Moncton 05879
Moore Museum, Mooretown 05932
Moose Factory Centennial Museum, Kirkland Lake 05693
Moose Jaw Museum and Art Gallery, Moose Jaw 05934
Moosehorn Heritage Museum, Moosehorn 05936
Moreton's Harbour Museum, Moreton's Harbour 05941
Morris and District Centennial Museum, Morris 05943
Morse Museum, Morse 05945
Mossbank and District Museum, Mossbank 05946
Multicultural Heritage Centre, Stony Plain 06494
Musée Acadien, Gloucester 05496
Musée Acadien, Miscouche 05864
Musée Acadien, Moncton 05880
Musée Acadien de Pubnico-Ouest, West Pubnico 06772
Musée d'Aylmer, Aylmer 05029
Musée de Kamouraska, Kamouraska 05642
Musée de la Gaspésie, Gaspé 05478
Musée de Lachine, Lachine 05712
Musée de Saint-Pierre-Jolys, Saint-Pierre-Jolys 06372
Musée du Fjord, La Baie 05705
Musée du Haut-Richelieu, Saint-Jean-sur-Richelieu 06330
Musée François Pilote, La Pocatière 05707
Musée Girouxville, Girouxville 05489
Musée Héritage, Saint-Albert 06300
Musée Historique Charles Le Moyne, Longueuil 05776
Musée Historique du Madawaska, Edmundston 05396
Musée Le Pionnier, Saint-Malo 06365
Musée Maison Saint-Gabriel, Montréal 05923
Musée Namesokanjik, Lac Mégantic 05710
Musée Pointe des Chênes, Sainte-Anne 06381
Musée Regional d'Argenteuil, Saint-André-d'Argenteuil 06302
Musée Régional de la Côte-Nord, Sept-Iles 06422
Musée Régional de Rimouski, Rimouski 06272
Musée Régional de Vaudreuil-Soulanges, Vaudreuil 06702
Musée Saint-Brieux, Saint-Brieux 06308
Musée Saint-Georges, Saint-Georges, Manitoba 06319
Musée Saint-Joachim, La Broquerie 05706
Museum of Northern British Columbia, Prince Rupert 06189
Museum of Northern History at the Sir Harry Oakes Château, Kirkland Lake 05694
Museum of South East Alberta, Etzikom 05419
Museum of the Highwood, High River 05595
Muskoka Heritage Place, Huntsville 05610
Naicam Museum, Naicam 05954
Nakusp Museum, Nakusp 05957
Nanaimo District Museum, Nanaimo 05961
Naramata Museum, Naramata 05965
National Doukhobour Heritage Village, Verigin 06705
Nelson Museum, Nelson 05970
Nepean Museum, Nepean 05973
New Brunswick Museum, Saint John 06334
Niagara Historical Museum, Niagara-on-the-Lake 06003
Nicola Valley Museum, Merrit 05842
Nipawin and District Living Forestry Museum, Nipawin 06006
Nipigon Museum, Nipigon 06007
Nipissing Township Museum, Nipissing 06008
Nokomis and District Museum, Nokomis 06009
Nor' Wester and Loyalist Museum, Williamstown 06805
Norman Wells Historical Centre, Norman Wells 06011
North Atlantic Aviation Museum, Gander 05474
North Bay and Area Museum, North Bay 06017
North Hastings Heritage Museum, Bancroft 05040
North Highland Community Museum, Dingwall 05331
North Huron District Museum, Wingham 06815
North Lanark Regional Museum, Almonte 04980
North Pacific Cannery Village Museum, Port Edward 06161
North Thompson Museum, Barriere 05050
North Vancouver Museum, North Vancouver 06025
Northern Gateway Museum, Denare Beach 05324
Northwestern National Exhibition Centre, Hazelton 05591
Nose Creek Valley Museum, Airdrie 04969
Nova Scotia Museum, Halifax 05559
Nuantta Sunakkutaangit Museum, Iqaluit 05626
Nutimik Lake Museum, Seven Sisters Falls 06423
Oakville Museum at Erchless Estate, Oakville 06040
O'Dell Inn, Annapolis Royal 04997
Ogniwo Polish Museum, Winnipeg 06835
Old George's Authentic Collectibles, Whitewood 06796
Old Meeting House Museum, Barrington 05052
Oldman River Cultural Centre, Brocket 05137
Orillia Museum of Art and History, Orillia 06054
Osgoode Township Museum, Vernon, Ontario 06709
Oshawa Sydenham Museum, Oshawa 06060
Osler Historical Museum, Osler 06062
Osoyoos Museum, Osoyoos 06064
Outlook and District Heritage Museum and Gallery, Outlook 06086
Paipoonge Historical Museum, Thunder Bay 06547
Parkdale-Maplewood Community Museum, Barss Corner 05054
Parks Canada Visitor Reception Centre, Churchill 05251
Peachland Museum, Peachland 06103
Peel Heritage Complex, Brampton 05114
Pemberton Museum, Pemberton 06105
Pembina Lobstick Historical Museum, Evansburg 05420
Pembina Threshermen's Museum, Winkler 06816
Penetanguishene Centennial Museum, Penetanguishene 06108
Peninsula and Saint Edmunds Township Museum, Tobermory 06553
Perth Museum, Perth 06114
Petite Anglicane, Forestville 05433
Petrolia Discovery, Petrolia 06125
Pickering Museum Village, Pickering 06126
Pictou County Historical Museum, New Glasgow 05979
Pilot Mound Cenntenial Museum, Pilot Mound 06132
Pioneer Village Museum, Beauséjour 05066
Pitt Meadows Museum, Pitt Meadows 06134
Piulimatsivik - Nain Museum, Nain 05955
Placentia Area Museum, Placentia 06136
Plamondon and District Museum, Plamondon 06137
Plaster Rock Museum, Plaster Rock 06138
Plum Coulee and District Museum, Plum Coulee 06140
Police and Pioneer Museum, Shoal Lake 06446
Port Clements Museum, Port Clements 06157
Port Colborne Historical and Marine Museum, Port Colborne 06158
Port Hardy Museum, Port Hardy 06162
Port Hastings Museum, Port Hastings 06163
Port-la-Joye-Fort Amherst, Charlottetown 05229
Port Moody Station Museum, Port Moody 06167
Port Union Museum, Port Union 06170
Pouch Cove Museum, Pouch Cove 06175
Prairie Panorama Museum, Czar 05300
Prairie Pioneer Museum, Craik 05285
Prairie River Museum, Prairie River 06177
Prairie West Historical Centre, Eston 05416
Presqu'ile Provincial Park Museum, Brighton 05133
Prince Albert Historical Museum, Prince Albert 06184
Princeton and District Museum, Princeton 06192
Provincial Museum of Alberta, Edmonton 05384
Quaco Museum and Archives, Saint Martins 06366
Queens County Museum, Liverpool 05759
Queens County Museum, Tilley House and Court House, Gagetown 05472
Quesnel and District Museum, Quesnel 06216
Railway Station Museum, Castlegar 05215
Rainy Hills Historical Society Pioneer Exhibits, Iddesleigh 05611
Rapid City Museum, Rapid City 06217
Raymore Pioneer Museum, Raymore 06218
Red Lake Museum, Red Lake 06223
Redcliff Museum, Redcliff 06224
Redwater and District Museum, Redwater 06225
Regina Plains Museum, Regina 06240
Restigouche Regional Museum, Dalhousie 05301
Reston and District Historical Museum, Reston 06252
Revelstoke Museum, Revelstoke 06254

Reynold Rapp Museum, Spalding 06479
Richibucto River Museum, Richibucto 06258
Richmond County Historical Society Museum, Melbourne 05832
Richmond Museum, Richmond 06264
Rideau District Museum, Westport 06776
Ridge House Museum, Ridgetown 06267
R.N. Atkinson Museum, Penticton 06110
Rocanville and District Museum, Rocanville 06280
Rose House Museum, Picton 06128
Rose Valley and District Heritage Museum, Rose Valley 06282
Rosebud Centennial Museum, Rosebud 06283
Rosetown Museum and Art Center, Rosetown 06285
Ross Thomson Museum, Halifax 05562
Rossburn Museum, Rossburn 06286
Rouleau and District Museum, Rouleau 06290
Roulston Museum, Carstairs 05212
Roy Whalen Regional Heritage Centre, Deer Lake 05317
Royal Ontario Museum, Toronto 06607
Rusty Relics Museum, Carlyle 05209
Saanich Pioneer Log Cabin Museum, Saanichton 06296
Sachs Harbour Museum, Sachs Harbour 06297
Saint Catharines Museum, Saint Catharines 06311
Saint Claude Museum, Saint Claude 06312
Saint Elie Pioneer Church Museum, Inglis 05618
Saint Joseph Island Museum Village, Richards Landing 06257
Saint Mary's Museum of Maxstone, Assiniboia 05015
Saint Norbert Provincial Heritage Park, Winnipeg 06843
Saint Patrick's Museum, Sydney 06528
Saint Walburg and District Historical Museum, Saint Walburg 06380
Salmo Museum, Salmo 06386
Saskatchewan River Valley Museum, Hague 05540
Saskatchewan Western Development Museum, Yorkton 06873
Sault Sainte Marie Museum, Sault Sainte Marie 06413
Scarborough Historical Museum, Scarborough 06414
Scugog Shores Historical Museum, Port Perry 06168
Seal Island Light Museum, Barrington 05053
Sedgewick Museum and Gallery, Sedgewick 06417
Selkirk College Mansbridge Kootenay Collection, Castlegar 05216
Shades of the Past, Carbonear 05203
Shamrock Museum, Shamrock 06426
Sharon Temple Historic Site, Sharon 06427
Shawnigan Lake Historical Museum, Shawnigan Lake 06431
Shelburne County Museum, Shelburne 06436
Shell Lake Museum, Shell Lake 06437
Sicamous and District Museum, Sicamous 06447
Sidney Historical Museum, Sidney 06449
Siksika Nation Museum, Siksika 06452
Simcoe County Museum, Minesing 05857
Simeon Perkins House, Liverpool 05760
Sioux Lookout Museum, Sioux Lookout 06459
Sipalaseequtt Museum, Pangnirtung 06093
Sir Alexander Galt Museum, Lethbridge 05747
Smith's Cove Historical Museum, Smith's Cove 06464
Sooke Region Museum, Art Gallery and Historic Moss Cottage, Sooke 06470
South Cariboo Historical Museum, Clinton 05258
South Grey Museum and Historical Library, Flesherton 05427
South Rawdon Museum, South Rawdon 06475
South Simcoe Pioneer Museum, Alliston 04978
South Similkameen Museum, Keremeos 05663
Southey and District Museum, Southey 06478
Southwestern Ontario Heritage Village, Kingsville 05690
Southwestern Saskatchewan Oldtimer's Museum, Maple Creek 05811
Spruce Row Museum, Waterford 06749
Squamish Valley Museum, Garibaldi Heights 05476
S.S. Moyie National Historic Site, Kaslo 05647
Star City Heritage Museum, Star City 06487
Stettler Town and Country Museum, Stettler 06490
Stone Shop Museum, Grimsby 05533
Stony Plain and District Pioneer Museum, Stony Plain 06495
Story of People, Yorkton 06874
Stoughton and District Museum, Stoughton 06496
Strasbourg and District Museum, Strasbourg 06497
Strathclair Museum, Strathclair 06501
Strathcona County Heritage Foundation Museum, Sherwood Park 06444
Strathroy Middlesex Museum, Strathroy 06503
Sturgis Station House Museum, Sturgis 06506
Summerland Museum, Summerland 06513
Sunrise Trail Museum, Tatamagouche 06535
Sunshine Coast Museum, Gibsons 05485
Surrey Museum, Surrey 06520
Swan Valley Historical Museum, Swan River 06523
Taber and District Museum, Taber 06530
Tabusintac Centennial Museum, Tabusintac 06531
Teeterville Pioneer Museum, Delhi 05320
Tehkummah Township Museum, Tehkummah 06537
Telkwa Museum, Telkwa 06538
Teulon and District Museum, Teulon 06541
Thelma Miles Museum, Matheson 05823
Thunder Bay Historical Museum Society, Thunder Bay 06549
Tignish Cultural Centre Museum, Tighish 06551
Timber Village Museum, Blind River 05085
Timmins Museum, South Porcupine 06474
Tofield Historical Museum, Tofield 06554
Torbay Museum, Torbay 06557
Trail Museum, Trail 06630
Transcona Historical Museum, Winnipeg 06848
Treherne Museum, Treherne 06631
Trepassey Area Museum, Trepassey 06632
Trinity Interpretation Centre, Trinity 06635
Trochu and District Museum, Trochu 06637
Tweed and Area Heritage Centre, Tweed 06651
Two Hills and District Museum, Two Hills 06653
Ukrainian Cultural Heritage Museum, Sandy Lake 06389
United Counties Museum, Cornwall 05278
United Empire Loyalist Museum, Bloomfield 05086
Unity and District Heritage Museum, Unity 06655
Upper Canada Village, Morrisburg 05944
Uxbridge-Scott Museum, Uxbridge 06657
Valemount and Area Museum, Valemount 06662
Valley Museum, McBride 05793
Vancouver Museum, Vancouver 06696
Vanderhoof Community Museum, Vanderhoof 06699
Vanguard Centennial Museum, Vanguard 06700
Vegreville Regional Museum, Vegreville 06703
Verwood Community Museum, Verwood 06711
Victoria County Historical Society Museum, Lindsay 05756
Viking Historical Museum, Viking 06732
Village Historique Acadien, Caraquet 05199
Village Québecois d'Antan, Drummondville 05345
Waba Cottage Museum, White Lake 06788
Wabowden Historical Museum, Wabowden 06737
Wadena and District Museum and Gallery, Wadena 06738
Wagon Wheel Regional Museum, Alix 04975
Wainwright Museum, Wainwright 06739
Wakaw Heritage Museum, Wakaw 06741
Wallace Area Museum, Wallace Bridge 06742
Wanuskewin Heritage Park, Saskatoon 06408
Waskada Museum, Waskada 06747
Wasyl Negrych Pioneer Homestead, Gilbert Plains 05486
Watson Crossley Community Museum, Grandview 05522
Wawota and District Museum, Wawota 06760
Welland Historical Museum, Welland 06762
Wellington Community Historical Museum, Wellington, Ontario 06763
Wellington County Museum, Fergus 05423
Wells Museum, Wells 06766
West Parry Sound District Museum, Parry Sound 06097
West Vancouver Museum, West Vancouver 06775
Western Development Museum, Saskatoon 06409
Wetaskiwin and District Museum, Wetaskiwin 06780
Whitbourne Museum, Whitbourne 06785
White Fox Museum, White Fox 06787
White Rock Museum, White Rock 06790
Whitewood Historical Museum, Whitewood 06797
Wilkie and District Museum, Wilkie 06801
William D. Lawrence House, Halifax 05566
Williams Lake Museum, Williams Lake 06804
Willoughby Historical Museum, Niagara Falls 05999
Willow Bunch Museum, Willow Bunch 06807
Windermere Valley Museum, Invermere 05622
Windsor's Community Museum, Windsor, Ontario 06813
Winnipegosis Museum, Winnipegosis 06856
Wolseley Community Museum, Wolseley 06859
Wolverine Hobby and Historical Society Museum, Spy Hill 06485
Woodlands Pioneer Museum, Woodlands 06862
Woodstock Museum, Woodstock 06865
Workers Arts and Heritage Centre, Hamilton 05577
Wynyard and District Museum, Wynyard 06866
Yester-Year Artifacts Museum, Rowley 06293
Yester-Years Community Museum, Dinsmore 05332
Ymir Museum, Ymir 06871
York Sunbury Historical Society Museum, Fredericton 05469

Chad

Musée d'Abeche, Abeche 06882
Musée National de Sarh, Sarh 06885
Musée N'Djamena, N'Djamena 06884

Chile

Museo de Antofagasta, Antofagasta 06888
Museo Regional de Iquique, Iquique 06897
Proed, Santiago de Chile 06920

China, People's Republic

Anqing Municipal Museum, Anqing 06933
Anshan City Museum, Anshan 06934
Anyang Yin Xu Bo Wu Yuan, Anyang 06935
Bangbu City Museum, Bangbu 06937
Bayin Guoleng Zhou Museum, Kuerle 07145
Beijing Museum, Beijing 06951
Benxi City Museum, Benxi 06999
Boer Tala Zhou Museum and Gallery, Bole 07000
Bozhou City Museum, Bozhou 07001
Caidian District Museum, Wuhan 07279
Changji Mulei County Museum, Changji 07006
Changjizhou Museum, Changji 07007
Changqing County Museum, Jinan 07129
Changsha City Museum, Changsha 07009
Changshu City Museum, Changshu 07012
Chaoyang City Museum, Chaoyang 07016
Chengdu City Museum, Chengdu 07020
China Nationalities Museum of Inner Mongolia, Tongliao 07272
Chongming County Museum, Shanghai 07210
Dagu Paotai Yi Zhi Museum, Tianjin 07261
Dahe Village Yi Zhi Museum, Zhengzhou 07326
Doumen County Museum, Zhuhai 07335
Fenghua Xikou Museum, Fenghua 07048
Fengxian Museum, Shanghai 07212
Foshan City Museum, Foshan 07049
Fujian Province Museum, Fuzhou 07056
Fushun City Museum, Fushun 07053
Fuxin City Museum, Fuxin 07054
Fuyang Museum, Fuyang 07055
Gansu Provincial Museum, Lanzhou 07147
Guangxi Provincial Museum, Guilin 07073
Guangzhou Liwan District Museum, Guangzhou 07065
Guangzhou Museum, Guangzhou 07067
Guilin City Museum, Guilin 07074
Guizhou Provincial Museum, Guiyang 07077
Hong Kong Heritage Museum, Hong Kong 07095
Hong Kong Museum of History, Hong Kong 07097
Huangshan City Museum, Huangshan 07116
Huhehot City Museum, Huhehot 07118
Huichang County Museum, Huichang 07120
Huludao City Museum, Huludao 07121
Inner Mongolia Museum, Huhehot 07119
Jiading District Museum, Shanghai 07213
Jian City Museum, Jian 07122
Jiangmen Museum, Jiangmen 07123
Jiangning County Museum, Nanjing 07178
Jiangyin City Museum, Jiangyin 07124
Jiaonan City Museum, Jiaonan 07126
Jilin City Wenmiao Museum, Jilin 07127
Jimo City Museum, Jimo 07128
Jinan City Museum, Jinan 07130
Jinshan Museum, Shanghai 07214
Jinzhou District Museum, Dalian 07036
Jixian Display Center, Jixian 07142
Kaifeng Municipal Museum, Kaifeng 07143
Kang Xicao Museum, Beijing 06969
Kazuo County Museum, Chaoyang 07017
Landlord's Manor House Museum, Dayi 07043
Lanzhou City Museum, Lanzhou 07148
Liaoning Provincial Museum, Chinchow 07028
Liaoyang City Museum, Liaoyang 07150
Licheng District Museum, Jinan 07132
Linan Museum, Hangzhou 07084
Lingyuan City Museum, Lingyuan 07151
Lintong County Museum, Xian 07294
Lishui County Museum, Nanjing 07180
Lishui County Museum, Zaicheng 07323
Liuhe County Display Center, Liucheng 07154
Longquanyi District Museum, Chengdu 07022
Lu Xun Museum In Shaoxing, Shaoxing 07232
Luchou Museum, Luchou 07155
Lugouqiao Display Center, Beijing 06971
Luoyang City Museum, Luoyang 07159
Lushun Museum, Dalian 07037
Mingcheng Yuan Shi Museum, Nanjing 07181
Museum of Datong, Datong 07042
Museum of Shanxi Province, Taiyuan 07257
Museum of the Linxia Autonomous Region, Linxia 07152
Museum of the Tujia and Miao Autonomous Prefecture in Western Hunan, Jishou 07140
Nanchang City Museum, Nanchang 07173
Nanhai Museum, Foshan 07050
Nankang County Museum, Ganzhou 07058
Nanning City Museum, Nanning 07191
Nantong Museum, Nantong 07193
Nanyang Hanhua Guan, Nanyang 07194
Ningbo Baoguo Si Display Center, Ningbo 07195
Ningbo Museum, Ningbo 07196
Pingdu City Museum, Pingdu 07198
Pixian Museum, Pixian 07199
Pulandian City Museum, Dalian 07040
Qingdao Municipal Museum, Qingdao 07204
Qingpu Museum, Shanghai 07218
Revolutionary Museum of the Jinggang Mountains, Jinggang Mountains 07139
Shanghai Museum, Shanghai 07221
Shenzhen Museum, Shenzhen 07242
Shi Liao Display Center, Nanjing 07187
Shicheng County Museum, Ganzhou 07059
Shihezi Junken Museum, Shihezi 07245
Shijiazhuang City Museum, Shijiazhuang 07247
Siping City Museum, Siping 07249
Songjiang County Museum, Shanghai 07225
Tai Hao Ling Museum, Zhoukou 07333
Taichang City Museum, Taichang 07255
Tianjin History Museum, Tianjin 07265
Tieling City Museum, Tieling 07271
Tongan County Museum, Xiamen 07291
Tongzhou District Museum, Beijing 06992
Wafangdian City Museum, Wafangdian 07277
Wan Zhou District Museum, Chongqing 07033
Wuhan City Museum, Wuhan 07281
Wuhou Museum, Chengdu 07027
Wujiang Museum, Wujiang 07284
Wuxi City Museum, Wuxi 07286
Xiamen City Museum, Xiamen 07292
Xian Beilin Museum, Xian 07301
Xiangtan City Museum, Xiangtan 07305
Xianyang City Museum, Xianyang 07306
Xiaoshan City Museum, Xiaoshan 07308
Xuchang City Museum, Xuchang 07311
Xuzhou Museum, Xuzhou 07312
Yangliuqing Museum, Tianjin 07270
Yangzhou Museum, Yangzhou 07315
Yichang City Museum, Yichang 07318
Yingkou City Museum, Yingkou 07320
Yongfeng County Museum, Enjiang 07047
Zengcheng City Museum, Zengcheng 07324
Zhangqiu Museum, Jinan 07137
Zhengding County Display Center, Shijiazhuang 07248
Zhengzhou Museum, Zhengzhou 07329
Zhenjiang Museum, Zhenjiang 07330
Zhongshan Museum, Zhongshan 07332
Zhou Hejing County Museum, Hejing 07092
Zhuhai Museum, Zhuhai 07336
Zibo City Museum, Zibo 07339

Colombia

Casa-Museo Jorge Eliécer Gaitán, Bogotá 07383
Casa Natal de Aquileo Parra, Barichara 07373
Museo Academia de Historia Leonardo Tascón, Buga 07440
Museo Alejandro Galvis, Tona 07606
Museo Anzoátegui, Pamplona 07541
Museo Arqueológico de Muzo, Muzo 07531
Museo Cardenal Crisanto Luque, Tenjo 07604
Museo de Historia Natural, Manizales 07508
Museo de la Casa de la Cultura, Pinchote 07560
Museo de la Sal, Zipaquirá 07628
Museo de los Andes, Socha 07595
Museo de Tradiciones Populares de Aguadas, Aguadas 07361
Museo del Centro de Historia de Tuluá, Tuluá 07607
Museo del Disco, Zipacón 07627
Museo del Samán, Guacarí 07487
Museo Ethnohistórico, Soatá 07594
Museo Histórico, El Carmen de Bolívar 07472
Museo Histórico Anton García de Bonilla, Ocaña 07537
Museo Histórico de Antioquia, Medellín 07522
Museo Histórico y Arqueológico, Belén de Umbría 07380
Museo Hotel Marquetá, Mariquita 07512
Museo Jorge Eliécer Gaitán, Puerto Gaitán 07570
Museo Jubanguana, Santa Fe de la Janguana 07584
Museo Municipal de Historia, Necolí 07532
Museo Nacional del Sombrero, Aguadas 07362
Museo Quevedo Zornoza, Zipaquirá 07629
Museo Regional Guayupe de Puerto Santander, Puerto Santander 07571

Congo, Democratic Republic

Musée de Butemo, Butemo 07631
Musée de Mayombe, Kinshasa 07635
Musée Ethnolopique Provincial, Tshikappa 07644
Musée National de Kananga, Kananga 07633
Musée National de Lubumbashi, Lumumbashi 07641
Musées Universitaire, Kinshasa 07638

Costa Rica

Museo Histórico La Casona de Santa Rosa, Liberia 07650

Côte d'Ivoire

Musée de Bonoua, Bonoua 07669
Musée de Vavoua, Vavoua 07673
Musée Don Bosco, Duekoue 07670
Musée K. Raphaël, Vavoua 07675
Musée Régional Bieth d'Abengourou, Abengourou 07665
Musée Régional Charles Combes, Bingerville 07667
Musée Régional de Bondoukou, Bondoukou 07668
Musée Régional Peleforo Gbon Coulibaly, Korhogo 07672

Croatia

Archeological and Natural History Museum, Brijuni 07684
Bakar Local History Museum, Bakar 07676
Dakovština Museum, Dakovo 07692
Delekovec Local History Collection, Delekovec 07693
Dr. Ljudevit Gaj Museum, Krapina 07727
Gradski Muzej, Križevci 07730
Gradski Muzej Karlovac, Karlovac 07713
Gradski Muzej Varaždin, Varaždin 07797
Kaštela Gradski Muzej, Kaštel Lukšić 07714
Knežev Dvor, Cavtat 07689
Lapidarij - Klaustar Samostana Sv. Domenika, Trogir 07793
Muzej Belišće, Belišće 07678
Muzej Brdovec, Savski Marof 07768
Muzej Grada Trogira, Trogir 07794
Muzej Grada Zagreba, Zagreb 07830
Muzej Kninske Krajine, Knin 07716
Muzej Korčula, Korčula 07722
Muzej Prigorja, Sesvete 07771
Muzej Turopolja, Velika Gorica 07799
Muzejska Zbirka, Imotski 07709
Muzejska Zbirka Jastrebarsko, Jastrebarsko 07711
Novi Vinodolski Regional Museum, Novi Vinodolski 07746
Općinski Muzej, Mali Lošinj 07738
Samobor Museum, Samobor 07767
Virje Local History Museum and Fine Arts Gallery, Virje 07800
Zavičajni Muzej, Buzet 07686
Zavičajni Muzej, Nova Gradiška 07745
Zavičajni Muzej, Ogulin 07747
Zavičajni Muzej Našice, Našice 07741
Zavičajni Muzej Ozlja, Ozalj 07753
Zavičajni Muzej Poreštine, Poreč 07755

Cuba

Antiguo Ayuntamiento y Cárcel de Bejucal, Bejucal 07863
Museo Casa Natal de Antonio Maceo, Santiago de Cuba 08131
Museo Comunidad Las Terrazas, San Cristobal 08101
Museo de Bahía de Cochinos, Playa Girón 08081
Museo de Frank País, Holguín 08006
Museo de la Ciudad de La Habana, La Habana 07961
Museo de la Constitución, Guáimaro 07912
Museo de la Piratería, Santiago de Cuba 08140
Museo de la Provincia de Granma, Bayamo 07859
Museo de los Combates contra los Bandidos, Trinidad 08161
Museo Historia Municipal, Antilla 07851
Museo Histórico, Pinar del Río 08073
Museo Historico, San Antonio de los Baños 08099
Museo Histórico Municipal de Regla, Regla 08089
Museo Historico Provincial, Cienfuegos 07893
Museo Histórico Provincial, Sancti-Spíritus 08112
Museo Histórico Provincial de Guantánamo, Guantánamo 07917
Museo Isabel Rubio, Isabel Rubio 08010
Museo Melia Cayo Coco y Museo Tryp Colonial, Cayo Coco 07884
Museo Municipal, Ciego de Avila 07888
Museo Municipal, Holguín 08008
Museo Municipal, Sancti-Spíritus 08113
Museo Municipal Alex Urquiola, El Salvador 08095
Museo Municipal de 10 de Octubre, La Habana 07978
Museo Municipal de Abreus, Abreus 07846
Museo Municipal de Aguada de Pasajeros, Aguada de Pasajeros 07847
Museo Municipal de Alto Songo y La Maya, Alto Songo 07848
Museo Municipal de Amancio, Amancio 07850
Museo Municipal de Báguano, Báguano 07852
Museo Municipal de Bahía Honda, Bahía Honda 07853
Museo Municipal de Baraguá, Baraguá 07856
Museo Municipal de Bartolomé Masó, Bartolomé Masó 07857
Museo Municipal de Bayamo, Bayamo 07861
Museo Municipal de Bolivia, Bolivia 07865
Museo Municipal de Buey Arriba, Buey Arriba 07866
Museo Municipal de Cabaiguán, Cabaiguán 07867
Museo Municipal de Cacomun, Cacomun 07868
Museo Municipal de Caibarién, Caibarién 07869
Museo Municipal de Caimanera, Caimanera 07870
Museo Municipal de Calimete, Calimete 07872
Museo Municipal de Camajuaní Hermanos Vidal Caro, Camajuaní 07878
Museo Municipal de Campechuela, Campechuela 07879
Museo Municipal de Candelaria, Candelaria 07880
Museo Municipal de Carlos Manuel de Céspedes, Carlos Manuel de Céspedes 07882
Museo Municipal de Cauto Cristo, Cauto Cristo 07883
Museo Municipal de Chambas, Chambas 07885
Museo Municipal de Cifuentes, Cifuentes 07894
Museo Municipal de Ciro Redondo, Ciro Redondo 07895
Museo Municipal de Colón José R. Zulueta, Colón 07897
Museo Municipal de Consolación del Sur, Consolación del Sur 07898
Museo Municipal de Contramaestre, Contramaestre 07899
Museo Municipal de Corralillo, Corralillo 07900
Museo Municipal de Cruces, Cruces 07901
Museo Municipal de Cueto, Cueto 07903
Museo Municipal de Cumanayagua, Cumanayagua 07904
Museo Municipal de Esmeralda, Esmeralda 07905
Museo Municipal de Florencia, Florencia 07906
Museo Municipal de Florida, Florida 07907
Museo Municipal de Fomento, Fomento 07908
Museo Municipal de Gibara, Gibara 07911
Museo Municipal de Guamá, La Plata 08080
Museo Municipal de Guane, Guane 07914
Museo Municipal de Guantánamo - Antigua Cárcel, Guantánamo 07918
Museo Municipal de Guisa, Guisa 07919
Museo Municipal de Habana del Este, La Habana 07980
Museo Municipal de Imías, Playitas y Cajobabo, Cajobabo 07871
Museo Municipal de Jagüey Grande, Jagüey Grande 08012
Museo Municipal de Jesús Menéndez, Jesús Menéndez 08015
Museo Municipal de Jiguaní, Jiguaní 08016
Museo Municipal de Jovellanos Domingo Mujica, Jovellanos 08019
Museo Municipal de la Lisa, La Habana 07981
Museo Municipal de La Sierpe, La Sierpe 08156
Museo Municipal de La Yaya, La Yaya 08182
Museo Municipal de Lajas, Lajas 08020
Museo Municipal de Los Arabos Clotilde García, Los Arabos 08021
Museo Municipal de Los Palacios, Los Palacios 08022
Museo Municipal de Maisí, Maisí 08024
Museo Municipal de Majagua, Majagua 08025
Museo Municipal de Majibacoa, Majibacoa 08026
Museo Municipal de Manatí Jesús Suárez Gayol, Manatí 08027
Museo Municipal de Manicaragua, Manicaragua 08028
Museo Municipal de Mantua, Mantua 08029
Museo Municipal de Manuel Tames, Manuel Tames 08030
Museo Municipal de Manzanillo, Manzanillo 08033
Museo Municipal de Marianao, La Habana 07982
Museo Municipal de Martí, Martí 08034
Museo Municipal de Mayarí, Mayarí 08044
Museo Municipal de Media Luna, Media Luna 08046
Museo Municipal de Minas, Minas 08047
Museo Municipal de Minas de Matahambre, Minas de Matahambre 08048
Museo Municipal de Moa, Moa 08049
Museo Municipal de Morón, Morón 08051
Museo Municipal de Najasa, Sibanicú 08154
Museo Municipal de Niceto Pérez, Niceto Pérez 08052
Museo Municipal de Niquero, Niquero 08053
Museo Municipal de Nuevitas, Nuevitas 08063
Museo Municipal de Palma Soriano, Palma Soriano 08065
Museo Municipal de Pedro Betancourt, Pedro Betancourt 08067
Museo Municipal de Perico, Perico 08068
Museo Municipal de Pilón, Pilón 08069
Museo Municipal de Placetas, Placetas 08079
Museo Municipal de Poblado de Jimaguayú, Jimaguayú 08017
Museo Municipal de Primero de Enero, Primero de Enero 08082
Museo Municipal de Quemado de Güines, Quemado de Güines 08086
Museo Municipal de Rafael Freyre, Rafael Freyre 08087
Museo Municipal de Río Cauto, Río Cauto 08091
Museo Municipal de Rodas, Rodas 08092
Museo Municipal de Sagua de Tánamo, Sagua de Tánamo 08093
Museo Municipal de Sagua la Grande, Sagua la Grande 08094
Museo Municipal de San Cristobal, San Cristobal 08102
Museo Municipal de San Juan y Martínez, San Juan y Martínez 08104
Museo Municipal de San Luis 29 de Abril, San Luis 08105
Museo Municipal de San Miguel del Padrón, La Habana 07983
Museo Municipal de Sandino, Sandino 08116
Museo Municipal de Santa Cruz del Sur, Santa Cruz del Sur 08126
Museo Municipal de Santo Domingo, Santo Domingo 08153
Museo Municipal de Sibanicú, Sibanicú 08155
Museo Municipal de Sierra de Cubitas, Cubitas 07902
Museo Municipal de Taguasco, Taguasco 08158
Museo Municipal de Trinidad, Trinidad 08162
Museo Municipal de Unión de Reyes Juan G. Gómez, Unión de Reyes 08164
Museo Municipal de Urbano Noris, Urbano Noris 08165
Museo Municipal de Varadero, Varadero 08166
Museo Municipal de Vedado, La Habana 07984
Museo Municipal de Venezuela, Venezuela 08167
Museo Municipal de Vertientes, Vertientes 08168
Museo Municipal de Viñales Adela Azcuy Labrador, Pinar del Río 08075
Museo Municipal de Yaguajay, Yaguajay 08179
Museo Municipal de Yara, Yara 08180
Museo Municipal de Yateras, Yateras 08181
Museo Municipal del Cerro, La Habana 07985
Museo Municipal Emilio Daudinot, San Antonio del Sur 08100
Museo Municipal Fernando García Grave de Peralta, Puerto Padre 08085
Museo Municipal Francisco Javier Balmaseda, Santa Clara 08123
Museo Municipal Jatibonico, Jatibonico 08014
Museo Municipal Juan M. Ameijeiras, El Salvador 08096
Museo Municipal Nueva Gerona, Nueva Gerona 08061
Museo Municipal Roberto Rojas Tamayo, Colombia 07896
Museo Municipal Rosendo Arteaga, Jobabo Dos 08018
Museo Oscar María de Rojas, Cárdenas 07881
Museo Pedrin Troya, San Nicolás de Bari 08106
Museo Polivalente de Palmira, Palmira 08066
Museo Presidio Modelo, Nueva Gerona 08062
Museo Provincial, Ciego de Avila 07889
Museo Provincial de Holguín La Periquera, Holguín 08009
Museo Provincial de Matanzas, Matanzas 08042
Museo Provincial de Villa Clara y Museo Municipal, Santa Clara 08125
Museo Provincial Don Emilio Bacardí Moreau, Santiago de Cuba 08151
Museo Provincial General Vicente García, Victoria de las Tunas 08174
Museo Provincial Ignacio Agramonte, La Vigía 08176
Museo San Miguel del Padrón, La Habana 07997

Cyprus

Palaepaphos Museum, Kouklia 08187
Thalassa - Aghia Napa Municipal Museum, Aghia Napa 08184

Czech Republic

Chebský Hrad, Cheb 08307
Fričovo Muzeum, Lázně Bělohrad 08443
Galerie Ludvíka Kuby, Březnice 08260
Horácké Muzeum, Nové Město na Moravě 08503
Hrad Roštejn, Telč 08675
Jihočeské Muzeum v Českých Budějovicích, České Budějovice 08299
Karlovarské Muzeum, Karlovy Vary 08401
Karlovské Muzeum, Velké Karlovice 08711
Kotulova Dřevěnka, Havířov 08344
Krajské Muzeum Cheb, Cheb 08308
Krkonošské Muzeum, Vrchlabí 08725
Malé Máslovické Muzeum Másla, Vodochody 08723
Masarykovo Muzeum, Hodonín 08354
Měnínská Brána, Brno 08269
Městské a Textilni Muzeum, Dvůr Králové nad Labem 08337
Městské Muzeum, Bílovec 08249
Městské Muzeum, Budyně nad Ohří 08285
Městské Muzeum, Bystřice nad Pernštejnem 08286
Městské Muzeum, Chrast u Chrudimě 08317
Městské Muzeum, Chrastava 08318
Městské Muzeum, Dobruška 08329
Městské Muzeum, Frenštát pod Radhoštěm 08339
Městské Muzeum, Horažďovice 08358
Městské Muzeum, Klobouky u Brna 08415
Městské Muzeum, Králíky 08428
Městské Muzeum, Ledeč nad Sázavou 08445
Městské Muzeum, Letohrad 08447
Městské Muzeum, Nejdek 08494
Městské Muzeum, Nepomuk 08497
Městské Muzeum, Nové Město nad Metují 08504
Městské Muzeum, Nový Bydžov 08508
Městské Muzeum, Přelouč 08621
Městské Muzeum, Přibyslav 08627
Městské Muzeum, Protivín 08630
Městské Muzeum, Rýmařov 08649
Městské Muzeum, Sadská 08650
Městské Muzeum, Sedlčany 08651
Městské Muzeum, Skuteč 08653
Městské Muzeum, Slapanice 08655
Městské Muzeum, Strážnice 08665
Městské Muzeum, Valašské Klobouky 08705
Městské Muzeum, Velká Bíteš 08709
Městské Muzeum, Vimperk 08718
Městské Muzeum, Žamberk 08737
Městské Muzeum, Zbiroh 08740
Městské Muzeum, Moravský Krumlov 08487
Městské Muzeum, Polička 08555
Městské Muzeum a Galerie, Břeclav 08259
Městské Muzeum a Galerie, Lomnice nad Popelkou 08461
Městské Muzeum a Galerie, Svitavy 08671
Městské Muzeum a Galerie, Vodňany 08722
Městské Muzeum a Památník Jakuba Jana Ryby, Rožmitál pod Třemšínem 08641
Městské Vlastivědné Mudruňkovo Muzeum, Říčany u Prahy 08634
Milevské Muzeum, Milevsko 08478
Místní Muzeum, Kopidlno 08419
Místní Muzeum, Libáň 08448
Místní Muzeum, Městec Králové 08474
Místní Muzeum, Mladá Vožice 08482
Místní Muzeum, Netolice 08498
Muzeum, Bzenec 08287
Muzeum a Galerie, Hranice 08370
Muzeum a Galerie Severního Plzeňska, Kralovice 08429
Muzeum Betlémů, Karlštejn 08404
Muzeum Blansko, Blansko 08251
Muzeum Boskovicka, Boskovice 08253
Muzeum Bučovice, Bučovice 08283
Muzeum Českého Krasu v Berouně - pobačka muzeum v Žebráku, Žebrák 08745
Muzeum Chodska, Domažlice 08332
Muzeum Dr. Bohuslava Horáka, Rokycany 08636
Muzeum Fojtství, Kopřivnice 08420
Muzeum - Františkánský klaster, Kadaň 08397
Muzeum Hlavního Města Prahy, Praha 08596
Muzeum Husitstvi, Žlutice 08754
Muzeum Jihovýchodní Moravy, Zlín 08751
Muzeum Jindřicha Simona Baara, Klenčí pod Čerchovem 08413
Muzeum Jindřicho Hradecka, Jindřichův Hradec 08394
Muzeum Klimkovice, Klimkovice 08414
Muzeum Kralupy, Kralupy nad Vltavou 08430
Muzeum Krnov, Krnov 08434
Muzeum Krupka, Krupka 08436
Muzeum Litovel, Litovel 08459
Muzeum Marie Gardavské, Kojetín 08416
Muzeum Města Brna, Brno 08273
Muzeum Města Ústí nad Labem, Ústí nad Labem 08703
Muzeum Orlických Hor, Rychnov nad Kněžnou 08647
Muzeum Podkrkonoší, Trutnov 08692
Muzeum Polná, Polná 08558
Muzeum Prostějovska, Prostějov 08629
Muzeum Regionu Valšsko ve Vsetíně - Zámek Vsetín, Vsetín 08730
Muzeum Rumburk, Rumburk 08646
Muzeum Strojíren Poldi, Kladno 08409
Muzeum Telč, Telč 08676
Muzeum Těšínska, Český Těšín 08305
Muzeum Těšínska, Havířov 08345
Muzeum Třešť, Třešť 08690
Muzeum Třineckých Železáren, Třinec 08691
Muzeum Týn nad Vltavou, Týn nad Vltavou 08696
Muzeum ve Štramberku, Štramberk 08664
Muzeum Vysočiny Jihlava, Jihlava 08390
Odděleni Oblastni Muzeum Jihovýchodni Moravy, Napajedla 08493
Okresní Muzeum, Děčín 08326
Okresní Muzeum, Ivančice 08376
Okresni Muzeum, Litoměřice 08456
Okresní Muzeum, Louny 08466
Okresní Muzeum, Mělník 08473
Okresní Muzeum, Rakovník 08633
Okresní Muzeum, Vlašim 08721
Okresní Muzeum a Galerie, Jičín 08388
Okresní Muzeum Praha-východ, Brandýs nad Labem 08255
Okresní Vlastivědné Muzeum, Český Krumlov 08303
Okresní Vlastivědné Muzeum, Šumperk 08668
Orlické Muzeum, Choceň 08313
Památník Bible Kralické, Kralice nad Oslavou 08427
Památník Města, Police nad Metují 08552
Památník Venkovského Lidu, Žumberk 08759
Památník Životické Tragedie, Havířov 08346
Podještědské Muzeum Karoliny Světlé, Český Dub 08301
Podlipanské Museum, Český Brod 08300
Prachatické Muzeum, Prachatice 08562
Prácheňské Muzeum, Písek 08540
Regionální Muzeum, Mikulov na Moravě 08476
Regionální Muzeum, Náchod 08492
Regionální Muzeum, Žďár nad Sázavou 08744
Regionální Muzeum K.A. Polánka, Žatec 08738
Regionální Muzeum v Chrudimi, Chrudim 08321
Regionální Muzeum v Teplicích, Teplice 08677
Slezské Zemské Muzeum, Opava 08522
Smrčkův Dům, Soběslav 08659
Stará Škola, Police nad Metuji 08553
Starý Zámek, Jevišovice 08387
Státní Hrad a Zámek, Frýdlant v Čechách 08341
Sucharduv Dům, Nová Paka 08501
Vlastivědné Muzeum, Bělá pod Bezdězem 08244
Vlastivědné Muzeum, Horšovský Týn 08363
Vlastivědné Muzeum, Kamenice nad Lipou 08398
Vlastivědné Muzeum, Kyjov 08441
Vlastivědné Muzeum, Žirovnice 08749
Vlastivědné Muzeum, Broumov 08280
Vlastivědné Muzeum Dr. Hostaše v Klatovech, Klatovy 08412
Výstavní síň Muzeum Těšínska, Jablunkov 08381
Wax Museum Český Krumlov, Český Krumlov 08304
Weisův Dům, Veselí nad Lužnicí 08716
Zámek Kinských, Valašské Meziříčí 08706
Zámek Lemberk, Jablonné v Podještědí 08380
Zámek Manětín, Manětín 08471
Západomoravské Muzeum v Třebíči - Muzeum Jemnice, Jemnice 08384
Znojemský Hrad, Znojmo 08758

Denmark

Amagermuseet, Dragør 08795
Anne Hvides Gård, Svendborg 09083
Århus Bymuseum, Århus 08768
Ballerup Egnsmuseet, Ballerup 08782
Bangsbo Museum, Frederikshavn 08828
Blicheregnens Museum, Kjellerup 08918
Blichermuseet på Herningsholm, Herning 08865
Brahetrolleborg Skolemuseum, Faaborg 08812
Brande Museum, Brande 08789
Brønshøj Museum, Brønshøj 08791
Bymuseet, Skjern 09062
Bymuseet Møntergården, Odense 09005
Dragør Museum, Dragør 08796
Familien Ernsts Samlingers Fond, Assens 08778
Fanø Museum, Fanø 08818
Farvergården, Kerteminde 08913
Frederiksværk Bymuseum, Frederiksværk 08833
Gilleleje Museum, Gilleleje 08836
Greve Museum, Greve 08842
Haderslev Museum, Haderslev 08849
Hadsund Egns Museum, Hadsund 08853
Haslev Museum, Haslev 08855
Heltborg Museum, Hurup Thy 08904
Historisk Museum, Slangerup 09072
Hørsholm Egns Museum, Hørsholm 08900
HTS-Museum, Rødovre 09035
Kalundborg og Omegns Museum, Kalundborg 08911
Karlebo Museum, Kokkedal 08958
Københavns Bymuseum, København 08933
Køge Museum, Køge 08956
Korsør By- og Overfartsmuseum, Korsør 08964
Læsø Museum, Læsø 08967
Lemvig Museum Vesterhus, Lemvig 08972
Løkken Museum, Løkken 08977
Middelfart Museum, Middelfart 08985
Morslands Historiske Museum, Nykøbing Mors 09000
Museerne i Fredericia, Fredericia 08825
Museet Færgegaarden, Jægerspris 08908
Museet for Varde By og Omegn, Varde 09101
Museet Holmen, Løgumkloster 08976
Museet på Sønderskov, Brørup 08792
Museet Tikøb Frysehus, Tikøb 09092
Museum Falsters Minder, Nykøbing Falster 08996
Næstved Museum, Næstved 08987
Nexø Museum, Nexø 08988
Nordfyns Museum, Bogense 08787
Nordsjaellandsk Folkemuseum, Hillerød 08874
Nyborg og Omegns Museer, Nyborg 08995
Odder Museum, Odder 09004
Odsherreds Museum, Asnæs 08777
Ølgod Museum, Ølgod 09019
Øregaard-Museum, Hellerup 08858
Østsjællands Museum, Stevns Museum, Store Heddinge 09080
Otterup Museum, Otterup 09021
Ringe Museum, Ringe 09031
Ringkøbing Museum, Ringkøbing 09032

Ringsted Museum, Ringsted 09033
Roskilde Museum, Roskilde 09043
Sæby Museum and Sæbygaard Manor Museum, Sæby 09051
Skagen By- og Egnsmuseum, Skagen 09057
Skanderborg Museum, Skanderborg 09059
Sorø Amts Museum, Sorø 09076
Sporvejsmuseet Skjoldenæsholm, Jystrup Midtsj 08910
Sundby Samling Bryggergården, Nørresundby 08993
Sundby Samling Raschgården, Nørresundby 08994
Svendborg og Omegns Museum, Svendborg 09087
Sydsjællands Museum, Vordingborg 09115
Tåsinge Skipperhjem og Folkemindesamling, Svendborg 09088
Try Museum, Dronninglund 08798
Værløse Museum, Værløse 09098
Vejle Museum, Vejle 09105

Dominican Republic
Museo Alcázar de Colón, Santo Domingo 09119
Museo Juan Pablo Duarte, Santo Domingo 09126

East Timor
Museum Istana Sultan Ternate, Maluku Utara 09133
Museum Negeri Timor-Timur, Dili 09131

Ecuador
Casa de la Cultura Benjamín Carrion, Cuenca 09148
Museo Aurelio Espinosa Polit, Cotocollao 09147
Museo Aurelio Espinoza Pólit, Quito 09195
Museo Balseros del Mar del Sur, Salango 09225
Museo Cultural Iijdio Guaranga, Guaranga 09167
Museo David Paltán, San Gabriel 09227
Museo de Arte Alberto Mena Caamaño, Quito 09201
Museo de la Ciudad, Quito 09207
Museo de la Comunidad de Agua Blanca, Puerto López 09192
Museo de la Comunidad de Chordeleg, Chordeleg 09145
Museo del Banco Central, Cuenca 09160
Museo del Banco Central, Loja 09185
Museo Historico, Riobamba 09224
Museo Historico Bae Calderon, Guayaquil 09175
Museo María Augusta Urrutia, Quito 09214
Museo Municipal Casa de Alfaro, Montecristi 09189
Museo Quinta Casa de Juan Montalvo, Ambato 09135
Museo Quinta Juan Leon Mera, Ambato 09136
Museo Víctor Alejandro Jaramillo, Ibarra 09184

Egypt
Antiquities Museum, Alexandria 09237
Hadiqat al-Asmak Museum, Zamalek 09308
Mallawy Museum, Mallawy 09301
Municipal Museum, Alexandria 09242
Port-Said Museum, Port Said 09303
Qasr Ali Ibrahim, Zamalek 09309
Saad Zaghlul Museum, Munira 09302
Sharia Museum, Cairo 09288
Tanta Museum, Tanta 09307

Estonia
Aavikute Majamuuseum, Kuressaare 09335
Eesti Vabaõhumuuseum, Tallinn 09365
Harjumaa Muuseum, Keila 09332
Heimtali Koduloomuuseum, Heimtali 09322
Heliloojate Kappide Majamuuseum, Suure-Jaani 09352
Helme Kihelkonnamuuseum, Helme 09323
Hiiumaa Muuseum, Kärdla 09328
Iisaku Muuseum, Iisaku 09325
Järvamaa Muuseum, Paide 09345
Läänemaa Muuseum, Haapsalu 09318
Mahtra Talurahvamuuseum, Juuru 09327
Mart Saare Majamuuseum, Suure-Jaani 09353
Mihkli Talumuuseum, Kihelkonna 09333
Mõisaküla Muuseum, Mõisaküla 09338
Mõniste Muuseum, Kuutsi 09337
Narva Muuseum, Narva 09341
Olustvere Muuseum, Olustvere 09342
Pärnu Muuseum, Pärnu 09344
Palamuse O. Lutsu Kihelkonnakoolimuuseum, Palamuse 09346
Põltsamaa Muuseum, Põltsamaa 09347
Põlva Talurahvamuuseum, Karilatsi 09329
Rakvere Linnus-Muuseum, Rakvere 09349
Ruhnu Muuseum, Ruhnu 09351
Saaremaa Muuseum, Kuressaare 09336
Tallinna Linnamuuseum, Tallinn 09372
Tartu Linnamuuseum, Tartu 09384
Tartumaa Muuseum, Elva 09316
Tarvastu Kihelkonnamuuseum, Tarvastu 09390
Valga Muuseum, Valga 09392
Viljandi Muuseum, Viljandi 09395
Võrumaa Muuseum, Võru 09397

Ethiopia
Castle Museum, Gonder 09404
City Museum, Yirgalem 09406

Finland
Abraham Ojanperän Museo, Liminka 09786
Äänekosken Kaupunginmuseo, Äänekoski 09410
Ähtärin Kotiseutumuseo, Ähtäri 09411
Aleksis Kiven Syntymäkoti, Palojoki 09905
Artjärven Kotiseutumuseo, Artjärvi 09418
Asikkalan Kotiseutumuseo, Asikkala 09419
Ekenäs Museum, Ekenäs 09425
Elimäen Kotiseutumuseo ja Koulumuseo, Elimäki 09428
Espoon Kaupunginmuseo, Espoo 09431
Etelä-Karjalan Museo, Lappeenranta 09760
Glims Talomuseo, Espoo 09434
Hämeenlinnan Kaupungin Historiallinen Museo, Hämeenlinna 09449
Halosenniemi Museo, Tuusula 10143
Haminan Kaupunginmuseo, Hamina 09459
Hauhon Esinemuseo, Hauho 09466
Hausjärven Kotiseutumuseo, Hausjärvi 09468
Heinolan Kaupunginmuseo, Heinola 09469
Helsingin Kaupunginmuseo, Helsinki 09488
Himangan Kotiseutumuseo, Himanka 09550
Itä-Hämeen Museo, Hartola 09465
Jakobstads Museum, Jakobstad 09573
Jalasjärven Museo, Jalasjarvi 09577
Joroisten Kotiseutumuseo, Joroinen 09585
Kaarlelan Kotiseutumuseo, Kokkola 09682
Kalajoen Kotiseutumuseo, Kalajoki 09614
Kalvolan Kunnan Kotiseutumuseo, Iittala 09560
Karkkila Högforsin Työläismuseo, Karkkila 09627
Kaskö Hembygdsmuseum, Kaskinen 09635
Kaurilan Koulumuseo, Tohmajärvi 10108
Keravan Museo, Kerava 09656
Kesälahden Museo, Kesälahti 09659
Keski-Suomen Museo, Jyväskylä 09601
Klaavola Museo, Tuusula 10145
Konneveden Kotiseutumuseo, Konnevesi 09688
Kuddnäs Z. Topeliuksen Lapsuudenkoti, Uusikaarlepyy 10150
Kuhmoisten Kotiseutumuseo, Kuhmoinen 09715
Kuopion Korttelimuseo, Kuopio 09719
Kuusiston Kartano, Kuusisto 09733
Lääninkivalteri Aschanin Talo, Heinola 09470
Lahden Kaupunginmuseo, Lahti 09743
Lemin Kotiseutumuseo, Lemi 09773
Lohilammen Museo, Sammatti 10019
Lohjan Museo, Lohja 09792
Loviisan Kaupungin Museo, Loviisa 09799
Mäntsälän Kotiseutumuseo, Mäntsälä 09808
Malmska Gården, Jakobstad 09574
Maskun Museo, Masku 09821
Matilda Roslin-Kalliolan Kirjailijakoti, Merikarvia 09824
Merimiehenkotimuseo, Oulu 09890
Möhkön Ruukki, Möhkö 09836
Muhoksen Kotiseutumuseo, Muhos 09838
Muonion Kotiseutumuseo, Muonio 09843
Myllysaaren Museo, Valkeakoski 10172
Närpes Hembygdsmuseum, Närpes 09855
Nurmeksen Museo, Nurmes 09873
Nyslotts Landskapsmuseum, Nyslott 09877
Paltamon Kotiseutumuseo, Paltamo 09906
Parainen District Museum, Parainen 09907
Parainen Industrial Museum, Parainen 09908
Peltolan Mäkitupalaismuseo, Tammijärvi 10073
Pieksämäen Museo, Pieksämäki 09925
Pöytyän Kotiseutumuseo, Pöytyä 09936
Pohjanmaan Museo, Vaasa 10161
Pohjois-Karjalan Museo, Joensuu 09581
Pohjois-Pohjanmaan Museo, Oulu 09897
Punkaharjun Kotiseutumuseo, Punkaharju 09963
Rantasalmen Museo, Rantasalmi 09976
Riihimäen Kaupunginmuseo, Riihimäki 09993
Saarijärven Museo, Saarijärvi 10012
Säkylän Kotiseutumuseo, Säkylä 10015
Sagalunds Museum, Kimito 09669
Saukkojärven Kotiseutu- ja Koulumuseo, Ranua 09979
Savonlinnan Maakuntamuseo, Savonlinna 10026
Skyttalan Museo, Parainen 09909
Suur-Savon Museo, Mikkeli 09834
Taalintehtaan Ruukinmuseo, Dalsbruk 09422
Teiskon Kotiseutumuseo, Tampere 10095
Turun Maakuntamuseo, Turku 10134
Vantaan Kaupunginmuseo, Vantaa 10183
Vihdin Museo, Vihti 10195
Wolkoffin Talomuseo, Lappeenranta 09765
Ylä-Savon Kotiseutumuseo, Iisalmi 09558

France
L'Archéodrome de Bourgogne, Meursault 12962
Catacombes, Paris 13479
Château de Tarascon, Tarascon (Bouches-du-Rhône) 14859
Château des Baux, Les Baux-de-Provence 12522
Château-Musée de Lantheuil, Lantheuil 12336
Château-Musée du Rhône, Tournon-sur-Rhône 14963
Cité des Métiers de Tradition, Saint-Laurent-de-la-Plaine 14307
Collections d'Art et d'Histoire, Clermont (Oise) 11328
Conservation Départementale Musées des Pays de l'Ain, Bourg-en-Bresse 10852
Domaine National de Chambord, Chambord 11146
Ecomusée de Hauteluce, Hauteluce 12001
Ecomusée de la Brenne, Le Blanc 12380
Ecomusée de la Communauté Le Creusot Montceau-les-Mines, Le Creusot 12407
Ecomusée de la Forêt Méditerranéenne, Gardanne 11839
Ecomusée de la Sainte-Baume, Plan-d'Aups 13747
Ecomusée de l'Ile-de-Groix, Ile-de-Groix 12046
Ecomusée Départemental de la Vendée, Les Épesses 12533
Ecomusée des Monts d'Arrée, Commana 11368
Ecomusée des Monts d'Arrée, Saint-Rivoal 14459
Ecomusée du Mont-Lozère, Le Pont-de-Montvert 12470
Ecomusée du Pays de Rennes, Rennes (Ille-et-Vilaine) 13939
Écomusée du Val de Saône, Seurre 14734
Écomusée Sauvegarde du Vieil Auzon, Auzon 10517
Faïences et Emaux, Longwy 12657
Familistère de Guise, Guise 11978
Maison de Pays, Pont-sur-Sambre 13820
Maison du Pays Roussillonnais, Roussillon (Isère) 14063
Maison du Vieil Alby, Albi 10274
Musée, Quiberon 13892
Musée Adrien-Mentienne, Bry-sur-Marne 10952
Musée Agathois, Agde 10228
Musée Agro-Pastoral d'Aussois, Aussois 10495
Musée Alpin, Chamonix-Mont-Blanc 11148
Musée André Dunoyer-de-Ségonzac, Boussy-Saint-Antoine 10877
Musée Archéologique, Mormoiron 13166
Musée Archéologique Hôtel Dieu, Cavaillon 11095
Musée Augustin-Bernard, Bourbon-l'Archambault 10847
Musée Basque et de l'Histoire de Bayonne, Bayonne 10621
Musée Bigouden, Pont-l'Abbé 13812
Musée Bigourdan du Vieux Moulin, Bagnères-de-Bigorre 10559
Musée Biochet-Brechot, Caudebec-en-Caux 11087
Musée Bonaparte, Auxonne 10513
Musée Bonnevallais, Bonneval 10797
Musée Bourguignon Perrin de Puycousin, Tournus 14964
Musée Briard et de la Crypte Mérovingienne, Jouarre 12091
Musée Calbet, Grisolles 11958
Musée Carnavalet - Histoire de Paris, Paris 13539
Musée-Centre de Documentation Alfred Desmasures, Hirson 12027
Musée Charles-de-Bruyères, Remiremont 13936
Musée Château du Bucheneck, Soultz-Haut-Rhin 14795
Musée Ciotaden, La Ciotat 12156
Musée Communal, Clérac 11316
Musée d'Archéologie Bargoin, Clermont-Ferrand 11321
Musée d'Art et d'Archéologie, Hyères 12041
Musée d'Art et d'Histoire, Cholet 11298
Musée d'Art et d'Histoire, Frontignan 11823
Musée d'Art et d'Histoire, Grézolles 11954
Musée d'Art et d'Histoire, Kaysersberg 12112
Musée d'Art et d'Histoire, Livry-Gargan 12637
Musée d'Art et d'Histoire, Nice 13311
Musée d'Art et d'Histoire, Poissy 13784
Musée d'Art et d'Histoire, Rueil-Malmaison 14074
Musée d'Art et d'Histoire, Saint-Julien-du-Sault 14297
Musée d'Art et d'Histoire, Rochefort (Charente-Maritime) 13999
Musée d'Art et d'Histoire de Toul, Toul 14924
Musée d'Art et d'Histoire des Côtes d'Armor, Saint-Brieuc 14132
Musée d'Art et d'Histoire Louis Senlecq, L'Isle-Adam 12626
Musée d'Art et d'Histoire Roger Rodière, Montreuil-sur-Mer 13144
Musée d'Art et Historique, Montbéliard 13059
Musée d'Art et Traditions Populaires, Binic 10737
Musée d'Arts et de Traditions Populaires, Palinges 13458
Musée d'Arts et de Traditions Populaires, Saint-Paul-de-Fenouillet 14400
Musée d'Assier, Feurs 11729
Musée de Biot, Biot 10739
Musée de Borda, Dax 11486
Musée de Bouxwiller et du Pays de Hanau, Bouxwiller 10880
Musée de Cervières, Cervières 11118
Musée de Charroux et de son Canton, Charroux-d'Allier 11191
Musée de Cognac, Cognac 11342
Musée de Cosne, Cosne-Cours-sur-Loire 11416
Musée de Dol, Dol-de-Bretagne 11540
Musée de France de Berck-sur-Mer, Berck-sur-Mer 10686
Musée de Jouques, Jouques 12094
Musée de la Bonneterie, Troyes 15005
Musée de la Corbillière, Mer 12941
Musée de la Correrie, Saint-Pierre-de-Chartreuse 14411
Musée de la Mairie de Crécy, Crécy-la-Chapelle 11452
Musée de la Résistance en Zone Interdite, Denain 11495
Musée de la Roue Tourne, La Mothe-Achard 12209
Musée de la Tour aux Puces, Thionville 14888
Musée de la Tour de l'Abbaye, Jouarre 12092
Musée de la Vie Bourguignonne Perrin-de-Puycousin, Dijon 11525
Musée de la Vie en Bassin Minier, Escaudain 11641
Musée de la Ville de Saverne, Saverne 14662
Musée de la Ville de Strasbourg, Strasbourg 14825
Musée de l'Academie de la Val d'Isère, Moutiers (Savoie) 13199
Musée de l'Alta Rocca, Lévie 12572
Musée de l'Ancien Havre, Le Havre 12424
Musée de l'Auditoire, Sainte-Suzanne 14553
Musée de l'Eau de Vie et des Vieux Métiers, Valognes 15071
Musée de l'Histoire Vivante Parc Montreau, Montreuil (Seine-Saint-Denis) 13143
Musée de l'Historire de Rosny, Rosny-sous-Bois 14041
Musée de l'Hôpital, Yssingeaux 15330
Musée de l'Hôtel de Vermandois, Senlis 14711
Musée de l'île d'Oleron Aliénor d'Aquitaine, Saint-Pierre-d'Oléron 14417
Musée de l'Ostrévant, Bouchain 10827
Musée de Maison-Alfort, Maisons-Alfort 12775
Musée de Montmartre, Paris 13582
Musée de Morlaix et Maison du 9 Grand Rue, Morlaix 13163
Musée de Nogent, Nogent-sur-Marne 13352
Musée de Salon et de la Crau, Salon-de-Provence 14590
Musée de Sarreguemines, Sarreguemines 14623
Musée de Suresnes René-Sordes, Suresnes 14845
Musée de Verrières-le-Buisson, Verrières-le-Buisson 15142
Musée de Vieux Sallèles, Sallèles-d'Aude 14577
Musée d'Entrecasteaux, Entrecasteaux 11619
Musée Départemental de Flandre, Cassel 11067
Musée Départemental Ignon-Fabre, Mende 12925
Musée des Alpilles, Saint-Rémy-de-Provence 14451
Musée des Amis de Thann, Thann 14880
Musée des Amis du Vieux Saint-Étienne, Saint-Étienne 14201
Musée des Arts et Traditions Populaires, Bressuire 10905
Musée des Canonniers Sédentaires de Lille, Lille 12600
Musée des Flûtes du Monde, Bollène 10790
Musée des Mines d'Argent des Gorges du Fournel, L'Argentière-la-Bessée 12344
Musée des Traditions Locales, Sainte-Maxime 14544
Musée d'Ethnographie Corse, Bastia 10603
Musée d'Histoire de la Ville et d'Ethnographie du Pays Malouin, Saint-Malo (Ille-et-Vilaine) 14341
Musée d'Histoire de Marseille, Marseille 12865
Musée d'Histoire et d'Art, Mirande 12991
Musée d'Histoire Local, Maubourguet 12891
Musée d'Histoire Locale, Saint-Paul-de-Vence 14402
Musée d'Histoire Locale, Saint-Renan 14455
Musée d'Histoire Locale et des Vieux Métiers, Saint-Ciers-sur-Gironde 14153
Musée d'Orbigny-Bernon, La Rochelle 12243
Musée du Château, Flers 11745
Musée du Château, Fougères (Ille-et-Vilaine) 11793
Musée du Château de Dourdan, Dourdan 11569
Musée du Château de Vitré, Vitré 15275
Musée du Château d'Henri IV, Nérac 13281
Musée du Château Paul Pastre, Marsillargues 12873
Musée du Château Saint-Jean, Nogent-le-Rotrou 13351
Musée du Châtillonnais, Châtillon-sur-Seine 11243
Musée du Compagnonnage, Paris 13600
Musée du Débarquement à Utah Beach, Sainte-Marie-du-Mont 14542
Musée du Dessin et de l'Estampe Originale, Gravelines 11929
Musée du Dolder, Riquewihr 13978
Musée du Donjon de la Toque, Huriel 12039
Musée du Florentinois, Saint-Florentin 14217
Musée du Léon, Lesneven 12562
Musée du Noyonnais, Noyon 13374
Musée du Patrimoine, Roquebrune-sur-Argens 14026
Musée du Patrimoine, Six-Fours-les-Plages 14756
Musée du Patrimoine des Pères de Bétharram, Lestelle-Bétharram 12565
Musée du Patrimoine et de la Dentelle, Chantilly 11165
Musée du Pays Brignolais, Brignoles 10931
Musée du Pays de Thônes, Thônes 14894
Musée du Pays Vaurais, Lavaur 12368
Musée du Pilori, Niort 13345
Musée du Présidial, Castelnaudary 11078
Musée du Ranquet, Clermont-Ferrand 11323
Musée du Rethélois e du Porcien, Rethel 13947
Musée du Saut du Tarn, Saint-Juéry 14293
Musée du Sceau Alsacien, La Petite-Pierre 12219
Musée du Temps qui Passe, Carquefou 11061
Musée du Terroir, Villeneuve-d'Ascq 15221
Musée du Terroir Bressan, Montpont 13136
Musée du Textile et de la Vie Sociale, Fourmies 11800
Musée du Trièves, Mens 12932
Musée du Val-de-Cher, Selles-sur-Cher 14699
Musée du Valois, Vez 15151
Musée du Vieil Argenteuil, Argenteuil 10407
Musée du Vieux Brest, Brest 10911
Musée du Vieux Clairac, Clairac 11308
Musée du Vieux Figeac, Figeac 11733
Musée du Vieux Granville, Granville 11912
Musée du Vieux Lambesc, Lambesc 12312
Musée du Vieux Nîmes, Nîmes 13341
Musée du Vieux Pérouges, Meximieux 12966
Musée du Vieux Toulon, Toulon (Var) 14930
Musée du Vieux Toulouse, Toulouse 14948
Musée du Vieux-Tréport, Le Tréport 12488
Musée du Vieux Warcq, Warcq 15302
Musée du Village, Saint-Sorlin-d'Arves 14478
Musée du Vivarais Protestant, Pranles 13864
Musée Edmond Rostand, Cambo-les-Bains 11009
Musée et Pavillon Flaubert, Croisset 11462
Musée Ethnologique Intercommunal du Vermandois, Vermand 15136
Musée Eugène Farcot, Sainville 14565
Musée Friry, Remiremont 13937
Musée Gadagne, Lyon 12745
Musée-Galerie Alexis et Gustave-Adolf Mossa, Nice 13319
Musée Galerie Honoré Camos, Bargemon 10591
Musée Gallé-Juillet, Creil 11453

Musée Gardanne Autrefois, Gardanne 11840
Musée Georges Borias, Uzès 15035
Musée Gletton, Vaiges 15040
Musée Greuze, Tournus 14965
Musée Guillion, Romanèche-Thorins 14014
Musée Henri-Barre, Thouars 14903
Musée Henri Boez, Maubeuge 12890
Musée Henri Dupuis, Saint-Omer 14388
Musée Historique, Gourdon (Alpes-Maritimes) 11893
Musée Historique, Haguenau 11986
Musée Historique, Strasbourg 14835
Musée Historique de Troyes et de la Champagne, Troyes 15006
Musée Historique du Bailliage de Rouffach, Rouffach 14057
Musée Historique du Centre-Var, Le Luc 12432
Musée Historique et Lapidaire, Morlaas 13161
Musée Historique et Militaire, Huningue 12036
Musée-Hôtel Le Vergeur, Reims 13932
Musée J.B. Mathon et André Durand, Neufchâtel-en-Bray 13285
Musée Jeanne d'Arc, Chinon 11291
Musée Johannique, Vaucouleurs 15097
Musée Joseph Denais, Beaufort-en-Vallée 10637
Musée la Muse, Mérindol 12945
Musée Labenche d'Art et d'Histoire, Brive-la-Gaillarde 10939
Musée Louis-Braille, Coupvray 11429
Musée Louis-Jourdan, Saint-Paul-de-Varax 14401
Musée Maçonnique de la Grande Loge de France, Paris 13625
Musée Maison des Templiers, Salers 14570
Musée Marc Deydier, Cucuron 11468
Musée Maurice Poignant, Bourg-sur-Gironde 10859
Musée Montebello, Trouville-sur-Mer 14999
Musée Municipal, Amboise 10314
Musée Municipal, Châtellerault 11233
Musée Municipal, Conques 11396
Musée Municipal, Cusset 11477
Musée Municipal, Forcalquier 11785
Musée Municipal, Mazan 12903
Musée Municipal, Saint-Calais 14137
Musée Municipal, Saint-Germain-Laval 14245
Musée Municipal, Villandraut 15170
Musée Municipal A.G. Poulain, Vernon 15140
Musée Municipal Albert Marzelles, Marmande 12828
Musée Municipal Apt, Apt 10387
Musée Municipal Auguste Grasset, Varzy 15092
Musée Municipal Bar-sur-Seine, Bar-sur-Seine 10584
Musée Municipal Bourbon-Lancy, Bourbon-Lancy 10846
Musée Municipal Châteaubriant, Châteaubriant 11212
Musée Municipal de Cambrai, Cambrai 11013
Musée Municipal de Civray, Civray 11306
Musée Municipal de Draguignan, Draguignan 11577
Musée Municipal de la Vie Sauvage, Le Bugue 12393
Musée Municipal de l'Évêché, Limoges 12616
Musée Municipal de Montmorillon, Montmorillon 13113
Musée Municipal de Saint-Gaudens, Saint-Gaudens 14226
Musée Municipal de Sault, Sault (Vaucluse) 14639
Musée Municipal des Beaux Arts et d'Histoire Naturelle, Châteaudun 11214
Musée Municipal des Capucins, Coulommiers 11427
Musée Municipal d'Histoire et d'Archéologie, Harnes 11991
Musée Municipal d'Orbec, Orbec 13414
Musée Municipal du Château, Gannat 11836
Musée Municipal du Présidial, Bazas 10624
Musée Municipal Frédéric Blandin, Nevers 13304
Musée Municipal Gautron du Coudray, Marzy 12885
Musée Municipal Georges Turpin, Parthenay 13662
Musée Municipal Paul Lafran, Saint-Chamas 14143
Musée Municipal Robert Dubois-Corneau, Brunoy 10949
Musée Municipal Urbain-Cabrol, Villefranche-de-Rouergue 15204
Musée National d'Enéerune, Nissan-lez-Ensérune 13348
Musée Oberlin, Waldersbach 15299
Musée Percheron, Mortagne-au-Perche 13171
Musée Pierre-Gaudin, Puteaux 13886
Musée Pigeard, Magny-en-Vexin 12764
Musée Pillon, Chaumont-en-Vexin 11248
Musée Quentovic, Etaples 11667
Musée Raymond Peynet, Brassac-les-Mines 10893
Musée Régional d'Auvergne, Riom 13973
Musée Régional de Fouras, Fouras 11798
Musée Régional de l'Orléanais, Beaugency 10638
Musée Régional Dupuy-Méstreau, Saintes 14559
Musée Roybet Fould, Courbevoie 11431
Musée Saint-Remi, Reims 13933
Musée Sainte-Croix, Poitiers 13787
Musée Serret, Saint-Amarin 14101
Musée Suffren et du Vieux Saint-Cannat, Saint-Cannat 14138
Musée Tour Saint-Michel, Guérande 11966
Musée Vauban, Neuf-Brisach 13284
Musée Vendéen, Fontenay-le-Comte 11772
Musée Victor Aubert, Maule 12892
Musée Villageois d'Orgon, Orgon 13425
Musée Villeneuvien, Villeneuve-sur-Yonne 15238
Musées de Sens, Sens 14715
Musées des Colombiers Cauchois, Oherville 13390
Museo Départemental A. Demard, Le-Haut-du-Them-Château-Lambert 12422
Palais Bénédictine, Fécamp 11713
Parc Château de Valencay, Valençay 15048
Réserve Géologique de Haute-Provence, Digne-les-Bains 11515
Sainte Maison de la Flocellière, La Flocellière 12182
Site Gallo-Romain de Grand, Grand 11901
Village-Musée, Fos-sur-Mer 11789

Georgia

State Museum of Abkhasia, Suchumi 15357

Germany

Abteilung Handwerk und dörfliches Leben des Heimatmuseums Neu-Ulm, Neu-Ulm 19006
Ahler Kråm - Volkskundliche Sammlung, Partenstein 19351
Albgaumuseum, Ettlingen 16974
Alexander-Mack-Museum, Bad Berleburg 15607
Allgäu-Museum, Kempten 18059
Alt-Arnstorf-Haus, Arnstorf 15515
Alt-Freden-Sammlung, Freden 17095
Alt-Stade im Baumhaus, Stade 20021
Alte Oberamtei, Gerabronn 17249
Das Alte Zollhaus Heimatmuseum, Hitzacker 17770
Altes Amtshaus, Werne 20524
Altes Haus, Greifenstein 17384
Altes Rathaus, Lüneburg 18554
Altonaer Museum in Hamburg, Hamburg 17527
Amrumer Heimatmuseum, Nebel 18983
Amtsturm-Museum, Lüchow, Wendland 18547
Archäologische Sammlung mit Heimatvertriebenenstube und Kruk-Sammlung, Königsbrunn 18172
Auberlehaus, Trossingen 20217
August-Holländer-Museum, Emsdetten 16866
Ausstellung Juden in Buttenhausen, Münsingen 18928
Aventinus-Museum, Abensberg 15389
Bachgau-Museum, Großostheim 17435
Bad Schwalbacher Kur-Stadt-Apotheken-Museum, Bad Schwalbach 15737
Badhaus Museum und Galerie, Kulmbach 18265
Badisches Landesmuseum Karlsruhe, Karlsruhe 17991
Bartholomäus-Schmucker-Heimatmuseum, Ruhpolding 19714
Bauernhausmuseum Knechtenhofen, Oberstaufen 19207
Bauernstube, Ellwangen 16835
Berg- und Stadtmuseum, Obernkirchen 19188
Bergbau- und Heimatmuseum, Goldkronach 17345
Bergwinkelmuseum, Schlüchtern 19804
Besucherbergwerk Vereinigt Zwitterfeld zu Zinnwald, Zinnwald-Georgenfeld 20757
Bezirksmuseum, Buchen 16386
Bezirksmuseum Dachau, Dachau 16522
Bezirksmuseum Marzahn-Hellersdorf, Berlin 15921
Bismarck-Museum, Bad Kissingen 15674
Blaues Schloß, Obernzenn 19191
BLM Bauernhaus-Museum Bortfeld, Wendeburg 20509
Bodenheimer Heimatmuseum, Bodenheim 16207
Börde-Heimatmuseum, Lamstedt 18298
Bördenheimatmuseum Heeslingen, Heeslingen 17658
Bomann-Museum Celle, Celle 16452
Braith-Mali-Museum, Biberach an der Riß 16138
Brandenburgisches Textilmuseum Forst, Forst, Lausitz 17023
Braunauer Heimatmuseum, Forchheim, Oberfranken 17019
Braunschweigisches Landesmuseum, Braunschweig 16293
Brensbach Museum und Galerie im alten Rathaus, Brensbach 16354
Breuberg-Museum, Breuberg 16358
Brünner Heimatmuseum, Schwäbisch Gmünd 19860
Brüxer und Komotauer Heimatstuben, Erlangen 16916
Brunnenmuseum, Bad Vilbel 15758
s'Buchholze Hisli, Schuttertal 19856
Buchholzer Heimatmuseum, Buchholz in der Nordheide 16389
Burg Beeskow, Beeskow 15867
Burg Hagen, Hagen bei Bremerhaven 17477
Burg-Museum, Parsberg 19350
Burg- und Schloßmuseum Allstedt, Allstedt 15434
Burg- und Stadtmuseum Königstein, Königstein im Taunus 18181
Burg Vischering, Lüdinghausen 18552
Burghofmuseum, Soest 19978
Burgmuseum, Lenzen, Elbe 18441
Burgmuseum, Wolfsegg 20666
Burgmuseum Bad Bodenteich, Bad Bodenteich 15618
Burgmuseum Waldeck, Waldeck, Hessen 20357
Burgturm Davert, Ascheberg, Westfalen 15535
Buxtehude Museum für Regionalgeschichte und Kunst, Buxtehude 16439
Christian-Wolff-Haus, Halle, Saale 17508
Denkmalhof Rauchhaus Möllin, Möllin 18764
Detlefsen-Museum, Glückstadt 17304
Dithmarscher Landesmuseum, Meldorf 18695
Dörpmuseum Münkeboe, Südbrookmerland 20118
Dokumentation Obersalzberg - Orts- und Zeitgeschichte, Berchtesgaden 15884
Domowniski muzej Dešno, Dissen, Niederlausitz 16625
Dorf- und Heimatmuseum, Winterbach bei Schorndorf 20614
Dorfmuseum, Bad Alexandersbad 15590
Dorfmuseum, Gahlenz 17189
Dorfmuseum, Kienberg, Oberbayern 18082
Dorfmuseum, Schönbach 19822
Dorfmuseum Alter Forsthof, Wetter, Hessen 20549
Dorfmuseum Altkirchen, Altkirchen 15458
Dorfmuseum Daniel-Martin-Haus, Rauschenberg 19504
Dorfmuseum Delligsen, Delligsen 16566
Dorfmuseum Günzach, Günzach 17454
Dorfmuseum im Greifenhaus, Hausen, Oberfranken 17646
Dorfmuseum Mertingen, Mertingen 18715
Dorfmuseum Ostheim, Nidderau 19090
Dorfmuseum Tündern, Hameln 17574
Dorfmuseum Weckbach, Weilbach 20441
Dorfmuseum Wilsenroth, Dornburg, Westerwald 16649
Dorfstube Münchholzhausen, Wetzlar 20550
Dotzheimer Museum, Wiesbaden 20570
Dr.-Bauer-Heimatmuseum, Bad Rothenfelde 15720
Dr. Eisenbarth- und Heimatmuseum, Oberviechtach 19213
Dreieich-Museum, Dreieich 16673
Drilandmuseum Gronau, Gronau, Westfalen 17414
Dümmer-Museum, Lembruch 18428
Egerländer-Elbogner Heimatstuben, Illertissen 17885
Egerland-Museum, Marktredwitz 18652
Ehemaliges Schlossvorwerk, Bremervörde 16348
Eichsfelder Heimatmuseum, Heilbad Heiligenstadt 17684
Eidelstedter Heimatmuseum, Hamburg 17535
Eiderstedter Heimatmuseum, Sankt Peter-Ording 19757
Eifelmuseum Blankenheim, Blankenheim, Ahr 16179
Elbschiffahrtsmuseum mit stadtgeschichtlicher Sammlung, Lauenburg 18350
Elsenzer Heimatstuben, Eppingen 16878
Emslandmuseum Lingen, Lingen 18482
Emslandmuseum Schloß Clemenswerth, Sögel 19974
Erbacher Heimatzimmer, Eltville 16841
Ernst-Moritz-Arndt-Museum, Garz, Rügen 17205
Erzgebirgisches Heimatmuseum Hospital Sankt Johannis, Sayda 19763
Die Eulenburg, Rinteln 19617
Fehnmusuem Eiland, Großefehn 17427
Felsberg-Museum, Lautertal, Odenwald 18362
Felsenmeer-Museum, Hemer 17708
Feringa Sach - Ortsgeschichte und heimatkundliche Sammlung, Unterföhring 20268
Festung Marienberg mit Fürstenbaumuseum, Würzburg 20692
Fichtelgebirgsmuseum, Wunsiedel 20708
Fischer- und Webermuseum Steinhude, Steinhude 20053
Flößer- und Heimatmuseum, Wolfach 20647
Focke-Museum, Bremen 16321
Fossilien- und Heimatmuseum, Messel 18718
Fränkische-Schweiz-Museum, Pottenstein 19438
Fränkisches Bauern- und Handwerkermuseum Kirchenburg Mönchsondheim, Iphofen 17914
Frankenwaldmuseum, Kronach 18244
Franziskanermuseum, Villingen-Schwenningen 20316
Frau Holle Expreß, Hessisch-Lichtenau 17745
Frauen Museum Wiesbaden, Wiesbaden 20572
Freilichtmuseum am Kiekeberg, Rosengarten, Kreis Harburg 19648
Freilichtmuseum "Frelsdorfer Brink", Frelsdorf 17126
Freilichtmuseum Rhöner Museumsdorf, Tann, Rhön 20141
Friesisches Heimatmuseum, Niebüll 19092
Froaschgass-Museum, Wettenberg 20546
Fürstenzimmer im Schloß Kirchheim, Kirchheim unter Teck 18095
Fürstlich Leiningensche Sammlungen - Heimatmuseum, Amorbach 15485
Gäubodenmuseum, Straubing 20077
Gaildorfer Stadtmuseum im Alten Schloß, Gaildorf 17192
Galerie Biebertal, Biebertal 16146
Gemeinde-Heimatmuseum Harsum, Harsum 17621
Gemeindemuseum im Historischen Rathaus, Seeheim-Jugenheim 19918
Geroldsecker-Museum im Storchenturm, Lahr, Schwarzwald 18289
Glashaus-Derneburg, Holle 17822
Glasmuseum Weisswasser, Weisswasser 20503
Glauberg-Museum, Glauburg 17297
Goethe-Gedenkstätte im Amtshaus, Ilmenau 17890
Goslarer Museum, Goslar 17349
Goslarer Zinnfiguren-Museum, Goslar 17350
Grafschafter Museum im Moerser Schloß, Moers 18776
Grafschaftsmuseum, Wertheim 20532
Graslitzer Gedenk- und Informationsraum, Aschaffenburg 15523
Greifensteiner Burgmuseum, Greifenstein 17386
Grenzland- und Trenckmuseum, Waldmünchen 20371
Grenzlandheimatstuben des Heimatkreises Marienbad, Neualbenreuth 19011
Hällisch-Fränkisches Museum, Schwäbisch Hall 19864
Härtsfeld-Museum, Neresheim 18994
Haidhausen-Museum, München 18854
Haimatmuseum Ginsheim-Gustavsburg, Ginsheim-Gustavsburg 17290
Haimatmuseum Großenlüder, Großenlüder 17430
Hallertauer Heimat- und Hopfenmuseum, Mainburg 18594
Hallertauer Hopfen- und Heimatmuseum, Geisenfeld 17216
Hamaland-Museum und Westmünsterländische Hofanlage, Vreden 20335
Hanauer Museum, Kehl 18047
Handwerksmuseum Groß-Gerau, Gross-Gerau 17415
Haniel Museum, Duisburg 16749
Haus am Kleistpark, Berlin 15984
Haus der Heimat, Olbernhau 19248
Haus der Ortsgeschichte, Schwäbisch Hall 19866
Haus der Stadtgeschichte, Offenbach am Main 19240
Haus der Stadtgeschichte, Donauwörth 16637
Haus des Gastes mit heimatkundlicher Sammlung, Gößweinstein 17331
Haus Kickelhain, Mosbach, Baden 18793
Haus Rottels, Neuss 19064
Haus zum Stockfisch - Stadtmuseum, Erfurt 16903
Hausenhäusl, Reit im Winkl 19554
Heidemuseum Dat ole Huus, Bispingen 16173
Heidemuseum Rischmannshof Walsrode, Walsrode 20383
Heiliggeistkirche, Landshut 18309
Heimat Museum Amöneburg, Amöneburg 15484
Heimat-Museum Maintal, Maintal 18597
Heimat- und Bauernmuseum, Bruck, Oberpfalz 16371
Heimat- und Bergbaumuseum, Nentershausen, Hessen 18993
Heimat- und Brauereimuseum, Pleinfeld 19414
Heimat- und Braunkohlemuseum, Steinberg, Oberpfalz 20046
Heimat- und Buddelmuseum, Osten 19289
Heimat- und Dorfmuseum Pfaffenwiesbach, Wehrheim 20421
Heimat- und Grimmelshausenmuseum, Oberkirch 19180
Heimat- und Humboldtmuseum, Eibau 16796
Heimat- und Industriemuseum, Kolbermoor 18199
Heimat- und Industriemuseum, Wackersdorf 20336
Heimat- und Schiffahrtsmuseum, Heinsen 17698
Heimat- und Ski-Museum, Braunlage 16291
Heimat- und Torfmuseum, Gröbenzell 17407
Heimat- und Uhrenmuseum, Villingen-Schwenningen 20317
Heimat- und Wallfahrtsmuseum, Xanten 20728
Heimatdiele Kutenholz, Kutenholz 18278
Heimatecke am Seifenbach, Beierfeld 15868
Heimatgeschichtliches Museum, Modautal 18760
Heimathaus, Nesselwang 19000
Heimathaus Alte Mühle, Schladen 19788
Heimathaus Aying, Aying 15581
Heimathaus De Theeshof, Schneverdingen 19820
Heimathaus der Stadt Lauingen, Lauingen 18357
Heimathaus der Stadt Warendorf, Warendorf 20400
Heimathaus des Rupertiwinkels und Heimatstube der Sudetendeutschen, Tittmoning 20182
Heimathaus Dingden, Hamminkeln 17580
Heimathaus Greven Worth, Selsingen 19936
Heimathaus Mehedorf, Bremervörde 16349
Heimathaus Neuchl-Anwesen, Hohenschäftlarn 17812
Heimathaus Pfarrkirchen, Pfarrkirchen 19386
Heimathaus Sittensen, Sittensen 19973
Heimathaus Sonthofen, Sonthofen 20001
Heimathaus Wendelstein, Wendelstein, Mittelfranken 20511
Heimathausanlage Schafstall, Bremervörde 16350
Heimatkabinett Westerholt, Herten 17740
Heimatkundliche Sammlung, Elzach 16844
Heimatkundliche Sammlung, Heideck 17661
Heimatkundliche Sammlung, Heroldsbach 17732
Heimatkundliche Sammlung, Isen 17919
Heimatkundliche Sammlung, Lich 18453
Heimatkundliche Sammlung, Pfronten 19392
Heimatkundliche Sammlung Bergendorf, Holzheim bei Rain, Lech 17828
Heimatkundliche Sammlung des Heimatdienstes Hindelang, Bad Hindelang 15662
Heimatkundliche Sammlung und Ausstellung, Hermannsburg 17724
Heimatkundliches Museum, Friedeburg, Ostfriesland 17140
Heimatmuseum, Adelsdorf 15394
Heimatmuseum, Aidlingen 15413
Heimatmuseum, Aken 15415
Heimatmuseum, Allendorf, Lumda 15431
Heimatmuseum, Angermünde 15492
Heimatmuseum, Arneburg 15511
Heimatmuseum, Bad Rodach 15719
Heimatmuseum, Bad Schandau 15733
Heimatmuseum, Blindheim 16187
Heimatmuseum, Camburg 16450
Heimatmuseum, Dahlen, Sachsen 16529
Heimatmuseum, Dietenhofen 16602
Heimatmuseum, Eibelstadt 16797
Heimatmuseum, Elsenfeld 16839
Heimatmuseum, Eltmann 16840
Heimatmuseum, Ergoldsbach 16908
Heimatmuseum, Falkensee 16984
Heimatmuseum, Falkenstein, Vogtland 16986
Heimatmuseum, Frankenberg, Sachsen 17027
Heimatmuseum, Friedland bei Neubrandenburg 17142
Heimatmuseum, Gerstungen 17264
Heimatmuseum, Grabow, Mecklenburg 17366
Heimatmuseum, Greußen 17397
Heimatmuseum, Großröhrsdorf, Oberlausitz 17437
Heimatmuseum, Großzschepa 17444
Heimatmuseum, Haimhausen 17493
Heimatmuseum, Haynsburg 17653
Heimatmuseum, Karlstein am Main 18010
Heimatmuseum, Kirchdorf auf Poel 18090
Heimatmuseum, Kölleda 18126
Heimatmuseum, Lengenfeld, Vogtland 18435
Heimatmuseum, Leupahn 18446
Heimatmuseum, Luckenwalde 18509
Heimatmuseum, Markranstädt 18641

Heimatmuseum, Mering 18710
Heimatmuseum, Möckmühl 18762
Heimatmuseum, Moosburg an der Isar 18788
Heimatmuseum, Neustadt in Sachsen 19082
Heimatmuseum, Oberndorf am Neckar 19185
Heimatmuseum, Osterwieck 19297
Heimatmuseum, Perleberg 19376
Heimatmuseum, Polling, Kreis Weilheim 19426
Heimatmuseum, Radeburg 19472
Heimatmuseum, Rattenberg 19497
Heimatmuseum, Reichenau an der Pulsnitz 19541
Heimatmuseum, Rötha 19636
Heimatmuseum, Sandhausen 19741
Heimatmuseum, Sternberg 20061
Heimatmuseum, Strausberg 20078
Heimatmuseum, Treuenbrietzen 20202
Heimatmuseum, Weisendorf 20487
Heimatmuseum, Wiesenbach, Baden 20577
Heimatmuseum, Wilsdruff 20602
Heimatmuseum, Mülheim an der Ruhr 18815
Heimatmuseum Ahlem, Hannover 17595
Heimatmuseum Ahrbergen, Giesen 17276
Heimatmuseum Aichach, Aichach 15408
Heimatmuseum Algermissen, Algermissen 15430
Heimatmuseum Alter Pfarrhof, Raisting 19479
Heimatmuseum Altes Rathaus, Angelburg 15490
Heimatmuseum Altes Rathaus, Böhl-Iggelheim 16215
Heimatmuseum Altes Schulhaus, Böhl-Iggelheim 16216
Heimatmuseum Amt Blankenstein, Gladenbach 17293
Heimatmuseum Aschen, Diepholz 16597
Heimatmuseum Auetal, Auetal 15547
Heimatmuseum Bad Aibling, Bad Aibling 15589
Heimatmuseum Bad Eilsen, Bad Eilsen 15635
Heimatmuseum Bad Endbach, Bad Endbach 15639
Heimatmuseum Bad König, Bad König 15676
Heimatmuseum Bad Laer, Bad Laer 15686
Heimatmuseum Bad Lauterberg, Bad Lauterberg 15689
Heimatmuseum Bad Münder, Bad Münder 15695
Heimatmuseum Bad Oldesloe, Bad Oldesloe 15711
Heimatmuseum Balingen, Balingen 15798
Heimatmuseum Bammental, Bammental 15820
Heimatmuseum Battenberg-Laisa, Battenberg, Eder 15829
Heimatmuseum Baunach, Baunach 15831
Heimatmuseum Beratzhausen, Beratzhausen 15882
Heimatmuseum Berching mit Ritter-v.-Gluck-Archiv, Berching 15883
Heimatmuseum Bergen-Enkheim, Frankfurt am Main 17050
Heimatmuseum Berkatal, Berkatal 15904
Heimatmuseum Berkatal, Berkatal 15905
Heimatmuseum Betzenstein, Betzenstein 16132
Heimatmuseum Biebesheim, Biebesheim 16148
Heimatmuseum Biebesheim, Biebesheim 16149
Heimatmuseum Biebrich, Wiesbaden 20574
Heimatmuseum Bislich, Wesel 20534
Heimatmuseum Blankenau, Hosenfeld 17844
Heimatmuseum Bleicherode, Bleicherode 16185
Heimatmuseum Bockwindmühle, Lebusa 18364
Heimatmuseum Börgerende-Rethwisch, Börgerende 16219
Heimatmuseum Boizenburg, Boizenburg 16224
Heimatmuseum Boxberg, Boxberg, Baden 16267
Heimatmuseum Breckerfeld, Breckerfeld 16308
Heimatmuseum Brigachtal, Brigachtal 16360
Heimatmuseum Brüssow, Brüssow 16381
Heimatmuseum Brunsbüttel, Brunsbüttel 16383
Heimatmuseum Buchenau, Dautphetal 16555
Heimatmuseum Buchenberg, Buchenberg bei Kempten 16387
Heimatmuseum Buchloe, Buchloe 16390
Heimatmuseum Büddenstedt, Büddenstedt 16395
Heimatmuseum Bühl, Baden, Bühl, Baden 16399
Heimatmuseum Bürgeln, Cölbe 16488
Heimatmuseum Burgau, Burgau, Schwaben 16414
Heimatmuseum Carl Swoboda, Schirgiswalde 19784
Heimatmuseum Charlottenburg-Wilmersdorf, Berlin 15988
Heimatmuseum Crumstadt, Riedstadt 19603
Heimatmuseum Dahme, Mark, Dahme, Mark 16531
Heimatmuseum Debstedt, Langen bei Bremerhaven 18320
Heimatmuseum der Gemeinde Dossenheim, Dossenheim 16669
Heimatmuseum der Marktgemeinde Wiggensbach, Wiggensbach 20584
Heimatmuseum der Stadt Bad Tölz, Bad Tölz 15754
Heimatmuseum der Stadt Gernsheim, Gernsheim 17257
Heimatmuseum der Stadt Herrnhut, Herrnhut 17737
Heimatmuseum der Stadt Hückeswagen, Hückeswagen 17851
Heimatmuseum der Stadt Marsberg, Marsberg 18658
Heimatmuseum der Stadt Northeim, Northeim 19127
Heimatmuseum der Stadt Rheinau in Freistett, Rheinau 19588
Heimatmuseum der Stadt Vohenstrauß, Vohenstrauß 20330
Heimatmuseum des Landkreises Regensburg, Altenthann 15456
Heimatmuseum des Nordböhmischen Niederlandes, Böblingen 16213
Heimatmuseum Dietzenbach, Dietzenbach 16606
Heimatmuseum Dirlewang, Dirlewang 16622
Heimatmuseum Dohna, Dohna 16631
Heimatmuseum Duderstadt, Duderstadt 16716
Heimatmuseum Dykhus, Borkum 16260
Heimatmuseum Ebenhausen, Oerlenbach 19230
Heimatmuseum Ebermannstadt, Ebermannstadt 16764
Heimatmuseum Ebern, Ebern 16765
Heimatmuseum Echzell, Echzell 16774
Heimatmuseum Eggenstein-Leopoldshafen, Eggenstein-Leopoldshafen 16789
Heimatmuseum Eisenbach, Obernburg 19182
Heimatmuseum Ellrich, Ellrich 16832
Heimatmuseum Elze, Elze 16845
Heimatmuseum Emskirchen, Emskirchen 16869
Heimatmuseum Epfenbach, Epfenbach 16877
Heimatmuseum Erbenheim, Wiesbaden 20575
Heimatmuseum Eschenburg, Eschenburg 16932
Heimatmuseum Eschwege, Eschwege 16936
Heimatmuseum Eversberg e.V., Meschede 18716
Heimatmuseum Finsterbergen, Finsterbergen 17004
Heimatmuseum Freiamt, Freiamt 17097
Heimatmuseum Freigericht, Freigericht 17119
Heimatmuseum Freudenstadt, Freudenstadt 17129
Heimatmuseum Freudenthal, Memmingen 18704
Heimatmuseum Friedewald, Friedewald, Hessen 17141
Heimatmuseum Friedrichsdorf-Seulberg, Friedrichsdorf, Taunus 17144
Heimatmuseum Friedrichshain, Berlin 15989
Heimatmuseum für Stadt und Kreis Gelnhausen, Gelnhausen 17223
Heimatmuseum für Stadt- und Landkreis, Kirchheimbolanden 18098
Heimatmuseum Gadebusch, Gadebusch 17188
Heimatmuseum Gadernheim, Lautertal, Odenwald 18363
Heimatmuseum Garbenheim, Wetzlar 20553
Heimatmuseum Garbsen, Garbsen 17195
Heimatmuseum Geisa, Geisa 17213
Heimatmuseum Geislingen, Geislingen an der Steige 17218
Heimatmuseum Gemünden, Weilrod 20452
Heimatmuseum Gensungen, Felsberg 16993
Heimatmuseum Geretsried, Geretsried 17250
Heimatmuseum Gersfeld, Gersfeld 17261
Heimatmuseum Giesen, Giesen 17277
Heimatmuseum Glonn, Glonn 17302
Heimatmuseum Görwihl, Görwihl 17328
Heimatmuseum Gößnitz, Gößnitz, Thüringen 17329
Heimatmuseum Grafing, Grafing bei München 17375
Heimatmuseum Grafling, Grafling 17376
Heimatmuseum Grafschaft Hoya, Hoya 17845
Heimatmuseum Gransee, Gransee 17377
Heimatmuseum Greene, Kreiensen 18230
Heimatmuseum Greversdorf, Geversdorf 17272
Heimatmuseum Grimmen "Im Mühlentor", Grimmen 17406
Heimatmuseum Grötzingen, Aichtal 15410
Heimatmuseum Großseelheim, Kirchhain 18092
Heimatmuseum Hähnlein, Alsbach-Hähnlein 15436
Heimatmuseum Haiger, Haiger 17487
Heimatmuseum Haiterbach, Haiterbach 17498
Heimatmuseum Hallstadt, Hallstadt 17525
Heimatmuseum Hebertsfelden, Hebertsfelden 17654
Heimatmuseum Heidelsheim, Bruchsal 16366
Heimatmuseum Heiligenhafen, Heiligenhafen 17694
Heimatmuseum Heinrich Zoller, Wittelshofen 20619
Heimatmuseum Heuchelheim-Kinzenbach, Heuchelheim, Kreis Gießen 17750
Heimatmuseum Heusenstamm, Heusenstamm 17751
Heimatmuseum Hochzeitshaus, Homberg, Efze 17835
Heimatmuseum Höchstädt an der Donau, Höchstädt an der Donau 17779
Heimatmuseum Hoheneggelsen, Söhlde 19975
Heimatmuseum Hohenroda, Hohenroda 17811
Heimatmuseum Hohenschönhausen, Berlin 15990
Heimatmuseum Hohenwestedt, Hohenwestedt 17818
Heimatmuseum Hornburg, Hornburg, Kreis Wolfenbüttel 17843
Heimatmuseum Hüttenberg, Hüttenberg 17862
Heimatmuseum Hus tu Löwenberg, Löwenberg 18492
Heimatmuseum im Alten Kloster, Erbendorf 16889
Heimatmuseum im Alten Rathaus, Bruchköbel 16363
Heimatmuseum im Berchtoldshof, Uhingen 20255
Heimatmuseum im Fünfeckigen Turm, Neckarbischofsheim 18985
Heimatmuseum im Herrenhaaus, Burghaun 16417
Heimatmuseum im Hintermeierhaus, Donauwörth 16638
Heimatmuseum im Neuen Spielhaus, Bruchköbel 16364
Heimatmuseum im Oberen Torturm, Lauchheim 18347
Heimatmuseum im Schelfenhaus, Volkach 20332
Heimatmuseum im Schloß, Zörbig 20766
Heimatmuseum im Schloß zu Werdorf, Aßlar 15539
Heimatmuseum im Unteren Turm, Leutershausen 18449
Heimatmuseum im Wachtturm, Geyer 17273
Heimatmuseum im Weserrenaissance Schloß, Bevern, Kreis Holzminden 16135
Heimatmuseum in der Windmühle Gettorf, Gettorf 17271
Heimatmuseum Ittersbach, Karlsbad 17986
Heimatmuseum Karlsdorf, Karlsdorf-Neuthard 17987
Heimatmuseum Kefenrod, Kefenrod 18046
Heimatmuseum Keltern, Keltern 18055
Heimatmuseum Kirberg, Hünfelden 17859
Heimatmuseum Kirchhain, Kirchhain 18093
Heimatmuseum Kirchheim, Heidelberg 17667
Heimatmuseum Kirchheim, Schwaben, Kirchheim, Schwaben 18094
Heimatmuseum Klosterlangheim, Lichtenfels, Bayern 18455
Heimatmuseum Königsdorf, Königsdorf, Oberbayern 18175
Heimatmuseum Köpenick, Berlin 15991
Heimatmuseum Kornburg, Nürnberg 19142
Heimatmuseum Kraiburg am Inn, Kraiburg am Inn 18215
Heimatmuseum Lahnau-Waldgirmes, Lahnau 18286
Heimatmuseum Lampertheim, Lampertheim 18296
Heimatmuseum Lamspringe, Lamspringe 18297
Heimatmuseum Landau, Landau an der Isar 18299
Heimatmuseum Langelsheim, Langelsheim 18317
Heimatmuseum Langenau, Langenau, Württemberg 18326
Heimatmuseum Langenseifen, Bad Schwalbach 15738
Heimatmuseum Langenselbold, Langenselbold 18337
Heimatmuseum Langenzenn, Langenzenn 18338
Heimatmuseum Laubach, Laubach, Hessen 18344
Heimatmuseum Lauda-Königshofen, Lauda-Königshofen 18348
Heimatmuseum Lauenau, Lauenau 18349
Heimatmuseum Leeheim, Riedstadt 19604
Heimatmuseum Leer, Leer 18366
Heimatmuseum Leipheim, Leipheim 18381
Heimatmuseum Lenggries, Lenggries 18438
Heimatmuseum Lette, Coesfeld 16490
Heimatmuseum Leutershausen, Leutershausen 18450
Heimatmuseum Lichtenberg, Berlin 15992
Heimatmuseum Lorch, Lorch, Württemberg 18504
Heimatmuseum Luditzer Kreis, Bad Sooden-Allendorf 15746
Heimatmuseum Lübbecke, Lübbecke 18531
Heimatmuseum Lügde, Lügde 18553
Heimatmuseum Lütgendortmund, Dortmund 16659
Heimatmuseum Magstadt, Magstadt 18590
Heimatmuseum Marktl, Marktl, Inn 18647
Heimatmuseum Marner Skatklub von 1873, Marne 18657
Heimatmuseum Maßbach, Maßbach 18662
Heimatmuseum Meerane, Meerane 18671
Heimatmuseum Meerholz, Gelnhausen 17224
Heimatmuseum Meinhard, Meinhard 18684
Heimatmuseum Mellrichstadt, Mellrichstadt 18700
Heimatmuseum Melsungen, Melsungen 18702
Heimatmuseum-Menton, Teningen 20159
Heimatmuseum Merkendorf, Merkendorf, Mittelfranken 18711
Heimatmuseum Michelbacher Schlößchen, Alzenau 15476
Heimatmuseum Miesbach, Miesbach 18735
Heimatmuseum Mindelheim, Mindelheim 18741
Heimatmuseum mit Hugo-Geißler-Saal, Tuttlingen 20237
Heimatmuseum mit ostdeutscher Heimatstube, Hanerau-Hademarschen 17589
Heimatmuseum Mitterfels, Mitterfels 18755
Heimatmuseum Münchingen, Korntal-Münchingen 18211
Heimatmuseum Münsingen, Münsingen 18930
Heimatmuseum Nauheim, Nauheim 18977
Heimatmuseum Naumburg, Naumburg, Hessen 18978
Heimatmuseum Naunheim, Wetzlar 20554
Heimatmuseum Neu-Ulm-Pfuhl, Neu-Ulm 19009
Heimatmuseum Neuenwalde, Langen bei Bremerhaven 18321
Heimatmuseum Neukirchen, Neukirchen, Knüllgebirge 19041
Heimatmuseum Neunkirchen, Neunkirchen bei Mosbach 19054
Heimatmuseum Neureichenau, Neureichenau 19058
Heimatmuseum Neuried, Neuried, Ortenaukreis 19059
Heimatmuseum Neustadt an der Aisch, Neustadt an der Aisch 19071
Heimatmuseum Neustadtgödens, Sande, Kreis Friesland 19740
Heimatmuseum Nidda, Nidda 19089
Heimatmuseum Nied, Frankfurt am Main 17051
Heimatmuseum Niemes und Prachatitz, Ingolstadt 17907
Heimatmuseum Nüdlingen, Nüdlingen 19129
Heimatmuseum Nürnberg, Nürnberg 19143
Heimatmuseum Obbornhofen, Hungen 17868
Heimatmuseum Obergünzburg mit Südseesammlung, Obergünzburg 19175
Heimatmuseum Oberndorf am Lech, Oberndorf am Lech 19184
Heimatmuseum Obernfeld, Obernfeld 19187
Heimatmuseum Oberstdorf, Oberstdorf 19210
Heimatmuseum Ochsenfurt, Ochsenfurt 19217
Heimatmuseum Oettingen, Oettingen 19236
Heimatmuseum Pankow, Berlin 15993
Heimatmuseum Papenburg, Papenburg 19346
Heimatmuseum Peldemühle, Wittmund 20630
Heimatmuseum Pfaffenhausen, Pfaffenhausen 19380
Heimatmuseum Pfarrscheuer, Römerstein 19633
Heimatmuseum Philippsburg, Philippsburg 19398
Heimatmuseum Postbauer-Heng, Postbauer-Heng 19429
Heimatmuseum Pressath, Pressath 19444
Heimatmuseum Prien, Prien 19450
Heimatmuseum Rain am Lech, Rain am Lech 19477
Heimatmuseum Rauchkate, Zetel 20747
Heimatmuseum Raunheim, Raunheim 19503
Heimatmuseum Rauschenberg, Rauschenberg 19505
Heimatmuseum Reiderland, Weener 20417
Heimatmuseum Reilingen, Reilingen 19549
Heimatmuseum Reinheim, Reinheim 19553
Heimatmuseum Reinickendorf, Berlin 15994
Heimatmuseum Reischenau, Dinkelscherben 16618
Heimatmuseum Reiterhaus, Neusalza-Spremberg 19062
Heimatmuseum Reutlingen, Reutlingen 19576
Heimatmuseum Rhüden, Seesen 19922
Heimatmuseum Rieneck, Rieneck 19608
Heimatmuseum Rodenberg, Rodenberg, Deister 19622
Heimatmuseum Rodenstein, Fränkisch-Crumbach 17024
Heimatmuseum Rodewald, Rodewald 19623
Heimatmuseum Römstedthaus, Bergen, Kreis Celle 15894
Heimatmuseum Rötz, Rötz 19638
Heimatmuseum Ronnenberg, Ronnenberg 19645
Heimatmuseum Rotenburg, Rotenburg, Wümme 19671
Heimatmuseum Runder Turm, Sigmaringen 19957
Heimatmuseum Sankt Laurentius, Dahlenburg 16530
Heimatmuseum Schermbeck, Schermbeck 19774
Heimatmuseum Schifferstadt, Schifferstadt 19777
Heimatmuseum Schliersee, Schliersee 19802
Heimatmuseum Schlitz, Schlitz 19803
Heimatmuseum Schloß Brenz, Sontheim an der Brenz 19999
Heimatmuseum Schloß Schönebeck, Bremen 16326
Heimatmuseum Schloß Tenneberg, Waltershausen 20386
Heimatmuseum Schloss Wildeck, Zschopau 20769
Heimatmuseum Schloß Wolkenstein, Wolkenstein 20670
Heimatmuseum Schnaittach, Schnaittach 19815
Heimatmuseum Schöneck, Schöneck, Vogtland 19829
Heimatmuseum Schöningen, Schöningen 19835
Heimatmuseum Schwanfeld, Schwanfeld 19875
Heimatmuseum Schwanheim, Frankfurt am Main 17052
Heimatmuseum Schwarza, Schwarza, Suhl 19879
Heimatmuseum Seeg, Seeg 19916
Heimatmuseum Seelze, Seelze 19920
Heimatmuseum Siegbach, Siegbach 19943
Heimatmuseum Simbach am Inn, Simbach am Inn 19959
Heimatmuseum Spangenberg, Spangenberg 20008
Heimatmuseum Sprendlingen, Sprendlingen 20017
Heimatmuseum Stade, Stade 20023
Heimatmuseum Stadt Bernstadt an der Eigen, Bernstadt auf dem Eigen 16130
Heimatmuseum Stadt Nagold-Steinhaus, Nagold 18971
Heimatmuseum Stadt Starnberg, Starnberg 20036
Heimatmuseum Stadt und Landkreis Neudek im Erzgebirge, Augsburg 15557
Heimatmuseum Stadtsteinach, Stadtsteinach 20035
Heimatmuseum Staufenberg, Staufenberg, Hessen 20039
Heimatmuseum Steinach, Steinbach, Taunus 20045
Heimatmuseum Steinfischbach, Waldems 20358
Heimatmuseum Steinwiesen, Steinwiesen 20055
Heimatmuseum Stockstadt am Main, Stockstadt am Main 20063
Heimatmuseum Tempelhof, Berlin 15995
Heimatmuseum Tiergarten, Berlin 15996
Heimatmuseum Todtmoos, Todtmoos 20183
Heimatmuseum - Traktoren- und Landmaschinenmuseum, Großengottern 17428
Heimatmuseum Trebur, Trebur 20197
Heimatmuseum Treptow, Berlin 15997
Heimatmuseum Uetze, Uetze 20251
Heimatmuseum und Archiv des Heimatvereins für den Bezirk Steglitz, Berlin 15998
Heimatmuseum und Dokumentationszentrum zur Deutschen Nachkriegsgeschichte, Wanfried 20391
Heimatmuseum und Galerie Neue Diele, Jork 17961
Heimatmuseum und Gedenkstätte Bützow, Bützow 16409
Heimatmuseum und Hedwig Courths-Mahler Archiv, Nebra 18984
Heimatmuseum und Karl-August-Forster-Bienenmuseum, Illertissen 17886
Heimatmuseum und Klosterruine, Arendsee, Altmark 15510
Heimatmuseum und Stadtarchiv, Flörsheim am Main 17015
Heimatmuseum und Textil-Schauwerkstatt, Greiz 17392
Heimatmuseum Unterboihingen, Wendlingen am Neckar 20513
Heimatmuseum Usingen, Usingen 20278
Heimatmuseum Usseln, Willingen, Upland 20600
Heimatmuseum Varel, Varel 20286
Heimatmuseum Velburg, Velburg 20296
Heimatmuseum Viernheim, Viernheim 20312
Heimatmuseum Vietze, Höhbeck 17782
Heimatmuseum Vilsbiburg - Kröninger Hafnermuseum, Vilsbiburg 20322
Heimatmuseum Wächtersbach, Wächtersbach 20338
Heimatmuseum Waldbrunn, Waldbrunn, Westerwald 20355
Heimatmuseum Waldthurn, Waldthurn 20374
Heimatmuseum Walldorf, Mörfelden-Walldorf 18774
Heimatmuseum Waltrop, Waltrop 20387
Heimatmuseum Wandsbek, Hamburg 17543
Heimatmuseum Wanna, Wanna 20398
Heimatmuseum Wedding, Berlin 15999
Heimatmuseum Wedel, Wedel 20415

Heimatmuseum Wehlen, Stadt Wehlen 20028
Heimatmuseum Wemding, Wemding 20508
Heimatmuseum Wennigsen, Wennigsen 20514
Heimatmuseum Wertach, Wertach 20530
Heimatmuseum Westerhausen, Westerhausen 20541
Heimatmuseum Wiedensahl, Wiedensahl 20564
Heimatmuseum Windeck, Windeck 20605
Heimatmuseum Winterberg im Böhmerwald, Freyung 17133
Heimatmuseum Wippra, Wippra 20616
Heimatmuseum Wißmar, Wettenberg 20548
Heimatmuseum Witten, Witten 20621
Heimatmuseum Wolfratshausen, Wolfratshausen 20657
Heimatmuseum Wolfskehlen, Riedstadt 19605
Heimatmuseum Wommelshausen, Bad Endbach 15640
Heimatmuseum Zarrentin, Zarrentin, Mecklenburg 20733
Heimatmuseum Zehlendorf, Berlin 16000
Heimatmuseum Zorge, Zorge 20767
Heimatmuseum Zusmarshausen, Zusmarshausen 20772
Heimatscheune, Zschepplin 20768
Heimatstube, Altenstadt an der Waldnaab 15454
Heimatstube Adlergebirge, Waldkraiburg 20368
Heimatstube Alfeld, Alfeld, Leine 15426
Heimatstube Altenau, Altenau, Harz 15445
Heimatstube Am Grevendiek, Sprockhövel 20020
Heimatstube Arenborn, Oberweser 19215
Heimatstube Bliedersdorf, Bliedersdorf 16186
Heimatstube Bredenbeck, Wennigsen 20515
Heimatstube Crostau, Crostau 16515
Heimatstube der Stadt Saaz, Roth, Mittelfranken 19673
Heimatstube Eime, Eime 16811
Heimatstube Elbingerode, Elbingerode, Harz 16828
Heimatstube Endersbach, Weinstadt 20485
Heimatstube Freiwaldau-Bieletal, Kirchheim unter Teck 18096
Heimatstube Fröndenberg, Fröndenberg 17155
Heimatstube Gräfenhain/ Nauendorf, Georgenthal 17240
Heimatstube Groß Nemerow, Groß Nemerow 17418
Heimatstube Großbodungen, Großbodungen 17425
Heimatstube Gutenberg, Oberostendorf 19193
Heimatstube Hänigsen, Uetze 20252
Heimatstube Haiger, Haiger 17488
Heimatstube Hinternah, Hinternah 17766
Heimatstube Hohenhameln, Hohenhameln 17807
Heimatstube im "Spieker Anno 1754", Tarmstedt 20144
Heimatstube Langenaubach, Haiger 17489
Heimatstube Lichtenstadt, Zirndorf 20758
Heimatstube Mühlbach mit Philipp-Neubrand-Gedächtnisstube, Eppingen 16879
Heimatstube Münstedt, Lahstedt 18291
Heimatstube Offenbach, Mittenaar 18752
Heimatstube Röckwitz, Röckwitz 19627
Heimatstube Röhrnbach-Kaltenbach, Röhrnbach 19632
Heimatstube Rohrbach, Eppingen 16880
Heimatstube Schlesien, Kaufbeuren 18039
Heimatstube Sperenberg, Sperenberg 20010
Heimatstube Stadt und Landkreis Saaz, Georgensgmünd 17238
Heimatstube Tribsees, Tribsees 20204
Heimatstube Trochtelfingen, Bopfingen 16252
Heimatstube Untere Baranya, Gingen 17288
Heimatstube Usedom, Usedom 20276
Heimatstube Wahrenbrück, Wahrenbrück 20347
Heimatstube Wehrstedt, Bad Salzdetfurth 15726
Heimatstuben, Ellrich 16833
Heimatstuben, Volkmarsen 20334
Heimatstuben im Arresturm, Spalt 20007
Heimatstuben im Oberen Tor, Scheinfeld 19771
Heimatstuben Schlesien, Vilsbiburg 20323
Heimatstuben Weipert und Erzgebirgsschau, Gunzenhausen 17463
Hellweg-Museum der Stadt Unna, Unna 20264
Hennebergisches Museum, Kloster Veßra 18115
Herborner Heimatmuseum, Herborn, Hessen 17715
Hermann-Grochtmann-Museum Datteln, Datteln 16553
Hermann-Hesse-Höri-Museum, Gaienhofen 17190
Herz'sche Heimatstiftung Hilgerhof, Pittenhart 19409
Hessisches Forst-Kulturhistorisches Museum, Biebergemünd 16145
Heuson-Museum im Rathaus, Büdingen 16398
Hexenbürgermeisterhaus, Lemgo 18429
Hinterlandmuseum Schloss Biedenkopf, Biedenkopf 16150
Hirschberger Heimatstuben, Alfeld, Leine 15427
Historiengewölbe, Rothenburg ob der Tauber 19677
Historische Sammlung Eltville, Eltville 16843
Historische Sammlungen im Gesundheitspark, Bad Gottleuba 15651
Historische Turmstuben, Winnenden 20611
Historisches Heimatmuseum, Östringen 19234
Historisches Museum am Hohen Ufer, Hannover 17597
Historisches Museum am Strom - Hildegard von Bingen, Bingen am Rhein 16164
Historisches Museum Aurich, Aurich 15578
Historisches Museum Bayreuth, Bayreuth 15846
Historisches Museum Bremerhaven, Bremerhaven 16340
Historisches Museum Frankfurt am Main, Frankfurt am Main 17055
Historisches Museum im Spital, Dinkelsbühl 16615
Historisches Museum Saar, Saarbrücken 19724
Historisches Museum Schloß Gifhorn, Gifhorn 17285
Historisches Museum Verden, Verden 20302
Hochrheinmuseum, Bad Säckingen 15723
Hof Haina mit Heimatmuseum, Biebertal 16147
Hofmarkmuseum, Eggenfelden 16786
Hofmarkmuseum Schloß Eggersberg, Riedenburg 19596
Hohenlohe-Museum, Neuenstein, Württemberg 19029
Hohenzollerisches Landesmuseum, Hechingen 17656
Hohhaus-Museum, Lauterbach, Hessen 18361
Holler Heimatmuseum, Holle 17823
Holstentor-Museum, Lübeck 18536
Hülser Heimatstuben, Krefeld 18226
Hufschmiede Museum Frehrking, Neustadt am Rübenberge 19068
Huldigungssaal und Rathaus, Goslar 17351
Hunsrück-Museum, Simmern, Hunsrück 19961
Huttermuseum, Erdweg 16892
Inselmuseum im Alten Leuchtturm, Wangerooge 20397
Inselmuseum Spiekeroog, Spiekeroog 20014
Isergebirgs Museum Neugablonz, Kaufbeuren 18040
Jägerndorfer Heimatstuben, Ansbach 15502
Jakob-Philipp-Hackert Ausstellung, Prenzlau 19442
Jerusalemhaus mit Verwaltung der Städtischen Sammlungen Wetzlar, Wetzlar 20555
Johann-Friedrich-Danneil-Museum, Salzwedel 19739
John-Wagener-Haus Sievern, Langen bei Bremerhaven 18322
Jüdisches Museum Georgensgmünd, Georgensgmünd 17239
Kaiserdom-Museum, Königslutter 18179
Kaiserstühler Heimatmuseum, Endingen 16871
Karasek-Museum, Seifhennersdorf 19928
Karrasburg Museum Coswig, Coswig bei Dresden 16499
Kelnhof-Museum, Bräunlingen 16270
Ketterer-Haus-Museum, Biberach, Baden 16142
Kirchengeschichtliches Museum in der Pfalzkapelle, Bad Wimpfen 15769
Klaus-Groth-Museum und Neue Museumsinsel Lüttenheid, Heide, Holstein 17660
Klettgau-Museum, Waldshut-Tiengen 20373
Kloster-Museum, Sankt Märgen 19753
Kloster zum Heiligen Kreuz, Rostock 19663
Kölnisches Stadtmuseum, Köln 18150
Königspesel, Hooge 17838
Korallen- und Heimatmuseum, Nattheim 18975
Kornhaus-Museum, Weiler-Simmerberg 20447
Das Kranichhaus, Otterndorf 19322
Kreis-Heimatmuseum, Bad Frankenhausen 15642
Kreis- und Heimatmuseum, Bogen 16222
Kreis- und Stadtmuseum, Dieburg 16596
Kreis- und Universitätsmuseum Helmstedt, Helmstedt 17704
Kreisheimatmuseum, Frankenberg, Eder 17025
Kreisheimatmuseum Striediecks Hof, Bünde 16404
Kreisheimatstube, Ellzee 16837
Kreismuseum, Neuwied 19085
Kreismuseum, Osterburg 19290
Kreismuseum Bad Liebenwerda, Bad Liebenwerda 15692
Kreismuseum Bitterfeld, Bitterfeld 16175
Kreismuseum der Heimatvertriebenen, Seligenstadt 19933
Kreismuseum Finsterwalde, Finsterwalde 17005
Kreismuseum Geilenkirchen, Geilenkirchen 17212
Kreismuseum Heinsberg, Heinsberg 17697
Kreismuseum Herzogtum Lauenburg, Ratzeburg 19500
Kreismuseum Jerichower Land, Genthin 17237
Kreismuseum Lodron-Haus, Mühldorf am Inn 18803
Kreismuseum Oranienburg, Oranienburg 19265
Kreismuseum Peine mit Kreisarchiv, Peine 19366
Kreismuseum Prinzeßhof, Itzehoe 17934
Kreismuseum Schönebeck, Schönebeck, Elbe 19827
Kreismuseum Syke, Syke 20131
Kreismuseum Walderbach, Walderbach 20363
Kreuzberg Museum, Berlin 16018
Krippenmuseum, Telgte 20155
Kultur- und Stadthistorisches Museum Duisburg, Duisburg 16751
Kulturgeschichtliches Museum Bügeleisenhaus, Hattingen 17634
Kulturgeschichtliches Museum Osnabrück, Osnabrück 19280
Kulturhistorische Sammlung, Iphofen 17916
Kulturhistorisches Museum Barockhaus, Görlitz 17323
Kulturhistorisches Museum Franziskanerkloster, Zittau 20761
Kulturhistorisches Museum Kaisertrutz/Reichenbacher Turm, Görlitz 17324
Kulturhistorisches Museum Prenzlau im Dominikanerkloster, Prenzlau 19443
Kulturhistorisches Museum Schloss Köthen, Köthen, Anhalt 18190
Kulturzentrum Hans-Reiffenstuel-Haus, Pfarrkirchen 19387
Kulturzentrum Ostpreußen, Ellingen, Bayern 16830
Kunst- und Heimathaus, Paderborn 19336
Kunst- und Heimatmuseum, Lorch, Rheingau 18503
Kunstgußmuseum Hirzenhain, Hirzenhain 17768
Ländliches Heimatmuseum, Lahntal 18288
Landesmuseum für Kunst und Kulturgeschichte, Schleswig 19794
Landesmuseum für schaumburg-lippische Geschichte, Landes- und Volkskunde, Bückeburg 16394
Landlmuseum Sulzbürg, Mühlhausen, Oberpfalz 18804
Landschaftsmuseum, Seligenstadt 19934
Landschaftsmuseum der Dübener Heide, Bad Düben 15629
Landschaftsmuseum Obermain, Kulmbach 18268
Landschaftsmuseum Westerwald, Hachenburg 17471
Landwirtschaftsmuseum Lüneburger Heide, Suderburg 20117
Langbeinmuseum, Hirschhorn, Neckar 17767
Langsdorfer Heimatmuseum, Lich 18454
Lechfeldmuseum, Königsbrunn 18173
Leib'sches Haus, Abteilung Stadtgeschichte und Volkskunde, Gießen 17281
Liebenberger Schloß Museum, Liebenberg 18461
Lilienhof, Lilienthal 18465
Lindenfelser Museum, Lindenfels 18480
Lippisches Landesmuseum, Detmold 16589
Lovriner Stube, Donauwörth 16640
Märkisches Museum, Berlin 16040
Marine-Museum Limburg, Limburg an der Lahn 18471
Markgräfler Museum Müllheim, Müllheim, Baden 18819
Markgrafenmuseum Ansbach, Ansbach 15503
Meininger Museen, Meiningen 18686
Mies-Pilsner-Heimatmuseum, Dinkelsbühl 16616
Mineralien- und Heimatmuseum, Pleystein 19416
Mittelschwäbisches Heimatmuseum Krumbach, Krumbach, Schwaben 18251
Möllner Museum Historisches Rathaus, Mölln 18766
Mörfelden Museum, Mörfelden-Walldorf 18775
Mörsbacher Museum, Mörsbach 18779
Montfort-Museum, Tettnang 20164
Mühlenhof-Freilichtmuseum Münster, Münster 18942
Mühlenmuseum, Woldegk 20646
Mühlenmuseum Mitling-Mark mit Sammlung Omas Küche, Westoverledingen 20544
Münchhausen-Museum, Bodenwerder 16209
Münchner Stadtmuseum, München 18880
Murgtal-Museum, Forbach 17018
Museen Alte Bischofsburg, Wittstock, Dosse 20632
Museen der Stadt Bad Kösen, Bad Kösen 15679
Museen im Kulturzentrum, Rendsburg 19570
Museum, Coswig, Anhalt 16498
Museum, Waldheim 20364
Museum Abodiacum, Denklingen 16573
Museum Adorf, Adorf, Vogtland 15399
Museum Altes Gymnasium, Schweinfurt 19890
Museum Altes Land, Jork 17962
Museum Altes Rathaus, Gerolzhofen 17259
Museum Altomünster, Altomünster 15470
Museum Alzey, Alzey 15477
Museum am Dannewerk, Dannewerk 16537
Museum am Lindenplatz, Weil am Rhein 20436
Museum am Markt, Schiltach 19782
Museum am Mühlturm, Isny 17930
Museum am Thie, Göttingen 17335
Museum Amelinghausen, Amelinghausen 15480
Museum Amtspforte Stadthagen, Stadthagen 20029
Museum Auerbach, Auerbach, Vogtland 15546
Museum auf der Osterburg, Weida 20424
Museum Bad Abbach, Bad Abbach 15588
Museum Bad Arolsen, Bad Arolsen 15591
Museum Bayerisches Vogtland, Hof, Saale 17793
Museum Bernhard Brühl, Landsberg bei Halle, Saale 18307
Museum Bickenbach, Bickenbach, Bergstraße 16143
Museum Bischofsheim, Bischofsheim bei Rüsselsheim 16170
Museum Blauer Anger, Bergen, Chiemgau 15892
Museum Brückenkopf, Jülich 17964
Museum Burg Brome, Brome 16361
Museum Burg Frankenberg, Aachen 15377
Museum Burg Mylau, Mylau 18966
Museum Burg Posterstein, Posterstein 19430
Museum Burg Pottenstein, Pottenstein 19439
Museum Burg Ronneburg, Ronneburg, Hessen 19644
Museum der Barbarossastadt Gelnhausen, Gelnhausen 17226
Museum der Donauschwaben, Herbrechtingen 17718
Museum der Elbinsel Wilhelmsburg, Hamburg 17556
Museum der Grafschaft, Barmstedt 15825
Museum der Stadt Alfeld (Leine), Alfeld, Leine 15428
Museum der Stadt Aue, Aue, Sachsen 15543
Museum der Stadt Bad Berleburg, Bad Berleburg 15609
Museum der Stadt Bad Gandersheim, Bad Gandersheim 15650
Museum der Stadt Bad Neuenahr-Ahrweiler, Bad Neuenahr-Ahrweiler 15703
Museum der Stadt Bad Staffelstein, Bad Staffelstein, Oberfranken 15748
Museum der Stadt Bensheim, Bensheim 15880
Museum der Stadt Boppard, Boppard 16255
Museum der Stadt Borna, Borna bei Leipzig 16263
Museum der Stadt Butzbach im Solms-Braunfelser Hof, Butzbach 16437
Museum der Stadt Calw, Calw 16449
Museum der Stadt Dommitzsch, Dommitzsch 16632
Museum der Stadt Dorsten, Dorsten 16653
Museum der Stadt Ehingen, Ehingen, Donau 16792
Museum der Stadt Eschborn, Eschborn 16931
Museum der Stadt Ettlingen, Ettlingen 16975
Museum der Stadt Gladbeck, Gladbeck 17291
Museum der Stadt Güstrow, Güstrow 17457
Museum der Stadt Hagenow, Hagenow 17485
Museum der Stadt Kraichtal, Kraichtal 18217
Museum der Stadt Lahnstein im Hexenturm, Lahnstein 18287
Museum der Stadt Lahr, Lahr, Schwarzwald 18290
Museum der Stadt Langen, Langen in Hessen 18323
Museum der Stadt Lünen, Lünen 18562
Museum der Stadt Nauen, Nauen 18976
Museum der Stadt Neu-Isenburg Haus zum Löwen, Neu-Isenburg 19004
Museum der Stadt Neustadt an der Weinstraße, Neustadt an der Weinstraße 19077
Museum der Stadt Neutraubling - Ortsgeschichtliche Dokumentation, Neutraubling 19084
Museum der Stadt Parchim, Parchim 19349
Museum der Stadt Pegau, Pegau 19364
Museum der Stadt Ratingen, Ratingen 19494
Museum der Stadt Schopfheim, Schopfheim 19842
Museum der Stadt Sinsheim, Sinsheim 19969
Museum der Stadt Troisdorf, Troisdorf 20216
Museum der Stadt Waiblingen, Waiblingen 20350
Museum der Stadt Weinheim, Weinheim, Bergstraße 20480
Museum der Stadt Wolgast, Wolgast 20667
Museum der Stadt Worms, Worms 20678
Museum der Westlausitz Kamenz, Kamenz 17979
Museum des ehemaligen Kreises Stuhm/Westpr., Bremervörde 16352
Museum des Haager Landes, Haag, Oberbayern 17469
Museum des Handwerks Bremerhaven-Wesermünde in Bederkesa, Bad Bederkesa 15596
Museum des Heimatkundlichen Vereins, Scheßlitz 19775
Museum des Historischen Vereins Freising, Freising 17122
Museum des Vereins für Heimatkunde im Landkreis Birkenfeld, Birkenfeld, Nahe 16166
Museum Dingolfing-Herzogsburg, Dingolfing 16614
Museum Eckernförde, Eckernförde 16776
Museum Flederwisch, Furth im Wald 17181
Museum-Freundschaften, Ostseebad Binz 19310
Museum Friesenheim, Ludwigshafen am Rhein 18519
Museum für Bergedorf und die Vierlande, Hamburg 17557
Museum für das Fürstentum Lüneburg, Lüneburg 18559
Museum für Hamburgische Geschichte, Hamburg 17558
Museum für Höchster Geschichte, Frankfurt am Main 17063
Museum für Kloster- und Heimatgeschichte, Harsefeld 17620
Museum für Kunst und Kulturgeschichte der Stadt Dortmund, Dortmund 16662
Museum für Schnitzkunst und Kulturgeschichte, Oberammergau 19168
Museum für Stadtgeschichte, Alpirsbach 15435
Museum für Stadtgeschichte, Breisach am Rhein 16312
Museum für Stadtgeschichte, Neuenburg am Rhein 19022
Museum für Stadtgeschichte, Freiburg im Breisgau 17114
Museum für Stadtgeschichte Dessau, Dessau 16580
Museum für Stadtgeschichte im Adam-und-Eva-Haus, Paderborn 19337
Museum für Stadtgeschichte und Volkskunde, Heppenheim 17712
Museum für Weinbau und Stadtgeschichte, Edenkoben 16779
Museum Garching an der Alz, Garching an der Alz 17196
Museum Goch, Goch 17309
Museum Goldener Steig, Waldkirchen, Niederbayern 20367
Museum Grossauheim, Hanau 17585
Museum Großkrotzenburg, Großkrotzenburg 17433
Museum Gülden Creutz, Worbis 20676
Museum Haldensleben, Haldensleben 17506
Museum Halle, Halle, Westfalen 17524
Museum Hameln, Hameln 17575
Museum Heimathaus Irmintraut, Ottersberg 19325
Museum Heimathaus Münsterland, Telgte 20156
Museum Helferhaus, Backnang 15586
Museum Hessenstube, Baunatal 15832
Museum Hofmühle, Immenstadt 17896
Museum Hohenzollern in Franken, Kulmbach 18269
Museum Huthaus Zinnwald, Altenberg, Erzgebirge 15448
Museum im alten Brauhaus, Homberg, Ohm 17836
Museum im Alten Rathaus, Mönchberg 18769
Museum im Alten Rathaus, Neckargemünd 18987
Museum im Alten Rathaus, Schmitten 19813
Museum im Alten Schloß, Neckarbischofsheim 18986
Museum im Ammes Haus, Hatzfeld 17640
Museum im Amtshausschlüpfla, Erlangen 16920
Museum im Astorhaus, Walldorf, Baden 20376
Museum im Blaahaus am Unteren Römerweg, Kiefersfelden 18070
Museum im Boyneburgischen Schloß, Sontra 20003
Museum im 'Fressenden Haus' - Burgkasten Weißenstein, Regen 19515
Museum im Gotischen Haus, Bad Homburg v.d.Höhe 15665
Museum im Heimathaus, Traunstein 20190
Museum im Herrenhaus, Hausach 17643
Museum im Kloster - Museum des Landkreises Osnabrück, Bersenbrück 16131

Museum im Kreuzgang, Landshut 18310
Museum im Malhaus, Wasserburg, Bodensee 20410
Museum im Markgrafen-Schloss, Emmendingen 16855
Museum im Marstall, Winsen, Luhe 20613
Museum im Mesnerhaus, Pfaffenhofen an der Ilm 19383
Museum im Pflegschloss, Schrobenhausen 19853
Museum im Prediger, Schwäbisch Gmünd 19862
Museum im Rathaus Möhringen, Tuttlingen 20238
Museum im Ritterhaus, Offenburg 19242
Museum im Ritterhaus, Osterode am Harz 19296
Museum im Schäferhaus, Wahlsburg 20346
Museum im Schloß Bad Pyrmont, Bad Pyrmont 15713
Museum im Schloß Wolfenbüttel, Wolfenbüttel 20654
Museum im Stadtturm, Groitzsch bei Pegau 17412
Museum im Steinhaus, Bad Wimpfen 15770
Museum im Steintor, Anklam 15494
Museum im Steintorturm, Brandenburg an der Havel 16285
Museum im Strumpferhaus, Oberstaufen 19209
Museum im Tuchmacherhaus, Thammhausen 20169
Museum im Wittelsbacher Schloss Friedberg, Friedberg, Bayern 17137
Museum im Zeughaus, Vechta 20290
Museum in der Adler-Apotheke, Eberswalde 16771
Museum in der Alten Schule, Efringen-Kirchen 16783
Museum in der Burg, Coppenbrügge 16495
Museum in der Präparandenschule, Höchberg 17777
Museum in der Remise, Bad Harzburg 15656
Museum in der Scheuergasse, Zwingenberg, Bergstraße 20783
Museum in Schweizer Hof, Bretten 16357
Museum Kleines Schloß, Blankenburg, Harz 16177
Museum Kloster Bentlage, Rheine 19590
Museum Kloster Zeven, Zeven 20753
Museum Leben am Meer, Esens 16940
Museum Leuchtenburg, Seitenroda 19929
Museum Löffingen, Löffingen 18489
Museum Malerwinkelhaus, Marktbreit 18644
Museum Neukirchen-Vluyn, Neukirchen-Vluyn 19042
Museum Neukölln, Berlin 16064
Museum Neuruppin, Neuruppin 19061
Museum Nienburg, Nienburg, Weser 19102
Museum Niesky, Niesky 19104
Museum Nikolaikirche, Berlin 16066
Museum Nordenham, Nordenham 19115
Museum NordJura, Weismain 20488
Museum Ober-Ramstadt, Ober-Ramstadt 19167
Museum Oberes Donautal, Fridingen 17136
Museum Otto Ludwig, Eisfeld 16827
Museum Petersberg, Petersberg bei Halle, Saale 19377
Museum Reichenau, Reichenau, Baden 19542
Museum Sankt Wendel, Sankt Wendel 19758
Museum Schloss Colditz, Colditz 16493
Museum Schloß Delitzsch, Delitzsch 16564
Museum Schloß Ehrenstein, Ohrdruf 19246
Museum Schloss Hellenstein, Heidenheim an der Brenz 17682
Museum Schloß Hohenlimburg, Hagen, Westfalen 17482
Museum Schloss Netzschkau, Netzschkau 19002
Museum Schloß Neu-Augustusburg, Weißenfels 20499
Museum Schloß Ratibor, Roth, Mittelfranken 19675
Museum Schloß Rochlitz, Rochlitz 19620
Museum Schloß Steinheim, Hanau 17586
Museum Schwarzes Ross, Hilpoltstein 17762
Museum Soltau, Soltau 19993
Museum Stadt Bad Hersfeld, Bad Hersfeld 15660
Museum Steinarbeiterhaus, Hohburg 17803
Museum Tegernseer Tal, Tegernsee 20151
Museum und Archiv der Stadt Gronau (Leine), Gronau, Leine 17413
Museum und Galerie der Stadt, Schwabmünchen 19858
Museum Uslar, Uslar 20280
Museum Viechtach, Viechtach 20308
Museum Villa Stahmer, Georgsmarienhütte 17242
Museum Voswinckelshof, Dinslaken 16619
Museum Wasserburg, Wasserburg am Inn 20408
Museum Wasserburg Anholt, Isselburg 17933
Museum Wiesbaden, Wiesbaden 20576
Museum Wildberg, Wildberg, Württemberg 20586
Museum Wurzen mit Ringelnatzsammlung, Wurzen 20720
Museum Wustrow, Wustrow, Niedersachsen 20724
Museum Zella-Mehlis, Zella-Mehlis 20745
Museum zur Geschichte von Christen und Juden, Laupheim 18359
Museumsanlage Kulturstiftung Landkreis Osterholz, Osterholz-Scharmbeck 19294
Museumsdorf Cloppenburg, Cloppenburg 16479
Museumshäuschen, Krebes 18222
Museumshof, Roßtal 19656
Museumshof am Sonnenlück, Erkner 16913
Museumshof Emmerstedt, Helmstedt 17705
Museumshof Historischer Moorhof Augustendorf, Gnarrenburg 17307
Museumslandschaft Deilbachtal, Essen 16960
Museumsstube Obermeiser, Calden 16444
Museumszentrum Lorsch, Lorsch 18505
Museumszentrum-Rehau, Rehau 19538
Natur- und Heimatmuseum Vellberg, Vellberg 20298
Naturhistorisches Museum Schloss Bertholdsburg, Schleusingen 19799
Neisser Haus - Heimathaus und Archiv, Hildesheim 17759
Neues Schloß, Schloßmuseum, Tettnang 20165
Neues Stadtmuseum Landsberg am Lech, Landsberg am Lech 18305
Neustädter Rathaus, Hanau 17587
Niederbergisches Museum Wülfrath, Wülfrath 20688
Niederebersdorfer Heimat- und Archivstuben, Tutzing 20241
Niederlausitz-Museum und Karl-Liebknecht-Gedenkstätte, Luckau, Niederlausitz 18508
Nordfriesisches Museum Ludwig-Nissen-Haus, Husum, Nordsee 17870
Nordhannoversches Bauernhaus-Museum, Isernhagen 17926
Nordpfälzer Heimatmuseum, Rockenhausen 19621
Oberhausmuseum Passau, Passau 19358
Oberlausitzer Sechsstädtebund- und Handwerksmuseum Löbau, Löbau 18488
Oberrheinisches Bäder- und Heimatmuseum Bad Bellingen, Bad Bellingen 15597
Oberschlesisches Landesmuseum, Ratingen 19495
Oma-Freese-Huus, Dornum 16652
Oranien-Nassau-Museum Oranienstein, Diez 16607
Ordenmuseum, Neuffen 19030
Original-Dorfschmiede Ehlen, Habichtswald 17470
Ortsgeschichtliche Sammlung, Bovenden 16266
Ortsgeschichtliches Museum, Siegenburg 19952
Ortskundliche Sammlung Bargteheide, Bargteheide 15824
Ortssammlung Wettelsheim, Treuchtlingen 20200
Ostdeutsche Heimatstube, Bad Zwischenahn 15784
Ostdeutsche Kultur- und Heimatstuben mit Schönbacher Stube, Heppenheim 17713
Osterzgebirgsmuseum, Lauenstein 18351
Das Ostfriesische Teemuseum und Norder Heimatmuseum, Norden 19113
Ostfriesisches Landesmuseum und Emder Rüstkammer, Emden 16850
Ostholstein-Museum, Eutin 16979
Ostholstein-Museum Neustadt, Neustadt in Holstein 19081
Ostpreußisches Landesmuseum, Lüneburg 18561
Otto-Schwabe-Museum, Hochheim am Main 17774
Otto-von-Guericke-Museum in der Lukasklause, Magdeburg 18586
Patenschaftsmuseum Goldap in Ostpreußen, Stade 20025
Peter-Wiepert-Museum, Burg auf Fehmarn 16410
Pfalzmuseum, Forchheim, Oberfranken 17020
Pfingstritt-Museum Kötzting, Kötzting 18192
Philipp Schäfer II Museum, Riedstadt 19606
Potsdam-Museum, Potsdam 19436
Priental-Museum, Aschau im Chiemgau 15534
Probstei-Museum, Schönberg, Holstein 19824
Quadrat Bottrop, Bottrop 16265
Rangau-Handwerkermuseum, Markt Erlbach 18643
Rangau-Heimathaus, Cadolzburg 16440
Rathausmuseum Nieder-Ohmen, Mücke 18798
Reblandmuseum, Baden-Baden 15789
Regionales Heimatmuseum für das Renchtal, Oppenau 19260
Regionalgeschichtliches Museum, Lutherstadt Eisleben 18573
Regionalmuseum, Stockstadt am Rhein 20064
Regionalmuseum Alte Schule, Kaufungen, Hessen 18045
Regionalmuseum Fritzlar, Fritzlar 17154
Regionalmuseum Neubrandenburg, Neubrandenburg 19013
Regionalmuseum Reichelsheim Odenwald, Reichelsheim, Odenwald 19540
Regionalmuseum Xanten, Xanten 20729
Reichenberger Heimatstube und Archiv, Augsburg 15565
Reichsdorf-Museum Gochsheim, Gochsheim 17310
Reichsstadtmuseum, Rothenburg ob der Tauber 19681
Reichsstadtmuseum im Ochsenhof, Bad Windsheim 15777
Reichsstadtmuseum Weißenburg, Weißenburg in Bayern 20492
Reichsstädtisches Archiv, Rathaushalle und Ratsstube, Mühlhausen, Thüringen 18809
Reiss-Engelhorn-Museen, Mannheim 18615
Rhein-Museum Koblenz, Koblenz 18123
Rheinisches Landes Museum Bonn, Bonn 16246
Rhön-Museum, Fladungen 17010
Rieck-Haus / Vierländer Freilichtmuseum, Hamburg 17564
Riesengebirgsmuseum, Marktoberdorf 18651
Riesengebirgsstube, Würzburg 20702
Rittergut Haus Laer, Bochum 16199
Römer und Bajuwaren Museum Burg Kipfenberg, Kipfenberg 18085
Römerbad, Schwangau 19876
Rohnstädter Heimatstube, Weilmünster 20451
Rosgartenmuseum, Konstanz 18206
Roter Haubarg, Witzwort 20639
Rothmühler Heimatmuseum und Archiv, Oestrich-Winkel 19232
Rügen-Museum, Ostseebad Binz 19314
Ruhrtalmuseum, Schwerte 19903
Rundlingmuseum Wendlandhof-Lübeln, Küsten 18263
Samson-Haus, Leer 18367
Sandauer Heimatstube, Arzberg, Oberfranken 15516
Sandelsches Museum, Kirchberg an der Jagst 18087
Sangerberger Heimatstube, Regenstauf 19535
Sauerland-Museum, Arnsberg 15512
Schlesisches Museum zu Görlitz, Görlitz 17325
Schliekau-Museum, Bad Bevensen 15614
Schloss Agathenburg, Agathenburg 15400
Schloß Bürgeln, Schliengen 19800
Schloss Ehrenburg, Coburg 16486
Schloß Marienburg, Pattensen 19361
Schloss Neuburg, Neuburg an der Donau 19018
Schloß Strünkede, Herne 17729
Schloß- und Spielkartenmuseum, Altenburg, Thüringen 15452
Schloßbergmuseum, Chemnitz 16472
Schloßmuseum, Höchstädt, Oberfranken 17781
Schloßmuseum, Ortenburg 19271
Schloßmuseum, Schrozberg 19855
Schloßmuseum, Quedlinburg 19464
Schloßmuseum Ismaning, Ismaning 17928
Schloßmuseum Jagsthausen, Jagsthausen 17936
Schloßmuseum Rimpar, Rimpar 19615
Schloßparkmuseum, Bad Kreuznach 15682
Schützenhaus Glaucha, Halle, Saale 17520
Schullandheim Sassen, Sassen, Vorpommern 19760
Schulmuseum Fronau, Roding 19626
Schwälmer Dorfmuseum, Schrecksbach 19849
Schwarzachtaler Heimatmuseum, Neunburg vorm Wald 19049
Sebnitzer Kunstblumen- und Heimatmuseum Prof. Alfred Meiche, Sebnitz 19908
Sensen- und Heimatmuseum, Achern 15391
Serbski muzej/ Wendisches Museum, Cottbus 16505
Serpentinsteinmuseum Zöblitz, Zöblitz 20765
Sieben-Schwaben-Museum, Türkheim 20234
Siebenbürgisches Museum Gundelsheim, Gundelsheim, Württemberg 17462
Siebengebirgsmuseum, Königswinter 18185
Sindringer Heimatmuseum - Stadtmühle, Forchtenberg 17022
Smiterlöwsche Sammlung, Franzburg 17086
Spengler-Museum, Sangerhausen 19743
Staatlicher Schloßbetrieb Schloß Nossen / Kloster Altzella, Nossen 19128
Stadt- und Brauereimuseum, Pritzwalk 19452
Stadt- und Burgmuseum, Eppstein 16884
Stadt- und Dampfmaschinenmuseum, Werdau, Sachsen 20517
Stadt- und Fachwerkmuseum Alte Universität, Eppingen 16882
Stadt- und Heimatmuseum der Stadt Marl, Marl, Westfalen 18656
Stadt- und Heimatmuseum mit Galerie, Waischenfeld 20351
Stadt- und Hochstiftmuseum, Dillingen an der Donau 16612
Stadt- und Industriemuseum-Lottehaus, Wetzlar 20561
Stadt- und Kreisgeschichtliches Museum, Hünfeld 17858
Stadt- und Kulturgeschichtliches Museum, Torgau 20186
Stadt- und Manfred-Kyber-Museum, Löwenstein 18493
Stadt- und Parkmuseum, Bad Muskau 15698
Stadt- und Regionalmuseum Landshut, Landshut 18313
Stadt- und Turmmuseum, Bad Camberg 15623
Stadt- und Wallfahrtsmuseum, Walldürn 20379
Stadtarchiv mit städtischen Sammlungen, Lauf an der Pegnitz 18353
Stadtgeschichtliche Sammlung, Velbert 20295
Stadtgeschichtliches Museum, Pfullingen 19394
Stadtgeschichtliches Museum, Tangermünde 20140
Stadtgeschichtliches Museum im Landrichterhaus, Karlstadt 18009
Stadtgeschichtliches Museum Leipzig, Leipzig 18419
Stadtgeschichtliches Museum Schabbellhaus, Wismar 20618
Stadtgeschichtliches Museum Spandau, Berlin 16101
Stadtgeschichtliches Museum Weißensee, Berlin 16102
Stadtgeschichtliches Zentrum, Lutherstadt Wittenberg 18578
Stadtgeschichts- und Schradenmuseum, Ortrand 19272
Stadtgeschichtsmuseum Schwerin, Schwerin 19900
Stadtmuseum, Apolda 15509
Stadtmuseum, Baunatal 15833
Stadtmuseum, Freilassing 17120
Stadtmuseum, Penzberg 19373
Stadtmuseum, Rothenburg, Oberlausitz 19686
Stadtmuseum "Alte Burg" Wittenberge, Wittenberge 20625
Stadtmuseum Alte Post, Ebersbach an der Fils 16767
Stadtmuseum Amberg, Amberg, Oberpfalz 15478
Stadtmuseum Amtsturm, Lübz 18546
Stadtmuseum Andernach, Andernach 15488
Stadtmuseum Bad Bergzabern, Bad Bergzabern 15603
Stadtmuseum Bad Berneck, Bad Berneck 15612
Stadtmuseum Bad Cannstatt, Stuttgart 20107
Stadtmuseum Bad Soden, Bad Soden am Taunus 15745
Stadtmuseum Bad Wildungen, Bad Wildungen 15766
Stadtmuseum Baden-Baden, Baden-Baden 15791
Stadtmuseum Bautzen, Bautzen 15836
Stadtmuseum Beckum, Beckum 15865
Stadtmuseum Bergkamen, Bergkamen 15902
Stadtmuseum Bonn, Bonn 16247
Stadtmuseum Brakel, Brakel 16272
Stadtmuseum Breuberg-Neustadt, Breuberg 16359
Stadtmuseum Burgdorf, Burgdorf, Kreis Hannover 16416
Stadtmuseum Burgstädt, Burgstädt 16431
Stadtmuseum Colditz, Colditz 16494
Stadtmuseum Cottbus, Cottbus 16506
Stadtmuseum Cuxhaven, Cuxhaven 16519
Stadtmuseum Damme, Damme, Dümmer 16534
Stadtmuseum Deggendorf, Deggendorf 16560
Stadtmuseum Delmenhorst, Delmenhorst 16569
Stadtmuseum der Landeshauptstadt Düsseldorf, Düsseldorf 16743
Stadtmuseum Ditzingen, Ditzingen 16626
Stadtmuseum Döbeln/Kleine Galerie, Döbeln 16628
Stadtmuseum Dresden, Dresden 16712
Stadtmuseum Eilenburg, Eilenburg 16810
Stadtmuseum Eisenberg, Eisenberg, Thüringen 16822
Stadtmuseum Erlangen, Erlangen 16923
Stadtmuseum Esslingen, Esslingen 16970
Stadtmuseum Fellbach, Fellbach 16992
Stadtmuseum Fürstenfeldbruck, Fürstenfeldbruck 17161
Stadtmuseum Fürth, Fürth, Bayern 17167
Stadtmuseum Gehrden, Gehrden, Hannover 17210
Stadtmuseum Geithain, Geithain 17220
Stadtmuseum Gera, Gera 17248
Stadtmuseum Gerlingen - Gerlinger Heimatmuseum - Museum der Deutschen aus Ungarn, Gerlingen 17252
Stadtmuseum Giengen, Giengen an der Brenz 17275
Stadtmuseum Göhre, Jena 17952
Stadtmuseum Grafenau, Grafenau, Niederbayern 17369
Stadtmuseum Groß-Gerau, Groß-Gerau 17416
Stadtmuseum Gütersloh, Gütersloh 17460
Stadtmuseum Gunzenhausen, Gunzenhausen 17465
Stadtmuseum Hagen, Hagen, Westfalen 17483
Stadtmuseum Hattingen, Hattingen 17637
Stadtmuseum Haus Kupferhammer, Warstein 20404
Stadtmuseum Herzogenaurach, Herzogenaurach 17744
Stadtmuseum Hildburghausen, Hildburghausen 17753
Stadtmuseum Hofgeismar, Hofgeismar 17798
Stadtmuseum Hofheim am Taunus, Hofheim am Taunus 17799
Stadtmuseum Holzminden, Holzminden 17832
Stadtmuseum Horb, Horb 17841
Stadtmuseum Hornmoldhaus, Bietigheim-Bissingen 16160
Stadtmuseum im Alten Forstamt, Stockach 20062
Stadtmuseum im Augustinerkloster, Bad Langensalza 15687
Stadtmuseum im Knochenhauer-Amtshaus, Hildesheim 17761
Stadtmuseum im Prinz-Max-Palais, Karlsruhe 18004
Stadtmuseum im Spital, Crailsheim 16507
Stadtmuseum Ingolstadt im Kavalier Hepp, Ingolstadt 17911
Stadtmuseum Iserlohn, Iserlohn 17922
Stadtmuseum Kassel, Kassel 18031
Stadtmuseum Kaufbeuren, Kaufbeuren 18044
Stadtmuseum Killingerhaus, Idstein 17882
Stadtmuseum Klostermühle, Bad Urach 15757
Stadtmuseum Leimen - Sankt Ilgen, Leimen, Baden 18374
Stadtmuseum Leonberg, Leonberg, Württemberg 18443
Stadtmuseum Leun, Leun 18445
Stadtmuseum Lichtenfels, Lichtenfels, Bayern 18457
Stadtmuseum Ludwigshafen, Ludwigshafen am Rhein 18522
Stadtmuseum Lüdenscheid, Lüdenscheid 18551
Stadtmuseum Meersburg, Meersburg 18678
Stadtmuseum Meppen, Meppen 18709
Stadtmuseum Mosbach, Mosbach, Baden 18796
Stadtmuseum Mühlberg, Elbe, Mühlberg, Elbe 18802
Stadtmuseum Mühlheim, Mühlheim am Main 18811
Stadtmuseum Münster, Münster 18946
Stadtmuseum Mutzschen, Mutzschen 18965
Stadtmuseum Naumburg, Naumburg, Saale 18981
Stadtmuseum Neumarkt, Neumarkt, Oberpfalz 19047
Stadtmuseum Neuötting, Neuötting 19056
Stadtmuseum Nittenau, Nittenau 19106
Stadtmuseum Nördlingen, Nördlingen 19110
Stadtmuseum Norderstedt, Norderstedt 19118
Stadtmuseum Nürtingen, Nürtingen 19166
Stadtmuseum Obermühle, Braunfels 16289
Stadtmuseum Oldenburg, Oldenburg, Oldenburg 19259
Stadtmuseum Pulsnitz, Pulsnitz 19454
Stadtmuseum Quakenbrück, Quakenbrück 19456
Stadtmuseum Rastatt, Rastatt 19490
Stadtmuseum Saalfeld im Franziskanerkloster, Saalfeld, Saale 19721
Stadtmuseum Sachsenheim, Sachsenheim 19730
Stadtmuseum Schleswig, Schleswig 19796
Stadtmuseum Schloß Hoyerswerda, Hoyerswerda 17848
Stadtmuseum Schloss Wolfsburg, Wolfsburg 20663
Stadtmuseum Schongau, Schongau 19841
Stadtmuseum Schramberg, Schramberg 19848
Stadtmuseum Schwabach, Schwabach 19857
Stadtmuseum Schwandorf mit Falkenauer Heimatstube, Schwandorf 19874
Stadtmuseum Schwedt, Schwedt 19887
Stadtmuseum Siegburg, Siegburg 19945
Stadtmuseum Sindelfingen, Sindelfingen 19965
Stadtmuseum Stadtoldendorf, Stadtoldendorf 20033
Stadtmuseum Steinfurt, Steinfurt 20047
Stadtmuseum Stubenhaus, Staufen 20038
Stadtmuseum Sulzbach-Rosenberg, Sulzbach-Rosenberg 20126
Stadtmuseum Teterow, Teterow 20162

Stadtmuseum Trostberg, Trostberg 20219
Stadtmuseum Tübingen, Tübingen 20229
Stadtmuseum Waldkraiburg, Waldkraiburg 20369
Stadtmuseum Weimar, Weimar, Thüringen 20474
Stadtmuseum Zweibrücken, Zweibrücken 20773
Stadttormuseum, Wehrheim 20422
Städtische Kunstsammlung Schloß Salder, Salzgitter 19735
Städtische Museen Heilbronn, Heilbronn 17692
Städtische Museen Junge Kunst und Viadrina, Frankfurt/Oder 17085
Städtisches Heimatmuseum, Ballenstedt 15802
Städtisches Heimatmuseum, Höchstadt an der Aisch 17778
Städtisches Heimatmuseum, Mengen 18707
Städtisches Heimatmuseum, Meßkirch 18719
Städtisches Heimatmuseum, Naila 18972
Städtisches Heimatmuseum, Reinfeld, Holstein 19552
Städtisches Heimatmuseum Erding, Erding 16891
Städtisches Heimatmuseum im Waldemarturm, Dannenberg, Elbe 16536
Städtisches Hellweg-Museum, Geseke 17269
Städtisches Museum, Bad Reichenhall 15718
Städtisches Museum, Bruchsal 16370
Städtisches Museum, Eisenhüttenstadt 16826
Städtisches Museum, Halberstadt 17504
Städtisches Museum, Iserlohn 17924
Städtisches Museum, Kitzingen 18105
Städtisches Museum, Menden 18706
Städtisches Museum, Pfungstadt 19396
Städtisches Museum, Überlingen 20245
Städtisches Museum, Welzheim 20507
Städtisches Museum, Werl 20522
Städtisches Museum, Wiesloch 20582
Städtisches Museum Abtshof, Jüterbog 17967
Städtisches Museum/ Daniel-Pöppelmann-Haus, Herford 17720
Städtisches Museum Einbeck, Einbeck 16813
Städtisches Museum Engen galerie, Engen 16874
Städtisches Museum Fürstenwalde, Fürstenwalde, Spree 17163
Städtisches Museum Göppingen im Storchen, Göppingen 17321
Städtisches Museum Göttingen, Göttingen 17341
Städtisches Museum Hann. Münden, Hann Münden 17591
Städtisches Museum im ehemaligen Heiliggeistspital, Munderkingen 18957
Städtisches Museum im Hospital, Nidderau 19091
Städtisches Museum im Kornhaus Bad Waldsee, Bad Waldsee 15759
Städtisches Museum Ludwigsburg, Ludwigsburg, Württemberg 18514
Städtisches Museum Peterskirche, Vaihingen 20282
Städtisches Museum Rosenheim, Rosenheim 19654
Städtisches Museum Seesen, Seesen 19923
Städtisches Museum Simeonstift, Trier 20215
Städtisches Museum Sprucker Mühle, Guben 17451
Städtisches Museum Tuttlinger Haus, Tuttlingen 20239
Städtisches Museum Wesel, Wesel 20538
Städtisches Propsteimuseum mit Römerthermen, Zülpich 20770
Stickereimuseum Eibenstock, Eibenstock 16798
Stiftlandmuseum, Waldsassen 20372
Stiftung Scheibler-Museum Rotes Haus, Monschau 18787
Stoltze-Turm und Stoltze-Museum der Frankfurter Sparkasse, Frankfurt am Main 17077
Storchenturm-Museum, Zell am Harmersbach 20741
Stuhlbau- und Heimatmuseum, Rabenau, Sachsen 19466
Südsauerlandmuseum, Attendorn 15540
Sülchgau-Museum, Rottenburg am Neckar 19691
Sylter Heimatmuseum, Sylt-Ost 20133
Tauberfränkisches Landschaftsmuseum, Tauberbischofsheim 20145
Teplitz-Schönauer Heimatmuseum, Frankfurt am Main 17079
Torhaus Dölitz, Leipzig 18422
Torhaus-Museum, Siegburg 19946
Trachten- und Heimatmuseum, Weiltingen 20453
Troadkasten, Sauerlach 19762
Tüshaus-Mühle, Dorsten 16655
Turmmuseum Schloß Mengerskirchen, Mengerskirchen 18708
Turmmuseum Stadt Blankenberg, Hennef 17711
Turmuhren- und Heimatmuseum Bockenem, Bockenem 16204
Uckermärkisches Volkskundemuseum Templin, Templin 20158
Überseemuseum Bremen, Bremen 16336
Uffenheimer Gollachgaumuseum, Uffenheim 20253
Ur-Donautal-Museum, Wellheim 20506
Vestisches Museum, Recklinghausen 19514
Vielstedter Bauernhaus, Vielstedt 20310
Völkerschlachtdenkmal und Forum 1813, Museum zur Geschichte der Völkerschlacht, Leipzig 18424
Vogelsberger Heimatmuseum, Schotten 19845
Vogteimuseum mit Blumenauer Heimatstube, Aurach 15577
Vogtländisches Dorfmuseum, Erlbach 16926
Vogtländisches Freilichtmuseum, Erlbach 16927
Volkskundliche Sammlung, Mömbris 18768
Volkskundliche Sammlung des Fichtelgebirgsvereins, Weidenberg 20428
Wagstädter Heimatstube, Bad Neustadt an der Saale 15707
Waldmuseum Dr. Kanngiesser, Braunfels 16290
Waldmuseum Göhrde, Göhrde 17312
Waldnaabtal-Museum in der Burg Neuhaus, Windischeschenbach 20607
Wallfahrts- und Heimatmuseum, Altötting 15467
Wassermühle Kuchelmiß, Kuchelmiß 18256
Wassertor-Museum, Isny 17932
Weberhaus Marlesreuth, Naila 18973
Weinbau- und Heimatmuseum, Klingenberg am Main 18110
Weißenhorner Heimatmuseum, Weißenhorn 20501
Werberger Stuben, Motten 18797
Westallgäuer Heimatmuseum, Weiler-Simmerberg 20448
Westfälisches Landesmuseum für Kunst und Kulturgeschichte Münster, Münster 18950
Wetterau-Museum, Friedberg, Hessen 17139
Wilhelm Fabry-Museum, Hilden 17756
Wilhelmsturm Dillenburg Museum, Dillenburg 16610
Wilmersdorf Archiv, Berlin 16116
Windmühle Vahrel, Varel 20288
Winser Museumshof, Winsen, Aller 20612
Wittenberger Freilichtmuseum, Edewecht 16782
Wixhäuser Dorfmuseum, Darmstadt 16551
Wolfsteiner Heimatmuseum im Schramlhaus, Freyung 17135
Zuckmantler Heimatstube, Bietigheim-Bissingen 16162

Ghana

Upper East Region Museum, Bolgatanga 20790
Volta Regional Museum, Ho 20793

Greece

Archipelagos Cultural Center, Athinai 20848
Collection of the Panagia Tourliani, Ano Mera 20827
Ecclesiastical Museum of Alexandroupolis, Alexandroupolis 20815
Gallery of the Society for Epirot Studies, Ioannina 20968
Historical and Ethnological Museum of Cappadocia, Kavala 21011
Historical and Ethnological Museum of the Mani, Kranae 21037
Historical and Folk Art Museum of Gavalohori, Chania 20917
Historical, Folk Art and Natural History Museum of Kozani, Kozani 21036
Historical Museum of Arta, Arta 20838
Manos Faltaits Museum, Euboea 20948
Municipal Gallery of Samos, Samos 21148
Municipal Museum of Kavala, Kavala 21012
Museum Chora, Amorgos 20819
Museum Megalopolis, Megalopolis 21061
Museum of Komotini, Komotini 21026
Museum of Postindependence Athens, Athinai 20887
Museum of the City of Athens, Athinai 20890
Museum of the History and Art of the Holy City of Missolonghi, Mesolongion 21065
Museum of the Statesman Eleftherios Venizelos and the Corresponding Historical Period, Athinai 20891
Museum of Works by Theophilos, Mytilini 21085
Nature-Study and Folk Art Museum of Loutra Almopias, Loutraki 21056
Spetses Museum, Spetses 21168
Tactual Museum, Kallithea 20990
Thessaloniki Museum for the Macedonian Struggle, Thessaloniki 21194

Greenland

Aasiaat Katersugaasiviat Museum, Aasiaat 21228
Avanersuup Katersugaasivia, Qaanaaq 21236
Ilulissat Katersugaasiviat, Ilulissat 21229
Maniitsup Katersugaasivia, Maniitsoq 21231
Nanortallip Katersugaasivia, Nanortalik 21232
Narsaq Museum, Narsaq 21233
Nunatta Katersugaasivia Allagaateqarfialu, Nuuk 21234
Paamiune Katersugausivik, Paamiut 21235
Qaqortup Katersugaasivia, Qaqortoq 21237
Qasigiannguit Katersugaasiviat, Qasigiannguit 21238
Qeqertarsuaq Museum, Qeqertasuaq 21239
Sisimiut Katersugaasiviat, Sisimiut 21240
Tasiilap Katersugaasivia, Tasiilaq 21241
Upernavik Museum, Upernavik 21242
Uummannap Katersugaasivia, Uummannaq 21243

Guadeloupe

Ecomusée de Marie Galante, Grand Bourg 21245
Musée Municipal de Saint-Barthélemy, Saint-Barthélemy 21251

Guam

Faninadahen Kosas Guahan, Adelup 21255
Guam Museum, Agana 21256
War in the Pacific National Historical Park, Piti 21259

Guatemala

Museo de Casa Popenoe, Antigua 21261
Museo del Palacio Nacional, Guatemala 21269
Museo Quezaltenango, Quezaltenango 21277
Museo Silvanus G. Morley y de las Estelas, El Petén 21265

Guinea

Musée Préfectoral de Boké, Boké 21279
Musée Préfectoral de Kissidougou, Kissidougou 21284
Musée Préfectoral de Koundara, Koundara 21285
Musée Préfectoral de N'Zerekore, N'Zerekore 21286

Hungary

Abony Lajos Falumúzeum, Abony 21305
Báthory István Múzeum, Nyírbátor 21491
Beregi Múzeum, Vásárosnamény 21605
Csongrádi Múzeum, Csongrád 21397
Damjanich János Múzeum, Szolnok 21585
Dráva Múzeum, Barcs 21316
Espersit Ház, Makó 21467
Fekete-Ház, Szeged 21547
Helytörténeti Múzeum, Pápa 21500
Hortobágyi Pásztormúzeum, Hortobágy 21433
Intercisa Múzeum, Dunaújváros 21405
Janus Pannonius Múzeum Igazgatòsàga, Pécs 21506
Kiscelli Múzeum, Budapest 21350
Klapka György Múzeum, Komáron 21464
Obudai Helytörténeti Gyűjtemény, Budapest 21368
Pákozdi Csata Emlékmüve, Pákozd 21496
Pékmúzeum, Sopron 21536
Pesterzsébeti Múzeum, Budapest 21377
Semsey Andor Múzeum, Balmazujváros 21315
Somogyi Megyei Múzeumok Igazgatósága, Kaposvár 21442
Tájház, Mezőkövesd 21472
Tatabánya Múzeum, Tatabánya 21595
Tessedik Sámuel Múzeum, Szarvas 21544
Tokaji Múzeum, Tokaji 21599
Town Museum, Gödöllő 21416
Vármúzeum, Esztergom 21414
Városi Múzeum, Kőszeg 21466
Várostörténeti Kiállitás, Sopron 21538
Várostörténeti Múzeum, Székesfehérvár 21563
Vay Adám Múzeum, Vaja 21603

Iceland

Arbæjarsafn, Reykjavík 21648
Byggðasafn, Vestmannaeyjar 21673
Byggðasafn Akraness og Nærsveita, Akranes 21618
Byggðasafn Árnesinga, Eyrarbakki 21631
Byggðasafn Austur-Skaftafellssýslu, Höfn 21638
Byggðasafn Borgarfjardar, Borgarnes 21625
Byggðasafn Dalvíkurbyggdar, Dalvík 21628
Byggðasafn Hafnarfjarðar, Hafnarfjörður 21633
Byggðasafn Rangæinga, Skogar 21670
Byggðasafn Reykjanesbaejar, Reykjanesbaer 21646
Byggðasafn Skagfirdinga, Varmahlid 21672
Byggðasafn Snæfellinga og Hnappdæla, Stykkishólmur 21671
Byggðasafn Vestfjarda, Isafjörður 21641
Byggðasafnid Grenjadarstad, Húsavík 21639
David Stefánsson Memorial Museum, Akureyri 21619
Minjasafn Austurlands, Egilsstadir 21629
Minjasafn Egils Ólafssonar, Patreksfjörður 21645
Minjasafnida å Akureyri, Akureyri 21620
Nonnahůs, Akureyri 21622
P^BDjóðminjasafn Islands, Reykjanik 21647
Safnahusid Húsavík, Húsavík 21640
Sigurhaedir - Hús Skáldsins Museum, Akureyri 21623

India

Akshaya Kumar Maitreya Museum, Siliguri 22025
City Museum, Ahmedabad 21678
DakshinaChitra Museum, Muttukadu 21956
District Museum, Darrang 21757
Gaya Museum, Gaya 21810
Geological Museum, Guwahati 21822
Manjusha Museum, Dharmasthala 21791
Municipal Museum Gwalior, Gwalior 21830
Museum and Art Gallery, Hooghly 21841
Museum of Kerala History, Edapally 21797
Pondicherry Museum, Pondicherry 21983
Prabhas Patan Museum, Prabhas Patan 21984
Sangli State Museum, Sangli 22009
Sardar Patel University Museum, Vallabhvidyanagar 22053
Uttar Pradesh State Museum, Lucknow 21932

Indonesia

Museum Adam Malik, Jakarta 22110
Museum Bahari, Jakarta 22114
Museum Balanga, Palangkaraya 22167
Museum Bangga Lore, Poso 22180
Museum Brawijaya, Malang 22153
Museum Bundo Kandung, Bukittinggi 22092
Museum Daerah Bangkalan, Bangkalan 22077
Museum Daerah Sumenep, Sumenep 22197
Museum Diponegoro, Magelang 22150
Museum Gayo, Aceh Tengah 22062
Museum Gedung Joang '45, Jakarta 22115
Museum Huta Bolon Simanindo, Samosir 22183
Museum Indonesia, Jakarta 22116
Museum Istant Siak Sri Indapura, Bengkalis 22083
Museum Kalimantan Tengah, Palangkaraya 22168
Museum Kartini, Jepara 22143
Museum Kartini Rembang, Rembang 22182
Museum Loka Budaya, Jayapura 22141
Museum Malikusaleh, Aceh Utara 22064
Museum Negeri Bali, Denpasar 22096
Museum Negeri Jambi, Jambi 22140
Museum Negeri Jawa Barat, Bandung 22075
Museum Negeri Kalimantan Barat, Pontianak 22179
Museum Negeri Lampung, Bandarlampung 22069
Museum Negeri Nusa Tenggara Barat, Mataram 22156
Museum Negeri of Bengkulu, Bengkulu 22084
Museum Negeri of Irian Jaya, Jayapura 22142
Museum Negeri Propinsi Sumatera Selatan Balaputra Dewa, Palembang 22169
Museum Negeri Sulawesi Tenggara, Kendari 22146
Museum Negeri Sulawesi Utara, Manado 22154
Museum Pemirintah Daerah Grobogan, Purwodadi Grobogan 22181
Museum Perjuangan, Yogyakarta 22225
Museum Perjuangan Bukit Barisan, Medan 22159
Museum Prabu Geusan Ulun, Sumedang 22196
Museum Purbakala Mojokerto, Mojokerto 22161
Museum Sepakat Segenap, Aceh Tenggara 22063
Museum Simalungun, Pematangsiantar 22177
Museum Suaka Budaya, Surakarta 22206
Museum Sulawesi Tengah, Palu 22172
Puri Gamelan Suar Agung, Denpasar 22098
Tridaya Eka Dharma Museum, Bukittinggi 22093

Iran

Abadan Museum, Abadan 22229
Azarbayezan Museum, Tabriz 22283
Birjand Museum, Birjand 22234
Chehel-Sotoon Museum, Qazvin 22273
Chehel-Sotoon Palace Museum, Isfahan 22245
Contemporary History Museum, Teheran 22292
Gorgan Museum, Gorgan 22239
Haft Tappeh Museum, Haft Tappeh 22241
Iran Bastan Museum, Teheran 22304
Islamic Museum, Teheran 22306
Maragheh Museum, Maragheh 22263
Miyandoab Museum, Miyandoab 22270
Muséyé Kerman, Kerman 22252
Rakhtshuy-Khaneh Museum, Zanjan 22338
Shohada Museum, Ghazvin 22237
Zahedan Museum, Zahedan 22337

Ireland

Ballybunion Heritage Museum, Ballybunion 22368
Belcarra Eviction Cottage, Castlebar 22387
Burren Centre, Kilfenora 22485
Cape Clear Heritage Centre, Skibbereen 22539
Carlow County Museum, Carlow 22383
Cavan County Museum, Ballyjamesduff 22372
Celebration of Irish Museum, Carrickmacross 22384
Clare Heritage Centre, Corofin 22407
Clonfert Museum, Clonfert 22397
Cobh Museum, Cobh 22399
Connemara History and Heritage Centre, Clifden 22394
Cork Public Museum, Cork 22402
County Museum, Sligo 22541
County Museum Dundalk, Dundalk 22463
De Valera Library and Museum, Ennis 22467
Donegal County Museum, Letterkenny 22503
Dublin Civic Museum, Dublin 22422
Dungarvan Museum, Dungarvan 22464
Glencolmcille Folk Village Museum, Glencolmcille 22477
Hillview Museum, Bagenalstown 22364
Inniskeen Folk Museum, Inniskeen 22482
Irish Palatine Association Museum, Rathkeale 22533
Kilmallock Museum, Kilmallock 22494
Kinlough Folk Museum, Kinlough 22497
Kinsale Regional Museum, Kinsale 22499
Knappogue Castle, Quin 22530
Limerick Museum, Limerick 22508
MacSwiney Memorial Museum, Kilmurry 22496
Millmount Museum and Tower, Drogheda 22412
Millstreet Local Museum, Millstreet 22519
Monaghan County Museum, Monaghan 22521
Nenagh District Heritage Centre, Nenagh 22527
North Kerry Museum, Ballyduff 22369
Old Barracks Heritage Centre, Cahersiveen 22382
Quaker Museum, Ballytore 22373
Reginalds Tower, Waterford 22554
Roscommon County Museum, Roscommon 22534
Rothe House Museum, Kilkenny 22488
Saint Mullins Heritage Centre, Saint Mullins 22538
Saint Peter's Church Museum, Kanturk 22483
South Tipperary County Museum, Clonmel 22398
Tullow Museum, Tullow 22550
Valentia Island Heritage Centre, Knightstown 22501
Waterford Treasures at the Granary, Waterford 22555
West Cork Regional Museum, Clonakilty 22396

Israel

Antiquities Museum of Tel Aviv-Yafo, Tel Aviv 22745
Beit Hankin, Kfar Yehoshua 22677
Beit Shturman Museum, Kibbutz Ein Harod 22684
Bialik-Museum, Tel Aviv 22750
Corin Maman Ashdod Museum, Ashdod 22572
Ekron - The Philistine City and it's Culture, Shiqmim 22744
Founders Room, Raanana 22729
Geological Museum, Mizpe Ramon 22716
Gush Ezyon Museum, Gush Ezyon 22594
Haifa City Museum, Haifa 22604
Meir Dizengoff Museum, Tel Aviv 22768
Museum of Acre, Acre 22563
Museum of the History of Tel Aviv-Yafo, Tel Aviv 22770
Museum of the History of Tiberias and the Lake Kinnereth, Tiberias 22782
Old Courtyard Museum, Kibbutz Ein Shemer 22685
Ramla Museum, Ramla 22738
Sharon Museum, Emek Hefer 22591
Shephela Museum, Kibbutz Kfar Menahem 22692
Sturman Institute Museum of Regional Science, Afula 22565
Tel Hai Museum, Tel-Hai 22779

Italy

Antiquarium, Crotone 23688
Antiquarium, Ravello 25076
Antiquarium Civico, Vico del Gargano 25998
Casa Museo Francesco Baracca, Lugo 24238
Casa Museo G. Mazzarino, Pescina 24879
Casa Museo R. Bendandi, Faenza 23749

Civico Museo, Cairo Montenotte 23257
Civico Museo Dianese, Diano Marina 23715
Civico Museo e Antiquarium Comunale, Lanuvio 24139
Civico Museo Flaminio Massetano, Massa Martana 24328
Civico Museo G. Galletti, Domodossola 23719
Civico Museo Morpurgo, Trieste 25816
Civico Museo Storico, Palmanova 24783
Civico Studio Museo Francesco Messina, Milano 24378
Collezione Civica d'Arte, Pinerolo 24926
Enoteca Regionale del Monferrato, Vignale Monferrato 26009
Mostra Permanente della Cultura Materiale, Levanto 24182
Mostra Permanente della Resistenza, Lugo 24239
Musei Civici - Museo della Città, Monza 24558
Musei della Cultura Popolare Radana, San Benedetto Po 25337
Museo Alessandro Minuziano, San Severo 25415
Museo Archeologico di Morgantina, Aidone 22820
Museo Bernardo de Muro, Tempio Pausania 25683
Museo Camillo Leone, Vercelli 25959
Museo Camuno e Biblioteca Civica, Breno 23197
Museo Casa Galimberti, Cuneo 23695
Museo Cervi, Gattatico 23963
Museo Civico, Aci Castello 22797
Museo Civico, Agrigento 22817
Museo Civico, Airola 22822
Museo Civico, Alatri 22827
Museo Civico, Argenta 22925
Museo Civico, Atina 22978
Museo Civico, Bardonecchia 23015
Museo Civico, Belluno 23048
Museo Civico, Bisacquino 23085
Museo Civico, Borgo Velino 23174
Museo Civico, Caprino Veronese 23336
Museo Civico, Casamicciola Terme 23371
Museo Civico, Castel Bolognese 23386
Museo Civico, Castelleone 23410
Museo Civico, Castelnovo Bariano 23416
Museo Civico, Castelnuovo Scrivia 23423
Museo Civico, Cittadella 23583
Museo Civico, Collelongo 23614
Museo Civico, Conversano 23641
Museo Civico, Cori 23651
Museo Civico, Crema 23676
Museo Civico, Crotone 23690
Museo Civico, Cuneo 23696
Museo Civico, Ferentino 23776
Museo Civico, Foggia 23892
Museo Civico, Fondi 23904
Museo Civico, Fornovo San Giovanni 23923
Museo Civico, Fratta Polesine 23935
Museo Civico, Fucecchio 23941
Museo Civico, Gangi 23958
Museo Civico, Larciano 24150
Museo Civico, Licata 24184
Museo Civico, Lodi 24201
Museo Civico, Maddaloni 24257
Museo Civico, Manerbio 24279
Museo Civico, Mattinata 24336
Museo Civico, Medicina 24341
Museo Civico, Mirandola 24431
Museo Civico, Osimo 24708
Museo Civico, Pegognaga 24833
Museo Civico, Pieve di Cento 24919
Museo Civico, Pontecorvo 24997
Museo Civico, Putignano 25057
Museo Civico, San Ferdinando di Puglia 25358
Museo Civico, San Severo 25416
Museo Civico, Trinitapoli 25833
Museo Civico, Vasanello 25902
Museo Civico, Bormio 23179
Museo Civico, San Cesario di Lecce 25346
Museo Civico, Luino 24241
Museo Civico, Rende 25103
Museo Civico, Canneto sull'Oglio 23314
Museo Civico A. Giacomelli, Montagnana 24489
Museo Civico A. Tubino, Masone 24312
Museo Civico A.E. Baruffaldi, Badia Polesine 22997
Museo Civico Alta Val Brembana, Valtorta 25888
Museo Civico Archeologico, Arona 22936
Museo Civico Archeologico, Barbarano Romano 23012
Museo Civico Archeologico, Montalto Marche 24493
Museo Civico Archeologico, Rosignano Marittimo 25284
Museo Civico Archeologico, Salò 25323
Museo Civico Archeologico Trebula Mutesca, Monteleone Sabino 24530
Museo Civico Borbonico, Salle 25322
Museo Civico C. Verri, Biassono 23077
Museo Civico Chiusa, Chiusa 23552
Museo Civico del Castello, Conegliano 23638
Museo Civico del Risorgimento, Modena 24440
Museo Civico della Torre, Treviglio 25801
Museo Civico di Merano - Stadtmuseum Meran, Merano 24352
Museo Civico di Palazzo Te, Mantova 24284
Museo Civico di Santa Maria della Consolazione, Altomonte 22864
Museo Civico Didattico Gian Andrea Irico, Trino 25834
Museo Civico Diocesano La Castellina, Norcia 24636
Museo Civico e d'Arte Sacra, Colle di Val d'Elsa 23609
Museo Civico E. Nardi, Poggio Mirteto 24977
Museo Civico F. L. Belgiorno, Modica 24451
Museo Civico F. Rittatore Von Willer, Farnese 23765
Museo Civico Filippo Meli, Ciminna 23563
Museo Civico G. Ugonia, Brisighella 23215
Museo Civico-Galleria di Palazzo Pretorio, Prato 25044
Museo Civico Giacomo Rodolfo, Carignano 23347
Museo Civico Gonzaga, Novellara 24655
Museo Civico Guiseppe Fiorelli, Lucera 24233
Museo Civico Luigi Dalla Laita, Ala 22823
Museo Civico P. A. Garda, Ivrea 24111
Museo Civico P. Rosario, Ascoli Satriano 22956
Museo Civico Padre Michele Jacobelli, Casalvieri 23369
Museo Civico Preistorico, Pofi 24972
Museo Civico Storico ed Etnografico, Primaluna 25053
Museo Communale Antiquarium, Atena Lucana 22977
Museo Complesso della Collegiata, Castiglione Olona 23436
Museo Comunale della Valle del Sarno, Sarno 25476
Museo Comunale E. Durio, Civiasco 23587
Museo Correr, Venezia 25927
Museo de Ra Regoles, Cortina d'Ampezzo 23661
Museo degli Alpini, Bassano del Grappa 23038
Museo dei Grandi Fiumi, Rovigo 25297
Museo dei Vigili Urbani, Cosenza 23666
Museo del Capriolo, San Donato Val di Comino 25356
Museo del Centro Caprense Ignazio Cerio, Capri 23334
Museo del Lavoro, Follonica 23900
Museo del Lavoro Contadino, Brisighella 23216
Museo del Lavoro Povero e della Civiltà Contadina, Livraga 24196
Museo del Lino, Pescarolo 24871
Museo del Modellismo Storico, Voghiera 26047
Museo del Risorgimento, Castelfidardo 23394
Museo del Risorgimento, Imola 24087
Museo del Risorgimento, Lucca 24229
Museo del Risorgimento, Villafranca 26017
Museo del Risorgimento, Piacenza 24891
Museo del Risorgimento Aurelio Saffi, Forli 23909
Museo del Risorgimento F. Tanara, Langhirano 24137
Museo del Territorio, Foggia 23893
Museo del Territorio, Longiano 24210
Museo del Territorio, San Severino Marche 25413
Museo del Territorio, Finale Emilia 23816
Museo del Territorio dell'Alta Valle dell'Aulella, Casola in Lunigiana 23376
Museo del Villaggio, Chiusa 23553
Museo della Antica Civiltà Locale, Bronte 23217
Museo della Biblioteca Maldotti, Guastalla 24073
Museo della Casa Carsica, Monrupino 24481
Museo della Città, Aquino 22910
Museo della Città, Udine 25848
Museo della Città, Rimini 25115
Museo della Città e del Territorio, Monsummano Terme 24486
Museo della Civiltà Contadina, Barolo 23034
Museo della Civiltà Contadina, Bastiglia 23042
Museo della Civiltà Contadina D. Bianco, Sammichele di Bari 25330
Museo della Civiltà Romana, Roma 25195
Museo della Civiltà Solandra, Malé 24268
Museo della Civitella, Chieti 23546
Museo della Figurina di Gesso e dell'Emigrazione, Coreglia Antelminelli 23649
Museo della Misericordia, San Miniato 25399
Museo della Nostra Terra, Pieve Torina 24923
Museo della Resistanza e della Civiltà Contadina, Pietrabruna 24909
Museo della Resistenza e del Folclore Valsabbino, Pertica Bassa 24844
Museo della Società di Studi Patri, Gallarate 23953
Museo della Società Storia del Novese, Novi Ligure 24657
Museo della Stampa, Jesi 24114
Museo della Val Gardena, Ortisei 24698
Museo della Valchiavenna, Chiavenna 23535
Museo delle Arti e delle Tradizioni di Puglia, Latiano 24157
Museo delle Tradizioni Locali, Zoppè di Cadore 26060
Museo dell'Intreccio Mediterraneo, Castelsardo 23425
Museo dello Studio, Bologna 23120
Museo di Criminologia Medievale, San Gimignano 25364
Museo di Prali e della Val Germanasca, Prali 25034
Museo di Rievocazione Storica, Mondavio 24471
Museo di Rocca Fregoso, Sant'Agata Feltria 25447
Museo di Rodoretto, Prali 25035
Museo di Storia della Mezzadria, Senigallia 25536
Museo di Storia e Arte, Gorizia 24035
Museo di Storia e Cultura della Val del Biois, Vallada Agordina 25878
Museo di Storia Locale, Velturno 25908
Museo di Storia Quarnese, Quarna Sotto 25058
Museo Diefenbach, Capri 23335
Museo Dolomythos di San Candido, San Candido 25343
Museo e Certosa di San Martino, Napoli 24600
Museo elle Arti e Tradizioni Contadine, Roccasecca dei Volsci 25142
Museo elle Genti delle Valli di Lanzo, Ceres 23479
Museo Emidiano, Agnone 22812
Museo Eritreo Bottego, Parma 24809
Museo Etnografico di Servola, Trieste 25828
Museo Etnografico Don Luigi Pellegrini, Castiglione di Garfagnana 23435
Museo Etnografico e Tradizioni Contadine Borgo Antico, Torricella Sicura 25778
Museo F. Renzi, Borghi 23167
Museo Hans Multscher e Museo Civico, Vipiteno 26028
Museo Illichiano, Castell'Arquato 23408
Museo Ladino di Fassa, Pozza di Fassa 25032
Museo Lapidario, Urbino 25860
Museo Lapidario del Duomo di Sant' Eufemia, Grado 24043
Museo Leoniano, Carpineto Romano 23356
Museo Luigi Varoli, Cotignola 23673
Museo Manzoniano, Lesa 24180
Museo Memorie Pollentine, Pollenza 24981
Museo Montemartini, Roma 25229
Museo Nazionale Archeologico, Civitavecchia 23596
Museo Nazionale della Residenza Napoleonica dei Mulini, Portoferraio 25021
Museo Nazionale di Casa Giusti, Monsummano Terme 24488
Museo Nazionale Garibaldino, La Maddalena 24118
Museo Parrocchiale e Museo P. Mascagni, Bagnara di Romagna 23002
Museo Pietro Micca e dell'Assedio, Torino 25760
Museo Pomposiano, Codigoro 23603
Museo Preistorico N. Lamboglia e Val Varatello, Toirano 25716
Museo Quattroruote, Rozzano 25300
Museo Regionale di Camarina, Ragusa 25069
Museo Risorgimentale, Montichiari 24554
Museo Risorgimentale, Pieve di Cadore 24918
Museo Rudolf Stolz, Sesto in Pusteria 25558
Museo Sacrario Galileo Ferraris, Livorno Ferraris 24195
Museo Sardo di Antropologia ed Etnografia, Cagliari 23253
Museo Statale, Mileto 24424
Museo Storico, Montese 24547
Museo Storico Alpino, Antrodoco 22897
Museo Storico C. Musazzi, Parabiago 24790
Museo Storico Cappuccino, Camerino 23290
Museo Storico Civico Cuggionesie, Cuggiono 23693
Museo Storico del Forte, Osoppo 24711
Museo Storico Dittico Alto Livenza, Sacile 25308
Museo Storico Etnografico, Sampeyre 25331
Museo Storico Lisotti Maria, Gradara 24038
Museo Storico Michele Ghislieri, Vicoforte 26002
Museo Storico Navale, Venezia 25944
Museo Storico Novarese Aldo Rossini, Novara 24651
Museo Sveviano, Trieste 25832
Museo Territoriale del Lago di Bolsena, Bolsena 23148
Museo Vallivo, Valfurva 25875
Museo Valtellinese di Storia e Arte, Sondrio 25603
Museo Virgiliano, Virgilio 26030
Museum Passeier - Andreas Hofer, San Leonardo in Passiria 25381
Parco Nazionale delle Incisioni Rupestri, Capo di Ponte 23328
Pinacoteca Civica, Imola 24092
Pinacoteca e Musei Comunali, Macerata 24251
Raccolta Civica, Città di Castello 23582
Raccolta Comunale, Acquasparta 22801
Raccolta Comunale, Celenza Valfortore 23471
Raccolta Comunale, Sigillo 25580
Sala A. De Carolis, Montefiore dell'Aso 24524
Santa Giulia - Museo della Città, Brescia 23210

Jamaica
Jamaica Folk Museum, Kingston 26070
Jamaican People's Museum of Craft and Technology, Spanish Town 26082
Seville Great House and Heritage Park, Ocho Rios 26080

Japan
Aikawa Folk Museum and Exhibition Hall of Folk Crafts, Aikawa 26087
Akadomari-mura Folk Museum, Akadomari 26091
Akita-kenritsu Hakubutsukan, Akita 26094
Aomori-kenritsu Kyodokan, Aomori 26099
Arai-shiritsu Hakubutsukan, Arai 26101
Chiba-kenritsu Kazusa Hakubutsukan, Kisarazu 26337
Chofu Museum, Shimonoseki 26751
Chofu-shiritsu Hakabutsukan, Chofu 26130
Chojagahara Kokokan, Itoigawa 26265
Department of Historical Manuscripts, Tokyo 26840
Echizen-No-Sato Museum, Takefu 26813
Ehime-kenritsu Rekishi Minzoku Shiryokan, Matsuyama 26485
Fukui-kenritsu Hakubutsukan, Fukui 26144
Fukuoka-shi Hakubutsukan, Fukuoka 26147
Fukushima-kenritsu Hakubutsukan, Aizuwakamatsu 26090
Funabashi Hakubutsukan, Funabashi 26154
Gifu-ken Hakubutsukan, Seki 26729
Hachijo Municipal Museum, Hachijo 26161
Hachioji-shi Hakubutsukan, Hachioji 26164
Hagi Municipal Museum, Hagi 26168
Hakodate-shiritsu Hakubutsukan, Hakodate 26172
Hamamatsu-shiritsu Hakubutsukan, Hamamatsu 26180
Hamura-shiritsu Hakubutsukan, Hamura 26181
Hara Castle Memorial Hall, Minamiarima 26490
Higashi-Murayama Municipal Museum of Provincial History, Higashi-Murayama 26188
Higashi-Osaka-shiritsu Kyodo Hakubutsukan, Higashi-Osaka 26189
Higashi-yamate District Historic Preservation Center, Nagasaki 26546
Hirano-go Folk Museum, Osaka 26646
Hirata Kinenkan, Takayama 26808
Hiratsuka-shi Hakubutsukan, Hiratsuka 26208
Hirosaki-shiritsu Hakubutsukan, Hirosaki 26209
Hitachi Kyodo Hakubutsukan, Hitachi 26224
Hokkaido Bungakukan, Sapporo 26710
Hokumouken Kita-mi Bunka, Kita-mi 26339
Hyogo-kenritsu Rekishi Hakubutsukan, Himeji 26196
Ichikawa Municipal Museum, Ichikawa 26236
Iida-shi Bijutsu Hakubutsukan, Iida 26237
Ishikawa-kenritsu Rekishi Hakubutsukan, Kanazawa 26309
Ishikawa Takuboku Memorial Museum, Tamayama 26818
Itami-shiritsu Hakubutsukan, Itami 26262
Itsutsubashikan, Sendai 26730
Iwakuni Municipal Museum, Iwakuni 26272
Iwate-kenritsu Hakubutsukan, Morioka 26515
Joetsu-shiritsu Hakubutsukan, Joetsu 26282
Kagoshima-kenritsu Hakubutsukan, Kagoshima 26288
Kamada Local Museum, Sakaide 26701
Kamiina Museum, Ina 26246
Kanagawa-kenritsu Rekishi Hakabutsukan, Yokohama 27015
Kanai-machi Hakabutsukan, Kanai 26303
Kawasaki-shi Shimin Hakubutsukan, Kawasaki 26328
Kii Fudoki-No-Oka Museum, Wakayama 26996
Kitakamakura Museum, Kamakura 26295
Kitakami Municipal Museum, Kitakami 26341
Kiyose-shi Kyodo Hakubutsukan, Kiyose 26344
Koan Collection, Hadano 26167
Kobe-shiritsu Hakubutsukan, Kobe 26350
Kokubunji Cultural Exhibition Center, Kokubunji 26365
Komatsu Shiritsu Hakubutsukan, Komatsu 26368
Kosanji Temple Museum, Toyota, Hiroshima 26975
Kumamoto-shiritsu Hakubutsukan, Kumamoto 26378
Kunisaki-machi Rekishi Minzoku Shiryokan, Kunisaki 26379
Kuramayama Museum, Kyoto 26417
Kushiro City Museum, Kushiro 26391
Kyoto-fu Kyoto Bunka Hakubutsukan, Kyoto 26422
Machida-shiritsu Hakubutsukan Machida City Museum, Machida 26463
Matsudo Museum, Matsodo 26469
Matsumoto-shiritsu Hakubutsukan, Matsumoto 26477
Matsushima Kanrantei Museum, Matsushima 26481
Mie-kenritsu Hakubutsukan, Tsu 26977
Minami-yamate District Historic Preservation Center, Nagasaki 26548
Minowa Museum, Minowa 26493
Miyazaki-ken Sogo Hakubutsukan, Miyazaki, Miyazaki-ken 26511
Morioka City Local Hall, Morioka 26517
Musashimurayama City Rekishi Minzoku Shiryo-kan, Musashimurayama 26523
Museums Abashirikangoku, Abashiri 26085
Nagaoka-shiritsu Hakabutsukan, Nagaoka 26534
Nagasaki City Museum of History and Folklore, Nagasaki 26552
Nagoya-shi Hakubutsukan, Nagoya, Aichi 26569
Nakano Historical Museum, Tokyo 26896
Nerima Home Town Museum, Tokyo 26898
Niigata City Folk Museum, Niigata 26592
Niigata-kenritsu Rekishi Hakubutsukan, Nagaoka 26537
Ningyo no Ie, Kyoto 26439
Nippon Kokeshi Museum, Naruko 26588
Okayama-kenritsu Hakubutsukan, Okayama 26627
Okayama-kenritsu Kibiji Local Museum, Soja 26772
Okinawa-kenritsu Hakubutsukan, Naha 26572
Ome-shiritsu Hakubutsukan, Ome 26636
Osaka Museum of History, Osaka 26666
Otaru-shi Hakubutsukan, Otaru 26679
Prefectural Assembly Memorial Hall, Niigata 26597
Ryotsu Folk Museum, Ryotsu 26687
Sado Hakabutsukan, Sawata 26727
Sado-koku Ogi Folk Museum, Ogi 26620
Saga-kenritsu Hakubutsukan, Saga 26691
Saijo Municipal Local Museum, Saijo 26692
Saitama-kenritsu Hakubutsukan, Omiya 26639
Sakai-shiritsu Hakubutsukan, Sakai 26699
Sendai-shi Hakubutsukan, Sendai 26736
Shenshu-Bunko Museum, Tokyo 26918
Shibayama Haniwa Hakubutsukan, Shibayama 26743
Shiga-kenritsu Omi Fudoki-No-Oka Shiryokan, Azuchi 26116
Shikoku Minka Hakubutsukan, Takamatsu 26792
Shimosuwa Museum, Shimosuwa 26755
Shin-Yokohama Ramen Hakubutsukan, Yokohama 27018
Shinagawa Historical Museum, Tokyo 26919
Shitamachi Museum, Tokyo 26921
Shoko Shuseikan Historical Museum, Kagoshima 26290
Shokokan Museum, Mito 26505
Snow Country Tree Museum, Shiozawa 26761
Soma Gyofu Kinenkan, Itoigawa 26268
Sukagawa-shiritsu Hakubutsukan, Sukagawa 26777
Tama Seiseki Kinenkan, Tama 26816
Tochigi-kenritsu Hakubutsukan, Utsunomiya 26994
Tokushima Prefectural Local Culture Hall, Tokushima 26827
Tottori-kenritsu Hakubutsukan, Tottori 26964
Urahoro-cho Kyodo Hakubutsukan, Urahoro 26992
Uwajima-shiritsu Date Hakubutsukan, Uwajima 26995

Village Museum of Local History, Chihaya-Akasa 26126
Wakayama-kenritsu Hakubutsukan, Wakayama 26997
Yaeyama Museum, Ishigaki 26258
Yakage Museum, Yakage 27001
Yamaguchi-kenritsu Hakubutsukan, Yamaguchi 27005
Yanaga Hokkaido Museums, Sapporo 26723
Yuzawa History and Folk Museum, Yuzawa 27039

Jordan
Al-Karak Museum for Archaeology and Folklore, Al-Karak 27041
Madaba Archaeology Museum, Ajloun 27040
Petra Museum, Petra 27065

Kazakhstan
Čimkentskij Istoriko-Kraevedčeskij Muzej, Čimkent 27078
Džambul Historical and Regional Museum, Džambul 27080
East Kazakhstan Historical and Regional Museum, Ust-Kamenogorsk 27099
Gurievskij Istoriko-Kraevedčeskij Muzej, Guriev 27084
Istoriko-Kraevedčeskij Muzej, Arkalyk 27075
Istoriko-Kraevedčeskij Muzej, Karaganda 27085
Istoriko-Kraevedčeskij Muzej, Temirtau 27097
Istoriko-Kraevedčeskij Muzej Džezkazgana, Džezkazgan 27083
Istoriko-Kraevedčeskij Muzej Kokčetava, Kokčetav 27086
Istoriko-Kraevedčeskij Muzej Kzyl-Orda, Kzyl-Orda 27087
Istoriko-Kraevedčeskij Muzej Mangyšlaka, Ševčenko 27095
Istoriko-Kraevedčeskij Muzej Vostočnogo Kazachstana, Petropavlovsk 27090
Memorialnyj Muzej Alii Moldagulovoj, Geroiny Sovetskogo Sojuza, Aktöbe 27070
Muzej Prezidentskogo Centra Kultury Respubliki Kazachstan, Astana 27077
Pavlodarskij Istoriko-Kraevedčeskij Muzej, Pavlodar 27089
Semipalatinskij Istoriko-Kraevedčeskij Muzej, Semey 27093
Uralskij Istoriko-Kraevedčeskij Muzej, Uralsk 27098

Kenya
Kabarnet Museum, Kabarnet 27103
Kisumu Museum, Kisumu 27105
Lamu Museum, Lamu 27107
Meru Museum, Meru 27108

Korea, Democratic People's Republic
Myohyang-san Museum, Hyangsan 27118
Shinchon Museum, Shinchon 27124

Korea, Republic
Busan Museum, Busan 27137
Cheongju National Museum, Cheongju 27149
Chungju Museum, Chungju 27152
Chungnam University Museum, Daejeon 27159
Daegu National Museum, Daegu 27154
Dongguk University Museum, Seoul 27230
Gangneung Municipal Museum, Gangneung 27168
Gangwon Folk Museum, Cheongil 27147
Geochang Museum, Geochang 27171
Geoje Museum, Geoje 27172
Gwangju Municipal Folk Museum, Gwangju 27182
Gwangju National Museum, Gwangju 27183
Gyemyung University Museum, Daegu 27156
Gyeongbuk National University Museum, Daegu 27157
Gyeonggi Provincial Museum, Yongin 27299
Gyeongju National Museum, Gyeongju 27185
Hong-ik University Museum, Seoul 27238
Incheon Metropolitan City Museum, Incheon 27191
Jeonju Municipal Museum, Jeonju 27199
Jeonju National Museum, Jeonju 27200
Korea University Museum, Seoul 27246
Kyunghee University Museum, Seoul 27255
Mireuksa Temple Museum, Iksan 27188
Miryang Municipal Museum, Miryang 27211
Museum of Daejeon History, Daejeon 27162
Sungjon University Museum, Seoul 27286
Yeongil Folk Museum, Pohang 27218

Kyrgyzstan
Istoriko-Kraevedčeskij Muzej, Tokmok 27316
Osškij Objedinennyj Istoriko-Kulturnyj Muzej-Zapovednik, Oš 27312
Przhevalsk Regional Museum, Prževalsk 27314

Laos
Musée Kaysone Phomvihane, Vientiane 27320

Latvia
Aizkraukles Vēstures un Mākslas Muzejs, Aizkraukle 27328
Bauskas Novadpētniecības un Mākslas Muzejs, Bauska 27334
Daugavpils Muzeja, Daugavpils 27345
Liepājas Muzeja, Liepāja 27378
Rīgas Vēstures un Kuģniecības muzejs, Rīga 27441

Liechtenstein
DoMuS - Museum und Galerie der Gemeinde Schaan, Schaan 27510
Liechtensteinisches Landesmuseum, Vaduz 27516
Walser Heimatmuseum, Triesenberg 27513
Wohnmuseum Schellenberg, Schellenberg 27512

Lithuania
Šiauliai Aušros Museum, Šiauliai 27531
Trakai Historical Museum, Trakai 27534
Žeimelis Žiemgalos Museum, Žeimelis 27540

Luxembourg
A. Schiiwesch Musée Rural, Binsfeld 27544
Musée d'Histoire de la Ville de Luxembourg, Luxembourg 27565
Musée Local, Brandenbourg 27545
Musée Local, Weiler-la-Tour 27581
Musée Municipal, Dudelange 27551

Macedonia
Muzej-Galerija Kavadarci, Kavadarci 27585
Muzej i Galerija Bitola, Bitola 27584
Naroden Muzej, Ohrid 27587
Pokrajinski Muzej, Strumica 27596
Zavod za Zaštita na Spomenicite na Kulturata, Prirodnite Retkosti i Muzej, Strumica 27597

Madagascar
Musée de l'Université de Fianarantsoa, Fianarantsoa 27606
Musée Régional du Cerel, Toamasina 27609

Malawi
Lake Malawi Museum, Mangochi 27612
Mzuzu Regional Museum, Mzuzu 27613

Malaysia
Istana Batu, Kota Bharu 27629
Lembaga Muzium Negeri, Pulau Pinang 27681
Museum of History and Ethnography Negeri, Melaka 27667
Muzium Alor Gajah, Melaka 27668
Muzium Darul Ridzwan, Ipoh 27622
Muzium Negeri Perlis, Kangar 27625
Muzium Negeri Selangor, Shah Alam 27687
Muzium Negeri Trengganu, Kuala Terengganu 27656
P. Ramlee Memorial, Kuala Lumpur 27649
Public Service Memorial, Kuala Lumpur 27650
Pucuk Rebung Royal Gallery Museum, Kuala Lumpur 27651
Royal Museum Sri Menanti, Seremban 27685
Sultan Abu Bakar Museum Pahang, Pekan 27679
Tin Museum - Gedung Raja Abdullah, Kelang 27627
Tunku Abdul Rahman Memorial, Kuala Lumpur 27655

Maldives
National Museum, Malé 27690

Mali
Musée Régional de Sikasso, Sikasso 27693
Musée Régional du Sahel, Gao 27692

Mauritania
Musée de Ouadane, Nouakchott 27730

Mauritius
Vieux Grand Port Archaeological Site, Old Grand Port 27736

Mexico
Casa de Hidalgo, Dolores Hidalgo 27891
Ex Convento de Santo Domingo de Guzman, Oaxtepec 28280
Museo Anenecuilco, Ayala 27785
Museo Antzetik Ta Jtelum, Zinacantán 28656
Museo Bahía de los Angeles, Ensenada 27912
Museo Balaa Xte Guech Gulal, Teotitlán del Valle 28484
Museo Benito Juárez, José Azueta 28034
Museo Bernabé de las Casas, Mina 28218
Museo Campamento Irritila, San Pedro 28419
Museo Casa de la Cultura, Montemorelos 28228
Museo Casa de Morelos, Ecatepec de Morelos 27902
Museo Casa de Morelos, Morelia 28243
Museo Casa del Deán, Puebla 28321
Museo Casa del Diego, Celaya 27808
Museo Casa del Dr. Mora, Comonfort 27851
Museo Casa Francisco Villa, Hidalgo del Parral 27991
Museo Casa Mata, Matamoros 28073
Museo Casa Maya, Cancún 27804
Museo Cerro de la Campana, Santiago Suchilquitongo 28439
Museo Cerro de los Huizaches, San Pablo Huixtepec 28418
Museo Ciénaga de San Pedro, Madera 28065
Museo Coahuila y Texas, Monclova 28225
Museo Comunitario, Mineral del Monte 28220
Museo Comunitario, Puente de Ixtla 28346
Museo Comunitario Altagracia de Arauz, Ensenada 27913
Museo Comunitario Amuzgo de Xochistlahuaca, Xochistlahuaca 28625
Museo Comunitario Colonia Vicente Guerrero, Colonia Vicente Guerrero 27843
Museo Comunitario Concuemitl, Cuencamé 27872
Museo Comunitario Coronela Amelia La Güera Robles, Xochipala 28624
Museo Comunitario Crónica y Arte Agropecuario de la Sierra Gorda, Landa de Matamoros 28050
Museo Comunitario Cuarenta Casas, Valentín Gómez Farías 28581
Museo Comunitario de Antropología e Historia, Apatzingán 27774
Museo Comunitario de Atoyac, Atoyac 27783
Museo Comunitario de Carrillo Puerto, Alvaro Obregón 27769
Museo Comunitario de Ciudad Lerdo, Lerdo 28058

Museo Comunitario de Historia de San José de Gracia, San José de Gracia 28387
Museo Comunitario de Huitzapula, Huitzapula 28007
Museo Comunitario de Ixtlahuacán, Ixtlahuacán 28018
Museo Comunitario de la Ballena, La Paz 28042
Museo Comunitario de Las Varas, Compostela 27852
Museo Comunitario de Pejelagartero, Huimanguillo 28005
Museo Comunitario de Pipillola, Españita 27921
Museo Comunitario de San Andrés Mixquic, México 28120
Museo Comunitario de San Nicolás Zoyatlán, San Nicolás Zoyatlán 28416
Museo Comunitario de Santa Eulalia, Santa Euralia 28433
Museo Comunitario de Santa Martha, Mulegé 28257
Museo Comunitario de Tototepec, Tototepec 28564
Museo Comunitario de Xalisco, Xalisco 28619
Museo Comunitario de Xolalpan, Ixtacamaxtitlán 28016
Museo Comunitario del Valle de Guadalupe, Ensenada 27914
Museo Comunitario El Rosario, El Rosario 27907
Museo Comunitario Felipe Carrillo Puerto, Motul 28255
Museo Comunitario Francisco I. Madero, Francisco I. Madero, Coahuila 27924
Museo Comunitario Hicupa, Tehuacán 28473
Museo Comunitario Hitalulu, San Martín Huamelulpan 28408
Museo Comunitario Huitza Chilin, San Pedro 28420
Museo Comunitario Iluikatlachiyalistli, Yahualica 28628
Museo Comunitario Ismael Girón González, Pánuco, Zacatecas 28302
Museo Comunitario Itzmal Kauil, Izamal 28020
Museo Comunitario Ji, Ocosingo 28284
Museo Comunitario Jna Niingui, San Miguel Tequixtepec 28413
Museo Comunitario Joyonaque, Tuxtla Gutiérrez 28570
Museo Comunitario Juan García Aldama de la Comunidad Cucapá, El Mayor Indígena 27905
Museo Comunitario Kumkuy Ys Untzi, Copainalá 27855
Museo Comunitario Maika, Poanas 28315
Museo Comunitario Note Ujía, Santa María Asunción Tlaxiaco 28434
Museo Comunitario Nu-kuiñe, Cuquila 27887
Museo Comunitario Rubén Jaramillo, Tlaquiltenango 28531
Museo Comunitario Serafín Olarte, Papantla 28303
Museo Comunitario Shan-Dany, Santa Ana del Valle 28426
Museo Comunitario sin Paredes Colonia Orizaba, Mexicali 28089
Museo Comunitario Snuuvico, San Juan Mixtepec Juxtlahuaca 28396
Museo Comunitario Tejamen, Nuevo Ideal 28270
Museo Comunitario Tzakualli, Zacualpan 28645
Museo Comunitario Unión y Progreso, Cuatrocienegas 27869
Museo Comunitario Xiximes, Gómez Palacio 27935
Museo Comunitario Xolalpan Calli, Hueyapan 28002
Museo Comunitario Ya Nñädi Yu Nohño Los Conocimientos de los Otomíes, Tolimán 28539
Museo Comunitario Yucu-Iti, Santa María Yucu-Iti 28435
Museo Comunitario Ze Acatl Topiltzin Quetzalcoatl, Tepoztlán 28501
Museo Contalpa de Nombre de Dios, Nombre de Dios 28269
Museo Costumbrista de Sonora, Alamos 27765
Museo de Acaponeta, Acaponeta 27746
Museo de Aguascalientes, Aguascalientes 27754
Museo de Ahumada, Villa Ahumada y Anexas 28603
Museo de Akil Uyotoch Cah, Akil 27764
Museo de Ameca, Vetagrande 28596
Museo de Antropología e Historia de Allende, Allende 27767
Museo de Antropología e Historia de Santiago Papasquiaro, Santiago Papasquiaro 28438
Museo de Atoyac, Atoyac de Alvarez 27784
Museo de Ayutla, Ayutla de los Libres 27786
Museo de Batopilas, Francisco I. Madero, Coahuila 27925
Museo de Bermejillo, Bermejillo 27792
Museo de Buenos Aires, Tacotalpa 28448
Museo de Campeche, Campeche 27796
Museo de Ciudades Hermanas, Guadalajara 27950
Museo de Cochoapa, Ometepec 28289
Museo de Colón, Colón 27841
Museo de Conkal, Conkal 27854
Museo de Cosautlán de Carvajal, Cosautlán de Carvajal 27861
Museo de Coscomatepec, Coscomatepec de Bravo 27862
Museo de Cuajinicuilapa, Cuajinicuilapa 27866
Museo de El Pueblito, Corregidora 27859
Museo de Emiliano Zapata, Emiliano Zapata 27909
Museo de General Zaragoza, General Zaragoza 27933
Museo de Guadalupe, Guadalupe 27962
Museo de Guamúchil de Salvador Alvarado, Guamúchil 27966
Museo de Historia de Ensenada, Ensenada 27916
Museo de Historia de Higueras, Higueras 27992
Museo de Historia de Lampazos de Naranjo y las Armas Nacionales, Lampazos de Naranjo 28049

Museo de Historia de Linares, Linares 28062
Museo de Historia Regional de Pánuco, Pánuco, Veracruz 28301
Museo de Historia Regional de Sabinas Hidalgo, Sabinas Hidalgo 28362
Museo de Hostotipaquillo, Hostotipaquillo 27993
Museo de Jala, Jala 28021
Museo de Jamapa, Jamapa 28026
Museo de la Casa de Cultura de Zacapú, Zacapu 28633
Museo de la Casa de la Cultura, San Luis Potosí 28400
Museo de la Casa del Risco, México 28135
Museo de La Cerería, Tlayacapan 28536
Museo de la Ciudad, Campeche 27797
Museo de la Ciudad, Guadalajara 27951
Museo de la Ciudad, Mérida 28083
Museo de la Ciudad, Tecate 28466
Museo de la Ciudad de Chetumal, Chetumal 27816
Museo de la Ciudad de Córdoba, Córdoba 27857
Museo de la Ciudad de Irapuato, Irapuato 28013
Museo de la Ciudad de León, León 28055
Museo de la Ciudad de México, México 28137
Museo de la Ciudad de Querétaro, Querétaro 28353
Museo de la Ciudad de Sombrerete, Sombrerete 28446
Museo de la Ciudad de Tepatitlán de Morelos, Tepatitlán de Morelos 28485
Museo de la Ciudad de Veracruz, Veracruz 28594
Museo de la Ciudad Tuxtlán, Tuxtla Gutiérrez 28571
Museo de la Colonia Siete de Marzo, Juan Aldama 28035
Museo de la Iguana, Tecomán 28469
Museo de la Isla de Cozumel, Cozumel 27865
Museo de la Labranza, Francisco I. Madero, Hidalgo 27928
Museo de la Tortuga, Aquila 27778
Museo de la Villa de Ahome, Ahome 27760
Museo de Lagos de Moreno, Lagos de Moreno 28048
Museo de las Culturas de la Huasteca Potosina Tamuantzán, Valles 28587
Museo de los Altos de Chiapas, San Cristóbal de las Casas 28378
Museo de Maní y Museo del Convento San Miguel Arcángel, Maní 28067
Museo de Mexticacan, Mexticacán 28215
Museo de Mier y Noriega, Mier y Noriega 28217
Museo de Minería e Historia de Cosala, Cosalá 27860
Museo de Paracho, Paracho 28305
Museo de Pungarabato, Pungarabato 28351
Museo de Ruiz, Ruiz 28361
Museo de San Juan Raya, Zapotitlán Salinas 28650
Museo de San Juan Tlacotenco, San Juan Tlacotenco 28397
Museo de San Miguel, Tlaxiaco 28535
Museo de San Pablo, San Pablo Huitzo 28417
Museo de San Pedro, Navolato 28265
Museo de San Pedro, San Pedro Lagunillas 28423
Museo de Sayula Juan Rulfo, Sayula 28443
Museo de Susticacán, Susticacán 28447
Museo de Tacuichamona, Culiacán 27884
Museo de Tahdziú, Tahdziú 28450
Museo de Tapalpa, Tapalpa 28456
Museo de Taximaroa, Hidalgo 27990
Museo de Tepeticpa, Tepeticpa 28491
Museo de Texcalyacac, Texcalyacac 28507
Museo de Tlahualilo, Tlahualilo de Zaragoza 28521
Museo de Tlalancaleca, San Matías Tlalancaleca 28409
Museo de Tlapa, Tlapa de Comonfort 28527
Museo de Tlayacapan, Tlayacapan 28537
Museo de Totolapan, Totolapan 28563
Museo de Tultitlán, Tultitlán de Mariano Escobedo 28566
Museo de Velardeña, Velardeña 28591
Museo de Xiutetelco, Xiutetelco 28622
Museo de Xochitepec, Xochitepec 28626
Museo de Xolalpancalli, Zacapoaxtla 28632
Museo de Yautepec, Yautepec 28629
Museo del Centro Cultural Joaquín Arcadio Pagaza, Valle de Bravo 28583
Museo del Centro Cultural La Cantera, Jonacatepec 28032
Museo del Centro Cultural Sor Juana Inés de la Cruz, Tepetlixpa 28492
Museo del Centro Histórico, San Juan del Río 28393
Museo del Cuale, Puerto Vallarta 28349
Museo del Ejidatario, Guasave 27979
Museo del Estado, Morelia 28251
Museo del Pueblo, Guanajuato 27974
Museo del Tequila, Tequila 28504
Museo del Valle de Tehuacán, Tehuacán 28475
Museo del Valle de Xico, Valle de Chalco 28584
Museo Dr. José Gómez Panaco, Balancán 27790
Museo El Centenario, Garza García 27930
Museo El Pariancito, San Luis Potosí 28404
Museo Escolar y Comunitario de Acamalín, Xico 28620
Museo Filemón Gutiérrez Ramírez, Ameca 27771
Museo Fin de la Tierra, Francisco I. Madero, Coahuila 27926
Museo Fuentes de Loreto y Guadalupe, Palmar de Bravo 28300
Museo Fundación Estero Beach, Ensenada 27917
Museo General Porfirio Rubio, Landa de Matamoros 28051
Museo Gonzalo Carrasco, Otumba 28291
Museo Hacienda San Pedro, General Zuazua 27934

Museo Hermenegildo Galeana, Tecpan de Galeana 28470
Museo Histórica Ex Convento de Tepoztlán, Tepoztlán 28503
Museo Histórico de Acapulco, Acapulco 27747
Museo Histórico de Ayotzinapa, Tixtla de Guerrero 28517
Museo Histórico de Guachinango, Guachinango 27938
Museo Histórico de la Ciudad, Torreón 28557
Museo Histórico de Múzquiz, Múzquiz 28259
Museo Histórico de Reynosa, Reynosa 28357
Museo Histórico de San Miguel de Allende, San Miguel de Allende 28410
Museo Histórico de San Nicolás de los Garza, San Nicolás de los Garza 28415
Museo Histórico Municipal, Ocotlán 28286
Museo Histórico Municipal, Taxco de Alarcón 28462
Museo Histórico Regional Ex Cuartel de la Compañía Fija, Ensenada 27918
Museo Huehuetla-tolli, Comala 27846
Museo Hunucmá de Sisal, Hunucmá 28008
Museo Irineo Germán, Azoyú 27787
Museo José María Luis Mora, Ocoyoacac 28287
Museo José y Tomás Chávez Morado, Silao 28445
Museo Juárez e Historia de Mapimí y Ojuela, Mapimí 28070
Museo Juarista de Congregación Hidalgo, Entronque Congregación Hidalgo 27919
Museo La Chole, Petatlán 28309
Museo La Flor de Jimulco, Torreón 28558
Museo La Pesca, Benito Juárez 27791
Museo Local de Acámbaro, Dolores Hidalgo 27893
Museo Local de Antropología e Historia de Compostela, Compostela 27853
Museo Local de Valle de Santiago, Valle de Santiago 28585
Museo Local Tuxteco, Santiago Tuxtla 28441
Museo Lucio Balderas Márquez, Landa de Matamoros 28052
Museo Manuel Ojinaga, Manuel Ojinaga 28068
Museo Metropolitano de Monterrey, Monterrey 28238
Museo Mohicca, Mohicca 28223
Museo Morelos, Carácuaro 27806
Museo Municipal, Mier 28216
Museo Municipal de Historia Malitzín de Huiloapan, Huiloapan de Cuauhtémoc 28004
Museo Municipal de Historia y Arqueología, González 27937
Museo Municipal IV Centenario, Pinos 28312
Museo Municipal Jesús González Herrera, Matamoros 28074
Museo Municipal Jesús H. Salgado, Teloloapan 28476
Museo Municipal José Reyes Meza, Altamira 27768
Museo Municipal Los Guachimontones y Museo de Arquitectura Prehispánica, Teuchitlán 28506
Museo Municipal Quetzalpapalotl, Teotihuacán 28483
Museo Nezahualcóyotl Acomiztli, Nezahualcóyotl 28267
Museo Ñiace, Tepelmeme de Morelos 28490
Museo Nuestro Pueblo y Museo Etnográfico de Tecpatán, Tecpatán 28471
Museo Parroquial, San Sebastián del Oeste 28425
Museo Peñón Blanco, Peñón Blanco 28308
Museo Petatlán, Petatlán 28310
Museo Peten Ak, Valladolid 28582
Museo Prof. Arturo Reyes Viramontes, Jalpa 28023
Museo Prof. Moisés Sáenz Garza, Apodaca 27777
Museo Prof. Ricardo Vega Noriega, San Ignacio 28386
Museo Raíces de Satevó, Satevó 28442
Museo Regional, San Juan Bautista Tuxtepec 28389
Museo Regional Comunitario Altepepialcalli, México 28197
Museo Regional Cuauhnáhuac, Cuernavaca 27876
Museo Regional de Acambay, Acambay 27744
Museo Regional de Aldama, Aldama 27766
Museo Regional de Arte e Historia, Jerez de García Salinas 28030
Museo Regional de Campeche, Campeche 27800
Museo Regional de Chiapas, Tuxtla Gutiérrez 28575
Museo Regional de Cuetzalan, Cuetzalán 27879
Museo Regional de Durango y Museo del Niño, Durango 27901
Museo Regional de Guanajuato Alhóndiga de Granaditas, Guanajuato 27977
Museo Regional de Guerrero, Chilpancingo 27832
Museo Regional de Hidalgo, Pachuca 28297
Museo Regional de Historia de Colima, Colima 27838
Museo Regional de Iguala, Iguala de la Independencia 28012
Museo Regional de la Laguna, Torreón 28560
Museo Regional de las Culturas Occidente, Guzmán 27982
Museo Regional de Mascota, Mascota 28072
Museo Regional de Nayarit, Tepic 28499
Museo Regional de Nuevo León, Monterrey 28239
Museo Regional de Puebla, Puebla 28342
Museo Regional de Querétaro, Querétaro 28355
Museo Regional de Río Verde, Río Verde 28359
Museo Regional de Sinaloa, Culiacán 27886
Museo Regional de Sonora, Hermosillo 27988
Museo Regional de Tierra Caliente, Coyuca de Catalán 27864
Museo Regional de Tlaxcala, Tlaxcala 28534
Museo Regional de Yucatán, Mérida 28085
Museo Regional del Valle del Fuerte, Ahome 27761
Museo Regional El Fuerte, El Fuerte 27903
Museo Regional Huasteco, Valles 28588
Museo Regional Lázaro Cárdenas, Tlapehuala 28528
Museo Regional Luciano Márquez, Zacatlán 28644
Museo Regional Michoacano, Morelia 28253
Museo Regional Potosino, San Luis Potosí 28407
Museo Regional Rescate de Raíces, Ahualulco de Mercado 27763
Museo Regional Rufino Muñiz Torres, Ocampo 28283
Museo Regional Valparaíso, Valparaiso 28589
Museo San José el Mogote, San José el Mogote 28388
Museo San Juan en la Historia, San Juan del Río 28395
Museo San Miguel Teotongo, México 28200
Museo Senen Mexic, Acatlán de Osorio 27750
Museo Tarike, Chihuahua 27828
Museo Taurino, Huamantla 27995
Museo Tepeapulco, Tepeapulco 28488
Museo Tetetzontlilco, Tizayuca 28519
Museo Tlallán, Tala 28451
Museo Tohue, Vicente Guerrero, Durango 28600
Museo Tomaskitla, Epazoyucan 27920
Museo Tomochic, Vicente Guerrero 28599
Museo Tonallán, Tonalá, Jalisco 28554
Museo Tonatiuh, Zempoala 28653
Museo Towi, Guachochi 27941
Museo Wakuatay, Playas de Rosarito 28314
Museo Xochiltepec, Magdalena 28066
Museo Xólotl, San Bartolo Tenayuca 28376
Museo Yoloxúchitl, Cuernavaca 27877
Museo Zacatecano, Zacatecas 28642
Museo Zoloxúchitl, Zacualpan 28646
Recinto Casa Benito Juárez, Saltillo 28372

Mongolia
Ulaanbaatar City Museum, Ulaanbaatar 28687

Morocco
Musée du Batha, Fèz 28695
Musée Sidi Med Ben Abdellah, Essaouira 28693

Mozambique
Fondaçao-Museu Chissano, Matola 28728
Museu de Nampula, Nampula 28729
Museum Municipal, Beira 28718

Myanmar
National Museum of Mandalay, Mandalay 28733
Pathein Museum, Pathein 28741
Rakhine State Museum, Sitture 28743
Shan State Museum, Taunggyi 28745
State Library and Museum, Mawlamyine 28737

Namibia
Gobabis Museum, Gobabis 28754
Grootfontein Museum Das Alte Fort, Grootfontein 28755
Helmeringhausen Museum, Helmeringhausen 28756
Keetmanshoop Museum, Keetmanshoop 28757
Kolmanskop Museum, Kolmanskop 28758
Lizauli Cultural Village, Lizauli 28759
Lüderitz Museum, Lüderitz 28760
Nakambale Museum, Ondangwa 28766
Omaruru Museum, Omaruru 28764
Ombalantu Baobab Tree, Ombalantu 28765
Outjo Museum, Outjo 28768
Rehoboth Museum, Rehoboth 28769
Sperrgebiet Museum, Oranjemund 28767
Swakopmund Museum, Swakopmund 28773
Tsumeb Museum, Tsumeb 28776
Walvis Bay Museum, Walvis Bay 28777

Nepal
Memorial Museum King Tribhuvan, Kathmandu 28787

Netherlands
Aldfaers Erf Route, Allingawier 28807
Aldheidskeamer Uldrik Bottema, Aldeboarn 28801
Amerongs Historisch Museum/ Tabaksmuseum, Amerongen 28817
Amsterdams Historisch Museum, Amsterdam 28836
Archeologisch en Paleontologisch Museum Hertogsgemaal, 's-Hertogenbosch 29402
Archeologisch Museum Haarlem, Haarlem 29322
De Baracquen Museum voor Bourtanger Bodemvondsten, Bourtange 29009
Biesbosch Museum, Werkendam 29993
Brabants Museum Oud Oosterhout, Oosterhout 29670
Breda's Museum, Breda 29020
Brouws Museum, Brouwershaven 29031
Cultuur-Historisch Museum Sorgdrager, Hollum 29431
Cultuurhistorisch Museum Valkenswaard, Valkenswaard 29922
Dongha Museum, Dongen 29166
Dorpsmuseum de Kleuskes, Liempde 29539
Dorpsmuseum De Kluis, Eext 29203
Dorpsmuseum in de Drie Snoeken, Oud-Gastel 29690
Drenthe's Veste Stedelijk Museum, Coevorden 29057
Driels Oudheidkundig Museum, Kerkdriel 29479
Edams Museum, Edam 29191
Enkhuizer Almanak Museum, Enkhuizen 29231
Epema-State, IJsbrechtum 29460
Gemeentelijk Historisch Museum Ouder-Amstel, Ouderkerk aan de Amstel 29699
Gemeentelijke Expositieruimte Kampen, Kampen 29470
Gemeentemuseum, Weesp 29990
Gemeentemuseum De Tiendschuur, Weert 29988
Gemeentemuseum Het Markiezenhof, Bergen op Zoom 28983
Gemeentemuseum 't Behouden Huijs, Terschelling-West 29868
Gemeentemuseum 't Sterkenhuis, Bergen, Noord-Holland 28981
Gevangenismuseum Veenhuizen, Veenhuizen 29930
Het Gildenhuys, Blokzijl 28990
Goois Museum, Hilversum 29419
Goors Historisch Museum, Goor 29289
Gorcums Museum, Gorinchem 29291
Heemerf De Schutsboom, Goirle 29288
Heemkundemuseum Beek, Beek 28966
Heemkundig Museum, Ommeren 29663
Heemschuur Maasland, Heesch 29370
De Heksenwaag, Oudewater 29702
Historisch Museum Arnhem, Arnhem 28935
Historisch Museum de Bevelanden, Goes 29286
Historisch Museum De Tien Malen, Putten 29718
Historisch Museum Den Briel, Brielle 29028
Historisch Museum Deventer, Deventer 29145
Historisch Museum Hedel, Hedel 29356
Historisch Museum Het Kleine Veenlo, Veenendaal 29928
Historisch Museum Het Palthe Huis, Oldenzaal 29657
Historisch Museum Oald Hengel, Hengelo, Overijssel 29398
Historisch Museum Piet Dorenbosch, Boxtel 29013
Historisch Museum Ter Aar, Ter Aar 28796
Historisch Museum Tweestromenland, Beneden Leeuwen 28975
Historisch Museum Wolfheze, Wolfheze 30017
Historisch Muzeum Hazerswoude, Hazerswoude Dorp 29355
Historisch Openluchtmuseum Eindhoven, Eindhoven 29211
Hof van Hessen, Huissen 29453
Home of History, Rotterdam 29753
Huis Verwolde, Laren, Gelderland 29497
Huize Keizer, Denekamp 29139
Huizer Museum Het Schoutenhuis, Huizen 29456
Kapiteinshuis Pekela, Nieuwe Pekela 29618
Katwijks Museum, Katwijk aan Zee 29477
't Kiekhuus, Wolvega 30018
Kijk en Luister Museum, Bennekom 28976
De Klomphoek, Beilen 28970
Koornmarktspoort, Kampen 29472
Het Land van Strijen, Strijen 29858
Het Land van Thorn/ Panorama Thorn, Thorn 29870
Liemers Museum, Zevenaar 30055
Limburgs Miniatuurmuseum, Sint Geertruid 29820
Limburgs Museum, Venlo 29939
Limburgs Openluchtmuseum Eynderhoof, Nederweert Eind 29608
Loosduins Museum De Korenschuur, Den Haag 29102
Maarten van Rossum Museum, Zaltbommel 30044
Marker Museum, Marken 29580
Martinustoren, Losser 29550
Middendorpshuis, Den Ham 29131
Minimuseum, Groningen 29310
Molen van Frans Expositie, Mander (Tubbergen) 29577
Museum Ceuclum, Cuijk 29060
Museum de 5000 Morgen, Hoogeveen 29437
Museum De Koloniehof, Frederiksoord 29263
Museum De Schilpen, Maasland 29561
Museum de Speeltoren, Monnickendam 29601
Museum de Stratemakerstoren, Nijmegen 29631
Museum de Striid tsjin it Wetter, Wommels 30020
Museum de Trije Gritenijen, Grou 29319
Museum Delfzijl, Delfzijl 29088
Museum Dorestad, Wijk bij Duurstede 30004
Museum Dorpsbehoud Papendrecht, Papendrecht 29710
Museum Echt, Echt 29190
Museum Elisabeth Weeshuis, Culemborg 29063
Museum Flehite Amersfoort, Amersfoort 28824
Museum Freriks, Winterswijk 30014
Museum Frerikshuus, Aalten 28795
Museum Gesigt van't Dok, Hellevoetsluis 29390
Museum Havezate Mensinge, Roden 29740
Museum Het Groot Graffel, Warnsveld 29979
Museum Het Petershuis, Gennep 29275
Museum Het Schip, Amsterdam 28877
Museum Het Verscholen Dorp, Vierhouten 29944
Museum in 't Houtenhuis, De Rijp 29069
Museum Kempenland, Eindhoven 29215
Museum Maarssen, Maarssen 29557
Museum Meerenberg, Bloemendaal 28989
Museum Nagele, Nagele 29607
Museum Orvelte, Orvelte 29680
Museum Oud-Asperen, Asperen 28946
Museum Oud Overschie, Rotterdam 29761
Museum Oud-Rijnsburg, Rijnsburg 29732
Museum Oud Soest, Soest 29842
Museum Palthehof, Nieuwleusen 29624
Museum Rijswijk Het Tollenshuis, Rijswijk, Zuid-Holland 29735
Museum Schietkamp-Harskamp, Harskamp 29349
Museum Slag bij Heiligerlee, Heiligerlee 29377
Museum Stad Appingedam, Appingedam 28931
Museum Stedhûs Sleat, Sloten 29835
Museum Swaensteyn, Voorburg 29962
Museum 't Coopmanshûs, Franeker 29261
Museum voor Heemkunde Almelo, Almelo 28809
Museum Wierdenland, Ezinge 29258
Museum Willem van Haren, Heerenveen 29363
Museum Yerseke, Yerseke 30030
Museum Zwaantje Hans Stockman's Hof, Schoonebeek 29811
Museumboerderij, Leens 29504
Museumboerderij Eungs Schöppe, Markelo 29579
Museumboerderij Tante Jaantje, Callantsoog 29052
Museumboerderij Vreeburg, Schagen 29795
Museumboerderij Westfrisia, Hoogwoud 29440
Museumsboerderij Oud Noordwijk, Noordwijk, Zuid-Holland 29645
Museumwinkel Albert Heijn, Zaandam 30036
Nationaal Coöperatie Museum, Schiedam 29803
Natuur Historisch Museum en Heemkunde Centrum, Meerssen 29586
De Nieuwe Toren, Kampen 29473
Het Noorderhuis, Zaandam 30038
De Notelaer, Hingene 29423
Openluchtmuseum De Duinhuisjes, Rockanje 29738
De Oude Aarde, Giethoorn 29282
Het Oude Raadhuis, Oud-Beijerland 29689
Het Oude Raadhuis, Urk 29892
Het Oude Stadhuis, Hasselt 29350
Oudheidkamer, Den Burg 29089
Oudheidkamer, Koudekerk 29492
Oudheidkamer, Steenwijk 29852
Oudheidkamer, Wijngaarden 30005
Oudheidkamer Bleiswijk, Bleiswijk 28987
Oudheidkamer Boerderij Strunk, Raalte 29721
Oudheidkamer Brederwiede, Vollenhove 29960
Oudheidkamer Buisjan Enter, Enter 29244
Oudheidkamer Dantumadeel, Zwaagwesteinde 30078
Oudheidkamer de Oude Pastory, Heiloo 29378
Oudheidkamer Doorn, Doorn 29168
Oudheidkamer Eemnes, Eemnes 29199
Oudheidkamer Geervliet, Geervliet 29266
Oudheidkamer Hellevoetsluis, Hellevoetsluis 29392
Oudheidkamer Hoolt'n, Holten 29434
Oudheidkamer IJsselstreek, Wijhe 30003
Oudheidkamer Leiderdorp, Leiderdorp 29528
Oudheidkamer Lemster Fiifgea, Lemmer 29536
Oudheidkamer Leshuis, Dedemsvaart 29073
Oudheidkamer Lunteren, Lunteren 29552
Oudheidkamer/ Museum Mr. Andreae, Kollum 29488
Oudheidkamer Nunspeet, Nunspeet 29651
Oudheidkamer Renswoude, Renswoude 29727
Oudheidkamer Ridderkerk, Ridderkerk 29731
Oudheidkamer Rozenburg, Rozenburg 29782
Die Oudheidkamer tot Medenblick, Medemblik 29585
Oudheidkamer Wassenaar, Wassenaar 29984
Oudheidkamer Wieringerwaard het Polderhuis, Wieringerwaard 30001
Oudheidkundige Verzameling, Schinveld 29806
Oudheidkundig Museum Arnemuiden, Arnemuiden 28933
Pasmans Huus, Ruinen 29784
Purmerends Museum, Purmerend 29717
Regthuis Oudkarspel, Oudkarspel 29703
't Rieuw, Nuis 29649
Rijssens Museum, Rijssen 29734
Roerstreekmuseum, Sint Odiliënberg 29822
De Schotse Huizen, Veere 29932
Slaait'n Hoes, Onstwedde 29665
Slag van de Somme Museum, Schagen 29797
Sliedrechts Museum, Sliedrecht 29830
Spakenburgs Museum 't Vurhuus, Bunschoten Spakenburg 29039
Stadsmuseum Doetinchem, Doetinchem 29162
Stadsmuseum Groenlo, Groenlo 29303
Stadsmuseum IJsselstein, IJsselstein 29462
Stadsmuseum Woerden, Woerden 30016
Stadsmuseum Zoetermeer, Zoetermeer 30064
Stedelijk Museum Amsterdam, Amsterdam 28902
Stedelijk Museum Het Domein, Sittard 29827
Stedelijk Museum Kampen, Kampen 29474
Stedelijk Museum Zutphen, Zutphen 30077
Stedelijke Oudheidkamer De Roos, Geertruidenberg 29265
Streekheemmuseum den Aanwas, Ossendrecht 29685
Streekhistorisch Centrum, Stadskanaal 29849
Streekmuseum De Groote Sociëteit, Tiel 29875
Streekmuseum de Moennik, Helden 29383
Streekmuseum De Vier Ambachten, Hulst 29457
Streekmuseum Goeree en Overflakkee, Sommelsdijk 29845
Streekmuseum Het Admiraliteitshuis, Dokkum 29164
Streekmuseum Het Dorp van Bartje, Rolde 29744
Streekmuseum Het Land van Axel, Axel 28956
Streekmuseum Jan Anderson, Vlaardingen 29947
Streekmuseum Land van Valkenburg, Valkenburg, Limburg 29920
Streekmuseum Leudal, Haelen 29336
Streekmuseum Oudheidkamer Reeuwijk, Reeuwijk 29724
Streekmuseum Stevensweert/ Ohé en Laak, Stevensweert 29857
Streekmuseum Volkssterrenwacht, Burgum 29047
Streekmuseum West Zeeuws-Vlaanderen, IJzendijke 29463
Themapark Openluchtmuseum De Spitkeet, Harkema 29344
Torenmuseum, Goedereede 29285
De Turfschuur, Kolhorn 29487
Het Veenkoloniaal Museum, Veendam 29926
Veenmuseum het Vriezenveense Veld, Vriezenveen 29968
Veluws Museum Nairac, Barneveld 28965
Vestingmuseum Oudeschans, Oudeschans 29700
Visserij- en Cultuurhistorisch Museum, Woudrichem 30026
Het Vlaemsche Erfgoed, Groede 29302
Voerman Museum Hattem, Hattem 29353
Volendams Museum, Volendam 29958
Volksbuurtmuseum Wijk, Utrecht 29912
Volkskundig Educatie Museum, Susteren 29862

Vughts Historisch Museum, Vught 29972
Het Waalres Museum, Waalre 29973
Waterland Neeltje Jans, Vrouwenpolder 29969
Werkspoor Museum, Amsterdam 28914
Westfries Museum, Hoorn 29446
Zaanlandse Oudheidkamer Honig Breet Huis, Zaandijk 30043
Zaans Museum, Zaandam 30041
De Zaanse Schans, Zaandam 30042
Zandvoorts Museum, Zandvoort 30046
Zuiderzeemuseum, Enkhuizen 29234

Netherlands Antilles
Curaçao Museum, Curaçao 30088
Museum Kura Hulanda, Curaçao 30089

New Caledonia
Musée Historique, Bourail 30090

New Zealand
Alexandra Museum, Alexandra 30093
Amuri Historical Museum, Waiau 30270
Aratoi Wairarapa Museum of Art and History, Masterton 30197
Ashburton Museum, Ashburton 30097
Auckland Museum and Auckland War Memorial Museum, Auckland 30104
Belfast Museum, Christchurch 30123
Brain-Watkins House, Tauranga 30258
Brayshaw Museum Park, Blenheim 30117
Cambridge Museum, Cambridge 30119
Catlins Historical Museum, Owaka 30224
Central Hawke's Bay Settlers Museum, Waipawa 30276
Chatham Islands Museum, Tuku Rd, Waitangi 30269
Cheviot Museum, Cheviot 30120
Clyde Historical Museum, Clyde 30136
Cobblestones Museum, Greytown 30171
Coromandel School of Mines Museum, Coromandel 30137
Cromwell Museum, Cromwell 30138
Cust Museum, Cust 30139
Dargaville Museum, Dargaville 30141
Eketahuna and Districts Museum, Eketahuna 30156
Far North Regional Museum, Kaitaia 30191
Featherston Heritage Museum, Featherston 30157
Featherston Memorabilia Museum, Featherston 30158
Firth Tower Historical Reserve, Matamata 30202
Flaxbourne Settlers Museum, Ward 30288
Forrester Gallery, Oamaru 30217
Founders Historic Park, Nelson 30209
Foxton Museum, Foxton 30162
Golden Bay Museum and Gallery, Golden Bay 30165
Gore Historical Museum and Hokonui Heritage Research Centre, Gore 30168
Havelock Museum, Havelock 30175
Hawke's Bay Museum, Napier 30207
Helensville and District Pioneer Museum, Helensville 30178
Hororata Historic Museum, Darfield 30140
Howick Historical Village, Pakuranga 30228
Hurworth Cottage, New Plymouth 30214
Journey's End Cottage and Laishley House, Auckland 30111
Kaikohe Pioneer Village and Museum, Kaikohe 30189
Kaikoura District Museum, Kaikoura 30190
Kapiti Coast Museum Waikanae, Wellington 30295
Karamea Centennial Museum, Karamea 30192
The Kauri Museum, Matakohe 30201
Kawhia Regional Museum Gallery, Kawhia 30193
Lyttelton Historical Museum, Christchurch 30129
Marton Historic Village Museum, Marton 30196
Mercury Bay and District Museum, Whitianga 30317
Morrin Museum, Morrinsville 30204
Motueka District Museum, Motueka 30205
Mount Bruce Pioneer Museum, Masterton 30198
Murchison Museum, Murchison 30206
Museum of Wellington, City and Sea, Wellington 30299
Nelson Provincial Museum, Nelson 30210
North Otago Museum, Oamaru 30218
Ongaonga Old School Museum, Ongaonga 30220
Opotiki Museum, Opotiki 30221
Otago Settlers Museum, Dunedin 30152
Otakou Marae Museum, Dunedin 30154
Otautau and District Local History Museum, Otautau 30222
Oxford Museum, Oxford 30225
Paeroa and District Historical Society Museum, Paeroa 30226
Pahiatua and District Museum, Pahiatua 30227
Papakura and District Historical Society Museum, Papakura 30232
Pataka, Porirua 30240
Picton Community Museum, Picton 30236
Pioneer Village, Silverdale 30254
Piopio and District Museum, Piopio 30237
Plains Vintage Railway and Historical Museum, Ashburton 30100
Pleasant Point Railway and Historical Society Museum, Pleasant Point 30238
Port Chalmers Museum, Port Chalmers 30242
Puhoi Historical Society Museum, Puhoi 30243
Raglan and District Museum, Raglan 30245
Rakiura Museum, Stewart Island 30255
Rangiora Museum, Rangiora 30246
Renwick Museum, Renwick 30247
Russell Museum, Russell 30253
South Canterbury Museum, Timaru 30265
South Taranaki District Museum, Patea 30235
Southland Museum and Art Gallery, Invercargill 30186
Sumner/Redcliffs Historical Museum, Christchurch 30133
Taieri Historical Museum, Outram 30223
Taihape and District Museum, Taihape 30256
Tairawhiti Museum, Gisborne 30164
Tauranga Museum, Tauranga 30259
Tawhiti Museum, Hawera 30177
Te Amorangi Trust Museum, Rotorua 30250
Te Awamutu Museum, Te Awamutu 30260
Te Kuiti and District Historical Society Museum, Te Kuiti 30261
Te Manawa Life Mind, Palmerston North 30231
Te Whare Taonga O Akaroa, Akaroa 30092
Te Whare Whakaaro o Pito-one, Hutt City 30183
Temuka Courthouse Museum, Temuka 30262
Teviot District Museum, Roxburgh 30251
Tokomairiro Historical Society Museum, Milton 30203
Tuatapere Bushmans Museum, Tuatapere 30268
Upper Waitaki Pioneer Museum and Art Gallery, Kurow 30195
Vallance Cottage, Alexandra 30094
Waiheke Island Historical Society Museum, Waiheke Island 30271
Waikato Museum of Art and History, Hamilton 30174
Waikouaiti Museum, Waikouaiti 30273
Waipukurau Museum, Waipukurau 30278
Wairoa Museum Kopututanga, Wairoa 30279
Wallace Early Settlers Museum, Riverton 30248
Warkworth and District Museum, Warkworth 30290
West Coast Historical Museum, Hokitika 30179
Whanganui Regional Museum, Wanganui 30286
Whangarei Museum, Whangarei 30316
Whangaroa County Museum, Kaeo 30187
Woodville Pioneer Museum, Woodville 30318
Wyndham Museum, Wyndham 30319

Nicaragua
Museo Gregorio Aguilar Barea, Chontales 30320
Museo Tenderi, Masaya 30323

Niger
Musée Régional de Zinder, Zinder 30325

Nigeria
Aaragon Museum, Ilupeju 30345
Didi Museum, Abuja 30328
Esie Museum, Esie 30337
National Museum Bauchi, Bauchi 30333
National Museum Ibadan, Ibadan 30340
National Museum, Lagos, Onikan 30354
National Museum Makurdi, Makurdi 30351
National Museum Minna, Minna 30352
National Museum of Calabar, Calabar 30335
National Museum of Enugu, Enugu 30336
National Museum of Ilorin, Ilorin 30344
National Museum of Port Harcourt, Port Harcourt 30361
National Museum of the Imo State, Owerri 30359
National Museum of the Ogun State, Abeokuta 30327
National Museum of the Ondo State, Akure 30330
National Museum Uyo, Uyo 30364
Odinani Museum, Awka 30332
Owo Museum, Owo 30360
University Museum, Port Harcourt 30362

Norfolk Island
Norfolk Island Museum, Kingston 30366

Norway
Ålen Bygdetun, Ålen 30373
Alta Museum, Alta 30378
Alvdal Museum, Alvdal 30379
Andrøymuseet, Andenes 30386
Arendal Bymuseum, Arendal 30389
Atnabrufossen Vannbruksmuseum, Atna 30403
Aust-Agder Museet, Arendal 30390
Austefjord Museum, Austefjorden 30405
Austråttborgen, Trondheim 30936
Ballangen Bygdemuseum, Ballangen 30410
Bamble Museum, Langesund 30626
Bautahaugen Samlinger, Hedalen 30541
Bjarkøy Museum, Bjarkøy 30432
Bjugn Bygdatun, Bjugn 30436
Blakstad Sykehus Museum, Asker 30400
Blokkodden Villmarksmuseet, Engerdal 30480
Bokn Bygdemuseet, Bokn 30442
Bommen Elvemuseum, Vennesla 30984
Bomsholmen Museum, Arendal 30391
Borgarsyssel Museum, Sarpsborg 30829
Brandval Museum, Brandval 30449
Breidablikk, Stavanger 30879
Brevik Bymuseum, Brevik 30451
Burøsund Bygdemuseum, Vannareid 30971
Bymodellen, Oslo 30729
Cudrio Kystmuseum, Langesund 30627
Dalsgaard Museum, Geilo 30510
Dalane Folkemuseum, Egersund 30466
Dåsettunet, Lyngdal 30659
Dikemark Sykehus Museum, Asker 30401
Dølmo Bygdetun, Tolga 30923
Dønna Bygdesamling, Dønna 30461
Drammens Museum for Kunst og Kulturhistorie, Drammen 30463
Dyrøy Bygdemuseum, Tennevoll 30917
Eidsberg og Mysen Historielag, Eidsberg 30471
Eidskog Museum, Eidskog 30472
Eidsvoll Bygdemuseet, Eidsvoll Verk 30475
Eiktunet Kulturhistorisk Museum, Gjøvik 30513
Elingaard Museum, Gressvik 30518
Elvarheim Museum, Åmli 30381
Enebakk Bygdetun, Trysil 30947
Evje og Hornnes Museum, Evje 30482
Fedrenes Minne, Hidrasund 30548
Finnkroken Bygdemuseum, Tromsdalen 30931
Fjordane Forsvarsmuseum, Nordfjordeid 30709
Fjøsangersamlingene, Fjøsanger 30493
Flatanger Bygdemuseum, Flatanger 30494
Folldal Bygdetun, Folldal 30499
Forsand Bygdemuseum, Forsand 30503
Fosnes Bygdemuseum, Jøa 30585
Fredrikstad Museum, Fredrikstad 30504
Frosta Bygdemuseet, Frosta 30506
Frøya Bygdemuseum, Sistranda 30838
Gildeskål Bygdesamling, Gildeskål 30511
Gjesdal Bygdemuseum, Ålgård 30376
Godøy Kystmuseum, Godøy 30514
Grong Bygdamuseum, Grong 30521
Gruetunet Museum, Kirkenær i Solør 30593
Guovdageainnu Gilisillju, Kautokeino 30592
Hå Bygdemuseum, Varhaug 30975
Hamarøy Bygdetun, Harmarøy 30532
Hardanger Folkemuseum, Lofthus 30647
De Heibergske Samlinger - Sogn Folkemuseum, Kaupanger 30591
Hemne Bygdemuseum, Kyrksæterøra 30624
Herdla Museum, Herdla 30544
Herøy Bygdesamling, Herøy 30545
Herøy Kystmuseum, Herøy 30547
Holdhus Skulemuseum, Eikelandsosen 30476
Holmestova, Frekhaug 30505
Holmestrand Museum, Holmestrand 30554
Høvåg Museum, Høvåg 30569
Hurdal Bygdetun, Hurdal 30573
Indre Sør-Troms Distriktsmuseum, Tennevoll 30918
Iveland og Vegusdal Bygdemuseum, Vatnestrom 30979
Karmsund Folkemuseum, Haugesund 30538
Klæbu Bygdemuseum, Klæbu 30597
Klepp Bygdemuseum, Kleppe 30598
Klokkergården Bygdetun Lyngdal Misjonsmuseum, Lyngdal 30660
Økomuseum Grenseland, Sarpsborg 30830
Krambuvika Bygdemuseum, Tennevoll 30919
Kystmuseet i Nord-Trøndelag, Rørvik 30807
Laudal Museum, Marnardal 30667
Leirfjord Bygdesamlinger, Leirfjord 30633
Leksvik Bygdesamling, Leksvik 30636
Levanger Museum, Levanger 30639
Lier Bygdetun, Tranby 30928
Lindesnes Bygdemuseum, Sør-Audnedal 30864
Lista Museum, Vanse 30972
Lom Bygdamuseum, Lom 30650
Lund Bygdemuseum, Moi 30684
Måbødalen Kulturlandskapsmuseum, Eidfjord 30470
Malla Bleikvasslis Samlinger, Bleikvasslia 30437
Marnardal Museum, Marnardal 30668
Meløy Bygdemuseum, Ørnes 30720
Midttunet, Skei i Jølster 30844
Miljømuseet Dokken, Haugesund 30539
Namsskogan Bygdatun, Namsskogan 30702
Nes Lensemuseum, Skiptvet 30848
Nord-Troms Museum, Sørkjosen 30866
Norddal Museum, Valldal 30970
Nordli Bygdemuseum, Nordli 30711
Nordmøre Museum, Kristiansund 30618
Nore og Uvdal Bygdetun, Uvdal i Numedal 30964
Norsk Kjøretøyhistorisk Museum, Lillehammer 30643
Norsk Tindemuseum, Åndalsnes 30384
Oddentunet, Os i Østerdalen 30722
Ofoten Museum, Narvik 30705
Øksnes Bygdemuseum, Alsvåg 30377
Orkdal Bygdemuseum, Svorkmo 30912
Osbane Museet, Fana 30486
Osen Bygdetun, Steinsdalen 30895
Oslo Bymuseum, Oslo 30758
Petran Museum, Haltdalen 30527
Porsanger Museum, Lakselv 30625
Porsgrunn Bymuseum, Porsgrunn 30780
Rabekk Museum, Moss 30693
Rælingen Bygdetun, Fjerdingby 30492
Rana Museum, Mo i Rana 30674
Randaberg Bygdemuseum, Randaberg 30786
Rennesøy Bygdemuseum, Rennesøy 30790
Rindal Bygdemuseum, Rindal 30791
Rød Bygdetunet, Uskedalen 30961
Røldal Bygdemuseum, Røldal 30800
Rørosmuseet, Røros 30806
Røyrvik Bygdatun, Limingen 30645
Ryfylkemuseet, Sand 30819
Rygnestadtunet, Rysstad 30813
Salangen Bygdetun, Sjøvegan 30839
Saltdal Museum, Rognan 30799
Sandefjord Bymuseum, Sandefjord 30823
Sandefjordmuseene, Sandefjord 30825
Sandnesmuseet, Sandnes 30826
Sandtorg Bygdetun, Sørvik 30871
Sannidal Bygdetun, Sannidal 30828
Sauda Museum, Sauda 30832
Sekken Museum, Sekken 30833
Selbu Strikkemuseum, Selbu 30835
Singsås Museum, Singsås 30837
Sjukehusmuseet i Skien, Skien 30846
Skånland Museum, Evenskjer 30481
Skaun Bygdamuseum, Børsa 30445
Skiptvet Bygdemuseum, Skiptvet 30849
Smøla Museum, Smøla 30856
Snåsa Bygdamuseum, Snåsa 30857
Soknedal Bygdemuseum, Soknedal 30860
Sømna Bygdetun, Sømna 30863
Sør-Senja Museum, Stonglandseidet 30899
Stavanger Museum, Stavanger 30890
Stokke Bygdetun og Galleri Bokeskogen, Stokke 30897
Straumsnes Bygdemuseum, Kanestraum 30588
Sund Bygdemuseum, Skogsvåg 30851
Sunndal Bygdemuseum, Sunndalsøra 30907
Sunnmøre Museum, Ålesund 30375
Surnadal Bygdemuseum, Surnadal 30908
Svalbard-Museum, Longyearbyen 30655
Svelvik Museum, Svelvik 30910
Tana Museum, Tana 30915
Time Bygdemuseum, Undheim 30960
Tørvikbygd Bygdemuseum, Tørvikbygd 30927
Toten Økomuseum, Kapp 30589
Træe, Bryne 30454
Tresfjord Museum, Tresfjord 30929
Trondarnes Distriktmuseum, Harstad 30535
Tune Bygdemuseum, Sarpsborg 30831
Tvedestrand Museum, Tvedestrand 30953
Tveit Bygdemuseum, Tveit 30954
Tveitens Samlinger, Eggedal 30469
Tydal Museum, Tydal 30955
Ullensaker Bygdemuseum, Jessheim 30582
Vadsø Museum - Ruija Kvenmuseum, Vadsø 30966
Varanger Museum Sør, Kirkenes 30595
Varden Redningsmuseum, Narbø 30703
Varteig Bygdemuseum, Varteig 30977
Vefsn Museum, Mosjøen 30692
Vega Bygdemuseum, Vega 30981
Vegårshei Bygdetun, Vegårshei 30982
Vektermuseet i Valbergtårnet, Stavanger 30892
Verran Museum, Malm 30661
Vest-Telemark Museum, Dalen i Telemark 30459
Vestvågøy Museum, Leknes 30635
Vingelen Kirke- og Skolemuseum, Vingelen 30995
Woksengs Samlinger, Rørvik 30808
Yrjar Heimbygdslag, Opphaug 30718

Pakistan
Lahore Fort Museum, Lahore 31037
Lahore Museum, Lahore 31038
Peshawar Museum, Peshawar 31051
Sind Provincial Museum, Hyderabad 31021

Palestine
Armenian Museum, Jerusalem 31068
Darl At Tifl Museum, Jerusalem 31069
Municipality Museum, Hebron 31067

Panama
Museo Belisario Porras, Panamá City 31078

Papua New Guinea
Madang Museum, Yomba 31092

Peru
Centro Andino de Tecnología Tradicional y Cultura de la Comunidades, Ollantaytambo 31233
Museo Antonio Raimondi, La Merced 31194
Museo Arqueológico e Histórico de Andahuaylas, Andahuaylas 31111
Museo Arqueológico Municipal y Museo Municipal Miguel Justino Ramírez, Piura 31238
Museo de Abancay, Abancay 31109
Museo de Arqueología e Historia Natural de Yungay, Yungay 31271
Museo de Etnohistoria de Suyo, Suyo 31252
Museo de Sitio de la Pampa Galeras, Quinua 31245
Museo Etnográfico, Cajamarca 31129
Museo General, Yanahuanca 31269
Museo Histórico Andrés Avelino Cáceres, Ayacucho 31122
Museo Histórico de Chacamarka, Chacamarka 31140
Museo Histórico Municipal Guillermo Zegarra Meneses, Arequipa 31115
Museo Histórico Regional de Tacna, Tacna 31257
Museo Municipal, Iquitos 31187
Museo Municipal de Cabana, Cabana 31124
Museo Municipal de Huaytará, Huaytará 31178
Museo Municipal de Nazca y Casa Museo María Reiche, Nazca 31232
Museo Orve, Chaupimascos 31142
Museo Regional Amazónico, Iquitos 31188
Museo Regional Daniel Hernández Morillo, Huancavelica 31167
Museo Regional de Arqueología, Huamanga 31166
Museo Regional de Casma Max Uhle, Casma 31137
Museo Regional de Ica María Reiche Gross Newman, Ica 31182
Museo Regional de San Martín, Moyobamba 31230
Museo Salesiano, Huancayo 31170
Museo Técnico Pedagógico de la Región de Pasco, San Juan 31246

Philippines
Aera Memorial Museum, San Pablo 31441
Asian Center Museum, Quezon City 31428
Aurelio Sevilla Alvero Library and Museum, Pasay 31410
Baguio-Mountain Provinces Museum, Baguio 31282
Benguet Museum, La Trinidad 31339
Bohol Museum, Tagbilaran 31455
Bolinao National Museum, Bolinao 31289
Bontoc Museum, Bontoc, Ifugao 31291
Butuan City Museum, Butuan 31294
Butuan National Museum, Butuan 31296
Cagayan Museum, Tuguegarao 31460
Casagwa National Museum, Daraga 31323
Cebu City Museum, Cebu 31310

Davao Museum, Davao 31325
Ford Museum, Dumalag 31327
Hiyas ng Bulakan Museum, Malolos 31361
Iligan Museum, Iligan 31328
Kabayan National Museum, Kabayan 31334
Kiangan National Museum, Kiangan 31338
Laoag Museum, Vigan 31464
Legaspi City Museum, Legaspi 31340
Magsingal National Museum, Magsingal 31350
Museo de Tarlac, Tarlac 31458
Museo del Seminario Conciliar de Nueva Caceres, Naga 31406
Museo Iloilo, Iloilo 31329
Museo Negrense, Bacolod 31278
Museo ng Batangas, Lipa 31342
Museo ng Katipunan, Lipa 31343
Museo ng Manila, Manila 31385
The Negros Museum, Bacolod 31279
Padre Burgos National Museum, Vigan 31465
Palawan Museum, Puerto Princesa 31424
Palawan National Museum, Quezon 31426
Philippine Presidential Museum, Malacañang 31358
Pila Museum, Pila 31422
Quezonia Museum, Manila 31395
Santa Fe Community Museum, Santa Fe 31443
Southwestern University Museum, Cebu 31317
Teodoro P. Resurreccion Memorial Museum, Luna 31348
University of Northern Philippines Museum, Vigan 31466
Vargas Museum and Art Gallery, Mandaluyong 31366
Vigan House Museum, Vigan 31467
Xavier University Museum (Museo de Oro), Cagayan de Oro City 31300

Poland
Dom Eskenów, Toruń 32049
Dwór w Dołędze, Tarnów 32040
History of Grudziądz, Grudziądz 31610
Izba Muzealna im. Antoniego Krajewskiego, Lanckorona 31747
Jan Kochanowski Muzeum, Czarnolas 31541
Martyrologiczny Punkt Upamiętnienia - Rotunda, Zamość 32211
Museum Okręgowe im. Stanisława Staszica, Piła 31880
Muzeum Biblioteki Kórnickiej, Kórnik 31673
Muzeum Dawnego Kupiectwa, Świdnica 32014
Muzeum Dom Urbańczyka, Chrzanów 31535
Muzeum Filumenistyczne, Bystrzyca Kłodzka 31518
Muzeum Historii Katowic, Katowice 31646
Muzeum Historii Miasta, Zduńska Wola 32216
Muzeum Historii Miasta Łodzi, Łódź 31770
Muzeum Historii Miasta Lublina, Lublin 31790
Muzeum Historii Miasta Poznania, Poznań 31904
Muzeum Historii Przemysłu, Opatówek 31854
Muzeum Historii Włocławka, Włocławek 32162
Muzeum Historyczne, Przasnysz 31919
Muzeum Historyczne Miasta Gdańska, Gdańsk 31571
Muzeum Historyczne Miasta Starego Warszawy, Warszawa 32101
Muzeum Historyczne Miasta Tarnobrzega, Tarnobrzeg 32039
Muzeum Historyczne w Wrocławiu, Wrocław 32178
Muzeum Historyczno-Archeologiczne, Ostrowiec Świętokrzyski 31866
Muzeum im. Edmunda Bojanowskiego w Grabonogu, Grabonóg 31608
Muzeum im. Michąla Kajki w Ogródku, Ogródek 31844
Muzeum im. Nałkowskich, Wołomin 32170
Muzeum im. Stanisława Staszica, Hrubieszów 31615
Muzeum im. Wiktora Stachowiaka, Trzcianka 32057
Muzeum im. Władysława St. Reymonta, Lipce Reymonotowskie 31763
Muzeum-Kaszubski Park Etnograficzny w Wdzydzach Kiszewskich, Wdzydze Kiszewskie 32147
Muzeum Kaszubskie, Kościerzyna 31675
Muzeum Kościuszkowskie Dworek Zacisze, Miechów 31800
Muzeum Kultury Łemkowskiej w Zyndranowej, Tylawa 32062
Muzeum Martyrologii, Bielsk Podlaski 31491
Muzeum Miasta Gdyni, Gdynia 31586
Muzeum Miasta i Rzeki Warty, Warta 32145
Muzeum Miasta Kołobrzegu, Kołobrzeg 31669
Muzeum Miasta Ostrowa Wielkopolskiego, Ostrów Wielkopolski 31865
Muzeum Miasta Zgierza, Zgierz 32218
Muzeum Miejskie, Świętochłowice 32016
Muzeum Miejskie im. Maksymiliana Chroboka, Ruda Śląska 31953
Muzeum Nadwiślańskie, Kazimierz Dolny 31649
Muzeum Narodowe Ziemi Przemyskiej, Przemyśl 31921
Muzeum Oddział im. Albina Makowskiego, Chojnice 31529
Muzeum Okręgowe, Ciechanów 31537
Muzeum Okręgowe, Konin 31672
Muzeum Okręgowe, Krosno 31736
Muzeum Okręgowe, Nowy Sącz 31835
Muzeum Okręgowe, Ostrołęka 31864
Muzeum Okręgowe, Sieradz 31973
Muzeum Okręgowe, Tarnów 32043
Muzeum Okręgowe, Zaborów 32198
Muzeum Okręgowe w Chełmie, Chełm 31523
Muzeum Okręgowe w Lesznie, Leszno 31757
Muzeum Okręgowe w Toruniu, Toruń 32054
Muzeum Pamięci Narodowej lata 1939 -1956, Kielce 31659
Muzeum Parafialne, Pakość 31875
Muzeum Pienińskie im. Józefa Szalaya, Szczawnica 32022
Muzeum Podhalańskie PTTK, Nowy Targ 31837
Muzeum Południowego Podlasia, Biała Podlaska 31484
Muzeum Pomorza Środkowego, Słupsk 31980
Muzeum Pożarnictwa, Lidzbark 31760
Muzeum Prawa i Prawników Polskich, Katowice 31647
Muzeum Puszczy Kampinoskiej, Kampinos 31639
Muzeum Regionalne, Barlinek 31478
Muzeum Regionalne, Biecz 31490
Muzeum Regionalne, Biłgoraj 31497
Muzeum Regionalne, Brodnica 31510
Muzeum Regionalne, Brzeziny 31512
Muzeum Regionalne, Człuchów 31549
Muzeum Regionalne, Głogówek 31596
Muzeum Regionalne, Iłża 31616
Muzeum Regionalne, Jasło 31623
Muzeum Regionalne, Jawor 31625
Muzeum Regionalne, Kościan 31674
Muzeum Regionalne, Kozienice 31680
Muzeum Regionalne, Kutno 31745
Muzeum Regionalne, Lubań 31784
Muzeum Regionalne, Miechów 31801
Muzeum Regionalne, Mielec 31806
Muzeum Regionalne, Nowe Miasto nad Pilicą 31831
Muzeum Regionalne, Ojców 31846
Muzeum Regionalne, Opoczno 31856
Muzeum Regionalne, Ostrzeszów 31867
Muzeum Regionalne, Pińczów 31882
Muzeum Regionalne, Pułtusk 31933
Muzeum Regionalne, Siedlce 31970
Muzeum Regionalne, Sławków 31977
Muzeum Regionalne, Środa Śląska 31993
Muzeum Regionalne, Sucha Beskidzka 32004
Muzeum Regionalne, Wągrowiec 32070
Muzeum Regionalne, Wronki 32194
Muzeum Regionalne, Słupca 31979
Muzeum Regionalne, Kraśnik 31731
Muzeum Regionalne, Łęczna 31750
Muzeum Regionalne, Pszczew 31925
Muzeum Regionalne, Radzyn Chełmiński 31942
Muzeum Regionalne, Myślibórz 31817
Muzeum Regionalne im. Adama Fastnachta, Brzozów 31513
Muzeum Regionalne im. Albina Nowickiego, Ryn 31956
Muzeum Regionalne im. Antoniego Minkiewicza, Olkusz 31850
Muzeum Regionalne im. Dzieci Wrzesińskich, Września 32195
Muzeum Regionalne im. Marcina Rożka, Wolsztyn 32171
Muzeum Regionalne im. Władysława Kowalskiego, Dobczyce 31553
Muzeum Regionalne im Wojciechy Dutkiewicz, Rogoźno 31951
Muzeum Regionalne Polskiego Towarzystwa Turystyczno-Krajoznawczego, Grodzisk Mazowiecki 31609
Muzeum Regionalne PTTK, Puławy 31932
Muzeum Regionalne PTTK, Starachowice 31996
Muzeum Regionalne PTTK w Zagórzu Śląskim Zamek Grodno, Zagórze Śląskie 32203
Muzeum Regionalne Siemiatycki Ośrodek Kultury, Siemiatycze 31972
Muzeum Regionalne w Stęszewie, Stęszew 32001
Muzeum Regionalne w Świebodzinie, Świebodzin 32015
Muzeum Regionalne Ziemi Limanowskiej, Limanowa 31762
Muzeum Regionalne Ziemi Sadowieńskiej, Sadowne 31961
Muzeum Rybołówstwa Morskiego, Świnoujście 32019
Muzeum Sejmu, Warszawa 32125
Muzeum Skansen, Pszczyna 31926
Muzeum Skansen Kolejnictwa, Kościerzyna 31676
Muzeum Śląska Cieszyńskiego w Cieszynie, Cieszyn 31540
Muzeum Śląska Opolskiego, Opole 31859
Muzeum Śląskie, Katowice 31648
Muzeum Sopotu, Sopot 31988
Muzeum Społeczne, Strzyżów 32003
Muzeum Śremskie, Śrem 31992
Muzeum Tatrzańskie im. Tytusa Chałubińskiego, Zakopane 32209
Muzeum Tkactwa Dolnośląskiego, Kamienna Góra 31637
Muzeum Tradycji i Perspektyw Huty im. B. Bieruta, Częstochowa 31547
Muzeum w Bielsku Podlaskim, Bielsk Podlaski 31492
Muzeum w Chorzowie, Chorzów 31534
Muzeum w Elblągu, Elbląg 31560
Muzeum w Gliwicach, Gliwice 31593
Muzeum w Gostyniu, Gostyń 31607
Muzeum w Grudziądzu, Grudziądz 31611
Muzeum w Grudziądzul w Klasztorna, Grudziądz 31612
Muzeum w Kętach, Kęty 31656
Muzeum w Łęczycy, Łęczyca 31751
Muzeum w Nysie, Nysa 31840
Muzeum w Rybniku, Rybnik 31955
Muzeum w Stargardzie, Stargard 31997
Muzeum w Szklarskiej Porębie Hoffmanna, Szklarska Poręba 32035
Muzeum w Tarnowskich Górach, Tarnowskie Góry 32045
Muzeum w Tykocinie, Tykocin 32061
Muzeum w Wodzisławiu Śląskim, Wodzisław Śląski 32167
Muzeum w Żywcu, Żywiec 32228
Muzeum Walk o Wał Pomorski przy Miejsko-Gminnym Ośrodku Kultury, Mirosławiec 31809
Muzeum Warmii i Mazur, Olsztyn 31852
Muzeum Warmińskie, Lidzbark Warmiński 31761
Muzeum Westerplatte Sucharskiego, Gdańsk 31577
Muzeum Wnętrz Zabytkowych, Dębno 31552
Muzeum Woli, Warszawa 32135
Muzeum Zagłębia, Będzin 31480
Muzeum Zamek, Baranów Sandomierski 31475
Muzeum-Zamek w Bolkowie, Bolków 31509
Muzeum Zamek w Łańcucie, Łańcut 31748
Muzeum Ziemi Augustowskiej, Augustów 31473
Muzeum Ziemi Dobrzyńskiej, Rypin 31957
Muzeum Ziemi Kłodzkiej, Kłodzko 31664
Muzeum Ziemi Kociewskiej, Starogard Gdański 31998
Muzeum Ziemi Krajeńskiej, Nakło nad Notecią 31819
Muzeum Ziemi Lubawskiej, Nowe Miasto Lubawskie 31830
Muzeum Ziemi Mrągowskiej, Mrągowo 31813
Muzeum Ziemi Pałuckiej, Żnin 32224
Muzeum Ziemi Prudnickiej, Prudnik 31917
Muzeum Ziemi Puckiej, Puck 31929
Muzeum Ziemi Sochaczewskiej, Sochaczew 31987
Muzeum Ziemi Sulmierzyckiej im. S.F. Klonowica, Sulmierzyce 32006
Muzeum Ziemi Wałeckiej, Wałcz 32074
Muzeum Ziemi Wschowskiej, Wschowa 32196
Muzeum Ziemi Zaborskiej i Galeria Sztuki Ludowej, Wiele 32152
Muzeum Ziemi Złotowskiej, Złotów 32222
Ośrodek Historii Dęblińskiego Węzła Kolejowego, Dęblin 31551
Pałac w Dobrzycy, Dobrzyca 31556
Pałac w Rogalinie, Świątniki 32012
Pomorskie Muzeum Wojskowe, Bydgoszcz 31516
Prywatne Muzeum Etnograficzno-Historyczne, Bielsk Podlaski 31493
Regionalna Izba Muzealna, Poddębice 31888
Regionalne Muzeum Młodej Polski - Rydlówka, Kraków 31727
Stała Ekspozycja Muzealna Ziemi Sierakowickiej, Sierakowice 31974
Szpitalki, Puck 31930
Wielkopolskie Muzeum Pożarnictwa PTTK, Rakoniewice 31943
Wojewódzkie Muzeum Pożarnictwa, Włocławek 32164
Zbiory Historyczno-Etnograficzne, Oświęcim 31869

Portugal
Casa-Museu Teixeira Lopes, Vila Nova de Gaia 32358
Museu de Angra do Heroísmo, Angra do Heroísmo 32237
Museu de Aveiro, Aveiro 32239
Museu de Carlos Machado, Ponta Delgada 32327
Museu de Francisco Tavares Proença Júnior, Castelo Branco 32251
Museu de Leiria, Leiria 32283
Museu Municipal, Alcochete 32231
Museu Municipal de Portalegre, Portalegre 32328
Museu Municipal de Santarém, Santarém 32341
Museu Municipal de Viana do Castelo, Viana do Castelo 32356
Museu Municipal do Seixal Núcleo Sede, Seixal 32345
Museu Municipal Dr. José Formosinho, Lagos 32280
Museu Municipal Dr. Santos Rocha, Figueira da Foz 32273
Museu Municipal Pedro Nunes, Alcácer do Sal 32230
Museu Municipal Quinta do Conventinho, Loures 32318
Museu Regional de Arqueologia D. Diogo de Sousa, Braga 32243
Museu Restauraçao, Lisboa 32316
Santiago do Cacém Museu Municipal, Santiago do Cacém 32342

Puerto Rico
Caparra Ruins Historical Museum, Guaynabo 32373
Casa Rosada Abelardo Díaz Alfaro, Caguas 32366
Dr. Jose Celso Barbose Museum, Bayamón 32363
Hacienda Buena Vista, Ponce 32377
Museo Casa Blanca, San Juan 32392
Museo de Arte, Historia y Cultura Casa Alonso, Vega Baja 32411
Museo de Coamo, Coamo 32371
Museo de la Historia de Ponce, Ponce 32381
Museo Fuerte Conde de Mirasol de Vieques, Vieques 32412
San Juan National Historic Site, San Juan 32409

Qatar
Al Zubara Fort, Doha 32415

Réunion
Musée Historique de Saint-Gilles-les-Hauts, Saint-Paul 32423

Romania
Colecţia Muzeală de Istorie, Săcueni 32585
Complexul Muzeal Arad, Arad 32430
Complexul Muzeal Bucovina, Suceava 32600
Muzeal de Istorie, Târgovişte 32602
Muzeul Banatului, Timişoara 32614
Muzeul Banatului Montan, Reşiţa 32581
Muzeul Brăilei, Brăila 32444
Muzeul Bran, Bran 32445
Muzeul Câmpiei Băileştitor, Băileşti 32436
Muzeul de Artă şi Artă Populară, Calafat 32478
Muzeul de Istorie, Bicaz 32439
Muzeul de Istorie, Oneşti 32559
Muzeul de Istorie, Târgu Jiu 32606
Muzeul de Istorie Augustin Bunea, Blaj 32441
Muzeul de Istorie, Etnografie şi Artă Plastică, Lugoj 32544
Muzeul de Istorie Gherla, Gherla 32526
Muzeul de Istorie Locală şi Etnografie, Brad 32443
Muzeul de Istorie şi Arheologie, Tulcea 32619
Muzeul de Istorie şi Etnografie, Târgu Neamţ 32612
Muzeul de Istorie Sighişoara, Sighişoara 32595
Muzeul de Istorie Turda, Turda 32621
Muzeul de Istorie Valea Hârtibaciului, Agnita 32425
Muzeul Dunării de Jos, Călăraşi 32479
Muzeul Etnografic Ioan Tugui, Câmpulung Moldovenesc 32485
Muzeul Grăniceresc Năsăudean, Năsăud 32553
Muzeul Haáz Rezsö, Odorheiu Secuiesc 32557
Muzeul în Aer Liber, Negreşti-Oaş 32555
Muzeul Judeţean Bistriţa-Năsăud, Bistriţa 32440
Muzeul Judeţean Botoşani, Botoşani 32442
Muzeul Judeţean Buzău, Buzău 32477
Muzeul Judeţean de Istorie, Galaţi 32524
Muzeul Judeţean de Istorie şi Arheologie Iulian Antonescu Bacău, Bacău 32433
Muzeul Judeţean de Istorie şi Artă, Slatina 32598
Muzeul Judeţean de Istorie şi Artă Zalău, Zalău 32626
Muzeul Judeţean de Istorie Teleorman, Alexandria 32429
Muzeul Judeţean Ialomiţa, Slobozia 32599
Muzeul Judeţean Maramureş, Baia Mare 32435
Muzeul Judeţean Mureş, Târgu Mureş 32608
Muzeul Judeţean Satu Mare, Satu Mare 32587
Muzeul Judeţean Ştefan cel Mare, Vaslui 32624
Muzeul Judeţean Teohari Antonescu, Giurgiu 32527
Muzeul Judeţean Vâlcea, Râmnicu Vâlcea 32578
Muzeul Maramureşului, Sighetu Marmaţiei 32594
Muzeul Municipal, Huşi 32531
Muzeul Municipal, Râmnicu Sărat 32577
Muzeul Municipal Câmpulung, Câmpulung 32482
Muzeul Municipal Curtea de Argeş, Curtea de Argeş 32509
Muzeul Municipal de Istorie, Roşiorii de Vede 32584
Muzeul Municipal Dej ş Galeria de Artă, Dej 32510
Muzeul Municipal Ioan Raica Sebeş, Sebeş 32589
Muzeul Municipal Medias, Mediaş 32549
Muzeul Municipiului Bucureşti, Bucureşti 32461
Muzeul National Secuisec, Sfântu Gheorghe 32590
Muzeul Olteniei, Craiova 32507
Muzeul Orăşanesc Fălticeni, Fălticeni 32519
Muzeul Orăşenecs de Istorie şi Etnografie, Beiuş 32438
Muzeul Orăşenesc, Carei 32489
Muzeul Orăşenesc, Tecuci 32613
Muzeul Orăşenesc de Istorie, Aiud 32427
Muzeul Orăşenesc Molnar Istvan, Cristuru Secuiesc 32508
Muzeul Regiunii Porţilor de Fier, Drobeta-Turnu Severin 32516
Muzeul Romanaţiului, Caracal 32486
Muzeul Sătesc, Cornu 32504
Muzeul Secuiesc al Ciucului, Miercurea-Ciuc 32550
Muzeul Ţării Crişurilor, Oradea 32562
Muzeul Ţării Oaşului, Negreşti-Oaş 32556
Muzeul Tarisznyás Márton, Gheorghieni 32525
Muzeul Vasile Pârvan, Bârlad 32437
Muzeul Vrancei, Focşani 32521

Russia
Adlerskij Kraevedčeskij Muzej - Muzej Istorii Adlerskogo Rajona, Soči 33539
Adygejskij Respublikanskij Kraevedčeskij Muzej, Majkop 33003
Aginskij Okružnoj Kraevedčeskij Muzej im. G. Cybikova, Aginskoe 32630
Altajskij Gosudarstvennyj Kraevedčeskij Muzej, Barnaul 32671
Altajskij Respublikanskij Kraevedčeskij Muzej im. A.V. Anochina, Gorno-Altajsk 32808
Amurskij Gorodskoj Kraevedčeskij Muzej, Amursk 32637
Amurskij Oblastnoj Kraevedčeskij Muzej im. G.S. Novikova-Daurskogo, Blagoveščensk 32691
Archangelskij Literaturnyj Muzej, Archangelsk 32647
Archangelskij Oblastnoj Kraevedčeskij Muzej, Archangelsk 32648
Architekturno-ėtnografičeskij Muzej Angarskaja Derevnja, Bratsk 32702
Arzamasskij Istoriko-chudožestvennyj Muzej, Arzamas 32656
Astrachanskij Gosudarstvennyj Obedinennyj Istoriko-architekturnyj Muzej-zapovednik, Astrachan 32659
Astrachanskij Kraevedčeskij Muzej, Astrachan 32660
Astrachanskij Kreml, Astrachan 32661
Azovskij Kraevedčeskij Muzej, Azov 32668
Balachninskij Kraevedčeskij Muzej, Balachna 32669
Barabinskij Kraevedčeskij Muzej, Barabinsk 32670
Belgorodskij Gosudarstvennyj Istoriko- Kraevedčeskij Muzej, Belgorod 32676
Belinskij Rajonnyj Kraevedčeskij Muzej, Belinskij 32678
Belozerskij Istoriko-chudožestvennyj Muzej, Belozersk 32680
Bereznikovskij Istoriko-kraevedčeskij Muzej, Berezniki 32685

Bijskij Kraevedčeskij Muzej V.V. Bianki, Bijsk 32687
Bolšemuraškinskij Gosudarstvennyj Istoriko-chudožestvennyj Muzej, Bolšoe Muraškino 32697
Borisoglebskij Kraevedčeskij Muzej, Borisoglebsk 32698
Bratskij Gorodskoj Objedinennyj Muzej Istorii Osvoenija Angary, Bratsk 32704
Brjanskij Gosudarstvennyj Obedinennyj Kraevedčeskij Muzej, Brjansk 32706
Buguruslanskij Istoriko-kraevedčeskij Muzej, Buguruslan 32712
Bujnakskij Istoriko-kraevedčeskij Muzej, Bujnaksk 32713
Buzulukskij Gorodskoj Istoriko-kraevedčeskij Muzej, Buzuluk 32714
Čajkovskij Kraevedčeskij Muzej, Čajkovskij 32716
Čeljabinskij Oblastnoj Kraevedčeskij Muzej, Čeljabinsk 32725
Čerdynskij Kraevedčeskij Muzej A.S. Puškina, Čerdyn 32728
Čerkechskij Muzej Jakutskaja Političeskaja Ssylka, Čerkech 32735
Chabarovskij Kraevoj Kraevedčeskij Muzej im. N.I. Grodekova, Chabarovsk 32737
Chakasskij Respublikanskij Kraevedčeskij Muzej, Abakan 32627
Chvalynskij Kraevedčeskij Muzej, Chvalynsk 32747
Čukotskij Okružnoj Kraevedčeskij Muzej, Anadyr' 32638
Čuvašskij Nacionalnyj Muzej, Čeboksary 32719
Dagestanskij Gosudarstvennyj Objedinennyj Istoriko-architekturnyj Muzej, Machačkala 32995
Diorama Kurskaja Bitva - Belgorodskoe Napravlenie, Belgorod 32677
Dobrjanskij Istoriko-kraevedčeskij Muzej, Dobrjanka 32759
Dom-muzej N.N. Chochrjakova, Kirov 32916
Dom-muzej Dekabristov, Kurgan 32970
Dom-muzej E.M. Jaroslavskogo, Jakutsk 32840
Dom-muzej M.B. Grekova, Novočerkassk 33232
Dom-muzej im. T.N. Granovskogo, Orël 33260
Dom-muzej V.I. Lenina, Kazan 32886
Dom-muzej V.I. Lenina, Samara 33370
Dom-muzej M.K. Ammosova, Jakutsk 32841
Dom-muzej N.S. Muchina, Joškar-Ola 32857
Dom-muzej Semji Lopatinych, Stavropol 33560
Dom-muzej V.A. Rusanova, Orël 33262
Domik Petra I, Sankt-Peterburg 33391
Donskoj Istoriko-kraevedčeskij Muzej, Donskoe 32761
Dzeržinskij Gorodskoj Kraevedčeskij Muzej, Dzeržinsk 32765
Ėkspozicija "Ivanovskaja starina", Ivanovo 32827
Elabužskij Gosudarstvennyj Istoriko-architekturnyj i Chudožestvennyj Muzej-zapovednik, Elabuga 32785
Enisejskij Kraevedčeskij Muzej, Enisejsk 32796
Essentukskij Gorodskoj Kraevedčeskij Muzej im. V.P. Špakovskogo, Essentuki 32798
Ėtnografičeskij Muzej pod Otkrytym Nebom Torum Maa, Chanty-Mansijsk 32742
Gatčinskij Kraevedčeskij Muzej - Prioratskij Dvorec, Gatčina 32800
Gatčinskij Literaturno-memorialnyj Muzej-usadba P.E. Ščerbova, Gatčina 32801
Glazovskij Kraevedčeskij Muzej, Glazov 32805
Gorodskoj Kraevedčeskij Muzej, Elec 32792
Gorodskoj Muzej Boevoj Slavy, Kaluga 32876
Gosudarstevnnyj Istoriko-architekturnyj i Chudožestvennyj Muzej-zapovednik Drevnij Derbent, Derbent 32756
Gosudarstvennyj Istoričeskij Zapovednik Gorki Leninskie, Gorki Leninskie 32807
Gosudarstvennyj Istoriko-architekturnyj i Prirodno-landšaftnyj Muzej Zapovednik Izborsk, Izborsk 32834
Gosudarstvennyj Istoriko-ėtnografičeskij i Architekturnyj Muzej-zapovednik Staraja Sarepta, Volgograd 33714
Gosudarstvennyj Istoriko-ėtnografičeskij Muzej-zapovednik Šušenskoe, Šušenskoe 33569
Gosudarstvennyj Istoriko-memorialnyj Zapovednik Rodina V.I. Lenina, Uljanovsk 33656
Gosudarstvennyj Muzej Istorii Sankt-Peterburga - Petropavlovskij Sobor, Sankt-Peterburg 33404
Gosudarstvennyj Muzej-zapovednik S.A. Esenina, Konstantinovo 32937
Gosudarstvennyj Okružnoj Muzej Prirody i Čeloveka Goroda Chanty-Mansijsk, Chanty-Mansijsk 32744
Igarskij Kraevedčeskij Kompleks Muzej Večnoj Merzloty, Igarka 32811
Ingušskij Gosudarstvennyj Muzej Kraevedenija im. T.Ch. Malsagova, Nazran 33203
Irkutskij Oblastnoj Kraevedčeskij Muzej, Irkutsk 32814
Iskitimskij Kraevedčeskij Muzej, Iskitim 32822
Istoriko-chudožestvennyj Muzej, Uglič 33649
Istoriko-ėtnografičeskij Muzej Usadba Galskich, Čerepovec 32731
Istoriko-Kraevedčeskij Muzej, Ivanovo 32828
Istoriko-kraevedčeskij Muzej g. Kronštadta, Kronštadt 32964
Istoriko-kulturnyj Muzej-zapovednik Idnakar, Glazov 32806
Istoriko-memorialnyj i Architurno-chudožestvennyj Muzej, Tichvin 33600
Jakutskij Gosudarstvennyj Muzej Istorii i Kultury Narodov Severa im. Jaroslavskogo, Jakutsk 32843
Jamalo-Neneckij Okružnoj Kraevedčeskij Muzej im. I.S. Šemanovskogo, Salechard 33364
Jaroslavskij Istoriko-architekturnyj i Chudožestvennyj Muzej-zapovednik, Jaroslavl 32849
Jaroslavskij Muzej Boevoj Slavy, Jaroslavl 32850
Jurjeveckij Kraevedčeskij Muzej, Jurjevec 32864
Kaliningradskij Oblastnoj Istoriko-chudožestvennyj Muzej, Kaliningrad 32870
Kaliningradskij Oblastnoj Kraevedčeskij Muzej, Kaliningrad 32871
Kalužskij Oblastnoj Kraevedčeskij Muzej, Kaluga 32879
Kamčatskij Oblastnoj Kraevedčeskij Muzej, Petropavlovsk-Kamčatskij 33310
Kamčatskij Voenno-istoričeskij Muzej, Petropavlovsk-Kamčatskij 33311
Kargopolskij Gosudarstvennyj Istoriko-Architekturnyj i Chudožestvennyj Muzej, Kargopol 32884
Kemerovskij Istoriko-architekturnyi Muzej Krasnaja Gorka, Kemerovo 32911
Kemerovskij Oblastnoj Kraevedčeskij Muzej, Kemerovo 32912
Kirovskij Oblastnoj Kraevedčeskij Muzej, Kirov 32920
Kislovodskij Istoriko-kraevedčeskij Muzej Krepost', Kislovodsk 32928
Kizljarskij Kraevedčeskij Muzej im. P.I. Bagrationa, Kizljar 32932
Klinskoe Muzejnoe Obedinenie, Klin 32934
Komi-Permjackij Okružnoj Kraevedčeskij Muzej im. Subbotina-Permjaka, Kudymkar 32968
Komi Respublikanskij Istoriko-Kraevedčeskij Muzej, Syktyvkar 33573
Korablinskij Kraevedčeskij Muzej, Korablino 32938
Kraevedčeskij Muzej Evrejskoj Avtonomnoj Oblasti, Birobidžan 32689
Kraevedčeskij Muzej g. Lomonosova, Lomonosov 32990
Kraevedčeskij Muzej g. Puškina, Puškin 33337
Kraevedčeskij Muzej g. Puškino, Puškino 33341
Kraevedčeskij Muzej Novgorodskogo Rajona, Velikij Novgorod 33677
Kraevoj Muzej Istorii Literatury, Iskusstva i Kultury Altaja, Barnaul 32673
Krasnojarskij Kraevoj Kraevedčeskij Muzej, Krasnojarsk 32952
Krasnojarskij Kulturno-istoričeskij Muzejnyj Kompleks, Krasnojarsk 32953
Krasnokamskij Kraevedčeskij Muzej, Krasnokamsk 32959
Krasnoturinskij Kraevedčeskij Muzej, Krasnoturinsk 32960
Kungurskij Kraevedčeskij Muzej, Kungur 32969
Kurganskij Oblastnoj Kraevedčeskij Muzej, Kurgan 32972
Kurskij Gosudarstvennyj Oblastnoj Kraevedčeskij Muzej, Kursk 32974
Lgovskij Gosudarstvennyj Kraevedčeskij Muzej, Lgov 32981
Lipeckij Oblastnoj Kraevedčeskij Muzej, Lipeck 32984
Literaturnyj Muzej im. K.V. Ivanova, Čeboksary 32720
Magnitogorskij Kraevedčeskij Muzej, Magnitogorsk 33002
Malojaroslaveckij Istoriko-kraevedčeskij Muzej, Malojaroslavec 33006
Malojaroslaveckij Muzej Voennoj Istorii 1812 Goda, Malojaroslavec 33007
Memorialnyj Dom-muzej Podpolnaja Tipografija Permskogo Komiteta RSDRP 1906 g., Perm 33303
Memorialnyj Dom-Muzej I.I. Šiškina, Elabuga 32786
Memorialnyj Dom-muzej Uljanovych, Astrachan 32663
Memorialnyj Muzej Jurija Gagarina, Gagarin 32799
Memorialnyj Muzej-kabinet M.V. Frunze, Ivanovo 32830
Memorialnyj Muzej-kvartira M.S. Spiridonova, Čeboksary 32721
Michajlovskij Istoričeskij Muzej, Michajlov 33011
Mineralovodskij Kraevedčeskij Muzej, Mineral'nye Vody 33012
Minusinskij Regionalnyj Kraevedčeskij Muzej im. N.M. Martjanova, Minusinsk 33016
Murmanskij Oblastnoj Kraevedčeskij Muzej, Murmansk 33189
Muzei Permskogo Gosudarstvennogo Universiteta, Perm 33304
Muzej A Muzy ne Molčali, Sankt-Peterburg 33426
Muzej Alpinizma, Turizma i Istorii Kurorta Teberda, Teberda 33597
Muzej Arsenal - Muzej Velikoj Otečestvennoj Vojny, Voronež 33731
Muzej Boevogo i Trudovogo Podviga 1941-1945, Saransk 33498
Muzej Boevoj Slavy, Astrachan 32664
Muzej V.I. Čapaeva, Čeboksary 32722
Muzej Cerkov Dekabristov, Čita 32751
Muzej Dekabristov, Minusinsk 33017
Muzej Dekabristov - Dom Trubeckogo, Irkutsk 32816
Muzej Ėtnografii, Istorii i Kultury Narodov Baškortostana, Ufa 33646
Muzej Goroda Jurjevca, Jurjevec 32865
Muzej Goroda Penzy, Penza 33288
Muzej Gorodskaja Duma, Tjumen 33604
Muzej Gradostroitelstva i Byta Taganroga, Taganrog 33583
Muzej Istorii Aksaja, Aksaj 32631
Muzej Istorii Burjatii im. M.N. Changalova, Ulan-Udė 33653
Muzej Istorii Ekaterinburga, Ekaterinburg 32775
Muzej Istorii g. Stavropolja, Stavropol 33562
Muzej Istorii Goroda Irkutska, Irkutsk 32818
Muzej Istorii Goroda Joškar-Oly, Joškar-Ola 32859
Muzej Istorii Goroda-Kurorta Soči, Soči 33541
Muzej Istorii Goroda Naberežnye Čelny, Naberežnye Čelny 33192
Muzej Istorii Goroda Šlisselburga, Šlisselburg 33525
Muzej Istorii Goroda Tjumeni, Tjumen 33606
Muzej Istorii i Kultury Goroda Votkinska, Votkinsk 33738
Muzej Istorii i Kultury Moskovskogo Rajona, Nižnij Novgorod 33210
Muzej Istorii i Kultury Srednego Prikamja, Sarapul 33503
Muzej Istorii Izučenija i Osvoenija Evropejskogo Severa, Apatity 32645
Muzej Istorii Jaroslavlja, Jaroslavl 32853
Muzej Istorii Kolskich Saamov, Lovozero 32993
Muzej Istorii Kraja, Belozersk 32683
Muzej Istorii Moskvy, Moskva 33109
Muzej Istorii Orenburga, Orenburg 33269
Muzej Istorii Otečestvennogo Predprinimatelstva, Moskva 33110
Muzej Istorii Permskogo Rajona, Perm 33306
Muzej Istorii Političeskoj Ssylki, Bratsk 32705
Muzej Istorii Politssylki v Jakutii, Jakutsk 32844
Muzej Istorii Priokskogo Rajona, Nižnij Novgorod 33214
Muzej Istorii Rossijskogo Gosudarstvennogo Pedagogičeskogo Universiteta im A.I. Gercena, Sankt-Peterburg 33443
Muzej Istorii Teatrov Dagestana, Machačkala 32998
Muzej Konspiritavnaja Kvartira Simbirskoj Gruppy RSDRP 1904-1906, Uljanovsk 33661
Muzej Kraevedenija g. Elabuga, Elabuga 32787
Muzej Kronštadtskaja Krepost, Kronštadt 32966
Muzej Kultury Astrachani, Astrachan 32666
Muzej Kupečeskogo Byta, Ekaterinburg 32778
Muzej-kvartira A.M. Gorkogo, Nižnij Novgorod 33215
Muzej Literatury Burjatii im. Choca Namsaraeva, Ulan-Udė 33654
Muzej Meterologičeskaja Stancija Simbirska, Uljanovsk 33662
Muzej Mologskogo Kraja, Rybinsk 33361
Muzej Moskovskoj Konservatorii, Moskva 33136
Muzej Narodnoje Obrazovanie Simbirskoj Gubernii v 70-80 gody 19 veka, Uljanovsk 33664
Muzej Nekropol' Demidovych i Vystavočnyj Zal Tulskij Metall, Tula 33627
Muzej Nižegorodskij Ostrog, Nižnij Novgorod 33218
Muzej Nižegorodskoj Intelligencii, Nižnij Novgorod 33219
Muzej Oktjabrskogo Vooružennogo Vosstanija, Voronež 33733
Muzej Russko-Armjanskoj Družby, Rostov-na-Donu 33357
Muzej Simbirskaja Čuvašskaja Škola - Kvartira I.Ja. Jakovleva, Uljanovsk 33665
Muzej Simbirskaja Klassičeskaja Gimnazija, Uljanovsk 33666
Muzej Smolenščina v Gody Velikoj Otečestvennoj Vojny 1941 -1945, Smolensk 33530
Muzej Sovremennoj Istorii i Kultury Severnoj Osetii, Vladikavkaz 33689
Muzej A.V. Suvorova, Velikij Novgorod 33679
Muzej Uezdnogo Goroda, Čistopol 32749
Muzej-usadba N.A. Durovoj, Elabuga 32788
Muzej Vladimira Raevskogo, Bogoslovka 32695
Muzej-zapovednik Dmitrovskij Kreml, Dmitrov 32758
Muzejno-vystavočnyj Centr, Ivanovo 32833
Muzejno-vystavočnyj Centr - Diorama, Kirov 32923
Muzejno-vystavočnyj Centr Tul'skie Drevnosti, Tula 33630
Muzejno-vystavočnyj Kompleks Volokolamskij Kreml, Volokolamsk 33726
Nacionalnyj Muzej Kabardino-Balkarskoj Respubliki, Nalčik 33197
Nacionalnyj Muzej Respubliki Marij Ėl im. T. Evseeva, Joškar-Ola 32861
Nacionalnyj Muzej Respubliki Tatarstan, Kazan 32907
Nacionalnyj Muzej Udmurtskoj Respubliki im. K. Gerda, Iževsk 32836
Narodnyj Istoriko-kraevedčeskij Muzej Tatarska, Tatarsk 33596
Narovčatskij Rajonnyj Kraevedčeskij Muzej, Narovčat 33201
Neneckij Okružnoj Kraevedčeskij Muzej, Narjan-Mar 33198
Nižegorodskij Gosudarstvennyj Istoriko-architekturnyj Muzej-zapovednik, Nižnij Novgorod 33223
Nižnetagilskij Muzej-Zapovednik Gornozavodskogo Dela Srednego Urala, Nižnij Tagil 33228
Novokuzneckij Kraevedeskij Muzej, Novokuzneck 33237
Novorossijskij Gosudarstvennyj Istoričeskij Muzej Zapovednik, Novorossijsk 33238
Novotroickij Istoriko-kraevedčeskij Muzej, Novotroick 33247
Oblastnoj Kraevedčeskij Muzej, Ekaterinburg 32782
Oblastnoj Kraevedčeskij Muzej im A.A. Kuznecova, Čita 32752
Oloneckij Nacionalnyj Muzej Karelov-Livvikov im. N.T.Prilukin, Olonec 33252
Omskij Gosudarstvennyj Istoriko-kraevedčeskij Muzej, Omsk 33255
Orenburgskij Oblastnoj Kraevedčeskij Muzej, Orenburg 33270
Orlovskij Oblastnoj Kraevedčeskij Muzej, Orël 33267
Orskij Istoriko-kraevedčeskij Muzej, Orsk 33272
Osinskij Kraevedčeskij Muzej, Osa 33273
Penzenskij Gosudarstvennyj Obedinennyj Kraevedčeskij Muzej, Penza 33294
Pjatigorskij Kraevedčeskij Muzej, Pjatigorsk 33322
Pskovskij Gosudarstvennyj Istoričesko-architekturnyj i Chudožestnennyj Muzej-zapovednik, Pskov 33332
Pskovskij Memorialnyj Muzej V.I. Lenina, Pskov 33333
Pustozerskij Kompleksnyj Istoriko-prirodnyj Muzej, Narjan-Mar 33199
Roslavlskij Istoriko-chudožstvennyj Muzej, Roslavl 33353
Samarskij Oblastnoj Istoriko-kraevedčeskij Muzej im. P.V. Alabina, Samara 33378
Saratovskij Ėtnografičeskij Muzej, Saratov 33509
Saratovskij Gosudarstvennyj Muzej Boevoj Slavy, Saratov 33510
Saratovskij Kraevedčeskij Muzej, Saratov 33511
Šeltozerskij Vepsskij Ėtnografičeskij Muzej, Šeltozero 33515
Semenovskij Gosudarstvennyj Kraevedčeskij Istoriko-chudožestvennyj Muzej, Semenov 33516
Sergačskij Kraevedčeskij Muzej, Sergač 33518
Severo-osetinskij Gosudarstvennyj Obedinennyj Muzej Istorii, Architektury i Literatury, Vladikavkaz 33690
Šlisselburgskaja Krepost Orešek, Šlisselburg 33526
Smolenskij Istoričeskij Muzej, Smolensk 33535
Smolenskij Muzej-Zapovednik, Smolensk 33536
Solikamskij Gorodskoj Kraevedčeskij Muzej, Solikamsk 33543
Staroladožskij Istoriko-Architekturnyj i Archeologičeskij Muzej-Zapovednik, Staraja Ladoga 33553
Starooskolskij Kraevedčeskij Muzej, Staryj Oskol 33559
Starorusskij Kraevedčeskij Muzej, Staraja Russa 33555
Stavropolskij Kraevedčeskij Muzej im. G.N. Prozriteleva i G.K. Prave, Stavropol 33563
Syzranskij Gorodskoj Kraevedčeskij Muzej, Syzran 33581
Taganrogskij Kraevedčeskij Muzej, Taganrog 33587
Tajmyrskij Okružnoj Kraevedčeskij Muzej, Dudinka 32762
Tambovskij Oblastnoj Kraevedčeskij Muzej, Tambov 33591
Tarskij Istoriko-kraevedčeskij Muzej, Tara 33592
Tarusskij Kraevedčeskij Muzej, Tarusa 33594
Troickij Sobor, Serpuchov 33523
Tuapsinskij Kraevedčeskij Muzej im. N.G. Poletaeva, Tuapse 33622
Tulskij Oblastnoj Kraevedčeskij Muzej, Tula 33633
Tuvinskij Respublikanskij Kraevedčeskij Muzej im. Aldan Maadyr, Kyzyl 32979
Tverskoj Gosudarstvennyj Obedinennyj Muzej, Tver 33639
Uljanovskij Oblastnoj Kraevedčeskij Muzej im. I.A. Gončarova, Uljanovsk 33669
Valaamskij Naučno-issledovatelskij Cerkovno-archeologičeskij i Prirodnyj Muzej-zapovednik, Sortavala 33548
Velikolukskij Kraevedčeskij Muzej, Velikie Luki 33676
Vetlužskij Kraevedčeskij Muzej, Vetluga 33685
Vjatskaja Kunstkamera, Kirov 32924
Volgogradskij Memorialno-istoričeskij Muzej, Volgograd 33717
Volgogradskij Oblastnoj Kraevedčeskij Muzej, Volgograd 33719
Vorkutinskij Mežrajonnyj Kraevedčeskij Muzej, Vorkuta 33728
Voronežskij Oblastnoj Kraevedčeskij Muzej, Voronež 33736
Vserossijskij Istoriko-ėtnografičeskij Muzej, Toržok 33620
Vsevoložskij Gosudarstvennyj Istoriko-kraevedčeskij Muzej, Vsevoložsk 33740
Vyborgskij Kraevedčeskij Muzej, Vyborg 33742
Vystavočnyj Zal, Vologda 33725
Vystavočnyj Zal Spasskaja Cerkov, Irkutsk 32821

St. Pierre and Miquelon

Musée-Archives de Saint-Pierre, Saint-Pierre 33756

San Marino

Museo di Stato, San Marino 33765

Senegal

Musée Régional Ex-Dixième Riaom, Thiès 33785

Serbia-Montenegro

Gradski Muzej, Kosovska Mitrovica 33847
Gradski Muzej, Sremski Karlovci 33915
Gradski Muzej i Galerija, Bečej 33791
Gradski Muzej - Városi Muzeum, Subotica 33918
J.U. Polimski Muzej, Berane 33822
Memorijalni Muzeji Bela Crkva i Stolice, Krupanj 33856
Muzej Budva, Budva 33826
Muzej Grada Novog Sada, Novi Sad 33870
Muzej Jovana Jovanovića-Zmaja, Sremska Kamenica 33911
Muzej Krajine Negotin, Negotin 33862
Muzej Srema, Sremska Mitrovica 33913
Muzej u Smederevu, Smederevo 33906
Muzej Ulcinj, Ulcinj 33923
Narodni Muzej, Pančevo 33880
Narodni Muzej, Zaječar 33930
Narodni Muzej Crne Gore, Cetinje 33833
Narodni Muzej Valjevo, Valjevo 33926
Nikšićki Muzej, Nikšić 33863
Njegošev Muzej, Cetinje 33834
Opštinski Muzej, Sremska Mitrovica 33914

Regionali Muzej, Djakovica 33836
Spomen-Muzej Prosvetitelja i Pisca Kirila Pejčinovića, Lesak kod Tetova 33858
Spomen-Park Kragujevački Oktobar, Kragujevac 33854
Vojvodjanski Muzej, Novi Sad 33875
Zavičajni Muzej, Bileća 33823
Zavičajni Muzej, Danilovgrad 33835
Zavičajni Muzej, Doboj 33837
Zavičajni Muzej, Herceg-Novi 33841
Zavičajni Muzej, Jaša Tomić 33843
Zavičajni Muzej, Pljevlja 33885
Zavičajni Muzej, Trebinje 33922
Zavičajni Muzej, Ulcinj 33924
Zavičajni Muzej u Jagodini, Jagodina 33842
Zavičajni Muzej Zemuna, Zemun 33931

Singapore
Fort Siloso, Singapore 33938
Singapore History Museum at Riverside Point, Singapore 33943

Slovakia
Gemersko-Malohontské Múzeum, Rimavská Sobota 34051
Krajanské Múzeum MS Bratislava, Bratislava 33968
Kysucke Múzeum, Čadca 33984
L. Novomeský Múzeum, Senica 34057
LDM-Múzeum Andreja Sládkoviča Krupina, Krupina 34009
Lubovnianske Múzeum - Hrad, Stará Lubovňa 34065
Malokarpatské Múzeum v Pezinku, Pezinok 34041
Městské Múzeum, Ilava 34000
Městské Múzeum Filakovo, Filakovo 33993
Městské Múzeum L. Štúra, Uhrovec 34077
Městské Múzeum Michala Tillnera, Malacky 34020
Městské Múzeum Poltár, Poltár 34044
Městské Múzeum Rajec, Rajec 34050
Mestské Múzeum v Bratislave, Bratislava 33970
Misijné Múzeum Nitra, Nitra 34034
Múzeum a Galéria Hont Šahy, Šahy 34056
Múzeum Bábkarských Kultúr a Hračiek Hrad Modry Kameň, Modrý Kameň 34031
Múzeum Krompachy, Krompachy 34008
Múzeum Ludovita Štúra, Modra 34030
Múzeum Madarskej Kultúry a Podunajska, Komárno 34003
Múzeum Michala Greisigera, Spišská Béla 34061
Múzeum Spiša, Spišská Nová Ves 34064
Múzeum v Kežmarku, Kežmarok 34002
Múzeum vo Svätý Antone, Svätý Anton 34068
Novohradské Múzeum, Filakovo 33994
Novohradské Múzeum, Lučenec 34019
Podjavorinské Múzeum, Nové Mesto nad Váhom 34038
Pohronské Múzeum v Novej Bani, Nová Baňa 34037
Ponitrianske Múzeum, Nitra 34035
Považské Múzeum, Žilina 34079
Šarišské Múzeum, Bardejov 33952
Slovenské Banské Múzeum, Banská Štiavnica 33951
Spišské Múzeum, Levoča 34012
Stredoslovenské Múzeum, Banská Bystrica 33950
Tekovské Múzeum v Leviciach, Levice 34010
Trenčianske Múzeum, Trenčín 34074
Vlastivedné a Literárne Múzeum, Svätý Jur 34069
Vlastivedné Múzeum, Prešov 34049
Vlastivedné Múzeum v Galante, Galanta 33995
Zemplínske Múzeum, Michalovce 34029
Žitnoostrovské Múzeum, Dunajská Streda 33992

Slovenia
Dolenjski Muzej Novo Mesto, Novo Mesto 34136
Goriški Muzej, Nova Gorica 34135
Loški Muzej, Škofja Loka 34148
Mestni Muzej Idrija, Idrija 34091
Muzej na Blejskem Gradu, Bled 34085
Muzej Velenje, Velenje 34162
Muzejska Zbirka Laško, Laško 34103
Pokrajinski Muzej, Maribor 34127
Ribniški Muzej, Ribnica na Dolenjskem 34146
Rojstna Hiša Simona Gregorčiča, Vrsno 34165
Sokličev Muzej, Slovenj Gradec 34151
Tolminski Muzej, Tolmin 34155
Triglavska Muzejska Zbirka, Mojstrana 34132
Tržiški Muzej, Tržič 34160

Solomon Islands
Soloman Island National Museum and Cultural Centre, Honiara 34167

South Africa
Albany Museum, Grahamstown 34249
Aliwal North Museum and Church Plein Museum, Aliwal North 34171
Arend Dieperink Museum, Potgietersrus 34339
Barkley East Museum, Barkley East 34175
Bartolomeu Dias Museum Complex, Mossel Bay 34311
Beaufort West Museum, Beaufort West 34177
Bergtheil Museum, Westville 34403
Bethlehem Museum, Bethlehem 34179
Burgersdorp Cultural Historical Museum, Burgersdorp 34197
Calvinia Regional Museum, Calvinia 34199
Colesberg/Kemper Museum, Colesberg 34218
C.P. Nel Museum, Oudtshoorn 34319
District Six Museum, Cape Town 34205
Drostdy Museum, Uitenhage 34393
East London Museum, East London 34236
Elgin Apple Museum, Grabouw 34248
First Raadsaal Museum, Bloemfontein 34183
Freshford House Museum, Bloemfontein 34184
George Museum, George 34244
Graaf-Reinet Museum, Graaff-Reinet 34246
Great Brak River Museum, Great Brak River 34255
Hartenbos Museum, Hartenbos 34259
Heritage Collection Catherina Brand, Ladybrand 34300
History Museum, Grahamstown 34250
Howick Museum, Howick 34264
Julius Gordon Africana Centre, Riversdale 34368
Kalahari-Oranje Museum, Upington 34395
Klerksdorp Museum, Klerksdorp 34297
Knysna Museum, Knysna 34298
Kwa Muhle Museum, Durban 34228
Lichtenburg Museums and Art Gallery, Lichtenburg 34301
McGregor Museum and Duggan Cronin Gallery, Kimberley 34290
Mafikeng Museum, Mafikeng 34304
Mary Moffat Museum, Griquatown 34258
Messina Museum, Messina 34307
Michaelis Collection, Cape Town 34207
Museum Africa, Johannesburg 34280
Museum Caledon River, Smithfield 34378
Museum Chris Van Niekerk, Boshof 34194
Museum Transgariep, Philippolis 34323
Old Court House Museum, Durban 34229
Paarl Museum, Paarl 34321
Parys Museum, Parys 34322
Pellisier House Museum, Bethulie 34180
Pilgrim's Rest Museum, Pilgrim's Rest 34330
P.W. Vorster Museum, Middelburg Cape 34308
Rhodes Cottage Museum, Muizenberg 34313
Robben Island Museum, Robben Island 34369
Roodepoort Museum, Florida Park 34240
Saint Vincent Church Museum, Isandlwana 34265
Schoemansdal Museum, Louis Trichardt 34302
Simon's Town Museum, Simon's Town 34376
South African Police Service Museum, Pretoria 34356
Sterkstroom Museum, Sterkstroom 34388
Talana Museum and Heritage Park, Dundee 34222
Township Museum, Lwandle 34303
Vaal Teknorama Cultural Museum, Vereeniging 34396
Village Museum, Stellenbosch 34387
Voortrekker Monument Heritage Site, Pretoria 34364
Vryburg Museum, Vryburg 34399
Welkom Museum, Welkom 34402

Spain
Casa Museo Alegre de Sagrera, Terrassa 35523
Casa Museo Ignacio Zuloaga, Zumaia 35739
Casa-Museu Pare Manyanet, Tremp 35573
Casa-Museu Prat de la Riba, Castellterçol 34696
Casa-Museu Torres Amat, Sallent 35367
Casa Natal de Sant Antoni María Claret, Sallent 35368
Castell Cartoixa Vallparadis, Terrassa 35524
Colleció de la Unió Excursionista de Catalunya, Olesa de Montserrat 35168
Colleció d'Autòbils de Salvador Claret Sargatal, Sils 35495
Colleció de la Tossa de Montbui, Santa Margarida de Montbui 35421
Fundación Municipal de Cultura Luis Ortega Brú, San Roque 35390
Museo Arqueológico de Úbeda, Ubeda 35583
Museo Arqueológico Etnológico Municipal, Guardamar de Segura 34889
Museo Biblioteca La Casona, Tudanca 35577
Museo Carlos Maside, Sada 35352
Museo Comarcal Reus, Reus 35312
Museo de Albacete, Albacete 34419
Museo de Cáceres, Cáceres 34641
Museo de Cádiz, Cádiz 34647
Museo de Cuenca, Cuenca 34764
Museo de Historia de Tenerife y Archivo Insular, La Laguna 34937
Museo de Historia y Cultura Casa Pedrilla, Cáceres 34642
Museo de la Ciudad, Vinaròs 35691
Museo de la Guardia Civil, Madrid 35026
Museo de la Paeria, Lleida 34967
Museo de la Rioja, Logroño 34981
Museo de la Sociedad Amigos de Laguardia, Laguardia 34935
Museo de Menorca, Mahón 35067
Museo de San Isidro, Madrid 35029
Museo de Segovia, Segovia 35465
Museo de Zamora, Zamora 35714
Museo de Zaragoza, Zaragoza 35721
Museo del Almudín, Xàtiva 35704
Museo del Castillo de Odna, Onda 35179
Museo Etnografico Extremeño González Santana, Olivenza 35171
Museo Histórico de la Ciudad, Valencia 35607
Museo Histórico de Requena y su Comarca, Requena 35311
Museo Histórico Municipal de Écija, Ecija 34783
Museo Historico Munipal, Montilla 35137
Museo Lara, Ronda 35340
Museo Militar Regional de Burgos, Burgos 34635
Museo Municipal, Algeciras 34445
Museo Municipal, Alzira 34460
Museo Municipal, Calatayud 34654
Museo Municipal, Carmona 34681
Museo Municipal, Melilla 35108
Museo Municipal, Nerva 35159
Museo Municipal, Reus 35313
Museo Municipal, Vélez-Málaga 35641
Museo Municipal de Madrid, Madrid 35040
Museo Municipal de Vigo Quiñones de León, Vigo 35655
Museo Municipal Eduard Camps Cava, Guissona 34895
Museo Municipal Elisa Cendrero, Ciudad Real 34723
Museo Municipal Ulpiano Checa, Colmenar de Oreja 34729
Museo Nájerillense, Nájera 35154
Museo Provincial, Teruel 35530
Museu Arxiu Comarcal, Moià 35118
Museu-Arxiu de Santa María de Mataró, Mataró 35099
Museu Arxiu de Vilassar de Dalt, Vilassar de Dalt 35671
Museu-Arxiu Municipal, Tortosa 35569
Museu-Arxiu Municipal de Calella, Calella 34659
Museu Biblioteca Fundació Mauri, La Garriga 34839
Museu Cerdà, Puigcerdà 35303
Museu Comarcal, Tárrega 35518
Museu Comarcal de Berga, Berga 34602
Museu Comarcal de la Conca de Barberà, Montblanc 35129
Museu Comarcal de l'Anoia, Igualada 34914
Museu Comarcal de Manresa, Manresa 35082
Museu de Badalona, Badalona 34520
Museu de Bellvís, Bellvís 34596
Museu de Coses del Poble, Collbató 34728
Museu de Gavà, Gavà 34842
Museu de Gelida, Gelida 34843
Museu de Granollers, Granollers 34883
Museu de la Vila, Vilar-Rodona 35670
Museu de l'Adet, Torelló 35554
Museu de l'Aigua Colleció Gavarró, Vilanova del Camí 35663
Museu de Llaberia, Tivissa 35533
Museu de Llavaneres, Sant Andreu de Llavaneres 35394
Museu de Lloret de Mar, Lloret de Mar 34977
Museu de Mallorca, Palma de Mallorca 35233
Museu de Mataró, Mataró 35100
Museu de Montgrí i del Baix Ter, Torroella de Montgrí 35566
Museu de Sant Joan de Mediona, Mediona 35106
Museu de Sant Pol de Mar, Sant Pol de Mar 35407
Museu de Torrebesses, Torrebesses 35559
Museu de Torrellebreta, Malla 35076
Museu de Torroja, Torroja del Priorat 35567
Museu d'El Bruc, El Bruc 34624
Museu del Càntir, Argentona 34483
Museu del Montsec, Artesa de Segre 34491
Museu del Montsià, Amposta 34464
Museu del Pagès, Torroella de Fluvià 35565
Museu del Pastor, Fornells de la Muntanya 34823
Museu d'Història, Sabadell 35348
Museu d'Història Casa Castellarnau, Tarragona 35513
Museu d'Història de la Ciutat, Barcelona 34573
Museu d'Història de la Ciutat, Girona 34856
Museu d'Historia de Tarragona Pretori Romà, Tarragona 35514
Museu Els Cups, Montbrió del Camp 35131
Museu Etnologic d'Era Val d'Aran, Vielha 35654
Museu Històric Municipal, Riudoms 35327
Museu Historic Municipal de Polinyà, Polinyà 35278
Museu la Granja, Espai Cultural, Santa Perpètua de Mogoda 35427
Museu Manolo Hugué, Caldes de Montbui 34657
Museu Municipal, Alcover 34437
Museu Municipal, Guimerà 34894
Museu Municipal, Llivia 34976
Museu Municipal, Manlleu 35081
Museu Municipal, Palafrugell 35210
Museu Municipal, Riudecanyes 35326
Museu Municipal Can Xifreda, Sant Feliu de Codines 35399
Museu Municipal d'Agramunt, Agramunt 34410
Museu Municipal de la Pagesia, Castellbisbal 34690
Museu Municipal de Nàutica, El Masnou 35097
Museu Municipal de Pallejà, Pallejà 35218
Museu Municipal Joan Pal i Gras, Llinars del Vallés 34974
Museu Municipal Miquel Soldevila, Prats de Lluçanès 35293
Museu Rocaguinarda, Oristà 35190
Museu Sentronà, Tiana 35532
Museu Vallhonrat, Rubí 35343
Palacio Real la Almudaina, Palma de Mallorca 35235
Sala de Trofeos del Duque de Arión, Plasencia 35275
Zerain Cultural Park, Zerain 35735

Sri Lanka
Galle National Museum, Galle 35754
Jaffna National Museum, Jaffna 35756
Kandy National Museum, Kandy 35757
Ratnapura National Museum, Ratnapura 35760

Sudan
El-Barkai Museum, Khartoum 35764
Khalif's House Museum, Khartoum 35768
Sultan Ali Dianr Museum, El-Fasher 35761

Suriname
Openluchtmuseum Nieuw Amsterdam, Nieuw Amsterdam 35776
Surinaams Museum, Paramaribo 35778

Sweden
Åhus Museum, Åhus 35788
Ajtte Museum, Jokkmokk 35981
Åkers Hembygdsmuseum, Strängnäs 36300
Alingsås Museum, Alingsås 35789
Åmåls Hembygdsmuseum, Åmål 35793
Arboga Museum, Arboga 35806
Årsunda Viking Museum, Årsunda 35812
Arvidsjaurs Hembygdsmuseum, Arvidsjaur 35813
Åsavallen, Edsbro 35857
Aspö-Tosterö Hembygdsmuseum, Strängnäs 36301
Åtvidabergs Bruks- och Facitmuseum, Åtvidaberg 35824
Bergartsmuséet, Sandviken 36176
Berte Museum, Slöinge 36204
Bjärnums Museum, Bjärnum 35832
Blekinge Museum, Karlskrona 35998
Bohusläns Museum, Uddevalla 36342
Bollnäs Konsthallen, Bollnäs 35837
Borås Museum, Borås 35841
Borgsjö Hembygdsgård, Erikslund 35868
Broby Hembygdspark, Broby 35847
Bruksmuseet Smedsgården, Sandviken 36177
Brunskogs Hembygdsgård, Brunskog 35848
Ekomuseum Gränsland och Strømstad Museum, Strømstad 36303
Eksjö Museum med Albert Engströms Samlingarna, Eksjö 35860
Enköpings Museum, Enköping 35866
Eriksbergs Museum, Tranås 36330
Eslövs Stadsmuseum, Eslöv 35874
Falbygdens Museum, Falköping 35880
Falsterbo Museum, Falsterbo 35881
Filipstads Bergslags Hembygdsgård, Filipstad 35887
Fredriksdals Friluftsmuseum, Helsingborg 35949
Frejamuséet, Kil 36006
Friluftsmuseet i Apladalen, Värnamo 36376
Frösö Hembygdsmuseum, Frösön 35896
Gamla Linköping, Linköping 36040
Gamla Skeninge, Skänninge 36190
Gammelgården Friluftsmuseet, Bengtfors 35829
Glommersträsks Hembygdsmuseum, Glommersträsk 35905
Göteborgs Stadsmuseum, Göteborg 35913
Grangärde Hembygdsgården, Grangärde 35929
Grassagården Miljömuseum, Strängnäs 36302
Hembygdsgården, Bjurholm 35833
Hembygdsgården i Kristvalla, Nybro 36125
Hembygdsmuseet i Korsberga, Korsberga 36015
Höganäs Museum och Konsthall, Höganäs 35956
Högarps Bymuseum, Vetlanda 36402
Hörby Museum, Hörby 35959
Huskvarna Stadsmuseum, Huskvarna 35969
Jämtlands Läns Museum, Östersund 36146
Jönköpings Läns Museum, Jönköping 35977
Kalix Flottningsmuseum, Kalix 35986
Kalmar Läns Museum, Kalmar 35988
Karlshamns Museum, Karlshamn 35992
Katrineholms Hembygdsmuseet, Kristineholm 36021
Kläppgården Hembygdsmuseum, Harads 35945
Köpings Museum, Köping 36010
Kortedala Museum, Göteborg 35914
Kristinehamns Museum, Kristinehamn 36020
Kungsudden Local Museum, Kungsör 36025
Länsmuseet Västernorrland, Härnösand 35935
Länsmuseet Varberg, Varberg 36395
Landskrona Museum, Landskrona 36029
Lesjöforsmuseum, Lesjöfors 36030
Lima Hembygdsgård, Lima 36036
Lindesbergsmuseum, Lindesberg 36038
Ljungby Gamla Torg Hembygdsmuseum, Ljungby 36044
Ljusdalsbygdens Museum, Ljusdal 36045
Ljusterö Hembygdsmuseum, Ljusterö 36046
Måleriyrkets Museum, Stockholm 36257
Målilla Hembygdspark, Målilla 36067
Malmö Museer, Malmö 36077
Malungs Hembygdsgård, Malung 36082
Mariefreds Hembygdsmuseum, Mariefred 36085
Markarydsortens Hembygdsmuseum, Markaryd 36092
Masonry Museum Vånevik and Näset, Påskallavik 36156
Mjölby Hembygdsgård, Mjölby 36094
Mölndals Museum, Mölndal 36097
Motala Museum, Motala 36106
Museet Näktergalen, Vimmerby 36411
Museum Åsättra, Ljusterö 36047
Museum Skänninge Rådhus, Skänninge 36191
Njudungs Hembygdsmuseum, Vetlanda 36403
Nordhallands Hembygdsförening, Kungsbacka 36023
Norrbyskärs Museum, Hörnefors 35960
Österlens Museum, Simrishamn 36189
Övertorneå Hembygdsmuseum, Övertorneå 36151
Olofsfors Bruksmuseum, Nordmaling 36114
Ornunga Museum, Vårgårda 36398
Pengsjö Nybyggarmuseum, Vännäs 36375
Piteå Museum, Piteå 36157
Regionmuseet Kristianstad, Kristianstad 36018
Regionmuseet Västra Götaland, Vänersborg 36373
Rörbäcksnäs Hembygdsgård, Lima 36037
Roslagsmuseet, Norrtälje 36124
Säters Hembygdsmuseum, Säter 36170
Samegården med Museum, Tärnaby 36320
Sigtuna Rådhus, Sigtuna 36184
Skövde Stadsmuseum, Skövde 36199
Skogsmuseet i Lycksele, Lycksele 36066
Söderbärke Hembygdsgård, Söderbärke 36208
Söderhamns Stadsmuseum, Söderhamn 36209
Sölje Bygdegård, Glava 35903
Sölvesborgs Museum, Sölvesborg 36215
Sörmlands Museum, Nyköping 36128
Sörmlandsgården, Eskilstuna 35872

Sollefteå Museum, Sollefteå 36216
Solna Hembygdsmuseum, Solna 36222
Stadsmuseet i Gråbrödraklostret, Ystad 36422
Stadsmuseet och Ahlbergshallen, Östersund 36148
Stafsjö Bruksmuseum, Falkenberg 35878
Stockholms Länsmuseum, Stockholm 36287
Stockholms Stadsmuseum, Stockholm 36290
Strømstads Museum, Strømstad 36304
Sundbybergs Museum, Sundbyberg 36306
Sundsbergs Gård Museum och Konsthall, Sunne 36312
Sundsvalls Museum, Sundsvall 36309
Swensbylijda, Svensbyn 36317
Tibro Museum, Tibro 36323
Tidaholms Museum, Tidaholm 36325
Torekällbergets Museum, Södertälje 36213
Trollhättans Museum och Saab Museum, Trollhättan 36337
Tumbergs Skol- och Hembygdsmuseum, Vårgårda 36399
Tunabygdens Gammelgård, Borlänge 35846
Ulricehamns Museum, Ulricehamn 36345
Ulrika museum, Ulrika 36346
Upplandsmuseet, Uppsala 36361
Vadsbo Museum, Mariestad 36091
Vadstena Stadsmuseum, Vadstena 36370
Vämöparken, Karlskrona 36001
Vänersborgs Museum, Vänersborg 36374
Värmlands Museum, Karlstad 36003
Väsby Kungsgård, Sala 36174
Västerbottens Museum, Umeå 36349
Västergötlands Museum, Skara 36194
Västerviks Museum, Västervik 36387
Västra Göinge Hembygdsmuseum, Hässleholm 35937
Vetlanda Museum, Vetlanda 36405
Viktor Rydbergsmuseet, Jönköping 35980

Switzerland

Bergsturz-Museum Goldau, Goldau 36768
Bibliothèque Publique et Universitaire, Genève 36728
Birsfelder Museum, Birsfelden 36572
Büecheler-Hus, Kloten 36828
Ciäsa Granda, Stampa 37201
Dichter- und Stadtmuseum/ Herwegh-Archiv, Liestal 36876
Dörflihaus-Museum, Spiringen 37194
Dorfmuseum, Bennwil 36535
Dorfmuseum, Birr 36571
Dorfmuseum, Bönigen 36575
Dorfmuseum, Ettingen 36695
Dorfmuseum, Feldbrunnen 36698
Dorfmuseum, Fislisbach 36700
Dorfmuseum, Gontenschwil 36769
Dorfmuseum, Hombrechtikon 36807
Dorfmuseum, Hüntwangen 36810
Dorfmuseum, Konolfingen 36831
Dorfmuseum, Langendorf 36845
Dorfmuseum, Rupperswil 37078
Dorfmuseum, Schwanden (Glarus) 37147
Dorfmuseum, Therwil 37239
Dorfmuseum, Wiesen 37317
Dorfmuseum, Zeihen 37356
Dorfmuseum, Ziefen 37360
Dorfmuseum Bellach, Bellach 36525
Dorfmuseum Graberhaus, Strengelbach 37219
Dorfmuseum Kirchbözberg, Unterbözberg 37260
Dorfmuseum Maschwanden, Maschwanden 36929
Dorfmuseum Melihus, Möhlin 36942
Dorfmuseum Schlossweid, Ringgenberg 37065
Dürstelerhaus, Ottikon (Gossau) 37017
Ecomuseum Simplon, Simplon Dorf 37170
Ente Museo Poschiavino, Poschiavo 37030
Entlebucher Heimatmuseum, Schüpfheim 37146
Freilichtmuseum Säge Buch, Buch 36595
Fricktaler Museum, Rheinfelden 37054
Gandahus, Vals 37281
Das Gelbe Haus, Flirns Dorf 36704
Gemeindemuseum, Krauchthal 36833
Gemeindemuseum, Regensdorf 37048
Gemeindemuseum Rothus, Oberriet 37002
Heimat- und Posamentermuseum Sissach, Sissach 37177
Heimatkundliche Sammlung, Richterswil 37056
Heimatmuseum, Brugg 36591
Heimatmuseum, Donzhausen 36663
Heimatmuseum, Grindelwald 36781
Heimatmuseum, Grüningen 36782
Heimatmuseum, Hallau 36790
Heimatmuseum, Küssnacht am Rigi 36841
Heimatmuseum, Rothrist 37073
Heimatmuseum, Wald, Zürich 37299
Heimatmuseum, Waltensburg 37304
Heimatmuseum Aarburg, Aarburg 36430
Heimatmuseum Adelboden, Adelboden 36432
Heimatmuseum am Pfäffikersee, Pfäffikon (Zürich) 37021
Heimatmuseum Arnold Bärtschi, Dulliken 36667
Heimatmuseum der Talschaft Lauterbrunnen, Lauterbrunnen 36868
Heimatmuseum Elgg, Elgg 36678
Heimatmuseum Grächen, Grächen 36772
Heimatmuseum Kreuzlingen, Kreuzlingen 36836
Heimatmuseum Leuk Stadt, Leuk Stadt 36872
Heimatmuseum Oltingen-Wenslingen-Anwil, Oltingen 37012
Heimatmuseum Prättigau, Grüsch 36784
Heimatmuseum Prestegg, Altstätten 36452
Heimatmuseum Rheinwald, Splügen 37196
Heimatmuseum Schinznach-Dorf, Schinznach Dorf 37134
Heimatmuseum Schwarzbubenland, Dornach 36664
Heimatmuseum Seehof, Buonas 36604
Heimatmuseum Seon, Seon 37164
Heimatmuseum Spittel, Büren an der Aare 36599
Heimatmuseum Spycher, Rickenbach (Luzern) 37058
Heimatmuseum Stein, Stein am Rhein 37213
Heimatmuseum Suhr, Suhr 37222
Heimatmuseum Trimmis, Trimmis 37254
Heimatmuseum Trubschachen, Trubschachen 37255
Heimatmuseum Weesen, Weesen 37308
Heimatmuseum Wiedlisbach, Wiedlisbach 37315
Historische Sammlung im Zeitturm, Mellingen 36937
Historisches Museum Aargau, Lenzburg 36870
Historisches Museum der Stadt Baden, Baden 36485
Historisches Museum des Kantons Thurgau, Frauenfeld 36706
Historisches Museum Heiden, Heiden 36798
Historisches Museum Obwalden, Sarnen 37123
Historisches Museum Olten, Olten 37008
Historisches Museum Uri, Altdorf, Uri 36447
Historisches Museum Wiedlisbach, Wiedlisbach 37316
Ital Reding-Haus, Schwyz 37151
Ittinger Museum, Warth 37306
Kultur-Historisches Museum Grenchen, Grenchen 36778
Kulturmühle Lützelflüh, Lützelflüh 36896
Lötschentaler Museum, Kippel 36826
Maison Buttin-de Loës, Grandvaux 36777
La Maison du Blé et du Pain, Echallens 36670
Maison Tavel, Genève 36738
March-Museum, Vorderthal 37296
Musée, Le Landeron 36844
Musée Alpin d'Anzère, Anzère 36460
Musée d'Art et d'Histoire Neuchâtel, Neuchâtel 36984
Musée de Carouge, Carouge 36613
Musée de la Confrérie des Vignerons, Vevey 37286
Musée de l'Areuse, Boudry 36581
Musée de l'Evéché, Sion 37175
Musée des Haudères, Les Haudères 36793
Musée d'Estavayer, Estavayer-le-Lac 36693
Musée d'Orbe, Orbe 37013
Musée du Grand-Lens, Lens 36869
Musée du Pays et Val de Charmey, Charmey (Gruyère) 36624
Musée du Tour Automatique et d'Histoire de Moutier, Moutier 36959
Musée du Vieux-Baulmes, Baulmes 36523
Musée du Vieux-Bex, Bex 36561
Musée du Vieux-Monthey, Monthey 36945
Musée du Vieux-Montreux, Montreux 36947
Musée du Vieux-Pays, Le Châble 36621
Musée du Vieux-Saxon, Saxon 37128
Musée Gruérien, Bulle 36603
Musée Historique de Lausanne, Lausanne 36864
Musée Historique de Vevey, Vevey 37288
Musée Isérables, Isérables 36815
Musée La Sagne, La Sagne 37083
Musée Rural Jurassien, Les Genevez 36756
Musée Sonvilier, Sonvilier 37191
Musée Vissoie, Vissoie 37294
Musehum.BL, Liestal 36880
Museo Casa del Padre, Orselina 37016
Museo del Malcantone, Curio 36651
Museo di Blenio, Lottigna 36892
Museo di Leventina, Giornico 36761
Museo di Val Verzasca, Sonogno 37189
Museo Elisarion, Minusio 36941
Museo Epper, Ascona 36471
Museo Moesano, San Vittore 37098
Museo Nazionale del San Gottardo, Airolo 36442
Museo Onsernonese, Loco 36891
Museo Regionale della Centovalli e del Pedemonte, Intragna 36814
Museo Storico, Lugano 36903
Museo Vallerano Bregagliotto, Stampa 37202
Museum Alpin, Pontresina 37026
Museum Amden, Amden 36454
Museum auf der Burg, Raron 37045
Museum Bischofszell, Bischofszell 36574
Museum Burghalde, Lenzburg 36871
Museum Chornhuus, Gränichen 36773
Museum der Landschaft Hasli, Meiringen 36934
Museum der Winterthur-Versicherungen, Winterthur 37334
Museum des Landes Glarus, Näfels 36978
Museum Herisau, Herisau 36802
Museum im Bellpark, Kriens 36839
Museum im Kirchhoferhaus, Sankt Gallen 37104
Museum im Schulhaus, Niederrohrdorf 36991
Museum im Stockalperschloß, Brig 36588
Museum im Thomas Legler-Haus, Diesbach 36659
Museum im Zendenrathaus, Ernen 36690
Museum in der Burg Zug, Zug 37428
Museum Langenthal, Langenthal 36846
Museum Laufental, Laufen 36848
Museum Lindwurm, Stein am Rhein 37215
Museum Löwenburg, Ederswiler 36671
Museum Neuhaus, Biel, Kanton Bern 36564
Museum Regional, Savognin 37126
Museum Regiunal Surselva Casa Carniec, Ilanz 36813
Museum Salzbütte, Huttwil 36811
Museum Sarganserland, Sargans 37119
Museum Wolfhalden, Wolfhalden 37349
Museum zu Allerheiligen, Schaffhausen 37132
Museum zum Schiff, Laufenburg 36850
Nidwaldner Museum, Stans 37205
Obersimmentaler Heimatmuseum, Zweisimmen 37432
Ortsgeschichtliche Sammlung, Oberrieden 37001
Ortsgeschichtliche Sammlung Rebstein, Rebstein 37046
Ortsmuseum, Amriswil 36457
Ortsmuseum, Andwil 36459
Ortsmuseum, Bergün 36536
Ortsmuseum, Binningen 36569
Ortsmuseum, Bülach 36598
Ortsmuseum, Bütschwil 36601
Ortsmuseum, Häggenschwil 36789
Ortsmuseum, Jona 36821
Ortsmuseum, Laax 36843
Ortsmuseum, Liesberg 36875
Ortsmuseum, Meilen 36933
Ortsmuseum, Merenschwand 36939
Ortsmuseum, Oftringen 37007
Ortsmuseum, Rafz 37040
Ortsmuseum, Roggwil 37067
Ortsmuseum, Rüti, Zürich 37077
Ortsmuseum, Sankt Stephan 37116
Ortsmuseum, Schänis 37129
Ortsmuseum, Thalwil 37237
Ortsmuseum, Unterengstringen 37261
Ortsmuseum, Untersiggenthal 37266
Ortsmuseum, Vaz 37282
Ortsmuseum, Vnà 37295
Ortsmuseum, Wängi 37298
Ortsmuseum, Walenstadt 37301
Ortsmuseum Altstetten, Altstetten 36453
Ortsmuseum Beringen, Beringen 36537
Ortsmuseum Brittnau, Brittnau 36589
Ortsmuseum Dietikon, Dietikon 36661
Ortsmuseum Erlenbach, Erlenbach (Zürich) 36686
Ortsmuseum Frenkendorf, Frenkendorf 36710
Ortsmuseum für Heimatkunde, Schlieren 37138
Ortsmuseum Kefiturm, Belp 36534
Ortsmuseum Kilchberg, Kilchberg, Zürich 36825
Ortsmuseum Küsnacht, Küsnacht 36840
Ortsmuseum Mollis, Mollis 36943
Ortsmuseum Mühle, Maur 36932
Ortsmuseum Neunkirch, Neunkirch 36988
Ortsmuseum Oberes Bad, Marbach (Sankt Gallen) 36921
Ortsmuseum Oberuzwil, Oberuzwil 37003
Ortsmuseum Oetwil, Oetwil am See 37005
Ortsmuseum Rüschlikon, Rüschlikon 37076
Ortsmuseum Schleitheim, Schleitheim 37136
Ortsmuseum Schmitten, Schmitten (Albula) 37140
Ortsmuseum Spreitenbach, Spreitenbach 37197
Ortsmuseum Steinmaur, Sünikon 37221
Ortsmuseum Trotte, Arlesheim 36468
Ortsmuseum Urdorf, Urdorf 37269
Ortsmuseum Vechigen, Boll 36576
Ortsmuseum Wallisellen, Wallisellen 37302
Ortsmuseum Weiach, Weiach 37309
Ortsmuseum Wila, Wila 37321
Ortsmuseum Wilchingen, Wilchingen 37322
Ortsmuseum Wilderswil, Wilderswil 37324
Ortsmuseum Wollishofen, Zürich 37403
Ortsmuseum zur Farb, Stäfa 37200
Ortsstube, Bolligen 36577
Privatmuseum Im Blauen Haus, Appenzell 36464
Rathausmuseum, Sempach Stadt 37161
Regionalmuseum Binn, Binn 36567
Regionalmuseum Schwarzwasser, Schwarzenburg 37148
Reiat-Museum, Thayngen 37238
Saaser Museum, Saas Fee 37079
Safier Heimatmuseum, Safien 37082
Schamser Talmuseum, Zillis 37362
Schatzturm zu Schwyz, Schwyz 37152
Schloß Mörsburg, Stadel (Winterthur) 37199
Schloß Sargans, Sargans 37120
Schlossmuseum, Burgdorf 36608
Sensler Museum, Tafers 37228
Simon Gfeller-Gedenkstube, Heimisbach 36800
Sontg Hippolytus, Veulden 37284
Städtisches Ortsmuseum Schwamendingen, Zürich 37409
Staufferhaus - Sammlung Alt Unterentfelden, Unterentfelden 37262
Stiftung Rebhaus Wingreis, Twann 37258
Stiftung Stadtmuseum Sursee, Sursee 37227
Tal-Museum, Engelberg 36682
Talmuseum Chasa Jaura, Valchava 37276
Talmuseum Ursern, Andermatt 36458
Textil- und Heimatmuseum, Sennwald 37162
Toggenburger Museum, Lichtensteig 36874
Touristik-Museum, Unterseen 37264
Weberei- und Heimatmuseum Ruedertal, Schmiedrued 37139
Weissenstein-Museum, Weissenstein bei Solothurn 37310

Syria

Aleppo National Museum, Aleppo 37433
Hama National Museum, Hama 37439

Tajikistan

Chorožskij Istoriko-Kraevedčeskij Muzej, Chorog 37444
Chudžandskij Istoriko-Kraevedčeskij Muzej, Chudžand 37445
Isfara Historical and Regional Museum, Isfara 37447
Istoriko-Kraevedčeskij Muzej Ura Tjube, Ura-Tjube 37451
Kuljabskij Istoriko-Kraevedčeskij Muzej, Kuljab 37448
Respublikanskij Istoriko-Kraevedčeskij Muzej im. Rudaki Abuabdullo, Pendžikent 37450

Tanzania

Peace Memorial Museum, Zanzibar 37470
Shinyanga Mazingira Museum, Shinyanga 37465
Singida Museum, Singida 37466

Thailand

Benchamabophit National Museum, Bangkok 37478
Chaiya National Museum, Surat Thani 37542
Chiang Saen National Museum, Chiang Rai 37504
Chumbhot-Punthip Museum, Bangkok 37480
Hariphunchai National Museum, Lampun 37512
In Buri National Museum, Sing Buri 37536
Kamphaeng Phet National Museum, Kamphaeng Phet 37506
Kao Chong, Trang 37544
Kao Luang, Nakhon Si Thammarat 37518
Kao Ta Phet, Sukhothai 37538
Kao Yai, Saraburi 37535
Lan Sang, Tak 37543
Maha Wirawong National Museum, Nakhon Ratchasima 37517
Matchimawas National Museum, Songkhla 37537
Nam Nao, Petchabun 37523
National Museum, Bangkok 37491
Ob Luang, Chiang Mai 37502
Phe, Rayong 37531
Phra Borommathat National Museum, Nakhon Si Thammarat 37520
Phra Chetuponwimonmangkhalaram National Museum, Bangkok 37493
Phra Phuttachinnarat National Museum, Phitsanulok 37528
Phukradung, Loei 37513
Phupan, Sakon Nakhon 37532
Sam Roi Yod, Phachuab Khiri Khan 37525
Sawanworanayok National Museum, Sukhothai 37540
Thrai Kao, Battani 37500
Ton Sak Yai, Uttaradit 37545
Ton Trai, Phuket 37530
Tung Salaeng Luang, Phitsanulok 37529
Wachiraprasat Museum, Phetchaburi 37526
Wat Ko Museum, Phetchaburi 37527
Wat Phra Thart Lampang Luang Museum, Lampang 37511

Togo

Musée d'Histoire et d'Ethnographie, Aneho 37546
Musée Régional de Kara, Kara 37548
Musée Régional de Sokadé, Sokadé 37550
Musée Régional des Savanes, Dapaong 37547

Tunisia

Musée Chemtou, Jendouba 37564
Musée Dar Ayed, Ksar Hellal 37567
Musée Dar-Chraiet, Tozeur 37589
Musée Dar-Hammamet, Hammamet 37562
Musée de Sousse, Sousse 37586
Musée de Tabarka, Tabarka 37587
Musée du 18 Novembre 1939, Téboursouk 37588
Musée Sbeïtla, Sbeïtla 37578
Musée Sidi Bou Saïd, Sidi Bou Saïd 37584
Musée Sidi Zitouni, Houmt Souk 37563

Turkey

Antalya Müzesi, Antalya 37623
Manisa Müzesi, Manisa 37756
Şehir Müzesi, Beşiktaş 37634

Turkmenistan

Čelekenskij Muzej, Čeleken 37814
Ethnographical Museum, Turkmenbashi 37821
Historical and Ethnographical Museum, Turkmenabat 37820
Kunja-Urgench Historical Site Museum, Keneurgench 37815
Tačauz Muzej, Tačauz 37819

Ukraine

Černivci Local Museum, Černivci 37839
Chersonskij Kraevedčeskij Muzej, Cherson 37843
Doneckij Oblastnoj Kraevedčeskij Muzej, Doneck 37851
Kirovograd Regional Museum of Local History, Art and Nature, Kirovograd 37861
Krasnojarskij Istoričeskij Muzej Memorial Pobedy, Krasnojarsk 37865
Krymski Respublikanskij Kraevedčeskij Muzej, Simferopol 37904
Local History Museum, Krivoj Rog 37866
Local Museum of History and Culture, Lugansk 37881
Muzej Kraevedenija, Jalta 37855
Nikolaevsk Local Museum, Nikolaev 37890
Odessa Local History Museum, Odessa 37894
Regional Museum, Žytomyr 37914
Rivnenski Museum of Regional Studies, Rivne 37899
Ternopil Local Museum, Ternopil 37907
Usman Jusupov Memorial Museum, Jalta 37856
Vinnitsa Museum of Local Lore, Vinnica 37911
Vladimir-Volynski Local Museum, Vladimir-Volynski 37912
Volynskyj Krajeznavčyj Muzej, Luck 37880
Zaporožeskij Kraevedčeskij Muzej, Zaporože 37913

United Arab Emirates

Dubai Museum, Dubai 37916
Fujairah Museum, Fujairah 37918
Sharjah Heritage Museum, Sharjah 37923

United Kingdom

Abbey House Museum, Leeds 39440
Abbeydale Industrial Hamlet, Sheffield 40481
Abbotsford House, Melrose 39931
Aberconwy House, Conwy 38626
Abergavenny Museum, Abergavenny 37948
Abernethy Museum, Abernethy 37950
Abertillery Museum, Abertillery 37951
Abingdon Museum, Abingdon 37957
Abington Museum, Northampton 40081
Aldeburgh Museum, Aldeburgh 37962
Alderney Society Museum, Alderney 37964
Aldershot Military Museum and Rushmoor Local History Gallery, Aldershot 37966
Alford Heritage Centre, Alford, Aberdeenshire 37972
Alford Manor House Museum, Alford, Lincolnshire 37974
Allhallows Museum of Lace and Antiquities, Honiton 39259
Almond Valley Heritage Centre, Livingston 39533
Almonry Heritage Centre, Evesham 38953
Alyth Museum, Alyth 37994
Amersham Museum, Amersham 37998
An Iodnlann, Isle-of-Tiree 39319
An Tairbeart Museum, Tarbert 40673
Ancient House Museum, Thetford 40694
Andover Museum, Andover 38000
Angus Folk Museum, Glamis 39036
Anne of Cleves House Museum, Lewes 39483
Arbroath Museum, Arbroath 38012
Arbuthnot Museum, Peterhead 40191
Armadale Community Museum, Armadale 38015
Armagh County Museum, Armagh 38017
Arran Heritage Museum, Brodick 38372
Arthur Cottage, Ballymena 38068
Arundel Museum and Heritage Centre, Arundel 38024
Ashburton Museum, Ashburton 38026
Ashby-de-la-Zouch Museum, Ashby-de-la-Zouch 38027
Ashford Museum, Ashford 38028
Ashton Court Visitor Centre, Bristol 38348
Ashwell Village Museum, Ashwell 38036
Athelstan Museum, Malmesbury 39882
Atholl Country Life Museum, Blair Atholl 38252
Auld Kirk Museum, Kirkintilloch 39395
Avoncroft Museum of Historic Buildings, Bromsgrove 38376
Axbridge Museum, Axbridge 38044
Axminster Museum, Axminster 38045
Ayscoughfee Hall Museum, Spalding 40562
Bagshaw Museum, Batley 38127
Baird Institute Museum, Cumnock 38686
Ballycastle Museum, Ballycastle 38065
Ballymena Museum, Ballymena 38069
Ballymoney Museum, Ballymoney 38071
Banbury Museum, Banbury 38075
Banchory Museum, Banchory 38077
Banff Museum, Banff 38079
Bangor Museum and Art Gallery, Bangor, Gwynedd 38081
Bantock House, Wolverhampton 40915
Barnet Museum, London 39575
Bassetlaw Museum and Percy Laws Memorial Gallery, Retford 40310
Battle Museum of Local History, Battle 38130
Bayle Museum, Bridlington 38327
Baysgarth House Museum, Barton-upon-Humber 38098
The Beacon Whitehaven, Whitehaven 40856
Beaminster Museum, Beaminster 38134
Beamish, the North of England Open Air Museum, Beamish 38136
Beccles and District Museum, Beccles 38140
Beck Isle Museum of Rural Life, Pickering 40201
Beckford's Tower and Museum, Bath 38111
Bedale Museum, Bedale 38142
Bedford Museum, Bedford 38146
Bellaghy Bawn, Magherafelt 39871
Bennie Museum, Bathgate 38126
Berkswell Village Museum, Berkswell 38170
Bersham Heritage Centre and Ironworks, Wrexham 40939
Berwick Borough Museum and Art Gallery, Berwick-upon-Tweed 38173
Bexhill Museum, Bexhill-on-Sea 38186
Bexley Museum, London 39579
Bishop Bonner's Cottage Museum, East Dereham 38840
Bishop's Stortford Local History Museum, Bishop's Stortford 38239
Bishops Waltham Museum, Bishop's Waltham 38241
Bitterne Local History Centre, Southampton 40543
Blackridge Community Museum, Blackridge 38247
Blackwater Valley Museum, Benburb 38164
Blake Museum, Bridgwater 38324
Blandford Forum Museum, Blandford Forum 38255
Blickling Hall, Norwich 40089
Bloxham Village Museum, Bloxham 38261
Bodmin Town Museum, Bodmin 38264
Bognor Regis Museum, Bognor Regis 38268
Bo'ness Heritage Area, Bo'ness 38275
Borough Museum and Art Gallery, Newcastle-under-Lyme 40031
Boscobel House, Shropshire 40513
Bourne Hall Museum, Ewell 38954
Bradford-on-Avon Museum, Bradford-on-Avon 38301
Braintree District Museum, Braintree 38308
Brander Museum, Huntly 39279
Brandon Heritage Museum, Brandon 38310
Braunton and District Museum, Braunton 38311
Brechin Museum, Brechin 38314
Brecknock Museum and Art Gallery, Brecon 38316
Bredy Farm Old Farming Collection, Bridport 38330
Brentwood Museum, Brentwood 38319
Brewery Chapel Museum, Halstead 39158
Brewhouse Yard Museum, Nottingham 40104
Bridewell Museum, Norwich 40090
Bridgnorth Northgate Museum, Bridgnorth 38321
Bridport Museum, Bridport 38331
Brightlingsea Museum, Brightlingsea 38336
Brighton Museum and Art Gallery, Brighton 38340
Bristol City Museum and Art Gallery, Bristol 38351
Bromsgrove Museum, Bromsgrove 38377
Broughton House and Garden, Kirkcudbright 39392
Broughty Castle Museum, Dundee 38797
Bruce Castle Museum, London 39589
Buckfast Abbey, Buckfastleigh 38380
Buckinghamshire County Museum, Aylesbury 38046
Bude-Stratton Museum, Bude 38389
Bungay Museum, Bungay 38394
Burghead Museum, Burghead 38396
Burnham Museum, Burnham-on-Crouch 38397
Burntisland Museum, Burntisland 38403
Burton Court, Eardisland 38834
Burwell Museum, Burwell 38410
Bury Art Gallery and Museum, Bury, Lancashire 38411
Bushey Museum and Art Gallery, Bushey 38421
Buxton Museum and Art Gallery, Buxton 38427
Cadeby Experience, Cadeby 38429
Caernarfon Maritime Museum, Caernarfon 38432
Caithness District Museum, Wick 40867
The Calgach Centre, Derry 38722
Callendar House, Falkirk 38968
Cambridge and County Folk Museum, Cambridge 38450
Campbeltown Museum, Campbeltown 38468
Canolfan Y Plase, Bala 38061
Canolfan Y Plase, Y Bala 40949
Canterbury Heritage Museum, Canterbury 38471
Cardigan Heritage Centre, Cardigan 38486
Carew Manor and Dovecote, Beddington 38144
Carisbrooke Castle Museum, Newport, Isle of Wight 40053
Carlisle Collection of Miniature Rooms, Nunnington 40119
Carmarthen Heritage Centre, Carmarthen 38492
Castle Combe Museum, Castle Combe 38500
Castle Museum, Clitheroe 38590
Castleton Village Museum, Castleton 38505
Castletown Museum, Gerston 39030
Cater Museum, Billericay 38200
Cathcartston Visitor Centre, Dalmellington 38693
Ceredigion Museum, Aberystwyth 37955
Champs Chapel Museum, East Hendred 38842
Chard and District Museum, Chard 38522
Charlbury Museum, Charlbury 38525
Charnwood Museum, Loughborough 39829
Charterhouse School Museum, Godalming 39087
Chatelherault, Ferniegair 38986
Chelmsford Museum, Chelmsford 38537
Chepstow Museum, Chepstow 38546
Chertsey Museum, Chertsey 38548
Chesham Town Museum, Chesham 38549
Chesterfield Museum and Art Gallery, Chesterfield 38554
Chesterholm Museum Roman Vindolanda, Hexham 39237
Chichester District Museum, Chichester 38559
Chiltern Open Air Museum, Chalfont Saint Giles 38519
Chippenham Museum and Heritage Centre, Chippenham 38568
Chipping Norton Museum of Local History, Chipping Norton 38570
Church Farmhouse Museum, London 39607
Cirencester Lock-Up, Cirencester 38583
City Museum, Leeds 39443
City Museum and Art Gallery, Gloucester 39080
City Museum and Art Gallery, Plymouth 40209
City Museum and Records Office, Portsmouth 40249
Clackmannshire Council Museum, Alloa 37979
Clan Donnachaidh Museum, Pitlochry 40204
Clan Gunn Museum, Latheron 39427
Clare Ancient House Museum, Clare 38585
Clink Prison Museum, London 39610
Clive House Museum, Shrewsbury 40507
Clun Local History Museum, Clun 38592
Coggeshall Heritage Centre and Museum, Coggeshall 38607
Coldstream Museum, Coldstream 38616
Colne Valley Museum, Golcar 39089
Colzium Museum, Kilsyth 39365
Combe Martin Museum, Combe Martin 38620
Commandery Museum, Worcester 40928
Corinium Museum, Cirencester 38584
Cothey Bottom Heritage Centre, Newport, Isle of Wight 40054
Country Life Museum, Yeovil 40955
Countryside Museum, East Budleigh 38837
County Museum Technical Centre, Halton 39159
Court Hall Museum, Sittingbourne 40520
Court House and Museum, Pevensey 40199
Cowbridge and District Museum, Cowbridge 38648
Crail Museum, Crail 38656
Cranbrook Museum, Cranbrook 38658
Craven Museum, Skipton 40527
Crawfordjohn Heritage Venture, Biggar 38195
Crawley Museum Centre, Crawley 38659
Creetown Exhibition Centre, Creetown 38661
Crewkerne and District Museum, Crewkerne 38667
Cricklade Museum, Cricklade 38669
Cromer Museum, Cromer 38672
Croydon Museum, Croydon 38677
Croydon Natural History and Scientific Society Museum, Croydon 38678
Crystal Palace Museum, London 39618
Cuckfield Museum, Cuckfield 38679
Cumbernauld Museum, Cumbernauld 38684
Cynon Valley Museum, Aberdare 37928
Dacorum Heritage, Berkhamsted 38169
Dales Countryside Museum, Hawes 39193
Daniel Owen Museum, Mold 39972
Dartford Borough Museum, Dartford 38700
Dartmouth Museum, Dartmouth 38702
Daventry Museum, Daventry 38705
Dawlish Museum, Dawlish 38706
Deal Maritime and Local History Museum, Deal 38709
Dean Heritage Museum, Soudley 40532
Denbigh Museum and Gallery, Denbigh 38714
Derby Museum and Art Gallery, Derby 38716
Derrymore House, Bessbrook 38178
Dewey Museum, Warminster 40785
Dewsbury Museum, Dewsbury 38728
Dingwall Museum, Dingwall 38731
Discovery Museum, Newcastle-upon-Tyne 40035
Diss Museum, Diss 38734
Ditchling Museum, Ditchling 38735
Dollar Museum, Dollar 38738
Doncaster Museum and Art Gallery, Doncaster 38741
Dorchester Abbey Museum, Dorchester-on-Thames 38754
Dorman Memorial Museum, Middlesbrough 39948
Dorney Court, Windsor 40899
Dornoch Heritage Museum, Dornoch 38758
Dorset County Museum, Dorchester 38748
Douglas Heritage Museum, Douglas, Lanarkshire 38761
Dover Museum, Dover 38766
Down County Museum, Downpatrick 38773
Drenewydd Museum, Bute Town 38426
Drumlanrig's Tower, Hawick 39194
Dualchas-Museum Bharraigh Agus Bhatarsaidh, Isle-of-Barra 39314
Dumfries Museum, Dumfries 38788
Dunbar Town House Museum, Dunbar 38793
Dunblane Museum, Dunblane 38796
Dunfermline Museum, Dunfermline 38809
Dunkeld Cathedral Chapter House Museum, Dunkeld 38814
Dunrobin Castle Museum, Golspie 39091
Duns Area Museum, Duns 38819
Dunwich Museum, Dunwich 38823
Durham Heritage Centre and Museum, Durham 38825
Earls Barton Museum of Local Life, Earls Barton 38835
Easdale Island Folk Museum, Easdale Island 38836
East Surrey Museum, Caterham 38512
Eastbourne Heritage Centre, Eastbourne 38852
Eastleigh Museum, Eastleigh 38860
Eden Valley Museum, Edenbridge 38867
Egham Museum, Egham 38922
Elmbridge Museum, Weybridge 40841
Ely Museum, Ely 38933
Emsworth Museum, Emsworth 38936
Erewash Museum, Ilkeston 39286
Erith Museum, Erith 38946
Exmouth Museum, Exmouth 38960
Eyam Museum, Eyam 38962
Fairlynch Museum, Budleigh Salterton 38390
Fakenham Museum of Gas and Local History, Fakenham 38966
Fawley Court Historic House and Museum, Henley-on-Thames 39219
Feering and Kelvedon Local History Museum, Kelevedon 39331
Fermanagh County Museum at Enniskillen Castle, Enniskillen 38939
Fernhill House, Belfast 38152
Fetlar Interpretive Centre, Fetlar 38988
Fife Folk Museum, Ceres 38518
Filey Museum, Filey 38990
First Garden City Heritage Museum, Letchworth 39480
Five Council Museums East Headquarters, Cupar 38687
Fleur de Lis Heritage Centre, Faversham 38984
Flintham Museum, Flintham 38996
Fochabers Folk Museum, Fochabers 38998
Folkestone Museum and Art Gallery, Folkestone 39000
Folklife Display, Lisnaskea 39511
Forty Hall Museum, Enfield 38937
Fossil Grove, Glasgow 39044
Fraserburgh Museum, Fraserburgh 39015
Gairloch Heritage Museum, Gairloch 39022
Galashiels Museum, Galashiels 39023
The Galleries, Woking 40913
Gallery Oldham, Oldham 40128
German Underground Hospital, Saint Lawrence 40411
Gillingham Museum, Gillingham, Dorset 39031
Gladstone Court Museum, Biggar 38196
Glastonbury Lake Village Museum, Glastonbury 39071
Glencoe and North Lorn Folk Museum, Glencoe 39074
Glenesk Folk Museum, Glenesk 39075
Glossop Heritage Centre, Glossop 39078
Gloucester Folk Museum, Gloucester 39081
Godalming Museum, Godalming 39088
Goole Museum and Art Gallery, Goole 39094
Gosport Museum, Gosport 39099
Gower Heritage Centre, Gower 39106
Grace Darling Museum, Bamburgh 38074
Grange Museum of Community History, London 39647
Grangemouth Museum, Grangemouth 39108
Grantham Museum, Grantham 39111
Granton Centre, Edinburgh 38886
Grantown Museum, Grantown-on-Spey 39113
Gravesham Museum, Gravesend, Kent 39116
Great Bardfield Cage, Great Bardfield 39119
Great Bardfield Cottage Museum, Great Bardfield 39120
Greenwich Heritage Centre, London 39649
Greenwich Local History Centre, London 39650
Grosvenor Museum, Chester 38552
The Guards Museum, London 39652
Guernsey Museum and Art Gallery, Saint Peter Port 40424
Guildford Museum, Guildford 39138
Guildhall, Beverley 38182
Guildhall Museum, Carlisle 38489
Guildhall Museum, Chichester 38562
Guildhall Museum, Sandwich 40446
Gwynedd Education and Culture, Caernarfon 38433
Hackney Museum, London 39657
Hailsham Heritage Centre, Hailsham 39146
Halesworth and District Museum, Halesworth 39148
Hallaton Museum, Hallaton 39157
Halliwell's House Museum, Selkirk 40468
Ham House, Richmond, Surrey 40318
Hamilton Low Parks Museum, Hamilton 39160
Hampstead Museum, London 39659
Handsworth Saint Mary's Museum, Sheffield 40485
Hanseatic Booth or The Pier House, Symbister 40669
Harborough Museum, Market Harborough 39915
Harbour Life Exhibition, Bridport 38332
Harbour Museum, Londonderry 39816
Harlow Museum, Harlow 39163
Harris Museum and Art Gallery, Preston 40266
Harrow Museum, Harrow 39173
Hartland Quay Museum, Bideford 38192
Hartland Quay Museum, Hartland 39174
Havant Museum, Havant 39189
Haverhill and District Local History Centre, Haverhill 39192
Hawick Museum, Hawick 39195
Hedon Museum, Hedon 39207
Helena Thompson Museum, Workington 40934
Helston Folk Museum, Helston 39214
Henfield Museum, Henfield 39218
Heptonstall Museum, Heptonstall 39222
Herbert Art Gallery and Museum, Coventry 38643
Herne Bay Museum and Gallery, Herne Bay 39232
Hertford Museum, Hertford 39234
Hinckley and District Museum, Hinckley 39246
Hindley Museum, Hindley 39247
Historic Resources Centre, Annan 38003
History Shop, Wigan 40870
Hitchin Museum and Art Gallery, Hitchin 39248
Holsworthy Museum, Holsworthy 39255
Honeywood Heritage Centre, London 39667
Hornsea Museum of Village Life, Hornsea 39261
Horsforth Village Museum, Leeds 39446
House on Crutches Museum, Bishop's Castle 38238
Howell Harris Museum, Brecon 38317
Huntly House Museum, Edinburgh 38889
Hythe Local History Room, Hythe, Kent 39283
Iceni Village and Museums, Cockley Cley 38606
Ilchester Museum, Ilchester 39284
Ilfracombe Museum, Ilfracombe 39285
Ingatestone Hall, Ingatestone 39290
Inverkeithing Museum, Inverkeithing 39297
Inverness Museum and Art Gallery, Inverness 39300
Iona Heritage Centre, Isle-of-Iona 39316
Irish Linen Centre and Lisburn Museum, Lisburn 39510
Ironbridge Gorge Museum, Ironbridge 39308
Isles of Scilly Museum, Saint Mary's 40415
Islington Museum, London 39675
Jane Welsh Carlyle's House, Haddington 39142
Jersey Museum, Saint Helier 40401
Jewel Tower, London 39676
John Hastie Museum, Strathaven 40632
John McDouall Stuart Museum, Dysart 38832
The Judge's Lodging, Presteigne 40265
Kegworth Museum, Kegworth 39326
Kelham Island Museum, Sheffield 40486
Kelso Museum and Turret Gallery, Kelso 39334
Kendal Museum, Kendal 39337
Keswick Museum and Art Gallery, Keswick 39344
Kilsyth's Heritage, Kilsyth 39366
Kilwinning Abbey Tower, Kilwinning 39368
Kingston Museum, Kingston-upon-Thames 39385
Kinross Museum, Kinross 39390
Kirkcaldy Museum and Art Gallery, Kirkcaldy 39391
Kirkleatham Museum, Redcar 40300
Kirriemuir Gateway to the Glens Museum, Kerriemuir 39341
Knaresborough Castle and Old Courthouse Museum, Knaresborough 39400
Knutsford Heritage Centre, Knutsford 39404
Kyle and Carrick District Library and Museum, Ayr 38050
Kyngston House Museum, Saint Albans 40373
Laing Museum, Newburgh 40027

Lanark Museum, Lanark 39410
Lancaster City Museum, Lancaster 39414
Lanman Museum, Framlingham 39014
Largs Museum, Largs 39425
Larne Museum, Larne 39426
Larrybane and Carrick-A-Rede, Ballycastle 38066
Lauderdale House, London 39684
Lawrence House Museum, Launceston 39431
Laxfield and District Museum, Laxfield 39434
Leamington Spa Art Gallery and Museum, Leamington Spa 39436
Leatherhead Museum of Local History, Leatherhead 39437
Leighton Hall, Carnforth 38494
Leominster Folk Museum, Leominster 39477
Lichfield Heritage Centre, Lichfield 39491
Lindfield Parvise Museum, Haywards Heath 39201
Linlithgow Story, Linlithgow 39508
Litcham Village Museum, Litcham 39512
Little Houses, Dunkeld 38815
Littlehampton Museum, Littlehampton 39514
Llancaiach Fawr Living History Museum, Nelson 40007
Llandudno Museum and Art Gallery, Llandudno 39541
Llanidloes Museum, Llanidloes 39556
Lleyn Historical and Maritime Museum, Nefyn 40006
Lochwinnoch Community Museum, Lochwinnoch 39561
London Borough of Bromley Museum, Orpington 40135
Long Eaton Town Hall, Long Eaton 39820
Lossiemouth Fisheries and Community Museum, Lossiemouth 39826
Lostwithiel Museum, Lostwithiel 39827
Louth Museum, Louth 39834
Lower Methil Heritage Centre, Lower Methil 39836
Lowestoft Museum, Lowestoft 39839
Lowewood Museum, Hoddesdon 39251
Ludlow Museum, Ludlow 39842
Lydd Town Museum, Lydd 39850
Lyme Regis Philpot Museum, Lyme Regis 39853
Lyn and Exmoor Museum, Lynton 39856
Lytham Heritage Centre, Lytham Saint Anne's 39859
Macclesfield Silk Museum, Macclesfield 39865
McKechnie Institute, Girvan 39034
McManus Galleries, Dundee 38800
Maldon District Museum, Maldon 39880
Mallaig Heritage Centre, Mallaig 39881
Malvern Museum, Great Malvern 39122
Manor Cottage Heritage Centre, Southwick 40560
Manor House Museum, Kettering 39348
Manor House Museum and Art Gallery, Ilkley 39287
Mansfield Museum and Art Gallery, Mansfield 39906
Manx Museum, Douglas, Isle of Man 38760
Margrove - South Cleveland Heritage Centre, Boosbeck 38278
Market Lavington Village Museum, Market Lavington 39917
Marlipins Museum, Shoreham-by-Sea 40503
Maxwelton House Museum, Moniaive 39976
Measham Museum, Measham 39928
Medway Heritage Centre, Chatham 38531
Mellerstain House, Gordon 39096
Melton Carnegie Museum, Melton Mowbray 39933
Merchant's House Museum, Plymouth 40210
Mere Museum, Mere 39935
Mersea Island Museum, West Mersea 40827
Methil Heritage Centre, Methil 39940
Midsomer Norton and District Museum, Radstock 40277
Mildenhall and District Museum, Mildenhall, Suffolk 39952
Milford Haven Museum, Milford Haven 39953
Milton Keynes Museum, Milton Keynes 39962
Minster Abbey Gatehouse Museum, Sheerness 40480
Moat Park Heritage Centre, Biggar 38198
Moffat Museum, Moffat 39970
Motherwell Heritage Centre, Motherwell 39988
Moyse's Hall Museum, Bury Saint Edmunds 38417
Much Wenlock Museum, Much Wenlock 39993
Mull Museum, Tobermory 40713
The Museum, Newton Stewart 40065
Museum and Art Gallery, Forfar 39005
Museum and Art Gallery, Letchworth 39481
Museum and Art Gallery, Newport, Gwent 40051
Museum and Art Gallery, Nuneaton 40118
The Museum in the Park, Stroud 40639
Museum Nan Eilean, Sgoil Lionacleit, Benbecula 38163
Museum Nan Eilean, Steornabhagh, Stornoway 40615
Museum of Ambleside, Ambleside 37996
Museum of Barnstaple and North Devon, Barnstaple 38093
Museum of Berkshire Aviation, Woodley 40923
Museum of Cannock Chase, Hednesford 39206
Museum of Dartmoor Life, Okehampton 40126
Museum of Island History, Newport, Isle of Wight 40055
Museum of Islay Life, Port Charlotte 40231
Museum of Lakeland Life, Kendal 39338
Museum of Lancashire, Preston 40267
Museum of Lincolnshire Life, Lincoln 39500
Museum of Local History, Hastings 39185
Museum of London, London 39718
Museum of North Craven Life, Settle 40473
Museum of Oxford, Oxford 40148
Museum of Reading, Reading 40296
Museum of Richmond, Richmond, Surrey 40320
Museum of Saint Albans, Saint Albans 40375
Museum of South Somerset, Yeovil 40956
Museum of South Yorkshire Life, Doncaster 38743
Museum of Speed, Pendine 40173
Museum of the Cumbraes, Millport 39956
Museum of the Holmesdale Natural History Club, Reigate 40307
Museum of the Isles, Armadale 38016
Museum of the Manchesters, Ashton-under-Lyne 38033
Museum of Victorian Whitby, Whitby 40851
Nairn Fishertown Museum, Nairn 39996
Nantwich Museum, Nantwich 39999
National Fairground Museum, Northampton 40083
National Horseracing Museum, Newmarket 40050
Navan Centre, Armagh 38019
Neath Museum, Neath 40005
Ness Historical Society Museum, Port-of-Ness 40232
New Hall, Dymchurch 38831
Newham Heritage Centre, London 39734
Newhaven Heritage Museum, Edinburgh 38902
Newport Pagnell Historical Society Museum, Newport Pagnell 40058
Newry and Mourne Arts Centre and Museum, Newry 40061
Newry Museum, Newry 40062
Newton Abbot Town and Great Western Railway Museum, Newton Abbot 40063
Nidderdale Museum, Harrogate 39170
Normanton Church Museum, Oakham 40120
North Ayrshire Museum, Saltcoats 40439
North Berwick Museum, North Berwick 40078
North Cornwall Museum and Gallery, Camelford 38467
North Down Heritage Centre, Bangor, County Down 38080
North Lincolnshire Museum, Scunthorpe 40460
North Somerset Museum, Weston-super-Mare 40835
Northland Viking Centre, Auckengill 38039
Norton Conyers, Near Ripon 40003
Norwood Museum, Holm 39253
Old Bell Museum, Montgomery 39980
The Old Byre Heritage Centre, Dervaig 38724
Old Gaol Museum, Buckingham 38387
Old Guildhall Museum, Looe 39825
Old Haa, Yell 40952
Old House Museum, Bakewell 38059
Old Post Office Museum, Turriff 40734
Old Town Hall, Hemel Hempstead 39217
Old Town Hall Museum, Margate 39912
Oriel Ynys Môn, Llangefni 39550
Otley Museum, Otley 40138
Oundle Museum, Oundle 40139
The Oxfordshire Museum, Woodstock 40925
Padstow Museum, Padstow 40157
Paisley Museum and Art Gallery, Paisley 40161
Parc Howard Museum and Art Gallery, Llanelli 39546
Parnham House, Beaminster 38135
Peacock Heritage Centre, Chesterfield 38556
Pendle Heritage Centre, Barrowford 38097
Penlee House Gallery and Museum, Penzance 40181
Penrhos Cottage, Llanycefn 39558
Penrith Museum, Penrith 40176
The People's Museum, Belfast 38157
Perranzabuloe Folk Museum, Perranporth 40183
Petersfield Museum, Petersfield 40194
Pewsey Heritage Centre, Pewsey 40200
Pittencrieff House Museum, Dunfermline 38810
Plas Mawr, Conwy 38627
The Police Museum, Belfast 38158
Pontefract Museum, Pontefract 40218
Pontypool Museums, Pontypool 40221
Pontypridd Museum, Pontypridd 40223
Porthcawl Museum, Porthcawl 40240
Portland Basin Museum, Ashton-under-Lyne 38034
Potland Museum, Basildon 38100
Potters Bar Museum, Potters Bar 40262
Prescot Museum, Prescot 40264
Priest's House, Easton-on-the-Hill 38863
Priest's House Museum, Wimborne Minster 40879
Prittlewell Priory Museum, Southend-on-Sea 40553
Public Library and Museum, Herne Bay 39233
Pumphouse Educational Museum, London 39750
Purton Museum, Swindon 40663
Queensferry Museum, South Queensferry 40536
Raasay Heritage Museum, Kyle 39407
Radnorshire Museum, Llandrindod Wells 39539
Ramsgate Museum, Ramsgate 40283
Red House Museum, Gomersal 39092
Reigate Priory Museum, Reigate 40308
Rhayader and District Museum, Rhayader 40311
Rhondda Heritage Park, Trehafod 40725
Rhondda Museum, Llwynypia 39560
Rhyl Library, Museum and Arts Centre, Rhyl 40313
Richmondshire Museum, Richmond, North Yorkshire 40317
River and Rowing Museum, Henley-on-Thames 39220
Robin Hood's Bay and Fylingdale Museum, Robin Hood's Bay 40331
Rochdale Art and Heritage Centre, Rochdale 40332
Rossendale Museum, Rawtenstall 40293
Royston and District Museum, Royston 40348
Rozelle House Galleries, Ayr 38052
Ruddington Village Museum, Ruddington 40352
Rustington Heritage Exhibition Centre, Rustington 40360
Rutland County Museum, Oakham 40122
Rydal Mount, Ambleside 37997
Rye Castle Museum, Rye 40364
Rye Heritage Centre Town Model, Rye 40365
Saffron Walden Museum, Saffron Walden 40368
Saint Andrews Museum, Saint Andrews 40384
Saint Andrews Preservation Museum, Saint Andrews 40385
Saint Barbe Museum and Art Gallery, Lymington 39854
Saint Margaret's Museum, Saint Margaret's Bay 40413
Saint Neots Museum, Saint Neots 40416
Saint Patrick's Trian, Armagh 38021
Salford Museum and Art Gallery, Salford 40432
Saltash Heritage Centre, Saltash 40438
Sanquhar Tolbooth Museum, Sanquhar 40449
Scalloway Museum, Scalloway 40453
Scolton Manor Museum, Haverfordwest 39191
Seaford Museum of Local History, Seaford 40461
Segedunum Roman Fort, Baths and Museum, Wallsend 40769
Sevenoaks Museum and Gallery, Sevenoaks 40475
Shaftesbury Town Museum, Shaftesbury 40478
Shambles Museum, Newent 40044
Sherborne Museum, Sherborne 40495
Sheringham Museum, Sheringham 40498
Sherrier Resources Centre, Lutterworth 39848
Shetland Museum, Lerwick 39479
Shirehall Museum, Little Walsingham 39513
Shotts Heritage Centre, Shotts 40505
Shrewsbury Museum and Art Gallery, Shrewsbury 40511
Shugborough Estate Museum, Milford, Staffordshire 39954
Sidmouth Museum, Sidmouth 40515
Sir Henry Jones Museum, Llangernyw 39551
Sir Walter Scott's Courtroom, Selkirk 40471
Sittingbourne Heritage Museum, Sittingbourne 40523
Skye and Lochalsh Area Museums, Portree 40246
Sledmere House, Sledmere 40529
Slough Museum, Slough 40530
Somerset County Museum, Taunton 40677
Souter Johnnie's House, Kirkoswald 39396
South Ribble Museum and Exhibition Centre, Leyland 39488
South Shields Museum and Art Gallery, South Shields 40538
Southend Central Museum, Southend-on-Sea 40555
Southwold Museum, Southwold 40561
Spalding Gentlemen's Society Museum, Spalding 40564
Spelthorne Museum, Staines 40573
Sperrin Heritage Centre, Plumridge 40208
Stamford Museum, Stamford 40577
Stevenage Museum, Stevenage 40583
Stewart Collection, Pocklington 40214
Stewarton and District Museum, Stewarton 40585
The Stewartry Museum, Kirkcudbright 39393
Steyning Museum, Steyning 40586
Stirling Smith Art Gallery and Museum, Stirling 40595
Stockport Museum, Stockport 40598
Stranraer Museum, Stranraer 40622
Stratfield Saye House and Wellington Exhibition, Basingstoke 38103
Strathnaver Museum, Thurso 40708
Stromness Museum, Stromness 40638
Sue Ryder Museum, Cavendish 38513
Summerlee Heritage Park, Coatbridge 38600
Sunderland Museum, Sunderland 40650
Surrey Heath Museum, Camberley 38446
Sutton Windmill and Broads Museum, Sutton, Norwich 40651
Swaffham Museum, Swaffham 40653
Swalcliffe Barn, Swalcliffe 40654
Swansea Museum, Swansea 40661
Swindon Museum and Art Gallery, Swindon 40668
Tamworth Castle Museum, Tamworth 40671
Teignmouth and Shaldon Museum, Teignmouth 40681
Tenbury and District Museum, Tenbury Wells 40683
Tenby Museum and Art Gallery, Tenby 40684
Tenterden and District Museum, Tenterden 40688
Tewkesbury Museum, Tewkesbury 40692
Thirsk Museum, Thirsk 40698
Thomas Muir Museum, Bishopbriggs 38237
Thornbury and District Museum, Thornbury, Gloucestershire 40699
Thorney Heritage Centre, Thorney 40700
Three Rivers Museum and Local History, Rickmansworth 40323
Thurrock Museum, Grays 39117
Thurso Heritage Museum, Thurso 40709
Time Machine, Weston-super-Mare 40836
Timespan Museum and Art Gallery, Helmsdale 39210
Tiptree Museum, Tiptree 40711
Tiverton Museum of Mid Devon Life, Tiverton 40712
Toad Hole Cottage Museum, Ludham 39841
Tolbooth Museum, Stonehaven 40613
Tolhouse Museum and Brass Rubbing Centre, Great Yarmouth 39127
Tolsey Museum, Burford 38395
Tolson Memorial Museum, Huddersfield 39274
Tomintoul Museum, Tomintoul 40716
Topsham Museum, Topsham 40717
Torfaen Museum, Pontypool 40222
Torquay Museum, Torquay 40718
Torrington Museum, Torrington 40721
Totnes Elizabethan Museum, Totnes 40724
Tower Museum, Londonderry 39818
Town and Crown Exhibition, Windsor 40904
Town House, Culross 38683
Town Museum, East Grinstead 38841
Towneley Hall Art Gallery and Museums, Burnley 38401
Traditional Heritage Museum, Sheffield 40491
Tudor House, Margate 39913
Tudor House Museum, Southampton 40549
Tugnet Ice House, Spey Bay 40567
Tullie House - City Museum and Art Gallery, Carlisle 38490
Tunbridge Wells Museum and Art Gallery, Tunbridge Wells 40732
Tweeddale Museum, Peebles 40166
Ty Gwyn and Ty Crwn, Barmouth 38086
Ullapool Museum, Ullapool 40747
Upperlands Eco-Museum, Derry 38723
Uttoxeter Heritage Centre, Uttoxeter 40754
Vale and Downland Museum, Wantage 40782
Valence House Museum and Art Gallery, Dagenham 38690
The Valiant Soldier, Buckfastleigh 38382
Ventnor Heritage Museum, Ventnor 40756
Vestry House Museum, London 39793
Victoria Jubilee Museum, Cawthorne 38516
Wakefield Museum, Wakefield 40765
Wallingford Museum, Wallingford 40767
Walsall Local History Centre, Walsall 40775
Walsall Museum, Walsall 40776
Walton Hall Heritage Centre, Warrington 40788
Walton Maritime Museum, Walton-on-the-Naze 40779
Wandsworth Museum, London 39799
Ware Museum, Ware 40783
Wareham Town Museum, Wareham 40784
Warrington Museum and Art Gallery, Warrington 40789
Watford Museum, Watford 40803
Weardale Museum, Weardale 40805
Weaver's Cottage, Kilbarchan 39355
Wednesbury Museum and Art Gallery, Wednesbury 40806
Welholme Galleries, Grimsby 39134
Wellingborough Heritage Centre, Wellingborough 40811
Wellington Aviation Museum, Moreton-in-Marsh 39985
West Berkshire Museum, Newbury 40030
West Highland Museum, Fort William 39011
West Kilbride Museum, West Kilbride 40825
Westbury Manor Museum, Fareham 38976
Weymouth Museum, Weymouth 40846
Whitburn Community Museum, Whitburn 40849
Whitby Museum, Whitby 40854
Whitehall, Cheam 38534
Whittlesey Museum, Whittlesey 40864
Whitworth Historical Society Museum, Whitworth 40866
Wick Heritage Centre, Wick 40868
Wigan Pier, Wigan 40872
Wightwick Manor, Wolverhampton 40917
Willenhall Museum, Willenhall 40874
Willis Museum, Basingstoke 38105
Wilson Museum of Narberth, Narberth 40001
Wiltshire Heritage Museum and Gallery, Devizes 38726
Wimbledon Society Museum of Local History, London 39811
Wincanton Museum, Wincanton 40880
Winchcombe Folk and Police Museum, Winchcombe 40882
Winchelsea Museum, Winchelsea 40884
Winchester City Museum, Winchester 40896
Wirral Museum, Birkenhead 38208
Wisbech and Fenland Museum, Wisbech 40907
Witney and District Museum and Art Gallery, Witney 40911
Wollaston Heritage Museum, Wollaston 40914
Woodbridge Museum, Woodbridge 40920
Woodchurch Village Life Museum, Woodchurch 40921
Woodhall Spa Cottage Museum, Woodhall Spa 40922
Woolpit and District Museum, Woolpit 40927
Worcester City Museum and Art Gallery, Worcester 40932
Worcestershire County Museum, Kidderminster 39353
Worksop Museum, Worksop 40936
World of Glass, Saint Helens 40398
Worthing Museum and Art Gallery, Worthing 40937
Wotton Heritage Centre, Wotton-under-Edge 40938
Wrexham County Borough Museum, Wrexham 40944
Wycombe Museum, High Wycombe 39241
Wymondham Heritage Museum, Wymondham 40948
York Story, York 40972

Uruguay

Museo de Piria, Piriápolis 41033
Museo Ernesto Laroche, Montevideo 41003
Museo Histórico Municipal, Salto 41038
Museo Martin Perez, Montevideo 41009
Museo Municipal Cabildo de Montevideo, Montevideo 41010
Museo Municipal de Historia y Arqueología, Rivera 41037
Museo Regional de San Carlos, San Carlos 41039
Museo Regional Francisco Mazzoni, Maldonado 40982
Museo y Biblioteca Blanco Acevedo, Montevideo 41026

U.S.A.

The 1811 Old Lincoln County Jail and 1839 Jailer's House Museum, Wiscasset 48714

1859 Jail-Marshal's Home and Museum, Independence 44199
1914 Plant City High School Community Exhibition, Plant City 46542
Academy Hall Museum of the Rocky Hill Historical Society, Rocky Hill 46980
Acorn Hall House Museum, Morristown 45504
Adam Thoroughgood House, Virginia Beach 48243
Adams County Historical Museum, Decatur 42835
Adams County Historical Society Museum, Gettysburg 43661
Adams County Historical Society Museum, Lind 44802
Adams County Museum, Brighton 41899
Adams Museum, Deadwood 42820
Adams Old Stone Grist Mill, Bellows Falls 41605
Adena State Memorial, Chillicothe 42378
Adirondack Center Museum, Elizabethtown 43134
Adirondack Museum, Blue Mountain Lake 41758
Agecroft Hall, Richmond 46869
Aiken County Historical Museum, Aiken 41068
A.J. Snyder Estate, Rosendale 47007
Akwesasne Museum, Hogansburg 44047
Alabama History Museum, Montgomery 45465
Alamo Township Museum-John E. Gray Memorial, Kalamazoo 44376
Alaska State Museum, Juneau 44368
Albany Historical Museum, Sabetha 47044
Albany Regional Museum, Albany 41090
Albion Academy Historical Museum, Edgerton 43084
Alden Historical Society Museum, Alden 41114
Alden House Museum, Duxbury 43027
Alexandria Black History Resource Center, Alexandria 41121
Alger County Heritage Center, Munising 45559
Alice Austen House Museum, Staten Island 47779
Alice T. Miner Colonial Collection, Chazy 42268
Allan Shivers Museum, Woodville 48746
Allegan County Historical and Old Jail Museum, Allegan 41141
Allegany County Historical Museum, Cumberland 42724
Allegany County Museum, Belmont 41610
Allen County-Fort Wayne Historical Society Museum, Fort Wayne 43474
Allen County Historical Museum, Iola 44243
Allen County Museum, Lima 44772
Amador-Livermore Valley Museum, Pleasanton 46552
Amelia Island Museum of History, Fernandina Beach 43314
American Labor Museum, Haledon 43872
American Swedish Historical Museum, Philadelphia 46389
American West Heritage Center, Wellsville 48503
Americana Manse, Whitney-Halsey Home, Belmont 41611
Americana Museum, Terra Alta 47982
Amherst County Museum, Amherst 41184
Amherst History Museum, Amherst 41176
Amherst Museum, Amherst 41183
Amity and Woodbridge Historical Society Museum, Woodbridge 48727
Amory Regional Museum, Amory 41186
Anacortes Museum, Anacortes 41189
Anadarko Philomathic Museum, Anadarko 41190
Anaheim Museum, Anaheim 41194
Anderson County Historical Museum, Garnett 43627
Anderson County Museum, Anderson 41205
Andover Historical Society Museum, Andover 41208
Andrew County Museum, Savannah 47488
Androscoggin Historical Society Museum, Auburn 41372
Animas Museum, Durango 43014
Anna Miller Museum, Newcastle 45912
The Anne Spencer Memorial Foundation, Lynchburg 45002
Annie E. Woodman Institute, Dover 42972
Annie Riggs Memorial Museum, Fort Stockton 43461
Anoka County Historical and Genealogical Museum, Anoka 41232
Anson County Historical Society Museum, Wadesboro 48272
Antelope County Historical Museum, Neligh 45646
The Appaloosa Museum and Heritage Center, Moscow 45517
Appomattox Court House, Appomattox 41242
A.R. Bowman Memorial Museum, Prineville 46707
Arbor Lodge, Nebraska City 45641
Arcade Historical Museum, Arcade 41244
Arcadia Township Historical Museum and Furniture Museum, Arcadia 41245
Archer County Museum, Archer City 41249
Arches Museum of Pioneer Life, Winona 48695
Archibald Graham McIlwaine House, Petersburg 46371
Arizona Hall of Fame Museum, Phoenix 46471
Arizona Historical Society Museum, Tempe 47969
Arizona Historical Society Pioneer Museum, Flagstaff 43328
Arkansas Post Museum, Gillett 43668
Arlington Heights Historical Museum, Arlington Heights 41268
Arlington Historical Museum, Arlington 41264
Arlington Historical Society, Arlington 41257
Arlington House - The Robert E. Lee Memorial, Arlington 41265
Arlington Museum, Birmingham 41704
Arms Family Museum of Local History, Youngstown 48806
Artesia Historical Museum and Art Center, Artesia 41272
Arthurdale Heritage Museum, Arthurdale 41273
Asa Packer Mansion, Jim Thorpe 44343
Ash Lawn-Highland, Charlottesville 42246
Ashland Historical Museum, Ashland 41288
Ashland Historical Society Museum, Ashland 41299
Ashtabula County Historical Society Museum, Geneva-on-the-Lake 43646
Ashton Villa, Galveston 43606
Aspen Historical Society Museum, Aspen 41306
Astors' Beechwood-Victorian Living History Museum, Newport 45923
Atascadero Historical Society Museum, Atascadero 41313
Atchison County Historical Society Museum, Atchison 41315
Atlanta History Museum, Atlanta 41333
Atlanta Museum, Atlanta 41335
Atlantic City Historical Museum, Atlantic City 41365
Atlantic County Historical Society Museum, Somers Point 47668
Attmore-Oliver House, New Bern 45665
Au Glaize Village, Defiance 42853
Audrain Historical Museum, Graceland Museum, Mexico 45280
Auglaize County Historical Society Museum, Saint Marys 47144
Augusta Historical Museum, Augusta 41387
Augusta Museum of History, Augusta 41380
Aurora Historical Museum, Aurora 41394
Aurora Historical Society Museum, Aurora 41402
Aurora History Museum, Aurora 41393
Austin History Center, Austin 41405
Avery County Museum, Newland 45919
Avon Historical Society Museum, Avon 41428
Aztalan Museum, Jefferson 44326
Aztec Museum and Pioneer Village, Aztec 41429
Bacon's Castle, Surry 47894
Badger Mine and Museum, Shullsburg 47621
Baker-Cederberg Museum, Rochester 46938
Baldwin County Heritage Museum, Elberta 43126
Baldwin Historical Society Museum, Baldwin 41442
Baldwin-Reynolds House Museum, Meadville 45214
Baltimore County Historical Museum, Cockeysville 42507
Bangor Historical Society Museum, Bangor 41492
Banner County Historical Museum, Harrisburg 43921
Banning Residence Museum, Wilmington 48647
Bannock County Historical Museum, Pocatello 46570
Bar Harbor Historical Society Museum, Bar Harbor 41498
Baranov Museum, Kodiak 44525
Barn Museum and Rail Depot Museum, Troutdale 48066
Barnes County Historical Museum, Valley City 48187
Barnet Historical Society Museum, Barnet 41507
Barnwell County Museum, Barnwell 41510
Barre Historical Museum, Barre 41511
Barrington Area Historical Museum, Barrington 41512
Barron County Historical Society's Pioneer Village Museum, Cameron 42068
Bartholomew County Historical Museum, Columbus 42577
Bartlesville Area History Museum, Bartlesville 41513
The Bartlett Museum, Amesbury 41174
Barton County Historical Society Village and Museum, Great Bend 43779
Bartow History Center, Cartersville 42121
Bartow-Pell Mansion Museum, Bronx 41913
Bassett Hall, Williamsburg 48625
Batavia Depot Museum, Batavia 41520
Batsto Village, Hammonton 43890
Baxter Springs Heritage Center and Museum, Baxter Springs 41542
Bay Area Museum, Seabrook 47522
Bay View Historical Museum, Bay View 41545
Beacon Historical Society Museum, Beacon 41551
Bear Butte State Park Visitors Center, Sturgis 47864
Beaufort Historic Site, Beaufort 41557
Beaufort Museum, Beaufort 41559
Beauvais Heritage Center, Clark 42430
Beaver Island Historical Museum, Beaver Island 41574
Beck Cultural Exchange Center, Knoxville 44512
Becker County Historical Museum, Detroit Lakes 42938
Bedford City/County Museum, Bedford 41583
Bedford Historical Society Museum, Bedford 41581
Behringer-Crawford Museum, Covington 42680
Belhaven Memorial Museum, Belhaven 41587
The Belknap Mill Museum, Laconia 44564
Bell County Museum, Belton 41618
Belle Grove Plantation, Middletown 45319
Belle Meade Plantation, Nashville 45612
Belleville Area Museum, Belleville 41592
Bellflower Genealogical and Historical Society Museum, Bellflower 41600
Bellport-Brookhaven Historical Society Museum, Bellport 41607
Beloit Historical Society Museum, Beloit 41614
Beltrami County Historical Museum, Bemidji 41621
Bement-Billings Farmstead, Newark Valley 45900
Benicia Historical Museum, Benicia 41624
Benjamin Patterson Inn Museum Complex, Corning 42635
Bennett Place State Historic Site, Durham 43017
The Bennington Museum, Bennington 41629
Benton County Historical Museum, Philomath 46469
Benton County Historical Museum, Prosser 46712
The Benton Homestead, Tolland 48022
Benzie Area Historical Museum, Benzonia 41634
Bergen County Historical Society Museum, River Edge 46909
Bergen Museum of Local History, Bergen 41638
Berkeley Plantation, Charles City 42201
Berkshire County Historical Society Museum at Arrowhead, Pittsfield 46531
The Berkshire Museum, Pittsfield 46532
Berlin Art and Historical Collections, Berlin 41651
Berlin Historical Society Museum of Local History, Berlin 41652
Bernard Historical Museum, Delton 42867
Bernice Pauahi Bishop Museum, Honolulu 44072
Bessemer Hall of History, Bessemer 41658
Bethel Historical Society's Regional History Center, Bethel 41661
Bethlehem Historical Association Museum, Selkirk 47562
Betsey Williams Cottage, Providence 46715
Betts House Research Center, Cincinnati 42398
Beverly Historical Museum, Beverly 41671
Bexley Historical Society Museum, Bexley 41678
Bidwell House, Monterey 45460
Big Springs Museum, Caledonia 42032
Bigelow House Museum, Olympia 46139
Billings Farm and Museum, Woodstock 48742
Biltmore Estate, Asheville 41276
Birmingham Historical Museum, Birmingham 41713
Bisbee Mining and Historical Museum, Bisbee 41714
Bishop Hill Colony, Bishop Hill 41716
Bishop Hill Heritage Museum, Bishop Hill 41717
The Bishop's Palace, Galveston 43607
Black Kettle Museum, Cheyenne 42296
Black River Academy Museum, Ludlow 44996
Black River Historical Society of Lorain Museum, Lorain 44883
Blackberry Farm-Pioneer Village, Aurora 41396
Blackman Museum, Snohomish 47659
Blackstone Valley Historical Society Museum, Lincoln 44797
Blaine County Historical Museum, Hailey 43868
Blaine County Museum, Chinook 42385
Blaine House, Augusta 41388
Blewitt-Harrison-Lee Museum, Columbus 42580
Bloomington Historical Museum, Bloomington 41752
Blount Mansion, Knoxville 44513
Blue Earth County Historical Museum, Mankato 45119
Blue Licks Battlefield Museum, Mount Olivet 45533
Boal Mansion Museum, Boalsburg 41762
Boca Raton Historical Society Museum, Boca Raton 41764
Bolduc House Museum, Sainte Genevieve 47183
Bolinas Museum, Bolinas 41775
Bolivar Hall, San Antonio 47245
Bolton Historical Museum, Bolton 41777
Bonner County Historical Museum, Sandpoint 47382
Bonnet House, Fort Lauderdale 43408
Booker T. Washington National Monument, Hardy 43911
Boone County Historical Society Museum, Belvidere 41619
The Boorman House, Mauston 45206
Boothbay Railway Village, Boothbay 41790
Bordentown Historical Society Museum, Bordentown 41793
Boulder History Museum, Boulder 41833
Bowen House/ Roseland Cottage, Woodstock 48737
Bowie Railroad Station and Huntington Museum, Bowie 41845
Bowne House, Flushing 43352
Boyer Museum and National Marbles Hall of Fame, Wildwood 48620
The Boyle House - Hot Spring County Museum, Malvern 45086
Boys Town Hall of History Father Flanagan House, Boys Town 41856
Bradford County Historical Society Museum, Towanda 48042
Bradford Historical Society Museum, Bradford 41865
Bragg-Mitchell Mansion, Mobile 45417
Braintree Historical Society Museum, Braintree 41867
Brattleboro Museum and Art Center, Brattleboro 41872
Brazoria County Historical Museum, Angleton 41210
Brevard Museum, Cocoa 42508
Brick House, Montgomery 45469
Brick Store Museum, Kennebunk 44434
Bridgehampton Historical Society Museum, Bridgehampton 41886
Bridgton Historical Museum, Bridgton 41896
Brigham Young's Winter Home, Saint George 47090
Brimstone Museum, Sulphur 47874
Bristol Historical and Preservation Society Museum, Bristol 41904
Bronck Museum, Coxsackie 42685
Bronx County Historical Society Museum, Bronx 41914
Brookfield Museum, Brookfield 41929
Brookings County Museum, Volga 48256
Brookline Historical Society Museum, Brookline 41934
Brooklyn Historical Society Museum, Brooklyn 41953
Brooks Academy Museum, Harwich 43954
Brookside Saratoga County Historical Society, Ballston Spa 41445
Broome County Historical Society Museum, Binghamton 41698
Broward County Historical Museum, Fort Lauderdale 43409
Brown County Historical Society Museum, New Ulm 45748
Brown County Historical Society Pioneer Museum, Nashville 45610
Brownella Cottage, Galion 43602
Brownville Historical Society Museum, Brownville 41966
Brunswick Town State Historic Site, Winnabow 48691
Brush Country Museum, Cotulla 42670
Buccleuch Mansion, New Brunswick 45676
Bucksport Historical Museum, Bucksport 41977
Bucyrus Historical Society Museum, Bucyrus 41978
Buena Park Historical Society Museum, Buena Park 41979
Buffalo and Erie County Historical Society Museum, Buffalo 41983
Buffalo Bill Cody Homestead, Princeton 46695
Buffalo Trails Museum, Epping 43197
Bureau County Historical Society Museum, Princeton 46696
Burgwin-Wright Museum, Wilmington 48658
Burke County Historical Powers Lake Complex, Powers Lake 46681
Burleson County Historical Museum, Caldwell 42031
Burlington County Historical Society Museum, Burlington 42004
Burlington Historical Museum, Burlington 42000
Burlington Historical Museum, Burlington 42001
Burnham Tavern, Machias 45027
Burritt on the Mountain, Huntsville 44172
Burrowes Mansion Museum, Matawan 45203
Burt County Museum, Tekamah 47967
Bush House Museum and Bush Barn Art Center, Salem 47207
Bushwhacker Museum, Nevada 45652
Butler County Historical Museum, Allison 41149
Butler County Museum, Hamilton 43883
Butler County Museum and Kansas Oil Museum, El Dorado 43107
Byron Historical Museum, Byron 42021
Cabot Historical Society Museum, Cabot 42023
Caddo-Pine Island Oil and Historical Society Museum, Oil City 46105
Cades Cove Open-Air Museum, Townsend 48044
Calaveras County Museum, San Andreas 47238
Caleb Pusey House, Upland 48156
Calhoun County Museum, Port Lavaca 46600
Calhoun County Museum, Rockwell City 46978
Calhoun County Museum, Saint Matthews 47148
Callahan County Pioneer Museum, Baird 41434
Calumet County Historical Society Museum, New Holstein 45703
Cambria County Historical Society Museum, Ebensburg 43077
Cambria Historical Society Museum, New Providence 45744
Cambridge Historical Museum, Cambridge 42039
Cambridge Museum, Cambridge 42052
Camden Archives and Museum, Camden 42063
Camden County Historical Society Museum, Camden 42059
Camp Floyd, Fairfield 43269
Camp Hancock, Bismarck 41719
Campbell County Rockpile Museum, Gillette 43670
Campbell House Museum, Saint Louis 47113
Campus Martius Museum, Marietta 45147
Camron-Stanford House, Oakland 46061
Canaan Historical Society Museum, Canaan 42073
Canadian County Historical Museum, El Reno 43125
Canal Fulton Heritage Society Museum, Canal Fulton 42075
Canby Depot Museum, Canby 42078
Caney Valley Historical Society Museum, Caney 42079
Cannon Falls Area Historical Museum, Cannon Falls 42080
Cannon Village Visitor Center, Kannapolis 44389
Canon City Municipal Museum, Canon City 42081
Canterbury Shaker Village, Canterbury 42083
Canton Historical Museum, Canton 42084
Cape Cod National Seashore Museum, Wellfleet 48497
Cape Henry Lighthouse, Virginia Beach 48245
Cape May County Historical Museum, Cape May Court House 42098
Cape Vincent Historical Museum, Cape Vincent 42100
Captain Nathaniel B. Palmer House, Stonington 47828
Carbon County Museum, Rawlins 46802
Carl Sandburg Home, Flat Rock 43335
Carlsbad Museum and Art Center, Carlsbad 42109
Carlton County Historical Museum and Heritage Center, Cloquet 42502
Carlyle House, Alexandria 41123
Carnegie Center for Art History, New Albany 45657
Carnegie Historical Museum, Fairfield 43266
Carnifex Ferry Battlefield State Park and Museum, Summersville 47875
Carnton Plantation, Franklin 43521
Carriage House Museum, Camden 42062
Carson County Square House Museum, Panhandle 46280
Carter County Museum, Ekalaka 43103
The Carter House, Franklin 43522
Carteret County Museum of History and Art, Morehead City 45495

Caryl House, Dover 42970
Casa Adobe de San Rafael, Glendale 43688
Casa Amesti, Monterey 45452
Casa Grande History Museum, Casa Grande 42127
Casey Farm, Saunderstown 47471
Cass County Historical Society Museum, Logansport 44846
Cass County Historical Society Museum, Plattsmouth 46550
Cass County Historical Society Museum, West Fargo 48521
Cassia County Museum, Burley 41994
Casteel-Linn House and Museum, Princeton 46698
The Castle, Marietta 45148
Castle Museum of Saginaw County History, Saginaw 47062
Castleton Historical Society Museum, Castleton 42137
Catalina Island Museum, Avalon 41426
Catawba County Museum of History, Newton 45945
The Catlin House Museum, Scranton 47516
Cattaraugus Area Historical Center, Cattaraugus 42142
Cattle Raisers Museum, Fort Worth 43483
Cauthorn Memorial Depot and Sutton County Jail, Sonora 47677
Cayuga Museum, Auburn 41373
Cayuga-Owasco Lakes Historical Society Museum, Moravia 45492
Cedar Falls Historical Museum, Cedar Falls 42148
Cedar Grove Historical Society Museum, Cedar Grove 42152
Cedar Key Historical Society Museum, Cedar Key 42153
Cedar Key State Park Museum, Cedar Key 42154
Cedar Valley Memories, Osage 46199
Centerville Historical Museum, Centerville 42170
Central Missouri State University Archives and Museum, Warrensburg 48315
Central Montana Historical Association Museum, Lewistown 44732
Central Nevada Museum, Tonopah 48030
Central Texas Area Museum, Salado 47186
Centre County Historical Society Museum, State College 47778
Centre County Library Historical Museum, Bellefonte 41589
Centre Hill Mansion, Petersburg 46372
Chagrin Falls Historical Society Museum, Chagrin Falls 42181
Chalet of the Golden Fleece, New Glarus 45688
Chamizal National Memorial, El Paso 43114
Champaign County Historical Museum, Champaign 42186
Champaign County Historical Museum, Urbana 48165
Chandler Museum, Chandler 42190
Chapman Historical Museum, Glens Falls 43692
Chappell Hill Historical Society Museum, Chappell Hill 42199
Charles A. Grignon Mansion, Kaukauna 44418
Charles A. Weyerhaeuser Memorial Museum, Little Falls 44818
Charles B. Aycock Birthplace, Fremont 43554
Charles Carroll House of Annapolis, Annapolis 41226
Charles Gates Dawes House, Evanston 43237
The Charleston Museum, Charleston 42211
Charlotte Museum of History and Hezekiah Alexander Homesite, Charlotte 42238
Charnley-Persky House Museum, Chicago 42312
Chase County Museum, Cottonwood Falls 42666
Chatillon-DeMenil Mansion, Saint Louis 47114
Chattanooga Regional History Museum, Chattanooga 42259
Chelan County Historical Museum, Cashmere 42128
Chelan County Public Utility District, Wenatchee 48504
Chelmsford Historical Museum, Chelmsford 42270
Chelmsford Historical Society Museum, South Chelmsford 47689
Chemung Valley History Museum, Elmira 43170
Chenango County Historical Society Museum, Norwich 46038
Cheney Homestead, Manchester 45092
Cheraw Lyceum Museum, Cheraw 42272
Cherokee County Historical Museum, Murphy 45571
Cherokee Strip Land Rush Museum, Arkansas City 41256
Cherokee Strip Museum, Alva 41161
Cherry County Historical Society Museum, Valentine 48183
Cherry Valley Museum, Cherry Valley 42279
Chesapeake Beach Railway Museum, Chesapeake Beach 42281
Cheshire County Museum, Keene 44425
Chester County Historical Society Museum, West Chester 48517
Chester County Museum, Chester 42286
Chesterfield Historical Society of Verginia Museum, Chesterfield 42291
Chetopa Historical Museum, Chetopa 42295
Chickasaw County Historical Society Museum, Bradford Village, Nashua 45607
Chico Museum, Chico 42371
Childress County Heritage Museum, Childress 42375
Chimney Point Tavern, Addison 41064
Chippewa County Historical Society Museum, Montevideo 45463
Chippewa Valley Museum, Eau Claire 43074
Chisholm Trail Historical Museum, Waurika 48462
Chisholm Trail Museum, Kingfisher 44486
Christian C. Sanderson Museum, Chadds Ford 42176
Christiansted National Historic Site, Saint Croix 47087
CHTJ Southard House Museum, Richmond 46866
Churchill County Museum and Archives, Fallon 43285
Cincinnati Museum Center, Cincinnati 42402
City County Pioneer Museum, Sweetwater 47903
City Island Nautical Museum, Bronx 41917
City Museum, Saint Louis 47115
City of Bowie Museums, Bowie 41846
City of Ketchikan Museum, Ketchikan 44458
City of Las Vegas and Rough Riders Memorial Museum, Las Vegas 44662
City of Wayne Historical Museum, Wayne 48475
Claremont Museum, Claremont 42421
Clark County Historical Museum, Vancouver 48199
Clark County Historical Society Museum, Springfield 47756
Clark County Museum, Marshall 45176
Clark House Museum Complex, Wolfeboro 48722
Clarke County Historical Museum, Berryville 41657
Clarke House Museum, Chicago 42319
Clarke Memorial Museum, Eureka 43230
Clarkson Historical Museum, Clarkson 42432
Clarksville-Montgomery County Museum-Customs House Museum, Clarksville 42435
Clausen Memorial Museum, Petersburg 46369
Clawson Historical Museum, Clawson 42439
Clay County Historical Museum, Liberty 44765
Clay County Museum, Moorhead 45487
Clear Lake Area Historical Museum, Clear Lake 42449
Clearfield County Historical Society Museum, Clearfield 42450
Clearwater County Historical Museum, Shevlin 47605
Clearwater Historical Museum, Orofino 46194
Cleo Redd Fisher Museum, Loudonville 44957
Clermont State Historic Site, Clermont 42460
Cleveland County Historical Museum, Shelby 47595
Clewiston Museum, Clewiston 42487
Clifton Community Historical Society, Clifton 42488
Clinton County Historical Museum, Plattsburgh 46547
Clinton County Historical Society Museum, Saint Johns 47097
Clinton County Museum, Frankfort 43506
Cliveden House, Philadelphia 46401
Cloud County Historical Museum, Concordia 42607
Coastal Heritage Museum, Crystal River 42716
Cocalico Valley Museum, Ephrata 43194
Codington County Heritage Museum, Watertown 48444
Coe Hall, Oyster Bay 46247
Cokato Museum and Akerlund Photography Studio, Cokato 42516
Cole County Historical Museum, Jefferson City 44327
Coleman House Museum, Ainsworth 41070
Coley Homestead and Barn Museum, Weston 48566
Colleton Museum, Walterboro 48294
Collier County Museum, Naples 45601
Colonel Davenport Historical Foundation, Rock Island 46954
Colonial Burlington Foundation, Burlington 42005
Colonial Industrial Quarter, Bethlehem 41665
Colonial Pennsylvania Plantation, Media 45222
Colonial Williamsburg, Williamsburg 48627
Colorado Springs Museum, Colorado Springs 42536
Colorado University Heritage Center, Boulder 41835
Colton Area Museum, Colton 42545
Colton Hall Museum, Monterey 45453
Columbia County Historical Museum, Lake City 44583
Columbia County Historical Society Museum, Kinderhook 44482
Columbia County Historical Society Museum, Saint Helens 47093
Columbia County Museum, Bloomsburg 41753
Columbia George Interpretive Center, Stevenson 47809
Columbiana-Fairfield Township Museum, Columbiana 42573
Comanche Crossing Museum, Strasburg 47845
Community Historical Museum, Maxwell 45207
Community Historical Museum of Mount Holly, Belmont 41612
Community Memorial Museum of Sutter County, Yuba City 48814
Comstock Historic House, Moorhead 45488
Con Foster Museum, Traverse City 48049
Concord Museum, Concord 42598
Confederate Memorial Hall-Bleak House, Knoxville 44514
Confederate Memorial State Historic Site, Higginsville 44013
Conference House, Staten Island 47780
Conklin Reed Organ and History Museum, Hanover 43906
Connecticut Historical Society Museum, Hartford 43938
Connecticut Valley Historical Museum, Springfield 47745
Conrad Mansion Museum, Kalispell 44383
Conrad Weiser Homestead, Womelsdorf 48725
Constitution Convention Museum, Port Saint Joe 46602
Constitution Island Association Museum, West Point 48542
Cook County Historical Museum, Grand Marais 43751
Cook Inlet Historical Society Museum, Anchorage 41198
Cooper Regional History Museum, Upland 48155
The Coopersville Area Historical Society Museum, Coopersville 42621
Coos County Historical Society Museum, North Bend 45981
Copper Village Museum and Arts Center, Anaconda 41188
Copshaholm House Museum and Historic Oliver Gardens, South Bend 47679
Coquille River Museum, Brandon 41869
Cordova Historical Museum, Cordova 42632
Cornelius Low House/Middlesex County Museum, Piscataway 46501
Cornwall Historical Museum, Cornwall 42640
Coronado-Quivira Museum, Lyons 45013
Corpus Christi Museum of Science and History, Corpus Christi 42645
Corry Area Historical Society Museum, Corry 42649
Cortland County Historical Society Museum, Cortland 42654
Cottage Grove Museum, Cottage Grove 42664
Cottage Lawn, Oneida 46156
Courthouse Museum, Berrien Springs 41654
Courthouse Museum, Exira 43254
Courthouse Museum, Newport 45920
Courthouse Square Museum, Charlotte 42235
The Cowley County Historical Museum, Winfield 48689
Cowlitz County Historical Museum, Kelso 44430
Cracker Country Museum, Tampa 47941
Crailo State Historic Site, Rensselaer 46840
Cranbrook House and Gardens Auxiliary, Bloomfield Hills 41739
Cranbury Historical and Preservation Society Museum, Cranbury 42688
Cravens House, Lookout Mountain 44881
Crawford County Historical Museum, Pittsburg 46503
Crazy Mountain Museum, Big Timber 41685
Crestline Shunk Museum, Crestline 42697
Cripple Creek District Museum, Cripple Creek 42702
Crocker House, Mount Clemens 45525
Crockett County Museum, Ozona 46251
Crockett Tavern Museum, Morristown 45512
Crook County Museum and Art Gallery, Sundance 47883
Crosby County Pioneer Memorial Museum, Crosbyton 42709
Crow Wing County Historical Museum, Brainerd 41866
Crown Gardens Museum, Dalton 42766
Crystal Lake Falls Historical Museum, Barton 41517
Culberson County Historical Museum, Van Horn 48195
Culbertson Museum, Culbertson 42720
Cullman County Museum, Cullman 42722
Cumberland County Historical Society Museum, Greenwich 43834
Cupertino Historical Museum, Cupertino 42729
Curry Historical Society Museum, Gold Beach 43710
Cushing House Museum, Newburyport 45909
Custer County 1881 Courthouse Museum, Custer 42734
Custer County Historical Society Museum, Broken Bow 41911
Custom House Maritime Museum, Newburyport 45910
Cuyuna Range Museum, Crosby 42707
Cyrus H. McCormick Memorial Museum, Steeles Tavern 47800
Dacotah Prairie Museum and Lamont Art Gallery, Aberdeen 41045
Dakota Territorial Museum, Yankton 48777
Dakotaland Museum, Huron 44180
Dal-Paso Museum, Lamesa 44614
Dallam-Hartley XIT Museum, Dalhart 42741
Dallas Historical Society Museum, Dallas 42749
Dan O'Laurie Canyon Country Museum, Moab 45416
Danbury Museum, Danbury 42770
Daniel Boone Homestead, Birdsboro 41702
Daniels County Museum and Pioneer Town, Scobey 47504
Danvers Historical Society Exhibition, Danvers 42774
Dar-Hervey Ely House, Rochester 46940
Darnall's Chance, Upper Marlboro 48157
Daughters of Utah Pioneers Pioneer Memorial Museum, Salt Lake City 47230
David Bradford House, Washington 48416
David Crawford House, Newburgh 45904
David Nichols-Captain John Wilson House, Cohasset 42514
Davidson County Historical Museum, Lexington 44752
Dawes County Historical Society Museum, Chadron 42178
Dawson County Historical Museum, Lexington 44754
Dayton Historical Depot Society Museum, Dayton 42809
De Mores State Historic Site, Bismarck 41720
De Smet Depot Museum, De Smet 42818
Deaf Smith County Museum, Hereford 43998
Dearborn Historical Museum, Dearborn 42823
Death Valley National Park Visitor Center and Museum, Death Valley 42826
Dedham Historical Museum, Dedham 42840
Deer Isle-Stonington Historical Society Museum, Deer Isle 42843
Deerfield Beach Historical Society Museum, Deerfield Beach 42851
DeKalb Historical Society Museum, Decatur 42830
Del Norte County Historical Society Museum, Crescent City 42695
Delano Heritage Park, Delano 42861
Delaware Agricultural Museum, Dover 42968
Delaware Museum, Wilmington 48650
Delaware State Museums, Dover 42969
Delta County Historical Society Museum, Escanaba 43205
Delta County Museum, Delta 42865
Dennison Railroad Depot Museum, Dennison 42872
Denton County Historical Museum, Denton 42875
Depot Museum and Fort Sedgwick Museum, Julesburg 44364
Depot Museum Complex, Condon 42608
The Depot Museum Complex, Henderson 43992
Depot Park Museum, Sonoma 47675
Des Plaines Historical Museum, Des Plaines 42913
Deschutes County Historical Society Museum, Bend 41622
Desha County Museum, Dumas 43004
Detroit Historical Museum, Detroit 42923
Devils Tower Visitor Center, Devils Tower 42939
Dewey Hotel, Dewey 42940
DeWitt County Historical Museum, Cuero 42719
DeWitt Historical Society Museum, Ithaca 44270
Dexter Area Museum, Dexter 42943
Dexter Historical Society Museum, Dexter 42942
Dickinson County Heritage Center, Abilene 41048
Discover Houston County Visitors Center-Museum, Crockett 42704
Discovery Center, Fresno 43557
Divide County Historical Society Museum, Crosby 42708
Dodge County Historical Museum, Mantorville 45128
Dodge County Historical Society Museum, Beaver Dam 41573
Donald G. Trayser Memorial Museum, Barnstable 41508
Door County Museum, Sturgeon Bay 47861
Dorchester County Historical Society Museum, Cambridge 42050
Doric House, Flemington 43337
Dorothea B. Hoover Historical Museum, Joplin 44361
Dorothy G. Page Museum, Wasilla 48425
Dossin Great Lakes Museum, Detroit 42927
Douglas County Historical Society Museum, Superior 47889
Douglas County Museum Complex, Armour 41270
Douglas County Museum of History and Natural History, Roseburg 47003
The Downers Grove Park District Museum, Downers Grove 42979
Downieville Museum, Downieville 42981
Dr. Increase Mathews House, Zanesville 48820
Dr. William Robinson Plantation, Clark 42429
Drake House Museum, Plainfield 46538
Drake Well Museum, Titusville 48014
Drayton Hall, Charleston 42214
Drew County Historical Museum, Monticello 45471
Driebe Freight Station, Stroudsburg 47853
Drummond Home, Hominy 44070
Drummond Island Historical Museum, Drummond Island 42988
Dry Falls Interpretive Center, Coulee City 42672
Dublin-Laurens Museum, Dublin 42989
Duluth Children's Museum, Duluth 42998
Duncan Cottage Museum, Metlakatla 45277
Dundee Township Historical Society Museum, Dundee 43009
Dundy County Historical Society Museum, Benkelman 41626
Dunedin Historical Society Museum, Dunedin 43011
Dunham Tavern Museum, Cleveland 42472
Dunklin County Museum, Kennett 44439
DuPont Historical Museum, DuPont 43013
Durham Center Museum, East Durham 43038
Durham Historic Association Museum, Durham 43026
Durham Western Heritage Museum, Omaha 46145
Duxbury Rural and Historical Society, Duxbury 43029
Dyer Memorial Library, Abington 41056
Eagle Historical Society and Museums, Eagle City 43032
The Earle-Harrison House, Waco 48263
Earle Wightman Museum, Oyster Bay 46248
Earlyworks Museum Complex, Huntsville 44173
East Brunswick Museum, East Brunswick 43037
East Hampton Historical Society Museum, East Hampton 43044
East Jersey Olde Towne, Piscataway 46502
East Jordan Portside Art and Historical Museum, East Jordan 43052
East Poultney Museum, East Poultney 43058
East Tennessee Historical Society Museum, Knoxville 44517
Eastchester Historical Society Museum, Bronxville 41927
Eastern Arizona Museum, Pima 46488
Eastern California Museum, Independence 44197
Eastern Oregon Museum on the Old Oregon Trail, Haines 43871
Ebenezer Maxwell Mansion, Philadelphia 46404
Echo Historical Museum, Echo 43079
Eckley Miners' Village, Eckley 43080
Edgar Allan Poe Cottage, Bronx 41918
Edgar Allan Poe Museum, Richmond 46876
Edgar County Historical Museum, Paris 46284
Edison Plaza Museum, Beaumont 41567
Edmond Historical Society Museum, Edmond 43091
Edmonds South Snohomish County Historical Society Museum, Edmonds 43093
Edna Historical Museum, Edna 43094

Edsel and Eleanor Ford House, Grosse Pointe Shores 43844
Edwards County Historical Museum, Kinsley 44500
Edwin Wolters Memorial Museum, Shiner 47607
Eells-Stow House, Milford 45337
Ehrman Mansion, Tahoma 47928
Eisenhower Birthplace, Denison 42870
El Dorado County Historical Museum, Placerville 46537
El Monte Historical Society Museum, El Monte 43109
El Pueblo Museum, Pueblo 46738
El Rancho de Las Golondrinas Museum, Santa Fe 47417
Elberton Granite Museum, Elberton 43127
Eleanor Roosevelt National Historic Site, Hyde Park 44186
Elk Grove Farmhouse Museum, Elk Grove Village 43136
Elkhart County Historical Museum, Bristol 41902
Ella Sharp Museum, Jackson 44276
Elliott Museum, Stuart 47857
Ellis County Museum, Waxahachie 48469
Ellsworth County Museum, Ellsworth 43162
Elmhurst Historical Museum, Elmhurst 43166
Emmett Kelly Historical Museum, Sedan 47556
Empire Area Heritage Group - History Museum, Empire 43181
Enfield Historical Society Museum, Enfield 43188
Enfield Shaker Museum, Enfield 43189
Ephraim Foundation Museums, Ephraim 43193
Ephrata Cloister, Ephrata 43195
Erie Canal Museum, Syracuse 47907
Erie Canal Village, Rome 46995
Erie History Center, Erie 43201
Erwin Museum, Painted Post 46263
Essex Historical Museum, Essex 43212
Essley-Noble Museum, Aledo 41115
Estes Park Area Historical Museum, Estes Park 43216
Eugene Field House and Saint Louis Toy Museum, Saint Louis 47120
Eureka Pioneer Museum of McPherson County, Eureka 43233
Eureka School House, Springfield 47759
Evansville Museum of Arts and Science, Evansville 43245
Excelsior-Lake Minnetonka Historical Museum, Excelsior 43250
The Executive Mansion, Frankfort 43507
Ezra Meeker Mansion, Puyallup 46751
Fairbanks Museum and Planetarium, Saint Johnsbury 47098
Fairfield County Museum, Winnsboro 48694
Fairport Historical Museum, Fairport 43275
Fairview Museum of History and Art, Fairview 43277
Faith Trumbull Chapter Museum, Norwich 46035
Fall River County Historical Museum, Hot Springs 44110
Fall River Historical Society Museum, Fall River 43282
Falmouth Historical Museum, Falmouth 43287
The Farmers' Museum, Cooperstown 42618
Farmington Museum, Farmington 43299
Farrar-Mansur House and Old Mill Museum, Weston 48571
Faulkner County Museum, Conway 42612
Fayette County Historical Museum, West Union 48549
Fayette County Museum, Washington Court House 48422
Fayette Heritage Museum, La Grange 44545
Felix Valle State Historic Site, Sainte Genevieve 47184
Fenton History Center-Museum and Library, Jamestown 44311
Fillmore County Historical Museum, Fountain 43496
Fillmore Historical Museum, Fillmore 43320
The Filson Historical Society Museum, Louisville 44965
The Finley House, Wayne 48480
Finney County Kansas Historical Museum, Garden City 43617
Firelands Historical Society Museum, Norwalk 46034
Fisher Grove Country School, Frankfort 43516
Fitchburg Historical Society Museum, Fitchburg 43327
Fleming Historical Museum, Fleming 43336
Flint House, Scotia 47506
Flood Museum, Johnstown 44352
Florence Griswold Museum, Old Lyme 46133
Florence Price Pioneer Museum, Florence 43346
Florewood State Park, Greenwood 43836
Florida Adventure Museum, Punta Gorda 46746
Florida International Museum, Saint Petersburg 47172
Floyd County Historical Museum, Charles City 42200
Follett House Museum, Sandusky 47383
Folsom History Museum, Folsom 43358
Forbes Mill Museum of Regional History, Los Gatos 44955
Ford County Historical Society Museum, Paxton 46319
The Forges and Manor of Ringwood, Ringwood 46902
Former Governors' Mansion, Bismarck 41721
Fort Abercrombie Historic Site, Abercrombie 41044
Fort Bedford Museum, Bedford 41582
Fort Bend Museum, Richmond 46867
Fort Benton Museum of the Upper Missouri, Fort Benton 43367
Fort Bridger State Museum, Fort Bridger 43373
Fort Buenaventura, Ogden 46098
Fort Collins Museum, Fort Collins 43380
Fort Crawford Museum, Prairie du Chien 46682
Fort Croghan Museum, Burnet 42010
Fort Crook Historical Museum, Fall River Mills 43284
Fort Dodge Historical Museum, Fort Dodge 43389
Fort Hill Museum, Hillsboro 44026
Fort Hill - The John C. Calhoun House, Clemson 42456
Fort Hunter Mansion, Harrisburg 43923
Fort Jones Museum, Fort Jones 43405
Fort Klock Historic Restoration, Saint Johnsville 47100
Fort Leaton, Presidio 46691
Fort Leavenworth Historical Museum and Post Museum, Fort Leavenworth 43415
Fort Lee Historic Park and Museum, Fort Lee 43417
Fort Mackinac, Mackinac Island 45029
Fort Morgan Museum, Fort Morgan 43432
Fort Myers Historical Museum, Fort Myers 43436
Fort Nisqually Living History Museum, Tacoma 47917
Fort Osage, Sibley 47623
Fort Plain Museum, Fort Plain 43443
Fort Richardson, Jacksboro 44275
Fort Saint Joseph Museum, Niles 45954
Fort Sisseton, Lake City 44585
Fort Smith Museum of History, Fort Smith 43458
Fort Stanwix, Rome 46996
Fort Totten State Historic Museum, Fort Totten 43464
Fort Vancouver, Vancouver 48200
Fort Walla Walla Museum, Walla Walla 48285
Fort Washington Museum, Fort Washington 43471
Fort Wilkins Historic Complex, Copper Harbor 42624
Fort Winnebago Surgeons Quarters, Portage 46612
Fossil Country Museum, Kemmerer 44431
Fossil Museum, Fossil 43494
Fossil Station Museum, Russell 47033
Fostoria Area Historical Museum, Fostoria 43495
Four Rivers Cultural Center, Ontario 46166
Fox Island Historical Society Museum, Fox Island 43499
Fox Lake Historical Museum, Fox Lake 43500
Framingham Historical Society and Museum, Framingham 43502
Francis Land House, Virginia Beach 48247
Francisco Fort Museum, La Veta 44559
Frank H. McClung Museum, Knoxville 44519
Frank Lloyd Wright's Pope-Leighey House, Mount Vernon 45545
Frank Phillips Home, Bartlesville 41514
Frankenmuth Historical Museum, Frankenmuth 43505
Frankfort Area Historical Museum, West Frankfort 48523
Franklin County Historical Museum, Pasco 46307
Franklin County Museum, Brookville 41958
Franklin County Old Jail Museum, Winchester 48678
Franklin Historical Society Museum, Franklin 43518
Fraunces Tavern Museum, New York 45801
Fredericksburg Area Museum and Cultural Center, Fredericksburg 43535
Freeborn County Historical Museum, Albert Lea 41094
Freeport Historical Society Museum, Freeport 43552
Freestone County Historical Museum, Fairfield 43268
Fremont County Pioneer Museum, Lander 44632
French Azilum, Towanda 48043
Fresno Metropolitan Museum, Fresno 43559
Friendship Hill National Historic Site, Point Marion 46574
Frisco Historical Society Museum, Frisco 43564
Front Street Museum, Ogallala 46095
Frontier Museum, Williston 48640
Frontier Village Museum, Jamestown 44307
Fruitlands Museums, Harvard 43952
Fullerton Museum Center, Fullerton 43572
Fulton County Historical Museum, Wauseon 48465
Fulton County Historical Society Museum, Rochester 46932
Fulton County Museum, Groversville 43849
Furnas-Gosper Historical Society Museum, Arapahoe 41243
Gadsby's Tavern Museum, Alexandria 41127
Gage County Historical Museum, Beatrice 41555
Gaineswood, Demopolis 42869
Galena-Jo Daviess County Historical Museum, Galena 43593
Galion Historical Museum, Galion 43603
Galloway House and Village, Fond du Lac 43360
Galveston County Historical Museum, Galveston 43609
Garden County Museum, Oshkosh 46203
Gardner House Museum, Albion 41098
Gardner Museum, Gardner 43623
Garibaldi and Meucci Museum, Staten Island 47781
Garnavillo Historical Museum, Garnavillo 43626
Garner Memorial Museum, Uvalde 48172
Garrett County Historical Museum, Oakland 46072
Garrett Historical Museum, Garrett 43629
Garst Museum, Greenville 43827
Gaston County Museum of Art and History, Dallas 42742
Gatekeeper's Museum and Marion Steinbach Indian Basket Museum, Tahoe City 47927
Gates House, Machiasport 45028
Gates Mills Historical Society Museum, Gates Mills 43634
Gateway to the Panhandle, Gate 43633
Geddes Historic District Village, Geddes 43637
General Adam Stephen House, Martinsburg 45191
General Crook House Museum, Omaha 46147
General Daniel Bissell House, Saint Louis 47122
General Sterling Price Museum, Keytesville 44478
Genesee Country Village and Museum, Mumford 45554
Geographical Center Historical Museum, Rugby 47027
George I. Ashby Memorial Museum, Copper Center 42623
George Taylor House, Catasauqua 42138
George Washington Birthplace National Monument, Colonial Beach 42532
Georgetown Museum, Columbus 42584
Georgia Historical Society Museum, Savannah 47479
Georgia Salzburger Society Museum, Rincon 46901
The Georgian, Lancaster 44621
Georgia's Stone Mountain Park, Stone Mountain 47827
Germantown Historical Society Museum, Philadelphia 46413
Gernon House and Blacksmith Shop, Russell 47034
Gig Harbor Peninsula Historical Society Museum, Gig Harbor 43667
Gila County Historical Museum, Globe 43700
Gilman Garrison House, Exeter 43252
Gilman Museum, Hellertown 43985
Gilman Town Hall Museum, Issaquah 44269
Gilpin History Museum, Central City 42173
Gilroy Historical Museum, Gilroy 43675
Glastonbury Museum, Glastonbury 43678
The Glebe House Museum, Woodbury 48729
Glenn H. Curtiss Museum, Hammondsport 43888
Glenview Area Historical Museum, Glenview 43695
Gloucester County Historical Society Museum, Woodbury 48731
Gnadenhutten Historical Park and Museum, Gnadenhutten 43707
Golden Ball Tavern Museum, Weston 48568
Golden Spike National Historic Site, Brigham City 41898
Goliad State Historical Park, Goliad 43722
Gomez Foundation for Mill House, Marlboro 45169
Gonzales Memorial Museum, Gonzales 43724
Goochland County Museum, Goochland 43725
Goochland County Museum, Goochland 43726
Gorgas House, Tuscaloosa 48114
Goschenhoppen Folklife Museum, Green Lane 43793
Goshen Historical Society Museum, Goshen 43732
Gouverneur Historical Association Museum, Gouverneur 43735
Governor Henry Lippitt House Museum, Providence 46719
Governor John Langdon House, Portsmouth 46648
Governor Printz Park, Essington 43214
Governor Ross Plantation, Seaford 47523
Governor Seay Mansion, Kingfisher 44487
Governor Stephen Hopkins House, Providence 46720
Governor's Mansion, Columbia 42560
Governor's Mansion, Sacramento 47052
Grace Hudson Museum and The Sun House, Ukiah 48134
Grace Museum, Abilene 41053
Graeme Park/Keith Mansion, Horsham 44107
Grafton Museum, Grafton 43737
Graham County Historical Museum, Safford 47060
Grand County Museum, Hot Sulphur Springs 44112
Grand Forks County Historical Society Museum, Grand Forks 43741
Grand Lake Area Historical Museum, Grand Lake 43750
Granger Homestead Society Museum, Canandaigua 42076
Grant County Historical Museum, Canyon City 42093
Grant County Historical Museum, Elbow Lake 43128
Grant County Historical Museum, Ephrata 43196
Grant County Museum, Elgin 43130
Grant County Museum, Hyannis 44185
Grant County Museum, Medford 45219
Grant County Museum, Sheridan 47601
Grant County Museum, Ulysses 48137
Grant's Birthplace State Memorial, Point Pleasant 46575
Granville County Historical Society Museum, Oxford 46240
Granville Historical Museum, Granville 43773
Graue Mill and Museum, Oak Brook 46050
Great Basin Museum, Delta 42866
Greater Harvard Area Historical Society, Harvard 43951
Greater Hazleton Historical Society Museum, Hazleton 43978
Greater Loveland Historical Society Museum, Loveland 44981
Greater Port Jefferson Museum, Port Jefferson 46598
Green Mountain Club, Waterbury Center 48428
Greenbelt Museum, Greenbelt 43796
Greene County Historical Museum, Waynesburg 48484
Greene County Historical Society Museum, Xenia 48772
Greenfield Historical Society Museum, Greenfield 43808
Greenfield Museum, Greenfield 43807
Greensboro Historical Museum, Greensboro 43813
Greenwood County Historical Society Museum, Eureka 43232
Gregg County Historical Museum, Longview 44878
Gresham History Museum, Gresham 43838
Greybull Museum, Greybull 43839
Grinnell Historical Museum, Grinnell 43842
Grinter Place, Kansas City 44393
Grosse Ile Historical Museum, Grosse Ile 43843
Grover Cleveland Birthplace, Caldwell 42029
Guernsey County Museum, Cambridge 42055
Gunn Memorial Library and Museum, Washington 48329
Gunnison County Pioneer and Historical Museum, Gunnison 43853
Gunston Hall Plantation, Mason Neck 45201
Gwinnett Historical Society Museum, Lawrenceville 44690
Gwinnett History Museum, Lawrenceville 44691
Haas-Lilienthal House, San Francisco 47319
Hackettstown Historical Society Museum, Hackettstown 43859
Hackley Hume Historic Site, Muskegon 45577
Haddonfield Museum, Haddonfield 43860
Hagadorn House Museum, Almond 41153
Hahns Peak Area Historical Museum, Clark 42428
Hahs Museum, Hattiesburg 43957
Haines Museum, Waukegan 48459
Hale Farm and Village, Bath 41524
Halifax Historical Museum, Daytona Beach 42810
Hall of Fame for Great Americans, Bronx 41920
Hamilton Library and Two Mile House, Carlisle 42104
Hamilton van Wogener Museum, Clifton 42489
Hamlin Garland Homestead, West Salem 48545
Hammond Historical Museum, Hammond 43886
Hampton County Historical Museum, Hampton 43893
Hampton Plantation, McClellanville 45019
Hana Cultural Center, Hana, Maui 43900
Hanby House, Westerville 48555
Hancock County Historical Museum, Carthage 42125
Hancock Historical Museum, Findlay 43323
Hancock Historical Society Museum, Hancock 43901
Hancock Shaker Village, Pittsfield 46533
Hannah Lindahl Children's Museum, Mishawaka 45399
Hanover Historical Society Museum, Hanover 43908
Hanover House, Clemson 42457
Har-Ber Village, Grove 43847
Hardin County Historical Museum, Kenton 44449
Harding Home and Museum, Marion 45162
Harding Museum, Franklin 43520
Hardwick Historical Museum, Hardwick 43910
Harney County Historical Museum, Burns 42011
Harold Warp Pioneer Village Foundation, Minden 45376
Harper City Historical Museum, Harper 43916
Harpers Ferry National Historical Park, Harpers Ferry 43918
Harris Art Gallery, James M. Lykes Maritime Gallery and Hutchings Gallery, Galveston 43610
Harrison County Historical Museum, Marshall 45182
Harrison House, Branford 41870
Hartsville Museum, Hartsville 43948
Harvard Historical Society Museum, Still River 47810
Harvey County Historical Museum, Newton 45943
The Haskell County Historical Museum, Sublette 47866
Hastings Museum, Hastings 43956
Hatton-Eielson Museum, Hatton 43959
Haverford Township Historical Society Museum, Havertown 43963
Haverhill Historical Museum, Haverhill 43961
Hawks Inn, Delafield 42859
Hawks Nest State Park, Ansted 41233
Headlund Museum, Hugo 44146
Healy House and Dexter Cabin, Leadville 44700
Hearst Castle, San Simeon 47377
Heart of West Texas Museum, Colorado City 42533
Heddon Museum, Dowagiac 42977
Heisey Museum, Lock Haven 44838
Held-Poage Memorial Home, Ukiah 48135
Helvetia Museum, Helvetia 43986
Hendrickson House Museum and Old Swedes Church, Wilmington 48653
Hennepin History Museum, Minneapolis 45384
Henry County Historical Museum, New Castle 45684
Henry County Museum and Cultural Arts Center, Clinton 42495
Henry Ford Estate, Dearborn 42824
Henry Guest House, New Brunswick 45677
The Henry Sheldon Museum of Vermont Histoy, Middlebury 45307
Heritage Center of Lancaster County, Lancaster 44624
Heritage Discover Center, Johnstown 44353
Heritage Farmstead Museum, Plano 46541
Heritage Hall Museum and Archives, Freeman 43548
Heritage Hill State Park, Green Bay 43789
Heritage House of Orange County Museum, Orange 46171
Heritage Museum, Idaho Springs 44192
The Heritage Museum, Astoria 41311
Heritage Museum and Potton House, Big Spring 41683
The Heritage Museum at Falfurrias, Falfurrias 43280
Heritage Museum Foundation of Tate County, Senatobia 47564
Heritage Museum of Northwest Florida, Valparaiso 48191
Heritage Plantation of Sandwich, Sandwich 47386
The Heritage Society Museum, Houston 44121
Heritage Square Museum, Ontario 46164
Heritage Village, Mountain Lake 45547
Heritage Village, Sharonville 47581
Heritage Village Museum, Woodville 48747
Heritage Village - Pinellas County Historical Museum, Largo 44654

Heritage Walk Museum, Escondido 43209
Herkimer County Historical Society Museum, Herkimer 44000
Herkimer Home, Little Falls 44820
The Hermitage - Home of President Andrew Jackson, Hermitage 44003
Hettinger County Historical Society Museum, Regent 46830
Heurich House Museum, Washington 48359
Hibbing Historical Museum, Hibbing 44005
Hickory Grove Rural School Museum, Ogden 46096
Hicksville Gregory Museum, Hicksville 44010
Hidalgo County Historical Museum, Edinburg 43088
Hiddenite Center, Hiddenite 44012
High Cliff General Store Museum, Sherwood 47604
High Plains Heritage Center, Great Falls 43781
High Plains Museum, McCook 45021
High Point Museum, High Point 44015
Highland House Museum, Hillsboro 44027
Highland Park Historical Museum, Highland Park 44020
Highlands, Fort Washington 43472
Highlands Museum and Discovery Center, Ashland 41287
Hildene, Manchester 45101
Hill Country Museum, Kerrville 44455
Hill-Hold Museum, Montgomery 45470
Hillsboro Area Historical Society Museum, Hillsboro 44029
Hillsboro Museum, Hillsboro 44024
Hinsdale Historical Society Museum, Hinsdale 44038
Historic Allaire Village, Allaire 41140
Historic Annapolis Foundation, Annapolis 41229
Historic Bath State Historic Site, Bath 41523
Historic Brattonsville, McConnells 45020
Historic Burlington County Prison Museum, Mount Holly 45531
Historic Camden Revolutionary War Site, Camden 42065
Historic Carson House, Marion 45161
Historic Charleston Foundation, Charleston 42219
Historic Charlton Park Village and Museum, Hastings 43955
Historic Columbia Foundation, Columbia 42562
Historic Crab Orchard Museum and Pioneer Park, Tazewell 47964
Historic Cragfont, Castalian Springs 42134
Historic Daniel Boone Home and Boonesfield Village, Defiance 42852
Historic Deerfield, Deerfield 42849
Historic Fallsington, Fallsington 43286
Historic Gardner's Basin, Atlantic City 41366
Historic General Dodge House, Council Bluffs 42673
Historic Georgetown, Georgetown 43648
Historic Governors' Mansion, Cheyenne 42298
Historic Halifax, Halifax 43873
Historic Hermann Museum, Hermann 44002
Historic Hope Foundation, Windsor 48683
Historic Houses of Odessa, Delaware, Odessa 46092
Historic Hudson Valley, Tarrytown 47957
The Historic Indian Agency House, Portage 46613
Historic Kenmore, Fredericksburg 43536
Historic Lincoln, Lincoln 44795
Historic Michie Tavern, Charlottesville 42248
Historic New Harmony, New Harmony 45692
The Historic New Orleans Collection, New Orleans 45727
Historic Northampton, Northampton 46014
Historic Occoquan, Occoquan 46083
Historic Palmyra, Palmyra 46270
Historic Pensacola Village, Pensacola 46342
Historic Pittsford, Pittsford 46534
Historic Preservation Association of Bourbon County, Fort Scott 43454
Historic Richmond Town, Staten Island 47782
Historic Rock Ford, Lancaster 44625
Historic Rugby, Rugby 47028
Historic Schaefferstown, Schaefferstown 47494
Historic Shepherdstown Museum, Shepherdstown 47600
Historic Smithfield, Blacksburg 41727
Historic Speedwell, Morristown 45506
Historic White Pine Village, Ludington 44995
Historical and Genealogical Society of Indiana County, Indiana 44210
Historical and Natural History Museum of Natick, South Natick 47699
Historical Museum at Fort Missoula, Missoula 45405
The Historical Museum at Saint Gertrude, Cottonwood 42665
Historical Museum of Bay County, Bay City 41543
Historical Museum of Cecil County, Elkton 43147
Historical Museum of Frederick County, Frederick 43527
Historical Museum of Old Randolph, Randolph 46789
Historical Museum of Palm Beach County, West Palm Beach 48537
Historical Museum of Talbot County, Easton 43067
Historical Society Museum, Hudson 44144
Historical Society Museum of Carroll County, Westminster 48563
Historical Society Museum of Ocean Grove, New Jersey, Ocean Grove 46086
Historical Society Museum of the Town of Greenwich, Greenwich 43832
Historical Society of Berks County Museum, Reading 46807
Historical Society of Bloomfield Museum, Bloomfield 41734
Historical Society of Kent County Museum, Chestertown 42292
Historical Society of Middletown and the Wallkill Precinct, Middletown 45317
Historical Society of Oak Park and River Forest, Oak Park 46054
Historical Society of Pennsylvania, Philadelphia 46417
Historical Society of Santuit and Cotuit, Cotuit 42669
History Museum for Springfield-Greene County, Springfield 47753
Hiwan Homestead Museum, Evergreen 43249
Hoard Historical Museum, Fort Atkinson 43365
Hobart Historical Society Museum, Hobart 44042
Hoiles-Davis Museum, Greenville 43823
Holland Historical Society Museum, Holland 44058
Holland Land Office Museum, Batavia 41521
Holland Museum, Holland 44056
Hollywood Heritage Museum, Los Angeles 44909
Holmes County Historical Society Museum, Millersburg 45346
Home of Franklin D. Roosevelt, Hyde Park 44188
Home of Stone, Dodge City 42955
Home Sweet Home Museum, East Hampton 43047
Homerville Museum, Homer 44069
Honolulu House Museum, Marshall 45178
Hood River County Historical Museum, Hood River 44095
Hope Historical Society Museum, Hope 44097
Hope Lodge and Mather Mill, Fort Washington 43473
Hopewell Museum, Hopewell 44098
Hopewell Museum, Paris 46285
Hopi Cultural Museum, Second Mesa 47553
Hopsewee Plantation, Georgetown 43653
Horace Greeley House, Chappaqua 42197
Horizons Unlimited Supplementary Educational Center, Salisbury 47219
Hornby Museum, Hornby 44104
Hoskins House, Burlington 42006
Houghton County Historical Museum Society, Lake Linden 44590
House in the Horseshoe, Sanford 47395
House of History, Malone 45085
House of Wickersham, Juneau 44369
The House on the Rock, Spring Green 47730
Howard County Historical Museum, Kokomo 44527
Howard County Historical Society Museum, Ellicott City 43158
Howell Historical Society Committee Museum, Howell 44139
Hudson River Museum of Westchester, Yonkers 48785
Humboldt County Historical Association Museum, Dakota City 42740
Humboldt County Historical Association Museum, Humboldt 44150
Humboldt Historical Museum, Humboldt 44151
Humpback Rocks Mountain Farm Visitor Center, Waynesboro 48483
Hunt-Morgan House, Lexington 44739
Hunter-Dawson State Historic Site, New Madrid 45715
Huntingdon County Museum, Huntingdon 44153
Huntington County Historical Society Museum, Huntington 44157
Huntington Historical Society Museum, Huntington 44162
Hurley Patentee Manor, Hurley 44177
Huron City Museums, Port Austin 46591
Hurricane Valley Heritage Park Museum, Hurricane 44181
Hutchinson County Museum, Borger 41794
Hutchinson House Museum, Waupaca 48461
Hyde Hall, East Springfield 43060
Illinois and Michigan Canal Museum, Lockport 44840
Illinois State Museum, Springfield 47737
Immigrant City Historical Museum of Lawrence and its People, Lawrence 44689
Imogene Herbert Historical Museum, Manistique 45113
Imperial Calcasieu Museum, Lake Charles 44582
Independence Historical Museum, Independence 44198
Independence National Historical Park, Philadelphia 46418
Indian Hill Historical Society Museum, Cincinnati 42408
Indian King Tavern Museum, Haddonfield 43861
Interlaken Historical Society Museum, Interlaken 44238
Iosco County Historical Museum, East Tawas 43061
Iowa Masonic Library and Museum, Cedar Rapids 42159
Ipswich Historical Society Museum, Ipswich 44251
Iredell Museum of Arts Heritage, Statesville 47794
Iron County Museum, Caspian 42132
Ironwood Area Historical Museum, Ironwood 44255
Ironworld Discovery Center, Chisholm 42388
Iroquois County Historical Society Museum, Watseka 48455
Isaac Farrar Mansion, Bangor 41494
Isabel Miller Museum, Sitka 47649
Isanti County Museum, Cambridge 42051
Ischua Valley Historical Society, Franklinville 43524
Island County Historical Society Museum, Coupeville 42677
Isle La Motte Historical Society Museum, Isle La Motte 44265
Isle of Wight Courthouse, Smithfield 47656
Isleford Historical Museum, Isleford 44266
Islesboro Historical Museum, Islesboro 44267
Itasca Heritage Center Museum, Grand Rapids 43762
Ivy Green, Tuscumbia 48120
J. Evetts Haley History Center, Midland 45325
Jack London State Historic Park, Glen Ellen 43681
Jackson County Historical Museum, Lakefield 44601
Jackson County Historical Museum, Maquoketa 45131
Jackson County Historical Society Museum, Black River Falls 41724
Jackson Hole Historical Museum, Jackson 44289
The Jackson Homestead, Newton 45944
Jackson-Washabaugh Historical Museum, Kadoka 44373
Jackson's Mill Historic Area, Weston 48572
Jacob Walden House, Walden 48281
Jaffrey Civic Center, Jaffrey 44302
James A. Garfield National Historic Site, Mentor 45256
James J. Hill House, Saint Paul 47157
The James Madison Museum, Orange 46174
James Madison's Montpelier, Montpelier Station 45480
James Mitchell Varnum House and Museum, East Greenwich 43040
James Monroe Museum and Memorial Library, Fredericksburg 43537
James W. Dillon House Museum, Dillon 42951
Jamestown Museum, Jamestown 44314
Jamestown Visitor Center Museum, Jamestown 44316
J.E. Reeves Home and Museum, Dover 42973
Jeff Matthews Memorial Museum, Galax 43592
Jefferson County Historical Association Museum, Steubenville 47806
Jefferson County Historical Museum, Madison 45057
Jefferson County Historical Museum, Pine Bluff 46490
Jefferson County Historical Society Museum, Watertown 48442
Jefferson Historical Museum, Jefferson 44325
Jefferson Patterson Museum, Saint Leonard 47110
Jekyll Island Museum, Jekyll Island 44331
Jemez State Monument, Jemez Springs 44332
Jennings-Brown House Female Academy, Bennettsville 41627
Jericho Historical Society Museum, Jericho Corners 44335
Jerome County Historical Society, Jerome 44337
Jersey City Museum, Jersey City 44340
Jesse Besser Museum, Alpena 41154
Jesse James Bank Museum, Liberty 44767
Jesse James Farm and Museum, Kearney 44420
Jesse James Home Museum, Saint Joseph 47106
Jewell County Historical Museum, Mankato 45118
Jim Gatchell Museum, Buffalo 41991
Jim Thorpe Home, Yale 48775
J.J. Jackson Memorial Museum, Weaverville 48486
J.M. Davis Arms and Historical Museum, Claremore 42422
John Abbott II House, Hamilton 43880
John E. Conner Museum, Kingsville 44499
John G. Voigt House, Plymouth 46568
The John Harris/Simon Cameron Mansion, Harrisburg 43924
John Humphrey House, Swampscott 47899
John Jay French House, Beaumont 41569
John Marshall House, Richmond 46880
John Paul Jones House Museum, Portsmouth 46649
John R. Jackson House, Winlock 48690
John Rains House, Rancho Cucamonga 46783
John Ralston Museum, Mendham 45249
John S. Barry Historical Society Museum, Constantine 42611
John Smart House, Medina 45225
John Stark Edwards House, Warren 48310
John Strong Mansion, Addison 41065
John Sydnor's 1847 Powhatan House, Galveston 43611
Johnson County Historical Society Museum, Coralville 42630
Johnson County Historical Society Museum, Tecumseh 47966
Johnson County Historical Society Museum, Warrensburg 48316
Johnson County History Museum, Franklin 43517
Johnson County Museums, Shawnee 47586
Johnson Ferry House Museum, Titusville 48013
Johnson Hall, Johnstown 44350
Johnson-Humrickhouse Museum, Coshocton 42662
Johnstown Historical Society Museum, Johnstown 44351
Joliet Area Historical Museum, Joliet 44355
Jonesborough-Washington County History Museum, Jonesborough 44360
Judge Roy Bean Visitor Center, Langtry 44638
Judith Basin County Museum, Stanford 47774
Julia A. Purnell Museum, Snow Hill 47661
Junction City Historical Society Museum, Junction City 44367
Juneau-Douglas City Museum, Juneau 44370
Justin Smith Morrill Homestead, Strafford 47844
J.W. Parmely Historical Home Museum, Ipswich 44252
Kake Tribal Heritage Foundation, Kake 44375
Kalamazoo Valley Museum, Kalamazoo 44380
Kalkaska County Historical Museum, Kalkaska 44385
Kaminski House Museum, Georgetown 43654
Kanabec History Center, Mora 45490
Kankakee County Historical Society Museum, Kankakee 44388
Kansas City Museum/Science City at Union Station, Kansas City 44400
Kauffman Museum, North Newton 45999
Kearney County Historical Museum, Minden 45377
Kearney Mansion Museum, Fresno 43560
Keeler Tavern Museum, Ridgefield 46897
Kell House Museum, Wichita Falls 48613
Kelley House Museum, Mendocino 45250
Kellogg Historical Society Museum, Kellogg 44428
Kelso House, Kent 44445
Kelton House Museum, Columbus 42589
Kemp-McCarthy Memorial Museum, Rowe 47020
Kenilworth Historical Society Museum, Kenilworth 44432
Kennebunkport Historical Museum, Kennebunkport 44435
Kenosha County Museum, Kenosha 44440
Kent-Delord House Museum, Plattsburgh 46548
Kentuck Museum and Art Center, Northport 46026
The Kentucky Museum, Bowling Green 41849
Kerbyville Museum, Kerby 44454
Kern County Museum, Bakersfield 41440
Kerr Place, Onancock 46154
Kershaw County Historical Society Museum, Camden 42066
Kewaunee County Historical Museum, Kewaunee 44460
Key West Lighthouse Museum, Key West 44467
Key West Museum of Art and History, Key West 44468
Keystone Area Museum, Keystone 44475
Kimball House Museum, Battle Creek 41538
Kimberly Crest House, Redlands 46821
Kimble County Historical Museum, Junction 44366
Kingman County Historical Museum, Kingman 44489
Kingman Tavern Historical Museum, Cummington 42727
Kingsland Homestead, Flushing 43354
Kinney Pioneer Museum, Clear Lake 42448
Kit Carson Historical Society Museum, Kit Carson 44506
Kitsap Museum, Bremerton 41879
Kittery Historical and Naval Museum, Kittery 44507
Kittson County History Center Museum, Lake Bronson 44578
Kiwanis Van Slyke Museum Foundation, Caldwell 42027
Klamath County Museum, Klamath Falls 44509
Klein Museum, Mobridge 45426
Klickitat County Historical Society Museum, Goldendale 43716
Klyne Esopus Historical Society Museum, Ulster Park 48136
Knife River Indian Villages National Historic Site, Stanton 47775
Knight Museum of High Plains Heritage, Alliance 41148
Knox County Museum, Benjamin 41625
Knox County Museum, Knoxville 44511
Koochiching County Historical Society Museum, International Falls 44240
Kotzebue Museum, Kotzebue 44528
Kruse House Museum, West Chicago 48518
Kuhlmann King Historical House and Museum, Boerne 41770
Kuser Farm Mansion, Hamilton 43881
Lac Qui Parle County Historical Museum, Madison 45060
Lacey Historical Society Museum, Forked River 43363
Lafayette Museum - Alexandre Mouton House, Lafayette 44570
Laguardia and Wagner Archives, Long Island City 44867
Lake County Discovery Museum, Wauconda 48457
Lake County Historical Museum, Tavares 47961
Lake County Historical Society Museum, Kirtland Hills 44505
Lake County Historical Society Museum, Mentor 45257
Lake County Museum, Lakeport 44605
Lake Forest-Lake Bluff Historical Society Museum, Lake Forest 44586
Lake George Historical Association Museum, Lake George 44588
Lake Guernsey Museum, Guernsey 43850
Lake Hopatcong Historical Museum, Landing 44633
Lake Hopatcong Historical Museum, Landing 44634
Lake of the Red Cedars Museum, Cedar Lake 42155
Lake of the Woods County Museum, Baudette 41541
Lake Placid-North Elba Historical Society Museum, Lake Placid 44594
Lake Wales Depot Museum, Lake Wales 44597
Lakewood's Heritage Culture and the Arts Galleries, Lakewood 44608
Lancaster County Museum, Lancaster 44627
Lancaster Historical Society Museum, Lancaster 44619
Lancaster Museum/Art Gallery, Lancaster 44616
Landis Valley Museum, Lancaster 44629
Lane County Historical Museum, Dighton 42947
Lane House, Roseburg 47004
Langlade County Historical Society Museum, Antigo 41234
Lansing Manor House Museum, North Blenheim 45984
Laramie Plains Museum, Laramie 44648
Larchmont Historical Society Museum, Mamaroneck 45088

Lars Noak Blacksmith Shop, Larsson/Ostlund Log Home One-Room Capitol School, New Sweden 45746
LaSalle County Historical Society Museum, Utica 48167
Lauder Museum, Amityville 41185
Laura Ingalls Wilder Museum, Walnut Grove 48292
The Laurel Museum, Laurel 44676
Laurence C. Jones Museum, Piney Woods 46496
Lawrence County Gray House Museum, Ironton 44254
Lawrence County Historical Museum, Bedford 41579
Layland Museum, Cleburne 42454
Le Roy House and Jell-o Gallery, Le Roy 44697
Le Sueur Museum, Le Sueur 44698
Leavenworth County Historical Society Museum, Leavenworth 44702
Lee Chapel and Museum, Lexington 44760
Lee County Historical Society Museum, Loachapoka 44837
Lee-Fendall House, Alexandria 41131
Leelanau Historical Museum, Leland 44714
Lefferts Homestead, Brooklyn 41945
Lehigh County Historical Society Museum, Allentown 41145
Lemee House, Natchitoches 45636
Lemhi County Historical Museum, Salmon 47224
Lesueur County Historical Museum, Elysian 43179
Leverett Historical Museum, Leverett 44719
Lewes Historical Society Museum, Lewes 44720
Lewis County Historical Museum, Chehalis 42269
Lewis County Historical Society Museum, Lowville 44989
Lewis County Historical Society Museum, Lyons Falls 45015
Lexington County Museum, Lexington 44756
Lexington Historical Society Exhibition, Lexington 44749
Libby Museum, Wolfeboro 48723
Liberty County Museum, Chester 42283
Liberty Hall Historic Center, Lamoni 44615
Libertyville-Mundelein Historical Society Museum, Libertyville 44768
Licking County Historical Museum, Newark 45894
Lightner Museum, Saint Augustine 47068
Lincoln County Historical Museum, Davenport 42788
Lincoln County Historical Society Museum, Lincoln 44775
Lincoln County Historical Society Museum, North Platte 46004
Lincoln County Historical Society Museum of Pioneer History, Chandler 42191
Lincoln County Pioneer Museum, Hendricks 43995
Lincoln Parish Museum, Ruston 47038
Lincoln Park Historical Museum, Lincoln Park 44799
The Lincoln-Tallman Restorations, Janesville 44318
Lincoln's New Salem Historic Site, Petersburg 46370
Linn County Historical Museum and Moyer House, Brownsville 41964
Linn County Historical Society Museum, Cedar Rapids 42160
Linn County Museum, Pleasanton 46553
Lisbon Historical Society Museum, Lisbon 44810
Lisle Station Park, Lisle 44812
Litchfield Historical Society Museum, Litchfield 44813
Little Compton Historical Society Museum, Little Compton 44817
Little Falls Historical Museum, Little Falls 44821
Little Traverse Historical Museum, Petoskey 46383
Littleton Historical Museum, Littleton 44828
Livingston County Historical Society Museum, Geneseo 43639
Livingston Depot Center, Livingston 44832
Lockehaven Schoolhouse Museum, Enfield 43190
Lockhouse-Friends of the Delaware Canal, New Hope 45705
Lockwood-Mathews Mansion Museum, Norwalk 46032
Log Cabin Village, Fort Worth 43488
Logan County Historical Society Museum, Bellefontaine 41588
Logan County Museum, Paris 46282
Lombard Historical Museum, Lombard 44848
Lompoc Valley Historical Society Museum, Lompoc 44851
Lon C. Hill Home, Harlingen 43913
Long Branch Historical Museum, Long Branch 44866
Longfellow's Wayside Inn Museum, South Sudbury 47703
Longmont Museum, Longmont 44877
Loop Museum and Art Center, Seagraves 47525
Lopez Island Historical Museum, Lopez Island 44882
Lorenzo State Historic Site, Cazenovia 42145
Los Alamos County Historical Museum, Los Alamos 44888
Los Nogales Museum, Seguin 47560
Lost City Museum, Overton 46224
Lou Holtz and Upper Ohio Valley Hall of Fame, East Liverpool 43055
Loudoun Museum, Leesburg 44710
Louis H. and Lena Firn Grover Museum, Shelbyville 47596
Louisa County Historical Museum, Louisa 44958
Louisiana State Exhibit Museum, Shreveport 47612
Loveland Museum and Gallery, Loveland 44980
Lowell Damon House, Wauwatosa 48466
Lowell National Historical Park, Lowell 44983
Lower Cape Fear Historical Society Museum, Wilmington 48661
Lowndes County Museum, Valdosta 48180
Luckhard Museum - The Indian Mission, Sebewaing 47550
Lummis Home El Alisal, Los Angeles 44925
Luna Mimbres Museum, Deming 42868
Lura Watkins Museum, Middleton 45312
Luther Burbank Home, Santa Rosa 47446
Lyman House Memorial Museum, Hilo 44032
Lynchburg Museum System, Lynchburg 45005
Lynden Pioneer Museum, Lynden 45009
Lyndhurst, Tarrytown 47958
Lyndon B. Johnson National Historical Park, Johnson City 44349
Lynn Museum, Lynn 45011
Lynnhaven House, Virginia Beach 48248
Lyon County Historical Society Museum, Marshall 45179
Lyon County Museum, Emporia 43183
The Lyons Redstone Museum, Lyons 45012
Mabry-Hazen House, Knoxville 44521
McCallum Museum, Sibley 47622
McClurg Mansion, Westfield 48559
McCone County Museum, Circle 42414
McConnell Mansion, Moscow 45518
McCoy House, Lewistown 44734
Macculloch Hall Historical Museum, Morristown 45507
McCutchen Overland Inn, McCutchenville 45023
McDade Museum, McDade 45024
Macedon Historical Society Museum, Macedon 45025
McFaddin-Ward House, Beaumont 41570
McFarland Historical Society Museum, McFarland 45026
Machan Museum, La Grange 44543
Machan Museum, Lagrange 44574
McHenry County Historical Society Museum, Union 48140
McHenry Museum, Modesto 45428
McIntosh County Historical Society Museum, Ashley 41300
Macktown Living History Site and Whitman Trading Post, Rockton 46974
McLean-Alanreed Area Museum, McLean 45039
McLean County Historical Society Museum, Washburn 48326
McLean County Museum of History, Bloomington 41744
McMinn County Living Heritage Museum, Athens 41327
Macon County Museum Complex, Decatur 42833
MacPheadris/Warner House, Portsmouth 46650
McPherson County Old Mill Museum, Lindsborg 44807
McPherson Museum, McPherson 45050
Madam Brett Homestead, Beacon 41553
Madeline Island Historical Museum, La Pointe 44554
Madera County Museum, Madera 45052
Madison County Historical Museum, Edwardsville 43097
Madison County Historical Society Museum, Winterset 48710
Madison Historical Society Museum, Madison 45053
Madison-Morgan Cultural Center Collection, Madison 45055
Magevney House, Memphis 45239
Magnolia Grove-Historic House Museum, Greensboro 43810
Magnolia Manor Museum, Cairo 42026
Magnolia Plantation, Charleston 42223
Magoffin Home, El Paso 43121
Maine Historical Society Museum, Portland 46624
Maine State Museum, Augusta 41390
Maitland Historical Museums, Maitland 45080
The Major General Frederick Funston Boyhood Home and Museum, Iola 44244
Malibu Lagoon Museum, Malibu 45084
Manassas Museum System, Manassas 45090
Manatee Village Historical Park Museum, Bradenton 41862
Manchester Historic Association Museum, Manchester 45098
Manchester Historical Society Museum, Manchester 45094
Manistee County Historical Museum, Manistee 45112
Mansfield Historical Society Museum, Storrs 47836
Maple Valley Historical Museum, Maple Valley 45130
Marathon County Historical Society Museum, Wausau 48464
Marble Historical Museum, Marble 45133
Marble Springs State Historic Farmstead Governor John Sevier Memorial, Knoxville 44522
Marblehead Historical Museum and J.O.J. Frost Folk Art Gallery, Marblehead 45136
Marcellus Historical Society Museum, Marcellus 45139
Marianna-Lee County Museum, Marianna 45141
Marias Museum of History and Art, Shelby 47594
Marietta House Museum, Glenn Dale 43691
Marietta Museum of History, Marietta 45144
Marilla Historical Society Museum, Marilla 45152
Marin History Museum, San Rafael 47375
Marinette County Historical Museum, Marinette 45154
Marion County Historical Society Museum, Marion 45163
Marion County Historical Society Museum, Salem 47209
Marion Heritage Center, Marion 45156
Marion Public Library Museum, Marion 45158
Marlboro County Historical Museum, Bennettsville 41628
Marlboro Museum, Marlboro 45170
Marquette County History Museum, Marquette 45173
Marquette County Museum, Westfield 48560
Marshall County Historical Museum, Plymouth 46558
Marshall County Museum, Marshalltown 45185
Marston House, San Diego 47278
Martha Berry Museum, Rome 46994
Martha's Vineyard Historical Society Exhibition, Edgartown 43082
Martin County Historical Museum, Stanton 47776
Marvin Newton House, Brookfield 41930
Mary Ball Washington Museum, Lancaster 44631
Mary McLeod Bethune House, Washington 48368
Mary Washington House, Fredericksburg 43539
Maryland Historical Society Museum, Baltimore 41477
Marymoor Museum of Eastside History, Redmond 46825
Mason County Museum, Mason 45199
Mason County Museum, Maysville 45208
The Masonic Library and Museum of Pennsylvania, Philadelphia 46426
Matagorda County Museum, Bay City 41544
Matheson Museum, Gainesville 43582
Mathias Ham House, Dubuque 42992
Mattapoisett Museum and Carriage House, Mattapoisett 45204
Matthews Museum of Maine Heritage, Union 48142
Matt's Museum, Lawtell 44694
Maturango Museum of the Indian Wells Valley, Ridgecrest 46895
May Museum and Park, Farmville 43303
Mayflower Society Museum, Plymouth 46560
Maymont, Richmond 46882
Mayville Area Museum of History and Genealogy, Mayville 45209
Mayville Historical Society Museum, Mayville 45211
Mazomanie Historical Society Museum, Mazomanie 45212
Meade County Historical Society Museum, Meade 45213
Meadow Brook Hall, Rochester 46934
Meadowcroft Museum of Rural Life, Avella 41427
Meadowlands Museum, Rutherford 47040
Meagher County Historical Association Castle Museum, White Sulphur Springs 48591
Mecosta County Historical Museum, Big Rapids 41682
Meeker County Museum and G.A.R. Hall, Litchfield 44815
Meeker Home Museum, Greeley 43785
Meeteetse Museums, Meeteetse 45228
Meigs County Museum, Pomeroy 46580
Mellette House, Watertown 48445
Mem-Erie Historical Museum, Erie 43199
Memorial Hall Museum, Deerfield 42850
Memorial Museum, Ada 41063
Memory Lane Museum at Seattle Goodwill, Seattle 47538
Mendocino County Museum, Willits 48641
Mennonite Heritage Center, Harleysville 43912
Menominee County Heritage Museum, Menominee 45253
Mentor Graham Museum, Blunt 41761
Merced County Courthouse Museum, Merced 45260
Mercer County Genealogical and Historical Society Museum, Princeton 46699
Mercer County Historical Museum, Celina 42165
Mercer County Museum, Mercer 45261
Meriden Historical Society Museum, Meriden 45263
Meriwether Lewis Dredge Museum, Brownville 41967
Merrill Historical Museum, Merrill 45267
Merrill Museum, Carrollton 42113
Miami County Museum, Peru 46364
Michel Brouillet House and Museum, Vincennes 48240
Michigan Historical Museum, Lansing 44643
Middle Border Museum of American Indian and Pioneer Life, Mitchell 45414
Middleborough Historical Museum, Middleborough 45304
Middlebury Historical Society Museum, Wyoming 48769
Middlesex Canal Collection, Lowell 44985
Middlesex County Historical Society Museum, Middletown 45315
Middletown Valley Historical Society Museum, Middletown 45316
Midland County Historical Museum, Midland 45322
Midland County Historical Museum, Midland 45327
Midway Museum, Midway 45332
Milam County Historical Museum, Cameron 42067
Milan Historical Museum, Milan 45334
Milford Historical Museum, Milford 45340
Milford Historical Society Museum, Milford 45338
Milford Museum, Milford 45339
Mill Race Historical Village, Northville 46030
Millard Fillmore House, East Aurora 43036
Miller Art Center, Springfield 47760
Miller-Cory House Museum, Westfield 48558
Miller House Museum, Hagerstown 43866
Mills County Museum, Glenwood 43698
Milton Historical Museum, Milton 45356
Milwaukee County Historical Society Museum, Milwaukee 45367
Mineral County Museum, Superior 47888
Minisink Valley Historical Society Museum, Port Jervis 46599
Minnilusa Pioneer Museum, Rapid City 46796
Mission Bell Museum, Coweta 42684
Mission Inn Museum, Riverside 46920
Mission Mill Museum, Salem 47210
Mission San Juan Capistrano Museum, San Juan Capistrano 47360
Mission San Luis Rey Museum, Oceanside 46089
Missisquoi Valley Historical Society Museum, North Troy 46009
Mississippi River Museum at Mud Island River Park, Memphis 45245
Mitchell County Historical Museum, Osage 46200
Modoc County Historical Museum, Alturas 41159
Moffatt-Ladd House, Portsmouth 46651
Mohave Museum of History and Arts, Kingman 44488
Mohonk Preserve, Gardiner 43622
Mondak Heritage Historical Museum and Art Gallery, Sidney 47624
The Monhegan Museum, Monhegan 45432
Monmouth County Historical Museum, Freehold 43547
Monmouth Museum, Lincroft 44801
Monroe County Heritage Museum, Monroeville 45447
Monroe County Historical Museum, Monroe 45443
Monroe County Historical Society, Bloomington 41747
Monroe County Local History Room and Library, Sparta 47714
Monroe Historical Society Museum, Monroe 45438
Montague Museum, Montague 45448
Montana Historical Society Museum, Helena 43984
Montclair Historical Society Museum, Montclair 45451
Monterey History and Art Association Museum, Monterey 45455
Montgomery County Historical Society Center, Dayton 42803
Montgomery County Historical Society Museum, Rockville 46977
Montgomery Museum and Lewis Miller Regional Art Center, Christiansburg 42391
Montrose County Historical Museum, Montrose 45482
Montville Township Historical Museum, Montville 45485
Moody County Museum, Flandreau 43334
Moore County Historical Museum, Dumas 43005
Moravian Museum of Bethlehem, Bethlehem 41668
Morgan Row Museum, Harrodsburg 43932
The Morris Museum, Morristown 45508
Morton Grove Historical Museum, Morton Grove 45516
Morton Homestead, Prospect Park 46711
Morton House Museum, Benton Harbor 41633
Morton Museum of Cooke County, Gainesville 43590
Moses Lake Museum and Art Center, Moses Lake 45520
Moses Myers House, Norfolk 45968
Mount Airy Museum of Regional History, Mount Airy 45523
Mount Desert Island Historical Museum, Somesville 47674
Mount Pleasant Historical Society Museum, Mount Pleasant 45538
Mount Prospect Historical Society Museums, Mount Prospect 45541
Mount Vernon Hotel Museum, New York 45836
Mountain Gateway Museum, Old Fort 46132
Murray-Lindsay Mansion, Lindsay 44805
Murrell Home, Tahlequah 47926
The Museum, Greenwood 43837
Museum of Amana History, Amana 41163
Museum of Anthracite Mining, Ashland 41298
Museum of Appalachia, Norris 45977
The Museum of Arts and Sciences, Daytona Beach 42811
Museum of Bronx History, Bronx 41923
Museum of Central Connecticut State University, New Britain 45673
The Museum of Clallam County Historical Society, Port Angeles 46588
Museum of Early Trades and Crafts, Madison 45063
Museum of History and Art, Morehead City 45496
Museum of History and Art, Ontario 46163
Museum of Maryland History, Baltimore 41483
Museum of Migrating People, Bronx 41924
Museum of Mobile, Mobile 45422
Museum of New Hampshire History, Concord 42605
The Museum of Newport History, Newport 45926
Museum of North Idaho, Coeur d'Alene 42511
Museum of Northern Arizona, Flagstaff 43329
Museum of Northwest Colorado, Craig 42687
Museum of Orient and East Marion History, Orient 46181
Museum of Seminole County History, Sanford 47393
The Museum of Southern History, Sugarland 47870
Museum of Surveying, Lansing 44644
Museum of Texas Tech University, Lubbock 44991
Museum of the Bedford Historical Society, Bedford 41580
Museum of the Berkeley Springs, Berkeley Springs 41650
Museum of the Big Bend, Alpine 41155
Museum of the Cherokee Strip, Enid 43192
Museum of the City of Lake Worth, Lake Worth 44598
Museum of the City of New York, New York 45847
Museum of the Great Plains, Lawton 44695
Museum of the Gulf Coast, Port Arthur 46590

Museum of the Historical Society of Trappe, Collegeville, Perkiomen Valley, Trappe 48048
Museum of the Llano Estacado, Plainview 46540
Museum of the Rockies, Bozeman 41858
The Museum of the South Dakota State Historical Society, Pierre 46484
Museum of the Southwest, Midland 45328
Museum of the Waxhaws and Andrew Jackson Memorial, Waxhaw 48471
Museum of the Weathersfield Historical Society, Weathersfield 48485
Museum of the Western Prairie, Altus 41160
Museum of the Weston Historical Society, Weston 48569
Museum of Western Colorado, Grand Junction 43748
Museum of Yarmouth History, Yarmouth 48778
Museum of York County, Rock Hill 46950
Museum Village, Monroe 45445
The Museums of Oglebay Institute, Wheeling 48587
Muskegon County Museum, Muskegon 45578
Musselshell Valley Historical Museum, Roundup 47019
Nantucket Historical Association Museum, Nantucket 45598
Napa Valley Museum, Yountville 48809
Narcissa Prentiss House, Prattsburgh 46687
Narragansett Historical Society Museum, Templeton 47978
Nathan Denison House, Forty Fort 43493
Nathaniel W. Faison Home and Museum, La Grange 44546
National Historic Oregon Trail Interpretive Center, Baker City 41437
National McKinley Birthplace Memorial, Niles 45955
National Route 66 Museum and Old Town Museum, Elk City 43135
National Steinbeck Center, Salinas 47216
National Women's Hall of Fame, Seneca Falls 47566
Nauvoo Historical Society Museum, Nauvoo 45639
Navarro County Historical Society Museum, Corsicana 42650
Nebraska Prairie Museum, Holdrege 44051
Neill-Cochran Museum House, Austin 41418
Neill Museum, Fort Davis 43385
Nemours Mansion and Gardens, Wilmington 48654
Neptune Township Historical Museum, Neptune 45651
Netherland Inn House Museum, Kingsport 44491
Nevada County Historical Society Museum, Nevada City 45655
Nevada State Museum, Las Vegas 44673
Neversink Valley Area Museum, Cuddebackville 42718
Neville Public Museum of Brown County, Green Bay 43792
New Bedford Whaling Museum, New Bedford 45662
The New Berlin Historical Society Museum, New Berlin 45664
New Braunfels Conservation Society Museum, New Braunfels 45669
New Canaan Historical Society Museum, New Canaan 45680
New Castle Historical Society Museum, New Castle 45683
New England Fire and History Museum, Brewster 41883
New Hampshire Antiquarian Society Museum, Hopkinton 44101
New Haven Colony Historical Society Museum, New Haven 45697
New Jersey Historical Society Museum, Newark 45891
New London County Historical Society Museum, New London 45711
New London Historical Society Museum, New London 45713
New London Public Museum, New London 45714
New Milford Historical Society Museum, New Milford 45717
New Sweden Historical Museum, New Sweden 45747
New Windsor Cantonment State Historic Site and National Purple Heart Hall of Honor, Vails Gate 48177
The New York Historical Society Museum, New York 45858
Newaygo County Museum, Newaygo 45902
Newell Museum, Newell 45915
Newport Mansions, Newport 45931
Newport State Park, Ellison Bay 43161
Newsome House Museum, Newport News 45938
Newton Museum, Newton 45942
Newtown Historic Museum, Newtown 45949
Nez Perce County Museum, Lewiston 44727
Niagara County Historical Center, Lockport 44842
Nici Self Museum, Centennial 42166
Ninety-Six National Historic Site, Ninety-Six 45956
Nishna Heritage Museum, Oakland 46071
No Man's Land Historical Museum, Goodwell 43728
Noah Webster House - Museum of West Hartford History, West Hartford 48527
Noank Historical Society Museum, Noank 45957
Nobleboro Historical Society Museum, Nobleboro 45958
Nordic Heritage Museum, Seattle 47541
Nordica Homestead Museum, Farmington 43298
Norfolk Historical Museum, Norfolk 45962
Norfolk Historical Society Museum, Norfolk 45970
Norman Cleveland County Historical Museum, Norman 45975
North Andover Historical Museum, North Andover 45979
North Castle Historical Society Museum, Armonk 41269
North Haven Historical Society Museum, North Haven 45995
North House Museum, Lewisburg 44726
North Lee County Historic Center and Santa Fe Depot Museum Complex, Fort Madison 43425
North Platte Valley Museum, Gering 43656
Northampton County Historical and Genealogical Society Museum, Easton 43070
Northborough Historical Museum, Northborough 46017
Northeast Mississippi Museum, Corinth 42634
Northeast Oakland Historical Museum, Oxford 46237
Northfield Historical Society Museum, Northfield 46021
Northland Historical Society Museum, Lake Tomahawk 44595
Northport Historical Society Museum, Northport 46027
The Northumberland County Historical Society Museum, Sunbury 47882
Northwest Museum of Arts and Culture, Spokane 47728
Norwich Historical Society Museum, Norwich 46042
Norwood Historical Association Museum, Norwood 46043
Novato History Museum, Novato 46046
Nowata County Historical Society Museum, Nowata 46047
O. Henry Home and Museum, Austin 41419
Oak Creek Pioneer Village, Oak Creek 46051
Oakdale Museum, Oakdale 46058
Oaklands Historic House Museum, Murfreesboro 45568
Oakleigh House, Mobile 45423
Oakley Pioneer Museum, Oakley 46073
Oatlands Plantation, Leesburg 44712
Oberlin Historical and Improvement Organization Museum, Oberlin 46077
Ocean City Historical Museum, Ocean City 46085
Ocean County Historical Museum, Toms River 48026
Oconto County Historical Society Museum, Oconto 46091
The Octagon House, Hudson 44145
Octagon House, Watertown 48446
Ogden Historical Society Museum, Spencerport 47723
Ogden House, Fairfield 43264
Ogden Union Station Museums, Ogden 46100
Ohio River Museum, Marietta 45151
Ojai Valley Museum, Ojai 46108
Okefenokee Heritage Center, Waycross 48472
Oklahoma Museum of History, Oklahoma City 46121
Oklahoma Route 66 Museum, Clinton 42500
Olana State Historic Site, Hudson 44143
Old Atwood House Museum, Chatham 42256
Old Bethpage Village Restoration, Old Bethpage 46129
Old Bohemia Historical Museum, Warwick 48319
Old Brown's Mill School, Chambersburg 42185
Old Brutus Historical Society Museum, Weedsport 48490
Old City Park - The Historical Village of Dallas, Dallas 42756
Old Conway Homestead Museum and Mary Meeker Cramer Museum, Camden 42058
Old Court House Museum-Eva Whitaker Davis Memorial, Vicksburg 48229
Old Courthouse Heritage Museum, Inverness 44242
Old Courthouse Museum, Santa Ana 47400
Old Cowtown Museum, Wichita 48607
Old Dorchester State Historic Site, Summerville 47876
Old Dutch Parsonage, Somerville 47672
Old Economy Village Museum, Ambridge 41168
Old Exchange and Provost Dungeon, Charleston 42225
Old Falls Village, Menomonee Falls 45254
Old Fort Bissell, Phillipsburg 46468
Old Fort Harrod Museum, Harrodsburg 43933
Old Fort Harrod State Park Mansion Museum, Harrodsburg 43934
Old Fort House Museum, Fort Edward 43392
Old Fort Johnson, Fort Johnson 43404
Old Fort Lauderdale Museum of History, Fort Lauderdale 43413
Old Fort Number 4 Associates, Charlestown 42234
The Old Governor's Mansion, Frankfort 43513
Old Greer County Museum and Hall of Fame, Mangum 45103
Old Iron County Courthouse Museum, Hurley 44178
The Old Jail Museum, Warrenton 48317
Old Jefferson Town, Oskaloosa 46209
Old Lighthouse Museum, Stonington 47829
Old Lincoln County Courthouse Museum, Lincoln 44796
Old Mill Museum, Cimarron 42395
Old Mill Museum, San Marino 47367
Old Salem, Winston-Salem 48702
Old Shawnee Town, Shawnee 47587
Old Stone Fort Museum Complex, Schoharie 47499
The Old Stone House, Washington 48388
The Old Stone House Museum, Brownington 41962
Old Stone House Museum, Windsor 48684
The Old Stone Jail Museum, Palmyra 46272
Old Sturbridge Village, Sturbridge 47859
The Old Tavern Museum, Tuscaloosa 48115
Old Town Hall Museum, Fifield 43319
Old Town Museum, Old Town 46135
Old Town San Diego, San Diego 47284
Old Village Hall Museum, Lindenhurst 44804
Old West Museum, Sunset 47887
Old Westbury Gardens, Old Westbury 46136
Old York Historical Museum, York 48792
Oldest Stone House Museum, Lakewood 44611
Oldham County History Center, La Grange 44544
Oliver House Museum, Penn Yan 46340
Oliver Kelley Farm, Elk River 43138
Oliver Tucker Historic Museum, Beverly 41672
Olmstead Place State Park, Ellensburg 43151
Oneida Community Mansion House, Oneida 46157
Oneida County Historical Society Museum, Utica 48171
Onondaga Historical Association Museum, Syracuse 47912
Onslow County Museum, Richlands 46857
Ontario County Historical Society Museum, Canandaigua 42077
Ontonagon County Historical Society Museum, Ontonagon 46167
Opelousas Museum, Opelousas 46168
Opus 40 and the Quarryman's Museum, Saugerties 47465
Orange County Historical Museum, Hillsborough 44030
Orange County Regional History Center, Orlando 46187
Orangetown Historical Museum, Pearl River 46323
Orcas Island Historical Museum, Eastsound 43071
Orchard Park Historical Society Museum, Orchard Park 46178
Oregon History Center, Portland 46637
Oregon-Jerusalem Historical Museum, Oregon 46179
Oregon Trail Museum, Gering 43657
Orland Historical Museum, Orland 46184
Oroville Chinese Temple, Oroville 46198
Osage County Historical Society, Lyndon 45010
Osage County Historical Society Museum, Pawhuska 46314
Osborn-Jackson House, East Hampton 43049
Oscar Anderson House Museum, Anchorage 41201
Oshkosh Public Museum, Oshkosh 46206
Ossining Historical Society Museum, Ossining 46212
Osterville Historical Museum, Osterville 46213
Oswego Historical Museum, Oswego 46214
Otoe County Museum of Memories, Syracuse 47905
Ottawa County Historical Museum, Port Clinton 46592
Otter Tail County Historical Museum, Fergus Falls 43313
Outagamie Museum and Houdini Historical Center, Appleton 41240
Overfield Tavern Museum, Troy 48073
Overholser Mansion, Oklahoma City 46122
Overland Trail Museum, Sterling 47803
Owensboro Area Museum of Science and History, Owensboro 46229
Owyhee County Historical Museum, Murphy 45570
Oxford Library Museum, Oxford 46235
Oxford Museum, Oxford 46236
Ozaukee County Historical Society Pioneer Village, Saukville 47468
Pacem in Terris, Warwick 48320
Pacific County Historical Museum, South Bend 47684
Packwood House Museum, Lewisburg 44722
Pajaro Valley Historical Museum, Watsonville 48456
Palace of the Governors, Santa Fe 47429
Palmer/Gullickson Octagon Home, West Salem 48546
Palmer House, Northfield 46024
Panhandle-Plains Historical Museum, Canyon 42092
Parishville Museum, Parishville 46287
Park City Museum, Park City 46289
Parris Island Museum, Parris Island 46296
Parsons Historical Society Museum, Parsons 46299
Parsonsfield-Porter History House, Porter 46619
Pasadena Historical Museum, Pasadena 46305
Pascack Historical Society Museum, Park Ridge 46293
Passaic County Historical Society Museum, Paterson 46310
Paterson Museum, Paterson 46311
Paul Laurence Dunbar State Memorial, Dayton 42805
Pawnee City Historical Society Museum, Pawnee City 46317
Peabody Essex Museum, Salem 47198
Pebble Hill Plantation, Thomasville 48001
Peekskill Museum, Peekskill 46327
Pejepscot Historical Society Museum, Brunswick 41973
Pella Historical Village, Pella 46329
Pembroke Historical Museum, Pembroke 46333
Pendarvis, Mineral Point 45379
Pennsbury Manor, Morrisville 45514
Pennyroyal Area Museum, Hopkinsville 44100
Pensacola Historical Museum, Pensacola 46344
Perkins County Historical Society Museum, Grant 43766
Peshtigo Fire Museum, Peshtigo 46365
Peter Conser House, Heavener 43980
Peter Rice Homestead, Marlboro 45168
Peter Wentz Farmstead, Worcester 48759
Peter Whitmer Sr. Home and Visitors Center, Waterloo 48437
Peter Yegen Jr. Yellowstone County Museum, Billings 41690
Peterborough Historical Society Museum, Peterborough 46368
The Petersburg Museums, Petersburg 46376
Petersham Historical Museum, Petersham 46381
Pettaquamscutt Museum, Kingston 44497
Pettis County Historical Society Museum, Sedalia 47555
P.H. Sullivan Museum and Genealogy Library, Zionsville 48825
Phi Kappa Psi Fraternity-Heritage Hall, Indianapolis 44233
Phillips County Museum, Helena 43982
Phillips County Museum, Holyoke 44064
Phillips Historical Society Museum, Phillips 46467
The Philmont Museum, Seton Memorial Library and Kit Carson Museum, Cimarron 42396
Phoenix Museum of History, Phoenix 46478
Piatt Castles, West Liberty 48533
Piatt County Museum, Monticello 45473
Pickens County Museum of Art History, Pickens 46481
Pike County Museum, Milford 45343
Pilgrim Hall Museum, Plymouth 46561
Pilgrim Monument and Provincetown Museum, Provincetown 46729
Pimeria Alta Historical Society Museum, Nogales 45960
Pine County Historical Society Museum, Askov 41304
Pine Grove Historic Museum, Pontiac 46585
Pinecrest Historical Village, Manitowoc 45115
Pioneer Corner Museum, New Holstein 45704
Pioneer Farm Museum and Ohop Indian Village, Eatonville 43073
Pioneer Heritage Center, Cavalier 42143
Pioneer-Krier Museum, Ashland 41285
Pioneer-Krier Museum, Ashland 41286
Pioneer Museum, Fabius 43256
Pioneer Museum, Fairmont 43272
Pioneer Museum, Wild Rose 48619
Pioneer Museum and Vereins Kirche, Fredericksburg 43532
Pioneer Museum of Alabama, Troy 48067
Pioneer Town, Wimberley 48674
Pioneer Village, Farmington 43302
Pittock Mansion, Portland 46640
Pittsford Historical Society Museum, Pittsford 46536
Plains Indians and Pioneers Museum, Woodward 48748
Plainsman Museum, Aurora 41401
Plantation Agriculture Museum, Scott 47509
Plantation Historical Museum, Plantation 46543
Plumas County Museum, Quincy 46756
Plymouth Antiquarian Society Museum, Plymouth 46563
Plymouth Historical Museum, Plymouth 46565
Pocahontas County Iowa Historical Society Museum, Laurens 44680
Pocahontas County Museum, Marlinton 45172
Point of Honor, Lynchburg 45007
Polk County Historical Museum, Cedartown 42164
Polk County Historical Museum, Crookston 42706
Polk County Historical Museum, Osceola 46202
Polk County Historical Society, Des Moines 42908
Polk County Memorial Museum, Livingston 44835
Polk County Museum, Balsam Lake 41446
Polson Park and Museum, Hoquiam 44102
Pony Express Museum, Saint Joseph 47108
Pope County Historical Museum, Glenwood 43699
Pope's Tavern Museum, Florence 43344
Poplar Grove Historic Plantation, Wilmington 48662
Port Gamble Historic Museum, Port Gamble 46593
Port Huron Museum, Port Huron 46597
Portage County Historical Society Museum, Ravenna 46800
Portage County Museum, Stevens Point 47808
La Porte County Historical Society Museum, La Porte 44555
Porter County Old Jail Museum, Valparaiso 48193
Portland Children's Museum Second Generation, Portland 46642
Portland Museum, Louisville 44974
Portsmouth Museum, Portsmouth 46658
Potsdam Public Museum, Potsdam 46669
Potter County Historical Society Museum, Coudersport 42671
Potts Inn Museum, Pottsville 46672
Pottsgrove Manor, Pottstown 46671
Pound Ridge Museum, Pound Ridge 46679
Powder Magazine, Charleston 42226
Powell County Museum, Deer Lodge 42848
Powers Museum, Carthage 42126
Prairie County Museum, Des Arc 42904
Prairie Homestead, Philip 46465
The Prairie Museum of Art and History, Colby 42517
Prairie Trails Museum of Wayne County, Corydon 42661
Prairie Village, Madison 45064
Pratt County Historical Society Museum, Pratt 46686
Pratt Museum, Homer 44068
President Chester A. Arthur Historic Site, Fairfield 43270
President's Cottage Museum, White Sulphur Springs 48592
Presque Isle County Historical Museum, Rogers City 46987
Prestwould Foundation, Clarksville 42438
Pricketts Fort, Fairmont 43273
Princeton Museum, Princeton 46702
Promont House Museum, Milford 45342

Prouty-Chew Museum, Geneva 43642
Provincetown Heritage Museum, Provincetown 46731
Public Museum of Grand Rapids, Grand Rapids 43759
Pueblo County Historical Society Museum, Pueblo 46739
La Puente Valley Historical Society Museum, La Puente 44558
Putnam Cottage, Greenwich 43833
Putnam County Historical Society and Foundry School Museum, Cold Spring 42518
Putnam County Historical Society Museum, Kalida 44382
Putney Historical Society Museum, Putney 46749
Queens Historical Museum, Flushing 43356
Quincy and Adams County Museum, Quincy 46759
Quincy Historical Museum, Quincy 46765
The Quincy Museum, Quincy 46761
Rachel Carson Homestead, Springdale 47734
Railroad House Historical Museum, Sanford 47396
Raleigh City Museum, Raleigh 46779
Ralls Historical Museum, Ralls 46781
Ralph Foster Museum, Point Lookout 46573
Ramsay House, Alexandria 41133
Ramsey House Museum Plantation, Knoxville 44523
Rancho Los Alamitos, Long Beach 44863
Rancho Los Cerritos, Long Beach 44864
Randall Library Museum, Stow 47841
Randolph County Historical Museum, Winchester 48676
Randolph County Museum, Beverly 41674
Randolph Historical Society Museum, Randolph 46791
Rankin House State Memorial, Ripley 46904
Rankin Museum, Rankin 46792
Ransom County Historical Society Museum, Fort Ransom 43446
Raton Museum, Raton 46799
Ravalli County Museum, Hamilton 43877
Rawhide Old West Museum, Scottsdale 47513
Ray E. Powell Museum, Grandview 43764
Raynham Hall Museum, Oyster Bay 46249
Rea Museum, Murfreesboro 45566
Reading Historical Society Museum, Reading 46805
Reading Historical Society Museum, Reading 46810
Readsboro Historical Society Museum, Readsboro 46812
Red Barn Museum, Morristown 45511
Red Clay State Historical Park, Cleveland 42486
Red Hill-Patrick Henry National Memorial, Brookneal 41955
Red Mill Museum Village, Clinton 42498
Red River and Northern Plains Regional Museum, West Fargo 48522
Red River Historical Society Museum, Clay City 42440
Redington Museum, Waterville 48448
Refugio County Museum, Refugio 46829
Regional Museum of Spartanburg County, Spartanburg 47716
Reitz Home Museum, Evansville 43246
Remick Country Doctor Museum and Farm, Tamworth 47948
Reno County Museum, Hutchinson 44184
Rensselaer County Historical Society Museum, Troy 48071
Renton Museum, Renton 46841
Renville County Historical Society Museum, Mohall 45429
Republic County Historical Society Museum, Belleville 41591
Reynolds Homestead, Critz 42703
Rhode Island Black Heritage Society Museum, Providence 46725
Rhode Island Historical Society Exhibition, Providence 46726
Rialto Museum, Rialto 46850
Rice County Museum of History, Faribault 43294
Richard Salter Storrs House, Longmeadow 44876
Richardson-Bates House Museum, Oswego 46216
Richey Historical Museum, Richey 46851
Richey Historical Society, Richey 46852
Richland County Historical Museum, Wahpeton 48274
Richland County Museum, Lexington 44755
Richmond Museum of History, Richmond 46860
Rifle Creek Museum, Rifle 46900
Riley County Historical Museum, Manhattan 45110
Rimrocker Historical Museum of West Montrose County, Naturita 45637
Rio Grande Valley Museum, Harlingen 43914
Riordan Mansion, Flagstaff 43331
Ripley County Historical Society Museum, Versailles 48224
Ripon Historical Society Museum, Ripon 46907
Rittman Historical Society Museum, Rittman 46908
River Museum, Wellsville 48502
Riverdale Mansion, Riverdale Park 46913
Riverside Municipal Museum, Riverside 46922
Riverside Museum, La Crosse 44538
Riverton Museum, Riverton 46925
Riverview at Hobson Grove, Bowling Green 41851
Robbins Hunter Museum, Granville 43774
Robert E. Lee Memorial Association, Stratford 47851
Robert Mills Historic House and Park, Columbia 42565
Robert Newell House, Saint Paul 47168
Robert S. Kerr Museum, Poteau 46668
Roberts County Museum, Miami 45296
Rochester Hills Museum at Van Hoosen Farm, Rochester Hills 46949
Rochester Historical Society Museum, Rochester 46943
Rock County Historical Society Museum, Janesville 44319
Rock Creek Station State Historic Park, Fairbury 43259
Rock House Museum, Wytheville 48770
Rock Island County Historical Museum, Moline 45431
Rock Springs Historical Museum, Rock Springs 46958
Rockbridge Historical Society Museum, Lexington 44762
Rockingham Free Museum, Bellows Falls 41606
Rockland County Museum, New City 45687
Rockwood Museum, Wilmington 48655
Rocky Ford Historical Museum, Rocky Ford 46979
Rocky Mount Museum, Piney Flats 46495
Roger Williams National Memorial, Providence 46727
Rogers Historical Museum, Rogers 46985
Rokeby Museum, Ferrisburgh 43316
Rollo Jamison Museum, Platteville 46546
Rome Historical Society Museum, Rome 46998
Roosevelt County Museum, Portales 46618
Root House Museum, Marietta 45146
Rose Center Museum, Morristown 45513
Rose Hill Mansion, Geneva 43643
Rose Hill Museum, Bay Village 41548
Rosebud County Pioneer Museum, Forsyth 43364
Rosemount Museum, Pueblo 46740
Ross County Historical Society Museum, Chillicothe 42381
Roswell Museum and Art Center, Roswell 47016
The Rotunda, Charlottesville 42250
Rowley Historical Museum, Rowley 47021
Roxbury Historical Museum, Roxbury 47023
Royal Arts Foundation, Newport 45933
The Royal Governor's Mansion, Perth Amboy 46361
Royalton Historical Society Museum, Royalton 47026
R.P. Strathearn Historical Park, Simi 47636
Ruddick's Folly, Suffolk 47867
Rundlet-May House, Portsmouth 46653
Rural Life Museum and Windrush Gardens, Baton Rouge 41534
Rush County Historical Society Museum, Rushville 47031
Rusk County Historical Society Museum, Ladysmith 44565
Rye Historical Society Museum, Rye 47043
Sachem Historical Society Museum, Holbrook 44049
Sacramento Mountains Historical Museum, Cloudcroft 42504
Safety Harbor Museum of Regional History, Safety Harbor 47058
Saguache County Museum, Saguache 47064
Saint Albans Historical Museum, Saint Albans 47065
Saint Augustine Historical Society Museum, Saint Augustine 47071
Saint Charles County Museum, Saint Charles 47081
Saint Charles Heritage Center, Saint Charles 47077
Saint Clair County Historical Museum, Belleville 41590
Saint James' House, Fredericksburg 43542
Saint John's Church and Parish Museum, Hampton 43897
Saint Louis County Historical Museum, Duluth 43002
Saint Lucie County Historical Museum, Fort Pierce 43441
Saint Marys and Benzinger Township Museum, Saint Marys 47145
Saint Paul Museum, Randleman 46788
Saint Petersburg Museum of History, Saint Petersburg 47175
Saint Simons Island Lighthouse Museum, Saint Simons Island 47182
Sainte Genevieve Museum, Sainte Genevieve 47185
Sainte Marie among the Iroquois, Liverpool 44830
Salem 1630 Pioneer Village, Salem 47200
Salem County Historical Society Museum, Salem 47204
Salem Historical Society Museum, Salem 47205
Salem Museum, Salem 47211
Salida Museum, Salida 47212
Saline County Historical Society Museum, Dorchester 42959
Salisbury Historical Society Museum, Salisbury 47222
Salisbury Mansion, Worcester 48755
Salmon Brook Historical Society Museum, Granby 43739
Sam Houston Historical Schoolhouse, Maryville 45198
The Sam Rayburn Museum, Bonham 41780
Samuel F.B. Morse Historic Site, Poughkeepsie 46677
San Antonio Missions Visitor Center, San Antonio 47259
San Buenaventura Mission Museum, Ventura 48209
San Diego Historical Society Museum, San Diego 47289
San Dieguito Heritage Museum, Encinitas 43187
San Fernando Historical Museum, Mission Hills 45400
San Jacinto Museum, San Jacinto 47348
San Joaquin County Historical Museum, Lodi 44843
San Juan Bautista State Historic Park, San Juan Bautista 47359
San Juan County Historical Museum, Silverton 47635
San Juan County Museum, Bloomfield 41735
San Juan Historical Society Museum, Friday Harbor 43561
San Luis Obispo County Historical Museum, San Luis Obispo 47363
San Mateo County Historical Museum, Redwood City 46826
Sanchez Adobe Historic Site, Pacifica 46255
Sand Springs Cultural and Historical Museum, Sand Springs 47378
Sandown Historical Museum, Sandown 47381
Sandpoint Lighthouse, Escanaba 43206
Sands-Willets House, Port Washington 46611
Sandwich Historical Society Museum, Center Sandwich 42168
Sandwich Historical Society Museum, Sandwich 47385
Sandy Bay Historical Museums, Rockport 46970
Sandy Spring Museum, Sandy Spring 47392
Sanford Museum, Cherokee 42274
Sanford Museum, Sanford 47394
Sanilac County Historical Museum, Port Sanilac 46603
Santa Barbara Historical Museum, Santa Barbara 47403
Santa Fe Trail Museum, Larned 44656
Santa Fe Trail Museums of Gray County, Ingalls 44236
Santa Maria Valley Historical Society Museum, Santa Maria 47437
Sapulpa Historical Museum, Sapulpa 47449
Saratoga Museum, Saratoga 47458
Saratoga Springs Museum, Saratoga Springs 47462
Sarpy County Historical Museum, Bellevue 41594
Satterlee Clark House, Horicon 44103
Sauk County Historical Museum, Baraboo 41502
Sauk Prairie Area Historical Society Museum, Prairie du Sac 46685
Saunders County Historical Museum, Wahoo 48273
Sawin Memorial Building, Dover 42971
Sawyer's Sandhills Museum, Valentine 48184
Sayville Historical Society Museum, Sayville 47490
Scantic Academy Museum, East Windsor 43064
Scarborough Historical Museum, Scarborough 47491
Scarsdale Historical Society Museum, Scarsdale 47492
Schenectady County Historical Society Museum, Schenectady 47497
Schenectady Museum, Schenectady 47498
Schminck Memorial Museum, Lakeview 44607
Schoenbrunn Village State Memorial, New Philadelphia 45742
Schoharie Colonial Heritage Association Museum, Schoharie 47500
Schoolhouse Museum, Ridgewood 46899
Schuyler County Historical Society Museum, Montour Falls 45475
Schuyler Jail Museum, Rushville 47030
Schuyler Mansion, Albany 41086
Schwenkfelder Library and Heritage Center, Pennsburg 46341
Science Museum of Minnesota, Saint Paul 47166
Scituate Historical Museum, Scituate 47502
Scotland Heritage Chapel and Museum, Scotland 47508
Scurry County Museum, Snyder 47662
Seaford Historical Museum, Seaford 47524
Searcy County Museum, Marshall 45175
Sedgwick-Brooklin Historical Museum, Sedgwick 47557
Senator George Norris State Historic Site, McCook 45022
Senator John Heinz Pittsburgh Regional History Center, Pittsburgh 46525
Seneca County Museum, Tiffin 48006
Seneca Falls Historical Society Museum, Seneca Falls 47567
Sequoyah Cabin, Sallisaw 47223
Serra Museum, San Diego 47296
Seward County Historical Society Museum, Goehner 43708
Seward House, Auburn 41375
Seward Museum, Seward 47572
Seymour Community Museum, Seymour 47575
Shaftsbury Historical Society Museum, Shaftsbury 47577
Shaker Heritage Society Museum, Albany 41087
Shaker Historical Society Museum, Shaker Heights 47578
Shaker Museum, Old Chatham 46131
Shaker Village of Pleasant Hill, Harrodsburg 43935
Shandy Hall, Geneva 43645
Sharlot Hall Museum, Prescott 46689
Sharpsteen Museum, Calistoga 42034
Shasta College Museum, Redding 46820
Shaw Island Historical Society Museum, Shaw Island 47584
Shawano County Museum, Shawanao 47585
Sheboygan County Historical Museum, Sheboygan 47590
Shelburne Museum, Shelburne 47593
Shelter House, Emmaus 43180
Shelter Island Historical Society Museum, Shelter Island 47599
Shenandoah Valley Folk Art and Heritage Center, Dayton 42808
Sherburne County Historical Museum, Becker 41576
Sherman House, Lancaster 44622
Sherwood-Davidson House, Newark 45897
Sherwood Forest Plantation, Charles City 42202
Shippensburg Historical Society Museum, Shippensburg 47609
Shirley Plantation, Charles City 42203
Shoreline Historical Museum, Seattle 47547
Shorter Mansion Museum, Eufaula 43219
Sibley County Historical Museum, Henderson 43989
Sidney Historical Association Museum, Sidney 47626
Sidney Lanier Cottage, Macon 45047
Silas Wright Jr. Historic House, Canton 42087
Siloam Springs Museum, Siloam Springs 47627
Silver City Museum, Silver City 47629
Silver Cliff Museum, Silver Cliff 47631
Silver River Museum, Ocala 46082
Silvercreek Museum, Freeport 43550
Simon Paneak Memorial Museum, Anaktuvuk Pass 41195
Simsbury Historical Society Museum, Simsbury 47637
Sioux City Public Museum, Sioux City 47639
Siouxland Heritage Museums, Sioux Falls 47646
Siskiyou County Museum, Yreka 48813
Sitka National Historical Park, Sitka 47651
Skagit County Historical Museum, La Conner 44533
Skagway City Museum, Skagway 47652
Skinner Museum of Mount Holyoke College, South Hadley 47694
Slabsides, West Park 48541
Slate Run Living Historical Farm, Ashville 41303
Slate Valley Museum, Granville 43771
Slaughter Ranch Museum, Douglas 42962
Slifer House, Lewisburg 44723
Sloan Museum, Flint 43340
Smith County Historical Society Museum, Tyler 48131
Smith-McDowell House Museum, Asheville 41282
Smith's Fort Plantation, Surry 47896
Smithsonian Institution, Washington 48393
Smithtown Historical Society Museum, Smithtown 47657
Smyth County Museum, Marion 45165
Snake River Heritage Center, Weiser 48492
Snake River Heritage Center, Weiser 48493
Snoqualmie Valley Historical Museum, North Bend 45982
Snug Harbor Cultural Center, Staten Island 47787
The Snyder County Historical Society Museum, Middleburg 45306
Snyder Museum and Creative Arts Center, Bastrop 41519
Sod House Museum, Aline 41139
Sod House Museum, Gothenburg 43734
Sodus Bay Historical Society Museum, Sodus Point 47664
Somers Historical Society Museum, Somers 47667
Somers Mansion, Somers Point 47669
Somerset Historical Center, Somerset 47670
Somerset Place, Creswell 42701
Somervell County Museum, Glen Rose 43685
Somerville Museum, Somerville 47671
Somesville Museum, Mount Desert 45527
Sonoma County Museum, Santa Rosa 47448
Sonoma State Historic Park, Sonoma 47676
Sophienburg Museum, New Braunfels 45670
South Bannock County Historical Center, Lava Hot Springs 44683
South Boston-Halifax County Museum of Fine Arts and History, South Boston 47687
South Carolina State Museum, Columbia 42569
South Charleston Museum, South Charleston 47688
South County Museum, Narragansett 45605
South Florida Museum, Bradenton 41863
South Hero Bicentennial Museum, South Hero 47696
South Holland Historical Museum, South Holland 47697
South Milwaukee Historical Society Museum, South Milwaukee 47698
South Park City Museum, Fairplay 43274
South Pass City State Historic Site, South Pass City 47701
South River Meeting House, Lynchburg 45008
South Texas Museum, Alice 41138
South Wood County Historical Museum, Wisconsin Rapids 48719
Southampton Historical Museum, Southampton 47708
Southeast Museum, Brewster 41884
Southern Oregon Historical Society Museum, Medford 45221
Southold Historical Society Museum, Southold 47710
Space Farms Zoological Park and Museum, Sussex 47897
Spanish Governor's Palace, San Antonio 47261
Spencer-Peirce-Little Farm, Newbury 45907
Spindletop and Gladys City Boomtown Museum, Beaumont 41571
SPLIA Gallery, Cold Spring Harbor 42519
Split Rock Lighthouse Historic Site, Two Harbors 48128
Spotsylvania Historical Museum, Spotsylvania 47729
Spring Mill State Park Pioneer Village and Grissom Memorial, Mitchell 45411
Spring Street Historical Museum, Shreveport 47618
Springfield Historical Society Museum, Springfield 47755
Springfield Museum, Springfield 47758
Springfield Museum of Old Domestic Life, High Point 44016
Springs Museum, Springs 47761
Staatsburgh State Historic Museum, Staatsburg 47765
Stacy's Tavern Museum and Glen Ellyn Historical Society, Glen Ellyn 43682
Stagecoach Inn Museum Complex, Newbury Park 45908
Stamford Historical Society Museum, Stamford 47767
Stanley-Whitman House, Farmington 43297
Stanly County Historic Museum, Albemarle 41093

Stanton County Museum, Pilger 46486
Starved Rock State Park, Utica 48168
State Historical Society of Iowa Museum, Des Moines 42911
State Historical Society of North Dakota Museum, Bismarck 41722
Staten Island Historical Society Museum, Staten Island 47790
Staten Island Institute of Arts and Sciences, Staten Island 47791
Stauth Memorial Museum, Montezuma 45464
Steamboat Dock Museum, Keyport 44472
Steele County Museum, Hope 44096
Steilacoom Historical Museum, Steilacoom 47801
Stengel-True Museum, Marion 45164
Stephens County Historical Society Museum, Duncan 43008
Stephenson County Historical Society Museum, Freeport 43551
Stephenville Museum, Stephenville 47802
Sterling Historical Society Museum, Sterling 47805
Sterling-Rock Falls Historical Society Museum, Sterling 47804
Sterne-Hoya Museum, Nacogdoches 45590
Steuben House Museum, River Edge 46910
Stevens County Historical Society Museum, Morris 45503
Stevens Museum, Salem 47189
Stockholm Historical Society Museum, Stockholm 47822
Stone Fort Museum, Nacogdoches 45591
Stonehouse Museum, Vale 48182
Stoughton Historical Museum, Stoughton 47839
Stow House, Goleta 43721
Stow West 1825 School Museum, Stow 47842
The Stoy Museum of the Lebanon County Historical Society, Lebanon 44705
Stranahan House, Fort Lauderdale 43414
Strasburg Museum, Strasburg 47849
The Stratford Historical Society and Catherine B. Mitchell Museum, Stratford 47850
Strawbery Banke, Portsmouth 46654
Stroud Mansion, Stroudsburg 47856
Stuhr Museum of the Prairie Pioneer, Grand Island 43746
Sturdivant Hall, Selma 47563
Stutsman County Memorial Museum, Jamestown 44308
Suffolk County Historical Society Museum, Riverhead 46916
Suffolk Resolves House, Milton 45354
Sullivan County Historical Society Museum, Hurleyville 44179
Summit County Historical Society Museum, Akron 41075
The Sumter County Museum, Sumter 47879
Sun Prairie Historical Museum, Sun Prairie 47881
Sunnyside Historical Museum, Sunnyside 47884
Sunnyvale Historical Museum, Sunnyvale 47886
Susan B. Anthony House, Rochester 46947
Susquehanna County Historical Society, Montrose 45484
Susquehanna Museum of Havre de Grace, Havre de Grace 43967
Sussex County Historical Society Museum, Newton 45946
Sutter's Fort, Sacramento 47054
Sutton-Ditz House Museum, Clarion 42426
Swarthout Memorial Museum, La Crosse 44539
Sweet Briar Museum, Sweet Briar 47902
Sweetwater County Historical Museum, Green River 43794
Swenson Memorial Museum of Stephens County, Breckenridge 41877
Swift County Historical Museum, Benson 41631
Swisher County Museum, Tulia 48102
Swiss Historical Village, New Glarus 45689
Switzerland County Historical Society Museum, Vevay 48226
Table Rock Historical Society Museum, Table Rock 47914
Talkeetna Historical Society Museum, Talkeetna 47930
Tallahassee Museum of History and Natural Science, Tallahassee 47938
Tama County Historical Museum, Toledo 48017
Tampa Bay History Center, Tampa 47945
Tante Blanche Museum, Madawaska 45051
Taos Historic Museums, Taos 47953
Tappantown Historical Society Museum, Tappan 47954
Tarpon Springs Cultural Center, Tarpon Springs 47956
Tarrytowns Museum, Tarrytown 47959
T.B. Ferguson Home, Watonga 48453
Teackle Mansion, Princess Anne 46694
Temecula Valley Museum, Temecula 47968
Tempe Historical Museum, Tempe 47975
Temperance Tavern, Newcomerstown 45913
Ten Broeck Mansion, Albany 41088
Tenino Depot Museum, Tenino 47980
Terrace Hill Historic Site and Governor's Mansion, Des Moines 42912
Territorial Capital-Lane Museum, Lecompton 44707
Territorial Statehouse State Museum, Fillmore 43321
Territory Town USA, Old West Museum, Okemah 46109
Terwilliger Museum, Waterloo 48438
Teutopolis Monastery Museum, Teutopolis 47989
Texana Museum, Edna 43095
Texarkana Museums System, Texarkana 47991
Texas Governor's Mansion, Austin 41420
The Little Cowboy Bar and Museum, Fromberg 43567
Thetford Historical Society Museum, Thetford 47997
This Is The Place Heritage Park, Salt Lake City 47233
Thomas Clarke House-Princeton Battlefield, Princeton 46706
Thomas-Foreman Home, Muskogee 45583
Thomas Hart Benton Home and Studio, Kansas City 44410
Thomas J. Boyd Museum, Wytheville 48771
Thomas Price House, Woodruff 48734
Thomas T. Taber Museum, Williamsport 48632
Thomas Warne Historical Museum, Old Bridge Township 46130
Thomaston Historical Museum, Thomaston 47999
Thornhill Historic Site and 19th Century Village, Chesterfield 42290
Thornton W. Burgess Museum, Sandwich 47389
Three Rivers Museum, Muskogee 45584
Three Village Historical Society Museum, Setauket 47570
Thronateeska Heritage Foundation, Albany 41082
Thunderbird Museum, Merrillan 45268
Tillamook County Pioneer Museum, Tillamook 48008
Tinley Park Historical Society Museum, Tinley Park 48010
Tintic Mining Museum, Eureka 43234
Tioga County Historical Society Museum, Owego 46226
Tioga Point Museum, Athens 41326
Tippecanoe County Historical Museum, Lafayette 44569
Tipton County Museum, Covington 42683
Tipton-Haynes Museum, Johnson City 44348
Tobacco Farm Life Museum, Kenly 44433
Tobias Community Historical Society Museum, Tobias 48015
Tolland County Jail and Warden's Home Museum, Tolland 48023
Tom Mix Museum, Dewey 42941
Tomball Community Museum Center, Tomball 48024
Tonawandas Museum, Tonawanda 48028
Tongass Historical Museum, Ketchikan 44459
Top of Oklahoma Historical Museum, Blackwell 41730
Toppenish Museum, Toppenish 48036
Topsfield Historical Museum, Topsfield 48037
Torrington Historical Society Museum, Torrington 48040
Town of Clarence Museum, Clarence 42424
Town of Manlius Museum, Manlius 45122
Town of North Hempstead Museum, Westbury 48551
Town of Ontario Historical and Landmark Preservation Society Museum Complex, Ontario 46165
Town of Warwick Museum, Warwick 48321
Traill County Historical Society Museum, Hillsboro 44025
Trapezium House, Petersburg 46379
Travellers Rest Historic House Museum, Nashville 45627
Trenton City Museum, Trenton 48059
Trenton Historical Museum, Trenton 48051
Tri-Cities Museum, Grand Haven 43745
Tri-County Historical Society and Museum, Herington 43999
Troxell-Steckel House and Farm Museum, Egypt 43102
Troy Museum and Historic Village, Troy 48068
Tsa Mo Ga Memorial Museum, Plains 46539
TU-Endie-Wei State Park, Point Pleasant 46576
Tuck Museum, Hampton 43892
Tucumcari Historical Research Institute Museum, Tucumcari 48099
Tulare County Museum, Visalia 48254
Tularosa Basin Historical Society Museum, Alamogordo 41078
Twin Falls County Museum, Twin Falls 48125
Twin Falls Museum, Mullens 45553
Twinsburg Historical Society Museum, Twinsburg 48126
Tybee Museum and Tybee Island Light Station, Tybee Island 48129
Ukrainian-American Archives and Museum, Hamtramck 43899
Ulster County Historical Society Museum, Marbletown 45137
Umatilla County Historical Society Museum, Pendleton 46335
Union County Heritage Museum, New Albany 45660
Union County Historical Complex, Creston 42698
Union County Historical Foundation Museum, Union 48147
Union County Historical Society Museum, Blairsville 41731
Union County Historical Society Museum, Marysville 45195
Union County Museum, Lewisburg 44724
Union County Museum, Union 48145
University Museum, Martin 45189
University of Colorado Museum, Boulder 41837
Upham Mansion, Marshfield 45187
Upper Musselshell Historical Society Museum, Harlowtown 43915
Upper Paxton Township Museum, Millersburg 45347
Upper Snake River Valley Historical Museum, Rexburg 46847
Utica Museum, Hobson 44045
Vacaville Museum, Vacaville 48173
Vaile Mansion - Dewitt Museum, Independence 44208
The Valdez Museum, Valdez 48179
Valentown Museum, Victor 48232
Vallejo Naval and Historical Museum, Vallejo 48185
Valley Community Historical Society Museum, Valley 48186
Valley County Pioneer Museum, Glasgow 43677
Van Buren County Historical Society Museum, Keosauqua 44453
Van Nostrand-Starkins House, Roslyn 47010
Van Riper-Hopper House, Wayne 48479
Van Wyck Homestead Museum, Fishkill 43325
Vanderbilt Mansion National Museum, Hyde Park 44189
Vashon Maury Island Heritage Museum, Vashon 48206
Ventura County Maritime Museum, Oxnard 46245
Ventura County Museum of History and Art, Ventura 48211
The Verdier House, Beaufort 41561
Vermilion County Museum, Danville 42777
Vermont Historical Society Museum, Montpelier 45478
The Vermont State House, Montpelier 45479
Vernon County Museum, Viroqua 48253
Vernon Historical Museum and Pond Road Chapel, Vernon 48219
Vernonia Historical Museum, Vernonia 48221
Vest-Lindsey House, Frankfort 43515
Vestal Museum, Vestal 48225
Victor Valley Museum and Art Gallery, Apple Valley 41237
Vigo County Historical Museum, Terre Haute 47987
Villa Louis Historic Site, Prairie du Chien 46683
Villa Montezuma Museum, San Diego 47300
Village Historical Society Museum, Harrison 43929
Village of Elsah Museum, Elsah 43173
The Vinalhaven Historical Society Museum, Vinalhaven 48237
Virginia Air and Space Center, Hampton 43898
Virginia Baptist Historical Society Museum, Richmond 46889
Virginia City Madison County Historical Museum, Virginia City 48251
Volendam Windmill Museum, Milford 45341
Wabaunsee County Historical Museum, Alma 41152
Wahkiakum County Historical Museum, Cathlamet 42140
Wakefield Historical Museum, Wakefield 48279
Wakefield House Museum, Blue Earth 41755
Wakefield Museum, Wakefield 48278
Wallace House, Somerville 47673
Wallingford Historical Society Museum, Wallingford 48288
Wallis Museum at Connors State College, Warner 48305
Walt Whitman Birthplace State Historic Site, Huntington Station 44170
Walt Whitman House, Camden 42061
Walter Elwood Museum, Amsterdam 41187
Waltham Historical Society Museum, Waltham 48299
The Waltham Museum, Waltham 48300
Walton House Museum, Centerville 42171
Wanapum Dam Heritage Center, Beverly 41673
Wapello County Historical Museum, Ottumwa 46222
Ward County Historical Society Museum, Minot 45398
Warner Museum, Springville 47762
Warren County Historical Society Museum, Lebanon 44704
Warren County Museum, Warren 48313
Warren Historical Museum, Warren 48307
Warrick County Museum, Boonville 41789
Warsaw Historical Museum, Warsaw 48318
Wasco County Historical Museum, The Dalles 42763
Washakie Museum, Worland 48760
Washburn County Historical Society Museum, Shell Lake 47598
Washburn Historical Museum, Washburn 48327
Washington County Historical Association Museum, Fort Calhoun 43375
Washington County Historical Society Museum, Portland 46644
Washington County Historical Society Museum, Washington 48413
Washington County Historical Society Museum, Washington 48419
Washington County Historical Society Museum, West Bend 48512
Washington County Museum, Akron 41071
Washington County Museum, Sandersville 47380
Washington Historical Museum, Washington 48412
Washington Museum, Washington 48414
Washington State Capital Museum, Olympia 46142
Washington State Historical Society Museum, Tacoma 47924
Washington's Lands Museum and Sayre Log House, Ravenswood 46801
Water Mill Museum, Water Mill 48426
Waterford Historical Museum, Waterford 48429
Watertown Historical Society Museum, Watertown 48439
Watkins Community Museum of History, Lawrence 44688
Watkins Museum, Taylorsville 47963
Watson-Curtze Mansion, Erie 43204
Watters Smith, Lost Creek 44956
Wauconda Township Museum, Wauconda 48458
Waukesha County Museum, Waukesha 48460
Wayland Historical Museum, Wayland 48474
Wayne County Historical Museum, Richmond 46863
Wayne County Historical Society Museum, Lyons 45014
Wayne County Historical Society Museum, Wooster 48751
Wayne County Museum, Honesdale 44071
Weaverville Joss House, Weaverville 48487
The Webb-Deane-Stevens Museum, Wethersfield 48575
Webb House Museum, Newark 45898
Webster County Historical Museum, Red Cloud 46815
Webster House Museum, Elkhorn 43145
Weems-Botts Museum, Dumfries 43006
Weeping Water Valley Historical Society Museum, Weeping Water 48491
Wellesley Historical Society, Wellesley Hills 48496
Wellfleet Historical Society Museum, Wellfleet 48498
Wells County Historical Museum, Bluffton 41760
Wells County Museum, Fessenden 43318
Wenatchee Valley Museum, Wenatchee 48507
Weslaco Bicultural Museum, Weslaco 48509
West Allis Historical Society Museum, West Allis 48510
West Baton Rouge Museum, Port Allen 46587
West Chicago City Museum, West Chicago 48519
West of the Pecos Museum, Pecos 46325
West Overton Museums, Scottdale 47511
West Pasco Historical Society Museum, New Port Richey 45743
West River Museum, Philip 46466
West Virginia Independence Hall, Wheeling 48588
West Virginia Northern Community College Alumni Association Museum, Wheeling 48589
West Virginia State Museum, Charleston 42232
Western Hennepin County Pioneers Museum, Long Lake 44874
Western Heritage Center, Billings 41691
Western Museum, Abilene 41052
Western Reserve Historical Society Museum, Cleveland 42485
Western Rhode Island Civic Museum, Coventry 42679
Western Springs Museum, Western Springs 48553
Westminster Historical Society Museum, Westminster 48565
Westport Historical Museum, Westport 48573
Westport Maritime Museum, Westport 48574
Westville Historic Handicrafts Museum, Lumpkin 45000
Wethersfield Museum, Wethersfield 48576
Wexford County Historical Museum, Cadillac 42024
W.H. Over Museum, Vermillion 48216
The W.H. Stark House, Orange 46173
Wharton County Historical Museum, Wharton 48579
Whatcom Museum of History and Art, Bellingham 41604
Wheat Ridge Sod House Museum, Wheat Ridge 48580
Wheaton History Center, Wheaton 48585
Wheeler Historic Farm, Salt Lake City 47237
Whipple House Museum, Ashland 41294
White County Historical Museums, Carmi 42111
White County Historical Society Museum, Cleveland 42461
White County Historical Society Museum, Monticello 45474
White Deer Land Museum, Pampa 46275
White Pillars Museum, De Pere 42817
White Pine Public Museum, Ely 43176
White River Museum, Meeker 45227
White River Valley Museum, Auburn 41377
Whitefield House Museum, Nazareth 45640
Whitehead Memorial Museum, Del Rio 42858
Whitewater Historical Museum, Whitewater 48595
Whitingham Historical Museum, Whitingham 48596
Whitley County Historical Museum, Columbia City 42571
Wichita Falls Museum and Art Center, Wichita Falls 48614
Wichita-Sedgwick County Historical Museum, Wichita 48612
Wilbur D. May Museum, Reno 46838
Wilder Memorial Museum, Strawberry Point 47852
Wilderness Road Regional Museum, Newbern 45903
Wildwood Center, Nebraska City 45642
Wilkin County Historical Museum, Breckenridge 41876
Wilkinson County Museum, Woodville 48745
Willa Cather State Historic Site, Red Cloud 46816
William B. Ide Adobe State Historic Park, Red Bluff 46814
William Clark Market House Museum, Paducah 46257
William H. Harrison Museum/ Grouseland, Vincennes 48242
William Holmes McGuffey Museum, Oxford 46243
William S. Hart Museum, Newhall 45918
William Trent House, Trenton 48060
Williams County Historical Museum, Montpelier 45476
Williamson County Historical Society Museum, Marion 45157
Willoughby-Baylor House, Norfolk 45972
Wilmette Historical Museum, Wilmette 48646
Wilson County Historical Society Museum, Fredonia 43544
Wilson Historical Museum, Wilson 48670
Wilton Historical Museums, Wilton 48672
Wilton House Museum, Richmond 46892
Winchendon Historical Museum, Winchendon 48675

Winchester-Frederick County Historical Society Museum, Winchester 48679
Wind River Historical Center Dubois Museum, Dubois 42990
Windmill Island Municipal Park Museum, Holland 44057
Winedale Historical Center, Round Top 47018
Winnetka Historical Museum, Winnetka 48693
Wisconsin Historical Museum, Madison 45073
Wise County Heritage Museum, Decatur 42837
Wistariahurst Museum, Holyoke 44066
Wolcott House Museum Complex, Maumee 45205
Wolf Point Area Historical Society Museum, Wolf Point 48721
Wood County Historical Center, Bowling Green 41854
Woodlawn Museum, Ellsworth 43164
Woodlawn Plantation, Alexandria 41136
Woodside Store Historic Site, Woodside 48736
Woodson County Historical Museum, Yates Center 48781
Woodstock Historical Society Museum, Bryant Pond 41975
Woodstock Historical Society Museum, Woodstock 48738
Woodstock Historical Society Museum, Woodstock 48743
Woodstock Museum of Shenandoah County, Woodstock 48741
Worcester Historical Museum, Worcester 48758
Worthington Historical Society Museum, Worthington 48764
Wrather West Kentucky Museum, Murray 45573
Wray Museum, Wray 48765
Wright County Historical Museum, Buffalo 41980
Wright's Ferry Mansion, Columbia 42556
Wyandot County Historical Society Museum, Upper Sandusky 48161
Wyandotte County Museum, Bonner Springs 41782
Wyandotte Museum, Wyandotte 48767
Wyatt Earp Birthplace, Monmouth 45435
Wyoming Pioneer Home, Thermopolis 47996
Wyoming Pioneer Memorial Museum, Douglas 42965
Wyoming Territorial Park, Laramie 44651
Yakima Valley Museum, Yakima 48774
Ybor City State Museum, Tampa 47947
Yellow Medicine County Historical Museum, Granite Falls 43765
Yellowstone Gateway Museum of Park County, Livingston 44833
Yolo County Historical Museum, Woodland 48732
York County Museum, York 48796
Yorktown Historical Museum, Yorktown 48798
The Yosemite Museum, Yosemite National Park 48804
Ypsilanti Historical Museum, Ypsilanti 48811
Yturri-Edmunds Historic Site, San Antonio 47267
Yucaipa Adobe, Yucaipa 48816
Yugtarvik Regional Museum, Bethel 41660
Zelienople Historical Museum, Zelienople 48822
Zion Historical Museum, Zion 48823
Zoar State Memorial, Zoar 48826

Uzbekistan
Andižanskij Kraevedčeskij Muzej, Andižan 48829
Angrenskij Kraevedčeskij Muzej, Angren 48831
Bucharskij Gosudarstvennyj Muzej, Buchara 48832
Dom-muzej Hamza Hakim-zade Niazy, Kokand 48841
Ferganskij Oblastnoj Kraevedčeskij Muzej, Fergana 48836
Gosudarstvennyj Kraevedčeskij Muzej Karalpakii, Nukus 48845
Istoriko-Kraevedčeskij Muzej Kattagurgana, Kattakurgan 48840
Itčan Qala Davlat Muzej Qo'riqxonasi, Chiva 48834
Kaškadarinskij Kraevedčeskij Muzej, Karši 48839
Kraevedčeskij Muzej, Samarkand 48850
Kraevedčeskij Muzej Čirčika, Čirčik 48835
Kraevedčeskij Muzej Namangana, Namangan 48844
Muzej Hamza Hakim-Žade Niazy, Fergana 48837
Sadriddin Aini Memorial Museum, Samarkand 48851

Venezuela
Casa Museo Páez, Valencia 48966
Museo Biblioteca Nueva Cádiz y Casa Natal de Juan Bautista Arismendi, Nueva Cádiz 48958
Museo Colonial, El Tocuyo 48939
Museo Cuadra de Bolívar, Caracas 48909
Museo de Anzoátegui, Barcelona 48892
Museo de Barquisimeto, Barquisimeto 48895
Museo de Caracas, Caracas 48915
Museo de Ciudad Bolívar, Ciudad Bolívar 48934
Museo de la Ciudad de Píritu, Píritu 48960
Museo de los Llanos, Guanare 48943
Museo del Estado de Mérida, Mérida 48957
Museo Jacobo Borges, Caracas 48925

Vietnam
Bao Tàng Hai Phong, Hai Phong 48984
Ha Noi Museum, Ha Noi 48978
Hong Quang Museum, Hong-Gai 48995
Hung-Yen Museum, Hung-Yen 48996
Lam Dong Museum, Lam Dong 48997
Phu Khanh Museum, Phu Khanh 48999
Ton Duc Thang Museum, Ho Chi Minh City 48992

Zambia
Livingstone Museum, Livingstone 49017
National Archives of Zambia, Lusaka 49021
Nayuma Museum, Limulunga 49016

Zimbabwe
Mutare Museum, Mutare 49038

History, Maritime → Boats and Shipping

History, Medieval

Austria
Ateliersammlung Herbert Hiesmayr, Sankt Thomas am Blasenstein 02608
Emperor Maximilian of Mexico Museum, Hardegg 02002
Frühmittelaltermuseum Carantana, Rothenthurn 02527
Museum Kunst-Kultur-Kellerromantik, Schleinbach 02634
Ostarrichi-Kulturhof, Neuhofen an der Ybbs 02343

Bulgaria
Regionalen Istoričeski Muzej, Stara Zagora 04868

France
Château-Musée, Châteaudun 11213
Maison des Châteaux Forts, Obersteinbach 13384
Maison Natale de Jeanne d'Arc et Centre d'Interprètation, Domremy-la-Pucelle 11551
Musée Colette, Saint-Sauveur-en-Puisaye 14467
Musée des Temps Barbares, Marle 12825
Musée du Vieux-Château, Laval (Mayenne) 12361
Musée Municipal d'Avranches, Avranches 10542

Germany
Alte Kirche Friedensdorf, Dautphetal 16554
Ausstellung Haus Wysburg und Ruine Wysburg, Remptendorf 19563
Brückenhausmuseum, Erfurt 16896
Burgmuseum, Sulzberg 20127
Burgmuseum Schlossfreiheit, Tangermünde 20138
Dokumentationsraum für staufische Geschichte, Göppingen 17315
Fuggerei-Museum, Augsburg 15554
Gildehaus Bardowick, Bardowick 15823
Hexenmuseum, Ringelai 19616
Historisches Museum der Pfalz, Speyer 20011
Mittelalterliches Foltermuseum, Rüdesheim am Rhein 19706
Museum bei der Kaiserpfalz, Ingelheim am Rhein 17900
Museum Burg Scharfenstein, Scharfenstein 19765
Museumsdorf Düppel, Berlin 16069
Naturhistorisches Museum, Nürnberg 19155
Rheinisches Landesmuseum Trier, Trier 20212
Stadtmuseum Coesfeld und Städtische Turmgalerie, Coesfeld 16491

Iran
Azadi Museum, Teheran 22290

Italy
Museo del Sovrano Ordine Militare dei Cavalieri di Malta, Roma 25189
Palazzo del Senato, Pinerolo 24933

Japan
Japan-China Peace Negotiations Memorial Hall, Shimonoseki 26752

Netherlands
Museum Catharijneconvent, Utrecht 29901

Norway
Arkeologisk Museum i Stavanger, Stavanger 30877
Bryggens Museum, Bergen 30419
Erkebispegården, Trondheim 30937
Hedmarksmuseet og Domkirkeodden, Hamar 30528
Ledaal Museum, Stavanger 30880

Poland
Muzeum Mikołaja Kopernika, Toruń 32053
Muzeum Piastów Śląskich, Brzeg 31511

Romania
Complexul Monumental Curtea Domnească, Târgovişte 32601
Muzeul Judeţean Alexandru Ştefulescu, Târgu Jiu 32607

Russia
Aleksandrovskaja Sloboda - Gosudarstvennyj Istoriko-architekturnyj i Chudožestvennyj Muzej-zapovednik, Aleksandrov 32633
Gosudarstvennyj Istoriko-architekturnyj i Chudožestvennyj Muzej-zapovednik Drevnij Derbent, Derbent 32756
Gosudarstvennyj Voenno-istoričeskij i Prirodnyj Muzej-zapovednik Kulikovo Pole, Tula 33624
Gosudarstvennyj Voenno-istoričeskij Muzej-zapovednik Prochorovskoe Pole, Prochorovka 33328
Muzej Podviga Ivana Susanina, Susanino 33568
Soloveckij Gosudarstvennyj Istoriko-Architekturnyj i Prirodnyj Muzej-Zapovednik, Soloveckij 33546

Spain
Centro Cultural Torre de la Calahorra, Córdoba 34735
Monasterio de las Huelgas de Burgos, Burgos 34628
Museo Arqueológico y Etnológico Córdoba, Córdoba 34737
Museo Regional de Prehistoria y Arqueología de Cantabria, Santander 35433

Sweden
Historiska Museet, Lund 36057
Historiska Museet, Stockholm 36246
Statens Historiska Museum, Stockholm 36285
Stockholms Medeltidsmuseum, Stockholm 36288

Switzerland
Musée Jurassien d'Art et d'Histoire, Delémont 36657
Museum Kleines Klingental, Basel 36512

Turkmenistan
Historical and Ethnographical Museum, Mary 37818

United Kingdom
Bishop of Winchester's Palace Site, Witney 40909
Cistercian Museum, Hailes 39145
Old Gala House, Galashiels 39024
Provand's Lordship, Glasgow 39062
Saint John and Coningsby Medieval Museum, Hereford 39230

U.S.A.
Swords Into Plowshares Peace Center and Gallery, Detroit 42935

History, Modern

Algeria
Musee d'Ifri, Ifri 00066
Musée National du Moudjahid, El Madania 00062

Argentina
Museo Casa de Ricardo Rojas, Buenos Aires 00161
Museo de Aduanas y Puerto, Buenos Aires 00164
Museo de la Casa de Acuerdo de San Nicolás, San Nicolás de los Arroyos 00590
Museo de la Palabra, Villa Adelina 00658
Museo de la Reconquista, Tigre 00632
Museo Fuerte Independencia, Tandil 00629
Museo Histórico de la Ciudad de Buenos Aires Brigadier-General Cornelio de Saavedra, Buenos Aires 00210
Museo Historico del Norte, Salta 00541
Museo Histórico Nacional Casa del Virrey Liniers, Alta Gracia 00111
Museo Histórico Nacional del Cabildo de Buenos Aires y de la Revolucion de Mayo, Buenos Aires 00216
Museo Histórico Sarmiento, Buenos Aires 00217
Museo Mitre, Buenos Aires 00224
Museo Presidente José Evaristo Uriburu, Salta 00542
Museo Roca, Buenos Aires 00241
Museo y Archivo Histórico Localista Almirante Guillermo Brown, Adrogué 00107

Australia
Defence Services Museum, Adelaide 00705
Jewish Holocaust Centre, Elsternwick 01013
Parkside Cottage Museum, Narrandera 01305
Powder Magazine, Beechworth 00785
Sydney Jewish Museum, Darlinghurst 00969
Vietnam Veterans Museum, San Remo 01442

Austria
Einsiedelei Erzherzog Maximilians des Deutschmeisters, Innsbruck 02063
Erzherzog Franz-Ferdinand Museum, Artstetten 01681
Gedenkräume im Schloß Hartheim, Alkoven 01654
Gedenkraum 1945, Hochwolkersdorf 02035
Heimathaus Sankt Georgen an der Gusen, Sankt Georgen an der Gusen 02564
Heimatvertriebenen-Stuben, Traun 02737
KZ-Gedenkstätte Mauthausen, Mauthausen 02289
KZ-Gedenkstätte und Zeitgeschichte-Museum Ebensee, Ebensee 01781
Museum Aspern-Essling 1809, Wien 02935
Museum der Heimatvertriebenen, Wels 02813
Österreichisches Freimaurermuseum, Rosenau Schloß 02525
Weg des Friedens, Purgstall an der Erlauf 02465

Belgium
Boerenkrijgmuseum, Overmere 03684
Breendonk Fort National Memorial, Willebroek 03840
In Flanders Fields Museum, Ieper 03515
Joods Museum van Deportatie en Verzet, Mechelen 03615
Musée Ducal, Bouillon 03233
Musée Napoleon, Ligny 03590
Sanctuary Wood Museum - Hill 62, Zillebeke 03853
Talbot House, Poperinge 03688

Bolivia
Casa de la Libertad, Sucre 03904

Brazil
Memorial do Imigrante, São Paulo 04497
Museu do Monumento Nacional aos Mortos da Segunda Guerra Mundial, Rio de Janeiro 04372
Museu Imperial, Petrópolis 04263
Museu José Bonifácio, São Paulo 04539

Bulgaria
Gradski Istoričeski Muzej, Nova Zagora 04744
Gradski Istoričeski Muzej, Peruštica 04760
Istoričeski Muzej, Dimitrovgrad 04651
Istoričeski Muzej Belogradčik, Belogradčik 04617
Kăšta-muzej Chadži Dimităr, Sliven 04818
Kăšta-muzej Georgi Dimitrov, Kovačevci 04721
Kăšta-muzej Mitko Palauzov, Gabrovo 04669
Kăšta-muzej Nikola Parapunov, Razlog 04799
Kăšta-muzej Panaët Chitov, Sliven 04821
Kăšta-muzej Rajna Knjaginja, Panagjurište 04751
Kăšta-muzej Todor Kableškov, Koprivštica 04715
Muzej Glavna Kvartira na Ruskata Armija 1877-1878, Pordim 04785
Muzej na Septemvrijskoto Văstanie, Michajlovgrad 04739
Muzej Osvoboždenieto na Pleven 1877, Pleven 04767
Muzej Vasil Levski, Karlovo 04691
Muzej Vasil Levski, Loveč 04729
Muzej za Istorija na Varna, Varna 04903
Okražen Istoričeski Muzej, Pernik 04759
Okražen Muzej na Văzraždaneto i Nacionalno-osvoboditelnite Borbi, Plovdiv 04781
Regionalen Istoričeski Muzej, Ruse 04807
Regionalen Istoričeski Muzej, Stara Zagora 04868

Canada
Adelaide Hunter Hoodless Homestead, Saint George 06318
Bytown Historical Museum, Ottawa 06066
Centre Commémoratif de l'Holocauste à Montréal, Montréal 05895
Elgin County Pioneer Museum, Saint Thomas 06374
Grenfell House Museum, Saint Anthony 06305
Langham Cultural Centre Galleries, Kaslo 05646
Mackenzie House, Toronto 06590
Memorial Library and Art Gallery, Saskatoon 06399
Memorial War Museum, Bathurst 05057
Nicolas Denys Museum, Saint Peters 06371
Ross Thomson House Museum, Shelburne 06435
Salmon Arm Museum, Salmon Arm 06387
Settlers' Museum, Mahone Bay 05799
Trembowla Cross of Freedom Museum, Dauphin 05310
William Henry Steeves House, Hillsborough 05597

China, People's Republic
Changning District Revolutionary Display Center, Shanghai 07208
Changshu Mausoleum of Fallen Heroes, Changshu 07014
Dr. Sun Yat Sen Memorial House, Macau 07160
Hunan Revolutionary Cemetery, Changsha 07011
Jilin Revolutionary Museum, Changchun 07004
Jinan Revolutionary Mausoleum of Fallen Heroes, Jinan 07131
Lushun Su Jun Mausoleum of Fallen Heroes, Dalian 07039
Museum of International Friendship, Beijing 06976
Museum of the History of Revolution, Lhasa 07149
Museum of the Revolution, Nanchang 07172
Museum of the Revolution, Yanan 07313
Northeast Martyrs Memorial Hall, Harbin 07090
Revolutionary History Museum, Guangzhou 07072
Simingshan Revolutionary Martyr Memory, Yuyao 07322
Taiping Museum, Nanjing 07188
Wuxi Revolutionary Display Center, Wuxi 07288
Xin Hai Shouyi Mausoleum of Fallen Heroes, Wuhan 07282
Zhabei Revolutionary Shi Liao Display Center, Shanghai 07227

Croatia
Gradski Muzej Makarska, Makarska 07736
Museum of Istrian History, Pula 07758
Muzej Grada Rijeke, Rijeka 07761
Muzej Radničkog Pokreta i NOB za Slavoniju i Baranju, Slavonski Brod 07778
Muzej Seljačkih Buna, Gornja Stubica 07703
Spomen Park-Kumrovec, Kumrovec 07731

Cuba
Casa Natal de Jesús Montané Oropesa, Nueva Gerona 08054
Granma Memorial, La Habana 07931
Museo 9 de Abril, Santa Clara 08118
Museo Antimperialista, Nueva Gerona 08055
Museo Antonio Maceo, San Pedro 08107
Museo Benito Juárez, La Habana 07937
Museo Casa de los Mártires, La Habana 07945
Museo Casa del Libertador Simón Bolívar, La Habana 07947
Museo Casa Natal de Camilo Cienfuegos, La Habana 07950
Museo Casa Natal de Frank País, Santiago de Cuba 08132
Museo Casa Natal de Ignacio Agramonte, Camagüey 07875
Museo Casa Natal de Pedro Martínez Brito, Ciego de Avila 07886
Museo Casa Natal de Serafín Sánchez, Sancti-Spíritus 08109
Museo de Granjita Siboney, Santiago de Cuba 08136
Museo de la Clandestinidad, Nueva Gerona 08057
Museo de la Lucha Clandestina, Nueva Gerona 08058
Museo de la Lucha Clandestina, Santiago de Cuba 08139
Museo de la Lucha Estudiantil Jesús Suárez Gayol, Camagüey 07876
Museo de la Revolución, La Habana 07962
Museo de la Revolución, Nueva Gerona 08059
Museo de las Luchas Obreras, Manzanillo 08031
Museo El Cañón, Puerto Boniato 08084
Museo Finca El Abra, Siguanea 08157
Museo Fragua Martiana, La Habana 07970

Museo Hermanas Giralt, Cienfuegos 07891
Museo Histórico de 26 de Julio, Santiago de Cuba 08147
Museo Marcha del Pueblo Combatiente, La Habana 07973
Museo Memorial 12 de Septiembre, La Habana 07976
Museo Memorial Antonio Guiteras Holmes, Pinar del Río 08074
Museo Memorial Ernesto Che Guevara, Santa Clara 08122
Museo Memorial Mártires de Barbados, Victoria de las Tunas 08172
Museo Napoleónico, La Habana 07993
Museo Ñico Lopez, Bayamo 07862
Museo Plaza de Revolución General Antonio Maceo, Santiago de Cuba 08150

Cyprus
Cyprus National Struggle Museum, Lefkosia 08199

Czech Republic
Historické Muzeum, Slavkov u Brna 08657
Magdeburská Kasárna, Terezín 08679
Památník Františka Palackého, Hodslavice 08355
Památník Josefa Hybeše, Dašice 08325
Památník Mohyla míru, Prace u Brna 08560
Památník Národní Svobody, Hrabyně 08366
Památník Terezín, Terezín 08680
Památník Životické Tragedie, Havířov 08346
Zámek, Jirkov 08395

Denmark
Besættelsessamlingen 1940-45, Grindsted 08843
Bunker Museet, Frederikshavn 08829
Frihedsmuseet, København 08929
Den Gamle By, Århus 08770

Dominican Republic
Casa-Fuerte de Ponce de León, Santo Domingo 09116

Ecuador
Museo Jacinto Jijón y Caamaño, Quito 09212

Estonia
Kaitseväe Ühendatud Õppeasutuste Muuseum, Tartu 09378
Okupatsioonimuuseum, Tallinn 09370

Finland
Lenin-Museo, Tampere 10080

France
Centre National Musée Jean-Jaurès, Castres 11082
Exposition Permanente Souvenir du Maréchal Lannes, Lectoure 12502
Historial de la Grande Guerre, Péronne 13698
Maison des Jardies-Musée Léon Gambetta, Sèvres 14738
Maison Natale du Maréchal Foch, Tarbes 14865
Maison Nationale Bonaparte, Ajaccio 10262
Mémorial de Vendée, Saint-Sulpice-le-Verdon 14481
Mémorial du Maréchal Leclerc de Hauteclocque et de la Libération de Paris et Musée Jean Moulin, Paris 13527
Musée Charles-Louis-Philippe, Cérilly 11111
Musée Communal de la Résistance et de la Déportation, Vénissieux 15120
Musée d'Argonne, Varennes-en-Argonne 15089
Musée de Cahors Henri-Martin, Cahors 10996
Musée de la Franc-Maçonnerie, Paris 13555
Musée de la Résistance, Limoges 12611
Musée de la Résistance Bretonne, Saint-Marcel (Morbihan) 14345
Musée de la Résistance et de la Déportation, Agen 10230
Musée de la Résistance et de la Déportation, Besançon 10700
Musée de la Résistance et de la Déportation, Montauban 13046
Musée de la Résistance et de la Déportation, Castelnau-le-Lez 11074
Musée de la Résistance Nationale, Champigny-sur-Marne 11157
Musée de la Révolution Française, Vizille 15280
Musée de l'Arc de Triomphe, Paris 13569
Musée de l'Ordre de la Libération, Paris 13579
Musée Departemental de la Résistance et de la Déportation, Forges-les-Eaux 11787
Musée des Troupes de Marine, Fréjus 11810
Musée d'Histoire Contemporaine, Paris 13594
Musée du Groupe Jovinien de Résistance Bayard, Joigny (Yonne) 12083
Musée du Maréchal Murat, Labastide-Murat 12282
Musée du Mur de l'Atlantique, Ouistreham 13445
Musée Émile-Jean, Villiers-sur-Marne 15258
Musée Haut Savoyard de la Résistance, Bonneville 10798
Musée-Hôtel Bertrand, Châteauroux (Indre) 11227
Musée Juin 1944, L'Aigle 12305
Musée Lénine, Paris 13624
Musée-Maison du Petit Poitou, Chaillé-les-Marais 11122
Musée Mémorial de la Bataille de Normandie, Bayeux 10618
Musée Mémorial de la Ligne Maginot du Rhin, Marckolsheim 12812
Musée Municipal, Richelieu 13963
Musée Napoléon Ier et Tresors des Eglises, Brienne-le-Château 10929
Musée Napoléonien, Ajaccio 10267
Musée National de la Coopération Franco-Américaine, Blérancourt 10766
Musée National des Châteaux de Malmaison et de Bois-Préau, Rueil-Malmaison 14075
Musée Naval et Napoléonien, Antibes 10375
Le Refuge de Grasla, Les Brouzils 12530

Germany
Alte Schule mit Clara-Zetkin-Gedächtnisstätte, Königshain-Wiederau 18178
Anti-Kriegs-Museum, Berlin 15913
Archiv Bürgerbewegung Leipzig e.V., Leipzig 18385
Archiv und Museum des Heimatkreises Leitmeritz, Fulda 17171
Ausstellung Faszination und Gewalt - Dokumentationszentrum Reichsparteitagsgelände, Nürnberg 19134
Bauernkriegsmuseum, Weinstadt 20482
Befreiungshalle Kelheim, Kelheim 18050
Bismarck-Museum, Friedrichsruh bei Hamburg 17150
Clara-Zetkin-Museum, Birkenwerder 16167
DenkStätte Weiße Rose am Lichthof der Universität München, München 18837
Deutsches Hugenotten-Museum, Bad Karlshafen 15672
Dokumentation Obersalzberg - Orts- und Zeitgeschichte, Berchtesgaden 15884
Dokumentations- und Informationszentrum Emslandlager (DIZ), Papenburg 19345
Dokumentationszentrum des Landes für die Opfer deutscher Diktaturen, Schwerin 19895
Erich Maria Remarque-Friedenszentrum, Osnabrück 19277
Erinnerungsstätte für die Freiheitsbewegungen in der deutschen Geschichte, Rastatt 19486
Forschungs- und Gedenkstätte Normannenstrasse - Stasi Museum, Berlin 15948
Freiland-Grenzmuseum Sorge, Sorge, Harz 20004
Friedenshistorisches Museum, Bad Hindelang 15661
Friedensmuseum, Meeder 18670
Gedenkstätte Bergen-Belsen, Lohheide 18496
Gedenkstätte Breitenau, Guxhagen 17468
Gedenkstätte Buchenwald, Weimar, Thüringen 20458
Gedenkstätte Erfurter Parteitag 1891, Erfurt 16902
Gedenkstätte für die Opfer politischer Gewaltherrschaft 1945-1989, Magdeburg 18580
Gedenkstätte Goldener Löwe, Eisenach 16815
Gedenkstätte Hadamar, Hadamar 17472
Gedenkstätte in der JVA Wolfenbüttel, Wolfenbüttel 20652
Gedenkstätte Museum in der Runden Ecke, Leipzig 18397
Gedenkstätte/Museum Seelower Höhen, Seelow 19919
Gedenkstätte Plötzensee für die Opfer des Nationalsozialismus, Berlin 15973
Gedenkstätte und Museum Sachsenhausen, Oranienburg 19264
Grenzland-Museum Bad Sachsa, Bad Sachsa 15722
Grenzlandmuseum, Schnackenburg 19814
Grenzlandmuseum Eichsfeld, Teistungen 20154
Grenzlandmuseum Swinmark, Schnega 19818
Grenzmuseum Philippsthal (Werra), Philippsthal, Werra 19399
Grenzmuseum Schifflersgrund, Asbach-Sickenberg 15520
Gustav-Adolf-Gedenkstätte, Lützen 18564
Haus der Ost- und Westpreußen, Oberschleißheim 19201
Haus Mährisch-Schönberg, Bad Hersfeld 15659
Heimat und Bildhauer Kern Museum, Forchtenberg 17021
Heimatmuseum Freudenthal, Memmingen 18704
Heimatmuseum Geisa, Geisa 17213
Heimatmuseum Günzburg, Günzburg 17455
Heimatmuseum und Gedenkstätte Bützow, Bützow 16409
Historisch-Technisches Informationszentrum, Peenemünde 19362
Jenny-Marx-Haus, Salzwedel 19738
Jüdisches Museum Georgensgmünd, Georgensgmünd 17239
KdF-Museum, Ostseebad Binz 19309
Kindheitsmuseum, Marburg 18628
Kreismuseum Wewelsburg, Büren, Westfalen 16405
KZ-Gedenk- und Begegnungsstätte, Ladelund 18282
KZ-Gedenkstätte - Dachau, Dachau 16524
KZ-Gedenkstätte Flossenbürg, Flossenbürg 17017
KZ-Gedenkstätte Mittelbau-Dora, Nordhausen 19121
KZ-Gedenkstätte Neuengamme, Hamburg 17553
Mahn- und Gedenkstätte Düsseldorf, Düsseldorf 16734
Mahn- und Gedenkstätte Isenschnibber-Feldscheune, Gardelegen 17198
Mahn- und Gedenkstätte Ravensbrück, Fürstenberg, Havel 17158
Mahn- und Gedenkstätte Steinwache, Dortmund 16660
Mahn- und Gedenkstätte Wernigerode, Wernigerode 20527
Mahn- und Gedenkstätten Wöbbelin, Wöbbelin 20640
Mauermuseum - Museum Haus am Checkpoint Charlie, Berlin 16042
Museen Alte Bischofsburg, Wittstock, Dosse 20632
Museum Berlin-Karlshorst, Berlin 16045
Museum Blindenwerkstatt Otto Weidt, Berlin 16047
Museum Burg Hohnstein, Hohnstein 17820
Museum des Todesmarsches im Belower Wald, Wittstock, Dosse 20633
Museum im Schloß Lützen, Lützen 18565
Museum im Stasi-Bunker, Machern 18579
Museum Schloß Kuckuckstein, Liebstadt 18463
Museumshof Lerchennest - Friedrich-der-Große-Museum, Sinsheim 19970
Nostalgie Museum, Brandenburg an der Havel 16286
Parlamentsausstellung des Deutschen Bundestages "Wege, Irrwege, Umwege", Berlin 16079
Pfinzgaumuseum, Karlsruhe 18000
Plan-Weseritzer Heimatstuben mit Archiv, Tirschenreuth 20179
Prora-Museum, Ostseebad Binz 19313
Reichspräsident-Friedrich-Ebert-Gedenkstätte, Heidelberg 17672
Reichstagsmuseum, Regensburg 19529
Ruhmeshalle und Bavaria, München 18902
Schwules Museum, Berlin 16094
Stauffenberg-Schloß und Stauffenberggedächtniszimmer, Albstadt 15423
Steinscher Hof Kirberg, Hünfelden 17860
Stiftung Bundeskanzler-Adenauer-Haus, Bad Honnef 15669
Stiftung Haus der Geschichte der Bundesrepublik Deutschland, Bonn 16248
Stiftung Haus der Geschichte der Bundesrepublik Deutschland, Leipzig 18420
Templerhaus, Amorbach 15487
Thomas-Müntzer-Gedenkstätte, Heldrungen 17700
Topographie des Terrors, Berlin 16107
Torhaus Markkleeberg, Markkleeberg 18638
Unterfränkisches Grenzmuseum, Bad Königshofen 15677
Währungsreform von 1948 und Konklave in Rothwesten, Fuldatal 17179
Walhalla, Donaustauf 16635
Zwangsarbeiter Gedenkstätte, Leipzig 18425

Greece
Historical Museum of Azogire, Azogire 20909
Historical Museum of the National Resistance of Rentina, Agrapha, Karditsa 21000
Museum of the Sacrifice of the People of Kalavryta, Kalavryta 20989
National Historical Museum, Athinai 20893

Honduras
Museo Nacional de Historia Colonial, Omoa 21300

Hungary
József Attila Múzeum, Makó 21468
Kossuth Lajos Emlékmúzeuma, Monok 21483
Nemzeti Történeti Emlékpark, Opusztaszer 21493

India
Gandhi Sangrahalaya, Patna 21977
Gandhi Smarak Sangrahalaya, Ahmedabad 21679
Gandhi Smarak Sangrahalaya, Sevagram 22015
National Gandhi Museum and Library, Delhi 21775
Nehru Memorial Museum and Library, Delhi 21781
Sarat Smriti Granthagar, Panitras 21974
Shaheed-e-Azam Bhagat Singh Museum, Khatkar Kalan 21888

Indonesia
Museum Joang '45, Surabaya 22199

Ireland
Pearse Museum, Dublin 22451
Thurles Famine Museum, Thurles 22546
War Memorial, Dublin 22456

Israel
Aaronson House, Zichron Yaakov 22789
Beit Hameiri, Zefat 22786
Beit Lohamei Haghetaot, Lohamei-Hageta'ot 22709
Dubrovin Farm Museum, Yisod Hama'ala 22784
Etzel Museum, Tel Aviv 22754
From Holocaust to Revival Museum, Chof Ashkelon 22584
Historical Museum, Jerusalem 22636
Jabotinsky Museum, Tel Aviv 22762
Jewish National Fund House, Tel Aviv 22763
Massua-Educational Museum on the Holocaust, Tel Yitzhak 22780
Mitzpe Revivim Museum, Kibbutz Revivim 22700
Museum Khan, Hadera 22595
Museum of the Underground Prisoners-Acre, Acre 22564
Rishon Le-Zion Museum, Rishon Le-Zion 22741
Shfela Museum, Kibbutz Kfar Menahem 22693
Underground Prisoners Museum, Jerusalem 22669
Village Museum, Kfar Tavor 22676
Yigal Allon Center, Ginnosar 22592

Italy
Civico Museo del Risorgimento e Sacrario Oberdan, Trieste 25812
Civico Museo della Risiera di San Sabba, Trieste 25813
Istituto per la Storia della Resistenza e della Societa Contemporanea nelle Province di Biella e Vercelli, Borgosesia 23176
Mostra Permanente della Resistenzo, Massa Marittima 24321
Musei Civici, Pavia 24822
Museo Cavour, Santena 25462
Museo Centrale del Risorgimento, Roma 25182
Museo Civico, Salemi 25316
Museo Civico del Risorgimemto, Bologna 23111
Museo del Risorgimento, Brescia 23203
Museo del Risorgimento, Genova 23991
Museo del Risorgimento, Massa Marittima 24323
Museo del Risorgimento e della Resistenza, Ferrara 23790
Museo del Risorgimento e della Resistenza, Vicenza 25994
Museo del Risorgimento e Raccolte Storiche, Milano 24396
Museo del Risorgimento L. Musini, Fidenza 23802
Museo della Repubblica Partigiana, Montefiorino 24525
Museo di Storia Contemporanea, Milano 24401
Museo e Biblioteca della Resistenza, Sansepolcro 25428
Museo Garibaldino, Caprera 23332
Museo Internazionale della Croce Rossa, Castiglione delle Stiviere 23433
Museo Napoleonico, Roma 25230
Museo Napoleonico, Tolentino 25722
Museo Napoleonico G. Antonelli, Arcole 22914
Museo Nazionale del Risorgimento Italiano, Torino 25758
Museo Nazionale della Residenza Napoleonica, Portoferraio 25020
Museo Palazzina Storica, Peschiera del Garda 24873
Museo Storico dei Granatieri di Sardegna, Roma 25249
Museo Storico del Nastro Azzurro, Salò 25324
Museo Storico della Città, Bergamo 23065
Museo Storico della Guardia di Finanza, Roma 25253
Museo Storico della Liberazione di Roma, Roma 25254
Museo Storico della Resistanza S. Maneschi, Neviano degli Arduini 24618
Museo Storico della Resistenza, Stazzema 25631
Museo Storico G. Garibaldi, Como 23630
Museo Storico in Trento Onlus, Trento 25796

Japan
26 Martyrs Museum, Nagasaki 26542
Hiroshima City Museum of Traditional Provincial Industry, Hiroshima 26215
Hiroshima Heiwa Kinen Shiryokan, Hiroshima 26216
Kyoto Museum for World Peace, Kyoto 26427
Memorial Museum of the Kanto Earthquake Disaster, Tokyo 26891
Nagasaki Atomic Bomb Museum, Nagasaki 26551
Osaka International Peace Center, Osaka 26663

Kenya
Kapenguria Museum, Kapenguria 27104

Korea, Democratic People's Republic
Korean Revolutionary Museum, Pyongyang 27122
Memorial Museum of the War of Liberation, Pyongyang 27123
Shinchon Museum, Shinchon 27124

Korea, Republic
Independence Hall of Korea, Cheonan 27146
Korea War Memorial, Seoul 27247

Lebanon
Musée Al Mathaf El Lubnani, Beiteddine 27487

Lithuania
Lithuanian State Museum, Vilnius 27538

Luxembourg
Musée Historique, Clervaux 27547
Musée National de la Résistance, Esch-sur-Alzette 27556

Malaysia
Cultural Museum, Melaka 27662

Mexico
Museo de la Lucha Obrera, Cananea 27801
Museo de la Resistencia Indígena, Ixcateopan de Cuauhtémoc 28015
Museo Mural Homenaje a Benito Juárez, México 28182
Museo Nacional de la Revolución, México 28191
Museo Nacional de las Intervenciones, México 28193

Monaco
Musée des Souvenirs Napoléoniens et des Archives du Palais, Monaco 28667

Mongolia
Friendship Museum, Darhan 28674
Museum for the Victims of Political Repression, Ulaanbaatar 28680
Muzej Revoljucionnogo Dvizenija, Altanbulag 28673

Mozambique
Museu da Revolução, Maputo 28720

Netherlands
Aaltense Oorlogs- en Verzetscollectie 1940-1945, Aalten 28794
Achterhoeks Museum 1940-1945, Hengelo, Gelderland 29397
Anne Frank Huis, Amsterdam 28838
Arnhems Oorlogsmuseum 1940-45, Arnhem 28934
Corpsmuseum van het Utrechtsch Studenten Corps, Utrecht 29898
Corrie ten Boomhuis, Haarlem 29323
Czaar Peterhuisje, Zaandam 30032
Expositie 40-45, Blitterswijk 28988
Ferdinand Domela Nieuwenhuis Museum, Heerenveen 29362
Herinneringscentrum Kamp Westerbork, Hooghalen 29439
De Hollandsche Schouwburg, Amsterdam 28860

Maas en Waals Museum 1939-1945, Winssen 30011
Museum 1940-1945, Dordrecht 29175
Museum '40-'45, Slochteren 29833
Museum Bevrijdende Vleugels, Best 28985
Museum de Maurits 1940-1945, Doesburg 29158
Museum Oorlog en Vrede, Breda 29022
Museum van de Twintigste Eeuw, Hoorn 29442
Museum voor Vrede en Geweldloosheid, Amsterdam 28880
Museum Watersnood 1953, Ouwerkerk 29705
Nationaal Oorlogs- en Verzetsmuseum, Overloon 29707
Oorlogs- en Verzetsmuseum Johannes Post, Ridderkerk 29730
Oorlogsmuseum Bezinning 1940-1945, Borculo 29000
Regionaal Museum 1940-1945 Schagen en Omstreken, Schagen 29796
Ridderhofstad Gunterstein, Breukelen 29027
Stichting Zeeland 1939-1945, 's-Heer Abtskerke 29358
Verzetsmuseum Amsterdam, Amsterdam 28912
Verzetsmuseum Friesland, Leeuwarden 29516
Verzetz Museum Zuid-Holland, Gouda 29299
Yi Jun Peace Museum, Den Haag 29129

Norway
Eidsvoll 1814 - Rikspolitisk Senter, Eidsvoll Verk 30474
Gamlehaugen, Paradis 30777
Gjenreisingsmuseet, Hammerfest 30531
Det Hanseatiske Museum og Schøtstuene, Bergen 30422
Jacob Breda Bullmuseet, Rendalen 30788
Nordland Røde Kors Krigsminnemuseum, Narvik 30704

Pakistan
Quaid-i-Azam Birthplace and Museum, Karachi 31032

Panama
Museo del Canal Interoceanico de Panamá, Panamá City 31087

Paraguay
Museo de la Casa de la Independencia, Asunción 31100

Peru
Museo Nacional de Antropología, Arqueología e Historia del Perú, Lima 31221

Philippines
Apolinario Mabini Birthplace Museum, Tanauan 31457
Apolinario Mabini Shrine and Museum, Manila 31367
José Rizal Shrine Museum, Calamba 31301
José Rizal Shrine Museum, Dapitan 31322
Wenceslao Vinzons Historical Landmark Museum, Vinzons 31468

Poland
Centralne Muzeum Jeńców Wojennych w Łambinowicach -Opolu, Opole 31857
Mauzoleum Walki i Męczeństwa 1939-1945, Warszawa 32085
Muzeum Byłego Obozu Zagłady w Chełmnie nad Narem, Chełmno 31524
Muzeum Byłego Obozu Zagłady w Sobiborze, Sobibór 31982
Muzeum Czynu Niepodległościowego, Kraków 31697
Muzeum Czynu Partyzanckiego, Polichno 31893
Muzeum Gross-Rosen, Wałbrzych 32071
Muzeum Historii Polskiego Ruchu Ludowego, Warszawa 32099
Muzeum Historyczne Miasta Krakowa - Oddział Pomorska, Kraków 31708
Muzeum im. Kazimierza Pułaskiego, Warka-Winiary 32075
Muzeum Martyrologii i Walki Radogoszcz, Łódź 31773
Muzeum Martyrologii Wielkopolan w Forcie VII, Poznań 31907
Muzeum Niepodległości, Warszawa 32116
Muzeum Powstania Warszawskiego, Warszawa 32120
Muzeum Regionalne PTTK im. J. Łukasiewicza, Gorlice 31605
Muzeum Ubezpieczeń, Kraków 31721
Muzeum Uzbrojenia - Cytadela Poznańska, Poznań 31912
Muzeum Walki i Męczeństwa w Treblince, Kosów Lacki 31677
Muzeum X Pawilonu Cytadeli Warszawskiej, Warszawa 32136
Państwowe Muzeum Gross-Rosen w Rogoźnicy, Rogoźnica 31950
Państwowe Muzeum na Majdanku, Lublin 31796
Państwowe Muzeum Stutthof, Sztutowo 32036
Państwowe Muzeum Stutthof w Sztutowie, Sopot 31989
Państwowe Muzeum w Oświęcimiu-Brzezince, Oświęcim 31868

Romania
Muzeul Doftana, Doftana 32512
Muzeul Memorial Avram Iancu, Avram Iancu 32431

Russia
Blindaž gde podpisan akt o kapituljacii, Kaliningrad 32867
Centralnyj Muzej Velikoj Otečestvennoj Vojny, Moskva 33027
Gosudarstvennyj Centralnyj Muzej Sovremennoj Istorii Rossii, Moskva 33050
Gosudarstvennyj Istoriko-memorialnyj Sankt-Peterburgskij Muzej Smolnyj, Sankt-Peterburg 33398
Gosudarstvennyj Memorialnyj Muzej Oborony i Blokady Leningrada, Sankt-Peterburg 33401
Gosudarstvennyj Muzej Oborony Moskvy, Moskva 33062
Gosudarstvennyj Muzej-panorama Stalingradskaja Bitva, Volgograd 33715
Gosudarstvennyj Muzej Političeskoj Istorii Rossii, Sankt-Peterburg 33405
Kraevedčeskij Muzej Evrejskoj Avtonomnoj Oblasti, Birobidžan 32689
Muzej 700 let - Landskrona, Nevskoe Ustje, Nienšanc, Sankt-Peterburg 33425
Muzej A Muzy ne Molčali, Sankt-Peterburg 33426
Muzej Diplomatičeskogo Korpusa, Vologda 33722
Muzej i Obščestvennyj Centr Mir, Progress, Prava Čeloveka im. Andreja Sacharova, Moskva 33104
Muzej im. S.M. Kirova, Sankt-Peterburg 33436
Muzej Kirovskogo Zavoda, Sankt-Peterburg 33446
Muzej Krejsera Avrora, Sankt-Peterburg 33447
Muzej V.I. Lenina, Moskva 33130
Muzej Revoljucii, Moskva 33149
Muzej Sovremennoj Istorii i Kultury Severnoj Osetii, Vladikavkaz 33689
Soloveckij Gosudarstvennyj Istoriko-Architekturnyj i Prirodnyj Muzej-Zapovednik, Soloveckij 33546

Serbia-Montenegro
Muzej Radničkog Pokreta i Narodne Revolucije, Novi Sad 33871
Muzej u Arandjelovcu, Arandjelovac 33787
Zaduzbina Kralja Petra I Karađorđevića, Topola 33921

Slovakia
Historické Múzeum, Bratislava 33964
Muzeum Slovenského Narodného Povstania, Banská Bystrica 33948
Podpolianske Múzeum Detva, Detva 33987

Slovenia
Muzej Ljudske Revolucije Slovenj Gradec, Slovenj Gradec 34150
Muzej Narodne Osvoboditve, Maribor 34126
Muzej Novejše Zgodovine Celje, Celje 34089
Muzej Novejše Zgodovine Slovenije, Ljubljana 34113
Muzeji Radovljiške Občine, Begunje na Gorenjskem 34084
Muzejska Zbirka NOB, Zagorje 34166
Pokrajinski Muzej, Murska Sobota 34134

South Africa
Cape Town Holocaust Centre, Cape Town 34202
Kruger Museum, Pretoria 34345
Mahatma Gandhi Museum, Verulam 34397
Nieuwe Republiek Museums - Vryheid, Vryheid 34400

Spain
Casa Natal de Legazpi, Zumárraga 35740
Museo de la Batalla de Vitoria, Vitoria-Gasteiz 35701
Museo-Palacio del Emperador Carlos V, Cuacos de Yuste 34760
Museo Simón Bolívar, Bolívar 34620

Sri Lanka
Dutch Period Museum, Colombo 35748

Switzerland
Kosciuszko-Museum, Solothurn 37184
Napoleon Museum, Salenstein 37092
Villa Kruger, Clarens 36638

Tanzania
Arusha Declaration Museum, Arusha 37452

Tunisia
Musée du Mouvement National, Tunis 37594

Turkey
Atatürk Kongre ve Etnografya Müzesi, Sivas 37788
Çanakkale Şehitleri Heykeli ve Savaş Müzesi, Çanakkale 37650

Ukraine
Charkivskij Istoričnij Muzej, Charkiv 37841

United Kingdom
Althorp Museum, Althorp 37989
Baden-Powell House, London 39570
Bletchley Park Exhibition, Bletchley 38259
Brenzett Aeronautical Museum, Romney Marsh 40339
British in India Museum, Colne 38619
Channel Islands Military Museum, Saint Ouen 40418
Cornwall Aero Park, Helston 39212
Eden Camp, Malton 39883
German Occupation Museum, Forest 39004
The Grand Lodge of Scotland Museum, Edinburgh 38885
Imperial War Museum, London 39671
John Knox's House, Edinburgh 38890
Kelvedon Hatch Secret Nuclear Bunker, Kelvedon Hatch 39335
Lloyd's Nelson Collection, London 39692
Noirmont Command Bunker, Saint Brelade 40391
Peace Museum, Bradford 38300
Robert Owen Memorial Museum, Newtown, Powys 40071
Rochdale Pioneers Museum, Rochdale 40333
Scotland's Secret Bunker, Saint Andrews 40387
Second World War Experience Centre, Leeds 39451
War Room and Motor House Collection, Harrogate 39172
Wellesbourne Wartime Museum, Wellesbourne 40809

U.S.A.
Abraham Lincoln Birthplace, Hodgenville 44046
Ainsley House, Campbell 42070
America's Black Holocaust Museum, Milwaukee 45358
Andrew Johnson National Historic Site, Greeneville 43801
Anne Frank Center USA, New York 45764
Arizona State Capitol Museum, Phoenix 46474
Atwater Kent Museum - The History Museum of Philadelphia, Philadelphia 46393
Bailey House Museum, Wailuku 48275
Bedingfield Inn Museum, Lumpkin 44999
Bidwell Mansion, Chico 42370
Black American West Museum and Heritage Center, Denver 42878
Bloomfield Academy Museum, Bloomfield 41737
Boscobel Restoration, Garrison 43630
Bowers Mansion, Carson City 42117
Bryant Cottage, Bement 41620
Cahokia Courthouse State Historic Site, Cahokia 42025
California State Capitol Museum, Sacramento 47047
Calvin Coolidge Memorial Room of the Forbes Library, Northampton 46013
Campbell Historical Museum, Campbell 42071
Carl Sandburg State Historic Site, Galesburg 43597
Carry A. Nation Home Memorial, Medicine Lodge 45223
Chieftains Museum, Rome 46993
Church-Waddel-Brumby House Museum, Athens 41317
City Hall Council Chamber Gallery, Charleston 42213
Clark County Museum, Henderson 43990
Collingwood Museum on Americanism, Alexandria 41124
Colonel William Jones House, Gentryville 43647
Columbia County Historical Society Museum, Kinderhook 44482
Columbus Cultural Arts Center, Columbus 42586
Confederate Museum, Crawfordville 42693
Conner Prairie Living History Museum, Fishers 43324
Crowley Museum, Sarasota 47452
Culbertson Mansion, New Albany 45659
Dallas Holocaust Memorial Center, Dallas 42750
Danville Museum of Fine Arts and History, Danville 42780
Davenport House Museum, Savannah 47477
The David Davis Mansion, Bloomington 41742
East Martello Museum, Key West 44463
Edward H. White II Memorial Museum, Brooks Air Force Base 41957
El Paso Holocaust Museum, El Paso 43115
Elfreth's Alley Museum, Philadelphia 46406
Ellwood House Museum, DeKalb 42855
Ernie Pyle House, Dana 42769
Eugene V. Debs Home, Terre Haute 47983
Evergreen House, Baltimore 41466
First Consolidated School in Minnesota, Saum 47470
Five Civilized Tribes Museum, Muskogee 45581
Flagler Museum, Palm Beach 46264
Florida Holocaust Museum, Saint Petersburg 47171
Fonthill Museum of the Bucks County Historical Society, Doylestown 42982
Franklin D. Roosevelt Library-Museum, Hyde Park 44187
Gene Stratton-Porter House, Rome City 46999
George C. Marshall Museum, Lexington 44759
Gibson House Museum, Boston 41808
Gilbert's Bar House of Refuge, Stuart 47858
Gunderson House, Kenyon 44450
Hampton-Preston Mansion, Columbia 42561
Harlan-Lincoln House, Mount Pleasant 45534
Hartford House Museum, Manhattan 45106
Hay House Museum, Macon 45044
Henry B. Plant Museum, Tampa 47942
Henry Ford Museum and Greenfield Village, Dearborn 42825
Historic Cherry Hill, Albany 41084
Historic Madison House, Madison 45056
Holocaust Documentation and Education Center, North Miami 45996
Holocaust Memorial Center of Central Florida, Maitland 45078
Holocaust Museum Houston, Houston 44122
Iredell Museum of Arts Heritage, Statesville 47794
James Buchanan Foundation for the Preservation of Wheatland, Lancaster 44626
Jane Addams' Hull-House Museum, Chicago 42336
John Fitzgerald Kennedy House, Brookline 41936
John Wesley Powell Memorial Museum, Page 46259
Juliette Gordon Low Birthplace, Savannah 47480
Kingsley Plantation, Jacksonville 44298
Klondike Gold Rush National Historical Park, Seattle 47537
The Lane Place, Crawfordsville 42691
Lanier Mansion, Madison 45058
Lapham-Patterson House, Thomasville 48000
Levi Coffin House, Fountain City 43497
Lincoln Home, Springfield 47738
Lincoln Log Cabin, Lerna 44717
The Little Brick House, Vandalia 48202
Little White House, Warm Springs 48303
Little White Schoolhouse, Ripon 46905
Long Island Museum of American Art, History and Cariages, Stony Brook 47830
Los Angeles Museum of the Holocaust, Los Angeles 44924
McNamara House Museum, Victoria 48233
Magnolia Mound Plantation, Baton Rouge 41531
Malabar Farm State Park, Lucas 44994
Mamie Doud Eisenhower Birthplace, Boone 41786
Mann-Simons Cottage, Columbia 42564
Mardi Gras Museum, Biloxi 41694
Martin Luther King jr. Center for Nonviolent Social Change, Atlanta 41350
Martin Luther King jr. National Historic Site and Preservation District, Atlanta 41351
Metamora Courthouse, Metamora 45275
Middleton Place Foundation, Charleston 42224
Mississippi University for Women Museum, Columbus 42583
Montauk, Clermont 42459
Moore Home, Lerna 44718
Morris-Jumel Mansion, New York 45835
Museum of Jewish Heritage - A Living Memorial to the Holocaust, New York 45842
National Civil Rights Museum, Memphis 45246
Nelson Pioneer Farm and Museum, Oskaloosa 46208
New Harmony State Historic Site, New Harmony 45694
Pacific Asia Museum, Pasadena 46303
Patterson Homestead, Dayton 42804
Paul Dresser Memorial Birthplace, Terre Haute 47985
Pierre Menard Home - State Historic Site, Ellis Grove 43160
Pitot House Museum, New Orleans 45738
Porterville Historical Museum, Porterville 46620
Queen Emma Summer Palace, Honolulu 44087
Ralph Waldo Emerson House, Concord 42602
Roosevelt Campobello, Lubec 44993
Saint Joseph Museum, Saint Joseph 47109
Salisbury House, Des Moines 42909
Sarguinetti Century House Museum, Yuma 48818
Shrewsbury Windle House, Madison 45059
Simon Wiesenthal Center, Los Angeles 44941
Simon Wiesenthal Center - Museum of Tolerance, Los Angeles 44942
Sixth Floor Museum at Dealey Plaza, Dallas 42757
Skowhegan History House, Skowhegan 47653
Spirit of '76 Museum, Elyria 43178
Stan Hywet Hall and Gardens, Akron 41074
The Supreme Court of the United States Museum, Washington 48396
Taylor-Grady House, Athens 41322
Thomas Sappington House Museum, Crestwood 42700
Traveler's Rest State Historic Site, Toccoa 48016
United States Grant's Home, Galena 43595
United States Holocaust Memorial Museum, Washington 48401
Valentine Richmond History Center, Richmond 46888
Vann House, Chatsworth 42257
Vizcaya Museum, Miami 45292
Walnut Grove Plantation, Roebuck 46983
Wayne County Museum, Honesdale 44071
W.C. Handy Home Museum, Florence 43345
The White House, Washington 48409
Wilbur Wright Birthplace and Interpretive Center, Hagerstown 43864
Wisconsin Maritime Museum, Manitowoc 45117
Wolf House Museum, Manhattan 45111
Woodrow Wilson House, Washington 48410
Worker's Home Museum, South Bend 47683

Uzbekistan
International Museum of Peace and Solidarity, Samarkand 48849

Vietnam
Ho Chi Minh Memorial House, Thua Thien Hue 49001
Ho Chi Minh Museum, Ha Noi 48979
Ho Chi Minh Museum, Ho Chi Minh City 48987
Ho Chi Minh Museum, Thua Thien Hue 49002
Nghe-Tinh Museum, Vinh 49004
Revolutionary Museum Ho Chi Minh City, Ho Chi Minh City 48989
Viet Nam Revolution Museum, Ha Noi 48982
War Remnants Museum, Ho Chi Minh City 48994

Yemen
Taizz Museum, Taizz 49013

History, Social → Social Conditions

Horology

Australia
Melbourne Clocks Museum, Hampton 01089

Austria
Eisenuhren- und Antikuhrenmuseum, Steyr 02682
Steirisches Uhren-, Musikalien- und Volkskundemuseum, Arnfels 01679
Uhrenmuseum, Wien 02996

Belgium
Astronomisch Compensatieuurwerk Kamiel Festraets, Sint-Truiden 03748
Klokkenmuseum, Hechtel 03487
Musées de l'Horlogerie Pater, Langueville 03552
Museum Woning voor antieke Horlogerie, Mechelen 03616
Zimmertoren, Lier 03588

Czech Republic
Muzeum Hodin, Šternberk 08662
Muzeum Správy Krnap, Vrchlabí 08726

Finland
Suomen Kellomuseo, Espoo 09438

France
Musée de l'Horlogerie, Pesmes 13715
Musée de l'Horlogerie Ancienne, Fougères (Ille-et-Vilaine) 11792
Musée de l'Horlogerie du Haut-Doubs, Morteau 13173
Musée Frédéric-Japy, Beaucourt 10636
Musée Horlogerie Automates Yves Cupillard, Morteau 13174
Musée Royaume de l'Horloge, Villedieu-les-Poêles 15195

Germany
Babls Uhrensammlung, Waffenbrunn 20340
Deutsches Uhrenmuseum, Furtwangen im Schwarzwald 17184
Fränkisches Turmuhrenmuseum, Mistelbach 18751
Grüttert Uhrenmuseum Bremen, Bremen 16325
Heimat- und Uhrenmuseum, Villingen-Schwenningen 20317
Heimatmuseum Kastl, Kastl bei Amberg 18034
Heimatstuben der Stadt, Titisee-Neustadt 20180
Mathematisch-Physikalischer Salon, Dresden 16696
Museum für Uhren und Schmuck, Frankfurt am Main 17068
Ruhlaer Uhrenmuseum, Ruhla 19711
Schwäbisches Turmuhrenmuseum, Mindelheim 18744
Turmuhrenmuseum, Naunhof 18982
Uhrenindustriemuseum, Villingen-Schwenningen 20321
Uhrenmuseum, Bad Grund 15655
Uhrenmuseum, Bad Iburg 15671
Uhrenmuseum, Regensburg 19533
Uhrenmuseum Glashütte, Glashütte, Sachsen 17295
Uhrentechnische Lehrschau Hennig, Kurort Hartha 18271
Wuppertaler Uhrenmuseum, Wuppertal 20718

Italy
Museo dell'Orologio da Torre G.B. Bergallo, Tovo San Giacomo 25781

Japan
Daimyo Tokei Hakubutsukan, Tokyo 26839
Fukuyama Auto and Clock Museum, Fukuyama 26150
Omi Shrine Clock Museum, Otsu 26682

Netherlands
Klokkengieterij Museum, Heiligerlee 29376
Klokkenmuseum, Frederiksoord 29262
Museum van het Nederlandse Uurwerk, Zaandam 30035
Nederlands Goud-, Zilver- en Klokkenmuseum, Schoonhoven 29812
Zandlopermuseum Glanerbrug, Enschede 29242

New Zealand
Claphams Clock Museum, Whangarei 30314

Poland
Muzeum Rzemiosł Artystycznych i Precyzyjnych, Warszawa 32123
Muzeum Zegarów Wieżowych, Gdańsk 31578
Państwowe Muzeum im. Przypkowskich, Jędrzejów 31628

Slovakia
Expozícia Historických Hodín, Bratislava 33960

Spain
Museo Castillo El Macho, Peñiscola 35264
Museo de Relojes, A Coruña 34752

Switzerland
Espace Horloger de la Vallée de Joux, Le Sentier 37163
Musée de l'Horlogerie et de l'Emaillerie, Genève 36744
Musée des Curiosités Horlogères, Puidoux 37036
Musée d'Horlogerie du Locle, Le Locle 36890
Musée International d'Horlogerie, La Chaux-de-Fonds 36630
Musée Longines, Saint-Imier 37086
Musée Régional d'Histoire et d'Artisanat du Val-de-Travers, Môtiers 36956
Museum für Uhren und mechanische Musikinstrumente, Oberhofen am Thunersee 36998
Museum Omega, Biel, Kanton Bern 36565
Patek Philippe Museum, Genève 36753
Uhrenmuseum Beyer, Zürich 37415
Uhrensammlung Kellenberger, Winterthur 37342

United Kingdom
Belmont Collection, Throwley 40706
Collection of the Worshipful Company of Clockmakers, London 39612
Coventry Watch Museum, Coventry 38642
John Gershom-Parkington Collection of Timekeeping Instruments, Bury Saint Edmunds 38416
Keith Harding's World of Mechanical Music, Northleach 40086
Library and Collection of the Worshipful Company of Clockmakers, London 39687
Mill House Cider Museum and Dorset Collection of Clocks, Owermoigne 40140
Museum of Clock and Watch Making, Prescot 40263
Prescot Museum, Prescot 40264
The Time Museum, Newark-on-Trent 40025
Tymperleys Clock Museum, Colchester 38614

U.S.A.
American Clock and Watch Museum, Bristol 41900
American Watchmakers-Clockmakers Institute, Harrison 43928
Bily Clock Museum and Antonin Dvorak Exhibition, Spillville 47724
The National Time Museum, Chicago 42351
National Watch and Clock Museum, Columbia 42555
Old Clock Museum, Pharr 46385
Willard House and Clock Museum, Grafton 43736

Horses

Australia
Australian Racing Museum, Caulfield 00902

Austria
Lipizzaner Museum, Wien 02927
Museum für Beschirrung und Besattelung, Hufbeschlag und Veterinär-Orthopädie, Wien 02943

Belgium
Musée Spadois du Cheval, Spa 03762

Bulgaria
Muzej na Bivolarstvoto i Konevădstvoto, Šumen 04875

Canada
Appaloosa Horse Club of Canada Senior Citizens Museum, Claresholm 05254

China, People's Republic
The Hong Kong Racing Museum, Hong Kong 07098

Czech Republic
Hippologické Muzeum, Slatiňany 08656

France
Musée de l'Horlogerie, Saint-Nicolas-d'Aliermont 14383
Musée du Cheval, Saumur 14648
Musée Vivant du Cheval, Chantilly 11166

Germany
Deutsches Pferdemuseum, Verden 20301
Gestütsmuseum Offenhausen, Gomadingen 17346

Hungary
Lipicai Múzeum, Szilvásvárad 21583

Ireland
Irish Horse Museum, Tully 22551

Japan
Equine Museum of Japan, Yokohama 27012
Horsemanship Museum of Takekoma Shrine, Natori 26591

Korea, Republic
Equine Museum, Gwacheon 27179

Poland
Muzeum Łowiectwa i Jeździectwa, Warszawa 32111

Russia
Muzej Konevodstva, Moskva 33118

Sweden
Nordiska Travmuseet i Årjäng, Årjäng 35809

Switzerland
Musée du Cheval, La Sarraz 37125
Pferdekuranstalt, Bern 36548

United Kingdom
National Horseracing Museum, Newmarket 40050
The Royal Mews, London 39765
Suffolk Punch Heavy Horse Museum, Woodbridge 40919
York Racing Museum, York 40971

U.S.A.
Aiken Thoroughbred Racing Hall of Fame and Museum, Aiken 41069
American Royal Museum, Kansas City 44395
American Saddlebred Museum, Lexington 44735
American Work Horse Museum, Lexington 44757
Hubbard Museum of the American West, Ruidoso Downs 47029
International Museum of the Horse, Lexington 44740
National Museum of the Morgan Horse, Shelburne 47592

Horticulture

Austria
Steirisches Obstbaumuseum, Puch bei Weiz 02458

Brazil
Sítio Roberto Burle Marx, Rio de Janeiro 04404

Canada
Lawn Heritage Museum, Lamaline 05721

Czech Republic
Národní Zemědělské Muzeum, Úsek Valtice, Valtice 08707

Denmark
Flynderupgård Museet, Espergærde 08811

Egypt
Agricultural Museum, Cairo 09253

Germany
Deutsches Gartenbaumuseum Erfurt, Erfurt 16897
Deutsches Kleingärtnermuseum, Leipzig 18391
Gärtner- und Häckermuseum, Bamberg 15807
Obstmuseum, Sörup 19977
Rosenmuseum Steinfurth, Bad Nauheim 15699
Wieland-Gartenhaus, Biberach an der Riß 16140

Netherlands
Betuws Fruitteelt Museum, Erichem 29249
Land- en Tuinbouwmuseum, Etten-Leur 29255
Museum Lammert Boerma, Borgercompagnie 29005
'T Olde Ras, Doesburg 29160

Norway
Gamle Hvam Museum, Årnes 30395
Våler Torvdriftsmuseum, Våler i Solør 30968
Vigatunet, Hjelmeland 30550

United Kingdom
Botanic Gardens Museum, Southport 40558
British Lawnmower Museum, Southport 40559
Harlow Carr Museum of Gardening, Harrogate 39168
National Museum of Gardening, Helston 39215
Rievaulx Abbay, Rievaulx 40324

U.S.A.
Barnes Foundation, Merion 45266

Household Articles

Australia
Cleve National Trust Museum, Cleve 00925

Austria
Europäisches Museum für Frieden, Stadtschlaining 02673
Privatsammlung Hermine Brandstetter, Ostermiething 02389

Belgium
Musée Communal, Xhoris 03848

Canada
Badger Creek Museum, Cartwright 05213
Heritage Farm Village, North Battleford 06014
New Denmark Memorial Museum, New Denmark 05974
Sombra Township Museum, Sombra 06469

Denmark
L. Lange's Ovnmuseum, Svendborg 09085

Finland
Lounais-Hämeen Museo, Forssa 09442
Tuomarinkylän Museo, Helsinki 09543
Varkauden Museo, Varkaus 10186

France
Musée d'Art et d'Histoire de Provence, Grasse 11917

Germany
Besenmuseum Galerie, Ehingen, Donau 16791
Bürsten- und Heimatmuseum, Schönheide 19834
Deutsches Pinsel- und Bürstenmuseum, Bechhofen 15864
Erstes Nachttopf-Museum der Welt, München 18843
Feuerstätten-Ausstellung im Lausitzer Bergbaumuseum, Hoyerswerda 17846
Gerbermuseum, Bretten 16355
Miele-Museum, Gütersloh 17459
Ortsmuseum Ursulastift, Gerstetten 17262
Sammlung Berger, Amorbach 15486
Schloß Neunhof, Nürnberg 19158
Stadtmuseum Lüdenscheid, Lüdenscheid 18551
Uckermärkische Heimatstuben, Fürstenwerder 17164
Wäscherei-Museum Omas Waschküche, Berlin 16115

Greece
Historical and Folklore Museum, Kalamata 20984

Ireland
Castle Brand Visitor Centre, Nenagh 22526

Italy
Museo del Coltello Sardo, Arbus 22912
Museo della Bilancia, Campogalliano 23307
Museo della Civiltà Contadina ed Artigiana, Ripatransone 25124
Museo della Fondazione Ugo da Como, Lonato 24207

Japan
Sanuki Folk Art Museum, Takamatsu 26790

Korea, Republic
Jeju Folklore Museum, Jeju 27196

Lebanon
Beiteddine Museum, Shouf 27494

Netherlands
Boerderij Klein Hulze, Almen 28811
Gemeentelijk Museum 't Oude Slot, Veldhoven 29934
Grietje Tump Museum, Landsmeer 29496
Grootmoeders Keukenmuseum, Nijmegen 29630
Museum - Herberg de Ar, Westerbork 29995
Museum voor het Kruideniersbedrijf, Utrecht 29903
Nederlands Strijkijzer-Museum, Noordbroek 29643
Oudheidkamer, Bruinisse 29032
Oudheidkamer Willem Van Strijen, Zevenbergen 30058

New Zealand
North Otago Museum, Oamaru 30218
Waimate Historical Museum, Waimate 30274

Norway
Sandnesmuseet, Sandnes 30826

Philippines
Museo ng Kalinangang Pilipino, Manila 31384
Zaldivar Museum, Albuera 31273

Russia
Muzej Tul'skie Samovary, Tula 33628

South Africa
Free State Voortrekker Museum, Winburg 34404
Sammy Marks Museum, Pretoria 34355

Sweden
Kronbloms Kök, Örebro 36135

Switzerland
Collection d'Etains, Sierre 37165

United Kingdom
Biscuit Tin Museum, Duns 38818
Bygones at Holkham, Wells-next-the-Sea 40813
Dalmeny House, South Queensferry 40534
Fan Museum, London 39633
Hornsea Museum of Village Life, Hornsea 39261
The Museum of the Home, Pembroke 40169
Priest House, West Hoathly 40824
Railway Village Museum, Swindon 40664
Session Cottage Museum, Turriff 40735
Swinford Museum, Filkins 38991

Hunting

Austria
Heimat-Jagdmuseum, Prigglitz 02455
Jagdmuseum Brandhof, Gollrad 01905
Museum Kaiser Franz Joseph I. und die Jagd, Neuberg an der Mürz 02340
Oberösterreichisches Jagdmuseum, Sankt Florian 02562
Sammlung Jagdkunde, Graz 01932
Trophäensaal, Altenfelden 01662

Croatia
Lovački Muzej, Zagreb 07827

Czech Republic
Lesnické, Myslivecké a Rybářské Muzeum, Hluboká nad Vltavou 08352
Muzeum T.G. Masaryk's House, Čejkovice 08291
Zámek Budišov, Budišov u Třebíče 08284

Denmark
Dansk Jagt- og Skovbrugsmuseum, Hørsholm 08899
Fjordmuseet, Jyllinge 08909
Spillemands-Jagt og Skovbrugsmuseet i Rebild, Skørping 09067

Finland
Ålands Jakt och Fiskemuseum, Eckerö 09424
Tyrvään Seudun Museo, Vammala 10176

France
Musée de la Chasse et de la Nature, Paris 13551
Musée de la Vénerie et des Spahis, Senlis 14710
Musée International de la Chasse, Gien 11860

Germany
Deutsches Jagd- und Fischereimuseum, München 18838
Forstliche und Jagdkundliche Lehrschau Grillenburg, Grillenburg 17399
Gräfliche Sammlungen und Afrikanisches Jagdmuseum, Erbach, Odenwald 16888
Jagd- und Falknereimuseum, Riedenburg 19597
Jagd- und Fischereimuseum, Adelsdorf 15395

Jagd- und Fischereimuseum Schloss Tambach, Weitramsdorf 20505
Jagd- und Naturkunde Museum, Niederstetten 19098
Jagd- und Naturkundemuseum, Brüggen, Niederrhein 16374
Jagd- und Schloßmuseum Spangenberg, Spangenberg 20009
Jagdhaus Gabelbach, Ilmenau 17891
Jagdkundemuseum, Dischingen 16624
Jagdmuseum, Buschow 16432
Jagdschau im Jagdschloss Springe, Springe 20018
Jagdschloß Granitz, Ostseebad Binz 19308
Jagdschloß Paulinzella, Rottenbach 19689
Museum Burg Falkenstein, Pansfelde 19344
Museum des Oberbergischen Kreises, Nümbrecht 19131
Museum für Jagdtier- und Vogelkunde des Erzgebirges, Augustusburg 15573
Museum für ländliches Kulturgut, Landwirtschaft, Forsten und Jagd, Ulrichstein 20262
Museum Jagd und Wild auf Burg Falkenstein, Falkenstein, Oberpfalz 16985
Museum Jagdschloß Kranichstein, Darmstadt 16546
Museum Schloss Moritzburg, Moritzburg 18791
Schloss Ludwigslust, Ludwigslust 18527
Schloß Wolfstein mit Jagd- und Fischereimuseum und Galerie Wolfstein, Freyung 17134
Tier- und Jagdmuseum, Bad Dürrheim 15634

Hungary
Mátra Múzeum, Gyöngyös 21417

Netherlands
Landbouw- en Juttersmuseum Swartwoude, Buren, Friesland 29041
Museum voor Natuur- en Wildbeheer, Doorwerth 29172
Stinzenmuseum, Beers 28968

Norway
Norsk Skogbruksmuseum, Elverum 30478

Poland
Muzeum Łowiectwa i Jeździectwa, Warszawa 32111

Russia
Muzej Ochotovedenija, Irkutsk 32820
Muzej Ochoty i Rybolovstva, Moskva 33144

Slovakia
Múzeum vo Svätý Antone, Svätý Anton 34068

Slovenia
Tehniški Muzej Slovenije, Ljubljana 34122

Spain
Museo Nacional de Caza, Riofrío 35321

Sweden
Jaktvårdsmuseum, Eksjö 35863
Kungajaktmuseet, Vargön 36400
Nordvärmlands Jakt och Fiskemuseum, Sysslebäck 36318

Switzerland
Greb Jagd-Museum, Busswil (Thurgau) 36610
Museum Alpin, Pontresina 37026
Schweizer Museum für Wild und Jagd, Utzenstorf 37273

United Kingdom
Dog Collar Museum, Maidstone 39875
Dunrobin Castle Museum, Golspie 39091

U.S.A.
Atlantic Wildfowl Heritage Museum, Virginia Beach 48244
Morven Park Museum, Leesburg 44711

Hygiene → Medicine and Hygiene

Icons

Albania
Onufri Iconographic Museum, Bérat 00013

Austria
Österreichisches Ikonenmuseum, Potzneusiedl 02438

Bosnia and Herzegovina
Umjetnička galerija Bosne i Hercegovine, Sarajevo 03924

Bulgaria
Chudožestvena Galerija, Čirpan 04644
Chudožestvena Galerija Prof. Ilija Petrov, Razgrad 04796
Muzej-kripta Aleksandăr Nevski, Sofia 04839
Muzej na Văzroždenskata Ikona, Varna 04901
Muzej Văzroždenski Ikoni, Radomir 04794

Canada
Musée d'Art Néo-Byzantin, Montréal 05915

Croatia
Biskupska Pinakoteka, Dubrovnik 07694
Muzej Srpske Pravoslavne Crkve, Dubrovnik 07699

Cyprus
Byzantine Museum, Paphos 08213
Byzantine Museum and Art Galleries, Lefkosia 08194

Cyprus, Turkish Republic
Archangelos Mihail İkon Müzesi, Girne 08222
İskele İon Müzesi, İskele 08230
Maraş İkon Müzesi, Gazimağusa 08218
Saint Barnabas Icon and Archaeological Museum, Gazimağusa 08221
Saint Mamas Manastırı İkon Müzesi, Güzelyurt 08229

Egypt
Coptic Museum, Cairo 09258

Finland
Ortodoksinen Kirkkomuseo, Kuopio 09722

Germany
Ikonen-Museum, Recklinghausen 19512
Ikonen-Museum der Stadt Frankfurt am Main, Frankfurt am Main 17056
Ikonenmuseum, Autenried 15580
Ikonenmuseum Schloß Autenried, Ichenhausen 17878

Greece
Agathonos Monastery Collection, Ypati 21220
Agei Saranda Monastery, Spárti 21163
Agia Lovra Monastery, Kalavryta 20987
Agios Vissarion Monastery, Trikala 21201
Archeological Collection, Filiatra 20954
Byzantine Museum, Tinos 21199
Byzantine Museum of Katapoliani, Paros 21111
Byzantine Museum of the Metropolis of Samos and Ikaria, Samos 21147
Collection of Icons and Curch Heiröooms at Pyrgos, Thera 21177
Collection of the Evangelismos tis Theotokou, Skiathos 21159
Collection of the Mega Spileon Monastery, Kalavryta 20988
Collection of the Metropolis of Kefallinia, Argostolion 20834
Collection of the Metropolis of Monemvassia and Spárti, Spárti 21165
Collection of the Metropolis of Xanthi, Xanthi 21217
Collection of the Monastery of Saint Ignatios, Kalloni 20991
Collection of the Monastery of Saint John the Divine, Antissa 20828
Collection of the Saint John the Divine Monastery, Patmos 21112
Collection of the Tatarna Monastery, Karpenission 21002
Corgialenios Historical and Cultural Museum, Argostolion 20835
Ecclesiastical Museum, Komotini 21024
Ecclesiastical Museum of the Metropolis of Trikki and Stagoi, Trikala 21202
Kardamyla Cultural Centre of Michael and Stamatia Xylas, Ano Kardamyla 20826
Monastery of the Evangelistria, Skopelos 21160
Monastery of the Zoodochos Pigi or Agia, Batsi 20910
Museum of Epirot Folk Art, Metsovon 21071
Museum of Sacred Icons, Athinai 20888
Museum of the Metropolis of Messinia, Kalamata 20985
Preveli Monastery, Myrthios 21081

India
Museum of Icons and Art Objects, Gangtok 21804

Italy
Museo di Dipinti Sacri Ponte dei Greci, Venezia 25936

Macedonia
Muzej na Makedonija - Arceološki, Etnološki i Istoriski, Skopje 27590

Mexico
Museo Iconográfico del Quijote, Guanajuato 27976

Netherlands
Odigia Ikonen-Museum, Den Haag 29120

Romania
Muzeul de Artă, Iaşi 32532

Russia
Aleksandrovskaja Sloboda - Gosudarstvennyj Istoriko-architekturnyj i Chudožestvennyj Muzej-zapovednik, Aleksandrov 32633
Belgorodskij Gosudarstvennyj Chudožestvennyj Muzej, Belgorod 32675
Bereznikovskij Istoriko-kraevedčeskij Muzej, Berezniki 32685
Centralnyj Muzej Drevnerusskoj Kultury i Isskustva im. Andreja Rubleva, Moskva 33024
Chudožestvenno-memorialnyj Muzej K.S. Petrova-Vodkina, Chvalynsk 32746
Chudožestvenno-vystavočnyj Kompleks, Sarapul 33501
Čitinskij Oblastnoj Chudožestvennyj Muzej, Čita 32750
Gosudarstvennaja Tretjakovskaja Galerja, Moskva 33046
Gosudarstvennyj Muzej Palechskogo Iskusstva, Palech 33282
Gosudarstvennyj Russkij Muzej, Sankt-Peterburg 33407
Gosudarstvennyj Vladimiro-Suzdalskij Istoriko-architekturnyj i Chudožestvennyj Muzej-zapovednik, Vladimir 33692
Irkutskij Oblastnoj Chudožestvennyj Muzej im. V.P. Sukačeva, Irkutsk 32813
Jaroslavskij Chudožestvennyj Muzej - Gubernatorskij Dom, Jaroslavl 32848
Kargopolskij Gosudarstvennyj Istoriko-Architekturnyj i Chudožestvennyj Muzej, Kargopol 32884
Kirillo-Belozerskij Istoriko-Architekturnyj i Chudožestvennyj Muzej-Zapovednik, Kirillov 32915
Kostromskoj Gosudarstvennyj Istoriko-architekturnyj Muzej-zapovednik, Kostroma 32942
Kostromskoj Gosudarstvennyj Obedinennyj Chudožestvennyj Muzej, Kostroma 32943
Krasnojarskij Chudožestvennyj Muzej im. V.I. Surikova, Krasnojarsk 32950
Mitropolіčji Palaty - Muzej Drevnerusskogo Iskusstva, Jaroslavl 32852
Muzej Istorii i Kultury Srednego Prikamja, Sarapul 33503
Muzej Izobrazitelnych Iskusstv Karelii, Petrozavodsk 33318
Muzej Tul'skij Kreml', Tula 33629
Novokuzneckij Chudožestvennyj Muzej, Novokuzneck 33236
Pereslavl-Zalesskij Gosudarstvennyj Istoriko-architekturnyj i Chudožestvennyj Muzej-zapovednik, Pereslavl-Zalesskij 33299
Permskaja Gosudarstvennaja Chudožestvennaja Galereja, Perm 33307
Pokrovskij Sobor-chram Vasilija Blažennogo, Moskva 33173
Rostovskij Kreml - Gosudarstvennyj Muzej-zapovednik, Rostov (Jaroslavskaja obl.) 33355
Samarskij Eparchialnyj Cerkovno-istoričeskij Muzej, Samara 33376
Sergievo-Posadskij Gosudarstvennyj Istoriko-chudožestvennyj Muzej Zapovednik, Sergiev Posad 33521
Solikamskij Gorodskoj Kraevedčeskij Muzej, Solikamsk 33543
Staročerkasskij Istoriko-architekturnyj Muzej-zapovednik, Staročerkassk 33556
Staroladožskij Istoriko-Architekturnyj i Archeologičeskij Muzej-Zapovednik, Staraja Ladoga 33553
Stavropolskij Muzej Izobrazitelnych Iskusstv, Stavropol 33564
Svijažskij Architekturno-chudožestvennyj Muzej, Svijažsk 33570
Tjumenskij Oblastnoj Muzej Izobrazitelnych Iskusstv, Tjumen 33611
Tomskij Oblastnoj Chudožestvennyj Muzej, Tomsk 33616
Udmurtskij Respublikanskij Muzej Izobrazitelnych Iskusstv, Iževsk 32837
Uspenskij Sobor, Moskva 33182

Serbia-Montenegro
Zbirka Crkve Sv. Nikole, Perast 33883

Ukraine
Kiev-Pechersky National Museum, Kyïv 37872
Muzej Volynskoj Ikony, Luck 37879
National Art Museum of Ukraine, Kyïv 37875
The Bleschunov Municipal Museum of Personal Collections, Odessa 37896

Incunabula → Books, Book Art and Manuscripts

Indian Artifacts

Australia
Tiagarra Aboriginal Culture Centre and Museum, Devonport 00980

Brazil
Museu de Índio, Uberlândia 04576
Museu do Índio, Lagoa Seca 04165
Museu do Índio, Manaus 04191

Canada
Alberni Valley Museum, Port Alberni 06148
Algonquin Culture and Heritage Centre, Golden Lake 05499
Beothuk Interpretation Centre, Boyd's Cove 05106
Buffalo Nations Luxton Museum, Banff 05042
Campbell River Museum, Campbell River 05187
Enook Galleries, Waterloo 06754
Fort Whoop-Up Centre, Lethbridge 05745
Fraser-Fort George Regional Museum, Prince George 06186
F.T. Hill Museum, Riverhurst 06274
George Johnston Tlingit Indian Museum, Teslin 06540
Grey County Museum, Owen Sound 06088
Historical Museum of Saint James-Assiniboia, Winnipeg 06827
Joseph Brant Museum, Burlington 05147
McGillis Pioneer Home, Saint Victor 06378
Museum of the North American Indian Travelling College, Cornwall 05277
Porcupine Plain and District Museum, Porcupine Plain 06147
Port-au-Choix Site, Port-au-Choix 06151
Salmon Arm Museum, Salmon Arm 06387
Sam Waller Museum, The Pas 06098
Strasbourg and District Museum, Strasbourg 06497
Thunder Bay Historical Museum Society, Thunder Bay 06549

Malaysia
Orang Asli Museum, Melaka 27676

Sweden
Djusa Indianmuseum, Dala Husby 35849

Switzerland
Nordamerika Native Museum, Zürich 37400

U.S.A.
Ah-Tah-Thi-Ki Museum, Big Cypress Seminole Indian Reservation 41679
Angel Mounds Historic Site, Evansville 43244
Appalachian Center for Crafts, Smithville 47658
Ataloa Lodge Museum, Muskogee 45580
Black Hawk State Historic Site, Rock Island 46953
Blackwater Draw Museum, Portales 46614
Buffalo Bill Museum of Le Claire, Iowa, Le Claire 44696
California State Indian Museum, Sacramento 47048
Cherokee Heritage Centre, Tahlequah 47925
Chickasaw Council House Museum, Tishomingo 48011
Chief Plenty Coups Museum, Pryor 46737
Colorado River Indian Tribes Museum, Parker 46294
Creek Council House Museum, Okmulgee 46125
Elizabeth D. Walters Library, Stroudsburg 47854
Favell Museum of Western Art and Indian Artifacts, Klamath Falls 44508
Five Civilized Tribes Museum, Muskogee 45581
Flathead Indian Museum, Saint Ignatius 47095
Fort Recovery Museum, Fort Recovery 43447
Frisco Native American Museum and Natural History Center, Frisco 43565
Gadsden Museum, Mesilla 45273
Grand Mound History Center, International Falls 44239
Hopewell Culture National Historic Park, Chillicothe 42379
Indian Museum of Lake County-Ohio, Painesville 46262
Indian Museum of the Carolinas, Laurinburg 44682
Indian Pueblo Cultural Center, Albuquerque 41101
Ka-Do-Ha Indian Village Museum, Murfreesboro 45565
Marin Museum of the American Indian, Novato 46045
Mitchell Museum of the American Indian, Evanston 43242
Moundbuilders State Memorial and Museum, Newark 45895
Murrell Home, Park Hill 46290
Museum of the Cherokee Indian, Cherokee 42276
Museum of the Plains Indian, Browning 41960
Museum of the Red River, Idabel 44190
National Hall of Fame for Famous American Indians, Anadarko 41192
National Museum of the American Indian, New York 45852
Native American Exhibit, Fonda 43361
Native American Heritage Museum at Highland Mission, Highland 44017
Native American Resource Center, Pembroke 46334
Navajo Nation Museum, Window Rock 48682
Old Log Jail and Chapel Museums, Greenfield 43806
Olde Colonial Courthouse, Barnstable 41509
School of Nations Museum, Elsah 43172
Seminole Nation Museum, Wewoka 48577
Seneca-Iroquois National Museum, Salamanca 47188
Serpent Mound Museum, Peebles 46326
Sheldon Museum, Haines 43870
Six Nations Indian Museum, Onchiota 46155
Southern Plains Indian Museum, Anadarko 41193
Southold Indian Museum, Southold 47711
Starved Rock State Park, Utica 48168
Stewart Indian Cultural Center, Carson City 42120
Tantaquidgeon Indian Museum, Uncasville 48138
Town Creek Indian Mound Historic Site, Mount Gilead 45530
Ute Indian Museum, Montrose 45483
Walker Wildlife and Indian Artifacts Museum, Walker 48283
Wolf Point Area Historical Society Museum, Wolf Point 48721
Woodruff Museum of Indian Artifacts, Bridgeton 41894

Industry

Argentina
Museo del Patrimonio Histórico, Buenos Aires 00202

Australia
Historical Woolscour Blackall, Blackall 00807
Kandos Bicentennial Industrial Museum, Kandos 01133
Museum of Transportation and Rural Industries, Boyanup 00824

Austria
Fabrikmuseum Johann Nemetz, Wiener
Neustadt 03015
Montanmuseum, Hieflau 02028

Belgium
Musée Bruxellois de l'Industrie et du Travail,
Bruxelles 03292
Musée du Coticule, Vielsalm 03813

Bulgaria
Muzej na Morskoto Stopanstvo, Varna 04899

Canada
British Columbia Orchard Industry Museum,
Kelowna 05650
Centre d'Exposition sur l'Industrie des Pâtes et
Papiers, Trois-Rivières 06639
Industrial Heritage Complex, Smiths Falls 06466
Musée J. Armand Bombardier, Valcourt 06661
Museum of Industry, Stellarton 06489
Shand House Museum, Windsor, Nova Scotia 06809

Cuba
Museo de la Industria Azucarera, Abel
Santamaría 07845

Denmark
Cathrinesminde Teglværksmuseum, Broager 08790

Finland
Askon Museo, Lahti 09739
Parainen Industrial Museum, Parainen 09908
Rosenlew-museo, Pori 09946

France
Atelier des Produits Résineux Vidal, Luxey 12717
Cité des Sciences et de l'Industrie, Paris 13484
Ecomusée du Pays de Rennes, Rennes (Ille-et-
Vilaine) 13939
Musée Campanaire, L'Isle-Jourdain 12627
Musée d'Art et d'Industrie, Saint-Étienne 14198
Musée de la Contrefaçon, Paris 13553
Musée de la Houille Blanche et de ses Industries,
Lancey 12315
Musée de l'Aventure Industrielle, Apt 10386
Musée du Papier Le Nil, Angoulême 10357
Musée Régional de l'Alsace Bossue, Sarre-
Union 14621

Germany
Bayerisches Moor- und Torfmuseum, Grassau,
Chiemgau 17378
Deutsches Schuhmuseum, Hauenstein 17641
Fabrikmuseum Nordwolle, Delmenhorst 16567
Heimat- und Industriemuseum, Kolbermoor 18199
Heimat- und Industriemuseum, Wackersdorf 20336
Historischer Ausstellungsraum im Heizkraftwerk
Moabit, Berlin 16001
Historisches Zentrum, Wuppertal 20713
Industrie Museum Lauf, Lauf an der Pegnitz 18352
Industrie- und Filmmuseum Wolfen, Wolfen 20650
Industriemuseum Elmshorn, Elmshorn 16838
Industriemuseum Lohne, Lohne, Oldenburg 18498
Museum für Industrie- und Technikgeschichte,
Frankfurt am Main 17064
Museum Ziegelei Lage, Lage, Lippe 18285
Neugablonzer Industrie- und Schmuckmuseum im
Isergebirgs-Museum, Kaufbeuren 18042
Rheinisches Industriemuseum, Engelskirchen 16873
Rheinisches Industriemuseum, Oberhausen,
Rheinland 19178
Sammlung industrielle Gestaltung, Berlin 16088
Stadt- und Dampfmaschinenmuseum, Werdau,
Sachsen 20517
Stadt- und Festungsmuseum im Ludwigstor,
Germersheim 17254
Stadtmuseum Povelturm, Nordhorn 19124
Tabakspeicher, Nordhausen 19122
Westfälisches Industriemuseum, Petershagen,
Weser 19379
Westfälisches Industriemuseum, Hattingen 17639
Westfälisches Industriemuseum, Dortmund 16666
Westfälisches Industriemuseum, Bochum 16202
Wetsfälisches Industriemuseum Zeche Nachtigall,
Witten 20623
Zeittunnel Wülfrath, Wülfrath 20689
Ziegel- und Kalkmuseum, Winzer 20615
Ziegeleipark Mildenberg, Mildenberg 18737

Hungary
Húsipari Múzeum, Budapest 21345
Országos Alumíniumipari Múzeum,
Székesfehérvár 21558

Italy
Ecomuseo dell'Archeologia Industriale, Schio 25526
Ecomuseo di Archeologia Industriale E. CrumiSre,
Villar Pellice 26021
Museo del Patrimonio Industriale, Bologna 23114
Museo del Tessile e della Tradizione Industriale, Busto
Arsizio 23239
Museo della Plastica, Pont Canavese 24988
Museo dell'Arte e della Tecnologia Confetteria,
Sulmona 25647
Museo delle Ferrovie, Monserrato 23249
Museo delle Ferrovie in Sardegna, Cagliari 23249
Museo dell'Ingegno e della Tecnologia Preindustriale,
Colorno 23619

Japan
Hiroshima City Museum of Traditional Provincial
Industry, Hiroshima 26215
Kouseiroudoushou Sangyo Anzen Gijutsukan,
Tokyo 26876
Museum of the Nagasaki Heavy Industries,
Nagasaki 26549
Nagaoka-shiritsu Kogyo Hakurankai, Nagaoka 26535

Mexico
Museo Industrial de Santa Catarina El Blanqueo,
Santa Catarina 28430
Museo Mexitlán, Tijuana 28513
Museo Textil La Trinidad, Santa Cruz Tlaxcala 28431

Netherlands
Industrieel Museum, Sas van Gent 29792
Ons Museum, Giessendam 29277
Techniekmuseum Heim, Hengelo, Overijssel 29399
Verfmolen de Kat, Zaandam 30040

Norway
Birkenes Bygdemuseum, Birkeland 30431
Hydro Industripark-Museum, Porsgrunn 30779
Kistefos-museet, Jevnaker 30584
Klevfos Industrimuseum, Ådalsbruk 30368
Norsk Fiskeindustrimuseum, Melbu 30670
Norsk Hermetikkmuseum, Stavanger 30884
Norsk Vasskraft- og Industristadmuseum,
Tyssedal 30958

Pakistan
Mughal Museum, Lahore 31039

Philippines
The Coca-Cola Pavillion, Santa Cruz 31442

Poland
Muzeum Przemysłu, Warszawa 32122
Muzeum Przemysłu i Techniki, Wałbrzych 32072

Portugal
Museu da Cerâmica de Sacavém, Loures 32317

Réunion
Muséum Agricole et Industriel de Stella Matutina,
Piton-Saint-Leu 32419

Russia
Kemerovskij Istoriko-architekturnyi Muzej Krasnaja
Gorka, Kemerovo 32911
Muzej AO Petrozavod, Sankt-Peterburg 33428
Muzej Istorii Architektury i Promyšlennoj Techniki
Urala, Ekaterinburg 32774
Muzej Kronštadtskogo Morskogo Zavoda,
Kronštadt 32967
Sankt-Peterburgskij Muzej Chleba, Sankt-
Peterburg 33480

Spain
Museo Cemento Rezola, Donostia-San
Sebastián 34776

Sweden
Arbetets Museum, Norrköping 36115
Åssamuséet, Åtvidaberg 35823
Bofors Industrimuseum, Karlskoga 35993
Forsviks Industriminnen, Forsvik 35893
Gåröströms Industrimuseum, Gnosjö 35906
Huseby Bruk, Grimslöv 35930
Hylténs Industrimuseum, Gnosjö 35907
Iggesunds Bruksmuseum, Iggesund 35971
Industrimuséet C.W. Thorstensons Mekaniska
Verkstad, Åmål 35797
Järnvägs- och Industrimuseum, Hagfors 35938
Mariestads Industrimuseum, Mariestad 36090
Nobelmuseet och Bofors Industrimuseum,
Karlskoga 35996
Repslagarmuseet, Älvängen 35783
Stickmaskinsmuseum, Glemminebro 35904
Töllstorps Industrimuseum, Gnosjö 35908

Switzerland
Museum im Greuterhof, Islikon 36816

United Kingdom
Abbeydale Industrial Hamlet, Sheffield 40481
Amberley Working Museum, Amberley 37995
Bersham Heritage Centre and Ironworks,
Wrexham 40939
Black Country Living Museum, Dudley 38781
Bradford Industrial Museum and Horses at work,
Bradford 38295
Bridewell Museum, Norwich 40090
Bristol Industrial Museum, Bristol 38352
Corfe Castle Museum, Corfe Castle 38632
Dalbeattie Museum, Dalbeattie 38691
Derby Industrial Museum, Derby 38715
Engine House Project, Chelmsford 38538
Etruria Industrial Museum, Stoke-on-Trent 40604
Frome Museum, Frome 39019
Green Dragon Museum, Stockton-on-Tees 40599
Industrial Museum, Nottingham 40108
Kelham Island Museum, Sheffield 39019
Kidwelly Industrial Museum, Kidwelly 39354
Langton Matravers Museum, Langton
Matravers 39422
Llwernog Silver-Lead Mine Museum,
Ponterwyd 40219
Long Warehouse, Coalbrookdale 38595
Museum of Local Crafts and Industries,
Burnley 38399

Museum of Science and Industry in Manchester,
Manchester 39898
Port Sunlight Heritage Centre, Port Sunlight 40236
Riverside Museum at Blake's Lock, Reading 40298
Somerset Brick and Tile Museum, Bridgwater 38325
Wandle Industrial Museum, Mitcham 39969
Workshop and Stores, Grangemouth 39109

U.S.A.
Alexander and Baldwin Sugar Museum,
Puunene 46750
American Precision Museum, Windsor 48685
American Textile History Museum, Lowell 44982
Antique Gas and Steam Engine Museum, Vista 48255
Arkansas Museum of Natural Resources,
Smackover 47655
Attleboro Area Industrial Museum, Attleboro 41367
Baltimore Museum of Industry, Baltimore 41455
Charles River Museum of Industry, Waltham 48296
Cornwall Iron Furnace, Cornwall 42641
Crane Museum, Dalton 42767
Crystal Lake Falls Historical Museum, Barton 41517
Dr Pepper Museum and Free Enterprise Institute,
Waco 48262
Drake Well Museum, Titusville 48014
East Ely Railroad Depot Museum, Ely 43175
Fossil Station Museum, Russell 47033
Frye's Measure Mill, Wilton 48673
Grand Portage, Grand Marais 43752
Hamburg State Park Museum, Mitchell 45410
Herschell Carrousel Factory Museum, North
Tonawanda 46008
Historic Madison House, Madison 45056
Hopewell Furnace National Historic Site,
Elverson 43174
Industrial and Agricultural Museum, York 48795
The Invention Factory, Trenton 48055
Lightner Museum, Saint Augustine 47068
Liquid Paper Correction Fluid Museum, Santa
Fe 47422
Lowell National Historical Park, Lowell 44983
Maramec Museum, Saint James 47096
Maritime and Seafood Industry Museum, Biloxi 41695
Mission Mill Museum, Salem 47210
Museum of History and Industry, Seattle 47540
Pacific Lumber Company Museum, Scotia 47505
Racine Heritage Museum, Racine 46768
Rough and Tumble Engineers Museum, Kinzers 44501
RV/MH Heritage Foundation, Elkhart 43143
Slater Mill Historic Site, Pawtucket 46318
Sloss Furnaces National Historic Landmark,
Birmingham 41708
Texas City Museum, Texas City 47992
Venango Museum of Art, Science and Industry, Oil
City 46106
The Waltham Museum, Waltham 48300
Watermen's Museum, Yorktown 48800
Watkins Woolen Mill, Lawson 44693
Windham Textile and History Museum,
Willimantic 48637

Inscriptions and Epitaphs

Austria
Museumsfriedhof Tirol, Kramsach 02153

France
Musée Lapidaire, Carpentras 11058

Greece
Epigraphical Museum, Athinai 20859

India
Rajputana Museum, Ajmer 21685

Italy
Antiquarium, Fondi 23903
Antiquarium del Teatro Greco-Romano,
Taormina 25671
Museo Civico Archeologico, Camerino 23283
Museo di Santo Stefano, Bologna 23132
Museo R. Campelli, Pievebovigliana 24925

Philippines
Divine Word University Museum, Tacloban 31452

Turkey
Medrese Müzesi, Akşehir 37606

Vatican City
Galleria Lapidaria, Città del Vaticano 48871
Museo Pio Cristiano, Città del Vaticano 48880

Insects

Argentina
Museo Entomológco Mariposas del Mundo, San
Miguel 00579

Australia
Carnaby Collection of Beetles and Butterflies, Boyup
Brook 00825

Austria
Naturmuseum, Neuberg an der Mürz 02341

Belgium
Natuurpunt Museum, Turnhout 03804

Bulgaria
Prirodonaučen Muzej, Černi Osăm 04638

Canada
Insectarium de Montréal, Montréal 05906
J.B. Wallis Museum of Entomology, Winnipeg 06829
Spencer Entomological Museum, Vancouver 06690

Chile
Luis E. Peña G. Collection, Santiago de Chile 06907

Costa Rica
Museo de Insectos de la Universidad de Costa Rica,
San José 07656

Czech Republic
Entomologické Oddělení, Praha 08573

France
Musée des Papillons, Fuveau 11828

Germany
Museum G. Frey des Entomologischen Instituts,
Tutzing 20240
Naturkundemuseum Erfurt, Erfurt 16907
Staatliches Naturhistorisches Museum,
Braunschweig 16304
Zoologische Staatssammlung, München 18926

Hungary
Mátra Múzeum, Gyöngyös 21417

Israel
Sharon Museum Emek Hefer, Midreshet
Ruppin 22714

Italy
Collezione Entomologica, Sassari 25484
Collezioni del Dipartimento di Entomologia e Zoologia
Agraria, Portici 25010
Museo Civico di Storia Naturale, Carmagnola 23348
Museo degli Insetti, Bisegna 23088

Japan
Entomological Museum of Fujikyu, Fujiyoshida 26140
Osaka-kenritsu Chu Hakabutsukan, Mino 26491

Jordan
Insects Museum, Amman 27050

Macedonia
Prirodonaučen Muzej na Makedonija, Skopje 27592

Oman
Oman Natural History Museum, Muscat 31006

Panama
Museo de Ciencias Naturales, Panamá City 31081

Philippines
Jumalon Museum and Art Gallery, Cebu 31313

Poland
Muzeum Regionalne, Lubartów 31785

Romania
Muzeul Naţional de Istorie Naturala Grigore Antipa,
Bucureşti 32468

Slovenia
Prirodoslovni Muzej Slovenije, Ljubljana 34118

South Africa
Queenstown and Frontier Museum,
Queenstown 34365

Switzerland
Papiliorama-Nocturama Foundation, Kerzers 36823
Tierwelt-Panorama, Ebikon 36668

Thailand
Forest Entomology Museum, Bangkok 37483

United Kingdom
Booth Museum of Natural History, Brighton 38338
National Dragonfly Biomuseum, Ashton,
Oundle 38031
Oxford University Museum of Natural History,
Oxford 40151
Worldwide Butterflies and Lullingstone Silk Farm,
Sherborne 40496

U.S.A.
Entomology Research Museum, Riverside 46918
Essig Museum of Entomology, Berkeley 41642
The Frost Entomological Museum, University
Park 48152
May Natural History Museum and Museum of Space
Exploration, Colorado Springs 42539
R.M. Bohart Museum of Entomology, Davis 42795

Instruments of Torture

Austria
Folterkammer mit Heimatmuseum, Pöggstall 02424
Foltermuseum, Wien 02883

France
Tour des Voleurs, Riquewihr 13979

Germany
Burg Stolpen, Stolpen 20069
Hexenmuseum, Ringelai 19616
Kriminal- und Foltermuseum Henke, Brandenburg an der Havel 16282
Museum im Zwinger, Goslar 17354

Italy
Museo delle Armi, Armature e Strumenti di Tortura, Ischia Ponte 24101

Spain
Museu de l'Institut de Criminología, Barcelona 34567

United Kingdom
Museum of Witchcraft, Cornwall 38634

Ironwork → Metalwork

Ivory

Belgium
Trésor de la Cathedrale Notre-Dame, Tournai 03797

France
Musée de la Céramique et de l'Ivoire, Commercy 11373
Musée des Ivoires, Yvetot 15332

Germany
Deutsches Elfenbeinmuseum Erbach, Erbach, Odenwald 16887
Domschatz, Trier 20208
Elfenbein-Museum, Michelstadt 18728
Elfenbeinmuseum, Walldürn 20377

Iran
Golestan Palace Museum, Teheran 22300

Italy
Civiche Raccolte d'Arte Applicata, Milano 24374

Jewellery → Precious Stones

Judaica

Argentina
Museo Judío de Buenos Aires Dr. Salvador Kibrick, Buenos Aires 00221

Australia
Jewish Holocaust Centre, Elsternwick 01013
Jewish Museum of Australia, Saint Kilda, Victoria 01434
Sydney Jewish Museum, Darlinghurst 00969

Austria
Jüdisches Museum der Stadt Wien, Wien 02903
Jüdisches Museum Hohenems, Hohenems 02041
Museum Judenplatz Wien, Wien 02948
Österreichisches Jüdisches Museum, Eisenstadt 01810

Bosnia and Herzegovina
Muzej Jevreja Bosne i Hercegovine, Sarajevo 03921

Canada
Beth Tzedec Reuben and Helene Dennis Museum, Toronto 06563
Saint John Jewish Historical Museum, Saint John 06336
Silverman Heritage Museum, Toronto 06612

Czech Republic
Židovské Muzeum v Praze, Praha 08620

France
Musée d'Art et d'Histoire du Judaïsme, Paris 13546
Musée d'Art Juif, Paris 13547
Musée d'Arts et Traditions Populaires, Marmoutier 12831
Musée Judéo-Alsacien, Bouxwiller 10881
Musée Juif Comtadin, Cavaillon 11097

Germany
Aktives Museum Südwestfalen, Siegen 19947
Alte Synagoge, Hechingen 17655
Alte Synagoge, Essen 16944

August-Gottschalk-Haus, Esens 16938
Berend Lehmann Museum, Halberstadt 17499
Braunschweigisches Landesmuseum, Braunschweig 16293
Ehemalige Synagoge Erfelden, Riedstadt 19602
Ehemalige Synagoge mit Ausstellung Juden auf dem Lande- Beispiel Ichenhausen, Ichenhausen 17877
Emslandmuseum Lingen, Lingen 18482
Gedenkstätte Ehemalige Synagoge, Adelsheim 15396
Gedenkstätte Synagoge, Dornum 16651
Heine-Haus, Hamburg 17544
Jüdische Gedenkstätte und ehemalige Synagoge, Wallhausen, Württemberg 20381
Jüdisches Kulturmuseum, Augsburg 15558
Jüdisches Kulturzentrum, Fulda 17176
Jüdisches Museum, Frankfurt am Main 17057
Jüdisches Museum, Göppingen 17316
Jüdisches Museum, München 18859
Jüdisches Museum Berlin, Berlin 16009
Jüdisches Museum Emmendingen, Emmendingen 16854
Jüdisches Museum Franken in Fürth, Fürth, Bayern 17165
Jüdisches Museum Franken in Schnaittach, Schnaittach 19816
Jüdisches Museum im Raschi-Haus, Worms 20677
Jüdisches Museum Rendsburg und Dr.-Bamberger-Haus, Rendsburg 19569
Landesrabbiner Dr. I.E. Lichtgfeld-Museum, Michelstadt 18729
Museum in der Präparandenschule, Höchberg 17777
Museum Judengasse, Frankfurt am Main 17069
Museum Synagoge Gröbzig, Gröbzig 17408
Museum zur Geschichte der Juden in Kreis und Stadt Heilbronn, Obersulm 19211
Städtische Dauerausstellung zur Geschichte der Aschaffenburger Juden, Aschaffenburg 15532
Synagoge und Jüdisches Museum Ermreuth, Neunkirchen am Brand 19052

Greece
Evraiko Mouseio tis Ellados, Athinai 20861
Jewish Museum of Thessaloniki, Thessaloniki 21184

Hungary
Középkori O-Zsinagóga, Sopron 21533
Országos Zsidó Vallási és Történeti Gyüjtemény, Budapest 21376

Ireland
Irish Jewish Museum, Dublin 22434

Israel
Babylonian Jewry Museum, Or Yehuda 22725
Bar David Museum, Kibbutz Bar Am 22679
Beit-Alfa Ancient Synagogue, Kibbutz Chefzi-bah 22680
Beit Hatefutsoth, Tel Aviv 22748
Capharnaum Ancient Synagogue, Kfar Nahum 22674
Central Archives for the History of the Jewish People, Jerusalem 22628
Institute for Jewish Studies Gallery, Jerusalem 22638
Isaak Kaplan Old Yishuv Coourt Museum, Jerusalem 22640
Israel Museum, Jerusalem, Jerusalem 22643
Kook Museum, Jerusalem 22645
Mishkan Le'Omanut, Ein Harod 22589
Museum of Ethnography and Folklore, Tel Aviv 22769
Museum of Jewish Art, Jerusalem 22647
Schocken Institute of Jewish Research, Jerusalem 22661
Sholem Asch House, Bat Yam 22578
Sir Isaac and Lady Edith Wolfson Museum, Jerusalem 22664
Ticho House, Jerusalem 22666
The U. Nahon Museum of Italian Jewish Art, Jerusalem 22668

Italy
Museo della Comunità Ebraica, Venezia 25932

Latvia
Ebreji Latvijã, Rïga 27404

Mexico
Museo Histórico Judío y del Holocausto Tuvie Maizel, México 28175

Netherlands
Joods Historisch Museum, Amsterdam 28862
Synagoge, Bourtange 29010

Poland
Muzeum Dzieje i Kultura Żydów, Kraków 31699
Muzeum Sztuki Cmentarnej, Wrocław 32185
Muzeum Żydowskiego Instytutu Historycznego w Polsce, Warszawa 32138

Portugal
Museu Luso-Hebraico de Albraão Zacuto, Tomar 32353

Romania
Muzeul de Istorie a Evreilor din România, Bucureşti 32456

Serbia-Montenegro
Jevrejski Istorijski Muzej, Beograd 33800

Slovakia
Múzeum Židovskej Kultúry, Bratislava 33976

South Africa
South African Jewish Museum, Cape Town 34211

Spain
Museo Sefardí, Toledo 35545

Suriname
Stichting Joden Savanna, Paramaribo 35777

Sweden
Judiska Museet i Stockholm, Stockholm 36249

Switzerland
Jüdisches Museum der Schweiz, Basel 36501

United Kingdom
Jewish Museum, London 39677
Jewish Museum Finchley, London 39678
Manchester Jewish Museum, Manchester 39893
Scottish Jewish Museum, Glasgow 39068

U.S.A.
American Jewish Historical Museum, New York 45758
Benjamin and Dr. Edgar R. Cofeld Judaic Museum of Temple Beth Zion, Buffalo 41982
The Ernest W. Michel Historical Judaica Collection, New York 45797
Gershon Rebecca Fenster Museum of Jewish Art, Tulsa 45814
Herbert and Eileen Bernard Museum, New York 45814
Hillel Jewish Student Center Gallery, Cincinnati 42407
Jane L. and Robert H. Weiner Judaic Museum, Rockville 46975
The Jewish Museum, New York 45821
Jewish Museum of Florida, Miami Beach 45299
Jewish Museum of Maryland, Baltimore 41472
Judaica Museum of Central Synagogue, New York 45823
Judaica Museum of the Hebrew Home for the Aged at Riverdale, Bronx 41921
Lillian and Albert Small Jewish Museum, Washington 48366
The Magnes Museum, Berkeley 41645
The Magnes Museum, San Francisco 47323
Museum of Jewish Heritage - A Living Memorial to the Holocaust, New York 45842
Museum of the Southern Jewish Experience, Jackson 44283
National Museum of American Jewish Military History, Washington 48377
Philadelphia Museum of Judaica-Congregation Rodeph Shalom, Philadelphia 46443
Sylvia Plotkin Judaica Museum, Scottsdale 47515
Temple Museum of Religious Art, Cleveland 42483
William Breman Jewish Heritage Museum, Atlanta 41362
Zimmer Children's Museum, Los Angeles 44952

Keys → Locks and Keys

Lace → Needlework

Lacquerwork

France
Musée des Beaux-Arts et de la Dentelle, Alençon 10281

Germany
Museum für Lackkunst, Münster 18943

Japan
Hachiga Minzoku Bijutsukan, Takayama 26802
Hida Takayama Museum, Takayama 26806
Hida Takayama Shunkei Kaikan, Takayama 26807
Kaisendo Museum, Kaminoyama 26297

Mexico
Museo de Laca, Chiapa de Corzo 27818

Myanmar
Lacquerware Museum, Pagan 28740

Russia
Dom-muzej A.A. Dydkina, Palech 33279
Dom-muzej I.I. Golikova, Palech 33280
Dom-Muzej P.D. Korina, Palech 33281
Dom-muzej N.M. Zinovjeva, Djagilevo 32757
Gosudarstvennyj Muzej Palechskogo Iskusstva, Palech 33282

Lamps and Lighting

Australia
Firelight Museum, Leongatha 01174
Lighthouse Keepers Cottage, Carnarvon 00899
Narooma Lighthouse Museum, Narooma 01303

Belgium
Lampenmuseum, Wezemaal 03839
Musée de l'Éclairage, Liège 03580

Canada
Cap-de-Bon-Désir, Bergonnes 05075
Cape Bonavista Lighthouse, Bonavista 05094
Mississagi Strait Lighthouse Museum, Meldrum 05833
Point Amour Lighthouse, Saint John's 06347
West Point Lighthouse Museum, O'Leary 06051

Czech Republic
Muzeum Svitidel a Chladičů, Nový Jičín 08510

Germany
Museum Gunnar-Wester-Haus, Schweinfurt 19892
Zentrum für Internationale Lichtkunst, Unna 20266

Iran
Aineh va Roshananal Museum, Yazd 22334

Ireland
Wexford County Museum, Enniscorthy 22469

Japan
Himezaki Lighthouse Museum, Ryotsu 26686

Korea, Republic
Janggigot Lighthouse Museum, Pohang 27217

Mexico
Museo de la Luz, México 28140

Poland
Muzeum Latarnia Morska, Władysławowo 32159

Spain
Casita del Príncipe, El Pardo 35252

United Kingdom
Museum of Lighting, Edinburgh 38894
Museum of Scottish Lighthouses, Fraserburgh 39016
Pendeen Lighthouse, Pendeen 40172
Skerryvore Museum, Hynish 39282
Smeaton's Tower, Plymouth 40213
Withernsea Lighthouse Museum, Withernsea 40908

U.S.A.
Key West Lighthouse Museum, Key West 44467
Lightship Museum and Naval Shipyard Museum, Portsmouth 46663
Magic Lantern Castle Museum, San Antonio 47254
Montauk Point Lighthouse Museum, Montauk 45449
National Packard Museum, Warren 48311
Neustadt Museum of Tiffany Art, New York 45854
Ponce DeLeon Inlet Lighthouse, Ponce Inlet 46583

Language and Literature

Argentina
Museo Almafuerte, La Plata 00385
Museo Areneo de Estudios Históricos de Nueva Pompeya, Buenos Aires 00157
Museo de Arte Español, Buenos Aires 00167
Museo Histórico José Hernández-Chacra Pueyrredón, Villa Ballester 00660
Museo y Centro Cultural Victoria Ocampo, Mar del Plata 00429

Armenia
Charents Literary Memorial Museum, Erevan 00679
Isahakians Museum, Erevan 00682
Tumanyans Museum, Erevan 00693

Australia
Henry Kendall Cottage and Historical Museum, Gosford 01067
Henry Lawson Centre, Gulgong 01077
Nutcote Museum, Neutral Bay 01313
Palma Rosa Museum, Hamilton, Brisbane 01086
Tom Collins House, Swanbourne 01488

Austria
Adalbert-Stifter-Haus, Linz 02225
Anton Wildgans-Haus, Mödling 02308
Bezirksmuseum Alsergrund, Wien 02850
Bezirksmuseum Döbling, Wien 02852
Franz Xaver Gruber-Gedächtnishaus, Ach 01640
Georg Rendl-Museum, Sankt Georgen bei Salzburg 02566
Georg Trakl-Forschungs- und Gedenkstätte, Salzburg 02539
Hanrieder-Gedenkraum, Putzleinsdorf 02467
Heimatmuseum und Klöpferhaus, Eibiswald 01798
Hermann Broch-Museum, Teesdorf 02718
Internationales Esperanto-Museum der Österreichischen Nationalbibliothek, Wien 02901
Josef Weinheber-Museum, Kirchstetten 02115
Joseph Misson-Gedenkstätte, Mühlbach am Mannhartsberg 02325
Karl Heinrich Waggerl-Haus, Wagrain 02781
Kernstock-Museum, Bruck an der Lafnitz 01751
Österreichische Nationalbibliothek, Wien 02955
Österreichisches Sprachinselmuseum, Wien 02962
Paul Anton Keller-Museum, Lockenhaus 02247
Paul Ernst-Gedenkstätte, Sankt Georgen an der Stiefing 02565

Peter Handke-Ausstellung, Griffen 01943
Raimund-Gedenkstätte, Gutenstein 01978
Richard Billinger-Gedenkraum, Sankt Marienkirchen bei Schärding 02584
Robert Hamerling - Museum, Kirchberg am Walde 02110
Robert Musil-Literatur-Museum, Klagenfurt 02132
Sterbehaus Ferdinand Raimunds, Pottenstein 02437
Strindberg-Museum Saxen, Saxen 02622
Unser kleines Museum, Gries im Pinzgau 01941
Wystan Hugh Auden-Dokumentationsräume, Kirchstetten 02116

Azerbaijan
Nizami Ganjavi, Baku 03068

Belarus
Litaraturny muzej Janki Kupaly, Minsk 03117
Literary History Museum, Minsk 03118
Maksim Bogdanovich Literature Museum, Minsk 03119

Belgium
AMVC-Letterenhuis, Antwerpen 03135
Archives et Musée de la Littérature, Bruxelles 03270
Centre Provincial d'Hébergement Le Caillou, Roisin 03708
Emile Verhaeren Museum, Sint-Amands 03734
Guido Gezellemuseum, Brugge 03254
Literair Museum, Hasselt 03480
Musée Adolphe Hardy, Dison 03393
Musée Camille Lemonnier, Bruxelles 03293
Musée Émile Verhaeren, Honnelles 03501
Musée Guillaume Apollinaire, Stavelot 03766
Museum Arnold Vander Haeghen, Gent 03443
Stedelijk Museum Huize Ernest Claes, Scherpenheuvel 03728
Timmermans-Opsomerhuis, Lier 03587
Uilenspiegel Museum, Damme 03371

Bosnia and Herzegovina
Muzej Književnosti i Pozorišne Umjetnosti Bosne i Hercegovine i Galerija MAK, Sarajevo 03922

Brazil
Academia Brasileira de Letras, Rio de Janeiro 04313
Museu Castro Alves, Salvador 04424

Bulgaria
Dom-muzej Čudomir, Kazanlăk 04698
Dom-muzej Elin Pelin, Bajlovo 04608
Dom-muzej Penjo Penev, Dimitrovgrad 04649
Dom-muzej Ivan Vazov, Sopot 04861
Dom-muzej Konstantin Veličkov, Pazardžik 04754
Istoričeski Muzej, Bansko 04613
Kăšta-muzej Angel Karalijčev, Sofia 04828
Kăšta-muzej Christo Botev, Kalofer 04686
Kăšta-muzej Christo Smirnenski, Sofia 04829
Kăšta-muzej Dimcho Debeljanov, Koprivštica 04712
Kăšta-muzej Dimităr Dimov, Sofia 04831
Kăšta-muzej Dobri Čintulov, Sliven 04819
Kăšta-muzej Dobri Voinikov, Šumen 04871
Kăšta-muzej Emilijan Stanev, Veliko Tărnovo 04914
Kăšta-muzej Ërdan Ëovkov, Žeravna 04933
Kăšta-muzej Geo Milev, Stara Zagora 04866
Kašta-muzej Ivan Vazov, Berkovica 04622
Kăšta-muzej Ivan Vazov, Sofia 04833
Kăšta-muzej Lamartine, Plovdiv 04779
Kăšta-muzej Ljuben Karavelov, Koprivštica 04714
Kăšta-muzej Nikola Ënkov Vapcarov, Bansko 04615
Kăšta-muzej Nikola Vapcarov, Sofia 04834
Kăšta-muzej Pejo Javorov, Sofia 04835
Kăšta-muzej Pejo K. Javorov, Čirpan 04646
Kăšta-muzej Petko i Pencho Slavejkovi, Sofia 04836
Kăšta-muzej s Dom-pametnik Jordan Jovkov, Dobrič 04656
Kăšta-muzej Slavejkovi, Trjavna 04887
Nacionalen Literaturen Muzej, Sofia 04847

Canada
Anne of Green Gables Museum, Kensington 05657
Benares Historic House, Mississauga 05868
Chiefswood Museum, Ohsweken 06043
Donnelly Homestead, Lucan 05785
Ivan Franko Museum, Winnipeg 06828
McCrae House, Guelph 05537
Stephansson House, Edmonton 05386
Stephen Leacock Museum, Orillia 06055

Chile
Museo Gabriela Mistral de Vicuña, Vicuña 06929

China, People's Republic
Guangzhou Lu Xun Museum, Guangzhou 07066
Museum in Memory of Lu Xun, Beijing 06974
National Museum of Modern Chinese Literature, Beijing 06981
Shanghai Luxun House, Shanghai 07220

Colombia
Colección del Poeta Baudilio Montoya, Clarcá 07464
Museo Eduardo Carranza, Villavicencio 07626

Croatia
Muzej Hrvatske Književnosti i Kazališne Umjetnosti, Zagreb 07831

Cuba
Casa de Dulce María Loynaz, La Habana 07920
Casa de José Jacinto Milanés, Matanzas 08035
Casa Natal de Regino Boti, Guantánamo 07915
Museo Alejo Carpentier, Camagüey 07873
Museo Andrés Cué, Amancio 07849
Museo Casa de la Poesía, La Habana 07944
Museo Casa Natal de José María Heredia, Santiago de Cuba 08133
Museo Casa Natal de José Martí, La Habana 07951
Museo del Humor, San Antonio de los Baños 08098
Museo Ernest Hemingway, San Francisco de Paula 08103
Museo José Martí, La Habana 07972
Museo Quinta Amalia Simoni, Camagüey 07877

Cyprus, Turkish Republic
Namık Kemal Zindanı ve Müzesi, Gazimağusa 08219

Czech Republic
Městské Muzeum Antonína Sovy, Pacov 08531
Muzeum Aloise Jiráska, Hronov 08371
Muzeum Aloise Jiráska a Mikoláše Alše, Praha 08592
Muzeum Boženy Němcové, Česká Skalice 08295
Muzeum Bratří Čapků, Malé Svatoňovice 08470
Muzeum Josefa Dobrovského a pamětní síň Jaroslava Kvapila, Chudenice 08322
Muzeum Prostějovska, Prostějov 08629
Muzeum J.V. Sládka, Zbiroh 08741
Památník Boženy Němcové, Červený Kostelec 08293
Památník Bratří Křičků, Kelč 08408
Památník Bratří Mrštíků, Diváky 08327
Památník Karla Čapka, Stará Huť u Dobříše 08661
Památník Karla Havlíčka Borovského, Havlíčkův Brod 08348
Památník Karla Hynka Máchy, Doksy 08330
Památník Karla Jaromíra Erbena, Miletin 08477
Památník Karla Václava Raise, Lázně Bělohrad 08444
Památník Národního Písemnictví (Muzeum České Literatury), Praha 08609
Památník Petra Bezruče, Kostelec na Hané 08422
Památník Petra Bezruče, Opava 08520
Památník Romànu Aloise Jiráska Skály, Teplice nad Metují 08678
Památník Svatopluka Čecha, Obříství 08513
Památník Svatopluka Čecha, Ostředek 08529
Památník Terezy Novákové, Proseč u Skutče 08628
Památník Václava Beneše Třebízského, Třebíz 08689
Památník Václava Beneše Třebízského a Svatopluka Čecha, Liten 08454
Rodný Domek Adalberta Stiftera, Horní Planá 08361
Rodný Domek Aloise Jiráska, Hronov 08372
Rodný Domek Otokara Březiny, Počátky 08549

Denmark
Bakkemuseet, Frederiksberg 08826
Digterhuset, Farsø 08821
Drachmanns Hus, Skagen 09054
E. Bindstouw, Viborg 09109
Hans Christian Andersen Museum, Odense 09011
Hans Christian Andersens Barndomshjem, Odense 09012
Jenle Museum, Roslev 09047
Johannes Jørgensens Mindestuer, Svendborg 09084
Karen Blixen Museet, Rungsted Kyst 09049
Skjoldborgs Barndomshjem, Vesløs 09106
Struer Museum og Johs. Buchholtz Hus, Struer 09081
Tersløsegaard, Dianalund 08794
Wesselstuerne, København 08954

Egypt
Manuscript Museum, Alexandria 09241
Shawqi Museum, Cairo 09289

Estonia
Eesti Kirjandusmuuseum, Tartu 09374
Karl Ristikivi Majamuuseum, Tartu 09380
Oskar Luts Majamuuseum, Tartu 09381

Finland
Danielson-Kalmarin Huvila, Vääksy 10165
Einari Vuorelan Kirjailijakoti, Keuruu 09660
J.L. Runebergin Koti, Porvoo 09951
Juhani Ahon Museo, Iisalmi 09557
Paikkarin Torppa, Sammatti 10020
Putkinotko, Savonlinna 10025
Westmansmors stugan, Jakobstad 09576

France
Bibliothèque-Musée Valéry-Larbaud, Vichy 15159
Galerie Bovary, Ry 14079
Maison de Balzac, Paris 13521
Maison de Victor Hugo, Paris 13524
Maison d'Elsa Triolet et Louis Aragon, Saint-Arnoult-en-Yvelines 14116
Maison Jacques Prévert, Omonville-la-Petite 13406
Maison Littéraire de Victor Hugo, Bièvres 10731
Maison-Souvenir de George Sand, Nohant-Vic 13354
Maison Stendhal, Grenoble 11939
Memorial Goethe, Sessenheim 14727
Musée Adam Mickiewicz, Paris 13528
Musée Alexandre Dumas, Villers-Cotterêts 15242
Musée Alphonse Daudet, Fontvieille 11783
Musée Arthur Rimbaud, Charleville-Mézières 11177
Musée Balzac, Saché 14082
Musée Barbey d'Aurévilly, Saint-Sauveur-le-Vicomte 14469
Musée-Bibliothèque François Pétrarque, Fontaine-de-Vaucluse 11759
Musée Charles Milcendeau-Jean Yole, Soullans 14793
Musée Corneille, Rouen 14046
Musée d'Art et d'Histoire, Saint-Denis (Seine-Saint-Denis) 14180
Musée de la Musique Mécanique, Les Gets 12539
Musée de Pierre Corneille, Le Petit-Couronne 12462
Musée de Vulliod Saint-Germain, Pézenas 13724
Musée des Charmettes, Chambéry 11140
Musée-École du Grand Meaulnes, Épineuil-le-Fleuriel 11634
Musée Émile-Guillaumin, Ygrande 15328
Musée Espéranto a Gray, Gray 11935
Musée Flaubert et d'Histoire de la Médecine, Rouen 14052
Musée Frédéric Mistral, Maillane 12769
Musée George Sand et de la Vallée Noire, La Châtre 12153
Musée Historique et Erckmann-Chatrian, Phalsbourg 13727
Musée J.-E.-Blanche, Offranville 13387
Musée Jean de la Fontaine, Château-Thierry 11210
Musée Jean-Jacques Rousseau, Montmorency 13111
Musée Joachim du Bellay, Liré 12620
Musée Jules Verne, Nantes 13259
Musée Lamartine, Mâcon 12758
Musée Maison de Clemenceau, Saint-Vincent-sur-Jard 14507
Musée-Maison Marcel Proust, Illiers-Combray 12056
Musée Maurice et Eugénie de Guérin, Andillac 10335
Musée Memorial Alain, Mortagne-au-Perche 13170
Musée Paul Valéry, Sète 14731
Musée Pierre-Loti, Rochefort (Charente-Maritime) 14001
Musée Rabelais, Seuilly 14733
Musée Schiller-Goethe, Châlons-en-Champagne 11132
Musée Stendhal, Grenoble 11946
Musée Verlaine, Juniville 12105
Musée Victor-Hugo, Villequier 15239

Georgia
Ilja Čavčavadze Memorial Museum, Tbilisi 15363
State Literature Museum of Georgia, Tbilisi 15365

Germany
Agnes-Miegel-Haus, Bad Nenndorf 15702
Ausstellung Fontane und Hankels Ablage, Zeuthen 20751
Ausstellung Max-Kommerell, Münsingen 18929
Berthold-Auerbach-Museum, Horb 17840
Brecht-Weigel-Gedenkstätte, Berlin 15929
Brechthaus, Augsburg 15551
Brehm-Gedenkstätte, Renthendorf 19572
Brüder Grimm-Haus Steinau, Steinau an der Straße 20042
Brüder Grimm-Museum Kassel, Kassel 18012
Buddenbrookhaus, Lübeck 18534
Büchnerhaus, Riedstadt 19601
Deutsches Eichendorff-Museum, Wangen im Allgäu 20392
Deutsches Märchen- und Wesersagenmuseum, Bad Oeynhausen 15708
Dichtermuseum Joseph Maria Lutz, Pfaffenhofen an der Ilm 19381
Dorfmuseum Hausen im Wiesental, Hausen im Wiesental 17644
Droste-Museum, Münster 18936
Droste-Museum, Havixbeck 17651
Droste-Museum im Fürstenhäusle, Meersburg 18675
Ehm Welk-Haus, Bad Doberan 15624
Ehm-Welk-Literaturmuseum, Angermünde 15491
Erich Kästner Museum Dresden, Dresden 16680
Ernst-Moritz-Arndt-Haus, Bonn 16235
E.T.A. Hoffmann-Haus mit Sammlung, Bamberg 15805
Faust-Museum, Knittlingen 18118
Freies Deutsches Hochstift/ Frankfurter Goethe-Museum mit Goethe-Haus, Frankfurt am Main 17046
Friedrich-Rückert-Gedächtnisstätte, Coburg 16481
Friedrich-Wilhelm-Weber-Museum, Bad Driburg 15626
Fritz-Reuter-Literaturmuseum, Reuterstadt Stavenhagen 19574
Gellert-Museum, Hainichen, Sachsen 17496
Gerhart-Hauptmann-Haus, Kloster, Hiddensee 18113
Gerhart-Hauptmann-Museum, Erkner 16912
Das Gleimhaus, Halberstadt 17501
Goethe-Gedenkstätte, Jena 17942
Goethe-Museum Düsseldorf, Düsseldorf 16725
Goethe-Museum Stützerbach mit Museum zur Geschichte des technischen Glases, Stützerbach 20081
Goethes Gartenhaus - Goethe-Nationalmuseum, Weimar, Thüringen 20460
Goethes Wohnhaus mit Goethe-Nationalmuseum, Weimar, Thüringen 20461
Gottfried-August-Bürger-Museum, Molmerswende 18784
Günter Grass-Kulturstiftung Hansestadt Lübeck, Lübeck 18535
Gustav-Freytag-Archiv und Museum, Wangen im Allgäu 20393
Gustav-Freytag-Gedenkstätte, Gotha 17359
Hans-Fallada-Haus, Feldberg, Mecklenburg 16987
Hansjakobmuseum im Freihof, Haslach 17626
Hebbel-Museum, Wesselburen 20539
Heimatmuseum und Hedwig Courths-Mahler Archiv, Nebra 18984
Heinrich-Heine-Institut-Museum, Düsseldorf 16726
Heinrich-Hoffmann-Museum, Frankfurt am Main 17053
Hermann-Allmers-Haus, Sandstedt 19742
Hermann-Hesse-Museum, Calw 16447
Hölderlinturm, Tübingen 20224
Hoffmann-von-Fallersleben-Museum, Wolfsburg 20660
Jagdhaus Gabelbach, Ilmenau 17891
James-Krüss-Turm, München 18858
Jean-Paul-Museum der Stadt Bayreuth, Bayreuth 15848
Jean-Paul-Zimmer in der Rollwenzelei, Bayreuth 15849
Justinus-Kerner-Haus, Weinsberg 20481
Karl-May-Haus, Hohenstein-Ernstthal 17813
Karl-May-Museum, Radebeul 19469
Kirms-Krackow-Haus, Weimar, Thüringen 20462
Klaus-Groth-Museum und Neue Museumsinsel Lüttenheid, Heide, Holstein 17660
Kleist-Museum, Frankfurt/Oder 17083
Klopstock Museum, Quedlinburg 19462
Kolbenheyer-Archiv und Gedenkstätte, Geretsried 17251
Kraszewski-Museum, Dresden 16687
Kügelgenhaus, Dresden 16688
Kurt-Tucholsky-Gedenkstätte, Rheinsberg 19591
Lessing-Museum, Kamenz 17978
Literaturarchiv Sulzbach-Rosenberg, Sulzbach-Rosenberg 20125
Literaturhaus, Magdeburg 18583
Literaturium / Micro Hall Art Center, Edewecht 16781
Literaturmuseum Brecht-Weigel-Haus, Buckow, Märkische Schweiz 16391
Literaturmuseum im Baumbachhaus, Meiningen 18685
Literaturmuseum Theodor Storm, Heilbad Heiligenstadt 17685
Ludwig-Thoma-Haus, Tegernsee 20149
Mahn- und Gedenkstätten Wöbbelin, Wöbbelin 20640
Maxim-Gorki-Gedächtnisstätte, Seebad Heringsdorf 19913
Michael-Ende-Museum, München 18875
Mörikehaus Ochsenwang, Bissingen an der Teck 16174
Münchhausen-Museum, Bodenwerder 16209
Museum Friedrichshagener Dichterkreis, Berlin 16052
Museum für Literatur am Oberrhein, Karlsruhe 17997
Museum Neuruppin, Neuruppin 19061
Museum Raabe-Haus, Eschershausen 16933
Museum Wolfram von Eschenbach, Wolframs-Eschenbach 20656
Museum Wurzen mit Ringelnatzsammlung, Wurzen 20720
Nietzsche-Haus, Naumburg, Saale 18980
Novalis-Museum, Wiederstedt 20566
Platenhäuschen, Erlangen 16922
Polenz-Museum, Cunewalde 16518
Profanierte Marienkapelle, Ludwigsstadt 18529
Raabe-Haus, Braunschweig 16303
Reuterhaus mit Richard-Wagner-Sammlung, Eisenach 16817
Romantikerhaus, Jena 17948
Schiller-Museum, Bauerbach 15830
Schiller-Nationalmuseum und Deutsches Literaturarchiv, Marbach am Neckar 18619
Schillerhäuschen, Dresden 16707
Schillerhaus, Ludwigshafen am Rhein 18520
Schillerhaus, Leipzig 18415
Schillerhaus, Goethe-Nationalmuseum, Weimar, Thüringen 20471
Schillers Gartenhaus der Friedrich-Schiller-Universität, Jena 17950
Schillers Geburtshaus, Marbach am Neckar 18620
Schloß Kochberg mit Liebhabertheater, Großkochberg 17432
Serbski muzej - Sorbisches Museum, Bautzen 15835
Stefan-George-Museum im Stefan-George-Haus, Bingen am Rhein 16165
Stiftung für Konkrete Kunst, Reutlingen 19582
Theodor-Storm-Haus, Husum, Nordsee 17873
Till-Eulenspiegel-Museum, Schöppenstedt 19840
Tobias-Mayer-Museum, Marbach am Neckar 18621
Waldschmidt-Ausstellung, Eschlkam 16934
Wieland-Archiv, Biberach an der Riß 16139
Wieland-Gartenhaus, Biberach an der Riß 16140
Wieland-Gedenkzimmer, Achstetten 15392
Wielandgut Ossmannstedt mit Wieland-Gedenkstätte, Ossmannstedt 19287
Wilhelm-Busch-Geburtshaus, Wiedensahl 20565
Wilhelm-Busch-Gedenkstätte, Seesen 19924

Greece
Kazantzakis Museum, Iráklion 20976
Museum of Dionysios Solomos and Eminent Zakynthians, Zakynthos 21221
Palamas Museum, Athinai 20899
Solomos Museum, Corfu 20934

Guadeloupe
Musée Municipal Saint-John-Perse, Pointe-à-Pitre 21248

Hungary
Ady Endre Emlékmúzeum, Budapest 21322
Babits Mihály Emlékház, Szekszárd 21564
Gárdonyi Géza Emlékmúzeum, Eger 21408
Jókai Mór Emlékmúzeum, Balatonfüred 21311
József Attila Emlékmúzeum, Balatonszárszó 21312
Kisfaludy Emlékmúzeum, Sümeg 21541
Petőfi Irodalmi Múzeum, Budapest 21378
Petőfi Emlékmúzeum, Kiskőrös 21456
Petőfi Múzeum, Aszód 21307
Vörösmarty Mihály Emlékmúzeum, Kapolnásnyék 21439

Iceland
Sigurhaedir - Hús Skáldsins Museum, Akureyri 21623
Stofnun Arna Magnússonar, Reykjavík 21667

India
Ghalib Museum, Delhi 21770
Rabindra Bharati Museum, Kolkata 21910
Rabindra Bhavana, Santiniketan 22011

Indonesia
Literary Documentation Centre H.B. Yasin, Jakarta 22107

Iran
Hessaby Museum, Teheran 22302
Shahryar Museum, Tabriz 22286

Ireland
James Joyce Centre, Dublin 22438
James Joyce Museum, Dublin 22439
Munster Literature Centre, Cork 22404
Newman House, Dublin 22449
Nora Barnacle House Museum, Galway 22475
Writers Museum, Dublin 22460
Yeats Tower - Thoor Ballylee, Gort 22479

Israel
Nahum Gutman's Museum, Tel Aviv 22771
Shalom Aleichem Museum, Tel Aviv 22774
Sholem Asch House, Bat Yam 22578

Italy
Casa del Boccaccio, Certaldo 23486
Casa dell'Ariosto, Ferrara 23783
Casa di Goethe, Roma 25150
Casa di Petrarca, Arquà Petrarca 22942
Casa di Pirandello, Agrigento 22815
Casa di Pirandello, Roma 25151
Casa Leopardi, Recanati 25085
Casa Museo di Dante, Firenze 23826
Casa Museo Giovanni Verga, Catania 23444
Casa Natale di Giosuè Carducci, Pietrasanta 24911
Keats-Shelley House, Roma 25169
Manzoni Villa, Lecco 24170
Museo Alfieriano, Asti 22972
Museo Carducci - Biblioteca e Casa, Bologna 23108
Museo Casa Natale G. D'Annunzio, Pescara 24866
Museo Cerlogne, Saint Nicolas 25310
Museo Dantesco, Ravenna 25080
Museo del Tasso, Roma 25190
Museo Deleddiano, Nuoro 24662
Museo della Guerra, Gardone Riviera 23959
Museo della Tipografia, Città di Castello 23579
Museo Manzoniano, Milano 24405

Japan
Hermann Hesse Museum, Hiroshima 26211
Hokkaido Museum of Literature, Sapporo 26713
Koizumi Yakumo Kinenkan, Matsue 26470
Matsuyama Municipal Shiki Kinen Museum, Matsuyama 26486
Nihon Kindai Bungakukan, Tokyo 26905
Niigata-shiritsu Aizu Yaichi Kinenkan, Niigata 26594
Suzuki Bokushi Kinenkan, Shiozawa 26762

Kazakhstan
Džambulskij Literaturnyj Memorialnyj Muzej, Džambul 27081
Memorialnyj Literaturnyj Muzej F.M. Dostoevskogo, Semey 27091
National Literary and Memorial Museum-Complex of Sabit Mukanov and Gabit Musrepov, Almaty 27074
Respublikanskij Literaturnyij Memorialnyj Muzej Abaja, Semey 27092

Kenya
Karen Blixen Museum, Nairobi 27110

Korea, Republic
Sung-Am Archives of Classical Literature, Seoul 27284

Kyrgyzstan
Gumbez Manace Literary Ethnographic Museum, Taš-Aryk 27315

Latvia
Jaņa Rozentāla un Rūdolfa Blaumaņa Muzejs, Rīga 27409
Literature, Theatre and Music Museum, Rīga 27429
Raiņa Literatūras un Mākslas Vēstures Muzejs, Rīga 27435

Lithuania
Maironis Lithuanian Literature Museum, Kaunas 27520
Poet Jovaras House, Šiauliai 27529

Luxembourg
Musée Littéraire Victor Hugo, Vianden 27579

Malaysia
Muzium Sastera, Melaka 27673

Mauritius
Robert Edward Hart Memorial Museum, Souillac 27741

Mexico
Casa Museo Amado Nervo, Tepic 28494
Casa Museo Carlos Pellicer Cámara, Villahermosa 28604
Casa Museo Maestro Manuel Altamirano, Tixtla de Guerrero 28516
Museo Casa de Ramón López Velarde, Jerez de García Salinas 28029
Museo del Recuerdo de la Academia Mexicana de la Lengua, México 28161
Museo Elías Nandino, Cocula 27835
Museo José Fernando Ramírez, Durango 27900
Museo Othoniano, San Luis Potosí 28406
Museo Ramón López Velarde, México 28196

Mongolia
Natsagdorj Museum, Ulaanbaatar 28684

Netherlands
A.M. de Jonghuis, Nieuw Vossemeer 29615
Bilderdijkmuseum, Amsterdam 28846
Frysk Letterkundich Museum, Leeuwarden 29510
It Gysbert Japicxhûs Museum, Bolsward 28994
Multatuli Museum, Amsterdam 28874
Theo Thijssen Museum, Amsterdam 28909
Tresoar, Frysk Histoarysk en Letterkundich Sintrum, Leeuwarden 29515

Norway
Aulestad, Follebu 30501
Bjørgan Prestegård, Kvikne 30622
Henrik Ibsen Museum, Skien 30845
Ibsen-museet, Oslo 30737
Ibsenhuset og Grimstad Bymuseet, Grimstad 30519
Ivar Aasen-tunet, Hovdebygda 30570
Kittelsenhuset, Kragerø 30610
Knudaheio - Garborgheimen, Undheim 30959
Nørholm, Homborsund 30557
Petter Dass-Museet på Alstahaug, Sandnessjøen 30827
Ratvolden, Røros 30805
Sagstua Skolemuseum, Sagstua 30815
Vinjestoga, Vinje 30997

Pakistan
Iqbal Museum, Lahore 31036

Philippines
Ayala Museum, Vigan 31463

Poland
Dom Gerharta Hauptmanna, Jelenia Góra 31629
Jan Kochanowski Muzeum, Czarnolas 31541
Muzeum Andrzeja Struga, Warszawa 32088
Muzeum Biograficzne Władysława Orkana, Poręba Wielka 31894
Muzeum Bolesława Prusa, Nałęczów 31820
Muzeum-Dworek Wincentego Pola, Lublin 31789
Muzeum Emila Zegadłowicza, Wadowice 32068
Muzeum Henryka Sienkiewicza, Wola Okrzejska 32168
Muzeum Henryka Sienkiewicza w Oblęgorku, Oblęgorek 31841
Muzeum im. Adama Mickiewicza w Śmiełowie, Żerków 32217
Muzeum im. Aleksandra Świętochowskiego, Gołotczyzna 31601
Muzeum Jana Kasprowicza, Zakopane 32206
Muzeum Józefa Ignacego Kraszewskiego, Romanów 31952
Muzeum Kornela Makuszyńskiego, Zakopane 32208
Muzeum Lat Szkolnych Stefana Żeromskiego, Kielce 31657
Muzeum Literackie Henryka Sienkiewicza, Poznań 31906
Muzeum Literackie im. Józefa Czechowicza, Lublin 31792
Muzeum Literatury im. Adama Mickiewicza, Warszawa 32110
Muzeum Literatury im. Jarosława Iwaszkiewicza, Sandomierz 31964
Muzeum Marii Konopnickiej w Żarnowcu, Jedlicze 31627
Muzeum Mazowsza Zachodniego, Żyradów 32226
Muzeum Okręgowe, Suwałki 32010
Muzeum Piśmiennictwa i Muzyki Kaszubsko-Pomorskiej, Wejherowo 32149
Muzeum-Pracownia Literacka Arkadego Fiedlera, Puszczykowo 31934
Muzeum Romantyzmu, Opinogóra 31855
Muzeum Stanisława Staszica, Piła 31881
Muzeum Stefana Żeromskiego, Nałęczów 31821
Muzeum Władysława Broniewskiego, Warszawa 32132
Oddział Literacki im. Marii Dąbrowskiej w Russowie, Russów 31954
Regionalne Muzeum Młodej Polski - Rydlówka, Kraków 31727

Portugal
Casa-Oficina de António Carneiro, Porto 32332

Romania
Casa Memorială Vasile Alecsandri, Mireşti 32551
Memorialul Ipoteşti-Centrul Naţional de Studii Mihai Eminescu, Ipoteşti 32542
Muzeul Brăilei, Brăila 32444
Muzeul Literaturii Române, Iaşi 32536
Muzeul Memorial Ady Endre, Oradea 32560
Muzeul Memorial Bojdeuca Ion Creangă, Iaşi 32537
Muzeul Memorial Emil Isac, Cluj-Napoca 32493
Muzeul Memorial George Coşbuc, Coşbuc 32505
Muzeul Memorial Iosif Vulcan, Oradea 32561
Muzeul Memorial Liviu Rebreanu, Năsăud 32554
Muzeul Memorial Octavian Goga, Ciucea 32490
Muzeul Memorial Petőfi Sándor, Coltau 32497
Muzeul Mihai Eminescu, Iaşi 32538
Muzeul National al Literaturii Române, Bucureşti 32462

Russia
Aleksandrovskij Literaturno-chudožestvennyj Muzej Mariny i Anastasii Cvetaevych, Aleksandrov 32635
Archangelskij Literaturnyj Muzej, Archangelsk 32647
Arzamasskij Gosudarstvennyj Literaturno-Memorialnyj Muzej A.P. Gajdara, Arzamas 32655
Brjanskij Literaturnyj Muzej, Brjansk 32707
Dom-muzej L.N. Andreeva, Orël 33259
Dom-muzej A.P. Čechova, Moskva 33036
Dom-muzej K.I. Čukovskogo, Peredelkino 33296
Dom-muzej M.I. Cvetaevoj, Moskva 33037
Dom-muzej F.M. Dostoevskogo, Staraja Russa 33554
Dom-muzej N.V. Gogolja, Moskva 33039
Dom-muzej A.S. Grina, Kirov 32917
Dom-muzej V.G. Korolenko, Gelendžik 32803
Dom-muzej M.Ju. Lermontova, Moskva 33040
Dom-muzej N.S. Leskova, Orël 33261
Dom-muzej N.S. Muchina, Olikjal 33250
Dom-muzej N.S. Muchina, Joškar-Ola 32857
Dom-muzej N.A. Nekrasova, Čudovo 32753
Dom-muzej I.S. Nikitina, Voronež 33730
Dom-muzej A.N. Ostrovskogo, Moskva 33041
Dom-muzej B.L. Pasternaka, Peredelkino 33297
Dom-muzej M.M. Prišvina, Dunino 32763
Dom-muzej M.E. Saltykova-Ščedrina, Kirov 32918
Dom-muzej Semji Cvetaevych, Novo-Talicy 33231
Dom-muzej Tukaevych, Košlauč 32941
Dom-muzej G.I. Uspenskogo, Sjabrenicy 33524
Dom-muzej Velimira Chlebnikova, Astrachan 32662
Dom-Muzej V.V. Veresaeva, Tula 33623
Dom Poėta A.N. Širjaevca - Muzej Krestjanskogo Byta, Žigulevsk 33748
Eleckij Literaturno-memorialnyj Muzej Pisatelja I.A. Bunina, Elec 32791
Ėžvinskij Literaturnyj Muzej, Syktyvkar 33571
Gatčinskij Literaturno-memorialnyj Muzej-usadba P.E. Ščerbova, Gatčina 32801
Gosudarstvennyj Istoriko-kulturnyj i Prirodnyj Muzej-zapovednik A.S. Griboedova - Chmelita, Chmelita 32745
Gosudarstvennyj Istoriko-literaturnyj i Prirodnyj Muzej-zapovednik A.A. Bloka, Solnečnogorsk 33544
Gosudarstvennyj Istoriko-literaturnyj Muzej-Zapovednik A.S. Puškina s usadbami Vjazemy i Zacharovo, Bolšie Vjazemy 32696
Gosudarstvennyj Literaturno-memorialnyj Muzej Anny Achmatovoj v Fontannom Dome, Sankt-Peterburg 33399
Gosudarstvennyj Literaturno-memorialnyj Muzej N.A. Dobroljubova, Nižnij Novgorod 33206
Gosudarstvennyj Literaturno-memorialnyj Muzej im. M.Ju. Lermontova, Pjatigorsk 33321
Gosudarstvennyj Literaturno-memorialnyj Muzej N. Ostrovskogo, Soči 33540
Gosudarstvennyj Literaturno-memorialnyj Muzej A.N. Radiščeva, Radiščevo 33346
Gosudarstvennyj Literaturno-memorialnyj Muzej-zapovednik A.P. Čechova, Melichovo 33009
Gosudarstvennyj Literaturno-memorialnyj Muzej-zapovednik N.A. Nekrasova "Karabicha", Karabicha 32883
Gosudarstvennyj Literaturnyj Muzej, Moskva 33057
Gosudarstvennyj Literaturnyj Muzej A.M. Gorkogo, Nižnij Novgorod 33207
Gosudarstvennyj Literaturnyj Muzej im. I.S. Turgeneva, Orël 33263
Gosudarstvennyj Memorialnyj Dom-muzej Bulata Okudžavy, Peredelkino 33298
Gosudarstvennyj Memorialnyj i Prirodnyj Muzej-zapovednik A.N. Ostrovskogo - Ščelykovo, Ščelykovo 33513
Gosudarstvennyj Memorialnyj i Prirodnyj Muzej-zapovednik I.S. Turgeneva 'Spasskoe Lutovinovo', Spasskoe-Lutovinovo 33550
Gosudarstvennyj Memorialnyj Muzej-usadba V.G. Belinskogo, Belinskij 32679
Gosudarstvennyj Muzej K.A. Fedina, Saratov 33506
Gosudarstvennyj Muzej A.I. Kuprina, Narovčat 33200
Gosudarstvennyj Muzej V.V. Majakovskogo, Moskva 33060
Gosudarstvennyj Muzej A.S. Puškina, Moskva 33063
Gosudarstvennyj Muzej L.N. Tolstogo, Moskva 33065
Gosudarstvennyj Muzej L.N. Tolstogo, Moskva 33066
Gosudarstvennyj Muzej L.N. Tolstogo "Jasnaja Poljana", Jasnaja Poljana (Tula) 32856
Gosudarstvennyj Muzej-zapovednik S.A. Esenina, Konstantinovo 32937
Gosudarstvennyj Muzej-zapovednik M.A. Šolochova, Vešenskaja 33683
Istoriko-literaturnyj Muzej I.A. Gončarova, Uljanovsk 33657
Istoriko-memorialnyj Muzej M.V. Lomonosova, Lomonosovo 32992
Jaroslavskij Istoriko-architekturnyj i Chudožestvennyj Muzej-zapovednik, Jaroslavl 32849
Kirovskij Oblastnoj Kraevedčeskij Muzej, Kirov 32920
Kraevoj Muzej Istorii Literatury, Iskusstva i Kultury Altaja, Barnaul 32673
Kulturnyj Centr-muzej V.S. Vysockogo, Moskva 33071
Lermontovskij Gosudarstvennyj Muzej-zapovednik Tarchany, Lermontovo 32980
Lgovskij Literaturno-memorialnyj Muzej A.P. Gajdara, Lgov 32982
Lgovskij Literaturno-memorialnyj Muzej N.N. Aseeva, Lgov 32983
Literaturno-chudožestvennyj Muzej-usadba Prijutino, Vsevoložsk 33739
Literaturno-memorialnyj Dom-Muzej D.N. Mamina-Sibirjaka, Ekaterinburg 32769
Literaturno-memorial'nyj Dom-Muzej F.M. Rešetnikova, Ekaterinburg 32770
Literaturno-memorialnyj Dom-muzej Sulejmana Stalskogo, Ašaga-Stalsk 32657
Literaturno-memorialnyj Muzej F.M. Dostoevskogo, Novokuzneck 33235
Literaturno-memorialnyj Muzej F.M. Dostoevskogo, Sankt-Peterburg 33414
Literaturno-memorialnyj Muzej Vasilija Erošenko, Staryj Oskol 33558
Literaturno-memorialnyj Muzej F.A. Abramova, Verkola 33682
Literaturno-memorialnyj Muzej M. Gorkogo, Samara 33372
Literaturno-memorialnyj Muzej im. A.M. Gorkogo, Kazan 32892
Literaturno-memorialnyj Muzej Stancionnyj Smotritel, Vyra 33743
Literaturno-memorialnyj Muzej M.M. Zoščenko, Sankt-Peterburg 33415
Literaturno-teatralnyj Muzej N.M. Djakonova, Syktyvkar 33574
Literaturnyj Muzej, Krasnojarsk 32954
Literaturnyj Muzej, Penza 33286
Literaturnyj Muzej Abakumcevo, Abakumcevo 32628
Literaturnyj Muzej-centr K.G. Paustovskogo, Moskva 33072
Literaturnyj Muzej Goroda Nalčik, Nalčik 33194
Literaturnyj Muzej im. K.V. Ivanova, Čeboksary 32720
Literaturnyj Muzej Instituta Russkoj Literatury, Sankt-Peterburg 33416
Literaturnyj Muzej F.I. Tjutčeva, Ovstug 33278
Memorialnaja Muzej-kvartira N.A. Nekrasova, Sankt-Peterburg 33417
Memorialno-literaturnyj Muzej A.P. Bondina, Ekaterinburg 32771
Memorialnyj Dom-muzej S.T. Aksakova, Ufa 33642
Memorialnyj Dom-muzej Gercena, Moskva 33075
Memorialnyj Dom-muzej Marko Vovčok, Nalčik 33195
Memorialnyj Dom-muzej Mažita Gafuri, Ufa 33643
Memorialnyj Dom-Muzej P.P. Bažova, Ekaterinburg 32772
Memorialnyj Kompleks G. Tukaja, Novyj Kyrlaj 33249
Memorialnyj Muzej-dača A.S. Puškina, Puškin 33338
Memorialnyj Muzej-kvartira A.A. Šogencukova, Nalčik 33196
Memorialnyj Muzej-kvartira A.S. Puškina, Moskva 33079
Memorialnyj Muzej Licej, Puškin 33339
Memorialnyj Muzej A.G. Malyškina, Mokšan 33018
Memorialnyj Muzej B.L. Pasternaka, Čistopol 32748
Michajlovskoe - Gosudarstvennyj Memorialnyj Istoriko-literaturnyj i Prirodno-landšaftnyj Muzej-Zapovednik A.S. Puškina, Puškinskie Gory 33344
Moskovskij Gosudarstvennyj Muzej S.A. Esenina, Moskva 33087
Moskovskij Literaturnyj Muzej-Centr K.G. Paustovskogo, Moskva 33089
Municipalnyj Objedinennyj Muzej Pisatelej Urala, Ekaterinburg 32773
Municipalnyj Muzej Anna Achmatova - Serebrjannyj vek, Sankt-Peterburg 33424
Muzej E.A. Boratynskogo, Kazan 32895
Muzej-čitalnja N.V. Fëdorova, Moskva 33093
Muzej-čitalnja na Nacionalnych Jazykach, Penza 33287
Muzej V.I. Dalja, Moskva 33094
Muzej Detstva A.M. Gorkogo - Domik Kaširina, Nižnij Novgorod 33209
Muzej Ekslibrisa, Moskva 33096
Muzej Gabdulla Tukaja, Kazan 32896
Muzej A.M. Gorkogo, Moskva 33098
Muzej I.A. Bunina, Orël 33265
Muzej im. N.A. Ostrovskogo, Moskva 33106
Muzej Istorii Teatrov Dagestana, Machačkala 32998
Muzej Kajuma Nasyri, Kazan 32899
Muzej A. Kolcova, Voronež 33732
Muzej Kukol i Detskoj Knigi Strana Čudes, Ekaterinburg 32777
Muzej Kultury Astrachani, Astrachan 32666
Muzej-kvartira A.M. Gorkogo, Moskva 33121
Muzej-kvartira M.I. Cvetaevoj v Bolševo, Korolev 32940
Muzej-kvartira F.M. Dostoevskogo, Moskva 33123
Muzej-kvartira A.M. Gorkogo, Nižnij Novgorod 33215
Muzej-kvartira G.D. Krasilnikova, Iževsk 32835
Muzej-kvartira Lunačarskogo, Moskva 33125
Muzej-kvartira V.S. Mejercholda, Moskva 33126
Muzej-kvartira A. Puškina, Sankt-Peterburg 33453
Muzej-kvartira T.G. Ševčenko, Sankt-Peterburg 33455
Muzej-kvartira A.N. Tolstogo, Moskva 33129
Muzej-kvartita Musa Džalilja, Kazan 32902
Muzej Literaturnaja Žizn' Urala XIX Veka, Ekaterinburg 32779
Muzej Literaturnoj Žizni Jaroslavskogo Kraja, Jaroslavl 32854
Muzej Literatury Burjatii im. Choca Namsaraeva, Ulan-Udė 33654
Muzej-nekropol Literatorskie Mostki, Sankt-Peterburg 33460
Muzej Pisatelej-orlovcev, Orël 33266
Muzej Pisatelja A.P. Bibika, Mineral'nye Vody 33013
Muzej Poėta S. Orlova, Belozersk 32684
Muzej A.S. Puškina, Toržok 33619
Muzej A.S. Puškina v Bernove, Bernov 32686

Muzej M.E. Saltykova-Ščedrina, Tver 33636
Muzej Šarifa Kamala, Kazan 32905
Muzej Sceničeskogo Iskusstva im. V.E. Mejercholda, Penza 33292
Muzej A.K. Tolstogo, Krasnyj Rog 32963
Muzej L.N. Tolstogo na stancii Lev Tolstoj, Stancija Lev Tolstoj 33552
Muzej-usadba N.G. Černyševskogo, Saratov 33508
Muzej- Usadba F.M. Dostoevskogo Darovoe, Darovoe 32755
Muzej-usadba N.A. Durovoj, Elabuga 32788
Muzej-usadba L.N. Tolstogo Nikol'skoe Vjazemskoe, Nikol'skoe-Vjazemskoe 33204
Muzej-usadba "Muranovo" im. F.I. Tjutčeva, Lugovskoe 32994
Muzej-usadba Ostafjevo "Russkij Parnas", Ostafjevo 33274
Muzej-usadba poéta D. Venevitinova, Novoživotinnoe 33248
Muzej-usadba Roždestveno, Roždestveno 33359
Muzej-usadba A.N. Tolstogo, Samara 33374
Muzej-usadba L.N. Tolstogo v Chamovnikach, Moskva 33157
Muzej Vladimira Raevskogo, Bogoslovka 32695
Muzej-zapovednik Abramcevo, Abramcevo 32629
Muzej-zapovednik Pisatelja S.T. Aksakova, Aksakovo 32632
Nižnetagilskij Muzej-Zapovednik Gornozavodskogo Dela Srednego Urala, Nižnij Tagil 33228
Novorossijskij Gosudarstvennyj Istoričeskij Muzej Zapovednik, Novorossijsk 33238
Omskij Gosudarstvennyj Literaturnyj Muzej im. F.M. Dostoevskogo, Omsk 33256
Polibinskij Memorialnyj Muzej-usadba S.V. Kovalevskoj, Polibino 33327
Sankt-Peterburgskij Muzej V.V. Nabokova, Sankt-Peterburg 33482
Severo-osetinskij Literaturnyj Muzej im. K.L. Cetagurova, Vladikavkaz 33691
Taganrogskij Gosudarstvennyj Literaturnyj i Istoriko-architekturnyj Muzej-zapovednik, Taganrog 33586
Taganrogskij Muzej im. A.P. Čechova, Taganrog 33588
Tarusskij Muzej Semji Cvetaevych, Tarusa 33595
Vserossijskij Memorialnyj Muzej-zapovednik V.M. Šukšina, Srostki 33551
Vserossijskij Muzej Puškina, Sankt-Peterburg 33489
Vystavočnye Zaly v Dome Aksakovych, Moskva 33184

Samoa
Robert Louis Stevenson Museum, Vailima 33758

Serbia-Montenegro
Memorijalni Muzej Džuro Jakšić, Srpska Crnja 33916
Vukov i Dositejev Muzej, Beograd 33820

Slovakia
Literárna Expozícia - Múzeum Janka Jesenského, Bratislava 33969
Museum of Literature and Music, Banská Bystrica 33947
Múzeum Bábkarských Kutúr a Hračiek Hrad Modrý Kameň, expozícia Dolná Strhová, Dolná Strehová 33988
Múzeum Janka Krála, Liptovský Mikuláš 34015
Múzeum Ludovíta Štúra, Modra 34030
Oravské Múzeum Pavla Országha Hviezdoslava, Dolný Kubín 33990
Slovenské Múzeum A.S. Puškina, Brodzany 33983
Slovenské Národné Literárne Múzeum, Martin 34026
Vlastivedné a Literárne Múzeum, Svätý Jur 34069

Slovenia
Kurnikova Hiša, Tržič 34158
Prešernov Spominski Muzej, Kranj 34101
Rojstna Hiša Pesnika Otona Župančiča, Vinica 34163
Spominska Zbirka Pisatelja Ivana Cankarja, Vrhnika 34164

South Africa
Afrikaanse Taalmuseum, Paarl 34320
Nasionale Afrikaanse Letterkundige Museum en Navorsingsentrum, Bloemfontein 34188
National English Literary Museum, Grahamstown 34251
Olive Schreiner House, Cradock 34221

Spain
Casa de Zorrilla, Valladolid 35616
Casa-Museo Antonio Machado, Segovia 35462
Casa-Museo Azorín, Monóvar 35127
Casa Museo de Cervantes, Valladolid 35617
Casa-Museo de Lope de Vega, Madrid 34990
Casa-Museo de Unamuno, Salamanca 35357
Casa Museo Federico García Lorca, Fuente Vaqueros 34831
Casa-Museo Menéndez Pelayo, Santander 35430
Casa-Museo Rosalía de Castro, Padrón 35208
Casa-Museo Tomás Morales, Moya 35142
Casa-Museo Zenobia-Juan Ramón, Moguer 35115
Casa-Museu del Poeta Verdaguer, Folgueroles 34820
Centro de Mesonero Romanos, Madrid 34992
Museo Casa Natal de Cervantes, Alcalá de Henares 34427
Museu-Casa Verdaguer, Vallvidrera 35639
Museu Víctor Balaguer, Vilanova i la Geltrú 35668

Sweden
Alsters Herrgård, Karlstad 36002
C.M. Bellman Museum, Stockholm 36237
Dan Andersson Museum, Ludvika 36051
Engströmsgården, Hult 35967

Eyvind Johnson-Stugan, Boden 35834
Ivar Lo-Museet, Stockholm 36248
Mårbacka Manor, Östra Ämtervik 36149
Orgelmuseet i Fläckebo, Salbohed 36175
Sandellmuseet, Ramkvilla 36160
Strindbergsmuseet Blå Tornet, Stockholm 36292
Vättehult - Pälle Nävers Diktarstuga, Vetlanda 36404

Switzerland
Ausstellung Heinrich Federer, Sachseln 37080
Bibliothèque Publique et Universitaire, Salle Rousseau, Neuchâtel 36982
Dichter- und Stadtmuseum/ Herwegh-Archiv, Liestal 36876
Fondation Martin Bodmer, Cologny 36641
Fondation Rainer Maria Rilke, Sierre 37166
Gotthelf-Stube, Lützelflüh 36895
Institut et Musée Voltaire, Genève 36737
Johanna-Spyri-Museum im Alten Schulhaus, Hirzel 36805
Musée de la Science-Fiction, de l'Utopie et des Voyages Extraordinaires, Yverdon-les-Bains 37353
Musée Jean-Jacques Rousseau, Genève 36749
Musée Jean-Jacques Rousseau, Môtiers 36954
Musée Sherlock Holmes, Lucens 36894
Museo Hermann Hesse, Montagnola 36944
Museum Casa Anatta, Casa Selma und Klarwelt der Seligen, Ascona 36472
Sherlock Holmes-Museum, Meiringen 36935
Strauhof Zürich, Zürich 37411
Thomas-Mann-Archiv, Zürich 37412

Turkey
Aşiyan Müzesi, Bebek 37631
Cahit Sıtkı Tarancı Müzesi, Diyarbakır 37660
İstanbul Divan Edebiyatı Müzesi, İstanbul 37704
Sait Faik Müzesi, Burgaz Adası 37642
Yunus Emre Müzesi, Yunus Emre 37809

Ukraine
Černigiv Mykhailo Kotsiubynsky Literary Museum, Černigiv 37837
Istoriko-memorialnyj Muzej Semji Fadeevyh-Chan-Blavackij, Dnepropetrovsk 37849
Kiev Lesya Ukrainka State Literature Museum, Kyïv 37870
Kiev Taras Shevchenko National Museum, Kyïv 37873
Literaturno-Memoralnyj Muzej N.A Ostrovskogo, Šepetovka 37900
Literaturno-memorialny Muzei A.S. Puškina i P.I. Čajkovskogo, Kamenka 37858
Literaturno-memorialny Muzej Ivana Franko, Lviv 37884
Literaturno-Memorialny Muzej Lesi Ukrayinky, Kolodjažne 37862
Memorial Museum The Grave of T.G. Shevchenko, Kanev 37859
Memorijalnyj Dom-muzej Javornickogo, Dnepropetrovsk 37850
Poltava State Museum, Poltava 37898
Velikosoročinskij literaturno-memorialnyj muzej im N.V. Gogolja, Velikie Soročintsy 37910
Yu.A. Fedkovich Memorial Museum, Černivci 37840

United Kingdom
Abbotsford House, Melrose 39931
Bachelor's Club, Tarbolton 40674
Barrie's Birthplace, Kirriemuir 39399
Bateman's Kipling's House, Burwash 38409
Bleak House, Broadstairs 38365
Brontë Parsonage Museum, Haworth 39199
Broughton House and Garden, Kirkcudbright 39392
Brownsbank Cottage, Biggar 38194
Burns Cottage Museum, Alloway 37980
Burns House Museum, Mauchline 39925
Carlyle's House, London 39598
Ceiriog Memorial Institute, Glyn Ceiriog 39086
Charles Dickens Birthplace Museum, Portsmouth 40248
Charles Dickens Centre, Rochester 40334
Coleridge Cottage, Nether Stowey 40010
Cowper and Newton Museum, Olney 40130
D.H. Lawrence Birthplace Museum, Eastwood 38864
The Dickens House Museum, London 39624
Dickens House Museum Broadstairs, Broadstairs 38367
Dove Cottage and the Wordsworth Museum, Grasmere 39114
Dr. Johnson's House, London 39625
Dylan Thomas Boathouse, Laugharne 39429
Elstow Moot Hall, Bedford 38148
Hardy's Cottage, Higher Bockhampton 39242
Hauteville House, Saint Peter Port 40425
Hill Top, Sawrey 40451
Izaak Walton's Cottage, Shallowford 40479
James Hogg Exhibition, Selkirk 40469
Jane Austen's House, Chawton 38533
Jerome K. Jerome Birthplace Museum, Walsall 40772
John Buchan Centre, Tweedoale 40737
John Bunyan Museum, Bedford 38149
John Creasey Museum, Salisbury 40434
John Moore Countryside Museum, Tewkesbury 40690
Keats House, London 39679
Michael Bruce Cottage Museum, Kinnesswood 39389
Milton's Cottage, Chalfont Saint Giles 38520
Newstead Abbey, Ravenshead 40290
Richard Jefferies Museum, Swindon 40665
Robert Burns Centre, Dumfries 38791
Robert Burns House, Dumfries 38792
Ruskin Library, Lancaster 39418

Samuel Johnson Birthplace Museum, Lichfield 39492
Shandy Hall, Coxwold 38652
Shaw's Corner, Ayot-Saint-Lawrence 38048
Thomas Carlyle's Birthplace, Ecclefechan 38866
Tobias Smollett Museum, Alexandria 37971
Ty Mawr Wybrnant, Dolwyddelan 38739
Vennel Gallery, Irvine 39313
Wordsworth House, Cockermouth 38605
The Writers' Museum, Edinburgh 38921

U.S.A.
Berkshire County Historical Society Museum at Arrowhead, Pittsfield 46531
Curwood Castle, Owosso 46232
Dickinson Homestead, Amherst 41177
Edgar Allan Poe House, Philadelphia 46405
Edgar Allan Poe House and Museum, Baltimore 41464
Edgar Allan Poe Museum, Richmond 46876
Ernest Hemingway House Museum, Key West 44464
Hemingway Museum, Oak Park 46053
John G. Neihardt Center, Bancroft 41490
John Greenleaf Whittier Home, Amesbury 41175
The Kate Chopin House and Bayou Folk Museum, Cloutierville 42505
Knott House Museum, Tallahassee 47932
Limberlost State Historic Site, Geneva 43641
Museum of the Alphabet, Waxhaw 48470
My Old Kentucky Home, Bardstown 41503
National Steinbeck Center, Salinas 47216
Orchard House - Home of the Alcotts, Concord 42601
Pearl S. Buck Birthplace, Hillsboro 44023
Robert Louis Stevenson Memorial Cottage, Saranac Lake 47450
Sarah Orne Jewett House, South Berwick 47686
Scholte House Museum, Pella 46330
Vachel Lindsay Home, Springfield 47743
Wadsworth-Longfellow House, Portland 46629
William Cullen Bryant Homestead, Cummington 42728
Wren's Nest House Museum, Atlanta 41363
Zane Grey Museum, Lackawaxen 44561

Uzbekistan
Literaturnyj Muzej Alisher Navoj, Taškent 48855
Literaturnyj Muzej Andižana, Andižan 48830
Literaturnyj Muzej G. Guliama iz Fergana, Kokand 48842
Sadriddin Aini Memorial Museum, Samarkand 48851

Venezuela
Casa de Andrés Eloy Blanco, Cumaná 48936
Casa Natal de José Antonio Ramos Sucre, Cumaná 48937
Museo Alberto Arvelo Torrealba, Barinas 48894

Germany
Deutsches Schloss-und Beschlägemuseum,
Velbert 20293

Netherlands
LIPS Slotenmuseum, Dordrecht 29174

United Kingdom
Neville Blakey Museum of Locks, Keys and Safes,
Brierfield 38333
Willenhall Lock Museum, Willenhall 40873

U.S.A.
Lock Museum of America, Terryville 47988

Lumber → Forest Products

Machines and Machinery

Australia
Boiler House Steam and Engine Museum,
Kurwongbah 01155
Booleroo Steam and Traction Museum, Booleroo
Centre 00812
Chinchilla and District Historical Society Museum,
Chinchilla 00915
Cobdogla Irrigation and Steam Museum,
Cobdogla 00932
Corrigin Museum, Corrigin 00948
Manjimup Timber Museum, Manjimup 01206
Morphett's Enginehouse Museum, Burra 00866
National Motor Museum, Birdwood 00806
Rushworth Museum, Rushworth 01429

Belgium
Nationaal Borstelmuseum, Izegem 03522
Nationaal Schoeiselmuseum, Izegem 03523
Nationaal Vlas-, Kant- en Linnenmuseum,
Kortrijk 03542

Canada
Rocanville and District Museum, Rocanville 06280

Czech Republic
Technické Muzeum v Brně, Brno 08277

Denmark
Arbejder-, Håndværker- og Industrimuseet,
Horsens 08894

Finland
Rosenlew-museo, Pori 09946

France
Ecomusée la Cité des Abeilles, Saint-Faust 14212
Galerie Bovary, Ry 14079
Musée des Automates, La Rochelle 12240
Musée des Automates, Sauclières 14629
Musée du Moteur, Saumur 14649
Musée Industriel Corderie Vallois, Notre-Dame-de-
Bondeville 13365

Germany
Ausstellung Historischer Elektromaschinenbau,
Leipzig 18386
Bayerisches Moor- und Torfmuseum, Grassau,
Chiemgau 17378
Deutsches Baumaschinen-Modellmuseum,
Weilburg 20443
Gerätemuseum des Coburger Landes, Ahorn, Kreis
Coburg 15405
Industriemuseum Chemnitz, Chemnitz 16465
Landesmuseum Koblenz, Koblenz 18120
MAN Museum, Augsburg 15560
Molkerei-Museum, Bernbeuren 16124
Museum Industriekultur mit Motorradmuseum,
Nürnberg 19154
Sammlung Gauselmann, Espelkamp 16942
Sammlung historischer Maschinen und Geräte,
Calau 16442
Stadtmuseum, Apolda 15509
Technisches Museum der Pforzheimer Schmuck- und
Uhrenindustrie, Pforzheim 19391
Werksmuseum der MTU, München 18923

Ireland
The Steam Museum, Straffan 22543
Strabally Steam Museum, Stradbally 22542

Italy
Museo All'Aperto di Storia dell'Agricoltura,
Sassari 25485
Museo Archeologico dell'Arte della Lana,
Arpino 22939
Museo dei Tasso e della Storia Postale, Camerata
Cornello 23282

Japan
Kawaguchi-ko Motor Museum, Narusawa 26589

Netherlands
De Brede, Maasbree 29560
Museumwerf 't Kromhout, Amsterdam 28883
Naaimachine Museum, Dordrecht 29176
Nederlands Stoommachinemuseum,
Medemblik 29583

Noord-Hollands Motoren Museum, Nieuwe
Niedorp 29617
Poldermuseum, Puttershoek 29719
Poldermuseum de Hooge Boezem Achter Haastrecht,
Haastrecht 29335
Racemotormuseum Lexmond, Lexmond 29537
Stoomhoutzagerij, Groenlo 29304

New Zealand
Otago Vintage Machinery Club Museum,
Dunedin 30153
Pigeon Valley Steam Museum, Wakefield 30283
Tokomaru Steam Engine Museum, Tokomaru 30267

Norway
Bergens Tekniske Museum, Bergen 30418

Russia
Muzej Istorii Architektury i Promyšlennoj Techniki
Urala, Ekaterinburg 32774

Spain
Museu dels Autòmats, Barcelona 34572

Sweden
Faktoriet, Eskilstuna 35870
Fornminnesgården, Eksjö 35861
Museum för Utombordsmotorer, Varberg 36396
Rubens Maskinhistoriska Samlingar, Götene 35924

Switzerland
Musée Suisse de la Machine à Coudre,
Fribourg 36717
Nähmaschinen-Museum, Steckborn 37210
Schweizerisches Dampfmaschinenmuseum
Vaporama, Thun 37242

United Kingdom
Bolton Steam Museum, Bolton 38270
Brunel Engine House, London 39591
Cheddleton Flint Mill, Cheddleton 38536
Coleham Pumping Station, Shrewsbury 40508
Cornish Mines, Engines and Cornwall Industrial
Discovery Centre, Pool 40225
Corris Railway Museum, Machynlleth 39868
The Crossness Engines, London 39617
Dingles Steam Village, Lifton 39495
Doune Motor Museum, Doune 38762
Eastney Beam Engine House, Portsmouth 40251
Etruria Industrial Museum, Stoke-on-Trent 40604
Forncett Industrial Steam Museum, Forncett Saint
Mary 39006
Garlogie Mill Power House Museum, Garlogie 39025
Haynes Motor Museum, Sparkford 40565
Hobbies Museum of Fretwork, Dereham 38721
Hollycombe Steam Collection, Liphook 39509
House Mill, London 39669
Kew Bridge Steam Museum, Kew 39349
Lark Lane Motor Museum, Liverpool 39519
Lewis Textile Museum, Blackburn, Lancashire 38244
Middleton Top Engine House, Middleton-by-
Wirksworth 39951
Midland Motor Museum, Bridgnorth 38323
Motor Museum, Ramsgate 40282
Museum of Bath at Work, Bath 38117
Museum of the Welsh Woollen Industry,
Llandysul 39543
National Tramway Museum, Matlock 39922
Newcomen Engine House, Dartmouth 38703
Papplewick Pumping Station, Ravenshead 40291
Pinchbeck Marsh Engine and Land Drainage Museum,
Spalding 40563
Ruddington Framework Knitters' Museum,
Ruddington 40351
Ryhope Engines Museum, Sunderland 40648
Shore Road Pumping Station, Birkenhead 38206
Stretham Old Engine, Stretham 40636
Waterworks Museum - Hereford, Hereford 39231
West Wycombe Motor Museum, West
Wycombe 40829
Westonzoyland Pumping Station Museum,
Bridgwater 38326
Workshop and Stores, Grangemouth 39109

U.S.A.
Carpenter Museum of Antique Outboard Motors,
Gilmanton 43673
Hidalgo Pumphouse Heritage, Hidalgo 44011
Museo Abarth, Marietta 45145
Steam Engine Museum, Mabel 45016

Majolica → Porcelain and Ceramics

Mammals

Australia
Whaleworld Museum, Albany 00726

Belgium
Natuurpunt Museum, Turnhout 03804

Bulgaria
Prirodonaučen Muzej, Černi Osăm 04638

Canada
Agawa Bay Exhibition Centre, Wawa 06758
Sidney Marine Museum, Sidney 06450

Czech Republic
Zámek Budišov, Budišov u Třebíče 08284

Finland
K.E. Kivirikon Lintu- ja Nisäkäskokoelma,
Helsinki 09500

India
Zoology Museum, Lucknow 21933

Italy
Museo di Storia Naturale della Maremma,
Grosseto 24058

Japan
Shiretoko Museum, Shari 26742

Netherlands
Natuurmuseum Rotterdam, Rotterdam 29766

Poland
Muzeum Lasu i Drewna przy Lesnym Zakładzie
Doświadczalnym SGGW, Rogów 31949

Puerto Rico
Caribbean Primate Research Center Museum, San
Juan 32387

Romania
Muzeul Naţional de Istorie Naturala Grigore Antipa,
Bucureşti 32468

Slovenia
Prirodoslovni Muzej Slovenije, Ljubljana 34118

South Africa
Amathole Museum, King William's Town 34295

Switzerland
Museum Stemmler, Schaffhausen 37131

Man, Prehistoric

Argentina
Museo de Antropología, Córdoba 00292

Brazil
Museu Nacional, Rio de Janeiro 04388

Colombia
Museo Universitario, Medellín 07524

Croatia
Hrvatski Prirodoslovni Muzej, Zagreb 07823

Ecuador
Museo de Antropología, Ibarra 09181
Museo de Sitio Arqueologico el Mongote Real Alto,
Guayaquil 09172

Germany
Neanderthal Museum, Mettmann 18725
Urmensch-Museum, Steinheim an der Murr 20051

Greece
Anthropological-Ethnological Museum, Athinai 20847

Iran
Mardom-shenasi-ye Kavir, Nayin 22271

Italy
Museo Preistorico Balzi Rossi, Ventimiglia 25956

Mexico
Museo de Antropología, Tecolotlán 28467
Museo de Antropología de Xalapa, Xalapa 28615
Museo Regional de Antropología J. Jesús Figueroa
Torres, Sayula 28444

U.S.A.
Wayne State University Museum of Anthropology,
Detroit 42936
William S. Webb Museum of Anthropology,
Lexington 44748
Zion National Park Museum, Springdale 47735

Manuscripts → Books, Book Art and
Manuscripts

Maps → Cartography

Marine Archaeology

Australia
Museum of Tropical Queensland, Townsville 01546
Western Australian Maritime Museum,
Fremantle 01038

Brazil
Espaço Cultural da Marinha, Rio de Janeiro 04323

Bulgaria
Archeologičeski Muzej, Burgas 04631

Cameroon
Cameroon Maritime Museum, Douala 04953

Canada
Sidney Marine Museum, Sidney 06450

Cyprus, Turkish Republic
Batik Gemi Müzesi, Girne 08223

Dominican Republic
Museo de las Atarazanas, Santo Domingo 09123

France
Conservatoire Maritime Basque, Ciboure 11304
Musée Conservatoire Maritime et Rural,
Narbonne 13266
Musée de la Mer, Cannes 11026
Musée de la Mer OCEAM, Les Sables-d'Olonne 12554
Musée d'Istres, Istres 12065
Musée Maritime de l'île de Tatihou, Saint-Vaast-la-
Hougue 14495

Germany
Museum für Unterwasserarchäologie, Saßnitz 19761
Nationalpark-Haus, Butjadingen 16434

Iran
Military Marine Museum, Bandar-Anzali 22233

Israel
Clandestine Immigration and Naval Museum,
Haifa 22601
National Maritime Museum, Haifa 22609

Italy
Museo della Marineria dell'Alto e Medio Adriatico,
Cesenatico 23511
Museo Navale Romano, Albenga 22834

Korea, Republic
Korea Maritime University Museum, Busan 27142

Malaysia
Maritime Archaeology Museum, Melaka 27664

Norway
Stavanger Maritime Museum, Stavanger 30889

Qatar
Al Khor Museum, Al Khor 32413
Al Wakra Museum, AL Wakra 32414

South Africa
Port Elizabeth Museum, Port Elizabeth 34333

Spain
Museo Militar Regional de Sevilla, San
Fernando 35374
Museo Naval de Cartagena, Cartagena 34686
Museu d'Arqueològia Submarina, Pals 35246

Sweden
Vasamuseet, Stockholm 36298

Turkey
Bodrum Sualti Arkeolojisi Müzesi, Bodrum 37637

United Kingdom
Dartmouth Museum, Dartmouth 38702
National Maritime Museum, London 39731

Marine Biology → Oceanography

Masks

Belgium
Musée International du Carnaval et du Masque,
Binche 03217

Burkina Faso
Musée de la Bendrologie, Manéga 04939

Denmark
Radio- og Motorcykel Museet, Stubbekøbing 09082

Germany
Deutsches Fastnachtmuseum, Kitzingen 18104
Narrenschopf, Bad Dürrheim 15632

Japan
Shishi Kaikan, Takayama 26810

Korea, Republic
Galchon Mask Museum, Goseong 27178
Hahoedong Mask Museum, Andong 27129

Mexico
Museo de la Máscara, Morelia 28249
Museo Nacional de la Máscara, San Luis
Potosí 28405

Sri Lanka
Ambalangoda Mask Museum, Ambalangoda 35742

Switzerland
Musée Suisse de la Marionette, Fribourg 36718

Mass Media

Argentina
Museo de Medios de Comunicación, Resistencia 00508
Museo del las Comunicaciones de Mar del Plata, Mar del Plata 00425
Museo Radiofónico de la Ciudad de Boulogne, Boulogne 00142

Australia
City Park Radio Museum, Launceston 01167

Austria
Ars Electronica Center, Linz 02226
Erstes Österreichisches Funk- und Radiomuseum, Wien 02879
Museum in Progress, Wien 02947

Brazil
Museu da Imprensa, Brasília 03998
Museu do Rádio, Juiz de Fora 04157

Canada
CBC Museum, Toronto 06570
CBC Radio Museum, Saint John's 06342
Manitoba Amateur Radio Museum, Brandon 05123

Finland
Keskisuomalaisen Museo, Jyväskylä 09603
Radio- ja TV-Museo, Lahti 09747

France
Musée de la Publicité, Paris 13563
Musée de la Radio Galletti, Saint-Maurice-de-Rotherens 14363
Musée de Radio France, Paris 13584
Musée Municipal, Louhans 12678

Germany
Bremer Rundfunkmuseum, Bremen 16319
Deutsches Film- und Fototechnik Museum, Deidesheim 16561
Internationales Radiomuseum, Bad Laasphe 15685
Internationales Zeitungsmuseum der Stadt Aachen, Aachen 15373
Photographisch-optisches Museum, Biedenkopf 16151
Radiomuseum, Bad Bentheim 15600
Radiomuseum, Rottenburg an der Laaber 19693
Radiomuseum, Waldbronn 20354
Rundfunkmuseum der Stadt Fürth, Fürth, Bayern 17166
Rundfunkmuseum Schloß Brunn, Emskirchen 16870

Italy
Museo Civico della Media Valle del Liri, Sora 25606
Museo della Guerra Adamellina, Spiazzo 25618

Japan
Koto-ku Fukagawa Edo Siryokan, Tokyo 26874
Newsstand Museum, Osaka 26659
NHK Hoso Hakubutsukan, Tokyo 26901
Teishin Sogo Hakubutsukan, Tokyo 26931

Korea, Republic
Korean Magazine Museum, Seoul 27250
Samsung Museum of Publishing, Seoul 27269

Lithuania
Radio and Television Museum, Šiauliai 27530

Mexico
Museo Casa de León Trotsky, México 28115
Museo del Retrato Hablado, México 28162

Netherlands
Museum Radio-Wereld, Diever 29154
Museum voor het Radiozendamateurisme Jan Corver, Budel 29035
Omroepmuseum en Smalfilmmuseum, Hilversum 29420
Persmuseum, Amsterdam 28892
Radio Amateur Museum, Reusel 29728
Radio- en Speelgoed Museum, Onstwedde 29664
Rotterdams Radio Museum, Rotterdam 29773

Russia
Centralnyj Muzej Svjazi im. A.S. Popova, Sankt-Peterburg 33386
Muzej-studija Radioteatra, Moskva 33152

Sweden
Radiomuseet i Göteborg, Göteborg 35918
Sveriges Rundradiomuseum, Motala 36107

Switzerland
Musée Au Filament Rouge, Perrefitte 37019
Musée National Suisse de l'Audiovisuel, Montreux 36948

Turkey
Basin Müzesi Sanat Galerisi, İstanbul 37695

United Kingdom
Museum of Entertainment, Whaplode 40848
Museum of the Moving Images, London 39721
National Arts Education Archive, Wakefield 40760
Orkney Wireless Museum, Kirkwall 39398
Vintage Wireless Museum, London 39797

U.S.A.
American Museum of the Moving Image, Astoria 41307
French Cable Station Museum in Orleans, Orleans 46191
Lum and Abner Museum and Jot 'Em Down Store, Pine Ridge 46491
The Museum of Broadcast Communications, Chicago 42343
Museum of Television and Radio, Beverly Hills 41677
Museum of Television and Radio, New York 45845
The Newseum, Arlington 41266
Radio-Television Museum, Bowie 41847
Robert R. McCormick Museum at Cantigny, Wheaton 48584

Venezuela
Museo Audiovisual, Caracas 48907

Medals → Numismatics

Medicine and Hygiene

Afghanistan
Pathology Museum, Kabul 00005

Argentina
Museo Casa de Bernardo A. Houssay, Buenos Aires 00160
Museo de Ciencias Morfológicas, Rosario 00526
Museo de Historia de la Medicina y de la Cirugía Vincente A. Risolía, Buenos Aires 00179
Museo de la Psicología Experimental Argentina Horacio G. Piñero, Buenos Aires 00190
Museo de Patología, Buenos Aires 00194
Museo de Urología, Buenos Aires 00197
Museo del Médico, Santa Fé 00602
Museo Houssay de Historia de la Ciencia y Técnología, Buenos Aires 00220
Museo Odontológico Dr. Jorge E. Dunster, Corrientes 00323
Museo Pedro Ara, Córdoba 00309
Museum Oculorum, Buenos Aires 00250

Australia
Childers Pharmaceutical Museum, Childers 00909
Dr. Arratta Memorial Museum, Muttaburra 01297
Geoffrey Kaye Museum of Anaesthetic History, Melbourne 01227
Marks-Hirshfeld Museum of Medical History, Herston 01095
Medical History Museum, Hobart 01101
Medical History Museum, Melbourne 01236
Mooroopna Hospital, Mooroopna 01271
The Museum of Nursing, Camperdown 00883
Museum of Pathology, Sydney 01503
Old Springsure Hospital Museum, Springsure 01471
Royal Flying Doctor Service Visitors Centre, Edge Hill 01007
Tracy Maund Historical Collection, Carlton South 00898
Western Australian Medical Museum, Subiaco 01483
Wide Bay Hospital Museum, Maryborough 01218

Austria
Anatomisches Museum, Innsbruck 02060
Dokumentation des ehemaligen Heilbades, Bad Pirawarth 01716
Erstes Österreichisches Rettungsmuseum, Hohenems 02040
Institut Zeileis, Gallspach 01865
Medizinhistorisches Museum, Wien 02930
Museum für Medizin-Meteorologie, Zwettl, Niederösterreich 03060
Museum Mödling, Mödling 02312
Pathologisch-anatomisches Bundesmuseum, Wien 02971
Sanitärmuseum, Wien 02984
Sigmund Freud-Museum, Wien 02989

Belgium
Hôpital Notre-Dame de la Rose, Lessines 03561
Musée de la Médecine, Bruxelles 03305
Museum Dr. Guislain, Gent 03444
Museum voor Anesthesie Verantare, Antwerpen 03158
Museum voor Geschiedenis van de Geneeskunde, Gent 03446

Brazil
Museu da Faculdade de Odontologia, Araraquara 03954
Museu de Images do Inconsciente, Rio de Janeiro 04360
Museu de Medicina, Curitiba 04071
Museu de Odontologia Professor Salles Cunha, Rio de Janeiro 04362
Museu de Patologia do Instituto Oswaldo Cruz, Rio de Janeiro 04363
Museu Inaldo de Lyra Neves-Manta, Rio de Janeiro 04386

Bulgaria
Muzej Čovek i negovoto Zdrave, Varna 04896
Muzej za Istorija na Medicinata, Varna 04902

Canada
Alberta Association of Registered Nurses Museum, Edmonton 05368
Alberta Hospital Museum, Ponoka 06145
British Columbia Congenital Heart Museum, Vancouver 06666
British Columbia Medical Association Museum, Vancouver 06668
Centennial Museum of the Nanaimo Regional General Hospital, Nanaimo 05959
Dental Museum, Edmonton 05372
Hamilton Psychiatric Hospital Museum St. Joseph's Mountain Site, Hamilton 05573
Hillary House and Koffler Museum of Medicine, Aurora 05022
History of Contraception Museum, Toronto 06583
James J. O'Mara Pharmacy Museum, Saint John's 06345
Lillian Stevenson Nursing Archives Museum, Saint John's 06346
Museum of Health Care, Kingston 05685
Museum of Mental Health Services, Toronto 06597
New Brunswick Healthcare Museum, Fredericton 05464

China, People's Republic
China Tradition Medicine Museum, Chongqing 07030
Chinese Medicine Museum, Hangzhou 07082
Museum of Medical History, Shanghai 07217
Museum of Medical Sciences, Hong Kong 07105

Colombia
Museo Bernardo Samper Sordo, Bogotá 07393
Museo de Historia de la Medicina, Bogotá 07403

Croatia
Muzej Kliničke Psihijatrijske Bolnice Vrapče, Zagreb 07832

Cuba
Museo Casa Alejandro de Humboldt, La Habana 07938
Museo Casa de Sais Montes de Oca Hermanos, Pinar del Río 08072
Museo Casa Natal de Hermanos Ameijeiras, Pueblo Viejo 08083
Museo de Medicina Tropical Carlos J. Finlay, La Habana 07964

Czech Republic
České Zdravotnické Muzeum, Praha 08568
U Zlaté Koruny, Brno 08278

Denmark
Medicinsk-Historisk Museum, København 08938
Museet Psykiatrisk Hospital i Århus, Risskov 09034

Ecuador
Museo de la Medicine, Cuenca 09155
Museo Nacional de Historia de la Medicina Eduardo Estrella, Quito 09215

Egypt
Anatomy and Pathology Museum, Alexandria 09236
Museum of Hygiene, Cairo 09273

Estonia
Eesti Tervishoiu Muuseum, Tallinn 09364

Finland
Hammaslääketieteen Museo, Helsinki 09483
Helsingin Yliopistomuseo, Helsinki 09491
Helsingin Yliopiston Lääketieteen Historian Laitos ja Museo, Helsinki 09493
Keski-Suomen Sairaanhoitopiirin Sairaalamuseo, Jyväskylä 09602
Sairaalamuseo, Lahti 09749
Sotilaslääketieteen Museo, Lahti 09750
Turun Terveydenhuoltomuseo, Turku 10136

France
Ancienne École de Médecine Navale, Rochefort (Charente-Maritime) 13996
Musée Albert Schweitzer, Kaysersberg 12111
Musée Arménien de France, Paris 13530
Musée Claude Bernard, Saint-Julien-en-Beaujolais 14299
Musée d'Anatomie Delmas-Orfila-Rouvière, Paris 13544
Musée d'Anatomie Normale, Strasbourg 14819
Musée de l'Assistance Publique-Hôpitaux de Paris, Paris 13572
Musée de l'Histoire de la Médecine, Vandœuvre-les-Nancy 15078
Musée de l'Histoire de la Médecine de Toulouse, Toulouse 14943
Musée de Matière Médicale, Paris 13580
Musée des Hospices Civils de Lyon, Lyon 12737
Musée d'Histoire de la Médecine, Paris 13595
Musée d'Histoire de la Médecine et de la Pharmacie, Lyon 12743
Musée Dupuytren, Paris 13610
Musée Flaubert et d'Histoire de la Médecine, Rouen 14052
Musée Ollier, Les Vans 12560
Musée Pasteur, Dole 11542
Musée Pasteur, Calmette et Guérin, Lille 12604
Musée Pierre Fauchard, Paris 13645

Germany
Albert-Schweitzer-Gedenk- und Begegnungsstätte, Weimar, Thüringen 20454
Anatomische Sammlung, Erlangen 16914
Berliner Medizinhistorisches Museum der Charité, Berlin 15918
Deutsches Hygiene-Museum, Dresden 16679
Deutsches Medizinhistorisches Museum, Ingolstadt 17906
Deutsches Orthopädisches Geschichts- und Forschungsmuseum, Frankfurt am Main 17037
Deutsches Röntgen-Museum, Remscheid 19564
Historische Arztpraxis, Burgstädt 16430
Karthaus-Prüll Museen des Bezirksklinikums Regensburg, Regensburg 19525
Krankenhaus-Museum am Zentralkrankenhaus Bremen-Ost, Bremen 16327
Krankenhausmuseum, Nürnberg 19149
Medizin- und Pharmaziehistorische Sammlung Kiel der Christian-Albrechts-Universität, Kiel 18077
Medizinhistorische Sammlung der Ruhr-Universität Bochum, Bochum 16197
Medizinhistorische Sammlungen, Chemnitz 16467
Museum Anatomicum, Marburg 18631
Psychiatrie-Museum, Emmendingen 16856
Psychiatrie Museum im Philippshospital, Riedstadt 19607
Psychiatriemuseum Haina, Haina, Kloster 17494
Robert-Koch-Museum, Berlin 16083
Rot-Kreuz-Museum, Regenstauf 19534
Rotkreuz-Museum, Nürnberg 19157
Rotkreuz-Museum Berlin, Berlin 16084
Rotkreuzmuseum, Hofheim, Unterfranken 17801
Sächsisches Apothekenmuseum Leipzig, Leipzig 18413
Sächsisches Psychiatriemuseum, Leipzig 18414
Sanitätsmuseum, Großpösna 17436
Spitalmuseum, Aub 15541
Stadtmuseum Gütersloh, Gütersloh 17460
Strigel-Museum und Antoniter-Museum, Memmingen 18705
Zahnärztliches Museum, Tübingen 20231
Zahnhistorische Sammlung, Coburg 16487

Greece
International Hippocratic Foundation of Kos, Kos 21032

Hungary
Katona József Múzeum, Kecskemét 21448
Semmelweis Orvostörténeti Múzeum, Budapest 21382

Iceland
Nesstofusafn, Seltjarnarnes 21668

India
Anatomy Museum, Chennai 21740
Anatomy Museum, Mumbai 21945
Gauhati Medical College Museum, Gauhati 21809
Grant Medical College Museum, Mumbai 21948
Guwahati Medical Museum, Guwahati 21823
Health Museum, Hyderabad 21843
Medical College Museum, Vadodara 22050
Museum of the Medical College, Mysore 21962
Pathology and Bacteriology Museum, Lucknow 21929
Pathology Museum, Mumbai 21953
State Ayurvedic College Museum, Hardwar 21836
State Health Institute Museum, Lucknow 21931
Sulabh International Museum of Toilets, Delhi 21784

Indonesia
Museum Anatomy FK UI, Jakarta 22111
Museum Kedokteran, Jakarta 22118

Ireland
Royal College of Surgeons in Ireland Museum, Dublin 22454

Israel
Medicine and Pioneers Museum, Menahimiya 22711

Italy
Donazione Putti Biblioteca, Bologna 23102
Musei Anatomici, Modena 24436
Museo Anatomia Veterinaria, Napoli 24576
Museo Anatomico, Pisa 24948
Museo Anatomico, Siena 25568
Museo Anatomico G. Tumiati, Ferrara 23785
Museo Comunale La Malaria e la sua Storia, Pontinia 25001
Museo dei Ferri Chirurgici, Pistoia 24959
Museo delle Cere Anatomiche Luigi Cattaneo, Bologna 23118
Museo dell'Istituto di Anatomia Patologica, Padova 24738
Museo dell'IstitutoCentral di Patologia, Roma 25205
Museo di Anatomia Comparata, Bologna 23121
Museo di Anatomia Comparata Battista Grassi, Roma 25206
Museo di Anatomia Patologica, Roma 25207
Museo di Anatomia Patologica C. Taruffi, Bologna 23122
Museo di Anatomia Patologica Veterinaria, Ozzano dell'Emilia 24724
Museo di Anatomia Umana, Torino 25744
Museo di Anatomia Umana, Napoli 24586
Museo di Anatomia Umana Normale, Parma 24804
Museo di Anatomia Umana Normale, Bologna 23123

Museo di Anatomia Veterinaria, Napoli 24587
Museo di Antropologia Criminale, Torino 25746
Museo di Etnomedicina, Piazzola sul Brenta 24903
Museo di Scienze Naturali del Collegio, Lodi 24203
Museo di Storia della Medicina, Roma 25219
Museo Organologico Didattico, Cremona 23682
Museo Ostetrico, Bologna 23142
Museo Ostetrico, Padova 24747
Museo Storico dell'Arte Sanitaria, Roma 25258
Raccolte del Dipartimento di Scienze Radiologiche,
 Roma 25267
Raccolte dell'Istituto di Clinica delle Malattie Tropicali
 e Subtropicali, Roma 25268
Raccolte dell'Istituto di Clinica Otorinolaringoiatrica,
 Roma 25269
Raccolte dell'Istituto di Clinica Urologica,
 Roma 25270

Japan
Chiba-kenritsu Sonan Hakubutsukan, Isumi 26260
Dr. Hideyo Noguchi Memorial Hall, Inawashiro 26247
Toyama Museum, Toyama 26971

Jordan
Medical Museum, Amman 27057

Korea, Republic
Gacheon Museum, Incheon 27190

Kuwait
Educational Science Museum, Kuwait 27305

Latvia
Paula Stradiņa Medicīnas Vēstures Muzejs,
 Rīga 27434

Malaysia
Biomedical Museum, Kuala Lumpur 27640

Mexico
Museo Antiguo Palacio de la Medicina Mexicana,
 México 28106
Museo de Medicina Maya, San Cristóbal de las
 Casas 28379
Museo de Medicina Tradicional y Herbolaria,
 Cuernavaca 27874
Museo de Odontología, México 28146
Museo del Pueblo-Hospital, Quiroga 28356
Museo Estatal de Patología, Puebla 28339
Sala Histórica de la Facultad de Medicina,
 Mitras 28222

Myanmar
Health Museum, Yangon 28750

Netherlands
Anatomisch Museum, Groningen 29306
Anatomisch Museum, Utrecht 29895
Anatomisch Museum Nijmegen, Nijmegen 29629
Anatomisch Museum van de Rijksuniversiteit Leiden,
 Leiden 29518
Historische Verzameling Militair Geneeskundige
 Dienst, Loosdrecht 29545
Medisch Farmaceutisch Museum de Griffioen,
 Delft 29080
Museum Boerhaave, Leiden 29521
Museum De Kluis, Boekel 28993
Museum Duin en Bosch, Castricum 29056
Museum GGZ-Drenthe, Assen 28951
Museumproject AZG, Groningen 29312
Nationaal Ambulance- en Eerste Hulpmuseum,
 Winschoten 30009
Oorlogs- en Verzetsmuseum Johannes Post,
 Ridderkerk 29730
Parkzicht, Ermelo 29252
Tuberculosemuseum Beatrixoord, Appelscha 28930
Verpleegkundig Historisch Bezit, Amersfoort 28827
Ziekenhuis- en Verpleegkundig Museum,
 Deventer 29147

New Zealand
Anatomy Museum, Dunedin 30144
Ernest and Marion Davis Medical History Museum,
 Auckland 30106
Order of Saint John Museum, Christchurch 30130
Porirua Hospital Museum, Porirua 30241
Royal New Zealand Army Medical Corps Museum,
 Christchurch 30131

Norway
Lepramuseet Sant Jørgens Hospital, Bergen 30424
Redningsselskapets Museum, Horten 30567
Sand Bakkens Medisinske Museum,
 Flekkefjord 30496
Sykepleiemuseum, Oslo 30766
Trastad Samlinger, Borkenes 30444
Ullevål Sykehus Museum, Oslo 30768

Peru
Museo Arqueológico de Cajamarca y Museo Médico,
 Cajamarca 31126

Philippines
Philippine Radiation Science Museum, Manila 31391

Poland
Muzeum Akademii Medycznej, Poznań 31897
Muzeum Historii Medycyny i Farmacji,
 Szczecin 32026
Muzeum Pamięci Narodowej, Kraków 31717
Muzeum Polskiej Wojskowej Służby Zdrowia,
 Łódź 31774

Russia
Dom-muzej Akademika E.N. Pavlovskogo,
 Borisoglebsk 32699
Memorialnyj Muzej-usadba Akademika I.P. Pavlova,
 Rjazan 33350
Muzej Istorii Razvitija Mediciny, Astrachan 32665
Muzej Obščestva Krasnogo Kresta Rossii,
 Moskva 33141
Muzej Zdravoochranenija, Sankt-Peterburg 33469
Voenno-medicinskij Muzej, Sankt-Peterburg 33488

Slovenia
Pharmaceutical and Medical Museum of Bohuslav
 Lavička, Ljubljana 34116

South Africa
Adler Museum of Medicine, Johannesburg 34267
African Herbalist Shops, Johannesburg 34268
Brebner Surgical Museum, Johannesburg 34274
Pathology Museum, Pretoria 34352

Spain
Colección Anatomía, Madrid 34994
Museo Retrospectivo de Farmacia y Medicina, El
 Masnou 35096

Sweden
Ersta Diakonimuseum, Stockholm 36239
Hospitalsmuseet, Vadstena 36367
Landstingsmuseet, Örebro 36137
Målilla Sanatoriums Museum, Målilla 36069
Medicinhistoriska Museet, Göteborg 35915
Medicinhistoriska Museet, Linköping 36041
Medicinhistoriska Museet, Lund 36063
Medicinhistoriska Museet, Vänersborg 36372
Medicinhistoriska Museet Eugenia, Stockholm 36261
Mentalvårdsmuseet Säter, Säter 36169
Psykiatrihistoriska Museet, Uppsala 36359
Psykiatrihistoriska Museet, Växjö 36389
Sveriges VVS-Museum, Katrineholm 36005
Tandläkarmuseum, Sunne 36313
Uppsala Medicinhistoriska Museum, Uppsala 36363

Switzerland
Anatomisches Museum Basel, Basel 36494
Henry-Dunant-Museum, Heiden 36797
Medizinhistorisches Museum, Zürich 37388
Moulagensammlung des Universitätsspitals und der
 Universität Zürich, Zürich 37391
Psychiatrie-Museum, Bern 36549

Thailand
Congdom Anatomical Museum, Bangkok 37481
Forensic Medicine Museum, Bangkok 37482
Museum of Medical Equipment, Bangkok 37489

United Kingdom
Alexander Fleming Laboratory Museum,
 London 39564
Anaesthetic Museum, London 39566
Army Medical Services Museum, Aldershot 37967
Bethlem Royal Hospital Archives and Museum,
 Beckenham 38141
BOC Museum, London 39581
British Dental Association Museum, London 39583
British Red Cross Museum and Archives,
 London 39588
Chamberlain Museum of Pathology,
 Birmingham 38219
Crichton Museum, Dumfries 38786
The Crossness Engines, London 39617
Florence Nightingale Museum, London 39636
Freud Museum, London 39639
George Eliot Hospital Museum, Nuneaton 40117
Gordon Museum, London 39645
Hunter House, East Kilbride 38844
Hunterian Museum, London 39670
Jenner Museum, Berkeley 38168
Manchester University Medical School Museum,
 Manchester 39897
Mervyn Quinlan Museum, Benenden 38165
Museum of Anatomy, Glasgow 39055
Museum of Dentistry, Liverpool 39524
Museum of the Royal College of Surgeons of
 Edinburgh, Edinburgh 38896
Museum of the Royal Pharmaceutical Society of Great
 Britain, London 39724
National Hearing Aid Museum, London 39730
Old Operating Theatre, Museum and Herb Garret,
 London 39737
Port Sunlight Heritage Centre, Port Sunlight 40236
Royal Army Dental Corps Historical Museum,
 Aldershot 37969
Royal College of Obstetricians and Gynaecologists
 Collection, London 39761
Royal London Hospital Archives and Museum,
 London 39764
Saint Bartholomew's Hospital Museum,
 London 39770
Saint Bernard's Hospital Museum and Chapel,
 Southall 40541
Stephen G. Beaumont Museum, Wakefield 40763
Sunnyside Museum, Hillside 39244
Thackray Museum, Leeds 39454
TWO 10 Gallery, London 39792

U.S.A.
Alumni Museum, Catonsville 42141
American Red Cross Museum, Washington 48331
Carter-Coile Country Doctors Museum,
 Winterville 48713
Children's Health Museum, Charlottesville 42247
Clara Barton Home, Glen Echo 43680
Clendening History of Medicine Library and Museum,
 Kansas City 44392
The Country Doctor Museum, Bailey 41432
Crawford W. Long Museum, Jefferson 44321
DeWitt Stetten Jr. Museum of Medical Research,
 Bethesda 41662
Dittrick Museum of Medical History, Cleveland 42471
Dr Daniel W. Kissam House, Huntington 44160
Dr. Francis Medical and Apothecary Museum,
 Jacksonville 44291
Dr. John Harris Dental Museum, Bainbridge 41433
Dr. Samuel D. Harris National Museum of Dentistry,
 Baltimore 41463
East Tennessee Discovery Center, Knoxville 44516
Feet First: The Scholl Story, North Chicago 45987
Fort Winnebago Surgeons Quarters, Portage 46612
Global Health Odyssey, Atlanta 41347
Glore Psychiatric Museum, Saint Joseph 47105
Health Adventure, Asheville 41281
Health Museum of Cleveland, Cleveland 42474
Heartland - The California Museum of the Heart,
 Rancho Mirage 46786
History of Medicine Collections, Durham 43022
Hospitals and Clinics Medical Museum, Iowa
 City 44245
Indiana Medical History Museum, Indianapolis 44223
International Museum of Surgical Science,
 Chicago 42335
The John Q. Adams Center for the History of
 Otolaryngology - Head and Neck Surgery,
 Alexandria 41130
Joseph A. Tallman Museum, Cherokee 42273
Kansas Health Museum, Halstead 43875
Macaulay Museum of Dental History,
 Charleston 42222
McDowell House and Apothecary Shop,
 Danville 42779
Menczer Museum of Medicine and Dentistry,
 Hartford 43941
Mobile Medical Museum, Mobile 45420
Montgomery County Historical Society Museum,
 Rockville 46977
Museum at Mountain Home, Johnson City 44347
Museum of Health and Medical Science,
 Houston 44130
The Museum of Nursing History, Philadelphia 46431
Museum of the University of Connecticut Health
 Center, Farmington 43296
The Museum of Vision, San Francisco 47331
Mutter Museum, Philadelphia 46432
National Museum of Civil War Medicine,
 Frederick 43529
National Museum of Health and Medicine,
 Washington 48378
New Orleans Pharmacy Museum, New Orleans 45736
The Pearson Museum, Springfield 47741
Sioux Empire Medical Museum, Sioux Falls 47645
Stabler-Leadbeater Apothecary Museum,
 Alexandria 41134
Still National Osteopathic Museum, Kirksville 44503
Transylvania Museum, Lexington 44745
United States Army Medical Department Museum,
 Fort Sam Houston 43452
University Medical Museum, Charleston 42228
Wood Library-Museum of Anesthesiology, Park
 Ridge 46292

Uzbekistan
Muzej Obščestvennogo Zdorovja Uzbekistana,
 Taškent 48858

Metals and Metallurgy

Australia
New England Brass and Iron Lace Foundry Museum,
 Uralla 01564

Austria
Hochofen-Museum Bundschuh, Thomatal 02730
Hochofenmuseum Radwerk IV, Vordernberg 02778
Metallmuseum, Tullnerbach-Lawies 02748
Montanmuseum, Gußwerk 01975
Stadt- und Steirisches Eisenmuseum, Eisenerz 01802
Volkskundemuseum Spiralschmiede, Lasberg 02192

Belgium
Maison de la Metallurgie et de l'Industrie de Liège,
 Liège 03569
Musée du Fer et de la Métallurgie Ancienne, Saint-
 Hubert 03722

Canada
Musée du Bronze d'Inverness, Inverness 05624

China, People's Republic
Huangshi Municipal Museum, Huangshi 07117

Czech Republic
Museum of Vitkovice, Ostrava 08526
Muzeum Dr. Bohuslava Horáka, Dobřiv 08328
Muzeum Strojíren Poldi, Kladno 08409
Technické Muzeum v Brně, Brno 08277

Finland
Suomen Valimomuseo ja Högforsin Masuuni,
 Karkkila 09628

France
Ecomusée Industriel de Lochrist-Inzinzac, Lochrist-
 Inzinzac 12642
Musée de la Grosse Forge, Aube 10457
Musée de l'Histoire du Fer, Jarville 12075

Germany
Aurnhammer-Sammlung, Treuchtlingen 20199
Deutsches Kaltwalzmuseum, Hagen, Westfalen 17478
Eisenhammer Dorfchemnitz, Dorfchemnitz bei
 Sayda 16644
Gesenkschmiede Lubenbach, Zella-Mehlis 20744
Hammer- und Waffenschmiede-Museum Hexenagger,
 Altmannstein 15459
Historische Ausstellung Krupp, Essen 16951
Historische Hammerschmiede, Blaubeuren 16181
Industriemuseum Brandenburg, Brandenburg an der
 Havel 16280
Mansfeld-Museum Hettstedt, Hettstedt, Sachsen-
 Anhalt 17747
Maxhütten-Museum, Bergen, Chiemgau 15891
Museum Eisenhüttenwerk Peitz, Peitz 19370
Museum Saigerhütte Olbernhau- Kupferhammer,
 Olbernhau 19249
Museum Wasseralfingen, Aalen 15383
Schmiedemuseum Bremecker Hammer,
 Lüdenscheid 18550
Technisches Denkmal Kupferhammer, Thießen bei
 Dessau 20173
Technisches Denkmal Neue Hütte,
 Schmalkalden 19809
Technisches Schaudenkmal Gießerei Heinrichshütte,
 Wurzbach 20719

Hungary
Központi Kohászati Múzeum, Miskolc 21477
Öntödei Múzeum, Budapest 21371

Japan
Nihon Kinzoku Gakkai Fuzoku Kinzoku Hakubutsukan,
 Sendai 26733
Wako Hakubutsukan, Yasugi 27010

Netherlands
Het Behouden Blik, Uithuizermeeden 29890

Poland
Muzeum Starożytnego Hutnictwa Świętokrzyskiego
 im. prof. M. Radwana, Nowa Słupia 31828
Zabytkowa Huta Żelaza, Chlewiska 31525
Zabytkowa Kuźnia Wodna w Starej Kuźnicy, Stara
 Kuźnica 31995

Russia
Muzej Istorii Architektury i Promyšlennoj Techniki
 Urala, Ekaterinburg 32774
Nižnetagilskij Muzej-Zapovednik Gornozavodskogo
 Dela Srednego Urala, Nižnij Tagil 33228

Serbia-Montenegro
Muzej Rudarstva i Metalurgije, Bor 33824

Sweden
Hälleforsnäs Gjuterimuseum, Hälleforsnäs 35934
Hudiksvalls Bruksminnen, Hudiksvall 35966
Rademachersmedjorna, Eskilstuna 35871

Switzerland
Toggenburger Schmiede- und Handwerksmuseum,
 Bazenheid 36524

United Kingdom
Brass Rubbing Centre, Edinburgh 38871
London Brass Rubbing Centre, London 39693

U.S.A.
Iron and Steel Museum of Alabama, McCalla 45018

Metalwork

Austria
Alte Marktschmiede, Lasberg 02190
Freilichtmuseum Fürstenhammer, Lasberg 02191
Freilichtmuseum Hammerschmiede, Bad Wimsbach-
 Neydharting 01722
Karlinger-Schmiede, Unterweißenbach 02756
Montanmuseum, Gußwerk 01975
Prof. Gerstmayr-Museum, Mauthausen 02290
Schaumuseum Alte Huf-und Wagenschmiede, Gmünd,
 Niederösterreich 01892

Canada
Lieu Historique National des Forges du Saint-Maurice,
 Trois-Rivières 06641

Czech Republic
Železářské Muzeum, Komárov u Horovic 08418

Finland
Fiskars Museum, Fiskars 09439

France
Musée-Atelier du Cuivre et de l'Argent, Paris 13531
Musée de la Grosse Forge, Aube 10457

Germany
Blankschmiede Neimke, Dassel 16552
Deutsches Drahtmuseum, Altena 15442
Deutsches Klingenmuseum Solingen, Solingen 19984
Domschatzkammer, Essen 16948
Eisenkunstgussmuseum, Büdelsdorf 16396
Fabrikmuseum der Leonischen Industrie, Roth, Mittelfranken 19672
Glockenschmiede, Ruhpolding 19715
Gold- und Silberschmiedemuseum, Mülsen-Sankt-Jakob 18821
Hammerschmiede und Stockerhof, Neuburg an der Kammel 19020
Heinrich-Blickle-Museum, Sammlung gußeiserner Ofenplatten, Rosenfeld 19647
Historische Schlosserei Pelzer, Jena 17944
Historischer Eisenhammer, Roth, Mittelfranken 19674
Hüttenmuseum Thale, Thale 20166
Museum der Grafschaft Mark, Altena 15443
Museum für Eisenkunstguß, Hirzenhain 17769
Ofenplattensammlung der Schwäbische Hüttenwerke, Aalen 15384
Original-Dorfschmiede Ehlen, Habichtswald 17470
Rheinisches Eisenkunstguss Museum, Bendorf, Rhein 15875
Rheinisches Industriemuseum, Solingen 19986
Sayner Gießhalle, Bendorf, Rhein 15876
Schaudenkmal Gaszentrale, Unterwellenborn 20271
Schmiedemuseum Kirchlauter, Kirchlauter 18099
Südharzer Eisenhüttenmuseum, Bad Lauterberg 15691
Voithenberghammer, Furth im Wald 17182

Iceland
Sjóminja- og Vélsmiðjusafn, Reykjavík 21666

Italy
Museo Civico d'Arte Industriale e Galleria Davia Bargellini, Bologna 23110
Museo degli Usi e Costumi della Gente Trentina, San Michele all'Adige 25396
Museo del Ferro e della Ghisa, Follonica 23899
Museo Etnografico Comunale, Premana 25052

Netherlands
H.J. van de Kamp Museum, Sint Oedenrode 29824
Oale Smederie, Hellendoorn 29388
Smederij Museum Wijlen dhr Verkley, Nieuwkoop 29623

Norway
Næs Jernverksmuseum, Tvedestrand 30952

Poland
Muzeum Kowalstwa w Warszawie, Warszawa 32108

Slovenia
Muzeji Radovljiške Občine, Kropa 34102

Sweden
Gislöfs Smidesmuseum, Simrishamn 36186

Switzerland
Gewerbemuseum, Winterthur 37328
Musée du Fer et du Chemin de Fer, Vallorbe 37279

Turkey
Vakıf Inşaat ve Sanat Eserleri Müzesi, İstanbul 37713

United Kingdom
East Carlton Steel Heritage Centre, East Carlton 38838
Museum of Iron and Darby Furnace, Coalbrookdale 38596
Wortley Top Forge, Thurgoland 40707

U.S.A.
National Ornamental Metal Museum, Memphis 45247

Meteorites

Argentina
Museo de Mineralogía y Geología Dr. Alfredo Stelzner, Córdoba 00297
Museo del Cielo, Villa Carlos Paz 00661

Denmark
Geologisk Museum, København 08930

Finland
Kivimuseo, Helsinki 09502

France
Musée de la Météorite, L'Aigle 12303

Germany
Meteorkrater-Museum, Steinheim am Albuch 20049
Mineralogische Schau- und Lehrsammlung, Tübingen 20228

Italy
Museo di Scienze Naturali, Brescia 23205

Japan
Museum of Unearthed Artifacts, Nagasaki 26550

U.S.A.
Big Well, Greensburg 43820
Cernan Earth and Space Center, River Grove 46912
Craters of the Moon, Arco 41250
Institute of Meteoritics Meteorite Museum, Albuquerque 41102

Military History

Algeria
Musée de l'Armée, Alger 00041
Musée National du Djihad, Alger 00047

Angola
Museu Central das Forças Armadas, Luanda 00095

Argentina
Museo Belgraniano, La Plata 00386
Museo de la Policía Federal Argentina, Buenos Aires 00189
Museo Historiador Hernández Galiano, Tostado 00638
Museo Histórico del Regimiento de Granaderos a Caballo General San Martín, Buenos Aires 00214
Museo Municipal Histórico Regional Almirante Brown, Bernal 00140
Museo Naval Puerto Belgrano, Puerto Belgrano 00488
Sala Histórica del Regimiento de Infantería Mecanizado 24, Río Gallegos 00518
Sala Historica General Savio, Buenos Aires 00253

Australia
Alice Springs RSL War Museum, Alice Springs 00733
Anzac Cottage Museum, Mount Hawthorn 01282
Army Museum, Paddington, New South Wales 01350
Army Museum of South Australia, Keswick 01142
Army Museum of Western Australia, Perth 01362
Australian War Memorial, Campbell 00879
Dubbo Military Museum, Dubbo 00990
Fort Glanville, Semaphore Park 01446
Fort Queenscliff Museum, Queenscliff 01400
Frank Partridge V.C. Military Museum, Bowraville 00823
Garrison Gallery, Historical and Military Museum, Millers Point 01256
Hassett's Uralla Military Museum, Uralla 01562
HMAS Castlemaine - Museum Ship, Williamstown 01600
Melbourne Tank Museum, Narre Warren North 01306
Merredin Military Museum, Merredin 01248
Milne Bay Military Museum, Toowoomba 01540
New South Wales Lancers Memorial Museum, Parramatta 01358
Queensland Military Memorial Museum, Fortitude Valley 01032
Returned Services League War Museum, Stawell 01475
Royal Australian Corps of Transport Museum, Puckapunyal 01396
Royal Australian Infantry Corps Museum, Singleton 01453
Tatura Irrigation and Wartime Camps Museum, Tatura 01521

Austria
Freilichtmuseum des Gebirgskrieges, Kötschach-Mauthen 02149
Heeresgeschichtliches Museum im Arsenal, Wien 02895
Militärgeschichtliche Ortssammlung, Schnifis 02636
Militärgeschichtliches Museum, Ardagger 01677
Museum 1915-1918, Kötschach-Mauthen 02150
Radetzky-Gedenkstätte Heldenberg, Kleinwetzdorf 02136
Rainermuseum Salzburg, Salzburg 02547
Truppenmuseum, Straß in Steiermark 02704
Vorarlberger Militärmuseum, Bregenz 01747

Belarus
Belorusskij Gosudarstvennyj Muzej Istorii Velikoj Otečestvennoj Vojny, Minsk 03113
Kobrinski Voenno-istoričeski Muzej im. A.V. Suvorova, Kobrin 03112

Belgium
Boerenkrijgmuseum, Overmere 03684
Musée de la Ligne Koningshooikt-Wavre, Chaumont 03357
Musée des Chasseurs à Pied, Charleroi 03352
Musée Royal de l'Armée et d'Histoire Militaire, Bruxelles 03336
Musée Wellington, Waterloo 03830
Museum Slag der Zilveren Helmen, Halen 03466
Museum van de Boerenkrijg, Berlare 03214
Museum van het Kamp van Beverlo, Leopoldsburg 03560
Panorama de la Bataille de Waterloo, Braine-l'Alleud 03237
Rietgaverstede, Nevele 03656

Bermuda
Bermuda National Trust Museum, Saint George's 03886

Brazil
Army Museum and Fort Copacabana, Rio de Janeiro 04315
Museu da Brigada Militar, Porto Alegre 04276
Museu da Força Expedicionária Brasileira, Rio de Janeiro 04347
Museu da Polícia Militar de Pernambuco, Recife 04297
Museu de Armas Major Lara Ribas, Florianópolis 04090
Museu de Polícia Militar, São Paulo 04523
Museu Militar do Forte do Brum, Recife 04306

Bulgaria
Gradski Istoričeski Muzej, Klisura 04711
Istoričeski Muzej - Preminavane na Ruskite Vojski pri Svištov, Svištov 04881
Istoričeskij Muzej, Tutrakan 04892
Muzej Rumănski Voin, Pordim 04786
Muzej Vojniško Văstanie 1918, Radomir 04795
Nacionalen Voennoistoričeski Muzej, Sofia 04855
Panorama Plevenska Epopeja 1877, Pleven 04769
Voenno-istoričeski Muzej, Gorna Studena 04676
Voenno-istoričeski Muzej, Pleven 04772
Voenno-istoričeski Muzej Osvoboditelna Vojna 1877-1878, Bjala 04623

Canada
12 Vancouver Service Battalion Museum, Richmond 06259
15th Field Artillery Regiment Museum, Vancouver 06664
26th Field Artillery Regiment Museum, Brandon 05115
Base Borden Military Museum, Borden 05098
British Columbia Regiment Museum, Vancouver 06669
Calgary Highlanders Museum, Calgary 05163
Cameron Highlanders of Ottawa Regimental Museum, Ottawa 06067
Canadian Airborne Forces Museum, Petawawa 06115
Canadian Military Studies Museum, Limehouse 05754
Canadian Scottish Regiment Museum, Victoria 06715
CFB Esquimalt Naval Museum and Military Museum, Victoria 06717
Currahee Military Museum, Virden 06734
Discovery Harbour, Penetanguishene 06107
Elgin Military Museum, Saint Thomas 06375
First Hussars Citizen Soldiers Museum, London 05765
Fort Beauséjour National Historic Site, Aulac 05020
Fort-Chambly, Chambly 05221
Fort Edward, Grand-Pré 05517
Fort Garry Horse Regimental Museum, Winnipeg 06825
Fort George, Niagara-on-the-Lake 06000
Fort Henry, Kingston 05675
Fort Normandeau, Red Deer 06221
Fort Saint Joseph, Richards Landing 06256
Fort Wellington, Prescott 06179
Governor General's Foot Guards Regimental Museum, Ottawa 06081
Guard House and Soldiers Barracks, Fredericton 05461
Halifax Citadel, Halifax 05552
Hamilton Military Museum, Hamilton 05571
HMCS Haida, Toronto 06584
Lorne Scots Regimental Museum, Brampton 05113
Loyal Edmonton Regiment Military Museum, Edmonton 05379
Musée du Royal 22e Régiment, Québec 06207
Musée Militaire du 12e Régiment Blindé du Canada, Trois-Rivières 06644
Musée Régimentaire les Fusiliers de Sherbrooke, Sherbrooke, Québec 06443
Musée Stewart au Fort de Ile Sainte-Hélène, Montréal 05926
Museum of the Regiments, Calgary 05173
Museum of the Royal Regiment of Canada, Toronto 06598
Museum of The Royal Westminster Regiment Historical Society, New Westminster 05985
Northern Lights Military Museum, Goose Bay 05501
Parc de l'Artillerie, Québec 06210
Perth Regiment Museum, Stratford 06500
The Prince Edward Island Regiment Museum, Charlottetown 05231
Prince of Wales Martello Tower, Halifax 05561
Princess Patricia's Canadian Light Infantry Museum, Calgary 05178
Queen's Own Rifles of Canada Regimental Museum, Toronto 06603
Queen's York Rangers Regimental Museum, Toronto 06604
Quidi Vidi Battery, Saint John's 06349
RCMP Centennial Celebration Museum, Fairview 05421
Reynolds Museum, Wetaskiwin 06779
Rocky Mountain Rangers Museum, Kamloops 05640
Royal Canadian Military Institute Museum, Toronto 06606
Royal Canadian Ordnance Corps Museum, Montréal 05929
Royal Hamilton Light Infantry Heritage Museum, Hamilton 05575
Saskatchewan Military Museum, Regina 06245
Seaforth Highlanders of Canada Regimental Museum, Vancouver 06688
Thunder Bay Military Museum, Thunder Bay 06550
Toronto Scottish Regimental Museum, Toronto 06619
Uniacke Estate Museum, Mount Uniacke 05949
Vancouver Naval Museum, West Vancouver 06774
Veterans'Memorial Military Museum, Kensington 05659
York Sunbury Historical Society Museum, Fredericton 05469

Chile
Museo Histórico Nacional, Santiago de Chile 06915

China, People's Republic
Dandong Museum on the War to resist U.S. Aggression and Aid Korea, Dandong 07041
Military Museum, Macau 07166
Museum of the Chinese People's Revolutionary Military Affairs, Beijing 06977
Old Zhi Display Center, Xing Si Army, Nanchang 07174

China, Republic
Armed Forces Museum, Taipei 07343

Colombia
Museo Militar de Colombia, Bogotá 07427

Cuba
Museo Antiguo Cuartel de Caballería del Ejército Español, Camagüey 07874
Museo de Ejército Oriental, Holguín 08005
Museo Fortaleza de San Carlos de la Cabaña, La Habana 07969
Museo Máximo Gómez, La Habana 07975

Czech Republic
Armádní Muzeum Žižkov, Praha 08563
Expozice České Lidové Armády, Praha 08575
Památník Bitvy 1813, Chlumec u Ústi nad Labem 08311
Památník Bitvy 1866 na Chlumu, Všestary 08729
Vojenské Technické Muzeum, Krhanice 08433

Denmark
Blaavandshuk Egnsmuseum, Oksbøl 09016
Tirpitz-Stillingen, Blåvand 08786
Varde Artillerimuseum, Varde 09102

Ecuador
La Casa de los Tratados, Girón 09165
Museo Templete de los Heros Nacionales, Quito 09218

Egypt
Military Museum, El-Alamein 09292
Port-Said Museum, Port Said 09303

Finland
Artillery Museum of Finland, Hämeenlinna 09447
Hanko Front Museum, Hanko 09462
Ilmavoimien Viestikoulun Perinnehuone, Tikkakoski 10105
Lylyn Viestivarikon Museo, Lyly 09807
Maneesi Sotamuseo, Helsinki 09513
Päämajamuseo, Mikkeli 09833
Panssarimuseo, Parola 09913
Pioneerimuseo, Koria 09690
Rajamuseo, Imatra 09566
Rannikkotykistömuseo, Helsinki 09523
Reserviupseerikoulun Museo, Hamina 09460
Sotamuseo, Helsinki 09529
Sukellusvene Vesikko, Helsinki 09530
Viestimuseo, Riihimäki 09998

France
L'Argonaute, Paris 13469
Militarial Musée Mémorial pour la Paix, Boissezon 10788
Musée 2ème Guerre Mondiale, Ambleteuse 10306
Musée 39-45, Roscoff 14033
Musée à Flot de l'Escorteur d'Escadre, Nantes 13250
Musée Août-1944, Falaise 11701
Musée Bernadotte, Pau 13666
Musée d'Arromanches, Arromanches-les-Bains 10432
Musée d'Art Militaire, Vincey 15266
Musée de la Bataille, Fontenoy-en-Puisaye 11776
Musée de la Bataille du 6 Août 1870, Woerth 15321
Musée de la Batterie de Merville, Merville 12950
Musée de la Figurine, Toulon (Var) 14927
Musée de la Figurine Historique, Compiègne 11376
Musée de la Guerre de Vendée, Les Sables-d'Olonne 12553
Musée de la Libération, Cherbourg 11276
Musée de la Ligne Maginot, Hunspach 12037
Musée de la Ligne Maginot, Lembach 12510
Musée de la Mémoire et de la Paix, Clerval 11332
Musée de la Première Guerre Mondiale, Villeneuve-les-Convers 15230
Musée de la Seconde Guerre Mondiale, Digne-les-Bains 11511
Musée de l'Armée, Paris 13570
Musée de l'Empéri, Salon-de-Provence 14589
Musée de l'Infanterie, Montpellier 13125
Musée des Troupes de Marine, Fréjus 11810
Musée du Débarquement en Provence, Toulon (Var) 14929
Musée du Lycée Militaire de Saint-Cyr, Saint-Cyr-l'École 14170
Musée du Service de Santé des Armées, Paris 13606
Musée du Souvenir, Guer 11964
Musée du Souvenir du Génie, Angers 10348
Musée Fort de Sucy, Sucy-en-Brie 14841
Musée Guerre et Paix en Ardennes, Novion-Porcien 13368
Musée Historique et Erckmann-Chatrian, Phalsbourg 13727
Musée Historique et Militaire, Huningue 12036
Musée la Perçée du Bocage 1944, Saint-Martin-des-Besaces 14353

Musée Libertador du Général San Martin, Boulogne-sur-Mer 10840
Musée Militaire des Gloires et Souvenirs du Périgord, Périgueux 13694
Musée Militaire Faller, Mars-la-Tour 12835
Musée Municipal, Cusset 11477
Musée Natiocional des Deux Victoires, Mouilleron-en-Pareds 13183
Musée Naval et Napoléonien, Antibes 10375
Musée No.4 Commando, Ouistreham 13446
Musée Pierre Noël, Saint-Dié-des-Vosges 14187
Musée Serret, Saint-Amarin 14101
Musée sur l'Artillerie, la Cavalerie et l'Infanterie, Seclin 14688
Musée Vauban, Neuf-Brisach 13284
Musée Wagon de l'Armistice, Compiègne 11379
Musée Westercamp, Wissembourg 15319
Salle de Traditions de la Garde Républicaine, Paris 13659

Germany
Armeemuseum 'Friedrich der Große', Kulmbach 18264
Blüchermuseum, Kaub 18035
Deutsches Panzermuseum Munster, Munster 18958
Eurocenter Sächsische Militärgeschichte, Kossa 18214
First Infantry Division Museum, Würzburg 20693
Garnisonmuseum Nürnberg, Nürnberg 19138
Gebirgsjägermuseum, Sonthofen 20000
Gneisenau-Gedenkstätte, Gneisenaustadt Schildau 17308
Heimatmuseum, Friedland bei Neubrandenburg 17142
Heimatmuseum, Karlstein am Main 18010
Historisches Museum im Marstall, Paderborn 19335
Krell'sche Schmiede, Wernigerode 20526
Kultur- und Militärmuseum, Grafenwöhr 17374
Luftwaffenmuseum der Bundeswehr, Berlin 16038
Militär- und Jagdgeschichtliche Sammlung, Bad Wildungen 15765
Militärhistorisches Museum der Bundeswehr, Dresden 16697
Museum 1806, Cospeda 16497
Museum für historische Wehrtechnik, Röthenbach an der Pegnitz 19637
Museum für Militär- und Zeitgeschichte, Kolitzheim 18200
Museum für Waffentechink, Ausrüstung, Auszeichnungswesen, Vilshofen 20325
Museum im Zeughaus, Vechta 20290
NVA-Museum, Ostseebad Binz 19312
Osthofentor-Museum, Soest 19979
Rottauer Museum für Fahrzeuge, Wehrtechnik und Zeitgeschichte bis 1948, Pocking 19424
Schloß Höchstädt, Höchstädt an der Donau 17780
Stadt- und Festungsmuseum im Ludwigstor, Germersheim 17254
Stadtmauermuseum Nördlingen, Nördlingen 19109
Städtisches Museum/ Daniel-Pöppelmann-Haus, Herford 17720
Völkerschlachtdenkmal und Forum 1813, Museum zur Geschichte der Völkerschlacht, Leipzig 18424
Wehrgeschichtliches Museum Rastatt, Rastatt 19492
Westwallmuseum Gerstfeldhöhe, Pirmasens 19404

Greece
Historical and Ethnological Museum of Patras, Patrai 21115
Polemiko Mouseio, Athinai 20902

Guadeloupe
Fort Fleur d'Epée, Le Gosier 21246

Guam
War in the Pacific National Historical Park, Asan 21257
War in the Pacific National Historical Park, Piti 21259

Hungary
Hadtörténeti Múzeum, Budapest 21341
Római Kötár, Szentendre 21574

India
Bishnu Museum, Shillong 22016
Indian War Memorial Museum, Delhi 21771

Indonesia
Museum Dirgantara Mandala, Yogyakarta 22221
Museum Mandala Wangsit Siliwangi, Bandung 22073
Museum Militer, Jakarta 22123
Museum Palagan, Ambarawa 22066
Museum Tni A.L. Loka Jala Carana, Surabaya 22201

Iran
Military Marine Museum, Bandar-Anzali 22233
Military Museum, Teheran 22312

Ireland
Dublin Castle, Dublin 22421
Military Heritage Tours, Longford 22510

Israel
Battle Museum, Kibbutz Gesher 22687
Haghna Museum, Tel Aviv 22756
Israel Defense Forces History Museum, Tel Aviv 22760
Israeli Air Force Museum, Hatzerim 22615
Jewish Battalions Museum, Ahivil 22566
Museum Zahal, Hakirya 22614

Italy
Musée du Regiment GG.FF., Firenze 23850
Museo dei Combattenti, Soncino 25600
Museo dei Reperti Bellici e Storici della Guerra 1915-1918, Capovalle 23330
Museo dei Soldati del Montello, Nervesa della Battaglia 24615
Museo dei Soldatino e della Figurina Storica, Calenzano 23266
Museo del Combattente, Modena 24441
Museo del Reggimento "Giovani Fascisti", Ponti sul Mincio 24999
Museo del Risorgimento, Solferino 25596
Museo della Battaglia, Vittorio Veneto 26040
Museo della Battaglia di Marengo, Alessandria 22848
Museo della Battaglia di Marengo, Spinetta Marengo 25621
Museo delle Armi Antiche e Fortezza Medievale, Acquaviva Picena 22803
Museo delle Truppe Alpine Mario Balocco, Biella 23081
Museo di Architettura Militare, Bologna 23125
Museo Ferrucciano, Gavinana 23965
Museo Sacrario delle Bandiere, Roma 25247
Museo Storico degli Truppe Alpini, Trento 25795
Museo Storico dei Bersaglieri, Roma 25248
Museo Storico della Motorizzazione Militare, Roma 25255
Museo Storico delle Armi, Civitella del Tronto 23598
Museo Storico Militare, Comun Nuovo 23634
Museo Storico Militare e Sacrario die Redipuglia, Fogliano Redipuglia 23896
Museo Storico Militare Umberto I, Turate 25843
Museo Storico Nazionale di Artiglieria, Torino 25762

Jamaica
Military Museum, Kingston 26072

Japan
Yamamoto Isoroku Kinenkan, Nagaoka 26539

Jordan
Martyr's Memorial at Sports City, Amman 27056

Korea, Republic
Military Academy Museum, Seoul 27257

Kyrgyzstan
Memorialnyj Dom-Muzej M.V. Biškek, Biškek 27308

Lebanon
Moussa Castle Museum, Beiteddine 27486

Lithuania
Vytautas The Great War Museum, Kaunas 27523

Luxembourg
Musée de la Bataille des Ardennes, Wiltz 27582
Musée des Enrôles de Force, Dudelange 27550
Musée National d'Histoire Militaire, Diekirch 27549

Malaysia
Muzium Angkatan Tentera, Kuala Lumpur 27643
Muzium Tentera Laut Diraja Malaysia, Melaka 27674
Royal Malaysian Navy Museum, Lumut 27659

Mexico
Casa Museo Cadete Juan Escutia, Tepic 28495
Casa Museo Coronel Gregorio Méndez Magaña, Jalpa de Méndez 28024
Museo Casa del General Alvaro Obregón, Huatabampo 27998
Museo Cuartel de Emiliano Zapata, Tlaltizapán 28526
Museo Cuartel Zapatista, México 28121
Museo de la Guerra de Castas, Felipe Carrillo Puerto 27923
Museo de la No Intervención Fuerte de Loreto, Puebla 28330
Museo del Ejército y Fuerza Aérea Bethlemitas, México 28155
Museo del Ejército y Fuerza Aérea Mexicanos Cuartel Colorado, Guadalajara 27956
Museo General Ignacio Zaragoza, Puebla 28340
Museo Histórico Naval Central, México 28176
Museo Teniente José Azuela, Zihuatanejo 28655
Museo Toma de Zacatecas o Cerro de la Bufa, Zacatecas 28640

Mongolia
Military Museum, Ulaanbaatar 28677

Mozambique
Museu Histórico Militar, Maputo 28723

Myanmar
War Museum, Yangon 28753

Netherlands
Airborne Museum Hartenstein, Oosterbeek 29666
Gelders Schuttersmuseum, Didam 29148
Generaal Maczek Museum, Breda 29021
Historische Genie Verzameling, Vught 29970
Historische Verzameling Aan- en Afvoertroepen, Stroe 29859
Historische Verzameling Intendance, Bussum 29049
Historische Verzameling Korps Nationale Reserve, Harskamp 29347
Historische Verzameling Luchtdoelartillerie, Ede 29193
Historische Verzameling Regiment van Heutsz, Arnhem 28937
Infantierie Museum, Harskamp 29348
Kazemattenmuseum, Oosterend 29668
Kazemattenmuseum Kornwerderzand, Kornwerderzand 29491
Koninklijk Nederlands Leger- en Wapenmuseum, Delft 29079
Koninklijk Tehuis voor Oud-Militairen en Museum Bronbeek, Arnhem 28940
Mariniersmuseum, Rotterdam 29757
Militair Historisch Museum De Veteraan, Eefde 29196
Museum Brigade en Garde Prinses Irene, Oirschot 29653
Museum Nederlandse Cavalerie, Amersfoort 28826
Museum 't Schilderhuis, Driebergen-Rijsenburg 29181
Museumschip Mercuur, Den Haag 29116
Nationaal Bevrijdingsmuseum 1944-1945, Groesbeek 29305
Nederlands Artillerie Museum, 't Harde 29339
Nederlands Militair Kustverdedigingsmuseum, Hoek van Holland 29427
Oorlogsverzetsmuseum Rotterdam, Rotterdam 29771
Traditiekamer Regiment Stoottroepen, Assen 28953
Vesting Bourtange, Bourtange 29011
Vischpoort en Kazematten, Elburg 29226

New Zealand
Air Force Museum, Christchurch 30121
Auckland Museum and Auckland War Memorial Museum, Auckland 30104
Otago Military Museum, Dunedin 30150
Royal New Zealand Army Medical Corps Museum, Christchurch 30131
Royal New Zealand Navy Museum, Devonport 30142

Nigeria
National War Museum of Umauhia, Umauhia 30363

Norway
Arquebus Krigshistorisk Museum, Haugesund 30536
Austrått Fort, Brekstad 30450
Bjørn West-Museet, Matredal 30669
Blodveimuseet, Rognan 30798
Falstadminnet, Levanger 30638
Flyhistorisk Museum, Sola 30861
Forsvarsmuseet, Oslo 30733
Gudbrandsdal Krigsminnesamling, Kvam 30621
Kristiansand Kanonmuseum, Kristiansand 30613
Lofoten Krigsminnemuseum, Svolvær 30911
Marinemuseet, Horten 30565
Nordland Røde Kors Krigsminnemuseum, Narvik 30704
Nordsjøfartmuseet, Tælavåg 30914
Norges Hjemmefrontmuseum, Oslo 30748
Okkupasjonsmuseet, Eidsvoll 30473
Senjehesten Kystforsvarsmuseum, Moen 30682

Oman
Sultan's Armed Forces Museum, Muscat 31008

Pakistan
PAF Museum, Karachi 31031
Pakistan Air Force Museum Peshawar, Peshawar 31050

Paraguay
Colección Carlos Alberto Pusineri Scala, Asunción 31095
Museo Histórico Militar, Asunción 31103

Peru
Museo Andrés Avelino Cáceres, Lima 31199
Museo de los Combatientes del Morro de Arica, Lima 31212
Museo de Sitio de la Pampa Galeras, Quinua 31245
Museo de Sitio del Campo de la Alianza, Tacna 31255
Museo Histórico Militar Real Felipe, Callao 31133

Philippines
Armed Forces of the Philippines Museum, Quezon City 31427
Miguel Malvar Museum, Santo Tomas 31445
Philippine Army Museum, Makati 31355
Philippine Navy Museum, Cavite 31305

Poland
Muzeum 1 Pułku Strzelców Podhalańskich Armii Krajowej, Szczawa 32021
Muzeum 24 Pułku Ułanów, Kraśnik 31730
Muzeum 7 Pułku Ułanów Lubelskich, Mińsk Mazowiecki 31808
Muzeum Armii Krajowej, Kraków 31696
Muzeum Armii Poznań, Poznań 31900
Muzeum Bitwy Legnickiej, Legnickie Pole 31755
Muzeum Broni Pancernej, Poznań 31901
Muzeum Czynu Niepodległościowego, Kraków 31697
Muzeum Czynu Powstańczego, Leśnica 31756
Muzeum Czynu Zbrojnego Pracowników Huty im. Tadeusza Sendzimira, Kraków 31698
Muzeum Historyczne - Pałac w Dukli, Dukla 31558
Muzeum im. Orła Białego, Skarżysko-Kamienna 31976
Muzeum Martyrologii Alianckich Jeńców Wojennych, Żagań 32202
Muzeum Oręża Polskiego, Kołobrzeg 31670
Muzeum Wojska, Białystok 31488
Pomorskie Muzeum Wojskowe, Bydgoszcz 31516
Wielkopolskie Muzeum Wojskowe, Poznań 31915

Portugal
Museu da Liga dos Combatentes da Grande Guerra, Lisboa 32295
Museu Militar, Coimbra 32261

Puerto Rico
Fortín San Jerónimo del Boquerón, San Juan 32390
San Juan National Historic Site, San Juan 32409

Romania
Muzeul de Etnografie şi a Regimentului de Graniţă, Caransebeş 32488
Muzeul Marinei Române, Constanţa 32502
Muzeul Militar Naţional, Bucureşti 32460

Russia
Centralnyj Muzej Federalnoj Pograničnoj Služby RF, Moskva 33025
Centralnyj Muzej Vooružennych Sil, Moskva 33028
Diorama Kurskaja Bitva - Belgorodskoe Napravlenie, Belgorod 32677
Dom-muzej S.M. Budennogo, Proletarsk 33329
Fort N5 - Muzej Istorii Velikoj Otečestvennoj Vojny, Kaliningrad 32868
Gorodskoj Muzej Boevoj Slavy, Kaluga 32876
Gosudarstvennyj Borodinskij Voenno-istoričeskij Muzej-zapovednik, Borodino 32701
Gosudarstvennyj Memorialnyj Muzej im. A.V. Suvorova, Sankt-Peterburg 33400
Gosudarstvennyj Muzej-panorama Stalingradskaja Bitva, Volgograd 33715
Gosudarstvennyj Voenno-istoričeskij i Prirodnyj Muzej-zapovednik Kulikovo Pole, Tula 33624
Gosudarstvennyj Voenno-istoričeskij Muzej-zapovednik Prochorovskoe Pole, Prochorovka 33328
Istoričeskaja Usadba Botik Petra I, Veskovo 33684
Istoriko-memorialnyj Kompleks Gerojam Stalingradskoj Bitvy na Mamaevom Kurgane, Volgograd 33716
Jaroslavskij Muzej Boevoj Slavy, Jaroslavl 32850
Kamčatskij Voenno-istoričeskij Muzej, Petropavlovsk-Kamčatskij 33311
Malojaroslaveckij Muzej Voennoj Istorii 1812 Goda, Malojaroslavec 33007
Memorialnaja Gvardejskaja Krasnoznamënnaja Podvodnaja Lodka S-56 1939 g., Vladivostok 33699
Memorialnyj Muzej-kabinet M.V. Frunze, Ivanovo 32830
Muzej Arsenal - Muzej Velikoj Otečestvennoj Vojny, Voronež 33731
Muzej Boevoj Slavy, Astrachan 32664
Muzej V.I. Čapaeva, Čeboksary 32722
Muzej-Diorama Orlovskaja Nastupatelnaja Operacija, Orël 33264
Muzej Istorii Vojsk Moskovskogo Voennogo Okruga, Moskva 33112
Muzej-panorama Borodinskaja Bitva, Moskva 33145
Muzej Pograničnoj Ochrany, Moskva 33147
Muzej Štab-kvartira V.K. Bljuchera, Tjumen 33608
Muzej-usadba A.V. Suvorova, Končanskoe-Suvorovskoe 32936
Muzejno-vystavočnyj Kompleks Volokolamskij Kreml, Volokolamsk 33726
Muzj Istorii Rossijskich Voennych Učilišč, Sankt-Peterburg 33472
Novorossijskij Gosudarstvennyj Istoričeskij Muzej Zapovednik, Novorossijsk 33238
Saratovskij Gosudarstvennyj Muzej Boevoj Slavy, Saratov 33510
Storoževoj Korabl' 'Krasnyj Vympel' 1911 g., Vladivostok 33710
Voenno-istoričeskij Muzej Artillerii, Inženernych Vojsk i Vojsk Svjazi, Sankt-Peterburg 33487
Voenno-istoričeskij Muzej Tichookeanskogo Flota, Vladivostok 33712
Volgogradskij Memorialno-istoričeskij Muzej, Volgograd 33717

Slovakia
Dukelské Múzeum, Svidník 34070

South Africa
Castle Military Museum, Cape Town 34203
Magersfontein Battlefields Museum, Kimberley 34291
Military Museum Fort, Bloemfontein 34186
Oorlogsmuseum, Bloemfontein 34193
South African National Museum of Military History, Saxonwold 34374
Talana Museum and Heritage Park, Dundee 34222

Spain
Museo del Ejército, Madrid 35032
Museo Específico de la Legión, Ceuta 34712
Museo Militar de Menorca, Es Castell 34689
Sala de Recuerdos de la Escuela Militar de Montaña, Jaca 34921

Sweden
Armémuseum, Stockholm 36232
Beredskapsmuseet, Viken 36407
Eda Skans Museum, Åmotfors 35798
Eldnäset Flottningsmuseum, Ånge 35803
Fästningsmuseet Karlsborg, Karlsborg 35991
Garnisonsmuseet, Boden 35835
Husarmuseum, Eksjö 35862
Limhamns Museum, Malmö 36074
Marinmuseum, Karlskrona 35999
Museet Malmahed, Malmköping 36070
Pansarmuséet, Axvall 35827
Smålands Militärhistoriska Museum, Eksjö 35864

Switzerland
Festungsmuseum Heldsberg, Sankt Margrethen 37111
Festungsmuseum Reuenthal, Reuenthal 37053
Musée Cantonal d'Histoire Militaire, Saint-Maurice 37087
Musée Militaire, Colombier 36644

Thailand
Armed Forces Survey Department Museum, Bangkok 37474
Army Museum of Infantry Center, Phachuab Khiri Khan 37524
Museum of the Royal Thai Air Force, Bangkok 37490

Tunisia
Musée Militaire Ligne Mareth, Mareth 37572
Musée Militaire National, Manouba 37571

Turkey
Askeri Müze ve Kültür Sitesi Komtuanlığı^BE, İstanbul 37691
Deniz Müzesi, İstanbul 37698

Ukraine
Krasnojarskij Istoričeskij Muzej Memorial Pobedy, Krasnojarsk 37865

United Kingdom
100th Bomb Group Memorial Museum, Dickleburgh 38729
390th Bomb Group Memorial Air Museum and British Resistance Organisation Museum, Framlingham 39013
448th Bomb Group Memorial Museum, Seething 40464
A Soldier's Life, Newcastle-upon-Tyne 40032
Adjutant General's Corps Museum, Winchester 40885
Airborne Forces Museum, Aldershot 37965
Army Physical Training Corps Museum, Aldershot 37968
Aylmer Military Collection, Brading 38303
Ayrshire Yeomanry Museum, Ayr 38049
Beatty Museum, Newport Pagnell 40057
Bedfordshire and Hertfordshire Regiment Association Museum Collection, Luton 39843
Berwick Barracks, Berwick-upon-Tweed 38172
Bosworth Battlefield Visitor Centre and Country Park, Market Bosworth 39914
Buffs Museum, Canterbury 38469
Castle and Regimental Museum, Monmouth 39977
Castle Cornet Military and Maritime Museums, Saint Peter Port 40422
Channel Islands Military Museum, Saint Ouen 40418
D-Day Museum and Overlord Embroidery, Portsmouth 40250
Dartmouth Castle, Dartmouth 38701
Divisional Kohima Museum, York 40961
Duke of Cornwall's Light Infantry Museum, Bodmin 38265
East Essex Aviation Society and Museum of the 40's, Saint Osyth 40417
Essex Regiment Museum, Chelmsford 38540
Fawley Court Historic House and Museum, Henley-on-Thames 39219
Five Council Museums East Headquarters, Cupar 38687
Fort Amherst Heritage Museum, Chatham 38528
Fort Grey and Shipwreck Museum, Saint Peter Port 40423
Fort Widley, Portsmouth 40252
Fusiliers London Volunteers' Museum, London 39640
Fusiliers Museum of Northumberland, Alnwick 37984
Gordon Highlanders Museum, Aberdeen 37937
Grand Shaft, Dover 38768
Green Howards Museum, Richmond, North Yorkshire 40316
Gurkha Museum, Winchester 40888
Hamilton Low Parks Museum, Hamilton 39160
HMS Belfast, London 39665
Houghton Hall Soldier Museum, Houghton 39267
Imperial War Museum Duxford, Cambridge 38456
Inns of Court and City Yeomanry Museum, London 39672
Kent Battle of Britain Museum, Hawkinge 39197
King's Own Royal Regiment Museum, Lancaster 39413
King's Own Yorkshire Light Infantry Regimental Museum, Doncaster 38742
The King's Royal Hussars Museum, Winchester 40889
Leith Hall, Huntly 39280
Light Infantry Museum, Winchester 40890
Liverpool Scottish Regimental Museum, Liverpool 39521
London Irish Rifles Regimental Museum, London 39697
London Scottish Regimental Museum, London 39698
Military Heritage Museum, Lewes 39485
Military Vehicle Museum, Newcastle-upon-Tyne 40039
Muckleburgh Collection, Weybourne 40839
Museum of Army Transport, Beverley 38183
Museum of Military Intelligence, Chicksands 38566
Museum of the 40's, Point Clear Bay 40215
Museum of The Duke of Wellington's Regiment, Halifax 39153
Museum of the Manchesters, Ashton-under-Lyne 38033
Museum of the Northamptonshire Regiment, Northampton 40082
Museum of the Percy Tenantry Volunteers 1798-1814, Alnwick 37986
Museum of the Royal Leicestershire Regiment, Leicester 39465
Museum of the Worcestershire Regiment, Worcester 40930
National Army Museum, London 39728
National Army Museum, Camberley 38443
National Army Museum Sandhurst Departments, Sandhurst, Berkshire 40442
Newhaven Fort, Newhaven 40046
Noirmont Command Bunker, Saint Brelade 40391
North Weald Airfield Museum and Memorial, Epping 38943
Nothe Fort Museum of Coastal Defence, Weymouth 40843
The Police Museum, Belfast 38158
Princess of Wales's Royal Regiment and Queen's Regiment Museum, Dover 38769
Quebec House, Westerham 40832
Queen's Lancashire Regiment Museum, Preston 40269
Queen's Own Royal West Kent Regimental Museum, Maidstone 39878
Queen's Royal Irish Hussars Museum, Eastbourne 38855
The Queen's Royal Lancers Regimental Museum, Grantham 39112
Queen's Royal Surrey Regiment Museum, Guildford 39141
Queen's Royal Surrey Regiment Museum, West Clandon 40823
Regimental Museum of 1st The Queen's Dragoon Guards, Cardiff 38482
Regimental Museum of the 13th/18th Royal Hussars and Kent Dragoons, Cawthorne 38515
Regimental Museum of the 9th/12th Royal Lancers, Derby 38719
Regimental Museum of the Black Watch, Perth 40186
Regimental Museum of the Oxfordshire and Buckinghamshire Light Infantry, Oxford 40154
Regimental Museum of the Royal Dragoon Guards and the Prince of Wales's Own Regiment of Yorkshire, York 40967
Regimental Museum of the Royal Scots Dragoon Guards, Edinburgh 38908
Regimental Museum of the Sherwood Foresters, Nottingham 40114
REME Museum of Technology, Arborfield 38009
Royal Anglian Regiment Museum, Duxford 38830
Royal Berkshire Yeomanry Cavalry Museum, Windsor 40902
Royal Fusiliers Regimental Museum, London 39762
Royal Green Jackets Museum, Winchester 40891
Royal Hampshire Regiment Museum, Winchester 40892
Royal Highland Fusiliers Regimental Museum, Glasgow 39064
Royal Inniskilling Fusiliers Regimental Museum, Enniskillen 38941
Royal Irish Regiment Museum, Ballymena 38070
Royal Lincolnshire Regiment Museum, Lincoln 39502
Royal Logistic Corps Museum, Deepcut 38712
Royal Marines Museum, Portsmouth 40257
Royal Military Academy Sandhurst Collection, Camberley 38444
Royal Military Police Museum, Chichester 38565
Royal Navy Submarine Museum, Gosport 39102
Royal Norfolk Regimental Museum, Norwich 40099
Royal Observer Corps Museum, Eastleigh 38861
Royal Regiment of Fusiliers Museum, Warwick 40792
Royal Welch Fusiliers Regimental Museum, Caernarfon 38434
Royal Wiltshire Yeomanry Museum, Swindon 40666
Saint Peter's Bunker, Saint Peter 40421
Scapa Flow Museum, Hoy 39271
Shropshire Regimental Museum, Shrewsbury 40512
Soldiers of Gloucestershire Museum, Gloucester 39085
Somme Heritage Centre, Newtownards 40075
South Nottinghamshire Hussars Museum, Bulwell 38392
South Wales Borderers and Monmouthshire Regimental Museum of the Royal Regiment of Wales, Brecon 38318
Staffordshire Regiment Museum, Lichfield 39493
Suffolk Regiment Museum, Bury Saint Edmunds 38418
Sussex Combined Services Museum, Eastbourne 38857
Tank Museum, Bovington 38289
Tilbury Fort, Tilbury 40710
Ugbrooke House, Chudleigh 38580
War Memorial Carillon Tower and Military Museum, Loughborough 39832
The Welch Regiment Museum (41st/ 69th Foot) of the Rpyal Regiment of Wales, Cardiff 38485
Westminster Dragoons Museum, London 39806
York and Lancaster Regimental Museum, Rotherham 40346

Uruguay
Museo de Armas, Montevideo 40994

U.S.A.
103rd Ohio Volunteer Infantry Memorial, Sheffield Lake 47591
45th Infantry Division Museum, Oklahoma City 46110
4th Infantry Division Museum, Fort Hood 43397
82nd Airborne Division War Memorial Museum, Fort Bragg 43371
Air Force Armament Museum, Eglin Air Force Base 43101
Air Force Flight Test Center Museum, Edwards Air Force Base 43096
Air Heritage Museum of Santa Barbara/Goleta, Goleta 43719
Air Power Park and Museum, Hampton 43894
Airborne and Special Operations Museum, Fayetteville 43309
Airmen Memorial Museum, Suitland 47872
Alamance Battleground, Burlington 42003
The Alamo, San Antonio 47243
Allied Air Force Museum, Allentown 41144
American Airpower Heritage Museum, Midland 45324
The American Historical Foundation Museum, Richmond 46870
American Military Museum, Charleston 42207
Ancient and Honorable Artillery Company Museum, Boston 41796
Antietam National Battlefield, Sharpsburg 47582
Artillery Company of Newport Military Museum, Newport 45922
Baltimore Civil War Museum, Baltimore 41452
Battleship North Carolina, Wilmington 48656
Battleship South Dakota Memorial, Sioux Falls 47641
Battleship Texas, La Porte 44556
Baxter Springs Heritage Center and Museum, Baxter Springs 41542
Beauvoir, Biloxi 41693
Benicia Historical Museum, Benicia 41624
Bentonville Battleground State Historic Site, Four Oaks 43498
Big Hole National Battlefield, Wisdom 48720
Brandywine Battlefield, Chadds Ford 42174
Bremerton Naval Museum, Bremerton 41878
Bushy Run Battlefield Museum, Jeannette 44320
Cairo Museum, Vicksburg 48227
Casemate Museum, Fort Monroe 43431
Castle Air Museum, Atwater 41369
Chickamauga-Chattanooga National Military Park, Fort Oglethorpe 43438
Civil Engineer Corps and Seabee Museum, Port Hueneme 46595
Civil War Museum of Lone Jack, Jackson County, Lone Jack 44855
Columbus-Belmont Civil War Museum, Columbus 42579
Combat Air Museum, Topeka 48032
Command Museum, San Diego 47274
Confederate Museum, New Orleans 45721
Cowpens National Battlefield, Chesnee 42282
Crown Point State Historic Site, Crown Point 42715
Custer Battlefield Museum, Garryowen 43631
Desoto National Memorial, Bradenton 41861
Dey Mansion, Wayne 48478
Don F. Pratt Museum, Fort Campbell 43376
Drum Barracks Civil War Museum, Wilmington 48648
Emil A. Blackmore Museum of the American Legion, Indianapolis 44218
Exchange Hotel Civil War Museum, Gordonsville 43729
Fifth Maine Regiment Center, Peaks Island 46322
First Cavalry Division Museum, Fort Hood 43398
The First Division Museum at Cantigny, Wheaton 48583
First Michigan Museum of Military History, Holland 44054
Fort Atkinson State Historical Park, Fort Calhoun 43374
Fort Belknap Museum, Newcastle 45911
Fort Bliss Museum, Fort Bliss 43369
Fort Bowie, Bowie 41842
Fort Buford State Historic Site, Williston 48638
Fort Caspar Museum, Casper 42129
Fort Christmas, Christmas 42392
Fort Clatsop National Memorial, Astoria 41310
Fort Dalles Museum, The Dalles 42762
Fort Davidson State Historic Site, Pilot Knob 46487
Fort Davis, Fort Davis 43384
Fort de Chartres Museum, Prairie du Rocher 46684
Fort Delaware Society Museum, Delaware City 42862
Fort Dix Museum, Fort Dix 43387
Fort Dobbs State Historic Site, Statesville 47793
Fort Dodge Historical Museum, Fort Dodge 43389
Fort Donelson National Battlefield Museum, Dover 42975
Fort Douglas Military Museum, Fort Douglas 43390
Fort Fetterman State Museum, Douglas 42964
Fort Frederick, Big Pool 41681
Fort George G. Meade Museum, Fort Meade 43426
Fort Gibson Historic Site, Fort Gibson 43395
Fort Harker Museum, Kanopolis 44390
Fort Hartsuff, Burwell 42014
Fort Hays, Hays 43969
Fort Huachuca Museum, Fort Huachuca 43399
Fort Inglish, Bonham 41779
Fort Jackson Museum, Fort Jackson 43401
Fort Kearney Museum, Kearney 44421
Fort Kearny State Historical Park, Kearney 44422
Fort King George Historic Site, Darien 42783
Fort Knox State Historic Site, Stockton Springs 47826
Fort Laramie, Fort Laramie 43407
Fort Larned, Larned 44655
Fort Laurens State Memorial, Bolivar 41776
Fort Lewis Military Museum, Fort Lewis 43422
Fort McAllister, Richmond Hill 46893
Fort MacArthur Museum, San Pedro 47371
Fort McKavett State Historic Park, Fort McKavett 43423
Fort Mackinac, Mackinac Island 45029
Fort Meigs State Memorial, Perrysburg 46357
Fort Mifflin, Philadelphia 46410
Fort Morgan Museum, Gulf Shores 43852
Fort Morris, Midway 45331
Fort Necessity National Battlefield, Farmington 43300
Fort Ontario, Oswego 46215
Fort Phil Kearny, Story 47838
Fort Pike, New Orleans 45724
Fort Pitt Museum, Pittsburg 46505
Fort Polk Military Museum, Fort Polk 43444
Fort Pulaski, Savannah 47478
Fort Recovery Museum, Fort Recovery 43447
Fort Robinson Museum, Crawford 42689
Fort Sam Houston Museum, Fort Sam Houston 43451
Fort Savannah Museum, Lewisburg 44725
Fort Selden State Monument, Radium Springs 46770
Fort Sidney Museum and Post Commander's Home, Sidney 47625
Fort Sill, Fort Sill 43455
Fort Spokane Visitor Center and Museum, Davenport 42787
Fort Stewart Museum, Fort Stewart 43460
Fort Sumter National Monument, Sullivan's Island 47873
Fort Tejon, Lebec 44706
Fort Ticonderoga, Ticonderoga 48005
Fort Towson Military Park, Fort Towson 43465
Fort Union National Monument, Watrous 48454
Fort Ward Museum and Historic Site, Alexandria 41125
Fort Washington, Fort Washington 43469
Fort Washita, Durant 43016
Fort William Henry Museum, Lake George 44587
Fort Zachary Taylor, Key West 44465
Fredericksburg and Spotsylvania National Military Park, Fredericksburg 43534
Frontier Army Museum, Fort Leavenworth 43416
General Douglas L. McBride Museum, Roswell 47014
General Douglas MacArthur Memorial, Norfolk 45964
General Jacob Brown Historical Museum, Brownville 41968
General Lewis B. Hershey Museum, Angola 41211
General Patton Memorial Museum, Chiriaco Summit 42387
General Sweeney's Museum, Republic 46844
Georgia Veterans Memorial Museum, Cordele 42631
Gettysburg National Military Park, Gettysburg 43663
Grand Army of the Republic Civil War Museum, Philadelphia 46415
Grand Army of the Republic Memorial and Veteran's Military Museum, Aurora 41397
Grand Gulf Military State Park Museum, Port Gibson 46594
Great Lakes Naval Memorial and Museum, Muskegon 45576
Grissom Air Museum, Peru 46363
Guilford Courthouse National Military Park, Greensboro 43815
Hampton Roads Naval Museum, Norfolk 45965
Harbor Defense Museum of New York City, Brooklyn 41942
Hill Aerospace Museum, Hill Air Force Base 44021
Historic Fort Snelling, Saint Paul 47156
Historic Fort Steilacoom, Tacoma 47918
Historic Fort Stockton, Fort Stockton 43462
History and Traditions Museum, Lackland Air Force Base 44562
Homerville Museum, Homer 44069
Horseshoe Bend National Military Park, Daviston 42796
Illinois Citizen Soldier Museum, Galesburg 43599
Indiana War Memorials Museum, Indianapolis 44225
Jean Lafitte National Historical Park and Preserve, New Orleans 45728
Jefferson Barracks, Saint Louis 47124
JFK Special Warfare Museum, Fort Bragg 43372
John Brown House, Osawatomie 46201
Kalamazoo Aviation History Museum, Kalamazoo 44378
Kennesaw Mountain National Battlefield Park, Kennesaw 44438
Kentucky Military History Museum, Frankfort 43510
Kings Mountain National Military Park, Blacksburg 41725
Knox's Headquarters State Historic Site, Vails Gate 48176
Korean War Veterans National Museum, Tuscola 48118
Lansing Veterans Memorial Museum, Lansing 44640
Little Bighorn Battlefield Museum, Crow Agency 42712
Lone Star Flight Museum/Texas Aviation Hall of Fame, Galveston 43612
Louisiana Naval War Memorial U.S.S. Kidd, Baton Rouge 41528
Manassas National Battlefield Park, Manassas 45091
March Field Museum, Riverside 46919
Medal of Honor Museum of Military History, Chattanooga 42264
Memorial Day Museum of Waterloo, Waterloo 48436
Military Historians Museum, Westbrook 48550
Military Medal Museum, San Jose 47352
Military Museum of Southern New England, Danbury 42771
Military Veterans Museum, Oshkosh 46205
Moores Creek National Battlefield, Currie 42732
Morristown National Historical Park, Morristown 45509
Motts Military Museum, Groveport 43848
Museum at Mountain Home, Johnson City 44347
The Museum of the Confederacy, Richmond 46883
Muskogee War Memorial Park and Military Museum, Muskogee 45582
National Cryptologic Museum, Fort Meade 43427
National D-Day Museum, New Orleans 45732

National Infantry Museum, Fort Benning 43366
National Museum of American Jewish Military History, Washington 48377
National Museum of Naval Aviation, Pensacola 46343
Naval War College Museum, Newport 45929
The Navy Museum, Washington 48386
New Jersey Naval Museum, Hackensack 43858
New Market Battlefield State Historical Park, New Market 45716
New Mexico Wing-Commemorative Air Force, Hobbs 44044
Old Barracks Museum, Trenton 48058
Old Fort Garland, Fort Garland 43394
Old Fort Jackson, Savannah 47481
Old Fort Meade Museum, Fort Meade 43428
Old Fort Niagara, Youngstown 48805
The Old Guard Museum, Fort Myer 43433
Oldest House Museum Complex, Saint Augustine 47069
Olustee Battlefield, Olustee 46138
Oregon Military Museum, Clackamas 42416
Oriskany Battlefield, Oriskany 46183
Pamplin Park Civil War Site, Petersburg 46374
Patriots Point Naval and Maritime Museum, Mount Pleasant 45540
Patton Museum of Cavalry and Armor, Fort Knox 43406
Pea Ridge National Military Park, Garfield 43625
Pennsylvania Military Museum and 28th Division Shrine, Boalsburg 41763
Perryville Battlefield Museum, Perryville 46358
Petersburg National Battlefield, Petersburg 46377
Phillips County Museum, Helena 43982
Port Columbus National Civil War Naval Center, Columbus 42576
Port Townsend Marine Science Center, Port Townsend 46606
Portsmouth Museum of Military History, Portsmouth 46664
Presidio La Bahia, Goliad 43723
Puget Sound Coast Artillery Museum at Fort Worden, Port Townsend 46607
Rankin Museum, Ellerbe 43154
Richmond National Battlefield Park, Richmond 46885
Rock Island Arsenal Museum, Rock Island 46956
Sackets Harbor Battlefield State Historic Site, Sackets Harbor 47045
Saint John's Northwestern Military Academy Museum, Delafield 42860
San Juan Island National Historical Park, Friday Harbor 43562
Saratoga National Historical Park, Stillwater 47812
Shiloh National Military Park and Cemetery, Shiloh 47606
Siege Museum, Petersburg 46378
Smallwood's Retreat, Marbury 45138
Soldiers' Memorial Military Museum, Saint Louis 47138
Soldiers National Museum, Gettysburg 43665
Sons of the American Revolution, Roselle 47006
South Carolina Military Museum, Columbia 42568
South Carolina National Guard Museum, Sumter 47878
Springfield Armory Museum, Springfield 47749
Stones River National Battlefield, Murfreesboro 45569
Stony Point Battlefield State Historic Site, Stony Point 47833
Strategic Air Space Museum, Ashland 41291
Submarine Force Museum and Historic Ship Nautilus, Groton 43845
Texas Heritage Museum, Hillsboro 44028
Texas Military Forces Museum, Austin 41422
Third Cavalry Museum, Fort Carson 43377
Thomas Clarke House-Princeton Battlefield, Princeton 46706
UDT-SEAL Museum, Fort Pierce 43442
Ukrainian-American Museum, Warren 48308
United States Air Force Academy Museum, El Paso 43110
United States Air Force Museum, Wright-Patterson Air Force Base 48766
United States Army Air Defense Artillery Museum, Fort Bliss 43370
United States Army Aviation Museum, Fort Rucker 43450
United States Army Center of Military History, Fort McNair 43424
United States Army Chaplain Museum, Fort Jackson 43402
United States Army Communications-Electronics Museum, Fort Monmouth 43430
United States Army Engineer Museum, Fort Leonard Wood 43420
United States Army Finance Corps Museum, Fort Jackson 43403
United States Army Heritage and Education Center, Carlisle 42106
United States Army Museum of Hawaii, Fort DeRussy 43386
United States Army Ordnance Museum, Aberdeen Proving Ground 41047
The United States Army Quartermaster Museum, Fort Lee 43418
United States Army Signal Corps and Fort Gordon Museum, Fort Gordon 43396
United States Army Transportation Museum, Fort Eustis 43393
United States Army Women's Museum, Fort Lee 43419
United States Brig Niagara, Homeport Erie Maritime Museum, Erie 43203
United States Cavalry Museum, Fort Riley 43449
United States Marine Corps Air-Ground Museum, Quantico 46753
United States Marine Corps Museum, Washington 48402
United States Navy Supply Corps Museum, Athens 41323
US Army Military Police Corps Museum, Fort Leonard Wood 43421
USS Alabama Battleship Memorial Park, Mobile 45425
USS Arizona Memorial, Honolulu 44092
USS Bowfin Submarine Museum, Honolulu 44093
USS Constitution Museum, Boston 41831
USS Lexington Museum on the Bay, Corpus Christi 42647
Varnum Memorial Armory and Military Museum, East Greenwich 43042
Vicksburg National Military Park-Cairo Museum, Vicksburg 48230
Vietnam Era Educational Center, Holmdel 44063
Virginia Military Institute Museum, Lexington 44763
The Virginia War Museum, Newport News 45941
Warren ICBM and Heritage Museum, Frances E. Warren Air Force Base 43503
Warren Rifles Confederate Museum, Front Royal 43568
Washington's Headquarters, Newburgh 45905
The Watervliet Arsenal Museum, Watervliet 48449
West Point Museum, West Point 48543
Wilson's Creek National Battlefield, Republic 46845
Wings of Freedom, Huntington 44158
Wisconsin National Guard Memorial Library and Museum, Camp Douglas 42069
Wisconsin Veterans Museum King, King 44484
Wisconsin Veterans Museum Madison, Madison 45075
Wright Museum, Wolfeboro 48724
Yankee Air Museum, Belleville 41593

Venezuela
Museo Urdaneta Histórico Militar, Maracaibo 48951

Vietnam
Anti-Aircraft Museum, Ha Noi 48971
Bao Tàng Quan Doi, Ha Noi 48973
South-East Armed Force Museum, Ho Chi Minh City 48990

Yemen
Military Museum, Sanaa 49010

Mills

Australia
Berkshire Mill Museum, Moora 01269
Chinchilla and District Historical Society Museum, Chinchilla 00915
Quorn Mill Museum, Quorn 01406

Austria
Alte Mühle Schrattenberg, Schrattenberg 02639
Freilichtmuseum Apriacher Stockmühlen, Heiligenblut 02015
Freilichtmuseum Katzensteiner Mühle, Weyer 02827
Freilichtmuseum Kugelmühle, Seeham 02657
Freilichtmuseum Ledermühle, Sankt Oswald bei Freistadt 02591
Freilichtmuseum Oberlienz, Oberlienz 02369
Grasselmühle, Reichenthal 02497
Hausmühle, Steinbach am Attersee 02678
Heimathaus Wenigzell, Wenigzell 02820
Hundsmarktmühle, Thalgau 02726
Kürbismühlenmuseum, Preding 02449
Leithenmühle, Windhaag bei Freistadt 03037
Museum Furthmühle, Pram 02445
Museum Stoffels Säge-Mühle, Hohenems 02042
Obermühle Hochburg-Ach, Ach 01641
Ramitscheder-Mühle, Edlbach 01787
Schattleitenmühle, Garsten 01870
Wastlmühle, Lainbach 02177
Windmühle, Retz 02509

Belgium
Mercator Graventoren-Watermolen, Rupelmonde 03717
Mola- het Provinciaal Molenmuseum, Wachtebeke 03823
Molenmuseum, Sint-Amands 03735
Sint-Janshuismolen en Koeleweimolen, Brugge 03267

Canada
Balmoral Grist Mill, Tatamagouche 06534
Bell Rock Mill Museum, Verona 06710
Delta Mill and Old Stone Mill Museum, Delta 05322
Flour Mill Museum, Sudbury 06510
Grist Mill, Keremeos 05662
Historic Babcock Mill, Odessa 06042
Hope Water Powered Saw Mill, Peterborough 06118
Kingston Mills Blockhouse, Elgin 05400
Lang Water Powered Grist Mill, Peterborough 06120
McDougall Mill Museum, Renfrew 06251
McLean Mill, Port Alberni 06149
MacPherson's Mill and Farm Homestead, New Glasgow 05978
Moulin de Beaumont, Beaumont 05065
Moulin Fleming, LaSalle 05729
Moulin Légaré, Saint-Eustache 06315
Mountain Mills Museum, Saint Catharines 06309
Museum of South East Alberta, Etzikom 05419
Old Hastings Mill Store Museum, Vancouver 06685
La Pulperie de Chicoutimi, Chicoutimi 05247
Sutherland Steam Mill, Denmark 05326
Todmorden Mills Heritage Museum and Arts Centre, Toronto 06614
Watson's Mill, Manotick 05808
Wile Carding Mill Museum, Bridgewater 05131

Czech Republic
Větrný Mlýn, Rudice 08645

Denmark
Højer Mølle- og Marskmuseum, Højer 08883
Kaleko Mølle, Faaborg 08816
Skjern Vindmølle, Skjern 09066
Tadre Mølle, Hvalsø 08905

France
Maison de la Meunerie, Nieul-sur-l'Autise 13331
Moulin à Papier Vallis-Clausa, Fontaine-de-Vaucluse 11757
Les Moulins, Sagy 14085
Musée du Moulin, Saint-Jean-Saint-Nicolas 14291
Musée Moulin de Maupertuis, Donzy 11554

Germany
Altmühltaler Mühlenmuseum, Dietfurt 16603
Bockwindmühle Brehna, Brehna 16310
Bockwindmühlenmuseum, Trebbus 20194
Buchholzer Heimatmuseum, Buchholz in der Nordheide 16389
Freilichtmuseum Scherzenmühle Weidenberg, Weidenberg 20427
Furthmühle, Egenhofen 16785
Heimatmuseum Bockwindmühle, Lebusa 18364
Heimatmuseum Elze, Elze 16845
Heimatmuseum Vollmers Mühle, Seebach, Baden 19910
Internationales Wind- und Wassermühlenmuseum, Gifhorn 17286
Klopfermühle mit Mühlenmuseum, Lengenfeld, Vogtland 18436
Klostermühlenmuseum, Thierhaupten 20172
Lassaner Mühle, Lassan 18343
Lindigtmühle am Lindenvorwerk, Kohren-Sahlis 18196
Linnenschmidt'sche Vormals Landesherrliche Mühle zu Venne, Ostercappeln 19292
Moisburger Mühlenmuseum, Moisburg 18782
Mühlen- und Landwirtschaftsmuseum, Jever 17956
Mühlen- und Landwirtschaftsmuseum, Westfehmarn 20543
Das Mühlendorf, Ottenhöfen 19321
Mühlenfachmuseum, Aurich 15579
Mühlenmuseum, Pfullingen 19393
Mühlenmuseum, Sontra 20002
Mühlenmuseum, Woldegk 20646
Mühlenmuseum Haren (Ems), Haren 17618
Mühlenmuseum Katzbrui, Apfeltrach 15506
Mühlenmuseum Mitling-Mark mit Sammlung Omas Küche, Westoverledingen 20544
Museum für Mühlenbautechnik, Syrau 20135
Museum Moorseer Mühle, Nordenham 19114
Museum Neue Mühle, Erfurt 16906
Museumsmühle Hasbergen, Delmenhorst 16568
Museumsmühle mit heimatkundlicher Sammlung, Varel 20287
Ölmühle Michelau, Rudersberg 19699
Produktionsmuseum Klostermühle, Boitzenburg 16223
Schiffmühle Höfgen, Grimma 17403
Schleifmühle Schwerin, Schwerin 19898
Schwarzwälder Mühlenmuseum, Grafenhausen 17372
Städtisches Museum Sprucker Mühle, Guben 17451
Strötzbacher Mühle, Mömbris 18767
Technisches Denkmal Neumannmühle, Ottendorf bei Sebnitz 19320
Teichmühle, Steinwiesen 20056
Volkskunde- und Mühlenmuseum, Waltersdorf bei Zittau 20385
Wassermühle Höfgen, Grimma 17405
Wassermühle Kuchelmiß, Kuchelmiß 18256
Weicheltmühle, Reichenau bei Dippoldiswalde 19544
Wilhelm-Busch-Mühle, Ebergötzen 16763

Greece
Mykonos Folklore Museum, Mykonos 21078

Hungary
Szélmalom, Szeged 21553

Ireland
Tuam Mill Museum, Tuam 22549

Lithuania
Žaliūkių Windmill, Šiauliai 27533

Netherlands
Gitstappermolen, Vlodrop 29957
De Grafelijke Torenmolen, Zeddam 30047
Koren en Pel Molen De Eendracht, Anjum 28921
Koren en Pelmolen De Noordstar, Noordbroek 29642
Korenmolen de Hoop, Hellendoorn 29385
Korenmolen de Hoop, Klarenbeek 29483
Korenmolen de Phenix, Nes 29610
Korenmolen de Zandhaas, Santpoort 29789
Molen van Sloten, Amsterdam 28873
Molenmuseum, Koog aan de Zaan 29489
Molenmuseum de Assumburg, Nieuw Vossemeer 29616
Molenmuseum De Valk, Leiden 29520
Molenmuseum De Wachter, Zuidlaren 30070
Museum De Doornboom, Hilvarenbeek 29416
Museum-Gemaal de Hoogte, Nieuwolda 29626
Museum van Zwerfstenen in de Rosmolen, Zeddam 30048
Museumgemaal Caners, 's- Hertogenbosch 29406
Museummolen, Schermerhorn 29799
Museummolen Jan Pol, Dalen 29065
Nederlands Graanmuseum/Olie- en Korenmolen Woldzigt, Roderwolde 29742
Oliemolen de Zoeker, Zaandam 30039
Oliemolen Het Pink, Koog aan de Zaan 29490
Oudheidkamer Weststellingwerf, Wolvega 30019
Poldermuseum Het Grootslag - Nationaal Saet en Cruytmuseum, Andijk 28920
Stoomgemaal Halfweg, Halfweg 29337
Stoomgemaal Hertog Reijnout en Bezoekerscentrum Arkemheen, Nijkerk 29628
Stoomgemaal Mastenbroek, Genemuiden 29273

Norway
Aremark Historielag, Aremark 30388
Fotland Bygdemølle, Bryne 30452

Poland
Muzeum Historii Młynarstwa i Wodnych Urządzeń Przemysłu Wiejskiego w Jaraczu, Jaracz 31620
Muzeum Młynarstwa Powietrznego, Będzia 31482

Spain
Conjunto de la Ferrería y Molinos de Agorregi, Aia 34415
Molino-Museo Gregorio Prieto, Valdepeñas 35590

Sweden
Frövifors Pappersbruksmuseum, Frövi 35897
Kulla Gunnarstorps Mölla, Helsingborg 35953
Pålsjö Kvarn, Helsingborg 35954
Skogsmuseum, Åsele 35820

Switzerland
Moulins Souterrains du Col-des-Roches, Le Locle 36888
Mühlenmuseum Brüglingen, Münchenstein 36965
Mühlerama, Zürich 37392

United Kingdom
Arlington Mill Museum, Bibury 38188
Bembridge Windmill Museum, Mottistone 39989
Blackgang Sawmill and Saint Catherine's Quay, Blackgang 38245
Blackpool Mill, Narberth 40000
Bradford Industrial Museum and Horses at work, Bradford 38295
Bromham Mill and Art Gallery, Bromham 38375
Bunbury Watermill, Bunbury 38393
Bursledon Windmill, Bursledon 38404
Calbourne Water Mill and Rural Museum, Calbourne 38437
Caudwell's Mill Craft Centre, Matlock 39920
Charney Basset Mill, Wantage 40781
Coldharbour Mill, Uffculme 40745
Crabble Corn Mill, Dover 38764
Crakehall Water Mill, Crakehall 38657
Cromford Mill, Cromford 38675
Dalgarven Mill, Kilwinning 39367
Dell Mill, Isle-of-Lewis 39317
Ford End Watermill, Ivinghoe 39321
Green's Mill and Science Centre, Nottingham 40107
Heatherslaw Mill, Cornhill-on-Tweed 38633
Heckington Windmill, Heckington 39205
Heron Corn Mill and Museum of Papermaking, Beetham 38150
Hornsbury Mill, Chard 38524
Ifield Watermill, Crawley 38660
King's Mill Visitor Centre, Wrexham 40942
Leeds Industrial Museum, Leeds 39447
Lytham Windmill Museum, Lytham Saint Anne's 39861
Meopham Windmill, Meopham 39934
Mill Green Museum and Mill, Hatfield 39188
Muncaster Watermill, Ravenglass 40286
North Leverton Windmill, North Leverton 40079
Otterton Mill Centre and Working Museum, Budleigh Salterton 38391
Patterson's Spade Mill, Templepatrick 40682
Quarry Bank Mill, Styal 40640
Queen Street Mill Textile Museum, Burnley 38400
Sarehole Mill, Birmingham 38227
Saxtead Green Post Mill, Saxtead 40452
Skidby Windmill and Museum of East Riding Rural Life, Skidby 40525
Stansted Mountfitchet Windmill, Stansted Mountfitchet 40580
Stevington Windmill, Stevington 40584
Stott Park Bobbin Mill, Ulverston 40749
Stretton Water Mill, Farndon 38979
Swanton Mill, Ashford 38029
Thwaite Mills Watermill, Leeds 39455
Trader Windmill, Sibsey 40514
Upminster Mill, Upminster 40750
Wellbrook Beetling Mill, Cookstown 38630
West Blatchington Windmill, Hove 39270
White Mill Rural Heritage Centre, Sandwich 40448

Wimbledon Windmill Museum, London 39812
Windmill and Milling Museum, Polegate 40216
Worsbrough Mill Museum, Barnsley, South Yorkshire 38092

U.S.A.
Burwell-Morgan Mill, Millwood 45351
Champion Mill, Champion 42189
Crane Museum, Dalton 42767
Fabyan Villa Museum and Dutch Windmill, Geneva 43640
Frye's Measure Mill, Wilton 48673
Graue Mill and Museum, Oak Brook 46050
Hamburg State Park Museum, Mitchell 45410
Hanford Mills Museum, East Meredith 43057
Historic Bowens Mills and Pioneer Park, Middleville 45320
Historic Mill Creek, Mackinaw City 45034
McPherson County Old Mill Museum, Lindsborg 44807
Mayflower Gold Mill, Silverton 47634
Neligh Mills, Neligh 45647
Old Schwamb Mill, Arlington 41258
Pennypacker Mills, Schwenksville 47501
Praters Mill, Varnell 48204
Saugus Iron Works, Saugus 47466
Union Mills Homestead and Grist Mill, Westminster 48564

Mineralogy

Argentina
Centro de Exposiciónes de Geologia y Mineria, Buenos Aires 00145
Museo de Ciencias Naturales Luma, Tanti 00631
Museo de Mineralogía y Geología Dr. Alfredo Stelzner, Córdoba 00297
Museo Municipal de Historia Natural, General Alvear 00352
Museo Provincial de Historia Natural de La Pampa, Santa Rosa 00613

Australia
Ashworths Treasures of the Earth, Home Hill 01108
Crystal Kingdom, Coonabarabran 00944
Echuca Gem Club Collection, Echuca 01002
House of Bottles, Kinglake 01148
School of Earth Sciences Museum, Townsville 01548
West Coast Pioneer's Memorial Museum, Zeehan 01635

Austria
Bergbaumuseum, Hall in Tirol 01991
Bergbaumuseum mit Mineralienschau und Schaubergwerk, Hüttenberg 02050
Felsenmuseum, Bernstein, Burgenland 01734
Heimathaus Richard Eichinger und Steinmuseum, Enzenkirchen 01820
Kristalle und Edle Steine Turracher Höhe, Ebene Reichenau 01779
Landesmuseum Joanneum, Graz 01922
Marmormuseum, Adnet 01645
Museum Bramberg "Wilhelmgut", Bramberg 01743
Paläontologisches Museum, Offenhausen 02384
Stadtmuseum Schladming, Schladming 02632

Belgium
Mineralogisch Museum, Merksem 03624
Musée Communal de la Pierre de Sprimont, Sprimont 03763
Musée de Minéralogie et de Géologie, Bruxelles 03313
Schoolmuseum Michel Thiery, Gent 03449

Bolivia
Museo Mineralogico, La Paz 03898

Bosnia and Herzegovina
Zavičajni Muzej, Travnik 03926

Brazil
Museu Amsterdam Sauer de Pedras Preciosas, Rio de Janeiro 04330
Museu de Ciências da Terra - DNPM, Rio de Janeiro 04357
Museu de Geologia, Porto Alegre 04281
Museu de Minerais e Rochas, Uberlândia 04577
Museu de Mineralogia, Congonhas 04050
Museu de Mineralogia Luiz Englert, Porto Alegre 04282
Museu H. Stern, Rio de Janeiro 04380

Bulgaria
Prirodonaučen Muzej, Burgas 04636

Canada
Bancroft Mineral Museum, Bancroft 05039
Fundy Geological Museum, Parrsboro 06095
Mineral and Gem Geological Museum, Parrsboro 06096
Musée Minéralogique d'Asbestos, Asbestos 05010
Musée Minéralogique et Minier de Thetford Mines, Thetford Mines 06542
New Brunswick Mining and Mineral Interpretation Centre, Petit-Rocher 06124
Princeton and District Museum, Princeton 06192
R.B. Ferguson Museum of Mineralogy, Winnipeg 06838

Chile
Museo de Historia Natural de Valparaíso, Valparaíso 06927

Colombia
Colección de Minerales y Arqueología, Villanueva 07625
Museo de Historia Natural, Alta Suiza 07365
Museo de Minerales del Instituto Geofísico, Bogotá 07410
Museo Mineralógico Salón Tulio Ospina, Medellín 07523
Museo Mineralógico y Antropológico, Ibagué 07498
Museo Vitaliano Zuccardi, Sincelejo 07593

Croatia
Hrvatski Narodni Zoološki Muzej, Zagreb 07821
Mineraloško-Petrografski Muzej, Zagreb 07828
Muzej Krapinskog Pračovjeka, Krapina 07728

Czech Republic
Dietrichsteinský Palác, Brno 08264
Krajské Muzeum Sokolov, Sokolov 08660
Městské Muzeum, Radnice u Rokycan 08632
Městské Muzeum, Stříbro 08666
Městské Muzeum, Volyně 08724
Městské Muzeum v Mariánských Lázních, Mariánské Lázně 08472
Muzeum Českého Ráje, Turnov 08694
Okresni Muzeum, Most 08489
Okresni Vlastivědné Muzeum, Nový Jičín 08511
Ostravské Muzeum, Ostrava 08527
Rožmberský Dům, Soběslav 08658
Sládečkovo Vlastivědné Muzeum v Kladně, Kladno 08410

Denmark
Geologisk Museum, København 08930

Ecuador
Museo del Colegio Nacional Pedro Vicente Maldonado, Riobamba 09223
Museo Petrográfico del Servicio Nacional de Geología y Minería, Quito 09217
Museo Vásquez Fuller, Otavalo 09190

Finland
Geologian museo, Helsinki 09481
Geologian Tutkimuskeskuksen Kivimuseo, Espoo 09433
Kivimuseo, Helsinki 09502
Kivimuseo, Tampere 10078
Kultamuseo Tankavaara, Tankavaara 10099

France
Espace Minéralogique Minéraux Couleur Nature, Eymoutiers 11688
Expositions Pipe et Diamant, Saint-Claude 14158
Galerie de Minéralogie, Paris 13506
Maison de la Pierre de Volvic, Volvic 15287
Maison des Minéraux, Crozon 11463
Musée de la Mine de Cap Garonne, Le Pradet 12472
Musée de la Pierre, Trambly 14983
Musée de Minéralogie de l'Ecole des Mines de Paris, Paris 13581
Musée des Minéraux et Fossiles des Ardennes, Bogny-sur-Meuse 10784
Musée d'Histoire Naturelle, Nantes 13257
Musée Minéralogique, Nîmes 13342
Musée Minéralogique de la Société Industrielle, Mulhouse 13215
Musée Municipal, Saint-Dizier 14191
Musée Pierre Borrione, Aime-en-Tarentaise 10243
Muséum d'Histoire Naturelle, Le Havre 12428
Petit Musée Minéraux et Faune de l'Alpe, Bourg-Saint-Maurice 10857

Germany
Bartholomäus-Schmucker-Heimatmuseum, Ruhpolding 19714
Bergbau- und Mineralienmuseum, Oberwolfach 19216
Geologisches Museum der DSK-Saar, Saarbrücken 19723
Geologisches und Mineralogisches Museum der Christian-Albrechts-Universität, Kiel 18072
GeoMuseum der Universität, Köln 18139
Geosammlung der Technischen Universität Clausthal, Clausthal-Zellerfeld 16475
Geowissenschaftliche Sammlungen, Freiberg, Sachsen 17099
Heimatmuseum Betzenstein, Betzenstein 16132
Heimatmuseum im Alten Kloster, Erbendorf 16889
Heimatstube Langenaubach, Haiger 17489
Höhlenmuseum Kubacher Kristallhöhle und Freilicht-Steinemuseum, Weilburg 20445
Kali-Bergbaumuseum Volpriehausen, Uslar 20279
Kristallmuseum, Viechtach 20307
Marienglashöhle Friedrichroda, Friedrichroda 17143
Mineralien-Fossilien-Museum, Neckartenzlingen 18991
Mineralien-Kabinett der TU Braunschweig, Braunschweig 16300
Mineralien-Sammlung, Hohenwarth 17817
Mineralien- und Heimatmuseum, Pleystein 19416
Mineralienmuseum Essen, Essen 16957
Mineralienmuseum Pforzheim-Dillweißenstein, Pforzheim 19388
Mineraliensammlung, Lauingen 18358
Mineralienschau, Vohenstrauß 20331
Mineralogisch-Geologische Gesteins-Sammlung, Schwarzenfeld 19885
Mineralogische Sammlung, Erlangen 16919
Mineralogische Schau- und Lehrsammlung, Tübingen 20228
Mineralogisches Museum der Philipps-Universität Marburg, Marburg 18630
Mineralogisches Museum der Universität, Würzburg 20698
Mineralogisches Museum der Universität Bonn, Bonn 16244
Mineralogisches Museum der Universität Hamburg, Hamburg 17554
Mineralogisches Museum (Kristalle und Gesteine), Münster 18941
Museum für Geologie und Paläontologie am Geowissenschaftlichen Zentrum der Universität Göttingen, Göttingen 17337
Museum für Mineralogie und Geologie, Dresden 16700
Museum für Naturkunde der Humboldt-Universität zu Berlin, Berlin 16056
Museum im Hollerhaus, Dietfurt 16604
Museum Reich der Kristalle, München 18884
Naturkunde-Museum, Bielefeld 16159
Naturkunde-Museum Bamberg, Bamberg 15813
Privatmuseum Hans Klein, Prichsenstadt 19448
Schwarzwälder Mineralienmuseum, Neubulach 19016
Stadthistorisches Museum, Bad Salzdetfurth 15728
Stadtmuseum Nittenau, Nittenau 19106
Stadtmuseum Stadtoldendorf, Stadtoldendorf 20033
Stein- und Fossiliensammlung Albert, Sulzdorf 20129
Urwelt-Museum Oberfranken, Bayreuth 15860
Urweltmuseum Aalen, Aalen 15386
Waldmuseum, Mehlmeisel 18681
Zinngrube Ehrenfriedersdorf, Ehrenfriedersdorf 16795

Greece
Mineralogical Museum of Kamarzia, Attica 20907
Mineralogical Museum of Lavrion, Lavrion 21045
Museum of Mineralogy, Petrology and Geology, Zografou 21226

Hungary
Herman Ottó Múzeum, Miskolc 21475

India
Central College Museum, Bangalore 21702
Geography Museum, Faizabad 21801
Geological Museum, Lucknow 21925
Our India Project Museum, Narendrapur 21966

Ireland
James Mitchell Museum, Galway 22473

Italy
Frasassi- le Grotte, Genga 23974
Mineralogy, Petrography and Volcanology Museum, Catania 23445
Mostra della Giudaica e Raccolta di Minerali, Laino Borgo 24128
Mostra Permanente della Tradizione Mineraria, Tarvisio 25675
Museo A. Ricci dei Minerali Elbani, Rio nell'Elba 25121
Museo Carlo Venturini, Massa Lombarda 24317
Museo Civico, Finale Emilia 23815
Museo Civico A. Klitsche de la Grange, Allumiere 22859
Museo Civico di Scienze Naturali, Voghera 26044
Museo Civico di Storia Naturale, Ferrara 23787
Museo Comunale A. Mendola, Favara 23770
Museo dei Fossili e dei Minerali, Smerillo 25591
Museo dei Fossili e di Storia Naturale, Montefalcone Appennino 24518
Museo dei Fossili e Minerali del Monte Nerone, Apecchio 22903
Museo dei Minerali e della Miniera, Oltre il Colle 24677
Museo dei Minerali Elbani, Rio Marina 25120
Museo dell'Ardesia, Cicagna 23560
Museo di Geologia e Paleontologia, Pavia 24824
Museo di Minerali e Fossili, Montefiore Conca 24522
Museo di Mineralogia, Massa Marittima 24326
Museo di Mineralogia, Palermo 24770
Museo di Mineralogia, Roma 25215
Museo di Mineralogia, di Petrologia e Geologia, Modena 24444
Museo di Mineralogia e Paleontologia, Saint Vincent 25312
Museo di Mineralogia e Petrografia, Pavia 24825
Museo di Mineralogia e Petrografia, Parma 24806
Museo di Mineralogia e Petrografia L. Bombicci, Bologna 23127
Museo di Mineralogia L. De Prunner, Cagliari 23250
Museo di Paleontologia e di Mineralogia, Valdagno 25872
Museo di Paleontologia e Mineralogia, Campomorone 23310
Museo di Storia Naturale, Cremona 23681
Museo di Storia Naturale - Sez Mineralogia, Firenze 23871
Museo Mineralogico, Bortigiadas 23181
Museo Mineralogico, Valle Aurina 25880
Museo Mineralogico Campano, Vico Equense 26001
Museo Mineralogico e Naturalistico, Bormio 23180
Museo Mineralogico e Paleontologico delle Zolfare, Caltanissetta 23277
Museo Mineralogico Permanente, Carro 23362
Museo Mineralogico Sardo, Iglesias 24082
Museo Minerario Alpino, Cogne 23607
Museo P. Calderini, Varallo Sesia 25891
Museo Storico Minerario, Perticara 24845
Real Museo Mineralogico, Napoli 24607

Japan
Akita Daigaku Kozangakubu Fuzok u Kogyo Hakubutsukan, Akita 26093
Ikuno Kobutsukan, Ikuno, Hyogo 26242
Tanakami Mineral Museum, Otsu 26684

Luxembourg
Collection Eugène Pesch, Oberkorn 27572

Mexico
Museo de Mineralogía, Pachuca 28294
Museo de Mineralogía, Guanajuato 27973
Museo de Mineralogía Dr Miguel Romero Sánchez, Tehuacán 28474
Museo de Mineralogía y Geología Ing. Luis Silva Ruelas, Morelia 28250
Museo Ora Ton, Chamula 27814

Mozambique
Museu Nacional de Geologia, Maputo 28726

Netherlands
Geo Inn, Oosterbeek 29667
Mineralogisch-Geologisch Museum, Delft 29081
Mineralogisch Museum, Grou 29318

New Zealand
Crystal Mountain - Crystal Mineral Gallery Museum, Auckland 30105
Geology Museum, Auckland 30108
Thames School of Mines and Mineralogical Museum, Thames 30263

Poland
Muzeum Mineralogiczne, Szklarska Poręba 32034
Muzeum Mineralogiczne, Wrocław 32180
Muzeum Mineralogicznego Uniwersytetu Wrocławskiego, Wrocław 32181

Portugal
Museu de História Natural, Porto 32334
Museu Mineralógico e Geológico, Coimbra 32262

Romania
Muzeul de Mineralogie Baia Mare, Baia Mare 32434

Russia
Angarskij Muzej Mineralov, Angarsk 32642
Geologičeskij Muzej, Vorkuta 33727
Geologo-mineralogičeskij Muzej, Kazan 32888
Geologo-mineralogičeskij Muzej im. A.I. Kozlova, Vladivostok 33697
Gornyj Muzej, Sankt-Peterburg 33396
Gosudarstvennyj Geologičeskij Muzej im V.I. Vernadskogo, Moskva 33053
Mineralogičeskij Muzej, Apatity 32644
Mineralogičeskij Muzej im. A.E. Fersmana Rossijskoj Akademii Nauk, Moskva 33084
Mineralogičeskij Muzej im. A.V. Sidorova, Irkutsk 32815
Muzei Permskogo Gosudarstvennogo Universiteta, Perm 33304
Muzej Geologii, Čeljabinsk 32727
Muzej Samocvety Bajkala, Sljudjanka 33527
Muzejno-vystavočnyj Centr, Dal'negorsk 32754
Udivitelnoe v Kamne - Muzej Mineralov, Rud, Samocvetov, Teberda 33598

Serbia-Montenegro
Zbirka Rudnika Majdanpek, Majdanpek 33860

Spain
Colección de Geología, Vilajüiga 35660
Museo de Ciencias Naturales, Pontevedra 35283
Museo Geominero, Madrid 35037
Museu Mollfulleda de Mineralogia, Arenys de Mar 34481

Sri Lanka
Museum of Gems and Minerals, Ratnapura 35759

Sweden
Evolutionsmuseet, Paleontologi, Uppsala 36354
Jokkmokks Stencenter, Jokkmokk 35983
Mineral- och Gruvmuseet, Holsbybrunn 35964
Skottvångs Gruva, Mariefred 36087
Tykarpsgrottan Kalkmuseum, Hässleholm 35936

Switzerland
Alpines Museum, Zermatt 37357
Collezione di Minerali e Fossili, Semione 37160
Geologisch-Mineralogische Ausstellung der Eidgenössischen Technischen Hochschule Zürich, Zürich 37376
Kristallmuseum, Guttannen 36788
Mineralien Museum, Seedorf (Uri) 37156
Musée des Minéraux et des Fossiles, Rougemont 37074
Museum Alpin, Pontresina 37026
Museum La Truaisch, Sedrun 37155
Steinmuseum, Solothurn 37188

Tanzania
Mineral Resources Divisional Museum, Dodoma 37460

Thailand
Mineralogy Museum, Bangkok 37488

United Kingdom
Abbey and Stones Museum, Margam 39909
Camborne School of Mines Geological Museum and Art Gallery, Pool 40224
Cornwall Geological Museum, Penzance 40179
Creetown Gem Rock Museum, Creetown 38662
Geological Museum and Art Gallery, Redruth 40303
Killhope, the North of England Lead Mining Museum, Weardale 40804
Planet Earth Museum, Newhaven 40047
Royal Cornwall Museum, Truro 40730
Royal Pump Room Museum, Harrogate 39171
Welsh Slate Museum, Llanberis 39536

U.S.A.
A.E. Seaman Mineral Museum, Houghton 44113
Arizona Mining and Mineral Museum, Phoenix 46472
California State Mining and Mineral Museum, Mariposa 45166
Colburn Gem and Mineral Museum, Asheville 41278
Colorado School of Mines Geology Museum, Golden 43714
Cranbrook Institute of Science, Bloomfield Hills 41740
Gillespie Museum of Minerals, De Land 42815
Idaho Museum of Mining and Geology, Boise 41773
Lizzadro Museum of Lapidary Art, Elmhurst 43167
Meadowlands Museum, Rutherford 47040
Miles Mineral Museum, Portales 46616
Mineral and Lapidary Museum of Henderson County, Hendersonville 43994
Mineral Museum, Butte 42018
Mineralogical Museum of Harvard University, Cambridge 42046
Mousley Museum of Natural History, Yucaipa 48815
Museum of North Carolina Minerals, Spruce Pine 47764
New Mexico Bureau of Mines Mineral Museum, Socorro 47663
Post Rock Museum, La Crosse 44535
Stone Museum, Monroe Township 45446
Tri-State Mineral Museum, Joplin 44363
University of Arizona Mineral Museum, Tucson 48094
W.M. Keck Museum, Reno 46839

Vietnam
Geological Museum, Ho Chi Minh City 48985

Zimbabwe
Macgregor Museum, Harare 49030

Miniature Painting

France
Collections de l'Ecole Nationale Supérieure des Beaux-Arts, Paris 13494

India
Government Museum and Art Gallery, Chandigarh 21738
Maharaja Sawai Man Singh II Museum, Jaipur, Rajasthan 21863
M.C. Mehta Gallery, Ahmedabad 21680

Netherlands
Reflex Miniatuur Museum voor Hedendaagse Kunst, Amsterdam 28896

Switzerland
Patek Philippe Museum, Genève 36753

United Kingdom
Impossible Microworld Museum, Bath 38116
Sherborne Castle, Sherborne 40494

Mining Engineering

Argentina
Museo del Cielo, Villa Carlos Paz 00661

Australia
Acland Coal Mine Museum, Acland 00697
Burra Mine Open Air Museum, Burra 00865
Emmaville Mining Museum, Emmaville 01017
Grubb Shaft Gold and Heritage Museum, Beaconsfield 00780
Gwalia Historical Museum, Leonora 01175
Gympie and District Historical and Gold Mining Museum, Gympie 01082
Hannans North Tourist Mine, Kalgoorlie 01132
Herons Reef Historic Gold Diggings, Fryerstown 01040
Morphett's Enginehouse Museum, Burra 00866
Richmond Main Mining Museum, Pelaw Main 01359
Sovereign Hill, Ballarat 00765
State Coal Mine Museum, Wonthaggi 01614
Umoona Opal Mine and Museum, Coober Pedy 00941

Austria
Arsenik-Schauhütte des Bezirksheimatmuseums Spittal im Pöllatal, Rennweg 02506
Ausstellungszentrum Heft, Hüttenberg 02049
Bergbau- und Heimatmuseum, Gloggnitz 01883
Bergbaumuseum, Grünbach am Schneeberg 01965
Bergbaumuseum, Mühlbach am Hochkönig 02324
Bergbaumuseum Klagenfurt, Klagenfurt 02122
Bergbaumuseum Leogang, Leogang 02212
Bergbaumuseum mit Mineralienschau und Schaubergwerk, Hüttenberg 02050
Bergbaumuseum Pöllau, Neumarkt in Steiermark 02352
Bergbaumuseum und Schaustollen, Fohnsdorf 01840
Bergbauschaustollen, Pölfing-Brunn 02429
Böcksteiner Montanmuseum Hohe Tauern, Böckstein 01742
Eisenmuseum, Murau 02331
Historische Silbergruben - Schaubergwerk und Museum, Oberzeiring 02381
Museum Bramberg "Wilhelmgut", Bramberg 01743
Rauriser Talmuseum, Rauris 02492
Schaubergwerk Barbarastollen, Leogang 02213
Schaubergwerk Grillenberg, Payerbach 02394
Schaubergwerk Kupferplatte, Jochberg 02090
Schaubergwerk Seegrotte, Hinterbrühl 02029
Schloß- und Goldbergbaumuseum, Großkirchheim 01954
Schwazer Silberbergwerk, Schwaz 02650
Tiroler Bergbau- und Hüttenmuseum, Brixlegg 01750
Untersbergmuseum Fürstenbrunn, Grödig 01945

Belgium
Musée de la Mine, Musée de la Clouterie, Musée du Gazomètre, Fontaine-l'Evêque 03420
Vlaams Mijnmuseum, Beringen 03212

Brazil
Museu do Ouro, Sabará 04416
Museu Mineralógico da Escola de Minas, Ouro Preto 04240

Canada
Baie Verte Peninsula Miners' Museum, Baie Verte 05037
Barkerville Historic Town, Barkerville 05046
Black Nugget Museum, Ladysmith 05714
British Columbia Museum of Mining, Britannia Beach 05135
Cape Breton Miners' Museum, Glace Bay 05490
Cobalt's Northern Ontario Mining Museum, Cobalt 05261
Elliot Lake Nuclear and Mining Museum, Elliot Lake 05404
Fernie and District Historical Museum, Fernie 05424
Frank Mills Outdoor Mining Machinery Museum, Silverton 06455
Historic Atlas Coal Mine, East Coulee 05361
Inverness Miners Museum, Inverness 05623
Jack Lynn Memorial Museum, Horsefly 05605
Jack Miner Museum, Kingsville 05689
Keno City Mining Museum, Keno City 05655
Leitch Collieries, Crowsnest Pass 05292
Lynn Lake Mining Town Museum, Lynn Lake 05791
Musée Régional des Mines et des Arts de Malartic, Malartic 05803
New Brunswick Mining and Mineral Interpretation Centre, Petit-Rocher 06124
Rossland Historical Museum, Rossland 06287
Saint Lawrence Memorial Miner's Museum, Saint Lawrence 06362
Sandon Museum, New Denver 05975
Silver Ledge Hotel Museum, Ainsworth Hot Springs 04968
Springhill Miner's Museum, Springhill 06482
Stewart Historical Museum, Stewart 06491
Village Minier de Bourlamaque, Val d'Or 06659

Croatia
Narodni Muzej Labin, Labin 07734
Tehnički Muzej, Zagreb 07838

Czech Republic
Hornické Muzeum OKD, Ostrava 08525
Hornické Muzeum Příbram, Příbram 08625
Hornický Skanzen důl Mayrau, Vinařice u Kladna 08719
Muzeum Českého granátu, Třebenice 08685
Muzeum Jáchymovského Hornictví a Lázeňství, Jáchymov 08382
Okresní Muzeum v Kutné Hoře - Hradek, Kutná Hora 08439

Denmark
Søby Brunkulslejer og Brunkulsmuseet, Herning 08870

Estonia
Kohtla Kaevanduspark-muuseum, Ida 09324

Finland
Leppävirran Kotiseutumuseo, Leppävirta 09779
Outokummun Kaivosmuseo, Outokumpu 09900

France
Caves Muséalisées Byrrh, Thuir 14907
Centre de Culture scientifique la Rotonde Ecole des Mines, Saint-Étienne 14196
Centre Minier de Faymoreau, Faymoreau-les-Mines 11710
Ecomusée des Bruneaux, Firminy 11737
Maison de Pays, Sainte-Marie-aux-Mines 14540
La Mine-Image, La Motte-d'Aveillans 12210
Mine Témoin d'Alès, Alès 10285
Musée de la Mine, Brassac-les-Mines 10892
Musée de la Mine, La Machine 12206
Musée de la Mine, Saint-Étienne 14200
Musée de la Mine, Gréasque 11936
Musée de la Mine et de Meunerie-Moulin de Marcy, Le Molay-Littry 12449
Musée de la Mine et des Hommes, Blanzy 10762
Musée de la Mine Lucien-Mazars, Aubin 10465
Musée de la Mine Marcel Maulini, Ronchamp 14022
Musée de l'Ardoise, Renazé 13938
Musée des Mines d'Argent des Gorges du Fournel, L'Argentière-la-Bessée 12344
Musée des Mines de Fer de Lorraine, Neufchef 13287
Musée du Fer et du Fil, Dompierre (Orne) 11548
Musée du Mineur, La Grand-Combe 12192

Germany
Bergbau- und Greifenstein-Museum, Ehrenfriedersdorf 16794
Bergbau- und Heimatmuseum Paulushof, Essen 16946
Bergbau- und Industriemuseum Ostbayern, Kümmersbruck 18257
Bergbau- und Stadtmuseum Weilburg, Weilburg 20442
Bergbaumuseum, Altenberg, Erzgebirge 15447
Bergbaumuseum, Hausham 17647
Bergbaumuseum, Oelsnitz, Erzgebirge 19227
Bergbaumuseum Achthal, Teisendorf 20153
Bergbaumuseum im Besucherbergwerk Tiefer Stollen, Aalen 15380
Bergbaumuseum Peißenberg, Peißenberg 19368
Bergbaumuseum Schachtanlage Knesebeck, Bad Grund 15654
Bergisches Museum für Bergbau, Handwerk und Gewerbe, Bergisch Gladbach 15896
Bergmännisches Traditionskabinett mit Besucherbergwerk, Breitenbrunn, Erzgebirge 16314
Bergwerksmuseum, Penzberg 19372
Bergwerksmuseum Schacht Mehren, Mehren 18682
Besucher-Bergwerk Hüttenstollen, Salzhemmendorf 19737
Besucherbergwerk Finstertal, Asbach bei Schmalkalden 15519
Besucherbergwerk Grube Fortuna, Solms 19988
Besucherbergwerk Grube Gustav, Meißner 18694
Besucherbergwerk Schiefergrube Christine, Willingen, Upland 20598
Deutsches Bergbau-Museum, Bochum 16193
Erzstollen Silbergründle, Seebach, Baden 19909
Feld- und Grubenbahnmuseum, Solms 19989
Forum Fränkischer Hof, Bad Rappenau 15714
Fossilien- und Heimatmuseum, Messel 18718
Granitabbaumuseum, Königshain 18177
Grube Alte Hoffnung Erbstolln, Mittweida 18757
Haniel Museum, Duisburg 16749
Heimat- und Bergbaumuseum, Lugau, Erzgebirge 18566
Heimat- und Bergbaumuseum, Nentershausen, Hessen 18993
Heimat- und Braunkohlemuseum, Steinberg, Oberpfalz 20046
Heimatmuseum, Markranstädt 18641
Heimatmuseum, Scharfenberg bei Meißen 19764
Heimatmuseum Friedewald, Friedewald, Hessen 17141
Heimatstube Offenbach, Mittenaar 18752
Hessisches Braunkohle Bergbaumuseum, Borken, Hessen 16257
Historischer Schieferbergbau Lehesten, Lehesten, Thüringer Wald 18370
Historisches Bergamt Bad Wildungen-Bergfreiheit, Bad Wildungen 15762
Historisches Erzbergwerk im Silberbergwerk Bodenmais, Bodenmais 16208
Historisches Kabinett - Sammlung für Bergbaukunde, Modellsammlung, Winkler-Gedenkstätte und Karzer, Freiberg, Sachsen 17100
Historisches Schmucksteinbergwerk Silberschacht, Bach an der Donau 15584
Historisches Silberbergwerk "Hella-Glücksstollen", Neubulach 19015
Informationszentrum Schloss Paffendorf, Bergheim, Erft 15895
Institut für Wissenschafts- und Technikgeschichte, Kustodie, Freiberg, Sachsen 17101
Kali-Bergbaumuseum Volpriehausen, Uslar 20279
Kunstsammlungen Zwickau, Zwickau 20776
Landesbergbaumuseum Baden-Württemberg, Sulzburg 20128
Lausitzer Bergbaumuseum Knappenrode, Hoyerswerda 17847
Lehr- und Schaubergwerk Frisch Glück, Johanngeorgenstadt 17960
Lehr- und Schaubergwerk Herkules Frisch Glück, Beierfeld 15869
Luisenhütte, Balve 15803
Maffeischächte der Grube Auerbach-Nitzlbuch, Auerbach, Oberpfalz 15544
Mansfeld-Museum Hettstedt, Hettstedt, Sachsen-Anhalt 17747
Mansfelder Bergwerksbahn e.V., Benndorf 15878
Mineralien-Museum Andreas Gabrys, Lam 18294
Museum der Stadt Aue, Aue, Sachsen 15543
Museum der Stadt Gladbeck, Gladbeck 17291
Museum Huthaus Einigkeit, Brand-Erbisdorf 16276
Museum Industriekultur, Osnabrück 19283
Museum Schloß Schwarzenberg, Schwarzenberg, Erzgebirge 19884
Museum und Besucherbergwerk, Goslar 17355
Museum und Besucherbergwerk der Graphit Kropfmühl AG, Hauzenberg 17648
Museumspark, Rüdersdorf bei Berlin 19703
Niedersächsisches Bergbaumuseum, Langelsheim 18319
Niedersächsisches Museum für Kali- und Salzbergbau, Ronnenberg 19646
Oberharzer Bergwerksmuseum, Clausthal-Zellerfeld 16476
Oberpfälzer Flußspat-Besucherbergwerk Reichhart-Schacht, Stulln 20082
Saarländisches Bergbaumuseum, Bexbach 16137
Sächsischer Lehr- Besucherbergwerk-Himmelfahrt-Fundgrube, Freiberg, Sachsen 17103
Sandsteinmuseum Kloster Cornberg, Cornberg 16496
Schaubergwerk Büchenberg, Elbingerode, Harz 16829
Schaubergwerk Teufelsgrund, Münstertal 18954
Schaubergwerk Zum Tiefen Molchner Stolln, Pobershau 19422
Schiefermuseum, Ludwigsstadt 18530
Schwarzwälder Mineralienmuseum, Neubulach 19016
Silbereisenbergwerk Gleißinger Fels, Fichtelberg 17000
Silberstollen Geising, Geising 17217
Stadt- und Bergbaumuseum Freiberg, Freiberg, Sachsen 17104
Stadt- und Heimatmuseum, Marienberg 18634
Städtische Sammlungen Freital, Freital 17125
Steinkohlen-Besucherbergwerk Rabensteiner Stollen, Ilfeld 17884
Technisches Denkmal Museumkalkwerk Lengefeld, Lengefeld, Erzgebirge 18433
Technisches Denkmal Tobiashammer, Ohrdruf 19247
Werra-Kalibergbau-Museum, Heringen, Werra 17723
Zinngrube Ehrenfriedersdorf, Ehrenfriedersdorf 16795

Hungary
Alapítvány Érc és Ásványbányászati Múzeum, Rudabánya 21519
Központi Bányászati Múzeum, Sopron 21534
Mecseki Bányászati Múzeum, Pécs 21509
Tatabánya Múzeum, Tatabánya 21595

Italy
Collezione P. Mariani, Desio 23714
Museo Antica Miniera di Talco Brunetta, Cantoira 23319
Museo dei Minerali e della Miniera, Oltre il Colle 24677
Museo della Miniera, Cesena 23501
Museo della Miniera, Massa Marittima 24324
Museo della Miniera, Prata di Pordenone 25038
Museo della Miniera, Schilpario 25524
Museo della Miniera Aurifera della Guia, Macugnaga 24254
Museo della Miniera di Zolfo di Cabernardi, Sassoferrato 25496
Museo dell'Arte Mineraria, Iglesias 24081
Museo delle Miniere, Valle Aurina 25879
Museo di Arte e Giacimenti Minerari, Latina 24159
Museo di Arte e Storia delle Miniere, Massa Marittima 24325
Museo Storico dell'Oro Italiano, Silvano d'Orba 25582
Museo Storico Minerario di Perticara, Novafeltria 24642
Parco Museo Minerario, Abbadia San Salvatore 22793

Japan
Nogata-shi Sekitan Kinenkan, Nogata 26609
Sekitan Kinenkan, Ube 26982

Korea, Republic
Boryeong Coal Museum, Boryeong 27133

Luxembourg
Musée National des Mines Fer Luxembourgeoisie, Rumelange 27575

Mexico
Museo de Historia de la Minería de Santa Rosalía, Mulegé 28258
Museo de la Minería, San Juan de Guadalupe 28391
Museo de la Minería del Estado de México, El Oro 27906
Museo de la Minería José de la Borda, Taxco de Alarcón 28459
Museo de Minería de la Compañía Real del Monte, Pachuca 28295
Museo de Minería e Historia de Cosala, Cosalá 27860
Museo Dr. Atl, Pihuamo 28311
Museo El Minero, Santa Bárbara 28429

Namibia
Kolmanskop Museum, Kolmanskop 28758

Netherlands
Industrion Museum for Industry and Society, Kerkrade 29480
Steenkolenmijn Daalhemergroeve, Valkenburg, Limburg 29919

New Zealand
Alexandra Museum, Alexandra 30093
Brunner Mine Site, Dobson 30143
Coromandel School of Mines Museum, Coromandel 30137
Lakes District Museum, Arrowtown 30095
Waihi Arts Centre and Museum Association, Waihi 30272

Norway
Folldal Gruver, Folldal 30500
Gammelgruva, Løkken Verk 30648
Hadeland Bergverksmuseum, Grua 30522
Museum Blaafarveværket, Åmot i Modum 30382
Norsk Bergverksmuseum, Kongsberg 30605
Sulitjelma Gruvemuseum, Sulitjelma 30905
Sunnhordland Folkemuseum og Sogelag, Stord 30900

Poland
Muzeum Geologiczne, Kraków 31704
Muzeum Górnictwa i Hutnictwa Kopalina Złota, Złoty
 Stok 32223
Muzeum Górnictwa i Hutnictwa Rud Żelaza,
 Częstochowa 31546
Muzeum Górnictwa Podziemnego, Nowa Ruda 31826
Muzeum Górnictwa Węglowego, Zabrze 32199
Muzeum Górnicze, Bogatynia 31503
Muzeum Przemysłu i Techniki, Wałbrzych 32072
Muzeum Żup Krakowskich, Wieliczka 32153
Skansen Górniczy Królowa Luiza, Zabrze 32201

Romania
Muzeul Mineritului, Petroşani 32564

Russia
Gornyj Muzej, Sankt-Peterburg 33396
Kemerovskij Istoriko-architekturnyi Muzej Krasnaja
 Gorka, Kemerovo 32911
Memorialnyj Istoriko-biografičeskij Dom-muzej
 Akademika N.V. Melnikova, Sarapul 33502

Serbia-Montenegro
Mineraloška Zbirka Rudnika Trepča, Stari Trg 33917
Muzej Rudarstva i Metalurgije, Bor 33824

Slovakia
Banícke Múzeum, Gelnica 33996
Banicke Múzeum, Rožňava 34052
Slovenské Banské Múzeum, Banská Štiavnica 33951

Slovenia
Koroški Muzej Ravne na Koroškem, Ravne na
 Koroškem 34144
Muzej Jesenice, Jesenice 34092

South Africa
Barberton Museum, Barberton 34174
Pilgrim's Rest Museum, Pilgrim's Rest 34330
Talana Museum and Heritage Park, Dundee 34222

Spain
Museo Histórico Minero Don Felipe de Borbón y
 Grecia, Madrid 35038

Sweden
Ådelfors Gruvmuseum, Holsbybrunn 35963
Bruksmuseet i Robertsfors, Robertsfors 36161
Bruksmuseum, Eksjö 35859
Ebbamåla Bruk, Kyrkhult 36026
Gamla Brukets Muséer, Munkfors 36108
Gruvmuseet, Sala 36172
Kopparberget Gruvmuseum, Falun 35883
LKAB Gruvmuseum, Kiruna 36007
Ludvika Gammelgård och Gruvmuseum,
 Ludvika 36052
Mineral- och Gruvmuseet, Holsbybrunn 35964
Siggebohyttans Bergmansgård, Nora 36112

Switzerland
Bergbaumuseum, Horgen 36808
Bergbaumuseum Graubünden mit Schaubergwerk,
 Davos Platz 36653
Gonzen-Museum, Sargans 37117

United Kingdom
Big Pit National Mining Museum of Wales,
 Blaenavon 38250
Cefn Coed Colliery Museum, Neath 40004
Chatterley Whitfield Mining Museum, Stoke-on-
 Trent 40603
Cleveland Ironstone Mining Museum,
 Skinningrove 40526
D.H. Lawrence Heritage Centre, Eastwood 38865
Dunaskin Open Air Museum, Patna 40163
Florence Mine Heritage Centre, Egremont 38924
Geevor Tin Mining Museum, Pendeen 40171
Gloddfa Ganol Slate Mine, Blaenau Ffestiniog 38248
Great Laxey Wheel and Mines Trail, Laxey 39432
Hartham Park - Underground Quarry Museum,
 Corsham 38637
Minera Lead Mines, Minera 39965
Morwellham Quay Historic Port Copper Mine,
 Tavistock 40680
Museum of Lead Mining, Wanlockhead 40780
Museum of Yorkshire Dales Lead Mining, Earby 38833
National Coal Mining Museum for England,
 Wakefield 40761
Nenthead Mines Heritage Centre, Nenthead 40008
Peak District Mining Museum, Matlock 39923
Poldark Mine and Heritage Complex, Helston 39216
Prestongrange Museum, Prestongrange 40270
Scottish Mining Museum, Newtongrange 40066
South Wales Miner's Museum, Port Talbot 40238
Sygun Copper Mine, Beddgelert 38143
Tar Tunnel, Coalport 38598
Threlkeld Quarry and Mining Museum,
 Threlkeld 40705
Tolgus Tin Mill and Streamworks, Redruth 40404
Welsh Slate Museum, Llanberis 39536
Woodhorn Colliery Museum, Ashington 38030

Uruguay
Museo Geológico del Uruguay, Montevideo 41004

U.S.A.
Alabama Mining Museum, Dora 42958
Argo Gold Mine and Mill Museum, Idaho
 Springs 44191
Arizona Mining and Mineral Museum, Phoenix 46472
Big Thunder Gold Mine, Keystone 44474
Bisbee Mining and Historical Museum, Bisbee 41714
Black Hills Mining Museum, Lead 44699
California State Mining and Mineral Museum,
 Mariposa 45166
Coal Miners' Museum, Van Lear 48196
Comer Museum, Morgantown 45498
Coppertown U.S.A., Calumet 42035
Dahlonega Courthouse Gold Museum,
 Dahlonega 42739
Dugger Coal Museum, Dugger 42994
Fort Wilkins Historic Complex, Copper Harbor 42624
Franklin Mineral Museum, Franklin 43519
Galena Mining and Historical Museum, Galena 43596
Grand Encampment Museum, Encampment 43186
Idaho Museum of Mining and Geology, Boise 41773
Iron Mountain Iron Mine, Vulcan 44258
Ironworld Discovery Center, Chisholm 42388
Jerome State Historic Park, Jerome 44336
Lafayette Miners Museum, Lafayette 44567
Miners Foundry Cultural Center, Nevada City 45654
The Mining Museum, Platteville 46545
Museum of Anthracite Mining, Ashland 41298
North Star Mining Museum, Grass Valley 43776
Reed Gold Mine, Midland 45323
Reed Gold Mine State Historic Site, Stanfield 47771
Slate Valley Museum, Granville 43771
Sterling Hill Mining Museum, Ogdensburg 46102
Tintic Mining Museum, Eureka 43234
Underhill Museum, Idaho Springs 44193
Vermont Marble Museum, Proctor 46709
Wallace District Mining Museum, Wallace 48287
The Walsenburg Mining Museum and Fort Francisco
 Museum of La Veta, Walsenburg 48293
Western Museum of Mining and Industry, Colorado
 Springs 42542
World Museum of Mining, Butte 42019
Yesteryear House-Central Mine, Clarkston 42433

Zambia
Copperbelt Museum, Ndola 49024

Zimbabwe
National Mining Museum, Kwekwe 49035

Mollusks

France
Musée du Coquillage, Le Lavandou 12430
Musée Maison de l'Huître, Gujan-Mestras 11980

Greece
Moschakeion, Moschato 21075

Italy
Museo Zoologico Cambria, Messina 24365

Netherlands
Natuurmuseum Rotterdam, Rotterdam 29766

Russia
Muzej Instituta Biologii Morja, Vladivostok 33704
Zoologičeskij Muzej, Vladivostok 33713

Spain
Museo Nacional de Ciencias Naturales, Madrid 35045
Museu de Malacología Cau del Cargol, Vilassar de
 Dalt 35672

Monasteries

Austria
Kartause Gaming, Gaming 01866

Bangladesh
Archaeological Museum, Mainamati 03097

Belgium
Musée de l'Abbaye d'Orval, Villers-devant-
 Orval 03815
Museum van de Abdij van Roosenberg,
 Waasmunster 03821

Bulgaria
Nacionalen Muzej Rilski Manastir, Rilski
 Manastir 04800

Cambodia
The Angkor Conservation, Siem Reap 04951

Denmark
Danmarks Kloster Museum, Ry 09050

France
Musée-Abbaye Saint-Germain, Auxerre 10509

Germany
Deutsches Kartausen-Museum, Buxheim bei
 Memmingen 16438
Kloster Altenberg, Solms 19990
Kloster Irsee, Irsee 17917
Klosteranlage mit Klostermuseum, Maulbronn 18665
Klostermuseum Heggbach, Maselheim 18661
Klostermuseum Hirsau, Calw 16448
Klostermuseum Jerichow, Jerichow 17954
Kornhaus Georgenthal-Klosterruinen,
 Georgenthal 17241
Missionsmuseum, Schwarzach am Main 19880
Museum Abtei Liesborn, Wadersloh 20337
Museum Höxter-Corvey, Höxter 17790
Museum Kloster Zinna, Kloster Zinna 18116
Museum Sankt Blasien, Sankt Blasien 19747
Museum zur Kloster- und Stadtgeschichte, Steinheim
 an der Murr 20050
Prignitz-Museum Havelberg, Havelberg 17650
Prunkräume in der Residenz, Kempten 18064
Sammlungen der Benediktiner-Abtei Braunau, Rohr,
 Niederbayern 19641
Schloss Salem, Salem, Baden 19733
Torbogenmuseum, Königsbronn 18171

Greece
Karyes-Protaton, Agion Oros 20806

Ireland
Adare Trinity Museum, Adare 22358

Italy
Museo della Collegiata, Castell'Arquato 23406
Museo dell'Opera di Santa Croce, Firenze 23861

Japan
Treasure House of the Eiheiji Temple, Eiheiji 26135

Netherlands
Museum Kloster Ter Apel, Ter Apel 28922

Norway
Klostertunet, Halsnøy Kloster 30525
Rissa Bygdemuseum, Rissa 30794
Utstein Kloster, Mosterøy 30694

Peru
Monasterio de Santa Catalina, Arequipa 31112

Russia
Gosudarstvennyj Istoriko-architekturnyj i Prirodno-
 landšaftnyj Muzej Zapovednik Izborsk,
 Izborsk 32834
Novodevičij Monastyr, Moskva 33164
Svjatogorskij Monastyr, Puškinskie Gory 33345

Serbia-Montenegro
Manastirski Muzej, Cetinje 33832
Riznica Manastira Studenica, Raška 33900

Slovakia
Múzeum Červený Kláštor, Červený Kláštor 33986

Spain
Monasterio de la Encarnación, Madrid 35010
Monasterio de la Santa Cruz, Sahagún 35355
Monasterio de las Descalzas Reales, Madrid 35011
Monasterio de las Huelgas de Burgos, Burgos 34628
Monasterio de San Juan de los Reyes, Toledo 35536
Monasterio de San Pedro, San Pedro de
 Cardeña 35388
Monasterio de Sant Cugat, Sant Cugat del
 Vallès 35397
Monasterio de Santa María, Ripoll 35324
Monasterio de Santa María, Santa María de
 Huerta 35422
Monasterio de Santa María la Real, Nájera 35153
Monasterio de Santes Creus, Santes Creus 35435
Museo del Monasterio de Santa María de la Vid, La
 Vid 35653
Museu de Poblet, Monestir de Poblet 35122
Museu Monàstic, Vallbona de les Monges 35631

Switzerland
Klostermuseum Sankt Georgen, Stein am
 Rhein 37214

United Kingdom
Beaulieu Abbey Exhibition of Monastic Life,
 Brockenhurst 38370
Bede's World, Jarrow 39323
Glastonbury Abbey Museum, Glastonbury 39070

U.S.A.
Teutopolis Monastery Museum, Teutopolis 47989

Money → Numismatics

Mosaics

France
Musée de la Mosaïque et des Émaux, Briare 10923

Greece
Refectory of the Hosios Loukas Monastery,
 Boeotia 20911

Italy
Antiquarium e Mosaico Romano, Bevagna 23073
Musei Civici agli Eremitani, Padova 24733
Museo del Battistero, Albenga 22832
Museo di Torcello, Venezia 25939
Pinacoteca Comunale d'Arte Antica e Moderna,
 Faenza 23757

Japan
Mokuzo-gan Gallery, Odawara 26614

Portugal
Museu Monográfico de Conimbriga, Condeixa-a-
 Nova 32266

Spain
Museo Municipal, Alcázar de San Juan 34432

Switzerland
Pro Urba, Orbe 37014

Tunisia
Musée de Sousse, Sousse 37586
Musée National du Bardo, Bardo 37553

Turkey
Büyük Saray Mozaik Müzesi, İstanbul 37697
İstanbul Arkeoloji Müzeleri, İstanbul 37702
Silifke Mozaik Müzesi, Narlıkuyu 37765

Ukraine
Saint Sophia of Kiev, Kyïv 37876

United Kingdom
Aldborough Roman Town Museum,
 Boroughbridge 38280
Roman Villa Museum at Bignor, Pulborough 40274

Mummies

Egypt
Elephantine Island's Museum, Aswan 09249

Germany
Bleikeller, Bremen 16318
Petrefaktensammlung, Bad Staffelstein,
 Oberfranken 15749

Italy
Museo delle Mummie, Ferentillo 23775

Mexico
Museo de las Momias, Guanajuato 27972
Museo de Momias de Celaya, Celaya 27810

Poland
Muzeum im. Władysława Orkana, Rabka 31936

Mural Painting and
Decoration

Belgium
Sint-Baafskathedraal Gent, Gent 03450

Bulgaria
Muzej na Rezbarskoto i Zografsko Izkustvo,
 Trjavna 04888

Canada
Canadian Museum of Animal Art, Bolton 05091

France
Musée Palais Lascaris, Nice 13324

Germany
Fürstlich Ysenburg- und Büdingensches
 Schloßmuseum, Büdingen 16397
Leitheimer Schloß-Museum, Kaisheim 17973
Museum für Vor- und Frühgeschichte,
 Saarbrücken 19725
Torhalle Frauenchiemsee und Vikarhaus,
 Chiemsee 16474

Greece
Kitsos Makris Folk Art Center, Volos 21212

Italy
Cappella degli Scrovegni, Padova 24731
Cenacolo di Sant'Apollonia, Firenze 23829
Chiesa di Santa Maria Maddalena de Pazzi,
 Firenze 23830
Chiostro dello Scalzo, Firenze 23831
Convento dell'ex-Convento di Sant'Onofrio detto di
 Fuligno, Firenze 23834
Fondazione Romano nel Cenacolo di Santo Spirito,
 Firenze 23835
Libreria Sansoviniana, Venezia 25921
Museo Benedettino Nonantolano e Diocesano di Arte
 Sacra, Nonantola 24635
Museo Civico, Sansepolcro 25427
Museo Civico, Siena 25572
Museo Civico A. Parazzi, Viadana 25983
Museo Civico di Schifanoia, Ferrara 23786
Museo d'Arte Sacra, Colle di Val d'Elsa 23610
Museo degli Argenti, Firenze 23854

Museo del Camposanto Vecchio e dell'Opera, Pisa 24949
Museo del Castello Colleoni Porto, Thiene 25704
Museo della Villa Bettoni, Bogliaco 23095
Museo dell'Opera del Duomo, Prato 25047
Museo di Palazzo Vecchio, Firenze 23868
Museo di Pittura Murale, Prato 25048
Museo di San Marco, Firenze 23869
Museo Diocesano, Gaeta 23947
Museo Diocesano Albani, Urbino 25859
Museo e Chiostri Monumentali di Santa Maria Novella, Firenze 23874
Palazzo Medici Riccardi, Firenze 23883
Pinacoteca Civica, Spello 25616
Pinacoteca e Museo Civici, Camerino 23291
Rocca Borromeo, Angera 22890
Villa Farnesina, Roma 25271

Japan
Horyuji Kondo Hekiga Mosha Tenjikan, Nagakute 26525
Nagoya Castle Treasure House, Nagoya, Aichi 26566
Takamatsuzuka Wall Painting Museum, Asuka 26113
Yaegaki-jinja Treasure Storehouse, Matsue 26475

Mexico
Casa Museo La Moreña, La Barca 28041
Museo de la Pintura Mural y Museo Manuel Gamio, Teotihuacán 28481
Museo de la Sep, México 28144

Serbia-Montenegro
Galerija Freska, Beograd 33796

Spain
Museo de Navarra, Pamplona 35249
Museo Real Colegiata de San Isidoro, León 34951
Museu Diocesà d'Urgell, La Seu d'Urgell 35470

Switzerland
Klostermuseum, Müstair 36970

Turkey
Göreme Açıkhava Müzesi, Nevşehir 37766

Ukraine
Saint Sophia of Kiev, Kyïv 37876

United Kingdom
Plas Newydd, Llanfairpwll 39549

U.S.A.
Gallery of Prehistoric Paintings, New York 45804

Museology

Brazil
Museu de Arqueologia e Etnologia da Universidade de São Paulo, São Paulo 04512

Chile
Museo Histórico y Antropológico de la Universidad Austral de Chile, Valdivia 06925

United Kingdom
Conservation Centre Presentation, Liverpool 39516

Venezuela
Museo Armando Reverón, Macuto 48950

Music and Musical Instruments

Argentina
Museo Areneo de Estudios Históricos de Nueva Pompeya, Buenos Aires 00157
Museo de Instrumentos Musicales, Buenos Aires 00182
Museo de la Partitura Historica, Rosario 00527
Museo de SADAIC Vicente López y Planes, Buenos Aires 00195
Museo del Tango Roberto Firpo, Salto 00544
Museo del Teatro y la Música de Córdoba Cristobal de Aguilar, Córdoba 00301
Museo Manuel de Falla, Alta Gracia 00112

Armenia
Khachatrians Museum, Erevan 00684
Spendiarians Museum, Erevan 00689

Australia
Grainger Museum, Parkville, Victoria 01357
Historic and Ethnic Instrument Collection, Nedlands 01311
McCrae Homestead Museum, McCrae 01191
Miniature English Village and Brass Rubbing Centre, Flaxton 01027
Museum of Lillydale, Lilydale 01176
Das Neumann Haus Museum, Laidley 01159
Organ Historical Trust of Australia, Camberwell, Victoria 00877
Waltzing Matilda Centre and Qantilda Museum, Winton 01606

Austria
Anton Bruckner-Museum, Ansfelden 01676
Arnold Schönberg Center, Wien 02835
Beethoven Eroicahaus, Wien 02845
Beethoven-Gedenkstätte in Floridsdorf, Wien 02846
Beethoven Heiligenstädter Testament, Wien 02847
Beethoven Pasqualatihaus, Wien 02848
Beethovenhaus, Krems 02155
Beethovenhaus " Haus der Neunten", Baden bei Wien 01726
Blasmusik-Museum, Ratten 02489
Brucknerzimmer, Kronstorf 02166
Franz Schmidt Museum, Perchtoldsdorf 02399
Franz Xaver Gruber-Museum, Lamprechtshausen 02179
Haydn-Geburtshaus, Rohrau 02521
Haydn-Gedenkstätte mit Brahms-Gedenkraum, Wien 02894
Haydn-Haus Eisenstadt, Eisenstadt 01809
Hugo Wolf-Haus, Perchtoldsdorf 02400
Ignaz J. Pleyel Museum, Großweikersdorf 01964
Johann Michael Haydn-Gedenkstätte, Salzburg 02541
Johannes Brahms-Museum, Mürzzuschlag 02329
Kammerhofmuseum der Stadt Gmunden, Gmunden 01896
Komponierstube Gustav Mahlers, Steinbach am Attersee 02680
Lehár-Villa, Bad Ischl 01707
Lisztmuseum, Raiding 02477
Mozart Figarohaus, Wien 02932
Mozart-Gedenkstätte im Bezirksgericht, Sankt Gilgen 02570
Mozart Wohnhaus, Salzburg 02543
Mozarts Geburtshaus, Salzburg 02544
Museum des Wiener Männergesang-Vereins, Wien 02942
Museum Franz Schubert und sein Freundeskreis, Atzenbrugg 01688
Museum für mechanische Musik und Volkskunst, Haslach 02007
Musica Kremsmünster, Kremsmünster 02162
Pater Peter Singer-Museum, Salzburg 02546
Robert Stolz Museum Graz, Graz 01931
Schönberg-Haus in Mödling, Mödling 02314
Schubert Geburtshaus und Adalbert Stifter-Gedenkräume, Wien 02987
Schubert Sterbewohnung, Wien 02988
Stadtmuseum Oberwölz und Österreichisches Blasmusikmuseum, Oberwölz 02380
Steirisches Uhren-, Musikalien- und Volkskundemuseum, Arnfels 01679
Stiftssammlungen des Zisterzienserstiftes Rein, Gratwein 01908
Stille Nacht-Museum, Hallein 01999
Stoani Haus der Musik, Gasen 01873
Strauß Gedenkstätte, Wien 02992
Wilhelm Kienzl-Museum, Waizenkirchen 02789

Belgium
AMVC-Letterenhuis, Antwerpen 03135
Harmonium-Art-Museum, Schelle 03725
Musée des Instruments de Musique, Bruxelles 03317
Musée Grétry, Liège 03584
Muziekinstrumenten-Museum, Peer 03685
Peter Benoitmuseum, Harelbeke 03476
Stedelijk Museum voor Heemkunde en Folklore, Aarschot 03126
Vleeshuis, Antwerpen 03177

Brazil
Carlos Gomes Museum, Campinas 04021
Centro de Pesquisas Folclóricas, Rio de Janeiro 04320
Museu da Imagem e do Som, Rio de Janeiro 04348
Museu Villa-Lobos, Rio de Janeiro 04397

Bulgaria
Etnografska Ekspozicija, Pazardžik 04755

Burkina Faso
Musée de la Musique de Ouagadougou, Ouagadougou 04942

Canada
Anne Murray Centre, Springhill 06481
Guy Lombardo Museum, London 05768
Hank Snow Country Music Centre, Liverpool 05758
Musée de l'Accordéon, Montmagny 05885
Sounds of Yesteryear, Winnipeg 06847

China, People's Republic
National Museum of Music, Beijing 06982

Colombia
Colleccíon de Instrumentos Musicales "Monsenór José Ignacio Perdomo Escobar", Bogotá 07389
Museo de la Parroquia de Gámbita, Gámbita 07483
Museo Organológico Folklórico Musical, Bogotá 07431

Croatia
Zbirka Umjetnina KAIROS, Trogir 07796

Cuba
Casa de Miguel Failde Pérez, Matanzas 08036
Museo de la Música Alejandro García Caturla, Santa Clara 08120
Museo de la Música Rodrigo Prats, Santa Clara 08121
Museo Nacional de la Música, La Habana 07991

Czech Republic
Dům Pánů z Kunštátu, Brno 08265
Muzeum Antonína Dvořáka, Praha 08593
Muzeum Bedřicha Smetany, Praha 08594
Muzeum České Hudby, Praha 08595
Muzeum Středniho Pootavi, Strakonice 08663
Muzikologické Pracoviště, Opava 08519
Památník Antonína Dvořáka, Nelahozeves 08495
Památník Antonína Dvořáka, Vysoká u Příbrami 08732
Památník Antonína Dvořáka, Zlonice 08753
Památník Bedřicha Smetany, Jabkenice 08377
Památník Bohuslava Martinů, Polička 08556
Památník Dr. Emila Axmana, Chropyně 08319
Památník Josefa Suka, Křečovice 08432
Památník Leoše Janáčka, Hukvaldy 08373
Památník Leoše Janáčka, Brno 08275
Památník W.A. Mozarta a Manželů Duškových, Praha 08610
Památník Zdeňka Fibicha, Všeborice 08728
Starý Zámek, Jevišovice 08387

Denmark
Carl Nielsen Museet, Odense 09006
Carl Nielsens Barndomshjem, Årslev 08775
Musikhistorisk Museum og Carl Claudius' Samling, København 08941

Ecuador
Museo de Instrumentos Musicales Pablo Traversari, Quito 09205

Estonia
August Kitzbergi Tubamuuseum, Karksi 09330
Eesti Teatri- ja Muusikamuuseum, Tallinn 09363

Finland
Ainola, Järvenpää 09571
Sibelius Museum, Turku 10127
Suomen Kansansoitinmuseo, Kaustinen 09643

France
Maison de la Musique Mécanique, Mirecourt 12993
Maison du Luthier-Musée, Jenzat 12079
Moulin à Musique Mécanique, Mormoiron 13165
Musée Claude Debussy, Saint-Germain-en-Laye 14240
Musée de la Musique, Anduze 10339
Musée de la Musique, Paris 13558
Musée de la Musique Mécanique, Crillon-le-Brave 11461
Musée de l'Art Forain et de la Musique Mécanique, Conflans-en-Jarnisy 11391
Musée de Rouget de Lisle, Lons-le-Saunier 12661
Musée des Instruments de Musique à Vent, La Couture-Boussey 12165
Musée des Musiques Populaires, Montluçon 13103
Musée du Phonographe et de la Musique Mécanique, Sainte-Maxime 14545
Musée Edith Piaf, Paris 13611
Musée Hector Berlioz, La Côte-Saint-André 12161
Musée Maurice Ravel, Montfort-l'Amaury 13086
Musée-Placard d'Erik Satie, Paris 13647
Musée Pyrénéen, Lourdes 12698

Germany
Albert-Schweitzer-Gedenk- und Begegnungsstätte, Weimar, Thüringen 20454
Archiv und Kollektion Paul Kaiser-Reka, Brandenburg an der Havel 16278
Bach-Gedenkstätte im Schloß Köthen, Köthen, Anhalt 18189
Bach-Museum, Leipzig 18389
Bachhaus Eisenach, Eisenach 16814
Beatles Museum, Halle, Saale 17507
Beethoven-Haus, Bonn 16231
Brahmshaus, Heide, Holstein 17659
Carl-Maria-von-Weber-Museum, Dresden 16678
Carl Orff Museum, Dießen am Ammersee 16599
Deutsches Harmonikamuseum, Trossingen 20218
Deutsches Musikautomaten Museum, Bruchsal 16365
Deutsches Phonomuseum, Sankt Georgen im Schwarzwald 19749
Ellermeiers Burgmannshof, Hardegsen 17616
Elztalmuseum - Regionalgeschichte und Orgelbau, Waldkirch 20366
Erstes Deutsches Museum für mechanische Musikinstrumente, Rüdesheim am Rhein 19704
Franz-Liszt-Museum der Stadt Bayreuth, Bayreuth 15845
Gebrüder-Lachner-Museum, Rain am Lech 19476
Geigenbau-Museum, Bubenreuth 16385
Geigenbaumuseum, Mittenwald 18754
Händel-Haus, Halle, Saale 17513
Harmonium-Museum, Hennef 17710
Haus zum Palmbaum - Bachausstellung Arnstadt, Arnstadt 15513
Heinrich-Schütz-Haus, Bad Köstritz 15680
Heinrich-Schütz-Haus Weißenfels, Weißenfels 20498
Liszthaus - Goethe-Nationalmuseum, Weimar, Thüringen 20464
Little Cavern, Biebelnheim 16144
Louis Spohr-Gedenk- und Forschungsstätte, Kassel 18023
Mauersberger-Museum, Großrückerswalde 17439
Max-Reger-Gedächtniszimmer, Brand, Oberpfalz 16277
Mozarthaus, Augsburg 15562
Museum Bürgstadt, Bürgstadt 16407
Museum der Stadt Füssen, Füssen 17168
Museum für Blasmusikinstrumente, Kürnbach 18262
Museum Gottfried Silbermann, Frauenstein 17090
Musik- und Wintersportmuseum, Klingenthal 18111
Musikhistorische Sammlung Jehle, Albstadt 15420
Musikinstrumenten-Ausstellung des Händel-Hauses, Halle, Saale 17517
Musikinstrumenten-Museum, Markneukirchen 18640
Musikinstrumenten-Museum, Berlin 16070
Musikinstrumenten-Museum der Universität Leipzig (Interim), Leipzig 18410
Musikinstrumenten- und Puppenmuseum, Goslar 17356
Musikinstrumentenmuseum, München 18888
Musikinstrumentenmuseum Lißberg, Ortenberg, Hessen 19270
Musikinstrumentensammlung, Erlangen 16921
Musikinstrumentensammlung der Universität, Göttingen 17338
Musikinstrumentensammlung Hans und Hede Grumbt Wasserburg Haus Kemnade, Hattingen 17635
Neues Schloß und Instrumentenmuseum, Kißlegg 18103
Orgelbaumuseum, Ostheim vor der Rhön 19299
Orgelmuseum Altes Schloß, Valley 20284
Orgelmuseum Borgentreich, Borgentreich 16256
Orgelmuseum Kelheim, Kelheim 18051
Private Sammlung Mechanischer Musikinstrumente, Wohlhausen 20645
Reuterhaus mit Richard-Wagner-Sammlung, Eisenach 16817
Richard-Wagner-Museum, Bayreuth 15858
Richard-Wagner-Museum Graupa, Pirna 19406
Robert-Schumann-Haus Zwickau, Zwickau 20778
Sängermuseum, Feuchtwangen 16999
Sammlung historischer Tasteninstrumente Neumeyer-Junghanns-Tracey, Bad Krozingen 15684
Schumann-Haus, Leipzig 18417
Schwarzwald-Museum, Triberg 20203
Silcher-Museum Schnait, Weinstadt 20486
Stadtmuseum im Spital, Crailsheim 16507
Stiftung Kloster Michaelstein/Museum, Blankenburg, Harz 16178
Technik Museum Speyer, Speyer 20013
Thürmer Pianoforte-Museum, Meißen 18693
Trompetenmuseum, Bad Säckingen 15725
Werner-Egk-Begegnungsstätte, Donauwörth 16642
Zungeninstrumenten-Sammlung Zwota, Zwota 20787

Greece
Anoyanakis Collection, Athinai 20846
Mouseio Laikon Organon, Athinai 20877
Museum of Greek Musical Instruments, Thessaloniki 21190

Hungary
Bartók Béla Emlékház, Budapest 21329
Beethoven Emlékmúzeum, Martonvásár 21469
Liszt Ferenc Emlékmúzeum és Kutatóközpont, Budapest 21354
Zenetörténeti Múzeum, Budapest 21392

India
TTD Museum, Tirupati 22040

Iran
Sabā's House, Teheran 22324

Ireland
Ceol - Irish Traditional Music Centre, Dublin 22416
Irish Music Hall of Fame, Dublin 22437

Israel
Music Box of Zami Museum, Metula 22712
Musical Instruments Museum, Jerusalem 22654

Italy
Casa Museo dei Puccini, Pescaglia 24864
Casa Natale di G. Verdi, Busseto 23234
Casa Natale di Toscanini, Parma 24794
Casa Natale G. Donizetti, Bergamo 23059
Castello D'Albertis, Genova 23977
Civico Museo Bibliografico Musicale, Bologna 23100
Civico Museo degli Strumenti Musicali, Milano 24377
Collezione di Violini, Cremona 23678
Galleria dell'Accademia, Firenze 23842
House of Music-Parma, Parma 24800
Museo Casa Busoni, Empoli 23728
Museo Casa Natale Giacomo Puccini, Lucca 24227
Museo Casa Pascoli, Barga 23017
Museo Casa Rossini, Pesaro 24858
Museo Civico Belliniano, Catania 23446
Museo degli Strumenti Musica Populare Sardi, Tadasuni 25664
Museo degli Strumenti Musicali, Cesena 23498
Museo degli Strumenti Musicali Meccanici, Savio 25505
Museo degli Strumenti Musicali Meccanici, Sestola 25559
Museo del Conservatorio die Napoli, Napoli 24582
Museo del Jazz G. Dagnino, Genova 23990
Museo del Pianoforte Antico, Ala 22824
Museo della Canzone e della Riproduzione Sonora, Vallecrosia 25881
Museo della Liuteria, Arpino 22940
Museo della Pipa, Gavirate 23966
Museo della Zampogna, Scapoli 25518
Museo di Strumenti del Conservatorio Statale di Musica Giuseppe Verdi, Torino 25751
Museo Donizettiano, Bergamo 23064
Museo Etnomusicale I Gigli di Nola, Nola 24632
Museo Francesco Cilea, Palmi 24787
Museo G. Spontini, Maiolati Spontini 24263
Museo Internazionale della Fisarmonica, Castelfidardo 23395
Museo Musicale d'Abruzzo, Ortona 24700

Museo Nazionale degli Strumenti Musicali, Roma 25232
Museo Nazionale degli Strumenti per il Calcolo, Pisa 24951
Museo Pucciniano, Torre del Lago Puccini 25772
Museo Storico della Filarmonica Sestrese, Genova 24008
Museo Stradivariano, Cremona 23683
Raccolta di Fisarmoniche d'Epoca, Camerano 23281
Tempietto Rossiniano della Fondazione Rossini, Pesaro 24862
Villa Museo Puccini, Viareggio 25986
Villa Verdi, Villanova sull'Arda 26019

Jamaica
Bob Marley Museum, Kingston 26065

Japan
Drum Museum Taikokan, Tokyo 26841
Gakki Hakubutsukan, Tokyo 26849
Gakkigaku Shiryôkan, Tachikawa 26781
Kyoto Arashiyama Music Box Museum, Kyoto 26418
Sendai Music Box Museum, Sendai 26735

Kazakhstan
Muzej Narodnych Muzykalnych Instrumentov Kazachstana, Almaty 27073

Korea, Republic
Chamsori Gramophone and Audio Science Museum, Gangneung 27166
Museum of Korean Traditional Music, Seoul 27261

Latvia
Literature, Theatre and Music Museum, Rīga 27429
Music Museum, Rīga 27432

Luxembourg
Musée d'Instruments Anciens et d'Archives au Conservatoire de Musique, Luxembourg 27566

Malta
Cathedral Museum, Mdina 27697

Mexico
Guitar Museo Ex Teresa Arte Actual, México 28104
Museo Casita Blanca de Agustín Lara, Boca del Río 27793
Museo de la Canción Yucateca, Mérida 28082
Museo de la Casa de la Música Mexicana, México 28134
Museo de la Música Grabada, Zapotlanejo 28652
Museo Silvestre Vargas, Tecalitlán 28465

Netherlands
Accordeon en Harmonica Museum, Malden 29576
Christ Boelens Jukeboxen Museum, Sint Oedenrode 29823
Draaiorgelmuseum, Assen 28949
Gaviolizaal, Helmond 29393
Kijk en Luister Museum, Bennekom 28976
Museum Musica, Stadskanaal 29847
Muziekinformatie- en documentatiecentrum Ton Stolk, Vlaardingen 29946
Muziekinstrumentenmakersmuseum, Tilburg 29878
Nationaal Historisch Orgelmuseum Elburg, Elburg 29224
Nationaal Museum van Speelklok tot Pierement, Utrecht 29904
Pianola Museum, Amsterdam 28894
Rock 'n Roll Museum Arum, Arum 28945

Nigeria
National Museum Ibadan, Ibadan 30340

Norway
Edvard Grieg Museum, Paradis 30776
Jacob Breda Bullmuseet, Rendalen 30788
Kirsten Flagstad Museum, Hamar 30529
Myllarheimen, Rauland 30787
Prøysenhuset, Rudshøgda 30811
Ringve Museum, Trondheim 30941
Siljustøl Museum, Paradis 30778

Philippines
Sala Piano Museum, Cebu 31315

Poland
Biblioteka, Muzeum i Archiwum Warszawskiego Towarzystwa Muzycznego im. Stanisława Moniuszki, Warszawa 32076
Dom Urodzenia Fryderyka Chopina, Warszawa 32081
Muzeum Feliksa Nowowiejskiego, Barczewo 31476
Muzeum Fryderyka Chopina, Warszawa 32096
Muzeum Fryderyka Chopina w Żelazowej Woli, Sochaczew 31985
Muzeum Instrumentów Muzycznych, Poznań 31905
Muzeum Ludowych Instrumentów Muzycznych, Szydłowiec 32038
Muzeum Piśmiennictwa i Muzyki Kaszubsko-Pomorskiej, Wejherowo 32149
Salon Muzyczny im. Fryderyka Chopina, Antonin 31472
Salonik Chopinów, Warszawa 32141

Portugal
Museu da Música Portuguesa, Estoril 32268
Museu Instrumental, Lisboa 32304

Puerto Rico
Museo Pablo Casals, San Juan 32403

Romania
Casa Memorială Gheorghe Dima, Braşov 32446
Muzeul Memorial George Enescu, Dorohoi 32514
Muzeul Național George Enescu, Bucureşti 32469

Russia
Častnyj Muzej Grammofonov i Fonografov, Sankt-Peterburg 33382
Dača Šaljapina - Gosudarstvennyj Istoriko-kulturnyj Muzej, Kislovodsk 32927
Dom-Muzej T.N. Chrenikova, Elec 32789
Dom-Muzej S.V. Rachmaninova, Ivanovka 32824
Dom-muzej F.I. Šaljapina, Moskva 33042
Gosudarstvennaja Kollekcija Unikalnych Muzykalnych Instrumentov, Moskva 33045
Gosudarstvennyj Centralnyj Muzej Musykal'noj Kultury im. M.I. Glinki, Moskva 33049
Gosudarstvennyj Dom-muzej P.I. Čajkovskogo, Klin 32933
Gosudarstvennyj Memorialnyj Dom-muzej N.A. Rimskogo-Korsakova, Tichvin 33599
Gosudarstvennyj Muzej-usadba P.I. Čajkovskogo, Votkinsk 33737
Kamernyj Šaljapinskij Zal, Kazan 32889
Kraevoj Muzej Istorii Literatury, Iskusstva i Kultury Altaja, Barnaul 32673
Memorialnyj Dom-muzej L.V. Sobinova, Jaroslavl 32851
Memorialnyj Muzej I.S. Ključnikova-Palantaja, Joškar-Ola 32858
Memorialnyj Muzej-kvartira Rimskogo-Korsakova, Sankt-Peterburg 33421
Memorialnyj Muzej-kvartira Vadima Alekseeviča Kozina, Magadan 33000
Memorialnyj Muzej A.N. Skrjabina, Moskva 33082
Memorialnyj Muzej-usadba M.P. Musorgskogo, Naumovo 33202
Memorialnyj Muzej-zapovednik N.A. Rimskogo-Korsakova Ljubensk-Večaša, Pljussa 33326
Muzej Istorii Peterburgskoj Konservatorii, Sankt-Peterburg 33440
Muzej-kvartira Dirižëra N.S. Golovanov, Moskva 33122
Muzej-kvartira Naziba Žiganova, Kazan 32901
Muzej-kvartira F.I. Šaljapina, Sankt-Peterburg 33454
Muzej Moskovskoj Konservatorii, Moskva 33136
Muzej Muzykalnoj i Teatralnoj Kultury na Kavkazskich Mineralnyh Vodach, Kislovodsk 32930
Muzej Muzykalnych Instrumentov, Sankt-Peterburg 33459
Muzej N.G. Rubinstejna, Moskva 33140
Muzej S.S. Prokofjeva, Moskva 33148
Muzej Russkoj Pesni im. A. Averkina, Sasovo 33512
Muzej Salicha Sajdaševa, Kazan 32904
Muzej S.I. Taneeva v Djutkovo, Zvenigorod 33750
Muzej-usadba M.I. Glinki, Novospasskoe 33246
Muzyka i Vremja - Častnyj Muzej Džona Mostoslavskogo, Jaroslavl 32855
Šeremetevskij Dvorec - Fontannyj Dom, Sankt-Peterburg 33483

Slovakia
Hudobná Expozícia - Rodný Dom J.N. Hummela, Bratislava 33965
Hudobné Múzeum, Bratislava 33966
Museum of Literature and Music, Banská Bystrica 33947
Nábytkové Múzeum, Markušovce 34021

South Africa
Afrikaans Music Museum, Bloemfontein 34182
National Music Museum, Bloemfontein 34190

Spain
Casa Museo Julián Gayarre, Roncal 35336
Casa-Museo Manuel de Falla, Granada 34866
Museo de la Gaita, Gijón 34845
Museu de la Música, Barcelona 34562
Museu Pau Casals, El Vendrell 35645

Sweden
Carl Jularbo Museum, Avesta 35826
Hobby- och Leksaksmuseum, Stockholm 36247
Jazzens Museum, Kolbäck 36012
Jussi Björlingmuseet, Borlänge 35845
Musikmuseet, Stockholm 36264
Smålands Bil, Musik och Leksaksmuseum, Rydaholm 36165
Smetanamuseet, Göteborg 35921
Stiftelsen Musikkulturens Främjande, Stockholm 36286

Switzerland
Ausstellung der Schweizerischen Geigenbauschule, Brienz, Bern 36586
Blasinstrumenten-Sammlung, Zimmerwald 37363
Fredy's Mechanisches Musikmuseum, Lichtensteig 36873
Harmonium-Museum, Liestal 36878
Mechanisches Musikmuseum, Sursee 37225
Musée Baud, L'Auberson 36476
Musée de Boîtes à Musique et Automates, Sainte-Croix 37090
Musée de Musiques, L'Auberson 36477
Musée Paderewski, Morges 36952
Musée Suisse de l'Orgue, Roche 37066
Museum für Musikautomaten, Seewen 37158
Museum für Uhren und mechanische Musikinstrumente, Oberhofen am Thunersee 36998
Musikmuseum, Basel 36513
Nostalgisches Musikparadies, Oberhasli 36997
Richard Wagner-Museum, Luzern 36916
Sammlung Heinrich Brechbühl, Steffisburg 37212
Schweizer Jazzmuseum, Uster 37271
Streichinstrumentemsammlung, Einsiedeln 36677

Tunisia
Ennejma Ezzahra-Palais du Baron d'Erlanger, Sidi Bou Saïd 37582

Turkey
Aynalıkavak Kasrı, İstanbul 37694
İstanbul Divan Edebiyatı Müzesi, İstanbul 37704

Ukraine
Literaturno-memorialny Muzei A.S. Puškina i P.I. Čajkovskogo, Kamenka 37858
Museum of Theatrical, Musical and Cinematographic Art of Ukraine, Kyïv 37874
Muzej Igora Stravinskogo, Ustyloog 37908

United Kingdom
Chantry Bagpipe Museum, Morpeth 39987
Dean Castle, Kilmarnock 39361
Edinburgh University Collection of Historic Musical Instruments, Edinburgh 38880
The Elgar Birthplace Museum, Lower Broadheath 39835
Fenton House, London 39634
Finchcocks, Goudhurst 39105
Handel House Museum, London 39660
Holst Birthplace Museum, Cheltenham 38545
Horniman Museum, London 39668
Joseph Parry's Cottage, Merthyr Tydfil 39938
Keith Harding's World of Mechanical Music, Northleach 40086
Mechanical Music and Doll Collection, Chichester 38563
Mechanical Music Museum and Bygones, Cotton 38639
Museum of Instruments, London 39717
Museum of Piping, Glasgow 39056
Museum of the Royal Military School of Music, Twickenham 40740
Museum of Victorian Reed Organs and Harmoniums, Shipley 40501
Musical Museum, London 39726
Piano Museum Collection, Hereford 39229
Renishaw Hall Museum and Art Gallery, Renishaw 40309
Russell Collection of Early Keyboard Instruments, Edinburgh 38913
Saint Albans Organ Museum, Saint Albans 40377

U.S.A.
Alabama Music Hall of Fame, Tuscumbia 48119
American Classical Music Hall of Fame and Museum, Cincinnati 42397
American Jazz Museum, Kansas City 44394
America's National Music Museum, Vermillion 48214
Bagpipe Music Museum, Ellicott City 43156
Boswell Museum of Music, East Springfield 43059
Buddy Holly Center, Lubbock 44990
Center for American Music, Stephen Foster Memorial, Pittsburgh 46513
Conklin Reed Organ and History Museum, Hanover 43906
Country Music Hall of Fame and Museum, Nashville 45614
Delta Blues Museum, Clarksdale 42431
Eubie Blake National Jazz Museum and Cultural Center, Baltimore 41465
Experience Music Project, Seattle 47533
Fort Morgan Museum, Fort Morgan 43432
Georgia Music Hall of Fame, Macon 45043
Gospel Music Hall of Fame and Museum, Detroit 42928
Graceland, Memphis 45238
Hollywood Bowl Museum, Los Angeles 44907
International Bluegrass Music Museum, Owensboro 46228
Liberace Museum, Las Vegas 44671
Lockwood-Mathews Mansion Museum, Norwalk 46032
Louisiana Country Music Museum, Marthaville 45188
Mario Lanza Museum, Philadelphia 46425
Motown Historical Museum, Detroit 42933
Museum of the American Piano, New York 45846
The Music House, Acme 41061
Musical Box Society International Museum, Norwalk 46033
Musical Wonder House, Wiscasset 48717
The Rock and Roll Hall of Fame and Museum, Cleveland 42479
The Roy Rogers-Dale Evans Museum, Victorville 48235
Sarasota Classic Car Museum, Sarasota 47454
Stearns Collection of Musical Instruments, Ann Arbor 41221
Texas Music Museum, Austin 41423
Yale University Collection of Musical Instruments, New Haven 45701
Yesteryear Museum, Pamplin 46276

Uzbekistan
Mouhtar Ashrafi Museum, Taškent 48856

Naive Art → Folk Art

Natural History

Afghanistan
Science Museum, Kabul 00006

Albania
Muzeu i Shkencave Natyrore, Tiranë 00035

Algeria
History and Natural History Museum, Alger 00040

Angola
Museu Nacional de História Natural, Luanda 00100

Argentina
Museo Argentino de Ciencias Naturales Bernardino Rivadavia, Buenos Aires 00158
Museo de Antropología y Ciencias Naturales, Concordia 00287
Museo de Ciencias Antropológicas y Naturales, Santiago del Estero 00616
Museo de Ciencias Naturales Augusto G. Schulz, Resistencia 00506
Museo de Ciencias Naturales Bartolomé Mitre, Córdoba 00294
Museo de Ciencias Naturales de Oberá, Oberá 00460
Museo de Ciencias Naturales del Departamento San Cristóbal, San Cristóbal 00554
Museo de Ciencias Naturales e Historia, Posadas 00482
Museo de Ciencias Naturales Rvdo. P. Antonio Scasso, San Nicolás de los Arroyos 00589
Museo de Ciencias Naturales y Antropológicas Juan Cornelio Moyano, Mendoza 00435
Museo de Ciencias Naturales y Antropológicas Prof. Antonio Serrano, Paraná 00465
Museo de Ciencias Naturales y Misional del Colegio San José, Esperanza 00342
Museo de Historia Natural Dr. Ricardo S. Vadell, Suipacha 00624
Museo de Instituto Antártico Argentino, Buenos Aires 00180
Museo de la Facultad de Ciencias Naturales y del Instituto Miguel Lillo, San Miguel de Tucumán 00584
Museo de la Región de Ansenuza Aníbal Montes, Miramar 00448
Museo de la Selva Juan Forster, Miramar 00449
Museo del Agua y del Suelo, Viedma 00657
Museo del Colegio Nacional Justo José de Urquiza, Paraná 00467
Museo del Parque Nacional Los Alerces, Villa Futalaufquen 00667
Museo El Hombre y la Naturaleza, San Juan 00571
Museo Histórico y Natural de Lavalle, Lavalle Villa Tulumaya 00406
Museo Interactivo de Ciencias Naturales, Ituzaingó 00370
Museo Jorge Pasquini López, San Salvador de Jujuy 00597
Museo Marcelo López del Instituto Hellen Keller, Córdoba 00305
Museo Municipal de Ciencias, Bahía Blanca 00129
Museo Municipal de Ciencias Naturales Carlos Ameghino, Mercedes 00445
Museo Municipal de Ciencias Naturales Carlos Darwin, Punta Alta 00493
Museo Municipal de Historia Natural, San Rafael 00594
Museo Paleontológico Egidio Feruglio, Trelew 00639
Museo Participativo de Ciencias, Buenos Aires 00236
Museo Provincial de Ciencias Naturales Dr. Angelo Gallardo, Rosario 00532
Museo Provincial de Ciencias Naturales Florentino Ameghino, Santa Fé 00609
Museo Provincial de Ciencias Naturales y Oceanográfico, Puerto Madryn 00491
Museo Provincial de Historia Natural de La Pampa, Santa Rosa 00613
Museo Regional de Ciencias Naturales Tomás Santa Coloma, Tres Arroyos 00642

Australia
Albany Residency Museum, Albany 00721
Australian Museum, Sydney 01492
Lake Broadwater Natural History Museum, Dalby 00965
Museum of Central Australia, Alice Springs 00735
Museum of Tropical Queensland, Townsville 01546
Papua New Guinea Display Centre, Crafers 00951
Queen Victoria Museum and Art Gallery, Launceston 01170
Rottnest Island Museum, Rottnest Island 01427
South Australian Museum, Adelaide 00713
Western Australian Museum Geraldton, Geraldton 01049
Wildlife Wonderlands Giant Worm Museum, Bass 00771

Austria
inatura- Erlebnis Naturschau Dornbirn, Dornbirn 01769
Lobaumuseum, Wien 02928
Museum Mödling, Mödling 02312
Naturhistorisches Museum, Wien 02951
Naturkunde- und Feuerwehrmuseum, Dobersberg 01765

Naturwissenschaftliche Sammlungen, Innsbruck 02076
Niederösterreichisches Landesmuseum, Sankt Pölten 02603

Bahrain
Bahrain National Museum, Manama 03078

Belarus
Beloveżskaja Pušča Muzej, Beloveżskaja Pušča 03110

Belgium
Musée de la Montagne Saint-Pierre, Lanaye 03550
Musée de l'Histoire de la Forêt d'Ardenne, Saint-Hubert 03720
Musée d'Histoire Naturelle de Mons, Mons 03634
Natuurwetenschappelijk Museum, Antwerpen 03164

Belize
Belize Audubon Society, Belize City 03863
Chaa Creek Natural History Centre, San Ignacio 03870
Natural History Museum, Las Cuevas 03868

Bermuda
Bermuda Natural History Museum, Flatts 03880

Bolivia
Museo del Litoral Boliviano, La Paz 03896

Bosnia and Herzegovina
Zemaljski Muzej, Sarajevo 03925

Botswana
Nhabe Museum, Nhabe 03938

Brazil
Centro de Educação Ambiental Gralha Azul e Museu de História Natural, Cascavel 04043
Ecomuseu, Rio de Janeiro 04322
Ecomuseu da Fazenda Boa Vista, Roseira 04414
Ecomuseu do Rabeirão do Ilha, Florianópolis 04088
Laboratário de Ensino de Ciências, Ribeirão Preto 04309
Museu Arquediocesano Dom Joaquim, Brusque 04012
Museu Civico-Religioso Padre Cicero, Juazeiro do Norte 04154
Museu de Ciência e Técnica da Escola de Minas, Ouro Preto 04239
Museu de Ciências Naturais, Guarapuava 04120
Museu de Ciências Naturais, Porto Alegre 04279
Museu de Ciências Naturais, Recife 04299
Museu de Ciências Naturais PUC Minas, Belo Horizonte 03985
Museu de História e Ciências Naturais, Além Paraíba 03941
Museu de História Natural, Belo Horizonte 03986
Museu de História Natural, Campinas 04026
Museu de História Natural Prof. Antonio Pergola, Atibaia 03962
Museu de Paleontologia, Monte Alto 04208
Museu e Biblioteca do Instituto Geográfico e Histórico do Amazonas, Manaus 04192
Museu Nacional, Rio de Janeiro 04388
Museu Paraense Emílio Goeldi, Belém 03978
Museu Parque Malwee, Jaraguá do Sul 04144
Museu Zoobotânico Augusto Ruschi, Passo Fundo 04248
Museus de História Natural e Etnologia Indígena, Juiz de Fora 04159

Brunei
Muzium Brunei, Bandar Seri Begawan 04598

Bulgaria
Nacionalen Prirodonaučen Muzej, Sofia 04853
Prirodonaučen Muzej, Burgas 04636
Prirodonaučen Muzej, Kotel 04720
Prirodonaučen Muzej, Plovdiv 04782
Prirodonaučen Muzej, Belogradčik 04619

Canada
Abernethy Nature Heritage Museum, Abernethy 04965
Banff Park Museum, Banff 05041
Big Beaver Nature Centre and Museum, Big Beaver 05077
Biodôme de Montréal, Montréal 05892
B.J. Hales Museum of Natural History, Brandon 05118
Canadian Museum of Nature, Ottawa 06072
Cape Breton Centre for Heritage and Science, Sydney 06525
Centre d'Interpretation du Parc de l'Île-Bonaventure-et-du Rocher-Percé, Percé 06111
Centre d'Interprétation du Patrimoine de Sorel, Sorel-Tracy 06471
Centre Muséographique, Québec 06195
Chatham-Kent Museum, Chatham, Ontario 05237
Écomusée de la Haute-Beauce, Saint-Evariste 06317
Garden of the Gulf Museum, Montague 05883
Grand Coteau Heritage and Cultural Centre, Shaunavon 06428
Kluane Museum of Natural History, Burwash Landing 05153
Lac LaRonge Museum, LaRonge 05728
Living Prairie Museum, Winnipeg 06830
MacBride Museum, Whitehorse 06792
McLurg Museum, Wilkie 06800
Manitoba Museum of Man and Nature, Winnipeg 06833
Miramichi Natural History Museum, Miramichi 05861
Mountain View Doukhobor Museum, Grand Forks 05515
Musée des Sciences Naturelles, Vaudreuil 06701
Musée du Séminaire de Sherbrooke, Sherbrooke, Québec 06442
Nova Scotia Museum of Natural History, Halifax 05560
Ovens Museum, Riverport 06275
Park House Museum, Amherstburg 04989
Point Pelee Natural History Museum, Leamington 05740
Presqu'ile Provincial Park Museum, Brighton 05133
Prince Albert National Park Nature Centre, Waskesiu Lake 06748
Quetico Provincial Park Heritage Pavilion, Atikokan 05018
Rondeau Provincial Park Visitor Centre, Morpeth 05942
Royal British Columbia Museum, Victoria 06729
Royal Saskatchewan Museum, Regina 06243
Sam Waller Museum, The Pas 06098
Saskatchewan Wildlife Federation Museum, North Battleford 06015
Transcona Historical Museum, Winnipeg 06848
Whiteshell Natural Historic Museum, Seven Sisters Falls 06424

Chad
Musée National, N'Djamena 06883

Chile
Museo de Historia Natural de Concepción, Concepción 06892
Museo de Historia Natural de San Pedro Nolasco, Santiago de Chile 06912
Museo de Historia Natural de Valparaíso, Valparaíso 06927
Museo Dillmann S. Bullock, Angol 06886
Museo Regional Salesiano Maggiorino Borgatello, Punta Arenas 06905

China, People's Republic
Chongqing Natural Museum, Chongqing 07032
Dalian Natural History Museum, Dalian 07035
Guangxi Natural Museum, Nanning 07189
Jilin Natural Museum, Changchun 07003
Shanghai Natural History Museum, Shanghai 07222
Shanghai Science Technology Museum, Shanghai 07223
Tianjin Museum of Natural History, Tianjin 07266
Zhejiang Natural Museum, Hangzhou 07088

China, Republic
Taiwan Museum, Taipei 07359

Colombia
Instituto Geográfico Agustín Codazzi, Bogotá 07391
Museo Casa de la Cultura de Barichara, Barichara 07375
Museo de Ciencias Naturales Federico Carlos Lehmann, Cali 07448
Museo de Geología, Manizales 07507
Museo de Geología y Suelos, Armenia 07371
Museo de Historia Natural, Popayán 07564
Museo de la Diversidad Biológica y Cultural del Pacífico, Quibdó 07572
Museo del Carbón, Lenguazaque 07504
Museo del Mar El Rodadero, Santa Marta 07589
Museo Gabriel Mateus, Sabanagrande 07580
Museo Gemológico, Bogotá 07421
Museo Geológico Petrolero, Neiva 07534
Museo Luis Alberto Acuña, Villa de Leyva 07621
Museo Nacional del Petróleo Samuel Schneider Uribe, Barrancabermeja 07376
Museo Natural, Pensilvania 07556
Museo Universitario, Medellín 07524
Museo y Parque Nacional, Montenegro 07530

Congo, Republic
Musée National du Congo, Brazzaville 07645

Croatia
Archeological and Natural History Museum, Brijuni 07684
Prirodoslovni Muzej, Rijeka 07764
Prirodoslovni Muzej, Split 07785

Cuba
Museo Ciencias Naturales, Nueva Gerona 08056
Museo Ciencias Naturales Carlos de la Torre, Sancti-Spíritus 08110
Museo de Ciencias Naturales Carlos de la Torre, Holguín 08004
Museo de Ciencias Naturales Tomás Romay, Santiago de Cuba 08135
Museo de Historia Natural Felipe Poey, La Habana 07960
Museo de Historia Natural Valle de la Prehistoria, Santiago de Cuba 08137
Museo Historia de las Ciencias Carlos J. Finlay, La Habana 07971
Museo Nacional de Historia Natural, La Habana 07988
Tranquilino Sandalio de Noda Museo de Ciencias Naturales, Pinar del Río 08078

Cyprus, Turkish Republic
Güzelyurt Müzesi, Güzelyurt 08228

Czech Republic
Hrad Roštejn, Telč 08675
Jihomoravské Muzeum ve Znojmě, Znojmo 08756
Městské Muzeum a Galerie, Hlinsko v Čechách 08350
Moravské Zemské Muzeum, Brno 08272
Muzeum, Litvínov 08460
Muzeum Regionu Valšsko ve Vsetině - Zámek Vsetín, Vsetín 08730
Muzeum v Bruntále, Bruntál 08282
Muzeum Východních Čech v Hradci Králové, Hradec Králové 08368
Muzeum Vysočiny Jihlava, Jihlava 08390
Národní Muzeum, Praha 08602
Okresní Muzeum, Hořovice 08362
Památník Prokopa Diviše, Znojmo 08757
Polabské Muzeum, Poděbrady 08551
Přírodovědecké Muzeum, Praha 08613
Přírodovědecké Oddělení, Opava 08521
Středočeské Muzeum, Roztoky u Prahy 08643
Vlastivědné Muzeum v Olomouci, Olomouc 08516
Zámek Kinských, Valašské Meziříčí 08706
Západočeské Muzeum, Plzeň 08547

Denmark
Wellings Landsbymuseum, Lintrup 08974

Ecuador
Museo del Santuario de la Virgen de Agua Santa, Baños 09142
Museo Ecuatoriano de Ciencias Naturales, Quito 09209
Museo Farallón Dillon, Ballenita 09140
Vivarium, Quito 09220

El Salvador
Museo de Historia Natural de El Salvador, San Salvador 09312

Estonia
Eesti Loodusmuuseum, Tallinn 09359
Karl Ernst von Baeri Muuseum, Tartu 09379

Faroe Islands
Føroya Náttúrugripasavn, Tórshavn 09408

Finland
Forssan Luonnonhistoriallinen Museo, Forssa 09441
Jyväskylän Yliopiston Museo - Keski-Suomen Luontomuseo, Jyväskylä 09598
Kuopion Luonnontieteellinen Museo, Kuopio 09720
Luonnonhistoriallinen Museo, Porvoo 09952
Luonnontieteellinen Museo, Helsinki 09511
Pohjanmaan Museo, Vaasa 10161
Seinäjoen Luonto-Museo, Seinäjoki 10029
Tampereen Luonnontieteellinen Museo, Tampere 10090
Tieteelliset Kokoelmat, Forssa 09443

France
Centre d'Hébergement, d'Étude sur la Nature et l'Environnement, Allouville-Bellefosse 10294
Château-Musée, Tourrette-Levens 14967
Éco Musée Vivant de Provence, La Gaude 12190
Ecomusée de la Crau, Saint-Martin-de-Crau 14349
Ecomusée des Appeaux et de la Faune, Saint-Didier 14183
Maison de la Loire, Montlouis-sur-Loire 13101
Maison de la Réserve Naturelle du Lac de Remoray, Labergement-Sainte-Marie 12284
Maison de la Rivière, de l'Eau et de la Pêche, Sizun 14758
Maison de l'Environnement et de la Chasse, Sault (Vaucluse) 14638
Maison du Parc Naturel Régional du Luberon, Apt 10385
Maison-Musée des Sciences, Lettres et Arts de Cholet et de sa Région, Cholet 11297
Musée d'Allard, Montbrison 13062
Musée de Cerdagne d'Eyne, Eyne 11692
Musée des Sciences Naturelles, Orléans 13433
Musée d'Histoire Naturell, Auxerre 10510
Musée d'Histoire Naturelle, Aix-en-Provence 10253
Musée d'Histoire Naturelle, Angers 10347
Musée d'Histoire Naturelle, Chambéry 11141
Musée d'Histoire Naturelle, Gray 11934
Musée d'Histoire Naturelle, La Rochelle 12242
Musée d'Histoire Naturelle, Perpignan 13707
Musée d'Histoire Naturelle, Rouen 14050
Musée d'Histoire Naturelle, Amnéville-les-Thermes 10327
Musée d'Histoire Naturelle, Dijon 11528
Musée d'Histoire Naturelle de Toulon, Toulon (Var) 14928
Musée d'Histoire Naturelle et de Géologie, Lille 12601
Musée d'Histoire Naturelle et de la Préhistoire, Nîmes 13340
Musée d'Histoire Naturelle et d'Ethnographie, Colmar 11359
Musée d'Histoire Naturelle et d'Histoire Locale, Elbeuf 11607
Musée d'Histoire Naturelle Gabriel-Foucher, Bourges 10863
Musée d'Initiation à la Nature de Normandie, Caen 10984
Musée du Biterrois, Béziers 10719
Musée du Château des Ducs de Wurtemberg, Montbéliard 13060
Musée du Château d'Oigny-en-Valois, Oigny-en-Valois 13392
Musée du Granit, Saint-Michel-de-Montjoie 14370
Musée Harmas Jean-Henri Fabre, Sérignan-du-Comtat 14719
Musée Joseph Durand, Saint-Clément-des-Baleines 14159
Musée Lecoq, Clermont-Ferrand 11325
Musée-Maison de la Nature, Samer 14597
Musée Municipal des Beaux Arts et d'Histoire Naturelle, Châteaudun 11214
Musée Océanographique, L'Ile-Rousse 12594
Musée Pasteur, Paris 13643
Musée Requien, Avignon 10534
Musée Vert, Le Mans 12439
Musée Vivant d'Histoire Naturelle, Nancy 13244
Muséem d'Histoire Naturelle, Marseille 12871
Muséum des Volcans, Aurillac 10492
Muséum d'Histoire Naturelle, Autun 10500
Museum d'Histoire Naturelle, Blois 10775
Muséum d'Histoire Naturelle, Chartres 11195
Muséum d'Histoire Naturelle, Gras 11916
Muséum d'Histoire Naturelle, Grenoble 11947
Muséum d'Histoire Naturelle, Lyon 12750
Muséum d'Histoire Naturelle, Nice 13326
Muséum d'Histoire Naturelle, Troyes 15008
Muséum d'Histoire-Naturelle, Cherbourg 11279
Muséum d'Histoire Naturelle de Bordeaux, Bordeaux 10820
Muséum d'Histoire Naturelle de la Ville de Bayonne, Bayonne 10623
Muséum d'Histoire Naturelle de Toulouse, Toulouse 14953
Muséum d'Histoire Naturelle de Tours, Tours 14977
Nature en Provence, Riez 13967
Rhinopolis, Gannat 11837

French Guiana
Musée Départemental Alexandre Franconie, Cayenne 15340

French Polynesia
Musée du Coquillage, Papara 15344

Georgia
State Museum of Adjar, Batumi 15353
State Museum of the South-Ossetian Autonomous District, Chinvali 15354

Germany
Adelhausermuseum, Natur- und Völkerkunde, Freiburg im Breisgau 17105
Alpines Museum des Deutschen Alpenvereins, München 18823
Bayerisches Moor- und Torfmuseum, Grassau, Chiemgau 17378
Bodensee-Naturmuseum, Konstanz 18202
Carl-Schweizer-Museum, Murrhardt 18963
Darß-Museum, Ostseebad Prerow 19316
Dillhäuser Fachwerkhaus im Tiergarten Weilburg, Weilburg 20444
Elbschloss Bleckede, Bleckede 16184
Emsland-Moormuseum, Geeste 17208
Felsendome Rabenstein, Chemnitz 16463
Fuhlrott-Museum, Wuppertal 20711
Harzmuseum, Wernigerode 20525
Haus der Natur, Eichendorf 16800
Haus der Natur, Willingen, Upland 20599
Heimat- und Bauernmuseum, Bruck, Oberpfalz 16371
Heimat- und Naturkunde-Museum Wanne-Eickel, Herne 17728
Heimatmuseum der Insel Hiddensee, Kloster, Hiddensee 18114
Heimatmuseum und Naturalienkabinett, Waldenburg, Sachsen 20360
Informationsstelle des Naturparks Fichtelgebirge, Zell, Oberfranken 20742
Kinder-Akademie Fulda Werkraummuseum, Fulda 17177
Korallen- und Heimatmuseum, Nattheim 18975
Kreis-Heimatmuseum, Bad Frankenhausen 15642
Landesmuseum für Natur und Mensch, Oldenburg, Oldenburg 19257
Landschaftsmuseum Obermain, Kulmbach 18268
Lippisches Landesmuseum, Detmold 16589
Mauritianum, Altenburg, Thüringen 15451
Moor- und Fehnmuseum, Barßel 15827
Moormuseum Moordorf, Südbrookmerland 20119
Müritz-Museum, Waren 20399
Museum am Schölerberg, Osnabrück 19282
Museum Bayerisches Vogtland, Hof, Saale 17793
Museum der heimischen Tierwelt, Nabburg 18967
Museum der Stadt Gladbeck, Gladbeck 17291
Museum für Naturkunde, Chemnitz 16468
Museum für Naturkunde, Magdeburg 18585
Museum für Naturkunde, Düsseldorf 16737
Museum für Naturkunde und Völkerkunde Julius Riemer, Lutherstadt Wittenberg 18577
Museum für Naturkunde und Vorgeschichte, Dessau 16579
Museum im Umweltschutz-Informationszentrum Oberfranken mit Kinder-Erlebnis-Museum, Bayreuth 15856
Museum Mensch und Natur, München 18883
Natureum Niederelbe, Balje 15801
Naturhistorisches Museum, Heilbronn 17689
Naturhistorisches Museum Schloss Bertholdsburg, Schleusingen 19799
Naturkunde-Museum, Coburg 16484
Naturkundemuseum, Reutlingen 19578
Naturkundemuseum Freiberg, Freiberg, Sachsen 17102
Naturkundemuseum im Marstall, Paderborn 19339
Naturkundemuseum im Ottoneum, Kassel 18027
Naturkundemuseum Leipzig, Leipzig 18411
Naturkundemuseum Ludwigslust, Ludwigslust 18526
Naturkundemuseum Niebüll, Niebüll 19093

Naturkundliches Bildungszentrum, Ulm 20259
Naturkundliches Museum, Wiesenfelden 20579
Naturkundliches Museum und Schulungsstätte "Alte Schmiede", Handeloh 17588
Naturmuseum der Stadt Augsburg, Augsburg 15563
Naturwissenschaftliche Sammlungen, Berlin 16072
Naturwissenschaftliches Museum, Aschaffenburg 15526
Naturwissenschaftliches Museum der Stadt Flensburg, Flensburg 17013
Naturwissenschaftliches Museum Duisburg, Duisburg 16755
Niedersächsisches Landesmuseum Hannover, Hannover 17607
Pfalzmuseum für Naturkunde (POLLICHIA-Museum), Bad Dürkheim 15630
Potsdam-Museum, Potsdam 19436
Reiss-Engelhorn-Museen, Mannheim 18615
Römisches Museum und Naturkunde-Museum, Kempten 18065
Ruhrlandmuseum Essen, Essen 16962
Senckenberg-Forschungsinstitut und Naturmuseum, Frankfurt am Main 17072
Staatliches Museum für Naturkunde, Karlsruhe 18003
Staatliches Museum für Naturkunde Görlitz, Görlitz 17327
Staatliches Museum für Naturkunde Stuttgart, Stuttgart 20105
Stadtmuseum Schloß Hoyerswerda, Hoyerswerda 17848
Städtisches Naturkundliches Museum, Göppingen 17322
Torfmuseum, Neustadt am Rübenberge 19070
Überseemuseum Bremen, Bremen 16336
Vylym-Hütte, Userin 20277
Waldmuseum, Burg, Dithmarschen 16411
Waldmuseum, Furth im Wald 17183
Waldmuseum Wassermühle, Wingst 20608
Westfälisches Museum für Naturkunde, Münster 18951

Greece
Mouseion Goulandri Fysikis Istorias, Kifissia 21015
Museum of Natural History and Historical Photography, Polygyros 21132
Museum of the White Mountains of Samaria, Chania 20918
Natural History Museum of Amarousio, Amarousio 20817
Natural History Museum of Cephalonia and Ithaca, Argostolion 20836
Natural History Museum of Elassona, Elassona 20943
Natural History Museum of Oeta, Ipati 20973
Zakynthos Museum of the Natural Heritage, Zakynthos 21223

Guatemala
Museo de Historia Natural, Guatemala 21268
Museo Quezaltenango, Quezaltenango 21277

Hungary
Bakonyi Természettudományi Múzeum, Zirc 21617
Janus Pannonius Múzeum Természettudományi Osztálya, Pécs 21507
Magyar Természettudományi Múzeum, Budapest 21362
Országos Műszaki Múzeum, Budapest 21373
Savaria Múzeum, Szombathely 21587

Iceland
Byggðasafn Austur-Skaftafellssýslu, Höfn 21638
Fiska- og Náttúrngripasafn Vestmannaeyja, Vestmannaeyjar 21674
Náttúrufrædaistofnun Islands, Akureyrarsetur, Akureyri 21621
Natturufrædistofa Kopavogs, Kópavogur 21643
Náttúrufræðistofnun Íslands, Reykjavík 21658
Náttúrugripasafnid i Neskaupstad, Neskaupstadur 21644

India
Baroda Museum and Picture Gallery, Vadodara 22048
Bengal Natural History Museum, Darjeeling 21755
Birbal Sahni Institute of Palaeobotany Museum, Lucknow 21922
Goa Science Centre, Panaji 21972
Government Museum, Thiruvananthapuram 22035
Government Museum, Udaipur 22044
Municipal Museum Gwalior, Gwalior 21830
National Museum of Natural History, Delhi 21777
Natural History Museum of Bombay Natural History Society, Mumbai 21951
North Bengal Science Centre, Siliguri 22026
Regional Museum of Natural History, Bhopal 21723
Regional Science Centre, Guwahati, Assam 21827
Saint Joseph's College Museum, Tiruchirappalli 22037
State Museum, Trichur 22042

Iran
Eastern Azarbaijan Province History Museum, Tabriz 22285
Natural History Museum, Gorgan 22240
Natural History Museum, Ilam 22243
Natural History Museum, Teheran 22320
Natural History Museum, Urmieh 22332
Natural History Museum, Yazd 22335
Natural History Museum, Khorram-Abaad 22258
Taymori Hall, Isfahan 22247
Zoological Museum, Teheran 22329

Iraq
Iraq Natural History Research Centre and Museum, Baghdad 22345

Ireland
Ballyheigue Maritime Centre, Ballyheigue 22371
Museum of Natural History, Dublin 22445

Israel
Bet Pinhas Museum of Nature, Haifa 22599
Hebrew University Collections of Natural History, Jerusalem 22634
Natural Sciences Museum, Hulata 22622
Neot Kedumim, Lod 22708
Sharon Museum, Emek Hefer 22591
Sturman Institute Museum of Regional Science, Afula 22565

Italy
Centro di Scienze Naturali e Raccolta Natura ed Arte, Prato 25041
Civico Museo di Scienze Naturali, Domodossola 23718
Civico Museo di Storia Naturale della Lombardia, Jerago con Orago 24112
Civico Museo Insubrico di Storia Naturale, Induno Olona 24097
Civico Museo Naturalistico, Ovada 24722
Collezione di Farfalle, Guardia Sanframondi 24069
Domus Galilaeana, Pisa 24945
Musei Civici, Reggio Emilia 25096
Museo Aldrovandiano, Bologna 23105
Museo Berenziano, Cremona 23679
Museo Brandolini e Giol, Oderzo 24664
Museo Brembano di Scienze Naturali, San Pellegrino Terme 25405
Museo Civico, Ragogna 25066
Museo Civico, Finale Emilia 23815
Museo Civico A. Klitsche de la Grange, Allumiere 22859
Museo Civico delle Scienze, Pordenone 25008
Museo Civico di Scienze Naturali, Faenza 23751
Museo Civico di Storia Naturale, Casalnuovo Monterotaro 23368
Museo Civico di Storia Naturale, Chies d'Alpago 23542
Museo Civico di Storia Naturale, Cittanova 23585
Museo Civico di Storia Naturale, Crocetta del Montello 23686
Museo Civico di Storia Naturale, Milano 24387
Museo Civico di Storia Naturale, Morbegno 24563
Museo Civico di Storia Naturale, Taino 25668
Museo Civico di Storia Naturale, Trieste 25823
Museo Civico di Storia Naturale, Venezia 25926
Museo Civico di Storia Naturale, Verona 25971
Museo Civico di Storia Naturale del Liceo Glassico N. Machiavelli, Lucca 24228
Museo Civico Didattico di Scienze Naturali, Pinerolo 24927
Museo Civico E. Barba, Gallipoli 23955
Museo Civico Naturalistico, Maserada sul Piave 24311
Museo Civico Naturalistico dei Monti Prenestini, Capranica Prenestina 23331
Museo Civico Naturalistico Severo Sini, Villa d'Almè 26012
Museo Civico P. A. Garda, Ivrea 24111
Museo Civico per la Preistoria del Monte Cetona, Cetona 23514
Museo Civicodi Scienze Naturali, Randazzo 25072
Museo Civicodi Storia Naturale, Stazzano 25630
Museo degli Alpini, Savignone 25504
Museo dei Fossili e di Storia Naturale, Montefalcone Appennino 24518
Museo del Capriolo, Bisegna 23089
Museo del Fungo e di Scienze Naturali, Boves 23190
Museo del Lupo Appenninico, Civitella Alfedena 23597
Museo del Regio Esercito Italiano, Orta 24696
Museo del Sottosuolo P. Parenzan, Latiano 24155
Museo della Bonifica, Argenta 22926
Museo della Flora, Fauna e Mineralogia, Auronzo di Cadore 22987
Museo dell'Avifauna Appenninica, Sarnano 25473
Museo delle Scienze della Terra e del Lavoro Contadino, Piandimeleto 24896
Museo delle Valli d'Argenta, Argenta 22927
Museo di Ecologia e Storia Naturale, Marano sul Panaro 24294
Museo di Preistoria e Protostoria della Valle del Fiume Fiora, Manciano 24275
Museo di Scienze Naturale e Umane, L'Aquila 24143
Museo di Scienze Naturali, Belvi 23051
Museo di Scienze Naturali, Bolzano 23155
Museo di Scienze Naturali, Cesena 23505
Museo di Scienze Naturali, Città della Pieve 23574
Museo di Scienze Naturali, Malnate 24269
Museo di Scienze Naturali, Pavia 24826
Museo di Scienze Naturali, Camerino 23288
Museo di Scienze Naturali L. Paolucci, Offagna 24668
Museo di Scienze Naturali Tommaso Salvadori, Fermo 23779
Museo di Storia Naturale, Follonica 23901
Museo di Storia Naturale, Macerata 24248
Museo di Storia Naturale, Merate 24356
Museo di Storia Naturale, Perugia 24855
Museo di Storia Naturale, Piacenza 24894
Museo di Storia Naturale, Senna Lodigiana 25539
Museo di Storia Naturale, Stroncone 25644
Museo di Storia Naturale, Sulmona 25648
Museo di Storia Naturale, Parma 24807
Museo di Storia Naturale, Parma 24808
Museo di Storia Naturale A. Orsini, Ascoli Piceno 22952
Museo di Storia Naturale A. Stoppani, Venegono Inferiore 25911
Museo di Storia Naturale Aquilegia, Assemini 22960
Museo di Storia Naturale del Cilento, Laureana Cilento 24162
Museo di Storia Naturale Don Bosco, Torino 25750
Museo di Storia Naturale e del Territorio, Calci 23260
Museo di Storia Naturale e dell'Uomo, Carrara 23358
Museo di Storia Naturale Faraggiana-Ferrandi, Novara 24646
Museo di Storia Naturale S. Ferrari, Bedonia 23046
Museo di Storia Naturali e Archeologia, Montebelluna 24505
Museo Didattico, Niscemi 24623
Museo Etnografico e di Scienze Naturali, Torino 25754
Museo Friulano di Storia Naturale, Udine 25850
Museo G. Scarabelli, Imola 24090
Museo Marinaro Tommasino-Andreatta, San Colombano Certenoli 25351
Museo Mineralogico e Naturalistico, Bormio 23180
Museo Missionario Cinese e di Storia Naturale, Lecce 24165
Museo Naturali e Appennino, Revi nel Lazio 25106
Museo Naturalistica-Archeologico, Vicenza 25995
Museo Naturalistico, Champdepraz 23518
Museo Naturalistico, Lesina 24181
Museo Naturalistico, Pescasseroli 24872
Museo Naturalistico, Picinisco 24905
Museo Naturalistico, Portoferraio 25019
Museo Naturalistico, Chieri 23540
Museo Naturalistico Archeologico M. Locati, Lama dei Peligni 24130
Museo naturalistico del Frignano, Pavullo nel Frignano 24831
Museo Naturalistico e della Civiltà Contadina, Berceto 23058
Museo Naturalistico F. Minà Palumbo, Castelbuono 23393
Museo Naturalistico G. Zanardo, Tambre 25670
Museo Naturalistico Libero Gatti, Copanello 23642
Museo Naturalistico Missionario, Chiusa Pesio 23554
Museo Naturalistico N. De Leone, Penne 24838
Museo Naturalistico O. Perini, Borca di Cadore 23162
Museo Naturalistico P. Barrasso, Caramanico Terme 23341
Museo Ornitologico e di Scienze Naturali, Ravenna 25082
Museo Pavese di Scienze Naturali, Pavia 24827
Museo Regionale di Scienze Naturali, Saint Pierre 25311
Museo Regionale di Scienze Naturali, Torino 25761
Museo Storico dela Caccia e del Territorio, Cerreto Guidi 23484
Museo Tridentino di Scienze Naturali, Trento 25797
Raccolta dell'Avifauna delle Marche, Montefortino 24527
Raccolta Naturalistica, Tagliolo Monferrato 25667
Raccolta Paleontologica e Preistorica, Narni 24612
Villa Godi Malinverni, Lugo di Vicenza 24240

Jamaica
Institute of Jamaica, Kingston 26069
Natural History Museum, Kingston 26076

Japan
Agricultural Museum, Miyazaki, Miyazaki-ken 26510
Ainu Museum, Sapporo 26708
Akiyoshidai Kagaku Hakubutsukan, Shuuhou 26770
Chiba-kenritsu Chuo Hakubutsukan, Chiba 26122
Ehime-kenritsu Hakubutsukan, Matsuyama 26484
Fukui City Natural Science Museum, Fukui 26141
Gifu-ken Hakubutsukan, Seki 26729
Hiwa Museum for Natural History, Hiwa 26225
Horaiji-san Shizenkagaku Hakubutsukan, Hourai 26233
Institute of Nature Study, Tokyo 26860
Kagoshima-ken Bunka Center, Kagoshima 26287
Kagoshima-kenritsu Hakubutsukan, Kagoshima 26288
Kenritsu Kagakukan Joetsu, Joetsu 26283
Kokuritsu Kagaku Hakubutsukan, Tokyo 26872
Miyazaki-ken Sogo Hakubutsukan, Miyazaki, Miyazaki-ken 26511
Nagaoka Municipal Science Museum, Nagaoka 26533
Okinawa-kenritsu Hakubutsukan, Naha 26572
Omachi Alpine Museum, Omachi 26633
Ryuga-Do Cave Museun, Tosayamada 26962
Saga-kenritsu Hakubutsukan, Saga 26691
Saitama-kenritsu Shizenshi Hakubutsukan, Nagatoro 26562
Towada Natural History Museum, Towadako 26966
The University Museum, Tokyo 26953
Yokosuka-shi Hakubutsukan, Yokosuka 27027

Jordan
Children's Heritage and Science Museum, Amman 27047
Jordan Natural History Museum, Irbid 27063

Korea, Republic
Jeju-do Folklore and Natural History Museum, Jeju 27194
Kyunghee University Museum, Seoul 27255
National Science Museum of Korea, Daejeon 27163
Seoul National Science Museum, Seoul 27275

Kuwait
Educational Science Museum, Kuwait 27305

Laos
Maison de Boua Kang Bung, Luang Prabang 27317

Latvia
Latvijas Dabas Muzejs, Rīga 27414

Lebanon
Musée de Préhistoire Libanaise, Beirut 27482

Lesotho
Lesotho National Museum, Maseru 27495

Liberia
Natural History Museum of Liberia, Monrovia 27500

Luxembourg
Musée National d'Histoire Naturelle, Luxembourg 27568

Malawi
Museum of Malawi, Blantyre 27611

Malaysia
Jabatan Muzium Sabah, Kota Kinabalu 27631
Muzium Negara, Kuala Lumpur 27644

Malta
Ghar Dalam Cave and Museum, Birzebbuga 27695
National Museum of Natural History, Mdina 27698
Natural Science Museum, Victoria 27710

Mauritius
Natural History Museum, Port Louis 27740

Mexico
Museo de Ciencia, Cuernavaca 27873
Museo de Ciencias de Ensenada, Ensenada 27915
Museo de Ciencias Explora, León 28054
Museo de Ciencias Naturales, Toluca 28543
Museo de Historia Natural, Mérida 28081
Museo de Historia Natural, México 28131
Museo de Historia Natural, Villahermosa 28610
Museo de Historia Natural, Zapotlán del Rey 28651
Museo de Historia Natural, La Paz 28043
Museo de Historia Natural Alfredo Dugès, Guanajuato 27970
Museo de Historia Natural del Ateneo Fuente, Saltillo 28365
Museo de Historia Natural Dr. Manuel M. Villada, Toluca 28545
Museo de Historia Natural Dr. Manuel Martínez Solórzano, Morelia 28248
Museo de Historia Natural José Vilet Brullet, Mexquitic 28214
Museo de Historia Natural Regional, Lerdo 28059
Museo de la Fauna y Ciencias Naturales, Monterrey 28233
Museo de los Altos de Chiapas, San Cristóbal de las Casas 28378
Museo del Desierto, Saltillo 28368
Museo Interactivo de Ciencia, Tecnología y Medio Ambiente Sol del Niño, Mexicali 28090
Museo Laguna del Caimán, Tlahualilo de Zaragoza 28522
Museo Miguel Álvarez del Toro, Tuxtla Gutiérrez 28574
Museo Parque de la Cristianía, Chapala 27815
Museo Universitario de Ciencias y Artes, Roma, México 28207

Moldova
Muzeul National de Etnografie si Istorie Naturala, Chişinău 28659

Mongolia
Natural History Museum, Ulaanbaatar 28685
Ulsyn Töw Muzei, Ulaanbaatar 28688

Morocco
Museum National d'Histoire Naturelle, Rabat 28708

Mozambique
Museu de História Natural, Maputo 28722
Museu Monstruário de Manica, Manica 28719

Myanmar
Natural History Museum, Yangon 28752

Namibia
Möwe Bay Museum, Möwe Bay 28762
National Museum of Namibia, Windhoek 28781
Okaukuejo Museum, Okaukuejo 28763
Swakopmund Museum, Swakopmund 28773

Netherlands
Bezoekerscentrum de Meinweg, Herkenbosch 29400
Bezoekerscentrum Mijl Op Zeven, Ospel 29681
Centrum voor Natuur en Landschap, Terschelling-West 29867
Collectie Anderson, Losser 29549
Ecodrome Zwolle, Zwolle 30083
EcoMare, De Koog 29067
Fort Kijkduin, Castricum 29055
Fries Natuurmuseum, Leeuwarden 29509
Missiemuseum Steyl, Steijl 29853
Museon, Den Haag 29106
Nationaal Natuurhistorisch Museum Naturalis, Leiden 29522
Natuurhistorisch en Volkenkundig Museum, Oudenbosch 29697
Natuurhistorisch Museum de Peel, Asten 28955

Natuurhistorisch Museum het Diorama, Nunspeet 29650
Natuurmuseum Ameland, Nes 29611
Natuurmuseum Brabant, Tilburg 29879
Natuurmuseum de Wielewaal, Lopik 29547
Natuurmuseum E. Heimans, Zaandam 30037
Natuurmuseum Enschede, Enschede 29238
Natuurmuseum het Drents-Friese Woud, Wateren 29985
Natuurmuseum Mar en Klif, Oudemirdum 29696
Natuurmuseum Nijmegen, Nijmegen 29635
De Noordwester, Vlieland 29954
Pieter Vermeulen Museum, Ijmuiden 29458
Regionaal Natuurmuseum Westflinge, Sint Pancras 29826
Tute-Natura, Bennekom 28977
Zeeuws Biologisch Museum, Oostkapelle 29673
Zomerkoestal uut 't Wold, Ruinerwold 29788

New Zealand
Auckland Museum and Auckland War Memorial Museum, Auckland 30104
Canterbury Museum, Christchurch 30124
South Canterbury Museum, Timaru 30265
Te Kauri Lodge Museum, Hamilton 30173
Te Papa, Wellington 30311

Niger
Musée National du Niger, Niamey 30324

Nigeria
National Museum, Oshogbo 30358
Natural History Museum, Ife 30343

Norway
Agder Naturmuseum, Kristiansand 30611
Bergen Museum, Bergen 30415
Massnes Villmarksmuseum, Bjordal 30434
Naturhistoriske Samlinger, Bergen 30425
Norsk Fjellmuseum, Lom 30651
Rana Museum, Mo i Rana 30675
Stabbursnes Naturhus og Museum, Indre Billefjord 30578
Sykkylven Naturhistorisk Museum, Sykkylven 30913
Vitenskapsmuseet, Trondheim 30946
Zoologisk Museum, Oslo 30772

Pakistan
Bahawalpur State Museum, Bhawalpur 31014
Dam Site Museum, Mangla 31045
Natural History Museum, Karachi 31030
Natural History Museum, Lahore 31041
Pakistan Museum of Natural History, Islamabad 31026

Panama
Museo Nacional de Panamá, Panamá City 31088

Papua New Guinea
Papua New Guinea National Museum and Art Gallery, Boroko 31090

Paraguay
Museo de Ciencias Naturales, Asunción 31098
Museo de Historia Natural del Paraquay, Asunción 31099

Peru
Museo de Arqueología e Historia Natural de Yungay, Yungay 31271
Museo de Ciencias, Huánuco 31171
Museo de Ciencias Naturales, Cusco 31153
Museo de Historia de Ciencias Naturales, Chuquimarca 31148
Museo de Historia Natural de la Universidad Antenor Orrego, Trujillo 31261
Museo de Historia Natural Javier Prado, Lima 31210
Museo de Historia Natural Víctor Vaca Aguinaga, Lambayeque 31196
Museo Multidisciplinario del Colegio La Salle, Lima 31220
Museo Municipal de Nazca y Casa Museo María Reiche, Nazca 31232
Museo Universitario y Museo de Anatomía General, Yanacancha 31268
Museos de la Universidad Nacional de Cajamarca, Cajamarca 31130

Philippines
Museum of Natural History, Los Baños 31345
Natural Science Museum, Marawi 31400
University of San Carlos Biological Museum, Cebu 31319
University of Santo Tomas Museum of Arts and Sciences, Manila 31398
University of Southern Philippines Museum, Cebu 31320

Poland
Jacek Malczewski Muzeum, Radom 31938
Muzeum Borów Tucholskich, Tuchola 32059
Muzeum Częstochowskie, Częstochowa 31545
Muzeum Ewolucji Instytutu Paleobiologii PAN, Warszawa 32094
Muzeum im. prof. Władysława Szafera, Ojców 31845
Muzeum Łowiectwa i Jeździectwa, Warszawa 32111
Muzeum Miejskie, Nowa Sól 31829
Muzeum Przyrodnicze, Jelenia Góra 31631
Muzeum Przyrodnicze, Kazimierz Dolny 31650
Muzeum Przyrodnicze Babiogórskiego Parku Narodowego, Zawoja 32214
Muzeum Przyrodnicze Bieszczadzkiego Parku Narodowego, Ustrzyki Dolne 32063
Muzeum Przyrodnicze Karkonoskiego Parku Narodowego, Jelenia Góra 31632
Muzeum Przyrodnicze Uniwersytetu Łódzkiego, Łódź 31775
Muzeum Przyrodnicze Uniwersytetu Wrocławskiego, Wrocław 32184
Muzeum Przyrodnicze Wolińskiego Parku Narodowego im. Prof. Adama Wodziczki, Międzyzdroje 31804
Muzeum Przyrodniczo-Leśne Słowińskiego Parku Narodowego, Smołdzino 31981
Muzeum Regionalne w Świebodzinie, Świebodzin 32015
Muzeum w Gorzowie Wielkopolskim, Gorzów Wielkopolski 31606
Muzeum w Wałbrzychu, Wałbrzych 32073
Muzeum Wiedzy o Środowisku, Poznań 31913
Muzeum Ziemi Piskiej, Oddział Muzem Okręgowego w Suwałkach, Pisz 31884
Muzeum Zoologiczne Instytutu Zoologii Uniwersytetu Jagiellońskiego, Kraków 31723
Ośrodek Muzealno-Dydaktyczny Wielkopolskiego Parku Narodowego, Mosina 31812

Portugal
Museu de História Natural, Coimbra 32259
Museu Nacional de História Natural, Lisboa 32309

Réunion
Muséum d'Histoire Naturelle, Saint-Denis 32421

Romania
Complexul Muzeal de Stiinţe ale Naturii Constanţa, Constanţa 32498
Complexul Muzeal de Stiintele Naturii Ion Borcea, Bacău 32432
Muzeul de Istorie Naturală din Sibiu, Sibiu 32592
Muzeul de Istorie Naturală Iaşi, Iaşi 32534
Muzeul de Ştiinţele Naturii, Dorohoi 32513
Muzeul de Ştiinţele Naturii, Focşani 32520
Muzeul de Stiinţele Naturii, Roman 32583
Muzeul de Ştiinţele Naturii Aiud, Aiud 32426
Muzeul de Şttiinte Naturale, Tulcea 32620
Muzeul Judeţean Argeş, Piteşti 32569
Muzeul Judeţean de Ştiinţele Naturii Prahova, Ploieşti 32573
Muzeul Judeţean Mureş-Secţia de St^Biinţele Naturii, Târgu Mureş 32611
Muzeul Naţional de Istorie Naturala Grigore Antipa, Bucureşti 32468

Russia
Brjanskij Gosudarstvennyj Obedinennyj Kraevedčeskij Muzej, Brjansk 32706
Chvalynskij Kraevedčeskij Muzej, Chvalynsk 32747
Darvinovskij Muzej, Moskva 33034
Kurskij Gosudarstvennyj Oblastnoj Kraevedčeskij Muzej, Kursk 32974
Lipeckij Oblastnoj Kraevedčeskij Muzej, Lipeck 32984
Miasskij Kraevedčeskij Muzej, Miass 33010
Muzej Brjanskij Les, Brjansk 32710
Muzej Gosudarstvennogo Prirodnogo Nacionalnogo Parka Losinogo Ostrova, Moskva 33102
Muzej-kvartira K.A. Timirjazeva, Moskva 33128
Muzej Prirody Burjatii, Ulan-Udė 33655
Muzej Zemlevedenija Moskovskogo Gosudarstvennogo Universiteta M.V. Lomonosova, Moskva 33160
Nižnetagilskij Muzej-Zapovednik Gornozavodskogo Dela Srednego Urala, Nižnij Tagil 33228
Novorossijskij Gosudarstvennyj Istoričeskij Muzej Zapovednik, Novorossijsk 33238
Novosibirskij Oblastnoj Kraevedčeskij Muzej, Novosibirsk 33244
Osinskij Kraevedčeskij Muzej, Osa 33273
Pjatigorskij Kraevedčeskij Muzej, Pjatigorsk 33322
Primorskij Gosudarstvennyj Muzej im. V.K. Arseneva, Vladivostok 33709
Pustozerskij Kompleksnyj Istoriko-prirodnyj Muzej, Narjan-Mar 33199
Sebežskij Muzej Prirody, Sebež 33514
Tajmyrskij Okružnoj Kraevedčeskij Muzej, Dudinka 32762

St. Pierre and Miquelon
Musée-Archives de Saint-Pierre, Saint-Pierre 33756

Senegal
Centre de Recherches et de Documentation du Sénégal, Saint-Louis 33784

Serbia-Montenegro
Gradski Muzej Vršac, Vršac 33928
Narodni Muzej Sabac, Sabac 33902
Prirodnjački Muzej, Beograd 33816
Prirodnjački Muzej Crne Gore, Podgorica 33890

Seychelles
National Museum, Victoria 33934

Slovakia
Městské Múzeum, Sabinov 34055
Městské Múzeum, Zlaté Moravce 34080
Múzeum Andreja Kmeťa, Martin 34025
Múzeum Madarskej Kultúry a Podunajska, Komárno 34003
Múzeum Spiša, Spišská Nová Ves 34064
Podtatranské Múzeum, Poprad 34045
Prírodovedné Múzeum, Bratislava 33977
Vlastivedné Múzeum v Hlohovci, Hlohovec 33997
Záhorské Múzeum, Skalica 34058

South Africa
Durban Natural Science Museum, Durban 34226
East London Museum, East London 34236
Natal Museum, Pietermaritzburg 34327
National Museum Bloemfontein, Bloemfontein 34189
Stevenson-Hamilton Memorial Information Centre, Skukuza 34377

Spain
Centre d'Interpretació p.n. d'Aigüestortes i Estany de Sant Maurici, Espot 34805
Collección de Arte y Ciencias Naturales, Ciudad Real 34719
Museo de Ciencias Naturales, Pamplona 35248
Museo de Ciencias Naturales de Alava, Vitoria-Gasteiz 35700
Museo de Ciencias Naturales de Tenerife, Santa Cruz de Tenerife 35414
Museo del Colegio Costa y Llobera, Port de Pollença 35288
Museo del Seminario Diocesano, Burgos 34633
Museo Valenciano de Historia Natural, Valencia 35612
Museu Darder d'Història Natural, Banyoles 34528
Museu de Ciències Naturals de Barcelona, Barcelona 34557
Museu de Granollers-Ciències Naturals, Granollers 34884
Museu de Vilafranca-Museu del Vi, Vilafranca del Penedès 35659
Museu Municipal Guilleries, Sant Hilari Sacalm 35402
Museu Regional d'Artá, Artá 34489

Sri Lanka
National Museum of Natural History, Colombo 35751

Sudan
Natural History Museum, Medani 35771
Natural History Museum, Port Sudan 35774

Sweden
Ájtte - Svenskt Fjäll- och Samemuseum, Jokkmokk 35982
Fjärilshuset Haga Tradgard, Stockholm 36241
Gotlands Naturmuseum, Visby 36415
Naturens Hus, Stockholm 36266
Naturhistoriska Museet, Malmö 36078
Naturhistoriska Museet i Göteborg, Göteborg 35916
Naturhistoriska Riksmuseet, Stockholm 36267
Naturum Stendörren, Nyköping 36127
Nordens Ark, Hunnebostrand 35968
Rättviks Konstmuseum och Naturmuseum, Rättvik 36159
Regionmuseet Kristianstad, Kristianstad 36018

Switzerland
Bündner Natur-Museum, Chur 36633
Collection d'Histoire Naturelle, Le Locle 36887
Musée Cantonal d'Histoire Naturelle, Sion 37174
Musée de la Banderette, Travers 37252
Musée d'Histoire Naturelle, La Chaux-de-Fonds 36629
Musée d'Histoire Naturelle, Fribourg 36716
Musée Jurassien des Sciences Naturelles, Porrentruy 37029
Museo Cantonale di Storia Naturale, Lugano 36899
Museum, Zofingen 37366
Muséum d'Histoire Naturelle, Genève 36752
Muséum d'Histoire Naturelle, Neuchâtel 36986
Nationalparkhaus, Zernez 37359
Natur-Museum Luzern, Luzern 36914
Naturama Aargau, Aarau 36427
Naturhistorisches Museum, Heiden 36799
Naturhistorisches Museum Basel, Basel 36514
Naturhistorisches Museum der Burgergemeinde Bern, Bern 36547
Naturkundemuseum, Altdorf, Uri 36449
Naturmuseum, Sankt Gallen 37106
Naturmuseum Solothurn, Solothurn 37186
Naturwissenschaftliche Sammlung, Stans 37204
Naturwissenschaftliche Sammlungen der Stadt Winterthur, Winterthur 37338
Naturwissenschaftliche Sammlungen des Kantons Glarus, Engi 36683
Schweizerisches Alpines Museum, Bern 36552

Tanzania
Manyara Museum, Manyara 37461
Mikumi Museum, Mikumi 37463
Ngurdoto Gate Museum, Arusha 37454
Serengeti Museum, Arusha 37455

Thailand
Nonthaburi Natural History Museum, Nonthaburi 37522
Parasite Museum, Bangkok 37492

Trinidad and Tobago
National Museum and Art Gallery of Trinidad and Tobago, Port-of-Spain 37552

Uganda
Game and Fisheries Museum, Entebbe 37822
Uganda Museum, Kampala 37829

Ukraine
Ivano-Frankovsk Local Museum, Ivano-Frankovsk 37854
Khmelnitski Regional Museum, Chmelnickij 37844
Kirovograd Regional Museum of Local History, Art and Nature, Kirovograd 37861
State Museum of Natural History of NAS of Ukraine, Lviv 37889
Vinnitsa Museum of Local Lore, Vinnica 37911
Zakarpatskij Kraeznavčij Muzej, Užgorod 37909

United Arab Emirates
Sharjah Natural History Museum, Sharjah 37925

United Kingdom
At-Bristol, Bristol 38349
Bath Royal Literary and Scientific Institution, Bath 38110
Bournemouth Natural Science Society Museum, Bournemouth 38285
Bracken Hall Countryside Centre, Baildon 38057
City Museum and Art Gallery, Plymouth 40209
Cliffe Castle Museum, Keighley 39327
College Museum, Epsom 38944
Dorman Memorial Museum, Middlesbrough 39948
Down House, Downe 38771
Dunnet Pavilion, Castletown 38507
Edinburgh University Natural History Collections, Edinburgh 38881
Eton College Natural History Museum, Eton 38950
Fleetwood Museum, Fleetwood 38995
Giants Causeway Visitor Centre, Bushmills 38425
Guernsey Museum and Art Gallery, Saint Peter Port 40424
Hancock Museum, Newcastle-upon-Tyne 40036
Horniman Museum, London 39668
Ipswich Museum, Ipswich 39305
John Dony Field Centre, Bushmead 38422
John Moore Countryside Museum, Tewkesbury 40690
King's Lynn Museum, King's Lynn 39370
Kinneil Museum and Roman Fortlet, Bo'ness 38276
Landmark Forest Heritage Park, Carrbridge 38496
Maidstone Museum and Bentlif Art Gallery, Maidstone 39877
Museum and Art Gallery Leicester, Leicester 39464
Museum of Lancashire, Preston 40267
Museum of the Holmesdale Natural History Club, Reigate 40307
Natural History Department, Hitchin 39250
Natural History Museum, Colchester 38613
Natural History Museum, London 39733
Natural History Museum, Nottingham 40111
Natural History Museum, Portsmouth 40256
North Lincolnshire Museum, Scunthorpe 40460
The Old Byre Heritage Centre, Dervaig 38724
The Oxfordshire Museum, Woodstock 40925
Perth Museum and Art Gallery, Perth 40185
Phillips Countryside Museum, Brokerswood 38374
Royal Albert Memorial Museum and Art Gallery, Exeter 38957
Royal Naval Museum Portsmouth, Portsmouth 40258
SEARCH-Centre, Gosport 39103
Sound Visitor Centre, Port Saint Mary 40234
University Museum, Dundee 38805
Warwickshire Museum, Warwick 40796
Wiltshire Heritage Museum and Gallery, Devizes 38726
Wood End Museum, Scarborough 40457
Yorkshire Museum, York 40973

Uruguay
Museo Antártico, Montevideo 40992
Museo Antonio Lussich, Punta Ballena 41034
Museo de Mercedes, Mercedes 40983
Museo Fernando García, Canelones 40976
Museo Nacional de Historia Natural y Antropología, Montevideo 41018

U.S.A.
Academy of Natural Sciences of Philadelphia Museum, Philadelphia 46386
A.D. Buck Museum of Natural History and Science, Tonkawa 48029
Alabama Museum of Natural History, Tuscaloosa 48112
Alaska Museum of Natural History, Eagle River 43034
American Museum of Natural History, New York 45759
Anniston Museum of Natural History, Anniston 41231
Arizona-Sonora Desert Museum, Tucson 48081
The Art Museum of Los Gatos and the Nature Museum of Los Gatos, Los Gatos 44954
Austin Nature and Science Center, Austin 41407
Bailey-Matthews Shell Museum, Sanibel 47397
Bear Mountain Trailside Museums Wildlife Center, Bear Mountain 41554
Bergen Museum of Art and Science, Hackensack 43857
Bernice Pauahi Bishop Museum, Honolulu 44072
Biology Department Teaching Museum, Muncie 45556
Black Hills Museum of Natural History, Hill City 44022
Blue Hills Trailside Museum, Milton 45352
Bluestone Museum, Hinton 44039
Bolin Wildlife Exhibit and Antique Collection, McKinney 45036
Boone County Historical Center, Boone 41783
Boonshoft Museum of Discovery, Dayton 42799
Bowers Science Museum, Cortland 42653
Bradbury Science Museum, Los Alamos 44887
Branigan Cultural Center, Las Cruces 44657
Brazos Valley Museum of Natural History, Bryan 41974
Brazosport Museum of Natural Science, Brazosport 41873
Brazosport Museum of Natural Science, Clute 42506
Brevard Museum, Cocoa 42508
Buckhorn Museum, San Antonio 47246

Buffalo Museum of Science, Buffalo 41985
Burke Museum of Natural History and Culture, Seattle 47529
Burpee Museum of Natural History, Rockford 46959
Burritt on the Mountain, Huntsville 44172
Cable Natural History Museum, Cable 42022
Cairo Museum, Vicksburg 48227
California Academy of Sciences Museum, San Francisco 47312
Call of the Wild Museum, Gaylord 43636
Callkins Field Museum, Iowa Falls 44250
Calvert Marine Museum, Solomons 47665
Cape Cod Museum of Natural History, Brewster 41882
Cape Fear Museum, Wilmington 48659
Capitol Reef National Park Visitor Center, Torrey 48039
Carl G. Fenner Nature Center, Lansing 44641
Carlsbad Caverns National Park, Carlsbad 42108
Carnegie Museum of Natural History, Pittsburgh 46511
Carrie Weedon Natural Science Museum, Galesville 43600
Castine Scientific Society Museum, Castine 42136
Cedar Key State Park Museum, Cedar Key 42154
The Centennial Museum at the University of Texas at El Paso, El Paso 43113
Central Missouri State University Archives and Museum, Warrensburg 48315
Charles R. Conner Museum, Pullman 46743
The Chicago Academy of Sciences Peggy Notebaert Nature Museum, Chicago 42313
Children's Discovery Museum of Central Illinois, Bloomington 41741
Children's Museum of History, Natural History and Science at Utica, New York, Utica 48169
Chiricahua Museum, Willcox 48623
Cincinnati Museum Center, Cincinnati 42402
Cleveland Museum of Natural History, Cleveland 42467
College of Eastern Utah Prehistoric Museum, Price 46693
Connecticut State Museum of Natural History, Storrs 47835
Conner Prairie Living History Museum, Fishers 43324
Cosi Toledo, Toledo 48019
Cottonlandia Museum, Greenwood 43835
Cracker Trail Museum, Zolfo Springs 48827
Crane Point Hammock Museum, Marathon 45132
Crowley Museum, Sarasota 47452
Cumberland Science Museum, Nashville 45615
Cylburn Nature Museum, Baltimore 41462
D. Ralph Hostetter Museum of Natural History, Harrisonburg 43930
Dallas Museum of Natural History, Dallas 42752
Death Valley National Park Visitor Center and Museum, Death Valley 42826
Delano Heritage Park, Delano 42861
Delaware Museum of Natural History, Wilmington 48651
Delbridge Museum, Sioux Falls 47642
Denver Museum of Nature and Science, Denver 42887
Diablo Valley College Museum, Pleasant Hill 46551
The Dinosaur Museum, Saint Louis 47119
The Discovery Museum, Bridgeport 41890
Discovery Place, Charlotte 42239
East Tennessee Discovery Center, Knoxville 44516
East-West Center, Honolulu 44075
Eastern California Museum, Independence 44197
EcoTarium, Worcester 48752
Ehrhart Museum, Antwerp 41235
Ehrman Mansion, Tahoma 47928
El Campo Museum of Natural History, El Campo 43105
Elgin Public Museum, Elgin 43129
Environmental Education Center, Basking Ridge 41518
Everhart Museum of Natural History, Science and Art, Scranton 47517
Exhibit Museum of Natural History, Ann Arbor 41216
Fairbanks Museum and Planetarium, Saint Johnsbury 47098
Fairfax Museum and Visitor Center, Fairfax 43260
Fernbank Museum of Natural History, Atlanta 41341
Field Museum, Chicago 42325
Field Museum of Natural History, Chicago 42326
Flint Ridge State Memorial Museum, Glenford 43690
Florida Museum of Natural History, Gainesville 43581
Forest History Center, Grand Rapids 43761
Fort Ancient Museum, Oregonia 46180
Fort Caroline Memorial Museum, Jacksonville 44294
Fort Hancock Museum, Sandy Hook 47391
Fort Raleigh, Manteo 45126
Fort Roosevelt Natural Science and History Museum, Hanford 43903
Frank H. McClung Museum, Knoxville 44519
Fresno Metropolitan Museum, Fresno 43559
George B. Dorr Museum of Natural History, Bar Harbor 41499
George Washington Carver Museum, Tuskegee Institute 48122
Georgia Museum of Natural History, Athens 41319
Georgia Southern University Museum, Statesboro 47792
Georgia's Stone Mountain Park, Stone Mountain 47827
Gilman Museum, Hellertown 43985
Glacier National Park Museum, West Glacier 48524
Glen Helen Ecology Institute Trailside Museum, Yellow Springs 48783
Great Lakes Science Center, Cleveland 42473
Great Valley Museum of Natural History, Modesto 45427
Gunnison Museum of Natural History, Pawling 46315
Hands on Children's Museum, Olympia 46141
Hands-on House, Lancaster 44623
Harbor Branch Oceanographic Institution, Fort Pierce 43440
Harvard Museum of Natural History, Cambridge 42041
Hastings Museum, Hastings 43956
Heard Natural Science Museum, McKinney 45038
Herrett Center for Arts and Science, Twin Falls 48124
Hi-Desert Nature Museum, Yucca Valley 48817
High Desert Museum, Bend 41623
Hinchman House, Nantucket 45596
Horizons Unlimited Supplementary Educational Center, Salisbury 47219
Houston Museum of Natural Science, Houston 44124
Howard B. Owens Science Center, Lanham-Seabrook 44639
Humboldt State University Natural History Museum, Arcata 41246
Idaho Museum of Natural History, Pocatello 46571
Illinois State Museum, Springfield 47737
Imagination Station Science Museum, Wilson 48669
Imagisphere Children's Museum, North Richland Hills 46005
Indian City U.S.A., Anadarko 41191
Indian Springs State Park Museum, Flovilla 43351
Indiana State Museum, Indianapolis 44224
International Wildlife Museum, Tucson 48090
Iredell Museum of Arts Heritage, Statesville 47794
James A. McFaul Environmental Center of Bergen County, Wyckoff 48768
James Ford Bell Museum of Natural History, Minneapolis 45387
James R. Slater Museum of Natural History, Tacoma 47919
Jean Lafitte National Historical Park and Preserve, New Orleans 45728
John Burroughs Memorial, Roxbury 47024
John Hutchings Museum of Natural History, Lehi 44713
Joseph Moore Museum, Richmond 46861
Jurica Nature Museum, Lisle 44811
Kansas City Museum/Science City at Union Station, Kansas City 44400
Kenosha Public Museum, Kenosha 44441
Kingman Museum of Natural History, Battle Creek 41539
Kirkpatrick Science and Air Space Museum at Omniplex, Oklahoma City 46114
Lafayette Natural History Museum, Lafayette 44571
Lake Erie Nature and Science Center, Bay Village 41547
Lake Meredith Aquatic and Wildlife Museum, Fritch 43566
Lanier Museum of Natural History, Buford 41992
Las Vegas Natural History Museum, Las Vegas 44670
Laura Ingalls Wilder Museum, Burr Oak 42012
Lava Beds National Monument, Tulelake 48101
Lawrence Hall of Science, Berkeley 41644
L.C. Bates Museum, Hinckley 44034
Libby Museum, Wolfeboro 48723
Limberlost State Historic Site, Geneva 43641
Lindsay Wildlife Museum, Walnut Creek 48291
Living Museum at Tulsa Zoo, Tulsa 48105
Lora Robins Gallery of Design from Nature, Richmond 46881
McKinley Museum and McKinley National Memorial, Canton 42090
Mary Brogan Museum of Art and Science, Tallahassee 47935
Massacre Rocks State Park Museum, American Falls 41169
Maturango Museum of the Indian Wells Valley, Ridgecrest 46895
May Natural History Museum and Museum of Space Exploration, Colorado Springs 42539
Mayborn Museum, Waco 48265
Memphis Pink Palace Museum, Memphis 45244
Michigan State University Museum, East Lansing 43054
Mill Grove, The Audubon Wildlife Sanctuary, Audubon 41379
Milton J. Rubenstein Museum of Science and Technology, Syracuse 47910
Milwaukee Public Museum, Milwaukee 45368
Mississippi Museum of Natural Science, Jackson 44281
Mississippi River Museum at Mud Island River Park, Memphis 45245
Mohonk Preserve, Gardiner 43622
Monte L. Bean Life Science Museum, Provo 46735
Monterey State Historic Park, Monterey 45457
Montshire Museum of Science, Norwich 46041
Morningside Nature Center, Gainesville 43583
Morro Bay State Park Museum of Natural History, Morro Bay 45515
Morrow Mountain State Park Museum, Albemarle 41092
Mount Washington Museum, North Conway 45989
Mousley Museum of Natural History, Yucaipa 48815
Murie Museum, Kelly 44429
Museum of Cultural and Natural History, Mount Pleasant 45536
Museum of Long Island Natural Sciences, Stony Brook 47831
Museum of Natural History, Marshall 45180
Museum of Natural History, Providence 46722
The Museum of Natural History, Stevens Point 47807
Museum of Natural History, Urbana 48163
Museum of Natural History, Eugene 43224
Museum of Natural Science, Baton Rouge 41532
Museum of Science and Industry, Chicago 42349
Museum of Southwestern Biology, Albuquerque 41105
Museum of Texas Tech University, Lubbock 44991
Museum of the Hudson Highlands, Cornwall-on-Hudson 42642
Museum of Western Colorado, Grand Junction 43748
Napa Valley Museum, Yountville 48809
Natchez Trace Parkway Study Collection, Tupelo 48109
National Museum of Natural History, Washington 48379
Natural History Museum, Portales 46617
Natural History Museum, Lawrence 44685
Natural History Museum of Los Angeles County, Los Angeles 44934
Natural Science Center of Greensboro, Greensboro 43818
Nature Museum, Charlotte 42245
Nature Museum at Grafton, Grafton 43738
Nevada State Museum, Carson City 42118
Neversink Valley Area Museum, Cuddebackville 42718
New Canaan Nature Center, New Canaan 45681
New Jersey State Museum, Trenton 48057
New Mexico Museum of Natural History and Science, Albuquerque 41107
North Carolina Museum of Life and Science, Durham 43024
North Carolina Museum of Natural Sciences, Raleigh 46777
The North Museum of Natural History and Science, Lancaster 44630
Northeastern Nevada Museum, Elko 43146
Nylander Museum, Caribou 42103
Oakland Museum of California, Oakland 46067
Ojai Valley Museum, Ojai 46108
Oregon Museum of Science and Industry, Portland 46638
The Oyster and Maritime Museum of Chincoteague, Chincoteague 42383
Pacific Grove Museum of Natural History, Pacific Grove 46253
Palm Springs Desert Museum, Palm Springs 46267
Paterson Museum, Paterson 46311
Peabody Museum of Natural History, New Haven 45698
Pember Museum of Natural History, Granville 43770
Petaluma Wildlife and Natural Science Museum, Petaluma 46367
Pinnacles National Monument, Paicines 46261
Pittsburg State University Natural History Museum, Pittsburg 46504
Portland Children's Museum Second Generation, Portland 46642
The Pratt Museum of Natural History, Amherst 41181
Princeton University Museum of Natural History, Princeton 46704
Putnam Museum of History and Natural Science, Davenport 42786
The Quincy Museum, Quincy 46761
Raymond M. Alf Museum of Paleontology, Claremont 42420
Reading Public Museum and Art Gallery, Reading 46809
Red Rock Museum, Church Rock 42394
Redding Museum of Art and History, Redding 46819
Richard H. Schmidt Museum of Natural History, Emporia 43185
River Hills Park Museum, Chesterfield 42289
River Legacy Living Science Center, Arlington 41262
Robert A. Vines Environmental Science Center, Houston 44134
Robert Toombs House, Washington 48411
Rochester Museum, Rochester 46944
Rocky Mountain National Park Museum, Estes Park 43217
Roger Tory Peterson Institute of Natural History Museum, Jamestown 44313
Saint Joseph Museum, Saint Joseph 47109
Sam Noble Oklahoma Museum of Natural History, Norman 45976
San Bernardino County Museum, Redlands 46824
San Diego Natural History Museum, San Diego 47295
Santa Barbara Museum of Natural History, Santa Barbara 47405
Santa Cruz Museum of Natural History, Santa Cruz 47414
Schiele Museum of Natural History, Gastonia 43632
Science and Technology Museum of Atlanta, Atlanta 41358
Science Center of Pinellas County, Saint Petersburg 47177
Science Center of West Virginia, Bluefield 41759
Science Museum of Minnesota, Saint Paul 47166
Science Museum of Western Virginia, Roanoke 46930
Sciworks, Winston-Salem 48704
Scriver Museum of Montana Wildlife and Hall of Bronze, Browning 41961
Smithsonian Institution, Washington 48393
South Florida Museum, Bradenton 41863
South Florida Museum of Natural History, Dania Beach 42773
Southern Oregon University Museum of Vertebrate Natural History, Ashland 41297
Southern Vermont Natural History Museum, Marlboro 45171
Spartanburg Science Center, Spartanburg 47719
Springfield Science Museum, Springfield 47750
Spurlock Museum, Urbana 48164
Squam Lakes Natural Science Center, Holderness 44050
Stamford Museum and Nature Center, Stamford 47768
Stephen C. Foster State Park, Fargo 43289
Stephens Museum, Fayette 43307
Sternberg Museum of Natural History, Hays 43971
Strecker Museum Complex, Waco 48268
Sulphur Creek Nature Center, Hayward 43974
Tallahassee Museum of History and Natural Science, Tallahassee 47938
Texas Memorial Museum of Science and History, Austin 41421
Thames Museum, Newport 45934
Thornton W. Burgess Museum, Sandwich 47389
Trailside Nature and Science Center, Mountainside 45550
Trailside Nature Center and Museum, Cincinnati 42411
Trailside Nature Museum, Cross River 42711
Tucker Tower Nature Center Park Museum, Ardmore 41253
University of Alaska Museum, Fairbanks 43258
University of Colorado Museum, Boulder 41837
University of Iowa Museum of Natural History, Iowa City 44249
University of Nebraska State Museum, Lincoln 44793
UNLV Barrick Museum, Las Vegas 44674
Utah Field House of Natural History State Park, Vernal 48217
Utah Museum of Natural History, Salt Lake City 47235
Virginia Living Museum, Newport News 45940
Virginia Museum of Natural History, Martinsville 45193
Voyageurs National Park Museum, International Falls 44241
Wagner Free Institute of Science, Philadelphia 46462
Walker Wildlife and Indian Artifacts Museum, Walker 48283
Wayne State University Museum of Natural History, Detroit 42937
Weinberg Nature Center, Scarsdale 47493
Westmoreland Sanctuary, Bedford Corners 41584
Weymouth Woods-Sandhills Nature Preserve Museum, Southern Pines 47709
W.H. Over Museum, Vermillion 48216
Whitaker Center for Science and the Arts, Harrisburg 43927
White Memorial Conservation Center, Litchfield 44814
White Pine Public Museum, Ely 43176
Willamette Science and Technology Center, Eugene 43229
William Pryor Letchworth Museum, Castile 42135
Wind River Historical Center Dubois Museum, Dubois 42990
World Museum of Natural History, Riverside 46924
The Yosemite Museum, Yosemite National Park 48804
Youth Science Institute, San Jose 47358

Uzbekistan
Respublikanskij Prirodovedčeskij Muzej, Taškent 48859

Venezuela
Museo de Ciencias, Caracas 48916

Needlework

Armenia
State Folk Art Museum of Armenia, Erevan 00690

Australia
Embroiderers Guild Museum, Mile End 01253

Belgium
Musée de la Dentelle, Marche-en-Famenne 03608

Czech Republic
Městské a Textilni Muzeum, Dvůr Králové nad Labem 08337
Muzeum Krajky, Prachatice 08561
Muzeum Krajky, Vamberk 08708
Okresní Muzeum, Chomutov 08314

Finland
Rauman Museo, Rauma 09983

France
150 ans de Couture, Aix-les-Bains 10258
Musée de la Coutellerie, Nogent-en-Bassigny 13350
Musée de la Dentelle, Caudry 11091
Musée de la Dentelle à la Main, Arlanc-en-Livradois 10412
Musée de la Dentelle au Point d'Alençon, Alençon 10280
Musée des Manufactures de Dentelles, Retournac 13950

Musée-Maison des Dentelles et du Point d'Argentan, Argentan 10406

Germany
Das Deutsche Stickmuster-Museum Celle, Celle 16453
Fingerhutmuseum, Creglingen 16509
Klöppelmuseum und Heimatkundliche Sammlung, Abenberg 15387
Museum der Schwalm, Schwalmstadt 19871
Museum Klingelbeutel, Gaukönigshofen 17207
Museum Schloß Schwarzenberg, Schwarzenberg, Erzgebirge 19884
Nadlerhaus, Hundshübel 17867
Plauener Spitzenmuseum, Plauen 19412

Greece
Binos Collection, Mytilini 21084
Folklore Museum of Avlon, Avlon 20908
Monastery of the Taxiarchs, Aigion 20814

Hungary
Csipkeház, Kiskunhalas 21459
Tájház, Buzsák 21394

Italy
Museo del Merletto, Offida 24670
Museo del Merletto, Venezia 25929

Korea, Republic
Museum of Korean Embroidery, Seoul 27260

Netherlands
Museum voor Naaldkunst, Wedde 29987
Naaimachinemuseum, Nieuweschans 29621
Vingerhoedmuseum, Veenendaal 29929

Réunion
Musée-Ecole de Broderie, Cilaos 32418

Spain
Museu Marès de la Punta, Arenys de Mar 34480

Switzerland
Textilmuseum, Sankt Gallen 37108

United Kingdom
Allhallows Museum of Lace and Antiquities, Honiton 39259
Cowper and Newton Museum, Olney 40130
Embroiderers' Guild Museum Collection, East Molesey 38847
Forge Mill Needle Museum and Bordesley Abbey Visitor Centre, Redditch 40302
Guildford Museum, Guildford 39138
Hardwick Hall, Chesterfield 38555
London Sewing Machine Museum, London 39699
Luton Museum and Art Gallery, Luton 39845
Manor Cottage Heritage Centre, Southwick 40560
Moravian Museum, Pudsey 40272
Museum of Costume and Textiles, Nottingham 40109
Museum of Nottingham Lace, Nottingham 40110
Rachel Kay Shuttleworth Textile Collections, Padiham 40156
Shellin Antiques and Irish Lace Museum, Enniskillen 38942
Traquair House, Innerleithen 39291

U.S.A.
Barbara Fritchie House, Frederick 43525

Numismatics

Argentina
Museo del Banco Provincia de Córdoba, Córdoba 00300
Museo del Pasado Cuyano, Mendoza 00437
Museo Numismático Dr. José Evaristo Uriburu, Buenos Aires 00234

Australia
Banking and Currency Museum, Kadina 01128

Austria
Heimatkundehaus und Münzkabinett, Sankt Marien 02582
Münzensammlung, Graz 01925
Notgeld-Sammlung 1918/20, Bad Wimsbach-Neydharting 01724
Salzburger Museum Carolino Augusteum, Salzburg 02551

Belgium
Cabinet des Médailles, Bruxelles 03277
Munt- en Penningkabinet van de Provincie Limburg, Tongeren 03782
Musée de la Banque Nationale de Belgique, Bruxelles 03303

Bolivia
Museo de la Casa Nacional de la Moneda, Potosí 03903

Brazil
Centro Cultural Banco do Brasil, Rio de Janeiro 04319
Museu da Fazenda Federal, Rio de Janeiro 04346
Museu de Arqueologia e Etnologia da Universidade de São Paulo, São Paulo 04512
Museu de Valores, Rio de Janeiro 04365
Museu de Valores do Banco Central do Brasil, Brasília 04001
Museu do Banco de Crédito Real de Minas Gerais, Juiz de Fora 04156
Museu Dom Inocencio, Campanha 04019
Museu e Arquivo Histórico do Centro Cultural Banco do Brasil, Rio de Janeiro 04379
Museu Histórico do Piaú, Teresina 04566
Museu Numismático e Filatélico, Rio de Janeiro 04392

Canada
Currency Museum of the Bank of Canada, Ottawa 06079
Royal Canadian Mint, Winnipeg 06841

China, People's Republic
Ancient Coins Museum, Beijing 06941
Nansong Qian Currency Museum, Hangzhou 07086
Suzhou National Treasure Numismatics Museum, Suzhou 07253

Colombia
Colección Numismática, Bogotá 07387
Museo Casa de la Moneda, Mariquita 07511
Museo de Historia Económica, Bogotá 07404

Costa Rica
Museo de Numismática, San José 07657

Croatia
Arheološki Muzej Zagreb, Zagreb 07809

Cuba
Museo Numismático, La Habana 07994

Cyprus
Museum of the History of Cypriot Coinage, Lefkosia 08204

Czech Republic
Muzeum Prostějovska, Prostějov 08629
Východočeské Muzeum, Pardubice 08534

Denmark
Den Kongelige Mønt- og Medaillesamling, København 08934

Ecuador
Museo Manuela Sáenz, Quito 09213

Ethiopia
Ethnographic Museum, Addis Ababa 09398

Finland
Raha- ja Mitalikokoelma, Helsinki 09521

France
Cabinet des Medailles et Antiques, Paris 13478
Cabinet des Monnaies et Médailles, Marseille 12845
Cabinet des Monnais et Médailles du Revest-les-Eaux, Le Revest-les-Eaux 12477
Institut Tessin, Paris 13517
Musée Archéologique, Lectoure 12503
Musée de la Monnaie, Paris 13557
Musée Gallo-Romain d'Aoste, Aoste 10382
Musée Numismatique J. Puig, Perpignan 13709

Germany
Akademisches Münzkabinett, Jena 17937
Allgäu-Museum, Kempten 18059
Burg Neuhaus, Wolfsburg 20658
Finanzgeschichtliche Sammlung der Bundesfinanzakademie, Brühl, Rheinland 16376
Geldgeschichtliches Museum, Köln 18138
Geldmuseum der Deutschen Bundesbank, Frankfurt am Main 17048
Johann-David-Köhler-Haus, Colditz 16492
Kestner-Museum, Hannover 17599
Münzkabinett, Dresden 16698
Münzkabinett, Berlin 16044
Münzkabinett der Preussag AG, Hannover 17605
Münzkabinett im Stadtarchiv Mainz, Mainz 18603
Museum am Mühlturm, Isny 17930
Niedersächsisches Münzkabinett der Deutschen Bank, Hannover 17608
Orientalisches Münzkabinett Jena, Jena 17946
Sammlung Dr. Berkowitz, Hannover 17610
Siegelmuseum Schloß Waldenburg, Waldenburg, Württemberg 20362
Staatliche Münzsammlung, München 18913
Stadtmuseum Schongau, Schongau 19841
Städtische Münzsammlung im Archiv der Hansestadt Lübeck, Lübeck 18543
Universitätssammlung antiker und nachantiker Münzen und Medaillen, Tübingen 20230

Greece
Kyrou Collection, Athinai 20870
Museum of Banknotes of the Ionian Bank, Corfu 20933
Numismatic Museum, Athens, Athinai 20897

Haiti
Unité Musée Numismatique, Port-au-Prince 21296

Hungary
Banknote and Coin Collection of the National Bank of Hungary, Budapest 21328

Iceland
Myntsafn Sedlabanka og Thjódminjasafns, Reykjavík 21657

India
Aithasic Puratatva Sangrahalaya, Delhi 21763
Archaeological Museum, Gorakhpur 21811
Archaeological Museum, Pune 21986
Chattishgarh Mudra Sangrahalaya, Katora Talab 21885
Government Museum, Chennai 21744
Governmental Educational Museum, Muzaffarnagar 21957
Rajkiya Sangrahalaya, Udaipur 22045

Iran
Sekkeh Museum, Kerman 22254

Israel
Kadman Numismatic Pavilion, Tel Aviv 22764

Italy
Musei Civici agli Eremitani, Padova 24733
Museo Alessi, Enna 23732
Museo Berenziano, Cremona 23679
Museo Bottacin, Padova 24736
Museo Carlo Venturini, Massa Lombarda 24317
Museo della Fondazione Mandralisca, Cefalù 23466
Museo dell'Accademia di Sant'Anselmo, Aosta 22902
Museo di Archeologia, Pavia 24823
Museo Numismatico della Zecca, Roma 25240
Piccolo Museo della Moneta, Vicenza 25996
Pinacoteca e Museo Civico, Volterra 26053

Jamaica
Money Museum, Kingston 26073

Japan
Mint Museum, Osaka 26655
Nihon Ginko Kin'yu Kenkyujo Kahei Hakubutsukan, Tokyo 26904

Jordan
Coins Museum, Amman 27048

Malaysia
Bak Negara Muzium Matawang, Kuala Lumpur 27638
Muzium Numismatik Maybank, Kuala Lumpur 27645

Malta
Cathedral Museum, Mdina 27697

Mexico
Museo de Numismática del Estado de México, Toluca 28548
Museo Pedro Coronel, Zacatecas 28638

Monaco
Musée des Timbres et des Monnaies, Monaco 28668

Myanmar
State Library and Museum, Kyaukpyu 28732

Nepal
Numismatic Museum, Kathmandu 28790

Netherlands
Het Koninklijk Penningkabinet, Leiden 29519
Munt- en Penningkabinet van de Spaar- en Voorschotbank, Surhuisterveen 29860
Museum van de Kanselarij der Nederlandse Orden, Apeldoorn 28926
Nederlands Economisch Penningkabinet, Rotterdam 29768
Het Nederlands Muntmuseum, Utrecht 29905
Veluws Museum van Oudheden - Stadsmuseum, Harderwijk 29342

Norway
Den Kongelige Mynts Museum, Kongsberg 30601
Løten Bankmuseum, Løten 30656
Myntkabinett, Oslo 30745
Sparebankmuseet, Oslo 30763

Peru
Museo Numismático del Banco Continental, Arequipa 31116
Museo Numismático del Banco Wiese, Lima 31223
Museo Provincial José María Morante, Arequipa 31117

Poland
Gabinet Numizmatyczny Mennicy Państwowej, Warszawa 32083
Muzeum Emeryka Hutten-Czapskiego, Kraków 31700
Muzeum Sztuki Medalierskiej, Wrocław 32187
Muzeum w Chorzowie, Chorzów 31534
Zakład Narodowy im. Ossolińskich, Wrocław 32193

Portugal
Museu Eng. António de Almeida, Porto 32337
Museu Numismático Português, Lisboa 32313

Russia
Chakasskij Respublikanskij Kraevedčeskij Muzej, Abakan 32627
Gosudarstvennyj Okružnoj Muzej Prirody i Čeloveka Goroda Chanty-Mansijsk, Chanty-Mansijsk 32744
Regionalnyj Muzej Severnogo Priladožja, Sortavala 33547

Slovakia
NBS-Múzeum Mincí a Medailí, Kremnica 34007

South Africa
ABSA Group Museum, Johannesburg 34266
South African Mint Museum-Coin World, Centurion 34216

Spain
Colección de Numismática, Vitoria-Gasteiz 35696
Gabinete Numismático de Cataluña, Barcelona 34542
Museo de la Fabrica nacional de Moneda y Timbre, Madrid 35024
Museo de Palencia, Palencia 35214
Museu Episcopal de Vic, Vic 35652
Sala d'Arqueologia i Gabinet Numismàtic, Lleida 34972
Yacimiento-Museo Arqueológico, Garray 34838

Sweden
Kungl. Myntkabinettet, Stockholm 36251
Uppsala Universitet Myntkabinett, Uppsala 36364

Switzerland
Glücksspielmuseum, Saxon 37127
Münzkabinett und Antikensammlung der Stadt Winterthur, Winterthur 37332
Musée Monetaire Cantonal, Lausanne 36865
Musée Romain, Lausanne 36867

United Kingdom
Bank of England Museum, London 39571
The British Museum, London 39586
Fitzwilliam Museum, Cambridge 38454
Museum on the Mound, Edinburgh 38897
Royal Mint Sovereign Gallery, London 39766

Uruguay
Museo del Gaucho y de la Moneda, Montevideo 41001

U.S.A.
American Numismatic Society Museum, New York 45760
Franklin Mint Museum, Franklin Center 43523
Museum of the American Numismatic Association, Colorado Springs 42540
United States Army Finance Corps Museum, Fort Jackson 43403
United States Mint-Philadelphia, Philadelphia 46459

Uzbekistan
Surchondarë Vilojati Archeologija Muzeji, Termiz 48864

Oceanography

Argentina
Museo del Lago Gutiérrez, Bariloche 00137
Museo Provincial de Ciencias Naturales y Oceanográfico, Puerto Madryn 00491

Brazil
Museu Oceanográfico do Valo do Itajaí, Itajaí 04129

Bulgaria
Muzej na Morskoto Stopanstvo, Varna 04899
Prirodonaučen Muzej, Varna 04906

Canada
Marine Museum of the Great Lakes, Kingston 05681
Sidney Marine Museum, Sidney 06450

Chile
Museo Comparativo de Biología Marina, Viña del Mar 06930

Cyprus
Museum of Marine Life of Cyprus, Aghia Napa 08183

Egypt
Aquatics Museum - Institute of Oceanography and Fisheries, Suez 09306

Estonia
Eesti Meremuuseum, Tallinn 09360

France
Centre de la Mer, Paris 13481
Fondation Océanographique, Six-Fours-les-Plages 14755
Musée de la Mer, Biarritz 10725
Musée-Marinarium du Haut Lavédan, Pierrefitte-Nestalas 13734
Musée Mer et Désert, Villerville 15246
Musée Océanographique, Arcachon 10395
Musée Océanographique, Bonifacio 10793
Musée Océanographique, Kingersheim 12114
Musée Océanographique de l'Odet, Ergué-Gabéric 11637
Nausicaa, Boulogne-sur-Mer 10841
Océanopolis, Brest 10914
Océarium du Croisic, Le Croisic 12409

Germany
Deutsches Meeresmuseum, Stralsund 20073
Internationales Muschelmuseum, Wangerland 20396
Muschel- und Schneckenmuseum, Norden 19112
Nationalpark-Haus, Butjadingen 16434
Nordseemuseum, Bremerhaven 16343

Guadeloupe
Musée International du Coquillage, Saint-Barthélemy 21250

India
District Science Centre, Tirunelveli 22038

Israel
Red Sea Maritime Museum, Eilat 22588

Italy
Museo del Mare, Furci Siculo 23945
Museo del Mare, Ischia Ponte 24100
Museo del Mare, Pesaro 24859
Museo del Mare, Piombino 24937
Museo del Mare, Pizzo 24969
Museo del Mare, Pollica 24982
Museo di Biologia Marina, Porto Cesareo 25012
Museo di Biologia Marina, Taranto 25673
Museo di Biologia Marina, Fano 23763
Museo Didattico del Mare, Napoli 24597
Museo Navale Archeologico N. Lamboglia, La
  Maddalena 24117
Museo Paleomarino, Reggio Calabria 25092

Japan
Futtsu Oceanographic Museum of Chiba Prefecture,
  Kimitsu 26334
Mukaishima Marine Biological Station,
  Mukaishima 26519
Shima Marineland, Ago 26086
Shimoda Marine Biological Station, Kamo, Izu 26301
Suma Aqualife Museum, Kobe 26352
Umi-no Hakubutsukan, Toba 26823

Korea, Republic
National Maritime Museum, Mokpo 27212

Lebanon
Les Merveilles de la Mer, Jdeidet El-Metn 27491

Madagascar
Musée de la Mer, Nosy-Bé 27607

Mexico
Museo del Mar, Mazatlán 28078

Monaco
Musée Océanographique de Monaco, Monaco 28671

Mozambique
Museum of Inhaca Island, Maputo 28727

Netherlands
Brouws Museum, Brouwershaven 29031
Miramar Zeemuseum, Vledder 29949
Sealife Scheveningen, Den Haag 29125
Zeemuseum, Den Haag 29130

New Zealand
New Zealand Marine Studies Centre, Dunedin 30149

Panama
Museo de Ciencias Naturales, Panamá City 31081

Poland
Muzeum Morskie, Szczecin 32028
Muzeum Oceanograficzne Mir, Gdynia 31587
Szkolne Muzeum Morskie, Bolesławiec 31508

Portugal
Museu do Mar - Rei D. Carlos, Cascais 32250
Museu Municipal do Funchal (História Natural),
  Funchal 32276
Museu Oceanográfico, Setúbal 32347

Puerto Rico
Marine Sciences Museum, Mayagüez 32376

Russia
Gosudarstvennyj Severnyj Morskoj Muzej,
  Archangelsk 32651
Morskoj Muzej, Petrozavodsk 33317
Morskoj Muzej-Akvarium, Vladivostok 33702
Muzej Mirovogo Okeana, Kaliningrad 32873
Muzej Priroda Morja i eë Ochrana, Vladivostok 33707
Naučnyj Morskoj Muzej, Kaliningrad 32874

Senegal
Musée de la Mer, Gorée 33782

Serbia-Montenegro
Ribarsko-Biološka Zbirka, Novi Dojran 33866

Spain
Palacio del Mar, Donostia-San Sebastián 34779

Sweden
Aquaria Vattenmuseum, Stockholm 36230

Tunisia
Musée Océanographique Dar-El-Hout de Salammbô,
  Salammbô 37577

United Kingdom
Robertson Museum and Aquarium, Millport 39957
Scottish Maritime Museum, Irvine 39312

Uruguay
Museo del Mar, La Barra 40977

U.S.A.
Calvert Marine Museum, Solomons 47665
Chesapeake Bay Maritime Museum, Saint
  Michaels 47149
Custom House Maritime Museum,
  Newburyport 45910
East Hampton Town Marine Museum, East
  Hampton 43045
Kendall Whaling Museum, Sharon 47579
Maine Maritime Museum, Bath 41522
Marine Museum at Fall River, Fall River 43283
Marineland Ocean Museum, Marineland 45153

Mel Fisher Maritime Heritage Museum, Key
  West 44469
The MIT Museum, Cambridge 42048
Museum of Yarmouth History, Yarmouth 48778
Niagara Gorge Discovery Center, Niagara Falls 45950
North Carolina Maritime Museum, Beaufort 41558
North Wind Undersea Institute, Bronx 41925
Penobscot Marine Museum, Searsport 47527
Ponce DeLeon Inlet Lighthouse, Ponce Inlet 46583
Shore Village Museum, Rockland 46967
South Street Seaport Museum, New York 45874
Suffolk County Vanderbilt Museum, Centerport 42169
Texas Maritime Museum, Rockport 46973
Treasures of the Sea Exhibit, Georgetown 43650
Ventura County Maritime Museum, Oxnard 46245
Virginia Marine Science Museum, Virginia
  Beach 48250
William Scarbrough House, Savannah 47486
Woods Hole Oceanographic Institution Exhibit Center,
  Woods Hole 48735

Venezuela
Museo del Mar, Boca de Río 48896

Vietnam
Oceanographic Museum, Nhatrang 48998

Oenology → Wines and Spirits

Office Equipment

Austria
Büromaschinen-Museum, Aspang 01683
Kopiergerätemuseum, Wien 02911

Finland
Suomen Tietojenkäsittelymuseo, Jyväskylä 09605

Germany
Büromuseum, Mülheim an der Ruhr 18814
Computermuseum Aachen, Aachen 15370
Deutsches Schreibmaschinenmuseum,
  Bayreuth 15843
Museum der Kommunikations- und Bürogeschichte,
  Bamberg 15811
Telefonmuseum Hittfelder Bahnhof, Seevetal 19925

Italy
Museo di Informatica e Storia del Calcolo,
  Pennabilli 24834

Mexico
Museo de Telefonía, Delicias 27890

Switzerland
Schreibmaschinen-Museum, Pfäffikon (Zürich) 37022
Schreibmaschinenmuseum Baggenstos,
  Wallisellen 37303

Oil → Petroleum Industry and Trade

Opera → Performing Arts

Optics

Canada
Museum of Visual Science and Optometry,
  Waterloo 06755

France
Musée de l'Optique, Biesheim 10729
Musée Pierre Marly, Paris 13646

Germany
Fotomuseum CAMERAMA, Bad Soden am
  Taunus 15744
Holowood - Holographiemuseum Bamberg,
  Bamberg 15809
Kreismuseum, Rathenow 19493
Leica Stammbaum and Museum, Solms 19991
Museum für Holographie und neue Medien,
  Pulheim 19453
Optisches Museum, Oberkochen 19181
Optisches Museum der Ernst-Abbe-Stiftung Jena,
  Jena 17945
Sammlung historischer Mikroskope von Ernst Leitz,
  Wetzlar 20560
Zeiler Foto- und Filmmuseum, Zeil am Main 20736

Netherlands
Nationaal Brilmuseum Amsterdam, Amsterdam 28884
Universiteitsmuseum Utrecht, Utrecht 29911

Slovakia
Oddelenie Technické Múzeum Košice, Spišská
  Béla 34062

Switzerland
Illusoria-Land, Ittigen 36818

Musée Suisse de l'Appareil Photographique,
  Vevey 37290

United Kingdom
British Optical Association Museum, London 39587
Buckingham Movie Museum, Buckingham 38386

Ornithology → Birds

Painted and Stained Glass

France
Musée de l'Hospice Saint-Roch, Issoudun 12062

Germany
Deutsches Glasmalerei-Museum Linnich,
  Linnich 18484
Museum für bäuerliche und sakrale Kunst,
  Ruhpolding 19717
Museum für Zeitgenössische Glasmalerei, Langen in
  Hessen 18324

Japan
Hamamatsu City Museum of Art, Hamamatsu 26179

Switzerland
Musée Suisse du Vitrail, Romont 37069

Painting

Argentina
Casa Museo Bruzzone, Mar del Plata 00424
Estudio Museo Ramoneda, Humahuaca 00364
El Fogon de los Arrieros, Resistencia 00505
Museo Atelier Antonio Ortiz Echagüe, Carro
  Quemado 00266
Museo Austral de Pintura Primitiva Moderna Naif,
  Esquel 00345
Museo Maurice Minkowski, Buenos Aires 00222
Museo Municipal de Arte Angel María de Rosa,
  Junín 00373
Museo Municipal de Arte Juan Carlos Castagnino, Mar
  del Plata 00427
Museo Municipal de Artes Visuales, Quilmes 00495
Museo Municipal de Artes Visuales, Santa Fé 00607
Museo Nacional de Bellas Artes, Buenos Aires 00228
Museo Provincial de Bellas Artes, Corrientes 00324
Museo Provincial de Bellas Artes Dr. Pedro E.
  Martínez, Paraná 00470
Palacio del Mate, Posadas 00486
Pinacoteca, Córdoba 00313

Armenia
Avetisians Museum, Erevan 00678
Jottos Museum-Workshop, Erevan 00683
M. Sarians Museum, Erevan 00685

Australia
Brauhinia Shire Bicentennial Art Gallery,
  Springsure 01470
Dalby Regional Gallery, Dalby 00964
Harvery Art Gallery, Harvey 01090
McCrae Homestead Museum, McCrae 01191
Murilla Shire Art Gallery, Miles 01255
National Gallery of Victoria, Melbourne 01237
Tamworth City Gallery, Tamworth 01515
Tweed River Regional Art Gallery,
  Murwillumbah 01294
Wollongong City Gallery, Wollongong East 01610

Austria
Alfons Graber-Museum, Steinach 02677
Ausstellungszentrum Heiligenkreuzer Hof,
  Wien 02839
Europäisches Museum für Frieden,
  Stadtschlaining 02673
Franz Zeh-Museum, Heidenreichstein 02010
Galerie Günther Frey, Radenthein 02473
Galerie im Teisenhoferhof der Malschule Motiv
  Wachau, Weißenkirchen in der Wachau 02803
Gauermann-Museum, Miesenbach 02297
Kunstsammlung des Benediktinerstifts Seitenstetten,
  Seitenstetten 02658
Liechtenstein Museum, Wien 02926
Museum des Augustiner-Chorherrenstifts,
  Reichersberg 02498
Museum Kaiser Franz Joseph I. und die Jagd,
  Neuberg an der Mürz 02340
Prof. Eidenberger-Museum, Niederwaldkirchen 02363
Riesenrundgemälde Schlacht am Bergisel,
  Innsbruck 02077
Sammlung Essl - Kunst der Gegenwart,
  Klosterneuburg 02142
Schloß Ambras, Innsbruck 02079
Schloßmuseum Niederleis, Niederleis 02360
Stiftsmuseum Praemonstratenser-Chorherren Stift
  Schlägl, Aigen-Schlägl 01652
Stiftung Aratym, Gutenstein 01979

Belarus
Chagall Museum, Vitebsk 03123

Belgium
Broelmuseum, Kortrijk 03540
Bruggemuseum - Onthaalkerk van Onze-Lieve-Vrouw,
  Brugge 03251
Collections Artistiques de l'Université de Liège,
  Liège 03568
Eugeen Van Mieghem Museum, Antwerpen 03142
Gemeentelijk Museum Gustaaf de Smet,
  Deurle 03380
Hôpital Notre-Dame de la Rose, Lessines 03561
Koninklijk Museum voor Schone Kunsten Antwerpen,
  Antwerpen 03146
Maison Vincent Van Gogh, Cuesmes 03365
Musée Alexandre-Louis Martin, Carnières 03346
Musée Constantin Meunier, Bruxelles 03297
Musée de l'Art Wallon, Liège 03579
Musée de l'Assistance Publique, Bruxelles 03308
Musée des Beaux-Arts Charleroi, Charleroi 03351
Musée des Beaux-Arts de la Ville de Mons,
  Mons 03633
Musée d'Ixelles, Bruxelles 03319
Musée du Vieux-Cimetière, Soignies 03756
Musée Ducal, Bouillon 03233
Musée Léon de Smet, Deurle 03381
Museum Constant Permeke, Jabbeke 03526
Museum Félix de Boeck, Drogenbos 03395
Museum Jakob Smits, Mol 03629
Museum Maagdenhuis, Antwerpen 03150
Museum Mayer van den Bergh, Antwerpen 03151
Museum Modest Huys, Zulte 03859
Museum Onze-Lieve-Vrouw ter Potterie,
  Brugge 03260
Museum Smidt van Gelder, Antwerpen 03154
Museum Tysmans, Houthalen 03508
Provinciaal Museum Stijn Streuvels, Ingooigem 03519
Rockoxhuis, Antwerpen 03171
Stadhuis van Antwerpen, Antwerpen 03174
Stedelijk Museum Hoogstraten, Hoogstraten 03502
Timmermans-Opsomerhuis, Lier 03587

Brazil
Coleção do Palácio do Governo de Campos do Jordão,
  Campos de Jordão 04035
Museu Alfredo Andersen, Curitiba 04064
Museu de Arte Contemporânea da Universidade de
  São Paulo, São Paulo 04514
Museu de Arte Sacra Dom Ranulfo, Maceió 04182
Museu Internacional de Arte Naïf do Brasil, Rio de
  Janeiro 04387
Pinacoteca do Estado de São Paulo, São Paulo 04545

Bulgaria
Chudožestvena Galerija, Čirpan 04644
Chudožestvena Galerija, Veliko Tărnovo 04913
Chudožestvena Galerija, Žeravna 04932
Chudožestvena Galerija Ruse, Ruse 04802
Kăšta-muzej Stanislav Dospevski, Pazardžik 04756
Muzej Georgi Velčev, Varna 04898
Okrăžna Chudožestvena Galerija, Burgas 04635
Okrăžna Chudožestvena Galerija, Pleven 04768
Okrăžna Chudožestvena Galerija, Vidin 04927
Okrăžna Chudožestvena Galerija Vladimir Dimitrov-
  Majstora, Kjustendil 04709
Sofijska Gradska Chudožestvena Galerija,
  Sofia 04859

Canada
Art Gallery of Ontario, Toronto 06561
Art Gallery of Peterborough, Peterborough 06116
Centre d'Art de Cowansville, Cowansville 05283
Centre d'Exposition l'Imagier, Aylmer 05028
Chapel Gallery, North Battleford 06013
Legislative Building Art Galleries, Regina 06236
Leighton Foundation Collection, Calgary 05170
Mind and Matter Gallery, White Rock 06789
Oak Hall, Niagara Falls 05996
Perrault's Museum, Val Marie 06660
Vancouver Art Gallery, Vancouver 06693
Ziska Gallery, Bracebridge 05109

Chile
Casa del Arte de la Universidad de Concepción,
  Concepción 06891
Museo de Bellas Artes, Viña del Mar 06931
Museo Nacional de Bellas Artes de Santiago de Chile,
  Santiago de Chile 06916
Pinacoteca de la Universidad de Concepción,
  Concepción 06894

China, People's Republic
Lin San Zhi Art Display Center, Zhujiang 07337
Museum of Fine Arts, Beijing 06975
Qingdao Painting Gallery, Qingdao 07205
Quanzhou Painting Gallery, Quanzhou 07207
Shaanxi Chinese Painting Gallery, Xian 07297
Shandong Painting Gallery, Jinan 07133
Shanxi Painting Gallery, Taiyuan 07258
Shenzhen Painting Gallery, Shenzhen 07243
Taiyuan Painting Gallery, Taiyuan 07259
Tianjin Painting Gallery, Tianjin 07267
Xinjiang Painting Gallery, Urumchi 07276

China, Republic
Hwa Kang Museum, Taipei 07347
Ran-In-Ting Museum, Taipei 07355

Colombia
Museo de Arte Colonial, Bogotá 07396

Museo de Arte Contemporáneo, Bogotá 07397
Museo Efrain Martínez Zambrano, Popayán 07566

Croatia
Galerija Slika, Motovun 07740
Galerija Umjetnina, Split 07781
Ivan Meštrović Gallery, Split 07782
Muzej za Umjetnost i Obrt, Zagreb 07834
Zavičajni Muzej Grada Rovinja, Rovinj 07766

Cuba
Casa Natal del Pintor Wifredo Lam, Santa Clara 08117
Mariano Rodríguez Gallery, La Habana 07932
Museo Casa de Carmen Montilla, La Habana 07941
Museo Concha Ferrant, La Habana 07954
Museo de La Imagen, Vista Alegre 08177
Museo El Hurón Azul, La Habana 07968

Cyprus
Byzantine Museum and Art Galleries, Lefkosia 08194
Limassol Municipal Art Gallery, Lemesos 08211

Cyprus, Turkish Republic
Güzel Sanatlar Müzesi, Girne 08226

Czech Republic
Egon Schiele Art Centrum, Český Krumlov 08302
Expozice Mladý Gustav Mahler a Jihlava, Jihlava 08389
Galerie Antonína Chittussiho, Ronov nad Doubravou 08637
Galerie Felixe Jeneweina, Kutná Hora 08437
Klášter Sv. Anežky České, Praha 08584
Muzeum Aloise Jiráska, Hronov 08371
Muzeum Umění, Benešov 08246
Památník Adolfa Kaspara, Loštice 08463

Denmark
Ballerup Egnsmuseet, Ballerup 08782
Faaborg Museum for Fynsk Malerkunst, Faaborg 08813
Fanø Kunstsamling, Fanø 08817
Jugendhuset, Varde 09100
Michael og Anna Anchers Hus og Saxilds Gaard, Skagen 09056
Mølsteds Museum, Dragør 08797
Museet på Koldinghus, Kolding 08959
Randers Kunstmuseum, Randers 09026
Skagens Museum, Skagen 09058
Skovgaard Museet i Viborg, Viborg 09111
Statens Museum for Kunst, København 08950
Storm P.-Museet, Frederiksberg 08827
Vejle Kunstmuseum, Vejle 09104

Dominican Republic
Galería Nacional de Bellas Artes, Santo Domingo 09118
Museo Bellapart, Santo Domingo 09120

Egypt
Museum of Fine Arts and Cultural Center, Alexandria 09243

Estonia
Johann Köleri Muuseum, Vastemõisa 09393
Kristjan Raud Museum, Tallinn 09367

Finland
Nelimarkka Museo . Etelä-Pohjanmaan Aluetaidemuseo ja Nelimarkka-resedenssi, Alajärvi 09413
Särestöniemi-Museo, Kaukonen 09641
Taidemuseo, Kokkola 09685

France
Centre d'Art Contemporain, Istres 12064
Collection Historial Cognacq-Jay, Paris 13488
Collections de la Fondation Roger-van-Rogger, Bandol 10576
Collections de l'Ecole Nationale Supérieure des Beaux-Arts, Paris 13494
Fondation Le Corbusier, Paris 13504
Fondation Van-Gogh Arles, Arles 10414
Galerie de Nesle - Exposition, Paris 13507
Maison-Musée Ted Jacobs, Les Cerqueux-sous-Passavent 12532
Maison Natale du Maréchal Foch, Tarbes 14865
Musée Adzak, Paris 13529
Musée Antoine Lécuyer, Saint-Quentin (Aisne) 14434
Musée Arménien de France, Paris 13530
Musée Arteum, Châteauneuf-le-Rouge 11219
Musée Baron Gérard, Bayeux 10615
Musée Bourdelle, Paris 13538
Musée Calvet, Avignon 10528
Musée Charles Léandre, Domfront 11544
Musée Condé, Chantilly 11164
Musée d'Art et d'Archéologie, Aurillac 10490
Musée d'Art et d'Archéologie, Senlis 14709
Musée d'Art et d'Histoire, Dreux 11579
Musée d'Art et d'Histoire Romain Rolland, Clamecy 11311
Musée d'Art Naïf, Nice 13313
Musée Daubigny, Auvers-sur-Oise 10504
Musée de Grenoble, Grenoble 11942
Musée de Pont-Aven, Pont-Aven 13803
Musée de Région Auguste Chabaud, Graveson 11931
Musée de Vulliod Saint-Germain, Pézenas 13724
Musée Départemental d'Art Ancien et Contemporain, Épinal 11633
Musée des Arts et Traditions Populaires, Locronan 12644
Musée des Augustins, Toulouse 14946
Musée des Beaux-Arts, Arras 10429
Musée des Beaux-Arts, Béziers 10718
Musée des Beaux-Arts, Blois 10774
Musée des Beaux-Arts, Brest 10910
Musée des Beaux-Arts, Carcassonne 11043
Musée des Beaux-Arts, Chambéry 11139
Musée des Beaux-Arts, Marseille 12862
Musée des Beaux-Arts, Menton 12938
Musée des Beaux-Arts, Mirande 12990
Musée des Beaux-Arts, Nantes 13256
Musée des Beaux-Arts, Quimper 13901
Musée des Beaux-Arts, Rouen 14049
Musée des Beaux-Arts, Strasbourg 14832
Musée des Beaux-Arts, Tourcoing 14961
Musée des Beaux-Arts, Saintes 14557
Musée des Beaux-Arts, Mulhouse 13209
Musée des Beaux-Arts de Dunkerque, Dunkerque 11585
Musée des Beaux-Arts et d'Archéologie, Besançon 10701
Musée des Beaux-Arts et d'Archéologie, Libourne 12582
Musée des Beaux-Arts et d'Archéologie, Rennes (Ille-et-Vilaine) 13943
Musée des Beaux-Arts et de la Dentelle, Calais 11003
Musée du Centre de Recherches sur les Monuments Historiques, Paris 13598
Musée du Château, Flers 11745
Musée du Faouët, Le Faouët 12413
Musée du Louvre, Paris 13603
Musée du Luxembourg, Paris 13604
Musée du Pastel, Magrin 12767
Musée Duplessis, Carpentras 11057
Musée en Herbe, Paris 13613
Musée Eugène Boudin, Honfleur 12030
Musée Fabre, Montpellier 13132
Musée Fesch, Ajaccio 10265
Musée Francisque Mandet, Riom 13972
Musée François Desnoyer, Saint-Cyprien 14167
Musée Garinet, Châlons-en-Champagne 11130
Musée Garret, Vesoul 15149
Musée Grobet-Labadié, Marseille 12869
Musée Hardy, Clécy 11314
Musée Historique, Mont-Saint-Michel 13032
Musée Hyacinthe Rigaud, Perpignan 13708
Musée Jeanne d'Aboville, La Fère 12168
Musée Langlois, Beaumont-en-Auge 10645
Musée Louis-Cornu, Wassigny 15306
Musée Magnin, Dijon 11530
Musée Malraux, Le Havre 12427
Musée Moralès, Port-de-Bouc 13837
Musée Morice Lipsi, Rosey 14037
Musée Municipal, Bernay 10693
Musée Municipal, Coutances 11443
Musée Municipal, La Roche-sur-Yon 12233
Musée Municipal, Lons-le-Saunier 12662
Musée Municipal, Vire 15270
Musée Municipal de la Chartreuse, Douai 11560
Musée Municipal des Beaux-Arts, Valence (Drôme) 15051
Musée Municipal Paul Lafran, Saint-Chamas 14143
Musée National des Arts Asiatiques Guimet, Paris 13633
Musée National Ernest Hébert, Paris 13639
Musée Paul-José Gosselin, Saint-Vaast-la-Hougue 14496
Musée Raoul Dastrac, Aiguillon 10240
Musée Saint-Vic, Saint-Amand-Montrond 14098
Musée Simon-Segal, Aups 10485
Musée Thomas-Henry, Cherbourg 11278
Musées de la Cour d'Or, Metz 12958

Georgia
Georgian State Picture Gallery, Tbilisi 15361

Germany
Allgäu-Museum, Kempten 18059
Anhaltische Gemäldegalerie, Dessau 16576
August Macke Haus, Bonn 16230
Bilder-Galerie, Ostseebad Binz 19305
Braith-Mali-Museum, Biberach an der Riß 16138
Brasilianische Botschaft, Berlin 15926
C.O. Müller-Galerie, Eichstätt 16803
Edwin Scharff Museum am Petrusplatz, Neu-Ulm 19008
Erstes Imaginäres Museum - Sammlung Günter Dietz, Wasserburg am Inn 20406
Friedrich-Eckenfelder-Galerie, Balingen 15797
Fürstliches Schloß mit Gemäldegalerie, Mausoleum, Bückeburg 16392
Gablonzer Archiv Museum, Kaufbeuren 18038
Galerie im Alten Rathaus, Prien 19449
Galerie im Ermelerspeicher, Schwedt 19886
Galerie im Kulturhaus Spandau, Berlin 15961
Galerie Skell, Schmiedeberg, Osterzgebirge 19812
Gaudnek-Museum, Altomünster 15469
Gemäldegalerie, Berlin 15974
Gemäldegalerie Alte Meister, Kassel 18017
Gemäldesammlung, Erlangen 16917
Gentilhaus, Aschaffenburg 15522
Heimatmuseum Scheeßel, Scheeßel 19768
Heimatmuseum Stadt Starnberg, Starnberg 20036
Herkomer-Museum am Mutterturm, Landsberg am Lech 18303
Hudetz-Turm, Wiesent 20580
Jakob-Philipp-Hackert Ausstellung, Prenzlau 19442
Künstlerhaus Walter Helm, Aschaffenburg 15524
Kulturhaus der Otto-Hellmeier-Stiftung, Raisting 19480
Ludwig-Doerfler-Galerie, Schillingsfürst 19779
Mainfränkisches Museum Würzburg, Würzburg 20696
Malerstübchen Willingshausen, Willingshausen 20601
Mansfeldgalerie im Kulturhaus, Lutherstadt Eisleben 18569
Museen im Alten Rathaus, Pirmasens 19401
Museum am Burghof, Lörrach 18490
Museum Burg Falkenstein, Pansfelde 19344
Museum der Stadt Ettlingen, Ettlingen 16975
Museum Folkwang Essen, Essen 16959
Museum Gasteiger-Haus, Utting 20281
Museum Rolf Werner, Seebad Bansin 19912
Neue Residenz, Bamberg 15814
Olaf-Gulbransson-Museum, Tegernsee 20152
Otto-Dill Museum, Neustadt an der Weinstraße 19078
Otto-Dix-Haus, Gera 17247
Paul-Röder-Museum, Marktoberdorf 18650
Podium Kunst, Schramberg 19847
Rathausgalerie, Bad Harzburg 15657
Schiffahrtsmuseum Nordfriesland, Husum, Nordsee 17871
Schloß Weissenstein, Pommersfelden 19427
Schloßmuseum Murnau, Murnau 18962
Schlossmuseum Oranienburg, Oranienburg 19266
Staatliche Kunsthalle Karlsruhe, Karlsruhe 18002
Staatsgalerie in der Benediktiner-Abtei, Ottobeuren 19328
Stadtmuseum Bautzen, Bautzen 15836
Städtische Galerie, Schieder-Schwalenberg 19776
Städtische Gemäldegalerie, Füssen 17170
Städtische Kunstgalerie im Deutschordenshaus, Donauwörth 16641
Städtische Wessenberg-Galerie, Konstanz 18207
Strübhaus-Haus der Malkunst, Veringenstadt 20304
Wallraf-Richartz-Museum - Fondation Corboud, Köln 18168

Greece
Alex Mylonas Museum, Athinai 20845
Angelos and Angeliki Giallina Gallery, Corfu 20927
Gounaropoulos Museum of Zografou, Zografou 21224
N. Hadjikyriakos-Ghikas Gallery, Athinai 20892
Tellogleion Foundation, Thessaloniki 21193

Guam
Isla Center for the Arts at the University of Guam, Mangilao 21258

Hungary
Hincz Gyula Állandó Gyüjtemény, Vác 21601
Kohán Múzeum, Gyula 21424
Munkácsy Mihály Múzeum, Békéscsaba 21319
Rippl-Rónai Emlékház, Kaposvár 21441
Szönyi István Emlék Múzeum, Zebegény 21616
Zettl Langer gyüjtemény, Sopron 21539
Zichy Mihály Emlékmúzeum, Zala 21612

Iceland
Listasafn Einars Jónssonar, Reykjavík 21653

India
Academy of Fine Arts Museum, Kolkata 21896
Bhuri Singh Museum, Chamba 21737
Central Museum, Bhopal 21720
Sri Chitra Art Gallery, Thiruvananthapuram 22034
Dogra Art Museum, Jammu 21865
Folklore Museum, Mysore 21959
Government Museum, Udaipur 22044
Government Museum Vellore, Vellore 22059
Indian Museum, Kolkata 21905
Institute Menezes Braganza, Panaji 21973
Sri Jayachamarajendra Art Gallery, Mysore 21960
Maharaja Fate Singh Museum, Vadodara 22049
Museum of Art and Archaeology, Dharwad 21792
Mutua Museum, Imphal 21855
Salar Jung Museum, Hyderabad 21846
Sangli State Museum, Sangli 22009
TTD Museum, Tirupati 22040
Victoria Memorial Hall, Kolkata 21914

Indonesia
Gunarsa Museum, Klungkung 22148
Museum Le Mayeur, Sanur 22184
Neka Museum and Gallery, Gianyar 22102

Ireland
Bantry House, Bantry 22375
Glebe House and Gallery, Church Hill 22393
Limerick City Gallery of Art, Limerick 22507
The Maritime Museum, Dublin 22441

Israel
Glichenstein Museum, Zefat 22787
Uri and Rami Nechushtan, Kibbutz Ashdot Yaakov 22678
Zetlin Museum, Ramat Gan 22735

Italy
Casa Natale Leonardo da Vinci, Vinci 26024
Cenacolo di Sant'Apollonia, Firenze 23829
Ciruito Museale Urbano, Cascia 23373
Civico Museo d'Arte Moderne, Anticoli Corrado 22895
Convento dell'ex-Convento di Sant'Onofrio detto di Fuligno, Firenze 23834
Galleria Accademia Albertina di Belle Arti, Torino 25733
Galleria Civica, Valdagno 25870
Galleria di Palazzo Rosso, Genova 23983
Galleria Regionale d'Arte Moderna e Contemporanea, Sassoferrato 25493
Mostra Permanente della Biblioteca Estense, Modena 24435
Museo Alessi, Enna 23732
Museo Archeologico e Pinacoteca, Piacenza 24890
Museo Archeologico G. Moretti, San Severino Marche 25412
Museo Baroffio e del Santuario del Sacro Monte sopra Varese, Varese 25896
Museo Berenziano, Cremona 23679
Museo Borromeo, Isola Bella 24104
Museo Carlo Venturini, Massa Lombarda 24317
Museo Civico, Casale Monferrato 23364
Museo Civico, Siena 25572
Museo Civico, Rieti 25110
Museo Civico Ala Ponzone, Cremona 23680
Museo Civico d'Arte, Pordenone 25007
Museo Civico e d'Arte Sacra, Colle di Val d'Elsa 23609
Museo Civico e Pinacoteca, Fano 23762
Museo Civico e Pinacoteca Basilio Cascella, Pescara 24867
Museo Civico Il Correggio, Correggio 23656
Museo Civico Rocca Flea, Gualdo Tadino 24066
Museo d'Arte Antica, Milano 24389
Museo d'Arte Sacra, San Leo 25380
Museo degli Affreschi G.B. Cavalcaselle, Verona 25972
Museo del Cenedese, Vittorio Veneto 26039
Museo del Paesaggio, Pallanza 24782
Museo della Civiltà Contadina, Sassocorvaro 25491
Museo della Fondazione Giovanni Scaramangà di Altomonte, Trieste 25827
Museo di Capodimonte, Napoli 24589
Museo di Castelvecchio, Verona 25974
Museo di Palazzo Ducale, Mantova 24289
Museo di Sant'Agostino, Genova 23998
Museo Domenicani, Taggia 25665
Museo e Pinacoteca Civica, Alessandria 22849
Museo e Pinacoteca Civici, Vasto 25903
Museo e Pinacoteca della Basilica di San Paolo, Roma 25221
Museo e Pinacoteca S. Gentili, San Ginesio 25368
Museo Francesco Borgogna, Vercelli 25960
Museo Lodovico Pogliaghi, Varese 25897
Museo Missionario delle Grazie, Rimini 25118
Museo Pinacoteca A. Salvucci, Molfetta 24459
Museo-Pinacoteca Comunale, Mogliano Marche 24455
Museo Poldi Pezzoli, Milano 24409
Museo Sant'Andrea, Clusone 23600
Museo Storico Aloisiano, Castiglione delle Stiviere 23434
Palazzo Attems-Petzenstein, Gorizia 24036
Pinacoteca, Ploaghe 24971
Pinacoteca, Teramo 25688
Pinacoteca Capitolina, Roma 25264
Pinacoteca Chiesa di San Tomaso Becket, Padova 24751
Pinacoteca Civica, Cento 23474
Pinacoteca Civica, Imperia 24096
Pinacoteca Civica, Monza 24560
Pinacoteca Civica, Pieve di Cento 24921
Pinacoteca Civica, Fermo 23782
Pinacoteca Civica A. Ricci, Monte San Martino 24500
Pinacoteca Civica Carlo Servolini, Collesalvetti 23615
Pinacoteca Civica Melozzo degli Ambrogi, Forlì 23917
Pinacoteca Comunale, Spoleto 25626
Pinacoteca Comunale, Ravenna 25084
Pinacoteca Comunale, Massa Marittima 24327
Pinacoteca Comunale Alberto Martini, Oderzo 24666
Pinacoteca Comunale d'Arte Antica e Moderna, Faenza 23757
Pinacoteca Comunale Foresiana, Portoferraio 25022
Pinacoteca del Duomo, Cittadella 23584
Pinacoteca della Chiesa di San Francesco, Mercatello sul Metauro 24359
Pinacoteca dell'Accademia dei Concordi e del Seminario, Rovigo 25298
Pinacoteca e Musei Civici, Jesi 24116
Pinacoteca e Musei Comunali, Macerata 24251
Pinacoteca G. A. Levis, Racconigi 25063
Pinacoteca Giovanni e Marella Agnelli, Torino 25766
Pinacoteca Giovanni Morscio, Dolceacqua 23717
Pinacoteca M. Cascella, Ortona 24701
Pinacoteca Manfrediana, Venezia 25949
Pinacoteca Nazionale, Siena 25578
Pinacoteca Nazionale, Cagliari 23255
Pinacoteca Parrocchiale, Corridonia 23658
Pinacoteca Repossi, Chiari 23528
Quadreria Cesarini, Fossombrone 23929

Jamaica
Institute of Jamaica, Kingston 26069

Japan
Akita Prefectural Art Gallery, Akita 26095
Bridgestone Bijutsukan, Tokyo 26832
Chiba City Museum of Art, Chiba 26120
Eisei Bunko Museum, Tokyo 26843
Hiroshima Bijutsukan, Hiroshima 26212
Hokkaidoritsu Asahikawa Bijutsukan, Asahikawa 26106
Ibaraki Daigaku Izura Bijutsu Bunka Kenkyujo, Kitaibaraki 26340
Kawanabe Kyosai Memorial Museum, Warabi 26999
Kuroda Kinenshitsu, Tokyo 26880
Kushiro Art Museum, Kushiro 26390
Meiji Memorial Picture Gallery, Tokyo 26890
Narukawa Bijutsukan, Hakone 26177
Ryushi Memorial Hall, Tokyo 26914
Shinshu-shinmachi Art Museum, Shinshiyuushin 26756
Takasaki-shi Bijutsukan, Takasaki 26800

Tenri Gallery, Tokyo 26932
Torajiro Kojima Memorial Hall, Kurashiki 26385
Tsuchida Bakusen Bijutsukan, Sawata 26728
Ueno Royal Museum, Tokyo 26951
Yamagata Bijutsukan, Yamagata 27002

Korea, Republic
Onggi Folk Museum and Institute, Seoul 27265
Woljeon Art Museum, Seoul 27290

Lebanon
Daheshite Museum, Beirut 27480
Gibran Museum, Bsharri 27488

Luxembourg
Villa Vauban, Luxembourg 27570

Malaysia
Ibrahim Hussein Foundation Museum, Pulau Langkawi 27680
Kedah State Art Gallery, Alor Setar 27617

Malta
Zabbar Sanctuary Museum, Zabbar 27718

Mexico
Galería de Arte Jaguar Despertado, Villahermosa 28606
Galería de la Escuela de Diseño y Artesanias del Instituto Nacional de Bellas Artes, México 28097
Museo Casa de Agustín Arrieta, Puebla 28319
Museo Centro de la Imagen, México 28118
Museo de la Acuarela del Estado de México, Toluca 28546
Museo de las Pinturas Rupestres de San Ignacio, Pueblo de San Ignacio 28345
Museo Franco Lázaro, Chiapa de Corzo 27819
Museo Galería Manuel Lepe, Puerto Vallarta 28350
Museo Nacional de la Acuarela, México 28189
Museo Rubén Herrera, Saltillo 28370

Morocco
American Legation Museum, Tanger 28710

Myanmar
Mon State Museum, Mawlamyine 28736

Nepal
Picture Gallery, Bhaktapur 28785

Netherlands
Expositieruimte De Weem, Westeremden 29997
Familie Vrouwenhofje - Hofje van Aerden, Leerdam 29505
Frans Hals Museum, Haarlem 29324
Kijk- en Luistermuseum, Bant 28962
Marc Chagall Kunsthuis, Amsterdam 28871
Museum Paul Tétar Van Elven, Delft 29085
Museum Slager, 's-Hertogenbosch 29404
Museum Ton Schulten, Ootmarsum 29676
Museum Veluwezoom, Doorwerth 29171
Museum voor Moderne Kunst, Arnhem 28941
Oudheidkamer Heerde, Heerde 29359
Panorama Mesdag, Den Haag 29121
Ruurd Wiersma Hûs, Burdaard 29040
Schilder- en Bakkerijmuseum 't Steenhuis, Niebert 29612
Sikkens Schildersmuseum, Sassenheim 29793
Tentoonstellingsruimte 't Oute Hus, Burgh-Haamstede 29046
Het Tromp's Huys, Vlieland 29955
Het Vrouwenhuis, Zwolle 30087

New Zealand
Auckland Art Gallery - Toi o Tāmaki, Auckland 30103
Christchurch Art Gallery Te Puna o Waiwhetu, Christchurch 30126

Pakistan
Shakir Ali Museum, Lahore 31043
Tasneem Arts Gallery, Peshawar 31052

Peru
Casa Museo Mario Urteaga, Cajamarca 31125
Museo de Arte e Historia, Lima 31206
Museo de San Jerónimo, Cusco 31155
Museo de Sitio de Chinchero, Urubamba 31266
Museo San Juan de Letrán, Chucuito 31145
Pinacoteca Municipal Ignacio Merino, Lima 31227

Philippines
Blanco Family Museum, Angono 31275
Jorge B. Vargas Museum and Filipiana Research Center, Quezon City 31434
Juan Luna Shrine Museum, Badoc 31281
Lopez Memorial Museum, Pasig 31420
Vicente Manansala Museum, Binangonan 31288

Poland
Dom Józefa Mehoffera, Kraków 31683
Kamienica Szołayskich, Kraków 31691
Miejska Galeria Sztuki, Łódź 31767
Muzeum Mazowieckie w Płocku, Płock 31887
Muzeum Narodowe w Kielcach, Kielce 31658
Muzeum Narodowe w Poznaniu, Oddział w Rogalinie, Rogalin 31947
Muzeum Uniwersytetu Jagiellońskiego - Collegium Maius, Kraków 31722
Muzeum w Grudziądzu, Grudziądz 31611

Portugal
Casa-Museu de Almeida Moreira, Viseu 32360
Fundação Ricardo do Espírito Santo Silva, Lisboa 32287
Museu de Evora, Evora 32269
Museu de Grão Vasco, Viseu 32361
Museu de Lamego, Lamego 32282
Museu de Roque Gameiro, Minde 32320
Museu Nacional de Soares dos Reis, Porto 32338

Puerto Rico
Museo de Arte de Ponce, Ponce 32380
Museum of History, Anthropology and Art, San Juan 32405

Romania
Muzeul Hrandt Avakian, Bucureşti 32457
Muzeul Memorial Nicolae Grigorescu, Câmpina 32481
Muzeul Theodor Aman, Bucureşti 32473

Russia
Belozerskij Muzej Narodnogo Dekorativno-prikladnogo Iskusstva, Belozersk 32681
Bolšoj Dvorec, Lomonosov 32986
Chudožestvenno-memorialnyj Muzej K.S. Petrova-Vodkina, Chvalynsk 32746
Chudožestvennyj Muzej im. M.S. Tuganova, Vladikavkaz 33686
Dalnevostočnyj Chudožestvennyj Muzej, Chabarovsk 32739
Dom-Muzej I.N. Kramskogo, Ostrogožsk 33275
Dom-muzej Narodnogo Chudožnika V.A. Igoševa, Chanty-Mansijsk 32741
Dom-muzej Osipovych-Vul'f v Trigorskom, Puškinskie Gory 33343
Ekaterinburgskij Muzej Izobrazitelnych Iskusstv, Ekaterinburg 32766
Ekatermininskij Dvorec - Gosudarstvennyj Muzej Carskoje Selo, Puškin 33336
Gosudarstvennaja Tretjakovskaja Galerja, Moskva 33046
Gosudarstvennyj Chudožestvenno-architekturnyj Dvorcovo-parkovyj Muzej-zapovednik Oranienbaum, Lomonosov 32988
Gosudarstvennyj Chudožestvenno-architekturnyj Dvorcovo-parkovyj Muzej-zapovednik Pavlovsk, Pavlovsk 33285
Gosudarstvennyj Chudožestvennyj Istoriko-architekturnyj i prirodno-landšaftnyj Muzej-zapovednik Kolomenskoe, Moskva 33052
Gosudarstvennyj Istoriko-architekturnyj i Prirodno-landšaftnyj Muzej Zapovednik Izborsk, Izborsk 32834
Gosudarstvennyj Memorial'nyj Istoriko-chudožestvennyj i Prirodnyj Muzej-zapovednik V.D. Polenova, Strachovo 33566
Gosudarstvennyj Muzej Vadima Sidura, Moskva 33064
Gosudarstvennyj Muzej-usadba Archangelskoe, Archangelskoe 32654
Gosudarstvennyj Muzej Zapovednik Petergof, Sankt-Peterburg 33406
Gosudarstvennyj Russkij Muzej, Sankt-Peterburg 33407
Gosudarstvennyj Russkij Muzej, Sankt-Peterburg 33408
Gosudarstvennyj Vystavočnyj Zal Zamoskvorec^Bie, Moskva 33069
Jaroslavskij Chudožestvennyj Muzej - Gubernatorskij Dom, Jaroslavl 32848
Kartinnaja Galerija im. P.I. Šolochova, Borisoglebsk 32700
Memorialnyj Dom-muzej P.D. Korina, Moskva 33076
Memorialnyj Dom-muzej V.M. Vaznecova, Moskva 33077
Meždunarodnyj Centr-Muzej im. N.K. Rericha, Moskva 33083
Moskovskaja Gosudarstvennaja Kartinnaja Galereja A. Šilova, Moskva 33085
Moskovskij Gosudarstvennyj Vystavočnyj Zal Malyi Manež, Moskva 33088
Muzej Istorii Moskvy, Moskva 33109
Muzej-kvartira A.I. Kuindži, Sankt-Peterburg 33452
Muzej-usadba im. N.K. Rericha, Izvara 32839
Novosibirskaja Kartinnaja Galereja, Novosibirsk 33242
Orlovskij Oblastnoj Muzej Izobrazitelnych Iskusstv, Orël 33268
Ostrogožskij Rajonnyj Istoriko-chudožestvennyj Muzej im. I.N. Kramskogo, Ostrogožsk 33276
Primorskaja Kraevaja Kartinnaja Galereja, Vladivostok 33708
Regionalnyj Muzej Severnogo Priladožja, Sortavala 33547
Rostovskij Kreml - Gosudarstvennyj Muzej-zapovednik, Rostov (Jaroslavskaja obl.) 33355
Rybinskij Gosudarstvennyj Istoriko-architekturnyj i Chudožestvennyj Muzej-zapovednik, Rybinsk 33362
Tobolskaja Kartinnaja Galereja, Tobolsk 33612
Tomskij Oblastnoj Chudožestvennyj Muzej, Tomsk 33616
Uljanovskij Oblastnoj Chudožestvennyj Muzej, Uljanovsk 33668
Valaamskij Naučno-issledovatelskij Cerkovno-archeologičeskij i Prirodnyj Muzej-zapovednik, Sortavala 33548

Serbia-Montenegro
Galerija Matice Srpske, Novi Sad 33869
Galerija Srpske Akademije Nauka i Umetnosti, Beograd 33798
Gradski Muzej, Kosovska Mitrovica 33847
Memorijalna Galerija Veliša Lekovića, Bar 33789
Umjetnička Galerija Josip-Bepo Benkovic, Herceg-Novi 33840

Singapore
Tan Oe Pang Art Studio, Singapore 33945

Slovakia
Gáleria Marie Medvedckej, Tvrdošín 34076
Galéria Mesta Bratislavy, Bratislava 33963
Novohradská Galéria, Lučenec 34018
Oravská Galéria, Dolný Kubín 33989
Tatranská Galéria, Poprad 34046

Slovenia
Muzejska Zbirka, Rogoška Slatina 34147

South Africa
Rupert Museum, Stellenbosch 34382
William Fehr Collection, Cape Town 34215
William Humphreys Art Gallery, Kimberley 34294

Spain
Basílica de Nuestra Señora del Pilar, Zaragoza 35715
Casa de los Tiros, Granada 34865
Casa-Museu Castell Gala Dalí, La Pera 35265
Casa-Museu de Salvador Dalí de Cadaqués, Cadaqués 34643
Colección de la Caja de Ahorros, Valencia 35598
Colección de Pintura y Recuerdos Históricos del Castell de Balsareny, Balsareny 34525
Colección Krekovic, Palma de Mallorca 35223
Colección Osuna, Sevilla 35475
Convento de San Antonio el Real, Segovia 35463
Museo de Almería, Almería 34454
Museo de la Colegiata San Luis, Villagarcía de Campos Valladolid 35680
Museo de la Fundación Duque de Lerma, Toledo 35540
Museo de la Real Academia de Bellas Artes de San Fernando, Madrid 35027
Museo de Málaga, Málaga 35073
Museo de Murcia, Murcia 35147
Museo del Monasterio de San Joaquín y Santa Ana, Valladolid 35622
Museo del Patriarca, Valencia 35604
Museo Diocesà, Tarragona 35511
Museo Diocesano, Salamanca 35364
Museo Lázaro Galdiano, Madrid 35039
Museo Municipal, Ayllón 34509
Museo Municipal de Bellas Artes, Santa Cruz de Tenerife 35416
Museo Municipal de San Telmo, Donostia-San Sebastián 34778
Museo Municipal de Vigo Quiñones de León, Vigo 35655
Museo Municipal Manuel Torres, Marín 35092
Museo Nacional del Prado, Madrid 35048
Museo Naval de Cartagena, Cartagena 34686
Museo Néstor, Las Palmas de Gran Canaria 35243
Museo Parroquial, Paradas 35251
Museo Pecharromán, Pasarón de la Vera 35255
Museu Cau Ferrat, Sitges 35497
Museu Maricel de Mar, Sitges 35498
Palacio Real de El Pardo, El Pardo 35253
San Antonio Abad, Madrid 35063

Sri Lanka
Lionel Wendt Art Gallery, Colombo 35749
National Art Gallery, Colombo 35750
Sapumal Foundation Gallery, Colombo 35752

Sweden
Aguélimuseet, Sala 36171
Bildmuseet, Umeå 36347
Måleriyrkets Museum, Stockholm 36257
Nordiska Akvarellmuseet, Skärhamn 36192

Switzerland
Alexej von Jawlensky-Archiv, Locarno 36884
Centre d'Art Contemporain, Genève 36730
Hans Erni Museum, Luzern 36909
Kunstmuseum, Solothurn 37185
Kunstmuseum Olten, Olten 37009
Kunstmuseum Winterthur, Winterthur 37331
Museo d'Arte, Tenero 37231
Museo Hermann Hesse, Montagnola 36944
Schweizerisches Alpines Museum, Bern 36552
Wocher-Panorama der Stadt Thun um 1810, Thun 37244

Tanzania
Kibo Art Gallery, Marangu 37462

Turkey
Resim ve Heykel Müzesi, İstanbul 37705

Ukraine
National Aivazovsky Picture Gallery, Feodosija 37853
National Art Museum of Ukraine, Kyïv 37875
The Bleschunov Municipal Museum of Personal Collections, Odessa 37896

United Kingdom
Arbroath Art Gallery, Arbroath 38011
Atkinson Art Gallery, Southport 40557
Bingham Library Trust Art Collection, Cirencester 38582
Brantwood, Coniston 38624
Brighton Museum and Art Gallery, Brighton 38340
Burrell Collection, Glasgow 39039
Buscot House, Buscot 38420
Castell y Waun, Chirk 38571
Castle Douglas Art Gallery, Castle Douglas 38502
CCA-Centre for Contemporary Arts, Glasgow 39040
Christ Church Picture Gallery, Oxford 40145
Corsham Court, Corsham 38636
Courtauld Institute Gallery, London 39615
Cyfarthfa Castle Museum and Art Gallery, Merthyr Tydfil 39937
De Morgan Centre, London 39620
Drumlanrig's Tower, Hawick 39194
Dulwich Picture Gallery, London 39627
Edwin Young Collection, Salisbury 40433
Glynn Vivian Art Gallery, Swansea 40658
Gracefield Arts Centre, Dumfries 38789
Hagley Hall, Hagley 39144
Hastings Museum and Art Gallery, Hastings 39184
Hawick Museum, Hawick 39195
Heaton Hall, Manchester 39888
Hopetoun House, South Queensferry 40535
The John Southern Gallery, Dobwalls 38736
Kirkcaldy Museum and Art Gallery, Kirkcaldy 39391
Lanhydrock, Bodmin 38266
Leamington Spa Art Gallery and Museum, Leamington Spa 39436
Leighton Hall, Carnforth 38494
Lillie Art Gallery, Milngavie 39958
Long Eaton Town Hall, Long Eaton 39820
Loseley House, Guildford 39140
The Lowry Gallery, Salford 40430
Lytham Hall, Lytham Saint Anne's 39858
McKechnie Institute, Girvan 39034
McLean Museum and Art Gallery, Greenock 39131
Marble Hill House, Twickenham 40738
Mellerstain House, Gordon 39096
Mercer Art Gallery, Harrogate 39169
Mirehouse, Keswick 39345
Painters's Hall, London 39739
Penwith Galleries, Saint Ives, Cornwall 40407
Perth Museum and Art Gallery, Perth 40185
Peter Anson Gallery, Buckie 38385
Polesden Lacey, Dorking 38756
POSK Gallery, London 39748
The Queen's Gallery, London 39752
Rockingham Castle, Market Harborough 39916
Royal Academy of Arts Gallery, London 39754
Royal Cambrian Academy of Art, Conwy 38628
Royal Cornwall Museum, Truro 40730
Royal Museum and Art Gallery, Canterbury 38474
Scarborough Art Gallery, Scarborough 40456
Sir Alfred Munnings Art Museum, Dedham 38711
Sir Max Aitken Museum, Cowes 38650
Smith Art Gallery, Brighouse 38335
Southside House, London 39781
Stockport Art Gallery, Stockport 40597
Sutton Park, Sutton-on-the-Forest 40652
Talbot Rice Gallery, Edinburgh 38920
Towneley Hall Art Gallery and Museums, Burnley 38401
Trevithick Cottage, Camborne 38449
Upton House, Banbury 38076
Usher Gallery, Lincoln 39503
Westgate Museum, Winchester 40894
Williamson Art Gallery and Museum, Birkenhead 38207
Woburn Abbey, Woburn 40912

Uruguay
Museo de Bellas Artes Departamental de San José, San José de Mayo 41041
Museo Municipal de Bellas Artes Juan Manuel Blanes, Montevideo 41011
Museo Nacional de Bellas Artes, Montevideo 41017

U.S.A.
Americas Society Art Gallery, New York 45761
Artists' Cooperative Gallery, Omaha 46143
Arts and Science Center for Southeast Arkansas, Pine Bluff 46489
Atrium Gallery, Fort Worth 43481
Barnes Foundation, Merion 45266
Baycrafters, Bay Village 41546
Blair Museum of Lithophanes, Toledo 48018
Boatmen's National Bank Art Collection, Saint Louis 47112
The Coffin School Museum, Nantucket 45595
Crane Collection Gallery, Wellesley 48494
Eastern Shore Art Center, Fairhope 43271
Edward Hopper House, Nyack 46048
Free Public Library Collection, New Bedford 45661
Gallery at the Wharf, Coupeville 42676
Gallery One, Ellensburg 43150
Haverhill Public Library Special Collections, Haverhill 43962
John G. Johnson Collection, Philadelphia 46421
Jose Drudis-Biada Art Gallery, Los Angeles 44916
Joseph A. Driscoll Art Gallery, Brockton 41910
Kaji Aso Studio Gallery Nature and Temptation, Boston 41813
Klemm Gallery, Adrian 41066
Laguna Art Museum, Laguna Beach 44575
Miller Art Center, Springfield 47760
Morton J. May Foundation Gallery, Saint Louis 47129
Museum of History and Art, Ontario 46163
North Lee County Historic Center and Santa Fe Depot Museum Complex, Fort Madison 43425
Ocean City Art Center, Ocean City 46084
Orlando Brown House, Frankfort 43514
The Parthenon, Nashville 45622
Piedra Lumbre Visitors Center, Abiquiu 41058
Pittock Mansion, Portland 46640
Plastic Club, Philadelphia 46444
Print and Picture Collection, Philadelphia 46447

Saint Johnsbury Athenaeum, Saint Johnsbury 47099
Southwestern Utah Art Gallery, Saint George 47091
Taft Museum of Art, Cincinnati 42410
Union County Public Library Union Room,
Monroe 45444
University Gallery, Boca Raton 41769
Vance Kirkland Museum, Denver 42902
Weyers-Sampson Art Gallery, Greenville 43828
Wynn Collection, Las Vegas 44675

Vanuatu
Michoutouchkine Pilioko Foundation, Port Vila 48865

Vatican City
Pinacoteca Vaticana, Città del Vaticano 48885

Venezuela
Museo de Arte Colonial, Caracas 48911

Painting, 17th C.

Austria
Salzburger Barockmuseum, Salzburg 02550

France
Maison Natale de Claude Gellée, Chamagne 11134
Musée des Beaux-Arts, Dole 11541

Germany
Deutsche Barockgalerie, Augsburg 15552

Italy
Casino dell'Aurora Pallavicini, Roma 25153
Museo Didattico, Tivoli 25711
Palazzo Borromeo, Stresa 25643
Pinacoteca Civica F. Duranti, Montefortino 24526
Quadreria dei Girolamini, Napoli 24605
Quadreria della Cassa Depositi e Prestiti,
Roma 25265

Netherlands
Museum Het Rembrandthuis, Amsterdam 28876

Russia
Cerkov Troicy v Nikitnikach, Moskva 33033

South Africa
Michaelis Collection, Cape Town 34207

United Kingdom
Brodie Castle, Forres 39007

Painting, 18th C.

Austria
Salzburger Barockmuseum, Salzburg 02550

Belgium
Château d'Aigremont, Seraing 03730

Germany
Deutsche Barockgalerie, Augsburg 15552
Gotisches Haus, Wörlitz 20641
Museum Schloss Luisium, Dessau 16581
Schloss Mosigkau, Dessau 16583
Schloss Wörlitz und Englisches Landhaus,
Wörlitz 20642
Staatsgalerie im Neuen Schloß,
Oberschleißheim 19206

Italy
Fondazione Museo Glauco Lombardi, Parma 24798
Museo Diego Aragona Pignatelli Cortes, Napoli 24598

Japan
Ike Taiga Museum of Art, Kyoto 26404

Russia
Gosudarstvennyj Vladimiro-Suzdalskij Istoriko-
architekturnyj i Chudožestvennyj Muzej-zapovednik,
Vladimir 33692

Painting, 19th C.

Austria
Kunstkammer des Innsbrucker Servitenkloster,
Innsbruck 02071
Wachaumuseum, Weißenkirchen in der
Wachau 02804

Belgium
Musée Antoine Wiertz, Bruxelles 03290
Musée Provincial Félicien Rops, Namur 03651

Croatia
Moderna Galerija Rijeka - Muzej Moderne i
Suvremene Umjetnosti, Rijeka 07760
Umjetnička Galerija, Dubrovnik 07702

Czech Republic
Památník Josefa Mánesa, Čechy pod Košířem 08290
Památník Mikoláše Alše, Mirotice 08479

Denmark
Ordrupgaard, Charlottenlund 08793

Finland
Cygnaeuksen Galleria, Helsinki 09476
Gösta Serlachiuksen Taidemuseo, Mänttä 09810
Reitzin Säätiön Kokoelmat, Helsinki 09524

France
Atelier Paul Cézanne, Aix-en-Provence 10249
Espace d'Exposition Minal, Héricourt 12012
Musée-Atelier Werner-Lichtner-Aix, Sérignan-du-
Comtat 14718
Musée Claude Monet, Giverny 11871
Musée d'Art Américain, Giverny 11872
Musée d'Art et d'Histoire de Lisieux, Lisieux 12621
Musée de Melun, Melun 12923
Musée du Docteur Faure, Aix-les-Bains 10260
Musée Ingres, Montauban 13048
Musée Marmottan Claude Monet, Paris 13627
Musée National Eugène Delacroix, Paris 13640
Musée Paul Gauguin, Pont-Aven 13804
Musée Petiet, Limoux 12619
Musée Renoir, Cagnes-sur-Mer 10991
Musée Toulouse-Lautrec, Albi 10276

French Polynesia
Musée Paul Gauguin, Papeete 15347

Germany
Behnhaus/ Drägerhaus, Lübeck 18533
Fürst Pückler Museum - Park und Schloß Branitz,
Cottbus 16501
Gemäldegalerie Dachau, Dachau 16523
Hans-Thoma-Gedächtnisstätte und
Vortaunusmuseum, Oberursel 19212
Hans-Thoma-Museum, Bernau, Baden 16121
Jakob-Grünenwald-Gedächtnisstätte, Ebersbach an
der Fils 16766
Kunstmuseum Hohenkarpfen, Hausen ob
Verena 17645
Lenbachmuseum, Schrobenhausen 19852
Leonhardi-Museum, Dresden 16694
Max-Klinger-Gedenkstätte, Naumburg, Saale 18979
Museum Bad Arolsen, Bad Arolsen 15591
Museum Villa Stuck, München 18887
Neue Pinakothek, München 18889
Schack-Galerie, München 18904
Schloss Oranienbaum, Oranienbaum 19263
Slevogthof Neukastel, Leinsweiler 18379
Staatsgalerie in der Kunsthalle, Augsburg 15570
Stadtmuseum Hüfingen, Hüfingen 17853
Stiftung B.C. Koekkoek-Haus, Kleve 18108

Greece
Art Gallery of the Municipality and Town of
Mesolongion, Mesolongion 21064

Italy
Collezione Jucker, Milano 24380
Museo Bottega della Tarsia Lignea, Sorrento 25610
Museo Civico Giovanni Fattori, Livorno 24191
Pinacoteca Comunale V. Bindi, Giulianova 24031

Japan
Ehime-kenritsu Bijutsukan, Matsuyama 26483
Ishibashi Museum of Art and Asian Gallery,
Kurume 26388
Yamatane Bijutsukan, Tokyo 26958

Netherlands
Museum Mesdag, Den Haag 29112
Van Gogh Documentatiecentrum, Nuenen 29648
Van Gogh Museum, Amsterdam 28911

New Zealand
Aigantighe Art Museum, Timaru 30264
The Suter, Te Aratoi o Whakatu, Nelson 30211

Norway
Oscarshall Slott, Oslo 30757

Russia
Bogorodickij Dvorec-muzej i Park, Bogorodick 32694
Chudožestvenno-memorialnyj Muzej K.S. Petrova-
Vodkina, Chvalynsk 32746
Dom-muzej P.P. Čistjakova, Puškin 33335
Muzej-kvartira A.I. Kuindži, Sankt-Peterburg 33452

Spain
Museu d'Art Modern 'Jaume Morera, Lleida 34970

Sweden
Carl Larsson-Gården, Sundborn 36305
Prins Eugens Waldemarsudde, Stockholm 36274

Switzerland
Aargauer Kunsthaus, Aarau 36424
Kunstmuseum, Sankt Gallen 37102
Museum Oskar Reinhart am Stadtgarten,
Winterthur 37337
Ortsmuseum mit Karl-Jauslin-Sammlung,
Muttenz 36977
Pinacoteca Cantonale Giovanni Züst, Rancate 37041
Segantini-Museum, Sankt Moritz 37115
Stiftung Sammlung E.G. Bührle, Zürich 37410

United Kingdom
Birmingham Museum and Art Gallery,
Birmingham 38214

Hartlepool Art Gallery, Hartlepool 39175
Haworth Art Gallery, Accrington 37959

Painting, 20th C.

Algeria
Musée Emile Aubry, Béjaïa 00051

Australia
Canberra School of Art Gallery, Acton 00699
Nolan Gallery, Tharwa 01529

Austria
Dokumentationszentrum Prof. Sepp Mayrhuber,
Pöchlarn 02420
Fritz Fröhlich-Sammlung im Stift Wilhering,
Wilhering 03032
Galerie im Nachtwächterhaus, Poysdorf 02440

Belgium
Musée de Louvain-la-Neuve, Louvain-la-
Neuve 03600
Museum Ensorhuis, Oostende 03668
Museum Paul Delvaux, Sint-Idesbald 03737

Bulgaria
Chudožestvena Galerija, Pernik 04758

Canada
Art Gallery of Sudbury, Sudbury 06507
Emily Carr Arts Centre Museum, Victoria 06719

Croatia
Memorijalna Galerija Djure Tiljka, Komiža 07717
Moderna Galerija Rijeka - Muzej Moderne i
Suvremene Umjetnosti, Rijeka 07760
Spomen Muzej Stojana Araliče, Otočac 07751
Umjetnička Galerija, Dubrovnik 07702

Czech Republic
Galerie Výtvarného Umění, Roudnice nad
Labem 08838
Národní Dům na Smíchově, Praha 08601
Zámek Moravský Krumlov - Galerie Slovanská Epopej
Alfonse Muchy, Moravský Krumlov 08488

Denmark
Carl-Henning Pedersen og Else Alfelts Museum,
Herning 08866
Jens Søndergaard Museet, Lemvig 08971

Finland
Didrichsenin Taidemuseo, Helsinki 09478
Gallen-Kallela Museum, Espoo 09432
Gösta Serlachiuksen Taidemuseo, Mänttä 09810
Imatran Taidemuseo, Imatra 09564
Lahden Taidemuseo, Lahti 09744
Sara Hildénin Taidemuseo, Tampere 10084
Tampereen Nykytaiteen Museo, Tampere 10091
Wäinö Aaltosen Museo, Turku 10138

France
Halle Saint-Pierre Museum, Paris 13515
Musée d'Art Moderne Richard Anacréon,
Granville 11911
Musée de Peinture Mario Prassinos, Saint-Rémy-de-
Provence 14450
Musée des Années 30, Boulogne-Billancourt 10837
Musée des Beaux-Arts Denys Puech, Rodez 14007
Musée Emmanuel de la Villéon, Fougères (Ille-et-
Vilaine) 11794
Musée Mathurin Méheut, Lamballe 12311
Musée Matisse, Le Cateau-Cambrésis 12396
Musée Municipal d'Art Naïf, Noyers (Yonne) 13371
Musée Pol Mara, Gordes 11888
Musée Toulouse-Lautrec, Albi 10276
Musée Utrillo-Valadon, Sannois 14603

French Polynesia
Musée Paul Gauguin, Papeete 15347

Germany
Bauhaus-Archiv, Berlin 15916
Brücke Museum, Berlin 15931
Diözesanmuseum, Freising 17121
Franz-Marc-Museum, Kochel am See 18124
Fritz-Best-Museum, Kronberg 18247
Galerie Am Markt, Bad Saulgau 15731
Galerie Neue Meister, Dresden 16682
Gemäldegalerie Dachau, Dachau 16523
Große Kunstschau, Worpswede 20683
Kunsthalle Bielefeld, Bielefeld 16156
Kunsthalle Mannheim, Mannheim 18612
Kunsthalle Würth, Schwäbisch Hall 19868
Kunstmuseum, Mülheim an der Ruhr 18816
Kunstmuseum Hohenkarpfen, Hausen ob
Verena 17645
Kunstsammlungen der Ruhr-Universität Bochum,
Bochum 16196
Molerhiisli, Hausach 17642
Museum am Ostwall, Dortmund 16661
Museum im Kulturspeicher, Würzburg 20700
Museum Langenargen/ Bodensee,
Langenargen 18325
Museum Theo Kerg, Schriesheim 19850
Museum Würth, Künzelsau 18259
Neues Schloß Meersburg, Meersburg 18677
Nolde-Museum, Neukirchen bei Niebüll 19039

Otto-Dix-Haus Hemmenhofen, Gaienhofen 17191
Otto Modersohn Museum, Ottersberg 19326
Saarland Museum, Saarbrücken 19727
Schloß Villa Ludwigshöhe mit Max-Slevogt-Galerie,
Edenkoben 16780
Staatsgalerie in der Kunsthalle, Augsburg 15570
Staatsgalerie moderner Kunst in der Pinakothek der
Moderne, München 18917
Städtische Galerie, Ettlingen 16976
Städtische Galerie im Rathauspark, Gladbeck 17292
Städtische Kunstsammlung, Murrhardt 18964
Wilhelm-Morgner-Haus, Soest 19981

Greece
Art Gallery of the Municipality and Town of
Mesolongion, Mesolongion 21064
Museum of Contemporary Greek Painters,
Amfissa 20818
Papadopoulos Picture Gallery, Tinos 21200

Hungary
Czóbel Béla Múzeum, Szentendre 21569
Vasarely Múzeum, Pécs 21517

India
Baroda Museum and Picture Gallery, Vadodara 22048

Ireland
Crawford Municipal Art Gallery, Cork 22403

Israel
Chagall House, Haifa 22600
Haifa Museum of Art, Haifa 22605
Janco-Dada Museum, Ein Hod 22590
Municipal Museum, Dimona 22586
Rubin Museum, Tel Aviv 22773
Ticho House, Jerusalem 22666

Italy
Civica Galleria d'Arte Moderna, Gallarate 23950
Galleria Civica d'Arte Moderna, Spoleto 25622
Galleria d'Arte Moderna e Contemporanea R. Guttuso,
Bagheria 22998
Museo d'Arte C. Barbella, Chieti 23545
Museo Depero, Rovereto 25292
Museo di Arte Moderna e Contemporanea di Trento e
Rovereto, Rovereto 25293
Peggy Guggenheim Collection, Venezia 25948

Japan
Abashiri Kyodo Bijutsukan, Abashiri 26083
Aichi-ken Bijutsukan, Nagoya, Aichi 26563
Ikeda 20-seiki Bijutsukan, Ito 26263
Kurayoshi Museum, Kurayoshi 26386
Morioka Hashimoto Museum of Art, Morioka 26518
Niigata-kenritsu Kindai Bijutsukan, Nagaoka 26536
Yamatane Bijutsukan, Tokyo 26958

Jordan
Jordan National Gallery of Fine Arts, Amman 27055

Netherlands
Chabot Museum, Rotterdam 29748
Gemeentemuseum Den Haag, Den Haag 29095
Museum De Wieger, Deurne 29141
Stedelijk Museum Amsterdam, Amsterdam 28902

New Zealand
Aigantighe Art Museum, Timaru 30264

Norway
Henie Onstad Kunstsenter, Høvikodden 30571
Mons Breidvik Galleries, Norheimsund 30713

Philippines
Ateneo Art Gallery, Quezon City 31429

Portugal
Museu de Ovar, Ovar 32325
Museu Municipal Amadeo de Souza-Cardoso,
Amarante 32235

Russia
Galereja Forum, Sankt-Peterburg 33394
Kartinnaja Galereja Pejzažej P.M. Grečiškina,
Stavropol 33561
Memorialnyj Dom-muzej P.D. Korina, Moskva 33076
Muzej-kvartira I.I. Brodskogo, Sankt-Peterburg 33449
Muzej-usadba I.E. Repina, Repino 33347
Udmurtskij Respublikanskij Muzej Izobrazitelnych
Iskusstv, Iževsk 32837

Serbia-Montenegro
Savremena Galerija Umetničke Kolonije Ečka,
Zrenjanin 33933

Slovenia
Mestna Galerija Ljubljana, Ljubljana 34110
Napotnikova Galerija, Šoštanj 34153
Umetnostna Galerija Maribor, Maribor 34129

Spain
Museu d'Art Modern 'Jaume Morera, Lleida 34970

Switzerland
Adolf-Dietrich-Haus, Berlingen 36538
Kirchner Museum Davos, Davos Platz 36654
Musée de Pully, Pully 37039
Picasso-Museum, Luzern 36915

Turkey
Ayşe ve Ercümend Kalmık Vakfı-Müzesi,
Gümüşsuyu 37685

United Kingdom
Dean Gallery, Edinburgh 38876
Grundy Art Gallery, Blackpool 38246
Hartlepool Art Gallery, Hartlepool 39175
Middlesbrough Art Gallery, Middlesbrough 39949
Scottish National Gallery of Modern Art Gallery, Edinburgh 38916

Venezuela
Museo de Bellas Artes de Caracas, Caracas 48914

Painting, English

Belgium
Arentshuis, Brugge 03246

India
Birla Academy of Art and Culture Museum, Kolkata 21900

Ireland
Fota House, Carrigtwohill 22385

New Zealand
Dunedin Public Art Gallery, Dunedin 30145

United Kingdom
Alfred East Art Gallery, Kettering 39346
Burton Agnes Hall, Burton Agnes 38407
The Burton Art Gallery and Museum, Bideford 38191
Bury Art Gallery and Museum, Bury, Lancashire 38411
Buscot Park House, Faringdon 38977
Cartwright Hall Art Gallery, Bradford 38296
Derby Museum and Art Gallery, Derby 38716
Falkland Palace and Garden, Falkland 38970
Falmouth Art Gallery, Falmouth 38972
Gainsborough's House, Sudbury, Suffolk 40642
Gallery Oldham, Oldham 40128
Guildhall Art Gallery, London 39654
Huddersfield Art Gallery, Huddersfield 39272
Lady Lever Art Gallery, Port Sunlight 40235
Laing Art Gallery, Newcastle-upon-Tyne 40038
Lotherton Hall, Aberford 37947
Pencarrow House, Bodmin 38267
Pollok House, Glasgow 39060
Rochdale Art and Heritage Centre, Rochdale 40332
Royal Holloway College Picture Gallery, Egham 38923
Sewerby Hall Art Gallery and Museum, Bridlington 38329
Shipley Art Gallery, Gateshead 39028
Southampton City Art Gallery, Southampton 40546
Stanley Spencer Gallery, Cookham 38629
Sudley House, Liverpool 39528
Tate Britain, London 39787
Temple Newsam House, Leeds 39452
Towner Art Gallery and Local Museum, Eastbourne 38858
Tunbridge Wells Museum and Art Gallery, Tunbridge Wells 40732
Wakefield Art Gallery, Wakefield 40764
Watts Gallery, Compton, Surrey 38621
Wednesbury Museum and Art Gallery, Wednesbury 40806
Wolverhampton Art Gallery, Wolverhampton 40918

Painting, European

Australia
Bendigo Art Gallery, Bendigo 00794
New Norcia Museum and Art Gallery, New Norcia 01314

Austria
Gemäldegalerie der Akademie der Bildenden Künste, Wien 02886
Residenzgalerie Salzburg, Salzburg 02548
Tiroler Landesmuseum Ferdinandeum, Innsbruck 02082

Belgium
Musée David et Alice Van Buuren, Bruxelles 03301

Brazil
Museu de Arte de São Paulo Assis Chateaubriand, São Paulo 04515

Canada
MacKenzie Art Gallery, Regina 06238

Czech Republic
Galerie Výtvarného Umění, Ostrava 08524
Klašter Sv. Jiří, Praha 08585
Oblastní Galerie, Liberec 08450
Okresní Muzeum Kroměřížska, Kroměříž 08435
Památník Otakara Štáfla, Havlíčkův Brod 08349
Strahovská Obrazárna, Praha 08616

Estonia
Tartu Kunstimuuseum, Tartu 09383

France
Institut Tessin, Paris 13517
Musée Boleslaw Biegas, Paris 13535
Musée Bonnat, Bayonne 10622
Musée d'Art et d'Histoire, Bergues 10691
Musée d'Art et d'Histoire, Narbonne 13267
Musée des Beaux-Arts, Angers 10346
Musée des Beaux-Arts, Caen 10983
Musée des Beaux-Arts, Lille 12599
Musée des Beaux-Arts, Lyon 12736
Musée des Beaux-Arts, Nancy 13241
Musée des Beaux-Arts, Orléans 13432
Musée des Beaux-Arts, Pau 13668
Musée des Beaux-Arts, Tours 14970
Musée des Beaux-Arts de Bordeaux, Bordeaux 10812
Musée des Beaux-Arts Jules Chéret, Nice 13317
Musée des Ursulines, Mâcon 12757
Musée Jacquemart-André, Paris 13621
Musée Manoir de Kerazan, Loctudy 12646
Musée Municipal de l'Évêché, Limoges 12616

Germany
Alte Pinakothek, München 18824
Bayerische Staatsgemäldesammlungen, München 18832
Gemäldegalerie Alte Meister, Dresden 16684
Hamburger Kunsthalle, Hamburg 17541
Herzog Anton Ulrich-Museum, Braunschweig 16297
Jagdschloß Grunewald, Berlin 16007
Kunsthalle Bremen, Bremen 16328
Kunsthalle zu Kiel der Christian-Albrechts-Universität, Kiel 18075
Kunstsammlung der Universität Göttingen, Göttingen 17334
Kunstsammlungen, Schwerin 19896
Kurpfälzisches Museum der Stadt Heidelberg, Heidelberg 17668
Martin-von-Wagner-Museum der Universität Würzburg, Würzburg 20697
Museum Corps de Logis, Düsseldorf 16735
Museum für Europäische Gartenkunst, Düsseldorf 16736
Neue Galerie, Staatliche und Städtische Kunstsammlungen, Kassel 18028
Schloss und Schlosspark Charlottenburg mit Schinkelpavillon, Belvedere und Mausoleum, Berlin 16092
Schloßmuseum, Weimar, Thüringen 20472
Das Städel, Frankfurt am Main 17074
Städtische Galerie im Lenbachhaus und Kunstbau, München 18918
Von der Heydt-Museum, Wuppertal 20717

Greece
Ethniki Pinakothiki Mouseio Alexander Soytzoy, Athinai 20860

Ireland
National Gallery of Ireland, Dublin 22446

Italy
Fondazione Magnani Rocca, Mamiano di Traversetolo 24273
Galleria Civica Anna e Luigi Parmiggiani, Reggio Emilia 25094
Galleria Nazionale d'Arte Antica Palazzo Corsini, Roma 25163
Galleria Spada, Roma 25166

Luxembourg
Jean-Pierre Pescatore Collection Villa Vauban, Luxembourg 27561

Netherlands
Huis Singraven, Denekamp 29138
Rijksmuseum Twenthe, Enschede 29240

Norway
Hagan, Eggedal 30468
Holmsbu Billedgalleri, Holmsbu 30556
Munchs Hus, Åsgårdstrand 30398
Rogaland Kunstmuseum, Stavanger 30887
Trondheim Kunstmuseum, Trondheim 30944

Poland
Galeria Sztuki Polskiej XIX w. w Sukiennicach, Kraków 31689
Jacek Malczewski Muzeum, Radom 31938

Portugal
Casa-Museu dos Patudos, Alpiarça 32233
Museu Nacional de Arte Antiga, Lisboa 32307

Russia
Gosudarstvennyj Ėrmitaž, Sankt-Peterburg 33397
Muzej Dvorec A.D. Menšikova, Sankt-Peterburg 33433
Smolenskij Muzej-Zapovednik, Smolensk 33536
Voronežskij Chudožestvennyj Muzej im. I.N. Kramskogo, Voronež 33735

Slovenia
Narodna Galerija, Ljubljana 34114

Spain
Collecio Thyssen-Bornemisza, Barcelona 34537
Museo de los Reyes Católicos, Granada 34877

Sweden
Göteborgs Konstmuseum, Göteborg 35912
Kungliga Akademien för de Fria Konsterna, Stockholm 36252

Switzerland
Fondazione Thyssen-Bornemisza, Castagnola 36616
Kunstmuseum Basel, Basel 36505
Musée Cantonal des Beaux-Arts de Lausanne, Lausanne 36860
Museo Civico di Belle Arti, Lugano 36900
Museum Briner und Kern, Winterthur 37333
Sammlung Oskar Reinhart 'Am Römerholz', Winterthur 37339

Turkey
Erzurum Resim ve Heykel Müzesi, Erzurum 37673
İzmir Resim ve Heykel Müzesi, İzmir 37719

United Kingdom
The Bowes Museum, Barnard Castle 38087
Buscot Park House, Faringdon 38977
Cooper Gallery, Barnsley, South Yorkshire 38091
Glasgow Art Gallery and Museum, Glasgow 39046
Hampton Court Palace, East Molesey 38848
Hatton Gallery, Newcastle-upon-Tyne 40037
National Gallery, London 39729
National Gallery of Scotland, Edinburgh 38898
The New Art Gallery Walsall, Walsall 40773
Tabley House Collection, Knutsford 39405
The Walker, Liverpool 39531
The Wallace Collection, London 39798
Weston Park, Weston-under-Lizard 40837
York City Art Gallery, York 40969

Painting, French

Belgium
Musée d'Art Moderne et d'Art Contemporain, Liège 03576

France
L'Annonciade, Saint-Tropez 14491
Musée Albert André, Bagnols-sur-Cèze 10565
Musée Baron Martin, Gray 11933
Musée de la Vie Romantique, Paris 13568
Musée Départemental de l'Oise, Beauvais 10655
Musée des Beaux-Arts, Beaune 10648
Musée des Beaux-Arts, La Rochelle 12241
Musée des Beaux-Arts, Valenciennes 15054
Musée des Peintres de l'Ecole de Murol, Murol 13223
Musée Gustave Moreau, Paris 13618
Musée Jean-Honoré Fragonard, Grasse 11923
Musée-Maison Natale Gustave Courbet, Ornans 13438
Musée Matisse, Nice 13321
Musée Municipal de l'École de Barbizon - Auberge Ganne, Barbizon 10586
Musée Municipal Gautron du Coudray, Marzy 12885
Musée National de l'Orangerie, Paris 13632
Musée National Eugène Delacroix, Paris 13640
Musée National Jean-Jacques Henner, Paris 13641
Musée National Message Biblique Marc Chagall, Nice 13322
Musée Picasso, Antibes 10377
Musée Pissarro, Pontoise 13832
Musée Toulouse-Lautrec, Naucelle 13274
Musée Utrillo-Valadon, Sannois 14603
Musée Yves-Brayer, Cordes 11407

Germany
Staatsgalerie in der Residenz, Ansbach 15505

Switzerland
Museum Langmatt, Baden 36488
Petit Palais, Genève 36754

Painting, German

Germany
Atelier Otto Niemeyer-Holstein, Koserow 18213
Conzen-Sammlung, Düsseldorf 16719
Künstlerhaus Exter, Übersee 20246
Kunstforum Ostdeutsche Galerie, Regensburg 19527
Kunsthalle Rostock, Rostock 19665
Museum der Stadt Pasewalk und Künstlergedenkstätte Paul Holz, Pasewalk 19353
Pahl Museum, Mainhardt 18595
Staatsgalerie im Hohen Schloß, Füssen 17169
Toni-Merz-Museum, Sasbach bei Achern, Baden 19759

Italy
Museo Hans Multscher e Museo Civico, Vipiteno 26028

Painting, Italian

Austria
Graf Harrach'sche Familiensammlung, Rohrau 02520

France
Musée Départemental de l'Oise, Beauvais 10655
Musée des Beaux-Arts Denys Puech, Rodez 14007

Germany
Staatsgalerie in der Residenz Würzburg, Würzburg 20706

Italy
Ca'Rezzonico Museo del Settecento Veneziano, Venezia 25913
Casa Buonarroti, Firenze 23825
Casa di Giorgione, Castelfranco Veneto 23400
Casa Natale di Raffaello, Urbino 25856
Cenacolo del Ghirlandaio, Firenze 23828
Cenacolo Vinciano, Milano 24370
Centro Culturale Polivalente, Bagnacavallo 23001
Galleria Alberoni, Piacenza 24887
Galleria Colonna, Roma 25158
Galleria Comunale d'Arte, Cagliari 23244
Galleria d'Arte Moderna, Firenze 23839
Galleria d'Arte Moderna Ricci-Oddi, Piacenza 24888
Galleria degli Uffizi, Firenze 23840
Galleria dell'Accademia, Firenze 23842
Galleria dell'Accademia Tadini, Lovere 24223
Galleria di Palazzo Bianco, Genova 23982
Galleria Doria Pamphilj, Roma 25161
Galleria Estense, Modena 24434
Galleria M. Rizzi, Sestri Levante 25561
Galleria Municipale, Francavilla al Mare 23930
Galleria Nazionale, Parma 24799
Galleria Nazionale d'Arte Antica Palazzo Barberini, Roma 25162
Galleria Nazionale dell'Umbria, Perugia 24848
Galleria Nazionale di Palazzo Spinola, Genova 23984
Galleria Palatina, Firenze 23844
Galleria Regionale di Palazzo Bellomo, Siracusa 25585
Galleria Sabauda, Torino 25735
Gallerie dell'Accademia, Venezia 25920
Musei Civici agli Eremitani, Padova 24733
Museo Bandini, Fiesole 23805
Museo B.Gigli, Recanati 25086
Museo Canonica, Roma 25181
Museo Canonicale, Verona 25970
Museo Civico, Pescia 24875
Museo Civico di San Francesco, Montefalco 24517
Museo Civico e Diocesano d' Arte Sacra, Montalcino 24491
Museo Civico e Pinacoteca P.F. Crociani, Montepulciano 24538
Museo Civico Giulio Ferrari, Carpi 23353
Museo Civico Luigi Bailo, Treviso 25804
Museo Correr, Venezia 25927
Museo del Risorgimento Vittorio Emanuele Orlando, Palermo 24768
Museo della Civiltà Locale, Trevi 25799
Museo della Collegiata, Chianciano Terme 23523
Museo della Collegiata di Santa Andrea, Empoli 23730
Museo della Fondazione Querini Stampalia, Venezia 25934
Museo della Magnifica Comunità di Cadore, Pieve di Cadore 24915
Museo della Scuola Grande del Carmini, Venezia 25935
Museo della Società di Esecutori di Pie Disposizioni, Siena 25573
Museo di Arte Medioevale e Moderna, Arezzo 22921
Museo di Bevagna, Bevagna 23074
Museo di Casa Vasari, Arezzo 22922
Museo di San Giuseppe, Bologna 23130
Museo di Santa Maria delle Grazie, San Giovanni Valdarno 25375
Museo Didattico Giuseppe Pellizza, Volpedo 26048
Museo Diocesano, Cortona 23664
Museo Diocesano, Pienza 24908
Museo Giannettino Luxoro, Genova 24005
Museo Giovanni Boldini, Ferrara 23795
Museo Morandi - Collezioni Comunali d'Arte, Bologna 23140
Museo Novarese d'Arte e Storia R. Fumagalli, Novara 24649
Museo Regionale, Messina 24364
Museo Renato Brozzi, Traversetolo 25786
Museo Storico e Topografico, Firenze 23882
Museo Vanvitelliano, Caserta 23374
MUTEC Museo Pinacoteca Comunale, Barletta 23033
Palazzo Ducale, Venezia 25946
Pinacoteca, Castelfiorentino 23397
Pinacoteca Civica, Ascoli Piceno 22955
Pinacoteca Civica, Iesi 24080
Pinacoteca Civica, San Gimignano 25367
Pinacoteca Civica Francesco Podesti e Galleria Comunale d'Arte Moderna, Ancona 22885
Pinacoteca Comunale, Cesena 23507
Pinacoteca Comunale, Città di Castello 23581
Pinacoteca Comunale, Massa Fermana 24316
Pinacoteca Comunale, Assisi 22969
Pinacoteca del Pio Monte della Misericordia, Napoli 24604
Pinacoteca dell'Accademia Carrara, Bergamo 23066
Pinacoteca di Brera, Milano 24417
Pinacoteca e Museo Civico, Bettona 23072
Pinacoteca e Museo Civico, Volterra 26053
Pinacoteca e Museo de Napoli, Terlizzi 25689
Pinacoteca Giuseppe Stuard, Parma 24812
Pinacoteca, Museo delle Ceramiche, Pesaro 24861
Pinacoteca Nazionale, Bologna 23145

Pinacoteca Nazionale, Ferrara 23800
Pinacoteca Provinciale Corrado Giaquinto, Bari 23029
Pinacoteca Zelantea, Acireale 22798
Scuola Dalmata dei Santi Giorgio e Trifone, Venezia 25950
Scuola Grande Arciconfraternita di San Rocco, Venezia 25951
Scuola Grande di San Giovanni Evangelista, Venezia 25952
Studio-Museo di Giuseppe Pellizza, Volpedo 26049

Peru
Museo de Arte Italiano, Lima 31207

U.S.A.
Clowes Fund Collection, Indianapolis 44216

Painting, Latin American

Argentina
Museo Municipal de Artes Plásticas, Olavarría 00462
Museo Municipal de Bellas Artes Lucas Braulio Areco, Posadas 00484
Museo Regional de Pintura José Antonio Terry, Tilcara 00637

Bolivia
Museo del Ateneo de Bellas Artes, Sucre 03908

Brazil
Museu Antonio Parreiras, Niterói 04225
Museu Dom João VI, Rio de Janeiro 04377

Cuba
Museo Wifredo Lam, La Habana 08001

Mexico
Casa Museo José Clemente Orozco, Guadalajara 27942
Museo Casa Diego Rivera, Guanajuato 27968
Museo Casa Estudio Diego Rivera y Frida Kahlo, México 28116
Museo del Palacio de Bellas Artes, México 28160
Museo Frida Kahlo, México 28172
Museo Nacional de Arte, México 28185
Pinacoteca Virreinal de San Diego, México 28212

Puerto Rico
Popular Arts Museum, San Juan 32407

Painting, Medieval

Austria
Alte Galerie, Graz 01909
Museum des Chorherrenstifts Klosterneuburg, Klosterneuburg 02141

Czech Republic
Klašter Sv. Jiří, Praha 08585

France
Musée d'Unterlinden, Colmar 11361

Germany
Staatsgalerie in der Burg, Burghausen, Salzach 16423
Staatsgalerie in der Neuen Residenz, Bamberg 15818

Hungary
Keresztény Múzeum, Esztergom 21412

India
Birla Academy of Art and Culture Museum, Kolkata 21900

Italy
Museo Civico, Pistoia 24957
Museo Emilio Greco, Orvieto 24705

Macedonia
Umjetnička Galerija, Skopje 27593

Russia
Centralnyj Muzej Drevnerusskoj Kultury i Isskustva im. Andreja Rubleva, Moskva 33024
Rjazanskij Gosudarstvennyj Istoriko-architekturnyj Muzej-zapovednik, Rjazan 33351

Spain
Instituto Amatller de Arte Hispánico, Barcelona 34545
Museo Diocesano de Huesca, Huesca 34908

Painting, Netherlandish

Belgium
Emile Van Doren Museum, Genk 03430
Memlingmuseum Sint Janshospitaal, Brugge 03257
Musée des Beaux-Arts de Tournai, Tournai 03794
Musée des Beaux-Arts et Céramique, Verviers 03810
Museum van het Heilig Bloed, Brugge 03263
Museum Wuyts-Van Campen en Baron Caroly, Lier 03586
Rubenshuis, Antwerpen 03173
Schatkamer van de Sint-Salvatorskathedraal, Brugge 03266
Stedelijk Museum, Oudenaarde 03678
Stedelijk Museum Van der Kelen-Mertens, Leuven 03565

Germany
Staatsgalerie in der Residenz, Ansbach 15505

Italy
Galleria di Palazzo Bianco, Genova 23982
Galleria Sabauda, Torino 25735

Netherlands
Dordrechts Museum, Dordrecht 29173
Frans Walkate Archief/ SNS Historisch Archief, Kampen 29469
Groninger Museum, Groningen 29309
Jopie Huisman Museum, Workum 30021
Mauritshuis, Den Haag 29105
Museum Bredius, Den Haag 29108
Museum Het Prinsenhof, Delft 29082
Museum Kempenland, Eindhoven 29215
Museum voor Moderne Kunst, Arnhem 28941
Oudheidkundige Verzameling, Sluis 29836
Peter Van den Braken Centrum, Sterksel 29856
Rijksmuseum, Amsterdam 28898
Schilderijenzaal Prins Willem V, Den Haag 29123
Singer Museum, Laren, Noord-Holland 29499
Stedelijk Museum De Lakenhal, Leiden 29526
Ton Smits Huis, Eindhoven 29220

South Africa
Groot Constantia Manor House and Wine Museum, Constantia 34219

United Kingdom
Breamore House Museum, Breamore 38313
Raby Castle, Darlington 38698
Shipley Art Gallery, Gateshead 39028

Painting, Renaissance

Belgium
Da Vinci-Museum, Tongerlo 03783

Canada
Imhoff Art Gallery, Saint Walburg 06379

France
Musée du Clos-Lucé, Amboise 10313

Germany
Albrecht-Dürer-Haus, Nürnberg 19133
Burg Trausnitz, Landshut 18308
Städtisches Museum Schloß Rheydt, Mönchengladbach 18773

Italy
Castello d'Issogne, Issogne 24108
Galleria Nazionale delle Marche, Urbino 25857
Museo Casa Natale di Tiziano Vecellio, Pieve di Cadore 24914
Museo del Cenacolo di Andrea del Sarto a San Salvi, Firenze 23856
Pinacoteca Comunale, Sarnano 25475

Portugal
Museu de Setúbal - Convento de Jesus - Galeria de Arte Quinhentista, Setúbal 32346

Painting, Spanish

Austria
Graf Harrach'sche Familiensammlung, Rohrau 02520

France
Musée Goya, Castres 11084

Spain
Casa-Museo José Benlliure, Valencia 35596
Casa National de Goya, Fuendetodos 34827
Casa y Museo de El Greco, Toledo 35535
Colección de Arte Carmen Rodríguez Acosta, Granada 34867
Colección de la Facultad de Filosofía y Letras, Madrid 34999
Colección del Banco de España, Madrid 35003
Colección Veri, Marratxinet 35093
Ermita de San Antonio de la Florida y Museo Panteón de Goya, Madrid 35006
Museo Barrau, Santa Eulària des Riu 35417
Museo de Bellas Artes, Badajoz 34518
Museo de Bellas Artes, Córdoba 34738
Museo de Bellas Artes de Granada, Granada 34875
Museo de Bellas Artes de Santander, Santander 35431
Museo de Reproducciones de El Greco, Yecla 35709
Museo Evaristo Valle, Gijón 34847
Museo Gustavo de Maeztu, Estella 34807
Museo Jovellanos, Gijón 34848
Museo Julio Romero de Torres, Córdoba 34740
Museo Municipal Mariano Benlliure, Crevillente 34759
Museo Nicanor Piñole, Gijón 34849
Museo Romántico, Madrid 35053
Museo Sorolla, Madrid 35055
Museo Zabaleta, Quesada 35305
Museu Nacional d'Art de Catalunya, Barcelona 34585

United Kingdom
Pollok House, Glasgow 39060

Paleontology → Fossils

Paper

Australia
Tamworth City Gallery, Tamworth 01515

Belgium
Musée National du Papier, Malmedy 03607

Canada
Centre d'Exposition sur l'Industrie des Pâtes et Papiers, Trois-Rivières 06639

Czech Republic
Papírna Muzeum, Velké Losiny 08712

Denmark
Bruunshåb Gamle Papfabrik, Viborg 09107

Finland
Myllysaaren Museo, Valkeakoski 10172
Paperimuseo, Espoo 09436
Verlan Tehdasmuseo, Verla 10191

France
Musée Au fil du papier, Pont-à-Mousson 13799
Musée de la Bande Dessinée, Angoulême 10354
Musée du Papier Le Nil, Angoulême 10357
Musée Historique du Papier, Ambert 10304
Musée Historique du Papier, Couze-et-Saint-Front 11447

Germany
Firmenmusemum Novatech, Reutlingen 19575
Museum Papiermühle Homburg, Triefenstein 20205
Papiergeschichtliche Sammlung, Bergisch Gladbach 15898
Papiermuseum, Düren 16718
Rheinisches Industriemuseum Bergisch Gladbach, Bergisch Gladbach 15899
Sammlung für Papier- und Druckgeschichte, Frankenberg, Sachsen 17028
Wilhelm-Hack-Museum Ludwigshafen am Rhein, Ludwigshafen am Rhein 18523

Italy
Museo Civico della Carta, Cairate 23256
Museo del Papiro, Siracusa 25587
Museo della Carta, Amalfi 22870
Museo della Carta e della Filigrana, Fabriano 23746
Museo della Carta e della Filigrana, Pioraco 24940
Museo della Cartolina S. Nuvoli, Isera 24102
Museo della Filigrana, Campo Ligure 23300

Japan
Kami no Hakubutsukan, Tokyo 26866

Malaysia
Muzium Layang Layang, Melaka 27671

Mexico
Museo del Molino de Papel, México 28158

Netherlands
Museum van Knipkunst, Westerbork 29996
Papiermolen de Schoolmeester, Westzaan 29999

Norway
Norsk Emballasje Museum, Oslo 30749

Poland
Muzeum Papiernictwa, Duszniki Zdrój 31559

Spain
Museo Molino Papelero de Capellades, Capellades 34674

Switzerland
Basler Papiermühle, Basel 36498

United Kingdom
Heron Corn Mill and Museum of Papermaking, Beetham 38150
The Whitworth Art Gallery, Manchester 39904

U.S.A.
Liquid Paper Museum, Nambe 45593
Robert C. Williams American Museum of Papermaking, Atlanta 41356

Peasant Life and Traditions

Argentina
Museo Posta de Yatasto, Metán 00447

Australia
Blacksmith's Cottage, Bacchus Marsh 00757
Carboolture Historical Village and Museum, Caboolture 00871
Chiverton House Museum, Northampton 01330
City of Gosnells Museum, Gosnells 01068
Clifton and District Historical Museum, Clifton 00928
Cottage Blundell's, Canberra 00885
Hunter Valley Museum of Rural Life, Scone 01444
Kalamunda History Village, Kalamunda 01130
Murchison Settlement Museum, Mullewa 01287

Austria
Alte Wassermühlen und Museum Des Bauern Sach und Zeug, Maria Luggau 02267
Bauernmühle-Dorfmuseum, Finkenstein 01838
Bauernmuseum Großklein, Großklein 01955
Bauernmuseum Guntersdorf, Guntersdorf 01972
Bauernmuseum Lanzenkirchen, Lanzenkirchen 02189
Bauernmuseum Osternach, Ort im Innkreis 02385
Bauernmuseum Spannberg, Spannberg 02667
Bergbauernmuseum, Wildschönau 03029
Denkmalhof Arler, Abtenau 01639
Familienmuseum im Altbauernhaus, Göstling an der Ybbs 01900
Freilichtmuseum Historische Volkskunde Kalte Kuchl, Rohr im Gebirge 02519
Freilichtmuseum Tiroler Bauernhöfe, Kramsach 02152
Heimathaus Litzelsdorf, Litzelsdorf 02245
Holzknechtmuseum im Salzkammergut, Bad Goisern 01701
Holzknechtmuseum Trübenbach im Naturpark Ötscher-Tormäuer, Wienerbruck 03023
Mentlhof-Bergbauernmuseum, Heiligenblut 02016
Museum für bäuerliche Arbeitsgeräte, Imst 02055
Museum Humanum, Waldkirchen 02790
Museum im Tabor, Feldbach 01827
Oberösterreichisches Freilichtmuseum Sumerauerhof, Sankt Florian 02561
Paznauner Bauernmuseum, Mathon 02279
Tiroler Bauernhausmuseum, Kitzbühel 02119
Volkskundlich-Landwirtschaftliche Sammlung, Stainz 02674
Waldviertler Bauernhaus-Museum, Weitra 02809
Waldviertler Bauernhof-Museum, Gföhl 01878

Belgium
Musée de la Vie Paysanne, Dampicourt 03372
Musée de la Vie Rurale en Wallonie, Saint-Hubert 03719
Museum een Eeuw Landelijk Leven, Torhout 03785
Stedelijk Museum-Hoevemuseum, Sint-Truiden 03753
Zwischen Venn und Schneeifel, Saint-Vith 03724

Brazil
Museu de Comunicação Social Hipólito José da Costa, Porto Alegre 04280

Canada
Fishermen's Life Museum, Jeddore Oyster Ponds 05632
Red Deer and District Museum, Red Deer 06222
Whitchurch-Stouffville Museum, Gormley 05503

Cuba
Museo El Piñero, Nueva Gerona 08060
Museo Municipal de Boyeros, La Habana 07979

Czech Republic
Valašské Muzeum v Přírodě, Rožnov pod Radhoštěm 08642

Denmark
Ærø Museum, Ærøskøbing 08764
Als Hjemstavnsmuseum, Hadsund 08852
Frilandsmuseet, Kongens Lyngby 08962
Odsherreds Kulturhistorike Museum, Højby 08882

Estonia
Mulgi Külamuuseum, Halliste 09320

Finland
Herttoniemen Museo, Helsinki 09495
Hollolan Kotiseutumuseo, Hollola 09551
Juvan Museo, Juva 09591
Kainuun Museo, Kajaani 09610
Kangasniemen Museo, Kangasniemi 09619
Kokemäen Ulkomuseo, Kokemäki 09680
Merimiehen Koti, Uusikaupunki 10154
Museokylä Kalluntalo, Laukaa 09770
Nivalan Museo Katvala, Nivala 09865
Oriveden Pitäjänmäen Museo, Orivesi 09888
Pielaveden Kotiseutumuseo, Pielavesi 09928
Porlammin Kotiseutumuseo, Porlammi 09948
Rovaniemen Kotiseutumuseo, Rovaniemi 10003
Saamelaismuseo Siida, Inari 09569
Saloisten Kotiseutumuseo, Arkkukari 09417
Seurasaaren Ulkomuseo, Helsinki 09527
Talomuseo, Kuortane 09725
Työväenasuntomuseo, Helsinki 09544

Vihannin Kotiseutumuseo, Vihanti 10194
Ypäjän Kotiseutumuseo, Ypäjä 10219

France
Ecomusée d'Alsace, Ungersheim 15026
Écomusée de la Bourrine du Bois Juquaud, Saint-Hilaire-de-Riez 14261
Ecomusée des Pays de l'Oise, Beauvais 10653
Ecomusée d'Hannonville, Hannonville-sous-les-Côtes 11988
Maison de l'Eclusier, Saint-Malo-de-Guersac 14339
Musée Alice Taverne, Ambierle 10305
Musée Conservatoire Maritime et Rural, Narbonne 13266
Musée d'Arts et Traditions Populaires, Marmoutier 12831
Musée d'Arts et Traditions Populaires, Yssingeaux 15329
Musée de Kerhinet, Saint-Lyphard 14333
Musée de la Ferme d'Antan, Jugon-lès-Lacs 12100
Musée de la Goubaudière, Cholet 11299
Musée de la Paysannerie, Baguer-Morvan 10567
Musée de la Vie Rurale, Steenwerck 14802
Musée de l'Habitat rural en Pays d'Aigues, La Tour-d'Aigues 12267
Musée de Pays de Seine-et-Marne, Saint-Cyr-sur-Morin 14175
Musée des Petits Métiers de la Ferme, Wervicq-Sud 15311
Musée des Tradition de l'île, Noirmoutier-en-l'Ile 13358
Musée des Vieux Métiers, Saissac 14566
Musée du Bugey-Valmorey, Lochieu 12641
Musée du Charroi Rural, Salmiech 14586
Musée du Monde Rural, Rettel 13951
Musée Ferme d'Autrefois et Matériel Artisanal, Thourie 14904
Musée-Maison de la Vie Rurale, La Flocellière 12181
Musée Mnemosina, Prunelli-di-Fium'Orbu 13882
Musée Pastoral le Monde Paysan d'Autrefois, Saint-Pé-de-Bigorre 14408
Musée Rural, Foucherans 11790
Musée Rural, Saint-André-d'Embrun 14106
Musée Rural de la Sologne Bourbonnaise, Beaulon 10641
Musée Rural du Porzay, Plomodiern 13764
Musée Villageois d'Orgon, Orgon 13425

Germany
Ackerbürgermuseum Haus Leck, Grebenstein 17380
Agrarmuseum Wandlitz, Wandlitz 20390
Bäuerliches Museum im Achentaler Heimathaus, Rohrdorf 19642
Bauern- und Handwerker-Museum, Malgersdorf 18608
Bauernhaus-Museum, Wolfegg 20649
Bauernhausmuseum, Bad Füssing 15646
Bauernhausmuseum Altburg, Calw 16446
Bauernhausmuseum Hohenstein, Württemberg, Hohenstein, Württemberg 17816
Bauernhausmuseum Schniderlihof, Oberried 19195
Bauernmuseum, Zahna 20732
Bauernmuseum Blankensee, Trebbin 20193
Bauernmuseum Inzigkofen, Inzigkofen 17913
Bauernmuseum Zabeltitz, Zabeltitz 20731
BLM Bauernhaus-Museum Bortfeld, Wendeburg 20509
Börde-Museum Burg Ummendorf, Ummendorf 20263
Brandenburgisches Freilichtmuseum Altranft, Altranft 15472
Bürger- und Bauernmuseum, Hilzingen 17764
Burg- und Mühlenmuseum Pewsum, Krummhörn 18254
Dorfmuseum Ahnenhaus, Pliezhausen 19417
Dorfmuseum Buchenberg, Königsfeld im Schwarzwald 18176
Dorfmuseum Deckenpfronn, Deckenpfronn 16556
Dorfmuseum Dettingen/Iller, Dettingen an der Iller 16594
Dorfmuseum Poppenweiler, Ludwigsburg, Württemberg 18511
Fränkische Hopfenscheune mit heimatkundlicher Sammlung, Neunkirchen am Sand 19053
Fränkisches Freilandmuseum Fladungen, Fladungen 17009
Freilichtmuseum Beuren, Beuren bei Nürtingen 16133
Freilichtmuseum Dorfstube Ötlingen, Weil am Rhein 20434
Freilichtmuseum Neuhausen ob Eck, Neuhausen ob Eck 19035
Fürstenbergerhof, Zell am Harmersbach 20739
Heimatmuseum, Buttstädt 16436
Heimatmuseum, Höpfingen 17787
Heimatmuseum, Neckargerach 18989
Heimatmuseum, Nellingen 18992
Heimatmuseum, Neukirch, Lausitz 19038
Heimatmuseum, Schöneiche bei Berlin 19830
Heimatmuseum Altmannstein, Altmannstein 15460
Heimatmuseum Flacht, Weissach, Württemberg 20490
Heimatmuseum Ihringen, Ihringen 17883
Heimatmuseum im Vogteigebäude, Hüttlingen 17863
Heimatmuseum Mehrstetten, Mehrstetten 18683
Heimatmuseum Obere Mühle, Loßburg 18507
Heimatmuseum Seßlach, Seßlach 19941
Heimatmuseum Untergrombach, Bruchsal 16367
Heimatstube Fischbach, Niedereschach 19097
Heimatstube Mühlhausen, Villingen-Schwenningen 20318
Heimatstube Neuhaus-Schiernitz, Neuhaus-Schierschnitz 19034
Heimatstuben, Waldbronn 20353
Heimatstuben der Csávolyer im Beinsteiner Torturm, Waiblingen 20349
Hohenloher Freilandmuseum, Schwäbisch Hall 19867
Karpatendeutsches Museum, Karlsruhe 17994
Kreisheimatmuseum, Grimma 17401
Mönchguter Museen im Ostseebad Göhren, Göhren, Rügen 17313
Museum, Mühlacker 18801
Museum Alte Lateinschule Großenhain, Großenhain, Sachsen 17429
Museum im Adler, Benningen 15879
Museum Im Dorf, Reutlingen 19577
Museum im Seelhaus, Bopfingen 16253
Museum Kalt-Heiß, Deckenpfronn 16557
Museumsdorf Bayerischer Wald, Tittling 20181
Museumsdorf Cloppenburg, Cloppenburg 16479
Museumshof, Bad Oeynhausen 15709
Museumshof auf dem Braem, Gescher 17266
Niederlausitzer Heidemuseum, Spremberg 20016
Niederrheinisches Freilichtmuseum, Grefrath 17383
Oberschwäbisches Museumsdorf Kreisfreilichtmuseum Kürnbach, Bad Schussenried 15736
Odenwälder Freilandmuseum, Walldürn 20378
Reubacher Heimatmuseum, Rot 19669
Rheinisches Freilichtmuseum und Landesmuseum für Volkskunde Kommern, Mechernich 18669
Rhön-Museum, Fladungen 17010
Rieser Bauernmuseum, Maihingen 18592
Schwäbisches Bauern- und Technikmuseum, Eschach 16930
Schwarzwälder Freilichtmuseum Vogtsbauernhof, Gutach, Schwarzwaldbahn 17467
Stadt-und Wagenmuseum Oschatz, Oschatz 19273
Städtische Museen Wangen im Allgäu, Wangen im Allgäu 20395
Städtisches Museum, Korbach 18210
Stormarnsches Dorfmuseum, Altes Bauernhaus am Thie, Hoisdorf 17821
Ungarn-deutsche Heimatstuben, Langenau, Württemberg 18328
Vilstaler Bauernmuseum, Eichendorf 16801
Vogtländisches Freilichtmuseum Landwüst, Landwüst 18315
Volkskunde-Museum, Rudolstadt 19701
Volkskunde- und Freilichtmuseum, Konz 18208
Waldhufen-Heimatmuseum Salmbach, Engelsbrand 16872
Westfälisches Freilichtmuseum Detmold, Detmold 16590

Hungary
Göcseji Falumúzeum, Zalaegerszeg 21613
Sóstói Múzeumfalu, Sóstógyógyfürdő 21540
Szabadtéri Néprajzi Gyűjtemény, Szenna 21566
Szabadtéri Néprajzi Múzeum, Szentendre 21575
Vasi Múzeumfalu, Szombathely 21590

Italy
Casa Museo A. Uccello, Palazzolo Acreide 24759
Cascina Museo della Civiltà Contadina, Cremona 23677
Galleria del Maggio, Villa Minozzo 26014
Mostra della Civiltà Contadina, Massa Marittima 24320
Museo Contadino, Varese Ligure 25900
Museo del Lavoro Contadino, Campobello di Mazara 23305
Museo del Lavoro e della Tradizioni Popolari della Versilia Storica, Seravezza 25542
Museo della Canape e della Vita Contadina, Bentivoglio 23055
Museo della Civiltà Contadina, Novellara 24656
Museo della Civiltà Contadina, Moio della Civitella 24456
Museo della Civiltà Contadina del Cilento, Montecorice 24516
Museo della Civiltà Contadina dell'Alto Monferrato e della Bassa Langa, Castagnole delle Lanze 23384
Museo della Civiltà Rurale del Vicentino, Malo 24271
Museo della Rocca, Dozza 23723
Museo dell'Agricoltura e del Mondo Rurale, San Martino in Rio 25390
Museo delle Contadinerie, Costigliole d'Asti 23672
Museo di Civiltà Contadina, Castelnuovo Calcea 23419
Museo di Storia e Cultura Contadina, Genova 23999
Museo Etnografico Coumboscuro della Civiltà Provenzale in Italia, Sancto Lucia de Coumboscuro 25422
Museo Etnografico Romagnolo Benedetto Pergoli, Forlì 23914
Museo Ettore Pomarici Santomasi, Gravina di Puglia 24050
Museo Provinciale della Vita Contadina, San Vito al Tagliamento 25419
Raccolta d'Arte Ubaldiana, Piandimeleto 24897

Korea, Republic
Jungmun Folklore Museum, Seogwipo 27220

Lebanon
Saint Sharbel Museum, Annaya 27479

Malaysia
Wedding and Custom Museum, Kuah 27635

Mexico
Museo del Campesino, Xochitepec 28627

Netherlands
Allerhande, Hippolytushoef 29424
Het Oale Meestershuus, Slagharen 29828
Openluchtmuseum Het Hoogeland, Warffum 29978
De Sfeer van Weleer, Rekken 29725
Themapark Openluchtmuseum De Spitkeet, Harkema 29344

Norway
Agatunet, Nå 30697
Bø Museum, Bø i Telemark 30438
Hemnes Museum, Bjerka 30433
Inderøy Museums- og Historielag, Inderøy 30576
Lesja Bygdatun, Lesja 30637
Oppdal Bygdemuseum, Oppdal 30716
Rollag Bygdetun, Rollag 30801
De Samiske Samlinger, Karasjok 30590
Søgne Bygdemuseum, Søgne 30859
Stor-Elvdal Museum, Koppang 30607
Sunnhordland Folkemuseum og Sogelag, Stord 30900
Tingvoll Museum, Tingvoll 30921
Tynset Bygdemuseum, Tynset 30957
Valdres Folkemusum, Fagernes 30484

Poland
Muzeum Przyrodniczo-Leśne Świętokrzyskiego Parku Narodowego, Święty Krzyż 32018
Muzeum Wsi Lubelskiej, Lublin 31795

Romania
Muzeul Țăranului Român, București 32470

Russia
Gosudarstvennyj Istoriko-ėtnografičeskij Muzej-zapovednik Šušenskoe, Šušenskoe 33569
Ibresinskij Ėtnografičeskij Muzej pod Otkryrym Nebom, Ibresi 32810
Oloneckij Nacionalnyj Muzej Karelov-Livvikov im. N.T.Prilukin, Olonec 33252
Osinskij Kraevedčeskij Muzej, Osa 33273
Šeltozerskij Vepsskij Ėtnografičeskij Muzej, Šeltozero 33515

Spain
Museu dels Raiers, El Pont de Claverol 35280

Sweden
Ekehagens Forntidsby, Åsarp 35819
Hägnan Friluftsmuseet i Gammelstad, Gammelstad 35902
Örnsköldsviks Museum, Örnsköldsvik 36144

Switzerland
Bauernhaus-Museum, Muttenz 36975
Bauernmuseum Althuus, Gurbü 36786
Heimatmuseum, Oberweningen 37004
Heimatmuseum Bucheggberg, Buchegg 36596
Heimatmuseum der Albert-Edelmann-Stiftung, Ebnat-Kappel 36669
Musée Paysan et Artisanal, La Chaux-de-Fonds 36631
Museo della Civiltà Contadina del Mendrisiotto, Stabio 37198
Museum Stammertal, Unterstammheim 37267
Museum zur Ronmühle, Schötz 37144
Orts- und Wohnmuseum, Marthalen 36922
Ortsmuseum Hinwil, Hinwil 36804
Ortsmuseum zur Hohlen Eich, Wädenswil 37297
Schweizerisches Freilichtmuseum für ländliche Kultur, Brienz, Bern 36587

United Kingdom
Auchindrain Museum of Country Life, Inveraray 39292
Blists Hill Victorian Town Open Air Museum, Madeley 39870
Breamore Countryside Museum, Breamore 38312
Calbourne Water Mill and Rural Museum, Calbourne 38437
Cotswold Heritage Centre, Northleach 40085
Folk Museum, Câtel 38511
Glenesk Folk Museum, Brechin 38315
Great Barn Museum of Wiltshire Rural Life, Avebury 38042
Grove Rural Life Museum, Ramsey, Isle of Man 40280
Lackham Museum of Agriculture and Rural Life, Lacock 39409
Mesolithic Museum, Abinger Common 37958
Mullach Ban Folk Museum, Mullach Ban 39994
Museum of East Anglian Life, Stowmarket 40618
Museum of Kent Life, Sandling 40443
Perry's Cider Mills, Ilminster 39288
Roots of Norfolk at Gressenhall, Gressenhall 39132
Rural Life Centre, Farnham 38983
Stanmer Rural Museum, Brighton 38345
Usk Rural Life Museum, Usk 40753
Wayside Folk Museum, Zennor 40975
White House Museum of Buildings and Country Life, Aston Munslow 38037

U.S.A.
Ashland Logging Museum, Ashland 41289
Battles Museums of Rural Life, Girard 43676
Blue Ridge Institute and Museum, Ferrum 43317
Calvin Coolidge State Historic Site, Plymouth Notch 46569
Coggeshall Farm Museum, Bristol 41905
Forest Capital State Museum, Perry 46354
Fred Dana Marsh Museum, Ormond Beach 46192
Frontier Culture Museum, Staunton 47795
Georgia Agrirama, Tifton 48007
Gibbs Museum of Pioneer and Dakotah Life, Falcon Heights 43279
Hans Herr House and Museum, Willow St 48644
Independence Visitors Center, Independence 44204
Lum and Abner Museum and Jot 'Em Down Store, Pine Ridge 46491
Midway Village and Museum, Rockford 46961
Mountain Life Museum, London 44853
Museum of Rural Life, Denton 42873
Naper Settlement Museum, Naperville 45600
Patten Lumberman's Museum, Patten 46312
South County Museum, Narragansett 45605
The Spanish Quarter Museum, Saint Augustine 47074
Storrowton Village Museum, West Springfield 48548
Stuttgart Agricultural Museum, Stuttgart 47865
Volo Antique Auto Museum and Village, Volo 48257
Watson Farm, Jamestown 44315

Performing Arts

Argentina
Museo de Instituto Nacional de Estudios de Teatro, Buenos Aires 00181
Museo de la Casa del Teatro, Buenos Aires 00184
Museo del Teatro Colón, Buenos Aires 00203
Museo del Teatro y la Música de Córdoba Cristobal de Aguilar, Córdoba 00301

Australia
Performance Space, Redfern 01410
Performing Arts Collection of South Australia, Adelaide 00712
Performing Arts Museum, Melbourne 01239

Austria
Kinder-Knürstl-Museum, Götzis 01902
Museum der Wahrnehmung, Graz 01926
Museum Sensenwerk, Deutschfeistritz 01760
Österreichisches Circus- und Clown-Museum, Wien 02956
Österreichisches Theatermuseum, Wien 02963
Puppentheatermuseum, Mistelbach an der Zaya 02302

Belgium
AMVC-Letterenhuis, Antwerpen 03135
Archives et Musée de la Littérature, Bruxelles 03270
Musée du Théâtre Royal de Toone, Bruxelles 03328

Brazil
Museu de Arte Mágica e Ilusionismo João Peixoto dos Santos, São Paulo 04516
Museu de Bonecos e Ventrílocos, São Paulo 04519
Museu de Cartão, São Paulo 04520
Museu dos Teatros do Rio de Janeiro, Rio de Janeiro 04378
Museu Teatro, Rio de Janeiro 04395

Bulgaria
Muzej na Naroden Teatar Ivan Vazov, Sofia 04842
Muzej na Narodnata Opera, Sofia 04843

China, People's Republic
Beijing Animation Art Museum, Beijing 06944
Beijing Opera Museum, Beijing 06953
Sanying Pagoda and Museum of Dinosaur, Shaoguan 07230
Tianjin Drama Museum, Tianjin 07264

Costa Rica
Galeria Teatro Nacional Enrique Echandi y Joaquín García Monge, San José 07653

Cyprus
Nikos Nikolaides Theatrical Archives, Lemesos 08212

Czech Republic
Měninská Brána, Brno 08269
Moravské Zemské Muzeum, Brno 08272

Denmark
Teatermuseet i Hofteatret, København 08951

Estonia
Eesti Teatri- ja Muusikamuuseum, Tallinn 09363

Finland
Teatterimuseo, Helsinki 09540

France
Bibliothèque-Musée de la Comédie-Française, Paris 13475
Manoir de Veygoux, Scénomusée des Combrailles, Charbonnières-les-Varennes 11173
Musée de l'Opéra National de Paris, Paris 13578
Musée du Cirque, Vatan 15096
Musée du Cirque, Wasquehal 15305
Musée du Théâtre, Couilly-Pont-aux-Dames 11424
Musée Humoristique Albert Dubout, Palavas-les-Flots 13457
Musée Jean-Gabin, Mériel 12943
Musée Kwok-On, Paris 13623

Georgia
State Theatrical Museum, Tbilisi 15367

Germany
Artistenmuseum, Marburg 18623
Augsburger Puppentheatermuseum Die Kiste, Augsburg 15550
Brecht-Weigel-Gedenkstätte, Berlin 15929

Chaplin-Archiv, Frankfurt am Main 17033
Deutsches Theatermuseum, München 18841
Ekhof-Theater, Gotha 17357
Erstes Circusmuseum in Deutschland, Preetz, Holstein 19440
Fastnachtsmuseum, Herbstein 17719
Filmmuseum Bendestorf, Bendestorf 15874
Freiburger Fasnetmuseum, Freiburg im Breisgau 17109
Historische Kuranlagen und Goethe-Theater Bad Lauchstädt, Bad Lauchstädt 15688
Karnevalmuseum, Mönchengladbach 18771
König Ludwig II.-Museum, Herrenchiemsee 17733
Markt- und Schaustellermuseum, Essen 16956
Museum für Puppentheater, Lübeck 18540
Neuberin-Museum, Reichenbach, Vogtland 19546
Puppentheatersammlung, Radebeul 19470
Stadtmuseum Rottweil, Rottweil 19698
Theatergeschichtliche Sammlung und Hebbel-Sammlung, Kiel 18080
Theatermuseum der Landeshauptstadt, Düsseldorf 16744
Theatermuseum Hannover, Hannover 17612
Theatermuseum in der Reithalle, Meiningen 18688
Theaterwissenschaftliche Sammlung, Köln 18167
Valentin-Karlstadt Musäum, München 18922
Zirkus und Varieté Archivsammlung Reinhard Tetzlaff, Hamburg 17572

Greece
Hellenic Theatre Museum and Study Center, Athinai 20866
Katina Paxinou Museum, Athinai 20868
Marika Kotopouli Museum, Zografou 21225
Museum of Delphic Celebrations of Angelos and Eva Sikellianou, Athinai 20885
Panos Aravantinos Theatrical Museum of Painting and Stage Design, Piraeus 21125
Spathareion Museum of the Shadow Theatre, Maroussi 21058

Hungary
Bajor Gizi Emlékmúzeum, Budapest 21327
Országos Színháztörténeti Múzeum és Intézet, Budapest 21375

Israel
Israel Children's Museum, Holon 22621
Israel Goor Theater Archive and Museum, Jerusalem 22642

Italy
Civico Museo Biblioteca dell'Attore del Teatro, Genova 23979
Civico Museo Setificio Monti, Abbadia Lariana 22792
Civico Museo Teatrale di Fondazione Carlo Schmidl, Trieste 25819
Collezione Minici Zotti, Padova 24732
Collezione Titta Ruffo, Pisa 24942
Mostra dei Pupi Siciliani, Caltagirone 23271
Museo del Teatro, Faenza 23753
Museo del Teatro, Spoleto 25624
Museo del Teatro dell'Aquila, Fermo 23778
Museo del Teatro Municipale, Piacenza 24892
Museo del Teatro Romagnolo, Forlì 23910
Museo dell'Attore Napoletano, Napoli 24583
Museo delle Marionette, Campomorone 23309
Museo dell'Opera di Santa Niccolao, Buggiano 23227
Museo di Peppone e Don Camillo, Brescello 23200
Museo Rodolfo Valentino, Castellaneta 23404
Museo Teatrale alla Scala, Milano 24412
Museo Teatrale del Burcardo, Roma 25261

Japan
Osaka-kenritsu Waha Kamigata Bungeikan, Osaka 26664
Sado Nohgaku-no-sato, Ryotsu 26688
Waseda Daigaku Tsubouchi Hakushi Kinen Engeki Hakubutsukan, Tokyo 26954
Yoshimoto Bungeikan, Osaka 26675

Latvia
Literature, Theatre and Music Museum, Rīga 27429

Mexico
Museo Teatro La Casa de los Títeres, Monterrey 28240

Mongolia
Mongolian Theatre Museum, Ulaanbaatar 28679

Netherlands
Dickens Museumtheater, Bronkhorst 29030
Gouds Poppentheater en Museum, Gouda 29293
Kermis- en Circusmuseum Steenwijk, Steenwijk 29851
Oeteldonks Gemintemuzejum, 's-Hertogenbosch 29408
Poppen en Poppenhuis Museum 't Duvelke, Breda 29024
Theater Museum, Amsterdam 28908

Norway
Fritzøe Museum, Larvik 30629
Norsk Barnemuseum, Stavanger 30882
Teatermuseet i Oslo, Oslo 30767

Pakistan
Faqir Khana Museum, Lahore 31034

Poland
Muzeum Teatralne, Warszawa 32128
Muzeum Teatralne, Kraków 31720

Portugal
Museu Nacional do Teatro, Lisboa 32310

Romania
Muzeul Teatrului, Iași 32540
Muzeul Teatrului Național, București 32471

Russia
Dom-Muzej A.L. Durova, Voronež 33729
Dom-muzej M.N. Ermolovoj, Moskva 33038
Dom-muzej F.I. Šaljapina, Moskva 33042
Dom-muzej K.S. Stanislavskogo, Moskva 33043
Gorodskoj Muzej Teatralnogo Iskusstva, Omsk 33254
Gosudarstvennyj Centralnyj Teatralnyj Muzej im. Bachrušina, Moskva 33051
Gosudarstvennyj Muzej Detskich Teatrov, Moskva 33059
Kulturnyj Centr-muzej V.S. Vysockogo, Moskva 33071
Literaturno-teatralnyj Muzej N.M. Djakonova, Syktyvkar 33574
Memorialnyj Muzej-kvartira Aktërov Samojlovych, Sankt-Peterburg 33418
Muzej A Muzy ne Molčali, Sankt-Peterburg 33426
Muzej Cirkovogo Iskusstva, Sankt-Peterburg 33430
Muzej Etnografičeskogo Kostjuma na Kuklach, Moskva 33097
Muzej Gosudarstvennogo Akademičeskogo Bolšogo Teatra Rossii, Moskva 33099
Muzej Gosudarstvennogo Akademičeskogo Malogo Teatra, Moskva 33100
Muzej Gosudarstvennogo Akademičeskogo Marijnskogo Teatra Opery i Baleta, Sankt-Peterburg 33434
Muzej Gosudarstvennogo Akademičeskogo Teatra Opery i Baleta imeni Mussorgskogo, Sankt-Peterburg 33435
Muzej Istorii Teatrov Dagestana, Machačkala 32998
Muzej-kvartira Dirižëra N.S. Golovanov, Moskva 33122
Muzej-kvartira V.S. Mejercholda, Moskva 33126
Muzej-kvartira V.I. Nemiroviča-Dančenko, Moskva 33127
Muzej-kvartira F.I. Šaljapina, Sankt-Peterburg 33454
Muzej Moskovskogo Chudožestvennogo Akademičeskogo Teatra, Moskva 33135
Muzej Moskovskoj Konservatorii, Moskva 33136
Muzej Muzykalnoj i Teatralnoj Kultury na Kavkazskich Mineralnyh Vodach, Kislovodsk 32930
Muzej N.G. Rubinstejna, Moskva 33140
Muzej Sceničeskogo Iskusstva im. V.È. Mejercholda, Penza 33292
Muzej Teatra, Sankt-Peterburg 33467
Muzej Teatra Operetty, Moskva 33153
Muzej Teatralnoj Kukly A.A Veselova, Voronež 33734
Muzej-zapovednik Abramcevo, Abramcevo 32629
Sankt-Peterburgskij Muzej Teatralnogo i Musykalnogo Iskusstva, Sankt-Peterburg 33481
Teatralnyj Muzej, Kazan 32909

Serbia-Montenegro
Muzej Pozorišne Umetnosti Srbije, Beograd 33809

Slovenia
Slovenski Gledališki Muzej, Ljubljana 34120

South Africa
National Theatre Museum, Bloemfontein 34191

Spain
Museo del Teatro, Almagro 34451
Museu de les Arts Escèniques, Barcelona 34565

Sweden
Dansmuseet, Stockholm 36238
Gripes Modeltheatremuseum, Nyköping 36126
Marionettmuseet, Stockholm 36258
Smetanamuseet, Göteborg 35921
Sveriges Teatermuseum, Nacka 36110

Switzerland
Schweizerische Theatersammlung, Bern 36551

Ukraine
Museum of Theatrical, Musical and Cinematographic Art of Ukraine, Kyiv 37874

United Kingdom
Cabaret Mechanical Theatre, London 39594
Ellen Terry Memorial Museum, Tenterden 40686
Georgian Theatre Royal Museum, Richmond, North Yorkshire 40315
Greenwich Theatre Art Gallery, London 39651
Mander and Mitchenson Theatre Collection, London 39704
Museum of Entertainment, Whaplode 40848
Royal Shakespeare Company Collection, Stratford-upon-Avon 40629
Theatre Museum, London 39790
University of Bristol Theatre Collection, Bristol 38361

U.S.A.
American Museum of Magic, Marshall 45177
Arts and Science Center for Southeast Arkansas, Pine Bluff 46489
Barnum Museum, Bridgeport 41889
Bloomington Art Center, Bloomington 41751
Center for Puppetry Arts, Atlanta 41337
Central City Opera House Museum, Central City 42172
Charles B. Goddard Center for Visual and Performing Arts, Ardmore 41251
Circus City Festival Museum, Peru 46362
Circus World Museum, Baraboo 41500
Cumberland Theatre Arts Gallery, Cumberland 42725
Diverse Works, Houston 44120
Emmett Kelly Historical Museum, Sedan 47556
Ford's Theatre, Washington 48355
Hampden-Booth Theatre Museum, New York 45812
Hocking Valley Museum of Theatrical History, Nelsonville 45648
Hollywood Bowl Museum, Los Angeles 44907
Houdini Museum, Scranton 47518
International Clown Hall of Fame and Research Center, Milwaukee 45365
The John and Mable Ringling Museum of Art, Sarasota 47453
Laura and Paul Mesaros Galleries, Morgantown 45499
Marcella Sembrich Opera Museum, Bolton Landing 41778
The Museum of Vision, San Francisco 47331
National Museum of Dance, Saratoga Springs 47460
New York Public Library for the Performing Arts, New York 45859
Palm Springs Desert Museum, Palm Springs 46267
Rose Museum at Carnegie Hall, New York 45865
Tabor Opera House Museum, Leadville 44701
The Roy Rogers-Dale Evans Museum, Branson 41871
Vent Haven Museum, Fort Mitchell 43429
Visual Arts Center, Portsmouth 46667
Western Gallery, Bellingham 41603
Wexner Center for the Arts, Columbus 42593
Yerba Buena Center for the Arts, San Francisco 47346

Petroleum Industry and Trade

Argentina
Museo Nacional del Petróleo, Comodoro Rivadavia 00282

Australia
Sagasco Historical Group Museum, Brompton 00848

Austria
Erdölmuseum, Neusiedl an der Zaya 02358
Freilichtmuseum Erdöl- und Erdgaslehrpfad, Prottes 02457

Canada
Oil Museum of Canada, Oil Springs 06045
Oil Sands Discovery Centre, Fort McMurray 05446
Petrolia Discovery, Petrolia 06125
Ralph Allen Memorial Museum, Oxbow 06091
Turner Valley Gas Plant, Turner Valley 06650

France
Musée du Pétrole, Merkwiller-Pechelbronn 12947

Germany
Deutsches Erdölmuseum Wietze, Wietze 20583
ESWE Technicum, Wiesbaden 20571
Gaseum, Essen 16950
Heimatstube Hänigsen, Uetze 20252

Hungary
Magyar Olajipari Múzeum, Zalaegerszeg 21615

India
Regional Science Centre, Guwahati, Assam 21827

Japan
Gasu no Kagakukan, Takaishi 26788

Oman
Oil and Gas Exhibition Centre, Qurm 31010

Poland
Muzeum Przemysłu Naftowego w Bóbrce, Chorkówka 31531

Romania
Muzeul Național al Petrolului, Ploiești 32574

Switzerland
Öle-Museum, Münsingen 36967

United Kingdom
Aberdeen Maritime Museum, Aberdeen 37931
Biggar Gasworks Museum, Biggar 38193
Flame!, Carrickfergus 38497
The National Gas Museum, Leicester 39466

U.S.A.
Butler County Museum and Kansas Oil Museum, El Dorado 43107
California Oil Museum, Santa Paula 47443
East Texas Oil Museum at Kilgore College, Kilgore 44479
Historic Pithole City, Pleasantville 46557
Norman No. 1 Oil Well Museum, Neodesha 45649
Oil Patch Museum, Russell 47036

Pets

Austria
KiK - Kultur im Kloster, Klostermarienberg 02138

France
Musée du Chien, Villeneuve-les-Convers 15231

Netherlands
Hondenmuseum, Eindhoven 29212
Katten Kabinet, Amsterdam 28867

United Kingdom
Dog Collar Museum, Maidstone 39875

Pewter

Czech Republic
Muzeum Mladoboleslavska, Mladá Boleslav 08480

France
Musée du Terroir Marseillais, Marseille 12867

Germany
Heimatmuseum im Wachtturm, Geyer 17273
Kreismuseum Zons, Dormagen 16646
Torhaus Dölitz, Leipzig 18422
Völkerschlachtdenkmal und Forum 1813, Museum zur Geschichte der Völkerschlacht, Leipzig 18424
Weygang-Museum, Öhringen 19226

Netherlands
Het Zakkendragershuisje, Rotterdam 29781

Pharmacy

Argentina
Museo de la Farmacia Dra. D'Alessio Bonino, Buenos Aires 00188

Australia
Medical History Museum, Melbourne 01236

Austria
Destillier- und Drogenmuseum, Pernegg 02404
Grazer Stadtmuseum, Graz 01916

Belgium
Hôpital Notre-Dame de la Rose, Lessines 03561
Museactron, Maaseik 03602

Brazil
Museu Antonio Lago, Rio de Janeiro 04332
Museu da Farmáciada Santa Casa da Misericórdia do Rio de Janeiro, Rio de Janeiro 04344
Museu de Farmácia, São Paulo 04521

Canada
Niagara Apothecary, Niagara-on-the-Lake 06001
Saskatchewan Pharmacy Museum, Regina 06246

Cuba
Farmacia Museo Taquechel, La Habana 07927
Museo Farmacéutico, Matanzas 08039

Finland
Apteekkimuseo ja Qwensel, Turku 10118

France
Ancienne École de Médecine Navale, Rochefort (Charente-Maritime) 13996
Apothécairerie de l'Hôtel Dieu-le-Comte, Troyes 15000
Musée de la Pharmacie, Montpellier 13122
Musée de la Pharmacie, Tence 14873
Musée de la Pharmacie Albert Ciurana, Montpellier 13123
Musée de L'Hôpital Général de Dijon, Dijon 11526
Musée d'Histoire de la Médecine et de la Pharmacie, Lyon 12743
Musée Moissan, Paris 13628

Germany
Apotheken-Museum, Schiltach 19781
Apothekenmuseum, Hofgeismar 17795
Bad Schwalbacher Kur-Stadt-Apotheken-Museum, Bad Schwalbach 15737
Deutsches Apotheken-Museum im Heidelberger Schloß, Heidelberg 17664
Krankenhausmuseum, Nürnberg 19149
Löwen-Drogerie und Museum, Oelsnitz, Vogtland 19229
Medizin- und Pharmaziehistorische Sammlung Kiel der Christian-Albrechts-Universität, Kiel 18077
Niederlausitzer Apothekenmuseum, Cottbus 16504
Stiftung Kohl'sche Einhorn-Apotheke, Weißenburg in Bayern 20496

Hungary
Arany Sas Patika, Budapest 21325

Fekete Sas Patikamúzeum, Székesfehérvár 21556
Patikamúzeum, Kőszeg 21465

Italy
Farmacia Conventuale, Venezia 25915
Farmamuseo Sa Potecaria, Villacidro 26016
Museo della Farmacia Picciola, Trieste 25826
Raccolta di Vasi da Farmacia, Roccavaldina 25143

Japan
Dosho-machi Pharmaceutical and Historical Museum,
  Osaka 26642
Health Science Museum, Hiroshima 26210
Naito Kinen Kusuri Hakubutsukan, Kawashima,
  Gifu 26331

Netherlands
Kruidentuin de Groene Kruidhof, Elburg 29223
Medisch Farmaceutisch Museum de Griffioen,
  Delft 29080
Nederlands Drogisterij Museum, Maarssen 29558

New Zealand
Ernest and Marion Davis Medical History Museum,
  Auckland 30106

Norway
Ibsenhuset og Grimstad Bymuseet, Grimstad 30519
Norsk Farmasihistorisk Museum, Oslo 30750

Poland
Muzeum Farmacji, Warszawa 32095
Muzeum Farmacji, Kraków 31702
Muzeum Historii Medycyny i Farmacji,
  Szczecin 32026

Romania
Colecția de Istorie a Farmaciei Cluj-Napoca, Cluj-
  Napoca 32491

Russia
Farmacevtičeskij Muzej, Moskva 33044

Slovakia
Farmaceutická Expozícia, Bratislava 33962

Slovenia
Pharmaceutical and Medical Museum of Bohuslav
  Lavička, Ljubljana 34116

South Africa
Adler Museum of Medicine, Johannesburg 34267

Spain
Museo Arqueológico y de Historia Natural, Santo
  Domingo de Silos 35457
Museo de Farmacia, Llivia 34975
Museo de Farmacia, Peñaranda de Duero 35263
Museo de la Farmacia Hispana, Madrid 35025
Museo Retrospectivo de Farmacia y Medicina, El
  Masnou 35096
Museu Farmàcia de l'Hospital de Santa Catarina,
  Girona 34858
Real Cartuja, Valldemosa 35633

Sweden
Stranda Hembygdsförening, Mönsterås 36098

Switzerland
Pharmazie-Historisches Museum der Universität
  Basel, Basel 36516

United Kingdom
Museum of the Royal Pharmaceutical Society of Great
  Britain, London 39724
Pharmaceutical Society Late Victorian Pharmacy,
  Edinburgh 38905

U.S.A.
New Orleans Pharmacy Museum, New Orleans 45736
Texas Pharmacy Museum, Amarillo 41167

Philately → Postage Stamps

Philosophy

Austria
Gsellmanns Weltmaschine, Edelsbach bei
  Feldbach 01785
Ludwig Wittgenstein-Dauerausstellung, Kirchberg am
  Wechsel 02111
Sigmund Freud-Museum, Wien 02989

Belgium
Maison d'Erasme, Bruxelles 03287

Czech Republic
Památník Jana Ámoše Komenského, Bílá
  Třemešná 08248
Památník Jana Ámoše Komenského, Horní
  Branná 08360
Památník Jana Ámoše Komenského, Fulnek 08342
Pamětní Síň Jana Ámoše Komenského, Brandýs nad
  Orlicí 08257

France
Musée Jean-Jacques Rousseau, Montmorency 13111

Germany
Albert-Schweitzer-Gedenk- und Begegnungsstätte,
  Weimar, Thüringen 20454
Deutsches Freimaurermuseum, Bayreuth 15842
Ernst-Bloch-Zentrum, Ludwigshafen am Rhein 18517
Freimaurermuseum der Großen Landesloge der
  Freimaurer von Deutschland, Sankt
  Michaelisdonn 19754
Friedrich-Engels-Haus, Wuppertal 20710
Hegelhaus, Stuttgart 20095
Karl-Marx-Haus, Trier 20210
Museum Barockschloß Rammenau,
  Rammenau 19481
Nietzsche-Archiv, Weimar, Thüringen 20467
Novalis-Museum, Wiederstedt 20566
Wilhelm-Ostwald-Gedenkstätte, Großbothen 17426

Greece
Theophilos Kairis Museum, Andros 20825

Italy
Museo Mario Praz, Roma 25228

Lebanon
Gibran Museum, Bsharri 27488

Netherlands
Het Spinozahuis, Rijnsburg 29733

Russia
Ėkspozicija "Čelovek. Duša. Duchovnost.",
  Ivanovo 32826
Muzej-usadba poèta D. Venevitinova,
  Novoživotinnoe 33248

Spain
Museo Balmes, Vic 35650

Switzerland
Museum Casa Anatta, Casa Selma und Klarwelt der
  Seligen, Ascona 36472
Nietzsche-Haus, Sils in Engadin 37169

Turkey
Ziya Gökalp Müzesi, Diyarbakır 37663

Ukraine
Istoriko-memorialnyj Muzej Semji Fadeevyh-Chan-
  Blavackij, Dnepropetrovsk 37849

United Kingdom
Museum of Freemasonry, London 39713

U.S.A.
Orchard House - Home of the Alcotts, Concord 42601

Uzbekistan
Memorialnyj Muzej Abu Ali Ibn Sina, Afčona 48828

Photography

Argentina
Museo de la Fotografía, Rafaela 00497
Museo Municipal Histórico Fotográfico de Quilmes,
  Quilmes 00496

Australia
Australian Centre for Photography, Paddington, New
  South Wales 01351
Beatties Historic Photograph Museum, Dodges
  Ferry 00983
Centre for Contemporary Photography, Fitzroy 01024
City Exhibition Space, Sydney 01494
Eric Thomas Galley Museum, Queenstown 01403
Horsham Regional Art Gallery, Horsham 01110
Latrobe Court House Museum, Latrobe 01166
Monash Gallery of Art, Wheelers Hill 01596

Austria
Albertina, Wien 02830
Bild- und Tonarchiv, Graz 01911
Fotoforum West, Innsbruck 02064
Galerie im Rathaus, Bad Aussee 01690
Oberösterreichische Fotogalerie, Linz 02239
Palais Palffy, Wien 02968
Photomuseum des Landes Oberösterreich, Bad
  Ischl 01710
Sammlung Essl - Kunst der Gegenwart,
  Klosterneuburg 02142

Belgium
Archives et Musée de la Littérature, Bruxelles 03270
Fotomuseum Provincie Antwerpen, Antwerpen 03144
Musée de la Photographie, Charleroi 03350

Brazil
Museu Histórico, Pará de Minas 04243

Canada
Canadian Museum of Contemporary Photography,
  Ottawa 06071
Dazibao, Montréal 05902
Photographers Gallery, Saskatoon 06403
Presentation House Gallery, North Vancouver 06027
Saint Marys Museum, Saint Marys 06367
VU Centre de Diffusion et de Production de la
  Photographie, Québec 06212

Chile
Sala Sergio Larrain, Santiago de Chile 06921

Cuba
Fototeca de Cuba, La Habana 07928

Czech Republic
České Centrum Fotografie, Praha 08566
Muzeum Umění, Benešov 08246
Uměleckoprůmyslové Muzeum v Praze, Praha 08617

Denmark
Danmarks Fotomuseum, Herning 08867
Museet for Fotokunst, Odense 09015
Det Nationale Fotomuseum, København 08942

Estonia
Raevangla Fotomuuseum, Tallinn 09371

Finland
Helsingin Kaupungin Taidemuseo, Meilahti,
  Helsinki 09486
Suomen Valokuvataiteen Museo, Helsinki 09535

France
Centre de Photographie de Lectoure, Lectoure 12501
Centre National de la Photographie, Paris 13483
Centre Photographique d'Ile-de-France, Pontault-
  Combault 13823
Centre Régional de la Photographie Nord-Pas-de-
  Calais, Douchy-les-Mines 11565
Le Château d'Eau, Toulouse 14937
Fondation Van-Gogh Arles, Arles 10414
Galerie Nationale du Jeu de Paume, Paris 13511
Maison Européenne de la Photo, Paris 13526
Musée Adzak, Paris 13529
Musée Arménien de France, Paris 13530
Musée Charles Cros, Fabrezan 11698
Musée de la Photographie, Mougins 13179
Musée du Centre de Recherches sur les Monuments
  Historiques, Paris 13598
Musée Français de la Photographie, Bièvres 10733
Musée Municipal, La Roche-sur-Yon 12233
Musée National des Arts Asiatiques Guimet,
  Paris 13633

Germany
Agfa Photo-Historama, Köln 18128
Bildarchiv Foto Marburg, Marburg 18624
Camera Obscura, Hainichen, Sachsen 17495
Deichtorhallen Hamburg, Hamburg 17530
Deutsches Film- und Fototechnik Museum,
  Deidesheim 16561
Foto-Museum, Essen 16949
Fotogalerie Alte Feuerwache, Mannheim 18611
Fotografie Forum international, Frankfurt am
  Main 17041
Fotomuseum im Münchner Stadtmuseum,
  München 18850
Die Galerie in der Alten Schule, Berlin 15966
Haus der Fotografie - Dr. Robert-Gerlich-Museum,
  Burghausen, Salzach 16420
Heimatmuseum Glonn, Glonn 17302
Holowood - Holographiemuseum Bamberg,
  Bamberg 15809
Industrie- und Filmmuseum Wolfen, Wolfen 20650
Internationales Haus der Photographie,
  Hamburg 17546
Kamera- und Fotomuseum Leipzig, Leipzig 18400
Kunstsammlungen der Ruhr-Universität Bochum,
  Bochum 16196
Kupferstich-Kabinett, Dresden 16692
Münchner Stadtmuseum, München 18880
Museum Folkwang Essen, Essen 16959
Museum für Gegenwartskunst Siegen, Siegen 19949
Museum für Photographie, Braunschweig 16302
Museum Galgenhaus, Berlin 16060
Orientalisches Münzkabinett Jena, Jena 17946
Photographisch-optisches Museum,
  Biedenkopf 16151
Reiss-Engelhorn-Museen, Mannheim 18615
Städtische Galerie Iserlohn, Iserlohn 17923

Hungary
Magyar Fotográfiai Múzeum, Kecskemét 21450

Iceland
Ljósmyndasafn Reykjavíkur Grófarhús,
  Reykjavík 21656

India
Gandhi Museum, Bhavnagar 21718

Ireland
Irish Architectural Archive, Dublin 22433

Israel
Israeli Museum of Photography, Tel-Hai 22778

Italy
Civica Raccolta delle Stampe Achille Bertarelli,
  Milano 24372
Gabinetto Fotografico, Firenze 23837
Istituto di Fotografia Alpina Vittorio Sella, Biella 23078
Museo-Archivio di Fotografia Storica, Roma 25177
Museo del Foto Gabinetto die Fisica, Urbino 25858
Museo della Fotografia Storica e Contemporanea,
  Torino 25740
Museo dell'Immagine, Cesena 23504
Museo di Storia della Fotografia Fratelli Alinari,
  Firenze 23870
Museo Ken Damy di Fotografia Contemporanea,
  Brescia 23207

Museo Nazionale del Cinema, Torino 25757
Museo Nazionale della Fotografia, Brescia 23208

Japan
Hirano Image Library, Osaka 26648
Ken Domon Museum of Photography, Sakata 26704
Kiyosato Museum of Photographic Arts,
  Takane 26794
Kodak Gallery Hiroshima, Hiroshima 26219
Kushiro Art Museum, Kushiro 26390
Midorikawa Yoishi Shashin Bijutsukan,
  Okayama 26625
Minolta Photo Space Hiroshima, Hiroshima 26220
Nakagawa Photo Gallery, Kyoto 26438
Namikawa Banri Bukkyo Bijutsu Shashin Gallery,
  Hiroshima 26221
Nara City Museum of Photography, Nara 26579
Nihon Camera Hakubutsukan, Tokyo 26902
Nikon Gallery, Hiroshima 26222
Shirahata Shiro World Mountains Photograph
  Collection, Yuzawa 27038
Shoji Ueda Museum of Photography, Kishimoto 26338
Tokyo-to Shashin Bijutsukan, Tokyo 26946
Tsuwano Gendai Photo Gallery, Tsuwano 26981

Lithuania
Photography Museum, Šiauliai 27528

Luxembourg
Musée Municipal, Dudelange 27551
Villa Vauban, Luxembourg 27570

Mauritius
Musée de la Photographie, Port Louis 27739

Mexico
Centro Fotográfico Álvarez Bravo, Oaxaca 28271
Museo de la Fotografía, Pachuca 28293
Museo del Cine y la Fotografía, Puebla 28338
Museo Fotográfico de Nanchital, Nanchital de Lázaro
  Cárdenas del Río 28261

Netherlands
Ter Beziens, Kolhorn 29486
Foam Fotografiemuseum Amsterdam,
  Amsterdam 28853
Fotomuseum Den Haag, Den Haag 29094
Huis Marseille, Amsterdam 28861
Museum Kempenland, Eindhoven 29215
Nederlands Foto Instituut, Rotterdam 29769
Omroepmuseum en Smalfilmmuseum,
  Hilversum 29420
Oudheidkamer/ Museum Mr. Andreae, Kollum 29488
Prentenkabinet Universiteit Leiden, Leiden 29523
Spaarnestad Fotoarchief, Haarlem 29330
Stedelijk Museum Het Domein, Sittard 29827

New Zealand
Albertland and Districts Museum, Wellsford 30312
City Gallery Wellington, Wellington 30292
Nelson Provincial Museum, Nelson 30210
New Zealand Centre for Photography,
  Wellington 30301

Norway
Levanger Museum, Levanger 30639
Norsk Museum for Fotografi - Preus Fotomuseum,
  Horten 30566

Poland
Fotograficzny Muzeum Regionalnego w Mielcu,
  Mielec 31805
Fotoplastikon, Warszawa 32082
Gdańska Galeria Fotografii, Gdańsk 31567
Muzeum Historii Fotografii, Kraków 31705
Muzeum Historii Fotografii im. Prof. Władysława
  Bogackiego, Kraków 31706

Russia
Fotografičeskij Muzej Dom Metenkova,
  Ekaterinburg 32767
Moskovskij Dom Fotografii, Moskva 33086
Objedinenie Fotocentr Sojuza Žurnalistov,
  Moskva 33165
Russkij Muzej Fotografii, Nižnij Novgorod 33225

Slovenia
Arhitekturni Muzej Ljubljana, Ljubljana 34104

South Africa
Bensusan Museum of Photography,
  Johannesburg 34270

Spain
Metrònom, Barcelona 34546
Museo de Reproducciones Artísticas, Bilbao 34613

Sweden
Alingsås Museum, Alingsås 35789
Bildens Hus, Sundsvall 36307
Erna och Victor Hasselblads Fotografiska Centrum,
  Göteborg 35910
Fotomuséet i Osby, Osby 36152
Fotomuseet Olympia, Falkenberg 35877
Moderna Museet, Stockholm 36262

Switzerland
Centre de la Photographie Genève, Genève 36731
Fotomuseum Winterthur, Winterthur 37327
Musée de l'Elysée, Lausanne 36863
Museum im Bellpark, Kriens 36839

United Kingdom
British Photographic Museum, Totnes 40722

Cambridge University Collection of Air Photographs, Cambridge 38452
Dimbola Lodge, Freshwater 39017
Focal Point Gallery, Southend-on-Sea 40552
Fox Talbot Museum, Lacock 39408
HMS Ganges Association Museum, Ipswich 39304
Impressions Gallery of Photography, York 40963
Jersey Photographic Museum, Saint Helier 40402
Kildonan Museum, Kildonan 39356
Kirklees Collection of Photographs, Huddersfield 39273
Leigh Heritage Centre, Leigh-on-Sea 39472
National Museum of Photography, Film and Television, Bradford 38299
Nelson Tower, Forres 39009
Open Eye Photography Gallery, Liverpool 39526
Peacock, Aberdeen 37941
Photographers' Gallery, London 39744
Postcard Museum, Holmfirth 39254
The Royal Photographic Society Octagon Galleries, Bath 38122
Sutcliffe Gallery, Whitby 40852
Vintage Museum of Photography, London 39796

U.S.A.
Abrons Arts Center, New York 45751
The African American Museum in Philadelphia, Philadelphia 46387
Agnes Gallery, Birmingham 41703
The Albin O. Kuhn Gallery, Baltimore 41447
Aperture Photo Gallery and EMU Art Gallery, Eugene 43220
Arthur Griffin Center for Photographic Art, Winchester 48677
Baldwin Photographic Gallery, Murfreesboro 45567
Blue Sky, Portland 46631
Burden Gallery, New York 45774
California Museum of Photography, Riverside 46917
Center for Creative Photography, Tucson 48083
Center for Photography at Woodstock, Woodstock 48739
Cokato Museum and Akerlund Photography Studio, Cokato 42516
Dorothea C. Witham Gallery, Lewiston 44729
Folk Art and Photography Galleries, Atlanta 41343
The Friends of Photography at the Ansel Adams Center, San Francisco 47317
Gallery at the Wharf, Coupeville 42676
Historical Society of Oak Park and River Forest, Oak Park 46054
International Center of Photography, New York 45817
International Museum of Photography and Film, Rochester 46941
J. Paul Getty Museum, Los Angeles 44913
Japanese American National Museum, Los Angeles 44914
Los Angeles Center for Photographic Studies, Los Angeles 44919
The Lyons Redstone Museum, Lyons 45012
Main Gallery of Henry Street Settlement, New York 45829
The Museum of Contemporary Photography, Chicago 42345
Museum of Photographic Arts, San Diego 47283
Photographic Investments Gallery, Atlanta 41355
Photographic Resource Center, Boston 41824
Ruddell Gallery, Spearfish 47721
Santa Ana College Art Gallery, Santa Ana 47401
Silver Eye Center for Photography, Pittsburgh 46526
Society for Contemporary Photography, Kansas City 44408
Southeast Museum of Photography, Daytona Beach 42812
Video Museum and Theater, Grass Valley 43777
Visual Arts Museum, New York 45885
Washington Center for Photography, Washington 48405
White Gallery, Portland 46645

Physics

Argentina
Fundación Solar Rietti, Buenos Aires 00153
Museo de Física de la Universidad Nacional de La Plata, La Plata 00390

Belgium
Atomium, Bruxelles 03271
Museum voor de Geschiedenis van de Wetenschappen, Gent 03445

Bulgaria
Palata na Fizikata, Kazanlăk 04703

Canada
Ontario Science Centre, Toronto 06600

Germany
Faszinosum, Borna bei Leipzig 16262
Naturkundliche Sammlung, Altusried 15475
Röntgen-Gedächtnisstätte, Würzburg 20703

Israel
Bloomfield Science Museum Jerusalem, Jerusalem 22626

Italy
Domus Galilaeana, Pisa 24945
Museo di Fisica, Bologna 23126
Museo Torricelliano, Faenza 23756
Tempio Voltiano, Como 23632

Mexico
Museo de Ciencias Explora, León 28054
Museo de Física Recreativa, Puebla 28328
Museo de la Radiodifusión, Puebla 28331

Philippines
Philippine Radiation Science Museum, Manila 31391

Poland
Muzeum Marii Skłodowskiej-Curie, Warszawa 32113

Portugal
Museu de Física, Coimbra 32258

Sweden
Nora Museum, Gyttorp 35933
Observatoriemuseet, Stockholm 36270

United Kingdom
Aberdeen University Natural Philosophy Museum, Aberdeen 37933
Fox Talbot Museum, Lacock 39408
Liverpool Museum, Liverpool 39520
Michael Faraday's Laboratory and Museum, London 39708

U.S.A.
Louisville Science Center, Louisville 44970
Regional Science and Discovery Center, Horseheads 44106
Science Discovery Center of Oneonta, Oneonta 46160
Science Imaginarium, Waterloo 48433
Whitaker Center for Science and the Arts, Harrisburg 43927

Pipes, Tobacco → Tobacco

Plaster Casts

Germany
Abguss Sammlung antiker Plastik, Berlin 15907
Gipsformerei, Berlin 15976
Knauf-Museum, Iphofen 17915
Museum Kloster Asbach, Rotthalmünster 19694

India
Government Educational Museum, Deoria 21787

Italy
Gipsoteca Canoviana e Casa del Canova, Possagno 25027
Gipsoteca del Castello Normanno Svevo, Bari 23019
Gipsoteca Istituto d'Arte, Firenze 23847
Museo del Palazzo del Podestà e Gipsoteca Libero Andreotti, Pescia 24877

Spain
Museo del Azulejo, Onda 35178
Museo del Castillo de Odna, Onda 35179

Switzerland
Gipsmuseum Oberwiesen, Schleitheim 37135

United Kingdom
House of the Binns, Linlithgow 39506

Uruguay
Museo del Azulejo, Montevideo 40999

Playing Cards

Belgium
Nationaal Museum van de Speelkaart, Turnhout 03803

France
Musée du Vieux Marseille, Marseille 12868

Germany
Deutsches Spielkartenmuseum, Leinfelden-Echterdingen 18375
Schloß- und Spielkartenmuseum, Altenburg, Thüringen 15452

Spain
Museo Fournier de Naipes de Alava, Vitoria-Gasteiz 35702

Police → Criminology

Politics and Government

Argentina
Antiguo Recinto del Congreso Nacional, Buenos Aires 00143
Museo de la Casa de Gobierno, San Miguel de Tucumán 00582
Museo de la Casa Rosada, Buenos Aires 00185
Museo Nuestra Señora de Carrodilla, Luján de Cuyo 00418
Museo Roberto Noble, Buenos Aires 00240
Museo Senador Domingo Faustino Sarmiento, Buenos Aires 00243

Australia
Chifley Home, Bathurst 00775
Government House, Sydney 01495
Hawke House, Bordertown 00815
Museum of Sydney, Sydney 01504
Old Government House, Belair 00790
Old Government House, Brisbane 00839
Old Parliament House, Canberra 00888
Vaucluse House, Vaucluse 01565

Austria
Zeitreise - Renner Villa Gloggnitz, Gloggnitz 01885

Benin
Musée d'Histoire, Ouidah 03875

Bulgaria
Kăšta-muzej Dimităr Blagoev, Bankja 04612
Kăšta-muzej Dimităr Blagoev, Sofia 04830
Kăšta-muzej Dimitar Pešev, Kjustendil 04706
Kăšta-muzej Vasil Kolarov, Šumen 04874
Muzeen Kat Parva Socialističeska Sbirka, Veliko Tărnovo 04916
Muzej na Ministerstvoto na Vnatrešnite raboti, Sofia 04841
Nacionalen Muzej Georgi Dimitrov, Sofia 04849

Canada
Bellevue House, Kingston 05673
Commissariat House, Saint John's 06343
Cossit House Museum, Sydney 06526
Diefenbaker House, Prince Albert 06181
Domaine Cataraqui, Sillery 06453
Government House Museum and Heritage Property, Regina 06235
Haliburton House Museum, Windsor, Nova Scotia 06808
John G. Diefenbaker Replica Law Office, Wakaw 06740
Musée Laurier, Victoriaville 06731
Old Government House, Fredericton 05466
Rutherford House, Edmonton 05385
Vancouver Holocaust Education Centre, Vancouver 06694
William Henry Steeves House, Hillsborough 05597

China, People's Republic
Museum at the Site of the First National Congress of the Communist Party of China, Shanghai 07216
Museum of the former Residence of Comrade Mao Zedong at Shaoshan, Shaoshan 07231
Rongyu Guan, Jiangyin 07125

Colombia
Museo Casa Rafael Núñez, Cartagena 07455

Costa Rica
Museo Historico Dr. Rafael Angel Calderón Guardia, San José 07660

Cuba
Museo Casa Natal de Celia Sanchez Manduley, Media Luna 08045
Museo Nacional del Ministerio del Interior, La Habana 07992

Denmark
Reventlow-Museet Pederstrup, Horslunde 08901

Egypt
Museum of the People's Assembly, Cairo 09277

Finland
Urho Kekkonen Museo Tamminiemi, Helsinki 09545

France
Musée Georges Clemenceau, Paris 13616

Germany
Bismarck-Museum, Schönhausen, Elbe 19833
Deutsch-Deutsches Museum Mödlareuth, Töpen 20184
Grenzland-Museum Bad Sachsa, Bad Sachsa 15722
Reichstagsmuseum, Regensburg 19529
Residenz Ellingen, Ellingen, Bayern 16831
Unterfränkisches Grenzmuseum, Bad Königshofen 15677

Greece
Alexandros Papanastassiou Museum, Levidion 21046
Capodistria Museum, Koukouritsa, Evropouli 21033

Honduras
Museo de Historia Republicana, Tegucigalpa 21303

Hungary
Bajcsy-Zsilinszky Emlékmúzeum, Veszprém 21607
Széchenyi Emlékmúzeum, Nagycenk 21485
Szoborpark, Budapest 21384
Vay Adám Múzeum, Vaja 21603

India
Chandradhari Museum, Darbhanga 21754
Gandhi Memorial Museum, Madurai 21934
Gandhi Museum, Bhavnagar 21718
Gandhi Museum, Lucknow 21924
Gandhi Smarak Sangrahalaya, Barrackpore 21710
National Gandhi Museum and Library, Delhi 21775
Netaji Museum, Kolkata 21909
V.K. Krishna Menon Museum and Art Gallery, Kozhikode 21917

Iran
Constitution Museum, Tabriz 22284

Ireland
Avondale House, Rathdrum 22531
Custom House Visitor Centre, Dublin 22418
Parnell Museum, Rathdrum 22532

Israel
Ben-Gurion House, Tel Aviv 22749

Italy
Casa Museo A. Gramsci, Ghilarza 24020
Domus Mazziniana, Pisa 24946
Museo G. Marconi, Pontecchio Marconi 24996

Japan
Gaimusho, Gaiko Shiryokan, Tokyo 26848
Osaka Human Rights Museum, Osaka 26662
Parliamentary Memorial Museum, Tokyo 26913
Yoshizawa Kinenkan, Joetsu 26285

Jordan
Political Life Museum, Amman 27059

Korea, Republic
Diplomatic History Museum, Seoul 27229

Madagascar
Musée du Palais de la Reine, Antananarivo 27602

Malaysia
Muzium Tuan Yang Terutama Melaka, Melaka 27675

Mexico
Casa Museo López Portillo, Guadalajara 27943
Casa Museo Silvestre Rodríguez, Nacozari de García 28260
Museo Abraham González, Vicente Guerrero 28598
Museo Adolfo López Mateos, Atizapán de Zaragoza 27781
Museo Casa de Carranza, Cuatrocienegas 27868
Museo Casa del General Alvaro Obregón, Huatabampo 27998
Museo de Sitio Casa de Juárez, Oaxaca 28278
Museo Isidro Fabela, Atlacomulco 27782
Museo Legislativo los Sentimientos de la Nación, México 28180
Museo Luis Donaldo Colosio, Francisco I. Madero, Coahuila 27927
Museo-Sala de los Símbolos Patrios, Hermosillo 27989
Sala Melchor Ocampo, Morelia 28254

Netherlands
't Oude Raadhuis, Beek en Donk 28967
Theo Thijssen Museum, Amsterdam 28909

Norway
Johan Nygaardsvold Museum, Hommelvik 30559
Politimuseet i Oslo, Oslo 30759

Peru
Museo Tribunal de la Santa Inquisición y del Congreso, Lima 31226

Philippines
CAP Art Center and Price Mansion, Tacloban 31451
Carlos P. Garcia Memorabilia, Manila 31372
Earist Museum, Manila 31377
Jose P. Laurel Memorial Museum, Manila 31378
José P. Laurel Monument Museum, Santo Tomas 31444
Kaban ng Hiyas ng Lungsod ng Mandaluyong, Mandaluyong 31364
Manuel L. Quezon Memorial Shrine Museum, Quezon City 31435
Marcos Museum, Batac 31285
Museum of Philippine Political History, Manila 31388
Ramón Magsaysay Memorabilia Museum, Manila 31396
Redoña Residence Museum, Tacloban 31453
Sarrat Museum, Sarrat 31446
Vigan House Museum, Vigan 31467

Poland
Muzeum Hymnu Narodowego, Nowy Karczma 31833

Puerto Rico
Casa Jesús T. Piñero, Canóvanas 32369
Luis Muñoz Rivera Museum, Barranquitas 32362
Museo Casa Blanca, San Juan 32392

Romania
Muzeul Memorial Octavian Goga, Ciucea 32490

Russia
Aleksandrovskij Dvorec - Gosudarstvennyj Muzej Carskoje Selo, Puškin 33334
Bunker Stalina, Samara 33366
Centralnyj Muzej MVD Rossii, Moskva 33026
Čerkechskij Muzej Jakutskaja Političeskaja Ssylka, Čerkech 32735
Dom-muzej Istorii Molodežnogo Dviženija, Rjazan 33349
Dom-muzej M.K. Ammosova, Jakutsk 32841
Gosudarstvennyj Istoriko-memorialnyj Zapovednik Rodina V.I. Lenina, Uljanovsk 33656
Kraevedčeskij Muzej Evrejskoj Avtonomnoj Oblasti, Birobidžan 32689
Memorialnyj Dom-muzej G.V. Plechanova, Lipeck 32985
Memorialnyj Muzej Karima Chakimova, Ufa 33644
Memorialnyj Muzej-Kvartira S.M. Kirova, Vladikavkaz 33688
Muzej Dekabristov - Dom Trubeckogo, Irkutsk 32816
Muzej Dekabristov - Dom Volkonskich, Irkutsk 32817
Muzej Diplomatičeskogo Korpusa, Vologda 33722
Muzej i Obščestvennyj Centr Mir, Progress, Prava Čeloveka im. Andreja Sacharova, Moskva 33104
Muzej Istorii Političeskoj Polcii Rossii - Gorochovaja 2, Sankt-Peterburg 33441
Muzej Istorii Političeskoj Ssylki, Bratsk 32705
Muzej Istorii Politssylki v Jakutii, Jakutsk 32844
Muzej Istorii Revoljucionno-demokratičeskogo Dviženija 1880-1890 gg, Sankt-Peterburg 33442
Muzej Istorii UVD Kalužskoj Oblasti, Kaluga 32880
Muzej-kvartira Alliluevych, Sankt-Peterburg 33448
Muzej-kvartira A.D. Sacharova, Nižnij Novgorod 33216
Podpolnaja Tipografija CK RSDRP, Moskva 33172
Pskovskij Memorialnyj Muzej V.I. Lenina, Pskov 33333

Serbia-Montenegro
Muzej Istorije Jugoslavije, Beograd 33805

South Africa
Goetz/Fleischack Museum, Potchefstroom 34334
Kruger Museum, Pretoria 34345
Museum Presidency, Bloemfontein 34187
President Pretorius Museum, Potchefstroom 34336
Rhodes Cottage Museum, Muizenberg 34313

Spain
Casa-Museo León y Castillo, Telde 35521
Museo Documental, Guernica y Luno 34892

Sri Lanka
Bandaranaike Museum, Colombo 35746

Sweden
Skånska Lasses Hus, Mjölby 36095

Turkey
Anıtkabir-Atatürk ve Kurtuluş Müzesi, Ankara 37613
Atatürk Evi, Trabzon 37796
Atatürk Köşkü, Diyarbakır 37659
Atatürk Müzesi, Bursa 37643
Atatürk Müzesi, İzmir 37717
Atatürk Müzesi, Konya 37739
Atatürk Museum, Samsun 37776
Atatürk ve Etnografya Müzesi, Akşehir 37605
Ataürk Müzesi, Şişli 37786
Dolmabahçe Sarayı Müzesi, İstanbul 37699
Eskişehir Atatürk ve Kültür Müzesi, Eskişehir 37675

United Kingdom
Apsley House, London 39567
Ballance House, Glenavy 39073
Benjamin Franklin House, London 39578
Cabinet War Rooms, London 39595
Chartwell House, Chartwell 38527
Commonwealth Institute, London 39614
Cromwell Museum, Huntingdon 39277
Greenhill Covenanter's House, Biggar 38197
Hughenden Manor, High Wycombe 39240
Lloyd George Museum and Highgate, Llanystumdwy 39559
Milton's Cottage, Chalfont Saint Giles 38520
Old House of Keys, Castletown 38510
Pankhurst Centre, Manchester 39901
Rhodes Memorial Museum and Commonwealth Centre, Bishop's Stortford 38240
War and Peace Exhibition, Oban 40124
Washington Old Hall, Washington, Tyne and Wear 40800

U.S.A.
Allison-Antrim Museum, Greencastle 43800
Andrew Johnson National Historic Site, Greeneville 43801
Anti-Saloon League Museum, Westerville 48554
CIA Museum, McLean 45040
Dan Quayle Center and Museum, Huntington 44156
Edmonston House, Vails Gate 48175
First Territorial Capitol of Kansas, Fort Riley 43448
Franklin D. Roosevelt Library-Museum, Hyde Park 44187
George Bush Presidential Library and Museum, College Station 42525
George Washington's Ferry Farm, Stafford County 47766
Georgia Capitol Museum, Atlanta 41344
Harry S. Truman Little White House Museum, Key West 44466
Harry's Truman Farm Home, Grandview 43763
Hiram Smith Octagon House, Neenah 45644
Humphrey Forum, Minneapolis 45385
James K. Polk Memorial, Pineville 46494
King Manor, Jamaica 44305
McConnell Mansion, Moscow 45518
Meadow Garden Museum, Augusta 41385
Monticello, Home of Thomas Jefferson, Charlottesville 42249
Museum of American Political Life, West Hartford 48526
Museum of American Presidents, Strasburg 47848
Museum of the Waxhaws and Andrew Jackson Memorial, Waxhaw 48471
National Liberty Museum, Philadelphia 46435
New Jersey State House, Trenton 48056
Old Constitution House, Windsor 48686
Old South Meeting House, Boston 41821
Old State Capitol, Springfield 47740
Quincy and Adams County Museum, Quincy 46759
Ronald Reagan Boyhood Home, Dixon 42953
Sewall-Belmont House, Washington 48391
Tudor Place Museum, Washington 48398
Varner-Hogg Plantation, West Columbia 48520
The White House, Washington 48409
Woodrow Wilson Birthplace and Museum, Staunton 47799
Zebulon B. Vance Birthplace, Weaverville 48488

Porcelain and Ceramics

Australia
Colac Otway Shire Hammerton Bottle Collection, Colac 00935
Devonport Gallery and Arts Centre, Devonport 00977
Erica Underwood Gallery, Bentley 00797
Fusions Gallery, Fortitude Valley 01031
National Museum of Australian Pottery, Wodonga 01608
Northcote Pottery, Thornbury 01533
Orange Regional Gallery, Orange 01347
Shepparton Art Gallery, Shepparton 01451

Austria
Mühlviertler Keramikwerkstätte Hafnerhaus, Leopoldschlag 02216
Novum Forum, Neumarkt in Steiermark 02353
Schloß Weyer, Gmunden 01897
Sommerhuber-Kachelofenmuseum, Steyr 02690
Töpfermuseum, Stoob 02702
Wiener Porzellanmanufaktur Augarten, Wien 03006
Zsolnay-Keramik-Porzellan-Museum, Potzneusiedl 02439

Belgium
Broelmuseum, Kortrijk 03540
Hôpital Notre-Dame de la Rose, Lessines 03561
Hotel-Museum Arthur Merghelynck, Ieper 03514
Musée de la Céramique d'Andenne, Andenne 03129
Musée d'Histoire et des Arts Décoratifs, Tournai 03795
Musée du Vieux Nimy, Mons 03636
Museum Maagdenhuis, Antwerpen 03150
Museum van het Abtenhuis, Geraardsbergen 03458
Pavillon Chinois et Tour Japonaise, Bruxelles 03340
Töpfereimuseum Raeren, Raeren 03691

Bermuda
Verdmont Historic House Museum, Smith's Parish 03890

Brazil
Museu Barão de Mauá, Mauá 04201

Bulgaria
Muzej na Chudožestvenite Zanajati i Priložnite Izkustva, Trojan 04890

Canada
Burlington Art Centre, Burlington 05145
Canadian Clay and Glass Gallery, Waterloo 06751
Clay Products Interpretive Centre, Medicine Hat 05830
Gallery of British Columbia Ceramics, Vancouver 06677
George R. Gardiner Museum of Ceramic Art, Toronto 06580

Chile
Museo Histórico de Osorno, Osorno 06901

China, People's Republic
Flagstaff House Museum of Tea Ware, Hong Kong 07094
Jingdezhen Porcelain Museum, Jingdezhen 07138
University Museum and Art Gallery, Hong Kong 07114
Xi Bao Celadon Museum, Shenzhen 07244
Yixing Porcelain Corporation Museum, Yixing 07321

China, Republic
Hwa Kang Museum, Taipei 07347

Colombia
Museo del Oro, Bogotá 07415

Cuba
Farmacia Museo Taquechel, La Habana 07927
Museo Nacional de la Cerámica, La Habana 07990

Czech Republic
Havelkovo Muzeum, Loštice 08462
Městské Muzeum, Kožlany 08426
Místní Muzeum, Netvořice 08499
Muzeum Českého Porcelánu, Klášterec nad Ohří 08411
Muzeum Hrnčířstvi a Keramiky, Kostelec nad Černými lesy 08423
Muzeum Keramiky, Bechyně 08243
Muzeum Mladaboleslavska, Mladá Boleslav 08480
Muzeum Olomučanské Keramiky, Olomučany 08517
Muzeum Porcelánu Pirkenhammer, Březová u Karlových Var 08261
Muzeum Tynecké Keramiky, Týnec nad Sázavou 08697
Muzeum Vyškovska, Vyškov 08731

Denmark
Bornholms Museum, Rønne 09037
Den Gamle Gaard, Faaborg 08814
Hammerichs Hus, Ærøskøbing 08766
Mariager Museum, Mariager 08979
Vejen Kunstmuseum, Vejen 09103

Finland
Arabia Museum-Gallery, Helsinki 09472

France
Galerie Terra Viva, Saint-Quentin-la-Poterie 14438
Maison de la Faïence, Desvres 11503
Musée Agathois, Agde 10228
Musée Archéologique, Lectoure 12503
Musée Arménien de France, Paris 13530
Musée Benoît de Puydt, Bailleul 10569
Musée Charles-VII, Mehun-sur-Yèvre 12915
Musée-Château, Grignan 11956
Musée Comtois, Besançon 10698
Musée d'Allauch, Allauch 10291
Musée d'Art et d'Histoire, Narbonne 13267
Musée d'Art et d'Histoire de Toul, Toul 14924
Musée de Bible et Terre Sainte, Paris 13550
Musée de Biot, Biot 10739
Musée de la Céramique, Digoin 11516
Musée de la Céramique, Lezoux 12576
Musée de la Céramique, Rouen 14047
Musée de la Céramique et de l'Ivoire, Commercy 11373
Musée de la Faïence, Forges-les-Eaux 11786
Musée de la Faïence, Marseille 12855
Musée de la Faïence, Montereau-Fault-Yonne 13076
Musée de la Faïence et des Arts de la Table, Samadet 14594
Musée de la Faïence Jules Verlingue, Quimper 13897
Musée de la Glace, Mazaugues 12904
Musée de la Mode Retrovée, Digoin 11517
Musée de la Porcelaine, Saint-Yrieix-la-Perche 14511
Musée de la Poterie de Grès, Betschdorf 10710
Musée de la Poterie et de la Céramique, Sadirac 14083
Musée de la Reine Bérengère, Le Mans 12436
Musée de l'Hospice Comtesse, Lille 12598
Musée de Traditions Populaires et d'Archéologie, Chauvigny 11255
Musée Départemental Breton, Quimper 13900
Musée Départemental de l'Oise, Beauvais 10655
Musée Départemental des Hautes-Alpes, Gap 11838
Musée des Arts Décoratifs, Bordeaux 10811
Musée des Arts Décoratifs, Strasbourg 14831
Musée des Beaux-Arts et d'Archeologie Joseph Déchelette, Roanne 13985
Musée des Faïences Anciennes de la Tour d'Aigues, La Tour-d'Aigues 12268
Musée des Faïences de Varages, Varages 15085
Musée des Ivoires, Yvetot 15332
Musée du Château de Lunéville, Lunéville 12712
Musée Gallé-Juillet, Creil 11453
Musée Haviland, Limoges 12614
Musée Historique de la Faïence, Moustiers-Sainte-Marie 13195
Musée la Faïencerie, Ancy-le-Franc 10333
Musée Léon Marès, Lovagny 12706
Musée Magnelli, Vallauris 15060
Musée Maison du Potier, Le Fuilet 12416
Musée Mathurin Méheut, Lamballe 12311
Musée Municipal de la Poterie, La Chapelle-aux-Pots 12140
Musée Municipal de Louviers, Louviers 12704
Musée Municipal de Saint-Gaudens, Saint-Gaudens 14226
Musée National Adrien Dubouché, Limoges 12617
Musée National de Céramique, Sèvres 14739
Musée National de la Renaissance, Ecouen 11599
Musée National des Arts Asiatiques Guimet, Paris 13633
Musée Paul Charnoz, Paray-le-Monial 13465
Musée Privé Saint-Jean l'Aigle, Herserange 12016
Musée Sarret de Grozon, Arbois 10392

Germany
Antikensammlung der Friedrich-Alexander-Universität Erlangen-Nürnberg, Erlangen 16915
Coburger Puppen-Museum, Coburg 16480
Deutsches Porzellanmuseum, Hohenberg an der Eger 17805
Emslandmuseum Schloß Clemenswerth, Sögel 19974
Erkenbert-Museum, Frankenthal, Pfalz 17029
Erstes Nachttopf-Museum der Welt, München 18843
Europäisches Industriemuseum für Porzellan und Europäisches Museum für Technische Keramik, Selb 19930
Glashütte, Bad Reichenhall 15717
Großherzoglich-Hessische Porzellansammlung, Darmstadt 16539
Heimat- und Hafnermuseum, Heidenheim, Mittelfranken 17683
Heimat- und Keramikmuseum, Kandern 17982
Heimatmuseum Büddenstedt, Büddenstedt 16395
Heimatmuseum Luditzer Kreis, Bad Sooden-Allendorf 15746
Heimatmuseum Oettingen, Oettingen 19236
Heimatmuseum Vilsbiburg - Kröninger Hafnermuseum, Vilsbiburg 20322
Heimatmuseum Wächtersbach, Wächtersbach 20338
Heimatstuben, Volkmarsen 20334
Henneberg-Museum, Münnerstadt 18927
Hetjens-Museum, Düsseldorf 16727
Internationales Keramik-Museum, Weiden, Oberpfalz 20425
Kaffeekannenmuseum, Schöppenstedt 19839
Kelsterbacher Museum für Porzellan, Kelsterbach 18054
Keramik-Museum, Bürgel 16406
Keramik-Museum Berlin, Berlin 16014
Keramik Museum Mettlach, Mettlach 18724
Keramikmuseum Schloss Obernzell, Obernzell 19190
Keramikmuseum Staufen, Staufen 20037
Keramikmuseum Westerwald, Höhr-Grenzhausen 17784
Kronberger Haus, Frankfurt am Main 17060
Krüge-Museum, Creußen 16512
Märkisches Ziegelei-Museum Glindow, Glindow 17301
Meißener Porzellan-Sammlung Stiftung Ernst Schneider, Oberschleißheim 19203
Meißner Porzellan-Kabinett, Bad Soden 15743
Merkelbach-Museum, Höhr-Grenzhausen 17785
Museum, Coswig, Anhalt 16498
Museum der Staatlichen Porzellan-Manufaktur Meissen, Meißen 18691
Museum für islamische Fliesen und Keramik, Tegernsee 20150
Museum im Schloß, Frohburg 17156
Museum im Schloss, Fürstenberg, Weser 17159
Museum in der Majolika-Manufaktur, Karlsruhe 17999
Museum Kellinghusen, Kellinghusen 18052
Museum Leuchtenburg, Seitenroda 19929
Museum Otto Ludwig, Eisfeld 16827
Museum Schloß Ratibor, Roth, Mittelfranken 19675
Nachttopf-Museum, Kreuth 18236
Neues Schloß Bayreuth, Bayreuth 15857
Neues Schloss Wallerstein, Wallerstein 20380
Nymphenburger Porzellan-Sammlung Bäuml, München 18891
Ofen- und Keramikmuseum Velten, Velten 20300
Ortssammlung Wettelsheim, Treuchtlingen 20200
Das Ostfriesische Teemuseum und Norder Heimatmuseum, Norden 19113
Porzellanmuseum, Rödental 19629
Porzellanmuseum Reichmannsdorf, Reichmannsdorf 19548
Porzellansammlung, Dresden 16704
Rokokomuseum Schloß Belvedere, Weimar, Thüringen 20470
Sammlung Ernst Schneider, Düsseldorf 16741
Sammlung Ludwig in Bamberg, Bamberg 15815
Schloßmuseum, Ellwangen 16836
Schloßmuseum Mespelbrunn, Mespelbrunn 18717
Stadtmuseum Nittenau, Nittenau 19106
Stadtmuseum Schorndorf, Schorndorf, Württemberg 19844
Stiftung Aschenbrenner, Garmisch-Partenkirchen 17203
Stiftung Keramion, Frechen 17094
Stiftung Schloß Ahrensburg, Ahrensburg 15407
Teplitz-Schönauer Heimatmuseum, Frankfurt am Main 17079
Töpferei und Museum im Kannenofen, Höhr-Grenzhausen 17786
Töpfereimuseum, Langerwehe 18340
Töpfermuseum, Duingen 16745
Töpfermuseum, Kohren-Sahlis 18198
Töpfermuseum, Rödermark 19631
Töpfermuseum Im alten Kannenofen, Ransbach-Baumbach 19484
Töpfermuseum Thurnau, Thurnau 20174
Werksmuseum der Waechtersbacher Keramik, Brachttal 16268

Ghana
Prempeh II Jubilee Museum, Kumasi 20797

Greece
Antonopouleion Archeological Museum, Pylos 21134
Archeological Collection, Agios Kirikos 20809
Archeological Collection, Tanagra 21171
Archeological Museum, Tegea 21172
Archeological Museum, Thera 21176
Archeological Museum, Vathy 21207
Centre for the Study of Greek Traditional Pottery, Athinai 20854
Georgiou Collection, Lindos 21050
Ioannidis Collection, Lindos 21051
Kaskines Collection, Lindos 21052
Museum Agios Nikolaos, Agios Nikolaos 20810
National Folk Museum of Lesbos, Mytilini 21086

Hungary
Herendi Porcelánművészeti, Herend 21426
Kovács Margit Kerámiagyűjtemény, Szentendre 21573

Porcelánmúzeum, Hollóháza 21429
Zsolnay Kerámia Kiállitás, Pécs 21518

India
Abhai Smarak Panchal Sangrahalaya, Bareilly 21707
Government Educational Museum, Bulandshahar 21733
Tamralipta Museum and Research Center, Tamluk 22031

Indonesia
Museum Asserajah El Hasyimiah Palace, Bengkalis 22082
Museum Seni Rupa dan Keramik, Jakarta 22132

Iran
Abgineh Va Sofalineh, Teheran 22287
Golestan Palace Museum, Teheran 22300

Italy
Antiquarium, Prato 25039
Civica Raccolta di Terraglia, Laveno Mombello 24164
Civiche Raccolte d'Arte Applicata, Milano 24374
Museo Archeologico e della Ceramica, Montelupo Fiorentino 24533
Museo Artistico Industriale F. Palizzi, Napoli 24578
Museo Carlo Venturini, Massa Lombarda 24317
Museo Civico della Ceramica, Nove 24654
Museo Civico e della Ceramica, Cerreto Sannita 23485
Museo Civico e Pinacoteca, Urbania 25853
Museo Comunale della Ceramica, Cutrofiano 23705
Museo della Ceramica, Bassano del Grappa 23040
Museo della Ceramica, Castellamonte 23403
Museo della Ceramica, Fiorano Modenese 23820
Museo della Ceramica, Patti 24818
Museo della Ceramica, Salerno 25318
Museo della Ceramica, Vietri 26005
Museo della Ceramica del Castello, Salerno 25319
Museo della Ceramica di Castelli, Castelli 23412
Museo dell'Agro Falisco, Civita Castellana 23592
Museo delle Ceramiche, Forlì 23911
Museo delle Ceramiche, Tolentino 25719
Museo delle Ceramiche Abruzzesi, Loreto Aprutino 24218
Museo delle Porcellane, Firenze 23860
Museo dell'Opera del Santuario, Tolentino 25720
Museo di Santa Restituta, Lacco Ameno 24126
Museo Didattico delle Maioliche, Grottaglie 24061
Museo Duca di Martina, Napoli 24599
Museo Internazionale delle Ceramiche, Faenza 23754
Museo Nazionale Archeologico, Ferrara 23798
Museo Regionale della Ceramica, Caltagirone 23273
Museo Regionale della Ceramica, Deruta 23709
Museo Richard Ginori della Manifattura di Doccia, Sesto Fiorentino 25557
Museo Selinuntino, Castelvetrano 23429
Pinacoteca, Museo delle Ceramiche, Pesaro 24861
Raccolta delle Piastrelle di Ceramica, Sassuolo 25498

Japan
Aichi-ken Toji Siryokan, Seto 26739
Arita Toji Bijutsukan, Arita 26102
Asahi-yaki Pottery Museum, Uji, Kyoto 26988
Bizen Pottery Traditional and Contemporary Art Museum, Bizen 26118
Ehime Bunkakan, Imabari 26243
Fukui-ken Togeikan, Miyazaki, Fukui 26508
Gifu-ken Toji Shiryokan, Tajimi 26787
Hachiga Minzoku Bijutsukan, Takayama 26802
Hakone Souunzan Bijutsukan, Hakone 26176
Hayashibara Bijutsukan, Okayama 26624
Hyogo-ken Togeikan, Kobe 26346
Idemitsu Bijutsukan, Tokyo 26859
Kawai Kanjiro's House, Kyoto 26408
Kei Fujiwara Art Museum, Bizen 26119
Kibi Archaeological Collection, Soja 26771
Kikusui Handicraft Museum, Kawanishi 26326
Kurita Bijutsukan, Ashikaga 26108
Masaki Art Museum, Osaka 26654
Mashiko Sankokan, Mashiko 26468
Mizuno Old Ceramics House, Miyazaki, Fukui 26509
Osaka-shiritsu Toyo Toji Bijutsukan, Osaka 26671
Raku Museum, Kyoto 26446
Saga-kenritsu Kyushu Toji Bunkakan, Arita 26103
Saitama-kenritsu Sakitama Shiryokan, Gyoda 26160
Seto-shi Rekishi Minzoku Shiryokan, Seto 26740
Seto Tojiki, Seto 26741
Tokoname Togei Kenkyujyo, Tokoname 26824
Tomimoto Kenkichi Memorial Museum, Ando 26098
Tottori Folk Art Museum, Tottori 26963
Ukiyo-e and Pottery Museum, Osaka 26674

Korea, Republic
Celamuse - Porcelain Museum, Seoul 27224
Ewha Yoja Taehakkyo Pakmulgwan, Seoul 27232
Haegang Ceramics Museum, Icheon 27187
Hongsan Museum, Seoul 27239
Horim Museum, Seoul 27240
Onggi Folk Museum and Institute, Seoul 27265
Sojun Art Museum, Siheung 27292

Latvia
Rīgas Vēstures un Kugniecības muzejs, Rīga 27441

Luxembourg
Musée de la Poterie, Nospelt 27571

Mexico
Museo Nacional de la Cerámica, Tonalá, Jalisco 28553
Museo Pantaleón Panduro, Tlaquepaque 28529
Museo Regional de la Cerámica, Tlaquepaque 28530

Morocco
Musée National de la Céramique, Safi 28709

Netherlands
Aardewerkvermuseum Petrus Pegout, Noordbroek 29640
Fini's Hoeve, Vriezenveen 29966
Harlinger Aardewerk Museum, Harlingen 29346
't Huijs Dever, Lisse 29542
Keramiekcentrum Tiendschuur, Tegelen 29864
Keramisch Museum Goedewaagen, Nieuw Buinen 29613
Mobach Keramiek Museum, Utrecht 29899
Museum De Ghulden Roos, Roosendaal 29745
Museum De Moriaan, Gouda 29296
Museum Het Prinsenhof, Delft 29082
Museum Lambert Van Meerten, Delft 29083
Museum Mesdag, Den Haag 29112
Museum Paul Tétar Van Elven, Delft 29085
Museum voor Hedendaagse Kunst, 's-Hertogenbosch 29405
Museum voor Keramiek Pablo Rueda Lara, Rotterdam 29763
Nationaal Spaarpottenmuseum, Amsterdam 28885
Nederlands Kachelmuseum, Alkmaar 28805
Oudheidkamer Beilen, Beilen 28971
Porselein Dierenpark, Wildervank 30006
Pottenbakkerij De Brinksteen, Dwingeloo 29187
Pottenbakkerij Het Ovenhuis, Ruinerwold 29787
Pottenbakkerij Museum, Kattendijke 29476
Princessehof Leeuwarden, Leeuwarden 29514
Purmerends Museum, Purmerend 29717
Tassenmuseum Hendrikje, Amstelveen 28833
Warkums Erfskip, Workum 30024

New Zealand
The Suter, Te Aratoi o Whakatu, Nelson 30211

Norway
Egersund Fayancemuseum, Egersund 30467

Paraguay
Museo de Cerámica y Bellas Artes Julián de la Herreria, Asunción 31097
Museo del Barro, Asunción 31101

Peru
Museo Nacional de Antropología, Arqueología e Historia del Perú, Lima 31221

Philippines
MPG Town Gallery, Odiongan 31408
Puerto Galera National Museum, Puerto Galera 31423

Poland
Muzeum Ceramiki, Bolesławiec 31507
Muzeum Ceramiki Kaszubskiej Neclów, Chmielno 31526
Muzeum Technik Ceramicznych, Koło 31668
Muzeum Ziemi Kujawskiej i Dobrzyńskiej, Włocławek 32163
Pałac Radziwiłłów w Nieborowie, Nieborów 31822

Portugal
Museu Arqueológico, Lisboa 32291
Museu da Cerâmica de Sacavém, Loures 32317
Museu de Olaria, Barcelos 32241
Museu Monográfico de Conimbriga, Condeixa-a-Nova 32266
Museu Nacional de Soares dos Reis, Porto 32338

Russia
Gosudarstvennyj Chudožestvenno-architekturnyj Dvorcovo-parkovyj Muzej-zapovednik Pavlovsk, Pavlovsk 33285
Muzej Keramiki i Usadba Kuskovo XVIII Veka, Moskva 33114
Omskij Oblastnoj Muzej Izobrazitelnych Iskusstv im. M.A. Vrubelja, Omsk 33257
Rybinskij Gosudarstvennyj Istoriko-architekturnyj i Chudožestvennyj Muzej-zapovednik, Rybinsk 33362

Slovakia
Múzeum Ludovíta Štúra, Modra 34030
Novohradská Galéria, Lučenec 34018

South Africa
Engelenburg House Art Collection, Pretoria 34342
Koopmans-De Wet House Museum, Cape Town 34206
Van Tilburg Collection, Pretoria 34363

Spain
Centro Agost, Museo de Alfarería, Agost 34408
Museo de Almería, Almería 34454
Museo de Cerámica de la Cartuja, Salteras 35370
Museo de Cerámica Ruiz de Luna, Talavera de la Reina 35508
Museo de Farmacia Militar, Madrid 35021
Museo de Zaragoza, Zaragoza 35722
Museo Municipal de Cerámica, Paterna 35257
Museo Nacional de Artes Decorativas, Madrid 35044
Museo Nacional de Cerámica y de las Artes Suntuarias González Martí, Valencia 35608
Museo Zuloaga, Segovia 35468
Museu de Cerâmica, Barcelona 34556
Museu de Ceràmica de Manises, Manises 35080
Museu Municipal, Tona 35551
Palacio Real de El Pardo, El Pardo 35253

Sweden
Gamla Krukmakarverkstaden, Arvika 35816
Gustavsbergs Porslinmuseum, Gustavsberg 35932
Höganäs Museum och Konsthall, Höganäs 35956
State Apartments of the Royal Palace, Stockholm 36284
Törngrens Krukmakeri, Falkenberg 35879

Switzerland
Gewerbemuseum, Winterthur 37328
Glasmuseum, Hergiswil, Nidwalden 36801
Heimatmuseum Alt-Falkenstein, Balsthal 36492
Heimatmuseum Klus, Klus 36829
Keramik-Museum, Triengen 37253
Musée Historique et des Porcelaines, Nyon 36994
Ortsmuseum Kilchberg, Kilchberg, Zürich 36825
Thaler Keramikmuseum und Maria-Felchin-Sammlung, Matzendorf 36930
Zunfthaus zur Meisen, Zürich 37422
Zunfthaus zur Meisen Keramiksammlung, Zürich 37423

Ukraine
The Bleschunov Municipal Museum of Personal Collections, Odessa 37896

United Kingdom
Allen Gallery, Alton 37990
Art Gallery and Museum, Bootle 38279
Barlow Collection of Chinese Ceramics, Bronzes and Jades, Brighton 38337
The Burton Art Gallery and Museum, Bideford 38191
Castle Museum, Norwich 40091
The Ceramic Collection, Aberystwyth 37954
Clevedon Court, Clevedon 38589
Cleveland Crafts Centre, Middlesbrough 39947
Clifton Park Museum, Rotherham 40344
Coalport China Museum, Coalport 38597
Collection of Martinware Pottery, Southall 40540
Croydon Museum, Croydon 38677
De Morgan Centre, London 39620
Gladstone Working Pottery Museum, Stoke-on-Trent 40607
Glynn Vivian Art Gallery, Swansea 40658
Goss and Crested China Centre, Horndean 39260
Guildhall Museum, Carlisle 38489
Harlow Museum, Harlow 39163
Hastings Museum and Art Gallery, Hastings 39184
Hull University Art Collection, Kingston-upon-Hull 39381
Jackfield Tile Museum, Jackfield 39322
Kirkcaldy Museum and Art Gallery, Kirkcaldy 39391
Melrose Abbey Museum, Melrose 39932
Mill Green Museum and Mill, Hatfield 39188
Minton Museum, Stoke-on-Trent 40608
Museum of the Royal Pharmaceutical Society of Great Britain, London 39724
Museum of Worcester Porcelain, Worcester 40931
Nantgarw China Works Museum, Nantgarw 39998
Penwith Galleries, Saint Ives, Cornwall 40407
Percival David Foundation of Chinese Art, London 39742
Peter Scott Gallery, Lancaster 39416
Pitzhanger Manor-House and Gallery, London 39745
The Potteries Museum and Art Gallery, Stoke-on-Trent 40609
Raby Castle, Darlington 38698
Roman Villa Museum at Bignor, Pulborough 40274
Royal Crown Derby Museum, Derby 38720
School of Art Gallery and Museum, Aberystwyth 37956
Sherborne Castle, Sherborne 40494
Sir Henry Doulton Gallery, Stoke-on-Trent 40610
Spode Museum, Stoke-on-Trent 40611
Sunderland Museum, Sunderland 40650
Upton House, Banbury 38076
Wedgwood Museum, Stoke-on-Trent 40612
Wisbech and Fenland Museum, Wisbech 40907

U.S.A.
A.L. Fetterman Educational Museum, Fort Valley 43466
The Bradford Museum of Collector's Plates, Niles 45953
Butter Pat Museum, Bigfork 41686
Central Iowa Art Museum, Marshalltown 45184
China Institute Gallery, New York 45783
Clay Studio, Philadelphia 46400
Goodman Museum, Tyler 48130
Houston Harte University Center, San Angelo 47241
The Jones Museum of Glass and Ceramics, Sebago 47549
Lladro Museum, New York 45825
Museum of Ceramics, East Liverpool 43056
National Museum of Ceramic Art and Glass, Baltimore 41484
North Carolina Pottery Center, Seagrove 47526
Ohio Ceramic Center, Roseville 47008
Pewabic Pottery Museum, Detroit 42934
The Ross C. Purdy Museum of Ceramics, Westerville 48556
The Scein-Joseph International Museum of Ceramic Art, Alfred 41137
Touchstone Center for Crafts, Farmington 43301
The World Organization of China Painters, Oklahoma City 46124

Venezuela
Museo de Cerámica y Loza Popular, Falcón 48941

Portraits

Colombia
Museo de Arte Religioso Presbítero Antonio María Franco, Supía 07602

Denmark
Det Nationalhistoriske Museum på Frederiksborg, Hillerød 08873

Germany
Burg Hohenzollern, Bisingen 16172
Stiftung Schloß Eutin, Eutin 16981

Greece
Municipal Gallery of Samos, Samos 21148

Italy
Quadreria Comunale, Prato 25049

Netherlands
Ter Beziens, Kolhorn 29486
Dekema State Portrettengalerij, Jelsum 29465
Hofje Van Gratie, Delft 29078

New Zealand
New Zealand Portrait Gallery, Wellington 30303

Serbia-Montenegro
Zbirka Eparhije Banatski, Vršac 33929

Spain
Galerie de Catalans Illustres, Barcelona 34544

Sweden
Svenska Statens Porträttsamling, Mariefred 36088

United Kingdom
Beningbrough Hall, York 40959
The Blairs Museum, Aberdeen 37935
Bodelwyddan Castle Museum, Bodelwyddan 38262
Djanogly Art Gallery, Nottingham 40105
Fyvie Castle, Fyvie 39020
Goodwood House, Chichester 38561
Library Drawings Collection, London 39688
National Portrait Gallery, London 39732
Parham Elizabethan House Gardens, Pulborough 40273
Scottish National Portrait Gallery, Edinburgh 38917
Ugbrooke House, Chudleigh 38580

U.S.A.
Cecil Clark Davis Gallery, Marion 45160
The Gilbert Stuart Museum, Saunderstown 47472
John Jay Homestead, Katonah 44415
Redwood Library and Athenaeum, Newport 45932

Postage Stamps

Brazil
Museu Numismático e Filatélico, Rio de Janeiro 04392

Canada
Musée Canadien de la Poste, Gatineau 05483

China, People's Republic
China Stamp Museum, Beijing 06963

Cuba
Museo Postal Cubano, La Habana 07995

Egypt
Postal Museum, Cairo 09284

France
Musée de la Poste, Paris 13561
Musée Régional du Timbre et de la Philatélie, Le Luc 12433

French Polynesia
Centre Philatélique de Polynésie Française, Papeete 15345

Germany
Archiv für Philatelie der Museumsstiftung Post und Telekommunikation, Bonn 16227
Briefmarkenmuseum im Kloster Bardel, Bad Bentheim 15599

Greece
Tahydromiko Moyseio, Athinai 20904

Hungary
Bélyegmúzeum, Budapest 21330

India
National Philatelic Museum, Delhi 21778

Iran
Museum of Post and Telecomunication Mokhaberat, Teheran 22316

Israel
Postal and Philatelic Museum, Tel Aviv 22772

Italy
Gabinetto delle Stampe, Roma 25156
Gabinetto Stampe e Disegni, Venezia 25916
Museo della Stampa, Soncino 25601

Japan
Kitte no Hakubutsukan, Tokyo 26869

Jordan
Postal Museum, Amman 27060

Liechtenstein
Postmuseum des Fürstentums Liechtenstein, Vaduz 27517

Mexico
Museo de Filatelia de Oaxaca, Oaxaca 28275

Monaco
Musée des Timbres et des Monnaies, Monaco 28668

Peru
Museo Postal y Filatélico del Perú, Lima 31224

Philippines
Postal Museum and Philatelic Library, Manila 31393

San Marino
Museo Postale, Filatelico-Numismatico, San Marino 33767

Spain
Museo Postal y Telegráfico, Madrid 35052

U.S.A.
The Collectors Club, New York 45785
National Postal Museum, Washington 48383
Spellman Museum of Stamps and Postal History, Weston 48570

Zambia
National Archives of Zambia, Lusaka 49021

Postal Services

Andorra
Museu Postal d'Andorra, Ordino 00086

Argentina
Museo de Telecomunicaciones, Buenos Aires 00196
Museo Postal y Telegráfico Doctor Ramon J. Carcano, Buenos Aires 00238

Australia
Telstra Museum Brisbane, Clayfield 00922
Wireless Hill Telecommunications Museum, Applecross 00745

Botswana
Postal Museum Botswana, Gaborone 03935

Brazil
Museu de Telecomunicações, Rio de Janeiro 04364
Museu do Telephone, Rio de Janeiro 04375
Museu Postal e Telegráfico da ECT, Brasília 04007

Canada
Bell Canada Telephone Historical Collection, Montréal 05891
Maison de la Poste, Montréal 05911
Musée Canadien de la Poste, Gatineau 05483
Poste de Traite Chauvin, Tadoussac 06533
Ross House Museum, Winnipeg 06840
Telephone Historical Collection, Halifax 05564
Telephone Pioneer Museum, Saint John 06338
Telorama, Regina 06249
Toronto's First Post Office, Toronto 06621

China, People's Republic
Beijing Telephone History Museum, Donghuang 07045

China, Republic
Postal Museum, Taipei 07354

Colombia
Museo Filatélico del Banco de la República, Medellín 07520
Museo Postal Eduardo Santos, Bogotá 07432

Croatia
Hrvatski Muzej Pošte i Telekomunikacija, Zagreb 07820

Czech Republic
Poštovní Muzeum, Praha 08612
Poštovní Muzeum, Vyšší Brod 08735

Denmark
Post Tele Museum, København 08947
Telefonmuseet, Hellerup 08859

Estonia
Eesti Postimuuseum, Tartu 09375

Finland
Postimuseo, Helsinki 09520

France
Musée de la Communication en Alsace, Riquewihr 13976

Musée de la Poste, Amélie-les-Bains-Palalda 10318
Musée de la Poste, Paris 13561
Musée de la Poste, Prunelli-di-Fium'Orbu 13881
Musée de la Poste, Saint-Flour (Cantal) 14220
Musée de la Poste des Pays de Loire, Nantes 13252
Musée du Téléphone, Nancy 13242
Musée du Téléphone Narbonne, Narbonne 13269
Musée Postal d'Aquitaine, Saint-Macaire 14336
Musée Régional des Télécommunications en Flandres, Marcq-en-Barœul 12814

Germany
Museum für Kommunikation Berlin, Berlin 16055
Museum für Kommunikation Frankfurt, Frankfurt am Main 17065
Museum für Kommunikation Hamburg, Hamburg 17559
Museum für Kommunikation Nürnberg im Verkehrsmuseum, Nürnberg 19152
Museumsstiftung Post und Telekommunikation, Bonn 16245
Philipp-Reis-Gedächtnisstätte, Friedrichsdorf, Taunus 17145
Postmuseum Mettingen, Mettingen 18722
Postmuseum Rheinhausen, Oberhausen-Rheinhausen 19176
Telefonmuseum Hittfelder Bahnhof, Seevetal 19925

Greece
Museum of Telecommunications, Néa Kifissia 21097

Hungary
Postamúzeum, Balatonszemes 21313
Postamúzeum, Budapest 21379

Iceland
Póstminjasafn Íslands, Hafnarfjörður 21636
Símaminjasafnið, Reykjavík 21665

Indonesia
Museum Pos Giro, Bandung 22076

Iran
Museum of Post and Telecomunication Mokhaberat, Teheran 22316

Israel
Postal and Philatelic Museum, Tel Aviv 22772

Italy
Museo dei Tasso e della Storia Postale, Camerata Cornello 23282
Museo Internazionale dell'Immagine Postale, Belvedere Ostrense 23050
Museo Storico delle Poste e Telecomunicazioni, Roma 25259

Japan
Maejima Memorial Museum, Joetsu 26284

Korea, Republic
Chungnam Telecommunication Museum, Daejeon 27158
Communications Monument, Seoul 27226
Postal Museum, Seoul 27266

Latvia
Lattelekom Muzejs, Rīga 27411

Liechtenstein
Postmuseum des Fürstentums Liechtenstein, Vaduz 27517

Luxembourg
Musée des Postes et Telecommunications, Luxembourg 27563

Malawi
Mtengatenga Postal Museum, Namaka 27614

Mauritius
Mauritius Postal Museum, Port Louis 27738

Mexico
Museo Biblioteca Palacio Postal, México 28111
Museo de las Telecomunicaciones, México 28145
Museo Regional de Telecomunicaciones Tomás Guzmán Cantú, La Paz 28046
Museo Telefónico Victoria, México 28205

Morocco
Musée Postal, Rabat 28707

Norway
Kjerringøy Gamle Handelssted, Bodø 30439

Peru
Museo Postal y Filatélico del Perú, Lima 31224

Poland
Muzeum Poczty i Telekomunikacji, Wrocław 32183
Muzeum Poczty i Telekomunikacji Oddział w Gdańsku, Gdańsk 31574

Portugal
Museu das Comunicações, Lisboa 32296

Russia
Centralnyj Muzej Svjazi im. A.S. Popova, Sankt-Peterburg 33386
Literaturno-memorial'nyj Dom-Muzej F.M. Rešetnikova, Ekaterinburg 32770

Serbia-Montenegro
PTT Muzej Zajednice Jugoslavenskih Pošta, Telegrafa i Telefona, Beograd 33817

South Africa
Stampwise Info Square, Pretoria 34358

Spain
Museo de las Telecomunicaciones, Madrid 35028
Museo Postal y Telegráfico, Madrid 35052
Museu Gabinet Postal, Barcelona 34580

Sweden
Bodaskogs Affärs- och Postmuseum, Aneby 35800
Postal Museum, Stockholm 36273

Switzerland
Musée des Téléphones de Genève, Plan-les-Ouates 37025
Museum für Kommunikation, Bern 36546
Museum-Telefonzentrale, Magden 36919
Telefonmuseum im Greuterhof, Islikon 36817

Tunisia
Musée Postal, Tunis 37595

United Kingdom
Bath Postal Museum, Bath 38109
British Telecom Museum, Oxford 40143
Heritage Royal Mail Collection, London 39663
Museum of Communication, Bo'ness 38277
National Wireless Museum, Seaview 40463
Timeball Tower, Deal 38710

U.S.A.
Arkansas Post National Memorial, Gillett 43669
Fort Leavenworth Historical Museum and Post Museum, Fort Leavenworth 43415
Maitland Historical Museums, Maitland 45080
National Postal Museum, Washington 48383
Spellman Museum of Stamps and Postal History, Weston 48570

Posters

Finland
Julistemuseo, Lahti 09741

Germany
Kleines Plakatmuseum, Bayreuth 15851
Puppentheatermuseum, Kaufbeuren 18043

Switzerland
Museum für Gestaltung Zürich, Zürich 37397

United Kingdom
Centre for the Magic Arts, London 39601

Pottery, Earthenware → Porcelain and Ceramics

Precious Stones

Argentina
Museo de Mineralogía y Geología Dr. Alfredo Stelzner, Córdoba 00297

Australia
Australian Pearling Exhibition, Darwin 00971
Berlins Gem and Historical Museum, South Nanango 01461
Griffith Regional Art Gallery, Griffith 01076
Kealley's Gemstone Museum, Nannup 01299
Opal and Gem Museum, Ballina 00767
Port Stephens Shell Museum, Corlette 00946

Austria
Kristalle und Edle Steine Turracher Höhe, Ebene Reichenau 01779
Perlmuttdrechslerei, Riegersburg, Niederösterreich 02514
Schmuckmuseum Gablonzer Industrie, Enns 01819
Swarovski Kristallwelten, Wattens 02797

Belgium
Diamantmuseum, Antwerpen 03140
Diamantmuseum, Grobbendonk 03463
Musée Curtius, Liège 03571

Brazil
Museu Amsterdam Sauer de Pedras Preciosas, Rio de Janeiro 04330
Museu de Geologia, Porto Alegre 04281
Museu do Diamante, Diamantina 04080
Museu H. Stern, Rio de Janeiro 04380

Costa Rica
Museo del Jade, San José 07659

Croatia
Etnografski Muzej Split, Split 07780

Cyprus
Cyprus Jewellers Museum, Lefkosia 08197

Czech Republic
Městské Muzeum Klenotnice, Nová Paka 08500
Muzeum Českého Ráje, Turnov 08694

Egypt
Palace of Royal Jewelleries, Zizinia 09311
Royal Jewelry Museum, Alexandria 09246

Finland
Jalokivi Galleria, Kemi 09648
Ylämaan Jalokivimuseo, Ylämaa 10212

France
Espace d'Exposition Minal, Héricourt 12012
Musée de l'Ardoise, Trélazé 14993

Germany
Bernsteinmuseum, Ostseebad Sellin 19318
Deutsches Edelsteinmuseum, Idar-Oberstein 17879
Grünes Gewölbe, Dresden 16685
Kristallmuseum Riedenburg, Riedenburg 19598
Museum Idar-Oberstein, Idar-Oberstein 17880

Greece
Gouriotis Collection, Lárissa 21044
Ilias Lalaounis Jewelry Museum, Athinai 20867
Mouseio Kompologiou, Nafplion 21091

Iran
Javaherat, Teheran 22307

Israel
Harry Oppenheimer Diamond Museum, Ramat Gan 22731

Italy
Museo del Bijou, Casalmaggiore 23367
Museo della Pietra Serena, Firenzuola 23888

Jordan
Jordan Folklore Museum, Amman 27053

Morocco
Musée des Oudaïa, Rabat 28706

Netherlands
Edelsteenslijperij de Steenarend, Eindhoven 29210
Museum voor Moderne Kunst, Arnhem 28941

Poland
Muzeum Kamieni Szlachetnych, Polanica Zdrój 31892

Russia
Almaznyj Fond, Moskva 33019
Geologo-mineralogičeskij Muzej im. A.I. Kozlova, Vladivostok 33697
Mineralogičeskij Muzej im. A.V. Sidorova, Irkutsk 32815
Muzej Prirody Burjatii, Ulan-Udé 33655
Muzej Samocvety Bajkala, Sljudjanka 33527

Sweden
Porfyrmuseet, Älvdalen 35785

Switzerland
Musée de l'Horlogerie et de l'Emaillerie, Genève 36744

United Kingdom
The Crypt - Town Hall Plate Room, Oxford 40146
Her Majesty Tower of London, London 39662
Museum of the Jewellery Quarter, Birmingham 38225
Town and Crown Exhibition, Windsor 40904

U.S.A.
Crater of Diamonds State Park Museum, Murfreesboro 45564
Touchstone Center for Crafts, Farmington 43301
Turquoise Museum, Albuquerque 41110

Prehistory and Early History

Argentina
Museo Municipal C.I.P.A.S., Salto 00545
Museo Paleontológico, Arqueológico e Histórico de la Ciudad de Deán Funes, Deán Funes 00328

Australia
Hawkesbury Museum, Windsor 01605

Austria
Archäologisches Pilgermuseum Hemmaberg-Juenna, Globasnitz 01882
Archiv für die Waldviertler Urgeschichtsforschung, Horn 02047
Ateliersammlung Herbert Hiesmayr, Sankt Thomas am Blasenstein 02608
Ausgrabungsdokumentation 6000 Jahre Wohnberg Oberleis, Ernstbrunn 01821
Burgmuseum für Vor- und Frühgeschichte, Deutschlandsberg 01762
Erstes Urgeschichtliches Freilichtmuseum der Steiermark, Kulm bei Weiz 02171
Grenzlandmuseum Raabs an der Thaya, Raabs an der Thaya 02470
Heimatmuseum Steyregg, Steyregg 02693
Höbarth- und Madermuseum der Stadt Horn, Horn 02048
Keltenmuseum, Hallein 01997
Kulturerbe Hallstatt, Hallstatt 02000

Museum für Frühgeschichte des Landes Niederösterreich, Traismauer 02733
Museum für Ur- und Frühgeschichte, Stillfried 02696
Museum für Ur- und Frühgeschichte, Wieselburg an der Erlauf 03025
Museum für Urgeschichte, Koblach 02145
Museum für Urgeschichte des Landes Niederösterreich, Asparn an der Zaya 01685
Museum Großklein, Großklein 01956
Österreichisches Felsbildermuseum, Spital am Pyhrn 02668
Salzburger Museum Carolino Augusteum, Salzburg 02551
Stadtmuseum Wiener Neustadt, Wiener Neustadt 03021
Tiroler Landesmuseum Ferdinandeum, Innsbruck 02082
Ur- und frühgeschichtliche Eisenindustrie im Bezirk Oberpullendorf - Schauraum, Oberpullendorf 02375
Urgeschichtliche Sammlung, Engerwitzdorf 01817
Urzeitmuseum Nußdorf ob der Traisen, Traismauer 02735

Belgium
Archeologisch Museum van de Universiteit, Gent 03433
Domus Romana, Aubechies 03191
Heemkundig Museum Slag van Lafelt, Vlijtingen 03820
Musée Archéologique Régional d'Orp-le-Grand, Orp-le-Grand 03675
Musée de la Préhistoire, Gesves 03460
Musée de la Préhistoire en Wallonie, Flémalle 03419
Musée d'Ourthe-Ambléve, Comblain-au-Pont 03359
Musée Historique et Préhistorique Van den Steen, Jehay-Amay 03528
Musée Régional d'Histoire et d'Archéologie, Visé 03819
Ondergronds Museum, Kanne 03532
Voorhistorisch Museum, Zonhoven 03855

Brazil
Museu de Arqueologia e Artes Populares, Paranaguá 04245
Museu de Pré-História Professora Márcia Angelina Alves, Perdizes 04259

Bulgaria
Nacionalen Muzej Zemjata i Chorata, Sofia 04851

Canada
Musée d'Histoire et d'Archéologie, La Sarre 05709
Powell River Historical Museum, Powell River 06176

China, People's Republic
Regional Museum, Xinhui 07310

Colombia
Museo Luis Alberto Acuña, Villa de Leyva 07621

Congo, Democratic Republic
Musée de Préhistoire, Kinshasa 07636

Croatia
Arheološki Muzej Zagreb, Zagreb 07809

Cuba
Museo de Historia Natural Valle de la Prehistoria, Santiago de Cuba 08137

Cyprus
Leventis Municipal Museum of Nicosia, Lefkosia 08202

Czech Republic
Archeologické Pracoviště, Opava 08518
Melicharovo Městské Muzeum, Unhošt 08700
Regionální Muzeum K.A. Polánka, Žatec 08738

Denmark
Esbjerg Museum, Esbjerg 08807
Haderslev Museum, Haderslev 08849
Moesgård Museum, Højbjerg 08880
Ringkøbing Museum, Ringkøbing 09032
Skive Museum, Skive 09061
Skjern-Egvad Museum, Skjern 09065
Søllerød Museum, Holte 08892
Vesthimmerlands Museum, Års 08774

Egypt
National Museum for Civilization, Cairo 09280

Equatorial Guinea
Museo Etnológico Misional C.M.F., Santa Isabel 09314

Finland
Ålands Museum, Mariehamn 09815

France
Collection Préhistorique Pagès, Le Moustier 12457
Dinosauria - Musée des Dinosaures, Espéraza 11652
Ecomusée de la Vallée du Galeizon, Cendras 11102
Exposition de la Préhistoire, Mazières-en-Mauges 12911
Expostion Grotte Chauvet Pont d'Arc, Vallon-Pont-d'Arc 15066
Musée Archéologique, Martizay 12882
Musée Archéologique, Sainte-Bazeille 14520
Musée Archéologique de Site, Liffol-le-Grand 12586
Musée-Château des Adhémar, Montélimar 13073
Musée d'Archéologieque, Saint-Ciers-sur-Gironde 14152
Musée d'Art et d'Histoire, Saint-Antonin-Noble-Val 14112
Musée de la Pierre à Fusil, Meusnes 12964
Musée de la Préhistoire, Le Mas-d'Azil 12442
Musée de la Préhistoire, Saint-Porchaire 14424
Musée de la Préhistoire-Le Cairn, Saint-Hilaire-la-Forêt 14265
Musée de l'Avallonnais, Avallon 10521
Musée de l'Homme de Néandertal, La Chapelle-aux-Saints 12141
Musée de Paléontologie, Menat 12924
Musée de Paléontologie Humaine de Terra Amata, Nice 13315
Musée de Préhistoire, Aurignac 10489
Musée de Préhistoire Amédée Lemozi, Cabrerets 10969
Musée de Préhistoire des Gorges du Verdon, Quinson 13904
Musée de Préhistoire d'île-de-France, Nemours 13280
Musée de Préhistoire James Miln-Zacharie le Rouzic, Carnac 11053
Musée de Préhistoire Régionale, Menton 12937
Musée de Ventabren, Ventabren 15123
Musée Départemental Breton, Quimper 13900
Musée Départemental de la Préhistoire, Le Grand-Pressigny 12418
Musée Départemental de Préhistoire, Solutré-Pouilly 14767
Musée Départemental de Préhistoire Corse, Sartène 14626
Musée des Arts et Traditions Populaires, Esse 11655
Musée des Bujoliers, Saint-Cezaire 14141
Musée des Corbières, Sigean 14751
Musée du Vieil Auvillar, Auvillar 10506
Musée Municipal de Préhistoire, Les Matelles 12545
Musée Municipal de Préhistoire Régionale, Saint-Pons-de-Thomières 14423
Musée Municipal des Beaux Arts et d'Histoire Naturelle, Châteaudun 11214
Musée National de Préhistoire, Les Eyzies-de-Tayac-Sireuil 12538
Musée Préhistorique Charles Nardin, Sainte-Foy-la-Grande 14532
Musée Préhistorique Finistérien, Penmarch 13685
Musée Régional de Préhistoire, Orgnac-l'Aven 13423
Musée Sundgauvien, Altkirch 10297
Parc de la Préhistoire, Tarascon-sur-Ariège 14864
Parc de Préhistoire de Bretagne, Malansac 12781
Plaine des Dinosaures, Mèze 12972
Le Préhistorama, Rousson 14065
Tour-Musée de Velaux, Velaux 15109

Germany
Alamannenmuseum Ellwangen, Ellwangen 16834
Altmärkisches Museum, Stendal 20057
Archäologie-Museum, Heilbronn 17686
Archäologische Staatssammlung München, München 18827
Archäologisches Landesmuseum, Wünsdorf 20690
Archäologisches Museum, Frankfurt am Main 17031
Archäologisches Museum des Historischen Vereins für Oberfranken, Bayreuth 15840
Archäologisches Museum Neu-Ulm, Neu-Ulm 19007
Archäologisches Zentrum Hitzacker, Hitzacker 17771
Audorfer Museum im Burgtor, Oberaudorf 19169
Ausstellung zur Erd- und Vorgeschichte, Breitscheid, Hessen 16316
Bachmann-Museum Bremervörde, Bremervörde 16346
Braith-Mali-Museum, Biberach an der Riß 16138
Braunschweigisches Landesmuseum, Wolfenbüttel 20651
Dischinger Heimatmuseum, Dischingen 16623
Dr.-Carl-Haeberlin-Friesen-Museum, Wyk auf Föhr 20726
Festungsanlage-Museum Senftenberg, Senftenberg 19938
Geschichtlich-heimatkundliche Sammlung, Aschheim 15537
Goldberg-Museum, Riesbürg 19610
Haffmuseum Ueckermünde, Ueckermünde 20247
Heimat- und Handfeuerwaffenmuseum, Kemnath 18056
Heimat- und Torfmuseum, Gröbenzell 17407
Heimatmuseum, Allensbach 15433
Heimatmuseum, Camburg 16450
Heimatmuseum, Grabow, Mecklenburg 17366
Heimatmuseum, Prieros 19451
Heimatmuseum Blaubeuren, Blaubeuren 16180
Heimatmuseum der Stadt Rerik, Ostseebad Rerik 19317
Heimatmuseum Ebersbach in der Humboldt-Baude, Ebersbach, Sachsen 16768
Heimatmuseum Garbsen, Garbsen 17195
Heimatmuseum Gensungen, Felsberg 16993
Heimatmuseum Maßbach, Maßbach 18662
Heimatmuseum Osterhofen, Osterhofen 19293
Heimatmuseum Riedlingen, Riedlingen 19600
Heimatmuseum Uelzen mit Gläsersammlung Röver, Uelzen 20248
Helms-Museum, Hamburg 17545
Herborner Heimatmuseum, Herborn, Hessen 17715
Hürten-Heimatmuseum, Bad Münstereifel 15697
Jesuitenkolleg, Mindelheim 18742
Karl-Wagenplast-Museum, Schwaigern 19870
Kreisheimatmuseum Weißes Haus, Rotenburg an der Fulda 19670
Kulturgeschichtliches Museum Osnabrück, Osnabrück 19280
Kulturhistorisches Museum Schloß Merseburg, Merseburg 18713
Landesmuseum für Natur und Mensch, Oldenburg, Oldenburg 19257
Landesmuseum für Vorgeschichte, Dresden 16693
Landesmuseum für Vorgeschichte Sachsen-Anhalt, Halle, Saale 17515
Lobdengau-Museum, Ladenburg 18284
Ludwig-Roselius-Museum für Ur- und Frühgeschichte, Worpswede 20685
Museum Alzey, Alzey 15477
Museum Burg Eisenhardt, Belzig 15873
Museum Burg Ranis, Ranis 19483
Museum der Stadt Lauffen am Neckar, Lauffen am Neckar 18356
Museum der Stadt Schkeuditz, Schkeuditz 19786
Museum der Stadt Wolgast, Wolgast 20667
Museum des Ohrekreises, Wolmirstedt 20671
Museum für die Archäologie des Eiszeitalters, Neuwied 19086
Museum für Naturkunde des Zittauer Landes, Zittau 20762
Museum für Naturkunde und Vorgeschichte, Dessau 16579
Museum für Ur- und Frühgeschichte, Freiburg im Breisgau 17115
Museum für Ur- und Frühgeschichte, Eichstätt 16807
Museum für Ur- und Frühgeschichte Thüringens, Weimar, Thüringen 20465
Museum für Vor- und Frühgeschichte, Gunzenhausen 17464
Museum für Vor- und Frühgeschichte, Langenau, Württemberg 18327
Museum für Vor- und Frühgeschichte, Berlin 16059
Museum für Vor- und Frühgeschichte, Saarbrücken 19725
Museum für Vor- und Frühgeschichte sowie Stadtgeschichte, Egeln 16784
Museum im Kräuterkasten, Albstadt 15419
Museum im Marstall, Winsen, Luhe 20613
Museum im Vorderen Schloss, Mühlheim an der Donau 18812
Museum Reichenfels, Hohenleuben 17808
Museum Schloss Hellenstein, Heidenheim an der Brenz 17682
Museum Schloß Klippenstein, Radeberg 19468
Museum Schloß Moritzburg, Zeitz, Elster 20738
Niederbayerisches Vorgeschichtsmuseum, Landau an der Isar 18300
Niedersächsisches Landesmuseum Hannover, Hannover 17607
Oderlandmuseum, Bad Freienwalde 15645
Peter-Wiepert-Museum, Burg auf Fehmarn 16410
Pfahlbaumuseum Unteruhldingen, Uhldingen-Mühlhofen 20256
Prähistorische Siedlung Pestenacker, Weil am Lech 20433
Prähistorisches Heimatmuseum, Veringenstadt 20303
Quadrat Bottrop, Bottrop 16265
Rheinisches Landesmuseum Trier, Trier 20212
Roemer- und Pelizaeus-Museum, Hildesheim 17760
Römermuseum Kastell Boiotro, Passau 19360
Römermuseum Weißenburg, Weißenburg in Bayern 20493
Römisch-Germanisches Zentralmuseum, Mainz 18606
Römische Villa Rustica Möckenlohe, Adelschlag 15393
Sammlung Irmgard Friedl, Bad Griesbach im Rottal 15653
Schloss Neuburg, Neuburg an der Donau 19018
Schloßmuseum, Quedlinburg 19464
Siegerlandmuseum mit Ausstellungsforum Haus Oranienstraße, Siegen 19950
Spengler-Museum, Sangerhausen 19743
Spreewald-Museum Lübbenau/Lehde, Lübbenau 18532
Stadtmuseum Erlangen, Erlangen 16923
Stadtmuseum Mutzschen, Mutzschen 18965
Stadtmuseum Tharandt, Tharandt 20171
Städtisches Heimatmuseum, Taucha bei Leipzig 20146
Städtisches Museum, Bad Reichenhall 15718
Städtisches Museum Ludwigsburg, Ludwigsburg, Württemberg 18514
Städtisches Zentrum für Geschichte und Kunst, Riesa 19609
Steinsburg-Museum, Römhild 19635
Steinzeitmuseum, Korb 18209
Südschwäbisches Archäologiemuseum im Jesuitenkolleg, Mindelheim 18745
Uffenheimer Gollachgaumuseum, Uffenheim 20253
Ulmer Museum, Ulm 20261
Ur- und Frühgeschichtliche Sammlung, Erlangen 16925
Urgeschichtliches Museum und Galerie Vierzigtausend Jahre Kunst, Blaubeuren 16183
Urweltmuseum, Pirna 19408
Volkskundemuseum, Schönberg, Mecklenburg 19826
Vor- und Frühgeschichtliche Sammlung, Kassel 18033
Vor- und Frühgeschichtliches Museum, Thalmässing 20168
Vorgeschichtsmuseum der Oberpfalz, Amberg, Oberpfalz 15479
Vorgeschichtsmuseum im Grabfeldgau, Bad Königshofen 15678
Wallenfels'sches Haus, Abteilung Vor- und Frühgeschichte, Archäologie und Völkerkunde, Gießen 17284
Zeittunnel Wülfrath, Wülfrath 20689

Greece
Archeological Collection, Liknades 21047
Archeological Collection, Maroneia 21057
Archeological Collection, Siatista 21153
P. and Al. Canellopoulos Museum, Athinai 20898

Guinea
Musée Annexe de Youkounkoun, Youkounkoun 21287
Musée National de Conakry, Conakry 21282
Musée Préfectoral de Kissidougou, Kissidougou 21284

Hungary
Vértesszőlősi Bemutatóhely, Vértesszőllős 21606

India
Archaeological Museum, Pune 21986
Archaeological Museum, Udaipur 22043
Archaeology Museum, Allahabad 21690
Baripada Museum, Baripada 21708
University Museum of Science and Culture, Aligarh 21687

Israel
Bet Gordon, Deganya Aleph 22585
Huleh Valley Regional Prehistoric Museum, Kibbutz Maayan Baruch 22696
Museum of Prehistory, Jerusalem 22649
Museum of Prehistory, Shaar Hagolan 22742

Italy
Antiquarium Forense, Roma 25148
Centro Camuno di Studi Preistorici, Capo di Ponte 23326
Civiche Raccolte Archeologiche e Numismatiche, Milano 24373
Civico Museo Archeologico e di Scienze Naturali Federico Eusebio, Alba 22829
Istituto Italiano di Paleontologia Umana, Roma 25168
Mercati Dr. Traiano, Roma 25170
Museo Archeologico Eoliano, Lipari 24187
Museo Archeologico G. Moretti, San Severino Marche 25412
Museo Archeologico Statale, Ascoli Piceno 22950
Museo Civico, Erba 23735
Museo Civico, Mazara del Vallo 24337
Museo Civico, Rovereto 25291
Museo Civico A. Klitsche de la Grange, Allumiere 22859
Museo Civico Archeologico Etnologico, Modena 24438
Museo Civico Archeologico U. Granafei, Mesagne 24362
Museo Civico B. Romano, Termini Imerese 25692
Museo Civico della Val Fiorentina Vittorino Cazzetta, Selva di Cadore 25531
Museo Civico di Archeologia Ligure, Genova 23986
Museo Civico di Paleontologia e Archeologia, Ugento 25851
Museo Civico di Paleontologia e Paletnologia, Borgosesia 23177
Museo Civico e Pinacoteca, Sassoferrato 25495
Museo Civico per la Preistoria del Monte Cetona, Cetona 23514
Museo d'Arte Preistorica, Pinerolo 24928
Museo delle Origini, Roma 25203
Museo delle Palafitte, Molina di Ledro 24461
Museo di Antichita, Torino 25745
Museo di Paleontologia e Paletnologia, Maglie 24261
Museo di Preistorico e Paleontologico, Sant'Anna d'Alfaedo 25454
Museo Fiorentino di Preistoria, Firenze 23876
Museo Nazionale di Santa Maria delle Monanche e Paleolitico, Isernia 24103
Museo Nazionale Domenico Ridola, Matera 24335
Museo Nazionale Preistorico ed Etnografico Luigi Pigorini, Roma 25238
Museo Preistorico e Lapidario, Verucchio 25979
Museo Sella e Mosca, Alghero 22855
Villa Mirabello, Varese 25899

Japan
Gifu-ken Hakubutsukan, Seki 26729
Idojiri Kokokan, Fujimi 26138
Kokubunji-shi Bunkazai Hozonkan, Kokubunji 26366
Meiji-Daigaku Kouko Hakubutsukan, Tokyo 26887
Tohoku Daigaku, Kokoshiryoshitsu, Sendai 26737

Kenya
Kariandusi Prehistoric Site Museum, Gilgil 27101
National Museum Nairobi, Nairobi 27112
Olorgesailie Prehistoric Site Museum, Olorgesailie 27114

Korea, Republic
Yonsei University Museum, Seoul 27291

Luxembourg
Musée de Préhistoire, Echternach 27553

Malta
Ggantija Prehistoric Temples, Xaghra 27714

Mexico
Museo Prehistórico de Tepexpan, Tepexpan 28493
Museo Regional Doctor Leonardo Oliva, Ahualulco de Mercado 27762

Monaco
Musée d'Anthropologie Préhistorique, Monaco 28665

Morocco
Musée Archéologique, Rabat 28704

Netherlands
Archeologiemuseum, Stein 29854
Eicha-Museum, Bergeijk 28980
Historiekamer Hardenberg, Hardenberg 29340
Museum Oud Vriezenveen, Vriezenveen 29967
Museum Smallingerland, Drachten 29179
Nationaal Hunebedden Infocentrum, Borger 29004
Noordbrabants Museum, 's-Hertogenbosch 29407
Openluchtmuseum Erve Kots, Lievelde 29541
Streekmuseum De Oude Wolden, Bellingwolde 28974
Streekmuseum Schippersbeurs, Elsloo 29227
Veluws Museum Nairac, Barneveld 28965

Norway
Arkeologisk Museum i Stavanger, Stavanger 30877
Universitetets Oldsaksamling, Oslo 30769

Portugal
Museu Geológico, Lisboa 32303
Museu Municipal Abade Pedrosa, Santo Tirso 32343
Museu Nacional de Arqueologia, Lisboa 32306

Russia
Muzej Archeologii, Syktyvkar 33575

Serbia-Montenegro
Muzej Kosova, Priština 33895
Muzejska Zbirka, Knić 33846
Školska Zbirka Odžaci, Odžaci 33878
Zavičajni Muzej, Nikšić 33864

South Africa
Bushman Site Museum, Estcourt 34239
Stevenson-Hamilton Memorial Information Centre, Skukuza 34377
Victoria West Regional Museum, Victoria West 34398

Spain
Museo Arqueológico d'Eivissa i Formentera, Eivissa 34785
Museo Arqueológico Municipal, Jerez de la Frontera 34928
Museo Arqueológico Provincial, Huesca 34907
Museo Arqueológico Provincial, Ourense 35198
Museo Arqueológico y Etnológico Córdoba, Córdoba 34737
Museo Arqueológico y Etnológico de Granada, Granada 34873
Museo Cantábrico, Comillas 34732
Museo de Bellas Artes, Mahón 35066
Museo de Jaén, Jaén 34924
Museo de las Excavaciones de Torralba, Ambrona 34461
Museo de León, León 34949
Museo de Lluc, Escorca 34801
Museo de Murcia, Murcia 35146
Museo de Navarra, Pamplona 35249
Museo de Prehistoria y Servicio de Investigación Prehistórica, Valencia 35603
Museo Diaz-Caneja de Arte Contemporaneo, Palencia 35215
Museo Didáctico de Prehistoria, Alba de Tormes 34417
Museo Municipal, Amposta 34463
Museo Municipal, Aroche 34486
Museo Municipal, Tárrega 35517
Museo Municipal de Calahorra, Calahorra 34650
Museo Nacional y Centro de Investigación de Altamira, Santillana del Mar 35453
Museo Provincial, Lugo 34987
Museo Regional de Prehistoria y Arqueología de Cantabria, Santander 35433
Museu d'Arqueologia de Catalunya Girona, Girona 34854
Museu de Prehistòria i de les Cultures de València, Valencia 35613
Museu Diocesà i Comarcal, Solsona 35502

Sweden
Historiska Museet, Lund 36057

Switzerland
Collezione Preistorica, Castaneda 36618
Heimatmuseum Rapperswil, Rapperswil, Sankt Gallen 37043
Historische Ortssammlung, Reigoldswil 37050
Historisches Museum Sankt Gallen, Sankt Gallen 37100
Musée Cantonal d'Archéologie et d'Histoire, Lausanne 36857
Museum, Zofingen 37366
Museum Appenzell, Appenzell 36462
Museum für Urgeschichte(n), Zug 37427
Museum im Kornhaus, Rorschach 37072
Pfahlbautenmuseum, Pfyn 37023
Préhisto-Parc et Grottes, Réclère 37047

Syria
Homs Museum, Homs 37440

United Kingdom
Alexander Keiller Museum, Avebury 38041
Hull and East Riding Museum, Kingston-upon-Hull 39379
Jewry Wall Museum, Leicester 39462
Museum of Ancient Culture, Kilmartin 39363
Museum of the Iron Age, Andover 38001
Poldowrian Museum of Prehistory, Coverack 38647
Rotunda Museum of Archaeology and Local History, Scarborough 40455

U.S.A.
Edisto Island Historic Preservation Society Museum, Edisto Island 43090
Maturango Museum of the Indian Wells Valley, Ridgecrest 46895
Wyoming Dinosaur Center, Thermopolis 47995

Venezuela
Museo de Arte e Historia Casa de Los Celis, Valencia 48967

Zambia
Victoria Falls Information Centre, Livingstone 49019

Zimbabwe
Children's Library Museum, Marondera 49036
Matopos National Park Site Museums, Bulawayo 49026

Press → Mass Media

Printing

Australia
Melbourne Museum of Printing, Footscray 01029
Pinnaroo Printing Museum, Pinnaroo 01369
Wagga Wagga Art Gallery, Wagga Wagga 01570

Austria
Buchdruckmuseum, Rohrbach in Oberösterreich 02523
Druckmuseum Graz, Graz 01913
Historischer Handblaudruck Wagner, Bad Leonfelden 01713

Belgium
Dagbladmuseum Abraham Verhoevenhuis, Antwerpen 03139
Museum Plantin-Moretus, Antwerpen 03152
Nationaal Museum van de Speelkaart, Turnhout 03803

Brazil
Museu de Arte Contemporânea da Universidade de São Paulo, São Paulo 04514

Czech Republic
Muzeum Knihy, Žďár nad Sázavou 08743
Památník Jiřího Melantricha z Aventýna, Roždalovice 08640

Denmark
Bogtrykmuseet, Esbjerg 08805
Danmarks Mediemuseum, Odense 09008

Finland
Keskisuomalaisen Museo, Jyväskylä 09603

France
Atelier-Musée Livre et Typographie, Grignan 11955
Musée Champenois de l'Imprimerie, Épernay 11625
Musée de l'Imprimerie, Nantes 13253
Musée du Luxembourg, Paris 13604
Musée Renaudot, Loudun 12675

Germany
Druckereimuseum, Hatten, Oldenburg 17631
Druckereimuseum, Wildeshausen 20589
Gutenberg-Gedenkstätte, Eltville 16842
Gutenberg-Museum, Mainz 18600
Heimatmuseum Buchloe, Buchloe 16390
Kupferstichkabinett - Sammlung der Zeichnungen und Druckgraphik, Berlin 16033
Lichtdruck-Werkstatt-Museum, Dresden 16695
Lithographiesteinarchiv und druckhistorische Werkstätte, München 18871
MAN Museum, Augsburg 15560
Museen im Kulturzentrum, Rendsburg 19570
Museum für Druck, Mosbach, Baden 18795
Museum für Druckkunst, Leipzig 18406
Museum für visuelle Kommunikation, Köln 18159
Ottmar-Mergenthaler-Museum, Bad Mergentheim 15694
Werksmuseum Koenig Bauer AG, Würzburg 20707

Hungary
Kner Nyomdaipari Múzeum, Gyomaendrőd 21418

Ireland
Dublin Print Museum, Dublin 22423
National Print Museum, Dublin 22447

Italy
Museo Bodoniano, Parma 24803

Korea, Republic
Cheongju Early Printing Museum, Cheongju 27148
Samsung Museum of Publishing, Seoul 27269

Lebanon
Qozhaya Museum, Qozhaya 27492

Netherlands
Drukkerijmuseum Meppel, Meppel 29589
Grafisch Historisch Centrum - Drukkerijmuseum, Etten Leur 29253
Grafisch Musem-Atelier in den Groenen Zonck, Wouw 30027
Grafisch Museum Zutphen, Zutphen 30075
Museum de Historische Drukkerij, Maastricht 29566
Museum Enschedé, Haarlem 29327
Museum Lettergieten 1983, Westzaan 29998
Museum Oude Boekdrukkunst, Almen 28812
Nederlands Steendrukmuseum, Valkenswaard 29924

New Zealand
Yaldhurst Museum of Transport and Science, Christchurch 30134

Norway
Norsk Grafisk Museum, Stavanger 30883

Philippines
Museo Rosendo Mejica, Iloilo 31330

Romania
Muzeul Tiparului și al Cạrtii Vechi Românești, Târgoviște 32604

Russia
Muzej Istorii Pečati Sankt-Peterburga, Sankt-Peterburg 33439

Sweden
Rosenlöfs Tryckerimuseum, Kungsgården 36024

Switzerland
Centre d'Edition Contemporaine, Genève 36732
Druckereimuseum, Freienbach 36709
Gutenberg Museum, Fribourg 36714
Heimatmuseum und Buchdruckerstube, Beromünster 36557

United Kingdom
Gray's Printing Press, Strabane 40619
Guildford House Gallery, Guildford 39137
Guildford House Gallery, Guildford 39137
John Jarrold Printing Museum, Norwich 40095
Oxford University Press Museum, Oxford 40152
Peacock, Aberdeen 37941
Printing House Museum, Cockermouth 38604
Strang Print Room, London 39784
Thomas Bewick's Birthplace, Mickley 39943

U.S.A.
American Printing House for the Blind, Callahan Museum, Louisville 44961
Museum of Printing History, Houston 44131
The Printing Museum, Carson 42115
State Capital Publishing Museum, Guthrie 43856
University of Kansas Ryther Printing Museum, Lawrence 44687
Wooden Nickel Historical Museum, San Antonio 47266

Prints → Graphic Arts

Prisons → Criminology

Puppets → Dolls and Puppets

Radio → Mass Media

Railroads

Argentina
Museo de Ferrocarriles en Miniatura Werner Dura, La Falda 00379
Museo Ferroviario de Gualeguaychú, Gualeguaychú 00362
Museo Histórico Ferroviario Escribano Alfredo Rueda, Rueda 00534
Museo La Vieja Estación, María Teresa 00430
Museo Nacional y Centro de Estudios Históricos Ferroviarios, Buenos Aires 00232

Australia
Adelaide River Railway Heritage Precinct, Adelaide River 00718
Alpenrail Swiss Model Village and Railway, Claremont, Tasmania 00917
Australian Railway Museum, Melbourne 01223
Beta Railway Station Historic Museum, Alpha 00741
Bundaberg Railway Museum, Bundaberg 00862
Don River Railway Museum, Devonport 00979
Dorrigo Steam Railway and Museum, Dorrigo 00986
Gisborne Steam Park, Gisborne 01053
Jamestown Museum, Jamestown 01123
Merredin Railway Station Museum, Merredin 01249
National Railway Museum, Port Adelaide 01373
Old Canberra Tram Company Museum, Dickson 00982
Old Railway Station Museum, Northam 01329
Onslow Goods Shed Museum, Onslow 01345
Pinnaroo Heritage Museum, Pinnaroo 01368
Platform 1 Heritage Farm Railway, Littlehampton 01181
Puffing Billy Steam Museum, Menzies Creek 01246
Queensland Pioneer Steam Railway, Blackstone 00809
Rail Transport Museum, Bassendean 00772
Railco Museum, Ravenshoe 01407
Railway Station Museum, Wonthaggi 01613
Richmond Vale Railway Museum, Pelaw Main 01360
Serviceton Historic Railway Station, Serviceton 01448
Station House, Culcairn 00960
Sulphide Street Station Railway and Historical Museum, Broken Hill 00847
Sydney Tramway Museum, Loftus 01182
Tramway Museum, Bendigo 00796
Trentham Agricultural and Railway Museum, Trentham 01551
Walkaway Station Museum, Walkaway 01573
West Coast Pioneer's Memorial Museum, Zeehan 01635
West Torrens Railway, Signal Telegraph and Aviation Museum, Brooklyn Park 00850
Yass Railway Museum, Yass 01631

Austria
Eisenbahnmuseum, Deutsch Wagram 01758
Eisenbahnmuseum Strasshof - Das Heizhaus, Strasshof 02706
Erzbergbahn- und Wintersportmuseum, Vordernberg 02777
Feld- und Industriebahnmuseum (FIM), Freiland 01848
Florianerbahn, Sankt Florian 02560
Localbahnmuseum, Innsbruck 02073
Museumsbahn Steyrtal, Steyr 02688
Museumseisenbahn Payerbach-Hirschwang, Hirschwang 02031
Pferde-Eisenbahn Museum, Rainbach im Mühlkreis 02478
Salzkammergut-Lokalbahn-Museum, Mondsee 02322
Schmalspurbahn-Museum, Frojach 01857
Tramway-Museum Graz, Graz 01935
Verkehrsmuseum Sankt Veit an der Glan, Sankt Veit an der Glan 02615
Wälderbähnle, Bezau 01737
Waldviertler Eisenbahnmuseum, Sigmundsherberg 02663
Zahnradbahnschuppen, Puchberg 02459

Belgium
Musée des Chemins de Fer Belges, Bruxelles 03315
Spoorwegmuseum van Miniatuurmodellen, Heist-op-den-Berg 03490
Trammuseum, Schepdaal 03727

Brazil
Centro Ferroviário de Cultura, Volta Grande 04594
Museu da Estrada de Ferro Madeira-Mamoré, Porto Velho 04291
Museu do Trem, Rio de Janeiro 04376

Canada
Alberta Central Railway Museum, Wetaskiwin 06777
Alberta Railway Museum, Edmonton 05370
British Columbia Forest Discovery Centre, Duncan 05352
Calgary and Edmonton Railway Museum, Edmonton 05371
Canadian Museum of Rail Travel, Cranbrook 05287
Canadian Railway Museum, Saint Constant 06313
Carbonear Railway Station, Carbonear 05202
Chatham Railroad Museum, Chatham, Ontario 05238
Cochrane Railway and Pioneer Museum, Cochrane 05263
Elmira Railway Museum, Elmira 05405
End of Steel Heritage Museum, Hines Creek 05598
Fort Erie Railroad Museum, Fort Erie 05435
Hillsborough Railway Museum, Hillsborough 05596
Kaatza Station Museum, Lake Cowichan 05719
Kettle River Museum, Midway 05848
Komoka Railway Museum, Komoka 05704
Kwinitsa Station Railway Museum, Prince Rupert 06188
Ladysmith Railway Museum, Ladysmith 05715
Melville Railway Museum, Melville 05839
Musquodoboit Railway Museum, Musquodoboit Harbour 05953
Orangedale Railway Museum, Orangedale 06053
Owen Sound Marine and Rail Museum, Owen Sound 06089
Pacific Great Eastern Station, North Vancouver 06026
Port-aux-Basques Railway Heritage Centre, Port-aux-Basques 06154
Railway and Forestry Museum, Prince George 06187
Ralph Allen Memorial Museum, Oxbow 06091
Revelstoke Railway Museum, Revelstoke 06255
Smiths Falls Railway Museum of Eastern Ontario, Smiths Falls 06467
Streetcar and Electric Railway Museum, Milton 05855
Sydney and Louisburg Railway Museum, Louisbourg 05783

China, People's Republic
Beijing Gu Guanxiang Station, Beijing 06950
Hong Kong Railway Museum, Hong Kong 07099
Jiaozhuang Hu Didao Station, Beijing 06968

Colombia
Museo Historia del Ferrocarril de Antioquia, Medellín 07521

Cuba
Estación Ferrocarril Bejucal, Bejucal 07864

Czech Republic
Městské Muzeum, Česká Třebová 08297

Denmark
Danmarks Jernbanemuseum, Odense 09007
Museet på Gudhjem Station, Gudhjem 08848

Egypt
Egyptian National Railways Museum, Cairo 09262

Estonia
Eesti Muuseumraudtee, Haapsalu 09317
Eesti Muuseumraudtee Lavassaare Muuseum, Tallinn 09361

Finland
Jokioisten Museorautatie ja Kapearaidemuseo, Jokioinen 09582
Pietarin Radan Museo, Lahti 09746
Suomen Rautatiemuseo, Hyvinkää 09556
Veturimuseo, Toijala 10111

France
Collection de Locomotives à Vapeur, Obermodern 13380
Collection de Matériel Ferroviaire, Burnhaupt-le-Haut 10959
Espace du Cheminot, Nîmes 13334
Musée Collection Ferroviaire, Miramas 12988
Musée de la Machine Agricole et à Vapeur, Ambert 10302
Musée des Tramways à Vapeur et des Chemins de Fer Secondaires Français, Butry-sur-Oise 10963
Musée des Transports, Pithiviers-le-Vieil 13743
Musée du Rail, Cajarc 11000
Musée du Rail, Dinan 11535
Musée du Train, Clairac 11307
Musée du Train et du Jouet, Arpaillargues-et-Aureillac 10424
Musée Ferroviaire de Saint-Géry, Saint-Géry 14250
Musée Français du Chemin de Fer, Mulhouse 13213
Musée Régional du Chemin de Fer, Rosny-sous-Bois 14042

Germany
Bayerisches Eisenbahnmuseum, Nördlingen 19107
Berliner S-Bahn-Museum, Potsdam 19432
Dampflok-Museum, Hermeskeil 17726
DB Museum im Verkehrsmuseum Nürnberg, Nürnberg 19135
Deutsches Dampflokomotiv-Museum, Neuenmarkt 19028
Deutsches Feld- und Kleinbahnmuseum, Deinste 16563
Eisenbahn-Museum Lokschuppen Aumühle, Aumühle bei Hamburg 15576
Eisenbahnmuseum, Vienenburg 20311
Eisenbahnmuseum Bayerischer Bahnhof zu Leipzig, Leipzig 18392
Eisenbahnmuseum Bochum-Dahlhausen, Bochum 16195
Eisenbahnmuseum Darmstadt-Kranichstein, Darmstadt 16538
Eisenbahnmuseum Historischer Wasserturm, Bebra 15862
Eisenbahnmuseum Neustadt an der Weinstraße, Neustadt an der Weinstraße 19074
Eisenbahnmuseum - Sammlung Frey, Seifhennersdorf 19927
Eisenbahnmuseum Schwarzenberg, Schwarzenberg, Erzgebirge 19883
Eisenbahnmuseum Vienenburg, Bad Zwesten 15781
Feld- und Grubenbahnmuseum, Solms 19989
Frankfurter Feldbahnmuseum, Frankfurt am Main 17043
Frau Holle Expreß, Hessisch-Lichtenau 17745
Härtsfeldbahn-Museum, Neresheim 18995
Historischer Straßenbahnhof Leipzig-Möckern, Leipzig 18399
Localbahnmuseum Bayerisch Eisenstein, Bayerisch Eisenstein 15838
Museumseisenbahn Schwalm-Knüll, Fritzlar 17153
Niedersächsisches Kleinbahn-Museum Bruchhausen-Vilsen, Bruchhausen-Vilsen 16362
Oberweißbacher Bergbahn, Mellenbach-Glasbach 18699
Regionales Eisenbahnmuseum der Museumseisenbahn Hamm im Maximilianpark, Hamm, Westfalen 17578
Sächsisches Eisenbahnmuseum, Chemnitz 16471
Sächsisches Schmalspurbahn-Museum Rittersgrün, Rittersgrün 19618
Trambahn-Museum, München 18920
Verkehrsmuseum Dresden, Dresden 16715
Westfälisches Feldbahnmuseum, Lengerich, Westfalen 18437

Greece
Mouseio Trenon, Athinai 20879

Hungary
Közlekedési Múzeum, Budapest 21352

India
National Rail Museum, Delhi 21779

Indonesia
Museum Kereta, Ambarawa 22065

Ireland
County Donegal Railway Heritage Centre, Donegal 22411
Fry Model Railway, Demesne 22408
Fry Model Railway Museum, Malahide 22515
The Steam Museum, Straffan 22543
West Cork Model Railway Village, Clonakilty 22395

Israel
Israel Railway Museum, Haifa 22607

Italy
Museo Ferrovario, Trieste 25829
Museo Ferroviario, Cuneo 23697
Museo Ferroviario del Verbano, Luino 24242
Museo Ferroviario Piemontese, Savigliano 25500
Museo Nazionale Ferroviario, Napoli 24602

Korea, Republic
BuGok Railroad Exhibition Hall, Uiwang 27296
Seoul Station Hall, Seoul 27278

Mexico
Museo Comunitario de Estación Coahuila, Mexicali 28087
Museo de la Antigua Estación Ferroviaria, Teocelo 28480
Museo del Ferrocarril, Aguascalientes 27757
Museo del Ferrocarril, Guadalajara 27957
Museo del Ferrocarril, Monterrey 28234
Museo del Ferrocarril, Torreón 28556
Museo Ferrocarrilero, Empalme 27910
Museo la Antigua Casa del Agua, Hunucmá 28009
Museo Nacional de Ferrocarriles Mexicanos, Puebla 28341
Museo Nacional de los Ferrocarriles Mexicanos, México 28194
Museo Toma de Zacatecas o Cerro de la Bufa, Zacatecas 28640

Namibia
TransNamib Museum, Windhoek 28784

Netherlands
Blokwachterswoning Waterhuizen, Waterhuizen 29986
Gelderse Smalspoor Museum, Erlecom 29250
Het Gols-Station, Winterswijk 30013
Industrieel Smalspoor Museum, Erica 29248
Museum Buurt Spoorweg, Haaksbergen 29320
Museum Stoomdepot, Rotterdam 29762
Museumspoorlijn Star, Stadskanaal 29848
Museumstoomtram Hoorn-Medemblik, Hoorn 29443
Nationaal Smalspoormuseum - Stoomtrein Valkenburgse Meer, Valkenburg, Zuid-Holland 29921
Nederlands Spoorwegmuseum, Utrecht 29906
NZH Vervoers Museum, Haarlem 29328
Rijdend Electrisch Tram Museum, Amsterdam 28897
Spoor- en Tramweg Verzameling, Loppersum 29548
Stoomtrein Goes-Borsele, Goes 29287
Streekmuseum Alphen, Alphen, Noord-Brabant 28814
Zuid-Limburgse Stoomtreinmaatschappij, Simpelveld 29817

New Zealand
Fell Locomotive Museum, Featherston 30159
Founders Historic Park, Nelson 30209
Paekakariki Railway Museum, Wellington 30306
Plains Vintage Railway and Historical Museum, Ashburton 30100
Pleasant Point Railway and Historical Society Museum, Pleasant Point 30238
Silver Stream Railway Museum, Hutt City 30182

Norway
Bergens Tekniske Museum, Bergen 30418
Krøderbanen, Krøderen 30620
Lommedalsbanen, Rykkinn 30812
Norsk Jernbanemuseum, Hamar 30530
Osbane Museet, Fana 30486
Setesdalsbanen Stiftelsen, Vennesla 30985
Sporveismuseet Vognhall 5, Oslo 30764
Thamshavnbanen, Løkken Verk 30649
Urskog-Hølandsbanen, Sørumsand 30868

Peru
Museo Ferroviario, Tacna 31256

Poland
Muzeum Kolei Wąskotorowej, Sochaczew 31986
Muzeum Kolejnictwa, Warszawa 32106

Russia
Centralnyj Muzej Oktjabrskoj Železnoj Dorogi, Sankt-Peterburg 33384
Centralnyj Muzej Železnodorožnogo Transporta, Sankt-Peterburg 33387
Muzej Železnodorožnoj Techniki, Sankt-Peterburg 33470

Serbia-Montenegro
Zeleznički Muzej, Beograd 33821

Slovenia
Koroški Muzej Ravne na Koroškem, Ravne na Koroškem 34144

South Africa
Railway Station Museum, Uitenhage 34394
South African National Railway Museum, Auckland Park 34173

Spain
Ferrería de Mirandaola, Legazpia 34944
Museo del Ferrocarril de Madrid, Madrid 35033
Museo Vasco del Ferrocarril, Azpeitia 34514
Museu del Ferrocarril, Vilanova i la Geltrú 35666

Sweden
Åmåls Järnvägsmuseum, Åmål 35794
Anten-Gräfsnäs Järnväg, Alingsås 35790
Banmuseet, Ängelholm 35786
Grängesbergsbanornas Järnvägsmuseum, Grängesberg 35926
Järnvägs- och Industrimuseum, Hagfors 35938
Järnvägsmuseet, Kristianstad 36017
Museisällskapet Jädraås-Tallås Järnväg, Jädraås 35973
Museispårvägen Malmköping, Malmköping 36071
Norrbottens Järnvägsmuseum, Luleå 36053
Nynäshamns Järnvägsmuseum, Nynäshamn 36130
Östra Södermanlands Museijärnväg, Mariefred 36086
Ohsabanan museijärnväg, Växjö 36388
Rallarmuseet, Moskosel 36104
Risten-Lakviks Järnväg, Åtvidaberg 35825
Skara Järnvägsmuseum, Skara 36193
Sveriges Järnvägsmuseum, Gävle 35901

Switzerland
Chemin de Fer-Musée Blonay-Chamby, Lausanne 36851
Musée du Fer et du Chemin de Fer, Vallorbe 37279
Tram Museum Zürich, Zürich 37414

United Kingdom
Amberley Working Museum, Amberley 37995
Bala Like Railway Museum, Bala 38060
Birmingham Railway Museum, Birmingham 38216
Bluebell Railway, Uckfield 40743
Bodmin and Wenford Railway, Bodmin 38263
Bo'ness and Kinneil Railway, Bo'ness 38274
Bowes Railway Heritage Museum, Gateshead 39026
Buckinghamshire Railway Centre, Quainton 40275
Cadeby Light Railway, Cadeby 38430
Colonel Stephens Railway Museum, Tenterden 40685
Conwy Valley Railway Museum, Betws-y-coed 38180
Crampton Tower Museum, Broadstairs 38366
Darlington Railway Centre and Museum, Darlington 38697
Didcot Railway Centre, Didcot 38730
Downpatrick Railway Museum, Downpatrick 38774
East Anglian Railway Museum, Colchester 38609
Elham Valley Railway Museum, Folkestone 38999
Embsay Bolton Abbey Steam Railway, Skipton 40528
Errol Station Railway Heritage Centre, Blairgowrie 38254
Foyle Valley Railway Museum, Londonderry 39815
Giant's Causeway and Bushmills Railway, Bushmills 38424
Glenfinnan Station Museum, Fort William 39010
Gloucestershire Warwickshire Railway, Toddington 40714
Great Central Railway Museum, Loughborough 39830
Groudle Glen Railway, Onchan 40133
Gwili Steam Railway, Bronwydd 38378
Haig Colliery Mining Museum, Whitehaven 40857
Immingham Museum, Immingham 39289
Ingrow Loco Museum, Keighley 39329
Irchester Narrow Gauge Railway Museum, Wellingborough 40810
Isle of Wight Steam Railway and Isle of Wight Railway Heritage Museum, Havenstreet 39190
John Sinclair Railway Collection, Killingworth 39360
Keighley and Worth Valley Railway Museum, Haworth 39200
Kent and East Sussex Railway, Tenterden 40687
Kidderminster Railway Museum, Kidderminster 39352
Lappa Valley Steam Railway, Newquay 40059
Leighton Buzzard Railway, Leighton Buzzard 39474
Llanberis Lake Railway, Llanberis 39535
Mangapps Farm Railway Museum, Burnham-on-Crouch 38398
Maud Railway Museum, Maud 39926
Mid Hampshire Railway Museum, Alresford 37987
Midland Railway Centre, Ripley, Derbyshire 40325
Monkwearmouth Station Museum, Sunderland 40644
Museum of Rail Travel, Keighley 39330
Museum of the Mid-Suffolk Light Railway, Wetheringsett 40838
Narrow Gauge Railway Museum, Tywyn 40742
National Railway Museum, York 40966
Nene Valley Railway, Stibbington 40587
Newton Abbot Town and Great Western Railway Museum, Newton Abbot 40063
Norchard Railway Centre, Lydney 39851
North Norfolk Railway Museum, Sheringham 40497
North Woolwich Old Station Museum, London 39735
North Yorkshire Moors Railway, Pickering 40202
Northampton and Lamport Railway, Chapel Brampton 38521
Paignton and Dartmouth Steam Railway, Paignton 40160
Peak Rail Museum, Matlock 39924
Penrhyn Castle, Bangor, Gwynedd 38083
Pontypool and Blaenavon Railway, Blaenavon 38251
Railway Age, Crewe 38666
Railway Museum, Ravenglass 40287
Railworld, Peterborough 40189
Romney Toy and Model Museum, New Romney 40016
Rutland Railway Museum, Cottesmore 38638
Scottish Industrial Railway Centre, Dalmellington 38694
Severn Valley Railway, Bewdley 38185
Sittingbourne and Kemsley Light Railway, Sittingbourne 40522
Somerset and Dorset Railway Trust Museum, Washford 40798
South Devon Railway, Buckfastleigh 38381
South Tynedale Railway Preservation Society, Alston 37988
STEAM Museum of the Great Western Railway, Swindon 40667
Steamtown Railway Museum, Carnforth 38495
Stephenson Railway Museum, North Shields 40080
Strathspey Railway, Aviemore 38043
Swanage Railway, Swanage 40655
Teifi Valley Railway, Llandysul 39544
Thursford Collection, Fakenham 38967
Timothy Hackworth Victorian Railway Museum, Shildon 40500
Tiverton Museum of Mid Devon Life, Tiverton 40712
Wells Walsingham Light Railway, Wells-next-the-Sea 40814
Welsh Highland Railway Museum, Porthmadog 40243
Welshpool and Llanfair Light Railway, Llanfair Caereinion 39548
West Somerset Railway, Minehead 39964
Winchcombe Railway Museum, Winchcombe 40883
Wylam Railway Museum, Wylam 40947

Uruguay
Museo del Círculo de Estudios Ferroviarios del Uruguay, Montevideo 41000

U.S.A.
The Age of Steam Railroad Museum, Dallas 42744
Alabama Mining Museum, Dora 42958
Ashland Railroad Station Museum, Ashland 41292
The B O Railroad Museum, Baltimore 41450
B O Railroad Station Museum, Ellicott City 43155
Baltimore Streetcar Museum, Baltimore 41457
Barn Museum and Rail Depot Museum, Troutdale 48066
Baycrafters, Bay Village 41546
Berkshire Scenic Railway Museum, Lenox 44716
Best Friend of Charleston Museum, Charleston 42209
Boothbay Railway Village, Boothbay 41790
Bowie Railroad Station and Huntington Museum, Bowie 41845
Branchville Railroad Shrine and Museum, Branchville 41868
Brunswick Railroad Museum, Brunswick 41970
Burlington-Rock Island Railroad and Historical Museum, Teague 47965
California State Railroad Museum, Sacramento 47049
Casey Jones Home and Railroad Museum, Jackson 44287
Casey Jones Museum, Vaughan 48207
Catawissa Railroad Museum, Catawissa 42139
Chesapeake Beach Railway Museum, Chesapeake Beach 42281
Choctaw Museum, Hugo 44147
Cimarron Valley Railroad Museum, Cushing 42733
Colorado Railroad Museum, Golden 43713
Comanche Crossing Museum, Strasburg 47845
Conneaut Railroad Museum, Conneaut 42609
Conway Scenic Railroad, North Conway 45988
Cookeville Depot Museum, Cookeville 42615
Dennison Railroad Depot Museum, Dennison 42872
East Ely Railroad Depot Museum, Ely 43175
East Troy Electric Railroad Museum, East Troy 43062
End-O-Line Railroad Museum, Currie 42731
Florida Gulf Coast Railroad Museum, Parrish 46297
Fox Lake Historical Museum, Fox Lake 43500
Fox River Trolley Museum, South Elgin 47692
Garrett Historical Museum, Garrett 43629
Gold Coast Railroad Museum, Miami 45284
Harmar Station, Marietta 45150
Huntington Railroad Museum, Huntington 44166
Illinois Railway Museum, Union 48139
Indiana Transportation Museum, Noblesville 45959
Iowa Railroad Historical Museum, Boone 41784
Kare Shelley Railroad Museum, Boone 41785
Kennesaw Civil War Museum, Kennesaw 44437
Kentucky Railway Museum, New Haven 45702
Lake Shore Railway Museum, North East 45992
Lake Superior Railroad Museum, Duluth 43001
Laws Railroad Museum, Bishop 41715
Lincoln Train Museum, Gettysburg 43664
Livingston Depot Center, Livingston 44832
Mid-Continent Railway Museum, North Freedom 45994
Monticello Railway Museum, Monticello 45472
National Capital Trolley Museum, Silver Spring 47633
National New York Central Railroad Museum, Elkhart 43141
National Railroad Museum, Green Bay 43791
National Railroad Museum and Hall of Fame, Hamlet 43885
Nevada State Railroad Museum, Carson City 42119
Newark Valley Depot Museum, Newark Valley 45901
North Carolina Transportation Museum, Spencer 47722
Northwest Railway Museum, Snoqualmie 47660
Ohio Railway Museum, Worthington 48763
Old Dominion Railway Museum, Richmond 46884
Oregon Electric Railway Historical Society Museum, Lake Oswego 44592
Pennsylvania Trolley Museum, Washington 48418
Railroad and Heritage Museum, Temple 47976
Railroad Museum of Long Island, Riverhead 46915
Railroad Museum of Pennsylvania, Strasburg 47847

Railroader's Memorial Museum, Altoona 41158
The Railway Exposition, Covington 42681
Railway Heritage Network, Linden 44803
Rockhill Trolley Museum, Rockhill Furnace 46966
Salamanca Rail Museum, Salamanca 47187
San Diego Model Railroad Museum, San Diego 47292
Shore Line Trolley Museum, East Haven 43050
South Coast Railroad Museum at Goleta Depot, Goleta 43720
Southeast Museum, Brewster 41884
Southeastern Railway Museum, Duluth 42996
Southern California Chapter Railway and Locomotive Museum, Los Angeles 44944
Tennessee Central Railway Museum, Nashville 45624
Tennessee Valley Railroad Museum, Chattanooga 42266
Transportation Exhibits, Nevada City 45656
Tri-County Historical Society and Museum, Herington 43999
Trolley Museum of New York, Kingston 44495
Wabash Frisco and Pacific Association Museum, Glencoe 43686
The Western Railway Museum, Suisun City 47871
Wilmington Railroad Museum, Wilmington 48664

Zambia
Railway Museum, Livingstone 49018

Zimbabwe
National Railways of Zimbabwe Museum, Raylton 49039

Rare Books → Books, Book Art and Manuscripts

Religious Art and Symbolism

Argentina
Museo de Arte Religioso Juan de Tejeda, Córdoba 00293
Museo de Arte Sacro de La Rioja, La Rioja 00396
Museo de Arte Sacro San Francisco, Salta 00538
Museo Histórico de Corrientes Manuel Cabral de Mayo y Alpoín, Corrientes 00322
Museo Histórico de la Iglesia, Buenos Aires 00213
Museo Histórico de San Francisco, Santa Fé 00604
Museo Jesútico Nacional de Jesús María, Jesús María 00371
Museo Sacro de la Catedral, San Miguel de Tucumán 00588

Austria
Augustinermuseum, Rattenberg, Inn 02490
Benediktinerstift und Stiftssammlungen, Altenburg 01661
Diözesan-Museum, Sankt Pölten 02600
Diözesanmuseum Graz, Graz 01912
Dommuseum zu Salzburg, Salzburg 02533
Ehemaliges Benediktinerinnenstift Göß, Leoben 02208
Eisenerzer Krippenhaus, Eisenerz 01801
Erzbischöfliches Dom- und Diözesanmuseum, Wien 02880
Klostersammlung der Benediktinerabtei, Michaelbeuern 02293
Kunstkammer des Innsbrucker Servitenkloster, Innsbruck 02071
Museum des Zisterzienserstifts mit Margret Bilger-Galerie, Schlierbach 02635
Museum Innviertler Volkskundehaus und Galerie der Stadt Ried, Ried im Innkreis 02512
Pater Peter Singer-Museum, Salzburg 02546
Prämonstratenser-Chorherrenstift mit Stiftssammlungen, Geras 01874
Salvatorianerkloster, Gurk 01974
Sammlung Religiöser Volkskunst, Wien 02982
Sammlungen des Stiftes Sankt Lambrecht, Sankt Lambrecht 02579
Schatzkammer, Frauenkirchen 01847
Schatzkammer der Wallfahrtskirche Maria Dreieichen, Stockern 02700
Schatzkammer der Wallfahrtskirche Maria Schutz, Maria Schutz am Semmering 02271
Stift Dürnstein, Dürnstein, Niederösterreich 01776
Stift Melk, Melk 02292
Stiftsmuseum, Millstatt 02299
Stiftsmuseum Schatzhaus Kärntens, Sankt Paul 02597
Stiftsmuseum Steyr-Gleink, Steyr-Gleink 02692
Stiftssammlungen des Zisterzienserstiftes Rein, Gratwein 01908
Votivsammlung der Wallfahrtskirche Maria Kirchental, Sankt Martin bei Lofer 02587
Wallfahrtsbasilika Mariazell, Mariazell 02276
Wallfahrtsmuseum, Maria Taferl 02273
Zisterzienserstift und Stiftssammlungen, Stams 02675

Belarus
Muzej Staražytna Belaruskaj Kultury, Minsk 03120

Belgium
Béguinage d'Anderlecht, Bruxelles 03273
Heemmuseum Bystervelt, Schelle 03726
Kunsthal Sint-Pietersabdij, Gent 03441
Musée d'Art Religieux et d'Art Mosan, Liège 03577
Musée Diocésain et Trésor de la Cathédrale Saint-Aubain, Namur 03649
Musée Marial de Beauraing, Beauraing 03203
De Schatkammer van de Ouze-Lieve-Vrouwekerk, Sint-Truiden 03752
Trésor de la Collegiale Sainte-Waudru, Mons 03637
Trésor de l'Eglise Primaire Saint-Sebastien, Stavelot 03767

Bosnia and Herzegovina
Muzej-riznica Stare Srpske Pravoslavne Crkve, Sarajevo 03923

Brazil
Museu da Curia Metropolitana, Porto Alegre 04277
Museu da Imagem, Campinas 04024
Museu da Imagem e do Som de Alagoas, Maceió 04181
Museu da Imagem e do Som de Campinas, Campinas 04025
Museu da Imagem e do Som de Campos, Campos dos Goitacazes 04036
Museu da Imagem e do Som de Cascavel, Cascavel 04044
Museu da Imagem e do Som de Curitiba, Curitiba 04067
Museu da Imagem e do Som de e da Imprensa da Bahia, Salvador 04425
Museu da Imagem e do Som de Goiás, Goiás 04114
Museu da Imagem e do Som de Piracicaba, São Paulo 04506
Museu da Imagem e do Som de Resende, Resende 04307
Museu da Imagem e do Som de Santa Catarina, Florianópolis 04089
Museu da Imagem e do Som de São Paulo, São Paulo 04507
Museu da Imagem e do Som de Taubaté, Taubaté 04557
Museu da Imagem e do Som do Ceará, Fortaleza 04098
Museu da Imagem e do Som do Pará, Belém 03971
Museu da Imagem e do Som do Paraná, Curitiba 04068
Museu da Venrável Ordem Terceira de São Francisco da Penitência, Rio de Janeiro 04353
Museu das Alfaias da Paróquia da Cachoeira, Cachoeira 04014
Museu de Arte e História Racioppi, Belo Horizonte 03984
Museu de Arte Religiosa, Vitória 04591
Museu de Arte Sacra, Rio de Janeiro 04355
Museu de Arte Sacra, Salvador 04429
Museu de Arte Sacra, São Paulo 04518
Museu de Arte Sacra da Catedral-Basílica, Salvador 04430
Museu de Arte Sacra de Santos, Santos 04453
Museu de Arte Sacra Padre Roberto Barbalho, Recife 04298
Museu de Imagem e do Som de Pernambuco, Recife 04300
Museu de Nossa Senhora da Glória do Outeiro, Rio de Janeiro 04361
Museu Dom Vital, Recife 04305
Museu Henriqueta Catharino, Salvador 04437
Museu Municipal de Arte e História, Nova Era 04227

Bulgaria
Bachkovski Manastir muzej, Bachkovo 04607
Muzej-kripta Aleksandăr Nevski, Sofia 04839
Muzej na Ikonata v Carkvata Sv. Nikolai, Pleven 04766
Muzej na Văzraždaneto, Varna 04900
Nacionalen Muzej Bojanska Crkva, Sofia 04848

Cambodia
Musée Poveal, Battambang 04947

Cameroon
Petit Musée d'Art Camerounais, Yaoundé 04963

Canada
Basilique Notre-Dame de Montréal, Montréal 05889
Chapelle des Indiens, Tadoussac 06532
Mennonite Heritage Museum, Rosthern 06289
Musée d'Art Religieux, Wellington, Prince Edward Island 06764
Musée de l'Eglise Notre-Dame, Montréal 05916
Musée de Sainte-Anne, Sainte-Anne-de-Beaupré 06382
Musée des Augustines de l'Hôpital Général de Québec, Québec 06205
Musée du Frère André, Montréal 05921
Musée Marguerite Bourgeoys, Montréal 05925
Musée Pierre Boucher, Trois-Rivières 06645
Old Saint Edward's Anglican Church, Clementsport 05256
Saint-Laurent Art Museum, Montréal 05930
Saint Michael's Historical Museum, Chatham, New Brunswick 05236
Saint Volodymyr Museum, Winnipeg 06844

Chile
Museo de Arte Colonial de San Francisco, Santiago de Chile 06909

China, People's Republic
China Museum of Buddhist Literature and Heritage, Beijing 06960
Museum of Sacred Art, Macau 07168
Saint Dominic Church Museum, Macau 07169

Colombia
Biblioteca Luis-Angel Arango, Bogotá 07381
Museo Arquidiocesano de Arte Religioso, Pamplona 07542
Museo Arquidiocesano de Arte Religioso de Popayán, Popayán 07561
Museo Convento del Desierto de la Candelaria, Ráquira 07574
Museo Convento Santo Ecce Homo, Sutamarchán 07603
Museo de Arte Religioso de Girón, Girón 07485
Museo de Arte Religioso de la Catedral de San Nicolás, Rionegro 07577
Museo de Arte Religioso de Monguí, Monguí 07528
Museo de Arte Religioso Julio Franco Arango, Duitama 07471
Museo de Arte Religioso Tiberio de J. Salazar y Herrera, Sonsón 07599
Museo de Arte Religioso y Colonial, Cali 07447
Museo de la Parroquia de Gámbita, Gámbita 07483
Museo de Santa Clara, Bogotá 07412
Museo del Carmen, Villa de Leyva 07620
Museo del Milagroso, Buga 07441
Museo Iberoamericano de Arte Moderno de Popayán, Popayán 07567
Museo Juan Lorenzo Lucero, Pasto 07548
Museo Medardo Burbano, Pasto 07552
Museo Nacional Mariano, Chiquinquira 07463
Museo Parroquial de Arte Religioso, Turmequé 07615
Museo Raíces, Jesús María 07502
Museo Religioso de Guatavita, Guatavita 07493
Museo Religioso y Colonial de San Francisco, Cali 07452
Museo Santa Clara la Real, Tunja 07614
Museo-Santuario de San Pedro Claver, Cartagena 07458
Sala de Memorias Culturales, Mogotes 07526

Croatia
Dijecezanski Muzej Zagrebačke Nadbiskupije, Zagreb 07812
Fine Arts Collection of the Franciscan Monastery, Orebić 07748
Galerija Zavjetnih Slika Brodova, Dubrovnik 07696
Izložbena Dvorana Sv. Mihovila, Korčula 07721
Katedralna Zbirka, Hvar 07706
Museum Collection and Old Pharmacy of the Friars Minor, Dubrovnik 07698
Muzej Dominikanskog Samostana, Bol 07683
Muzej Franjevačkog Samostana, Rovinj 07765
Muzejska Zbirka Franjevačkog Samostana, Imotski 07710
Muzejska Zbirka Kapucinskog Samostana, Karlobag 07712
Opatska Riznica Sv. Marka, Korčula 07723
Permanent Exhibition of Votive Pictures Sanctuary of our Lady of Trsat, Rijeka 07762
Riznica Katedrala, Split 07787
Riznica Katedrala, Trogir 07795
Riznica Samostana Svetog Frane, Zadar 07808
Riznica Zagrebačke Katedrala, Zagreb 07836
Riznica Župne Crkve, Nin 07744
Sakralna Baština Muzej, Senj 07769
Zbirka Bratovštine Gospe od Utjehe, Korčula 07724
Zbirka Bratovštine Sv. Roka, Korčula 07725
Zbirka Crkvene Umjetnosti, Šibenik 07773
Zbirka Franjevačkog Samostana Visovac, Visovac 07802
Zbirka Ikona Bratovštine Svih Svetih, Korčula 07726
Zbirka Umjetnina Franjevačkog Samostana, Hvar 07708
Zbirka Umjetnina KAIROS, Trogir 07796
Zupski Muzej Lopud, Lopud 07735

Cuba
Museo de Arte Religioso, La Habana 07958

Czech Republic
Kaple Sv. Kříže, Praha 08583

Denmark
Davids Samling, København 08928
Møns Museum, Stege 09079
Museet for Religiøs Kunst og Bodil Kaalund Samlingerne, Lemvig 08973
Roskilde Domkirkemuseum, Roskilde 09042

Ecuador
Museo de Arte Religioso Concepción, Riobamba 09221
Museo de Arte Religioso la Concepción, Baños 09141
Muséo de Las Conceptas, Cuenca 09157
Museo Diocesano de Arte Religioso Nuestra Señora del Cisne, Loja 09186
Museo Manuela Sáenz, Quito 09213
Museo Mariano Acosta, Ibarra 09183
Museo Santuario Nuestra Señora Natividad del Guayco, La Magdalena 09187

Ethiopia
Museum of the Holy Trinity Church of Ethiopia, Addis Ababa 09399

Finland
Kirkkomuseo, Mikkeli 09831
Lähetysmuseo, Helsinki 09507
Rautalammin Museo, Rautalampi 09988

France
Collection d'Art Religieux Ancien, Prunay-en-Yvelines 13880
Dépôt-Musée Diocésain, Metz 12955
Galeries du Panthéon Bouddhique du Japon et de la Chine, Paris 13513
Maison Natale de Saint-Vincent-de-Paul, Saint-Vincent-de-Paul 14505
Musée d'Allauch, Allauch 10291
Musée d'Art Religieux, Blois 10772
Musée d'Art Sacré, Dijon 11523
Musée d'Art Sacré, Gramat 11898
Musée d'Art Sacré de Fourvière, Lyon 12730
Musée d'Art Sacré de la Cathédrale Saint-Siffrein, Carpentras 11056
Musée d'Art Sacré du Gard, Pont-Saint-Esprit 13817
Musée de l'Abbaye de Port-Royal, Magny-lès-Hameaux 12765
Musée de l'Abbaye Saint-Vigor, Cérisy-la-Forêt 11113
Musée de l'Oeuvre Notre-Dame, Strasbourg 14827
Musée Départemental d'Art Religieux, Sées 14691
Musée des Santons des Baux, Les Baux-de-Provence 12525
Musée Diocésan d'Art Religieux, Lille 12602
Musée du Santon, Generagues 11848
Musée du Santon, Le Val 12492
Musée du Santon, Marseille 12866
Musée du Santon et des Traditions de Provence, Fontaine-de-Vaucluse 11762
Musée du Vieux Marseille, Marseille 12868
Musée François-Pompon, Saulieu 14636
Musée Lambinet, Versailles 15144
Musée Pierre de Luxembourg, Villeneuve-lès-Avignon 15229
Musée Saint-Jacques, Moissac 13002
Musée Vivant Denon, Chalon-sur-Saône 11127
Trésor de la Cathédrale de Troyes, Troyes 15010

Germany
Bilder und Zeichen der Frömmigkeit - Sammlung Rudolf Kriss, Straubing 20076
Bischöfliches Diözesanmuseum für christliche Kunst, Münster 18934
Bischöfliches Dom- und Diözesanmuseum Mainz, Mainz 18598
Buxtehude Museum für Regionalgeschichte und Kunst, Buxtehude 16439
Diözesanmuseum, Bamberg 15804
Diözesanmuseum, Freising 17121
Diözesanmuseum Sankt Afra, Augsburg 15553
Diözesanmuseum Sankt Ulrich, Regensburg 19518
Dom-Museum, Fulda 17173
Dom-Museum Bremen, Bremen 16320
Dom-Museum Hildesheim, Hildesheim 17757
Dom und Domschatz Halberstadt, Halberstadt 17500
Domkammer der Kathedralkirche Sankt Paulus zu Münster, Münster 18935
Dommuseum, Brandenburg an der Havel 16279
Dommuseum, Frankfurt am Main 17038
Domschatz, Würzburg 20691
Domschatz der Sankt Servatius-Stiftskirche, Quedlinburg 19457
Domschatz- und Diözesan-Museum Eichstätt, Eichstätt 16804
Domschatz- und Diözesanmuseum, Passau 19354
Domschatz und Museum des Sankt Petri-Domes, Fritzlar 17152
Domschatzkammer, Aachen 15372
Domschatzkammer Sankt Petri, Bautzen 15834
Domschatzkammer und Diözesanmuseum, Osnabrück 19275
Domvorhalle, Goslar 17348
Erstes Schutzengel-Museum der Welt, Kreuth 18235
Erzbischöfliches Diözesanmuseum Köln, Köln 18135
Erzbischöfliches Diözesanmuseum und Domschatzkammer, Paderborn 19333
Europäische Glasmalerei- und Krippenausstellung, Schramberg 19846
Felix-Müller-Museum im Zehntspeicher, Neunkirchen am Brand 19051
Fränkische Galerie, Kronach 18243
Heimatmuseum Aichach, Aichach 15408
Helmstedter Freundeskreis für Paramentik und christliche Kunst, Helmstedt 17702
Henneberg-Museum, Münnerstadt 18927
Herzog Anton Ulrich-Museum, Braunschweig 16297
Jesuitenkolleg, Mindelheim 18742
Kloster Ebstorf, Ebstorf 16772
Kloster Isenhagen, Hankensbüttel 17590
Kloster Lüne, Lüneburg 18558
Kloster Mariensee, Neustadt am Rübenberge 19069
Kloster Medingen, Bad Bevensen 15613
Kloster Sankt Marienberg, Helmstedt 17703
Kloster Walsrode, Walsrode 20384
Kloster Wienhausen, Wienhausen 20568
Klostermuseum, Roggenburg 19640
Klostermuseum der Benediktiner-Abtei, Ottobeuren 19327
Klostermuseum der Sankt Josefskongregation, Ursberg 20274
Klostermuseum in der Pfarrkirche Sankt Magnus, Bad Schussenried 15735
Kunstkammer der Pfarrkirche Sankt Georg, Bocholt 16189
Kunstsammlung des Herzoglichen Georgianums, München 18868
Kunstsammlung Lorenzkapelle Rottweil, Rottweil 19696
Kunstsammlung Sankt Nicolai-Kirche, Kalkar 17974

Laufener Stiftsschatz, Laufen, Salzach 18354
Museum Abtei Liesborn, Wadersloh 20337
Museum der Cistercienserinnen-Abtei Lichtenthal, Baden-Baden 15788
Museum für bäuerliche und sakrale Kunst, Ruhpolding 19717
Museum für Niederrheinische Sakralkunst, Kempen 18057
Museum für Sakrale Kunst und Liturgie, Heidelberg 17669
Museum Haus Löwenberg, Gengenbach 17236
Museum Kirche zum Heiligen Kreuz, Zittau 20763
Museum Klingelbeutel, Gaukönigshofen 17207
Pfarrmuseum, Dießen am Ammersee 16601
Pfarrmuseum, Flintsbach 17014
Sankt Patrokli-Dom-Museum Soest, Soest 19980
Schatzkammer, Altötting 15465
Schatzkammer der Basilika Sankt Ludgerus, Essen 16963
Schatzkammer der Evangelisch-Lutherischen Sankt Andreaskirche, Weißenburg in Bayern 20495
Schatzkammer des Münsters, Reichenau, Baden 19543
Schatzkammer Kloster Sankt Marienstern, Panschwitz-Kuckau 19343
Schloss Johannisburg mit Schlossgarten, Aschaffenburg 15529
Schloß Lichtenstein, Lichtenstein, Württemberg 18459
Schloss Neuburg, Neuburg an der Donau 19018
Schloßmuseum, Ellwangen 16836
Städtisches Kramer-Museum, Kempen 18058
Staurothek, Domschatz und Diözesanmuseum Limburg, Limburg an der Lahn 18473
Stift Fischbeck, Hessisch Oldendorf 17746
Stiftskirchenmuseum, Himmelkron 17765
Stiftsmuseum, Bad Buchau 15622
Turmmuseum Sankt Magnus, Esens 16941
Vom Kloster zum Dorf, Creglingen 16510
Wallfahrtsmuseum, Legau 18368
Wallfahrtsmuseum, Neukirchen beim Heiligen Blut 19040
Wallfahrtsmuseum, Bruckmühl 16372

Greece
Agion Panton Church Museum, Metéora 21067
Agios Andreas Monastery Museum, Agios Andreas 20807
Agios Stephanos Monastery, Metéora 21068
Arkadi Monastery Collection, Rethymnon 21138
Church of the Holy Apostles Collection, Parga 21109
Collection of the Proussou Monastery, Karpenission 21001
Folk Art Museum of the Metropolis of Kos, Kos 21031
Gonias Monastery, Kolymvari 21022
Metamorphosis Church Museum, Metéora 21069
Néa Moni Collection, Chios 20924
Panachrantos Monastery, Falika 20950
Saint George Epanosifis Monastery, Iráklion 20978
Timios Stavros Monastery, Mavradzei 21060

Honduras
Museo de Arte Religioso Colonial, Comayagua 21299

Hungary
Budavári Mátyás Templom Egyházmüvészeti Gyüjteménye, Budapest 21332
Dunamelléki Református Egyházkerület Biblia Múzeuma, Budapest 21334
Dunamelléki Református Egyházkerület Ráday Múzeuma, Kecskemét 21445
Dunántúli Református Egyházkerület Tudományos Gyüjteményei Múzeum, Pápa 21498
Evangélikus Országos Múzeum, Budapest 21337
Magyar Ortodox Múzeum, Miskolc 21478
Pannonhalmi Főapátság Gyűjteménye, Pannonhalma 21497
Református Kollégiumi és Egyházművészeti Múzeum, Debrecen 21400
Római Katolikus Egyházi Gyűjtemény, Sárospatak 21525
Sárospataki Református Kollégium Tudományos Gyüjteményei Múzeum, Sárospatak 21526
Szerb Egyházy Múzeum, Szentendre 21577

India
Hindi Sangrahalaya, Allahabad 21692
Phulsanda Religious Arts Museum, Phulsanda 21980

Iran
Holy Defense Museum, Kerman 22251

Ireland
Ecclesiastical Museum, Mullingar 22524
Saint Mel's Diocesan Museum, Longford 22511

Israel
Crusader Church, Abu Ghosh 22562
Israel Bible Museum, Zefat 22788
Museum of Psalms, Jerusalem 22650
Wolfson Museum, Jerusalem 22671

Italy
Basilica Collegiata di Santa Maria Assunta, San Gimignano 25360
Capella Brancacci, Firenze 23823
Complesso Museale di Santa Chiara, Napoli 24574
Galleria d'Arte Sacra dei Contemporanei, Milano 24384
Galleria degli ex Voto del Santuario, Livorno 24190
Galleria dello Spedale degli Innocenti, Firenze 23843
Musei Sistini del Piceno, San Benedetto del Tronto 25332
Museo Alessi, Enna 23732
Museo Alfonsiano, Pagani 24754
Museo Archeologico Attrezzato e Cattedrale di San Zeno, Pistoia 24955
Museo Aurelio Marena, Bitonto 23091
Museo Badia di San Gemolo, Valganna 25876
Museo Beato Angelico, Vicchio 25990
Museo Cabriniano, Sant'Angelo Lodigiano 25450
Museo Canonicale, Verona 25970
Museo Capitolare, Assisi 22962
Museo Capitolare di San Lorenzo, Perugia 24851
Museo Christiano, Cividale del Friuli 23589
Museo d'Arte Sacra, Camaiore 23280
Museo d'Arte Sacra, Ponzone 25003
Museo d'Arte Sacra, San Gimignano 25363
Museo d'Arte Sacra, Asciano 22947
Museo d'Arte Sacra Cardinale Agnifili, Rocca di Mezzo 25136
Museo d'Arte Sacra della Insigne Collegiata di San Lorenzo, Montevarchi 24550
Museo d'Arte Sacra della Santa Maria Assunta, Gallarate 23951
Museo d'Arte Sacra della Val d'Arbia, Buonconvento 23229
Museo d'Arte Sacro San Martino, Alzano Lombardo 22868
Museo degli Arazzi delle Madrice, Marsala 24306
Museo degli Arredi Sacri, Castel Sant'Elia 23390
Museo del Duomo, Massa 24314
Museo del Duomo, Ravello 25078
Museo del Int. Presepio in Miniatura Guido Colitti, Campobasso 23303
Museo del Santuario di Santa Maria Santissima della Fontenuova, Monsummano Terme 24485
Museo del Tesoro della Cattedrale, Aosta 22901
Museo del Tesoro Santuario della Misericordia, Savona 25511
Museo della Basilica, Gandino 23957
Museo della Basilica, Santa Maria degli Angeli 25437
Museo della Basilica di San Michele Arcangelo, Monte Sant'Angelo 24503
Museo della Basilica di San Nicola, Bari 23021
Museo della Basilica di Santa Maria del Colle, Pescocostanzo 24881
Museo della Basilica di Santa Maria della Passione, Milano 24397
Museo della Basilica Patriarcale S. Maria degli Angeli, Assisi 22965
Museo della Cattedrale, Barletta 23031
Museo della Cattedrale, Chiusi Città 23556
Museo della Cattedrale, Monopoli 24478
Museo della Certosa, Certosa di Pavia 23488
Museo della Pieve di San Pietro, Prato 25046
Museo delle Cripte, Poggiardo 24974
Museo dell'Opera del Duomo, Perugia 24853
Museo di Arte Religiosa, Oleggio 24675
Museo di San Domenico, Bologna 23129
Museo di San Petronio, Bologna 23131
Museo di Santa Maria di Castello, Genova 23997
Museo di Sant'Antonino, Piacenza 24893
Museo Diocesano, Acerenza 22795
Museo Diocesano, Agrigento 22818
Museo Diocesano, Albenga 22833
Museo Diocesano, Andria 22888
Museo Diocesano, Ascoli Piceno 22953
Museo Diocesano, Bari 23025
Museo Diocesano, Cassano allo Jonio 23381
Museo Diocesano, Empoli 23731
Museo Diocesano, Gubbio 24074
Museo Diocesano, Mantova 24290
Museo Diocesano, Mazara del Vallo 24338
Museo Diocesano, Osimo 24709
Museo Diocesano, Piazza Armerina 24900
Museo Diocesano, Recanati 25088
Museo Diocesano, San Miniato 25400
Museo Diocesano, Trani 25783
Museo Diocesano, Velletri 25906
Museo Diocesano, Pistoia 24960
Museo Diocesano, Imola 24089
Museo Diocesano A. Bernareggi, Bergamo 23063
Museo Diocesano Antonio Bergamaschi, Pennabilli 24836
Museo Diocesano d'Arte Sacra, Brescia 23206
Museo Diocesano d'Arte Sacra, Nicotera 24621
Museo Diocesano d'Arte Sacra, Orte 24697
Museo Diocesano d'Arte Sacra, Rossano 25288
Museo Diocesano di Arte Sacra, Lodi 24204
Museo Diocesano di Arte Sacra, Palermo 24773
Museo Diocesano di Arte Sacra, Volterra 26051
Museo Diocesano di Arte Sacra del Duomo, Arezzo 22923
Museo Diocesano di Arte Sacra San Gregorio Barbarigo, Padova 24744
Museo Diocesano e Gallerie del Tiepolo, Udine 25849
Museo Diocesano Inercomunale di Arte Sacra, Castignano 23437
Museo Diocesano Inercomunale di Arte Sacra, Rotella 25289
Museo Diocesano Intercomunale di Arte Sacra, Comunanza 23635
Museo Diocesano Intercomunale di Arte Sacra, Grottammare 24062
Museo Diocesano Intercomunale di Arte Sacra, Monteprandone 24537
Museo Diocesano Intercomunale di Arte Sacra, Ripatransone 25126
Museo Diocesano Teatino, Chieti 23547
Museo Diocesano Tridentino, Trento 25794
Museo e Archivio Capitolare, Assisi 22967
Museo e Chiostri Monumentali di Santa Maria Novella, Firenze 23874
Museo e Pinacoteca Diocesana, Camerino 23289
Museo Ecclesiastico, Caorle 23321
Museo Francescano, Roma 25224
Museo Francescano - Raccolta d'Arte, Gubbio 24076
Museo Orientale, Tagliacozzo 25666
Museo Parrocchiale, Castell'Arquato 23409
Museo Parrocchiale, Mogliano Marche 24454
Museo Parrocchiale della Chiesa Collegiata, Mercatello sul Metauro 24358
Museo Parrocchiale di Arte Sacra, Ponte in Valtellina 24991
Museo Parrocchiale e Museo P. Mascagni, Bagnara di Romagna 23002
Museo Pio IX, Senigallia 25537
Museo Tesoro Basilica di San Francesco, Assisi 22968
Museo Tesoro della Collegiata di San Lorenzo, Chiavenna 23536
Museo Tipologico del Presepe, Macerata 24250
Pinacoteca Comunale, Castiglion Fiorentino 23430
Pinacoteca Diocesana di Arte Sacra, Senigallia 25538
Pinacoteca Parrocchiale, Buonconvento 23230
Raccolta d'Arte, Città della Pieve 23575
Raccolta d'Arte, Roccalbegna 25140
Raccolta dell'Opera del Duomo, Oristano 24693

Japan
Amanosan Kongo-ji Treasure House, Kawachi-Nagano 26320
Amida-ji Treasure Storehouse, Hofu 26226
Atsuta-Jingu Museum, Nagoya, Aichi 26564
Chikubushima Treasure House, Shiga 26747
Chikurin-ji Treasure House, Kochi 26353
Chusonji Sankozo, Hiraizumi 26202
Daigo-ji Treasure Hall, Kyoto 26393
Daihoon-ji Treasure House, Kyoto 26394
Hakone-Jinja Homotsuden, Hakone 26175
Hiraizumi Museum, Hiraizumi 26203
Horyuji Daihozoden Treasure Museum, Ikoma 26240
Hosyokan Byodoin Museum, Uji, Kyoto 26989
Hotoko Ninomiya Jinja Homotsuden, Odawara 26612
Ichijo-ji Treasure House, Kasai 26314
Itsukushima-jinja Homotsukan, Hatsukaichi 26184
Izumo Taisha Shrine Treasure, Taisha 26784
Izumo Taisha Treasure House, Izumo 26279
Kakurin-ji Treasure House, Kakogawa 26292
Kamakura Kokuhokan, Kamakura 26293
Kamakuragu Homotsu Chinretsujo, Kamakura 26294
Kanshin-ji Reihokan, Kawachi-Nagano 26321
Kashima-jingu Treasure House, Kashima, Ibaraki 26318
Kasuga Taisha, Nara 26576
Katori-jingu Treasure House, Sawara 26726
Kikuchi-Rekishikan, Kikuchi 26333
Kitano Temman-gu Treasure House, Kyoto 26410
Kofukuji Kokuhokan, Nara 26577
Koryu-ji Reihoden, Kyoto 26415
Koyasan Reihokan, Koya 26373
Kumano Nachi Taisha Treasure House, Nachikatsuura 26524
Kyoto Kokuritsu Hakubutsukan, Kyoto 26424
Minobusan Homotsukan, Minobu 26492
Mishima Taisha Treasure House, Mishima 26496
Motsu-ji Storage House, Hiraizumi 26204
Munakata Taisha Shinpōkan, Genkai 26156
Myōhōin Homotsukan, Kyoto 26437
Naritasan History Museum, Narita 26587
Nata-dera Homotsukan, Komatsu 26369
Nikko Futarasan Jinja Hakubutsukan, Nikko 26602
Nikko Toshogu Treasure Museum, Nikko 26603
Ninna-ji Temple Treasure House, Kyoto 26440
Nyoirin-ji Treasure House, Yoshino 27032
Oyamazumi-jinja Kokuhokan, Omishima 26638
Rinno-ji Jokodo Treasure House, Nikko 26604
Rokuharamitsu-ji Treasure House, Kyoto 26448
Rokuonji, Kyoto 26449
Saikyo-ji Treasure Hall, Hirado 26201
Sanjusangendo, Kyoto 26452
Senko-ji Treasure House, Ono 26640
Shido-dera Treasure House, Shido 26745
Shido-ji Homotsukan, Shido 26746
Shingen-Ko Treasure House, Enzan 26136
Shiogama Shrine Museum, Shiogami 26757
Shoren-in Treasure House, Kyoto 26457
Shosoin Treasure Repository, Nara 26583
Sumiyoshi-jinja Treasure House, Shimonoseki 26754
To-ji Homotsukan, Kyoto 26458
Todai-ji Treasure Hall, Nara 26584
Toshodai-ji Treasure House, Nara 26585
Uesugi Shrine Treasure House, Yonezawa 27031
Yahiko-jinja Treasure House, Yahiko 27000
Yakushi-ji Treasure House, Nara 26586
Yamaguchi Hoshun Memorial Hall, Hayama 26186
Yamanouchi-jinja Treasure History Hall, Kochi 26357
Yogen-In Homotsukan, Kyoto 26461
Yutoku Shrine Museum, Kashima, Saga 26319
Zenko-ji Tendai Sect Treasure House, Nagano 26530
Zuigan-ji Hakabutsukan, Matsushima 26482

Korea, Republic
Moka Buddhist Museum, Gangcheon 27164
Museum of Korean Buddhist Art, Seoul 27259

Lebanon
Qozhaya Museum, Qozhaya 27492

Malta
Saint John's Co-Cathedral and Museum, Valletta 27706
Zabbar Sanctuary Museum, Zabbar 27718

Mexico
Museo de Arte Religioso, Huaquechula 27997
Museo de Arte Religioso de Santa Mónica, Puebla 28327
Museo de Arte Religioso Ex Convento Franciscano, Huejotzingo 28000
Museo de Arte Sacro, Chihuahua 27824
Museo Ex Convento Agustino de San Pablo, Yuriria 28631
Museo Virreinal de Zinacantepec, San Miguel Zinacantepec 28414

Mongolia
Museum of Religious History, Ulaanbaatar 28682

Myanmar
The Buddhist Art Museum, Yangon 28748
Museum of the Shwenawdaw Pagoda, Bago 28731

Netherlands
Breda's Museum, Breda 29020
Centrum voor Heiligenbeelden, Kranenburg 29493
Gaudete, Museum voor Volksdevotie, Boxtel 29012
Gemeentemuseum voor Religieuze Kunst Jacob van Horne, Weert 29989
Kerkmuseum Janum, Janum 29464
Museum Amstelkring, Amsterdam 28875
Museum in de Stiftkerk, Thorn 29872
Museum Sacrum, Tiel 29874
Museum Van Gerwen-Lemmens, Valkenswaard 29923
Museum voor Kerkelijke Kunst, Workum 30022
Museum voor Religieuze Kunst, Uden 29884
Schatkamer Sint Walburgis Basiliek, Arnhem 28944
Schatkamer van de Basiliek van Onze Lieve Vrouwe, Maastricht 29571
Schatkamer van de Sint-Servaasbasiliek, Maastricht 29572
Sint Jansmuseum De Bouwloods, 's-Hertogenbosch 29410
Sint-Plechelmusbasiliek met Schatkamer, Oldenzaal 29659
Stichting Santjes en Kantjes, Maastricht 29574
't Stift, Susteren 29861
Wilhelmietenmuseum, Huijbergen 29452
Zwanenbroedershuis, 's-Hertogenbosch 29411

Norway
Heddal Bygdetun, Notodden 30714
Stiklestad Nasjonal Kultursenter, Verdal 30987

Panama
Museo de Arte Religioso, Parita 31089
Museo de Arte Religioso Colonial, Panamá City 31080

Paraguay
Museo Iconográfico, Itaugua 31107
Museo Mons Juan Sinforiano Bogarin, Asunción 31104

Peru
Museo de Arte Religioso Convento de San Francisco, Cajamarca 31128
Museo de Arte Religioso de la Catedral, Lima 31209
Museo de Arte Religioso de Piura, Piura 31239
Museo del Convento de La Merced, Mantas 31228
Museo del Convento de los Descalzos, Lima 31217
Museo del Convento de San Francisco, Lima 31218
Museo del Convento de Santa Catalina, Cusco 31156
Museo Lítico de Pukara, Pukara 31243
Palacio Arzobispal, Cusco 31161
Pinacoteca Carmelita del Convento del Carmen, Trujillo 31265

Philippines
Barasoain Church Museum, Malolos 31359
San Agustin Museum Intramuros, Manila 31397
University of San Carlos Anthropology Museum, Cebu 31318
Xavier University Museum (Museo de Oro), Cagayan de Oro City 31300

Poland
Muzeum Archidiecezjalne, Katowice 31645
Muzeum Archidiecezjalne, Poznań 31899
Muzeum Archidiecezjalne, Przemyśl 31920
Muzeum Archidiecezjalne, Wrocław 32174
Muzeum Archidiecezjalne Lubelskie, Lublin 31787
Muzeum Diecezjalne, Tarnów 32041
Muzeum Diecezjalne Sztuki Kościelnej, Sandomierz 31962
Muzeum Diecezji Pelplińskiej, Pelplin 31877
Muzeum Katedralne Jana Pawła II, Kraków 31711
Muzeum Klasztorne OO Cystersów, Szczyrzyc 32031
Muzeum Parafialne, Dobra 31554
Muzeum Parafialne, Krynica 31741
Muzeum Sztuki Cmentarnej, Wrocław 32185
Muzeum Sztuki Sakralnej, Bardo 31477
Parafia Ewangelicko - Augsburska Wang, Karpacz 31642
Zabytkowa Cerkiew w Bartnem, Bartne 31479
Zbiory Sztuki na Jasnej Górze, Częstochowa 31548

Portugal
Museu Antonino, Faro 32271
Museu de Arte Sacra da Universidade, Coimbra 32257

Museu de Aveiro, Aveiro 32239
Museu de São Roque, Lisboa 32299
Museu Diocesano de Arte Sacra, Funchal 32275
Museu Nacional de Machado de Castro, Coimbra 32264
Museu Paroquial de Óbidos, Óbidos 32323
Núcleo Museológico do Santuário do Senhor Jesus da Pedra, Óbidos 32324
Palácio Nacional de Mafra, Mafra 32319
Tesouro-Museu da Sé de Braga, Braga 32244

Puerto Rico
Museo de Arte Religioso Porta Coeli, San Juan 32395

Romania
Colcția Muzeală a Mănăstirii Lainici, Bumbești-Jiu 32475

Russia
Archangelskij Sobor, Moskva 33020
Blagoveščenskij Sobor, Moskva 33021
Centralnyj Muzej Drevnerusskoj Kultury i Isskustva im. Andreja Rubleva, Moskva 33024
Cerkov Pokrova v Filjach, Moskva 33031
Cerkov Položenija riz Presvjatoj Bogorodicy, Moskva 33032
Gosudarstvennaja Tretjakovskaja Galerja, Moskva 33046
Isaakevskij Sobor - Memorialnyj Muzej-pamjatnik, Sankt-Peterburg 33410
Mitropolični Palaty - Muzej Drevnerusskogo Iskusstva, Jaroslavl 32852
Muzej Cerkov Petra i Pavla, Tjumen 33601
Muzej Chrama Christa Spasitelja, Moskva 33092
Muzej Istorii Burjatii im. M.N. Changalova, Ulan-Udė 33653
Muzej Spasskaja Cerkov, Tjumen 33607
Novodevičij Monastyr, Moskva 33164
Patrijaršie Palaty, Moskva 33171
Soloveckij Gosudarstvennyj Istoriko-Architekturnyj i Prirodnyj Muzej-Zapovednik, Soloveckij 33546
Svjato-Troickij Sobor, Sankt-Peterburg 33485
Svjatogorskij Monastyr, Puškinskie Gory 33345
Valaamskij Naučno-issledovatelskij Cerkovno-archeologičeskij i Prirodnyj Muzej-zapovednik, Sortavala 33548
Vystavočnyj Zal Spasskaja Cerkov, Irkutsk 32821

Serbia-Montenegro
Crkva-Muzej na Oplencu, Oplenac kod Topole 33879
Franjevački Samostan, Fojnica 33839
Muzej Srpske Pravoslavne Crkve, Beograd 33813
Zbirka Crkve Gospe od Skrpjela, Perast 33882
Zbirka Eparhije Banatski, Vršac 33929
Zbirka Župne Crkve, Prčanj 33894

Spain
Arxiu del Monestir, Sant Joan de les Abadesses 35403
Casa de las Dueñas, Sevilla 35472
Colección Parroquial, Colmenar Viejo 34730
Colección Parroquial, Gascueña 34840
Colección Parroquial, San Mateo 35384
Colección Parroquial, Traiguera 35571
Collećión Parroquial, Albocácer 34423
Hospital-Santuario de Nuestra Señora de la Caridad, Illescas 34916
Monasterio de Dominicas, Quejana 35304
Monasterio de la Encarnación, Osuna 35195
Monasterio de San Millán de Suso, San Millán de Suso 35386
Monasterio de Santa Clara, Zafra 35710
Museo Arciprestal, Morella 35140
Museo Catedral, Palma de Mallorca 35230
Museo Catedralicio, Almería 34453
Museo Catedralicio, Badajoz 34517
Museo Catedralicio, Burgo de Osma 34627
Museo Catedralicio, Burgos 34629
Museo Catedralicio, Cádiz 34646
Museo Catedralicio, Ciudad Real 34720
Museo Catedralicio, Eivissa 34786
Museo Catedralicio, Guadix 34888
Museo Catedralicio, Jaén 34922
Museo Catedralicio, León 34946
Museo Catedralicio, Málaga 35070
Museo Catedralicio, Palencia 35213
Museo Catedralicio, Santo Domingo de la Calzada 35456
Museo Catedralicio, Segovia 35464
Museo Catedralicio, Sigüenza 35493
Museo Catedralicio, Tortosa 35568
Museo Catedralicio-Diocesano, León 34947
Museo Catedralicio Diocesano, Pamplona 35247
Museo Conventual, Medina de Pomar 35101
Museo das Peregrinacións, Santiago de Compostela 35439
Museo de Arte Sacro, Monforte de Lemos 35123
Museo de Arte Sacro, Osuna 35197
Museo de Arte Sacro de la Colegiata de Iria Flavia, Padrón 35209
Museo de la Catedral de Santiago de Compostela, Santiago de Compostela 35443
Museo de la Colegiata, Belmonte 34597
Museo de la Colegiata, Medinaceli 35105
Museo de la Santa Iglesia Catedral, Avila 34503
Museo de los Caminos, Astorga 34495
Museo de los Condestables de Castilla, Medina de Pomar 35102
Museo de los Corporales, Daroca 34766
Museo de Semana Santa, Zamora 35713
Museo Diocesano, Lleida 34968
Museo Diocesano, Lugo 34986
Museo Diocesano, Tudela 35579
Museo Diocesano-Catedralicio, Cuenca 34765
Museo Diocesano-Catedralicio, Ourense 35200
Museo Diocesano-Catedralicio, Segorbe 35458
Museo Diocesano-Catedralicio, Valladolid 35624
Museo Diocesano-Catedralicio, Barbastro 34530
Museo Diocesano Catedralicio de Arte Sacro, Orihuela 35187
Museo Diocesano de Arte Antiguo, Sigüenza 35494
Museo Diocesano de Arte Sacro, Las Palmas de Gran Canaria 35241
Museo Diocesano de Arte Sacro, Teruel 35529
Museo Municipal, Antequera 34468
Museo Municipal de Bellas Artes, Xàtiva 35705
Museo Parroquial, Alquezar 34458
Museo Parroquial, Barco de Avila 34592
Museo Parroquial, Bocairente 34619
Museo Parroquial, Celanova 34704
Museo Parroquial, Medina de Rioseco 35104
Museo Parroquial, Roda de Isábena 35329
Museo Parroquial, Santa Gadea del Cid 35419
Museo Parroquial, Santa María del Campo 35425
Museo Parroquial de San Félix, Girona 34852
Museo Parroquial de Santa Eulalia, Paredes de Nava 35254
Museo Parroquial de Zurbarán, Marchena 35091
Museo Parroquial Santa María La Real, Xunqueira de Ambia 35706
Museo Sor María de Jesús de Agreda, Agreda 34411
Museo-Tesoro Catedralicio, Córdoba 34742
Museo-Tesoro Catedralicio, Lugo 34988
Museo-Tesoro Catedralicio, Plasencia 35274
Museo-Tesoro Catedralicio, Toledo 35548
Museo-Tesoro de la Basílica de la Macarena, Sevilla 35489
Museo-Tesoro de la Cofradía de la Expiración, Málaga 35075
Museo-Tesoro de la Santina, Covadonga 34756
Museo-Tesoro del Templo del Cristo del Gran Poder, Sevilla 35490
Museo-Tesoro Parroquial, Arcos de la Frontera 34477
Museo-Tesoro Parroquial de Santiago, Orihuela 35188
Museo Virgen de la Portería, Avila 34507
Museo y Archivo Histórico Diocesano, Tui 35580
Museu-Arxiu de Santa María de Mataró, Mataró 35099
Museu Capitular, Lleida 34969
Museu d'Art, Girona 34855
Museu Diocesà de Barcelona, Barcelona 34574
Museu Diocesà de Mallorca, Palma de Mallorca 35234
Museu Històric de la Seu, Manresa 35084
Museu Parroquial, Castellò d'Empúries 34692
Museu Parroquial, Santa Pau 35426
Museu Parroquial Palau Solitar, Palau de Plegamans 35212
Museu-Tresor Parroquial, Verdú 35648
Palau Ducal dels Borja, Gandía 34837
Real Casa del Labrador, Aranjuez 34473
Real Monasterio de Santa María de El Puig, El Puig de Santa María 35302
Valle de los Caídos, Valle de Cuelgamuros 35634

Switzerland
Dommuseum, Chur 36635
Domschatz Sankt Ursen Kathedrale, Solothurn 37181
Kirchenschatz, Bremgarten (Aargau) 36584
Kirchenschatz, Glarus 36763
Kirchenschatz-Museum, Baden 36486
Kirchenschatz Sankt Pelagius Kirche, Bischofszell 36573
Klostermuseum Disentis, Disentis 36662
Musée de Payerne et Abbatiale, Payerne 37018
Musée du Grand Saint-Bernard, Le Grand-Saint-Bernard 36775
Musée sur l'Ordre de Malte, Compesières 36645
Museo di Santa Maria degli Angioli, Lugano 36902

Tunisia
Musée d'Art Islamique du Ribat, Monastir 37575
Musée d'Art Islamique Raqqada, Kairouan 37565

United Arab Emirates
Sharjah Islamic Museum, Sharjah 37924

United Kingdom
The Blairs Museum, Aberdeen 37935
Cathedral Treasury Museum, Carlisle 38488
Christ Church Cathedral Treasury, Oxford 40144
Guildford Cathedral Treasury, Guildford 39136
Lincoln Cathedral Treasury, Lincoln 39498
Rievaulx Abbey, Rievaulx 40324
Saint Andrews Cathedral Museum, Saint Andrews 40383
Saint Augustine's Abbey, Canterbury 38475
Saint Mungo Museum of Religious Life and Art, Glasgow 39065
Saint Peter Hungate Church Museum, Norwich 40101
Saint Vigeans Museum, Arbroath 38013
Wesley's House and Museum, London 39804
Westminster Abbey Museum, London 39805
York Minster Undercroft Treasury and Crypt, York 40970

U.S.A.
Badè Institute of Biblical Archaeology and Howell Bible Collection, Berkeley 41639
Biblical Arts Center, Dallas 42746
Bob Jones University Museum and Gallery, Greenville 43829
Dadian Gallery, Washington 48343
Gallery at the American Bible Society, New York 45803
Glencairn Museum, Bryn Athyn 41976
Jane L. and Robert H. Weiner Judaic Museum, Rockville 46975
Lutheran Brotherhood Gallery, Minneapolis 45389
The Magnes Museum, Berkeley 41645
The Magnes Museum, San Francisco 47323
Mizel Museum of Judaica, Denver 42891
Mormon Visitors Center, Independence 44206
Museum of Church History and Art, Salt Lake City 47231
Museum of Contemporary Religious Art, Saint Louis 47130
National Museum of Catholic Art and History, New York 45851
Rothko Chapel, Houston 44135
Samuel S. Fleisher Art Memorial, Philadelphia 46455
San Carlos Cathedral Museum, Monterey 45459
Siskin Museum of Religious and Ceremonial Art, Chattanooga 42265
Temple Museum of Religious Art, Beachwood 41550
Upper Room Chapel Museum, Nashville 45628

Vatican City
Cappelle Sistina, Sala e Gallerie Affrescate, Città del Vaticano 48868
Collezione d'Arte Religiosa Moderna, Città del Vaticano 48869
Museo Pio Cristiano, Città del Vaticano 48880

Venezuela
Museo Diocesano Lucas Guillermo Castillo, Falcón 48942

Religious History and Traditions

Argentina
Museo Catedral de La Plata, La Plata 00387
Museo Histórico Franciscano, San Salvador de Jujuy 00596
Museo Jesuítico de Sitio, Yapeyú 00675
Museo Jesuitico Nacional de Jesus María, Córdoba 00304
Museo Jesútico Nacional de Jesús María, Jesús María 00371
Museo Monseñor José Fagnano, Río Grande 00519
Museo Obispo Fray José Antonio de San Alberto, Córdoba 00308
Museo Padre Coll, Buenos Aires 00235

Australia
Bishop's Lodge Museum, Hay 01093
Christmas Museum Gallery, Horsley Park 01111
Goold Catholic Museum, East Melbourne 00999
Linton and District Museum, Linton 01177
Lit Sing Kwang Chinese Temple, Innisfail 01121
Mary MacKillop Pilgrimage Centre, Fitzroy 01026
Mary Mackillop Place Museum, North Sydney 01328
Monsignor Hawes Priest House Museum, Mullewa 01286
Steiglitz Court House, Steiglitz 01477

Austria
Diözesanmuseum Eisenstadt, Eisenstadt 01807
Diözesanmuseum Graz, Graz 01912
Diözesanmuseum Linz, Linz 02230
Evangelisches Diözesanmuseum, Fresach 01852
Evangelisches Diözesanmuseum, Murau 02332
Evangelisches Diözesanmuseum im Burgenland, Stoob 02701
Evangelisches Museum in Wien, Wien 02881
Evangelisches Museum Oberösterreich, Rutzenmoos 02529
Kaplanstöckl, Hohenzell 02043
Kartause Aggsbach, Aggsbach Dorf 01648
KiK - Kultur im Kloster, Klostermarienberg 02138
Kirchenhäusl, Sankt Oswald bei Freistadt 02592
Konventmuseum der Barmherzigen Brüder, Wien 02910
Krippensammlung, Großraming 01960
Prämonstratenser-Chorherrenstift mit Stiftssammlungen, Geras 01874
Provinzmuseum der Franziskaner, Wien 02974
Sakraler Austellungsraum, Groß Sieghart 01950
Salvatorianerkloster, Gurk 01974
Schatzkammer - Turmmuseum der Pfarrkirche, Sankt Wolfgang im Salzkammergut 02621
Stiftsmuseum, Garsten 01871
Stiftsmuseum, Mattsee 02283
Stiftsmuseum, Zwettl, Niederösterreich 03062
Stiftssammlungen Lambach, Lambach 02178
Wallfahrtsmuseum, Maria Enzersdorf am Gebirge 02265
Zisterzienserabtei Mehrerau, Bregenz 01748
Zisterzienserstift, Lilienfeld 02224

Belgium
Abdij Museum, Sint-Truiden 03747
Begijnhofkerk, Sint-Truiden 03749
Monasterium De Wijngaard, Brugge 03258
Musée Gaspar, Arlon 03184
Musée Saint-Rémy, Cuesmes 03366
Museum Abdij Mariënlof, Kerniel 03534
Museum Godshuis Belle, Ieper 03516
Museum Grootseminarie, Brugge 03259
Museum Kerkschat Sint-Katharinakerk, Maaseik 03603
Museum Pater Valentinus Paquay-Heilig Paterke, Hasselt 03481
Museum van de Onze-Lieve-Vrouwkerk, Brugge 03262
Museum Vlaamse Minderbroeders, Sint-Truiden 03751
Oudheidkundig Museum van het Begijnhof, Turnhout 03805
Sint-Godelievemuseum, Gistel 03461
Ten Duinen 1138, Koksijde 03537
Trésor de la Basilique Saint-Materne, Walcourt 03825

Brazil
Espaço dos Anjos, Leopoldina 04173
Museu e Arquivo Municipal, Bom Jesus 03993
Museu Municipal Padre Antônio Ribeiro Pinto, Urucânia 04581
Museu Sacro São José de Ribamar, Aquiraz 03949

Brunei
Exhibition Gallery of the Islamic Dáwah Centre, Bandar Seri Begawan 04597

Bulgaria
Nacionalen Cărkoven Istoriko-archeologičeski Muzej, Sofia 04844
Pametnik na Kulturata Zemenski Manastir, Zemen 04931
Troyanski Manastir, Orešak 04748

Canada
Anglican Cathedral Museum, Saint John's 06339
Basilian Fathers Museum, Mundare 05950
Biblical Museum of Canada, Vancouver 06665
Christ Church Community Museum, Lakefield 05720
Father Pandosy Mission, Kelowna 05651
Martyrs' Shrine, Midland 05847
Musée Bon-Pasteur, Québec 06201
Musée de l'Oratoire Saint-Joseph, Montréal 05917
Musée des Papes, Grand-Anse 05507
Musée des Religions, Nicolet 06005
Musée des Soeurs de Sainte-Anne, Lachine 05713
Musée des Soeurs Grises de Montréal, Montréal 05919
Musée des Ursulines, Québec 06206
Musée Marie-Rose Durocher, Longueuil 05777
Musée Sainte-Marie, Church Point 05249
Museum Dom Benoît, Notre-Dame-de-Lourdes 06036
Norwich and District Museum, Norwich 06035
Saint Angela's Museum, Prelate 06178
Saint Thomas' Old Garrison Church Museum, Saint John's 06352
Sarcee People's Museum, Calgary 05179
Sharon Temple Historic Site, Sharon 06427
Trembowla Cross of Freedom Museum, Dauphin 05310
Vieille Maison des Jésuites, Québec 06211

China, People's Republic
Wen Tianxiang Temple, Beijing 06993

Côte d'Ivoire
Musée du Prophète Djouman Mihin, Vavoua 07674

Cuba
Museo Abel Santamaría, La Habana 07933
Museo Arquidiocesano, Santiago de Cuba 08130
Museo del Parque Abel Santamaría Cuadrado, Santiago de Cuba 08143

Cyprus, Turkish Republic
Bellapais Manastiri, Girne 08224

Czech Republic
Expozice Dominikánský Klášter, Jablonné v Podještědí 08379
Galerie a Muzeum Litoměřické Diecéze, Litoměřice 08455
Husitské Muzeum v Táboře, Tábor 08673
Památník Bible Kralické, Kralice nad Oslavou 08427
Památník Mistra Jana Husa, Husinec 08375

Denmark
Museerne i Fredericia, Fredericia 08825
Museet ved Sct. Ansgar Kirke, København 08940

Ecuador
Museo Diocesano de Arte Religioso Nuestra Señora del Cisne, Loja 09186
Museo Religioso Santa Domingo, Bolivar 09144

Egypt
Islamic Museum, Abbasiya 09232
Islamic Museum, Cairo 09267

Estonia
Dominiiklaste Kloostrimuuseum, Tallinn 09355

Finland
Turun Tuomiokirkkomuseo, Turku 10137

France
Abbaye de Flaran, Valence-sur-Baise 15052
Basilique Royale Saint-Denis, Saint-Denis (Seine-Saint-Denis) 14179
Maison d'Abraham Mazel à Falguières, Mialet 12974
Maison du Protestantisme, Nîmes 13336
Musée Archéologique, Lectoure 12503
Musée-Bibliothèque de l'Histoire du Protestantisme, Joigny (Yonne) 12082
Musée Calvin, Noyon 13372

Musée Comtois, Besançon 10698
Musée d'Art Sacré, Hambye 11987
Musée d'Art Sacré, Le Val 12490
Musée d'Art Sacré Copte et Byzantin Scete, Le Revest-les-Eaux 12478
Musée d'Art Sacré - Francis Poulenc, Rocamadour 13987
Musée d'Art Sacré Occidental, Le Revest-les-Eaux 12479
Musée d'Arte Sacré, Lorgues 12665
Musée de Germigny et Grange Germignonne, Germigny-des-Prés 11854
Musée de la France Protestante de l'Ouest, Monsireigne 13023
Musée de la Société de l'Histoire du Protestantisme Français, Paris 13565
Musée de la Vie Monastique, Saint-Hilaire-du-Harcouët 14263
Musée de Notre-Dame-de-Paris, Paris 13583
Musée des Patenôtriers, Brain-sur-Allonnes 10885
Musée des Pénitents Blancs, Marsac-en-Livradois 12836
Musée du Désert, Mialet 12975
Musée du Patrimoine des Pères de Bétharram, Lestelle-Bétharram 12565
Musée du Protestantisme Dauphinois, Le Poët-Laval 12467
Musée du Protestantisme en Haut Languedoc, Ferrières (Tarn) 11725
Musée Ernest Renan, Tréguier 14989
Musée Notre Dame de la Pierre, Sarrance 14619
Musée Rochelais d'Histoire Protestante, La Rochelle 12251
Musée Saint-François-Régis, La Louvesc 12204
Petit Musée de la Chartreuse Saint-Hugon, Arvillard 10442

Germany
Alte Kirche Friedensdorf, Dautphetal 16554
Altes Schloß Schleißheim, Oekumenische Sammlung Gertrud Weinhold "Das Gottesjahr und seine Feste", Oberschleißheim 19198
Bibelgalerie Meersburg, Meersburg 18672
Bibelmuseum, Münster 18933
Bruder-Konrad-Museum, Altötting 15462
Crescentia-Gedenkstätte, Kaufbeuren 18036
Dauerausstellung des Missionswerkes, Neuendettelsau 19023
Deutschordensmuseum Bad Mergentheim, Bad Mergentheim 15693
Dioramenschau Altötting, Altötting 15463
Domschatzkammer, Köln 18132
Doppelkapelle Sankt Crucis, Landsberg bei Halle, Saale 18306
Ehemalige Benediktinerabtei, Seligenstadt 19932
Die Franckeschen Stiftungen zu Halle, Halle, Saale 17509
Geburtshaus des heiligen Konrad von Parzham, Bad Griesbach im Rottal 15652
Heimatmuseum Lamspringe, Lamspringe 18297
Henri-Arnaud-Haus - Waldensermuseum, Ötisheim 19235
Hochstift Meissen, Meißen 18690
Hugenotten-Museum, Berlin 16002
Hus-Museum, Konstanz 18203
Jagdschloß Paulinzella, Rottenbach 19689
Johanniter-Museum, Krautheim, Jagst 18221
Johanniter- und Maltesermuseum, Heitersheim 17699
Kaiserdom-Museum, Königslutter 18179
Kartäusermuseum Tückelhausen, Ochsenfurt 19218
Katharina-Luther-Stube, Torgau 20185
Kirchenmuseum, Marienhafe 18635
Kleines Kirchengeschichtsmuseum Sankt Gumbertus, Illesheim 17887
Kloster Mariensee, Neustadt am Rübenberge 19069
Kornhaus Georgenthal-Klosterruinen, Georgenthal 17241
Krippenmuseum, Glattbach 17296
Landeskirchliches Museum, Ludwigsburg, Württemberg 18512
Leonhardi-Museum Aigen, Bad Füssing 15648
Luther-Stube Mansfeld, Mansfeld, Südharz 18617
Lutherhaus, Eisenach 16816
Lutherhaus Wittenberg, Lutherstadt Wittenberg 18575
Lutherkirche und Lutherzimmer im Dorfgemeinschaftshaus, Möhra 18763
Martin Luthers Geburtshaus, Lutherstadt Eisleben 18570
Melanchthonhaus Bretten, Bretten 16356
Melanchthonhaus Wittenberg, Lutherstadt Wittenberg 18576
Missions-Museum der Pallottiner Limburg, Limburg an der Lahn 18472
Missionsmuseum Bug, Bamberg 15810
Museum Altomünster, Altomünster 15470
Museum für klösterliche Kultur, Bad Wurzach 15780
Museum im Kloster Grafschaft, Schmallenberg 19810
Museum Jerusalem Panorama Kreuzigung Christi, Altötting 15464
Museum Kartause Astheim, Volkach 20333
Museum Kloster Hude, Hude, Oldenburg 17850
Museum Kloster Zeven, Zeven 20753
Museum Nikolaikirche, Berlin 16066
Museum Stift Börstel, Berge bei Quakenbrück 15890
Museumszentrum Lorsch, Lorsch 18505
Ordensmuseum Abtei Kamp, Kamp-Lintfort 17981
Praedicantenbibliothek der Nikolaikirche, Isny 17931
Religionskundliche Sammlung der Philipps-Universität, Marburg 18632
Sakrale Kunst in der Sankt-Anna-Kapelle, Cham 16459
Sankt Matthäus-Kirche im Kulturforum, Berlin 16089
Schatzkammer der Kath. Pfarrkirche Sankt Servatius, Siegburg 19944
Schatzkammer der Wallfahrtskirche, Hohenpeißenberg 17810
Schatzkammer Grafenrheinfeld, Grafenrheinfeld 17373
Stadt- und Wallfahrtsmuseum, Walldürn 20379
Stift Fischbeck, Hessisch Oldendorf 17746
Stiftsmuseum und Domschatzkammer, Xanten 20730
Stiftung Stift Neuzelle, Neuzelle 19088
Synagogen-Museum, Urspringen 20275
Wallfahrtsmuseum, Steingaden 20048
Wallfahrtsmuseum, Bruckmühl 16372
Wallfahrtsmuseum Inchenhofen, Inchenhofen 17897
Zisterziensermuseum Riddagshausen, Braunschweig 16306

Greece
Ayios Dimitrios Crypt Museum, Thessaloniki 21180
Bible Museum, Trilofo 21203
Collection of the Church of Koimissis tis Theotokou, Panagitsa Pellis 21106
Collection of the Church of the Evangelistria, Kastron Agiou Georgiou 21009
Collection of the Church of the Pangia, Agiassos 20805
Collection of the Monastery of Agios Andreas, Peratata 21118
Ecclesiastical Collection, Naoussa 21093
Ecclesiastical Museum of Alexandroupolis, Alexandroupolis 20815
Historical Museum of Anthiros, Karditsa 20998
Historical Museum of Portitsa, Karditsa 20999
Monastery of the Panagia Xenia, Almyros 20816

Hungary
Okeresztény Mauzóleum, Pécs 21513

India
Central Sikh Museum, Amritsar 21697

Iran
Armenian Cathedral and Museum, Isfahan 22244
Astan-e-Qods-e Razavi Museums, Mashad 22265
Holy Defense Museum, Kerman 22251

Ireland
Brother Rice Museum, Waterford 22552
Heritage Centre of Saint Louis Convent, Monaghan 22520
Knock Folk Museum, Knock 22502

Israel
Islamic Museum, Jerusalem 22641
Neot Kedumim, Lod 22708

Italy
Conservatorio di Santa Chiara, San Miniato 25397
Museo Casa Natale di San Pio X, Riese Pio X 25109
Museo del Duomo, Udine 25847
Museo del Santuario di Crea, Serralunga di Crea 25546
Museo del Tesoro della Cattedrale, Savona 25510
Museo della Collegiata, San Candido 25342
Museo dell'Abbazia di Santa Maria in Sylvis, Sesto al Reghena 25554
Museo delle Anime dei Defunti, Roma 25200
Museo delle Sinopie, Pisa 24950
Museo dell'Opera del Santuario, Tolentino 25720
Museo di Santa Cecilia, San Lazzaro di Savena 25378
Museo Diocesano, Spoleto 25625
Museo Diocesano d'Arte Sacra, Scaria 25519
Museo Diocesano d'Arte Sacra, Treviso 25807
Museo Diocesano d'Arte Sacra Santa Apollonia, Venezia 25940
Museo Diocesano e Tesoro della Cattedrale, Troia 25838
Museo Marciano, Venezia 25942
Museo Missionario, Padova 24746
Museo Missionario Cinese e di Storia Naturale, Lecce 24165
Museo Parrocchiale del Santuario del Santissimo Crocifisso, Buggiano 23228
Museo Provinciale Campano, Capua 23339
Museo Valdese della Balziglia, Massello 24330
Piccolo Museo Parrocchiale, Torgnon 25728
Piccolo Museo Parrocchiale, Valsavarenche 25885
Pinacoteca dell'Abbazia di Novacello, Varna 25901
Roccolta d'Arte Sacra, San Piero a Sieve 25406
Santuario Casa Santa Caterina, Siena 25579

Japan
Amakusa Kirishitankan, Hondo 26230
Confucian Shrine and Chinese Museum, Nagasaki 26544
Kaieji Buddhist Temple Site Museum, Sennan 26738
Museum of the Grove of the Village Shrine, Osaka 26656
Rengebu-ji Temple, Ogi 26618

Jordan
Islamic Museum, Amman 27051
Mazar Islamic Museum, Al-Mazar 27042

Korea, Republic
Jikjiseongbo Museum, Gimcheon 27173
Tongdosa Museum, Yangsan 27298

Malta
Gozo Cathedral Museum, Victoria 27709

Mexico
Galería Episcopal, Zacatecas 28634
Museo a la Bandera y Santuario de la Patria, Iguala de la Independencia 28011
Museo Altar de la Patria, Ixcateopan de Cuauhtémoc 28014
Museo Católico Peninsular, Mérida 28079
Museo Coltzin, Culiacán 27881
Museo Creadores, San Fernando 28384
Museo Cristero Señor Cura Cristóbal Magallanes, Totatiche 28561
Museo de la Basílica de Guadalupe, México 28132
Museo de la Evangelización, Huejotzingo 28001
Museo de la Purísima Concepción, Celaya 27809
Museo de las Misiones Jesuitas, Loreto 28063
Museo de Maní y Museo del Convento San Miguel Arcángel, Maní 28067
Museo de Nuestra Señora del Rosario, Talpa de Allende 28452
Museo de Oxolotán, Tacotalpa 28449
Museo de San Esteban Tetelpa, Zacatepec de Hidalgo 28643
Museo de San José María de Yermo y Parres, Puebla 28336
Museo de Todos los Santos, La Paz 28044
Museo del Ex Convento de Culhuacán, México 28156
Museo Ex Convento Agustino Siglo XVI, México 28168
Museo Ex-Convento de San Juan Bautista, Tlayacapan 28538
Museo Ex Convento del Carmen, Guadalajara 27960
Museo Ex Templo de San Agustín, Zacatecas 28636
Museo Ex Votos Sr. de la Misericordia, Tepatitlán de Morelos 28486
Museo Félix de Jesús, México 28169
Museo Kan Pepen, Teabo 28463
Museo Mariano Matamoros, Jantetelco 28028
Museo Rafael Coronel, Zacatecas 28639
Museo Regional Doctor Leonardo Oliva, Ahualulco de Mercado 27762
Museo Virgen de Zapopan, Zapopan 28649

Mongolia
Chojin Lama Museum, Ulaanbaatar 28675
Palace Museum, Ulaanbaatar 28686

Namibia
Schmelenhaus Museum, Windhoek 28783

Netherlands
Baarle's Museum, Baarle-Hertog 28958
Bijbels Museum, Amsterdam 28845
Gaudete, Museum voor Volksdevotie, Boxtel 29012
Heemkamer Barthold Van Hessel, Aarle Rixtel 28798
In de Zevende Hemel, Apeldoorn 28925
Kapucijnenmuseum, 's-Hertogenbosch 29403
Mannenzaal van het Sint Pieters en Bloklands Gasthuis, Amersfoort 28822
Missiemuseum Steyl, Steijl 29853
Museum Abdijkerk, Thorn 29871
Museum Catharijneconvent, Utrecht 29901
Museum der Katakombenstichting, Valkenburg, Limburg 29918
Museum Sint Bernardushof, Aduard 28800
Museum Sint Sellian, Sellingen 29816
Museum Stapelen, Boxtel 29014
Nederlands Zouavenmuseum, Oudenbosch 29698
Religieus Museum Kijk-je Kerk-Kunst, Gennep 29276
Schatkamer Sint Lambertuskerk, Horst 29450

New Zealand
The Salvation Army Territorial Archives and Museum, Wellington 30309

Norway
Hans Nielsens Hauges Minne, Rolvsøy 30802
Jødisk Museum, Trondheim 30938
Misjonsmuseet, Stavanger 30881
Misjonsmuseet på Fjellhaug, Oslo 30742
Rygge Museum, Larkollen 30628

Palestine
Islamic Museum, Jerusalem 31070

Peru
Museo de la Catedral, Cusco 31154
Museo de la Catedral, Trujillo 31262
Museo de la Iglesia de la Compañía de Jesús, Ica 31181
Museo de la Iglesia de San Pedro, Chucuito 31144
Museo de la Recoleta, Yanahuara 31270
Museo de Sitio Arqueológico Kuntur Wasi, San Pablo 31247
Museo de Sitio Huaca El Dragón, La Esperanza 31193
Museo del Convento de Santo Domingo, Cusco 31157
Museo Santuarios Andinos de la Universidad Católica de Santa María, Arequipa 31118

Philippines
Archdiocesan Museum of Manila, Manila 31368
Baclayon Church Museum, Baclayon 31277
Basilica del Santo Niño Museum, Cebu 31306
Butuan Diocesan Museum, Butuan 31295
Cebu Archdiodesan Museum, Cebu 31309
Christ the King College Museum, Calbayog 31302
Iglesia ni Cristo Museum and Gallery, Quezon City 31433
Jorge Barlin National Monument, Baao 31276
Monsignor Yatco Ecclesiastical Museum, Batangas 31287
Museo de Santa Monica, Panay 31409
Museo del Seminario Conciliar de Nueva Caceres, Naga 31406
Museo It Akean, Kalibo 31335
Museo Recoleto, Quezon City 31436
P. Jacinto Zamora Historical Museum, Manila 31389
Puerta de Isabel II Gallery, Manila 31394
Santo Niño Shrine and Heritage Museum, Tacloban 31454

Poland
Galeria Okręgowe, Biała Podlaska 31483
Muzeum Archidiecezjalne, Szczecin 32024
Muzeum Archidiecezjalne w Krakowie, Kraków 31695
Muzeum Archidiecezji Łódzkiej, Łódź 31769
Muzeum Archidiecezji Warszawskiej, Warszawa 32089
Muzeum Cystersów, Wąchock 32066
Muzeum Diecezjalne, Płock 31886
Muzeum Diecezjalne, Siedlce 31969
Muzeum Diecezjalne w Opolu, Opole 31858
Muzeum Martyrologii (Sonnenburg), Słońsk 31978
Muzeum Misyjne, Czerna 31542
Muzeum Misyjne, Krosno 31735
Muzeum Misyjne Misjonarzy Oblatów MN, Święty Krzyż 32017
Muzeum Parafialne, Widawa 32151
Muzeum Parafialne, Bobowa 31500
Muzeum Parafialne, Rzepiennik Strzyżewski 31958
Muzeum Parafialne, Tropie 32056
Muzeum Parafialne, Grybów 31613
Muzeum Parafialne, Złota 32221
Muzeum Parafialne im. Jana Wnęka w Odporyszowie, Odporyszów 31843
Muzeum Parafialne im. Ks. Edwarda Nitki, Paszyn 31876
Muzeum Reformacji Polskiej, Mikołajki 31807
Parafialne Muzeum Regionalne, Krasnobród 31732

Portugal
Museu Antoniano, Lisboa 32290
Museu D. Lopo de Almeida, Abrantes 32229
Museu do Santuário de Nossa Senhora da Abadia, Amares 32236

Puerto Rico
Museo de Arte Religioso Santo Domingo de Porta Coeli, San Germán 32385

Russia
Cerkov Pokrova v Filjach, Moskva 33031
Dom-muzej Tukaevych, Košlauč 32941
Ėkspozicija "Čelovek. Duša. Duchovnost.", Ivanovo 32826
Gosudarstvennyj Muzej Istorii Religii, Sankt-Peterburg 33403
Kraevedčeskij Muzej Evrejskoj Avtonomnoj Oblasti, Birobidžan 32689
Muzej Cerkov Petra i Pavla, Tjumen 33601
Muzej Chrama Christa Spasitelja, Moskva 33092
Muzej Istorii Burjatii im. M.N. Changalova, Ulan-Udė 33653
Oloneckij Nacionalnyj Muzej Karelov-Livvikov im. N.T.Prilukin, Olonec 33252
Samarskij Eparchialnyj Cerkovno-istoričeskij Muzej, Samara 33376
Troickij Sobor, Serpuchov 33523
Valaamskij Naučno-issledovatelskij Cerkovno-archeologičeskij i Prirodnyj Muzej-zapovednik, Sortavala 33548
Vystavočnyj Zal Spasskaja Cerkov, Irkutsk 32821

South Africa
Genadendal Museum, Genadendal 34243
Macrorie House Museum, Pietermaritzburg 34326
Missionary Museum, King William's Town 34296
Missionary Museum of the N.G. Kerk, Stellenbosch 34381
S.P. Engelbrecht Museum of the Nederduitsch Hervormde Kerk van Afrika, Pretoria 34357
Transgariep Museum, Philippolis 34324

Spain
Casa Natal de San Ignacio, Azpeitia 34511
Casa Santuario de San Pedro Claver, Verdú 35646
Caserío de Errecarte, Azpeitia 34512
Castillo de Javier, Javier 34927
Collección del Santo Rosario, Aroche 34485
Convento y Museo de de las Úrsulas, Salamanca 35358
Madres Dominicanas - Monasterio Sancti Spiritus, Toro 35557
Museo Arqueológico y Etnológico de Granada, Granada 34873
Museo Catedralicio, Salamanca 35360
Museo Catedralicio-Diocesano, Valencia 35600
Museo Catedralico y Giralda, Sevilla 35480
Museo de la Coria, Trujillo 35576
Museo de la Iglesia, Oviedo 35205
Museo de la Real Capilla, Arenas de San Pedro 34479
Museo de las Madres Benedictinas, Sahagún 35356
Museo de Terra Santa, Santiago de Compostela 35445
Museo del Convento de San Esteban, Salamanca 35362
Museo del Convento de Santa Clara, Salamanca 35363
Museo del Monasterio de Tulebras, Tulebras 35581
Museo Diocesano de San Sebastián, Donostia-San Sebastián 34777

Museo Diocesano Regina Coeli, Santillana del Mar 35452
Museo Parroquial, Espejo 34803
Museo Teresiano, Alba de Tormes 34418
Museo y Archivo Histórico Diocesano, Tui 35580
Museu-Arxiu Parroquial, Canet de Mar 34670
Museu de la Catedral, Barcelona 34559
Museu del Temple Expiatori de la Sagrada Familia, Barcelona 34571
Museu Parroquial, Altafulla 34459
Museu Parroquial, Calonge de Mar 34662
Museu Parroquiali, Vimbodí 35689

Sweden
Burlövs Gamla Prästgård, Arlöv 35811
Helge Ands Kyrkoruin, Visby 36416
Missionsmuséet, Vårgårda 36397
Sancta Birgitta Klostermuseum, Vadstena 36368
Sankta Karins Kyrkoruin, Visby 36417

Switzerland
Hausmuseum Kloster Kreuzlingen, Kreuzlingen 36835
Kirchenschatz-Museum Sankt Martin, Altdorf, Uri 36448
Musée de l'Ordre de Malte, Bardonnex 36493
Museum Bruder Klaus, Sachseln 37081
Museum der Schweizer Kapuzinerprovinz, Sursee 37226
Ritterhaus Bubikon, Bubikon 36594
Zwingligeburtshaus, Wildhaus 37325

Turkey
Aya İrini Kilisesi üzesi, İstanbul 37692

United Kingdom
All Hallows Undercroft Museum, London 39565
Ancient Order of Foresters, Southampton 40542
Bath Abbey Heritage Vaults, Bath 38107
Birkenhead Priory and Saint Mary's Tower, Birkenhead 38204
Byland Abbey, Coxwold 38651
Cardinal Ó Fiaich Heritage Centre, Cullyhanna 38680
Cathedral Treasury, Chichester 38558
Forde Abbey, Chard 38523
Infirmary Museum, Saint Ronan's Church Museum and Columba Centre, Isle-of-Iona 39315
Monks' Dormitory Museum, Durham 38827
Museum of Methodism, London 39720
Museum of Primitive Methodism, Englesea Brook, Crewe 38665
Museum of the Order of Saint John, London 39722
Peel Castle, Peel 40168
Reading Abbay Gateway, Reading 40297
Rosslyn Chapel, Roslin 40342
Rushen Abbey, Ballasalla 38063
Saint Asaph Cathedral Treasury, Saint Asaph 40388
Saint Michael's Loft Museum, Christchurch 38579
Saint Nicholas Priory, Exeter 38958
Saint Peter's Church, Sunderland 40649
Saint Robert's Cave, Knaresborough 39401
Salomons Memento Rooms, Southborough 40550
Tintern Abbey, Chepstow 38547
Whithorn - Cradle of Christianity, Whithorn 40860
William Carey Museum, Leicester 39470

U.S.A.
American Baptist Museum, Rochester 46937
American Catholic Historical Society Museum, Philadelphia 46388
American Jewish Historical Museum, New York 45758
Archaeological Museum, Louisville 44962
Archives Museum - Temple Mickve Israel, Savannah 47476
The Arthur J. Moore Methodist Museum, Saint Simons Island 47178
Beehive House, Salt Lake City 47226
Beth Ahabah Museum and Archives, Richmond 46873
Biedenharn Museum and Gardens, Monroe 45439
Billy Graham Center Museum, Wheaton 48581
Bishop Martin Museum, Natchitoches 45634
Catholic Historical Society of the Roanoke Valley Museum, Roanoke 46928
Chinese House Museum, Echo 43078
Community of Christ Musuem, Independence 44200
Concordia Historical Institute Museum, Saint Louis 47116
Disciples of Christ Historical Society Museum, Nashville 45616
Eldridge Street Project, New York 45796
Father Marquette National Memorial and Museum, Saint Ignace 47094
Fifth Meeting House, Lancaster 44618
Gustav Jeeninga Museum of Bible and Near Eastern Studies, Anderson 41203
Hebrew Union College-Jewish Institute of Religion Skirball Museum, Cincinnati 42406
Hill Cumorah Visitors Center and Historic Sites, Palmyra 46269
Historic Liberty Jail Visitors Center, Liberty 44766
History Center of the United Methodist Church, Madison 45062
Holyland Exhibition, Los Angeles 44911
The Joseph A. Callaway Archaeological Museum, Louisville 44966
Judaica Museum of Central Synagogue, New York 45823
Judaica Museum of the Hebrew Home for the Aged at Riverdale, Bronx 41921
Kateri Galleries, Auriesville 41392
Kirtland Temple Historic Center, Kirtland 44504
Knights of Columbus Museum, New Haven 45696
Living Word National Bible Museum, Aledo 41116
Longyear Museum, Chestnut Hill 42293
Lovely Lane Museum, Baltimore 41475
Luckhard Museum - The Indian Mission, Sebewaing 47550
Marian and Religious Museum, Brooklyn 41947
Mennonite Heritage Center, Harleysville 43912
Mennonite Library and Archives Museum, North Newton 46000
The Mission House, Stockbridge 47818
Mission Houses Museum, Honolulu 44084
Mission San Carlos Borromeo del Rio Carmelo, Carmel 42110
Mission San Diego de Alcala, San Diego 47280
Mission San Luis Obispo de Tolosa, San Luis Obispo 47361
Mission San Miguel, San Miguel 47370
Mississippi Baptist Historical Commission Museum, Clinton 42496
Moravian Museum of Bethlehem, Bethlehem 41668
Museum of Church History and Art, Salt Lake City 47231
Museum of the Southern Jewish Experience, Jackson 44283
Museum of the Western Jesuit Missions, Hazelwood 43977
Museum of Waldensian History, Valdese 48178
National Museum of American Jewish History, Philadelphia 46436
National Museum of Catholic Art and History, New York 45851
National Yiddish Book Center, Amherst 41180
Native American Exhibit, Fonda 43361
Nebraska Conference United Methodist Historical Center, Lincoln 44789
Old Bohemia Historical Museum, Warwick 48319
Old Cathedral Museum, Saint Louis 47133
Old Mission Santa Ines, Solvang 47666
Old Saint Ferdinand's Shrine, Florissant 43350
Oroville Chinese Temple, Oroville 46198
Perry County Lutheran Historical Society Museum, Altenburg 41156
Philadelphia Museum of Judaica-Congregation Rodeph Shalom, Philadelphia 46443
Presbyterian Historical Society Museum, Montreat 45481
Presbyterian Historical Society Museum, Philadelphia 46446
La Purisima Mission, Lompoc 44852
Quaker Yearly Meeting House, Mount Pleasant 45539
Rose Lawn Museum, Cartersville 42123
Saint George's United Methodist Church Museum, Philadelphia 46453
Saint Photios Greek Orthodox National Shrine, Saint Augustine 47073
Salvation Army Southern Historical Museum, Atlanta 41357
San Antonio Missions Museum, Jolon 44357
San Fernando Historical Museum, Mission Hills 45400
San Gabriel Mission Museum, San Gabriel 47347
San Miguel Mission Church, Santa Fe 47430
Santuario de Nuestra Senora de Guadalupe, Santa Fe 47432
Scotland Heritage Chapel and Museum, Scotland 47508
Siskin Museum of Religious and Ceremonial Art, Chattanooga 42265
Spertus Museum, Chicago 42363
Temple Museum of Religious Art, Beachwood 41550
Texas Baptist Historical Center Museum, Brenham 41880
Thomas L. Kane Memorial Chapel, Kane 44387
Tome Parish Museum, Tome 48025
Trinity Museum of the Parish of Trinity Church, New York 45883
Vasa Lutheran Church Museum, Vasa 48205
Washington National Cathedral, Washington 48407
Whitefield House Museum, Nazareth 45640
William A. Quayle Bible Collection, Baldwin City 41444
World Methodist Museum, Lake Junaluska 44589
Yeshiva University Museum, New York 45887

Vatican City
Museo Sacro, Città del Vaticano 48882

Venezuela
Museo Diocesano, Valle del Espíritu Santo 48968
Museo Sacro de Caracas, Caracas 48927

Reptiles

Bulgaria
Prirodonaučen Muzej, Černi Osăm 04638

Romania
Muzeul Național de Istorie Naturala Grigore Antipa, București 32468

U.S.A.
Rattlesnake Museum, Albuquerque 41108

Rescue Equipment → Fire Fighting and Rescue Work

Rocks → Mineralogy

Salt

Austria
Salzwelten Altaussee, Altaussee 01660
Salzwelten Salzburg-Bad Dürrnberg, Hallein 01998

China, People's Republic
Museum of the History of the Salt Industry, Zigong 07340

France
Musée Claude Nicolas Ledoux Saline Royale, Arc-et-Senans 10394
Musée des Marais Salants, Batz-sur-Mer 10604
Musée du Sel, Marsal 12839

Germany
Alte Saline Bad Reichenhall, Bad Reichenhall 15715
Besucherbergwerk Bad Friedrichshall-Kochendorf, Heilbronn 17687
Borlach-Museum, Bad Dürrenberg 15631
Deutsches Salzmuseum - Industriedenkmal Saline Lüneburg, Lüneburg 18556
Forum Fränkischer Hof, Bad Rappenau 15714
Saline- und Heimatmuseum, Bad Sulza 15753
Salinenmuseum Unteres Bohrhaus, Rottweil 19697
Salzbergwerk Berchtesgaden, Berchtesgaden 15887
Salzmuseum, Bad Nauheim 15700
Salzmuseum, Bad Sooden-Allendorf 15747
Soleleitungsmuseum Brunnhaus Klaushäusl, Grassau, Chiemgau 17379
Stadthistorisches Museum, Bad Salzdetfurth 15728
Technisches Halloren- und Salinenmuseum, Halle, Saale 17522

Italy
Museo Storico delle Saline, Margherita di Savoia 24297

Japan
Shio-no-michi Hakabutsukan, Itoigawa 26267
Tabako to Shio no Hakubutsukan, Tokyo 26929

Mexico
Museo Comunitario de la Sal, Armería 27780

Netherlands
Zoutmuseum Delden, Delden 29075

Portugal
Museu Municipal, Alcochete 32231

Russia
Bereznikovskij Istoriko-kraevedčeskij Muzej, Berezniki 32685

Spain
Museu de Sal de Josep Arnau, Cardona 34679

Switzerland
Mines de Sel de Bex, Bex 36560

United Kingdom
Lion Salt Works, Northwich 40087
Pilchard Works, Newlyn 40048
Salt Museum, Northwich 40088

U.S.A.
Salt Museum, Liverpool 44831

Sarcophagi → Tombs

Scientific Apparatus and Instruments

Argentina
Exploratorio, San Isidro 00564
Museo de Ciencia y Técnica, Buenos Aires 00176
Museo de los Niños Abasto, Buenos Aires 00192
Museo Interactivo de Ciencias, Paraná 00469
Museo Meteorológico Nacional Dr. Benjamín A. Gould, Córdoba 00306

Australia
Museum of the History of Science, Sydney 01505
Physics Museum, Brisbane 00840
Sydney Children's Museum, Merrylands 01251

Austria
Fotohistorische Sammlung, Penk 02396
Sanitärmuseum, Wien 02984

Brazil
Espaço Museu da Vida, Rio de Janeiro 04324

Canada
Saskatchewan Science Centre, Regina 06247
Science North, Sudbury 06512

China, People's Republic
Nanjingdi Zhen Science Museum, Nanjing 07185

Croatia
Tehnički Muzej, Zagreb 07838

Czech Republic
Technické Muzeum v Brně, Brno 08277

Denmark
Steno Museet, Århus 08773

Egypt
Science Museum, Alexandria 09247

Finland
Helsingin Yliopistomuseo, Helsinki 09491

France
Musée de l'Horlogerie et du Décolletage, Cluses 11337
Musée du Temps, Besançon 10703

Germany
Deutsches Museum, München 18839
Deutsches Museum - Verkehrszentrum, München 18840
Mathematikum, Gießen 17283
Mathematisch-Physikalischer Salon, Dresden 16696
Museum "Vermessen in Bayern - von der Messlatte zur Antenne", München 18886
Otto-von-Guericke-Museum in der Lukasklause, Magdeburg 18586
Philipp-Matthäus-Hahn-Museum, Albstadt 15422
Rhein-Museum Koblenz, Koblenz 18123

Hungary
Eötvös Loránd Emlékkiállítás, Budapest 21335

India
Bardhaman Science Centre, Bardhaman 21706
Dhenkanal Science Centre, Dhenkanal 21794
District Science Centre, Purulia 21996

Israel
National Museum of Science, Planning and Technology, Haifa 22610

Italy
Istituto e Museo di Storia della Scienza, Firenze 23848

Korea, Republic
National Science Museum of Korea, Daejeon 27163

Mexico
Museo Universitario de Ciencias, Zacatecas 28641

Netherlands
Historical Collection Electronical Engineering, Delft 29077
Museum Boerhaave, Leiden 29521
NEMO, Amsterdam 28889
Teylers Museum, Haarlem 29331

Philippines
Philippine Science Centrum, Manila 31392

Portugal
Museu de Física, Coimbra 32258

Romania
Muzeul Științei și Tehnicii Ștefan Procopiu, Iași 32539

Russia
Angarskij Muzej Časov, Angarsk 32641
Biljarskij Gosudarstvennyj Istoriko-Architekturnyj i Prirodnyj Muzej-Zapovednik, Biljarsk 32688
Centr Istorii Aviacionnych Dvigatelej im. N.D. Kuznecova, Samara 33367
Centralnyj Muzej Svjazi im. A.S. Popova, Sankt-Peterburg 33386
Dom-muzej K.É. Ciolkovskogo, Kaluga 32875
Muzej Istorii Razvitija Mediciny, Astrachan 32665
Muzej K. É. Ciolkovskogo, Aviacii i Kosmonavtiki, Kirov 32921
Muzej M.V. Lomonosova, Sankt-Peterburg 33456
Muzej Meteorologii Glavnoj Geofizičeskoj Observatorii im. A.I. Voejkova, Sankt-Peterburg 33457
Muzej Meterologičeskaja Stancija Simbirska, Uljanovsk 33662
Muzej Nižegorodskaja Radiolaboratorija, Nižnij Novgorod 33217
Muzej Radio im. A.S. Popova, Ekaterinburg 32780

Serbia-Montenegro
Muzej Nikole Tesle, Beograd 33808

Singapore
Singapore Science Centre, Singapore 33944

Spain
Casa de las Ciencias, A Coruña 34746
Cosmocaixa, Alcobendas 34434
Museo del Observatorio Astronómico Nacional, Madrid 35035
Museo Interactivo de Ciencias, Granada 34879
Museo Nacional de la Ciencia y la Tecnología, Madrid 35046

Sweden
Berzeliusmuseet, Stockholm 36234

United Arab Emirates
Sharjah Science Museum, Sharjah 37926

United Kingdom
Barometer World Museum, Merton 39939
Cavendish Laboratory, Cambridge 38453

Collins Gallery, Glasgow 39042
Hunterian Museum, Glasgow 39051
Museum of the History of Science, Oxford 40149
Saint Andrews University Museum Collections, Saint Andrews 40386
Satrosphere, Aberdeen 37944
University Museum, Dundee 38805
Whipple Museum of the History of Science, Cambridge 38465
Whowhatwherewhenwhy W5, Belfast 38161

U.S.A.
American Museum of Science and Energy, Oak Ridge 46055
Arizona Science Center, Phoenix 46473
A.W.A. Electronic-Communication Museum, Bloomfield 41736
Baltimore Public Works Museum, Baltimore 41456
Berea College Burroughs Geological Museum, Berea 41635
Black Hills Museum of Natural History, Hill City 44022
Bowers Science Museum, Cortland 42653
Brazosport Museum of Natural Science, Brazosport 41873
Brevard Museum of Art and Science, Melbourne 45229
California Science Center, Los Angeles 44894
Carnegie Science Center, Pittsburgh 46512
Carter House Natural Science Museum, Redding 46818
Catawba Science Center, Hickory 44006
Center for Meteorite Studies, Tempe 47971
The Children's Science Center, Cape Coral 42094
Cincinnati Museum Center, Cincinnati 42402
Coastal Discovery Museum, Hilton Head Island 44033
Columbia River Exhibition of History, Science and Technology, Richland 46855
Cranbrook Institute of Science, Bloomfield Hills 41740
Detroit Science Center, Detroit 42926
Diablo Valley College Museum, Pleasant Hill 46551
Discovery Center of Idaho, Boise 41772
Discovery Center Science Museum, Fort Collins 43379
Discovery Museum History Center, Sacramento 47051
Discovery Park, Safford 47059
Discovery Science Center of Central Florida, Ocala 46080
Discovery World - The James Lovell Museum of Science, Economics and Technology, Milwaukee 45361
Don Harrington Discovery Center, Amarillo 41166
East Tennessee Discovery Center, Knoxville 44516
Edison and Ford Winter Estates, Fort Myers 43434
Everhart Museum of Natural History, Science and Art, Scranton 47517
Explora Science Center and Children's Museum, Albuquerque 41100
The Exploratorium, San Francisco 47316
Fernbank Science Center, Atlanta 41342
Flandrau Science Center, Tucson 48087
Fort Worth Museum of Science and History, Fort Worth 43485
The Franklin Institute, Philadelphia 46411
Geology Museum, Huntington 44164
George Washington Carver House, Diamond 42944
Harbor Branch Oceanographic Institution, Fort Pierce 43440
Hicksville Gregory Museum, Hicksville 44010
Houston Museum of Natural Science, Houston 44124
Insights - El Paso Science Center, El Paso 43119
Iredell Museum of Arts Heritage, Statesville 47794
Kansas City Museum/Science City at Union Station, Kansas City 44400
Kauai Children's Discovery Museum, Kapaa 44413
Lakeview Museum of Arts and Sciences, Peoria 46349
Louisiana Arts and Science Center, Baton Rouge 41527
McAllen International Museum, McAllen 45017
McKinley Museum and McKinley National Memorial, Canton 42090
McWane Center, Birmingham 41707
Mary Brogan Museum of Art and Science, Tallahassee 47935
Maryland Science Center, Baltimore 41479
Maxwell Museum of Anthropology, Albuquerque 41104
Miami Museum of Science, Miami 45291
Monte L. Bean Life Science Museum, Provo 46735
Museum of Arts and Sciences, Macon 45045
Museum of Discovery and Science, Fort Lauderdale 43412
Museum of Geology, Rapid City 46797
Museum of Robotics, Orinda 46182
Museum of Science, Boston 41818
Museum of Science and History of Jacksonville, Jacksonville 44299
National Inventors Hall of Fame, Akron 41073
National Museum of Natural History, Washington 48379
New Mexico Museum of Natural History and Science, Albuquerque 41107
New York Hall of Science, Flushing 43355
North Carolina Museum of Life and Science, Durham 43024
The North Museum of Natural History and Science, Lancaster 44630
Omnisphere and Science Center, Wichita 48608
The Oyster and Maritime Museum of Chincoteague, Chincoteague 42383
Pacific Science Center, Seattle 47543
Paterson Museum, Paterson 46311
Petaluma Wildlife and Natural Science Museum, Petaluma 46367
Porter Thermometer Museum, Onset 46162
Reading Public Museum and Art Gallery, Reading 46809
Red River Valley Museum, Vernon 48218
Reuben H. Fleet Science Center, San Diego 47285
Roberson Museum and Science Center, Binghamton 41700
Rochester Museum, Rochester 46944
Saint Louis Science Center Museum, Saint Louis 47136
Sci-Port Discovery Center, Shreveport 47617
Sci-Tech Center of Northern New York, Watertown 48443
Science Center of Connecticut, West Hartford 48529
Science Center of Iowa, Des Moines 42910
Science Museum, Upton 48162
Science Museum of Long Island, Manhasset 45104
Science Museum of Minnesota, Saint Paul 47166
Science Museum of Virginia, Richmond 46886
Science Museum of Western Virginia, Roanoke 46930
Science Spectrum, Lubbock 44992
Science Station Museum, Cedar Rapids 42162
Sciencenter, Ithaca 44274
Sony Wonder Technology Lab, New York 45873
South Dakota Discovery Center, Pierre 46485
Southwest Museum of Science and Technology, Dallas 42759
Southwestern Michigan College Museum, Dowagiac 42978
Virginia Living Museum, Newport News 45940
Weather Dicovery Center, North Conway 45990

Scientific Expeditions

Australia
Australian Antarctic Division Display, Kingston 01150
Bligh Museum of Pacific Exploration, Bruny Island 00855
Sturt House, Grange 01073

Austria
Heinrich Harrer-Museum, Hüttenberg 02051

Belgium
Africa-Museum, Tervuren 03772

Canada
Champlain Trail Museum, Pembroke 06106

Czech Republic
African Safari and Veteran Car Museum, Dvůr Králové nad Labem 08336
Památník Dr. Emila Holuba, Holice v Čechách 08357

Denmark
Hauchs Physiske Cabinet, Sorø 09075
Knud Rasmussens Hus, Hundested 08903

France
Musée des Sciences, Laval (Mayenne) 12359

Germany
Abenteuermuseum Saarbrücken - Sammlung Heinz Rox-Schulz, Saarbrücken 19722
Alfred-Wegener-Gedenkstätte, Zechlinerhütte 20734

Italy
Museo Aerospaziale Monte di Apollo, Perugia 24849
Museo dell'Aeronautica G. Caproni, Trento 25793

Kyrgyzstan
Memorialnyj Muzej N.M. Prževalskogo, Prževalsk 27313

Latvia
Gaidu un Skautu Muzejs, Ogre 27390

New Zealand
Canterbury Museum, Christchurch 30124

Norway
Ishavsmuseet Aarvak, Brandal 30448
Olav Bjaaland Museum, Morgedal 30690
Polarmuseet, Andenes 30387
Roald Amundsens Hjem Uranienborg, Svartskog 30909
Roald Amundsens Minne, Borge Sarpsborg 30443

South Africa
Hartenbos Museum, Hartenbos 34259

Spain
Casa-Museo de Colón, Valladolid 35618
Monasterio de Santa María de la Rábida, Palos de la Frontera 35245
Museo Casa de Colón, Las Palmas de Gran Canaria 35240

Sweden
Andréemuseet, Gränna 35927
Ostindiefararen Götheborg, Göteborg 35917

United Kingdom
Captain Cook Birthplace Museum, Middlesbrough 39946
Captain Cook Memorial Museum, Whitby 40850
Captain Cook Schoolroom Museum, Great Ayton 39118
David Livingstone Centre, Blantyre 38258
Gilbert White's House and the Oates Museum, Selborne 40465
John McDouall Stuart Museum, Dysart 38832
Royal Research Ship Discovery, Dundee 38804
Scott Polar Research Institute Museum, Cambridge 38461

Uruguay
Museo de Descubrimiento, Montevideo 40997

U.S.A.
Captain Nathaniel B. Palmer House, Stonington 47828
John Woolman Memorial, Mount Holly 45532
Johnson Collection of Photographs, Movies and Memorabilia, Chanute 42193
Lawrence L. Lee Scouting Museum, Manchester 45097
Lewis and Clark Center, Saint Charles 47080
Martin and Osa Johnson Safari Museum, Chanute 42194
North Star Scouting Memorabilia, West Saint Paul 48544

Sculpture

Argentina
El Fogon de los Arrieros, Resistencia 00505
Museo al Aire Libre, Buenos Aires 00156
Museo Casa de Yrurtia, Buenos Aires 00162
Museo Municipal de Bellas Artes Lucas Braulio Areco, Posadas 00484

Australia
City of Melbourne Collection, Melbourne 01225

Austria
Anton Hanak-Museum, Langenzersdorf 02186
Atelier Augarten - Zentrum für zeitgenössische Kunst der Österreichischen Galerie Belvedere, Wien 02838
Dokumentation des ehemaligen Heilbades, Bad Pirawarth 01716
Freilichtmuseum Römersteinbruch, Sankt Margarethen 02581
Galerie im Bildhauerhaus und Skulpturenwanderweg, Einöde 01799
Künstlergarten Alfred Kurz, Lichtenau 02218
Liechtenstein Museum, Wien 02926
Museum des Augustiner-Chorherrenstifts, Reichersberg 02498
Museum für zeitgenössische Metallplastik, Sankt Pantaleon 02595
Othmar Jaindl-Museum, Villach 02760
Palais Surreal, Wien 02969
Sammlung Essl - Kunst der Gegenwart, Klosterneuburg 02142
Schloß und Gurschner Museum, Pram 02446
Schloßmuseum Niederleis, Niederleis 02360
Schwarzenberger Skulpturenpark, Schwarzenberg am Böhmerwald 02644
Siegfried Charoux-Museum, Langenzersdorf 02188
Skulpturenpark Kramsach, Kramsach 02154
Tiroler Kunstpavillon Kleiner Hofgarten, Innsbruck 02081

Belgium
Gallery Sculpturama, Bornem 03227
Musée Communal du Comte de Jette, Bruxelles 03296
Musée Constantin Meunier, Bruxelles 03297
Musée de l'Art Wallon, Liège 03579
Musée de l'Assistance Publique, Bruxelles 03308
Musée des Beaux-Arts de la Ville de Mons, Mons 03633
Musée du Vieux-Cimetière, Soignies 03756
Musée en Plein Air du Sart-Tilman, Liège 03583
Musées Royaux d'Art et d'Histoire, Bruxelles 03337
Museum Mayer van den Bergh, Antwerpen 03151
Openluchtmuseum voor Beeldhouwkunst Middelheim, Antwerpen 03166
Schatkamer van de Sint-Salvatorskathedraal, Brugge 03266
Stedelijk Museum Het Toreke, Tienen 03778
Steenmuseum, Gent 03453
Taxandriamuseum, Turnhout 03806

Brazil
Museu de Arte Contemporânea da Universidade de São Paulo, São Paulo 04514
Museu de Artes Plásticas, Taubaté 04559
Museu Internacional de Arte Naïf do Brasil, Rio de Janeiro 04387

Bulgaria
Sofijska Gradska Chudožestvena Galerija, Sofia 04859

Canada
Art Gallery of York University, North York 06029
Canadian Sculpture Centre, Toronto 06568
Dofasco Gallery, Dundas 05354
John Weaver Sculpture Museum, Hope 05604
Mind and Matter Gallery, White Rock 06789
Robert Tait McKenzie Memorial Museum and Mill of Kintail, Almonte 04981
Toronto Sculpture Garden, Toronto 06620
Ziska Gallery, Bracebridge 05109

China, People's Republic
Art Museum of Dazu Rock Carvings in Chongqing, Chongqing 07029

China, Republic
Juming Museum, Taipei 07348

Congo, Democratic Republic
Musée des Beaux-Arts, Kinshasa 07637

Croatia
Atelier Ivan Meštrović, Zagreb 07810
Galerija Antuna Augustinčića, Klanjec 07715
Ivan Meštrović Gallery, Split 07782
Muzej za Umjetnost i Obrt, Zagreb 07834
Umjetnička Galerija, Dubrovnik 07702

Cuba
Museo Artes Plásticas, Pinar del Río 08071
Museo Oscar Fernandez Morera, Sancti-Spíritus 08115
Museo Taller de Escultura, Victoria de las Tunas 08175

Cyprus
Limassol Municipal Art Gallery, Lemesos 08211
Pierides Sculpture Garden, Larnaka 08192

Cyprus, Turkish Republic
Taş Eserler Müzesi - Lapidari, Lefkoşa 08240

Czech Republic
Klášter Sv. Anežky České, Praha 08584
Městské Muzeum a Galerie, Hořice v Pokrkonoší 08359
Městské Muzeum a Galerie Otakara Spaniela a Josefa Wágnera, Jaroměř 08383
Muzeum Umění, Benešov 08246
Státní Galerie Výtvarného Umění, Cheb 08309

Denmark
Faaborg Museum for Fynsk Malerkunst, Faaborg 08813
Hammerichs Hus, Ærøskøbing 08766
Louisiana Museum of Modern Art, Humlebæk 08902
Ny Carlsberg Glyptotek, København 08944
Randers Kunstmuseum, Randers 09026
Rudolph Tegners Museum, Dronningmølle 08800
Statens Museum for Kunst, København 08950
Thingbaek Kalkminer Bundgaards Museum, Skørping 09068
Thorvaldsens Museum, København 08952
Thorvaldsens Samlingen på Nysø, Præstø 09024
Vejen Kunstmuseum, Vejen 09103

Dominican Republic
Museo Bellapart, Santo Domingo 09120

Egypt
Mukhtar Museum, Cairo 09271

Finland
Emil Wikström Museo, Valkeakoski 10170
Gösta Serlachiuksen Taidemuseo, Mänttä 09810
Huittisten Museo, Huittinen 09552
Lapinlahden Taidemuseo ja Eemil Halosen Museo, Lapinlahti 09759
Mikkelin Taidemuseo, Mikkeli 09832
Wäinö Aaltosen Museo, Turku 10138
Walter Runebergin Veistoskokoelma, Porvoo 09955
Yrjö Liipolan Taidekokoelma, Koski 09698

France
Centre d'Art Contemporain, Istres 12064
Château de Fleurigny, Thorigny-sur-Oreuse 14902
Collections de l'Ecole Nationale Supérieure des Beaux-Arts, Paris 13494
Espace Salvador Dalí, Paris 13500
Fondation François-Brochet, Auxerre 10508
Fondation Le Corbusier, Paris 13504
Fondation Van-Gogh Arles, Arles 10414
Galerie Beaubourg, Vence 15114
Halle Saint-Pierre Museum, Paris 13515
Institut Tessin, Paris 13517
Musée Adzak, Paris 13529
Musée André Abbal, Carbonne 11039
Musée Arménien de France, Paris 13530
Musée Bartholdi, Colmar 11357
Musée Boleslaw Biegas, Paris 13535
Musée Bouchard, Paris 13536
Musée Bourdelle, Paris 13538
Musée Calvet, Avignon 10528
Musée d'Art et d'Archéologie, Aurillac 10490
Musée d'Art et d'Histoire, Meudon 12959
Musée de la Bohème, Yviers 15335
Musée de la Société Archéologique et Historique de la Charente, Angoulême 10355
Musée de la Vie Romantique, Paris 13568
Musée de Provins et du Provinois, Provins 13878
Musée de Région Auguste Chabaud, Graveson 11931
Musée de Statues d'Enfants, Les Mages 12544
Musée Départemental d'Art Ancien et Contemporain, Épinal 11633
Musée Départemental de l'École Publique, Chevregny 11284

Musée Départemental de l'Oise, Beauvais 10655
Musée des Amis de Thann, Thann 14880
Musée des Années 30, Boulogne-Billancourt 10837
Musée des Arts Décoratifs, Saumur 14645
Musée des Augustins, Toulouse 14946
Musée des Beaux-Arts, Angers 10346
Musée des Beaux-Arts, Arras 10429
Musée des Beaux-Arts, Béziers 10718
Musée des Beaux-Arts, Marseille 12862
Musée des Beaux-Arts, Pau 13668
Musée des Beaux-Arts, Valenciennes 15054
Musée des Beaux-Arts de Bordeaux, Bordeaux 10812
Musée des Bois Sculptes, Cancale 11018
Musée Despiau Wlérick, Mont-de-Marsan 13027
Musée du Centre de Recherches sur les Monuments
  Historiques, Paris 13598
Musée du Luxembourg, Paris 13604
Musée du Prieuré, Charolles 11187
Musée du Prieuré de Graville, Le Havre 12425
Musée du Santon, Pierrefeu-du-Var 13733
Musée François-Pompon, Saulieu 14636
Musée Garinet, Châlons-en-Champagne 11130
Musée Henri Chapu, Le Mée-sur-Seine 12445
Musée-Jardin Paul-Landowski, Boulogne-
  Billancourt 10838
Musée Jules Desbois, Parçay-les-Pins 13466
Musée Lapidaire, Avignon 10532
Musée Lapidaire de la Cité, Carcassonne 11045
Musée Lapidaire de Mozac, Mozac 13204
Musée Louis-Cornu, Wassigny 15306
Musée Magnin, Dijon 11530
Musée Moralès, Port-de-Bouc 13837
Musée Morice Lipsi, Rosey 14037
Musée Municipal, Lons-le-Saunier 12662
Musée Municipal de la Chartreuse, Douai 11560
Musée Municipal de l'Évêché, Limoges 12616
Musée Municipal de Vendôme, Vendôme 15117
Musée Municipal Nicolas Poussin, Les Andelys 12516
Musée National Auguste Rodin, Meudon 12960
Musée National des Arts Asiatiques Guimet,
  Paris 13633
Musée P. Dubois-A. Boucher, Nogent-sur-Seine 13353
Musée René Davoine, Charolles 11188
Musée Rude, Dijon 11531
Musée Santons du Monde, Clermont-l'Hérault 11327
Musée Zadkine, Paris 13649
Villa Arson, Nice 13328

Germany
Akademisches Kunstmuseum der Universität,
  Bonn 16225
Albrechtsburg, Meißen 18689
Alf Lechner Museum, Ingolstadt 17902
Antiken- und Abgußsammlung des Archäologischen
  Seminars, Marburg 18622
Antikensammlung der Friedrich-Alexander-Universität
  Erlangen-Nürnberg, Erlangen 16915
Edwin Scharff Museum am Petrusplatz, Neu-
  Ulm 19008
Ernst Barlach Haus, Hamburg 17536
Ernst Barlach Museum, Ratzeburg 19499
Ernst Barlach Stiftung Güstrow, Güstrow 17456
Europäischer Skulpturenpark, Willebadessen 20596
Fritz-Best-Museum, Kronberg 18247
Gerhard-Marcks-Haus, Bremen 16323
Heimatmuseum Stadt Starnberg, Starnberg 20036
Karl-Seckinger-Ausstellung, Karlsruhe 17993
Klostergalerie, Zehdenick 20735
Kulturzentrum Sinsteden des Kreises Neuss,
  Rommerskirchen 19643
Kunsthalle Bremen, Bremen 16328
Kunsthalle Würth, Schwäbisch Hall 19868
Kunstmuseum Kloster Unser Lieben Frauen,
  Magdeburg 18582
Kunstsammlung Lorenzkapelle Rottweil,
  Rottweil 19696
Kunstsammlungen der Ruhr-Universität Bochum,
  Bochum 16196
Lapidarium, Berlin 16036
Mainfränkisches Museum Würzburg, Würzburg 20696
Museum am Ostwall, Dortmund 16661
Museum Bad Arolsen, Bad Arolsen 15591
Museum Corps de Logis, Düsseldorf 16735
Museum für Abgüsse Klassischer Bildwerke,
  München 18882
Museum für Kunst in Steatit, Frankfurt am
  Main 17066
Museum Gasteiger-Haus, Utting 20281
Museum Würth, Künzelsau 18259
Nationalgalerie Friedrichswerdersche Kirche -
  Schinkelmuseum, Berlin 16071
Prof.-Fritz-Behn-Museum, Bad Dürrheim 15633
Sammlung Mittelalterliche Kunst in Thüringen,
  Eisenach 16818
Sammlungen des Archäologischen Instituts der
  Universität, Göttingen 17340
Schloß Seehof, Memmelsdorf 18703
Schlossmuseum Oranienburg, Oranienburg 19266
Skulpturen-Museum, Heilbronn 17691
Skulpturenhain vor Marleben, Trebel 20195
Skulpturenmuseum Glaskasten Marl, Marl,
  Westfalen 18655
Skulpturenmuseum im Hofberg, Landshut 18312
Skulpturenpark, Bad Nauheim 15701
Skulpturensammlung, Dresden 16709
Skulpturensammlung und Museum für Byzantinische
  Kunst, Berlin 16096
Skulpturenweg, Emmendingen 16858
Städtische Galerie im Rathauspark, Gladbeck 17292

Städtische Galerie Liebieghaus, Frankfurt am
  Main 17075
Städtisches Museum Simeonstift, Trier 20215
Stiftsmuseum der Stadt Aschaffenburg,
  Aschaffenburg 15533
Stiftung Hans Arp und Sophie Taeuber-Arp,
  Remagen 19562
Stiftung Wilhelm Lehmbruck Museum,
  Duisburg 16757
Suermondt-Ludwig-Museum, Aachen 15378
Von der Heydt-Museum, Wuppertal 20717
Walhalla, Donaustauf 16635

Greece
A. Sohos Museum, Tinos 21197
Alex Mylonas Museum, Athinai 20845
Archeological Collection, Drama 20940
Archeological Collection, Serrai 21151
Archeological Collection, Symi 21170
Archeological Collection, Tanagra 21171
Christos Capralos Museum, Aegina 20804
Christos Capralos Museum, Agrinion 20812
Christos Capralos Museum, Athinai 20855
Historical Museum of Crete, Iráklion 20975
Monemvasia Archeological Collection,
  Monemvasia 21074
Museum of Sculpture and Figurines of Loukia
  Georganti, Athinai 20889
N. Hadjikyriakos-Ghikas Gallery, Athinai 20892
Nikolaos Perantinos Museum of Sculpture,
  Athinai 20896
Skironio Centrum Kifissa, Néa Kifissia 21098
Yiannoulis Halepas Museum and Museum of Tinian
  Artists, Panormos Tinou 21107

Guam
Isla Center for the Arts at the University of Guam,
  Mangilao 21258

Hungary
Finta Múzeum, Túrkeve 21600
Hincz Gyula Allandó Gyüjtemény, Vác 21601
Szoborpark, Budapest 21384

Iceland
Ásmundarsafn, Reykjavík 21649
Listasafn Einars Jónssonar, Reykjavík 21653
Listasafn Sigurjóns Ólafssonar, Reykjavík 21654

India
Archaeological Museum, Konarak 21915
Archaeological Museum, Vaisali 22052
Archaeological Museum, Varanasi 22055
Assam State Museum, Gauhati 21807
Bangiya Sahitya Parisad Museum, Kolkata 21899
Belkhandi Museum, Belkhandi 21711
Bhagalpur Museum, Bhagalpur 21712
Birla Museum, Bhopal 21719
Bundelkhand Chhatrasal Museum, Banda 21700
District Museum, Guntur 21817
District Museum, Shivpuri 22022
Dr. Raj Bali Pandey Puratatva Sangrahalaya,
  Deoria 21786
Government Museum, Bharatpur 21714
Government Museum, Kodagu 21893
Government Museum, Mathura 21940
Government Museum, Mount Abu 21944
Government Museum, Udaipur 22044
Government Museum and Art Gallery,
  Chandigarh 21738
Himachal State Museum, Shimla 22020
History Museum, Ahmednagar 21683
I.V.K. Rajwade Sanshodhan Mandal Museum,
  Dhule 21795
Khajana Buildings Museum, Hyderabad 21844
Khiching Museum, Khiching 21889
Mahatma Gandhi Hindi Sangrahalaya, Kalpi 21879
Mahatma Gandhi Memorial College Museum,
  Udupi 22046
Mehrangarh Museum, Jodhpur 21875
Museum of Art and Archaeology, Dharwad 21792
Mutua Museum, Imphal 21855
Puratatva Sangrahalaya, Gorakhpur 21813
Purvattatva Sangrahalaya Madhya Pradesh Shasan,
  Damoh 21753
Rani Laxmi Bai Palace Sculpture Collection,
  Jhansi 21873
Sahitya Parishad Museum, Midnapore 21943
Sikar Museum, Sikar 22024
Sir Choturam Memorial Museum, Sangaria 22008
State Kala Akademi Museum, Imphal 21858
State Museum, Bhopal 21725
Thanjavur Art Gallery, Thanjavur 22032
TTD Museum, Tirupati 22040
Tulsi Sangrahalaya Ramvan, Satna 22014
Watson Museum, Rajkot 22002
Zilla Samgrahasala, Purulia 21997

Ireland
Bogwood Sculpture Artists, Newtowncashel 22529

Italy
Antiquarium Sestinale, Sestino 25553
Casa Buonarroti, Firenze 23825
Casa Museo Fantoni, Rovetta 25295
Cripta e Museo di Sant'Anastasio, Asti 22971
Fondazione Magnani Rocca, Mamiano di
  Traversetolo 24273
Galleria d'Arte Moderna, Firenze 23839
Galleria d'Arte Moderna Carlo Rizzarda, Feltre 23771
Galleria dell'Accademia, Firenze 23842

Galleria e Mostra del Presepe nel Mondo, Santuario di
  Montevergine 25468
Galleria Regionale di Palazzo Bellomo,
  Siracusa 25585
Galleria Rinaldo Carnielo, Firenze 23845
Giardino di Boboli, Firenze 23846
Musei Civici, Pavia 24822
Musei Civici agli Eremitani, Padova 24733
Museo Archeologico e della Collegiata, Casole
  d'Elsa 23379
Museo Arcivescovile, Ravenna 25079
Museo Bardini, Firenze 23853
Museo Barracco, Roma 25179
Museo Berenziano, Cremona 23679
Museo Canonica, Roma 25181
Museo Canonicale, Verona 25970
Museo Civico Antonio Cordici, Erice 23739
Museo d'Arte Antica, Milano 24389
Museo degli Affreschi G.B. Cavalcaselle,
  Verona 25972
Museo del Duomo, Milano 24394
Museo della Figurina, Modena 24443
Museo delle Statue - Stele Lunigianesi,
  Pontremoli 25002
Museo dell'Opera di Santa Maria del Fiore,
  Firenze 23862
Museo di Castelvecchio, Verona 25974
Museo di Sant'Agostino, Genova 23998
Museo di Sculture Iperspaziali, Bomarzo 23157
Museo di Villa Carlotta, Tremezzo 25789
Museo Dupré, Fiesole 23807
Museo G. Manzù, Ardea 22915
Museo Galleria di Villa Borghese, Roma 25225
Museo Lapidario e del Tesoro del Duomo,
  Modena 24447
Museo Lapidario Marsicano, Avezzano 22993
Museo Lodovico Pogliaghi, Varese 25897
Museo Michelangelo, Caprese 23333
Museo Nazionale, Ravenna 25081
Museo Nazionale del Bargello, Firenze 23879
Parco Monumentale di Pinocchio, Collodi 23617
Pinacoteca dell'Accademia di Belle Arti,
  Carrara 23359
Pinacoteca Giovanni e Marella Agnelli, Torino 25766
Villa San Michele, Anacapri 22878

Japan
Asakura Sculpture Gallery, Tokyo 26829
Chokoku no Mori Bijutsukan, Hakone 26174
Iwate-kenritsu Hakubutsukan, Morioka 26515
Museum of Contemporary Sculpture, Tokyo 26894
Rokuzan Bijutsukan, Hotaka 26232
Sapporo Sculpture Museum, Sapporo 26719
Utsukushigahara Kogen Bijutsukan, Takeshi 26814

Korea, Republic
Mok Am Museum of Art, Koyang 27206
Moran Open-air Museum, Namyangju 27216

Lebanon
Rachana Open Air Museum, Rachana 27493

Liberia
Tubman Centre of African Culture, Cape Mount 27497

Lithuania
Europos Parkas, Vilnius 27535

Malaysia
Ibrahim Hussein Foundation Museum, Pulau
  Langkawi 27680

Mexico
Galería de la Escuela Nacional de Artes Plásticas,
  México 28098
Museo de la Escultura Mexica Eusebio Dávalos,
  Acatitlán 27749
Museo Escultórico de Geles Cabrera, México 28166
Museo Universitario Alejandro Rangel Hidalgo,
  Nogueras 28268

Morocco
Forbes Museum, Tanger 28711

Nepal
Woodwork Museum, Bhaktapur 28786

Netherlands
Museum Beelden aan Zee, Den Haag 29107
Museum Jacobs van den Hof, Amersfoort 28825
Museum Theo Jans, Klarenbeek 29484
Odapark, Venray 29942
Het Oude Slot Heemstede, Heemstede 29357
Pier Pander Museum, Leeuwarden 29513

Nigeria
National Museum Esie, Esie 30338

Norway
Anders Svors Museet, Hornindal 30563
Anne Grimdalens Minne, Dalen i Telemark 30458
Erkebispegården, Trondheim 30937
Nils Aas Kunstverksted, Inderøy 30577
Vigeland-Museet, Oslo 30770

Peru
Pinacoteca Municipal de la Provincia de Corongo,
  Corongo 31150

Poland
Centrum Rzeźby Polskiej, Oronsko 31862
Muzeum Kamienica Łozińskich, Kraków 31710

Portugal
Casa-Museu Teixeira Lopes e Galerias Diego de
  Macedo, Porto 32331
Museu de Alberto Sampaio, Guimarães 32278
Museu Municipal de Santarém, Santarém 32341

Puerto Rico
Museo de Arte de Ponce, Ponce 32380
Popular Arts Museum, San Juan 32407

Romania
Colecţia de Artă Plastică Fr. Storck şi Cecilia Cecilia
  Cuţescu Stock, Bucureşti 32451
Muzeul Cornel Medrea, Bucureşti 32453
Muzeul de Artă, Drobeta-Turnu Severin 32515
Muzeul de Artă, Târgu Jiu 32605

Russia
Chudožestvennyj Muzej im. M.S. Tuganova,
  Vladikavkaz 33686
Dom-muzej Skulptora A.S. Golubkinoj, Zarajsk 33745
Gosudarstvennyj Muzej-masterskaja Skulptora A.S.
  Golubkinoj, Moskva 33061
Gosudarstvennyj Muzej Vadima Sidura,
  Moskva 33064
Memorialnyj Muzej-Masterskaja Skulptora S.T.
  Konenkova, Moskva 33081
Meždunarodnyj Centr-Muzej im. N.K. Rericha,
  Moskva 33083
Muzej Skulptury, Sankt-Peterburg 33465
Muzej Skulptury S.T. Konenkova, Smolensk 33529
Muzej-usadba im. N.K. Rericha, Izvara 32839
Park-muzej im. A.K. Tolstogo, Brjansk 32711
Permskaja Gosudarstvennaja Chudožestvennaja
  Galereja, Perm 33307

Serbia-Montenegro
Galerija Matice Srpske, Novi Sad 33869
Galerija Srpske Akademije Nauka i Umetnosti,
  Beograd 33798

Slovakia
Galéria Mesta Bratislavy, Bratislava 33963

Slovenia
Gorenjski Muzej Kranj, Kranj 34100

South Africa
Rupert Museum, Stellenbosch 34382

Spain
Cason del Buen Retiro, Madrid 34991
Chillida Leku, Hernani 34900
Museo Antón, Candás 34667
Museo Casa Murillo, Sevilla 35479
Museo de Huelva, Huelva 34906
Museo del Sacromonte, Granada 34878
Museo Diocesano-Catedralicio, Astorga 34497
Museo Lorenzo Coullaut-Valera, Marchena 35090
Museo Municipal, Ayllón 34509
Museo Municipal Mateo Hernández, Béjar 34594
Museo Nacional de Escultura, Valladolid 35626
Museo Salzillo, Murcia 35150
Museu Clarà, Barcelona 34549
Museu d'Art, Girona 34855
Museu Frederic Marès, Barcelona 34578

Sudan
Merowe Museum, Merowe 35772

Sweden
Carl Eldhs Ateljémuseum, Stockholm 36236
Dalahästmuseum, Dala-Järna 35850
Döderhultarmuseet, Oskarshamn 36153
Gustav III.'s Antikmuseum, Stockholm 36244
Millesgården, Lidingö 36032
Skulpturens Hus, Stockholm 36282
Vitlycke Museum, Tanumshede 36322

Switzerland
Antikensammlung, Bern 36539
Kirchner Museum Davos, Davos Platz 36654
Kunstmuseum, Solothurn 37185
Kunstmuseum Winterthur, Winterthur 37331
Lapidarium, Sankt Gallen 37103
Museo Vela, Ligornetto 36882
Museum der Klosterruine mit Lapidarium,
  Rüeggisberg 37075
Museum Erwin Rehmann, Laufenburg 36849
Museum Kleines Klingental, Basel 36512
Paul Gugelmann-Museum, Schönenwerd 37142
Skulpturhalle Basel, Basel 36522

Turkey
Resim ve Heykel Müzesi, İstanbul 37705

United Kingdom
Andrew Logan Museum of Sculpture,
  Welshpool 40815
Barbara Hepworth Museum and Sculpture Garden,
  Saint Ives, Cornwall 40406
Bolton Museum and Art Gallery, Bolton 38269
The Burton Art Gallery and Museum, Bideford 38191
Courtauld Institute Gallery, London 39615
Furness Abbey, Barrow-in-Furness 38096
Henry Moore Institute, Leeds 39445
New Art Centre, East Winterslow 38851
The New Art Gallery Walsall, Walsall 40773
Penwith Galleries, Saint Ives, Cornwall 40407
Royal British Society of Sculptors, London 39758
William Lamb Memorial Studio, Montrose 39984
Winchester Cathedral Triforium Gallery,
  Winchester 40895

Wrest Park, Silsoe 40518
Wysing Arts, Bourn 38284
Yorkshire Sculpture Park, West Bretton 40820

Uruguay
Museo de Artes Plásticas, Madonado 40978

U.S.A.
Angel Orensanz Foundation Center for the Arts, New
York 45763
Brookgreen Gardens, Murrells Inlet 45574
Casa Amesti, Monterey 45452
Chapel Gallery, West Newton 48535
Crane Collection Gallery, Wellesley 48494
DeCordova Museum and Sculpture Park,
Lincoln 44777
Gallery II, Kalamazoo 44377
Gallery of Art, Overland Park 46223
Ginny Williams Family Foundation, Denver 42889
Grounds For Sculpture, Hamilton 43878
International Sculpture Center, Hamilton 43879
Irving Arts Center, Irving 44259
James and Meryl Hearst Center for the Arts, Cedar
Falls 42150
Johnson Atelier, Mercerville 45262
Joseph A. Cain Memorial Art Gallery, Corpus
Christi 42646
Krasl Art Center, Saint Joseph 47102
Laumeier Sculpture Park and Museum, Saint
Louis 47126
Mitchell Museum at Cedarhurst, Mount Vernon 45544
Myra Powell Art Gallery and Gallery at the Station,
Ogden 46099
Nathan Manilow Sculpture Park, University
Park 48151
National Liberty Museum, Philadelphia 46435
The North Shore Arts Association, Gloucester 43704
Sculpture Center, Long Island City 44872
Socrates Sculpture Park, Long Island City 44873
Umlauf Sculpture Garden and Museum, Austin 41424

Vatican City
Museo Gregoriano Profano, Città del Vaticano 48876

Venezuela
Museo de Arte Contemporáneo Francisco Narvárez,
Porlamar 48962

Vietnam
National Museum of Cham Sculpture, Da Nang 48969

Shells

Australia
Big Shell Museum, Tewantin 01524
Griffiths Sea Shell Museum and Marine Display, Lakes
Entrance 01161
Port Stephens Shell Museum, Corlette 00946
Rosewall Memorial Shell Museum, Port Lincoln 01384

Brazil
Museu Oceanográfico Prof. Eliézer de C. Rios, Rio
Grande 04408

China, People's Republic
Lushun Snakes Dao Natural Museum, Dalian 07038

Croatia
Malakološki Muzej, Makarska 07737

France
Museum du Coquillage, Les Sables-d'Olonne 12556

Germany
Buddelschiff-Museum, Wedel 20413
Internationales Muschelmuseum, Wangerland 20396
Muschel- und Schneckenmuseum, Norden 19112

Greece
Corfu Museum of Shells, Kastellanoi Mesis 21004
Museum of Shells of the Greek Seas, Néa
Moudiana 21099

Italy
Museo Conchiliologico e della Carta Moneta, Bellaria
Igea Marina 23047

Japan
Chiba-shi Kasori Kaizuka Hakubutsukan, Chiba 26123

Mozambique
Museu Ferreira de Almeida, Nampula 28730

Netherlands
Gloria Maris Schelpengalerie, Giethoorn 29281
Miramar Zeemuseum, Vledder 29949
Schelpen Museum, Zaamslag 30031

New Zealand
Picton Community Museum, Picton 30236

Oman
Oman Natural History Museum, Muscat 31006

United Kingdom
Glandford Shell Museum, Glandford 39038

Shipping → Boats and Shipping

Shoes

Austria
Stiefelmachermuseum, Rechnitz 02495

Belgium
Nationaal Schoeiselmuseum, Izegem 03523

Canada
Bata Shoe Museum, Toronto 06562

Czech Republic
Obuvnické Muzeum, Zlín 08752

France
Musée de la Cordonnerie, Alby-sur-Chéran 10278
Musée de l'Industrie Régionale de la Chaussure,
Saint-André-de-la-Marche 14105
Musée du Sabot, Buironfosse 10954
Musée du Sabotier, Soucht 14782
Musée International de la Chaussure, Romans-sur-
Isère 14016

Germany
Deutsches Schuhmuseum, Hauenstein 17641
Deutsches Schustermuseum, Burgkunstadt 16426
DLM - Deutsches Ledermuseum/ Schuhmuseum
Offenbach, Offenbach am Main 19239
Heimatmuseum Buchenberg, Buchenberg bei
Kempten 16387
Historisches Schuhmuseum, Landsberg am
Lech 18304
Museen im Alten Rathaus, Pirmasens 19401
Museum Schloß Neu-Augustusburg,
Weißenfels 20499

Italy
Museo della Bonifica, San Donà di Piave 25355
Museo della Calzatura, Sant'Elpidio a Mare 25461
Museo della Calzatura d'Autore di Rossimoda,
Strá 25638
Museo della Calzatura P. Bertolini, Vigevano 26007

Japan
Japan Footwear Museum, Fukuyama 26153

Mexico
Museo del Calzado El Borceguí, México 28153

Namibia
Leather Museum, Swakopmund 28771

Netherlands
Klompenmuseum De Platijn, Best 28984
Klompenmuseum Gebr. Wietzes, Eelde 29197
Klompenmuseum 't Oale Ambacht, Goor 29290
Klompenmuseum 't Schöpke Enter, Enter 29243
Museum de Klompenmaker, Keijenborg 29478
Nederlands Leder- en Schoenenmuseum,
Waalwijk 29974
Scherjon's Klompenmakerij en Museum,
Noardburgum 29639

Spain
Museo del Calzado, Elda 34795

Sweden
Skoindustrimuseet, Kumla 36022

Switzerland
Bally Schuhmuseum, Schönenwerd 37141

United Kingdom
Northampton Museum and Art Gallery,
Northampton 40084
Rossendale Footware Heritage Museum,
Rawtenstall 40292
Shoe Museum, Street 40635

Silk

China, People's Republic
China Silk Museum, Hangzhou 07080
Suzhou Silk Museum, Suzhou 07254

France
Atelier Municipal de Passementerie, Lyon 12723
Atelier-Musée de la Soie, Taulignan 14871
Chemin de la Soie, Molière-Cavaillac 13004
Musée de la Soie, Monoblet 13018
Musée des Vallées Cévenoles, Saint-Jean-du-
Gard 14289
Musée du Fil de Soie, Vierzon 15165
Musée du Mont-de-Piété et de la Condition des Soies,
Avignon 10530
Musée du Tissage et de la Soierie, Bussières 10960
Musée Maison de la Soie, Saint-Hippolyte-du-
Fort 14267

Germany
Haus der Seidenkultur, Krefeld 18224
Stadtmuseum Pirna, Pirna 19407

Greece
Silk Museum, Soufli 21162

India
Mysore Silk Museum, Bangalore 21704

Italy
Museo della Seta Abegg, Garlate 23962
Museo dell'Arte della Seta, Catanzaro 23452
Museo dell'Artigianato Tessile e della Seta, Reggio
Calabria 25090
Museo Didattico della Seta, Como 23628

Japan
Okaya Sericultural, Equipment and Literature and Silk
Museum, Okaya 26623
Silk Hakubutsukan, Yokohama 27019

Korea, Republic
Silk Museum, Gangnae 27165

Netherlands
Zijdemuseum, Meliskerke 29588

Spain
Museo del Tejido Sedero Valenciano, Valencia 35605

Sweden
Sidenväveri Museum, Stockholm 36279

United Kingdom
Macclesfield Silk Museum, Macclesfield 39865
Paradise Mill Silk Industry Museum,
Macclesfield 39866
Whitchurch Silk Mill, Whitchurch, Hampshire 40855

U.S.A.
Wistariahurst Museum, Holyoke 44066

Silver → Gold and Silver

Skeletons → Bones

Social Conditions

Angola
Museu da Escravatura, Luanda 00096

Argentina
De los Viejos Colonos, Bariloche 00135
Museo Comunitario de Villa Regina, Villa
Regina 00673
Museo Histórico Comunal y de la Colonización Judía
Rabino Aaron H. Goldman, Moisés Ville 00451
Museo Social Argentino de Universidad, Buenos
Aires 00244

Australia
ANZAC Memorial, Sydney 01489
History House, Portland 01390
Hou Wang Chinese Temple and Museum,
Atherton 00754
Immigration Museum, Melbourne 01234
Longreach Power House Museum, Longreach 01185
Meroogal House, Nowra 01336
Mulgrave Settlers Museum, Gordonvale 01066
Mundubbera and District Historical Museum,
Mundubbera 01289
National Museum of Australia, Canberra 00887
National Pioneer Women's Hall of Fame, Alice
Springs 00736
Vaucluse House, Vaucluse 01565
Wangaratta Exhibitions Gallery, Wangaratta 01576

Austria
Erstes Österreichisches Museum für
Alltagsgeschichte, Neupölla 02356
Museum Arbeitswelt Steyr, Steyr 02685
Museum der Gewerkschaft Agrar-Nahrung-Genuß,
Wien 02937
Museum im Hof, Sankt Pölten 02601
Österreichisches Gesellschafts- und
Wirtschaftsmuseum, Wien 02959

Belgium
Archief en Museum van het Vlaams Leven te Brussel,
Bruxelles 03269
Daensmuseum en Archief van de Vlaamse Sociale
Strijd, Aalst 03124
Museum van het Vlaams Studentenleven,
Leuven 03562
Pelgrom Museum Poorterswoning, Antwerpen 03167
Sint-Dimpna en Gasthuismuseum, Geel 03427

Benin
Musée d'Histoire, Ouidah 03875

Brazil
Memorial Pontes de Miranda da Justiça do Trabalho
em Alagoas, Maceió 04177
Museu da Terra e da Vida, Mafra 04186
Museu das Reduções, Ouro Preto 04237
Museu Histórico Visconde de São Leopoldo, São
Leopoldo 04475

Bulgaria
Okrăžen Istoričeski Muzej, Plovdiv 04780

Burkina Faso
Musée Provincial du Poni, Gaoua 04937

Canada
Hanna Pioneer Museum, Hanna 05581
Salvation Army George Scott Railton Museum,
Toronto 06608
Westfield Heritage Village, Rockton 06281

China, People's Republic
Museum of Dr. Sun Yat-Sen, Zhongshan 07331

Croatia
Muzej Grada Splita, Split 07783

Czech Republic
Muzeum a Pojizerská Galerie, Semily 08652
Památník Selského Povstáni, Rtyně v
Podkrkonoši 08644

Denmark
Arbejdermuseet, København 08921
Kvindemuseet i Danmark, Århus 08771
Socialmuseet Det Gamle Syge-Plejehjem,
Hinnerup 08875

Estonia
Heino Lubja Kaalumuuseum, Mustvee 09339

Finland
Amurin Työläismuseokortteli, Tampere 10075
Kauppilanmäen Museo, Valkeakoski 10171
Pelastusarmeijan Museo, Helsinki 09519
Rakennuskulttuuritalo Toivo ja Korsmanin talo,
Pori 09945
Teollisuustyöväen Asuntomuseo, Imatra 09568
Työväen Keskusmuseo, Tampere 10096
Vaajakosken Työläiskotimuseo, Jyväskylä 09606

France
CEDIAS Musée Social, Paris 13480
Familistère de Guise, Guise 11978
Maison de l'Outil et de la Pensée Ouvrière,
Troyes 15002
Musée d'Histoire 1939-1945 L'Appel de la Liberté,
Fontaine-de-Vaucluse 11761
Musée du Travail Charles-Peyre, Montfermeil 13081

Germany
Badisches Landesmuseum Karlsruhe,
Karlsruhe 17991
Blindenmuseum, Berlin 15924
Friedrich-Engels-Haus, Wuppertal 20710
Hans-Böckler-Geburtshaus, Trautskirchen 20192
Heimatmuseum, Friedland bei
Neubrandenburg 17142
Heimatmuseum, Herbrechtingen 17717
Historisches Museum Bielefeld, Bielefeld 16155
Industriemuseum Chemnitz, Chemnitz 16465
Karl-Marx-Haus, Trier 20210
Löhe-Zeit-Museum, Neuendettelsau 19024
Museum der Arbeit, Hamburg 17555
Museum der Stadt Rüsselsheim, Rüsselsheim 19708
Museum Der Kunststall, Dahlem 16528
Museum Malerwinkelhaus, Marktbreit 18644
Museum Schloss Lichtenberg, Fischbachtal 17007
Rheinisches Industriemuseum, Ratingen 19496
Ruhrlandmuseum Essen, Essen 16962
Schnarch-Museum Alfeld, Alfeld, Leine 15429
Schulze-Delitzsch-Haus, Delitzsch 16565
Speicherstadtmuseum, Hamburg 17567
Werra-Kalibergbau-Museum, Heringen, Werra 17723
Westfälisches Industriemuseum, Petershagen,
Weser 19379
Westfälisches Industriemuseum, Hattingen 17639
Westfälisches Industriemuseum, Dortmund 16666
Westfälisches Industriemuseum, Bochum 16202
Wetsfälisches Industriemuseum Zeche Nachtigall,
Witten 20623
Willi Dickhut Museum, Gelsenkirchen 17231

Hungary
Nógrádi Történeti Múzeum, Salgótarján 21523

Ireland
Custom House Visitor Centre, Dublin 22418
Irish Labour History Society Museum, Dublin 22435
The Kerry Bog Village Museum, Glenbeigh 22476

Italy
Museo del Lavoro, Castelmagno 23414
Museo delle Scienze della Terra e del Lavoro
Contadino, Piandimeleto 24896
Museo dell'Emigrante Casa Giannini, Favale di
Malvaro 23769
Museo dell'Emigrazione G.B. Scalabrini, Francavilla
Angitola 23931
Museo dell'Uomo e dell'Ambiente, Terra del
Sole 25698

Japan
Nagaoka Municipal Science Museum, Nagaoka 26533

Mauritius
Folk Museum of Indian Immigration, Moka 27734

Mexico
Museo Nacional de Culturas Populares, México 28187
Museo Niño Minero, Vetagrande 28597

Moldova
Muzeul Pedagogic Republican, Chişinău 28661

Namibia
Alte Feste, Windhoek 28778
Owela Display Centre, Windhoek 28782

Netherlands
Burger Weeshuis, Zierikzee 30059
Erotisch Museum, Amsterdam 28851
Museum Jannink, Enschede 29237
Museum voor Communicatie, Den Haag 29115
Nationaal Museum Verpleging en Verzorging, Zetten 30054
Nationaal Vakbondsmuseum De Burcht, Amsterdam 28886
Sexmuseum Amsterdam Venustempel, Amsterdam 28901
Westzaanse Bodemvondsten Kok-Voogt, Westzaan 30000
Woonbootmuseum, Amsterdam 28916

New Zealand
Catlins Historical Museum, Owaka 30224
Engine House, Dunedin 30147
Museum of Wellington, City and Sea, Wellington 30299
Otago Settlers Museum, Dunedin 30152
South Canterbury Museum, Timaru 30265

Norway
Funnefoss Industriarbeidermuseum, Årnes 30394
Labråten, Hvalstad 30575
Norsk Industriarbeidermuseet, Rjukan 30795
Trastad Samlinger, Borkenes 30444
Vesterålsmuseet, Melbu 30671

Poland
Muzeum Okregowe, Żyradów 32227
Muzeum Tradycji Niepodległościowych, Łódź 31778

Puerto Rico
Museo de Nuestra Raíz Africana, San Juan 32397

Romania
Punct Muzeal Gospodăria Tărănească, Enisala 32517

Russia
Centralnyj Muzej Vserossijskogo Obščestva Slepych, Moskva 33029
Muzej Nižegorodskoj Intelligencii, Nižnij Novgorod 33219
Muzej Obščestva Krasnogo Kresta Rossii, Moskva 33141
Muzej Obščestvennogo Pitanija, Moskva 33143
Ogni Moskvy - Muzej Istorii Gorodskogo Osveščenija, Moskva 33166

Senegal
Maison des Esclaves, Gorée 33781

Serbia-Montenegro
Muzej Kulturne Istorije, Požarevac 33892

Slovenia
Muzej Ljudske Revolucije Trbovlje, Trbovlje 34156

South Africa
Kimberley Mine Museum, Kimberley 34289

Spain
Museo Comarcal, Zalduondo 35711

Sweden
Arbetets Museum, Norrköping 36115
Emigrantmuseet, Kisa 36008
Gråbo Minnenas Museum, Karlskoga 35994
Säfsnäs Arbetarmuseum och Hembygdsgård, Fredriksberg 35894
Statarmuseum Mejeriet, Örebro 36140

United Kingdom
Bexhill Museum of Costume and Social History, Bexhill-on-Sea 38187
Blaise Castle House Museum, Bristol 38350
Buckleys Yesterday's World, Battle 38131
Cogges Manor Farm Museum, Witney 40910
Cookworthy Museum of Rural Life in South Devon, Kingsbridge 39374
East Carlton Steel Heritage Centre, East Carlton 38838
Elizabethan House Museum, Great Yarmouth 39123
Epping Forest District Museum, Waltham Abbey 40777
Heatherbank Museum of Social Work, Glasgow 39049
Highland Museum of Childhood, Strathpeffer 40633
Imperial War Museum North, Manchester 39890
Iona Heritage Centre, Isle-of-Iona 39316
Lancaster City Museum, Lancaster 39414
Landmark Forest Heritage Park, Carrbridge 38496
Langton Matravers Museum, Langton Matravers 39422
Luton Museum and Art Gallery, Luton 39845
Millgate Museum, Newark-on-Trent 40020
Montrose Museum and Art Gallery, Montrose 39983
Museum of Liverpool Life, Liverpool 39525
Museum of Smuggling History, Ventnor 40755
National Museum of Labour History, Manchester 39899
Patterson Heritage Museum and Family History Centre, Birchington 38202
People's History Museum, Manchester 39902
People's Story Museum, Edinburgh 38904
Pickford's House Museum, Derby 38718
Powysland Museum and Montgomery Canal Centre, Welshpool 40817
Prescot Museum, Prescot 40264
Ragged School Museum, London 39753
Saint John's House, Warwick 40793
Salvation Army International Heritage Centre, London 39772
Scaplen's Court Museum, Poole 40229
South Wales Miner's Museum, Port Talbot 40238
Summerlee Heritage Park, Coatbridge 38600
Swaledale Folk Museum, Reeth 40305
Tain and District Museum, Tain 40670
Town House Museum of Lynn Life, King's Lynn 39372
Ulster-American Folk Park, Omagh 40131
Waterfront Museum, Poole 40230
West Berkshire Museum, Newbury 40030
West Somerset Rural Life Museum, Allerford 37976
Weymouth Museum, Weymouth 40846

U.S.A.
Birmingham Civil Rights Institute Museum, Birmingham 41705
Black Heritage Museum, Miami 45282
Chesapeake and Ohio Canal Tavern Museum, Sharpsburg 47583
Cotting-Smith-Assembly-House, Salem 47191
The David Davis Mansion, Bloomington 41742
George Meany Memorial Exhibition, Silver Spring 47632
International Museum of Gay and Lesbian History, Los Angeles 44912
Prudence Crandall Museum, Canterbury 42082
The Sandor Teszler Gallery, Spartanburg 47717
Stone's Tavern Museum, Ligonier 44769
Tunica-Biloxi Native American Museum, Marksville 45167
Wapello County Historical Museum, Ottumwa 46222
Wenham Museum, Wenham 48508

Speleology

Austria
Höhlenmuseum, Obertraun 02377
Höhlenmuseum Eisensteinhöhle, Bad Fischau 01697
Höhlenmuseum in der Lurgrotte, Peggau 02395
Karst- und Höhlenkundliche Abteilung, Wien 02907
Obir-Tropfsteinhöhlen, Bad Eisenkappel 01695

Belgium
Natuurhistorisch Museum Boekenbergpark, Antwerpen 03163

Bulgaria
Muzej na Rodopskija Karst, Čepelare 04637

China, People's Republic
Art Museum of Dazu Rock Carvings in Chongqing, Chongqing 07029

France
Grotte de Rouffignac, Rouffignac-Saint-Cernin 14059
Grottes Préhistoriques de Sare-Lezea, Sare 14608
Musée Archeologique, Azé 10552
Musée de Spéléologie, Fontaine-de-Vaucluse 11760
Musée Français de Spéléologie, Gagny 11832
Musée Grotte de Limousis, Limousis 12618
Parc Préhistorique des Grottes de Fontirou, Castella 11070

Germany
Höhlenkundemuseum Dechenhöhle, Iserlohn 17921
Höhlenmuseum, Frasdorf 17087
Museum für Höhlenkunde, Laichingen 18292
Saalfelder Feengrotten, Saalfeld, Saale 19720

Italy
Museo Civico Geo-Speleologico, Garessio 23960
Museo Civico Speleo-Archeologico, Nuoro 24660
Museo di Paleontologia e Speleologia E.A. Martel, Carbonia 23345
Museo di Speleologia, Borgo Grotta Gigante 23171
Museo di Speleologia e Carsismo A. Parolini, Valstagna 25886
Museo di Speleologia Vincenzo Rivera, L'Aquila 24144
Museo Speleopaleontologico, Genga 23976
Museo Speologico, Sgonico 25565

Malta
Ghar Dalam Cave and Museum, Birzebbuga 27695

Mexico
Museo de la Cueva del Señor del Calvario, México 28138

New Zealand
Waitomo Museum of Caves, Waitomo Caves 30281

Slovakia
Slovenské Múzeum Ochrany Prírody a Jaskyniarstva, Liptovský Mikuláš 34017

Slovenia
Notranjski Muzej Postojna, Postojna 34139

South Africa
Cango Caves Interpretive Centre, Oudtshoorn 34318

Switzerland
Höhlenmuseum, Sundlauenen 37224
Musée Suisse de Spéléologie, Chamoson 36623

United Kingdom
Dan-yr-Ogof Showcaves Museum, Abercrave 37927
Llechwedd Slate Caverns, Blaenau Ffestiniog 38249
Wookey Hole Cave Diving and Archaeological Museum, Wookey Hole 40926

Spirits → Wines and Spirits

Sports and Recreation

Argentina
Museo del Deporte Pierre de Coubertin, La Falda 00380
Museo Municipal del Deporte, San Fernando del Valle de Catamarca 00558
Primer Museo Permanente del Boxeo Argentino, Buenos Aires 00252

Australia
Australian Gallery of Sport and Olympic Museum, Jolimont 01126
Golf Australia House, Melbourne 01230
Museum of Western Australian Sport, Claremont, Western Australia 00920
National Motor Racing Museum, Bathurst 00776

Austria
Alpenverein-Museum, Innsbruck 02059
Eisstockmuseum, Sankt Georgen im Attergau 02568
Internationales FIS Wintersport- und Heimatmuseum, Mürzzuschlag 02328
Jenbacher Museum, Jenbach 02086
Österreichisches Olympia- und Sportmuseum, Wien 02961
Österreichisches Wandermuseum, Alpl 01657
Salzburger Landes-Skimuseum, Werfenweng 02823
Ski- und Heimatmuseum, Sankt Anton am Arlberg 02558

Belgium
Sportmuseum Vlaanderen, Hofstade 03500

Brazil
Museu de Esportes Mané Garrincha, Rio de Janeiro 04358

Bulgaria
Nacionalen Muzej na Fizičeskata Kultura i Sport, Sofia 04850

Canada
Alberta Sports Hall of Fame and Museum, Red Deer 06220
Aquatic Hall of Fame, Winnipeg 06819
British Columbia Golf House Museum, Vancouver 06667
British Columbia Sports Hall of Fame and Museum, Vancouver 06670
Canada's Sports Hall of Fame, Toronto 06565
Canadian Baseball Hall of Fame, Toronto 06566
Canadian Football Hall of Fame and Museum, Hamilton 05568
Canadian Golf Hall of Fame, Oakville 06037
Canadian Golf Museum, Aylmer 05027
Canadian Lacrosse Hall of Fame, New Westminster 05983
Canadian Olympic Hall of Fame, Ottawa 06073
Canadian Scouting Museum, Ottawa 06074
Canadian Ski Museum, Ottawa 06075
Glengarry Sports Hall of Fame, Maxville 05826
Hockey Hall of Fame, Toronto 06585
International Ice Hockey Federation Museum, Kingston 05677
Manitoba Sports Hall of Fame and Museum, Winnipeg 06834
Musée Gilles-Villeneuve, Berthierville 05076
New Brunswick Sports Hall of Fame, Fredericton 05465
Northwestern Ontario Sports Hall of Fame, Thunder Bay 06545
Olympic Hall of Fame and Museum, Calgary 05177
Royal Saint John's Regatta Museum, Saint John's 06351
Saint John Sports Hall of Fame, Saint John 06337
Saskatchewan Baseball Hall of Fame and Museum, Battleford 05062
Saskatchewan Sports Hall of Fame and Museum, Regina 06248
Sports Hall of Memories, Trail 06629

China, People's Republic
China Sports Museum, Beijing 06962

Croatia
Hrvatski Sportski Muzej, Zagreb 07825

Cuba
Museo Casa Natal Juan Manuel Márquez, La Habana 07952
Museo de História del Deporte, La Habana 07959
Museo del Deporte, Cienfuegos 07890
Museo del Deporte, Holguín 08007

Cyprus
Cyprus Olympic Committee Museum, Lefkosia 08200

Czech Republic
Muzeum Tělovýchovy a Sportu, Praha 08597

Estonia
Eesti Spordimuuseum, Tartu 09377

Finland
Hiihtomuseo, Lahti 09740
Suomen Jääkiekko-Museo, Tampere 10085
Suomen Jalkapallomuseo, Valkeakoski 10173
Suomen Nyrkkeilymuseo, Tampere 10087
Suomen Urheilumuseo, Helsinki 09534
Varalan Liikuntamuseo, Tampere 10098

France
Musée des Ballons, Balleroy 10572
Musée des Cultures Taurines, Nîmes 13339
Musée des XVIes Jeux Olympiques d'Hiver, Albertville 10272
Musée du Ski, Besse-en-Chandesse 10706
Musée National du Sport, Paris 13638

Germany
Billardmuseum, München 18834
Deutsches Boxsport-Museum, Sagard 19731
Deutsches Skimuseum, Planegg 19410
Deutsches Sport- und Olympia-Museum, Köln 18130
Fischinger Heimathaus mit Schimuseum, Fischen im Allgäu 17008
Frankfurter Sportmuseum, Frankfurt am Main 17045
Friedrich-Ludwig-Jahn-Museum, Freyburg 17130
Grünauer Wassersportmuseum, Berlin 15979
Heimat- und Ski-Museum, Braunlage 16291
Motor-Sport-Museum Hockenheimring, Hockenheim 17775
Museum im Goetz-Haus, Leipzig 18408
Museum im Klösterle, Peiting 19369
Musik- und Wintersportmuseum, Klingenthal 18111
Schwäbisches Schützenmuseum, Kronburg 18250
Ski- und Heimatmuseum, Kurort Oberwiesenthal 18273
Ski- und Heimatmuseum Upfingen, Sankt Johann, Württemberg 19752
Skimuseum, Oberreute 19194
Sportmuseum Berlin, Berlin 16097
Sportmuseum Leipzig, Leipzig 18418
Stadtmuseum Teterow, Teterow 20161
Tennismuseum Gasber, Oberhausen, Rheinland 19179

Hungary
Testnevelési és Sportmúzeum, Budapest 21385

India
Mountaineering Museum, Darjeeling 21756
National Sportsmuseum, Patiala 21976

Israel
International Jewish Sports Hall of Fame, Netanya 22722
Pierre Gildesgame Maccabi Sports Museum, Ramat Gan 22734

Italy
Museo della SAT, Trento 25792
Museo Nazionale della Montagna Duca degli Abruzzi, Torino 25759

Japan
Chichibunomiya Kinen Supohtsu Hakubutsukan, Tokyo 26835
Hirano Hakabutsukan, Osaka 26647
Japanese Ski Memorial Museum, Joetsu 26281
Sapporo Winter Sports Museum, Sapporo 26721
Sports Car Museum of Japan, Gotemba 26159
Sumo Hakubutsukan, Tokyo 26927
Yakyu Taiiku Hakubutsukan, Tokyo 26957

Korea, Republic
Gukgiwon Taekwondo Museum, Seoul 27235
Korean Ski Museum, Ganseong 27170
Seoul Olympic Museum, Seoul 27277

Latvia
Latvijas Sporta Muzejs, Rīga 27421

Liechtenstein
Skimuseum, Vaduz 27518

Mexico
Museo Casa de la Bola, México 28114
Museo Comité Olímpico, México 28119
Museo del Deporte, Pabellón de Arteaga 28292
Salón de la Fama del Beisbol Profesional de México, Monterrey 28242

Netherlands
Ajax Museum, Amsterdam 28834
Het Eerste Friese Schaatsmuseum, Hindeloopen 29421
Groninger Schaatsmuseum, Sappemeer 29791
Kaatsmuseum, Franeker 29260
Max Euwe Centrum, Amsterdam 28872
Nationaal Schaakmuseum, Den Haag 29118
Het Nederlands Sportmuseum Olympion, Lelystad 29532

New Zealand
Bowls New Zealand Museum, New Plymouth 30212
National Scout Museum of New Zealand, Kaiapoi 30188
New Zealand Cricket Museum, Wellington 30302

New Zealands Rugby Museum, Palmerston
North 30229
Olympic Museum, Wellington 30305

Norway
Kongsberg Ski Museum, Kongsberg 30602
Norges Olympiske Museum, Lillehammer 30642
Skimuseet, Oslo 30762
Sondre Nordheimstova, Morgedal 30691

Poland
Muzeum Sportu i Turystyki, Łódź 31776
Muzeum Sportu i Turystyki, Warszawa 32126
Muzeum Sportu i Turystyki Regionu Karkonoszy,
Karpacz 31640
Muzeum Sportu i Turystyki Ziemi Gdańskiej,
Gdańsk 31575

Puerto Rico
Museo Puertorriqueño del Deportes, Salinas 32383

Russia
Muzej Grebnych Vidov Sporta, Moskva 33103
Muzej Istorii Poljarnych Olimpiad, Murmansk 33190
Muzej Obščestva Sporta Dinamo-Moskva,
Moskva 33142
Muzej Sporta v Lužnikach, Moskva 33150

South Africa
Rugby Museum, Newlands 34314

Spain
Museu Futbol Club Barcelona President Núñez,
Barcelona 34579
Museu i Centre d'Estudis de l'Esport Dr. Melcior Colet,
Barcelona 34582

Sweden
Borås Idrottsmuseum, Borås 35839
Helsingborgs Idrottsmuseum, Helsingborg 35950
Idrottsmuseet, Malmö 36073
Nordiska Travmuseet i Årjäng, Årjäng 35809
Sveriges Riksidrottsmuseum, Farsta 35886
Västerbottens Museum, Umeå 36349
Vasalopps Museet Mora, Mora 36102
Vasalopps Museet Sälen, Transtrand 36331

Switzerland
Alpines Ballonsport-Museum, Mürren 36969
Musée Olympique Lausanne, Lausanne 36866
Schweizerisches Alpines Museum, Bern 36552
Schweizerisches Schützenmuseum, Bern 36553
Schweizerisches Sportmuseum, Basel 36521
Wintersport-Museum, Davos Platz 36656

Turkey
Turkish Sports Museum, Şişli 37787

United Kingdom
Anfield Museum, Liverpool 39515
Artemis Archery Collection, Oldland 40129
British Cycling Museum, Camelford 38466
British Golf Museum, Saint Andrews 40381
Deep Sea Adventure and Diving Museum,
Weymouth 40842
Donington Grand Prix Collection, Castle
Donington 38501
James Gilbert Rugby Football Museum, Rugby 40355
Jim Clark Room, Duns 38820
Leicestershire CCC Museum, Leicester 39463
Manchester United Museum and Tour Centre,
Manchester 39896
MCC Museum, London 39706
Millwall FC Museum, London 39709
Museum of Rugby, Twickenham 40739
River and Rowing Museum, Henley-on-
Thames 39220
Rugby Art Gallery and Museum, Rugby 40356
Rugby School Museum, Rugby 40357
Scottish Football Museum, Glasgow 39067
Scottish Rugby Union Museum, Edinburgh 38918
Somerset Cricket Museum, Taunton 40678
Wimbledon Lawn Tennis Museum, London 39810

U.S.A.
Aiken Thoroughbred Racing Hall of Fame and
Museum, Aiken 41069
American Quarter Horse Heritage Center and
Museum, Amarillo 41165
American Sport Art Museum and Archives,
Daphne 42781
Babe Didrikson Zaharias Museum, Beaumont 41564
Babe Ruth Birthplace Museum, Baltimore 41451
Black Legends of Professional Basketball Museum,
Detroit 42915
College Football Hall of Fame, South Bend 47678
Colorado Ski Museum and Ski Hall of Fame,
Vail 48174
Don Garlits Museum of Drag Racing, Ocala 46081
Golf Museum, Far Hills 43288
Golf Museum, Newport News 45936
Green Bay Packer Hall of Fame, Green Bay 43788
Greyhound Hall of Fame, Abilene 41050
Harness Racing Museum and Hall of Fame,
Goshen 43733
Huntington Beach International Surfing Museum,
Huntington Beach 44169
Indiana Basketball Hall of Fame, New Castle 45685
Indianapolis Motor Speedway Hall of Fame Museum,
Indianapolis 44227
International Bowling Museum and Hall of Fame, Saint
Louis 47123

International Motor Racing Research Center, Watkins
Glen 48451
International Sport Aviation Museum, Lakeland 44602
International Swimming Hall of Fame, Fort
Lauderdale 43410
International Tennis Hall of Fame Museum,
Newport 45925
Kentucky Derby Museum, Louisville 44968
The Lacrosse Museum and National Hall of Fame,
Baltimore 41474
Legends of the Game Baseball Museum,
Arlington 41261
Lou Holtz and Upper Ohio Valley Hall of Fame, East
Liverpool 43055
Louisville Slugger Museum, Louisville 44971
Michigan Sports Hall of Fame, Detroit 42932
Naismith Memorial Basketball Hall of Fame,
Springfield 47748
National Art Museum of Sport, Indianapolis 44232
National Baseball Hall of Fame and Museum,
Cooperstown 42620
National Football Museum, Canton 42091
National Fresh Water Fishing Hall of Fame,
Hayward 43976
National Museum of Polo and Hall of Fame, Lake
Worth 44599
National Museum of Racing and Hall of Fame,
Saratoga Springs 47461
National Museum of Roller Skating, Lincoln 44788
National Museum of the Morgan Horse,
Shelburne 47592
The National Soccer Hall of Fame, Oneonta 46159
National Softball Hall of Fame and Museum Complex,
Oklahoma City 46117
National Wrestling Hall of Fame, Stillwater 47814
New England Ski Museum, Franconia 43504
Oregon Sports Hall of Fame and Museum,
Portland 46639
Paul W. Bryant Museum, Tuscaloosa 48116
Peter J. McGovern Little League Baseball Museum,
South Williamsport 47706
Pro Rodeo Hall of Fame and Museum of the American
Cowboy, Colorado Springs 42541
San Diego Hall of Champions Sports Museum, San
Diego 47288
Sanford Museum, Sanford 47394
Schwartz Collection of Skiing Heritage, Tiburon 48004
South Carolina Tennis Hall of Fame, Belton 41617
South Dakota Amateur Baseball Hall of Fame, Lake
Norden 44591
The Sports Museum of New England, Boston 41828
Texas Sports Hall of Fame, Waco 48270
United States Hockey Hall of Fame, Eveleth 43248
United States National Ski Hall of Fame and Museum,
Ishpeming 44263
Virginia Sports Hall of Fame and Museum,
Portsmouth 46666
Water Ski Hall of Fame, Polk City 46578
World Figure Skating Museum and Hall of Fame,
Colorado Springs 42543
World Golf Hall of Fame, Saint Augustine 47075
Yogi Berra Museum, Little Falls 44819

Venezuela
Museo del Beisbol, Caracas 48922

Stained Glass → Painted and Stained Glass

Stelae → Tombs

Stoves

Belgium
Musées Gaumais, Virton 03817

Germany
Egge-Museum Altenbeken, Altenbeken 15446
Eisenkunstgußmuseum, Witzenhausen 20636
Museum für Eisenkunstguß, Hirzenhain 17769

Netherlands
Haags Openbaar Vervoer Museum, Den Haag 29097
Haardplatenmuseum Klarenbeek, Klarenbeek 29482

Stucco

Germany
Kleines Stuck-Museum, Freiburg im Breisgau 17110
Schloss Salem, Salem, Baden 19733

Sugar

Austria
Österreichisches Zuckermuseum, Tulln 02746

Barbados
Sir Frank Hutson Sugar Museum, Saint James 03106

Canada
British Columbia Sugar Museum, Vancouver 06671
Maple Sugar Museum, Art Gallery and Pioneer Home,
Sundridge 06517
Redpath Sugar Museum, Toronto 06605

Cuba
Museo de la Industria Azucarera, Abel
Santamaría 07845

Germany
Zucker-Museum, Berlin 16119

Guadeloupe
Ecomusée de Marie Galante, Grand Bourg 21245

Indonesia
Museum Gula, Klaten 22147

Puerto Rico
Museo Castillo Serrallés, Ponce 32379

U.S.A.
The Judah P. Benjamin Confederate Memorial at
Gamble Plantation, Ellenton 43153
New England Maple Museum, Pittsford 46535

Tapestries

Belgium
Musée de la Tapisserie, Enghien 03405
Stedelijk Museum, Oudenaarde 03678
De Wit - Royal Manufacturers of Tapestries,
Mechelen 03622

France
Château d'Angers, Angers 10341
Château de Langeais, Langeais 12323
Château-Musée de la Grange, Manom 12792
Château-Musée du XVe et XVIIIe Siècle,
Commarin 11371
Galerie Nationale de la Tapisserie et de l'Art Textile,
Beauvais 10654
Musée d'Arts et d'Histoire, Hesdin 12018
Musée de la Tapisserie Contemporaine, Angers 10344
Musée de la Tapisserie de Bayeux, Bayeux 10616
Musée Départemental de la Tapisserie,
Aubusson 10467
Musée Jean-Lurçat, Angers 10349
Musée Leblanc-Duvernoy, Auxerre 10511
Musée Réattu, Arles 10417
Musée Sobirats, Carpentras 11059
Villa et Jardins Ephrussi de Rothschild, Saint-Jean-
Cap-Ferrat 14271

Italy
Museo Pinacoteca Santa Casa, Loreto 24215
Museo Storico della Tappezzeria, Bologna 23144
Pinacoteca Civica Bruno Molajoli, Fabriano 23748

Malaysia
Textile Museum, Kuala Lumpur 27653

Netherlands
Museumboerderij New Greenwich Village, Zuidwolde,
Drenthe 30072
Vierschaar Museum, Veere 29933

Spain
Museo Catedralicio, Lleida 34966
Museo Catedralicio, Zamora 35712
Museo Catedralicio de La Seo de Zaragoza,
Zaragoza 35719
Museo de Tapices, Oncala 35176
Museo Diocesano de Albarracín, Albarracín 34421
Museo Parroquial, Pastrana 35256
Real Fábrica de Tapices, Madrid 35061

Switzerland
Schloßmuseum Thun, Thun 37241

Tunisia
Ennejma Ezzahra-Palais du Baron d'Erlanger, Sidi Bou
Saïd 37582

United Kingdom
Hampton Court Palace, East Molesey 38848
Lanhydrock, Bodmin 38266
Lyme Hall, Disley 38732
Occupation Tapestry Gallery and Maritime Museum,
Saint Helier 40404
Upton House, Banbury 38076

Vatican City
Galleria degli Arazzi, Città del Vaticano 48870

Tea and Coffee

Angola
Museu do Café, Luanda 00098

Brazil
Museu do Café Cel. Francisco Schmidt, Ribeirão
Preto 04310

France
Musée du Thé, Paris 13607

Germany
Museum für Kaffeetechnik, Emmerich 16859
Museum Zum Arabischen Coffe Baum, Leipzig 18409
Das Ostfriesische Teemuseum und Norder
Heimatmuseum, Norden 19113

Iran
Muséyé Chay-e Lahijan, Lahijan 22261

Ireland
Bewley's Café Museum, Dublin 22415

Korea, Republic
Busan Woman's College Tea-ceremony Museum,
Busan 27139

Mauritius
Tea Museum, Bois-Cheri 27732

Mexico
Museo del Café, San Cristóbal de las Casas 28381

Netherlands
Geels Co. Koffie- en Theemuseum,
Amsterdam 28854
Koffie- en Theemuseum, Amsterdam 28867
Koffie- en Winkelmuseum, Pieterburen 29713
Museum Joure, Joure 29466
De Theefabriek, Houwerzijl 29451

Switzerland
Johann Jacobs Museum, Zürich 37382

United Kingdom
Bramah Tea and Coffee Museum, London 39582

Technology

Argentina
Museo Faryluk, Aristóbulo del Valle 00118
Museo Houssay de Historia de la Ciencia y
Técnología, Buenos Aires 00220
Museo Tecnológico Ingeniero Eduardo Latzina, Buenos
Aires 00245

Australia
Excell Blacksmith and Engineering Workshop
Museum, Tumby Bay 01554
Museum Victoria, Carlton South 00897
Powerhouse Museum, Ultimo 01558
Provan's Mechanical Museum, Colac 00936
Questacon The National Science and Technology
Centre, Canberra 00890
Scienceworks, Spotswood 01468
Scienceworks Museum, Melbourne 01242

Austria
Heizungsmuseum Wien, Wien 02896
Österreichisches Tonbandmuseum, Wien 02964
Technisches Museum Wien, Wien 02993

Bangladesh
Science Museum, Dhaka 03093

Belgium
Museum voor de Oudere Technieken,
Grimbergen 03462
Museum voor Industriele Archeologie en Textiel,
Gent 03447
Stedelijke Musea, Sint-Niklaas 03744
Technopolis, Mechelen 03621

Brazil
Museu da Energia, Itu 04138
Museu da Escola de Engenharia, Rio de
Janeiro 04342
Museu de Ciência e Tecnologia, Salvador 04431
Museu do Gás, Rio de Janeiro 04368
Museu Municipal, Cachoeira do Sul 04016
Museu Naval de Amazônia, Belém 03977
Museu Técnico-Científico do Instituto Oscar Freire,
São Paulo 04544

Bulgaria
Nacionalen Politechničeski Muzej, Sofia 04852

Canada
Alexander Graham Bell National Historic Site,
Baddeck 05031
Bell Homestead, Brantford 05124
Calgary Science Centre, Calgary 05165
Canada Science and Technology Museum,
Ottawa 06070

Heart's Content Cable Station, Heart's Content 05593
London Regional Children's Museum, London 05770
Ontario Science Centre, Toronto 06600

China, People's Republic
Hong Kong Science Museum, Hong Kong 07100
Shanghai Science Technology Museum, Shanghai 07223

Colombia
Museo de la Ciencia y el Juego, Bogotá 07406
Museo de los Niños, Bogotá 07407
Museo Mundocaña, Cali 07451
Museo Mundocaña, Palmira 07540
Museo Siderúrgico de Colombia, Nobsa 07535

Croatia
Tehnički Muzej, Zagreb 07838

Czech Republic
Hornické Muzeum OKD, Ostrava 08525
Hornický Skanzen důl Mayrau, Vinařice u Kladna 08719
Národní Technické Muzeum, Praha 08603
Stará Huť v Josefovském Údolí, Adamov 08241
Technické Muzeum, Petřvald u Karviné 08538
Technické Muzeum Tatra, Kopřivnice 08421
Textilní Muzeum TIBA, Česká Skalice 08296
Vojenské Technické Muzeum, Krhanice 08433
Výstavní Síň Muzea Těšínska, Orlová 08523

Denmark
Burmeister Wain's Museum, København 08924
Carlsberg Museum Valby, Valby 09099
Danmarks Tekniske Museum, Helsingør 08860
Elmuseet, Bjerringbro 08783
Experimentarium, Hellerup 08857

Egypt
Science Museum, Giza 09296
Science Museum, Alexandria 09247

Estonia
Õisu Tehnikumi Muuseum, Halliste 09321

Finland
Altia Oyj, Rajamäki 09975
Heureka - The Finnish Science Centre, Vantaa 10180
Polyteekkarimuseo, Espoo 09437
Strömforsin Teollisuusmuseo, Ruotsinpyhtää 10006
Tekniikan Museo, Helsinki 09541

France
Cité des Sciences et de l'Industrie, Paris 13484
Maison-Musée des Sciences, Lettres et Arts de Cholet et de sa Région, Cholet 11297
Musée de la Monnaie, Paris 13557
Musée de l'Automate et de la Robotique, Souillac 14787
Musée de l'Holographie, Paris 13575
Musée des Automates, Neuilly-sur-Seine 13291
Musée des Egouts de Paris, Paris 13589
Musée des Sciences, Laval (Mayenne) 12359
Musée Municipal de Millau, Millau 12980
Palais de la Découverte, Paris 13651

Germany
Arithmeum, Bonn 16228
ARP Museum Bahnhof Rolandseck, Remagen 19558
Ausstellungen im Bosch-Archiv, Stuttgart 20084
Automatik-Museum, Leipzig 18388
Computermuseum Aachen, Aachen 15370
Deutsches Museum, München 18839
Deutsches Museum - Verkehrszentrum, München 18840
Deutsches Technikmuseum Berlin, Berlin 15940
Erstes Tretauto-Museum der Welt, München 18845
Forum am Deutschen Museum, München 18849
Grammophonmuseum, Bad Urach 15755
Hanf-Museum, Berlin 15983
Hebezeug-Museum, Witten 20620
Heinz Nixdorf MuseumsForum, Paderborn 19334
Heizungsmuseum der Buderus Heiztechnik, Lollar 18501
Historisches Museum Bielefeld, Bielefeld 16155
Hütten- und Technikmuseum Ilsenburg, Ilsenburg 17892
Kellergedenkstätte Krippen, Bad Schandau 15734
Kinder-Akademie Fulda Werkraummuseum, Fulda 17177
Landesmuseum für Technik und Arbeit in Mannheim, Mannheim 18613
Märchenofen, Neu-Ulm 19010
Museum 3. Dimension, Dinkelsbühl 16617
Museum der Stadt Rüsselsheim, Rüsselsheim 19708
Museum für Astronomie und Technikgeschichte, Kassel 18024
Museum für Landtechnik und Landarbeit, Emmerthal 16863
Museum für Waage und Gewicht, Balingen 15799
Museum Ober-Ramstadt, Ober-Ramstadt 19167
Museum zum Anfassen, Ostseebad Binz 19311
Philipp-Reis-Gedächtnisstätte, Friedrichsdorf, Taunus 17145
Rechnermuseum der Gesellschaft für wissenschaftliche Datenverarbeitung, Göttingen 17339
Rheinisches Industriemuseum, Ratingen 19496
Rundfunkmuseum der Stadt Fürth, Fürth, Bayern 17166
Sammlungen der Technischen Universität Dresden, Dresden 16706
Siemens-Forum in Berlin, Berlin 16095
Silberwaren- und Bijouteriemuseum, Schwäbisch Gmünd 19863
Technik anno dazumal - Museum Kratzmühle, Kinding 18083
Technik Museum Speyer, Speyer 20013
Technik- und Verkehrsmuseum, Stade 20027
Technikmuseum Magdeburg, Magdeburg 18589
Technische Sammlungen der Stadt Dresden, Dresden 16713
Technisches Landesmuseum, Schwerin 19901
Universitätssammlungen Kunst Technik, Dresden 16714
Weltkulturerbe Völklinger Hütte, Völklingen 20328
Werksmuseum der Firma Linke-Hofmann-Busch, Salzgitter 19736

Ghana
Museum of Science and Technology, Accra 20789

Greece
Science Center of Thessaloniki and Technology Museum, Thessaloniki 21192

Hungary
Országos Műszaki Múzeum, Budapest 21373

India
Alpha Museum, Bangalore 21701
Bardhaman Science Centre, Bardhaman 21706
Birla Industrial and Technological Museum, Kolkata 21901
Birla Museum, Pilani 21981
District Science Centre, Purulia 21996
Goa Science Centre, Panaji 21972
Kurukshetra Panorama Science Centre, Kurukshetra 21918
Museum of the College of Engineering, Chennai 21747
National Science Centre, Delhi 21780
Nehru Science Centre, Mumbai 21952
Regional Science Centre, Tirupati 22039
Sanjay Sharma Museum, Jaipur, Rajasthan 21864
Visvesvaraya Industrial and Technological Museum, Bangalore 21705

Indonesia
Museum Science and Technology, Jakarta 22130

Iran
Time Museum, Teheran 22328

Ireland
College Museum, Maynooth 22518
Ireland's Historic Science Centre, Birr 22377

Israel
Bloomfield Science Museum Jerusalem, Jerusalem 22626
Havayeda Museum, Holon 22620
National Museum of Science, Planning and Technology, Haifa 22610

Italy
Museo degli Strumenti della Riproduzione del Suono, Roma 25185
Museo della Bonifica, Argenta 22926
Museo della Tecnica e del Lavoro MV Agusta, Samarate 25328
Museo dell'Informazione, Senigallia 25535
Museo di Informatica e Storia del Calcolo, Pennabilli 24834
Museo Leonardiano, Vinci 26026
Museo Nazionale della Scienza e della Tecnica Leonardo da Vinci, Milano 24408
Museo Postale e Telegrafico della Mitteleuropa, Trieste 25830

Japan
Gallery Abarth, Yamanakako 27006
Hirano Soundscape Museum, Yamatokoriyama 27007
Hiroshima Children's Museum, Hiroshima 26214
Ikomayama Uchu Kagakukan, Ikoma 26241
Kagaku Gijutsukan, Tokyo 26864
Kouseiroudoushou Sangyo Anzen Gijutsukan, Tokyo 26876
Kyoto Yuzen Bunka Kaikan, Kyoto 26432
Nagaoka Cog Museum, Nagaoka 26532
Nagasaki Science Museum, Nagasaki 26556
Nagoya-shi Kagakukan, Nagoya, Aichi 26570
Niigata Science Museum, Niigata 26593
NTT InterCommunication Center, Tokyo 26908
Osaka Science Museum, Osaka 26668
Otaru-shi Seishonen Kagakugijutsukan, Otaru 26680
Sendai Music Box Museum, Sendai 26735
Shiseido Art House, Kakegawa 26291
Tepia, Kikai Sangyo Kinenkan, Tokyo 26934
Tokyo Noko Daigaku Kogakubu Fuzoku Sen'i Hakubutsukan, Koganei 26364
Toshiba Kagakukan, Kawasaki 26330
The University Museum, Tokyo 26953

Korea, Republic
Museum of Chungju National University, Chungju 27153
Seoul National Science Museum, Seoul 27275

Latvia
Rīgas Motormuzejs, Rīga 27439

Mexico
Centro de Ciencia y Tecnología, Guadalajara 27944
Descubre Museo Interactivo de Ciencia y Tecnología, Aguascalientes 27753
Imagina-Museo Interactivo Puebla, Puebla 28316
Museo Casa de la Tecnología, Monterrey 28229
Museo de Ciencia, Cuernavaca 27873
Museo de Ciencia y Tecnología del Estado de Veracruz, Xalapa 28616
Museo de Ciencias de Ensenada, Ensenada 27915
Museo El Chapulín, Saltillo 28369
Museo Histórico de la Educación Tecnológica en México, Chilpancingo 27830
Museo Interactivo de Ciencia, Tecnología y Medio Ambiente Sol del Niño, Mexicali 28090
Museo Interactivo del Centro de Ciencias de Sinaloa, Culiacán 27885
Museo Interactivo El Rehilete, Pachuca 28296
Universum, Museo de las Ciencias de la UNAM, México 28213

Netherlands
De Dijk Te Kijk, Petten 29712
Explorion, Heerlen 29366
Expo Haringvliet, Stellendam 29855
Expozee, Lauwersoog 29500
Modelbouwmuseum, Wassenaar 29983
Museum De Cruquius, Cruquius 29058
Nationaal Baggermuseum, Sliedrecht 29829
NEMO, Amsterdam 28889
Nieuw Land Poldermuseum, Lelystad 29533
Poldermuseum Den Huijgen Dijck, Heerhugowaard 29365
Radiomuseum, Borculo 29002
Techniek Museum Delft, Delft 29087
Telefoonmuseum, Drouwen 29184

New Zealand
East Coast Museum of Technology, Gisborne 30163
Ferrymead Heritage Park, Christchurch 30128
Kaikohe Pioneer Village and Museum, Kaikohe 30189
Te Manawa Life Mind, Palmerston North 30231

Norway
Cementmuseet Slemmestad, Slemmestad 30855
Kongsberg Våpenfabrikks Museum, Kongsberg 30603
Norsk Teknisk Museum, Oslo 30754
Norsk Telemuseum - Kristiansand, Kristiansand 30614
Norsk Telemuseum - Lødingen, Lødingen 30646
Norsk Telemuseum - Sørvågen, Sørvågen 30870
Norsk Telemuseum - Stavanger, Stavanger 30886
Norsk Telemuseum - Trondheim, Trondheim 30940

Pakistan
National Museum of Science and Technology, Lahore 31040

Peru
Museo de Ciencias, Huánuco 31171

Philippines
Normisist Folk Inventions Museum, Butuan 31297
Rizal Technological and Polytechnic Institute Museum, Morong 31402
The Science Museum, Cebu 31316
Science Works!, Marikina 31401

Poland
Muzeum Budownictwa i Techniki Wiejskiej, Bogdaniec 31504
Muzeum Drukarstwa Warszawskiego, Warszawa 32093
Muzeum Gazownictwa, Paczków 31874
Muzeum Gazownictwa, Sobótka 31983
Muzeum Gazownictwa przy Gazowni Warszawskiej, Warszawa 32097
Muzeum Inżynierii Miejskiej, Kraków 31709
Muzeum Kolei Wąskotorowej w Wenecji, Wenecja 32150
Muzeum Okręgowe Zabytków Techniki, Tarnów 32044
Muzeum Politechniki Warszawskiej, Warszawa 32119
Muzeum Pożarnictwa Ziemi Olkuskiej, Olkusz 31849
Muzeum przy Zakładach Metalowych im. Hipolita Cegielskiego, Poznań 31910
Muzeum Techniki w Warzawie, Warszawa 32129
Muzeum Wikliniarstwa i Chmielarstwa, Nowy Tomyśl 31838
Muzeum Wojsk Inżynieryjnych, Wrocław 32191
Muzeum Zagłębia Staropolskiego w Sielpi, Sielpia 31971
Statek-Muzeum Dar Pomorza, Gdańsk 31581
Statek-Muzeum Dar Pomorza, Gdynia 31590
Statek-Muzeum Sołdek, Gdańsk 31582
Zabytkowa Kuźnia Wodna, Gdańsk 31584

Portugal
Museu Nacional da Ciência e da Técnica, Coimbra 32263

Romania
Muzeul Naţional al Petrolului, Ploieşti 32574
Muzeul Ştiinţei şi Tehnicii Ştefan Procopiu, Iaşi 32539

Russia
Memorialnyj Muzej-laboratorija A.S. Popova, Kronštadt 32965
Memorialnyj Muzej A.S. Popova, Sankt-Peterburg 33422
Memorialnyj Muzej A.S. Popova - Izobretatelja Radio, Krasnoturinsk 32961
Muzej Radio im. A.S. Popova, Ekaterinburg 32780
Politechničskij Muzej, Moskva 33174

Serbia-Montenegro
Muzej Nauke i Tehnike, Beograd 33807

Singapore
Singapore Science Centre, Singapore 33944

Slovakia
Slovenské Technické Múzeum, Košice 34005

Slovenia
Tehniški Muzej Slovenije, Ljubljana 34122

South Africa
Museum of Science and Technology, Pretoria 34349
South African National Museum of Military History, Saxonwold 34374

Spain
Colección del Observatorio de Cartuja, Granada 34868
Domus - Casa del Hombre, A Coruña 34748
Miramon Kutxaespacio de la Ciencia, Donostia-San Sebastián 34775
Museo de l'Enginyeria de Catalunya, Barcelona 34547
Museo Elder, Las Palmas de Gran Canaria 35242
Museo Lara, Ronda 35340
Museo Nacional de la Ciencia y la Tecnología, Madrid 35046
Museu de la Ciència i de la Tècnica de Catalunya, Terrassa 35527

Sweden
Dalénmuseet, Stenstorp 36228
Hogia PC-Museum, Stenungsund 36229
Innovatum Kunskapens Hus, Trollhättan 36335
Kareum - Gamla Bilsalongen, Sparreholm 36224
Observatoriemuseet, Stockholm 36270
Radiomuseet i Jönköping, Jönköping 35978
Rolf Bergendorffs Radio Museum, Lessebo 36031
Säffle Marinmotor Museum, Säffle 36167
Sveriges Rundradiomuseum, Motala 36107
Teknikens Hus, Luleå 36055
Teknikens och Sjöfartens Hus, Malmö 36080
Tekniska Kvarnen, Örebro 36141
Tekniska Museet, Stockholm 36293
Telemuseum, Stockholm 36294
Universeum, Göteborg 35923
Xperiment Huset, Växjö 36393

Switzerland
Einstein-Haus, Bern 36540
Musée d'Histoire des Sciences, Genève 36746
Museum-Telefonzentrale, Magden 36919
Technorama, Winterthur 37341

Thailand
Science Centre for Education, Bangkok 37495

United Kingdom
Abbey Pumping Station Museum, Leicester 39458
Alderney Railway - Braye Road Station, Alderney 37963
Amberley Working Museum, Amberley 37995
At-Bristol, Bristol 38349
Bletchley Park Exhibition, Bletchley 38259
Bressingham Steam Museum, Diss 38733
British Balloon Museum, Newbury 40029
British Engineerium, Hove 39268
Cambridge Museum of Technology, Cambridge 38451
Carshalton Water Tower, Carshalton 38498
Charney Bassett Mill, Charney Basset 38526
Discovery Museum, Newcastle-upon-Tyne 40035
Great Orme Tramway, Llandudno 39540
Inspire - Hands-on Science Centre, Norwich 40094
Ironbridge Tollhouse, Ironbridge 39309
Jodrell Bank Science Centre and Arboretum, Macclesfield 39864
John King Workshop Museum, Pinxton 40203
Kirkaldy Testing Museum, London 39682
Llangollen Railway, Llangollen 39554
Long Shop Museum, Leiston 39475
Look Out Discovery Centre, Bracknell 38292
Museum of Science and Industry in Manchester, Manchester 39898
National Space Centre, Leicester 39467
Oliver Cromwell's House, Ely 38934
Oswestry Transport Museum, Oswestry 40137
Porthcurno Telegraph Museum, Porthcurno 40241
Prickwillow Drainage Engine Museum, Prickwillow 40271
Railway Preservation Society of Ireland, Whitehead 40858
Royal Air Force Air Defence Radar Museum, Norwich 40098
Royal Engineers Museum, Chatham 38532
Science Museum, London 39773
Techniquest, Cardiff 38484
Thinktank, Birmingham 38230
Tower Bridge Exhibition, London 39791
Wilton Windmill, Wilton, Marlborough 40877

U.S.A.
American Museum of Radio, Bellingham 41601
American Museum of Science and Energy, Oak Ridge 46055
American Precision Museum, Windsor 48685
Ann Arbor Hands-On Museum, Ann Arbor 41214
Arkansas Museum of Natural Resources, Smackover 47655
A.W.A. Electronic-Communication Museum, Bloomfield 41736
The B O Railroad Museum, Baltimore 41450

Baker-Cederberg Museum, Rochester 46938
The Bakken, Minneapolis 45381
Baltimore Museum of Industry, Baltimore 41455
Betty Brinn Children's Museum, Milwaukee 45359
Boulder City-Hoover Dam Museum, Boulder City 41839
California Science Center, Los Angeles 44894
Carnegie Science Center, Pittsburgh 46512
Catawba Science Center, Hickory 44006
Charles River Museum of Industry, Waltham 48296
Children's Discovery Museum of Central Illinois, Bloomington 41741
Children's Museum of History, Natural History and Science at Utica, New York, Utica 48169
The Children's Science Center, Cape Coral 42094
Cle Elum Telephone Museum, Cle Elum 42447
Coca-Cola Memorabilia Museum of Elizabethtown, Elizabethtown 43133
Columbia River Exhibition of History, Science and Technology, Richland 46855
COSI Columbus, Columbus 42588
Cosi Toledo, Toledo 48019
CTS Turner Museum, Elkhart 43139
Cumberland Science Museum, Nashville 45615
Discovery Center, Fresno 43557
Discovery Center of Springfield, Springfield 47752
Discovery Center Science Museum, Fort Collins 43379
Discovery Museum History Center, Sacramento 47051
The Discovery Museums, Acton 41062
Discovery Park, Safford 47059
Discovery Place, Charlotte 42239
Discovery Science Center of Central Florida, Ocala 46080
Discovery World - The James Lovell Museum of Science, Economics and Technology, Milwaukee 45361
Don Harrington Discovery Center, Amarillo 41166
Eli Whitney Museum, Hamden 43876
Elwood Haynes Museum, Kokomo 44526
Essex Shipbuilding Museum, Essex 43213
Explora Science Center and Children's Museum, Albuquerque 41100
Fort Discovery, Augusta 41382
The Franklin Institute, Philadelphia 46411
Franklin Mint Museum, Franklin Center 43523
Frontiers of Flight Museum, Dallas 42753
Great Explorations, Saint Petersburg 47173
Great Lakes Science Center, Cleveland 42473
Gulf Coast Exploreum, Mobile 45419
The Hagley Museum, Wilmington 48652
Hands on Children's Museum, Olympia 46141
Healdton Oil Museum, Healdton 43979
Hicksville Gregory Museum, Hicksville 44010
Hidalgo Pumphouse Heritage, Hidalgo 44011
Historical Electronics Museum, Linthicum 44809
Hoover Historical Center, North Canton 45986
Hudson Valley Children's Museum, Nanuet 45599
The Imaginarium, Anchorage 41200
Imaginarium Hands-On Museum, Fort Myers 43437
Imagination Station Science Museum, Wilson 48669
Imagisphere Children's Museum, North Richland Hills 46005
The Invention Factory, Trenton 48055
Jefferson Telephone Museum, Jefferson 44322
John Gorrie Museum, Apalachicola 41236
John Rivers Communications Museum, Charleston 42220
Kalamazoo Valley Museum, Kalamazoo 44380
Lawrence Hall of Science, Berkeley 41644
Long Island Museum of Science and Technology, Garden City 43620
Louisiana Tech Museum, Ruston 47039
Louisville Science Center, Louisville 44970
McWane Center, Birmingham 41707
Margaret Hutchinson Compton Gallery, Cambridge 42045
Maryland Science Center, Baltimore 41479
Memphis Pink Palace Museum, Memphis 45244
Mercer Museum of the Bucks County Historical Society, Doylestown 42985
Michigan State Trust for Railway Preservation, Owosso 46233
Mid-America Science Museum, Hot Springs 44109
Milton J. Rubenstein Museum of Science and Technology, Syracuse 47910
The MIT Museum, Cambridge 42048
Motorola Museum, Schaumburg 47495
Mount Vernon Museum of Incandescent Lighting, Baltimore 41482
Museum of Anthracite Mining, Ashland 41298
Museum of Independent Telephony, Abilene 41051
Museum of Radio and Technology, Huntington 44167
Museum of Robotics, Orinda 46182
Museum of Science, Boston 41818
Museum of Science and Industry, Chicago 42349
Museum of Science and Industry, Tampa 47943
National Canal Museum, Easton 43069
National Inventors Hall of Fame, Akron 41073
New England Wireless and Steam Museum, East Greenwich 43041
New Mexico Museum of Space History, Alamogordo 41077
New York Hall of Science, Flushing 43355
Oregon Museum of Science and Industry, Portland 46638
Orlando Science Center, Orlando 46189
Outagamie Museum and Houdini Historical Center, Appleton 41240
Pacific Science Center, Seattle 47543
The Petroleum Museum, Midland 45329
Real World Computer Museum, Boothwyn 41792
Remington Firearms Museum and Country Store, Ilion 44195
Reuben H. Fleet Science Center, San Diego 47285
Rocky Reach Dam, Wenatchee 48506
Rosalie House, Eureka Springs 43235
Saint Louis Science Center Museum, Saint Louis 47136
Schenectady Museum, Schenectady 47498
Sci-Port Discovery Center, Shreveport 47617
Sci-Tech Center of Northern New York, Watertown 48443
Science and Technology Museum of Atlanta, Atlanta 41358
Science Center of Connecticut, West Hartford 48529
Science Center of Iowa, Des Moines 42910
Science Center of West Virginia, Bluefield 41759
Science Discovery Center of Oneonta, Oneonta 46160
The Science Factory, Eugene 43227
Science Museum of Minnesota, Saint Paul 47166
Science Museum of Virginia, Richmond 46886
Science Spectrum, Lubbock 44992
Sciencenter, Ithaca 44274
Scitech, Aurora 41399
Sciworks, Winston-Salem 48704
Sloane-Stanley Museum and Kent Furnace, Kent 44444
Sloss Furnaces National Historic Landmark, Birmingham 41708
Smithsonian Institution, Washington 48393
Sony Wonder Technology Lab, New York 45873
South Dakota Discovery Center, Pierre 46485
South Florida Science Museum, West Palm Beach 48540
Southwest Museum of Science and Technology, Dallas 42759
Space Center Houston, Houston 44138
Spartanburg Science Center, Spartanburg 47719
SPC Pioneer Museum, San Francisco 47341
Springfield Science Museum, Springfield 47750
Stevens County Gas and Historical Museum, Hugoton 44148
Telephone Pioneer Museum of New Mexico, Albuquerque 41109
Thomas Edison House, Louisville 44977
Thomas Newcomen Museum, Exton 43255
Titan Missile Museum, Green Valley 43795
United States Army Aviation Museum, Fort Rucker 43450
United States Army Communications-Electronics Museum, Fort Monmouth 43430
US Patent and Trademark Office - Museum, Arlington 41267
Vestal Museum, Vestal 48225
Western Museum of Mining and Industry, Colorado Springs 42542
Wheels O' Time Museum, Peoria 46351
Willamette Science and Technology Center, Eugene 43229
The Works, Newark 45899

Venezuela
Museo de Ciencias, Caracas 48916

Telecommunications → Postal Services

Television → Mass Media

Terracotta

Brazil
Museu da Bacia do Paraná, Maringá 04199

Italy
Collezione di Ceramiche Mostra Permanente, Fiorano Modenese 23819
Mostra Permanente della Ceramica, San Lorenzello 25382
Museo Civico delle Ceramiche, Santo Stefano di Camastra 25465
Museo della Ceramica A. Ribezzi, Latiano 24156
Museo della Tecnica e del Lavoro MV Augusta, Trequanda 25798
Museo Ocarina e degli Strumenti in Terracotta, Budrio 23225

Vatican City
Museo Gregoriano Etrusco, Città del Vaticano 48875

Textiles

Australia
Ararat Gallery, Ararat 00746
Frances Burke Textile Resource Centre, Melbourne 01226
Tamworth City Gallery, Tamworth 01515

Austria
Lebendes Textilmuseum, Groß Siegharts 01949
Modesammlung, Wien 02931
Textildruckmuseum Mittelweiherburg, Hard, Vorarlberg 02001
Textilmuseum Firma Franz Pischl, Telfs 02721
Wien Museum Hermesvilla mit Schauräumen der Modesammlung, Wien 03000

Belgium
Kant- en Textielcentrum, Diest 03385
Modemuseum Provincie Antwerpen, Antwerpen 03149
Musée de la Rubanerie Cominoise, Comines 03360
Museum van Hedendaagse Kantwerken, Sint-Truiden 03750
Stedelijk Textielmuseum, Ronse 03713

Bulgaria
Muzej na Tekstilnata Industrija, Sliven 04822

Canada
Barrington Woolen Mill Museum, Barrington 05051
Clothing and Textiles Museum, Winnipeg 06821
Mississippi Valley Textile Museum, Almonte 04979
Musée Beaulne, Coaticook 05260
Musée Marsil, Saint-Lambert 06359
Museum for Textiles, Toronto 06595
Red Deer and District Museum, Red Deer 06222
Ukrainian Museum of Canada, Saskatoon 06407
Ukrainian Museum of Canada - Ontario Branch, Toronto 06623
Wile Carding Mill Museum, Bridgewater 05131

Czech Republic
Městské Muzeum, Moravská Třebová 08485
Muzeum, Zábřeh na Moravě 08736
Muzeum Krnov, Krnov 08434
Památník Jiráskova Pokladu, Potštejn 08559
Textilní Muzeum TIBA, Česká Skalice 08296

Denmark
Textilforum, Herning 08871

France
Atelier-Musée des Tisserands et de la Charentaise, Varaignes 15086
Ecomusée du Roannais, Roanne 13984
Maison de Pays, Sainte-Marie-aux-Mines 14540
Maison du Lin, Routot 14066
Musée Arménien de France, Paris 13530
Musée de la Soierie, Charlieu 11181
Musée de la Viscose, Échirolles 11596
Musée de l'Impression sur Etoffes, Mulhouse 13208
Musée Departemental du Textile, Lavelanet 12370
Musée des Tapisseries, Aix-en-Provence 10252
Musée des Tissus, Lyon 12741
Musée du Costume Comtois, Montgesoye 13089
Musée du Fer et du Fil, Dompierre (Orne) 11548
Musée du Feutre, Mouzon 13202
Musée du Textile des Vosges, Ventron 15124
Musée du Textile et du Peigne en Corne, Lavelanet 12371
Musée du Textilen, La Labastide-Rouairoux 12203
Musée Municipal de la Toile de Jouy, Jouy-en-Josas 12096
Musée National des Arts Asiatiques Guimet, Paris 13633
Musée Souleïado Charles Demery, Tarascon (Bouches-du-Rhône) 14862
Musée Textile de Haute-Alsace, Husseren-Wesserling 12040
Musées de La Poëslerie et de la Dentelle, Villedieu-les-Poêles 15196

Germany
Brandenburgisches Textilmuseum Forst, Forst, Lausitz 17023
Deutsches Damast- und Frottiermuseum Großschönau, Großschönau, Sachsen 17440
Deutsches Textilmuseum Krefeld, Krefeld 18223
Erstes Deutsches Strumpfmuseum, Gelenau, Erzgebirge 17222
Flachsmuseum Beeck, Wegberg 20419
Heimatmuseum Fronfeste, Limbach-Oberfrohna 18468
Kreismuseum Zons, Dormagen 16646
Leinen- und Spitzenmuseum Haigerseelbach, Haiger 17490
Maschenmuseum, Albstadt 15418
Museum auf dem Burghof, Springe 20019
Museum Haus Martfeld, Schwelm 19894
Museumshof, Rahden 19475
Oberfränkisches Textilmuseum, Helmbrechts 17701
Rheinisches Industriemuseum Euskirchen, Euskirchen 16977
Schraube Museum, Halberstadt 17503
Textilmuseum, Neumünster 19048
Textilmuseum Die Scheune, Nettetal 19001
Textilmuseum im Jesuitenkolleg, Mindelheim 18746
Textilmuseum Max Berk im Kurpfälzischen Museum der Stadt Heidelberg, Heidelberg 17676
Tuchmacher-Museum Bramsche, Bramsche 16273
Westfälisches Industriemuseum, Textilmuseum, Bocholt 16191
Westsächsisches Textilmuseum Crimmitschau, Crimmitschau 16514

Greece
Corgialenios Historical and Cultural Museum, Argostolion 20835

Guatemala
Museo Ixchel del Traje Indigena, Guatemala 21270

Hungary
Textilmúzeum, Budapest 21386

Iceland
Heimilisidnardarsafnid Halldórustofa, Blönduós 21624

India
Calico Museum of Textiles, Ahmedabad 21677
College of Textile Technology Museum, Hooghly 21840
Kachchh Museum, Bhuj 21728
Sardar Vallabhbhai Patel Museum, Surat 22030
State Kala Akademi Museum, Imphal 21858
TTD Museum, Tirupati 22040

Indonesia
Museum Batik, Pekalongan 22174
Museum Takstil, Jakarta 22134

Italy
Museo dei Damaschi, Lorsica 24221
Museo del Tessile, Chieri 23538
Museo del Tessuto, Prato 25045
Museo di Palazzo Mocenigo, Venezia 25938

Japan
Bunka Gakuen Fukushoku Hakabutsukan, Tokyo 26833
Kanebo Museum of Textiles, Osaka 26650
Kenji Igarashi Memorial Museum, Tokyo 26868
Nishijin Textile Center, Kyoto 26441
Oriamu Museum, Izumiotsu 26278
Orinasukan, Kyoto 26445

Mexico
Museo Textil La Trinidad, Santa Cruz Tlaxcala 28431

Netherlands
Art of Velvet Gallery De Stierenstal, Montfoort 29602
Nederlands Textielmuseum, Tilburg 29880
De Wascht en Strekt, Gilze 29284

Norway
Norsk Trikotasjemuseum, Salhus 30817
Råde Bygdetun, Råde 30783

Poland
Centralne Muzeum Włókiennictwa, Łódź 31765

Portugal
Museu de Francisco Tavares Proença Júnior, Castelo Branco 32251

Russia
Muzej Ivanovskogo Sitca, Ivanovo 32831

Spain
Centre de Documentació i Museu Tèxtil, Terrassa 35525
Museo Etnográfico Textil Pérez Enciso, Plasencia 35273
Museo Etnológico de Morella y del Meastrazgo, Morella 35141
Museu de l'Estampació de Premià de Mar, Premià de Mar 35295

Sweden
Dock- och Textilmuseum, Katrineholm 36004
Lövångers Sockenmuseum, Lövånger 36049
Norrköpings Stadsmuseum, Norrköping 36121
Regionmuseet Kristianstad, Kristianstad 36018
Rydals Museum, Rydal 36166
Skattkammaren - Uppsala Domkyrkas Museum, Uppsala 36360
Textilarkivet Västernorrland, Sollefteå 36217
Textilmuseet, Borås 35843
Textilmuseet Högbo, Sandviken 36181

Switzerland
Freiämter Strohmuseum, Wohlen (Aargau) 37348
Musée des Toiles Peintes, Colombier 36643
Museum Bellerive, Zürich 37395
Ortsmuseum Diessenhofen, Diessenhofen 36660
Textil- und Heimatmuseum, Sennwald 37162
Textilmaschinenmuseum Neuthal, Bäretswil 36490
Textilmuseum, Hauptwil 36794

Turkey
Vakıf Kilim ve Düz Dokuma Yaygılar Müzesi, İstanbul 37714

United Kingdom
Andrew Carnegie Birthplace Museum, Dunfermline 38808
Bankfield Museum, Halifax 39149
Childhood and Costume Museum, Bridgnorth 38322
Colour Museum, Bradford 38297
Eyhorne Manor Laundry Museum, Hollingbourne 39252
Falkland Palace and Garden, Falkland 38970
Friary Art Gallery, Lichfield 39489
Guildford House Gallery, Guildford 39137
Helmshore Textile Museums, Helmshore 39211
Irish Linen Centre and Lisburn Museum, Lisburn 39510
Lewis Textile Museum, Blackburn, Lancashire 38244
Newarke Houses Museum, Leicester 39468

Paulise de Bush Costume Collection, Broadclyst — 38364
Ruddington Framework Knitters' Museum, Ruddington — 40351
Saddleworth Museum and Art Gallery, Uppermill — 40752
Scottish Museum of Woollen Textiles, Walkerburn — 40766
Textile Conservation Centre, Winchester — 40893
Totnes Costume Museum, Totnes — 40723
Trowbridge Museum, Trowbridge — 40729
Verdant Works, Dundee — 38807
Weavers' Triangle Visitor Centre, Burnley — 38402

U.S.A.
Ace of Clubs House, Texarkana — 47990
American Textile History Museum, Lowell — 44982
Big Red Barn Gallery, Clearmont — 42451
Dar American First Ladies of Texas Historic Costumes Collection, Denton — 42874
The Design Center at Philadelphia University, Philadelphia — 46402
Elizabeth Sage Historic Costume Collection, Bloomington — 41745
The Fabric Workshop and Museum, Philadelphia — 46408
The Goldstein Museum of Design, Saint Paul — 47154
Grovewood Gallery, Asheville — 41280
Gustafson Gallery, Fort Collins — 43381
Helen Louise Allen Textile Collection, Madison — 45068
Lace Museum, Sunnyvale — 47885
Liberace Museum, Las Vegas — 44671
Mattye Reed African Heritage Center, Greensboro — 43817
Milan Historical Museum, Milan — 45334
Museum of the American Quilter's Society, Paducah — 46256
New England Quilt Museum, Lowell — 44986
Quilters Hall of Fame, Marion — 45159
Reuel B. Pritchett Museum, Bridgewater — 41895
Rocky Mountain Quilt Museum, Golden — 43715
San Jose Museum of Quilts and Textiles, San Jose — 47357
Scalamandre Archives, Long Island City — 44871
Slater Mill Historic Site, Pawtucket — 46318
South Carolina Cotton Museum, Bishopville — 41718
The Textile Museum, Washington — 48397
Wilmette Historical Museum, Wilmette — 48646
Windham Textile and History Museum, Willimantic — 48637

Theatre → Performing Arts

Tin Figures → Lead and Tin Figures

Tobacco

Australia
Tobacco Museum, Texas — 01528

Austria
Art Cult Center - Tabakmuseum, Wien — 02836
Heimatmuseum und Pfeifenmuseum, Sankt Aegyd am Neuwalde — 02556
Stadtmuseum Wienertor Hainburg, Hainburg an der Donau — 01988
Tabakmuseum, Oberzeiring — 02382

Belgium
Historisch Pijp en Tabaksmuseum, Sint-Niklaas — 03739
Musée du Cheval, de la Vie Rurale et du Tabac, Thuillies — 03776
Musée du Vieux Nimy, Mons — 03636
National Tobacco Museum, Wervik — 03835
Stedelijk Museum voor Pijp en Tabak, Harelbeke — 03477

Canada
Delhi Ontario Tobacco Museum Heritage Centre, Delhi — 05319

Cuba
Museo Casa de Puerto Rico y Sala del Tabaco, La Habana — 07946

France
Musée d'Intérêt National du Tabac, Bergerac — 10689

Germany
Deutsches Tabak- und Zigarrenmuseum, Bünde — 16402
Deutsches Tabakpfeifenmuseum, Oberelsbach — 19174
Oberrheinisches Tabakmuseum, Mahlberg — 18591
Schnupftabakmuseum, Grafenau, Niederbayern — 17368
Tabak-Museum der Stadt Hockenheim, Hockenheim — 17776
Tabakhistorische Sammlung Reemtsma, Hamburg — 17570
Tabakmuseum, Lorsch — 18506

Japan
Tabako to Shio no Hakubutsukan, Tokyo — 26929

Netherlands
Amerongs Historisch Museum/ Tabaksmuseum, Amerongen — 28817
Kamper Tabaksmuseum, Kampen — 29471
Museum De Moriaan, Gouda — 29296
Museum Joure, Joure — 29466
Niemeyer Tabaksmuseum, Groningen — 29314
Pijpenkabinet Smokiana, Amsterdam — 28895

Puerto Rico
Museo del Tabaco Herminio, Caguas — 32368

Slovenia
Tobačni Muzej, Ljubljana — 34123

Sweden
Tobaks- och Tändstickmuseum, Stockholm — 36296

United Kingdom
Clay Tobacco Pipe Museum, Broseley — 38379

Tombs

Australia
Camperdown Cemetery, Newtown — 01320
Sexton's Cottage Museum, Crows Nest — 00956

Austria
Freilichtmuseum Spätbronzezeitlicher Hügelgräber, Siegendorf — 02660
Kaisergruft, Wien — 02905
Wiener Bestattungsmuseum, Wien — 03002

China, People's Republic
Beijing Dabaotai Western Han Tomb Museum, Beijing — 06948
Lei Cheng Uk Han Tomb Museum, Hong Kong — 07104
Municipal Museum, Jiuquan — 07141

Croatia
Muzej Hvarske Baštine, Hvar — 07707

Cuba
Museo Chorro de Maita, Yaguajay — 08178

Cyprus, Turkish Republic
Canbulat Türbe ve Müzesi, Gazimağusa — 08217

Denmark
Ladbyskibsmuseet, Kerteminde — 08916

Germany
Archäologisches Museum im Rathaus, Weichering — 20423
Bajuwarenmuseum Waging am See, Waging — 20343
Heimatkundliche Sammlung Burg Rheinfels, Sankt Goar — 19750
Museum Burg Linn, Krefeld — 18228
Museum für Sepulkralkultur, Kassel — 18025
Museum Kloster Asbach, Rotthalmünster — 19694

Greece
Archeological Collection, Feres — 20953

Israel
Dominus Flevit, Jerusalem — 22630

Italy
Ipogeo dei Volumni, Ponte San Giovanni — 24993
Museo Civico, Troia — 25837
Museo Civico Aufidenate De Nino, Alfedena — 22851
Museo della Badia Benedettina, Cava dei Tirreni — 23458
Museo di Archeologia Sacra e Profana, Roma — 25210
Museo Nazionale Archeologico, Tarquinia — 25674
Tombe Reali di Casa Savoia, Torino — 25767

Mexico
Museo de la Muerte, San Juan del Río — 28392
Museo de Momias de Celaya, Celaya — 27810

Spain
Museo Provincial, Lugo — 34987
Museu i Necròpolis Paleocristians, Tarragona — 35515

Sweden
Sundsvalls Museum, Sundsvall — 36309

Switzerland
Museo Plebano, Agno — 36436
Museum im Turmhof, Steckborn — 37209
Sammlung Friedhof Hörnli, Riehen — 37062

Turkey
Çifte Minareli Medrese Müzesi, Erzurum — 37670
Selçuk Müzesi, Konya — 37745
Sırçalı Medrese Müzesi, Konya — 37746

United Kingdom
Infirmary Museum, Saint Ronan's Church Museum and Columba Centre, Isle-of-Iona — 39315

Vatican City
Museo Pio Cristiano, Città del Vaticano — 48880

Tools

Australia
Excell Blacksmith and Engineering Workshop Museum, Tumby Bay — 01554
Norseman Historical and Geological Collection, Norseman — 01324
Victoria's First Hardware Museum, Sorrento — 01457

Canada
City of York Museum, York — 06872

Denmark
Give-Egnens Museum, Give — 08837
Mariager Museum, Mariager — 08979

Finland
Jokioisten Naulamuseo, Jokioinen — 09583
Rosenlew-museo, Pori — 09946

France
Ecomusée de Saint-Dégan, Brech — 10899
Maison de l'Outil et de la Pensée Ouvrière, Troyes — 15002

Germany
Deutsches Werkzeugmuseum, Remscheid — 19565
Heimat- und Schmiedemuseum, Widdern — 20563
Heimatmuseum Hossingen, Meßstetten — 18720
Heimatmuseum in der Scheune, Mössingen — 18780
Holzgerätemuseum, Schlüchtern — 19805
Museum Würth, Künzelsau — 18259
Resenhof, Bernau, Baden — 16122

Guadeloupe
Musée Municipal de Saint-Barthélemy, Saint-Barthélemy — 21251

Ireland
Macroom Museum, Macroom — 22514
Tullow Museum, Tullow — 22550
Willie Monks Museum, Lusk — 22513

Israel
Man and His Work Center in Memory of S. Avitsur, Tel Aviv — 22767

Italy
Museo del Chiodo, Forno di Zoldo — 23922
Museo dell'Opificio delle Pietre Dure, Firenze — 23863
Museo dell'Utensileria, Lanzo Torinese — 24141

Japan
Hida Minzoku-mura, Takayama — 26804
Sakai-shiritsu Hamono Hakubutsukan, Sakai — 26700

Netherlands
Gereedschap Museum Mensert, Delft — 29076
Koperslagersmuseum Van de Beele, Horst — 29448
Stedelijke Oudheidkamer, Genemuiden — 29272

New Zealand
Museum of Woodwork and Ornamental Turning, Ashburton — 30099

Norway
Roparshaugsamlinga, Isdalstø — 30580

Romania
Muzeul Tehnic Prof. Ing. Dimitrie Leonida, Bucureşti — 32472

Sweden
Kvarnbacken Prylmuseum, Sandviken — 36179
Penselmuseet i Bankeryd, Bankeryd — 35828
Skogs- och Motorsågsmuseum, Sunne — 36311

Switzerland
Schreinereimuseum, Ibach — 36812

United Kingdom
Forge Museum, Much Hadham — 39991
Longdale Craft Centre and Museum, Ravenshead — 40289
Moira Furnace, Moira — 39971
Museum of Bath at Work, Bath — 38117
Pinchbeck Marsh Engine and Land Drainage Museum, Spalding — 40563
Ryedale Folk Museum, Hutton-le-Hole — 39281
Swinford Museum, Filkins — 38991
Usk Rural Life Museum, Usk — 40753
W. Hourston Smithy Museum, Saint Margaret's Hope — 40414
Weald and Downland Open Air Museum, Singleton — 40519
Workshop and Stores, Grangemouth — 39109

U.S.A.
American Cotton Museum, Greenville — 43831
Sloane-Stanley Museum and Kent Furnace, Kent — 44444
W. Henry Duvall Tool Museum, Upper Marlboro — 48158
World O' Tools Museum, Waverly — 48467

Tourism

Argentina
Exposición Roberto J. Mouras, Carlos Casares — 00264

Finland
Suomen Matkailumuseo, Imatra — 09567

Russia
Muzej Istorii Turizma, Sankt-Peterburg — 33445

Switzerland
Hotelmuseum, Flims Waldhaus — 36703
Museum Schweizer Hotellerie und Tourismus, Zürich — 37399

U.S.A.
Eagle Tavern Museum, Watkinsville — 48452
Hotel de Paris Museum, Georgetown — 43649

Toys and Games

Algeria
Musée de l'Enfance, Alger — 00042
Musée du Mont Riant, Alger — 00043

Australia
Australian Toy Museum, Collingwood — 00939
Brierly Jigsaw Gallery, Bridgetown — 00834
Doll and Bear Museum, Manunda — 01208

Austria
Badener Puppen- und Spielzeugmuseum, Baden bei Wien — 01725
Museum für Billard- und Kaffeehauskultur, Wien — 02944
Österreichisches Spiele Museum, Leopoldsdorf im Marchfelde — 02217
Puppen- und Spielzeugmuseum, Wien — 02975
Salzburger Museum Carolino Augusteum, Salzburg — 02551
Spielkartensammlung Piatnik, Wien — 02991
Spielzeugmuseum, Loosdorf, Bez. Melk — 02252

Belgium
Speelgoedmuseum Mechelen, Mechelen — 03617

Canada
Aunt Margaret's Museum of Childhood, Dufresne — 05349
Elliott Avedon Museum and Archives of Games, Waterloo — 06753
Museum of Childhood, Toronto — 06596

Cuba
Museo Gran Casino, Bayamo — 07860

Czech Republic
Městské Muzeum a Galerie, Hořice v Pokrkonoší — 08359
Museum Hraček, Praha — 08591
Východočeské Muzeum, Pardubice — 08534

Estonia
Tartu Mänguasjamuuseum, Tartu — 09385

Finland
Linnanmäen Museo, Helsinki — 09510
Nukkemuseo Suruton, Savonlinna — 10024
Suomenlinnan Lelumuseo, Helsinki — 09538

France
Espace-Jouets, Firminy — 11738
Musée Comtois, Besançon — 10698
Musée d'Allard, Montbrison — 13062
Musée de la Figurine Historique et du Jouet Ancien, Le Val — 12491
Musée de l'Automobile Miniature et des Poupées Anciennes, Nointel (Oise) — 13355
Musée du Jeu de l'Oie, Rambouillet — 13910
Musée du Jouet, Moirans-en-Montagne — 12999
Musée du Jouet, Poissy — 13785
Musée du Jouet Ancien "Atlantrain", Saint-Just-Luzac — 14301
Musée du Modèle Réduit, Varces — 15088
Musée la Vie des Jouets, Mauleon — 12893
Musée Municipal Département Jouet, La Ferté-Macé — 12170
Musée Rambolitrain, Rambouillet — 13912
Nef des Jouets, Soultz-Haut-Rhin — 14796

Germany
Boxenstopmuseum Auto-Zweirad-Spielzeug, Tübingen — 20221
Deutsches Spiele-Archiv, Marburg — 18626
Deutsches Spielemuseum, Chemnitz — 16461
Deutsches Spielzeugmuseum, Sonneberg, Thüringen — 19997
Erzgebirgisches Spielzeugmuseum, Kurort Seiffen — 18276
Fränkisches Spielzeugmuseum, Gößweinstein — 17330
Heimatmuseum Rieneck, Rieneck — 19608
Kindergartenmuseum, Bruchsal — 16368
Kindheitsmuseum, Marburg — 18628

Das kleine Spielzeugmuseum, Baden-Baden 15787
Märklin-Museum, Göppingen 17319
Margarete-Steiff-Museum, Giengen an der Brenz 17274
Modellbahnmuseum-Muggendorf, Wiesenttal 20581
Museum im Schloß, Frohburg 17156
Musikinstrumenten- und Puppenmuseum, Goslar 17356
Norddeutsches Spielzeugmuseum, Soltau 19994
Puppen- und Spielzeugmuseum, Holzminden 17831
Puppen- und Spielzeugmuseum, Lichtenstein, Sachsen 18458
Puppen- und Spielzeugmuseum Sammlung Katharina Engels, Rothenburg ob der Tauber 19680
Puppenmuseum im Kunsthof, Herten 17741
Schloßmuseum Aulendorf-Kunst des Klassizismus-Altes Spielzeug, Aulendorf 15575
Spielzeug anno dazumal - Museum Beilngries, Beilngries 15871
Spielzeug-Museum Bad Herrenalb, Bad Herrenalb 15658
Spielzeugmuseum, Bad Lauterberg 15690
Spielzeugmuseum, Görlitz 17326
Spielzeugmuseum, Hemau 17707
Spielzeugmuseum, Michelstadt 18733
Spielzeugmuseum, Schkeuditz 19787
Spielzeugmuseum, Trier 20213
Spielzeugmuseum, Zwiesel 20780
Spielzeugmuseum, Nürnberg 19161
Spielzeugmuseum, Ingolstadt 17910
Spielzeugmuseum Alsfeld, Alsfeld 15438
Spielzeugmuseum Bebra, Bebra 15863
Spielzeugmuseum im Alten Rathausturm, München 18910
Spielzeugmuseum im Alten Schloß, Sugenheim 20120
Stadtmuseum Baden-Baden, Baden-Baden 15792
Stadtmuseum Sindelfingen, Sindelfingen 19965
Städtisches Heimatmuseum, Lippstadt 18485
Städtisches Museum Zirndorf, Zirndorf 20759
Steinhuder Spielzeugnuseum, Steinhude 20054
Verlagsmuseum der Unternehmensgruppe Ravensburger, Ravensburg 19509

Greece
Museum of the History of Children's Games and Books, Myrina 21080

Hungary
Szórakaténusz Játékmúzeum, Kecskemét 21452

Ireland
The Berkeley Costume and Toy Museum, New Ross 22528

Italy
Museo del Cavallo Giocattolo, Grandate 24046
Museo del Giocattolo, Palermo 24767
Museo del Giocattolo, Sezze 25564

Japan
Japanese Rural Toy Museum, Kurashiki 26380
Kyodo Gangu-kan, Takayama 26809
Little Sweets Museum, Osaka 26652
Nihon Gangu Shiryokan, Tokyo 26903
Osaka Lottery Dream Museum, Osaka 26665

Luxembourg
Musée du Jouet, Clervaux 27546
Musée Folklorique et Viticole à Possen, Bech-Kleinmacher 27542

Malta
Pomskizillious Museum of Toys, Xaghra 27715

Mexico
Museo del Juguete Tradicional Mexicano, San Francisco de los Romo 28385

Netherlands
Koffie- en Winkelmuseum, Pieterburen 29713
Matchboxmuseum Latent, Prinsenbeek 29715
Museum Kinderwereld, Roden 29741
Museum voor Klederdracht en Oud Speelgoed, Warnsveld 29980
Het Nationaal Autominiaturen Museum, Asperen 28947
Nationaal Modelspoor Museum, Sneek 29839
Nederlands Kansspelmuseum, Den Haag 29119
Oude Ambachten en Speelgoedmuseum, Terschuur 29869
Poppen- en Speelgoedmuseum, Tilburg 29882
Poppenhuis Carmen, Utrecht 29909
Radio- en Speelgoed Museum, Onstwedde 29664
Speelgoedmuseum De Kijkdoos, Hoorn 29445
Speelgoedmuseum Deventer, Deventer 29146
Toy-Toy Museum, Rotterdam 29777
TV Toys Dieren, Dieren 29152

Poland
Muzeum Zabawek ze Zbiorow Henryka Tomaszewskiego, Karpacz 31641
Muzeum Zabawkarstwa, Kielce 31661

Russia
Chudožestvenno-pedagogičeskij Muzej Igruški - Kulturno-delovoj Centr, Sergiev Posad 33519

Slovakia
Múzeum Bábkarských Kultúr a Hračiek Hrad Modry Kameň, Modrý Kameň 34031

South Africa
Toy and Miniature Museum, Stellenbosch 34384

Spain
Museu del Joguet de Catalunya, Figueres 34818
Museu Valencia del Joguet, Ibi 34911

Sweden
Hobby- och Leksaksmuseum, Stockholm 36247
Leksaksmuseet, Stockholm 36254
Rallarmuseet, Moskosel 36104
Smålands Bil, Musik och Leksaksmuseum, Rydaholm 36165

Switzerland
Erzgebirgisches Spielzeugmuseum, Liestal 36877
Musée Suisse du Jeu, La Tour-de-Peilz 37249
Puppenhausmuseum, Basel 36517
Spielzeugmuseum, Davos Platz 36655
Spielzeugmuseum, Dorf- und Rebbaumuseum, Riehen 37063
Spielzeugmuseum - Sammlung Depuoz, Zürich 37408
Zürcher Spielzeugmuseum, Zürich 37421

United Kingdom
Arundel Toy Museum Dolls House, Arundel 38025
Bear Museum, Petersfield 40192
Broadway Magic Experience, Broadway 38368
The Corgi Heritage Centre, Heywood 39239
Cumberland Toy and Model Museum, Cockermouth 38603
Eureka! The Museum for Children, Halifax 39152
Hollytrees Museum, Colchester 38611
House on the Hill Museums Adventure, Stansted Mountfitchet 40578
Judges' Lodgings, Lancaster 39412
Lilliput Antique Doll and Toy Museum, Brading 38305
London Toy and Model Museum, London 39700
Museum of Childhood, Sudbury, Derbyshire 40641
Museum of Childhood at Bethnal Green, London 39712
Museum of Childhood Memories, Beaumaris 38139
Old Toy Show, Lincoln 39501
Penshurst Place and Toy Museum, Penshurst 40178
Pollock's Toy Museum, London 39747
Romney Toy and Model Museum, New Romney 40016
Rottingdean Grange Art Gallery and National Toy Museum, Brighton 38343
Vina Cooke Museum of Dolls and Bygone Childhood, Newark-on-Trent 40026
Vintage Toy and Train Museum, Sidmouth 40516

U.S.A.
Creatabilitoys! - Museum of Advertising Icons, Coral Gables 42626
Crossroads of America, Bethlehem 41663
Eugene Field House and Saint Louis Toy Museum, Saint Louis 47120
The Heritage Museum of Fine Arts for Youth, Detroit 42929
House of a Thousand Dolls, Loma 44847
Lancaster Antique Toy and Train Collection, Portsmouth 46662
Matchbox Road Museum, Newfield 45917
Milan Historical Museum, Milan 45334
Milano Model and Toy Museum, Elmhurst 43168
Museum of Carousel Art and History, Sandusky 47384
National Farm Toy Museum, Dyersville 43030
The National Toy Train Museum, Strasburg 47846
Pauline E. Glidden Toy Museum, Ashland 41293
Toy and Miniature Museum of Kansas City, Kansas City 44412
Trainland U.S.A., Colfax 42521
Washington Dolls House and Toy Museum, Washington 48406
Wenham Museum, Wenham 48508
World Kite Museum and Hall of Fame, Long Beach 44865
Yesteryears Doll and Toy Museum, Sandwich 47390

Trades and Guilds

Australia
Alexandra Timber Tramway and Museum, Alexandra 00730
Brennan and Geraghty's Store Museum, Maryborough 01215

Austria
Alte Huf- und Wagenschmiede, Dietmanns 01764
Erstes Kärntner Handwerksmuseum, Baldramsdorf 01732
Erstes Österreichisches Tischler-Museum, Pöchlarn 02421
Färbermuseum, Gutau 01976
Freilichtmuseum Handwerkerhaus Stegwagner, Windhaag bei Freistadt 03034
Freilichtmuseum Sägehammer Hofwies, Windhaag bei Freistadt 03035
Holztriftanlage Mendlingtal, Göstling an der Ybbs 01901
Kaufmannsmuseum des Heimatvereins Haslach, Haslach 02006
Museum Alte Schmiede, Wien 02934
Österreichisches Werbemuseum, Wien 02965
Pulkauer Gewerbemuseum, Pulkau 02462
Sammlungen des Marktamtes, Wien 02983
Schmiede im Hammergraben, Helfenberg 02018
Volkskundliches Berufe- und Handwerker-Museum, Aspang 01684

Belgium
Koninklijke Hoofdgilde Sint-Sebastiaan, Brugge 03256
Museum van de Kruisbooggilde Sint-Joris, Brugge 03261

Canada
Commanda General Store Museum, Commanda 05270
Dickson Store Museum, Spruce View 06484
Forwarders' Museum, Prescott 06180
Hyman and Sons General Store, Gaspé 05477
Site-Historique du Banc-de-Paspébiac, Paspébiac 06099

Czech Republic
Expozice Řemesel, Moravské Budějovice 08486

Denmark
Roskilde Museums Købmandsgård, Roskilde 09044
Slagelse Museum for Handel, Håndværk og Industri, Slagelse 09071
Slagterbutikken anno 1920, Roskilde 09045

Finland
Hotelli- ja Ravintolamuseo, Helsinki 09496
Jakobstads Museum, Jakobstad 09573
Kurikan Museo, Kurikka 09726
Naantalin Museo, Naantali 09853

Germany
Bäckereimuseum, Rimpar 19614
Bauern- und Handwerker-Museum, Malgersdorf 18608
Christophs Friseur-Museum, Leipheim 18380
Deutsches Fleischermuseum, Böblingen 16211
Drechsler- und Metalldrücker-Museum, Wendelstein, Mittelfranken 20510
Fränkisches Museum, Feuchtwangen 16997
Freiburger Fasnetmuseum, Freiburg im Breisgau 17109
Gildehaus Bardowick, Bardowick 15823
Gothaer Haus der Versicherungsgeschichte, Gotha 17358
Handwerk Gewerbe Museum, Krauschwitz 18220
Handwerksmuseum am Mühlenberg, Suhlendorf 20123
Heimat-und Handwerkermuseum, Leutershausen 18448
Heimatmuseum Calau, Calau 16441
Heimatmuseum der Stadt Herrnhut, Herrnhut 17737
Heimatmuseum der Stadt Ketzin, Ketzin 18067
Heimatstube Ansprung, Zöblitz 20764
Historische Gesellenherberge, Blankenburg, Harz 16176
Historischer Saal der Fischerzunft, Würzburg 20695
Historisches Museum Bamberg, Bamberg 15808
Kreismuseum Finsterwalde, Finsterwalde 17005
Krell'sche Schmiede, Wernigerode 20526
Lechflößermuseum, Lechbruck am See 18365
Museum auf der Osterburg, Weida 20424
Museum der Stadt Mittweida "Alte Pfarrhäuser", Mittweida 18758
Museum in der Burg, Coppenbrügge 16495
Museum Wurzen mit Ringelnatzsammlung, Wurzen 20720
Museumsstadl, Bernried, Niederbayern 16127
Schmiede Burg Schlitz, Burg Schlitz 16412
Schmiedemuseum Arfeld, Bad Berleburg 15611
Schwarzwald-Museum, Triberg 20203
Stadtmuseum Naumburg, Naumburg, Saale 18981
Stadtmuseum Pforzheim, Pforzheim 19390
Steinhauermuseum, Randersacker 19482

Ireland
Findlater Museum, Dublin 22425

Italy
Museo del Cappello, Montappone 24496
Museo di Merceologia, Roma 25214

Korea, Republic
Museum of Korean Commercial History, Yongin 27302

Malta
Gharb Folklore Museum, Gharb 27696

Netherlands
Museummolen de Nieuwe Palmboom, Schiedam 29802
Stadhuismuseum, Zierikzee 30062
Tattoo Museum, Amsterdam 28907

New Zealand
Briar Herb Factory Museum, Clyde 30135

Norway
Samvirkemuseet, Gjettum 30512

Pakistan
Mughal Museum, Lahore 31039

Russia
Muzej Kupečeskogo Byta, Ekaterinburg 32778

Slovakia
Považské Múzeum, Žilina 34079

Sweden
Johanna Museet, Skurup 36202
Slöinge Lanthandelsmuseum, Slöinge 36205

Switzerland
Wertpapier-Museum, Zürich 37417

United Kingdom
Aberystwyth Yesterday, Aberystwyth 37953
Guildhall Museum, Rochester 40335
Her Majesty Customs and Excise National Museum, Liverpool 39518
Museum of Net Manufacture, Dorset 38759
Museum of Shops, Eastbourne 38853
Orkney Museum, Kirkwall 39397
Riverside Museum at Blake's Lock, Reading 40298
Stephens Collection, London 39783
Stockwood Craft Museum and Mossman Gallery, Luton 39846
Mr. Straw's House, Worksop 40935
W.H. Smith Museum, Newtown, Powys 40072

U.S.A.
Blacksmith Shop Museum, Dover-Foxcroft 42976
Forts Folle Avoine Historic Park, Danbury 42772
Grand Island Trader's Cabin, Munising 45560
Hubbell Trading Post, Ganado 43616
Jefferds Tavern, York 48788
John Hancock Warehouse, York 48789
John Ward House, Salem 47196
Old Market House, Galena 43594
Phelps Store Museum, Palmyra 46271
South Sutton Old Store Museum, South Sutton 47704
Wells Fargo History Museum Old Sacramento, Sacramento 47057
Zippo and Case Visitors Center Company Museum, Bradford 41864

Transport

Argentina
Museo de Transportes, Luján 00415
Museo Histórico del Transporte Carlos Hillner Decoud, Quilmes 00494
Museo Rural de la Posta de Sinsacate, Jesús María 00372

Australia
Australian Electric Transport Museum, Saint Kilda, South Australia 01432
Brisbane Tramway Museum, Ferny Grove 01023
D.A. Wurfel Grain Collection, Pinnaroo 01367
Museum of Transportation and Rural Industries, Boyanup 00824
Victoria's Tramway Museum, Bylands 00869

Austria
Gipfelmuseum, Ehrwald 01796
Mödlinger Stadtverkehrsmuseum, Mödling 02311
Weinviertler Oldtimermuseum Poysdorf, Poysdorf 02442
Wiener Straßenbahnmuseum, Wien 03009
Wiener Tramwaymuseum, Wien 03011

Belgium
Musée des Transports en Commun du Pays de Liège, Liège 03581
Musée du Transport Urbain Bruxellois, Bruxelles 03329
Vlaams Tram- en Autobusmuseum, Berchem 03211

Brazil
Museu do Bonde, Rio de Janeiro 04366
Museu do Trem da Cidade de Recife, Recife 04304
Museu dos Transportes Públicos Gaetano Ferolla, São Paulo 04532

Bulgaria
Nacionalen Muzej na Transporta i Săobščenijata, Ruse 04806

Canada
1910 Boomtown, Saskatoon 06393
Cumberland House, Regina 06229
History of Transportation, Moose Jaw 05933
Pouce Coupe Museum, Pouce Coupe 06174
Yukon Transportation Museum, Whitehorse 06794

China, People's Republic
Xian Highway Display Center, Xian 07303

China, Republic
Chung-Cheng Aviation Museum, Taipei 07346

Czech Republic
Muzeum Velké Meziříčí, Velké Meziříčí 08713
Ústecká Bus Historické Muzeum, Chlumec u Ústi nad Labem 08312

Denmark
Lolland-Falsters Traktor- og Motormuseum, Eskildstrup 08810

Egypt
Transportation Museum, Cairo 09290

Finland
Keski-Suomen Tieliikennemuseo, Kintaus 09671

Mobilia, Kangasala 09617
Raitioliikennemuseo, Helsinki 09522
Saimaan Kanavan Museo, Lappeenranta 09764

France
Espace du Cheminot, Nîmes 13334
Mémoire de la Nationale 7, Piolenc 13738
Musée de la Poste et des Voyages, Amboise 10311
Musée de l'Automobile de Vendée, Talmont-Saint-Hilaire 14850
Musée des Arts et Metiers, Paris 13587
Musée des Télécoms, Pleumeur-Bodou 13758
Musée des Transports, du Tourisme et des Communications, Toulouse 14947
Musée des Voitures Anciennes, Landivisiau 12318
Musée du Canal, Ecuisses 11601

Germany
Bremerhavener Versorgungs- und Verkehrsmuseum, Bremerhaven 16338
DB Museum im Verkehrsmuseum Nürnberg, Nürnberg 19135
Deutsches Straßenmuseum, Germersheim 17253
Deutsches Technikmuseum Berlin, Berlin 15940
Eisenbahnmuseum Lehmann, Hofheim, Unterfranken 17800
Flößerei- und Verkehrsmuseum, Gengenbach 17234
Hannoversches Straßenbahn-Museum, Sehnde 19926
Heimat- und Flößermuseum Calmbach, Bad Wildbad 15761
Historisches Straßenbahn-Depot Sankt Peter, Nürnberg 19146
Museum für Nummernschilder, Verkehrs- und Zulassungsgeschichte, Großolbersdorf 17434
Museum Industriekultur mit Motorradmuseum, Nürnberg 19154
Nutzfahrzeugmuseum, Hartmannsdorf 17623
Technik Museum Speyer, Speyer 20013
Technik- und Verkehrsmuseum, Stade 20027
Unterfränkisches Verkehrsmuseum, Gemünden am Main 17233
Verkehrsmuseum, Frankfurt am Main 17080
Verkehrsmuseum Dresden, Dresden 16715
Verkehrsmuseum Karlsruhe, Karlsruhe 18006

Hungary
Közlekedési Múzeum, Budapest 21352
Millenniumi Földalatti Vasúti Múzeum, Budapest 21363
Városi Tömegközlekedési Múzeum, Budapest 21389

Israel
Egged Museum of Passengers Traffic, Holon 22619

Italy
Museo dei Trasporti, Ranco 25071

Japan
Chikatetsu Hakabutsukan, Tokyo 26837
Kotsu Hakubutsukan, Tokyo 26875
Kotsu Kagaku Hakubutsukan, Osaka 26651
Umekoji Steam Locomotive Museum, Kyoto 26459

Lithuania
Bicycle Museum, Šiauliai 27526

Luxembourg
Musée des Tramway et Autobus, Luxembourg 27564

Mexico
Museo de Historia del Transporte, Guadalupe 27963

Namibia
TransNamib Museum, Windhoek 28784

Netherlands
Amsterdams Openbaar Vervoer Museum, Amsterdam 28837
Museum Stichting van het Rotterdamsche Tramweg Maatschappij, Ouddorp 29693
Nationaal Smalspoormuseum - Stoomtrein Valkenburgse Meer, Valkenburg, Zuid-Holland 29921
Openbaar Vervoer Museum, Borculo 29001
Openbaar Vervoer Museum, Rotterdam 29772
Tram Museum Rotterdam, Rotterdam 29778

New Zealand
East Coast Museum of Technology, Gisborne 30163
Ferrymead Heritage Park, Christchurch 30128
Museum of Transport and Technology, Auckland 30113
Yaldhurst Museum of Transport and Science, Christchurch 30134

Norway
Birkenes Bygdemuseum, Birkeland 30431
Haldensvassdragets Kanalmuseum, Ørje 30719
Kristianhus Motormuseum, Vik i Sogn 30992
Norsk Emballasje Museum, Oslo 30749
Norsk Vegmuseum, Fåberg 30483
Vegmuseet - Rogaland, Stavanger 30891

Poland
Okręgowe Muzeum Techniki Drogowej i Mostowej Okręgu Lubelskiego przy Zarządzie Dróg w Zamościu, Zamość 32213

Portugal
Museu do Carro Eléctrico, Porto 32336
Museu dos Transportes, Coimbra 32260

Russia
Konjušenny Muzej -Muzej Avtomobil'nogo Transporta, Sankt-Peterburg 33412
Muzej Avtomobilnogo Transporta, Kursk 32976
Muzej Istorii Moskovskogo Metropolitena, Moskva 33108
Muzej Morskogo Flota, Moskva 33134

South Africa
Heidelberg Motor Museum, Heidelberg 34260
James Hall Museum of Transport, Johannesburg 34278
Outeniqua Railway Museum, George 34245

Sweden
Holmgrens Volkswagenmuseum, Pålsboda 36155
Kanalmuseet Skantzen, Hallstahammar 35939
Norrbottens Järnvägsmuseum, Luleå 36053

Switzerland
Verkehrshaus der Schweiz, Luzern 36918

United Kingdom
Aston Manor Transport Museum, Birmingham 38210
Aycliffe and District Bus Preservation Society, Newton Aycliffe 40064
Birkenhead Tramways and Taylor Street Large Object Collections, Birkenhead 38205
Bournemouth Transport Museum, Christchurch 38575
Brattle Farm Museum, Staplehurst 40581
Bury Transport Museum, Bury, Lancashire 38412
Castle Point Transport Museum, Canvey Island 38477
Cobham Bus Museum, Cobham 38602
Cotswold Motoring Museum and Toy Collection, Bourton-on-the-Water 38287
Dover Transport Museum, Whitfield 40859
East Anglia Transport Museum, Carlton Colville 38491
Grampian Transport Museum, Alford, Aberdeenshire 37973
Ipswich Transport Museum, Ipswich 39306
Kennet and Avon Canal Trust Museum, Devizes 38725
Launceston Steam Railway, Launceston 39430
Lincolnshire Road Transport Museum, Lincoln 39499
Llangollen Motor Museum, Llangollen 39553
London's Transport Museum, London 39701
Manchester Museum of Transport, Manchester 39895
Museum of Transport, Glasgow 39057
National Motor Museum, Brockenhurst 38371
Nottingham Transport Heritage Centre, Ruddington 40350
Oxford Bus Museum Trust, Long Hanborough 39822
Pendon Museum, Long Wittenham 39824
Saint Helens Transport Museum, Saint Helens 40397
Sandtoft Transport Centre, Doncaster 38744
Sheffield Bus Museum, Sheffield 40488
Snibston Discovery Park, Coalville 38599
Stondon Museum, Lower Stondon 39837
Streetlife Museum, Kingston-upon-Hull 39383
Ulster Folk and Transport Museum, Holywood 39258
War Room and Motor House Collection, Harrogate 39172
Workshop and Stores, Grangemouth 39109

U.S.A.
American Bicycle and Cycling Museum, Santa Fe 47415
Ashland Logging Museum, Ashland 41290
Atchinson, Topeka and Santa Fe Depot, Alden 41113
Baltimore Streetcar Museum, Baltimore 41457
Canal Society of New York State Museum, Syracuse 47906
Carriage House Museum, Colorado Springs 42534
Central Texas Museum of Automotive History, Rosanky 47001
Cole Land Transportation Museum, Bangor 41493
Connecticut Trolley Museum, East Windsor 43063
Cookeville Depot Museum, Cookeville 42615
Delaware and Hudson Canal Museum, High Falls 44014
Estes-Winn Antique Automobile Museum, Asheville 41279
Forest Park Museum, Perry 46355
Forney Transportation Museum, Denver 42888
The Franklin Museum, Tucson 48088
Genesee Country Village and Museum, Mumford 45554
Great Plains Transportation Museum, Wichita 48602
Hollenberg Pony Express Station Museum, Hanover 43905
Indiana Transportation Museum, Noblesville 45959
Lake Waccamaw Depot Museum, Lake Waccamaw 44596
Larz Anderson Auto Museum, Brookline 41937
Long Island Museum of American Art, History and Cariages, Stony Brook 47830
Michigan State Trust for Railway Preservation, Owosso 46233
Michigan Transit Museum, Mount Clemens 45526
Minnesota Transportation Museum, Saint Paul 47164
Miracle of America Museum, Polson 46579
Museum of Transportation, Saint Louis 47132
National Road/Zane Grey Museum, Norwich 46040
New York Museum of Transportation, West Henrietta 48530
New York Transit Museum, Brooklyn 41948
Orange Empire Railway Museum, Perris 46353
Owls Head Transportation Museum, Owls Head 46231
Pate Museum of Transportation, Cresson 42696
Patee House Museum, Saint Joseph 47107
Pioneer Auto Museum, Murdo 45563
Portholes Into the Past, Medina 45226
Railways to Yesterday, Rockhill Furnace 46965
R.E. Olds Transportation Museum, Lansing 44645
Schoharie Crossing, Fort Hunter 43400
Seashore Trolley Museum, Kennebunkport 44436
Shore Line Trolley Museum, East Haven 43050
Sloan Museum, Flint 43340
Southern Museum of Flight, Birmingham 41709
Stanley Museum, Kingfield 44485
Steamtown National Historic Site, Scranton 47521
Studebaker National Museum, South Bend 47682
Swigart Museum, Huntingdon 44155
Transportation Exhibits, Nevada City 45656
Travel Town Museum, Los Angeles 44947
United States Army Transportation Museum, Fort Eustis 43393
Virginia Museum of Transportation, Roanoke 46931
Wade House and Wesley Jung Carriage Museum, Greenbush 43797
Wells Fargo History Museum, Minneapolis 45395
Wells Fargo History Museum, Sacramento 47056
West Chicago City Museum, West Chicago 48519
Wheels O' Time Museum, Peoria 46351
Whitewater Canal Historic Site, Metamora 45276
Wisconsin Automotive Museum, Hartford 43946
Yankee Candle Car Museum, South Deerfield 47691

Venezuela
Museo del Transporte Guillermo José Schael, Caracas 48924

Travel → Tourism

Treasuries

Austria
Museum und Schatzkammer des Deutschen Ordens, Wien 02950

Belgium
Krypte en Schatkamer van de O.L.V. Basiliek, Halle 03469
Trésor de la Cathedrale Notre-Dame, Tournai 03797
Trésor et Musée de la Collegiale Sainte-Begge, Andenne 03130

Croatia
Riznica Franjevačkog Samostana Split, Split 07786
Riznica Katedrala, Dubrovnik 07701

Denmark
Rosenborg Slot, København 08948

France
Musée-Abbaye de Charroux, Charroux 11190
Musées de Sens, Sens 14715
Palais du Tau, Reims 13934

Germany
Domschatz, Trier 20208
Domschatzmuseum, Regensburg 19519
Kirchenschatz im Sankt Fridolinsmünster, Bad Säckingen 15724
Schatzkammer der Residenz München, München 18905

Italy
Museo del Tesoro del Duomo, Monza 24559
Museo del Tesoro del Duomo, Rieti 25111
Museo del Tesoro del Duomo, Veroli 25965
Museo del Tesoro della Cattedrale, Anagni 22880
Museo del Tesoro della Cattedrale di San Lorenzo, Genova 23992
Museo delle Rimembranze, Cosenza 23667
Museo Diacesano, Enna 23734
Tesoro del Duomo, Messina 24366
Tesoro del Duomo, Vigevano 26008
Tesoro della Chiesa di San Pietro, Calascibetta 23258
Tesoro della Santa Maria della Scala, Chieri 23541

Japan
Honda Museum, Kanazawa 26305
Meiji Jingu Homotsuden, Tokyo 26889
Suifu Meitokukai Foundation Tokugawa Museum, Mito 26506

Netherlands
Schatkamer van de Kathedrale Basiliek Sint-Bavo, Haarlem 29329

Russia
Almaznyj Fond, Moskva 33019

Serbia-Montenegro
Riznica Srpske Pravoslavne Crkve u Kotoru, Kotor 33849

Spain
Museo Catedralicio, Granada 34874
Museo-Tesoro Catedralicio y Diocesano, Calahorra 34651
Museu-Tresor Parroquial, Olot 35174
Tresor de la Catedral, Girona 34860

Sweden
Skattkammaren, Stockholm 36281

Switzerland
Klostermuseum, Muri (Aargau) 36972
Museum Münster, Münster 36968
Trésor de la Cathédrale Notre-Dame-du-Glarier, Sion 37176

Turkey
Topkapı Sarayı Müzesi, İstanbul 37709

United Kingdom
Christ Church Cathedral Treasury, Oxford 40144
Durham Cathedral Treasures of Saint Cuthbert, Durham 38824

Typography → Books, Book Art and Manuscripts

Uniforms, Military

Belgium
Bastogne Historical Center, Bastogne 03198
Museum Slag der Zilveren Helmen, Halen 03466

Brazil
Museu da Força Expedicionária Brasileira, Rio de Janeiro 04347
Museu do Monumento Nacional aos Mortos da Segunda Guerra Mundial, Rio de Janeiro 04372

Canada
Black Watch of Canada Regimental Memorial Museum, Montréal 05893
Canadian Force Base Gagetown Military Museum, Oromocto 06056
Canadian War Museum, Ottawa 06076
Jamieson Museum, Moosomin 05937
Lord Strathcona's Horse Museum, Calgary 05171
Military Communications and Electronics Museum, Kingston 05682
Queen's Own Cameron Highlanders of Canada Regimental Museum, Winnipeg 06837
Royal Canadian Artillery Museum, Shilo 06445
The Royal Canadian Regiment Museum, London 05773
Royal Military College of Canada Museum, Kingston 05687

Denmark
Forsvarsmuseet på Bornholm, Rønne 09039
Tøjhusmuseet, København 08953

Finland
Mannerheim Museo, Helsinki 09514
Ratsuväkimuseo, Lappeenranta 09763

France
Musée de la Cavalerie, Saumur 14643
Musée de la Gendarmerie, Melun 12922
Musée de la Seconde Guerre Mondiale, Tourcoing 14960
Musée International des Polices et des Gendarmeries, Charvieu-Chavagneux 11196

Germany
Mindener Museum für Geschichte, Landes- und Volkskunde, Minden, Westfalen 18749
Ordenmuseum, Neuffen 19030
Städtisches Museum Abtshof, Jüterbog 17967

Ghana
Ghana Armed Forces Museum, Kumasi 20795

India
Army Medical Corps Centre Museum, Lucknow 21920
Fort Saint George Museum, Chennai 21743

Indonesia
Museum Abri Satriamandala, Jakarta 22109

Iran
Military Museum, Teheran 22312

Ireland
Mullingar Military Museum, Mullingar 22525

Italy
Museo Civico della Navigazione Fluviale, Battaglia Terme 23043
Museo della Battaglia, San Martino della Battaglia 25388
Museo della Cultura Marinara, Tortoreto Lido 25780
Museo delle Armi e delle Uniformi, Urbisaglia 25863
Museo Storico della Fanteria, Roma 25252
Museo Storico dell'Arma del Genio, Roma 25257

Netherlands
Historisch Museum Grenadiers en Jagers, Arnhem 28936
Marinemuseum, Den Helder 29134
Slag van de Somme Museum, Schagen 29797
Traditiekamer Regiment Stoottroepen, Assen 28953

New Zealand
Queen Elizabeth II Army Memorial Museum, Waiouru 30275

Pakistan
Pakistan Army Museum, Rawalpindi 31056

Poland
Muzeum Bitwy Grunwaldzkiej, Stębark 32000

Puerto Rico
Museum of Military and Naval History, San Juan 32406

Russia
Centralnyj Voenno-morskoj Muzej, Sankt-Peterburg 33388
Voenno-istoričeskij Muzej Tichookeanskogo Flota, Vladivostok 33712

Serbia-Montenegro
Muzej Stara Livnica, Kragujevac 33851

South Africa
Castle Military Museum, Cape Town 34203

Spain
Museo de Farmacia Militar, Madrid 35021

Thailand
Royal Thai Navy Museum, Samut Prakan 37534

United Kingdom
Aldershot Military Museum and Rushmoor Local History Gallery, Aldershot 37966
Argyll and Sutherland Highlanders Regimental Museum, Stirling 40589
Bankfield Museum, Halifax 39149
Border Regiment and King's Own Royal Border Regiment Museum, Carlisle 38487
Cheshire Military Museum, Chester 38550
Duke of Cornwall's Light Infantry Museum, Bodmin 38265
Durham Light Infantry Museum and Durham Art Gallery, Durham 38826
Fusiliers' Museum Lancashire, Bury, Lancashire 38413
Herefordshire Light Infantry Regimental Museum, Hereford 39226
Household Cavalry Museum, Windsor 40901
Kent and Sharpshooters Yeomanry Museum, Edenbridge 38869
King's Own Scottish Borderers Regimental Museum, Berwick-upon-Tweed 38174
Military Museum of Devon and Dorset, Dorchester 38750
National War Museum of Scotland, Edinburgh 38900
Queen's Own Hussars Museum, Warwick 40791
Regimental Museum The Highlanders, Inverness 39301
Royal Army Educational Corps Museum, Beaconsfield 38133
Royal Army Veterinary Corps Museum, Aldershot 37970
Royal Irish Fusiliers Museum, Armagh 38020
Royal Scots Regimental Museum, Edinburgh 38911
Royal Signals Museum, Blandford Forum 38257
Royal Sussex Regiment Museum, Eastbourne 38856
Royal Ulster Rifles Regimental Museum, Belfast 38159
Somerset Military Museum, Taunton 40679
South Wales Borderers and Monmouthshire Regimental Museum of the Royal Regiment of Wales, Brecon 38318
Wiltshire Regiment Museum, Devizes 38727
Winchcombe Folk and Police Museum, Winchcombe 40882
Worcestershire Yeomanry Cavalry Museum, Worcester 40933

U.S.A.
Admiral Nimitz National Museum of the Pacific War, Fredericksburg 43531
Military Historians Museum, Westbrook 48550

Vehicles

Andorra
Museu Nacional de l'Automòbil, Encamp 00083

Argentina
Museo Argentino de Motos Antiguas, Mendoza 00433
Museo del Automóvil, Buenos Aires 00198
Museo del Automóvil, Luján 00416
Museo del Automóvil Club Argentino, Buenos Aires 00199
Museo del Automóvil de Santa Teresita, Santa Teresita 00615
Museo del Automovilismo Juan Manuel Fangio, Balcarce 00130
Museo Ramos Generales, Villa María 00671

Australia
Australian Electric Transport Museum, Saint Kilda, South Australia 01432
Binalong Motor Museum, Binalong 00802
Canberra Bicycle Museum, Dickson 00981
Chiltern Motor Museum, Chiltern 00913
Cobb and Co Museum, Toowoomba 01539
Gippsland Heritage Park, Moe 01262
H. B. Lamb Early Transport Buggy Museum, Camperdown 00882
Latrobe Bicycle Race Club Museum, Latrobe 01165
Motorcycle Haven, Adelaide River 00719
National Automobile Museum of Tasmania, Launceston 01169
National Motorcycle Museum, Mitchell 01261
Pine Ridge Car Museum, Main Ridge 01197
Powerhouse House and Car Museum, Portland 01393
Raverty's Motor Museum, Echuca 01004
Serpentine Vintage Tractors and Machinery Museum, Serpentine 01447

Austria
Automobil-Museum Siegfried Marcus, Stockerau 02698
Automobil- und Motorradmuseum Austria, Mitterndorf an der Fischa 02305
Automobilhistorisches Museum, Linz 02227
Automobilmuseum, Aspang 01682
Fahrradmuseum, Ybbs 03045
Kutschenmuseum, Laa an der Thaya 02174
Motorrad-Museum Krems-Egelsee, Krems 02159
Motorradmuseum, Neunkirchen, Niederösterreich 02355
Motorradmuseum, Sulz 02709
Museum Fahrzeug-Technik-Luftfahrt, Bad Ischl 01709
Nostalgie auf Rädern - Fahrzeugmuseum, Großklein 01957
Das Österreichische Motorradmuseum, Eggenburg 01793
Österreichisches Straßenbahn- und Lokalbahnbetriebsmuseum, Mariazell 02275
Oldtimermuseum, Ardagger 01678
Oldtimermuseum im Schloß, Blindenmarkt 01740
Porsche Automuseum Helmut Pfeifhofer, Gmünd, Kärnten 01890
Radmuseum anno dazumal, Altmünster 01667
Tauernstraßen-Museum, Eben im Pongau 01777
Traktorveteranensammlung Dorf an der Pram, Wendling 02818
Villacher Fahrzeugmuseum, Villach 02763

Barbados
Mallalieu Motor Museum, Christ Church 03104

Belgium
Automuseum Old Timer, Lo-Reninge 03592
Autoworld, Bruxelles 03272
Musée du Circuit de Spa-Francorchamps, Stavelot 03765
Nationaal Wielermuseum, Roeselare 03703

Bulgaria
Muzej Ford i Bălgarija, Sofia 04838

Canada
Canadian Automotive Museum, Oshawa 06059
Car Life Museum, Bonshaw 05097
Cosmodôme, Laval 05733
Gervais Wheels Museum, Alida 04974
Heaman's Antique Autorama, Carman 05211
Manitoba Automobile Museum, Elkhorn 05403
Musée Automobile, Saint-Jacques 06324
Musée Jean-Hotte, Saint-Eustache 06316
Reynolds Museum, Wetaskiwin 06779
Spoke Wheel Car Museum, Charlottetown 05233
Streetcar and Electric Railway Museum, Milton 05855
Trev Deeley Motorcycle Museum, Richmond 06266

Chile
Auto Museum Moncopulli, Osorno 06900

China, People's Republic
Grand Prix Museum, Macau 07162

Cuba
Depósito del Automóvil, La Habana 07926

Czech Republic
African Safari and Veteran Car Museum, Dvůr Králové nad Labem 08336
Automuseum E.R. Prihoda, Praha 08564
Muzeum Bicyklů, Rokycany 08635
Muzeum Historických Motocyklů, Kašperské Hory 08406
Muzeum Motocyklů, Lesná u Znojma 08446
První České Muzeum Velocipédu, Chotěboř 08316
Škoda Auto Museum, Mladá Boleslav 08481
Technické Muzeum Tatra, Kopřivnice 08421
Ústecká Bus Historické Muzeum, Chlumec u Ústi nad Labem 08312

Denmark
Aalholm Automobil Museum, Nysted 09003
Danmarks Cykelmuseum, Ålestrup 08767
Egeskov Veteranmuseum, Kværndrup 08966
Jysk Automobilmuseum, Gjern 08838
Radio- og Motorcykel Museet, Stubbekøbing 09082

Finland
Espoon Automuseo, Espoo 09430
Helsingin Automuseo, Helsinki 09484
Tiemuseo, Helsinki 09542
TS-Auto- Viestintämuseo, Turku 10131

France
Collection de l'Aventure Automobile, Poissy 13783
Collection Schlumpf, Mulhouse 13207
Espace Automobiles Matra, Romorantin-Lanthenay 14019
Galerie des Transports, Marseille 12851
Manoir Automobile, Lohéac 12649
Musée Auto Moto Vélo, Châtellerault 11232
Musée Automobile, Saint-Germain-Laval 14243
Musée Automobile de la Sarthe, Le Mans 12435
Musée de la Chartreuse et Fondation Bugatti, Molsheim 13005
Musée de la Voiture à Cheval, Les Épesses 12535
Musée de l'Automobile, Grenoble 11944
Musée de l'Automobile, Orgon 13424
Musée de l'Automobile, Valençay 15047
Musée de l'Automobile, Velaine-en-Haye 15108
Musée de l'Automobile de Vendée, Talmont-Saint-Hilaire 14850
Musée de l'Automobile Française, Reims 13927
Musée de l'Automobile La Belle Époque, Pont-l'Évêque 13815
Musée de l'Automobile Miniature, Fontenay-sur-Mer 11774
Musée de l'Automobile Sportive, Sanary-sur-Mer 14599
Musée de l'Automobiliste, Mougins 13180
Musée de l'Estérel, Les Adrets-de-l'Estérel 12515
Musée de Voitures Anciennes et Sellerie, Menetou-Salon 12929
Musée des Arts et Metiers, Paris 13587
Musée du Poids Lourd et des Véhicules Anciens, Mondoubleau 13010
Musée du Souvenier, Seillans 14694
Musée du Vélo, Labastide-d'Armagnac 12280
Musée du Vélo, Periers 13690
Musée du Vélocipède, Cadouin 10977
Musée et Salon Permanent de l'Automobile de Sport Prestige et Collection, Chauffailles 11247
Musée Exposition la Voiture à Travers les Âges, Chamblanc 11144
Musée Henri Malartre, Rochetaillée-sur-Saône 14003
Musée Militaire, Clères 11318
Musée National de la Voiture et du Tourisme, Compiègne 11377
Le Petit Musée de la Bicyclette, La Batie-Montgascon 12124

Germany
Audi Museum Mobile, Ingolstadt 17903
August Horch Museum Zwickau, Zwickau 20774
Auto Museum Dr. Carl Benz, Ladenburg 18283
Auto-Museum Fritz B. Busch, Wolfegg 20648
Auto Technik Museum, Sinsheim 19968
Auto- und Motorradmuseum, Witzenhausen 20635
Automobil-Museum, Asendorf bei Bruchhausen-Vilsen 15538
Automobil-Veteranen-Salon, Gundelfingen an der Donau 17461
Automobilmuseum Dresden, Dresden 16675
Automuseum Engstingen, Engstingen 16876
Automuseum Störy, Bockenem 16203
Auwärter-Museum, Stuttgart 20085
BMW Museum, München 18835
Boxenstopmuseum Auto-Zweirad-Spielzeug, Tübingen 20221
DDR-Motorradmuseum, Borna bei Leipzig 16261
Deutsches Automuseum Schloss Langenburg, Langenburg 18329
Deutsches Zweirad- und NSU-Museum, Neckarsulm 18990
EFA Museum für Deutsche Automobilgeschichte, Amerang 15482
Erstes Deutsches Motorroller-Museum, Aschaffenburg 15521
Erstes Niederbayerisches Automobil- und Motorrad-Museum, Adlkofen 15398
Fahrradmuseum der Fahrrad-Veteranen-Freunde-Dresden 1990, Dresden 16681
Fahrzeugmuseum Marxzell, Marxzell 18660
Fahrzeugmuseum Suhl, Suhl 20121
Heinrich-Büssing-Haus, Wolfsburg 20659
Historische Fahrzeugsammlung, Simmelsdorf 19960
Horster Motorrad-Museum, Gelsenkirchen 17227
Landwirtschaftliches Museum Wetzlar, Wetzlar 20556
Luftfahrt- und Technik-Museumspark, Merseburg 18714
Mercedes-Benz Museum, Stuttgart 20100
Motor-Sport-Museum Hockenheimring, Hockenheim 17775
Motorrad-Museum, Augustusburg 15572
Motorrad Museum, Ibbenbüren 17874
Motorrad-Veteranen- und Technikmuseum, Großschönau, Sachsen 17441
Motorradmuseum, Michelstadt 18730
Museum für Kutschen, Chaisen, Karren, Heidenheim an der Brenz 17680
Museum für Sächsische Fahrzeuge, Chemnitz 16469
Niederrheinisches Motorradmuseum, Moers 18777
Niedersächsisches Kutschenmuseum, Lilienthal 18466
Norddeutsches Auto- und Motorrad-Museum, Bad Oeynhausen 15710
Nutzfahrzeugmuseum, Hartmannsdorf 17623
Oldenburger Fahrradmuseum, Oldenburg, Oldenburg 19258
Porsche Museum, Stuttgart 20103
Rosso Bianco-Auto Museum, Aschaffenburg 15528
Rübesams Da Capo Oldtimermuseum, Leipzig 18412
Schlepper-, Auto- und Gerätemuseum Hesse, Aidhausen 15411
Schnauferlstall, Ruhpolding 19718
Stiftung AutoMuseum Volkswagen, Wolfsburg 20665
Werksmuseum Achse, Rad und Wagen, Wiehl 20567
Westfalia-Auto-Museum, Rheda-Wiedenbrück 19586

Iran
Air Force Museum, Teheran 22289

Ireland
An Dun Transport and Heritage Museum, Ballinahown 22365
Celbridge Motor Museum, Celbridge 22392
Fethard Park and Folk Museum, Fethard 22470
Museum of Irish Transport, Killarney 22492
National Transport Museum, Dublin 22448
Rathgory Transport Museum, Dunleer 22465

Israel
Israeli Air Force Museum, Hatzerim 22615
Yad Lashiryon Museum, Latrun 22707

Italy
Archivio Storico Fiat, Torino 25729
Museo del Motociclo, Rimini 25114
Museo del Motociclo Moto Guzzi, Mondello del Lario 24473
Museo della Carrozza, Macerata 24247
Museo dell'Automobile, San Martino in Rio 25391
Museo dell'Automobile Carlo Biscaretti di Ruffia, Torino 25743
Museo dell'Automobile e della Tecnica, Farra d'Isonzo 23767
Museo dell'Automobile L. Bonfanti, Romano d'Ezzelino 25274
Museo delle Carrozze, Trani 25782
Museo Storico Alfa Romeo, Arese 22917

Japan
Bicycle Culture Center, Tokyo 26831
Ferrari Museum, Gotemba 26158
Fukuyama Auto and Clock Museum, Fukuyama 26150
Hirano Hakabutsukan, Osaka 26647
Honda Collection Hall, Suzuka 26780
Jitensha Bunka, Tokyo 26863
Jitensha Hakubutsukan Saikuru Senta, Sakai 26696
Mitsubishi Automobile Gallery, Okazaki 26630
Motor Car Museum of Japan, Futatsunashi 26155
Sports Car Museum of Japan, Gotemba 26159
Toyota Automobile Museum, Nagakute 26526

Luxembourg
Musée d'Automobiles en Miniature - Den Dinky, Vianden 27577

Mexico
Museo de Autos y del Transporte Humberto Lobo Villarreal, Monterrey 28231
Museo del Automóvil, México 28152
Museo del Automóvil Puebla, Puebla 28337
Museo del Transporte, Garza García 27929

Monaco
Collection de Voitures Anciennes de S.A.S. Le Prince de Monaco, Monaco 28663

Netherlands
American Motorcycle Museum, Raalte 29720
Het Amsterdams Automuseum, Zwanenburg 30079
Automusa, Bergeijk 28979
Automuseum Deventer, Deventer 29142
Automuseum Histo-Mobil, Giethoorn 29279
Automuseum Schagen, Schagen 29794
Autotron, Rosmalen 29746
Bromfietsmuseum De Peel, Ospel 29682
DAF Automobiel Museum, Eindhoven 29209
Den Hartogh Ford Museum, Hillegom 29415
Eerste Nederlandse Opel Automuseum, Tijnje 29876
Indian Museum, Lemmer 29535
Kinderwagenmuseum, Nieuwolda 29625
Klein Saab Museum d'Oude Bolneus, Woerden 30015
Louwman Collection - Het National Automobilmuseum, Raamsdonksveer 29722
Nationaal Fietsmuseum Velorama, Nijmegen 29634
Noordelijk Busmuseum, Winschoten 30010
Oldtimercentrum Select, Joure 29467
Oldtimermuseum De Rijke, Oostvoorne 29674
Oldtimermuseum De Ronkel, Kloosterburen 29485
Portanje's Vespa Scooter en Nostalgie Collectie, Bunnik 29037
Rijwiel- en Bromfietsmuseum, Zoutkamp 30067
Tweewielermuseum Tankstop, Workum 30023
Wagenmakersmuseum, Leiden 29527

New Zealand
Ashburton Vintage Car Club Museum, Ashburton 30098
Dr. Heins Classic Car Collection, Christchurch 30127
Shantytown, Greymouth 30170
Southward Museum, Paraparaumu 30234

Norway
Flyhistorisk Museum, Sola 30861
Hølonda Skimuseum of Bygdasamling, Gåsbakken 30509
Horten Bilmuseum, Horten 30564
Motormuseet, Strømmen 30903
Norsk Luftfartsmuseum, Bodø 30441
Rogaland Bilmuseum, Vigrestad 30991
Søndhordland Motormuseum, Valevåg 30969

Poland
Muzeum Dworu Polskiego, Plochocin 31885
Muzeum Motoryzacji, Otrębusy 31870
Muzeum Motoryzacji Automobilklubu Wielkopolski, Poznań 31908
Zbiory Sprzętu Ratowniczego Kolejowego, Poznań 31916

Portugal
Museu do Caramulo, Caramulo 32247

Russia
Konjušenny Muzej -Muzej Avtomobil'nogo Transporta, Sankt-Peterburg 33412
Lomakovskij Muzej Starinnych Avtomobilei i Motociklov, Moskva 33073
Muzej Avtomobilnogo Transporta, Kursk 32976
Muzej Zavoda Moskvič, Moskva 33159

San Marino
Museo Auto d'Ecopa, San Marino 33760

Spain
Museu de Cera, Barcelona 34555
Museu de l'Automòbil, Barcelona 34563

Sweden
Arvika Fordonmuseum, Arvika 35815
Bergslagens Motormuseum, Grängesberg 35925
Eds MC- och Motormuseum, Ed 35856
Laganland Bilmuseum, Lagan 36027
Målilla Motormuseum, Målilla 36068
MC-Museum Gyllene Hjulet, Surahammar 36314
Skokloster Motormuseum, Skokloster 36200
Smålands Bil, Musik och Leksaksmuseum, Rydaholm 36165
Spårvägsmuseet, Stockholm 36283
Svedinos Bil- och Flygmuseum, Slöinge 36206
Svenska Transportmuseet, Huskvarna 35970
Torsby Fordonsmuseum, Torsby 36329
Trollhättans Museum och Saab Museum, Trollhättan 36337
Vagnshistoriska Museet, Fristad 35895

Switzerland
Automobil Museum Alte Garage, Rorschach 37071
Historicum, Sargans 37118
Monteverdi Car Collection, Binningen 36568
Motorradmuseum, Gossau (Sankt Gallen) 36771
Musée Automobile, Genève 36741
Musée de l'Automobile, Martigny 36927
Musée de l'Automobile, Muriaux 36973
Musée de l'Automobile, Plan-les-Ouates 37024
Musée International de l'Automobile, Le Grand-Saconnex 36774
Musée Jean Tua, Genève 36750
Oldtimer-Museum, Arbon 36467
Oldtimer Museum, Rheinfelden 37055
Zielhaus am Klausenpass, Spiringen 37195
Zweiradmuseum Bühler, Wolfhausen 37350

United Kingdom
Alex Brown Cycle History Museum, Thornhill, Dumfriesshire 40703
Archaeology Unit and Transport Museum, Gloucester 39079
Atwell-Wilson Motor Museum, Calne 38440
Automobilia, Hebden Bridge 39204
Battlesbridge Motorcycle Museum, Battlesbridge 38132
Benson Veteran Cycle Museum, Benson 38166
Betws-y-coed Motor Museum, Betws-y-coed 38179
British Commercial Vehicle Museum, Leyland 39487
British Cycling Museum, Camelford 38466
Brooklands Museum, Weybridge 40840
Bugatti Trust, Cheltenham 38542
Cars of the Stars Motor Museum, Keswick 39342
Christchurch Tricycle Museum, Christchurch 38576
C.M. Booth Collection of Historic Vehicles, Rolvenden 40338
Donington Grand Prix Collection, Castle Donington 38501
First Penny Farthing Museum, Knutsford 39403
Geeson Brothers Motor Cycle Museum, South Witham 40539
Glenluce Motor Museum, Glenluce 39076
Haynes Motor Museum, Sparkford 40565
Heritage Motor Centre, Gaydon 39029
Hooton Park Exhibition Centre, Ellesmere Port 38927
Jaguar Daimler Heritage Trust, Allesley 37977
Lakeland Motor Museum, Grange-over-Sands 39107
Lawn, Lincoln 39497
London Motorcycle Museum, Greenford 39129
Mark Hall Cycle Museum, Harlow 39164
Motor Museum, Filching 38989
Mouldsworth Motor Museum, Mouldsworth 39990
Murray's Motorcycle Museum, Laxey 39433
Museum of British Road Transport, Coventry 38645
Myreton Motor Museum, Aberlady 37949
National Cycle Collection, Llandrindod Wells 39538
National Motor Museum, Brockenhurst 38371
National Motorcycle Museum, Bickenhill 38189
Newburn Hall Motor Museum, Newburn 40028
Patrick Collection Motor Museum, Birmingham 38226
REME Museum of Technology, Arborfield 38009
Romany Folklore Museum and Workshop, Selborne 40466
Royal Signals Museum, Blandford Forum 38257
Sammy Miller Motorcycle Museum, New Milton 40014
Sandringham House Museum, Sandringham 40445
Shackerstone Railway Museum, Shackerstone 40476
Shuttleworth Collection, Old Warden 40127
Sir Henry Royce Memorial Foundation, Paulerspury 40164
Stanford Hall Motorcycle Museum, Lutterworth 39849
Worcestershire County Museum, Kidderminster 39353
World of Country Life, Exmouth 38961
Yorkshire Museum of Carriages and Horse Drawn Vehicles, Wensleydale 40819

Uruguay
Museo del Automóvil, Montevideo 40998

U.S.A.
Antique Auto and Race Car Museum, Bedford 41578
Ark-La-Tex Antique and Classic Vehicle Museum, Shreveport 47611
Auburn-Cord-Duesenberg Museum, Auburn 41370
Automotive Hall of Fame, Dearborn 42822
Belair Stable Museum, Bowie 41844
Bicycle Museum of America, New Bremen 45671
Boyertown Museum of Historic Vehicles, Boyertown 41855
C. Grier Beam Truck Museum, Cherryville 42280
Canton Classic Car Museum, Canton 42088
Car and Carriage Museum, Pittsburgh 46509
Classic Cars Museum, Salt Lake City 47229
Crawford Auto-Aviation Museum, Cleveland 42470
Dixie Gun Works' Old Car Museum, Union City 48148
Ellingson Car Museum, Rogers 46986
Elwood Haynes Museum, Kokomo 44526
Four Wheel Drive Foundation, Clintonville 42501
Gilmore-CCCA Museum, Hickory Corners 44009
Hall of Fame and Classic Car Museum, Weedsport 48489
Hartung's Auto and License Plate Museum, Glenview 43696
Henry H. Blommel Historic Automotive Data Collection, Connersville 42610
International Motor Racing Research Center, Watkins Glen 48451
Joe Weatherly Museum, Darlington 42784
Mac's Antique Car Museum, Tulsa 48106
Memoryville USA, Rolla 46991
Miracle of America Museum, Polson 46579
Motorcycle Hall of Fame Museum, Pickerington 46482
Museum of Automobile History, Syracuse 47911
Museum of Automobiles, Morrilton 45502
National Automobile Museum, Reno 46833
National Automotive and Truck Museum of the United States, Auburn 41371
National Corvette Museum, Bowling Green 41850
National Packard Museum, Warren 48311
National Sprint Car Hall of Fame and Museum, Knoxville 44510
Northeast Classic Car Museum, Norwich 46039
Pacific Northwest Truck Museum, Brooks 41956
Roaring Twenties Antique Car Museum, Hood 44094
S. Ray Miller Auto Museum, Elkhart 43144
San Diego Automotive Museum, San Diego 47287
Sarasota Classic Car Museum, Sarasota 47454
Towe Auto Museum, Sacramento 47055
Volo Antique Auto Museum and Village, Volo 48257
Walter P. Chrysler Boyhood Home and Museum, Ellis 43159
Walter P. Chrysler Museum, Auburn Hills 41378
Wells Auto Museum, Wells 48501

Veterinary Medicine

Austria
Museum des Veterinäramtes, Wien 02941
Museum für Beschirrung und Besattelung, Hufbeschlag und Veterinär-Orthopädie, Wien 02943

Finland
Helsingin Yliopistomuseo - Eläinlääketieteen Historian Museo, Helsinki 09492

France
Musée Fragonard de l'Ecole Nationale Vétérinaire d'Alfort, Maisons-Alfort 12776

Germany
Veterinärmedizinhistorisches Museum der Tierärztlichen Hochschule Hannover, Hannover 17613
Zoologisches und Tiermedizinisches Museum der Universität Hohenheim, Stuttgart 20116

India
Museum of Animal Husbandary and Veterinary, Guwahati 21824
Museum of Veterinary, Guwahati 21825

Netherlands
Museum Diergeneeskunde, Utrecht 29902

Norway
Norsk Veterinærmedisinsk Museum, Oslo 30756

Poland
Muzeum Weterynarii, Ciechanowiec 31539

South Africa
Arnold Theiler Museum for African Diseases, Onderstepoort 34315
Onderstepoort Veterinary History Museum, Onderstepoort 34316

Sweden
Veterinärhistoriska Museet, Skara 36195

United Kingdom
Army Medical Services Museum, Aldershot 37967
Veterinary Museum, London 39794

Viticulture → Wines and Spirits

Voyages of Discovery → Scientific Expeditions

Wallpaper

France
Maison du Patrimoine de Saint-Chef, Saint-Chef 14144
Musée du Papier Peint, Rixheim 13983

Germany
Deutsches Tapetenmuseum, Kassel 18014

Italy
Museo Bottega della Tarsia Lignea, Sorrento 25610

Water

Australia
Waterwheel Museum, Salisbury 01440

Austria
Wasserleitungsmuseum, Reichenau an der Rax 02496
Wasserleitungsmuseum, Wildalpen 03027

Belgium
L'Amusette, Mesvin 03627

Canada
Toronto's Waterfront Museum, Toronto 06622

Finland
Maanmittausmuseo, Helsinki 09512
Saimaan Kanavan Museo, Lappeenranta 09764

France
Centre de la Mer, Paris 13481
La Maison de l'Eau, Mallièvre 12786
Maison de l'Eau et de la Pêche, Besse-en-Chandesse 10705
Maison de l'Eau et de la Pêche, Neuvic (Corrèze) 13292
Musée de l'Eau, Pont-en-Royans 13810

Germany
Aquarius Wassermuseum, Mülheim an der Ruhr 18813
EAM-live-Museum Lippoldsberg, Wahlsburg 20345
EAM-live-Museum Wasserkraftwerk Merkenbach, Dillenburg 16608
EAM-live-Museum Wasserkraftwerk Wülmersen, Kassel 18016
ESWE Technicum, Wiesbaden 20571
Inn-Museum, Rosenheim 19651
Museum der Stadtwerke, Pirmasens 19403
Museum im Wasserwerk, Berlin 16061
Siedlungswerk der Hamburger Stadtentwässerung, Hamburg 17566
Technisches Museum Alte Wasserkunst, Bautzen 15837
Wasserkunst von 1535, Bad Arolsen 15593
Wasserwelt Erlebnismuseum, Ostseebad Binz 19315

Greece
Open-Air Water-Power Museum, Dimitsana 20938

Hungary
Magyar Környezetvédelmi és Vízügyi Múzeum, Esztergom 21413
Szabadtéri Vízügyi Múzeum, Szolnok 21586

India
Regional Science Centre, Lucknow 21930

Iran
Iranian National Museum of Water, Teheran 22305

Israel
Inland-Water Ecological Laboratory Collection, Jerusalem 22637

Japan
Osaka-kenritsu Sayamaike Hakubutsukan, Osaka-Sayama 26677
Sapporo Waterworks Memorial Museum, Sapporo 26720

Korea, Republic
Dongjin Irrigation Folk Museum, Gimje 27174
Tong-Jin Irrigation Folk Museum, Kimje 27204

Mexico
Museo Casa del Agua, Tehuacán 28472
Museo Hidráulico del Sistema de Drenaje Profundo, México 28174
Museo la Antigua Casa del Agua, Hunucmá 28009

Netherlands
Milieucentrum De Grote Rivieren, Heerewaarden 29364
Museum De Cruquius, Cruquius 29058

Nederlands Waterleidingmuseum, Utrecht 29907
Poldermuseum, Puttershoek 29719
Poldermuseum de Hooge Boezem Achter Haastrecht, Haastrecht 29335

Norway
Fetsund Lenser Fløtingsmuseum, Fetsund 30489
Hydro Industripark-Museum, Porsgrunn 30779
Norsk Bremuseum, Fjærland 30491
Norsk Vasskraft- og Industristadmuseum, Tyssedal 30958
Vassdragsmuseet Labro, Skollenborg 30852

Portugal
Museu da Agua da Epal, Lisboa 32293

Russia
Muzej Mir Vody Sankt-Peterburga, Sankt-Peterburg 33458
Muzej Vody, Moskva 33158

Sweden
Tom Tits Experiment, Södertälje 36212

Switzerland
BKW-Museum, Mühleberg 36961
Zürcher Abwassermuseum Kläranlage Werdhölzli, Zürich 37420

United Kingdom
Basingstoke Canal Exhibition, Mytchett 39995
Brindley Bank Pumping Station and Museum, Rugeley 40358
Carshalton Water Tower, London 39599
Coultershaw Beam Pump, Petworth 40196
Finch Foundry Working Museum, Okehampton 40125
Kew Bridge Steam Museum, Kew 39349
Lagan Lookout Centre, Belfast 38153
Strathpeffer Spa Pumping Room Exhibition, Strathpeffer 40634
Water Supply Museum, Weymouth 40845
Waterways Museum, Goole 39095

U.S.A.
The Aquary Museum, Tucson 48078

Yemen
The Tanks of Aden, Aden 49008

Wax, Molded

Argentina
Museo Histórico de Cera, Buenos Aires 00209

Australia
World in Wax Museum, Echuca 01005

Canada
Louis Tussaud's Waxworks Museum, Niagara Falls 05991
Movieland Wax Museum of the Stars, Niagara Falls 05994
Royal Atlantic Wax Museum, Hunter River 05609
Royal London Wax Museum, Victoria 06730

Czech Republic
Muzeum Voskových Figurín České Historie, Praha 08598
Muzeum Voskových Figurín České Historie, Praha 08599
Wax Museum Český Krumlov, Český Krumlov 08304
Wax Museum Karlštejn, Karlštejn 08405

Denmark
Louis Tussaud Wax Museum, København 08937

France
Musée Grévin, Paris 13617
Musée Historique, Mont-Saint-Michel 13032

Germany
Lebzelterei- und Wachsziehereimuseum, Pfaffenhofen an der Ilm 19382

Ireland
Wax Museum, Dublin 22458

Italy
Museo delle Cere, Roma 25201

Lebanon
Wax Museum, Byblos 27490

Mexico
Museo Ceramoteca, Salamanca 28363
Museo de Cera, Guadalajara 27949
Museo de Cera de la Ciudad de México, México 28127
Museo de Cera de la Villa, México 28128
Museo de Cera de Tijuana, Tijuana 28511
Museo de La Cerería, Tlayacapan 28536

Monaco
Musée de Cires, Monaco 28666

Netherlands
Madame Tussaud's Amsterdam, Amsterdam 28870

Russia
Muzej Voskovych Figur, Sankt-Peterburg 33468
Otraženie - Muzej Voskovych Figur, Moskva 33169

Spain
Museo del Doctor Olavide, Madrid 35031

United Kingdom
Isle of Wight Wax Works, Brading 38304
Madame Tussaud's, London 39702

U.S.A.
Great Blacks in Wax Museum, Baltimore 41468
Hollywood Wax Museum, Los Angeles 44910
John Brown Wax Museum, Harpers Ferry 43919
Madame Tussaud's Wax Museum, New York 45828
Old West Wax Museum, Thermopolis 47994
Parade of Presidents Wax Museum, Keystone 44477

Weapons → Arms and Armour

Weaving

Australia
Elizabeth Farm, Rosehill 01424
National Wool Museum, Geelong 01046
Tasmanian Wool Centre, Ross 01426

Austria
Erstes Waldviertler Webereimuseum, Waidhofen an der Thaya 02782
Museum Alte Textilfabrik, Weitra 02807
Webereimuseum, Haslach 02008
Webermuseum, Heidenreichstein 02014

Canada
Musée les Retrouvailles, Saint-Jean-Port-Joli 06329

France
Musée du Tissage et de la Soierie, Bussières 10960
Le Musée du Tisserand Dauphinois, La Batie-Montgascon 12123

Germany
Fischer- und Webermuseum Steinhude, Steinhude 20053
Handweberei Henni Jaensch-Zeymer, Geltow 17232
Heimatmuseum, Sohland 19982
Heimatmuseum Alte Weberstube, Niedercunnersdorf 19096
Heimatstube Wilthen, Wilthen 20604
Historische Weberei, Braunsdorf 16307
Stadtmuseum Povelturm, Nordhorn 19124
Teppich und Heimatmuseum, Oelsnitz, Erzgebirge 19228
Textilmuseum Die Scheune, Nettetal 19001
Weberei- und Heimatmuseum, Laichingen 18293
Webereimuseum, Breitenberg, Niederbayern 16313
Weberhausmuseum, Schauenstein 19767
Weberstube Jonsdorf, Kurort Jonsdorf 18272

Greece
Ioannina Museum, Ioannina 20969
Nomikos Collection, Pyrgos 21135
Vlachos Collection, Mytilini 21089

Japan
Shiozawa Tsumugi Commemorative Museum, Shiozawa 26760

Netherlands
Museumboerderij, Staphorst 29850
Museumboerderij Vreeburg, Schagen 29795
Weverijmuseum, Geldrop 29269

Norway
Sjølingstad Uldvarefabrik, Mandal 30666

Poland
Muzeum Okręgowe, Bielsko-Biała 31494

Sweden
Textilmuseet, Borås 35843

Switzerland
Weberei- und Heimatmuseum Ruedertal, Schmiedrued 37139

United Kingdom
Bancroft Mill Engine Trust, Barnoldswick 38089
Mill Trail Visitor Centre, Alva 37993
Newtown Textile Museum, Newtown, Powys 40069
Paisley Museum and Art Gallery, Paisley 40161
Weaver's Cottage, Kilbarchan 39355

U.S.A.
Handweaving Museum and Arts Center, Clayton 42444
Watkins Woolen Mill, Lawson 44693

Weights and Measures

Germany
Adam-Ries-Museum, Annaberg-Buchholz 15496
Stadt-und Wagenmuseum Oschatz, Oschatz 19273
Zirkelmuseum, Wilhelmsdorf, Mittelfranken 20590

Netherlands
Weegmuseum de Oude Waag, Someren 29844

Poland
Muzeum Miar - Zbiory Metrologiczne Głównego Urzędu Miar, Warszawa 32114

United Kingdom
Avery Historical Museum, Smethwick 40531
Westgate Museum, Winchester 40894

U.S.A.
Degenhart Paperweight and Glass Museum, Cambridge 42054

Whaling → Fishing and Fisheries

Wines and Spirits

Australia
Grapevine Museum, Chiltern 00914
Pioneer Rum Museum, Beenleigh 00788
Tasmania Distillery Museum, Hobart 01105

Austria
Bezirksmuseum Döbling, Wien 02852
Erstes Oberösterreichisches Schnapsmuseum, Sankt Oswald bei Freistadt 02590
Galerie und Weinmuseum Schloß Gamlitz, Gamlitz 01867
Heimatmuseum, Grafenwörth 01906
Kellermuseum, Falkenstein 01823
Mostmuseum, Neumarkt im Mühlkreis 02351
Mostmuseum, Sankt Leonhard am Forst 02580
Pulkautaler Weinbaumuseum, Hadres 01986
Retzer Erlebniskeller, Retz 02508
Schlumberger Wein- und Sektkellerei, Wien 02986
Stadtmuseum mit Weinmuseum, Bad Vöslau 01721
Weinbau- und Landwirtschaftsmuseum, Hadersdorf 01985
Weinbaumuseum, Reidling 02502
Weinmuseum, Güssing 01970
Weinmuseum Kitzeck, Kitzeck im Sausal 02120
Weinmuseum Prellenkirchen, Prellenkirchen 02452
Weinstadtmuseum Krems, Krems 02160
Winzerhaus, Poppendorfberg 02435

Belgium
Nationaal Jenevermuseum, Hasselt 03483
Wijnklder Soniën, Overijse 03683

Canada
The Wine Museum, Kelowna 05654

China, People's Republic
Macau Wine Museum, Macau 07164

Cuba
Museo del Ron, Santiago de Cuba 08144
Museo del Ron Havana Club, La Habana 07966

Finland
Altia Oyj, Rajamäki 09975

France
Caveau-Musée Les Vignerons de Roueïre, Quarante 13889
Château de Monbazillac, Monbazillac 13007
Château du Clos de Vougeot, Vougeot 15292
Collection d'Outillage Ancien de Tonnellerie, Cussac-Fort-Médoc 11473
Collection Vini-Viticole et de Tonnellerie, Zellenberg 15339
Ecomusée de la Pomme au Calvados, Le Sap 12480
Ecomusée de la Vigne et du Vin, Gradignan 11895
Ecomusée du Libournais, Montagne 13036
Ecomusée du Pay de la Cerise de Fougerolles, Fougerolles (Haute-Saône) 11796
Exposition Universelle des Vins et Spiritueux, Bandol 10577
Hameau en Beaujolais, Romanèche-Thorins 14012
Musée Animé du Vin et de la Tonnellerie, Chinon 11288
Musée-Château de Pommard, Pommard 13792
Musée de la Cave des Champagnes de Castellane, Épernay 11626
Musée de la Distillerie, Pontarlier 13821
Musée de la Distillerie Combier, Saumur 14644
Musée de La Glacerie, La Glacerie 12191
Musée de la Mémoire de la Vigne et du Vin, Saint-Pierre-de-Mézoargues 14416
Musée de la Pomme et du Cidre, Pleudihen-sur-Rance 13755
Musée de la Pomme et du Cidre, Vaudeurs 15098
Musée de la Pomme et du Cidre et des Métiers Traditionnels, Rosay 14031
Musée de la Tonnellerie, Generac 11847
Musée de la Tonnellerie et du Vin, Aloxe-Corton 10296
Musée de la Tradition Champenoise, Épernay 11627
Musée de la Vie Rurale, Desaignes 11501
Musée de la Vigne, Boën-sur-Lignon 10779
Musée de la Vigne, Gornac 11889
Musée de la Vigne, Verzenay 15148
Musée de la Vigne et du Vin, Aubière 10461
Musée de la Vigne et du Vin, Gruissan 11959
Musée de la Vigne et du Vin, Le Mesnil-sur-Oger 12448
Musée de la Vigne et du Vin, Lézignan-Corbières 12575
Musée de la Vigne et du Vin, Lods 12648
Musée de la Vigne et du Vin, Pierreclos 13730
Musée de la Vigne et du Vin d'Anjou, Saint-Lambert-du-Lattay 14303
Musée de la Vigne et du Vin de Franche-Comté, Arbois 10391
Musée de l'Alambic, Saint-Desirat 14182
Musée de l'Armagnac, Condom 11390
Musée des Vins de Touraine, Tours 14971
Musée du Calvados et des Métiers Anciens de Pont-l'Évêque, Pont-l'Évêque 13816
Musée du Château de Cassaigne, Cassaigne 11066
Musée du Cidre, Montaure 13049
Musée du Cidre Breton, Argol 10409
Musée du Cidre du Pays d'Othe, Eaux-Puiseaux 11592
Musée du Donjon de la Toque, Huriel 12039
Musée du Mont Corbier, Saint-Jean-de-Maurienne 14284
Musée du Pays du Der, Sainte-Rémy-en-Bouzemont 14550
Musée du Terroir et de la Volaille, Romenay 14018
Musée du Vieux Pressoir et de la Vigne, Coulanges-la-Vineuse 11425
Musée du Vigneron, Chaumont-le-Bois 11251
Musée du Vigneron, Wuenheim 15323
Musée du Vigneron Paul Coulon et Fils, Rasteau 13914
Musée du Vignoble et des Vins d'Alsace, Kientzheim 12113
Musée du Vignoble Nantais, Le Pallet 12459
Musée du Vin, Brem-sur-Mer 10902
Musée du Vin, Paris 13609
Musée du Vin, Saint-Hilaire-de-Loulay 14260
Musée du Vin, Châteauneuf-du-Pape 11218
Musée du Vin dans l'Art, Pauillac 13674
Musée du Vin de Bourgogne, Beaune 10649
Musée du Vin de Bourgogne, Beaune 10650
Musée du Vin de Champagne Piper-Heidsieck, Reims 13930
Musée du Vin de la Batellerie et de la Tonnellerie, Bergerac 10690
Musée Historique du Cidre, Melleray-la-Vallée 12921
Musée Regional de la Vigne et du Vin, Montmélian 13109
Musée Régional du Cidre et du Calvados, Valognes 15074
Musée Vigneron, Vendres 15118
Musée Viticole, Saint-Yzans-de-Médoc 14512
Musée Viticole Charles-Bernard, Fixin 11741
Terra-Vinea, Portel-des-Corbières 13848
Vinorama - Musée du Vin, Bordeaux 10821

Germany
Baierweinmuseum, Bach an der Donau 15583
Brennereimuseum Haselünne, Haselünne 17624
Dampfkornbranntweinbrennerei-Museum, Wildeshausen 20588
Deutsches Weinbaumuseum, Oppenheim 19261
Dorfmuseum, Pfaffenweiler 19385
Dorfmuseum Hanweiler, Winnenden 20609
Erstes Korkenziehermuseum der Welt, Kreuth 18234
Frankfurter Äpfelwein-Museum, Frankfurt am Main 17042
Grenzwald-Destillation Museum, Crottendorf 16516
Heimat-Museum Maintal, Maintal 18597
Heimatmuseum Dornstetten, Dornstetten 16650
Historisches Museum der Pfalz, Speyer 20011
Hohenloher Freilandmuseum, Schwäbisch Hall 19867
Kaiserstühler Weinbaumuseum, Vogtsburg 20329
Kelter- und Weinbaumuseum, Niederstetten 19099
Kölner Weinmuseum, Köln 18148
Kupferberg-Museum, Mainz 18601
Markgräfler Museum Müllheim, Müllheim, Baden 18819
Mittelmoselmuseum im Barockhaus Böcking, Traben-Trarbach 20187
Museum Bürgstadt, Bürgstadt 16407
Museum für Weinbau und Stadtgeschichte, Edenkoben 16779
Museum für Weinkultur, Deidesheim 16562
Neckarschiffahrts-Museum und Weinbau, Stadt- und Industriegeschichte, Heilbronn 17690
Rheingauer Weinmuseum Brömserburg, Rüdesheim am Rhein 19707
Schnapsmuseum, Kötzting 18193
Schwäbisches Schnapsmuseum, Bönnigheim 16218
Sieben-Keltern-Museum, Metzingen 18726
Stadtmuseum Herrenmühle, Hammelburg 17579
Tauberländer Dorfmuseum, Weikersheim 20432
Vinarium, Cleebronn 16478
Wein- und Heimatmuseum, Durbach 16758
Weinbau- und Heimatmuseum, Klingenberg am Main 18110
Weinbaumuseum, Flörsheim-Dalsheim 17016
Weinbaumuseum Alte Kelter, Erlenbach, Kreis Heilbronn 16928
Weinbaumuseum der Winzergenossenschaft, Ortenberg, Baden 19268
Weinbaumuseum im Herrenhof, Neustadt an der Weinstraße 19079
Weinbaumuseum Meersburg, Meersburg 18679
Weinbaumuseum Stuttgart-Uhlbach, Stuttgart 20112
Weinmuseum, Vaihingen 20283
Weinmuseum Schlagkamp-Desoye Senheim, Senheim 19940
Winzermuseum Rauenberg, Rauenberg 19502

Hungary
Présház, Tokaji 21598
Tokaji Múzeum, Tokaji 21599

Ireland
Desmond Castle, Kinsale 22498
Locke's Distillery Museum, Kilbeggan 22484
The Old Jameson Distillery, Dublin 22450

Italy
Enoteca Regionale Permanente la Serenissima, Gradisca d'Isonzo 24039
Museo Agricolo e del Vino Ricci Curbastro, Capriolo 23337
Museo Bersano delle Contadinerie e Stampe antiche del Vino, Nizza Monferrato 24624
Museo del Vino, Caldaro 23262
Museo del Vino, Torgiano 25726
Museo del Vino e della Donna, Ciliverghe 23562
Museo della Liquirizia, Rossano 25287
Museo della Vite e del Vino, Carmignano 23350
Museo della Vite e del Vino, Rufina 25301
Museo della Viticoltura, Prarostino 25037
Museo dell'Arte del Vino, Staffolo 25628
Museo dell'Enoteca Regionale Piemontese, Grinzane Cavour 24052
Museo di Storia dell'Agricoltura, Cesena 23506
Museo Enologico Grasso, Milazzo 24422
Museo Martini di Storia dell'Enologia, Chieri 23539
Museo Martini di Storia dell'Enologia, Pessione 24882
Museo Ratti dei Vini d'Alba, La Morra 24119
Museo Sella e Mosca, Alghero 22855
Poli Museo della Grappa, Bassano del Grappa 23041

Japan
Fureai Minatokan, Osaka 26645
Ponshu-kan-Echigo Sake Museum, Yuzawa 27036
Yoshinogawa Sake Museum Hisago-tei, Nagaoka 26540

Luxembourg
Freilichtmuseum Schwebsingen, Bech-Kleinmacher 27541
Musée du Vin, Ehnen 27554

Mexico
Museo de la Sidra Copa de Oro, San Andrés Cholula 28374
Museo Francisco Javier Sauza, Tequila 28505

Netherlands
Doesburgsch Mosterd- en Azijnmuseum, Doesburg 29157
Het Gedistilleerd Museum, Schiedam 29800
Nationaal Likeur- en Frisdrankenmuseum Isidorus Jonkers, Hilvarenbeek 29418
Nederlands Wijnmuseum, Arnhem 28943
Het Wijnkopersgildehuys, Amsterdam 28915
Wijnmuseum Maastricht, Cadier en Keer 29051

Poland
Muzeum Ziemi Lubuskiej, Zielona Góra 32220

Portugal
Museu Rural e do Vinho do Concelho, Cartaxo 32248

Puerto Rico
Museo Castillo Serrallés, Ponce 32379

Slovakia
Malokarpatské Múzeum v Pezinku, Pezinok 34041

South Africa
Groot Constantia Manor House and Wine Museum, Constantia 34219

Spain
Cortijo Bacardi, Málaga 35069

Sweden
Vin- och Sprithistoriska Museet, Stockholm 36299

Switzerland
Argauisch Kantonales Weinbaumuseum, Tegerfelden 37230
Haus zum Torggel, Berneck 36555
Heimat- und Rebbaumuseum, Spiez 37192
Musée de la Vigne et du Vin, Aigle 36438
Musée International de l'Etiquette, Aigle 36439
Musée Régional d'Histoire et d'Artisanat du Val-de-Travers, Môtiers 36956
Musée Valaisan de la Vigne et du Vin, Sierre 37167
Orts- und Weinbaumuseum, Neftenbach 36979
Ortsmuseum Höngg, Zürich 37402
Rebbaumuseum am Bielersee, Ligerz 36881
Schaffhauser Weinbaumuseum, Hallau 36791
Walliser Reb- und Weinmuseum, Salgesch 37093
Weinbau-Museum, Chur 36637

Weinbaumuseum am Zürichsee, Au, Zürich 36475
Weinbaumuseum Jenins, Jenins 36820

United Kingdom
Cider Museum, Hereford 39224
Glenfarclas Distillery Museum, Ballindalloch 38064
Glenfiddich Distillery Museum, Dufftown 38784
Harvey's Wine Museum, Bristol 38357
Lindisfarne Wine and Spirit Museum, Berwick-upon-Tweed 38176
Mill House Cider Museum and Dorset Collection of Clocks, Owermoigne 40140
Scotch Whisky Heritage Centre, Edinburgh 38914
Sheppy's Farm and Cider Museum, Bradford-on-Tone 38302

U.S.A.
Browntown Museum, Lake City 44584
Oscar Getz Museum of Whiskey History, Bardstown 41504
Rodgers Tavern, Perryville 46359
Wine Museum of Greyton H. Taylor, Hammondsport 43889

Wood → Forest Products

Wood Carving

Armenia
State Folk Art Museum of Armenia, Erevan 00690
State Fretwork Museum, Erevan 00691

Bulgaria
Muzej na Rezbarskoto i Zografsko Izkustvo, Trjavna 04888

Canada
Musée des Anciens Canadiens, Saint-Jean-Port-Joli 06328

France
Galerie Europeenne de la Forêt et du Bois, Dompierre (Orne) 11547
Musée des Tourneurs, Aiguines 10241
Musée National Picasso La Guerre et la Paix, Vallauris 15061

Germany
Städtische Galerie, Traunstein 20191

Greece
Nikou Collection, Mytilini 21087

Ireland
Clonfert Diocesan Museum, Loughrea 22512

Italy
Mostra Permanente di Xilografie di Pietro Parigi, Firenze 23849
Museo della Xilografia, Carpi 23354
Museo dell'Arte della Tornitura del Legno, Pettenasco 24886
Museo Diocesano e Collezione dei Presepi, Bressanone 23211
Museo Etnografico del Pinerolese e Museo del Legno, Pinerolo 24930

Japan
Nihon Ukiyo-e Hakubutsukan, Matsumoto 26479

Netherlands
Museumboerderij New Greenwich Village, Zuidwolde, Drenthe 30072

New Zealand
Museum of Woodwork and Ornamental Turning, Ashburton 30099
Puke Ariki, New Plymouth 30215

Nigeria
National Museum Oron, Oron 30355

Russia
Architekturno-étnografičeskij Muzej Derevjannogo Zodčestva Chochlovka, Perm 33300
Muzej Narodnogo Derevjannogo Zodčestva Vitoslavlicy, Velikij Novgorod 33678
Permskaja Gosudarstvennaja Chudožestvennaja Galereja, Perm 33307
Tomskij Muzej Derevjannogo Zodčestva, Tomsk 33615

Switzerland
Ausstellung der Kantonalen Schnitzerschule, Brienz, Bern 36585

Thailand
Kamthieng House, Bangkok 37487

Turkey
Vakıf İnşaat ve Sanat Eserleri Müzesi, İstanbul 37713

United Kingdom
Florence Nightingale Museum, Aylesbury 38047
Little Moreton Hall, Congleton 38623
Thomas Bewick's Birthplace, Mickley 39943
William Lamb Memorial Studio, Montrose 39984

U.S.A.
Alaska Indian Arts, Haines 43869
Barnegat Bay Decoy and Baymen's Museum, Tuckerton 48077
Crafts Museum, Mequon 45259
Hoo-Hoo International Forestry Museum, Gurdon 43854
Jim Savage Art Gallery and Museum, Sioux Falls 47644
Longboat Key Center for the Arts, Longboat Key 44875
Museum of Woodcarving, Shell Lake 47597
National Museum of Woodcarving, Custer 42735
Trinity Heights - Saint Joseph Center-Museum, Sioux City 47640
Wendell Gilley Museum, Southwest Harbor 47712

Zoology

Argentina
Museo de Animales Venenosos, Buenos Aires 00165
Museo de Zoología, Córdoba 00299
Museo Histórico Municipal Alfredo E. Múlgura, General Belgrano 00353
Museo Municipal de Ciencias Naturales Lorenzo Scaglia, Mar del Plata 00428
Museo Natural Dr. Carlos A. Marelli, Colón 00281

Armenia
Zoological Museum of the Institute of Zoology, Erevan 00695

Australia
Tasmanian Museum and Art Gallery, Hobart 01106
Western Australian Museum, Perth 01364
Zoology Museum, Brisbane 00844

Austria
Biologiezentrum des Oberösterreichischen Landesmuseums, Linz 02228
Kynologisches Museum, Wien 02922
Landesmuseum Joanneum, Graz 01922
Naturhistorisches Museum, Admont 01644
Robert Hytha-Museum, Oberwölbling 02379

Belgium
Aquarium Dubuisson et Musée de Zoologie de l'Université de Liège, Liège 03566
Koninklijke Maatschappij voor Dierkunde van Antwerpen, Antwerpen 03147
Musée de Zoologie Auguste Lameere, Bruxelles 03314
Musée d'Histoire Naturelle de Mons, Mons 03634
Musée d'Histoire Naturelle et Vivarium, Tournai 03796

Brazil
Inpa Coleções Zoológicas, Manaus 04188
Museu de Zoologia, São Paulo 04526
Museu Regional da Fauna e Flora do Itatiaia, Itatiaia 04136

Canada
Aasland Museum Taxidermy, Cranbrook 05286
Adams Igloo Wildlife Museum, Smithers 06461
Cowan Vertebrate Museum, Vancouver 06675
Frames Northern Museum, Creighton 05288
Grizzly Bear Prairie Museum, Wanham 06743
International Fox Museum, Summerside 06515
Museum of Zoology, Edmonton 05383
UBC Fish Museum, Vancouver 06691
University of Calgary Museum of Zoology, Calgary 05181
Zoology Museum, Winnipeg 06855

Colombia
Museo de Ciencias Naturales del Colegio de San José, Medellín 07516
Museo de Historia Natural, Pereira 07558
Museo de História Natural, Tunja 07612
Museo de Historia Natural, Bucaramanga 07438
Museo Vitaliano Zuccardi, Sincelejo 07593

Croatia
Hrvatski Narodni Zoološki Muzej, Zagreb 07821

Czech Republic
Biskupský Dvůr, Brno 08262
Lesnické, Myslivecké a Rybářské Muzeum, Hluboká nad Vltavou 08352
Muzeum Úsov, Úsov 08702
Rožmberský Dům, Soběslav 08658
Zámek Budišov, Budišov u Třebíče 08284

Denmark
Zoologisk Museum, København 08955
Zoologisk Museum Svendborg, Svendborg 09089

Egypt
Giza Zoological Museum, Giza 09294
Scientific Researches Museum, Cairo 09287

Estonia
Tartu Ülikooli Zooloogiamuuseum, Tartu 09389

Ethiopia
Zoological Museum, Addis Ababa 09402

Finland
Eläinmuseo, Helsinki 09480
K.E. Kivirikon Lintu- ja Nisäkäskoelma, Helsinki 09500
Luontotalo Arkki, Pori 09943
Ostrobothnia Australis, Vaasa 10160
Oulun Yliopiston Eläinmuseo, Oulu 09893
Turun Biologinen Museo, Turku 10132

France
Maison de la Baie du Mont Saint-Michel, Vains 15041
Musée Césaire Phisalix, Mouthier-Haute-Pierre 13196
Musée d'Anatomie Normale, Strasbourg 14819
Musée de la Vallée de l'Ubaye, Barcelonnette 10587
Musée d'Histoire Naturelle, Nantes 13257
Musée du Loup, Le Cloître-Saint-Thégonnec 12401
Musée et Atelier d'Art Animalier, La Chapelle-Thouarault 12151
Musée Océanographique, Arcachon 10395
Musée Zoologique de l'Université Louis Pasteur et de la Ville de Strasbourg, Strasbourg 14838
Museum-Aquarium de Nancy, Nancy 13245
Muséum d'Histoire Naturelle, Nice 13326
Muséum National d'Histoire Naturelle, Paris 13650
Parc Zoologique Arche de Noé et Amazonia, Saint-Clément-des-Baleines 14160

Germany
Brehm-Gedenkstätte, Renthendorf 19572
Dillhäuser Fachwerkhaus im Tiergarten Weilburg, Weilburg 20444
Dinosaurier-Freilichtmuseum Münchehagen, Rehburg-Loccum 19539
Dr.-Carl-Haeberlin-Friesen-Museum, Wyk auf Föhr 20726
Ernst-Haeckel-Haus, Jena 17938
Fehn- und Schiffahrtsmuseum, Rhauderfehn 19583
Forst- und Jagdmuseum, Hofgeismar 17796
Forstmuseum Heringen, Heringen, Werra 17722
Jagd- und Naturkunde Museum, Niederstetten 19098
Münchner Tiermuseum, München 18881
Museum der Natur, Gotha 17360
Museum der Stadt Alfeld (Leine), Alfeld, Leine 15428
Museum für Naturkunde der Humboldt-Universität zu Berlin, Berlin 16056
Museum für Naturkunde der Stadt Gera, Gera 17245
Museum für Tierkunde, Dresden 16702
Naturhistorisches Museum, Mainz 18605
Naturkunde-Museum Bamberg, Bamberg 15813
Naturkundemuseum Erfurt, Erfurt 16907
Naturkundemuseum Ostbayern, Regensburg 19528
Phyletisches Museum, Jena 17947
Rhöner Naturmuseum, Tann, Rhön 20142
Staatlicher Schloßbetrieb Schloß Nossen / Kloster Altzella, Nossen 19128
Staatliches Naturhistorisches Museum, Braunschweig 16304
Tiermuseum, Lenggries 18439
Zoologische Sammlungen des Institutes für Zoologie, Halle, Saale 17523
Zoologische Schausammlung, Tübingen 20233
Zoologische Staatssammlung, München 18926
Zoologisches Forschungsinstitut und Museum Alexander Koenig, Bonn 16250
Zoologisches Museum der Universität, Göttingen 17343
Zoologisches Museum der Universität Hamburg, Hamburg 17573
Zoologisches Museum der Universität Heidelberg, Heidelberg 17768
Zoologisches Museum zu Kiel, Kiel 18081
Zoologisches und Tiermedizinisches Museum der Universität Hohenheim, Stuttgart 20116

Ghana
Zoology Museum, Legon 20801

Greece
Animal and Fish Museum, Evros 20949
Zoological Museum, Zografou 21227

Guatemala
Museo Nacional y Zoológico La Aurora, Guatemala 21274

India
Agharkar Museum, Allahabad 21688
Biodiversity Museum, Dehradun 21758
Government J.T.C. Museum, Faizabad 21802
Government Museum, Chennai 21744
Madras Christian College Museum, Chennai 21746
Mahatma Gandhi Museum, Mangalore 21938
Museum of Arthropoda, Pune 21993
Zoological Museum, Faizabad 21803
Zoological Museum, Gorakhpur 21814
Zoological Museum, Hardwar 21837
Zoological Museum, Jaunpur 21869
Zoological Museum, Meerut 21942
Zoology and Botany Museum, Ernakulam 21798
Zoology Museum, Annamalai Nagar 21698
Zoology Museum, Kanpur 21883
Zoology Museum, Muzaffarnagar 21958

Indonesia
Museum Kebun Raya Bogor, Bogor 22088
Museum Komodo, Jakarta 22120
Museum Taman Laut Ancol, Jakarta 22135
Zoological Museum, Pematangsiantar 22178

Iran
Zoological Museum at Agricultural College, Karaj 22249

Ireland
Museum of Natural History, Dublin 22445
University College Zoological Museum, Cork 22405
Zoological Museum, Dublin 22461

Israel
Bet Gordon, Deganya Aleph 22585
Ussishkin House, Kibbutz Dan 22681
Zoological Museum, Tel Aviv 22777

Italy
Gabinetto Geologico e Botanico Piccinini, Pergola 24841
Museo Alpino Duca degli Abruzzi, Courmayeur 23674
Museo Apistico, Bologna 23106
Museo Civico di Storia Naturale, Ferrara 23787
Museo Civico di Storia Naturale Giacomo Doria, Genova 23987
Museo Civico di Zoologia, Roma 25183
Museo dell'Orso, Villavallelonga 26023
Museo di Anatomia Comparata Battista Grassi, Roma 25206
Museo di Scienza della Terra, Bari 23023
Museo di Storia Naturale dell'Accademia dei Fisocritici, Siena 25576
Museo di Storia Naturale - Sez Zoologica La Specola, Firenze 23872
Museo di Zoologia, Bari 23024
Museo di Zoologia, Napoli 24596
Museo di Zoologia, Bologna 23133
Museo di Zoologia, Roma 25220
Museo di Zoologia e Mineralogia, Siddi 25567
Museo di Zoologia Pietro Doderlein, Palermo 24772
Museo di Zoologico, Catania 23449
Museo di Zoologico e di Anatomia, Torino 25752
Museo Didattico Zoologico, Oria 24688
Museo Zoologico, Padova 24749
Museo Zoologico degli Vertebrati, Avellino 22990
Museo Zoologico dell'Istituto Nazionale per la Fauna Selvatica, Ozzano dell'Emilia 24725
Museo Zoologico G. Scarpa, Treviso 25808

Jamaica
Zoology Museum, Kingston 26077

Japan
Hieizan Natural History Museum, Kyoto 26403
Meguro Kiseichukan, Tokyo 26884
Odawara Crustacea Museum, Tokyo 26910

Jordan
Animal Museum, Amman 27043

Madagascar
Musée d'Orstom, Antananarivo 27601

Mexico
Museo de la Fauna, Aguascalientes 27756
Museo de la Fauna de Veracruz, Xalapa 28617
Museo de la Fauna y Ciencias Naturales, Monterrey 28233
Museo de la Vida Animal Herpetario, Puebla 28333
Museo de Zoología Alfonso L. Herrera, México 28151
Museo Zoologico César Dominguez Flores, Tuxtla Gutiérrez 28576

Netherlands
Kikkermuseum, Den Haag 29099
Museonder, Otterlo 29687
Schoonewelle, Zwartsluis 30080
Zoölogisch Museum Amsterdam, Amsterdam 28917

New Zealand
Kahutara Canoes and Taxidermy Museum, Featherston 30160
Otago Museum, Dunedin 30151

Nigeria
Zoology Museum, Ibadan 30341

Norway
Natural History Museum, Oslo 30747

Pakistan
Islamia College Museum, Peshawar 31049
Zoological Museum, Lahore 31044

Peru
Museo de Zoología Juan Ormea, Trujillo 31264
Museo Forestal de la Policía Ecológica, Jesús María 31190
Museo Mirador de Quistococha, Iquitos 31186

Philippines
Quest - Center for Earth Science And Discovery, Makati 31356
Zamboanga National Museum, Zamboanga 31470

Poland
Muzeum i Instytut Zoologii PAN, Warszawa 32102
Muzeum Lasu i Drewna przy Lesnym Zakładzie Doświadczalnym SGGW, Rogów 31949
Muzeum Przyrodnicze Instytutu Systematyki i Ewolucji Zwierząt, Kraków 31718

Portugal
Museu de História Natural, Porto 32334
Museu Zoológico, Coimbra 32265

Romania
Complex Muzeal de Ştiinţele Naturii, Galaţi   32522
Muzeul Naţional de Istorie Naturala Grigore Antipa, Bucureşti   32468
Muzeul Zoologic al Universităţii Babeş-Bolyai, Cluj-Napoca   32496

Russia
Gosudarstvennyj Muzej Životnovodstva im Akademika E.F. Liskuna, Moskva   33067
Muzei Permskogo Gosudarstvennogo Universiteta, Perm   33304
Muzej 'Archeologija, Ètnografija i Èkologija Sibiri' Kemerovskogo Gosudarstvennogo Universiteta, Kemerovo   32914
Muzej Instituta Biologii Morja, Vladivostok   33704
Muzej Košek, Moskva   33119
Muzej Priroda Morja i eë Ochrana, Vladivostok   33707
Novosibirskij Muzej Prirody, Novosibirsk   33243
Samarskij Zoologičeskij Muzej, Samara   33379
Zoologičeskij Muzej, Vladivostok   33713
Zoologičeskij Muzej, Kazan   32910
Zoologičeskij Muzej, Syktyvkar   33580
Zoologičeskij Muzej Kafedry Zoologii Pozvonočnych, Sankt-Peterburg   33493
Zoologičeskij Muzej Moskovskogo Gosudarstvennogo Universiteta M.V. Lomonosova, Moskva   33186
Zoologičeskij Muzej Rossijskogo Gosudarstvennogo Pedagogičeskogo Universiteta im. A.I. Gercena, Sankt-Peterburg   33494

Zoologičeskij Muzej Rossijskoj Akademii Nauk, Sankt-Peterburg   33495
Zoologičeskij Muzej Tomskogo Gosudarstvennogo Universiteta, Tomsk   33618

Slovakia
Múzeum Tatranského Národného Parku, Tatranská Lomnica   34073
Ponitrianske Múzeum, Nitra   34035

South Africa
Albany Museum, Grahamstown   34249
Port Elizabeth Museum, Port Elizabeth   34333
South African Museum, Cape Town   34213
Transvaal Museum, Pretoria   34359
Zoology Museum, Johannesburg   34286

Spain
Museo de Ciencias Naturales, Pamplona   35248
Museo de Historia Natural, Santiago de Compostela   35442
Museo Nacional de Ciencias Naturales, Madrid   35045

Sweden
Ånge Zoologiska Museum, Ånge   35802
Evolutionsmuseet, Uppsala   36353
Zoologiska Museet, Lund   36065
Zoologiska Utställingar, Uppsala   36366

Switzerland
Hasenmuseum, Bubikon   36593

Musée Cantonal de Zoologie, Lausanne   36859
Musée des Grenouilles, Estavayer-le-Lac   36692
Tierwelt-Panorama, Ebikon   36668
Zoologisches Museum der Universität Zürich, Zürich   37419

Uganda
Department of Zoology Museum, Kampala   37825
Murchison Falls National Park Museum, Murchison Falls   37832
Queen Elizabeth National Park Museum, Lake Katwe   37830
Wildlife Education Centre, Entebbe   37824

Ukraine
The Benedykt Dybowsky Zoological Museum, Lviv   37883

United Kingdom
Bell Pettigrew Museum, Saint Andrews   40380
Birmingham Nature Centre, Birmingham   38215
Cole Museum of Zoology, Reading   40294
Grant Museum of Zoology and Comparative Anatomy, London   39648
Hunterian Museum, Zoology Section, Glasgow   39052
Loch Ness 2000 Exhibition, Drumnadrochit   38778
Natural History Museum, Bangor, Gwynedd   38082
Natural History Museum, Belfast   38154
Oxford University Museum of Natural History, Oxford   40151

University Museum of Zoology, Cambridge   38464
Walter Rothschild Zoological Museum, Tring   40728

Uruguay
Museo Zoológico Dámaso A. Larrañaga, Montevideo   41029

U.S.A.
Las Cruces Museum of Natural History, Las Cruces   44658
Museum of Science at the Toledo Zoo, Toledo   48020
Museum of Vertebrate Zoology, Berkeley   41647
Museum of Zoology, Amherst   41179
Museum of Zoology, Ann Arbor   41220
National Museum of Wildlife Art, Jackson   44290
New Bedford Whaling Museum, New Bedford   45662
Palo Alto Junior Museum, Palo Alto   46274
Philip L. Wright Zoological Museum, Missoula   45408
Space Farms Zoological Park and Museum, Sussex   47897
University of North Dakota Zoology Museum, Grand Forks   43744
University of Northern Iowa Museum Museums Collections, Cedar Falls   42151
University of Wisconsin Zoological Museum, Madison   45072

Zimbabwe
Natural History Museum of Zimbabwe, Bulawayo   49028

List of Advertisers

co + operate solutions + co, Dresden, **Germany** .... Front pages

Collections de la Salle des Martyrs-Chapelle-Crypte: Missions Etrangères de Paris, **France** 220

Deffner & Johann, Röthlein, **Germany** .... Front pages

Gallerie di Palazzo Leoni Montanari, Vicenza, **Italy** 425

Gosudarstvennyj istoričeskij Muzej (State Historical Museum), Moskva, **Russia** 445

Kunstmuseum Wolfsburg, **Germany** .... Front pages

Musée Suisse, Zürich, **Switzerland** 621

Musées royaux des Beaux-Arts de Belgique, Brussels, **Belgium** .... Front pages

Museo Amparo, Puebla, **Mexico** 463

Museo Castillo Serrallés, Ponce, **Puerto Rico** 531

Museo d'Arte Provincia di Nuoro, **Italy** V

Museum Georg Schäfer, Schweinfurt, **Germany** 330

Museum Jerusalem Panorama Kreuzigung Christi, Altötting, **Germany** 250

Museum voor Schoone Kunsten, Gent, **Belgium** 62

Neues Stadtmuseum Landsberg am Lech, **Germany** II

Soundgarden Audioguidance GmbH, Eching, **Germany** .... 3rd cover page

Staatsgalerie Stuttgart, **Germany** 333

Städtische Galerie Karlsruhe, **Germany** 295

Stedelijke Musea, Brugge, **Belgium** .... 2nd cover page

Turaidas Muzejrezervats, Sigulda, **Latvia** 450

Media-Agentur Schaefer

You are interested by an advertisement in Museums of the World?

Than please contact us. We advice you with pleasure and create your advertisement free of charge if you wish.

Museums of the World is the standard work for museums, the art trade, centres of cultural studies, libraries and anybody searching for a specific museum for private, academic or business reasons.

Advertising agency

Media-Agentur Schaefer
Dr. Frauke Schaefer
Inselstraße 20, D-04103 Leipzig
Tel.: ++49 341/30 10 620
Fax: ++49 341/30 10 621
info@media-schaefer.de
www.media-schaefer.de

w w w . m e d i a - s c h a e f e r . d e